The Almanac of American Politics 2016

**Members of Congress and Governors:
their Profiles and Election Results,
their States and Districts**

Richard E. Cohen

James A. Barnes

with
Keating Holland

Introductions by
Charlie Cook
Michael Barone

Columbia Books & Information Services
National Journal

ISBN-13: 978-1-938518-29-4 (cloth)

ISBN-13: 978-1-938518-30-0 (paper)

ISBN-13: 978-1-938518-31-7 (e-book)

THE ALMANAC OF AMERICAN POLITICS
2016

Chief Author	Richard E. Cohen
Co-author	James A. Barnes
Managing Editor	Lisa L. Lang
Senior Contributing Authors	Charlie Cook Michael Barone (Founding Author)
Senior Authors	Louis Jacobson, Louis Peck
Senior Editor	John Bicknell
Data Editor	Keating Holland
Writers	Chuck McCutcheon, Cam Newton, Kirk Victor, David Wasserman
Editors	Karlyn Bowman, Jennifer Duffy, Jim Welch
Researchers	Colin O'Keefe (chief of researchers), Charles Aull (writer-researcher), Jaime Arsenault, Jessica Dravecky, Audrey Faber, Chris Lee, Andy Bechhoefer (data)
Proofers	Jaime Arsenault, Chris Lee
Production Assistant	Lori Sullivan
Election Results, Maps	Ballotpedia, Polidata
Campaign Finance	The Center for Responsive Politics

Columbia Books & Information Services
President: Joel Poznansky

About the Authors

Richard E. Cohen brings to the Almanac four decades of experience covering Capitol Hill, chiefly for *National Journal*. He was co-author of the Almanac from 2001 through 2010. He was the 1990 winner of the Everett McKinley Dirksen Award for distinguished reporting on Congress. Cohen is an active author of books about Congress, including a biography of former House Ways and Means Committee chairman Dan Rostenkowski.

James A. Barnes is a senior writer for Ballotpedia.org and a consultant to CNN, where he has projected the outcomes of presidential, congressional and gubernatorial races for its election night and primary night coverage. He was the chief political correspondent for *National Journal* for more than 20 years and founder of the *National Journal* Insiders Poll. He was a contributor to *The State of American Politics*.

Acknowledgements

The authors owe a debt of gratitude to several people and organizations that have contributed to the 2016 edition of *The Almanac of American Politics* and sustained it for decades. Most notably, Michael Barone authored the original 1972 *Almanac*, and since then his insights have been the heart and soul of this essential work on the American polity. John Fox Sullivan, the former president and publisher of *National Journal* magazines and David Bradley, the owner of *National Journal*'s parent company, Atlantic Media, have nurtured the *Almanac* for many years and worked to see it continue. Ballotpedia and its publisher, Leslie Graves, provided research and editorial support to the 2016 *Almanac*, without which this edition would not have been possible. Charlie Cook and his staff at the Cook Political Report also made significant contributions to this latest edition. The Center for Responsive Politics provided a unique compilation of data that contributes to readers' understanding of campaign finance in federal elections. Clark Benson, at Polidata, contributed updated congressional district maps. We also are grateful to Sue Lloyd-Novak, Brittany Carter, Duncan Bell, James Cameron, Adem Gokturk, Jamie Herring, Maggie Aland, Julie Pietrzak and the Columbia Books staff for their efforts getting this book to print.

TABLE OF CONTENTS

Guide to Usage xiii
Abbreviations xix
Political Overview 1
   By Charlie Cook
Voting in Divided Government 19
   By Michael Barone
President and Vice President 24
Leadership 2051
Senate Seniority 2053
House Seniority 2054
Committee Listings (Senate) 2059
Committee Listings (House) 2067
Profile List 2081

ALABAMA 25
Gov. Robert Bentley (R) 30

SENATORS
Richard Shelby (R) 32
Jeff Sessions (R) 36

REPRESENTATIVES, (6R, 1D)
1. Bradley Byrne (R) 39
2. Martha Roby (R) 42
3. Mike Rogers (R) 44
4. Robert Aderholt (R) 48
5. Mo Brooks (R) 51
6. Gary Palmer (R) 54
7. Terri Sewell (D) 57

ALASKA 61
Gov. Bill Walker (I) 66

SENATORS
Lisa Murkowski (R) 68
Dan Sullivan (R) 72

REPRESENTATIVE-AT-LARGE, (1R)
Don Young (R) 74

ARIZONA 78
Gov. Doug Ducey (R) 83

SENATORS
John McCain (R) 85
Jeff Flake (R) 92

REPRESENTATIVES, (5R, 4D)
1. Ann Kirkpatrick (D) 94
2. Martha McSally (R) 97
3. Raúl Grijalva (D) 100
4. Paul Gosar (R) 103
5. Matt Salmon (R) 106
6. David Schweikert (R) 109
7. Ruben Gallego (D) 112
8. Trent Franks (R) 115
9. Kyrsten Sinema (D) 118

ARKANSAS 121
Gov. Asa Hutchinson (R) 125

SENATORS
John Boozman (R) 126
Tom Cotton (R) 129

REPRESENTATIVES, (4R)
1. Rick Crawford (R) 131
2. French Hill (R) 134
3. Steve Womack (R) 136
4. Bruce Westerman (R) 139

CALIFORNIA 142
Gov. Jerry Brown (D) 151

SENATORS
Dianne Feinstein (D) 154
Barbara Boxer (D) 158

REPRESENTATIVES, (14R, 39D)
1. Doug LaMalfa (R) 162
2. Jared Huffman (D) 165
3. John Garamendi (D) 168
4. Tom McClintock (R) 170
5. Mike Thompson (D) 173
6. Doris Matsui (D) 176
7. Ami Bera (D) 179
8. Paul Cook (R) 182
9. Jerry McNerney (D) 184
10. Jeff Denham (R) 187
11. Mark DeSaulnier (D) 191
12. Nancy Pelosi (D) 193
13. Barbara Lee (D) 201
14. Jackie Speier (D) 205
15. Eric Swalwell (D) 208
16. Jim Costa (D) 211
17. Mike Honda (D) 214
18. Anna Eshoo (D) 217
19. Zoe Lofgren (D) 220
20. Sam Farr (D) 223
21. David Valadao (R) 226
22. Devin Nunes (R) 229
23. Kevin McCarthy (R) 232
24. Lois Capps (D) 236
25. Steve Knight (R) 239
26. Julia Brownley (D) 241
27. Judy Chu (D) 244
28. Adam Schiff (D) 247
29. Tony Cárdenas (D) 250
30. Brad Sherman (D) 253
31. Pete Aguilar (D) 256
32. Grace Napolitano (D) 259
33. Ted Lieu (D) 261
34. Xavier Becerra (D) 264
35. Norma Torres (D) 267
36. Raul Ruiz (D) 270

37. Karen Bass (D) 272
38. Linda Sánchez (D) 275
39. Ed Royce (R)................................. 278
40. Lucille Roybal-Allard (D) 281
41. Mark Takano (D)........................... 284
42. Ken Calvert (R)............................. 286
43. Maxine Waters (D)........................ 289
44. Janice Hahn (D)............................ 293
45. Mimi Walters (R).......................... 296
46. Loretta Sanchez (D) 298
47. Alan Lowenthal (D) 301
48. Dana Rohrabacher (R)................... 304
49. Darrell Issa (R) 307
50. Duncan D. Hunter (R)................... 311
51. Juan Vargas (D) 314
52. Scott Peters (D)............................ 316
53. Susan Davis (D) 319

COLORADO 323
Gov. John Hickenlooper (D) 327

SENATORS
Michael Bennet (D) 330
Cory Gardner (R)................................... 333

REPRESENTATIVES, (4R, 3D)
1. Diana DeGette (D) 335
2. Jared Polis (D)............................... 338
3. Scott Tipton (R)............................. 341
4. Ken Buck (R).................................. 345
5. Doug Lamborn (R) 347
6. Mike Coffman (R)........................... 350
7. Ed Perlmutter (D)......................... 353

CONNECTICUT.................... 357
Gov. Dannel Malloy (D).......................... 361

SENATORS
Richard Blumenthal (D) 364
Chris Murphy (D).................................. 366

REPRESENTATIVES, (5D)
1. John Larson (D) 369
2. Joe Courtney (D)........................... 372
3. Rosa DeLauro (D) 375
4. Jim Himes (D)............................... 378
5. Elizabeth Esty (D) 381

DELAWARE 385
Gov. Jack Markell (D)............................. 389

SENATORS
Thomas Carper (D) 391
Christopher Coons (D) 394

REPRESENTATIVE-AT-LARGE, (1D)
John Carney (D).................................... 397

DISTRICT OF COLUMBIA 399

DELEGATE, 1(D)
Eleanor Holmes Norton (D)................... 401

FLORIDA 404
Gov. Rick Scott (R)................................ 411

SENATORS
Bill Nelson (D)...................................... 415
Marco Rubio (R) 418

REPRESENTATIVES, (17R, 10D)
1. Jeff Miller (R)............................... 422
2. Gwen Graham (D)......................... 425
3. Ted Yoho (R) 428
4. Ander Crenshaw (R) 430
5. Corrine Brown (D) 433
6. Ron DeSantis (R) 437
7. John Mica (R)............................... 439
8. Bill Posey (R)............................... 443
9. Alan Grayson (D) 446
10. Daniel Webster (R)....................... 449
11. Richard Nugent (R)....................... 452
12. Gus Bilirakis (R).......................... 455
13. David Jolly (R) 458
14. Kathy Castor (D).......................... 460
15. Dennis Ross (R)............................ 463
16. Vern Buchanan (R) 466
17. Tom Rooney (R)............................ 469
18. Patrick Murphy (D) 472
19. Curt Clawson (R) 474
20. Alcee Hastings (D) 477
21. Ted Deutch (D) 480
22. Lois Frankel (D)........................... 483
23. Debbie Wasserman
    Schultz (D)................................... 486
24. Frederica Wilson (D).................... 490
25. Mario Diaz-Balart (R)................... 493
26. Carlos Curbelo (R) 496
27. Ileana Ros-Lehtinen (R) 499

GEORGIA 503
Gov. Nathan Deal (R)............................. 508

SENATORS
Johnny Isakson (R) 510
David Perdue (R)................................... 513

REPRESENTATIVES, (10R, 4D)
1. Buddy Carter (R) 515
2. Sanford Bishop (D) 517
3. Lynn Westmoreland (R)................. 520
4. Hank Johnson (D)......................... 522
5. John Lewis (D) 525
6. Tom Price (R)............................... 528
7. Rob Woodall (R)............................ 531
8. Austin Scott (R)............................ 534
9. Doug Collins (R)........................... 536
10. Jody Hice (R) 539
11. Barry Loudermilk (R) 541
12. Rick Allen (R) 543
13. David Scott (D)............................. 545
14. Tom Graves (R) 548

HAWAII 552
Gov. David Ige (D) 557

SENATORS
Brian Schatz (D)................................ 559
Mazie Hirono (D)............................... 561

REPRESENTATIVES, (2D)
  1. Mark Takai (D)............................ 563
  2. Tulsi Gabbard (D)........................ 565

IDAHO 569
Gov. Butch Otter (R)........................... 573

SENATORS
Mike Crapo (R).................................. 575
James Risch (R)................................. 578

REPRESENTATIVES, (2R)
  1. Raúl Labrador (R)........................ 580
  2. Mike Simpson (R) 583

ILLINOIS.............................. 587
Gov. Bruce Rauner (R) 593

SENATORS
Richard Durbin (D) 595
Mark Kirk (R)................................... 599

REPRESENTATIVES, (7R, 10D, 1 VACANT)
  1. Bobby Rush (D)........................... 602
  2. Robin Kelly (D) 606
  3. Daniel Lipinski (D) 609
  4. Luis Gutierrez (D)........................ 612
  5. Mike Quigley (D).......................... 615
  6. Peter Roskam (R).......................... 618
  7. Danny Davis (D) 621
  8. Tammy Duckworth (D) 624
  9. Jan Schakowsky (D) 627
 10. Bob Dold (R).............................. 630
 11. Bill Foster (D)............................ 632
 12. Mike Bost (R) 635
 13. Rodney Davis (R) 637
 14. Randy Hultgren (R) 640
 15. John Shimkus (R) 643
 16. Adam Kinzinger (R)...................... 646
 17. Cheri Bustos (D) 649
 18. Vacant.................................... 652

INDIANA 655
Gov. Mike Pence (R) 660

SENATORS
Dan Coats (R).................................... 662
Joe Donnelly (D)................................. 665

REPRESENTATIVES, (7R, 2D)
  1. Peter Visclosky (D)...................... 667
  2. Jackie Walorski (R) 670
  3. Marlin Stutzman (R) 673
  4. Todd Rokita (R).......................... 676
  5. Susan Brooks (R) 679
  6. Luke Messer (R) 681
  7. André Carson (D)......................... 684
  8. Larry Bucshon (R) 687
  9. Todd Young (R)........................... 690

IOWA................................ 693
Gov. Terry Branstad (R) 699

SENATORS
Charles Grassley (R)............................. 701
Joni Ernst (R)................................... 706

REPRESENTATIVES, (3R, 1D)
  1. Rod Blum (R)............................. 708
  2. Dave Loebsack (D) 710
  3. David Young (R) 713
  4. Steve King (R)........................... 716

KANSAS 720
Gov. Sam Brownback (R) 724

SENATORS
Pat Roberts (R).................................. 726
Jerry Moran (R)................................. 730

REPRESENTATIVES, (4R)
  1. Tim Huelskamp (R) 733
  2. Lynn Jenkins (R).......................... 736
  3. Kevin Yoder (R) 739
  4. Mike Pompeo (R).......................... 741

KENTUCKY 745
Gov. Steve Beshear (D).......................... 749

SENATORS
Mitch McConnell (R)............................. 752
Rand Paul (R)................................... 758

REPRESENTATIVES, (5R, 1D)
  1. Ed Whitfield (R) 761
  2. Brett Guthrie (R)........................ 764
  3. John Yarmuth (D) 767
  4. Thomas Massie (R) 770
  5. Harold Rogers (R) 773
  6. Andy Barr (R)............................ 777

LOUISIANA 780
Gov. Bobby Jindal (R)........................... 785

SENATORS
David Vitter (R)................................. 788
Bill Cassidy (R) 792

REPRESENTATIVES, (5R, 1D)
  1. Steve Scalise (R) 794
  2. Cedric Richmond (D) 799
  3. Charles Boustany (R) 802
  4. John Fleming (R) 805
  5. Ralph Abraham (R)....................... 808
  6. Garret Graves (R) 810

MAINE.............................. 813
Gov. Paul LePage (R)............................ 817

SENATORS
Susan Collins (R)................................ 819
Angus King (I)................................... 823

REPRESENTATIVES, (1R, 1D)
1. Chellie Pingree (D) 826
2. Bruce Poliquin (R)...................... 829

MARYLAND 832
Gov. Larry Hogan (R) 837

SENATORS
Barbara Mikulski (D)........................... 840
Ben Cardin (D) 844

REPRESENTATIVES, (1R, 7D)
1. Andy Harris (R) 847
2. Dutch Ruppersberger (D) 850
3. John Sarbanes (D) 853
4. Donna Edwards (D) 856
5. Steny Hoyer (D) 860
6. John Delaney (D) 864
7. Elijah Cummings (D)................... 867
8. Chris Van Hollen (D) 871

MASSACHUSETTS 876
Gov. Charlie Baker (R)........................... 881

SENATORS
Elizabeth Warren (D)........................... 883
Edward Markey (D) 887

REPRESENTATIVES, (9D)
1. Richard Neal (D) 890
2. James McGovern (D) 893
3. Niki Tsongas (D) 896
4. Joe Kennedy (D)......................... 899
5. Katherine Clark (D)..................... 902
6. Seth Moulton (D) 904
7. Michael Capuano (D) 906
8. Stephen Lynch (D) 910
9. William Keating (D)..................... 913

MICHIGAN 916
Gov. Rick Snyder (R) 922

SENATORS
Debbie Stabenow (D)............................ 924
Gary Peters (D) 928

REPRESENTATIVES, (9R, 5D)
1. Dan Benishek (R)........................ 930
2. Bill Huizenga (R) 933
3. Justin Amash (R) 936
4. John Moolenaar (R) 939
5. Dan Kildee (D) 941
6. Fred Upton (R).......................... 944
7. Tim Walberg (R) 948
8. Mike Bishop (R) 951
9. Sander Levin (D)........................ 953
10. Candice Miller (R)...................... 956
11. Dave Trott (R).......................... 960
12. Debbie Dingell (D) 962
13. John Conyers (D) 964
14. Brenda Lawrence (D).................... 968

MINNESOTA 972
Gov. Mark Dayton (D) 977

SENATORS
Amy Klobuchar (D) 980
Al Franken (D) 983

REPRESENTATIVES, (3R, 5D)
1. Tim Walz (D) 986
2. John Kline (R) 990
3. Erik Paulsen (R)........................ 993
4. Betty McCollum (D)..................... 996
5. Keith Ellison (D) 999
6. Tom Emmer (R) 1002
7. Collin Peterson (D)..................... 1004
8. Rick Nolan (D) 1008

MISSISSIPPI........................ 1012
Gov. Phil Bryant (R) 1016

SENATORS
Thad Cochran (R) 1018
Roger Wicker (R) 1021

REPRESENTATIVES, (3R, 1D)
1. Trent Kelly (R) 1025
2. Bennie Thompson (D) 1027
3. Gregg Harper (R)....................... 1031
4. Steven Palazzo (R) 1033

MISSOURI 1037
Gov. Jay Nixon (D)............................... 1041

SENATORS
Claire McCaskill (D) 1044
Roy Blunt (R)................................... 1048

REPRESENTATIVES, (6R, 2D)
1. William Lacy Clay (D) 1052
2. Ann Wagner (R)......................... 1056
3. Blaine Luetkemeyer (R) 1058
4. Vicky Hartzler (R)...................... 1061
5. Emanuel Cleaver (D) 1064
6. Sam Graves (R).......................... 1067
7. Billy Long (R)............................ 1070
8. Jason Smith (R) 1073

MONTANA 1076
Gov. Steve Bullock (D)......................... 1080

SENATORS
Jon Tester (D) 1081
Steve Daines (R)................................ 1085

REPRESENTATIVE-AT-LARGE, (1R)
Ryan Zinke (R) 1086

NEBRASKA 1088
Gov. Pete Ricketts (R).......................... 1092

SENATORS
Deb Fischer (R).................................. 1094
Ben Sasse (R).................................... 1097

REPRESENTATIVES, (2R, 1D)
1. Jeff Fortenberry (R) 1099
2. Brad Ashford (D)........................ 1102
3. Adrian Smith (R) 1105

NEVADA............................ 1108
Gov. Brian Sandoval (R)........................1113

SENATORS
Harry Reid (D)................................ 1115
Dean Heller (R) 1119

REPRESENTATIVES, (3R, 1D)
1. Dina Titus (D) 1121
2. Mark Amodei (R)........................ 1124
3. Joe Heck (R) 1127
4. Cresent Hardy (R)....................... 1130

NEW HAMPSHIRE 1134
Gov. Maggie Hassan (D)...................... 1140

SENATORS
Jeanne Shaheen (D) 1142
Kelly Ayotte (R) 1146

REPRESENTATIVES, (1R, 1D)
1. Frank Guinta (R) 1149
2. Ann McLane Kuster (D) 1152

NEW JERSEY...................... 1156
Gov. Chris Christie (R) 1162

SENATORS
Robert Menendez (D) 1165
Cory Booker (D).............................. 1170

REPRESENTATIVES, (6R, 6D)
1. Donald Norcross (D) 1173
2. Frank LoBiondo (R) 1176
3. Tom MacArthur (R) 1179
4. Chris Smith (R).......................... 1181
5. Scott Garrett (R) 1185
6. Frank Pallone (D) 1188
7. Leonard Lance (R) 1191
8. Albio Sires (D)........................... 1194
9. Bill Pascrell (D) 1197
10. Donald Payne Jr. (D)................. 1200
11. Rodney Frelinghuysen (R).......... 1202
12. Bonnie Watson Coleman (D) 1206

NEW MEXICO...................... 1208
Gov. Susana Martinez (R)................... 1212

SENATORS
Tom Udall (D)................................ 1214
Martin Heinrich (D)......................... 1217

REPRESENTATIVES, (1R, 2D)
1. Michelle Lujan Grisham (D) 1219
2. Steve Pearce (R).......................... 1222
3. Ben Ray Luján (D)....................... 1225

NEW YORK.......................... 1228
Gov. Andrew Cuomo (D) 1236

SENATORS
Charles Schumer (D)........................... 1240
Kirsten Gillibrand (D)......................... 1246

REPRESENTATIVES, (9R, 18D)
1. Lee Zeldin (R)............................ 1250
2. Peter King (R) 1253
3. Steve Israel (D) 1256
4. Kathleen Rice (D)....................... 1259
5. Gregory Meeks (D)...................... 1262
6. Grace Meng (D)......................... 1265
7. Nydia Velázquez (D) 1268
8. Hakeem Jeffries (D)..................... 1271
9. Yvette Clarke (D)........................ 1273
10. Jerrold Nadler (D)...................... 1277
11. Daniel Donovan (R) 1280
12. Carolyn Maloney (D).................. 1283
13. Charles Rangel (D) 1287
14. Joseph Crowley (D)..................... 1291
15. José Serrano (D)......................... 1295
16. Eliot Engel (D) 1298
17. Nita Lowey (D)........................... 1301
18. Sean Patrick Maloney (D) 1304
19. Chris Gibson (R) 1307
20. Paul Tonko (D) 1310
21. Elise Stefanik (R)....................... 1313
22. Richard Hanna (R)...................... 1315
23. Tom Reed (R)............................. 1318
24. John Katko (R) 1321
25. Louise Slaughter (D)................... 1323
26. Brian Higgins (D)........................ 1326
27. Chris Collins (R) 1329

NORTH CAROLINA............ 1332
Gov. Pat McCrory (R) 1337

SENATORS
Richard Burr (R) 1340
Thom Tillis (R) 1344

REPRESENTATIVES, (10R, 3D)
1. G.K. Butterfield (D)..................... 1346
2. Renee Ellmers (R)........................ 1349
3. Walter Jones (R).......................... 1352
4. David Price (D)............................ 1355
5. Virginia Foxx (R)......................... 1358
6. Mark Walker (R) 1361
7. David Rouzer (R).......................... 1363
8. Richard Hudson (R) 1366
9. Robert Pittenger (R)..................... 1368
10. Patrick McHenry (R).................... 1371
11. Mark Meadows (R)....................... 1375
12. Alma Adams (D)........................... 1378
13. George Holding (R)...................... 1380

NORTH DAKOTA 1383
Gov. Jack Dalrymple (R) 1387

x   **Contents**

SENATORS
John Hoeven (R)...................................... 1389
Heidi Heitkamp (D) 1392

REPRESENTATIVE-AT-LARGE, (1R)
Kevin Cramer (R)................................. 1395

OHIO 1398
Gov. John Kasich (R) 1404

SENATORS
Sherrod Brown (D) 1406
Rob Portman (R)................................... 1410

REPRESENTATIVES, (12R, 4D)
1. Steve Chabot (R)........................... 1414
2. Brad Wenstrup (R)...................... 1417
3. Joyce Beatty (D) 1420
4. Jim Jordan (R) 1423
5. Bob Latta (R)............................... 1426
6. Bill Johnson (R) 1429
7. Bob Gibbs (R) 1432
8. John Boehner (R) 1435
9. Marcy Kaptur (D) 1441
10. Mike Turner (R) 1444
11. Marcia Fudge (D) 1447
12. Pat Tiberi (R)............................... 1450
13. Tim Ryan (D)................................ 1453
14. David Joyce (R) 1456
15. Steve Stivers (R) 1459
16. Jim Renacci (R) 1461

OKLAHOMA 1465
Gov. Mary Fallin (R)............................. 1469

SENATORS
James Inhofe (R) 1471
James Lankford (R)............................... 1474

REPRESENTATIVES, (5R)
1. Jim Bridenstine (R) 1476
2. Markwayne Mullin (R) 1479
3. Frank Lucas (R) 1482
4. Tom Cole (R)................................ 1485
5. Steve Russell (R)......................... 1489

OREGON 1492
Gov. Kate Brown (D) 1496

SENATORS
Ron Wyden (D)..................................... 1498
Jeff Merkley (D) 1502

REPRESENTATIVES, (1R, 4D)
1. Suzanne Bonamici (D) 1505
2. Greg Walden (R)......................... 1508
3. Earl Blumenauer (D).................. 1511
4. Peter DeFazio (D)....................... 1514
5. Kurt Schrader (D)....................... 1517

PENNSYLVANIA 1521
Gov. Tom Wolf (D) 1527

SENATORS
Robert Casey Jr. (D) 1528
Pat Toomey (R) 1532

REPRESENTATIVES, (13R, 5D)
1. Robert Brady (D)......................... 1536
2. Chaka Fattah (D) 1539
3. Mike Kelly (R) 1542
4. Scott Perry (R)........................... 1545
5. Glenn Thompson (R) 1548
6. Ryan Costello (R) 1551
7. Pat Meehan (R) 1553
8. Mike Fitzpatrick (R) 1556
9. Bill Shuster (R) 1559
10. Tom Marino (R)........................... 1562
11. Lou Barletta (R) 1565
12. Keith Rothfus (R) 1567
13. Brendan Boyle (D) 1570
14. Mike Doyle (D) 1572
15. Charlie Dent (R)......................... 1575
16. Joe Pitts (R)................................ 1578
17. Matt Cartwright (D) 1580
18. Tim Murphy (R) 1583

RHODE ISLAND................ 1586
Gov. Gina Raimondo (D) 1590

SENATORS
Jack Reed (D) 1592
Sheldon Whitehouse (D) 1595

REPRESENTATIVES, (2D)
1. David Cicilline (D) 1599
2. Jim Langevin (D) 1602

SOUTH CAROLINA............ 1605
Gov. Nikki Haley (R) 1610

SENATORS
Lindsey Graham (R)............................. 1613
Tim Scott (R) 1617

REPRESENTATIVES, (6R, 1D)
1. Mark Sanford (R) 1620
2. Joe Wilson (R) 1624
3. Jeff Duncan (R) 1627
4. Trey Gowdy (R) 1629
5. Mick Mulvaney (R) 1633
6. James Clyburn (D)....................... 1636
7. Tom Rice (R)................................ 1640

SOUTH DAKOTA 1643
Gov. Dennis Daugaard (R) 1648

SENATORS
John Thune (R)..................................... 1650
Mike Rounds (R)................................... 1654

REPRESENTATIVE-AT-LARGE, (1R)
Kristi Noem (R) 1656

TENNESSEE 1659
Gov. Bill Haslam (R)........................... 1664

SENATORS
Lamar Alexander (R) 1667
Bob Corker (R).................................. 1671

REPRESENTATIVES, (7R, 2D)
  1. Phil Roe (R) 1675
  2. John Duncan (R) 1678
  3. Charles Fleischmann (R)............ 1681
  4. Scott DesJarlais (R) 1684
  5. Jim Cooper (D) 1687
  6. Diane Black (R)........................... 1690
  7. Marsha Blackburn (R) 1693
  8. Stephen Fincher (R).................... 1696
  9. Steve Cohen (D) 1698

TEXAS 1702
Gov. Greg Abbott (R) 1710

SENATORS
John Cornyn (R) 1712
Ted Cruz (R) 1717

REPRESENTATIVES, (25R, 11D)
  1. Louie Gohmert (R) 1720
  2. Ted Poe (R) 1723
  3. Sam Johnson (R)........................ 1726
  4. John Ratcliffe (R) 1729
  5. Jeb Hensarling (R)...................... 1731
  6. Joe Barton (R) 1735
  7. John Culberson (R)..................... 1738
  8. Kevin Brady (R) 1741
  9. Al Green (D) 1744
 10. Michael McCaul (R) 1747
 11. Mike Conaway (R)....................... 1750
 12. Kay Granger (R) 1754
 13. Mac Thornberry (R) 1757
 14. Randy Weber (R) 1760
 15. Rubén Hinojosa (D)..................... 1763
 16. Beto O'Rourke (D) 1766
 17. Bill Flores (R)............................. 1769
 18. Sheila Jackson Lee (D) 1772
 19. Randy Neugebauer (R) 1775
 20. Joaquin Castro (D)...................... 1778
 21. Lamar Smith (R).......................... 1781
 22. Pete Olson (R) 1784
 23. Will Hurd (R).............................. 1787
 24. Kenny Marchant (R).................... 1790
 25. Roger Williams (R)...................... 1792
 26. Michael Burgess (R).................... 1795
 27. Blake Farenthold (R) 1798
 28. Henry Cuellar (D) 1801
 29. Gene Green (D) 1804
 30. Eddie Bernice Johnson (D)......... 1807
 31. John Carter (R) 1810

 32. Pete Sessions (R)........................ 1812
 33. Marc Veasey (D)......................... 1816
 34. Filemon Vela (D) 1819
 35. Lloyd Doggett (D)........................ 1821
 36. Brian Babin (R)........................... 1824

UTAH................................. 1828
Gov. Gary Herbert (R) 1833

SENATORS
Orrin Hatch (R) 1835
Mike Lee (R) 1839

REPRESENTATIVES, (4R)
  1. Rob Bishop (R) 1842
  2. Chris Stewart (R)....................... 1845
  3. Jason Chaffetz (R)...................... 1848
  4. Mia Love (R)............................... 1852

VERMONT 1855
Gov. Peter Shumlin (D) 1859

SENATORS
Patrick Leahy (D).............................. 1862
Bernie Sanders (I).............................. 1866

REPRESENTATIVE-AT-LARGE, (1D)
Peter Welch (D).................................. 1871

VIRGINIA...........................1874
Gov. Terry McAuliffe (D) 1879

SENATORS
Mark Warner (D)................................ 1882
Tim Kaine (D).................................... 1886

REPRESENTATIVES, (8R, 3D)
  1. Rob Wittman (R) 1889
  2. Scott Rigell (R) 1892
  3. Bobby Scott (D) 1895
  4. Randy Forbes (R) 1898
  5. Robert Hurt (R).......................... 1901
  6. Bob Goodlatte (R)....................... 1903
  7. Dave Brat (R) 1907
  8. Don Beyer (D)............................. 1909
  9. Morgan Griffith (R) 1912
 10. Barbara Comstock (R) 1915
 11. Gerald Connolly (D).................... 1917

WASHINGTON................... 1921
Gov. Jay Inslee (D)............................. 1926

SENATORS
Patty Murray (D)................................ 1928
Maria Cantwell (D) 1932

REPRESENTATIVES, (4R, 6D)
  1. Suzan DelBene (D)...................... 1936
  2. Rick Larsen (D).......................... 1939
  3. Jaime Herrera Beutler (R) 1942
  4. Dan Newhouse (R) 1945
  5. Cathy McMorris Rodgers (R) 1947

6. Derek Kilmer (D) 1950
7. Jim McDermott (D).................... 1953
8. Dave Reichert (R)...................... 1956
9. Adam Smith (D)......................... 1959
10. Denny Heck (D).......................... 1962

WEST VIRGINIA................. 1965
Gov. Earl Ray Tomblin (D) 1969

SENATORS
Joe Manchin (D) 1971
Shelley Moore Capito (R).................... 1975

REPRESENTATIVES, (3R)
1. David McKinley (R) 1976
2. Alex Mooney (R)........................ 1979
3. Evan Jenkins (R) 1982

WISCONSIN 1985
Gov. Scott Walker (R) 1990

SENATORS
Ron Johnson (R) 1994
Tammy Baldwin (D)............................ 1997

REPRESENTATIVES, (5R, 3D)
1. Paul Ryan (R) 1999
2. Mark Pocan (D)........................... 2004
3. Ron Kind (D) 2006
4. Gwen Moore (D) 2009

5. Jim Sensenbrenner (R).............. 2012
6. Glenn Grothman (R).................. 2016
7. Sean Duffy (R)........................... 2018
8. Reid Ribble (R).......................... 2021

WYOMING......................... 2025
Gov. Matt Mead (R) 2029

SENATORS
Michael Enzi (R)................................. 2031
John Barrasso (R)............................... 2033

REPRESENTATIVE-AT-LARGE, (1R)
Cynthia Lummis (R) 2036

THE INSULAR TERRITORIES

AMERICAN SAMOA 2039
Aumua Amata Coleman
Radewagen (R) 2040

GUAM 2041
Madeleine Bordallo (D)....................... 2042

NORTHERN MARIANA ISLANDS..... 2043
Gregorio Kilili Camacho Sablan (D) ... 2045

PUERTO RICO 2046
Pedro Pierluisi (D).............................. 2048

VIRGIN ISLANDS 2048
Stacey Plaskett (D) 2050

GUIDE TO USAGE

The following guide explains the information sources used by *The Almanac of American Politics*. Major sources of information include the U.S. Census Bureau, Ballotpedia, the Center for Responsive Politics, *The Cook Political Report* and the Almanac's writers and researchers. The 2016 *Almanac* offers significant updates from the previous edition of the book, published in 2013. Figures released by the Census Bureau may vary slightly from those used by the Almanac due to different methods of data aggregation or tabulation. Percentages used in the book may not add up to 100% because of rounding.

Biography

This section lists the date each governor, senator, and representative was elected or appointed, the date and place of birth, academic degrees earned, religion, marital status, and, if applicable, spouse's name and number of children. Also provided is a brief outline of the subject's past elected offices, professional career and military service, and office addresses, telephone numbers, and websites. Committee and subcommittee assignments are current as of May 2015. (Note: On many committees, the chairman and ranking minority member are ex officio members of subcommittees. Leaders in the House typically do not serve on committees.

Vote Ratings

Group Ratings: The congressional ratings by 10 interest groups provide insight into a legislator's general ideology and the degree to which he or she reflects the group's point of view. Some organizations provided just one rating for 2013 and 2014, the two sessions of the 113th Congress.

ADA: Americans for Democratic Action
   Liberal: Since its founding in 1947, ADA has pushed for less defense spending and greater protection of civil liberties and human rights. The ADA selects 20 key votes a year for its analysis.

ACLU: American Civil Liberties Union
   Pro-individual liberties: ACLU seeks to protect individuals from what it views as legal, executive, and congressional infringements on civil liberties. The ACLU compiles a combined score for each two-year Congress. (C = Combined)

AFL-CIO: American Federation of Labor Congress of Industrial Organizations
   Liberal labor: The AFL-CIO is a federation of 56 unions representing some 12.5 million members that advocates for social and economic justice and improved working conditions through collective bargaining. Its analysis is based on roll call votes in 2013. Its 2014 analysis was not available at press time.

LCV: League of Conservation Voters
   Environmental: Formed in 1970, LCV is the arm of the environmental movement that works to elect pro-environmental protection candidates to Congress. LCV ratings are based on key votes on energy, environment, and natural resources legislation in 2013 and 2014.

ITI: Information Technology Industry Council
   High-tech industry: ITI represents the leading U.S. providers of information technology products and services. It compiles a combined score for each two-year Congress. (C = Combined)

COC: U.S. Chamber of Commerce
   Pro-business: Founded in 1912, COC represents local, regional, and state chambers of commerce in addition to trade and professional organizations. It promotes free market policies and ranks members of Congress for key business votes.

HAFA: Heritage Action for America
   Conservative: HAFA advocates for conservative policies, many of which are developed by its sister organization, the Heritage Foundation. Key votes in this rating encompass a broad range of conservative issues. It compiles a combined score for each two-year Congress. (C = Combined)

ACU: American Conservative Union

Conservative: Since 1971, ACU ratings have provided a means of gauging the conservatism of members of Congress on foreign policy, social, and budget issues. Its scores are annual.

CFG: Club for Growth

Pro-tax limitation: CFG supports limited government, lower taxes, and policies it deems favorable to economic growth. CFG's annual ratings are based on key votes on taxes, trade, and the economy.

FRC: Family Research Council

Social conservative: The FRC promotes traditional marriage and family and advocates for policies that uphold Judeo-Christian values. Its annual ratings are based on votes on abortion and family issues. It compiles a combined score for each two-year Congress. (C = Combined)

National Journal Ratings

National Journal's rating system is a method of analyzing congressional voting. Every year, the magazine compiles a list of congressional roll call votes and classifies them as economic, social, or foreign policy-related. The votes in each issue area are subjected to a principal-components analysis, a statistical procedure designed to determine the degree to which each vote resembles other votes in the same category (the same members of Congress tending to vote together). The analysis also reveals which "yea" votes correlated with which "nay" votes within each issue area (members voting yea on certain issues tended to vote nay on others). The yea and nay positions on each roll call are then identified as conservative or liberal. Each roll call vote is assigned a weight from one (lowest) to three (highest), based on the degree to which it correlates with other votes in the same issue area. A higher weight means that vote is more strongly correlated with other votes and is therefore a better test of economic, social, or foreign policy ideology. Members of Congress who participate in at least half of the votes in an area receive ratings. Members who miss more than half the votes are not scored (shown as *). Absences and abstentions are not counted.

Members of Congress are then ranked according to relative liberalism and conservatism. Finally, they are assigned percentiles showing their rank relative to others in the chamber. The liberal percentage score means that the member's votes were more liberal than that percentage of his or her colleagues' votes in that issue area in the year indicated. The conservative score means that the member's votes were more conservative than that percentage of his or her colleagues' votes in that issue area. The composite score is an average of a member's three issue-based scores. *National Journal* did not conduct an analysis of 2014 roll call votes.

Key Votes

The key votes section presents the positions of Senators and House members on important issues. The following key votes, selected by the Almanac staff, took place during the 113th Congress (2013-14). There are 12 votes in the Senate and 12 votes in the House, which are split among economic, foreign policy, and social issues. A member who was absent or declined to vote receives NV for "not voting." The letter P signifies a vote of "present." No listings are provided for members who were not in office at the time. Roll-call data were obtained from www.thomas.com, which receives information from the Clerk of the House and Secretary of the Senate.

Senate Votes

- **Sandy storm spending:** (Senate Vote 4, HR 152) A bill to provide about $50 billion for communities that suffered from Superstorm Sandy in October 2012. Jan. 28, 2013. Passed 62-36. (D: 52-0; R: 9-36; I: 1-0)
- **Chuck Hagel Confirmation:** (Senate Vote 24) Confirmation of Chuck Hagel of Nebraska to be Secretary of Defense. Feb. 26, 2013. Approved 58-41. (D: 52-0; R: 4-41; I: 2-0)
- **Gun Background Checks:** (Senate Vote 97, S 649) Amendment to expand the background check system to include firearms purchased at gun shows or on the Internet. April 17, 2013. Defeated 54-46. (60 votes were required for approval. D: 48-5; R: 4-41; I: 2-0)

- **Immigration Reform:** (Senate Vote 168, S 744) A bill to overhaul U.S. immigration policies, including an incremental path to citizenship for most illegal immigrants in the nation. June 27, 2013. Passed 68-32. (D: 52-0; R: 14-32; I: 2-0)
- **Student Loan Rates:** (Senate Vote 185, HR 1911) A bill to adjust federal student loan interest rates after July 1, 2013. July 24, 2013. Passed 81-18. (D: 35-16; R: 45-1; I: 1-1)
- **Employee Non-discrim'n Act:** (Senate Vote 232, S 815) A bill to prohibit employers and other organizations from discriminating against employees or applicants on the basis of their sexual orientation or gender identity. Nov. 7, 2013. Passed 64-32. (D: 52-0; R: 10-32; I: 2-0)
- **Senate Vote on Judgeships:** (Senate Vote 242) Judgment on a ruling of the Senate presiding officer on a point of order to that cloture motions on most nominations are subject to a majority vote. Nov. 21, 2013. Rejected 48-52. (D: 3-50; R: 45-0; I: 0-2)
- **Defense Dept. Spending:** (Senate Vote 245, S 1197) Cloture motion on a bill to set Pentagon spending limits for Fiscal 2014. Nov. 21, 2013. Defeated 51-44. (60 votes required for approval. D: 49-2; R: 0-46; I: 2-0)
- **Bipartisan Budget Deal:** (Senate Vote 281, H.J. Res 59) A resolution to increase spending caps in Fiscal 2014 and 2015 for domestic and defense spending. Dec. 18, 2013. Passed 64-36. (D: 53-0; R: 9-36; I: 2-0)
- **Farm Bill Conference Rept.:** (Senate Vote 21, HR 2642) Conference report to reauthorize most farm and nutrition programs through 2018. Feb. 4, 2014. Passed 68-32. (D: 44-9; R: 22-23; I: 2-0)
- **Unempl. Comp. Extension:** (Senate Vote 101, HR 3979) A bill to extend eligibility for expanded unemployment benefits through May 2014. April 7, 2014. Passed 59-38. (D: 51-0; R: 6-38; I: 2-0)
- **Keystone Pipeline:** (Senate Vote 280, S 2280) A bill to expedite construction and maintenance of the Keystone XL pipeline without further Executive Branch review. Nov. 18, 2014. Defeated 59-41. (60 votes were required for approval. D: 14-39; R: 45-0; I: 0-2)

House Votes

- **Sandy storm spending:** (House Vote, 23, HR 152) A bill to provide about $50 billion for communities that suffered from Superstorm Sandy in October 2012. Jan. 15, 2013. Passed 241-180. (R: 49-179; D: 192-1)
- **Violence Against Women Act:** (House Vote 55, S 47) A bill to reauthorize the Violence Against Women Act, with additional protections to victims of domestic violence, sexual assault and stalking. Feb. 28, 2013. Passed 286-138. (R: 87-138; D: 199-0)
- **Guantanamo Bay Detainees:** (House Vote 185, HR 4486) An amendment to permit prisoners at Guantanamo Bay Cuba to be house at a facility in the United States. April 30, 2014. Defeated 168-249. (R: 4-221; D: 164-28)
- **Abortion 20-week ban:** (House Vote 251, HR 1797) A bill to ban abortions after 20 weeks, with limited exceptions. June 18, 2013. Passed 228-196. (R: 222-6; D: 6-190)
- **Medical Marijuana:** (House Vote 258, HR 4660) An amendment to prohibit the Justice Department from preventing states to implement their laws on the use, distribution, possession or cultivation of medical marijuana. May 30, 2014. Passed 219-189. (R: 49-172; D: 170-17)
- **Farm Bill:** (House Vote 286, HR 1947) A bill to reauthorize most farm and nutrition programs through 2018. June 20, 2013. Defeated 195-234. (R: 171-62; D: 24-172)
- **Afghanistan Combat:** (House Vote 332, HR 4870) An amendment to prohibit funds to conduct combat operations in Afghanistan after December 2014. June 20, 2014. Defeated 153-260. (R: 20-207; D: 133-53)
- **NSA Phone Data Collection:** (House Vote 412, HR 2397) An amendment to restrict funds to execute court orders under the Foreign Intelligence Surveillance Act that pertain to individuals. July 24, 2013. Defeated 205-217. (R: 94-134; D: 111-83)
- **Syrian Rebels Training:** (House Vote 507, H.J. Res 124) An amendment to authorize the Defense Department to train and equip Syrian rebels to secure territory controlled by the Syrian opposition and to defend against the Islamic State. Sept. 17, 2014. Passed 273-156. (R: 159-71; D: 114-85)
- **Keystone pipeline:** (House Vote 519, HR 5682) A bill to expedite construction and maintenance of the Keystone XL pipeline without further Executive Branch review. Nov. 14, 2014 Passed 252-161. (R: 221-0; D: 31-161)

- **Immigration Exec. Action:** (House Vote 550, HR 5759) A bill to prohibit the Executive Branch from failing to deport immigrants who are unlawfully in the United States. December 4, 2014. Passed 219-197. (R: 216-7; D: 3-190)
- **Bipartisan budget deal:** (House Vote 640, H.J. Res 59) A resolution to increase spending caps in Fiscal 2014 and 2015 for domestic and defense spending. Dec. 12, 2013. Passed 332-94. (R: 169-62; D: 163-32)

NOTE: Freshman members of the House, because they took office in January 2015, do not have key votes or vote scores from the interest groups and *National Journal* for the 113th Congress (2013-14). Freshman senators have vote scores if they served in the House. Freshmen who won in a special election to fill a vacancy may have some key votes and vote scores from some interest groups.

Election Results

The most recent election results are listed for senators and governors. For House members, the results are from the 2014 primary and general elections, as well as any runoffs in 2014 or special elections held since November 2014. Candidates in primaries receiving less than 5% (before rounding) of the total vote and candidates in general elections receiving less than 2% (before rounding) of the total were excluded. Election results were supplied by Ballotpedia and Secretary of State websites.

Prior Winning Percentages: The incumbent's winning percentages in earlier elections.

Campaign Finance

Campaign finance data in the *Almanac* were provided by the non-profit, non partisan Center for Responsive Politics, the leading campaign finance watch-dog and research organization based in Washington D.C. The campaign spending data for federal candidates are based on information reported to the Federal Election Commission. The first column of information following the percentage of the vote that the candidate received in the general election represents the amount of money that the candidate's campaign spent in that election cycle (two years for House candidates and six years for Senate candidates). The second column of information shows what outside entities—Super Pacs, social welfare 501(c)(4) organizations, trade associations, unions, political parties, corporations, individuals or other groups—spent *on behalf* of that candidate in that election cycle. The third column shows what outside entities spent *against* that candidate. The spending figures cited are what outside entities were required to report to the FEC; it may not account for all the outside money spent in a race, because some outside spending is not subject to federal campaign finance disclosure rules. Spending figures of less than $1,000 are not included in this section.

Demographics

Population: Figures are from the 2013 American Community Survey (ACS) one-year estimates reported by the U.S. Census Bureau.

Urban/suburban/rural population: Figures are based on an analysis of population counts for zip-code tabulation areas (ZCTAs) from the 2012 ACS. This analysis used a traditional definition of urbanity based on the principal cities and counties assigned by the federal government to Metropolitan Statistical Area (MSAs). Each zip code in a congressional district was coded as urban, suburban or rural based on the place name of the post office associated with that zip code. A zip code with the place name of a principal city of an MSA was defined as urban; zip codes located in a county within an MSA but not in a principal city were defined as suburban, and zip codes not located in a county assigned to an MSA were defined as rural. Figures in this section are not based on numbers reported by the U.S. Census Bureau, which does not offer any data on suburban population.

Land area: Size of district in square miles, excluding water.

Born in state: Percent of entire population of the district that was born in the state in which that district is located.

Race and ethnicity: Figures are from the 2012 ACS reported by the Census Bureau. As defined by the Census Bureau, race reflects individual respondents' perception of their racial identity. Latino origin is defined as an ethnicity. The Census Bureau initially reports data for whites, blacks, and other racial groups that include both Latinos and non-Latinos, but traditionally will follow this initial report with figures that breaks racial and ethnic data into results that are more useful for political analysis. As a result, the 2016 version of the Almanac uses the following definitions:

White refers to people who describe their race as white and who say they are not of Latino ancestry or descent.

Black refers to people who describe their race as black or African-American and who say they are not of Latino ancestry or descent.

Latino refers to people who say they are of Latino or Hispanic ancestry, regardless of how they answer questions about their racial identity.

Asian refers to people who describe their race as Asian and who say they are not of Latino ancestry or descent.

Amer. Indian refers to people who describe their race as American Indian or Alaska Native and who say they are not of Latino ancestry or descent.

Pac. Island refers to people who describe their race as black or Native Hawaiian or "other Pacific Islander" and who say they are not of Latino ancestry or descent.

Two races refer to people who choose more than one racial category (white, black, Asian, American Indian or Pacific Islander) to describe themselves. This does not include people who describe themselves as Latino.

Only the top four racial and ethnic groups in each district (or state) are displayed, as well as the number who choose more than one race. For the nation, more categories on race and ethnicity are included. This information is based on the 2013 ACS survey.

White Ethnic: The Census Bureau asks respondents to describe their ethnic ancestry and lists over 30 countries or regions of origin. "White Ethnic" refers to the number of people in each district who describe themselves as Irish, Italian, Polish, Hungarian, Lithuanian, Ukrainian, Czech, Slovak, Russian, Greek, French (except Basque), French-Canadian and Portuguese.

Education: *H.S. grad or less* refers to people who did not attend college. *Some college* refers to people who attended college but did not receive a diploma, or who received an associate's degree but not a bachelor's degree. *College degree, 4 yr.* refers to people who received a bachelor's degree but did not receive a graduate or professional degree after attending college. *Post-grad study* refers to people who received a graduate or professional degree. All groups are a percentage of people 25 years and older.

Veterans/active duty: This category includes both men and women in the civilian population who served in the U.S. military and men and women currently employed in the U.S. armed forces.

Median income: This figure represents the median income (not the average income) for all households in the congressional district (or state) for 2013. The numbers in parentheses immediately below indicates where the district ranks among all 435 districts, with the richest district indicated by *(1 of 435)* and the poorest by *(435 of 435)*.

Income: Each category represents the number of households in each district (or state) with a reported income that fell within that bracket in 2013.

Poverty rate: This figure indicates the poverty rate computed by the Census Bureau for 2013 for each district using the definition outlined in the Office of Management and Budget's (OMB) Statistical Policy Directive 14.

Work: The Census Bureau asks all respondents over the age of 16 who are employed in the civilian workforce about their occupation and assigns each respondent to one of five occupation codes defined by the federal government. *White collar* refers to civilian workers assigned to the category titled "Management, Business, Science and Arts occupations." *Blue collar* refers to workers assigned to two categories: "Natural Resources, Construction and Maintenance occupations" and "Production, Transportation and Material Moving occupations." *Sales and service* refers to workers assigned to the final two categories: "Service occupations" and "Sales and Office occupations."

Govt. workers: This category shows the percentage of respondents over the age of 16 who are employed in the civilian government workforce.

Language: This is percentage of households in the nation speaking a certain language as a percentage of people 5 years and older. The abbreviation *other European* refers to other Indo-European languages.

Place of Birth: The Census asks people if they are native or foreign born, and if they currently reside in the state in which they were born or if they were born in a different state.

Foreign-born Citizenship Status: This category shows the percentage of foreign-born residents in the U.S. who are citizens.

Region of Foreign Born: This category shows the regions of the world where foreign-born residents were born.

Other Data

Voter Turnout Box: The shares of the total estimated citizen voting age population that voted in the 2014 congressional election in a district and the 2012 presidential election in the district. Cook Political Report House Editor David Wasserman compiled the election data. The authors did the calculation. In Congressional races in Florida and Oklahoma, the Secretary of State website does not report election results for House candidates who run unopposed, and thus no turnout figure can be calculated. For states, 2014 election data for the turnout ratio is based on the statewide race with the highest voter turnout compiled by United States Elections Project.

Legislature: A breakdown of the membership of the state's legislature by party affiliation compiled by Ballotpedia. Figures reflect the partisan tally in June 2015. An "I" stands for independent, a "V" means there was a vacancy.

Congress Line-Up: A breakdown of the House delegation by party affiliation, based on the 2014 and 2012 election results.

Presidential Vote Box: This estimates the presidential vote by congressional district from information that Polidata, a Virginia-based political statistics and demographics firm, collects from state and local election offices. Some states readily provide district-level presidential vote data. By necessity, other results are aggregated from precinct-level returns. Voting data from districts with split precincts and centrally counted absentee votes should be considered estimates; the allocation of these unassigned votes is determined by Polidata. The 2008 presidential results by congressional district are extrapolations showing how the district would have voted for president that year if the current, post-2010 census boundaries had been in place. This information was used in the 2014 edition of the *Almanac*.

Cook Partisan Voting Index: Developed in 1997 by political analyst Charlie Cook, the partisan voting index (PVI) is designed to provide an overall assessment of a state or congressional district's generic partisan strength. The PVI measures a state or district's recent partisan performance at the presidential level (district value) against that of the nation as a whole (national value). For this volume, the calculations are based on an average of 2008 and 2012 presidential election data for each district, based on the congressional district boundaries that were in place in November 2012. Both years carry equal weight. Only votes for major party nominees are considered. The national Democratic value is roughly 52.8% (an average of Barack Obama's 53.7% share in 2008 and 52% share in 2012) and the national Republican value is about 47.2%. Thus, if Obama won an average of 57.8% of the two-party vote in a given district, the district's PVI would be D+5, because it voted 5 percentage points more Democratic than the national average. A PVI value of "even" indicates an evenly balanced district.

Abbreviations

ACLU	American Civil Liberties Union	IAP	Independent American Party (NV)
ACU	American Conservative Union	IC	Independent Conservative
ADA	Americans for Democratic Action	ID	Independent Democrat
AFDC	Aid to Families with Dependent Children	IG	Independent Green
		Ind	Independence Party
AFL-CIO	American Federation of Labor and Congress of Industrial Organizations	ITI	Information Technology Industry Council
AID	Agency for International Development	IVP	Independent Voters Party
		LCV	League of Conservation Voters
ANWR	Arctic National Wildlife Refuge	LHOB	Longworth House Office Building
BL	Better Life Party	Lib	Libertarian Party
C	Conservative Party (NY)	Mod	Moderate Party
CAFE	Corporate Average Fuel Economy	NAFTA	North American Free Trade Agreement
CAFTA	Central America Free Trade Agreement	NARAL	NARAL Pro-Choice America
CFG	Club for Growth	NL	Natural Law Party
CHMN	Chairman	NP	Non-Partisan
CHOB	Cannon House Office Building	NPA	No Party Affiliation
CIA	Central Intelligence Agency	NRCC	National Republican Congressional Committee
CNP	Constitution Party		
COC	United States Chamber of Commerce	NRSC	National Republican Senatorial Committee
COLA	Cost of Living Adjustment		
D	Democratic Party	NSA	National Security Agency
DCCC	Democratic Congressional Campaign Committee	NTU	National Taxpayers Union
		PF	Peace and Freedom Party
DCS	District of Columbia Statehood	PNP	New Progressive Party (PR) (Spanish: *Partido Nuevo Progresista*)
DFL	Democratic-Farmer-Labor Party (MN)		
DLC	Democratic Leadership Council	POP	Populist Party
DNC	Democratic National Committee	PPD	Popular Democratic Party (PR) (Spanish: *Partido Popular Democrático*)
DSCC	Democratic Senatorial Campaign Committee		
DSOB	Dirksen Senate Office Building	PRG	Progressive Party
EMILY	EMILY's List (Early Money is Like Yeast)	R	Republican Party
		Ref	Reform Party
ERISA	Employee Retirement Income Security Act	RHOB	Rayburn House Office Building
		RMM	Ranking Minority Member
FEC	Federal Election Commission	RNC	Republican National Committee
FERC	Federal Energy Regulatory Commission	RSOB	Russell Senate Office Building
		RTL	Right-to-Life Party
FRC	Family Research Council	S	Capitol Building Room (Senate side)
GOP	Republican Party (Grand Old Party)		
G	Green Party	SOC	Socialist Party
H	Capitol Building Room (House side)	SW	Socialist Workers Party
HAFA	Heritage Action for America	UAW	United Auto Workers
HSOB	Hart Senate Office Building	UMJ	United States Marijuana Party
I	Independent	WF	Working Families

The Shifting Politics of 2016, An Overview

By Charlie Cook

Every four years, we inevitably hear people say the upcoming presidential election will be "the most important in American history." Some of those expressing this sentiment are candidates or campaign staffers; at least for them, this may very well feel like "the most important election." With others, the statement is more a reflection of a frame of reference that may not reach very far back into American political history. The fact is, every presidential election is important; not just to Americans, but around the world.

Arguably, "open" presidential elections—those without an incumbent seeking re-election—take on larger importance, simply because sitting presidents usually win. Since the end of World War II, all eight incumbent presidents who sought re-election (who managed to avoid a significant challenge to their re-nomination) won. The three who lost, Presidents Gerald Ford in 1976 (who was not actually elected in his own right), Jimmy Carter in 1980 and George H.W. Bush in 1992, all had real challenges to their nominations from Ronald Reagan, Edward Kennedy and Pat Buchanan, respectively. So, an open presidential race presents more of a fork in the road for the country than an incumbent re-elect cycle.

Another reason why 2016 may be more interesting than many others is that this is likely to be a very close race. Since 1960, we have seen five of the eight closest presidential elections in American history take place. After the razor-thin Kennedy victory over Nixon in 1960, we have seen incredibly close races (ranked by percent-age margin of victory) in 2000, 1968, 1976, and 2004 (2012 was the 12th closest in American history). The increasingly polarized nature of our electorate almost ensures close elections at this point. Each of the two major parties has a relatively narrow trading range in terms of support, high floors and low ceilings.

Through the first half of 2015 it appeared that both major parties were behaving contrary to their recent tendencies. Republicans typically have had a fight, perhaps even a big fight, prior to finally choosing whoever's turn it is to be the next GOP nominee. In a very hierarchical fashion, they typically nominate either the sitting president, a current or former vice president, one of the top runners-up in the immediate past presidential nomination fight, the commanding general of the most recently fought world war, or the son of a former president. With the nomination of Sen. Barry Goldwater in 1964 the notable exception to this rule, there has been a certain amount of deference to the party establishment in nomination decisions. If Republicans behave the way they normally do, there will be an intra-party fight, and eventually former Florida Gov. Jeb Bush will win the GOP nomination.

Typically, unless there is a popular incumbent seeking re-election, Democrats have a real donnybrook on their hands, with resulting nomination outcomes only about half the time what one might have predicted two years prior to the convention. At press time it might be changing, but up until mid-summer 2015, it seemed that while Democrats may or may not have been falling in love with former Secretary of State Hillary Clinton, at a minimum they were falling in line behind her. At least early on, it certainly appeared that Democrats were behaving more like Republicans historically have.

Conversely, Republicans seem to be acting more like Democrats traditionally have behaved. While Jeb Bush may still win the GOP nomination, he has encountered considerable resistance, indeed ideological headwinds far stronger than what his father or brother experienced or than many anticipated as well as a bit of Bush Fatigue, akin to the Clinton Fatigue that we are seeing as well. A strong and growing outsider, angry, anti-establishment, anti-politician mood began taking hold in the GOP, thrusting businessman Donald Trump into first place in both national and early state polling and boosting Dr. Ben Carson. We obviously saw some of those sentiments during the 2012 GOP nomination fight as well. Bush's nomination is far from the sure thing that many assumed a year or two earlier. With arguably the largest field of Republican contenders in history, and little deference paid earlier to Bush (i.e. the GOP nominee who most likely fits the traditional GOP nomination pattern) at this point, Republicans seemed to be behaving the way Democrats normally do while Democrats suddenly began behaving more like Democrats again. This will be fascinating to watch and a surprisingly volatile situation in both parties.

However, as anyone reading the *Almanac of American Politics* already appreciates, presidential elections are far from the only elections of importance. The party controlling the House or holding a majority in the Senate, and the strength and durability of those majorities, are just as significant. Stalemate is too often the current status quo in Washington, which has resulted in a great deal of power devolving to the state capitals, where governors and state legislatures are forced to resolve critical issues. In short, there is a lot that is important and necessary to pay attention to beyond the presidential race.

There is also a natural tendency among people looking at a presidential race, and even at down-ballot elections, to focus immediately on the personalities and images of the best-known candidates. Unfortunately, and too often, the conversation never moves beyond that. While public perceptions of a candidate are certainly important, it's better to start off by examining the fundamental factors and forces that, independent of said candidate, have a great impact on the outcome of each election. I would suggest, as a start, looking at these elections from the top down, beginning at 50,000 feet with those over-arching dynamics before gradually getting to the ground level, where the hand-to-hand combat in American politics takes place.

Vast Majority of Voters are Already 'Baked into the Cake'

A few electoral observations are in order. First, consider that the vast majority of voters in general elections are not truly "up for grabs." Historically, roughly 90 percent of people who consider themselves Democrats routinely vote for Democratic candidates, just as 90 percent of those who call themselves Republicans can be counted upon to vote reliably for GOP candidates.

According to Edison Research's 2012 national exit poll for the five networks and the Associated Press, 92 percent of self-described Democrats voted for President Obama with the same percentage voting for the Democratic candidate for the House. On the other side, 93 percent of self-identified Republicans cast their ballots for Mitt Romney and 94 percent for the GOP candidate for the House in their district.

In 1992, during an unusual three-way contest between President George H.W. Bush, Arkansas Gov. Bill Clinton, and businessman H. Ross Perot, 73 percent of Republicans voted for Bush, and 77 percent of Democrats voted for Clinton. Since then, in 1996, Clinton pulled 84 percent of the vote among Democrats while Sen. Robert Dole won 80 percent of the vote from Republicans. In that 2000 cliffhanger election, Vice President Al Gore carried 86 percent of the vote from Democrats. Texas Gov. George W. Bush did even better, winning 90 percent of the vote of self-described Republicans. Four years later, with Bush running for re-election, he pulled 93 percent of his fellow Republicans while Sen. John Kerry received 89 percent of the vote among Democrats. In 2008, Sens. Barack Obama and John McCain carride 89 and 90 percent of their fellow party members, respectively. There is little uncertainty in how most partisans cast their ballots.

Exit polls have shown that the proportion of voters identifying themselves as independents have ranged in the last six presidential elections from as low as 26 percent in 1996 and 2004, to 29 percent in 2008 and 2012. But, even most of those who call themselves independents do not actually behave that independently. According to the American National Election Study (a series of national surveys supervised by political scientists led by the University of Michigan and Stanford University taken immediately before and after presidential elections), 87 percent of independents who, when pushed, conceded they feel closer to the Democratic Party voted for President Obama in 2012. The same percentage of independents who say they felt closer to the Republican Party cast their ballot for Romney the same year. In 2008, Obama captured 91 percent of the Democratic-leaning independents, while McCain won 82 percent of the Republican-leaning independents. Four years earlier, 88 percent of Democratic-leaning independents voted for Kerry, while 85 percent of Republican-leaning independents voted for President George W. Bush. Simply put, some people self-identify as independents but are, for all intents and purposes, partisans, voting almost as partisan as those who simply label themselves Democrats or Republicans.

"Pure" or "hard" independents, those who do not lean toward either party, made up only 5 percent of the 2012 electorate (they preferred Romney over Obama, 54 percent to 46 percent), according to the ANES survey. In 2008, these voters accounted for 6.5 percent of the electorate (breaking for Obama, 55 percent to 45 percent) and 5.5 percent in 2004 (siding with Kerry, 56 percent to 44 percent). Note that in two of those three elections, the pure independents actually favored the losing candidate—and in each case, against the incumbent party—reminding us that precisely who votes and the turnout percentage among partisans and partisan-leaning independents are awfully important.

Unfortunately, the exit polls taken on Election Day don't try to push independents to lean one direction (thus the dependence on the ANES on this question), but they can break out the ideology of independents. Independents who self-identify as liberal behave much like Democratic-leaning independents, while independents who call themselves conservative behave pretty much like Republican-leaning independents.

Pollsters often refer to "swing voters," though what exactly they mean varies from one survey-taker to another. Most include all self-identified independents—pure independents as well as partisan-leaners—along with "soft (or weak) Democrats" and "soft (or weak) Republicans" thrown in for good measure. Soft or weak partisans are those who identify with one party but, when asked if they consider themselves a "strong" Democrat or Republican, or a "not very strong" Democrat or Republican, choose the "not very strong" option. The ANES surveys show that even those "soft partisans" toe the line pretty closely: 86 percent of the weak Democrats voted for Kerry in 2004, with the same for Obama in 2008. Eighty-five percent were for Obama in 2012. Ninety percent of weak Republicans voted for Bush in 2004, 88 percent for McCain in 2008, with the same percentage for Romney in 2012.

In both presidential and congressional voting, there has been a general trend of greater partisan polarization as each party has become more ideologically cohesive. There are fewer moderate and conservative Democrats than in the days of Bill Clinton's presidency, just as there are fewer moderate and liberal Republicans as in those days as well. This diminished ideological diversity in each party translates into more straight-line voting. As a result, our system increasingly behaves in a more parliamentary manner, where the party is more important than the candidates. Turnout has become as or more important than persuasion.

Another overlooked fact is that the vast majority of voters make up their minds long before Election Day. The 2012 exit polls indicated 69 percent of voters made up their minds before September, 9 percent during September, 11 percent in October , only 6 percent "in the last few days" and just 3 percent on Election Day.

There are increasingly large proportions of voters who are effectively "baked into the cake" well before the candidates are selected and the campaigns are waged. The most meaningful voter variable is whether they show up to vote, although this is less of a factor in presidential election years when turnout is generally high and the electorate is broad, diverse and looks more or less like the country as a whole. In midterm election years, however, the participation rate is not only considerably lower but tends to be older, whiter, more conservative and more Republican. In recent years, this has yielded quite different results from balloting in presidential years. In this changing political landscape and increased polarization, it takes something pretty significant—for example, the unpopularity of the Iraq war in 2006—to turn midterm elections ugly for Republicans.

These patterns among voters are reflected in the membership of Congress as well. Ideological ratings of members of both the House and Senate now show that not a single Democrat in the House is more conservative than a single Republican in the chamber (and vice versa). The same is true in the Senate. This is partially the product of increasingly ideological primaries on each side; moderate to liberal Republicans are either no longer getting elected in the first place, or are eliminated in primaries when they seek higher office. In the same breath, moderate to conservative Democrats are increasingly winnowed out of races by primary challenges from the far left. The reality in Congress today is that most members on either side are more concerned about losing a primary to the extreme wings of their own party or simply having a tough primary than they are about losing the general election. General elections, however, have also taken their toll on centrists in both parties. When giant partisan waves hit, it is the moderates who usually pay the price in the general (if they make it that far), not the ideologues, who tend to represent safe districts and states and most often easily survive the general election.

Emory University political scientist Alan Abramowitz theorizes that partisan voters are motivated by opposition to candidates of the other party or contempt for the opposite party as much, if not more than, they are motivated by casting ballots in support of a specific candidate or affinity for their own party. It gives credence to the view that hate is often a stronger motivating force in politics than love.

2016 Presidential Election Footprint

Just as there are few swing voters, there are even fewer swing states. In reality, only a dozen states are decisive by Election Day. Democrats have won 18 states plus the District of Columbia in six consecutive elections, while Republicans have carried 13 states six times in a row. With 31 states plus D.C. consistently voting the same way in every election since 1992, there is a lot less uncertainty than some imagine; a state that has voted for one party six times in a row is very likely to vote that way a seventh time.

In recent presidential elections, the attention has generally centered on just a dozen states: Colorado, Florida, Iowa, Michigan, Minnesota, Nevada, New Hampshire, North Carolina, Ohio, Pennsylvania, Virginia and Wisconsin. Indiana made it a baker's dozen in 2008, voting Democratic for the first time since Lyndon Johnson's victory in 1964. Hoosiers returned to the GOP fold in 2012 and the state looks likely to stay there for the foreseeable future.

Narrowing it down even further, a case can be made that the 2016 election will depend on Republicans' ability to flip a handful of states Obama won by the slimmest of margins. In 2012, Obama won seven states with less than 53 percent of all major party votes: Colorado, Florida, Iowa, New Hampshire, Ohio, Pennsylvania and Virginia. Together, these states account for 99 Electoral College votes, far more than the 64 additional votes Republicans would need over 2012 to win a majority. Of these states, only Pennsylvania has voted for Democrats in the past six elections. Conversely, the only state that Republicans barely won in 2012 was North Carolina.

However, if Republicans were to flip only the states where Obama won less than 52 percent of all major party votes in 2012, they would tack on only Florida, Ohio and Virginia and win 60 additional Electoral votes, falling four short of an Electoral College majority. By rank order of Obama's 2012 margins, the next state in line would be Pennsylvania, perhaps making the Keystone State the "tipping point state" of the 2016 election, to borrow a term from political analyst Nate Silver. Colorado would be very close behind. Fundamentally, there is a very thin line between victory and defeat, and in a very close election, a split between the popular vote and the Electoral College, as occurred in 2000, is still possible. My colleague David Wasserman points out that Obama won just 690 out of 3,141 counties, 121 fewer than Michael Dukakis did in 1988 and that just three counties—Broward in Florida, Cuyahoga in Ohio and Philadelphia in Pennsylvania—provided Obama's victories in those three states and effectively tipped the election in his favor.

Just as "Deep Throat" told the Washington Post's Bob Woodward and Carl Bernstein to "follow the money" in the Watergate scandal, watching where money is being spent will tell you precisely which states are the most competitive in 2016. According to figures from political television ad-tracking firm Kantar Media CMAG, of the $896 million spent on broadcast television during the 2012 general election, 84 percent was spent in just seven states: Florida ($173 million), Virginia ($151 million), Ohio ($150 million), North Carolina ($97 million), Colorado ($73 million), Iowa ($57 million), and Nevada ($55 million). Strikingly, 53 percent of the total was spent in just three states: Florida, Virginia, and Ohio. The 2016 swing state footprint is not likely to be very different from the last one.

Key Dynamics for 2016

So, what are the dynamics going to be in the 2016 presidential election? Certainly, events here at home or abroad, of an economic or national security nature, could change the fundamental forces shaping the election. For the moment, it appears there are two main narratives competing for national dominance: "Time for a Change" versus "Changing American Demographics."

Time for a Change

There is considerable validity to the saying often (but not universally) attributed to Mark Twain, that "history does not repeat itself but it does rhyme." There are certain rhymes and rhythms to American politics. American voters tend to vote for change after one party has the White House for two consecutive terms. Since the end of World War II, a party has occupied the White House for two consecutive terms six times: in five out of six, that same party's bid for a third term failed.

In 1960, after eight years under Dwight Eisenhower, Americans voted Republicans out of the White House. They did the same to Democrats in 1968 after two terms under John Kennedy and Lyndon Johnson. Again in 1976, after eight years with Richard Nixon and Gerald

Ford, Americans opted for change. This pattern repeated itself in 2000 as well, after eight years of Bill Clinton, and again in 2008 after George W. Bush's two terms. During that period, voters granted a third term only in 1988, when President Ronald Reagan's job approval ratings were (unusually) high after eight years. In that case his vice president, George H.W. Bush, was able to prevail over Democratic Gov. Michael Dukakis of Massachusetts.

Five times out of six is a persuasive pattern. It makes sense that over eight years there can be an accumulation of voter grievances with the party in power. The lack of trust that many voters have with the political parties can potentially provide an incentive to kick a party out of power after eight years to prevent it from becoming too powerful or too complacent. It should be noted that four of those five elections (1960, 1968, 1976 and 2000) were among our closest presidential elections in history.

To a certain extent, the "time for a change" dynamic is a function of presidential job approval. Emory University's Abramowitz suggests that to the extent that a president has an approval rating below 50 percent at the end of eight years, it means the "time for a change" dynamic is strong. An approval rating of the sitting president over 50 percent, Abramowitz suggests, can indicate a weaker incentive for change. As a result, it is certainly worth keeping an eye on Obama's job approval rating between now and November 2016, even though his name will never again appear on a ballot. Events of domestic terrorism or civil unrest could fuel an even stronger change dynamic in 2016 as well.

But this time for a change dynamic should not just be seen in the partisan context of keeping Democrats in or throwing them out of the White House. The rise of the Tea Party movement in 2009 and 2010 that signaled important changes in the Republican Party, along with the deference to the mainstream and establishment leaders and the preference for stability and predictability having disappeared, there suddenly became a time for a change within the GOP as well. At the same time, the rise of the Occupy Wall Street movement and canonization of Sen. Elizabeth Warren became the most visible elements of a move to the left in the Democratic Party and a push-back against the centrist elements of the party and more business-friendly interests that led to Bill Clinton's election to the White House in 1992. Thus, the time for a change sentiment was becoming palpable within the Democratic Party as well.

A rise in populism, anger at the party establishments and hostility to Washington and career politicians have created a volatility that has made our politics even more turbulent than normal. They have fueled the early surges of both Donald Trump and Bernie Sanders.

Changing American Demographics

During the period from Nixon's election in 1968 through George H.W. Bush's victory in 1988, Republicans won five out of six presidential elections. The only exception was Carter's win in 1976, after the Watergate scandal and following Ford's controversial pardon of Nixon. During that time, Democratic political analyst Horace Busby, a former White House aide to Johnson, coined the idea of a "Republican lock on the Electoral College." It may not have been a lock, but Republicans were clearly on a roll.

Looking at the most recent elections from 1992 through 2012, however, Democrats won the popular vote in five out of six and the Electoral College in four of those. (The difference there being Gore's popular vote advantage that was trumped by George W. Bush's Electoral vote advantage in 2000.) Democrats have now won 300 or more Electoral votes in four of the last six elections; Republicans last won 300 or more in 1988. Democrats have won 18 states plus the District of Columbia six times in a row, totaling 242 Electoral votes or 89 percent of the 270 needed to win. Conversely, the Republican base of 13 states that the GOP has won six times in a row adds up to 102 Electoral votes, just 38 percent of the 270 needed. Some Democrats (prematurely, in my judgment), are now referring to their party's "Blue Wall" of states that they believe makes Democrats a strong favorite in the 2016 presidential election. That's a pretty bold statement; however, it does suggest that something has changed during the half dozen elections between 1968 and 1988 and the following six from 1992 and 2012.

The difference, simply put, is demographics. When Bill Clinton won in 1992, white voters cast 87 percent of the total vote. By 2012, that share had dropped 15 points to 72 percent. This explains how Romney won 59 percent of the white vote and still lost the election by almost four points. Until 2012, winning 59 percent or more of the white vote was tantamount to victory. Losing the African-American vote by an 87-point margin, the Latino vote by a 44-point margin, and the Asian-American vote by a 47-point margin made the arithmetic pretty difficult for Romney, despite his lock on the white vote.

Demographics have never before been this bad for Republicans. As recently as 2004—the last election before the immigration issue flared up—Bush won re-election with 44 percent of the Latino vote (according to Election Night exit polls). It is important to note that some political scientists, including some involved in the network exit poll, believe that number overstated Bush's support among Latinos. They estimate that the actual Bush share of the Latino vote was more like 40 percent. However, whether Bush garnered 40 percent or 44 percent, his percentage of the Latino vote remains much higher than the 27 percent that Romney pulled in, or the 31 percent that McCain won in 2008.

The Asian-American vote was never really perceived as a partisan voting bloc until very recently. In fact, Clinton lost the Asian-American vote in 1992 and tied when running for re-election in 1996. It's pretty hard to explain Obama winning that group by 73 percent to 26 percent in 2012. Taken together, whites constituted 89 percent of Romney's total vote, Latinos 6 percent, blacks 2 percent, Asians 1 percent, and "other" at 2 percent. Obama's support was considerably more diverse, with whites making up 56 percent of his vote, blacks 23 percent, Latinos 14 percent, Asian Americans 4 percent, and "other" 2 percent. One of those looks more like the country than the other.

Again citing the House Editor of the Cook Political Report and resident statistics whiz, David Wasserman has looked closely at the 2012 national exit polls as well as the Census Bureau's American Community Survey in an attempt to ascertain how the 2016 electorate in each state will be different from 2012, based on population trends. Wasserman came up with three takeaways for each party. Democrats should find reason for optimism on three points. First, that the white share of the 2016 electorate may fall about two points from 2012, dropping from 72 percent to 70 percent, with 13 percent African American, 11 percent Latino and 6 percent Asian/Other. Second, if each demographic group votes the same way in 2016 as in 2012, the Democratic margin will be about 1.5 points higher; Obama's margin would be something like 5.4 percent compared to the 3.85 percent final margin in 2012. According to Wasserman's projections, this would not be enough to swing any state that fell into the Romney column last time, but Romney's two-point margin in North Carolina would slip to about three-tenths of a percent. Third, even among white voters, Republicans' best-performing segment is whites without college degrees, and that sub-demographic could decline from 36 percent of the electorate to 33 percent.

Wasserman's additional findings (which might encourage Republicans) are, first, that even with these demographic trends, states like Arizona and Georgia will still not be in play in 2016 for Democrats. The white share of the vote is dropping in both states, but not fast enough for Democrats in 2016. Second, there is no magic number that Republicans need to hit among Latinos, or any other group, to win the White House. Because so many Latino voters, Wasserman found, are concentrated in non-swing states like California, Texas and New York, they are under-represented in swing states. Even if Romney won a 10-percent higher share of Latinos in every state, it would only have gained him one state, Florida, taking the Republican from 206 to 237 Electoral votes, still short of the 270 needed to win. Even with a 10-percent increase in the Latino share of the vote, Romney would not have been able to prevail in Colorado, Nevada or New Mexico. On this point, Wasserman concludes, "While Republicans badly want to win over more Latinos; the task is not paramount to their success as often thought." Finally, he argues that "the 'target numbers' Republicans need to win among each group to win the White House are achievable for the right candidate." Rather than doing better among specific groups, Republicans need to do better across the board. Walking through both college-educated and non-college educated whites, African Americans, Latinos and Asians/Others, both nationally and in swing states, Wasserman points to what Republicans need to do, noting that their proportions in these groups were attained by the GOP in the 2014 election and in past elections by both Jeb Bush and Marco Rubio.

It wouldn't be terribly reliable to project current population trends all the way out to the 2024 elections at this point. But, presumably, some currently red, safe Republican states like Arizona, Georgia and Texas have the strong potential to become purple/swing states. When this happens, if Republicans haven't improved their reputation with minority voters, the Electoral College math becomes very difficult for the GOP moving forward. Some Republican strategists seem to hope that older, working-class, white voters, particularly in the Great Lakes states, could make up for some of those losses, but that will not be easy.

While opposition to immigration reform explains a considerable degree of the problem facing Republicans, it definitely does not tell the whole story. Many minority voters perceive a lack of respect from the GOP. They see a Republican Party that is dominated by old white men, many of whom don't seem to like anyone who doesn't look like them. While this absolutely is an inaccurate and unfair portrayal of most Republicans, the extent to which this is a common image of the GOP among minority voters is an enormous problem for the Republican Party. Sometimes, symbolism is as important as, or perhaps even more important, than substance itself. Simply making the immigration issue go away wouldn't solve Republican problems with minority voters, but it would be a start toward gaining their support.

The Age Challenge

The challenge facing Republicans with young voters is only slightly less daunting. While Romney's strongest vote was among voters 65 years of age and older, ultimately winning that group by 12 points, Obama's most potent support group was 18- to 29-year-olds, whom he won by a 23-point margin. For the two age cohorts in-between, 30- to 44-year-olds favored Obama by a seven point margin, whereas 45- to 64-year-olds favored Romney by just four points. Although those 65 and older have a higher voter participation rate than those under 30, 19 percent of the 2012 electorate was under 30, and just 16 percent was 65 or older.

One rather blunt way of looking at it is that people under 40 years old, particularly those under 30, are the future. Looking in the mirror (I am 61) and at others over 60, we are kind of the "pre-dead." Republicans are doing very well with the pre-dead, not so well with the future. To be sure, some voters change their ideological and partisan stripes as they get older. People's political attitudes when young are somewhat fluid, and often begin to jell as they get older.

The window for Republicans to reach out to millennial voters in particular is not going to stay open forever. While most millennials don't hate government the way that most conservatives and many Republicans do, they do not instinctively love big government in the way most liberals and many Democrats do. Millennials are skeptical about the effectiveness of government in solving big problems. They are open to alternative solutions to solving problems outside of established institutions. The challenge for the Republican Party is that so many millennials are—pick your term—moderate, liberal, tolerant, or libertarian on social and cultural issues. Many hit the mute button when they hear Republicans and conservatives talking about cultural issues, and they often never even hear economic or national security arguments that are made when the conversation pivots away from social issues. This is a real challenge for Republicans.

In his terrific recent book, "2016 and Beyond: How Republicans Can Elect a President in the New America," GOP pollster Whit Ayres lays out the demographic and arguably existential crisis facing the Republican Party. If it doesn't change, it will, at least in presidential races, become a non-competitive party.

The Midterm Difference

As dire as the national picture seems for Republicans heading into 2016, the picture is considerably different for the party below the presidential level. As previously stated, presidential-year electorates are big, broad and diverse, while midterm electorates are older, whiter, more conservative, and more Republican. Given the huge differences in voting patterns between younger and older, minority and white voters, these two vastly different electorates tend to produce very different results.

Fortunately for the GOP, the vast majority of governorships and state legislative seats are up in midterm elections when Republicans have a natural turnout advantage. Considering congressional and state legislative redistricting, as well as the fact that down-ballot offices like the state legislature provide the farm teams for the two major parties in terms of future candidate development, this is no small advantage.

Republicans also benefited in 2010 and 2014, each a midterm election under a Democratic president with sagging approval ratings throughout the campaign season. Keep in mind that the party holding the White House has lost ground in the House in all but three midterm elections since 1862. In 1934, President Franklin Roosevelt's first-term, midterm election, voters were still not finished blaming ousted President Herbert Hoover and the Republican Party for the onset of the Great Depression. Democrats gained seats in 1998 as a backlash against a Republican Congress successfully impeaching and unsuccessfully attempting to remove Clinton from office. The pattern was again bucked in 2002, the first election after the September 11 attacks, with Bush's popularity still sky high. (Worth noting, in 1902, Republicans held the White House and gained nine seats, but the House had expanded by 25 seats with the reapportionment that year, and Republicans lost ground while technically gaining seats)

This relatively recent Republican midterm election advantage was obviously offset in 2006. George W. Bush's second-term, midterm election was a notoriously bad situation for a White House party, particularly at a time when the Iraq War had become enormously unpopular. Bush's Gallup approval rating at the time of the election had plummeted to 38 percent. An unpopular president waging a very unpopular war provided the exception to the pattern.

Republicans were unusually fortunate in the 2010 election after suffering punishing losses in 2006 and 2008. As 2010 was the last election before redistricting, huge gains in governorships and state legislative seats boosted Republican strength in the state capitals going into the 2011 remapping, thus giving the GOP its strongest redistricting situation in modern history. The 2010 win has the unique potential to pay long-term dividends for the Republican Party.

All of this has resulted in a boom-and-bust cycle that we have seen in the last four elections. Democrats feasted in the two presidential elections and suffered famine in the two midterms. For Republicans, the pattern was reversed. In both parties, their two victory years provided a balm for their loss years, providing plenty of fodder for rationalizing that their party's problems were not really so bad.

2016 Democratic Presidential Nomination

By the time this Almanac reaches bookstores and mailboxes, the first caucuses and primaries will be just a few months away, making prognostications about the nomination fights highly problematic. Early in 2015, once Sen. Elizabeth Warren made clear that she was not running, it was certainly plausible that the only person who could beat Hillary Clinton for the Democratic nomination was Hillary Clinton.

Clinton seemed to be situated similarly to then-Vice President Al Gore in 2000. Some Democrats were excited about the prospect of Gore as the nominee, others were fine, and still others simply resigned to the inevitability of it. Sen. Bill Bradley mounted an outsider challenge to Gore that never amounted to a whole lot and Gore went on to win every primary and caucus and the nomination handily. Going into 2015, it seemed that for Democratic voters, Clinton was a package, one that came with assets and liabilities, strengths and weaknesses. The totality of that package will be assessed. If she is perceived as energetic, passionate, with big, bold ideas and is future oriented, the nomination is locked up. To the extent that these characteristics are not projected or perceived, or that four or eight years of another Clinton Presidency would be as much of a roller coaster as the last one, or that she was seen as unelectable, then there would be some question as to whether she might lose the nomination.

As 2015 unfolded, two things occurred that raised some doubts. First, Sen. Bernie Sanders began attracting big crowds and improving poll numbers both nationally and in key early states like Iowa and New Hampshire. It appeared to be little more than the support that past insurgent, outsider Democratic candidates often mount in presidential nomination contests, dating back to California Gov. Jerry Brown against Jimmy Carter in 1976, Sen. Gary Hart to former Vice President Walter Mondale in 1984, Bradley against Gore in 2000 and former Vermont Gov. Howard Dean to Sens. John Kerry and John Edwards in 2004. There seems to be a natural outsider vote against all but the most popular, sitting incumbent Democrats, with Sanders capturing that, coalescing those who initially pined for Warren and backed the Occupy Wall Street movement-Democrats uncomfortable with the close ties between the Clintons and Wall Street and business interests. In and of itself, this didn't seem to be a threatening problem to Clinton.

The second was a series of unflattering news stories about the Clinton Foundation fundraising, President Clinton's honoraria and potentially more serious allegations that as Secretary of State, Clinton used a private computer server and that classified information was (or wasn't) included in emails, possibly even some classified as Top Secret. Even Republican polling was showing that the attack on Americans in Benghazi was not registering as a problem for her among anyone but Republicans and conservatives who never liked her to begin with. The original question was whether the issue evolved from one of judgment, opting to use a private server as opposed to more conventional official channels, playing into the narrative that Clinton played by different rules than everyone else. But when allegations arose that some of the emails may have included classified, and even Top Secret information, the potential grew for the story to evolve from simply questioning her judgment to one of breaking Federal laws, ones that have tripped up former Directors of Central Intelligence, John Deutch and David Petraeus, both of whom faced significant legal problems from their handling of classified materials, underscoring the potential severity of this kind of situation. At this writing, these questions were not resolved.

While Clinton's favorable or positive ratings remained quite high in the summer of 2015, her plummeting ratings among independents since leaving the State Department triggered a decline in her general election trial heat matchups nationally and in swing states causing Democrats to begin worrying about her electability in November 2016. Before this drop, even among Democrats who were less than infatuated with Clinton, there had been a presumption that she was highly electable. Now that is less sure. Thus any problems she has in terms of nomination relate to her general election viability, not so much about her individually.

Is Clinton's hold on the Democratic nomination in jeopardy and if so, from threats inside or outside the current field of candidates? Among those currently running, Sanders, former Rhode Island Gov. Lincoln Chafee, former Maryland Gov. Martin O'Malley and former Sen. Jim Webb of Virginia, very few give Chafee or Webb any chance of becoming serious contenders, leaving Sanders and O'Malley as theoretical threats.

Though it isn't hard to see the attraction of Sanders among liberal activists, it's harder to see him as an existential threat to Clinton's nomination. First there is age, Sanders will be turning 75 in September 2016, he would be 79 at the end of a first term and if re-elected, 83 at the end of a second. While there is certainly no maximum age in the Constitution, Ronald Reagan was 69 when he was first elected, the same age that Hillary Clinton will turn a week before the 2016 election. My guess is that many would see 69 or 70 as at or near the high end of the scale for acceptable age for a newly elected president, most would be skeptical of 75. But for the very reason that the most liberal wing of the Democratic Party has become enamored with Sanders is also a pretty good reason that they should be hesitant about nominating him. On most issues, Sanders operated on the fringe of Senate Democrats and had an exceedingly modest record of accomplishment in the Senate. Sanders generally chose to take a stand on his principles rather than being an impact player in the House and more recently in the Senate. Finally, ideologically Sanders may fit what the Left sees as perfection, he certainly does not fit the profile of successful Democratic presidential nominees, having a fighting chance at winning voters between the two ideological 40-yard lines. At least to this observer, if Sanders could win a presidential general election, it simply meant that a Democrat was destined to win the general election, that the Republican Party had imploded, it nominated an unelectable ticket or that a third party candidate was going to disproportionately siphon votes out of the GOP column. In other words, if Donald Trump's name appeared nationwide on the general election ballot as either the nominee or an independent candidate.

Among the candidates as of the Summer of 2015, Martin O'Malley seemed to be the alternative to Clinton who fit a profile that has worked in the past, in terms of positions held (Baltimore Mayor and Governor of Maryland), age (turning 53 in January 2016), and ideology (left of Center but not outside the normal mainstream of the Democratic Party). While at this point O'Malley is showing little sign of progress and it is debatable whether he could have won a third term as governor, if he had been allowed to do so. If someone in the field could give her a real race, it would likely be O'Malley.

That raises the question of whether it is too late for someone else to jump in and effectively give Clinton a run. At this writing Vice President Joe Biden (who will turn 74 two weeks after the 2016 election) had opened the door to a possible run while others have suggested former Vice President Al Gore, Secretary of State John Kerry while others are touting Warren. One outside the box suggestion has been former New York Mayor Michael Bloomberg. He certainly could write a single check and fund a campaign entirely, but the Sanders-Warren-Occupy Wall Street Crowd would probably be apoplectic over a candidate from Wall Street. It is questionable whether a campaign could be built from scratch this late. It almost certainly would require a candidate who is either a self-funder or already possess very high national name recognition, a coast to coast network and very strong fundraising potential. If anything has changed, it is the advent of Superpacs and the ability of unlimited spending on behalf of candidates through these various forms of political committees and tax exempt entities. At least theoretically that cracks open a door, but this would seem pretty unlikely unless Clinton's legal challenges prove very real and appear very quickly.

It seems unlikely that someone five or six years older than Clinton—as Vice President Biden or Sen. Sanders will be, respectively, in November 2016 would be able to capture a nomination or win a general election.

Given concerns over whether Clinton has suddenly become unelectable, it would seem far-fetched that Democrats would find Sanders more electable, or for that matter two of the other rivals, former Rhode Island Gov. Lincoln Chafee or former Sen. Jim Webb of Virginia.

Thus, Sanders became a vehicle for anyone with objections to Clinton, those who want to send her a message, or those trying to move the party toward the left, or prevent it from sliding toward the middle. It has been argued that the fact that Sanders isn't a particularly plausible nominee makes him a safe vehicle for individuals wanting to send a message. Despite his failure to make headway as of mid-summer 2015, O'Malley is likely the current rival that the Clinton camp would rather not see gaining any ground. If Sanders is sucking all of the oxygen from the more liberal wing of the party, there is less available for a more probable alternative like O'Malley.

2016 Republican Presidential Nomination

As very little is simple about politics anymore, one potentially useful way of looking at the Republican Party is to think on three levels. First, the traditional Left-Right ideological axis, although admittedly there is very little remaining, has become more Center Right to Right. A second is inside-outside, with the inside reflecting the more establishment and conventional Republican Party in which a career in politics is not necessarily pejorative and the outside wants to shake things up, devaluing experience or who would change the process and policy more. The third is priorities, with some placing a greater emphasis on economic issues, whether from the conventional or from the Tea Party perspective, other social and cultural concerns, with Pro-Life, evangelical and home school advocates populating much of this and a third, foreign policy, whether from traditional internationalist or Neo-Conservative points of view.

As suggested earlier, Republicans normally behave in a very hierarchical fashion, nominating whoever's turn it is to head the top of the ticket. This pattern indicates the deference that GOP voters have historically given to the party establishment, the so-called 'mainstream' element of the party. But with the Republican Party's movement more to the right and, more importantly, the rise of an element that is decidedly anti-establishment—underscored by the 2009 and 2010 rise of the Tea Party movement—that deference to entrenched party leaders means less than before. Whether it is enough to cost Jeb Bush the GOP nomination remains to be seen, but this change has presented the former Florida governor with headwinds, both ideological and personal, that neither his brother nor father faced. That's what makes this nomination less predictable than GOP contests in the past. While few believe that Donald Trump can actually win a Republican nomination, few thought he actually would run, that he could make it to first place in national and key early state polling and, for that matter, stay in the top slot for more than a few weeks. But the fact that Trump did all of that speaks to the passion that the anti-establishment faction of the GOP has in this campaign, and underscores the resistance to making a more conventional choice and the difficulty in predicting anything. At the time of this writing, for example, the top two places in national polling for the GOP nomination are held by Trump and Carson, the two representing pretty much the antithesis of the kind of nominees Republicans usually choose. While neither is likely to end up with the nomination, it is an indicator that something is going on in the GOP, just as Herman Cain's brief ascendency represented something highly unorthodox four years ago.

A gigantic field of candidates means that some—like New Jersey Gov. Chris Christie, former Hewlett Packard CEO Carly Fiorina, Ohio Gov. John Kasich, Sen. Marco Rubio of Florida, and Wisconsin Gov. Scott Walker and perhaps former Texas Gov. Rick Perry—are more acceptable to the traditional Republican establishment. Others—like former Arkansas Gov. Mike Huckabee, Louisiana Gov. Bobby Jindal, and former Sen. Rick Santorum—are preferred by Republicans who remain more narrowly focused on social and cultural issues, including but not limited to those with a more religious bent in their politics. Still others appeal to the more ideologically inclined and tea party-oriented Republicans—like Dr. Ben Carson of Maryland, Sens. Ted Cruz of Texas and Rand Paul of Kentucky. In one sense, different candidates have been fishing in different pools for different kinds of GOP voters. Some have likened the choices to walking into a Baskin-Robbins ice cream shop with 31 flavors, something for everyone.

There are as many theories as to what will happen as there are political aficionados speculating, and it seems plausible that the more establishment-oriented candidates will fight it out for one or perhaps two slots with the more renegade or ideological candidates maneuvering for another, from the outside. History argues for the GOP establishment ultimately prevailing. But, that looks far less certain than in the past.

Senate

Nationally, Senate election outcomes are a function of two things: the political climate and partisan exposure. Obviously, the popularity (or lack thereof) of a president or a party at the time of any election is a major factor in the results. However, the level of exposure each party has to losses is also a driving force. If one party has a huge class of seats up for election that cycle, it carries more opportunity for losses than does the party with only a few seats up. When one party has a great Senate year in one election, they will almost inevitably have more Senators up for election six years later, thus facing greater exposure to potential losses. Freshmen who take over seats from the other party often find themselves facing reelection six years later in a state that is not naturally hospitable to their party. The more eventful an election year is, the greater the exposure. Conversely, when a party has a horrific year in the Senate, sometimes losing most, if not all, of their competitive seats in difficult states, they enter the election six years later with fewer potentially vulnerable seats and more opportunities for gains. Additionally, how a state performs in the previous presidential election is becoming a very good predictor of how that state will vote in a Senate race. Presidential performance is not a perfect predictor, particularly when trying to anticipate the outcome in a midterm election, largely because of the different turnout dynamics of a general vs. midterm. But increasingly it is a better model than any other metric.

In 2014, Democrats faced a double-barrel assault. It was a second-term, midterm election—historically, a notoriously bad situation for the incumbent party in the White House, particularly with an incumbent with low presidential job approval numbers. While midterm elections are usually bad for the party in the White House, the second-term midterm elections are often the worst. The notable exception to that pattern was Clinton's presidency. Democrats under Clinton suffered their own partisan bloodbath during his first-term, midterm election. Democrats lost their majority in the House for the first time in 40 years, as well as the Senate majority (something they held for 34 of the previous 40 years). However, in Clinton's second midterm election, largely because of a public backlash against his impeachment and attempted removal from office, Democrats managed to break even in the Senate and gained five seats in the House. But they were much less fortunate in 2014. The week before the midterm election, Obama had a 42 percent job approval rating in the Gallup Poll; it was 40 percent the week of the election, far below Clinton's 66 percent approval at the comparable six-year election mark during his administration.

The other half of the Democrats' dire situation in 2014 was exposure. Because of strong gains six years earlier, Democrats entered the cycle with 21 seats at risk, compared with just 15 for Republicans. More important, Democrats found themselves defending seven seats in states that Romney carried just two years earlier. Four of those seats were in states that Romney won by 15 points or more; incumbents Mark Pryor (Arkansas) and Mary Landrieu (Louisiana), plus two open seats in South Dakota and West Virginia. Democrats had to defend two more states that Romney carried by 14 points: incumbent Mark Begich (Alaska) and what became an open seat in Montana. Finally, Democrats had Kay Hagan in North Carolina, a state that Romney won by just two points in 2012 but clearly tilted right in a midterm election. Conversely, the GOP only had one seat in an Obama-carried state, Susan Collins (Maine), who faced no serious competition. Beyond Maine, Republicans didn't have to defend any other seats in states that Romney carried by less than eight points. Democrats lost all seven of the Democratic seats in Romney states, plus two more: incumbent Mark Udall (Colorado) and an open seat in Iowa. These were both states that Obama won two years earlier by five and six points, respectively. It's important to remember that the different composition of the electorate in a midterm can flip states that tilted toward Obama in a presidential year.

The combination of a tough political environment and disproportional Democratic exposure was a lethal combination for the party in 2014. Hence, we saw the continuation of the pattern of "boom-bust" cycles for the two parties that we experienced in 2006, 2008, 2010 and 2012. It is enough to make any political aficionado dizzy.

Also relevant is that until a party can count on 60 Senate votes (enough to invoke clo-ture and cut off a filibuster), they are not truly in control of the upper chamber. Even so, a majority of fewer than 60 seats still matters in the Senate. The current Republican Senate Majority Leader, Mitch McConnell, is running the chamber in a very different way than did his predecessor, Democrat (now Minority Leader) Harry Reid. Reid was inclined to shut the Senate down if he encountered any problems. McConnell is much more of an institutional-ist, believing whenever possible in regular order: committee hearings and reporting out bills or amendments allowed by either side on the floor whenever possible. Yet, it is important to note that McConnell tends to be heavy handed when he sees Democrats becoming overly obstinate. New Yorker Chuck Schumer is a lock to be elected Democratic leader after Reid's retirement at the end of this Congress. While there are few members as partisan as Schumer, the New Yorker seems to have become more focused today on cutting deals and getting legis-lation moving—of course with his imprint on the content—than he was during the years he was chairman of the Democratic Senatorial Campaign Committee. It is a decent bet that the McConnell-Schumer relationship will have its ups and downs and involve plenty of fights, but ultimately it will be smoother than the poisonous McConnell-Reid pairing. These two people clearly loathe one another and make little effort to hide it.

2016 Senate Races

At this writing, Republicans hold 54 Senate seats while Democrats have 44, plus two independents who caucus with (and are effectively) Democrats, Angus King of Maine and Bernie Sanders of Vermont. To win the majority, Democrats need a four-seat net gain if they hold the White House (the incoming vice president would break the tie) or five seats if they don't. Keep in mind that in presidential years, such as 2016, voter turnout is big, broad and diverse, and looks more or less like the country as opposed to midterm elections when the electorate is smaller, older, more conservative and more Republican.

As we said, the political climate and exposure to loss are the two primary differentials in Senate elections. While the political environment in the fall of 2016 is impossible to pinpoint, the exposure part of the equation is already quite clear. In 2016, Republicans find them-selves defending 24 seats to only 10 for Democrats. Obama carried seven of the GOP-held states in 2012. Conversely there are no Democratic Senate seats up in 2016 in states that Romney won.

It has been noted earlier that when a party scores big in the Senate in one election, six years later, they are usually over-exposed to losses with that class of seats comes back around. As this 2016 crop of Senate seats were last up in 2010, a great year for Republicans who were able to score a net gain of six Senate seats (and 63 in the House), that means that Republicans up this time last won with a very strong wind at their back, a favorable environ-ment that may well not exist in 2016.

As Jennifer Duffy, the senior editor of The Cook Political Report has noted, while Repub-licans certainly face a challenging environment in 2016, it is arguably less difficult than the one Democrats faced in 2014. Republicans are defending only one seat found deep in enemy territory: Illinois, a state that is as tough as those that Democrats faced defending Landrieu, Pryor and the open seats in South Dakota and West Virginia. In Illinois, Mark Kirk will have to face a state that Obama won by 17 points in 2012, the same margin that Romney carried Landrieu's Louisiana—though not quite as difficult as Begich's Alaska or Pryor's Arkansas were for Democrats in 2014. Republicans have six other shaky seats, but all in states that Obama won by seven points or less. Republican incumbent Ron Johnson is up in Wisconsin, a state that Obama won by seven points; Chuck Grassley (Iowa) and Kelly Ayotte (New Hampshire) are both in states that Obama won by six points; Pat Toomey in Pennsylvania, a state Obama carried by five points; Rob Portman in Ohio, an Obama three-point state; and an open seat in Florida, which Obama carried by one point.

Conversely, the open seat in Nevada represents the only obvious shot the GOP has to pick up a seat in this upcoming cycle. Efforts to come up with a first- or second-tier challenger in Colorado to Michael Bennet have been unsuccessful thus far. Republicans will clearly try to come up with a strong challenge to a Democrat somewhere else, if for no other reason than to stretch Democratic resources thinner by making them defend more territory and thus be unable to spend virtually all of their money on offense.

Realistically, Democrats have no shot against Grassley, so long as he is running for re-election (as he appears to be at the time of this writing). Democratic chances against Ayotte hinge largely on Gov. Maggie Hassan challenging the incumbent, which is no more than a 50 percent prospect and maybe less. These seven Republican-held seats, along with incumbent Richard Burr's (North Carolina), represent the primary level of Republican expo-sure. After that are long-shot campaigns against John McCain in Arizona and Roy Blunt in Missouri, as well as an open seat in Indiana.

It is an exaggeration to say that Democrats have to run the table to win a Senate majority in 2016, but it isn't a particularly outlandish exaggeration. They would need a highly favor-able political environment, a strong turnout among young and minority voters, and some breaks in individual states to pull it off, or perhaps Donald Trump's name somewhere on the ballot. We have certainly seen plenty of these in both directions over the last four elections.

In 2018, the tables again are turned. Democrats will be defending 25 seats, five of which are in states that Romney carried—all by nine points or more. In this case, it isn't so much that Democrats did well six years earlier in 2012, they picked up only two seats that year, but that six years before that in 2006, was a banner year for Democrats, gaining six seats that year with the Iraq War and President George W. Bush radioactive. Freshman Democratic incumbent Heidi Heitkamp will be up in North Dakota, a state Romney won by 20 points. Another freshman, Democrat Joe Manchin, is up in West Virginia, a state Romney swept by 27 points. Second-term Democrat Claire McCaskill will be up in Missouri, a plus-nine point Romney state. Two more Democrats, Joe Donnelly (Indiana) and Jon Tester (Montana) will face re-election in 2018 in states that Romney won by ten and 14 points, respectively. Nevada's Dean Heller is the only Republican up in an Obama state (Romney lost the Silver State by seven points).

2018 is a midterm election and as previously discussed, turnout dynamics have favored Republicans in the last such elections. However, the party and approval rating of the next president will obviously matter. Midterm elections are almost always referenda on the incumbent president, or an opportunity for voters to vent their spleens. In midterms, presi-dents are rarely popular, so who wins in 2016 will be important in knowing which side would potentially be on the defensive, at least within the framework of the political climate. Ulti-mately, a Democratic presidential victory in 2016 potentially overexposes the party in terms of seats and renders it vulnerable to an unfavorable political climate. A GOP presidential victory could mean a potentially unfavorable climate offsetting any usual Republican advan-tage on midterm election turnout

The 2020 Senate contest will flip the situation yet again. Republicans have 22 seats up that year, compared to just 11 for Democrats. With Republicans picking up nine seats in 2014, there is more exposure for the GOP although the gains for Republican seats that year were largely in states that Romney had carried in 2012, thus not exactly enemy territory for the GOP. Being a presidential year, the turnout will likely favor Democrats more than Republicans, but obviously the popularity and strength of the incumbent president will be a big factor as well. The GOP Senate exposure in 2020 appears now to be more theoretical than real. Only three GOP seats are up in Obama states: Susan Collins in Maine (Obama +15), Cory Gardner in Colorado (Obama +5) and Joni Ernst in Iowa (Obama +6). First-term Sen. Thom Tillis in North Carolina (Romney +2) will also be up. No Democrats are up in Romney states. Potentially the most vulnerable Democratic seat will be Mark Warner's in Virginia, as the state has moved out of the red, Republican leaning category to become a swing state.

Such lopsided Senate classes are produced by the exposure and political climate of elec-tions six and sometimes even 12 years earlier when that particular class of seats was last up for consideration by the American public. Increasingly, we are seeing voting behavior more akin to a parliamentary system, where two political parties with high floors and low ceilings are operating in a relatively evenly divided and exceedingly polarized environment. While there aren't many swing voters up for grabs, there are enough, and most are looking to send a message to the candidates of the party they are most upset with at that moment. The result is essentially a political aftershock.

2016 House Races

With the House currently split between 247 Republicans and 188 Democrats, for House control to change hands, Democrats would need a net gain of 30 seats, a feat that is extremely unlikely. Given the normal ebb and flow of congressional elections, Democrats should pick up seats in 2016. However, if they are able to cover even half that 30-seat gain necessary, it would be a good night for them. Keep in mind, in 2014, Democrats only lost 13 seats and that only 16 of 247 House Republican victors won their races by less than 10 points—that's a pretty astonishing lack of obvious exposure.

To get to 218, Democrats would effectively have to win each of the nine Republican seats currently rated as Toss Up by the Cook Political Report, win all 13 of the races in the Lean Republican column, and capture eight out of the 15 GOP-held seats in the Likely Republican category (a category considered non-competitive but worth watching), while simultaneously holding onto all three Democratic-held Toss Up seats, all four of the Lean Democratic seats, as well as 12 of the Likely Democratic seats and all 169 seats rated as Solid Democrat. In short, it would take a tsunami wave for Democrats to win a majority in 2016.

Keeping in mind the large re-election advantage that House incumbents generally have (the re-election rate in the House runs substantially higher than in the Senate), how many open seats each party has, and which seats are open (whether in safe or competitive districts) is important. However, it is unlikely that there will be enough Republican retirements to make a difference this time around. Indeed, given the uphill odds that House Democrats appear to be facing in 2016, the challenge has been keeping their own members from retiring more than looking for places to take advantage of GOP retirements.

While such partisan waves periodically happen, they almost always occur in midterm, not presidential election years, with the incumbent President's party only very rarely the beneficiary. A total of 35 national elections have taken place since the end of World War II; 10 have resulted in a net gain of 30 or more seats by one party. Of those, just three were in presidential election years. The party in the White House gained at least 30 seats in 1948, when Harry Truman was elected, and again in 1964 when Lyndon Johnson won, both rather extraordinary circumstances, the winning president in each case succeeding their deceased predecessors. In 1980, Democrats suffered massive losses when President Jimmy Carter lost to Ronald Reagan by a 10-point margin. None of these previous circumstances should give House Democrats any hope in 2016. It would seem plausible that Democrats might gain back, more or less, those 13 seats but gains much more or a lot less than that would seem somewhat unlikely in the absence of some major political wave. Court-ordered redistricting in several states could benefit Democrats to the tune of a handful of seats but does not significantly reduce the magnitude of their challenge in trying to regain the House in 2016.

2021-22 Reapportionment and Redistricting

After the 2020 decennial Census results are released, there will be a reapportionment of congressional seats across all 50 states. Then, the redistricting process will take place within each state (some erroneously use the terms reapportionment and redistricting interchangeably). According to a December 2014 report by Election Data Services' Kim Brace, given current population trends, Texas will likely gain three House seats with Florida, North Carolina, Colorado, California and Virginia each gaining an additional seat. Pennsylvania, Michigan, Illinois, Rhode Island, West Virginia, Ohio, Minnesota and Alabama will each lose one seat. Given fluctuating population patterns, some of these estimates could change.

Oregon, Arizona, and Montana are the closest to gaining an additional seat each. New York came the closest to losing a seat, and Pennsylvania could lose a second seat.

Many Democrats blame redistricting for their problems in the House. No doubt, Republican governors and state legislators were able to create the most GOP-friendly map in modern history, and this is certainly much of the reason why the House has grown to be almost out of reach for Democrats. David Wasserman, House editor for the Cook Political Report, argues that while Democrats have been able to do well in presidential and Senate elections, at least in non-midterm election years, many of those statewide Democratic wins are driven by non-white voters who are clustered in a relatively few, mostly urban congressional districts, while Republican voters are spread out and more efficiently allocated in many more districts. This distribution of voters, for the time being, gives the GOP an advantage at the House level.

While some of this concentration of minority—and, we could add, younger voters in districts with major universities—is clearly partisan design by mapmakers, much of it is simply a product of where people choose to live. Republican voters tend to prefer to live in suburban, exurban, small town, and rural areas and these are places where the GOP is able to win more districts by somewhat lesser margins. Democrats, on the other hand, are more successful at running up massive majorities in fewer districts. Some African-American and Latino incumbents, almost all Democrats, have exacerbated this problem by lobbying, often colluding with Republican governors, legislators and mapmakers, to get heavily minority, safe districts, effectively bleaching out adjacent districts, making them overwhelmingly white, more conservative and more Republican, and thus giving the GOP more districts.

Over the last few decades, the redistricting standard of "compact and contiguous" has given way to simply contiguous, the result of a change in interpretation of the Voting Rights Act. We went from a direction under the VRA of 'creating a minority district if you can,' to one of almost of 'if there is any way to create one, you have to and the more minority that district is, the better.' Thus a classic and needed piece of legislation, passed by a Democratic Congress and president, has contributed to the un-doing of Democratic majorities.

Democrats appear highly unlikely to capture a House majority in 2016. However, given this heavy concentration of Democratic voters into a minority of districts, is there any hope of the party winning 218 or more seats before the 2021 redistricting? This seems unlikely, with any chance of Democratic victory largely predicated on a Republican winning the presidency in 2016 and becoming massively unpopular by the time of the 2018 midterm, or perhaps the 2020 re-election.

Most Likely House Seats Gains and Losses after 2020

1. Texas (+3)	1. Pennsylvania (-1)
2. Florida (+1)	2. Michigan (-1)
3. North Carolina (+1)	3. Illinois (-1)
4. Colorado (+1)	4. Rhode Island (-1)
5. California (+1)	5. West Virginia (-1)
6. Virginia (+1)	6. Ohio (-1)
	7. Minnesota (-1)
	8. Alabama (-1)

Possible House Seats Gains and Losses after 2020

1. Oregon (+1)	1. New York (-1)
2. Arizona (+1)	2. Pennsylvania (-2)
3. Montana (+1)	3. Wisconsin (-1)

As Wasserman has written, "A vicious cycle is underway for Democrats. In more than two-thirds of states, state legislatures control the redistricting process. And at that level, Democrats are suffering from the same woes as in Congress—except on a more massive scale. Democratic voters' over-concentration in cities means they win inefficiently large majorities in their own safe state legislative seats, and enable Republicans to pack them into small minorities in plenty of state houses."

The University of Virginia's Center of Politics' Larry Sabato and Geoffrey Skelley calculated in early 2015 that Democrats have lost 913 state legislative seats since Obama took office. Taking note of that, the Cook Political Report's National Editor Amy Walter argues that Democrats will lock themselves out of a House majority for another 10 years if they don't start paying more attention to state-level races.

Wasserman concludes "in many state legislatures (particularly in the South and Midwest), Democrats are so deep in the minority that gaining one or both chambers to earn a seat at the redistricting table isn't a realistic goal. That leaves Democrats with only two strategic options: either win more gubernatorial seats to earn veto power and send more maps to the courts, or get behind reform movements to establish more bipartisan or nonpartisan redistricting commissions." Alternatively, in a tongue-in-cheek spirit, Wasserman has suggested that Democrats begin a massive effort to encourage Democratic voters to relocate from urban areas to suburban, small town and rural areas to make the party competitive in more districts.

Governors

Gubernatorial races follow a predictable pattern: three governorships (Kentucky, Louisiana and Mississippi) are always up in the year preceding a presidential election; 11 are up in the presidential year; New Jersey and Virginia are on the ballot the year following a presidential year; and 36 come up in the midterm cycle. New Hampshire and Vermont, the remaining states with two-year terms, are up both in midterm and presidential election years. But if the pattern is predictable, it is often volatile, particularly in mid-term cycles.

For the overall 2013-2014 gubernatorial cycle, Democrats suffered a net loss of two governorships, Republicans and independents gained one seat each. In 2013, with Clinton-confidant Terry McAuliffe's win, Democrats picked up the Virginia governorship from Republicans while incumbent Chris Christie held onto New Jersey for GOP. That Democratic victory in Virginia actually broke a historic pattern. From 1977 under Carter onward, the party holding the White House had always lost the Virginia governorship.

2015-2018 Governor's Races

2015-2016	2017-2018	
Obama States	**Obama States**	**Romney States**
Shumlin (D-VT) +36	Ige (D-HI) +43	Deal (R-GA) +8
Markell (D-DE) +19	Shumlin (D-VT) +36	Ducey (R-AZ) +9
Inslee (D-WA) +15	Brown (D-CA) +28	Haley (R-SC) +10
Brown (D-OR) +12	Raimondo (D-RI) +27	Walker (I-AK) +14
Hassan (D-NH) +6	Cuomo (D-NY) +26	Abbott (R-TX) +16,
Romney States	Hogan (R-MD) +26	Daugaard (R-SD) +18
McCrory (R-NC) +2	Baker (R-MA) +23	Haslam (R-TN) +20
Nixon (D-MO) +9	Christie (R-NJ) +17	Bentley (R-AL) +22
Pence (R-IN) +10	Mallory (D-CT) +17	Brownback (R-KS) +22
Bryant (R-MS) +12	Rauner (R-IL) +17	Ricketts (R-NE) +22
Bullock (D-MT) +14	LePage (R-ME) +15	Hutchinson (R-AR) +24
Jindal (R-LA) +17	Brown (D-OR) +12	Otter (R-ID) +32
Darlymple (R-ND) +20	Snyder (R-MI) +10	Fallon (R-OK) +34
Beshear (D-KY) +23	Martinez (R-NM) +10	Mead (R-WY) +41
Tomblin (D-WV) +27	Dayton (D-MN) +8	
Herbert (R-UT) +48	Sandoval (R-NV) +7	
	Walker (R-WI) +7	
	Branstad (R-IA) +6	
	Hassan (D-NH) +6	
	Hickenlooper (D-CO) +5	
	Wolf (D-PA) +5	
	McCauliffe (D-VA) +4	
	Kasich (R-OH) +3	
	Scott (R-FL) +1	

Note: This chart shows upcoming governors' races in the states that Barack Obama and Mitt Romney carried in the 2012 election. The plus sign indicates the percentage point margin of victory for Obama or Romney in each state. Shading indicates that the current governor is of a different party than the presidential winner.

Then in 2014, Democrats suffered a loss of four governorships; Gov. Pat Quinn in Illinois and open seats in Arkansas, Maryland and Massachusetts. Republicans lost the open seat in Pennsylvania and saw Alaska Gov. Sean Parnell lose to independent Bill Walker. Republicans finished the cycle with 31 governorships to 18 for Democrats and one independent.

Given the increased devolution of power from the federal to state governments, control of the governorships has never been more important. That makes it significant that there could well be as many as 30 open governorships between 2015 and 2018. Considering term limits, as well as incumbents who opt not to seek reelection, it is possible that 60 percent of our nation's governorships are likely to get new occupants over the next three years. There are two open governorships in 2015, and another four (and possibly even five) in 2016. Both governorships up in 2017—New Jersey and Virginia—will be open, bringing the number to eight before getting to the mega-class of 36 governorships up in 2018. Of this class, 16 incumbents are term limited, bringing the number of open governorships to 24. Plus, there are a number of incumbents who are eligible to run because they represent states without term limits, but may opt to retire, like Republican Butch Otter of Idaho and Democrat Andrew Cuomo of New York. That group could add as many as six more open seats, bringing the total number to 30. That is an extraordinary degree of volatility.

2015-2016 Gubernatorial Races

In 2015, Republicans are defending Louisiana and Mississippi, while Democrats are trying to hold onto Kentucky. At this writing in the summer of 2015, Republicans are well-positioned to hold the open seat in Louisiana and Mississippi Gov. Phil Bryant should win a second term easily. The surprise is the Democratic-held open seat in Kentucky, a state that has become increasingly more Republican, at least at the federal level. Republicans started the cycle as favorites to pick up the seat, but Matt Bevin, a tea party-backed business-man won the GOP nomination. He is certainly not the strongest candidate the party could have nominated, it is possible the state has changed enough to make up for his shortcomings. At this writing, the race remains a toss up.

Just as it is important when considering Senate races nationally to look at the outcomes six years earlier and in the House two-years back, the same holds true for the 48 states on four-year term cycles. In the case of 2016 governorships, only one gubernatorial race in 2012 resulted in party switch, North Carolina shifting from Democrat to Republican. This suggests, at least for now, that this is not a terribly volatile class of governorships up. But, sometimes looks can be deceiving.

Democrats' challenge in 2016 is their open seats in Missouri and West Virginia. Mitt Romney carried those states in 2012 by nine and 27 points, respectively, even though Democratic incumbents were able to get re-elected. It will be much more difficult for the party to hold onto these seats now that they are open. If New Hampshire Gov. Maggie Hassan opts to run for the Senate rather than reelection, add that seat to the list of very competitive Democratic-held gubernatorial races. It's possible that Montana Gov. Steve Bullock could find himself in a tough race against a wealthy Republican businessman.

Democrats have one more seat to defend in a special election in Oregon. Upon Gov. John Kitzhaber's resignation in February of 2015, Secretary of State Kate Brown assumed the state's highest office. She must run in 2016 for the right to finish the last two years of Kitzhaber's term. Assuming she is successful, Brown would then have to run in 2018 for a full four-year term. Obama carried Oregon by 12 points in 2012, which makes Brown the favorite in 2016. If Republicans had an opportunity to pick up this seat, it was in 2014 against the vulnerable Kitzhaber.

Republicans appear to have less exposure. North Carolina Gov. Pat McCrory will certainly face an extremely competitive race against Democratic Attorney General Roy Cooper, the presumptive Democratic nominee, while Indiana Gov. Mike Pence starts as the favorite, but is going to have to work for a second term. The other two GOP seats up in 2016—North Dakota and Utah—won't be competitive.

The end result is that Republicans might actually add a seat or two to their current lineup of 31 governorships.

2017-2018 Gubernatorial Races

As far as governors are concerned, it's the 2017-2018 cycle that is of critical importance, both in terms of the sheer numbers and open seats, as well as the implications for congressional and state legislative redistricting in many states. Almost half of the nation's governor-ships will be vacated after this election, which combined with the redistricting angle, make this cycle something of a political Powerball that may give one party or another a decisive advantage.

In 2017, each party has a seat up. Republicans will defend an open seat in New Jersey, while Democrats will attempt to hold onto an open seat in Virginia. Obama carried both states in 2012.

In 2018, Republicans will have 24 seats up, including 14 incumbents who will be term limited. Eleven of the GOP governorships up in 2018 are in states that Obama won in 2012. Democrats have only half as many governors up, 11, with just two incumbents termed out. None of the Democratic seats is in a state that Romney carried. Alaska's Bill Walker, an independent, is also up for reelection

As has been noted, part of the problem for Republicans has to do with the cycle. The GOP had a fantastic 2010 midterm election up and down the ballot, scoring a net gain of six governorships, then picking up two more in the 2014 midterms, giving Republicans considerable exposure in 2018. This is the dark lining behind a silver cloud, as it were.

Both parties know what is at stake in governors' races in 2018, to the point that 2016 is seen as something of an afterthought. The party committees are already strategizing, recruiting and raising money for that 2018 cycle.

Conclusion

A considerable degree of humility is necessary in contemplating upcoming elections. First, voting is nothing more than human behavior, something that is unpredictable by its very nature. Second, events can and often do change the circumstances surrounding an election, yielding an unexpected outcome. But that is what makes the study of elections interesting and fun. No matter who you are, how closely you are paying attention, or how much data you examine, the unexpected will happen.

* * * *

On a personal note, as a senior in high school, I walked into a bookstore in my hometown of Shreveport, Louisiana and bought a copy of a new, hot-off-the-press book, the Almanac of American Politics. That year was 1972, and as soon as subsequent editions have been published, I have bought and devoured each one. I now own two complete sets: one at the office, another at home. This has truly become the bible of American politics. The Almanac of American Politics has become as essential to the lives of true political aficionados as utility companies are to homes. It's an honor for me to contribute to The Almanac and play a role in its continuation. The political world owes a debt of gratitude to Joel Poznansky and his colleagues at Columbia Books, as well as Richard Cohen for their tireless efforts to keep this important work alive and improving in its fifth decade.

Straight-Ticket Voting in Divided Government

By Michael Barone

American politics seems stuck in a rut. In the 20 years heading into the 2016 elections there has been relatively little movement in partisan preferences in either presidential or congressional elections, at least as counted by the popular vote.

Democrats have won four of the last six presidential elections, starting in 1992, and won a plurality of the popular vote in a fifth. But the variance between outcomes has been, by historical standards, small. The Ross Perot candidacies made the partisan percentages in the 1992 and, to a lesser extent, the 1996 elections incommensurate with those to follow, but starting with 1996 every Democratic nominee has won between 48% and 53% of the popular vote and starting with 2000 every Republican nominee has won between 46% and 51% of the popular vote. (If Bob Dole had won the votes of the two-thirds of Perot supporters who said he was their second choice, he would have won 45% in 1996, almost within the same range.) There has not been such narrow variation in partisan percentages in successive presidential elections since the three elections of the 1880s, which was also the last time the winner of the popular vote lost in the Electoral College.

The same trend is apparent in congressional elections, as measured by each party's percentage of the popular vote for House of Representatives, which in the last 20 years has suddenly become again, as it was in the second half of the 19th and first half of the 20th century, a pretty accurate barometer of party support.

Starting with 1994, Republicans have won majorities in the House in nine of 11 elections, and have won popular vote pluralities in every one except 2012, when Democrats had a 49%-48% edge. Republican majorities owe something to the advantages the party had in redistricting following the 2000 and 2010 censuses, but those advantages, as political scientists have argued, were marginal and in any case proved to be unavailing in 2006 and 2008, the two years when Democrats won House majorities.

These psephological facts seem to be an anomaly: in an era of increasing straight-ticket voting, the results have produced divided government—with one party holding the White House and the other party holding a majority in at least one house of Congress—70% of the time, for six years during Bill Clinton's presidency, three and one-half of George W. Bush's and six of Barack Obama's. This anomaly is largely the result of demographic clustering, the fact that heavily Democratic voting groups—blacks, Hispanics (in many states) and gentry liberals—tend to be clustered in most central cities, many sympathetic suburbs and most university towns, while Republican voters are spread more evenly around the rest of the country.

This gives Democrats an advantage in the Electoral College, where those clusters tend to render safe Democratic states and the District of Columbia with about 170 electoral votes, while Republicans have a similar advantage in states with only about 105. But clustering helps Republicans in elections held in equal-population districts, since Democratic votes are clustered in relatively few districts and Republican votes are more evenly spread around in the rest.

The results were apparent in the 2012 election. Barack Obama, with 51% of the popular vote, won 332 electoral votes; by contrast, George W. Bush with 51% of the popular vote in 2004 won 286. But Obama carried only a minority of congressional districts, 209, while Bush carried 255. The effect of increasing straight-ticket voting is apparent in the House results in those years. Bush's party won 232 House seats in 2004, 23 seats fewer than Bush carried, while Obama's party won 201 House seats in 2012, only eight seats fewer than he carried. In 2012 there were only 26 districts that voted for the president of one party and a representative of the other—the lowest number since 1920.

It has often been argued that Democrats will have an increasing advantage in presidential elections because of the inevitably increasing percentage of non-white voters, who amounted to 25% of the electorate in 2008 and 28% in 2012. That percentage is expected to increase to 30% in 2016. There is much merit in this view, and in the argument that Republicans will be disadvantaged by increases in the non-white percentage of the electorate.

But there are also some caveats to be noted. It is unlikely that Hillary Clinton or any other Democratic nominee will have quite as large a percentage advantage among black voters as the first black president won, and it is possible that a Republican nominee will do better among Hispanics than John McCain did in 2008 (31%) or Mitt Romney in 2012 (27%). In addition, Hispanics are not a nationally uniform group, either in national origin or in political proclivities. They tend to vote very heavily Democratic in already heavily Democratic states and to have often given Republicans higher percentages than nationally in the relatively few target states in which they are significant shares of the electorate (Colorado, Florida, Nevada, New Mexico). Exit polls showed Asians voting heavily for Obama in 2012 but split evenly between House Democrats and Republicans in 2014. They are an even more diverse group than Hispanics, and the exit poll is not designed to provide a reliable sample of such small segments of the national electorate. In addition Asians are concentrated in heavily Democratic states and account for more than 3% of voters in only one target state, Virginia.

There are other ways to slice the electorate. One is to distinguish what might be called Coastal states—the Northeast minus Pennsylvania and the four Pacific states of California, Oregon, Washington and Hawaii—and the Heartland. About 30% of the nation's votes are cast in the Coastal states, 31% in the 2008 and 2012 presidential elections, 32% and 29% in the 2010 and 2014 House elections. The Coastal states are heavily Democratic and include only one target state, New Hampshire; they voted 61%-37% for Obama in 2008 and 60%-38% in 2012, and Democrats' share of their votes for House of Representatives increased from 54% in 2010 to 57% in 2012. All of their electoral votes, 173 (including the District of Columbia) in 2008 and 170 in 2010 were cast for Obama.

The overwhelming share of the nation's contested turf, in both presidential and congressional elections, is in the Heartland. And here the Democratic margins have been declining. Obama ran essentially even with John McCain in these states (less than 4,000 votes behind) in 2008 and carried 192 of their electoral votes to McCain's 173. In 2012 the Heartland voted 51%-47% for Mitt Romney and he carried 206 of their electoral votes to Obama's 162, which included 47 electoral votes in Florida and Ohio, which voted 50% and 51% for Obama. Romney won 3% more popular votes in these states than McCain, while Obama won 6% fewer popular votes than he had four years before. In the 2010 and 2014 House elections, the Heartland voted 56%-41% Republican, and Republican House candidates won majorities or pluralities of the popular vote in states with 330 and 317 electoral votes. Some analysts point out that Democrats have carried states with 240 electoral votes in six straight presidential elections. But they carried several of them by very narrow margins in one or more of those races; if this is a "blue wall," it is one with many not heavily concealed gaps and crevasses. Small shifts in the balance of national opinion could produce quite different results.

The increasing non-white percentage of the electorate is often treated as the result of rising voter turnout. And the increase in the black percentage of the electorate from the 10% or 11% in 1996, 2000 and 2004 to 13% in 2008 and 2012 undoubtedly reflected an increasing number of blacks choosing spontaneously or being prompted by campaign activity to vote for the first black major party nominee for president, since the black percentage of total population has increased only very marginally in recent decades. But overall turnout has not increased during the years of the Obama presidency, as it did during George W. Bush's presidency. Presidential year turnout increased from 105 million in 2000 to 122 million in 2004 and 131 million in 2008.

Thus the largest turnout increase, in percentage and absolute numbers, occurred in 2004, as John Kerry received 16% more popular votes than Al Gore and George W. Bush received 23% more votes than he had four years before (the largest such increase since Franklin Roosevelt in 1936). In contrast, presidential turnout declined from 131 million in 2008 to 129 million in 2012. Some 59% of that turnout decline was accounted for by declines in New York and New Jersey, which were uncontested presidentially and struck by superstorm Sandy a week before the election, and California, which was also uncontested presidentially and had no seriously contested statewide contests. But most other states registered turnout declines, and turnout increased primarily in target states where both parties worked to maximize their own turnout—though turnout was down significantly even in Ohio, a target state for the fourth consecutive presidential election with little population growth. If enthusiasm, both for and against Bush in 2004 and for Obama in 2008, helped to drive turnout, such enthusiasm seemed to be lacking in 2012. Similarly, turnout in congressional elections declined from 86.5 million in 2010 to 78.1 million in 2012, a 10% decline.

All these trends are potentially operative in 2016, a campaign year when the parties seem to be playing opposite to type. Republicans, seen as typically anointing the candidate next in line, instead in mid-2015 had a field of more than a dozen candidates, with none consistently running significantly ahead (and only a few behind) in national and early-contest state polls. Democrats, who historically have had rollicking nomination fights featuring candidates with substantial differences on issues, were mostly looking forward to the nomination of Hillary Clinton, who in almost all polls enjoyed leads that would have been welcome to incumbent Democratic presidents in some earlier cycles.

Another dynamic, however, seemed to be in play: the tendency of party's wingers—right-wing Republicans, left-wing Democrats—to become restive in the second term of their party's presidency. Such restiveness resulted in Ronald Reagan's and Edward Kennedy's challenges to Gerald Ford and Jimmy Carter in their first (and, it turned out, only) presidential terms. It was not apparent in the second term of Ronald Reagan's presidency, during almost all of which his job approval remained over 50%. But it flared brightly in George H. W. Bush's presidency—the first time a party held the office for a third consecutive term since the 1940s—as House Republican Whip Newt Gingrich opposed Bush's proposal for a tax increase and Patrick Buchanan launched a spirited challenge to Bush in the primaries. The trend was apparent at the end of Bill Clinton's presidency, when contrary to wide expectations a significant third-party vote went not to Buchanan—discontent with the Bush record having abated—but to Ralph Nader, running on a left-wing platform, who won 2.7% of the popular vote and, in the minds of many, deprived Al Gore of the electoral votes that would have put him in the White House. It was apparent to some extent in the Republican nominating race in 2008 and came into full flower with the emergence in 2009 of the tea party movement, many of whose followers emphasized their discontent with George W. Bush's record as much as with the policies of the Obama Democrats.

This partisan restiveness is a natural and rational phenomenon. Partisan wingers tend to take their parties' presidents' achievements for granted, to resent his inevitable compromises and to lament the roads not taken to further goals. They fear that those goals will become even more remote if, as usually happens, their party is turned out of power. By the second half of the second Obama term, many Democrats were lamenting that not all troops had been pulled out of the Middle East and Afghanistan, that the detention center at Guantanamo Bay was not closed, that the large banks' market share was increasing and had not been capped, that programs like universal pre-kindergarten and Social Security benefit increases were not under serious consideration. Such concerns were reflected in mid-2015 by unexpectedly large poll numbers and large, enthusiastic crowds for Vermont Sen. Bernie Sanders in New Hampshire and Iowa. But even weak showings by Clinton in these two states' early contests seemed unlikely to weaken her hold on voters who are black (whom she largely lost to Barack Obama in 2008) and Hispanic (whom she carried by wide margins over Obama), who tend to dominate the next contests in South Carolina and Nevada and who make up large minorities of primary voters in the big state contests to come. But by mid-2015 the primary and caucus schedule was not finalized, filing deadlines were far in the future and it was possible better known politicians (Joe Biden? Elizabeth Warren?) could enter the race. Left-wing Democrats, like right-wing Republicans, are often attracted by candidates who support policies that are thought to be opposed by a majority of general election voters. But Democrats, like Republicans, rarely nominate such candidates for president.

In congressional races, Democrats have a serious chance of reversing the Republicans' 54-46 margin in the Senate. The reason is that the lineup of seats up for election in the 2016 cycle favors Democrats, just as the lineup of seats up in 2014 favored Republicans. In mid-2015 Republicans held 24 of the Senate seats up in 2016 and Democrats held only 10. None of the Democratic seats are in states carried by Romney and only two (Colorado, Nevada) are in target states. In contrast, seven of the 24 Republican seats up in 2016 are in states carried in 2012 by Barack Obama (Florida, Iowa, New Hampshire, Ohio, Pennsylvania, Wisconsin) and another in the one target state carried, narrowly, by Romney (North Carolina).

This looks to be as steep a challenge to Republicans as Democrats faced in 2014, when they went into the Senate races holding seats in 21 states, including seven carried by Obama in 2012, versus only 15 for Republicans. Democrats lost all seven seats in the Romney states, plus two others in target states carried by Obama (Colorado, Iowa). But there is a difference between the Democrats' plight in 2014 and the Republicans' plight in 2016. Obama lost by double-digit margins in six of the seven Democratic seats in Romney states up in 2014; Democrats had to run far ahead of the president, and in a straight-ticket voting era, to hold them. In contrast, only one of the Republican seats up in 2016 in Obama states was carried by the president by double-digits (Illinois). The other six are in target seats Obama won by margins under 10%. It is certainly possible for Democrats to win each of these seats, except probably in Iowa if Charles Grassley runs for a sixth term. But it is also possible for Republicans to retain each of them and the North Carolina seat as well.

But it should be added that, as in 2014, a handful of incumbents might be beaten in primaries, with a resulting change in the outlook in such seats. And of course if one party wins several seats by very narrow margins, the partisan balance in the Senate could be altered in a way considered unlikely at the beginning of the electoral cycle.

Republican control of the House of Representatives seems unlikely to be in jeopardy. Republicans emerged from the 2014 election with 247 House members—fewer than Democrats had after the 2008 election but more than Republicans had won in any election since 1928. In order to win a majority, Democrats will have to run well ahead of Obama's showing in 2012, when he carried only 209 House districts and Mitt Romney carried 226. In a broader perspective, over the last 20 years there has been a striking continuity in House elections, in terms of seats won and percentages of the popular vote, with the exception of the elections of 2006 and 2008. In those two campaign cycles Republicans were running uphill, as George W. Bush had the lowest job approval ratings of any president of the last 20 years. Democrats carried the House popular vote by 53%-45% in 2006 and 54%-43% in 2008. These were their best results since 1990, when voters, especially but not only in the South, frequently split their tickets, more often in favor of Democrats than Republicans in House races. They also equaled or exceeded the widest House popular vote margins Republicans have won since 1994—and left them with enough House seats that they were able to pass the 2009 stimulus package and the 2010 heath care law.

But aside from those two elections, conducted in a unique political atmosphere, the results of House elections starting with 1994 have been eerily similar. Republicans have received between 48% and 52% of the House popular vote, and Democrats have received between 44% and 49% of the House popular vote. Republicans have won between 221 and 247 House seats, and Democrats have won between 1;88 and 214. Only once in these elections, in 2012, did Democrats win a plurality of the popular vote, by a 49%-48% margin, and two-thirds of that margin came from California, where a new primary system meant that there was no Republican candidate in eight of the 53 seats.

Such continuity in House election results is not unusual in recent times, especially if one sets aside, as here, a couple of elections that appear to be partisan outliers. In the 18 elections from 1958 to 1992, excluding the heavily Democratic years 1964 and 1974, Republicans won between 43% and 48% of the popular vote while Democrats won between 50% and 56%. Republicans won between 152 and 195 House seats, Democrats won between 240 and 283 House seats. In none of these elections did Republicans win either a majority of seats or a plurality of the popular vote. This was the period during which political scientists declared that Democrats had a lock on the House of Representatives and when they said, starting with 1968, Republicans had a lock on the presidency. In the 10 elections between 1938 and 1956, setting aside the heavily Republican year 1946, the competition was closer. Republicans won between 45% and 51% of the popular vote and Democrats won between 46% and 52%. Republicans won between 162 and 221 seats, Democrats between 213 and 267. In only one of these years, 1952, did Republicans win a majority of House seats, while in only two years, 1942 and 1950, did Republicans win a plurality of the popular vote.

The relative continuity of House elections, relative that is to wider variations in results in presidential elections, owes something to the popularity of often long-serving incumbents, reflecting their prowess at providing benefits for their districts and voting in accord with local sentiment. But there were differences between these three periods. In the 1938-56 period, a time of straight-ticket voting, there was a close correlation between presidential popularity and partisan voting. The fact that Democrats' rather narrow leads in popular votes tended to produce Democratic majorities is accounted for by the South, which voted heavily Democratic but had low general election turnout (because of poll taxes, exclusion of blacks from voting and lack of suspense about general election outcomes); the South cast only 11% to 17% of the nation's votes then, compared with 19% to 32% since passage of the Voting Rights Act, outlawing of the poll tax in the 1960s and increased partisan competition over the years. In the 1958-92 period, a time of increasing split-ticket voting, House Democrats benefited from the ancestral Democratic proclivities of many white Southerners who voted Republican (or for George Wallace in 1968) in presidential elections. Democrats also benefited from the assiduous constituency-courting of the young liberal Democrats elected in non-Southern Republican-leaning districts in the years from 1970 to 1976: the Vietnam-Watergate generation.

None of these factors has been in play since the early 1990s. The Vietnam-Watergate generation has faded from the scene. Senior Southern Democrats left the House or were defeated and replaced by Republicans. In 1992, for the first time since Reconstruction, Republicans won a larger percentage of the House vote in the South (defined as the 11 Confederate states plus West Virginia, Kentucky and Oklahoma) than outside the South, even as the Republican president was going down to defeat. Starting in 1994, Republicans have won a majority of the House popular vote in the South every year. And, as previously noted, in an era when political partisanship is closely linked to cultural issues and personal moral values, Americans have moved from split-ticket voting to straight-ticket voting.

A quarter-century ago it was widely believed that Republicans had a huge advantage in presidential elections and Democrats a huge advantage in congressional elections. Statistics supported that belief. Republicans won five of the previous six presidential elections and by an average popular vote margin of 10%. Democrats won majorities of the House in every election from 1954 to 1992 and, between 1958 and 1992, never elected fewer than 243 members, 25 more than the majority of 218. In the America headed toward the 2016 election, the partisan advantages seem reversed. Democrats, thanks to demographic clustering, have an advantage in presidential elections while Republicans, because of the same dynamic, have an advantage in House elections. But Democrats' popular vote majority averages only 4% and Republicans, until the 2014 election, never won more than 242 House seats. Even in an era of straight-ticket voting and considerable continuity in election results, nothing is inevitable in contemporary American politics.

President

Barack Obama (D)

Elected 2008, term expires Jan. 2017, 2nd term; b. Aug. 4, 1961, Honolulu, HI; Attended Occidental Col., 1979-81, Columbia U., B.A. 1983, Harvard U., J.D. 1991; Christian; married (Michelle); 2 children.

Elected Office: IL Senate, 1996-2004; U.S. Senate, 2005-08.

Professional Career: Dir., Illinois Project Vote!, 1992; Practicing atty., 1993-2004; Lecturer, U. of Chicago, 1992-2004.

Vice President

Joe Biden (D)

Elected 2008, term expires Jan. 2017, 2nd term; b. Nov. 20, 1942, Scranton, PA; U. of DE, B.A. 1965, Syracuse U., J.D. 1968; Catholic; married (Jill); 4 children (2 deceased).

Elected Office: New Castle Cnty. Cncl., 1970-72; U.S. Senate, 1973-2009.

Professional Career: Practicing atty., 1969-72.

Population		
Total (2013 census):	316,497,531	
% change since 2000:	Up 2.5%	
Land area (sq. miles):	3,531,905	
Pop. per sq. mile:	90	

Race and Ethnicity		
White:	63.3%	
Latino:	16.6%	
Black:	12.2%	
Asian:	4.8%	
American Indian:	0.7%	
Pacific Islander:	0.2%	
Some other race:	0.2%	
Two or more races:	2.0%*	
White ethnic:	26.9%	
Mexican:	10.7%	
Puerto Rican:	1.6%	
Cuban:	0.6%	
Other Latino or Hispanic:	3.7%	
*excluding some other race		

Language		
English only:	79.3%	
Spanish:	12.9%	
Other European:	3.7%	
Asian:	3.3%	

Place of Birth		
Native:	87.1%	
Born in United States:	85.7%	
State of residence:	58.7%	
Different state:	26.9%	
Puerto Rico, U.S. Islands or abroad to American parent:	1.4%	
Foreign born:	12.9%	

Foreign-born Citizenship Status		
Naturalized U.S. citizen:	45.1%	
Not a U.S. citizen:	54.9%	

Region of Foreign Born		
Latin America:	52.5%	
Asia:	28.8%	
Europe:	11.9%	
Africa:	4.1%	
Northern America:	2.0%	
Oceania:	0.6%	

Education		
H.S. grad. or less:	42.0%	
Some college:	20.0%	
Bachelor's degree:	18.0%	
Post-grad study:	10.8%	

Military		
Veterans/active duty:	9.4%	

Age Groups		
Infant to 17:	23.7%	
18 to 34:	23.4%	
55 to 64:	39.5%	
Over 64:	13.4%	

18 years and over		
Male:	48.6%	
Female:	51.4%	

65 years and over		
Male:	43.4%	
Female:	56.6%	

Income		
Median income:	$53,046	
Under $50,000:	47.3%	
$50,000-$99,999:	30.1%	
$100,000-$199,999:	17.8%	
$200,000 or more:	4.8%	
Poverty Rate:	15.4%	

Work		
White collar:	36.2%	
Blue collar:	21.1%	
Sales and service:	42.7%	
Gov't workers:	14.9%	

2012 Presidential Vote

Barack Obama (D)	65,907,124	(51%)
Mitt Romney (R)	60,931,731	(47%)

2008 Presidential Vote

Barack Obama (D)	69,498,215	(53%)
John McCain (R)	59,948,240	(46%)

★ ALABAMA ★

The past hangs over Alabama like its tall yellow pines: Refrains from decades-old civil rights struggles recur in the debate on gay marriage and the state's manufacturing base has once again been built with the help of outsiders. And while Alabama's dominant political party has changed, populists and "big mules" remain.

The French founded Mobile near the Gulf of Mexico in 1702, but the interior of Alabama remained Indian country until 1814, when Andrew Jackson defeated the Red Stick band of the Creek Indians at Horseshoe Bend, ending the two-year Creek War. Jackson imposed a treaty on the Red Sticks and on his own Indian allies, expropriating almost all of what five years later became the state of Alabama. With the Indians removed, the first white settlers poured in. Farmers from Tennessee swept into the red clay hills in the north, bringing the folkways of the Scots-Irish, with their hot-spirited willingness and fierce determination to avenge any perceived insult or threat. The second wave of settlement came a decade later, when entrepreneurial planters brought slaves to pick cotton in the fertile Black Belt (named for its soil) in south central Alabama. The interplay between the yeomen farmers and the plantation grandees has run through Alabama politics ever since. Both sought secession after the election of Abraham Lincoln, and the first Confederate Congress assembled in Montgomery in February 1861, where Jefferson Davis took the oath of office as president of the Confederacy in the Greek Revival state capitol atop Goat Hill.

After the Civil War and Reconstruction, Alabama, like other Southern states, became solidly Democratic, with an angry populist accent. With its solid-iron Red Mountain, steel manufacturing grew up around Birmingham in the late 1880s, thanks to northern bankers who helped finance it, and Yankee engineers who built the blast furnaces. Birmingham, site of Dixie's first steel production, became known as the "Pittsburgh of the South" and the industry's growth gave birth to the nearby city of Bessemer and later Fairfield, a company town of U.S. Steel.

In the first half of the 20th century, Alabama politics pitted Black Belt planters, timber barons and economic potentates in Birmingham and Mobile called "the Big Mules," against populists who favored the New Deal. The latter included some influential and colorful figures: Gov. Bibb Graves, Supreme Court Justice Hugo Black, Lister Hill, who authored Tennessee Valley Authority legislation in the House of Representatives, 1952 vice presidential nominee John Sparkman, and Gov. James E. "Big Jim" Folsom Sr.

Alabama went on to become, kicking and screaming, one of the birthplaces of the civil rights movement. From the Dexter Avenue King Memorial Baptist Church, the 26-year-old Martin Luther King Jr. led the Montgomery bus boycott after seamstress Rosa Parks refused to sit in the back of the public transit. A hundred miles north in Birmingham, two weeks after King penned his *Letter from Birmingham Jail* in 1963, Birmingham Police Commissioner Eugene "Bull" Connor, then Alabama's Democratic National Committeeman who had helped lead the walkout of southern delegates at the party's 1948 national convention, ordered police dogs and fire hoses to be turned on peaceful demonstrators. Four months later, four girls were killed when a bomb exploded in Birmingham's 16th Street Baptist Church. (The bombers were convicted in 1977, 2001 and 2002.) In March 1965, scores of some 600 marchers, catalyzed by the murder of civil rights advocate Jimmie Lee Jackson in Marion, were severely beaten by police at Selma's Edmund Pettus Bridge en route to Montgomery.

These events had reverberations far beyond Alabama. In June 1963, President John Kennedy endorsed what would become the Civil Rights Act of 1964, and in July 1965, Congress passed the Voting Rights Act. Fifty years later, the movie "Selma" generated headlines for its treatment of President Lyndon Johnson as too cautious on civil rights and the paucity of Academy Award nominations the film garnered. Actor David Oyelowo, who portrayed King, accused Hollywood of preferring "subservient" black narratives.

While Alabamians like Parks and King were leading the nation forward on race, Alabama's most prominent politician of the time, George Wallace, was pushing back. During his first term as governor, Wallace made national news in June 1963 by standing in the schoolhouse door at the University of Alabama to defy a federal court desegregation order. In 1964, Wallace ran in the Democratic presidential primaries and got surprising support in Indiana, Maryland and Wisconsin. In 1968, as a third-party candidate, he won 13.5% of the popular vote and carried five southern states and 46 electoral votes. He ran in the Democratic

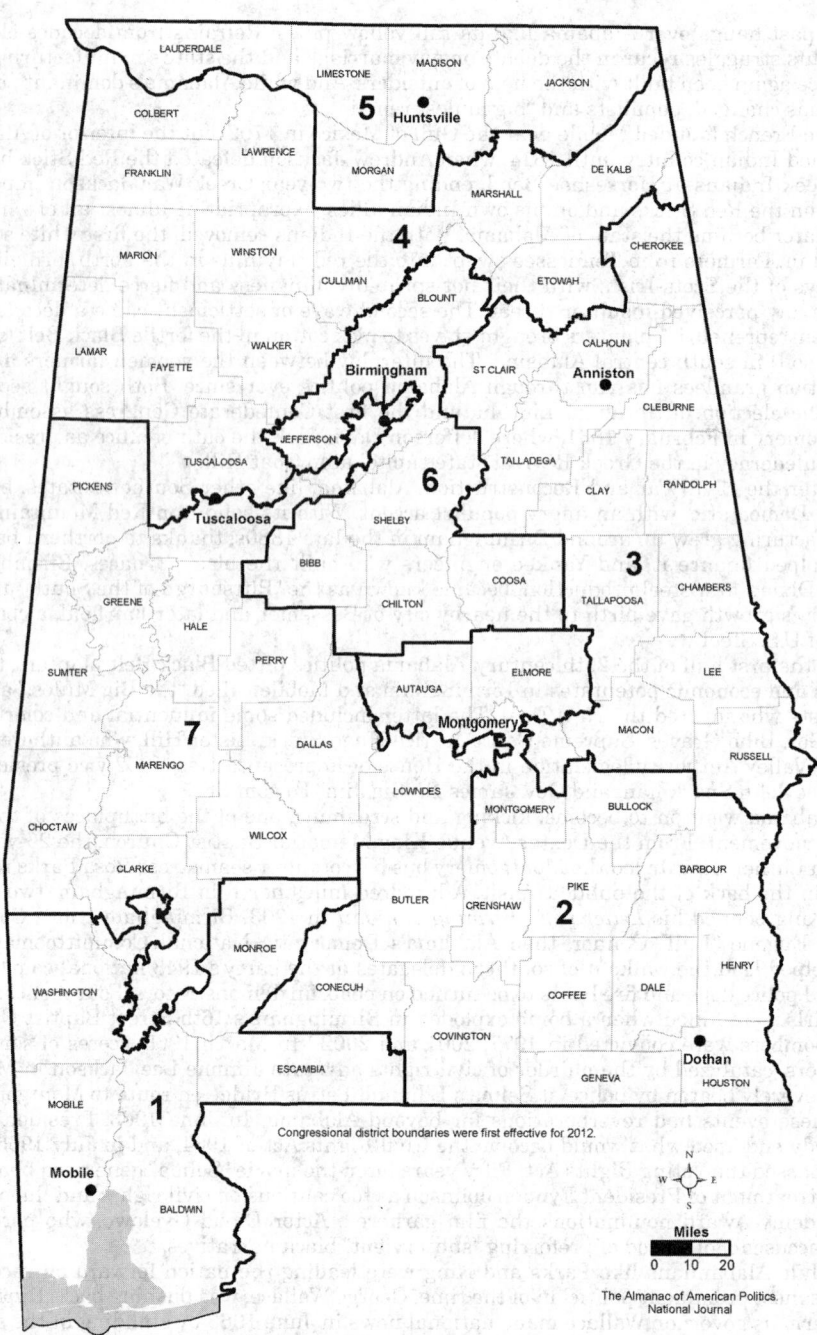

Congressional district boundaries were first effective for 2012.

Miles
0 10 20

The Almanac of American Politics.
National Journal

primaries again in 1972, and was shot and partially paralyzed while campaigning in Laurel, Maryland. He remained a formidable figure nationally until Jimmy Carter beat him in the 1976 Florida Democratic primary. He dominated Alabama politics, winning the governorship in 1962, running his wife to succeed him in 1966 (she died midterm), regaining the governorship in 1970 and 1974, then running and winning one last time in 1982. He spent his final years apologizing for his acts and met with Vivian Malone Jones, one of the students he tried to block from attending the University of Alabama, professing, "The South has changed, and for the better." He died in 1998. Jones, the sister-in-law of former Attorney General Eric H. Holder Jr., died in 2005.

Today civil rights tourism is a major business. Montgomery boasts sculptor-architect Maya Lin's circular Civil Rights Memorial, Troy University's Rosa Parks Museum, and the Dexter Parsonage. The Selma to Montgomery National Historic Trail runs along U.S. Highway 80. The Alabama Civil Rights Museum Trail includes the Tuskegee Airmen National Historic Site and the 16th Street Baptist Church.

Economically, Alabama has been making up ground lost during the Wallace years. While Atlanta was peacefully desegregating and beginning decades of white-collar growth, Birmingham was violently resisting the civil rights movement, only to see its blue-collar base in the steel industry shrink and its most talented residents of all races flee to calmer climes.

Automobiles have played a major part in Alabama's manufacturing revival, and as with the steel industry a century before, outsiders helped fuel the rebirth. Mercedes opened its first American assembly line in 1997, outside of Tuscaloosa while Honda has a major plant in Lincoln and Hyundai has one in Montgomery. These operations spawned dozens of auto supplier and subcontractor firms. According to the Center for Business and Economic Research at the University of Alabama, since 2011 the state has attracted more than 200 auto-related businesses involving $4 billion in investment and some 17,000 new jobs and ranks 5th in U.S. vehicle production.

ThyssenKrupp built a huge $5 billion steel and processing facility north of Mobile that opened in 2010 and was sold to Luxembourg's ArcelorMittal and Japan's Nippon Steel & Sumitomo Metal in 2013. Airbus selected Mobile for its first U.S. assembly plant where A320 aircraft were due to roll out in 2015. Pennsylvania-based Carpenter Technologies built a premium metals plant near Huntsville to provide alloy steel products for aerospace engines and medical devices. As demand for Alabama autos rebounded, the state's unemployment fell to a seasonally adjusted rate of 6.1% at the end of 2014, down from a recession high 10.5% in fall 2009. But the labor force participation rate also sunk to 56.5% in 2014—compared to 62.9% nationally—its lowest level since 1976.

Unions have not succeeded in organizing these new plants, and an investigative report by ProPublica and NPR found that Alabama had among the lowest workers' compensation benefits in the country. Still, more than one in ten of the state's workers still hold a union card, a rate that is by far the highest for states of the old Confederacy. Most members are public employees, like teachers in the politically potent Alabama Education Association.

The highest median family income in the state can be found in the Huntsville area, an engineering hotbed, where the U.S. Army Redstone Arsenal and Marshall Space Flight Center have been big job generators, and Raytheon opened a missile integration facility in 2012. Other wealthy turfs, with even faster population growth, are the Mobile suburbs and resort communities of Baldwin County. Birmingham is now a major commercial hub in the South. But that prosperity has largely eluded rural Alabama, where joblessness and grinding poverty persist. An *AL.com* analysis of the $5.4 billion in new business investment in the state in 2012, found that 76% flowed to the state's 15 urban counties, while the rest went to Alabama's 52 rural counties, and 11 of those saw no new funds at all.

In the 30-plus years since George Wallace's name last appeared on an Alabama ballot, the state has become solidly Republican in national politics. But for many years, most talented state politicians were Democrats who, along with their allies—the AEA, major black political associations, and trial lawyers—still beat less experienced Republicans. Gradually, even these canny Democratic survivors were overcome: Gov. Don Siegelman was defeated for a second term in 2002 and convicted on corruption charges in 2006; Lt. Gov. Jim Folsom Jr.—a former governor in the 1990s—got swamped by the 2010 Republican wave; a year later, legendary AEA political chief Paul Hubbert stepped down at the age of 76; and in 2012, Alabama's last Democratic statewide elected official, Lucy Baxley, 74, saw her political career end when she lost her reelection bid for Public Service Commission president to Twinkle Cavanaugh.

At the same time, the local Democratic machinery atrophied and the party's longstanding control of the state legislature also disappeared in 2010, when midterm voters propelled Republicans to almost a two-to-one advantage in the state Senate and a 27-seat upper hand in the state House—the first GOP majorities in Montgomery since Reconstruction. Two of the prime movers in that victory, state Rep. Mike Hubbard,

Voter Turnout	
2013 Total Citizen 18+	3,630,233
2014 Turnout Highest Office	1,180,413
2014 Turnout as % CVAP	32.5%
2012 Turnout as % CVAP	57.6%

Legislature			
Senate:	26R	8D	1I
House:	72R	33D	

the Republican state party chairman, and state Sen. Del Marsh, president pro tem of that chamber, led a disciplined and relentless campaign. Just like national GOP strategists who learned long ago that the path to congressional majorities ran through conservative districts and states in the South that had reflexively elected centrist Democrats, Hubbard, in particular, aggressively backed candidates in seats that had previously been conceded to conservative Democratic legislators and were ripe for Republican takeover.

But power can be corrupting and in 2014 House Speaker Hubbard was indicted by a Lee County grand jury on 23 counts of using his office for personal gain and soliciting favors from the state's ruling class. In an email to a board member of the Business Council of Alabama, a financially pressed Hubbard complained, "I was the architect of putting a pro-business legislature in place yet businesses seem to want to avoid any personal association with me like the plague." Hubbard maintained his innocence and 99 of the 105 state House members re-elected him Speaker in 2015. His trial was scheduled for October.

In 2015, the state was roiled by the debate over gay marriage when federal Judge Callie Granade ruled unconstitutional the Sanctity of Marriage Amendment to the state constitution banning same-sex unions, which 81% of Alabama voters supported in 2006.

The two leading protagonists in this legal struggle were steeped in Alabama's judicial culture. Granade is the granddaughter of Richard Rives, a federal judge in Montgomery who belonged to the "Fifth Circuit Four," a group of federal judges whose civil rights rulings helped desegregate the South. She also served as the first female assistant U.S. Attorney in the Southern District of Alabama when that office was run by GOP Sen. Jeff Sessions, who enthusiastically backed her nomination to the federal bench in 2001. At her confirmation hearing, her former boss presented Granade to the Judiciary Committee and declared that she had "the temperament, integrity, and legal knowledge, as well as the experience, that will make her an outstanding jurist on the Federal bench."

Roy Moore, the chief justice of the Alabama Supreme Court, led the fight against gay marriage asserting that a lower federal court could not command local probate judges to issue marriage licenses to gay couples. That attitude was nothing new for Moore, a devout Baptist, who as chief justice defied a federal judge's order to remove a 5,280-pound granite monument to the Ten Commandments that he had installed in his Montgomery courthouse. A state ethics board removed Moore in 2003, but Alabama voters returned him to his judicial post in 2012.

The gay marriage controversy stirred memories of the state's civil rights strife: rancorous opposition to federal power and an aversion to social change. Native Alabamian Diane

Population		Race and Ethnicity		Income	
Total:	4,833,722	White	66.7%	Median income:	$41,381
Urban:	38.8%	Black	26.5%		(45 of 50)
Suburban:	26.3%	Latino	3.9%	Under $50,000	56.2%
Rural:	34.9%	Asian	1.1%	$50,000-$99,999:	28.0%
Land area:	50,645	Two races	1.2%	$100,000-$199,999:	13.2%
Pop/sq. mi.:	95.4	White Ethnic	14.3%	$200,000 or more:	2.6%
Born in state:	70.0%			Poverty Rate	16.7%
		Education			
Age Groups		H.S. grad or less:	46.5%	**Work**	
Under 18:	23.0%	Some college:	30.0%	White collar:	33.3%
18 to 34:	23.0%	College degree, 4 yr.:	14.8%	Blue collar:	25.7%
35 to 64:	39.1%	Post-grad study:	8.7%	Sales and service:	40.9%
Over 64:	14.9%			Govt. workers:	16.2%
		Military			
		Veterans/active duty:	9.5%		

McWhorter, who won a 2002 Pulitzer Prize for her book on Birmingham's racial struggles, "Carry Me Home," told *The New York Times*, "It's like our oxygen is defiance and our identity is aggrievement."

Presidential Politics   The last Democrat to carry Alabama in a presidential election was Jimmy Carter, a son of the South, in 1976. President Gerald R. Ford carried only seven of the state's 67 counties. Since then, Alabama has been solidly Republican in presidential politics. John McCain won it 60%-39% in 2008 and Mitt Romney won it four years later by a nearly identical 61%-38%. Nearly 100% of the state's African-Americans voted for Barack Obama and well over 80% of whites for the Republicans.

2012 Presidential Vote		
Mitt Romney (R)..............1,255,925	(61%)	
Barack Obama (D) 795,696	(38%)	
2012 Presidential Primary		
Rick Santorum (R) 214,572	(35%)	
Newt Gingrich (R)..............182,239	(29%)	
Mitt Romney (R)................180,308	(29%)	
2008 Presidential Vote		
John McCain (R) 1,266,546	(60%)	
Barack Obama (D) 813,479	(39%)	

With victories in Jefferson County (Birmingham) in 2008 and 2012, Obama became the first Democrat to carry the state's largest county since 1952. But the share of the statewide vote that Jefferson accounts for in presidential contests fell below 15% in 2012, down from more than 19% in 1980. That decline reflects the growth of Birmingham suburbs and exurbs in Shelby and St. Clair counties whose combined share of the statewide vote more than doubled and rose above 6% between those two elections. Other than Conecuh in 2012, the rest of the counties that Obama won in these two elections were in the Black Belt, the poorest and most Democratic area of the state.

Alabama moved its traditional June primary to Super Tuesday, February 5, for the 2008 cycle, in hopes of getting national attention. But it was predictably overshadowed by larger states voting that day. For the first time, more votes were cast for Republican candidates (552,000) than for Democrats (537,000). In 2008, Mike Huckabee, with big margins in Jacksonian northern counties of the Tennessee River Basin, bested McCain 41%-37%, with 18% for Romney. Among Democrats in 2008, Obama won 56%-42%. In 2012, Alabama Republicans again favored the candidate of the evangelical Right: In the second week of March, Rick Santorum won with 35% to 29% for Newt Gingrich who edged Romney by less than 2,000 votes for second place out of 622,084 votes cast. The 2012 GOP contest was irrelevant to the outcome of the presidential race, but it did have a big impact down ballot when Roy Moore—who had famously defied a federal judge's order to remove a monument to the Ten Commandments from a Montgomery courthouse—upset the incumbent Republican state Supreme Court Justice on the strength of conservative Christians voting in the primary.

Congressional Districts   Alabama's shift to its predominantly Republican delegation came more slowly than in other southern states. As recently as 2010, it was split between four Republicans and three Democrats. But that year's election eliminated the final white Democrats (in the Montgomery and Huntsville-area districts), and the subsequent redistricting further entrenched the Democrats' hold on the African-American 7th District by adding most of Montgomery's black precincts to its Birmingham-area black population. The prospect of a competitive partisan congressional election in the state is remote, at least until the next redistricting.

114th Congress Lineup	
6 R	1 D
113th Congress Lineup	
6 R	1 D

Another way in which the Alabama has contrasted to most of the South has been its shrinking number of House districts. As recently as 1960, it had nine seats. Current Census Bureau population forecasts project that it will drop to six seats after the 2020 reapportionment. That loss almost surely would be a Republican seat. With the likelihood of continued GOP districts based in Mobile, Montgomery, Birmingham and Huntsville, that likely would result in elimination of one of the mostly rural districts in the central part of Alabama, which have been held by veteran Reps. Mike Rogers and Robert Aderholt.

Governor

Robert Bentley (R)

Elected 2010, term expires Jan. 2019, 2nd term; b. Feb. 3, 1943, Columbiana, AL; U. of AL (Tuscaloosa), B.S. 1964; U. of AL (Birmingham), M.D. 1968; Southern Baptist; Married (Dianne); 4 children.

Military Career: U.S. Air Force, 1969-75.

Elected Office: AL House, 2002-10.

Professional Career: Residency, Carraway United Methodist Hospital, 1968-69; Residency, Dermatology, U. of AL, 1974; Founding partner/pres., AL Dermatology Assoc., 1974-present.

Office: 600 Dexter Ave., Montgomery, 36130; 334-242-7100; Fax: 334-353-0004; Website: www.governor.alabama.gov.

Election Results

2014 general	Robert Bentley (R)	750,231	(64%)
	Parker Griffith (D)	427,787	(36%)
2014 primary	Robert Bentley (R)	388,247	(89%)
	Stacy George (R)	25,134	(6%)

Prior winning percentage: 2010 (58%)

Republican Robert Bentley joked that not even his wife gave him a chance when he launched his campaign for governor of Alabama in 2010. Indeed, Bentley has frequently had trouble earning the respect of his fellow Republican lawmakers in Montgomery. But by the beginning of his second term, Bentley appeared to be a more confident chief executive, determined to move his state beyond the legacy of its past.

Bentley grew up in rural Columbiana, southeast of Birmingham, where his father worked at a sawmill. Neither of his parents got past the ninth grade, but Bentley drove himself to succeed academically, becoming president of the student body, a state debate champion and valedictorian of his class at Shelby County High School. He put himself through college at the University of Alabama, majoring in chemistry and biology and earning a bachelor's degree in three years. Fulfilling a childhood dream to become a doctor, he went on to Alabama's medical school and received his M.D. in 1968. It was the height of the Vietnam era, and Bentley joined the Air Force. He was commissioned as a captain and served as a general medical officer at Pope Air Force Base at Fort Bragg in North Carolina. After completing his three-year residency, he moved to Tuscaloosa to start what became a very successful dermatology practice.

Bentley entered politics in 1998, but lost a state Senate race by 57 votes. Four years later he handily captured a seat in the state House of Representatives. He advocated for conservative causes, such as lowering taxes, and he was the driving force in revising the state's organ donor laws. Never known as a rhetorical firebrand, Bentley opted for a low-key, mild-mannered style. He was reelected in 2006 and in his second term introduced a constitutional amendment to freeze property taxes for homeowners.

As Bentley prepared to retire from his dermatology practice, he told his family in late 2008 that he was going to run for governor to succeed term-limited GOP incumbent Bob Riley. He announced his candidacy in May 2009, promising to develop better relations with state legislators than Riley had. He played up his medical credentials, using the slogan "Alabama is sick, and we need a doctor." But he struggled to raise money and had to loan his campaign nearly $800,000 out of his personal fortune. He faced two better-known and better-funded Republican primary opponents—businessman Tim James, the son of former Gov. Fob James, and Bradley Byrne, a former state senator and chancellor of the Alabama Community College System who was first elected as a Democrat but switched to the GOP in 1997 and was backed by Riley. Three other Republicans also vied for the nomination, including former state Supreme Court Justice Roy Moore, who drew national attention for his refusal to remove a monument of the Ten Commandments from his state courthouse in defiance of a federal judge's order.

In the June primary, Byrne received 28% of the vote while Bentley and James were tied with 25% each. Bentley had a slim advantage over James of fewer than 200 votes out of almost half a million cast. The results set up a runoff between Byrne and Bentley. Besides Riley, Byrne won endorsements from GOP Reps. Jo Bonner, Spencer Bachus and Mike Rogers. Bentley campaigned as an outsider vowing, "to clean up Montgomery and it's going to start with the governor's office." He also portrayed Byrne as less Republican than himself, citing Byrne's votes for Democrats Bill Clinton and Michael Dukakis in previous presidential elections. Bentley was helped in the run-off by the shadowy intervention of the Alabama Teachers Association. Byrne was bombarded with misleading negative ads paid for by the Conservative Coalition for Alabama, an innocuous political committee that was covertly and entirely funded by the AEA, which had long battled with the college chancellor. Bentley prevailed in the runoff with 56% of the vote.

Bentley's opponent in the general election was Democrat Ron Sparks, the state agriculture commissioner, who relentlessly advocated for a vote to legalize and tax gambling to fund education and state services. Bentley accused Sparks of taking money from gambling interests who faced indictment in a federal public corruption investigation. He too supported a public vote on gambling, but said there were better ways to bolster the state's finances. Given the unpopularity of President Barack Obama and congressional Democrats in Alabama and across much of the country in 2010, Bentley won with ease, 58%-42%. There were no hard feelings after the race and Bentley asked his vanquished foe to become director of the Alabama Rural Development Office.

Entering the governorship, Bentley tried to focus on his campaign pledges to make government more efficient and to create jobs, but he faced some daunting obstacles, topped by a projected shortfall in state revenue of some $450 million. In March 2011, he announced cuts of as much as 15% to many state departments. The next month, more than a dozen Alabama counties were devastated by tornadoes, killing 253 people and causing more than $2 billion in property damage. In part because of the disaster, the state's fiscal problems worsened, prompting Bentley to shear another $188 million from the budget in 2012. The reductions gashed the state's already stretched-to-the-limit social services, including agencies for public health and mental health.

In 2011, Bentley embraced a brutally harsh anti-immigration measure passed by the state legislature that included making medical professionals prove they were citizens to maintain their licenses to practice, allowing police to stop anyone on reasonable suspicion they are in the country illegally, and requiring K-12 school administrators to determine the legal status of new students. At the signing ceremony, Bentley boasted, "I campaigned for the toughest immigration laws and I'm proud of the legislature for working tirelessly to create the strongest immigration bill in the country." But the new law quickly started to cause problems for the state. Agribusiness and construction firms complained of labor shortages. Police detained a foreign worker and a visiting executive with the state's Honda and Mercedes auto assembly plants, respectively, who couldn't prove their legal status. Charges were later dropped. When Alabama business leaders expressed concerns that foreign investments could dry up, Bentley said he personally reassured the state's overseas partners that "our people and communities are as inviting and welcoming as we've always been." But in an interview with Associated Press, Bentley acknowledged that the severe law could conjure up negative images of the state's past. "It's going to take us a long time to outlive those stereotypes that are out there among people that Alabama is living in the '50s and '60s," he said.

Dealing with the assertive new GOP majority in the legislature was not Bentley's forte. During the 2012 regular session, lawmakers overrode his vetoes and proposed amendments six times and complained he was not sufficiently engaged with them. The relationship was such that when the legislature sent Bentley another tough immigration measure that year he threatened to veto it and called on the lawmakers to revise its controversial provisions in a special session. They ignored Bentley's concerns and he backed down, signed the bill, claiming it still improved the state's immigration law. Some Republicans publicly wondered if the governor had what it takes to be the state's chief executive, and the Mobile *Press-Register* said in an editorial: "Although liked by all, (Bentley) is playing too passive a role to be truly influential." The governor didn't hide his disdain for the Republican-run statehouse either. As the 2014 Alabama legislative session came to close, he told a Chamber of Commerce gathering in Huntsville that the Legislature had a lot in common with professional wrestling because it was "90 percent fake and 10 percent real."

Bentley had far less difficulty negotiating his 2014 reelection. He faced token opposition in the GOP primary and his opponent in the general election was former Democratic Rep.

Parker Griffith, a retired oncologist who was elected in 2008 to represent the Huntsville-based 5th district in northern Alabama, switched parties in hopes of holding the Republican-oriented seat, and was defeated in the 2010 GOP primary. Minutes before the registration deadline, he filed papers to seek the 2014 Democratic gubernatorial nomination. Among the ranks of Republican governors, Bentley had been one of the most vociferous opponents of Medicaid expansion under the 2010 Affordable Care Act, and Griffith tried to make that opposition the centerpiece of his campaign. But the issue never took hold, Griffith was woefully underfunded and Bentley cruised to a 64%-36% victory.

In his second inaugural address, Bentley declared, "If we are continually looking behind, focused on our past, whether good or bad, we can't see where we are going in our future." And there was reason to be optimistic: Since Bentley took office in January 2011, the unemployment rate in Alabama had fallen from 8.9% to 6.0%. But the rest of the state's finances had not similarly rebounded and at the start of his second term Bentley faced a $700 million shortfall in the state budget. Confronted with the options of raising taxes or cutting state agencies and social services even further, Bentley, who had opposed revenue hikes throughout his political career, chose the former. Most of the governor's proposed increases came from raising taxes on cigarettes and tobacco and on automobiles. Bentley tried to rally support for his plan by stumping for it across the state. "This is a real crisis," he frequently insisted. To drive home his message, Bentley's office would typically release specific budget cuts for the communities where he spoke unless taxes were raised. Even though conservative commentators pilloried him over his tax stance and Republicans in the legislature gave a cold shoulder to the governor's proposals, Bentley displayed a purpose and determination in the budget debate that were not always so evident in his first term. "After four years of uneven efforts, [Bentley] appears to have found his voice and is leading," observed veteran Alabama journalist Charles J. Dean.

The state's body politic was also upended in early 2015, when U.S. District Judge Callie Granade struck down its ban on same-sex marriage and ordered Alabama county probate judges to start granting marriage licenses to gay and lesbian couples. That ignited a legal showdown with state Supreme Court Justice Moore who told the local magistrates that they need not comply with Granade's decree. After the U.S. Supreme Court denied a request by Alabama authorities to block Granade's ruling, and with memories of the negative fallout from the state's hardline stance on immigration policy still fresh, Bentley sought to defuse the controversy. In so doing, he consciously juxtaposed himself with the state's legendary governor, George Wallace, whose hostility towards desegregation and the federal judges who sought to enforce it dominated the state's politics in the 1960s. "I'm going to do everything I can to make sure people across the country and people across the world realize that Alabama is a different state and that we respect the rule of law," Bentley said at a press conference. "It's important for people across the country to realize that the governor of Alabama today is not the governor of Alabama 50 years ago."

Senior Senator

Richard Shelby (R)

Elected 1986, term expires Jan. 2017, 5th term; b. May 6, 1934, Birmingham; U. of AL, B.A. 1957; U of AL School of Law, LL.B. 1963; Presbyterian; married (Annette Nevin); 2 children.

Elected Office: AL Senate, 1970-78; U.S. House, 1979-87.

Professional Career: Practicing atty., 1963-78; City prosecutor, Tuscaloosa, 1963-71; U.S. magistrate, 1966-70; Spec. asst. to Alabama atty. gen., 1969-71.

DC Office: 304 RSOB, 20510, 202-224-5744; Fax: 202-224-3416; Website: shelby.senate.gov.

State Offices: Birmingham, 205-731-1384; Huntsville, 256-772-0460; Mobile, 251-694-4164; Montgomery, 334-223-7303; Tuscaloosa, 205-759-5047.

Committees: *Appropriations:* Commerce, Justice, Science & Related Agencies (Chmn); Defense; Energy & Water Development; Homeland Security; Labor, HHS, Education & Related Agencies; Transportation, HUD, & Related Agencies. *Banking, Housing & Urban Affairs* (Chmn): Ex-officio member of each subcommittee. *Rules & Administration.*

Group Ratings

	ADA	ACLU	AFL-CIO	LCV	ITI	COC	HAFA	ACU	CFG	FRC
2014	15%	0%	–	20%	33%	88%	75%	88%	76%	93%
2013	10%	C	22%	23%	C	50%	C	76%	82%	C

National Journal Ratings

	2013 LIB — 2013 CONS	
Economic	32% —	67%
Social	9% —	90%
Foreign	21% —	76%
Composite	22% —	79%

Key Votes of the 113th Congress

1. Sandy storm spending	Y	5. Student Loan Rates	Y	9. Bipartisan Budget Deal	N
2. Chuck Hagel Confirmation	Y	6. Employee Non-Discrim'n Act	N	10. Farm Bill Conference Rept.	N
3. Gun Background Checks	N	7. Senate Vote on Judgeships	Y	11. Unempl. Comp. Extension	N
4. Immigration Reform	N	8. Defense Dept. Spending	N	12. Keystone Pipeline	Y

Election Results

2010 general	Richard Shelby (R)............................968,181	(65%)	$2,647,169	$1,479
	William Barnes (D) 515,619	(35%)	$5,871	
2010 primary	Richard Shelby (R)..........................405, 398	(84%)		
	N.C. 'Clint' Moser (R).........................75,190	(16%)		

Prior winning percentages: 2004 (68%), 1998 (63%), 1992 (65%), 1986 (50%); House: 1984 (97%), 1982 (97%), 1980 (73%), 1978 (94%)

Alabama senior Sen. Richard Shelby is a Republican who has tangled with the nation's spy chiefs, battled over Wall Street regulation, and in 2015 returned as chairman of the Banking, Housing and Urban Affairs Committee. But the issue for which he may be best known at home is spending. Adept at securing federal funds, he has five buildings at Alabama's public universities named for him. And he has the distinction of being the only current Senator to win election to that office as a Democrat (twice) and a Republican (three times), proof of his political dexterity in the state.

Shelby grew up in Birmingham, the son of a steelworker. After earning two degrees from the University of Alabama, he stayed in Tuscaloosa and practiced law with Walter Flowers, who was later a conservative Democratic congressman. Shelby, a Democrat at that time, was elected to the state Senate in 1970 at age 36. When Flowers ran, unsuccessfully, for the Senate in 1978, Shelby ran for his House seat. The critical contest was the Democratic runoff against Chris McNair, an African-American state legislator whose daughter, Denise, was one of the four young girls killed in the 1963 Birmingham church bombing. Although the district had the highest black percentage in Alabama at the time, Shelby won 59%-41%. In the House, Shelby had a conservative voting record, opposing the Voting Rights Act extension and the Martin Luther King Jr. holiday. He ran for the Senate in 1986 and won the Democratic primary with 51% of the vote after then-Secretary of State (and later governor) Don Siegelman withdrew. In the general election, he ran ads against incumbent Republican Jeremiah Denton, a retired admiral who had been a prisoner of war in Vietnam, for voting to cut Social Security and for owning two Mercedes-Benz cars. Shelby won by 7,000 votes.

A deft politician, he is quick to backslap with colleagues and recount war stories during downtime. But when it comes to legislation, Shelby is a notoriously tough negotiator, known for keeping his cards close to his chest and preserving his options for as long as possible. Such tactics can frustrate participants on and off Capitol Hill, and, at times, nearly thwart would-be deals. Shelby believes the 2010 Dodd-Frank financial reforms overreached in setting rules for regional and smaller banks.

As one of a half a dozen or so conservative Southern Democrats in the Senate in the mid-1980s, Shelby at first attracted little notice. In 1992, he was reelected 65%-33%, breaking a jinx on a seat that before Shelby's election in 1986 had had four different occupants in 10 years. Soon after President Bill Clinton took office in 1993, Shelby broke ranks with the Democratic Party. At a meeting with Vice President Al Gore, he turned to the assembled Alabama television cameras and opposed the Clinton program as "high on taxes, low on spending cuts." In response, the administration announced that a multimillion-dollar space facility would be built not in Alabama but in Texas (although it eventually was built in Alabama). The more he defied Clinton, the better Shelby's favorable ratings were at home. The day after Republicans regained control of the Senate in 1994, Shelby announced he was switching parties, increasing the GOP majority to 53-47. Republicans happily allowed him to keep his seniority on the Banking Committee and gave him seats on Appropriations and its Defense Subcommittee.

Shelby got a seat on the Intelligence Committee as well, putting him on a course to become its chairman in 1997. One of his first acts was to scuttle the nomination of Clinton National Security Adviser Anthony Lake to be Director of the Central Intelligence Agency. By the time of the Sept. 11 attacks, the Senate was back in Democratic hands, but Shelby, as the ranking Republican on the Intelligence panel, was an important player in the ensuing weeks and months. He had adopted an adversarial posture toward the intelligence agencies during the Clinton and Bush presidencies, and soon after the terrorist attacks, Shelby stopped just short of calling for the resignation of CIA Director George Tenet. In June 2004, when Tenet announced his resignation, Shelby said, "What was a surprise was that he held onto the job as long as he did."

Aside from his positions on the intelligence agencies, Shelby was mostly supportive of the Bush administration's conduct of the war on terrorism. In December 2001, he was one of 10 senators to sign a letter calling for a plan "to eliminate the threat from Iraq." But he clashed with the two Intelligence Committee chairmen, Democratic Sen. Bob Graham and Republican Rep. Porter Goss, both of Florida. He helped push aside their choice of staff director for the joint congressional probe of intelligence agencies, and he installed his own candidate. At first, he opposed the appointment of an independent Sept. 11 commission as unnecessary, but relented in 2002. He was out front in calling for the creation of a director of national intelligence after the intelligence community, in his view, was unable to share information. That position was later upheld by the 9/11 Commission and adopted in the intelligence bill approved by Congress in 2004. That bill included a Shelby proposal to give the DNI ombudsman access to all intelligence for analytical reviews, but he was displeased that the new director would not be a Cabinet member.

On domestic issues, Shelby has compiled a conservative record. But he is not a free market purist. Despite his party switch, he has remained friendly with trial lawyers, who usually support Democrats in Alabama. Lawyers and law firms have been his biggest source of campaign contributions, according to the Center for Responsive Politics. He opposed Alabama colleague Jeff Sessions' amendment to cap lawyers' fees in tobacco cases and insisted tort reform was a state issue. He voted against a 2004 bill to protect gun manufacturers from liability for actions of users of their products. He was the only Senate Republican to vote against financial services deregulation in 1999, and he opposed allowing federally insured banks to sell real estate or insurance. In 2013, Shelby was one of only five Senate Republicans to oppose the New Year's Eve fiscal cliff agreement, saying that the bipartisan deal on taxes and spending "falls far short of the measures necessary to promote job creation, economic growth, and fiscal stability."

Between 2003 and the end of 2012, Shelby was either the chairman or the ranking minority member of the Banking Committee, and from that perch, was at the center of congressional attempts to stem problems in the mortgage and financial industries. On a hotly lobbied issue in 2003, Shelby supported defining stock options as expenses, a measure opposed by the high technology industry. The same year, he presciently quizzed Federal Reserve Chairman Alan Greenspan about the increasing number of home loans to borrowers with weak credit histories, a trend that led to the home mortgage market collapse. In 2008, Democratic chairman Christopher Dodd of Connecticut pushed a compromise-housing bill that would allow bankruptcy judges to restructure mortgages and another proposal to refinance mortgages for millions of homeowners at risk of defaulting. Consumer groups pushed for both, but could not get by Shelby.

He also opposed the $700 billion rescue of the financial markets in September 2008, though President Bush was pushing the legislation. Two months later, he protested the massive government loan for the Big Three domestic automakers, which he called "dinosaurs." He threatened to filibuster and the bill did not pass the Senate, though President Barack Obama proceeded with a successful administrative version. When Shelby was accused of defending foreign automakers with plants in Alabama, he pointed out that he had voted against an earlier bailout of Chrysler long before the plants were built. In 2010, Shelby again came under fire for blocking the nomination of economist Peter Diamond to the board of the Federal Reserve. He insisted Diamond lacked experience and knowledge in monetary economics, comments that were derided by national media outlets after Diamond won the Nobel Prize in economics in October of that year. Diamond withdrew his nomination in 2011.

Shelby was a key player in efforts to reform the nation's financial regulatory system in 2009-2010. He and Dodd agreed, in theory, to the creation of a consumer financial protection division or agency. However, a persistent sticking point surfaced over the details of creating the new entity. While Dodd and Obama wanted the new consumer protection agency to be housed within the Federal Reserve and given more independence, Shelby called for creating a consumer protection division within the FDIC. His substitute failed 61-38. He expressed other reservations about the bill, including its failure to address Fannie Mae and Freddie Mac, the quasi-governmental mortgage agencies that received substantial rescue funds. When the financial services reform bill was passed by the Senate in May 2010, Shelby voted against it. Despite his objections to the creation of the Troubled Asset Relief Program to assist failing banks, Shelby drew praise from the program's special inspector general, Neil Barofsky. In a 2012 book criticizing Congress and the Treasury Department for its handling of the issue, Barofsky singled out Shelby for being more interested in substance than were many of his colleagues. In one briefing with the senator, he wrote, "I probably covered more in fifteen minutes of rapid-fire questions and answers than in most hour-long meetings with other members of Congress."

Working with new Banking committee chairman Tim Johnson of South Dakota in 2011, Shelby remained at the forefront of Republican efforts to delay the Obama administration's implementation of the new consumer protection bureau. He demanded changes to the bureau's structure before he would consider approving a director to lead it; the objections by him and other Republicans eventually prompted Obama to circumvent the Senate in January 2012 and make a recess appointment of former Ohio Attorney General Richard Cordray.

His term limit on the panel forced him to step aside in January 2013 in favor of Idaho's Mike Crapo, and he became the ranking minority member on Appropriations. As an appropriator, Shelby has looked out for Alabama's interests. When it comes to earmarking, the special provisions tucked into spending bills by individual lawmakers, Shelby has "made a kind of art form out of it," former Alabama GOP Rep. Jack Edwards told the Mobile *Press-Register*. He's obtained hundreds of millions of dollars for Alabama's universities as well as funds for refurbishing the Vulcan statue on Birmingham's Red Mountain—a favorite target of Sen. John McCain of Arizona, who has crusaded against earmarks. Shelby was critical of the Senate's earmark ban adopted in November 2010, saying it would put a significant crimp in his long-term goal of securing $1 billion for science, engineering, and research projects at the state's colleges.

One example of Shelby's legislative talents came in 2014 when his liberal Democratic colleague from Maryland, Senate Appropriations chairwoman Barbara Mikulski, agreed to boost spending for the Space Launch System, an important project at the Marshall Space Flight Center in Huntsville. Critics have derided SLS as a "rocket to nowhere," asserting that its technology is outmoded and much costlier than using private alternatives to propel heavy payloads into space. But Shelby and Mikulski, with her own home-state interest at the Goddard Space Flight Center, worked collaboratively to fund NASA programs. Said Mikulski at a hearing that year, "He's a true partner."

But Mississippi Republican Thad Cochran's re-election in 2014 led him to claim the Appropriations chairmanship, sending Shelby back to Banking. Because of Senate GOP rules that allow chairmen to serve for six years total (he previously held the gavel from 2003-2006), Shelby can expect to serve in that job for only two years, adding to the already difficult task. He also has to work with a new ranking Democrat on the committee, the liberal populist Sherrod Brown of Ohio. Brown and other Democrats expressed concerns over Shelby's handling of legislation to ease banking regulations and make changes at the Federal Reserve.

Shelby's party switch in 1994 caused him no trouble in increasingly Republican Alabama, in part because he routinely raises significant amounts of money to discourage serious challengers. In 1998, he was reelected 63%-37% over a retired ironworker who mortgaged his pickup truck to pay the $2,672 filing fee. For the 2004 election, his Democratic opponent was Wayne Sowell, Alabama's first black Senate nominee and a telephone claims representative for the Social Security Administration in Birmingham. Shelby spent only $2.3 million of the $11 million he had stockpiled for the contest, and won 68%-32%, losing only nine black-majority counties in the Black Belt. He easily won reelection in 2010 against Democrat William Barnes, a Birmingham lawyer.

Shelby announced in January 2015 that he would run again in 2016 when he would be 82. To frighten off any would-be challengers from the tea party or elsewhere, he had already amassed a campaign war chest of close to $18 million by the end of 2014. Many have chastised Shelby for hoarding all that cash and not sharing more of it with other deserving GOP candidates. But as chairman of the Banking Committee, and determined as ever, he was unlikely to let up on the fundraising until he secured a sixth term.

Junior Senator

Jeff Sessions (R)

Elected 1996, term expires Jan. 2021, 3rd term; b. Dec. 24, 1946, Selma; Huntingdon Col., B.A. 1969, U. of AL, J.D. 1973; Methodist; married (Mary Blackshear Sessions); 3 children.

Military Career: Army Reserves, Captain, 1973-86.

Elected Office: AL atty. gen., 1994-96.

Professional Career: Practicing atty., 1973-75, 1977-81, 1993-94; Asst. U.S. atty., 1975-77; U.S. atty., 1981-93.

DC Office: 326 RSOB, 20510, 202-224-4124; Fax: 202-224-3149; Website: sessions.senate.gov.

State Offices: Birmingham, 205-731-1500; Huntsville, 256-533-0979; Mobile, 251-414-3083; Montgomery, 334-244-7017; Wiregrass, 334-792-4924.

Committees: *Armed Services:* Airland; SeaPower; Strategic Forces (Chmn). *Budget. Environment & Public Works:* Clean Air & Nuclear Safety; Fisheries, Water, & Wildlife; Transportation & Infrastructure. *Judiciary:* Immigration & the National Interest (Chmn); Crime & Terrorism; Oversight, Agency Action, Federal Rights & Federal Courts.

Group Ratings

	ADA	ACLU	AFL-CIO	LCV	ITI	COC	HAFA	ACU	CFG	FRC
2014	5%	0%	–	0%	0%	57%	85%	96%	98%	100%
2013	10%	C	18%	15%	C	50%	C	88%	88%	C

National Journal Ratings

	2013 LIB	—	2013 CONS
Economic	15%	—	80%
Social	16%	—	83%
Foreign	15%	—	84%
Composite	17%	—	84%

Key Votes of the 113th Congress

1. Sandy storm spending	N	5. Student Loan Rates	Y	9. Bipartisan Budget Deal	N
2. Chuck Hagel Confirmation	N	6. Employee Non-Discrim'n Act	NV	10. Farm Bill Conference Rept.	N
3. Gun Background Checks	N	7. Senate Vote on Judgeships	Y	11. Unempl. Comp. Extension	N
4. Immigration Reform	N	8. Defense Dept. Spending	N	12. Keystone Pipeline	Y

Election Results

2014 general	Jeff Sessions (R)......................... unopposed	$2,013,832	$14,042
2014 primary	Jeff Sessions (R)......................... unopposed		

Prior winning percentages: 2008 (63%), 2002 (59%), 1996 (52%)

In Republican Jeff Sessions, Alabama's junior senator since 1997, one can hear echoes from the state's populist past and Gov. "Big Jim" Folsom railing against the "monopolists, brass hats, Wall Street lawyers [and], tea sippers," who had little in common with the "peace loving, God-fearing people of the Cotton Belt." He is arguably the Senate's most outspoken critic of illegal immigration, whom the conservative *National Review* dubbed "amnesty's worst enemy."

Sessions grew up along the state's Black Belt, the son of a country store owner, and recalls seeing many farm families go bankrupt. "They got crushed by debt, and the lesson was clear: You simply cannot live above your means or it will catch up to you," he told the Mobile *Press-Register* in 2012. He graduated from Huntingdon College and the University of Alabama Law School and practiced law in a small town near the Tennessee Valley and later in Mobile. He was appointed U.S. attorney in Mobile in 1981, at age 35, and became known as a tough, aggressive prosecutor over the next dozen years. In 1985, he was nominated for a federal judgeship but was attacked by liberals including Massachusetts Sen. Ted Kennedy, a senior Democrat on the Judiciary Committee, who called Sessions "a throwback to a shameful era" on racial matters. With Alabama's Democratic Sen. Howell Heflin voting against him in the committee, his nomination never went to the Senate floor.

In 1994, Sessions challenged state Attorney General Jimmy Evans, a Democrat who had successfully prosecuted Republican Gov. Guy Hunt the year before, and won 57%-43%. In March 1995, when Heflin announced his retirement, Sessions ran for his seat. In the contested GOP primary against long-distance phone carrier executive Sid McDonald, who spent more than $1 million on his campaign, Sessions relied on his base in southern Alabama, territory that not so long ago cast almost no Republican primary votes. From Birmingham north, the race was a close race: McDonald led 30%-29%. But in the rest of the state, Sessions led 48%-12%, for a 38%-22% statewide margin. In the runoff, McDonald extended his lead north of Birmingham to 54%-46%. But almost half the total votes were cast farther south, and there Sessions led 73%-27%, for a 59%-41% win.

The Democratic nominee, trial lawyer and state Sen. Roger Bedford, was financed by trial lawyers and endorsed by key public employee unions and African-American organizations. In the general election, Bedford was competitive in fundraising and was the better campaigner. He opposed abortion rights, gun control, and gays in the military. Sessions avoided debates and attacked his opponent as a "Ted Kennedy" Democrat, which implied that Bedford was too far to the left for Alabama. Sessions won 52%-45%, running best in suburban counties. Bedford carried the Black Belt and other rural counties.

Sessions has a very conservative voting record in the Senate. On the Budget Committee, he has assailed President Barack Obama for being unwilling to seriously address the growing national debt. He also complained about the unwillingness of his Democratic counterparts on the committee to pass a budget plan and said GOP Rep. Paul Ryan's controversial House-passed budget "lays the foundation for an American renaissance." He often travels around Alabama giving detailed presentations, complete with charts, about the mounting debt, using much the same manner as he did in his days as a prosecutor, laying out the facts and asking people to judge. He teamed with Missouri Democrat Claire McCaskill in 2010 on an amendment to impose multi-year caps on discretionary spending. The pair offered the measure several times until it fell just one vote short of the 60 required to pass. When Senate Budget Chairman Patty Murray of Washington struck a deal with her House counterpart, Ryan, on a bipartisan budget in December 2013, Sessions was among those refusing to endorse it. He opposed raising discretionary spending above the level agreed to in the 10-year Budget Control Act period, and opposed using trust-fund savings to increase that spending. He is a leading Senate critic of earmarks, the special provisions inserted into spending bills by lawmakers for their districts or states. Nevertheless, Sessions supports major projects with an impact on Alabama.

On the Judiciary Committee, Sessions has been a reliable voice against the "activist judiciary" and many of President Obama's judicial nominees whom he deems too liberal. "It seems if you have the ACLU DNA, you get a pretty good leg up to being nominated by this president," declared Sessions on the Senate floor in 2010. Sessions opposed Obama's nomination of Loretta Lynch to be Attorney General, though he voted in 2009 for her predecessor Eric Holder, of whom Sessions would later become a sharp critic. On a few occasions, Sessions has worked with Democrats on criminal reform legislation. Sessions' tenacious manner as a lawmaker can contradict his genial demeanor, and former Kennedy spokesman Jim Manley said that despite the Alabamian's bruising judicial confirmation fight, he never betrayed any personal animosity towards his boss. "Say what you will about him, he was always nice to Kennedy and other Democrats as well," recalled Manley.

Sessions became a leader against illegal immigration because, he said, no one else was willing to do so. In 2006, Sessions emerged as one of the most vocal opponents of the bipartisan immigration bill sponsored by Sens. Kennedy and John McCain of Arizona He staunchly opposed a provision granting immigrants who had entered the country illegally a process to achieve citizenship. Over the next two years, as Congress debated changes in immigration policy, Sessions was a major roadblock to proposals easing immigration restrictions. In January 2007, he got the Senate to pass a bill banning federal contracts for 10 years to contractors who do not use the E-Verify system and hire illegal immigrants. Later in the year, he fought a bill that came to the floor that created a guest-worker program for illegal immigrants. Sessions derided the bi-partisan group of Senators "who met in secret" to craft the immigration bill and ultimately beat them, delivering a significant defeat to President George W. Bush who supported the measure.

As calls grew four years later for Congress to act on immigration, he was unyielding on the need for tighter enforcement above all else: "Securing the border, and enforcing immigration law, is especially important in these difficult economic times. Illegal labor depresses wages and makes it more difficult for out-of-work Americans to find good-paying jobs," he said. More recently, Sessions has been a skeptic of the H1-B visa program which facilitates foreign workers with science, technology, engineering and math know-how to join high-tech firms.

Sessions bitterly but unsuccessfully opposed the Senate's 2013 bipartisan immigration reform bill, sending around policy proposals to undecided members and criticizing the news media for what he called its bias in favor of the proposal. When an influx of Central American refugees on the U.S.-Mexico border led Congress to take up a bill trying to control the border in July 2014, Sessions again was among those leading the charge against it. He raised a point of order against the Senate's $3.6 billion border funding bill; Democrats fell 10 votes short of defeating it. When he took to the Senate floor that year, Sessions often seemed to channel the populist resentments of Alabama's "Big Jim" Folsom. "I know who I work for, and that is the hard-working people of Alabama and the United States," thundered Sessions. "A small group of CEOs don't get to set immigration policy for the country, no matter how much money they have." On another occasion, Sessions sneered at the cooperation between the Obama White House and corporate leaders to further immigration. "The administration is meeting with the elite, the cosmopolitan set, who scorn and mock the concerns of everyday Americans," Sessions decried. "These great and powerful citizens of the world, we know, don't care much about old-fashioned things like national boundaries..."

Although Sessions has sponsored few major bills, he has had considerable success inserting into other legislation provisions he favors that set new federal policy. He typically targets bills that are likely to pass, an effective strategy. When the Medicare prescription drug bill came to the floor in 2003, Sessions added a provision for higher Medicare reimbursement for rural hospitals and threatened to vote against the final version of the bill unless it stayed in. It did, sending $738 million to Alabama, more than any other state save Texas and Florida. He also is unafraid to block legislation he dislikes. For several months in 2011, he held up passage of the Generalized System of Preferences, a trade agreement that opens the United States to up to 5,000 products from 127 developing countries, in an unsuccessful bid to make changes to protect a sleeping bag maker in his state from foreign competition.

Sessions has been a staunch defender of the oil, gas, and nuclear power industries. After the BP oil spill in 2010, he joined Louisiana Republican David Vitter on a bill to limit the damages for spill-related losses apart from cleanup costs. He rejected the idea that BP should lead the cleanup effort, saying the government should take on that role. Sessions is a climate change skeptic. When Sen. Barbara Boxer told him at an August 2012 hearing that 98 percent of scientists agree that humans are responsible for climate change, he scoffed, "I am offended by that ... I don't believe that's correct."

On the Armed Services Committee, Sessions has been a big advocate for missile defense, and he has focused on building up defense installations in Alabama. He supported the Bush administration on the Iraq war and was one of nine senators to vote against an amendment banning "cruel, inhuman, or degrading treatment" of prisoners. He has criticized the Obama administration's fight against terrorism, calling former Attorney General Holder "too soft" on the issue and wrote in a *Washington Post* op-ed in 2011: "This administration has lost sight of the reality that actionable intelligence—not criminal prosecution—is the only way our country can detect and foil the next al-Qaida plot."

In his 2002 reelection bid, Sessions faced Democrat Susan Parker, the state auditor and a fundraiser for colleges. She had the support of teachers' unions, but Sessions outspent her 4-to-1 and won 59%-40%. He raised early money in advance of the 2008 election, warding off possible challenges by prominent Democrats—Artur Davis, then a House member, and Ron Sparks, the state agriculture commissioner. His opponent was state Sen. Vivian Davis Figures of Mobile. Sessions spent $3.8 million, while Figures spent $331,000. Sessions won 63%-37%. He secured a fourth term in 2014, running unopposed.

Upon returning to Washington, Sessions suffered a setback when he lost a bid for the Budget Committee chairmanship to his more temperate GOP colleague from Wyoming, Mike Enzi. Both Sessions and Enzi were elected to the Senate in 1996, but Enzi maintained seniority due to a rare party procedure: They drew lots after they were both first elected to determine their ranking among all Republican Senators, most of whom are reluctant to buck the seniority system. Sessions ultimately deferred to Enzi, but some observers believe he would have lost a showdown had the matter been put to a vote, because of his willingness to discomfort the GOP leadership in prosecuting his case against immigration. As a consolation prize of sorts, Sessions became chairman of the Judiciary Committee's immigration panel from which he has continued to champion his cause.

FIRST DISTRICT

Bradley Byrne (R)

Elected 2013, 1st full term. b: Feb. 16, 1955, Mobile; University Military School, 1973; Duke University, B.A. 1977; U. of AL, J.D. 1980; Episcopalian; married (Rebecca); 4 children.

Elected Office: AL state Senate, 2002-2007.

Professional Career: Practicing atty., 1980-94, 2010-13; AL State Bd. of Ed., 1994-2002; Chancellor of AL Dept. of Postsecondary Ed., 2007-09.

DC Office: 119 CHOB, 20515, 202-225-4931; Fax: 202-225-0562; Website: byrne.house.gov.

State Offices: Mobile, 251-690-2811; Summerdale, 251-989-2664.

Committees: *Armed Services:* Emerging Threats & Capabilities; Seapower & Projection Forces. *Education & the Workforce:* Health, Employment, Labor, & Pensions; Higher Education & Workforce Training. *Natural Resources.*

Group Ratings (House)

	ADA	ACLU	AFL-CIO	LCV	ITI	COC	HAFA	ACU	CFG	FRC
2014	0%	0%	–	0%	100%	85%	63%	88%	77%	100%
2013	–	C	–	–	C	–	C	–	–	C

Key Votes of the 113th Congress (House)

1. Guantanamo Bay Detainees N	3. Afghanistan Combat N	5. Keystone Pipeline Y
2. Medical Marijuana N	4. Syrian Rebels Training Y	6. Immigration Exec. Action Y

Election Results

2014 general	Bradley Byrne (R)............................	103,758	(68%)	$1,655,999	$261,707
	Burton LeFlore (D)	48,278	(32%)	$35,603	
2014 primary	Bradley Byrne (R)...................... unopposed				

Prior winning percentage: 2013 special (71%)

Population		Race and Ethnicity		Income	
Total:	695,176	White:	65.6 %	Median income:	$42,309
Urban:	52.5%	Black:	28.0%		*(352 of 435)*
Suburban:	27.1%	Latino:	2.8%	Under $50,000:	56.7%
Rural:	20.4%	Asian:	1.3%	$50,000-$99,999:	28.3%
Land area:	6,067	Two races:	1.1%	$100,000-$199,999:	12.5%
Pop/sq. mi.:	91.4	White Ethnic:	15.9%	$200,000 or more:	2.4%
Born in state:	68.0%			Poverty Rate:	19.8%
		Education			
Age Groups		H.S. grad or less:	45.9%	**Work**	
Under 18:	23.7%	Some college:	31.2%	White collar:	31.1%
18 to 34:	22.0%	College degree, 4 yr.:	15.7%	Blue collar:	24.6%
35 to 64:	38.8%	Post-grad study:	7.2%	Sales and service:	44.3%
Over 64:	15.5%			Govt. workers:	13.5%
		Military			
		Veterans/active duty:	10.1%		

Southwest Alabama: Mobile Bay

Mobile, the port where the Tombigbee and Alabama rivers flow into the Gulf of Mexico, was a strategic point on the American frontier. Spanish after the Revolutionary War, it was wrested away by threats of war from Secretary of State John Quincy Adams. During the Civil War, it was one of the major Confederate ports. In 1864, Admiral David Farragut, while steaming into the harbor lashed to his mast, cried, "Damn the torpedoes! Full speed ahead." Today, Mobile is full of graceful signs of its exotic past.

Voter Turnout	
2013 Total Citizen 18+	522,389
2014 House Turnout	152,234
2014 Turnout as % CVAP	29.1%
2012 Turnout % CVAP	58.1%

Behind the docks and rail lines are downtown buildings and old houses with Spanish motifs, French accents, or tropical Art Deco lines. Further inland are neighborhoods with spacious houses, often with double porches, overhung by huge live oaks graced with Spanish moss. Mobile is a Gulf Coast version of Charleston or a smaller, more comfortable New Orleans, with a taste for shellfish and spicy food and an even older Mardi Gras, which the locals have been celebrating since 1703. As befits a frontier city with a martial past, Mobile is bristling with arms: One of the city's proudest possessions is the battleship *USS Alabama*, moored at the head of Mobile Bay, with its guns aimed out toward the Gulf. Mobile's economy was based originally on docks and shipyards, factories and terminals, but with a determination to impose touches of beauty on its hot, flat landscape. The capital improvements include Mobile's State Docks, which serve Alabama's booming Mercedes, Honda, and Hyundai auto factories. Mobile's $300 million container terminal opened in 2008 and immediately more than doubled annual shipments with an alternative shipping route to Midwest markets. With the expansion of the Panama Canal and European aircraft manufacturer Airbus opening a new assembly line in Mobile for its A320 airline, the city's port is attracting more business, including for Alabama's robust aerospace industry. The nearby Daphne-Fairhope-Foley area in Baldwin County ranked second among the fastest growing "micropolitan" areas in the country from 2010 to 2011, according to the Census Bureau.

In August 2005, Hurricane Katrina struck Mobile and its beaches with Category 4 intensity. On Dauphin Island, the 14-mile spit of land south of Mobile Bay, 300 homes were swept away, and a one-mile gash created a new island. Elsewhere in Mobile and Baldwin counties, Katrina caused major damage to pecan, peanut, and cotton crops. Disaster struck the area again in 2010. After the explosion of BP's Deepwater Horizon offshore drilling rig, oil washed up on beaches and into Mobile Bay, prompting concerns that neighboring Louisiana was receiving more cleanup attention. The Mobile Bay National Estuary Program created a priority list of local clean-up projects.

Mobile is the focus of Alabama's 1st Congressional District, which extends north along the usually lazy Tombigbee and Alabama rivers, with their old forts and mansions. Monroeville is the home of Harper Lee, whose classic *To Kill a Mockingbird* and her best-selling 2015 novel *Go Set a Watchman*, are set here. Her childhood playmate was noted author Truman Capote. There are also surviving backcountry settlements of blacks and Cajuns (who may or may not be descended from Louisiana Cajuns) and Creek Indians. Once cotton fields, this is now timberland, a major contributor to Alabama's economy.

East of Mobile Bay, along the shores of the Gulf of Mexico, are condominium communities in Baldwin County. The area hosts the annual National Shrimp Festival, and its glorious Gulf beaches are one of the South's best-kept secrets.

For years, this southern seaboard of the Confederacy has been among the most hawkish parts of America, and today it is solidly Republican in national elections.

2012 Presidential Vote		
Mitt Romney (R)	184,743	(62%)
Barack Obama (D)	111,712	(37%)
2008 Presidential Vote		
John McCain (R)	183,754	(61%)
Barack Obama (D)	115,981	(38%)
Cook Partisan Voting Index:	R+15	

But in 2005, in elections held after Katrina, Mobile elected its first African-American mayor, Sam Jones, a liberal Democrat who served with 2008 GOP presidential nominee John McCain during the Vietnam War. After he was reelected in 2009 running unopposed, Jones lost in 2013 to Republican businessman Sandy Stimpson. Turnout in African-American precincts declined, and Jones was outspent 4-to-1.

Bradley Byrne (R)

Republican Bradley Byrne was elected to Congress in December 2013 in a special election to replace Jo Bonner, who resigned after 11 years to accept a position as vice chancellor at the University of Alabama. Byrne was born and raised in Mobile, where he practiced law for

14 years. He began his political career in 1994, successfully seeking a seat on the Alabama State Board of Education. He ran as a Democrat but left to join the Republican Party in 1997. "I learned there was no place for a conservative in the Alabama Democratic Party," Byrne told a reporter in November 2013. After serving a second term on the state's Board of Education, he was elected to two terms in the state Senate. He stepped aside in 2007 when he was appointed chancellor of the Alabama Community College System, where he drew high marks for cleaning up a corrupt system. A previous chancellor had been indicted on federal bribery charges, as part of widespread criminal violations.

Byrne didn't stay away from electoral politics for long, resigning in 2009 to launch a campaign for governor in 2010. With much of the state's Republican establishment and business community behind him, Byrne was the early frontrunner. He finished first in a tight four-way June Republican primary with 28 percent of the vote. Byrne lost the runoff to state Rep. Robert Bentley, 56%-44%. He returned to practicing law in Mobile. But he didn't hide his itch to seek elected office again. In May 2013, Byrne got the opening he needed when Bonner, coincidentally, took a high-ranking state education post.

Once again, Byrne entered the race as the favorite with strong support from the business community and Mobile-area establishment, given his past political experience. In a nine-candidate Republican field, he finished first with 35 percent of the primary vote. His opponent in the Republican run-off was businessman Dean Young, an outspoken social conservative, who got 23 percent. In the weeks following the first round of voting, Byrne picked up endorsements from Bonner, the U.S. Chamber of Commerce, and two vanquished primary opponents: conservative commentator Quin Hillyer and state Rep. Chad Fincher. The chamber spent more than $185,000 on direct mail and digital ads to boost Byrne less than a week before the run-off vote.

Little separated Byrne and Young in terms of policy, but the differences in their respective campaign styles were stark. Young, who challenged Bonner in the 2012 primary, stirred up controversy on the campaign trail. He called for President Barack Obama's impeachment, said he would not support House Speaker John Boehner, and objected to "homosexuals pretending like they're married." Byrne, meanwhile, kept his focus on attacking Obama and a dysfunctional Congress, while touting his own record as a public official. In an unexpectedly narrow outcome, the far better-funded Byrne won the November 2013 runoff, 52.5%-47.5%. A month later, Byrne handily won the general election with 71 percent of the vote in a low-turnout contest against real-estate agent Burton LeFlore, grandson of Alabama civil-rights leader John LeFlore. In 2014, Byrne won his first full term over LeFlore. He got 68 percent, with a turnout of three times as many voters.

In the House, Byrne won committee assignments consistent with his local and personal interests: Armed Services, Natural Resources, and Education and the Workforce. With his insider credentials, he quickly got to work. He teamed with other Republicans on reforms in elementary and secondary education that would restore local control and empower parents and teachers. In February 2015, the House passed his bill to repeal—not for the first time—President Obama's Affordable Care Act. The proposal also called for House committees to prepare health-care alternatives. Following an intensive push by Mobile business interests, Byrne praised outgoing Defense Secretary Chuck Hagel's decision to resume procurement of an updated version of the Navy's Littoral Combat Ships, relatively small vessels that are built at the Austral Shipyard in Mobile.

On other local issues, Byrne responded to constituent concerns by helping to create and becoming a co-chair of the bipartisan Congressional Coastal Communities Caucus. The group was organized to help address often controversial policy issues, including weather-related disasters, marine habitats, erosion, and tourism. When the Obama administration in January 2015 released recommendations for off-shore oil and gas leasing, Byrne applauded the decision to open new areas off the Atlantic Coast, but he advocated additional sites for exploration.

The 1st Congressional District has had a tradition in the past half-century of electing Republicans who become hard-working and politically secure. Byrne could fit that mold. But his career potentially faces two questions: Might he eventually face a well-organized tea party challenge in a primary? And would he be interested in making another bid for statewide office, either for the Senate or in Montgomery?

SECOND DISTRICT

Martha Roby (R)

Elected 2010, 3rd term; b. July 26, 1976, Montgomery; New York U., B.A. 1998, Samford U., J.D. 2001; Presbyterian; Married (Riley); 2 children.

Elected Office: Montgomery City Cncl., 2003-10.

Professional Career: Practicing atty., 2002-04.

DC Office: 428 CHOB, 20515, 202-225-2901; Fax: 202-225-8913; Website: roby.house.gov.

State Offices: Andalusia, 334-428-1129; Dothan, 334-794-9680; Montgomery, 334-277-9113.

Committees: *Appropriations:* Commerce, Justice, Science & Related Agencies; Labor, HHS, Education & Related Agencies; Military Construction, Veterans Affairs & Related Agencies. *Select Benghazi Committee.*

Group Ratings

	ADA	ACLU	AFL-CIO	LCV	ITI	COC	HAFA	ACU	CFG	FRC
2014	0%	0%	–	3%	80%	93%	47%	56%	46%	100%
2013	0%	C	14%	0%	C	77%	C	64%	59%	C

National Journal Ratings

	2013 LIB	—	2013 CONS
Economic	38%	—	61%
Social	16%	—	74%
Foreign	24%	—	68%
Composite	29%	—	71%

Key Votes of the 113th Congress

1. Sandy storm spending	N	5. Medical Marijuana	N	9. Syrian Rebels Training	Y
2. Violence Against Women Act	N	6. Farm Bill	Y	10. Keystone pipeline	Y
3. Guantanamo Bay Detainees	N	7. Afghanistan Combat	N	11. Immigration Exec. Action	Y
4. Abortion 20-week ban	Y	8. NSA Phone Data Collection	N	12. Bipartisan budget deal	Y

Election Results

2014 general	Martha Roby (R)	113,103	(67%)	$793,565
	Erick Wright (D)	54,692	(33%)	$10,473
2014 primary	Martha Roby (R)	unopposed		

Prior winning percentages: 2012 (64%), 2010 (51%)

Population		Race and Ethnicity		Income	
Total:	690,074	White	63.8%	Median income:	$41,862
Urban:	31.0%	Black	29.6%		*(360 of 435)*
Suburban:	18.1%	Latino	3.3%	Under $50,000	57.5%
Rural:	50.9%	Asian	0.9%	$50,000-$99,999:	28.9%
Land area:	10,142	Two races	1.8%	$100,000-$199,999:	11.8%
Pop/sq. mi.:	68.9	White Ethnic	12.0%	$200,000 or more:	1.8%
Born in state:	68.9%			Poverty Rate	19.6%
		Education			
Age Groups		H.S. grad or less:	49.1%	**Work**	
Under 18:	23.5%	Some college:	30.5%	White collar:	29.9%
18 to 34:	23.0%	College degree, 4 yr.:	12.5%	Blue collar:	27.7%
35 to 64:	38.5%	Post-grad study:	7.9%	Sales and service:	42.3%
Over 64:	15.1%			Govt. workers:	19.5%
		Military			
		Veterans/active duty:	13.1%		

Southeast Alabama: Montgomery, Dothan

Thick green countryside blankets southern Alabama. Even in Montgomery, the stone and brick buildings of the downtown district do not mask the contours of the hills or hide the lush foliage. One can look downhill from the restored Greek Revival capitol toward Dexter Avenue King Memorial Baptist Church, where the young Martin Luther King Jr. was pastor in the 1950s, or out past the impressive Carolyn Blount Theatre, host of the Alabama Shakespeare Festival, toward new subdivisions and shopping malls, and easily imagine when this land was covered with cotton fields and pine trees and a young Wilson Pickett, the legendary soul singer, was still performing in Baptist

Voter Turnout	
2013 Total Citizen 18+	519,145
2014 House Turnout	167,952
2014 Turnout as % CVAP	32.4%
2012 Turnout % CVAP	57%

church choirs in Prattville. The atmosphere is especially rural in southeast Alabama's Wiregrass region, named for the stiff native grass. There is the fishing town of Eufaula, along the Chattahoochee River; the Army's Fort Rucker, the home of Army aviation flight training; and Enterprise, site of the Boll Weevil Monument that commemorates the insect that destroyed two-thirds of the cotton crop in 1915 and then spread throughout the South. Timber is an important resource here, and peanuts have replaced cotton as the main crop in the area surrounding Dothan, which calls itself the "peanut capital of the world." Each fall, Dothan holds the National Peanut Festival, the largest of its kind, to celebrate peanut growers and the harvest season. A statue of peanut innovator George Washington Carver can be found here.

The area's industrial diversification has been led by the automobile industry. Hyundai, the world's fifth largest automaker, built its first U.S. assembly plant in southwest Montgomery County, with about 3,000 local jobs and annual production capacity of 400,000 cars. The company calls the facility one of the most advanced in the North American auto industry, producing the new design, safety technologies, and eco-friendly features of the new Sonata Sedan. Hyundai Heavy Industries opened a $90 million plant to manufacture large power transformers here in 2011, hiring about 500 people when it opened.

The 2nd Congressional District of Alabama covers 12 counties in the southeast corner of the state. It also includes a thin link in the heart of Montgomery, but shares the surrounding metropolitan area with the 3rd and 7th districts to the east and west. In the 2011 redistricting, the more heavily black precincts in west Montgomery, as well as mostly African-American Lowndes County, were moved into a new corner of the sprawling majority-minority 7th. The remaining Montgomery County precincts in the district, plus suburban Elmore and Autauga counties, vote heavily Republican, as does

2012 Presidential Vote		
Mitt Romney (R)	182,146	(63%)
Barack Obama (D)	105,636	(36%)
2008 Presidential Vote		
John McCain (R)	188,634	(64%)
Barack Obama (D)	102,625	(35%)
Cook Partisan Voting Index:	R+17	

Houston County in the Wiregrass region. These areas outvote the district's "Black Belt" counties, including Bullock, with a large black majority, and Barbour on the Georgia border, which was George Wallace's home base. The district is solidly Republican.

Martha Roby (R)

Alabama 2nd District Republican Martha Roby has won notice as an articulate and more visible conservative in a party trying to reach out to women voters. Although she continues to draw some flak from the tea party wing for being insufficiently committed to its agenda, she is young enough to chart her course to increased influence in the House or potentially a Senate seat.

Roby is the daughter of Joel Dubina, a judge on the U.S. Court of Appeals for the 11th Circuit. She grew up in Montgomery and received a bachelor's degree in music from New York University in 1998. After earning a law degree from Samford University in Birmingham, she returned to her hometown to practice law. In 2003, she was elected to the Montgomery City Council. In that role, she led efforts to adopt an ordinance barring city businesses from hiring undocumented workers. In 2007, she won a second term with 82 percent of the vote.

Immigration emerged as a major issue in her 2010 House challenge to freshman Democratic Rep. Bobby Bright. A former mayor of Montgomery, Bright criticized Roby for moving too slowly on her undocumented workers initiative. Roby and the Republicans kept Bright on the partisan defensive. He felt it necessary to become the first Democrat to announce he would not vote again to elect California liberal Nancy Pelosi as speaker of the House. In one campaign ad, Bright boasted of having voted with then-House Minority Leader John Boehner of Ohio 80 percent of the time. He also played up his endorsements from the National Rifle Association and the National Right to Life PAC. He sometimes campaigned in a "Fire Congress" T-shirt. The Democratic Congressional Campaign Committee spent about $1 million for Bright. But Roby pulled out a close win, 51%-49%.

On the Armed Services Committee during her first term, she advocated for the Maxwell-Gunter Air Force Base and Army post at Fort Rucker in her district. After a bipartisan deal was reached between the Republican leadership and President Barack Obama to raise the debt ceiling, Roby said she voted against final passage because she feared it could lead to severe defense cuts. "This bill goes much too far," she said in a statement, arguing that it could result in "devastating and unjustified cuts to our national security." *Politico* named her the most underrated member of the freshman class, saying, "If she's able to win reelection, she could be a leader of her party." Recognizing her appeal to younger voters, Mitt Romney's presidential campaign brought Roby to North Carolina to appear on his behalf at a September 2012 rally. But a few conservative activists weren't satisfied with some of her votes. Erick Erickson of the influential *RedState.com* charged, "She has carried water for the leadership" and "betrayed her conservative constituents."

After the 2012 election, Roby made a bid to join the House Republican leadership as GOP conference vice chair. But she lost to the slightly more senior Lynn Jenkins of Kansas. She got an impressive consolation prize in 2013 when Boehner and other GOP leaders tapped Roby for the opening on the Appropriations Committee created by the resignation of fellow Alabamian Jo Bonner. She also displayed her conservative credentials by gaining a seat on the Select Committee on Benghazi, where she criticized the State Department's failure to upgrade security at its Libyan facility. She remained a hawk on defense, joining with Democratic Rep. Tulsi Gabbard of Hawaii to warn of the "devastating" effect if automatic military spending cuts took effect in 2016. Roby was outspoken in her criticism of mismanagement by the Veterans Affairs Department, and led the call for top officials to resign. On a local issue, she told Labor Secretary Thomas Perez that he should apologize for criticizing the safety record of the Hyundai plant in Montgomery. Two days later, the Labor Department clarified that Perez was referring to Hyundai suppliers.

Roby co-sponsored the March 2015 commemoration of the 50th anniversary of the Selma to Montgomery civil rights march. She organized significant participation by other House Republicans, plus former President George W. Bush. Collaborating with 7th District Democratic Representative Terri Sewell, Roby passed legislation giving the Congressional Gold Medal to the 1965 marchers.

The decision by Republican redistricters in Alabama to shift the most heavily black Montgomery precincts from the 2nd District to the 7th District ensured that no Democrat, not even Bright, would have a chance there for another decade. In her next two campaigns, Roby sailed to reelection with 64 percent and 67 percent of the vote. In her 2014 campaign against first-time candidate Erick Wright, she received 50 percent of the vote in the portion of Montgomery County that remained in the 2nd District. That was a big improvement over 2010, when she got 41 percent in the county. She led by more than 3-to-1 in the next three largest counties: Houston (Dothan), plus Elmore and Autauga in the metro Montgomery area. With her firm base in the state's southeast corner and her consensus-building style, she could stake a claim when a Senate seat becomes available.

THIRD DISTRICT

Mike Rogers (R)

Elected 2002, 7th term. b: July 16, 1958, Hammond, IN; Jacksonville State U, B.A. 1981, M.P.A. 1984; Birmingham Schl of Law, J.D. 1991; Baptist; married (Beth); 3 children.

Elected Office: Calhoun Cnty. Commission, 1986-90; AL House, 1994-2002; Min. ldr., 1998-2000.

Professional Career: Practicing atty., 1991-2002.

DC Office: 324 CHOB, 20515, 202-225-3261; Fax: 202-226-8485; Website: mikerogers.house.gov.

State Offices: Anniston, 256-236-5655; Opelika, 334-745-6221.

Committees: *Armed Services:* Readiness; Strategic Forces (Chmn). *Agriculture:* Commodity, Exchanges, Energy, & Credit; General Farm Commodities & Risk Mgmt. *Homeland Security:* Border & Maritime Security; Transportation Security.

Group Ratings

	ADA	ACLU	AFL-CIO	LCV	ITI	COC	HAFA	ACU	CFG	FRC
2014	0%	0%	–	0%	100%	79%	58%	84%	70%	88%
2013	0%	C	19%	0%	C	77%	C	60%	53%	C

National Journal Ratings

	2013 LIB — 2013 CONS	
Economic	42% —	58%
Social	0% —	87%
Foreign	24% —	68%
Composite	26% —	75%

Key Votes of the 113th Congress

1. Sandy storm spending	N	5. Medical Marijuana	Y	9. Syrian Rebels Training	Y
2. Violence Against Women Act	N	6. Farm Bill	Y	10. Keystone pipeline	Y
3. Guantanamo Bay Detainees	N	7. Afghanistan Combat	N	11. Immigration Exec. Action	Y
4. Abortion 20-week ban	Y	8. NSA Phone Data Collection	N	12. Bipartisan budget deal	Y

Election Results

2014 general	Mike Rogers (R)	103,558	(66%)	$936,332
	Jesse Smith (D)	52,816	(34%)	$9,000
2014 primary	Mike Rogers (R)	50,372	(76%)	
	Thomas Casson (R)	15,999	(24%)	

Prior winning percentages: 2012 (64%), 2010 (59%), 2008 (53%), 2006 (59%), 2004 (61%), 2002 (50%)

Population		Race and Ethnicity		Income	
Total:	697,761	White	69.3%	Median income:	$40,990
Urban:	32.5%	Black	25.6%		*(377 of 435)*
Suburban:	23.8%	Latino	2.5%	Under $50,000	58.3%
Rural:	43.7%	Asian	1.2%	$50,000-$99,999:	27.7%
Land area:	7,544	Two races	1.0%	$100,000-$199,999:	11.8%
Pop/sq. mi.:	100.2	White Ethnic	12.0%	$200,000 or more:	2.2%
Born in state:	65.8%			Poverty Rate	19.9%
Age Groups		**Education**			
		H.S. grad or less:	49.4%	**Work**	
Under 18:	22.2%	Some college:	29.6%	White collar:	31.7%
18 to 34:	24.7%	College degree, 4 yr.:	12.2%	Blue collar:	27.8%
35 to 64:	38.7%	Post-grad study:	8.9%	Sales and service:	40.5%
Over 64:	14.4%				
		Military		Govt. workers:	18.9%
		Veterans/active duty:	10.3%		

Eastern Alabama: Auburn, Anniston

Voter Turnout	
2013 Total Citizen 18+	530,775
2014 House Turnout	156,620
2014 Turnout as % CVAP	29.5%
2012 Turnout % CVAP	53.1%

The 3rd Congressional District of Alabama is centered geographically and philosophically in Lineville. The small town's progress from Ku Klux Klan country to an integrated community where crowds regularly cheer mixed black and white high school teams and people of all races work together echoes that of America's most integrated institution, the military. Lineville produced more men and women per capita for Operation Desert Storm than any other community in the nation. When the United States invaded Iraq in 2003, Alabama was the nation's top contributor of National Guard personnel. The local military presence is unmistakable: Calhoun County is home to the Anniston Army Depot. Horseshoe Bend is where Andrew Jackson won a climactic battle against the Upper Creek Indians. Fort Mitchell, a 19th-century frontier military outpost, is the site of a national military cemetery sometimes referred to as the "Arlington of the South." Phenix City, across the Chattahoochee River from Georgia's Fort Benning, served as a "sin city" in the 1940s and 1950s, with virtually every imaginable vice for pleasure-seeking soldiers, a place so sleazy that Gen. George Patton threatened to level it with his tanks. Today, the huge military installation plays a more constructive role in the local economy.

There are other places of distinction in the district: Tuskegee is the home of Booker T. Washington's Tuskegee Institute (now Tuskegee University), the training ground for the Tuskegee Airmen, the first black pilots trained to fly for the U.S. military. Auburn is the home of Auburn University and its renowned sports teams and veterinary school. Talladega is the site of

2012 Presidential Vote		
Mitt Romney (R)................174,620	(62%)
Barack Obama (D) 103,089	(37%)
2008 Presidential Vote		
John McCain (R)................177,136	(63%)
Barack Obama (D) 103,458	(37%)
Cook Partisan Voting Index: R+16		

the Alabama Institute for the Deaf and Blind, and is perhaps America's most user-friendly city for people with disabilities. NASCAR fans know it as the home of a famed speedway and for the International Motorsports Hall of Fame—the Cooperstown of auto racing.

This looks and feels like rural country, though few people here make a living off their farms. Rather, they work at Tyson Foods or Wal-Mart or in dozens of small and medium-sized factories. An economy once dependent on cotton mills is today more diverse, and interstates have brought in new businesses, including a huge Honda assembly plant in Talladega County that employs more than 4,000. In 2012, residents of the county also managed to temporarily halt a Bureau of Land Management and Forest Service plan to auction 43,000 acres of land parcels in the Talladega National Forest, which they feared would lead to hydraulic fracturing or "fracking," and cause environmental damage to the forest. Energy companies backed away from drilling, though they have been discouraged that initial tests failed to meet production expectations.

Politically, this was long one of the heartlands of the conservative wing of the Democratic Party, the home of white Democrats who are patriotic supporters of the military and cautious supporters of some domestic programs. There is also a large population of African-American descendants of slaves from plantations. But the area has become Republican, except for Tuskegee's Macon County. St. Clair County is solidly Republican. From 2000 to 2010, the county grew by 29 percent, almost four times faster than the population growth rate of the state, and it is almost 89 percent white and largely conservative-leaning.

Democrats have remained competitive in some state elections. In the old incarnation of the district, George W. Bush won 52 percent here in 2000, and 58 percent in 2004. Barack Obama increased black turnout in 2008, but John McCain still won with 56 percent of the vote. With the redistricting changes, Democrats have had a more difficult time competing here.

Mike Rogers (R)

With the 2014 retirement of House Intelligence Committee chairman Mike Rogers of Michigan, the Mike Rogers of Alabama has become the most prominent Republican representative with that name who focuses on national security and legislative initiatives to protect the homeland.

Rogers is a fifth-generation resident of Calhoun County, the son of a textile worker and a fireman. At the age of 28 in 1986, he was the first Republican elected to the county commission. In 1994, he won a seat in the Alabama House, and in his second term, he became minority leader. In 2002, after Republican Bob Riley gave up the 3rd District seat to run for governor, Rogers easily won the GOP nomination to succeed him. But in the general election, he had stiff competition from Democrat Joe Turnham Jr., who served three years as state party chairman and challenged Riley unsuccessfully in 1998. Turnham and Rogers tried to "out-bubba" each other, with Turnham calling for a congressional auto racing caucus and demanding that Rogers prove he had hunting and fishing licenses. Rogers touted his working-class values and support from the National Rifle Association. He also emphasized his opposition to abortion rights and support for a constitutional amendment permitting prayer in the public schools. Though both national parties targeted the race, Turnham did not risk bringing in national Democrats to campaign for him in the socially conservative district, while Rogers got frequent visits from national Republican leaders. The contrast in national party support was evident in Rogers's big fundraising advantage. Still, Rogers won, but only 50%-48%. He did well in his base, Calhoun County, where he got 60 percent of the vote. In contrast, Turnham lost Lee County, his home, 52%-46%, but carried the district's portion of Montgomery County 57%-42%.

Rogers has sought to enhance Alabama's role in domestic protection against terrorism. His district includes the Federal Emergency Management Agency's Center for Domestic Preparedness. In 2010, he spoke out against President Barack Obama's proposal to combine several FEMA grant programs, including those for a corps of citizen volunteers and for interoperable communications systems for first-responders. He has been highly critical of the Transportation Security Administration, saying that the aviation security agency must become "smarter, leaner, and tougher." After the 2012 election, he competed to fill a vacancy as chairman of the House Homeland Security Committee. He lost narrowly to Rep. Mike McCaul of Texas, who was supported by Speaker John Boehner. The House's term limits for committee chairmen could give Rogers another opportunity after the 2018 election.

On the Armed Services Committee, Rogers is chairman of the Strategic Forces Subcommittee. He seeks to protect Anniston Army Depot as well as Maxwell-Gunter Air Force Base and Fort Benning just across the state line in Georgia. Like other Alabama Republicans, he has supported having the power to earmark spending bills to protect those and other state interests. He is a leading House Republican hawk on defense issues. At a hearing of his subcommittee, he said that the growing nuclear-weapons threat to the United States from overseas, especially Russia, should force increased attention to missile defense. After Sen. Dianne Feinstein in 2014 said that current spending for nuclear weapons is "unsustainable," Rogers wrote a letter to *The Washington Post* that her comment shows a disregard for reality. "Nuclear weapons are not undermining other national security priorities—they are undergirding them."

Rogers has been outspoken in describing security threats facing the nation and potential responses. With the Islamic State, he said during a meeting in his district, "Let's go over there and kill them and get out. ... We cannot ignore this problem. We can't put our head in the sand because all of us are tired of war. We're tired of Iraq, we're tired of Afghanistan, we're tired of all of these little nuts around the world ... but the fact is, the threats [ISIL] has are going to hit us."

Rogers occasionally shows populist leanings on economic issues. He bucked the Bush administration and won local praise by opposing the free trade agreement with Morocco on the grounds that it would reduce local textile and apparel jobs. In 2009, he proposed allowing new car buyers a tax deduction of up to $7,500. But he has been a reliable Republican vote since the GOP regained the majority. That shows his growing electoral confidence in what had been a "yellow dog" Democratic bastion.

In this ancestrally Democratic district with 27 percent African-American population, Rogers has worked hard to entrench himself and raise money to discourage Democratic opposition. In 2008, he faced a serious contest with Josh Segall, a 29-year-old Montgomery bankruptcy lawyer who stuck with Democratic doctrine on most issues except gay rights and gun control, spent more than $1 million, and had the support of the Democratic Congressional Campaign Committee. He attacked Rogers for backing the $700 billion government rescue of the financial markets, and also accused him of harming the local textile industry with his support of the Central America Free Trade Agreement. Rogers attacked Segall for his "Hollywood and New York" campaign contributions and his liberal views that "don't reflect east Alabama's conservative values." Segall won Montgomery County 62%-38% and three nearby counties, but Rogers prevailed 53%-47% overall. He has made himself a fixture ever since.

FOURTH DISTRICT

Robert Aderholt (R)

Elected 1996, 10th term; b. July 22, 1965, Haleyville; Birmingham-Southern Col., B.A. 1987, Samford U., J.D. 1990; Congregationalist Baptist; married (Caroline); 2 children.

Professional Career: Haleyville Municipal Judge, 1992-95; Asst. legal advisor, Gov. Fob James, 1995-96.

DC Office: 235 CHOB, 20515, 202-225-4876; Fax: 202-225-5587; Website: aderholt.house.gov.

State Offices: Cullman, 256-734-6043; Gadsden, 256-546-0201; Jasper, 205-221-2310; Tuscumbia, 256-381-3450.

Committees: *Appropriations:* Agriculture, Rural Development, FDA & Related Agencies (Chmn); Commerce, Justice, Science & Related Agencies (VChmn).

Group Ratings

	ADA	ACLU	AFL-CIO	LCV	ITI	COC	HAFA	ACU	CFG	FRC
2014	0%	0%	–	3%	100%	91%	56%	61%	64%	100%
2013	0%	C	15%	4%	C	75%	C	67%	60%	C

National Journal Ratings

	2013 LIB	—	2013 CONS
Economic	37%	—	63%
Social	16%	—	74%
Foreign	15%	—	77%
Composite	26%	—	74%

Key Votes of the 113th Congress

1. Sandy storm spending	N	5. Medical Marijuana	N	9. Syrian Rebels Training	N
2. Violence Against Women Act	N	6. Farm Bill	Y	10. Keystone pipeline	Y
3. Guantanamo Bay Detainees	N	7. Afghanistan Combat	N	11. Immigration Exec. Action	NV
4. Abortion 20-week ban	Y	8. NSA Phone Data Collection	N	12. Bipartisan budget deal	Y

Election Results

2014 general	Robert Aderholt (R)..................... unopposed	$909,881
2014 primary	Robert Aderholt (R)..................... unopposed	

Prior winning percentages: 2012 (74%), 2010 (99%), 2008 (75%), 2006 (70%), 2004 (75%), 2002 (87%), 2000 (61%), 1998 (56%), 1996 (50%)

Population		Race and Ethnicity		Income	
Total:	685,175	White	84.5%	Median income:	$39,993
Urban:	16.1%	Black	7.2%		*(390 of 435)*
Suburban:	18.7%	Latino	5.6%	Under $50,000	60.4%
Rural:	65.2%	Amer. Indian	0.7%	$50,000-$99,999:	27.9%
Land area:	8,889	Two races	1.4%	$100,000-$199,999:	10.0%
Pop/sq. mi.:	82.8	White Ethnic	16.2%	$200,000 or more:	1.7%
Born in state:	74.8%			Poverty Rate	17.5%
		Education			
Age Groups		H.S. grad or less:	53.3%	**Work**	
Under 18:	22.7%	Some college:	30.7%	White collar:	29.2%
18 to 34:	20.6%	College degree, 4 yr.:	9.8%	Blue collar:	33.1%
35 to 64:	40.0%	Post-grad study:	6.1%	Sales and service:	37.7%
Over 64:	16.7%				
		Military		Govt. workers:	15.2%
		Veterans/active duty:	8.4%		

North-Central Alabama: Gadsden

The Appalachian Mountains' corduroy ridges, dividing the Atlantic coast from the interior, make up America's coal-and-steel industrial spine, from the black coal country of western Pennsylvania to the red hill country of northern Alabama. Here rose America's two premier steel cities, Pittsburgh and Birmingham. Around both, and for many miles in between, is

countryside settled by feisty Scots-Irish farmers in
the years between the Revolution and the Civil War.
In valley land accessible to railroads, great steel factories were built in the 80 years after the Civil War,
along with smaller factories that produced socks,
tires, glass, and chemicals, and butchered chickens.

Voter Turnout	
2013 Total Citizen 18+	508,346
2014 House Turnout	134,752
2014 Turnout as % CVAP	26.5%
2012 Turnout % CVAP	54.1%

Northern Alabama was solidly Democratic through the 1950s. It was populist on economics,
conservative on cultural issues. Since then, the region has moved toward the Republicans,
even though it has benefited from massive federal public works programs. The movement is
most pronounced in counties close to Birmingham and along the interstates.

Alabama's 4th Congressional District is a collection of small towns—Cullman, Jasper,
Russellville, Fort Payne, and Albertville. The last is the home of a military helicopter plant
and other aerospace facilities. Sandwiched between Huntsville to the north and Birmingham to the south, the 4th District crosses the state and the Appalachian ridges, from the
Georgia state line to the Mississippi line. Decades of coal mining scarred 150 square miles
of landscape, about one-fourth of which has been reclaimed, with pockets of jobs. Gritty
Gadsden (pop. 37,000) is the biggest city, with a large Goodyear tire plant built in 1929—
with more than 1,000 workers and daily production exceeding 20,000 tires. Plant managers
in 2014 introduced a new tire for the Ford F-150 aluminum body truck and said that their
future was bright. The plant's most famous employee was activist Lilly Ledbetter, who, after
discovering that her salary was much lower than men in similar positions, waged a nine-
year battle on behalf of equal pay for women. Her case became a cause celebre for Democrats, and President Barack Obama in 2009 signed into law the Lilly Ledbetter Fair Pay Act
extending the statute of limitations on equal-pay discrimination lawsuits.

This area was hard hit by deadly tornadoes that struck Alabama on April 27, 2011. Of
the 253 people who died statewide, 122 lived in northwest Alabama. The Category EF-5
twister, the strongest there is, cleared a three-quarter-mile wide path 25 miles long, killing
over 70 people. In the small town of Hackleburg in Marion County, there weren't enough
body bags for the dead, and officials were forced to store some of them in a refrigerated truck.
Hackleburg was already struggling with nearly 13 percent unemployment when the storm
destroyed a Wrangler jeans distribution center. Two years later, Hackleburg and Wrangler
celebrated the opening of a new 369,000 square-foot plant, with a conveyer system capable of
handling 27 million pairs of jeans annually along two miles of belts. The $31 million facility
is the largest employer in town, with about 200 workers. The Hackleburg city hall and fire
and police stations were rebuilt.

The 4th is Alabama's premier Scots-Irish district, with the lowest African-American
population percentage of the state's seven congressional districts. Though family income is low
and poverty above national averages, high marriage rates provide some social stability. There
are few vestiges of its Democratic heritage. The more traditionally Democratic Shoals region
in the northwest has moved into the 4th District. That shift has had little impact on the 4th's
strong conservative leanings. Under the old boundaries, George W. Bush won here with 71
percent in 2004. John McCain won many of these counties with more than 70 percent of the
vote in 2008. Mitt Romney's 75 percent made
this district his 7th-best performance in the
nation in 2012 and his best in Alabama.

Census Bureau mid-decade population
estimates project that Alabama will lose a
seat in the reapportionment following the
2020 Census. The 4th district could be at
risk because it's the only one in Alabama
without an urban population center.

2012 Presidential Vote
Mitt Romney (R)................205,589   (75%)
Barack Obama (D) 65,852   (24%)

2008 Presidential Vote
John McCain (R)................205,680   (73%)
Barack Obama (D) 72,152   (26%)

Cook Partisan Voting Index: R+28

Robert Aderholt (R)

Robert Aderholt, a Republican first elected in 1996, is a mild-mannered conservative and a
senior member of the Appropriations Committee who is positioned to chair the panel within
a few years. He considers obtaining federal money for the state to be an essential part of his
job, and he often takes a constituent-based approach.

Aderholt is from Winston County, the one ancestrally Republican county in north Alabama; it opposed secession in the Civil War and declared itself the Free State of Winston.

His father was a circuit judge for more than 30 years; his wife's father was a state senator and state commissioner of Agriculture and Industry. In 1992, Aderholt was appointed Haleyville municipal judge. Three years later, he became a top aide to Republican Gov. Fob James. With that pedigree, he decided to run for Congress when 30-year veteran Rep. Tom Bevill, a Democrat and a pork-barrel spending appropriator, retired. As the Republican nominee, he faced state Sen. Bob Wilson Jr., who called himself a Democrat "in the Tom Bevill tradition." In this culturally conservative district, Aderholt emphasized cultural issues, opposing abortion rights, gun control, same-sex marriage, and prohibitions against school prayer. "We want to go to Washington to deliver a message, and that is, don't mess with our traditional family values," he said. He also attacked Wilson for his support from labor unions and trial lawyers. This was a nationally targeted race, seriously contested, and Aderholt won 50%-48%. The outcome was a landmark in the Republican takeover of rural southern districts.

Aderholt's voting record is generally conservative, and he was among the first House Republicans to join the Tea Party Caucus in July 2010. But he often sides with labor and economic populists on trade issues, mainly because of local imperatives. He has supported quotas on steel imports and sponsored a bill assessing additional antidumping duties on foreign steel. He voted against normalizing trade relations with China and opposed free-trade agreements with Chile, Morocco, and Singapore. In 2005, however, he was a crucial vote for the Central America Free Trade Agreement after he got a last-minute letter from President George W. Bush delaying the phase-out of tariffs on socks. In another populist leaning, he was the only House member from Alabama in 2008 to vote against the $700 billion rescue of the financial markets. He cited public "discontent" with the plan and the need for a more market-based approach.

He regularly goes to bat for the region's aerospace industry. He has worked with delegation members to have a new NASA heavy-lift rocket designed to carry astronauts into deep space built at Huntsville's Marshall Space Flight Center. In 2013, he demanded that NASA make plans to return to the moon, with both human and robotic missions, to assure "that we lead from the front."

Recognizing Aderholt's electoral vulnerability when he took office, Republican leaders put him on the Appropriations Committee, where he has secured more highway and water projects money than most of his GOP colleagues. He worked his way up through the ranks. After Republicans assumed control of the House in 2011, he was given the chairmanship of the Appropriations Subcommittee on Homeland Security. When a tornado hit his district hard that year, he increased spending on disaster relief while offsetting the cost with other cuts to the Homeland Security and Energy department budgets. He made his social views known in May 2012 when he added an amendment to the department's spending bill specifying that none of the funds provided to Immigration and Customs Enforcement (ICE) could be used to pay for an abortion, except under certain circumstances. The provision went nowhere in the Democratic-controlled Senate.

In 2013, Aderholt became chairman of the Agriculture Subcommittee at Appropriations, which tends to the interests of many of his constituents. He took credit for staying within budget limits, and more than 2 percent below President Barack Obama's spending request of about $20 billion. His panel faces the limitation that about $120 billion under its control is for "mandatory" programs—chiefly food stamps—and therefore subject to limited appropriations tinkering. He lists his priorities as "cutting edge" agricultural research, vibrant rural communities, nutrition for the most vulnerable, competitive markets in the global economy, and the safest food and drug supply in the world. He also is mindful of agri-business needs. He scored a legislative coup in the 2014 "lame-duck" omnibus spending bill when House-Senate conferees adopted his modified plan to limit federal standards advocated by first lady Michelle Obama that would require more whole grains in school foods. When a federal advisory panel urged consideration of the environmental impacts of nutrition plans, Aderholt criticized "politically motivated" steps such as taxes on certain foods that he said were at odds with sound science.

At Appropriations, he retained his interest in social issues. In response to Obama's executive actions on immigration, he prepared House Republican legislation in January 2015 that would nullify presidential action and toughen enforcement against undocumented immigrants, especially the surge of unaccompanied children who crossed the southern border in 2014. Earlier that year, the House approved his plan to make it more difficult for other countries to deport unaccompanied children. The American people were looking to Republicans for leadership on the issue, he said. When Alabama Chief Justice Roy Moore called for a new law to prevent federal judges from interfering with public displays of the Ten Commandments, Aderholt sponsored legislation toward that goal. "The acknowledgment of God is not a legitimate subject of review by the federal courts," Aderholt said.

Aderholt faced serious challenges in his first two reelections, but has won easily since. With his relative youth and as the third-ranking Republican on House Appropriations, he is positioned for the chairmanship of the full committee. The chief obstacle standing in his way might be that Alabama's prospective loss of a House seat after the 2020 census could place at risk his rural district—with its lack of a population center.

FIFTH DISTRICT

Mo Brooks (R)

Elected 2010, 3rd term; b. April 29, 1954, Charleston, SC; Duke U., B.A. 1975, U. of AL, J.D. 1978; Non-denominational Christian; Married (Martha); 4 children.

Elected Office: AL House, 1983-92; Madison Cnty. Commissioner, 1996-2010.

Professional Career: Tuscaloosa Cnty. prosecutor, 1978-80; Clerk, Circuit Ct. Judge John Snodgrass, 1980-82; Madison Cnty. district atty., 1991-93; AL special asst. atty. gen., 1995-2002; practicing atty., 1993-2010.

DC Office: 1230 LHOB, 20515, 202-225-4801; Fax: 202-225-4392; Website: brooks.house.gov.

State Offices: Decatur, 256-355-9400; Huntsville, 256-551-0190; Florence, 256-718-5155.

Committees: *Armed Services:* Emerging Threats & Capabilities; Strategic Forces. *Foreign Affairs:* Asia & the Pacific; Europe, Eurasia, & Emerging Threats. *Science, Space, & Technology:* Energy; Space (VChmn).

Group Ratings

	ADA	ACLU	AFL-CIO	LCV	ITI	COC	HAFA	ACU	CFG	FRC
2014	0%	0%	–	3%	80%	71%	75%	84%	88%	63%
2013	0%	C	14%	4%	C	62%	C	84%	80%	C

National Journal Ratings

	2013 LIB	—	2013 CONS
Economic	34%	—	65%
Social	0%	—	87%
Foreign	15%	—	77%
Composite	20%	—	80%

Key Votes of the 113th Congress

1. Sandy storm spending	N	5. Medical Marijuana	Y	9. Syrian Rebels Training	N
2. Violence Against Women Act	N	6. Farm Bill	Y	10. Keystone pipeline	Y
3. Guantanamo Bay Detainees	N	7. Afghanistan Combat	N	11. Immigration Exec. Action	Y
4. Abortion 20-week ban	Y	8. NSA Phone Data Collection	N	12. Bipartisan budget deal	N

Election Results

2014 general	Mo Brooks (R)	115,338	(74%)	$299,838
	Mark Bray (I)	39,005	(25%)	$26,438
2014 primary	Mo Brooks (R)	49,117	(80%)	
	Jerry Hill (R)	12,038	(20%)	

Prior winning percentages: 2012 (65%), 2010 (58%)

Population		Race and Ethnicity		Income	
Total:	701,220	White	73.8%	Median income:	$49,974
Urban:	44.6%	Black	17.4%		*(243 of 435)*
Suburban:	39.5%	Latino	4.9%	Under $50,000	50.0%
Rural:	16.0%	Asian	1.3%	$50,000-$99,999:	28.9%
Land area:	3,677	Two races	1.8%	$100,000-$199,999:	17.8%
Pop/sq. mi.:	181.9	White Ethnic	15.7%	$200,000 or more:	3.3%
Born in state:	61.7%			Poverty Rate	15.8%
		Education			
Age Groups		H.S. grad or less:	41.4%	**Work**	
Under 18:	22.5%	Some college:	29.0%	White collar:	38.5%
18 to 34:	22.6%	College degree, 4 yr.:	19.1%	Blue collar:	23.8%
35 to 64:	40.2%	Post-grad study:	10.5%	Sales and service:	37.7%
Over 64:	14.8%			Govt. workers:	16.9%
		Military			
		Veterans/active duty:	10.5%		

North Alabama: Huntsville, Decatur

After the Soviets put up Sputnik in 1957, the Redstone Arsenal in Huntsville became the nation's foremost missile development center. Then a sleepy town huddled around a well-preserved, early-19th-century settlement, Huntsville grew to become Alabama's fourth-largest city and the center of its northern tier.

Voter Turnout	
2013 Total Citizen 18+	529,049
2014 House Turnout	154,974
2014 Turnout as % CVAP	29.3%
2012 Turnout % CVAP	57.2%

Residents are fond of referring to their hometown as "Rocket City." The first of the large U.S. ballistic missiles were developed here. On the grounds of Redstone, NASA built its Marshall Space Flight Center in the 1960s, and the Huntsville-Decatur area soon achieved high-tech critical mass. With leadership from Wernher von Braun and other German engineers, Redstone and Marshall built Explorer 1, the first American orbiting satellite; the Mercury-Redstone vehicle that boosted astronaut Alan Shepard into suborbital flight; and the Saturn V rocket that sent men to the moon. In the 1970s, Marshall produced Skylab and developed the space shuttle's main engines and solid-rocket boosters. The Boeing research center here, in a consortium with Lockheed Martin, produces the Delta IV heavy rocket booster at its factory in Decatur, about 20 miles west of Huntsville.

With the retirement of the space shuttle, NASA expected that Marshall would have a major role in preparing the next generation of space vehicles, including the Ares I rocket and the Constellation project aimed at returning humans to the moon. But the Obama administration, wary of large-scale space exploration programs funded entirely by the government, scuttled the Constellation program and officials estimated that it cost the area 1,500 contractor jobs. But Congress and the Obama White House remained committed to NASA's new heavy-lift rocket developed in Huntsville. The Redstone Arsenal has more than 35,000 employees, including more than 1,000 active-duty military.

Huntsville has done a smart job of diversifying its high-tech economy in recent years, and has been able to weather setbacks like Constellation better than most cities its size. Space-related jobs have evolved with a broader defense focus. In 2005, the Pentagon base-closing commission moved 1,800 jobs in the Missile Defense Agency from northern Virginia to Redstone. More than two dozen aerospace companies subsequently moved or expanded to Huntsville to remain close to the agency. A Verizon Wireless call center now employs 1,300 people in the city, mostly for customer service. Other companies that have expanded their operations include Boeing, Toyota and Remington. Over several decades, city leaders carefully cultivated the Cummings Research Park, now home to 300 companies specializing in technology-based manufacturing, biotechnology and pharmaceuticals. It calls itself the second-largest research and development park in the nation and "a model for transforming research into business success." In addition to the usual tax incentives and grants, the city took the novel approach of offering to train or retrain high-tech manufacturing employees at city facilities for free.

The city and surrounding area were dealt a serious economic setback on April 27, 2011, when deadly tornadoes struck Alabama. At least six ripped through Madison County, which includes Huntsville, killing nine people and injuring 82. Huntsville gained a new kind of identity in early 2015 when a federal judge ruled that same-sex marriages were legal in

Alabama. Unexpectedly, the city became a destination wedding spot for gays in the South. Like high-tech centers in places like Cambridge Massachusetts, Austin Texas, and California's Silicon Valley, Huntsville has attracted many educated and motivated people who also are socially liberal, though they haven't done much to change the area's conservative politics.

2012 Presidential Vote		
Mitt Romney (R)................189,838		(64%)
Barack Obama (D) 103,601		(35%)
2008 Presidential Vote		
John McCain (R)................184,654		(62%)
Barack Obama (D) 107,223		(36%)
Cook Partisan Voting Index: R+17		

The 5th Congressional District of Alabama takes in most of the space counties. For years, most voters here were staunch New Deal Democrats, liberal on economics and not much interested in race issues, like longtime Sen. John Sparkman, the party's vice presidential nominee in 1952. But professional and technical people in the space business tended to be conservative, and this made much of northern Alabama marginal-to-Republican country in the 1990s. The district has voted Republican for president since 1980, but hadn't elected a Republican to Congress until 2010. Parker Griffith was elected as a Democrat in 2008, and switched to the GOP a year later.

In the 2011 redistricting, Republicans dropped Barack Obama's share of the district vote in 2008 from 38 percent to 36 percent. For now, this has become a safe Republican district.

Mo Brooks (R)

Mo Brooks, the 5th District congressman, in 2010 became the first Republican to be elected to the seat since 1868. As a boisterous member of that year's freshman GOP class, he occasionally has drawn Democratic barbs for his blunt speaking style.

Brooks was born in Charleston, South Carolina. His father, Jack Brooks, was raised "dirt poor" in Chattanooga, Tennessee, and his mother, Betty Brooks, grew up without electricity or indoor plumbing. "Out of that poverty, my parents learned that you'd better work, and work hard," Brooks said. In 1963, when Mo was 9, the family moved to Huntsville, where Jack worked as an electrical engineer and Betty taught high school economics and government. Brooks was a student at Grissom High School during the Vietnam War, and he says the experience influenced his decision to make a career in government. He quit the basketball team to join the debate team and wound up participating in two state-championship debates. Brooks studied economics and political science at Duke University, graduating in three years, and got his law degree from the University of Alabama. After meeting his future wife, Martha Jenkins, of Ohio at a fraternity event, they married and moved to Huntsville, where he landed a circuit court clerkship. In 1982, he ran for the Alabama House, becoming one of only 11 Republicans out of 147 legislators. Brooks gained the No. 1 ranking from the Alabama Taxpayers' Defense Fund for his efforts to fight tax increases. Republican Gov. Guy Hunt appointed him Madison County district attorney in 1991. He succeeded Democrat Bud Cramer, who had been elected to the U.S. House. Brooks lost the D.A.'s job two years later, hampered by Cramer's endorsement of his Democratic opponent. He returned to public office in 1996, on the Madison County Commission.

Brooks won his House seat following hard-fought primary and general election battles. He defeated one-term Rep. Parker Griffith in the Republican primary. Griffith had been elected as a Democrat, but switched parties in December 2009 and said he would seek reelection in 2010 as a Republican. During their primary contest, Brooks campaigned on the theme that the district "deserves a congressman who acts honorably." He won with 51 percent of the vote to Griffith's 33 percent. In the general election, Brooks' opponent was Steve Raby, the longtime chief of staff to former Sen. Howell Heflin of Alabama. The Democrat shunned his party label in most of his ads, focusing almost exclusively on local issues. Brooks, for his part, took on hot-button issues, declaring that he favored repealing President Barack Obama's health care legislation and deporting all illegal immigrants. He said that the country was veering dangerously toward socialism and that the trend must be reversed. Brooks won 58%-42%.

Within four months of taking the seat, he charged in a House floor speech that the United States is at "risk of insolvency and bankruptcy because the socialist members of this body choose to spend money that we do not have." After Democrats protested, Brooks asked that his remarks be stricken from the record, but did not apologize for them. Several months later, at a forum back home, Brooks said he supported any measure "short of shooting them" to force illegal immigrants back to their home countries. Latino lawmakers and groups condemned his remarks.

When he circulated a letter in November 2011 urging House GOP leaders to hold a vote on a Senate-passed Chinese currency manipulation measure, the conservative anti-tax group Club for Growth assailed Brooks for "standing with Senate liberals like [Democratic Sens.] Sherrod Brown and Chuck Schumer." Brooks was unapologetic: "Americans cannot stand idly by and watch Communist China undermine our economy via unfair trade practices," he said.

Brooks landed in an even bigger controversy in August 2014. Asked by conservative radio host Laura Ingraham about a statement that the Republican Party was alienating non-white voters, Brooks responded: "This is a part of the war on whites that's being launched by the Democratic Party. And the way in which they're launching this war is by claiming that whites hate everybody else. It's a part of the strategy that Barack Obama implemented in 2008, continued in 2012, where he divides us all on race, on sex, greed, envy, class warfare, all those kinds of things." Ingraham responded that the characterization was "a little out there," and numerous Democrats blasted Brooks for playing the race card. But he was unapologetic. On a regular basis, Brooks said a few days later, Democrats "appeal to specific racial groups by saying we will protect you, that particular racial group—well, who are they talking about protecting them from? Well, they're talking about protecting them from Republicans."

Brooks has committee assignments that match up well with his district: Armed Services, and Science, Space and Technology, where he is vice-chair of the Space Subcommittee. He has been part of a bipartisan coalition that has sought to reorient space policy with a stepping stone approach to exploration. That plan seeks a capability to access the International Space Station so American astronauts can rely on American rockets. It also makes long-term plans to take astronauts to deep-space destinations like Mars. On defense spending, he makes the case that the United States should spend what it takes to fight terrorism. If the Europeans "choose to be halfhearted about it, if our interests are at stake and the security of the American people is at stake, then I think we gotta be there," he said. "I don't think you put a price tag on it."

Although he has been outspoken in criticism of House Republican leaders, Brooks supported John Boehner for Speaker in 2015 because, he said, "there was no better option before me," and the alternative would be chaos. He said that he had unsuccessfully encouraged credible House conservatives to challenge Boehner.

In what had been an entrenched Democratic district less than a decade ago, Brooks has secured his House seat. In the 2012 primary, he dispatched Griffith again in the Republican primary with 71 percent of the vote, winning each of the district's five counties. In his November reelections, he won 65 percent and 74 percent of the vote.

SIXTH DISTRICT

Gary Palmer (R)

Elected 2014, 1st term; b. May 14, 1954, Haleyville; U. of AL, B.S. 1977; Presbyterian; married (Ann); 3 children.

Professional Career: Engineer, 1977-89; Founder/pres., AL Policy Institute (formerly AL Family Alliance), 1989-2013; Founding board member, State Policy Network, 1992-98.

DC Office: 206 CHOB, 20515, 202-225-4921; Fax: 202-225-2082; Website: palmer.house.gov.

State Offices: Birmingham, 205-968-1290; Clanton, 205-280-6846; Oneonta, 205-274-2136.

Committees: *Budget. Oversight & Gov't Reform:* Interior. *Science, Space, & Technology:* Environment; Research & Technology.

Election Results

2014 general	Gary Palmer (R)	135,945	(76%)	$1,690,309	$46,182
	Mark Lester (D)	42,291	(24%)	$165,465	
2014 primary runoff	Gary Palmer (R)	47,491	(64%)		
	Paul DeMarco (R)	27,295	(36%)		
2014 primary	Paul DeMarco (R)	30,894	(33%)		
	Gary Palmer (R)	18,655	(20%)		
	Scott Beason (R)	14,451	(15%)		
	Chad Mathis (R)	14,420	(15%)		
	Will Brooke (R)	13,130	(14%)		

Population		Race and Ethnicity		Income	
Total:	697,436	White	78.0%	Median income:	$57,367
Urban:	39.8%	Black	13.8%		*(148 of 435)*
Suburban:	41.3%	Latino	5.5%	Under $50,000	43.4%
Rural:	18.9%	Asian	1.8%	$50,000-$99,999:	32.1%
Land area:	4,171	Two races	0.6%	$100,000-$199,999:	19.2%
Pop/sq. mi.:	186.6	White Ethnic	19.6%	$200,000 or more:	5.2%
Born in state:	70.9%			Poverty Rate	11.5%
		Education			
Age Groups		H.S. grad or less:	36.8%	**Work**	
Under 18:	23.9%	Some college:	28.4%	White collar:	41.4%
18 to 34:	21.4%	College degree, 4 yr.:	21.3%	Blue collar:	18.3%
35 to 64:	40.3%	Post-grad study:	13.4%	Sales and service:	40.3%
Over 64:	14.4%				
		Military		Govt. workers:	13.4%
		Veterans/active duty:	8.9%		

Central Alabama: Birmingham Suburbs, Shelby County

Birmingham, once one of America's booming industrial cities, was better known in the middle of the
20th century as a bastion of white resistance to the
civil rights movement. Its prospects in the 21st century have been more hopeful. This is a new city by
Southern standards. Before the Civil War, there was

Voter Turnout	
2013 Total Citizen 18+	513,367
2014 House Turnout	178,449
2014 Turnout as % CVAP	34.8%
2012 Turnout % CVAP	62.5%

nothing here but a few creeks running below Red Mountain. But Red Mountain is almost
pure iron ore. With the additional mining of coal, Birmingham—the self-styled Magic City—
had by 1890 the South's largest steel mills. In the early 20th century, as the statue of Vulcan, the Roman god of fire and metalworking, looked out over the smokestack-filled valley,
Birmingham seemed the most progressive city in the South. But the worldwide overcapacity of steel and technological obsolescence at home sent the American steel industry into
long-term decline starting in the 1950s. Meanwhile, Birmingham's political leaders plotted
to avoid desegregation, and the city's violent reaction to the civil rights movement made
a vivid impression on the rest of the country, which watched it unfold on the increasingly
inter-connected medium of television. Police Commissioner (and Democratic National Committeeman at the time) Bull Connor set dogs and fire hoses against peaceful demonstrators,
and Ku Klux Klansmen bombed the 16th Street Baptist Church, killing four young girls
in 1963. Those images haunted Birmingham for a generation. As the more civic-minded
Atlanta became the new heart of the South, Birmingham also suffered from uninspired
business leadership. An example remains its mid-sized airport terminal, which is dwarfed
by Atlanta's Hartsfield-Jackson Airport.

In recent years, Birmingham has worked to improve race relations and develop a new
economic base. Health care is a major industry. The city has some of the largest and most
advanced medical care centers in the South, and is especially renowned for its sports medicine facilities and specialists who tend to the ailments of famous athletes. Banking is also
important. While Atlanta's banks foundered and were acquired by outsiders, Birmingham
became the largest Southern banking center outside Charlotte, North Carolina. But city
leaders have worried that the viability of the downtown area and white movement to newer
suburbs have caused an uptick in racial polarization.

The city's population has declined by 100,000 since 1960 and was 73 percent African-
American in 2010. Whites have been moving out of Birmingham's Jefferson County southeast to Shelby County, which grew 44 percent in the 1990s and 36 percent in the next
decade—the fastest growth in the state. (The migration to Shelby has not been entirely
white flight. Its African-American population has increased as well, though the county is
about 90 percent white.) Shelby County has been economically productive, with the lowest
unemployment rate in the state in recent years. Jefferson County, once more Republican
than most of Alabama, votes Democratic in close statewide elections, while Shelby County
is overwhelmingly Republican. Metropolitan planners project an 85 percent population
increase for Shelby County from 2005 to 2035, but only a 2 percent increase for Jefferson,
whose physical expansion is limited by its hills.

Shelby County played a vital role in a recent civil rights debate, to the dismay of many local and national activists, when it argued that it no longer engages in racially discriminatory practices in elections and challenged the constitutionality of the federal rule that most southern states are required to report ballot changes under the Voting Rights Act. In a landmark 2013 ruling that overturned a central provision of that law, the U.S. Supreme Court agreed with Shelby County that it was no longer required to get Justice Department approval of each voting change—which, in this case, removed a black-majority district in the small town of Calera. On behalf of the 5-4 majority, Chief Justice John Roberts wrote that the formula for determining which jurisdictions are covered by the law was unconstitutional and that the "preclearance" requirement was no longer required. "Things have changed dramatically" for the better in the South, he said, and "these improvements are in large part because of the Voting Rights Act." Critics of Congress blamed lawmakers for the bipartisan failure to update the law—both before and after the ruling. Although some proposals were discussed, neither party viewed the update as a priority and legislation failed to move from committees. Absent congressional action, the Roberts majority has determined the relevance and scope of the long-standing statute.

The 6th Congressional District of Alabama, which once included all of Birmingham and most of Jefferson County, is now the suburban Birmingham-area district and strongly Republican. It includes Shelby County and parts of Jefferson County, such as prosperous Mountain Brook with upscale shopping malls, and stretches southwest toward Tuscaloosa and south along Interstate 65 halfway to Montgomery. Its largest city, Hoover, houses the corporate offices of Blue Cross and Blue Shield of Alabama. Parts of Jefferson County have moved into the mostly African-American 7th District. Jefferson retains a slight majority of the district vote. This has been one of the most Republican districts in the nation. Under its previous borders, it voted 74 percent for George W. Bush in 2000—his second-best district outside Texas. The new district lines also gave 74 percent to Mitt Romney in 2012, his ninth-best district in the nation.

2012 Presidential Vote		
Mitt Romney (R).................233,803	(74%)
Barack Obama (D) 77,235	(25%)
2008 Presidential Vote		
John McCain (R).................236,543	(74%)
Barack Obama (D) 80,357	(25%)
Cook Partisan Voting Index: R+28		

Gary Palmer (R)

Republican Gary Palmer was elected to Congress in 2014 by sweeping the runoff of his party's primary as a political outsider in one of the nation's strongest Republican districts. He succeeded retiring GOP Rep. Spencer Bachus, a former chairman of the House Financial Services Committee and ally of Speaker John Boehner. Palmer didn't take long to show his independent credentials, when he was one of 25 Republican members—including five freshmen—who opposed giving Boehner a new term as the House's top officer.

Palmer grew up on a small farm in Hackleburg, Ala. He was the first in his family to go to college, where he studied engineering. He started his career in the private sector before cofounding the Alabama Policy Institute (API) in 1989. As president of the think tank with ties to the right-leaning American Legislative Exchange Council (ALEC), Palmer has been engaged for years in state-level policy issues, including tax and regulatory affairs.

In 2012, API joined a coalition that successfully campaigned against a public referendum on a measure to transfer money from the Alabama Trust Fund—which collects royalties from offshore gas exploration—into the state's cash-strapped General Fund, which covers many social services. Palmer and other conservatives argued that a "no" vote on the transfer would force the state government to downsize and allocate its spending more efficiently. Palmer also recommended a proposal to congressional Republicans that any debt-ceiling deal should contain language allowing oil and gas exploitation on federal lands as a way to pay down the national debt.

Palmer's path to victory focused on the party primary, which began with a seven-candidate field. He came in second in the initial June vote, trailing GOP state Rep. Paul DeMarco, 33%-19%. DeMarco led the field in each of the district's seven counties. In the run-off, the Club for Growth weighed in for Palmer after deeming DeMarco pro-tax. Palmer got the Club's endorsement, along with $250,000 for ads that helped him go on the offensive. He also won the backing of nationally known Republicans such as Indiana Gov. Mike Pence and former presidential candidate Rick Santorum. Palmer won the July runoff handily, 64%-36%. In this district, he didn't need to break a sweat with his general election victory over Democrat Mark Lester, with 76 percent of the vote.

Even before taking office, Palmer joined several incoming GOP members who said they would not back Boehner for a third term as Speaker. In a debate before the runoff, Palmer told the audience: "I cannot in good conscience support John Boehner because I think he lost his legitimacy to lead" after bringing to the House floor bills that most Republican members opposed. Palmer later said he regretted making that pledge because it could threaten his ability to land good committee assignments. But he said he had told Boehner before the election that he would need to keep his word to his constituents—unlike some other freshmen who reneged on their campaign promises. As he later recounted his conversation with the Speaker, "not only would I lose their confidence, but I would lose his. I think he respected that." Instead, Palmer voted for Alabama Sen. Jeff Sessions; under the Constitution, the Speaker does not need to be a member of the House.

As he predicted, Palmer fell short on influential committee posts. In a delegation where each of the other five Republicans serves on either the Appropriations or Armed Services Committee, Palmer was assigned to Science, Space and Technology (potentially useful for Alabama), plus the Budget and Oversight and Government Reform panels. He was outspoken on the House floor during early debates in 2015. In March, he opposed the bipartisan agreement to fund the Homeland Security Department. Instead, he urged another three days of debate to drive a tougher compromise on the measure, which already had consumed two months.

In this district, Palmer's only reelection concern is a Republican primary challenge from a more "establishment" candidate. His political start-up showed his skillfulness in seeking a balance at home.

SEVENTH DISTRICT

Terri Sewell (D)

Elected 2010, 3rd term; b. Jan. 1, 1965, Selma; Princeton U., B.A. 1986, Oxford U., M.A. 1988, Harvard U., J.D. 1992; African Methodist Episcopal; Single.

Professional Career: Clerk, U.S. District Court judge, 1993-94; practicing atty., 1994-2010.

DC Office: 1133 LHOB, 20515, 202-225-2665; Fax: 202-226-9567; Website: sewell.house.gov.

State Offices: Birmingham, 205-254-1960; Montgomery, 334-262-1919; Selma, 334-877-4414; Tuscaloosa, 205-752-5380.

Committees: *Financial Services:* Capital Markets & Gov't Sponsored Enterprises; Monetary Policy & Trade. *Intelligence (Select).*

Group Ratings

	ADA	ACLU	AFL-CIO	LCV	ITI	COC	HAFA	ACU	CFG	FRC
2014	70%	72%	–	77%	80%	69%	10%	8%	2%	38%
2013	65%	C	95%	75%	C	62%	C	13%	15%	C

National Journal Ratings

	2013 LIB	—	2013 CONS
Economic	61%	—	39%
Social	63%	—	36%
Foreign	59%	—	41%
Composite	61%	—	39%

Key Votes of the 113th Congress

1. Sandy storm spending	Y	5. Medical Marijuana	N	9. Syrian Rebels Training	Y
2. Violence Against Women Act	Y	6. Farm Bill	N	10. Keystone pipeline	Y
3. Guantanamo Bay Detainees	N	7. Afghanistan Combat	N	11. Immigration Exec. Action	N
4. Abortion 20-week ban	N	8. NSA Phone Data Collection	N	12. Bipartisan budget deal	Y

Election Results

2014 general	Terri Sewell (D)........................... unopposed		$1,468,013	$2,918
2014 primary	Terri Sewell (D)................................74,830	(84%)		
	Tamara Harris Johnson (D)...............14,345	(16%)		

Prior winning percentages: 2012 (76%), 2010 (72%)

Population		Race and Ethnicity		Income	
Total:	666,880	Black	64.0%	Median income:	$31,953
Urban:	55.7%	White	32.0%		*(431 of 435)*
Suburban:	14.5%	Latino	2.5%	Under $50,000	67.8%
Rural:	29.8%	Asian	0.8%	$50,000-$99,999:	22.1%
Land area:	10,156	Two races	0.6%	$100,000-$199,999:	8.7%
Pop/sq. mi.:	81.4	White Ethnic	5.8%	$200,000 or more:	1.4%
Born in state:	80.2%			Poverty Rate	27.6%
		Education			
Age Groups		H.S. grad or less:	50.0%	**Work**	
Under 18:	22.3%	Some college:	31.0%	White collar:	29.4%
18 to 34:	26.8%	College degree, 4 yr.:	12.3%	Blue collar:	26.2%
35 to 64:	37.2%	Post-grad study:	6.7%	Sales and service:	44.4%
Over 64:	13.7%				
		Military		Govt. workers:	16.3%
		Veterans/active duty:	7.7%		

Central Alabama: Birmingham, Tuscaloosa

Alabama has learned to celebrate its black heritage, building striking memorials to the civil rights movement in Montgomery and Birmingham, acknowledging its history as ground zero of white resistance to the empowerment of blacks in the 1950s and 1960s.

Voter Turnout	
2013 Total Citizen 18+	507,162
2014 House Turnout	135,899
2014 Turnout as % CVAP	26.8%
2012 Turnout % CVAP	61.1%

Blacks first came here as slaves. The last slave ship to the United States, the *Clotilde*, docked in Mobile in 1859, where its cargo was then set free. Blacks were part of the great migration into the cotton lands after the Jacksonians swept the Indians out of the Southeast and sent them on their Trail of Tears to what is now Oklahoma. Today, Alabama's rural African-Americans are still clustered in the Black Belt of fertile dark soil across the center of the state. In Selma, founded by Alabama's one vice president, William Rufus King, Sheriff Jim Clark's troops beat up peaceful marchers on the Edmund Pettus Bridge in demonstrations that led to the march on Montgomery and the 1965 Voting Rights Act. All 11 of Alabama's majority-black counties are in the rich farm country of the Black Belt, but most Alabama blacks now live in urban areas—one-quarter of them in metropolitan Birmingham.

After decades of urban decline, Birmingham has undergone a renaissance in recent years. The city pulled itself out of the spiral of abandoned neighborhoods, soaring joblessness, and crime through the savvy use of public-private partnerships and other incentives. Numerous vacant and boarded up buildings have been supplanted by lofts and cafes for young professionals and empty-nesters, slowing the trend of migration to the suburbs. The industrial flats of downtown Birmingham are reemerging as a population center. Crime zones like the Metropolitan Gardens public housing project were leveled and replaced with mixed-income apartments. In January 2015, Mayor William Bell touted the opening of new hotels and an entertainment district downtown, and urged action on a new domed football stadium.

But change has come too slowly to stem the exodus from the city entirely, and Birmingham's population declined 12.6 percent from 2000 to 2010. In late 2009, the city took it hard on the chin when its controversial mayor, Larry Langford, was convicted of accepting $230,000 in bribes for steering millions of dollars of Jefferson County sewer bond business to an investment banker buddy when Langford headed the county commission. That and other shady deals with large investment houses on Wall Street forced the county to the brink of bankruptcy, dealing Birmingham both a tough financial and public relations blow to the civic optimism that had fueled its revival. Compounding the city's financial woes were recovery efforts after a deadly series of tornadoes touched down in Alabama on April 27, 2011, destroying entire neighborhoods in the Birmingham and Tuscaloosa metro areas.

The 7th Congressional District of Alabama was created in 1992 as a majority African-American district, which sprawls from Birmingham and Tuscaloosa nearly to Mobile County. In 2011 redistricting, the legislature needed to add about 79,000 people here. Heavily black Lowndes County and western black precincts of Montgomery were moved to the 7th. All of this made the

2012 Presidential Vote		
Barack Obama (D) 228,468	(73%)
Mitt Romney (R)...................85,106	(27%)
2008 Presidential Vote		
Barack Obama (D) 231,758	(72%)
John McCain (R)...................90,138	(28%)
Cook Partisan Voting Index: D+20		

2nd and 3rd districts whiter and safer for the GOP, and further solidified the 7th for the Democrats. Some Democratic legislators protested these moves because they made it harder for the party to compete in the rest of the state.

The Alabama River flows on the district's eastern edge, while the Tombigbee River straddles the western border. The area is filled with old plantations and a thriving catfish industry. The district takes in part of Tuscaloosa, home of the University of Alabama, and nearby Vance, site of a Mercedes factory. In 2014, company officials announced plans to expand production capacity at the Vance plant by more than 60 percent, featuring a new SUV model. Even with some recent economic progress, this remains one of the poorest districts in the nation.

The district has become 64 percent African-American and solidly Democratic—the only district in Alabama where Democrats have an expectation of victory. In 2008, Barack Obama swept each of the Black Belt counties by large margins. Overall, he won this district, 73%-27%.

In March 2015, Obama spoke in Selma to commemorate the 50th anniversary of the bloody march to Montgomery. In comments that were more a celebration than a policy prescription, he said that the 1965 protest had created a great legacy in the nation's march to civil rights. "We gather here to honor the courage of ordinary Americans willing to endure billy clubs and the chastening rod; tear gas and the trampling hoof; men and women who despite the gush of blood and splintered bone would stay true to their North Star and keep marching toward justice." Few of those 1965 protesters could have imagined that an African-American president would lead the festivities a half-century later.

Terri Sewell (D)

Democrat Terri Sewell, the congresswoman from the 7th District, in 2010 became the first African-American woman elected to Congress from Alabama. A personable consensus builder, Sewell was lauded by *The Washington Post* as "the breakout star" of the Congressional Black Caucus.

Sewell was born in Huntsville and raised in Selma, a hotbed of activity for the civil rights movement. She grew up near the famed Edmund Pettus Bridge, the site of the "Bloody Sunday" clash between protest marchers and state troopers. Sewell's family offered shelter for wayward travelers making the famed march from Selma to Montgomery in 1965. Hailing from such a place, "you appreciate the significance of your elders' fight for voting rights and civil rights," said Sewell, who was two months old during the march. Her mother, Nancy Sewell, was the first African-American woman elected to the Selma City Council. Her father was the high school basketball coach at Selma High School, where Sewell was the first black valedictorian. "Well, when you can get no dates because your daddy is a coach, all you can really do is study, right?" she joked.

Sewell earned her undergraduate degree from Princeton University. During that time, she took part in a Big Sister program and drew inspiration from the mentor assigned to her, Michelle Robinson, now first lady Michelle Obama. While Sewell was writing her senior thesis at Princeton, she also met former Democratic Rep. Shirley Chisholm of New York, the first African-American woman elected to Congress and later a candidate for president, who was retired by then and teaching at Mount Holyoke College. "I don't know if anybody could ever follow in Shirley Chisholm's footsteps, but I can tell you that I was inspired by her whole life story," Sewell said.

Sewell later studied politics at Oxford University on a scholarship, earning a master's degree. A theater buff, she dabbled in drama while at Oxford, directing and starring in the play *For Colored Girls Who Have Considered Suicide When the Rainbow is Enuf* by Ntozake

Shange. Later, while earning her law degree from Harvard, Sewell was a classmate of future President Barack Obama. At Harvard, she took a year off to turn her master's thesis into a book called *Black Tribunes: Race and Representation in British Politics*.

After graduating, Sewell clerked for a U.S. District Court judge in Birmingham, then in 1994 moved to New York City to work as a lawyer on Wall Street. But she returned home to Alabama to help care for her ailing father after he suffered several strokes. She was a bond lawyer and a partner in a Birmingham law firm.

When Democratic Rep. Artur Davis decided to leave the House after four terms to run for governor, Sewell jumped into the primary contest against eight other candidates. They included prominent local figures Earl Hilliard Jr., son of former Rep. Earl Hilliard, and Jefferson County Commissioner Shelia Smoot. Sewell had lower name recognition than Hilliard or Smoot, but she made up for it by outraising the other candidates with both a local and national fund-raising network. She finished first in the Democratic primary with 37% of the vote. Smoot snagged second place with 29%, setting up a runoff. Smoot got the endorsement of House Majority Whip James Clyburn, but Sewell outspent Smoot by nearly $1 million. In a relatively congenial runoff, Sewell bested Smoot, 55%-45%. She won easily that November. The *Montgomery Advertiser*, in endorsing her in 2012, called her "one of the most impressive newcomers in Congress."

In the House, Sewell has been more of a centrist than many of her more liberal Black Caucus colleagues. She hit it off with her classmate from Alabama, Republican Martha Roby. As first-term members of the Agriculture Committee, they worked together on a bill to reduce some of the most fertile acreage eligible for the federal Conservation Reserve Program in response to farmers who say that too much cropland is being lost to the program. On the Science, Space, and Technology Committee, Sewell joined Alabama Republicans in looking out for the state's NASA installations. But she also showed her loyalty to her party. When Davis switched parties and was chosen as a speaker at the 2012 Republican National Convention, Sewell blasted him for being "out of touch" and "never connected to the best interests of this district."

With increased seniority, Sewell gained assignments to two influential House committees: Financial Services and Intelligence. In 2014, she joined the Financial Services panel's bipartisan support of legislation to preserve access to financing for manufactured housing, especially for low-income rural Americans. She sought to ensure that the maximum allowable interest rate would be reasonable and fair. In 2015, Sewell became the ranking Democrat on the Intelligence subcommittee with oversight of Pentagon agencies. On other issues, she worked with a bipartisan group to file the Voting Rights Amendment Act of 2015, which was designed to restore a key section of the law that the Supreme Court had overturned in 2013. "I am pleased that both Democrats and Republicans recognize the need to strengthen federal voter protections," she said, while voicing regret that the limited proposal would not restore full Justice Department review of election-law changes in Alabama. Sewell voiced regret when U.S. Steel announced layoffs at its Fairfield Works, and said "Congress must do more to help companies like U.S. Steel and others in the manufacturing sector grow and create more jobs for Americans." She broke with Obama in supporting construction of the Keystone XL pipeline.

Sewell gained national prominence and an emotional personal moment during the March 2015 50th anniversary commemoration in Selma of the march to Montgomery, which she and Roby helped to organize. The parade across the Edmund Pettus Bridge was led by the Obamas and their two teen-aged daughters. In an interview with *Roll Call,* Sewell said that her life story disproves the title of Thomas Wolfe's 1940 novel *You Can't Go Home Again.* She embraced her "season of service," but said that she doesn't expect further career moves in politics. "This is it for me."

★ ALASKA ★

Alaska often chafes at its relationship with Washington and maintains an individualistic culture that has responded to unique conditions with creativity not always seen in the lower 48, or what Alaskans sometimes refer to as "Outside." But the state faces ongoing challenges in harnessing its energy resources and replacing lost oil revenues.

The father of Alaska was Secretary of State William Seward who took advantage of an opportunity in 1867 to create an American Pacific empire by purchasing the region from Russia for $7.2 million. The Alaska territory owes much of its early growth to federal decisions. While the state burst into national consciousness the Klondike Gold Rush of 1897, its largest city, Anchorage, had its beginnings in 1914 as the chief worksite for the federal government's Alaska Railroad, completed in 1923. Its famous sled dog race, the Iditarod, started in 1973 on a trail originally cleared and graded by the Army after Congress established the Alaska Road Commission in 1905. The race honors the 1925 emergency 20-team relay that delivered medicine from Nenana over almost 700 miles to icebound Nome in 127 hours, saving hundreds of lives from a diphtheria outbreak, a feat that generated headlines in the lower 48. Alaska became strategic territory in World War II, when the Aleutian Islands of Attu and Kiska were invaded by a small force of Japanese, the only part of the United States occupied by a foreign enemy since the War of 1812. Alaska, with only 72,000 people when the war began, was connected to the states by the Army's Alcan Highway, completed in 1942; by 1943, there were 152,000 troops in the territory. Alaska is the only state abutting Russia, across the Bering Strait and over the North Pole—there actually is a part of Alaska where you can see Russian land—and the state maintains a strategic geographic position. The military is a major presence at Joint Base Elmendorf-Richardson near Anchorage (which dispatched humanitarian aid to Nepalese earthquake victims in 2015) and at Fort Wainwright and Eielson Air Force Base near Fairbanks, with interceptors for the national missile defense system not far to the south at Fort Greely. Indeed, with the U.S. "pivot to Asia," military spending continues to flow to the state. Pending an environmental review, the Pentagon announced in 2015 that Clear Air Force Station in Anderson was slated for a billion-dollar Long- Range Discrimination Radar system to better detect missile threats from countries such as North Korea. The state also has the highest per capita rate of military veterans in the nation.

The least densely populated state, Alaska has less than one-quarter of one percent of the nation's population, but it has almost one-sixth of its land area. If superimposed on the continental United States, Alaska would stretch from Florida to California. The westernmost Aleutians are closer to Tokyo than to Juneau and farther west than Wellington, New Zealand. Many Alaskans have no access to state roads and are reachable only by boat or airplane. Only 736,000 people live in Alaska, and about two-thirds reside in Anchorage and the nearby Kenai Peninsula and Matanuska-Susitna Valley. This plus the Fairbanks metro, about one-eighth of the population, are the fastest-growing parts of Alaska. The Panhandle, with about one-tenth of the population, is the old Alaska, its towns settled by Russians built up against steep mountains on inlets from the Pacific. It includes the state capital of Juneau, which is inaccessible by road or highway—you have to ferry or fly in. The rest of the population lives in the Bush and the Aleutians, scattered in small towns, Native settlements and the wilderness.

Alaska became a state in January 1959, which technically ended federal dominance. But Alaska has remained a state intertwined with the government, an independent-minded society dependent on federal spending, subsidies and special treatment, and at the same time, resentful of what it considers Washington's meddling and intervention. Washington remains the largest landowner in Alaska with roughly 60 percent of the state's total area under the supervision of more than a dozen federal agencies including national parks, wildlife refuges, national forests, military bases and the North Slope National Petroleum Reserve. In 1959, Alaska's economy depended on fishing, oil production in Cook Inlet around Anchorage and the military—all federally regulated or controlled—and they continue to be important. A 2014 Pew Charitable Trusts study found that Alaska ranked third in the nation in terms of per capita total federal spending in the states, trailing only Maryland and Virginia, home to legions of federal employees. In federal grants alone, Alaska ranked number one. Alaskans continue to seek federal subsidies for intrastate air service, loan guarantees for the fishing

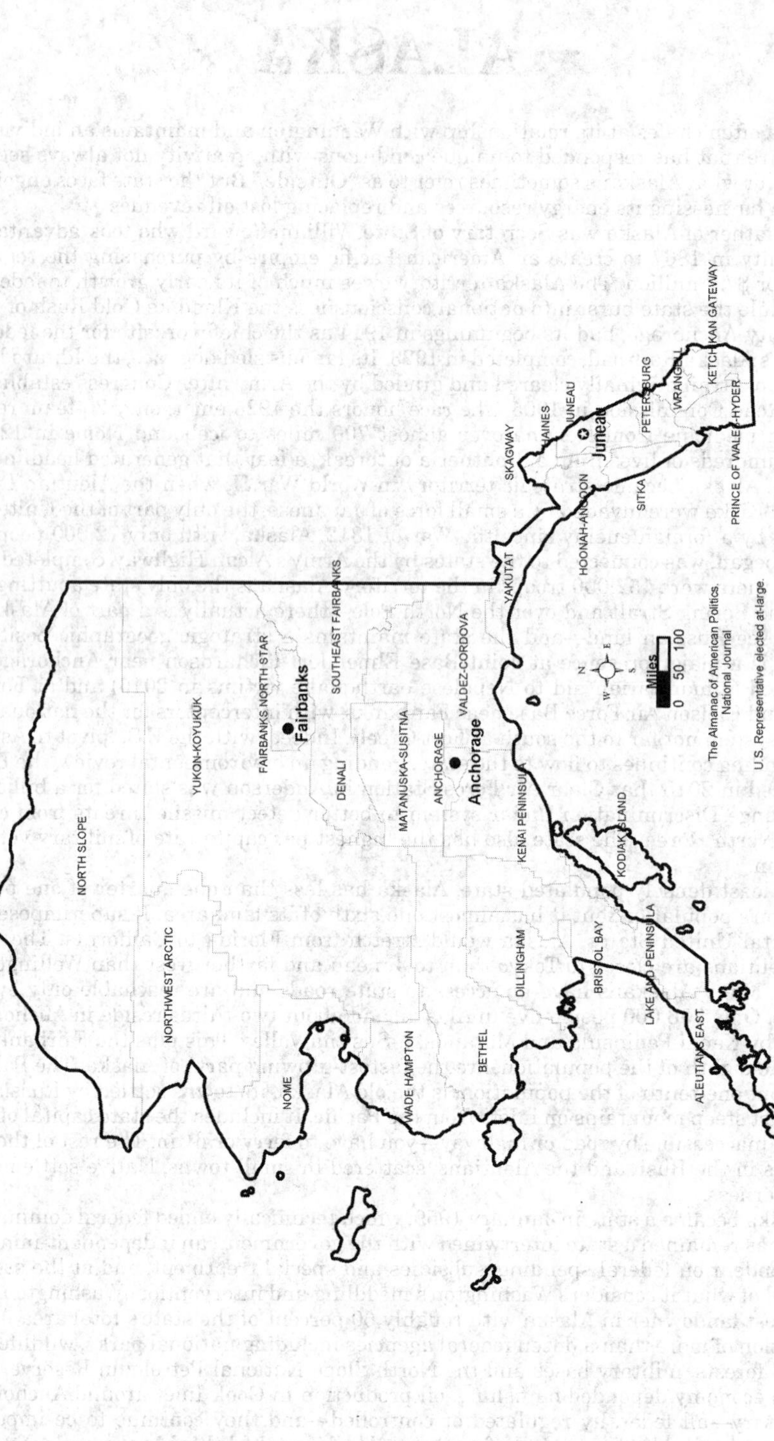

SKAGWAY

HAINES

JUNEAU

Juneau

HOONAH-ANGOON

YAKUTAT

SITKA

PETERSBURG

WRANGELL

KETCHIKAN GATEWAY

PRINCE OF WALES-HYDER

NORTH SLOPE

YUKON-KOYUKUK

FAIRBANKS NORTH STAR

Fairbanks

SOUTHEAST FAIRBANKS

DENALI

MATANUSKA-SUSITNA

VALDEZ-CORDOVA

ANCHORAGE

Anchorage

NORTHWEST ARCTIC

NOME

WADE HAMPTON

BETHEL

DILLINGHAM

KENAI PENINSULA

KODIAK ISLAND

BRISTOL BAY

LAKE AND PENINSULA

ALEUTIANS EAST

N
W   E
S

Miles
0   50   100

The Almanac of American Politics
National Journal

U.S. Representative elected at-large

industry and funding for the Alaska Railroad. The state's special needs, its longtime Sen. Ted Stevens used to argue, justify its special treatment.

But something else has transformed Alaska, something unforeseen by those who successfully obtained statehood in 1959. Less than a decade later, Alaska's economy and public life were reshaped by the discovery of North Slope oil. It began suddenly, almost accidentally, as Arco chief executive Robert Anderson, after seven dry wells on Prudhoe Bay, decided to use a nearby drilling rig to make another try—and as a natural gas flare shot 30 feet in the air discovered the 12-billion barrel North Slope oil field. This was the greatest single oil strike in U.S. history and the beginning of much of today's Alaska.

Finding oil in Prudhoe Bay was somewhat akin to finding it on the moon. It was not clear in 1968 who owned the oil or how it could be taken out. The Statehood Act of 1959 gave the state the right to choose its own public lands, but only after settling Native land claims. The only feasible way to get the oil out—the Arctic Ocean ice breaks up in late July for only six weeks—was a pipeline. But environmentalists opposed that option for fear that it would destroy the delicate permafrost and interfere with caribou migrations. Development-minded Alaskans got a pipeline bill through Congress in 1973, but the pipeline had to be built on stilts and wasn't opened until 1977. Then in 1980, after astute lobbying by environmentalists, Congress passed—over the objections of Alaska's two senators and Rep. Don Young—the Alaska National Interest Lands Conservation Act (ANILCA), which set aside 159 million acres as national parks, national monuments or wilderness: one-third of the state was protected (or barred) from development. Much, if not all of this, turned out to be for the best. The pipeline came on line just as oil prices were approaching a peak, thus generating maximum revenues to the state, which gets most of the royalties. The environment was protected far better than it would have been without the safeguards. With fluctuations, the Western Arctic herd of caribou grew from 75,000 in 1976 to 235,000 in 2013, and Native Alaskans got more autonomy than the non-Native majority of Alaskans would have given them. With oil providing some 85 percent of its revenue, the state government abolished its income tax in 1980—it doesn't have a state sales tax either—and created a low-tax regime. Wisely, Alaska did not squander its windfall. In 1976, Republican Gov. Jay Hammond persuaded the legislature to establish a Permanent Fund for most of the oil revenues. Each year, it presents every resident with a dividend based on a five-year rolling average of the Permanent Fund's financial performance, which is now largely generated by stock, bond and real estate investments, not oil revenue. In 2014, that dividend was $1,884, the third-largest check issued since the yearly distributions to Alaskans began in 1982. In 2015, the market value of the Permanent Fund reached almost $55 billion.

But the petro-fueled hayride Alaskans have enjoyed for many years has become quite bumpy. North Slope oil production has been falling for decades, peaking in 1988 at almost 2 million barrels a day. By 2014, production was down to less than 500,000 barrels a day. That decline, however, was cushioned by the relatively steady rise in the global demand and price for oil. Then the wellhead price for Alaskan crude began its long slide in 2014, causing a drop in the oil royalties the state received, which shrunk the amount of money going into its coffers. At the same time, receipts from the corporate, production and property taxes that the state levies on oil companies also tumbled. Overall, the state received roughly $4.7 billion in oil revenue in fiscal 2014 for its unrestricted general fund (out of $5.4 billion in total revenue), which pays for state discretionary spending on government operations, basic services and capital improvements. In 2015 those oil revenues were expected to plunge to less than $1.7 billion. The Alaska Department of Revenue warned in the spring of 2015 that the "state requires much higher oil prices and/or significantly increasing oil production" in order to stabilize its finances. Neither of those options seems likely to happen any time soon. Alaska's Permanent Fund has been walled off from the state's operating budget and in the past voters have rejected proposals to tap the fund's investment income, let alone it's capital. But given the collapse in oil revenues, lawmakers in Juneau have looked for ways to access parts of that bankroll to help pay the state's bills.

Over the years, Alaskans' efforts to develop energy resources outside of the North Slope have been frustrated. Its congressional delegation, despite its relative seniority, was unable to overcome the opposition of environmental groups to oil drilling in the Arctic National Wildlife Refuge (ANWR) east of Prudhoe Bay. ANWR was estimated to have 9 to 16 billion barrels, and horizontal drilling techniques meant that the drilling footprint could be reduced to the size of Washington's Dulles Airport. Congress was on the verge of approving ANWR drilling in 1989 when the *Exxon Valdez* ran aground in Prince William Sound near the pipeline terminus at Valdez. The ensuing uproar over environmental damage stalled the drilling issue, and Democrats managed to block its approval in subsequent Congresses. Then in January 2015, President Obama proposed the largest ever wilderness designation in ANWR, which would place its potentially oil-rich coastal plain and millions of additional acres off-limits to future oil and gas development. Republican Sena-

Voter Turnout	
2013 Total Citizen 18+	526,769
2014 Highest Statewide Turnout	282,382
2014 Turnout as % CVAP	53.6%
2012 Turnout as % CVAP	57.4%

Legislature			
Senate:	14R	6D	
House:	23R	16D	1I

tors Lisa Murkowski and Dan Sullivan described the president's plan as an "attack" and "war" on Alaska. Independent Gov. Bill Walker said that the Obama administration was "taking our economy away from us piece by piece." The month prior to his announcement on ANWR, the president had ordered an indefinite ban on oil and gas drilling in Alaska's Bristol Bay.

Although the North Slope's oil has been pumped out through a pipeline since 1977, there has not been a way to get its vast quantities of natural gas out. In addition to more than 30 trillion cubic feet of known gas reserves, the U.S. Geological Survey estimates that there are another 85 trillion cubic feet of undiscovered gas on the Slope. For years, Alaska lawmakers and energy concerns had focused on building a pipeline from the North Slope to Alberta Canada where it would connect to other North American pipelines to send natural gas to the U.S. But advances in horizontal fracturing—known as fracking—significantly increased natural gas production in the lower 48 and made the Alberta pipeline economically far less feasible. Now there is momentum behind the Alaska LNG Project, which would transport gas from Prudhoe Bay and Point Thomson on the North Slope through an 800-mile pipeline to a plant in Nikiski on the Kenai Peninsula, where it would be liquefied for shipment primarily to markets in Asia. A consortium of ExxonMobil, BP, ConnocoPhillips and TransCanada, working with the Alaska Gasline Development Corporation, a public corporation representing the state's interests in natural gas development on the North Slope, is backing the project which is expected to cost $45-to-$65 billion to construct and will not be up and running before 2025. The Obama administration backed this plan to develop Alaska's energy resources: In May 2015, the Department of Energy approved a conditional license permitting Alaska LNG to export to countries in Asia with which the U.S. has not had a free trade agreement, such as China, Japan and India, vastly expanding the potential customers for Alaska's natural gas.

Alaska's forbidding terrain is responsible for some of its economic assets: It has more aircraft per capita than any other state, and a PricewaterhouseCoopers study found that general aviation in Alaska supported 5,800 jobs in 2013 and contributed more than $1.1 billion to the state's total economic output that year. Private contractors provide much of the Post Office's service to the Bush. Alaska's fisheries accounted for more than half of the nation's seafood harvest in 2012, according to a report by the National Marine Fisheries Service. Tourism, the No. 2 private employer, has been on the rise, with cruise ships prowling the intra-coastal inlets amid glaciers and grizzlies, docking in Anchorage for side trips to the Denali National Park and Preserve. Alaska has major mines producing gold,

Population		Race and Ethnicity		Income	
Total:	735,132	White	63.6%	Median income:	$61,137
Urban:	47.5%	AI/AN	13.8%		(10 of 50)
Suburban:	13.2%	Latino	5.8%	Under $50,000	32.9%
Rural:	39.3%	Asian	5.3%	$50,000-$99,999:	33.9%
Landarea:	570,641	Tworaces	7.4%	$100,000-$199,999:	27.2%
Pop/sq.mi.:	1.3	White Ethnic	20.6%	$200,000 or more:	6.0%
Borninstate:	42.9%			Poverty Rate	9.3%
		Education			
Age Groups		H.S. grad or less:	36.2%	Work	
Under 18:	25.6%	Some college:	35.8%	White collar:	35.8%
18 to 34:	26.9%	College degree, 4 yr.:	18.2%	Blue collar:	40.7%
35 to 64:	38.5%	Post-grad study:	9.8%	Sales and service:	23.4%
Over 64:	8.9%				
		Military		Govt. workers:	23.5%
		Veterans/active duty:	14.0%		

copper, coal and zinc in operation. Twelve Native corporations created by the Alaska Native Claims Act have proved to be successful, not only in providing dividend income, elderly benefits and scholarships and employment opportunities for Natives, but also in helping them preserve Native traditions and adapt to Alaska's market economy at their own pace. The corporate model allows more continuity in office for the Alaska Native corporations' managers—although some have made bad decisions and been thrown out. This cumulative voting method, by which a minority can get a seat on the board, has produced management that is sensitive to all opinions. Huge windfalls are avoided because all corporations share 70 percent of profits from mineral sales. In 2010, the Native corporations had gross revenues of more than $8 billion and employed some 16,000 Alaskans. But not all is rosy. Native villages in the Bush have little in the way of a private-sector economy, and alcoholism and suicide rates remain high.

In partisan terms, Alaska has proved to be pretty solidly Republican: it did not elect a Democrat to the Senate between 1974 and 2008, when Nick Begich was elected for one term. Family or fate has often connected the state's congressional delegation. Sen. Lisa Murkowski, who survived defeat in the 2010 Republican primary to win as a write-in candidate, is the daughter of Frank Murkowski, who served in the Senate from 1980 to 2002 and then was elected governor. Begich is the son of Nick Begich, the last Alaska Democrat to serve in the House, who died in a plane crash with House Majority Leader Hale Boggs in 1972. And Rep. Don Young was the Republican chosen to replace the elder Begich in a 1973 special election, and reelected ever since. In the statehouse, the former mayor of Wasilla, Sarah Palin, beat Frank Murkowski in the 2006 GOP primary and then former Democratic Gov. Tony Knowles in November. But Palin, after her run as the Republican vice presidential nominee in 2008, resigned in July 2009, complaining of media attention and the spurious charges filed against her under an ethics law she had supported. Lt. Gov. Sean Parnell succeeded her. Parnell was elected in his own right in 2010, after beating Anchorage attorney Bill Walker in the GOP primary and in the general election Democratic legislator Ethan Berkowitz, who had run against Parnell as Knowles' running mate in 2006. It was supposed to be an easy reelection bid for Parnell, but Walker, who had better luck running as an independent, defeated him. Meanwhile, Republican Dan Sullivan thwarted Begich's reelection bid, giving Alaska an unusual political exacta in 2014—dumping an incumbent Governor and Senator of different parties in the same general election. According to the Smart Politics website at the Humphrey School of Public Affairs, the last time that happened was in 1990, in Minnesota. To top it off, the state's voters approved a ballot measure legalizing marijuana use for persons 21 years of age or older. But nothing should surprise in this small state with a Libertarian bent and unique characteristics: Alaska can be quirky, and its politics are not always congruent with politics Outside.

Presidential Politics   When Alaska and Hawaii were admitted to the union in 1959, it was expected that Alaska would vote Democratic and Hawaii Republican. It has turned out to be the other way around. Alaska has voted for the GOP standard bearer in every presidential election except for 1964, the LBJ landslide year. Rural areas in the northern and western regions of the state, including hundreds of tiny settlements of Native Alaskans are the most Democratic, while Republicans are strongest in the "Mat-Su" territory (short for the borough of Matansuka-Susitna), the fastest growing area of the state, containing the northern suburbs of Anchorage. Roughly 40 percent of the state's population lives in Anchorage, its largest city, which tends to vote Republican, but Democrats have some bastions there as well.

In 1992, third-party candidate Ross Perot won 28 percent here, his second-best showing in the country. In 2000, George W. Bush won 59%-28%, but Ralph Nader got 10 percent of the vote, Nader's best showing. In 2004, Bush got 61 percent and John Kerry improved on Al Gore's showing with

2012 Presidential Vote		
Mitt Romney (R)................164,676	(55%)
Barack Obama (D)..............122,640	(41%)
Gary Johnson (Lib)................7,392	(2%)
2012 Presidential Caucus	
Mitt Romney (R)....................4,554	(32%)
Rick Santorum (R)................4,254	(30%)
Ron Paul (R)...........................3,410	(24%)
Newt Gingrich (R) 1,878	(13%)
2008 Presidential Vote	
John McCain (R).................193,841	(59%)
Barack Obama (D)..............123,594	(38%)

36 percent, after Nader's vote sunk below 2 percent. In the 2008 Democratic caucus, with fewer than 9,000 participants, Barack Obama beat Hillary Clinton 75%-25%. It was one of many caucuses that year where the Obama forces out-organized Clinton's, and for a time it looked like his campaign might be competitive in the general election. By August, Obama had scores of paid staffers in the state, and his volunteers were busy canvassing voters in the long hours of summer daylight. But McCain's selection of then Gov. Sarah Palin as his running mate tucked Alaska safely into the Republican column. (In Alaska's 2008 GOP caucuses, McCain finished fourth, far behind the winner, Mitt Romney, as well as behind Mike Huckabee and Ron Paul.) Four years later, Romney again won the March 2012 caucuses, but only narrowly over Rick Santorum. Ron Paul failed to capitalize on state's libertarian streak and finished third. That fall, Romney handily won, but Obama's 41 percent showing was the best for a Democrat since Hubert Humphrey won 42 percent in 1968. And while he still lost there, Alaska was the state where, on the margin, Obama improved the most over his performance in 2008.

One memorable footnote for Alaska in presidential politics is the trip that Richard Nixon made there in 1960, two days before Election Day, in order to fulfill his pledge to campaign in all 50 states. The distant stop on the presidential trail consumed precious time on Nixon's closing days' schedule that might have been better spent stumping in Texas or Illinois, states with far more Electoral Votes which Nixon lost by a whisker.

Governor

Bill Walker (I)

Elected 2014, term expires Dec. 2018, 1st full term; b. April 16, 1951, Fairbanks; Lewis and Clark College, B.S. 1973, U. of Puget Sound, J.D. 1983; Christian; married (Donna); 4 children.

Elected Office: Valdez City Cncl., 1977-79; Valdez mayor, 1979.

Professional Career: Commercial fisherman, 1969; Construction worker, 1970-74; Owner, Bill Walker Construction Company, 1975-80; Practicing atty., 1983-95; Owner/atty., Walker and Levesque LLC/ Walker Richards LLC Law Firm, 1995-present.

Office: Alaska State Capitol Building, Third Fl., Juneau, 99811-0001, 907-465-3500; Fax: 907-465-3532; Website: gov.state.ak.us

State Offices: Anchorage, 907-269-7450; Fairbanks, 907-451-2920; Mat-Su, 907-761-5690

Election Results

2014 general	Bill Walker (I)	134,658	(48%)
	Sean Parnell (R)	128,435	(46%)
	Carolyn "Care" Clift (L)	8,985	(3%)
	J.R. Myers (CNP)	6,987	(3%)

Bill Walker won the governor's seat in November 2014 as an independent, defeating Republican incumbent Sean Parnell in a campaign that was unconventional, even by Alaska's eccentric political standards. And as he began his statehouse tenure, Walker, a former Republican, continued to display a feisty independence in his dealings with the GOP-controlled state legislature.

Walker was born in Fairbanks, the youngest of four children, and raised in Delta Junction and Valdez. His father, a World War II veteran, was working in home construction when the 1964 earthquake struck, destroying the family's home and much of the town of Valdez. At 12, Walker helped provide for the family by working as a janitor at the local post office. He worked his way through Lewis and Clark College in Portland, Oregon, as a carpenter and laborer on the Trans-Alaska Pipeline and joined the family construction trade after graduating from college with a B.S. in business administration. He won a seat on the Valdez City Council in 1977 and two years later, at the age of 27, was elected the city's the youngest-ever mayor. After one term he went to law school and after graduating in 1983, joined an old-line Anchorage firm. He founded his own firm, Walker Richards, in 1995, which had a primary focus on oil and gas and municipal law. He represented several local communities and served as general counsel to the Alaska Gasline Port Authority. Walker ran for the governor in 2010, but lost to incumbent Gov. Sean Parnell in the GOP primary. He began another attempt to replace Parnell for the Republican gubernatorial nod, but dropped out of the primary race in 2013 to run as an independent and head directly to the general election.

Although his popularity was ebbing in 2014, Parnell looked like a reasonable bet to win a three-way race with Walker and Democrat Byron Mallott, the former mayor of Juneau. But the contest was upended in September when Mallott dropped his bid for governor and agreed to become Walker's running mate on a "unity ticket," something the independent had been urging in order to have a better chance at dislodging Parnell. This was not the first time Mallott had backed an independent—in 2010 he strayed from the party line and signed on to co-chair Lisa Murkowski's independent Senate bid. The Alaska Democratic state central committee, eager to oust Parnell, endorsed Mallott's switch and an Anchorage judge subsequently upheld his pairing with Walker. The fusion ticket did not agree on everything— Walker was pro-life and Mallott was pro-choice—but the two vowed to work together on the major issues confronting the state.

Parnell was weakened with the release of a federal report in September about a sexual-assault scandal in the Alaska National Guard. The report detailed many cases of ethical misconduct and years of alleged cover-ups. Parnell then fired several Guard officers, but many, including Walker, said the governor's actions came too late. In the fall campaign Walker opposed Parnell on his decision to sign legislation in 2013 that significantly lowered the oil-production taxes that had been raised by GOP Gov. Sarah Palin, whom Parnell had served with as lieutenant governor. Walker, echoing Palin's populism, declared he would not bow to oil companies' interests to gain votes. The independent also supported expanding Medicaid coverage in Alaska, which Parnell opposed. And when a U.S. District Court struck down the state's ban on same-sex marriage in October, Walker criticized Parnell for pledging to appeal the ruling. Walker said he did not agree with same-sex marriage but would "uphold the laws of the land," and warned that spending state resources on an appeal was unwise. The race was already one of the most exotic contests of 2014, when in the waning days of the campaign, tea party heroine Palin endorsed Walker and accused Parnell, her ex-running mate, of "caving" to Big Oil. The Walker-Mallott ticket won by about 6,200 votes out of 285,000 cast, making it one of the closest elections in state history.

Walker's initial nominations to head up state agencies lacked partisan direction. Of his first seven major selections, only one, Craig Richards, Walker's former law partner and his pick for attorney general, was a registered Republican. His choices to run the departments of health and social services, environmental conservation, labor, natural resources, revenue, and public safety were not enrolled in either of the two major parties. Some of Walker's key advisers, like his chief of staff and his legislative director were Republicans, but that hardly eased GOP suspicions of the new governor's team. Not long after he took office, Walker booted three energy careerists off the Alaska Gasline Development Corporation, the public entity that is working with major oil companies to build a pipeline to transport natural gas from the North Slope to the Kenai Peninsula for export overseas. Walker's management of the corporation rankled Republican House Speaker Mike Chenault, who had personally backed one of the booted commissioners, a veteran Texas-based pipeline construction consultant. Walker said he was a "strong believer in local hire[s]." The early jousting between Walker and Chenault, seemed to foreshow a rocky relationship between the two leaders. It didn't help matters that Chenault's chief of staff had been Parnell's campaign manager.

In March, Chenault introduced legislation that blocked Walker from using the Development Corp. to come up with alternatives to the Alaska LNG Project Pipeline. Walker seemed to take Chenault's move as an affront to his authority. At press conference he brandished a copy of the bill and asked, in an annoyed tone, "Are you kidding me?". A month later, he carried out his promise to veto the measure. In May, the Republican-run House Finance committee effectively tabled Walker's Medicaid expansion proposal. A few days later, Walker returned the favor, and he vetoed most elements of a budget passed by Republican lawmakers, because it was woefully underfunded, a result of the collapse in oil revenues coming into the state coffers. It was an inauspicious start for the new governor who said in his first week in office that he wanted to set "a tone of working together" with the legislature.

Senior Senator

Lisa Murkowski (R)

Appointed Dec. 2002, term expires 2016, 2nd full term; b. May 22, 1957, Ketchikan; Willamette U., 1975-77, Georgetown U., B.A. 1980, Willamette U., J.D. 1985; Catholic; married (Verne Martell); 2 children.

Elected Office: AK House, 1998-2002.

Professional Career: Anchorage Dist. Court Clerk's Office, atty., 1987-89; Practicing atty., 1989-98.

DC Office: 709 HSOB, 20510, 202-224-6665; Fax: 202-224-5301; Website: murkowski.senate.gov.

State Offices: Anchorage, 907-271-3735; Fairbanks, 907-456-0233; Juneau, 907-586-7277; Kenai, 907-283-5808; Ketchikan, 907-225-6880; Matsu, 907-376-7665.

Committees: *Appropriations:* Commerce, Justice, Science & Related Agencies; Defense; Energy & Water Development; Homeland Security; Interior, Environment & Related Agencies (Chmn); Military Construction, Veterans Affairs & Related Agencies. *Energy & Natural Resources* (Chmn). *Health, Education, Labor & Pensions:* Primary Health & Aging. *Indian Affairs.*

Group Ratings

	ADA	ACLU	AFL-CIO	LCV	ITI	COC	HAFA	ACU	CFG	FRC
2014	30%	80%	–	0%	66%	100%	23%	41%	27%	46%
2013	30%	C	69%	38%	C	71%	C	38%	52%	C

National Journal Ratings

	2013 LIB	—	2013 CONS
Economic	43%	—	56%
Social	46%	—	53%
Foreign	43%	—	56%
Composite	45%	—	56%

Key Votes of the 113th Congress

1. Sandy storm spending	Y	5. Student Loan Rates	Y	9. Bipartisan Budget Deal	Y
2. Chuck Hagel Confirmation	N	6. Employee Non-Discrim'n Act	Y	10. Farm Bill Conference Rept.	N
3. Gun Background Checks	N	7. Senate Vote on Judgeships	Y	11. Unempl. Comp. Extension	Y
4. Immigration Reform	Y	8. Defense Dept. Spending	N	12. Keystone Pipeline	Y

Election Results

2010 general	Lisa Murkowski (WI)	101,091	(39%)	$4,605,972	$1,1761,254	$280,332
	Joe Miller (R)	90,839	(35%)	$1,487,872	$1,911,679	$22,469
	Scott McAdams (D)	60,045	(23%)	$1,268,031	$227,743	$252,792
2010 primary	Joe Miller (R)	55,878	(51%)			
	Lisa Murkowski (R)	53,872	(49%)			

Prior winning percentage: 2004 (49%)

Lisa Murkowski, Alaska's senior senator, is a Republican who was appointed to the Senate in 2002 by her father, then-Gov. Frank Murkowski, to fill the vacancy created when he resigned to become governor. Two years later, she won a full term to become the first woman elected to Congress from Alaska. But when Murkowski sought re-election in 2010, she was upended in the GOP primary by a Tea Party-backed candidate, Joe Miller. Murkowski refused to accept defeat. She engineered a remarkable comeback, becoming the first senator to win a write-in campaign since Strom Thurmond of South Carolina in 1954.

Murkowski, the first Alaskan-born Senator, grew up in Ketchikan in Alaska's Panhandle and in Fairbanks. She attended Willamette University in Salem, Oregon, for two years, and graduated from Georgetown University in 1980, the year her father was first elected to the Senate. Murkowski went on to get a law degree from Willamette University College of Law in 1985, after which she served as an Anchorage District Court attorney, worked for an Anchorage law firm for eight years and later started her own law practice. In 1998, she was elected to the state House from a district that includes north Anchorage.

Early on as a state legislator, Murkowski showed a streak of independence that she has displayed throughout her career. At times, it has put her on a collision course with stalwart conservatives. For example, when Alaska was facing a $1.1 billion budget shortfall in 2002, Murkowski was a leader in the bipartisan Fiscal Policy Caucus that pushed for a tax hike, including raising the alcohol tax from 3 cents to 10 cents a drink. That position put Murkowski at odds with her father, who was running for governor on a pledge of no new taxes. Her bill was enacted, making Alaska the state with the highest alcohol tax in the country. Some conservatives derisively referred to her and her allies as "RIMs"—Republican Invertebrate Moderates.

Those positions took a political toll. Murkowski barely eked out a victory in her re-election bid in 2002 against conservative Nancy Dahlstrom. Murkowski won by only 57 votes, but, afterwards, she was chosen to be the state's House Majority Leader. That year, Alaskans also elected her father governor, though he had two years left in his Senate term. (Republican state legislators saw to it that he—not outgoing Democratic Gov. Tony Knowles—appointed a successor. Earlier in the year, they passed, over Knowles' veto, a law barring a governor from appointing a successor until five days after the vacancy occurred.) Frank Murkowski compiled an impressive list of possible successors and said he was looking for someone whose views on Alaska issues were in sync with his and who had legislative experience and was young enough to serve many years. He chose Lisa Murkowski.

It was the first time a governor had appointed his or her child to the Senate and provoked plenty of controversy. While most Republicans and many Democrats praised Murkowski's abilities, others said her selection was all about nepotism. Lisa Murkowski stressed that she and her father kept separate political lives. "We have always maintained very separate identities, at least for the time I have been in the legislature," she said. "I haven't called him for counseling, and typically he doesn't offer."

Still, Murkowski knew that as she completed her father's Senate term, critics would be watching to see if she was up to the job. She wasted no time in using political skills that she had honed in the Alaska legislature, winning committee assignments that put her at the center of issues of great importance to the state. No perch was more important than a seat on the Energy Committee, given the state's heavy reliance on oil and mineral-related revenue.

In learning the ropes, Murkowski got much help from the state's long-time senator, Ted Stevens, a formidable figure, whose senior position on the Appropriations Committee made him one of Capitol Hill's most influential lawmakers. For example, Murkowski pushed through a bill, with Stevens' help, that included federal loan guarantees for a 3,500-mile pipeline that would bring natural gas from the North Slope to the lower 48—a major venture for the state. Stevens, in his characteristic blunt manner, praised Murkowski's work, and said she "is a hell of a lot better senator than her Dad ever was." (She returned that loyalty in 2009 by asking President George W. Bush to pardon Stevens after he was convicted for concealing $250,000 in gifts from an oil executive. Bush declined, but Stevens' conviction was tossed out because of prosecutorial misconduct.)

No Alaska Republican senator had ever been defeated for reelection, but as Murkowski entered the 2004 campaign, she was vulnerable. She had primary opposition from conservative former legislator Mike Miller, who attacked her stands on abortion, gun rights, and taxes. Miller was even supported by her father's lieutenant governor, Loren Leman. But Murkowski was better financed and had the support of Stevens and irascible, long-time Rep. Don Young. She easily prevailed in the primary 58%-37%.

In the general election, she faced a tough race against Knowles, the most successful Democrat in the state at the time. A Vietnam veteran and Yale classmate and friend of George W. Bush, Knowles ran a restaurant in Anchorage and had twice been elected the city's mayor and twice won gubernatorial races. The nepotism issue loomed over the campaign. Fifty thousand voters signed a ballot measure to ban governors from appointing new senators, and it later passed with 56 percent of the vote. Stevens campaigned for Murkowski, stressing that Alaska would be hurt if Democrats gained a Senate majority and that Murkowski, at age 47, would have a chance of amassing more seniority than would 61-year-old Knowles. This strong red state voted to give the GOP junior senator a full term, 49%-46%.

Returned to Capitol Hill, Murkowski established a moderate voting record, considerably closer to the middle of the road than her father's conservative slant. She also assumed a much larger role in the Senate on Alaska-centric issues after Stevens lost his bid for reelection in 2008 amid the corruption scandal. Like her mentor, she secured a seat on the Appropriations Committee, a critical post for a state so dependent on federal spending. Republican leaders helped her in other ways. She joined the GOP Senate leadership as a counsel to Minority Leader Mitch McConnell. When Nevada Republican John Ensign stepped down as

Republican Policy Committee chairman in 2009 after acknowledging an extramarital affair, Murkowski replaced South Dakota's John Thune as the conference vice chair while Thune moved into Ensign's old slot.

Even as her star was rising on Capitol Hill, Murkowski had to deal with an ethics controversy prompted by a real estate purchase that she and her husband made in late 2006. They bought an acre of waterfront land on Alaska's Kenai River from developer Bob Penney, a friend of Stevens. An ethics watchdog group charged that the $179,500 the couple paid was well below the market value of approximately $350,000. Penney told local newspaper reporters that he had sold Murkowski the land, next to property he owned on the river, for the assessed value. However, in early 2007, just weeks after the sale, the assessed value on the lot went up to $215,000. In July 2007, Murkowski called the deal "nothing nefarious or underhanded," but she decided to sell the land back to Penney for the purchase price of $179,500.

Meanwhile, she aggressively pushed for the state delegation's long-standing goal of opening up the Alaska National Wildlife Refuge to oil and gas exploration—a popular idea in the state but one that has been rebuffed repeatedly in Washington. While the area houses a wide array of wildlife, it also is thought to hold large oil and gas reserves. Murkowski has battled the Obama Administration repeatedly over the issue. She was especially incensed when President Barack Obama said in 2015 that he would ask Congress to designate some 12 million of ANWR's 19 million acres as wilderness. She blasted the move as "a stunning attack on our sovereignty."

Murkowski has been effective in working across the aisle as was demonstrated right after she took the reins of the Energy and Natural Resources Committee in 2015. New Senate Majority Leader Mitch McConnell made the Keystone XL pipeline bill his first major legislative priority. Murkowski worked closely with Democrat Maria Cantwell of Washington, the panel's ranking member, on the bill even though Cantwell opposed the measure. The two senators dealt with nearly 250 amendments, a large number that reflected McConnell's pledge to allow free-wheeling debate. The bill passed 62-36, and even though Obama vetoed the legislation, the collaborative work of the two senators won their colleagues' praise. Murkowski had displayed that style before, when, as the committee's ranking member, she maintained an amicable working relationship with Democrat Mary Landrieu of Louisiana, the chairman.

Murkowski has an acrimonious relationship with Interior Secretary Sally Jewell, who rejected construction of a one-lane emergency access road in the Izembek National Wildlife Refuge that she and other state lawmakers had long sought as a critical medical link to facilitate access to an all-weather airport at Cold Bay for the isolated village of King Cove. Environmentalists countered that such development threatened sensitive wildlife. Murkowski also rebuked Jewell at a hearing in February 2015, when she charged the Obama Administration was shutting off development on the North Slope by starving the trans-Alaska pipeline of oil. "You're depriving us of jobs, revenue security and prosperity," Murkowski said.

Murkowski showed her legislative skills—and political savvy—in June 2012 when President Obama signed into law her bill settling a longstanding dispute between Alaska Natives and the state and federal government over fishing and hunting land around Salmon Lake. The new law designated more than 14,000 acres of land in the area to the locally-controlled Bering Straits Native Corporation, while allowing the Bureau of Land Management to own nine acres of Salmon Lake campground. That resolution likely reinforced Murkowski's strong standing with Alaska Natives, whose solid support for her write-in campaign was a key to her 2010 reelection.

Despite those legislative skills, Murkowski has continued to take stances over the years that alienate some conservative Republicans in her state. She joined just three other Republican senators to seek more civil liberties protections in the USA Patriot Act after President Bush had asked Congress to reauthorize it. She also joined Iowa Democratic Sen. Tom Harkin in 2007 on an amendment to the farm bill to raise nutritional standards for food and beverages sold in school vending machines and cafeterias.

Her work on state issues, as well as frequent trips home to showcase her growing influence did not stave off Miller's vigorous challenge in 2010. A Fairbanks attorney and self-described "constitutional conservative," Miller charged that Murkowski was a Washington insider who had abandoned Republican values by supporting abortion rights and higher taxes. His candidacy was backed by the then popular former Governor and former GOP vice presidential nominee Sarah Palin, who had defeated Frank Murkowski in the GOP gubernatorial primary in 2006. Palin's followers in the tea party movement flocked to Miller's camp. Miller's challenge also was boosted by an anti-abortion referendum on the ballot, which brought thousands of voters to the polls.

Murkowski's ads touting her record of accomplishment were insufficient to overcome conservative skepticism. Miller narrowly prevailed 51 percent to 49 percent. After conceding, Murkowski decided to pursue a long-shot write-in campaign. With the slogan "Let's Make History," she waged a spirited campaign, pointing to the considerable seniority that federally-dependent Alaska would lack if she lost. Her GOP colleagues in the Senate, who were prohibited by party rules from endorsing her as an Independent, lined up behind Miller because, they said, Republican voters had spoken in the primary. But many were not enthusiastic.

Miller's campaign suffered from various missteps, and when Murkowski won, he challenged ballots on which Murkowski's name was not spelled clearly. State court rejected that move and held that voter intent sufficed. Murkowski prevailed with 39 percent of the vote in the three-way contest in which Miller garnered 35 percent and Democrat Scott McAdams gained about 23 percent.

After that successful write-in campaign, there was some question about whether Murkowski would steer a moderate course and continue to show her independent bent or seek out issues to appease her conservative critics. It seemed challenging for her to find the best path forward. For example, in March 2011, *The New York Times* ran a story highlighting Murkowski's support for a bill to cut $2 billion from Head Start, a preschool program for impoverished children that she had supported in the past. Murkowski defended her vote to *The Times,* saying, "I did not get caught up in the individual cuts....My vote was a marker for moving towards a greater degree in a reduction in spending." In May 2011, Murkowski was one of just five Republican senators to vote against a House-passed budget bill by Republican Rep. Paul Ryan of Wisconsin, that included a sweeping plan to revamp Medicare.

Her independent streak continued when she was the only Republican to join Democrats in voting to break a filibuster on the nomination of Caitlin Halligan to the U.S. Court of Appeals for the District of Columbia Circuit. Judicial nominees should receive up-or-down votes without being filibustered, she said. (Halligan's nomination never reached the floor and she withdrew in 2013.) Murkowski also was the only Republican to oppose a GOP filibuster of another controversial Obama nominee to the appellate court, Goodwin Liu. In 2014, the Club for Growth, a political action group that strongly favors tax cuts and reductions in federal government spending, rated Murkowski the least fiscally conservative Republican in the Senate. Murkowski was one of only seven GOP senators not to sign an open letter in March 2015 to Iran's leaders warning them that regardless of a nuclear deal they might strike with Obama, the president would be leaving office in 2017. Their clear message was that any agreement with Obama could subsequently be reversed.

While such independent stances will likely invite a primary challenge in 2016, Murkowski has helped her standing at home as a strong advocate for Alaska interests as chairman of the Energy Committee. She is seeking faster permitting and environmental reviews of new projects as well as aggressively pushing for expanded drilling on federal lands and waters. Her agenda also includes boosting funding for nuclear power and providing greater oversight for Energy Department loan-guarantee programs to avoid controversies like the Solyndra Co. "green technology investment" that became a scandal when the solar panel manufacturer went bankrupt in 2011, costing taxpayers hundreds of millions of dollars.

Support for local interests will be important if, as appears likely, Murkowski's independence will provide ammunition for another challenge in the Republican primary.

Junior Senator

Dan Sullivan (R)

Elected 2014, term expires 2020, 1st full term; b. November 13, 1964, Fairview Park, OH; Harvard U., 1987, Georgetown U., M.S./J.D. 1993; married (Julie); 3 children.

Military Career: U.S Marine Corps, 1993-97, U.S. Marine Corps Reserves, 1997-present.

Professional Career: Law clerk, U.S. Court of Appeals for the Ninth Circuit, 1997-98; Law clerk, AK Supreme Court, 1998-99; Asst. Secretary of State for Economic, Energy, and Business Affairs, U.S. Dept. of State, 2006-2009; AK Atty. General, 2009-2010; Commissioner, AK Dept. of Natural Resources, 2010-2013.

DC Office: 702 HSOB, 20510, 202-224-3004; Fax: 202-224-6501; Website: sullivan.senate.gov.

State Offices: Anchorage, 907-271-5915; Fairbanks, 907-456-0261; Juneau, 907-586-7277; Kenai, 907-283-4000; Ketchikan, 907-225-6880; Matsu, 907-376-9956.

Committees: *Environment & Public Works:* Fisheries, Water & Wildlife (Chmn); Superfund, Waste Management & Regulatory Oversight. *Armed Services:* Airland; Personnel; SeaPower. *Commerce, Science & Transportation:* Aviation Operations, Safety & Security; Communications, Technology, Innovation & the Internet; Oceans, Atmosphere, Fisheries & Coast Guard; Space, Science & Competitiveness; Surface Transportation and Merchant Marine Infrastructure, Safety & Security. *Veterans' Affairs.*

Election Results

2014 general	Dan Sullivan (R)	135,445	(48%)	$7,797,250	$4,548,858	$15,791,064
	Mark Begich (D)	129,431	(46%)	$11,082,246	$7,103,335	$13,709,045
	Mark Fish (Lib)	10,512	(4%)			
	Ted Gianoutsos (I)	5,636	(2%)			
2014 primary	Dan Sullivan (R)	44,7740	(40%)			
	Joe Miller (R)	35,904	(32%)			
	Mead Tredwell (R)	27,807	(25%)			

Alaska's new junior senator, Dan Sullivan, who formerly was the state's attorney general, was elected in 2014, narrowly defeating Democratic Sen. Mark Begich after a bruising contest. A Marine with a long résumé of state and federal jobs, Sullivan proved too formidable a challenger for Begich in a very bad year for Democrats. A key to Sullivan's victory was his ability to nationalize the race and make it about Begich's ties to President Obama, who is very unpopular in Alaska. Despite Begich's aggressive moves to distance himself from the President and from the national Democratic Party, he still could not overcome Alaska's strong Republican tilt.

Sullivan grew up in Ohio and graduated from Harvard with a bachelor's degree in economics and then earned a joint law and foreign service degree from Georgetown University. After a clerkship with Alaska Supreme Court Chief Justice Warren Matthews, he joined the Anchorage office of the Seattle-based Perkins Coie law firm. He has served in the Marines since 1993, both on active duty and in the reserves.

Sullivan worked in the National Security Council during George W. Bush's administration and later became an assistant secretary of State for economic, energy, and business affairs. Alaska Gov. Sarah Palin appointed him attorney general in 2009, and her successor, Sean Parnell, named him head of the state's Department of Natural Resources. During Sullivan's term in office, he was deployed to Afghanistan for six weeks.

National Republicans made the Alaska Senate race a priority as they sought to defeat Begich, who had narrowly toppled longtime Republican Sen. Ted Stevens in 2008 after Stevens was indicted on corruption charges that eventually were dismissed. As a Democrat from a deep-red state, Begich focused intensely on parochial issues and worked to show his independence from Obama. Begich even boasted to *The Washington Post* that he was "a thorn in his [backside]." In a controversial move, he also tried to make himself appear nonpartisan by running a campaign ad that featured the image of his Republican Senate colleague Lisa Murkowski and touted their close relationship. Murkowski told him to stop using it, and made clear that she supported Sullivan.

Still, Begich stressed his independence from national Democrats on a number of issues. He was one of only four Senate Democrats to oppose a bill ending tax breaks for oil companies and he opposed a ban on earmark spending as a measure that would hurt his state's economy.

But the prospect of the GOP retaking Senate control prompted conservative interest groups to pull out the stops. They decided to throw their efforts behind Sullivan in a GOP primary that included Lieutenant Governor Mead Treadwell and tea party favorite Joe Miller, who had defeated Murkowski in the 2010 primary before she won the general election as a write-in candidate. The Club for Growth, a group that backs fiscal conservatives, endorsed Sullivan, as did the U.S. Chamber of Commerce. They were betting that Sullivan had the best shot to defeat Begich. He won the primary with 40 percent of the vote, topping Miller's 32 percent and Treadwell's 25 percent.

Begich's campaign also apparently saw Sullivan as the toughest opponent in the general election, as Democrats began attacking the Ohio native during the GOP primary, trying to paint him as an outsider—a carpetbagger who did not have deep Alaska roots. It was a theme that they would continue to sound until Election Day.

Begich's campaign made a misstep with an ad attacking Sullivan, the former attorney general, for the early release of a sex offender who was later charged with murdering an elderly couple and raping their two-year-old granddaughter. It featured a former Anchorage police officer making the charge, but Begich waited a few days until he finally took it down amid a backlash, including a demand from the victims' family that it be withdrawn and a Sullivan response ad that charged that it was "shameful" that Begich used "heinous crimes for political gain."

Sullivan also had an early gaffe when he criticized Begich in an ad filmed atop an Anchorage convention center, saying Alaskans wanted someone who delivered real results. Construction of the center was considered a significant achievement for Begich when he was mayor, and he implored his opponent to visit some of the other locales on which the senator had worked. But, otherwise, Sullivan ran a carefully managed campaign whose overriding goal was to tie Begich to Obama at every opportunity.

One issue that clearly separated the candidates was Begich's support for the Affordable Care Act—a stance that was stressed by Sullivan and conservative groups in ads against the Democratic senator. While Begich said the law had flaws and needed fixing, he also maintained that it had provided greater access to health care coverage for Alaskans. Sullivan campaigned that it should be repealed.

Ultimately, the bitter battle consumed about $60 million—the most expensive race in Alaska history. Despite Begich's skills as a campaigner and the Democrats' good ground game, Republicans had a superior ground game. This red state simply was not going to return Begich during a national Republican wave that swept the GOP into Senate control and solidified the party's hold on the House.

Once on Capitol Hill, Sullivan snared assignments that he had sought, including to the Commerce, Science and Transportation Committee; the Armed Services Committee; the Environment and Public Works Committee; and the Veterans Affairs' Committee. He is chairman of the Environment Subcommittee on Fisheries, Water and Wildlife. He said in a speech in March to a joint session of the Alaska legislature—a traditional oration for senators in the state—that his priorities include combatting what he sees as overreach by the federal government and maintaining a strong military presence in Alaska.

Sullivan, as the only military reservist in the Senate (long-time Reserve members Lindsay Graham and Mark Kirk recently have retired), quickly made it clear that he would bring his hawkish views to the debate over defense issues. In an Armed Services hearing in March, Sullivan described Obama's view as an "almost delusional view of the world environment" when the President suggested in his State of the Union address that the shadow of crisis had passed in various threats, from ISIL's advance to Russia's aggression and Iran's nuclear program. In another hearing in May, Sullivan said that the President should level with the public that the war against ISIS is going to be protracted. It appears that such tough talk will be a standard part of Sullivan's rhetoric as he settles in on Capitol Hill.

REPRESENTATIVE-AT-LARGE

Don Young (R)

Elected March 1973, 21st full term; b. June 9, 1933, Meridian, CA; Yuba Jr. Col., A.A. 1952, Chico St. Col., B.A. 1958; Episcopalian; married (Anne); 2 children.

Military Career: Army, 1955-57.

Elected Office: Fort Yukon City Cncl., 1960-64; Fort Yukon mayor, 1964-68; AK House, 1966-70; AK Senate, 1970-73.

Professional Career: Schl. teacher, Fort Yukon, 1960-68; Riverboat captain, 1968-72.

DC Office: 2314 RHOB, 20515, 202-225-5765; Fax: 202-225-0425; Website: donyoung.house.gov.

State Offices: Anchorage, 907-271-5978; Fairbanks, 907-456-0210.

Committees: *Natural Resources:* Indian, Insular & Alaska Native Affairs (Chmn); Water, Power & Oceans; Federal Lands. *Transportation & Infrastructure:* Coast Guard & Maritime Transportation; Highways & Transit; Aviation.

Group Ratings

	ADA	ACLU	AFL-CIO	LCV	ITI	COC	HAFA	ACU	CFG	FRC
2014	10%	0%	–	3%	80%	93%	35%	52%	39%	63%
2013	20%	C	53%	4%	C	83%	C	42%	40%	C

National Journal Ratings

	2013 LIB	—	2013 CONS
Economic	48%	—	52%
Social	52%	—	48%
Foreign	24%	—	76%
Composite	41%	—	59%

Key Votes of the 113th Congress

1. Sandy storm spending	Y	5. Medical Marijuana	Y	9. Syrian Rebels Training	Y
2. Violence Against Women Act	NV	6. Farm Bill	Y	10. Keystone pipeline	Y
3. Guantanamo Bay Detainees	N	7. Afghanistan Combat	N	11. Immigration Exec. Action	Y
4. Abortion 20-week ban	Y	8. NSA Phone Data Collection	Y	12. Bipartisan budget deal	Y

Election Results

2014 general	Don Young (R)	142,572	(51%)	$809,039	$9,275
	Forrest Dunbar (D)	114,602	(41%)	$230,089	$32, 881
	Jim McDermott (Lib)	21,290	(8%)	$7,877	
2014 primary	Don Young (R)	79,393	(74%)		
	John Cox (R)	14,497	(14%)		
	David Seaward (R)	7,604	(7%)		
	David Dohner (R)	5,373	(5%)		

Prior winning percentages: 2012 (64%), 2010 (69%), 2008 (50%), 2006 (57%), 2004 (71%), 2002 (75%), 2000 (70%), 1998 (63%), 1996 (59%), 1994 (57%), 1992 (47%), 1990 (52%), 1988 (63%), 1986 (57%), 1984 (55%), 1982 (71%), 1980 (74%), 1978 (55%), 1976 (71%), 1974 (54%), 1973 special (51%)

Don Young has been Alaska's congressman-at-large since 1973 and is now the most-senior Republican in the House. By December 2015, he will have served longer than any House Republican other than former Speaker Joe Cannon, who retired in 1923 after

Voter Turnout	
2013 Total Citizen 18+	526,769
2014 House Turnout	279,725
2014 Turnout as % CVAP	53.1%
2012 Turnout as % CVAP	57.4%

46 years. Young's long political career was nearly destroyed by an influence-peddling scandal in 2008, when he narrowly survived reelection. He remains a forceful figure in Washington. But after having served six years each as chairman of two House committees that are vital to his home state, he has lost much of his internal clout.

Young grew up on his family's farm in the Sacramento Valley of California, served in the Army, and graduated from college. He had a thirst for adventure and the rugged outdoors: He remembers that *The Call of the Wild* by Jack London was a favorite book growing up. He moved to Alaska in 1959, the year that the vast, untamed U.S. territory became a state. Young worked in construction, fishing, trapping, and gold prospecting. He taught elementary school to indigenous Alaskan children in Fort Yukon, population 700. After spring thaws, he worked as a tugboat captain on the Yukon. He is a licensed mariner, which, in his words, is definitely not a typical profession of "one of these smooth, namby-pamby politicians." Young was elected mayor of Fort Yukon in 1964, to the state House in 1966, and to the state Senate in 1970. He ran for Congress in 1972. His opponent, incumbent Democrat Nick Begich, was killed in a plane crash in October and reelected posthumously. Young won the March 1973 special election to succeed him. Young is not a free-market conservative and has recently voted with liberals on some cultural issues, but he is a consistent, fierce advocate for Alaska's interests. He is temperamental and salty-tongued. To critics who once proposed shifting money for Alaska bridges to Hurricane Katrina recovery efforts, he said, "They can kiss my ear."

Soon after taking his seat in the House, Young voted for building the Alaska oil pipeline. But he often found that his aggressive pursuit of economic development for his state conflicted with the environmental lobby and its interest in preserving wildlife. On what was then the Interior Committee, he called his critics a "self-centered bunch, the wafflestomping, Harvard-graduating, intellectual idiots." When Republicans have controlled the House, Young occupied power positions that allowed him to work around his adversaries. He chaired the Resources Committee from 1995 to 2001 and the Transportation and Infrastructure Committee from 2001 to 2007. In each case, his tenure was limited by the House GOP term-limits rule for committee chairmen. He steered to House passage bills allowing oil drilling in the Arctic National Wildlife Refuge in 1995, 2001, and 2006, only to see them defeated or bottled up in the Senate. His attempts to roll back environmental rulings, such as allowing logging in the Tongass National Forest, were frustrated in the 1990s by Democratic President Bill Clinton or by adverse votes cast by Republicans from the Northeast, Arizona, and Florida. But on both committees, Young also proved capable of forging bipartisan consensus. In 2000, he got Congress to pass the Conservation and Reinvestment Act to dedicate royalties from offshore oil and gas wells to state purchases of land.

At the Transportation and Infrastructure Committee, he led arguably the most bipartisan panel in the House because its chairmen traditionally larded their bills to make sure every cooperating committee member received plenty of highway or mass transit projects for his or her district. In 2003, Young proposed a surface transportation bill with $375 billion in spending, financed with a gas tax increase. But the Bush administration and the House Republican leadership were stoutly opposed to any such hike. In 2005, he tried again and got the House to pass a $284 billion bill in March. But there was mounting criticism of the bill's earmarks—special projects for certain lawmakers—particularly of two bridges in Alaska. One was from Anchorage to the largely uninhabited land across the Knik Arm; the other was from the town of Ketchikan (pop. 14,000) to the island of Gravina (pop. 50), whose airport could be reached by local ferry. They were derisively dubbed the "bridges to nowhere." In July, both chambers passed by near-unanimous votes a $286 billion bill with more than 6,300 earmarks. They included $230 million for the Knik Arm bridge and $220 million for the Ketchikan-Gravina bridge. The bill contained about $941 million for Young's Alaska, more than any other state except California, Illinois, and New York.

That likely would have been the end of the earmark controversy, except that Hurricane Katrina struck the Gulf Coast in August. Suddenly, there were demands that money be shifted from Alaska's "bridges to nowhere" to New Orleans and other parts of the devastated region. "That is the dumbest thing I ever heard," Young said. But for the next year, criticism of earmarks and the bridges continued. Conservative Republicans as well as Democrats chimed in, and profligate spending, symbolized by the two spans, emerged as an issue in the 2006 election. It was among the factors that helped wipe out the Republican majorities that year.

For an incumbent with his lengthy seniority, Young has had a bumpy history with Alaska voters and has frequently drawn serious challengers. In recent years, his acerbic personality has been accompanied by ethical problems. In April 2007, a former Young aide pleaded guilty to accepting cash from disgraced lobbyist Jack Abramoff in exchange for inside government information. Records showed 120 contacts between Young and his staff with Abramoff and his clients. The next month, Rick Smith, an associate of Young's and a former lobbyist with the oil services firm VECO, a major Young contributor since 1989, pleaded guilty to bribing Alaska state legislators. *The New York Times* published a story about a Young staffer altering the 2005 transportation bill to add $10 million for an interstate interchange in Florida that would help real estate developer Daniel Aronoff, who had raised $40,000 for the law-maker. Young dismissed the allegations, telling the *Anchorage Daily News* that it was just "a recycled story." Plus, he said, Florida Gulf Coast University supported the Coconut Road interchange. In April 2008, Democratic Speaker Nancy Pelosi ordered an ethics investiga-tion, and the Justice Department conducted its own review. Following lengthy inquiries, no charges were lodged against Young.

Former Alaska House Minority Leader Ethan Berkowitz, a Democrat, ran against him in the general election in 2008, and Republican Lt. Gov. Sean Parnell announced he would challenge Young in the primary. Parnell was endorsed by GOP Gov. Sarah Palin. Polls in the summer of 2008 showed Young trailing both Parnell and Berkowitz, but he professed to be unfazed, saying he was used to tough reelections. During a debate with Parnell, he said: "I've been accused of being arrogant, being a bully, and sometimes I'll plead to being both of those. Most of the time and every time I've done that is because I'm fighting for this state." Parnell spent $572,000, with strong support from the anti-tax Club for Growth. "We're tired of being the nation's symbol of excess and greed," Parnell said in an August debate. Young beat Parnell by just 304 votes.

His battle was far from over, however. Berkowitz was well funded, with $1.6 million, while Young's resources were depleted by legal fees and by the primary contest. The Demo-cratic Congressional Campaign Committee spent $1.4 million on ads charging that Young was the subject of multiple investigations. Berkowitz and Young were not far apart on the issues. Berkowitz framed the choice as one of style, contrasting his consensus-building approach to Young's tendency to "bully and intimidate." He said he would seek earmarks if communities and citizens asked for them, but not for lobbyists. Young responded during a debate, tongue in cheek, that he is "one of the nicest, kindest persons in the world." He added, "But when you mess with the state, you're messing with me." Young defeated Berkowitz 50%-45%. Young ran only even in usually Republican Anchorage and carried the Fairbanks area 50%-44%, thanks largely to support from his hometown of Fort Yukon.

Young returned to Washington, but he remained under a political cloud. He lost the ranking minority member position on Resources, the committee on which he had served for 36 years. Young issued a press release saying he would regain the post when "my name is cleared." He remained as feisty as ever. When the GOP caucus voted to hold a moratorium on special-interest earmark requests, Young scoffed at the idea. "To do that would be turn-ing my back on the state that I love while handing over control to President Obama and his appointed government officials," he wrote in a *Daily News* column. He also drew bipartisan criticism when he argued the massive BP oil spill in the Gulf of Mexico was "not an environ-mental disaster" but "a natural phenomenon." Ethics problems lingered for Young. In 2011, the House Ethics Committee looked into the legal defense fund Young set up for the Justice Department probe, but the panel subsequently cleared him of wrongdoing. In June 2014, the committee rebuked him for "improperly accepting nearly $60,000 in hunting trips, rides on private planes and other gifts and failing to report them on his financial disclosure forms." The gifts dated back to 2001. Young repaid the donors of the gifts, plus his campaign account. "I've been under a cloud all my life," Young told reporters in Juneau. "It's sort of like living in Juneau. It rains on you all the time. You don't even notice it."

In the House, Young has remained an active legislator. He got a provision attached to the 2012 Interior appropriations bill that forbids the National Park Service from regulating waters in Alaska's Yukon-Charley Rivers National Preserve. In 2011, the House passed two Young-sponsored bills of local interest: one to authorize hydroelectricity projects in part of the Denali National Park & Preserve, and another to authorize funds for coastal mapping and hydrographic surveys of the Arctic region. In an effort to protect the fishing industry, Young forged an unlikely alliance that year with liberal Democratic Rep. Lynn Woolsey of California, on a bill that passed the House to bar the Food and Drug Administration from spending money on bioengineered salmon. Young also introduced a sweeping bill—with long odds of passage and designed to make a political point—that would require the Obama administration to review and justify every regulation implemented in the past 20 years. After Interior Secretary Sally Jewell rejected what Young viewed as a potentially life-saving road through an Alaska refuge, he wagged his finger at her and told her at an April 2014 committee hearing, "I think your decision stunk."

Young has remained as feisty and vocal as ever. At a Natural Resources Committee hear-ing in November 2011 with Interior Secretary Ken Salazar, Young wore a propeller cap on his head that read "Obama's Energy Plan." He told Salazar that the Obama administration had no energy program and facetiously said he was in support of the non-existent Obama plan. In a March 2013 radio interview in Alaska, he referred to Latino immigrants as "wetbacks." Other Republicans who were keen on making political inroads with Hispanic voters swiftly condemned him, and Young apologized for what he acknowledged was an "insensitive" term. During a March 2015 hearing with Jewell, during which he objected to placing gray wolves on the endangered species list, Young said that wolves could be put to good use in many areas. "You wouldn't have a homeless problem anymore," he said.

Young was reelected in November 2014 with 51 percent of the vote to 41 per cent for Democrat Forrest Dunbar, and received the largest vote total of any statewide candidate in Alaska. He has no plans to retire. "The only time I'll retire is when people want to retire me," Young told the *Daily News* the next month. "The people decide I can't serve them anymore, they'll get rid of me. It's that simple." His real enthusiasm is no longer legislation, he added, but "helping people that have problems."

★ ARIZONA ★

Growing and changing more rapidly in recent decades than most states, Arizona is also home to America's oldest continuous community, the Hopi Indians, who have lived as shepherds on the plateaus east of the Grand Canyon for more than 900 years. They have spurned Christianity since 1680, when they killed the local Franciscan priests and burned their churches. Their land disputes with the more numerous Navajo have dragged on for centuries. Efforts by federal government to get the two tribes to share lands came to naught, and it has cost more than $500 million to relocate primarily the Navajos to new homes. Separately, the Obama Administration agreed in 2014 to a record $544 million tribal settlement with the Navajo Nation over claims that its reservation had been mismanaged by the government for decades.

Besides the Native American population, the rugged desert, mountains, and forested lands of Arizona were sparsely populated when the United States obtained them after the Mexican War in 1848 to provide land for the planned transcontinental railroad. Arizona was made a separate territory in 1863 after some locals tried to join the Confederacy. Nearly half a century later, in 1912, it became the 48th state.

Back then few imagined that Arizona would transcend its frontier roots. For decades it relied on the five Cs, memorialized in the state seal. The first C was copper: The dome of the state Capitol is encased in copper, and one of the state's leading public figures was Lewis Douglas, scion of a prominent Arizona mining family, a congressman, Franklin D. Roosevelt's first budget director, and Harry Truman's ambassador to Britain. The second C was cattle: As late as the mid-1960s, a dozen or so cattle barons ran the state legislature. The third C was cotton: the signature achievement of Carl Hayden, a Democratic senator from 1927 to 1969, was the Central Arizona Project, a massive irrigation program that brought cotton farms to the flatlands around Phoenix. The water also helped with the fourth C: citrus. The fifth C was climate; dry, clear air drew visitors seeking its therapeutic benefits, as well as tourists, but the scorching summer heat deterred permanent transplants for many years.

Then came air conditioning. In the years after World War II, Arizona became less dependent on federal largesse, except for its military bases and defense contracts. Businessmen, lawyers, developers, and water companies, notably the Salt River Project, built Arizona and fostered an environment that welcomed new technological ideas. Their political champion was Barry Goldwater, a Phoenix City Council member, Senator and the 1964 GOP presidential nominee who was the nation's most recognizable conservative for much of the 1950s and 1960s. He helped to make Arizona solidly Republican, the only state to vote Republican for president in every election from 1952 to 1992. (An eight-foot bronze likeness of the father of the modern conservative movement was unveiled in the U.S. Capitol's Statuary Hall in 2015.)

For years, Arizona's growth was based more on high tech and low taxes than the influx of retirees. Phoenix started attracting high-tech industries when Motorola built a research center for military electronics there in 1948. Other major employers, Honeywell, Raytheon, Intel, Avnet and General Dynamics, followed. Defense industries are important here, especially the manufacture of unmanned aircraft. Arizona lawmakers had hoped to lure a Federal Aviation Administration drone research facility in 2013, but the state was not selected for a site. Still, it counts two Air Force bases and a Marine air station, plus the huge Barry M. Goldwater Range, where many of America's pilots have been trained. The technology sector has also given a boost to clean energy jobs in the state. Over three square miles of the desert near Gila Bend, the new Solana solar plant is able to make electricity without direct sunlight and to generate power at night. The state can use the juice: 25 percent of the energy consumed in Arizona homes is for air conditioning, about four times the national average, according to the U.S. Energy Information Agency Residential Energy Consumption Survey. Arizona's Renewable Energy Standard requires 15 percent of the state's electricity consumption to come from renewables by 2025. In 2014, 2.8 percent of its electricity generation came from solar. In 2015, Apple Inc. announced it plans to locate a global data networks center in Mesa, a $2 billion investment over 10 years that local officials hope will foster a new tech hub in the area.

Arizona has been one of the nation's boom states and its population nearly doubled from 3.7 million in 1990 to 6.7 million in 2014. Second to Nevada, it grew faster than any other

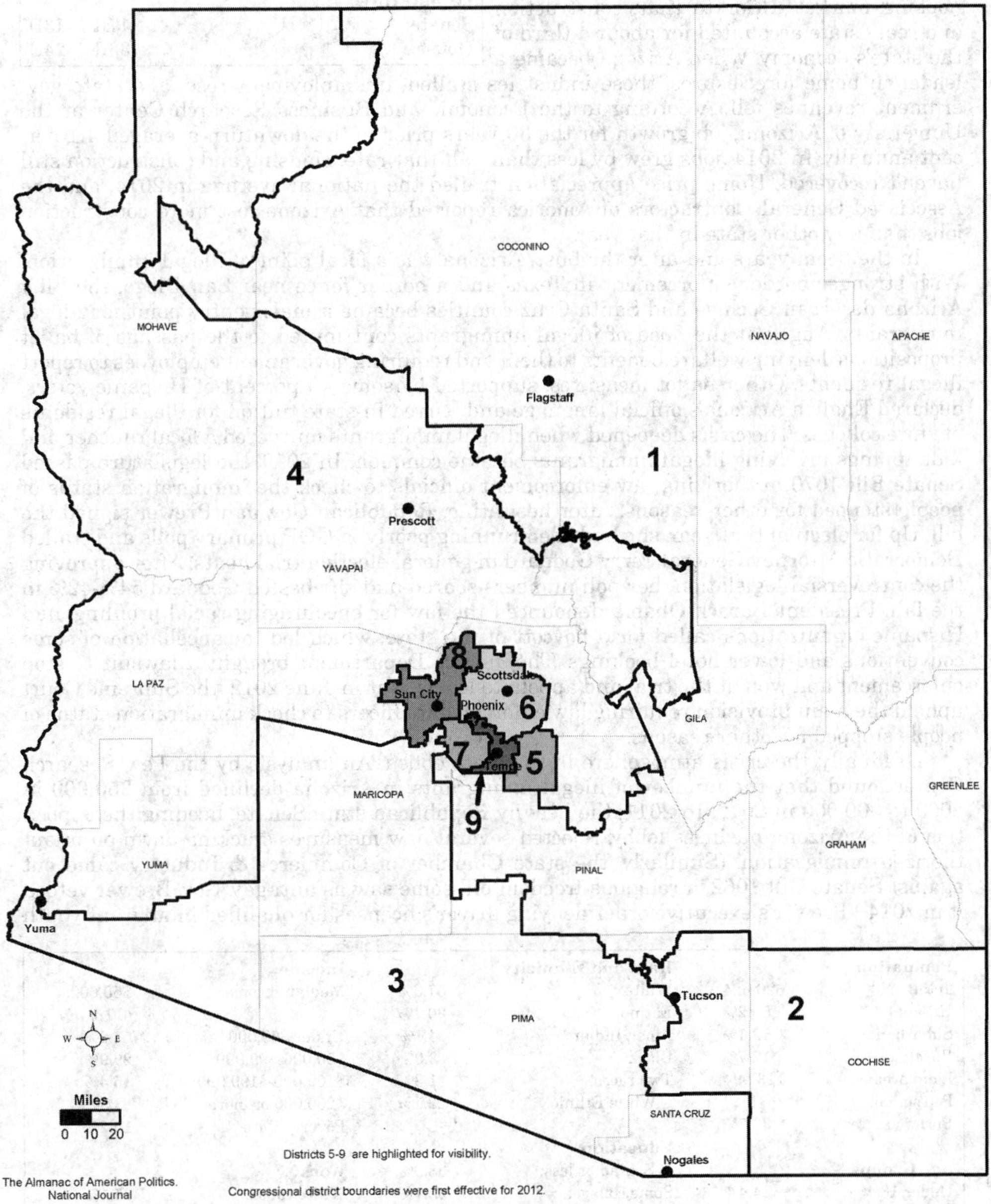

COCONINO

MOHAVE

NAVAJO

APACHE

Flagstaff

4

1

Prescott

YAVAPAI

8

Scottsdale

Sun City

Phoenix

6

GILA

LA PAZ

7

Tempe

5

MARICOBA

9

GREENLEE

YUMA

PINAL

GRAHAM

Yuma

3

Tucson

2

PIMA

COCHISE

SANTA CRUZ

Nogales

Miles

0 10 20

Districts 5-9 are highlighted for visibility.

The Almanac of American Politics.
National Journal

Congressional district boundaries were first effective for 2012.

state from 2000 to 2010. That kind of growth led developers to buy out the cotton farms, and the Valley of the Sun around Phoenix lost nearly half its farmland between 1975 and 2000. But Arizona's boom took a major blow with the Great Recession and collapse of the housing market. Prior to that, construction and real estate accounted for about a third of the state's economy. When Arizona became a

Voter Turnout	
2013 Total Citizen 18+	4,502,052
2014 Highest Statewide Turnout	1,506,416
2014 Turnout as % CVAP	33.5%
2012 Turnout as % CVAP	51.7%

Legislature		
Senate:	17R	13D
House:	36R	24D

leader in home foreclosures, those industries stalled, unemployment rose, and state government revenues fell. According to the Economic and Business Research Center at the University of Arizona, job growth for the 30 years prior to the downturn averaged 4.1 percent annually. In 2014, jobs grew by less than half that rate. Housing and construction still haven't recovered: Home price appreciation trailed the national average in 2014, and the Associated General Contractors of America reported that Arizona lost more construction jobs than any other state in that year.

In the boom years and after the bust, Arizona was a focal point of illegal immigration. With stronger border enforcement in Texas and a border fence near San Diego, the hilly Arizona desert in Cochise and Santa Cruz counties became a major entry point for illegal immigrants. Anger at the flood of illegal immigrants contributed to the passage of ballot propositions denying welfare benefits to them and requiring government employees to report illegal residents. Other ballot measures, supported by some 40 percent of Hispanic voters, declared English Arizona's official language and barred in-state tuition for illegal residents at state colleges. The crisis deepened when illegal immigrants murdered a local rancher and kidnappings involving illegal immigrants became common. In 2010, the legislature passed Senate Bill 1070 authorizing law enforcement officials to check the immigration status of people stopped for other reasons. After hesitating, Republican Gov. Jan Brewer signed the bill. Up for election that year, she had been running poorly in GOP primary polls and trailed Democratic Attorney General Terry Goddard in general election trial heats. After approving the controversial legislation, her poll numbers soared and she bested Goddard 54%-42% in the fall. President Barack Obama denounced the law for encouraging racial profiling, and Hispanic organizations called for a boycott of the state, which led to cancellation of some conventions and lower hotel bookings. The Justice Department brought a lawsuit to stop enforcement and won at the trial and appellate levels. But in June 2012, the Supreme Court upheld the main provision requiring law enforcement officers to check immigration status of people stopped for other reasons.

Gradually, the crisis atmosphere in the state ebbed. An analysis by the Pew Research Center found that the number of illegal immigrants in Arizona declined from 350,000 in 2009 to 300,000 in 2012. In 2011, the heavily Republican state Senate, heeding the opposition of the Arizona business lobby, rejected several new measures cracking down on unauthorized immigration. (Similarly, the state Chamber of Commerce & Industry came out against Senate Bill 1062, a religious-freedom bill some saw as anti-gay. Gov. Brewer vetoed it in 2014.) Brewer's executive order denying driver's licenses for qualified immigrant youth

Population		Race and Ethnicity		Income	
Total:	6,626,624	White	57.3%	Median income:	$50,602
Urban:	55.2%	Latino	30.1%		(30 of 50)
Suburban:	32.1%	Amer. Indian	4.1%	Under $50,000	51.2%
Rural:	12.7%	Black	3.9%	$50,000-$99,999:	29.9%
Land area:	113,594	Two races	1.8%	$100,000-$199,999:	15.4%
Pop/sq. mi.:	58.3	White Ethnic	22.1%	$200,000 or more:	3.5%
Born in state:	38.7%			Poverty Rate	15.2%
		Education			
Age Groups		H.S. grad or less:	38.9%	**Work**	
Under 18:	24.4%	Some college:	33.7%	White collar:	35.1%
18 to 34:	23.3%	College degree, 4 yr.:	17.1%	Blue collar:	46.1%
35 to 64:	36.9%	Post-grad study:	10.3%	Sales and service:	18.8%
Over 64:	15.4%				
		Military		Govt. workers:	14.7%
		Veterans/active duty:	9.9%		

under the Deferred Action for Childhood Arrivals, or "DACA" program, was upended in 2014 when the Supreme Court upheld a lower court ruling that overturned her order. Also that year, a federal judge ruled that Arizona authorities could no longer enforce the state's 2005 immigrant smuggling law, signed into law by Democratic Gov. Janet Napolitano, which local officials like Maricopa County Sheriff Joe Arpaio embraced to fight illegal immigration.

The state has been a source of other headaches for the Obama Administration. The Justice Department's Operation Fast and Furious, the misbegotten gun-trafficking investigation by the Bureau of Alcohol, Tobacco, Firearms and Explosives, began in Arizona in 2009 and led to the killing of border Patrolman Brian Terry in 2010. In the wake of the fiasco, the acting director and the deputy director of the ATF resigned their posts. The Phoenix VA Health Care System was the epicenter of the 2014 Veterans Health Administration scandal.

Politically, Arizona has seemed on the verge of becoming less Republican and more competitive—but not quite getting there. Democrats have posted a few notable victories: Bill Clinton carried the state 47%-44% in 1996, and Janet Napolitano was elected governor in 2002 and 2006. Indeed, from 1997 until 2015, the state had only women governors: Republican Jane Hull took office when GOP incumbent Fife Symington resigned after he was convicted of defrauding lenders as a commercial real estate developer, and Brewer replaced Napolitano after she stepped down to become Homeland Security secretary in 2009. In terms of partisan alignment, both parties have been losing ground to independents. From 2004 to 2014, Democratic registration fell from 34.6 percent to 28.9 percent of the statewide total and GOP registration dropped from 39.9 percent to 34.5 percent. At the same time, the number of registered independents rose by more than half a million and their share of the Arizona electorate jumped from 24.8 percent to 35.8 percent.

Democrats have hoped that the increasing Hispanic population—30 percent in the 2010 Census—would tip the state their way in presidential contests, but John Kerry and Barack Obama lost by almost identical margins, even as the Latino share of the vote rose from 12 percent in 2004 to 18 percent in 2012. The immigration issue seems to have made Latinos more Democratic and whites more Republican. Mitt Romney lost Latinos by 74%-25%, but he carried whites, 66%-32%, running ahead of the 59 percent white vote for George W. Bush in 2004 and John McCain in 2008. Bush and McCain both captured more than 40 percent of the Hispanic vote. While Arizona has attracted retiring white seniors, minorities, who are mostly Hispanics, now make up about 45 percent of the state's population. The 2015 study "States of Change" by the American Enterprise Institute, Brookings Institution and Center for American Progress, estimates that by 2023, the state will have a majority-minority population. But it won't be until 2038 that minorities are expected to constitute a majority of Arizona's eligible voters.

Presidential Politics Except for Bill Clinton's success in 1996, Republican nominees have carried Arizona in 15 of the last 16 presidential elections—a stretch that extends back to 1952. And in 1996, third-party candidate Ross Perot appears to have siphoned a few more GOP votes from Bob Dole, than Democrats from Clinton. When George W. Bush squared off against Al Gore four years later, the GOP hit its targets in vote-rich Maricopa County and elsewhere around the state.

Maricopa, which contains metro Phoenix

2012 Presidential Vote		
Mitt Romney (R)	1,233,654	(54%)
Barack Obama (D)	1,025,232	(45%)
2012 Presidential Caucus		
Mitt Romney (R)	239,167	(47%)
Rick Santorum (R)	138,031	(27%)
Newt Gingrich (R)	81,748	(16%)
Ron Paul (R)	43,952	(9%)
2008 Presidential Vote		
John McCain (R)	1,230,111	(54%)
Barack Obama (D)	1,034,707	(45%)

with fast-growing suburbs and exurbs such as Surprise, Buckeye, Goodyear and Gilbert, and large cities such as Glendale, Mesa and Scottsdale, cast 60 percent of the state's votes in the last two presidential races. The county is reliably Republican, but Tempe, home to Arizona State University, provides some Democratic votes. Pima County, dominated by Tucson, the state's second largest city, is a Democratic center, but less than one-fifth of the state's ballots are cast there. The rest of Arizona's largely rural territory used to be home to conservative ranchers and others who were known as "Pinto" or "Goldwater" Democrats. But today it is GOP turf, except for Apache County with its tribal reservations; Coconino County, with Flagstaff and the Northern Arizona University; and Santa Cruz County where four-out-of-five residents is Hispanic. In order to prevail, a Democratic presidential candidate needs to battle a Republican at least close to a draw in Maricopa, score a big turnout in Pima, and hold down the losses in the rest of the state. That was essentially the Clinton formula in 1996.

Arizona has tried every so often to make itself another Iowa or New Hampshire in presidential politics, but with little success. In 1972, it had an early Democratic primary, and the improbable winner was Republican-turned-Democrat Mayor John Lindsay of New York. His campaign went nowhere from there. In 1996, Arizona wanted to set its primary on the same date as New Hampshire's; but settled for one week later. The state became a battleground between Kansas Sen. Bob Dole, who had John McCain's support; conservative commentator Pat Buchanan; and magazine publisher Steve Forbes, who spent lavishly on ads boosting his flat tax and attacking Washington politicians. Forbes won 33 percent and all the delegates, after which his campaign, like that of his fellow Easterner Lindsay a quarter-century earlier, went nowhere. Dole managed to squeeze out a second-place finish over Buchanan, 30%-28%, but the night was not without a scare for the Senator: three of the television networks, ABC, CBS and CNN, incorrectly projected that Dole would finish third, a showing that would have undercut his bid for the nomination he eventually captured.

In 2000, Arizona tried again. McCain had irritated local Republicans enough that Gov. Jane Hull and other party leaders endorsed George W. Bush. McCain, however, won a solid victory in his home state in the February primary, but it was overshadowed by his victory the same day in Michigan. In 2006, Arizona Democrats made a bid to have their state designated as the site for a caucus election soon after Iowa, but the Democratic National Committee picked Nevada instead. So in 2008, Arizona joined more than a dozen Super Tuesday states holding their contests on the first Tuesday in February. The Republican primary was a foregone conclusion, but having antagonized some conservatives, McCain only beat Mitt Romney 47%-35%. Romney carried the area including Mesa and Chandler and rural Graham County, both with large Mormon populations, as well as Apache and Navajo. On the Democratic side, Hillary Clinton, with heavy support from Latinos, bested Obama 50%-42%. Obama carried the upscale area of Scottsdale and Tempe plus Coconino and Yavapai counties. In 2012, Romney won the February 28 primary handily over Rick Santorum.

Congressional Districts Arizona has become a competitive battleground for House seats. Its nine-member delegation includes four solidly Republican districts, two solidly Democratic districts (with large Hispanic majorities), and three districts that could remain "toss-up" for the remainder of the decade.

114th Congress Lineup	
5 R	4 D
113th Congress Lineup	
4 R	5 D

Those three districts—now represented by two Democrats and one Republican, all of them women—are based in the sprawling rural eastern part of the state, Tempe and Tucson.

That map was drawn by a five-member Independent Redistricting Commission, which was created by a statewide referendum in 2000. Its members include two Democrats, two Republicans and an independent picked by the other four. The commission's map resulted in a delegation of six Republican and two Democrats after the 2002 election, but it shifted to five Democrats and three Republicans in 2008. The GOP wave of 2010 restored Republicans to a 5-3 majority. When Arizona gained a seat from the 2010 census, replicating its pattern of increasing its delegation by at least one seat following each decennial count since 1960, Democrats unexpectedly emerged from a state dominated by a Republican governor and legislature with the map of their dreams and five of the state's nine House seats.

The Democrats' good fortune resulted when the commission's Republicans agreed to select as the panel's chair Colleen Coyle Mathis, a Tucson health care administrator who described herself as a "post-partisan" ex-Republican. She quickly sided with the commission's Democrats on the need to draw more competitive districts. The result was a plan that sought to protect the two heavily Hispanic districts in the Phoenix area plus the Democratic-leaning 2nd district in Tucson. The commission also drew two others that Democrats could win: a new 9th District anchored by the university bastion of Tempe, and an altered Northern Arizona 1st District linking the feuding Hopi and Navajo tribes, who had agreed to consolidate their votes after years of being split into different districts.

The map infuriated Republicans: Not only did it maximize Democratic opportunities, it forced Republicans David Schweikert and Ben Quayle to run against each other even though the state was gaining a seat. GOP Gov. Jan Brewer chose to void the map and accused

Mathis of "gross misconduct." The state Senate then removed her from the commission on a 21-6 vote, with several Democrats abstaining in protest. The *Arizona Republic* slammed Brewer for running "roughshod over the public."

The spectacle further escalated into a game of one-upmanship when the commission's lawyers challenged Brewer's actions before the Arizona Supreme Court. Less than three weeks after Mathis' removal, Arizona's top court rebuked Brewer and reinstated Mathis. The commission voted to re-pass the map in January 2012. Republicans' worst fears were confirmed when Schweikert and Quayle were forced to duel in an ugly August primary and Democrats picked up both the 1st and 9th districts in November. In 2014, Democrats retained those two districts but they narrowly lost the 2nd district.

The Republican-controlled legislature, meanwhile, challenged the map in federal court. Its lawyers contended that the 2000 referendum violated the Constitution by removing its authority over the congressional district map. A three-judge federal court ruled against the legislature in February 2014, with two of the judges dismissing the complaint on the grounds that the Arizona constitution reserved the initiative power to its people, and that the federal Constitution permits "legislative" power to be exercised through a referendum.

The U.S. Supreme Court agreed to review that ruling. In a 5-4 decision, the court held that Arizona voters had the authority to create a redistricting commission. Its ruling could encourage citizen referenda in other states, though both political parties likely will remain reluctant to relinquish their control.

Governor

Doug Ducey (R)

Elected 2014, term expires 2018, 1st term; b. April 9, 1964, Toledo, OH; Arizona State U., B.S. 1986; Catholic; married (Angela); 3 children.

Elected Office: AZ Treasurer, 2010-14.

Professional Career: Beer distributorship marketing coordinator, Hensley & Co., 1982-86; Sales and marketing exec., Proctor & Gamble, 1986-93; CEO and chairman, Cold Stone Creamery, 1996-2007; Chairman, iMemories, 2008-12.

Office: Arizona State Capitol Building, Phoenix, 85007, 602-542-433; Website: azgovernor.gov

State Offices: Tucson, 520-628-6580.

Election Results

2014 general	Doug Ducey (R)	805,062	(53%)
	Fred DuVal (D)	626,921	(42%)
	Barry J. Hess (L)	57,337	(4%)
2014 primary	Doug Ducey (R)	200,607	(37%)
	Scott Smith (R)	119,107	(22%)
	Christine Jones (R)	89,922	(17%)
	Ken Bennett (R)	62,010	(12%)
	Andrew Thomas (R)	43,822	(8%)

Republican Doug Ducey is the self-professed "conservative ice cream guy" who won the governorship in 2014 succeeding GOP incumbent, Jan Brewer, whose tenure had a habit of attracting negative headlines. As governor, Ducey has largely conformed to that description, especially when it comes to state spending and taxes, but he has also avoided confrontation on some social issues.

Ducey grew up in Toledo Ohio and graduated from St. John's Jesuit High School in 1982. He drove west in his Datsun B210, leaving his recession-ravaged state to attend Arizona State University and seek his fortune in the Sunbelt. He found it in a Tempe ice cream store. After graduating with a degree in finance in 1986, and a brief stint in marketing at Procter & Gamble, Ducey joined up with the founder of Cold Stone Creamery and helped turn a single-scoop shop into a global brand with more than 1,400 stores. He eventually became CEO. In 2007, at the age of 43, Ducey helped engineer a merger with another Arizona franchising heavyweight, Kahala Corp. He got very rich in the process, but that corporate marriage didn't work out, an experience Ducey described to *Bloomberg Business* as "incredibly frustrating and disappointing, but equally liberating all at once." Ducey took some time off, refocused, and became the lead investor and chairman of the board of iMemories, a friend's technology startup in Scottsdale, which helps people digitize their home movies and share them online. "As an entrepreneur, you're constantly navigating your way through a proverbial hallway of new opportunities," said Ducey. "Identifying and capitalizing on the right open door defines your success."

A new opportunity knocked in 2010, when Ducey made his first foray into elective politics and sought the state treasurer's post, vowing to bring his business background to state government to help promote jobs and economic growth. That's not a core function of the state treasurer, and at the time, many viewed his bid for the treasurer's job as a warm-up for a Senate or gubernatorial run. Nevertheless, with his connections to the Phoenix business elite, Ducey significantly outraised and outspent his more credentialed GOP opponents including a conservative favorite, and he handily won the primary and prevailed in the fall. While he was Treasurer, Ducey raised his political profile by leading a successful fight to defeat a 2012 ballot initiative that would have made a temporary one-cent sales tax increase permanent. In 2014, in a spirited Republican contest to replace Brewer, Ducey played up his business know-how again, but this time he had plenty of backing from prominent conservatives including Sen. Ted Cruz of Texas, former Alaska Gov. Sarah Palin, and immigration hardliner Maricopa County Sheriff Joe Arpaio, who had supported one of Ducey's GOP primary rivals four years prior. Brewer backed former Mesa Mayor Scott Smith in the primary, and another opponent, Christine Jones, the former legal counsel of GoDaddy, the Scottsdale Internet domain company, spent $5.4 million of her own money on the race and was aided by another $2 million independent effort funded by the company's founder. Ducey's stewardship of Cold Stone Creamery was criticized for a high default rate on Small Business Administration loans used to finance franchises, but he easily captured the primary.

In the general election, Ducey then faced former Board of Regents member Fred DuVal, a centrist Democrat, Clinton White House staffer and long-time adviser to former Arizona Democratic Gov. Bruce Babbitt. Ducey campaigned as the champion of business, favoring cuts in state regulations and dramatic reductions in business and personal income taxes. With looming state deficits, DuVal called Ducey's tax plans unrealistic and stressed more state funding for education to improve the Arizona workforce as a way to attract and expand business. Ducey campaigned against Common Core education standards, favored limiting the definition of marriage to that between a man and a woman, and opposed benefits to domestic partners of gay state employees, but added that he would always comply with the law. The campaign had its low points including minor infractions in both candidates' driving records that came under scrutiny. Republicans painted DuVal as a career lobbyist with sinister clients, while liberals touted stories linking some of Ducey's Italian-American relatives in Ohio to organized crime. Ducey pumped about $5 million of his own money into his campaign, which, along with allied groups, spent more than $10 million on the election compared to some $3 million spent by DuVal and his outside backers. Ducey won by nearly 12 percentage points while his party swept every statewide office, and Arizonans extended a streak dating back to 1982 of not electing a governor who was a native of the state.

In office, and confronting a yawning state deficit, Ducey pushed through an austere budget that cut nearly $100 million in funding to higher education, borrowed more than $100 million from the state's rainy day fund and clawed back some $220 million in unspent agency funds. Ducey had proposed raising the state vehicle registration fee, but GOP lawmakers in Phoenix balked and rejected the governor's argument that a fee increase was not a tax hike. The state legislature did adopt a one-year lifetime cap on Temporary Assistance to Needy Families, making the state's support program for low-income families with children among the most tightfisted in the nation. Doctors and hospitals were also slated for a five percent cut in state Medicaid reimbursements. Ducey backed off a plan to prune non-classroom K-12 education spending and negotiated a deal with legislators giving schools more flexibility in this regard. While K-12 escaped the budget ax, Arizona's aid to public school students still ranks near the bottom of the states. Ducey has vowed not to raise state taxes to pay for increased education funding and reportedly warned business leaders in a private meeting that he would fight any ballot measure that tried to accomplish that goal.

Ducey also steered clear of some controversial topics, which hardly pleased his more conservative backers. He rejected their demands for scrapping Common Core standards and instead asked the Arizona Board of Education to review, modify and possibly replace some of the K-12 learning benchmarks. Ducey called a bill prohibiting the use of Common Core standards in Arizona, which had been approved by the state House of Representatives, "unnecessary," and the state Senate voted the measure down. When Ducey learned that the Arizona Department of Child Safety had stopped granting joint foster care licenses and adoptions for same-sex couples while the U.S. Supreme Court was weighing the issue of same sex marriage—the U.S. Court of Appeals for the 9th Circuit had overturned Arizona's ban on it in 2014—the governor quickly stepped in and ordered the state agency to allow all legally married couples in Arizona to serve as foster parents and adopt. Ducey displayed an efficient leadership style during his early days in office and an *Arizona Republic* analysis found that when the Legislature concluded its work, it had held its shortest regular session—81 days—since 1968.

Senior Senator

John McCain (R)

Elected 1986, term expires 2016, 5th term; b. Aug. 29, 1936, Panama Canal Zone; U.S. Naval Acad., B.S. 1958, Natl. War Col., 1973-74; Episcopalian; married (Cindy); 7 children.

Military Career: Navy, 1958-80 (Vietnam).

Elected Office: U.S. House, 1982-86.

Professional Career: Dir., Navy Senate Liaison Office, 1977-81.

DC Office: 241 RSOB, 20510, 202-224-2235; Fax: 202-228-2862; Website: mccain.senate.gov.

State Offices: Phoenix, 602-952-2410; Prescott, 928-445-0833; Tempe, 480-897-6289; Tucson, 520-670-6334.

Committees: *Armed Services* (Chmn: ex officio member of each subcommittee). *Homeland Security & Governmental Affairs:* Investigations (Permanent); Regulatory Affairs & Federal Management. *Indian Affairs. Intelligence (Select).*

Group Ratings

	ADA	ACLU	AFL-CIO	LCV	ITI	COC	HAFA	ACU	CFG	FRC
2014	5%	53%	–	20%	66%	86%	49%	91%	88%	79%
2013	20%	C	33%	31%	C	88%	C	52%	71%	C

National Journal Ratings

	2013 LIB	—	2013 CONS
Economic	38%	—	61%
Social	41%	—	58%
Foreign	39%	—	60%
Composite	40%	—	60%

Key Votes of the 113th Congress

1. Sandy storm spending N	5. Student Loan Rates Y	9. Bipartisan Budget Deal Y
2. Chuck Hagel Confirmation N	6. Employee Non-Discrim'n Act Y	10. Farm Bill Conference Rept. N
3. Gun Background Checks Y	7. Senate Vote on Judgeships Y	11. Unempl. Comp. Extension N
4. Immigration Reform Y	8. Defense Dept. Spending N	12. Keystone Pipeline Y

Election Results

2010 general	John McCain (R)	1,005,615	(59%)	$22,247,415	$302,089
	Rodney Glassman (D)	592,011	(35%)	$1,328,686	
	David Nolan (Lib)	80,097	(5%)		
2010 primary	John McCain (R)	333,744	(56%)		
	J. D. Hayworth (R)	190,229	(32%)		
	Jim Deakin (R)	69,328	(12%)		

Prior winning percentages: 2004 (77%), 1998 (69%), 1992 (56%), 1986 (60%); House: 1984 (78%), 1982 (66%)

John McCain, Arizona's senior senator, was once the Democrats' ideal Republican—fiercely independent and unafraid to cross the aisle to work on issues such as campaign finance and immigration reform. Since losing to Barack Obama in the 2008 presidential race, however,

McCain has rebranded himself as the GOP's chief critic of Obama's national security policies, using his celebrity status to advocate a hawkish approach in the Middle East and elsewhere.

McCain was born in the Canal Zone, the son and grandson of Navy admirals. (His married-to-the-military mother, Roberta McCain, at age 96, was one of his hardest-working campaign supporters; she danced at the podium at the Republican National Convention celebrating his nomination.) McCain graduated from the Naval Academy, fifth from the bottom of his class academically and high in demerits, but trained to be a fighter pilot. He volunteered for service in Vietnam, and flew ground-attack aircraft from carriers at sea. In July 1967, he was severely injured in a flight-deck explosion on the carrier USS *Forrestal*. McCain could have returned home but refused. He continued to fly bombing runs over North Vietnam. That October, on his 23rd bombing mission, his A-4E Skyhawk was shot down by a missile, and McCain ejected from the plane, breaking both of his arms and a leg in a fall into Truc Bach Lake near Hanoi. After pulling him from the water, his North Vietnamese "rescuers" crushed one of his shoulders with a rifle butt, bayoneted him, then refused him medical treatment during his stay at a prison dubbed the Hanoi Hilton by U.S. soldiers.

He spent the next five and a half years in prisoner-of-war camps, most of it in suffering as a result of repeated torture by his Communist captors. He spent two of those years in solitary confinement. That chapter of McCain's life is recounted in Robert Timberg's *The Nightingale's Song* and in McCain's 1999 best-seller *Faith of My Fathers*. When he was offered release because of his father's rank, he refused to be let out ahead of those who had been imprisoned longer. He returned to the United States in March 1973 with other POWs.

McCain recovered in military hospitals, and despite intensive physical therapy, suffered permanent injuries, including restricted movement of his arms. On top of the many medals and commendations he received, his heroism was rewarded with a final assignment in a high-profile role as the Navy's liaison to the Senate in 1977. McCain says the job launched his career in politics. He became close to several senators, including Republicans John Tower of Texas and William Cohen of Maine and Democrat Gary Hart of Colorado. On the personal front, McCain's first marriage failed. In 1980, he remarried, to Cindy Lou Hensley, the wealthy daughter of a beer distributor from Phoenix. Two years later, he ran for an open House seat in Arizona. Attacked as an outsider, he responded, "The longest place I ever lived in was Hanoi." He won a four-way primary with 32%, and then the general election in November. In 1986, he easily defeated former Arizona state legislator Democrat Richard Kimball to win the Senate seat of conservative icon Barry Goldwater, who was retiring.

For all of the attention he now commands, McCain kept a low profile during his early years in Congress. Though a strong supporter of the Reagan administration, McCain, as a newly-elected House member, showed his independence by taking a remarkable stance for such a junior lawmaker by opposing the president's dispatch of troops to Lebanon in 1982, arguing they were too few to be effective and too vulnerable to attack. He was vindicated when a truck bomb blasted Marine barracks and killed 241 U.S. servicemen—a stunning loss that led Reagan to withdraw troops.

Later, after being elected to the Senate in 1986, he backed President George H.W. Bush's war in the Persian Gulf in 1990 and even his controversial decision not to oust Iraqi leader Saddam Hussein. In the 1990s, McCain worked with Massachusetts Sen. John Kerry, a Democrat and also a decorated Vietnam veteran, to end the trade embargo on Vietnam, and pressed for establishing diplomatic relations. He supported air strikes against Serbia in 1999 but criticized the Clinton administration for ruling out ground troops in Bosnia and for not using "all necessary force" against the Serbs.

McCain strongly supported President George W. Bush in the war on terrorism after September 11 and in his later decision to go to war with Iraq. McCain repeatedly pushed for more ground troops in Afghanistan and signed a letter urging that Iraq be the next target. He called for a special commission to investigate intelligence failures before the terrorist attacks. The final version of the law provided, at the insistence of relatives of 9/11 casualties, that McCain and Republican Richard Shelby of Alabama get a veto over appointees to the commission. When Bush decided to invade Iraq in 2003, McCain continually pushed for a larger army and more troops to get the job done. He clashed frequently with Defense Secretary Donald Rumsfeld. McCain finally concluded that the administration's handling of the war "will go down as one of the worst" mistakes in U.S. military history.

McCain built a reputation in Congress as someone who refused to engage in business as usual, making him a popular figure outside of Washington. But at one time, engaging in business as usual nearly ended his career. In the late-1980s, McCain was one of the Keating Five senators investigated for allegedly pressuring regulators on behalf of Charles Keating's Arizona savings and loan. Ultimately, he got a slap on the wrist for exercising poor judgment but there was no finding of improper conduct. Vindicated by his reelection in 1992, McCain reinvented himself as a reformer.

When Republicans won control of Congress two years later, McCain sought out Democrat Russ Feingold of Wisconsin, a champion of reform who had a bill to clamp down on campaign finance abuses. For the next several years, the McCain-Feingold bills went through several transformations. Key features included prohibitions on soft money—the large, unregulated contributions to political parties that were ripe for abuse—and limits on advertising by independent organizations within 60 days of an election. The changes were fiercely opposed as an infringement on free speech and as a threat to the Republican Party by the assertive Mitch McConnell of Kentucky, who used threats of filibusters to prevent the bill from coming to a vote. McCain threatened to tie up the Senate in early 2001 unless Majority Leader Trent Lott of Mississippi set aside time for debate on the issue. In March 2001, after two weeks of spirited debate, during which McCain and Feingold fended off several poison-pill amendments, the legislation passed April 2 on a 59-41 vote. The House passed its version in February 2002, and the bill became law.

For years, it withstood multiple court challenges. But then in January 2010, the Supreme Court, reversing earlier precedents, struck down a key reform when it ruled in *Citizens United vs. Federal Election Commission* that curbs on political spending by corporations are an unconstitutional infringement on free speech. The 2002 law had banned the broadcast, cable, or satellite transmission of election messages paid for by corporations or labor unions from their general funds 30 days before a presidential primary and 60 days before the general elections. "I think there will be scandals associated with the worst decision of the United States Supreme Court in the 21st century," McCain said in June 2012. He cited the justices' inability to understand the realities of campaigning and added, "I just wish one of them had run for county sheriff." But he refused to join Democrats in supporting the DISCLOSE Act aimed at correcting *Citizens United*, calling it "closer to a clever attempt at political gamesmanship than actual reform."

Another of his legislative crusades was a war on earmarks, the practice among lawmakers of slipping high-dollar projects into bills to benefit a particular congressional district or state. Each year, McCain highlighted the pork-barrel spending he found in appropriations bills, to the growing irritation of his colleagues in both parties, who were accustomed to using earmarks to curry favor with voters back home. But eventually McCain's lonely campaign was joined by conservatives in the House, and both chambers in 2011 adopted an earmark ban.

McCain's generally conservative voting record has as many quirks as the man himself. He supported funding of embryonic stem cell research, in opposition to most other Republicans. With liberal Democrat Kerry, he proposed fuel efficiency standards of 36 miles per gallon for cars and light trucks by 2015. And with independent Sen. Joe Lieberman of Connecticut, he co-authored a bill to reduce carbon dioxide emissions. McCain opposed the constitutional amendment to ban same-sex marriage as "antithetical in every way to the core philosophy of Republicans" to respect states' rights to govern themselves.

His biggest act of ideological heresy came on immigration. "The truth is, border enforcement alone does not work," McCain said, as most conservatives were pursuing tougher enforcement strategies. He opposed Arizona's Proposition 200, which would cut off public benefits to illegal immigrants, arguing that it would "delay, possibly derail, the search for a solution." In 2005, McCain and liberal Sen. Edward Kennedy of Massachusetts sponsored an immigration bill that gave illegal immigrants a path to legalization, allowing them to obtain two three-year visas and then "get in the back of the line" of legal immigrants. "Some Americans believe we must find all these millions, round them up, and send them back to the countries they came from. I don't know how you do that. And I don't know why you would want to," McCain said. But a comprehensive bill failed in 2006 and again in 2007.

When immigration resurfaced as a front-burner issue after the 2012 elections, he joined a bipartisan group that crafted a proposal. That required working closely with New York Sen. Charles Schumer, one of the few Democrats whose ubiquitous media presence rivals that of McCain's. Schumer told *The New Yorker* that McCain came to him after they worked on a deal to protect the Senate's filibuster rules. "He said, 'You know? You're a much different person than I thought you were,'" Schumer recalled.

The so-called "Gang of Eight" got a comprehensive bill that combined a path to citizenship for illegal immigrants with extremely tough border-security measures through the Senate in 2013, but the Republican-controlled House refused to take up that or any other broad-ranging measure. When a disgusted Obama issued an executive order on immigration in November 2014, McCain complained it was "a cynical action that means that the president isn't that interested in comprehensive reform. He's only interested in placating his base." McCain was so angered by what he saw as an unconstitutional act that he opposed Loretta Lynch's nomination to be attorney general in 2015, even as he said she is very well-qualified. "We have to send a message to the president that we will not agree to his nominees who endorse his unconstitutional behavior," he told reporters.

McCain's quest for the presidency began with the 2000 election. In 1999, he decided to skip the caucuses in dovish and ethanol-loving Iowa (McCain had long denounced ethanol subsidies as pork barrel spending) to concentrate on the primary in New Hampshire, where he traveled around in his "Straight Talk Express" bus. At first, only a few reporters traveled with him and crowds were sparse. But McCain struck a chord. To increasingly large and more enthusiastic crowds, he told his personal story in self-deprecating terms, and pledged, "I will never tell you a lie." He talked about defense and foreign-policy issues—the only candidate to spend much time doing so—and invariably called for campaign finance regulation.

McCain did not have much support from his colleagues, and *The Arizona Republic* wrote editorials warning of McCain's "volcanic" temper. But the strength of feeling among his ever-larger crowds was real, and on Feb. 1, McCain beat George W. Bush in New Hampshire by an impressive margin, 49%-30%. Suddenly he became, if not the front-runner, at least the front-runner's most serious opponent.

From there, the "Straight Talk Express" had mixed success. It went to South Carolina, where both the Republican establishment and Christian conservatives lined up with Bush. The campaigning got negative, but what hurt even more was McCain's failure to win over self-identified Republicans. His emphasis on campaign finance regulation and his criticisms of Bush's tax cuts for giving too much to the rich helped with independents but sounded like enemy talk to Republicans. On Feb. 18, Bush won 53%-42% in South Carolina, in what turned out to be a decisive victory. The race continued, with McCain running way ahead of Bush among independents, but way behind among Republicans in Southern states. McCain's most striking win was in Michigan that February, where he prevailed 50%-43%, among an atypical electorate: Seventeen percent of Republican primary voters were self-identified Democrats, 35% were independents, and only a minority were Republicans. On Super Tuesday, March 7, McCain won in Massachusetts, Connecticut, Rhode Island, and Vermont. But he lost in New York, Ohio, and California. He suspended his campaign in March and two months later grudgingly endorsed Bush.

Four years later, as Bush headed into his 2004 reelection campaign, McCain was a major national figure, with high positive ratings among Republicans and very low negatives among Democrats. Always enchanted with him, the press—which McCain would laughingly refer to as his base—provided lavish coverage. As Kerry, his fellow Vietnam veteran, clinched the Democratic nomination in March 2004, there even was speculation that he might ask McCain to be his vice presidential nominee. After some days of speculation, McCain firmly rejected the idea. "I am a pro-life, deficit-hawk, free-trade Republican," he said. Subsequently, the Bush and McCain camps made peace. But McCain also maintained his relationship with fellow vet Kerry. When the Swift Boat Veterans for Truth ads appeared against Kerry, McCain called them "dishonorable" and said they should be dropped from the air.

As the 2008 presidential contest neared, McCain voiced more frequently and fervently his long-standing opposition to abortion rights. Even so, many conservatives were not enthusiastic about McCain, given his stands on campaign finance, immigration, and carbon dioxide emissions. Their skepticism doomed McCain's early strategy in 2007, which was to campaign as the next-in-line Republican for the presidential nomination. By late June, the McCain campaign was broke. Its opulent headquarters closed, and the campaign's top managers were fired, replaced with McCain stalwart Rick Davis and Bush-Cheney veteran Steve Schmidt. Backed into a corner, McCain adopted the campaign strategy that some of the best consultants rely on: Campaign on what you believe. His backup strategy was: Wait for the other candidates' strategies to fail.

They both worked. After a spring trip to Iraq, McCain commented in July 2007 that he was convinced the controversial troop surge strategy was working and praised the outcome.

In September, he launched his "No Surrender" tour. In the GOP primary debates, McCain was treated respectfully and uncritically by his opponents, while he was quick to jab at any who expressed skepticism about the surge. Only Mike Huckabee, the former minister and Arkansas governor, exceeded expectations, running second in the Iowa straw poll in August 2007, and first, ahead of the free-spending Romney, in the Iowa caucuses on Jan. 3, 2008. As in 2000, McCain had written off dovish Iowa, with its love of ethanol subsidies. He focused on New Hampshire, where his maverick ways were embraced, and campaigned very hard in the Granite State. On Jan. 8, he beat Romney, who owned a vacation home in New Hampshire and had been governor in neighboring Massachusetts, 37%-32%. "Mac is back," the crowd chanted on Election Night.

Next up was Michigan, where Romney had grown up and where his father was governor 40 years before. Romney promised to bring back jobs to the state's important automobile industry, while McCain, in his classic "straight talk" said bluntly that many jobs would never return. With fewer crossovers than in 2000, Romney prevailed with 39 percent of the vote to McCain's 30 percent. After Michigan, attention turned to South Carolina, where McCain had lost decisively to Bush in 2000. This was the one, real four-way Republican contest in 2008. McCain, with 33%, finished ahead of Huckabee, with 30%. In critical and always baffling Florida on Jan. 29, GOP Gov. Charlie Crist delivered a surprise endorsement of McCain. The result was a 36%-31% victory for McCain over Romney. A few days later on Super Tuesday, Feb. 5, McCain effectively sewed up the nomination, winning absolute majorities (his first) in New York, New Jersey, and Connecticut, while eking out a 1% victory over Huckabee in Missouri. He also racked up victories in states as diverse as California, Illinois, Oklahoma, and Delaware. Two days later, Romney withdrew. Huckabee remained in the race for another month.

By late spring, McCain had consolidated the Republican base, but it was smaller than in 2004, and not sufficiently motivated to come anywhere close to matching the fundraising feats of Democrat Barack Obama. McCain faced difficult political dynamics, including Bush's low job rating, an increasing Democratic advantage in party identification, doubts about the course of the economy, the continuing unpopularity of the war in Iraq, and the enthusiasm among young, Hispanic and black voters for Obama. The Arizona senator also was hampered by his own campaign finance law. Obama eschewed federal funding and was able to massively outspend McCain, who had little choice but to take public financing.

Given these circumstances, it's perhaps surprising that McCain made a contest of it at all and that he actually was leading during part of the fall campaign. He sought to portray himself more than Obama as an agent of change, even though the Democratic nominee's whole campaign was built around the change he would bring to the White House. After Obama chose 36-year Senate veteran Joe Biden of Delaware as his running mate, McCain chose the two-year governor of Alaska, Sarah Palin. Her initial appearance in Ohio and her speech before the Republican National Convention sparked great enthusiasm among the Republican base. The campaign was finally able to muster volunteer and fundraising efforts competitive with Obama's. For about two weeks, the McCain-Palin ticket actually led Obama-Biden by narrow margins. But it became apparent that Palin was unprepared for the rigors of a national campaign. News articles depicted her as lacking knowledge about a range of issues, and her rambling interviews and verbal gaffes provided fodder for *Saturday Night Live* and late-night comics. She also was mercurial in temperament, clashing with McCain's aides and eventually overshadowing the senator's own campaign.

Then, on Sept. 15, Lehman Brothers, a global financial services firm, went into bankruptcy, precipitating a far-reaching crisis. The same day, McCain said, "The fundamentals of our economy are strong." Four days later, Treasury Secretary Henry Paulson and Federal Reserve Chairman Ben Bernanke called for a $700 billion rescue of the financial markets. Obama's campaign scoffed at McCain's "strong" comment, surged in the polls, and never relinquished the lead after that. On Sept. 24, McCain announced he was suspending his campaign, pulling his television ads, and returning to the Capitol to work on the financial industry bill. He said he might not appear at the first presidential debate scheduled two days later. Obama coolly observed that a president has to tend to more than one thing at a time, and the debate went off. When the House initially rejected the financial rescue on Sept. 29, McCain was blamed for not bringing along a sufficient number of House Republicans.

In the rhetoric war, McCain attacked Obama sharply on taxes, energy, and other issues. But he also subtly raised questions about Obama's character, asking voters whether they knew the "real Barack Obama" and could trust him. When fringe activists started loudly protesting that Obama might be a socialist or a terrorist and perhaps was not even an American citizen, McCain modulated his comments, saying on Oct. 10, "I want to be president of the United States and obviously I do not want Senator Obama to be, but I have to tell you, I have to tell you he is a decent person, and a person that you do not have to be scared of as president of the United States." He criticized Obama for saying he wanted to "spread the wealth around," but when asked in a debate about the economy, McCain fell back on his determination to stop spending on earmarks—hardly a comprehensive economic agenda. Obama won 53%-46%, the best Democratic percentage since 1964. Obama got 95% support from African-American voters, and he won 66%-32% among voters under age 30. Among those older than 30, McCain lost by only a point, 50%-49%. On Election Night, McCain made a gracious concession speech, saying, "Senator Obama has achieved a great thing for himself and for his country."

After the election, McCain went through a difficult period in which he was often angry and during which he displayed that volcanic temper that had erupted from time to time throughout his career. "It took me three years of feeling sorry for myself," Mr. McCain said to a group of reporters in 2012. After his defeat, he resumed playing the prominent role that had characterized much of his Senate career, though he took a more conservative line than he had in earlier years. He called for a payroll tax cut in January 2009 and opposed the Democrats' $787 billion economic stimulus bill. In April 2009, despite his support of past legislation to reduce carbon emissions, he called the Democrats' cap-and-trade bill irresponsible and said the plan to auction all emissions credits was "bad economic policy that would cost businesses billions of dollars and allow for little to no transition into a low carbon system."

McCain remained heavily involved in defense issues. He worked with Armed Services Committee Chairman Carl Levin of Michigan to support Defense Secretary Robert Gates' decision in 2009 to end production of the F-22 fighter. And, after his many criticisms of Bush's handling of the Iraq war, he gave the former president credit for ending it well. "Though most Democrats still cannot bear to admit it, the war in Iraq is ending successfully because the surge worked," he told *The Wall Street Journal*. McCain supported Obama's decisions to send more troops to Afghanistan in March and December 2009 but criticized the president's call for troop reductions starting by July 2011. He also spoke out strongly against repeal of the ban on openly gay military personnel.

McCain's positive image with the public had been built on his tendency toward political independence, but that image acquired chinks during his reelection campaign in 2010. He disappointed many of his longtime supporters when, faced with a primary challenge in his reelection, McCain backed away from some of his earlier stances and told *Newsweek* in April 2010, "I never considered myself a maverick."

One of his most telling changes of heart was on immigration. McCain retreated from his earlier out-front support for a path to citizenship and other elements of a bipartisan approach to illegal immigration. He said, bluntly, that voters had spoken and that the border must be protected first, before any comprehensive bill would be passed. Most Republican primary voters in Arizona and practically all talk radio hosts there strongly opposed legalization as a form of amnesty, and McCain, no doubt, was angling to eliminate an easy line of attack for his primary opponent, conservative talk radio host J.D. Hayworth, a former House member. In March 2009, McCain snipped to a Hispanic group, "You people made your choice during the election," a reference to exit polls that showed he lost Latinos to Obama 67%-31%. He also supported Arizona's controversial new law allowing police to look into the immigration status of people stopped for other reasons.

With his long Senate career on the line, McCain campaigned nonstop and beat Hayworth in the August primary 56%-32%, a solid victory. A third candidate who claimed tea party affiliation got 12%. In the general election campaign, Democratic nominee Rodney Glassman, the former vice mayor of Tucson, could attract little funding in a year in which many other Democratic Senate candidates were struggling, and he never became well-known in the Phoenix market. McCain won, 59%-35%.

The Republican gains in the 2010 elections appeared to whet McCain's inclinations toward partisanship, leaving his onetime Democratic allies disappointed. "I just hope he goes back to his roots," Senate Majority Whip Dick Durbin of Illinois told *The New York Times* in July 2012. On international issues, he called for airstrikes on Syrian forces attempting to put down a popular rebellion, and repeatedly blasted the Obama administration's "feckless foreign policy that abandons American leadership." He also criticized the administration's handling of the attack on the U.S. consulate in Libya and called for an active U.S. role in brokering Middle East peace in the wake of Israel's fight with Hamas in Gaza in fall 2012.

When Obama won reelection in 2012 and considered nominating United Nations Ambassador Susan Rice as Secretary of State, McCain and his close ally Sen. Lindsey Graham of South Carolina emerged as Rice's most full-throated critics. McCain called her "unqualified," citing her erroneous public statements about the September terrorist attack in Benghazi and prompting an angry Obama to retort, "If Senator McCain and Senator Graham and others want to go after somebody, they should go after me." The senators, however, won the battle when Rice withdrew her name in December, though she later became Obama's National Security Advisor. The two senators next began raising concerns about the fitness of their former Senate colleague, Nebraska's Chuck Hagel, to become Defense Secretary, questioning his loyalty to Israel and willingness to intervene militarily overseas. They were unable to stop Hagel from being confirmed.

McCain became chairman of the Armed Services Committee in 2015, a perch from which he said he hoped to shape his legacy as someone who played "a significant role in defeating the forces of radical Islam that want to destroy America." Right out of the gate he harshly criticized what he saw as Obama's weaknesses that have failed in the Middle East. He charged the President had "lost touch with reality" and blistered his lack of strategy on CBS in January just as he was settling into his role atop the Committee. "It is delusional for them to think that what they're doing is succeeding," he charged and called for more of a military presence to combat the Islamic State of Iraq and Syria (ISIS). He also blasted the White House's deteriorating relationship with Israel.

He told the Associated Press in January 2015, "You will see, probably, the busiest Senate Armed Services Committee that you've ever seen." He promised to address how the Pentagon is structured as a follow-up to the 1986 Goldwater-Nichols Department of Defense Reorganization Act, which his role model Goldwater cosponsored. But above all else, he pushed aggressively for an expanded U.S. military presence in the Middle East. He had caused a stir in 2013 when he ventured into Syria to meet with opposition leaders whom he hoped could topple Bashar al-Assad. Twelve of the fifteen Syrian commanders with whom he met subsequently died. "We are probably in the most serious period of turmoil in our lifetime," he told *The Washington Post*.

He flashed his legendary temper at a group of Code Pink anti-war protestors who shouted for the arrest of former Secretary of State Henry Kissinger during a hearing in January 2015. "Get out of here, you lowlife scum!" he barked in an exchange that immediately went viral. Bringing in luminaries such as Kissinger, who was testifying along with former Secretaries of State George Shultz and Madeleine Albright, was part of McCain's mission to educate his more-junior colleagues about America's historic role in the world. "I think John's legacy is that he never quits," Vice President Joe Biden, a longtime Senate colleague, told the AP.

In 2015, McCain made clear that he planned to run for a sixth term in 2016, when he would be 80. "I still think I have a lot to do," he told the AP. Hard-charging conservatives, angered by his "maverick" stances and skeptical of his moves on immigration, targeted McCain. Some potential GOP challengers kept the door open but failed to launch a campaign. The less-experienced state Sen. Kelli Ward formed an exploratory committee. Democratic Rep. Ann Kirkpatrick announced that she would seek the Senate seat, too. McCain never has taken a race for granted. Sitting atop the Armed Services Committee as the critic-in-chief of President Obama, McCain prepared for an election that likely would be dominated by national security.

Junior Senator

Jeff Flake (R)

Elected 2012, term expires 2018, 1st term; b. Dec. 31, 1962, Snowflake; Brigham Young U., B.A. 1986, M.A. 1987; Mormon; married (Cheryl); 5 children.

Elected Office: U.S. House, 2000-12.

Professional Career: Owner, public affairs firm, 1987; Exec. dir., Foundation for Democracy (Namibia), 1989-90; Exec. dir., Goldwater Inst., 1992-99.

DC Office: 413 RSOB, 20515, 202-224-4521; Fax: 202-228-0515; Website: flake.senate.gov.

State Offices: Phoenix, 602-840-1891; Tucson, 520-575-8633.

Committees: *Aging (Special). Energy & Natural Resources:* Energy; Public Lands, Forests & Mining; Water & Power. *Foreign Relations:* Africa & Global Health Policy (Chmn); East Asia, the Pacific & International Cybersecurity Policy; Multilateral International Development, Multilateral Institutions & International Economic, Energy & Environmental Policy; Western Hemisphere, Transnational Crime, Civilian Security, Democracy, Human Rights & Global Women's Issues. *Judiciary:* Privacy, Technology & the Law (Chmn); Crime & Terrorism; Oversight, Agency Action, Federal Rights & Federal Courts.

Group Ratings

	ADA	ACLU	AFL-CIO	LCV	ITI	COC	HAFA	ACU	CFG	FRC
2014	10%	53%	–	20%	66%	75%	59%	92%	90%	79%
2013	15%	C	28%	23%	C	88%	C	71%	84%	C

National Journal Ratings

	2013 LIB	—	2013 CONS
Economic	23%	—	76%
Social	40%	—	59%
Foreign	40%	—	59%
Composite	35%	—	65%

Key Votes of the 113th Congress

1. Sandy storm spending	N	5. Student Loan Rates	Y
2. Chuck Hagel Confirmation	N	6. Employee Non-Discrim'n Act	Y
3. Gun Background Checks	N	7. Senate Vote on Judgeships	Y
4. Immigration Reform	Y	8. Defense Dept. Spending	N

9. Bipartisan Budget Deal	N
10. Farm Bill Conference Rept.	N
11. Unempl. Comp. Extension	N
12. Keystone Pipeline	Y

Election Results

2012 general	Jeff Flake (R)	1,104,457	(49%)	$9,557,420	$4,606,334	$8,514,069
	Richard Carmona (D)	1,036,542	(46%)	$6,373,544	$1,138,072	$8,035,923
	Marc Victor (Lib)	102,109	(5%)			
2012 primary	Jeff Flake (R)	357,360	(69%)			
	Will Cardon (R)	110,150	(21%)			
	Clair Van Steenwyk (R)	29,159	(6%)			

Prior winning percentages: House: 2010 (66%), 2008 (62%), 2006 (75%), 2004 (79%), 2002 (66%), 2000 (54%)

Republican Jeff Flake was elected Arizona's junior senator in 2012 to replace retiring GOP Sen. Jon Kyl. Flake had served six terms in the House and has faithfully followed the libertarian-leaning conservative principles of former Arizona Sen. Barry Goldwater, even when it has meant sometimes alienating his GOP colleagues.

A fifth-generation Arizonan, Flake is a Mormon who was born and raised on a ranch in Snowflake, a town named after his great-great-grandfather. The fifth of 11 children, he graduated with a degree in international studies from Brigham Young University and did missionary work in South Africa and Zimbabwe. In 1989, he moved to Namibia to become executive director of the Foundation for Democracy, which monitored democratic progress in that country. After Namibia gained independence in 1990, Flake returned to Arizona and became executive director of the Goldwater Institute, where he led the fight for Arizona's charter school law.

In 2000, when conservative Republican Matt Salmon kept his pledge to serve only three terms in the House, he picked Flake to succeed him. Flake faced four opponents in a hard-fought September primary, in which he ran as the most conservative candidate and won. In the general election, Flake easily defeated Democrat David Mendoza, a longtime lobbyist for public employees.

Flake promised to "continue to rock the boat" as Salmon had as a principled conservative who bucked the Republican leadership. He became the House's leading opponent of earmarking and regularly tried to amend legislation to ban such special-interest funding provisions from being added to spending bills. His willingness to take on special projects in the districts of fellow Republicans and Democrats made him a darling of conservative groups such as the Club for Growth, which favors limiting federal government spending. After Republicans regained control of the House in 2010, he won a spot on the Appropriations Committee, whose members strongly favored earmarks.

Flake also has not hesitated to show an independent streak. During President George W. Bush's administration, Flake voted against the new Republican President's 2001 No Child Left Behind education overhaul and the 2003 law extending Medicare benefits for prescription drugs. In 2010, he was one of only three Republicans to oppose a bill overhauling how the Defense Department buys goods and services through expanding the Pentagon's acquisition authority.

At the same time, Flake's beliefs on occasion led him to support Democratic measures that many Republicans abhorred. He supported a 2007 bill to prohibit workplace discrimination against gays, although he said in 2010 that he wouldn't support a revised version because of its expansion to include transgender rights. He also joined Democrats in calling for an end to the 1962 trade embargo with Cuba, a blockade that many staunchly anti-Communist Republicans support.

When Kyl decided against seeking a fourth term, Flake joined the race. He faced a primary challenge from real estate investor Wil Cardon, and the two men waged an acrimonious campaign. Cardon inveighed against "career politicians" and ran an ad using Flake's own words to highlight his broken pledge not to serve more than three House terms. "What can I say? I lied," Flake joked in an interview with Reason TV. Flake won easily, although Cardon outspent him, 2-to-1. But the late-August primary meant that he had less time to focus on the fall campaign against Democrat Richard Carmona, a former U.S. surgeon general.

Carmona stressed doing more to assist veterans and took the middle ground on many issues, including immigration and health care. Flake, meanwhile, emphasized his fiscal conservatism. His campaign ran one of the most explosive ads of the 2012 election cycle in which Cristina Beato, Carmona's former boss at the Health and Human Services Department, alleged that he twice angrily banged on her door and yelled at her in the middle of the night after workplace disputes. Carmona's campaign denied the charges and released its own spot featuring Cecilia Rosales, a University of Arizona professor, who called her former colleague "respectful and supportive of his coworkers."

Carmona closed the gap in polls but could not overcome Arizona's Republican tilt. Flake won the endorsement of *The Arizona Republic*, which wrote, "With the exception of Rep. Paul Ryan, perhaps no candidate for federal office in this election cycle is more committed to forcing sanity back into the nation's finances." Flake narrowly prevailed, 49%-46%, with Libertarian Marc Victor drawing the remaining 5%. Although Carmona took Tucson's Pima County 55%-42% and Flagstaff's Coconino County 57%-38%, Flake managed to hold onto Phoenix's Maricopa County 50%-45% and piled up larger margins in the state's rural areas.

Having been so outspoken for so many years in advocating for an end to travel and trade restrictions with Cuba, it is perhaps no surprise that the Obama Administration asked him, in December 2014, to be the only Republican in a secret delegation that flew to Cuba. In a prisoner swap, the group brought Alan P. Gross, a jailed U.S. government contractor who had worked with the U.S. Agency for International Development, back home. Even as most other Republicans lambasted the Cuban government as tyrannical and repressive and opposed Obama's move to normalize diplomatic relations with the Communist island, Flake has consistently seen issues involving the two countries in terms of freedom, including the freedom to travel.

Flake also parted company with most of his Senate Republican colleagues in supporting the nomination of Loretta Lynch to be Attorney General. He voted for her as a member of the Judiciary Committee and, again, when her nomination came to the Senate floor in April 2015. Similarly, Flake was one of only seven Republicans who declined to sign a letter to Iran's leaders that warned that an agreement with Obama without congressional approval was nothing more than an executive agreement that could be short-lived since it could be undone by a future President or Congress.

Each of those stances—favoring the move to open diplomatic relations with Cuba, backing the Lynch nomination and declining to sign the letter to the Iranian leaders—put Flake at odds with Arizona's senior senator, John McCain. But the two senators have worked together on other issues, including in 2013, when as members of the so-called bipartisan Gang of Eight, they sought to move a comprehensive immigration bill.

FIRST DISTRICT

Ann Kirkpatrick (D)

Elected 2012, 3rd term; b. March 14, 1950, McNary; U. of AZ, B.A. 1972, J.D. 1979; Catholic; married (Roger Curley); 2 children.

Elected Office: AZ House, 2004-07; U.S. House, 2009-11.

Professional Career: Coconino deputy cnty. atty., 1980-81; Pima deputy cnty. atty., 1981-85; Sedona city atty., 1990-91; Instructor, Coconino Comm. Col., 2005; Practicing lawyer, 2011-12.

DC Office: 201 CHOB, 20515, 202-225-3361; Fax: 202-225-3462; Website: kirkpatrick.house.gov.

State Offices: Casa Grande, 520-316-0839; Flagstaff, 928-213-9981; Globe, 928-425-3231; Marana, 520-382-2663; Show Low, 928-537-5657.

Committees: *Agriculture:* Commodity Exchanges, Energy & Credit; Conservation & Forestry; General Farm Commodities & Risk Management. *Transportation & Infrastructure:* Aviation; Highways & Transit; Water Resources & Environment.

Group Ratings

	ADA	ACLU	AFL-CIO	LCV	ITI	COC	HAFA	ACU	CFG	FRC
2014	50%	61%	–	69%	80%	57%	13%	13%	12%	13%
2013	55%	C	100%	61%	C	62%	C	23%	13%	C

National Journal Ratings

	2013 LIB	—	2013 CONS
Economic	58%	—	42%
Social	58%	—	42%
Foreign	57%	—	43%
Composite	58%	—	42%

Key Votes of the 113th Congress

1. Sandy storm spending	NV	5. Medical Marijuana	Y	9. Syrian Rebels Training	Y
2. Violence Against Women Act	Y	6. Farm Bill	N	10. Keystone pipeline	N
3. Guantanamo Bay Detainees	N	7. Afghanistan Combat	NV	11. Immigration Exec. Action	N
4. Abortion 20-week ban	N	8. NSA Phone Data Collection	N	12. Bipartisan budget deal	Y

Election Results

2014 general	Ann Kirkpatrick (D)	97,391	(53%)	$3,323,325	$337,132	$5,745,763
	Andy Tobin (R)	87,723	(47%)	$1,377,528	$792,123	$5,213,031
2014 primary	Ann Kirkpatrick (D) ....unopposed				

Prior winning percentages: 2012 (49%), 2008 (56%)

Population		Race and Ethnicity		Income	
Total:	723,969	White	51.2%	Median income:	$46,894
Urban:	18.5%	Amer. Indian	22.6%		*(283 of 435)*
Suburban:	29.0%	Latino	20.4%	Under $50,000	52.2%
Rural:	52.4%	Black	2.3%	$50,000-$99,999:	31.6%
Land area:	49,206	Two races	1.8%	$100,000-$199,999:	14.4%
Pop/sq. mi.:	14.7	White Ethnic	17.8%	$200,000 or more:	1.9%
Born in state:	51.4%			Poverty Rate	22.3%
		Education			
Age Groups		H.S. grad or less:	41.3%	**Work**	
Under 18:	24.7%	Some college:	35.8%	White collar:	33.3%
18 to 34:	23.1%	College degree, 4 yr.:	13.9%	Blue collar:	43.6%
35 to 64:	36.1%	Post-grad study:	8.9%	Sales and service:	23.1%
Over 64:	16.1%				
		Military		Govt. workers:	23.6%
		Veterans/active duty:	10.6%		

Northeast/Central Arizona: Southern Phoenix, Northern Tucson Suburbs

Beyond Phoenix, Arizona is a vast state of stunning beauty: the awe-inspiring Grand Canyon, the subtle pastel hues of the Painted Desert, the sheer cliff walls of Canyon de Chelly, the still waters of Lake Powell, the mountainous pine forests around Flagstaff, and the rust-and-rose red rocks of Sedona. It

Voter Turnout	
2013 Total Citizen 18+	519,299
2014 House Turnout	184,114
2014 Turnout as % CVAP	35.6%
2012 Turnout as % CVAP	50.3%

also has man-made landmarks. The celebrated U.S. 66, now mostly superseded by Interstate 40, traverses the district, and it's dotted with old copper mining towns like Globe.

All of these places are in the 1st Congressional District in northeastern Arizona, an area larger than Pennsylvania. It encompasses Flagstaff, a university town and growing retirement mecca that has lured snowbirds with its climate and well-priced housing. But the boom in home construction made the city vulnerable to the housing bust of the late 2000s; the median home value in Flagstaff was $252,000 in 2012, down $127,000 from its peak in 2006. By January 2015, the median value had returned to $315,000. There have been ample signs of economic recovery in the district. Investors are buying up land to develop shopping centers and housing in fast-growing Pinal County. In Casa Grande, a Pinal County town between Phoenix and Tucson, Phoenix Mart was scheduled to open in late 2015 as a 1.6 million-square-foot commercial complex, with 4 million square feet of support facilities, that styles itself as "a 21st Century global commerce center that connects manufacturers, distributors, wholesalers and retailers." In Flagstaff, Northern Arizona University continued its rapid growth. The city was designated in August 2014 as an International Dark Sky City, which permits lighting to be controlled.

The 1st is also home to the nation's largest Indian population. A full 23 percent of its residents identify themselves as Native Americans, who outnumber Hispanics in the district. Redistricting after the 2010 census united the Navajo and Hopi reservations in the same congressional district for the first time in the state's history. The two tribes, historic enemies, concluded they could wield more political clout together than apart. Other tribes with a presence here are the Fort Apache, San Carlos, Havasupai, Hualapai, Kaibab, Gila River, and Zuni.

By far the largest is the Navajo Nation. Most of the Navajo are in Apache County, with the rest in Navajo and Coconino counties and others on parts of the reservation that extend into New Mexico and Utah. There are about 174,000 Navajo in the three states, of whom an estimated 71 percent speak the language, and many still practice the traditional Navajo lifestyle. They have a history of fiercely contested tribal elections and considerable social problems. Unemployment recently has been close to 50 percent. A large number of dwellings are without telephone service, and 21 percent of homes lack complete plumbing systems. Alcoholism and drug abuse are rampant, violent crime is a problem, and there is little economic development. Following a failed decades-long, $500 million effort to encourage the Navajo and Hopi to share land, the federal government in 2015 planned to remove members of each tribe from the property of the other.

The 1st District was drawn to be competitive politically. With its diversity and huge size, it is one of the most difficult in the nation to manage. Although Democrats still hold a 10-point voter registration advantage, the district has leaned slightly Republican in recent presidential elections. The copper mining counties of Greenlee, Graham, and Gila are historically Demo-

2012 Presidential Vote		
Mitt Romney (R)................131,115	(50%)
Barack Obama (D) 124,550	(48%)
2008 Presidential Vote		
John McCain (R)................131,209	(51%)
Barack Obama (D) 123,077	(48%)
Cook Partisan Voting Index: R+4		

cratic and still register that way, but they tend to vote Republican for president. Apache County, with its Navajo majority, is heavily Democratic. Coconino County is increasingly Democratic. But Pinal County, which has the most voters, leans Republican.

Ann Kirkpatrick (D)

Democrat Ann Kirkpatrick has won two tight elections, and lost another in 2010, in a diverse and swing district. In seeking to give Native Americans a greater voice in Washington, she literally tries to speak their language; she grew up speaking Apache and took lessons to learn Navajo. In May 2015, she became the leading Democratic challenger to Sen. John McCain for the 2016 campaign.

Kirkpatrick hails from the White Mountain Apache Nation reservation in eastern Arizona. Her father owned a general store and her mother was a public school teacher. Her uncle, William Bourdon, served in the state legislature, and Kirkpatrick campaigned for him while she was still in elementary school. After earning her bachelor's degree from the University of Arizona, she spent two years teaching in Tucson. She subsequently earned a law degree and worked as a prosecutor for the Coconino County Attorney's Office, specializing in drug crime cases. She later served as the city attorney of Sedona. In 2004, Kirkpatrick was elected to the state House of Representatives. At the time, conventional wisdom held that a non-Indian could not be elected from her district, where two-thirds of the registered voters were Native Americans. Undeterred, Kirkpatrick challenged incumbent Rep. Sylvia Laughter, a Navajo and political independent. Kirkpatrick campaigned door-to-door and won. In office, she worked to provide Indian tribes with money to build communications infrastructure.

When allegations of misconduct by Republican Rep. Rick Renzi surfaced in 2007, the Democratic Congressional Campaign Committee identified the seat as a top target in 2008. Kirkpatrick resigned from the state legislature to campaign for the Democratic nomination. (Renzi opted not to seek reelection and was convicted in 2013 on charges related to a land deal that allegedly benefited one of his former business partners.) Kirkpatrick won a four-way Democratic primary with 47 percent of the vote, and the DCCC helped with a fall advertising campaign. In the general election, she soundly defeated GOP antitax activist Sydney Hay. In the House, Kirkpatrick mostly supported President Barack Obama's agenda, voting for the $787 billion economic stimulus bill and the 2010 health care law.

Running for reelection in 2010, Kirkpatrick was challenged by Republican Paul Gosar, a dentist and political newcomer. Gosar attacked her support of the health care law and took a hard line on immigration, touting his endorsement from controversial Maricopa County Sheriff Joe Arpaio, known for his crackdowns on illegal immigrants. Kirkpatrick refused to follow many other Democrats in tight reelection contests that year who distanced themselves from the Obama administration, and she lost the race, 50%-44%. During the intervening two years, Kirkpatrick practiced law out of her home. She also dealt with tragedy after her mentor and good friend, Democratic Rep. Gabrielle Giffords, and 18 others were shot, six of them fatally, by a gunman in front of a Tucson grocery store. "I was devastated and grieved for a long time," Kirkpatrick said.

By 2012, redistricting had altered the 1st District to make it more favorable to a Democrat, but still very competitive. Gosar decided to run for reelection in the newly created and GOP-friendly 4th District. Kirkpatrick told *National Journal,* "I kind of looked around to see if there was anybody else in the district who was interested and who could win, and basically it boiled down to, 'We'll give it another try.'"

In mounting her comeback, Kirkpatrick faced Republican Jonathan Paton, an Iraq War veteran and former state legislator, in the rejiggered 1st District. Both candidates had to travel extensively to campaign, and the district's sizable Native American population worked to Kirkpatrick's advantage. Democrats attacked Paton for the brief work he did as a lobbyist for the payday-lending industry, while he hammered Kirkpatrick for spending too much tax-payer money on her staff. But 2012 proved to be a better year for Democrats than 2010, and Kirkpatrick pulled out a 49%-45% win over Paton, with Libertarian Kim Allen getting 6%.

In the House, Kirkpatrick struck up a surprisingly congenial working relationship with former foe Gosar. The two worked closely on legislation that affects their adjoining districts, including a plan to generate new jobs with the creation of a copper mine. It required federal approval of a land swap with mine operator Resolution Copper Mining Co., but the plan drew opposition from environmentalists. They co-sponsored a town hall meeting in Superior to drum up support for the mine. Kirkpatrick stood to benefit politically from taking a bipartisan approach.

In the fall of 2013, the National Republican Congressional Committee began running ads that again slammed her for supporting Obamacare. But Kirkpatrick argued that the law's expansion of Medicaid is popular with the district's poor, rural voters and maintains that any opponent who campaigns for repeal of Obamacare "is really out of step with this district." Her Republican opponent in 2014 was another state lawmaker, House Speaker Andy Tobin, who sought to make the campaign a referendum on Obama. But Tobin was hindered by his responsibilities as Speaker, and his primary contest was nasty and unexpectedly tight. Kirkpatrick this time placed more emphasis on her bipartisanship. In a surprising outcome, given the strong Republican performance nationwide, Kirkpatrick prevailed 52%-48%. Her victory margin in Coconino was roughly equal to Tobin's combined lead in Pinal and Pima (Tucson) counties. Kirkpatrick's lead of more than 10,000 votes in Apache County accounted for her overall margin of victory.

Starting her third term in the House in 2015, Kirkpatrick took a seat on the Agriculture Committee—the first House member from Arizona to serve on that panel since 1952. With Reps. Patrick Murphy of Florida and Collin Peterson of Minnesota, she is one of three surviving non-freshman House Democrats serving districts that Mitt Romney won in 2012. Not surprisingly, the NRCC in February 2015 placed her on its initial list of targets for 2016. Subsequently, Kirkpatrick entered the contest to oppose McCain. Other Democratic candidates could emerge with a Phoenix base. The contest for her House seat will be competitive, with perhaps a slight edge to Republicans, depending on the nominees.

SECOND DISTRICT

Martha McSally (R)

Elected 2014, 1st term; b. March 22, 1966, Warwick, RI; Air Force Academy, B.S. 1988, Harvard U, M.P.P. 1990, U.S. Air War College, M.S. 2007; Protestant; single.

Military Career: U.S. Air Force, 1988-2010 (Iraq: Afghanistan).

Professional Career: Legislative fellow, 1999-2000; National Security Studies professor, George C. Marshall Ctr, 2011-12.

DC Office: 1029 LHOB, 20515, 202-225-2542; Fax: 202-225-0378; Website: mcsally.house.gov.

State Offices: Sierra Vista, 520-459-3115; Tucson, 520-881-3588.

Committees: *Armed Services:* Oversight & Investigations; Tactical Air & Land Forces. *Homeland Security:* Emergency Preparedness, Response & Communications (Chmn); Border and Maritime Security.

Election Results

2014 general	Martha McSally (R)	109,704	(50%)	$4,466,678	$1,262,228	$4,855,268
	Ron Barber (D)	109,543	(50%)	$3,610,617	$441,559	$4,367,078
2014 primary	Martha McSally (D)	45,492	(69%)			
	Chuck Wooten (D)	14,995	(23%)			
	Shelley Kais	5,103	(8%)			

Population		Ethnicity		Income	
Total:	717,970	White	63.8%	Median income:	$45,176
Urban:	82.3%	Latino	26.5%		*(318 of 435)*
Suburban:	5.8%	Black	3.6%	Under $50,000	54.5%
Rural:	11.9%	Asian	2.9%	$50,000-$99,999:	28.0%
Land area:	7,070	Two races	2.1%	$100,000-$199,999:	14.2%
Pop/sq. mi.:	101.6	White Ethnic	27.5%	$200,000 or more:	3.3%
Born in state:	35.8%			Poverty Rate	17.1%
		Education			
Age Groups		H.S. grad or less:	31.6%	**Work**	
Under 18:	20.7%	Some college:	35.8%	White collar:	37.8%
18 to 34:	23.9%	College degree, 4 yr.:	18.6%	Blue collar:	46.7%
35 to 64:	36.4%	Post-grad study:	14.0%	Sales and service:	15.5%
Over 64:	19.0%				
		Military		Govt. workers:	19.5%
		Veterans/active duty:	14.3%		

Southeast Arizona: Tucson Metro

Arizona's first frontier was just south of today's Tucson, where Franciscan friars built Mission San Xavier del Bac in the 18th century. To the east, the late-19th century mining towns of Tombstone and Bisbee sprang up on mountainsides, where miners dug up gold, silver, and much of America's copper. In

Voter Turnout	
2013 Total Citizen 18+	531,047
2014 House Turnout	219,351
2014 Turnout as % CVAP	41.3%
2012 Turnout as % CVAP	55.8%

those wild and wicked mining days, the Earp brothers waged their famous gunfight against a gang of outlaws at the O.K. Corral in Tombstone. A 1957 movie starring Burt Lancaster and Kirk Douglas told that tale and helped to put the city on the tourism map. Cochise County, where Tombstone and Bisbee are located, was the most populous county when Arizona became the 48th state in 1912. Here the white man finally quashed the rebellion of the land-starved American Indian, when the Apache leader Geronimo faced the Army in 1900.

In recent years, Cochise County became an active frontier again. After the Border Patrol reduced illegal crossings in California and Texas, Mexicans trying to enter the United States illegally began coming to Agua Prieta, just across the border from the town of Douglas. There they fan out, cross the border, and use the area's numerous roads, mountain trails, and ranch lands to get to Tucson and Phoenix. The Border Patrol's Tucson sector has become the most active on the border in both apprehensions and illegal drug seizures. Stepped-up border enforcement and a reduced flow of illegal immigrants have resulted in decreases in these metrics—the 123,000 arrests in 2010 marked the lowest number in the Tucson sector since 1993. But the bodies of many who don't make it are still found in the mountains and in the desert. Border Patrol agent Brian Terry was killed in December 2010 as he patrolled in nearby Santa Cruz County. His death attracted widespread attention after two weapons from the shooting were traced to the Bureau of Alcohol, Tobacco, Firearms, and Explosives' failed "Fast and Furious" gun-trafficking operation. Drug trafficking remains active. In February 2015, when police in Cochise County seized nearly 4,800 pounds of marijuana, they subsequently located an elaborate drug-smuggling tunnel in the border town of Naco.

One immigrant destination is Tucson, Arizona's second metropolis. It is much smaller and politically less conservative than Phoenix. Tucson is a high-tech city and home to the University of Arizona. Defense giant Raytheon Co. has a huge missile plant at Tucson International Airport, which is in the 3rd District. Other companies have flocked to the city in recent years to work on solar energy projects. It is also a tourist destination, with famed resorts. Tucson does not share the wealth of Phoenix. In February 2015, the Census Bureau reported that Tucson was the nation's fifth-poorest city, with one in four residents in poverty.

For nearly 40 years, Tucson was the political base of the brothers Udall: Stewart, a House member in the 1950s and Interior secretary in the 1960s; and Morris, a House member for 30 years and a pioneering environmentalist who died in 1998. Stewart's son Tom Udall represents New Mexico in the Senate; a cousin, Stephen Udall, finished second in the 2002 Democratic primary in Arizona's 1st District.

The 2nd Congressional District includes most of Tucson, except the Latino-dominated west and south sides. It also includes the eastern half of surrounding Pima County and much southeastern Arizona high desert real estate, including all of mountainous Cochise County, the small, border-crossing town of Douglas, and the city of Sierra Vista near Fort Huachuca, the site of the Army Military Intelligence Center, where military interrogators are trained. Politically, it is very closely divided, voting for Arizona GOP favorite son John McCain by less than

2012 Presidential Vote		
Mitt Romney (R)................149,651	(50%)
Barack Obama (D) 144,966	(48%)
2008 Presidential Vote		
John McCain (R)................153,730	(50%)
Barack Obama (D) 150,896	(49%)
Cook Partisan Voting Index: R+3		

a percentage point in 2008 and for Republican Mitt Romney by just two points in 2012. After redistricting, the district shed some Republican suburbs north of Tucson. But this remains among the most competitive districts in the nation, a place where political centrism can be rewarded.

Martha McSally (R)

Republican Martha McSally, elected in 2014, made history by being the first woman to fly and command an Air Force squadron in combat. Two years after narrowly losing to Democratic Rep. Ron Barber, she campaigned on her extensive military background to win a rematch that wasn't officially decided for more than six weeks.

A Rhode Island native, McSally came to Arizona in the early 1990s when she was assigned to Davis-Monthan Air Force Base in Tucson. She had graduated from the Air Force Academy in 1988 with a biology degree. Two years later, she received a master's in public policy from Harvard University. In 1999, McSally was selected for a Washington, D.C.-based fellowship program. Through the program, she served as a national security adviser to Republican Sen. Jon Kyl of Arizona.

McSally retired as a colonel in the Air Force with more than 2,600 flight hours. She served multiple tours in the Middle East and supervised the execution of an air campaign based in Saudi Arabia for Operation Iraqi Freedom. She also led a combat deployment to Afghanistan for Operation Enduring Freedom. In 2007, McSally received her second master's degree from the Air Force Air War College.

She drew national attention after she filed—and won—a 2001 lawsuit against the Defense Department to overturn a policy that required U.S. servicewomen based in Saudi Arabia to wear a body-covering Muslim *abaya* and headscarf. In an interview on CBS's *60 Minutes*, she criticized what she called other forms of discrimination in the conservative Saudi culture. "I can fly a single-seat aircraft in enemy territory, but [in Saudi Arabia] I can't drive a vehicle," she said.

Barber, a former aide to Rep. Gabrielle Giffords who was injured alongside the former congresswoman in a 2011 mass shooting in Tucson, won a 2012 special election to fill her vacated seat. McSally finished second among five candidates in the Republican primary for the special election, but handily won the 2012 primary for the two-year term. Barber's general-election race against McSally drew controversy: The Democratic-backed House Majority PAC changed an ad that showed McSally in a kitchen cooking "a recipe for disaster" after she called it sexist. Meanwhile, McSally was criticized for saying, "I resemble Gabby Giffords more than the man who worked for her." Barber prevailed with a 2,454-vote margin out of more than 292,000 votes cast.

In their rematch, Barber and McSally fought another contentious battle. At one debate, they sparred over stricter gun-control laws, with McSally criticizing an ad by Giffords' Americans for Responsible Solutions political committee that said the Republican "opposes making it harder for stalkers to get a gun." McSally, who revealed she was a victim of stalking, called the ad "horrendous." Giffords's group ended up spending more than $2 million on behalf of Barber, in what turned out to be one of the most expensive House races of the year. McSally raised about $4.8 million compared with $4 million for Barber. Spending by outside groups exceeded $10 million, and was roughly equal for each side.

Election night didn't end the skirmishing between the candidates. Just over a week after the election, McSally held a lead of fewer than 200 votes and declared victory. But the narrow margin triggered a mandatory recount under Arizona law. Barber, meanwhile, sought several ways to get additional provisional and early ballots counted, but failed each time. On December 17, Maricopa County Superior Court Judge Katherine Cooper ruled McSally ahead by 167 votes, settling the election. In Cochise County, which cast 16 percent of the total vote, McSally won by 7,060 votes. Barber took Pima by 6,893 votes. *National Journal* wrote that McSally's military background shaped her politically "not only because it cultivated toughness, but because it made her an expert in refusing to take no for an answer."

In the House, McSally won her coveted seat on the Armed Services Committee even before she was declared the election winner. Following her committee selection, she vowed to be a strong voice for both the military and for Raytheon's weapons programs in Tucson. In January 2015, she praised the Pentagon's decision to lift its ban on women soldiers taking on combat roles as "long overdue." In contrast to the other four House Republicans in the Arizona delegation, she voted with party leaders in March 2015 to support full-year funding of the Homeland Security Department.

The recent history of this district makes it likely that McSally will face a competitive challenge in 2016.

THIRD DISTRICT

Raúl Grijalva (D)

Elected 2002, 7th term; b. Feb. 19, 1948, Tucson; U. of AZ, B.A. 1986; Catholic; married (Ramona); 3 children.

Elected Office: Tucson Unified Schl. Dist. Governing Bd., 1974-86; Pima Cnty. Bd. of Supervisors, 1988-2002.

Professional Career: Asst. dean of Hispanic Affairs, U. of AZ., 1987.

DC Office: 1511 LHOB, 20515, 202-225-2435; Fax: 202-225-1541; Website: grijalva.house.gov.

State Offices: Avondale, 623-536-3388; Somerton, 928-343-7933; Tucson, 520-622-6788.

Committees: *Education & the Workforce:* Early Childhood, Elementary & Secondary Education; Higher Education & Workforce Training. *Natural Resources* (RMM: ex officio member of each subcommittee).

Group Ratings

	ADA	ACLU	AFL-CIO	LCV	ITI	COC	HAFA	ACU	CFG	FRC
2014	100%	88%	–	97%	20%	29%	17%	12%	17%	0%
2013	100%	C	100%	89%	C	23%	C	17%	16%	C

National Journal Ratings

	2013 LIB	—	2013 CONS
Economic	86%	—	14%
Social	93%	—	0%
Foreign	86%	—	14%
Composite	90%	—	11%

Key Votes of the 113th Congress

1. Sandy storm spending	Y	5. Medical Marijuana	Y	9. Syrian Rebels Training	N
2. Violence Against Women Act	Y	6. Farm Bill	N	10. Keystone pipeline	N
3. Guantanamo Bay Detainees	N	7. Afghanistan Combat	Y	11. Immigration Exec. Action	N
4. Abortion 20-week ban	N	8. NSA Phone Data Collection	Y	12. Bipartisan budget deal	N

Election Results

2014 general	Raúl Grijalva (D) 58,192	(56%)	$560,866	$4,458
	Gabriela Saucedo Mercer (R) 46,185	(44%)	$103,441	
2014 primary	Raul Grijalva (D) ....unopposed			

Prior winning percentages: 2012 (58%), 2010 (50%), 2008 (63%), 2006 (61%), 2004 (62%), 2002 (59%)

Population		Race and Ethnicity		Income	
Total:	722,963	Latino	61.1%	Median income:	$39,843
Urban:	52.8%	White	28.0%		*(392 of 435)*
Suburban:	28.1%	Amer. Indian	4.3%	Under $50,000	60.1%
Rural:	19.1%	Black	4.2%	$50,000-$99,999:	28.7%
Land area:	8,448	Two races	0.8%	$100,000-$199,999:	9.9%
Pop/sq. mi.:	85.6	White Ethnic	12.2%	$200,000 or more:	1.3%
Born in state:	46.5%			Poverty Rate	23.4%
		Education			
Age Groups		H.S. grad or less:	53.9%	**Work**	
Under 18:	27.7%	Some college:	30.9%	White collar:	26.0%
18 to 34:	26.8%	College degree, 4 yr.:	9.8%	Blue collar:	47.1%
35 to 64:	35.0%	Post-grad study:	5.4%	Sales and service:	26.9%
Over 64:	10.4%				
		Military		Govt. workers:	19.0%
		Veterans/active duty:	8.0%		

Southwest Arizona: Tucson West, Western Phoenix Exurbs

Southern Arizona, although technically part of Mexico for hundreds of years, was never a home to Latin American civilization the way northern New Mexico has been. Here the hot desert land was inhabited mainly by Native American tribes such as the Apache and Cocopah. They kept their culture and language alive in the region until they were uprooted by English-speaking whites who came in on cavalry horses and in miners' wagons and railroad cars in the late 19th century. In 1854, the Gadsden Purchase—$10 million to Mexico for 30,000 square miles of desert—cleared the way for a southern transcontinental railroad. Today's Hispanic Arizonans are mostly descendants of later emigrants from Mexico, some of whom came over the border in the sleepier days before World War II, when *la frontera* was scarcely patrolled. Many more came in the 1980s to partake in the dazzling economic growth in the region that lasted over a quarter-century. That immigration pattern has slowed considerably in recent years, with the collapse of the real estate market in Arizona and stronger enforcement along the Mexican border.

Voter Turnout	
2013 Total Citizen 18+	434,790
2014 House Turnout	104,428
2014 Turnout as % CVAP	24%
2012 Turnout as % CVAP	41.6%

The 3rd Congressional District is one of the state's two Hispanic-majority districts, with a population that is 61 percent Hispanic. One of the two overwhelmingly Democratic districts in the state, it is geographically huge, sharing 293 miles of border with Mexico. The district is a collection of four distant communities connected by many square miles of uninhabited Sonoran desert.

One is the suburb of Avondale west of downtown Phoenix, home to Phoenix International Raceway. Avondale is also the site of the Palo Verde Nuclear Generating Station, the nation's largest nuclear generation facility and the only one not located by a large body of water. The second community is the heavily Latino and mostly low-income west and south sides of Tucson, where the University of Arizona, the largest employer in southern Arizona, is located. The third is the Mexican border town of Nogales, which is 95 percent Hispanic and located near many maquiladora plants. It is one of the busiest cargo terminals along the Mexican border, but it also has long been an entry point for the drug trade and the scene of many illegal border crossings in recent years. The twin smuggling tides—drugs and people—have inflicted damage on the fragile desert ecosystem. The federal government has responded with money-laundering restrictions that have adversely affected the dealings of some banks with produce companies. The fourth is Yuma, located on the California border at a Colorado River crossing in an irrigated agricultural valley that is often the hottest place in the country. The lower Colorado produces much of the nation's lettuce and in the winter is a magnet for RV campers.

Out in the desert you find the Organ Pipe Cactus National Monument, the Sonoran Desert National Monument, the Tohono O'odham Indian Reservation, and the Barry M. Goldwater Air Force Range, the largest aerial gunnery range after

2012 Presidential Vote
Barack Obama (D) 108,902   (61%)
Mitt Romney (R)...................65,482   (37%)

2008 Presidential Vote
Barack Obama (D) 102,735   (58%)
John McCain (R)...................71,883   (41%)

Cook Partisan Voting Index: D+8

Nevada's Nellis Air Force Range. However, 95 percent of it is not used for target practice in order to protect the habitat of the endangered Sonoran pronghorn antelope. Near Nogales, other unique forms of wildlife are found in the Tumacacori Highlands, including endangered species such as the jaguar, peregrine falcon, Chiricahua leopard frog and the Mexican spotted owl. With its brutal desert heat, the Baboquivari trail that runs north to the Tohono O'odham Nation has been the deadliest immigrant crossing in the nation. In early 2015, a decrease in crime led Border Patrol officials to reopen to the public all 516 square miles of the Organ Pipe park.

Raúl Grijalva (D)

Raúl Grijalva, a Democrat first elected in 2002, is one of the House's most liberal members. He took over in 2015 as ranking Democrat on the Natural Resources Committee, which gives him a platform for his outspoken progressive views that often feature a border perspective.

Grijalva was born and grew up in Tucson, the son of a *bracero*, or guest worker, who emigrated from Mexico in 1945. He says his personal hero is Robert F. Kennedy because of "his vision and his love for this country, and his care and compassion for all Americans." He graduated from the University of Arizona and has deep roots in the immigrant community on the city's southwest side. He was director of El Pueblo Neighborhood Center and assistant dean for Hispanic student affairs at the university. In 1974, he was elected to the Tucson school board and served 12 years. In 1988, he was elected a Pima County supervisor and served 14 years. As supervisor, he backed an effort to extend medical and dental benefits to same-sex domestic partners of county employees and focused on affordable health care, family and children services, and economic growth. Developers and builders helped elect him to office, but his support for planned growth and impact fees later alienated them.

In the House, his rhetoric often matches the fervor of his voting record. In 2008, Grijalva was elected co-chair of what was then the 75-member Progressive Caucus. In that position, he initially insisted that any health care overhaul include a government-run insurance option to compete with private insurers, but he later backed away from that demand. He also espoused a "war tax" that year to finance military operations in Afghanistan, an effort he considered immoral. Speaking in opposition to GOP plans to repeal President Barack Obama's Affordable Care Act, he said in February 2012, "We must protect the American people from the Republican 'No Care' agenda. Their agenda for America is simple: No care if you lose your job. No care if you or your child has a preexisting condition." In December 2014, he spoke out against the bipartisan omnibus spending bill and said that Democrats need to do a better job of defining where they stand.

Much of his effort has been focused on immigration policy. He has co-sponsored bills to raise the number of low-skill visas from 5,000 to 400,000 and to allow legalization for some illegal immigrants, provided they pay a $500 civil fine. After Arizona state lawmakers passed a controversial immigration bill in 2010 expanding law enforcement's powers to detain suspected immigrants, Grijalva took the unusual step of urging a boycott of his state, calling on sympathetic organizations to refrain from using Arizona as a convention site. He abandoned the boycott idea after a federal judge halted implementation of most of the immigration law. In 2014, he encouraged the efforts of Republican Mario Diaz-Balart of Florida to find common ground on a bipartisan plan to approve immigration changes that he viewed as "low-hanging fruit." But Diaz-Balart failed to secure support from Republican leaders. When a federal judge in Texas in February 2015 ordered a stop to Obama's executive order aimed at protecting some illegal immigrants, Grijalva said: "This injunction is not the result of sound legal action—it is the result of a lawsuit shopped around by attorneys general and governors intent on undermining the president's efforts."

His initial focus on environmental and energy issues was popular at home. He worked to stop uranium mining in the Kaibab National Forest and on federal lands near the Grand Canyon, and he was behind efforts to create a Sonoran Desert conservation system, which would protect 3.3 million acres and 56 miles of trails. Grijalva sponsored legislation creating a Public Lands Service Corps to train federal land managers as well as to protect parts of Pima and Santa Cruz counties from future mining claims, and he has stuck up for the San Carlos Apache Tribe in battling copper-mining operations around its lands. Combining his interests in the environment and immigration, he has implored Homeland Security Department officials to take into account protecting native plants and species when building fences and other security checkpoints at the border.

At the Natural Resources Committee, Grijalva became the ranking Democrat in January 2015. Grace Napolitano of California decided not to seek the position even though she had more seniority. Two years earlier, Grjalva had stirred the pot when he unsuccessfully challenged the far more senior Peter DeFazio of Oregon for the top post. When documents were released in February 2015 that suggested fossil-fuel companies were underwriting the research of climate-change skeptics, Grijalva wrote to seven universities requesting detailed records. He worked with Democratic leaders in opposing House Republican efforts to require approval of the Keystone XL pipeline. He planned hearings across the country to seek the views of Hispanics and other minority groups on environmental issues.

Despite the strongly Democratic foundation of his district, Grijalva has faced reelection challenges. In 2010, Republican Ruth McClung, a 28-year-old physicist, voiced the slogan "Boycott Grijalva, not Arizona." She got help from tea party groups, along with a televised endorsement from Republican Sen. John McCain, and pulled nearly even in polls. At the same time, Grijalva's abandonment of the boycott did not help him with his Hispanic base of supporters. But national Democrats raced to his assistance with ads, and he eked out a 50%-44% victory. Two years later, he had a far easier time against Republican Gabriela Saucedo Mercer, a conservative activist who described him as a "Marxist." He won 58%-37%.

When the *Arizona Republic* reported in January 2014 that Grijalva had missed 13 percent of the previous year's congressional votes, giving him one of the worst attendance records in Congress, he shrugged it off. "I had perfect attendance in the fifth grade," he told the newspaper. "That didn't make me the smartest kid in the class." In a rematch with Saucedo Mercer, he won with 56 percent. In Pima County, which cast nearly half of the total vote, Grijalva led 61%-39%. But he trailed narrowly in Maricopa County and barely led in Yuma. Saucedo Mercer spent only $103,000. Even with his solid Democratic base, those numbers suggest that Grijalva could be at risk to an aggressive challenger, or when the state has redistricting changes.

FOURTH DISTRICT

Paul Gosar (R)

Elected 2010, 3rd term; b. Nov. 27, 1958, Rock Springs, WY; Creighton U., B.S. 1981, D.D.S. 1985; Catholic; married (Maude); 3 children.

Professional Career: Owner, dental practice.

DC Office: 504 CHOB, 20515, 202-225-2315; Fax: 202-226-9739; Website: gosar.house.gov.

State Offices: Gold Canyon, 480-882-2697; Prescott, 928-445-1683.

Committees: *Natural Resources:* Energy & Mineral Resources; Indian, Insular & Alaskan Native Affairs; Water, Power & Oceans (VChmn). *Oversight & Government Reform:* Interior; Information Technology.

Group Ratings

	ADA	ACLU	AFL-CIO	LCV	ITI	COC	HAFA	ACU	CFG	FRC
2014	10%	33%	–	3%	40%	58%	77%	92%	93%	100%
2013	10%	C	10%	4%	C	69%	C	92%	83%	C

National Journal Ratings

	2013 LIB	—	2013 CONS
Economic	12%	—	87%
Social	13%	—	84%
Foreign	50%	—	50%
Composite	26%	—	74%

Key Votes of the 113th Congress

1. Sandy storm spending		N	5. Medical Marijuana	N	9. Syrian Rebels Training	N
2. Violence Against Women Act	N	6. Farm Bill	Y	10. Keystone pipeline	Y
3. Guantanamo Bay Detainees	N	7. Afghanistan Combat	N	11. Immigration Exec. Action	P
4. Abortion 20-week ban	Y	8. NSA Phone Data Collection	Y	12. Bipartisan budget deal	N

Election Results

2014 general	Paul Gosar (R)............................122,560	(70%)	$401,797
	Mikel Weisser (D) 45,179	(26%)	$32,624
	Chris Rike (Lib) 7,440	(4%)	
2014 primary	Paul Gosar (R)......................unopposed		

Prior winning percentages: 2012 (67%), 2010 (50%)

Population		Race and Ethnicity		Income	
Total:	732,689	White	74.5%	Median income:	$43,436
Urban:	25.9%	Latino	19.4%		*(339 of 435)*
Suburban:	42.7%	Amer. Indian	1.8%	Under $50,000	56.9%
Rural:	31.4%	Black	1.5%	$50,000-$99,999:	31.4%
Land area:	21,669	Two races	1.9%	$100,000-$199,999:	10.0%
Pop/sq. mi.:	33.8	White Ethnic	26.0%	$200,000 or more:	1.7%
Born in state:	27.3%			Poverty Rate	17.4%
		Education			
Age Groups		H.S. grad or less:	45.5%	**Work**	
Under 18:	21.2%	Some college:	37.2%	White collar:	28.8%
18 to 34:	17.2%	College degree, 4 yr.:	10.8%	Blue collar:	48.9%
35 to 64:	37.5%	Post-grad study:	6.5%	Sales and service:	22.2%
Over 64:	24.0%				
		Military		Govt. workers:	15.4%
		Veterans/active duty:	14.8%		

Central/Western Arizona: Eastern Phoenix Exurbs, Lake Havasu City

Beyond the cities of Phoenix and Tucson, much of Arizona looks as it did a century ago. Some places maintain a timeless Western look, like Wickenburg, the oldest Arizona town north of Tucson. Others preserve antiquated ways of life, such as the polygamist community of Colorado City, just south of Utah. In

Voter Turnout	
2013 Total Citizen 18+	541,385
2014 House Turnout	175,179
2014 Turnout as % CVAP	32.4%
2012 Turnout as % CVAP	48.6%

some cases, nature and settlement juxtapose jarringly: The real London Bridge has been transplanted to Lake Havasu City, a retirement community on the Colorado River and a popular spring break destination for college students.

Approximately the size of Massachusetts, the expansive 4th Congressional District stretches from the Hoover Dam and Lake Mead in the northwest corner of the state down all the way to the outskirts of Yuma and nearly to the border of Mexico, and it spans east to Prescott and beyond to the Phoenix exurbs in Pinal County. The district covers La Paz County, most of Mohave and Yavapai counties, and parts of Yuma, Gila, and Pinal counties, along with a tiny slice of Maricopa. Its population center is in fast-growing Prescott, the place where Barry Goldwater announced his presidential campaign in 1964. Once a gold mining camp, Prescott has been home since 1888 to America's oldest annual rodeo and it retains the charming markers of an older city. Its Yavapai County Courthouse Plaza has been called one of America's Great Public Spaces by the American Planning Association, which described it as "a majestic, man-made urban forest in the heart of a historic commercial district." The plaza is a popular local gathering spot for everything from music festivals to campaign kick-offs. In 2014, city leaders drafted a General Plan for the future of Prescott, which focused on issues such as land use, growth management and open space. Affordable housing remained a prime concern.

The district's economy is fueled by tourism, with visitors coming to explore Western folklore. Jerome, a mining town built improbably on hillside stilts, has been reborn as an artist colony. Bullhead City is home to the annual River Regatta, where

2012 Presidential Vote		
Mitt Romney (R).................173,394	(67%)	
Barack Obama (D) 80,035	(31%)	
2008 Presidential Vote		
John McCain (R).................161,081	(64%)	
Barack Obama (D) 86,282	(34%)	
Cook Partisan Voting Index: R+20		

participants take an eight-mile float down the Colorado. The district is a retirement haven, and also a mecca for second homes. Prescott and Lake Havasu are among the most popular retirement destinations in the country. According to the Census Bureau, Lake Havasu has become the "remarriage capital" of the nation; in this self-styled "party town," 42 percent of women and 41 percent of men have married at least twice. The number of retirees, along with upwardly striving, family-oriented young migrants, infuse the area with a cultural and political conservatism, helping to make the newly drawn 4th the most Republican in the state and in the top 10 percent nationwide.

Paul Gosar (R)

Republican Paul Gosar, after surviving two competitive elections, has settled into the Republican-friendly 4th District, and he has signed on with party renegades in the House.

Gosar grew up in Pinedale Wyoming, a town of fewer than 2,000 residents near the headwaters of the Green River. Gosar's father, a geologist with Belco Petroleum and Union Pacific, was often away working on rigs, and an uncle, who was a dentist, stepped in as a role model during those absences. Gosar went on to study dentistry at Creighton University with the expectation that he would return to Wyoming to enter practice with his uncle. His father, however, advised him to seek a more vibrant economy. "My dad took me aside and said, 'I don't think the right time is here. I think the minerals, the oil, and gas are going to crash,'" Gosar recalled. After receiving his D.D.S. in 1985, Gosar landed in Flagstaff, Ariz. Appealing to a local banker for financing to launch his practice in 1985, Gosar says he emphasized his frugality, vowing to eat nothing but peanut-butter-and-jelly sandwiches until his business was established.

When he decided to challenge freshman 1st District Democratic Rep. Ann Kirkpatrick in the 2010 election, Gosar was motivated by his contempt for the health care overhaul that the Democratic Congress enacted. In his campaign, Gosar sharply criticized her votes for President Barack Obama's agenda in Congress. He also took a hard line on immigration, touting his endorsement from Maricopa County Sheriff Joe Arpaio, who has aggressively pursued illegal immigrants in Arizona. Kirkpatrick refused to distance herself from the administration. Her ads highlighted her support for Obama's initiatives and cast Gosar as an irresponsible millionaire who was late paying business and property taxes 12 times. Going into the closing weeks of the contest, Kirkpatrick had $870,000 to spend, compared with Gosar's $49,000. But he received help from the American Dental Association and other medical groups that opposed the health care law. He also got help from tea party activists. The national GOP wave in high-growth areas like this district helped to seal his 50%-44% victory.

In Washington, Gosar immediately made clear his contempt for Washington's typical ways. He told a reporter that the formal swearing-in ceremony on the House floor felt awkward, and that Congress should have held a barbecue with legislators serving people. On the Oversight and Government Reform Committee in 2011, he became one of the first House members to call on Attorney General Eric Holder to resign because of the failed "Operation Fast and Furious," a program that facilitated the sale of thousands of weapons to Mexican drug cartels. In an interview with *The Daily Caller*, he accused Holder and other government officials of possibly being "accessories to murder" for their roles. Gosar continued to lead attacks on Holder, which resulted in the House vote in June 2012 to cite the attorney general for contempt of Congress. The vote was 255-67, with 108 Democrats not voting.

On the Natural Resources Committee, Gosar enacted a law aimed at eliminating red tape on a dam project spanning the Coconino and Tonto national forests. In 2014, Congress approved as part of its annual defense spending bill his proposal to swap 2,400 acres of Tonto forest land—which includes the San Carlos Apache reservation—to make way for a new $4 billion copper mine. In exchange, the Resolution Copper Company gave up land scattered across the state. Sen. John McCain of Arizona strongly backed that proposal, which removed land restrictions that had been imposed in 1955. Gosar spoke out against the administration's management of national forests and grasslands, saying that constituents were left "vulnerable to catastrophic wildfires." He unsuccessfully tried to amend legislation on the

House floor to abolish Davis-Bacon Act requirements that federal contractors pay a prevailing union wage, calling them onerous for businesses.

Concerned over his reelection prospects, and faced with new redistricting lines that bolstered Democrats, Gosar in January 2012 announced he would move out of his Flagstaff home and run in the more Republican-leaning 4th District. (Kirkpatrick would win back the 1st District seat.) Pinal County Sheriff Paul Babeu, a hard-liner on illegal immigration, initially was considered the front-runner, but his campaign's momentum halted when a former boyfriend (and illegal immigrant) accused him of threatening deportation to keep their relationship quiet. Babeu came out as gay but denied the allegations, and he was reelected as sheriff.

That left Gosar with two challengers in the August 2012 GOP primary: state Sen. Ron Gould of Lake Havasu City and radio station owner Rick Murphy of Bullhead City. Gould, regarded as one of the Arizona legislature's most conservative members, waged an aggressive campaign against Gosar, attacking him for being the only Republican in Arizona's House delegation to support the 2011 deal to raise the nation's debt limit. The anti-tax group Club for Growth contributed heavily to Gould's campaign, but the American Dental Association's political action committee countered with help for a fellow dentist. Gosar won with 51% to Gould's 32% and Murphy's 17%. Gosar won easily in November against a largely unknown Democrat. In 2014, he breezed to reelection without a GOP primary.

On the opening day of Congress in January 2015, Gosar was one of 25 House Republicans who opposed giving John Boehner another term as Speaker. Instead, he voted for Rep. Daniel Webster of Florida. "Our leadership in D.C. should be bold and determined," Gosar said in a statement. "We do not need more status quo." Two months later, Gosar blamed Senate Republicans for congressional failure to stand firm against Obama's executive action on immigration, and conceded that Boehner was not entirely at fault. He became an active participant in the House GOP's Freedom Caucus, which prepared conservative policy alternatives.

FIFTH DISTRICT

Matt Salmon (R)

Elected 2012, 5th term; b. Jan. 21, 1958, Salt Lake City, UT; AZ St. U., B.A. 1981, Brigham Young U., M.P.A. 1986; Mormon; married (Nancy); 4 children.

Elected Office: AZ Senate, 1990-94; U.S. House, 1995-2001.

Professional Career: Public affairs mgr., US West, 1981-94; Chmn., AZ Republican Party, 2004-07; Lobbyist, Greenberg Traurig, 2005-07; Pres., COMPTEL, 2008-09; Pres., Upstream Consulting, 2003-present.

DC Office: 2349 RHOB, 20515, 202-225-2635; Fax: 202-226-4386; Website: salmon.house.gov.

State Offices: Gilbert, 480-699-8239.

Committees: *Education & the Workforce:* Health, Employment, Labor & Pensions; Higher Education & Workforce Training. *Foreign Affairs:* Asia & the Pacific (Chmn); Western Hemisphere.

Group Ratings

	ADA	ACLU	AFL-CIO	LCV	ITI	COC	HAFA	ACU	CFG	FRC
2014	20%	5%	–	3%	60%	50%	94%	96%	98%	100%
2013	5%	C	10%	7%	C	69%	C	100%	100%	C

National Journal Ratings

	2013 LIB	—	2013 CONS
Economic	3%	—	96%
Social	16%	—	74%
Foreign	44%	—	56%
Composite	23%	—	77%

Key Votes of the 113th Congress

1. Sandy storm spending		5. Medical Marijuana	N	9. Syrian Rebels Training	N
2. Violence Against Women Act	N	6. Farm Bill	N	10. Keystone pipeline	Y
3. Guantanamo Bay Detainees	N	7. Afghanistan Combat	N	11. Immigration Exec. Action	Y
4. Abortion 20-week ban	Y	8. NSA Phone Data Collection	Y	12. Bipartisan budget deal	N

Election Results

2014 general   Matt Salmon (R) 124,867   (70%) $574,359

                  James Woods (D)........................ 54,596   (30%) $56,750

2014 primary   Matt Salmon (R) .... unopposed

Prior winning percentages: 2012 (67%), 1998 (65%), 1996 (60%), 1994 (56%)

Population		Race and Ethnicity		Income	
Total:	759,102	White	71.2%	Median income:	$65,288
Urban:	49.0%	Latino	18.4%		*(80 of 435)*
Suburban:	51.0%	Asian	3.8%	Under $50,000	38.4%
Rural:	0.0%	Black	3.4%	$50,000-$99,999:	32.3%
Land area:	346	Tworaces	2.1%	$100,000-$199,999:	24.5%
Pop/sq. mi.:	2,194.3	WhiteEthnic	22.2%	$200,000 or more:	4.9%
Born in state:	36.2%			Poverty Rate	9.1%
		Education			
Age Groups		H.S. grad or less:	29.0%	**Work**	
Under 18:	27.4%	Some college:	35.9%	White collar:	43.4%
18to34:	19.4%	College degree, 4yr.:	22.4%	Blue collar:	41.7%
35to64:	38.2%	Post-gradstudy:	12.7%	Sales and service:	14.9%
Over64:	15.0%				
		Military		Govt. workers:	11.4%
		Veterans/activeduty:	9.9%		

Eastern Phoenix Suburbs: Eastern Mesa, Gilbert

The city of Phoenix is exceedingly young. Conservative trailblazer Barry Goldwater, born in 1909, grew up knowing people who remembered when the Valley of the Sun—or the Valley, as most people say—was virtually empty, with a few parched settlements set above a dry riverbed. As late as 1950, only 107,000

Voter Turnout	
2013 Total Citizen 18+	517,305
2014 House Turnout	179,463
2014 Turnout as % CVAP	34.7%
2012 Turnout as % CVAP	57.5%

people lived in Phoenix and 332,000 in all of Maricopa County. But the air conditioner and military technology transformed Phoenix into today's high-rise studded metropolis, with 1.5 million city dwellers and slightly more than 4 million people in Maricopa County, as of 2013. From 2000 to 2011, Maricopa's population grew by 26 percent. The growth slowed to 5 percent from 2010 to 2013, thanks to the collapse of the local housing market and the state's crackdowns on illegal immigration. Still, many parts of the nation would welcome such an increase. Gilbert's population doubled to 208,543 from 2000 to 2010 and passed Tempe in Arizona's population rankings. This is not, as some people think, a giant retirement village, nor is it overrun by crooked land salesmen and fast-buck artists, though Phoenix has attracted its share of each.

Maricopa's second-largest city is Mesa, south of the Salt River and east of Phoenix. It was founded by Mormons in 1878 on one square mile and was laid out Salt Lake City-style on broad streets with large lots. A gleaming white Mormon temple was built in 1927, one of the few in the United States then. In 1950, Mesa had 17,000 people, and more than half of its residents earned their living from farming, primarily citrus and cotton. In 2013, it had 457,000 people, more than Minneapolis and St. Louis. A former Air Force base is now the Phoenix-Mesa Gateway Airport, with plans for it to become a major multimodal center for passengers and freight. Despite earlier hopes to grow beyond small carriers, its recent passenger traffic has been chiefly with Allegiant Air. In February 2012, the Mesa Arts Center hosted the final nationally televised Republican presidential debate. In March 2015, the state Supreme Court approved creative plans to use existing highway funds to finance expansion of light rail in Mesa.

The 5th Congressional District of Arizona is made up of Phoenix's East Valley suburbs, namely Mesa, Chandler, Gilbert, and Queen Creek. Nicknamed the Silicon Desert, Chandler has become one of the fastest-growing high-tech centers in the country, with companies drawn to relatively cheap real estate and semiconductor chip maker Intel's longstanding presence. Intel, the largest employer in the region, maintains its second-biggest facility in Chandler and the company has completed a neighboring manufacturing facility, known as Fab 42, which was expected to employ 1,000 additional workers. But that planned 2013 opening was delayed by a drop in personal computer sales; two existing Intel facilities were retrofitted as temporary steps. Houston-based data center operator CyrusOne plans a 1 million-square-foot data center, slated to be the largest of its kind in the U.S. In February 2015, Apple announced that it will build a $2 billion data center in Mesa, which will serve as the control center

2012 Presidential Vote		
Mitt Romney (R)................187,304		(64%)
Barack Obama (D) 101,511		(35%)
2008 Presidential Vote		
John McCain (R)................179,647		(63%)
Barack Obama (D) 104,100		(36%)
Cook Partisan Voting Index: R+17		

for Apple's four other U.S.-based data operations. It will be powered entirely by renewable energy.

The 5th includes some high-income precincts, but the district's cultural tone is resolutely middle class. It is the second most heavily Republican district in the state, giving presidential nominee Mitt Romney 64 percent of the vote in 2012.

Matt Salmon (R)

Republican Matt Salmon has been a conservative activist during his two stints in the House, which were separated by a 12-year hiatus following his self-imposed, three-term pledge. In each case, he has not been reticent to challenge his party leaders.

Salmon was born in Salt Lake City. His father worked for Mountain Bell Telephone, and a promotion led the family to relocate to Albuquerque. The Salmons eventually settled near Mesa, where he was president of his high school student body. As a Mormon, Salmon did his missionary work in Taiwan from 1977 to 1979. "We spoke Mandarin every day, and after six months there, I was dreaming in Chinese," he recalled. In 1981, he graduated from Arizona State University. He later worked in public affairs for telecommunications company US West. Salmon was elected to the Arizona Senate in 1990 and rose to become assistant majority leader.

In 1994, he ran for Congress as part of the Newt Gingrich-led group of Republicans who called themselves revolutionaries and campaigned on a national agenda called the "Contract With America." In the general election, he faced off against Democratic state Sen. Chuck Blanchard, a former clerk for Supreme Court Justice Sandra Day O'Connor. Blanchard took some moderate positions and ran a tough campaign. But Salmon still won, 56%-39%, and Republicans took control of the House for the first time in 40 years.

During his first tour in the House, Salmon served on the International Relations Committee, since renamed the Foreign Affairs Committee. He took a keen interest in issues related to China, criticizing the communist government for human rights violations. After meeting with Chinese President Jiang Zemin, he helped secure the release of imprisoned academic Song Yongyi. One of Salmon's accomplishments was coauthoring "Aimee's Law," which used financial measures to discourage states from releasing incarcerated rapists and murderers. Among Republicans, he was a leading rebel—not only against the previous 40 years of Democratic policies but, often vociferously, against Speaker Newt Gingrich. In 1997, he was a supporter of the attempted "coup" against Gingrich. After the election the next year, Gingrich quit under pressure—with Salmon among the first who publicly urged him to go. Unlike many of the Republicans elected in the 1994 class, he was faithful to a self-imposed term limit on his service.

Salmon ran an unsuccessful bid for governor against Janet Napolitano in 2002, and later became chairman of the Arizona Republican Party. He also registered to lobby, working on telecommunications issues and serving as president of the high-tech trade association COMPTEL.

In 2011, Salmon launched his campaign to return to Congress, emphasizing the need to curb the national debt. "My feeling is, if guys like me that can make a difference don't try, then shame on us," he said. The GOP primary pitted the more youthful former state House Speaker Kirk Adams against the more experienced Salmon. In a debate, Adams characterized Salmon as past his prime, while Salmon countered that seniority is important in Washington. Republican Gov. Jan Brewer and former Florida Gov. Jeb Bush endorsed Salmon, while Adams got the support of Rep. Jeff Flake and Republican Sens. John McCain and Jon Kyl of Arizona. Salmon also won endorsements from the anti-tax group Club for Growth and *The Arizona Republic*.

The two candidates agreed on most issues, pushing for less regulation and lower taxes. Adams ran an ad accusing Salmon of lobbying for pharmaceutical companies that supported President Barack Obama's health care law. Salmon said the drug companies were only looking for a small provision in the law and that he vehemently opposed the legislation. Salmon prevailed in the primary, 52%-48%. In the solidly Republican district, the general election was a foregone conclusion; Salmon easily dispatched Democratic community activist Spencer Morgan, 67%-33%.

On his return to the House, it seemed like déjà vu. Salmon got a seat on Foreign Affairs. He clashed with party leaders. House Republicans struggled to do business with a Democratic president. And he proposed a constitutional amendment limiting House members to six years. In January 2015, Salmon became chairman of the Asia and the Pacific Subcommittee. He cited his experience as a missionary nearly four decades earlier, and said "there is a clear need for continued U.S. engagement and leadership" in the region. A month later, he worked with the committee to approve legislation to strengthen sanctions against North Korea. Salmon was a founding member of the Freedom Caucus, which advocates limited government. He filed a bill requiring food-stamp recipients to show photo ID when claiming the benefits.

Despite encouragement from Maricopa County Republicans to challenge McCain in the 2016 Republican primary, Salmon in February 2015 told an independent fund-raising group to stop its advocacy on his behalf. But the pleas to run became more widespread. During the spring, he said that he was giving serious consideration to a campaign. By summer, he had backed off again.

SIXTH DISTRICT

David Schweikert (R)

Elected 2010, 3rd term; b. March 3, 1962, Los Angeles, CA; Scottsdale Comm. Coll., A.A. 1985, AZ St. U., B.S. 1988, M.B.A. 2005; Catholic; married (Joyce).

Elected Office: AZ House, 1989-94; Treasurer, Maricopa Cnty., 2004-06.

Professional Career: Member, AZ State Board of Equalization, 1995-2003; Owner, Sheridan Equities & Sheridan Equities Holdings.

DC Office: 409 CHOB, 20515, 202-225-2190; Fax: 202-225-0096; Website: schweikert.house.gov.

State Offices: Scottsdale, 480-946-2411.

Committees: *Financial Services:* Monetary Policy & Trade; Capital Markets & Government Sponsored Enterprises.

Group Ratings

	ADA	ACLU	AFL-CIO	LCV	ITI	COC	HAFA	ACU	CFG	FRC
2014	5%	11%	–	3%	100%	64%	92%	100%	94%	63%
2013	5%	C	10%	7%	C	85%	C	100%	100%	C

National Journal Ratings

	2013 LIB	—	2013 CONS
Economic	0%	—	98%
Social	16%	—	74%
Foreign	44%	—	56%
Composite	22%	—	78%

Key Votes of the 113th Congress

1. Sandy storm spending	N	5. Medical Marijuana	Y	9. Syrian Rebels Training	Y
2. Violence Against Women Act	N	6. Farm Bill	N	10. Keystone pipeline	Y
3. Guantanamo Bay Detainees	N	7. Afghanistan Combat	N	11. Immigration Exec. Action	Y
4. Abortion 20-week ban	Y	8. NSA Phone Data Collection	Y	12. Bipartisan budget deal	N

Election Results

2014 general	David Schweikert (R)	129,578	(65%)	$533,363
	John Williamson (D)	70,198	(35%)	
2014 primary	David Schweikert (R)	unopposed		

Prior winning percentages: 2012 (61%), 2010 (52%)

Population		Race and Ethnicity		Income	
Total:	737,884	White	74.9%	Median income:	$61,200
Urban:	87.7%	Latino	15.1%		*(111 of 435)*
Suburban:	12.1%	Asian	4.2%	Under $50,000	40.9%
Rural:	0.2%	Black	2.3%	$50,000-$99,999:	29.7%
Land area:	845	Two races	1.9%	$100,000-$199,999:	20.8%
Pop/sq. mi.:	873.7	White Ethnic	32.5%	$200,000 or more:	8.6%
Born in state:	31.3%			Poverty Rate	11.2%
		Education			
Age Groups		H.S. grad or less:	26.8%	**Work**	
Under 18:	21.1%	Some college:	31.6%	White collar:	43.6%
18 to 34:	21.4%	College degree, 4 yr.:	26.2%	Blue collar:	45.5%
35 to 64:	41.2%	Post-gradstudy:	15.4%	Sales and service:	11.0%
Over 64:	16.3%				
		Military		Govt. workers:	10.2%
		Veterans/activeduty:	8.9%		

Northeastern Phoenix Suburbs: Scottsdale

In May 1998, conservative trailblazer Barry Goldwater died at his home in the Phoenix suburb of Paradise Valley. His life had spanned the whole history of the state of Arizona. He was born on New Year's Day 1909, when Arizona was still a territory, and he could remember when it was the "baby state," with

Voter Turnout	
2013 Total Citizen 18+	534,140
2014 House Turnout	199,776
2014 Turnout as % CVAP	37.4%
2012 Turnout as % CVAP	59.6%

fewer people than any state except Delaware, Wyoming, and Nevada. When he returned from military service in World War II, Paradise Valley was still undeveloped, and Phoenix— founded after the Civil War as a hay market for cavalry horses at Fort McDowell—was not much more than a tiny outpost of American civilization, a metropolitan area of fewer than 300,000 in the sizzling desert. By 2013, there were 4 million people in metropolitan Phoenix. And the city had been transformed from a frontier outpost to a diversified high-tech center, an example of how creativity and ingenuity can build a sophisticated city even in the most unwelcoming environs.

Like Los Angeles and San Francisco, Phoenix is dotted with mountains that rise grandly from the plains and are preserved as undeveloped parkland. Some, such as Shaw Butte, contain archaeological evidence that Indians used them as a base for sophisticated astronomical observations. From the landmark Camelback Mountain, 1,800 feet above Phoenix and Paradise Valley, one can get with equal awe a sense of what the land was originally like and an understanding of how impressively Phoenix has grown.

Over the mountains, east of the affluent part of Phoenix and north of Tempe and the Salt River Indian Reservation, is Scottsdale, a city that grew in population from 130,000 in 1990 to 227,000 in 2013. Scottsdale is home to Frank Lloyd Wright's Taliesin West, the architect's onetime winter home and studio, which when built in the McDowell Mountain foothills in the 1940s was beyond the reach of electricity and telephone lines. Today, the city boasts luxury shopping malls, resorts, the renowned WestWorld equestrian center and the most expensive real estate market in Arizona. Local politicians argue over whether Scottsdale should keep marketing itself as a Western town or emphasize its new live-work downtown. The city also likes to tout its importance in the Cactus League of warm-weather cities that host spring training camps for Major League Baseball, and its reputation as one of the most retiree-friendly cities in the country. Twenty percent of its residents are 65 and older, the largest percentage among cities with 100,000 or more people.

The 6th Congressional District of Arizona includes the northern part of Phoenix, most of Scottsdale, plus Paradise Valley and other communities to the north, including Cave Creek and Carefree, so named in 1955 by developers who hoped to lure snow-

2012 Presidential Vote		
Mitt Romney (R)	186,537	(60%)
Barack Obama (D)	121,661	(39%)

2008 Presidential Vote		
John McCain (R)	182,681	(58%)
Barack Obama (D)	130,379	(41%)

Cook Partisan Voting Index: R+12

bird retirees. As with four other Arizona districts, the 6th is contained entirely in Maricopa County, but it has the most college graduates and is the only one that borders each of the other four. This is an affluent and heavily Republican district that attracted the notice of former Alaska governor Sarah Palin when she was looking for a lower-48 home. The 2008 GOP vice presidential nominee purchased in 2011 a $1.7 million property in Scottsdale.

David Schweikert (R)

Republican David Schweikert won his seat by defeating a two-term House Democrat and kept it two years later by defeating a fellow freshman Republican in a nasty redistricting-created primary. Then, he was stripped of his prime House committee assignment because he flaunted his independence of the GOP leadership. Despite that brass-knuckle background, Schweikert is a wonkish fiscal conservative who "enjoys poring over a spreadsheet the way most people dive into a good novel," *The Arizona Republic* said when it endorsed him when he was first elected in 2010.

Schweikert was born in a Catholic home for unwed mothers in downtown Los Angeles; he was adopted and raised by a family in Arizona. As a young man in Scottsdale, he was involved in sports and joined a club for Republican teens. He credits his early affinity for politics to former President Ronald Reagan. "We had a president [Jimmy Carter], who would go on television wearing a sweater and demanding that we adjust our thermostats because we were living in a world of shortages," Schweikert recalled. Along came Reagan, who galvanized a "wave of young people," he said. As an undergraduate at Arizona State University, Schweikert focused on finance and real estate. "I have spent almost all my life within a 20-mile radius," he said. But he was "fiercely independent," refusing to accept his parents' help to finance his education. He acquired a real estate license at the age of 18 and worked full-time while taking classes at night. He graduated in six years.

He ventured into the political arena at age 26, when he lost a bid for the Arizona House. Two years later, he was elected to an open seat in the Scottsdale area, and at the end of his freshman term, he became majority whip. He was 30 and one of the youngest whips in state history. He worked to pass legislation that laid the foundation for tax cuts, tort reform, and charter schools, as well as a bill shortening the legislative session from 170 to 98 days. In the course of his public service, Schweikert returned to ASU to get a master's degree in business administration. He next ran for Maricopa County treasurer and won. In that role, from 2004 to 2007, he managed a $4 billion budget, created a program to help low-income seniors pay their property taxes, and corrected thousands of deed errors.

In 2008, Schweikert was the Republican nominee to challenge Democratic Rep. Harry Mitchell, who took a GOP seat two years earlier. Schweikert lost by 9 percentage points in an inhospitable year for Republicans. Two years later, their rematch told the larger tale of the 2010 election. It featured an incumbent under fire for supporting the Obama administration agenda and a conservative challenger touting his outsider credentials. Schweikert made Mitchell's vote for President Barack Obama's $787 billion economic stimulus bill a central theme, and his campaign signs called Mitchell a "lap dog" for liberal House Speaker Nancy Pelosi. Mitchell countered that he had been among the Democrats most likely to buck his party. The incumbent raised about twice as much money. But Schweikert won, 53%-42%. A Libertarian candidate got 5%.

In the House, Schweikert became known for his studiousness; he told *The Washington Post* in May 2011 that he spent five hours a day learning the workings of government-sponsored mortgage giants Fannie Mae and Freddie Mac as a member of the Financial Services Committee. He worked with Republican Jeb Hensarling of Texas on a measure to phase out the dollar bill for the dollar coin, saying it could save the government about $5.5 billion over 30 years. In the summer of 2011, he strongly opposed raising the federal debt ceiling. He accused Treasury Secretary Tim Geithner of having "his hair on fire. ... It's absolutely silly. We have plenty of cash flow to pay debt." In January 2012, he introduced a bill proposing a constitutional amendment that would force Congress to get approval from a majority of the states before increasing the debt limit in the future. But he ultimately agreed to a final compromise that was signed into law.

After the 2010 census, the state's independent redistricting commission lumped Schweikert in a district with Rep. Ben Quayle, the son of former Vice President Dan Quayle. The younger Quayle represented two-thirds of the new district. House Republican leaders and outgoing Arizona Sen. Jon Kyl lined up to support Quayle, whom they considered the more loyal Republican. Schweikert portrayed himself as a reformer up against the GOP establishment, which he said his opponent embodied. He also cast Quayle as immature, reviving allegations from 2010 that his opponent had made offensive comments on a racy nightlife website, DirtyScottsdale.com. Quayle at first denied any connection with the site, but later in their campaign acknowledged that he had done some writing for it.

Quayle labeled Schweikert "Dishonest Dave" and accused him of being the source of a *Politico* story alleging that Quayle was one of the GOP congressmen who took a late-night swim in the Sea of Galilee during a 2011 trip to Israel. (Quayle said he took a brief swim and brought home some of the water to baptize his daughter.) The acrimony peaked when Schweikert's campaign sent out a mailer claiming that Quayle "goes both ways" on conservative issues. Quayle and his supporters, including Sen. John McCain, angrily accused Schweikert of sexual innuendo, a charge that the congressman denied. Schweikert prevailed, 51%-49%. The general-election race was a formality in this comfortably Republican district.

In the new Congress, House Republican leaders took the rare step of booting Schweikert off Financial Services; Schweikert's aides claimed it was because of his willingness to challenge the leadership, although the bitterness of his race with Quayle also may have been a factor. He also left the House Republican whip team. Still, Schweikert did not make a complete break. He was not among the 10 House Republicans who voted against John Boehner for Speaker. He moved to the Science, Space, and Technology Committee, returning to work without public complaint, and reestablished his party credentials. He voted in 2013 and 2014 for the annual budget resolution, even though other conservatives left the reservation. After the 2014 election, he regained his seat on Financial Services, though his earlier seniority was not restored. Then, Schweikert again voted for Boehner for Speaker—despite continued objections to his leadership. The appropriate time to challenge his Speakership would have been in the private meetings of the Republican Conference, not in a public vote where his opponent was Nancy Pelosi, he told reporters.

Conservative activists urged him to oppose McCain in the 2016 Republican primary. In February 2015, Schweikert didn't close the door, but said that he was leaning against the contest and that his wife thought that it was a bad idea. In a distinctive feature of his career, he won reelection in 2014 without breaking a sweat.

SEVENTH DISTRICT

Ruben Gallego (D)

Elected 2014, 1st term; b. Nov 20, 1979, Chicago, IL; Harvard U., A.B. 2004; Catholic; married (Kate).

Military Career: U.S. Marine Corps, 2002-06 (Iraq).

Elected Office: AZ House, 2010-14.

Professional Career: Public affairs consultant 2007-08; Delegate, DNC 2008; Vice chair, AZ Democratic Party, 2009.

DC Office: 1218 LHOB, 20515, 202-225-4065; Website: rubengallego. house.gov.

State Offices: Phoenix, 602-256-0551.

Committees: *Armed Services:* Readiness; Tactical Air & Land Forces. *Natural Resources:* Energy & Mineral Resources; Water, Power & Oceans; Oversight & Investigations.

Election Results

2014 general	Ruben Gallego (D)	54,235	(75%)	$911,026	$248,969
	Joe Cobb (Lib)	10,715	(15%)	$1,288	
	Rebecca DeWitt (AE)	3,858	(5%)		
	Jose Penalosa (I)	3,496	(5%)		
2014 primary	Ruben Gallego (D)	14,936	(49%)		
	Mary Rose Wilcox	11,077	(36%)		
	Randy Camacho	2,330	(8%)		
	Jarrett Maupin	2,199	(7%)		

Population		Race and Ethnicity		Income	
Total:	749,222	Latino	65.9%	Median income:	$32,372
Urban:	88.3%	White	19.9%		*(430 of 435)*
Suburban:	11.7%	Black	8.5%	Under $50,000	68.7%
Rural:	0.0%	Asian	2.3%	$50,000-$99,999:	23.0%
Landarea:	309	Two races	0.9%	$100,000-$199,999:	7.4%
Pop/sq.mi.:	2,425.1	White Ethnic	8.2%	$200,000 or more:	0.9%
Borninstate:	47.6%			Poverty Rate	37.0%
		Education			
		H.S. grad or less:	60.8%	**Work**	
Age Groups		Some college:	26.0%	White collar:	20.3%
Under 18:	31.6%	College degree, 4 yr.:	9.0%	Blue collar:	50.1%
18 to 34:	28.5%	Post-grad study:	4.2%	Sales and service:	29.6%
35 to 64:	33.5%				
Over 64:	6.3%	**Military**		Govt. workers:	9.6%
		Veterans/activeduty:	5.1%		

Central and Western Phoenix

Phoenix is a relatively new American metropolis. It has grown to a big city just in the past generation. Yet it is also an ancient city, or, built on top of one. The Arizona Canal, several miles north of downtown Phoenix, runs along the route of a canal built about 600 years ago by the Hohokam aboriginal people.

Voter Turnout	
2013 Total Citizen 18+	373,469
2014 House Turnout	72,454
2014 Turnout as % CVAP	19.4%
2012 Turnout as % CVAP	39.3%

They distributed irrigated water diverted from the Salt River in its wet moments to farmers in what today is called the Valley of the Sun, and they made sophisticated astronomical observations from the mountains that jut up from the plains. This society disappeared for reasons unknown less than half a century before the Spaniards arrived in North America. So, today's Phoenix is the second civilization to prosper in this desert region. Maricopa County had 332,000 people in 1950 and more than 4 million by 2010. Half a century ago, Phoenix spread six miles north, west, and east of the downtown and only a few miles south. Downtown was its only office district and its main shopping area, and people blew fans over boxes of ice to cool off. Today, the view from downtown Phoenix's office towers stretches as far as the eye can see, toward groupings of other office towers to the north, northeast, and northwest.

The city opened its first light rail transit line in December 2008, connecting residents of the Tempe and Mesa suburbs to downtown Phoenix on a 20-mile line. Trains travel at the posted speed limits for those roads. Annual ridership increased from 5 million in 2009 to 14 million in 2014. Local officials estimated that the initial $1.4 billion cost has generated $7 billion in economic investment. Separate three-mile extensions at each end were delayed when the state's economy collapsed, but they got underway in 2013. In March 2015, the city council approved a 35-year, $32 billion transportation plan for 40 more miles of light rail across the area, plus additional bus service, with financing from a sales tax hike. Also that month, the federal government approved the $1.9 billion, 22-mile Loop 202 highway extension between downtown Phoenix and Chandler on Interstate 10. The controversial project shares financing from the sales tax.

The 7th Congressional District of Arizona is centered in downtown Phoenix and is based entirely in Maricopa County. It covers the capitol, in a rundown neighborhood a couple of miles to the west, and busy Sky Harbor International Airport, situated in an industrial corridor several miles east. It includes most of southern Phoenix, and its boundaries follow approximately the southern and western city limits. It stretches south into Guadalupe and northwest into parts of Glendale. Geographically, the district covers most of the land between South Mountain and Camelback Mountain.

The area was hit extremely hard by the economic downturn in the late-2000s. The median existing home price in the metropolitan Phoenix area fell from $245,000 in September 2006 to $115,000 in September 2011. By March 2015, about half of that dip had been recovered. Tourism also declined during those years, after activists urged boycotts of the state because of its aggressive crackdown against illegal immigrants. The Phoenix Suns basketball team wore "Los Suns" jerseys during the controversy to show support for area Hispanics, and pro-immigrant demonstrators protested at the 2011 baseball All-Star Game at Phoenix's Chase Field. In early 2015, area housing remained "in the doldrums," the *Arizona Republic* reported, with new housing starts having dropped from more than 40,000 annually to less than 10,000. But recent job growth has been the third fastest rate in the nation, according to the *Republic*. In 2014, the local veterans' hospital became the unfortunate symbol of the

2012 Presidential Vote		
Barack Obama (D) 101,028	(72%)
Mitt Romney (R)...................37,353	(27%)

2008 Presidential Vote		
Barack Obama (D) 86,034	(65%)
John McCain (R)..................45,336	(34%)

Cook Partisan Voting Index: D+16

nationwide failure of the Veterans Affairs Department's health system: delayed or inadequate care, fabricated records, and flawed management. During a March 2015 visit to the hospital, President Barack Obama said that the care was "outstanding," but that there was a need to restore "trust and confidence" in the VA and that he was creating another committee to review how veterans' needs could be met.

The district is one of Arizona's two Hispanic districts; its population is 66 percent Hispanic. Most are Mexican, but there has been an influx of Guatemalans in recent years. Politically, this is a solidly Democratic district.

Ruben Gallego (D)

Democrat Ruben Gallego, a first-generation American, was the first in his family to go to college. In a swift rise to influence, he was easily elected in 2014 to represent Arizona's 7th District. His impressive bio drew quick attention, including from President Barack Obama—who has bonded with Gallego on their separate experiences in Chicago and at Harvard. Two days after he took office, he joined Obama on an Air Force One flight from Phoenix back to Washington.

Gallego's biography is made for a political candidate, including a hardscrabble upbringing, a Harvard degree, and military service in Iraq. Born in Chicago to Hispanic immigrant parents, Gallego and his family struggled after his father left home, something Gallego has said helps him relate to the low-income people in his district. He got his undergraduate degree in international relations. While attending Harvard, he enlisted in the Marine Corps. He served in Iraq as an assistant machine gunner and fought in more than 10 combat operations in urban areas; his best friend died in combat. That experience, including his anger over the poor quality of the troops' equipment, led him to get involved in politics and to help veterans.

Gallego was elected to the Arizona Senate in 2010, rising to assistant minority leader in 2012. When 12-term Democratic Rep. Ed Pastor decided to retire, Gallego left the legislature to run. In this ultra-blue district, where Obama got 72 percent in 2012 and the Democratic nominee was considered a shoo-in, the true contest came in the August primary. His chief competitor was Mary Rose Wilcox, who is Hispanic and had high name recognition as a Maricopa County supervisor. She was endorsed by Pastor, but may have suffered because she was 30 years older than Gallego.

Gallego appealed to Latino voters, noting his opposition to the Arizona law requiring police officers in some circumstances to determine the immigration status of arrested or detained persons. Gallego also founded Citizens for Professional Law Enforcement, which sought to recall Maricopa County Sheriff Joe Arpaio. The controversial sheriff has been criticized for alleged racial profiling and for investigating Obama's birth certificate. A Wilcox supporter challenged Gallego's nominating petitions for not using his legal name. The suit was withdrawn when Gallego explained he had changed his name in 2008 from Ruben Marinelarena (his father's name) to Ruben Marinelarena Gallego to honor the mother who raised him. He combined a social media presence with aggressive door-to-door campaigning, and out-raised Wilcox by about $300,000.

In the five-candidate field, Gallego won with 48.4% to 35.9% for Wilcox. In November, he won without Republican opposition. His success, he said, is "living proof that the American Dream still exists." His wife Kate is a member of the Phoenix city council. They met during a fraternity date auction in college.

Gallego pledged to work on veterans' issues, education, and income inequality. He said that he hoped to serve his career in the House. "I'll be trying to work my way fast into leadership," he told a local reporter. "As a congressman, you can do more for your state the more seniority you have, the better committees you get." With seats on the Armed Services and

Natural Resources Committee, he was off to a good start. He opposed additional U.S. military action in Iraq, which he described as "a horrible sequel to a horrible movie." He cited the many men and women who had died because of the decisions of officials in Washington and at the Pentagon, and said that additional steps to assist Iraq should not come with the risk of losing more American lives. The United States "should support our allies in the region, but limit the scope of our involvement on the ground," he said in response to Obama's request to authorize the use of force against the Islamic State. Gallego joined a new congressional caucus of lawmakers who had served in the military since 2001. At home, he opposed Republican lawsuits that have challenged Obama's authority to assist undocumented immigrants. Instead, he said, they penalize communities that "work legally here, pay their taxes, raise their families and become part of the social fabric of America." At Gallego's request, the Federal Aviation Administration agreed to review flight paths at Sky Harbor Airport to limit the noise over local neighborhoods.

EIGHTH DISTRICT

Trent Franks (R)

Elected 2002, 7th term; b. June 19, 1957, Uravan, CO; Ottawa U., 1989-90; Baptist; married (Josie); 2 children.

Elected Office: AZ House, 1984-86.

Professional Career: Dir., AZ Gov.'s Office for Children, 1987-88; Exec. dir., AZ Family Research Inst., 1989-93; Writer-commentator, AZ radio station KTKP; Co-owner, Franks Brothers Independent Drilling; Pres.-CEO, Liberty Petroleum Corp.

DC Office: 2435 RHOB, 20515, 202-225-4576; Fax: 202-225-6328; Website: franks.house.gov.

State Offices: Glendale, 623-776-7911.

Committees: *Armed Services*: Emerging Threats & Capabilities (VChmn); Strategic Forces. *Judiciary*: Constitution & Civil Justice (Chmn); Courts, Intellectual Property & the Internet.

Group Ratings

	ADA	ACLU	AFL-CIO	LCV	ITI	COC	HAFA	ACU	CFG	FRC
2014	5%	0%	–	6%	80%	57%	96%	100%	98%	100%
2013	0%	C	10%	11%	C	85%	C	96%	100%	C

National Journal Ratings

	2013 LIB	—	2013 CONS
Economic	0%	—	98%
Social	13%	—	84%
Foreign	0%	—	95%
Composite	6%	—	94%

Key Votes of the 113th Congress

1. Sandy storm spending	N	5. Medical Marijuana	N	9. Syrian Rebels Training	Y
2. Violence Against Women Act	N	6. Farm Bill	N	10. Keystone pipeline	Y
3. Guantanamo Bay Detainees	N	7. Afghanistan Combat	N	11. Immigration Exec. Action	Y
4. Abortion 20-week ban	Y	8. NSA Phone Data Collection	N	12. Bipartisan budget deal	N

Election Results

2014 general	Trent Franks (R)	128,710	(76%)	$369,181
	Stephen Dolgos (AE)	41,066	(24%)	
2014 primary	Trent Franks (R)	53,771	(73%)	
	Clair Van Steenwyk	19,629	(27%)	

Prior winning percentages: 2012 (63%), 2010 (65%), 2008 (59%), 2006 (59%), 2004 (59%), 2002 (60%)

Population		Race and Ethnicity		Income	
Total:	741,374	White	73.2%	Median income:	$56,025
Urban:	16.4%	Latino	18.0%		*(158 of 435)*
Suburban:	83.1%	Black	3.3%	Under $50,000	43.6%
Rural:	0.5%	Asian	2.8%	$50,000-$99,999:	34.6%
Land area:	1,008	Two races	2.0%	$100,000-$199,999:	18.7%
Pop/sq. mi.:	735.4	White Ethnic	26.5%	$200,000 or more:	3.1%
Born in state:	34.4%			Poverty Rate	11.1%
		Education			
Age Groups		H.S.grad or less:	35.2%	**Work**	
Under 18:	22.9%	Somecollege:	36.3%	White collar:	36.3%
18 to 34:	18.7%	College degree, 4 yr.:	18.3%	Blue collar:	47.2%
35 to 64:	37.2%	Post-grad study:	10.1%	Sales and service:	16.5%
Over 64:	21.2%				
		Military		Govt. workers:	13.3%
		Veterans/activeduty:	13.3%		

Western Phoenix Suburbs: Glendale, Peoria

In 1938, when most of Phoenix's West Valley was barren, desert landscape, Flora Mae Statler paid 35 cents an acre to acquire land on the site of what became the city of Surprise. Statler chose the name, she later recalled, because she'd "be surprised if this town ever amounted to much." But the city got the last laugh on

Voter Turnout	
2013 Total Citizen 18+	538,625
2014 House Turnout	169,776
2014 Turnout as % CVAP	31.5%
2012 Turnout as % CVAP	55.4%

Statler: Over the last half-century, it has become one of the fastest-growing cities in rapidly growing Maricopa County.

Once a haven for retirees looking for warmer climates, Surprise and Phoenix's surrounding western suburbs have been booming, although the collapse of the housing market slowed the tempo. Astride Grand Avenue, the only diagonal street in the rigorous grid of metro Phoenix, is the suburb of Glendale, not so long ago just a crossroads but now home to 235,000 people. The Phoenix Coyotes hockey stadium went up in Glendale in 2003. That was followed in 2006 by the University of Phoenix Stadium, which has a retractable roof and capacity of more than 78,000, and has hosted major national sports events, including the 2015 Super Bowl. Nearby Westgate City Center is now one of several edge cities in Phoenix's Valley of the Sun. Tucked between Surprise and Glendale is Peoria, as middle-American as its namesake in Illinois, and Sun City, a huge retirement community started in the 1950s. Peoria has spent close to $100 million to revive its older community as an historic area. The planned community of Anthem, 30 miles north of downtown and established in 1998, has about 22,000 residents.

All of these cities are part of the 8th Congressional District of Arizona, which covers Phoenix's West Valley. Because this has been an area of rapid growth, it was particularly hard hit by the housing bust and subsequent economic downturn in the mid-2000s. But recovery is slowly arriving: Work was completed in 2014 on the Loop 303 interchange with Interstate 10 in Goodyear, which improves access to cities in the West Valley. Real estate values are again on the rise, with home values in Surprise increasing 50 percent from 2011 to 2014. A casino under construction in Glendale has stirred strong opposition from mayors elsewhere in West Valley. Also in the district is Luke Air Force Base, which has the largest fighter training wing in the Air Force and the only active duty F-16 training

2012 Presidential Vote		
Mitt Romney (R)................179,555		(62%)
Barack Obama (D) 107,335		(37%)
2008 Presidential Vote		
John McCain (R).................174,731		(61%)
Barack Obama (D) 110,760		(38%)
Cook Partisan Voting Index: R+15		

base in the United States. The Pentagon is preparing Luke as the main operational training base for pilots of the F-35A Lightning II fighter jets, which will replace the F-16 fleet.

This is conservative territory, one of four districts redrawn to elect Republicans after the 2010 census. The district grew much more compact in redistricting, shedding counties along the Colorado River.

Trent Franks (R)

Trent Franks, a Republican first elected in 2002, is best known for his fervent opposition to abortion rights. He has unsuccessfully pushed a measure that would criminalize abortions based on the sex or gender of the fetus. As chairman of a House Judiciary subcommittee that handles such issues, he is positioned to move such legislation. But some Republican leaders and rank-and-file members object to his agenda as bad politics.

Franks grew up in Colorado, attended college briefly, and started his own oil-and-gas exploration business. His political career began when he won a single term in the Arizona House in 1984. There, he was known for wearing a tie tack in the shape of the feet of a fetus, as a constant reminder of his anti-abortion views. In 1987, he was the director of the Governor's Office for Children under Evan Mecham, a conservative Republican who was later impeached. In 1989, Franks became executive director of the Arizona Family Research Institute, an organization associated with James Dobson's Focus on the Family, and he was a consultant to conservative Pat Buchanan's presidential campaign. On another social conservative priority, Franks designed the state's 1997 scholarship tax credit legislation, a much litigated measure that ultimately was upheld by the U.S. Supreme Court. The plan provides tax credits for donations to nonprofit organizations to help families pay for private education.

In the House since 2002, Franks has accumulated a conservative voting record while emerging as a fierce rhetorical firebrand. He was among the first House Republicans to join the Tea Party Caucus in 2010. Despite the House Republican majority's desire to focus on economic rather than social issues, he has continued to seek votes on abortion-related bills. In May 2012, the leadership brought to the floor his measure to criminalize abortions based on the fetus' sex or gender, on the heels of a similar new Arizona state law. It needed two-thirds to pass under the House rule for handling that bill, but it fell 30 votes short on the 246-168 roll call. In June 2013, the House passed his Pain Capable Unborn Child Protection Act, which was designed to prevent an abortion after five months of pregnancy; the Senate took no action. In January 2015, he was preparing to bring to the House floor a similar bill, but the measure stirred objections from a group of House Republican women, including newly elected members, and GOP leaders pulled the bill from debate. Franks responded that he was disappointed, and that party leaders had assured him that he would have another opportunity. The House passed the bill a few months later with minor tweaks.

Franks has been highly critical of a provision in the Voting Rights Act empowering the Justice Department to approve or challenge changes to voting laws in states such as Arizona. He said it was "ludicrous" that his state had to get preclearance before new congressional redistricting maps could take effect. The Supreme Court agreed in a 2014 challenge to the law brought by Shelby County Alabama. In February 2015, he joined leading conservatives participating in a documentary that contended that gay rights threaten Christianity.

On the Armed Services Committee, Franks has strongly supported missile defense as well as protecting against electromagnetic pulse (EMP) attacks. Such attacks involve a powerful shock wave that can disrupt magnetic fields and potentially damage electric systems. In December 2014, the House approved a bill that would strengthen protection for the nation's electric grid.

Franks first ran for a House seat in 1994 but lost to John Shadegg in the Republican primary, 43%-30%. In 2002, Republican Rep. Bob Stump announced he was retiring and endorsed Lisa Atkins, his chief of staff. Franks was not thought to be in the top tier of candidates, but his base of Christian conservatives and abortion opponents, plus his spending of $300,000 of his own money, made him a contender. He called for overturning the Supreme Court's *Roe v. Wade* decision legalizing abortion and for constitutional protection for fetuses. He endorsed a flat tax to replace the federal income tax, supported individual investment accounts in Social Security, and called for tougher enforcement of immigration laws. His base of activists made the difference. He finished first with 28% of the vote, only 797 votes ahead of Atkins, who got 26%. In November, he won 60%-37%. He has not faced a serious reelection threat since then.

His strong rhetoric has caused him occasional problems. In 2010, Franks angered African Americans when he declared that their population has been decimated more by abortions than by slavery. Discussing President Barack Obama's reelection prospects, he said in

March 2011, "He is a left-wing ideologue of the first magnitude, and if we don't understand that now, then I'm afraid that somehow he may get back in in two years, and I don't know that the country can survive that."

On a personal note, he has encouraged public awareness of facial deformity similar to the one he has battled. Franks has had multiple surgeries to correct a cleft palate.

NINTH DISTRICT

Kyrsten Sinema (D)

Elected 2012, 2nd term; b. July 12, 1976, Tucson; Brigham Young U., B.A. 1995, AZ St. U., M.A. 1999, J.D. 2004, Ph.D. 2012; no religious affiliation; single.

Elected Office: AZ House, 2004-10; AZ Senate, 2010-12.

Professional Career: Social worker, 1995-2002; Practicing lawyer, 2005-present; Instructor, Ctr. for Progressive Leadership, 2006-present.

DC Office: 1530 LHOB, 20515, 202-225-9888; Fax: 202-2259731; Website: sinema.house.gov.

State Offices: Phoenix, 602-956-2285.

Committees: *Financial Services*: Financial Institutions & Consumer Credit; Oversight & Investigations.

Group Ratings

	ADA	ACLU	AFL-CIO	LCV	ITI	COC	HAFA	ACU	CFG	FRC
2014	40%	61%	–	83%	100%	71%	12%	8%	19%	0%
2013	50%	C	90%	79%	C	77%	C	24%	14%	C

National Journal Ratings

	2013 LIB	—	2013 CONS
Economic	57%	—	42%
Social	57%	—	42%
Foreign	55%	—	45%
Composite	57%	—	43%

Key Votes of the 113th Congress

1. Sandy storm spending	Y	5. Medical Marijuana	Y	9. Syrian Rebels Training	Y
2. Violence Against Women Act	Y	6. Farm Bill	Y	10. Keystone pipeline	N
3. Guantanamo Bay Detainees	N	7. Afghanistan Combat	N	11. Immigration Exec. Action	N
4. Abortion 20-week ban	N	8. NSA Phone Data Collection	N	12. Bipartisan budget deal	Y

Election Results

2014 general	Kyrsten Sinema (D) 88,609	(55%)	$3,458,415	$651,931	$36,000
	Wendy Rogers (R) 67,841	(42%)	$1,328,059	$18,030	$453,411
	Powell Gammill (Lib).................... 5,612	(4%)			
2014 primary	Kyrsten Sinema (D) ....unopposed				

Prior winning percentage: 2012 (49%)

Population		Race and Ethnicity		Income	
Total:	741,451	White	58.6%	Median income:	$49,487
Urban:	75.9%	Latino	26.3%		(249 of 435)
Suburban:	24.1%	Black	5.6%	Under $50,000	50.4%
Rural:	0.0%	Asian	4.4%	$50,000-$99,999:	28.9%
Land area:	256	Two races	2.5%	$100,000-$199,999:	16.2%
Pop/sq.mi.:	2,894.6	White Ethnic	23.0%	$200,000 or more:	4.5%
Born in state:	37.8%			Poverty Rate	19.4%
		Education			
Age Groups		H.S. grad or less:	31.9%	**Work**	
Under 18:	22.0%	Some college:	32.1%	White collar:	39.9%
18 to 34:	31.0%	College degree, 4 yr.:	22.3%	Blue collar:	45.7%
35 to 64:	36.8%	Post-grad study:	13.7%	Sales and service:	14.4%
Over 64:	10.2%			Govt. workers:	13.1%
		Military			
		Veterans/activeduty:	6.9%		

Central and Eastern Phoenix Suburbs: Western Mesa

As metropolitan Phoenix has expanded in the Valley of the Sun over the past half century, it has absorbed the crossroads towns that were once separate and distinct. One such town is Tempe, east of downtown Phoenix. It was founded in 1871 as Hayden's Ferry by the father of future Democratic Sen. Carl Hayden,

Voter Turnout	
2013 Total Citizen 18+	511,992
2014 House Turnout	162,062
2014 Turnout as % CVAP	31.7%
2012 Turnout as % CVAP	51.4%

who held that office from 1927 to 1969, and it was renamed in 1879 for an ancient Greek vale. The old town centered on Arizona State University, and both the town and the university have expanded greatly over the decades. The campus sits astride a rise with a fine view of much of metropolitan Phoenix; the school now has the largest enrollment of any U.S. four-year public university at more than 80,000 students. The Mayo Clinic has formed a partnership with the university to develop the Mayo Medical School, scheduled to open in 2017. Located near the Mayo Hospital campus in North Scottsdale, the medical school plans to emphasize innovative, patient-centered care. It will be accompanied by a new biosciences center.

Tempe is relatively affluent, with 168,000 people in 2013, up from 142,000 in 1990. That growth has been slow compared with nearby Scottsdale and Chandler, which has become a booming corporate center. Tempe has nine stations along Phoenix's original 20-mile light rail system. Its Mill Avenue district across from the Arizona State campus is a pedestrian-friendly downtown featuring red brick sidewalks and turn-of-the-century buildings. The city is also headquarters to US Airways, the fifth-largest airline in the country before it merged with Fort-Worth based American Airlines to become the largest in the nation. The day before college football's Fiesta Bowl in Glendale, Tempe hosts a parade and block party.

The 9th Congressional District of Arizona includes Tempe and parts of Scottsdale, Mesa, Chandler, and Phoenix. It was drawn to be the only politically competitive district based in the Phoenix area, but its demographic characteristics are favorable for Democrats. Republicans held a 34%-31% registration advantage in the 2012 presidential election. But the district contains high shares of college graduates and high-income households, drawn to Democrats on cultural issues. President Barack Obama won here with 51 percent in both 2008 and 2012. Outside of Arizona's two majority-minority districts, the 9th contains the largest concentration of Hispanics, at 27 percent.

2012 Presidential Vote		
Barack Obama (D)	135,244	(51%)
Mitt Romney (R)	123,263	(47%)
2008 Presidential Vote		
Barack Obama (D)	140,444	(51%)
John McCain (R)	129,813	(47%)
Cook Partisan Voting Index:	R+1	

Kyrsten Sinema (D)

Democrat Kyrsten Sinema won the newly created 9th District seat in 2012. She has a compelling personal history, which illustrates the major cultural changes that have taken place in Arizona. She also has quickly established her mark in the House.

Sinema grew up in Tucson Arizona. Her parents divorced, and her mother remarried a teacher. When her stepfather lost his job, the family took shelter for two years in an abandoned gas station without running water or electricity. They eventually moved into a home, but remained poor. At 16, Sinema graduated as her high school's valedictorian and went on to earn a bachelor's degree in social work from Brigham Young University, followed by a master's degree in social work, a law degree, and a doctorate in justice studies from Arizona State University—all while working full-time. After graduating from BYU at 18, she became a social worker in a central Phoenix school district. Before her election to Congress, she worked as a lawyer, an adjunct professor at Arizona State, and an instructor at the Center for Progressive Leadership, a Washington-based institute that trains activists in progressive policies.

Sinema, who says she overcame adversity by using Helen Keller as a role model, was motivated to enter politics to assist people with backgrounds similar to hers. "I'm a Democrat today … because they taught me the best of both ideas: help each other when you're struggling, but work very hard on your own," she told *National Journal*. After losing her first bid for the Arizona House as an independent in 2002, she ran as a Democrat and won in 2004. She served there until 2010, when she was elected to the state Senate. Sinema was known in the legislature for her liberal politics. She sponsored several bills aimed at reining in the tough tactics of Maricopa County Sheriff Joe Arpaio on illegal immigration. But she also earned a reputation for working with Republicans to pass legislation on human trafficking and other issues. Sinema, who is the first openly bisexual member of Congress, also has promoted gay rights issues. She has run more than 10 marathons, including Boston in 2014.

Saying she was frustrated with the partisan divide in Congress, Sinema quit the Senate in January 2012 to run for the new 9th District seat, which had no incumbent. She won the Democratic primary with 41% of the vote; state Sen. David Schapira got 30% and former Arizona Democratic Party Chairman Andrei Cherny, a former speechwriter for President Bill Clinton, got 29%. Her general election opponent was Vernon Parker, a former Paradise Valley mayor who served in both Bush administrations. He won the Republican primary with 22 percent of the vote in a seven-candidate field.

Sinema and Parker fiercely competed for the independent vote, with each painting the other as extreme in attack ads. Sinema echoed President Barack Obama's call to develop an economy "that rewards those who work hard and play by the rules," calling for closing corporate tax loopholes and protecting payroll tax cuts for working families. Parker followed the national GOP playbook in vowing to repeal the health care law and rein in runaway spending. Even as they ran negative ads, each promised to be the more bipartisan lawmaker. The *Arizona Republic* endorsed Sinema, saying that her nonpartisan style was a better fit. "For Sinema, it's always about the issue, not the personalities," the newspaper wrote. On Election Night, the race was undecided because election authorities failed to count more than one-quarter of the votes. Six days later, Sinema had won a 49%-45% victory, with Libertarian Powell Gammill getting the remainder.

In the House, Sinema took the oath of office on a copy of the Constitution, not the Bible. She said that she was not affiliated with a religion. As a member of the Financial Services Committee, she worked on housing and consumer issues. Her legislative actions have sometimes been unpredictable. She has joined organizations of moderate Democrats, occasionally has criticized Obama and has worked across the aisle with House Republicans. She co-founded the United Solutions Caucus, a bipartisan group of House freshmen working on solutions for both parties. "I'm just doing my thing," she told *Roll Call* in February 2015. "I know my thing's a little bit different than other people, but I don't think there's anything wrong with that at all. And, you know what? I don't mind if some people like it or don't like it. That's OK."

After the 2014 election, Minority Whip Steny Hoyer named Sinema a chief deputy whip. He said she brought "dynamism and fresh ideas that will surely enhance the work of the whip operation." In February 2015, she was one of five Democratic co-chairs of the congressional LGBT equality caucus who objected to the prospective Asian-Pacific trade pact on the grounds that LGBT people can be caned and imprisoned for up to 20 years under Malaysian law. Based on her teaching experience, she has worked on legislation to provide additional protections to the victims of sexual violence on campus. At home, Sinema appeared to have settled in politically. In 2014, she fared better than many other Democrats in competitive seats, including in Arizona. In a contest that had been expected to be tight, she defeated Wendy Rogers, 55%-42%. Sinema spent $3.5 million to $1.4 million for Rogers, who doubted the constitutionality of Social Security. Sinema benefited from another $700,000 of party spending on her behalf. She has been mentioned as a potential challenger to Sen. John McCain in 2016, which likely would be an uphill challenge. She has dismissed the possibility, though she created a leadership PAC that would be a useful fundraising vehicle.

She may have other opportunities for a statewide bid, which would draw national support from the LGBT community.

★ ARKANSAS ★

Arkansas, like its greatest politician, Bill Clinton, began life without many advantages. It consists of the land left over when Louisiana and Missouri were carved out of the Louisiana Purchase and what is now Oklahoma was fenced off as Indian Territory. In area, it is the second-smallest state from the Mississippi River to the Pacific Ocean. In population, it is the smallest Southern state except for West Virginia. Arkansas was not blessed with great natural resources, unless you count bauxite, once the main source of aluminum, or flame-retarding bromine. Historically, it was home to no major industry. Its first two senators could not agree on how to pronounce the state's name, but since 1881, it's been illegal to call it *ar-KAN-sas*. Settled by poor farmers with large families, few slaves, and little cash, Arkansas has had no major city like Atlanta, Dallas, or even Memphis, and over the years it has had one of the lowest income levels and percentages of college graduates of any state. Arkansas was settled more by Scots-Irish dirt farmers than by grand plantation owners. It fought for the Confederacy, except for a few Union men in the northwest, and followed other Southern states in establishing government-enforced racial segregation. It is the birthplace of Pentecostal denominations like the Church of God in Christ, which had roots in late 1800s Little Rock, and the Assemblies of God, founded in Hot Springs in 1914 and now headquartered in Springfield, Missouri.

When Clinton returned to the state from Yale Law School in 1973, the dominant figure in Arkansas, as far as most Americans were concerned, was Orval Faubus, governor from 1954 to 1966. Faubus was famous for blocking desegregation of Little Rock's Central High School in 1957 until President Eisenhower sent in federal troops to enforce the court order. And Arkansas was one of five states to vote for segregationist George Wallace for president in 1968. But Arkansas was changing, culturally and economically, in ways that made Clinton's career possible. Faubus had been succeeded by governors who repudiated his legacy: Republican Winthrop Rockefeller in 1966 and Democrat Dale Bumpers in 1970. Their politics made Clinton, then 28, a plausible candidate in the Republican-dominated third Congressional District in 1974. He narrowly lost to the incumbent Republican but probably came to the notice of leading entrepreneurs in the northwest corner of Arkansas, none of whom had quite yet achieved national fame: Sam Walton, whose first Wal-Mart had opened only a dozen years before; Don Tyson of chicken-producing Tyson Food; and J. B. Hunt and his trucking firm. In less than two decades, Walton was America's richest man, and Clinton was elected president.

Arkansas still ranks low on many national indexes—its median household income is the nation's second-lowest and one-in-five residents is in poverty—but it has achieved above-average population growth over the past two decades. Educational achievement is hit-and-miss—higher-than-average high-school graduation rates but lower-than-average rates of college degrees. Arkansas lost some manufacturing jobs in the 2007-09 recession, including Whirlpool's closure of a big appliance factory in Fort Smith, but its unemployment rate has stayed below the national average. There has been a natural gas boom in the Fayetteville area. Arkansas continues to lead the nation in rice production and is No. 2 in chickens, No. 3 in cotton and No. 4 in timber. State government finances have been in good shape thanks to budget reforms instituted after the state defaulted on bonds in the 1930s (its bank balance in January 1933 was supposedly $4.80). Spending programs are rated A, B, and C, and each category is funded only to the extent revenue flows in. Bonded debt and pension obligations have been kept low. Little Rock has become a vibrant regional center, with exurban growth spreading out past the Pulaski County line, and it has been attracting tourists thanks to the William J. Clinton Presidential Center, the nation's largest presidential library. (It is the first presidential library to feature electronic records as well as paper documents, with links to what the 42nd president considers his greatest achievements, along with a treatment of "the politics of persecution"—his take on his 1998 impeachment.) Northwest Arkansas has been booming even more, including Bentonville (where Wal-Mart's headquarters are housed and where Sam Walton's daughter, Alice Walton, opened in 2011 the Crystal Bridges museum, with a magnificent collection of American art) and the University of Arkansas, along with the research and technology firms its presence has midwifed.

Politically, Arkansas was long solidly Democratic, with Republican pockets in the mountains of the northwest. For years, it produced Democratic politicians who accumulated

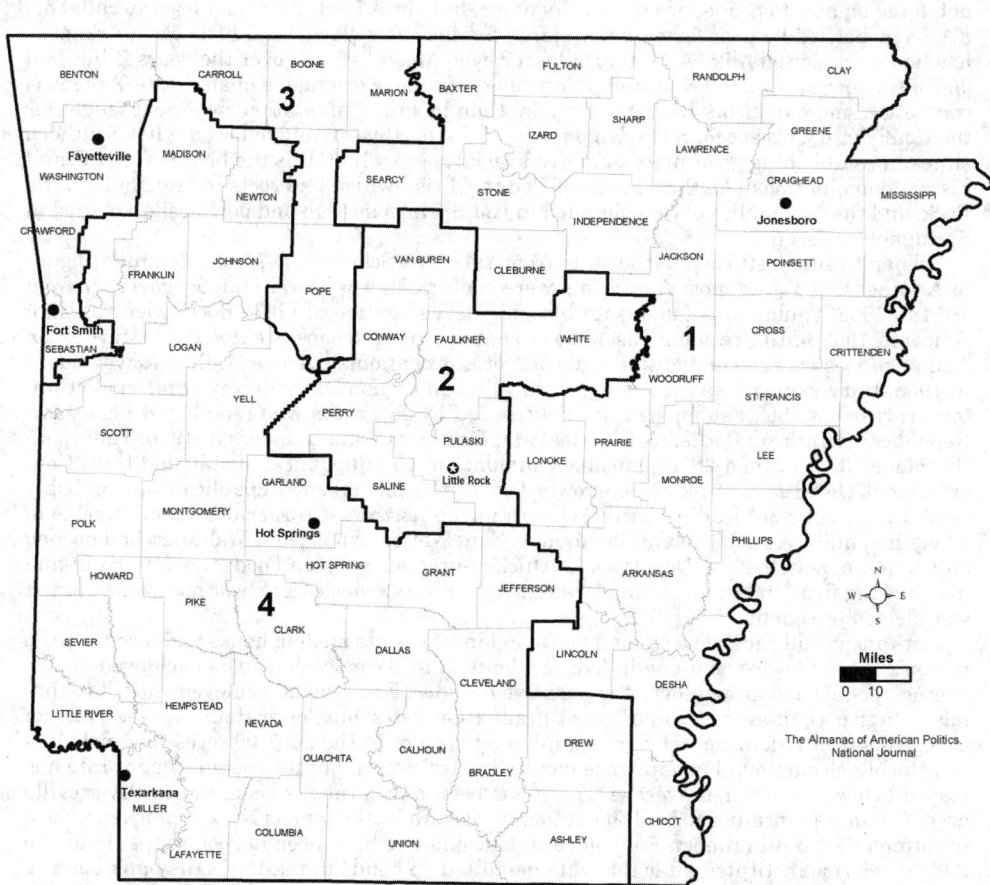

Congressional district boundaries were first effective for 2012.

The Almanac of American Politics.
National Journal

great seniority and power in Washington: longtime House Ways and Means Chairman Wilbur Mills; Sens. John McClellan and William Fulbright, who represented the state for a total of 65 years from the 1940s to the 1970s; and Sens. Dale Bumpers and David Pryor, who served a total of 42 years from the 1970s to the 1990s. Republicans won some governor races—Winthrop Rock-efeller in the 1960s, Frank White in 1980

Voter Turnout			
2013 Total Citizen 18+			2,165,783
2014 Highest Statewide Turnout			848,592
2014 Turnout as % CVAP			39.2%
2012 Turnout as % CVAP			49.5%
Legislature			
Senate:		24R	11D
House:		63R	36D 1I

(when he beat Clinton), and Mike Huckabee in 1998 and 2002—and John Paul Hammer-schmidt amassed influence in the House, serving from 1967 to 1993. Still, as late as the 1990s, Arkansas remained one of the most Democratic states in the South in presidential and congressional elections.

Not so any more. In 1999, Hillary Clinton decided to run for the Senate in New York, and she and Bill Clinton moved to Westchester County. The Clintons remain popular in Arkansas; Hillary Clinton got 70 percent of the vote in the 2008 Democratic presidential primary there, more than in any other state. But the Democratic Party at large has not remained popular, despite a few exceptions, such as Democratic Gov. Mike Beebe, the nation's only Democratic governor to be reelected by a wide margin in 2010. In presidential races, Arkansas voted 51 percent Republican in 2000, when President Clinton was still in office, and 61 percent Republican in 2012, when President Barack Obama was seeking a second term. As throughout the Scots-Irish belt of America, which runs from western Pennsylvania south-west along the Appalachian chain and west to Texas, Obama has been unpopular, both in the Democratic primaries in 2008 and in the general elections of 2008 and 2012.

In the Obama era, Arkansas has trended decidedly Republican. In 2010, the GOP claimed the offices of lieutenant governor, secretary of state, and land commissioner, even as Beebe was reelected. Democratic Sen. Blanche Lincoln was defeated 58%-37% by Republican Rep. John Boozman. Two of the state's three Democratic congressmen retired rather than run for reelection, and both were replaced by Republicans. The third retired in 2012 and was replaced by Republican Tom Cotton. Finally, in 2014, Mark Pryor, a second-generation Democratic senator and the only Democrat left in the Arkansas delegation—lost big to Cotton, 57%-40%, despite a major Democratic voter-turnout effort. Credible Democratic candidates for several House seats lost, including respected former FEMA head James Lee Witt, who was trounced by double digits. Meanwhile, the state legislature, heavily Democratic since Reconstruction, is now Republican: The GOP emerged from the 2014 election with majorities of 24-11 in the Senate and 64-36 in the House. After gaining control, the GOP steered the legislature to the right, voting to cut $140 million in taxes by fiscal 2016 and passing a raft of socially conservative legislation, including a measure declaring that life begins at conception and a ban on most abortions at 12 weeks.

There is a residual strain of populism in Arkansas—even during the 2014 Republican wave, voters approved a three-phase minimum-wage hike. Still, the trends for Arkansas Democrats are grim. Other southern states, such as North Carolina and Virginia, have

Population		Race and Ethnicity		Income	
Total:	2,959,373	White	74.3%	Median income:	$39,919
Urban:	29.5%	Black	15.7%		(49 of 50)
Suburban:	25.1%	Latino	6.5%	Under $50,000	59.4%
Rural:	45.4%	Asian	1.2%	$50,000-$99,999:	27.3%
Land area:	52,035	Two races	1.7%	$100,000-$199,999:	11.1%
Pop/sq. mi.:	56.9	White Ethnic	16.3%	$200,000 or more:	2.2%
Born in state:	62.2%			Poverty Rate	15.9%
		Education			
Age Groups		H.S. grad or less:	50.9%	**Work**	
Under 18:	24.0%	Some college:	28.5%	White collar:	31.9%
18 to 34:	22.7%	College degree, 4 yr.:	13.4%	Blue collar:	27.1%
35 to 64:	38.0%	Post-grad study:	7.2%	Sales and service:	41.0%
Over 64:	15.3%				
		Military		Govt. workers:	16.0%
		Veterans/active duty:	9.6%		

turned purple due to an influx of liberal-leaning outsiders, but in Arkansas, the fastest growth has occurred in the historically Republican northwest and in the GOP-leaning Little Rock exurbs. Population in rural, Democratic-friendly areas has stagnated or shrunk. "Arkansas may be past the point where Democrats are viable candidates for federal office," the *Cook Political Report's* David Wasserman wrote after the 2014 election.

Presidential Politics Like most Southern states, Arkansas voted more Democratic than the nation as a whole in presidential elections from Reconstruction to 1960. Since then, it has done so only when Jimmy Carter and Bill Clinton were atop the Democratic ticket. In the last four elections, it has voted 51 and 54 percent for George W. Bush, 59 percent for John McCain, and 61 percent for Mitt Romney. Between the presidential elections of 2000 and 2012, only in West Virginia has the Democratic percentage declined more precipitously than it has in Arkansas. In 1996, Clinton carried all but nine of the state's 75 counties, and in 2012, Obama won just nine. The Democratic

2012 Presidential Vote		
Mitt Romney (R)................647,744	(61%)
Barack Obama (D) 394,409	(37%)
2012 Presidential Primary		
Barack Obama (D) 94,936	(58%)
John Wolfe (D) 67,711	(42%)
2012 Presidential Primary		
Mitt Romney (R)................104,200	(68%)
Ron Paul (R) 20,399	(13%)
Rick Santorum (R) 20,308	(13%)
2008 Presidential Vote		
John McCain (R)................638,017	(59%)
Barack Obama (D) 422,310	(39%)

stronghold in presidential contests is Pulaski County, home to Little Rock, the state's largest city and capital. More than a third of the county's residents are African-American. Jefferson County (Pine Bluff) and rural counties of the Mississippi Delta also lean Democratic. Northwest Arkansas, the Ozark Mountain region, is historically Republican and home to the corporate headquarters of Wal-Mart in Bentonville. Asa Hutchinson, the state's newly minted GOP governor, represented this area when he was a congressman. Relatively fast growing suburban counties of Falkner and Saline around Little Rock are also GOP strengths.

In presidential primaries, Arkansas' preferences have been unequivocal. In 2008, when it voted on Super Tuesday, February 5, both parties had candidates with Arkansas experience, and both won handily. Hillary Clinton won by 70%-26% over Obama, and Huckabee won by 60%-20% over John McCain. For 2012, Arkansas reverted to its usual May primary date, and Romney, who had clinched the Republican nomination, won 68%-13% over Ron Paul. On the Democratic side, Obama beat John Wolfe, a Chattanooga lawyer and perennial candidate for office in Tennessee, by 58%-42%. Wolfe, who called Obama a "creature of Wall Street," carried 36 counties.

Congressional Districts The rapid Republican takeover of Arkansas since 2010, when it was the last remaining Southern state where Democrats still held the governorship and both houses of the legislature, has also extended to the congressional delegation. When Republicans that year flipped Democrats' usual

114th Congress Lineup
4 R   0 D
113th Congress Lineup
4 R   0 D

3-to-1 seat majority by picking up the open 1st and 2nd districts, national Democratic strategists applied pressure on their Arkansas counterparts to radically revamp the state's map by creating a solidly Democratic black influence district linking Little Rock with the state's Delta region.

But what party strategists in Washington wanted fell on deaf ears in Little Rock, where Democrats' first order of business was protecting sole surviving Blue Dog Democrat Mike Ross in the southern 4th District. Complicating matters was the need to shift voters from fast-growing Northwest Arkansas' heavily Republican 3rd District to the slow-growing 4th District. In April 2011, Gov. Mike Beebe signed off on a map that barely changed the 1st and 2nd districts but pushed the 4th District north to take a big bite of rural Republican counties out of the 3rd District, which in turn assumed a mangled arch shape to hang onto Republican Steve Womack's Russellville birthplace. Three months later, Ross announced his retirement, and Democrats lost the 4th District in a landslide, embarrassingly locking them out of the state's House delegation for the first time since Reconstruction.

In 2014, Democrats made strong bids for the 2nd and 4th districts, both of which had been opened by retirements. But Republicans comfortably won those two seats, and Ross suffered a double-digit loss in his bid for governor.

Governor

Asa Hutchinson (R)

Elected 2014, term expires Jan. 2019, 1st term; b. Dec. 3, 1950, Bentonville; Bob Jones U., B.S. 1972; U of AR (Fayetteville), J.D. 1975; Christian; Married (Susan); 4 children

Elected Office: U.S. House, 1997-2001.

Professional Career: Bentonville city atty., 1977-78; U.S. atty., 1982-85; Chairman, AR Republican Committee, 1990-95; Director, DEA, 2001-03; Under Secretary for Border & Transportation Security, Dept. Homeland Security, 2003-05.

Office: 500 Woodlane St., Little Rock, 72201; 501-682-2345; Website: governor.arkansas.gov.

Election Results

2014 general	Asa Hutchinson (R)	470,429	(55%)
	Mike Ross (D)	352,115	(42%)
2014 primary	Asa Hutchinson (R)	130,752	(73%)
	Curtis Coleman (R)	48,473	(27%)

Republican Asa Hutchinson was elected governor in 2014, succeeding Democrat Mike Beebe. After three unsuccessful tries for statewide office, Hutchinson prevailed over fellow former Rep. Mike Ross.

Hutchinson grew up on a farm with his brother Tim who later became a senator. Their parents also operated a Christian radio station and school. After graduating from Bob Jones University, Asa Hutchinson attended the University of Arkansas law school at the same time that Bill Clinton started teaching there. He became U.S. attorney in western Arkansas and prosecuted Clinton's half-brother, Roger, for cocaine possession.

He lost a long-shot 1986 bid for the Senate against Democrat Dale Bumpers, then ran for attorney general in 1990 and lost again. He spent the next five years as the state GOP chairman.

Hutchinson easily won election to the House in 1996 to succeed his brother, who moved to the Senate. He combined a conservative voting record with a pleasant demeanor to become an important player in a short time. In 1998, he served as one of the House's impeachment managers against Clinton. When George W. Bush became president, he tapped Hutchinson to head the Drug Enforcement Administration, then as undersecretary for transportation and border security in the new Homeland Security Department. Hutchinson returned to Arkansas to run for governor in 2006, but lost.

After the 2012 mass shooting in Newtown, Connecticut—when National Rifle Association executive vice president Wayne LaPierre decisively rejected national pressure to moderate the group's stance against gun control—LaPierre offered his solution, which was to ensure the presence of guns in schools as a defensive measure. LaPierre tapped Hutchinson to head a "multifaceted" education and training program "available to every school in America free of charge."

With Beebe term-limited, Hutchinson prepared for a race in 2014. He ended up facing Ross, who in 12 years in the House had been a Blue Dog with the kind of moderate voting record that could make him competitive in the Republican-trending state, including a vote against the Affordable Care Act. Hutchinson took less ideological stands during the campaign than he had in the past: He backed a November ballot measure to increase the state minimum wage and to provide additional funding for early-childhood education, two proposals that Democrats nationally have favored. He also aired an ad targeting women that featured his school-age granddaughter, who helped him advocate a plan to put computer-science classes in every high school and to help women compete for high-tech jobs.

Backed by $6.2 million from the Republican Governors Association aimed at tying Ross to President Barack Obama and other national Democrats, Hutchison prevailed, 55%-42%. Once in office—and leading the state's first unified Republican government since Reconstruction—Hutchinson succeeded in getting much of his proposed agenda passed, including a middle-class tax cut, scaled back from $100 million to $80 million.

Two legislative battles stood out. One was the latest chapter in the fight over the state's "private option"—Beebe's creative way of getting a red state to accept Medicaid expansion under the Affordable Care Act, by applying federal funds for Medicaid-eligible residents toward securing them private health coverage. Approved narrowly in 2013 and reauthorized even more narrowly in 2014, the program was a policy success, signing up more than 200,000 people, but its continued survival was in doubt given fierce conservative opposition in the legislature. After taking office, Hutchinson took something of a middle course, keeping the program in place through the end of 2016 as a task force drew up recommendations for a possible new direction after that.

The other conflict Hutchinson had to grapple with was a religious freedom measure that blew up shortly after a similar bill in Indiana drew fire for potentially enabling businesses to refuse to serve gays and lesbians. As in Indiana, disapproval from the business community was critical in forestalling the measure; in Arkansas, the key opposition came from Wal-Mart, and Hutchinson's son Seth attracted notice for signing a petition urging the governor to cast a veto. Hutchinson rejected the first version he received from lawmakers, ordering up changes to the most controversial provisions. The legislature complied, and Hutchinson signed the revised measure.

Senior Senator

John Boozman (R)

Elected 2010, term expires Jan. 2017, 1st term; b. Dec. 10, 1950, Shreveport, LA; U. of AR, 1969-72, Southern Col. of Optometry, O.D. 1977; Baptist; married (Cathy); 3 children.

Elected Office: Rogers Schl. Bd., 1994-2001; U.S. House, 2001-11.

Professional Career: Optometrist, Boozman-Hof Regional Eye Clinic, 1977-2001.

DC Office: 141 HSOB, 20510, 202-224-4843; Fax: 202-228-1371; Website: boozman.senate.gov.

State Offices: El Dorado, 870-863-4641; Ft. Smith, 479-573-0189; Jonesboro, 870-268-6925; Little Rock, 501-372-7153; Lowell, 479-725-0400; Mountain Home, 870-424-0129; Stuttgart, 870-672-6941.

Committees: *Agriculture, Nutrition & Forestry:* Commodities, Markets, Trade & Risk Management (Chmn); Conservation, Forestry & Natural Resources; Nutrition, Specialty Crops, & Agricultural Research. *Appropriations:* Commerce, Justice, Science & Related Agencies; Financial Services & General Gov't (Chmn); Military Construction & Veterans Affairs, & Related Agencies; State, Foreign Operations, & Related Programs; Transportation, HUD & Related Agencies. *Environment & Public Works:* Fisheries, Water, & Wildlife; Superfund, Waste Mgmt., & Regulatory Oversight; Transportation & Infrastructure. *Rules & Administration. Veterans' Affairs. Commission on Security & Cooperation in Europe.*

Group Ratings

	ADA	ACLU	AFL-CIO	LCV	ITI	COC	HAFA	ACU	CFG	FRC
2014	0%	0%	–	20%	33%	100%	68%	79%	65%	100%
2013	10%	C	28%	15%	C	75%	C	80%	70%	C

National Journal Ratings

	2013 LIB	—	2013 CONS
Economic	27%	—	72%
Social	0%	—	92%
Foreign	21%	—	76%
Composite	18%	—	82%

Key Votes of the 113th Congress

1. Sandy storm spending	N	5. Student Loan Rates	Y	9. Bipartisan Budget Deal	N
2. Chuck Hagel Confirmation	N	6. Employee Non-Discrim'n Act	N	10. Farm Bill Conference Rept.	Y
3. Gun Background Checks	N	7. Senate Vote on Judgeships	Y	11. Unempl. Comp. Extension	N
4. Immigration Reform	N	8. Defense Dept. Spending	N	12. Keystone Pipeline	Y

Election Results

2010 general	John Boozman (R)	451,618	(58%)	$3,666,798	$172,106	
	Blanche Lincoln (D)	288,156	(37%)	$12,662,526	$913,625	$3,514,725
	Trevor Drown (I)	25,234	(3%)			
2010 primary	John Boozman (R)	75,010	(53%)			
	Jim Holt (R)	24,826	(17%)			
	Gilbert Baker (R)	16,540	(12%)			
	Conrad Reynolds (R)	7,128	(5%)			

Prior winning percentages: House: 2008 (79%), 2006 (62%), 2004 (59%), 2002 (99%), 2001 special (56%)

Republican John Boozman is Arkansas' senior senator, having ousted two-term Democrat Blanche Lincoln in 2010 by one of the largest margins—more than 20 percent—of any Senate challenger over an incumbent. An amiable conservative, he generally hews to the party line though he also, occasionally, works across the aisle, as he did from time to time during his five terms in the House.

Boozman was born in Shreveport Louisiana and grew up in Fort Smith, the second-largest city in Arkansas. He credits his upbringing—his father was Air Force Master Sgt. Fay Boozman Jr.—for his appreciation of difficult issues that military families face. He graduated from Northside High School in Fort Smith and attended the University of Arkansas, where he played offensive guard on the football team. He left college after completing his pre-optometry requirements and went on to graduate from the Southern College of Optometry in 1977.

He opened the Boozman Eye Clinic in Rogers with his brother, Fay Boozman, an ophthalmologist. Their firm merged with another eye clinic in 1981 to form the Boozman-Hof Regional Eye Clinic. Boozman also established a low-vision program for the Arkansas School for the Blind and was a volunteer optometrist at a clinic that provides medical services to low-income families. He also raised Polled Hereford cattle that were competitive in the show ring.

His first experience in public office was on the Rogers School Board of Education—a seat he won in 1994. Four years later, he got a taste of a statewide campaign when he worked on his brother Fay's unsuccessful Senate race against Lincoln. After serving in the education post for seven years, Boozman in 2001 sought the seat vacated by Republican Rep. Asa Hutchinson, to head the Drug Enforcement Administration. Boozman won that special election, with the support of Governor Mike Huckabee. He distinguished himself as the only Republican in the contest to back President George W. Bush's push for limited federal funding of stem cell research. Boozman then easily defeated Mike Hathorn, a young Democratic state representative. Boozman had a strong grassroots organization and a sophisticated GOP get-out-the-vote operation.

When Boozman traveled to Capitol Hill to claim his seat, it marked his first trip to Washington, D.C. He worked with Republican Rep. Roy Blunt of Missouri on a water quality committee that steered money from the Environmental Protection Agency to the White and Elk Rivers, both of which are vital to local tourism and economic development. He also worked across the aisle on measures to improve benefits for veterans.

Boozman showed independence from the Bush White House by voting to end the trade embargo with Cuba and by backing a measure to allow the importation of prescription drugs from Canada. He opposed Bush's immigration proposal, calling it amnesty for illegal aliens. A devout evangelical Christian, Boozman sponsored measures to display the Ten Commandments in the House and Senate chambers, sought to weaken restrictions on churches' political activities and sponsored legislation to make English the country's official language.

Boozman made a misstep in 2005 by sponsoring and then withdrawing a bill to increase the maximum workday for truckers to 16 hours—a move sought by Wal-Mart but that was lambasted as a "sweatshop on wheels" that would have jeopardized safety. He also backed the controversial 2008 bill to rescue the U.S. financial system—an issue that tea party supporters used against some Republican incumbents in GOP primaries. He avoided that fate, when in his 2010 Senate race, former vice presidential nominee Sarah Palin backed him. When President Barack Obama took office, Boozman wasted no time in opposing the top White House initiatives.

In February 2010, he entered the Senate race. The political dynamics in the state had changed markedly. GOP presidential nominee John McCain had trounced Obama in 2008. Two House seats vacated by retiring Democrats also went Republican in 2010. Arkansas, one of the last Democratic holdouts in the South, clearly was joining the Dixie movement to the GOP.

In an eight-candidate field, Boozman secured the GOP nomination without a runoff. As the best-known candidate and having represented a district that was home to most of the state's Republican voters, Boozman captured 53 percent of the vote.

Lincoln's bid for a third term was hampered by a spirited primary challenge by Democratic Lt. Gov. Bill Halter, who not only made her drain her re-election funds but also forced her into a runoff. She narrowly won, but the battle left her weakened. Like other Republican Senate candidates in 2010, Boozman sought to exploit the state's disenchantment with Obama by nationalizing the battle and seeking to tie Lincoln to the White House.

Boozman blasted the two-term senator as out of step with the conservative values of the state and cited his endorsements from the National Rifle Association and Arkansas Right to Life. He sharply criticized Lincoln's vote for the economic stimulus and especially targeted her support of the sweeping health care legislation. "I listened to your concerns on `Obamacare,' fought for you in Washington, and voted against this bill," he said. "But the Senate has let you down. Arkansas did not have a voice in that chamber willing to stand up to" Obama and Democratic congressional leaders. Boozman said he would fight to repeal "Obamacare."

Lincoln tried to distance herself from Obama and to stress the importance to the state of her position as chair of the Agricultural Committee. But Republican Senate Leader Mitch McConnell helped Boozman by promising him that he would get a seat on that panel if he won. Lincoln criticized Boozman for hurting seniors with his support for privatizing Social Security and for cutting Medicare. Boozman countered that Lincoln was taking a card out of the old Democratic playbook by trying to scare seniors. When the votes were counted, the Senate race was no contest, as Boozman swept to a big win as part of the national GOP tide. He carried independents nearly 2 to 1 and even won a majority of older voters.

Boozman continued to compile a consistently conservative record. Right out of the gate, he introduced a measure to require parental notification at least four days before their minor daughter could have an abortion. He joined 34 other senators in opposing the farm bill because it did too little for Southern farmers, particularly rice and peanut growers.

Boozman joined several Republicans in withdrawing his support for legislation aimed at cracking down on the theft of Internet content after critics, including websites such as Google and Wikipedia and their users, said it would give the Justice Department the power to force Internet service providers to block access to sites accused of stealing intellectual property. As a member of the Veterans' Affairs panel, Boozman continued to advocate for greater veterans benefits, including by successfully pushing for a provision in a bill to give returning soldiers with brain injuries better mental and behavioral health services.

Boozman collaborated on important issues to the state with Democrat Sen. Mark Pryor, until his defeat in 2014. In June 2012, during the debate over reauthorizing the National Flood Insurance Program, they led a bipartisan group of senators who successfully opposed a proposal to mandate flood insurance for individuals residing near levees and other flood-control structures. They also sought to reverse an Air Force proposal to eliminate A-10 aircraft at the Arkansas Air National Guard's base in Fort Smith. Boozman reached across the aisle on veterans issues, teaming with Democrat Jon Tester of Montana in 2015 to introduce a measure to help combat homelessness among veterans.

As a stalwart conservative, Boozman opposed the Environmental Protection Agency for what he saw as an attack on coal, especially the agency's proposed rules to reduce carbon emissions at power plants—a move that he said would drive up costs in Arkansas.

Boozman had emergency heart surgery in 2014, but he recovered and is poised to seek a second term representing a state whose congressional delegation had had a huge shift since he was its lone Republican.

Junior Senator

Tom Cotton (R)

Elected 2014, term expires Jan. 2021, 1st term; b. May 13, 1977, Dardanelle; Harvard U., B.A. 1998, J.D. 2002; Christian; married (Anna); 1 child.

Military Career: U.S. Army, 2004-09 (Iraq).

Elected Office: U.S. House, 2012-14.

Professional Career: Clerk, U.S. Court of Appeals, 2002-03; Practicing atty., 2003-04; Mgmt. consultant, McKinsey & Co., 2010-11.

DC Office: 124 RSOB, 20510, 202-224-2353; Website: cotton.senate .gov.

State Offices: El Dorado, 870-864-8582; Jonesboro, 870-933-6223; Little Rock, 501-223-9081; Springdale, 479-751-0879.

Committees: *Armed Services:* Airland (Chmn); Emerging Threats & Capabilities; Personnel. *Banking, Housing, & Urban Affairs:* Economic Policy; Housing, Transportation, & Community Development; Nat'l Security & Int'l Trade & Finance. *Intelligence (Select). Aging (Special). Joint Economic Committee.*

Group Ratings (House)

	ADA	ACLU	AFL-CIO	LCV	ITI	COC	HAFA	ACU	CFG	FRC
2014	5%	15%	–	3%	80%	64%	82%	100%	96%	100%
2013	0%	C	19%	7%	C	92%	C	92%	92%	C

National Journal Ratings (House)

	2013 LIB	—	2013 CONS
Economic	18%	—	80%
Social	31%	—	67%
Foreign	34%	—	60%
Composite	29%	—	71%

Key Votes of the 113th Congress (House)

1. Sandy storm spending	N	5. Medical Marijuana	N	9. Syrian Rebels Training	Y
2. Violence Against Women Act	N	6. Farm Bill	N	10. Keystone Pipeline	Y
3. Guantanamo Bay Detainees	N	7. Afghanistan Combat	N	11. Immigration Exec. Action	Y
4. Abortion 20-week ban	Y	8. NSA Phone Data Collection	N	12. Bipartisan Budget Deal	N

Election Results

2014 general	Tom Cotton (R)	478,819	(57%)	$13,948,938	$8,004,645	$15,802,295
	Mark Pryor (D)	334,174	(40%)	$14,578,504	$987,646	$15,005,636
	Nathan LaFrance (Lib.)	17,210	(2%)			
	Mark Swaney (Green)	16,797	(2%)			
2014 primary	Tom Cotton (R)	20,899	(58%)			
	Beth Anne Rankin (R)	13,460	(37%)			
	John Cowart (R)	1,953	(5%)			

Prior winning percentage: House: 2012 (60%)

Republican Rep. Tom Cotton ousted incumbent Sen. Mark Pryor in one of 2014's most closely watched Senate races. Despite Pryor's reputation as one of the chamber's most conservative Democrats, Arkansas's increasingly rightward shift and President Obama's deep unpopularity there provided the opening for Cotton. Cotton's victory marked a milestone for the state, as it is the first time since Reconstruction that Republicans hold every seat in the state's congressional delegation.

A sixth-generation Arkansan, Cotton grew up on his family's cattle farm in Dardanelle. Even at a young age, Cotton's serious, studious demeanor made an impression, as did his growing interest in conservative thought and teachings. Friends remember him as a contrarian and a deep admirer of Winston Churchill. He studied government as an undergraduate at Harvard and went on to earn a degree from its law school. Cotton served as a judicial clerk for Judge Jerry Erwin Smith of the 5th Circuit Court of Appeals and later went to work at two law firms.

Cotton enlisted in the Army in December 2004, turning down an opportunity to join the Judge Advocate General Corps, preferring to serve in combat. He was deployed to

Baghdad in May 2006 as a platoon leader in the 101st Airborne Division, leading daily patrols through the city. His ferocity came through after his deployment when he wrote a letter in 2006 to *The New York Times* in response to a story the newspaper broke about the George W. Bush administration's program to trace financial transactions of people suspected of ties to terrorist organizations. "You may think you have done a public service," he wrote, "but you have gravely endangered the lives of my soldiers and all other soldiers and innocent Iraqis here." He went on: "Next time I hear that familiar explosion—or next time I feel it—I will wonder whether we could have stopped that bomb had you not instructed terrorists how to evade our financial surveillance. By the time we return home, maybe you will be in your rightful place: not at the Pulitzer announcements, but behind bars."

Though the *Times* chose not to publish the letter, Cotton had copied PowerLine, a conservative blog, which did publish it. His tough words made a big impression on some leading conservatives. William Kristol, the editor of *The Weekly Standard*, befriended Cotton and became his champion. In March 2007, Cotton joined the Old Guard at Arlington National Cemetery, the regiment that guards the Tomb of the Unknowns. The following year, he went to Afghanistan as an operations officer for a provincial construction team. After completing his military service, Cotton considered launching a campaign against Democratic Sen. Blanche Lincoln in 2010, but decided against it. Instead, he postponed pursuing political office and joined McKinsey & Co., a high-powered management consulting firm.

When Democratic Rep. Mike Ross announced in June 2011 that he would not seek reelection, Republicans saw a big opportunity. Cotton decided that this was the right time to take the plunge into politics. Hardly a natural politician, Cotton is more the cerebral, introverted, principled conservative than a back-slapper who enjoys mixing it up on the campaign trail. Still, his tough-minded conservatism caught the attention of national groups, earning endorsements from the anti-tax Club for Growth and the National Republican Congressional Committee, as well as from the state's major newspapers and from Sen. John McCain of Arizona, who shares Cotton's hawkish views. Cotton won the GOP primary with 58 percent of the vote, topping Beth Anne Rankin, a former aide to Republican Gov. Mike Huckabee. He then trounced Democratic state Rep. Gene Jeffress, racking up 60 percent of the vote.

In the House, Cotton quickly compiled a strongly conservative record and began to show an uncompromising streak. He opposed an initial version of the 2014 farm bill, which he scorned as a "food-stamp bill." He later backed a version that didn't contain food-stamp programs. He opposed disaster relief for folks who took a hit from Hurricane Sandy. He has been harshly critical of Obama on many issues related to the military and national security. After the April 2013 Boston Marathon bombing, he blasted the administration for "failing in its mission to stop terrorism before it reaches its targets in the United States." But Cotton didn't spare his party's anti-interventionist wing and, just months later, he joined with another veteran, Rep. Mike Pompeo of Kansas, to write an op-ed in *The Washington Post* urging fellow Republicans to support Obama's call for military intervention in Syria.

Given the state's growing GOP tilt and his military background and strong conservative credentials, Cotton was quickly seen as the party's best prospect to unseat Pryor. Though Republicans couldn't depict the centrist Pryor as a liberal Obama ally, they did hammer him for backing the Affordable Care Act. He also supported the administration's $787 billion economic stimulus bill and the Dodd-Frank Wall Street regulation bill. But he was one of a small number of Democrats who opposed additional background checks on gun purchases. He also parted company with the administration by backing the Keystone XL pipeline and, in 2012, he was the only Democrat to oppose the "Buffett rule" requiring millionaires to pay an effective 30% minimum tax rate. Pryor had a magical name in the state—as his dad held his Senate seat from 1979 until 1997. Republicans hadn't even bothered to field a candidate against him in 2008. But in the six years since then, the state's shift to the right invited a challenge. Polls showed an extremely tight race for months.

Right out of the gate, the Democratic strategy was to paint Cotton as an extremist, driven by ideological convictions that put him at odds with most Arkansans. They highlighted his vote against lower student loan interest rates—the only member of the state's delegation to oppose it—as well as his opposition to the farm bill. He countered that Obamacare had driven up the cost of student loans and should be repealed and that hometown banks should finance student loans rather than allowing the federal government to have a monopoly on that business.

Still, that Democratic tactic ultimately did not make a dent in the state's headlong trend toward backing GOP candidates. Cotton easily won, racking up a 57%-40% win. At 37, he became the youngest Member of the Senate. He quickly made his mark in advancing his hawkish views from the Armed Services Committee and as chairman of the Airland Subcommittee. Early on, Cotton made a big impression, grilling an Obama Defense Department official about Guantanamo—which Obama had promised to close during his campaign. "The only problem with Guantanamo Bay is that there are too many empty cells," Cotton said.

Shortly after that, the youthful senator made a splash that put him in national headlines when he authored a controversial letter to Iran's leaders in an attempt to head off what he saw as the White House negotiating a bad nuclear deal with Iran. Signed by 47 GOP senators, the letter warned Iran's leaders that striking an agreement with President Obama without congressional approval was nothing more than an executive agreement that could be short-lived since it could be undone by a future President or Congress. The letter infuriated White House officials as an inappropriate interference in the conduct of foreign policy. "The only thing unprecedented is an American president negotiating a nuclear deal with the world's leading state sponsor of terrorism without submitting it to Congress," Cotton countered on CNN. The Senate overwhelmingly approved the plan for congressional review of an agreement.

The letter, written after Cotton had been a senator for 65 days, underscored his outspoken, unapologetically bold approach, and made it clear that he is not willing to hold back despite his junior status.

FIRST DISTRICT

Rick Crawford (R)

Elected 2010, 3rd term; b. Jan. 22, 1966, Homestead Base, FL; AR St. U., B.S. 1996; Southern Baptist; married (Stacy); 2 children.

Military Career: U.S. Army, 1985-89 (Pakistan).

Professional Career: News anchor; Agri-reporter; Marketing mgr., John Deere; Owner, AgWatch Network.

DC Office: 1711 LHOB, 20515, 202-225-4076; Fax: 202-225-5602; Website: crawford.house.gov.

State Offices: Cabot, 501-843-3043; Jonesboro, 870-203-0540. Mountain Home, 870-424-2075.

Committees: *Agriculture:* General Farm Commodities & Risk Management (Chmn); Nutrition. *Transportation & Infrastructure:* Economic Development, Public Buildings & Emergency Management; Highways & Transit; Water Resources & Environment.

Group Ratings

	ADA	ACLU	AFL-CIO	LCV	ITI	COC	HAFA	ACU	CFG	FRC
2014	0%	0%	–	6%	40%	83%	58%	64%	61%	100%
2013	0%	C	25%	4%	C	75%	C	72%	60%	C

National Journal Ratings

	2013 LIB	—	2013 CONS
Economic	43%	—	56%
Social	0%	—	87%
Foreign	24%	—	68%
Composite	26%	—	74%

Key Votes of the 113th Congress

1. Sandy storm spending	Y	5. Medical Marijuana	N	9. Syrian Rebels Training	Y
2. Violence Against Women Act	N	6. Farm Bill	Y	10. Keystone pipeline	Y
3. Guantanamo Bay Detainees	N	7. Afghanistan Combat	N	11. Immigration Exec. Action	NV
4. Abortion 20-week ban	Y	8. NSA Phone Data Collection	N	12. Bipartisan budget deal	N

Election Results

2014 general	Rick Crawford (R)	124,139	(63%)	$665,075	$1,689
	Jackie McPherson (D)	63,555	(32%)	$279,781	
	Brian Scott Willhite (Lib)	8,562	(4%)		
2014 primary	Rick Crawford (R)	unopposed			

Prior winning percentages: 2012 (56%), 2010 (52%)

Population		Race and Ethnicity		Income	
Total:	729,971	White	76.8%	Median income:	$35,993
Urban:	14.0%	Black	18.3%		*(416 of 435)*
Suburban:	14.2%	Latino	2.8%	Under $50,000	64.4%
Rural:	71.8%	Asian	0.5%	$50,000-$99,999:	25.1%
Land area:	19,318	Two races	1.3%	$100,000-$199,999:	9.3%
Pop/sq. mi.:	38.5	White Ethnic	15.3%	$200,000 or more:	1.2%
Born in state:	66.6%			Poverty Rate	21.6%
		Education			
Age Groups		H.S. grad or less:	56.9%	**Work**	
Under 18:	23.6%	Some college:	28.0%	White collar:	29.2%
18 to 34:	21.0%	College degree, 4 yr.:	10.5%	Blue collar:	30.8%
35 to 64:	38.7%	Post-grad study:	4.6%	Sales and service:	40.0%
Over 64:	16.7%				
		Military		Govt. workers	15.9%
		Veterans/active duty:	10.5%		

Eastern Arkansas: The Delta, Jonesboro

The Mississippi Delta, the flat, mucky, river-crossed lowland on both sides of the great river, was some of the country's first industrial farmland. This land was uncultivated in most of the 19th century, when plows were still pulled by mules and muddy flatlands were impassable. Then, big landowners used machines to

Voter Turnout	
2013 Total Citizen 18+	550,148
2014 House Turnout	196,256
2014 Turnout as % CVAP	35.7%
2012 Turnout as % CVAP	46.2%

drain the marshlands and persuaded poor blacks to move here to tend fields of cotton, rice, and later, soybeans. The results were bountiful agriculture and impoverished people. Around 1940, the Delta began to slowly change: The first minimum-wage and war-industry jobs up North drew young people out of the Delta, and the introduction of the mechanical cotton picker idled many farm workers.

But this land—stretching flat as far as the eye can see, along ribbons of asphalt that shimmer in the heat—remains poor by national standards. The people are undereducated, and the area has substantial pockets of unemployment. Local rice farmers are among the largest recipients of federal farm subsidies. Riceland Foods, in the town of Stuttgart, is the world's largest rice miller and marketer and the largest recipient of subsidies in the United States, having received $554 million from 1995 to 2011. Producers Rice Mill, also in Stuttgart, ranked second in subsidies with $314 million over the same period. The local rice fields also attract ducks, helping put Arkansas on the map as the most productive state for mallard hunters.

The local economy suffered from the closing of major employers during the recession, but it is increasingly propped up by manufacturing. In 2010, Nordex USA, a German subsidiary, opened a turbine manufacturing plant in Jonesboro, with promises to employ 750 workers in a $40 million plant. That facility closed in 2013 as the result of "instability" in the U.S. wind energy market. In 2014, the factory was purchased by a rail-car manufacturer that planned to create 350 jobs. Another major rail manufacturing firm has factories a few miles away. Several big auto parts plants have been built in Marion, across the Mississippi River from Memphis.

The 1st Congressional District of Arkansas includes almost all of the state's Delta lands and stretches west to the cool, green Ozarks. The largest city in the district is Jonesboro, whose cheap labor and flat land have made it a hub for food-processing companies like Nestle and Frito-Lay. Jonesboro native John Grisham makes a number of references to the city in his book *A Painted House*. The district's natural beauty draws outdoorsmen to the sleepy Ozark town of Mountain Home, named *Outdoor Life* magazine's best place to live in 2008. The Delta, with its large African-American population, is the most Democratic part of Arkansas. Some of the hill counties are ancestrally Republican, and there is a Republican trend in

2012 Presidential Vote		
Mitt Romney (R)	154,551	(61%)
Barack Obama (D)	92,085	(36%)

2008 Presidential Vote		
John McCain (R)	151,947	(58%)
Barack Obama (D)	102,943	(39%)

Cook Partisan Voting Index: R+14

Jonesboro and in Lonoke County, which is part of the Little Rock metro area. The result is a district that leans Republican. Two Delta counties in the southeast, Chicot and Desha, are Democratic-leaning, but that may not be sufficient for the party to mount a successful challenge in the future.

Rick Crawford (R)

First District Rep. Rick Crawford in 2010 became the first Republican to win this northeastern Arkansas district since Reconstruction. A former news anchor and owner of an agricultural broadcasting business, he keeps an eye out for the region's cotton and rice farmers. Like the many Democrats who served this and similar districts in decades past, he is usually a loyalist who quietly produces farm and other legislation for party leaders.

Crawford was born in Florida on the former Homestead Air Force Base, where his father, a munitions expert, was stationed. Growing up in a military family meant a lot of "bouncing around," says Crawford, who attended a dozen schools as a child. The frequent uprooting provided a crash course in making friends quickly and adapting to new environments. After graduating from high school in Hudson, New Hampshire he enlisted in the Army, where he was trained as a bomb-disposal technician, disabling suspected live explosive devices. Crawford became a sergeant, did a tour of duty in Pakistan, and later served on U.S. Secret Service details for Presidents Ronald Reagan and George H.W. Bush.

When his military service ended, he enrolled at Arkansas State University, in Jonesboro, to study agribusiness and economics. He competed on the college rodeo circuit until injuries forced him to quit. In 1994, he declared personal bankruptcy, but he eventually found full-time employment—and discovered he had some skills—in rodeo announcing. He worked some 100 shows a year before finishing his degree. Working the rodeo-broadcasting gigs helped Crawford land a news-anchor job in Jonesboro after graduation. That eventually led him to agricultural broadcasting and to starting his own business called the AgWatch Network, a farm-news outlet that broadcast on dozens of radio stations in the mid-South, as well as on television stations in Little Rock and Jonesboro.

When Crawford decided to challenge seven-term Democratic Rep. Marion Berry for the 1st District seat, national Republicans were at first cool to the idea, hoping to recruit a more seasoned candidate. But Crawford gained traction after Berry announced he wouldn't run, which made the district ripe for a GOP takeover. Crawford coasted to an easy primary victory over 26-year-old congressional aide Princella Smith, and he launched a general election campaign with the theme that Democrats had lost touch with the region's rural and small-town conservative voters. In the general election campaign, Democrat Chad Causey, Berry's former chief of staff, made an issue of Crawford's personal bankruptcy, attacking the Republican for failing to release his financial records. Crawford, meanwhile, sought to portray Causey as a Washington insider beholden to national Democrats. The national parties jumped in with independent expenditures for ads. Former President Bill Clinton returned to his home state to help raise money for Causey, to no avail. Crawford won, 52%-44%.

In the House, Crawford sits on the Agriculture Committee, where he focuses on ways to protect farmers from what he considers overly burdensome regulations. In January 2015, he became chairman of the General Farm Commodities and Risk Management Subcommittee, which has jurisdiction over major commercial crops plus farm credit and crop insurance. That positioned him well to protect his district's interests on farm legislation. He cited improvements for crop insurance in the 2014 farm bill that have benefited his constituents, and promised close oversight of the Agriculture Department's implementation of the many complexities in the new law. He has filed a bill to protect bird hunters on farm lands from new federal penalties on baited fields.

His inclination to seek bipartisan consensus occasionally has caused problems for Crawford, including charges of flip-flopping. Although he has voted to repeal the Affordable Care Act, he has said that parts of it should remain in place. When he supported a 5 percent surtax on incomes exceeding $1 million to break a budget stalemate in 2012—but only if Congress first passed a balanced-budget constitutional amendment—Crawford told *The New York Times* that "many conservatives (are) calling for my head. ... But this does not deter me, because the alternative is economic calamity." He also urged his party to develop a more flexible approach on illegal immigration, arguing that immigrants are an important economic force.

Democrats in 2012 thought they might have a shot at unseating Crawford, claiming that redistricting had weakened him politically. But the national party's favored candidate, state Rep. Clark Hall, lost the primary to a little-known prosecutor. As a safeguard, Crawford announced that he would skip the Republican convention in Tampa to be at home "making sure farm families are getting the help they need from federal and state agencies." He won reelection with 56 percent of the vote. In 2014, he glided to reelection over Heber Springs Mayor Jackie McPherson, 63%-32%. Absent creative redistricting that might combine minority areas of Little Rock with parts of this district, Crawford appears to have become entrenched.

SECOND DISTRICT

French Hill (R)

Elected 2014, 1st term; b. Dec. 5, 1956, Little Rock; Vanderbilt U., B.S. 1979; Catholic; married (Martha); 2 children.

Professional Career: Staff, U.S. Senate Committee on Banking, Housing & Urban Affairs, 1982-84; Deputy asst., U.S. Treasury, 1989-91; Special asst., Economic Policy Council, 1991-93; Sr. advisor, Gov. Huckabee, 2008; Banker, Businessman.

DC Office: 1229 LHOB, 20515, 202-225-2506; Fax: 202-225-5903; Website: hill.house.gov.

State Offices: Conway, 501-358-3481; Little Rock, 501-324-5941.

Committees: *Financial Services:* Capital Markets & Gov't Sponsored Enterprises; Oversight & Investigations.

Election Results

2014 general	French Hill (R)	123,073	(52%)	$2,149,744	$662,534	$1,729,324
	Patrick Hays (D)	103,477	(44%)	$1,563,516	$110,521	$2,038,805
	Debbie Standiford (Lib)	10,590	(5%)			
2014 primary	French Hill (R)	29,916	(55%)			
	Ann Clemmer	12,400	(23%)			
	Conrad Reynolds	11,994	(22%)			

Population		Race and Ethnicity		Income	
Total:	751,463	White	69.9%	Median income:	$46,493
Urban:	53.3%	Black	21.8%		*(294 of 435)*
Suburban:	27.7%	Latino	4.9%	Under $50,000	53.4%
Rural:	19.0%	Asian	1.2%	$50,000-$99,999:	29.8%
Land area:	4,978	Two races	1.8%	$100,000-$199,999:	13.9%
Pop/sq. mi.:	134.3	White Ethnic	16.3%	$200,000 or more:	2.9%
Born in state:	68.0%			Poverty Rate	15.8%
		Education			
Age Groups		H.S. grad or less:	43.6%	**Work**	
Under 18:	23.8%	Some college:	29.4%	White collar:	35.6%
18 to 34:	24.7%	College degree, 4 yr.:	17.0%	Blue collar:	20.5%
35 to 64:	37.3%	Post-grad study:	10.0%	Sales and service:	43.9%
Over 64:	14.2%				
		Military		Govt. workers:	18.4%
		Veterans/active duty:	10.4%		

Central Arkansas: Little Rock, Pulaski

Little Rock has been the capital of Arkansas and also its largest city for more than a century. It is at the geographic center of an otherwise rural state, and it is home to the presidential library of Bill Clinton, the former Arkansas governor. The city was harshly criticized for its role at the dawn of the civil rights

Voter Turnout	
2013 Total Citizen 18+	555,044
2014 House Turnout	237,330
2014 Turnout as % CVAP	42.8%
2012 Turnout as % CVAP	52.7%

movement. In September 1957, Democratic Gov. Orval Faubus sent in the National Guard to block a desegregation order at Central High School. President Dwight D. Eisenhower sent

in U.S. troops and federalized the National
Guard to enforce the order, and Little Rock
became a synonym for bigotry around the
world. Forty years later, the Little Rock
Nine who had integrated the high school
returned for an anniversary commemoration with Clinton. "It was Little Rock that
made racial equality a driving obsession in
my life," he said. Today, Little Rock is still

2012 Presidential Vote		
Mitt Romney (R)................160,140	(55%)
Barack Obama (D) 125,527	(43%)
2008 Presidential Vote		
John McCain (R)................157,732	(54%)
Barack Obama (D) 129,888	(44%)
Cook Partisan Voting Index: R+8		

the political center of Arkansas, setting the tone of the public life of its state as do only a
few other state capitals—Boston, Providence, Atlanta, Denver, and Honolulu. It is home to
the *Arkansas Democrat-Gazette*, the feisty, conservative paper whose editor Paul Greenberg
saddled Clinton with "Slick Willie" in 1980. (Greenberg then worked for the *Pine Bluff Commercial*.) On the banks of the Arkansas River is the Clinton Presidential Center and Park,
opened in 2004 with his personal imprint. It has promoted local economic revitalization,
with architecture evocative of a "bridge to the 21st century."

The 2nd Congressional District of Arkansas includes Little Rock and North Little Rock,
a kind of industrial suburb across the Arkansas River and known informally for years as Dog
Town. The district also takes in Saline (named for its early salt works) and Faulkner (named
for fiddle player Sanford C. Faulkner, the original Arkansas Traveler) counties, which have
grown rapidly as people move farther out on the freeways. The Little Rock metropolitan
area has been economically resilient, and was among the areas in the nation that was least
affected by the recession in 2009. With its large shipping facilities, it is a robust market
for trade. Its $2.5 billion in exports were more than one-third of the state's total in 2013.
Welspun Corp, a Bombay India-based producer of large-diameter steel pipes, chiefly for oil
and gas companies, has employed more than 500 people at its Port of Little Rock plant. The
delay on the approval of the Keystone XL pipeline caused dozens of local job losses; Welspun
expects to produce half of the project's pipes.

This district's vote in presidential and statewide contests makes it the least conservative
of the state's four districts, slightly to the left among all seats held by Republicans. But it
continues to have a GOP lean. Pulaski County (Little Rock) includes a bit more than half of
the district voters and performs comfortably Democratic in competitive elections, such as the
2014 contests for governor and senator. But the outlying areas, led by Faulkner and Saline,
have become heavily Republican and they outweigh the Pulaski vote. This is the seat once
held by legendary Democratic Ways and Means Chairman Wilbur Mills, who retired in 1976.

French Hill (R)

French Hill, an investment banker and former senior policy adviser for President George H.W.
Bush, was elected in 2014 to replace retiring Rep. Tim Griffin, keeping the district in GOP
hands. Hill's race against former North Little Rock Mayor Patrick Henry Hays was competitive,
even though the district had voted for Mitt Romney by a 12-point margin in 2012.

A ninth-generation Arkansan, Hill's career has long intertwined his business acumen
with policy interests. The son and grandson of commercial and investment bankers, he earned
a bachelor's degree in economics from Vanderbilt University. He then worked as a banking
officer and senior financial analyst for Interfirst Bank in Dallas until 1982, when he moved to
Washington as a legislative aide for Republican Sen. John Tower of Texas. When Tower retired
two years later, Hill became director of the Dallas-based Mason Best Co., but he returned to
Washington in 1989 as a deputy assistant Treasury secretary. He then served as special assistant to Bush and the Economic Policy Council. He returned to investment banking in 1993
as chairman of First Commerce Trust and First Commercial Investments. Six years later he
joined with other investors to form Delta Trust & Bank in Little Rock, serving as its chairman.

In 2008, Hill served as senior adviser for former Arkansas Gov. Mike Huckabee's run
for the White House. The following year, GOP strategists hoped Hill would challenge Democratic Rep. Vic Snyder. When Snyder chose not to run, Hill instead contributed to Griffin's
successful campaign.

Hill sought the open House seat when Griffin ran successfully for lieutenant governor.
Against two credible opponents in the primary, he campaigned on a platform of fiscal conservatism that he highlighted in ads promoting "old Blue," a dusty 1998 Volvo. He took some
heat for failing to mention his other cars, including a BMW and Mercedes-Benz. He easily

won the primary with 55 percent of the vote, and took each of the seven counties. State Rep. Ann Clemmer, whose base was in Saline, ran second. In the general election, Hill advocated approval of the Keystone pipeline, the delay of which had adversely affected the Little Rock pipe-manufacturing firm Welspun. He pushed for a reduction in the corporate income tax while opposing efforts to hike the minimum wage—a stance he modified when voters approved a referendum to put the issue on the ballot.

National Democrats were enthusiastic about Hays. The Democratic Congressional Campaign Committee poured more than $1 million into the race. Former President Clinton also campaigned for Hays. Democrats slammed Hill for contributing to former state Treasurer Martha Shoffner, who "directed $700 million in taxpayer dollars to Hill's bank." Shoffner had been convicted in March 2014 on bribery and corruption charges. Pre-election polls showed a close contest. But Hill had a heavy fundraising advantage, particularly from the securities and investment industry. Hill ended up winning with 52 percent of the vote, slightly underperforming the district's recent vote history. Hays won 54 percent of the vote in Pulaski County, which cast 54 percent of the district vote. But that wasn't nearly enough to overcome Hill's big leads in the outlying counties, including 65 percent in Saline and 60 percent in Faulkner, the next two largest counties.

In the House, Hill was assigned to a post on the Financial Services Committee, where he has obvious expertise. He pledged to enhance transparency and accountability of federal agencies that deal with banking issues, "reduce the regulatory burden created by flawed policies like Dodd-Frank, and protect Arkansans from big-government overreach." He voiced concern that funds were being siphoned from the mortgage-assistance bankers Fannie Mae and Freddie Mac to support the Federal Housing Finance Agency. Democrats will watch Hill closely to see whether to target him in his first reelection bid.

THIRD DISTRICT

Steve Womack (R)

Elected 2010, 3rd term; b. Feb. 18, 1957, Russellville; AR Tech. U., B.A. 1979; Southern Baptist; married (Terri); 3 children.

Military Career: AR Army Natl. Guard, 1979-2009.

Elected Office: Rogers Mayor, 1998-2010.

Professional Career: Stn. mgr., KURM Radio, 1979-90; Rogers Cty. Council, 1983-84, 1997-98; Exec. officer, Army ROTC, U. of AR, 1990-96; Financial consultant, Merrill Lynch, 1996.

DC Office: 1119 LHOB, 20515, 202-225-4301; Fax: 202-225-5713; Website: womack.house.gov.

State Offices: Fort Smith, 479-424-1146; Harrison, 870-741-6900; Rogers, 479-464-0446.

Committees: *Appropriations:* Defense; Financial Services & General Gov't; Labor, HHS, Education & Related Agencies. *Budget.*

Group Ratings

	ADA	ACLU	AFL-CIO	LCV	ITI	COC	HAFA	ACU	CFG	FRC
2014	0%	0%	–	3%	100%	86%	52%	56%	51%	100%
2013	0%	C	14%	0%	C	92%	C	72%	63%	C

National Journal Ratings

	2013 LIB	—	2013 CONS
Economic	39%	—	60%
Social	0%	—	87%
Foreign	34%	—	60%
Composite	28%	—	72%

Key Votes of the 113th Congress

1. Sandy storm spending	N	5. Medical Marijuana	N	9. Syrian Rebels Training	Y
2. Violence Against Women Act	N	6. Farm Bill	Y	10. Keystone pipeline	Y
3. Guantanamo Bay Detainees	N	7. Afghanistan Combat	N	11. Immigration Exec. Action	Y
4. Abortion 20-week ban	Y	8. NSA Phone Data Collection	N	12. Bipartisan budget deal	Y

Election Results

2014 general Steve Womack (R)......................151,630   (79%) $574,944 $3,444
              Grant Brand (Lib).......................39,305   (21%)
2014 primary Steve Womack (R).................unopposed

Prior winning percentages: 2012 (76%), 2010 (72%)

Population		Race and Ethnicity		Income	
Total:	757,765	White	77.6%	Median income:	$44,405
Urban:	33.8%	Latino	12.7%		*(329 of 435)*
Suburban:	37.8%	Black	3.0%	Under $50,000	55.5%
Rural:	28.4%	Asian	2.5%	$50,000-$99,999:	28.6%
Land area:	6,987	Two races	2.4%	$100,000-$199,999:	12.6%
Pop/sq. mi.:	108.5	White Ethnic	17.3%	$200,000 or more:	3.4%
Born in state:	49.5%			Poverty Rate	19.0%
		Education			
Age Groups		H.S. grad or less:	48.0%	**Work**	
Under 18:	25.3%	Some college:	26.9%	White collar:	33.2%
18 to 34:	24.8%	College degree, 4 yr.:	15.8%	Blue collar:	40..3%
35 to 64:	36.6%	Post-grad study:	9.3%	Sales and service:	26.4%
Over 64:	13.2%				
		Military		Govt. workers	11.6%
		Veterans/active duty:	8.8%		

Northwest Arkansas: Fayetteville, Fort Smith

In the past decade, the northwest corner of Arkansas has become one of America's boom areas, with major corporate headquarters and dozens of small factories, tourist attractions, and retirement developments in the Ozarks. Anchoring the local economy are three major employers: Wal-Mart Stores, Tyson

Voter Turnout	
2013 Total Citizen 18+	522,105
2014 House Turnout	190,935
2014 Turnout as % CVAP	36.6%
2012 Turnout as % CVAP	49.4%

Foods, and J.B. Hunt Transport Services. The area has a rapidly growing population of Hispanics working at these companies, who make up more than 30 percent of the population of Springdale and Rogers. This is also home to the mountain-bound resort town of Eureka Springs and the handsome University of Arkansas in Fayetteville, where young lawyers Bill Clinton and Hillary Rodham married in the living room of a brick bungalow.

The friendly atmosphere, the prevalence of religious faith, and the natural backdrop of rounded green mountains and wide valleys in northwest Arkansas have been conducive to economic creativity and personal serenity. There have also been touches of genius. Sam Walton, who opened his first Wal-Mart on the town square of Bentonville (it's now a small museum), had the inspiration to build a retail chain in tradition-minded small towns and rural areas using sophisticated computerized management. It made him the richest man in America before he died in 1992, though he still drove a pickup truck and kept the corporate headquarters in a deliberately unglitzy building in Bentonville. The corporate headquarters are by far the largest employer in this corner of the state. Don Tyson built Tyson Foods, with headquarters outside Springdale, into the world's leading chicken producer and processor.

Other firms have flocked in, especially to do business with Wal-Mart, the world's largest food retailer. The region's unemployment is low, but local leaders worry about the area's aging workforce that often fails to meet demands for both skilled and entry-level positions, and its reliance on the three mainstay companies. They have launched an effort to diversify into professional services and tourism. Hospitality tax collections increased 15 percent in the fourth quarter of 2014. Fort Smith was dealt a blow in 2012 when Whirlpool closed its refrigerator production plant and shed 1,000 jobs. But that area too has strengthened, with increases in tech jobs and expanded commercial use of local waterways.

The 3rd Congressional District covers Northwest Arkansas, including Bentonville, Fayetteville, and Springdale, plus Fort Smith on the Oklahoma line. It extends as far east as Marion County, home to Ranger Boats, the renowned manufacturer of tournament-quality fishing boats. Politically, this area has been consistently the most Republican part of Arkansas since the Civil War. John Paul Hammerschmidt was elected to the House in 1966 as one of the first Republican congressmen from the South. He beat 28-year-old Bill Clinton in the Democratic year of 1974, ending Clinton's first bid for public office with a loss (although he got an impres-

2012 Presidential Vote		
Mitt Romney (R)..................168,703		(66%)
Barack Obama (D) 81,413		(32%)
2008 Presidential Vote		
John McCain (R)..................162,083		(64%)
Barack Obama (D) 85,993		(34%)
Cook Partisan Voting Index: R+19		

sive 48 percent of the vote). Lately, this area has become even more Republican, as Christian conservatives have entered politics, and new migrants and millionaires have voted heavily for the GOP.

As a result of post-census redistricting in 2011, the 3rd District shrank geographically, losing several Republican counties to the Pine Bluff-based 4th District. But it has remained the most Republican district in Arkansas..

Steve Womack (R)

Republican Steve Womack won the 2010 contest to fill the seat left vacant by GOP Rep. John Boozman, who ran successfully for the Senate. With his seat on the Appropriations Committee, he has become an active Republican lawmaker with a knack for both cutting deals and irritating Democrats.

Womack was born in Russellville Arkansas, and spent a good portion of his childhood in Moberly, Missouri. His father, a local radio broadcaster, introduced him to popular political figures in the region, including former Sens. Tom Eagleton and Stuart Symington and Gov. Warren Hearnes, all Missouri Democrats. "If I 'Dr. Phil' myself about what got me involved in public service, it's that I always admired political leaders," Womack said. After high school, Womack earned his bachelor's degree at Arkansas Tech University. He and his father subsequently established KURM Radio, which focused on community news, the weather, the county fair, and high school football and Little League baseball games. Womack covered local politics for the station. "I always would second-guess things, and say, 'Could I do that better?'" he recalled.

In 1990, Womack, by then a member of the Army National Guard, served as executive officer of the Army ROTC program at the University of Arkansas. In 2002, he led a peace-keeping task force of 500 troops in the Sinai Desert in Egypt—a mission established by the peace accords negotiated between Israel and Egypt in 1979. In 1998, Womack was elected mayor of Rogers, a city in the high-growth Fayetteville metropolitan area. He accurately anticipated a spike in demand for retail outlets in the area and worked to turn the city into a shopping destination, including the issuance of bonds to develop infrastructure to attract business. He also had a reputation for tough enforcement of immigration laws. Local Hispanic leaders were incensed when Womack maintained that a majority of crimes in the city were committed by illegal immigrants, which they said was untrue. In 2007, Womack directed city officials to cooperate with raids by federal immigration agents on a Northwest Arkansas Mexican restaurant chain. After Hispanic motorists filed a lawsuit charging racial profiling by Rogers and its police department, a settlement was reached without an award of damages or an admission of guilt; Womack formed a committee to build better relations with the immigrant community.

When Boozman challenged Democratic Sen. Blanche Lincoln, Womack stepped into a crowded field of Republicans interested in the seat. His chief opponent was Cecile Bledsoe, a state senator endorsed by former Alaska Gov. Sarah Palin and Asa Hutchinson, now the Arkansas governor. In a June runoff, the two candidates, who lived less than a mile apart, took to the airwaves in an unneighborly way. Bledsoe tried to portray herself as the true conservative in the race, promising to repeal President Barack Obama's health care overhaul. Womack touted his record of job creation and attacked Bledsoe for her votes to increase taxes when she was in the legislature. Womack eked out a victory, 52%-48%. In this solidly Republican district, which has not elected a Democrat to the House since 1967, the hard work was behind him. Womack defeated Democrat David Whitaker, a former assistant city attorney in Fayetteville, 72%-28%.

In the House, Womack established himself as a firmly conservative vote. To win a coveted slot on the Appropriations Committee as a freshman, he told Chairman Harold Rogers of Kentucky that being a mayor had taught him how to say "no." But he has been eager to say "yes" to local interests in their dealings with the federal government. With Democratic Rep. Jackie Speier of California, he filed a bill enabling Amazon and other online retailers to collect state sales taxes, something that benefitted brick-and-mortar retailers such as Arkansas' Wal-Mart, which already collect state sales taxes online. In March 2015, he joined with Rep. Jim Costa, another California Democrat, to create the Chicken Caucus; the poultry industry maintains more than 2,000 chicken houses in Benton County.

Womack's more controversial proposals have included an amendment to cancel funding for Obama's teleprompter, and to cancel congressional pay in the event of a federal shutdown. In January 2013, he was the only Arkansas Republican who supported the budget and tax deal to avoid across-the-board tax hikes. He showed his close connection to the GOP leadership when Speaker John Boehner invited him to join a 2014 delegation to Afghanistan. His rapid rise in seniority on the Appropriations Committee has moved him close to a subcommittee chairmanship.

Back home, Womack has achieved the impressive combination of avoiding a Republican primary and a Democratic challenger in both 2012 and 2014. He could face tea party opposition. But the strong corporate influence in this district likely would offer him some protection.

FOURTH DISTRICT

Bruce Westerman (R)

Elected 2014, 1st term; b. Nov. 18, 1967, Hot Springs; U. of AR, B.S. 1990; Yale Forestry School, M.F. 2001; Baptist; married (Sharon); 4 children.

Elected Office: AR House, 2010-14, min. ldr., 2012-13, maj. ldr., 2013-14.

Professional Career: Fountain Lake Schl. Bd., 2006-10, pres., 2009-10; Engineer, forester, Mid-South Engineering; Deacon, Walnut Valley Baptist Church.

DC Office: 130 CHOB, 20515, 202-225-3772; Fax: 202-225-1314; Website: westerman.house.gov.

State Offices: El Dorado, 870-864-8946; Hot Springs, 501-609-9796; Ozark, 501-295-9752; Pine Bluff, 870-536-8178.

Committees: *Budget. Natural Resources*: Federal Lands, Oversight & Investigations. *Science, Space, & Technology*: Environment (VChmn); Research & Technology.

Election Results

2014 general	Bruce Westerman (R)	110,789	(54%)	$938,240	$135,468	$72,401
	James Lee Witt (D)	87,742	(43%)	$1,189,667	$89,487	
	Ken Hamilton (Lib)	7,598	(4%)			
2014 primary	Bruce Westerman (R)	18,719	(54%)			
	Tommy Moll (R)	15,659	(46%)			

Population		Race and Ethnicity		Income	
Total:	720,174	White	72.8%	Median income:	$35,470
Urban:	15.8%	Black	19.5%		*(419 of 435)*
Suburban:	20.1%	Latino	5.5%	Under $50,000	64.3%
Rural:	64.1%	Asian	0.5%	$50,000-$99,999:	25.6%
Land area:	19,295	Two races	1.1%	$100,000-$199,999:	8.8%
Pop/sq. mi.:	37.3	White Ethnic	14.3%	$200,000 or more:	1.3%
Born in state	64.9%			Poverty Rate	22.6%
		Education			
Age Groups		H.S. grad or less:	55.0%	**Work**	
Under 18:	23.4%	Some college:	29.8%	White collar:	28.6%
18 to 34:	20.1%	College degree, 4 yr.	10.3%	Blue collar:	32.1%
35 to 64:	39.2%	Post-grad study:	4.8%	Sales and service:	39.3%
Over 64:	17.3%			Govt. workers	18.3%
		Military			
		Veterans/active duty:	9.9%		

Western Arkansas: Hot Springs, Pine Bluff

West from the Delta flatlands along the Mississippi River, where the water-soaked fields produce America's largest rice crop, are small cities like Pine Bluff and El Dorado and the Ouachita Mountains. Southern Arkansas might well be called the northwest corner of the Deep South. It includes the state's largest

Voter Turnout	
2013 Total Citizen 18+	538,486
2014 House Turnout	206,131
2014 Turnout as % CVAP	38.3%
2012 Turnout as % CVAP	49.7%

African-American population, a reminder that parts of southern Arkansas were once plantation country. There is also oil production, and the broiler-chicken industry looms large in these parts. The accent is clearly Arkansan: El Dorado, Nevada and Lafayette are all pronounced with long a's and accents on the penultimate syllable, and Ouachita, with a bow to the original French rendition of the Indian name, is *WASH-i-taw*.

The 4th Congressional District occupies much of the southern half of Arkansas, stretching from the eastern part of the state all the way west to Texarkana. It includes the little railroad-crossing, county-seat town of Hope, where former President Bill Clinton and his first White House chief of staff, Mack McLarty, were classmates in Miss Mary's kindergarten room and where former Gov. Mike Huckabee grew up a decade later. Hot Springs is the spa resort and gambling haven where Clinton's stepfather sold Buicks, his mother bet on the horses, and he excelled in high school. Established in 1832, Hot Springs National Park is the oldest federal reserve in the country, predating Yellowstone by 40 years (though Hot Springs was not declared a national park until much later).

To the east is Pine Bluff, where a century and a half ago Union soldiers withstood a Confederate attack on the fortified courthouse square. It is also the hometown of the late, legendary Green Bay Packer Don Hutson, often called the first modern National Football League wide receiver. Unemployment has been higher in Pine Bluff than in the rest of the state, despite the presence of poultry giant Tyson Foods, and the city's population declined nearly 11% from 2000 to 2010. The region has taken other hits to its economy lately, including the idling of 1,100 workers in 2010 at the Pine Bluff Chemical Agent Disposal Facility, which began operations in 2005 as part of an international effort to eradicate chemical weapons.

The 4th includes territory in the conservative northwest corner, including Madison, Johnson, and Franklin counties. The district leans substantially Republican.

2012 Presidential Vote		
Mitt Romney (R)	164,350	(62%)
Barack Obama (D)	95,384	(36%)
2008 Presidential Vote		
John McCain (R)	166,247	(60%)
Barack Obama (D)	103,478	(37%)
Cook Partisan Voting Index:	R+15	

Bruce Westerman (R)

Republican Bruce Westerman, with strong social conservative credentials and a pledge to reduce the size and scope of government, won Arkansas' 4th District in 2014 to succeed Rep. Tom Cotton—who ran successfully for the Senate—by persuading voters that he would be a better advocate for those values. With his defeat of James Lee Witt, who was the Federal Emergency Management Agency director in the Clinton administration, the former president's legacy in the area continued to diminish.

Born in Hot Springs, Westerman earned his B.S. in biological and agricultural engineering at the University of Arkansas, where he played for the Razorbacks football team. He completed his master's in forestry at Yale. He worked as a plant engineer for Riceland Foods and as an engineer and forester for Mid-South Engineering. Westerman was elected to the Arkansas House in 2010. When the GOP two years later took control of both chambers of the state Legislature for the first time since Reconstruction, Westerman became House majority leader. He had a solid record as a social and fiscal conservative, voting to override a gubernatorial veto of a voter ID law and to approve a bill banning abortions after 20 weeks. He supported legislation expanding gun rights; setting dress codes in public schools; and requiring that tests for driver's licenses be offered only in English. He was an architect of the "SIMPLE Plan" to reduce taxes and cut government regulation, a GOP agenda that has helped entrench a Republican majority, Westerman said. He opposed the so-called Private Option, Arkansas's expansion of Medicaid under the Affordable Care Act.

The 4th District, with its strong Old South flavor, had elected just two Republicans since Reconstruction—Cotton and Jay Dickey, a four-term congressman who lost in 2000 to Mike Ross after Dickey voted to impeach home-towner Bill Clinton, who remained popular in the district. In the 2014 primary, Westerman defeated energy businessman Tommy Moll 54%-46%. Westerman ran stronger in the southern part of the district, while Moll swept most of the northern counties. Westerman's 4,345-vote margin in Garland County (Hot Springs) accounted for his victory. Both candidates resided in that city.

Witt ran a vigorous and old-style campaign. He was one of the few prominent Democratic candidates across the nation who opposed gay marriage and abortion, and supported gun rights. But despite his continuing friendship with and a campaign visit from Clinton, and outspending his opponent by $250,000, Witt could not overcome the GOP tide in the district. Westerman won easily, 54%-42%. In the two largest counties, Westerman got 62 percent in Garland and Witt got 67 percent in Jefferson (Pine Bluff). Westerman won by big margins in the northwest counties.

In the House, he served on the Budget Committee and applauded the panel's 2016 budget plan, which sought to balance the budget in 10 years with no tax increases. "Our budget will respect the principle of federalism by returning authority to state and local leaders so they have the flexibility to better serve their unique communities," Westerman said. The first bill that he introduced would give state governments more flexibility to set work requirements for Medicaid beneficiaries.

★ CALIFORNIA ★

The Golden State—that is how Americans have long thought of California: as a distant and dreamy land initially, then as a shaper of culture and as a promised land for millions of Americans and immigrants for many decades. America's largest state in terms of population remains in many ways a great success story. But in some ways, it has failed to fulfill its promise. It is the birthplace of much of the world's most advanced technology, yet it has plenty of Third World neighborhoods. It is home to some of the world's most creative people and industries, but for five years it posted one of the nation's highest unemployment rates. Among the states, it has attracted the largest number of immigrants from Mexico, Latin America, and Asia, but it also has seen the largest exodus of citizens to other states.

In the middle of the 20th century, California was the promised land for an American middle class that supported the New Deal and liked Ike, that embraced and personified all-American values in 1940s movies and 1950s television. By the early 21st century, California had become a two-tiered society, with an affluent elite that embraces culturally liberal values—"gentry liberals" in Californian Joel Kotkin's inspired term—and immigrant masses living in Spanish-language neighborhoods and striving to hold onto low-paying jobs in a stagnant economy. California, we have been told for decades, is the America of the future—and for many years it was. But not necessarily any more. California's public policies were developed for a rapidly growing society with a large and growing upwardly mobile middle class. But today's California is no longer growing faster than the national average. Its middle class, far from expanding, has been fleeing to friendlier jurisdictions, leaving the state with downscale young age cohorts and an ever expanding public sector financed increasingly by high tax rates on the elite and by seemingly unsustainable levels of debt. What worked well for the middle class, Middle American California in the last century is not working for a two-tiered, culturally polarized California in this century.

With one out of eight people in America, California is a demographic giant, which means that its achievements—and problems—are the nation's. The 2010 census put California's population at 37 million, far ahead of second-place Texas, with 25 million. Metro Los Angeles had 13 million people, second only to metro New York City's 19 million. The San Francisco Bay Area had 8.2 million, not so far behind Chicagoland's 9.8 million. San Diego and Orange counties, with 3 million people each, are the nation's fifth and sixth largest counties. Latinos are poised to become the largest single ethnic or racial group in the state, at nearly 39 percent, making California the second state after New Mexico with that distinction; 14 percent of its residents are Asian and 7 percent are black. Between 2000 and 2010, the Asian population rose 31 percent and Hispanics rose 28 percent, while non-Hispanic whites declined more than 5 percent and blacks declined 1 percent.

Change has been a constant in California's history, and it owes its preeminence not only to its natural advantages, including its vast geographic area and pleasant climate, but also to its human ingenuity. California's economy has been transformed by one group of newcomers after another, and its politics are periodically transformed with the suddenness of an earthquake. In 1848, when California passed from Mexico to the United States by the Treaty of Guadalupe Hidalgo, it was sparsely populated, inhabited by a few thousand Indians and Mexicans and by a few hundred U.S. soldiers and men on the make. Then in 1848, gold was found in Sutter's Mill, and thousands of people arrived in the Gold Rush. Within months, San Francisco became one of America's 25 largest cities. The big money was made not by the miners but by the grocers and dry-goods merchants and transportation entrepreneurs who provisioned them, such as the Big Four—Crocker, Hopkins, Huntington and Stanford—who built the Central and Southern Pacific Railroads. Many of the laborers were Chinese, and California whites, angry at low-wage competition and fearful of an Asian tidal wave, were the impetus behind the aptly-named Chinese Exclusion Act of 1882, which suspended legal Chinese immigration and was not fully repealed until 1965.

The railroads sold off vast chunks of the Central Valley to large farming operations and enticed settlers with low fares to newly platted suburbs in the Los Angeles Basin. Engineers built great aqueducts that stretched hundreds of miles, from Yosemite to San Francisco and from the Owens River to Los Angeles, bringing water essential to the cities' growth. Early 20th century California was affluent and cultured, containing great museums, libraries, and

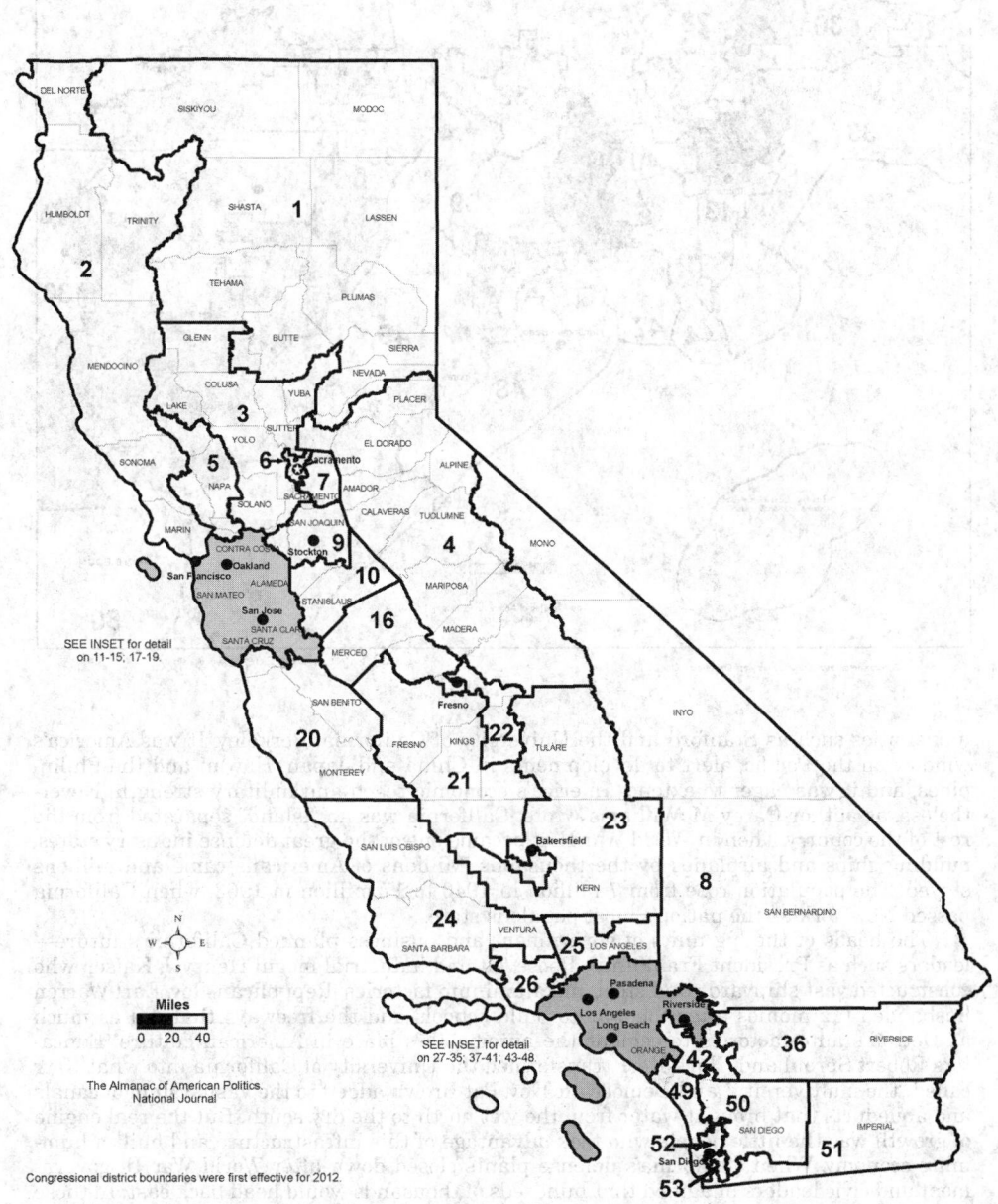

SEE INSET for detail
on 11-15; 17-19.

SEE INSET for detail
on 27-35; 37-41; 43-48.

Miles

0   20   40

The Almanac of American Politics.
National Journal

Congressional district boundaries were first effective for 2012.

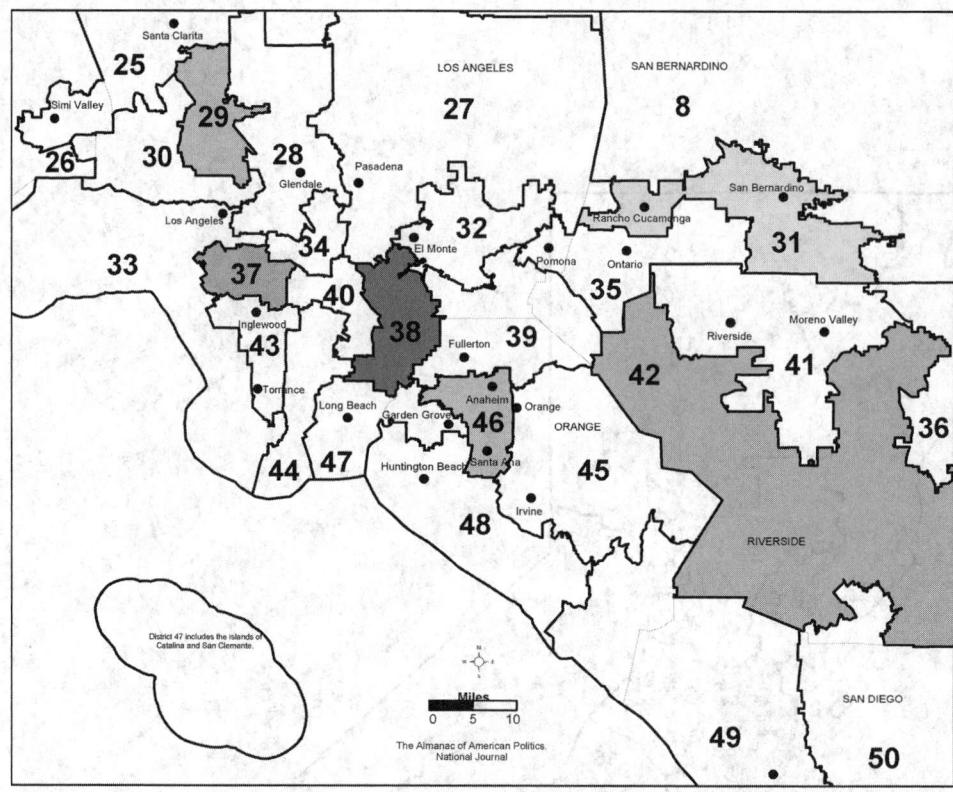

universities such as Stanford and the University of California, Berkeley. It was America's window on the Pacific, alert to developments in China and Japan, Hawaii and the Philippines, and it was eager to extend America's economic reach and military strength. Nevertheless, as author Carey McWilliams wrote, California was an "island" separated from the rest of the country. Then in World War II, it became one of the great defense industry states, building ships and airplanes by the thousands. Millions of Americans came and millions stayed. The population rose from 7 million in 1940 to 17 million in 1963, when California passed New York as the nation's most populous state.

The heads of the big units of government and business planned California's future— leaders such as President Franklin D. Roosevelt and industrial mogul Henry J. Kaiser, who constructed vast shipyards and steel and aluminum factories. Republican Gov. Earl Warren husbanded tax monies after the war to build schools and the freeways that did as much as Detroit's auto factories to cement the automobile's place in American culture. Educators Robert Sproul and Clark Kerr transformed the University of California into what Kerr called "the multiversity," and Democratic Gov. Pat Brown added to the vast system of canals and aqueducts that brought water from the wet north to the dry south. But the real engine of growth was the little people who took advantage of this infrastructure and built a humming economy. When California's defense plants closed down after World War II, government and civic leaders imagined that hundreds of thousands would head back east. In those days before universal air conditioning and thermal winter clothing, people had experienced a climate in which it was comfortable to be outdoors all year. They wanted to stay and so, as urbanologist Jane Jacobs pointed out, they created one-eighth of all the new jobs in the nation in the late 1940s in metro Los Angeles. This growth, multiplied thousands of times over, helped make California the nation's largest state.

The infusion of migrants transformed California politically. Before the war, it was a Republican state with progressive leanings. Political struggles took place inside the

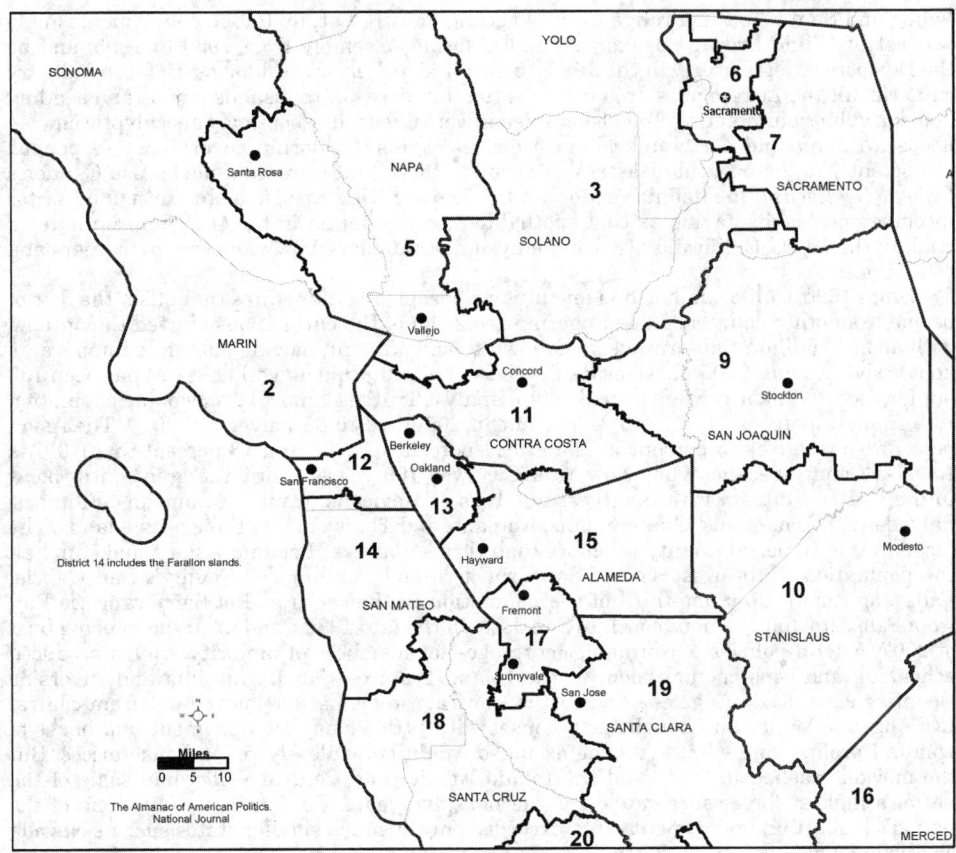

District 14 includes the Farallon islands.

The Almanac of American Politics.
National Journal

Congressional district boundaries were first effective for 2012.

Republican Party. The in-rush of the GI generation, with its allegiance to the New Deal, and the building of auto and steel factories with unionized workforces, transformed California into a two-party state. These new migrants were middle- and working-class, family men and women enjoying a life in suburbs in the lovely California climate. Warren's progressive Republicans remained dominant through the mid-1950s, but with Brown's election as governor in 1958, a group of talented liberal Democrats took over. Things turned sour in the mid-1960s, when student rebellions starting at Berkeley and the Watts riot upset the New Deal order. Californians responded by calling in a disillusioned New Dealer espousing the conformist cultural conservatism of the GI generation, Ronald Reagan. California was a harbinger: It showed the nation where it would go next in the 1980s.

In 1974, California elected Democrat Jerry Brown as governor, entranced for a time by his fresh vision of Baby Boomer liberalism. California's laid-back lifestyles became a magnet for highly educated Boomers, lawyers, scientists, techies, and show-biz types. But they were not the dominant force in the state's politics for some time. California voted Republican in every presidential election from 1968 to 1988. Brown's administration was not wholly successful on policy. Voters froze property taxes by passing Proposition 13 in 1978 and ousted three of his state Supreme Court justices in 1986. Republicans followed Brown in the governorship: George Deukmejian, elected in 1982 and 1986, and Pete Wilson, elected in 1990 and 1994.

In the 1980s, California's defense industry boomed, and Silicon Valley flowered south of San Francisco. Immigration continued in vast numbers, with newcomers living in the dirty stucco bungalows and garden apartments that white, blue-collar workers left behind in neighborhoods south and east of downtown Los Angeles. Large swaths of the San Fernando

Valley and Santa Ana in Orange County became mostly Latino. Public policy increasingly was set by Willie Brown, speaker of the California Assembly from 1980 to 1995, and by the Democratic legislature. In the 1990s, disaster struck in several forms. Defense industry cutbacks hit the Los Angeles area hard, costing hundreds of thousands of jobs and sending housing values plummeting. Television screens were filled with seemingly apocalyptic news—floods, wildfires and earthquakes, and riots and trials. California government responded competently to the natural disasters, less well to those that were man-made. Lou Cannon's *Official Negligence*, the definitive story of the Rodney King case, is a story of public-sector incompetence as dismaying as that spotlighted for the nation in the O.J. Simpson murder trial. In the 1990s, California also lost many of its trademark big businesses to mergers and relocations.

Since 1990, California has had an outflow of people to other states that offset the flow of people from other countries. The lingering recession of the early 1990s started the outflow, with about 2 million Californians, mostly white and affluent, moving out while immigrants kept arriving. Since 2005, the average flow between California and other states has been 133 out for each 100 in, according to real estate analyst Trulia. California's Hispanic population rose from 16 percent in 1980 to 32 percent in 2000 and to 38 percent in 2010. The Asian percentage rose from 5 percent in 1980 to 11 percent in 2000 and 13 percent in 2010. Los Angeles County became what New York City was 100 years before: the great entry point in the United States, with the largest numbers of Mexicans, Iranians, Samoans, Filipinos, Salvadorans, Armenians, Guatemalans, Koreans, and Thais outside their native lands. The farmlands of Imperial County are more than three-quarters Hispanic. Asians make up half the population of the west side of San Francisco and Los Angeles County's San Gabriel Valley, and more than one-third of the population in the south end of San Francisco Bay, from Palo Alto and Fremont south to San Jose. In the late 1990s, and until the housing bust of 2007, federal policies encouraging mortgages for members of minority groups produced a housing and construction boom in the Inland Empire—San Bernardino and Riverside Counties east of Los Angeles—and in the Central Valley. Latinos moved out from central Los Angeles County and bought new houses with little or no down payment and hopes of windfall profits from what everyone assumed would be endlessly rising house prices. But the market crashed in 2007, and the Inland Empire and Central Valley had some of the nation's highest foreclosure rates. For the next five years, California also had one of the nation's highest unemployment rates, exceeded only by much smaller states such as Nevada or Rhode Island.

In the decades after World War II, California was a politically marginal state, much targeted in national elections. In Ronald Reagan's time, it tilted Republican in presidential elections while usually tilting Democratic in congressional and state legislative contests. But starting in the early 1990s, it has become heavily Democratic in most elections. This was not immediately obvious. While Bill Clinton carried California 46%-33% in 1992 and proceeded to lavish attention on the state, Republican Gov. Pete Wilson won reelection in 1994 by emphasizing his support of Proposition 187, barring state aid to illegal immigrants. Wilson won 55%-41% and nearly 60% of all voters (and one-third of Hispanics) voted for Proposition 187. But ever afterward, California's increasing number of Latino voters have given Democrats enormous margins. That has helped the state's two Democratic senators, Dianne Feinstein and Barbara Boxer, both first elected in 1992, win reelection without difficulty.

Two other voting blocs have helped make California solidly Democratic. One is the gentry liberals—affluent, highly-educated whites living in lush corners of the big metropolitan areas, underpinned by the state's two resilient economic and cultural behemoths—Silicon Valley and Hollywood. They are liberal on cultural issues like abortion rights and same-sex marriage, more moderate on fiscal issues, and hostile to the religious conservatives who seem to dominate the national Republican party. They were similarly repelled by the conservative brand of California Republicans, who habitually denounced immigration and championed opposition to abortion rights. In the Reagan years, affluent neighborhoods, except for the heavily Jewish west side of Los Angeles, usually cast large Republican majorities; over the past two decades, they have become increasingly Democratic. This has helped Democrats maintain large majorities in California's House delegation and in both houses of the state legislature since 1996. The power of the public employee unions has exerted continued upward pressure on public spending, especially when California's progressive tax structure brings in gushers of revenue in prosperous years. When revenues plummet, as they did after the high-tech boom ended in 2000 or when the housing market crashed in 2007, the pressure is then to increase taxes. The second group increasingly bolstering Democratic fortunes is Asian-Americans. In 1992, they favored George H.W. Bush over Clinton, but they have moved heavily toward the Democratic party in the years since. They are an important factor in the lopsided margins by which Democrats carry the San Francisco Bay Area and Los Angeles County—both marginal areas when Reagan was running for governor.

California's two governors from 1998 to 2010, Democrat Gray Davis and Republican Arnold Schwarzenegger, tried to exert some discipline over this process, with limited success. Davis was not able to hold spending down enough and was blamed for electricity blackouts resulting from a flawed deregulation policy which he had no part in creating. Reelected by just 47%-42% in 2002, he faced a successful recall petition. Schwarzenegger, an Austrian immigrant bodybuilder-turned-movie-star, went on the *Tonight Show* to announce he was running. Two months later, Davis was recalled by a 55%-45% margin, and on the replacement ballot, Schwarzenegger finished first with 49%. Though others were initially cowed by Schwarzenegger's popularity, his frontal attack on the power structure in Sacramento— support for ballot measures giving the governor new powers to cut spending, to increase the time it took teachers to get tenure, and to create a redistricting commission—was rebuffed and his job rating fell below 50%. Schwarzenegger turned it around, backing liberal measures like carbon emissions reduction legislation and bonds for a high-speed rail line while trying, without great success, to hold down spending by the Democratic legislature. It was enough to easily win him reelection in 2006.

Even before the housing market crashed in 2007, California's economy was slowing down. From 1992 to 2000, the state gained 777,000 more jobs from startups than it lost in business closures; from 2000 to 2008, it lost 262,000 more jobs from closures than it gained from startups. Job creation in the 2000-10 decade in the San Francisco Bay area and Los Angeles County was minimal, while the job gains in those years in construction and real estate in the Inland Empire and Central Valley vanished when house prices slumped. One-third of California homeowners owed more on their mortgages than their houses are worth; the proportion hit 60 percent in parts of the Inland Empire. California's high taxes, stringent regulations, complex land use controls and high litigation risks have led critics to rank it at or near the bottom of states in business environment. Public employee unions' success in negotiating generous pension benefits has left the state government's once widely praised system underfunded and has led to municipal bankruptcies, in Vallejo in 2008 and Stockton and San Bernardino in 2012. California, with one-eighth the nation's population, has one-third of the nation's welfare recipients.

Seemingly adrift, California voters turned to a familiar face—Jerry Brown. In 2010, he defeated former eBay chief executive Meg Whitman for the governorship, despite her spending $141.5 million of her own money. In a strongly Republican year nationally, Brown won the same office he had won 36 and 32 years before by a solid 54%-41% margin. Once mocked as the flaky "Governor Moonbeam," Brown had by his third term matured into a moderate technocrat who knew the inside game and who, crucially, was at last undistracted by presidential ambitions. Task No. 1 was fixing the state's fiscal outlook; Brown made great strides, ultimately squeezing out an annual surplus that, while modest, would have been unthinkable a few years earlier. While the nation's overall economic comeback helped, Brown also played a role by successfully urging passage of a 2012 ballot measure that temporarily hiked income taxes on affluent voters and sales taxes.

Once upon a time, people used to analyze California politics by distinguishing between Northern California and Southern California. Northern California—the Central Valley and the North Coast as well as the San Francisco Bay Area—tended to vote for John F. Kennedy, Hubert Humphrey, Jimmy Carter, and other Democrats. Southern California—Los Angeles County as well as the smaller suburban and desert counties—tended to vote for Richard Nixon, Gerald Ford, and other Republicans. Today, the geographic divisions run the other way. The two sides are coastal California—all the counties that touch the ocean or San Francisco Bay—and interior California. Since 1990, coastal California has had a substantial inflow of immigrants and an even greater outflow of residents, most of them American but some of them immigrants as well. Most of those leaving have moved to places with lower housing prices and better public schools—to Arizona, Nevada, and other Rocky Mountain states, and to Texas. And from 2000 to 2007, large numbers of Latinos, both immigrants and citizens, moved to the Inland Empire and the desert to take advantage of cheap available mortgages and seemingly ever-rising home prices.

Coastal California, with its high housing prices and no-growth zoning restrictions, has had much more population, but much lower population growth, than interior California. And coastal California has had an increasingly two-tiered society economically, with not much of a middle class in between; San Francisco ranks as the second-most unequal metro area in the nation and saw the fastest growth

Voter Turnout	
2013 Total Citizen 18+	24,227,671
2014 Highest Statewide Turnout	7,317,581
2014 Turnout as % CVAP	30.2%
2012 Turnout as % CVAP	54.8%

Legislature		
Senate:	26D	14R
House:	52D	28R

in inequality in recent years, according to the Brookings Institution. Politically, its affluent elites and low-income immigrants remain united in voting Democratic. Coastal California voted 65%-33% for Barack Obama in 2008 and 64%-33% in 2012—better than he ran in any other state except his native Hawaii and tiny Vermont. The transformation of coastal California over the last generation can be measured another way: In 1984, Reagan lost the Bay Area 51%-48%; in 2012, Mitt Romney lost it 73%-24%. The Democratic trend is apparent in the far south coast. Orange County and San Diego County voted 75%-24% and 65%-33%, respectively, for Reagan. Romney carried Orange County by only 52%-46% and lost San Diego County by 53%-45%.

Interior California is a very different kind of place, with more native-born Americans moving in than immigrants. The income gap is not nearly as wide as in coastal California, and the cost of living is lower. But private-sector job creation was not stellar before 2007 and has been dismal since the housing collapse. In 2008, interior California trended Democratic, voting 50%-48% for Obama. In 2010, it swung Republican, voting 49%-45% for Meg Whitman and 53%-40% for Carly Fiorina over Sen. Barbara Boxer. In 2012, it gave Obama a 49%-48% margin over Romney. If interior California were a separate state, it would be very competitive in presidential elections and would have 19 electoral votes. But coastal California, more than twice as populous as interior California, is dominant politically.

The coalition of gentry liberals and low-income Hispanics—lost largely due to Wilson's immigration stances—has put the state far out of reach for Republicans. This isn't to say there aren't troubling signs for the dominant coalition: municipal bankruptcies and state pension woes, stagnant housing prices, public schools that yield some of the lowest test scores in the nation, community colleges with declining enrollments, and universities with rapidly rising tuitions. Still, even in the 2014 wave year for Republicans, California's GOP candidates for statewide office secured between 41 and 47 percent of the vote, and the Democrats who coasted to victory included not just Brown but several younger politicians with bigger ambitions—attorney general Kamala Harris, who is running to succeed Boxer in the Senate in 2016, and lieutenant governor Gavin Newsom, who is poised to run for governor in 2018.

Still, California, which has prided itself on setting trends for the rest of the country, is no longer always on the cutting edge. Its public policies, geared to a rapidly growing state with a rapidly growing middle class, are in danger of becoming dysfunctional as the state is increasingly polarized between rich and poor. Out-migration has meant that for the first time in the state's history, reapportionment in 2010 did not add any seats to its

Population		Race and Ethnicity		Income	
Total:	38,332,521	White	39.6%	Median income:	$57,528
Urban:	60.9%	Latino	38.1%		(14 of 50)
Suburban:	34.9%	Asian	13.0%	Under $50,000	42.6%
Rural:	4.2%	Black	5.7%	$50,000-$99,999:	28.7%
Land area:	155,779	Two races	2.6%	$100,000-$199,999:	21.0%
Pop/sq. mi.:	246.1	White Ethnic	17.5%	$200,000 or more:	7.7%
Born in state:	54.7%			Poverty Rate	13.2%
		Education			
Age Groups		H.S. grad or less:	39.1%	**Work**	
Under 18:	23.9%	Some college:	29.8%	White collar:	36.9%
18 to 34:	25.0%	College degree, 4 yr.:	19.5%	Blue collar:	42.8%
35 to 64:	38.5%	Post-grad study:	11.5%	Sales and service:	20.3%
Over 64:	12.5%			Govt. workers:	13.5%
		Military			
		Veterans/active duty:	6.2%		

House delegation. While California was ahead of the curve on same-sex marriage (and on electoral reform, including voter-backed experiments in non-partisan redistricting and top-two-finisher primaries), California is now the last Pacific Rim state not to make marijuana legal, due in part to Brown's opposition. And California must now conquer a record-setting drought that has ravaged the state and its huge agricultural industry, which, despite getting a fraction of the attention of Silicon Valley and Hollywood, produces half the nation's produce and nuts and a quarter of its milk. The Golden State may not glow with the same intensity it once did, but it remains too big to be ignored.

Presidential Politics California has 55 electoral votes, substantially more than any other state. That fact supposedly gave Republicans a near lock on the presidency from 1968 to 1988. Then, from 1992 to 2012, Democrats swept the state, giving them a structural advantage in the Electoral College. The state's vote for Democratic presidential candidates has grown from 46 percent in 1992 to 60 percent in 2012.

2012 Presidential Vote		
Barack Obama (D) 7,854,285		(60%)
Mitt Romney (R)..............4,839,958		(37%)
2012 Presidential Primary		
Mitt Romney (R)..............1,530,513		(80%)
Ron Paul (R) 199,246		(10%)
Rick Santorum (R) 102,258		(5%)
2008 Presidential Vote		
Barack Obama (D) 8,274,473		(61%)
John McCain (R)..............5,011,781		(37%)

Basically, Democrats are winning where the voters are: In the 10 counties that cast the highest number of total ballots in the 2012 presidential race, Barack Obama captured nine while Mitt Romney managed to win only Orange County. Collectively, Obama outpolled Romney in those top-10 counties by more 2.5 million votes, roughly 85 percent of his overall statewide margin of victory. Obama ran better than favorite son Ronald Reagan in 1984 and Democrat Lyndon Johnson in 1964, and won a higher percentage of votes than any presidential candidate since Franklin Roosevelt won 67 percent in California in 1936. And where there are lots of voters in California, the electorate is usually pretty diverse. In 2012, the exit poll found that 8 percent of California voters were African-American—lower than in any of the other 10 largest states but appreciably higher than blacks' 6 percent share of the California population. They voted 96 percent for Obama. Another 22 percent of the voters were Latinos, and they voted for Obama 72%-27%. Some 11 percent of the voters were Asian, and they went 79%-21% for Obama. These three groups, amounting to 41 percent of the electorate, gave Obama his entire margin and more; whites voted 53%-45% for Romney. The exit poll categories are not congruent, but it may be significant that the 50-64 year old age group, roughly approximating the Baby Boom generation, was reported as having voted 62 percent for Obama in 2008 and only 52 percent in 2012.

For years, California's June primary was a kingmaker. In 1964, the state was the center of national attention when Nelson Rockefeller lost here to Barry Goldwater in the GOP contest. California returned to the limelight in 1968; Robert Kennedy prevailed over Eugene McCarthy in the Democratic contest, but was assassinated by Palestinian terrorist Sirhan Sirhan on primary night. Four years later, George McGovern edged out Hubert Humphrey in the Democratic primary. The state's delegation was also the focus of a pivotal credentials fight at the Democratic National Convention where McGovern prevailed, assuring him the 1972 nomination. But the state lost its marquee status in four of the next five election cycles when both parties' nominations were essentially clinched long before California voted. For the 1996 campaign, California moved its presidential primary from the first week in June to March 26, which was still too late to make a difference. So in 2000 and 2004, California held its primary in the first week of March, and it became one of several states that clinched nominations for George W. Bush in 2000 and John Kerry in 2004. In 2008, California joined 14 other states holding primaries on February 5, Super Tuesday (eight other states conducted a caucus).

As it turned out in 2008, both parties' races were still competitive when Californians voted. But the state's leverage in the Democratic race was limited because all but 11 of its delegates were allotted by proportional representation within each of the 53 congressional districts. Democratic turnout was enormous—5 million, compared with 3 million in 2004. Hillary Clinton won 51%-43%. Obama narrowly lost the San Francisco Bay Area, while Clinton won 55 percent in Los Angeles County, the rest of Southern California and the Central Valley. Obama won among African-Americans, but Clinton carried the more numerous Latinos as well as Asians, 71%-25%. Obama's advantage among upscale liberals was marginal because Jewish voters in California, like those in New York and Florida, preferred Clinton. Clinton carried 42 congressional districts to Obama's 11, but proportional representation limited her delegate advantage to 204-166. If the Republican winner-take-all rules had been in force, she would have led 279-91, enough to have given her a solid lead in the delegate count and perhaps even the Democratic nomination.

The Republican primary attracted far fewer voters—2.9 million, only slightly more than the 2.8 million who voted in 2000. John McCain beat Mitt Romney 42%-35%. McCain's margin was widest, 53%-28% in the San Francisco Bay Area, 44%-35% in Los Angeles County and a narrow 40%-37% in the rest of Southern California. But McCain's overall 7 percent margin enabled him to carry 48 of the 53 congressional districts, which under Republican winner-take-all rules gave him a 155-15 delegate lead in the 53 congressional districts, which, along with strong McCain wins in other states, forced Romney to fold his campaign. For 2012, the legislature switched California's presidential primary to its traditional date in early June. By that time, Romney had wrapped up the GOP nomination, and he crushed Ron Paul by an 80%-10% margin.

Congressional Districts California has a rich tradition of partisan gerrymandering and incumbent protection: Republicans drew the lines to their advantage in the 1940s and 1950s, Democrats in the 1960s, 1970s, and 1980s. Democratic Rep. Phillip Burton, the former godfather of the process, used to defend

114th Congress Lineup	
14 R	39 D
113th Congress Lineup	
15 R	38 D

the drawing of safe seats by arguing it was inhumane to make congressmen catch red-eye flights to Washington every week. In 2001, consultant Michael Berman, the brother of then-Rep. Howard Berman, charged every incumbent Democrat $20,000 to draw a map that granted Democrats 33 and Republicans 20 safe seats.

In 2012, for the first time since it was admitted to the Union in 1850, California did not gain House seats following the decennial census. But thanks to 2010 voter approval, by 61%-39%, of a ballot proposition spearheaded by GOP Gov. Arnold Schwarzenegger, the state became the largest laboratory of redistricting reform yet. The Democratic-dominated legislature was forced to cede power to a 14-member Citizens Redistricting Commission forbidden from taking into account any partisan data or where incumbents live. Chosen by a byzantine application and lottery selection process, the commission included a chiropractor, a bookstore owner, and a businessman who just happened to be director of the U.S. Census Bureau under Presidents Richard Nixon and Gerald Ford.

After months of tedious meetings and mountains of public testimony, the commission in August 2011 adopted a new map that radically, and more logically, rearranged the state's 53 seats. Under the 2001 map, mangled lines had produced a delegation so safe that just one House seat changed partisan hands one time in 10 years' worth of elections. Moreover, clever incumbent protection had delayed advancements in Latino representation; in 2010, Latinos were 38 percent of California's population, but held just nine of the state's 53 seats. The new map threw 27 incumbents into 13 districts and created 14 seats with no resident incumbent. It also created three new or altered districts with functional majorities of Latino citizens: one in the fast-growing Central Valley, another in the San Fernando Valley, and a third anchored by San Diego.

Both parties worked frantically to adapt to the new order, pushing to avoid intra-party battles by awkwardly shoehorning affected members into nearby districts. Largely locked out of the process, some members had done their homework in advance by hiring consultants to drum up "grass-roots" community input before the commission, with some success: Orange County Democrat Loretta Sanchez's forces had convinced commissioners to keep her Latino base intact, and Democrat Brad Sherman was able to get a more advantageous district in advance of a showdown with San Fernando Valley neighbor Howard Berman. One incumbent, Republican Gary Miller, moved to (and won one term in) an entirely new district. Still, seven members—three Democrats and four Republicans—decided 2012 would be an ideal year to retire.

The end result was the most upheaval and loss of seniority California's delegation has ever seen. Not only did the new commission scramble the map, the state's new top-two jungle primary law meant candidates of the same party advanced to the November election in eight districts. In addition to retirees in 2012, plus 40-year Democratic veterans George Miller and Henry Waxman who retired after two more years, several senior members lost reelection, such as veteran Democrats Berman and Pete Stark and Republican Dan Lungren. What incumbents viewed as seniority, many voters saw as entrenchment, and reformers got the burst of competition and new blood they wanted.

Ironically, this "nonpartisan" map has turned out to be much more profitable for Democrats than the one the Democratic legislature passed in 2001. In 2014, spurred by House Majority Leader Kevin McCarthy of Bakersfield, Republicans waged a half-dozen competitive challenges. But, stunningly, every Democrat survived—a few by narrow margins. With the defeat of Republican Gary Miller, the Democrats increased their control of the delegation to 39-14. California has 12% of all House seats, but 21% of the Democratic Caucus, 22% of the House's women Members, and 39% of Hispanic members (including those of Portuguese ancestry). And California Democrats believe they can find ways to squeeze out a few more Republicans. They have made Phil Burton seem tame!

Governor

Jerry Brown (D)

Elected 2010, term expires Jan. 2019, 4th term; b. April 7, 1938, San Francisco; U. of CA Berkeley, B.A. 1961, Yale U., J.D. 1964; Catholic; married (Anne Gust).

Elected Office: Los Angeles Comm. Col. Bd. of Trustees, 1969-71; CA secy. of st., 1970-74; CA gov., 1974-82; Chmn., CA Dem. Party, 1989-91; Oakland mayor, 1998-2006; CA atty. gen., 2006-10.

Professional Career: Law clerk, CA Supreme Court; Practicing atty., Tuttle & Taylor; Practicing atty., Fulbright & Jaworski; Radio host, KPFA Berkeley, 1995-98.

Office: State Capitol, Suite 1173, Sacramento, 95814, 916-445-2841; Fax: 916-558-3160; Website: gov.ca.gov.

Election Results

2014 general	Jerry Brown (D)	4,388,368	(60%)
	Neel Kashkari (R)	2,929,213	(40%)
2014 primary	Jerry Brown (D)	2,354,769	(54%)
	Neel Kashkari (R)	839,767	(19%)
	Tim Donnelly (R)	643,236	(15%)

Prior winning percentages: 2010 (54%), 1978 (56%), 1974 (50%)

Only a few of today's top political figures have elective careers that go back further than that of Jerry Brown, a charismatic, independent-minded Democrat who was elected governor of California in 2010 and won an unprecedented fourth term in 2014. He first won statewide office as California's secretary of state in 1970, went on to serve two terms as governor, then was defeated in a bid for senator in 1982. He's also been the mayor of Oakland and a three-time presidential candidate.

Edmund G. Brown, Jr. grew up in San Francisco, in the upper-middle-class and heavily Catholic neighborhood of St. Francis Wood, the grandson of a cigar-store owner and a policeman, and the son of lawyer Edmund G. Brown, universally known as Pat. In 1943, when Jerry was five, Pat Brown ran for district attorney of the city and county of San Francisco and won. He went on to serve two terms as state attorney general, and, beginning in 1959, two terms as governor of California. With a liberal Democratic legislature, he embarked on a vast program of public spending—a water system transferring northern California water to the Central Valley and Los Angeles, a public university and state college system promising higher education for all who qualified, and a freeway program to connect the sprawling metropolitan areas that were growing up rapidly in the interstices between mountain ranges and the Pacific Ocean. Voters heartily endorsed this record when they reelected Pat Brown 52%-47% in 1962 over Richard Nixon, the future president.

At first, Pat Brown's son was uninterested in following his political heritage. A year after graduating from St. Ignatius High School in 1955, Jerry Brown entered the Sacred Heart Novitiate, a Jesuit seminary, where he set out to become a priest. But after several years, he changed course and entered the University of California, Berkeley, where he earned a degree in classics in 1961. This was before the tumultuous Berkeley rebellion of 1964, but Brown was something of a rebel against his father's policies. He championed the cause of Caryl Chessman, who was sentenced to death for rape. His father delayed the execution for a time but finally ordered it to go forward in 1960. After college, Brown went to Yale Law School, where he graduated in 1964 in the same class with future Sen. Gary Hart of Colorado.

After law school, Brown clerked for a state Supreme Court justice and then traveled in Latin America. When he returned to California, he settled not in his native San Francisco, but in Los Angeles. He worked for a large law firm, and in 1969, three years after his father was defeated by Republican Ronald Reagan 58%-42%, Brown ran for the board of trustees of Los Angeles Community College and finished first among 124 candidates. In 1970, he ran statewide for secretary of state and won easily, even as Reagan was winning a second term. The victory put Brown in position to run for governor in 1974, when it was presumed Reagan would retire (many presumed from political life forever) at the age of 63. In the Democratic primary, Brown had serious competition from San Francisco Mayor Joseph Alioto, state Assembly Speaker Bob Moretti and Rep. Jerome Waldie. He won with 38% of the vote to 19% for Alioto, 17% for Moretti and 8% for Waldie. It was a very favorable year for Democrats, but California then was not nearly as Democratic as it is now, and in the general election, Brown faced Controller Houston Flournoy, a moderate Republican. Brown won by only 50%-47%.

At age 36, Brown was governor of California. He turned out to be not at all the same kind of Democrat as his father. Brown refused to stay in the governor's mansion and instead hung out in a sparely furnished apartment. He refused to use the governor's limousine and drove around in a Plymouth. He largely stopped highway construction and tried to encourage mass transportation. He created a Wellness Commission and an Office of Appropriate Technology. Brown also legalized the practice of acupuncture. He opposed the death penalty, but his veto of a capital punishment bill was overridden by the legislature. If he was liberal on cultural issues, Brown was relatively conservative on economic issues. He was surprisingly tight-fisted on spending, but he also gave bargaining rights to public employee unions.

Brown's eccentricity and his unusual policy positions made him a regular subject of late-night comics' monologues. Still, in 1976, at age 38, he ran for president. In the primaries, he won his first victory in May in Maryland, 48%-37%, over front-runner Jimmy Carter of Georgia, with the help of San Francisco housewife and Democratic activist Nancy Pelosi, who later became Speaker of the House. One week later, he won in Nevada and ran a fairly close third to Frank Church of Idaho and Carter in dovish Oregon. Brown won 59 percent of the vote in the California primary, making him second in the national popular vote to Carter. But he was unable to stay ahead of Carter in subsequent contests, and he finished third at the 1976 Democratic convention with about 300 delegates.

His political career was not exactly washed up. In 1978, Brown won a second term as governor, defeating GOP state Attorney General Evelle Younger 56%-37%. That year, a taxpayers' revolt led to passage of Proposition 13 to freeze property taxes in a period of rapidly rising housing prices. Like most Democrats, Brown opposed it, but when it passed, he sounded like its biggest booster and set about cutting state spending in order to funnel revenue to localities. His second term is considered less successful than his first. For example, Brown in 1981 came under harsh attack by the state's important farm sector for refusing to order use of the pesticide malathion when California crops were hit by an infestation of medflies. But Brown was also ahead of his time in some ways. He appointed openly gay judges to the state courts, and he embraced satellite technology for emergency communications systems before it was common. His novel and sometimes far-fetched ideas inspired Chicago columnist Mike Royko to dub him "Governor Moonbeam," a nickname that, unfortunately for Brown, stuck. He ran for president again in 1980 and finished far behind Carter and Massachusetts Sen. Edward Kennedy everywhere, even in California. He won just 3 percent of the popular vote. In 1982, Brown ran for the Senate seat being vacated by Republican S. I. Hayakawa. He was far better known than his Republican opponent, San Diego Mayor Pete Wilson. But Wilson out-debated him and won 52%-45%. Brown carried Los Angeles County and the San Francisco Bay area narrowly, but lost in all but one county in the rest of the state.

In the mid-1980s, as Reagan was basking in public approval in the White House, Brown traveled to China, Japan, Russia, and India, where he worked with Mother Teresa's humanitarian projects. He practiced law in Los Angeles, and in 1989, embarked on a two-year stint as California Democratic chairman. In 1992, he ran for president a third time, refusing contributions over $100 and inviting listeners to call his 800 number to send him money. He finished a poor fifth in New Hampshire, but beat Arkansas' Bill Clinton and Massachusetts' Paul Tsongas in the Colorado and Connecticut primaries and in the caucuses in Maine, Vermont, and Nevada. He also aroused Clinton's ire by suggesting that there might be something improper about Hillary Clinton's work at the Rose Law Firm in Little Rock. By the time California voted in June, Clinton was the sure nominee, but he beat Brown there by only 47%-40%.

During most of the Clinton administration, Brown was utterly out of favor at the White House. In time, he moved to Oakland, and in 1998, ran for mayor of that troubled city. In an 11-candidate primary, he was elected with 59 percent of the vote. He won passage of a proposal creating a strong mayoral form of government, ordered innovative policing that sharply reduced crime, stimulated significant development in the bedraggled downtown and established both the Oakland School for the Arts and the Oakland Military Institute as an alternative high school option. He won a second term as mayor in 2002 with 64 percent of the vote.

In 2006, Brown, finishing his second term as Oakland mayor, ran for attorney general and won over state Sen. Chuck Poochigian 56%-38%. As attorney general, Brown in 2009 asked the Supreme Court to stay a three-judge federal court decision requiring the state to release 40,000 inmates from California prisons. He sued the city of San Bernardino for its zoning plan for encouraging sprawl. After voters in 2008 passed Proposition 8 overturning the state Supreme Court decision authorizing same-sex marriage, Brown initially promised to defend it in court but reversed himself in December, making the novel argument that the people could not revoke rights discovered by the courts to be "inalienable."

His most recent turn as the state's chief executive came about after actor-turned-politician Arnold Schwarzenegger was term-limited and California was mired in dire financial straits. The Republicans had a fierce primary between two Silicon Valley magnates, former eBay chief Meg Whitman and state Insurance Commissioner Steve Poizner. Spending some $60 million, Whitman won the primary 64%-27%. In the general election, Whitman ultimately spent $160 million, $141.5 million of it her own money. Whitman faced problems on immigration, as California Republicans have since 1996, and from seeming to mimic Schwarzenegger's agenda. Despite the national Republican tide, Brown beat Whitman, 54%-41%. In 2010, Brown won 63% of the vote in Los Angeles County and 67% in the San Francisco Bay area, way up from 53% in both places in 1974. He was modestly down elsewhere compared to 1974.

In his first weeks in office, Brown called for reductions in welfare programs, health care for the poor, community colleges, and a $1 billion cut from the budgets for the University of California and California State University systems. He followed with a state hiring freeze in February 2011 and then incensed mayors when he called for shutting down the state's nearly 400 municipal redevelopment agencies to save $1.7 billion. Brown ordered half of the state's employees to turn in their cell phones and directed all state departments to turn in non-essential vehicles and to halt all new auto purchases.

At the same time, Brown made several moves that went against the grain of other, less progressive states. He signed into law in April 2011 the nation's most aggressive clean-energy standard, which required the state's utilities to get one-third of their electricity from renewable sources, such as geothermal, wind, and solar, by 2020. Another bill he signed made California the first state to require that school textbooks and history lessons include the contributions of gay, lesbian, bisexual, and transgender Americans. Later that year, he signed a host of bills aimed at greater acceptance of immigrants, including one to allow thousands of undocumented students to apply for financial aid at state colleges and universities. And he enacted the nation's most far-reaching new gun laws by banning most residents from openly carrying unloaded handguns in public places and requiring that all rifles be registered. At the same time, though, he refused to sign a bill that would have required young skiers to wear helmets, decrying the "continuing and seemingly inexorable transfer of authority from parents to the state."

To show his commitment to personal frugality, Brown rented a loft apartment blocks from the Capitol and flew coach class—always taking the senior citizens' discount—without the security entourage that had surrounded Schwarzenegger. He further reinforced the unconventional politician image in June 2011 when he vetoed a state budget that was seen as laden with gimmicks. Unable to negotiate tax hikes with state Republicans, he eventually signed a budget that cut spending by $26.6 billion. At the end of the year, he announced nearly $1 billion in new budget cuts, slashing spending on higher education and eliminating funding for free school-bus service.

But Brown also had grander visions, saying, "At this stage, as I see many of my friends dying—I went to the funeral of my best friend a couple of weeks ago—I want to get (expletive) done." He unveiled a plan to build a $14 billion pair of tunnels—to be paid for by farmers and other water users—to move water from the north to the south to address the region's chronic water shortages. Environmentalists and Northern California lawmakers howled with outrage at the tunnel project, but Brown was unfazed. He also signed an $8 billion bill to kick off high-speed rail construction. Meanwhile, he pushed for voters to approve Proposition 30, an income tax hike on those earning at least $250,000, combined with a sales-tax increase. Thanks in large part to Brown's political skills, it ended up passing, 55%-45%. A jubilant Brown got more good news on Election Night 2012: Democrats gained a supermajority in both houses of the legislature, giving them the two-thirds majority needed to pass legislation to increase taxes. Brown announced plans to beef up education spending and balance the state's budget. The only thing spoiling his good fortune was his announcement in December 2012 that he was being treated for early-stage prostate cancer.

In the 2014 election—the first gubernatorial race using the state's top-two primary system—Brown's opponent in the general was Neel Kashkari, the U.S. Treasury Department official under President George W. Bush who spearheaded the Troubled Assets Relief Program, better known as the Wall Street bailout. Kashkari was more moderate on social issues and immigration than most state or national Republican officeholders, and he had enough money to compete. He actually ended up outspending Brown, $7.1 million to $5.9 million. But few voters gave him much thought (Brown only assented to one debate, aired alongside the U.S. Open in tennis and the NFL season opener), and Kashkari's week-long sojourn to Fresno, when he slept behind a dumpster while posing as a homeless job-seeker, only made the onetime Gov. Moonbeam seem sober by comparison. Most of Brown's reelection efforts consisted of advocating for two ballot measures—a $7.5 billion water bond and an effort to stabilize the state's budgetary rainy-day fund. Both measures passed—and, in what all but an afterthought, Brown defeated Kashkari, 60%-40%, to win an unprecedented fourth term (something the state constitution no longer allows).

While Brown continued to show flashes of quirkiness—at his 2014 State of the State address, Brown offered playing cards featuring his Welsh corgi, Sutter, and after winning reelection, he tweeted archly that he "didn't get here by being pusillanimous"—his fiscal achievements were hard to dismiss. Brown's combination of spending cuts and tax increases, bolstered by the nation's slow but steady economic recovery, helped turn the $26.6 billion deficit he inherited into billions of dollars of surplus by 2015. With the fiscal situation greatly improved, Brown moved aggressively on other fronts, including his three-decade quest for high-speed rail, which could cost as much as $68 billion; climate change, capped by an April 2015 proposal to cut carbon emissions to 40 percent below 1990 levels by 2030; and efforts to ease the state's historic drought, to which he imposed mandatory 25 percent cuts in water use and an effort to turn 50 million square feet of lawns into "drought-tolerant landscape." America's biggest state was, once again, facing California-sized challenges, with a dynamic septuagenarian once again leading it into the future.

Senior Senator

Dianne Feinstein (D)

Elected Nov. 1992, term expires Jan. 2019, 4th full term; b. June 22, 1933, San Francisco; Stanford U., B.A. 1955; Jewish; married (Richard C. Blum); 4 children.

Elected Office: San Francisco Bd. of Supervisors, 1970-78, pres., 1970-71, 1974-75, 1978; San Francisco mayor, 1978-88.

Professional Career: CA Women's Parole Bd., 1960-66; Director, Bank of CA, 1988-89.

DC Office: 331 HSOB, 20510, 202-224-3841; Fax: 202-228-3954; Website: feinstein.senate.gov.

State Offices: Fresno, 559-485-7430; Los Angeles, 310-914-7300; San Diego, 619-231-9712; San Francisco; 415-393-0707.

Committees: *Appropriations:* Agriculture, Rural Development, Food and Drug Administration & Related Agencies; Commerce, Justice, Science, & Related Agencies; Defense; Energy & Water Development (RMM); Interior, Environment & Related Agencies; Transportation, HUD & Related Agencies.

Intelligence (Select) (VChmn). *Judiciary:* Immigration & Nat'l Interest; Oversight, Agency Action, Federal Rights & Federal Courts; Privacy, Technology & the Law. *Rules & Administration.*

Group Ratings

	ADA	ACLU	AFL-CIO	LCV	ITI	COC	HAFA	ACU	CFG	FRC
2014	90%	93%	–	80%	100%	43%	2%	0%	0%	0%
2013	100%	C	100%	92%	C	50%	C	4%	2%	C

National Journal Ratings

	2013 LIB	—	2013 CONS
Economic	69%	—	30%
Social	73%	—	0%
Foreign	71%	—	0%
Composite	81%	—	20%

Key Votes of the 113th Congress

1. Sandy storm spending	Y	5. Student Loan Rates	Y	9. Bipartisan Budget Deal	Y
2. Chuck Hagel Confirmation	Y	6. Employee Non-Discrim'n Act	Y	10. Farm Bill Conference Rept.	Y
3. Gun Background Checks	Y	7. Senate Vote on Judgeships	N	11. Unempl. Comp. Extension	Y
4. Immigration Reform	Y	8. Defense Dept. Spending	Y	12. Keystone Pipeline	N

Election Results

2012 general	Dianne Feinstein (D)	7,864,624	(63%)	$12,152,230	$78,552
	Elizabeth Emken (R)	4,713,887	(37%)	$910,209	$17,851
2012 primary	Dianne Feinstein (D)	2,392,822	(49%)		
	Elizabeth Emken (R)	613,613	(13%)		
	Dan Hughes (R)	323,840	(7%)		

Prior winning percentages: 2006 (59%), 2000 (56%), 1994 (47%), 1992 special (54%)

Dianne Feinstein, California's senior senator, is a Democrat first elected in 1992. She is a respected pragmatist who can be a crucial ally to President Obama—particularly on gun control—as well as an annoyance to the White House with her blunt outspokenness on national-security matters.

Feinstein grew up in San Francisco in lush Presidio Heights, the daughter of a doctor who hoped she would follow him into the profession. In her first semester at Stanford University, Feinstein got a D in genetics and decided she did not have the aptitude for medicine. But she did love a class she took on American political thought. She graduated with a degree in criminology and then, while doing an internship, wrote a paper about post-conviction phases of the justice system that she thought contained valuable ideas for the state of California. Feinstein sent her paper to Gov. Pat Brown. Despite her youth—she was just 27—the governor appointed her to the California Women's Board of Terms and Parole. In 1969, she won her first election, to the San Francisco County Board of Supervisors. Feinstein went on to become president of the board and, in 1978, was suddenly catapulted to mayor when Mayor George Moscone and Supervisor Harvey Milk, the first openly gay man elected to public office in California history, were shot to death by former Supervisor Dan White. Feinstein discovered Moscone's body and, in the subsequent weeks, displayed a steadiness and a sense of command that calmed the city. She was elected to full terms in 1979 and 1983. Much later, when the film *Milk* was released to critical acclaim in 2008, Feinstein told *The New York Times* that she wasn't sure she'd ever be able to watch it. "It's very painful for me," she said.

In 1984, Democratic presidential candidate Walter Mondale seriously considered Feinstein for vice president but passed over her for Geraldine Ferraro because of qualms about the business dealings of Feinstein's husband, Richard Blum. She presided gracefully that year over the Democratic National Convention in San Francisco, while ironically, Ferraro juggled questions about her family's business dealings.

Ineligible for a third term, Feinstein left the mayor's office in 1987 and ran for governor in 1990. She won the Democratic primary impressively, then lost 49%-46% to Republican Pete Wilson. When Wilson appointed Orange County state Sen. John Seymour—an unknown and bland choice—to replace him in the Senate, Feinstein quickly announced for the seat. She defeated then-state Controller Gray Davis by 58%-33% in a heated primary that permanently soured her relationship with the future governor. Seymour struggled throughout the campaign, flip-flopping to support abortion rights and seeing his fear-mongering on illegal immigration and attacks on Feinstein's fundraising fall flat. Feinstein won 54%-38%, coming close even in Seymour's Southern California base.

In the Senate, Feinstein kept a distance from the Clinton administration, negotiating for changes before voting for its 1993 budget, voting against the North American Free Trade Agreement, and withdrawing her support of the Clinton health care plan. Feinstein's tough-on-crime background led her to sponsor a ban on assault weapons in 1994. When Idaho Republican Larry Craig argued that her definition of assault weapons was not rigorous enough and challenged her knowledge of firearms, she stopped the argument in its tracks by reminding the Senate of the horrific tragedy earlier in her political career. "I know something about what firearms can do," Feinstein said. "I came to be mayor of San Francisco as a product of assassination." In 2000, she sponsored an unsuccessful bill to require licensing of all guns and in 2004 pressed fervently for reauthorization of the 1994 assault-weapons ban. The act expired in September 2004. As the Democratic Party's support for gun control waned, Feinstein had a harder time convincing her colleagues to consider new gun restrictions. After a gunman at a Colorado movie theatre killed 12 people and injured 58 others in July 2012, Feinstein lamented that "there is no outrage out there" to spur a crackdown on guns.

The public mood changed just a few months later, with the December 2012 mass shooting of 26 small children and teachers at Sandy Hook Elementary School in Newtown Connecticut. Feinstein immediately became the point person in the Democratic-controlled Senate for legislation even tougher than the 1994 law; it would ban assault weapons and high-capacity magazines. Democratic leaders subsequently abandoned pushing for the new ban to focus on measures they hoped could draw more bipartisan support, such as expanding the criminal background check system and cracking down on so-called "straw purchasers" buying guns for criminals. After those proposals failed as well, Feinstein blamed the National Rifle Association for making colleagues afraid to vote on gun control legislation. "A fear has set in that if they vote for the bill they won't be re-elected. It's that plain, it's that simple," she told a San Francisco audience in April 2013.

Feinstein has had a moderate to liberal voting record and has differed on some issues from her colleague and Bay Area neighbor, Democratic Sen. Barbara Boxer. She supported the Bush tax cuts in 2001 and the Iraq war resolution in 2002, although two years later she said she had been misled into voting for the war by an exaggeration of the threat and regretted her vote. Feinstein supported the GOP's Medicare prescription drug bill in 2003 as well. With Republican Sen. Jon Kyl of Arizona, she co-sponsored a bill to bar entry to the United States for people from nations that sponsor terrorism, which became law in 2002.

In 2005, Feinstein was less bipartisan in the war over some of President Bush's judicial nominees, but she also was frequently willing to compromise in the end. With other Judiciary Democrats, she opposed several nominees to the federal appeals court. But then, with Boxer, she made an arrangement with the Bush administration to set up six-member panels to decide on the potential merits of federal trial judges in California. Three members were appointed by each side, and four votes were required to approve a nominee. In May 2005, Feinstein voted against the nomination of conservative nominee Priscilla Owen, but declined to take the harsher step of a filibuster. After an interview with Supreme Court nominee John Roberts in July 2005, she called him "very impressive" but opposed his confirmation nonetheless, out of concern that he might overturn the *Roe v. Wade* decision legalizing abortion. After Harriet Miers' nomination for the high court was withdrawn in October 2005, Feinstein said, "I don't believe they would have attacked a man the way she was attacked."

In recent years, Feinstein has become an outspoken proponent of gay rights. In February 2011, she introduced a bill to repeal the 1996 Defense of Marriage Act, which established that U.S. law recognizes only heterosexual marriages and prevented gay couples from receiving federal benefits. The Obama White House endorsed Feinstein's repeal effort. After those portions of DOMA were struck down by the Supreme Court in 2013, she reintroduced its full repeal in 2015 to eliminate the provision allowing states that had banned same-sex marriage to refuse to recognize gay marriages conducted in other states.

In 2009, Feinstein became chairman of the Senate Intelligence Committee and indicated she wanted to clean house at the intelligence agencies. "My view is that it's time for a new start," she said. "I want to see the Senate Intelligence Committee with much closer oversight and a much closer relationship with the intelligence community." When former Clinton White House Chief of Staff Leon Panetta was announced as Obama's choice for director of the Central Intelligence Agency, she said that she thought the president should have appointed "an intelligence professional." But after Vice President Joseph Biden said it was a mistake not to have informed her in advance of the appointment, she was conciliatory, saying, "I'm very respectful of the president's authority, and if this is the man he wants, then that means a lot to me."

When former National Security Agency contractor Edward Snowden leaked details of the NSA's domestic surveillance efforts in 2013, Feinstein was the Obama administration's most prominent Democratic defender. She accused Snowden of "treason" and took the agency to task for not being able to prevent him from accessing so much highly classified material, and defended the NSA's far-reaching covert collection of Americans' telephone call records. The situation caused her approval ratings among Californians to plummet, falling below Boxer's in January 2014 for the first time in 20 years. She shrugged it off. "Numbers go down, numbers go up," she told the *Los Angeles Times*, adding: "I don't think people understand" the NSA's work.

Feinstein doesn't hesitate to go her own way on the committee. In 2007, she supported immunity for telecommunications companies that had allowed the government to listen in on telephone calls from suspected terrorists abroad to persons in the United States, though many Democrats opposed immunity. Feinstein attached amendments to the 2007 and 2008 intelligence authorization bills to require that all government interrogations be conducted under the rules of the Army Field Manual, and she attempted to apply that standard to government contractors as well. In January 2009, she called for closing the detention camp at Guantanamo Bay, Cuba, which she called a "failed experiment." She later became engaged in protracted negotiations with the Obama administration over the public release of a report detailing the CIA's use of harsh interrogation techniques; she and other Democrats said the administration redacted far too much information. She also said the White House wasn't always prompt in notifying her about its decisions.

In late 2014 the Intelligence Committee released a report slamming the "deeply flawed" Bush-era approach to harsh interrogation methods by the CIA for detainees. Some Republicans ripped the report, which the CIA also derided, but Feinstein was defiant. "America is big enough to admit when it's wrong and confident enough to learn from its mistakes," she told CNN. "History will judge us by our commitment to a just society governed by law and the willingness to face an ugly truth and say: 'Never again.'"

No issue, however, drew as much attention as Feinstein's accusation in March 2014 that the CIA had secretly removed classified documents from her Intelligence Committee staff's computers in the middle of an oversight investigation. "I have asked for an apology and a recognition that this CIA search of computers used by its oversight committee was inappropriate. I have received neither," she said. After the agency conducted an investigation and apologized four months later, she said the probe and apology were "positive first steps," and stopped short of joining several of her colleagues in calling for CIA Director John Brennan to resign.

Feinstein disagreed with other Democrats who claimed the USA Patriot Act, the Bush administration's centerpiece anti-terrorism law, had led to violations of civil liberties, a statement cited by President Bush in pressing for renewal of the act. She also was the only Democrat on the committee to vote in 2006 for the amendment authorizing prosecutions for flag desecration. In spring 2015, as debate raged over reauthorizing the Patriot Act, she supported reauthorizing it while ending NSA's bulk collection of phone records, standing with Democrats and libertarian-leaning Republicans.

Feinstein repeatedly has prodded Obama to abandon his inherent cautiousness and pay more attention to global threats. In July 2014, she questioned whether he was spending too much time fundraising as conflicts raged between Israelis and Palestinians, between Russia and the Ukraine and in Iraq with the Islamic State terrorist group. "I'm not going to tell the president what to do, but I think the world would very much respect his increased attention on this matter, and I think there ought to be increased attention," she told MSNBC. A month later, when Obama said he lacked a strategy to deal with the Islamic State, she told NBC: "I think I've learned one thing about this president, and that is he's very cautious. Maybe in this instance, too cautious."

Feinstein frequently joins with Republicans in the increasingly anachronistic method of getting legislation passed through compromise. In 2009, she and conservative Sen. John Cornyn of Texas co-sponsored a bill to create a permanent commission to guarantee the financial viability of Social Security and Medicare. In March 2009, she and Judiciary Committee Chairman Patrick Leahy of Vermont hammered out a compromise creating clearer requirements in patent infringement cases. In 2010, she won wide agreement on a national registry for convicted arsonists and bombers. On the Senate Rules Committee, Feinstein has worked on institutional reforms, co-sponsoring a requirement that earmarks added to spending bills be posted on the Internet for at least 24 hours. As Rules chairman, she also presided over Obama's inauguration ceremonies on January 20, 2009.

With a seat on the powerful Appropriations Committee, Feinstein has sought public and private funding to protect old-growth redwoods in the Headwaters Forest and salt ponds in the San Francisco Bay area and to prohibit development, including solar plants and wind farms, on an additional 1 million acres in the Mojave Desert. She is more accommodating of trade ties with China than San Francisco neighbor Nancy Pelosi, the House minority leader. Feinstein has supported trade with China since she established a sister-city relationship in 1990 between San Francisco and Shanghai. She opposed Pelosi's efforts to impose penalties on China because of its human rights violations. In 2005, Feinstein called on China to crack down on piracy of intellectual property and to revalue its currency, but she opposed a bipartisan bill to impose 27.5% tariffs on Chinese goods if it did not revalue.

Feinstein has had only one serious challenge since she was elected to the Senate. In the Republican year of 1994. Rep. Michael Huffington spent $30 million of his own money running against her and pulled even in the polls in September. Huffington slipped when it was revealed that he and his wife, Arianna Huffington, employed an illegal alien as a nanny. (Arianna Huffington now runs the liberal *Huffington Post* news website.) On the Thursday before the election, it was revealed that Feinstein, despite her earlier denials, had employed a woman whose work permit had expired. Feinstein won narrowly, 47%–45%. She carried Los Angeles County 52%-40% and the San Francisco Bay Area 63%-30%, offsetting Huffington's margins in Southern California and the rest of the state.

In 2000, Republican Rep. Tom Campbell, a libertarian Stanford Law professor, challenged her. Feinstein far outspent him, $10.3 million to $4.4 million, and won 56%-37%, carrying all major regions of the state. In her 2006 reelection contest, Republicans nominated conservative former state Sen. Richard Mountjoy, who was never a serious threat, and she won, 59%-35%.

As she prepared to run again in 2012, a state poll showed that she was vulnerable; just 41% of voters approved of her job performance, and 44% of voters said they would not vote to reelect her. Compounding problems for Feinstein was a scandal involving her former campaign treasurer, Kinde Durkee, who was arrested for stealing huge sums from her California clients, including an estimated $4.5 million from Feinstein's campaign. Durkee is serving 8 years in prison. But her opponent, autism activist and perennial candidate Elizabeth Emken, failed to get traction. Emken raised just $914,000 to Feinstein's $9.8 million, and the incumbent won by 63%-37%.

Feinstein has sent mixed signals about retirement at the end of her term in 2018, when she will be 85.

Junior Senator

Barbara Boxer (D)

Elected 1992, term expires Jan. 2017, 4th term; b. Nov. 11, 1940, Brooklyn, NY; Brooklyn Col., B.A. 1962; Jewish; married (Stewart); 2 children.

Elected Office: Marin Cnty. Bd. of Supervisors, 1976-82; U.S. House, 1983-93.

Professional Career: Stockbroker & researcher, 1962-65; Journalist, *Pacific Sun*, 1972-74; Dist. aide, U.S. Rep. John Burton, 1974-76.

DC Office: 112 HSOB, 20510, 202-224-3553; Fax: 202-224-0454; Website: boxer.senate.gov.

State Offices: Fresno, 559-497-5109; Los Angeles, 213-894-5000; Oakland, 510-286-8537; Riverside, 951-684-4849; Sacramento, 916-448-2787; San Diego, 619-239-3884.

Committees: *Environment & Public Works (RMM).* Transportation & Infrastructure (RMM) (ex-officio member on all other subcommittees). *Ethics (Select)* (VChmn). *Foreign Relations:* East Asia, the Pacific, & the Int'l Cybersecurity Policy; Multilateral Int'l Development, Multilateral Institutions, & Int'l Economic, Energy, & Environmental Policy; State Dept. & USAID Mgmt., Int'l Operations, & Bilateral Int'l Development; Western Hemisphere, Transnational Crime, Civilian Security, Democracy, Human Rights, & Global Women's Issues (RMM).

Group Ratings

	ADA	ACLU	AFL-CIO	LCV	ITI	COC	HAFA	ACU	CFG	FRC
2014	85%	100%	–	80%	100%	29%	0%	4%	7%	0%
2013	100%	C	100%	100%	C	38%	C	4%	0%	C

National Journal Ratings

	2013 LIB	—	2013 CONS
Economic	93%	—	0%
Social	73%	—	0%
Foreign	64%	—	35%
Composite	83%	—	18%

Key Votes of the 113th Congress

1. Sandy storm spending	Y	5. Student Loan Rates	N	9. Bipartisan Budget Deal	Y
2. Chuck Hagel Confirmation	Y	6. Employee Non-Discrim'n Act	Y	10. Farm Bill Conference Rept.	Y
3. Gun Background Checks	Y	7. Senate Vote on Judgeships	N	11. Unempl. Comp. Extension	Y
4. Immigration Reform	Y	8. Defense Dept. Spending	Y	12. Keystone Pipeline	N

Election Results

2010 general	Barbara Boxer (D)	5,218,441	(52%)	$29,537,796	$5,808,977	$3,542,981
	Carly Fiorina (R)	4,217,366	(42%)	$21,338,700	$5,757,811	$1,501,494
2010 primary	Barbara Boxer (D)	1,957,920	(81%)			
	Brian Quintana (D)	338,442	(14%)			
	Robert Kaus (D)	123,573	(5%)			

Prior winning percentages: 2004 (58%), 1998 (53%), 1992 (48%); House: 1990 (68%), 1988 (73%), 1986 (74%), 1984 (68%), 1982 (52%)

Barbara Boxer, California's junior senator, is a Democrat first elected to the House in 1982 and a decade later to the Senate. She is the top Democrat on the Environment and Public Works Committee and one of the Senate's staunch liberals, well-known for her outspokenness and passion. She announced in January 2015 that she would not seek a fifth term, making her part of a major changing of the guard at the top of California Democratic politics alongside term-limited Gov. Jerry Brown, retired Reps. Henry Waxman and George Miller, and Sen. Dianne Feinstein, who is said to be mulling retirement in 2018.

Boxer grew up in Brooklyn. In 1962, she graduated from Brooklyn College, where she met her husband, Stewart. The couple moved to Marin County, in 1968. Boxer, a stockbroker, volunteered for Eugene McCarthy's presidential campaign that year. In 1970, she and some neighbors formed the Marin Alternative to oppose the Vietnam War. Marin County was only on its way to being trendy then; the overall political tone was liberal Republican, but heading left. In 1972, Boxer ran for the Board of Supervisors and lost to an incumbent Republican. She then went to work as an aide to Democratic Rep. John Burton. In 1976, she ran again for the county board and won. When Burton retired unexpectedly in 1982, Boxer ran for the House seat and was easily elected. In the House, she was known for her aggressive investigation into wasteful spending, unearthing the Air Force's $7,622 coffee pot in 1984, and for her vocal opposition to the Gulf War in the early 1990s. She also led a group of women House members in a march to the steps of the Senate to demand hearings into law professor Anita Hill's sexual-harassment allegations against Clarence Thomas, who was in the process of being confirmed to the Supreme Court.

In 1992, Boxer ran for the Senate. She started off as neither the best-known nor the best-financed candidate, but 1992 turned out to be the "Year of the Woman," in which the enthusiasm of the feminist left helped produce important victories for Democratic candidates. Boxer won the June primary with 44% of the vote, to 31% for Lt. Gov. Leo McCarthy and 22% for Rep. Mel Levine. In the general election, her opponent was Bruce Herschensohn, a Los Angeles television and radio commentator. The Boxer-Herschensohn race was a battle of opposites, the far left versus the far right of the ideological spectrum. Herschensohn opposed abortion rights and advocated a flat tax and offshore oil drilling. Boxer's positions were precisely the opposite. Her bid was helped by the poor showing of President George H.W. Bush's campaign in California and by the revelation late in the campaign that Herschensohn had frequented nightclubs that featured nude dancers. She won with 48% of the vote.

Boxer's voting record is among the most liberal in the Senate, and she has long been one of the chamber's most outspoken members, though in recent years she has shown an ability to work across the aisle with some of the Senate's most conservative members. Boxer is one of the strongest proponents of abortion rights in Congress and a prime sponsor of the Freedom of Choice Act, which would nullify all state restrictions on abortion, and its 2014 successor, the Women's Health Protection Act.

She was a staunch defender of President Bill Clinton during the impeachment proceedings in 1998, when the president was accused of lying about an extramarital affair with a White House intern. During the Clinton years, Boxer was frustrated when Republicans held up nominations to the Ninth Circuit Court of Appeals, long the most liberal in the country. So, during the George W. Bush years, she held up nominations of judges she considered too conservative, blocking the 2001 nomination of Rep. Christopher Cox of California to the Ninth Circuit and leading the charge in 2005 against the appointments of John Roberts and Samuel Alito to the Supreme Court. She was the lone senator to protest the awarding of Ohio's electoral votes to Bush in 2004, citing evidence of voter suppression.

Boxer has long concentrated on environmental issues. On the Environment and Public Works Committee during the years of Republican control of the Senate, she sparred continually with conservative chairman James Inhofe of Oklahoma over reducing carbon emissions to combat global warming. Inhofe famously said that the theory of human-caused global warming was a "hoax." The committee's emphasis changed abruptly when Democrats won the Senate majority in 2006. Boxer made addressing the causes of global warming her top legislative priority. "I really have two major goals," she said. "They are to protect the health of the American people. And the second is to make the environment a bipartisan issue again on Capitol Hill."

Her aggressive style did not always foster bipartisanship. In 2007, she harshly criticized then-Environmental Protection Agency chief Stephen Johnson for refusing to grant a waiver allowing California's tough carbon emissions law to go into effect. She sought access to an EPA staff document recommending a waiver and accused Johnson of lying. She fumed during the summer and fall of 2008 when he refused to appear before the committee to testify. Inhofe boycotted the hearings as well.

Boxer's primary goal was to enact a cap-and-trade system to reduce carbon emissions, which she has called "the greatest challenge of our generation." Such a system would allow companies to trade emissions "credits," depending on the amount of pollution they generate. In 2007, Boxer's committee took up a cap-and-trade bill sponsored by Connecticut independent Joe Lieberman and Virginia Republican John Warner, and in nearly 10 hours of hearings, she fended off more-restrictive amendments from independent Vermont Sen. Bernie Sanders and less-restrictive amendments from others. In May 2008, she advanced a version with changes she hoped would increase support. In early June, her bill attracted only 48 votes in the Senate, well short of the 60 needed to proceed.

In 2009, senators from states that are heavily dependent on coal-generated electricity wanted to stop any cap-and-trade bill that would put their states at a competitive disadvantage, but during the early months of the Obama administration, Boxer continued to push the legislation. As the year progressed, she ceded control of the issue to Lieberman and Massachusetts Democratic Sen. John Kerry, who unlike Boxer did not have to worry about reelection. Kerry and Lieberman enlisted South Carolina Republican Sen. Lindsey Graham in the hope that his support could bring aboard more Republicans. The three worked to develop a method of pricing carbon while increasing production of nuclear power, a compromise Boxer said she could accept. When Majority Leader Harry Reid proposed bringing up a comprehensive immigration bill for debate in April 2010, Graham said the climate bill was far closer to being ready and angrily accused Reid of catering to Hispanics in order to win his own reelection, essentially killing any deal.

In 2011, Boxer focused heavily on transportation and highway funding. Despite her earlier conflicts with Inhofe, she worked with him to iron out the details of a new federal transportation bill. The two-year bill had no spending earmarks and consolidated roughly 90 highway programs into 30. It passed the Senate, 76-22. Describing Boxer's role in the negotiations, the *San Francisco Chronicle* observed: "Tea Party conservatives have managed to transform (Boxer) into a paragon of bipartisanship." A version of the bill passed the House in 2012.

Boxer has continued to lead the charge against conservatives on major environmental issues—she has been a leading voice against building the Keystone XL oil pipeline in recent years—while finding some surprising bipartisan allies on less controversial topics in recent years. She cosponsored legislation with Republicans such as Kentucky Sen. Rand Paul to use overseas tax revenues to fund infrastructure programs. With Graham, she helped to pass an amendment that would allow victims of sexual assault in the military to opt out of testifying during the preliminary trial process and instead let them file sworn statements.

When conservative Sen. David Vitter of Louisiana took over as ranking member of the Environment committee in 2013, they started off on good footing, passing a major water infrastructure bill. But the relationship deteriorated by the end of the year amid personal acrimony over Obamacare and environmental issues. In 2015, Boxer again became ranking member of the committee, with Inhofe returning as chairman following Republicans' Senate takeover.

Boxer has long paid special attention to environmental issues at home. After complaints about pollution and odor in Mecca, Boxer asked the Environmental Protection Agency to investigate and appeared at a press event with environmental activist Erin Brockovich, who shot to prominence with a 2000 movie about her life starring Julia Roberts. The EPA forced a halt to all hazardous waste deliveries to the Western Environmental recycling plant and ordered the company to remove some contaminated soil. In February 2012, Boxer asked the Nuclear Regulatory Commission to do a full-scale review of the accident-prone San Onofre nuclear plant near San Diego. She also got a bill signed into law in May 2012 that enables the city of Tracy to buy land for a solar energy facility. In 2015 she sponsored bills to designate the Sacramento-San Joaquin delta a national heritage site and expand the John Muir National Historic Site.

Boxer pursued other bipartisan initiatives, working in 2007 with the Bush White House to increase the energy efficiency of federal buildings. She co-sponsored, with Republican John Ensign of Nevada, a bill to reduce the tax on corporate profits earned abroad if they were invested in creating American jobs. But after Congress' Joint Committee on Taxation pegged the revenue loss at $28 billion, the measure was not included in the president's February 2009 economic stimulus bill. Boxer has long been interested in enacting a "bill of rights" for stranded airline passengers, and in 2009 she joined Republican Sen. Olympia Snowe of Maine in seeking support for a measure allowing passengers to deplane after every three hours on the ground and to be given food, water, and other amenities while they wait. It was incorporated as part of a reauthorization bill for the Federal Aviation Administration that passed the Senate in 2010 but stalled in negotiations with the House. The Obama administration issued a rule modeled after their legislation that took effect in April of that year.

In 2007 and 2008, Boxer was entrusted with added institutional responsibilities when Reid appointed her to temporarily replace the disabled Tim Johnson of South Dakota as chairman of the Senate Ethics Committee. (Johnson suffered a brain hemorrhage in late 2006, but recovered.) In February 2008, she led the committee in admonishing Republican Larry Craig of Idaho for attempting to withdraw his guilty plea following his arrest in a gay sex sting in a Minneapolis airport men's room. Under Boxer, the panel also admonished New Mexico Republican Pete Domenici for contacting a federal prosecutor who was investigating state Democrats in a corruption case. In June 2008, after public revelations that Democrats Christopher Dodd of Connecticut and Kent Conrad of North Dakota had received favorable terms on home mortgages, committee members voted unanimously to require more disclosure of members' mortgage terms. She served as committee chair until Republicans won Senate control in 2015.

In 1998, Boxer was challenged by Republican state Treasurer Matt Fong. She raised $15 million and ran ads attacking Fong for what she called his ambiguous stances on issues like abortion rights. Fong attacked her for what he called the hypocrisy of her support for Clinton. (The president's brother-in-law, Tony Rodham, married Boxer's daughter.) But Fong failed to raise much money. Boxer won 53%-43%, an impressive performance for a Democrat dismissed a few years before as too left-wing for much of the state.

When she faced reelection in 2004, Boxer raised impressive amounts of money early, and well-known Republicans declined to make the race against her. Her opponent was Bill Jones, who had been elected secretary of state by narrow margins in 1994 and 1998 yet was not well known outside his home base in Fresno County. Boxer spent $16 million to Jones' $7 million. She won 58%-38%.

Carly Fiorina, the former chief executive officer of Hewlett-Packard, sought the GOP nomination to challenge Boxer in 2010. The well-connected former CEO had the potential to be a well-financed and formidable opponent, and after investing $5.5 million of her own savings, breezed past her Republican rivals in the June primary with 56% to former Rep. Tom Campbell's 22% and Assemblyman Chuck DeVore's 19%.

The political climate appeared ripe for Fiorina, with public distrust of Washington and its longtime inhabitants reaching a crescendo in the summer. Fiorina ran as an outsider with business experience, calling Boxer "one of the most bitterly partisan" senators and attacking her record of getting only a handful of original bills passed into law. She even was caught on an open microphone criticizing Boxer's hairstyle as "so yesterday." Fiorina embraced such conservative causes as opposing abortion rights and backing offshore drilling that alienated moderates and independents. Boxer attacked her opponent on those issues but focused on Fiorina's tenure at Hewlett-Packard, citing the company's decision to lay off 28,000 workers and move jobs overseas. Boxer refuted criticism of her thin legislative record, citing "1,000 Boxer provisions" enacted as amendments or other additions to legislation.

She got a boost from President Obama, whose popularity in the Golden State was above his national ratings and who campaigned for her. Boxer handily won a fourth term, 52%-42%. Boxer noted that Jerry Brown also was reelected and said, "I think as (voters) looked at Jerry and they looked at me, they said, 'you know, these are two imperfect people...but we trust them.'"

In 2005, Boxer published a novel called *A Time to Run* about a liberal, woman senator from California opposing a conservative Supreme Court nominee. Four years later, she came out with another *roman a clef* political thriller, *Blind Trust*, about the same senator battling a Republican White House on homeland security and civil liberties. She's also made numerous TV cameos including in "Parks and Recreation," "Gilmore Girls," "Curb Your Enthusiasm" and "Murphy Brown," pointing out the industry is a big one in her home state.

Boxer announced in a January 2015 web video with her grandson that she would retire at the end of her term. She said in a call with reporters that her greatest regrets were failing to stop the Iraq war, coming up short on legislation to remove military sexual assault cases from the chain of command, and failing to pass climate change legislation.

Boxer said it's "so critical" that her Senate seat "stays progressive"—and it looks like it may, with Democratic state Attorney General Kamala Harris the early front-runner to replace her. Harris scared off early Democratic alternatives who could have given her a tough run. Lt. Gov. Gavin Newsom and former Los Angeles Mayor Antonio Villaraigosa both showed more interest in the governor's race in 2018, and billionaire environmentalist Tom Steyer took a pass as well. Democratic Rep. Loretta Sanchez, who initially was Harris's only serious opponent, had a rocky campaign rollout. California's unusual "top two" primary law and its ever-growing Hispanic population could result in an unpredictable showdown in November 2016 between two Democratic candidates.

FIRST DISTRICT

Doug LaMalfa (R)

Elected 2012, 2nd term; b. July 2, 1960, Oroville; Cal Poly U. San Luis Obispo, B.S. 1982; Christian; married (Jill); 4 children.

Elected Office: CA Assembly, 2002-08; CA Senate, 2010-12.

Professional Career: Manager family rice farm.

DC Office: 322 CHOB, 20515, 202-225-3076; Website: lamalfa.house.gov.

State Offices: Auburn, 530-878-5035; Oroville, 530-534-7100; Redding, 530-223-5898.

Committees: *Agriculture:* Commodity Exchanges, Energy, & Credit; General Farm Commodities & Risk Management. *Natural Resources:* Federal Lands; Indian, Insular & Alaska Native Affairs; Water, Power & Oceans.

Group Ratings

	ADA	ACLU	AFL-CIO	LCV	ITI	COC	HAFA	ACU	CFG	FRC
2014	0%	0%	–	0%	100%	79%	67%	96%	79%	100%
2013	5%	C	14%	0%	C	77%	C	88%	67%	C

National Journal Ratings

	2013 LIB	—	2013 CONS
Economic	20%	—	80%
Social	0%	—	87%
Foreign	15%	—	77%
Composite	15%	—	85%

Key Votes of the 113th Congress

1. Sandy storm spending	N 5. Medical Marijuana	N 9. Syrian Rebels Training Y
2. Violence Against Women Act	N 6. Farm Bill	Y 10. Keystone pipeline Y
3. Guantanamo Bay Detainees	N 7. Afghanistan Combat	N 11. Immigration Exec. Action Y
4. Abortion 20-week ban	Y 8. NSA Phone Data Collection	Y 12. Bipartisan budget deal Y

Election Results

2014 general	Doug LaMalfa (R)	132,052	(61%)	$730,253
	Heidi Hall (D)	84,320	(39%)	$233,870
2014 primary	Doug LaMalfa (R)	75,317	(53%)	
	Heidi Hall (D)	42,481	(30%)	
	Gregory Cheadle (R)	13,909	(10%)	
	Dan Levine (D)	9,213	(7%)	

Prior winning percentage: 2012 (57%)

Population

Total:	707,992	White	78.4%	Median income:	$44,689
Urban:	32.4%	Latino	12.4%		(324 of 435)
Suburban:	25.8%	Asian	2.5%	Under $50,000	54.5%
Rural:	41.8%	Amer. Indian	1.5%	$50,000-$99,999:	28.7%
Land area:	19,074	Two races	3.6%	$100,000-$199,999:	13.7%
Pop/sq. mi.:	37.1	White Ethnic	27.5%	$200,000 or more:	3.2%
Born in state:	68.9%			Poverty Rate	18.6%

Age Groups / **Education** / **Work**

		H.S. grad or less:	36.8%	White collar:	33.2%
Under 18:	20.4%	Some college:	40.6%	Blue collar:	46.5%
18 to 34:	21.9%	College degree, 4 yr.:	14.7%	Sales and service:	20.3%
35 to 64:	38.9%	Post-grad study:	7.9%	Govt. workers:	19.2%
Over 64:	18.9%				
		Veterans/active duty:	10.8%		

Northeast: Butte, Shasta

Rising 14,000 feet over low foothills and the Central Valley, visible for 100 miles, is the snow-capped volcanic cone of Mount Shasta, one of a string of (supposedly) burnt-out volcanoes up and down the Pacific Coast. This is the far northern tier of California, where truck traffic on Interstate 5 is the only

Voter Turnout	
2013 Total Citizen 18+	542,159
2014 House Turnout	216,372
2014 Turnout as % CVAP	39.9%
2012 Turnout as % CVAP	55.9%

reminder of the choked metropolitan areas where most of the state's people live. This is lumber country mostly, where the mountains that rise on all sides—the Coast Range to the west, the Sierra Nevada to the east, the scattered mountains sealing off the Central Valley north of Redding—are thick with trees. It's rugged, flannel-shirt, two-lane-road country that was left behind economically when Los Angeles and San Francisco boomed after World War II. Since the 1980s, this northern end of California has been attracting people, mostly young families who come here to raise their children in a small-town environment, but also retirees looking for a calm atmosphere and low cost of living.

The 1st Congressional District of California is mountainous and mostly rural, with three major population areas. One is Redding, south of Mount Shasta, where increased high-altitude snowfall from Pacific Ocean moisture has allowed the Whitney Glacier to defy global warming trends by growing in the past century, the only glacier to do so. The second is farther south, at the edge of the Sierra foothills, around the Butte County communities of Paradise and Chico, home to a state university campus and Sierra Nevada Pale Ale. Between Redding and Chico is Red Bluff. This area was hit hard by the recession. Unemployment in Chico topped 15 percent in early 2011 before slowly declining to 7.5 percent in late 2014. Redding lost 600 construction jobs during the recession, a 20 percent drop; the recovery here was slower than the national average. The district also takes in thinly populated mountain counties like Modoc, site of a World War II detention facility for Japanese Americans. In September 2013, Modoc voted to secede from California—a statement of its alienation from the state's

2012 Presidential Vote		
Mitt Romney (R)................171,902		(56%)
Barack Obama (D) 122,379		(40%)
2008 Presidential Vote		
John McCain (R)................178,181		(55%)
Barack Obama (D).............140,368		(43%)
Cook Partisan Voting Index: R+10		

coastal dominance. Siskiyou County joined it in calling for a new state of Jefferson. Health care jobs have been a growing sector in the region. In 2014, the severe statewide drought fueled devastating fires in the mountains, which led to the evacuation of Weed and other neighboring towns.

The 1st District covers the northeast corner of California, sharing borders with Oregon to the north and Nevada to the east. Politically, it has a Democratic heritage but is culturally conservative and often angry at intrusions by urban environmentalists. Until 1980, the area elected rough-and-ready Democrats who pulled strings in Sacramento and Washington to build roads and dams. Since then, it has elected abstemious Republicans who have solidly conservative voting records and tend to local needs. The mountain areas have a stronger partisan lean. Chico, with its large state university, is more centrist. Overall, this is a Republican district.

Doug LaMalfa (R)

Republican Doug LaMalfa has settled into this isolated district, with the endorsement of his retired veteran predecessor Wally Herger. Like Herger, he has caused few ripples in Congress and has been satisfied to focus mostly on local issues.

LaMalfa hails from what he calls "the real California," a wide swath of rural country north of Sacramento, culturally removed from the liberal Bay Area. A fourth-generation rice farmer from Richvale in Butte County, he was born in Oroville and attended area schools. He later graduated with degrees in agriculture and business from California Polytechnic State University in San Luis Obispo. LaMalfa and his wife, Jill, operate the farm his great-grandfather started in 1931.

He served on various agricultural commissions before winning election in 2002 to the California Assembly, where he spent six years. In 2010, he was elected to the Senate, earning the most votes of any candidate for the legislature that year. LaMalfa made his name in Sacramento by promoting agricultural interests and fighting new government spending and regulation. He sought unsuccessfully to freeze funding for the state's voter-approved high-speed rail project, citing its cost overruns and curtailed route that eliminated service to San Diego and Sacramento. He also opposed a state-level Dream Act proposal giving financial aid to children of illegal immigrants. LaMalfa started "There Ought Not to Be a Law" contests, where citizens across California were invited to submit ideas for removing burdensome laws, with LaMalfa sponsoring the winning proposal.

Herger endorsed LaMalfa immediately after announcing his retirement, inviting criticism from those in Republican circles who objected to his "kingmaker" politics. The LaMalfa campaign also became embroiled in controversy when it was discovered that a staffer had set up an anonymous website attacking LaMalfa's chief Republican rival, former state Sen. Sam Aanestad. The site, which criticized Aanestad's record in the Senate and questioned whether he was truly a dentist, was taken down. In the primary, LaMalfa came in first under California's new all-party system, getting 38% of the vote. The second-highest vote getter was Democrat Jim Reed with 25%. Annestad finished third with 14%. By late summer, LaMalfa had amassed five times more money than Reed, with the largest sums coming from agricultural interests. He ran on a platform that heavily criticized excessive government spending, prompting critics to highlight the total $4.7 million in federal agricultural subsidies he received for his family's rice farm—including $188,570 in 2012. LaMalfa claimed the federal help was necessary for a small farm to comply with onerous federal regulations; rice farmers have long received sizable support. His 57%-43% win was less than stellar, but in line with the recent presidential vote in the district. He won all 11 counties, but had only 51% in Butte—which had the largest turnout.

In the House, LaMalfa won assignments to the district-related Agriculture and Natural Resources committees. He worked with neighboring Democratic Rep. John Garamendi on a bill to create a large new reservoir in Glenn and Colusa counties to serve northern California, mostly with state funding. LaMalfa said that private interests were ready to support the Sites Reservoir. In 2014, he worked on a Republican bill to assure that metropolitan water districts would receive all available water from the reservoir, but the measure was opposed by Democrats. He has called for shifting $3 billion from the state's high-speed rail project to pay for new water storage. An aide to LaMalfa said that she favored a local movement for Siskiyou County to secede from the state; LaMalfa encouraged the supporters but did not explicitly back their movement.

LaMalfa was reelected 61%-39% over Heidi Hall, a conservation expert with the state's Department of Water Resources, who promised to "break through the bitter partisanship" in Washington. She spent $233,000—not enough to be competitive in this sprawling district. LaMalfa increased his support in Butte County to 56%.

SECOND DISTRICT

Jared Huffman (D)

Elected 2012, 2nd term; b. Feb. 18, 1964, Independence, MO; U. of CA Santa Barbara, B.A. 1986, Boston Col., J.D. 1990; no religious affiliation; married (Susan); 2 children.

Elected Office: Bd. member, Marin Municipal Water Dist., 1994-2006; CA Assembly, 2006-12.

Professional Career: Atty., McCutchen, Doyle, Brown & Enersen, 1990-92; Managing partner, Boyd, Huffman & Williams, 1992-96; Managing partner, The Legal Solutions Group, 1996-2001; Sr. atty., Natural Resources Defense Cncl., 2001-06.

DC Office: 1630 LHOB, 20515, 202-225-5161; Website: huffman. house.gov.

Committees: *Natural Resources:* Federal Lands; Indian, Insular & Alaska Native Affairs; Water, Power & Oceans (RMM). *Transportation & Infrastructure:* Highways & Transit; Railroads, Pipelines, & Hazardous Materials (Chmn); Water Resources & Environment.

Group Ratings

	ADA	ACLU	AFL-CIO	LCV	ITI	COC	HAFA	ACU	CFG	FRC
2014	95%	88%	–	94%	40%	31%	13%	4%	4%	0%
2013	100%	C	95%	100%	C	31%	C	8%	16%	C

National Journal Ratings

	2013 LIB	—	2013 CONS
Economic	91%	—	0%
Social	93%	—	0%
Foreign	94%	—	0%
Composite	96%	—	4%

Key Votes of the 113th Congress

1. Sandy storm spending	Y	5. Medical Marijuana	Y	9. Syrian Rebels Training	N
2. Violence Against Women Act	Y	6. Farm Bill	N	10. Keystone pipeline	N
3. Guantanamo Bay Detainees	Y	7. Afghanistan Combat	Y	11. Immigration Exec. Action	N
4. Abortion 20-week ban	N	8. NSA Phone Data Collection	Y	12. Bipartisan budget deal	Y

Election Results

2014 general	Jared Huffman (D)	163,124	(75%)	$712,985	$4,364
	Dale Mensing (R)	54,400	(25%)	$5,462	
2014 primary	Jared Huffman (D)	99,186	(68%)		
	Dale Mensing (R)	32,614	(22%)		
	Andy Caffrey (D)	14,245	(10%)		

Prior winning percentage: 2012 (71%)

Population		Race and Ethnicity		Income	
Total:	713,816	White	72.1%	Median income:	$62,176
Urban:	12.8%	Latino	17.0%		*(97 of 435)*
Suburban:	49.1%	Asian	3.6%	Under $50,000	41.3%
Rural:	38.1%	Amer. Indian	1.9%	$50,000-$99,999:	26.9%
Land area:	9,687	Two races	3.2%	$100,000-$199,999:	21.8%
Pop/sq. mi.:	73.7	White Ethnic	33.2%	$200,000 or more:	10.0%
Born in state:	59.1%			Poverty Rate	13.7%
		Education			
Age Groups		H.S. grad or less:	28.4%	**Work**	
Under 18:	20.5%	Some college:	32.8%	White collar:	42.5%
18 to 34:	19.2%	College degree, 4 yr.:	23.5%	Blue collar:	40.7%
35 to 64:	42.9%	Post-grad study:	15.2%	Sales and service:	16.8%
Over 64:	17.4%			Govt. workers:	14.5%
		Military			
		Veterans/active duty:	8.3%		

Coastal North: Marin, Sonoma

The North Coast of California is unlike any other place in America. It is the only part of the lower 48 states first settled by Russians, who built Fort Ross in 1812. They sold it in 1841 to a Swiss pioneer named John Augustus Sutter; a Sutter employee's discovery of gold near Sacramento seven years

Voter Turnout	
2013 Total Citizen 18+	522,453
2014 House Turnout	217,524
2014 Turnout as % CVAP	41.6%
2012 Turnout as % CVAP	65.8%

later started the Gold Rush. It is the only part of the world with large numbers of redwood trees, shooting up hundreds of feet in the drizzly air. It is wet country, and for years it was one of America's prime lumbering areas. Coastal Eureka and smaller lumber towns are filled with filigreed Victorian houses and old mills, but also art galleries, hiking trails, pubs, and waterfront hotels.

Humboldt County is known for its quality marijuana fields, and the local economy relies heavily on the product, as depicted in the 2008 movie *Humboldt County*. Local voters that year in next-door Mendocino County pulled back from the nation's most liberal marijuana law by falling in line with the state limit of six plants per resident—instead of 24, which had been the county law since 2000—because of concern about non-medical abuses of the crop. The saturation of marijuana growers has led to a drop in prices, but increased production. In early 2015, Mendocino's economic recovery was solid, despite double-digit losses of manufacturing and construction jobs. Environmental groups are increasingly concerned about the impact pot growers are having on the region's salmon streams. Their farms consume enormous amounts of water while also spilling pesticides, fertilizers and other products into the Eel and Klamath Rivers, which historically have produced large salmon harvests. The problem has been compounded by California's extended drought, plus the proliferation of marijuana fields and the influx of young people from around the world who can get good pay and are eager to join in the harvest—typically from September to November. Local producers have begun to prepare for the possibility that use of weed might soon be legalized statewide.

The 2nd Congressional District of California runs from the Oregon border in the northwest corner of the state down through Marin County on San Francisco Bay. It includes the coastal counties of Del Norte, Humboldt, Mendocino, and Marin, which are connected by Highway 101, and inland Trinity County. The district also takes in part of Sonoma County, including Healdsburg, the Alexander Valley, and Simi Winery, one of the oldest boutique wineries in the state. In early 2015, Marin—which was experiencing a highly contagious measles outbreak—unexpectedly became the center for anti-vaccination advocates, especially among affluent and liberal families that have been known for being physically fit. Parents opposed to vaccinations often have resorted to self-medication, with the help of Internet sites and fear campaigns. Some public officials responded by denying access to public services for those who are

2012 Presidential Vote
Barack Obama (D) 230,212   (69%)
Mitt Romney (R)...................89,908   (27%)

2008 Presidential Vote
Barack Obama (D) 255,854   (72%)
John McCain (R)...................91,831   (26%)

Cook Partisan Voting Index: D+20

not vaccinated. The Marin County school board voted to end the vaccination exemption for personal beliefs.

The North Coast lumbering area, from Mendocino north, was once filled with rough-hewn working men, and was historically Democratic. Now the focus is on sustainable forestry and the area remains heavily Democratic, but with more socially liberal views. Inland is the wine-growing country around Healdsburg. President Barack Obama won Marin County in 2012 with a whopping 74% of the vote. In March 2015, the National Oceanic and Atmospheric Administration more than doubled the size of two large marine sanctuaries off the coast of Marin and Sonoma counties. That left NOAA with control of 350 miles off the California coast and the many species that thrive there.

Jared Huffman (D)

Democrat Jared Huffman, first elected in 2012, has stepped into the shoes of several activist lawmakers who recently retired from the California delegation. With his deep interest and expertise on resource issues, he has begun to have a policy impact in the Republican-controlled House, with both partisan and bipartisan initiatives.

Huffman was born in former President Harry Truman's hometown of Independence Missouri. He attended the University of California, Santa Barbara, on a volleyball scholarship, later becoming a three-time NCAA All-American. Three years later, Huffman earned his law degree and went to work on antitrust litigation at a San Francisco-based firm before opening his own practice. His interest in student athletics led to his involvement in a variety of Title IX cases, including a landmark case in which California State University agreed to guarantee gender equity in its men's and women's athletic programs.

In 1994, Huffman ran for and won a position on the board of the Marin Municipal Water District, an experience that led to a job as a senior attorney on water and fisheries issues with the Natural Resources Defense Council. In 2006, Huffman campaigned for the state Assembly, with a focus on environmental policy. He defeated Democratic front-runner Cynthia Murray, a 14-year Marin County supervisor, in the primary and won in November with 65 percent of the vote. During his three terms, he helped block efforts by Republican Gov. Arnold Schwarzenegger to construct a $356 million death row complex at San Quentin.

When he ran for the House in 2012, Huffman had the support of the district's retiring Rep. Lynn Woolsey and Rep. Mike Thompson of the neighboring 1st District, both Democrats, and a celebrity endorsement from Mickey Hart, former drummer for the Grateful Dead. At a fundraiser in Petaluma, Huffman performed Steven Van Zandt's "I Am a Patriot" with Hart. In California's jungle primary, eight Democrats split the progressive vote. Huffman finished first with 37 percent, and the splintered Democratic voting narrowly eliminated Norman Solomon, an antiwar activist and media critic who would have been Huffman's toughest opponent in the general election. Instead, the second spot went to Republican Daniel Roberts. In the solidly Democratic district, Huffman won 71%-29%.

In the House, Huffman serves on the Natural Resources and Transportation and Infrastructure committees. He quickly showed his activist stripes, with an initial focus on his district's diverse interests—including fishing and forestry. The House approved his bill to add Mendocino public lands to the California Coastal National Monument, and he worked with Republican Jamie Herrera Beutler of Washington on their bill to sustain Pacific coast fishing communities by reducing interest rates for ground-fish fishing boats. Huffman spoke out regularly on climate-change and raised options that might appeal to Republicans, such as energy efficiency and weather resiliency.

In January 2015, Huffman filed a bill to replace the 18.4 cents-per-gallon federal tax on gasoline with a carbon tax, which might average about 50 cents per gallon and be designed to finance highway and transit improvements. Despite their aversion to tax hikes, some Republicans have been open to changes in fuel taxes. In January 2015, he became the ranking Democrat on the influential Water, Power and Oceans Subcommittee, which handles local projects that are vital to many lawmakers. He said that he planned to use the post to tackle "the complex natural resource issues that we face in a constructive, problem-solving manner."

Huffman's hobby is winemaking, and his collection features his own "Homemade Hooch" wine. On the pop culture front, he held his own in a broadcast interview with Stephen Colbert, who enjoys mocking Congress. In 2014, he won reelection with minimal opposition from a Democratic and a Republican challenger.

THIRD DISTRICT

John Garamendi (D)

Elected Nov. 2009, 3rd full term; b. Jan. 24, 1945, Camp Blanding, FL; U. of CA Berkeley, B.A. 1966, Harvard U. M.B.A. 1974; Christian; married (Patti); 6 children.

Elected Office: CA Assembly, 1974-76; CA Senate, 1976-90; CA state ins. commissioner, 1991-94, 2002-06; CA lt. gov., 2007-09.

Professional Career: U.S. Peace Corps, Ethiopia, 1966-68; Deputy secy., U.S. Dept. of Interior, 1995-98.

DC Office: 2438 RHOB, 20515, 202-225-1880; Fax: 202-225-5914; Website: garamendi.house.gov.

State Offices: Davis, 530-753-5301; Fairfield, 707-438-1822; Yuba City, 530-329-8865.

Committees: *Armed Services:* Emerging Threats & Capabilities; Strategic Forces. *Transportation & Infrastructure:* Aviation; Coast Guard & Maritime Transportation (RMM); Water Resources & Environment.

Group Ratings

	ADA	ACLU	AFL-CIO	LCV	ITI	COC	HAFA	ACU	CFG	FRC
2014	55%	61%	–	77%	80%	64%	10%	4%	2%	0%
2013	75%	C	95%	96%	C	46%	C	12%	10%	C

National Journal Ratings

	2013 LIB	—	2013 CONS
Economic	67%	—	33%
Social	60%	—	39%
Foreign	77%	—	22%
Composite	68%	—	32%

Key Votes of the 113th Congress

1. Sandy storm spending	Y	5. Medical Marijuana	Y	9. Syrian Rebels Training	N
2. Violence Against Women Act	Y	6. Farm Bill	Y	10. Keystone pipeline	N
3. Guantanamo Bay Detainees	Y	7. Afghanistan Combat	Y	11. Immigration Exec. Action	N
4. Abortion 20-week ban	N	8. NSA Phone Data Collection	Y	12. Bipartisan budget deal	Y

Election Results

2014 general	John Garamendi (D)	79,224	(53%)	$1,290,607	$3,725
	Dan Logue (R)	71,036	(47%)	$815,768	$26,024
2014 primary	John Garamendi (D)	54,672	(53%)		
	Dan Logue (R)	47,560	(47%)		

Prior winning percentages: 2012 (54%), 2010 (59%), 2009 special (53%)

Population		Race and Ethnicity		Income	
Total:	714,407	White	48.7%	Median income:	$54,398
Urban:	36.9%	Latino	28.8%		*(174 of 435)*
Suburban:	49.6%	Asian	10.3%	Under $50,000	45.8%
Rural:	13.5%	Black	6.0%	$50,000-$99,999:	30.9%
Land area:	3,801	Two races	4.3%	$100,000-$199,999:	19.5%
Pop/sq. mi.:	188.0	White Ethnic	21.0%	$200,000 or more:	3.8%
Born in state	60.0%			Poverty Rate	16.3%
		Education			
Age Groups		H.S. grad or less:	40.6%	**Work**	
Under 18:	24.5%	Some college:	35.5%	White collar:	32.8%
18 to 34:	26.3%	College degree, 4 yr.:	14.9%	Blue collar:	42.8%
35 to 64:	36.8%	Post-grad study:	8.9%	Sales and service:	24.3%
Over 64:	12.4%				
		Military		Govt. workers:	21.5%
		Veterans/active duty:	10.8%		

North Central: Western Sacramento Suburbs, Solano

In California's Central Valley, north and west of Sacramento, are the farm counties of Colusa, Sutter, and Yuba. Marysville, the county seat of Yuba County, sits on the east bank of the Feather River. This heavily agricultural region includes locally cultivated rice hybrids from Colusa County, the

Voter Turnout	
2013 Total Citizen 18+	473,029
2014 House Turnout	150,260
2014 Turnout as % CVAP	31.8%
2012 Turnout as % CVAP	51.1%

leading rice-producing county in the nation. Sutter County is the nation's largest producer of prunes and the third-largest producer of walnuts. Yuba City is the headquarters for Sunsweet Growers, which operates a large dried fruit processing facility there. The local farm economy has suffered in recent years, however, and Colusa County has lost thousands of farm jobs and has had scant recovery. It retained the unwanted distinction in January 2015 of having the highest unemployment rate for any California county, at 23.2 percent. The setbacks in Colusa have been a lesson to rural Sutter and Yuba counties that agriculture is the foundation of their economy and that protection of natural resources is vital. The farm-based employment of those two counties dropped from 7,100 in 1997 to 4,600 in 2013.

By contrast, Solano, which is about midway between the Bay Area and Sacramento, has been thriving economically as an exurban commuter site and styles itself as "a place of opportunity." The Yuba City area has one of the largest Sikh populations in the United States. In 2014, a Sikh woman was elected to the city council—likely one of the first Sikh political victories in the nation. Davis is home to a branch of the University of California, with an activist faculty and student body. During the 2011 "Occupy Wall Street" protests, UC Davis became a flashpoint when a video of a university police officer pepper-spraying students sitting on the ground went viral on *YouTube*. Three police officers were suspended. Three years later, students staged a raucous protest against tuition hikes.

2012 Presidential Vote
Barack Obama (D) 131,237   (54%)
Mitt Romney (R).................104,145   (43%)

2008 Presidential Vote
Barack Obama (D) 142,789   (55%)
John McCain (R)..................110,142   (43%)

Cook Partisan Voting Index: D+3

The 3rd Congressional District of California includes Republican-leaning areas like Colusa, Sutter, and Yuba counties, along with a large portion of more Democratic Lake County. Its population center of Solano County leans Democratic. Politically, the 3rd District became competitive after the 2012 redistricting.

John Garamendi (D)

John Garamendi is one of the House's most politically seasoned Democrats, with a public service career spanning more than 40 years. A relative newcomer to the House and an active legislator, he was jolted when redistricting in 2011 moved him from a relatively secure seat to one where he may need to battle every two years to win reelection.

Garamendi was raised on his family's cattle ranch in Calaveras County. At the University of California, Berkeley, he was an All-American offensive guard in football and a competitive wrestler. After graduating, he joined the Peace Corps in Ethiopia, where his wife, Patti, also was a volunteer. The experience launched his career in public service. After returning to California, he won his first campaign in 1974 to the state Assembly. In 1976, he was elected to the state Senate, where he eventually became majority leader. During his career, he did two stints as the state's insurance commissioner and also was President Bill Clinton's deputy secretary of the Interior. But he failed twice in bids to become governor of California. In the 2006 Democratic primary for lieutenant governor, Garamendi narrowly defeated Jackie Speier. He went on to beat Republican Tom McClintock in the general election. Speier and McClintock now hold House seats from northern California. Garamendi was planning to seek an open seat for governor in 2010 when Ellen Tauscher resigned from the House in June 2009 to become President Barack Obama's undersecretary of State for arms control and international security.

In the jockeying before the all-party primary in September, state Sen. Mark DeSaulnier was an early favorite among Democrats and gained endorsements from Tauscher and Rep. George Miller, who held an adjoining district. DeSaulnier was better known locally, but Garamendi had higher name identification from his statewide campaigns, and he also was endorsed by Clinton and former Vice President Al Gore. In the September primary,

Garamendi prevailed among Democrats, winning 26% to DeSaulnier's 18%. But no candidate received the requisite 50% of the total vote, and Garamendi moved on to a runoff election against Republican attorney David Harmer. Harmer was competitive financially. Still, he faced an uphill battle in a suburban San Francisco district that tilted Democratic. Garamendi embraced Obama's agenda while Harmer opposed the president and his bailouts of the financial and auto industries. Garamendi won 53%-43%.

In the House, Garamendi has been an ardent environmentalist. He was among the strongest critics of offshore oil drilling in the wake of the BP oil spill in the Gulf of Mexico, pressing for his proposal to bar new federal drilling leases off the coasts of California, Oregon, and Washington. He has been outspoken in opposing Democratic Gov. Jerry Brown's ambitious plan to build two tunnels to pipe Sierra Nevada snowmelt to San Joaquin Valley farms and Southern California cities. On the Transportation and Infrastructure Committee, he became in 2013 the ranking minority member of the Coast Guard and Maritime Transportation Subcommittee, where he has sought to enhance farm and manufacturing exports.

California's independent redistricting commission put Garamendi's residence in the newly redrawn 3rd District, where 77 percent of voters were new to him, making him ripe for a GOP challenge in 2012. He was flipped from a mostly suburban Bay Area district to a more exurban and rural district, which shifted his focus to the water needs of drought-stricken farms. In the June primary, he got 51 percent of the vote, setting up a general election with Republican Kim Vann, a Colusa County supervisor. Vann sought to broaden her appeal by refusing to sign the Republicans' no-tax pledge and by embracing popular provisions in Obama's health care legislation. She ran a strong campaign and the U.S. Chamber of Commerce spent $600,000 on her behalf. But Garamendi won with 54 percent, precisely the district's vote for Obama.

In 2014, Garamendi faced another competitive reelection and was targeted by the National Republican Congressional Committee. After Vann decided against a rematch, his opponent was Assemblyman Dan Logue. In a head-to-head match-up, Garamendi won the June "all-party" primary with 53.5 percent of the vote. The general election rematch became a more intense version of a conventional conservative versus liberal contest. Logue opposed a minimum-wage hike and comprehensive immigration reform. Garamendi supported those two goals, plus high-speed rail for California. Both opposed Obama's handling of the war against the Islamic State. Garamendi had a fundraising advantage: $1.3 million to $800,000. In the November election, Logue easily won the more rural counties. But Garamendi won Lake, Solano and Yolo, including 67% in Yolo. Garamendi got 52.7% of the total vote. After Sen. Barbara Boxer announced her retirement in January 2015, Garamendi said that he was considering a run for her seat. But he sparked little interest.

FOURTH DISTRICT

Tom McClintock (R)

Elected 2008, 4th term; b. July 10, 1956, Bronxville, NY; U.C.L.A, B.A. 1988; Baptist; married (Lori); 2 children.

Elected Office: CA Assembly, 1982-92, 1996-2000; CA Senate, 2000-08.

Professional Career: Newspaper columnist, journalist, public policy analyst.

DC Office: 2331 RHOB, 20515, 202-225-2511; Fax: 202-225-5444; Website: mcclintock.house.gov.

State Offices: Roseville, 916-786-5560.

Committees: *Budget. Natural Resources:* Federal Lands (Chmn); Water, Power & Oceans.

Group Ratings

	ADA	ACLU	AFL-CIO	LCV	ITI	COC	HAFA	ACU	CFG	FRC
2014	10%	22%	–	6%	80%	50%	90%	100%	100%	63%
2013	10%	C	10%	7%	C	69%	C	100%	100%	C

National Journal Ratings

	2013 LIB	—	2013 CONS
Economic	2%	—	97%
Social	16%	—	74%
Foreign	51%	—	48%
Composite	25%	—	75%

Key Votes of the 113th Congress

1. Sandy storm spending	N	5. Medical Marijuana	Y	9. Syrian Rebels Training	N
2. Violence Against Women Act	N	6. Farm Bill	N	10. Keystone pipeline	Y
3. Guantanamo Bay Detainees	N	7. Afghanistan Combat	Y	11. Immigration Exec. Action	Y
4. Abortion 20-week ban	Y	8. NSA Phone Data Collection	Y	12. Bipartisan budget deal	N

Election Results

2014 general	Tom McClintock (R)	126,784	(60%)	$1,750,512	$36,043
	Art Moore (R)	84,350	(40%)	$196,522	
2014 primary	Tom McClintock (R)	80,999	(56%)		
	Art Moore (R)	32,855	(23%)		
	Jeffrey Gerlach (I)	30,300	(21%)		

Prior winning percentages: 2014 (60%), 2012 (61%), 2010 (61%), 2008 (50%)

Population		Race and Ethnicity		Income	
Total:	685,175	White	84.5%	Median income:	$39,993
Urban:	16.1%	Black	7.2%		*(390 of 435)*
Suburban:	18.7%	Latino	5.6%	Under $50,000	60.4%
Rural:	65.2%	Amer. Indian	0.7%	$50,000-$99,999:	27.9%
Land area:	8,279	Two races	1.4%	$100,000-$199,999:	10.0%
Pop/sq. mi.:	82.8	White Ethnic	16.2%	$200,000 or more:	1.7%
Born in state:	74.8%			Poverty Rate	17.5%
		Education			
Age Groups		H.S. grad or less:	53.3%	**Work**	
Under 18:	22.7%	Some college:	30.7%	White collar:	29.2%
18 to 34:	20.6%	College degree, 4 yr.:	9.8%	Blue collar:	37.7%
35 to 64:	40.0%	Post-grad study:	6.1%	Sales and service:	33.1%
Over 64:	16.7%				
		Military		Govt. workers:	15.2%
		Veterans/active duty:	8.4%		

East Central: Northern Sacramento Suburbs, Madera

California sprang into existence with the Gold Rush of 1849. Statehood and the creation of the first 27 counties followed in 1850. The new state's first boom area was the Mother Lode Country in the foothills of the Sierra Nevada above Sacramento.

Voter Turnout	
2013 Total Citizen 18+	528,174
2014 House Turnout	211,134
2014 Turnout as % CVAP	40%
2012 Turnout as % CVAP	64%

Mining camps the size of Eastern cities grew up almost overnight in vacant valleys locked amid steep hills, with thousands of would-be millionaires gathered to find gold. Most of those who actually got rich did so by providing goods and services that catered to miners' needs. In Placerville, John Studebaker had a buggy shop, Philip Armour ran a butcher shop, and Mark Hopkins had a dry goods store. The biggest mine in California was in Grass Valley in 1857 and was worked for half a century. But long before that, most of the Mother Lode Country emptied out, leaving ghost towns and villages with hundreds of deserted houses, an antique vacation country left behind in time.

When local residents celebrated the sesquicentennial, the area had been resurrected as a booming exurban and tourist mecca. Thousands of Californians—many of them families from smog-filled, middle-class suburbs of the Los Angeles Basin and the San Francisco Bay Area—went looking for a more pleasant, small-town, orderly environment and found it along fast-flowing creeks where the '49ers camped. Placer County, which includes Sacramento suburbs and part of the Mother Lode Country, grew 40 percent from 2000 to 2010, among the most rapid in California. It also ranks among its wealthiest counties. Its 5.2 percent unemployment rate in January 2015 was among the lowest in the state. Near Lake Tahoe, the development of ski resorts has promoted growth in Truckee. *USA Today* described the region this way: "The American River near Coloma becomes a virtual freeway of whooping rafters on summer weekends. The Mother Lode also offers modern-day prospectors an intriguing pastiche of bed-and-breakfast inns, musty antique stores and such blink-and-you'll-miss-'em outposts as Volcano, Fiddletown, Rough and Ready."

The 4th Congressional District of California takes in the Mother Lode counties of Mariposa and Tuolumne and a large share of

2012 Presidential Vote		
Mitt Romney (R)	195,388	(58%)
Barack Obama (D)	133,473	(40%)
2008 Presidential Vote		
John McCain (R)	191,700	(55%)
Barack Obama (D)	151,818	(43%)
Cook Partisan Voting Index: R+10		

Yosemite National Park. Placer County is the largest in the district. Many residents are concentrated in Sacramento suburbs like Roseville, which grew almost 49 percent from 2000 to 2010 and has become a major presence in the area. A swath of the district also has a large elderly population. In Amador, Calaveras, and Tuolumne counties, senior citizens make up 20 percent of the population, twice the state average, and one-third of them live on less than $20,000 a year. Calaveras County is perhaps best known as the setting for Mark Twain's famous short story about a jumping frog. This is the most solidly Republican district in northern California. Calaveras gained a different kind of attention in February 2015 when the American Civil Liberties Union filed a lawsuit against the county after its Board of Supervisors approved a resolution that invited young women to "test and see for themselves the many blessings that can come from living the teachings of Christ." According to the ACLU, the resolution unconstitutionally promotes one particular set of religious beliefs over all others.

Tom McClintock (R)

Republican Tom McClintock, who was first elected in 2008, is one of the California delegation's most conservative members, actively espousing his limited-government views in floor speeches, television interviews, and op-ed columns. In contrast to tea party and other junior House Republicans, he has spent most of his career in public office and he often pursues a separate course from the self-styled outsiders.

McClintock spent his early childhood in White Plains, New York. After graduating from the University of California, Los Angeles, he worked briefly as a political columnist and a state Senate aide before winning a seat in the California Assembly at age 26. From his earliest days in the legislature, McClintock was perhaps its most vocal, if not the most effective, budget hawk, railing against tax increases and high spending under Democratic and Republican administrations alike. Supporters saw an eloquent champion of conservative ideas, a policy wonk with a penchant for quoting Abraham Lincoln.

McClintock tested the limits of his statewide appeal in an increasingly liberal California through a relentless effort to win higher office. He ran for state controller in 1994 and again in 2002, narrowly losing both times. In 2006, he was unsuccessful as his party's nominee for lieutenant governor, even as Republican Gov. Arnold Schwarzenegger sailed to reelection. But no race elevated McClintock's profile in the state as much as his quixotic campaign for governor in the 2003 recall election. As star-struck Republicans lined up behind former actor Schwarzenegger, McClintock forged ahead, presenting himself as the true Republican in a field of hopefuls that at one point included political commentator Arianna Huffington and actor Gary Coleman. He finished with 13 percent.

Opportunity struck again for McClintock in 2008. After nine-term Republican Rep. John Doolittle announced he would step down from the 4th District seat amid a federal probe of disgraced Republican lobbyist Jack Abramoff, several Republicans in the district urged McClintock to run. He faced an intense, three-month primary campaign against former Rep. Doug Ose, a Republican moderate who held the neighboring 3rd District seat from 1999 to 2005. Ose, who also lived outside the district, attacked McClintock as a career politician and carpetbagger who had represented the Thousand Oaks areas in southern California during more than two decades in the Legislature. McClintock ran ads branding Ose as a liberal who had voted to raise taxes and had earmarked millions of dollars for federal projects in his district. McClintock won the primary 54%-39%.

In the general election, McClintock faced Democrat Charlie Brown, a retired Air Force officer who came within 10,000 votes of beating Doolittle in 2006. Brown, who raised his family in Roseville, renewed criticism of McClintock as an opportunist who didn't live in the district. McClintock ran ads calling attention to Brown's attendance at a 2005 protest by

Fifth District / **California**   173

Code Pink, the fiercely anti-war group, and asserted that Brown supported gay marriage but not the troops in Iraq. McClintock's expected easy victory actually took weeks to unfold. He won by precisely 1,800 votes, 50.2%-49.8%, and took six of the nine counties.

In the House, McClintock has proven to be a faithful conservative vote, though an occasionally nettlesome one to GOP leaders seeking to limit internal dissent. He promised to eschew spending earmarks for his district, and called for the earmarking process to be abolished instead of simply reformed. McClintock has consistently filed amendments to slash funding, even after Republicans took control of the House. In January 2013, he was an outspoken foe of spending for relief of individuals and local governments in New Jersey and New York that had been devastated by Hurricane Sandy three months earlier. Many Republicans agreed with him. The bill passed the House chiefly with Democratic votes. In March 2015, the House defeated his amendment to kill all funding for Amtrak. He criticized Congress for having "dutifully shoveled more money at [Amtrak] to keep it afloat."

From 2011 to 2014, McClintock chaired the Water and Power Subcommittee of the Natural Resources Committee. He complained that about half of the state's water supply is consumed to meet various environmental regulations, a particular problem during the state's frequent droughts. He was among the Golden State Republicans who worked on a House-passed bill in 2012 that directed the federal government to extract water from Northern California farms, fisheries, and cities to send to farmers further south. In 2015, he became chairman of the Federal Lands Subcommittee, which has jurisdiction over many large national forests and parks that are in or near McClintock's district.

After the redistricting changes in 2011, neighboring Rep. Dan Lungren considered a challenge to McClintock, but he ultimately ran and lost in the 7th District. McClintock has had no problem with Democrats in this district. But he faced an unusual election challenge in 2014, when his chief opponent was a moderate Republican who criticized McClintock as too conservative for his district.

Art Moore, a West Point graduate who had spent more than two years deployed overseas and then worked on intelligence issues as a consultant, voiced the conventional challenger's pitch against gridlock and dysfunction in Washington. Even if McClintock won, "he'll at least have gotten some competition that might make him rethink his role as a representative," Moore told *The New York Times*, and added that competition was good for the GOP. McClintock dismissed Moore as a Democratic front. He outspent the challenger, $1.75 million to about $200,000. Even with the endorsement of the *Sacramento Bee*, Moore underperformed. In the all-party primary, he trailed McClintock 56%-23% and barely made it to the general election ahead of a third-party contender. In November, Moore appeared to get little more than the standard opposition vote as he held McClintock to 60%, one percentage point less than his vote share in the two previous election wins.

FIFTH DISTRICT

Mike Thompson (D)

Elected 1998, 9th term; b. Jan. 24, 1951, St. Helena; CA St. U., B.A. 1982, M.A. 1996; Catholic; married (Janet); 2 children.

Military Career: U.S. Army 1969-72 (Vietnam).

Elected Office: CA Senate, 1990-98.

Professional Career: Supervisor, Beringer Winery; CA Assembly fellow, 1982-83; Chief of staff, CA Assemblyman Lou Papan, 1984-87; Chief of staff, CA Assemblywoman Jackie Speier, 1987-90; Owner, vineyard.

DC Office: 231 CHOB, 20515, 202-225-3311; Fax: 202-225-4335; Website: mikethompson.house.gov.

State Offices: Napa, 707-226-9898; Santa Rosa, 707-542-7182; Vallejo, 707-645-1888.

Committees: *Ways & Means:* Health; Select Revenue Measures.

Group Ratings

	ADA	ACLU	AFL-CIO	LCV	ITI	COC	HAFA	ACU	CFG	FRC
2014	80%	77%	–	94%	80%	43%	6%	4%	8%	0%
2013	85%	C	90%	96%	C	38%	C	13%	10%	C

National Journal Ratings

	2013 LIB	—	2013 CONS
Economic	91%	—	0%
Social	77%	—	23%
Foreign	90%	—	6%
Composite	88%	—	12%

Key Votes of the 113th Congress

1. Sandy storm spending	Y	5. Medical Marijuana	Y	9. Syrian Rebels Training	N
2. Violence Against Women Act	Y	6. Farm Bill	N	10. Keystone pipeline	N
3. Guantanamo Bay Detainees	Y	7. Afghanistan Combat	Y	11. Immigration Exec. Action	N
4. Abortion 20-week ban	N	8. NSA Phone Data Collection	N	12. Bipartisan budget deal	Y

Election Results

2014 general	Mike Thompson (D)........................	129,613	(76%)	$1,712,298	$2,536	$4,135
	James Hinton (I)...............................	41,535	(24%)			
2014 primary	Mike Thompson (D)........................	88,709	(80%)			
	James Hinton (I)...............................	12,292	(11%)			
	Douglas Van Raam (I)......................	9,279	(8%)			

Prior winning percentages: 2012 (74%), 2010 (63%), 2008 (68%), 2006 (66%), 2004 (67%), 2002 (64%), 2000 (65%), 1998 (62%)

Population		Race and Ethnicity		Income	
Total:	715,332	White	52.5%	Median income:	$62,432
Urban:	62.5%	Latino	25.9%		(96 of 435)
Suburban:	32.5%	Asian	10.5%	Under $50,000	39.5%
Rural:	5.1%	Black	6.5%	$50,000-$99,999:	31.9%
Land area:	1,613	Two races	3.3%	$100,000-$199,999:	22.3%
Pop/sq. mi.:	443.4	White Ethnic	25.9%	$200,000 or more:	6.3%
Born in state:	59.9%			Poverty Rate	13.0%
		Education			
Age Groups		H.S. grad or less:	34.7%	**Work**	
Under 18:	21.0%	Some college:	35.8%	White collar:	34.8%
18 to 34:	23.0%	College degree, 4 yr.:	19.7%	Blue collar:	45.0%
35 to 64:	40.7%	Post-grad study:	9.8%	Sales and service:	20.1%
Over 64:	15.3%				
		Military		Govt. workers:	13.8%
		Veterans/active duty:	8.2%		

Wine Country: Sonoma, Napa

In sunny valleys sealed off from the Coast Range, some of the nation's premium wine grapes are grown on ridges. Three decades ago, there were only 20 wineries in Napa Valley. Today, there are several hundred, with more just west of the ridges in Sonoma County. Wineries were a favorite invest-

Voter Turnout	
2013 Total Citizen 18+	501,756
2014 House Turnout	171,148
2014 Turnout as % CVAP	34.1%
2012 Turnout as % CVAP	59.8%

ment for Silicon Valley millionaires until the recession caused production cutbacks and thousands of job layoffs in 2008. But the vineyards continue to attract millions of visitors every year. The tourism industry in Sonoma County has had double-digit increases, with increased marketing of the region to foreign tourists. In Napa, the emphasis has turned from the vineyards to bottling and tourism; in 2014, more than two-thirds of the grapes used for wine were from outside the county. Olive trees are also grown here. Some of California's earliest literary haunts were in the region's beautiful, lush valleys. Robert Louis Stevenson took his honeymoon near Calistoga in Napa, and Jack London owned a giant house in Sonoma that mysteriously burned down in 1913. All is not mellow in wine country, though. Solano and Napa counties have persistently high rates of binge drinking and smoking, and Napa has had the highest obesity rate of the nine Bay Area counties, according to the UCLA Center for Health Policy Research.

Vallejo is named for a Mexican general and early member of the California Senate. From 1853 to 1996, Vallejo was the site of the giant Mare Island Naval Shipyard, where

41,000 people worked during World War II. When the shipyard closed, the city filed for bankruptcy in 2008, a dire turn of events also blamed on the huge public employee salaries and pensions the city was paying—292 of 411 city workers earned more than $100,000 a year. Although it emerged from bankruptcy, the city still has huge pension costs. In January 2015, unemployment in Solano County

2012 Presidential Vote		
Barack Obama (D) 199,924		(70%)
Mitt Romney (R)...................78,703		(27%)
2008 Presidential Vote		
Barack Obama (D) 217,090		(71%)
John McCain (R)...................82,366		(27%)
Cook Partisan Voting Index: D+19		

was 7 percent and jobs have rebounded. The Kaiser Permanente Medical Center in Vallejo had nearly 4,000 workers. Some of the shipyard's huge dry docks remain in operation for ship repair.

The 5th Congressional District includes all of Napa County and parts of Contra Costa, Lake, Solano, and Sonoma counties. Sonoma is the population center. In 2011, the state's redistricting commission aimed to unite much of California's wine-growing region. Santa Rosa, wine country's largest city, is situated in the west-central part of the district. The city is increasingly upscale, and laborers have become hard-pressed to find housing. Parts of Contra Costa, including Hercules and most of Martinez, were brought into the new 5th District. All of these areas are heavily Democratic, and the district is unlikely to be competitive any time soon.

Mike Thompson (D)

Democrat Mike Thompson, first elected in 1998, has a moderate voting record that has been among the least liberal of coastal Californians. But he is a trusted ally of Minority Leader Nancy Pelosi, a major fundraiser for his party, and a member of the powerful Ways and Means Committee.

Thompson grew up in the Napa Valley town of St. Helena, dropped out of high school, served in the Army in Vietnam, and earned a Purple Heart. Later, he got a bachelor's and master's degree from what is now California State University, Chico. He owned a vineyard and worked as a maintenance supervisor for Beringer, a big winery in the valley. From 1984 to 1990, he was chief of staff to two Assembly members from the Bay Area. In 1990, he was elected to the state Senate, where he chaired the Budget Committee. In 1998, he ran for the House seat of Republican Frank Riggs, who planned to challenge Democratic Sen. Barbara Boxer that year. Thompson faced weak opposition and had support from almost every interest group that matters in the district: unions, medical providers, vintners, oil and timber interests, environmental advocates, law enforcement groups, and fishermen. His issue stands—opposition to oil drilling off the California coast, support of abortion rights and the death penalty—were broadly popular. He won the primary 78%-22% and the general election 62%-33%. He has not been seriously challenged since. In the 2014 general, he won 76% of the vote, his highest share ever, against James Hinton, a third-party challenger who cited his tea party links.

In the House, Thompson joined both the centrist New Democrats and the Blue Dog Coalition of conservative Democrats. He agrees with Republicans on the need to abolish the estate tax, which he said unfairly burdens family farms. He co-founded the Congressional Wine Caucus, and wineries such as Gallo and Sutter Home have been among his largest campaign contributors. His leadership political action committee, the Victory in November Election PAC (VINE PAC), has raised at least $260,000 in each of the past five election cycles.

For several years, Thompson and the caucus have battled lawmakers allied with beer and alcohol wholesalers over a bill giving states new power to restrict sales over the Internet. When a bipartisan group of lawmakers in 2011 introduced a bill to ensure state governments can continue to regulate alcohol under the 21st Amendment, Thompson warned the bill would allow states to pass laws effectively banning direct shipping of spirits. "The federal government has no business picking winners and losers in the wine, beer, and distilled spirits industry," he said. The measure did not pass. In 2012, he joined GOP Rep. Ted Poe of Texas on a proposal to make it more attractive for private capital to invest in renewable energy. With neighboring California Democratic Rep. Jared Huffman, he filed a bill to strengthen criminal penalties for illegal marijuana farms.

He remains a reliable lieutenant for Pelosi. In December 2012, she named Thompson, a hunter and former chair of the Congressional Sportsmen's Caucus, to head a House Democratic task force to develop a response on gun issues following the deadly school massacre in

Newtown Connecticut. In March 2015, he filed an updated version of that proposal, which would close the Internet and gun-show loopholes in existing rules and expand background checks to all gun sales. He emphasized that his legislation protected hunters and gun owners. Earlier, Pelosi tapped him to coordinate redistricting efforts for Democrats following the 2010 census. He and Pelosi obtained Ethics Committee waivers to raise money for the National Democratic Redistricting Trust, which did not disclose its donors.

On the Ways and Means panel, he enacted a tax break for landowners who place their land under conservation easements, a way to preserve farmland. In 2007, he sponsored the Airline Passenger Bill of Rights, which requires airlines to provide basic necessities, like food, water, and well-ventilated facilities, when flights are delayed for long periods. Although it stalled in Congress, the Obama administration issued a rule modeled after the legislation in 2010, and it eventually was included in a 2012 bill to reauthorize the Federal Aviation Administration. After Republicans talked up increased domestic oil drilling, Thompson proposed a ban on drilling along California's North Coast, saying it makes little sense economically or environmentally.

In March 2015, Speaker John Boehner appointed him to a seat on the Migratory Bird Conservation Commission, which had long been held by Michigan Rep. John Dingell, who had retired. Whenever Pelosi leaves the House, that could signal Thompson's exit. It's unlikely that he would have nearly as close of a relationship with the next Democratic leader.

SIXTH DISTRICT

Doris Matsui (D)

Elected March 2005, 5th full term; b. Sept. 25, 1944, Poston, AZ; U. of CA Berkeley, B.A. 1966; United Methodist; widowed; 1 child.

Professional Career: Transition team, President-elect Bill Clinton, 1992-93; Deputy asst. to the pres., deputy dir. of public liaison, White House, 1993-98; Lobbyist, 1998-2005.

DC Office: 2311 RHOB, 20515, 202-225-7163; Fax: 202-225-0566; Website: matsui.house.gov.

State Offices: Sacramento, 916-498-5600.

Committees: *Energy & Commerce:* Communications & Technology; Health.

Group Ratings

	ADA	ACLU	AFL-CIO	LCV	ITI	COC	HAFA	ACU	CFG	FRC
2014	75%	88%	–	94%	60%	43%	6%	4%	4%	0%
2013	95%	C	95%	96%	C	31%	C	12%	12%	C

National Journal Ratings

	2013 LIB	—	2013 CONS
Economic	88%	—	11%
Social	93%	—	0%
Foreign	83%	—	15%
Composite	90%	—	10%

Key Votes of the 113th Congress

1. Sandy storm spending	Y	5. Medical Marijuana	Y	9. Syrian Rebels Training	N
2. Violence Against Women Act	Y	6. Farm Bill	N	10. Keystone pipeline	N
3. Guantanamo Bay Detainees	Y	7. Afghanistan Combat	Y	11. Immigration Exec. Action	N
4. Abortion 20-week ban	N	8. NSA Phone Data Collection	Y	12. Bipartisan budget deal	Y

Election Results

2014 general	Doris Matsui (D)	97,008	(73%)	$982,391
	Joseph McCray, Sr. (R)	36,448	(27%)	$20,950
2014 primary	Doris Matsui (D)	62,640	(74%)	
	Joseph McCray, Sr. (R)	22,465	(26%)	

Prior winning percentages: 2012 (75%), 2010 (72%), 2008 (74%), 2006 (71%), 2005 special (68%)

Population		Race and Ethnicity		Income	
Total:	729,428	White	38.6%	Median income:	$45,584
Urban:	88.3%	Latino	26.3%		*(307 of 435)*
Suburban:	10.2%	Asian	16.4%	Under $50,000	53.9%
Rural:	1.6%	Black	11.5%	$50,000-$99,999:	28.5%
Land area:	388	Two races	5.1%	$100,000-$199,999:	14.9%
Pop/sq. mi.:	1,882.1	White Ethnic	18.7%	$200,000 or more:	2.7%
Born in state:	59.6%			Poverty Rate	24.1%
		Education			
Age Groups		H.S. grad or less:	41.2%	**Work**	
Under 18:	25.0%	Some college:	33.4%	White collar:	33.7%
18 to 34:	27.4%	College degree, 4 yr.:	16.6%	Blue collar:	47.3%
35 to 64:	36.2%	Post-grad study:	8.8%	Sales and service:	19.0%
Over 64:	11.3%			Govt. workers:	21.0%
		Military			
		Veterans/active duty:	7.1%		

Sacramento

Sacramento, capital of the nation's most populous state, is the focus of California's third-largest media market. With its 72-mile light-rail system, it is no longer just a small city with a lot of civil servants and a vegetable-packing economy. It is a vibrant metropolis that has struggled recently

Voter Turnout	
2013 Total Citizen 18+	469,887
2014 House Turnout	133,456
2014 Turnout as % CVAP	28.4%
2012 Turnout as % CVAP	47.9%

along with the rest of the Golden State. Sacramento started as a port on the sluggish waters of the Sacramento and American rivers. It was the destination of many overland migrants, the site of Sutter's Fort, where workers for John Augustus Sutter found the gold that set off the Gold Rush of 1848, and the western terminus of the Pony Express in 1860. This was the natural choice at the time to be California's capital, halfway between San Francisco Bay and the Mother Lode Country in the foothills of the Sierras, and in the middle of California's vast valley. It has the world's largest almond processing plant, and agriculture continues to be important in Sacra-tomato, or Sacto, as some locals call it. In 2008, Sacramento elected its first African-American mayor, former NBA star Kevin Johnson. He won national recognition in 2014 when he became president of the U.S. Conference of Mayors. But he suffered a setback that year when local voters defeated a referendum to strengthen the authority of the mayor and weaken the city manager, who has been the executive officer; Johnson supported Measure L, which lost 56%-44%, the latest of several setbacks for advocates of such change.

In the old days, government was not a big business. Just a few lobbyists hung out in saloons on K or J streets, the governor's mansion was a musty antique, and the summers' 100-plus degree days emptied out what there was of the city. But air conditioning has replaced awnings, and freeways and shopping malls have followed the city's growth east and north toward the Sierra foothills. Platoons of lobbyists, lawyers, and consultants set up permanent shop, and new hotels have been built to serve them. Today, more than 1,750 registered lobbyists prowl the halls of the capitol, transforming the once working-class bastion. In the 1980s, metropolitan Sacramento grew by 35% and in the 1990s by 22%. From 2002 to 2012, it increased another 15% to 2.3 million people, about the same as metro Portland or San Antonio. Most of the growth has been outside the city. High-tech firms have moved east from Silicon Valley, with Intel and Hewlett-Packard maintaining large campuses. Bay Area refugees have welcomed less expensive living standards.

The growth has continued in recent years, but was temporarily slowed by housing shortages and the recession. In February 2015, job postings increased 25 percent over a year earlier. The future of the city's NBA franchise, the Kings, had been in jeopardy,

2012 Presidential Vote		
Barack Obama (D)	156,141	(69%)
Mitt Romney (R)	63,862	(28%)

2008 Presidential Vote		
Barack Obama (D)	163,592	(68%)
John McCain (R)	71,144	(30%)

Cook Partisan Voting Index: D+18

with threats that it might move to Seattle. But a deal was reached in 2013 for sale to new ownership and construction of a new arena in the city.

The 6th Congressional District of California consists of the city of Sacramento, West Sacramento in Yolo County, and parts of Sacramento County. It contains affluent neighborhoods and scattered low-income black and Latino neighborhoods, plus new condominiums north of the American River and middle-class subdivisions south of downtown. Its ethnically diverse communities include, among others, Hmong refugees from Laos, Vietnamese, Russians, and Ukrainians. This is the solidly Democratic part of greater Sacramento.

Doris Matsui (D)

Democrat Doris Matsui won a special election in 2005 to replace her late husband, Robert Matsui, a long-time member of the Ways and Means Committee. She lacks his flair in attracting attention, but may have matched him as a legislator with a choice seat on the Energy and Commerce panel.

Matsui, who was born in a Japanese internment camp in Arizona, was a well-known political figure during her husband's career in Congress. She grew up in Dinuba in Fresno County and graduated from the University of California, Berkeley. In Sacramento, she chaired the board of the local public television station and participated in many civic organizations. After working on Bill Clinton's presidential campaign, she joined his transition team and then served as deputy director of public liaison, where she worked on economic and budget issues. When she left the White House in 1998, she became a senior adviser at a Washington law firm.

Robert Matsui died of complications from a rare blood disorder in January 2005, after serving 13 terms. A few days after his memorial services, Doris Matsui announced that she would run in the special election. With urging from House Minority Leader Nancy Pelosi, other prominent Sacramento Democrats decided not to run. None of Matsui's 10 opponents in the nonpartisan contest had significant political experience or name recognition. Matsui emphasized her support for local water projects and her opposition to President George W. Bush's proposal for personal retirement accounts in Social Security. She also opposed the war in Iraq. Her investment in a partnership with a longtime friend who was a Sacramento land developer sparked a brief flurry of criticism, but she emphasized that her husband had nothing to do with the deal while he was in office and that there was no conflict of interest. Some called the contest a "coronation," but the lack of competition surely reflected the respect the Matsuis had won over the years. She won the all-party primary with 68% of the vote to 9% for the runner-up. She has not faced a competitive contest for reelection.

In the House, Matsui has a reliably liberal voting record. With her seat on Energy and Commerce, she has focused on telecommunications and consumer issues. In January 2015, she filed a bill that would ban companies from charging more for faster Internet access. The following month, she praised the decision by the Federal Communications Commission to approve a comparable approach with its "net neutrality" rules. She has filed legislation to remove roadblocks to health care technology. Matsui sometimes invokes her family's experience in internment camps to warn of potential civil liberties abuses in the war on terrorism. When President Barack Obama in February 2013 issued an executive order aimed at improving cybersecurity, she praised the decision to consider the implications for privacy.

When Congress in 2014 reauthorized the Coast Guard, it included a provision by Matsui to update crime data on passenger cruise ships, with more accessible information on their web sites. That strengthened a comparable law that she enacted in 2010. She joined Republican Rep. Randy Hultgren of Illinois in 2012 in lobbying conference committee members on the transportation reauthorization bill to strip out a provision, sought by Pennsylvania Democratic Sen. Bob Casey, that lowered the diesel/electric standard for new high-speed rail locomotives from 125 mph to 110 mph. They said the provision would make such trains less energy-efficient, and it was removed. In response to recent derailments, she urged federal regulators in February 2015 to implement stronger safety rules for trains carrying oil.

In January 2015, Matsui became co-chair of the Congressional Caucus on Women's Issues, with South Dakota Republican Kristi Noem.

SEVENTH DISTRICT

Ami Bera (D)

Elected 2012, 2nd term; b. March 2, 1965, Los Angeles; U. of CA Irvine, B.S. 1987, M.D. 1991; Unitarian; married (Janine); 1 child.

Professional Career: Prof., U. of CA Davis, 2004-12, assoc. dean, 2004-08; Chief med. officer, Sacramento Cnty. Dept. of Health & Human Services, 1999-2004; Med. dir., Mercy Healthcare Sacramento, 1998-99; MedClinic Med. Group, physician, 1999, asst. med. dir., 1997-98, chief of internal med. dept., 1996-97.

DC Office: 1535 LHOB, 20515, 202-225-5716; Website: bera.house.gov.

State Offices: Sacramento, 916-635-0505.

Committees: *Foreign Affairs:* Africa, Global Health, Global Human Rights, & Int'l Organizations. Asia & the Pacific. *Science, Space, & Technology:* Environment; Space.

Group Ratings

	ADA	ACLU	AFL-CIO	LCV	ITI	COC	HAFA	ACU	CFG	FRC
2014	55%	77%	–	89%	100%	64%	8%	0%	13%	0%
2013	50%	C	86%	93%	C	54%	C	8%	6%	C

National Journal Ratings

	2013 LIB	—	2013 CONS
Economic	60%	—	40%
Social	58%	—	42%
Foreign	61%	—	38%
Composite	60%	—	40%

Key Votes of the 113th Congress

1. Sandy storm spending	Y	5. Medical Marijuana	Y
2. Violence Against Women Act	Y	6. Farm Bill	Y
3. Guantanamo Bay Detainees	Y	7. Afghanistan Combat	N
4. Abortion 20-week ban	N	8. NSA Phone Data Collection	N

9. Syrian Rebels Training	Y
10. Keystone pipeline	N
11. Immigration Exec. Action	N
12. Bipartisan budget deal	Y

Election Results

2014 general	Ami Bera (D)	92,521	(50%)	$4,317,863	$711,714	$6,466,981
	Doug Ose (R)	91,066	(50%)	$5,114,546	$571,908	$5,949,035
2014 primary	Ami Bera (R)	51,878	(47%)			
	Doug Ose (R)	29,307	(26%)			
	Igor Birman (R)	19,431	(18%)			
	Elizabeth Emken (R)	7,924	(7%)			

Prior winning percentage: 2012 (52%)

Population		Race and Ethnicity		Income	
Total:	721,042	White	56.8%	Median income:	$60,735
Urban:	38.5%	Latino	17.2%		*(119 of 435)*
Suburban:	60.1%	Asian	12.1%	Under $50,000	40.9%
Rural:	1.4%	Black	7.3%	$50,000-$99,999:	31.7%
Land area:	544	Two races	4.6%	$100,000-$199,999:	22.0%
Pop/sq. mi.:	1,324.7	White Ethnic	26.6%	$200,000 or more:	5.3%
Born in state:	60.5%			Poverty Rate	13.9%
		Education			
Age Groups		H.S. grad or less:	32.0%	**Work**	
Under 18:	24.4%	Some college:	36.4%	White collar:	41.5%
18 to 34:	22.0%	College degree, 4 yr.:	20.7%	Blue collar:	43.4%
35 to 64:	40.0%	Post-grad study:	10.9%	Sales and service:	15.2%
Over 64:	13.7%				
		Military		Govt. workers:	21.3%
		Veterans/active duty:	8.9%		

Eastern Sacramento Suburbs

Until recently, Sacramento was chiefly the metropolis of a fertile valley that produced a marvelous variety of crops: rice, plums, almonds, olives, asparagus, pears, hops, beans, celery, onions, and potatoes, plus caviar-yielding sturgeon in pools of filtered water.

Voter Turnout	
2013 Total Citizen 18+	501,103
2014 House Turnout	183,587
2014 Turnout as % CVAP	36.6%
2012 Turnout as % CVAP	58.5%

The farmlands remain, and the capital city flourishes as a center of government. Until the recession struck in 2007, greater Sacramento was one of the fastest-growing metro areas in the country. Almost all of the growth was away from the floodplain of the Sacramento River, in the higher land east of the city that eventually turns into hills rising toward the Sierra Nevada. But home sales plunged and foreclosures soared in 2007, which led to service cutbacks in Sacramento County. The county's housing market has rebounded, with a 10 percent increase in both sales and prices in 2014. In Rancho Cordova, which won an All-America City award in 2010, local leaders created a New Urbanist development plan to replace aging strip malls with a traditional downtown. Voters there in November 2014 approved a half-percent increase in the sales tax to improve services and infrastructure. City officials soon found themselves uncertain how to spend the money.

The 7th Congressional District of California includes suburban Sacramento and much of Sacramento County outside the neighboring and mostly urban 6th District. All of its residents are in Sacramento County, in suburbs like Arden-Arcade and Carmichael. There is also the old town of Folsom, where Intel has a campus of about 6,300 employees with an average pay of $174,000, a prosperous company town that is moving beyond the image singer Johnny Cash created in his song, "Folsom Prison Blues." Intel calls the research lab its "nerve center," where engineers develop its core intellectual property. The company's chips are used in more than 80 percent of personal computers and laptops in the world, though its share has declined in recent years. Historically, Sacramento was Democratic. But Sacramento County, with its rapid growth, was more marginal in the early 2000s. In the 2004 presidential race, Democrat John Kerry won the county over George W. Bush by just 1,118 votes. But Barack Obama won the county convincingly in 2008 and 2012, beat-

2012 Presidential Vote		
Barack Obama (D)	145,147	(51%)
Mitt Romney (R)	133,888	(47%)
2008 Presidential Vote		
Barack Obama (D)	153,405	(52%)
John McCain (R)	137,313	(46%)
Cook Partisan Voting Index:	EVEN	

ing John McCain 59%-40% and Mitt Romney 58%-39%. Along with the 10th District, this is the most competitive political territory in northern California.

Ami Bera (D)

Democrat Ami Bera has had three consecutive tight elections, losing the first and winning the next two against a current and former House Republican member. He has continued to embrace President Barack Obama, and seems likely to remain in the Republican Party's crosshairs.

Bera was born in Hollywood, the son of parents who emigrated from India to the United States in the 1950s to attend college. His mother studied education and became a public elementary school teacher; his father paid for his engineering degree by ushering at Los Angeles Dodgers baseball games. The younger Bera said he grew up believing that he lived in a land of opportunity where "if you worked hard and played by the rules, you could reach your full potential." Bera excelled in science and math, and went to the University of California, Irvine, to study biology and then earn his medical degree. As a second-year medical student, he met his future wife, Janine, then an undergraduate and now also a physician. He told *National Journal* that the listening skills required for a good bedside manner have served him well in politics.

After several years practicing internal medicine, Bera became the medical director of care management for Mercy Healthcare Sacramento in 1998. There, he discovered the inefficiency within the health care sector and set about identifying and implementing "simple solutions" to reduce waste. In one project, his unit reviewed 911 calls that weren't actually emergencies and found that most originated from a small group of widows and widowers. By reaching out to that group, the unit dramatically reduced unnecessary calls. Realizing that other hospital groups in Sacramento County faced similar challenges, Bera became the county's chief medical officer in 1999. At the time, the county was unprepared to meet the demands of its uninsured population, which became a top priority for Bera. He said that Obama's Affordable Care Act "is not the direction I would have gone," but believes that the law offers a solid starting point to bring down spiraling medical costs.

In 2010, Bera challenged eight-term Republican Rep. Dan Lungren, who had a close election in 2008. Bera showed surprising strength as a fundraiser, drawing on donations from Indian Americans across the country. He accused Lungren of being out of touch with district voters, while the incumbent portrayed him as a rubber stamp for then-House Speaker Nancy Pelosi's liberal agenda. A late-breaking wave of nearly $700,000 in ads from GOP strategist Karl Rove's American Crossroads organization helped seal Lungren's win. Bera began almost immediately to make a second run. In 2012, he challenged Lungren in the post-redistricting 7th District, which was 3 percentage points more Democratic than Lungren's old district. In the primary, he won 41% of the vote to Lungren's 53%. In the general election, Bera benefited from a *Sacramento Bee* endorsement that said "Bera has matured, and Lungren has failed to meet local expectations." With turnout more than doubled from the spring, he defeated Lungren, 52%-48%.

In the House, Bera has been one of the California delegation's most moderate and politically attuned members. In June 2014 he was one of four California Democrats from competitive districts who voted against funding for the California high-speed rail project. A month later, he was one of 45 Democrats who joined most Republicans to raise the Child Tax Credit for higher-income taxpayers and reduce it for lower-income taxpayers. And he backed an unsuccessful version of the farm bill that cut $20 billion from the federal food stamp program, an amount that many of his fellow Democrats abhorred. He described the vote as a signal of his willingness to compromise. Bera sought opportunities to collaborate with House Republicans. In March 2015, he cosponsored with GOP Rep. Mark Meadows of North Carolina a bill to reduce the waiting time for patients at VA hospitals and to increase the number of visas allowed for doctors to practice at those hospitals.

On the Foreign Affairs Committee, Bera worked to improve ties between India and Afghanistan and spent a week in his parents' home region to encourage students there to attend California colleges. In January 2015, he was one of four congressional Democrats who accompanied Obama on his visit to India. He praised the civilian nuclear agreement that was reached with Prime Minister Narenda Modi. The deal "makes billions of dollars in trade possible for U.S. companies that want to build and invest in India [and] creates jobs in the U.S. and helps grow our economy," Bera said. Earlier, he spoke out against the Obama administration's contemplation of military action against Syria, preferring to let diplomacy work. And he worked on efforts to increase foreign exports of California's abundant agricultural products.

The closeness of the 2012 election and the favorable Republican climate in 2014 ensured that Bera would become a top GOP target. In the June primary, he led the pack with 47% of the vote, setting up a general-election race with former Rep. Doug Ose, who served six years before abiding by his term-limits pledge to retire in 2004. In the primary, Ose handily led Igor Berman, who was on leave as chief of staff to conservative Rep. Tom McClintock in the neighboring 4th District, and Elizabeth Emken, who got 37% in a long-shot challenge to Senator Dianne Feinstein in 2012. This became the most expensive House campaign in the 2014 cycle. National Republican groups poured more than $6 million into the general election on Ose's behalf, while Democrats spent more than $5 million for Bera. Ose spent $5.1 million from his own campaign treasury, compared with $4.3 million for Bera. The Democrat released an ad showing himself with patients and touting his decision to forego his salary during the 2013 government shutdown. In a contest that took several days to resolve, he eked out a win over Ose, 50.4%-49.6%.

Not surprisingly, Bera became an early Republican target for 2016. His support for the Trans-Pacific Partnership trade deal led organized labor to promise a Democratic primary challenge.

EIGHTH DISTRICT

Paul Cook (R)

Elected 2012, 2nd term; b. March 3, 1943, Meriden, CT; Southern CT St. U., B.S. 1966, CA St. U. San Bernadino, M.P.A. 1996, U. of CA Riverside, M.A. 2000; Catholic; married (Jeanne); 2 children.

Military Career: U.S. Marine Corps, Colonel, 1966-92 (Vietnam).

Elected Office: CA Assembly, 2006-12; Yucca Valley Town Cncl., Yucca Valley Mayor, 1998-2006.

Professional Career: Prof., U of CA Riverside, 2002-12; Asst. prof., Copper Mountain Col., 1998-2002; Exec. dir., Yucca Valley Chamber of Commerce, 1993-94.

DC Office: 1222 LHOB, 20515, 202-225-5861; Website: cook.house.gov.

State Offices: Apple Valley, 760-247-1815; Yucalpa, 909-797-4900.

Committees: *Armed Services:* Military Personnel; Seapower & Projection Forces; Tactical Air & Land Forces (VChmn); *Foreign Affairs:* Europe, Eurasia & Emerging Threats; Terrorism, Nonproliferation & Trade. *Natural Resources:* Energy & Mineral Resources; Indian, Insular & Alaska Native Affairs.

Group Ratings

	ADA	ACLU	AFL-CIO	LCV	ITI	COC	HAFA	ACU	CFG	FRC
2014	5%	5%	–	3%	100%	86%	61%	84%	74%	88%
2013	0%	C	33%	4%	C	92%	C	72%	72%	C

National Journal Ratings

	2013 LIB	—	2013 CONS
Economic	40%	—	60%
Social	43%	—	54%
Foreign	24%	—	68%
Composite	38%	—	63%

Key Votes of the 113th Congress

1. Sandy storm spending	N	5. Medical Marijuana	N
2. Violence Against Women Act	Y	6. Farm Bill	N
3. Guantanamo Bay Detainees	N	7. Afghanistan Combat	N
4. Abortion 20-week ban	Y	8. NSA Phone Data Collection	N

9. Syrian Rebels Training	Y
10. Keystone pipeline	Y
11. Immigration Exec. Action	Y
12. Bipartisan budget deal	Y

Election Results

2014 general	Paul Cook (R)	77,480	(68%)	$297,683	$9,209
	Bob Conaway (D)	37,056	(32%)	$6,104	
2014 primary	Paul Cook (R)	40,007	(58%)		
	Bob Conaway (D)	12,885	(19%)		
	Paul Hannosh (R)	9,037	(13%)		
	Odessia Lee (D)	6,930	(10%)		

Prior winning percentage: 2012 (57%)

Population		Race and Ethnicity		Income	
Total:	709,384	White	49.7%	Median income:	$45,976
Urban:	11.3%	Latino	35.9%		*(300 of 435)*
Suburban:	78.9%	Black	7.5%	Under $50,000	53.8%
Rural:	9.7%	Asian	3.2%	$50,000-$99,999:	29.7%
Land area:	7,964	Two races	2.2%	$100,000-$199,999:	14.4%
Pop/sq. mi.:	89.1	White Ethnic	18.0%	$200,000 or more:	2.1%
Born in state:	65.3%			Poverty Rate	21.8%
		Education			
Age Groups		H.S. grad or less:	46.7%	**Work**	
Under 18:	27.1%	Some college:	38.9%	White collar:	27.5%
18 to 34:	24.6%	College degree, 4 yr.:	8.6%	Blue collar:	46.7%
35 to 64:	36.1%	Post-grad study:	5.8%	Sales and service:	25.7%
Over 64:	12.2%				
		Military		Govt. workers:	21.4%
		Veterans/active duty:	10.7%		

High Desert: San Bernardino County

The eastern High Desert of California runs along the Nevada border, with a huge swath of land uninhabited for dozens of miles. In the west are the towns of Apple Valley and Victorville, a high-growth area that was once home to cowboy stars Roy Rogers and Dale Evans. Other San Bernardino

Voter Turnout	
2013 Total Citizen 18+	472,955
2014 House Turnout	114,536
2014 Turnout as % CVAP	24.2%
2012 Turnout as % CVAP	46%

County cities and towns dot the landscape: the heavily Hispanic city of Adelanto; Hesperia, a wayside on the Mormon Trail; and Needles, where the fictional Joad family stops soon after entering California in *The Grapes of Wrath*. To the north, off Interstate 15 heading to Las Vegas, are Barstow and the military training center at Fort Irwin. A fork splits Interstates 15 and 40, and both highways straddle the outskirts of the Mojave National Preserve before moving into Nevada. Like the rest of California, the Inland Empire struggled to climb out of the recession. The unemployment rate in San Bernardino County reached 14.8% in mid-2010 but dropped to 7% in December 2014. According to *The Press-Enterprise* newspaper, the county's food stamp usage rate was 17%, compared with 11% in Los Angeles County. Several economic development projects in the region are percolating, including a proposal by the Los Coyotes Band of Cahuilla Indians to build a casino in Barstow that could create 1,000 construction jobs. A plan for renewable energy projects in the desert has generated opposition from several counties, including San Bernardino, which has been partly based on the impact on private lands; some environmental groups and renewable-energy advocates object that the plan was poorly drafted. Proponents welcome the broad vision for land use in the plan, which would cover 22 million acres. San Bernardino has the most land of any county in the nation, but more than 80 percent of it is publicly owned.

The new 8th Congressional District of California covers Mono and Inyo counties, as well as most of San Bernardino County, though more than 90 percent of the population is in San Bernardino. Its geography is vast. It sweeps in the sleepy Mojave Desert and mountains, Death Valley (where the International Dark-Sky Association laments the visibility of lights from Las Vegas), and Owens Valley, the source of Los Angeles' water supply and the site of the California "Water Wars" that became the inspiration for the movie *Chinatown;* the conflict finally was resolved in 2014 when the county agreed on a new method to suppress the dust from the dry bed of Owens Lake. In 2014, Death Valley had more than 1 million visitors, the most in a decade. The district also includes Mammoth Lakes and

2012 Presidential Vote		
Mitt Romney (R)	118,278	(56%)
Barack Obama (D)	88,579	(42%)
2008 Presidential Vote		
John McCain (R)	124,020	(55%)
Barack Obama (D)	94,577	(42%)
Cook Partisan Voting Index:	R+10	

the Mammoth ski resort area in the Inyo National Forest. Despite pockets of Democratic support—Mono County voted for Barack Obama in the 2012 presidential race—this is strong Republican territory.

Paul Cook (R)

Republican Paul Cook, a 26-year Marine Corps veteran and Vietnam-era war hero, won this seat in 2012 at age 69. He became one of the most policy-focused and least publicity-minded of the GOP newcomers. His military and community backgrounds make him a throwback to an era when many Republicans styled themselves as representative of Main Street.

Cook, who moved to California at the end of his military career, grew up and attended school in the small manufacturing city of Meriden Connecticut. He studied education at Southern Connecticut State University, graduating in 1966, and joined the Marines that same year. His first assignment sent him to Vietnam, where he served as an infantry officer and platoon commander. During the war, he received the Bronze Star and two Purple Heart medals. He returned to the United States in 1968, eventually earning a promotion to captain while training infantry in North Carolina. He continued to rise through the ranks, and became a colonel in 1988 and the area commander for the Marine base at Camp Pendleton in California.

After his retirement from the military in 1992, Cook moved to Yucca Valley California, and was the executive director of the local Chamber of Commerce before heading back to school to earn degrees in public administration and political science. He taught political science and history at several California universities before earning tenure at Copper Mountain College, which has a close relationship with the local Marine base. Cook told *National Journal*, "When I retired from active duty, I still felt that I owed something to my community. That's why I pursued education. ... I still miss the classroom and recall those days fondly."

Cook won a seat on the Yucca Valley Town Council and ultimately served as the town's mayor. In 2006, Cook ran for the state Assembly, and unexpectedly won the seat against better-known candidates. As chairman of the Assembly's Veterans Affairs Committee (while serving in the minority party), he worked on issues related to retirement homes, child custody, higher education, and other services for veterans. He also worked to protect children from sexual predators, a legislative accomplishment of which he says he is particularly proud.

In his race for Congress, Cook enjoyed the support of a host of California Republicans, including former Gov. Pete Wilson and Reps. Darrell Issa and Jeff Denham. He was endorsed by the U.S. Chamber of Commerce and California Taxpayers Association. In a crowded field of 13 candidates, Cook trailed a newcomer tea party candidate, Gregg Imus, in the primary by just 237 votes; he was 240 votes ahead of third-place finisher Phil Liberatore, who also was a Republican. Cook picked up momentum in the general-election campaign, outraising Imus more than 5 to 1. He ran on promises not to raise taxes and to fight for veterans and military families, using the issues to distance himself from Democrats. "Military and veterans seem to be a low priority with this administration, but I won't let Washington replicate the past, where they forgot about veterans returning from Vietnam," he said. Under California's top-two, all-party primary system, Cook defeated his fellow Republican, 57%-43%.

In the House, Cook found a natural base on the Armed Services Committee. He filed a bill to permit continued pay checks to Pentagon employees furloughed during a government shutdown. He filed a bill in May 2013 to help homeless veterans find employment. In September 2014, he wrote in a column in the *San Bernardino Sun* that the Obama administration had "faltered in our commitment to Iraq," and he called for military action against the Islamic State in Iraq and Syria by arming proxy groups, but not with U.S. troops. He organized the Semper Fi PAC, which raised $75,000 in the 2013-2014 election cycle. In 2014, Cook breezed to reelection with 68 percent of the vote—this time against a Democrat, Bob Conway, who raised less than $6,000. He appears to be entrenched in his seat, at least until the next redistricting.

NINTH DISTRICT

Jerry McNerney (D)

Elected 2006, 5th term; b. June 18, 1951, Albuquerque, NM; U.S. Military Acad. West Point, attended 1969-71, U. of NM, B.S. 1973, M.S. 1975, Ph.D. 1981; Catholic; married (Mary); 3 children.

Professional Career: Natl. security contractor, Sandia Natl. Labs., 1979-85; Engineer, U.S. Windpower Kenetech, 1985-94; Energy consultant, 1994-99; CEO, start-up wind turbine manufacturer, 2000-06.

DC Office: 2265 RHOB, 20515, 202-225-1947; Fax: 202-225-4060; Website: mcnerney.house.gov.

State Offices: Antioch, 925-754-0716; Stockton, 209-476-8552.

Committees: *Energy & Commerce:* Communications & Technology; Energy & Power; Environment & the Economy. *Veterans' Affairs:* Economic Opportunity.

Group Ratings

	ADA	ACLU	AFL-CIO	LCV	ITI	COC	HAFA	ACU	CFG	FRC
2014	75%	77%	–	94%	60%	43%	6%	12%	6%	0%
2013	65%	C	95%	89%	C	38%	C	8%	6%	C

National Journal Ratings

	2013 LIB	—	2013 CONS
Economic	66%	—	34%
Social	58%	—	41%
Foreign	60%	—	40%
Composite	62%	—	39%

Key Votes of the 113th Congress

1. Sandy storm spending	Y	5. Medical Marijuana	Y	9. Syrian Rebels Training	Y
2. Violence Against Women Act	Y	6. Farm Bill	Y	10. Keystone pipeline	N
3. Guantanamo Bay Detainees	N	7. Afghanistan Combat	Y	11. Immigration Exec. Action	N
4. Abortion 20-week ban	N	8. NSA Phone Data Collection	N	12. Bipartisan budget deal	Y

Election Results

2014 general	Jerry McNerney (D)	63,475	(52%)	$1,109,115	$3,721
	Tony Amador (R)	57,729	(48%)	$62,058	$63,704
2014 primary	Jerry McNerney (D)	38,295	(49%)		
	Tony Amador (R)	20,424	(26%)		
	Steve Colangelo (R)	14,195	(18%)		
	Karen Mathews Davis (R)	4,637	(6%)		

Prior winning percentages: 2012 (56%), 2010 (48%), 2008 (55%), 2006 (53%)

Population		Race and Ethnicity		Income	
Total:	724,907	Latino	39.2%	Median income:	$52,739
Urban:	61.6%	White	35.6%		*(187 of 435)*
Suburban:	36.9%	Asian	12.9%	Under $50,000	47.3%
Rural:	1.5%	Black	7.5%	$50,000-$99,999:	28.4%
Land area:	1,534	Two races	3.7%	$100,000-$199,999:	21.0%
Pop/sq. mi.:	472.6	White Ethnic	17.5%	$200,000 or more:	3.3%
Born in state:	63.0%			Poverty Rate	19.8%
		Education			
Age Groups:		H.S. grad or less:	45.6%	**Work**	
Under 18:	27.8%	Some college:	35.4%	White collar:	27.7%
18 to 34:	22.9%	College degree, 4 yr.:	13.7%	Blue collar:	44.6%
35 to 64:	37.1%	Post-grad study:	5.3%	Sales and service:	27.7%
Over 64:	12.1%			Govt. workers:	15.3%
		Military			
		Veterans/active duty:	6.8%		

Central Valley: Stockton, San Joaquin

Voter Turnout	
2013 Total Citizen 18+	438,312
2014 House Turnout	121,204
2014 Turnout as % CVAP	27.7%
2012 Turnout as % CVAP	50.4%

California is often defined by its cosmopolitan cities, its gorgeous Pacific coastline, and its world-class vineyards. But beyond Beverly Hills and Nob Hill, there is another California that likes to get its hands dirty. This is an old part of the state, settled in the 1840s. When the Gold Rush fortune seekers departed, the land was left to a determined population of farmers. Crisscrossed with railroads and canals, the Central Valley became one of the world's greatest agricultural regions. The San Joaquin River channel was deepened to 37 feet, and Stockton today is the Central Valley's port. (The city is named after Robert Stockton, the second U.S. military governor of California, who captured Santa Barbara and Los Angeles from Mexico and proclaimed California U.S. territory.) The rich land attracted immigrants from all over: Mexicans came up Route 99 and joined North Dakotans flocking to the town of Lodi. Italian and Yugoslavian immigrants brought their Old World crops. Yankees and Okies brought their distinct churches and beliefs. Later, Southeast Asian refugees crowded into the old streets of Stockton. The region endures the usual plagues of a farm economy, such as the difficulty attracting migrant workers at harvest time, and some that are unique to California, such as chronic concerns about the water supply. A devastating drought that began in 2007 shrank the acreage of usable land. By March 2015, the federal government was prepared to deny water from its Central Valley Project reservoirs for a second year, and farmers feared they might need to shut down a million acres of production.

In recent decades, the Central Valley has also become a suburban zone. Because of the high cost of living in the San Francisco Bay Area, workers with modest incomes bought lower-priced houses around Tracy and Stockton and commute to work on Interstate 580, past the windmills of Altamont. Still, crime and unemployment remain barriers, and Stockton has become a poster child for urban dysfunction. *Forbes* magazine named Stockton the most miserable city in America in 2011. At the time, city officials tried to tackle mounting debt, slashing spending by $90 million and cutting police and fire department budgets. Their efforts fell short. In June 2012, facing close to $1 billion in long-term debt, Stockton became the biggest city in American history to declare bankruptcy; the following year, the record went to Detroit. Stockton also had the second-highest foreclosure rate in the country in 2012, and San Joaquin County's jobless

2012 Presidential Vote		
Barack Obama (D) 127,418	(58%)
Mitt Romney (R)..................88,403	(40%)
2008 Presidential Vote		
Barack Obama (D) 127,949	(57%)
John McCain (R)..................93,008	(41%)
Cook Partisan Voting Index: D+6		

rate remained at nearly 14 percent. In October 2014, a federal bankruptcy judge approved the city's bankruptcy plan, with higher taxes and slashed payments to bondholders, but little impact on public pensions. Stockton exited bankruptcy in February 2015. Its foreclosure and unemployment rates had dropped significantly by the end of 2014, but crime remained high.

The 9th Congressional District of California includes most of San Joaquin County and parts of Sacramento and Contra Costa counties. It contains all of Stockton, plus Lodi, a town with a sizable Muslim community and a thriving downtown. The district takes in Brentwood in Contra Costa County, the fastest-growing city in the Bay Area in the 2000s. Brentwood nearly doubled in population from 2000 to 2006, but growth has slowed considerably since the housing bust in 2007.

The creation of this district generated controversy. The state's nonpartisan redistricting commission was designed to preclude interference from elected and party officials. But a 2011 investigation by the online watchdog *ProPublica* found that Democratic Rep. Jerry McNerney hired a mapping consultant who set up a Facebook page called "OneSanJoaquin" to push for a San Joaquin-based district, which eventually came to pass. The district is more Democratic now and includes left-leaning voters from eastern Contra Costa County, but it is not overwhelmingly Democratic and could be competitive in the future, especially with continued economic woes.

Jerry McNerney (D)

Democrat Jerry McNerney has been one of the most politically vulnerable members of his party: In five successful elections since 2006, he has never won more than 56 percent of the vote. Though he is more moderate than most California Democrats, he has usually been a party loyalist and an ally of Minority Leader Nancy Pelosi.

McNerney's father was a union organizer in the 1930s and later worked for the U.S. Geological Survey in Albuquerque, where Jerry McNerney was born. Along with his twin brother, McNerney was sent to a military boarding school in Hays, Kan., and later won an appointment to the U.S. Military Academy. He left West Point after two years in the late 1960s because he opposed the war in Vietnam. He transferred to the University of New Mexico, where he eventually earned a doctoral degree in differential geometry. During that period, he was a passenger aboard a plane that was hijacked by three men who were wanted for the slaying of a New Mexico State Police officer. The hijackers let him off in Tampa before continuing on to Cuba. He spent several years as a contractor for Sandia National Laboratories, working on national security programs. In 1985, he moved to the private sector with U.S. Windpower and later was chief executive of a wind turbine firm. McNerney, who named his daughter Windy, claimed that his work contributed to saving the equivalent of 8.3 million tons of carbon dioxide.

In 2006, McNerney was an unlikely winner against Republican Rep. Richard Pombo, a local rancher in an area where he was so well known it was dubbed "Pombo Country." As the chairman of the House Resources Committee, Pombo was leader of the property-rights movement backed by ranchers and farmers. In the primary, the Democratic Congressional Campaign Committee endorsed Steve Filson, an airline pilot and political neophyte who turned out to be a disappointment. McNerney, endorsed by the state party and by local organized labor, soundly defeated Filson, 53%-28%. In the general election, Pombo outspent McNerney by nearly 2-to-1. McNerney managed nevertheless to turn the election into a referendum on Pombo, who was hated by national environmental groups, which called him an "eco-thug" and "Wildlife Enemy No. 1." Bolstered by a strong anti-Republican tide that year, McNerney won 53%-47%.

In the House, McNerney established a moderate voting record, especially on cultural issues. He joined a majority of Republicans in February 2011 in voting to extend several provisions of the 2001 anti-terrorism law known as the Patriot Act. He was vocal in publicly calling for President Barack Obama to take more action on housing foreclosures, and he introduced a measure in 2012 aimed at expediting short sales, which occur when lenders agree to allow a homeowner to sell property for less than what is owed on the mortgage. Energy has remained a prime interest, with a slot on the influential Energy and Commerce Committee. He won a provision regulating carbon emissions as part of a measure to encourage electric vehicle usage. He has shown some responsiveness to the economic peril in Stockton. In September 2014, he filed a bill to aid homeowners who may be facing foreclosure.

His history of tight reelection races has been beneficial, McNerney has said. "I have to be more moderate," he told *The Modesto Bee* in May 2012. "If I alienate Republicans, I can't win. If I alienate Democrats, I can't win." He has kept a low profile on Capitol Hill.

Republicans came after McNerney in 2010. They fielded a credible challenger in David Harmer, son of John Harmer, who was Ronald Reagan's lieutenant governor. The younger Harmer was a high-profile education activist and author, as well as a financial executive at JPMorgan Chase. Harmer promised to shun earmarks, calling them "the gateway drug of federal spending." Democratic interest groups attacked Harmer for a 2000 op-ed column calling for the abolition of public education. The race was so close, ballot-counting continued for days after the election. McNerney eked out a slim lead with 48 percent of the vote, as counties updated their counts, though Harmer refused to concede. Not until December 4 did his opponent throw in the towel.

In 2012, McNerney drew another strong opponent in Ricky Gill, an ambitious 25-year-old Indian American hailed as a rising GOP star. Gill graduated a semester early from law school in order to run for Congress. He raised nearly $3 million, and the National Republican Congressional Committee spent another $2.5 million on his behalf. As a Lodi native, Gill had ties to the area, while redistricting forced McNerney to move. Gill described himself as a "different kind of Republican," holding moderate stances on immigration and education. McNerney called Gill a novice who was propped up by his wealthy parents' business ties, and local newspapers echoed concerns about Gill's lack of real-world experience and endorsed McNerney. He also benefitted from Obama's strong showing in California to win, 56%-44%.

The 2014 election shaped up as an easier contest. Republican challenger Tony Amador was a former police officer and U.S. Marshal who had become a perennial political loser; he spent only $62,000 and had no national party assistance. But McNerney led by only 2,150 votes in San Joaquin, which cast two-thirds of the vote. He got a boost in the vote from Contra Costa, to win the district with 52.4 percent.

The outcome made clear that the economic turbulence in Stockton continues to roil local politics. And McNerney's repeated close contests might encourage more experienced challengers. Kathryn Nance, president of the local police union in Stockton, said she was planning a challenge in 2016.

TENTH DISTRICT

Jeff Denham (R)

Elected 2010, 3rd term; b. July 29, 1967, Hawthorne; CA Poly. St. U. San Luis Obispo, B.A. 1992; Presbyterian; married (Sonia); 2 children.

Military Career: U.S. Air Force, 1984-88; Air Force Reserves, 1988-2000 (Persian Gulf).

Elected Office: CA Senate, 2002-10.

Professional Career: Project mgr., Fresh Express, 1992-98; Almond rancher; Owner, Denham Plastics.

DC Office: 1730 LHOB, 20515, 202-225-4540; Fax: 202-225-3402; Website: denham.house.gov.

State Offices: Modesto, 209-579-5458.

Committees: *Agriculture:* Biotechnology, Horticulture, & Research. General Farm Commodities & Risk Mgmt. *Natural Resources:* Indian, Insular & Alaska Native Affairs; Water, Power & Oceans. *Transportation & Infrastructure:* Railroads, Pipelines & Hazardous Materials (Chmn); Highways & Transit; Water Resources & Environment.

Group Ratings

	ADA	ACLU	AFL-CIO	LCV	ITI	COC	HAFA	ACU	CFG	FRC
2014	5%	16%	–	3%	100%	93%	36%	58%	46%	88%
2013	0%	C	29%	4%	C	77%	C	60%	51%	C

National Journal Ratings

	2013 LIB	—	2013 CONS
Economic	43%	—	57%
Social	43%	—	54%
Foreign	44%	—	54%
Composite	44%	—	56%

Key Votes of the 113th Congress

1. Sandy storm spending	Y	5. Medical Marijuana	N	9. Syrian Rebels Training	Y
2. Violence Against Women Act	Y	6. Farm Bill	Y	10. Keystone pipeline	Y
3. Guantanamo Bay Detainees	N	7. Afghanistan Combat	N	11. Immigration Exec. Action	N
4. Abortion 20-week ban	Y	8. NSA Phone Data Collection	N	12. Bipartisan budget deal	Y

Election Results

2014 general	Jeff Denham (R)	70,582	(56%)	$1,753,321	$77,390	$14,358
	Michael Eggman (D)	55,123	(44%)	$1,291,436	$8,924	
2014 primary	Jeff Denham (R)	44,237	(59%)			
	Michael Eggman (D)	19,804	(26%)			
	Mike Barkley (D)	11,005	(15%)			

Prior winning percentages: 2012 (53%), 2010 (65%)

Population		Race and Ethnicity		Income	
Total:	722,266	White	46.2%	Median income:	$52,992
Urban:	52.9%	Latino	40.0%		(185 of 435)
Suburban:	43.7%	Asian	6.1%	Under $50,000	47.1%
Rural:	3.5%	Black	3.6%	$50,000-$99,999:	30.7%
Land area:	2,075	Two races	2.6%	$100,000-$199,999:	19.1%
Pop/sq. mi.:	348.1	White Ethnic	20.5%	$200,000 or more:	3.1%
Born in state:	66.3%			Poverty Rate	19.1%
		Education			
Age Groups		H.S. grad or less:	49.4%	**Work**	
Under 18:	28.1%	Some college:	34.1%	White collar:	27.0%
18 to 34:	24.2%	College degree, 4 yr.:	11.2%	Blue collar:	43.3%
35 to 64:	36.7%	Post-grad study:	5.3%	Sales and service:	29.7%
Over 64:	11.0%			Govt. workers:	13.5%
		Military			
		Veterans/active duty:	6.0%		

Central Valley: Modesto, Stanislaus

Voter Turnout	
2013 Total Citizen 18+	447,366
2014 House Turnout	125,705
2014 Turnout as % CVAP	28.1%
2012 Turnout as % CVAP	48.8%

The Central Valley of California is a miraculous landscape, an outdoor factory stretching as far as the eye can see. Nature created the vast flatlands, rimmed by mountains rising in the distant haze. In the 20th century, people disciplined the land with a remorseless mile-square grid of roads, the California Aqueduct, and dozens of arrow-straight canals. Pipes fitted with valves and gauges pump water, fertilizer, and pesticides to the fields in measured quantities with industrial precision. The crops grow in carefully spaced rows. The rich soil and the irrigated water were too precious to waste on decorative fountains or flower gardens. Throughout history, farming here has been a business, not a way of life. In the 19th century, the U.S. government did not give the land to 160-acre homesteaders but rather sold it to large enterprises in thousands-of-acres parcels. Among the most famous local capitalists were the Gallo brothers, Ernest and Julio, who started a winery in Modesto in 1933 with virtually no money. It now covers more than 10,000 acres of vineyards and produces about 80 million cases of wine each year.

In recent years, the Central Valley was one of California's surprise boom areas, not just for crops, but also for people. Middle-income workers in the San Francisco Bay Area drive east at the end of the day on Interstate 580, past surreal windmills whirling on the bare hills of Altamont Pass, to modestly priced homes in Modesto, the town immortalized (when it was much smaller) in the 1973 film *American Graffiti*. Warehouses and factories have sprung up on land that for all its farming value is cheaper than industrial land in the Bay Area. With drought and increases in water prices, some croplands have been given over to pasture. But there are costs: Traffic is

2012 Presidential Vote		
Barack Obama (D) 108,923		(51%)
Mitt Romney (R).................101,160		(47%)
2008 Presidential Vote		
Barack Obama (D) 111,656		(50%)
John McCain (R).................105,903		(48%)
Cook Partisan Voting Index: R+1		

a problem, air-pollution levels on bad days can be among the worst in the nation, and the pace of life has become more hectic. The over-pumping of groundwater has caused the Valley to sink a half-inch each month, the *Los Angeles Times* reported. Escalated by the drought, the result has been "cracking irrigation canals, buckling roads and permanently depleting storage space in the vast aquifer that underlies California's heartland." The aquifer extends 400 miles below the Valley. There have also been disputes with neighboring areas over water access. In 2012, negotiations over a water sale collapsed between San Francisco officials and the nonprofit Modesto Irrigation District, because of several internal disputes. In 2009 and 2010, the impact of the national recession on the Central Valley in some ways was more severe than elsewhere in the country, and extended drought reduced agricultural water supplies. For the second consecutive year, area farmers in 2015 were scheduled to receive no water for irrigation. Yet farming in Stanislaus County brought in $3.7 billion in revenue in 2013, with almonds, milk, and walnuts among the region's most profitable crops. Almonds were the leading crop, worth more than $1 billion.

The 10th Congressional District of California includes all of Stanislaus County and part of San Joaquin County, including Tracy, Ripon, and the almond center of Manteca. About three-fourths of the voters are in Stanislaus. It takes in Modesto, Oakdale, and Riverbank. The political tradition here had been Democratic. In the 1960s, Democrats in Washington and Democratic Gov. Pat Brown built the irrigation canals and authorized the water subsidies. This area produced two House Democratic whips, John McFall in the late 1970s and Tony Coelho in the 1980s. But the Central Valley, with the highest proportion of families and children in California, grew to be more culturally conservative than other parts of the state. In recent decades, it has trended Republican, and even the Latinos here are less solidly Democratic than those in Los Angeles. In the 2012 presidential election, Stanislaus County favored President Barack Obama over Mitt Romney by a slim margin, 51%-47%. The district as a whole narrowly leans Republican.

Jeff Denham (R)

Jeff Denham, a Republican elected in 2010, is a vocal fiscal conservative who has found that local economics and politics occasionally move in a separate track from his party, notably on agriculture and immigration. His background as an Air Force veteran and farmer has given him hands-on experience with many issues.

Denham was born near Los Angeles and lived in Indiana for five years, but he spent most of his childhood in the Northern California town of Pescadero. His parents divorced when he was in high school, and Denham spent much of his time at his grandparents' home. At age 17, Denham enlisted in the Air Force. He was a crew chief, preparing and maintaining aircraft such as F-4 fighter jets and C-5 transport planes. After transitioning to the Reserve for more than a dozen years, Denham attended community college and then transferred to Cal Poly, San Luis Obispo, where he was active in the College Republicans and received a bachelor's degree in political science. During the Persian Gulf War, he worked on an air base in Saudi Arabia. He also maintained aircraft in the peacekeeping mission in Somalia in 1992. Back home after his service, Denham became the manager of a packaged salad company, and in 1998, he founded his own business, Denham Plastics, an agricultural container supply firm. In 2004, he bought a ranch in Merced County, where he grows almonds.

Denham first ran for public office in 2000, losing a bid for the California Assembly. Two years later, he ran for the state Senate and eked out a victory in a district where Democrats held a 12-point registration advantage. His roommate for several years in Sacramento was Kevin McCarthy, now the House majority leader. As a state legislator, Denham sponsored a bill that would have required convicted pedophiles to wear electronic tracking devices for their entire lives. In 2007, during one of California's numerous budget crises, Democrats needed Republican support to approve a budget. Because of the makeup of Denham's district, Democratic leaders hoped that he would agree to a compromise that included spending cuts and tax increases. Denham refused, and as a result, Democratic Senate Leader Don Perata organized a recall campaign against him. In June 2008, a resounding 75 percent of district voters chose not to recall Denham.

When Republican Rep. George Radanovich retired in December 2009, he asked Denham to run. Denham did not have a clear path to Congress, however. Former Rep. Richard Pombo, who had been ousted in a neighboring district in 2006, and former Fresno Mayor Jim Patterson also ran in the 2010 primary. They criticized Denham for flying on a corporate jet with Republican strategist Karl Rove, a possible violation of federal election law, and for his ties to an Indian tribe that sponsored ads attacking his opponents. But with strong fundraising and the support of the popular Radanovich, Denham won the primary with 36%, ahead of Patterson, who finished with 31%. Pombo placed third with 21%. In the general election, Denham easily won, 65%-35%.

In the House, Denham got off to a shaky start when he ignored new Republican Speaker John Boehner's admonition to keep GOP inaugural celebrations austere, throwing a $2,500-a-person fundraiser featuring country singer LeAnn Rimes. But in recognition of his state legislative experience, he got the chairmanship of the Subcommittee on Economic Development, Public Buildings and Emergency Management at the Transportation and Infrastructure Committee. In 2012, the House agreed to his plan to create a commission to study whether federal offices were being used efficiently. He fought, unsuccessfully, to block plans to build a new $400 million courthouse in Los Angeles that was a priority for other California lawmakers, and he criticized the Securities and Exchange Commission for leasing 900,000 square feet of space, which he said was unneeded and cost the taxpayers $556 million. After the SEC's inspector general indicated the contract violated federal rules because of a noncompetitive bid, Denham and District of Columbia Del. Eleanor Holmes Norton wrote legislation preventing the agency from leasing property independently. On the defense spending bill in May 2014, he sought to add his "Enlist Act" to provide legal status to undocumented immigrants who serve in the military. Republican leaders blocked a vote on his plan, but the Defense Department four months later moved forward with a scaled-down version of his plan for a limited number of immigrants with language or medical skills. Denham praised the "step forward."

Denham in 2013 became chairman of the Railroads, Pipelines and Hazardous Materials Subcommittee, where he pursued numerous agriculture-related issues. He strongly opposed California's high-speed rail project, which Gov. Jerry Brown has pursued despite political and regional divisions in California. Following the January 2015 groundbreaking ceremony in Fresno, Denham complained, "California voters were promised jobs, ridership numbers, speeds and costs that look nothing like the current proposal. ... It's hard to celebrate breaking ground on what is likely to become abandoned pieces of track that never connect to a usable segment." In March 2015, the House passed his passenger rail bill with provisions to modernize the business operations of Amtrak. Denham included provisions that he said would prevent "another disaster like California high speed rail from wasting taxpayer dollars," including a requirement for state matching funds and deadlines for new projects. The bill won unanimous Democratic support, but only a slight majority of Republicans. With the nation's "unprecedented energy renaissance," he said, the nation's freight rails and pipelines have not kept pace with the increased demand.

In 2012, Denham finished first with 49 percent of the vote in the state's all-party primary, and then faced Democrat Jose Hernandez, a former astronaut, in the general. Hernandez criticized him for using taxpayers' money to stay in hotels near the district. Denham accused Hernandez of carpetbagging, since he had lived in Houston during the years he worked at NASA. The race tightened as Election Day drew nearer, but Denham pulled off a 53%-47% win. He had another competitive race in 2014 against beekeeper Michael Eggman, who spent $1.3 million. Denham spent $1.8 million, and benefited from a favorable Republican year. He won 56%-44%.

ELEVENTH DISTRICT

Mark DeSaulnier (D)

Elected 2014, 1st term; b. Mar. 31, 1952, Lowell, MA; Col. Holy Cross, B.A. 1974; Catholic; single; 2 children.

Elected Office: Concord City Cncl., 1991-94; Concord mayor, 1993; Contra Costa Cnty. Bd. Supervisors, 1994-2006, chair, 1994; CA Assembly 2006-08; CA Senate, 2008-14.

Professional Career: Deputy probation officer; Warehouse worker; Hotel service; Restauranteur; Business owner; Fellow, JFK School of Gov't, Harvard U., 2003.

DC Office: 327 CHOB, 20515, 202-225-2095; Fax: 202-225-5609; Website: desaulnier.house.gov.

State Offices: Richmond, 510-620-1000; Walnut Creek, 925-933-2660.

Committees: *Education & the Workforce:* Higher Education & Workforce Training; Workforce Protections. *Oversight & Gov't Reform:* Healthcare, Benefits & Administrative Rules; Transportation & Public Assets.

Election Results

2014 general	Mark DeSaulnier (D)	117,502	(67%)	$541,228
	Tue Phan-Quang (R)	57,160	(33%)	$113,194
2014 primary	Mark DeSaulnier (D)	59,605	(59%)	
	Tue Phan-Quang (R)	28,142	(28%)	

Population		Race and Ethnicity		Income	
Total:	733,916	White	48.4%	Median income:	$73,860
Urban:	20.0%	Latino	25.3%		*(47 of 435)*
Suburban:	79.9%	Asian	12.5%	Under $50,000	35.4%
Rural:	0.0%	Black	9.0%	$50,000-$99,999:	27.5%
Land area:	419	Two races	3.6%	$100,000-$199,999:	23.8%
Pop/sq. mi.:	1,751.4	White Ethnic	24.2%	$200,000 or more:	13.3%
Born in state:	54.1%			Poverty Rate	11.9%
		Education			
Age Groups		H.S. grad or less:	30.1%	**Work**	
Under 18:	22.7%	Some college:	28.9%	White collar:	41.8%
18 to 34:	21.8%	College degree, 4 yr.:	26.4%	Blue collar:	42.9%
35 to 64:	40.5%	Post-grad study:	14.7%	Sales and service:	15.3%
Over 64:	14.9%				
		Military		Govt. workers:	12.5%
		Veterans/active duty:	5.9%		

Outer East Bay: Concord, Richmond

The journey inward from the Pacific Ocean to the vast flatness of California's Central Valley passes through a wondrous variety of terrain. The traveler starts at the Golden Gate Bridge, with the lush green Presidio on one side and the bluffs of mountains in Marin County on the other. The journey

Voter Turnout	
2013 Total Citizen 18+	481,653
2014 House Turnout	174,662
2014 Turnout as % CVAP	36.3%
2012 Turnout as % CVAP	63.2%

continues through the San Francisco Bay, through the narrow Carquinez Strait to Suisun Bay, with its sloughs and marshes and ships ready for scrap, and finally past the mountains, to the flat, fertile expanse of California's great interior. This is not a journey most tourists make, but it was a familiar route to the first Americans in California, and it passes by much of the industrial base of the Bay Area. On the east side of the bay is Richmond, developed almost instantaneously during World War II when Henry J. Kaiser built a shipyard in its deep-water port and 91,000 people from all over the country were put to work building ships for the Pacific theater. What became known as Rosie the Riveter Memorial Park is now a national park.

The recession landed a severe blow here—median household earnings plummeted by more than $3,000 over the two years it lasted. The state Employment Development Department issued a report in March 2015 that the East Bay experienced in 2014 a robust jobs recovery. In recent years, Richmond citizens have begun harboring doubts about safety at a Chevron refinery plant, the

2012 Presidential Vote		
Barack Obama (D) 203,699	(68%)
Mitt Romney (R)...................90,226	(30%)
2008 Presidential Vote		
Barack Obama (D) 216,720	(69%)
John McCain (R)...................89,616	(29%)
Cook Partisan Voting Index: D+17		

scene of frequent fires and explosions. After an August 2012 fire at the plant, some residents blasted Chevron for causing high asthma rates and pollution, while business leaders defended the company as a jobs creator. The federal Chemical Safety Board issued a report in February 2015 that Chevron was responsible for the disaster because it failed to respond when experts warned of defects at the plant. In the 2014 election, Chevron fueled a backlash when it endorsed four candidates for the Richmond city council, and spent more than $3 million on their behalf. Independent Sen. Bernie Sanders of Vermont campaigned locally against the Chevron candidates. All of them lost. A local political science professor said the result showed that "ordinary people can defeat huge corporate power."

The 11th District of California includes most of Contra Costa County, including all of Richmond and Concord, which is the largest city in the county. Interstate 680 running north-south provides a spine for businesses and shopping centers up and down the San Ramon Valley, from burgeoning Concord to Walnut Creek. The district also takes in the "Lamorinda" area of Lafayette, Moraga, and Orinda. Officials in Concord lobbied the Pentagon to close the mostly unused Concord Naval Weapons Station so they could use the land for business and residential development. After California State University in 2014 dropped plans to build a new campus at the site, local officials began a search of additional options. The city is constrained physically by urban-growth limits that county voters imposed in 1990. It is solidly Democratic, but less culturally liberal than San Francisco.

Mark DeSaulnier (D)

In a solidly blue district, state lawmaker Mark DeSaulnier coasted to victory in 2014 after winning a six-candidate scrum in the June primary. It was DeSaulnier's second bid for the House, coming five years after he lost a special election in a neighboring district. He was strongly supported by his predecessor, Rep. George Miller, who retired after 40 years in the House, where he chaired the Education and the Workforce Committee.

DeSaulnier is a veteran of California politics with blue-collar bona fides. He had been a trucker, probation officer, and hotel worker before entering the restaurant business, eventually owning several Bay Area dining locales. A keen interest in local politics inspired him to run for Concord City Council in 1991, and he became mayor in 1993. In those early years, he was a Republican. Governor Pete Wilson appointed him to the influential state Air Resources Board in 1997. But, as he saw the GOP move to the right, he switched parties and became a Democrat. He was elected to the state Assembly in 2006 and the state Senate in 2008.

In January 2014, when Miller, a liberal leader and close ally of Minority Leader Nancy Pelosi, announced his retirement, DeSaulnier got his opening. He had lost an open-seat contest five years earlier to a better-known candidate, John Garamendi. This time, DeSaulnier made sure he was well positioned. Armed with the biggest war chest and a slew of endorsements (including the *San Francisco Chronicle*), DeSaulnier quickly became the front-runner. He used his day job in the state Senate, where he chaired the transportation committee, to advance liberal priorities. In May, he proposed a bill that would adjust the state corporate tax rate according to the wage disparity in each firm—a measure that resonated with Democrats but fell short of the required two-thirds majority to pass. He proposed another bill to set up a pilot project to reform the state's gasoline tax so that motorists pay based on mileage rather than by the gallon. That measure passed.

DeSaulnier has not always marched with his own party. He opposed proposals to revive California's troubled high-speed rail project, and he pledged to work with business groups to amend his corporate tax bill so it had a better chance of passage. By the June primary, however, DeSaulnier's dominance in the field trumped any concerns that liberals may have had. He collected 59 percent of the vote, well ahead of 28 percent for Republican Tue Phan-Quang. In the general election, he took 67 percent of the vote.

In the House, he won seats on the Education and Oversight and Government Reform committees. The first bill he introduced would expand the John Muir National Historic Site with private land in Martinez. Muir, a conservationist, was the father of the national parks. An earlier version of that bill passed the House in December 2014. After his long struggle to get to Congress, he likely will hold this seat as long as he wants it. His roommate in Washington is Democratic Rep. Jared Huffman, who represents the Marin County district across the Bay from DeSaulnier's district.

TWELFTH DISTRICT

Nancy Pelosi (D)

Elected June 1987, 14th full term; b. March 26, 1940, Baltimore, MD; Trinity Col., B.A. 1962; Catholic; married (Paul); 5 children.

Professional Career: CA Dem. Party, Northern chmn., 1977-81, St. chmn., 1981-83; DSCC finance chmn., 1985-86; PR exec., Ogilvy & Mather, 1986-87.

DC Office: 233 CHOB, 20515, 202-225-4965; Website: pelosi.house.gov.

State Offices: San Francisco, 415-556-4862.

Committees: House Minority Leader.

Group Ratings

	ADA	ACLU	AFL-CIO	LCV	ITI	COC	HAFA	ACU	CFG	FRC
2014	80%	88%	–	91%	60%	38%	11%	4%	4%	0%
2013	85%	C	90%	89%	C	31%	C	8%	12%	C

National Journal Ratings

	2013 LIB	—	2013 CONS
Economic	85%	—	15%
Social	77%	—	21%
Foreign	88%	—	12%
Composite	84%	—	16%

Key Votes of the 113th Congress

1. Sandy storm spending	Y	5. Medical Marijuana	Y	9. Syrian Rebels Training	Y
2. Violence Against Women Act	Y	6. Farm Bill	N	10. Keystone pipeline	N
3. Guantanamo Bay Detainees	Y	7. Afghanistan Combat	Y	11. Immigration Exec. Action	N
4. Abortion 20-week ban	N	8. NSA Phone Data Collection	N	12. Bipartisan budget deal	Y

Election Results

2014 general	Nancy Pelosi (D)	160,067	(83%)	$2,395,066
	John Dennis (R)	32,197	(17%)	$600,046
2014 primary	Nancy Pelosi (D)	79,816	(74%)	
	John Dennis (R)	12,922	(12%)	
	Barry Hermanson (Grn)	6,156	(6%)	

Prior winning percentages: 2012 (85%), 2010 (80%), 2008 (72%), 2006 (80%), 2004 (83%), 2002 (80%), 2000 (85%), 1998 (86%), 1996 (84%), 1994 (82%), 1992 (82%), 1990 (77%), 1988 (76%), 1987 special (63%)

Population		Race and Ethnicity		Income	
Total:	734,662	White	44.4%	Median income:	$77,577
Urban:	100.0%	Asian	30.7%		*(37 of 435)*
Suburban:	0.0%	Latino	15.0%	Under $50,000	36.2%
Rural:	0.0%	Black	5.6%	$50,000-$99,999:	22.7%
Land area:	41	Two races	3.2%	$100,000-$199,999:	24.5%
Pop/sq. mi.:	17,956.1	White Ethnic	23.6%	$200,000 or more:	16.6%
Born in state:	38.4%			Poverty Rate	13.9%
		Education			
Age Groups:		H.S. grad or less:	25.1%	**Work**	
Under 18:	13.3%	Some college:	20.8%	White collar:	54.0%
18 to 34:	30.7%	College degree, 4 yr.:	31.9%	Blue collar:	36.8%
35 to 64:	42.0%	Post-grad study:	22.2%	Sales and service:	9.2%
Over 64:	14.0%				
		Military		Govt. workers:	11.9%
		Veterans/active duty:	3.4%		

San Francisco

On Feb. 20, 1915, a crowd of 150,000 gathered on the grounds of the Panama-Pacific International Exposition to see the Spanish-Italian baroque-style structure built on reclaimed land in what was to become San Francisco's Marina district. The Expo-

Voter Turnout	
2013 Total Citizen 18+	543,133
2014 House Turnout	192,264
2014 Turnout as % CVAP	35.4%
2012 Turnout as % CVAP	61%

sition ostensibly celebrated the completion of the Panama Canal, but it was clearly intended to show off San Francisco's recovery from the 1906 earthquake. It also spotlighted the city as the central focus of America's efforts to open an economic door to the eastern part of the world, especially in light of the acquisition of Hawaii and the Philippines and of its interest in an open-door policy with China and trade with Japan. The Exposition established the physical style of San Francisco, encouraging the use of Mediterranean color, accent, and detail that characterizes many of the post-Victorian houses and commercial structures in The City, as the *San Francisco Examiner* called it for years. It set the tone for the picturesque Marina district, whose old buildings were among those damaged in the 1989 earthquake, and for Fisherman's Wharf and Ghirardelli Square. On a sunny day, San Francisco can look almost tropical, with brown mountains baking in the sun and light shining off the pastel stucco buildings. When the clouds scud in from the Pacific, it can look sinister, full of dark corners where a private detective's partner might be ambushed by a pretty woman. The buildings can be majestic, like the monumental Beaux-Arts City Hall, or tawdry, like the hotels of the Tenderloin district.

San Francisco grew from nothing to a major city in the single year of 1850, an instant product of the California Gold Rush. Within just a few years, culture was flourishing in the city, and San Francisco developed a parochial pride in the great writers who worked there—Jack London, Ambrose Bierce, Frank Norris—and in giving birth to the Arts and Crafts movement. Later, San Francisco newspaper scribe Herb Caen coined the term "beatnik" to describe the youthful penchant for freedom in the 1950s and wrote definitively about the hippies who thronged Haight-Ashbury in 1967. In the 1970s, the city was among the first to embrace the gay rights movement, in The Castro district. Gays lately have been moving to the suburbs and straights have been moving into the city. Perhaps surprisingly, a 2014 Gallup survey found that the overall metro area had the largest LGBT share of the population in the nation, at 6.2%, but the city itself was only 3.6%. Over the years, the city's booming economy—based initially on food processing, but now on finance, high-tech, and clothing (Levi Strauss, the Gap)—attracted talented newcomers, though its population is increasingly polarized between high-income and low-income. The dot-com crash in 2000 took

2012 Presidential Vote		
Barack Obama (D)	269,461	(84%)
Mitt Romney (R)	40,003	(13%)

2008 Presidential Vote		
Barack Obama (D)	288,455	(85%)
John McCain (R)	43,969	(13%)

Cook Partisan Voting Index: D+34

a brutal toll, but the city rallied in mid-decade, as new high-rise office buildings and condominiums sprang up on the waterfront and south of Market.

The housing bust in 2008 did not hit as hard here as in California's Central Valley subdivisions, where many modest-income Bay Area residents had been fleeing. The income inequality ratio in San Francisco is especially high chiefly because the wealthy are really wealthy, according to a February 2014 study by the Brookings Institution. Thanks to the flood of high-tech workers pouring into the city, many of whom commute daily to Silicon Valley on luxurious corporate buses ("Google buses"), the city's housing costs are so high that low-income persons have become virtually precluded from living in most parts of the city. This hyper-gentrification has led to economic stratification and has produced growing protests of activists and low-income groups that target the tech industry and developers. San Francisco has the lowest percentage of children, 16 percent, of any major city. Although it is proudly tolerant, San Francisco is one of California's whitest cities, with only about half as many black residents as it had in 1970. The population on the west side is nearly half Asian, but Asian communities are increasingly migrating to other parts of the Bay Area.

Politically, San Francisco was a progressive Republican town, like the two men who led the way into the Exposition: Mayor "Sunny Jim" Rolph and California Gov. Hiram Johnson. The sour-tempered Johnson made his name as a reformer, throwing out crooked city politicians. His administration gave California primary and recall elections, referenda, and strong civil-service laws. Rolph, mayor from 1911 to 1930 and then governor, built the civic center, parks, schools, streetcars, and the Hetch Hetchy aqueduct—the antique infrastructure of San Francisco today. Sympathetic to the conservation movement, willing to deal with organized labor in a union town that had America's only general strike in 1934, and tolerant of California's diversity, these progressive Republicans were the recognizable ancestors of the generally liberal San Franciscans of today.

More recently, the city has elected strong liberal politicians, notably Mayor George Moscone and the first openly gay supervisor, Harvey Milk. Both were shot to death in 1978 by Dan White, a former city supervisor, who was found guilty of the lesser crime of voluntary manslaughter. Over the next decade, the city's cultural liberalism was tempered by Democratic Mayor Dianne Feinstein, who vetoed a domestic partnership ordinance and opposed commercial rent control. In 1995, Willie Brown, ousted after 15 years as speaker of the state Assembly, returned home and was elected mayor. Brown's political flair was always in evidence, but high taxes and an increasing homeless population drove out middle-class families and immigrants.

As his successor, San Francisco installed Gavin Newsom, who in 2004 started issuing marriage licenses to same-sex couples, although California voters had outlawed same-sex marriage. The state Supreme Court ordered him to stop and voided the marriages. In 2008, Newsom was vindicated when the same court declared the ban on same-sex marriage unconstitutional. But his victory statement—"this door's wide open, it's going to happen, whether you like it or not"—was featured in ads for proponents of Proposition 8, which by a 52%-48% vote reversed the court's decision. The Supreme Court nullified that referendum in its seminal ruling in June 2013, when it ruled that supporters of the ballot measure had no standing to defend the referendum in court; earlier, a federal judge had ruled that Proposition 8 violated the Constitution. In November 2010, Newsom was elected California's lieutenant governor. The Board of Supervisors appointed City Administrator Ed Lee as interim mayor. Lee, the first Asian-American to serve in that office, won a four-year term in November 2011.

The 12th Congressional District of California takes in most of the city and county of San Francisco, except that the southwest corner is in the 14th District. It includes all of San Francisco's high-rise downtown area, the crowded and bustling Chinatown, Telegraph Hill, Nob Hill and Russian Hill, North Beach, Pacific Heights, and the Marina District (which does not have a very big marina). In the valleys are the Fillmore and Western Addition areas. The 12th also has Noe Valley; the Castro, still mainly gay; Haight-Ashbury, once the bedraggled center of hippie culture and now another gentrifying San Francisco neighborhood; and Potrero Hill, with its restored houses overlooking downtown. The district is 6% African American, 15% Hispanic, and 31% Asian, and it is overwhelmingly Democratic. James Fang, the city's only elected Republican office-holder, was defeated in 2014 after serving as a Bay Area Rapid Transit director for 24 years.

Nancy Pelosi (D)

Nancy Pelosi, speaker of the House from 2007 to 2011 and minority leader since Democrats lost control of the chamber, is one of the most polarizing figures in politics, with a positive and negative star quality reminiscent of the late Sen. Edward Kennedy of Massachusetts.

Detested by Republicans for her proudly liberal views and assertive style, she is beloved in her party for her legislative accomplishments as well as her fundraising and politicking, which continued unabated in her mid-70s. Pelosi was the first woman to achieve the speakership, and those four years were among the most productive for the House in the past century. Since then, she and her depleted Caucus have struggled.

Elected to Congress in June 1987, she has the energy and shrewdness of one who has handled the most delicate of political chores, and the charm and unflappability of one who is the mother of five and grandmother of nine. As minority leader, Pelosi's public image has receded since 2010, when Republicans ran thousands of ads vilifying her in their successful campaign to gain control of the House.

Democrats' dismal showings in the 2010 and 2014 midterm elections fueled speculation and some internal demands that it was time for her to step aside. But she has proven far too skilled at hauling in campaign funds; she collected more than $101 million, a personal record, during the 2014 cycle. Of that amount, more than $65 million went to the Democratic Congressional Campaign Committee, making up more than one-third of the DCCC's total. "I'm the one that brung everyone to the party by winning the House in the first place," she told *The Washington Post.* "I could have walked away, but we built something and then we want to take it to the next step"—winning back control of the House. For now, that goal seems unattainable, at least until redistricting for the 2022 election when she will be 82.

Pelosi did bow to the demands for new, younger faces in leadership by appointing fourth-term Rep. Ben Ray Luján of New Mexico, a Latino, to head the DCCC. And she installed Donna Edwards of Maryland, an African-American, as co-chair of the powerful Steering and Policy Committee along with longtime ally Rosa DeLauro of Connecticut. But her diminished influence was reflected in her inability to get her close friend and fellow Californian Anna Eshoo the ranking member post on the Energy and Commerce Committee. New Jersey's Frank Pallone, working with Minority Whip Steny Hoyer and other allies, beat out Eshoo for the job on a secret ballot. News reports have revealed growing unhappiness among younger rank-and-file members with what they saw as the entrenchment of longtime, and aging, figures in leadership and top committee slots. Most of them are Pelosi allies.

Hoyer also was part of a group that outmaneuvered Pelosi and other liberals in enacting a massive so-called "cromnibus" spending package in late 2014. Liberals had complained about language in the legislation that, among other things, loosened restrictions on Wall Street banks. But Hoyer helped to persuade 57 House Democrats to join Republicans in backing the measure, which President Barack Obama signed. In 2015, four House Democrats voted for an alternative to Pelosi. But, in March 2015, she worked with Speaker John Boehner in an impressive joint show of strength to win overwhelming House passage of a "doc fix" bill that solved long-standing problems with Medicare and health care laws.

Pelosi had another showdown with Obama in June 2015 when she joined with rank-and-file Democrats who mostly opposed the expedited congressional procedures on the prospective Trans-Pacific Partnership agreement that the President and his aides were negotiating with Asian allies and had become a centerpiece of his second-term agenda. Backers of the deal, including Speaker John Boehner, had worked to get support from Pelosi and other Democrats, at least on the "trade adjustment" worker assistance, which was an auxiliary part of the trade deal and had long been a signature part of the Democratic agenda. In effect, Pelosi abandoned the lame-duck President for the Democrats' steadfast allies in organized labor, even though Obama made a last-minute personal plea for support at a closed-door meeting of the Democratic Caucus. The resulting disarray among Democrats was a stark reminder of the limitations that Pelosi has faced in dealing with both Obama and congressional Republicans since she lost her gavel in 2010.

Earlier, Pelosi began the 112th Congress in January 2011 with 19 Democrats voting against her—the most defections that any party leader had suffered since 1913. Most of those votes were cast by the diminishing corps of moderate "Blue Dog" Democrats. As Republicans voted repeatedly to repeal the health care law that had been her signature achievement, she stood steadfastly against their criticisms.

Despite her furious fundraising, Pelosi and her lieutenants were unsuccessful in crafting a path to the majority that would circumvent the twin Democratic demons of redistricting and demographic shifts in many large metropolitan areas. In many parts of the nation, from Pennsylvania and Ohio to Florida and Texas, where Democrats once dominated the House delegations, her cultural liberalism and the relentless attacks of Republicans kept her from making credible appearances in public events on behalf of Democratic candidates or House members with whom she worked regularly at the Capitol. An early sign of that erosion of support came when her close ally, Rep. John Murtha of Pennsylvania, died in early 2010, and Pelosi's role was limited chiefly to fundraising assistance. In the southwest corner of Pennsylvania, the four House Democrats in 2002 shrunk to one a decade later. This pattern was repeated across the nation. Talk has occasionally circulated about whether she would continue as Democratic leader, and her daughter, Alexandra, in 2011 told a blogger that her mother was "done" with Washington and "wants to have a life," if her donors "didn't want her to stay so badly." Then, Pelosi announced she would indeed seek another term as party leader.

Pelosi grew up on Albemarle Street in Baltimore's Little Italy, just east of downtown. Her father, Thomas D'Alesandro Jr., served in the House from 1939 to 1947 and was mayor of Baltimore for 12 years after that. Her mother, Annunciata D'Alesandro, was an indefatigable political organizer, and her brother, Thomas, was mayor from 1967 to 1971. Pelosi says of her parents, "What I got from them was about economic fairness. That was the difference between Democrats and Republicans all those years ago." She graduated from Trinity University in Washington, D.C., where she met her husband Paul. After marrying, they moved to his hometown of San Francisco. There he became a successful real estate investor, and she raised their children and got into local Democratic politics.

In the 1970s, Pelosi struck rough-hewn Rep. John Burton of California as just another stylish hostess in a city that had many of them. But she soon got Burton's attention and that of his older brother, Rep. Phillip Burton, the de facto liberal leader of the House, who lost his race for majority leader to Texas Democrat Jim Wright by one vote in 1976. That year, Pelosi returned east to run the Maryland campaign of presidential candidate Jerry Brown, then and now once again governor of California. She was able to relate both to "Governor Moonbeam," as Brown was dubbed, and to the practical-minded politicians she had met through her parents. In 1977, she became chairman of the Northern California Democratic Party, and four years later, she became chairman of the California Democratic Party. The positions required a considerable amount of diplomacy, including dealing with fractious regional antagonisms. But Pelosi managed to remain on good terms with various warring Democrats and help the party hold majorities in the legislature.

Then in 1982, John Burton declined to run for reelection in a new Marin- and San Francisco-based district. Some Democrats sounded out Pelosi, whose Presidio Heights home was in the district, but she declined to run, and the seat went instead to Marin-based Democrat Barbara Boxer. Instead, Pelosi worked with Mayor Dianne Feinstein to land the 1984 Democratic National Convention for San Francisco. In 1985, she ran for Democratic National Chairman but lost to Paul Kirk. Before long, though, she had another opportunity. Phil Burton's widow, Sala Burton, was elected to succeed her husband after his death in 1983, but her health failed too. In 1987, as she was dying of cancer, she told her friends whom she wanted to succeed her: Nancy Pelosi.

Only two years before, Pelosi had told the press, "I won't be running for office." Her children were not yet grown, her husband's business interests kept him mostly in California, and their net worth was not yet such that she could afford to self-finance a campaign. (The couple eventually became extremely wealthy, with a home in San Francisco, a vineyard in the Napa Valley, a townhome in the Sierras, and a condominium in Washington.) Their diversified investments have placed Pelosi among the top five House members in their wealth, though she generally does not flaunt it in public. For her 75th birthday, she told reporters that she wanted a pool table. But she ran, moving her residence from Presidio Heights to a Pacific Heights rental apartment. Her chief opponent in the Democratic primary was San Francisco Supervisor Harry Britt, who had succeeded Harvey Milk after he was assassinated. San Francisco's gay community at that time was not as mainstream as it is now, but Britt, who was gay, had a good record in office, and Pelosi had to work hard to beat him, 35%-31%.

In her early days in Congress, Pelosi focused on important issues of local sensitivity. One was the Presidio. Burton had enacted a provision that transferred the Presidio from the military to the Interior Department. The problem was that it was so expensive to maintain, it threatened to exceed the National Park Service's budget. Through several Congresses, Pelosi worked to get bipartisan support for a funding source, and in 1997 created the Presidio Trust.

Another sensitive issue was human rights, especially in China. After the Tiananmen Square massacre in 1989, Pelosi sponsored an amendment to give Chinese students the right to remain in the United States, but President George H. W. Bush vetoed it. In 1991, she became the lead sponsor of the bill to make China's most-favored-nation status conditional on human rights reforms. The House overrode Bush's veto, but it was upheld in the Senate. After that, Pelosi led the annual fight against normalizing trade relations with China. She did all this at some political risk. Pelosi's position was by no means universally popular with Asian Americans in her district; many thought the United States should trade and negotiate quietly with China. One of her chief adversaries was her San Francisco neighbor, Feinstein; for many years, they lived in houses just a few blocks apart in Presidio Heights. Pelosi courted support from people on the opposite end of the ideological spectrum, especially religious conservatives in the Republican caucus who also wanted to remain vigilant on China's human rights record.

Pelosi rose to the position of senior Democrat on the Intelligence Committee. Following the September 11 attacks, she joined in the committee's conclusion that, while the intelligence community did not have specific evidence in advance, it did have information that was relevant to the attacks.

Her move into the leadership was persistent, shrewd, and well-organized. In 1997, as a member of the Ethics Committee, she doggedly pursued ethics charges against Republican Speaker Newt Gingrich and worked with Minority Whip David Bonior in using scorched-earth tactics against him. In 1999, she launched a campaign for majority whip, anticipating that Democrats would win a majority in 2000, which they nearly did. Her opponent was Hoyer. They were old acquaintances, having served as interns for Sen. Daniel Brewster of Maryland in the 1960s, but not confreres: there were considerable stylistic and ideological differences. Many of the Democratic women in the House felt there should be a woman in the leadership.

But in 2000, Republicans held on to their majority, and the race for majority whip was moot. Not for long, though. Michigan's Republican legislature, in drawing new congressional districts, put Bonior in a district that he could not win, and he decided to run for governor. He resigned as minority whip, and Pelosi was off and running against Hoyer. Some supporters played up her potential to become a celebrity—"a glamorous grandmother who knocks people off their feet," as then-Rep. Neil Abercrombie of Hawaii put it. With nearly unanimous support from the 32 California Democrats and from most women members, Pelosi started off with a strong base. Her support also crossed ideological lines. She was nominated by John Murtha, a mostly hawkish and culturally conservative Vietnam veteran from the coal country of western Pennsylvania, with a following among old-line Democrats. In October 2001, Pelosi won by a convincing 118-95.

As whip, Pelosi moved quickly to assert herself, sometimes independently from then-Minority Leader Dick Gephardt of Missouri. Her biggest conflict came in the fall of 2002, when she actively encouraged opponents of the resolution authorizing the use of force in Iraq, which Gephardt had enthusiastically endorsed. Pelosi contended that supporters had not made the case for using force and that she had seen no evidence that Iraq "poses an imminent threat to our nation." To the surprise of many, her efforts helped win 126 Democratic votes against the resolution, while only 81 backed Gephardt's position. In retrospect, the split signaled a transition in the caucus. Once the disappointing 2002 election results were in and Gephardt said that he was stepping down, Pelosi had all but locked up the support of a majority of the caucus. Rep. Martin Frost of Texas announced his candidacy with warnings that the selection of Pelosi might create a "permanent minority party." He withdrew from the contest a day later, conceding that he could not win, though he claimed substantial private support. Harold Ford of Tennessee made a belated, quixotic bid designed to appeal to a combination of blacks and New Democrats, but Pelosi won 177-29.

As the Democratic leader in the House, she brought a burst of energy—and favorable press coverage—to a party that badly needed both. She showed hands-on management in selecting members for committee vacancies and in developing a Democratic message criticizing the agenda of President George W. Bush. There were bruised feelings over some committee assignments, but even allies of Hoyer and Frost credited her with bringing a breath of fresh air and enthusiasm to party deliberations. As Republicans pressed their agenda, Pelosi declared that Democrats would take "a party position" in opposition to the Republican Medicare prescription-drug bill. But 16 Democrats voted for the final deal in November 2003, providing the critical margin for passage. She was largely silent about the renegades, many of whom were responding to local pressures favoring the bill.

Pelosi traveled the country in 2004 raising money and boosting local candidates. If she became speaker, Pelosi pledged, she would reform the House to give a greater voice to all members and to assure fairness. She cited Democratic gains of open seats in Kentucky and South Dakota in special elections in early 2004 as proof that the political tide was turning their way. But the three-seat loss in the November election that year turned out to be yet another disappointment for House Democrats, although Pelosi noted correctly that they won a net gain apart from the effects of the 2003 Texas redistricting. Bush's declining job approval ratings and the rising prospects of Democrats in the 2006 election helped Pelosi maintain party discipline.

Hoyer declared in the summer of 2006 that he had no intention of challenging Pelosi if once again Democrats failed to win a majority that fall. Just days later, Murtha announced he would run for majority leader if Democrats won, presumably against Hoyer. For months, House Democrats worked to come up with a platform for 2006 and after many postponements, emerged with a "Six for '06" program, including an increase in the minimum wage and approval of the remaining recommendations of the 9/11 Commission. Pelosi campaigned tirelessly across the country and was rewarded when Democrats gained 31 seats, enough for a Democratic majority, on Election Day.

As she assumed the office that put her second in line for the presidency, Pelosi said, "This is an historic moment, for Congress, and for the women of this country. It is a moment for which we have waited more than 200 years. For our daughters and granddaughters, today we have broken the marble ceiling. To our daughters and granddaughters, the sky is the limit." Much of her leadership team was already in place. Although she had vigorously supported Murtha for majority leader, Hoyer had the support of most of the conservative Blue Dog Democrats, most freshmen, and senior incoming committee chairmen. Hoyer won the No. 2 spot, 149-86. The third-ranking spot, majority whip, went to the well-liked James Clyburn of South Carolina, an African American who brought racial diversity to the new lineup. Influential Illinois Rep. Rahm Emanuel had wanted to be whip, but Pelosi persuaded him to take the fourth-ranking job, that of caucus chairman, with new responsibilities.

Beneath the velvet glove, Pelosi continued to operate with an iron fist. One of her key issues was reducing carbon dioxide emissions to curb global warming. So she announced the creation of a Select Committee on Energy Independence and Global Warming, to be headed by Energy and Commerce member Edward Markey of Massachusetts. Energy and Commerce Chairman John Dingell of Michigan protested that he was being sidelined, but Pelosi had her way.

She had some early and impressive legislative successes, but also some disappointments, especially when Democratic leaders in the closely divided Senate failed to rally the 60 votes needed to pass bills sent from the House. Her greatest frustration was being unable to end military involvement in Iraq. Pelosi conceded that she had underestimated the Republicans' willingness to stick with the president on the war, a position at odds with statements she said they had made to her privately and also at odds with the public mood in some Republican districts.

On domestic policy, Pelosi and her Democratic leadership ran a tight ship and were largely successful, at least in the House. The Democrats' bill to expand the State Children's Health Insurance Program was passed by both chambers, but Bush vetoed it. In 2008, she prevailed when she ignored the law giving the president broad authority over trade and refused to bring the Colombia Free Trade Agreement to the floor. When gasoline hit $4 a gallon and public opinion began to favor more offshore oil drilling, Pelosi refused to allow a roll call vote. "I'm trying to save the planet," she said. But Democrats too were coming under pressure to act on gas prices, and Pelosi agreed to allow a vote on a bill that gave the individual states a role in offshore drilling decisions.

Then, crisis struck, as the financial industry teetered on the verge of collapse, with the potential to send the United States into a second Great Depression. Treasury Secretary Henry Paulson and Federal Reserve Chairman Ben Bernanke confronted the House in September 2008 with a request for $700 billion to bail out big, failing financial firms. Pelosi, with Financial Services Committee Chairman Barney Frank of Massachusetts, decided to grant the request. But a few days later, it became clear that many Democrats were unwilling to vote for it. Pelosi announced she would bring Democrats along if 100 Republicans supported it as well. When the bill came to a vote on September 29, it was defeated, and Republicans blamed Pelosi for speaking harshly about Bush administration economic policies. The Senate changed some of the terms of the bill, and it passed on Oct. 1. The House took up the Senate version and, with some vote switches prompted by Pelosi, passed it two days later.

In the November 2008 election, Democrats gained 21 House seats, and Pelosi entered the 111th Congress in 2009 as the leader of 257 Democrats—the biggest majority a speaker had enjoyed since Democrat Thomas Foley of Washington in 1993-94. Pelosi made it plain to the new Obama administration that she expected it to work through her and not make side deals with Democratic factions, much less Republicans. As labor unions pressed for a card-check bill effectively abolishing the secret ballot in unionization elections, Pelosi let it be known that the Senate would have to act before she would ask Democrats in the House to cast what for some would be a politically dangerous vote. Pelosi went on to preside over a record of legislative accomplishments that many consider the most impressive since the Great Society Congress of 1965-66.

The first order of business was Obama's massive economic stimulus bill. Pelosi largely delegated the specifics to Appropriations Chairman David Obey of Wisconsin. The $819 billion measure was passed without a single Republican vote. The size of the stimulus was reduced in the Senate, and Pelosi negotiated hard to get the price tag to $787 billion. That amount was enacted in mid-February, less than a month after Obama's inauguration.

On Iraq, Pelosi said she was unhappy with Obama's decision to leave 50,000 troops there and also with the Justice Department's decision not to prosecute Bush administration officials for approving enhanced interrogation techniques. She was embarrassed in May 2009 when the Central Intelligence Agency released documents indicating that she had been present at a September 2002 briefing where water boarding was discussed. In a tense press conference, she said, "In that or any other briefing, we were not and, I repeat, were not told that water boarding or any of these other enhanced interrogation techniques were used"— only that they were legal. Republicans' call for an inquiry was rejected on partisan lines. Despite her hostility on Iraq, Pelosi worked with the administration to convince antiwar Democrats to help pass the $105.9 billion supplemental defense bill for the war.

As in the previous Congress, Pelosi pushed hard for legislation restricting carbon emissions, her signature issue. She quietly supported California Rep. Henry Waxman's successful campaign to replace Dingell as chairman of the Energy and Commerce, with prime jurisdiction over the issue. And she worked closely with Waxman and Markey of Massachusetts on the contents of the bill, including Waxman's concessions to win over conservative Democrats. She even met with 11 Republican moderates to get their support. In late June, the bill passed, 219-212, with eight Republicans voting yes. But the Senate did not act.

The other major initiative for Pelosi was Obama's health care overhaul. But finding agreement on complex and far-reaching changes to the medical insurance system, including a controversial proposal to let people opt into a federally sponsored plan, delayed the bill in committee for many weeks. As Pelosi had feared, opposition to the bill gained momentum at town hall meetings across the country during the August recess, including many in Democratic districts. Lawmakers were more skittish about the legislation when they returned. Pelosi agreed to changes in the controversial public option but refused to give in to pressure from conservative Democrats to drop it from the bill. And, in the 11th hour and to the dismay of feminists, she agreed to accept Michigan Rep. Bart Stupak's amendment barring coverage for abortions. A 1,990-page draft was unveiled on October 29 and the bill was passed 220-215 on November 7, with 39 Democrats voting no.

The public option proved to be an even tougher sell in the Senate, which ultimately voted on Christmas Eve for a health care overhaul minus the government insurance provision. Normally, a House and Senate conference committee would have begun immediately to hammer out a final version settling differences between the chambers. But on January 19, 2010, Republican Scott Brown won the special Senate election in Massachusetts for the seat vacated by the death of Kennedy. In his campaign, Brown had promised to be the 41st vote against the health care bill, denying Democrats the 60 votes they needed to stop a filibuster. The obstacles were great. But Pelosi characteristically braced for the fight. "We're in the majority," she told Obama. "We'll never have a better majority in your presidency in numbers than we've got right now. We can make this work."

Public opinion polls in early 2010 showed the public to be increasingly wary of the changes to the health care system. Pelosi agreed to drop a House-passed surtax on high-income earners, which was replaced by an excise tax on high-end insurance plans. She also got Stupak and other anti-abortion rights lawmakers to agree to changes to their provision that they had previously deemed unacceptable. On the day of the vote, March 21, Pelosi marched with fellow Democrats from their offices to the Capitol, while an angry crowd, held back by Capitol police, chanted "Kill the bill." Pelosi's attitude toward the anti-Obama health care forces was clear in a statement in January of that year: "We will go through the gate. If the gate is closed, we will go over the fence. If the fence is too high, we will pole vault in. If that doesn't work, we will parachute in. But we are going to get health care reform passed for the American people." The final roll call was 219-212, without a single Republican vote. The Senate acquiesced to the House changes and Obama signed the bill.

Its passage was the defining moment of Pelosi's speakership and showcased her skills at putting together complex legislation and rounding up reluctant votes, amid volatile public opinion. Polls around the country showed a disturbing number of incumbent Democrats trailing their Republican challengers. In September, she hoped to send Democrats home to campaign on a high note by having them vote to extend the Bush-era income tax cuts except for upper income-earners of $200,000 or more. But when it became clear the votes weren't there—a counter proposal to extend the cuts for everyone regardless of income was attracting Republicans and some Democrats—she moved to adjourn a week earlier than scheduled. It was acknowledgement that her ability to control a majority, after four years of doing so time and again, was now in the hands of a restless electorate in November.

That fall, Pelosi campaigned for Democrats across the country, but she was more a liability than an asset in conservative-leaning districts where Democratic incumbents were bombarded with GOP-orchestrated ads labeling them as "Pelosi-Reid Democrats." Even as Pelosi was expressing optimism publicly, the political tide was turning dramatically against Democrats who had voted for the health care bill and other elements of the Obama agenda. Democrats lost 63 seats, the most the party had lost since the 1938 election, and Republicans took majority control in January.

It was widely expected that Pelosi would relinquish her hold onto her leadership position. The last speakers to become minority leaders after their parties lost the majorities were Democrat Sam Rayburn and Republican Joseph Martin more than a half-century earlier. But after two days of prayer and conversations, Pelosi announced she wanted to run for minority leader again. She could not stop North Carolina's conservative Heath Shuler from launching a quixotic challenge. Pelosi prevailed in the caucus vote 150-43. When asked to explain why she won, she said, "Because I'm an effective leader, because we got the job done on health care and Wall Street reform and consumer protection, the list goes on. Because they know that I'm the person that can attract the resources, both intellectual and otherwise, to take us to victory because I have done it before." After two more elections, House Democrats held their smallest number of seats since 1928.

Back home, Pelosi has been overwhelmingly reelected. In 2008, antiwar protester Cindy Sheehan ran against her as an independent. Pelosi refused to debate or acknowledge Sheehan, who wound up getting 16% of the vote, more than the Republican nominee's 10%. Pelosi got 72%.

THIRTEENTH DISTRICT

Barbara Lee (D)

Elected April 1998, 9th full term; b. July 16, 1946, El Paso, TX; Mills Col., B.A. 1973, U. of CA Berkeley, M.S.W. 1975; Baptist; divorced; 2 children.

Elected Office: CA Assembly, 1991-97; CA Senate, 1997-98.

Professional Career: Chief of staff, U.S. Rep. Ron Dellums, 1975-87.

DC Office: 2267 RHOB, 20515, 202-225-2661; Fax: 202-225-9817; Website: lee.house.gov.

State Offices: Oakland, 510-763-0370.

Committees: *Appropriations:* Labor, HHS, Education & Related Agencies; Military Construction, Veterans Affairs, & Related Agencies; State, Foreign Operations & Related Programs. *Budget.*

Group Ratings

	ADA	ACLU	AFL-CIO	LCV	ITI	COC	HAFA	ACU	CFG	FRC
2014	90%	88%	–	91%	60%	31%	16%	8%	14%	0%
2013	100%	C	95%	96%	C	38%	C	20%	20%	C

National Journal Ratings

	2013 LIB	—	2013 CONS
Economic	91%	—	0%
Social	93%	—	0%
Foreign	79%	—	20%
Composite	91%	—	10%

Key Votes of the 113th Congress

1. Sandy storm spending	Y	5. Medical Marijuana	Y	9. Syrian Rebels Training	N
2. Violence Against Women Act	Y	6. Farm Bill	N	10. Keystone pipeline	N
3. Guantanamo Bay Detainees	Y	7. Afghanistan Combat	Y	11. Immigration Exec. Action	N
4. Abortion 20-week ban	N	8. NSA Phone Data Collection	Y	12. Bipartisan budget deal	N

Election Results

2014 general	Barbara Lee (D).................................168,491	(88%)	$1,100,730
	Dakin Sundeen (R)..............................21,940	(12%)	$4,790
2014 primary	Barbara Lee (D)..................................77,461	(83%)	
	Dakin Sundeen (R)................................9,533	(10%)	

Prior winning percentages: 2012 (87%), 2010 (84%), 2008 (86%), 2006 (86%), 2004 (85%), 2002 (81%), 2000 (85%), 1998 (83%), 1998 special (67%)

Population		Race and Ethnicity		Income	
Total:	732,753	White	34.1%	Median income:	$60,417
Urban:	92.7%	Asian	21.0%		*(124 of 435)*
Suburban:	7.3%	Latino	20.7%	Under $50,000	43.0%
Rural:	0.0%	Black	19.3%	$50,000-$99,999:	27.0%
Land area:	115	Two races	4.0%	$100,000-$199,999:	20.3%
Pop/sq. mi.:	6,344.3	White Ethnic	17.7%	$200,000 or more:	9.7%
Born in state:	49.7%			Poverty Rate	17.9%
		Education			
Age Groups:		H.S. grad or less:	30.6%	**Work**	
Under 18:	19.4%	Some college:	24.7%	White collar:	46.7%
18 to 34:	28.0%	College degree, 4 yr.:	23.9%	Blue collar:	38.3%
35 to 64:	40.0%	Post-grad study:	20.8%	Sales and service:	15.0%
Over 64:	12.6%				
		Military		Govt. workers:	16.7%
		Veterans/active duty:	4.5%		

East Bay: Oakland, Berkeley

On the East Bay opposite San Francisco, Oakland and Berkeley stand today on one of the lushest sites in America, overlooking the San Francisco-Oakland Bay Bridge and the Golden Gate Bridge and basking in the sunshine that is more common here than across the bay. Both cities host great

Voter Turnout	
2013 Total Citizen 18+	493,722
2014 House Turnout	190,431
2014 Turnout as % CVAP	38.6%
2012 Turnout as % CVAP	63.4%

institutions, but in different ways they are also museum pieces, antiques from a moment in the 1960s when both, especially Berkeley, gained identities that became hard to shake.

Berkeley was founded as a university town, named after the 18th-century Irish philosopher Bishop George Berkeley for his proclamation, "Westward the course of empire takes its way." Famous for years as the home of first-rate scholarship at the University of California, Berkeley became famous politically in 1964 as ground zero of student rebellion when an administrator's refusal to let students set up a table to sign up volunteers for Democrat Lyndon Johnson's presidential campaign led to months of riots, student strikes, and classroom confrontations. In 1969, students led protests at "People's Park," a lot owned by the university, and Republican Gov. Ronald Reagan sent in the National Guard to protect state property, an episode in which both sides relished the confrontation. Berkeley gave birth to a street culture that still exists. Its denizens made common cause with the quasi-political Black Panthers from nearby Oakland and smoked marijuana with the Hell's Angels motorcycle gang. With its view of the bay, the campus is beautiful, and old buildings like the shingled Claremont Hotel are grand, although construction of new offices and apartment buildings have created a more modern look in the past couple decades.

Oakland has a different history, centered on commerce. (Gertrude Stein was wrong: There is a there there.) It became the western terminus of the transcontinental railroad in 1870 and was connected by ferry to San Francisco. It has always had heavy industry, and its port today is the fifth-busiest in the country. The docks attracted young roustabouts like the writer Jack London, after whom a downtown square is named. Civic affairs were run by the local elite like the Knowland family, who owned the *Oakland Tribune*. With the Bay Area's largest black community, Oakland spawned the Black Panthers, a militant organization that came to define late 1960s radicalism. "The Black Panthers were mostly young activists whose personal lives and oftentimes limited professional opportunities were defined by Oakland's increasingly

2012 Presidential Vote		
Barack Obama (D) 268,093	(88%)
Mitt Romney (R)..................27,474	(9%)
2008 Presidential Vote		
Barack Obama (D) 283,183	(88%)
John McCain (R)..................32,359	(10%)
Cook Partisan Voting Index: D+37		

impoverished landscape," wrote Peniel Joseph in his history of the Black Power movement, *Waiting 'Til the Midnight Hour.* African-American leaders began to dominate city government in the 1970s and the *Tribune* came under black ownership in the 1980s.

Then Jerry Brown came on the scene. Governor of California 20 years earlier and an unsuccessful presidential candidate several times over, he ran an unorthodox campaign for mayor and won. Brown irritated local factions by firing department heads and ignoring long-standing alliances, but he seemed to take seriously his mission of propelling Oakland to prominence. With his tough talk on crime and advocacy of big commercial development projects that drove up rents, he sounded like a conservative. He even set up a military high school. Crime rates dropped, and the local economy thrived, partly with the growth of middle-income refugees from the exorbitant housing costs of San Francisco. But many longtime residents, especially African-Americans, complained about rising costs, and they in turn moved to the outskirts. The city's black population fell from 47 percent in 1980 to about 28 percent in 2010.

After Brown's departure, election and community leaders in 2007 created a public-private initiative called the Oakland Partnership, with the goal of attracting 10,000 jobs over five years. In its first two years, jobs were created, but the recession derailed much of the progress. Developers rushed to get entitlements to build condos and apartment complexes downtown, but many of the building plans failed to materialize, and the real estate market lagged behind much of the Bay Area. Although poverty has remained widespread in Oakland, the local real estate market was among the ten hottest in the nation in 2014 as prices surged by 26 percent, partly because they had become undervalued in the booming Bay Area. The anti-Wall Street "Occupy" movement was especially pronounced in Oakland, with a massive strike that shut down businesses and the city's bustling port in November 2011. Tense confrontations between city police and activists led to the use of tear gas and some 40 arrests. Recent racial tensions were buttressed by a 2014 police report that 62 percent of local police stops were made on blacks, who are 28 percent of the city's population.

The 13th Congressional District of California consists of Oakland and Berkeley; the suburb of San Leandro, originally settled by Portuguese immigrants; and the island city of Alameda. It also includes the Port of Oakland and Oakland International Airport. It's the most Democratic district in California and one of the most liberal in the nation.

Barbara Lee (D)

Democrat Barbara Lee, who won an April 1998 special election, is one of Congress' most liberal members, which has diminished her influence in a GOP-controlled House. From her prize seat on the Appropriations Committee, she seeks to help the poor while condemning U.S. military involvement overseas. Some of her proposals have gained a receptive ear from the Obama administration.

Lee spent her childhood in Texas and says her political thinking was shaped by her early exposure to race discrimination. While in labor with her, Lee's mother was at first denied treatment at an El Paso hospital. Lee attended a segregated school in that city until her parents sent their children to a Catholic school. In 1960, the family moved to Southern California, where Lee was the first black cheerleader in her high school, a distinction she won after enlisting the help of the local chapter of the NAACP. In 2008, Lee authored a memoir, *Renegade for Peace and Justice,* in which she discussed her experiences as a single welfare mother raising two children while attending college and her early days of social advocacy. "In order to go the policy front, I had to do the personal," she said. Lee graduated from Mills College in Oakland and got a degree in social work at the University of California, Berkeley. She started a community mental health center in Berkeley and then worked as a staffer for 12 years for Rep. Ron Dellums, who chaired the House Armed Services Committee. She was elected to the California Assembly in 1990 and to the Senate in 1996. After Dellums announced he was resigning, he endorsed Lee as his successor, and she won the special election with 67 percent of the vote. She has not faced a serious primary or general election challenge.

Lee agitates for a reduction in the nation's weapons stockpiles and sharp cuts in Pentagon spending. She has supported increased funding for international AIDS programs, and called for steps to end the 40-year trade embargo of Cuba. She was a founder of the Out of Iraq Caucus, a group of the most vocal antiwar House members. In July 2008, the House passed, 399-24, her bill to prevent permanent U.S. military bases in Iraq or U.S. control of Iraqi oil. In 2009, she led a delegation of Democrats to Cuba to discuss trade and other issues with its Communist-run government, and two years later helped to get charter passenger flights to the island nation from Oakland's airport. In January 2015, after President Barack Obama announced his plan to restore diplomatic relations with Cuba, the *San Francisco Chronicle* reported that she had a "gentlewoman's agreement" with Obama that she would become the ambassador to Havana. Lee denied the report, but she enthusiastically backed his efforts to lift the embargo and reach out to Cuba. In the six years since her first visit, she had been to Cuba 21 times and had met senior officials to facilitate relatively minor agricultural and tourist dealings and to encourage more trust. Lee's consistent opposition to military action occasionally has made her a lonely voice. As most Democrats voted to authorize the Clinton administration to bomb Serbia in 1999, Lee was the only House member to oppose a resolution supporting U.S. troops. In September 2001, she was the only member of Congress to vote against the resolution authorizing the use of force in response to the terrorist attacks. "If we rush to launch a counterattack, we run too great a risk that women, children, and other noncombatants will be caught in the crossfire," she said. Her vote brought a torrent of national attention, though her concern turned out to be valid. Lee received threats of violence, and the Capitol police provided her with 24-hour protection. But she had supportive rallies in her district. Years later, she defended her vote on the basis that the resolution had yielded "perpetual war." During the debate in October 2002 to authorize the use of force in Iraq, Lee offered an alternative calling for diplomatic action, which was defeated 355-72. As an alternative, she proposed in 2013 a new federal Department of Peacekeeping.

In 2007, House Speaker Nancy Pelosi gave Lee a seat on the Appropriations Committee. She was one of 14 Democrats to vote against the Iraq war funding bill on the House floor. "My conscience is that we can't put up more money to fund this war," Lee said. The House also passed her bill to encourage states to divest from companies that do business in Sudan, in protest of the genocide in the Darfur region. As the co-chair of the Progressive Caucus, she laid out an agenda with three priorities: economic justice and security, protection of civil rights and liberties, and promotion of global peace. As Republican criticism mounted over earmarked spending, Lee remained a staunch defender of the practice. "I'll tell them to come to my community and see what we can accomplish with whatever federal dollars we can get," she said in 2009.

After the 2008 election, Lee became chairwoman of the Congressional Black Caucus, which she calls "the conscience of the Congress." She and other caucus members lamented Obama's plans to add troops in Afghanistan, and they have pressured him to pay more attention to minorities. Unlike many other Black Caucus members who backed Hillary Rodham Clinton in 2008, Lee was an early supporter of Obama, in large part because of his opposition to the Iraq War.

After the 2012 election, she considered running for vice chair of the House Democratic Caucus. But such a bid might be difficult so long as the Democratic leader represents the district across the bay in San Francisco.

FOURTEENTH DISTRICT

Jackie Speier (D)

Elected April 2008, 4th full term; b. May 14, 1950, San Francisco; U. of CA Davis, B.A. 1972, U. of CA Hastings Schl. of Law, J.D. 1976; Catholic; married (Barry Dennis); 2 children.

Elected Office: San Mateo Cnty. Bd. of Supervisors, 1980-86; CA Assembly, 1986-98; CA Senate, 1998-2006.

Professional Career: Staff aide, Rep. Leo Ryan, 1973-78; Dir., gov. affairs, Community Gatepath, 1996-98; Dir., gov. affairs, Electronic Arts, 1996-98; Atty., 2007-08.

DC Office: 2465 RHOB, 20515, 202-225-3531; Fax: 202-226-4183; Website: speier.house.gov.

State Offices: San Mateo, 650-342-0300 or 415-566-5257.

Committees: *Armed Services:* Oversight & Investigations (RMM); Military Personnel. *Intelligence (Select):* Emerging Threats; NSA & Cybersecurity.

Group Ratings

	ADA	ACLU	AFL-CIO	LCV	ITI	COC	HAFA	ACU	CFG	FRC
2014	90%	77%	–	94%	60%	36%	18%	9%	13%	0%
2013	80%	C	89%	82%	C	42%	C	14%	20%	C

National Journal Ratings

	2013 LIB	—	2013 CONS
Economic	74%	—	26%
Social	93%	—	0%
Foreign	87%	—	12%
Composite	86%	—	14%

Key Votes of the 113th Congress

1. Sandy storm spending	NV	5. Medical Marijuana	Y	9. Syrian Rebels Training	N
2. Violence Against Women Act	Y	6. Farm Bill	N	10. Keystone pipeline	N
3. Guantanamo Bay Detainees	Y	7. Afghanistan Combat	NV	11. Immigration Exec. Action	N
4. Abortion 20-week ban	N	8. NSA Phone Data Collection	Y	12. Bipartisan budget deal	Y

Election Results

2014 general	Jackie Speier (D)	114,389	(77%)	$841,039
	Robin Chew (R)	34,757	(23%)	$24,652
2014 primary	Jackie Speier (D)	66,800	(77%)	
	Robin Chew (R)	19,482	(23%)	

Prior winning percentages: 2012 (79%), 2010 (76%), 2008 (75%), 2008 special (78%)

Population		Race and Ethnicity		Income	
Total:	721,245	White	35.5%	Median income:	$85,706
Urban:	73.7%	Asian	31.0%		(22 of 435)
Suburban:	26.3%	Latino	25.0%	Under $50,000	29.1%
Rural:	0.0%	Black	3.5%	$50,000-$99,999:	27.8%
Land area:	221	Two races	3.1%	$100,000-$199,999:	28.3%
Pop/sq. mi.:	3,258.7	White Ethnic	19.6%	$200,000 or more:	14.8%
Born in state:	47.2%			Poverty Rate	8.3%
		Education			
Age Groups		H.S. grad or less:	29.2%	**Work**	
Under 18:	20.1%	Some college:	27.1%	White collar:	42.8%
18 to 34:	22.8%	College degree, 4 yr.:	27.2%	Blue collar:	42.7%
35 to 64:	42.3%	Post-grad study:	16.5%	Sales and service:	14.5%
Over 64:	14.8%				
		Military		Govt. workers:	12.4%
		Veterans/active duty:	4.9%		

San Francisco Peninsula: San Mateo

The city of San Francisco sits at the tip of the San Francisco Peninsula on the California coast. This is geologically interesting country. The San Andreas Fault runs just east of the Coast Range, underneath the reservoirs that store San Francisco's water supply. To the west are green mountains running down

Voter Turnout	
2013 Total Citizen 18+	478,885
2014 House Turnout	149,146
2014 Turnout as % CVAP	31.1%
2012 Turnout as % CVAP	58%

to the ocean. To the east is a zone of flat land between mountain and bay, an unbroken chain of suburbs and urban settlement, with light industry and salt flats along the bay front. Daly City and Pacifica on the ocean are a kind of extension of San Francisco's old working-class districts, with boxy houses on streets looking out on the ocean or the freeway. Today, these neighborhoods are home to many of the Bay Area's Asian immigrants. Pacific Islanders are prominent, too. A large concentration of Samoans is in Daly City, and San Bruno is home to a sizable Tongan community. A strip of Highway 1 that winds along the coastal cliffs south of Pacifica passes through an area known as "Devil's Slide" for the mudslides that often follow heavy storms. A tunnel bypassing Devil's Slide opened in 2013.

On the Bay side is South San Francisco, where Herb Boyer and Bob Swanson sketched on a napkin their plans for the first biotechnology company, Genentech. They bought space in an old warehouse on the waterfront near a Bethlehem Steel plant. In 2009, Genentech was purchased by the Swiss pharmaceutical firm Roche and had a market capitalization exceeding $100 billion. The area is one large biotech campus overlooking the Bay, with lawns, parkways, and earth-toned office complexes, the center of the industry. *YouTube*, started in 2005, is headquartered in San Bruno. Oracle, a computer software company, is based in a cluster of gleaming glass buildings in Redwood City. In November 2014, Google bought a million square feet of office space in Redwood City. On the site of the former Bay Meadows racetrack near San Mateo, an 83-acre master-planned community is being developed.

Between the Bayshore Freeway and Interstate 280 are middle class suburbs that grew up to be cities with office complexes—Millbrae, Burlingame, San Mateo, and San Carlos. The area has also been the source of incredible athletic talent: Junipero Serra, an all-boys Catholic high school in San Mateo, enrolled both New England Patriots quarterback Tom Brady and former San Francisco Giants slugger Barry Bonds.

On September 9, 2010, a ruptured gas line in San Bruno caused a massive explosion that killed eight people and destroyed 38 homes. Federal investigators found cracks in welds that held sections of the pipe together, and it was revealed that pipeline owner Pacific Gas and Electric Co. had cut corners in its safety inspections. In September 2014, California regulators imposed $1.4 billion in penalties, its largest ever. PG&E responded that it was "deeply sorry" and that the penalty was appropriate. Bolstered by many large and creative local companies, the area weathered the recession better than most. In January 2015, the county's unemployment rate was 3.9 percent, the lowest in the state. The average monthly rent in 2014 for a two-bedroom apartment was $2,500. That is not so high, considering that the average tech worker in the county had a salary of $210,000—not counting the stock that Facebook founder Mark Zuckerberg sold that year.

The 14th Congressional District of California consists of these northern peninsula suburbs plus the southwest corner of San Francisco, which has less than 20 percent of the district population. It takes in about 80 percent of affluent San Mateo County. The 14th is 31 percent Asian and 25 percent Hispanic. The economic orientation here was historically toward San Francisco, then

2012 Presidential Vote		
Barack Obama (D)	200,343	(74%)
Mitt Romney (R)	63,589	(24%)
2008 Presidential Vote		
Barack Obama (D)	214,398	(75%)
John McCain (R)	68,555	(24%)
Cook Partisan Voting Index: D+23		

later toward Silicon Valley. But now the district has its own burgeoning biotech industry, and income levels are among the highest in California. Politically, the 14th District is overwhelmingly Democratic.

Jackie Speier (D)

Democrat Jackie Speier, who won a special election in April 2008, brought with her a unique experience as a young House aide and a continuing interest in national security.

An outspoken liberal, she has focused on consumer-protection issues as well as on exposing rapes and sexual assaults within the military.

Born in San Francisco's Sunset district, Speier graduated from the University of California, Davis, and got her law degree at UC Hastings College of the Law. While an undergraduate, she interned in Sacramento for Democratic Assemblyman Leo Ryan and later joined his staff after he was elected to Congress. In November 1978, Speier accompanied third-term Rep. Ryan to Jonestown, Guyana, to investigate claims that some of Ryan's constituents, who were members of a church called the Peoples Temple, were being held against their will by the Rev. Jim Jones of San Francisco. Some defectors from the church joined Ryan's entourage for the journey home, but the group made it only as far as the airport. Four assassins sent by Jones opened fire on the defenseless group. Ryan and four others, including two journalists, were killed. Speier was shot five times and left for dead on the airstrip, where she waited 15 hours before the Guyana police rescued her. In the meantime, Jones, back at his jungle camp, set in motion events that shocked the world. He forced his cult followers to commit "revolutionary suicide" by drinking poison-laced punch, which resulted in the deaths of more than 900 followers, some of them babies and children.

Once back in California, Speier underwent 10 surgeries, including skin grafts. Despite her injuries, she ran in the special election to succeed Ryan, gaining only 15 percent of the total vote and finishing third among Democrats in the primary. She then went local to build her political career, starting on the San Mateo County Board of Supervisors and serving 18 years in the state Legislature. Her pinnacle achievement was legislation protecting consumers' privacy from invasive practices by banks and insurance companies. In 2006, she unsuccessfully sought the nomination for lieutenant governor. A year later she joined three other women in co-authoring a book, *This Is Not the Life I Ordered: 50 Ways to Keep Your Head Above Water When Life Keeps Dragging You Down*.

When Democratic Rep. Tom Lantos, chairman of the House Foreign Affairs Committee and the only Holocaust survivor to serve in Congress, announced his retirement in January 2008, he endorsed Speier as his successor. He died in February of complications from cancer of the esophagus. Speier immediately became the front-runner. She won the all-party election with 75 percent of the vote against four little-known opponents.

Immediately after she took her oath of office, she caused a ruckus when she launched a sharp partisan attack on President George W. Bush's handling of the war in Iraq. "History will not judge us kindly if we sacrifice four generations of Americans because of the folly of one," she declared. Her remarks triggered a volley of boos among Republican members on the floor and prompted Republican Rep. Darrell Issa of California to walk out of the chamber, claiming she had violated House rules of decorum. Speier responded that she had been "forthright." Later, in March 2010, Speier joined 59 other Democrats in voting for a resolution requiring the withdrawal of troops from Afghanistan. Since then, as a member of the Armed Services Committee, she regularly has appeared on the House floor to speak about military men and women who have been raped or sexually assaulted, and she has taken a lead role in improving delivery of benefits to Bay Area veterans. She also would give women in the military access to free birth control and counseling. In 2015, she became ranking Democrat on the committee's oversight and investigations panel.

She drew attention in 2010 when she spent five days living on a food-stamp budget of $4.50 a day to call attention to rising poverty. That same year, she urged a recall of McDonald's glasses promoting the movie Shrek that were tainted with cadmium, a carcinogen, and called on the online classified ad site Craigslist to shut down its adult services section, which critics said was used to advertise sex with underage girls. During debate on a major financial services regulatory bill in 2009, Speier passed in the House an amendment requiring big banks to have at least $1 in capital for every $15 in assets. In the final bill, lawmakers watered down the requirement, giving federal regulators the option of enforcing the limit only if a firm posed a "grave threat" to financial stability.

After the massive 2010 pipeline explosion in her district killed eight people, Speier introduced a pipeline safety bill. The measure, signed into law in January 2012, doubles the maximum fine for safety violations to $2 million, authorizes more pipeline inspectors, and requires automatic shut-off valves on new or replaced pipelines.

In February 2011, during a House debate over funding for abortion providers, Speier emotionally discussed her own experience with abortion. She said that she had to terminate a pregnancy in the second trimester because of a serious medical complication, and she suggested that ardent anti-abortion rights Republican Rep. Chris Smith of New Jersey, was mischaracterizing the procedure she had. "For you to stand on this floor and to suggest, as you have, that somehow this is a procedure that is either welcomed or done cavalierly or done without any thought is preposterous," Speier said. Following reports of an increase in sexual assaults on college campuses, she was part of a bipartisan House group in 2014 that said one response should be to include the data for each school in the annual college rankings of *U.S. News & World Report*. "The issue has not been taken seriously enough," she said. Also that year, she called on NFL Commissioner Roger Goodell to resign because of his handling of domestic-violence cases involving several of the league's players.

Speier considered running for state attorney general in 2010 but opted to stay in the House. She has not faced a serious reelection challenge.

FIFTEENTH DISTRICT

Eric Swalwell (D)

Elected 2012, 2nd term; b. Nov. 16, 1980, Sac City, IA; U. of MD, B.A. 2003, J.D. 2006; Christian; single.

Elected Office: Dublin City Cncl., 2010-12.

Professional Career: Deputy dist. atty., Alameda Cnty., 2006-12.

DC Office: 129 CHOB, 20515, 202-225-5065; Website: swalwell.house .gov.

State Offices: Hayward, 510-370-3322; Pleasanton, 925-460-5100.

Committees: *Intelligence (Select):* CIA (RMM); Defense Intelligence & Overhead Architecture. *Science, Space, & Technology:* Energy; Research & Technology.

Group Ratings

	ADA	ACLU	AFL-CIO	LCV	ITI	COC	HAFA	ACU	CFG	FRC
2014	90%	77%	–	97%	100%	36%	14%	8%	11%	0%
2013	85%	C	100%	93%	C	46%	C	8%	13%	C

National Journal Ratings

	2013 LIB	—	2013 CONS
Economic	78%	—	21%
Social	87%	—	7%
Foreign	71%	—	27%
Composite	80%	—	20%

Key Votes of the 113th Congress

1. Sandy storm spending	Y	5. Medical Marijuana	Y	9. Syrian Rebels Training	N
2. Violence Against Women Act	Y	6. Farm Bill	N	10. Keystone pipeline	N
3. Guantanamo Bay Detainees	Y	7. Afghanistan Combat	Y	11. Immigration Exec. Action	N
4. Abortion 20-week ban	N	8. NSA Phone Data Collection	Y	12. Bipartisan budget deal	Y

Election Results

2014 general	Eric Swalwell (D)	99,756	(70%)	$1,669,314	$14,944
	Hugh Bussell (R)	43,150	(30%)	$16,477	
2014 primary	Eric Swalwell (D)	42,419	(49%)		
	Hugh Bussell (R)	22,228	(26%)		
	Ellen Corbett (D)	21,798	(25%)		

Prior winning percentage: 2012 (52%)

Population		Race and Ethnicity		Income	
Total:	734,837	White	36.5%	Median income:	$86,818
Urban:	31.0%	Asian	27.9%		*(18 of 435)*
Suburban:	68.9%	Latino	24.2%	Under $50,000	28.8%
Rural:	0.1%	Black	6.2%	$50,000-$99,999:	28.1%
Land area:	595	Two races	3.6%	$100,000-$199,999:	29.6%
Pop/sq. mi.:	1,235.2	White Ethnic	18.6%	$200,000 or more:	13.5%
Born in state:	51.2%			Poverty Rate	8.8%
		Education			
Age Groups		H.S. grad or less:	32.2%	**Work**	
Under 18:	24.3%	Some college:	27.4%	White collar:	44.4%
18 to 34:	21.5%	College degree, 4 yr.:	25.7%	Blue collar:	38.8%
35 to 64:	42.1%	Post-grad study:	14.7%	Sales and service:	16.9%
Over 64:	12.0%				
		Military		Govt. workers:	12.0%
		Veterans/active duty:	5.5%		

Southern East Bay: Hayward, Fremont

The East Bay is the workaday, unglamorous side of the San Francisco Bay Area—a narrow strip of land between the Bay and the surprisingly high mountains that rise just to the east. The shoreline is not picturesque, with its closed-down Navy bases and its docks, airports, and salt evaporators. The

Voter Turnout	
2013 Total Citizen 18+	458,000
2014 House Turnout	142,904
2014 Turnout as % CVAP	31.2%
2012 Turnout as % CVAP	56.2%

Bay Bridge cuts an inspiring figure, though it has required constant patching. A new span was opened in September 2013, but complaints continued about its safety. The San Mateo Bridge to the south is at best utilitarian. In World War II, when the shipyards of Richmond were buzzing, the East Bay south of Oakland was still largely uninhabited farm fields. After the war, the area filled up, south along old Route 17: Hayward, with its California State University campus and seafood industry; Union City, with its rail yards; and Newark, with dozens of industrial plants ranging from salt processing to computer network servers. Hit hard by the dot-com bust at the turn of the century, the East Bay revived with biotech, construction, and health care, only to be set back like the rest of California during the recession. Underneath the East Bay is the Hayward Fault, not as famous as the San Andreas, but just as dangerous. An earthquake there in 1868 registered about 7.0 on the Richter scale. Another rupture is overdue, and 7 million people in the region might be shaken significantly.

The 15th Congressional District of California is made up of East Bay towns in southern Alameda County and part of Castro Valley. It also includes a small slice of Contra Costa County near San Ramon. The district is racially and ethnically mixed. It includes Hayward, with its significant Asian and Hispanic populations, and Union City, which has become more than 50 percent Asian. In Pleasanton, developers in January 2015 announced plans for an Asian shopping center and office park. The district is home to the

2012 Presidential Vote		
Barack Obama (D)	177,243	(68%)
Mitt Romney (R)	77,748	(30%)
2008 Presidential Vote		
Barack Obama (D)	181,441	(68%)
John McCain (R)	81,938	(31%)
Cook Partisan Voting Index: D+16		

Lawrence Livermore National Laboratory, where the federal government conducts nuclear-warhead and energy research. Since the 1980s, anti-nuclear protestors have gathered at Livermore to commemorate historical events and denounce nuclear weapons. Politically, this is a safe Democratic district.

Eric Swalwell (D)

Democrat Eric Swalwell, whose defeat in 2012 of 40-year Democratic Rep. Pete Stark alarmed some Democrats who prefer the comfort of seniority, has mended fences with Minority Leader Nancy Pelosi and her team. With his youth and focus on tech and energy issues, Swalwell has brought some fresh thinking into the mostly retirement-age Democratic delegation in the Bay Area.

Born in Sac City, Iowa, Swalwell grew up in Dublin California, where he served on the city council. He attended the University of Maryland, where he was bitten by the political bug and graduated with a bachelor's in government and politics and then a law degree. He got his start in politics as an unpaid intern on Capitol Hill, working for then-Rep. Ellen Tauscher, a moderate Bay Area Democrat. To make ends meet, he worked two summer jobs around the Capitol, at the local gym and a restaurant, where he kept an eye out for members of Congress. "In the morning I would serve them gym towels," he said. "In the evening, I would serve them dinner." After graduation, Swalwell moved back to California and got a job as a prosecutor in the Alameda County district attorney's office, where he rose to the post of deputy district attorney. "I put a lot of bad guys away," he told voters on the campaign trail. In 2010, he ran successfully for city council in Dublin, an outer suburb of San Francisco.

Other prominent California Democrats had been patiently waiting for Stark to retire, including former Obama administration official Ro Khanna, who raised more than $1 million for a congressional bid. But as the 2012 election approached, Khanna and others opted to let Stark serve another term unchallenged. Swalwell jumped the line.

Much of the Democratic establishment backed Stark, including the state's two senators, leading labor unions, the state party, House Minority Leader Nancy Pelosi, the entire Bay Area congressional delegation, and President Barack Obama. Swalwell got support from a smattering of local officials, including Tauscher, his old boss. Swalwell began the campaign by pointedly competing in running races across the district, a series his campaign dubbed the "race for change." Beyond his hustle, Swalwell's campaign was largely fueled by Stark's own missteps.

During a debate, Stark wrongly accused Swalwell of taking bribes and had to apologize because it wasn't true. He accused a local newspaper columnist of donating to his opponent, and had to apologize because it wasn't true. And he threatened the family and livelihood of a local politician who endorsed Swalwell, but claimed he was provoked. After the slip-ups, the notoriously mercurial Stark was largely cloistered out of sight, instead relying on hard-hitting mailers, the rare scripted appearance, and his high name recognition after his decades of service.

Under California's new election rules, the two top vote-getters advance to the general election regardless of their party labels. Swalwell reached out to Republicans and independents dissatisfied with Stark's long liberal tenure. He didn't promise he would vote all that differently from Stark—he describes himself as a solid Democrat, though he believes "every human problem does not need a legislative solution"—but said that he would at least listen intently as their congressman. His 52%-48% victory in November was an ironic way for Stark to exit: Four decades earlier, Stark had made much the same argument in unseating the previous octogenarian congressman.

In the House, Swalwell took action on what he called a series of "small steps." He enacted his Philippines Charitable Giving Assistance Act, which permitted tax deductions for contributions to recovery in the Philippines following a typhoon that devastated the islands in November 2013. He attributed his success to bipartisan outreach. "The reason that the Bay Area, especially Silicon Valley, has led the way in innovation is that it's a collaborative environment," he told the *San Francisco Chronicle*, in reviewing his first term. In 2015, Swalwell joined the Intelligence Committee and became the ranking Democrat on its new CIA Subcommittee, which will oversee the agency's policy, activities and budget. Pelosi also gave him a political assignment to oversee Democratic outreach to young voters.

Swalwell began his reelection campaign with warnings from Stark and his allies that they planned to get even. His chief challenger was Democratic state Senate Majority Leader Ellen Corbett, whose district largely overlapped with the congressional district. She attacked Swalwell's inexperience and lack of Democratic credentials. Turning the tables, the incumbent claimed that the party establishment was supporting him, including House leaders and Obama. Swalwell benefited from a huge fundraising advantage. Despite Stark's earlier promise to give her a big boost, Corbett spent only $225,000 to Swalwell's $1.7 million for the cycle. Surprisingly, Corbett failed to survive the all-party primary. Swalwell got 49 percent of the total vote, and Corbett ran 430 votes behind Republican candidate Hugh Bussell. The general election immediately became an after-thought, with Swalwell winning, 70%-30%. During his apprenticeship, Swalwell appeared to have made all of the right moves, with some luck thrown in.

SIXTEENTH DISTRICT

Jim Costa (D)

Elected 2004, 6th term; b. April 13, 1952, Fresno; CA St. U. Fresno, B.A. 1974; Catholic; single.

Elected Office: CA Assembly, 1978-94; CA Senate, 1994-2002.

Professional Career: Consultant, 2002-04.

DC Office: 1314 LHOB, 20515, 202-225-3341; Website: costa.house.gov.

State Offices: Fresno, 559-495-1620; Merced, 209-384-1620.

Committees: *Agriculture:* General Farm Commodities & Risk Management; Horticulture, Research, Biotechnology & Foreign Agriculture; Livestock, Rural Development & Credit (RMM). *Natural Resources:* Energy & Mineral Resources; Water, Power & Oceans.

Group Ratings

	ADA	ACLU	AFL-CIO	LCV	ITI	COC	HAFA	ACU	CFG	FRC
2014	40%	66%	–	34%	60%	92%	16%	16%	18%	13%
2013	45%	C	79%	36%	C	69%	C	8%	11%	C

National Journal Ratings

	2013 LIB	—	2013 CONS
Economic	55%	—	44%
Social	58%	—	42%
Foreign	57%	—	43%
Composite	57%	—	43%

Key Votes of the 113th Congress

1. Sandy storm spending		5. Medical Marijuana	Y	9. Syrian Rebels Training	Y
2. Violence Against Women Act	Y	6. Farm Bill	Y	10. Keystone pipeline	NV
3. Guantanamo Bay Detainees	Y	7. Afghanistan Combat	N	11. Immigration Exec. Action	N
4. Abortion 20-week ban	N	8. NSA Phone Data Collection	N	12. Bipartisan budget deal	Y

Election Results

2014 general	Jim Costa (D)..	46,277	(51%)	$1,116,677	
	Johnny Tacherra (R).............................	44,943	(49%)	$342,204	$1,000
2014 primary	Jim Costa (D)..	25,586	(44%)		
	Johnny Tacherra (R).............................	12,542	(22%)		
	Steve Crass (R)..	8,877	(15%)		
	Mel Levey (R)...	4,565	(8%)		
	Joanna Garcia-Botelho (R)......................	3,827	(7%)		

Prior winning percentages: 2012 (57%), 2010 (52%), 2008 (74%), 2006 (100%), 2004 (53%)

Population		Race and Ethnicity		Income	
Total:	715,257	Latino	58.1%	Median income:	$36,190
Urban:	69.4%	White	24.4%		*(414 of 435)*
Suburban:	23.7%	Asian	9.0%	Under $50,000	63.9%
Rural:	6.9%	Black	5.5%	$50,000-$99,999:	25.4%
Land area:	2,702	Two races	2.0%	$100,000-$199,999:	9.3%
Pop/sq. mi.:	264.7	White Ethnic	10.4%	$200,000 or more:	1.4%
Born in state:	64.6%			Poverty Rate	32.8%
		Education			
Age Groups		H.S. grad or less:	57.4%	**Work**	
Under 18:	31.3%	Some college:	30.2%	White collar:	21.0%
18 to 34:	26.8%	College degree, 4 yr.:	8.1%	Blue collar:	41.9%
35 to 64:	32.4%	Post-grad study:	4.3%	Sales and service:	37.1%
Over 64:	9.4%			Govt. workers:	15.0%
		Military			
		Veterans/active duty:	5.5%		

Central Valley: Merced, Part of Fresno

Under orders from the Spanish governor of California to explore what lay beyond the coastal mountains, army officer Gabriel Moraga became one of the first Europeans to behold the Central Valley, a fertile expanse teaming with wildlife—heron, antelope, elk, and grizzly bears. He brought his soldiers

Voter Turnout	
2013 Total Citizen 18+	384,650
2014 House Turnout	91,220
2014 Turnout as % CVAP	23.7%
2012 Turnout as % CVAP	40.6%

through the Pacheco Pass, which would become the main route for exporting the natural riches of the Valley to the port cities springing up along the coast. During his travels in the early 1800s, Moraga bestowed Spanish names on the places and rivers he encountered. So the region he was inspired to call "Blessed Sacrament" became Sacramento. And, after one particularly long and dusty day, he stumbled on a much-welcomed river, which he called Merced, or, "River of Our Lady of Mercy." Like much of the rest of the valley, Merced grew to be a hub of agriculture. Located north of Fresno, the city incorporated in 1889, and its economy was long hitched to agribusiness. Harvest time attracted thousands of itinerant farmworkers from Mexico and elsewhere, and later, the region's affordable housing inspired new waves of migration. With the 2010 census, Latinos became a majority in surrounding Merced County. The empowered community approved a referendum in November 2014 switching local elections from at-large to district voting.

The 16th District of California encompasses all of Merced County and takes in parts of Madera and Fresno counties. Unemployment here in recent years has been among the nation's highest, and Merced County's jobless rate hit 20 percent in early 2012. In February 2015, the rate remained a painful 13.5 percent. That was relatively good news locally, with recent job growth in resources, tourism, education and health care. The University of California, Merced, which in 2005 opened as the 10th university in the vast UC system, has become a major employer. Highway 99 connects most of the key cities and towns in the district, with their shared agricultural and water interests: Livingston, Atwater, Merced, Chowchilla, Madera, and down to Fresno. But the drought became a new job

2012 Presidential Vote		
Barack Obama (D) 88,973		(59%)
Mitt Romney (R)...................59,808		(39%)
2008 Presidential Vote		
Barack Obama (D) 93,222		(58%)
John McCain (R)...................65,023		(40%)
Cook Partisan Voting Index:	D+7	

crippler, with the major cutbacks in water supply forcing many farmers to reduce their expenses or abandon their fields. In March 2015, Merced County restricted the export of its groundwater.

With its heavy concentration of Latinos and other immigrant groups, which respond to Voting Rights Act imperatives to provide fair Hispanic representation, Barack Obama won the new 16th with 58% in 2008 and 59% in 2012. But voter registration and turnout have been relatively low.

Jim Costa (D)

Democrat Jim Costa, elected in 2004, is a third-generation farmer who concentrates on the agricultural issues that affect his district's rural residents, often trying to find a middle ground between production and resource protection. For now, he is the only remaining Democrat from the Central Valley who fits the traditional mold of voting conservative on many economic and social policies but taking his party's side on most big issues.

Born in Fresno, he was raised on his family's dairy farm. He is the grandson of Portuguese immigrants who settled in the San Joaquin Valley near the turn of the 20th century. In 1978, Costa was elected to the state Assembly, where he was known as a moderate Democrat. In 2002, after he was forced to retire at age 50 because of term limits, Costa founded a consulting firm. Two years later, when Democratic Rep. Cal Dooley retired after 14 years, Costa entered the race with solid name recognition. His former state Senate district covered the entire congressional district. But in the March primary, he faced a bruising challenge from Lisa Quigley, Dooley's chief of staff. Quigley grew up in the Central Valley, but she hadn't lived in the district in nearly two decades. Costa questioned her residency and her agricultural credentials. Quigley was endorsed by Dooley and national abortion rights groups and she painted Costa as a special-interest lobbyist. In the campaign's final days, Quigley ran ads mentioning Costa's 1986 arrest for soliciting a prostitute and a 1994 incident in which police found drug paraphernalia in his home. Costa shrugged off the attacks and won the primary by an unexpectedly large 73%-27%.

In the general election, Costa began as a clear favorite in the Democratic-leaning district. But the Republican nominee, state Sen. Roy Ashburn, ran a formidable campaign. He criticized Costa for supporting tax policies that he said hurt low-income families. The National Republican Congressional Committee ran $1.5 million in ads saying, "Jim Costa—he's gonna cost ya." But Costa's lengthy legislative record didn't readily lend itself to the "liberal" label. In a relatively low turnout event, Costa won 53%-47%.

In the House, Costa got seats on the Agriculture and the Natural Resources committees, both important to his district. He and his close friend from the Valley and fellow Blue Dog Democrat Dennis Cardoza were among the last undecided votes on President Barack Obama's health care overhaul before agreeing to back it. Republicans charged that Cardoza and Costa were given extra public water allocations for their region, though both denied there was any connection. Costa was one of 10 Democrats to vote for California GOP Rep. Devin Nunes' House-passed bill in February 2012 to change California's system of water laws to benefit San Joaquin Valley farmers. The bill died in the Senate. Costa supported lifting the ban on oil drilling 50 to 100 miles off the nation's coast, but he sought to maintain the federal ban on drilling within 25 miles of shore.

Costa has bucked his party on fiscal issues that bring out his conservative impulses. He was one of 22 House Democrats to support a failed proposal in March 2012 to adopt the Simpson-Bowles commission's budget, which imposed politically painful spending reductions to balance the budget.

Costa did not face a significant reelection challenge until 2010. Republican rancher Andy Vidak did his best to blame Costa for the area's weak economy, running billboards depicting him as the pitchfork-holding "American Gothic" farmer with Speaker Nancy Pelosi at his side. Vidak surged in the polls, and in the closing weeks the race became a toss-up. Costa put in a month of heavy retail politicking, and he got last-minute help from the Democratic Congressional Campaign Committee. The Obama administration also chipped in: It announced a few days before the election that California would get an additional $715 million for high-speed rail, contingent on money being spent quickly on a San Joaquin Valley segment. In a recount that dragged on for three weeks, Costa won 52%-48%.

Following the 2012 redistricting, Costa moved to what seemed to be the favorable 16th District, though three-fourths of it was new political territory for him. National Republicans focused their attention elsewhere. But the 2014 election became a big surprise. In the first round of voting in June, Fresno County dairyman Johnny Tacherra easily led three other Republican candidates and moved into the general election with Costa. Before he decided to make the challenge, Tacherra met with Costa in his Washington office and pleaded for more water assistance for local farmers. But he felt rebuffed when the meeting ended. "I'm going to run for Congress against this guy because he does not represent us, he's not going to help us," Tacherra later recounted his reaction to *National Review*.

Running with no national-party assistance and one modestly paid campaign aide, Tacherra worked the grass roots to show his connection to the drought-stricken district, and he painted the incumbent as out of touch. Costa outspent the challenger by nearly 5-to-1. In contrast to 2010, he was so confident that he made contributions to endangered Democrats elsewhere during the closing weeks of the campaign. When the votes were tallied on election night, and for the following week, Tacherra shockingly held a narrow lead. He flew to Washington to join the bipartisan freshman orientation. But Costa pulled ahead in the official results just before Thanksgiving. He won by 1,334 votes on the strength of taking 64% of the Fresno County vote. Tacherra handily won Madera and Merced counties.

Following that scare, Costa sided with Republicans on multiple House votes, including support of the Keystone XL pipeline and new restrictions on Obama's regulatory authority. He may face the risk of inviting a Democratic challenger if he moves too far away from the party's base. Republicans, for their part, have begun to take this district more seriously.

SEVENTEENTH DISTRICT

Mike Honda (D)

Elected 2000, 8th term; b. June 27, 1941, Walnut Grove; San Jose St. U., B.A. 1968, M.A. 1974; Protestant; widowed; 2 children.

Elected Office: San Jose Unified Sch. Bd., 1981-90; Santa Clara Cnty. Bd. of Supervisors, 1990-96; CA Assembly, 1997-2000.

Professional Career: U.S. Peace Corps, El Salvador, 1965-67; Science teacher; Elem. schl. principal, 1978-90.

DC Office: 1713 LHOB, 20515, 202-225-2631; Fax: 202-225-2699; Website: honda.house.gov.

State Offices: Santa Clara, 408-436-2720.

Committees: *Appropriations:* Commerce, Justice, Science, & Related Agencies (RMM); Energy & Water Development, & Related Agencies.

Group Ratings

	ADA	ACLU	AFL-CIO	LCV	ITI	COC	HAFA	ACU	CFG	FRC
2014	95%	94%	–	94%	60%	38%	7%	8%	14%	0%
2013	95%	C	100%	89%	C	33%	C	5%	6%	C

National Journal Ratings

	2013 LIB	—	2013 CONS
Economic	91%	—	0%
Social	93%	—	0%
Foreign	94%	—	0%
Composite	96%	—	4%

Key Votes of the 113th Congress

1. Sandy storm spending	Y	5. Medical Marijuana	Y
2. Violence Against Women Act	Y	6. Farm Bill	NV
3. Guantanamo Bay Detainees	Y	7. Afghanistan Combat	Y
4. Abortion 20-week ban	N	8. NSA Phone Data Collection	Y

9. Syrian Rebels Training	N
10. Keystone pipeline	N
11. Immigration Exec. Action	N
12. Bipartisan budget deal	Y

Election Results

2014 general	Mike Honda (D)	69,561	(52%)	$3,447,979	$124,410	$372,286
	Ro Khanna (D)	64,847	(48%)	$4,427,101	$289,973	$83,777
2014 primary	Mike Honda (D)	43,607	(48%)			
	Ro Khanna (D)	25,384	(28%)			
	Vanila Singh (R)	15,359	(17%)			
	Joel Vanlandingham (R)	6,154	(7%)			

Prior winning percentages: 2012 (74%), 2010 (68%), 2008 (72%), 2006 (72%), 2004 (72%), 2002 (66%), 2000 (54%)

Population		Race and Ethnicity		Income	
Total:	732,118	Asian	48.6%	Median income:	$100,282
Urban:	58.4%	White	25.7%		*(6 of 435)*
Suburban:	41.6%	Latino	19.2%	Under $50,000	24.4%
Rural:	0.0%	Black	2.5%	$50,000-$99,999:	25.3%
Land area:	304	Two races	3.1%	$100,000-$199,999:	32.8%
Pop/sq. mi.:	2,409.8	White Ethnic	11.4%	$200,000 or more:	17.5%
Born in state:	39.6%			Poverty Rate	7.5%
		Education			
Age Groups		H.S. grad or less:	24.2%	**Work**	
Under 18:	22.2%	Some college:	21.6%	White collar:	57.9%
18 to 34:	24.9%	College degree, 4 yr.:	28.9%	Blue collar:	29.4%
35 to 64:	41.8%	Post-grad study:	25.3%	Sales and service:	12.6%
Over 64:	11.1%			Govt. workers:	7.3%
		Military			
		Veterans/active duty:	4.1%		

South Bay: San Jose suburbs, Central San Jose

A few decades ago, the broad valley of Santa Clara County around San Jose was mostly orchards and vineyards. Sheltered by mountains from the chilly ocean fogs, with soil incredibly fertile once it was irrigated, this valley produced peaches, plums, prunes, apricots, and grapes and made San Jose

Voter Turnout	
2013 Total Citizen 18+	430,628
2014 House Turnout	134,408
2014 Turnout as % CVAP	31.2%
2012 Turnout as % CVAP	56.7%

the nation's biggest fruit-packing center. Today, subdivisions, shopping centers, and office buildings have replaced the orchards, and the population of the county is close to 1.9 million. Its steady growth was stunted by the recession, but the recovery has had a strong bounce back: Real estate prices in Santa Clara County have been soaring. In March 2014, the average sales price for single-family homes climbed over $1,000,000, a 12 percent increase in the past year. The average monthly rental of a one-bedroom apartment exceeded $2,000. Nearby Fremont in Alameda County has experienced economic rejuvenation. A shuttered General Motors/Toyota plant was taken over by Tesla Motors, which has been building high-end electric cars there. With assembly line upgrades, the company planned to produce 100,000 cars in 2015. Fremont could become "the Detroit of the 21st century," gushed the newsletter *California Planning & Development Report*. Fremont is also home to the Little Kabul neighborhood of transplanted Afghans.

The 17th Congressional District consists of the city of Santa Clara and a northern wedge of Santa Clara County, the sixth biggest county in the state, with large numbers of Chinese, Vietnamese, and Mexican immigrants. The district also takes in a part of San Jose, part of Fremont, Newark, Sunnyvale, and Cupertino, where Steve Jobs started Apple in a garage in the 1970s and where the company is still based. Apple is expected to finish construction of its new headquarters in mid-2016, a state-of-the-art building that will house some 13,000 employees. The round building will have hallways that exceed one mile. Technology firms are an important driver of the district's economy. LinkedIn has plans for its new campus in Sunnyvale. And Twitter is moving some of its offices from San Francisco. On the less successful side of the ledger is Solyndra, the Fremont-based solar energy company that

2012 Presidential Vote		
Barack Obama (D) 163,862	(72%)
Mitt Romney (R)..................58,193	(26%)
2008 Presidential Vote		
Barack Obama (D) 169,756	(70%)
John McCain (R)..................68,528	(28%)
Cook Partisan Voting Index: D+20		

famously received economic stimulus money from the Obama administration and then went bankrupt in 2011. SolarCity, a California-based solar power company, has taken over its complex in Fremont.

Both Cupertino and Milpitas are more than 60 percent Asian, and this growing population has become a political force. The 17th District as a whole is almost 51 percent Asian American, by far the largest percentage of any district in California. Politically, it is solidly Democratic, as are its neighboring districts.

Mike Honda (D)

Democrat Mike Honda, first elected in 2000, is as liberal as any House member, but he is not as outspoken or confrontational as many of his like-minded colleagues. Instead of taking high-profile leadership roles, Honda prefers to put together coalitions for causes that might not otherwise get attention. "He really puts the K in 'Kumbaya,'" San Jose State University political scientist Larry Gerston told the *San Jose Mercury News*.

Honda's grandparents came to the United States from Japan's Kumamoto Prefecture, which served as the primary battleground for the Seinan Civil War in the 1870s (memorialized in the film *The Last Samurai*). Honda was born in Walnut Creek and spent 14 months as a youngster in a World War II internment camp in Colorado. In 2011, he recalled his father saying during that time "how the internment was unjust, unconstitutional, and, as a result, we just have to excel in everything we do." His wife, Jeanne, who died of cancer in 2004, was born in Hiroshima and survived the atomic attack before immigrating to the United States several years later. Honda received his bachelor's and master's degrees from San Jose State and served two years in the Peace Corps in El Salvador, where he became fluent in Spanish and gained a passion for teaching.

Honda worked as a science teacher, and was a principal at two area elementary schools from 1978 to 1986. During that period, he also served on the San Jose Unified School Board. He was then elected to the Santa Clara County Board of Supervisors. In 1996, he was elected to the California Assembly, where he worked to reduce classroom sizes and increase teacher benefits.

When Republican Rep. Tom Campbell decided to run against Democratic Sen. Dianne Feinstein, Honda initially was reluctant to run for the seat. But persuasive telephone calls from several leading House Democrats and, finally, from President Bill Clinton changed his mind. Honda won the primary over Bill Peacock, a venture capitalist, 67%-24%. His Republican opponent was Assemblyman Jim Cunneen, a Campbell protégé who was strongly supported by national GOP leaders and many Silicon Valley capitalists. Cunneen had liberal positions on cultural issues, and he tried to depict the contest as a referendum on the old economy versus the new. Honda, despite his close ties to unions, supported normal trade relations with China, a position strongly backed by the high-tech industry. He won 54%-42%, and has mostly coasted to reelection, with the steady disappearance of Republicans from the area.

Honda is among the most liberal House members, according to *National Journal's* rankings. As budget task force chairman of the Congressional Progressive Caucus, he offered an alternative spending plan in March 2012 calling for $2.4 trillion in job-creating projects; it was defeated 78-346. He has chaired the Congressional Asian Pacific American Caucus, which advocates for underrepresented groups on issues such as immigration. He helped to enact a cyber-security law that funds training and programs to protect computer data and networks. In 2007, with help from new House Speaker Nancy Pelosi, he got a seat on the powerful Appropriations Committee. He has focused on trying to win full funding for education programs, many of which are financed at levels well below the authorizing legislation.

An important cause for Honda is eliciting apologies for past abuses from Japan, and he has publicized the cause of American POWs in World War II who were transported on "hell ships" to work as slave laborers in Japan. In 2007, Honda won House passage of a resolution calling on Tokyo to apologize for forcing as many as 200,000 women into sexual slavery during the war. His efforts have generated controversy in Japan, and *The New York Times* referred to Honda as "one of the most famous American congressmen in his ancestral land." In February 2011, he joined the call for an official U.S. apology for the Chinese Exclusion Act of 1882, which suspended Chinese immigration and made Chinese in the United States ineligible for citizenship; the House passed the resolution the following year.

Another of Honda's passions is addressing low voter turnout in national elections, which he calls a "serious illness." In the 2012 election, he helped make the argument that Asian-Americans should reelect President Barack Obama. "I think his style is very Asian-American, thoughtful; he doesn't make snap decisions," Honda said. He also sought to persuade the technology industry to give the president another term. In the new 17th District in 2012, Honda was reelected with 74 percent of the vote.

In 2014, Honda faced a very competitive contest with Ro Khanna, a former Obama administration official, who earlier had set his eyes on the district held by veteran Democratic Rep. Pete Stark. But he was overtaken by Eric Stallwell, who unexpectedly ousted Stark in 2012 in the neighboring 15th District. In California's new election regime, the top two in the primary compete in the general election. In this strongly Democratic district, Honda and Khanna aptly expected that they would face off in November. But the 48%-28% advantage for Honda in June was unexpectedly large. Republican candidates took the remaining votes. Honda was endorsed by major Democratic leaders, including Obama and Pelosi. Khanna had some endorsements from local technology leaders. The views of the two candidates were similar, though Rhanna styled himself as more tech-friendly and half Honda's age. An intellectual-property lawyer and an economics lecturer at Stanford University, he had avid backing from the Indian community. "There's nothing wrong with Congressman Honda personally," Khanna told *The New Yorker*. "But there is something static about the political system, and I think the Valley gets that."

The November contest was much closer than the primary, with Honda prevailing 51.8%-48.2%. Khanna outspent Honda $4.4 million to $3.4 million, but learned the difficulty of ousting a generally popular incumbent. Honda said that he expected to serve more than one additional term. He spoke out to the high-tech community a month later with a column in *The Hill*, a Capitol Hill newspaper. Joining the criticism of employment practices in Silicon Valley, he wrote, "Imagine how much more could be done if women were full participants in the process."

EIGHTEENTH DISTRICT

Anna Eshoo (D)

Elected 1992, 12th term; b. Dec. 13, 1942, New Britain, CT; Canada Col., A.A. 1975; Catholic; divorced; 2 children.

Elected Office: San Mateo Cnty. Bd. of Supervisors, 1983-92, pres., 1986.

Professional Career: San Mateo Cnty. Dem. Party, 1980-92; Speaker pro tempore, CA assembly speaker, 1981-82.

DC Office: 241 CHOB, 20515, 202-225-8104; Fax: 202-225-8890; Website: eshoo.house.gov.

State Offices: Palo Alto, 650-323-2984, 408-245-2339, or 831-335-2020.

Committees: *Energy & Commerce:* Communications & Technology (RMM).

Group Ratings

	ADA	ACLU	AFL-CIO	LCV	ITI	COC	HAFA	ACU	CFG	FRC
2014	85%	83%	–	97%	60%	38%	10%	8%	14%	0%
2013	90%	C	95%	96%	C	31%	C	8%	12%	C

National Journal Ratings

	2013 LIB	—	2013 CONS
Economic	91%	—	0%
Social	79%	—	16%
Foreign	81%	—	18%
Composite	86%	—	14%

Key Votes of the 113th Congress

1. Sandy storm spending	Y	5. Medical Marijuana	Y	9. Syrian Rebels Training	N
2. Violence Against Women Act	Y	6. Farm Bill	N	10. Keystone pipeline	N
3. Guantanamo Bay Detainees	Y	7. Afghanistan Combat	Y	11. Immigration Exec. Action	N
4. Abortion 20-week ban	N	8. NSA Phone Data Collection	Y	12. Bipartisan budget deal	Y

Election Results

2014 general	Anna Eshoo (D).....................133,060	(68%)	$1,540,093	$7,311	
	Richard Fox (R)......................63,326	(32%)	$41,249	$82,674	
2014 primary	Anna Eshoo (D)......................81,295	(68%)			
	Richard Fox (R)......................27,111	(23%)			
	Bruce Anderson (R) 9,644	(8%)			

Prior winning percentages: 2012 (70%), 2010 (69%), 2008 (70%), 2006 (71%), 2004 (70%), 2002 (68%), 2000 (70%), 1998 (69%), 1996 (65%), 1994 (61%), 1992 (57%)

Population		Race and Ethnicity		Income	
Total:	731,201	White	57.6%	Median income:	$105,817
Urban:	65.2%	Asian	19.8%		(2 of 435)
Suburban:	34.1%	Latino	16.6%	Under $50,000	23.7%
Rural:	0.7%	Black	1.8%	$50,000-$99,999:	23.6%
Land area:	640	Two races	3.6%	$100,000-$199,999:	28.0%
Pop/sq. mi.:	1,141.7	White Ethnic	26.5%	$200,000 or more:	24.7%
Born in state:	48.2%			Poverty Rate	7.3%
		Education			
Age Groups		H.S. grad or less:	17.7%	**Work**	
Under 18:	22.8%	Some college:	22.3%	White collar:	59.3%
18 to 34:	20.1%	College degree, 4 yr.:	29.9%	Blue collar:	31.3%
35 to 64:	43.2%	Post-grad study:	30.1%	Sales and service:	9.4%
Over 64:	13.9%			Govt. workers:	9.6%
		Military			
		Veterans/active duty:	5.7%		

Silicon Valley: Western San Jose, Palo Alto

Silicon Valley is a place and a state of mind, an area that had no distinctive identity four decades ago but that people all over the world today recognize and imitate. In the 1980s and 1990s, Silicon Valley emerged as the center of America's computer industry, a place where creative minds developed

Voter Turnout	
2013 Total Citizen 18+	480,792
2014 House Turnout	196,386
2014 Turnout as % CVAP	40.8%
2012 Turnout as % CVAP	67.3%

products that large corporations never thought would sell. Its beginnings can be traced back to 1939, when William Hewlett and David Packard started their electronics firm in a Palo Alto garage, or perhaps even to 1891, when Stanford University was founded on the estate of a California governor and senator. Not every aspect of the computer business is centered here: Microsoft, routinely disparaged in every Palo Alto espresso shop and bar, is in Redmond Washington, and the downsized IBM is in Armonk New York. But Silicon Valley is where most of the giants and much of the creativity of the high-tech business—as well as many dot-coms—have been based, and where they continue to grow and generate extraordinary wealth.

How did Silicon Valley come to be where it is? One factor is Stanford, the students it attracts and produces, and its tradition of encouraging faculty members to pursue profit-making activity. Another key component is venture capital, widely available from innovation-minded old San Francisco money. A third ingredient is the presence of smart young innovators, attracted to the Valley's lifestyle. Elite law and medical school graduates head to the prestigious, high-salary jobs of central cities. But techies are free to live in this pleasant, healthy environment. Sheltered by hills from coastal fogs and rains, Silicon Valley boasts a sunny climate with perceptible but gentle seasons, perfect for year-round outdoor sports. These communities were rustic but never poor, rural but not small-minded, country-like but still easily accessible to urban luxuries. People here were ahead of the rest of the nation in fighting for the environment, in favoring natural over processed foods, and in incorporating regular exercise into busy lives.

The area has been quick to adapt to change. In the 1980s, in the face of threats from Japanese firms, Silicon Valley shifted to microprocessors and personal computers. In the 1990s, when PCs became a low-profit commodity business, Silicon Valley shifted to the Internet. Yahoo and Hotmail reportedly were conceived at Buck's restaurant, the networking nexus in Woodside. When the Internet bubble burst in 2000, Silicon Valley fell on hard times. By one estimate, the area lost 220,000 jobs, nearly two-thirds of the 350,000 created during the dot-com boom. Stock prices plummeted and real estate prices did too. Billions of dollars in paper wealth disappeared, and technology exports from California fell. In 2010, unemployment in the San Jose-Sunnyvale-Santa Clara region was above 11 percent. The question became whether Silicon Valley still had the ability to adapt. Recent signs point to a strong revival. In 2014, the Valley gained 58,000 jobs and 42,000 new residents, according to the Silicon Valley Index. Housing prices have roared back and are again among the highest in the nation, and there has been an accompanying surge in apartment construction. Innovation and investment opportunities have accelerated. In Menlo Park, where Facebook began work on its third local campus, voters rejected in November 2014 a referendum that would have capped local growth.

The 18th Congressional District of California includes large portions of Silicon Valley, along with Palo Alto and Stanford University. It includes a slice of San Jose and a slice of Menlo Park. Further south along El Camino Real are Mountain View and the 20,000 employees of Google, with ambitious plans for further expansion. There are some ultra-wealthy enclaves here: Woodside, with its mansions in the hills, and Los Altos Hills, with its stark contemporary homes overlooking San Francisco Bay. The district also takes in small San Jose-area cities such as Campbell, Los Gatos, and the increasingly Asian Saratoga. To the west is a long stretch of hills and wilderness areas, and Route 1 that overlooks the Pacific Ocean en route to Santa Cruz.

The area's political heritage is progressive, with a sort of environmentalist, dovish, culturally liberal but entrepreneurial Republicanism, typified until the 1990s by former Reps. Pete McCloskey and Tom Campbell. But that brand of Republican has become virtually extinct here, as in most of the nation.

2012 Presidential Vote		
Barack Obama (D)	218,082	(68%)
Mitt Romney (R)	92,457	(29%)

2008 Presidential Vote		
Barack Obama (D)	238,285	(71%)
John McCain (R)	92,539	(27%)

Cook Partisan Voting Index: D+18

Silicon Valley and the 18th District today are firmly Democratic.

Anna Eshoo (D)

Democrat Anna Eshoo, first elected in 1992, has much in common with her close friend Nancy Pelosi: Both are around the same age, Roman Catholic, wealthy East Coast transplants, and prodigious fundraisers for their party. Eshoo has had impressive accomplishments on a range of issues on the powerful Energy and Commerce Committee. But few, if any, House members could match the relentless pace and achievements of Pelosi.

Born in Connecticut, Eshoo is the only member of Congress of Assyrian descent. Her father, a jeweler and an FDR Democrat, sparked her interest in politics at a young age by taking her to political rallies. As a youngster, her mother briefly lived in Baghdad. The family moved to California. Eshoo married, had two children, and for a while was a stay-at-home mother working on a degree in English literature. (She later divorced.) Eshoo was active in civic groups, then chaired the San Mateo County Democratic Party and in 1982 was elected to the San Mateo Board of Supervisors. In 1988, she ran for the House against Republican Rep. Tom Campbell. The two spent a total of $2.5 million, which was big bucks in those days. Campbell won 52%-46%. In 1992, Campbell gave up his seat to run for the Senate, and Eshoo again ran. In the primary, she beat Assemblyman Ted Lempert, who had strong backing from environmentalists but lost ground by making unsubstantiated attacks against Eshoo. She prevailed 40%-36%. In what was still a swing district, Eshoo had a tough contest in November against Republican Tom Huening, the San Mateo supervisor who was backed by David Packard and other Silicon Valley business leaders. Eshoo won by a convincing 57%-39%. She has not had a serious challenge for reelection.

In the House, Eshoo's voting record has been mostly liberal, with more-moderate inclinations on issues such as taxes that affect high-income earners in her district. She has joined Republicans and high-tech interests in votes on securities litigation and normalizing trade relations with China. Eshoo also fought telecommunications legislation that would have allowed Internet carriers to have a two-tier pricing system, contending that it would put start-up firms at a disadvantage.

As a senior member of the Energy and Commerce Committee, Eshoo in 2011 defeated Illinois' Bobby Rush to take over the senior Democrat post on the panel's Subcommittee on Communications and Technology—a panel with obvious importance to her district. She has been a strong supporter of net neutrality, the concept that broadband providers should be prohibited from blocking certain traffic or setting up tiered pathways for Internet content. In February 2015, she praised the Federal Communications Commission for adopting net neutrality rules. "This is an epic battle between David and Goliath, and David won this round," Eshoo said. She has long argued in favor of ensuring that the FCC provides an adequate supply of spectrum that any company can use for free.

Eshoo has been active on health technology issues, and in 2009 prevailed over committee Chairman Henry Waxman in winning passage of a measure allowing makers of "biologic" drugs up to 12 years of protection from competition from the generic drug industry. In 2011, she enacted a bill to reduce the volume of television commercials. Other achievements include bills to increase Internet access for schools, to allow the use of electronic signatures in business transactions, and to require insurance companies to pay for reconstructive surgery for cancer patients.

Pelosi has had a close relationship with most House Democrats from the Bay Area. Those friendships have been especially strong on the Peninsula heading south from San Francisco and past San Jose, where the five Democratic members are stout Pelosi loyalists and defenders. Like her, those five have long seniority; their average age turned 70 in early 2015. Eshoo is the closest friend of Pelosi in the House. Confidants since they met at a Democratic event in the Bay Area in the early 1970s. Eshoo officiated at the marriage ceremony of Pelosi's daughter, Christine, in 2008. When the House passed the health care overhaul in 2010, Eshoo lauded her friend's political will in her dealings with Obama and Senate Majority Leader Harry Reid. "I think (Pelosi) is the one who has kept the steel in the president's back—and I think she represents that to Harry Reid too," Eshoo told *Politico*.

Following the 2014 election, Pelosi sought to return the favor when Eshoo moved to replace Waxman as the ranking Democrat on Energy and Commerce. But that proved to be a step too far. Eshoo was stymied by several factors: Rep. Frank Pallone of New Jersey had more seniority, and he emphasized that point. The secret vote became an opportunity for some Democrats to express unhappiness with Pelosi and their deepening minority status in the House. Plus, Pelosi and her allies stirred resentment with heavy-handed tactics to prevent Iraqi war veteran and double-amputee Rep. Tammy Duckworth from voting by proxy on the Pallone-Eshoo contest during her final weeks of pregnancy.

As other senior Democrats in Washington depart their positions after the 2016 election, it might not be long before the two Bay Area friends take their final working trip home.

NINETEENTH DISTRICT

Zoe Lofgren (D)

Elected 1994, 11th term; b. Dec. 21, 1947, San Mateo; Stanford U., B.A. 1970, U. of Santa Clara Schl. of Law, J.D. 1975; Protestant; married (John Marshall Collins); 2 children.

Elected Office: Santa Clara Bd. of Supervisors, 1980-94.

Professional Career: Staff asst., U.S. Rep. Don Edwards, 1970-78; Practicing atty., 1978-80; Prof., U. of Santa Clara Schl. of Law, 1977-80.

DC Office: 1401 LHOB, 20515, 202-225-3072; Website: lofgren.house. gov.

State Offices: San Jose, 408-271-8700.

Committees: *House Administration. Judiciary:* Courts, Intellectual Property & the Internet; Immigration & Border Security (RMM). *Science, Space, & Technology:* Oversight; Space. *Joint Committee on the Library.*

Group Ratings

	ADA	ACLU	AFL-CIO	LCV	ITI	COC	HAFA	ACU	CFG	FRC
2014	95%	88%	–	97%	60%	43%	10%	8%	11%	0%
2013	95%	C	90%	93%	C	31%	C	12%	13%	C

National Journal Ratings

	2013 LIB	—	2013 CONS
Economic	74%	—	26%
Social	79%	—	16%
Foreign	78%	—	21%
Composite	78%	—	22%

Key Votes of the 113th Congress

1. Sandy storm spending	Y	5. Medical Marijuana	Y	9. Syrian Rebels Training	N
2. Violence Against Women Act	Y	6. Farm Bill	N	10. Keystone pipeline	N
3. Guantanamo Bay Detainees	Y	7. Afghanistan Combat	Y	11. Immigration Exec. Action	N
4. Abortion 20-week ban	N	8. NSA Phone Data Collection	Y	12. Bipartisan budget deal	Y

Election Results

2014 general	Zoe Lofgren (D)	85,888	(67%)	$682,507	$3,142
	Robert Murray (D)	41,900	(33%)		
2014 primary	Zoe Lofgren (D)	63,845	(76%)		
	Robert Murray (D)	20,132	(24%)		

Prior winning percentages: 2012 (67%), 2010 (68%), 2008 (71%), 2006 (73%), 2004 (71%), 2002 (67%), 2000 (72%), 1998 (73%), 1996 (66%), 1994 (65%)

Population		Race and Ethnicity		Income	
Total:	746,071	Latino	41.3%	Median income:	$78,169
Urban:	81.4%	White	27.1%		(35 of 435)
Suburban:	18.0%	Asian	25.4%	Under $50,000	33.4%
Rural:	0.6%	Black	2.8%	$50,000-$99,999:	27.0%
Land area:	999	Two races	2.6%	$100,000-$199,999:	27.8%
Pop/sq. mi.:	746.8	White Ethnic	14.4%	$200,000 or more:	11.9%
Born in state:	49.8%			Poverty Rate	14.4%
		Education			
Age Groups		H.S. grad or less:	41.0%	**Work**	
Under 18:	24.6%	Some college:	28.1%	White collar:	37.2%
18 to 34:	24.8%	College degree, 4 yr.:	19.8%	Blue collar:	41.1%
35 to 64:	39.5%	Post-grad study:	11.2%	Sales and service:	21.7%
Over 64:	11.1%			Govt. workers:	10.2%
		Military			
		Veterans/active duty:	3.9%		

South Bay: Southern San Jose

With more people than San Francisco, a tradition of high-tech innovation, and a professional sports team, San Jose finally has claims on national attention and respect. Yet San Jose does not register on the national consciousness as it should. At the southern end of the Bay, it remains in the shadow of

Voter Turnout	
2013 Total Citizen 18+	445,153
2014 House Turnout	127,788
2014 Turnout as % CVAP	28.7%
2012 Turnout as % CVAP	53.6%

the city on the Golden Gate. San Francisco is every tourist's idea of a city: geographically compact, with picturesque housing; old and new immigrant groups; an economy historically based on heavy industry and sea trade; a large city bureaucracy; and a monumental City Hall. San Jose is quite different. It got its start as a farm-market town, with canneries and fruit-packing operations for the produce from the surrounding fertile plains. Farm labor icon Cesar Chavez settled with his family in the East San Jose barrio of Sal Si Puedes ("Get out if you can"). San Jose sits not on the Bay but on the Southern Pacific rail line above the marshes and salt evaporators. Its major transportation arteries are the freeways—U.S. 101, Interstates 280, 680, and 880, California 87—that encircle its revitalized downtown plus the larger Bay Area.

Starting in the 1950s, San Jose grew in every direction, with developers hopscotching across the farmland and at times putting up subdivisions faster than the few city employees could update the street maps. It now has a popular National Hockey League team, the San Jose Sharks. Its population passed 1 million in 2014, not far below San Francisco and Oakland combined. Economically, San Jose has been sustained by everything from its traditional agriculture to manufacturing to the high-tech businesses that are centered in Silicon Valley towns just to the west and north, and are omnipresent here: an American city, 21st-century style. In 2014, Santa Clara County had the highest median household income in the nation. The growth rate of the San Jose metro area economy ranked second in the nation to Houston a year earlier.

For many years, San Jose has been a focal point for immigration issues. It has Northern California's largest Mexican-American community, many of them farmworkers. Recent years have brought a diverse and substantial presence from Latin America and East and South Asia. Half of all Santa Clara County residents speak a language other than English at home, mostly Spanish, Vietnamese, or Chinese, and one in three is foreign born. Despite increased crime rates in recent years and a sizable cut in the city's budget, including for police, voters have endorsed most municipal leaders. Sam Liccardo, who had defended the cuts, took office as mayor in January 2015.

2012 Presidential Vote		
Barack Obama (D)	165,530	(71%)
Mitt Romney (R)	61,643	(27%)
2008 Presidential Vote		
Barack Obama (D)	158,588	(69%)
John McCain (R)	67,461	(29%)
Cook Partisan Voting Index:	D+19	

The 19th Congressional District of California consists of substantial portions of San Jose, including much of the city's downtown area and the neighborhoods of Alum Rock and East Foothills. The district takes in eastern and southern parts of Santa Clara County, including Morgan Hill, a traditional farming town that has branched into high tech. Near the southern edge of the district is Gilroy, which is 58 percent Hispanic, the garlic capital of the world and the home of the huge annual garlic festival. Politically, the district is solidly Democratic.

Zoe Lofgren (D)

The congresswoman from the 19th District is Zoe Lofgren, a Democrat first elected in 1994. She has been an active legislator on multiple issues, and perhaps the savviest defender of high technology's interests in the House.

Lofgren grew up in the Bay Area, where her father was a Teamsters truck driver and her mother worked for the Machinists Union. She graduated from Stanford University, and then moved to Washington to work for Democratic Rep. Don Edwards while he was a leader on the Judiciary Committee that voted to impeach President Richard Nixon. She stayed on for eight years as an aide to Edwards. She met her husband, a lawyer, one Election Night. Lofgren returned to California to get a law degree, and then specialized in immigration law. In 1980, she was elected to the Santa Clara County Board of Supervisors. When Edwards retired, Lofgren ran for his House seat. Her chief Democratic opponent, former San Jose Mayor Tom McEnery, was better known. But Lofgren raised twice as much money, with support from national women's organizations and women in the California delegation. She gained considerable recognition after she insisted on listing herself as a county supervisor/mother on the ballot. Election officials refused, and the national press covered the ensuing controversy. Lofgren won the primary 45%-42% and easily took the general election.

Lofgren's voting record, while mostly liberal, includes bipartisan free-market positions that often are responsive to local businesses and law enforcement. Working with Republicans, she won expanded allotments of visas for high-tech workers. She pushed for looser controls on encryption exports, securities litigation limitations, and relaxation of trade restraints on supercomputers, all big Silicon Valley causes. When the House split 210-210 on a proposal to restrict government access to library records, Lofgren was the only House member to vote "present." She said the amendment went too far in preventing legitimate law enforcement searches. In 2013, she introduced "Aaron's Law," in memory of Aaron Swartz, a young Harvard University professor and Internet entrepreneur who committed suicide after challenging book copyright rules and became the target of what Lofgren said were "disproportionate charges" by the Justice Department. Her proposal failed to get a House vote. With Republican Rep. Ted Poe of Texas, she filed a bill in February 2015 to prevent privacy intrusions by drones and other unmanned aircraft.

When Democrats won the majority in 2006, Lofgren, a trusted lieutenant of House Speaker Nancy Pelosi, became chairwoman of the Judiciary Subcommittee on Immigration and related issues. She hoped for a major overhaul of immigration policy, but the politically charged issue bogged down. When Republicans regained control of the House, Lofgren was an outspoken supporter of a bill that would change the visa system to allow more highly skilled immigrants from China and India to become permanent legal residents. In November 2011, the bill passed the House easily, with Lofgren joining forces with Judiciary Committee Chairman Lamar Smith of Texas. On another immigration-related measure, Lofgren was the chief sponsor of a bill to allow overseas military personnel and their spouses more time to file for permanent resident status through marriage. The bill was signed into law in 2011. With Republican Rep. Robert Goodlatte of Virginia, the Judiciary Committee chairman, she criticized in March 2015 the backlog of "green card" visa applications for talented foreign workers.

Lofgren emerged as one of the leading opponents of the controversial Stop Online Piracy Act, an intellectual property enforcement measure favored by movie studios and the recording industry but opposed by some of her Silicon Valley interests. It would give larger sites the power to kill rogue or upstart websites believed to be engaged in theft or copyright infringement. In October 2011, Lofgren told the tech media site *CNET* that the bill would signal "the end of the Internet as we know it." Google and Wikipedia helped push the debate by sponsoring an "Internet Black Out" day on Jan. 18, 2012. Later in the week, Smith, a bill sponsor, officially withdrew it.

In 2009, Lofgren took over as chairman of the House Ethics Committee just as it launched a politically sensitive inquiry of House Ways and Means Chairman Charles Rangel of New York, and questions were being raised about the connections of other senior Democrats to lobbyists. Lofgren's skills as a former staffer and law professor were tested by the politically combustible cases. She revealed in testimony before the House Administration Committee in early 2010 that at least 36 lawmakers—around 8 percent of the House—had been subjected to scrutiny for their dealings with special interests the previous year. Many were associated with the PMA Group lobbying firm, a group accused of exchanging campaign contributions for earmarks. She announced in February 2009 that she would return $7,000 in contributions from the firm. Her panel subsequently found that no House members colluded with the group.

Of the lawmakers under investigation, none proved more difficult than Rangel. She hoped to avoid a drawn-out and embarrassing ethics trial, but the defiant and crafty political veteran was unwilling to bargain. The case dragged on for months. Finally, just after the election, Rangel was afforded a trial but walked out in protest after complaining that he hadn't been granted enough time to hire a new attorney. Lofgren and the rest of the panel refused to back down, and a few days later voted 9-1 to censure him—a decision Lofgren called "quite wrenching."

In 2003, Lofgren tried to get a foothold in leadership by running for vice chair of the Democratic Caucus. But Pelosi, who is also from the Bay Area, had just been elected minority leader, and the Congressional Black Caucus pressed for one of its members to join the leadership. Lofgren got 53 votes to 95 for James Clyburn, an African American from South Carolina, who won the post. Lofgren has had no trouble winning reelection every two years.

TWENTIETH DISTRICT

Sam Farr (D)

Elected June 1993, 11th full term; b. July 4, 1941, San Francisco; Willamette U., B.S. 1963; Episcopalian; married (Shary); 1 child.

Elected Office: Monterey Cnty. Bd. of Supervisors, 1975-80, chmn. 1979; CA Assembly, 1980-93.

Professional Career: U.S. Peace Corps, Colombia, 1963-65; Staff, CA Assembly, 1965-75.

DC Office: 1126 LHOB, 20515, 202-225-2861; Fax: 202-225-6791; Website: farr.house.gov.

State Offices: Salinas, 831-424-2229; Santa Cruz, 831-429-1976.

Committees: *Appropriations:* Agriculture, Rural Development, FDA, & Related Agencies (RMM); Legislative Branch; Military Construction, Veteran Affairs, & Related Agencies.

Group Ratings

	ADA	ACLU	AFL-CIO	LCV	ITI	COC	HAFA	ACU	CFG	FRC
2014	80%	83%	–	91%	60%	62%	2%	4%	0%	0%
2013	100%	C	95%	86%	C	31%	C	4%	3%	C

National Journal Ratings

	2013 LIB	—	2013 CONS
Economic	91%	—	0%
Social	93%	—	0%
Foreign	94%	—	0%
Composite	96%	—	4%

Key Votes of the 113th Congress

1. Sandy storm spending	Y	5. Medical Marijuana	Y	9. Syrian Rebels Training	N
2. Violence Against Women Act	Y	6. Farm Bill	Y	10. Keystone pipeline	N
3. Guantanamo Bay Detainees	Y	7. Afghanistan Combat	Y	11. Immigration Exec. Action	N
4. Abortion 20-week ban	N	8. NSA Phone Data Collection	Y	12. Bipartisan budget deal	Y

Election Results

2014 general	Sam Farr (D)......................106,034	(75%)	$747,789	$1,656
	Ronald Paul Kabat (I) 35,010	(25%)	$15,488	
2014 primary	Sam Farr (D)................................67,528	(74%)		
	Ronald Paul Kabat (I) 23,950	(26%)		

Prior winning percentages: 2012 (74%), 2010 (67%), 2008 (74%), 2006 (76%), 2004 (67%), 2002 (68%), 2000 (69%), 1998 (65%), 1996 (59%), 1994 (52%), 1993 special (52%)

Population		Race and Ethnicity		Income	
Total:	725,199	Latino	51.5%	Median income:	$59,131
Urban:	51.1%	White	38.4%		(135 of 435)
Suburban:	32.6%	Asian	5.2%	Under $50,000	43.5%
Rural:	16.3%	Black	2.2%	$50,000-$99,999:	29.8%
Land area:	5,919	Two races	2.0%	$100,000-$199,999:	21.2%
Pop/sq. mi.:	122.5	White Ethnic	18.1%	$200,000 or more:	5.5%
Born in state:	57.8%			Poverty Rate	17.5%
		Education			
Age Groups		H.S. grad or less:	44.0%	**Work**	
Under 18:	25.4%	Some college:	30.2%	White collar:	30.9%
18 to 34:	26.6%	College degree, 4 yr.:	15.6%	Blue collar:	41.9%
35 to 64:	36.4%	Post-grad study:	10.3%	Sales and service:	27.3%
Over 64:	11.5%			Govt. workers:	15.2%
		Military			
		Veterans/active duty:	6.9%		

Central Coast: Monterey, Southern Santa Cruz

The California coast around Monterey Bay is for many a working definition of paradise. This kernel of California, site of the first state capital, still makes a fine living off the land and sea, as it has for 150 years. The inspiration for *The Grapes of Wrath* and many other John Steinbeck novels, the

Voter Turnout	
2013 Total Citizen 18+	422,281
2014 House Turnout	141,044
2014 Turnout as % CVAP	33.4%
2012 Turnout as % CVAP	57.3%

fields around Salinas provide much of the nation's lettuce and cauliflower. The area is often referred to as "the salad bowl of the world." Nearby, the farmlands around Castroville supply the country with its artichokes, and the vast greenhouses around Watsonville have been a popular supplier of roses. The fishing fleet and the 18 now-closed canneries of Monterey (the last sardines were canned in 1964) have generated a new industry. Once described by Steinbeck as "a poem, a stink, a grating noise, a quality of light, a tone, a habit, nostalgia, a dream," Cannery Row now is refurbished with upscale shops and hotels. The magnificent Monterey Bay Aquarium is one of California's top tourist destinations, and the National Marine Sanctuary holds more than 400 shipwrecks and ditched aircraft.

The Monterey Bay area calls itself the world's language-learning capital, with the Defense Language Institute, Language Line Services, and Cal State Monterey Bay's School of World Languages and Cultures. This area was also a magnet for the 1960s counterculture. The three-day Monterey Pop Festival in 1967 became the stuff of rock 'n' roll legend. Both The Who and Jimi Hendrix wanted to perform first. The Who won the deciding coin toss, and band members subsequently destroyed much of the stage after their set. Not to be outdone, Hendrix, during his performance, set his guitar on fire.

Perhaps the main attraction of the Monterey peninsula is the lush 17-Mile Drive along the Pacific Coast Highway, with Pebble Beach's golf courses, the Del Monte Lodge, and Carmel, whose restrictive laws—no house numbers, no door-to-door mail delivery, no stoplights, no wearing of high-heeled shoes without permits—reflect an effort to maintain the atmosphere of nearly a century ago, when it was an artists' colony. Monterey has suffered its own affordability gap. In 2014, only 27 percent of homes were affordable to residents with the median household income of $91,000, half the ratio of three years earlier. These days, the top-flight buyers include many investors from China, many of whom initially spent time in the area for language training. In February 2015, the county board approved the private development of a large solar farm, from which Apple Computer announced an $850 million agreement to purchase power.

The 20th Congressional District of California includes the entire coast of Monterey Bay and follows the stunning Big Sur coastline south along the steep slopes, taking in some of the most beautiful scenery in America. To the north along Monterey Bay, it runs past Watsonville to Santa Cruz. The district extends inland, into sunny valleys sheltered from ocean mists, and covers some of the nation's richest farmland. Most of the farmworkers are Latino, mainly Mexican. All of Monterey and San Benito counties are located here, and the district takes in portions of Santa Clara and Santa Cruz counties. About half of the population is in Monterey. Santa Cruz imposed strict water-rationing laws because of the drought.

The gap between rich and poor in Monterey County is wide. It has thousands of homes valued at more than $1 million but also usually ranks high in the share of households below the poverty line. Forty years ago, this was a solidly Republican area, dominated politically by the landowners in Salinas and the townspeople who sympathized with them, plus retirees in Santa Cruz and on the Monterey peninsula. But an influx of young people, attracted less by the economy than by the atmosphere, moved the coast to the left. Leon Panetta, whose career started as a Republican political aide and ended as a top official with two Democratic presidents, held this seat for 16 years; he now runs his family's large walnut farm in Carmel Valley. Monterey and Santa Cruz counties have become steadily more

2012 Presidential Vote		
Barack Obama (D)	168,956	(71%)
Mitt Romney (R)	62,427	(26%)
2008 Presidential Vote		
Barack Obama (D)	181,058	(72%)
John McCain (R)	64,803	(26%)
Cook Partisan Voting Index: D+21		

Democratic than the nation. In the 2012 presidential race, President Barack Obama got 75% of the vote from Santa Cruz and 67% from Monterey. This district is 51% Hispanic and is solidly Democratic.

Sam Farr (D)

Sam Farr, a Democrat first elected in June 1993, is an ardent liberal and a man of the sea. His chief responsibility in the House has been very much land-based: helping to write the annual farm spending bill.

A fifth-generation Californian, he grew up in Monterey County, where his father was a state senator for many years. Farr signed up for the Peace Corps after college, learned Spanish at the Monterey Institute of International Studies, and served two years in Colombia. He was a California Assembly staff member for a decade, became a Monterey County supervisor in 1975, and was elected to the Assembly in 1980. There, he wrote one of the nation's strictest oil spill liability laws. In 1993, when Democratic Rep. Leon Panetta resigned from the House to become director of the Office of Management and Budget, Farr ran for his seat. He entered the race as the overwhelming favorite, and won 26 percent of the vote in the all-party primary to defeat two other Democrats. But in the runoff, which came after President Bill Clinton's budget and tax increase had arrived in Congress, he struggled against Republican Bill McCampbell, whom Panetta had defeated 72%-24% seven months earlier. In an early warning of the political perils that Democrats faced a year later, Farr won, but by just 52%-43%.

In the House, Farr has a solidly liberal voting record. He is a close ally of Democratic Leader Nancy Pelosi and a longtime advocate of normalizing relations with Cuba; in 2009, he sent Obama a letter signed by 46 House members outlining a 10-step process for doing so. On the Appropriations Committee, Farr guards against Republican attempts to cut the National Oceanic and Atmospheric Administration's budget. In 2006, Farr helped to write the law revising rules for offshore fisheries, and in 2009, the House passed his bill to encourage a research and recovery program for endangered sea otters. The Obama administration issued an executive order in 2009 implementing a national ocean policy, and Farr urged lawmakers to pass legislation so that a future president couldn't overturn it. But he lamented the GOP's hostility to what has remained chiefly an idea. "Led by tea party conservatives, Republicans in Congress have launched a war on our oceans," he said in July 2012.

Farr looks out for his area's agricultural and tourism industries. He is the ranking Democrat on the House Appropriations subcommittee that handles the budget for the Department of Agriculture. This is especially useful, he notes, because his district's fertile coastal region grows more crops than any other state in the nation. He also focuses on rural development, especially to assure an adequate supply of housing for farmworkers. In May 2014, he lost a party-line vote on his attempt to defeat an amendment that allowed schools to defer the nutrition standards advocated by Michelle Obama. After the local spinach crop was affected by an E. coli outbreak in 2006, Farr pushed for $25 million to aid producers. Critics later stripped it from the bill. "It's easy to make fun of spinach," Farr said in defense of the subsidy. "But if we had eaten more of it, we would be a stronger society." He has called for more fruits and vegetables in school breakfasts and lunches. The omnibus spending bill that Congress approved after the 2014 election included an amendment that he prepared with Republican Dana Rohrabacher of California to prevent the Justice Department from targeting marijuana patients or providers in states that permit medical marijuana.

Congress passed in 2012 his bill to upgrade Pinnacles National Monument into a national park near Soledad, and he often talks up the need to control urban sprawl to protect tourism in Monterey County. "I tell people we sell scenery. Our job in the political world is to make sure that scenery is there," he told a local audience.

Farr has not been afraid to pursue his liberal views against prominent targets. In 2007, he co-sponsored a resolution calling for the impeachment of Vice President Dick Cheney, and in 2011 was among the Democratic lawmakers taking part in a "hunger fast" to protest what they said were proposed GOP budget cuts that would affect those living in poverty in the U.S. and abroad. Farr has been reelected easily. James Panetta, a Monterey County prosecutor and son of the former local Congressman, has publicly voiced interest in running for the seat when Farr retires.

TWENTY-FIRST DISTRICT

David Valadao (R)

Elected 2012, 2nd term; b. April 14, 1977, Hanford; Col. of the Sequoias, attended 1996-98; Catholic; married (Terra); 3 children.

Elected Office: CA Assembly, 2010-12.

Professional Career: Partner, Valadao Dairy and Triple V Dairy, 1992-present.

DC Office: 1004 LHOB, 20515, 202-225-4695; Website: valadao.house. gov.

State Offices: Bakersfield, 661-864-7736; Hanford, 559-582-5526.

Committees: *Appropriations:* Agriculture, Rural Development, FDA, & Related Agencies (VChmn); Energy & Water Development, & Related Agencies; Military Construction, Veteran Affairs, & Related Agencies.

Group Ratings

	ADA	ACLU	AFL-CIO	LCV	ITI	COC	HAFA	ACU	CFG	FRC
2014	10%	22%	–	3%	100%	100%	32%	44%	29%	88%
2013	5%	C	33%	0%	C	85%	C	56%	46%	C

National Journal Ratings

	2013 LIB	—	2013 CONS
Economic	46%	—	54%
Social	50%	—	49%
Foreign	34%	—	60%
Composite	45%	—	56%

Key Votes of the 113th Congress

1. Sandy storm spending	Y	5. Medical Marijuana	Y	9. Syrian Rebels Training	Y
2. Violence Against Women Act	Y	6. Farm Bill	Y	10. Keystone pipeline	Y
3. Guantanamo Bay Detainees	N	7. Afghanistan Combat	N	11. Immigration Exec. Action	N
4. Abortion 20-week ban	Y	8. NSA Phone Data Collection	N	12. Bipartisan budget deal	Y

Election Results

2014 general	David Valadao (R)	45,907	(58%)	$2,732,693	$715,020	$88,897
	Amanda Renteria (D)	33,470	(42%)	$1,690,530	$189,270	$24,767
2014 primary	David Valadao (R)	28,773	(63%)			
	Amanda Renteria (D)	11,682	(26%)			
	John Hernandez (D)	5,232	(12%)			

Prior winning percentage: 2012 (58%)

Population		Race and Ethnicity		Income	
Total:	711,414	Latino	72.1%	Median income:	$36,777
Urban:	47.3%	White	19.2%		*(410 of 435)*
Suburban:	42.0%	Black	3.7%	Under $50,000	63.2%
Rural:	10.7%	Asian	2.8%	$50,000-$99,999:	25.7%
Land area:	4,638	Two races	1.4%	$100,000-$199,999:	9.5%
Pop/sq. mi.:	153.4	White Ethnic	7.2%	$200,000 or more:	1.6%
Born in state:	60.7%			Poverty Rate	29.8%
		Education			
Age Groups		H.S. grad or less:	67.0%	**Work**	
Under 18:	32.0%	Some college:	24.7%	White collar:	16.8%
18 to 34:	27.7%	College degree, 4 yr.:	5.9%	Blue collar:	33.8%
35 to 64:	32.5%	Post-grad study:	2.4%	Sales and service:	49.3%
Over 64:	7.8%			Govt. workers:	14.7%
		Military			
		Veterans/active duty:	5.4%		

Central Valley: Southern Fresno Suburbs, Eastern Bakersfield

By car, California's Central Valley is a monotonous landscape: mile after mile of farmland with mile-square grid roads, intersected by railroads and canals, with an occasional cluster town. The land is hilly and gets more water near the Sierra Nevada mountains, and this is where the larger cities are.

Voter Turnout	
2013 Total Citizen 18+	336,180
2014 House Turnout	79,377
2014 Turnout as % CVAP	23.6%
2012 Turnout as % CVAP	35.6%

On the other side are the Westlands, where the land is flatter and the water scarcer. Its 600,000 acres are the nation's largest irrigation district. Here the land was always developed and sold in big plots; today, it has some of the world's largest farming operations. The land produces abundantly: alfalfa, cantaloupes, cotton, grapes, lima beans, olives, peaches, plums, raisins, sugar beets, tomatoes, walnuts, wheat. The landowners are a hardy and politically independent lot, but they have been happy to receive government help over the years, with money for crop price supports (in the case of cotton), agricultural research, irrigation systems, and, most important, subsidized and plentiful water.

Landowners have fought hard against liberals' efforts to change their way of life, from Democratic Gov. Jerry Brown's encouragement of Cesar Chavez's United Farm Workers in the 1970s to former House Natural Resources Committee Chairman George Miller's 1992 law to draw off more water to the Sacramento delta and charge higher prices for it in the valley. They have been stymied when conservatives in Congress have deadlocked on expansion of guest-worker programs pushed by valley farmers. Landowners also worry that Los Angeles users might outbid them for scarce water. In the Westlands, several hundred thousand acres have gone fallow. This region is a major contributor to California's oil production, and Kern County has the most oil wells in the state. Census Bureau data have shown that the population growth in Kings County has been heavily Hispanic, poor, and less likely to be married. Workers in the area's growing food-processing industry were often seasonal. Kings County planners provided some hope with proposals to create a new city, Quay Valley, with 75,000 people along Interstate 5. Skeptics questioned how developers would cope with decreased water availability, which already has adversely affected the local economy. The local farm communities have suffered a population drop since 2010.

The 21st Congressional District is very rural, includes large portions of the Westlands Water District, and links communities with similar agricultural and water interests. It takes in all of heavily Hispanic Kings County and parts of Fresno and Kern counties. The Naval Air Station Lemoore is home to the Strike Fighter Wing of the U.S. Pacific Fleet, and has plans to house a new wing of F-35 fighter jets. The town of Delano is Cesar Chavez's old headquarters, and at the southeastern foot of the district is the Latino part of Bakersfield, which is split between the 21st and the 23rd. The district is more than 70 percent Hispanic, but Hispanic voter registration and turnout are typically low. The district leans slightly Democratic. Barack Obama won 52% against John McCain and 55% against Mitt Romney, but a local Republican can win with the right background and political appeal.

2012 Presidential Vote		
Barack Obama (D)	65,146	(55%)
Mitt Romney (R)	51,917	(44%)

2008 Presidential Vote		
Barack Obama (D)	67,233	(52%)
John McCain (R)	59,549	(46%)

Cook Partisan Voting Index: D+2

David Valadao (R)

Former Republican state Assembly member David Valadao, a dairy farmer of Portuguese descent, has twice won the 21st District seat against credible Democratic opponents who under-performed their initial expectations. His skill and independence in addressing the area's agricultural issues have attracted attention from House Republicans.

Valadao's father emigrated to California from Portugal's Azores Islands and started a small dairy farm in Kings County in 1969. When Valadao was 8 years old, the family moved to Hanford. He recalls that he recalled riding in the car with his parents the day that all three voted for the first time. He was 18 and a registered Republican; his parents, who became naturalized citizens, were Democrats, although they later switched parties. Valadao worked on the family's farm, driving the tractor that carried feed for animals, and handling contracts and purchases. He was a part-time student at the College of the Sequoias but did not graduate. The single political science class he took "piqued my interest in politics, but I never considered running for office," he said. In 1992, he and his brother became partners in Valadao Dairy.

His appetite for politics was whetted when he was elected regional leadership council chairman of Land O'Lakes, a member-owned agricultural cooperative. Valadao began traveling to Sacramento and Washington, where he spoke with elected officials and groups on issues affecting dairy farmers, such as his region's aging water infrastructure. "The more I got involved in dairy and agricultural issues, the more I saw how much of an importance government and policies play in our lives," he said. He became active with the California Milk Advisory Board and the Western States Dairy Trade Association.

In 2010, Valadao was elected to the Assembly. He successfully sponsored legislation that eliminated millions of dollars in state funding to subsidize the production of corn-based ethanol. He also got a bill passed that placed restrictions on people with criminal convictions who care for the elderly or disabled.

In the 2012 race for this new House seat, Valadao got an early fundraising advantage, raising more than $400,000 in 2011. He finished first in the state's all-party primary, with 57% of the vote, while Democrat John Hernandez came in second with 22%. As the head of the Central California Hispanic Chamber of Commerce, Hernandez hoped he could make inroads with Latino voters. But he suffered from not living in the district and not having previously run for political office. The *Bakersfield Californian* endorsed Valadao, saying that the district's constituents "deserve a representative who has been tested politically a little more." In his surprisingly comfortable 58%-42% victory, Valadao led by large margins in Fresno and Kings counties, while Hernandez won narrowly in more urban Kern County.

With help from House GOP leader Kevin McCarthy, who represents a neighboring district, Valadao quickly showed his skills in the House when he secured a rare plum for a freshman: a seat on the Appropriations Committee, where he focused on securing funds for his district. He split with most Republicans on immigration legislation, by cosponsoring in 2013 the Democrats' sweeping reform plan and speaking positively about the bipartisan bill that passed the Senate that spring. He was one of six House Republicans to vote against an amendment by GOP Rep. Steve King of Iowa that would give immigration authorities wider discretion to deport undocumented immigrants. In discussing these proposals, he cited the immigration experience of his parents. The U.S. Chamber of Commerce gave Valadao its Spirit of Enterprise award for his work on immigration. In February 2014, he worked closely with California Republicans on a bill to reject an Obama administration decision to limit water supplies to home, farms and businesses in the Central Valley. Anyone voting against the bill, he said, was stating, "I want to raise the cost of food to everybody in the United States." The House passed the bill on a nearly party-line vote of 229-191.

In 2014, Democrats tried to learn from their flawed candidate in the previous cycle. They recruited and actively promoted Amanda Renteria, a Latina who had been chief of staff to Democratic Sen. Debbie Stabenow of Michigan. In the June primary, she easily defeated Hernandez, but Valadao got 63 percent of the total vote. That diminished some of the enthusiasm for Renteria, plus California Democrats were more focused on protecting their several vulnerable incumbents. In the general election, Vice President Joe Biden made a campaign appearance for Renteria. She raised an impressive $1.7 million, though much of her money came from outside the district and she fell short of Valadao's $2.7 million. Despite Democrats' expectations of a tighter race, Valadao had another 58%-42% victory, with a similar pattern in county returns as in 2012. Valadao benefited from his bipartisan legislative approach.

TWENTY-SECOND DISTRICT

Devin Nunes (R)

Elected 2002, 7th term; b. Oct. 1, 1973, Tulare; CA Poly. U., B.S. 1995, M.S. 1996; Catholic; married (Elizabeth); 3 children.

Elected Office: Col. of the Sequoias Governing Bd., 1996-2002.

Professional Career: Appt. dir., USDA Rural Dev., 2001.

DC Office: 1013 LHOB, 20515, 202-225-2523; Fax: 202-225-3404; Website: nunes.house.gov.

State Offices: Clovis, 559-323-5235; Visalia, 559-733-3861.

Committees: *Intelligence (Select):* (Chmn). *Ways & Means:* Health; Trade.

Group Ratings

	ADA	ACLU	AFL-CIO	LCV	ITI	COC	HAFA	ACU	CFG	FRC
2014	0%	0%	–	6%	100%	100%	37%	79%	51%	88%
2013	0%	C	26%	0%	C	85%	C	64%	56%	C

National Journal Ratings

	2013 LIB	—	2013 CONS
Economic	38%	—	62%
Social	41%	—	58%
Foreign	32%	—	67%
Composite	37%	—	63%

Key Votes of the 113th Congress

1. Sandy storm spending	NV	5. Medical Marijuana	N	9. Syrian Rebels Training	Y
2. Violence Against Women Act	Y	6. Farm Bill	Y	10. Keystone pipeline	Y
3. Guantanamo Bay Detainees	N	7. Afghanistan Combat	N	11. Immigration Exec. Action	Y
4. Abortion 20-week ban	Y	8. NSA Phone Data Collection	N	12. Bipartisan budget deal	Y

Election Results

2014 general	Devin Nunes (R)	96,053	(72%)	$1,456,624
	Suzanna Aguilera-Marrero (D)	37,289	(28%)	$36,799
2014 primary	Devin Nunes (R)	60,499	(68%)	
	Suzanna Aguilera-Marrero (D)	22,198	(25%)	
	John Catano (R)	6,403	(7%)	

Prior winning percentages: 2012 (62%), 2010 (unopposed), 2008 (68%), 2006 (67%), 2004 (73%), 2002 (70%)

Population		Race and Ethnicity		Income	
Total:	730,271	Latino	45.9%	Median income:	$50,389
Urban:	66.7%	White	41.9%		*(236 of 435)*
Suburban:	32.5%	Asian	7.0%	Under $50,000	49.6%
Rural:	0.8%	Black	2.5%	$50,000-$99,999:	30.3%
Land area:	1,825	Two races	1.9%	$100,000-$199,999:	16.0%
Pop/sq. mi.:	400.2	White Ethnic	15.7%	$200,000 or more:	4.1%
Born in state:	67.5%			Poverty Rate	22.5%
		Education			
Age Groups		H.S. grad or less:	43.9%	**Work**	
Under 18:	28.1%	Some college:	32.5%	White collar:	33.2%
18 to 34:	24.7%	College degree, 4 yr.:	14.9%	Blue collar:	41.8%
35 to 64:	35.3%	Post-grad study:	8.6%	Sales and service:	24.9%
Over 64:	11.8%				
		Military		Govt. workers:	18.3%
		Veterans/active duty:	6.3%		

Central Valley: Eastern Fresno City and Suburbs

In California's Central Valley, between the flat Westlands and the Sierras, is Fresno, a city that is both agricultural and industrial, middle American and ethnically diverse. Although it began as a farm-market center, the city has long since grown out to the north, east, and west from its downtown,

Voter Turnout	
2013 Total Citizen 18+	453,467
2014 House Turnout	133,342
2014 Turnout as % CVAP	29.4%
2012 Turnout as % CVAP	51.2%

and its economy has expanded to other sectors—construction, transportation, and financial services. It is in fact a creation of the Industrial Age and the Central Pacific Railroad. Historian Kevin Starr described the San Joaquin Valley, at the heart of the Central Valley, as "the most productive unnatural environment on Earth." Fresno's city fathers bred the local wine grape, developed the raisin industry, and introduced the Smyrna fig. These are among the area's 300-plus crops, which include cotton, lima beans, nectarines, almonds, tomatoes, cantaloupes, plums, peaches, and alfalfa. Dairy, however, is now the biggest commodity and Tulare County leads the nation in milk and dairy sales, with nearly a half million cows. Fresno County produces more farm products in dollar value than any other county in the United States. Those two counties, plus nearby Kern, have been exchanging places in recent years for the highest annual farm exports, with more than $6 billion each.

Central Valley agriculture is industrial in its thoroughness and in its ownership by large corporations. The vineyards outside Fresno radiate in mechanical precision, with vines just 10 feet apart and exposed to the relentless summer sun: nothing romantic or quaint about it. Until recently, times were good. The weak dollar boosted farm exports, large citrus groves benefited from losses in hurricane-plagued Florida, and nuts found new export markets. Then, the recession and severe drought hit the area hard. After having peaked at 16.7% in 2010, unemployment was still at 11% in 2014. Jobs in education and health services were up; farming was down. The 29% poverty rate was among the highest in the nation, and the share of high school graduates was below average. California voters in 2008 approved funding for a bullet train from San Francisco to Los Angeles that would run through the Central Valley. The plan has been fiercely opposed by local officials worried that it could attract too many people to the Fresno area, forcing residents out of single-family homes and into dense, urban communities. As the pace of rail construction increased, Gov. Jerry Brown hailed the prospect of concentrating new home development. "We can't keep paving over agricultural land," he said in February 2015.

The 22nd District covers large portions of Fresno and Tulare counties. The city of Fresno is split between the 22nd and the Hispanic majority 16th, based in Merced County. Route 99, the old Farm-to-Market Corridor, runs through the district and leads to the Hispanic-majority city of Tulare. In the northern part of the district is Clovis, billed as the "gateway to the Sierras." The central

2012 Presidential Vote		
Mitt Romney (R)	125,213	(57%)
Barack Obama (D)	92,005	(42%)
2008 Presidential Vote		
John McCain (R)	128,067	(56%)
Barack Obama (D)	98,176	(43%)
Cook Partisan Voting Index:	R+10	

area takes in the smaller city of Dinuba and Visalia, which is the district's largest city. It is a largely agricultural district that leans strongly Republican. Fresno County is one of the most conservative urban centers in the nation.

Devin Nunes (R)

Devin Nunes, a Republican first elected in 2002, is an influential conservative with ambitions within and beyond the House—he has briefly toyed with running for each home-state Senate seat. He was tapped by Speaker John Boehner as chairman of the House Intelligence Committee, and is an ardent ally of Paul Ryan and his desire to shrink government and reshape entitlement programs. He also works closely with Majority Leader Kevin McCarthy, who represents the adjacent 23rd District.

Nunes is the descendant of Portuguese immigrants from the Azores. His grandfather established the 600-acre-plus dairy farm that his parents ran when he was growing up in Tulare County. He graduated from California Polytechnic State University, San Luis Obispo, with degrees in agriculture, worked on the family farm, and married a local elementary schoolteacher whose family roots are also in Portugal. In 1998, at age 25, Nunes ran for the House in a neighboring district and finished second in the primary, 52%-48%. In 2000, he was the Tulare County campaign chairman for Republican Rep. Bill Thomas, who chaired the Ways and Means Committee before he retired. In 2001, with Thomas' help, Nunes was appointed California director of rural development for the U.S. Department of Agriculture. When California's redistricting plan was unveiled in September 2001, the 21st District was left without an incumbent, and Nunes moved quickly. He was supported by Thomas, whose deep-pocketed campaign contributors in the pharmaceutical and insurance industries agreed to help Nunes. At home, Nunes won the endorsement of the California Farm Bureau, the state's largest farm organization and a powerful voice in Central Valley politics.

But Nunes faced serious primary challenges from Jim Patterson, Fresno's conservative former mayor, who was backed by the anti-tax group Club for Growth, and California Assembly member Mike Briggs. There were few differences among them on policy. All three promised to seek new water sources for farmers about to lose the San Joaquin River as a primary source after environmentalists successfully lobbied to restore the river, which for years had been dammed for irrigation. The candidates also called for tax cuts, fewer federal regulations, and expanded guest-worker programs for immigrants. Nunes won with 37% of the vote to 33% for Patterson and 26% for Briggs. In November, Nunes won easily, 70%-26%. He has not been seriously challenged since.

Nunes has a mostly conservative voting record, although it tends to be more centrist on social issues. "I draw my inspiration from the Founding Fathers," he told *Time* magazine after being named one of its "40 Under 40" leaders in 2010. "... These political heroes brought us a republic form of government that centered on liberty. The struggle to preserve that liberty grows every time our federal government takes power and rights from the people." Nunes can deliver a cutting sound bite, once comparing government spending with the actions of "a broke gambler who desperately keeps doubling down in a vain effort to break even." He called libertarian Michigan GOP Rep. Justin Amash "al-Qaida's best friend in the Congress" for opposing tougher Republican positions on national security, and contributed to Amash's opponent in the 2014 primary. He said that conservative Republicans who were blamed by many for shutting down part of the government in 2013 because they opposed the Affordable Care Act were "lemmings with suicide vests."

Nunes is a frequent public defender of Boehner, and has challenged the speaker's Republican critics. So, it was little surprise that Boehner selected him as Intelligence Committee chairman in 2015. He revamped the panel's subcommittees, forming new ones to concentrate on scrutinizing the CIA, as well as the NSA and cybersecurity. In his early months as chairman, he promised to be an advocate for intelligence agencies and he kept a low profile— though he joined Boehner in a House GOP delegation to the Mideast. "My goal is to make sure we are getting our members out to every corner of the world," Nunes told McClatchy Newspapers. "You cannot conduct serious oversight work without getting on the ground and actually talking to the folks that are doing the work."

Legislatively, Nunes has dived into the district's most pressing issue: the use of water from the San Joaquin. He got a feasibility study for a new water reservoir near Temperance Flat, which would help farmers if the river was restored to its original flow. But he clashed with supporters of alternatives to increase water flow over the Friant Dam so salmon could be returned to the parched lower reaches of the San Joaquin. Nunes contended that the move would seriously deplete the area's water supply for irrigation. Leaders of such projects were like "communist politburo members who collect big checks and do nothing," he said.

As California's drought worsened in 2009, Nunes lashed out at the Obama administration for allying with "radical environmentalists" in preventing farmers from getting sufficient water for their crops. At a Natural Resources subcommittee hearing, he introduced a fishbowl of smelt for the record as a symbolic protest of how groups have used potential harm to fish to limit water deliveries for farming. He got a bill through the House in February 2012 to reshape California's water-rights system to deliver more San Joaquin water for farmers; Democrats condemned the move as a "water grab" and it did not move in the Senate, something Nunes attributed to Democratic Sens. Dianne Feinstein and Barbara Boxer defending "their environmental wacko friends."

As a member of Ways and Means, at the outset of the health care debate in 2009, Nunes joined Ryan in introducing a bill providing tax credits for people to buy insurance and ending the tax exemption for businesses providing workers with the benefit. Their strategy pre-empted Ways and Means' ranking Republican, Michigan's Dave Camp, who preferred to take more time to craft a plan. Nunes introduced his own bill in June 2012 to create a voluntary pilot program in which Medicare and Medicaid recipients would be given a debit-style "Medi-choice" card to buy health insurance. He outlined a proposal after the 2012 election to overhaul the tax code by replacing business taxes with a new system he said would create more economic growth.

Nunes has used his sizable contributions from dairy interests and other agricultural businesses to donate to colleagues' campaigns, thus increasing his growing internal clout. Either Nunes or Pat Tiberi of Ohio, another Boehner ally, is in line to be the top Republican at Ways and Means within the next decade.

TWENTY-THIRD DISTRICT

Kevin McCarthy (R)

Elected 2006, 5th term; b. Jan. 26, 1965, Bakersfield; CA St. U. Bakersfield, B.S. 1989, M.B.A. 1994; Baptist; married (Judy); 2 children.

Elected Office: Trustee, Kern Comm. Col. Bd., 2000-02; CA Assembly, 2002-07, min. ldr., 2004-06.

Professional Career: Owner, Kevin O's Deli, 1986-87, Mesa Marin Batting Range, 1991-92; Staff, U.S. Rep. Bill Thomas, 1987-2002.

DC Office: 2421 RHOB, 20515, 202-225-2915; Fax: 202-225-2908; Website: kevinmccarthy.house.gov.

State Offices: Bakersfield, 661-327-3611.

Committees: House Majority Leader.

Group Ratings

	ADA	ACLU	AFL-CIO	LCV	ITI	COC	HAFA	ACU	CFG	FRC
2014	0%	0%	–	3%	100%	100%	40%	76%	43%	88%
2013	0%	C	19%	0%	C	85%	C	72%	53%	C

National Journal Ratings

	2013 LIB	—	2013 CONS
Economic	42%	—	57%
Social	16%	—	74%
Foreign	44%	—	54%
Composite	36%	—	64%

Key Votes of the 113th Congress

1. Sandy storm spending	Y	5. Medical Marijuana	N	9. Syrian Rebels Training	Y
2. Violence Against Women Act	Y	6. Farm Bill	Y	10. Keystone pipeline	Y
3. Guantanamo Bay Detainees	N	7. Afghanistan Combat	N	11. Immigration Exec. Action	Y
4. Abortion 20-week ban	Y	8. NSA Phone Data Collection	N	12. Bipartisan budget deal	Y

Election Results

2014 general	Kevin McCarthy (R)	100,317	(75%)	$5,920,014
	Raul Garcia (D)	33,726	(25%)	$8,931
2014 primary	Kevin McCarthy (R)	58,334	(99%)	
	Raul Garcia (Write-in) (D)	313	(1%)	

Prior winning percentages: 2012 (73%), 2010 (99%), 2008 (100%), 2006 (71%)

Population		Race and Ethnicity		Income	
Total:	726,292	White	49.7%	Median income:	$52,207
Urban:	57.2%	Latino	35.4%		*(201 of 435)*
Suburban:	36.7%	Black	6.5%	Under $50,000	47.6%
Rural:	6.2%	Asian	5.0%	$50,000-$99,999:	31.0%
Land area:	5,207	Two races	2.2%	$100,000-$199,999:	17.5%
Pop/sq. mi.:	139.5	White Ethnic	17.2%	$200,000 or more:	3.8%
Born in state:	67.2%			Poverty Rate	19.8%
		Education			
Age Groups		H.S. grad or less:	45.6%	**Work**	
Under 18:	27.3%	Some college:	36.2%	White collar:	31.2%
18 to 34:	24.1%	College degree, 4 yr.:	12.2%	Blue collar:	43.4%
35 to 64:	37.1%	Post-grad study:	6.0%	Sales and service:	25.4%
Over 64:	11.5%				
		Military		Govt. workers:	20.5%
		Veterans/active duty:	9.2%		

Central Valley: Central and Western Bakersfield and Suburbs

Bakersfield, near the southern end of California's Central Valley, has been the focus of great migrations four times: in the gold rush of 1885; in the boomlet that followed the discovery of oil in 1899; in the 1930s flight of Dust Bowl refugees from Oklahoma, Kansas and Texas; and in a flood of

Voter Turnout	
2013 Total Citizen 18+	472,574
2014 House Turnout	134,043
2014 Turnout as % CVAP	28.4%
2012 Turnout as % CVAP	48.5%

newcomers in the last two decades, when Bakersfield and Kern County grew more rapidly than California's biggest metro areas. The migration that made the deepest imprint was in the 1930s. The Okies drove across a thousand miles of brown landscape, then through the Tehachapi Pass, and found this vast green valley, with its irrigated fields and its eucalyptus-shaded towns—the richest farming country in the world. The story is told vividly in novelist John Steinbeck's *The Grapes of Wrath* and in Dan Morgan's *Rising in the West*, which explains how the Okies' descendants prospered in California. As a result, the area around Bakersfield is the one Southern-accented part of California, the home of a thriving country-music scene that included singers Merle Haggard and the late Buck Owens.

People here are culturally conservative with little empathy for Los Angeles-style cultural liberalism. More recently, Latinos have been coming in large numbers for farm work. The result is that the Central Valley, including Bakersfield, has had both high population growth and high unemployment for a decade—with the latter climbing even higher when the housing market collapsed. Its 41 percent population increase from 2000 to 2010 placed Bakersfield among the top ten fastest-growing cities in the nation. The flip side was that unemployment for the Bakersfield-Delano area remained at 15.9 percent in early 2012. By the end of 2014, it dropped to a still high 10 percent.

The bad numbers spread across the board. Reduced oil prices, and the disincentive for drilling, became another hit to the local economy, which is home to the five most productive petroleum fields in California and relies on oil and gas for 7 percent of local jobs. In 2014, the American Lung Association gave "F"s to Bakersfield for all four of its smoking and tobacco-related grades. Access to clean water has been a persistent problem for some of the small Latino communities here. After *The New York Times* detailed the plight of tiny Seville, where pesticides and chemical fertilizers have made much of the water undrinkable, local organizations responded in 2015 with 60 water bottle filling stations that had filtered taps.

2012 Presidential Vote		
Mitt Romney (R)	139,816	(62%)
Barack Obama (D)	82,119	(36%)

2008 Presidential Vote		
John McCain (R)	145,527	(61%)
Barack Obama (D)	86,733	(37%)

Cook Partisan Voting Index: R+16

The 23rd Congressional District includes parts of Tulare and Kern counties. It includes part of Bakersfield, though the city spills into the Kings County-based 21st District too. The 23rd also covers the southern part of the Sierras, including Sequoia National Forest and Lake Isabella. Its southern end encompasses Edwards Air Force Base, where Chuck Yeager flew the X-1 and where the Space Shuttle has frequently landed, and the Naval Air

Weapons Station China Lake. This district dips south to take in part of Los Angeles County and Antelope Valley. About 80 percent of its voters are in Kern. This is the most Republican district in California.

Kevin McCarthy (R)

Kevin McCarthy, a gregarious former Capitol Hill staffer elected in 2006, rocketed to the No. 2 spot in the House GOP leadership with hard work, some luck, and the ability to reach across the party. In June 2014, he moved up to majority leader in the fallout from Virginia Rep. Eric Cantor's stunning primary defeat. He is the likely successor to John Boehner as House Speaker, though House Republican internal dynamics are highly unpredictable.

McCarthy grew up in Bakersfield, where his blue-collar family has lived for generations and often voted Democratic. He moved in the other direction. At 19, he won $5,000 in the state lottery and invested it in a deli, which helped pay for business school at Cal State, Bakersfield. In college, he was elected chairman of the California Young Republicans and later headed the national Young Republicans organization. After he sold the deli, he got a job in the local office of Rep. Bill Thomas, who was then on his way to chairing the powerful Ways and Means Committee. McCarthy eventually became Thomas' district director and protégé. In 2000, McCarthy was elected to the Kern County Community College Board, and in 2002 he was elected to the Assembly. He was immediately chosen Republican leader (which, because of California's term limits, is a little easier than it looks). McCarthy worked with Republican Gov. Arnold Schwarzenegger on the budget, workers' compensation issues, and redistricting procedures. His Republican colleague from the Central Valley, Rep. Devin Nunes, says that McCarthy "lives and breathes politics."

When Thomas announced his retirement in March 2006, just four days before the filing deadline, McCarthy was the obvious candidate to succeed him. He faced token opposition in the Republican primary. In November, he won 71%-29%. Looking ahead, he raised more than $1 million and traveled the country campaigning for other Republican congressional candidates. That attracted the attention of party leaders. After the election, which was a poor GOP performance nationwide, he was chosen the freshman representative on the Republican Steering Committee, a leadership arm that makes all-important committee assignments. He chaired the Platform Committee at the 2008 Republican National Convention, winning praise for soliciting a wide spectrum of views and uniting conservatives and moderates.

McCarthy landed a leadership position in 2009 when Minority Whip Cantor appointed him chief deputy whip—an unusual responsibility for a House member serving only his second term. On the night of President Barack Obama's inauguration that year, he reportedly implored a gathering of leading GOP lawmakers and activists plotting strategy to be aggressive. "If you act like you're the minority, you're going to stay in the minority," McCarthy said, according to Robert Draper's 2012 book *Do Not Ask What Good We Do: Inside the U.S. House of Representatives*. "We've gotta challenge them on every single bill and challenge them on every single campaign." In a sign of his media savvy, McCarthy cooperated extensively with Draper.

In the 2009-10 cycle, McCarthy wore multiple hats. He was the head of recruiting for the National Republican Congressional Committee, in what turned out to be a highly successful election for the GOP. He traveled widely looking for candidates, identifying people capable of taking on Democrats used to winning against weak opposition. Ultimately, Republicans had candidates in 430 of the 435 congressional districts, the highest number ever. Even after he recruited the candidates, McCarthy kept in constant contact with the top contenders, often with quick cell phone calls while he was heading to meet other prospects. With Cantor and Wisconsin Rep. Paul Ryan, he led the party's "Young Guns" program to spotlight and finance Republican challengers. Minority Leader John Boehner assigned McCarthy and Rep. Peter Roskam of Illinois to draw up a document similar to the House Republicans' 1994 Contract with America. They solicited ideas from the public on the Internet, and ultimately compiled the "Pledge to America" policy manifesto. Kept deliberately vague to deter Democratic attacks, it did not make as big an impression as the Contract, but it sought to commit incoming and veteran Republicans to a single set of policies, such as extending the Bush-era tax cuts and repealing Obama's health care overhaul.

McCarthy was rewarded for his impressive efforts for the party. When Cantor ascended to majority leader after Republicans won control of the House in 2010, McCarthy was the overwhelming choice for whip, the third-ranking position for the House majority. Rep. Pete

Sessions of Texas, another influential Republican, wanted the post, but was persuaded by Boehner to remain for a second term as chairman of the NRCC, clearing the way for McCarthy to run unopposed.

In his new job, McCarthy avoided the tensions with Boehner that Cantor experienced and employed a nice-guy approach in building trust. He mountain-biked with Republican members in the mornings and rounded up others in the evenings for group dinners, drawing them out by asking questions such as, "What's the most embarrassing thing that happened to you at college?" and "What was the first concert you went to?" He encouraged lawmakers to hang around his whip office on the first floor of the Capitol and he got acquainted with their families. "He knows everybody, and their spouse, and their kids," fellow California Republican Rep. John Campbell marveled in 2012.

"A conference united around policies creates better legislation than using intimidation," McCarthy told *The New York Times*. But he also did not go out of his way to build bridges to House Democrats, or senators of either party. "The Senate is like a country club, and the House is like stopping at a truck stop for breakfast," he told reporters at an August 2012 gathering. "We are a microcosm of society, and we reflect it first."

McCarthy paid particular attention to the often-rambunctious pack of tea party freshmen elected in 2010. He offered them advice, including telling them to vote their conscience at times even if it meant disagreeing with the leadership. Sometimes the results were disastrous—especially for the whip, whose job is to assure the majority party prevails. When the leadership decided in April 2011 to back a continuing resolution to keep the federal government operating, 59 Republicans defected. And at the height of the "fiscal cliff" negotiations in December 2012, when the two parties struggled against a deadline to reach agreement on spending and tax cuts, Boehner's "Plan B" proposal was pulled from the floor when it became clear that it lacked sufficient Republican votes.

McCarthy's whip operation continued to face periodic criticism for its failure to unite Republicans. But there was little second-guessing after Cantor quickly stepped down as majority leader following his 2014 primary defeat. With the support of friendly colleagues and the GOP's establishment wing, McCarthy geared up a campaign within hours to replace his fallen friend. Early on, there were rumblings that he might face stiff competition from two committee chairs from Texas who previously had served in leadership—Jeb Hensarling of Financial Services and Sessions of Rules. But neither pursued the clash, leaving Idaho maverick Raul Labrador as his only opponent. The secret ballot among House Republicans was held barely a week after Cantor's defeat. Labrador never stood a chance against McCarthy's formidable vote-counting operation.

As he prepared to start his new job, McCarthy laid out broad-based objectives that were designed to appeal across the board: a simpler and fairer tax code, energy independence, local control of education, and ending "the stale policies of the past." When it came to specifics, he quickly showed his allegiance to House conservatives. He endorsed closing the U.S. Export-Import Bank when its charter expired. McCarthy had voted in 2012 to renew the charter of the bank, which many conservatives contend engages in crony capitalism. After their big victories in the 2014 election, he showed a pragmatic side as well, warning donors that unless the Republican-controlled Congress could prove it could govern, the party would not capture the White House in 2016. He promised to overhaul how the House did its work by giving committee chairmen more autonomy, assuring that GOP leaders work more closely with their Senate counterparts, and finding issues to draw a clear contrast between the parties.

McCarthy moved to seize that big opportunity for Republicans in the early months of 2015. He helped create a working group of committee chairs to develop a Republican alternative to the Affordable Care Act. But after a month, Republicans were second-guessed for their occasional failure to get bills through the chamber. They picked what many saw as an unwinnable fight with Obama over immigration policy by trying to use a Department of Homeland Security spending bill to force an end to his executive order on the subject. At the last minute, the leadership jettisoned a planned vote on a controversial anti-abortion bill after some female Republican women lawmakers complained it was too harsh. With slight modifications, the House passed that bill a few months later.

McCarthy is no close friend of Democrats. But he makes an effort to have at least some relationships. At Obama's 2013 inauguration, McCarthy sat with liberal Supreme Court Justice Elena Kagan, and he once beseeched Vice President Joe Biden to call his mother on her birthday. In early 2015, he vowed to work closely with his home-state Democratic Sen. Dianne Feinstein to ease California's crippling drought. He has a far more adversarial relationship with California's other senator, Barbara Boxer; he blamed her for torpedoing a drought-relief bill the previous year. The tart-tongued Boxer said that when McCarthy made similar comments to her, she told him he was dreaming. Facing partisan criticism of scant Republican participation at the 50th anniversary celebration of civil rights protests in Selma, Ala., in March 2015, he made a last-minute decision to join the festivities.

McCarthy had no major party opposition in his first three reelection bids. In 2014, his Democratic opponent, Raul Garcia, was nominated as a write-in candidate and lost 75%-25% in November. But McCarthy suffered an embarrassing setback when several well-funded Republicans that year lost House challenges in California, often by excruciatingly close margins. McCarthy had promised that Republicans would gain seats in his home state. Instead, Republicans lost a seat in the Golden State, giving Democrats (and Nancy Pelosi) a 39-14 control of the state delegation. GOP problems in California certainly resulted from factors beyond his control. But their miseries are a continuing reminder of McCarthy's limitations at home—in contrast to GOP leaders who could cite their dominance of home-state delegations, for example, in Ohio, Virginia and Texas.

TWENTY-FOURTH DISTRICT

Lois Capps (D)

Elected March 1998, 9th full term; b. Jan. 10, 1938, Ladysmith, WI; Pacific Lutheran U., B.S. 1959, Yale U., M.A. 1964, U. of CA Santa Barbara, M.A. 1990; Lutheran; widowed; 3 children (1 deceased).

Professional Career: Staff nurse, Visiting Nurses Assn., 1963-64; Head nurse, Yale New Haven Hosp., 1960-63; Instructor, Santa Barbara City Col., 1983-95; Nurse, Santa Barbara Schl. Dist., 1979-96.

DC Office: 2231 RHOB, 20515, 202-225-3601; Fax: 202-225-5632; Website: capps.house.gov.

State Offices: San Luis Obispo, 805-546-8348; Santa Barbara, 805-730-1710; Santa Maria, 805-349-3832.

Committees: *Energy & Commerce:* Energy & Power; Environment & the Economy; Health. *Natural Resources:* Energy & Mineral Resources; Federal Lands.

Group Ratings

	ADA	ACLU	AFL-CIO	LCV	ITI	COC	HAFA	ACU	CFG	FRC
2014	80%	83%	–	94%	80%	43%	8%	4%	6%	0%
2013	80%	C	95%	96%	C	42%	C	12%	10%	C

National Journal Ratings

	2013 LIB	—	2013 CONS
Economic	80%	—	20%
Social	66%	—	32%
Foreign	83%	—	15%
Composite	77%	—	23%

Key Votes of the 113th Congress

1. Sandy storm spending	Y	5. Medical Marijuana	Y	9. Syrian Rebels Training	N
2. Violence Against Women Act	Y	6. Farm Bill	N	10. Keystone pipeline	N
3. Guantanamo Bay Detainees	Y	7. Afghanistan Combat	Y	11. Immigration Exec. Action	N
4. Abortion 20-week ban	N	8. NSA Phone Data Collection	Y	12. Bipartisan budget deal	Y

Election Results

2014 general	Lois Capps (D)	103,228	(52%)	$2,493,170	$255,867
	Chris Mitchum (R)	95,566	(48%)	$477,674	$170,381
2014 primary	Lois Capps (D)	58,198	(44%)		
	Chris Mitchum (R)	21,059	(16%)		
	Justin Fareed (R)	20,445	(15%)		
	Dale Francisco (R)	15,575	(12%)		
	Bradley Allen (R)	9,269	(7%)		

Prior winning percentages: 2012 (55%), 2010 (58%), 2008 (68%), 2006 (65%), 2004 (63%), 2002 (59%), 2000 (53%), 1998 (55%), 1998 special (55%)

Population		Race and Ethnicity		Income	
Total:	722,008	White	56.2%	Median income:	$60,796
Urban:	55.1%	Latino	34.7%		*(118 of 435)*
Suburban:	34.5%	Asian	4.4%	Under $50,000	42.2%
Rural:	10.3%	Black	1.8%	$50,000-$99,999:	29.7%
Land area:	5,642	Two races	2.2%	$100,000-$199,999:	21.5%
Pop/sq. mi.:	128.0	White Ethnic	22.9%	$200,000 or more:	6.6%
Born in state:	59.7%			Poverty Rate	15.8%
		Education			
Age Groups		H.S. grad or less:	34.2%	Work	
Under 18:	20.8%	Some college:	33.8%	White collar:	35.7%
18 to 34:	28.3%	College degree, 4 yr.:	19.8%	Blue collar:	43.1%
35 to 64:	35.9%	Post-grad study:	12.2%	Sales and service:	21.2%
Over 64:	15.0%				
		Military		Govt. workers:	17.0%
		Veterans/active duty:	8.2%		

Central Coast: Santa Barbara, San Luis Obispo

In a state where stunning coastal landscapes and charming small towns are a dime a dozen, Santa Barbara stands out as someplace special. It is a collection of red tile roofs and leafy live oaks, sheltered by towering mountains just above the sea.

Voter Turnout	
2013 Total Citizen 18+	492,092
2014 House Turnout	198,794
2014 Turnout as % CVAP	40.4%
2012 Turnout as % CVAP	59.7%

The impression is a bit misleading, for Santa Barbara has its problems. Most of its quaint white stucco buildings were put up not as part of 18th-century mission settlement, but after a 1925 earthquake leveled much of the town. Like Disneyland, it is not authentically old, but rather a bigger, more attractive, cleaner version of a historical artifact, one that is maintained not by a company, but by an architectural review board. The city has long been one of the nation's richest retirement communities, one comfortable with its high living costs and determined to preserve its pristine environment and serenity.

Both features came under threat spectacularly in 1969, when an underwater oil well ruptured, coating the beach with oil. Pictures of the oil slick in the channel, and of volunteers trying to wash oil off grounded birds, helped to launch the 1970s environmental movement. Almost all of the wells are closed now (though some old 19th-century wells mysteriously still wash up globs of oil to the beach at nearby Summerland). But the oil spill left a long-lasting residue in Santa Barbara's politics. This was once a mostly Republican community, uninterested in redistribution of wealth, but always concerned about the environment and having moderate-to-liberal impulses on cultural issues. Like most of coastal California, it has moved decisively to the left in the past decade. Despite that, 61 percent of voters opposed in November 2014 a Santa Barbara County referendum to impose a ban on fracking. Oil drilling has persisted for more than a century near Orcutt.

Much of the Santa Barbara coastline is occupied by Vandenberg Air Force Base, which launches unmanned government and commercial satellites into polar orbit. The largest towns in northern Santa Barbara County, like San Luis Obispo to the north, are pleasant, comfortable places, as untrendy as you can find in coastal California. One problem is that the cost of rental housing in both counties has become unaffordable for many local workers. In San Luis Obispo County, another challenge will be coping with future state budget cuts. California Polytechnic State University accounts for 12% of the county's jobs. San Luis Obispo County's economy grew by 4.1% in 2013 and its 5% unemploy-

2012 Presidential Vote		
Barack Obama (D) 158,119	(54%)
Mitt Romney (R).................126,049	(43%)
2008 Presidential Vote		
Barack Obama (D) 176,201	(57%)
John McCain (R).................127,748	(41%)
Cook Partisan Voting Index: D+4		

ment rate in February 2015 was one of the lowest in the state. For the first time in 20 years, strawberries overtook wine grapes in 2011 as the county's top crop.

The 24th Congressional District of California includes all of San Luis Obispo and Santa Barbara counties. Santa Maria is now the largest city in Santa Barbara County. It also brings in the northwest corner of Ventura County and a small coastal part of the city of San Buenaventura to the south, and encompasses much of the Los Padres National Forest. Politically, the district favors Democrats.

Lois Capps (D)

Lois Capps, a Democrat who first won her seat in 1998, is known for her pleasant disposition— she has been named "nicest House member" in *Washingtonian's* annual anonymous survey of Capitol Hill staffers. With her background as a nurse and a seat on the Energy and Commerce Committee, Capps has influenced multiple areas of health care policy. Her retirement announcement launched a likely competitive contest.

Capps grew up in Wyoming and Montana, the daughter of a Lutheran minister. She graduated from college with a nursing degree and was the head nurse at Yale New Haven Hospital when she met Walter Capps, a student at Yale Divinity School. In 1964, he became a professor at the University of California, Santa Barbara. Lois Capps became the head elementary school nurse for the Santa Barbara school system, director of the county's teenage pregnancy and parenting project, and a part-time instructor at Santa Barbara City Community College. In 1996, Walter Capps ran for the House and defeated Rep. Andrea Seastrand, a first-term conservative. He died of a heart attack in October 1997.

Lois Capps ran for his seat against Republican Assemblyman Tom Bordonaro, the favorite of Christian conservatives. Bordonaro, a paraplegic since a car accident in college, emphasized his "blue-collar roots and common values." Capps had help from labor unions and environmental groups. In the January 1998 primary, she finished first, 45%-29%. In the runoff, Bordonaro was hurt by divisions in the local GOP, and Capps won a surprisingly large 53%-45% victory.

She is a solid liberal, but has worked more successfully with Republicans than has the typical California Democrat. "I find it uncomfortable to be around people yelling at each other," she told the *Los Angeles Times* in October 2012. She worked with conservative Republican Rep. Darrell Issa of California in 2011 in asking U.S. Trade Representative Ron Kirk to support California flower growers in their efforts to compete with competitors in Colombia and other nations. Later, she teamed with Washington's Cathy McMorris Rodgers, a member of the GOP leadership, on a House-passed measure to bolster research on pediatric diseases, and with Adam Kinzinger of Illinois, on a measure assisting states to streamline certification of veterans with military medical training who want to continue careers as emergency medical technicians.

During the 2009-2010 health care overhaul debate, Capps emerged as a leading opponent of efforts by anti-abortion Democratic Rep. Bart Stupak of Michigan, to prevent federal subsidies to insurance carriers providing abortion coverage to women. She developed what she called "an abortion-neutral compromise" that would have barred direct payments of federal funds in most cases. But Stupak and his allies remained dissatisfied, contending that her proposal would have allowed indirect payments. They held up the final bill's fate until aides to President Barack Obama brokered a last-minute deal.

In keeping with her district's interests, Capps also focuses on environmental policy. She sought in 2011 to prevent the Nuclear Regulatory Commission from relicensing the Diablo Canyon nuclear power plant in her district until seismic studies were completed to address the area's vulnerability to earthquakes. She has opposed exploratory drilling in the Arctic Ocean, and an attempt by California Republicans to convert part of the Channel Islands into a private recreation area for the military. In March 2015, she filed a bill to research the impact that increasingly acidic oceans may have on the seafood industry. She has advocated stricter limits on guns, especially in cases of domestic violence, and she criticized Obama for not having "spent more time on" the broader issue in his 2015 State of the Union message.

After promising in 1998 to serve only three terms, Capps abandoned that pledge. She was not seriously challenged until 2012, when Republican Abel Maldonado ran against her. A former California state senator and lieutenant governor, Maldonado had a moderate voting record and drew interest from national Republicans who were thrilled to have a Latino candidate running in a district where 29% of voting age citizens were Latinos. But Capps outraised him by more than $1 million, and, in a year in which Obama won her district easily, she had no trouble winning, 55%-45%.

Two years later, she had an unexpectedly close reelection. Chris Mitchum, a former president of the Screen Actors Guild and son of the more renowned actor Robert Mitchum, emphasized free markets, lower taxes, and constitutional principles. In a strange twist, Mitchum opposed pork barrel spending, and told a group, "I do not intend to go to Washington, to represent the 24th District, to bring back baseball fields." In the final week of the campaign, Capps ran an ad that quoted those first 13 words, but dropped his obvious point. Mitchum responded, "To be honest, my first reaction was laughter." Capps outspent Mitchum by more than 5-to-1. But she was held to a 52%-48% victory, her tightest outcome ever. Three months later, Mitchum filed a defamation lawsuit against Capps, which was based on the misleading quote.

Capps announced in April 2015 that she would not seek reelection. Later that month, her daughter Laura, a former aide to President Bill Clinton and the wife of Democratic consultant Bill Burton, said that she had decided not to run. Competitive primaries already had taken shape in each party, with prominent local officials.

TWENTY-FIFTH DISTRICT

Steve Knight (R)

Elected 2014, 1st term; b. Dec. 17, 1966, Edwards Air Force Base, CA; Antelope Valley Col., A.A. 2006; Catholic; married (Lily); 2 children.

Military Career: U.S. Army, 1985-87; U.S. Army Reserve, 1987-93.

Elected Office: Palmdale City Cncl., 2005-08; CA Assembly, 2008-12, asst. min. ldr., 2010-12; Vice mayor, Palmdale; CA Senate 2012-14.

Professional Career: Police officer, 18 years.

DC Office: 1023 LHOB, 20515, 202-225-1956; Website: knight.house. gov.

State Offices: Palmdale, 661-441-0320; Santa Clarita, 661-255-5630; Simi Valley, 805-581-7130.

Committees: *Armed Services:* Military Personnel; Seapower & Projection Forces; Tactical Air & Land Forces. *Science, Space, & Technology:* Energy (VChmn); Space. *Small Business:* Contracting & Workforce; Investigations, Oversight & Regulations.

Election Results

2014 general	Steve Knight (R)	60,847	(53%)	$410,835	$5,488	$101,945
	Tony Strickland (R)	53,225	(47%)	$2,057,642	$171,854	$1,470
2014 primary	Tony Strickland (R)	19,090	(30%)			
	Steve Knight (R)	18,327	(28%)			
	Lee Rogers (D)	14,315	(22%)			
	Evan Thomas (D)	6,149	(10%)			
	Troy Castagna (R)	3,805	(6%)			

Population		Race and Ethnicity		Income	
Total:	716,815	White	43.1%	Median income:	$67,293
Urban:	7.5%	Latino	37.9%		*(72 of 435)*
Suburban:	90.3%	Asian	7.9%	Under $50,000	36.6%
Rural:	2.2%	Black	7.2%	$50,000-$99,999:	30.3%
Land area:	1,506	Two races	3.5%	$100,000-$199,999:	25.1%
Pop/sq. mi.:	476.1	White Ethnic	21.6%	$200,000 or more:	8.0%
Born in state:	60.8%			Poverty Rate	14.0%
		Education			
Age Groups:		H.S. grad or less:	37.7%	**Work**	
Under 18:	27.6%	Some college:	35.1%	White collar:	37.4%
18 to 34:	21.6%	College degree, 4 yr.:	17.7%	Blue collar:	44.7%
35 to 64:	40.1%	Post-grad study:	9.5%	Sales and service:	17.9%
Over 64:	10.7%			Govt. workers:	14.1%
		Military			
		Veterans/active duty:	6.3%		

Northern LA Exurbs: Santa Clarita

For decades, as the mild-temperature flatlands of the Los Angeles Basin and San Fernando Valley filled up with people, the rugged mountains and hot desert to the north in

Los Angeles County remained mostly empty. But as L.A. and the Valley filled up, people began moving north through the Newhall pass on Interstate 5 and northeast on Route 14 to the high desert country. Immediately north of the pass is Santa Clarita, with 180,000 residents, and the Six Flags Magic

Voter Turnout	
2013 Total Citizen 18+	457,306
2014 House Turnout	114,072
2014 Turnout as % CVAP	24.9%
2012 Turnout as % CVAP	56.4%

Mountain theme park. Northeast on Route 14, past the former gold-mining center of Acton, the mountains stop at the San Andreas Fault and the desert stretches out low and flat. This is Antelope Valley, with huge aerospace plants and military bases around Palmdale and Lancaster, where more than 300,000 people live. Not far from upscale shopping centers, there has been a resurgence of specialty farm crops such as baby carrots, organic onions, and parsnips. Access to health care has been a problem in Antelope Valley and the life expectancy of African Americans here has been four years shorter than for blacks in the rest of Los Angeles County. But completion in 2014 of the 15-acre High Desert Regional Health Center in Lancaster created optimism about a turnaround in medical care.

The Air Force Plant 42 is home to many defense contractors, with projects that include the B-2 Stealth Bomber, the F-117 Stealth Fighter, and the F-35 Joint Strike Fighter. The RQ-170 Sentinel, a next-generation drone reportedly used in stealth CIA operations, has been developed at Lockheed Martin's Skunk Works facility in Palmdale. In early 2015, the Pentagon had plans for a Long-Range Strike Bomber, which outgoing Defense Secretary Chuck Hagel said was "absolutely essential to keep our deterrent edge." Palmdale's large contractors quickly began to compete for the project. After several years as one of the fast-growing areas in California, with relatively cheap housing and easy mortgages, housing prices collapsed early during the Great Recession and this area had one of the nation's highest foreclosure rates. By 2013, the low prices resulted in some improvement of the housing market and a marked reduction of foreclosures. In a welcome diversification, Santa Clarita had become a favorite alternative production site for Hollywood studios.

The 25th Congressional District of California includes all of the Santa Clarita Valley and the high desert parts of Los Angeles County. The district extends to most of Simi Valley in Ventura County, including the Ronald Reagan Presidential Foundation and Library. Housed there are 55 million pages of presidential documents and a large piece of the Berlin Wall, which Reagan famously urged Soviet leader Mikhail Gorbachev to tear down. The 25th includes several state parks, including Castaic Lake State Recreation Area and Saddleback Butte State Park. The high desert, not surprisingly, suffered from

2012 Presidential Vote		
Mitt Romney (R)	125,258	(50%)
Barack Obama (D)	120,701	(48%)
2008 Presidential Vote		
Barack Obama (D)	124,377	(49%)
John McCain (R)	123,454	(49%)
Cook Partisan Voting Index: R+3		

the statewide drought. At Castaic Lake, water had to be pumped uphill in 2014 to get it to the local treatment plant. Beaches at the lake were closed and boats could no longer be launched from a trailer.

Politically, the district leans slightly Republican. Barack Obama won it by a sliver in 2008, and lost to Mitt Romney 50%-48% in 2012.

Steve Knight (R)

Steve Knight beat expectations in 2014 to defeat fellow Republican Tony Strickland in the 25th District, to replace retiring House Armed Services Committee Chairman Buck McKeon. The focus on personality and political base gave their contest elements of an election to the state Legislature, where each had served.

Knight was born into a military family and grew up in Palmdale. He enlisted in the Army after high school. After completing his military service, he joined the Los Angeles Police Department, where he served for 18 years. Citing the inspiration of his father—who had served in the state Assembly and Senate for 12 years—Knight successfully ran for the Palmdale City Council in 2005. He established a reputation as tough on crime and government spending. In 2008, he was elected to the Assembly, which was followed by a 2012 election to the state Senate. In those years, he compiled a solidly conservative record, especially on immigration and gun control.

Democrats were skeptical that McKeon's retirement gave them a pick-up opportunity. That became a certainty thanks to the state's all-party primary system. With eight candidates in the June primary, Strickland topped the field at 30 percent, Knight had 28 percent, and the top Democrat Lee Rogers got 22 percent. The four GOP candidates on the June ballot got a total of 65 percent of the vote. In the November run-off, Strickland was the early favorite, thanks to a big fundraising advantage and his lead in the primary.

Knight attacked Strickland as a carpetbagger from nearby Ventura County, where he lost a House bid in 2012, 53%-47%, in the blue-leaning 26th District against Democrat Julia Brownley. He contended that Strickland moved to the neighboring 25th only because he couldn't win in his own base. Knight played up his local roots and more socially conservative bona fides.

Knight encountered his own troubles, especially after he was one of only three state senators to vote against a bill banning Confederate symbols on state property. He ran his campaign on a shoestring budget while getting outspent by a 5-to-1 ratio. Knight suffered an embarrassing incident when Tim Donnelly, one of the most conservative Republicans in the State Assembly, made plans to campaign for him in Santa Clarita. But, the *Los Angeles Times* reported, Knight changed his mind when local political figures objected. The incident caused Democrat Rogers to rescind his endorsement of Knight. In the end, Strickland was unable to shake the label of opportunist. Knight won 53%-47%, less than a firm grip on his district.

In the House, Knight started on the right track when he won the lottery among all freshmen and got first choice in the selection of his office assignment. He took a seat on the Armed Services Committee near the bottom of the seniority list that McKeon had climbed over nearly two decades. The Small Business Committee in March approved Knight's bill to make it easier for small businesses to form joint ventures and compete for federal contracts. He faced the prospect of a significant Republican challenge to his reelection in 2016.

TWENTY-SIXTH DISTRICT

Julia Brownley (D)

Elected 2012, 2nd term; b. Aug. 28, 1952, Aiken, SC; Mount Vernon Col., B.A. 1975, American U., M.B.A. 1979; Episcopalian; divorced; 2 children.

Elected Office: CA Assembly, 2006-12; Santa Monica Malibu Schl. Bd., 1994-2006.

Professional Career: Product mgr., Steelcase, 1984-92; Sales mgr., Pitney Bowes, 1981-84; Sales mgr., Burroughs Corp., 1976-81.

DC Office: 1019 LHOB, 20515, 202-225-5811; Fax: 202-225-1100; Website: juliabrownley.house.gov.

State Offices: Oxnard, 805-379-1779; Thousand Oaks, 805-379-1779.

Committees: *Transportation & Infrastructure:* Aviation; Coast Guard & Maritime Transportation; Highways & Transit. *Veterans' Affairs:* Disability Assistance & Memorial Affairs; Health (RMM).

Group Ratings

	ADA	ACLU	AFL-CIO	LCV	ITI	COC	HAFA	ACU	CFG	FRC
2014	60%	77%	–	94%	100%	57%	6%	4%	13%	0%
2013	65%	C	90%	93%	C	54%	C	8%	3%	C

National Journal Ratings

	2013 LIB	—	2013 CONS
Economic	62%	—	38%
Social	69%	—	28%
Foreign	65%	—	35%
Composite	66%	—	34%

Key Votes of the 113th Congress

1. Sandy storm spending		Y	5. Medical Marijuana	Y	9. Syrian Rebels Training	Y
2. Violence Against Women Act		Y	6. Farm Bill	Y	10. Keystone pipeline	N
3. Guantanamo Bay Detainees		N	7. Afghanistan Combat	N	11. Immigration Exec. Action	N
4. Abortion 20-week ban		N	8. NSA Phone Data Collection	N	12. Bipartisan budget deal	Y

Election Results

2014 general	Julia Brownley (D) 87,176	(51%)	$3,364,754	$284,334	$1,242,981
	Jeff Gorell (R) 82,653	(49%)	$1,298,191	$252,279	$1,957,989
2014 primary	Julia Brownley (D) 38,854	(46%)			
	Jeff Gorell (R) 38,021	(45%)			
	Rafael Dagnesses (R) 6,536	(8%)			

Prior winning percentage: 2012 (53%)

Population		Race and Ethnicity		Income	
Total:	712,804	White	45.8%	Median income:	$76,679
Urban:	51.3%	Latino	43.5%		*(38 of 435)*
Suburban:	46.8%	Asian	6.5%	Under $50,000	32.9%
Rural:	1.9%	Black	1.9%	$50,000-$99,999:	29.3%
Land area:	1,089	Two races	2.0%	$100,000-$199,999:	27.2%
Pop/sq. mi.:	654.3	White Ethnic	20.3%	$200,000 or more:	10.6%
Born in state:	55.9%			Poverty Rate	13.1%
		Education:			
Age Groups		H.S. grad or less:	37.6%	**Work**	
Under 18:	25.0%	Some college:	30.8%	White collar:	35.7%
18 to 34:	23.7%	College degree, 4 yr.:	19.0%	Blue collar:	40.9%
35 to 64:	38.7%	Post-grad study:	12.6%	Sales and service:	23.4%
Over 64:	12.7%				
		Military		Govt. workers:	12.2%
		Veterans/active duty:	7.8%		

Southern Ventura: Oxnard, Thousand Oaks

The city of Simi Valley is a product of the 1960s, the expansive postwar years when migrants from points across the United States moved west to Los Angeles and then spread beyond city and county limits to fill up the valleys between the mountains.

Voter Turnout	
2013 Total Citizen 18+	449,335
2014 House Turnout	169,829
2014 Turnout as % CVAP	37.8%
2012 Turnout as % CVAP	61.2%

With their work ethic, varied skills, and appreciation of the local environment, they brought a distaste for the crime and civil strife that seemed all too common in Los Angeles during that turbulent decade in U.S. history. In the valleys of Ventura County, northwest of Los Angeles, people built communities in what had been orange and lemon groves. Like California overall, the Ventura County population has trended socially liberal and economically conservative. To the south is upscale Thousand Oaks, one of the safest large cities in the nation and the headquarters of biotechnology giant Amgen Inc. Farther west in Pleasant Valley is Camarillo, which is home to numerous technology firms.

In the inland valleys still farther west is Ojai. During the filming of the 1937 Frank Capra movie *Lost Horizon*, an aerial shot of the Ojai Valley was used to represent the mythical earthly paradise of Shangri-La. Also present here is the Santa Clara River Valley, with Fillmore, Piru, and Santa Paula. Fillmore, hoping to become a set destination for Hollywood movies, removed its palm trees in 2012 to make the town look less California and more universally American. Despite its affluence, the area did not escape the recession. Though the unemployment rate for the Oxnard-Thousand Oaks-Ventura metro area reached double digits in 2011, it dropped to 4.5 percent in December 2014. The local economy has a strong export market, including pharmaceuticals, semiconductors and citrus fruit. A downside is that the economic growth has created a shortage of housing for farm workers.

2012 Presidential Vote		
Barack Obama (D) 147,753	(54%)	
Mitt Romney (R).................119,677	(44%)	
2008 Presidential Vote		
Barack Obama (D) 162,181	(56%)	
John McCain (R).................118,793	(41%)	
Cook Partisan Voting Index: D+4		

The 26th Congressional District includes most of Ventura County, including its largest city, Oxnard. The district takes in Thousand Oaks and the Santa Clara River Valley. Simi Valley is split with the 25th, despite the objections of many residents who wanted a single district entirely in Ventura County Instead, the 26th has a thin slice of Los Angeles county. The 26th District leans Democratic, though it is more competitive than any Democratic-held district in L.A. County.

Julia Brownley (D)

Democrat Julia Brownley in 2012 took the Ventura County seat that had long been held by Republicans. With a political base that had been in Santa Monica south of the 26th District, she was slow to establish control of the district or her mark in the House.

Brownley grew up in Virginia in a Republican household. It wasn't until she went to Washington, D.C.'s all-girls Mount Vernon College (later incorporated into George Washington University) that she began to consider her personal politics. There, shaped by the emerging women's movement and the war in Vietnam, Brownley said she felt at home in the Democratic Party. After college, she pursued a career in marketing, earning a master's degree from American University and then working as a sales manager for several large companies. The career introduced her to her husband (they are now divorced) and brought her to California. Brownley's experiences with her children helped to push her into politics. Her daughter, Hannah, suffered from dyslexia. Working with the school system to improve Hannah's education inspired Brownley to run for the Santa Monica-Malibu school board in 1994. She stayed on the board for 12 years, and served as its president.

Frustrated with what she considered insufficient funding for the school district, Brownley in 2006 won a seat in the state Assembly. There, Brownley chaired the Education Committee, advocating higher spending on the state's schools at every level. She worked on legislation to prevent human trafficking, to improve the foster care system, and to reduce the prevalence of single-use plastic bags. She also worked to pass a state version of the Disclose Act that would require more disclosure of political donors.

In the contest for the open seat in the 26th District, Democrats had counted on Ventura County Supervisor Steve Bennett, but he dropped out before the filing deadline. Brownley moved up the coast from Santa Monica and prevailed in the primary over Linda Parks, a Republican-turned-independent hoping to steal moderate votes from Brownley. Nearly $1 million in advertising, including a $600,000 television buy from a Democratic super PAC, moved Brownley to the general election against state Sen. Tony Strickland. He led the primary with 44%, to 27% for Brownley and 18% for Parks.

In the general election, Strickland attacked Brownley for moving to the district, while emphasizing his own history in the area. The U.S. Chamber of Commerce and other groups contributed to his campaign, leading Brownley to call him a captive of "Washington special interests." The *Los Angeles Times* endorsed her, saying that the "ideologically rigid" Strickland lacked the "real-world pragmatism" of other Southern California Republicans. She won, 52.7%-47.3%. Ironically, Strickland in 2014 ran—and lost—in the adjacent Republican-leaning 25th District. Brownley had continuing problems in finding a comfort level with her new constituency. Her official House bio listed that she served on a school board for 12 years, for example, but it did not say where.

In the House, Brownley became active on the Veterans Affairs Committee, where she was ranking Democrat on the Health Subcommittee. She filed legislation to assure adequate housing for veterans who are terminally ill and to repeal the legislative provision enacted in 2013 that reduces the cost-of-living adjustment for veterans under 62. She pursued her interest in education issues by calling for increased funding of bilingual programs. In January 2015, she became co-chair with Republican Rep. Lamar Smith of Texas of the House Dyslexia Caucus.

Brownley faced another competitive campaign in 2014. This time, her opponent in November was Assemblyman Jeff Gorell, who showcased his moderate voting record in Sacramento. In September 2014, a Democratic official in Washington told *Roll Call* that, "This is a tight race and a difficult seat." Brownley was far better-funded, $3.4 million to $1.3 million, and also benefited in the expensive L.A. media market from more than $2 million in national party funding. She won narrowly, 51.3%-48.7%. It took more than a week to declare the winner.

The Democratic Congressional Campaign Committee included Brownley among the first 14 members of its Frontline program of House Democrats who are expected to be vulnerable in 2016. Brownley may be in a better position to survive with the higher turnout in a presidential election year.

TWENTY-SEVENTH DISTRICT

Judy Chu (D)

Elected July 2009, 3rd full term; b. July 7, 1953, Los Angeles; U.C.L.A., B.A. 1974, M.A. 1977; CA School of Professional Psychology, Ph.D. 1979; no religious affiliation; married (Mike Eng).

Elected Office: Garvey Schl. Bd., 1985-88; Monterey Park City Cncl., 1988-2001; Mayor, Monterey Park; CA Assembly, 2001-06; CA Bd. of Equalization, 2006-09, vice chmn., 2009.

Professional Career: Prof., Los Angeles City Col., Psychology Dept., 1981-88; E. Los Angeles Col., Psychology Dept., 1988-2001.

DC Office: 2423 RHOB, 20515, 202-225-5464; Fax: 202-225-5467; Website: chu.house.gov.

State Offices: Claremont, 909-625-5394; Pasadena, 626-304-0110.

Committees: *Judiciary:* Courts, Intellectual Property & the Internet; Crime, Terrorism, Homeland Security & Investigations. *Small Business:* Contracting & Workforce; Economic Growth, Tax & Capital Access (RMM); Health & Technology.

Group Ratings

	ADA	ACLU	AFL-CIO	LCV	ITI	COC	HAFA	ACU	CFG	FRC
2014	95%	72%	–	91%	40%	43%	13%	8%	11%	0%
2013	90%	C	100%	96%	C	31%	C	17%	18%	C

National Journal Ratings

	2013 LIB	—	2013 CONS
Economic	91%	—	0%
Social	93%	—	0%
Foreign	94%	—	0%
Composite	96%	—	4%

Key Votes of the 113th Congress

1. Sandy storm spending	Y	5. Medical Marijuana	Y	9. Syrian Rebels Training	Y
2. Violence Against Women Act	Y	6. Farm Bill	N	10. Keystone pipeline	N
3. Guantanamo Bay Detainees	Y	7. Afghanistan Combat	Y	11. Immigration Exec. Action	N
4. Abortion 20-week ban	N	8. NSA Phone Data Collection	Y	12. Bipartisan budget deal	N

Election Results

2014 general	Judy Chu (D)	75,728	(59%)	$737,543
	Jack Orswell (R)	51,852	(41%)	$159,259
2014 primary	Judy Chu (D)	50,203	(58%)	
	Jack Orswell (R)	20,868	(24%)	
	Bob Duran (R)	15,819	(18%)	

Prior winning percentages: 2012 (64%), 2010 (71%), 2009 special (62%)

Population		Race and Ethnicity		Income	
Total:	716,835	Asian	36.2%	Median income:	$68,053
Urban:	63.4%	White	30.8%		*(69 of 435)*
Suburban:	36.5%	Latino	26.1%	Under $50,000	37.2%
Rural:	0.1%	Black	4.2%	$50,000-$99,999:	30.0%
Land area:	512	Two races	2.2%	$100,000-$199,999:	23.9%
Pop/sq. mi.:	1,400.8	White Ethnic	11.3%	$200,000 or more:	8.8%
Born in state:	47.0%			Poverty Rate	13.8%
		Education			
Age Groups		H.S. grad or less:	31.9%	**Work**	
Under 18:	19.7%	Some college:	26.6%	White collar:	44.0%
18 to 34:	22.9%	College degree, 4 yr.:	25.4%	Blue collar:	42.4%
35 to 64:	41.3%	Post-grad study:	16.1%	Sales and service:	13.6%
Over 64:	16.2%				
		Military		Govt. workers:	14.1%
		Veterans/active duty:	4.1%		

San Gabriel Foothills: Pasadena, Alhambra

In the early part of the 20th century, when Los Angeles was growing rapidly and on its way to becoming one of America's major cities, its richest citizens settled not on the beach (too clammy and cold) or on the west side (too dusty and remote), but in communities they built at the base of the

Voter Turnout	
2013 Total Citizen 18+	482,342
2014 House Turnout	127,580
2014 Turnout as % CVAP	26.5%
2012 Turnout as % CVAP	53.7%

San Gabriel Mountains. Their snow-capped peaks, rising 10,000 feet above the city, are visible most of the year. The place to be was Pasadena, home of the Rose Bowl, Cal Tech, and a baroque-domed city hall. Pasadena and South Pasadena have carefully preserved their bungalow neighborhoods, and Pasadena preserved and rebuilt the 80-year-old curving Colorado Boulevard Bridge over Arroyo Seco. The economic downturn hit Pasadena's city government hard; its sales tax revenue dropped almost 24 percent in 2009. Still, the city pushed ahead with a $179 million renovation of the Rose Bowl, one of the area's economic mainstays. With the renovations complete ($30 million over budget), the Rose Bowl gained attention as a possible temporary stadium if a National Football League franchise returned to L.A. and awaited construction of a new stadium. More than 20 percent of all households in Pasadena have income below $25,000, which makes it difficult for them to find housing. Nearby is luxurious San Marino, the home of the Huntington Library, one of the world's great museums and scholarly institutions, with more than 150 acres of botanical gardens. In June 2014, San Marino Mayor Dennis Kneier resigned after a surveillance video revealed that he threw a bag of dog poop into his neighbor's yard. Arcadia has the Santa Anita Park racetrack and the Los Angeles County Arboretum & Botanic Garden. Wealthy Chinese have invested in business opportunities in the area.

Parts of this area have significant Asian populations. Chinese and other Asians are the majority in Monterey Park and 61 percent of the population in Rosemead. The late *New York Times* food maven R.W. Apple Jr. described "a memorable week in the gastronomic trenches" of the local Asian restaurant scene, and reported that "it is easier to buy bok choy than iceberg" in Monterey Park. In 2012, young Asian-Americans produced a *YouTube* rap video titled "626"—the area code for much of the San Gabriel Valley—and it went viral on the Internet.

The 27th Congressional District includes portions of Los Angeles County and much of the Pasadena area. It takes in San Marino and the San Gabriel foothills communities of Altadena, Glendora, Sierra Madre, and San Antonio Heights, which have similar water and fire-control issues. Wildfires in September 2012 burned more than 3,600 acres here and forced the evacuation of 12,000 people. Also in the district are San Gabriel, Temple City, and Claremont, dubbed "The City of Trees and PhD's" after its Claremont Colleges. Also in the district is a small indentation of San Bernardino County, near Upland, which leans Republican. With a large aging population, health services are the strongest employer in the San Gabriel Valley. Proposals to designate a large part of the San Gabriel Mountains as a national monument drew protests, especially from bikers, hunters and other recreational users. In November 2014, Claremont voters approved a referendum, 72%-

2012 Presidential Vote
Barack Obama (D)	161,528	(63%)
Mitt Romney (R)	90,278	(35%)

2008 Presidential Vote
Barack Obama (D)	160,486	(62%)
John McCain (R)	94,293	(36%)

Cook Partisan Voting Index: D+11

28%, allowing the city to seize its local water system by eminent domain and convert it to a municipal service. The 27th is 36% Asian American, the second-highest percentage of any California congressional district, and politically is solidly Democratic.

Judy Chu (D)

Democrat Judy Chu, who won a 2009 special election to succeed Democrat Hilda Solis, became the first Chinese-American woman in the House. She is a strong liberal and has been active in the Congressional Asian Pacific-American Caucus.

Chu grew up in Los Angeles as the daughter of an electrical technician who brought his wife over from China under the War Brides Act. The family moved to the Bay Area when she was in junior high school. She graduated from the University of California, Los Angeles, got a Ph.D. in psychology, and then taught for 13 years at East Los Angeles Community College.

She served on the Garvey School District board for three years and was mayor of Monterey Park for 12 years. In 2000, Chu was elected to the California Assembly, where she focused on criminal justice and environmental protection issues. As chairwoman of the Appropriations Committee, she sponsored a tax amnesty program that brought in significant sums for the state. In 2006, she was elected to the state Board of Equalization, where she worked on closing tax loopholes.

After Solis was appointed as President Barack Obama's first Secretary of Labor, the contest for the Democratic nomination became a race between Chu and state Sen. Gil Cedillo, the leading Hispanic candidate. Rather than simply an ethnic showdown between an Asian and a Latino, the race was more nuanced. Chu was endorsed by much of the Democratic establishment, including some prominent Hispanics, such as Los Angeles Mayor Anthony Villaraigosa and members of Solis' family. The Los Angeles County Labor Federation, which was impressed by Chu's support for farm workers, backed her, as did EMILY's List, the national advocacy group for pro-abortion rights Democratic women. A third candidate was also a Hispanic and siphoned off some likely Cedillo voters: political novice Emanuel Pleitez, a 26-year-old financial analyst who had worked on Obama's presidential campaign. Chu raised nearly $1 million, Cedillo more than $700,000, and Pleitez $200,000. Chu won with 32%, to 23% for Cedillo and 14% for Pleitez. Because Judy Chu failed to receive a majority of the total primary vote, she faced a runoff with Republican Betty Chu, a Monterey Park councilwoman who is Chu's distant cousin by marriage. The Democrat won by nearly 2-to-1, 62%-33%.

Chu continued Solis' strongly liberal voting record. She joined the Out of Afghanistan Caucus and voted against a 2010 spending bill to fund military operations there. After her nephew, a lance corporal in the Marines stationed in Afghanistan, committed suicide in 2011 after being beaten up by his fellow soldiers, she introduced an anti-military hazing bill. It was incorporated into the House-passed fiscal 2013 defense authorization bill. On the Judiciary Committee, she offered an amendment to a medical liability bill in 2011 to end health insurance companies' exemption from antitrust laws; it tied 13-13. She introduced a bill a few months later to limit employers' use of immigration law to thwart workers' efforts to protect their labor rights.

As chair of the Asian Pacific-American Caucus, Chu lobbied Asian Americans to support Obama's reelection in 2012. "No other U.S. president in history has had such a deep understanding of the vibrancy of Asia," she wrote in an op-ed piece shortly before the election. She sponsored a House-passed resolution in 2012 to have the United States apologize for the anti-immigrant Chinese Exclusion Act of 1882, telling colleagues that her grandfather was forced to carry a certificate of U.S. residence for about 40 years. "It is for my grandfather, and for all Chinese Americans who were told for six decades by the U.S. government that the land of the free wasn't open to them, that we must pass this resolution," she said. In May 2014, she unveiled for the caucus a package of immigration reforms, including a deferral of deportations for young undocumented immigrants.

On other issues, Chu has been a leading proponent of designating a large slice of the San Gabriel Mountains as a national park. In 2013, Chu was named by Minority Leader Nancy Pelosi to the Democratic Steering and Policy Committee. In December 2014, the House Standards of Official Conduct (Ethics) Committee issued Chu a letter of reproval after concluding that she interfered with the panel's investigation of whether her House aides had performed campaign work. "The committee acknowledged that my intention was to ease the staff member's anxiety and that I expressed regret for this one moment of contact," Chu said in a subsequent statement. In 2014, Republican Jack Orswell, a small business owner and former FBI agent, challenged Chu and got 40.6% of the vote. That was the first time that Chu was held below 60%, but she does not appear to be in jeopardy.

TWENTY-EIGHTH DISTRICT

Adam Schiff (D)

Elected 2000, 8th term; b. June 22, 1960, Framingham, MA; Stanford U., B.A. 1982, Harvard U., J.D. 1985; Jewish; married (Eve); 2 children.

Elected Office: CA Senate, 1996-2000.

Professional Career: Prosecutor, U.S. Atty. Gen. Office, L.A., 1987-93; Practicing atty., 1986-87, 1995-96.

DC Office: 2411 RHOB, 20515, 202-225-4176; Fax: 202-225-5828; Website: schiff.house.gov.

State Offices: Burbank, 818-450-2900; Hollywood, 323-315-5555.

Committees: *Intelligence (Permanent)* (RMM). *Select Benghazi Committee.*

Group Ratings

	ADA	ACLU	AFL-CIO	LCV	ITI	COC	HAFA	ACU	CFG	FRC
2014	80%	83%	–	97%	20%	46%	15%	8%	13%	0%
2013	85%	C	95%	96%	C	31%	C	16%	15%	C

National Journal Ratings

	2013 LIB	—	2013 CONS
Economic	76%	—	22%
Social	79%	—	16%
Foreign	79%	—	20%
Composite	79%	—	21%

Key Votes of the 113th Congress

1. Sandy storm spending	Y	5. Medical Marijuana	Y	9. Syrian Rebels Training	Y
2. Violence Against Women Act	Y	6. Farm Bill	N	10. Keystone pipeline	N
3. Guantanamo Bay Detainees	Y	7. Afghanistan Combat	Y	11. Immigration Exec. Action	N
4. Abortion 20-week ban	N	8. NSA Phone Data Collection	Y	12. Bipartisan budget deal	Y

Election Results

2014 general	Adam Schiff (D)	91,996	(77%)	$870,295
	Steve Stokes (I)	28,268	(24%)	$7,411
2014 primary	Adam Schiff (D)	46,004	(75%)	
	Steve Stokes (I)	11,078	(18%)	
	Sal Genovese (D)	4,643	(8%)	

Prior winning percentages: 2012 (77%), 2010 (65%), 2008 (69%), 2006 (63%), 2004 (65%), 2002 (63%), 2000 (53%)

Population		Race and Ethnicity		Income	
Total:	708,212	White	56.6%	Median income:	$52,887
Urban:	78.6%	Latino	25.3%		*(186 of 435)*
Suburban:	21.0%	Asian	13.3%	Under $50,000	47.1%
Rural:	0.4%	Black	2.1%	$50,000-$99,999:	26.4%
Land area:	268	Two races	2.1%	$100,000-$199,999:	17.6%
Pop/sq. mi.:	2,639.7	White Ethnic	20.5%	$200,000 or more:	8.9%
Born in state:	36.9%			Poverty Rate	16.6%
		Education			
Age Groups		H.S. grad or less:	29.9%	**Work**	
Under 18:	15.9%	Some college:	25.5%	White collar:	47.6%
18 to 34:	27.1%	College degree, 4 yr.:	30.1%	Blue collar:	41.4%
35 to 64:	42.8%	Post-grad study:	14.5%	Sales and service:	11.0%
Over 64:	14.2%				
		Military		Govt. workers:	9.1%
		Veterans/active duty:	3.6%		

Northern Los Angeles: Westside and Hollywood

The Westside (often written as one word) of Los Angeles is perhaps the most glamorous and flashiest concentration of affluence in the world. It is the heartland of one of America's most productive and creative industries and one of the nation's major exports, show business. The first moviemakers

Voter Turnout	
2013 Total Citizen 18+	484,815
2014 House Turnout	120,264
2014 Turnout as % CVAP	24.8%
2012 Turnout as % CVAP	55.5%

came here looking for a place to shoot silent films where the sunlight was more dependable than in Astoria, Queens, or Englewood, New Jersey. They found it in Hollywood, a suburb just annexed by burgeoning Los Angeles when the first movie studio was built in 1911. In 1923 came the "Hollywood" sign, overlooking the soon-famous intersection of Hollywood and Vine. By the 1930s, big studio lots were scattered around town, over the mountains in Burbank, or out toward the ocean in Westwood and Culver City. Miraculously, the studio bosses of that era—most of them Jewish immigrants with little ancestral experience of America—created a popular culture that was universally accessible and embodied the American spirit in a way that still rings true.

Beneath the Verdugo Mountains is Burbank, the "media capital of the world" and the headquarters for NBC Studios, ABC Studios, Warner Brothers, Universal Studios, and Disney, plus many small entertainment and multimedia companies. Millions of Americans recognize the name of Burbank from having watched "*The Tonight Show*," until Jimmy Fallon replaced Jay Leno as host and returned the show to Manhattan. The movie studios are an integral part of the local economy: In 2014, Warner Brothers employed 8,000 in Burbank, though recent industry downturns led to some cutbacks. More middle-class is Glendale, north of downtown Los Angeles, site of Forest Lawn Cemetery and DreamWorks Animation. Glendale, a diverse city with a large concentration of Armenians, recently has experienced a residential-building boom.

The entertainment industry here has pushed for greater protection of intellectual property and a crackdown on online piracy. The industry-favored Stop Online Piracy Act generated an "Internet Black Out" day of protest on Jan. 18, 2012, from Wikipedia and Google, and the controversy pitted Hollywood movie studios in Southern California against Northern California dot.coms and Silicon Valley. Marking the importance of the entertainment industry here, the aptly named Burbank Bob Hope Airport is located on North Hollywood Way. Plans have been explored to replace the aging terminal, which is too small and close to the runway. West Hollywood has a large gay community. It is also home to the Sunset Strip, a launching pad for many rock 'n' roll acts, including The Doors, Guns N' Roses, and Led Zeppelin. They played nightclubs like The Roxy, the Whisky a Go Go, and the now-shuttered London Fog, although these days the Strip attracts mostly lesser-known bands and cover acts.

2012 Presidential Vote		
Barack Obama (D)	187,441	(70%)
Mitt Romney (R)	70,757	(27%)
2008 Presidential Vote		
Barack Obama (D)	194,650	(71%)
John McCain (R)	73,510	(27%)
Cook Partisan Voting Index:	D+20	

The 28th Congressional District includes parts of the Westside and Los Angeles County, including La Crescenta-Montrose and La Cañada Flintridge, home of NASA's Jet Propulsion Laboratory. The largest cities are Glendale and Burbank, although part of the latter spills into the 30th District. Celebrity Kim Kardashian has expressed interest in becoming mayor of Glendale. This is a solidly Democratic district.

Adam Schiff (D)

Adam Schiff, a Democrat elected in 2000, has been an active and often independent voice on national security and intellectual property issues. He is more of a fiscal moderate than most Southern California Democrats, and repeatedly has called for Congress to provide more active oversight of the executive branch's national security actions.

Schiff's father was a traveling salesman and later owned a lumberyard. Schiff grew up throughout the country, graduating from high school in Northern California. He graduated from Stanford University and Harvard Law School. From 1987 to 1993, he worked in the U.S. attorney's office in Los Angeles. He ran for the California Assembly and lost three times. In 1996, he was elected to the state Senate. In his first two years, he enacted dozens of measures, including a bill guaranteeing up-to-date textbooks in classrooms and another reforming the child support system. Schiff also taught political science at Glendale Community College.

Schiff ran for the House in the first election following the 1998 impeachment of President Bill Clinton, when the issue became a factor in several races. Schiff challenged incumbent Republican James Rogan, who was a leader in the Judiciary Committee's deliberations and a persuasive voice for the case against Clinton, which centered on the president's lying under oath about an affair with a White House intern. Rogan had won reelection in 1998 by just 51%-46%, and Clinton pal and entertainment mogul David Geffen was promising to raise millions of dollars to oppose him. The Schiff-Rogan race became a fundraising marathon, and was then the most expensive House race on record. The candidates raised more than $10 million combined, and much more was spent independently by Clinton's supporters as well as his detractors. Rogan branded his opponent as a traditional tax-and-spend liberal, who would "run naked through the Treasury, spending everything he can." Schiff attacked Rogan for calling abortion a holocaust for the African-American community. Schiff won by an unexpectedly large 53%-44% vote, and has been easily reelected since.

In the House, Schiff joined the Blue Dog Coalition of moderate to conservative Democrats and has sometimes worked across party lines. But he also has been a party activist, contributing to the Democratic Congressional Campaign Committee's efforts by co-chairing a mentoring program for prime contenders.

Schiff served as co-chairman of the Congressional International Anti-Piracy Caucus. He joined Judiciary Committee Chairman Lamar Smith of Texas in sponsoring a bill to provide law enforcement and copyright holders with new tools to target websites based offshore that offer pirated music, movies, and other counterfeit goods. He was instrumental in bipartisan legislation that made identity theft a crime. And on a bill to implement recommendations of the 9/11 commission, he was the only Democrat voting with Judiciary Committee Republicans on added immigration restrictions. The final bill included his provisions to establish tougher penalties for developing a "dirty bomb," and to give new tools to law enforcement to crack down on weapons of mass destruction.

Schiff stirred complaints from liberal constituents when he supported the resolution approving the use of force in Iraq in 2002 and for voting for the USA Patriot Act, the anti-terrorism law that gave new powers to law enforcement. When the Justice Department's failed gun-tracking operation known as "Fast and Furious" became a political controversy in 2011, he called for implementing tougher penalties on straw-purchase gun buyers as an alternative to Republican demands for Attorney General Eric Holder's resignation. After the fatal police shooting of an unarmed black man in Ferguson Missouri in 2014, Schiff pushed Holder to help state and local law enforcement agencies acquire body-worn cameras.

His contribution to congressional ethics reform was a bill, passed by the House in 2007, preventing lawmakers from placing their spouses on campaign payrolls. After the Supreme Court in 2012 overturned a Montana law barring corporate spending in state elections, he worked with Harvard constitutional law scholar Laurence Tribe to introduce a constitutional amendment making it clear that Congress and the states have the authority to impose limitations on independent campaign expenditures.

On foreign policy, Schiff has pressed for recognition of the Armenian genocide as the responsibility of the Ottoman Empire, a move Turkey adamantly opposes. His resolution was approved by the House Foreign Affairs Committee in 2007, but he agreed to postpone further action after a strong response from Turkey. Schiff has been concerned that major national security actions should not be left solely to a president's discretion. He introduced a bill in 2013 to repeal the Authorization for Use of Military Force, which Congress passed after the 2001 attacks. He said it "was never intended to authorize a war without end, and it now poorly defines those who pose a threat to our country." When he offered an amendment based on the measure to the fiscal 2014 defense appropriations bill, it was defeated 185-236 after Republicans said it was dangerous to set a specific timeline for replacing the 2001 resolution.

When the terrorist group Islamic State of Iraq and Syria (ISIS) began capturing large swaths of territory in the Middle East in 2014, Schiff sought to call attention to the threat of Americans and Europeans carrying out attacks at home. "As with so much else in the post-9/11 era, the United States and its democratic allies must balance security and freedom as we seek to prevent our citizens from becoming radicalized and turning on us," he wrote in a *Los Angeles Register* op-ed column. Later, when Obama outlined a plan to deal with ISIS, Schiff became heavily involved in efforts to have Congress authorize the president's actions. "It's hard to explain the relative silence of my libertarian colleagues at a time when the president is about to announce a war effort that may take years," Schiff told *The Washington Post.* He also pressed for lawmakers to have a role in the administration's look at surveillance and privacy following revelations of the National Security Agency's domestic snooping. Schiff strongly objected to the Republican push to investigate the terrorist attacks on U.S. facilities in Benghazi, Libya. In May 2014, he told Fox News that a select committee on the matter was "a colossal waste of time" and that his party should boycott it—something that House leaders refused to do. He subsequently became a member of the select committee. Earlier, he was among the Democrats defending Obama adviser Susan Rice against Republican criticism that she had misled the public about terrorist attacks in Libya and Egypt.

Minority Leader Nancy Pelosi gave Schiff a significant niche on national security issues when she named him the ranking Democrat on the House Intelligence Committee in January 2015. "Schiff has been a vital voice on the most pressing national security challenges of our time, including counterterrorism efforts and challenges in the Middle East," she said. Schiff has brought to the table new proposals on intelligence policy. He has filed legislation to require greater transparency for the U.S. military drone program. He has opposed paying ransoms to free Americans held by rebel groups, such as ISIS. He also has advocated major changes in the National Security Agency's phone metadata surveillance program, which would require the government to request phone company records on a case-by-case basis.

Schiff, who has competed in triathlons, in 2014 participated in a week-long 545-mile bike ride down California's coast, on behalf of L.A.'s LGBT Center and the San Francisco AIDS Foundation. After Sen. Barbara Boxer in January 2015 said she would not seek reelection, Schiff said that he was "giving the matter serious consideration." The dynamics of California's top-two primary system might create an opportunity for a candidate with centrist credentials in a showdown against another Democrat. In May, he quietly announced that he would remain in the House, but he kept the door open to "other challenges in the future."

TWENTY-NINTH DISTRICT

Tony Cárdenas (D)

Elected 2012, 2nd term; b. March 31, 1963, Pacoima; U. of CA Santa Barbara, B.A. 1986; Christian; married (Norma); 4 children.

Elected Office: Los Angeles City Cncl., 2004-12; CA Assembly, 1996-2002.

Professional Career: Real-estate broker, 1987-96; Life ins. salesman, 1986-87; Electrical engineer, Hewlett-Packard, 1986.

DC Office: 1510 LHOB, 20515, 202-225-6131; Website: cardenas. house.gov.

State Offices: Panorama City, 818-781-7407.

Committees: *Energy & Commerce:* Commerce, Manufacturing, & Trade; Environment & the Economy; Health.

Group Ratings

	ADA	ACLU	AFL-CIO	LCV	ITI	COC	HAFA	ACU	CFG	FRC
2014	90%	77%	–	91%	80%	38%	15%	8%	16%	0%
2013	70%	C	95%	93%	C	42%	C	16%	12%	C

National Journal Ratings

	2013 LIB	—	2013 CONS
Economic	70%	—	29%
Social	69%	—	28%
Foreign	66%	—	32%
Composite	69%	—	31%

Key Votes of the 113th Congress

1. Sandy storm spending	Y	5. Medical Marijuana	Y	9. Syrian Rebels Training	Y
2. Violence Against Women Act	Y	6. Farm Bill	N	10. Keystone pipeline	N
3. Guantanamo Bay Detainees	Y	7. Afghanistan Combat	Y	11. Immigration Exec. Action	N
4. Abortion 20-week ban	N	8. NSA Phone Data Collection	Y	12. Bipartisan budget deal	Y

Election Results

2014 general	Tony Cárdenas (D)	50,096	(75%)	$953,305	$43,162
	William Leader (R)	17,045	(25%)		
2014 primary	Tony Cárdenas (D)	19,566	(63%)		
	William Leader (R)	8,025	(26%)		
	Venice Gamble (D)	3,542	(11%)		

Prior winning percentage: 2012 (74%)

Population		Race and Ethnicity		Income	
Total:	692,267	Latino	67.7%	Median income:	$45,233
Urban:	80.2%	White	19.0%		*(316 of 435)*
Suburban:	19.8%	Asian	8.0%	Under $50,000	54.3%
Rural:	0.0%	Black	3.6%	$50,000-$99,999:	29.4%
Land area:	165	Two races	1.2%	$100,000-$199,999:	14.2%
Pop/sq. mi.:	4,202.1	White Ethnic	6.3%	$200,000 or more:	2.2%
Born in state:	45.6%			Poverty Rate	22.6%
		Education			
Age Groups		H.S. grad or less:	58.1%	**Work**	
Under 18:	24.8%	Some college:	23.6%	White collar:	23.1%
18 to 34:	28.1%	College degree, 4 yr.:	13.8%	Blue collar:	48.9%
35 to 64:	38.3%	Post-grad study:	4.4%	Sales and service:	28.0%
Over 64:	8.9%			Govt. workers:	8.2%
		Military			
		Veterans/active duty:	2.7%		

Central San Fernando Valley: Van Nuys

A hiker looking north from the crest of the Santa Monica Mountains in 1912 would have seen a valley almost totally empty and barren, 20 miles long and 12 miles wide. Separated by the Cahuenga Pass from rapidly growing Los Angeles and Hollywood, the San Fernando Valley was bought up in

Voter Turnout	
2013 Total Citizen 18+	347,303
2014 House Turnout	67,141
2014 Turnout as % CVAP	19.3%
2012 Turnout as % CVAP	46.2%

massive tracts by civic leaders as they were urging city engineer William Mulholland to build a huge 250-mile aqueduct from the Owens Valley to bring water to Los Angeles and persuading the city in 1915 to annex 200 square miles of the Valley. In the years after World War II, this was modern suburbia, filled with *Leave It to Beaver* families. More recently, the San Fernando Valley became postmodern urban. The driver topping the crest saw office towers looming out over slightly hazy air, shopping centers, occasional palm trees, stucco subdivisions, and the squat factory and warehouse buildings that once made Los Angeles County a top manufacturing locale.

But many of the big plants have closed and the Valley has changed. The 1950s white families with stay-at-home moms have been replaced by Latino families with parents juggling two jobs and trying to raise children who will have a better chance than they had. Pacoima, at the northern end of the Valley, is mostly Latino. Farther south, in Van Nuys, Canoga Park, and Burbank, was the industrial base—the GM plants were mostly shut down in the 1980s, and the last large one to remain open, the Pratt and Whitney Rocketdyne plant, was sold to manufacturer GenCorp in 2012. The big factories have been

2012 Presidential Vote		
Barack Obama (D)	129,323	(77%)
Mitt Romney (R)	34,454	(21%)
2008 Presidential Vote		
Barack Obama (D)	135,455	(75%)
John McCain (R)	40,524	(23%)
Cook Partisan Voting Index: D+25		

supplanted by hundreds of small factories and multimedia plants. And the need for more water has become even more desperate for civic leaders.

The southern rim of the Valley, around the North Hollywood area, is still heavily Jewish and is attracting new families who often send their kids to religious schools. People with money cluster near the foot of the mountains around the Valley; those less well-off settle on the flatlands beyond. The Valley was hit hard when the housing bubble burst in 2007, with prices dropping 50 percent or more in some areas. This was a big area for subprime mortgages, which left homeowners, many of them Hispanic, underwater. The business and housing markets have improved in the past few years, with foreclosures down sharply, but times have remained tough. In 2014, Nestle and Sunkist closed plants, and adult film production plummeted. The Valley also has been plagued by increased crime, including gangs.

The 29th Congressional District of California consists of the eastern part of the San Fernando Valley in the city of Los Angeles. It includes affluent North Hollywood, as well as Van Nuys, North Hills, and Panorama City. The southeast part of the district takes in the NoHo Arts District. Parts of the northern end of the Valley, including economically declining Pacoima and the small city of San Fernando, are in the district. Whiteman Airport and Los Angeles Valley College are also here. The new 29th District is 68 percent Hispanic, and solidly Democratic.

Tony Cárdenas (D)

Democrat Tony Cárdenas, elected in 2012 as the first Latino congressman to represent Los Angeles's San Fernando Valley, has moved into prominent positions in the House and has been a player on issues that affect his district.

As the youngest of 11 children of Mexican immigrant parents, Cárdenas was born and raised in the Valley city of Pacoima. His father was a self-employed gardener who would take young Cárdenas and his brothers to work with him. While still a teenager, Cárdenas got his first paid job at San Fernando Valley's Boys & Girls Club through a summer work program. "Every time I got paid, I would give my parents money. I would save some money, and I would have a little money to spend," he recalled in an interview with *National Journal*. He earned a bachelor's degree in electrical engineering from the University of California, Santa Barbara in 1986. He subsequently went to work for Hewlett-Packard but left just five months later. "There has to be something different for me," he remembered thinking.

He returned home to Pacoima to live with his parents and sold life insurance for a year, then worked selling real estate for five years before opening his own brokerage firm in the San Fernando Valley. During that time, the Valley had become more Latino—but, he observed, political representation did not mirror that change. One day, a friend suggested that he run for political office. He did, and in 1996 became the first Latino to represent the Valley in the state Assembly. Cárdenas became known for his work to reform California's gang prevention and intervention programs. In 2000, the Legislature passed a bill he co-sponsored authorizing $121 million in annual funding for local juvenile justice programs in the state's 58 counties. Cárdenas says he became interested in gang-intervention programs after many of his childhood friends had run-ins with the law, lamenting, "They weren't exactly living a life that we had dreamed of."

In 2003, Cárdenas won a seat on the Los Angeles City Council, where he continued to work on gang prevention. He also worked to create opportunities for minority-owned businesses to compete for the city's bond underwriting work. And he pushed for policies to fight human trafficking and prevent the mistreatment of animals.

When he decided to run for Congress in a district with no incumbent, Cárdenas was a strong favorite among Democrats and he received 64 percent of the vote in the primary. His closest competitor was "No Party Preference" perennial candidate David Hernandez, an insurance adjuster and Vietnam veteran. Hernandez mocked Cárdenas for touting his Latino roots. A message on Hernandez's Facebook page said, "Tony Cárdenas wants to be the first Latino congressman from the San Fernando Valley. David Hernandez wants to be the congressman who represents and brings prosperity to the area which has … suffered under failed leadership." Those attacks barely resonated in the Democratic district, and Cárdenas won 74%-26%.

Cardenas has worn several hats in the House. He co-chaired the Crime Prevention and Youth Development Caucus with Rep. David Reichert of Washington, and the Congressional Student-Athlete Protection Caucus with Rep. Charlie Dent of Pennsylvania, both Republicans. In November 2014, he became chairman of BOLD PAC, the fundraising arm of the Congressional Hispanic Caucus. He also won a prized seat on the Energy and Commerce Committee.

Legislatively, he became one of the first House members to oppose the proposed merger of Comcast and Time Warner Cable, which he said would harm competition, raise costs, and "eliminate good jobs in California." He persistently sought votes on comprehensive immigration legislation, and told CNN in September 2014 that "the Latino community is frustrated with [President Obama] but pissed off with Republicans," over the delay. In December 2014, Congress passed the annual defense spending bill with his amendment that directed the Government Accountability Office to review the gaps and weaknesses in the Pentagon's cybersecurity, including their impact on businesses.

THIRTIETH DISTRICT

Brad Sherman (D)

Elected 1996, 10th term; b. Oct. 24, 1954, Los Angeles; U.C.L.A., B.A. 1974, Harvard U., J.D. 1979; Jewish; married (Lisa); 3 children.

Elected Office: CA Bd. of Equalization, 1990-95, chmn., 1991-95.

Professional Career: Practicing atty., Accountant, 1980-90.

DC Office: 2242 RHOB, 20515, 202-225-5911; Fax: 202-225-5879; Website: sherman.house.gov.

State Offices: Sherman Oaks, 818-501-9200.

Committees: *Financial Services:* Capital Markets & Gov't Sponsored Enterprises; Financial Institutions & Consumer Credit. *Foreign Affairs:* Asia & the Pacific (RMM); Terrorism, Nonproliferation & Trade.

Group Ratings

	ADA	ACLU	AFL-CIO	LCV	ITI	COC	HAFA	ACU	CFG	FRC
2014	75%	83%	–	97%	40%	50%	6%	0%	2%	0%
2013	70%	C	95%	96%	C	31%	C	20%	12%	C

National Journal Ratings

	2013 LIB	—	2013 CONS
Economic	68%	—	32%
Social	79%	—	16%
Foreign	62%	—	37%
Composite	71%	—	29%

Key Votes of the 113th Congress

1. Sandy storm spending	Y	5. Medical Marijuana	Y	9. Syrian Rebels Training	Y
2. Violence Against Women Act	Y	6. Farm Bill	N	10. Keystone pipeline	N
3. Guantanamo Bay Detainees	Y	7. Afghanistan Combat	N	11. Immigration Exec. Action	N
4. Abortion 20-week ban	N	8. NSA Phone Data Collection	Y	12. Bipartisan budget deal	Y

Election Results

2014 general	Brad Sherman (D)	86,568	(66%)	$842,754
	Mark Reed (R)	45,315	(34%)	$5,066
2014 primary	Brad Sherman (D)	40,787	(58%)	
	Mark Reed (R)	14,129	(20%)	
	Pablo Kleinman (R)	8,808	(13%)	
	Marc Litchman (D)	4,251	(6%)	

Prior winning percentages: 2012 (60%), 2010 (65%), 2008 (69%), 2006 (69%), 2004 (62%), 2002 (62%), 2000 (66%), 1998 (57%), 1996 (49%)

Population		Race and Ethnicity		Income	
Total:	744,617	White	50.9%	Median income:	$67,819
Urban:	76.3%	Latino	28.8%		*(70 of 435)*
Suburban:	23.7%	Asian	12.8%	Under $50,000	37.5%
Rural:	0.0%	Black	4.0%	$50,000-$99,999:	29.6%
Land area:	190	Two races	2.9%	$100,000-$199,999:	22.5%
Pop/sq. mi.:	3,916.8	White Ethnic	23.9%	$200,000 or more:	10.4%
Born in state:	46.4%			Poverty Rate	13.8%
		Education			
Age Groups		H.S. grad or less:	31.8%	Work	
Under 18:	20.9%	Some college:	28.3%	White collar:	45.6%
18 to 34:	23.9%	College degree, 4 yr.:	26.6%	Blue collar:	40.9%
35 to 64:	41.5%	Post-grad study:	13.3%	Sales and service:	13.5%
Over 64:	13.8%				
		Military		Govt. workers:	8.8%
		Veterans/active duty:	4.6%		

Southern San Fernando Valley: The Valley, Reseda

In the early 20th century, when the movie business was young, the San Fernando Valley was a vast expanse of empty land that had been annexed to Los Angeles in 1915. Moviemakers, looking for filming sites for a western, drove past the vacant lots of Westwood, up narrow roads through the

Voter Turnout	
2013 Total Citizen 18+	491,253
2014 House Turnout	131,883
2014 Turnout as % CVAP	26.8%
2012 Turnout as % CVAP	60.4%

Santa Monica Mountains, and into the vast Valley, sheltered from ocean breezes and rain-bearing clouds by the mountains. Since then, this big bowl of land has been transformed, first into 1950s suburbia, and then into a postmodern city of its own, economically vital and diversely ethnic. Even in its suburban years, the San Fernando Valley was not entirely residential. Big factories provided jobs. In those years, this was fast-growing, family-friendly territory. Plenty of upscale territory remains in the uplands of the Valley, in Granada Hills and Tarzana; and the office blocks and mini-malls show unmistakable signs of affluence. But in a not so family-friendly development, the Valley in recent years has been a hub for the adult-film industry. After Los Angeles County voters approved a measure in 2012 that required actors to wear condoms in sex scenes to control the spread of sexually transmitted disease, some adult-movie producers moved studio operations out of the region. What had been an annual total of about 500 permits for such motion pictures, television and commercial production across Los Angeles declined to about 40 in 2014, the *Los Angeles Daily News* reported. Other porn businesses diversified to new forms of technology and paraphernalia, and their headquarters remained in the area.

Parts of the Valley have been unhappy to be linked with the city of Los Angeles, whose City Council has imposed high taxes and irksome regulations. A secession movement arose, and the issue was put on the November 2002 ballot. The Valley voted 51%-49% for it, with stronger support here in the southern and western sections. But it needed a majority in all of Los Angeles to pass, and it failed. In 2013, partly in response to the secession movement, the L.A. City Council tightened rules on who can participate in such neighborhood elections, eliminating what had been called "Starbucks shareholders." After being hit hard by the recession, the Valley's economy began improving in 2010, thanks in part to a massive expansion in California's enterprise zone program. Nevertheless, many thousands of middle-class residents have relocated in recent years to less-costly places.

The 30th Congressional District covers the western and southern parts of the San Fernando Valley within Los Angeles. Along its southern border, the 30th includes Hidden Hills, Tarzana, and Encino. In the center of the district are industrial Canoga Park, Winnetka, and largely Hispanic Reseda. On the northern end is Granada Hills, where the San Fernando Valley's first oil well was drilled in 1916, and O'Melveny Park, one of

2012 Presidential Vote
Barack Obama (D) 186,301   (65%)
Mitt Romney (R)...................91,680   (32%)

2008 Presidential Vote
Barack Obama (D) 190,918   (66%)
John McCain (R)...................92,717   (32%)

Cook Partisan Voting Index: D+14

the largest parks in Los Angeles. Also in the district are Encino Hospital and California State University, Northridge. Although not as Hispanic as the neighboring 29th District, there is a strong Latino presence here and it is solidly Democratic territory.

Brad Sherman (D)

Brad Sherman, a Democrat first elected in 1996, has shown that he is a rough and ready political scrapper—on behalf of Israel and against Wall Street, for example. But his reelection brawl in 2012 against more senior Democrat Howard Berman left wounds that were slow to heal, especially with Minority Leader Nancy Pelosi.

Sherman grew up in Monterey Park, in the San Gabriel Valley east of Los Angeles. He started working on Democratic campaigns at age 6, stuffing envelopes for Rep. George Brown. He set up his own stamp-wholesaling firm at age 14. He graduated with high honors from the University of California at Los Angeles, worked as an accountant, and then went to Harvard Law School. He came back to the Los Angeles area to practice tax law, and he represented the Philippines in its successful effort to seize the assets of deposed President Ferdinand Marcos.

In 1990, Sherman was elected from Los Angeles County to the state Board of Equalization, which is a sort of tax court. He was known as a stickler for detail, a "tax nerd," as one former staffer said, who used the office with a keen scent for political advantage. He irritated cartoonists with a ruling that exempted artwork from the state tax but not illustrations. They took their revenge by setting up a website, the Sherman Gallery, where they vied in caricaturing the balding and bespectacled Sherman.

In 1996, Sherman moved his residence from Santa Monica to Sherman Oaks, where a House seat had opened. Both he and his Republican opponent, businessman Rich Sybert, were self-financers; Sherman spent $578,000 of his own money. And both stressed their moderation. Sherman campaigned against then-House Speaker Newt Gingrich and the Republican Congress, but he also supported the death penalty, called for phasing out racial quotas and preferences, and favored tough measures on illegal immigration. Sybert stressed his independence from Gingrich as well as his support of abortion rights and environmental protection. Sherman won 49%-44%.

In the House, his voting record has been more moderate than those of most other Los Angeles County Democrats, and he has shown occasional independence from party leaders. He drew national attention in June 2011 for introducing a bill to prevent cities from banning male circumcision—a response to a proposed ballot measure in San Francisco that would outlaw the circumcision of males under the age of 18. Sherman has taken an interest in some of the more arcane aspects of government. He sponsored bills for several years to overhaul the presidential succession process and another measure to set up a commission to reduce delays in processing Freedom of Information Act requests.

One of the few certified public accountants in Congress, Sherman serves on the Financial Services Committee, where his experience has been useful in congressional attempts to unravel recent corporate accounting scandals. In 2008, he was an outspoken foe of the bill creating the Troubled Assets Relief Program to bail out the financial services industry, dubbing it "cash for trash." He was regularly critical of Treasury Secretary Timothy Geithner's subsequent efforts on behalf of Wall Street, calling Geithner's proposal allowing the government to take over large firms "TARP on steroids." When domestic auto company executives testified in favor of a proposed bailout for that industry in November 2008, Sherman got them to concede that they had all flown separately to Washington in private airplanes, a revelation that sparked a public backlash. In 2009, he advocated a 70 percent surtax on all compensation exceeding $1 million for executives of financial institutions receiving large federal bailouts. Sherman helped form the new Consumer Financial Protection Bureau as part of the 2010 Dodd-Frank financial overhaul law. But one of the bill's namesakes, Rep. Barney Frank of Massachusetts, accused him of "arrogance" and of overstating his role after Sherman boasted that he had "more to do with Dodd-Frank than anyone except Dodd and Frank."

Sherman faced his first serious opposition when redistricting following the 2010 census lumped him together in 2012 with Howard Berman, a 30-year House veteran who had chaired the Foreign Affairs Committee. Berman had the backing of much of the state's Democratic establishment as well as the support of Hollywood elites for his work on anti-piracy legislation; even some prominent Republicans such as Rep. Darrell Issa of California and Sen. John McCain of Arizona came out publicly for him. But he was at a serious geographic disadvantage: The new 30th District covered twice as much of Sherman's old turf as Berman's base, which was in the new 29th District.

Both candidates raised plenty of money. The final tab for the race was $16.3 million, making it one of the nation's most expensive for the House. Sherman went on the attack, depicting Berman as a Washington insider who didn't understand constituents' concerns. The normally mild-mannered Berman followed suit, launching a weekly "BS Report" on his opponent and highlighting his inability to get more than a handful of bills into law, while criticizing him for loaning his campaigns money and then charging interest, an allegation that Sherman heatedly denied. The acrimony reached its peak at an October debate when the two loudly bickered over immigration legislation, and Sherman threw his arm around his opponent's shoulders and demanded, "You want to get into this?" A sheriff's deputy and a debate organizer stepped between them to prevent an escalation. Berman sent out a *YouTube* video of the incident accusing Sherman of trying to start a fight, prompting Sherman to apologize. But it was too little, too late for Berman. Sherman won easily, 60%-40%.

Sherman soon paid the price when Pelosi objected to his bid to become the senior Democrat on the Foreign Affairs Committee, where he had been next in line among Democratic members behind Berman; instead, Democrats selected Rep. Eliot Engel of New York. In a further dig, Sherman was denied the ranking Democrat position on the Middle East and North African Subcommittee, and that position went to far more junior Rep. Ted Deutch of Florida. Instead, he retained the top position on the Terrorism, Nonproliferation and Trade Subcommittee, where his priorities were preventing Iran from obtaining nuclear weapons and imposing tougher economic sanctions. He described as "preposterous" the Obama administration's search for a nuclear agreement with Iran. As a staunch Israel supporter, he contended that liberals suffer from "the David and Goliath inversion" regarding the Israel-Palestinian conflict. "Liberals always root for David, never Goliath," and they assume Israel is the aggressor, Sherman said. In 2015, he became the top Democrat on the Asia and the Pacific Subcommittee. He remained a staunch supporter of Israel and its prime minister, Benjamin Netanyahu. As part of the Israeli leader's controversial speech to Congress in March 2015, which many Democrats boycotted, Sherman said he was "honored" to serve on the escort committee that accompanied Netanyahu into the House chamber.

In 2014, Sherman had a much easier and less expensive reelection. Facing Republican small businessman Mark Reed, who finished third in the 2012 primary with 13% of the vote, Sherman this time won 66%-34%. His hold on this district appears secure.

THIRTY-FIRST DISTRICT

Pete Aguilar (D)

Elected 2014, 1st term; b. June 19, 1979, Fontana; U. of Redlands, B.S. 2001; Catholic; married (Alisha); 2 children.

Elected Office: Redlands City Cncl., 2006-14; Mayor, Redlands, 2010-14.

Professional Career: Business owner; Interim dir. & deputy dir., Inland Empire regional office of the Gov., 2001.

DC Office: 1223 LHOB, 20515, 202-225-3201; Fax: 202-226-6962; Website: aguilar.house.gov.

State Offices: Rancho Cucamonga, 909-980-1492.

Committees: *Agriculture:* Commodity Exchanges, Energy, & Credit; Nutrition. *Armed Services:* Emerging Threats & Capabilities; Strategic Forces.

Election Results

2014 general	Pete Aguilar (D)............................51,622	(52%)	$2,246,265	$618,460	$44,205
	Paul Chabot (R)............................48,162	(48%)	$469,542	$10,429	$1,299,986
2014 primary	Paul Chabot (R)............................14,163	(27%)			
	Pete Aguilar (D)..............................9,242	(17%)			
	Lesli Gooch (R)...............................9,033	(17%)			
	Eloise Reyes (D).............................8,461	(16%)			
	Joe Baca (D)...................................5,954	(11%)			
	Danny Tillman (D).........................4,659	(9%)			

Population		Race and Ethnicity		Income	
Total:	725,024	Latino	49.3%	Median income:	$52,503
Urban:	45.9%	White	29.0%		*(194 of 435)*
Suburban:	54.1%	Black	9.7%	Under $50,000	47.4%
Rural:	0.0%	Asian	7.3%	$50,000-$99,999:	29.9%
Land area:	325	Two races	3.8%	$100,000-$199,999:	18.4%
Pop/sq. mi.:	2,232.2	White Ethnic	12.6%	$200,000 or more:	4.4%
Born in state:	63.4%			Poverty Rate	21.2%
		Education			
Age Groups		H.S. grad or less:	43.2%	**Work**	
Under 18:	27.6%	Some college:	32.9%	White collar:	32.9%
18 to 34:	26.9%	College degree, 4 yr.:	14.9%	Blue collar:	44.9%
35 to 64:	36.1%	Post-grad study:	9.1%	Sales and service:	22.2%
Over 64:	9.4%				
		Military		Govt. workers:	17.7%
		Veterans/active duty:	6.2%		

Southwestern San Bernardino: Rancho Cucamonga

In the 1970s, as the coastal portions of the Los Angeles Basin became fully developed and in the 1980s, as real estate values skyrocketed, people with modest incomes and young families increasingly moved east, from the high-cost, high-crime coast to the smoggier, hotter valleys inland. There

Voter Turnout	
2013 Total Citizen 18+	449,619
2014 House Turnout	99,784
2014 Turnout as % CVAP	22.2%
2012 Turnout as % CVAP	46.6%

was a lot of empty, low-priced land in what people began calling the Inland Empire, defined usually as San Bernardino and Riverside counties, and even more in the desert to the north and east of the passes through the mountains that rim the Basin. This was a high-growth area, with a population that expanded from 1.6 million in 1980 to 4.2 million in 2010. In the century's first decade, there was a boom in commercial real estate, especially warehouses to store merchandise offloaded at the port of Los Angeles-Long Beach. The uptick in construction attracted many Latinos, both citizens and immigrants. San Bernardino has become the second-largest county in the nation—behind Miami-Dade in Florida—with a population that is majority Latino, a near tripling in Latino population to a total of 1.05 million from 1980 to 2012. New subdivisions sprang up and subprime mortgages were readily available with little or no money down.

Then in 2007 the housing bubble burst, and in the ensuing recession, commercial real estate went sour. Millions of square feet of warehouses stood empty. The Inland Empire had one of the nation's highest foreclosure rates and housing values fell by half. Many of the job losses were in the construction industry. Poverty has been a persistent challenge in the Inland Empire. Nowhere were the problems greater than in the city of San Bernardino, which a March 2012 Gallup survey declared one of the weakest metropolitan areas in the country for job creation. The city was criticized for carrying inflated pension costs and high government salaries, with nearly one in four city employees earning more than $100,000 a year in 2010. Facing a $45.8 million budget shortfall, San Bernardino voted to declare bankruptcy in July 2012.

Since then, conditions have stabilized in some cases and improved in others. In 2014, the city announced plans to repay fully its pension debt. Population growth in the Inland Empire slowed to 3.3 percent from 2010 to 2014. In January 2015, the financial website WalletHub ranked San Bernardino as the worst city in the nation to find a job. Rancho Cucamonga had improved to the top third of cities listed, and economic growth there had shut down most of the orange groves. Amazon opened a fulfillment center that employed 1,400. In 2014, private economic studies projected 4.2 percent annual economic growth for the Inland Empire, and 8.4 percent annual increase in the county's housing prices for the remainder of the decade.

2012 Presidential Vote		
Barack Obama (D) 118,043	(57%)
Mitt Romney (R)...................83,822	(41%)
2008 Presidential Vote		
Barack Obama (D) 122,691	(57%)
John McCain (R)...................89,376	(41%)
Cook Partisan Voting Index: D+5		

The 31st Congressional District covers some of the Inland Empire and is entirely within San Bernardino County. This includes the cities of Colton, Loma Linda, Redlands, and San Bernardino. Also here is Rancho Cucamonga. Its population had been soaring, but has been steady at about 170,000 since 2005. This city has a local baseball team, the Quakes, who play at the Epicenter. Rialto and Upland are split between this district and the 35th. The 31st was designed to comply with Voting Rights Act rules against racial discrimination. The district is about half Hispanic and politically leans Democratic. Barack Obama won 57 percent in each of his campaigns, though the area has been competitive locally.

Pete Aguilar (D)

Democrat Pete Aguilar's 2014 win returned the 31st District seat to the Democrats, who had long held it. The quirks of redistricting and an open primary gave the predominantly Hispanic district to the GOP in 2012, and the turbulent local politics remained unpredictable.

Aguilar was born in Fontana and grew up in San Bernardino. He earned undergraduate degrees in government and business administration at the University of Redlands. One of his first jobs was at the San Bernardino County Courthouse cafeteria, where his blind grandfather was the operator. In 2001, Gov. Gray Davis appointed Aguilar as deputy director of the Inland Empire Regional Office of the Governor. In 2006, Aguilar was appointed to the Redlands City Council, making him the youngest council member in the city's 140-year history. He ran successfully for two more terms and was elected mayor in 2010 by his fellow council members.

In 2012, he ran for Congress. Four Democrats divided the vote in the primary, with Aguilar the frontrunner among them with 23 percent of the total vote. But the two Republicans who sought the seat emerged at the top, with 27 and 25 percent. Rep. Gary Miller—who decided to run here for his eighth term, despite having not represented any of the district—won in November over fellow Republican Bob Dutton, 55%-45%.

Miller announced he would not seek reelection in 2014, and Aguilar again sought the seat. History almost repeated itself in June, as four Democrats faced off against three Republicans. GOP candidate Paul Chabot came in first with 27%, and Aguilar had 17% and hung onto a 209-vote lead over Republican Leslie Gooch. In late June, Gooch abandoned her quest for a recount. This time, the four Democratic candidates in the primary got 53% of the total vote. Former seven-term San Bernardino Democratic Rep. Joe Baca, who ran in the more strongly Democratic 35th District in 2012, finished fifth with only 11% of the vote.

Aguilar hammered Chabot for what he called his too-conservative views on education, immigration, and heath care. National Democratic ads referred to Chabot's support of Arizona's SB 1070, a controversial law that requires police in certain circumstances to determine the immigration status of detainees. Chabot, an Iraq war vet and Naval Reserve intelligence officer, focused on those experiences and how to combat terrorism. Aguilar won with 51% to Chabot's 49%. Aguilar out-spent Chabot, $2.2 million to $469,000, and was boosted by more than $1.5 million in national party money. Republicans seem to have missed an opportunity by steering clear of this contest, to Chabot's dismay.

In the House, Aguilar got seats on the Armed Services and Agriculture committees, where he said he will focus on issues relevant to the Inland Empire. He criticized President Barack Obama's executive action on immigration reform as not good enough. "To truly fix our broken immigration system and put our country on a path forward, Congress must pass a bill, much like the one passed by the Senate more than a year ago, that addresses all aspects of this issue," he wrote in a December 2014 op-ed. Republicans made him an early target for 2016, though presidential-year politics could be a boost for Aguilar. Chabot wrote an e-book about his campaign, and planned to run again in 2016.

THIRTY-SECOND DISTRICT

Grace Napolitano (D)

Elected 1998, 9th term; b. Dec. 4, 1936, Brownsville, TX; Brownsville H.S.; Catholic; married (Frank); 5 children.

Elected Office: Norwalk City Cncl., 1986-92; Norwalk mayor, 1990-92; CA Assembly, 1992-98.

Professional Career: Employee, Ford Motor Co., 1970-92.

DC Office: 1610 LHOB, 20515, 202-225-5256; Fax: 202-225-0027; Website: napolitano.house.gov.

State Offices: El Monte, 626-350-0150.

Committees: *Natural Resources:* Water, Power & Oceans. *Transportation & Infrastructure:* Highways & Transit; Railroads, Pipelines & Hazardous Materials; Water Resources & Environment (RMM).

Group Ratings

	ADA	ACLU	AFL-CIO	LCV	ITI	COC	HAFA	ACU	CFG	FRC
2014	95%	83%	–	83%	40%	38%	11%	8%	15%	0%
2013	100%	C	100%	86%	C	23%	C	16%	11%	C

National Journal Ratings

	2013 LIB	—	2013 CONS
Economic	91%	—	0%
Social	77%	—	21%
Foreign	90%	—	6%
Composite	89%	—	12%

Key Votes of the 113th Congress

1. Sandy storm spending	NV	5. Medical Marijuana	Y	9. Syrian Rebels Training	N
2. Violence Against Women Act	Y	6. Farm Bill	N	10. Keystone pipeline	N
3. Guantanamo Bay Detainees	Y	7. Afghanistan Combat	Y	11. Immigration Exec. Action	N
4. Abortion 20-week ban	N	8. NSA Phone Data Collection	Y	12. Bipartisan budget deal	Y

Election Results

2014 general	Grace Napolitano (D)	50,353	(60%)	$304,898
	Arturo Alas (R)	34,053	(40%)	$61,036
2014 primary	Grace Napolitano (D)	24,639	(60%)	
	Arturo Alas (R)	16,459	(40%)	

Prior winning percentages: 2012 (66%), 2010 (74%), 2008 (82%), 2006 (75%), 2004 (100%), 2002 (71%), 2000 (71%), 1998 (68%)

Population		Race and Ethnicity		Income	
Total:	706,167	Latino	61.9%	Median income:	$55,839
Urban:	70.6%	White	18.2%		*(159 of 435)*
Suburban:	29.4%	Asian	16.1%	Under $50,000	44.8%
Rural:	0.0%	Black	2.4%	$50,000-$99,999:	31.8%
Land area:	238	Two races	1.3%	$100,000-$199,999:	20.3%
Pop/sq. mi.:	2,972.4	White Ethnic	7.9%	$200,000 or more:	3.2%
Born in state:	56.4%			Poverty Rate	16.0%
		Education			
Age Groups		H.S. grad or less:	53.5%	**Work**	
Under 18:	23.7%	Some college:	26.7%	White collar:	27.3%
18 to 34:	26.1%	College degree, 4 yr.:	14.6%	Blue collar:	46.5%
35 to 64:	37.5%	Post-grad study:	5.2%	Sales and service:	26.2%
Over 64:	12.6%				
		Military		Govt. workers:	12.9%
		Veterans/active duty:	4.3%		

Eastern L.A. Suburbs: West Covina, La Puente

It was the great route west to California in the first half of the 20th century: Passengers on the Santa Fe railroad's *Super Chief* or motorists on U.S. 66, after hours and days in barren desert, would descend through the Cajon Pass into the Los Angeles Basin, and come upon orange groves and exotic plants thriving beneath the 10,000-foot snow-capped San Gabriel Mountains.

The railroad and highway ran through a line of towns built by Midwestern Protestants as independent communities. Foothills communities such as La Verne and San Dimas have horse trails and their own rodeos. In 2014, Azusa suffered both forest fires and mudslide threats from the nearby mountains.

Voter Turnout	
2013 Total Citizen 18+	430,615
2014 House Turnout	84,406
2014 Turnout as % CVAP	19.6%
2012 Turnout as % CVAP	47.8%

The area today has large and growing Hispanic and Asian populations. The western parts of the compact 32nd District—the areas closer to downtown Los Angeles—are heavily Latino: Covina, West Covina, and Azusa all are Hispanic-majority cities. In Baldwin Park, which is 80% Hispanic and 14% Asian, more than 80% of its population speaks a language other than English at home. Baldwin Park has had financial difficulties, but its bond rating was upgraded in September 2014. There have been other positive developments. Chinese investors have planned major investments in El Monte, including a Hilton hotel plus office and retail space. In October 2014, L.A. Metro announced an 11-mile extension of the Gold Line from Pasadena to Asuza, with a projected $2 billion cost.

In the small city of Irwindale, the city council in 2013 declared the Huy Fong Foods company a public nuisance because of the odor from Sriracha hot sauce production. The chili sauce has a devoted following. *Bon Appetit* has named it one of its favorite foods. David Tran, the company owner and a refugee from Vietnam, considered moving to a location elsewhere in California. Another food note: After an In-n-Out burger stand, which had been constructed in 1948, was demolished in Baldwin Park in 2011, public protests prompted the owner to build a 100-square-foot replica, with an antique Coldspot refrigerator, vintage fryers, and two-way speakers in the drive-through lane. That building was purely promotional. For food, customers were directed less than a mile near the site of the original stand, in the shadow of Interstate 10.

The 32nd District is nearly two-thirds Hispanic. Areas to the east, such as La Verne and San Dimas, have lower poverty rates and higher household incomes. The I-10 Freeway

2012 Presidential Vote		
Barack Obama (D)	133,061	(65%)
Mitt Romney (R)	66,269	(33%)
2008 Presidential Vote		
Barack Obama (D)	141,696	(62%)
John McCain (R)	80,808	(36%)
Cook Partisan Voting Index:	D+12	

connects the district to downtown Los Angeles. Glendora is split between this district and the Pasadena-based 27th District. The heavily Hispanic composition of this district makes it safe Democratic territory.

Grace Napolitano (D)

Grace Napolitano, a Democrat first elected in 1998, has concentrated on issues affecting lower-income Hispanics in her Southern California district, including jobs, water scarcity, and mental health. Her committee assignments have given her clout on pork-barrel projects, on both land and water.

Napolitano grew up in the lower Rio Grande Valley of Texas, married at age 18, and eventually had five children. When she was 23, the family moved to California. She got a job as a secretary at Ford Motor Co. and stayed for 22 years. After her first husband died, she married Frank Napolitano, and in 1980, they started a pizzeria. (*Washingtonian* magazine has praised her egg and tortilla hash, known as *migas*.) She served on the Norwalk City Council from 1986 to 1992, and also served one term as mayor, becoming the first Latino to hold the position. In 1992, she was elected to the California Assembly.

Term-limited in 1998, she got the opportunity to run for Congress when 16-year Democratic Rep. Esteban Torres announced three days before the filing deadline that he was retiring. Torres's surprise move was designed to promote the election of Jamie Casso, his son-in-law and chief of staff, who immediately announced his candidacy. Napolitano was not deterred, and got into the race. She criticized Casso for not living in the district, and he criticized an $180,000 loan she made to her campaign at an unusual 18% interest rate. Napolitano had the financial backing of national women's organizations, including EMILY's List, plus the benefit of higher name recognition. The two candidates had few differences on major issues. Napolitano signed a pledge to serve only three terms. She won the primary by 618 votes, and her victory in November was assured in the heavily Democratic district.

Napolitano has been among the most liberal members of the House. She is a former chairwoman of the Congressional Hispanic Caucus and has been more consensus-oriented on immigration legislation than some caucus members.

As a member of the Transportation and Infrastructure Committee, she has had an interest in rail safety. In work on the House-passed surface transportation bill in 2012, she defeated proposed changes in existing law that would have weakened safety measures, and she won an extension of a program to speed up transportation projects and lower costs by relieving California of the need for a review under the National Environmental Policy Act when a more stringent review already was completed. In 2015, she became the ranking Democrat on the Water Resources and Environment Subcommittee, where she said she would work to fix "our nation's crumbling water infrastructure."

On the Natural Resources Committee, she became chairwoman of the panel's Water and Power Subcommittee in 2007, with a focus on Southern California's acute need for an adequate water supply. She held hearings to examine possible long-term solutions to address water needs, and she called for continued funding of water desalination research in April 2012, saying, "Our water supply continues to be strained by population growth and climate change, and the ability to convert saltwater into drinking water is fast becoming a critical source of economic growth and international competition." In July 2014, she unveiled her "Water in the 21st Century" bill, which would provide $2 billion in loans and grants for water recycling, storm water capture and treatment, ground water management and water infrastructure projects. After the 2014 election, she decided not to seek the vacant post as senior Democrat on the full committee, which instead went to Rep. Raul Grijalva of Arizona.

Napolitano also gets involved in issues related to the mentally ill, an interest that was sparked by a report that one in three Hispanic girls contemplates suicide. "Mental health is treatable. But [the Latino community has] a stigma attached to it," Napolitano said. During the 2010 health care overhaul debate, she said affordable health care was "critical to the future of women who suffer in silence from mental illness." With Republican Rep. Chris Gibson, she filed in January 2015 a bill to authorize $200 million for school-based services that would offer early intervention and treatment for young people with mental health issues.

In February 2003, Napolitano abandoned her earlier pledge to serve only three terms. She has not been seriously challenged for reelection. In 2007, she was criticized by the watchdog group Citizens for Responsibility and Ethics in Washington for paying her daughter, Yolanda Dyer, and her daughter's consulting firm nearly $53,000 for work on her campaigns between 2002 and 2006. Napolitano said her daughter ran her campaigns. In 2012, she won with 66% of the vote in the redrawn 32nd District, in which more than 80% of voters were new to her. In 2014, she was held to 60% by Arturo Alas, a real estate agent who opposed the move by President Barack Obama to create a national monument in the San Gabriel Mountains. Alas, an immigrant from El Salvador, was part of what *Reuters* described as a group of "ethnically diverse young libertarians" who have sought to revive the Republican Party in Los Angeles.

THIRTY-THIRD DISTRICT

Ted Lieu (D)

Elected 2014, 1st term; b. March 29, 1969, Taipei, Taiwan; Stanford U., B.A. 1991, B.S. 1991, Georgetown U., J.D. 1994; Catholic; married (Betty); 2 children.

Military Career: U.S. Air Force, 1995-99; U.S. Air Force Reserve, 2000-present.

Elected Office: Torrance City Cncl., 2002-05; CA Assembly, 2005-10. CA Senate, 2011-14.

Professional Career: Clerk, U.S. Court of Appeals, 9th Circuit; Practicing atty..

DC Office: 415 CHOB, 20515, 202-225-3976; Website: lieu.house.gov.

State Offices: Los Angeles, 323-651-1040; Manhattan Beach, 310-321-7664.

Committees: *Budget. Oversight & Gov't Reform:* Information Technology; National Security.

Election Results

2014 general	Ted Lieu (D)	108,331	(59%)	$2,173,521	$20,474	$107,048
	Elan Carr (R)	74,700	(41%)	$1,575,540	$655,844	
2014 primary	Elan Carr (R)	23,476	(22%)			
	Ted Lieu (D)	20,432	(19%)			
	Wendy Greuel (D)	17,988	(17%)			
	Marianne Williamson (I)	14,335	(13%)			
	Matt Miller (D)	13,005	(12%)			
	Lily Gilani (R)	7,673	(7%)			

Population		Race and Ethnicity		Income	
Total:	717,954	White	66.4%	Median income:	$90,541
Urban:	78.7%	Asian	13.9%		*(11 of 435)*
Suburban:	21.3%	Latino	12.4%	Under $50,000	29.5%
Rural:	0.0%	Black	3.3%	$50,000-$99,999:	24.1%
Land area:	219	Two races	3.4%	$100,000-$199,999:	26.7%
Pop/sq. mi.:	3,272.8	White Ethnic	34.5%	$200,000 or more:	19.7%
Born in state:	45.6%			Poverty Rate	10.2%
		Education			
Age Groups		H.S. grad or less:	15.4%	**Work**	
Under 18:	18.9%	Some college:	23.0%	White collar:	60.2%
18 to 34:	23.3%	College degree, 4 yr.:	35.0%	Blue collar:	32.9%
35 to 64:	41.8%	Post-grad study:	26.6%	Sales and service:	6.9%
Over 64:	16.1%				
		Military		Govt. workers:	10.0%
		Veterans/active duty:	5.0%		

Coastal and Central L.A.: Santa Monica

Showbiz still sets the tone for the Westside of Los Angeles. It remains tremendously profitable, and not just for the big conglomerate-owned studios. There are tens of thousands of entrepreneurs, actors, writers, and craftsmen who are the best in the world at what they do and who tend to cluster

Voter Turnout	
2013 Total Citizen 18+	520,820
2014 House Turnout	183,031
2014 Turnout as % CVAP	35.1%
2012 Turnout as % CVAP	67.3%

on the Westside because so many others in the entertainment business work there. Not everyone is in show business, of course. The Westside is metro Los Angeles's biggest office center, with horrific traffic during the morning and evening rush hours. Most office workers can't afford to live in the limited and expensive neighborhoods nearby. The city's Purple Line subway is being extended to the Westside, a nine-mile extension from Wilshire/Western. Over the objections of Beverly Hills school district officials, who spent more than $3 million of taxpayer funds in their opposition, the $5.6 billion project includes a tunnel underneath Beverly Hills High School. Construction broke ground in November 2014 and is scheduled to be completed in 2023.

The area has a large and diverse Jewish community. Iranian Jews have poured in since 1979 and now make up almost one-quarter of the population of Beverly Hills, which elected an Iranian-American mayor in 2007. The old Fairfax district is home to many Russian Jewish immigrants and a number of corner delis, including the historic Canter's Deli that opened in 1931 and remains open 24/7. Beverly Hills and the Westside remain the locus of some of America's most expensive residential real estate, where people buy houses for millions of dollars, knock them down, and build new houses for many more millions. Rodeo Drive is one of the world's premier high-priced shopping areas. These communities experienced significant foreclosures following the housing bubble. Unlike in much of California, the average price for local real estate sales in February 2015 surpassed the earlier levels, including a return to some stratospheric prices, *Bloomberg News* reported. The L.A. City Council responded in March 2015 with

2012 Presidential Vote		
Barack Obama (D)	210,010	(61%)
Mitt Romney (R)	127,421	(37%)

2008 Presidential Vote		
Barack Obama (D)	220,825	(64%)
John McCain (R)	118,497	(34%)

Cook Partisan Voting Index: D+11

restrictions in 20 neighborhoods on what residents described as "mansionization," the building of mansion-like homes that are unusually large for their lots. In a somewhat separate move, the council has planned to close the Santa Monica airport, where actor Harrison Ford crash-landed following take-off in March 2015.

The 33rd Congressional District of California contains parts of Westside Los Angeles and the upscale cities of Beverly Hills, Bel Air, and Brentwood. It also takes in the campus of the University of California, Los Angeles and the J. Paul Getty Museum. Santa Monica is in the new 33rd, as is the whole 21 miles of Malibu on the Pacific Ocean. It dips down south of Santa Monica to take in Marina del Rey, which offers yacht moorings, and skirts along the ocean past Los Angeles International Airport to El Segundo, Manhattan Beach, and Redondo Beach. The southernmost point of the 33rd is Rancho Palos Verdes, where, on cliffs overlooking the ocean, is famed architect Frank Lloyd Wright's Wayfarers Chapel, also known as "The Glass Church." With a racial composition that is about three-fourths white, the district is less diverse than other congressional districts in greater Los Angeles. It is still solid Democratic territory, though with a more lofty average household income.

Ted Lieu (D)

Democrat Ted Lieu was elected in 2014 in one of the nation's richest and most liberal House districts. He replaced the iconic liberal Henry Waxman, who for 40 years played a major role in legislation ranging from health care to environmental protection and was aggressive at congressional oversight.

A Taiwanese American whose working-class family came to the United States when he was a toddler, he got his bachelor's degree from Stanford and a law degree from Georgetown University. Lieu's early career centered on law and military service. After four years of active duty in the Air Force, including a posting in the JAG Corps, he divided his time between working in the private sector and serving on the Torrance City Council. In 2005, he won a special election to serve in the state Assembly, followed by election to the state Senate in 2010 to represent much of the territory in the 33rd District. He backed a successful bill allowing undocumented immigrants to take the bar exam, as well as a measure calling for a state-wide referendum expressing opposition to the *Citizens United* ruling. On affirmative action, he staked out a more centrist position, opposing a bill that would have overturned the affirmative action ban at California state universities. That move drew criticism from black and Latino lawmakers.

When Waxman announced his retirement in 2013, he set off a primary fight that attracted no fewer than 18 candidates. Along with Lieu, the best known were Republican Elan Carr, who served with the Army in Iraq and was a deputy in the L.A. District Attorney's office, former L.A. mayoral candidate Wendy Greuel, and self-help guru Marianne Williamson, an independent. Some expected the contest would produce two Democratic front-runners under California's "jungle primary," in which the top two vote-getters advance regardless of party. Although Waxman in 2012 was held to a 54%-46% win over free-spending Independent businessman Bill Bloomfield, this is a comfortably Democratic district.

Lieu countered with an aggressive campaign that leveraged his deep political ties to the district, his liberal voting record in Sacramento, and a lineup of top Democratic endorsements, including L.A. Mayor Eric Garcetti, as well as the *Los Angeles Daily News*. Lieu also underscored the need for more Asian-American representation in Congress. In the June primary, he came in second to Carr, 21%-19%; Greuel was third with 17%. Lieu was set for an easy victory in a party stronghold, and his wealthy voters could help raise money for other Democrats. He won in November, 59%-41%. Carr announced plans to run for L.A. County Supervisor in 2016.

In the House, Lieu gained seats on the Budget Committee, and Oversight and Government Reform, which Waxman had chaired. He was the first House Democrat to announce his opposition to the request by President Barack Obama to authorize the use of military force against the Islamic State. "I do not believe the administration has made the case that ISIL represents a direct, grave threat to our nation," Lieu said. He joined several other junior House members in launching the bipartisan Post-9/11 Veterans Caucus. Noting that his district has one of the nation's largest populations of homeless veterans, plus a huge VA health care system, he emphasized the need for innovative solutions to the problems of returned service members. He opposed suggestions to privatize veterans' health care services. Lieu was elected president of the House Democrats' freshman class.

THIRTY-FOURTH DISTRICT

Xavier Becerra (D)

Elected 1992, 12th term; b. Jan. 26, 1958, Sacramento; Stanford U., B.A. 1980, J.D. 1984; Catholic; married (Carolina Reyes); 3 children.

Elected Office: CA Assembly, 1990-92.

Professional Career: Staff atty., Legal Assistance Corp. of Central MA; Dist. dir., CA Sen. Art Torres, 1986; CA deputy atty. gen., 1987-90.

DC Office: 1226 LHOB, 20515, 202-225-6235; Fax: 202-225-2202; Website: becerra.house.gov.

State Offices: Los Angeles, 213-481-1425.

Committees: *Ways & Means:* Social Security (RMM); Trade.

Group Ratings

	ADA	ACLU	AFL-CIO	LCV	ITI	COC	HAFA	ACU	CFG	FRC
2014	90%	88%	–	94%	40%	36%	10%	8%	13%	0%
2013	90%	C	95%	96%	C	23%	C	12%	12%	C

National Journal Ratings

	2013 LIB	—	2013 CONS
Economic	91%	—	0%
Social	84%	—	15%
Foreign	88%	—	11%
Composite	90%	—	11%

Key Votes of the 113th Congress

1. Sandy storm spending	Y	5. Medical Marijuana	Y	9. Syrian Rebels Training	Y
2. Violence Against Women Act	Y	6. Farm Bill	N	10. Keystone pipeline	N
3. Guantanamo Bay Detainees	Y	7. Afghanistan Combat	Y	11. Immigration Exec. Action	N
4. Abortion 20-week ban	N	8. NSA Phone Data Collection	Y	12. Bipartisan budget deal	Y

Election Results

2014 general	Xavier Becerra (D)	44,697	(73%)	$1,465,623	$2,073
	Adrienne Edwards (D)	16,924	(27%)		
2014 primary	Xavier Becerra (D)	22,878	(74%)		
	Adrienne Edwards (D)	4,474	(15%)		
	Howard Johnson (PF)	3,587	(12%)		

Prior winning percentages: 2012 (86%), 2010 (84%), 2008 (100%), 2006 (100%), 2004 (80%), 2002 (81%), 2000 (83%), 1998 (81%), 1996 (72%), 1994 (66%), 1992 (58%)

Population		Race and Ethnicity		Income	
Total:	712,425	Latino	66.5%	Median income:	$34,752
Urban:	99.3%	Asian	19.2%		*(422 of 435)*
Suburban:	0.7%	White	9.2%	Under $50,000	64.8%
Rural:	0.0%	Black	3.7%	$50,000-$99,999:	22.6%
Land area:	55	Two races	0.8%	$100,000-$199,999:	10.2%
Pop/sq. mi.:	13,031.4	White Ethnic	4.1%	$200,000 or more:	2.5%
Born in state:	41.7%			Poverty Rate	29.4%
		Education			
Age Groups		H.S. grad or less:	57.9%	**Work**	
Under 18:	22.1%	Some college:	19.8%	White collar:	24.9%
18 to 34:	30.1%	College degree, 4 yr.:	16.5%	Blue collar:	49.2%
35 to 64:	37.7%	Post-grad study:	5.9%	Sales and service:	25.8%
Over 64:	10.2%				
		Military		Govt. workers:	8.8%
		Veterans/active duty:	2.2%		

Downtown/Northeast L.A.

Surrounding downtown Los Angeles are neighborhoods built in the mid-20th century that are just now starting to take on the patina of the historic. Downtown L.A., with its pink cylinders jutting up to 70 stories from what was once a low-rise business district, has become surprisingly pedestrian-

Voter Turnout	
2013 Total Citizen 18+	340,309
2014 House Turnout	61,607
2014 Turnout as % CVAP	18.1%
2012 Turnout as % CVAP	45.2%

friendly, with attractive plazas like the one around the redesigned Los Angeles Public Library. But downtown L.A. remains detached from the ethnically diverse neighborhoods surrounding it. They seem to change character with every new immigration flow. South of downtown is the garment district, with factories in nondescript buildings, an economically vibrant area that has helped make Los Angeles one of the largest manufacturing cities in America today. As of 2014, the manufacturing workforce of 511,000 in the Los Angeles-Long Beach area was the largest in the nation; Chicago and New York City were next in line. Its products include apparel, chemicals, foods, furniture and electronics. But the Los Angeles County Economic Development Corporation worried that it has become difficult to find workers with sufficient education and skill sets. The number of workers has been declining as a result of a variety of factors, including the recession, automation, offshoring, improved productivity, local costs and paralyzing traffic. Only three Fortune 500 companies are based in the city. The city planned to release by the summer of 2015 a final plan to maximize water sources by capturing, filtering and storing more storm water.

To the north is Lincoln Heights, one of the oldest neighborhoods in the city and a heavily Hispanic area centered on the busy shopping street of North Broadway, where residents have been fighting gangs and graffiti with some success. Overall, crime in Los Angeles has dropped for 11 consecutive years through 2014, and reached its lowest level since 1959. Authorities credit the growing use of community policing. Highland Park and Eagle Rock, which were white middle-class enclaves 30 years ago, are now ethnically mixed and middle-class with large numbers of Latinos and Asians. Eagle Rock is the home of Occidental College, where President Barack Obama attended his first two years of college. West of downtown is Pico Union, an entry point for new immigrants where Greeks, Mexicans, and Central Americans co-mingle, united by their passion for soccer. Historic Filipinotown, known locally as Hi-Fi, was settled by Filipinos in the early 1900s and in recent years has become more of a polyglot.

These areas, plus Montecito Heights, Dodger Stadium, and Elysian Park, are parts of California's 34th Congressional District. The district also takes in Chinatown and Boyle Heights, once an entry neighborhood for Irish and Jewish immigrants and for the past 40 years predominantly Mexican-American. In Los Angeles' booming 1980s, these neighborhoods were suddenly thronged with immigrants, with small houses and garden apartments full of large families and many children. In the 1990s, the population surge stopped, and this became a slow-growing district, as the newcomers of the decade before moved out to middle-class neighborhoods and incoming immigrants spread more evenly around the Los Angeles Basin. Hip hop star will.i.am partnered with Chase Bank on an

2012 Presidential Vote		
Barack Obama (D)	127,510	(83%)
Mitt Romney (R)	21,739	(14%)
2008 Presidential Vote		
Barack Obama (D)	129,325	(79%)
John McCain (R)	29,966	(18%)
Cook Partisan Voting Index: D+30		

$8 million community development project in 2012 for his native Boyle Heights. The district is 66% Hispanic and 19% Asian. Politically, it is in the top 5% of Democratic districts in the nation.

Xavier Becerra (D)

Xavier Becerra, a Democrat first elected in 1992, became chairman of the House Democratic Caucus in late 2012, making him the most prominent Latino in the House. He also is a senior member of the powerful Ways and Means Committee. He has promising options, within the House and beyond.

Becerra grew up in Sacramento. His mother was a Mexican immigrant, and his father, who was born in the United States, supported the family with construction and other jobs.

He still wears his father's wedding ring as a reminder of his upbringing. Becerra worked his way through college and law school at Stanford University, becoming the first in his family to get a college degree. He married a Harvard Medical School graduate who became vice president of California's largest health care foundation. Becerra started his career at a legal services clinic in Massachusetts, doing work for mentally disabled clients. When he returned to California, Becerra was an aide to state Sen. Art Torres and then to Attorney General John Van de Kamp. In 1990, he was elected to the California Assembly.

In 1992, when Democratic Rep. Edward Roybal, California's first Latino congressman, announced his retirement, Becerra jumped into the race. His main competitor, Leticia Quezada, was a member of the Los Angeles school board. Becerra had the endorsements of Roybal and County Supervisor Gloria Molina. He won the primary with 32% of the vote to 22% for Quezada, and won the general election with 58% of the vote. Becerra has been overwhelmingly reelected ever since.

In the House, Becerra has been a consistent liberal. As a member of the House Democratic leadership, he has won praise for his hard-working, cerebral, and self-deprecating style. "I'm certainly not the best at politics," he likes to say. Some Congressional Hispanic Caucus members dubbed him "Harvard," although he did not attend that school. When Democrats won majority control of the House, fellow Californian and House Speaker Nancy Pelosi gave him the newly created position of assistant to the speaker, a post that gave him a role in setting the party's legislative agenda. In a 2008 leadership shuffle, Becerra ran for vice chairman of the Democratic Caucus, and with Pelosi's help defeated Marcy Kaptur of Ohio, 175-67. "When you're in leadership, you're in a different position than a rank-and-file member trying to push something, because you're having to convince your colleagues to go," Becerra told *Roll Call* in 2014. "I've learned to be pragmatic, but I don't sacrifice my principles, my values."

Pelosi also put Becerra on the presidential Simpson-Bowles deficit reduction panel in 2010 and the bipartisan congressional "super committee" that sought in vain to reach a deal on the issue a year later. But he has not always seen eye-to-eye with his mentor; she was reportedly angry in 2009 when he intimated to Progressive Caucus members that the leadership abandoned a government-run "public option" for the health care overhaul bill too quickly. "I understand I have tire tracks on my back from Xavier throwing me under the bus," Pelosi reportedly said.

President Barack Obama also recognized Becerra as a standout and offered him the post of U.S. trade representative. But Becerra declined after wisely deciding that trade policy would not be a major White House priority in Obama's early years. He has advocated tax changes to curtail the overseas exodus of jobs in the entertainment industry, including a tax credit for labor costs paid by independent film producers. He supported normalizing trade relations with China and won House approval of a resolution supporting reunification efforts between North and South Korea. His support for free trade deals with Chile and Singapore led to local protests by union activists, and he demanded improvements in the labor standards in the Central American Free Trade Agreement in return for his support. "Trade has to be sold as something that's good for us," he told *The Washington Post* in 2007.

Becerra had been Obama's campaign liaison to the Hispanic community and urged him to get behind a comprehensive immigration bill. He acknowledged in 2010 that Latinos regarded Obama with "a lot of suspicion" because of his failure to make the issue a priority in his first term. Campaigning for Obama in October 2012, however, Becerra laid the blame on House Republicans. "If it were up to the president and to Democrats, we'd have comprehensive immigration reform today," he told reporters on a conference call. He traveled the country to talk to Hispanic audiences on Obama's behalf, regularly pointing out Republican challenger Mitt Romney's tough stance against illegal immigrants and his support from immigration hard-liners like Arizona Gov. Jan Brewer and Iowa Rep. Steve King.

In 2013, Becerra was part of a bipartisan group of lawmakers that discussed immigration reform. He reportedly was slow to join a potential consensus within the group. He remained publicly upbeat about the prospects for a bill, but when Obama opted to issue a post-election executive order to provide temporary relief to some illegal immigrants, Becerra became a staunch administration defender. When Wyoming Republican Sen. John Barrasso complained on Fox News about the move, Becerra retorted: "I think the president has been very patient. He's been waiting a year and a half for the House Republicans to act on the bill that the Senate passed on a bipartisan basis."

Becerra was the first Hispanic to win a seat on Ways and Means, and in 2015 became the ranking-Democrat on the panel dealing with Social Security. In March 2015, with other committee Democrats, he proposed the Social Security Fraud Prevention Act, with cost-effective tools to combat fraud and errors. During the health care debate in 2009, he and Republican Charles Boustany of Louisiana convened a bipartisan group of lawmakers that tried and failed to find common ground on the issue. After Obama won reelection, Becerra lashed out at Republicans for being unwilling to accept tax increases on the highest earners during negotiations on a tax and spending bill aimed at avoiding the so-called fiscal cliff. "The Republican plan is almost as if the Republicans didn't watch the last two years of campaigning in the election," he told CNN.

He has been a leading advocate of establishing a commission to develop a national museum of the American Latino, which would be located on the National Mall and would be part of the Smithsonian Institution. The commission convened in 2009, and issued a set of recommendations that became the basis for a bill that Becerra and other prominent Hispanics introduced two years later. But the political muscle of the Latino community has been slow to coalesce behind the project, and discussions of design and financing have remained preliminary.

The one career setback for Becerra in recent years was his failed run for mayor of Los Angeles in 2001. He did not raise enough money to establish name recognition outside his district, and he was overshadowed by former Assembly Speaker Antonio Villaraigosa. In the primary, Becerra finished fifth, with just 6 percent of the vote. In January 2015, he said he was seriously considering a bid for retiring Democrat Barbara Boxer's Senate seat. In July, after veteran Rep. Loretta Sanchez stepped forward with her candidacy, he said that he will stay in the House. He voiced renewed interest in seeking a senior position in the post-Pelosi House Democratic leadership.

THIRTY-FIFTH DISTRICT

Norma Torres (D)

Elected 2014, 1st term; b. Apr. 4, 1965, Escuintla, Guatemala; National Labor Col., B.A. 2012; Catholic; married (Louis); 2 children.

Elected Office: Pomona City Cncl., 2000-06; Pomona mayor, 2006-08; CA Assembly, 2008-13; CA Senate, 2013-14.

Professional Career: Emergency dispatcher; Sales rep..

DC Office: 516 CHOB, 20515, 202-225-6161; Fax: 202-225-8671; Website: torres.house.gov.

State Offices: Ontario, 909-481-6474.

Committees: *Homeland Security:* Border & Maritime Security; Oversight & Mgmt. Efficiency. *Natural Resources:* Indian, Insular & Alaska Native Affairs; Water, Power & Oceans.

Election Results

2014 general	Norma Torres (D)	39,502	(63%)	$422,829
	Christina Gagnier (D)	22,753	(37%)	$83,829
2014 primary	Norma Torres (D)	17,996	(67%)	
	Christina Gagnier (D)	4,081	(15%)	
	Scott Heydenfeldt (D)	2,574	(10%)	
	Anthony Vieyra (D)	2,183	(8%)	

Population		Race and Ethnicity		Income	
Total:	728,298	Latino	70.0%	Median income:	$54,425
Urban:	59.9%	White	15.3%		*(173 of 435)*
Suburban:	40.1%	Black	6.5%	Under $50,000	45.8%
Rural:	0.0%	Asian	6.1%	$50,000-$99,999:	35.9%
Land area:	242	Two races	1.7%	$100,000-$199,999:	16.5%
Pop/sq. mi.:	3,012.9	White Ethnic	7.3%	$200,000 or more:	1.9%
Born in state:	59.9%			Poverty Rate	17.3%
		Education			
Age Groups		H.S. grad or less:	56.5%	**Work**	
Under 18:	28.1%	Some college:	28.6%	White collar:	21.8%
18 to 34:	27.4%	College degree, 4 yr.:	10.9%	Blue collar:	45.8%
35 to 64:	36.1%	Post-grad study:	4.0%	Sales and service:	32.4%
Over 64:	8.3%				
		Military		Govt. workers:	11.7%
		Veterans/active duty:	3.7%		

Inland Empire: Eastern L.A., Ontario

The gateway to the Los Angeles Basin for decades was San Bernardino. Passengers on the Santa Fe Railroad and motorists on U.S. 66 traveled from the hot and dusty desert, through the twisting, windy Cajon Pass, and wound up in the green, tree-lined Los Angeles Basin. This was an agricultural

Voter Turnout	
2013 Total Citizen 18+	403,422
2014 House Turnout	62,255
2014 Turnout as % CVAP	15.4%
2012 Turnout as % CVAP	41.9%

zone until World War II, when Henry J. Kaiser built the West Coast's first major steel mill between the Santa Fe and Southern Pacific rail lines in Fontana, just west of San Bernardino. Today, these lands have largely filled up. The Inland Empire, as it is called, may be where the smog piles up against the mountains, but it also has some of the lowest real estate prices in the Los Angeles Basin and an energetic small business economy. The large Kaiser steel mill closed in Fontana in 1994, but new businesses have moved in to supplant it. At this site, future California Gov. Arnold Schwarzenegger had a knock-down, drag-out fight with the enemy metal alloy machine in the 1991 blockbuster *Terminator 2: Judgment Day*.

Business growth has been spurred by huge distribution and warehouse centers that service overseas cargo from the Long Beach port. From 1990 to 2005, jobs in San Bernardino County grew from 408,000 to 643,000. But the recession hit hard in the Inland Empire, with home foreclosures among the highest in the nation and many residents fleeing the region. Partly because of the earlier excess of cheap credit, the foreclosure crisis and scarcity of bank loans remained major local problems long after conditions improved in most of the nation. In December 2013, the Inland Empire's unemployment rate dropped below 9 percent for the first time in more than five years. The unemployment rate in Fontana, which exceeded 11 percent two years earlier, fell below 8 percent at the end of 2014, with some help from the local California Steel plant that employed more than 1,000 workers. Like much of California, after Gov. Jerry Brown imposed statewide water restrictions in March 2015, local governments in this area imposed strict conservation measures. Despite these problems, a new entertainment district in downtown Pomona enlivened the nightlife.

The 35th District covers Pomona Valley and the city of Pomona in Los Angeles County. This district is mostly in San Bernardino County, taking in heavily Hispanic areas such as Fontana and Rialto. Fontana, which is 67 percent Hispanic, makes up the northern part of this district. The 35th also takes in Ontario and Ontario Mills, one of the

2012 Presidential Vote
Barack Obama (D) 108,983   (67%)
Mitt Romney (R)...................49,433   (31%)

2008 Presidential Vote
Barack Obama (D) 110,687   (65%)
John McCain (R)...................55,414   (33%)

Cook Partisan Voting Index: D+15

largest shopping malls in the United States. Also here is part of Chino, a meatpacking area. This is a safe Democratic district for the foreseeable future.

Norma Torres (D)

Democrat Norma Torres, a state lawmaker deeply involved in health care expansion and immigration debates, easily defeated another Democrat to take an open seat in 2014 after the incumbent decided to return home and seek a position in county government.

Torres was born in Guatemala but entered the United States at age 5, when her parents sent her to live with relatives in Whittier California, so that she would be safe from that country's bloody civil war. Her interest in community safety led to work as a 911 dispatcher in Pomona, where she soon developed a deeper interest in public service. One episode was particularly profound: In 1994, while she was handling other calls, a fellow dispatcher put a frantic Spanish-speaking woman on hold because no one else could speak with her. When Torres finally picked up, she heard a domestic dispute escalate on the other line, resulting in the shooting death of an 11-year-old. Shaken, she led a successful fight to compel the police to hire more bilingual dispatchers. She also helped to secure a $350,000 federal grant for improved technology. At age 47, she received her bachelor's degree in labor studies from the National Labor College in Silver Spring Maryland, where she took online courses.

Torres soon became involved in broader community issues, especially union organizing and immigrants' rights. She was elected to the Pomona City Council in 2000 and was elected mayor in 2006. The following year, when she returned for the first time to her hometown in Guatemala, she was treated like a celebrity. In 2008, her rise continued as she won a seat in the state Assembly.

Torres's next big opening came in a 2013 special election, after Gloria Negrete McLeod was elected to the House and gave up her state Senate seat. Torres won the Senate seat, and quickly became a busy lawmaker. She introduced two bills to increase diversity on the state board overseeing health care expansion, following a rollout period that many critics said underserved Latinos. She also championed a law to generate more revenue for programs that train and place doctors in medically underserved communities. To assist immigrants, she coauthored a successful measure that transferred $3 million to help unaccompanied minors fleeing Central America. She also pushed three bills cracking down on public corruption, one of which became law.

In February 2014, Negrete McLeod handed Torres yet another opportunity, announcing she would not seek reelection in the House and instead ran for a seat on the San Bernardino County Board of Supervisors, which she ultimately lost. In the blanket primary in June, Torres faced three other Democrats and a Republican. Bolstered by a sizable cash advantage, name recognition, and endorsements by major unions and women's groups, she got 67% to Christina Gagnier's 15%. Under California's "top two" rules, those two advanced to the general election in November, which proved another easy contest for Torres. During the full campaign, she outspent Gagnier $423,000 to $84,000, and won with 63%. More than three-fourths of that vote was cast in San Bernardino County.

In the House, she welcomed her seat on the Homeland Security Committee, with its opportunity to oversee ports of entry in her district's Ontario International Airport and the inland port serving the maritime ports of Los Angeles and Long Beach. In an interview with the *Inland Valley Daily Bulletin* about her initial weeks in the House, she said she was surprised and dismayed by the pervasive partisanship, including in her committee work. "Homeland Security, you think 'that's life and death,'" she said. "But we're not able to work together on this issue." She remained hopeful of finding common ground on some immigration issues. One new factor was serving in the congressional minority. In Pomona and Sacramento, she was in the majority party. Torres hoped for a lengthy tenure in the House.

THIRTY-SIXTH DISTRICT

Raul Ruiz (D)

Elected 2012, 2nd term; b. Aug. 25, 1972, Zacatecas, Mexico; U.C.L.A., B.S. 1994, Harvard U., M.D. M.P.P. 2001, M.P.H. 2007; Seventh-Day Adventist; single.

Professional Career: Emergency physician, Eisenhower Med. Ctr., 2007-2013; Assoc. dean, U. of CA Riverside Schl. of Med., 2011-2012.

DC Office: 1319 LHOB, 20515, 202-225-5330; Fax: 202-225-1238; Website: ruiz.house.gov.

State Offices: Palm Desert, 760-424-8888; Hemet, 951-765-2304.

Committees: *Natural Resources:* Indian, Insular & Alaska Native Affairs (RMM); Water, Power & Oceans. *Veterans' Affairs:* Disability Assistance & Memorial Affairs; Health.

Group Ratings

	ADA	ACLU	AFL-CIO	LCV	ITI	COC	HAFA	ACU	CFG	FRC
2014	60%	50%	–	89%	80%	64%	15%	23%	9%	13%
2013	60%	C	90%	86%	C	58%	C	28%	20%	C

National Journal Ratings

	2013 LIB	—	2013 CONS
Economic	59%	—	41%
Social	57%	—	43%
Foreign	55%	—	44%
Composite	57%	—	43%

Key Votes of the 113th Congress

1. Sandy storm spending	Y	5. Medical Marijuana	Y	9. Syrian Rebels Training	Y
2. Violence Against Women Act	Y	6. Farm Bill	N	10. Keystone pipeline	N
3. Guantanamo Bay Detainees	N	7. Afghanistan Combat	N	11. Immigration Exec. Action	N
4. Abortion 20-week ban	N	8. NSA Phone Data Collection	N	12. Bipartisan budget deal	Y

Election Results

2014 general	Raul Ruiz (D)	72,682	(54%)	$3,087,543	$436,036	$3,737
	Brian Nestande (R)	61,457	(46%)	$1,292,193	$176,159	$203,343
2014 primary	Raul Ruiz (D)	41,443	(50%)			
	Brian Nestande (R)	28,662	(35%)			
	Ray Haynes (R)	12,232	(15%)			

Prior winning percentage: 2012 (53%)

Population		Race and Ethnicity		Income	
Total:	722,653	Latino	47.9%	Median income:	$42,939
Urban:	0.0%	White	42.6%		*(344 of 435)*
Suburban:	93.4%	Black	3.6%	Under $50,000	55.7%
Rural:	6.6%	Asian	3.5%	$50,000-$99,999:	26.7%
Land area:	3,233	Two races	1.4%	$100,000-$199,999:	13.8%
Pop/sq. mi.:	223.5	White Ethnic	16.9%	$200,000 or more:	3.8%
Born in state:	54.8%			Poverty Rate	21.2%
		Education			
Age Groups		H.S. grad or less:	47.7%	**Work**	
Under 18:	25.0%	Some college:	31.9%	White collar:	25.7%
18 to 34:	20.8%	College degree, 4 yr.:	12.6%	Blue collar:	50.6%
35 to 64:	35.0%	Post-grad study:	7.9%	Sales and service:	23.7%
Over 64:	19.3%				
		Military		Govt. workers:	12.0%
		Veterans/active duty:	8.3%		

Eastern Riverside County: Indio, Palm Springs

From the air three decades ago, a night flight east from Los Angeles flew over the lights of homes of 10 million people and then into almost perfect darkness. The city then was a vast metropolis surrounded by almost uninhabited territory. Today, the sprinkled pattern of white lights has spread into the Inland Empire around Riverside and San Bernardino and is multiplying outward into the desert. Over the 10,000-foot-high San Jacinto Mountains, desert communities boomed: Palm Springs was once the lone winter resort for the stars but now is popu-

Voter Turnout	
2013 Total Citizen 18+	449,506
2014 House Turnout	134,139
2014 Turnout as % CVAP	29.8%
2012 Turnout as % CVAP	47.4%

lar for its retro architecture and as a destination for gay couples. It is one of a string of communities along Highway 111 and Frank Sinatra and Bob Hope drives. Among rich retirees, the coast's cachet lessened as beach cities filled up with roller-bladers and rent-control crusaders. The clean, dry, roomy desert, where the days are almost always crystal clear and the sky usually cloudless, became more attractive with the prevalence of air-conditioning. Two presidents retired to the desert here: Dwight Eisenhower, who wintered in Palm Desert, and Gerald Ford, who resided for 30 years after his presidency in nearby Rancho Mirage.

The population for Coachella Valley in 2008 was 443,000, including Indio and Coachella, the heavily Latino and fast-growing cities in the agricultural Coachella Valley. As with other parts of California, the mortgage crisis had an impact in the area. Area planners project stronger economic growth in Coachella Valley and a population of 600,000 by 2020. The valley produces roughly 95 percent of the dates consumed in the U.S. The annual music and arts festival in Coachella, which began in 1999, has become one of the leading music festivals in the nation and has drawn the largest revenue. In 2014, it sold out each of its six days of performance during two weekends in April, with daily sales of 96,500. That brought an estimated $90 million to the local economy. With its scenic location in the desert and a relatively short drive from Los Angeles, the event draws extensive attention in the entertainment world.

What will be the impact of water restrictions on the desert splendor of places like Rancho Mirage, with its cascading waterfalls and significantly larger water usage at many residences? Some local golf courses and homeowners associations contended that they might not be covered because they use private wells, according to *The Desert Sun*. As of 2013, tourist growth in the desert remained strong with a 12 percent increase in the previous two years. In March 2015, National Public Radio reported that Palm Springs had evolved to "Mad Men aesthetic," with abundant cocktail parties and vintage fashion.

2012 Presidential Vote		
Barack Obama (D) 107,914	(51%)
Mitt Romney (R)................101,156	(48%)
2008 Presidential Vote		
Barack Obama (D) 108,023	(51%)
John McCain (R).................101,599	(48%)
Cook Partisan Voting Index: R+1	

The 36th District covers eastern Riverside County. Interstate 10 runs through the district, taking in Banning and Beaumont on the western side and stretching all the way east to Blythe at the Nevada border. Among cities in the 36th are Coachella, Palm Springs, Rancho Mirage, and San Jacinto. Joshua Tree National Park, with its high-desert sands, is a popular tourist spot here (part of the park spills into the neighboring 8th District). This is a politically competitive district, which President Barack Obama won 51%-48% in each of his campaigns.

Raul Ruiz (D)

Emergency room doctor Raul Ruiz, a Democrat, narrowly defeated a veteran incumbent in 2012 in the 36th District. Ruiz effectively criticized the Republican's stance on Medicare and defended himself from attacks on his arrest while he was a student at medical school.

The son of farmworkers, Ruiz was born and raised in the Coachella Valley. He dreamed of being a doctor from a very young age. A family friend paid for Ruiz to apply to the University of California, Los Angeles, but he needed money for tuition. Ruiz went door-to-door in his hometown of Coachella with a handmade contract, asking neighbors and local businesses to contribute to his college fund in exchange for his future medical service to the community. He raised almost $2,000. After graduating from UCLA, Ruiz went to Harvard Medical School. As a student, he spent almost a year in Chiapas, Mexico, through a health and social justice organization, Partners in Health. The experience influenced Ruiz's views on health care. "I came out of there realizing the tremendous nature of poverty and how real policies can actually affect human lives," he later told *The Desert Sun* newspaper. After graduating from

Harvard with three degrees, Ruiz returned to the Coachella Valley and served in the emergency room of a nonprofit hospital. He returned to Chiapas in 2008 to work with the government on implementing health policy changes for the region. Two years later, Ruiz ventured to Haiti to help with recovery efforts after the catastrophic earthquake there.

Ruiz was Mary Bono Mack's first Hispanic opponent since she won the seat of her late husband, musician Sonny Bono, who died in a skiing accident in 1998. Ruiz had a demographic advantage in a newly redrawn district, where nearly 50% of voters are Latino. Ruiz and Bono Mack were the only two candidates for the district in the state's new jungle primary. Bono Mack won the first round, 58%-42%. But Ruiz got more than $1.1 million from the Democratic Congressional Campaign Committee, and the general election became a tight battle. Conservative super PACs supported Bono Mack, painting Ruiz as a minion of House Minority Leader Nancy Pelosi and attacking his support of President Barack Obama's health care legislation.

In the final weeks of the race, a local newspaper received an eight-page document from Bono Mack's campaign that outlined a Thanksgiving protest in which Ruiz was arrested and charged with two misdemeanors while attending Harvard. Both were dropped in a deal that also discharged claims of police brutality. At issue was Ruiz's participation in the National Day of Mourning, which takes place annually at Plymouth Rock to publicize the suffering of Native Americans since the Pilgrims' arrival in 1620.

Bono Mack's campaign cast Ruiz's participation in the event as anti-American and as left-wing extremism, and released a recording of a speech he gave at the protest. Ruiz characterized her efforts as desperate. Bono Mack also got backlash from tribal groups for calling Ruiz's actions unpatriotic. The pro-Democratic House Majority PAC ran ads accusing Bono Mack and her then-husband, Republican Rep. Connie Mack of Florida of benefiting from tax exemptions in Florida. Ruiz was endorsed by *The Desert Sun*, which said that Bono Mack had gotten too comfortable in Congress. Ruiz won by a surprisingly wide margin, 53%-47%.

In the House, the former emergency room doctor took on the logical issue of problems with veterans hospitals. He catalogued complaints of poor services, and filed legislation designed to reduce the claims backlog. In 2015, Ruiz became the senior Democrat on the Natural Resources Subcommittee on Indian, Insular, and Alaska Native Affairs. He pledged to work on improving health care, education, and economic growth for Native Americans.

In 2014, Ruiz was a top target of the National Republican Congressional Committee, which was counting on lower turnout in a midterm election. He benefited from unexpected events that drew extensive local media coverage, including two airplane flights during which he provided emergency service to other passengers. His opponent, Brian Nestande, a Republican Assemblyman and a former top aide to Bono Mack, proved to be a mediocre fundraiser. Ruiz out-spent him $3.1 million to $1.3 million. The NRCC contributed far less money to this contest than to its defense of Bono Mack in 2012. Ruiz won 54%-46%. Following the announcement by Sen. Barbara Boxer that she would not seek reelection in 2016, Ruiz did nothing to tamp down speculation that he might run. But the candidacy of Democratic Rep. Loretta Sanchez limited the option for Ruiz to rally Latino support.

THIRTY-SEVENTH DISTRICT

Karen Bass (D)

Elected 2010, 3rd term; b. Oct. 3, 1953, Los Angeles; U. of S. CA physician's asst. cert., CA St. U. Dominguez Hills, B.A. 1990; Baptist; divorced; 5 children (1 deceased).

Elected Office: CA Assembly, 2005-10, speaker, 2008-10.

Professional Career: Physician's asst., Los Angeles Cnty. Gen. Hosp.; Instructor, U. of S. CA; Exec. dir., Community Coalition, 1990-2004.

DC Office: 408 CHOB, 20515, 202-225-7084; Fax: 202-225-2422; Website: bass.house.gov.

State Offices: Los Angeles, 323-965-1422.

Committees: *Foreign Affairs:* Africa, Global Health, Global Human Rights, & Int'l Organizations (RMM). *Judiciary:* Courts, Intellectual Property, & the Internet; Crime, Terrorism, Homeland Security, & Investigations.

Group Ratings

	ADA	ACLU	AFL-CIO	LCV	ITI	COC	HAFA	ACU	CFG	FRC
2014	95%	77%	–	94%	60%	43%	13%	11%	13%	14%
2013	95%	C	95%	79%	C	31%	C	13%	19%	C

National Journal Ratings

	2013 LIB	—	2013 CONS
Economic	91%	—	0%
Social	93%	—	0%
Foreign	90%	—	10%
Composite	94%	—	6%

Key Votes of the 113th Congress

1. Sandy storm spending	Y	5. Medical Marijuana	N	9. Syrian Rebels Training	Y
2. Violence Against Women Act	Y	6. Farm Bill	N	10. Keystone pipeline	N
3. Guantanamo Bay Detainees	Y	7. Afghanistan Combat	Y	11. Immigration Exec. Action	N
4. Abortion 20-week ban	N	8. NSA Phone Data Collection	Y	12. Bipartisan budget deal	N

Election Results

2014 general	Karen Bass (D)	96,787	(84%)	$822,021
	Adam King (R)	18,051	(16%)	$14,693
2014 primary	Karen Bass (D)	47,639	(80%)	
	Adam King (R)	8,530	(14%)	
	Mervin Evans (D)	3,677	(6%)	

Prior winning percentages: 2012 (86%), 2010 (86%)

Population		Race and Ethnicity		Income	
Total:	732,610	Latino	39.4%	Median income:	$50,127
Urban:	100.0%	Black	24.0%		*(239 of 435)*
Suburban:	0.0%	White	23.3%	Under $50,000	49.9%
Rural:	0.0%	Asian	9.5%	$50,000-$99,999:	26.0%
Land area:	56	Two races	2.8%	$100,000-$199,999:	16.8%
Pop/sq. mi.:	13,108.1	White Ethnic	12.8%	$200,000 or more:	7.3%
Born in state:	47.5%			Poverty Rate	20.8%
		Education			
Age Groups		H.S. grad or less:	37.8%	**Work**	
Under 18:	21.0%	Some college:	25.3%	White collar:	40.7%
18 to 34:	29.6%	College degree, 4 yr.:	22.1%	Blue collar:	43.5%
35 to 64:	38.0%	Post-grad study:	14.8%	Sales and service:	15.8%
Over 64:	11.4%			Govt. workers:	10.6%
		Military			
		Veterans/active duty:	3.3%		

Western L.A./South L.A., Culver City

Voter Turnout	
2013 Total Citizen 18+	451,539
2014 House Turnout	114,838
2014 Turnout as % CVAP	25.4%
2012 Turnout as % CVAP	58.3%

Since the Los Angeles riots of 1992 and 1965, the city has had to live down its reputation as being inhospitable to African Americans, a problem exacerbated by racial tensions in the city's police department. This was the epicenter of L.A.'s two postwar riots, in the Watts district in 1965 and at the corner of Florence and Normandie in 1992. But by other measures—levels of income and degree of residential integration with non-blacks—blacks in Los Angeles had been doing better than those elsewhere in the United States. According to a 2011 National Urban League report, Los Angeles is the second-best city in the country for black-owned businesses. Job opportunities in Los Angeles—up to and including the office of mayor for 20 years—have been relatively good for blacks. And the long-simmering tension between the LAPD and the African-American community has been ameliorated by the region's changing demographics. Former Los Angeles Mayor Antonio Villaraigosa proudly noted that two-thirds of the city's police officers were non-white, though the command staff remains 55 percent white. Another, less positive side of the story has developed in recent years. Partly due to the high cost of housing, the black population in Los Angeles has dropped 8 percent since 2000, and the city ranks 40th out of 52 cities in the nation in terms of housing and income for blacks, according to L.A.-based urban-affairs scholar Joel Kotkin.

Baldwin Hills, where on clear days one can see the snow-capped San Gabriel Mountains, is a high-income, African-American neighborhood. Near View Park-Windsor Hills along Slauson Avenue are other comfortable black-majority neighborhoods. Crenshaw, an Art Deco neighborhood built in the 1920s and 1930s, is the birthplace of West Coast hip hop music. In one of the more rundown sections

2012 Presidential Vote		
Barack Obama (D) 222,329	(85%)
Mitt Romney (R)...................33,307	(13%)
2008 Presidential Vote		
Barack Obama (D) 229,434	(85%)
John McCain (R)...................35,230	(13%)
Cook Partisan Voting Index: D+34		

of Crenshaw, former L.A. Lakers basketball star Magic Johnson built his multiplex theaters. And the once desolate Culver City, which still features sprawling studios and media businesses, is experiencing a self-styled urban renaissance and is home to trendy new restaurants and a historically restored Culver Hotel.

These parts of Los Angeles are the heart of the 37th Congressional District, which is bisected by the Santa Monica Freeway. The district encompasses Century City, Ladera Heights, Baldwin Hills, and Hyde Park. It also includes the University of Southern California and the Los Angeles Memorial Coliseum, which has hosted two Olympics and, where the USC Trojans play football. It takes in several cultural landmarks, including the California Science Center, the Natural History Museum, and the California African American Museum. The 37th District is about 39% Latino and 24% black. It is one of the most Democratic districts in the nation. President Barack Obama got 85% of the local vote during each of his campaigns.

Karen Bass (D)

Karen Bass, elected in 2010, is a former California Assembly speaker and a Democratic up-and-comer who has drawn flattering comparisons to another Californian who once presided as speaker, House Minority Leader Nancy Pelosi. Although she has served only in the minority while in Congress, Bass has shown impressive leadership skills.

Bass was born and raised in Los Angeles. Her father was a letter carrier and her mother was a homemaker. Her father had moved to California from Texas after World War II; her mother was a Los Angeles native who learned to speak Spanish as a child. Bass told *National Journal* that the most influential part of her childhood was watching television news coverage of the civil rights movement with her father, which "absolutely, positively shaped who I am today and why I'm interested in politics." In middle school, Bass was a student representative on a committee overseeing integration of the school. At age 14, she got involved in Democratic Sen. Robert F. Kennedy's 1968 presidential campaign by signing up her mother as a precinct captain and then doing all the neighborhood canvassing herself. At her high school in West Los Angeles, Bass joined her teachers in protests against the Vietnam War. She attended San Diego State University and stayed active in community organizing. "School wound up being rather secondary for me," she said. Bass served on a committee that investigated accusations of police abuses in Los Angeles and participated in groups that advocated the end of apartheid in South Africa.

Bass ultimately received a nursing certificate from the University of Southern California and a bachelor's degree from California State University, Dominguez Hills. She was married in 1980 and had a daughter; the couple divorced in 1986. She and her ex-husband stayed in contact, cooperating on raising their daughter and four stepchildren. In 2006, Bass's daughter and son-in-law died in a car accident.

In 1990, Bass founded the Community Coalition, a nonprofit that works with African-American and Latino communities in South Los Angeles to combat drug use and gang violence by shutting down liquor stores and motels. The group also campaigned against Proposition 187, which sought to deny public services to illegal immigrants, and Proposition 209, which prohibited affirmative action admissions policies in public universities. Bass served as executive director of the organization for 14 years.

Bass won election to the state Assembly in 2004. In the legislature, she sponsored several bills aimed at reforming the state's foster care system and expanding health insurance programs for children. In her first term, she was the majority whip; in her second, she was majority leader; and in her third term, she became the first black female speaker of the Assembly. Trying to balance California's budget in the midst of a fiscal crisis consumed much of her tenure. She negotiated budget compromises that included deep cuts to education and social spending. Bass described her two years as speaker as "painful" and said, "I ran for office because I wanted to create, build, and expand programs, not tear them apart."

When Rep. Diane Watson announced she would retire, she supported Bass as her successor. Other prominent Democrats stayed out of the race, assuming that Bass would easily win on turf she had represented in the legislature. She won the June Democratic primary in 2010 with 85% of the vote; her nearest challenger was Felton Newell, a prosecutor with the Los Angeles city attorney's office, who finished with about 6%. In the general election, she easily defeated Republican lawyer James Andion.

In the House, Bass got seats on the Foreign Affairs and Budget committees and was made an assistant Democratic whip. She became co-chair of the Democratic Congressional Campaign Committee's Women LEAD program charged with recruiting more female candidates. Colleagues lauded her political skills, and she worked the talk-show circuit to articulate the party's message. *Politico* in December 2011 named her the freshman Democrat "most likely to succeed" and said she "looks more and more like a (Nancy) Pelosi-in-waiting each day." She gave up Budget and now sits on the Judiciary Committee. On Foreign Affairs, she is the senior Democrat on the Subcommittee on Africa, Global Health, Global Human Rights and International Organizations. Her work on Africa has included successful efforts to extend the African Growth and Opportunity Act. During the Ebola crisis in 2014, she joined Reps. Keith Ellison of Minnesota and Barbara Lee of California to urge President Barack Obama to send U.S. troops to care for Ebola patients in west Africa.

Bass maintained her advocacy of the poor and disadvantaged, introducing several bills to improve foster care. Speaking at the Democratic National Convention in 2012, she charged that GOP voter identification legislation was aimed at curtailing minorities' voting participation. "One of the darkest shadows of the past century is creeping into this one: one of our most basic rights—the right to vote, a right that we fought for and won—is under attack," she said. In January 2015, the House passed the bill she introduced with Republican Rep. John Kline of Minnesota, which was designed to connect child victims of trafficking to appropriate services and prevent further exploitation.

In addition to her legislative and political work, Bass drew attention for her avid interest in martial arts. She has brown belts in taekwondo and hapkido, a Korean self-defense technique. She likely won't need those skills to retain this seat.

THIRTY-EIGHTH DISTRICT

Linda Sánchez (D)

Elected 2002, 7th term; b. Jan. 28, 1969, Orange; U. of CA Berkeley, B.A. 1991, U.C.L.A., J.D. 1995; Catholic; married (James Sullivan); 4 children.

Professional Career: Practicing atty., 1995-98; Exec. secy. treas. of Orange Cnty. AFL-CIO, 2000-02.

DC Office: 2329 RHOB, 20515, 202-225-6676; Fax: 202-226-1012; Website: lindasanchez.house.gov.

State Offices: Cerritos, 562-860-5050.

Committees: *Ethics* (RMM). *Ways & Means:* Select Revenue Measures. *Select Benghazi Committee.*

Group Ratings

	ADA	ACLU	AFL-CIO	LCV	ITI	COC	HAFA	ACU	CFG	FRC
2014	80%	77%	–	91%	60%	43%	19%	8%	14%	0%
2013	95%	C	100%	100%	C	31%	C	8%	20%	C

National Journal Ratings

	2013 LIB	—	2013 CONS
Economic	91%	—	0%
Social	93%	—	0%
Foreign	90%	—	6%
Composite	95%	—	5%

Key Votes of the 113th Congress

1. Sandy storm spending	Y	5. Medical Marijuana	Y
2. Violence Against Women Act	Y	6. Farm Bill	N
3. Guantanamo Bay Detainees	Y	7. Afghanistan Combat	Y
4. Abortion 20-week ban	N	8. NSA Phone Data Collection	Y

9. Syrian Rebels Training	Y
10. Keystone pipeline	N
11. Immigration Exec. Action	N
12. Bipartisan budget deal	N

Election Results

2014 general	Linda Sánchez (D)	58,192	(59%)	$1,027,339
	Benjamin Campos (R)	40,288	(41%)	$5,247
2014 primary	Linda Sánchez (D)	27,149	(58%)	
	Benjamin Campos (R)	20,046	(42%)	

Prior winning percentages: 2012 (68%), 2010 (63%), 2008 (70%), 2006 (66%), 2004 (61%), 2002 (55%)

Population		Race and Ethnicity		Income	
Total:	725,481	Latino	61.2%	Median income:	$61,015
Urban:	88.8%	White	18.6%		*(115 of 435)*
Suburban:	11.2%	Asian	14.2%	Under $50,000	41.7%
Rural:	0.0%	Black	4.2%	$50,000-$99,999:	31.8%
Land area:	99	Two races	1.3%	$100,000-$199,999:	22.8%
Pop/sq. mi.:	7,349.2	White Ethnic	6.9%	$200,000 or more:	3.7%
Born in state:	61.1%			Poverty Rate	12.8%
		Education			
Age Groups		H.S. grad or less:	47.9%	**Work**	
Under 18:	24.2%	Some college:	30.5%	White collar:	29.4%
18 to 34:	24.3%	College degree, 4 yr.:	15.1%	Blue collar:	45.4%
35 to 64:	38.5%	Post-grad study:	6.5%	Sales and service:	25.2%
Over 64:	13.0%			Govt. workers:	15.0%
		Military			
		Veterans/active duty:	4.3%		

Eastern L.A. suburbs: Whittier, Norwalk

In the years just after World War II, much of southeast Los Angeles County was farmland—citrus groves and dairy farms. In the next two decades, housing subdivisions were built and new cities incorporated so that what had been a few towns separated by farmland became one continuous

Voter Turnout	
2013 Total Citizen 18+	465,178
2014 House Turnout	98,480
2014 Turnout as % CVAP	21.2%
2012 Turnout as % CVAP	50.9%

swath of suburbia. The towns were different in character. Whittier, founded by Midwestern Quakers, was the hometown of Richard Nixon, a young lawyer who decided to run for Congress in 1946. Lakewood, just north of Long Beach, used to be an area of lima bean fields. Developers built it up so rapidly in the 1950s that *Life* magazine featured it as one of the first mass-produced suburbs. Other towns were late-bloomers. There were still dairy farms in Cerritos in the 1970s, though few remain now.

Most of these communities are known as Gateway Cities in southeast Los Angeles County: Artesia, which Dutch and Portuguese dairy experts developed into a major dairy center for Southern California; Pico Rivera, which is 91% Hispanic; and La Mirada, named by Rand McNally Publishing founder Andrew McNally when he purchased 2,300 acres in the area in the late 1800s. The Hispanic share of Whittier's population grew from 56% in 2000 to 66% in 2010. Whittier has been ranked among the top cities to live in the United States. After World War Two, Montebello became a center of the large community of displaced Armenians. They built a monument to the Armenian genocide martyrs. Montebello also is home to blimp-maker Worldwide Aeros Corp. The company's original

2012 Presidential Vote		
Barack Obama (D)	149,141	(65%)
Mitt Romney (R)	75,780	(33%)

2008 Presidential Vote		
Barack Obama (D)	153,378	(62%)
John McCain (R)	90,643	(36%)

Cook Partisan Voting Index: D+12

nal plan for a new engineering facility to build a 120-mph aircraft to carry cargo loads for the military failed in 2013 when a large section of the ceiling collapsed and damaged the large experimental aircraft. Instead, in October 2014, the company dedicated a smaller version of the Goodyear blimp that was designed for use in advertising, tourism, or surveillance. But it needed adequate financing.

The 38th Congressional District encompasses Whittier, South Whittier, and some of the Gateway Cities in southeast Los Angeles County. It includes Norwalk, which is 70% Hispanic and the district's largest city; South El Monte; and Montebello. Lakewood is divided between this district and the Long Beach-based 47th. The 38th is more than 60% Hispanic and solidly Democratic.

Linda Sánchez (D)

Linda Sánchez, a Democrat first elected in 2002, is the junior member of the only pair of sisters elected to Congress; her sister is Loretta Sanchez, also of California, who is nine years older and a 2016 Senate candidate. With her legal background, Linda Sánchez has focused on judicial as well as international issues.

The sisters are two of the seven children of Mexican immigrant parents Ignacio Sánchez, a machinist, and Maria Macias, a bilingual education aide in an elementary school. Their parents met while trying to organize a union at a tire shop where they worked when they were young. Their mother once took little Linda to a rally to hear famed migrant farmworker organizer César Chávez speak. Linda Sánchez earned her bachelor's degree in Spanish literature at the University of California, Berkeley, and her law degree at the University of California, Los Angeles, working her way through school with jobs as a security guard, nanny, and teacher's aide. She became a civil rights lawyer and was executive secretary-treasurer of the Orange County Federation of Labor. "She's definitely the more liberal one," Loretta has said. She's also considered the funnier one. Sanchez has won kudos from Washington insiders for her routines at the D.C. Improv, a professional comedy club that often features members of Congress. At a dinner for journalists and their sources in 2012, she joked that well-tanned Republican House Speaker John Boehner's stewardship could be called "the Bronze Age."

When the new district lines were unveiled after the 2000 census, Linda Sánchez was one of six Democrats who ran for the seat. Her most important asset was her sister's support. She tapped Loretta's extensive fundraising network, walked precincts with her, and appeared in a television commercial with her. In a Spanish ad, their mother urged voters to send both of her daughters to Capitol Hill. All of this work gave Linda Sánchez an advantage over her two chief opponents, who were better known when the race began: two-term Assemblywoman Sally Havice and South Gate Councilman Hector De La Torre, a former legislative aide and Labor Department official. The three candidates differed very little on the issues.

Sánchez's ties to labor helped her build a strong voter-turnout operation. She also won the endorsement of then-House Minority Whip Nancy Pelosi of California. Her opponents noted that no Latino members of Congress endorsed Sánchez, and they charged that she was a political opportunist who changed her name and residence to run in the newly created district. Sánchez had used her non-Latino married name until she ran for the House. But she won the primary with 33% of the vote; De La Torre received 29% and Havice had 19%. In November, Republican Tim Escobar, a financial adviser and former Army helicopter pilot, called her an inexperienced liberal extremist. But Sánchez won 55%-41%, and she has been reelected easily since.

Sánchez has a strongly liberal voting record. She has sponsored popular Democratic bills to end the Social Security Administration's policy to deny benefits to same-sex couples and to establish a federal definition of school bullying to protect vulnerable students, including those who have been targeted because of their sexual orientation; the measures have not advanced. She can be quick to use her sharp tongue against political foes. Sanchez criticized conservative pundit Charles Krauthammer for suggesting Hispanics could be a natural Republican constituency if the GOP moderated its tone on illegal immigration. "If Mr. Krauthammer believes that all it will take for Republicans to win the Latino vote is to fix the GOP's offensive rhetoric on immigration, he truly doesn't understand that Latinos are not one-issue voters," she wrote in a *Huffington Post* column. In 2011, bloggers on the right derided her for saying on MSNBC that a potential government shutdown would hurt her financially. "I have to tell you that I live paycheck-to-paycheck, like most Americans," Sánchez said. "I'm still paying off my student loans. I have a 2-year-old son who I have to support, and I have to maintain residences on both coasts."

When Democrats won the majority in 2007, Sánchez gained influence as chairwoman of the Judiciary Committee's Commercial and Administrative Law Subcommittee, where she worked with senior Democrats on hearings to oversee the George W. Bush administration's allegedly politically motivated firings of U.S. attorneys around the country. When senior White House political adviser Karl Rove refused to cooperate, Sánchez initiated a contempt of Congress action. When Rove capitulated in March 2009, the House dropped its lawsuit against him.

As the top Democrat on the Ethics Committee, she found herself at the center of several thorny cases, including one involving California Democratic Rep. Maxine Waters. The panel ultimately did not pursue allegations that Waters arranged a 2008 meeting with Treasury Department officials to help steer financial bailout funds to a minority-owned bank in which her husband held a stake.

Sánchez has a plum assignment as the first Latina to serve on the Ways and Means Committee. As co-founder of the House Trade Working Group, she pledged tougher review of proposed international trade deals that she feared would ship jobs overseas, including the Trans-Pacific Partnership agreement that she strongly opposed. In 2015, she took over as head of the Congressional Hispanic Caucus, with plans to feature the group's junior members plus a more aggressive handling of immigration issues.

THIRTY-NINTH DISTRICT

Ed Royce (R)

Elected 1992, 12th term; b. Oct. 12, 1951, Los Angeles; CA St. U. Fullerton, B.A. 1977; Catholic; married (Marie).

Elected Office: CA Senate, 1983-92.

Professional Career: Tax mgr., 1979-82.

DC Office: 2310 RHOB, 20515, 202-225-4111; Website: royce.house .gov.

State Offices: Brea, 714-255-0101; Rowland Heights, 626-964-5123.

Committees: *Financial Services:* Capital Markets & Gov't Sponsored Enterprises; Housing & Insurance. *Foreign Affairs* (Chmn).

Group Ratings

	ADA	ACLU	AFL-CIO	LCV	ITI	COC	HAFA	ACU	CFG	FRC
2014	5%	0%	–	3%	80%	100%	66%	92%	70%	75%
2013	0%	C	11%	7%	C	77%	C	88%	89%	C

National Journal Ratings

	2013 LIB	—	2013 CONS
Economic	6%	—	93%
Social	27%	—	71%
Foreign	5%	—	86%
Composite	15%	—	85%

Key Votes of the 113th Congress

1. Sandy storm spending	N	5. Medical Marijuana	N
2. Violence Against Women Act	Y	6. Farm Bill	N
3. Guantanamo Bay Detainees	N	7. Afghanistan Combat	N
4. Abortion 20-week ban	Y	8. NSA Phone Data Collection	N

9. Syrian Rebels Training	Y
10. Keystone pipeline	Y
11. Immigration Exec. Action	Y
12. Bipartisan budget deal	Y

Election Results

2014 general	Edward Royce (R)	91,319	(69%)	$1,743,860
	Peter Anderson (D)	41,906	(31%)	$4,209
2014 primary	Edward Royce (D)	49,071	(71%)	
	Peter Anderson (R)	20,480	(29%)	

Prior winning percentages: 2012 (58%), 2010 (67%), 2008 (63%), 2006 (67%), 2004 (68%), 2002 (68%), 2000 (63%), 1998 (63%), 1996 (63%), 1994 (66%), 1992 (57%)

Population		Race and Ethnicity		Income	
Total:	721,014	Latino	34.6%	Median income:	$79,909
Urban:	49.7%	White	32.3%		*(33 of 435)*
Suburban:	50.3%	Asian	28.1%	Under $50,000	30.9%
Rural:	0.0%	Black	2.3%	$50,000-$99,999:	30.9%
Land area:	172	Two races	2.0%	$100,000-$199,999:	28.7%
Pop/sq. mi.:	4,184.0	White Ethnic	14.0%	$200,000 or more:	9.6%
Born in state:	53.0%			Poverty Rate	11.2%
		Education			
Age Groups		H.S. grad or less:	30.4%	**Work**	
Under 18:	22.3%	Some college:	30.4%	White collar:	42.4%
18 to 34:	24.1%	College degree, 4 yr.:	26.5%	Blue collar:	43.2%
35 to 64:	40.8%	Post-grad study:	12.7%	Sales and service:	14.5%
Over 64:	12.8%				
		Military		Govt. workers:	11.9%
		Veterans/active duty:	5.1%		

Northern Orange County: Fullerton, eastern Anaheim

During the Southern California land boom in the 1880s, Massachusetts grain merchants George and Edward Amerige headed west in search of new business opportunities. They went on a duck hunting trip near Anaheim and eventually opened a real estate business in the city. Through negotia-

Voter Turnout	
2013 Total Citizen 18+	481,250
2014 House Turnout	133,225
2014 Turnout as % CVAP	27.7%
2012 Turnout as % CVAP	57.4%

tions with railroad agent George Fullerton, the Ameriges eventually purchased 430 acres of land for $68,000 and allowed the railroad the right-of-way—provided of course that the railway's route include the new town they were developing. Local residents later voted to name the town Fullerton, and it developed as a prime source of juicy Valencia oranges. Today, Fullerton is home to its own college, California State University, Fullerton, which enrolls more than 38,000 students and has the largest business school in the state. The American Civil Liberties Union and an Asian-American civil rights group in March 2015 filed suit against the city of Fullerton on the basis that its at-large voting system prevented the Asian community from gaining a seat on the city council, even though 23 percent of the local population is Asian. Nearby is affluent Yorba Linda, which has a median income of $120,000 and is one of the wealthiest cities in the nation. In May 2015, voters soundly defeated recall petitions to remove the mayor and a council member who support high-density residential development.

The 39th Congressional District of California is based in northern Orange County and it includes the southeast corner of Los Angeles County and the southwest corner of San Bernardino County. More than two-thirds of the voters are in Orange County. In San Bernardino, it includes part of Chino, the site of a large youth prison that was closed in 2010. It also has large meatpacking plants, whose smell can carry across the valley on a windy day, and Chino Hills, incorporated in 1991 and full of subdivisions for commuters who battle the heavy traffic on Interstate 5.

In Los Angeles County, the 39th includes La Habra Heights and Diamond Bar, which is almost 53 percent Asian. In the Orange County section, it takes in a part of Anaheim and includes Yorba Linda, the birthplace of President Richard Nixon and the site of his presidential library. Only 40,000 people

2012 Presidential Vote		
Mitt Romney (R)..................133,742	(51%)
Barack Obama (D) 124,108	(47%)

2008 Presidential Vote		
John McCain (R).................135,930	(50%)
Barack Obama (D) 127,988	(48%)

Cook Partisan Voting Index: R+5

lived in Orange County in 1913 when Nixon was born; just over 3 million live there today. Other Orange County towns in the 39th are Brea and La Habra. Politically, the 39th leans Republican.

Ed Royce (R)

Ed Royce, a Republican first elected in 1992, is a hawkish conservative and fervent supporter of free trade. As chairman of the House Foreign Affairs Committee, he has actively asserted those views and sought to influence legislative actions and the policy debate.

Royce's profile almost precisely spans Orange County's. He grew up in Fullerton and belonged to the conservative Young Americans for Freedom at Cal State Fullerton. He was later the head of Youth for Reagan in California during Reagan's 1976 presidential primary challenge to Gerald Ford. Royce worked several years as a tax and capital projects manager for a cement company. In 1982, a group of conservative state legislators known as the "Cave Men" took him to a Black Angus restaurant—no avocado-and-sprout sandwiches for them—and persuaded him to run for the state Senate. He won at age 31. When the legislature refused to pass Royce's bill allowing crime victims to object to trial delays, giving grand juries more power, and ending "jury-shopping," he got the measure on the ballot as an initiative and it passed by a wide margin. He also wrote the first law making it a felony to stalk someone. In 1992, Royce ran for the House. With the blessing of Orange County Republican leaders, he was unopposed in the primary and easily won the general. He has been reelected by wide margins since.

In the House, Royce has a conservative voting record, and he has been a faithful fundraiser for Republicans, which helped him prevail over New Jersey Rep. Chris Smith in taking the helm at Foreign Affairs. As chairman, he has pursued aggressive oversight of President Barack Obama and his administration. He blasted what he called Obama's "unimaginative and moribund" handling of North Korea, and endorsed an alternative approach of cutting off money so that "the regime collapses." He called Iran's quest to attain nuclear weapons "a grave threat that demands constant attention and great pressure on Tehran." In February 2015, Royce told conservative talk-radio host Hugh Hewitt that giving the Obama administration explicit authority to strike Iran if it continued developing a nuclear weapon was "a good idea." Two months later, he voiced deep reservations about the framework of an agreement that Secretary of State John Kerry had reached with Iran. "I think when the ayatollah is calling for death to the little Satan, death to Israel, he's also calling for death to America, death to the great Satan," he said in an interview with PBS.

In 2014, Royce pressed for legislation providing aid to Ukraine while imposing sanctions on Russia. He brushed aside Senate Republicans' calls to include in the measure language to change how the United States provides money to the International Monetary Fund. "There isn't support in my committee on either side of the aisle for including this. We feel it should be handled separately," he told reporters. The provision eventually was dropped. He also called for more exports of American natural gas to Europe to compete with Russia in those markets. "Until we do something decisive on energy policy, until we have a strategy and a policy that actually is something that the Russians would really worry about long term, we don't have that hammer," Royce said.

Royce has developed a good working relationship with New York's Eliot Engel, the ranking Democrat on his committee. Both are staunch supporters of Israel. They have issued numerous joint news releases, and they appeared together on CNN in September 2014 to call for greater action against the Islamic State after the group released a video showing the beheading of an American hostage. Royce promised to develop closer ties with the Senate Foreign Relations Committee, saying on his blog, "It doesn't make a lot of sense to pass legislation in the House with little Senate support."

During the earlier Republican control of the House, Royce chaired the Subcommittee on Africa. Although he had never set foot in Africa, he was widely praised for getting up to speed on the issues. He was instrumental in getting bipartisan support to enact an Africa free trade bill. He also sponsored bills to encourage oil production, promote human rights, and condemn the genocide in Sudan. He was among the sponsors of a bipartisan bill in 2009 requiring Obama to develop a comprehensive plan to end the brutal two-decade war in Uganda.

In 2011, he became chairman of the Terrorism, Nonproliferation, and Trade Subcommittee, where he focused on the spread of radical Islam. He won enactment of a bill establishing Radio Free Afghanistan and another measure to promote nuclear nonproliferation in North Korea. He has also urged stronger strategic and trade relationships between the United States and India, and condemned discrimination against Hindus in Pakistan, Bangladesh, and Bhutan. He helped win the release of two journalists from a North Korean prison in 2009.

On other issues, Royce has been a vocal critic of the Obama administration's approach to immigration, calling for it to tightly enforce current laws rather than propose new ones. On the Financial Services Committee, he has worked with Democrats to expand lending authority for credit unions and to put them on an equivalent status with banks, something that puts him at odds with most Republicans, who align more closely with the banking industry. He enacted a bill in 2014 that expanded federal deposit insurance to include interest on lawyer trust accounts and similar escrow accounts housed within credit unions. During conference committee negotiations on the 2010 financial industry overhaul, he tried without success to persuade conferees to make major changes to government-backed mortgage giants Fannie Mae and Freddie Mac, arguing that reshaping the oft-criticized institutions was crucial to any reform effort.

Throughout his House career, Royce has been blessed with a solidly GOP district where, unlike other California Republicans, he has not had to worry about primaries or new voters.

FORTIETH DISTRICT

Lucille Roybal-Allard (D)

Elected 1992, 12th term; b. June 12, 1941, Boyle Heights; CA St. U. L.A., B.A. 1965; Catholic; married (Edward T. Allard III); 4 children.

Elected Office: CA Assembly, 1987-92.

Professional Career: Community relations; Nonprofit exec..

DC Office: 2330 RHOB, 20515, 202-225-1766; Fax: 202-226-0350; Website: roybal-allard.house.gov.

State Offices: Commerce, 323-721-8790.

Committees: *Appropriations:* Energy & Water Development, & Related Agencies; Homeland Security (RMM); Labor, HHS, Education, & Related Agencies.

Group Ratings

	ADA	ACLU	AFL-CIO	LCV	ITI	COC	HAFA	ACU	CFG	FRC
2014	85%	83%	–	97%	60%	43%	10%	8%	11%	0%
2013	100%	C	95%	89%	C	25%	C	8%	10%	C

National Journal Ratings

	2013 LIB	—	2013 CONS
Economic	91%	—	0%
Social	87%	—	7%
Foreign	90%	—	6%
Composite	93%	—	8%

Key Votes of the 113th Congress

1. Sandy storm spending	Y	5. Medical Marijuana	Y	9. Syrian Rebels Training	Y
2. Violence Against Women Act	Y	6. Farm Bill	N	10. Keystone pipeline	N
3. Guantanamo Bay Detainees	Y	7. Afghanistan Combat	Y	11. Immigration Exec. Action	N
4. Abortion 20-week ban	N	8. NSA Phone Data Collection	Y	12. Bipartisan budget deal	Y

Election Results

2014 general	Lucille Roybal-Allard (D)	30,208	(61%)	$498,231
	David Sanchez (D)	19,171	(39%)	
2014 primary	Lucille Roybal-Allard (D)	13,745	(66%)	
	David Sanchez (D)	6,968	(34%)	

Prior winning percentages: 2012 (59%), 2010 (77%), 2008 (77%), 2006 (77%), 2004 (74%), 2002 (74%), 2000 (85%), 1998 (87%), 1996 (82%), 1994 (81%), 1992 (63%)

Population		Race and Ethnicity		Income	
Total:	718,451	Latino	86.6%	Median income:	$38,981
Urban:	99.0%	Black	5.2%		*(398 of 435)*
Suburban:	1.0%	White	5.2%	Under $50,000	61.3%
Rural:	0.0%	Asian	2.1%	$50,000-$99,999:	27.8%
Land area:	64	Two races	0.4%	$100,000-$199,999:	9.3%
Pop/sq. mi.:	11,159.2	White Ethnic	2.2%	$200,000 or more:	1.5%
Born in state:	54.1%			Poverty Rate	29.3%
		Education			
Age Groups		H.S. grad or less:	71.6%	**Work**	
Under 18:	30.3%	Some college:	20.0%	White collar:	15.3%
18 to 34:	28.1%	College degree, 4 yr.:	6.1%	Blue collar:	46.8%
35 to 64:	34.0%	Post-grad study:	2.3%	Sales and service:	37.9%
Over 64:	7.6%				
		Military		Govt. workers:	8.9%
		Veterans/active duty:	2.1%		

Eastern Los Angeles: Bell Gardens, Downey

East Los Angeles is a piece of Latin America transplanted to California. Hard-working immigrants from Mexico and also from Central and South America come to find affordable housing, doubling and tripling up with other families in places that are close enough to drive an old car to work in fac-

Voter Turnout	
2013 Total Citizen 18+	308,276
2014 House Turnout	49,379
2014 Turnout as % CVAP	16%
2012 Turnout as % CVAP	47.5%

tories and warehouses south and east of downtown Los Angeles. The Gold Line extension of L.A.'s transit agency made their commutes considerably easier by bringing light rail service to the area. This part of Los Angeles includes the 1940s working-class suburb of Huntington Park, with its shopping strip on the wide Pacific Boulevard; and it includes Bell, Bell Gardens, Maywood, and Cudahy, all of which are now predominantly Latino. Maywood calls itself a "sanctuary city" for illegal immigrants.

The recession was brutal in an area already struggling to make ends meet as they dealt with the consequences of long-standing malfeasance. After Maywood laid off all but one of its public workers in 2010 and city services were performed by outsourced contractors, a plan for collaboration with neighboring Bell fell apart because of that city's corruption. The city's finances slowly improved, but have remained in jeopardy. Bell residents threw the bums out when they discovered in 2010 that their city manager was paid an annual salary of $787,000 and their police chief $457,000; both resigned their posts. Both pleaded guilty to corruption charges and were sentenced in 2014, as did several other former city officials. At his sentencing to 12 years, a Superior Court judge told former city manager Robert Rizzo, "you did some very, very bad things for a very long time." His successors said that taxpayers of the impoverished city continued to pay a "Rizzo tax." Cudahy also has been scandal-plagued; three city officials arrested on bribery charges in 2012 reached a plea deal, amid continuing investigations of corruption. Somewhat more affluent Bellflower is a formerly prime shopping area trying to make a comeback, and Downey is home to Raytheon's Public Safety Regional Technology Center, which won a contract to upgrade Los Angeles County's emergency dispatch system.

These are all communities in the 40th Congressional District of California, centered on East Los Angeles and located south of downtown L.A. Bisecting much of the district is the concrete-lined Los Angeles River. Environmentalists have pushed the city for years to clean it up and return it to a more natural condition, with adjacent parkland and bicycle paths, while preserving its flood-control assets. In 2014, federal and city officials agreed on a $1 billion plan for an 11-mile restoration that was designed to create an urban greenway from Glendale to downtown, with additional land that the city had purchased. The 40th District also takes in Paramount, where local businessmen Frank and Lawrence Zamboni invented refrigeration technology for the

2012 Presidential Vote		
Barack Obama (D)	115,637	(82%)
Mitt Romney (R)	23,446	(17%)

2008 Presidential Vote		
Barack Obama (D)	126,147	(79%)
John McCain (R)	31,510	(20%)

Cook Partisan Voting Index: D+29

dairy industry and the eventual Zamboni ice-resurfacing machine for skating rinks. With an 87 percent Latino population, this has become the most Hispanic district in California.

Lucille Roybal-Allard (D)

Lucille Roybal-Allard, first elected in 1992, was the first Mexican-American woman to be elected to Congress. Immigration reform is one of her main priorities, along with social programs serving the poor. As the ranking Democrat on the Appropriations Subcommittee on Homeland Security, she is well-positioned to oversee funding for that federal agency and immigration, though she maintains a low-profile approach.

Roybal-Allard grew up in the Los Angeles area, the daughter of longtime Democratic Rep. Edward Roybal, who was the first Latino to serve on the Los Angeles City Council. She dreamed of a show business career as a teenager and later worked as a department store clerk and for nonprofit organizations. After raising a family—two of her children are lawyers—she followed her father into politics when she was 45 years old. She was elected to the California Assembly in 1986. Six years later her father retired from the House, and she ran for the seat in a district that took in much of the territory he had represented for 30 years. Roybal-Allard won easily with 75% of the vote in the primary and 63% in the general election.

Roybal-Allard has compiled a solidly liberal voting record and has been among the Hispanic lawmakers pushing President Barack Obama to act boldly on immigration reform. One session between lawmakers and Obama domestic policy adviser Cecilia Munoz grew so testy that Roybal-Allard walked out, *The Washington Post* reported in April 2012. She called Obama's reelection a mandate to focus on a comprehensive immigration overhaul, predicting that opponents would revive "the usual scare tactics, misinformation, and misguided thinking. ... But the truth is that the facts are on our side, the majority of Americans are on our side, and the momentum is on our side."

She has a long history of advocacy for immigrants of all sorts. Among the immigration-related bills Roybal-Allard has introduced has been the Help Separated Families Act to ensure that children are not taken away from relatives because of a parent's immigration status, including deportation. When Senate Finance Committee Democrats proposed restrictions on illegal immigrants participating in health care programs as part of the 2010 overhaul, she joined a group of Hispanics who succeeded in modifying the provision. She is a co-sponsor of the DREAM Act, which would provide a path to legal immigration for college- or military-bound students. In the past, she pushed for in-state college tuition rates for illegal immigrants. Roybal-Allard also has filed legislation aimed at raising labor standards and protections for children of migrant farm workers to the same level as occupations outside of agriculture. Conservatives attacked the measure as an effort to give labor unions more power. When Obama in November 2014 posthumously gave the Presidential Medal of Freedom to her father, she recalled his success in working on bipartisan terms, including with Republican presidents, on behalf of undocumented immigrants.

As a member of the Appropriations Committee, Roybal-Allard championed a new federal courthouse in Los Angeles. After more than a decade of delay, ground was finally broken in August 2013 for the facility. She got a bill signed into law to coordinate federal programs and research on underage drinking as well as to fund a media campaign on its dangers. Another success was a new law in 2008 that authorized federal grants for newborn health screening for congenital, genetic, and metabolic disorders.

Roybal-Allard isn't as close to Minority Leader Nancy Pelosi and her inner circle as other Democratic women from California, which sometimes limits her leverage in the House. In 2006, Roybal-Allard seconded the nomination of Steny Hoyer of Maryland for majority leader, who opposed Pelosi's preferred candidate, John Murtha of Pennsylvania. Hoyer won the contest, so Roybal-Allard retained a friend or two in high places.

At home in 2012, under the state's new top-two, all-party primary rules, Roybal-Allard found herself with a Democratic challenger in November, college instructor David Sanchez. He held her to 59% of the vote, her lowest percentage ever, but she won reelection. They faced each other again in November 2014, when she won, 61%-39%. Sanchez did not report spending any campaign money in either contest.

FORTY-FIRST DISTRICT

Mark Takano (D)

Elected 2012, 2nd term; b. Dec. 10, 1960, Riverside; Harvard U., B.A. 1983, U. of CA Riverside, M.F.A. 2010; Methodist; single.

Elected Office: Bd. of Trustees, Riverside Comm. Col. Dist., 1990-2012, pres., 1992, 1997-8, 2005-06.

Professional Career: Teacher, Rialto Unified Schl. Dist., 1988-2013; Substitute teacher, Boston, 1984-85.

DC Office: 1507 LHOB, 20515, 202-225-2305; Website: takano.house .gov.

State Offices: Riverside, 951-222-0203.

Committees: *Education & the Workforce:* Early Childhood, Elementary, & Secondary Education; Health, Employment, Labor, & Pensions. *Science, Space, & Technology:* Environment. *Veterans' Affairs:* Economic Opportunity (RMM); Health.

Group Ratings

	ADA	ACLU	AFL-CIO	LCV	ITI	COC	HAFA	ACU	CFG	FRC
2014	100%	88%	–	97%	60%	36%	12%	8%	13%	0%
2013	90%	C	95%	96%	C	38%	C	12%	12%	C

National Journal Ratings

	2013 LIB	—	2013 CONS
Economic	91%	—	0%
Social	93%	—	0%
Foreign	75%	—	23%
Composite	89%	—	11%

Key Votes of the 113th Congress

1. Sandy storm spending	Y	5. Medical Marijuana	Y	9. Syrian Rebels Training	N
2. Violence Against Women Act	Y	6. Farm Bill	N	10. Keystone pipeline	N
3. Guantanamo Bay Detainees	Y	7. Afghanistan Combat	Y	11. Immigration Exec. Action	N
4. Abortion 20-week ban	N	8. NSA Phone Data Collection	Y	12. Bipartisan budget deal	Y

Election Results

2014 general	Mark Takano (D)	46,948	(57%)	$1,312,896
	Steve Adams (R)	35,936	(43%)	$230,976
2014 primary	Mark Takano (D)	19,648	(45%)	
	Steve Adams (R)	16,264	(37%)	
	Veronica Franco (D)	4,509	(10%)	
	Yvonne Girard (R)	3,581	(8%)	

Prior winning percentage: 2012 (59%)

Population		Race and Ethnicity		Income	
Total:	734,942	Latino	59.1%	Median income:	$52,546
Urban:	58.5%	White	23.8%		*(192 of 435)*
Suburban:	41.4%	Black	9.4%	Under $50,000	46.8%
Rural:	0.1%	Asian	5.2%	$50,000-$99,999:	34.2%
Land area:	422	Two races	1.8%	$100,000-$199,999:	15.9%
Pop/sq. mi.:	1,742.9	White Ethnic	10.0%	$200,000 or more:	3.0%
Born in state:	63.3%			Poverty Rate	20.2%
		Education			
Age Groups		H.S. grad or less:	52.4%	**Work**	
Under 18:	27.8%	Some college:	30.6%	White collar:	24.6%
18 to 34:	28.2%	College degree, 4 yr.:	10.8%	Blue collar:	45.7%
35 to 64:	35.4%	Post-grad study:	6.2%	Sales and service:	29.7%
Over 64:	8.6%				
		Military		Govt. workers:	15.6%
		Veterans/active duty:	5.7%		

Inland Empire: Central and Western Riverside, Moreno Valley

Riverside was a sleepy town of 34,000 people, a couple hours' drive from Los Angeles, when Richard and Pat Nixon were married there in 1940 at the Mission Inn, built in 1876 and, with its bell towers, fountains, and stained glass windows, an inspired setting for a wedding. Riverside was not

Voter Turnout	
2013 Total Citizen 18+	439,072
2014 House Turnout	82,884
2014 Turnout as % CVAP	18.9%
2012 Turnout as % CVAP	44.5%

much larger, with 46,000 people, when Ronald and Nancy Reagan spent their honeymoon at the Mission Inn a dozen years later, in 1952. Riverside then was a citrus center, a market town amid orange groves, where the local agricultural college developed, among other things, the navel orange. Today the Mission Inn is again doing business, after being shuttered from 1985 to 1992, but Riverside has changed completely. The city has grown to more than 310,000 people, and Riverside County has over 2 million, more than double its population in 1980. This has been a boom part of California, where modest-income families found new houses in inexpensive developments and small businesses found steady markets.

The Great Recession halted that progress, at least temporarily. Riverside County's unemployment rate dropped slowly from 12% in late 2012 to 7% two years later, higher than the statewide and national rates. The local economy has begun to turn around. In 2014, it surpassed the borough of Queens in New York and became the tenth largest county in the nation. The University of California opened a new medical school in Riverside. Its accreditation was delayed because of questions about the school's long-term funding, but it enrolled its first students in 2013. Moreno Valley added 4,000 jobs from 2009 to 2012. A 42-million-square-foot warehouse by World Logistics Center, which would be the largest in the nation and create perhaps 20,000 jobs, remained under review because of questions of possible illegal behavior. In 2014, population growth and housing starts accelerated in the county. A home developer began work on a 1,400-home project, which resumed construction that halted in 2008 and would be the largest development for Riverside in 20 years.

The newly created 41st District includes western parts of Riverside County and all of Riverside city, and the towns of Moreno Valley and Perris. This district also takes in the

2012 Presidential Vote		
Barack Obama (D)	114,040	(62%)
Mitt Romney (R)	67,314	(36%)

2008 Presidential Vote		
Barack Obama (D)	108,636	(59%)
John McCain (R)	70,547	(39%)

Cook Partisan Voting Index: D+9

area formerly covered by March Air Force Reserve Base. Politically, it leans comfortably Democratic. In 2012, President Barack Obama defeated Mitt Romney, 62%-36%.

Mark Takano (D)

Political newcomer Mark Takano, a Democrat elected in 2012, brought his experience as an inner-city schoolteacher to Capitol Hill. He also is the first openly gay person of color to hold a seat in Congress.

Born and raised in Riverside, Takano grew up in a self-described "typical Japanese-American family" with a strong emphasis on education, self-reliance, and public service. In his youth, he played junior football. He was fascinated by politics and remembers watching as a boy the televised Watergate hearings of the House Judiciary Committee, entranced by the opening remarks of Democratic Rep. Barbara Jordan of Texas. He earned a bachelor's degree in government from Harvard University. He was planning to go to law school but decided instead to try teaching, taking a job as a substitute teacher in the Boston area. The diverse region gave him the experience of working in wealthier districts like Brookline and also inner-city schools. He returned to school to get a teaching certificate, and took a job as an English and social studies teacher at the Rialto Unified School District. In 1990, Takano was elected to the Riverside Community College District's Board of Trustees. He became the board's longest-serving member, spending two separate terms as the board's president.

Takano made a bid for a House seat in 1992 but lost to Republican Ken Calvert in one of the closest elections in California history. Calvert defeated him again in 1994. He jokingly calls the ensuing time his "wilderness years," when he traveled to foreign countries while continuing to teach. Takano stayed active in his community, with roles on the California Community College Trustees board and the Board of the Chancellor's Asian Pacific Islander Community Advisory Center at the University of California, Riverside.

In June 2012, he ran in the redrawn 41st District in California's jungle primary, in which the top two finishers advance to the general election regardless of party affiliation. Republican John Tavaglione, a veteran Riverside County supervisor, came in first with 45% of the vote and Takano second, with 37%.

The district leans Democratic, giving Takano an edge in the general election. Tavaglione had a long history of working with Democrats in Riverside County, and he slightly outperformed Takano in fundraising. Tavaglione also took some moderate positions, declining to sign conservative activist Grover Norquist's "no new taxes" pledge. Takano ran as a populist, attacking lobbyists and oil and insurance companies. He stressed job creation, job training, and education reform. Neither candidate received much party financing. In the much higher turnout in November, Takano won 59%-41%. Takano said that he hoped his victory would be a breakthrough for LGBT rights.

Takano cited his teaching experience as integral to his membership on the Education and the Workforce Committee. As a minority-party freshman with modest influence in the House, Takano made creative use of social media and his communications skills to score rhetorical points and attempt to influence Washington debates. Invoking his background as a school teacher, he used a red pen to grade a letter that House Republicans had privately circulated among themselves about immigration. He gave the letter an "F," scrawled multiple comments in red, advised the GOP members to "See me after work," and posted the results on his Tumblr page. He took a similar approach and gave an "F" to Sen. Marco Rubio of Florida for his op-ed that was critical of the Federal Communications Commission's decision on "net neutrality." In November 2014, Takano criticized Sen. Rand Paul of Kentucky for comparing the overreach of President Barack Obama's executive actions on immigration to Franklin D. Roosevelt's internment of Japanese Americans during World War Two. Takano cited his Japanese-American parents, who were among those held prisoner, calling Paul's comment "insulting," and said that the action of Obama, in contrast to FDR, was designed to protect "vulnerable, hardworking immigrants." The Congressional Management Foundation named Takano one of 14 recipients of its "Golden Mouse" award for his engagement on social media.

In 2014, Takano faced a competitive challenger. Steve Adams, a Republican councilman from Riverside who called himself "apolitical" and said that an increase in the minimum wage would cost jobs. He took the unusual step for a Republican of advocating more spending on infrastructure, and said Obama had "fundamentally changed America, not for the good." Takano outspent Adams more than 5-to-1, and won 57%-43.

FORTY-SECOND DISTRICT

Ken Calvert (R)

Elected 1992, 12th term; b. June 8, 1953, Corona; San Diego St. U., B.A. 1975; Anglican/Episcopalian; divorced.

Professional Career: Restaurant owner, 1975-80; Real estate broker, 1980-92; Chmn., Riverside Cnty. Repub. Party, 1984-88.

DC Office: 2205 RHOB, 20515, 202-225-1986; Fax: 202-225-2004; Website: calvert.house.gov.

State Offices: Corona, 951-277-0042.

Committees: *Appropriations:* Defense; Energy, Water Development, & Related Agencies; Interior, Environment, & Related Agencies (Chmn).

Group Ratings

	ADA	ACLU	AFL-CIO	LCV	ITI	COC	HAFA	ACU	CFG	FRC
2014	0%	5%	–	3%	100%	100%	38%	68%	29%	88%
2013	0%	C	19%	0%	C	85%	C	64%	51%	C

National Journal Ratings

	2013 LIB	—	2013 CONS
Economic	40%	—	59%
Social	34%	—	62%
Foreign	34%	—	60%
Composite	38%	—	62%

Key Votes of the 113th Congress

1. Sandy storm spending N	5. Medical Marijuana	9. Syrian Rebels Training Y
2. Violence Against Women Act Y	6. Farm Bill Y	10. Keystone pipeline Y
3. Guantanamo Bay Detainees N	7. Afghanistan Combat	11. Immigration Exec. Action Y
4. Abortion 20-week ban Y	8. NSA Phone Data Collection N	12. Bipartisan budget deal Y

Election Results

2014 general	Ken Calvert (R)	74,540	(66%)	$1,206,751
	Tim Sheridan (D)	38,850	(34%)	$101,404
2014 primary	Ken Calvert (R)	37,506	(68%)	
	Tim Sheridan (D)	8,788	(16%)	
	Chris Marquez (D)	6,118	(11%)	
	Kerri Condley (D)	3,150	(6%)	

Prior winning percentages: 2012 (61%), 2010 (56%), 2008 (51%), 2006 (60%), 2004 (62%), 2002 (64%), 2000 (74%), 1998 (56%), 1996 (55%), 1994 (55%), 1992 (47%)

Population		Race and Ethnicity		Income	
Total:	746,215	White	48.8%	Median income:	$70,261
Urban:	15.7%	Latino	33.2%		*(62 of 435)*
Suburban:	83.9%	Asian	8.9%	Under $50,000	35.1%
Rural:	0.4%	Black	5.8%	$50,000-$99,999:	32.9%
Land area:	746	Two races	2.5%	$100,000-$199,999:	27.0%
Pop/sq. mi.:	1,000.5	White Ethnic	18.9%	$200,000 or more:	5.0%
Born in state:	59.5%			Poverty Rate	12.0%
		Education			
Age Groups		H.S. grad or less:	39.4%	**Work**	
Under 18:	27.5%	Some college:	36.3%	White collar:	35.8%
18 to 34:	22.9%	College degree, 4 yr.:	16.3%	Blue collar:	43.1%
35 to 64:	38.3%	Post-grad study:	8.0%	Sales and service:	21.1%
Over 64:	11.2%				
		Military		Govt. workers:	16.4%
		Veterans/active duty:	8.5%		

Inland Empire: Corona, West Riverside

The fastest growth in the Los Angeles metropolitan area over the past 25 years has been in the Inland Empire, at the eastern end of the Los Angeles Basin. Mostly orange groves and dairy farms a few decades ago, this territory is now the site of personal upward mobility and ethnic and cultural

Voter Turnout	
2013 Total Citizen 18+	476,425
2014 House Turnout	113,390
2014 Turnout as % CVAP	23.8%
2012 Turnout as % CVAP	49.1%

diversity. The main ingredient of the growth has been small entrepreneurial businesses, many of them started by people with Asian or Latino immigrant backgrounds. California has never been a land of leisure, as stereotype would have it, but rather a place for hard work, where the fertility of the soil and the productivity of the people have led to prosperity and, more recently, relative tolerance toward newcomers.

Anti-Asian sentiment expressed itself in the Chinese Exclusion Act of 1882 and the Japanese-American internment camps of 1942-45. Despite occasional tensions since World War II, this area otherwise has styled itself as a welcoming destination for immigrants. But that mindset may have changed or become more complex with the immigration problems on the southern border. In July 2014, local protestors in Murrietta surrounded and forced back three busses filled with immigration detainees who had been

2012 Presidential Vote		
Mitt Romney (R)	131,438	(57%)
Barack Obama (D)	96,212	(41%)

2008 Presidential Vote		
John McCain (R)	122,371	(55%)
Barack Obama (D)	97,426	(44%)

Cook Partisan Voting Index: R+10

sent from Texas and were approaching a local Border Patrol station. The local mayor said that protestors were worried whether the town could safely house the detainees.

During the Great Recession, the Inland Empire lost about 122,000 jobs by 2012, according to a report by Claremont McKenna College and the University of California, Los Angeles. The region had high foreclosure rates, with significant numbers of people moving out, rather than in, for the first time in decades. But the recovery recently has strengthened. The unemployment rate in Corona declined from 12% in 2010 to 5.4% in December 2014. Murrieta, which doubled in population from 2000 to 2010, is one of the fastest-growing locales in California. Its families are mostly young, with a 26% Hispanic share that is below the state average.

The 42nd Congressional District is based in the Inland Empire and includes part of Riverside County and the towns of Corona, Norco, and Murrieta. Lake Elsinore, the new city of Menifee, and part of Temecula are also in the district. The district is solidly Republican.

Ken Calvert (R)

Ken Calvert, a Republican first elected in 1992, is less conservative and outspoken than many of his firebrand colleagues from California, but he has been a Republican team player and an ally of GOP Speaker John Boehner, who put him on the leadership-run Steering Committee. He holds a plum spot on the Appropriations Committee, where he has become a "cardinal" who chairs a subcommittee.

Calvert grew up in Corona. While at San Diego State University, where he majored in economics, he was a congressional intern at the Senate Watergate hearings of 1973. Later, he ran the family restaurant back home and, in 1980, got into the commercial real estate business. In 1982, at age 29, he ran for Congress in a district that included almost all of Riverside County and lost a nine-candidate primary to Al McCandless by 868 votes. In 1992, he ran in a new district and won the GOP primary with 28 percent of the vote. His Democratic opponent was Mark Takano, a middle-school teacher who had the support of teachers' unions and Japanese Americans. Calvert beat Takano by 519 votes (Takano was elected to represent the neighboring 41st District in 2012.) Three decades after Calvert first ran, Riverside County has three entire districts in Congress, and a small corner of a fourth.

Soon after he was elected, Calvert ran into trouble at home when the Riverside *Press-Enterprise* reported that he had been stopped by police with a prostitute in his car. Calvert apologized and said that he was upset because his wife had divorced him the month before and his father had recently committed suicide. His opponents in 1994 used the incident against him. Calvert won the primary 51%-49%, with only an 884-vote margin, against business professor Joseph Khoury. Takano, running again in the general election, ran an ad that accused Calvert of "flagrant womanizing." But with the Republican tide that year, Calvert won 55%-38%.

In the House, Calvert has compiled a moderate-to-conservative voting record. He broke with most GOP colleagues in 2008 by supporting housing finance legislation, citing his district's high foreclosure rate. In March 2012, he committed Republican heresy by criticizing radio talk show host Rush Limbaugh, telling the Riverside *Press-Enterprise* that the broadcaster "put gas on the fire" by describing as a "slut" a Georgetown University law student who spoke favorably of contraception coverage under the 2010 health insurance law.

Calvert recently has introduced bills to open more of California's coast to offshore drilling, something many Democrats oppose. He has been a major backer of E-Verify, an online system he helped enact that allows employers to confirm the eligibility of new hires. Critics have faulted the system's accuracy, while farm groups have complained it has hurt their efforts to recruit workers. He has reacted to the immigration crisis of recent years by stating that migrants crossing the Mexican border illegally should be sent back, though with proper health procedures. In 2014, he called for a 15 percent reduction in the civilian workforce at the Pentagon to avoid more painful cuts in uniformed personnel.

Calvert had served on the Armed Services, Resources and Science committees, but left them in 2007 after snagging a coveted seat on Appropriations, where he aggressively sought spending earmarks for his district. In 2010, taxpayer groups criticized him for more than $33 million in solo provisions, the third-largest amount in the California delegation behind then-Speaker Nancy Pelosi and Appropriations ranking Republican Jerry Lewis.

Calvert took over in November 2013 the plum position as chairman of the Appropriations Subcommittee on Interior and the Environment. At the time, he said he was particularly interested in finding ways to strengthen domestic energy production on federal lands. He has been an enthusiastic supporter of the Keystone XL pipeline. In 2014, his subcommittee's bill became part of the omnibus spending bill. Calvert emphasized the funds in the bill for wildfire fighting and prevention programs, plus activities to reduce dead timber and other hazardous fuels in the forests, and funds for domestic energy production. In January 2015, to encourage the building of more infrastructure projects, he filed a bill to streamline highway construction timelines and eliminate the need for redundant environmental reviews.

In 2003, Calvert abandoned his 1992 pledge to serve only 12 years in Congress. He was reelected easily. In recent years, campaign opponents have called into question his ethics. In 2006, the *Los Angeles Times* reported that he and his real estate partner had bought a four-acre tract for $550,000, then sold it less than a year later for $985,000, after Calvert secured an $8 million spending earmark for expansion of a nearby freeway interchange. Calvert denied wrongdoing, noting that it was not illegal for a member of Congress to make personal investments. Conservative bloggers reacted angrily when he was named a year later to Appropriations.

In 2008, Calvert had a close contest against Democrat Bill Hedrick, a Corona-Norco school board member who was poorly funded and had no national party help. Hedrick benefited not just from Calvert's ethics problems, but also from Obama's success in the district. Calvert won by a little more than 6,000 votes, 51.2%-48.8%. Hedrick returned for a rematch in 2010. This time, he got help from the Democratic Congressional Campaign Committee, which ran ads slamming Calvert for voting against the economic stimulus bill, children's health legislation, and other initiatives. But the National Republican Congressional Committee stepped in to help Calvert, and the DCCC eventually turned its focus to more-winnable races in that strongly Republican year. Calvert won 56%-44%, spending more than $1.5 million to Hedrick's $493,000. Since then, he has been reelected handily against opponents with little or no financing.

FORTY-THIRD DISTRICT

Maxine Waters (D)

Elected 1990, 13th term; b. Aug. 15, 1938, St. Louis, MO; CA St. U. L.A., B.A. 1970; Christian; married (Sidney Williams); 2 children.

Elected Office: CA Assembly, 1977-91.

Professional Career: Head Start teacher, 1966; Deputy, City Councilman David Cunningham, 1973-76.

DC Office: 2221 RHOB, 20515, 202-225-2201; Fax: 202-225-7854; Website: waters.house.gov.

State Offices: Los Angeles, 323-757-8900.

Committees: *Financial Services* (RMM; ex-officio member of each subcommittee).

Group Ratings

	ADA	ACLU	AFL-CIO	LCV	ITI	COC	HAFA	ACU	CFG	FRC
2014	85%	83%	–	91%	40%	36%	16%	10%	17%	0%
2013	95%	C	95%	96%	C	31%	C	21%	22%	C

National Journal Ratings

	2013 LIB	—	2013 CONS
Economic	90%	—	9%
Social	68%	—	32%
Foreign	94%	—	0%
Composite	85%	—	15%

Key Votes of the 113th Congress

1. Sandy storm spending	Y	5. Medical Marijuana	NV	9. Syrian Rebels Training	Y
2. Violence Against Women Act	Y	6. Farm Bill	N	10. Keystone pipeline	N
3. Guantanamo Bay Detainees	Y	7. Afghanistan Combat	Y	11. Immigration Exec. Action	N
4. Abortion 20-week ban	N	8. NSA Phone Data Collection	Y	12. Bipartisan budget deal	N

Election Results

2014 general	Maxine Waters (D) 69,681	(71%)	$1,062,921	$2,572
	John Wood (R)...............................28,521	(29%)	$11,819	
2014 primary	Maxine Waters (D) 33,746	(67%)		
	John Wood (R)...............................16,440	(33%)		

Prior winning percentages: 2012 (71%), 2010 (79%), 2008 (83%), 2006 (84%), 2004 (81%), 2002 (78%), 2000 (87%), 1998 (89%), 1996 (86%), 1994 (78%), 1992 (83%), 1990 (79%)

Population		Race and Ethnicity		Income	
Total:	730,217	Latino	45.9%	Median income:	$47,145
Urban:	99.3%	Black	23.1%		(277 of 435)
Suburban:	0.7%	White	15.2%	Under $50,000	53.0%
Rural:	0.0%	Asian	12.5%	$50,000-$99,999:	28.1%
Land area:	72	Two races	2.3%	$100,000-$199,999:	15.3%
Pop/sq. mi.:	10,123.9	White Ethnic	7.6%	$200,000 or more:	3.5%
Born in state:	53.3%			Poverty Rate	21.4%
		Education			
Age Groups		H.S. grad or less:	46.8%	**Work**	
Under 18:	24.6%	Some college:	29.2%	White collar:	30.2%
18 to 34:	26.4%	College degree, 4 yr.:	16.9%	Blue collar:	48.4%
35 to 64:	38.0%	Post-grad study:	7.0%	Sales and service:	21.4%
Over 64:	11.0%				
		Military		Govt. workers:	12.7%
		Veterans/active duty:	4.3%		

Southern and Western L.A.: Inglewood, Torrance

In the years just after World War II, Los Angeles was the fastest-growing metropolitan area in America. LAX, today the world's fifth-busiest airport in the number of passengers, with eight central terminals, was then a small airfield amid open country. The mile-square grids east, north,

Voter Turnout	
2013 Total Citizen 18+	430,395
2014 House Turnout	98,202
2014 Turnout as % CVAP	22.8%
2012 Turnout as % CVAP	54.7%

and south of the airport were just filling up with subdivisions. Inglewood, just east of the airport around the Hollywood Park racetrack, attracted the young families of people who had moved to Los Angeles during the war—workers in the giant aircraft factories or in the small factories that every day were making California less dependent on goods from back East. In Hawthorne, near what has become the southeast corner of the airport, future celebrities were growing up—Sonny Bono, the Beach Boys, and during her early years, Marilyn Monroe. Gardena, east of Hawthorne, was known for its legal poker clubs and its Japanese-American residents, back from the wartime internment camps. Hawthorne had been home to a big Northrop Grumman plant. Space Exploration Technologies (Space X) is based in Hawthorne and is sending cargo shipments to the International Space Station, though the limited manned space flight by NASA is pushing Space X to seek out private contractors.

In this area is South Central or, more recently, South Los Angeles, after the City Council in 2003 officially renamed the community in an effort to rid it of the stigma of gang wars and race riots. In the days of residential segregation, much of this area was the home of Los Angeles' black community, its numbers greatly expanded by migration from the South during and after the war. As the nation's focus on civil rights receded in the 1980s and 1990s, this part of Los Angeles continued to deal with racial tensions. That led to chronic economic problems. An almost bankrupt Inglewood Unified School District was given $55 million as part of an emergency state takeover in 2012, with the school board voting to cut salaries by 15

2012 Presidential Vote		
Barack Obama (D) 173,342	(78%)
Mitt Romney (R)...................44,485	(20%)

2008 Presidential Vote		
Barack Obama (D) 180,881	(76%)
John McCain (R)...................52,350	(22%)

Cook Partisan Voting Index: D+26

percent to keep the school district afloat. Inglewood could have a brighter future as a potential site for the stadium that might house one or two franchises that the National Football League is eager to move to the nation's second largest television market.

The 43rd Congressional District covers much of this section of Los Angeles County, including Gardena, and the heavily Hispanic areas of Alondra Park, Hawthorne, and Lawndale. It also takes in part of Torrance, which is home to large Korean and Japanese communities and to the North American headquarters of Honda, though Toyota is moving its headquarters from Torrance to Plano Texas. On the northern end of the district is Inglewood and to the south is West Carson. The district takes in Los Angeles International Airport, though a narrow strip that separates the airport from the Pacific Ocean is in the 33rd District. It is safe Democratic territory

Maxine Waters (D)

Maxine Waters, a Democrat first elected in 1990, for years was known chiefly for her incendiary rhetoric and a protracted ethics controversy involving her husband. That changed in 2013, when she became ranking Democrat on the Financial Services Committee. She has settled into a substantive role, amid occasional clashes with the panel's conservative chairman, Jeb Hensarling of Texas.

Waters grew up in St. Louis, one of 13 children. She has said, "I know all about welfare. I remember the social workers peeking in the refrigerator and under the beds." She moved to California in 1961, worked in a garment factory, and raised two children. Waters got a sociology degree at California State University in Los Angeles and became an assistant Head Start teacher after the Watts riot of 1965. She likes to call herself "The Organizer" and has shown the capacity to draw big supportive crowds to her protests over the years. From 1973 to 1976, she worked on the staff of a Los Angeles city councilman. In 1976, she won a seat in the California Assembly, where she helped pass legislation divesting state pension funds from apartheid South Africa, setting up a child abuse prevention training program, and prohibiting police strip searches for nonviolent offenses. When Democratic Rep. Augustus Hawkins retired in 1990 after 28 years in the House, Waters was the obvious choice for the seat and won it easily. Her husband, Sidney Williams, a former professional football player and Mercedes-Benz salesman, became President Bill Clinton's ambassador to the Bahamas.

Having grown up in poverty and under segregation laws, Waters believes fervently in federal aid for the poor and for racial preferences to help blacks overcome the legacies of slavery, segregation, and discrimination. She has favored big reductions in defense spending in favor of domestic spending. She voted against the Gulf War resolution in 1991 and was a staunch opponent a decade later of the Iraq war as well as a subsequent troop buildup in Afghanistan. She has brought an intensity bordering on fury to her work, asserting herself regardless of protocol. Her anger is a political weapon she uses shrewdly to get both publicity and results. "I don't have time to be polite," Waters says.

She came to Washington shortly before the 1992 riots in L.A., which exemplified her best and worst moments. She flew home immediately and roused the Department of Water and Power to restore water to the riot area, and she was effective in adding provisions to the post-riot emergency act that were eventually signed into law. But she also suggested rioters were morally justified and claimed ominously, "Los Angeles is under siege. ... The violence could spill over to many other cities in this country."

Waters isn't afraid to step on toes. When House Appropriations Chairman David Obey of Wisconsin sought to ban spending earmarks named after members in 2009, she heatedly confronted him over his refusal to fund her request for the Maxine Waters Employment Preparation Center. Obey eventually prevailed. She pushed for federal loan guarantees to cities for economic and infrastructure development. In a rare legislative success in the Republican-controlled House, Waters sponsored an amendment to triple spending to erase the debts of poor nations, mostly in Africa. She has sponsored bills to repeal mandatory minimum sentences for drug crimes, and charges that the war on drugs has created "apartheid" in the U.S. In 2009, the House passed her bill to require the federal Bureau of Prisons to develop a program for inmate HIV/AIDS testing.

She has been an occasional thorn in the side of President Barack Obama. She endorsed Hillary Rodham Clinton over Obama during the 2008 Democratic presidential primaries. She and other Congressional Black Caucus members held up a vote on the financial services overhaul in November 2009 because they said the administration wasn't addressing the needs of segments of the black community. Waters repeatedly discussed the need to "educate" people advising Obama. At an Atlanta jobs fair in August 2011, she warned of growing disillusionment within minority communities over the unemployment rate, and she encouraged Obama to fight harder when negotiating with the GOP on budget matters and the economy. "The Congressional Black Caucus loves the president, too. We're supportive of the president, but we're getting tired," she said. "The unemployment is unconscionable. We don't know what the strategy is."

On the Financial Services Committee, she has a long history of working to address housing issues. She sponsored measures to overhaul discredited housing finance programs, expand affordable housing programs, and aid local governments to rehabilitate foreclosed homes. She harshly criticized the Federal Reserve Board and big bankers for their financing practices and the tight credit that resulted. She told a panel of banking executives in 2009, "to the captains of the universe sitting here before all of us, all of my political life I have been in disagreement with the banking industry." With Democratic Rep. Ron Klein of Florida, she got a bill through the committee in 2010 to crack down on fraudulent brokers and lenders, and she successfully amended the financial services bill to beef up protection for securities investors. When former committee Chairman Barney Frank retired in 2012, Waters succeeded him as the ranking member, giving her a larger platform to push her pro-regulatory, pro-consumer agenda.

As leader of Financial Services Committee Democrats, *Politico* reported in August 2014, Waters skillfully exploited divisions between conservative Republicans and big business. She had become "a sympathetic ally for corporate America"—notably on extension of the Export-Import Bank, which makes loans to businesses involved in trade. Her position has given her the opportunity to work with various interests, she said, "even if you've never worked with them before and even if you're never going to work with them again." In response to industry concerns about unintended consequences, she helped to tweak changes in flood-insurance regulations that she had helped to enact on a bipartisan basis in 2012. Waters remained a regulatory stalwart, as when she filed a bill in March 2015 to set limits on the Securities and Exchange Commission before it can grant waivers to those she called "bad actors" who have previously pled guilty to fraudulent activity. She also retained her focus on broader economic conflicts, including income inequality. In August 2014, she returned to her home town of St. Louis for the funeral of Michael Brown, whose shooting by police sparked riots in nearby Ferguson. She joined the community in "calling for justice."

In recent years, Waters' personal finances have become the target of watchdogs. In 2005, the liberal-leaning Citizens for Responsibility and Ethics in Washington criticized the fact that members of her family had made more than $1 million in eight years doing business with companies, candidates, and causes that she had helped in her official capacity. Her reply: "They do their business and I do mine." In March 2009, news stories raised the issue of whether Waters had urged federal regulators to give favorable treatment to a bank in which she and her husband had a financial interest. Federal regulators told *The New York Times* that Waters in 2008 helped set up a meeting with bankers, including one whose chief executive asked them for $50 million in government bailout funds. Waters defended her actions, saying, "I have been an outspoken advocate for minority communities and businesses in California and nationally for decades."

The House Ethics Committee launched an investigation in 2009 and subsequently charged her with three counts of breaking House rules barring lawmakers from taking actions in their own financial interest. Hoping to seize political advantage, Republicans clamored to have ethics trials of Waters and Charles Rangel of New York held before the November 2010 elections, and accused Ethics Chairwoman Zoe Lofgren of California of stalling. While Rangel's case went forward, Waters' trial was postponed when Lofgren and Alabama's Jo Bonner, the committee's ranking Republican, cited the discovery of additional evidence. Waters contended that the delay proved the case against her was weak. "I have been denied basic due process," she told reporters.

Meanwhile, it was revealed that two Ethics Committee lawyers on the case were placed on administrative leave. The highly secretive panel did not disclose the reason. Reports surfaced that the investigation was derailed over partisan infighting about the probe among committee members and staff. Veteran Washington lawyer Billy Martin was hired as an outside counsel to review the integrity of the committee's probe and decide whether the investigation of Waters should proceed. Martin determined that Waters' due process was not violated, and the committee resumed its investigation in June 2012. In response, Waters and 68 other Democrats asked the committee to release the Martin report, but the committee refused to make any of the documents public. In September 2012, the committee finally concluded its work and announced that Waters would not be charged with violating House ethics rules.

Waters is a force to be reckoned with in L.A. politics and she has been reelected without difficulty. The rising Hispanic percentage in her district has been viewed as the biggest threat to her career. In 2012, redistricting increased the Hispanic population to nearly a majority and reduced blacks to about one-fourth of her 43rd District. Still, she hasn't had much trouble keeping this seat. During the 2014 campaign, opponents plastered posters with a black-and-white illustration of Waters bordered with the words "Poverty Pimp," according to local news reports. John Wood, her Republican opponent, disavowed the activity. Waters won 71%-29%.

FORTY-FOURTH DISTRICT

Janice Hahn (D)

Elected July 2011, 2nd full term; b. March 30, 1952, Los Angeles; Abilene Christian U., B.S. 1974; Restorationist; divorced; 3 children.

Elected Office: L.A. City Charter Reform Commission, 1997-99; L.A. City Cncl., 2001-11.

Professional Career: Teacher, Good News Acad., 1974-78; Public affairs regional mgr., S. CA Edison Co., 1995-2000.

DC Office: 404 CHOB, 20515, 202-225-8220; Fax: 202-226-7290; Website: hahn.house.gov.

State Offices: Carson, 310-830-7600, ext. 1038; Compton, 310-605-5520; San Pedro, 310-831-1799; South Gate, 323-563-9562; Wilmington, 310-549-8282.

Committees: *Small Business:* Economic Growth; Tax and Capital Access. *Transportation & Infrastructure:* Coast Guard & Maritime Transportation; Highways & Transit; Railroads, Pipelines, & Hazardous Materials.

Group Ratings

	ADA	ACLU	AFL-CIO	LCV	ITI	COC	HAFA	ACU	CFG	FRC
2014	95%	83%	–	97%	60%	43%	10%	8%	13%	0%
2013	95%	C	95%	96%	C	38%	C	12%	12%	C

National Journal Ratings

	2013 LIB	—	2013 CONS
Economic	78%	—	21%
Social	79%	—	16%
Foreign	90%	—	6%
Composite	84%	—	16%

Key Votes of the 113th Congress

1. Sandy storm spending	Y	5. Medical Marijuana	Y	9. Syrian Rebels Training	N
2. Violence Against Women Act	Y	6. Farm Bill	N	10. Keystone pipeline	N
3. Guantanamo Bay Detainees	Y	7. Afghanistan Combat	Y	11. Immigration Exec. Action	N
4. Abortion 20-week ban	N	8. NSA Phone Data Collection	Y	12. Bipartisan budget deal	Y

Election Results

2014 general	Janice Hahn (D)	59,670	(87%)	$723,718
	Adam Shbeita (PF)	9,192	(13%)	
2014 primary	Janice Hahn (D)	25,641	(100%)	
	Adam Shbeita (PF)(write-in)	5	(0%)	

Prior winning percentages: 2012 (60%), 2011 special (55%)

Population		Race and Ethnicity		Income	
Total:	706,791	Latino	70.5%	Median income:	$44,909
Urban:	95.1%	Black	14.8%		*(322 of 435)*
Suburban:	4.9%	White	7.2%	Under $50,000	53.9%
Rural:	0.0%	Asian	4.6%	$50,000-$99,999:	29.4%
Land area:	71	Two races	2.1%	$100,000-$199,999:	14.9%
Pop/sq. mi.:	9,924.0	White Ethnic	3.0%	$200,000 or more:	1.8%
Born in state:	56.2%			Poverty Rate	24.3%
		Education			
Age Groups		H.S. grad or less:	62.3%	**Work**	
Under 18:	28.3%	Some college:	25.8%	White collar:	18.6%
18 to 34:	26.5%	College degree, 4 yr.:	8.5%	Blue collar:	47.3%
35 to 64:	35.9%	Post-grad study:	3.4%	Sales and service:	34.1%
Over 64:	9.3%				
		Military		Govt. workers:	11.8%
		Veterans/active duty:	3.1%		

Southern L.A.: San Pedro, Compton

Just five days after President Lyndon Johnson signed the landmark Voting Rights Act into law, a police arrest gone wrong led to the explosion of the Watts riots. Six days later, 34 people were dead, more than 1,000 were injured, and Los Angeles had a wound that would take years to heal. Postmodern

Voter Turnout	
2013 Total Citizen 18+	369,961
2014 House Turnout	68,862
2014 Turnout as % CVAP	18.6%
2012 Turnout as % CVAP	50.6%

novelist Thomas Pynchon, in a story about the riots in *The New York Times* magazine, wrote, "The heart of L.A.'s racial sickness is the coexistence of two very different cultures: one white and one black. Watts is country which lies, psychologically, uncounted miles further than most whites seem at present willing to travel." But the area also has a rich cultural heritage. In Compton, the Central Avenue entertainment district during the postwar years was filled with clubs and theaters hosting Ella Fitzgerald, Sarah Vaughan, Duke Ellington, and Louis Armstrong. In the mid-1990s, the Compton Cricket Club formed. Co-founded by political activist Ted Hayes as an alternative to street gangs, the team has toured England and Australia.

Still, Compton symbolizes many of the problems still facing South Los Angeles: high crime and gang violence, drugs, and poverty. The influential late 1980s rap group N.W.A. expressed the frustration of many city residents with the song *Straight Outta Compton*. In the past 20 years, Latinos have been arriving in increasing numbers, buying homes and opening businesses. The Bloods and Crips street gangs have been replaced by Hispanic counterparts such as Florencia 13, six of whose members were sentenced to life in prison in 2010 after a violent spell that left dozens of people dead. Today, Compton struggles with a poor economy and unemployment that topped 22% in 2011 and remained at 13% in December 2014. Crime rates are down, but have remained uncommonly high.

The once dominant blacks in Compton have been overtaken by Hispanics, 65% to 33%. The first Latino member of the city council was elected in 2013. Aja Brown, the black woman and urban planner who was elected mayor at age 31 in 2013, said after her election that she planned to take a Spanish class. *The Guardian* described her as "an incongruously youthful, glamorous figure at the helm of what many still consider one of America's murder capitals." Her timing may have been right. After taking office, Brown reached out to the gangs. The Bloods and Crips eventually reached a truce, which contributed to the crime reduction. At the same time, real estate prices in Compton began to soar, spurred partly by investors speculating on the long-term view.

The 44th Congressional District includes Carson, Compton, Willowbrook, and Rancho Dominguez, plus the overwhelmingly Hispanic South Gate and Lynwood—95% and 87% Latino, respectively. The district stretches south to include coastal areas, including San Pedro and some of Long Beach, which are urban in character and adjacent to

2012 Presidential Vote		
Barack Obama (D)	155,459	(85%)
Mitt Romney (R)	24,995	(14%)
2008 Presidential Vote		
Barack Obama (D)	164,768	(83%)
John McCain (R)	31,680	(16%)
Cook Partisan Voting Index:	D+32	

the massive ports of Los Angles and Long Beach. Politically, it is solidly Democratic. Barack Obama won 83% of the vote here in 2008 and 85% in 2012.

Janice Hahn (D)

Democrat Janice Hahn won an acrimonious July 2011 special election. The next year, she was pitted against another Democratic incumbent in a redrawn district, in what became a relatively easy victory. Hahn tossed all of that aside in February 2015 when she announced that she would run for the Los Angeles County Board of Supervisors in 2016. "With so much brinkmanship in Washington, I am confident that I can get more done for our region back here at home, serving in local government," she said.

Hahn's electoral successes can be attributed, in part, to her strong political pedigree. Her father, Kenneth Hahn, spent 40 years as a Los Angeles County supervisor after serving on L.A.'s City Council. A dominant figure among Democrats in the city, he helped persuade the Brooklyn Dodgers baseball team to relocate to Los Angeles in 1958. He was the only city politician to meet the late civil rights leader Rev. Martin Luther King Jr. at the airport during a visit to Los Angeles in the early 1960s, a fact his daughter later used in a campaign ad. Her uncle Gordon Hahn was a city councilman and served in the California Assembly. And her brother, James Hahn, was Los Angeles mayor from 2001 to 2005 after serving as city attorney. Janice Hahn's mother, Ramona, also was active in local politics.

Hahn received an education degree from Abilene Christian University in Texas, and taught at a private academy for four years. She later worked a series of jobs in the private sector, including as a public affairs manager at Southern California Edison and a vice president for Prudential Securities. She first ran for Congress in 1998, waging an unsuccessful campaign against Republican Rep. Steven Kuykendall, who won 49%-47%. She spent two years on the Los Angeles Charter Reform Commission before she was elected to the City Council in 2000. On the council, she cultivated the support of labor union members as a stalwart supporter of workers' rights, often opposing layoffs and furloughs for city workers. She developed a strong environmental record and was known as a tough advocate for her poor constituents.

In 2010, Hahn sought to parlay her experience on the council into California's lieutenant governor post. She was the initial front-runner, based on the strength of her last name. But San Francisco's mayor, Gavin Newsom, later entered the race. He proved more charismatic to voters and trounced Hahn in the Democratic primary by more than 20 points.

When veteran Democratic Rep. Jane Harman resigned her seat in Congress to head the Woodrow Wilson International Center for Scholars, Hahn quickly announced her candidacy. She vowed to work to "create new jobs, expand clean energy technologies, and ensure that local small business owners get the help and opportunities they need to flourish in a global economy." Hahn was unable to deter California Secretary of State Debra Bowen from jumping into the race. In the May primary of the special election, Bowen was unexpectedly nudged aside by Republican Craig Huey, a tea party-backed website publisher. He spent $500,000 from his own pocket on a "cut spending, grow jobs" campaign. Hahn finished first with 24.6%, and Huey finished second with 22.2%.

Hahn set the tone in the runoff with an ad highlighting what she termed Huey's "extremist right-wing agenda." An outside conservative group, Turn Right USA, tried to help Huey with an inflammatory *YouTube* video that portrayed Hahn as friendly with gang members. But the ad—which featured a white stripper—sparked accusations of racism and sexism, and Huey denounced it. He did, however, distribute a local news report that was based on the charges in the video. He also depicted Hahn as a career politician while playing up his devotion to fiscal austerity. National Republicans largely stayed out of the race, leaving Huey to self-finance much of his campaign, with more than $880,000 of his own money. Hahn, meanwhile, got fundraising help from House Minority Leader Nancy Pelosi. She won, 55%-45%.

In the House, Hahn was a reliable Democratic vote. She got a provision in the House-passed intelligence authorization bill in 2012 to ensure that coordination and training among spy agencies and local law enforcement agencies did not violate minorities' constitutional rights. On the Small Business Committee, she sought a reduction in the time required for a loan application through the Small Business Administration.

The 2012 redistricting left Hahn with little choice but to compete with three-term Rep. Laura Richardson. But Richardson was hurt by revelations about her finances, including her $454,000 debt, and more than $125,000 in legal bills stemming from a House ethics investigation into her staff's work on her behalf. Hahn, meanwhile, won the support of Los Angeles Mayor Antonio Villaraigosa, helping her make inroads among Latinos. Richardson's problems worsened when the House Ethics Committee recommended that she be formally reprimanded and pay a $10,000 fine for improperly using her legislative staff for campaign work, and then obstructing the investigation. Richardson had little opportunity to raise campaign funds and was outspent $2.5 million to $500,000. Hahn won, 60%-40%.

Hahn's decision to follow the family trail back home can be explained by both the influence of the county supervisors board, and the dim prospects for Democrats to make an early return to the House majority. She began her latest campaign as a favorite. The successor to her House seat almost certainly will be a Democrat, but is not likely to be white. The contest could shape up as a battle between blacks eager to regain a share of their fading influence in L.A. and surging Hispanics, who have suffered from relatively small voter registration and turnout. Hahn quickly endorsed Isadore Hall, a veteran African-American state senator, as her successor.

FORTY-FIFTH DISTRICT

Mimi Walters (R)

Elected 2014, 1st term; b. May 14, 1962, Pasadena; U.C.L.A., B.A. 1984; Catholic; married (David); 4 children.

Elected Office: Laguna Niguel City Cncl., 1996-2004, Laguna Mayor, 2000; CA Assembly, 2005-08; CA Senate, 2008-15.

Professional Career: Sales rep.; Investment exec., Drexel, Burnham, & Lambert; Kidder Peabody & Co..

DC Office: 236 CHOB, 20515, 202-225-5611; Fax: 202-225-9177; Website: walters.house.gov.

State Offices: Irvine, 949-263-8703.

Committees: *Judiciary:* Courts, Intellectual Property, & the Internet; Regulatory Reform, Commercial, & the Antitrust Law. *Transportation & Infrastructure:* Aviation, Highways & Transit; Railroads, Pipelines, & Hazardous Materials.

Election Results

2014 general	Mimi Walters (R)	106,083	(65%)	$1,323,770	$5,622
	Drew Leavens (D)	56,819	(35%)	$122,685	
2014 primary	Mimi Walters (R)	39,631	(45%)		
	Drew Leavens (D)	24,721	(28%)		
	Greg Raths (R)	21,284	(24%)		

Population		Race and Ethnicity		Income	
Total:	733,706	White	55.7%	Median income:	$90,318
Urban:	67.9%	Asian	20.9%		*(12 of 435)*
Suburban:	32.0%	Latino	18.7%	Under $50,000	26.8%
Rural:	0.1%	Black	1.4%	$50,000-$99,999:	27.6%
Land area:	266	Two races	2.7%	$100,000-$199,999:	31.7%
Pop/sq. mi.:	2,759.9	White Ethnic	21.6%	$200,000 or more:	13.8%
Born in state:	50.4%			Poverty Rate	8.3%
		Education			
Age Groups		H.S. grad or less:	21.2%	**Work**	
Under 18:	21.6%	Some college:	28.0%	White collar:	51.4%
18 to 34:	22.7%	College degree, 4 yr.:	30.9%	Blue collar:	38.7%
35 to 64:	41.9%	Post-grad study:	20.0%	Sales and service:	9.9%
Over 64:	13.8%				
		Military		Govt. workers:	10.7%
		Veterans/active duty:	5.8%		

Central Orange: Irvine, Lake Forest

Orange County is the sixth most populous county in the United States, having grown steadily from 130,000 people in 1940, to nearly 2 million in 1980, to 3.1 million in 2012. It narrowly trails its neighbor San Diego County. It is now a community with the patina of maturity, and in some respects, of an

Voter Turnout	
2013 Total Citizen 18+	507,168
2014 House Turnout	162,902
2014 Turnout as % CVAP	32.1%
2012 Turnout as % CVAP	64.5%

aging community fraying at the edges. In recent years, its economy has been constantly reshaped: Tourism remains key, but there is no single industry responsible for Orange County's prosperity. The region was hit hard by the defense spending cutbacks and recession of the early 1990s, but it bounced back, fueled by start-ups and small entrepreneurial successes. Orange County was again rocked by recession in 2008, when the hyperinflation of the local housing market abruptly burst and home values slid as much as 20 percent from 2007 levels. Rapid moves by local governments to cut costs and attract new projects, as well as continuing increases in alternative energy jobs such as solar power manufacturing, helped Orange County recover faster than other California counties. That growth has been steady, but slower than in recent decades. Unemployment for the county was a robust 4.4 percent in December 2014.

Always Republican, Orange County became a symbol of conservatism, first in California and then nationally. This was a solid base for Ronald Reagan in his campaigns for governor and president. In 1988, the district's 317,000-vote plurality for George H.W. Bush was his largest in any county in the nation. Over the years, Orange County has become racially and ethnically more diverse. The all-white Orange County stereotype is now thoroughly out of date, exemplified by the election in 2007 of the county's first Vietnamese-American supervisor. Nearly one-third of the county's residents were born in another country, and nearly half speak a language other than English at home. In 2004, Orange County gave George W. Bush a 222,000-vote margin, well below his father's margin 16 years before. The GOP advantage dwindled further in 2012, when Republican Mitt Romney beat President Barack Obama by about 70,000 votes.

The third-largest city in Orange County is Irvine. Irvine Ranch was purchased by Gold Rush merchant James Irvine from the Sepulveda and Yorba families. As Orange County grew up to the limits of the Irvine Ranch, the Irvine family was sitting on some immensely valuable territory, the last large plot of vacant land in metro Los Angeles. In 1959, the Irvines donated a site for the University of California, Irvine, which today exceeds 30,000 students. In the 1970s, they sold the rest to developers. Irvine was born as a planned community, with eight-lane parkways, huge office parks, shopping malls, and attractive subdivisions. It also attracted high-tech and high-growth businesses, highly educated and affluent people, and Asian immigrants. Its population is 39 percent Asian, and supports a Chinese supermarket and a Chinese-language library. A 2011 study by the *Business Insider* news website, using FBI crime statistics, found Irvine to be the safest city in the nation.

The 45th Congressional District is made up of central and south Orange County. It includes Irvine, Coto de Caza, and Rancho Santa Margarita, and also takes in parts of

2012 Presidential Vote
Mitt Romney (R)................169,489 (55%)
Barack Obama (D) 133,114 (43%)

2008 Presidential Vote
John McCain (R)................162,724 (51%)
Barack Obama (D) 148,791 (47%)

Cook Partisan Voting Index: R+7

Anaheim, Orange, and Mission Viejo, which is shared with the 49th District. It is 21% Asian and 19% Hispanic, and the district leans strongly Republican. This is one of three districts that are based entirely in Orange County, while three others are partly in the county.

Mimi Walters (R)

Republican Mimi Walters, first elected to represent California's heavily Republican 45th District in 2014, touted her long experience in public office. Her pro-business, anti-tax platform resonated in the district and initially played well with House GOP leaders.

Walters is the daughter of a Marine Corps captain who later became a major in the Marine Corps Reserve. She worked as a stockbroker and then for seven years as an investment executive before she won her first race in 1996 to the Laguna Niguel City Council.

She served as Laguna Niguel mayor before being elected to the state Assembly in 2004 and the state Senate in 2008. "When I first entered public service I firmly believed, and still do, that our prosperity does not come from government; it comes in spite of it," she said.

As a state senator, Walters joined other Republicans in opposing many of the measures backed by California Gov. Jerry Brown and his fellow Democrats. Those initiatives include a 2012 sales tax hike, and later, the governor's plan to redirect $250 million from the state's cap-and-trade program to high-speed rail. She also opposed efforts to raise the minimum wage. On environmental and immigration issues, by contrast, she staked out a more moderate approach.

Walters began planning her bid as soon as Republican Rep. John Campbell announced his retirement in 2013. Her tight connections among donors paid off as she entered the June primary with a 2-to-1 fundraising edge over all of her competitors combined. Unlike many other Republicans, Walters' association with the GOP establishment has helped rather than hurt her. At first, her strongest opposition came from fellow Republican Greg Raths, a retired Marine colonel. Walters focused her attacks on him rather than on any Democrat. The tactic paid off. She led Raths 45%-24%, and she was left to face Democrat Drew Leavens, who got 28%, in a district where Republicans hold a 15-point registration advantage.

After the primary, she pledged she would use her cash advantage to help those Republicans facing a tougher fight in the general election, and then use that political capital once elected to Congress. She outspent Leavens 10-to-1, and took 65 percent of the vote in the general.

In the House, her game plan initially proved successful. She was assigned to the Judiciary and Transportation and Infrastructure committees, which gave her an opportunity to work on an array of domestic issues. The freshman class selected Walters as its representative in the Republican leadership, the fifth woman on the leadership team. She said that Congress must become "solution-oriented," especially in creating jobs. On behalf of more than two dozen members of her class, she joined Republican Rep. Tom Emmer of Minnesota in sending a letter to President Barack Obama in March urging him to seek legislation granting him trade promotion authority. She was among several House Republican women who successfully urged GOP leaders to defer action in January on a bill restricting abortions, which subsequently was revised. As a "practical conservative," she told *The New York Times,* she wants to limit taxes and spending but added that "government's job is to sometimes help those people who need help—not to give them money to just give them money, but to give them tools to help bring them out of poverty."

FORTY-SIXTH DISTRICT

Loretta Sanchez (D)

Elected 1996, 10th term; b. Jan. 7, 1960, Lynwood; Chapman U., B.A. 1982, American U., M.B.A. 1984; Catholic; married (Jack Einwechter).

Professional Career: Mgr. & financial analyst, Orange Cnty. Transp. Auth., 1984-87; Asst. V.P., Fieldman Rolapp & Assoc., 1987-90; Assoc., Booz Allen & Hamilton, 1990-93; Principal, Amiga Advisors, 1993-96.

DC Office: 1211 LHOB, 20515, 202-225-2965; Fax: 202-225-5859; Website: lorettasanchez.house.gov.

State Offices: Garden Grove, 714-621-0102.

Committees: *Armed Services:* Strategic Forces; Tactical Air & Land Forces (RMM). *Homeland Security:* Border & Maritime Security; Cybersecurity, Infrastructure Protection, & Security Technologies.

Group Ratings

	ADA	ACLU	AFL-CIO	LCV	ITI	COC	HAFA	ACU	CFG	FRC
2014	75%	44%	–	97%	80%	43%	15%	21%	15%	0%
2013	75%	C	95%	96%	C	38%	C	13%	16%	C

National Journal Ratings

	2013 LIB	—	2013 CONS
Economic	79%	—	20%
Social	73%	—	24%
Foreign	61%	—	39%
Composite	72%	—	28%

Key Votes of the 113th Congress

1. Sandy storm spending	Y	5. Medical Marijuana	Y	9. Syrian Rebels Training	N
2. Violence Against Women Act	Y	6. Farm Bill	N	10. Keystone pipeline	N
3. Guantanamo Bay Detainees	N	7. Afghanistan Combat	Y	11. Immigration Exec. Action	N
4. Abortion 20-week ban	N	8. NSA Phone Data Collection	Y	12. Bipartisan budget deal	N

Election Results

2014 general	Loretta Sanchez (D) 49,738	(60%)	$1,284,392
	Adam Nick (R) 33,577	(40%)	$15,758
2014 primary	Loretta Sanchez (D) 20,172	(51%)	
	Adam Nick (R) 7,234	(18%)	
	John Cullum (R) 5,666	(14%)	
	Carlos Vazquez (R) 4,969	(13%)	

Prior winning percentages: 2012 (64%), 2010 (53%), 2008 (69%), 2006 (62%), 2004 (60%), 2002 (61%), 2000 (60%), 1998 (56%), 1996 (47%)

Population		Race and Ethnicity		Income	
Total:	726,686	Latino	67.4%	Median income:	$52,409
Urban:	100.0%	White	18.0%		*(198 of 435)*
Suburban:	0.0%	Asian	11.3%	Under $50,000	46.9%
Rural:	0.0%	Black	2.0%	$50,000-$99,999:	33.3%
Land area:	87	Two races	1.0%	$100,000-$199,999:	17.5%
Pop/sq. mi.:	8,334.1	White Ethnic	5.5%	$200,000 or more:	2.4%
Born in state:	50.8%			Poverty Rate	20.9%
		Education			
Age Groups		H.S. grad or less:	58.5%	**Work**	
Under 18:	26.9%	Some college:	24.8%	White collar:	22.7%
18 to 34:	28.5%	College degree, 4 yr.:	12.1%	Blue collar:	48.7%
35 to 64:	35.5%	Post-grad study:	4.6%	Sales and service:	28.6%
Over 64:	9.1%			Govt. workers:	8.3%
		Military			
		Veterans/active duty:	3.4%		

Northern Orange: Santa Ana, Central and Western Anaheim

When Walt Disney began planning Disneyland in the late 1940s, he did not have to drive far from downtown Los Angeles before finding undeveloped land. Dairy farms and orange groves covered most of southeast Los Angeles County and adjacent Orange County, which had only 216,000 people in

Voter Turnout	
2013 Total Citizen 18+	356,357
2014 House Turnout	83,315
2014 Turnout as % CVAP	23.4%
2012 Turnout as % CVAP	45.1%

1950. As Disneyland opened there in 1955 and became a great success, the area around it—a mass of flatland surrounded by mountains and sea—found itself directly in the path of the most explosively growing metropolitan area in the United States. Now, with 3.1 million people, Orange County is the nation's sixth-largest county, just a bit behind San Diego County.

Just as Orange County was once transformed by newcomers from Los Angeles County and the Midwest, so it is again being transformed by immigrants, from Mexico and other parts of Latin America, and from Vietnam, Taiwan, Korea, and other parts of East Asia. By 2010, the county was 34% Hispanic and 19% Asian. The county seat of Santa Ana is a major arrival point for immigrants from Mexico and is 78% Hispanic. Other immigrants have moved farther out, like so many Southern Californians before them, working multiple jobs, commuting on freeways, and living in stucco subdivisions. There are concentrations in various places—Latinos in Santa Ana and much of Anaheim and Vietnamese in Garden Grove, who constitute the largest Vietnamese community in the nation. But many of these new Californians are scattered throughout the county. Population growth has increased since a downturn during the recession, but those rates are lower than during the booming final three decades of the 20th century.

These demographic changes have made for some political wobble. Until the mid-1990s, Asians were split between the parties, and few Latinos were registered to vote. After the 1994 approval of Proposition 187, which sought to deny most social services to

2012 Presidential Vote		
Barack Obama (D) 95,479	(61%)
Mitt Romney (R)...................56,252	(36%)
2008 Presidential Vote		
Barack Obama (D) 92,591	(59%)
John McCain (R)...................61,861	(39%)
Cook Partisan Voting Index: D+9		

illegal immigrants, many more Latinos began voting, mostly Democratic. Asian voters have been less predictable. The area has faced significant challenges with crime. But crime rates declined in 2013, as did reports of gang activity. In 2014, Carlos Rojas took charge as the first Latino police chief in Santa Ana. The American Civil Liberties Union filed a lawsuit in 2012 against the city, claiming the at-large electoral system shuts out Hispanics from representation on the city council. In response, Anaheim voters in 2014 approved a referendum reorganizing the council to create district representation. In January 2015, Disneyland gained unwanted attention when it became the center of a highly infectious measles outbreak.

The 46th Congressional District covers central and western areas of Orange County. It takes in parts of Santa Ana, which is the second-largest city in Orange County, and Orange, which is split with the neighboring 45th. It also includes a significant portion of Anaheim, Orange County's largest city. The district comprises the strongly Democratic bastion of the county.

Loretta Sanchez (D)

Loretta Sanchez, a Democrat first elected in 1996, has been as well-known for her personal exploits—her wacky Christmas cards featuring her cat Gretzky always drew attention, as did her *YouTube*-captured dance to the 2012 hit song "Call Me Maybe"—as for her serious work on national security issues. She and her sister, Linda Sánchez, are the first sisters to serve in Congress. (Linda uses the accent mark with her surname; Loretta does not.) Her candidacy for an open Senate seat in 2016 provided her great opportunity, plus challenges.

Sanchez was raised in Anaheim. Her parents were Mexican immigrants; her father was a machinist and her mother worked to organize a union at the plant where she worked. She is nine years older than Linda. Sanchez graduated from Chapman University in Orange, and got an M.B.A. from American University in Washington, D.C. She worked as a financial analyst, providing advice on municipal finances to public agencies and private businesses, and started her own firm in the early 1990s. In 1994, she ran for the Anaheim City Council under her married name, Loretta Sanchez-Brixey, and lost.

In 1996, she ran for the House, this time as Loretta Sanchez, against one of the most vocal and veteran conservatives, Republican Rep. Robert Dornan. In the primary against three Anglo male Democrats, she won with 35%. That victory attracted little attention, not even from Dornan. But she shrewdly counted on increasing Latino turnout, plus attracting contributions from the many enemies that Dornan had made over a political career that went back to 1976. President Bill Clinton stumped for Sanchez in Santa Ana late in the campaign and may have made the difference. She won by 984 votes, 47%-46%. Dornan charged vote fraud, and, using the privileges afforded to former members, he regularly appeared on the Republican-controlled House floor trying to persuade his former colleagues to call for a special election. But in February 1998, the House Administration Committee upheld Sanchez's victory.

In the House, Sanchez's voting record has been in the Democratic middle, though she has been slightly more loyal to her party in recent years. The House-passed Violence Against Women Act included a provision of hers to update federal stalking laws, but she voted against the bill in May 2012 because she said it removed confidentiality protections for abused female immigrants. U.S.-Vietnam relations have been a focus for her. She accompanied Clinton on his 2000 visit there and met with dissidents to discuss human rights. In 2007, after three times having been denied a visa, she returned to Vietnam and again stirred controversy by attempting to meet with the wives of imprisoned dissidents and criticizing the government's lack of openness. She tried unsuccessfully in 2012 to amend a

Homeland Security spending bill to direct more money to anti-child exploitation and trafficking initiatives, citing them as particular problems for Vietnam. While sometimes critical of Vietnam's communist government, she embraced the reopening of diplomatic relations with communist Cuba. Her interest in diverse foreign policy issues helped to account for her membership in a record 140 House caucuses at the end of 2014. "We're generalists, as Congress-people," she said. "I'm so much more educated because I'm in those caucuses."

As the senior woman on the Armed Services Committee, she has tried to update the sexual assault crimes in the Uniform Code of Military Justice to comply with the way civilian sexual assault crimes are handled at the federal level. She has been a vocal advocate of allowing women to serve in combat. When that panel's top Democratic slot opened in 2010, she jockeyed for the spot. In the Steering and Policy Committee, she narrowly lost to Washington's Adam Smith, 28-23, but took the fight to the full Democratic caucus. Smith and Sanchez tied on the first ballot, but Smith prevailed, 97-86, on the second round. Sanchez is also the No. 2 Democrat on the Homeland Security Committee, where she has focused on port security, including her proposal for a secure, long-range automated vessel-tracking system.

Until 2010, Sanchez had been reelected comfortably. Voters had grown accustomed to her spirited and unconventional style, including her quirky Christmas cards, which featured Gretzky until his death in 2010. (Gretzky unexpectedly returned on Sanchez's card in 2014, wearing a red "Hillary 2016" cap.) Ever ambitious, Sanchez in 2009 briefly considered a run for governor. A year later, however, she found herself in a tough fight at home. Republican Assemblyman Van Tran, who fled Saigon with his family in 1975, raised more than $1 million. An independent candidate, Cecilia Iglesias, threatened to siphon off Hispanic voters while many Vietnamese were backing Tran. The situation irked Sanchez, who asserted on a Spanish-language Univision show in September that "the Vietnamese and the Republicans are, with an intensity, (trying) to take this seat." Tran responded that the district "belongs to the people and not an individual ethnicity." She recovered from that stumble, got party help—Bill Clinton headlined a rally for her—and raised more than $1.7 million. She won with 53% to Tran's 39% and Iglesias' 8%.

She had no such trouble in 2012 or 2014, although she irked conservatives when she said on MSNBC that GOP presidential candidate Mitt Romney "doesn't even want us [Latinos] to be here." Sanchez voiced strong interest in seeking the seat of retiring Sen. Barbara Boxer, but was hobbled by false starts in the spring of 2015. She jabbed at early Democratic frontrunner Attorney General Kamala Harris as inexperienced in Washington, especially on national security. Harris took an early fundraising lead, Sanchez was counting on strength with her Hispanic base in Southern California. But in her initial step as a candidate, she seemed to lack the polish that Harris had gained in previous statewide campaigns, and would need to establish more discipline and organization to reach out across the state.

FORTY-SEVENTH DISTRICT

Alan Lowenthal (D)

Elected 2012, 2nd term; b. March 8, 1941, New York, NY; Hobart Col., B.A. 1962, OH St. U., M.A. 1965, Ph.D. 1967; Jewish; married (Deborah); 2 children.

Elected Office: Long Beach City Cncl., 1992-98; CA Assembly, 1998-2004; CA Senate, 2004-2012.

Professional Career: Prof., CA. St. U. Long Beach, 1969-98.

DC Office: 108 CHOB, 20515, 202-225-7924; Fax: 202-225-7926; Website: lowenthal.house.gov.

State Offices: Long Beach, 562-436-3828.

Committees: *Foreign Affairs:* Asia & the Pacific; Europe, Eurasia & Emerging Threats; The Western Hemisphere. *Natural Resources:* Energy & Mineral Resources (RMM); Federal Lands; Water, Power & Oceans.

Group Ratings

	ADA	ACLU	AFL-CIO	LCV	ITI	COC	HAFA	ACU	CFG	FRC
2014	95%	88%	–	97%	40%	36%	12%	8%	11%	0%
2013	95%	C	100%	96%	C	33%	C	13%	12%	C

National Journal Ratings

	2013 LIB	—	2013 CONS
Economic	91%	—	0%
Social	93%	—	0%
Foreign	90%	—	6%
Composite	95%	—	5%

Key Votes of the 113th Congress

1. Sandy storm spending	Y	5. Medical Marijuana	Y	9. Syrian Rebels Training	N
2. Violence Against Women Act	Y	6. Farm Bill	N	10. Keystone pipeline	N
3. Guantanamo Bay Detainees	Y	7. Afghanistan Combat	Y	11. Immigration Exec. Action	N
4. Abortion 20-week ban	N	8. NSA Phone Data Collection	Y	12. Bipartisan budget deal	Y

Election Results

2014 general	Alan Lowenthal (D).......................69,091	(56%)	$506,597	$2,983
	Andy Whallon (R)..........................54,309	(44%)	$59,582	
2014 primary	Alan Lowenthal (D).....................44,019	(57%)		
	Andy Whallon (R)..........................33,093	(43%)		

Prior winning percentage: 2012 (57%)

Population		Race and Ethnicity		Income	
Total:	721,957	Latino	35.3%	Median income:	$56,829
Urban:	96.9%	White	32.6%		*(153 of 435)*
Suburban:	3.1%	Asian	19.9%	Under $50,000	43.8%
Rural:	0.0%	Black	7.9%	$50,000-$99,999:	30.7%
Land area:	132	Two races	3.0%	$100,000-$199,999:	20.0%
Pop/sq. mi.:	5,455.0	White Ethnic	15.5%	$200,000 or more:	5.5%
Born in state:	54.8%			Poverty Rate	17.8%
		Education			
Age Groups		H.S. grad or less:	38.8%	**Work**	
Under 18:	23.9%	Some college:	32.5%	White collar:	35.6%
18 to 34:	25.1%	College degree, 4 yr.:	18.7%	Blue collar:	44.1%
35 to 64:	39.1%	Post-grad study:	10.0%	Sales and service:	20.2%
Over 64:	11.9%				
		Military		Govt. workers:	11.9%
		Veterans/active duty:	5.2%		

Coastal L.A./Inland Orange: Long Beach, Garden Grove

With nearly 466,000 people, Long Beach would be a major metropolis almost anywhere but in Los Angeles County, where it seems just the largest of many suburbs. But it has an identity of its own. Founded as a beach resort in 1888, it soon became a port when Los Angeles civic leaders decided that

Voter Turnout	
2013 Total Citizen 18+	465,059
2014 House Turnout	123,400
2014 Turnout as % CVAP	26.5%
2012 Turnout as % CVAP	54.1%

if their town was to be a world-class city, it must have a world-class harbor. Since nature had not provided one, they built it where the Los Angeles River flows into the ocean at the western edge of Long Beach. By 1909, Los Angeles had annexed the harbor towns of San Pedro and Wilmington on the other side of the river. Over the next decades, the two cities persuaded the federal government to dredge channels and build a breakwater and turning basins. Long Beach was developing other businesses as well. It sprouted oil derricks in the 1920s and briefly became one of the nation's big oil producers. It was the site of major aircraft plants in the 1940s and beyond.

Since then, the Los Angeles-Long Beach port has become the nation's busiest cargo center, with huge steel-gray container ships pulling up to enormous automated loading facilities. The two ports in the complex compete with each other on business terms, but collaborate on many issues. The overall port, with 30,000 employees, handles the equivalent of 18,600, 20-foot containers daily docked at 10 piers and 80 berths. From there, cargo leaves by rail in more than 40 daily trains along the high-speed, 20-mile Alameda Corridor to the large rail yards near downtown Los Angeles. The recession reduced volume by almost a third in 2009, but the port has mostly rebounded. These facilities handle 43 percent of goods imported into the nation, and 27 percent of exports. The port was the scene of extended labor strife in 2012 after clerical workers with the International Longshore and Warehouse Union went on strike over the potential outsourcing of their jobs and other issues. After eight days, the strike at 10 of the 14 terminals was settled. A second labor dispute that had dragged on for months was settled in February 2015

2012 Presidential Vote		
Barack Obama (D) 147,456	(60%)
Mitt Romney (R)...................92,010	(38%)
2008 Presidential Vote		
Barack Obama (D) 146,518	(58%)
John McCain (R)...................98,637	(39%)
Cook Partisan Voting Index: D+8		

after mediation by Labor Secretary Thomas Perez, without a strike but with costly slowdowns in port operations.

The *Queen Mary*, converted into a floating hotel, is a big tourist attraction in Long Beach, and there are new high-rises and a huge aquarium along the beach. The city has also been a hot spot for West Coast hip hop, spawning frequent mentions from hometown star Snoop Dogg. Robert Garcia, a gay Latino, was elected in 2014 as the city's youngest mayor, with a promise to turn Long Beach into a mecca of innovation, "the Silicon Valley of the south." Still, the city has suffered from downsized manufacturing. In 2014, Boeing made plans to shut down production of its Globemaster III military transport plane, which had brought thousands of jobs. The Long Beach plant had been the last aircraft-manufacturing facility in California.

The 47th Congressional District is centered on Long Beach, and takes in Signal Hill, where oil rigs are still pumping. Parts are in Orange County, including Los Alamitos and Cypress, which has a large Asian-American population and is the birthplace of golfing great Tiger Woods. Parts of Garden Grove and Westminster, founded as a Presbyterian temperance colony in 1870, are shared with the 48th District. Politically, it leans strongly Democratic.

Alan Lowenthal (D)

Alan Lowenthal, a Democrat first elected in 2012, is a rare academician seeking to bring pragmatic problem-solving to Washington. With lengthy experience at home and in Sacramento, he has brought thoughtful ideas, though he has been limited as a junior member of the minority party.

Lowenthal was born in New York City and grew up in Queens. When he was about 12, the family moved to Long Island, where he went to high school. Lowenthal studied psychology at Hobart College, graduating with a bachelor's degree, and he continued his studies at Ohio State University, earning a master's degree and a doctorate. During his doctoral training, he had an internship in San Francisco and decided that he wanted to live in California. Lowenthal took a position at California State University, Long Beach, in 1969 as an assistant professor and settled in that city. In 1975, he joined Long Beach Area Citizens Involved, an umbrella group of community organizations trying to influence local government. He eventually became the group's president. He first ran for elected office in 1992, winning a seat on the Long Beach City Council. He was elected to the state Assembly in 1998, and to the state Senate six years later.

In the legislature, Lowenthal focused on reducing air pollution at California ports and protecting public health. "I wanted to make sure the community was livable and the port economically viable," he said. He counts his work on the ports of Los Angeles and Long Beach as achievements. He said he ran for Congress because he wanted to deal with national issues such as health care, retirement, and Social Security. "I have a strong value that the society needs to invest in people, and it needs to invest in the future," he said. "And it needs to be financially responsible."

Long Beach Councilman Gary DeLong, Lowenthal's opponent in 2012, ran as a moderate Republican who said he would not be bound by the decisions of the House Republican leadership. Even so, Lowenthal did his best to tie DeLong to the GOP establishment. He also seized on a comment DeLong made at a community event in which he said he had not seen scientific evidence that confirms the existence of climate change. DeLong had the edge in spending, $1.4 million to $1.2 million. But in this comfortably Democratic district, Lowenthal won 57%-43%.

In the House, Lowenthal, who claimed that his work in the Assembly helped to pave the way for the public referendum creating a citizens' redistricting commission in California, used his wider podium to urge the end to political gerrymandering and to the practice of politicians across the nation drawing their own districts. He filed a bill that would create redistricting panels in each state that would be based on the California model, and conceded that success would be much more difficult to achieve in Congress. He secured $13 million for dredging along the mouth of the Los Angeles River at the port. Serving on the House Foreign Affairs Committee, he focused especially on human-rights issues that have concerned his Vietnamese and other Asian constituents. In 2015, Lowenthal took over as senior Democrat on the Natural Resources Subcommittee on Energy and Mineral Resources, where he planned to focus on renewable energy development, especially on public lands, plus climate change. He also became a vice-chair of the House's LGBT Equality Caucus.

In the 2014 campaign, Republican Andy Whallon, a former aeronautical engineer, promised more job creation. But Whallon spent only $60,000, and Lowenthal's 56%-44% victory was close to his initial election.

FORTY-EIGHTH DISTRICT

Dana Rohrabacher (R)

Elected 1988, 14th term; b. June 21, 1947, Coronado; CA St. U. Long Beach., B.A. 1969, U. of S. CA, M.A. 1971; Christian; married (Rhonda); 3 children.

Professional Career: Radio & print journalist, 1970-80; Asst. press sect. Ronald Reagan, 1976, 1980; Sr. speechwriter, special asst. to Pres. Reagan, 1981-88.

DC Office: 2300 RHOB, 20515, 202-225-2415; Website: rohrabacher. house.gov.

State Offices: Huntington Beach, 714-960-6483.

Committees: *Foreign Affairs:* Asia & the Pacific; Europe, Eurasia & Emerging Threats (Chmn). *Science, Space, & Technology:* Energy; Space.

Group Ratings

	ADA	ACLU	AFL-CIO	LCV	ITI	COC	HAFA	ACU	CFG	FRC
2014	10%	11%	–	6%	40%	71%	75%	96%	90%	63%
2013	5%	C	10%	4%	C	62%	C	96%	90%	C

National Journal Ratings

	2013 LIB	—	2013 CONS
Economic	6%	—	93%
Social	27%	—	71%
Foreign	52%	—	48%
Composite	29%	—	71%

Key Votes of the 113th Congress

1. Sandy storm spending	N	5. Medical Marijuana	Y	9. Syrian Rebels Training	N
2. Violence Against Women Act	N	6. Farm Bill	N	10. Keystone pipeline	Y
3. Guantanamo Bay Detainees	N	7. Afghanistan Combat	Y	11. Immigration Exec. Action	Y
4. Abortion 20-week ban	Y	8. NSA Phone Data Collection	Y	12. Bipartisan budget deal	N

Election Results

2014 general	Dana Rohrabacher (R)	112,082	(64%)	$795,323
	Sue Savary (D)	62,713	(36%)	$111,839
2014 primary	Dana Rohrabacher (R)	52,431	(56%)	
	Sue Savary (D)	18,242	(20%)	
	Wendy Leece (R)	11,082	(12%)	
	David Burns (D)	6,142	(7%)	
	Robert Banuelos (D)	5,591	(6%)	

Prior winning percentages: 2012 (61%), 2010 (62%), 2008 (53%), 2006 (60%), 2004 (62%), 2002 (62%), 2000 (62%), 1998 (59%), 1996 (61%), 1994 (69%), 1992 (55%), 1990 (59%), 1988 (64%)

Population		Race and Ethnicity		Income	
Total:	723,140	White	58.2%	Median income:	$80,502
Urban:	80.0%	Latino	20.2%		*(31 of 435)*
Suburban:	20.0%	Asian	17.8%	Under $50,000	32.5%
Rural:	0.0%	Black	0.9%	$50,000-$99,999:	27.0%
Land area:	147	Two races	2.2%	$100,000-$199,999:	26.6%
Pop/sq. mi.:	4,921.3	White Ethnic	24.7%	$200,000 or more:	13.9%
Born in state:	51.4%			Poverty Rate	11.4%
		Education			
Age Groups		H.S. grad or less:	25.7%	**Work**	
Under 18:	21.0%	Some college:	30.5%	White collar:	44.4%
18 to 34:	22.3%	College degree, 4 yr.:	28.6%	Blue collar:	42.2%
35 to 64:	42.0%	Post-grad study:	15.1%	Sales and service:	13.4%
Over 64:	14.8%				
		Military		Govt. workers:	8.6%
		Veterans/active duty:	6.0%		

Coastal Orange: Huntington Beach, Costa Mesa

In the 1950s, when The Beach Boys were at Hawthorne High School in L.A., surfers would drive far down the coast to the vast expanse of Huntington Beach in Orange County to catch a wave. This was empty country then, vegetable fields and orange groves mainly, with nary a freeway or shopping

Voter Turnout	
2013 Total Citizen 18+	508,034
2014 House Turnout	174,795
2014 Turnout as % CVAP	34.4%
2012 Turnout as % CVAP	60.7%

center in sight. Today, the 42-mile shoreline of Orange County is pretty much filled in with pricey coastal resorts and other developments. Huntington Beach, a city of nearly 198,000, is a mixture of family subdivisions and garden apartments and home of the International Surfing Museum. Its eight miles of beach and self-depiction as Surf City make it a tourist draw in the summer. In 2015, city officials were exploring a new use for the ocean: a desalination plant to counter the state's water crisis.

To the north is Westminster, the center of a prominent Vietnamese-American community, with miles of shops with Vietnamese names and its own Vietnamese-language daily newspaper. Southeast along San Diego Freeway is Fountain Valley, the central focus of many Asian-owned high-technology businesses. Near the coast is Costa Mesa, site of South Coast Plaza's luxury stores and a grand performing arts center. Like other California cities, it experienced a huge influx of Hispanic immigrants in the past decade, and adapting has been rocky. The Costa Mesa City Council shut down a day-laborer center and declared itself a "rule of law city"—a message to illegal immigrants to stay away.

The 48th Congressional District takes in much of coastal Orange County and is anchored by Huntington Beach. It includes the oceanside cities of Laguna Beach, with its art galleries and cute shops, and Newport Beach, one of California's richest cities, which was rated in 2014 by Coldwell-Banker as the second-most expensive housing market in the country (behind Los Altos California), with an average listing of $1.9 million. Newport Beach was also the setting for the popular teen drama, *The O.C.* Westminster is split with the neighboring 47th District, but the area known as Little Saigon is in the 48th. With their entrepreneurial spirit, many of the Vietnamese communities compete with each other, for example, in celebrating the Lunar New Year ("Tet"), or in a more contentious battle between a Vietnamese newspaper publisher in Little Saigon and anti-Communist refugees who continue to fight the war that ended in 1975.

Parts of Garden Grove and Santa Ana are also in the district, as are Fountain Valley and Seal Beach and Leisure World, its large gated community for seniors. These coastal areas share many common interests in managing state beaches and coastal estuaries. Politically, this district leans firmly Republican.

2012 Presidential Vote		
Mitt Romney (R)	169,249	(55%)
Barack Obama (D)	133,103	(43%)
2008 Presidential Vote		
John McCain (R)	165,162	(51%)
Barack Obama (D)	148,929	(46%)
Cook Partisan Voting Index:	R+7	

Dana Rohrabacher (R)

A self-described "surfer Republican" who sports an American-flag surfboard on his lapel, Dana Rohrabacher likes to make waves in the House. Since coming to Capitol Hill in 1989, he has provoked people on both the left and right with his hyperbolic rhetoric and non-conformity. But he professes not to care, and says his motto is, "Fighting for freedom and having fun."

Rohrabacher grew up in Southern California, went to college and experimented with drugs, and once had a folk band called the Goldwaters. By the mid-1970s, he was on a far straighter path as a press aide in Ronald Reagan's 1976 and 1980 presidential campaigns. He wrote editorials for *The Orange County Register* and later was a speechwriter in the Reagan White House. He returned to Southern California in 1988, when GOP Rep. Dan Lungren was appointed acting state treasurer, leaving open a heavily Republican seat. Rohrabacher won the primary with 35% of the vote and prevailed in November with 64%. During the campaign, one of his volunteers, a surfer, entered him in a surfing contest. They later married and, in 2004, became the parents of triplets.

A self-styled free spirit, Rohrabacher formed friendships—based on their mutual love of tequila, he says—with actor John Wayne and rocker Sammy Hagar. His voting record can be unpredictable, especially on cultural issues. He supports the legal use of medical marijuana and joined with liberal Rep. Barney Frank of Massachusetts on a bill to decriminalize possession of less than 100 grams. He invited Frank, who is gay, and his partner, a surfer, to visit Huntington Beach. After the 2014 election, he doubled down in his support for legalization of marijuana, specifically in the District of Columbia. He told his fellow Republicans: "Wake up! ... The American people are shifting on this issue." With Democratic Rep. Earl Blumenauer of Oregon, he filed a bill to permit expanded use of medical marijuana by VA hospitals. In September 2013, *National Journal* profiled him as chairman of the Trolling Caucus, and added that he was "the country's most responsive social-media congressman, or an argument-junkie in need of a quick, online fix—or both."

Rohrabacher is a congressional skeptic of human-caused global warming. Although the threat increasingly troubles the scientific world, Rohrabacher told *Science* magazine in November 2012 that "in the global warming debate, we won. ... I think that after 10 years of debate, we can show that there are hundreds if not thousands of scientists who have come over to being skeptics." Rohrabacher has taken on some unusual causes. He has repeatedly sponsored a bill that would give District of Columbia residents full voting rights in Maryland but would maintain a separate District government.

Rohrabacher's other main focus has been the Foreign Affairs Committee, where he takes a special interest in efforts to fight the Taliban in Afghanistan. After the Sept. 11, 2001, attacks, he visited the exiled king of Afghanistan in Rome, encouraged him to return to Kabul, and promised that the United States would oust the Taliban and help rebuild the country. But he was a strong critic of former Afghan President Hamid Karzai, accusing him of having a "corrupt little clique." Karzai responded by refusing to let the congressman enter the country with a delegation in April 2012.

Another U.S. ally he has antagonized is Pakistan. After reports of widespread violations of human rights by Pakistan security forces in Baluchistan, Rohrabacher introduced a resolution in 2012 calling for a right of self-determination in the country's largest province. Government officials were incensed, but Rohrabacher said in a *Washington Post* op-ed, "We should not remain a silent partner to a Pakistani government that engages in monstrous crimes against its people." Rohrabacher also has been a longtime critic of China's rulers. He strongly opposed normal trade relations with China and has backed export controls to bar advanced technology from non-democratic governments, sometimes referring to the nation as "Red China." Rohrabacher has had an odd history with Russian leader Vladimir Putin. In the early 1990s, he claims to have arm-wrestled—and lost to—Putin in a Capitol Hill bar. In 2014, Rohrabacher defended Putin's invasion of Ukraine on the basis that post-Communist Russia had become a more open society.

For years, Rohrabacher has advocated stronger action against illegal immigration. In 2003, he delayed his support for the Republicans' Medicare prescription drug bill until GOP leaders, in exchange for his vote, gave him a vote on his bill to require hospitals to report potential illegal immigrants to the Homeland Security Department. He has led voter initiatives to remove illegal immigrants from California's welfare and school rolls, and he successfully urged President George W. Bush to commute the sentences of two former Border

Patrol agents who shot a Mexican drug dealer. After President Barack Obama's reelection, Rohrabacher charged on Twitter that the president's campaign orchestrated "giveaways to cronies who then donated ... to low-income citizens & illegals who then voted." In 2013, he said that if John Boehner brought an immigration bill to the House floor without the support of a majority of House Republicans, he should be removed as speaker.

As a maverick, Rohrabacher has been frustrated in his pursuit of a committee gavel. In 2006, he lost the top minority post on the full Science and Technology Committee to the more senior Ralph Hall of Texas. When Republicans regained the House majority in 2011, Hall became chairman. Rohrabacher sought again to chair the committee in 2013, but the slot went to Texas' Lamar Smith. Likewise, at the Foreign Affairs Committee, more junior members have surpassed him to become chairman. There have been a few other cases where senior House members have been denied chairmanships, but they are rare.

Rohrabacher usually has little trouble getting reelected, but in 2008, he faced Huntington Beach Mayor Debbie Cook, a Democratic lawyer and environmental activist who claimed he had done little during his time in Congress. With no help from the national party, she raised $482,000. Rohrabacher criticized Cook's opposition to more oil drilling and her support for the rescue of the financial markets. He won by a reduced 53%-43%. In the strongly Republican 2010, he won by a more customary, 62%-38%. In October 2011, *OC Weekly* reported that more than half of his campaign donations over a three-month period went to his wife, Rhonda, who was acting as his campaign manager. But voters have appeared not to care. Since then, he has been reelected with more than 60%.

FORTY-NINTH DISTRICT

Darrell Issa (R)

Elected 2000, 8th term; b. Nov. 1, 1953, Cleveland, OH; Siena Heights Col., B.A. 1976; Antioch Orthodox Christian; married (Kathy); 1 child.

Military Career: U.S. Army, 1970-72, 1976-80.

Professional Career: Founder & pres., Directed Electronics, 1982-99.

DC Office: 2269 RHOB, 20515, 202-225-3906; Fax: 202-225-3303; Website: issa.house.gov.

State Offices: Vista, 760-599-5000.

Committees: *Foreign Affairs:* The Middle East & North Africa; Terrorism, Nonproliferation, & Trade. *Judiciary:* Courts, Intellectual Property & the Internet (Chmn); Regulatory Reform, Commercial & Antitrust Law.

Group Ratings

	ADA	ACLU	AFL-CIO	LCV	ITI	COC	HAFA	ACU	CFG	FRC
2014	0%	5%	–	3%	80%	100%	54%	80%	51%	88%
2013	0%	C	24%	0%	C	92%	C	72%	62%	C

National Journal Ratings

	2013 LIB	—	2013 CONS
Economic	26%	—	73%
Social	16%	—	74%
Foreign	5%	—	86%
Composite	19%	—	81%

Key Votes of the 113th Congress

1. Sandy storm spending	N	5. Medical Marijuana	N	9. Syrian Rebels Training	Y
2. Violence Against Women Act	Y	6. Farm Bill	Y	10. Keystone pipeline	Y
3. Guantanamo Bay Detainees	N	7. Afghanistan Combat	N	11. Immigration Exec. Action	Y
4. Abortion 20-week ban	Y	8. NSA Phone Data Collection	N	12. Bipartisan budget deal	Y

Election Results

2014 general	Darrell Issa (R)	98,161	(60%)	$1,749,467	$1,316	$7,847
	Dave Peiser (D)	64,981	(40%)	$85,321		
2014 primary	Darrell Issa (R)	56,558	(62%)			
	Dave Peiser (D)	25,946	(28%)			
	Noboru Isagawa (D)	8,887	(10%)			

Prior winning percentages: 2012 (58%), 2010 (63%), 2008 (58%), 2006 (63%), 2004 (63%), 2002 (77%), 2000 (61%)

Population		Race and Ethnicity		Income	
Total:	717,823	White	62.0%	Median income:	$67,018
Urban:	30.9%	Latino	25.7%		(73 of 435)
Suburban:	69.1%	Asian	6.6%	Under $50,000	39.2%
Rural:	0.0%	Black	2.0%	$50,000-$99,999:	26.8%
Land area:	405	Two races	3.0%	$100,000-$199,999:	22.6%
Pop/sq. mi.:	1,774.0	White Ethnic	27.2%	$200,000 or more:	11.5%
Born in state:	50.1%			Poverty Rate	12.5%
		Education			
Age Groups		H.S. grad or less:	27.7%	**Work**	
Under 18:	22.1%	Some college:	32.0%	White collar:	43.8%
18 to 34:	23.9%	College degree, 4 yr.:	24.7%	Blue collar:	41.9%
35 to 64:	40.8%	Post-grad study:	15.7%	Sales and service:	14.3%
Over 64:	13.2%				
		Military		Govt. workers:	12.3%
		Veterans/active duty:	13.4%		

Northwest San Diego: Oceanside, Vista

The California coast between Los Angeles and San Diego has never entirely filled up with development—and never will as long as the Marine Corps retains custody of Camp Pendleton, the giant training base just south of the Orange-San Diego County line and the Corps' largest expedi-

Voter Turnout	
2013 Total Citizen 18+	499,082
2014 House Turnout	163,142
2014 Turnout as % CVAP	32.7%
2012 Turnout as % CVAP	61.3%

tionary training facility on the West Coast. The land along the coast and inland in northern San Diego County, usually referred to as North County, was largely empty territory a half-century ago—never fertile enough to produce a large farm community, never endowed with much manufacturing, never actively promoted as a retirement community. But North County has been growing rapidly since then. Today more than 800,000 people live here, and who can blame them? This is one of America's most beautiful and comfortable environments, with ocean and mountain scenery, sunny and warm weather, and low crime. Amid dry but not desert landscape, there are miles of rolling hills, with occasional sagebrush-like bushes. It has attracted thousands of new migrants—many, but by no means all—retirees. New construction and home sales fell off during the Great Recession, but the local economy has been on the upswing.

The 49th Congressional District covers the southernmost coastal area of Orange County, including Laguna Niguel and the heavily Republican San Clemente. Known as the "Spanish Village by the Sea," San Clemente is where Richard Nixon retired to write his memoirs after resigning the presidency. Nixon purchased his 5.5 acre estate in 1969, reportedly for a bit less than $1 million, though the financing was complicated and later controversial. He sold it in 1980. In April 2015, it was reported that the subsequent owner, the retired chief executive of Allergan pharmaceutical company, placed the property for sale for $75 million. The district also takes in parts of northern San Diego County and the North County, including Oceanside, Encinitas, and Carlsbad, home of the La Costa resort and a big tourist destination. The district has been the site of the San Onofre nuclear plant. But Southern California Edison announced in June 2013 the permanent shutdown of that facility because of the financial costs and regulatory uncertainty of restarting a reactor following discovery of a radiation leak in

2012 Presidential Vote		
Mitt Romney (R)	153,856	(52%)
Barack Obama (D)	134,447	(46%)
2008 Presidential Vote		
Barack Obama (D)	148,120	(50%)
John McCain (R)	144,815	(49%)
Cook Partisan Voting Index:	R+4	

January 2012, plus flaws in the plant's steam generators. In Carlsbad, a private company plans to open in late 2015 a $1 billion desalination plant, partly in response to the California water crisis. Many jurisdictions in this area had imposed water restrictions even before the statewide edict issued by Gov. Jerry Brown in April 2015.

The 49th District also takes in the northern edge of the city of San Diego. The district leans Republican.

Darrell Issa (R)

Darrell Issa is a Republican first elected in 2000. As chairman of the Oversight and Government Reform Committee from 2011 to January 2015, he made himself President Barack Obama's chief investigative nemesis. His aggressive, headline-grabbing pursuits of alleged waste, fraud, and abuse in the administration made him a hero to conservatives and the scourge of liberals. In his new post as chairman of the subcommittee in charge of patent policy, it's not likely that he will capture as much attention but he may wield influence.

Issa grew up in a working-class section of Cleveland, the son of an X-ray technician. Hampered by dyslexia, Issa found academics difficult, and he dropped out of high school to join the Army. After his service, the military paid for him to finish school, and he graduated from Siena Heights University in Michigan. A brother's run-ins with the law for car theft spurred Issa's idea for his first business venture. He invested all of his savings, some $7,000, in a car-alarm business in Cleveland, eventually taking it over with his wife, Kathy, and relocating the business to Vista California, north of San Diego. Their Directed Electronics became the nation's largest manufacturer of vehicle security systems, including the popular Viper system, and earned them a fortune. Issa became active in the high-technology lobby, serving as chairman of the Consumer Electronics Association. In 2010, the Center for Responsive Politics ranked Issa as the wealthiest member of Congress, with an estimated average net worth of $448 million. In January 2015, *Roll Call* reported that his net worth had dropped to $357 million, but he remained the wealthiest, with three times the net worth of the runner-up, Republican Rep. Michael McCaul of Texas.

In the early 1990s, Issa turned to politics, contributing to Republicans and chairing the 1996 campaign to pass Proposition 209, which banned the use of racial quotas and preferences in California. In 1998, he ran for the Republican nomination to challenge Sen. Barbara Boxer and spent $9.8 million of his own money. He lost the primary 45%-40% to Matt Fong. In November 1999, when Rep. Ron Packard announced his retirement, 10 candidates ran in the Republican primary. This turned into a contest between Issa and state Sen. Bill Morrow. Morrow questioned Issa's business practices, and Issa raised questions about Morrow's honesty. On most issues, the candidates took similar positions. Issa spent $1.5 million of his own money on the primary and beat Morrow 46%-30%. In the fall, the Democratic nominee abandoned his campaign after getting little national party support, and Issa won 61%-28%.

Issa's voting record has had occasional moderate notes, especially on foreign affairs. Of Lebanese descent, he has condemned the sponsorship of terrorism by Arab nations while urging the United States to build coalitions with friendly Arab nations. That earned him enemies among pro-Israel groups. Two members of the militant Jewish Defense League were charged with plotting to blow up Issa's office in San Clemente, a Culver City mosque, and a Muslim public affairs building. One of them died in 2002 and the other pleaded guilty to civil rights and weapons violations in 2005.

House Republican leaders chose Issa over several more senior Republicans after the 2008 election to be ranking member on Oversight and Government Reform, with broad authority to investigate the federal government. During the early days of the Republican Congress in 2011, he called the Obama administration "one of the most corrupt administrations ever." He later said that he meant it was guilty of overspending and inefficiency. He began his chairmanship by accusing the Department of Homeland Security of letting political appointees interfere with Freedom of Information Act requests, and subsequently made a regular point of describing the administration's refusal to release documents as inconsistent with its stated philosophy of openness. His committee issued a stinging report on the handling of the Deepwater Horizon oil spill disaster in the Gulf of Mexico, accusing Obama and his administration of giving BP too much control over cleanup operations and failing to ensure that affected Gulf Coast residents were paid fairly and quickly for their losses.

The so-called "Fast and Furious" investigation dominated the committee's agenda in 2011-12. The Bureau of Alcohol, Tobacco, Firearms, and Explosives operation, which began in 2009, allowed guns to be shipped illegally into Mexico in an effort to track them to drug cartels. Two of the guns were found a year later at the scene of the killing of a U.S. Border Patrol agent in Arizona. Issa and other committee Republicans repeatedly pressed the administration to discuss who at the Justice Department was aware of the operation, as well as who authorized it. Justice officials, citing executive privilege, said releasing material Issa sought could jeopardize ongoing investigations. The spat became a hot topic for the far right and conspiracy theories flourished, including one floated by Issa at a National Rifle

Association convention that the Obama administration deliberately lost the guns to later push for renewal of a ban on assault weapons.

Attorney General Eric Holder eventually landed in Issa's crosshairs. House Republicans voted in June 2012 to hold him in contempt of Congress for allegedly withholding information. Seventeen Democrats joined the GOP, immunizing the Republicans from accusations of pure partisanship. Still, the White House accused Issa and the GOP of a witch hunt against Holder. The Justice Department's inspector general issued a September 2012 report faulting ATF for misguided strategies and errors in judgment and management, which Issa said proved his point.

He turned his attention to the administration's handling of the Sept. 11, 2012, tragedy at the U.S. mission in Benghazi, Libya, in which four Americans were killed. Issa's office released 166 pages of "sensitive but unclassified" State Department communications related to Libya. But it did not redact identifying information about Libyans working with the United States. Ethics watchdog groups, who earlier had filed ethics complaints against Issa for releasing wiretap information related to Fast and Furious, joined Democrats in expressing outrage. Former Obama White House Chief of Staff Rahm Emanuel called Issa "reckless." Issa responded that, "Anything below 'Secret' (classification) is in fact just a name on a piece of paper." In May 2014, the House voted to create a select committee to investigate the events surrounding the attack in Benghazi, which superseded the work of the Issa committee. Issa backed down from his earlier demand that Secretary of State John Kerry testify before his panel.

Probably Issa's most highly charged inquiry was his panel's extended review in 2013-14 of the Internal Revenue Service and its allegedly unfair treatment of tea party groups that had applied for tax-exempt status. Issa and his staff documented examples of the IRS treating conservative activists with a double standard compared to their liberal counterparts. When Lois Lerner, the head of the IRS division on tax-exempt organizations, was discovered to have lost tens of thousands of files in her office computer, and Lerner then cited her Fifth Amendment right not to testify before the Issa committee because she might incriminate herself, the committee in May 2014 asked the Justice Department to investigate whether she had broken the law. Nearly a year later, the department concluded that there were not sufficient grounds on which to charge her. Lerner earlier was placed on administrative leave at the IRS.

Issa occasionally pursued investigations on a bipartisan basis, notably his review of misbehavior by Secret Service agents while they were supposedly on the job protecting Obama or incidents in which intruders ran loose on the White House grounds. With the Oversight Committee's ranking Democrat, Elijah Cummings of Maryland, Issa wrote that there was a "bipartisan apprehension about a series of dangerous security breaches." In a retrospective interview with the *Washington Examiner*, Issa cited his collaboration with Cummings on the enactment of several bills, including reform of federal information technology and greater transparency by the executive branch in its use of data.

In 2015, Issa became chairman of the Judiciary Subcommittee on Courts, Intellectual Property and Internet. He planned to pursue, in particular, patent reform issues. Drawing on his experience as a patent holder (he holds 37 of them), he had sponsored a bipartisan bill that became law in 2011 giving district court judges hearing patent cases access to clerks trained in patent law. He also has co-sponsored bipartisan legislation to create a review process of already-issued patents and to tighten rules for calculating damages in patent lawsuits. The technology industry had led the charge for patent reform, contending it has been held hostage by "patent trolls" who obtain patents solely for the purpose of launching infringement suits to cash in on multibillion-dollar damage awards. Issa also supported requiring radio stations to pay royalties to record companies and performers as well as to composers of music.

With ambitions for statewide office, Issa in 2003 spent $1.7 million of his own money to get the signatures needed for a recall election of Democratic Gov. Gray Davis. His hopes of getting unified GOP support as a replacement candidate were dashed when Arnold Schwarzenegger got in the race. Issa tearfully announced that he would not run. He has been reelected easily and his District is comfortably Republican, though less so than for other Southern Californians in the House GOP.

FIFTIETH DISTRICT

Duncan D. Hunter (R)

Elected 2008, 4th term; b. Dec. 7, 1976, San Diego; San Diego St. U., B.S. 2001; Baptist; married (Margaret); 3 children.

Military Career: U.S. Marine Corps, 2002-05 (Iraq); Marine Reserves, 2005-present (Afghanistan).

Professional Career: Business analyst, Cayenta Inc., 2000-02; Residential developer, 2005-07.

DC Office: 2429 RHOB, 20515, 202-225-5672; Fax: 202-225-0235; Website: hunter.house.gov.

State Offices: El Cajon, 619-448-5201; Temecula, 951-695-5108.

Committees: *Armed Services:* Emerging Threats & Capabilities; Seapower & Projection Forces (VChmn). *Education & the Workforce:* Early Childhood, Elementary & Secondary Education; Workforce Protections. *Transportation & Infrastructure:* Coast Guard & Maritime Transportation (Chmn); Highways & Transit; Water Resources & Environment.

Group Ratings

	ADA	ACLU	AFL-CIO	LCV	ITI	COC	HAFA	ACU	CFG	FRC
2014	5%	0%	–	0%	100%	79%	67%	88%	70%	50%
2013	0%	C	14%	4%	C	77%	C	78%	75%	C

National Journal Ratings

	2013 LIB	—	2013 CONS
Economic	16%	—	84%
Social	38%	—	62%
Foreign	14%	—	85%
Composite	23%	—	77%

Key Votes of the 113th Congress

1. Sandy storm spending	N	5. Medical Marijuana	Y	9. Syrian Rebels Training	N
2. Violence Against Women Act	Y	6. Farm Bill	Y	10. Keystone pipeline	Y
3. Guantanamo Bay Detainees	N	7. Afghanistan Combat	N	11. Immigration Exec. Action	Y
4. Abortion 20-week ban	NV	8. NSA Phone Data Collection	N	12. Bipartisan budget deal	Y

Election Results

2014 general	Duncan Hunter (R)	111,997	(71%)	$841,310
	James Kimber (D)	45,302	(29%)	$38,434
2014 primary	Duncan D. Hunter (R)	62,371	(70%)	
	James Kimber (D)	21,552	(24%)	
	Michael Benoit (L)	4,634	(5%)	

Prior winning percentages: 2012 (68%), 2010 (63%), 2008 (56%)

Population		Race and Ethnicity		Income	
Total:	730,427	White	58.1%	Median income:	$61,533
Urban:	8.4%	Latino	29.7%		*(105 of 435)*
Suburban:	89.6%	Asian	5.1%	Under $50,000	40.8%
Rural:	2.1%	Black	1.8%	$50,000-$99,999:	31.1%
Land area:	1,928	Two races	3.3%	$100,000-$199,999:	22.6%
Pop/sq. mi.:	378.9	White Ethnic	23.0%	$200,000 or more:	5.6%
Born in state:	55.5%			Poverty Rate	13.4%
		Education			
Age Groups		H.S. grad or less:	40.8%	**Work**	
Under 18:	23.8%	Some college:	34.9%	White collar:	31.6%
18 to 34:	23.5%	College degree, 4 yr.:	16.2%	Blue collar:	47.5%
35 to 64:	39.7%	Post-grad study:	8.1%	Sales and service:	21.0%
Over 64:	13.0%			Govt. workers:	12.2%
		Military			
		Veterans/active duty:	9.9%		

Inland San Diego: Escondido, El Cajon

San Diego began as a port, but today most metro-politan-area residents live out of sight of the sea, in hilltop neighborhoods that look out over distant ridges and freeways or in warm, sunny valleys amid the mountains that become dense and taller as one travels east from the Pacific Ocean. There is

Voter Turnout	
2013 Total Citizen 18+	477,505
2014 House Turnout	157,299
2014 Turnout as % CVAP	32.9%
2012 Turnout as % CVAP	59.2%

a discernible difference in attitudes and values between those who have settled inland and those who live nearer the ocean, part of the split between coastal California and interior California that has been at the heart of the state's political struggles and culture wars. Outside of the city of San Diego, both of these groups have tended to identify as Republicans. Coastal residents tend to be more affluent, and those who settle inland are more likely to be culturally traditional, supportive of the military, and dubious about the ability of government to help society's have-nots. Part of this can be explained by the large military presence there. A 2014 report estimated that the Pentagon accounts for about $39 billion in annual spending in San Diego County, which is about 20 percent of the local economy. That includes 56 ships home-ported in San Diego, and two aircraft carriers based in Coronado. Many veterans and military retirees have settled in the area.

North of San Diego on Interstate 15 is Escondido, a conservative city that is also nearly half Hispanic. Tensions between the Escondido political leadership and Latino activists have heightened in recent years, as the Escondido City Council passed several tough ordinances cracking down on illegal immigration. In response to a lawsuit against the city over its at-large electoral system that activists said was discriminatory against Latinos, the city agreed to divide its council into four districts, one of which had a Hispanic majority. In the November 2014 election, no Latino was elected and the council retained its conservative majority. The city has continued to suffer from what has been called a "cultural chasm." New housing and other growth in rural inland areas have been robust. The area's farmers said that the 2015 water restrictions were unfair because San Diego has been classified as an urban county.

The 50th Congressional District of California takes in much of the mountain and desert interior of San Diego County. Eastern parts of the district are lightly inhabited. In the mountains is tiny Alpine and in the desert is the town of Borrego Springs amid the giant Anza-Borrego Desert State Park. El Cajon, which is split between this district and the 51st, has the nation's second-largest community of Chaldeans, Catholic Arabs from Iraq. That Chaldean community has had conflicts with the church's international leadership over possible excommunication of local priests unless they recognized the authority

2012 Presidential Vote		
Mitt Romney (R)................165,104	(60%)
Barack Obama (D) 102,649	(38%)
2008 Presidential Vote		
John McCain (R)................161,222	(59%)
Barack Obama (D) 108,629	(40%)
Cook Partisan Voting Index: R+14	

in Baghdad. In January 2015, Pope Francis sided with the San Diego church. Politically, this is a solidly Republican district.

Duncan D. Hunter (R)

Republican Duncan D. Hunter, elected in 2008, holds the seat that his father, Duncan Hunter, former chairman of the House Armed Services Committee, held for 28 years before him. The younger Hunter is a Marine Corps veteran and just as much of a defense hawk as his father, even occasionally bucking his party on military issues.

The younger Hunter grew up in El Cajon and got a degree in business administration from San Diego State University, after having started a website design company with a friend during his sophomore year. He worked in the computer industry for several years during the technology boom of the late 1990s. He says that the Sept. 11, 2001, terrorist attacks prompted him to rethink his career plans. The next day, Hunter quit his job and enlisted in the Marine Corps. After completing officer training, Hunter was commissioned as a lieutenant. He was deployed to Iraq in 2003, served in Baghdad after the fall of the city, and in 2004 fought in the battle of Fallujah. In 2006, he was promoted to captain and placed on reserve status.

Though he earlier had shown little interest in following his father into politics, he said his battlefield experiences led him to reconsider public service. But shortly after announcing his candidacy in March 2007 for his retiring father's House seat, Hunter was again called to active duty, this time in Afghanistan. Hunter was prohibited from any campaign activities, including fundraising and planning, and held only one event before leaving. In his absence, the management of his nascent campaign fell to his wife, Margaret Hunter. She took over all appearances and campaign duties in addition to caring for their three young children. When Hunter called home from Afghanistan, it was illegal for him even to inquire how the campaign was going, and he remained largely in the dark until his duty ended in December 2007. He returned home to resume campaigning full-time.

In the June primary, Hunter faced Santee Councilman Brian Jones and San Diego Board of Education President Bob Watkins. Although both were well known locally and campaigned actively, Hunter and his family surrogates effectively ran on the basis of his military credentials. Hunter also benefited from his father's political and congressional connections, raising nearly three times as much as his Republican challengers. Hunter cruised to victory in the June primary with 72% percent of the vote. In the general election, Hunter faced another military veteran, retired Navy SEAL Commander Mike Lumpkin, a former Republican turned Democrat. He agreed with Hunter on many issues, including gun rights and the need for a fence along the U.S.-Mexico border. But national Democrats paid little attention to the contest, and Hunter prevailed, 56%-39%. He has won reelection with more than 60% since.

Hunter shares many of his father's political beliefs. On the Armed Services Committee, he cites national security as his top priority. "I can tell you what the guys on the ground, the men and women out there fighting, actually need," Hunter said. "We have a whole lot of brass out there at the Pentagon and in the DOD who haven't left their offices in six or seven years." He has been vocal about the need for more defense spending. In 2012, he said that the Obama administration should consider building fewer littoral combat ships that operate close to the shore, and use the savings to construct more traditional amphibious warships that could be used to support Marine Corps operations. The shortage of amphibious ships is "one of the most glaring gaps in the Navy," he said. He voted that year to restrict the Pentagon's ability to purchase alternative fuels, saying the military doesn't need them. He strongly opposed repealing the "don't ask, don't tell" policy prohibiting openly gay military personnel, telling National Public Radio that the bond between soldiers "is broken if you open up the military to transgenders, to hermaphrodites, to gays and lesbians."

Hunter pressed the Pentagon to do more to confront the threat posed by the Islamic State. He told Fox News in an October 2014 interview that their fighters had crossed the Mexican border into Texas. The Homeland Security Department firmly denied his claim. In June 2014, he complained that the United States was "scrambling" to fill intelligence gaps in Iraq that had led to what he called "misguided decisions." During a 2013 visit to the Syria-Jordan border, he said that President Barack Obama needed to provide additional support to rebel groups in Syria.

Hunter's other interests include tougher immigration laws and finding ways to halt the outflow of jobs overseas. In June 2014, he opposed the creation in Escondido of a shelter for children who had crossed the border illegally. On the Education and the Workforce Committee, he called for eliminating 43 education-related programs he deemed "unnecessary" and "wasteful," including initiatives dealing with teacher and school-leader training, arts, physical education, and mental health. It passed the committee in June 2011 but went no further. He co-authored an op-ed for *The Washington Post* in April 2013 in which he described management of veterans hospitals as a "quagmire," and that the Veterans Affairs Department's leadership was ill-serving veterans. A year later, VA Secretary Eric Shinseki resigned.

In 2013, Hunter took over as chairman of the Transportation and Infrastructure Subcommittee on Coast Guard and Maritime Transportation. This was especially useful for the San Diego region, where the Coast Guard has operated since 1937 and patrols for illegal immigration and drug enforcement. In December 2014, Congress completed action on an authorization bill that required a mission needs statement every four years for Coast Guard programs.

FIFTY-FIRST DISTRICT

Juan Vargas (D)

Elected 2012, 2nd term; b. March 7, 1961, National City; U. of San Diego, B.A. 1983, Fordham U., M.A. 1987, Harvard U., J.D. 1991; Catholic; married (Adrienne); 2 children.

Elected Office: San Diego City Cncl., 1993-2000; CA Assembly, 2000-06, asst. maj. ldr., 2000; CA Senate, 2010-2012.

Professional Career: Practicing atty., Luce, Forward, Hamilton, & Scripps; V.P., external affairs, Safeco Ins., 2006-08; V.P., corporate legal, Liberty Mutual Group, 2008-10.

DC Office: 1605 LHOB, 20515, 202-225-8045; Fax: 202-225-2772; Website: vargas.house.gov.

State Offices: Chula Vista, 619-422-5963; El Centro, 760-312-9900.

Committees: *Financial Services:* Financial Institutions & Consumer Credit; Oversight & Investigations. *House Administration. Joint Committee on Printing.*

Group Ratings

	ADA	ACLU	AFL-CIO	LCV	ITI	COC	HAFA	ACU	CFG	FRC
2014	85%	77%	–	94%	60%	50%	10%	8%	13%	13%
2013	65%	C	100%	89%	C	31%	C	12%	12%	C

National Journal Ratings

	2013 LIB	—	2013 CONS
Economic	70%	—	30%
Social	63%	—	36%
Foreign	64%	—	35%
Composite	66%	—	34%

Key Votes of the 113th Congress

1. Sandy storm spending	Y	5. Medical Marijuana	Y	9. Syrian Rebels Training	Y
2. Violence Against Women Act	Y	6. Farm Bill	N	10. Keystone pipeline	N
3. Guantanamo Bay Detainees	Y	7. Afghanistan Combat	N	11. Immigration Exec. Action	N
4. Abortion 20-week ban	N	8. NSA Phone Data Collection	N	12. Bipartisan budget deal	Y

Election Results

2014 general	Juan Vargas (D)..............................56,373	(69%)	$801,519	$12,413
	Stephen Meade (R).......................25,577	(31%)		
2014 primary	Juan Vargas (D)..............................35,812	(68%)		
	Stephen Meade (R).......................16,403	(31%)		

Prior winning percentage: 2012 (71%)

Population		Race and Ethnicity		Income	
Total:	743,982	Latino	69.1%	Median income:	$41,477
Urban:	72.9%	White	13.8%		*(368 of 435)*
Suburban:	14.5%	Black	7.6%	Under $50,000	58.1%
Rural:	12.6%	Asian	7.3%	$50,000-$99,999:	28.4%
Land area:	4,003	Two races	1.7%	$100,000-$199,999:	12.1%
Pop/sq. mi.:	185.9	White Ethnic	5.5%	$200,000 or more:	1.3%
Born in state:	52.5%			Poverty Rate	24.7%
		Education			
Age Groups		H.S. grad or less:	56.5%	**Work**	
Under 18:	28.3%	Some college:	30.1%	White collar:	21.1%
18 to 34:	28.1%	College degree, 4 yr.:	9.8%	Blue collar:	52.9%
35 to 64:	33.3%	Post-grad study:	3.6%	Sales and service:	26.0%
Over 64:	10.3%				
		Military		Govt. workers:	15.8%
		Veterans/active duty:	8.8%		

San Diego to Nevada: Eastern Chula Vista, Imperial

Anchoring a corner of the continental United States, San Diego not so long ago was a small Navy town known for its good harbor and splendid weather. It is now a major metropolis of 1.3 million people and the center of a county of 3.1 million. To

Voter Turnout	
2013 Total Citizen 18+	396,499
2014 House Turnout	81,950
2014 Turnout as % CVAP	20.7%
2012 Turnout as % CVAP	41%

its occasional discomfort, it is also one of the largest cities directly on an international border, situated between countries with strikingly different economic conditions, political systems, and cultural traditions. San Diego sits on the busiest border crossing in the world, and on a daily basis, agents for the Border Patrol play a sometimes violent cat-and-mouse game with people trying to cross illegally. The Great Recession slowed traffic considerably. Apprehensions in the San Diego sector, which numbered around 300,000 a year in the 1980s, dropped to 30,000 in 2014. The Homeland Security Department credits the decline to the large increase in Border Patrol officers. Local agents also seized 48 percent of the amphetamines and 38 percent of cocaine of the totals that were seized nationwide. Credit was due, in part, to the discovery of two tunnels that connected warehouses on the two sides of the border.

Thousands of legal workers cross the border daily to reach the industrial zone on San Diego's southern edge, in Otay Mesa and San Ysidro and the industrial suburbs of Chula Vista and National City. Many children from Mexico cross daily to attend public and private schools. Latinos pour billions of dollars into the San Diego economy and are scattered in various parts of the city. Oddly, there is not much evidence of Mexican style in San Diego— less than in Los Angeles.

The thinly-populated and agricultural Imperial County to the east has faced enormous economic adversity. Its unemployment rate is routinely the highest in California, earning that distinction again in February 2015 with a 20% jobless rate. El Centro, a center for lettuce growers, had the second-highest jobless rate of any city in the nation, with 21%. Only Yuma Arizona was higher. The county is 81% Hispanic. Its salvation may lie in energy innovation. The first solar energy project in the Imperial Valley opened in 2013. Others were under construction or in development. In 2014, officials failed to bring to the area a factory to build battery-operated Tesla cars; instead, that went to Las Vegas. They struck a more limited economic deal, with a large plant to draw lithium—used in electric car batteries—from the Salton Sea. Even in the desert, California's water shortage has had consequences. A plan to restore the Salton Sea made little progress in more than a decade of review. The sea, which was created when the Colorado River over-ran its dikes in 1905, has suffered because its disappearing wetlands and fish now attract fewer migrating birds. That

2012 Presidential Vote		
Barack Obama (D) 115,610	(69%)
Mitt Romney (R)...................48,108	(29%)

2008 Presidential Vote		
Barack Obama (D) 112,197	(66%)
John McCain (R)...................54,780	(32%)

Cook Partisan Voting Index:	D+16

makes the remaining sea even saltier, and will have consequences, in turn, for human activity. For now, Valley farmers have received sufficient water from the Colorado River. But they face growing pressure to share those resources with the rest of the state.

The 51st Congressional District of California covers California's entire border with Mexico, including the southeast corner of San Diego, and also National City and part of Chula Vista. It includes the Salton Sea basin in the eastern desert and the Tijuana River National Estuarine Research Reserve on the western coast. About one-fourth of the vote is cast in Imperial County. The district is 69 percent Hispanic, and solidly Democratic.

Juan Vargas (D)

Democrat Juan Vargas, first elected in 2012, has taken control of the district that he had sought for years.

Vargas was born in National City, just south of San Diego. He is the son of *braceros*, legal Mexican immigrants brought to the U.S. for cheap labor. Vargas grew up on a chicken ranch in an urbanized area. He calls it a "great upbringing, something very cool and different from my suburban neighbors." While other kids at school had dogs and cats, Vargas had pet ducks. "I used to fly them for exercise. I'd throw them in the air, and they'd fly around, and I'd catch them. The other kids thought this was the coolest thing," he told *National Journal*. Vargas considered entering the priesthood but said he was wary of going straight into a seminary. Instead, he attended the University of San Diego, graduating in 1983. After college, Vargas studied with the Jesuits, working with the poor, orphans, and refugees in El Salvador and elsewhere. The Jesuits sent him to Fordham University, where he studied philosophy and earned a master's degree. At Fordham, he met his future wife, Adrienne, a fellow student who worked with him at a soup kitchen in the Bronx. Vargas moved on to Harvard, where he earned a law degree in 1991 alongside a student named Barack Obama. Vargas guarded the future president in pickup basketball games and says Obama was the more talented player.

After law school, the Vargases settled in San Diego, where he briefly worked at a large corporate law firm. Vargas was elected to the San Diego City Council in 1993. In 2000, he won election to the California Assembly, where he stayed for six years. In 2010, he won election to the state Senate, where he took pro-union stances and advocated government support for children and the elderly. He sponsored a bill mandating the reporting of child abuse by athletic coaches in California, a direct response to the Pennsylvania State University sex abuse scandal.

Vargas ran three unsuccessful campaigns for Congress against Rep. Bob Filner in Democratic primaries before Filner retired and was elected mayor of San Diego. In their 2006 contest, both men ran intensely negative campaigns, but Filner prevailed thanks to strong support from Imperial County.

In 2012, political observers expected Vargas and fellow Latino Democrat Denise Moreno Ducheny to advance in California's new jungle primary, in which the top two finishers, regardless of party, compete in the general election. But Vargas lavished attention on the Republican candidate, Michael Crimmins, in order to help him slide into second place. Vargas refused to participate in a debate unless Crimmins was included. Meanwhile, Vargas hammered Ducheny for a previous drunken-driving arrest. Crimmins ultimately edged Ducheny 20%-15%, and went on to face Vargas in the fall election, when his defeat was all but assured in the strongly Democratic district that is two-thirds Latino. It was a smart strategy. Vargas won 71%-29%.

In the House, Vargas sought to provide a sympathetic ear to immigrants and refugees, no matter their circumstances. After protestors turned away busloads in Murrieta, he met with them the next day in El Centro in July 2014. Carrying a Bible, Vargas prayed with them and told them that they would be treated "fairly and with dignity." He did not promise that they would remain in the United States. In December 2013, he joined a day-long fast in Washington on behalf of immigration reform. With Republican Rep. Duncan Hunter, he filed a bill to provide protection and a "safe haven" for local Chaldean Christians who had been threatened by their religious leaders in Iraq.

Vargas had no trouble with reelection in 2014. His opponent, Stephen Meade, was 88 years old, spent no money, preferred to be called Stephanie and dressed like a woman (though he was married to a woman). The Republican Party gave him no assistance.

FIFTY-SECOND DISTRICT

Scott Peters (D)

Elected 2012, 2nd term; b. June 17, 1958, Springfield, OH; Duke U., B.A. 1980, NY U., J.D. 1984; Lutheran; married (Lynn Gorguze); 2 children.

Elected Office: San Diego City Cncl., 2000-08, pres., 2006-08.

Professional Career: Economist, U.S. Environmental Protection Agency, 1980-81; Deputy atty., San Diego City, 1991-96; Practicing atty., 1984-91, 1996-2000; CA Commission on Tax Policy in the New Economy, 2002-03; CA Coastal Commission, 2002-05; San Diego Unified Port District Commission, 2009-2012.

DC Office: 1122 LHOB, 20515, 202-225-0508; Website: scottpeters. house.gov.

State Offices: San Diego, 858-455-5550.

Committees: *Armed Services:* Readiness; Seapower & Projection Forces. *Judiciary:* Courts, Intellectual Property, & the Internet; Regulatory Reform, Commercial, & Antitrust Law.

Group Ratings

	ADA	ACLU	AFL-CIO	LCV	ITI	COC	HAFA	ACU	CFG	FRC
2014	60%	77%	–	86%	60%	64%	20%	4%	24%	0%
2013	50%	C	81%	100%	C	69%	C	24%	22%	C

National Journal Ratings

	2013 LIB	—	2013 CONS
Economic	58%	—	42%
Social	57%	—	43%
Foreign	64%	—	36%
Composite	60%	—	40%

Key Votes of the 113th Congress

1. Sandy storm spending	Y	5. Medical Marijuana	Y	9. Syrian Rebels Training	Y
2. Violence Against Women Act	Y	6. Farm Bill	N	10. Keystone pipeline	N
3. Guantanamo Bay Detainees	Y	7. Afghanistan Combat	N	11. Immigration Exec. Action	N
4. Abortion 20-week ban	N	8. NSA Phone Data Collection	N	12. Bipartisan budget deal	Y

Election Results

2014 general	Scott Peters (D)	98,826	(52%)	$4,504,003	$602,301	$2,985,437
	Carl DeMaio (R)	92,746	(48%)	$3,349,677	$550,991	$3,758,158
2014 primary	Scott Peters (D)	53,926	(42%)			
	Carl DeMaio (R)	44,954	(35%)			
	Kirk Jorgensen (R)	23,588	(19%)			

Prior winning percentage: 2012 (51%)

Population		Race and Ethnicity		Income	
Total:	713,904	White	59.6%	Median income:	$82,286
Urban:	81.2%	Asian	19.2%		*(26 of 435)*
Suburban:	18.8%	Latino	13.8%	Under $50,000	30.6%
Rural:	0.0%	Black	3.1%	$50,000-$99,999:	27.2%
Land area:	374	Two races	3.5%	$100,000-$199,999:	30.1%
Pop/sq. mi.:	1,909.1	White Ethnic	26.8%	$200,000 or more:	12.2%
Born in state:	42.1%			Poverty Rate	10.5%
		Education			
Age Groups		H.S. grad or less:	17.7%	**Work**	
Under 18:	20.0%	Some college:	27.2%	White collar:	56.1%
18 to 34:	29.1%	College degree, 4 yr.:	31.5%	Blue collar:	35.3%
35 to 64:	37.6%	Post-grad study:	23.6%	Sales and service:	8.6%
Over 64:	13.3%			Govt. workers:	13.8%
		Military			
		Veterans/active duty:	13.5%		

Northern San Diego: La Jolla, Mission Bay

When the United States was dictating the terms of the Treaty of Guadalupe Hidalgo in 1848 after its successful war with Mexico, it made sure the southern boundary of its new California territory was just south of the port of San Diego. This is one

Voter Turnout	
2013 Total Citizen 18+	509,614
2014 House Turnout	191,572
2014 Turnout as % CVAP	37.6%
2012 Turnout as % CVAP	61.7%

of three splendid natural harbors on the Pacific Coast, and in 1914, the Marine Corps established a base on North Island. This was just the first of many military bases in San Diego, with its mild climate, deep harbor, and plentiful land for aircraft maneuvers. Naval Base San Diego has been the major West Coast U.S. Navy base for more than 50 years, the second-largest Navy port behind Norfolk, and home to 117,000 active-duty personnel, split about evenly between the Navy and Marine Corps. Separate from the Naval facilities, the port generates more than 57,000 jobs and $7.6 billion in economic activity. Also located here are more than 240,000 veterans, and the retired aircraft carrier *Midway*.

The port and Navy base in the sheltered harbor remain the central focus of a rapidly growing metropolis that now stretches far inland and to the north. Downtown features post-modern buildings like the Horton Plaza amid a few well-preserved early-20th-century relics like the Spreckels Theatre. Across the harbor, on the sand spit that guards it against the ocean, is the white frame castle of the Hotel Del Coronado, with its surprisingly dark wooden interior—the U.S.'s largest wooden structure, opened in 1888 and a favored resort of past American presidents. The San Diego metro area economy has had slow, steady growth. Unemployment in San Diego County in December 2014 was 5.2 percent, below the statewide and national rates.

2012 Presidential Vote		
Barack Obama (D) 163,911	(52%)
Mitt Romney (R)................143,726	(46%)

2008 Presidential Vote		
Barack Obama (D) 183,911	(55%)
John McCain (R)................143,372	(43%)

Cook Partisan Voting Index: D+2

Growth in health sciences, biotech and telecommunications contribute to what San Diego calls its "innovation industry."

San Diego is not all Navy. To the north, the Pacific waves pound against the beach beneath erose cliffs of unique rock formations along the coast. Part of La Jolla is here, including the Scripps Institute of Oceanography. To the south are raffish Mission Beach; Ocean Beach, with its strong rip currents; and Point Loma, overlooking the entrance to the harbor. The weather—a sunny 70 degrees most of the time—lures tourists and new residents. The area's warm climate nourishes prodigious baseball talent. Boston Red Sox great Ted Williams grew up here. In his book *Moneyball*, author Michael Lewis says Rancho Bernardo High School in San Diego came to be known in baseball circles as "The Factory," because it produced so many big league prospects. San Diego is also home to Comic-Con International, a four-day comic book and pop culture event that caps its attendance at 130,000 people annually.

The 52nd Congressional District includes most of the city of San Diego. It is one of two districts that are entirely within San Diego County; three others are based largely in the county, but reach into adjacent counties. It runs along the west coast, taking in most of the city's Navy installations, ports, and beaches. Inland and north of San Diego, it includes high-income Poway. It shares La Jolla with the 49th District to its north. The district has a sizable liberal population and a growing Hispanic community. Politically, it has become a competitive congressional battleground, though it leans a bit Democratic in presidential contests.

Scott Peters (D)

Scott Peters, first elected in 2012 with help from a redrawn congressional district made four points more Democratic in redistricting, has survived two costly and tight campaigns against experienced local Republicans. That success has benefited from his occasional distancing from the liberal views of most congressional Democrats from California.

Peters is the son of a Lutheran minister who fought against redlining in Detroit in the 1960s, when African-Americans and Jews were prevented from buying homes in some neighborhoods. After a threat against his family sparked a police chief to suggest his father take them out of town for a week, Peters went on his first plane ride—a trip to Washington—at around age 8. He was "kind of taken by it," and got a book on the presidents and memorized their names in order. At age 14, while the family was briefly living in Chicago, Peters had his first taste of politics campaigning for Democrat George McGovern's unsuccessful 1972 presidential race. He studied political science and economics at Duke, taking a low-wage job cleaning pigeon cages for the psychology department to support himself. He went on to graduate from New York University's law school.

His wife, Lynn Gorguze, forged a successful career in private equity, and her work brought them to San Diego in 1988. She is the daughter of a wealthy La Jolla industrialist who was a contributor to Republican presidential candidate Mitt Romney. Peters had a wide-ranging, 16-year career as a lawyer handling environmental regulation, corporate taxes, and litigation at various firms; served as a deputy county counsel; and opened a private practice before being elected to the city council in 2000. During two back-to-back terms on the council—the last three years as president—Peters worked on reducing sewage spills, redeveloping neighborhoods to make them more walkable, boosting jobs with support for a downtown ballpark, and creating the city's first ethics commission. Peters also served on the San Diego Port Commission and California Coastal Commission. In January 2015, *Roll Call* ranked Peters as the eighth wealthiest member of Congress, with a net worth of $45 million.

In 2012, Peters endured a bruising primary battle against Lori Saldaña, a former state Assembly member. She drew support from a left-leaning coalition of environmentalists and other liberal activists, but Peters snagged endorsements from a host of Democratic officials, including local Rep. Bob Filner, a liberal firebrand. Despite outspending Saldaña by 5-to-1, Peters eked out a victory by just 700 votes.

Running against three-term Republican Rep. Brian Bilbray, Peters found himself on the defensive against GOP attacks that he underfunded public-employee pensions during his tenure on the council, something that had marred his unsuccessful race for city attorney in 2009. He responded by accusing Bilbray of talking as a moderate while voting as a conservative, and he regularly touted his desire not to be bound by ideology. "I'm just not a purist. You set goals and you have to work with everyone to figure out how to get what you can," he said.

Peters self-financed his campaign with more than $1 million and was one of the Democratic Congressional Campaign Committee's top "Red to Blue" candidates for picking up Republican-leaning seats. In an unusual pattern, Peters outspent the incumbent, $4.3 million to $2.8 million. He won with 51.2% of the vote to Bilbray's 48.8%.

In the House, he was among a small group of Democrats who voted with a majority of their party only about 80 percent of the time, according to an April 2015 analysis by *The New York Times*. He distanced himself from liberal icon Democratic Sen. Elizabeth Warren of Massachusetts by saying that he seeks to avoid "bashing business." He tried to remain a political outsider by creating and publicizing his #FixCongressNow plan of broad changes in how Congress and elections operate, including five-day work weeks. He said that Democrats "must move beyond economic fairness and now take the lead on creating an agenda for economic growth." But he also pursued some actions of a congressional insider, including his post as a senior whip with House Minority Whip Steny Hoyer. He lined up in favor of steps to combat climate change, protect seniors on Medicare, and promote immigration reform. On the House Armed Services Committee, he encouraged bipartisanship and protection of San Diego's Navy interests.

Even with all of these steps, he faced a difficult reelection in 2014 against Republican Carl DeMaio, a former member of the city council who had been praised for his efforts to improve the shaky finances of the city and narrowly lost a 2012 run for mayor of San Diego. DeMaio, who is openly gay, sought to move beyond traditional Republican support. In the first round of the election, Peters got 42% of the vote with DeMaio at 36%, and three Republicans divided the remainder. That was a clear sign that Peters was vulnerable.

DeMaio styled himself as a "next generation Republican," but Peters ran a tough ad campaign that focused on the challenger's sometimes abrasive style and hardline positions on the city council. DeMaio was put on the defensive by charges of sexual harassment and bribery that were made by a former campaign aide. In one of the most expensive House contests in the nation, Peters outspent DeMaio, $4.5 million to $3.4 million, and the two candidates split another $7 million in national party money. In a close count that was not settled until three days after the election, Peters won 51.6%-48.4%—very close to his 2012 outcome. Jacquie Atkinson, an openly lesbian Marine Corps combat veteran, voiced early interest in challenging Peters in 2016.

FIFTY-THIRD DISTRICT

Susan Davis (D)

Elected 2000, 8th term; b. April 13, 1944, Cambridge, MA; U. of CA Berkeley, B.A. 1965, U. of NC, M.S.W. 1968; Jewish; married (Steve); 2 children.

Elected Office: San Diego Schl. Bd., 1983-92, pres., 1989-92; CA Assembly, 1994-2000.

Professional Career: Devel. assoc., KPBS Radio, 1980-82.; Exec. dir., Aaron Price Fellows, 1990-94.

DC Office: 1214 LHOB, 20515, 202-225-2040; Fax: 202-225-2948; Website: susandavis.house.gov.

State Offices: San Diego, 619-280-5353.

Committees: *Armed Services:* Military Personnel (RMM); Readiness. *Education & the Workforce:* Early Childhood, Elementary & Secondary Education; Higher Education & Workforce Training.

Group Ratings

	ADA	ACLU	AFL-CIO	LCV	ITI	COC	HAFA	ACU	CFG	FRC
2014	75%	77%	–	97%	20%	50%	8%	0%	2%	13%
2013	75%	C	90%	96%	C	23%	C	12%	12%	C

National Journal Ratings

	2013 LIB	—	2013 CONS
Economic	76%	—	22%
Social	87%	—	7%
Foreign	77%	—	22%
Composite	82%	—	19%

Key Votes of the 113th Congress

1. Sandy storm spending	Y	5. Medical Marijuana	Y	9. Syrian Rebels Training	Y
2. Violence Against Women Act	Y	6. Farm Bill	N	10. Keystone pipeline	N
3. Guantanamo Bay Detainees	Y	7. Afghanistan Combat	N	11. Immigration Exec. Action	N
4. Abortion 20-week ban	N	8. NSA Phone Data Collection	N	12. Bipartisan budget deal	Y

Election Results

2014 general	Susan Davis (D)	87,104	(59%)	$541,155	
	Larry Wilske (R)	60,940	(41%)	$94,098	$3,366
2014 primary	Susan Davis (D)	50,041	(56%)		
	Larry Wilske (R)	18,384	(21%)		
	Wayne True (R)	9,182	(10%)		

Prior winning percentages: 2012 (61%), 2010 (62%), 2008 (68%), 2006 (68%), 2004 (66%), 2002 (62%), 2000 (50%)

Population		Race and Ethnicity		Income	
Total:	741,909	White	43.0%	Median income:	$61,021
Urban:	78.8%	Latino	32.3%		*(114 of 435)*
Suburban:	21.2%	Asian	13.1%	Under $50,000	40.9%
Rural:	0.0%	Black	7.0%	$50,000-$99,999:	32.8%
Land area:	168	Two races	3.8%	$100,000-$199,999:	21.6%
Pop/sq. mi.:	4,403.4	White Ethnic	19.8%	$200,000 or more:	4.8%
Born in state:	49.3%			Poverty Rate	14.1%
		Education			
Age Groups		H.S. grad or less:	31.1%	**Work**	
Under 18:	21.6%	Some college:	34.3%	White collar:	41.3%
18 to 34:	28.4%	College degree, 4 yr.:	21.6%	Blue collar:	44.1%
35 to 64:	38.2%	Post-grad study:	13.0%	Sales and service:	14.6%
Over 64:	11.8%				
		Military		Govt. workers:	18.3%
		Veterans/active duty:	12.7%		

East San Diego, La Mesa

Often thought of as California's most conservative, straight-arrow city because of its long association with the U.S. Navy and the military, San Diego is now a multi-ethnic metropolis, with a population that is roughly 30% Hispanic and 16% Asian. In a sense, the city is returning to its roots. Although it

Voter Turnout	
2013 Total Citizen 18+	509,208
2014 House Turnout	148,044
2014 Turnout as % CVAP	29.1%
2012 Turnout as % CVAP	56.4%

was the first European settlement in what is now California, San Diego was a part of newly independent Mexico in the early 1800s, and did not join the United States until after the Mexican-American War. It sits directly across the border from the Tijuana metropolitan area, and roughly 300,000 people a day cross from one city to the other.

San Diego recently has had a stormy and unconventional political history. In November 2012, the city elected 10-term Democratic Rep. Bob Filner as mayor. He was the city's first Democratic leader in 20 years. But he almost immediately ran into ethical problems and survived only seven months before he resigned under pressure and in the face of sexual harassment allegations by at least 18 women. He said he had been the victim of "the hysteria of a lynch mob." He later pleaded guilty to a false imprisonment charge, and served three months of home confinement. In February 2014, Republican Kevin Faulconer won a special election to fill Filner's term. Of all Republican mayors in the nation, he led the largest city. Faulconer had been a member of the city council and a public relations executive. The city is projected to continue its rapid growth rate, with a nearly 50 percent increase by 2050. Most of that likely will come from Hispanics.

2012 Presidential Vote		
Barack Obama (D) 174,616	(61%)	
Mitt Romney (R)................103,513	(36%)	

2008 Presidential Vote		
Barack Obama (D) 182,282	(62%)	
John McCain (R)................108,696	(37%)	

Cook Partisan Voting Index: D+10

The 53rd Congressional District is geographically the smallest San Diego-area district, taking in the eastern edge of the city and points inland to include the suburbs of Lemon Grove and Spring Valley. It includes La Mesa and La Presa, which is 47 percent Hispanic. Like the neighboring 52nd, this district has an active gay and lesbian presence. In 2012, the San Diego City Council renamed a street here after Harvey Milk, the gay San Francisco city official who was slain in office by a disgruntled former colleague. Milk, whose life was the subject of the 2008 biographical film *Milk*, lived in San Diego while serving in the Navy. The district has a number of parks, lakes, and open space preserves. In December 2014, a northern white rhinoceros died at the San Diego Zoo, leaving only five remaining in captivity. The zoo is among the 10 largest in the world.

Susan Davis (D)

Susan Davis, a Democrat first elected in 2000, is a low-profile member who avoids the media spotlight and splashy speeches for C-SPAN viewers in favor of working quietly behind the scenes on issues that range from women's health to allowing more voting by mail.

Davis grew up in Richmond California, the daughter of a pediatrician. She graduated from the University of California, Berkeley, and got a degree in social work at the University of North Carolina. After she married, she and her husband lived for a time in Japan while he served as an Air Force doctor during the Vietnam War. In 1972, they moved to San Diego. She was a producer for a local television station while also volunteering in civic groups, including as president of the local League of Women Voters. In 1983, she was elected to the San Diego school board. In 1994, she won the first of three terms in the California Assembly, where she chaired the Consumer Protection Committee.

Facing term limits, Davis in 2000 challenged Rep. Brian Bilbray, a Republican who had won three close elections. She portrayed him as too conservative for the district, though he took liberal and moderate positions on abortion rights and environmental protection. Bilbray had voted with conservatives to impeach President Bill Clinton in 1998, and Davis also attacked him for supporting bills that would deny citizenship to U.S.-born children of illegal immigrants. The AFL-CIO ran so much advertising on her behalf that Davis asked the union to stop. Davis won 50%-46%, and has been reelected without a serious challenge. Bilbray returned to Congress in June 2006 when he won a special election in the neighboring district, though he lost his seat a second time in 2012.

In the House, Davis has a liberal voting record but tends to be more centrist on foreign policy. Assigned to the Armed Services and Education and the Workforce committees, she set priorities that have included higher military pay, increased aid for school districts with a large military presence, increased student loans, and incentives for better teachers. She angered organized labor by voting to give President George W. Bush wide authority to negotiate international trade deals, which unions opposed. She called the vote "agonizing," but one that served the interests of a city that has been built on trade. Organized labor rescinded its endorsement of her. She has joined with several other Democrats to sponsor a bill ensuring that pregnant women are not forced out of jobs or denied reasonable job modifications that would allow them to continue working.

On Armed Services, she has been active on women's health issues. She sought to amend the fiscal 2012 defense authorization bill to cover abortions for military women who were victims of rape, but the Rules Committee blocked the move. She supported President Barack Obama's troop buildup in Afghanistan, but cautioned that greater civilian support and involvement from U.S. allies were essential. In 2009, as chairman of the Armed Services' Personnel Subcommittee, she helped secure a higher military pay raise than Obama requested.

Davis has been reelected with ease. She received an unusual amount of attention in 2012 when she filed a lawsuit to try to recover $160,000 in campaign funds that were siphoned by her one-time campaign treasurer, who pleaded guilty to stealing more than $7 million from Davis and other California lawmakers. The conflict was resolved in 2014 with a legal settlement that returned $90,000 to her campaign account. In July 2013, Davis urged San Diego Mayor Bob Filner to step down following mounting charges of sexual harassment. "His behavior, if not illegal, is reprehensible," she said of her former colleague in Congress and on the school board. He resigned a month later. In 2014, against modest Republican opposition, Davis posted weak reelection performances. In the first round, she got 56% of the vote against seven other candidates, none of them a Democrat. In November against Larry Wilske, whom she outspent by more than 5-to-1, Davis won with 59%. That was not immediate jeopardy, but her performance had weakened in a district where Barack Obama twice won more than 60% of the vote.

★ COLORADO ★

One summer day in 1893, Katherine Lee Bates, an English teacher at Colorado College, made her way by prairie wagon and mule up 14,114-foot Pikes Peak. Inspiration struck as she looked out over the spacious skies from the purple mountain's majesty to the amber waves of grain on the fruited plain, and she wrote the first version of *America the Beautiful*. Set to music, her words have resonated ever since, even though more than 90 percent of Americans up through World War II lived east of the Rockies, which rise above Denver, Boulder and Colorado Springs on the mile-high plateau. Colorado, the centennial state admitted to the Union in 1876, with its magnificent and contrasting landscapes, has long had a hold on the American imagination. And Colorado, as it has developed over the years, has been at the front edge of economic, cultural and political change. For all its scenery, it is demographically an urban state, with nearly half its 5 million people in metropolitan Denver and four-fifths in the urban strip paralleling the Front Range. And it is a healthy state, with the nation's lowest rates of obesity and highest rates of physical activity and health-club membership. You burn off more calories when you live, as most Coloradans do, around 5,000 feet above sea level.

Colorado started off with a boom, and its history has been one of occasional booms and long pauses of moderate growth. The first boom came after the Civil War, when gold and silver were discovered in the Rockies, and you can still see the grand opera houses and courthouses built in those years in Cripple Creek and Central City, Aspen and Telluride. But mining boom towns tend to go bust, and Denver, on the South Platte River just east of the mountains, soon became the region's leading city—a meatpacking, banking, and manufacturing center, the state capital and regional headquarters of the federal government. The state Capitol, standing exactly 5,280 feet above sea level, sports a dome of gold leaf, which was refurbished in 2011 and 2012 with a donation of 72 ounces of gold from the same mine in Cripple Creek that supplied the original gold.

To the north and west, the Capitol overlooks Denver's vigorous downtown, with skyscrapers built during the energy boom of the 1970s and the telecom boom of the 1990s. Off toward the usually dry river bed are the retro Coors Field baseball park and the Lower Downtown neighborhood with warehouses renovated into restaurants and clubs. Metro Denver stretches in all directions. To the east is the startling architecture of the Denver International Airport on the plains, its canopy suggesting the snow-capped Rockies, pioneers' covered wagons and Native American teepees. To the south is the sprawling Denver Tech Center, and all around are fast-growing tracts of subdivisions. Colorado has grown faster than the national average, but it has not had the explosive growth experienced by Arizona and Nevada in recent decades. Its housing bubble never inflated as much as theirs did, and foreclosure rates were much lower after housing prices crashed. Unemployment has tracked below the national average, peaking at 8.9 percent in the fall of 2010 and falling to 4.2 percent by March 2015. Colorado has attracted fewer retirees and low-skill immigrants than those states, and more young adults. Many of them have high education levels, and they are are eager to make a good living in what has generally been a growth economy, and to live in a state with a uniquely healthy, outdoors-minded environment. Coloradans like to jog, bike and of course, ski. Denver is famous for its large park system and many bike paths, and Boulder is a national center for bungee jumping, mountain biking, snowshoe running and hot-air ballooning. The public and local officials were angered in August 2015 by a spill of mining waste water at a site near Durango that federal officials had been cleaning up.

Most strikingly, Coloradans voted to make their state the first jurisdiction in the world to fully license the manufacture, cultivation and sale of marijuana. In its first year, 2014, marijuana became a $700 million industry, with hundreds of shops opening for recreational and medicinal sales, mostly in the highest-population areas. (Jurisdictions can choose whether to allow marijuana sales.) Unexpected problems emerged—difficulty in regulating "edibles," smaller-than-expected tax revenues due to the persistence of the black market—but with public opinion heading in a pro-marijuana direction, no one expected the clock to be turned back.

Colorado has been reshaped, economically and politically, by its successive waves of newcomers, who have increased the state's population from 1.7 million in 1960 to more than 5 million today. The conservative and boosterish Colorado of the 1960s was transformed in the 1970s by young liberal migrants who swept the state's politics by calling for environmental

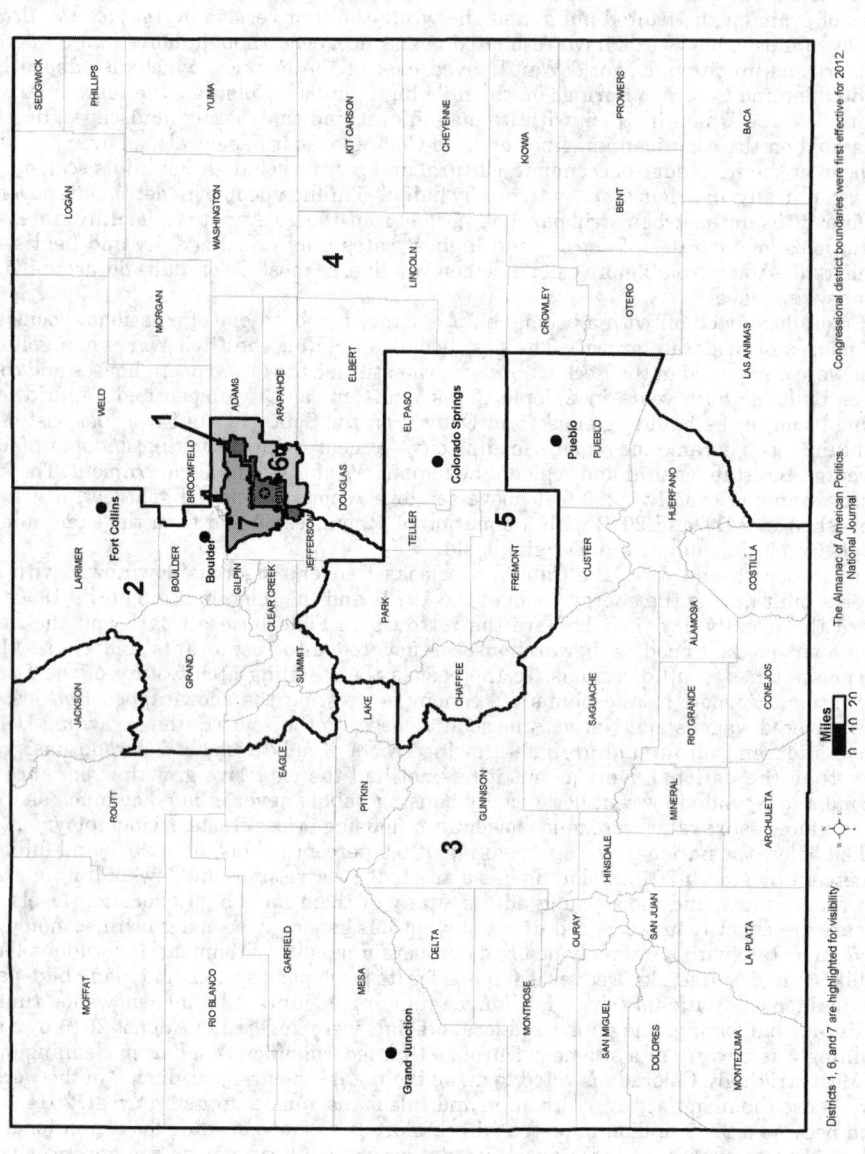

Districts 1, 6, and 7 are highlighted for visibility.

The Almanac of American Politics,
National Journal

Congressional district boundaries were first effective for 2012.

protections and slow growth. Its national leaders reflected this trend—Gov. Dick Lamm, Sen. Gary Hart, Rep. Patricia Schroeder, and Rep. Tim Wirth. Then in the 1990s, a new wave of migrants—tech-savvy, family-oriented cultural conservatives looking for an environment in which to prosper—moved Colorado's politics to the right. In that decade, private school enrollment was up 33 percent and the number of home-schooled children tripled. If the spirit of the 1970s newcomers was embodied in Boulder, with its pedestrian mall, outdoor sports shops, vegetarian restaurants, and politically dominant environmentalist liberals, the spirit of the 1990s newcomers was dominated by religious conservatives in Colorado Springs, the home of the Air Force Academy, Fort Carson, and Dr. James Dobson's Focus on the Family. Both of these politically divergent communities have some reason to believe that they exemplify the state. Colorado elections can be viewed as contests to determine which one actually does.

The victories of the liberal Democrats in the 1970s, starting with the 1972 referendum keeping the Winter Olympics out of Denver, were followed by a long period in which Republicans held control of the legislature and the state's congressional delegation. The victories of the conservative Republicans in the 1990s, starting with the 1990 referendum imposing term limits and the 1992 Taxpayers' Bill of Rights requiring referenda to raise taxes, were followed by a resurgence of the Democratic Party, led by liberal entrepreneurs such as Jared Polis, now the 2nd District representative, who was part of a "Gang of Four," including QuarkXPress founder Tim Gill, medical device heiress Patricia Stryker and geophysicist and MicroMAX software creator Rutt Bridges. The group nurtured a web of liberal activist organizations and shrewdly framed and targeted issues, ultimately reshaping the political landscape. They took advantage of favorable demographic trends. Colorado's Latino population now stands at 21 percent, the seventh-highest percentage of any state. The state also has one of the nation's youngest populations, with large university enclaves. In 2014, the *New York Times* pithily contrasted neighboring Weld County, GOP-dominated territory with 20,000 oil and gas wells, and Boulder, 15 miles to the west, "where a Buddhist-inspired university offers classes in yoga and the Tibetan language, and nature activists are working to carve out legal rights for ecosystems and wild species." Denver and Boulder attract young professionals imbued with liberal values; the ski resorts—Telluride, Aspen, Vail, Crested Butte, Steamboat Springs—are inhabited by the wealthy and the people who wait on them in boutiques and restaurants, and both groups lean Democratic.

Between 2002 and 2008, the polarities of power switched. Republicans were dominant in 2002, with majorities in both houses of the legislature, both Senate seats, and five of the seven House seats. Six years later, the Democrats were in charge. In 2008, Democrats held their convention in Denver, unbothered by the fact that their last national convention there, exactly 100 years before in 1908, nominated the losing ticket of William Jennings Bryan and John W. Kern. This time they nominated the winning ticket of Barack Obama and Joe Biden, and Colorado, not one of the most highly targeted states in 2004, gave the Democrats a solid majority in the general election.

The competition in 2010 and 2012 was closer. In 2010, Democrats prevailed at the top of the ticket, but with unimpressive percentages. Appointed Sen. Michael Bennet held on against tea party-supported Weld County District Attorney Ken Buck 48%-47%, and Democratic Denver Mayor John Hickenlooper succeeded fellow Democrat Bill Ritter with 51

Population		Race and Ethnicity		Income	
Total:	5,268,367	White	69.6%	Median income:	$63,371
Urban:	53.5%	Latino	20.9%		(5 of 50)
Suburban:	32.2%	Black	3.8%	Under $50,000	42.9%
Rural:	14.3%	Asian	2.7%	$50,000-$99,999:	31.4%
Land area:	103,642	Two races	2.2%	$100,000-$199,999:	20.3%
Pop/sq. mi.:	50.8	White Ethnic	26.9%	$200,000 or more:	5.4%
Born in state:	43.4%			Poverty Rate	11.4%
		Education			
Age Groups		H.S. grad or less:	31.1%	**Work**	
Under 18:	23.6%	Some college:	31.1%	White collar:	40.1%
18 to 34:	24.5%	College degree, 4 yr.:	23.8%	Blue collar:	41.6%
35 to 64:	39.7%	Post-grad study:	14.0%	Sales and service:	18.3%
Over 64:	12.2%				
		Military		Govt. workers:	13.8%
		Veterans/active duty:	10.0%		

percent of the vote in a three-way race. Further down the ballot, Republicans won all four statewide races, regained the 3rd and 4th district House seats they'd lost in 2006 and 2008, and secured a majority in the state House. Two years later, Democrats did a little better. Barack Obama carried the state 51%-46%, and Democrats won sufficient state House seats to secure unified control of the legislature. But Republicans held onto four of the seven U.S. House seats.

Voter Turnout	
2013 Total Citizen 18+	3,756,032
2014 Highest Statewide Turnout	2,041,020
2014 Turnout as % CVAP	54.3%
2012 Turnout as % CVAP	69.8%

Legislature			
Senate:	18R	17D	
House:	33D	31R	1V

In 2013 and 2014, Democrats were disabused of any sense of invincibility. The newly all-Democratic legislature ruffled feathers by enacting several liberal-leaning bills, most notably a gun control measure in the wake of the state's second firearm massacre, at a movie screening in the Denver suburb of Aurora. The measure imposed background checks for private gun sales and a cap on ammunition magazines of 15 rounds. In a low-turnout recall election, two Democratic lawmakers who had voted for the gun bill were ousted in a fight that drew in both the National Rifle Association and gun-control supporters like New York City Mayor Michael Bloomberg. Energy policy became a Democratic worry as well. In the run-up to the 2014 midterm election, Hickenlooper was sufficiently concerned about the risk to his party of ballot measures critical of fracking that he struck a deal to keep them (along with industry-backed measures) off the ballot, while also creating an 18-member task force to study the issue. On Election Day, Democratic Sen. Mark Udall, who began the election cycle seeming not especially vulnerable, lost to GOP Rep. Cory Gardner by 2 points after focusing excessively on abortion and other social issues; the GOP took over the state Senate and fell just short in the state House. Hickenlooper—like Gardner, buoyed by his personality—prevailed by 3 points. Udall underperformed in Pueblo County, a Democratic stronghold but one with blue-collar, religious, gun-friendly voters; he beat Gardner by a few hundred votes there, even though Bennet had carried it by almost 11,000 four years earlier. Meanwhile, Republican turnout rose in GOP-leaning counties such as El Paso and Douglas. The election demonstrated that, at a time when most states are dominated politically by one party, Colorado still preserves a vigorous two-party competition.

Presidential Politics When it comes to presidential contests, Colorado tends to swing from one political party to the other more than the nation as a whole: It cast higher percentages for Democrat Barack Obama and Republican George W. Bush than their national averages, as it did for Republicans Ronald Reagan, Richard Nixon and Dwight Eisenhower, and for Democrats Lyndon Johnson and Harry Truman.

2012 Presidential Vote		
Barack Obama (D)	1,323,101	(51%)
Mitt Romney (R)	1,185,243	(46%)

2012 Presidential Caucus		
Rick Santorum (R)	26,614	(40%)
Mitt Romney (R)	23,012	(35%)
Newt Gingrich (R)	8,445	(13%)
Ron Paul (R)	7,759	(12%)

2008 Presidential Vote		
Barack Obama (D)	1,288,576	(54%)
John McCain (R)	1,073,589	(45%)

Colorado wasn't always competitive: Between Johnson in 1964 and Obama in 2008 and 2012, the only Democrat to carry Colorado was Bill Clinton in 1992, and it's likely that independent candidate Ross Perot siphoned off enough Republican voters from George H.W. Bush to produce that outcome. But Democrats had Colorado in their sights when they selected Denver as the location for their 2008 national convention. Obama formally accepted the nomination in Mile High Stadium, the first outdoor venue for an acceptance speech since John F. Kennedy addressed Democratic delegates in the Los Angeles Coliseum in 1960. Colorado Democrats loved the show, and general election turnout was up from 2004 in heavily Democratic Denver and Boulder counties, despite low population growth. Turnout rose less in the heavily Republican Douglas County exurbs and Colorado Springs' El Paso County. Obama was the first Democrat since LBJ to capture the three large suburban counties around Denver: Adams, Arapahoe and Jefferson. The exit poll showed Obama carrying Latinos by 61%-38%, but also showed him winning whites, 50%-48%.

In 2012, Colorado was once again a target state. And it was again the scene of a significant campaign event, the first presidential debate at the University of Denver on October 3. Mitt Romney's strong performance gave him a boost, but the Obama campaign did an excellent job of getting its supporters to the polls, and he won narrower majorities in suburban Adams, Arapahoe and Jefferson. Fueled by the defection of college-educated whites, Obama lost whites overall to Romney, 54%-44%, according to the exit poll. But that survey also showed Obama sweeping Latinos 75%-23%—a big increase over 2008 and enough to account for his margin of victory in the state.

Colorado had an early March presidential primary from 1992 until 2000, which never attracted much national attention. In 2003, to save money, the legislature voted to eliminate the presidential primary and let the parties hold caucuses, and both chose to vote on Super Tuesday, February 5, in 2008. The Democratic caucuses attracted 120,000 voters, the Republican caucuses only 70,000, a harbinger for November's outcome. Enthusiasm for Obama and his campaign's superior organizational skills—demonstrated repeatedly in caucuses that year—produced a 67%-32% victory over Hillary Clinton. Mitt Romney, the only Republican to put much effort into the GOP caucuses, won with 60 percent of the vote; McCain got only 18 percent and Mike Huckabee 13 percent.

In 2012, Republicans held caucuses on February 7, and turnout slipped to 66,000. Romney won Denver and its upscale suburbs, and counties in the northwestern corner of the state with relatively high-paying coal jobs and resorts such as Steamboat Springs. But Rick Santorum carried much of the rest of the state including El Paso County—an evangelical stronghold where turnout was highest—by 47%-31%, and he won the state overall, 40%-35%.

Congressional Districts   After the 2010 census, the two parties had a lengthy and bitter stalemate in the state legislature that forced the federal courts to intervene. A Denver district judge chose a Democratic plan for the sake of making the Republican-held 6th District south of Denver more "com-

114th Congress Lineup	
4 R	3 D
113th Congress Lineup	
4 R	3 D

petitive." The outcome was similar to the 2001 redistricting, except that the battleground district in that showdown was the new 7th District north of Denver; Democrat Ed Perlmutter captured that seat in 2006 after it had initially been won by a Republican.

The latest map's biggest shift was to remove nearly all of heavily Republican Douglas County from the 6th District and replace it with increasingly Hispanic Aurora to the north, making Republican Mike Coffman's seat seven percentage points less Republican. But as in 2002, the payoff for Democrats has not been immediate. In 2012, Coffman escaped with a 48%-46% win after Democrats failed to recruit a strong candidate. Democrats ran a more credible challenger in 2014 with Andrew Romanoff, a former state House speaker. But Romanoff was the victim of the Republicans' nationwide surge, and Coffman stepped up his campaigning to take an unexpectedly strong 52%-43% victory.

With Colorado's history of shifting voter dynamics, competitive House contests could return soon to the 6th District and perhaps elsewhere. The state appears likely to gain an additional House seat after the 2020 census, which again could be located in competitive suburban or exurban areas outside Denver.

Governor

John Hickenlooper (D)

Elected 2010, term expires Jan. 2019, 2nd term; b. Feb. 7, 1952, Narberth, PA; Wesleyan U., B.A. 1974, M.A. 1980; Episcopalian; separated; 1 child.

Elected Office: Denver mayor, 2003-10.

Professional Career: Geologist, restaurateur, 1980-2003.

Office: 136 State Capitol Bldg, Denver, 80203-1792, 303-866-2471; Fax: 303-866-2003; Website: colorado.gov/governor.

Election Results

2014 General	John Hickenlooper (D)	1,006,433	(49%)
	Bob Beauprez (R)	938,195	(46%)
2014 Primary	John Hickenlooper (D)	unopposed	

Prior winning percentage: 2010 (51%)

Democrat John Hickenlooper, a beer entrepreneur with a penchant for reaching across the aisle, was elected governor of Colorado in 2010. During his first two years in office, his response to two major crises won him plaudits, and *Esquire* magazine named him one of its "Americans of the Year" in 2012. His approval rating subsequently plummeted, and though he found himself in a tough reelection fight, he managed to prevail in the strong GOP year of 2014.

"Hick," as he's known in Colorado newspaper headlines, grew up in the Philadelphia suburbs, raised by a frugal widowed mother. He is a descendant of the Revolutionary War financier Robert Morris "My great-grandparents were Quakers. And I tried to take that ethic into business. Quaker honesty, Quaker mindfulness, that effort to build community across differences," he told *The Philadelphia Inquirer*. He graduated from Wesleyan University, first studying English, and then getting a master's degree in geology. He moved to Colorado in 1981 and took a job in the oil industry. When oil prices fell in the 1980s, he was laid off. On a trip to the San Francisco Bay area, he stopped in at a brewpub, then a rarity. He thought the concept might work in Denver, and in 1988, he opened the Wynkoop Brewery, the first brewpub in Colorado, in the warehouse district northwest of downtown Denver. He ended up starting 14 restaurants and spearheaded development of the Lower Downtown as an entertainment district. Today LoDo is buzzing with activity.

Hickenlooper's business success got his friends talking about him running for mayor of Denver in 2003 to succeed term-limited incumbent Wellington Webb. Hickenlooper and city Auditor Don Mares were the top two finishers in a six-candidate field; their June 2003 runoff was noteworthy for its lack of vitriol. Hickenlooper refused to run negative ads and campaigned against "the nonsense of government," including parking meter rates. One television ad showed Hickenlooper with a change maker around his waist, thrusting quarters into meters. He also pledged to cut the city payroll by 4 percent. He beat Mares, 65%-35%.

As mayor, Hickenlooper reached out to suburban officials and to Republican Gov. Bill Owens. In 2004, he got all 32 mayors in metro Denver to support a ballot proposition instituting a 0.4% sales tax to raise $4.7 billion for a light rail system. He also got voters to approve the largest bond issue in the city's history, a permanent property tax increase and a tax increase for early childhood education. Hickenlooper also took control of the city's troubled public schools and installed his chief of staff, Michael Bennet, now a senator, as superintendent and charged him with using innovative ways to increase school performance. His 2005 program to increase energy efficiency and decrease carbon emissions reduced energy use per passenger by 11 percent at Denver International Airport and increased recycling in the city by 69 percent.

In 2007, Hickenlooper won a second term as mayor. When Democrat Bill Ritter was elected governor, the two worked together successfully to bring the 2008 Democratic National Convention to Denver. But they differed on other issues. Ritter favored restrictions on abortion rights, a position that put him at odds with many Democrats, and he favored limits on oil and gas drilling, which the business community opposed. Hickenlooper tended to take the opposite stands. In December 2008, when President Barack Obama appointed Democratic Sen. Ken Salazar as Interior secretary, it was widely expected that Ritter would appoint Hickenlooper to fill Salazar's Senate seat. Instead, Ritter appointed schools chief Bennet.

In January 2010, Ritter said he would not seek a second term. Obama called Hickenlooper and asked him to run. A week later, he agreed. While he quickly won Ritter's endorsement, he also criticized Ritter's rulemaking process and said he was "coming from a very different place" on oil and gas issues, saying he wanted to cut red tape, not increase it. Despite Hickenlooper's popularity in the Denver media market, which covers much of the state, Republicans seemed to have a serious chance to regain the office they lost in 2006. But one by one, their candidates imploded. In the spring of 2010, former Rep. Scott McInnis was competitive with Hickenlooper in the polls, but in July, it was revealed that a paper on water issues for which McInnis had been paid $300,000 by a think tank was in large part plagiarized. The narrow GOP primary winner, tea party-aligned businessman Daniel Maes, promptly fell into trouble for problems with his businesses and personal finances; then, newspaper reports indicated that he had seriously misstated his work as a police officer in Liberal, Kansas, some years before. Saying Maes was unacceptable, former U.S. Rep. Tom Tancredo, who had run a quixotic presidential campaign in 2008 as a hard-core opponent of illegal immigration, announced a bid on a third-party line. Blessed with such flawed opponents, Hickenlooper won with 51 percent, compared to 36 percent for Tancredo and just 11 percent for the Republican nominee, Maes.

Hickenlooper used the story of his work in converting Colorado Springs' old Cheyenne Hotel into a successful brewpub as a metaphor for how the state could emerge from the recession. He created an economic-development initiative that subsequently came out with a report called "the Colorado Blueprint," which called for creating a business-friendly environment. He submitted a spending plan that made $570 million in cuts on top of those that Ritter had proposed—with spending on elementary education taking the biggest hit—while raising the state's general fund reserve from 2 to 4 percent. An improved revenue forecast helped bring down the size of the education cuts, and Hickenlooper won positive marks for his willingness to broker differences between the Democratic-controlled Senate and the Republican-led House. The split between the chambers prevented bills on contentious issues such as gun rights and illegal immigration from reaching his desk. But he was able to get through a measure creating state health care exchanges as part of Obama's new federal health care law. Polls showed him with strong approval ratings among both Republicans and Democrats, and even conservative columnist George Will hailed him as an example for the Democratic Party to follow.

Entering his second year, Hickenlooper called for substantially increasing spending for economic development and announced plans to follow neighboring New Mexico in creating a "spaceport" for commercial rockets. He got into a tussle with Republicans over a property tax break for seniors that cost the state $100 million a year. Hickenlooper said suspending the tax break would help avoid further cuts to schools, while Republicans countered that the state should instead reduce spending on Medicaid. When revenues were forecast to come in an estimated $231 million higher than previously expected, the governor boosted spending on schools. But Hickenlooper was unable to overcome Republican resistance to a bill allowing civil unions for same-sex couples.

To deal with the wildfires that ravaged the state, he flew home from a trade mission to Mexico to be on the front lines, listening to rescue workers' requests. He subsequently called for more water storage and conservation to ease the effects of future droughts. His approval rating in polls reached 60 percent, prompting some in Colorado political circles to begin wondering if he would be a future presidential candidate. Despite a foray to New Hampshire, Hickenlooper downplayed such talk, saying he didn't feel like he was the right type of person for the job. In 2012, he amicably separated from his wife of 10 years, author Helen Thorpe; their announcement included the guidance, "Please feel free to include both of us in social gatherings as we will not find it awkward."

Ironically, Democratic legislative gains in the 2012 election helped dim Hickenlooper's popularity, as lawmakers from his own party pushed him to the left. Hickenlooper took heat for signing controversial gun control legislation in the wake of the movie theater massacre for which 24-year-old James Holmes in Aurora was convicted in July 2015, but spared the death penalty. He reportedly told an audience of county sheriffs that he regretted passing the measures because the uproar that they caused, and that he had not spoken to New York City Mayor Michael Bloomberg—a staunch backer of gun control—about the bills, though he acknowledged later that the two had talked. Hickenlooper also took heat for his stances on energy issues, especially his refusal to express an opinion about the Keystone XL pipeline project. "I've avoided taking a position because it's just going to piss off a lot of people in Washington that I don't need to piss off," he told the *Durango Herald*, "and my opinion is not going to change anybody's opinion there." Another unpopular move was his decision to grant what he called a "temporary reprieve" to Nathan Dunlap, a murderer convicted of the shooting deaths of four people at a Chuck E. Cheese in suburban Denver in 1993.

In 2014, former Rep. and 2006 gubernatorial nominee Republican Bob Beauprez was a late entrant into the race to challenge Hickenlooper's bid for a second term, but Beauprez managed to win the four-way GOP primary with 30 percent. By mid-September, polls showed the race tightening. Despite the Democrats' dismal showing nationally and in Colorado, Hickenlooper pulled off a 49%-46% victory. The win enabled Hickenlooper to, among other things, continue as chairman of the National Governors Association, a post he had assumed in July 2014.

By 2015, the state had completed the first year of voter-approved legalization of recreational marijuana, and while it quickly became a $700 million industry, with hundreds of shops opening for recreational and medicinal sales, it also brought public-safety challenges and lower-than-expected tax revenues for the state. Hickenlooper, who had opposed legalization from the beginning, said afterward that "If I could've waved a wand the day after the election, I would've reversed the election and said, 'This was a bad idea.'" His budget proposals for 2015 included a $480 million increase for K-12 education, $107 million more for higher education, a $30 million boost to the Colorado Opportunity Scholarship Initiative, and $6.6 million for child-welfare caseworkers. He also pushed a felony DUI bill (only three other states didn't have one) as well as efforts to expand bicycle infrastructure. After Hickenlooper's close electoral call in November 2014, his popularity rose again. In the spring of 2015, he had a 53%-37% job approval rating, much improved from the 48%-46% rating he had in July 2014.

Senior Senator

Michael Bennet (D)

Appointed Jan. 2009, term expires 2016, 1st full term; b. Nov. 28, 1964, New Delhi, India; Wesleyan U., B.A. 1987, Yale U., J.D. 1993; no religious affiliation; married (Susan Daggett); 3 children.

Professional Career: Dep. atty. gen., U.S. Dept. of Justice, 1995-97; Managing dir., Anschutz Investment Co., 1997-2003; Chief of staff, Denver Mayor John Hickenlooper, 2003-05; Superintendent, Denver Public Schl., 2005-09.

DC Office: 458 RSOB, 20510, 202-224-5852; Fax: 202-228-5097; Website: bennet.senate.gov.

State Offices: Alamosa, 719-587-0096; Colorado Springs, 719-328-1100; Denver, 303-455-7600; Durango, 970-259-1710; Fort Collins, 970-224-2200; Grand Junction, 970-241-6631; Pueblo, 719-542-7550.

Committees: *Agriculture, Nutrition & Forestry:* Conservation, Forestry & Natural Resources; Rural Development & Energy; Commodities, Risk Management & Trade; Nutrition, Specialty Crops, Food & Ag Research; *Finance:* Energy, Natural Resources & Infrastructure (RMM); Taxation & IRS Oversight; *Health, Education, Labor & Pensions:* Children & Families; Primary Health & Retirement Security.

Group Ratings

	ADA	ACLU	AFL-CIO	LCV	ITI	COC	HAFA	ACU	CFG	FRC
2014	90%	100%	–	60%	100%	38%	2%	4%	12%	0%
2013	85%	C	100%	92%	C	38%	C	8%	3%	C

National Journal Ratings

	2013 LIB	—	2013 CONS
Economic	62%	—	36%
Social	64%	—	34%
Foreign	66%	—	29%
Composite	66%	—	35%

Key Votes of the 113th Congress

1. Sandy storm spending	Y	5. Student Loan Rates	Y	9. Bipartisan Budget Deal	Y
2. Chuck Hagel Confirmation	Y	6. Employee Non-Discrim'n Act	Y	10. Farm Bill Conference Rept.	Y
3. Gun Background Checks	Y	7. Senate Vote on Judgeships	N	11. Unempl. Comp. Extension	Y
4. Immigration Reform	Y	8. Defense Dept. Spending	Y	12. Keystone Pipeline	Y

Election Results

2010 general	Michael Bennet (D)	851,590	(48%)	$13,082,057 $2,358,708 $11,777,405
	Ken Buck (R)	822,731	(46%)	$4,795,277 $3,839,471 $11,817,234
	Bob Kinsey (Green)	38,768	(2%)	
2010 primary	Michael Bennet (D)	184,714	(54%)	
	Andrew Romanoff (D)	156,419	(46%)	

Colorado's senior senator is Michael Bennet, a Democrat appointed by Gov. Bill Ritter in January 2009 to succeed Ken Salazar, who had been named Interior secretary by President Barack Obama. Though not well-known when he was selected, Bennett, still boyish-looking at 50, pulled off an impressive 2010 victory to win the seat in his own right. Two years later, he entered the leadership ranks as chairman of the Democratic Senatorial Campaign Committee. Bennet stepped aside in 2015 to concentrate on his 2016 reelection.

Bennet was born in New Delhi, India, where his father, Douglas Bennet, was an aide to Ambassador Chester Bowles. His mother and her family were Jews who emigrated from Poland after World War II. His younger brother, James, has been *The Atlantic*'s editor-in-chief since 2006. Michael grew up and attended private schools in Washington, D.C., while his father pursued his career in public service. Douglas Bennet was a staffer for Vice President Hubert Humphrey, an assistant secretary of state in the Carter administration and later president of National Public Radio.

The younger Bennet graduated from Wesleyan University and then went to work as an aide to Ohio Democratic Gov. Richard Celeste, a family friend. In 1990, Bennet entered Yale Law School, where he went on to be editor-in-chief of the *Yale Law Journal*. He clerked for a federal judge in Baltimore, where he met his wife, Susan Daggett, before joining Lloyd Cutler's influential law firm in Washington. In 1995, he was named counsel to Deputy Attorney General Jamie Gorelick in the Clinton administration and wrote speeches for Attorney General Janet Reno.

In 1997, he moved to Denver, where his wife, a natural resources lawyer, went to work for the Earthjustice Legal Defense Fund. Bennet took a job with the investment company headed by billionaire Philip Anschutz, a political conservative. Bennet had never read a balance sheet, and Anschutz told him to attend accounting school at night at his own expense. Eventually, Bennet landed big assignments, such as restructuring $3 billion in debt for several companies, including Forcenergy, Regal Cinemas, United Artists, and Edwards Theatres. He also oversaw the consolidation of the three theater chains into Regal Entertainment Group, the world's largest movie theater company.

In 2003, a fellow Wesleyan alumnus, John Hickenlooper, was elected Denver mayor and asked Bennet to be his chief of staff. Bennet says he gave up millions in stock options to accept "an opportunity that wouldn't come around again." He worked on balancing the budget, mediating a dispute between United and Frontier airlines at Denver International Airport, and brokering agreements with public-employee unions. "I have referred to him as the second mayor, the hidden mayor," Hickenlooper, who later became governor, told *The Denver Post*.

In 2005, the position of Denver Public Schools superintendent came open, and Bennet was among the 14 top candidates—even though he had no experience in education, had attended private schools, and was sending his daughter to a private kindergarten. The board picked him to head a system of 73,000 students, three-quarters of whom were Latino or African-American and two-thirds of them were eligible for the school lunch program. He instituted a "Denver Plan," which boosted performance standards in the schools and created workshops to teach principals how to lead schools to reform. An early childhood education program was put in place, and more than 90 percent of five-year-olds attended full-day kindergarten. By 2008, test scores were on the rise, but Denver schools still performed below statewide levels. Only 46 percent of Denver students showed proficiency in reading and 35 percent in math, compared to the statewide averages of 68 percent and 53 percent, respectively.

When Obama was running for president in 2008, Bennet co-hosted a fundraiser for the then-Illinois senator. He was later included in the Democratic candidate's weekly education conference calls, along with innovative big city school heads. After Obama was elected, Bennet was on the short list for Secretary of Education, although Obama ultimately chose Chicago schools chief Arne Duncan. Yet Bennet was not even considered a long shot to be selected Senator after Obama named Salazar his Interior secretary. Democratic Gov. Ritter had to appoint a replacement to serve until Salazar's Senate seat came up for reelection in 2010. Bennet had limited national experience that consisted mainly of a 2004 speech he gave to a group of business leaders denouncing the Iraq war and President George W. Bush.

The more obvious candidates were outgoing state House Speaker Andrew Romanoff, who had ties to Democratic politicians and activists across the state, and Hickenlooper, Bennet's mentor, who was well-known and popular throughout the state. On January 2, 2009, Ritter astonished just about everyone by naming Bennet, saying he was impressed with his record of bringing diverse interests together to solve problems and by his pragmatic approach to turning around troubled public and private enterprises. Republican leaders relished the prospect of taking on a candidate far less formidable electorally than Hickenlooper or Romanoff in 2010.

Once in office, Bennet tackled a number of government reforms, including measures to restrict the use of the filibuster and to tighten campaign finance rules. He dug into legislating with gusto. On the Health, Education, Labor, and Pensions Committee, he introduced a bill in August 2010 to strengthen the Food and Drug Administration's ability to identify and prevent tainted drugs from reaching consumers. The measure—one of the rare examples of bipartisan cooperation after the 2010 election—became law in July 2012. Drawing on his experience with Denver's schools, he added more than half a dozen proposals to the reauthorization of the No Child Left Behind education law, including tying new teacher licensing to performance and increasing the flexibility of school districts in spending federal money. During the fight over health insurance reform, he secured Senate passage of an amendment that established a deficit-neutral reserve fund to address inequities in Medicare and Medicaid reimbursements to providers. It also required Medicare savings to be invested back into the program.

As he prepared to seek election to the seat in his own right in 2010, he drew a fierce challenge in the Democratic primary from former state House Speaker Romanoff, who portrayed himself as the outsider in the race and attacked Bennet, a one-time investment banker, as a tool of Wall Street. He also accused Bennet of failing to support the public health insurance option component of health care reform, which liberals favored. Bennet proved to be a strong fundraiser and heavily outspent Romanoff. He insisted that he had supported the public option, which was left out of the final health care law because of opposition from party conservatives. He suffered a setback when *The New York Times* ran a story that said Bennet's efforts to eliminate a $400 million hole in the pension fund when he was Denver schools chief ended up forcing the school district further into debt. The article ran just four days before the primary, as Romanoff was surging in the polls. However, in a year that was widely viewed as tough for incumbents, Bennet defeated Romanoff 54% to 46%.

In November, Bennet faced another tough contest against Weld County District Attorney Ken Buck, who had won the GOP nomination over the establishment Republican candidate, former Lt. Gov. Jane Norton, with the backing of tea party activists. Buck portrayed Bennet as part of the problem in big-spending Washington, and attacked his votes for Obama's $787 billion economic stimulus bill and the health care legislation. Buck called for dismantling the Department of Education, advocated replacing the income tax with a national sales tax, and said he opposed abortion in all circumstances. He was also gaffe-prone. Bennet and the Democrats made an issue of his 2005 decision as district attorney not to prosecute an accused rapist because a jury would likely conclude that her complaint was a case of "buyer's remorse." In an appearance on *Meet the Press*, Buck compared homosexuality to alcoholism, saying, "I think that birth has an influence over it, like alcoholism and some other things. But I think that basically, you have a choice."

With $11.5 million in campaign funds, Bennet saturated the airwaves with Buck's missteps and portrayed him as too extreme for Colorado's independent-minded voters. Buck raised $5 million and had help from the GOP-friendly American Crossroads, which invested $5 million in negative ads against Bennet. But the Democrat held the upper hand in the air war in spite of his votes for major elements of the Obama agenda, which were hurting Democratic incumbents elsewhere. Colorado College political scientist Bob Loevy told *The Denver Post*, "To a very large extent, Bennet made the issue not about the national economy, but about the characteristics of Ken Buck."

Bennet won 48% to 46%. Exit polls showed that he was heavily favored by independent voters and benefited from a significant gender gap. Women voted for Bennet over Buck 56% to 40%; he carried unaffiliated voters 52% to 41%, and Hispanics by 2-to-1. None of this escaped the attention of Obama's reelection campaign, which used much the same strategy in 2012 against Republican Mitt Romney. "We did stitch together a winning coalition in 2010, and I think that coalition is part of the basis of what they are doing here in Colorado," Bennet told *The New York Times*.

Bennet is quick to join bipartisan coalitions. In recent years, he joined a group of senators to tackle comprehensive immigration reform, and he also worked with Tennessee Republican Lamar Alexander in trying to find a bipartisan way to escape the looming "fiscal cliff" in late 2012 through a package of tax cuts and deductions as well as entitlement reform. Bennet was one of only three Senate Democrats to oppose the final agreement on New Year's Eve 2013, saying it "does not put in place a real process to reduce the debt down the road." Also in 2012, Bennet was disappointed when his work to extend tax credits for wind energy stalled after running into Republican resistance. The difficulty of getting bills to the finish line prompted him to tell *The Washington Post* in March 2012, "My chief of staff said to me, 'You know it's not okay to hate your job.' And he's right. There's no point in wallowing in self-pity. No one's going to feel sorry for you."

Shortly after the 2012 election, Senate Majority Leader Harry Reid offered Bennet the DSCC chairmanship, but it took Bennet three weeks to agree to take the position. He was reluctant because he did not want the job if it would mean that it would interfere with his efforts to work across the aisle. Bennet decided to take up the challenge and, as compensation for the difficult task, he was awarded a coveted seat on the powerful Finance Committee. It turned out to be a disastrous election cycle for Democrats, who lost nine seats as well as control of the Senate. Among the political casualties was Bennett's good friend and Colorado colleague, Mark Udall, who ran a race similar to Bennet's in 2010, by stressing his opponent's "extreme" positions. The failure of that strategy surely will influence Bennet's game-plan in his reelection bid in 2016.

Despite the Democrats' dismal showing at the polls, Bennet seems to have largely escaped the second-guessing that inevitably follows such failures. Democrats, instead, quietly blamed the White House. At the same time, by serving in that DSCC job, Bennet got to know and work with the high-rollers in the party—folks who make big contributions and to whom Bennet can turn to for support in his reelection bid.

Bennet more recently showed his independence by joining only 13 other Democrats in the Senate to back construction of the controversial Keystone XL Pipeline. On the other hand, he came out forcefully against the letter signed by 47 Republicans, including his Colorado colleague Gardner, that warned Iran's leaders that reaching an agreement with President Obama without congressional approval was nothing more than an executive agreement that could be short-lived since it could be undone by a future President or Congress. The letter infuriated the White House and a number of Democratic senators, including Bennet, as an inappropriate interference in the conduct of foreign policy. "This letter is completely counterproductive and I cannot say enough about the seven Republicans who were wise enough not to sign it," Bennet said in a statement.

Still, after Gardner defeated Udall, the newly-elected Republican senator met with Bennet and they both stressed their desire to work together, especially on energy issues. They agreed not only on the Keystone Pipeline but also on the need for an "all of the above" approach to energy in which they favor renewable sources, such as wind, while they also have vowed to protect Colorado's liquid natural gas industry. At least part of Bennet's message going into his reelection campaign will likely be that he can work across the aisle and has the independence to split with his party.

Junior Senator

Cory Gardner (R)

Elected 2014, 1st term; b. Aug. 22, 1974, Yuma; CO St. U., B.A. 1997, U. of CO, J.D. 2001; Lutheran; married (Jaime); 3 children.

Elected Office: CO House, 2005-10; U.S. House, 2011-2015.

Professional Career: Communications dir., Natl. Corn Growers Assn., 2001-02; Staffer, Sen. Wayne Allard, 2002-05; Owner, Farmers Implement dealership.

DC Office: 354 RSOB, 20510, 202-224-5941; Fax: 202-224-6524; Website: http://www.gardner.senate.gov/HomePage.

State Offices: Denver, 303-391-5777; Greeley, 970-352-5546; Grand Junction, 970-245-9553; Pueblo, 719-543-1324; Yuma, 970-848-3095.

Committees: *Commerce, Science, and Transportation*: Communications & Technology & the Internet; Consumer Protection, Product Safety, & Insurance; Space, Science, & Competitiveness. *Energy & Natural Resources*: Energy; Public Lands, Forests, & Mining; Water & Power. *Foreign Relations*: East Asian, The Pacific, & International Cybersecurity Policy (Chmn); Europe & Regional Security Cooperation; Multilateral Institutions, & International Economic, Energy, & Environmental Policy; Western Hemisphere, Transnational Crime, Civilian Security, Democracy, Human Rights, & Global Women's Issues; *Small Business & Entrepreneurship*.

Group Ratings (House)

	ADA	ACLU	AFL-CIO	LCV	ITI	COC	HAFA	ACU	CFG	FRC
2014	5%	11%	–	3%	100%	93%	56%	76%	82%	75%
2013	5%	C	22%	4%	C	85%	C	85%	69%	C

National Journal Ratings (House)

	2013 LIB	—	2013 CONS
Economic	25%	—	75%
Social	34%	—	62%
Foreign	5%	—	86%
Composite	24%	—	77%

Key Votes of the 113th Congress (House)

1. Sandy storm spending	N	5. Medical Marijuana	N	9. Syrian Rebels Training	Y

1. Sandy storm spending   N   5. Medical Marijuana   N   9. Syrian Rebels Training   Y
2. Violence Against Women Act   Y   6. Farm Bill   Y   10. Keystone pipeline   Y
3. Guantanamo Bay Detainees   N   7. Afghanistan Combat   N   11. Immigration Exec. Action   Y
4. Abortion 20-week ban   Y   8. NSA Phone Data Collection Y   12. Bipartisan budget deal   N

Election Results

2014 general	Cory Gardner (R)	983,891	(48%)	$12,490,384	$9,012,838	$30,646,858
	Mark Udall (D)	944,203	(46%)	$20,463,869	$6,684,190	$23,665,575
	Gaylon Kent (Lib)	52,876	(3%)			
2014 primary	Cory Gardner (R)	unopposed				

Prior winning percentages: House: 2012 (58%), 2010 (52%)

Republican Cory Gardner toppled Democratic Sen. Mark Udall in 2014 by waging a well-executed, nimble campaign that the GOP hopes will serve as a blueprint for a comeback for the party in Colorado. The youthful, affable two-term Congressman, with an ever-present upbeat disposition, took advantage of plummeting ratings for Udall and President Obama, while he overcame criticism that he was too conservative for the state.

Gardner grew up in Yuma, a tiny farming and ranching town 150 miles east of Denver. After graduating from Colorado State University, summa cum laude, Gardner returned to Yuma in pursuit of a pastoral lifestyle. But his father urged him to consider a profession less closely tied to the vagaries of Colorado's Eastern Plains. In 2001, Gardner earned a law degree from the University of Colorado and took a job as communications director for the National Corn Growers Association. The following year, he became an aide to Sen. Wayne Allard, a Republican. In the summer of 2005, Gardner was appointed to fill a vacancy in the Colorado House, and a year later he won election to a full term.

Believing Democratic Rep. Betsy Markey to be vulnerable in early 2010, state Republicans coalesced around Gardner. They saw him as a rising star and emphasized his deep roots in the district's heavily Republican Eastern Plains. Gardner pounded Markey for supporting Obama's spending policies while he skirted the social issues that could have potentially alienated suburban voters. His strategy worked, as Markey was on the defensive after having supported Obama's $787 billion economic stimulus bill and his health insurance overhaul. At age 36, Gardner won with 52 percent of the vote.

In the House, Gardner was one of his freshman class's most faithful followers of the GOP leadership. He befriended House Budget Committee Chairman Paul Ryan of Wisconsin, often joining Ryan on the vice presidential campaign trail in 2012. Gardner received a choice seat on the Energy and Commerce Committee and frequently assisted in House Republican messaging on energy matters. But Gardner's moves weren't all partisan, as he formed an Energy Savings Performance Caucus with Vermont Democrat Peter Welch in 2012.

After easily winning reelection with 58 percent of the vote over Colorado Senate President Brandon Shaffer, Gardner decided to take on Udall by running as a political outsider who could get things done in Washington. By contrast, he charged that Udall was a rubber-stamp for Senate Majority Leader Harry Reid of Nevada and a captive of Washington. Udall quickly responded by painting Gardner as extreme on social issues and ran ads attacking him on birth control and abortion—a theme that he would sound relentlessly throughout the campaign.

But Udall was criticized for relying too heavily on those issues. His constant charges that Gardner held positions that were hostile to women, reinforced by outside groups that spent lavishly, saturated the airwaves. But he did little to make a positive case for his re-election.

That campaign strategy backfired. In a big blow to Udall, *The Denver Post,* the state's largest newspaper, which typically backs Democrats, endorsed Gardner. "Udall is trying to frighten voters rather than inspire them. His obnoxious one-issue campaign is an insult to those he seeks to convince," the editorial said. Noting that Congress is hardly functional, the newspaper said that it needs "fresh leadership, energy and ideas, and Cory Gardner can help provide them in the U.S. Senate. In every position the Yuma Republican has held over the years—from the state legislature to U.S. House of Representatives—he has quickly become someone to be reckoned with and whose words carry weight."

Gardner said that he listened to voters and changed his stance on a "personhood" bill that could have resulted in a ban on certain forms of birth control. That responsiveness to constituent desires is a move, he said, that "Udall and President Obama can't relate to." On energy policy—always important to Colorado voters—he noted that he had long supported renewable sources, including wind and solar. On another major issue, Gardner shifted his position on immigration and supported a move to give undocumented immigrants who serve in the armed forces a path to citizenship. He also was one of only a handful of House Republicans to oppose a bill that sought to prevent Obama from granting work permits to immigrants who were brought to the U.S. illegally as children.

Those moves appeared to reassure voters that he was not the inflexible ideologue that the Democrats charged he was. In his victory statement to supporters, Gardner happily proclaimed: "Tonight, we shook up the Senate—*you* shook up the Senate." He elaborated, saying, "We have signed up to be the tip of the spear, the vanguard of the movement that is sweeping our nation, to pick the shackle of gridlock and fundamentally change the dysfunction of Washington, D.C."

After taking his Senate seat, Gardner showed that he is not a rock-the-boat, hard-charging disrupter on the Right. Instead, while reliably conservative, Gardner also has taken a step to shoot down Democrats' charges that his policies constitute a "war on women." He followed through on his campaign promise and sponsored legislation to make certain forms of contraception available over the counter. "It's time to allow women the ability to make their own decisions about safe, effective, and long-established methods of contraception," Gardner said in a statement. "Most other drugs with such a long history of safe and routine use are available for purchase over the counter, and contraception should join them."

That stance shows that Gardner is not about to let Democrats pigeonhole him. He knows that Colorado's population growth is driven largely by immigrants from California. And he defeated Udall in a race in which self-identified moderates cast over one-third of the ballots. Given those political dynamics, Gardner is likely to continue to try to thread the needle of reassuring moderates and independents that he is no reflexive ideologue, while also maintaining the support of those on the Right, including the Tea Party.

FIRST DISTRICT

Diana DeGette (D)

Elected 1996, 10th term; b. July 29, 1957, Tachikawa, Japan; CO Col., B.A. 1979, N.Y.U., J.D. 1982; Presbyterian; married (Lino Lipinsky); 2 children.

Elected Office: CO House, 1992-96, asst. min. ldr., 1994-95.

Professional Career: Practicing atty., 1982-96.

DC Office: 2368 RHOB, 20515, 202-225-4431; Fax: 202-225-5657; Website: degette.house.gov.

State Offices: Denver, 303-844-4988.

Committees: *Energy & Commerce:* Communications & Technology; Environment & the Economy; Oversight & Investigations (RMM).

Group Ratings

	ADA	ACLU	AFL-CIO	LCV	ITI	COC	HAFA	ACU	CFG	FRC
2014	85%	88%	–	97%	40%	38%	13%	8%	12%	0%
2013	80%	C	95%	89%	C	33%	C	8%	18%	C

National Journal Ratings

	2013 LIB	—	2013 CONS
Economic	79%	—	21%
Social	93%	—	0%
Foreign	94%	—	0%
Composite	91%	—	9%

Key Votes of the 113th Congress

1. Sandy storm spending	Y 5. Medical Marijuana	Y 9. Syrian Rebels Training	Y
2. Violence Against Women Act	Y 6. Farm Bill	N 10. Keystone pipeline	N
3. Guantanamo Bay Detainees	Y 7. Afghanistan Combat	Y 11. Immigration Exec. Action	N
4. Abortion 20-week ban	N 8. NSA Phone Data Collection	Y 12. Bipartisan budget deal	Y

Election Results

2014 general	Diana DeGette (D)	183,281	(66%)	$1,068,909
	Martin Walsh (R)	80,682	(29%)	$16,325
	Frank Atwood (Lib)	9,292	(3%)	
2014 primary	Diana DeGette (D)	unopposed		

Prior winning percentages: 2012 (68%), 2010 (67%), 2008 (72%), 2006 (80%), 2004 (73%), 2002 (66%), 2000 (69%), 1998 (67%), 1996 (57%)

Population		Race and Ethnicity		Income	
Total:	772,255	White	56.7%	Median income:	$53,271
Urban:	86.6%	Latino	29.0%		(183 of 435)
Suburban:	13.4%	Black	8.3%	Under $50,000	46.6%
Rural:	0.0%	Asian	3.4%	$50,000-$99,999:	28.3%
Land area:	223	Two races	1.9%	$100,000-$199,999:	18.8%
Pop/sq. mi.:	3,458.6	White Ethnic	24.6%	$200,000 or more:	6.3%
Born in state:	42.4%			Poverty Rate	16.9%
		Education			
Age Groups		H.S. grad or less:	31.1%	**Work**	
Under 18:	21.0%	Some college:	24.9%	White collar:	44.0%
18 to 34:	29.4%	College degree, 4 yr.:	27.2%	Blue collar:	41.0%
35 to 64:	38.6%	Post-grad study:	16.7%	Sales and service:	15.1%
Over 64:	11.0%				
		Military		Govt. workers:	11.1%
		Veterans/active duty:	6.6%		

Denver Metro

Denver is serious about being the Mile-High City: There are three markers on the granite steps of the gold-domed Capitol that proclaim the elevation of 5,280 feet. Denver is situated a few miles from where the High Plains yield to the sharp peaks of the Front Range of the Rockies. With 650,000 peo-

Voter Turnout	
2013 Total Citizen 18+	547,312
2014 House Turnout	278,491
2014 Turnout as % CVAP	50.9%
2012 Turnout as % CVAP	70.1%

ple in 2013, the city for a century has been the economic and cultural capital of the Rocky Mountain region. On top of its Old West heritage and early-20th-century elegance, Denver has developed an exuberant postmodern style. The National Western Stock Show held here every year and the LoDo entertainment district along the South Platte River evoke the Old West. The Capitol, the spacious parks, the aspens that line the streets, give the city a lush, burnished air, in contrast to the dry plains and stark peaks.

Amid its downtown grid are the skyscrapers of the 1970s energy boom and the 1990s high-tech boom, plus Coors Field, where Major League Baseball's Colorado Rockies play, the Elitch Gardens Theme and Water Park, and the expanded Denver Museum of Nature & Science. Barack Obama claimed the Democratic presidential nomination at Mile High Stadium in 2008, with great expectations. Rather than losing population as many central cities have, Denver has gained people since 1990. In 2014, it ranked sixth among the nation's fastest-growing cities. Most of its neighborhoods have vitality, including the African-American neighborhoods of northeastern Denver, filled with neat 1950s bungalows, and the Hispanic quarter northwest of downtown. But more than three-quarters of the metro area's people now live in the suburbs, and Denver has disproportionate numbers of singles and cultural liberals who value an urban and physically active lifestyle in the gentrified areas south of the Capitol. Its gay and lesbian population is the eighth largest among the nation's metropolitan areas. In early 2015, a local bakery that had prepared many cakes for gay-themed events generated national attention when it refused

2012 Presidential Vote		
Barack Obama (D) 254,400	(69%)	
Mitt Romney (R).................106,334	(29%)	
2008 Presidential Vote		
Barack Obama (D) 238,308	(71%)	
John McCain (R)..................92,831	(28%)	
Cook Partisan Voting Index: D+18		

to prepare a cake with an anti-gay message. The customer filed a religious-discrimination complaint with the state's department of regulatory agencies.

Denver is the liberal heart of Colorado. The city remains majority Anglo, but has elected Hispanic and black mayors and is now 32 percent Latino. In the early 1970s, Denver liberals were hostile to growth and boosterism. Today's Denver has shown that growth can produce more of the distinctiveness that people here appreciate. Civic pride was rampant during the 2008 convention, with an emphasis on the city's alternative energy projects. There was good reason: Denver has been ranked among the nation's top 10 cities in business climate, livability, libraries, and bikeways. In March 2015, economic researchers reported that Denver was one of four cities in the nation where housing prices exceeded pre-recession levels.

The 1st Congressional District covers all of Denver and stretches northeast to include Denver International Airport. It includes affluent suburbs, long-settled Englewood and newly settled Cherry Hills Village in Arapahoe County. The district drops southwest to include suburban parts of Jefferson County, such as Columbine and Ken Caryl. Columbine High School was the location of one of the worst mass shootings in U.S. history, when two teenage boys killed 13 people in April 1999. In an era when cultural attitudes are a better clue to voting behavior than economic status, this district, which last elected a Republican in 1970, is the only solid Democratic district in the state. More than 80 percent of the voters are in Denver, which is far more Democratic than the district's outlying county precincts.

Diana DeGette (D)

Diana DeGette, first elected in 1996, is an energetic liberal and a chief deputy whip who has been among the House Democrats anxiously awaiting the chance to succeed the party's older, entrenched leaders. But the blockage at the top may have moved the succession to a younger generation of Democrats.

DeGette is a fourth-generation resident of Denver, though she was born on a military base in Japan. She says that she was inspired at age 13 by the television show *Storefront Lawyers* to "crusade for justice," and decided she would be a public interest lawyer. She attended New York University's law school on a full scholarship, and then returned to Denver to practice employment law. In 1992, at age 35, DeGette was elected to the Colorado House. Her signature accomplishment was the Bubble Bill, which was aimed at protecting women at abortion clinics by making it illegal for protesters to come within eight feet of a person entering or leaving a health care facility. The legal battle over its constitutionality eventually reached the U.S. Supreme Court, which upheld the law in a 6-3 decision. In 1995, when Rep. Patricia Schroeder, a pioneer of the feminist left, announced she was retiring after 24 years in the House, DeGette decided to run for the seat. Organizationally adept, legislatively creative and politically liberal, she proved a worthy successor to Schroeder, one of the most well-known figures in Colorado politics.

In both the minority and the majority, she has managed to achieve legislative successes in the House. On the Energy and Commerce Committee, she has focused on health care issues. She teamed with Republican Rep. Mike Castle of Delaware to establish a bipartisan coalition to expand federal funds for stem cell research, which employs excess embryos from in vitro fertilization. President George W. Bush opposed more money for such research, but in 2005, DeGette and Castle won majority support in the House, and the Senate passed the bill a year later. Bush vetoed the bill. Ultimately, President Barack Obama, using his executive powers, removed most federal restrictions on stem cell research in 2009. She wrote a book on the topic called *Sex, Science, and Stem Cells*. She explained that she was inspired to take on the cause after one of her daughters was diagnosed with diabetes at age 4.

On other health issues, she co-sponsored in 2009, with her congressional mentor John Dingell of Michigan, the Food Safety Enhancement Act. She secured two key provisions giving the Food and Drug Administration the power to mandate product recalls and authorizing the FDA to establish a food-tracking system. The bill was passed by the House but stalled in the Senate. Mandatory recall authority for the FDA became law in the Food Safety Modernization Act in 2011. During the health care overhaul debate in 2009 and 2010, DeGette played a major role in shaping the final abortion provisions in the legislation. With Republican Energy and Commerce Chairman Fred Upton of Michigan, she launched an initiative in February 2015 to reduce the time for getting "breakthrough drugs" into the hands of needy patients. Their goal, she said, is to make the United States "the health care innovation capital of the world." In July, the House overwhelmingly passed their 21st Century Cures Act. As the senior Democrat on the panel's Oversight and Investigations Subcommittee since 2011, she has pursued many health-care interests.

DeGette has been active on other issues affecting Colorado and the West. She introduced a measure in 2012 to provide health insurance to seasonal firefighters—an idea that Obama also implemented with an executive order. After Colorado and Washington state in 2012 passed laws legalizing marijuana, she joined GOP Rep. Mike Coffman of Colorado in filing a bill that bars the federal government from pre-empting such state laws. "My constituents have spoken, and I don't want the federal government denying money to Colorado or taking other punitive steps that would undermine the will of our citizens," she said.

DeGette has been active in House leadership politics, but has had setbacks. In 2001, she supported Maryland's Steny Hoyer in his unsuccessful bid for Democratic whip against California's Nancy Pelosi, who went on to become House Speaker. When Hoyer got the job as party whip in 2002, Hoyer added DeGette to his whip team, and she moved into the role of party strategist. When Democrats gained control of the House in 2007, Hoyer became majority leader, and DeGette seriously considered running for whip against South Carolina's James Clyburn. She said she ultimately decided that it would have been disruptive to have another internal struggle. Clyburn made DeGette his chief deputy whip. "If the opportunity arose I would love to be whip," DeGette said. "I love to whip!" According to *The Denver Post* in June 2012, DeGette insists that she be referred to as the dean of the Colorado delegation and permitted to speak publicly at any event she attends.

As a mother of two children, who were just 2 and 6 years old when she was elected, DeGette tries to help newer members of Congress with children find a balance between family and public life. She advises newcomers to "carve out family time" because while service in Congress is finite, family relationships last a lifetime. She has had limited campaign opposition. In 2002, Ramona Martinez, a 15-year member of the Denver City Council and a Democratic National Committeewoman, criticized her for having lost touch with the district. DeGette returned her family to Denver from the Maryland suburbs in 2001 and won impressively, 73%-27%. According to a Twitter study, DeGette's Twitter account ranks among the highest for elected officials in reaching across the aisle.

SECOND DISTRICT

Jared Polis (D)

Elected 2008, 4th term; b. May 12, 1975, Boulder; Princeton U., B.A. 1996; Jewish; partner (Marlon Reis); 2 children.

Elected Office: CO Bd. of Education, 2001-07, Chmn. 2004, Vice Chmn., 2005-06.

Professional Career: Entrepreneur, 1996-2008.

DC Office: 1433 LHOB, 20515, 202-225-2161; Fax: 202-226-7840; Website: polis.house.gov.

State Offices: Boulder, 303-484-9596; Frisco, 970-409-7301; Fort Collins, 970-226-1239.

Committee: *Education & the Workforce:* Higher Education & Workforce Training; Health, Employment, Labor, & Pensions (RMM); *Rules Committee:* Legislative and Budget Process.

Group Ratings

	ADA	ACLU	AFL-CIO	LCV	ITI	COC	HAFA	ACU	CFG	FRC
2014	85%	88%	–	77%	40%	38%	19%	13%	15%	0%
2013	65%	C	85%	82%	C	46%	C	25%	34%	C

National Journal Ratings

	2013 LIB	—	2013 CONS
Economic	61%	—	38%
Social	66%	—	32%
Foreign	78%	—	21%
Composite	69%	—	31%

Key Votes of the 113th Congress

1. Sandy storm spending	Y	5. Medical Marijuana	Y	9. Syrian Rebels Training	N
2. Violence Against Women Act	Y	6. Farm Bill	N	10. Keystone pipeline	N
3. Guantanamo Bay Detainees	Y	7. Afghanistan Combat	NV	11. Immigration Exec. Action	N
4. Abortion 20-week ban	N	8. NSA Phone Data Collection	Y	12. Bipartisan budget deal	Y

Election Results

2014 general	Jared Polis (D)	196,300	(57%)	$1,207,969	$83,590
	George Leing (R)	149,645	(43%)	$302,504	
2014 primary	Jared Polis (D)	unopposed			

Prior winning percentages: 2012 (56%), 2010 (57%), 2008 (63%)

Population		Race and Ethnicity		Income	
Total:	755,671	White	84.4%	Median income:	$68,653
Urban:	43.1%	Latino	9.8%		(67 of 435)
Suburban:	48.4%	Asian	2.6%	Under $50,000	37.5%
Rural:	8.5%	Black	0.8%	$50,000-$99,999:	30.3%
Land area:	6,440	Two races	2.1%	$100,000-$199,999:	24.0%
Pop/sq. mi.:	117.3	White Ethnic	33.5%	$200,000 or more:	8.2%
Born in state:	36.5%			Poverty Rate	11.8%
		Education			
Age Groups		H.S. grad or less:	20.8%	**Work**	
Under 18:	20.5%	Some college:	27.8%	White collar:	45.9%
18 to 34:	26.9%	College degree, 4 yr.:	29.8%	Blue collar:	39.4%
35 to 64:	40.4%	Post-grad study:	21.6%	Sales and service:	14.8%
Over 64:	12.2%			Govt. workers:	14.0%
		Military			
		Veterans/active duty:	7.7%		

Northern Front Range: Fort Collins, Boulder

Voter Turnout	
2013 Total Citizen 18+	573,111
2014 House Turnout	345,945
2014 Turnout as % CVAP	60.4%
2012 Turnout as % CVAP	77.2%

Nestled against the Front Range of the Rocky Mountains is Boulder, home of the 30,000-student University of Colorado, once billed by the city as "a combination of Lycra-clad athletes, New Age artists, and thoughtful intellectuals sipping cappuccinos." Boulder is one of the nation's leading centers for bungee jumping, mountain biking, snowshoeing, rock and ice climbing, downhill skiing, land surfing, and hot-air ballooning. It has been called the nation's No. 1 town for outdoor sports by *Outdoor* magazine, and in 2014 continued to top *Portfolio.com*'s list of mid-sized metropolitan areas with the best quality of life. Marathoners from around the world train in several camps here. It is also the home of Boulder College of Massage Therapy and the Buddhist Naropa University, where Allen Ginsberg helped start a poetry school in 1974.

All have come here because of the setting. The streets of Boulder look up at craggy peaks rising to 14,000 feet from a mile-high plain stretching farther east than the eye can see. It has become a magnet for technology firms dissatisfied with the more congested Silicon Valley. The economics also have been appealing. Unemployment in Boulder has been among the lowest in the nation: 2.8 percent in December 2014. *Business Insider* in 2015 ranked Boulder 4th best in the nation among city economies. The Fort Collins-Loveland area, which is north of Boulder, has had a steady inflow of Millennials since the recession, and was number-one in

2014 in Gallup's Well-Being index that measures emotional and physical health in U.S. cities. Fort Collins opened in May 2014 a new rapid transit line. But the city has faced some challenges. The demographic changes have widened the local income gap. And grassroots groups were displeased when a local judge in August 2014 overturned the Fort Collins moratorium on hydraulic fracking.

2012 Presidential Vote		
Barack Obama (D) 255,208	(58%)
Mitt Romney (R).................174,028	(40%)

2008 Presidential Vote		
Barack Obama (D) 255,225	(61%)
John McCain (R).................154,907	(37%)

Cook Partisan Voting Index: D+8

The 2nd Congressional District is centered in Boulder. Interstate 70 charts a scenically awesome course through the mountains as it takes in Rocky Mountain acreage, and it is often congested with cars loaded with skis and snowboards. The district includes the old coal mining town of Central City, which describes itself as "the richest square mile on earth" and has been home to more than 15 casinos. The lodges and resorts of Vail are farther west on Interstate 70. Once dependent on mining and agriculture, Vail evolved into an international resort city after the 10th Mountain Division ski troops were introduced to the Eagle River Valley in the 1940s. After World War II, a group of Army buddies returned and developed a ski resort. Larimer County, with Fort Collins and Loveland, is the largest county in the district.

The district is comfortably Democratic. Boulder County is a partisan hub for Democrats, but the rest of the district is relatively balanced politically.

Jared Polis (D)

Jared Polis, a Democrat first elected in 2008, is the first man who was openly gay when he was elected to Congress. The multi-talented multimillionaire entrepreneur has diverse policy interests plus partisan ambitions, and he has become an important fundraiser for his party.

Polis was born in Boulder, but grew up in San Diego. His mother, a poet, and his father, an artist, were both politically active during the anti-war movement of the late 1960s and early 1970s. Polis and his younger brother and sister frequently accompanied their parents to demonstrations and rallies. Their activism spurred Polis' interest in politics and liberal ideas. He graduated from high school in three years, and got his bachelor degree in political science at Princeton University. Also fascinated by technology and business, Polis banded together with two friends in their sophomore year to launch a start-up called American Information Systems, an Internet access provider. Soon afterward, he founded *bluemountainarts.com*, an electronic greeting card site that at its height was the eighth most popular on the Internet. His next venture was *Proflowers.com*, which enables customers to order fresh flowers directly from growers. All three were successful, and Polis sold them for profits of upwards of $300 million. (He has distributed business cards in which he calls himself a "retired florist.")

Financial security allowed Polis to focus on his other passions. "I was always interested in public service. Education is an issue I feel very passionately about, providing an opportunity to all Americans," he said. In 2000, he was elected to the Colorado State Board of Education when he was four years out of college, serving for six years and as chairman for one year. Polis was most proud of his advancement of school choice through charter schools and his work improving accountability standards for schools. In part with his own money, he founded two innovative charter schools in Colorado, which helped new immigrants assimilate, especially 16-to- 21-year-old immigrants with flexible day or evening programs, and teachers trained to help students learn English. "We really needed a school to cater to their unique needs," Polis said. At the same time, he partnered with three other Colorado multimillionaires—who were dubbed the "Gang of Four" in newspapers—and built a political fundraising operation that raised $3.6 million in 2004.

When Democratic Rep. Mark Udall in Colorado's 2nd District decided to seek an open Senate seat in 2008, Polis ran to replace him. In the Democratic primary, he faced former state Senate President Joan Fitz-Gerald and conservationist Will Shafroth. Most of the state's Democratic establishment backed Fitz-Gerald, based on her political seasoning. Pouring his own money into the campaign, Polis outspent his opponents 4-to-1. In the August primary, he got 42% of the vote, followed by Fitz-Gerald with 38% and Shafroth with 20%. At age 33, he breezed through the general election, 63%-34%. In the entire campaign, he spent $7 million, of which $6 million was his own. The nonpartisan watchdog Center for Responsive Politics ranked Polis in 2013 as the fourth-wealthiest member of the House, pegging his net worth in the range of $213 million, based on his financial disclosure reports.

In Washington, Democratic leaders gave Polis a seat on the influential Rules Committee, whose majority-party members control the terms of debate for major bills on the House floor. He has had a medley of interests. In 2009, Polis jumped into the health care debate, fighting a proposal by his own party that would pay for elements of the overhauled system with a tax on wealthy Americans. Polis maintained that the tax would hurt small business owners who aren't large enough to organize as corporations. The proposed surtax was dropped from the sweeping overhaul enacted in 2010. He introduced a bill in May 2012 to prevent pizza from being counted as a vegetable in school lunches after a similar Department of Agriculture proposal met with resistance from the frozen food industry. He has taken an interest in budget issues. He was one of 22 Democrats in April 2012 who voted for a plan that was based on the recommendations of President Barack Obama's Simpson-Bowles deficit-reduction commission. On gay rights, he was the chief House sponsor of the Employee Non-Discrimination Act. Responding to objections from gay-rights groups in July 2014, he narrowed the religious exemption in his proposal. In June 2015, he was one of 28 House Democrats who voted to give trade promotion authority to Obama.

At home, he clashed with state Democratic leaders in 2014 when he threatened to force public votes in November on two referenda that would limit hydraulic fracking for oil and gas in Colorado. Many Democrats feared that the move would backfire by increasing the turnout of conservative voters. Polis backed down at the August deadline after Gov. John Hickenlooper agreed to review alternative policy options. That clash was featured in a July 2014 *Politico* profile that called his career a political paradox: "He's had a remarkable string of successes while engendering serious scorn" for his ambition, the Colorado-based reporter wrote. "He very much fits the stereotype of the tech entrepreneur, possessing an awkward, savvy genius and lacking refinement."

Polis has displayed an impressive fundraising ability among House Democrats, collecting from liberal interest groups and investment companies while donating money to politically vulnerable colleagues through his Jared Polis Victory Fund. Redistricting made his district slightly less Democratic in 2012, when he picked up all of Larimer County, which has traditionally been a swing area. He won that year 56%-39% over state Sen. Kevin Lundberg. His 2014 contest was a comparable 57%-43% win over Republican George Leing, a lawyer who has worked on energy and finance issues and chaired the Boulder GOP. He suffered a setback following the 2014 election when Minority Leader Nancy Pelosi named Rep. Ben Ray Lujan of New Mexico to chair the Democratic Congressional Campaign Committee. Polis had openly sought the position, though he responded that he was "relieved" that he would not be taking on the partisan post. The outcome is not likely to quell his ambition. Polis and his husband, Marlon Reis, announced the birth of their second child in July 2014.

THIRD DISTRICT

Scott Tipton (R)

Elected 2010, 3rd term; b. Nov. 9, 1956, Española, NM; Fort Lewis Col., B.A. 1978; Anglican / Episcopal; married (Jean); 2 children.

Elected Office: CO House, 2009-11.

Professional Career: Owner, CEO, Mesa Verde Pottery.

DC Office: 218 CHOB, 20515, 202-225-4761; Fax: 202-226-9669; Website: tipton.house.gov.

State Offices: Alamosa, 719-587-5105; Durango, 970-259-1490; Grand Junction, 970-241-2499; Pueblo, 719-542-1073.

Committees: *Financial Services*: Financial Institutions & Consumer Credit; Oversight & Investigations.

Group Ratings

	ADA	ACLU	AFL-CIO	LCV	ITI	COC	HAFA	ACU	CFG	FRC
2014	0%	16%	–	6%	100%	86%	55%	77%	83%	88%
2013	10%	C	19%	4%	C	85%	C	72%	60%	C

National Journal Ratings

	2013 LIB	—	2013 CONS
Economic	33%	—	66%
Social	38%	—	59%
Foreign	41%	—	57%
Composite	38%	—	62%

Key Votes of the 113th Congress

1. Sandy storm spending	N	5. Medical Marijuana	N	9. Syrian Rebels Training	N
2. Violence Against Women Act	Y	6. Farm Bill	Y	10. Keystone pipeline	Y
3. Guantanamo Bay Detainees	N	7. Afghanistan Combat	NV	11. Immigration Exec. Action	Y
4. Abortion 20-week ban	Y	8. NSA Phone Data Collection	Y	12. Bipartisan budget deal	Y

Election Results

2014 general	Scott Tipton (R)	163,011	(58%)	$1,268,959	$8,453
	Abel Tapia (D)	100,364	(36%)	$290,205	$31,757
	Tisha Casida (I)	11,294	(4%)		
	Travis Mero (Lib)	6,472	(2%)		
2014 primary	Scott Tipton (R)	46,177	(75%)		
	David Cox (R)	15,773	(25%)		

Prior winning percentages: 2012 (53%), 2010 (50%)

Population		Race and Ethnicity		Income	
Total:	721,617	White	71.4%	Median income:	$47,419
Urban:	40.3%	Latino	24.3%		*(274 of 435)*
Suburban:	5.0%	Amer. Indian	1.3%	Under $50,000	51.9%
Rural:	54.7%	Black	0.8%	$50,000-$99,999:	30.7%
Land area:	58,818	Two races	1.5%	$100,000-$199,999:	14.7%
Pop/sq. mi.:	12.3	White Ethnic	24.4%	$200,000 or more:	2.8%
Born in state:	51.0%			Poverty Rate	16.3%
		Education			
Age Groups		H.S. grad or less:	38.8%	**Work**	
Under 18:	22.6%	Some college:	31.4%	White collar:	32.6%
18 to 34:	21.7%	College degree, 4 yr.:	19.5%	Blue collar:	44.0%
35 to 64:	40.1%	Post-grad study:	10.3%	Sales and service:	23.4%
Over 64:	15.6%			Govt. workers:	15.5%
		Military			
		Veterans/active duty:	9.7%		

Western Slope: Grand Junction, Pueblo

On a clear night from the air, they look like tiny mottled veins, thickest near Denver. These are the lights of the civilization Americans have built on the Western Slope of the Rockies in Colorado. The lights follow the trails of valley roads and mountainside switchbacks. The nodes mark the dozens of little

Voter Turnout	
2013 Total Citizen 18+	533,130
2014 House Turnout	281,141
2014 Turnout as % CVAP	52.7%
2012 Turnout as % CVAP	67.7%

towns built during mining boom years: the Gold Rush of the 1870s, the uranium boom of the 1950s, and the oil-shale boomlet of the 1970s. The Western Slope—everything west of the Front Range, with dozens of peaks over 14,000 feet—has always blocked east-west movement. Except for mining and skiing, few would have followed the Ute Indians and settled here. The miners who tracked gold and silver and lead ores also built Victorian towns with opera houses and gingerbread storefronts in Aspen and Telluride, in valleys and defiles scarcely accessible to the outside world. Now many of these towns have been restored by ski resort operators and joined by dozens of new condominiums and shopping malls. Cries of overdevelopment have followed. Tiny Woody Creek in Pitkin County is where famed gonzo journalist Hunter S. Thompson lived for most of his life. Of living near Aspen, Thompson once wrote, "They had left me alone, not hassled my friends ... and consistently ignored all rumors of madness and violence in my area." More than half of the area's iconic aspen trees have died in recent years due to fire or natural causes.

Amid the tourism, some resource development continues of gas deposits trapped beneath the Roan Plateau. In November 2014, following bipartisan encouragement by the Colorado congressional delegation, the federal government agreed with the state to permit limited drilling in designated areas of the plateau. The energy-rich Western Slope has suffered from the steep nationwide drop in natural gas prices. In northwest Colorado in 2012, there were only about 16 drilling rigs pushing into the sandstone and shale formations, down from 115 four years earlier, according to *The New York Times*. The industry slowdown has worsened since then.

The political map of the Western Slope is as diverse as its history. Aspen and Telluride are liberal and Democratic. The former coal mining centers of Crested Butte and Steamboat Springs, today sporting ski lodges, were formerly Republican, but are now Democratic as well. Durango, an old frontier town, has moved in the same direction. Republicans still have a voter registration edge in surrounding La Plata County, but Democrat Barack Obama won the county in the 2008 and 2012 presidential elections. Some areas are still heavily Republican and hostile to environmentalists and others of the liberal ilk: the rough-handed mining area around Grand Junction, where piles of tailings still crackle with radioactivity; and the northwest corner of the state, where people remember the oil shale boom with nostalgia. Generally on the Western Slope, the high-income areas, with lots of residents opposed to new oil and gas drilling, are the most Democratic, while more modest-income, working-class towns are the most Republican.

The 3rd Congressional District of Colorado includes most of the Western Slope, and occupies nearly half of Colorado. It takes in the small towns of Eagle and Gypsum, and it extends east of the Front Range to include the industrial city of Pueblo. There, on the banks of the Arkansas River, the Rockefellers built large steel factories before World War I to make barbed wire and rails. In March 2015, the Pueblo Chemical Depot began destroying the largest remaining stockpile of chemical weapons: more than 2,600 tons of a mustard gas agent. Today, the blue-collar town survives on large medical centers and some industrial plants. It suffered the highest unemployment rate in the state—11% in 2012—but that dropped to 6.4% in December 2014. At the same time, the county reported a record number of food stamp recipients. Pueblo is Democratic, as are most of the counties in the San Luis Valley to the south. (These inhabitants are Hispanics but not necessarily Mexican-Americans: Spanish-speaking people have been living here, as in northern New Mexico, for 350 years.) With the exception chiefly of counties toward the center of the state, the 3rd is a Republican-leaning district.

2012 Presidential Vote		
Mitt Romney (R)	185,459	(52%)
Barack Obama (D)	163,885	(46%)
2008 Presidential Vote		
John McCain (R)	171,171	(50%)
Barack Obama (D)	166,201	(49%)
Cook Partisan Voting Index: R+5		

Scott Tipton (R)

The congressman from the 3rd District is Scott Tipton, a conservative Republican elected in 2010 who has been known to buck his party's leadership and show occasional bipartisanship in dealing with local resource issues.

Tipton was born in Española New Mexico. His family moved to Cortez Colorado, three months after he was born. His father was a construction worker for a Denver-based company, but the family's finances were often strained by the medical needs of Tipton's brother, who was diabetic. "Until I was about 7 years old, we ate oatmeal every morning for breakfast," Tipton said. "It wasn't because we needed to lower our cholesterol." When Tipton enrolled in Fort Lewis College in Durango, he became the first member of his family to go beyond high school, an achievement he attributes to his stable home life.

After getting his degree, Tipton returned to his hometown to establish a production facility for Native American pottery and jewelry, employing childhood friends who belonged to the Ute and Navajo tribes. But his fledgling business was encumbered by onerous and redundant government paperwork, he says. "We spent hours filling out forms (asking) how many thousands of pounds of clays we went through each year," an experience that made Tipton a critic of government interference with small businesses.

In 2006, he mounted his first political campaign, challenging Democrat John Salazar, then a freshman. Salazar won handily, receiving 62 percent of the vote in a Democratic year, but Tipton's campaign increased his visibility. Two years later, the local Republican Party in nearby Montrose recruited him to run for the Colorado House, and he was soon on his way to Denver. As a Republican legislator, Tipton says he sometimes felt marginalized by the Democratic Party's hegemony in the state following the 2008 election.

In 2010, Tipton again challenged Salazar. In the GOP primary, retired Army lawyer Bob McConnell was the preferred candidate of tea party activists and Tipton's chief opponent. Some tea partiers viewed Tipton suspiciously as a member of the Republican establishment, but he refrained from criticizing McConnell. *The Pueblo Chieftain* newspaper dubbed Tipton's win a "bloodless victory." In the fall campaign, Tipton portrayed Salazar as too deferential to the Democratic leadership, slamming the incumbent for his votes in favor of President Barack Obama's $787 billion economic stimulus bill and the major health care overhaul. Of the 220 House supporters of the health care law, only 11 represented districts that were more Republican than Salazar's in 2010. Salazar also was perceived as having close ties to Obama because his younger brother, Ken Salazar, was the Interior secretary at the time. For his part, John Salazar deemphasized his party label, calling himself "An Independent Voice for Rural Colorado." The incumbent was well-funded, raising more than $2 million compared with Tipton's $1.2 million. The district's conservative voters were energized, and Tipton prevailed, 50%-46%.

Early in his first term, defying the House Republican leadership, Tipton voted against a major spending resolution in 2011 because he favored steeper spending cuts. He also joined other conservative freshmen in opposing House Speaker John Boehner's deal with the White House to raise the debt limit that year. Tipton also has worked on non-fiscal issues that play well at home. *The Denver Post* pointed out that he favored government funding for a local bicycle trail, a popular position in an environmentally conscious district that includes Aspen. He supported funding to preserve groundwater in the San Luis Valley, which is also in his district. In December 2014, when Congress was debating the addition of more than 100,000 acres of wilderness in Hermosa Creek near Durango, he won agreement to provide limited exemptions for continued use of snowmobile trails. On the other hand, Tipton has been eager to criticize excessive controls by federal regulators, such as the Environmental Protection Agency, who are not aware of local conditions. In January 2015, he proposed a 30-year plan for American energy that would rely on all energy sources without violating environmental rules.

Tipton was tripped up by some negative publicity about ethics in his first term. *Politico* reported that Tipton sent a letter apologizing to the House Ethics Committee after his daughter, who lobbied for a company named Broadnet, was dropping her father's name in order to get access to members of Congress. *The Denver Post* later reported that Tipton's office paid more than $7,700 for newsletters and a tele-town hall meeting to iConstituent and Constituent Services Inc., two businesses that do contract work with Broadnet, which is owned by Tipton's nephew, Steve Patterson. Tipton defended the payments, saying they were not made to Patterson's company directly. The incident had no residual impact.

Democrats targeted Tipton in 2012, backing the challenge of state Rep. Sal Pace. The National Republican Congressional Committee derided Pace as one of liberal House Minority Leader "Nancy Pelosi's hand-picked puppets," but he took some conservative positions, such as calling for a balanced budget amendment to the Constitution. Pace attacked Tipton's vote for Republican Rep. Paul Ryan's Medicare reform plan. "If you dare put an idea on the table you get demonized," Tipton complained during an August candidates' debate. Tipton slightly outspent Pace, $2.2 million to $1.9 million, and won, 53%-41%. In the 2014 Republican year, his victory margin grew to 58%-36% in an uncompetitive contest. Soon after that, Tipton voiced interest in challenging the reelection of Democratic Sen. Michael Bennet in 2016. He surely was encouraged by the 2014 success of then-Rep. Cory Gardner defeating Sen. Mark Udall in another match-up of a rural Republican and a metro Democrat. Colorado has a long history of partisan shifts in both statewide and congressional contests. But Tipton's caution indicated that he viewed a challenge to Bennet as uphill.

FOURTH DISTRICT

Ken Buck (R)

Elected 2014, 1st term; b. Feb. 16, 1959, Ossining, NY; Princeton U., A.B. 1981, U of WY-Laramie, J.D. 1985; Protestant; married (Perry); 2 children.

Elected Office: Weld County, CO, DA 2005-14.

Professional Career: Practicing atty., 1987-2002; Staff, U.S. Committee to Investigate Cover Arms Transactions with Iran, 1986-87.

DC Office: 416 CHOB, 20515, 202-225-4676; Fax: 202-225-5870; Website: https://buck.house.gov/

State Offices: Castle Rock, 720-639-9165; Greeley, 970-702-2136; Sterling, (970) 522-0915.

Committees: *Judiciary*: Crime, Terrorism, Homeland Security, & Investigations; Immigration & Border Security; *Oversight & Government Reform*: Government Operations; Interior.

Election Results

2014 general	Ken Buck (R)	185,292	(65%)	$1,248,049	$27,858
	Vic Meyers (D)	83,727	(29%)	$74,359	
	Jess Loban (Lib)	9,472	(3%)		
	Grant Doherty (I)	8,016	(3%)	$13,852	
2014 primary	Ken Buck (R)	32,714	(44%)		
	Scott Renfroe (R)	17,722	(24%)		
	Barbara Kirkmeyer (R)	12,155	(16%)		
	Scott Laffey (R)	11,433	(15%)		

Population		Race and Ethnicity		Income	
Total:	748,624	White	72.9%	Median income:	$64,525
Urban:	26.3%	Latino	21.8%		(82 of 435)
Suburban:	49.3%	Asian	2.0%	Under $50,000	39.1%
Rural:	24.4%	Black	1.2%	$50,000-$99,999:	32.1%
Land area:	25,966	Two races	1.6%	$100,000-$199,999:	22.4%
Pop/sq. mi.:	28.8	White Ethnic	24.3%	$200,000 or more:	6.4%
Born in state:	49.2%			Poverty Rate	11.1%
		Education			
		H.S. grad or less:	34.2%	**Work**	
Age Groups		Some college:	32.5%	White collar:	40.1%
Under 18:	25.8%	College degree, 4 yr.:	22.7%	Blue collar:	39.4%
18 to 34:	21.2%	Post-grad study:	10.5%	Sales and service:	20.5%
35 to 64:	40.9%				
Over 64:	12.1%			Govt. workers:	14.3%
		Military			
		Veterans/active duty:	9.1%		

Eastern Colorado: Weld, Douglas

The High Plains of eastern Colorado are dusty brown, gently rolling up toward the Rocky Mountains. The land is fertile, but dry. Rainfall is rare, the rivers are just a trickle most of the year, and in many places, groundwater is scarce. It is fine wheat country when irrigated, and one of the foremost

Voter Turnout	
2013 Total Citizen 18+	525,831
2014 House Turnout	286,507
2014 Turnout as % CVAP	54.5%
2012 Turnout as % CVAP	70.2%

beef cattle regions. But it has been squeezed in recent decades by declining prices for wheat, declining demand for beef and increased prices for water because of the high demand in Denver and along the Front Range. Bitter confrontations have erupted over who gets access to the South Platte River, leading to limitations on pumping from the basin. Local farmers have found that the value of their water rights to metro Denver far exceeds what they could hope to gain by farming. Their neighbors have condemned them for selling out and betraying a way of life. The prairie lands and small towns of the High Plains have small reminders of their past: the Pawnee National Grassland, where antelope, coyotes, and prairie dogs still roam, and Burlington's 1905 carousel, one of the few with the original paint. But the free market that once peopled the High Plains with farmers and ranchers and made it the scene of farm protests has caused it to empty out and revert to untamed land, ready again for increasingly numerous buffalo, elk, deer, and bighorn sheep.

2012 Presidential Vote		
Mitt Romney (R)..............210,019	(59%)
Barack Obama (D)............140,855	(39%)

2008 Presidential Vote		
John McCain (R)..............186,216	(56%)
Barack Obama (D)............138,610	(42%)

Cook Partisan Voting Index: R+11

This area stretches into the Denver suburbs, parts of which have become more populated in recent decades. Until the 1970s, Douglas County was a sparsely populated patch of the High Plains just east of the Front Range and south of Denver. From 2000 to 2010, it grew 62 percent, making it the fastest-growing county in the state. It largely avoided the housing slump, as young families moved into 35-acre "ranchettes," or to subdivisions around Castle Rock and Parker. In 2011, Douglas County was the ninth wealthiest in the nation with a median income of $93,573. This is Patio Land, as conservative writer David Brooks has described it: an area with a high-tech economy, a highly educated population with relatively conservative cultural values, and families looking for a safe environment for children, with the serenity—if not the close personal ties—of a small town, and the creativity of a metropolis.

The 4th Congressional District covers much of the Eastern Plains and the entire eastern half of the state, sharing borders with New Mexico, Oklahoma, Kansas, Nebraska, and Wyoming. It takes in most of Douglas County, including the city of Castle Rock, Elbert County, and Las Animas County. Douglas County, which has welcomed a surge of telecom and aerospace companies, has a significant Republican voter registration edge and voted for Mitt Romney over President Barack Obama, 62%-36%. Conservative activists in the county have pressed for a more free-enterprise approach to governance, including education; elementary schools compete for students. In 2014, the county ranked sixth in the nation in median household income. The 4th is a solidly Republican district.

The district has pockets of feisty conservatism. In January 2014, five small counties in the northeast corner of the state voted for a referendum to "pursue becoming the 51st state." Six other counties, including the larger Weld, defeated the proposal, which likely killed the immediate prospects for the plan. The movement was a cry of disenfranchisement for local officials and voters, which was directed especially at liberal rule in Denver. "We're tired of being ignored, we're tired of being politically disenfranchised," Sean Conway, a commissioner from oil-producing Weld County, told CNN. "But when you start imposing mandates different on other folks than yourself, that's the definition of tyranny." Others, citing energy regulation, said that they were fighting "a war on rural Colorado." Ironically, farmers in eastern Colorado, who have suffered from drought, depend heavily for their water supply on reservoirs and pipelines in the western part of the state, and officials have sought to increase that diversion.

Ken Buck (R)

Republican Ken Buck achieved a political revival in 2014 by trouncing Democrat Vic Meyers in Colorado's red-leaning 4th District race. He succeeded GOP Rep. Cory Gardner, who was elected to the Senate. Buck fell short of making it to Congress four years earlier when he narrowly lost a Senate contest to Democrat Michael Bennet that many expected Buck would win.

Buck cultivated his political chops early in his career. Fresh out of law school, he worked for then-Rep. Dick Cheney on the House's 1986-87 probe into the Iran-Contra scandal and later served as a trial attorney in the Justice Department. He returned to Colorado in the 1990s, when he was chief of the Criminal Division in the U.S. Attorney's Office. In 2005, he successfully ran for Weld County district attorney and was reelected twice. But his political hopes crashed in 2010. In the GOP primary, he attracted national attention by commenting that he would make a better candidate than his opponent, Lt. Gov. Jane Norton, because he didn't "wear heels." Further damage was done when he compared homosexuality to alcoholism on *Meet the Press*. He lost to Bennet by less than 2 percentage points, prompting many Republicans to view Colorado, along with Delaware and Nevada, as Senate pickup opportunities that the party squandered with weak candidates.

Sporting a more professional image and emphasizing his career in law enforcement, Buck launched another shot at the Senate in 2014 against first-term Democratic Sen. Mark Udall. But when Gardner threw his hat in the ring, Buck decided to step aside to compete for the 4th instead, where the turf is friendly for Republicans. GOP strategists expedited and cheered the move, encouraged by Gardner, who was viewed as having the better chance against Udall and was relieved to avoid a competitive primary. In the June primary for Gardner's House seat, Buck's name recognition and conservative reputation gave him a big edge over three GOP opponents, and he was largely immune from attacks from the right by state Sen. Scott Renfroe. He steered away from making controversial comments, even distancing himself from Washington Republicans who backed the government shutdown in 2013. Instead, he highlighted issues such as energy independence, touting his support for the Keystone XL pipeline. Boosted by endorsements from Gardner and other top Republicans, as well as the local newspaper, *The Greeley Tribune*, Buck topped the primary field with 44%, while Renfroe trailed by more than 20 points. In the general election, Buck easily beat Vic Meyers, 65%-29%. In this district, he seems secure.

He got a quick start in the House, with his election as president of the Republican freshman class. He said that he would focus on problem-solving, not partisanship. But he maintained his blunt-spoken style. In an op-ed for the *Colorado Springs Gazette* in which he defended police who had been accused of misconduct, he responded, "When was the last time you heard someone call 911 to report an intruder in their home and ask for a congressman to come help them?" Criticizing President Barack Obama for abusing his executive authority in February 2015, he said, "No more acting like King Barack."

FIFTH DISTRICT

Doug Lamborn (R)

Elected 2006, 5th term; b. May 24, 1954, Leavenworth, KS; U. of KS, B.S. 1978, J.D. 1985; Protestant; married (Jeanie); 5 children.

Elected Office: CO House, 1995-99; CO Senate, 1998-2006.

Professional Career: Practicing atty., 1987-2007.

DC Office: 2402 RHOB, 20515, 202-225-4422; Fax: 202-226-2638; Website: lamborn.house.gov.

State Offices: Buena Vista, 719-520-0055; Colorado Springs, 719-520-0055.

Committees: *Armed Services:* Strategic Forces; Emerging Threats & Capabilities. *Natural Resources:* Energy & Mineral Resources (Chmn); Oversight & Investigations. *Veterans' Affairs:* Disability Assistance & Memorial Affairs; Oversight & Investigations.

Group Ratings

	ADA	ACLU	AFL-CIO	LCV	ITI	COC	HAFA	ACU	CFG	FRC
2014	5%	11%	–	6%	100%	57%	84%	96%	98%	100%
2013	5%	C	10%	7%	C	77%	C	92%	84%	C

National Journal Ratings

	2013 LIB	—	2013 CONS
Economic	6%	—	94%
Social	13%	—	84%
Foreign	44%	—	54%
Composite	22%	—	78%

Key Votes of the 113th Congress

1. Sandy storm spending	N	5. Medical Marijuana	N	9. Syrian Rebels Training	Y
2. Violence Against Women Act	N	6. Farm Bill	N	10. Keystone pipeline	Y
3. Guantanamo Bay Detainees	N	7. Afghanistan Combat	N	11. Immigration Exec. Action	Y
4. Abortion 20-week ban	Y	8. NSA Phone Data Collection	Y	12. Bipartisan budget deal	Y

Election Results

2014 general	Doug Lamborn (R)	157,182	(60%)	$474,481
	Irv Halter (D)	105,673	(40%)	$833,436
2014 primary	Doug Lamborn (R)	38,741	(53%)	
	Bentley Rayburn (R)	34,967	(47%)	

Prior winning percentages: 2012 (65%), 2010 (66%), 2008 (60%), 2006 (60%)

Population		Race and Ethnicity		Income	
Total:	749,815	White	72.8%	Median income:	$55,295
Urban:	76.1%	Latino	14.8%		*(163 of 435)*
Suburban:	10.2%	Black	5.5%	Under $50,000	44.4%
Rural:	13.7%	Asian	2.5%	$50,000-$99,999:	32.9%
Land area:	8,509	Two races	3.5%	$100,000-$199,999:	18.9%
Pop/sq. mi.:	88.1	White Ethnic	27.3%	$200,000 or more:	3.8%
Born in state:	32.6%			Poverty Rate	11.2%
		Education			
Age Groups		H.S. grad or less:	28.1%	**Work**	
Under 18:	24.1%	Some college:	38.1%	White collar:	40.3%
18 to 34:	25.4%	College degree, 4 yr.:	20.7%	Blue collar:	42.6%
35 to 64:	38.3%	Post-grad study:	13.1%	Sales and service:	17.1%
Over 64:	12.2%			Govt. workers:	18.1%
		Military			
		Veterans/active duty:	22.9%		

Central Colorado: Colorado Springs

In 1893, Katherine Lee Bates took the cog railway up from Colorado Springs to the top of 14,110-foot Pikes Peak, and looking out at the purple mountain's majesty above amber waves of grain, she wrote the lines of "America the Beautiful." Pikes Peak, espied by Zebulon Pike in 1806, and Colorado

Voter Turnout	
2013 Total Citizen 18+	547,990
2014 House Turnout	262,855
2014 Turnout as % CVAP	48%
2012 Turnout as % CVAP	63.4%

Springs, with the Garden of the Gods and the Broadmoor hotel, have been tourist attractions for more than 100 years. In the second half of the 20th century, Colorado Springs, safe in the vastness of North America, also became a great American military fortress. During the height of the Cold War in the 1960s, the Pentagon constructed the North American Aerospace Defense Command more than 1,000 feet below Cheyenne Mountain, a fortified bunker theoretically able to survive a nuclear strike from a Soviet missile. The Pentagon, in part because of local traffic congestion, moved NORAD's surveillance operations to nearby Peterson Air Force Base, site of space-based defense research, with the option of a rapid return to secure Cheyenne Mountain in an emergency. Other military installations dominate the landscape as well: the Army installation at Fort Carson, the Air Force Academy, and Schriever Air Force Base, named for Gen. Bernard A. Schriever, a pioneer in the development of ballistic missile programs.

Colorado Springs has built a high-tech, innovative economy. In 2010, the city ranked sixth among medium-sized metropolitan areas in *Portfolio.com*'s best quality-of-life rankings. It must contend with occasional out-of-control fires that have become the bane of the West. A forest fire broke out here in June 2012 that destroyed 346 homes and forced the evacuation of about 35,000 people.

Led by the arrival of James Dobson's Focus on the Family in 1994, Colorado Springs has been a center of conservative Christianity, the home of Colorado's young conservatism and the counterpoint to Denver's

2012 Presidential Vote		
Mitt Romney (R)	200,558	(59%)
Barack Obama (D)	129,904	(38%)
2008 Presidential Vote		
John McCain (R)	188,391	(59%)
Barack Obama (D)	127,254	(40%)
Cook Partisan Voting Index:	R+13	

liberalism. This was the birthplace of Colorado's anti-tax initiatives and of Amendment 2, which in 1992 repealed the city's gay rights ordinances only to be later overturned by the U.S. Supreme Court. It is one of America's most Republican metropolitan areas. It was the birthplace of Wisconsin Gov. Scott Walker, a Republican whose union-busting made him a hero to movement conservatives.

The 5th Congressional District takes in Colorado Springs and El Paso County. It also includes Park, Teller, Fremont, and Chaffee counties, but more than 80% of the district's voters are in El Paso County. It is the strongest Republican district in Colorado. Still, its 59% for Mitt Romney in 2012 had less impact than did the 69% vote for Barack Obama in the 1st District (Denver), when Obama won statewide 51%-49%.

Doug Lamborn (R)

The congressman from the 5th District is Doug Lamborn, a conservative, tea party Republican first elected in 2006 and one of the party's fiercest partisans in the House. Despite the strong Republican lean of his district, he has not shut down competitive challenges from either party.

The son of a prison guard, Lamborn was born in Leavenworth, Kansas. He studied journalism at the University of Kansas and ultimately earned a law degree. He said he voted for Jimmy Carter in 1976, but was then drawn to the Republican politics of Ronald Reagan in the 1980s. In 1987, Lamborn moved his family to Colorado Springs, where he practiced business and real estate law and became an avid mountain climber. In 1994, he was elected to the state House, and he was appointed in 1998 to a Senate seat. During 12 years in the legislature, Lamborn compiled a firmly conservative record on social and fiscal issues.

When Republican Joel Hefley retired and created an open seat in 2006, he endorsed Jeff Crank, a former aide. Lamborn won the backing of the anti-tax Club for Growth and the Colorado Christian Coalition. At the May GOP convention, Crank won the delegate vote 46%-40%, but Lamborn had more than the 30% required to secure a place on the primary ballot. Lamborn emphasized his conservative voting record and vowed never to raise taxes. The state Christian Coalition sent a mailer suggesting Crank backed the "radical homosexual lobby." In the August primary, Crank won five of the district's six counties and appeared headed to victory. But the absentee ballot count flipped the results, and Lamborn won by 892 votes over Crank 27%-25%.

In November, Lamborn faced Democrat Jay Fawcett, an Air Force Academy graduate who won a Bronze star during the Persian Gulf War. In most years, the Democratic nominee would not have drawn a second look; no Democrat had won the seat since it was created in 1972. But the bruising Republican primary and a tough national environment for Republicans made for an unusually competitive general election. Hefley accused Lamborn of running a "sleazy" primary campaign and refused to endorse him. Fawcett purchased a newspaper ad featuring the names and photos of three dozen prominent local Republicans who also declined to endorse their party's nominee. Fawcett emphasized his military experience, a strong selling point in the military-oriented district. Despite October polls showing a dead heat, voters gave Lamborn a 60%-40% victory.

In the House, Lamborn became one of his party's most conservative members. He was an original member of the Tea Party Caucus. Lamborn overwhelmingly lost votes on amendments to eliminate funding for the National Endowment for the Arts and the Corporation for Public Broadcasting. During the 2011 debt and budget talks, he bucked Republican House Speaker John Boehner because he wanted President Barack Obama to agree to deeper cuts. But Lamborn has been enthusiastic about promoting more military spending in his district. In June 2011, he was criticized back home for supporting spending cuts for energy efficiency and renewable energy grants, including the National Renewable Energy Laboratory in Golden, Colo. Lamborn later explained to *The Denver Post* that he did not know that the program he was targeting included money for the Golden-based lab, and that he was not seeking that cut. "The bigger issue is, what is the government's role in renewable energy? There are some pitfalls we need to avoid," he told the newspaper.

Lamborn stepped into an even bigger morass during an interview with a Denver radio station in July 2011. Discussing Obama's budget policies, Lamborn said, "I don't even want to have to be associated with (Obama). It's like touching a tar baby." His use of the phrase "tar baby," which has a double meaning as a racial slur, brought condemnation from the NAACP and other civil rights groups. He quickly apologized to Obama and later apologized to a group of black leaders at a Baptist church in Fountain.

During the 2013 budget debate, Lamborn helped to prepare the budget plan of the conservative Republican Study Committee, which made further large cuts in domestic programs. He voiced concern that military cutbacks would affect personnel and missile programs in the Colorado Springs area. In December 2013, he called for cuts in Social Security, Medicare and farm programs to pay for increased defense spending. As chairman of the Natural Resources

Subcommittee on Energy and Mineral Resources, he said that he supported more development of all forms of energy. But his panel has not prepared major legislation.

Back home, lingering resentment over the 2006 primary led to a rematch with Crank in 2008. The challenger attacked Lamborn's job performance. This time, Lamborn won 44%-30%. He won easily in November against token Democratic opposition. In 2014, he faced unexpected problems. He barely won the GOP primary, 53%-47%, over Bentley Rayburn, a retired Air Force general who had challenged Lamborn in two earlier primaries. Bradley complained that Lamborn was "out of touch" with local concerns about possible military base closings in the area. Similar criticisms were raised in the general election by Democratic foe Irving Halter, also a retired Air Force general. Halter cited the district's large federal payroll in criticizing the incumbent as the only member of the Colorado delegation to vote for the government shutdown in October 2013. Lamborn kept a low profile during the campaign and he refused to debate, contending that his views were well-known and that Halter was trying to hide his. Halter raised $834,000 compared to only $490,000 for Lamborn, an unusual contrast for a veteran incumbent. Neither national party spent money on the contest. Lamborn won 60%-40%, which signaled Lamborn's personal weakness in a Republican year but probably is not enough to encourage Democrats that they can win this seat.

SIXTH DISTRICT

Mike Coffman (R)

Elected 2008, 4th term; b. March 19, 1955, Fort Leonard Wood, MO; U. of CO, B.A. 1979; Methodist; married (Cynthia).

Military Career: Army, 1972-79; Marine Corps, 1979-94, 2005-06 (Iraq).

Elected Office: CO House, 1988-94; CO Senate, 1994-98; CO treas., 1999-07 CO Secy. of State., 2007-08.

Professional Career: Property mgmt. firm owner, 1983-2000.

DC Office: 2443 RHOB, 20515, 202-225-7882; Fax: 202-226-4623; Website: coffman.house.gov.

State Offices: Aurora, 720-748-7514.

Committees: *Armed Services:* Military Personnel; Strategic Forces. *Veterans' Affairs:* Health; Oversight & Investigations (Chmn).

Group Ratings

	ADA	ACLU	AFL-CIO	LCV	ITI	COC	HAFA	ACU	CFG	FRC
2014	15%	16%	–	3%	100%	93%	62%	76%	71%	63%
2013	5%	C	19%	4%	C	92%	C	84%	75%	C

National Journal Ratings

	2013 LIB	—	2013 CONS
Economic	33%	—	66%
Social	34%	—	62%
Foreign	48%	—	52%
Composite	39%	—	61%

Key Votes of the 113th Congress

1. Sandy storm spending	N	5. Medical Marijuana	Y	9. Syrian Rebels Training	Y
2. Violence Against Women Act	Y	6. Farm Bill	N	10. Keystone pipeline	Y
3. Guantanamo Bay Detainees	N	7. Afghanistan Combat	N	11. Immigration Exec. Action	N
4. Abortion 20-week ban	Y	8. NSA Phone Data Collection	Y	12. Bipartisan budget deal	N

Election Results

2014 general	Mike Coffman (R)	143,467	(52%)	$4,708,362	$1,099,687	$3,899,822
	Andrew Romanoff (D)	118,847	(43%)	$5,145,370	$93,666	$4,238,939
	Norm Olsen (Lib)	8,623	(3%)			
	Gary Swing (G)	5,503	(2%)			
2014 primary	Mike Coffman (R)	unopposed				

Prior winning percentages: 2012 (48%), 2010 (66%), 2008 (61%)

Population		Race and Ethnicity		Income	
Total:	765,338	White	63.6%	Median income:	$65,987
Urban:	50.3%	Latino	19.6%		*(78 of 435)*
Suburban:	48.6%	Black	8.7%	Under $50,000	37.5%
Rural:	1.1%	Asian	4.9%	$50,000-$99,999:	32.2%
Land area:	906	Two races	2.6%	$100,000-$199,999:	24.1%
Pop/sq. mi.:	845.1	White Ethnic	23.8%	$200,000 or more:	6.3%
Born in state:	41.4%			Poverty Rate	11.7%
		Education			
Age Groups		H.S. grad or less:	29.0%	**Work**	
Under 18:	26.8%	Some college:	30.7%	White collar:	40.2%
18 to 34:	22.3%	College degree, 4 yr.:	25.7%	Blue collar:	43.1%
35 to 64:	40.6%	Post-grad study:	14.5%	Sales and service:	16.7%
Over 64:	10.4%				
		Military		Govt. workers:	12.2%
		Veterans/active duty:	8.8%		

Eastern and Southern Denver Suburbs: Aurora

Two generations ago, most people in metropolitan Denver lived in the city itself. At the city limits, the tree-shaded sidewalks gave way to the empty High Plains. Today, more than three-quarters of metro Denver residents live outside the city, some in long-settled suburbs, some in large new subdivisions

Voter Turnout	
2013 Total Citizen 18+	502,318
2014 House Turnout	276,440
2014 Turnout as % CVAP	72%
2012 Turnout as % CVAP	55%

raised up in the 1990s and 2000s on rolling land with magnificent views of the Rocky Mountains. Littleton, originally a small, long-settled suburb just south of Denver, now extends to vast new tracts. Other areas that surround Denver were once quite rural but have grown into modern suburbs. Just south of Littleton is fast-growing Douglas County and Highlands Ranch, whose 100,000 residents form one of the largest unincorporated communities in the nation. To the east of the now-closed Stapleton Airport is Aurora, with its huge regional mall and an increasing number of middle-class African Americans. The area has developed as a hub for alternative energy firms, including SloarATC, an 1,800-acre facility near Denver International Airport, where new technologies can be studied for their commercial value. Aurora-based Arapahoe County also is comfortable with the conventional energy industry, including nearly 2,800 jobs in 2012. In 2014, it had an 11 percent increase in its price for rental properties, which was the largest hike in the nation.

Aurora has been the site of not just innovation, but of unspeakable tragedy. At a July 2012 midnight showing of the movie *The Dark Knight Rises*, a mentally unstable gunman shot and killed 12 people and injured 58 others, an event that sparked an outpouring of public outrage and sympathy. In July 2015, James Holmes was found guilty of the murders. But the jury deadlocked and failed to impose the death penalty. That pain was compounded because Littleton remains known as the location of Columbine High School, which suffered in 1999 what had been the nation's worst school massacre when two teenagers killed 13 people

plus themselves. More recently, Aurora has gained another kind of infamy with reports that the cost of a VA hospital under construction has exceeded $1.7 billion, more than three times the estimate when ground was broken in 2009.

The 6th Congressional District covers Aurora, Littleton, and other south Denver suburbs. About 70 percent of the district is in Arapahoe County, with the remainder in

2012 Presidential Vote		
Barack Obama (D)	182,464	(52%)
Mitt Romney (R)	164,398	(47%)
2008 Presidential Vote		
Barack Obama (D)	175,487	(54%)
John McCain (R)	147,091	(45%)
Cook Partisan Voting Index: D+1		

small slices of Adams and Douglas counties. Aurora had long been a Republican-leaning city, but with more black and Latino residents moving in, it has been trending Democratic in recent years. The 6th has become one of the most competitive districts in one of the most competitive states. Barack Obama won this district twice, with 52% and then 54%, in his two presidential runs.

Mike Coffman (R)

The congressman from the 6th District is Mike Coffman, first elected as a conservative Republican in 2008. Following major redistricting shifts in 2012 that created a more competitive battleground, including a big increase in Hispanics, Coffman moderated his views and won two very competitive and expensive contests. That made him a hot property for GOP recruiters seeking a strong statewide contender.

The son of an Army doctor, Coffman enlisted in the Army before he finished high school and completed his diploma in the military. He went to the University of Colorado on the G.I. Bill, and then officers' school in the Marine Corps. After his active duty service ended, he started several Denver-area property management firms, which he sold in 2000. In 1988, Coffman was elected to the Colorado House. Two years later, he was called back to active duty with the Marines to serve in the first Gulf War. His colleagues draped his desk with a Marine Corps flag and yellow ribbons, and read his letters from the front lines on the House floor. After his service, Coffman returned to public life, first as a state senator and then as Colorado treasurer. Military duty called again in 2005. Coffman resigned as treasurer to deploy for six months in Iraq, where he helped establish local governments in the Western Euphrates River Valley. In 2006, he was elected secretary of state, touting his experience with the Iraqi elections. In that office, he drew criticism for taking several voting machines out of commission because of possible problems and not having replacement machines ready. The August 2008 primary was plagued with errors, and many voters did not receive absentee ballots.

In 2007, after five-term Republican Tom Tancredo retired from this House seat to wage a long-shot race for president, Coffman announced his candidacy. In the GOP primary, he was challenged by businessman Wil Armstrong, the son of former Republican Sen. Bill Armstrong, and state senators Ted Harvey and Steve Ward. The four were nearly uniformly conservative. All supported the Iraq war and, like Tancredo, were staunch opponents of giving citizenship to illegal immigrants. But Coffman had the highest name recognition, thanks to his statewide offices, and he also outraised his challengers. He won with 40% of the vote, with Armstrong coming in at 33%.

Amid his campaigning, Coffman was criticized for the alleged purging of thousands of names from voter rolls in a crucial swing state shortly before the November election because they were suspected of being duplicate or erroneous registrations. He disputed the number of names purged and said their removal was valid. Still, the Advancement Project, a national voting-rights group, sued Coffman over the purged registrations, and a judge four days before the election ordered him to reinstate 146 voters. The controversy apparently had no effect on Coffman's own campaign. In the general election, he cruised to victory against Democrat Hank Eng with 61% of the vote.

Once in Congress, Coffman opposed President Barack Obama's initiatives, telling the conservative publication *Human Events* in 2009 that "they are taking us down the road to a European-style social welfare state." Given his military background, he was appointed to the House Armed Services Committee. He got a bill through the House in March 2010 to extend re-employment protections for National Guard members. With the Republican takeover of the House in 2011, Coffman pushed for several internal reforms. He introduced a bill for a 10 percent salary reduction for members of Congress. He also sought to end their traditional pensions. He got an amendment attached to the 2012 defense authorization bill for a study of college tuition aid for military personnel.

In 2013, Coffman became chairman of the Veterans Affairs Subcommittee on Oversight and Investigations. For much of that time, the VA Department was widely criticized for inefficient and potentially criminal malfeasance in handling the health care problems of veterans, in addition to huge cost overruns of its hospital under construction in Aurora. Coffman aggressively pursued the problem. At a February 2015 hearing with VA Secretary Robert McDonald, Coffman asked when he would clean up the "corruption" and "incompetence" in his agency. The angry secretary, the former chief executive of Procter & Gamble, replied, "I've run a large company, sir. What have *you* done?"

Redistricting in 2012 more than doubled the Hispanic population of the district, and increased Obama's local vote share by 6 percent. Coffman took intensive Spanish training, and spent time in immigrant neighborhoods. As recently as August 2011, he had introduced legislation to allow communities to use English-only campaign ballots.

His opponent in November 2012 was Democrat Joe Miklosi, a state representative in the Denver suburbs. Miklosi highlighted his opponent's anti-abortion rights views and accused him of seeking to dismantle Medicare. Coffman was forced to apologize in May for telling supporters that "in his heart, [President Obama] is not an American." But Coffman fought back hard, criticizing Miklosi for supporting tax hikes and running what newspaper fact-checkers called misleading ads. "It is a different ballgame," Coffman acknowledged to *The New York Times*. "It is clearly a competitive district, and it is a big transition." Though the national Democratic Party targeted Coffman, he still outraised Miklosi, $3.4 million to $1.7 million. He squeaked out a victory, 48%-46%. He was one of 17 House Republicans who were elected that year even though Obama prevailed in their district.

After the election, Coffman softened his stance on immigration, with a bill to allow non-citizens, such as foreign students in the U.S. on visas, to serve in the military. "Like it did for my father and me, the prospect of military service would give these young people something to aspire to," he wrote in an op-ed column. He sponsored multiple bills aimed at helping the military and veterans, including a 2013 bill that became law to pay military officials during a government shutdown.

Coffman was one of the GOP's most vulnerable incumbents in 2014. He drew a top-tier challenger in Andrew Romanoff, a former state House speaker who had run for the Senate in 2010. Romanoff touted his bipartisan accomplishments as a state lawmaker while seeking to highlight public unhappiness with Congress and, by extension, with Coffman. "If we elect the same crowd to Congress, nothing is going to change and nothing is going to get done," Romanoff said at one debate. Coffman stressed his foreign-policy credentials and depicted himself as a workhorse. Both candidates and their national parties spent huge sums of money, a total of more than $17 million. Coffman won in a surprisingly comfortable 52%-43% outcome. He led in all three counties; Arapahoe and Adams were tight, but Douglas gave him 62%.

His impressive strength in his swing battleground district led Republican strategists to urge him to run against Sen. Michael Bennet in 2016. Coffman's wife, Cynthia, who was elected state attorney general in November 2014 after having served as deputy attorney general, was also touted as a potential challenger to Bennet. Other Republicans considered a bid, including Rep. Scott Tipton of the 3rd District. One factor for Mike Coffman was that he faced the prospect of continued intense challenges to retain his House seat, even with his two strong campaigns. In June 2015, he turned down a Senate challenge to the relief of House GOP campaign officials. Two weeks later, Cynthia Coffman made the same decision, but she was mentioned as a candidate for governor in 2018.

SEVENTH DISTRICT

Ed Perlmutter (D)

Elected 2006, 5th term; b. May 1, 1953, Denver; U. of CO, B.A. 1975, J.D. 1978; Protestant; married (Nancy); 3 children.

Elected Office: CO Senate, 1995-2003.

Professional Career: Practicing atty., 1979-2006.

DC Office: 1410 LHOB, 20515, 202-225-2645; Fax: 202-225-5278; Website: perlmutter.house.gov.

State Offices: Lakewood, 303-274-7944.

Committees: *Financial Services:* Capital Markets and Government Sponsored Enterprises; Monetary Policy & Trade. *Science, Space, & Technology:* Space; Energy.

Group Ratings

	ADA	ACLU	AFL-CIO	LCV	ITI	COC	HAFA	ACU	CFG	FRC
2014	70%	77%	–	77%	60%	62%	11%	4%	2%	0%
2013	70%	C	90%	82%	C	54%	C	12%	10%	C

National Journal Ratings

	2013 LIB	—	2013 CONS
Economic	62%	—	38%
Social	61%	—	38%
Foreign	61%	—	39%
Composite	62%	—	39%

Key Votes of the 113th Congress

1. Sandy storm spending	Y	5. Medical Marijuana	Y	9. Syrian Rebels Training	Y
2. Violence Against Women Act	Y	6. Farm Bill	N	10. Keystone pipeline	NV
3. Guantanamo Bay Detainees	Y	7. Afghanistan Combat	Y	11. Immigration Exec. Action	N
4. Abortion 20-week ban	N	8. NSA Phone Data Collection	Y	12. Bipartisan budget deal	Y

Election Results

2014 general	Ed Perlmutter (D)......................	148,225	(55%)	$1,891,892	$5,840
	Don Ytterberg (R)	120,918	(45%)	$298,112	$123,727
2014 primary	Ed Perlmutter (D).................unopposed				

Prior winning percentages: 2012 (54%), 2010 (53%), 2008 (63%), 2006 (55%)

Population		Race and Ethnicity		Income	
Total:	755,047	White	65.8%	Median income:	$58,609
Urban:	50.3%	Latino	27.1%		*(139 of 435)*
Suburban:	49.7%	Asian	3.1%	Under $50,000	42.7%
Rural:	0.0%	Black	1.4%	$50,000-$99,999:	34.1%
Land area:	524	Two races	2.0%	$100,000-$199,999:	19.1%
Pop/sq. mi.:	1,441.8	White Ethnic	26.5%	$200,000 or more:	4.1%
Born in state:	50.7%			Poverty Rate	11.6%
Age Groups		**Education**			
Under 18:	24.1%	H.S. grad or less:	35.9%	**Work**	
18 to 34:	24.3%	Some college:	32.8%	White collar:	35.9%
35 to 64:	39.2%	College degree, 4 yr.:	20.8%	Blue collar:	42.5%
Over 64:	12.4%	Post-grad study:	10.6%	Sales and service:	21.6%
		Military		Govt. workers:	12.9%
		Veterans/active duty:	8.6%		

Western and Northern Denver Suburbs: Arvada

The inner circle of suburbs around Denver was developed from the 1950s to the 1970s. West of Denver, on broad avenues running toward the mountains, is Lakewood, where growth was sparked by the Denver Federal Center. The suburbs are affluent in the south, and more marginal near the Denver city limits.

Voter Turnout	
2013 Total Citizen 18+	526,340
2014 House Turnout	269,143
2014 Turnout as % CVAP	51.1%
2012 Turnout as % CVAP	66.6%

To the west of the city is the town of Golden, with the old Colorado School of Mines and the Coors brewery. Denver's new light rail line extends 12 miles from downtown to Golden. To the north are Arvada and Wheat Ridge, middle-income suburbs with an increasing number of Latinos. To the northwest of Denver are Federal Heights, Northglenn, and Thornton, which experienced a 44% spurt in population from 2000 to 2010. Industrial Commerce City is here, with its large oil refinery. One of the civic jewels of the region is strong public education. Of the 50 largest school districts in the nation, Jefferson County was tied for the second-highest graduation rate in 2012.

The 7th Congressional District covers the suburbs north and west of Denver, sweeping in Arvada, Lakewood, Thornton, and Westminster, which are the district's largest cities. It also takes in the Rocky Mountain Arsenal National Wildlife Refuge, as well as other parks, lakes, and recreational spots. Jefferson County, which includes Golden and Lakewood, is perhaps Colorado's premier

2012 Presidential Vote		
Barack Obama (D) 196,386	(56%)
Mitt Romney (R).................144,446	(42%)

2008 Presidential Vote		
Barack Obama (D) 187,507	(57%)
John McCain (R).................132,985	(41%)

Cook Partisan Voting Index: D+5

political battleground. In the 2012 presidential race, President Barack Obama won Jefferson, 51%-46%. District-wide, he won, 56%-42%. The remaining one-third of the district population is in the western end of Adams County, extending just north of the airport. The district overall is comfortably Democratic.

Ed Perlmutter (D)

Ed Perlmutter, first elected in 2006, has been the most centrist member of Colorado's congressional delegation and a self-described "business-oriented Democrat." He usually backs his party on major issues, but regularly has sought out Republicans to work on financial, homeland security, and energy matters.

Perlmutter grew up in Jefferson County, walking precincts with his father on Democratic campaigns. He attended the University of Colorado and earned a law degree in 1978, and then went into private practice. In 1994, Perlmutter won election to the state Senate from a northern Jefferson County district that had not elected a Democrat in nearly 30 years. In the legislature, where he gained a reputation as a mediator, he chaired the renewable energy caucus and worked on legislation protecting consumer rights and promoting responsible growth. After serving two years as Senate president pro tem, he retired in 2002 when term limits forced him from office.

In 2002, Perlmutter was considered the early front-runner for the new 7th District seat in Congress. But he opted not to run, citing the time it would take him from his three daughters. The district elected Republican Bob Beauprez by just 121 votes. When Beauprez ran unsuccessfully for governor in 2006, Democrats immediately touted the 7th as one of their top pickup opportunities. This time, Perlmutter entered the race. His most significant primary opposition came from Peggy Lamm, a former state representative who used to be the sister-in-law of former Democratic Gov. Richard Lamm. Perlmutter campaigned in favor of embryonic stem cell research, and in his first commercial, his oldest daughter talked about how stem cell research might find a cure for her epilepsy. He won the primary by a solid 53%-38%.

In the general election, he faced Republican Rick O'Donnell, a rising star who had been executive director of the Colorado Department of Higher Education. At a time of multiple ethics scandals in Congress, O'Donnell argued that Perlmutter's marriage to a Denver lobbyist for a D.C.-based lobbying firm would lead to conflicts of interest. (They later divorced and he re-married to a school teacher.) The two candidates also debated illegal immigration. Perlmutter supported a guest worker program, while O'Donnell opposed it. By October, the two were closely matched in fundraising, each with well over $2 million. Beauprez's poor showing in the governor's race, and President George W. Bush's unpopularity worked against O'Donnell. Perlmutter won, 55%-42%.

In the House, Perlmutter has been a fairly consistent but not automatic Democratic vote. He split with other Colorado Democrats and immigration groups in 2011 in supporting Secure Communities, a federal program to speed up deportations of illegal immigrants convicted of crimes. He joined the centrist New Democrat Coalition and eventually became co-chair of its energy task force. In sync with local interests in energy, he sponsored a bill to offer incentives to lenders who create a market for energy-efficient buildings. He got a provision in the House-passed climate change bill in 2009 to benefit environmentally conscious banks, drawing criticism from Republicans when it was revealed that he was an investor in one of them.

Inspired by his daughter's struggles with epilepsy, Perlmutter won passage of a bill creating epilepsy centers for returning combat veterans. He repeatedly pushed the Department of Veterans Affairs to build a long-delayed local hospital, at one point threatening to show up at the site with veterans and shovels if construction didn't start as scheduled. (It did).

On the Financial Services Committee, Perlmutter worked with Republicans to add protections for taxpayers to the $700 billion government rescue of financial markets in 2008. He also worked with Colorado Republican Mike Coffman on legislation to temporarily allow small banks to amortize commercial real estate losses over seven years instead of writing them down all at once. In 2013, he filed a bill to permit banks to do business with marijuana retailers in states where they can operate legally. The legislation went nowhere in the Republican-controlled House. In June 2015, Perlmutter stuck with most House Democrats and opposed trade promotion authority for President Barack Obama.

In 2010, Perlmutter considered running for governor but decided against it. His reelection in a big Republican year proved considerably tougher than his initial contest. His challenger, Aurora GOP Councilman Ryan Frazier, an African-American Navy veteran, attacked him for contributing to government overspending. Perlmutter, meanwhile, accused his opponent's company, software developer Takara Systems, of outsourcing its consulting services. Frazier got considerable help from national Republicans and outside groups, but he couldn't keep pace financially with Perlmutter, who raised more than $2 million and won with 53% of the vote.

Perlmutter drew another formidable challenger two years later in Joe Coors, a wealthy heir to his family's brewing empire. Coors did not play up his beer-making background, emphasizing his record as a ceramics manufacturing executive. He sought to make an issue of Perlmutter's ex-wife's work as a lobbyist for California solar manufacturer Solyndra, which failed after getting significant federal help. Perlmutter fired back by accusing Coors of outsourcing jobs, which Coors denied. Perlmutter got last-minute help from the Democratic Congressional Campaign Committee and prevailed 53.5%-41%. In 2014, he out-spent former Jefferson County Republican chairman Don Ytterberg more than 6-to-1, and was not seriously threatened in his 55%-45% win. There was renewed speculation that he might run for governor in 2018, when John Hickenlooper is term-limited. Fun fact: Perlmutter often ends his local speeches with a cartwheel, to the delight of his audiences.

★ CONNECTICUT ★

Connecticut is in some respects America's highest achieving state, with the nation's top per capita personal income and great accumulations of wealth—but it is also a state with a yawning gap between the rich and poor, visible in the contrast between hedge fund managers' estates in Greenwich and the slums of Bridgeport not all that far away. It has higher percentages of college graduates and homeowners than the national average and higher percentages of people living in poverty. The state that is home to Yale University is in the upper tier of states competitive in the global knowledge economy, yet it has grown achingly slowly. By early 2015, employment in Connecticut remained below its 2008 peak, which itself barely exceeded what it was two decades earlier.

Connecticut was founded by Puritans who considered Massachusetts too lenient. Connecticut Yankees for years were flintier and more unyielding, more tightfisted and set in their ways than other New Englanders. Yet they were also open to certain reforms. In 1784, Connecticut voted for gradual emancipation of the state's slaves, one of the first societies anywhere to do so. Life here still bears the imprint of the 17th-century settlers, even though most Connecticut residents today are descendants of Catholic immigrants who arrived between 1840 and 1924. In 2010, 10 percent of the state's residents were black and 14 percent Hispanic. This small chunk of rocky terrain has been an odd duck politically, one of four states to back the Federalist Party in 1816 and one of the few to vote to reelect Herbert Hoover in 1932.

Connecticut's affluence came not from any windfall but from a knack for tinkering and making productive use of savings. George Washington called it the "provision state" for the supplies of food and cannon it provided his Revolutionary War forces. Connecticut made clocks, hats, combs, cigars, silk thread, pins, matches, brass and furniture. It invented and still manufactures Pez candy in the town of Orange, Nivea skin cream in Norwalk, and the Wiffle ball in Shelton. The quintessential Connecticut Yankee, Eli Whitney, was the inventor not only of the cotton gin but also of rifles with interchangeable parts. The state has been a major arms maker ever since Samuel Colt won a War Department contract to manufacture guns for the Mexican-American War; the company's disused, blue-onion-domed factory in Hartford received a National Park Service designation in 2014. (The state's longstanding gun connections caused tension following the 2012 shooting massacre at Sandy Hook Elementary School in Newtown; when Gov. Dan Malloy shepherded a tough anti-gun bill into law, he faced fierce opposition from the gun industry.)

During the Reagan defense buildup of the 1980s, Connecticut produced Air Force jets and Army helicopters and, in the Electric Boat Shipyard in New London, most of the Navy's nuclear submarines, continuing a long seafaring tradition memorialized at Mystic Seaport. These industries, like Connecticut's civilian manufacturers, depend heavily on meticulous work. Through decades of immigration, its workers never lost the Yankee knack: Connecticut ranks high in patents per capita. Over the years, the state has accumulated capital and invested shrewdly, with great skill at assessing risk. It has long been home to several of the nation's great insurance companies, and its laws are unusually friendly to creditors and harsh on debtors.

But Connecticut has been finding its success at wealth-accumulation hard to sustain. United Technologies Corp., which now owns Sikorsky Aircraft and Pratt & Whitney, remains the state's largest employer, but overall aerospace employment in the state has declined from 32,400 in 2008 to 29,200 in 2014. Connecticut's insurance companies have sustained casualty losses from natural disasters, and the state's small central cities—New Haven, Hartford and Bridgeport—have been plagued by crime and have been bleeding manufacturing jobs and people for years. In 1950, the three cities had 500,000 people in a state of 2 million; in 2010, they had 400,000 in a state of 3.6 million.

Connecticut's economic growth in the 1990s and 2000s was concentrated in two corners of the state, on opposite sides of the invisible divide that separates Yankee fans and Red Sox fans. (Bristol-based ESPN sits roughly along that line.) In the southeast are the Foxwoods Resort Casino, opened in 1992 and owned by the 900-member Mashantucket Pequot tribe, and its big competitor, Mohegan Sun, owned by the 1,700-member Mohegans. Collectively, the state's casinos employ about 20,000, but these are mostly lower-wage jobs, and the industry has faced struggles. New and expanded casinos in Pennsylvania, New York,

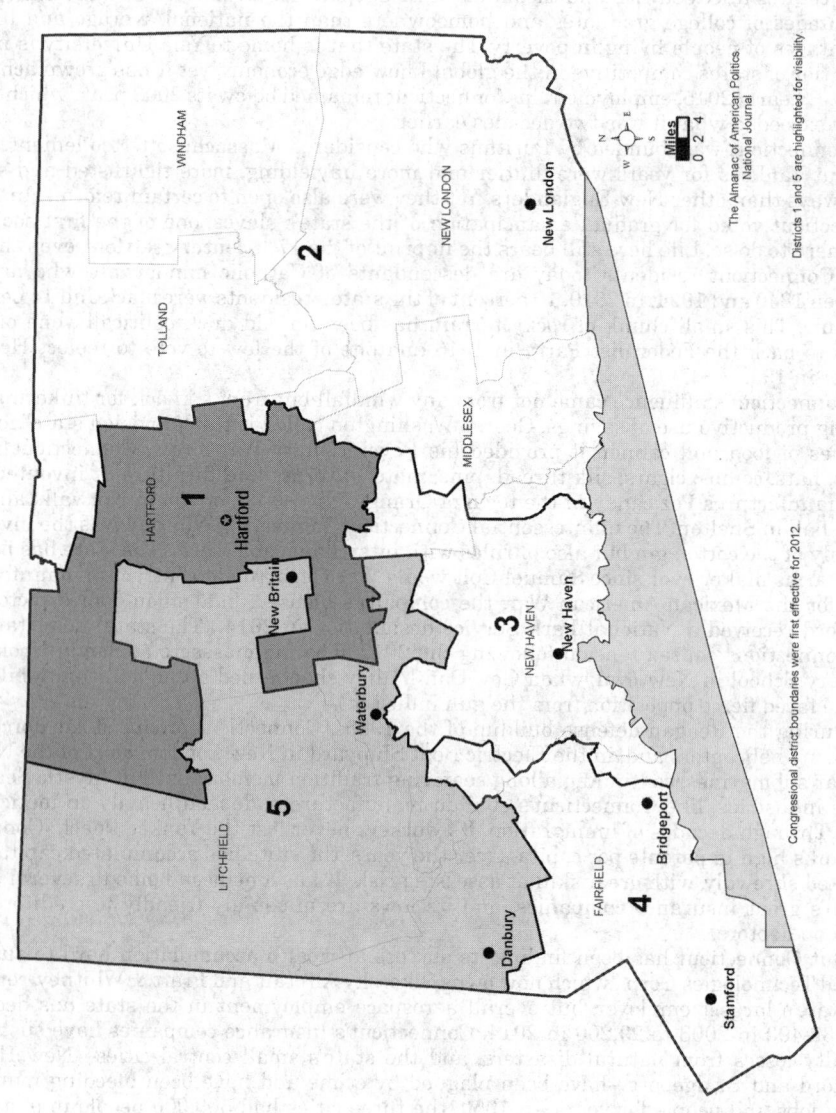

WINDHAM

NEW LONDON

New London

TOLLAND

MIDDLESEX

HARTFORD

1

Hartford

New Britain

NEW HAVEN

3

New Haven

Waterbury

LITCHFIELD

5

Bridgeport

FAIRFIELD

4

Danbury

Stamford

2

N
W   E
S

Miles
0 2 4

The Almanac of American Politics.
National Journal

Districts 1 and 5 are highlighted for visibility.

Congressional district boundaries were first effective for 2012.

Rhode Island and Maine have cut gross gambling revenues in Connecticut by an estimated 39 percent; in March 2012, saddled with $2 billion in debt, Foxwoods stopped payments to the Mashantuckets.

Meanwhile, in southwest Connecticut, Stamford and Greenwich have prospered from high finance, despite some setbacks after the Great Recession. But as Annie Lowrey noted in *New York* magazine, the shift from manufacturing to finance was not necessarily a boon for job creation: Bridgewater, a $150 billion hedge fund, employs only about 1,400 (very well-compensated) people. This has created what is by some measures the nation's most unequal state. One study found that members of Connecticut's top 1 percent averaged earnings of $2.7 million, compared to $52,000 for the remaining 99 percent—a ratio of more than 50 to 1. And the state's top 1 percent took 64 percent of all income growth from 1979 to 2007, the eighth-highest rate in the nation. "Get out of Greenwich, in other words, and you encounter lovely but stagnant suburbs—grist for so many ennui-afflicted short stories—studded with the occasional pocket of urban poverty," Lowrey wrote.

It's not clear that Connecticut's top-and-bottom work force, with many highly educated people and many with little education, is poised to spark growth. In recent years, its 18- to 34-year-old population has declined by about 200,000. An influx of immigrants from Mexico, Peru, the Dominican Republic and other parts of Latin America filled jobs that would otherwise go begging. Its state and local tax burden per capita is ranked third in the nation by the Tax Foundation, trailing only New York and New Jersey. High taxes, heavy regulation and requirements that health insurance policies cover every imaginable contingency have inhibited business growth. Meanwhile, in "Corrupticut," mayors of Waterbury and Bridgeport were sent to prison, and the mayor of Hartford was convicted on bribery charges in 2010. Republican Gov. John Rowland, elected three times, went to prison in 2005 for corruption. Then, in 2015, he was sentenced to 30 months in another political case altogether.

For much of the 20th century, Connecticut politics was an ethnic struggle between Yankee Republicans and Catholic Democrats. Slowly, as Catholic birthrates exceeded those of Protestants, Democrats gained ground. Their great leader was John Bailey, state party chairman from 1946 to 1975, a master legislative strategist and ticket-balancer, who was one of the first to endorse John F. Kennedy for president. The central cities and Catholic suburbs voted Democratic, and the WASP-y suburbs and rural towns voted Republican. But those days are gone. In the last three presidential elections, white Protestants and Catholics voted Republican; secular whites, blacks, and Latinos went heavily Democratic. Similar patterns appeared in the 2006 Senate Democratic primary between moderate incumbent Joe Lieberman and anti-Iraq war Democrat Ned Lamont, with many historically Republican areas favoring Lamont and historically Democratic areas favoring Lieberman. In 2008, Barack Obama got huge margins in central cities and did well in affluent suburbs, even carrying Greenwich, but lagged in ethnic and blue-collar areas that were once Democratic strongholds. In 2012, Obama lost ground in the most affluent suburbs while increasing his percentages in the central cities. Some polls showed the race close, but his statewide margin fell only from 61%-38% to 58%-41%.

Cultural issues have played a role in this. The state whose ban on contraceptives produced the U.S. Supreme Court's *Griswold* decision in 1965, the precursor of *Roe v. Wade*, now solidly supports abortion rights. In 2005, the legislature legalized civil unions for same-sex couples, and in 2008, the state Supreme Court converted all these into same-sex marriages. Connecticut legislators have also voted for in-state college tuition for children of illegal immigrants, for public financing of state legislative races, and for strict carbon emission reductions.

In congressional races, Connecticut has become solidly Democratic. For 22 years, its two senators were Democrats Christopher Dodd (himself son of a Democratic senator, Thomas Dodd) and Joe Lieberman, both of whom at one point ran for president. Lieberman was the Democratic vice presidential nominee in 2000, but his support of the Iraq war worked against him when he ran for president in 2004 and again in the 2006 Senate primary, which he lost to Lamont. He ran as an independent in the general election that year and beat Lamont 50%-40%, but he did not seek reelection in 2012. Dodd ran for president in 2008 and, although he spent much time in Iowa, he got few votes and dropped out. As chairman of the Senate Banking Committee, he helped put together the 2010 Dodd-Frank financial regulation legislation, but negative publicity about favorable home mortgage rates he received led to bad polling, and he decided not to run for reelection in 2010. In both 2010 and 2012, Republican Linda McMahon, head of World Wrestling Entertainment, spent lavishly

Population		Race and Ethnicity		Income	
Total:	3,596,080	White	70.7%	Median income:	$67,781
Urban:	27.7%	Latino	13.8%		(2 of 50)
Suburban:	66.7%	Black	9.5%	Under $50,000	37.6%
Rural:	5.6%	Asian	3.9%	$50,000-$99,999:	29.3%
Land area:	4,842	Two races	1.7%	$100,000-$199,999:	23.7%
Pop/sq. mi.:	742.7	White Ethnic	56.8%	$200,000 or more:	9.3%
Born in state:	55.1%			Poverty Rate	9.7%
		Education			
Age Groups		H.S. grad or less:	37.7%	**Work**	
Under 18:	21.8%	Some college:	25.1%	White collar:	40.4%
18 to 34:	21.8%	College degree, 4 yr.:	20.6%	Blue collar:	42.5%
35 to 64:	41.2%	Post-grad study:	16.6%	Sales and service:	17.1%
Over 64:	15.1%				
		Military		Govt. workers:	13.0%
		Veterans/active duty:	6.8%		

on television ads to try to win a Senate seat—some $100 million in those two races—but was unable to run far enough ahead of her party to win. In 2010, she lost 55%-43% to Richard Blumenthal, and in 2012 she lost 55%-40% to Rep. Chris Murphy. As recently as 2006, Republicans (albeit moderate ones) held a majority in the state's five-member U.S. House delegation. Since 2009, all five seats have been Democratic.

Oddly, though, Connecticut did not have a Democratic governor for two decades. Former liberal Republican Sen. Lowell Weicker, elected on the alphabetically advantaged "A Connecticut Party" line in 1990, pushed through the income tax in 1991 and retired in 1994. Rowland, elected with a plurality in 1994 and majorities in 1998 and 2002, sponsored mega-projects like a hockey arena in Hartford; after his resignation due to scandal, low-key Republican lieutenant governor Jodi Rell succeeded him and then won a full term by a wide margin in 2006. In 2010, Democrat Dan Malloy, longtime mayor of Stamford, defeated former Ambassador to Ireland Tom Foley by a hair. In office, Malloy and the Democratic legislature pushed through a thoroughgoing liberal program—a $1.5 billion tax increase; a 20-year, $1 billion economic development plan with state loans to biotech firms; looser marijuana laws; tough gun control initiatives; a state mandate for paid sick days; and a repeal of the death penalty. Malloy got public employee unions to agree to a two-year wage freeze and benefit cuts in return for a four-year promise of no layoffs. Running for reelection in 2014—another strongly Republican year—Malloy edged Foley a second time despite mediocre approval ratings, underscoring the state's resilient partisan leanings.

Voter Turnout

2013 Total Citizen 18+	2,576,393
2014 Highest Statewide Turnout	1,089,880
2014 Turnout as % CVAP	42.3%
2012 Turnout as % CVAP	60.9%

Legislature

Senate:	21D	15R
House:	87D	64R

Presidential Politics How could Barack Obama, who favored higher taxes on the rich, score victories in 2008 and 2012 in one of the nation's highest income states? Because liberal stands on cultural issues have trumped economic concerns among wealthy Connecticut voters and many of the state's white ethnics still cling to their Democratic roots. The wealthy "gold coast" towns of Greenwich, Stamford, New Canaan and Darien in Fairfield County, home to hedge fund executives and old WASP money, once a Republican bastion in the state, have been repelled by the influence of Christian evangelicals in the GOP. It's easy to forget that from 1972 to 1988, Republican presidential candidates carried the Nutmeg State. In 1988, Democratic nominee Michael Dukakis won only one of the state's eight counties, Hartford. In

2012 Presidential Vote

Barack Obama (D)	905,083	(58%)
Mitt Romney (R)	634,892	(41%)

2012 Presidential Primary

Mitt Romney (R)	40,171	(67%)
Ron Paul (R)	8,032	(13%)
Newt Gingrich (R)	6,135	(10%)
Rick Santorum (R)	4,072	(7%)

2008 Presidential Vote

Barack Obama (D)	997,772	(61%)
John McCain (R)	629,428	(38%)

1996, Democrat Bill Clinton swept them all. The legendary John Baily, who chaired the Connecticut Democratic Party from 1946 until his death in 1975, was a key early supporter of John F. Kennedy's 1960 presidential bid. Culturally conservative working-class Irish, Italian and Polish Catholics in Hartford, New Britain, Waterbury, New Haven, Bridgeport and New London, were the backbone of his Connecticut machine. Wall Street banker Prescott Bush of Greenwich—father and grandfather of future presidents—lost his first bid for the Senate in 1950 by 1,100 votes after the influential columnist Drew Pearson asserted on his radio show right before the election that Bush had been a treasurer of the Birth Control League.

Connecticut's primary has never had much impact on presidential nominations, typically overshadowed by its big neighbor to the west. Gary Hart in 1984, and Jerry Brown in 1992, won Connecticut, but each lost the subsequent New York primary. Two more recent Democratic White House hopefuls from Connecticut, Joe Lieberman in 2004 and Christopher Dodd in 2008, failed to keep their candidacies alive long enough to contest their home state. John McCain won the 2000 GOP Connecticut primary, but that year it was held on the same day as New York's, which George W. Bush comfortably won. Thanks to its "Gold Coast," Connecticut was an important stop on the 2008 fundraising circuit for Democratic and Republican contenders. That year, Democratic turnout was 355,000, far more than the past record of 241,000 in 1988. Obama won 51%-47%. He carried central cities and affluent suburbs, African-Americans and secular voters; Hillary Clinton carried ethnic areas and mill towns, Latinos and Catholics. The GOP primary attracted only 151,000 voters, less than the record 178,000 in 2000. McCain beat Romney, 52%-33%. In 2012, Connecticut voted after Rick Santorum had suspended his campaign, and Romney won with 67 percent of the vote.

Congressional Districts Connecticut has a bipartisan redistricting process. Two Republicans and two Democrats from each chamber of the legislature meet to draw the lines. If their map is approved by a two-thirds vote in both chambers, it becomes law. Otherwise, a ninth member is chosen by the other

114th Congress Lineup	
0 R	5 D
113th Congress Lineup	
0 R	5 D

eight, and they try to reach consensus. The customary collaboration didn't work in 2011, when Democrats controlled all five House seats. Republicans wanted to remove the heavily Democratic cities of Bridgeport and New Britain from the 4th and 5th districts respectively, in order to make both seats' boundaries smoother and more competitive. When the commission failed to meet its Supreme Court-extended deadline, the court stepped in and appointed Columbia Law Professor Nathaniel Persily as special redistricting master.

With instructions from the court to make minimal changes, Persily shifted only 28,975 residents between districts. In the subsequent two elections, Democrat Elizabeth Esty narrowly won the 5th District, with a big boost from New Britain. The long-time Republican success in western Connecticut districts has been relegated to the increasingly distant past.

Governor

Dannel Malloy (D)

Elected 2010, term expires Jan. 2019, 2nd term; b. July 21, 1955, Stamford; Boston Col., B.A. 1977, J.D. 1980; Catholic; married (Cathy); 3 children.

Elected Office: Stamford mayor, 1995-2009.

Professional Career: Asst. dist. atty., Brooklyn, NY, 1980-84; Partner, Abate & Fox, 1984-95.

Office: State Capitol, 210 Capitol Ave., Hartford, 06106, 860-566-4840; Fax: 860-524-7395; Website: portal.ct.gov/governor/.

Election Results

2014 general	Dannel Malloy (D)	554,314	(51%)
	Tom Foley (R)	526,295	(48%)

Prior winning percentage: 2010 (50%)

Democrat Dannel Malloy was elected governor of Connecticut in 2010. Like his better-known counterparts Andrew Cuomo of New York and Chris Christie of New Jersey, he is a former prosecutor; unlike them, he lacks the celebrity cachet of being a future presidential possibility, and he has had to contend with low approval ratings while navigating an arduous fiscal landscape. Nevertheless, he was able to win reelection narrowly in 2014.

Malloy, the youngest of eight children, grew up in Stamford with a learning disability; he had difficulties with reading and motor coordination and after several years was diagnosed as dyslexic. He graduated from Boston College and its law school, taking the bar exam orally. He was an assistant district attorney in Brooklyn from 1980 to 1984, and in that role, obtained 22 convictions in 23 felony cases. He moved back to Stamford to practice law. In 1995, he beat Republican incumbent Mayor Stanley Esposito and served in that job until 2009. In those years, Malloy recruited big financial houses to set up shop in Stamford, eventually generating about 5,000 new jobs. He sponsored citywide preschool and a Stamford Urban Transitway. The one blight on his record was an accusation of favoritism to campaign contributors and contractors who did work on his house. After a 17-month investigation, prosecutors said there was no evidence of wrongdoing.

Stamford is not Connecticut's biggest city, but it often casts a large number of votes, which was helpful for Malloy when he set his sights on statewide office. In 2006, he ran for governor, won the endorsement of the Democratic state convention by a single vote and then lost the Democratic primary to New Haven Mayor John DeStefano, 51%-49%. DeStefano went on to be defeated 63%-35% by Republican incumbent Jodi Rell, whose low-key approach was a relief to voters disgusted with Republican Gov. John Rowland, who resigned amid corruption-related charges that ultimately sent him to prison.

Rell announced in November 2009 she would not run again. In March 2010, Malloy got into the contest as an underdog in the Democratic primary against investor Ned Lamont, who had beaten Sen. Joe Lieberman in the 2006 Senate primary, but then lost to him when Lieberman ran as an independent in the general election. On the Republican side, a contest shaped up between Lt. Gov. Mike Fedele and former Ambassador to Ireland Tom Foley.

Lamont attacked Malloy for allegedly awarding no-bid contracts in Stamford, and Malloy attacked Lamont's business practices. Lamont spent $8.6 million of his own money, which triggered Connecticut's Citizens' Election Program and the allocation of $2.5 million in public funds to Malloy. He also had the support of public employee unions, which had backed DeStefano in 2006. That helped him beat Lamont by more than 2-to-1 at the May Democratic state convention. Although Lamont led in initial polls, Malloy won the August 10 primary, 57%-43%. At the same time, Foley edged Fedele in the Republican primary, 42%-39%.

There were sharp issue differences between the candidates in the fall 2010 campaign. Malloy opposed the death penalty, while Foley said he would follow Rell's lead and veto any bill repealing it. The issue was especially vivid because of the conviction in October of a career criminal for killing a mother and two daughters in a 2007 home invasion in Cheshire. "There is absolutely no connection between the death penalty and preventing or discouraging homicides from taking place," Malloy said.

Malloy also favored legalizing same-sex marriage and a union-backed bill to require companies with more than 50 employees to grant workers paid sick days. He called for requiring 20 percent of Connecticut's electricity to be produced from renewable sources by 2020 and presented a 12-point economic development plan. Foley promised no tax increases and called for $2 billion in spending cuts in the state budget. Malloy charged that Foley had driven a Georgia textile company into bankruptcy while earning $20 million himself from the firm. Foley said that Malloy misstated the facts and that he had lost control of the company before the bankruptcy.

By September, Foley had loaned his campaign $5.3 million, and Malloy became eligible for some $6 million in public financing. Malloy was well ahead in the polls in early fall, but the race tightened in October and the results were extremely close. Malloy was declared the winner the Friday after the election, 50%-49%.

In early 2011, his first order of business was figuring out ways to address a projected $3.5 billion budget shortfall. He took the politically unpopular step of asking the Democratic-controlled General Assembly for tax increases, saying, "It's what's right for my state. Connecticut would not be Connecticut if we cut $3.5 billion out of the budget." Lawmakers eventually approved a $40.2 billion budget that included $1.5 billion in tax hikes, including an increase in the general sales tax. They refused, however, to grant Malloy's request for a 3-cents-a-gallon gasoline tax increase, citing high gas prices.

He also had to battle the state's 45,000 unionized employees, who in June rejected his call for $1.6 billion in concessions to balance the budget. In response, he called for eliminating 6,500 jobs. After two months of negotiations, the unions agreed to a modified version of the deal. On a more positive note, he signed into law his campaign-promised bill to require companies to provide employees with paid sick leave. But his anemic approval rating in a June Quinnipiac University poll, 37 percent, reflected the public's unease over the tax hikes.

To promote economic development in a state that had no net gain in employment in more than two decades, Malloy unveiled a "First Five" plan that called for benefits for the first five companies to expand business in the state. NBC Sports accepted the deal and announced plans in October 2011 to add studio, production, and office space in Stamford in exchange for $20 million in tax breaks. He also got lawmakers to approve a $626 million package of hiring incentives, job training and infrastructure repair, with most of it intended to help small businesses. He took an optimistic tone in his January 2012 State of the State address, saying, "Make no mistake about it. We will end this year in the black." He also unveiled an ambitious education reform plan that drew fire from teachers' unions because of a proposal to make it easier for school districts to fire underperforming teachers with tenure. "I believe education reform is the civil rights issue of our time," he said in May 2012 after lawmakers passed his proposal. He also signed a bill the following month to legalize and regulate medical marijuana. But at the end of 2012, the state's finances remained precarious. After projecting a manageable $60 million deficit in November, state officials revised the number upward a month later to $363 million. And they warned that the deficit was expected to grow to $1.1 billion by 2014.

In all, Malloy, in concert with the heavily Democratic legislature, was able to implement one of the nation's most solidly liberal agendas—a $10.10 minimum wage, mandatory paid sick leave, a death penalty repeal, relaxed laws on marijuana, a ban on discrimination based on "gender identity or expression" and tougher gun control. In the process, Malloy gained a reputation for arrogance and combativeness, without a gift for schmoozing to smooth his rougher edges. "Malloy doesn't have one amino acid of Bill Clinton's charm DNA, and maybe he pays a big price for that," veteran Nutmeg State journalist Colin McEnroe told *The New York Times* in 2011. The silver lining was a certain steeliness and a cool-under-fire approach amid crises. Malloy gained respect for his handling of natural disasters, and he took a central role after the December 2012 massacre at Sandy Hook Elementary School in Newtown, when a troubled young man opened fire on small children and their teachers, killing 26, including 20 children. When Malloy arrived at the scene, he learned that it fell to him to inform anxious parents that their children had been killed; he decided to do so before awaiting formal identifications of the victims, a task he described afterward with great emotion. Later, he spearheaded a firm legislative response, pushing through a ban on assault weapons and high-capacity magazines in the face of fierce opposition from the gun industry, some of which has centuries-old ties to his state.

The reverberations from the tax hike and the state's zigzagging economic recovery left Malloy with weak approval ratings as he approached his reelection in 2014. For most of the election cycle, handicappers rated Malloy's rematch with Foley as a toss-up, despite Connecticut's increasingly blue hue in major races. In a brutal election year for Democrats, Malloy did something many other candidates in his party were unwilling to do—invite Barack Obama to campaign for him, which the president did in Bridgeport shortly before Election Day. Ultimately, though, there was enough of an economic recovery—tentative though it may have been—to save him. By a somewhat more comfortable margin than in 2010, Malloy defeated Foley, 51%-48% (with the remainder coming from the left-leaning Working Families Party ballot line). The *Hartford Courant* ascribed Malloy's win to incremental gains among affluent voters: Some of the "wealthiest sections of the state—greater Danbury, the Farmington Valley and the shoreline from I-91 to the Connecticut River—all swung toward Malloy as the economy improved for them."

After his reelection victory, Malloy kept the bold moves coming. He pushed for a $100 billion investment in highways and mass transit over 30 years, greater use of rooftop solar energy, and submitted a budget with a 3.3 percent increase in state spending in 2016 and a 3.1 percent increase for 2017, alongside cuts to the sales tax rate. When Indiana passed a law that critics said could allow businesses to discriminate against gays and lesbians—a law later modified under national pressure—Malloy signed an executive order barring state-funded travel to Indiana. One area where Malloy has hit the brakes is on gun control. In March 2015, the Sandy Hook Advisory Commission, a panel Malloy established, issued a

277-page report that recommended tighter laws on gun registration, expanded use of trigger locks, serial numbers for shell casings, and the ability of law enforcement to take firearms, ammunition and gun permits from those facing a restraining order. But Malloy threw cold water on the report, saying that "there's just not a big appetite for even talking about guns at the moment in the state of Connecticut." Malloy's profile could rise nationally as he takes the helm of the Democratic Governors Association during the presidential election year of 2016.

Senior Senator

Richard Blumenthal (D)

Elected 2010, term expires Jan. 2017, 1st term; b. Feb. 13, 1946, Brooklyn, NY; Harvard U., B.A. 1967, Yale U., J.D. 1973; Jewish; married (Cynthia); 4 children.

Military Career: U.S. Marine Corps Reserves, 1970-76.

Elected Office: CT House, 1984-87; CT Senate, 1987-90; CT atty. gen., 1991-2010.

Professional Career: Teacher, Washington D.C. public schl., 1968-69; Staff asst., White House Office of Econ. Opportunity, 1969-70; Clerk, Supreme Court Justice Harry Blackmun, 1974-75; Administrative asst., Sen. Abraham Ribicoff, 1975-76; U.S. atty. CT, 1977-81; Practing atty., 1981-90.

DC Office: 706 HSOB, 20510, 202-224-2823; Fax: 202-224-9673; Website: blumenthal.senate.gov.

State Offices: Bridgeport, 203-330-0598; Hartford, 860-258-6940.

Committees: *Aging (Special). Armed Services:* Airland; Personnel; SeaPower. *Commerce, Science & Transportation:* Aviation Operations, Safety, & Security; Communications, Technology, Innovation, & the Internet; Consumer Protection, Product Safety, Insurance, & Data Security (RMM); Oceans, Atmosphere, Fisheries & Coast Guard; Surface Transportation & Merchant Marine Infrastructure, Safety & Security. *Judiciary:* Antitrust, Competition Policy & Consumer Rights; Immigration & the National Interest; Oversight, Agency Action, Federal Rights & Federal Courts. *Veterans' Affairs (RMM).*

Group Ratings

	ADA	ACLU	AFL-CIO	LCV	ITI	COC	HAFA	ACU	CFG	FRC
2014	90%	100%	–	80%	100%	38%	3%	8%	17%	0%
2013	100%	C	100%	100%	C	50%	C	4%	2%	C

National Journal Ratings

	2013 LIB	—	2013 CONS
Economic	82%	—	80%
Social	73%	—	0%
Foreign	71%	—	0%
Composite	86%	—	14%

Key Votes of the 113th Congress

1. Sandy storm spending	Y	5. Student Loan Rates	N	9. Bipartisan Budget Deal	Y
2. Chuck Hagel Confirmation	Y	6. Employee Non-Discrim'n Act	Y	10. Farm Bill Conference Rept.	N
3. Gun Background Checks	Y	7. Senate Vote on Judgeships	N	11. Unempl. Comp. Extension	Y
4. Immigration Reform	Y	8. Defense Dept. Spending	Y	12. Keystone Pipeline	N

Election Results

2010 general	Richard Blumenthal (D)	636,040	(55%)	$8,716,686	$311,571	$68,087
	Linda McMahon (R)	498,341	(43%)	$50,181,464	$20,413	$2,171,714
2010 primary	Richard Blumenthal (D)	unopposed				

For two decades, Democrat Richard Blumenthal was Connecticut's aggressive, media-savvy attorney general, focusing on one high-profile consumer protection issue after another and becoming the state's most popular elected official in the process. Although seemingly unhesitant to take on corporate targets ranging from Big Tobacco to the nation's largest banks, Blumenthal earned a reputation for caution when it came to tackling his political future: He resisted repeated entreaties from fellow Democrats to run for governor of the Nutmeg State, a post occupied by Republicans during much of the time that he was the state's top lawyer.

Finally, just as Blumenthal finally seemed ready to take the plunge for higher office—eyeing a challenge to Democratic-turned-independent Sen. Joe Lieberman in 2012—an unexpected opening occurred. Veteran Democratic Sen. Christopher Dodd, at the height of his power on Capitol Hill but politically embattled at home over allegations that he had accepted political favors, abruptly announced his retirement at the beginning of 2010. Blumenthal switched from seeking re-election to run for Dodd's seat, and won by a double-digit margin—but only after being roughed up by a Republican opponent who had made a fortune thanks to professional wrestling.

Blumenthal was born in the New York City borough of Brooklyn; his father, Martin, had fled Nazi Germany in 1935 and became wealthy by trading commodities in his adopted country. (Blumenthal now regularly ranks among the top 10 wealthiest members of Congress—largely due to his wife, Cynthia, whose father, New York real estate magnate Peter Malkin, counts the iconic Empire State Building among his recent holdings.) After graduating from Harvard with a degree in political science, Blumenthal later attended Yale Law School, where he edited the *Yale Law Journal* and was a classmate of Hillary Rodham Clinton. Blumenthal's post-college list of employers reads like a Who's Who of the Washington elite in the 1970s. They included longtime *Washington Post* publisher Katharine Graham, future New York Sen. Daniel Patrick Moynihan when the latter was a top adviser in the Nixon White House, and Supreme Court Justice William Brennan—for whom Blumenthal clerked. After a two-year stint as a top aide to Sen. Abraham Ribicoff—who then held the seat Blumenthal now occupies—President Carter in 1977 appointed the 31-year old Blumenthal as U.S. attorney for Connecticut.

Entering private law practice in the early 1980s, Blumenthal—doing volunteer work for the NAACP Legal Defense Fund—gained further visibility by winning a stay of execution for a prisoner on Florida's death row just hours before it was to take place, and later convincing an appeals court to overturn the murder conviction against the prisoner, Joseph Green Brown. Later, Blumenthal said the Brown case changed his view of the death penalty "because it provided such a dramatic illustration of how the system could be fallible and cause the death of an innocent person." But the case came back to haunt Blumenthal after he was elected to the Senate: Brown's wife was found dead in September 2012, and Brown was arrested again and charged with first degree murder.

Elected to the Connecticut Assembly in 1984 and to the state Senate in 1987 before his successful run for attorney general in 1990, Blumenthal used the latter position to pursue lawsuits against health insurers and polluters as well as banks and tobacco companies. Detractors derided him as "Sue 'Em All Blumenthal," but voters elected him to five terms, never with less than 59 percent of the vote. When he finally got his shot to run for Senate in 2010, it initially looked like an electoral stroll in the park, given his popularity in a one-time swing state that had titled heavily blue. But it was also the year that the tea party took flight, and the Republican nominee, Linda McMahon—who, with her husband, Vince McMahon had started World Wrestling Entertainment—harnessed an upswing in GOP voter energy to make it a real contest.

The first sign things were not going to be easy for Blumenthal was his apparent exaggeration of his military service. A member of the Marine Corps Reserve from 1970 to 1975, Blumenthal claimed on several occasions to have served in Vietnam, though he never in fact was deployed. The McMahon campaign attacked him for distorting his record, putting a chink in his best asset: his image as a selfless crusader. Blumenthal apologized, but the episode sparked a nasty back-and-forth campaign, with Blumenthal's initial wide lead in the polls tightening considerably.

McMahon proved to be a tireless campaigner, and, to appeal to Democrats and independents, she billed herself as a centrist who supported abortion rights and the prerogative of states to decide the same-sex marriage issue. But her readiness for the job was called into question by revelations that she had failed to even vote in the two prior elections of 2006 and 2008. Blumenthal's camp went after McMahon over sexism and use of steroids in professional wrestling, where McMahon had earned a fortune as WWE president. By the end of the campaign, she had spent more than $50 million—almost six times as much as Blumenthal—with most of it coming from her own pocket. Blumenthal went after her, declaring that voters deserved "an election, not an auction." The *Hartford Courant* noted that McMahon "had persistent trouble winning over women voters, despite the fact she would have become the first female senator in the state's history. Some women were turned off by some of the racier images of WWE; others didn't like her aggressive advertising strategy." When the results were in, showing Blumenthal with a 55%-43% win, the *Courant* summed things up this way: "In the beginning, Richard Blumenthal looked unbeatable. At the end, he was. In between, there was quite a battle."

In his first term on Capitol Hill, Blumenthal picked up where he left off in Hartford— taking on the role of consumer advocate in high-profile controversies. Shortly after being sworn into office, he asked the Food and Drug Administration to ban the sale of menthol cigarettes, pointing out high usage rates among young people and minorities. More recently, he pressed General Motors to create a compensation fund for victims of defective ignition switches in the company's automobiles, and has pursued legislation to require repairs for recalled vehicles be performed before a renewed registration is granted. He has credited a bill that he sponsored with Republican Sen. John McCain of Arizona with pushing the Federal Communications Commission to change its rules on the blackout of televised sporting events—and, in late 2014, Blumenthal held a hearing on the incidence of domestic violence among National Football League players, followed by the NFL donating $25 million to a domestic violence hotline. "My friends at the hotline say it was a $25 million hearing," Blumenthal afterward told the *Connecticut Mirror*, adding: "One lesson to me is that legislation is only one lever to fight for benefits for the people of Connecticut. I can use my position to shine a light on problems."

With an eye toward his constituents, Blumenthal has pressured the Federal Railroad Administration to adopt new regulations after a series of accidents on Metro North, the commuter line that thousands of Connecticut residents ride to get to jobs in New York City. He has been less successful on what also became a key safety issue for many in his home state following the 2012 mass shooting at a Newtown elementary school in which 26 were killed, most of them children. In 2013, he helped lead the Senate effort that sought expanded background checks for gun owners; it was blocked by several moderate Democrats from red states.

Blumenthal's committee assignments include the Armed Services panel; the defense industry is a major employer in eastern Connecticut. In early 2015, Blumenthal became ranking Democrat on the Veterans Affairs Committee; his son, Matthew, is an officer in the Marine Corps Reserve and has served in Afghanistan. Legislation mandating more mental health resources for veterans, also co-authored with McCain, passed the Senate unanimously early in 2015. But, despite efforts to reach across the aisle, Blumenthal has for the most part been a reliable partisan.

Now the state's senior senator with the 2012 retirement of Lieberman, Blumenthal will be 70 when he is up for re-election in 2016. He has been actively raising money, and, despite his 2010 political bruising, his poll ratings since have been high. Former U.S. Comptroller General David Walker, who ran for lieutenant governor in the 2014 Republican primary, for a time considered taking on Blumenthal. But, in early 2015, Walker accepted a job in the Washington, D.C. area, leaving no obvious challenger in sight.

Junior Senator

Chris Murphy (D)

Elected 2012, term expires Jan. 2019, 1st term; b. Aug. 3, 1973, White Plains, NY; Williams Col., B.A. 1996, U. of CT, J.D. 2002; Protestant; married (Cathy Holahan); 2 children.

Elected Office: CT House, 1999-2003; CT Senate, 2003-06; U.S. House, 2007-13.

Professional Career: Southington CT Planning & Zoning Commission, 1997-99; Practicing atty., 2002-06.

DC Office: 136 HSOB, 20510, 202-224-4041; Fax: 202-224-9750; Website: murphy.senate.gov.

State Offices: Hartford, 860-549-8463.

Committees: *Appropriations:* Commerce, Justice, Science, & Related Agencies; Legislative Branch; Military Construction & Veterans Affairs, & Related Agencies; State, Foreign Operations, & Related Programs; Transportation, Housing, & Urban Development, & Related Agencies. *Foreign Relations:* Near East, South Asia, Central Asia, & Counterterrorism (RMM); Europe & Regional Security Cooperation; State Dept & USAID Mgmt., Int'l Operations, & Bilateral Int'l Development. *Health, Education, Labor & Pensions:* Primary Health & Retirement Security.

Group Ratings

	ADA	ACLU	AFL-CIO	LCV	ITI	COC	HAFA	ACU	CFG	FRC
2014	90%	100%	–	80%	100%	38%	3%	0%	10%	0%
2013	100%	C	100%	100%	C	50%	C	4%	2%	C

National Journal Ratings

	2013 LIB	—	2013 CONS
Economic	93%	—	0%
Social	73%	—	0%
Foreign	71%	—	0%
Composite	90%	—	11%

Key Votes of the 113th Congress

1. Sandy storm spending	Y	5. Student Loan Rates	Y	9. Bipartisan Budget Deal	Y
2. Chuck Hagel Confirmation	Y	6. Employee Non-Discrim'n Act	Y	10. Farm Bill Conference Rept.	N
3. Gun Background Checks	Y	7. Senate Vote on Judgeships	N	11. Unempl. Comp. Extension	Y
4. Immigration Reform	Y	8. Defense Dept. Spending	Y	12. Keystone Pipeline	N

Election Results

2012 general	Chris Murphy (D)	828,761	(55%)	$10,436,219	$1,879,868	$85,309
	Linda McMahon (R)	651,089	(43%)	$49,496,249	$1,022,818	$7,426,239
2012 primary	Chris Murphy (D)	94,424	(67%)			
	Susan Bysiewicz (D)	47,109	(33%)			

Prior winning percentages: House: 2010 (54%), 2008 (59%), 2006 (56%)

When it comes to foreign policy, there could hardly be a bigger contrast than the one between Connecticut's junior senator, Chris Murphy, and his predecessor, Joe Lieberman. Lieberman was long one of the Democratic Party's leading hawks: His support for the Iraq war ultimately pushed the party's 2000 vice-presidential nominee into the role of political independent. Murphy, since succeeding Lieberman in early 2013, has emerged as one of the Senate's most outspoken doves with regard to U.S. involvement in the Middle East. In the process, Murphy has found himself at odds with both President Barack Obama and Obama's 2008 Republican opponent, Arizona Sen. John McCain—the latter a close friend and ally for whom Lieberman bolted the Democratic Party to support in that year's presidential race. "The dominance of the President, Senator McCain, and Senator [Rand] Paul on foreign policy should trouble progressives," Murphy declared in an op-ed piece published in early 2015.

Murphy's foreign policy stance can be traced to the circumstances of his arrival on Capitol Hill nearly a decade ago. In 2006, he was elected to the House of Representatives from northwestern Connecticut at the age of 33, with his opposition to the war in Iraq helping him to oust a veteran Republican incumbent, Nancy Johnson. (It was the same year that Lieberman's strong support of the Iraq war cost him renomination in the Democratic primary; he went on to win the general election as an independent.) Raised in the Hartford suburb of Wethersfield—his father is managing partner of a large Hartford law firm—Murphy first took on Johnson in 1996. Just out of Williams College, he signed on as campaign manager for Charlotte Koskoff, who came within 1,600 votes of toppling Johnson. Two years later, Murphy ran for office himself, winning a seat in the state House when he was just 25. He also pursued a law degree, which he received in the spring of 2002; later that year, he won election to the state Senate.

In early 2005, Murphy moved into Johnson's 5th District, which had been significantly redrawn after Connecticut's loss of a House seat following the 2000 census, and announced plans to challenge her. Besides Iraq, the debate focused on the Medicare prescription drug benefit that Johnson, a moderate Republican, had helped design in 2003 as chairman of the House Ways and Means panel's Health Subcommittee. Murphy contended that the prescription drug program's enrollment deadlines penalized seniors, and spotlighted drug industry contributions to Johnson. Johnson, who had served in Congress for nearly a quarter of a century, counterattacked with ads accusing Murphy of voting to raise taxes 27 times, and outspent Murphy by 2-1. But, as the Democrats rode a national wave to retake the House majority, Murphy won easily, 56%-44%.

In the House, Murphy was a fairly loyal Democrat, although he boasted of his role in Center Aisle Caucus, which he described as "one of the few places in the House where Republicans and Democrats are…getting together to try and talk about the importance of civility." While his district was home to many insurance industry employees, he backed a government-run public option as part of the 2009-2010 health care overhaul to compete with private insurers. An ardent advocate for "buy American" requirements throughout his congressional career, he introduced bills to require federal contracting officials to accept and solicit information from businesses regarding how many U.S. jobs would be retained or created if their bid was chosen.

When Lieberman announced his retirement, Murphy faced a Democratic primary against former Connecticut Secretary of State Susan Bysiewicz, who ran a controversial TV ad seeking to link Murphy to Wall Street in the wake of the 2008 financial meltdown; it cited more than $700,000 in contributions to Murphy from Wall Street sources over a six-year period. But Bysiewicz found herself on the defensive after having to acknowledge that the ad had overstated Murphy's donations from hedge funds. Murphy triumphed in the primary by 2-1. The general election turned out to be *déjà vu*. Linda McMahon, the former professional wrestling magnate who had lost the 2010 Senate race to Democrat Richard Blumenthal, was again the Republican nominee. And, like Blumenthal two years earlier, Murphy struggled in the general election despite being an odds-on favorite at the start of the campaign.

While Blumenthal had stumbled due to inflated claims on his military record, Murphy was tripped up over revelations that he missed mortgage payments and been sued over failure to pay rent. Murphy blamed a busy schedule for the missed payments. McMahon's personal finances also were called into question after reports surfaced that she had been late on several property-tax bills. As she had in 2010, McMahon tapped into her personal wealth to float her campaign—burning through nearly $50 million. And, like two years earlier, she sought to move to the political center—but it prompted questions about her true ideological leanings. Murphy targeted McMahon on issues affecting seniors, arguing she would pose a threat to Social Security and Medicare. On Election Day, McMahon lost by the same 55%-43% spread by which she had come up short to Blumenthal in 2010.

Murphy was sworn into the Senate just weeks after the shootings at Newtown's Sandy Hook Elementary School, located in the congressional district that he represented. He and Blumenthal have pushed repeatedly, albeit unsuccessfully, for gun restrictions, while Murphy has actively sought to rankle the National Rifle Association by questioning its influence. In the wake of Newtown, he characterized Congress' failure to approve a bill for expanded background checks for gun owners the biggest disappointment of his political career. In his first year in the Senate, Murphy's voting record tied him for first (with fellow Democrats Charles Schumer of New York and Brian Schatz of Hawaii) as the chamber's most liberal member, according to *National Journal* rankings. In contrast to his senior in-state colleague, Murphy is among the Senate's poorer members: His 2014 financial disclosure form showed student loan debt of as much as $50,000. Murphy and Schatz in late 2013 teamed up on a bill to provide incentives to college administrators to bring down the cost of higher education.

On domestic policy, Murphy has been an outspoken defender of Obama's signature legislative achievement: the Affordable Care Act. A member of the Senate Health, Education, Labor and Pensions Committee, he volunteered to take the lead role among Senate Democrats in seeking to rebut relentless Republican criticism of "Obamacare." His willingness to perform this politically onerous task appears to have served him well with Democratic leaders: Murphy was given a coveted seat on the Appropriations Committee at the outset of the 114th Congress.

Murphy's relations with the White House on foreign policy have been another matter. He gained widespread attention in September 2013 when he told Obama—who had called Murphy at home—that he could not support the administration's plan to take military action against Syria. "I can't say that it was a comfortable position to be in, having a public dispute with the president so early in my freshman term," Murphy, who sits on the Senate Foreign Relations Committee, told the *Connecticut Mirror*. A year later, he also came out solidly against the Obama administration's efforts to train and arm Syrian rebels to fight the Islamic militant force ISIS. Murphy says he became wary of U.S. military involvements because of what he saw as the failures of wars in Iraq and Afghanistan. "I want ISIS defeated in Syria," he said in a floor speech. "But too much can go wrong, for not enough possible gain, for the U.S. to increase our involvement in the Syrian civil war."

Murphy has been more militant on Ukrainian independence—influenced, he says, by his Polish-American mother, a retired school teacher. As he was growing up, he recalls her relating the struggles of relatives in the old country living in the shadow of Russian power. He also represents a state with a significant Ukrainian-American community. In December 2013, Murphy traveled to Ukraine, where he and a Senate colleague stood in Kiev's Independence Square and addressed thousands of protesters seeking the ouster of Ukraine's Russian-backed president. The colleague who joined Murphy in Independence Square? None other than Joe Lieberman's old friend and ally, John McCain, with whom Murphy has struck up a friendship despite numerous differences.

Murphy was only 39 when elected to the Senate. Given his state's tilt toward the Democrats in recent years, he may be around long enough to accumulate a lot of seniority—and influence. He boasts he is the first Connecticut senator in almost 30 years to sit on the powerful Appropriations Committee, and longevity could make him chairman down the road. "I'm young. I only get a six-year term," Murphy told a reporter for the *Connecticut Post* in 2014, "but I'm planning to be around the Senate long enough to beat the gun lobby."

FIRST DISTRICT

John Larson (D)

Elected 1998, 9th term; b. July 22, 1948, Hartford; Central CT U., B.A. 1971; Catholic; married (Leslie); 3 children.

Elected Office: E. Hartford Bd. of Ed., 1977-79; E. Hartford Town Cncl., 1979-83; CT Senate, 1986-98, pres. pro-tem, 1990-98.

Professional Career: H.S. teacher, 1972-77; Ins. broker, 1977-98; Sr. fellow, Yale Bush Ctr., 1995-98.

DC Office: 1501 LHOB, 20515, 202-225-2265; Fax: 202-225-1031; Website: larson.house.gov.

State Offices: Hartford, 860-278-8888.

Committees: *Ethics. Ways & Means:* Select Revenue Measures; Social Security.

Group Ratings

	ADA	ACLU	AFL-CIO	LCV	ITI	COC	HAFA	ACU	CFG	FRC
2014	85%	77%	–	97%	80%	43%	14%	8%	13%	0%
2013	75%	C	95%	96%	C	31%	C	13%	12%	C

National Journal Ratings

	2013 LIB	—	2013 CONS
Economic	78%	—	22%
Social	87%	—	7%
Foreign	81%	—	18%
Composite	83%	—	17%

Key Votes of the 113th Congress

1. Sandy storm spending	Y	5. Medical Marijuana	Y	9. Syrian Rebels Training	N
2. Violence Against Women Act	Y	6. Farm Bill	N	10. Keystone pipeline	N
3. Guantanamo Bay Detainees	Y	7. Afghanistan Combat	Y	11. Immigration Exec. Action	NV
4. Abortion 20-week ban	N	8. NSA Phone Data Collection	Y	12. Bipartisan budget deal	Y

Election Results

2014 general	John Larson (D)	134,980	(62%)	$1,659,154	$8,211
	Matthew Corey (R)	78,112	(36%)	$32,291	
2014 primary	John Larson (D)	unopposed			

Prior winning percentages: 2012 (70%), 2010 (61%), 2008 (72%), 2006 (74%), 2004 (73%), 2002 (67%), 2000 (72%), 1998 (58%)

Population		Race and Ethnicity		Income	
Total:	716,580	White	64.5%	Median income:	$63,439
Urban:	30.6%	Latino	15.4%		*(90 of 435)*
Suburban:	63.2%	Black	13.3%	Under $50,000	39.5%
Rural:	6.1%	Asian	5.0%	$50,000-$99,999:	30.6%
Land area:	748	Two races	1.4%	$100,000-$199,999:	23.7%
Pop/sq. mi.:	958.1	White Ethnic	54.3%	$200,000 or more:	6.2%
Born in state:	59.3%			Poverty Rate	12.4%
		Education			
Age Groups		H.S. grad or less:	39.0%	**Work**	
Under 18:	**21.6%**	Some college:	25.2%	White collar:	42.1%
18 to 34:	21.9%	College degree, 4 yr.:	20.4%	Blue collar:	41.4%
35 to 64:	40.3%	Post-grad study:	15.4%	Sales and service:	16.6%
Over 64:	16.1%			Govt. workers:	14.6%
		Military			
		Veterans/active duty:	6.8%		

North-central Connecticut: Hartford

The Puritans who founded Hartford certainly never expected, or even hoped, that Connecticut's Yankees would turn out to be shrewd businessmen. Yet this is exactly what happened. Mark Twain moved to Hartford in 1871 to become director of an insurance company, and in time became the Connecticut

Voter Turnout	
2013 Total Citizen 18+	516,439
2014 House Turnout	217,696
2014 Turnout as % CVAP	42.2%
2012 Turnout as % CVAP	61%

capital's most famous citizen. Today, Connecticut has the second-largest concentration of financial and insurance firms in the nation, mostly in the Hartford area. Its merchants wrote fire insurance, using the capital they had accumulated in the Napoleonic Wars to finance their ventures. The native Samuel Colt played a foundational role in developing the state's armaments base; he conceived of the revolving-barrel pistol after watching the wheel of a ship spin while on a year-long voyage at sea. His gun factory, just south of downtown Hartford, became one of the nation's great arms plants. Thanks to the broad Connecticut River, Hartford also became a seaport.

Although each sector has downsized, insurance and armaments are still economic mainstays of Hartford, Connecticut's biggest metropolitan area. But many employers have moved out of Hartford itself, hastening the sad decline of this once rich city. The central core has been filled with bedraggled, high-crime neighborhoods littered with abandoned buildings. Downtown landmarks, such as the Broadcast House, have been demolished, while the Civic Center, renamed the XL Center in 2007, has suffered in its declining neighborhood. Where 177,000 people lived in 1950, there were about 124,800 residents in 2010. The population is 39% African-American and 43% Hispanic. There may be hope for a business turnaround. A developer has unveiled plans for a $350 million Downtown North with housing, retail, a brewery, and a 9,000-spectator minor league ballpark on long-vacant land.

The areas beyond the city lines of Hartford are more affluent and faring somewhat better. But insurance industry employment dropped to 47,000 statewide in 2014 from 50,000 in 2011. Across the river is the Pratt & Whitney jet engine plant in East Hartford, cornerstone of Connecticut-based United Technologies. Though its operations have been shrunk by Pentagon spending cutbacks and its local workforce is less than one-fourth its size in 1980, it still builds engines for more than 600 customers around the world. Hartford is also home to the nation's longest-circulating newspaper, the *Hartford Courant*, established in 1764.

The 1st Congressional District of Connecticut is centered on Hartford. In its present incarnation, it looks like a lobster claw. The top half of the claw passes first through Windsor, where Amy Archer-Gilligan's poisoning spree in the late 1910s at the retirement home she oversaw shocked the citizenry and inspired the play *Arsenic and*

2012 Presidential Vote
Barack Obama (D) 200,910   (63%)
Mitt Romney (R).................112,962   (36%)

2008 Presidential Vote
Barack Obama (D) 219,219   (66%)
John McCain (R).................109,658   (33%)

Cook Partisan Voting Index: D+13

Old Lace, and the film version that followed. The claw then swings west across the northern border of the state, excluding some affluent suburbs while taking in small towns and part of Torrington. The bottom half of the district swings southwest of Hartford. It includes Bristol, site of the sprawling headquarters of ESPN, the multimedia network that employs more than 4,200 people locally of its 8,000 worldwide. ESPN Plaza includes nearly 1.2 million square feet in 17 buildings on 123 acres. In 2015, Bristol gained national attention for its municipal fiber optic network that provides Internet access to the city's agencies and in public places.

The Hartford area has long been more Democratic than the rest of Connecticut. It owes some of its Democratic character to John Bailey, an old-fashioned political boss with a scandal-free career who promoted a raft of first-class candidates, including John F. Kennedy and his daughter Barbara Kennelly, the former 1st District Representative.

John Larson (D)

Democrat John Larson, first elected in 1998, has been an influential figure among House Democrats, popular with colleagues and active on the tax-writing Ways and Means Committee. Term limits removed him as chairman of the Democratic Caucus in 2012, but he remains a go-to figure in the Caucus.

One of eight children, Larson grew up in the Mayberry Village public-housing project in East Hartford, and is fond of saying that he is a "product of public housing, public education, and public service." His father was a fireman at Pratt & Whitney and also worked as an auto mechanic and butcher. His mother had a job at the state Capitol and served on the town council. Speaking at the 2012 Democratic National Convention, he said that his mother had dementia and required round-the-clock care, paid for in part through her Social Security benefits. "Don't ever tell me or any American that's a handout," he said. "It's the insurance they paid for." Larson's politics are a product of his upbringing. He says that he doesn't believe in big government or small government, but the "effective use of government on behalf of the people you are sworn to serve."

After graduating from Central Connecticut State University, Larson taught high school and coached athletics. He also worked in the hometown industry as an insurance agent. In 1982, at age 34, Larson was elected to the state Senate. Four years later, he earned a promotion to Senate president. He sponsored one of the nation's first family medical leave laws, a prototype for the federal bill sponsored by home-state Sen. Christopher Dodd and signed into law by President Bill Clinton in 1993.

Larson seemed headed for governor and, in 1994, won the party designation at the state convention. But Comptroller Bill Curry built an organization of unionists and liberal activists and beat him 55%-45% in the primary. When Democratic Rep. Barbara Kennelly decided to run for governor in 1998, Larson ran for her seat. In the primary, he raised impressive sums, built a local organization, campaigned door-to-door, and got help from Hartford Mayor Mike Peters. He won 46%-43% over Secretary of State Miles Rapoport. In the general election, he competed against Kevin O'Connor, a 31-year-old Securities and Exchange Commission lawyer who was endorsed by the *Hartford Courant.* Larson won 58%-41% and has not been seriously challenged since. He has generously donated campaign funds to colleagues, including $242,000 in 2014.

Larson's voting record places him near the center of his party. After Republicans regained the majority in 2011, he chided them for preaching balanced budgets while supporting tariff breaks, which cost the Treasury hundreds of millions of dollars in lost revenue every year. But he doesn't hesitate to work with Republicans on legislation, especially at Ways and Means—with Texas' Kevin Brady on a measure to make permanent a research and development tax credit; and with Louisiana's Charles Boustany on a bill to allow individuals to get back at the end of the year any unused funds in their medical savings accounts. He showed his bipartisan stripes on a local issue in 2013 when he became co-chairman of the Congressional Joint Strike Fighter Caucus, which backs the F-35, whose engines are made by Pratt & Whitney. In 2014, he won approval in the final version of the defense spending bill for a provision that designated Hartford's Coltsville as a national historical park, a 260-acre site along the river, which includes 19th century factories.

In 2003, Larson became the senior Democrat on the House Administration Committee, the congressional housekeeping panel that handles office space assignments and other perks of interest to colleagues. Among his legislative interests at the committee were campaign finance and election reform, including a proposal that would allow the federal government to match funds raised by a candidate who agrees to accept contributions of only $100 or less. He also has proposed a constitutional amendment that would give members of the House four-year terms with elections staggered every two years. Longer terms would make legislators more effective by allowing them to spend less time campaigning, Larson said.

Nancy Pelosi brought Larson into her circle of advisers, and his influence grew. In 2006, he won a hotly contested race for Democratic Caucus vice chairman. His competitors were the better-known Jan Schakowsky of Illinois and Joseph Crowley of New York. When Schakowsky finished third on the first ballot and was eliminated, she threw her support to Larson. With Schakowsky's former supporters, Larson prevailed on the second ballot 116-87 over Crowley, who was allied with Maryland's Steny Hoyer, Pelosi's arch-rival in leadership. In 2007, Larson planned to run for caucus chairman, but stepped aside when it became clear that Rahm Emanuel of Illinois had locked up support for the job. When Emanuel quit the House in November 2008 to become chief of staff to President-elect Barack Obama, then-Speaker Pelosi persuaded Chris Van Hollen of Maryland to remain as chairman of the Democratic Congressional Campaign Committee, clearing the field for Larson to finally become caucus chairman.

Larson took on a number of assignments for Pelosi, including dealing with party dissidents who complained that Pelosi's Iraq strategy was too accommodating to President George W. Bush and later coordinating the Democrats' strategy on energy policy. Some Democrats privately derided him as Pelosi's cheerleader, but he shrugged off such comments, saying that his "bottom-up, member's member" approach was very different from the imperious style Emanuel was known for, but no less effective.

When Democrats lost control of the House in 2010, Larson remained as caucus chairman. He drew scorn from conservatives when he likened the Occupy Wall Street protests to the Arab Spring grassroots movements in the Middle East. In 2011, he handled messaging for Obama's unsuccessful jobs plan, introducing the bill in the House along with related measures and leading a rally to call for a vote. But the caucus chairmanship position had a four-year limit, and because Democrats did not reclaim the majority in November 2012, there was no place for Larson to move up. He yielded to California's Xavier Becerra, the vice chairman. He continued to serve as a mentor to younger members and said that he would welcome a return to a position in party leadership.

SECOND DISTRICT

Joe Courtney (D)

Elected 2006, 5th term; b. April 6, 1953, West Hartford; Tufts U., B.A. 1975, U. of CT, J.D. 1978; Catholic; married (Audrey); 2 children.

Elected Office: CT House, 1987-94.

Professional Career: Practicing atty., 1978-2006; CT coordinator, John Edwards pres. campaign, 2004.

DC Office: 2348 RHOB, 20515, 202-225-2076; Fax: 202-225-4977; Website: courtney.house.gov.

State Offices: Enfield, 860-741-6011; Norwich, 860-886-0139.

Committees: *Armed Services:* Readiness; Seapower & Projection Forces (RMM). *Education & the Workforce:* Health, Employment, Labor & Pensions; Higher Education & Workforce Training.

Group Ratings

	ADA	ACLU	AFL-CIO	LCV	ITI	COC	HAFA	ACU	CFG	FRC
2014	80%	83%	–	94%	80%	50%	12%	8%	13%	0%
2013	75%	C	100%	93%	C	38%	C	8%	10%	C

National Journal Ratings

	2013 LIB	—	2013 CONS
Economic	78%	—	21%
Social	77%	—	21%
Foreign	69%	—	29%
Composite	76%	—	25%

Key Votes of the 113th Congress

1. Sandy storm spending	Y	5. Medical Marijuana	Y	9. Syrian Rebels Training	Y
2. Violence Against Women Act	Y	6. Farm Bill	N	10. Keystone pipeline	N
3. Guantanamo Bay Detainees	Y	7. Afghanistan Combat	Y	11. Immigration Exec. Action	N
4. Abortion 20-week ban	N	8. NSA Phone Data Collection	Y	12. Bipartisan budget deal	Y

Election Results

2014 general	Joe Courtney (D)....................... 140,731	(62%)	$1,127,170	$14,226
	Lori Hopkins-Cavanagh (R)........ 80,381	(36%)	$62,121	
2014 primary	Joe Courtney (D)....................unopposed			

Prior winning percentages: 2012 (68%), 2010 (60%), 2008 (66%), 2006 (50%)

Population		Race and Ethnicity		Income	
Total:	714,637	White	83.6%	Median income:	$67,614
Urban:	9.1%	Latino	6.9%		*(71 of 435)*
Suburban:	88.5%	Black	3.9%	Under $50,000	36.0%
Rural:	2.4%	Asian	2.8%	$50,000-$99,999:	32.5%
Land area:	2,037	Two races	2.4%	$100,000-$199,999:	25.1%
Pop/sq. mi.:	350.8	White Ethnic	66.9%	$200,000 or more:	6.4%
Born in state:	57.0%			Poverty Rate	8.5%
		Education			
Age Groups		H.S. grad or less:	38.5%	**Work**	
Under 18:	20.3%	Some college:	28.5%	White collar:	38.7%
18 to 34:	22.9%	College degree, 4 yr.:	18.3%	Blue collar:	42.3%
35 to 64:	41.5%	Post-grad study:	14.7%	Sales and service:	19.0%
Over 64:	15.3%				
		Military		Govt. workers:	16.4%
		Veterans/active duty:	10.2%		

Eastern Connecticut: New London, Tolland

When Puritans from Massachusetts and England arrived in eastern Connecticut, the flinty hills were the home of small Indian tribes, whose numbers had been decimated by warfare and even more by disease. Factories quickly developed around mills in little villages on the fast-flowing Quinebaug and

Voter Turnout	
2013 Total Citizen 18+	549,306
2014 House Turnout	227,750
2014 Turnout as % CVAP	41.5%
2012 Turnout as % CVAP	58.4%

Shetucket rivers. Soon, New London and Norwich were among the 13 colonies' leading workshops and ports. The infamous plot of Connecticut native Benedict Arnold to deliver West Point in New York to the British was uncovered during the American Revolution, but his company did succeed in burning New London to the ground in 1781 and sacking Fort Griswold. The region's deep vein of human industriousness sustained it into the 20th century, when new technology took over in shaping the area. Four nuclear power plants were built here, more than in any similarly populated part of the United States. In Groton, the "Submarine Capital of the World" situated across the Thames River from New London, is General Dynamics' Electric Boat company, which built its first submarines in 1915 and later, nuclear submarines.

The 1990s brought a serious downturn in the local economy. The end of the Cold War and accompanying reductions in military spending have been painful for the region. Although the Navy has contracted for additional production at Groton, the port is a constant target for base closure, and its long-term survival remains in doubt. Meanwhile, drug maker Pfizer Inc. in 2012 closed its research and development headquarters in New London and moved many of its workers to its manufacturing plant in Groton and others to Cambridge, Mass. In 2014, the local economy improved, and the unemployment rate moved closer to the national average. A national Coast Guard museum is scheduled to open in 2017 on the New London waterfront.

The area's economic base has shifted to entertainment, specifically to gambling. The Foxwoods Resort Casino, built by the 650-member Mashantucket Pequot tribe, is the largest casino in the Western Hemisphere. But its employees have dropped from 10,500 to 7,600 in 2014. Uncasville is the site of the Mohegan Sun casino, the second-largest in the Western Hemisphere with a slightly smaller payroll. But competition from nearby states and the slow national economy are stunting the growth of gaming in the area. Foxwoods has struggled to restructure billions of dollars in debt. The tribe has sought to diversify by opening a mall and seeking a new casino elsewhere.

2012 Presidential Vote		
Barack Obama (D) 177,522	(56%)
Mitt Romney (R).................135,212	(43%)

2008 Presidential Vote		
Barack Obama (D) 199,603	(59%)
John McCain (R).................136,086	(40%)

Cook Partisan Voting Index: D+5

The 2nd Congressional District includes most of the eastern part of the state, centering on the small cities of New London and Norwich and including mill towns and the University of Connecticut in Storrs. The northeastern edge of Windham County, long known as "Quiet Corner" for its small towns and dairy farms, has lured away many Rhode Island and Massachusetts residents looking to escape high taxes and housing prices. The district stretches west to the outskirts of Hartford and to antique-filled small towns like Essex and Old Lyme on Long Island Sound.

For many years, this was a politically marginal district, with close battles between Yankee Republicans and Catholic Democrats. More recently, it has trended comfortably Democratic.

Joe Courtney (D)

Democrat Joe Courtney, elected in 2006, has tirelessly promoted issues that are important to him, including education and defense. With his position as ranking member of the Armed Services Subcommittee on Seapower and Projection Forces, he is well-positioned as a vigilant guardian of General Dynamics' Electric Boat plant and the New London Naval Submarine Base.

Courtney was raised in West Hartford. He studied at Tufts University, graduated from the University of Connecticut law school and went into private practice. In 1986, he won the first of four terms in the state House, where he served as chairman of the public health and human services committees. He ran unsuccessfully for lieutenant governor in 1998, and then unsuccessfully against Republican Rep. Rob Simmons in 2002. Courtney ran on the Democratic themes of Social Security protection, better prescription drug coverage for seniors and opposition to President George W. Bush's tax cuts, but Simmons won 54%-46%.

Courtney returned for a rematch in 2006. Democrats worked diligently to nationalize the race by exploiting voter anger over the Iraq war and GOP ethics scandals in Congress. Simmons touted his independence by pointing to votes he took on partial-birth abortion and same-sex marriage in opposition to the administration's positions. He also touted his successful lobbying to keep the submarine base off the 2005 base-closing list. Courtney was the survivor of the closest House race of the 2006 elections, with a winning margin of 83 votes out of the more than 242,000 cast.

In the House, Courtney's new colleagues gave him a nickname, "Landslide Joe." But he also got a seat on Armed Services, where he could more effectively lobby for the Navy's shipbuilding program at Groton. He worked with other Connecticut and Rhode Island lawmakers in 2007 to successfully secure an extra $588 million in the defense appropriations bill for submarines, paving the way for the Navy to double its submarine production from one to two a year. That led to another nickname from colleagues: "Two Sub Joe." During negotiations on so-called "fiscal cliff" tax and spending legislation in late 2012, he told the *Hartford Courant* that he faithfully studied Electric Boat employment listings like baseball box scores, looking for signs of anxiety because of the threat of massive defense cuts.

Courtney took over as co-chair of the Congressional Shipbuilding Caucus and worked to prevent a one-year cut in submarine production in 2014 while protecting the appropriation for a "stretched" version of a Virginia-class sub with cruise-missile tubes, which was designed at the Electric Boat yard. In the 2014 defense spending bill, he secured as much as $3.5 billion for a "National Sea-Based Deterrence Fund" that would allow the Pentagon to pay for a new class of submarines that could be built by Electric Boat in Groton. He also successfully lobbied the Pentagon to include in its Quadrennial Defense Review the need for a future fleet of as many as 55 submarines, up from the 48 called for in 2006. In January 2015, Courtney aptly noted that his senior position on the Seapower Subcommittee is "not only vital to Connecticut, but to our nation's security today and in the future."

He has generally been a faithful Democrat. Representing a district that includes the University of Connecticut, he has been the leading champion of keeping interest rates low on federally backed college loans. With Sen. Elizabeth Warren of Massachusetts, he filed legislation in March 2015 to reverse rate hikes that were enacted in 2013. During the 2009 health care debate, Courtney led House Democratic opposition to a proposed "Cadillac tax" on high-cost health insurance plans, which he said would harm millions of middle-class people. He helped change it to a 3.8 percent tax on non-wage income. On an important local issue in 2008, Courtney won enactment of a bill giving environmental protection to 25 miles of the Eightmile River, bringing it under the Wild and Scenic Rivers Act. In a sign of his commitment to local prerogatives, Courtney noticed in early 2013 a histori-cal inaccuracy in Steven Spielberg's acclaimed movie *Lincoln*. The film wrongly depicted two Connecticut congressmen voting against the 13th Amendment abolishing slavery. The congressman asked Spielberg to correct the mistake for the DVD release of the film. The writer of the film responded that the film narrative served the larger story line. Courtney continued to press his point.

Unlike most Democrats elected in 2006, Courtney has had a much easier time keeping his office than he did in winning it, never receiving less than 60 percent of the vote.

THIRD DISTRICT

Rosa DeLauro (D)

Elected 1990, 13th term; b. March 2, 1943, New Haven; Marymount Col., B.A. 1964, Columbia U., M.A. 1966; Catholic; married (Stanley Greenberg); 3 children.

Professional Career: Exec. asst., New Haven Mayor Frank Logue, 1976-77; Exec. asst. & develop. admin., City of New Haven, 1977-79; Chief of staff, U.S. Sen. Christopher Dodd, 1981-87; Exec. dir., Count-down '87, 1987-88; Exec. dir., EMILY's List, 1989-90.

DC Office: 2413 RHOB, 20515, 202-225-3661; Fax: 202-225-4890; Website: delauro.house.gov.

State Offices: Derby, 203-735-5005; Middletown, 860-344-1159; Naugatuck, 203-729-0204; New Haven, 203-562-3718.

Committees: *Appropriations:* Agriculture, Rural Development, FDA, & Related Agencies; Labor, HHS, Education, & Related Agencies (RMM).

Group Ratings

	ADA	ACLU	AFL-CIO	LCV	ITI	COC	HAFA	ACU	CFG	FRC
2014	85%	88%	–	97%	40%	36%	16%	8%	13%	0%
2013	80%	C	95%	96%	C	23%	C	17%	16%	C

National Journal Ratings

	2013 LIB	—	2013 CONS
Economic	90%	—	10%
Social	87%	—	7%
Foreign	75%	—	23%
Composite	85%	—	15%

Key Votes of the 113th Congress

1. Sandy storm spending	Y	5. Medical Marijuana	Y	9. Syrian Rebels Training	N
2. Violence Against Women Act	Y	6. Farm Bill	N	10. Keystone pipeline	N
3. Guantanamo Bay Detainees	Y	7. Afghanistan Combat	Y	11. Immigration Exec. Action	N
4. Abortion 20-week ban	N	8. NSA Phone Data Collection	Y	12. Bipartisan budget deal	N

Election Results

2014 general	Rosa DeLauro (D)	140,485	(67%)	$1,236,492	$4,512
	James Brown (R)	69,454	(33%)	$6,837	
2014 primary	Rosa DeLauro (D)	unopposed			

Prior winning percentages: 2012 (75%), 2010 (65%), 2008 (77%), 2006 (76%), 2004 (72%), 2002 (66%), 2000 (72%), 1998 (71%), 1996 (71%), 1994 (63%), 1992 (66%), 1990 (52%)

Population		Race and Ethnicity		Income	
Total:	716,738	White	68.4%	Median income:	$59,165
Urban:	28.3%	Latino	13.2%		(134 of 435)
Suburban:	71.7%	Black	12.5%	Under $50,000	42.2%
Rural:	0.0%	Asian	3.9%	$50,000-$99,999:	29.0%
Land area:	492	Two races	1.5%	$100,000-$199,999:	23.0%
Pop/sq. mi.:	1,456.6	White Ethnic	58.6%	$200,000 or more:	5.9%
Born in state:	62.6%			Poverty Rate	11.9%
		Education			
Age Groups		H.S. grad or less:	40.1%	**Work**	
Under 18:	20.5%	Some college:	24.9%	White collar:	40.4%
18 to 34:	24.3%	College degree, 4 yr.:	19.3%	Blue collar:	43.2%
35 to 64:	39.7%	Post-grad study:	15.7%	Sales and service:	16.4%
Over 64:	15.5%				
		Military		Govt. workers:	12.8%
		Veterans/active duty:	6.7%		

South Central Connecticut: New Haven

The New Haven Colony was founded in 1637 by a group of Puritan settlers who opted to bypass the Massachusetts Bay Colony after concluding the religious practices near Boston weren't strict enough. Their new colony was successful and grew rapidly. More than 150 years later, a young Yale

Voter Turnout	
2013 Total Citizen 18+	531,167
2014 House Turnout	210,420
2014 Turnout as % CVAP	39.6%
2012 Turnout as % CVAP	57.8%

graduate named Eli Whitney won an order from the young U.S. government to produce 10,000 muskets at $13.40 each. Whitney had invented the cotton gin six years earlier, which had embroiled him in a lengthy patent suit. He was determined to make a quick profit on the musket contract, so he set up a system of interchangeable parts and invented a milling machine and gauges: the birth of standardized American manufacturing. For the next 150 years or so, New Haven mass-produced rifles, clocks, locks, hardware and toys—anything its tinkerers and entrepreneurs could fashion. Today, few factories remain in New Haven, and the area's defense contracts are modest compared to those of the city's heyday. The factory that produced Winchester rifles and guns for 140 years closed in 2006. In recent years, southern Connecticut around New Haven discovered a new source of prosperity in scores of small technology and biomedical firms.

But the city itself, with significant crime rates and many neighborhoods scarred by abandoned homes, has shrunk in population. In 2011, it had 130,000 people, down from 164,000 in 1950. Yale University, with its Gothic spires and red-brick halls, has always been the visual focus of New Haven and is now its largest employer. Some local revival was sparked by a state development program that turned old retail and office buildings into residences and by $1 billion in investments by biotech firms. In December 2014, unemployment in the New Haven area had dropped to 5.8%, but it stubbornly remained at 7.9% in the city. Racial minorities and immigrants have had an influential voice in New Haven. In 2007, it became the first city in the nation to issue resident identification cards, including for undocumented immigrants. In the

2012 Presidential Vote		
Barack Obama (D)	191,197	(63%)
Mitt Romney (R)	110,867	(36%)

2008 Presidential Vote		
Barack Obama (D)	198,837	(63%)
John McCain (R)	114,513	(36%)

Cook Partisan Voting Index: D+11

midst of the occasional urban chaos, the *Record Journal* in Meriden had a reassuring report in March 2015 about local nature: Two bald eagles nested along the Quinnipiac River in

Hampden, a sign the local bald eagle population was increasing. But there was no guarantee that the specific migratory birds would return to the area. The news story quoted a wildlife biologist that the return of the eagles was a sign that pollution of state waterways had decreased.

The 3rd Congressional District covers the New Haven metropolitan area, and extends to the outskirts of the former industrial cities of Bridgeport, Waterbury, and Meriden. The New Haven metropolitan area has long since spread beyond the narrow city limits into what were once Yankee villages and countryside. The suburb of Hamden has made it onto CNNMoney's list of the 100 best places to live. Politically, the 3rd used to be a marginal district, regularly changing partisan hands in the 1980s. But it is now strongly Democratic, though slightly less than the Hartford-based 1st District. President Barack Obama got 63 percent of the vote here in both 2008 and 2012.

Rosa DeLauro (D)

Rosa DeLauro, a Democrat first elected in 1990, is an outspoken liberal—"a live wire whose words rush out like sparks," *The New York Times* once wrote—who has been active on women's health as well as food safety issues. She is a senior House appropriator on domestic funding issues, and has a seat at the Democratic leadership table as co-chair of the Steering and Policy Committee.

DeLauro grew up in New Haven's Wooster Square. Both of her parents were New Haven aldermen. Her mother, Luisa DeLauro, retired from the Board of Aldermen in 1999 after 35 years, the longest tenure in New Haven history. A granite monument honoring the family was dedicated in Wooster Square Park in 2011. Rosa DeLauro's husband, Stanley Greenberg, was Bill Clinton's chief pollster from 1991 to 1994 and worked for Al Gore's presidential campaign in 2000 and John Kerry's in 2004. As Obama's White House chief of staff, Rahm Emanuel, a family friend, officiated at the wedding of Greenberg's daughter Anna, a political consultant, and lived for a while in the basement of DeLauro's Capitol Hill home.

DeLauro has been in politics nearly all of her life. She was a development administrator in New Haven in the 1970s, chief of staff to Democratic Sen. Christopher Dodd from 1980 to 1987, then spent a year working to stop U.S. military aid to Nicaraguan contras before she became director of EMILY's List, the women's campaign fundraising group that supports abortion rights. When the 3rd District seat opened in 1990, DeLauro prevailed 52%-48% over anti-tax and anti-abortion Republican state Sen. Tom Scott. Her last serious competition came in 1992, when she won a rematch against Scott, 66%-34%.

As a close ally of Minority Leader Nancy Pelosi of California, DeLauro is one of the Democratic leadership's most vocal champions in debate. Pelosi in 2011 admiringly described her as "a force of nature." She is an active and ardent supporter of feminist issues. A cancer survivor, she sponsored the law to require that patients and doctors, not insurance companies, decide on 48-hour hospital stays for mastectomies. She also lobbied for insurance coverage of early-detection tests for cervical cancer, and helped to enact "Johanna's Law" to increase awareness of gynecological cancers. In 2009, she introduced a bill to require employers to give workers seven paid sick days annually. Also that year, the House passed her bill, which eventually became law as the Lilly Ledbetter Fair Pay Act, that provided remedies to victims of wage discrimination, reversing a Supreme Court decision that had made it more difficult to ensure that women and men doing the same job are paid comparable wages.

As a former chair of the Appropriations Subcommittee on Agriculture, Rural Development, Food and Drug Administration, and Related Agencies, DeLauro has taken a keen interest in food safety, which she said should have the same priority as prescription drug and medical device safety. Her subcommittee in 2008 increased by $1.8 billion President George W. Bush's funding request for the FDA. But she said a year later that the agency remained "badly broken," and faulted the Obama administration for not doing enough to address food safety in its fiscal 2010 budget. After the Centers for Disease Control and Prevention released figures in late 2010 showing that food-borne disease remained a public health threat, she introduced a bill to create a single agency to regulate the food supply. She unsuccessfully tried in June 2011 to boost funding for the Center for Food Safety and Applied Nutrition by $1 million for protection against E. coli sickness. In 2011, she became ranking Democrat on the Labor, HHS and Education Subcommittee at Appropriations. But she has had less opportunity to place her imprint on that bill because Democrats have been in the minority.

In an unusual clash with President Barack Obama in early 2015, DeLauro was a leader among House Democrats in siding with unions to oppose a new Trans-Pacific Partnership trade agreement that the United States was negotiating with 11 nations. Despite the prospect of lower tariffs, her greater concern was that the deal would kill good-paying jobs. It was vital, she said, that "everyone who works hard and plays by the rules has a chance to succeed." She criticized Obama's trade advisers for making their case with "misleading" information. DeLauro embraced Obama's opening to Cuba following her February 2015 visit to the island, but cautioned that diplomatic progress would be slow. "No one has their head in the sand or is wearing rose-colored glasses," she said.

DeLauro is known for her strong-mindedness. In 2009, as Pelosi reluctantly announced her support for an amendment strictly limiting insurance coverage for abortions as part of the health care overhaul, DeLauro reportedly got into an angry confrontation with California Rep. George Miller, another trusted Pelosi ally who called for more pragmatism. When home-state Senate colleague Joe Lieberman, a political independent, held up the legislation a month later, DeLauro demanded that Lieberman be recalled; he retired three years later. In December 2014, she and Pelosi got into an awkward situation when they denied the request of Illinois Rep. Tammy Duckworth to vote by proxy in a Democratic Caucus leadership contest in which both were supporting California Rep. Anna Eshoo, another close ally. Duckworth, a double amputee, was at home in her final weeks of pregnancy and under doctor's orders not to travel. Duckworth was denied her request, but Eshoo fell short on the vote.

DeLauro has run twice for chairwoman of the Democratic Caucus and suffered two painfully close setbacks. In 1998, she lost 108-97 to Martin Frost of Texas; Minority Leader Richard Gephardt then named her an assistant leader in charge of the party's message. In 2002, she lost 104-103 to Robert Menendez of New Jersey after an intense year-long contest. DeLauro has been an active supporter of Pelosi in her leadership races, which helped cement the bond between the two Italian-American liberal women. Pelosi has leaned on DeLauro for important leadership roles and made her co-chair of the Steering Committee, which is instrumental in committee assignments. In 2004, she led the drafting of the Democratic platform when John Kerry was nominated for president. She remains an influential voice in the party, with her skillful blend of policy and politics.

FOURTH DISTRICT

Jim Himes (D)

Elected 2008, 4th term; b. July 5, 1966, Lima, Peru; Harvard U., B.A. 1988, Oxford U., M.Phil. 1990; Presbyterian; married (Mary); 2 children.

Elected Office: Greenwich Bd. of Estimate & Taxation, 2006-07.

Professional Career: Financial analyst & V.P., Goldman Sachs, 1990-2002; Chmn., Greenwich Housing Authority, 2003-06; V.P., Enterprise Community Partners, 2004-08.

DC Office: 1227 LHOB, 20515, 202-225-5541; Fax: 202-225-9629; Website: himes.house.gov.

State Offices: Bridgeport, 866-453-0028; Stamford, 203-353-9400.

Committees: *Financial Services:* Capital Markets & Gov't Sponsored Enterprises; Monetary Policy & Trade. *Intelligence (Permanent Select).*

Group Ratings

	ADA	ACLU	AFL-CIO	LCV	ITI	COC	HAFA	ACU	CFG	FRC
2014	85%	83%	–	94%	80%	57%	15%	4%	9%	0%
2013	75%	C	79%	96%	C	69%	C	12%	15%	C

National Journal Ratings

	2013 LIB	—	2013 CONS
Economic	61%	—	39%
Social	69%	—	28%
Foreign	83%	—	15%
Composite	72%	—	28%

Key Votes of the 113th Congress

1. Sandy storm spending	Y	5. Medical Marijuana	Y	9. Syrian Rebels Training	N
2. Violence Against Women Act	Y	6. Farm Bill	N	10. Keystone pipeline	N
3. Guantanamo Bay Detainees	Y	7. Afghanistan Combat	Y	11. Immigration Exec. Action	N
4. Abortion 20-week ban	N	8. NSA Phone Data Collection	N	12. Bipartisan budget deal	Y

Election Results

2014 general	Jim Himes (D)	106,690	(54%)	$2,101,453	$20,587	$20,000
	Dan Debicela (R)	92,080	(46%)	$1,273,921	$85,000	
2014 primary	Jim Himes (D)	unopposed				

Prior winning percentages: 2012 (60%), 2010 (52%), 2008 (50%)

Population		Race and Ethnicity		Income	
Total:	735,823	White	64.6%	Median income:	$86,007
Urban:	51.4%	Latino	17.5%		*(20 of 435)*
Suburban:	48.6%	Black	11.3%	Under $50,000	31.5%
Rural:	0.0%	Asian	4.9%	$50,000-$99,999:	24.3%
Land area:	470	Two races	1.3%	$100,000-$199,999:	23.6%
Pop/sq. mi.:	1,566.1	White Ethnic	47.7%	$200,000 or more:	20.6%
Born in state:	41.9%			Poverty Rate	10.0%
		Education			
Age Groups		H.S. grad or less:	30.8%	**Work**	
Under 18:	24.8%	Some college:	21.0%	White collar:	43.7%
18 to 34:	20.1%	College degree, 4 yr.:	26.2%	Blue collar:	41.9%
35 to 64:	41.4%	Post-grad study:	22.0%	Sales and service:	14.4%
Over 64:	13.6%				
		Military		Govt. workers:	8.9%
		Veterans/active duty:	5.0%		

Southwest Connecticut: Bridgeport, Stamford

No one in colonial America imagined that southern Connecticut would someday lodge one of the largest concentrations of wealth in the world. The soil was stony, the terrain unaccommodating, and the harbors not as convenient as those in New York, Rhode Island, and Massachusetts. For 200 years, this was

Voter Turnout	
2013 Total Citizen 18+	466,994
2014 House Turnout	198,719
2014 Turnout as % CVAP	42.6%
2012 Turnout as % CVAP	67.1%

the home of unnoticed Yankee farmers, sailors, and tinkerers. Before starting his famous circus, P.T. Barnum was involved in abolitionist causes and cast a vote for the 13th Amendment while representing Fairfield in the state legislature; he also served a term as Bridgeport's mayor. Around the same time, rich New Yorkers began taking the train north to country houses in Connecticut. In the 20th century, Greenwich and other Yankee villages clustered around commuter railroad stations became the home of New York's elite.

Starting in the 1950s, New York City-based executives, eager to minimize their commutes and avoid New York's income taxes, moved their headquarters to Greenwich and beyond, including General Electric in Fairfield and several firms in Stamford. Greenwich, sometimes referred to as "Wall Street by the Sea" for its proliferation of hedge fund offices and financial firms, is closest to New York and commands the highest commercial rents of all these places.

The 4th Congressional District is the wealthiest district in the nation's wealthiest state. The district covers most of the southwest corner of Connecticut along Long Island Sound, from industrial Bridgeport, now the state's largest city, to affluent Greenwich. The district's waterfront towns include bustling and pricey Stamford, woodsy Darien, modest Norwalk, artsy-craftsy Westport, and Fairfield. An odd duck, Bridgeport is a low-income town, although it got spruced up when the state-financed Harbor Yard sports complex opened for minor league baseball and a downtown revitalization ensued. This social disparity within Fairfield County has ranked the 4th District as the fifth highest in the nation in income inequality, according to a July 2014 *Bloomberg BusinessWeek* listing. The top four are in New York City, Philadelphia, Chicago, and Miami—each of which is an urban locale compared to this suburban district. In a step that might adjust the balance, local developers have sought to encourage more Millennials to move into the area. The state and city of Norwalk received a federal grant in 2014 to help pay the nearly $500 million cost to replace the swing Walk Bridge, which was built in the 19th century. The Norwalk bridge is one of four movable bridges on the main line to New Haven, all in need of major repair. Plans to upgrade and expand the Stamford train station could cost another $500 million.

2012 Presidential Vote		
Barack Obama (D) 170,827	(55%)
Mitt Romney (R).................136,527	(44%)

2008 Presidential Vote		
Barack Obama (D) 194,984	(60%)
John McCain (R).................130,129	(40%)

Cook Partisan Voting Index: D+5

For many years, the heavily affluent suburbs outvoted Bridgeport and elected moderate-to-liberal Republicans such as Clare Boothe Luce, Lowell Weicker, and Chris Shays to Congress. But the influence of Christian conservatives in the GOP repelled Episcopalians and other mainline Protestants, and they have been increasingly voting Democratic. At the same time, the district has been diversifying. It is now only 57% non-Hispanic white, the lowest percentage in the state. There is some evidence, however, that the Democratic tide may have receded. President Barack Obama's share of the vote here dropped from 60% in 2008 to 55% in 2012, his largest decline in the state. Republicans had hoped that Bridgeport would be moved out of the 4th during post-2010 redistricting. Ultimately, few changes were made. For now, the district remains comfortably Democratic.

Jim Himes (D)

Jim Himes, a Democrat elected in 2008, is a former investment banker who puts his understanding of Wall Street to use at the Financial Services Committee and in conversations with colleagues. Given the growing hostility of many Democrats to deep-pocket financiers—especially hedge funds, which are based predominantly in his district—that may impose some limits on his influence.

Though he represents one of the wealthiest areas of the country, Himes grew up in different surroundings. Born in Lima Peru, he spent his early years in Peru and Colombia, where his father worked for the Ford Foundation. Around the time of his 10th birthday, after his parents divorced, he came to the United States with his mother and two sisters and settled in Pennington, N.J. His early experience in Latin America had an enduring effect. He speaks fluent Spanish and maintains a deep interest in the region. Himes earned his undergraduate degree from Harvard University and was a Rhodes scholar at Oxford. When he returned to the United States, he worked for Goldman Sachs as a financial analyst. On Sept. 11, 2001, he was at his office in Lower Manhattan and did volunteer work with ambulance crews. After 12 years, he left the investment house in 2002 as a vice president. The following year, he joined Enterprise Community Partners, a Columbia Maryland-based nonprofit dedicated to alleviating urban poverty. Beginning in 2004, he managed its offices in the Northeast.

Like many other Wall Street executives, Himes moved in 1998 to the affluent suburb of Greenwich to raise a family with his wife, Mary. He became active in the town Democratic committee, and served as chairman from 2003 to 2007. He was a campaign volunteer in 2006 for Democrat Diane Farrell, who finished about 7,000 votes behind Rep. Christopher Shays, a moderate Republican who had withstood repeated Democratic campaign assaults. The following April, Himes announced his own challenge against Shays. Himes set a torrid fundraising pace, aided in large measure by his Wall Street connections. The Democratic Congressional Campaign Committee also made him a top prospect. After easily dispatching a minor challenger in the August primary, Himes focused on Shays and the George W. Bush administration and attempted to link the two over the Iraq war. Himes embraced the national Democratic establishment, frequently reminding voters that he was running with presidential nominee Barack Obama. In the past, Shays' moderate record and Capitol Hill seniority helped him weather political storms. But in 2008, the enthusiasm for Obama's candidacy provided a powerful final push that gave Himes a 51%-48% win. He comfortably took the district's urban centers and managed to stay competitive in the affluent suburbs that tend to break Republican.

Himes has taken a centrist approach in Congress, supporting Obama's major priorities but also asserting his independence on behalf of his district. He riled some Democratic leaders when he joined several other junior lawmakers in 2010 to form a working group to propose large spending cuts in defense, energy, housing, and agriculture. In March 2012, he was one of 22 Democrats who supported a failed amendment to implement the recommendations of the Simpson-Bowles deficit reduction commission. He declared his frustration in April 2011 with keeping a large U.S. military presence in Afghanistan, telling a town hall audience: "I've arrived at the point of view that we're not going to change Afghanistan. I'm done. I'm done."

On the Financial Services Committee, he has engaged on district-related issues. During the furor in 2009 over bonuses paid to executives at AIG International and other firms receiving federal rescue money, he cosponsored a measure requiring all future compensation to be performance-based; it passed the House but stalled in the Senate. When the committee took up a sweeping financial overhaul bill, he helped craft a provision regulating the complex financial instruments known as derivatives. Consumer advocates criticized Himes and other centrist Democrats, accusing them of watering down derivatives controls passed by the Senate in an effort to appease Wall Street. Himes argued that the legislation took significant steps to crack down on abuses at investment firms.

Himes routinely speaks with colleagues about the industry. "He can explain things like derivatives and credit default swaps in plain English so [members] can have some degree of fluency in this, which is extremely helpful," fellow Connecticut Democrat Joe Courtney told the *Connecticut Post* in 2012. At the same time, Himes tries to bring disaffected Wall Streeters back to the Democratic fold. "I do hear anger" from the investment industry, he told *The New York Times* in 2011. "Many of them know me from my previous life, and they do call me and say, 'What the hell is going on?'"

Republicans hoped that they would have a better shot at unseating Himes in 2010 without Obama on the ballot. But the GOP nominated state Sen. Dan Debicella of Shelton over the more moderate former state Sen. Rob Russo of Bridgeport. Himes wasted little time in portraying Debicella as an extremist and again relied on his industry connections to raise almost $3.7 million. Debicella tried again in 2014, and the outcome was similar. Himes won 54%-46%. Himes got 71% in Bridgeport and Norwalk, which cast 21% of the total vote. Debicella won seven of the other nine communities and hill towns, but that upscale vote was not enough to overcome the urban support for Himes.

Following the election, he failed in his active bid to be Nancy Pelosi's choice to chair the Democratic Congressional Campaign Committee. She gave the post to Rep. Ben Ray Lujan of New Mexico, who was more junior but represented a much lower income district than Himes, who had been the DCCC's finance chairman. An anti-Wall Street activist praised Pelosi for "rejecting the Wall Street wing of the Democratic Party." Himes has been one of the most avid congressional users of Twitter, often while commuting by train. When a follower declared him to be "the coolest congressman," Himes tweeted, "On the other hand, in the land of the blind ..."

FIFTH DISTRICT

Elizabeth Esty (D)

Elected 2012, 2nd term; b. Aug. 25, 1959, Oak Park, IL; Harvard U., B.A. 1981, Yale U., J.D. 1985; Congregationalist; married (Dan); 3 children.

Elected Office: Cheshire Town Cncl., 2005-08; CT House, 2008-10.

Professional Career: Clerk, Judge Robert Keeton of MA; Practicing atty., 1986-90; Adjunct prof., American U., 1991-92; Health care policy analyst, 1990-2002; Sr. research scholar, Yale Law Schl., 1994-2009.

DC Office: 405 CHOB, 20515, 202-225-4476; Fax: 860-225-7289; Website: esty.house.gov.

State Offices: New Britain, 860-223-8412.

Committees: *Science, Space, & Technology:* Research & Technology. *Transportation & Infrastructure:* Highways & Transit; Railroads, Pipelines & Hazardous Materials; Water Resources & Environment.

Group Ratings

	ADA	ACLU	AFL-CIO	LCV	ITI	COC	HAFA	ACU	CFG	FRC
2014	80%	88%	–	97%	80%	50%	14%	8%	13%	0%
2013	65%	C	95%	96%	C	54%	C	8%	14%	C

National Journal Ratings

	2013 LIB	—	2013 CONS
Economic	63%	—	37%
Social	73%	—	24%
Foreign	71%	—	27%
Composite	70%	—	30%

Key Votes of the 113th Congress

1. Sandy storm spending	Y	5. Medical Marijuana	Y	9. Syrian Rebels Training	N
2. Violence Against Women Act	Y	6. Farm Bill	N	10. Keystone pipeline	N
3. Guantanamo Bay Detainees	Y	7. Afghanistan Combat	Y	11. Immigration Exec. Action	N
4. Abortion 20-week ban	N	8. NSA Phone Data Collection	N	12. Bipartisan budget deal	Y

Election Results

2014 general	Elizabeth Esty (D)	107,930	(53%)	$2,807,776	$51,134	
	Mark Greenberg (R)	93,861	(46%)	$1,769,247	$3,665	$627,571
2014 primary	Elizabeth Esty (D)	unopposed				

Prior winning percentage: 2012 (51%)

Population		Race and Ethnicity		Income	
Total:	712,302	White	72.6%	Median income:	$65,384
Urban:	18.4%	Latino	15.9%		*(79 of 435)*
Suburban:	62.0%	Black	6.2%	Under $50,000	38.6%
Rural:	19.6%	Asian	2.8%	$50,000-$99,999:	30.0%
Land area:	1,151	Two races	2.0%	$100,000-$199,999:	23.2%
Pop/sq. mi.:	618.7	White Ethnic	57.2%	$200,000 or more:	8.1%
Born in state:	54.9%			Poverty Rate	10.8%
		Education			
Age Groups		H.S. grad or less:	39.8%	**Work**	
Under 18:	21.9%	Some college:	26.1%	White collar:	37.3%
18 to 34:	19.9%	College degree, 4 yr.:	19.0%	Blue collar:	43.7%
35 to 64:	43.1%	Post-grad study:	15.1%	Sales and service:	19.0%
Over 64:	15.2%			Govt. workers:	12.2%
		Military			
		Veterans/active duty:	6.7%		

Western and Central Connecticut: Litchfield

Over the years, Connecticut's stony soil has become home to some of the most affluent people in the world. This is true in the hills of northwest Connecticut, far from the interstates and from Connecticut's small urban capital of Hartford. In Litchfield County are exquisite Yankee towns like Washington and Kent, where Connecticut's ship owners once invested their accumulated capital in factories and mills. They now are considered the "anti-Hamptons," a country-home mecca for ultra-rich New Yorkers seeking to avoid the glitz of Southampton and East Hampton. Avon and Simsbury have become comfortable bedroom communities to Hartford.

Voter Turnout	
2013 Total Citizen 18+	512,487
2014 House Turnout	211,123
2014 Turnout as % CVAP	41.2%
2012 Turnout as % CVAP	60.9%

Not far away are small industrial cities like New Britain, America's ball-bearing capital for years; Meriden, which turned from making ivory combs, clocks, and cutlery to producing electrical signaling equipment, biotech filters, and nuclear instruments; and Waterbury, once the nation's largest producer of brass. Like many manufacturing centers, these towns have fallen on hard times. The unemployment rate in Waterbury, in double digits since 2009, was 11.1 percent in January 2015–the second-highest in the state behind Hartford. Danbury, a city of 82,000, was once the nation's leading producer of hats, and is now a budding center for clean energy technology. East of Danbury is the sad small town of Newtown, where gunman Adam Lanza shocked the nation and ignited a debate— but little action—over gun control, care for

2012 Presidential Vote		
Barack Obama (D)	164,627	(54%)
Mitt Romney (R)	139,324	(45%)
2008 Presidential Vote		
Barack Obama (D)	185,130	(56%)
John McCain (R)	139,043	(42%)
Cook Partisan Voting Index:	D+3	

the mentally ill, and the marketing of violence to children when he killed 26 people, 20 of them children, at Sandy Hook Elementary School, in December 2012.

The 5th Congressional District of Connecticut covers much of the northwestern corner of the state, including the northern towns of Fairfield County. It has two arms that reach into the hills of central Connecticut—one to Democratic Meriden and the other to the affluent and Republican-leaning Farmington Valley suburbs of Hartford. It is a Democratically leaning district. Barack Obama won it by 14 points in 2008, and by a narrower 54-45% margin in 2012. But Republicans have been competitive here.

Elizabeth Esty (D)

Democratic lawyer Elizabeth Esty, first elected in the 5th District in 2012, has been challenged by two tough campaigns and her representation of a town that suffered great tragedy and moved to the epicenter of a national debate on gun control. Esty is more of a policy wonk and has not sought the spotlight at home. National Democrats hope that she becomes more politically secure so they can spend campaign money elsewhere.

Esty was born in Oak Park Illinois, but moved around growing up because of her father's work as a construction engineer. She described herself as the latest in "a long line of feisty women" on her mother's side, including her grandmother, who lobbied for civil rights. After graduating from high school in Minnesota, she came east to attend Harvard University, where she met her husband, Dan. Esty attended Yale Law School, then worked as a law clerk for U.S. District Judge Robert Keeton of Massachusetts. She moved to Washington to work for the large law firm Sidley Austin, where she wrote legal briefs in several cases that defended abortion rights. She later taught and did policy work in the health care field. She moved to Connecticut in 1994 when her husband started an environmental law and policy program at Yale.

Her first elected position was on the Cheshire Town Council, where she sought to provide tax relief for senior citizens and reduce the town's debt. In 2008, Esty was elected as a state representative, only to have her career halted. She voted to abolish the death penalty after two convicts killed three people in Cheshire in one of the most high-profile crimes in state history. Esty lost her next election to a Republican who backed capital punishment.

When Rep. Chris Murphy left the House seat to run for the Senate in 2012, state House Speaker Chris Donovan was the early Democratic favorite. But a pay-to-play scandal engulfed two of Donovan's top aides. With the help of a $500,000 self-loan to her campaign, Esty brushed past Donovan and businessman Dan Roberti in the primary. She faced state Sen. Andrew Roraback in the general election. Her economic agenda promised infrastructure improvements, training of future manufacturers, and better access to credit for small businesses. The Democratic Congressional Campaign Committee quickly went on the attack, running ads saying that Roraback would "fit right in" with images of such conservatives as Reps. Allen West of Florida and Michele Bachmann of Minnesota. Roraback, who supported abortion rights and same-sex marriage, denounced the ads as "outright lies." Esty maintained an edge in fundraising and was endorsed by *The New York Times*, which pointed to her capital punishment vote in the state legislature as "the kind of political fortitude Washington desperately needs." She won, 51%-49%.

Just before Esty took office, she was confronted with a massive tragedy in her district: the December 2012 Sandy Hook school shooting in Newtown in which 26 people were killed, including 20 children. On the day of the shooting, she rushed to Newtown from a freshman orientation session at Harvard University. "It's refocused my agenda; I know that," she told *The Connecticut Mirror*. President Barack Obama attended a local prayer vigil two days later, and described that day as the worst of his presidency. In his State of the Union message two months later, he urged Congress to vote on several gun-control measures. A day after she took office, Esty was named one of 12 vice chairs of the House Democrats' Congressional Gun Violence Prevention Task Force. "The status quo is unacceptable, and action is long overdue," she said, and later added that she was "very encouraged" by Obama's commitment to "real, meaningful change." Among other steps, she cosponsored a bill requiring background checks for all commercial gun sales. But, as often has been the case with firearms legislation, nothing happened in Congress. Esty won praise inside Congress and by advocacy groups for her efforts. She voiced frustration over the stalemate. "We should be ashamed," she said two years later.

As a first-term member of the House minority party, she had few legislative accomplishments. After failed attempts in two previous sessions, Congress enacted her Collinsville Renewable Energy Production Act, which required the Federal Energy Regulatory Commission to reinstate expired licenses for hydropower dams at two old mills in the town on the Farmington River. "We have the opportunity to reinvent a dormant dam into a dam producing local, clean energy," she told the House.

Esty showed occasional independence from her party. When she voted in 2013 for a Republican bill to delay for one year the mandate for coverage in the Affordable Care Act, the liberal advocacy group moveon.org launched online petitions asking Esty and other Democrats to explain their vote. She said that she was responding to constituent requests for more time. In February 2015, Esty was among 33 Democrats who voted to make permanent certain tax breaks. " Predictability is important, which is why I voted to make these tax incentives permanent and give local business owners the peace of mind they deserve," she explained to the *Connecticut Mirror*.

In 2014, Esty faced another competitive opponent, wealthy Litchfield real-estate businessman Mark Greenberg, who lost the Republican primary in 2010 and 2012. She broadcast an ad claiming that Greenberg was seeking to end the Social Security guarantee, which the *Hartford Courant* determined was false. They disagreed on other issues, including the death penalty, abortion and gun control. Greenberg self-financed more than $1.1 million of his $1.8 million campaign. Esty spent nearly $3 million, and had more than $600,000 in national party aid. She won, 53%-46%—a larger margin than in 2012, but not enough to discourage further Republican challenges. She won nearly two-thirds of the combined vote in the urban centers of Meriden, New Britain, and Waterbury. During his three terms representing the district, Murphy had consistently higher victory margins.

⋆ DELAWARE ⋆

On December 7, 1787, 30 Delawareans met at the Golden Fleece Tavern in Dover and voted unanimously to ratify the Constitution. And thus, the second smallest state in area became, as it likes to boast, the First State. This small corner of America has a long history. The mouth of the Delaware River was explored by Henry Hudson, and the Dutch and Swedes built settlements on the west bank in the 1630s. But the three counties of Delaware owe their separate existence to the politics of the proprietors of William Penn's colony to the north and to Delawareans' determination even before July 4, 1776, to declare independence not only from Britain but also from Pennsylvania.

Throughout most of its history, Delaware has been unusually affluent. It had the nation's highest income levels during the early 20th century and still has high income levels. Home ownership was at nearly 76 percent even after the housing bust. The many members of the du Pont family maintain beautiful cobblestone mansions in its chateau country, and the charming Brandywine Valley, which spills across the 12-mile semicircular border with Pennsylvania, includes a trove of refined tourist attractions. The Mason-Dixon Line forms Delaware's western border with Maryland, and the state has both Northern and Southern heritages. It was still a slave state when the Civil War broke out, but 92 percent of its blacks were free; today, its population is 22 percent black, almost twice the national average, and 8 percent Hispanic, two points higher than neighboring Pennsylvania. On his train ride to Washington in January 2009, newly-elected President Barack Obama, joined by native son Joe Biden, paid tribute to Delaware's Underground Railroad and diplomatically did not mention that Abraham Lincoln, during his 1861 train ride to Washington, decided not to risk a stop in slaveholding Delaware.

The state today has immigrant communities in the Wilmington area, and it has Southern-accented farmers in Kent and Sussex counties, plus Latino migrants working in its chicken plants (chickens outnumber people by 300 to 1 and produce tons of processed chicken dung known as "broiler litter") as well as in its beach-tourism industry (residents of the Washington, D.C. area flock to such Atlantic Ocean resorts as Rehoboth Beach and Bethany Beach during the summer). Newark has grown from a country crossroads to a small city as the University of Delaware has expanded. Well-preserved 18th century buildings line the streets of New Castle, the capital from 1704 to 1777; it is the home of the First State National Historical Park, a collection of vintage buildings dedicated by Obama in 2013, making Delaware the last state to secure a National Park Service unit.

For much of the last two centuries, the central focus of Delaware's economy was the business started by Éleuthère Irénée du Pont, the practical-minded son of a dreamy, idealistic French immigrant. He built a gunpowder mill on the banks of Brandywine Creek in 1802—the first enterprise of the du Pont family. Over time it became one of America's great munitions and chemical companies. It switched from gunpowder to dynamite in the 1880s, and the company grew especially rapidly during World War I, generating so much capital that it bought a large share of General Motors stock in 1914 and for 30 years controlled GM, which was for much of that time the nation's largest corporation. DuPont capital also financed what was arguably the world's finest research and development program. In the years on either side of World War II, DuPont prospered by bringing to the consumer and industrial markets new synthetics and plastics such as rayon, nylon, synthetic dyes, cellophane, Lucite, Teflon, and Dacron: "Better Living Through Chemistry."

Business trends in Delaware have had an outsized impact on national policy. In the late 19th century, the state passed pioneering laws of incorporation, giving more flexibility and power to managers and owners. Most companies in the *Fortune* 500 and on the New York Stock Exchange and Nasdaq are incorporated in Delaware. Their legal births take place in a federal-style building near the Capitol in Dover, which means that much of the nation's corporate law, especially on mergers and acquisitions, is made in Delaware's Chancery Court. Delaware politicians of both parties take care in choosing judges and writing corporate law to produce a reliable legal environment. Recently the Chancery Court's jurisdiction has been extended to intellectual property, and the Wilmington bar has been practicing much corporate bankruptcy law.

In the quarter-century boom starting in the early 1980s, Delaware fostered a new industry: credit cards. In 1981, Republican Gov. Pete du Pont pushed through a law abolishing

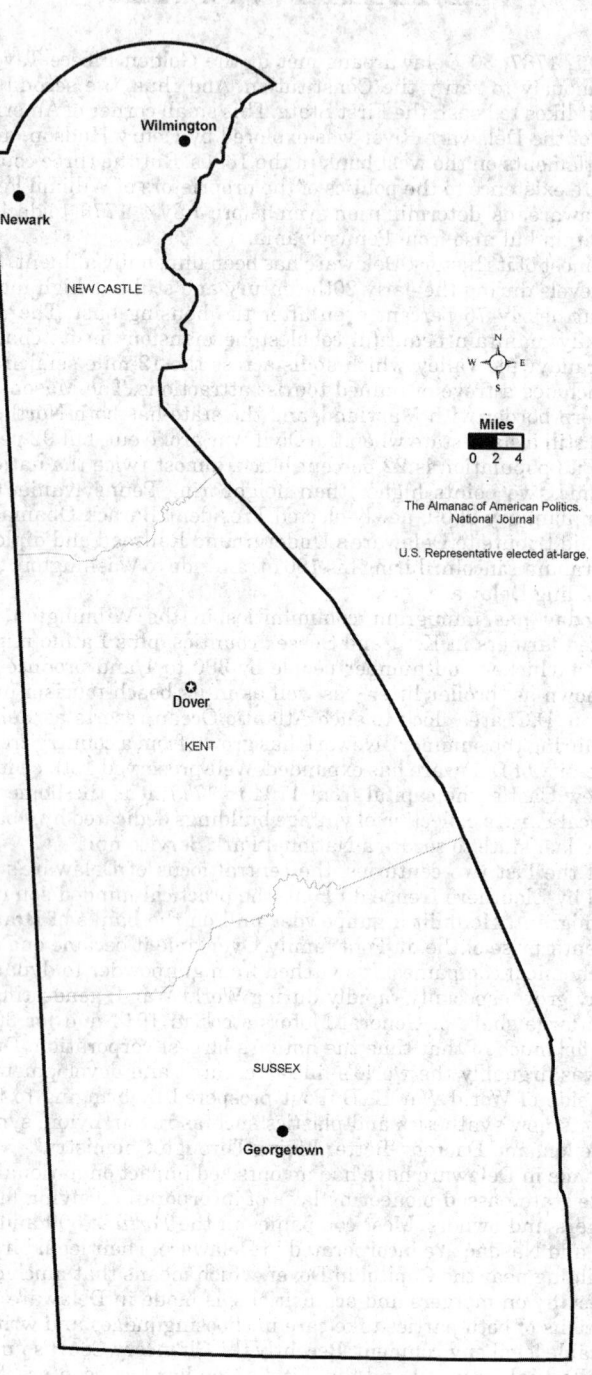

Wilmington

Newark

NEW CASTLE

W — N — E — S

Miles
0   2   4

The Almanac of American Politics.
National Journal

U.S. Representative elected at-large.

Dover

KENT

SUSSEX

Georgetown

Delaware's usury laws and lowering its bank franchise tax. Inflation was high, and banks were looking for a state with no limit on interest rates to locate their credit card operations. Although South Dakota abolished its usury law in 1980, it didn't have a labor force large enough to support many banks; Delaware did. MBNA Corporation moved there from Maryland in 1982, invented the affinity card in 1983, and became the nation's largest credit card issuer; its chief executive officer, Charles Cawley, replaced the du Pont family as Delaware's most visible philanthropist and community leader. Cawley retired in 2003, and Bank of America acquired MBNA in 2005. Two years later, the financial crisis hit the credit card business hard, helping to send Delaware into recession. The troubles in the domestic auto industry reverberated in the state as well. More than 1,000 people lost their jobs when Chrysler closed its plant in Newark at the end of 2008, and Obama administration efforts to locate the Fisker electric car plant there foundered. DuPont's employment rolls in the state have fallen by about two-thirds since 1990, and the company faces the prospect of further splintering amid global changes in the chemical sector. White-collar sectors have also lost thousands of jobs since 2001 due to corporate consolidation, and in 2012, personal income per capita in the state fell below the U.S. average for the first time since the Great Depression.

Advanced technology is helping replace some of those jobs—the Information Technology & Innovation Foundation has ranked Delaware second in the nation for its steps to create a "new economy"—and the state has continued to thrive by "exporting taxes." Journalist Jonathan Chait, irritated at the exorbitant tolls and traffic jams at the tollbooths on the Delaware Turnpike, wrote in *The New Republic,* "The organizing principle of Delaware government is to subsidize its people at the rest of the country's expense." State government gets 3 percent of its operating budget from the turnpike tolls (the highest per mile in the country: $4 for 11 miles), 22 percent from corporate and franchise taxes and 7 percent from the lottery and slot machines. It allows betting on football parley cards at racetracks, bars and restaurants. A 1993 U.S. Supreme Court decision sanctioned Delaware's tax on unclaimed property from other states. Exporting taxes has allowed Delaware to be one of the five states with no sales tax. And it has lowered its income tax several times in recent years, first under du Pont, then under Republican Gov. Michael Castle and Democratic Gov. Thomas Carper. Democratic Gov. Jack Markell, blessed with a budget surplus in spring 2011, called for lower business and banking taxes and a slight cut in the high income tax rate. Property taxes are low, with no reassessments for more than 25 years. Delaware boosters can argue that its state policies have provided credit to millions of people and businesses, enabled America's corporate economy to grow robustly and led the nation in a virtuous cycle of lowering taxes. Certainly Delaware has remained a draw; its population grew 18 percent in the 1990s and 15 percent from 2000 to 2010, including a flow of retirees from Pennsylvania, Maryland and New Jersey.

From the 1950s through the 1980s, the state produced robust two-party politics in which tiny Delaware's vote mirrored that of the nation. But in the 1990s, Delaware trended Democratic, and now it is virtually a one-party state. Delaware has not elected a Republican governor since 1988. Markell, then state treasurer, effectively clinched the race when he defeated Lt. Gov. John Carney in the 2008 Democratic primary and was easily reelected in 2012. From

Population		Race and Ethnicity		Income	
Total:	925,749	White	65.0%	Median income:	$52,219
Urban:	30.8%	Black	20.9%		(27 of 50)
Suburban:	68.3%	Latino	8.4%	Under $50,000	42.9%
Rural:	0.9%	Asian	3.3%	$50,000-$99,999:	32.6%
Land area:	1,949	Two races	2.1%	$100,000-$199,999:	19.7%
Pop/sq. mi.:	475.0	White Ethnic	35.7%	$200,000 or more:	4.9%
Born in state:	46.8%			Poverty Rate	12.4%
		Education			
Age Groups		H.S. grad or less:	42.9%	**Work**	
Under 18:	22.0%	Some college:	27.3%	White collar:	38.6%
18 to 34:	22.8%	College degree, 4 yr.:	17.2%	Blue collar:	43.4%
35 to 64:	39.3%	Post-grad study:	12.6%	Sales and service:	18.0%
Over 64:	15.9%			Govt. workers:	14.2%
		Military			
		Veterans/active duty:	9.6%		

1972 to 2000, Delaware's presence in the Senate was bipartisan, with Republican William Roth, first elected in 1970, getting along well with Democrat Biden, first elected in 1972 at age 29 (he turned the constitutional age of 30 before the term started). But Roth, at 79, was defeated in 2000 by former Gov. Tom Carper, who has been reelected twice with ease. After Biden won the vice presidency in 2008, his

Voter Turnout		
2013 Total Citizen 18+		681,862
2014 Highest Statewide Turnout		234,038
2014 Turnout as % CVAP		34.3%
2012 Turnout as % CVAP		61.2%
Legislature		
Senate:	13D	8R
House:	25D	16R

seat went to Democrat Chris Coons—unexpectedly at the time, but a harbinger of Democratic dominance. Rep. Mike Castle, a Republican moderate and former governor who had held statewide office since 1980, began as the favorite, but he lost the primary to eccentric conservative Christine O'Donnell, 53%-47%, on the strength of GOP tea party voters in the rural downstate. Also in 2010, Democrat John Carney won the state's single House seat by 57%-41%. That's just a little lower than the Obama-Biden ticket's margins of 62%-37% in 2008 and 59%-40% in 2012. The state House turned Democratic in 2008, joining the state Senate and the governorship for unified control. Neither chamber has been vulnerable to a switch in control since.

Delaware elections are not usually bitter contests (Castle's primary defeat was an exception). Thanks to the state's small size, politics remain intimate. Personal campaigning is important, and successful Delaware politicians are almost always nice people; they couldn't get elected otherwise. (This made Carper's decision to challenge the long-tenured Roth in 2000 a bold and atypical move.) Then there's Delaware's unique custom, dating back to 1792, of "Return Day." On the Thursday after an election, winning and losing candidates go to the Sussex County seat of Georgetown and ride together in carriages to receive the bipartisan cheers of the voters and, literally, bury a hatchet in a box of Lewes Beach sand. Not a bad example for the other 49 states.

Presidential Politics Delaware used to be a presidential bellwether: It had voted for every winner from 1952 to 1996, the longest winning streak of any state. But starting in 2000, this relatively wealthy state has been voting significantly more Democratic than the national average. New Castle County and its suburbs dominate the state's politics: three out of five ballots are cast in New Castle, while Kent and Sussex counties cast the rest. New Castle, like other affluent parts of major metropolitan areas, starting in the middle 1990s, tilted toward the Democrats

2012 Presidential Vote		
Barack Obama (D)	242,584	(59%)
Mitt Romney (R)	165,484	(40%)
2012 Presidential Primary		
Mitt Romney (R)	16,143	(56%)
Newt Gingrich (R)	7,742	(27%)
Ron Paul (R)	3,017	(11%)
Rick Santorum (R)	1,690	(6%)
2008 Presidential Vote		
Barack Obama (D)	255,459	(62%)
John McCain (R)	152,374	(37%)

and away from the Republicans on cultural issues, and it voted 2-to-1 or more for Obama in 2008 and 2012. Most Delaware voters still see plenty of ads, because in the past three elections, all candidates have targeted Pennsylvania, and New Castle and Kent are in the Philadelphia media market. (Sussex is in the Salisbury, Maryland market.)

In 2008, Delaware held its primary on February 5, Super Tuesday. Obama carried the state 53%-42%, winning by a big margin in both black neighborhoods and affluent suburbs in New Castle County. He also captured Kent. Hillary Clinton carried Southern-accented Sussex, which is rural, but also home to the state's popular beach towns. Some 96,000 Delawareans voted in the Democratic primary, while only 50,000 turned out for the Republican contest. John McCain won with 45 percent of the vote to 33 percent for Mitt Romney and 15 percent for Mike Huckabee. Less than 30,000 votes were cast in the April 24, 2012 GOP primary when the race was effectively over. Romney won 56%-27% over Newt Gingrich, who had hoped to revive his candidacy in the tiny state. Ron Paul received 11 percent.

Delaware has not produced many presidential hopefuls: both Democrat Joe Biden, who got his start on the New Castle County Council before he was elected Senator in 1972, and then GOP Gov. Pierre S. du Pont IV, unsuccessfully sought their parties' respective 1988 nominations. Biden took another stab in 2008, failed, but was tapped for the vice presidency.

Prior to 1988, the last presidential hopeful from Delaware was Sen. Thomas F. Bayard, Sr., a serious contender for the 1880 and 1884 Democratic nominations. Bayard's grandfather, James Asheton, Sr., was a Federalist member of the House of Representatives from Delaware in 1800 and cast a critical ballot to enable Democratic Republican Thomas Jefferson to win that famously contested election. The Bidens looked like they might become a political dynasty before the vice president's son Beau, an Iraq war veteran and former state Attorney General who was gearing up for a run for Governor and appeared to have unlimited potential, was tragically struck down by brain cancer in May 2015.

Governor

Jack Markell (D)

Elected 2008, term expires Jan. 2017, 2nd term; b. Nov. 26, 1960, Newark; Brown U., B.A. 1981, U. of Chicago, M.B.A. 1985; Jewish; married (Carla); 2 children.

Elected Office: DE treas., 1999-2008.

Professional Career: Officer, First Natl. Bank Chicago, 1982-86; Assoc., McKinsey & Co. Inc., 1986-88; Sr. V.P., Nextel, 1989-95; V.P., Comcast, 1996-98.

Office: Tatnall Bldg., 150 MLK Jr. Blvd., 2nd Fl., Dover, 19901, 302-744-4101; Fax: 302-739-2775; Website: state.de.us/governor.

Election Results

2012 general	Jack Markell (D)	275,993	(69%)
	Jeffrey Cragg (R)	113,793	(29%)
2012 primary	Jack Markell (D)	unopposed	

Prior winning percentage: 2008 (68%)

Democrat Jack Markell was elected governor of Delaware in 2008 and reelected with ease in 2012. A former telecommunications executive and self-described "card-carrying capitalist," he has become increasingly prominent in his party, chairing the Democratic Governors Association in 2010-2011 and the National Governors Association in 2012-2013.

Markell was raised in a split-level house in Newark Delaware, the youngest of three children. His father was a professor at the University of Delaware, and his mother was a state social worker. Growing up, Markell came to appreciate Delaware's small-town familiarity; he went to kindergarten with his future wife, Carla. His first foray into politics came at age 17, when he was elected president of his high school's student body. Later the same year, he accompanied his father on an overseas sabbatical, living half the year in Britain and half in New Zealand. After graduating from Brown University and earning an M.B.A. from the University of Chicago, Markell set off on a 16-year career in business. He worked for such big corporate players as Comcast, McKinsey and First Chicago Corp., but Markell is most closely identified with the telecommunications field. He was an early employee at a startup called Fleet Call, which grew into a major cellular service provider and rebranded itself as Nextel, a name Markell coined. He struck up a lasting friendship there with one of Fleet Call's early investors, Mark Warner, later governor of Virginia and now a senator. Markell touting his business acumen, defeated Republican state Treasurer Janet Rzewnicki in 1998 in his first campaign for public office; he won the office twice more.

Shortly after taking office, Markell sought to cut state spending by consolidating purchases across agencies. He helped pioneer a program that provides every state employee a detailed health assessment in an effort to provide better care while reducing the state's costs. Believing that most citizens knew relatively little about monetary issues, he sought to improve financial literacy in the state where most of the nation's credit cards are issued. Together with community and church leaders in Wilmington, he led a campaign to encourage eligible families to apply for the Earned Income Tax Credit.

When Democratic Gov. Ruth Ann Minner was barred by term limits from running again in 2008, Markell was a natural to get into the contest to succeed her. But there was someone of equal political stature ahead of him in line: John Carney, the lieutenant governor and Democratic favorite. In a small state where most elected officials are on personal terms with one another, office seekers defer to the wishes of party elders, who hoped to avoid the first contested Democratic gubernatorial primary since 1992. They urged Markell to run for lieutenant governor instead. But he was steadfast about wanting the top job. Deprived of his anticipated coronation, Carney lined up support from much of the party establishment, including Minner, state legislators and unions. But Markell campaigned tirelessly across the state and raised more than $4 million, including $725,000 of his own money, a record fundraising haul in a Delaware governor's race. Carney could not keep pace with Markell's fundraising, but he enjoyed the backing of the state party's executive committee, which ran ads against Markell. As Minner's popularity flagged after two terms in office, Markell subtly distanced himself from her by campaigning on a theme of change and, in June, released a detailed compendium of policy proposals called the "Blueprint for a Better Delaware." Still, Markell's victory in the September primary was a stunner. He took 51 percent of the vote to Carney's 49 percent, a margin of about 1,700 votes.

The party rallied behind Markell for the general election, where he faced Republican Bill Lee, a retired Superior Court judge making his third straight run for the office. On the campaign trail, Markell and Matt Denn, the Democratic candidate for lieutenant governor, touted a plan they claimed would save taxpayers more than $100 million while simultaneously balancing a state budget faced with a massive deficit. The 12-page document drew heavily on previous Markell proposals for health care, education and energy. The Republican Party tried to taint Markell with ads that referenced a 1994 lawsuit alleging that he and other Nextel executives had made false statements to boost the company's stock price. The executives settled the lawsuit for $27 million without admitting wrongdoing.

In the weeks leading up to the general election, few doubted that Markell would keep the governor's mansion in Democratic hands. He entered October with a commanding lead in the polls and 10 times as much money as his opponent. During a debate in late October, Lee pushed Markell to pledge not to levy any new taxes in order to fund his proposed programs. Markell refused, but still defeated Lee, 68%-32%.

Markell took office at a time of deepening economic uncertainty for the state, whose reliance on the financial services industry for its tax revenue left it disproportionately affected by volatility on Wall Street. Facing a budget deficit estimated at $800 million, Markell cut state workers' pay and raised taxes. Taking advantage of a provision in a 1992 federal law, he proposed legalizing sports betting in Delaware, as well as increasing the number of slot machines. The NCAA threatened a tournament boycott if betting were allowed on college games; a federal appeals court in August 2009 limited the betting to three-game parlays on NFL contests. Markell also promoted wind farms off the Delaware coast, in partnership with the governors of Maryland and Virginia, and got local utilities to commit to buying wind energy. In 2010, he signed a law requiring 25 percent of the state's electricity to come from renewable sources by 2025. He promoted a one-time tax amnesty in 2009 that netted $22 million and signed a bill in 2010 allowing mutual insurance companies headquartered in Delaware to demutualize, in line with Delaware's tradition of encouraging companies to incorporate in the state.

When General Motors announced in June 2009 that it would close the Boxwood Road plant, Markell encouraged Fisker Automotive to buy the facility. He enlisted Vice President Joe Biden's help, and in September got a $529 million loan from the Department of Energy on top of a $12.5 million state loan for infrastructure and other financial incentives. In October, the company announced it was moving in, and CEO Henrik Fisker told *The News Journal* of Wilmington, "The governor pulled (things) together faster than I can take my family of four people to dinner." Meanwhile, the state secured one of the first two funded Race to the Top grants for public schools as well as an Early Learning Challenge Grant to raise the percentage of high-need children in early-childhood programs. Markell also used his chairmanship of the NGA to promote job opportunities for people with physical and developmental disabilities.

With Delaware still in economic doldrums, Markell proposed a $3 billion budget in January 2011 that closed a $216 million budget shortfall without raising taxes, relying instead on a variety of measures that included the first layoffs of his administration. Within months, however, state officials found themselves with a projected $320 million surplus, the result of a sharp increase in abandoned property revenues. Meanwhile, in May, Markell signed into law bills that legalized civil unions for same-sex couples and legalized marijuana growing, distribution and use for limited medical purposes. A few months later, he announced an ambitious proposal to add a surcharge on Delmarva Power electric bills to help bring a fuel cell factory to Newark that could create 900 jobs and millions of dollars in economic development. The company opened a new factory in 2013, but was slow to meet its hiring goal.

Heading into a reelection year, Markell unveiled a $3.5 billion spending plan in January 2012 that was about 1 percent above current spending levels. Once again, though, higher-than-expected revenue projections enabled him to add money for unfunded retiree benefits and transportation projects. His general election opponent was Jeff Cragg, a little-known Republican former insurance executive. Cragg criticized the Fisker Automotive investment and campaigned with large signs reading "30,611," the number of unemployed workers in the state. But he was no match for a successful governor in a state where President Barack Obama coasted to victory. Markell won 69%-29%.

During his second term. Markell signed a bill to raise the state minimum wage to $8.25 an hour, and he launched an initiative called Pathways to Prosperity that offered high school students training in high-demand jobs that could earn them college credit. Markell has sought ways to curb the proliferation of testing in schools. In February 2014, Markell redoubled his efforts on gaming, announcing an agreement with Nevada's Republican governor, Brian Sandoval, to establish a landmark interstate compact on online poker, though the accord was slow to be implemented.

Markell is term-limited, and the 2016 race to succeed him should play out mainly on the Democratic side, given the party's growing dominance in the state. His likely successor was long presumed to be Beau Biden, the Vice President's son. The younger Biden, an Iraq War veteran, gave a high-profile nominating speech for his father at the 2012 Democratic National Convention, and as the state's elected attorney general, he attracted national attention for his work on sex crimes and gun control. With a magic last name for Delawareans, Biden would have been a virtual lock to win—but, after recovering from a stroke in 2010, Biden underwent brain surgery in 2013 and in May 2015, he died of brain cancer at age 46. The list of potential Democratic candidates includes Carney; Denn, who succeeded Biden as attorney general; and New Castle County executive Tom Gordon. The Republican bench is thin; the most commonly cited possible candidate is treasurer Ken Simpler, though he would have to give up a post he won for the first time in 2014.

Senior Senator

Thomas Carper (D)

Elected 2000, term expires Jan. 2019, 3rd term; b. Jan. 23, 1947, Beckley, WV; OH St. U., B.A. 1968, U. of DE, M.B.A. 1975; Presbyterian; married (Martha); 2 children.

Military Career: U.S. Navy, 1968-73 (Vietnam); Naval Reserves, 1973-91.

Elected Office: DE treas., 1976-83; U.S. House, 1983-93; DE gov., 1993-2001.

Professional Career: Industrial devel. specialist, DE Div. of Econ. Devel., 1975-76; Chmn, National Governors Association, 1998-99.

DC Office: 513 HSOB, 20510, 202-224-2441; Fax: 202-228-2190; Website: carper.senate.gov.

State Offices: Dover, 302-674-3308; Georgetown, 302-856-7690; Wilmington, 302-573-6291.

Committees: *Environment & Public Works:* Clean Air & Nuclear Safety (RMM); Fisheries, Water, & Wildlife; Superfund, Waste Mgmt., & Regulatory Oversight; Transportation & Infrastructure. *Finance:* Energy, Natural Resources, & Infrastructure; Taxation & IRS Oversight. *Homeland Security & Governmental Affairs* (RMM): Ex-officio member of all subcommittees.

Group Ratings

	ADA	ACLU	AFL-CIO	LCV	ITI	COC	HAFA	ACU	CFG	FRC
2014	85%	93%	–	80%	100%	50%	7%	4%	24%	0%
2013	80%	C	94%	92%	C	50%	C	4%	7%	C

National Journal Ratings

	2013 LIB	—	2013 CONS
Economic	59%	—	39%
Social	73%	—	0%
Foreign	71%	—	0%
Composite	77%	—	23%

Key Votes of the 113th Congress

1. Sandy storm spending	Y	5. Student Loan Rates	Y	9. Bipartisan Budget Deal	Y
2. Chuck Hagel Confirmation	Y	6. Employee Non-Discrim'n Act	Y	10. Farm Bill Conference Rept.	Y
3. Gun Background Checks	Y	7. Senate Vote on Judgeships	N	11. Unempl. Comp. Extension	Y
4. Immigration Reform	Y	8. Defense Dept. Spending	Y	12. Keystone Pipeline	Y

Election Results

2012 general	Thomas Carper (D)	265,415	(66%)	$5,324,026	$3,075
	Kevin Wade (R)	115,700	(29%)	$181,600	$10,000
	Alexander Pires (I)	15,300	(4%)	$413,774	
2012 primary	Thomas Carper (D)	43,587	(88%)		
	Keith Spanarelli (D)	6,028	(12%)		

Prior winning percentages: 2006 (70%), 2000 (56%); Governor: 1996 (70%), 1992 (65%); House: 1990 (66%), 1988 (68%), 1986 (66%), 1984 (59%), 1982 (52%)

Democrat Thomas Carper is arguably the most successful politician in the history of the First State: He has won 13 consecutive statewide elections, and has never lost a race in four decades in public office. Serving as state treasurer, House member and governor before his election to the Senate in 2000, Carper's reputation as a centrist consensus-builder has made him well-liked on both sides of the aisle on Capitol Hill as well as popular at home. Now Delaware's senior senator, he fits squarely into what the home state establishment refers to as the "Delaware Way": a low-key, pragmatic brand of politics favored in a pocket-sized state that often has the feel of an extended town, in which most of the key players know each other well. Carper's leading role on the Senate Governmental Affairs Committee— which he chaired in 2013-2014 and where he is now the ranking Democrat—has served to reinforce his image as a results-oriented legislator focused on issues outside of the political limelight, but important to the efficiency of government.

Carper grew up in Southside Virginia and attended Ohio State University on a Navy ROTC scholarship. He first came to Delaware as an ensign in the Navy; after service in Southeast Asia during the Vietnam War, where he was a mission commander piloting submarine-hunting planes, Carper returned to earn his M.B.A. at the University of Delaware. A year later, in 1976, he was elected state treasurer at age 29. In 1982, leading state Democrats—including Sen. Joe Biden—prodded Carper to leave his politically secure post to challenge Republican incumbent Thomas Evans for the state's at-large House seat. The ensuing race was a relatively rare detour from the Delaware Way; the tabloid *New York Post* labeled it as "the nation's dirtiest campaign" that year. Evans had been politically damaged by an acknowledged "association" with a young female lobbyist named Paula Parkinson, and the state of Carper's marriage was also dragged into the campaign. (Carper has since divorced and remarried.) Carper won with 52 percent, and the civility for which Delaware politics is known ultimately resurfaced: Carper and Evans became friendly, and Evans even contributed to Carper's campaign committee during the 2012 and 2014 election cycles.

After a decade in the House of accumulating a moderate voting record—his strong support of a constitutional amendment requiring a balanced budget set him apart from many fellow Democrats—Carper in 1992 was party to what is still referred to as "The Swap" by Delaware insiders. Carper and Republican Gov. Michael Castle were personal friends who, despite differing partisan affiliations, were considered near-ideological twins. Castle was term-limited and ran for the House, while Carper ran to succeed Castle as governor and won with nearly two-thirds of the vote. As governor, Carper pursued an agenda that was in many ways more conservative than liberal. He continued former Republican Gov. Pete du Pont's policy of cutting taxes, reducing income tax rates by about 10 per cent. Delaware's strong economy helped him keep the budget in the black, and he boosted the state's credit rating to a historic high even as state spending rose 40 percent in eight years. He also signed a bill authorizing charter schools.

After easily winning re-election in 1996, Carper—barred from seeking a third term in 2000—faced a possible interruption in a nearly quarter century of electoral success. Some thought Republican Sen. William Roth would retire after one-third of a century on Capitol Hill, and that Castle would run to succeed him; Carper went so far as to say publicly that, under such a scenario, he would have bowed out of politics, at least temporarily, rather than run against his friend Castle. But Roth decided to seek re-election, Castle shied away from a primary challenge to the incumbent, and Carper ran for the Senate.

In contrast to the Carper vs. Evans confrontation almost two decades earlier, this was a battle of positives. Both candidates had high approval ratings at home and were familiar figures to voters. Roth had a record of achievements that paid direct benefits to residents of this generally affluent state, starting with the Kemp-Roth tax cut of 1981. Later, as chairman of the Senate Finance Committee, he engineered the eponymous Roth IRA, enacted in 1997, as well as reform of the Internal Revenue Service. Roth's main problem was that he was 79 years old. The then 53-year-old Carper was careful not to campaign negatively against Roth, but his slogan, "A Senator for Our Future," spotlighted the generational contrast. While Carper regularly spent 16 hours per day campaigning, Roth stayed in Washington and made only a few appearances in the state. In October, Roth fainted twice on the campaign trail, once in full view of cameras, driving home the issue of age. On Election Day, Carper won by a solid 56-44 percent margin.

As was the case during his House tenure, Carper has amassed one of the more moderate voting records among Senate Democrats, and is often at the center of efforts to build bipartisan coalitions when important legislation bogs down, as illustrated by the push to pass a health care overhaul at the outset of the Obama administration. Carper bucked liberals in his party by opposing creation of a government-run insurance plan for those who could not afford private plans. But rather than attack the public option idea, he tried to broker a compromise he and other centrist Democrats could support. The public option was ultimately dropped from the final legislation, but Carper first sought to advance an alternative that would allow states to individually decide whether to offer a public option to compete with private insurers.

In addition to shaping health care policy, Carper has utilized his seat on the influential Finance Committee to strongly back free trade: In early 2015, as many of Congress' left-leaning Democrats were putting distance between themselves and President Barack Obama on a free trade agreement with 12 Asian nations, Carper was among those in his party to support not only the deal itself—but also a proposal to grant the president special authority to expedite negotiations of its provisions. In a May 2015 procedural vote on the matter in which Senate Democrats deserted Obama *en masse*, Carper was the sole Democrat to vote with the president.

Carper has been considered a budget hawk. In late 2012, he called for a deficit reduction blueprint similar to one developed earlier by the so-called Simpson-Bowles commission, which had backed proposals to overhaul the tax code and gradually raise the Medicare eligibility age. His affinity for Simpson-Bowles led him to be one of just three Senate Democrats to oppose a final budget deal on New Year's Eve 2013, intended to avert the so-called "fiscal cliff" of automatic tax hikes and spending cuts. More recently, he has pushed for a 12-cent gas tax increase to replenish the dwindling Highway Trust Fund, an idea to which his Republican colleagues have been cool. "I'm not going away. I think it's the right thing to do," Carper told the Wilmington *News Journal*. "We can't keep kicking the can down the road."

In his portfolio on the Governmental Affairs Committee, Carper has gotten legislation enacted beefing up protections against government payments to ineligible claimants of retiree or disability benefits, and requiring audits to identify billions lost through waste and fraudulent claims. He has been identified most with efforts to rescue the ailing Postal Service. He worked with a fellow centrist, Republican Susan Collins of Maine, in 2006 to pass the first major revision of Postal Service operations since 1970. (Delaware is a major center for the credit card industry, which accounts for about one-quarter of the Postal Service's mail.) As the Postal Service continued to run large deficits, Carper in 2012 engineered bipartisan Senate passage of legislation that allowed the service to offer buyout and early retirement incentives to 100,000 employees, while reducing six-day delivery to five days after giving officials time to come up with an alternative to save costs. But the bill stalled in the House, leaving Carper so frustrated that he created a Facebook page complaining about the lack of action. At the start of 2015, Carper vowed to keep pushing for Postal Service reform, while voicing optimism that it would finally happen.

A former chairman of the Environment and Public Works' subcommittees subpanel on clean air, Carper also has focused on legislation to reduce air pollution and halt climate change, while again reaching across the political aisle. With Republican Lamar Alexander of Tennessee as a partner, he authored legislation almost a decade ago to limit emissions of sulfur dioxide, nitrous oxide, mercury and carbon dioxide; the pair later pushed for another bill to substantially reduce emissions from power plants. Such efforts have made little headway on Capitol Hill, and Carper has been supportive of Obama administration efforts to accomplish such aims through EPA regulations. He has defended the EPA against Republican criticism, citing a 2012 American Lung Association study showing improvements in 18 of the 25 most pollution-plagued cities as evidence that "we can have a strong economy, clean air, and protect public health all at the same time."

Carper did run into blowback from environmentalists in January 2015, when he was one of just eight Democrats to join all Senate Republicans in an unsuccessful effort to override Obama's veto of legislation to construct the $8 billion Keystone XL pipeline. Carper said the controversy over the pipeline, designed to run from Canada through the Midwest, had "impeded our ability to work together and make progress even on issues that we're in agreement on," while declaring, "We need to address this issue and we need to move on." It bespeaks a broader frustration on the part of the former governor with the pace of getting things done on Capitol Hill. "My worst day as governor was better than my best day as a United States senator," he is said to have told colleagues. But Carper remains young by Senate standards—he will be 71 when next up for election in 2018—and the state has trended increasingly Democratic since he was first elected to his current post. In 2012, Republican engineer Kevin Wade, raised questions about Carper's health—which the senator called "baloney"—and blasted Carper's proposal to raise the gas tax. Carper responded by winning with 66 percent of the vote, down only slightly from his victory margin six years earlier.

Junior Senator

Christopher Coons (D)

Elected 2010, term expires Jan. 2021, 1st full term; b. Sept. 9, 1963, Greenwich, CT; Amherst Col., B.A. 1985, Yale U., J.D. 1992, Yale Divinity Schl., M.A.R. 1992; Presbyterian; married (Annie); 3 children.

Elected Office: Pres., New Castle Cnty. Cncl., 2001-05; New Castle Cnty. exec., 2005-10.

Professional Career: Practicing atty., W.L. Gore & Associates, 1996-2004.

DC Office: 127A RSOB, 20510, 202-224-5042; Website: coons.senate .gov.

State Offices: Dover, 302-736-5601; Wilmington, 302-573-6345.

Committees: *Appropriations:* Commerce, Justice, Science, & Related Agencies; Energy & Water Development; Financial Services & General Gov't (RMM); State, Foreign Operations, & Related Programs; Transportation, Housing & Urban Development, & Related Agencies. *Ethics (Select). Foreign Relations:* Africa & Global Health Policy; East Asia, the Pacific, & Int'l Cybersecurity Policy; State Dept. & USAID Mgmt., Int'l Operations, & Bilateral Int'l Development. *Judiciary:* Antitrust, Competition Policy & Consumer Rights; the Constitution; Oversight, Agency Action, Federal Rights & Federal Courts (RMM); Privacy, Technology & the Law. *Small Business & Entrepreneurship.*

Group Ratings

	ADA	ACLU	AFL-CIO	LCV	ITI	COC	HAFA	ACU	CFG	FRC
2014	90%	100%	–	80%	100%	43%	2%	4%	0%	0%
2013	85%	C	100%	92%	C	50%	C	4%	4%	C

National Journal Ratings

	2013 LIB	—	2013 CONS
Economic	70%	—	29%
Social	68%	—	29%
Foreign	66%	—	29%
Composite	70%	—	31%

Key Votes of the 113th Congress

1. Sandy storm spending	Y	5. Student Loan Rates	Y	9. Bipartisan Budget Deal	Y
2. Chuck Hagel Confirmation	Y	6. Employee Non-Discrim'n Act	Y	10. Farm Bill Conference Rept.	Y
3. Gun Background Checks	Y	7. Senate Vote on Judgeships	N	11. Unempl. Comp. Extension	Y
4. Immigration Reform	Y	8. Defense Dept. Spending	Y	12. Keystone Pipeline	N

Election Results

2014 general	Chris Coons (D)	130,655	(56%)	$8,958,014	$57,744
	Kevin Wade (R)	98,823	(42%)	$111,823	$72,702
2014 primary	Christopher Coons (D)	unopposed			

Prior winning percentage: 2010 (57%)

"Chris Coons may turn out to be the luckiest politician in America this year," CNN declared in mid-September of 2010. Indeed, at the outset of that year, Coons was hardly on the radar screen as a potential contender for the seat occupied for nearly four decades by Joe Biden. It took the biggest upset of the 2010 primary season—the Republican primary season, that is—to transform Coons from distinct underdog to overwhelming favorite to fill out the final four years of Biden's Senate term after the latter became vice president.

In style, Delaware's junior senator—easily re-elected to a full term in 2014—is a contrast to the voluble Biden; in substance, he has been a bipartisan-oriented, business-friendly Democrat in the mold of Virginia's Mark Warner, Colorado's Michael Bennet, and his home-state colleague, Thomas Carper. But, at times during his relatively brief tenure, Coons has shown an interest in taking on a more partisan role and moving up the Senate leadership ladder, including eyeing the chairmanship of the Democratic Senatorial Campaign Committee after the 2014 election.

Coons' family moved to Delaware during his early childhood; bankruptcy wiped out much of his father's business success, and his parents later divorced. His mother, Sally, a schoolteacher, later remarried: Coons' stepfather, Robert Gore, had played a key role in the founding of a highly successful family enterprise, Newark, Del.-based W.L. Gore and Associates. (Holder of the patent for water-resistant Gore-Tex fabric, the firm is among the top 200 privately held companies in the United States.) As a student at Wilmington's elite Tower Hill School, Coons considered himself a Republican and volunteered for Ronald Reagan's 1980 presidential campaign. His conversion to the Democratic Party came while he was a student at Amherst College. Studying in Kenya for a semester in 1984, Coons said that observing his host family changed the way he thought about poverty and free markets. It also led him to write a tongue-in-cheek column for the college newspaper, titled "Chris Coons: The Making of a Bearded Marxist," which would crop up as an issue in his Senate bid a quarter of a century later.

After graduating from Amherst with a dual major in chemistry and political science, Coons did relief work with a church group in South Africa before attending Yale Law School. He also enrolled in Yale's Divinity School, graduating from both programs in 1992. He initially worked with low-income students in New York City, but moved back to Delaware in 1996 after getting married—and went to work as an attorney for W.L. Gore, of which his stepfather was then president. Coons' first foray into politics came in 2000, when he was elected president of the New Castle County Council. Four years later, he was elected county executive on an anti-corruption platform; his predecessor had been dogged by corruption allegations. Despite promising in his campaign not to increase taxes, Coons wound up doing so to close a budget gap.

When Biden was elected vice president in 2008—winning re-election to the Senate at the same time—the heavy favorite on the Democratic side for the open seat was his son, state Attorney General Beau Biden. Ted Kaufman, a long-time aide to the elder Biden, received a temporary appointment to the job in late 2008, while ruling out running himself; it was seen as a move to keep the seat warm for the younger Biden until the 2010 election. But Beau Biden, who died in May 2015, declined to run, perhaps influenced by leading Democrats' appraisal that the race was, at best, an uphill battle against moderate-to-liberal Republican Rep. Michael Castle. Elected statewide 12 times in 30 years, Castle, also a former governor, was seen as a heavy favorite in the general election despite the state's increasingly Democratic tilt. But, in a year in which the tea party emerged as a major force in Republican politics, Castle lost the September GOP primary in a stunning upset to tea party-backed Christine O'Donnell, a consultant and TV commentator who had been defeated by Joe Biden by a 2-1 margin two years earlier.

Coons, seen as a heavy underdog against Castle, immediately catapulted to a double-digit lead over O'Donnell in the polls. Predictions that she would be a weak opponent were fulfilled in spades. O'Donnell was put on the defensive by old footage showing her condemning masturbation, and, most notably, claiming to have dabbled in witchcraft while an occasional guest more than a decade earlier on Bill Maher's nightly talk show, "Politically Incorrect". She was compelled to tape a now-famous campaign ad in which she reassured her supporters, "I am not a witch. I'm nothing you've heard. I am you." The ad accomplished little but to provide fodder for late-night comics. O'Donnell sought to focus on Coons' record of raising taxes as county executive, dubbing him "The Tax Man." Neither that nor Republican efforts to use his "Bearded Marxist" essay as a line of attack gained much traction. "I am a clean-shaven capitalist," Coons retorted. Mostly, Coons kept a low profile while O'Donnell's campaign came apart with one controversy after another. On Election Day, he won in a 57%-40% landslide, with exit polls showing him with a significant crossover vote from Republicans.

Even before winning the race, Coons' status as the electoral bulwark against an upstart tea party candidate won him a special place among national Democrats. "He's my favorite candidate. He's my pet," Majority Leader Harry Reid gushed to *The Hill* newspaper following the primary. But Coons also has made a determined effort to work with Republicans. He teamed with a fellow freshman, Florida Republican Marco Rubio, to introduce a jobs bill in 2011. He joined with Texas Republican John Cornyn on a bill to make the illegal streaming of television shows or movies a felony. As a member of the Energy and Natural Resources Committee, Coons worked with Republican James Inhofe of Oklahoma in a 2012 effort to scrutinize the renewable fuels standard, earlier mandated by Congress to increase production of biofuels. (Coons later gave up his seat on the energy panel when a coveted seat on the Appropriations Committee opened up.)

Following his 2010 election, Coons was given the chairmanship of Foreign Relations' Africa subcommittee in recognition of the time he spent on that continent. He struck up a friendship with the subcommittee's then ranking Republican, Georgia's Johnny Isakson, and they led the Senate's effort in 2012 to formally condemn Joseph Kony and his Lord's Resistance Army for its notorious reign of killings and child abductions across central Africa. Closer to home, Coons and Isakson teamed up to start the Senate Chicken Caucus, in recognition of the importance of the poultry industry to their home states. But Coons, who also serves on the Judiciary Committee, has found himself at odds with some leading congressional Republicans on the perennial issue of curbing patent abuses. A patent reform bill Coons introduced early in 2015—co-sponsored by Senate Minority Whip Dick Durbin of Illinois—was praised by university groups as well as the biotechnology and pharmaceutical industries. But it was criticized by the consumer electronics sector as doing little to restrain "patent trolls"—firms that purchase patents largely to seek financial settlements for infringement from other firms.

Defeating his Republican opponent, Kevin Wade—who unsuccessfully ran against Carper two years earlier—by 13 points in a difficult year for Democrats, Coons emerged with what he described as a rekindled appetite for campaigning. He expressed interest in heading the Senate Democrats' campaign arm, the DSCC, as the party began its quest to regain the Senate majority lost in the 2014 election. While success at the DSCC has often translated into an ascent into the top rungs of the Senate Democratic leadership, Coons ultimately withdrew from consideration, and the job went to Montana Sen. Jon Tester. "He ultimately decided it wasn't the right time for him to do it," said a spokesman, citing Coons' three teenage children at home and the punishing travel demands of the DSCC job. (Like Carper and, earlier, Biden, Coons commutes from Wilmington to Washington on most days when Congress is in session.) The Coons spokesman added, "He's also inherently a pretty bipartisan guy and was concerned it would be harder to make real progress on some of his legislative priorities while running the DSCC."

REPRESENTATIVE-AT-LARGE

John Carney (D)

Elected 2010, 3rd term; b. May 20, 1956, Wilmington; Dartmouth Col., B.A. 1978, U. of DE, M.P.A. 1987; Catholic; married (Tracey); 2 children.

Elected Office: DE secy. of finance, 1997-2000; DE lt. gov., 2001-09.

Professional Career: Staff, Sen. Joe Biden, 1986-89; Chief admin. officer, New Castle Cnty. Exec., 1989-94; Deputy chief of staff, Gov. Thomas Carper, 1994-97; Pres., COO, Transformative Technologies, 2009-10.

DC Office: 1406 LHOB, 20515, 202-225-4165; Website: johncarney. house.gov.

State Offices: Georgetown, 302-854-0667; Wilmington, 302-428-1902.

Committees: *Financial Services:* Capital Markets & Gov't Sponsored Enterprises; Monetary Policy & Trade.

Group Ratings

	ADA	ACLU	AFL-CIO	LCV	ITI	COC	HAFA	ACU	CFG	FRC
2014	70%	77%	–	77%	60%	55%	11%	0%	3%	0%
2013	65%	C	86%	93%	C	62%	C	20%	15%	C

National Journal Ratings

	2013 LIB	—	2013 CONS
Economic	62%	—	38%
Social	66%	—	32%
Foreign	74%	—	26%
Composite	68%	—	32%

Key Votes of the 113th Congress

1. Sandy storm spending	Y	5. Medical Marijuana	Y	9. Syrian Rebels Training	Y
2. Violence Against Women Act	Y	6. Farm Bill	N	10. Keystone pipeline	N
3. Guantanamo Bay Detainees	Y	7. Afghanistan Combat	Y	11. Immigration Exec. Action	N
4. Abortion 20-week ban	N	8. NSA Phone Data Collection	N	12. Bipartisan budget deal	Y

Election Results

2014 general	John C. Carney Jr. (D)	137,251	(59%)	$1,146,817	$50,035
	Rose Izzo (R)	85,146	(37%)	$21,926	
	Bernard August (G)	4,801	(2%)		
2014 primary	John Carney (D)	unopposed			

Prior winning percentages: 2012 (64%), 2010 (57%)

John Carney, first elected in 2010, is a centrist Democrat with an unusual devotion to bipartisanship—like his predecessor, nine-term Republican Rep. Michael Castle. Not long after taking office, he co-founded a policy group of Democrats and Republicans to calmly discuss finding common ground, and the group has achieved some results.

Voter Turnout	
2013 Total Citizen 18+	681,862
2014 House Turnout	231,617
2014 Turnout as % CVAP	34.0%
2012 Turnout as % CVAP	61.2%

Carney, the second of nine children born to two teachers, has lived in Wilmington for most of his life. He has been careful to stress his humble upbringing and the fact that he, his wife, and their two children live in a modest row house. Carney has spent nearly his entire adult life in public office, except for brief stints as president and chief operating officer of Transformative Technologies, a Delaware technology firm, and as executive vice president of a wind farm start-up called DelaWind. After getting a degree in English at Dartmouth College and a master's degree at the University of Delaware, Carney was an aide to Joe Biden, then a Democratic senator from Delaware. In the 1990s, he became a top aide to then Gov.

Thomas Carper, now a senator. Carney was the state secretary of finance under Carper from 1997 to 2000. That year, he won the first of two terms as lieutenant governor. In 2008, he lost a high-profile primary against Jack Markell for governor.

When Castle gave up the at-large House seat in a losing bid for the Senate, Carney earned the scorn of tea party activists who labeled him a "career politician" in his campaign against Republican Glen Urquhart. Carney ran on his support for renewable energy technology and jobs, and his opposition to oil drilling off the Delaware shoreline. Urquhart, a Rehoboth Beach developer, lambasted him for collecting government paychecks rather than creating jobs in the private sector. Urquhart also called attention to Carney's attempt to lobby the state for assistance in 2009, when he worked for DelaWind. But left-leaning Delaware was skittish about Urquhart's conservative positions. He said he would vote to repeal the Affordable Care Act and abolish the departments of Energy and Education. The Republican's social agenda and his lack of polish hurt him: In widely circulated comments, he compared liberals to Nazis while claiming that Hitler, not Thomas Jefferson, coined the phrase "separation of church and state." Carney declared Urquhart too "radical" and "extreme" to represent the neighborly state. He raised over $2 million, while Urquhart had $1.3 million, $1 million of it from his own pocket. Carney won, 57%-41%, a rare instance of a Democratic takeover of a seat in that GOP-friendly year.

In the House, Carney became the first freshman Democrat to pass an amendment in the House when he added a provision to a bill in May 2011 making rail security a priority for U.S. intelligence agencies. He was assigned to the Financial Services Committee and struck up a friendship with fellow freshman Jim Renacci, a Republican from Ohio, whom he admired for having a common sense approach to problems. They started a breakfast group that eventually grew to 14 lawmakers. "If our group can sit down, hear each other out, and come up with solutions we all agree on, that says something," Carney said in September 2011. "Can we move the needle nationally? I don't know, but it has to start somewhere." In 2014, the two proposed the Flexibility to Promote Reemployment Act, which would give states greater latitude to use federal unemployment insurance funds for programs such as worker retraining.

Carney joined another Republican, Stephen Fincher of Tennessee, in drafting legislation to make it easier for small and medium-sized companies to undertake an initial public offering and become a public company. Their measure passed the Financial Services Committee on a 54-1 vote in February 2012 and became law two months later after House Republicans included it in their job-creation agenda. In Delaware, corporate franchise and related fees are more than one-third of state revenue. Carney led another bipartisan effort to beseech President Barack Obama to consider a six-year transportation reauthorization bill and he introduced his own proposal for a balanced budget amendment, a concept normally pushed by Republicans. Neither proposal made any progress.

In two reelection campaigns, Carney has won easily. With the May 2015 death of Beau Biden, Carney became more likely to make another run for governor in 2016.

★ DISTRICT OF COLUMBIA ★

The capital of the most powerful and affluent nation in history, Washington is a physically beautiful city of great achievements and astonishing contrasts that go back more than 200 years. In 1787, the Constitution's framers, familiar with contemporary London and Paris mobs and remembering how unruly crowds had threatened the Continental Congress in Philadelphia, gave the new federal government control over the 10-mile-square that came to be called the District of Columbia. The Residence Act of 1790 located the District on the Potomac River along the borders of Maryland and Virginia, though in 1848 the portion west of the Potomac was retroceded to Virginia on the grounds that the federal government would never need it.

Over the years, Congress kept control of the District for its own advantage and, at times, out of distrust of the city's large African-American population. In the late 18th century, blacks made up one-quarter of Washington's residents. The city was a refuge for free blacks before the Civil War and right after emancipation. Radical Republicans gave the District self-government in 1871, but the experiment ended three years later after Gov. Alexander (Boss) Shepherd, in building great public works projects, spent the city into bankruptcy. In the 20th century, Washington's growth spurts, starting with the New Deal and World War II, resulted in the development of large, mostly white suburbs. It was at this time that African Americans became a larger percentage of the city's population, reaching a majority in the 1960 census. The civil rights movement brought about a change in the way that many District residents viewed their lack of voting rights. In 1961, Congress amended the Constitution to give District residents the right to vote for president; in 1968, residents began voting for the school board; in 1971, they received a non-voting delegate in Congress; and in 1973, the District of Columbia Home Rule Act allowed the city to elect a mayor and a city council.

For some time, self-government worked no better than it did in the 1870s. The Boss Shepherd of modern times was the late Marion Barry, a talented politician who proved to be a disastrous mayor. Barry held office for 16 of 20 years between 1978 and 1998. Under Barry, the District was a dysfunctional polity. Neighborhoods crumbled, the size of local government soared to 51,000 employees, and violent crime flourished. Barry nonetheless regularly won re-election, raising money from public employee unions and real estate developers and attacking critics as racists. In January 1990, District police arrested him at a D.C. hotel for cocaine possession. After a six-month stint in prison, he returned to city government. Barry was elected to the city council in 1992 and won a fourth term as mayor in 1994.

At that time, D.C. was experiencing a dire fiscal crisis, and Congress moved to wrest control of the government from Barry's hands. Republican House Speaker Newt Gingrich tasked Rep. Tom Davis, a Republican from Northern Virginia, with the job of stabilizing the District's finances. Working closely with D.C.'s elected delegate, Eleanor Holmes Norton, Davis set up a financial control board whose head, Anthony Williams, hacked away at the payroll and reformed management practices. In 1998, Barry chose not to run for a fifth term. Williams went on to win the Democratic primary and general election. The financial control board immediately relinquished power to the new mayor, and in 2000, a court returned control of most District departments to the city.

Beginning with William's tenure, the District's population started rising, from 572,000 in 2000 to 658,000 in 2014, with a substantial portion of this increase coming from well-educated, unmarried young people: 65% of the D.C. metropolitan area adult population has at least a bachelor's degree, while it is estimated that 70% are unmarried. Approximately 35% can be categorized as millennials. *The Washington Post* reported that in the November 2014 municipal elections, voters between the ages of 25 and 34 outnumbered senior citizens for the first time in 40 years. With youth and population growth have come gentrification and an exceptionally high cost of living. In 2012, District residents spent more on household-related expenditures than any other city in the country. High-rise condominiums and rental apartments targeted at singles were built in what had been high-crime areas. They sprouted new bars and trendy restaurants, rental bikes and bike lanes, food trucks and cupcake stores, dog parks and streetcar tracks. Meanwhile, the city's black population has continued to drop since its peak of 71% in 1970, as low-income black neighborhoods emptied out and middle-income blacks moved to majority-black suburbs. 2011 marked the first year in almost a half century that African Americans were not the majority in the District. The city's white population, on the other hand, grew more than 25% in the last decade. One corollary is that African Americans now cast barely half the votes in District elections. That made little difference in November 2012, when the District voted 91%-7% for President Barack Obama.

The District's economy has fluctuated in recent years. Federal spending and lobbying activity kept the city's economy buoyant throughout the recession. But as other cities moved into recovery, cuts to federal spending that began in 2010 slowed growth in D.C. and caused the area to lose many of its highest paying jobs. The hospitality and domestic tourism industries, however, have continued to prosper. More than 18 million Americans visited the capital in 2014, spending $6.8 billion on local transportation, hotels and restaurants.

Williams retired in 2006. Second-term councilman Adrian Fenty succeeded him, defeating Council President Linda Cropp in the Democratic primary 57%-31%. As mayor, Fenty's biggest initiative was improving the floundering public schools. For years D.C. schools, despite one of the highest per-pupil spending rates in the nation, had low achievement levels and plunging enrollments. In 2007, at Fenty's behest, the city council transferred control of the schools from an independent board of education to the mayor's office. He installed as his superintendent Michelle Rhee, an alumna of the Teach for America Program and founder of the New Teacher Project. Rhee closed nonperforming and underused schools and negotiated a contract with the union that gave teachers the option of earning merit pay and gave her the power to dismiss nonperforming teachers. Rhee also encouraged the charter school movement. Charter school enrollments in D.C. rose from 25% in 2006 to 44% in 2014, the third highest enrollment rate in the country.

In 2010, Fenty received a challenge for the Democratic nomination from Council President Vincent Gray. Building on African-American discontent with gentrification and Rhee's education policies and perceptions of Fenty as an aloof mayor, Gray won the primary 54%-44%. He carried almost every black-majority precinct and lost just about all the others. Shortly after the election, Rhee resigned. Gray replaced her with Kaya Henderson, who largely maintained Rhee's policies.

Gray continued many of the initiatives championed by his immediate predecessors, but problems emerged when two of his aides from the primary pleaded guilty to concealing contributions to a third candidate who flamboyantly attacked Fenty, apparently in an effort to dilute Fenty's support. Another aide pleaded guilty to funneling contributions from the city's largest contractor to a shadow campaign. These scandals set the stage for a grueling primary election in 2014. But things got much worse for Gray when federal prosecutors alleged that he was privy to the shadow campaign while it was happening. Unable to shake charges of corruption and criminal activity, Gray lost 44%-32% to Muriel Bowser, a second-term councilwoman with close ties to Fenty. Bowser went on to defeat David Catania, a Republican-turned-Independent councilman, in a contentious general election 54%-34%.

Often viewed as a cautious politician, Bowser has taken some risks as mayor, especially when it comes to the matter of District autonomy. In February 2015, Bowser defied Congress by allowing a voter-approved ballot measure that effectively legalized marijuana to take effect. House Republicans had previously attached a rider to the 2015 federal budget prohibiting the city from implementing the law. Bowser's administration ignored the

Population		Race and Ethnicity		Income	
Total:	646,449	Black	49.5%	Median income:	$65,830
Urban:	100.0%	White	35.8%		
Suburban:	0.0%	Latino	10.1%	Under $50,000	38.9%
Rural:	0.0%	Asian	1.8%	$50,000-$99,999:	25.3%
Land area:	61	Two races	2.6%	$100,000-$199,999:	23.8%
Pop/sq. mi.:	10,597.5	White Ethnic	18.4%	$200,000 or more:	12.0%
Born in state:	36.7%			Poverty Rate	20.7%
		Education			
Age Groups		H.S. grad or less:	28.5%	**Work**	
Under 18:	17.3%	Some college:	16.4%	White collar:	61.7%
18 to 34:	35.1%	College degree, 4 yr.:	22.7%	Blue collar:	5.8%
35 to 64:	36.2%	Post-grad study:	32.4%	Sales and service:	32.4%
Over 64:	11.4%				
		Military		Govt. workers:	25.0%
		Veterans/active duty:	5.8%		

rider by arguing that the measure had gone into effect before Congress passed the budget (though her office did refrain from setting up a framework for taxing and regulating marijuana in the city). Bowser also announced her support for the Budget Autonomy Act the city council passed in 2013. The

Voter Turnout	
2013 Total Citizen 18+	483,891
Highest District Turnout	175,071
2014 Turnout as % CVAP	36.2%
2012 Turnout as % CVAP	62.2%

act, which grants D.C. more control over its internal finances, had been tied up in courts since Gray's administration challenged it.

The District's liberalism has often made it a target for congressional conservatives. After the city council voted in favor of recognizing same-sex marriages performed within and outside the city in 2009, several Republicans filed bills to ban gay marriage in the District. In March 2015, Sen. Ted Cruz sought to overturn two D.C. laws: one aimed at prohibiting discrimination based on religious objections to abortion or birth control, and another that repealed an exemption for religious educational institutions from the city's LGBT anti-discrimination law. The following month,

Sen. Marco Rubio continued a decades-long battle between the District and gun-rights advocates by introducing a bill knocking down some of the city's restrictive firearms laws.

But there are some Republicans who have sympathized with the District's lack of budget autonomy and full voting rights. In May 2011, Oversight and Government Reform Chairman Darrell Issa of California surprised city residents by endorsing budget autonomy for the District. Issa said he felt "what the city does with city funds should be

2012 Presidential Vote		
Barack Obama (D)	267,070	(91%)
Mitt Romney (R)	21,381	(7%)
2012 Presidential Primary		
Mitt Romney (R)	3,577	(68%)
Ron Paul (R)	621	(12%)
Newt Gingrich (R)	558	(11%)
Jon Huntsman (R)	348	(7%)
2008 Presidential Vote		
Barack Obama (D)	245,800	(93%)
John McCain (R)	7,367	(7%)

primarily city decisions." Even more surprising was when conservative firebrand Louie Gohmert of Texas argued that requiring District residents to pay federal income taxes without full voting rights amounted to "taxation without representation," a phrase that has become the unofficial slogan of the D.C. statehood movement. He has proposed abolishing federal income taxes for District residents until they receive a full-voting representative in Congress.

DELEGATE

Eleanor Holmes Norton (D)

Elected 1990, 13th term; b. June 13, 1937, Washington, D.C.; Antioch Col., B.A. 1960, Yale U., M.A. 1963, LL.B. 1964; Episcopalian; divorced; 2 children

Professional Career: Clerk, Judge A. Leon Higginbotham, 1964-65; Asst. legal dir., ACLU, 1965-70; Adjunct asst. prof., NY U. Law School, 1970-71; Staff, NY mayor, 1971-74; Chair, NYC Human Rights Comm., 1970-77; Chair, US Equal Empl. Oppor. Comm., 1977-81; Sr. fellow, Urban Inst., 1981-82; Prof., Georgetown U. Law Ctr., 1982-90.

DC Office: 2136 RHOB, 20515, 202-225-8050; Fax: 202-225-3002; Website: norton.house.gov.

State Offices: NE Washington DC, 202-408-9041; SE Washington DC, 202-678-8900.

Committees: *Oversight & Gov't Reform:* Gov't Operations; Health Care, Benefits & Administrative Rules. *Transportation & Infrastructure:* Aviation; Economic Development, Public Buildings & Emergency Mgmt.; Highways & Transit (RMM); Water Resources & Environment.

Election Results

2014 general	Elenor Holmes Norton (D)	143,923	(81%)	$467,786
	Nelson Rimensnyder (R)	11,673	(7%)	$6,660
	Timothy Kreep (I)	9,101	(5%)	$9,890
	Natale Stracuzzi (DCS)	6,073	(4%)	
2014 primary	Elenor Holmes Norton (D)	..unopposed		

Prior winning percentages: 2012 (89%), 2010 (89%), 2008 (92%), 2006 (100%), 2004 (91%), 2002 (93%), 2000 (90%), 1998 (90%), 1996 (90%), 1994 (89%), 1992 (85%), 1990 (62%)

Eleanor Holmes Norton is a Democrat who was first elected delegate from the District of Columbia in 1990. The daughter of a District government employee and a school teacher, Norton graduated from Dunbar High School, and went on to get a law degree at Yale. She volunteered for the Student Nonviolent Coordinating Committee and traveled to Mississippi in 1963 to help register African-American voters. On June 11 of that year, she met with civil-rights activist Medgar Evers, who tried to convince her to move to Jackson and work as a civil rights lawyer. Just hours after Evers dropped her off at a bus station, a white supremacist shot and killed him in his driveway. Norton worked for the American Civil Liberties Union and the New York City Commission on Human Rights, and was head of the Equal Employment Opportunity Commission in the Carter administration. Afterward, she taught law at Georgetown University. When the delegate seat came open in 1990, she edged past Council Member Betty Anne Kane, 39%-33%, in the primary. Norton has been re-elected easily since.

In her early years in the House, she had the difficult task of responding to the fiscal collapse of the District government just as Republicans won control of Congress in 1995. But she quickly developed a reputation as hardworking, competent, intellectually honest, and able to get along with opponents as well as fellow partisans. Nonetheless, her relationship with congressional Republicans active on District matters has been mixed. She worked closely with former Republican Rep. Tom Davis of Virginia on several issues. In 1995, she collaborated with Davis and Speaker Newt Gingrich to create the fiscal control board that oversaw the District's financial recovery. In 1999, she and Davis also worked together to pass a law providing in-state tuition for District students at colleges and universities in any state. But Norton has often clashed with Republicans seeking to impose abortion restrictions on the District or repeal city laws on gun control and marijuana. When Maryland Rep. Andy Harris announced his intentions to challenge a voter-approved ballot measure decriminalizing marijuana in 2014, Norton stated, "D.C. residents can rest assured that when a mandate comes directly from the people, they haven't seen a fight like the fight I'm preparing to make against Rep. Andy Harris and any other member of Congress who attempts to undo our democratic process."

She has not always seen eye-to-eye with President Barack Obama either. In 2011, she was furious when he struck a budget deal with House Republicans that allowed conservatives to revive a school voucher program in the District and to prohibit the city from using its own funds to provide abortions for low-income women. She said both parties were using the District as a bargaining chip. She said, "It's time that the District of Columbia told the Congress to go straight to hell." The president drew her ire again during the partial government shutdown in 2013 by refusing to support a House-passed bill that would have allowed D.C. to tap local revenue sources to fund government operations. She has also criticized the Obama administration for what she called an "appalling lack of African-American representation" among the president's judicial nominees.

Norton has been frustrated in one of her top priorities: securing full voting rights for D.C. in the House, even after Democrats won majorities in both houses of Congress in 2006 and won the presidency in 2008. "We must never retreat from our full citizenship rights, and we must always seize any part of our rights that we can get," she told *The Washington Post*. Tom Davis came up with the idea of creating two new House seats, one for the District of Columbia and the other for the state entitled to the 436th district under the statutory reapportionment formula, which after the 2000 census happened to be heavily Republican Utah. That gave Republicans an incentive to vote for the bill. In 2007, the House passed her bill 241-177. But in the Senate, it fell three votes short of the 60 necessary to prevent a filibuster. In 2009, with increased Democratic majorities, Norton revived it and it was approved by the House Judiciary Committee in February 2009. In March, the Senate passed it, 61-37, but with an amendment sponsored by conservative Sen. John Ensign of Nevada overturning the District's gun control laws. Norton looked for a path to compromise, but then House conservatives added even more constraints on the District's ability to regulate guns and Norton threw up her hands. The legislation died soon thereafter. In January 2015, she introduced the New Columbia Admission Act, proposing to carve out a 51st state around the White House, Capitol, Supreme Court, and National Mall. Sen. Tom Carper of Delaware with 17 co-sponsors (all Democrats) filed a companion bill in the Senate.

Norton has had a number of successes on local issues, including the Southeast Federal Center Public-Private Development Act that promoted development around the Washington Navy Yard and the decision to place the Coast Guard headquarters on the grounds of the old St. Elizabeth's Hospital. And in 2007 she got the Democratic-controlled House to remove the ban on the District's needle exchange program intended to reduce AIDS transmission. In

2009, the House passed her bill freeing District employees from the federal Hatch Act limiting political activity once the District passed its own law on the subject. Her bill to allow the District to take over Kingman and Heritage islands in the Anacostia River passed the House as well, and her bill to restore retirement credits lost by District employees when their agency was transferred to the federal government became law. Democratic appropriators agreed to bar amendments affecting the District referendum authorizing medical marijuana and its ability to continue its needle exchange program. In addition, Norton got senators and the White House to recognize her recommendations for federal trial judges and the U.S. attorney for the District of Columbia. Norton's legislative agenda is not solely local, however. As the ranking member of the Highways and Transit Subcommittee, she has advocated increased funding for infrastructure and transportation projects. Norton also has a longstanding interest in nuclear disarmament. In every Congress since 1993, she has introduced a bill to dismantle the U.S. nuclear weapons program.

★ FLORIDA ★

More than 500 years ago, in March 1513, the Spanish conquistador Juan Ponce de León spied the coast of Florida. For the next 400 years, anyone sailing along Florida's 1,197 miles of coastline and 663 miles of beach would not have seen anything much different from what Ponce de Leon saw. But within the past century the state has been transformed, from a swampy, under-settled, mostly rural state of 1.5 million people (the smallest population in the South), to a metropolitan powerhouse of almost 20 million people. In 2014, the Census Bureau estimated that Florida had overtaken New York as the third most populous state in the country. The result is a heterogeneous nation-state, historically Southern, demographically Northeastern and Midwestern, and culturally, at least partly, Latin American. It has been economically vibrant for most of the past century, but vulnerable to sudden contractions, as in the mid-1920s when a hurricane abruptly ended the Miami real estate boom and during the Great Recession. But Florida has bounced back before, and it is growing again.

Florida is the only Atlantic Coast state that was not part of the colonial United States. In 1819, it was acquired from Spain, through the exertions of John Quincy Adams and Andrew Jackson. Adams thought that in foreign hands Florida could block the Gulf of Mexico and the Mississippi Valley, while Jackson saw it as a haven for runaway slaves and a launching pad for Indians to raid the farmers and planters of what was then the American Southwest. Florida was a minor agricultural state until the early 20th century, when its sunshine economy based on citrus production and tourism took hold. After the Civil War, orange groves sprang up along the St. John's River and outside of Tampa, but the "Great Freeze" of 1894-95 devastated the state's nascent citrus industry. Growers responded by expanding croplands further south and by 1915, citrus output in the state was roughly double its pre-freeze level. Florida's balmy winter climate inspired railroad barons Henry Flagler and Henry Plant to build grand resort hotels and accompanying rail lines (Flagler on the Atlantic coast and Plant on the Gulf) which not only brought vacationers to Florida, but also helped transport Florida oranges north to markets in Baltimore and Philadelphia in about a week. Later, auto entrepreneur Carl Fisher promoted tourism to Florida and the construction of the Dixie Highway, which in the 1920s helped millions of visitors travel to the state, many of whom decided to stay. Miami, founded in 1896, boomed until the hurricane hit in 1926 (and Fisher, who had become a local real estate magnate, lost his fortune). In the 1930s, New Yorkers started retiring to art deco apartments in Miami Beach. Empire State natives still make up about 1-in-12 Florida residents.

By the 1960s, retirees were flocking to the state looking for year-round sunshine after years of gray skies over factories and toil in urban street canyons. They joined agriculture and tourism as Florida's main economic drivers, but new industries, many related to the space program, also migrated to the state. In the 1980s and 1990s, the percentage of families with children as a share of Florida's population grew rapidly, lured by jobs and opportunities in communities that hadn't existed a generation earlier. The state's tourism sector, no longer dependent solely on beautiful beaches, was transformed and Orlando became the "Theme Park Capital of the World" with enough attractions to keep a vacationing family busy for weeks. The cruise business exploded, pumping more than $7 billion into Florida's economy by 2014. With more than five million passengers, Port Miami was the global leader for cruise travel while Port Canaveral, about an hour's drive east from Orlando, and Port Everglades, outside of Fort Lauderdale, have huge terminals as well. Normalizing relations with Cuba could eventually spur even more embarkations from the state's ports.

Florida is also an aviation industry hub and in 2014 civilian aircraft parts and engines were the state's leading export, exceeding all of its agricultural products destined for overseas markets. Brazilian manufacturer Embraer assembles executive jets in Melbourne, and recently added a new maintenance facility to its North American headquarters complex in Fort Lauderdale. Likewise, in 2014 the European turboprop maker ATR relocated its North American operations center to Miami Springs. Florida's "Space Coast" is seeing a revival after cutbacks in planetary exploration: Aerospace giant Northrop Grumman has invested heavily in its operations in Melbourne, building a new design center there and adding capacity to produce next-generation military aircraft. Boeing and SpaceX won a multi-billion dollar NASA deal to build capsules to transport astronauts to the space station and much of the work will be done at what was once the Orbiter processing facility at the Kennedy Space

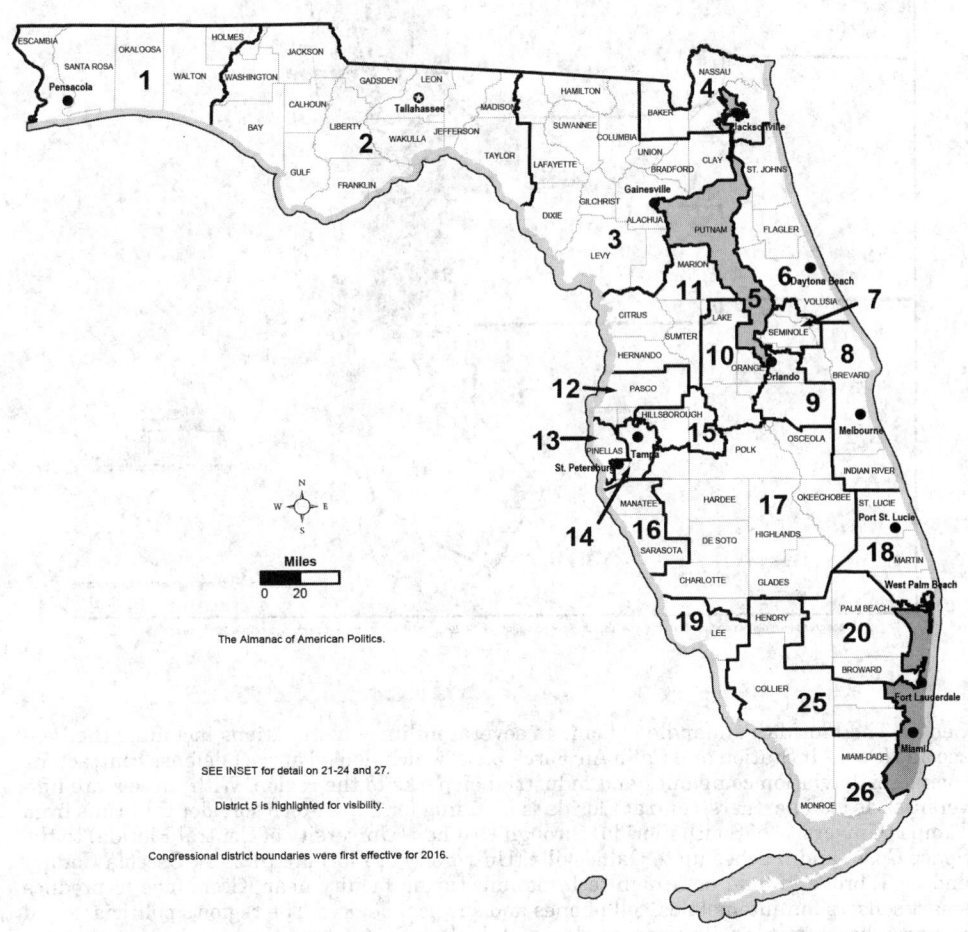

The Almanac of American Politics.

SEE INSET for detail on 21-24 and 27.

District 5 is highlighted for visibility.

Congressional district boundaries were first effective for 2016.

Miles
0   20

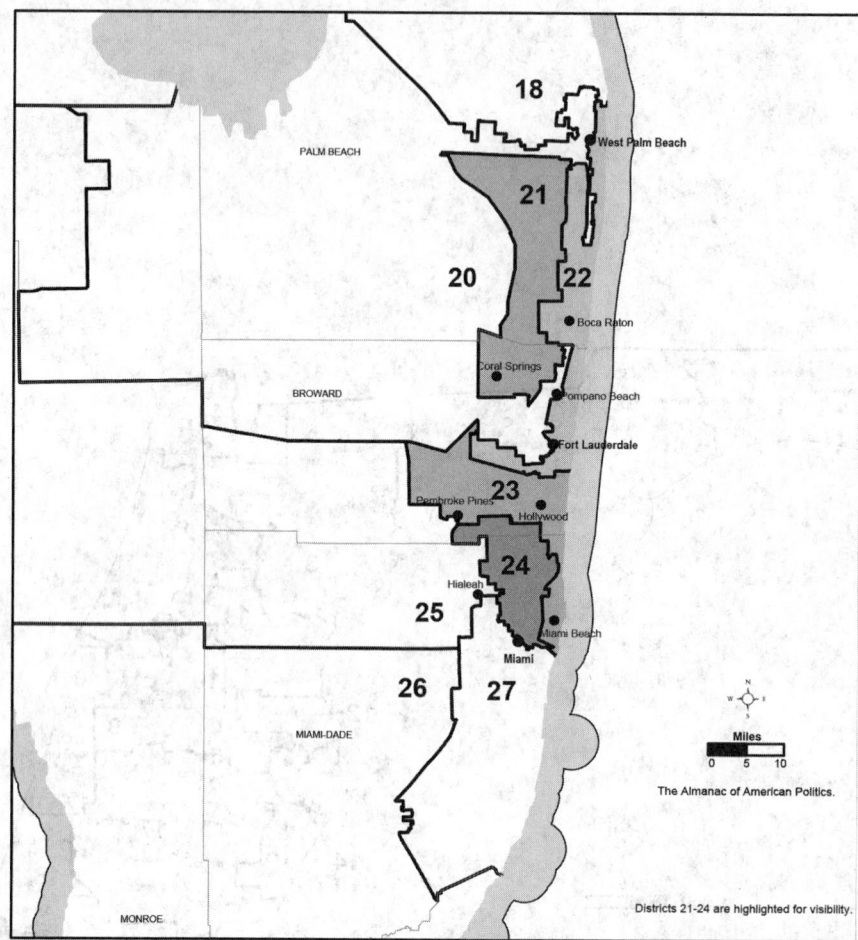

Districts 21-24 are highlighted for visibility.

Congressional district boundaries for these districts were first effective for 2012 and were unaffected by changes in the 2015 map..

Center. The Florida Panhandle is home to several military installations including the Pensacola Naval Air Station and Eglin Air Force Base, which helped attract defense contractors, commercial aviation companies and industrial airparks to the region. With three state universities as lead partners, central Florida is planning for a high-tech corridor that runs from Tampa (University of South Florida) through Orlando (University of Central Florida) to the Space Coast and reaches up to Gainesville (University of Florida). In 2014, Osceola County and UCF broke ground on a high tech manufacturing facility near Kissimmee to produce smart sensors for automobiles, cell phones and surgical devices. The region's politicians and business boosters hope its degree-holding skilled workforce and the state's favorable tax climate will attract startups and established companies alike. Further south, Google led an investment group that pumped more than half a billion dollars into the Dania Beach visual display startup Magic Leap in 2014.

But like other fast-growing states, Florida's economy has also been built on construction and real estate, which makes it subject to sudden downturns. The state's robust growth began to slow down in 2005, but the real estate speculators continued to gobble up houses and condos in Miami and Cape Coral, Orlando and Port St. Lucie on the assumption that good times would keep rolling and that they could turn a fast buck on heavily mortgaged properties, even as property taxes and insurance premiums rose. Then real estate values plummeted with the Great Recession: Median home prices fell from their peak of more than

$257,000 in 2006 to a low of about $122,000 in 2011. The foreclosure crisis hit few states as hard as it hit Florida. Many banks there compounded the problem by their inability to process the glut of distressed properties though the state's court system, and fraud was not uncommon. Local tax receipts, heavily dependent on property values and the construction industry, slumped. Unemployment rose from a seasonally adjusted rate of 3.5 percent in January 2007, to a peak of 11.2 percent in January 2010. During the recession, more Americans left Florida than moved there—for the first time since the end of World War II, when military personnel stationed in the state returned home and a series of major hurricanes hobbled agriculture production. The Great Recession lasted longer in Florida than most other states, and its economy didn't begin to recover until 2012. The median sales price for single-family homes stood at $175,000 in January 2015, and the increase in construction jobs was once again leading the state's economy, particularly in South Florida, while the unemployment rate statewide was 5.7 percent. Still, the housing sector remained troubled and 2015 began with more than 300,000 open foreclosure cases, and more than half a million mortgages were 90 days or more delinquent. Florida's recovery was evident in other ways: a steady rise in professional and business services from 2012 through 2014, primarily white collar jobs ranging from computer design to travel agencies, the second fastest growing employment sector. And between 2012 and 2013, Census figures showed that the state led the nation in creating self-employment, some 63,000 such jobs, almost one fourth of the nation's total of 270,000. Ironically, one of the state's original economic pillars, the citrus industry, has been crippled by a disease called greening, and orange harvests are down by more than half in the past decade. State and local government is likely to grow modestly as sales and property tax revenues increase with the rising economy and housing prices. Demand for services will rise as the state's population increases, but many public officials may be cautious in funding those needs, having just administered painful cuts following the bursting of the housing bubble.

And Florida's population trends are accelerating again. The Census reported that between 2010 and 2014, the state's population jumped 5.8 percent, compared to 3.3 percent for the nation as a whole. Retirees continue to come here and its 18.7 percent share of the population age 65 and older leads the nation, but the state's inhabitants are also increasingly diverse. The States of Change study by the American Enterprise Institute, the Brookings Institution and the Center for American Progress projects that Florida will have a majority-minority population by 2028. Already, more than half of its children are minorities, up from a little more than a third in 1980. For refugees from Cuba and Haiti and for immigrants from the Caribbean and Latin America, Florida has been a land of freedom from authoritarian and turbulent lands. Its population has been continually replenished with people from other states and foreign countries, and today, only a little more than one-third of Florida residents are natives. Miami has long been the economic and commercial capital of Latin America, as well as a mecca for its political exiles. You can fly nonstop from Miami to just about any place in Latin America, and both English and Spanish are common and Portuguese not unknown. (According to Visit Florida, a tourism industry marketing organization, more than 93 million people sojourned to the state in 2014. Canada led the list of international travelers

Population		Race and Ethnicity		Income	
Total:	19,552,860	White	57.3%	Median income:	$47,886
Urban:	59.1%	Latino	22.9%		(35 of 50)
Suburban:	34.8%	Black	15.3%	Under $50,000	53.4%
Rural:	6.1%	Asian	2.4%	$50,000-$99,999:	28.9%
Land area:	53,625	Two races	1.6%	$100,000-$199,999:	13.8%
Pop/sq. mi.:	364.6	White Ethnic	23.5%	$200,000 or more:	3.9%
Born in state:	36.2%			Poverty Rate	11.1%
		Education			
Age Groups		H.S. grad or less:	42.6%	**Work**	
Under 18:	20.6%	Some college:	30.2%	White collar:	33.6%
18 to 34:	21.6%	College degree, 4 yr.:	17.6%	Blue collar:	48.3%
35 to 64:	39.1%	Post-grad study:	9.7%	Sales and service:	18.1%
Over 64:	18.6%				
		Military		Govt. workers:	12.3%
		Veterans/active duty:	9.4%		

with more than 3.5 million followed by Brazil with some 1.6 million.) Large numbers of Puerto Ricans have been moving to Orlando and Osceola County; Mexicans are more prevalent in the state's verdant southwestern farmlands (Hendry, Collier and Hardee Counties). While Cubans still dominate Miami-Dade, they now make up less than a third of the state's overall

Voter Turnout		
2013 Total Citizen 18+		13,903,926
2014 Highest Statewide Turnout		5,951,561
2014 Turnout as % CVAP		42.8%
2012 Turnout as % CVAP		62.0%
Legislature		
Senate:	26R	14D
House:	81R	39D

Hispanic population. Central Florida—the I-4 corridor from Tampa-St. Petersburg through citrus and tourist centers to the Atlantic Coast—is mostly family country, although The Villages site in Sumter County is a haven for retirees and has been one of the fastest growing areas in the nation. A different example of the region's rapid rise is Lake Nona and its Medical City south of Orlando. What a decade ago was a downtrodden golf course and vacant land next to the airport is now a medical multiplex that includes Sanford-Burnham which conducts research in obesity and other diseases, the University of Central Florida's College of Medicine, Nemours Children's Hospital, and the massive new Orlando VA Medical Center. Along with surrounding pedestrian-friendly residential and commercial developments, this planned community aspires to be a global health services destination that *Fortune* magazine profiled in a 2014 cover story, "How to Build a Great American City." While the I-4 Corridor is expected to lead Florida's population growth in the coming decades, there is also the Gulf Coast with its affluent and burgeoning communities south of Tampa Bay, and the more modest retirement counties to the north. The western Panhandle, the so-called Redneck Riviera around Pensacola and Panama City, is culturally very Southern. State government is headquartered in Tallahassee, chosen because it was midway between the population centers of Jacksonville and Pensacola at a time when almost no one lived on the peninsula; Tallahassee and the university town of Gainesville are liberal bastions in a sea of conservatism.

Florida has a fragile civil society, and it can be chaotic and disorderly at times. Most people do not have deep roots in the state—most communities sprang into existence within living memory—and if Florida gives people more freedom and options than elsewhere, it also gives them more disruption and crime than many anticipated. Florida has more gun permits than any other state, and it pioneered the right for citizens to carry concealed weapons in 1987. The state's "stand-your-ground" law, which allows Floridians to use deadly force when they believe their lives are threatened, became a focal point in the tragic 2012 shooting death of an unarmed black teenager, Trayvon Martin, in Sanford. The subsequent legal proceedings were a staple on cable news and even President Barack Obama weighed in on the racial aspects of the case after an armed neighborhood watch volunteer of white and Latino descent who had confronted Martin was acquitted of any crime in July 2013.

The nation's other three largest states are one-sided politically, with California and New York heavily Democratic and Texas heavily Republican. Florida is, famously, closely divided. The state has been a battleground in every presidential race over the past two decades, including the recount of 2000 that lasted 36 days and was decided by the momentous United States Supreme Court case, *Bush v. Gore*. In the last two presidential contests, Floridians voted narrowly for Obama, who rallied the liberal Democratic base; then they flipped in the subsequent governor's races, electing and reelecting conservative Republican Rick Scott by even narrower margins. But the trend in state politics has been toward Republicans since the 1990s, when they captured the state House in 1994, the state Senate in 1996, and the governorship in 1998. Republicans in 2015 held all of the major elected statewide offices and had big majorities in the legislature. None of the Democratic candidates for Attorney General, Chief Financial Officer or Commissioner of Agriculture in the last election could muster more than 42 percent of the vote. Republican state legislators have been helped by term limits and redistricting: Democratic communities of African-Americans and Jews are concentrated in a few districts, while Republican voters are more evenly spread around. But Democrats have remained competitive in statewide contests, as the 2014 governor's race demonstrated. Perhaps it is a testament to the state's heterogeneous character that half a million more Floridians voted for a ballot measure to legalize medical marijuana than voted to reelect Scott, who personally opposed the proposal. (It still fell short of the 60 percent threshold required for passage.) Likewise, three-fourths of the state's voters in 2014 approved an amendment to the Florida constitution dedicating state funding for land and water conservation, a measure about which Scott was ambivalent and GOP leaders in the legislature opposed.

Presidential Politics On Election Night in 2012, none of the television networks called the outcome of the presidential race in Florida; they didn't need to. Once the polls had closed in California at 11:00 pm EST, Barack Obama was quickly awarded its 55 electoral votes. Then Ohio went his way, and by 11:25, NBC, CBS, CNN, FOX and ABC had declared the president reelected. Obama would end up carrying Florida by almost 75,000 votes, but in the early hours of Wednesday morning the contest appeared much closer and no one on the network deci-

2012 Presidential Vote		
Barack Obama (D) 4,237,756	(50%)
Mitt Romney (R).............4,163,447	(49%)
2012 Presidential Primary		
Mitt Romney (R)................776,159	(46%)
Newt Gingrich (R)..............534,121	(32%)
Rick Santorum (R) 223,249	(13%)
Ron Paul (R) 117,461	(7%)
2008 Presidential Vote		
Barack Obama (D) 4,282,074	(51%)
John McCain (R).............4,045,624	(48%)

sion desks wanted to risk making a bad call when the presidency had already been decided—and everyone remembered the networks' mishandling of the Florida call in 2000.

While the presidency doesn't always hang in the balance pending the results in Florida, the state will continue to be a critical battleground in the race for the White House. Florida has 29 electoral votes, the same number as New York; only California and Texas have more. The two major party nominees have received between 47 percent and 52 percent of the votes here in 2000, 2004, 2008 and 2012. The widest margin of victory was George W. Bush's 52%-47% win over John Kerry in 2004. The 2000 contest was excruciatingly close; and after 36 days, Bush was declared the winner by 537 votes out of nearly 6 million cast. The 2004 and 2008 contests saw surging turnout, rising to 7.6 million in 2004 and 8.4 million in 2008. In 2012, overall turnout in Florida rose only 1 percent, from 8.4 million to 8.5 million, as Obama edged Mitt Romney 50%-49%. The Obama team got its base vote out, especially Hispanics and blacks, in a year when enthusiasm was lower than it had been four years before. In Miami-Dade County, Obama made a net gain of 55,000 votes over his showing in 2008. In Osceola County, with its suburban Latino communities, Obama's net gain was almost 7,000 (but Miami-Dade had eight times as many registered voters as Osceola). The exit polls showed that Romney ran stronger than John McCain or Bush (in 2004) among all whites, white Protestants, white Catholics, Jews and the elderly, who were evidently not repelled by vice presidential nominee Paul Ryan's Medicare proposals. But whereas Bush carried Florida's Hispanics 56%-44%, and McCain lost them by 57%-42%, Romney lost Hispanics 60%-39%, losing 66%-34% among non-Cuban Hispanics and 49%-47% among Cuban-Americans. Younger Cubans evidently are not the strong Republicans their elders are as memories of pre-Castro Cuba fade into the past.

Florida's presidential primary was not crucial in determining a nomination between 1976, when Democrat Jimmy Carter defeated George Wallace and ended Wallace's career in national politics, and 2008, when McCain defeated Mitt Romney, a victory that propelled him to success one week later in the more than 20 states that held primaries or caucuses on Super Tuesday. McCain's victory in Florida came largely on the strength of independent-leaning Republicans and Hispanic Republicans, which gave McCain a taste of revenge since Romney had pummeled him for supporting immigration reform in the earlier Iowa caucuses. Seeking more clout, Florida's Republican legislature had moved the 2008 primary to January 29, a week before Super Tuesday. This violated Democratic Party rules, and in August 2007, the Democratic National Committee stripped Florida of its entire delegation; all major Democratic candidates agreed not to campaign there. Republicans were not so shy. Rudy Giuliani made his last stand in Florida, where he had led in early polls, but saw his standing sink after weak showings in earlier primaries and caucuses. Romney, fresh off victories in the Michigan primary and Nevada caucuses, campaigned as the conservative alternative to McCain. Mike Huckabee, who had lost South Carolina to McCain a week earlier, struggled to extend his appeal beyond evangelical Christians in a state with a more diverse Republican electorate. On the Saturday before the primary, then-GOP Gov. Charlie Crist, previously rumored to be for Giuliani, endorsed McCain. Turnout was large—1.9 million, nearly triple the 2000 turnout—and McCain won with 36 percent of the vote to 31 percent for Romney. Giuliani got 15 percent and Huckabee 14 percent. Democratic candidates mostly kept their promises to not campaign in Florida. Turnout in the primary was 1.75 million, more than double the 2004 turnout, and Hillary Clinton won 50 percent of the vote to 33 percent for Barack Obama and 14 percent for John Edwards. But with no delegates officially at stake, Clinton's victory was short-lived. The Clinton and Obama campaigns argued over the fate of Florida's convention delegation, and a few days before the end of the primary season a deal was brokered at a DNC meeting to seat a Florida delegation essentially split between the two contenders. That compromise did little for Clinton who still trailed Obama among pledged delegates.

In 2012, it was Romney's turn in the Sunshine State. Fresh off a loss to Newt Gingrich in the South Carolina primary, Romney needed to reestablish his momentum for the nomination, which he did with a solid 46%-32% victory over the former House Speaker. Romney and his Super PAC allies outspent Gingrich and his outside boosters by a margin of more than 4-to-1, a significant advantage in a state with 10 media markets. Gingrich had the support of ardent tea party supporters, white evangelicals and self-described "very conservative" voters, but that was hardly enough to prevail in Florida, even among Republicans. Romney swept the state except for the Panhandle region. He even won a majority of Hispanic Republicans who had sided with McCain four years earlier. Turnout dipped to 1.6 million, but that still represented more than two of every five registered Republicans. For the 2012 cycle, the GOP moved up its primary again to January 31. The Republican National Committee voted to deprive Florida of half its delegates (and gave the Florida delegation inconvenient hotel assignments for the national convention in Tampa). Apparently chastened, GOP lawmakers in Tallahassee passed legislation in 2015 to move the state's primary to March 15.

Congressional Districts   Florida has gained congressional districts after every census since 1930, when it elected just four House members. Its 15-seat gain since 1960 is more than any other state, including Texas, during that half-century. Follow-

114th Congress Lineup	
17 R	10 D
113th Congress Lineup	
17 R	10 D

ing the 2010 census, Florida gained two seats, to go from 25 to 27, leaving it with a delegation the same size as New York's. Republican Gov. Rick Scott's narrow victory and big GOP margins in the legislature after 2010 meant that Republicans controlled the redistricting process. But their growth opportunities were limited by two factors: Republicans' already robust 19-6 edge in the delegation following a banner year, and a new voter-approved law seeking to rein in the kind of gerrymandering that had created one of the strangest patchworks of districts in the country. In August 2015, the Legislature deadlocked on major changes in the redistricting map in response to a state Supreme Court ruling on that new law.

In November 2010, while four Florida Democrats lost their seats, voters simultaneously gave Democrats a silver lining by approving a set of ballot propositions backed by the reform group Fair Districts Florida. The Fair Districts amendments require legislators to draw compact districts conforming to county and city boundaries and prohibit them from taking into account partisan data or incumbent residences. Black Democrat Corrine Brown, whose district snakes through the North Florida swamp from Jacksonville to Orlando, as well as Cuban-American Republican Mario Diaz-Balart, whose party's interests were threatened by the new law, unsuccessfully sued in federal court to block the law, claiming it would harm minority voters.

Initially, Republican state legislators concluded that as long as they preserved the three grotesquely shaped minority-majority districts in North Florida (5th District), Tampa Bay (14th District), and South Florida (20th District) in the name of complying with the Voting Rights Act, they could keep Democratic voters sufficiently packed to hold onto a strong majority of neighboring seats—despite the state's overall partisan balance. So in February 2012, they passed a map keeping those three necessarily bizarre seats while neatly regularizing the boundaries of the rest. In a bid to protect their 2010 gains, they also drew the state's new seats in Democratic areas: the heavily Puerto Rican 9th District south of Orlando and the substantially Jewish 22nd District along the Gold Coast.

Allies of Democrats and the Fair Districts movement sued in state court to overturn the map, arguing Republicans had secretly used partisan data to preserve their edge. In particular, many Democrats (except Brown) would have liked for her egregiously shaped 5th District to be unpacked and for St. Petersburg's black neighborhoods to be reattached to the 13th District. But Republicans defended their handiwork by noting they had shoved two of their own, veteran John Mica and freshman Sandy Adams, into the same suburban Orlando seat. In April 2012, the Obama Justice Department granted the Republican map federal preclearance and a state circuit judge refused to block implementation of the map.

Fair Districts proponents continued to press for change. After Leon County Circuit Judge Terry Lewis ruled that the districts of Democrat Brown and Republican Daniel Webster failed to meet the Fair Districts standard, the legislature in August 2014 adopted a new map that altered seven of the state's districts and shifted nearly 400,000 voters in central and north Florida; that map took effect after the 2014 election. Judge Lewis approved the map, but the reformers appealed. In July 2015, the state Supreme Court threw out major pieces of the map across the state, ruling that it was a political gerrymander in violation of the 2010 referendum. The Court gave the Legislature explicit instructions on a new map.

In the two most recent elections, Democrats have retained the net gain of four House seats that they lost in 2010—leaving Republicans with 17-10 control of the delegation. In 2012, two flawed GOP freshmen lost their seats: often-inflammatory tea party activist Allen West, who had moved north to the open Treasure Coast 18th District, and David Rivera in the heavily Cuban-American 26th District, who was so tainted by various scandals that few House Republicans defended him. In 2014, each party lost one incumbent: Republican Steve Southerland in the 2nd, and Democrat Joe Garcia in the 26th. Pending further action, the July 2015 court order posed severe jeopardy to the seats of Democrat Gwen Graham and Republicans Daniel Webster and David Jolly, who decided to run for the Senate. Corinne Brown faced a likely primary challenge.

Governor

Rick Scott (R)

Elected 2010, term expires Jan. 2019, 2nd term; b. Dec. 1, 1952, Bloomington, IL; U. of MO, Kansas City, B.A. 1975, Southern Methodist U., J.D. 1978; Christian; married (Ann); 2 children.

Military Career: U.S. Navy, 1971-74.

Professional Career: Co-founder, chmn., & CEO, Columbia/HCA, 1987-97; Venture capitalist, 1997-2010; Practicing atty., Johnson & Swanson, Dallas.

Office: The Capitol, 400 S. Monroe St., Tallahassee, 32399-0001, 850-488-7146; Fax: 850-487-0801; Website: flgov.com.

Election Results

2014 general	Rick Scott (R)	2,865,343	(48%)
	Charlie Crist (D)	2,801,198	(47%)
	Adrian Wyllie (Lib)	223,356	(4%)
2014 primary	Rick Scott (R)	831,887	(88%)
	Elizabeth Cuevas-Neunder (R)	100,496	(11%)

Prior winning percentage: 2010 (49%)

Republican Rick Scott, a former healthcare CEO, mastered the art of running for high office, or at least prevailing in close contests, winning the governorship in 2010 and getting reelected in 2014 when many had counted him out. But those skills have not always translated to success in governing, and strained relations with lawmakers of his own party have at times marked his tenure in Tallahassee.

Scott grew up in Kansas City, Missouri, the son of a truck driver and JCPenney clerk. He enlisted in the Navy after one year of community college. After his military service, Scott enrolled at the University of Missouri-Kansas City, and, displaying an early entrepreneurial streak, financed his education by buying two donut shops and hiring his mother to manage them. Undergraduate degree in hand, he went to Southern Methodist University in Texas for a law degree. After college, he went to work for a large firm, where he specialized in health care mergers and acquisitions. In 1987, Scott put together a $6 billion bid to purchase Nashville-based HCA, the hospitals' firm founded by Drs. Thomas Frist and Thomas Frist, Jr., father and brother, respectively, of former GOP Sen. Bill Frist of Tennessee. When that offer was rejected, Scott and Texas billionaire Richard Rainwater started their own hospital company called Columbia with $125,000 in savings.

Columbia started off in 1988 with two hospitals in El Paso, and for the next nine years, bought up dozens of hospitals, many of them nonprofit operations, and offered ownership shares to doctors who made referrals. Columbia became highly profitable, and in 1994, made a successful bid for HCA. Scott worked to reduce costs and to require more accountability while opening heart bypass surgery facilities. By 1997, Columbia/HCA was the nation's largest health care company and its seventh largest employer, with 340 hospitals, $20 billion in revenues, and 285,000 employees. But the FBI was investigating charges that Columbia/HCA overbilled the Medicare and Medicaid programs, and twice raided the firm's hospitals seeking evidence. Nine days after the second raid, the board of directors ousted Scott, and Thomas Frist, Jr. was made chief executive officer. In settlements in 2000 and 2002, the firm pleaded guilty to federal fraud charges and paid $1.7 billion in fines. The company admitted to overcharging the government systematically by claiming marketing costs as reimbursable and by exaggerating the seriousness of the illnesses they were treating, among other abuses. In a deposition in a civil suit in which he was a witness, Scott invoked his Fifth Amendment right against self-incrimination 75 times rather than answer questions. His business associates told *The New York Times* at the time that Scott was a brilliant and incisive businessman who was undone by his fatal flaws, including arrogance and aggressiveness that had permeated the company. Still, Scott was richly rewarded for his work at Columbia/HCA, leaving with $10 million in cash and $300 million in stock and options. In rehabilitating his image later, Scott maintained that he was never charged with wrongdoing. "I learned very hard lessons from what happened, and those lessons have helped me become a better businessman and leader," he said. He went on to new business ventures. Scott bought control of America's Health Network cable channel, and in 2001 co-founded Solantic, which operates walk-in urgent care centers throughout Florida and specializes in patients without insurance. In 2003, he moved to Naples, Florida.

In March 2009, Scott cut a check for $5 million to found Conservatives for Patients' Rights, which ran TV ads featuring Scott criticizing President Barack Obama and congressional Democrats' healthcare reform bills, particularly the provision creating a government-financed insurance option. The Affordable Care Act passed in March 2010, and the next month, Scott announced that he was running for governor as a Republican to succeed Charlie Crist, who had opted to run for the Senate rather than seek a second term. Scott, who declared his net worth was $218 million, immediately spent $4.7 million on ads. The front-runner in the primary was Attorney General Bill McCollum, a former House member and the GOP nominee for the Senate in 2000, who was choice of the state's GOP establishment. But Scott's ad barrage sent McCollum tumbling in the polls. Scott called McCollum a career politician and attacked him for his connections to former state GOP Chairman Jim Greer, who was indicted on fraud charges. McCollum responded with ads recalling the Columbia/HCA problems and its record fine for fraud. Scott unveiled a catchy economic plan with seven steps to create 700,000 jobs in seven years, with corporate and property tax cuts, public payroll reductions, and the streamlining of government agencies. "Let's get to work" was the tag line on his ads. In all, Scott spent close to $50 million in the primary and beat McCollum 46%-44%. Soon afterward, he picked as his running mate GOP state Sen. Jennifer Carroll, the first African-American Republican woman elected to the Legislature. The fact that more votes were cast in the Republican primary than the Democratic primary, although there were more registered Democrats than Republicans in the state, boded well for Scott's general election campaign, as did the unpopularity of Obama among many Floridians. The Democratic nominee, the state's Chief Financial Officer Alex Sink, won her primary without serious opposition and with minimal spending. Her husband, Tampa lawyer Bill McBride, had beaten former Attorney General Janet Reno in the 2002 Democratic primary, and then lost the general election to incumbent Republican Gov. Jeb Bush. Sink had had a successful career in banking, rising to the position of head of Florida operations for the Bank of America. In 2006, she was elected to the new financial officer position, the only Democrat elected to statewide office that year other than Sen. Bill Nelson.

The Scott-Sink contest was one of the most negative races in the country. Democratic ads, some featuring law enforcement officials, attacked Scott for his conduct at Columbia/HCA. In their first debate, Sink said, "Rick, the people of Florida can't trust you." Scott painted Sink as a "Tallahassee insider" and a booster of Obama's policies. He said she would increase state spending by billions of dollars, while he would slash government. Perhaps the crucial moment came in the third debate on October 25. The campaigns had agreed not to allow the candidates to accept cell phone messages during the debate. But during a commercial break, an aide handed a Droid phone to Sink who read a message on it. Scott charged her with cheating, and the issue dominated news coverage for much of the last week of the campaign. Meanwhile, Scott ran ads featuring his mother, wife and adult daughters to soften his image from the highly negative portrayals by Democrats. Scott won another squeaker, 49%-48%. He carried Latinos 50%-48% and won 62% among whites without college degrees. Sink won 60 percent of the vote in the Gold Coast, but Scott ran just barely ahead of her in the I-4 Corridor, and won 55 percent of the vote in the rest of the state. Overall, his campaign and political committee spent $85 million on his election, $73 million of which he financed himself. Republicans also expanded their majorities in both houses of the legislature.

In his first year in office, Scott cut the state budget to just over $69 billion, about $1.3 billion smaller than in the previous fiscal year with large reductions in education spending. He also vetoed bills totaling a record $615 million; winning praise from tea party groups for cutting the Tallahassee lawmakers' prized earmark measures. Scott didn't shy away from taking on the state teachers' unions, and in the summer of 2011, he signed several education bills that expanded the use of school vouchers and increased enrollment at high-performing charter schools. He also rejected $2.4 billion in federal transportation funds for a high-speed train line between Tampa and Orlando. The project had been in the works for many years, and legislators from both parties criticized Scott's decision. Scott insisted that Florida tax-payers would ultimately be asked to pick up the tab for some of the construction costs. Scott enraged state Democrats with one of his most controversial moves: requiring welfare recipients to take drug tests. "While there are certainly legitimate needs for public assistance, it is unfair for Florida taxpayers to subsidize drug addiction," Scott said after signing the new law in May 2011. The law made national headlines and proved popular with conservatives in other states, but in late October, a U.S. District Court judge halted implementation on constitutional grounds and claimed that, contrary to data provided by the state, the program would not save money.

Scott also waded into Florida's knotty Cuba politics when he signed a bill in May 2012 cracking down on companies that do business with Cuba and Syria. He was initially praised by the Cuban exile community, but after he signed the bill, he issued a statement complaining that the law was unenforceable without support from the federal government. Republican state legislators and Cuban exiles complained that Scott had undermined the new policy, and Sen. Marco Rubio, R-Florida., publicly disagreed with the statement. As Scott prepared to run for re-election, he shifted toward the political center. He shed the tea party image of his first years in office and portrayed himself as a champion of education. In 2014, he signed a record $77 billion budget that increased funding for public schools, universities, child protection services and the environment. He also used a light touch with his veto pen, rejecting only $69 million in the legislators' priority items, a far cry from the ax he wielded on the 2011 budget. After vetoing a bill in 2013 to permit undocumented Florida residents to apply for a temporary drivers' license, he signed legislation providing in-state college tuition to them in 2014, over strong objections from some conservatives in his party.

Still, Scott's brash manner and an economy that was slow to recover disaffected many Floridians, and his poll standings sagged throughout 2011. While he had made good on most of his 2010 campaign promises—at least by the scoring of *The Tampa Bay Times*—by the middle of 2012, Scott's job approval rating sunk to 31 percent. The governor's vulnerability inspired former governor Charlie Crist to try for a comeback. The confrontation was one the marquee contests of the 2014 mid-term elections: the biggest state with the most competitive governor's race, featuring an embattled incumbent and a challenger who had become anathema to many conservative Republicans after he famously hugged President Obama in 2009, then lost a Senate race running as an independent in 2010, and now sought to return to Tallahassee as a Democrat. Crist readily adopted his new party's political playbook and criticized Scott for cutting education, restricting abortion, and vowing to raise the minimum wage. Scott promised to pump money into education, environmental protection, airports and seaport infrastructure and to cut taxes by up to $1 billion while maintaining his overall focus on creating jobs. Scott blamed Crist for leaving the state in poor financial shape and took credit for the subsequent economic turnaround. Crist sought to revive memories of Scott's troubled tenure at Columbia/HCA and his campaign ran ads highlighting the $1.7 billion in federal fraud fines the hospital company paid. Scott attacked Crist about his past friendship with Florida lawyer Scott Rothstein, who was convicted of investment fraud in a Ponzi scheme.

In one of the more bizarre episodes of political theater in any election, Scott refused to take the stage in a mid-October debate with Crist, because a small portable fan had been placed underneath the Democrat's podium in an apparent violation of the rules to which the candidates had agreed. After a flummoxed debate moderator tried for several minutes to explain the contretemps to a live television audience, Scott eventually walked onto the stage for his face-off with Crist. While he seemed a bit shaky at the outset, Scott more than held his own in the debate, but his performance was overshadowed by "fan-gate," and he was predictably skewered on late-night television. Scott didn't need to spend as much of his own money to win reelection as he had in 2010, but he didn't hesitate to open his wallet when he needed to: He contributed more than $12 million of his personal fortune to help pay for a TV ad blitz in the closing days of the campaign that Democrats believe tipped the election his way. Estimates vary, but between his campaign, his political committee and the money he steered to the state GOP, Scott's reelection bid was likely better funded than his previous campaign. Crist was hardly a pauper in the money race. His campaign spent more than $40 million and California billionaire environmentalist Tom Steyer's NextGen Climate political committee anted up roughly $20 million to defeat Scott. Crist won almost a quarter million more votes than Sink had four years earlier, but voting in the Democratic strongholds of Miami-Dade and Broward counties was ten and six percentage points, respectively, below the statewide turnout of registered voters. Higher turnout came in GOP bastions like Collier, St. John's, Manatee and Sumter Counties. The exit poll showed that Crist narrowly carried the under age 65 vote, but Scott handily won seniors. Scott carried white voters by a wide margin while Crist overwhelmingly won the votes of African Americans and easily carried Hispanics who had split their votes four years earlier between Scott and Sink. Crist even carried the Cuban vote, albeit by a slender margin.

Fresh off a hard-fought reelection victory that most political observers would have bet against a year earlier and looking at a projected $1 billion state surplus, Scott appeared well-positioned to start his second term and enact his agenda to increase spending on education and cut taxes. Instead, he seemed to stumble from the outset. He forced out the widely respected commissioner of the Florida Department of Law Enforcement (FDLE), Gerald Bailey, and had to backtrack from his initial claim that Bailey had resigned on his own. The revelation embarrassed Florida Cabinet members Attorney General Pam Bondi, state CFO Jeff Atwater and Agriculture Commissioner Adam Putman, all Republicans, who said they would not have rubber-stamped Scott's pick to replace Bailey had they known the true nature of his departure. Moreover, Bailey accused Scott's office of frequent political meddling in the FDLE's work, including requests to run interference in a federal money-laundering probe of a GOP donor and to implicate falsely an Orange County clerk in an investigation of a prison release scandal. Scott has denied Bailey's allegations. The Florida Society of News Editors filed a lawsuit against Scott and the Florida Cabinet for violating the state's Sunshine Law in Bailey's dismissal.

Then there was Scott's shifting stance on Medicaid expansion. Early in his first term, Scott, a long-time critic of the Affordable Care Act, opposed expanding the number of low-income people who could be covered by the program in exchange for having the federal government cover the costs for new enrollees. Scott said it was a bad deal for the state because it would eventually have to pick up some portion of the costs once the feds reduced their subsidy. After his mother died in an ICU unit and Obama had carried Florida for a second time, Scott reversed course and endorsed Medicaid expansion in early 2013, calling it a "compassionate, common-sense step forward." But Scott didn't push the idea, as the GOP-controlled state legislature remained hostile. Then in February 2015, the Centers for Medicare & Medicaid Services said it would not renew a Medicaid waiver that provided more than $1 billion as a "low income pool" for the state to compensate hospitals for treating uninsured and poor patients. That prompted the Republican majority in the state Senate to get behind Medicaid expansion to help state hospitals pay for uninsured care. But after Scott was unable to convince federal officials to extend the state's Medicaid waiver, he abruptly announced that he couldn't support Medicaid expansion saying the federal government couldn't be trusted to cover the costs. In an interview with Fox News, Scott likened the Obama administration to the TV mob family the Sopranos saying, "They're using bullying tactics to attack our state." Scott's Medicaid reversal antagonized Republican senators, who also complained that the governor was AWOL during much of the budget impasse—the worst since the GOP takeover of the statehouse in the mid-1990s—spending too much time on business recruiting trips or minor public events outside of Tallahassee. Republicans in the state House opposed the Senate's Medicaid expansion plans, and when Scott did try to intervene in the budget dispute, he was clumsy. At one point during the deadlock, Scott summoned individual Republican state senators to his office and threatened that he could veto their legislative priorities if they failed to pass his tax cut proposals. Several GOP lawmakers criticized the governor's tactics as counterproductive. State Sen. Don Gaetz, a former president of the chamber, said Scott's sessions with the lawmakers were likely to "lose him some ground in human relations."

Scott's persistent fundraising also chafed Republican legislators who felt he should have spent more time trying to broker a budget deal. Since the start of 2015, Scott's Let's Get to Work political committee had raised more $2 million. Consistent with his outsider's approach, Scott's committee aired TV spots touting his tax cut proposals while Republican lawmakers in both the state House and Senate tried to scale them back to help resolve their budget differences. Scott has reportedly told some of his top donors that he is interested in running for the Senate in 2018 when Bill Nelson's third term is up. The constant flow of fundraisers and ads, and his reversal on Medicaid expansion which would help protect his right flank in a GOP primary, suggest to many in Tallahassee that Scott has his eyes on moving to Washington.

Senior Senator

Bill Nelson (D)

Elected 2000, term expires Jan. 2019, 3rd term; b. Sept. 29, 1942, Miami; Yale U., B.A. 1965, U. of VA, J.D. 1968; Presbyterian; married (Grace Cavert); 2 children.

Military Career: U.S. Army, 1968-70; U.S. Army Reserves, 1965-71.

Elected Office: FL House, 1972-78; U.S. House, 1978-90; FL treasurer, insurance comm. & fire marshal, 1994-2000.

Professional Career: Practicing atty., 1970-79, 1991-94; Legis. asst., FL Gov. Reubin Askew, 1971; Crew member, Space Shuttle Columbia, 1986.

DC Office: 716 HSOB, 20510, 202-224-5274; Fax: 202-228-2183; Website: billnelson.senate.gov.

State Offices: Broward/Ft. Lauderdale, 954-693-4851; Fort Myers, 239-334-7760; Jacksonville, 904-346-4500; Miami-Dade/Coral Gables, 305-536-5999; Orlando, 407-872-7161; Tallahassee, 850-942-8415; Tampa, 813-225-7040; West Palm Beach, 561-514-0189.

Committees: *Aging (Special). Armed Services:* Emerging Threats & Capabilities (RMM); Seapower; Strategic Forces. *Commerce, Science & Transportation* (RMM: ex officio member of each subcommittee). *Finance:* Energy, Natural Resources & Infrastructure; International Trade, Customs & Global Competitiveness; Taxation & IRS Oversight.

Group Ratings

	ADA	ACLU	AFL-CIO	LCV	ITI	COC	HAFA	ACU	CFG	FRC
2014	85%	86%	–	80%	100%	50%	0%	0%	0%	0%
2013	85%	C	100%	85%	C	38%	C	4%	3%	C

National Journal Ratings

	2013 LIB	—	2013 CONS
Economic	66%	—	33%
Social	73%	—	0%
Foreign	71%	—	0%
Composite	80%	—	21%

Key Votes of the 113th Congress

1. Sandy storm spending	Y	5. Student Loan Rates	Y	9. Bipartisan Budget Deal	Y
2. Chuck Hagel Confirmation	Y	6. Employee Non-Discrim'n Act	Y	10. Farm Bill Conference Rept.	Y
3. Gun Background Checks	Y	7. Senate Vote on Judgeships	N	11. Unempl. Comp. Extension	Y
4. Immigration Reform	Y	8. Defense Dept. Spending	Y	12. Keystone Pipeline	N

Election Results

2012 general	Bill Nelson (D)	4,523,451	(55%)	$17,125,413	$3,790,749	$9,747,183
	Connie Mack (R)	3,458,267	(42%)	$7,508,151	$6,249,161	$3,598,471
2012 primary	Bill Nelson (D)	690,112	(79%)			
	Glen Burkett (D)	185,629	(21%)			

Prior winning percentages: 2006 (60%); 2000 (51%); House: 1988 (61%); 1986 (73%); 1984 (61%); 1982 (71%); 1980 (70%); 1978 (61%)

Bill Nelson, who was first elected to the Senate in 2000, is a careful centrist with a willingness to break from his party when he deems its interests diverge from those of his state. That moderation has helped him coast to reelection twice as other Democrats have struggled—he's the only Democrat holding statewide office in Florida.

Nelson grew up in Melbourne Florida. His mother was a schoolteacher, and his father was a lawyer and real estate investor who died when Bill was 14. Nelson likes to recall that his great-grandfather arrived in Florida from Denmark as a stowaway on a ship. From his family home in Rock Point, Nelson could see rockets blast off in the 1950s and 1960s from what is now the Kennedy Space Center. He was active in student government and has always been something of a straight arrow; he doesn't drink, smoke, or swear.

He attended the University of Florida for two years, and then graduated from Yale and the University of Virginia law school. After a two-year hitch in the Army, he returned to Melbourne where he briefly practiced law and worked on the staff of Democratic Gov. Reubin Askew. In 1972, at age 30, he was elected to the state House of Representatives.

In 1978, when Republican Rep. Louis Frey retired, Nelson ran for the House in a district that then included the Space Coast's Brevard County and most of Orlando's Orange County. His religious faith and traditional values, his indefatigable campaigning and folksy manner made him popular in an area that was trending Republican. He won the seat 61%-39%; in five succeeding elections, he captured 61% to 73% of the ballots in a district that voted just 29% for Democrat Michael Dukakis in the 1988 presidential race. In the House, he became chairman of the Science Committee's Space Subcommittee, obviously of prime importance to the district. Nelson not only boosted the space program in every possible way, but also rode the space shuttle Columbia himself, spending six days orbiting the Earth in early 1986. He still reminds people of his sojourn, noting that in space he saw no racial or political divides on Earth, just a single unified planet.

In 1989, with the support of leading Florida Democrats, Nelson set out to run against Republican Gov. Bob Martinez, who was not faring well in polls. But in early 1990, some Democrats became antsy about Nelson's prospects and persuaded Lawton Chiles, who had retired from the Senate in 1988 after three terms, to run. Chiles was always far ahead in their race and won the September primary, 70 percent to 31 percent. Nelson returned to his 77-acre oceanfront home in Melbourne, his political career seemingly over. But in 1994, he found an opening when state Insurance Commissioner Tom Gallagher, a Republican, ran for governor. Nelson was elected in November to an office whose full title was treasurer, insurance commissioner, and state fire marshal, and proceeded to compile an activist record.

Nelson's chance to run for higher office came in March 1999, when Republican Sen. Connie Mack said he would not run for reelection in 2000. Mack's retirement left a seat up for grabs in a state that, as Election Night 2000 returns would show, was closely divided between the parties. Republicans nominated 20-year, Orlando-based Rep. Bill McCollum, one of the House managers of the impeachment of President Bill Clinton.

Washington observers considered the race a contest about the wisdom of the impeachment, but mostly it was a battle of competing styles. Running his fourth statewide race in 10 years, Nelson's easygoing manner contrasted favorably with McCollum's stiff and sometimes caustic demeanor. With a long conservative record on abortion rights and gun control, McCollum attempted to moderate his positions, but only succeeded in antagonizing his base supporters. This was the most expensive Florida Senate race to that point, with the two candidates spending more than $15 million between them. Nelson won, 51 percent to 46 percent.

In the Senate, Nelson has become known as a deliberative lawmaker with a moderate-to-liberal voting record, usually siding with his party on major legislation. Some Republicans grouse that he prefers to tackle easy issues to tougher ones. "He is a connoisseur of low-hanging fruit," Florida Republican strategist J.M. "Mac" Stipanovich told *The Tampa Bay Times* in 2012. Nelson responded by citing his work against oil drilling and health care, among other issues. But gay-rights groups derided him for his cautiousness in 2012 after Obama declared his support for same-sex marriage: "I believe marriage should be left to the states," he said. "And Florida voted on same-sex marriage in 2008," the year voters approved a constitutional ban on gay marriage. Nelson flipped to supporting gay marriage in 2013, part of a groundswell of moderate Democrats who backed it ahead of a major Supreme Court decision that overturned parts of the Defense of Marriage Act.

Nelson is not especially well known nationally, but his activity on issues directly relevant to segments of Florida's population—including space, oil drilling, health care, national security, and restoring the Everglades—has raised his profile. He drew attention in May 2012, when former CIA official Jose Rodriguez said in a book that Nelson, as a member of the Intelligence Committee, had volunteered to be waterboarded to see what the controversial interrogation procedure was like. The agency declined. He was named in December 2012 as chairman of the Senate Special Committee on Aging, a panel that has no legislative authority but conducts oversight of issues relevant to senior citizens. He promised to expose financial scams and other abuses of the elderly. Nelson had long opposed warming relations with Cuba, holding up a $410 billion omnibus spending bill because of provisions that loosened travel and export restrictions in 2009, and relenting only after Treasury Secretary Timothy Geithner assured him in writing that the provisions would have little effect on current law. But in December of 2014, Nelson offered surprising if tepid support for the Obama administration's move to normalize relations with Cuba. "I'm as anti-Castro as they come, but it's time to move on," he told the Associated Press. "It's time to get into the 21st century."

Nelson was chairman of the Commerce subcommittee with jurisdiction over the space program from 2007 until Republicans retook Senate control in 2015. After the loss of the space shuttle Columbia, which disintegrated as it reentered Earth's atmosphere in 2003, killing seven crew members, Nelson called for accelerated development of a reusable space vehicle to ferry astronauts to the International Space Station. In 2004, he won passage of an amendment calling on NASA to report to Congress on the costs of extending the space shuttle program beyond 2010. When President Barack Obama took office, Nelson sharply criticized his administration's limited commitment to NASA and got a bill through the Senate providing enough money for another space shuttle flight in 2011, jump-starting NASA's new heavy-lift rocket. He and Republican Sen. Kay Bailey Hutchison of Texas, introduced a bill in December 2012 aimed at promoting greater international cooperation on human spaceflight. They got a scaled-down version into a Senate-passed bill that protects commercial space-launch operators against losses beyond what they insure. In spite of Nelson's boosterism, NASA has struggled in recent years as Republicans have fought for austerity and President Obama has shown limited interest in the program. Nelson lost his chairmanship when Democrats lost Senate control in 2015, but normally anti-government Republican Texas Sen. Ted Cruz has continued Hutchison's defense of their home-state program, and the Senate included a 2 percent bump for NASA spending in its 2015 budget.

Starting in 2005, Nelson worked with Republican colleague Mel Martinez of Florida to block oil and gas exploration in the eastern part of the Gulf of Mexico. After Republican Gov. Charlie Crist came out in favor of offshore drilling in June 2008, Nelson continued to oppose it. Then, in September 2008, Nelson said he would back a bipartisan deal allowing some offshore drilling in the gulf, provided it was limited to 125 miles, rather than 50 miles, from the Florida coast.

Then came the massive BP oil spill disaster in 2010. Nelson joined Democratic Sens. Bob Menendez and Frank Lautenberg of New Jersey in leading the opposition to expanded drilling along the East Coast and in the Gulf. Over objections from Republicans, Nelson also sought to increase the cap on damages from oil spills from $75 million to $10 billion. To discourage oil drilling in Cuban waters, Nelson and Menendez introduced a bill in November 2011 that would make it easier for Americans to sue foreign polluters for damages. In early 2015, Nelson succeeded in getting the Obama administration to ban drilling off Florida's coast through 2022.

As a member of the powerful Finance Committee, Nelson emerged as a player in the 2009-2010 health care debate. He amended an early version of the bill to lessen the impact of cuts to Medicare Advantage, a privatized Medicare program that covers more than 900,000 seniors in Florida. But Republicans castigated it as a backroom deal intended to benefit Florida, and his amendment was killed. He did successfully add an amendment to the Finance version of the bill exempting seniors from a hike in the itemized medical deduction limit. Since then, he has defended the law to those seeking its repeal. "Would you like me to repeal the part where you can keep your kid on your family policy until age 26?" he asked an angry constituent at a town hall meeting in August 2012. "Would you like me to repeal that part that says that the insurance company can't cancel you when you're in the middle of treatment?"

After returning to the Senate minority in 2015 Nelson turned his attention towards consumer advocacy, using his position as ranking member on the Senate Commerce Committee to question Verizon's use of "supercookies," calling their "snooping" on their customers "outrageous."

In June 2005, two-term Republican Rep. Katherine Harris announced she would challenge Nelson. Polling data indicated that Harris' prominent role as Florida secretary of state during the disputed 2000 presidential election had left her too unpopular to win, but she enjoyed celebrity status among many rank-and-file Republican voters, and other big-name Republicans declined to run. Nelson lost in the Panhandle but carried 57 of 67 counties, including Harris' home county of Sarasota.

Nelson drew another challenger in 2012—Florida Rep. Connie Mack IV, son of the senator who preceded Nelson. Mack won the Republican primary with nearly 60 percent of the vote. Nelson aggressively depicted Mack as a flawed candidate. The congressman had had several past brushes with the law, usually bar fights, as well as problems paying bills while going through a divorce, all of which figured prominently in Nelson's ads. Mack tried to paint Nelson as too liberal, but that line of attack failed to gain any traction. Republican groups spent heavily against him and polling showed a close race for a while, but Nelson won the endorsements of all of Florida's major newspapers and opened up a big lead in the closing months of the campaign, sailing to a 55 percent to 42 percent victory.

While Nelson has kept up collegial relations with most of his state's Republicans, he and Gov. Rick Scott have never gotten along well. Nelson has slammed the governor for refusing to expand the state's Medicaid program and ridiculed him for allegedly banning the term "climate change" in government documents. Nelson even introduced a Senate amendment that would prevent any ban on federal agencies and employees from talking about climate change.

Nelson weighed a run against Scott in 2014 but eventually deferred to Republican-turned-Democrat former Gov. Charlie Crist. Scott may be eying a run against Nelson in 2018, though there's no guarantee Nelson runs again.

Junior Senator

Marco Rubio (R)

Elected 2010, term expires Jan. 2017, 1st term; b. May 28, 1971, Miami; U. of FL, B.A. 1993, U. of Miami, J.D. 1996; Catholic; married (Jeanette); 4 children.

Elected Office: West Miami city commissioner, 1998-2000; FL House, 2000-08, Speaker, FL House, 2006-08.

Professional Career: Practicing atty., 1997-2010; Prof., FL Intl. U., 2009-10.

DC Office: 284 RSOB, 20510, 202-224-3041; Fax: 202-228-0285; Website: rubio.senate.gov.

State Offices: Jacksonville, 904-398-8586; Miami, 305-418-8553; Naples, 239-213-1521; Orlando, 407-254-2573; Palm Beach, 561-775-3360; Pensacola, 850-433-2603; Tampa, 813-977-6450; Tallahassee, 850-599-9100.

Committees: *Commerce, Science & Transportation:* Aviation Operations, Safety & Security; Communications, Technology, Innovation & the Internet; Oceans, Atmosphere, Fisheries & Coast Guard (Chmn); Space, Science & Competitiveness. *Foreign Relations:* Africa & Global Health Policy; East Asia, the Pacific & International Cybersecurity Policy; Near East, South Asia, Central Asia & Counterterrorism; Western Hemisphere, Transnational Crime, Civilian Security, Democracy, Human Rights & Global Women's Issues (Chmn). *Intelligence (Select). Small Business & Entrepreneurship.*

Group Ratings

	ADA	ACLU	AFL-CIO	LCV	ITI	COC	HAFA	ACU	CFG	FRC
2014	5%	40%	–	0%	33%	75%	82%	96%	92%	100%
2013	5%	C	6%	8%	C	71%	C	96%	91%	C

National Journal Ratings

	2013 LIB	—	2013 CONS
Economic	7%	—	92%
Social	34%	—	65%
Foreign	10%	—	89%
Composite	18%	—	83%

Key Votes of the 113th Congress

1. Sandy storm spending	N	5. Student Loan Rates	Y	9. Bipartisan Budget Deal N
2. Chuck Hagel Confirmation	N	6. Employee Non-Discrim'n Act	N	10. Farm Bill Conference Rept. N
3. Gun Background Checks	N	7. Senate Vote on Judgeships	Y	11. Unempl. Comp. Extension N
4. Immigration Reform	Y	8. Defense Dept. Spending	N	12. Keystone Pipeline Y

Election Results

2010 general	Marco Rubio (R)	2,645,743	(49%)	$21,638,315	$5,202,905	$244,840
	Charlie Crist (I)	1,607,549	(30%)	$13,608,676	$19,800	$1,604,852
	Kendrick Meek (D)	1,092,936	(20%)	$9,280,964	$500,155	
2010 primary	Marco Rubio (R)	1,069,936	(85%)			
	William Kogut (R)	112,080	(9%)			
	William Escoffery (R)	82,426	(7%)			

Marco Rubio, the junior senator from Florida, won a riveting contest in 2010 and is regarded as one of the Republicans with the best chance to reshape the GOP for the 21st century. He is a Latino in a party that is desperate to make inroads with that demographic group, an eloquent and telegenic public speaker with a compelling biography, and a consistent conservative with a deep interest in policy. These qualities made him a serious player as the 2016 race for the White House heated up.

Rubio was mostly brought up in a working-class Cuban-American neighborhood in Miami, the son of immigrants who left Cuba a few years before Fidel Castro took power. Rubio had said during his political rise that he was the "son of exiles" who were forced out by Castro's regime, though he used that expression less after accusations that he'd embellished their story. His parents had grown up poor and struggled to make ends meet. His father worked long days as a bartender, and his mother was a hotel maid with a second job at Kmart. The family moved to follow work; Rubio spent six years in Las Vegas while his parents worked in the hotel industry before returning to Miami for high school. At the encouragement of an aunt, he was baptized as a Mormon along with his mother and sister, only to convert back to Catholicism as a teenager. His upbringing is a cornerstone of his stump speech in public life, and he frequently references being "raised by people who know what it is like to lose their country."

Rubio initially was a Democrat, inspired by Massachusetts Sen. Edward Kennedy's famous "the dream shall never die" speech at the 1980 Democratic National Convention. But he said he soon joined his beloved grandfather in becoming a staunch Ronald Reagan supporter. "Reagan's election and my grandfather's allegiance to him were defining influences on me politically," Rubio wrote in his autobiography. "I've been a Republican ever since."

Rubio played football in high school, and despite his small stature, earned a football scholarship to Tarkio College in Missouri. He returned home after the school went bankrupt, spent a year at a junior college, and got his undergraduate degree in 1993 at the University of Florida. He then went to the University of Miami for a law degree. He interned for Republican Rep. Ileana Ros-Lehtinen, and in his last year of law school, ran the Dade County operation for Republican Sen. Bob Dole's presidential campaign in 1996. There, he met future Florida Gov. Jeb Bush, who became his political mentor and later his rival for the GOP presidential nomination. Bush has described him as "the best orator of American politics today ... He has managed to find a way to communicate a conservative message full of hope and optimism."

Rubio landed a position at the law firm of Al Cardenas, a prominent Republican and close Bush ally he got to know on the campaign trail. Around the same time, he met Jeanette Dousdebes, a former Miami Dolphins cheerleader, and they married in 1998. At age 26, he ran for city commissioner in West Miami, a tiny, heavily Cuban town just south of Miami International Airport, and beat an incumbent. Two years later, he won an open state House seat. Rubio quickly endeared himself to party leaders by working tirelessly on redistricting plans. In 2005, he became speaker of the Florida House, making him the youngest person and the first Hispanic to achieve that position. At the ceremony Bush presented him with a sword, a symbolic passing of the conservative torch in the state. Rubio toured the state, holding "idea-raisers" with voters to find budget-neutral ideas to improve the state. The 100 ideas he liked best were bundled into a book, which former House Speaker Newt Gingrich called "a work of genius." Many of the smaller proposals passed easily, but his personal favorite, replacing the state property tax with a sales tax, stalled.

His rise through Miami and statehouse politics corresponded with that of a close friend, David Rivera, with whom he bought a Tallahassee house. Rubio roomed with Rivera as well in their first two years in Washington, when he won a Senate seat and Rivera became a congressman, and stood by his friend through early ethics scandals. But he finally started looking for some distance when Rivera became embroiled in a federal investigation into whether he broke campaign finance laws and lost reelection.

In May 2009, Rubio announced his campaign for the Senate. He caught the tea party movement's lightning in its nascent days and used it to power his upstart primary campaign against then-popular Republican Gov. Charlie Crist, who had long been planning his bid for the Senate. Crist began the race with a huge cash and name recognition advantage, and the National Republican Senatorial Committee endorsed him early on. But Crist was never a favorite of conservatives, and his embrace of President Barack Obama's $787 billion economic stimulus bill (and his literal embrace of the president at a public event) infuriated many of them. Rubio received early support from Sen. Jim DeMint of South Carolina, a conservative stalwart who was backing insurgent GOP candidates, as well as quiet support from Bush and his allies. By the time Crist realized the conservative base was slipping away, it was too late. Rubio had gone from underdog to front-runner. On the verge of losing the primary, Crist quit the Republican Party in late April to run as an independent.

In the general election campaign, Rubio faced both Crist and Democratic nominee Kendrick Meek, a House member. Crist started off with an early lead in the polls, but his support plummeted as he got caught in the crossfire from Rubio on the right and Meek on the left, both of whom painted Crist as a political opportunist. Crist tried to become the de facto Democratic candidate with appeals to independents and moderate Republicans, but Meek refused to get out of the race, regularly polling at around 20% of the likely vote and denying Crist a one-on-one contest with Rubio.

Tea party activists, multiplying by the week, embraced Rubio's campaign and his theme of "Reclaim America." And although he benefited from the association, Rubio was careful not to come off as a firebrand like some of the movement's other stars. He stressed fiscal responsibility, although he sidestepped specific policy proposals. He indicated support for raising the eligibility age for Social Security beneficiaries and giving the president the line-item veto over spending bills. He opposed abortion rights and took a more conservative position than Crist on immigration, supporting Arizona's crackdown on illegal immigrants. Prominent Republicans got on board with Rubio, including former Vice President Dick Cheney, former Massachusetts Gov. Mitt Romney, and former Alaska Gov. Sarah Palin.

After August, Rubio did not trail in a single independent poll, and most polls showed him holding a double-digit lead. On Election Night, he won with 49 percent of the vote. Crist got 30 percent and Meek, 20 percent. At his victory celebration, Rubio made clear he would continue to be his own brand of Republican in the Senate, as he was in the campaign. "We make a great mistake if we believe that tonight these results are somehow an embrace of the Republican Party," he said. "What they are is a second chance, a second chance for Republicans to be what they said they were going to be not so long ago."

Early on, Rubio stuck to his theme of cutting government spending and came out against raising the debt ceiling. In a *Wall Street Journal* opinion piece in March 2011, Rubio wrote, "If we simply raise it once again, without a real plan to bring spending under control and get our economy growing, America faces the very real danger of a catastrophic economic crisis." But his voting pattern kept the movement happy; in his first year in the Senate, he was the 13th most conservative senator, with a perfect conservative score on social issues, according to *National Journal's* annual rankings. He also pleased tea party members by being one of just eight senators to oppose the New Year's Eve 2013 fiscal cliff deal; he contended it would complicate economic growth and job creation because employers would pass on the cost of the deal's tax hike to their employees.

As the Republican presidential primary candidates squabbled in early 2012, Rubio did his part to assist Mitt Romney, the former Massachusetts governor. He blasted Gingrich's campaign for airing a Spanish-language radio ad that described Romney as "the most anti-immigration candidate," and Gingrich pulled the spot. Even though Rubio had pledged to remain neutral during the primary season, when polls in March showed Obama beating Romney in Florida, the senator told Fox News: "I am going to endorse Mitt Romney. He offers such a stark contrast to the president's record." That triggered immediate speculation about his prospects for being included on the ticket.

At the same time, Rubio tried to offer his party a lifeline on immigration to bolster its low standing among Hispanics. He began talking about a potential compromise to the stalled DREAM Act aimed at helping children of illegal immigrants. His alternative called for extending legal residency to immigrant children bound for college or the military. The proposal came under sharp attack from the right, and he sought to characterize it as being less about immigration than about humanitarian relief for a group facing deportation. But Rubio's momentum came to a halt when Obama used his executive powers to put into place the major elements of Rubio's bill, leaving the senator grumbling that he deserved some credit.

As the vice-presidential guessing game reached a fever pitch in June of 2012, several news organizations, including the *Post*, ABC News, and *The New York Times*, quoted anonymous Romney advisers as saying the senator wasn't under serious consideration as a running mate. That prompted Romney to tell reporters. "Marco Rubio is being thoroughly vetted as part of our process." Even though Romney subsequently picked Rep. Paul Ryan of Wisconsin, all of the speculation benefited the senator. He elevated his national profile and sold more copies of *An American Son* while keeping a safe arm's length from a candidate many conservatives considered inauthentic.

Rubio was chosen to introduce Romney at the Republican National Convention in Tampa, and in his remarks, he criticized Obama for abandoning his positive message of 2008. "Hope and change has become divide and conquer," he complained. "…The story of our time will be written by Americans who haven't yet been born. Let's make sure they write that we did our part." Despite being overshadowed by actor Clint Eastwood's now-infamous rambling appearance, Rubio's speech drew widespread praise, with some pundits deeming it the best of the convention. He later campaigned heavily for Romney in Florida, but in the end, was unable to deliver his home state.

Following the election, Rubio gave several policy-oriented speeches, including one in which he mentioned the phrase "middle class" nearly three dozen times while discussing the need to close "the opportunity gap" between the wealthy and poor by reforming college Pell grants and student loan programs. As income inequality became an increasingly prominent issue, Rubio worked to come up with a conservative answer to the problem, focusing on college affordability.

By early 2013, he was being discussed as a presidential contender, and he was chosen to give the Republican response to Obama's State of the Union address that year. Although some people mocked him for awkwardly reaching for a water bottle midway through his remarks, he won favorable reviews for interweaving elements of his own story with criticism of the president for an "obsession" with raising taxes.

At the same time, Rubio was looking to help his party solve an issue that had cost it dearly in the 2012 elections: Immigration. After initially hesitating, he joined a bipartisan group crafting a comprehensive bill that would tighten border security while creating an eventual path to citizenship for many immigrants here illegally.

The push drew bipartisan praise and eventually passed the Senate by a wide margin, but stalled out in the GOP-controlled House. Rubio's involvement badly damaged his tea party standing, as right-wing radio turned on its onetime hero. Rubio, who had been leading early 2016 polls, saw his stock plummet. As he geared up for a presidential run he returned to his original stance on immigration, telling a crowd at the 2015 Conservative Political Action Conference that he'd learned voters won't approve of any pathway to citizenship until it's "proven to them that future illegal immigration will be controlled" and that immigration reform should be done in a piecemeal fashion with border security first.

As the immigration reform push collapsed, Rubio, using his perch on the Senate Foreign Relations Committee, leaned hard into criticizing Obama on foreign policy and calling for a more muscular, interventionist America. He drew headlines for attacking Obama's approach to Russia's meddling in Ukraine in 2014 and was a leading Senate voice calling for stronger opposition to Venezuela's government crackdowns on its people. And a cause near to his heart helped him start to recover in the conservative media—and make inroads with influential neoconservatives and the wealthy businessmen needed to win a presidential race. After Rubio railed against Cuba's communist regime in a February 2012 Senate floor speech, conservative radio host Rush Limbaugh said "We haven't had communism blasted like Rubio did it by an elected official in I don't know how long—certainly since the days of Reagan."

As Bush made an unexpected move towards a presidential bid in late 2014, many speculated that Rubio wouldn't challenge his former mentor. But he showed he wasn't going to back down, and immediately sought to capitalize on Obama's move to normalize relations with Cuba as a way to get his name back in the headlines.

Rubio announced his presidential campaign in April 2015, emphasizing his family's modest immigrant roots and seeking to draw a contrast with both Bush and former Secretary of State Hillary Clinton, the Democratic front-runner. "This election is a generational choice about what kind of country we will be," he said in his announcement speech in Miami.

His increased focus on foreign policy has helped him with hawkish GOP voters, and while some conservatives will never forgive him for his immigration apostasies, he was viewed as a serious challenger for the Republican nomination in the early stages of his presidential race. His decision not to seek a second term in the Senate opened the door to competitive primaries in each party in 2016.

FIRST DISTRICT

Jeff Miller (R)

Elected Oct. 2001, 7th full term; b. June 27, 1959, St. Petersburg; U. of FL, B.A. 1984; Baptist; married (Vicki); 2 children.

Elected Office: FL House, 1998-2001.

Professional Career: Real estate broker, Henry Co. homes; Owner, Jeff Miller Real Estate; Deputy sheriff.

DC Office: 336 CHOB, 20515, 202-225-4136; Fax: 202-225-3414; Website: jeffmiller.house.gov.

State Offices: Ft. Walton Beach, 850-664-1266; Pensacola, 850-479-1183.

Committees: *Armed Services:* Oversight & Investigations. *Intelligence (Select). Veterans' Affairs* (Chmn).

Group Ratings

	ADA	ACLU	AFL-CIO	LCV	ITI	COC	HAFA	ACU	CFG	FRC
2014	0%	0%	–	0%	100%	79%	72%	92%	77%	100%
2013	0%	C	10%	4%	C	85%	C	92%	81%	C

National Journal Ratings

	2013 LIB	—	2013 CONS
Economic	13%	—	87%
Social	27%	—	71%
Foreign	44%	—	54%
Composite	29%	—	71%

Key Votes of the 113th Congress

1. Sandy storm spending	N	5. Medical Marijuana	N	9. Syrian Rebels Training	N
2. Violence Against Women Act	N	6. Farm Bill	N	10. Keystone pipeline	Y
3. Guantanamo Bay Detainees	N	7. Afghanistan Combat	N	11. Immigration Exec. Action	Y
4. Abortion 20-week ban	Y	8. NSA Phone Data Collection	N	12. Bipartisan budget deal	Y

Election Results

2014 general	Jeff Miller (R)	165,086	(70%)	$543,974
	James Bryan (D)	54,976	(23%)	$14,533
	Mark Wichern (R)	15,281	(7%)	$207,773
2014 primary	Jeff Miller (R)	44,784	(75%)	
	John Krause (R)	14,660	(25%)	

Prior winning percentages: 2012 (70%), 2010 (80%), 2008 (70%), 2006 (69%), 2004 (77%), 2002 (75%), 2001 special (66%)

Population		Race and Ethnicity		Income	
Total:	729,553	White	74.6%	Median income:	$49,416
Urban:	51.1%	Black	12.9%		*(251 of 435)*
Suburban:	35.0%	Latino	5.4%	Under $50,000	50.4%
Rural:	13.9%	Asian	2.4%	$50,000-$99,999:	33.2%
Land area:	3,337	Two races	3.7%	$100,000-$199,999:	13.8%
Pop/sq. mi.:	218.6	White Ethnic	21.7%	$200,000 or more:	2.6%
Born in state:	39.4%			Poverty Rate	16.0%
		Education			
		H.S. grad or less:	38.8%	Work	
Age Groups		Some college:	35.9%	White collar:	32.2%
Under 18:	21.6%	College degree, 4 yr.:	16.3%	Blue collar:	49.0%
18 to 34:	24.5%	Post-grad study:	9.0%	Sales and service:	18.9%
35 to 64:	38.7%				
Over 64:	15.2%			Govt. workers:	16.4%
		Military			
		Veterans/active duty:	20.2%		

Western Panhandle: Pensacola, Fort Walton

The "Redneck Riviera" is the affectionate local name for the Gulf Coast beaches of Florida's Emerald Coast, stretching from Pensacola east to Destin. This has been military country ever since John Quincy Adams persuaded Spain to sell Florida to

Voter Turnout	
2013 Total Citizen 18+	558,825
2014 House Turnout	235,343
2014 Turnout as % CVAP	42.1%
2012 Turnout as % CVAP	64.3%

the United States in 1819, with the goal of gaining control of the port of Pensacola on the Gulf of Mexico. In October 1861, the Union defeated the Confederates in a battle to control Santa Rosa Island, the outermost spit of land protecting Pensacola Bay. In the 20th century, the Pensacola Naval Air Station was turned into the nation's first naval-aviation training base, giving birth to carrier aviation. Today, about 17,000 people are employed at Eglin Air Force Base, which spreads over three counties and, with approximately 100,000 square miles of airspace stretching over the Gulf to the Florida Keys, is considered the largest air base in the free world. The base is the Air Force center responsible for the development, acquisition, testing, deployment and sustainment of all air-delivered weapons, including the F-35 Joint Strike Fighter.

The western panhandle of Florida is culturally part of Dixie and lies closer to Houston than to Miami. A columnist for the *Pensacola News Journal* once recommended the creation of an independent commonwealth of West Florida. "We don't have much in common with the people inhabiting what I call peninsular Florida," wrote Jerry Maygarden. "I'm convinced that the further south you drive, the further north you get." Until recently, the panhandle was heavily dependent on the military and had little of its own economy. In January 2015, the Southern Co. utility announced ambitious plans to cooperate with three branches of the military to build a giant solar project, which could power 18,000 homes.

As the South has become more prosperous, the shore has attracted vacationing and retiring Southerners to its vast, fine-grained, white sand beaches and its pleasant, inlet-dotted bays. It has become a leading spring break destination for sometimes rowdy college students and the site of a large annual gay Memorial Day weekend party. The 4.9% unemployment rate in the Pensacola area in December 2014 was below the national and state average, and down significantly from the local 10.8% peak in January 2010.

The 1st Congressional District of Florida runs from Pensacola, adjoining the Alabama border, through Fort Walton Beach and Destin to Santa Rosa Beach. It is so far west, it is in the Central time zone. Inland, the 1st stretches farther east, taking in rural Walton and Holmes counties. The population here has grown steadily, with young civilians, not just military retirees, moving in and shifting attention to education and quality-of-life issues. The region has long been culturally and economically conservative, with a strong pro-military bent. It gave George Wallace (from neighboring Alabama) 61% of the vote in 1968; George McGovern managed only

2012 Presidential Vote
Mitt Romney (R)................242,950 (69%)
Barack Obama (D) 106,824 (30%)

2008 Presidential Vote
John McCain (R)................240,024 (67%)
Barack Obama (D) 114,887 (32%)

Cook Partisan Voting Index: R+21

16% of the vote here in 1972. John McCain had his best Florida showing in the district, with a 67%-32% lead over Barack Obama; four years later, Mitt Romney's 69%-30% showing was likewise his best in the state.

Jeff Miller (R)

The congressman from the 1st District is Jeff Miller, a Republican who took office in 2001 and quietly emerged a decade later as chairman of the House Veterans' Affairs Committee. He has been a forceful advocate for cleaning up waste and inefficiency at the troubled Veterans Affairs Department, working successfully with Democrats to cut deals.

The scion of a farm family that settled in central Florida in the mid-1800s, Miller grew up in Levy County, where his parents raised cattle. He graduated from the University of Florida, where he studied journalism (he worked as a TV weatherman for a time) and became an aide to the state's longtime agriculture commissioner, Democrat Doyle Conner. In 1998, he moved to Santa Rosa County, his wife's family home, and began to sell real estate. Having switched to the Republican Party the previous year, he won his first political campaign in 1998 against a Republican state representative who had received negative press after an altercation with a state trooper.

Two years later, the 1st District seat opened following the resignation of Republican Rep. Joe Scarborough, who became a talk-show host on the MSNBC cable network. Miller quickly became the favorite of national Republican leaders. Sensitive to coastal interests, Miller and the other serious contenders all claimed to be ardent environmentalists, an unusual twist in a GOP primary. Miller's best-known opponent was state Rep. Randy Knepper, chief of staff to the district's former Democratic representative, Earl Hutto, who retired in 1994. Scarborough endorsed Miller as "a strong voice for northwest Florida." In the six-candidate contest, Miller got 54% to 15% for Knepper. National Democrats made little effort to win a seat that had been their bastion for generations, and Miller won the general election, 66%-28%.

In the House, Miller has mostly compiled a conservative record. His occasional deviations from party dogma have chiefly been on local issues. A long-standing foe of oil and gas drilling in the eastern Gulf of Mexico, he relented in 2006, accepting a deal that opened up some offshore drilling but included a ban on drilling rigs in a military training range south of Fort Walton Beach. In 2013, he was one of 21 Republicans (mostly from Florida) who supported a Democratic amendment—which failed on a tie—ensuring that states have the right to regulate energy drilling beneath navigable waters within their boundaries.

In contrast to the voluble Scarborough, Miller gained a reputation for being soft-spoken and a good listener. He got seats on the Armed Services and Veterans' Affairs committees, obvious assignments for this district. He made multiple visits to U.S. troops in Afghanistan and Iraq and praised the conduct of the war at a time when Democrats were hammering President George W. Bush on the issue. He worked to protect local military facilities in the base-closing process. In 2008, he secured $54 million for an in-patient center at Eglin Hospital and pushed for a new veterans' hospital near the base to replace one destroyed by Hurricane Katrina in 2005. Congress in 2004 enacted Miller's bill to provide a 100 percent annuity to surviving military spouses.

When Democrats controlled the House, Miller was ranking Republican on the Armed Services Subcommittee on Terrorism and Unconventional Threats. In that role, he worked across the aisle to increase money for the military's Special Operations Command and for cybersecurity. With increasing focus on fiscal austerity at the Pentagon after the GOP regained House control, Miller fought to keep the F-35 Joint Strike Fighter program off the chopping block. During an Armed Services Committee hearing in 2011, he argued that the F-35 program directly or indirectly employed some 127,000 people. Pilots of the F-35s are trained at Eglin in Miller's district.

With the Republican takeover of the House in 2011, Miller became chairman of Veterans' Affairs. In a delegation with two former committee chairmen (John Mica, Ileana Ros-Lehtinen), he is the only Floridian who holds a gavel. He vowed to press the Veterans Affairs Department to reduce its significant backlog of benefit claims. He got two bills signed into law that year. His Restoring GI Bill Fairness Act authorized the VA to help pay tuition costs for student veterans at private colleges and universities in seven states. Miller later worked with Senate Veterans' Affairs Committee Chairman Patty Murray of Washington to find common ground on a bill to give companies a $2,400 tax credit for hiring a veteran previously unemployed for one month, $5,600 for hiring a veteran unemployed for at least six months, and up to $9,600 in tax credits for hiring unemployed veterans with service-connected disabilities. He also has targeted waste and mismanagement at the department. In October 2012, Miller and Republican Sen. Richard Burr of North Carolina called for the resignation of VA Chief of Staff John Gingrich over two training conferences in Orlando that cost more than $6 million. Gingrich remained in that position, but a critical inspector general report on spending at the conferences prompted the resignation of Assistant Secretary for Human Resources and Administration John Sepulveda.

When further scandals erupted in 2014 at the VA, whose $150 billion budget is the second largest among Cabinet departments, Miller demanded fixes but distanced himself from Republicans who sought to turn the problems into a political issue. He said he "couldn't have been more disappointed" with the slow response of President Barack Obama, but declined to call for the resignation of Secretary Eric Shinseki, who ultimately stepped down. "The secretary is a friend. I believe he is an honorable man who should be saluted for his service to this country," Miller told The *Tampa Bay Times*. "But he is head of an agency that has a mind and will of its own, and I'm hoping that changes can be made." In July, after weeks of exchanging charges and countercharges with his liberal Senate counterpart, Vermont Independent Bernie Sanders, they struck a deal on a sweeping reform of the agency. The $17 billion package included $10 billion in emergency funds to allow veterans to go to outside doctors if they live more than 40 miles from a VA facility or are forced to wait more than 14 days for an appointment.

In 2015, Miller was highly critical of Obama's VA budget, which asked for authority to reallocate money from the $10 billion program. Miller wanted the program to give veterans more care in private clinics. "If there's going to be any reallocation, it's going to be to further improve and strengthen the program itself and not address other unspecified needs," Miller said. He worked to get a bipartisan veteran suicide-prevention bill through the House. In March 2015, he accused the VA under new Secretary Robert McDonald of a lack of transparency and of impeding his committee's investigations. VA officials had challenged the need for some of the information he had requested, Miller said.

Miller also serves on the Select Intelligence Committee. He sought to take over as chairman following the retirement of Michigan's Mike Rogers in 2014. But Speaker John Boehner gave the gavel to his ally Devin Nunes of California, even though Miller had more national security experience.

At home, Miller faced a rematch in 2002 with decorated combat pilot Michael Francisco, an also-ran in the 2001 Republican primary, who criticized his lack of military experience. Miller won 64%-36%. Democrats have run only token challengers against him. In the Spring of 2015, he voiced public interest in running for the open senate seat in 2016. After other candidates announced and Miller did some polling, he dropped his interest.

SECOND DISTRICT

Gwen Graham (D)

Elected 2014, 1st term; b. Jan. 31, 1963, Miami Lakes; U. of North Carolina, Chapel Hill, B.A. 1984, American U., J.D. 1988; Episocopalian; married (Stephen Hurm); 3 children.

Professional Career: Legal counsel, Leon County schools, 2006-13.

DC Office: 1213 LHOB, 20515, 202-225-5235; Fax: 202-225-5615; Website: graham.house.gov.

State Offices: Panama City, 850-785-0812; Tallahassee, 850-891-8610.

Committees: *Agriculture:* Biotechnology, Horticulture & Research; General Farm Commodities & Risk Management. *Armed Services:* Oversight & Investigations; Seapower & Projection Forces; Tactical Air & Land Forces.

Election Results

2014 general	Gwen Graham (D)	126,096	(51%)	$3,663,383	$321,635	$2,462,833
	Steve Southerland (R)	123,262	(49%)	$2,971,841	$1,717,601	$4,155,510
2014 primary	Gwen Graham (D)	unopposed				

Population		Race and Ethnicity		Income	
Total:	710,751	White	65.6%	Median income:	$42,184
Urban:	59.3%	Black	24.2%		*(354 of 435)*
Suburban:	14.7%	Latino	5.5%	Under $50,000	57.2%
Rural:	25.9%	Asian	1.7%	$50,000-$99,999:	27.5%
Land area:	7,310	Two races	2.4%	$100,000-$199,999:	12.6%
Pop/sq. mi.:	97.2	White Ethnic	18.5%	$200,000 or more:	2.7%
Born in state:	55.9%			Poverty Rate	20.9%
		Education			
Age Groups		H.S. grad or less:	43.5%	**Work**	
Under 18:	19.8%	Some college:	30.3%	White collar:	36.2%
18 to 34:	28.5%	College degree, 4 yr.:	15.4%	Blue collar:	47.5%
35 to 64:	37.9%	Post-grad study:	10.8%	Sales and service:	16.3%
Over 64:	13.8%			Govt. workers:	27.2%
		Military			
		Veterans/active duty:	10.7%		

Eastern Panhandle: Tallahassee, Panama City

Tallahassee, Florida's capital, is situated in the middle of swampy lowlands 15 miles from the Gulf of Mexico. It's the opposite of the image people have of the typical booming Florida city, with endless miles of beach or a Magic Kingdom beckoning vacationing families. So how did it become the capital

Voter Turnout	
2013 Total Citizen 18+	552,243
2014 House Turnout	249,780
2014 Turnout as % CVAP	45.2%
2012 Turnout as % CVAP	62%

of the nation's third-largest state, as of December 2014? It was selected in the 19th century, when Florida's then-modest population lived mostly along the state's northern tier, placing Tallahassee, more or less, at its center of gravity. Ralph Waldo Emerson, visiting Tallahassee at the time, called it a "grotesque place, rapidly settled by public officers, land speculators, and desperadoes." Until fairly recently, it remained little more than a Spanish-mossed county seat with a pair of universities and a handsome Creole capitol, which was built in 1845 and preserved opposite its 1977 skyscraper replacement.

Since the 1980s, it has spread out and become a middling-sized city, with a tight-knit though sometimes fractious political and legal elite, bringing a taste of newly urbanized Florida to the state's north. In March 2015, the University of Toronto's Martin Prosperity Institute released a study that found Tallahassee the most segregated city in the United States in terms of economics, education and occupation. Tallahassee has not yet attained the critical mass of Sacramento, Austin, or Albany, but perhaps it is on its way. In 2014, WalletHub rated the city among the most afford-

able places to retire in the nation. There is certainly plenty of room for physical growth. The countryside around Tallahassee is still distinctly Dixie and is more reminiscent of southern Georgia than of southern Florida: The landscape is marked by cotton fields, soft pine stands, catfish farms, and small towns with big churches. A young Ray Charles grew up in tiny Greenville, on the northern bor-

2012 Presidential Vote		
Mitt Romney (R)	178,894	(52%)
Barack Obama (D)	158,651	(47%)
2008 Presidential Vote		
John McCain (R)	179,368	(52%)
Barack Obama (D)	162,346	(47%)
Cook Partisan Voting Index:	R+6	

der of the state; he began to take his first steps toward launching a revolution in music—and race relations—after hearing boogie woogie played at Mr. Wiley Pit's Red Wing Cafe in Greenville.

The 2nd Congressional District of Florida is centered in Tallahassee and extends along the Gulf Coast from west of Panama City and east to the Steinhatchee River, which empties into Deadman Bay off the Gulf. On its north end, it shares borders with Alabama and Georgia. Economic growth is spreading south from Tallahassee into Wakulla County. The opening of an airport in 2010 near Panama City, the first new international airport in the United States in more than a decade, spurred development of what already was a popular spring break destination along the state's pretty and underappreciated northwest beaches. This part of Florida had retained one of the highest percentages of native Floridians. But that is changing. In 2014, Panama City was the 19th fastest-growing metro area in the nation.

Historically, this was Democratic country. The area went for Jimmy Carter by 11 percentage points in 1980 and by 24 points in 1976, and it is still the most Democratic part of northern Florida. A large share of Tallahassee-area jobs are in city and state government, which has been a source of discomfort for the state's Republican rulers. The city's African-American population grew from about 25% in the 1990s to 35% in 2010. The district's liberal bent is also fueled by its two big universities, Florida State and Florida A&M. Tallahassee and Leon County have remarkably stable voting patterns, giving the Democratic presidential nominee 60-62% of the vote in four straight elections. Beyond Leon County, which casts about 40% of the district's votes, partisan performance is polarized. Gadsden County, the state's only black-majority county, is heavily Democratic, while the Gulf beach areas lately have voted strongly Republican. When most state officials in 2014 resisted same-sex marriage, Gadsden County kept its doors open to those couples. Barack Obama lost this district, 52%-47%, in his two presidential bids.

In most contests, the Gulf beach areas outvote the inland counties. But the margin is close enough to make this a swing district.

Gwen Graham (D)

First-time candidate Gwen Graham, in her narrow 2014 victory, benefited from the name recognition and popularity of her father Bob Graham, the state's former governor and senator. She was helped by a moderate political message that distanced herself from national Democrats. She was one of two Democrats who defeated an incumbent House Republican that year.

Graham was born in Miami Lakes and spent most of her childhood in the state capital of Tallahassee after her father was elected to the Florida House. After earning her law degree from American University in 1988, she worked on energy and environmental issues. With the birth of her first child in 1990, Graham left the private sector to care for her family for 13 years. She then returned to practice law in Tallahassee and to serve as director of employee relations for the Leon County School District.

Democrats were eager to take back the 2nd District, which Steve Southerland captured in the tea party wave of 2010. Southerland made the Democratic House Majority PAC's top 10 list of political targets, and Graham was included in her party's "Jumpstart" program to cultivate candidates in swing districts. Democrats have a voter registration edge in the district, but Republicans have done well there in presidential contests.

Graham touted herself as a centrist voice, determined to fix the "dysfunctional mess" in Washington. The onetime stay-at-home mom frequently derided members of Congress for "acting like children" in their inability to get along and get things done. While national Democratic-leaning groups such as EMILY's List backed Graham, she pointedly separated herself from the national party establishment. She said she disagreed with several aspects of the Affordable Care Act and distanced herself when asked if she would support Rep. Nancy Pelosi for minority leader, saying, "There needs to be new leadership on both sides of the aisle."

Graham reached out to liberals by making gender an issue. She pointed to a Southerland invitation to a men-only fundraising dinner that included the admonishment, "Tell the Mrs. not to wait up because the after-dinner whiskey and cigars will be smooth & the issues to discuss are many." Southerland responded to criticism by wondering aloud if Graham had ever been to a "lingerie shower." Graham was endorsed by the Blue Dog PAC and several labor unions, including the National Education Association. She won with 50.5% of the vote to Southerland's 49.3%. In the district's customary pattern, she took Leon County with 65%, but lost Bay (Panama City Beach), the second-largest county, with only 30%. She won 73% in Gadsden, the third-largest county. Graham outspent Southerland, $3.7 million to $2.9 million. Each national party added more than those amounts for its candidate—huge sums in a mostly rural district. She told supporters on Election Night, "I'm going to make sure that Congress is not dysfunctional, but is willing to work together."

In her first House vote, she kept her campaign pledge, as one of four Democrats voting for someone other than Pelosi in the vote for House Speaker. She cast her ballot for Tennessee Rep. Jim Cooper, a leading critic of the first woman Speaker. But party leaders did not hold that against her in giving Graham seats on Agriculture and Armed Services. She led House freshmen in cosponsoring bills that drew bipartisan support, and found herself drawing fire from both sides. When she voted for Republicans bills, such as support for the

Keystone XL pipeline and a roll-back of tighter Wall Street regulations, rank-and-file Democrats complained on social media. Republicans quickly listed her among their top campaign targets for 2016. Graham turned down suggestions that she should run for the Senate. The court-demanded redistricting changes appeared to leave her with no obvious base for reelection in 2016.

THIRD DISTRICT

Ted Yoho (R)

Elected 2012, 2nd term; b. April 13, 1955, Minneapolis, MN; Broward Comm. Coll., A.A. 1977, U. of FL, B.S.A. 1979, D.V.M. 1983; Catholic; married (Carolyn); 3 children.

Professional Career: Veterinarian, 1983-present

DC Office: 511 CHOB, 20515, 202-225-5744; Fax: 202-225-3973; Website: yoho.house.gov.

State Offices: Gainesville, 352-505-0838; Orange Park, 904-276-9626.

Committees: *Agriculture:* Horticulture, Research, Biotechnology & Foreign Agriculture; Livestock, Rural Development, & Credit; Nutrition. *Foreign Affairs:* Middle East & North Africa; Terrorism, Nonproliferation & Trade.

Group Ratings

	ADA	ACLU	AFL-CIO	LCV	ITI	COC	HAFA	ACU	CFG	FRC
2014	10%	22%	–	0%	60%	64%	72%	80%	69%	88%
2013	10%	C	10%	4%	C	54%	C	80%	76%	C

National Journal Ratings

	2013 LIB	—	2013 CONS
Economic	3%	—	96%
Social	0%	—	87%
Foreign	52%	—	48%
Composite	21%	—	79%

Key Votes of the 113th Congress

1. Sandy storm spending	N	5. Medical Marijuana	Y
2. Violence Against Women Act	N	6. Farm Bill	Y
3. Guantanamo Bay Detainees	N	7. Afghanistan Combat	Y
4. Abortion 20-week ban	Y	8. NSA Phone Data Collection	Y

9. Syrian Rebels Training	N
10. Keystone pipeline	Y
11. Immigration Exec. Action	Y
12. Bipartisan budget deal	Y

Election Results

2014 general	Ted Yoho (R) 148,691	(65%)	$791,907	$4,202	$218,743
	Marihelen Wheeler (D)............... 73,910	(32%)	$80,418		
	Howard Lawson (I) 6,208	(3%)			
2014 primary	Ted Yoho (R) 37,486	(79%)			
	Jake Rush (R)............................... 9,739	(21%)			

Prior winning percentage: 2012 (65%)

Population		Race and Ethnicity		Income	
Total:	707,112	White	73.7%	Median income:	$43,169
Urban:	32.4%	Black	13.1%		*(342 of 435)*
Suburban:	25.9%	Latino	8.1%	Under $50,000	56.3%
Rural:	41.7%	Asian	2.8%	$50,000-$99,999:	28.9%
Land area:	6,539	Two races	1.8%	$100,000-$199,999:	11.8%
Pop/sq. mi.:	108.1	White Ethnic	25.8%	$200,000 or more:	3.0%
Born in state:	50.5%			Poverty Rate	18.7%
		Education			
Age Groups		H.S. grad or less:	43.5%	**Work**	
Under 18:	21.4%	Some college:	32.7%	White collar:	34.1%
18 to 34:	25.5%	College degree, 4 yr.:	14.2%	Blue collar:	45.5%
35 to 64:	36.8%	Post-grad study:	9.5%	Sales and service:	20.4%
Over 64:	16.3%			Govt. workers:	21.1%
		Military			
		Veterans/active duty:	12.7%		

North Florida: Gainesville, Jacksonville Suburbs

The flat grasslands of central Florida, once bypassed by southbound tourists heading for the coastal resorts and cities, have become a prime growth area in this high-growth state. Central Florida's economy once depended on farming, on tourists getting off the interstate, and on state institutions, most

Voter Turnout	
2013 Total Citizen 18+	534,909
2014 House Turnout	228,809
2014 Turnout as % CVAP	42.8%
2012 Turnout as % CVAP	62.3%

notably the University of Florida in Gainesville. Then retirees began settling in places like the bluegrass country around Ocala, one of America's prime horse-breeding grounds, and the area began to share the development boom, growing by 19% from 2000 to 2007. But then the recession hit the region hard, with Ocala's unemployment rate soaring past 14% in 2010 and home foreclosures reaching record levels. By 2014, Ocala-based Marion County led the state in economic growth and foreclosures had declined, but the housing market remained soft. In March 2015, CSX announced plans to develop a major freight rail hub in Ocala. Farther north, the Suwannee River slowly winds its way from the Okefenokee Swamp in Georgia to the Gulf of Mexico. At one point, it cuts through limestone bedrock, creating a rare Florida whitewater rapid. North-central Florida is more like Georgia and the Deep South than the rest of the state, with voting patterns that have only recently solidified for the Republicans and that have partly offset the movement toward Democrats in South Florida.

The 3rd Congressional District of Florida is something of a "leftovers" district—portions of the state that were unassigned after the minority-majority 5th District was drawn to the east, and compact districts were carved out of Jacksonville, Tallahassee, and the exurbs of Orlando and Tampa. It can be viewed as four roughly evenly populated segments. The first segment consists of the bloc of rural counties north and northwest of Gainesville. This is the sleepiest part of the district, punctuated by small towns like White Springs, Lake City, and Raiford (home to a big state prison).

The second segment is centered on Orange Park and Middleburg, growing suburbs in Clay County southwest of Jacksonville. The third includes some parts of Gainesville and Alachua County. In 2012, Gainesville gained a brief flurry of attention as the "pirate capital" of the U.S. for the number of illegal music downloads that have taken place there. The fourth segment is made up of the western

2012 Presidential Vote		
Mitt Romney (R)..................200,965	(62%)
Barack Obama (D) 122,530	(38%)
2008 Presidential Vote		
John McCain (R).................196,557	(59%)
Barack Obama (D) 131,114	(40%)
Cook Partisan Voting Index: R+14		

suburbs of Ocala and the coastal counties that extend west to mostly undeveloped beaches on the Gulf of Mexico. Of the four, only the Gainesville segment is close to a swing area. The remainder of the district is solidly Republican.

Ted Yoho (R)

Republican Ted Yoho gained what probably will remain his proverbial 15 minutes of fame when he emerged as an unlikely candidate for Speaker in January 2015. He received some media buzz and got two votes—one of which was his own. His election to the House in 2012 likewise was unexpected, when he ran an outsider campaign with jabs at Washington politicians to defeat a veteran Republican incumbent.

Yoho was born in Minneapolis, the fifth of six sons. He moved with his family at age 11 to South Florida, where he graduated from high school. A star offensive tackle, Yoho landed a football scholarship at Florence State University (now the University of North Alabama), but quickly returned to Florida. He married his high school sweetheart, Carolyn, and decided to become a veterinarian. The couple moved to Gainesville, where he got a bachelor's degree in animal science at the University of Florida, then graduated from its veterinary college. Yoho built a successful large-animal veterinarian practice.

He first became interested in politics during President Bill Clinton's impeachment drama. Over time, he said he got fed up with politicians that either couldn't or wouldn't fix "the mess" in Washington that many of them helped to create. He sold his veterinary practice and launched his campaign. "One political consultant told us this race would be a good 'practice run,'" he recalled with amusement.

In the 2012 Republican primary, Yoho was not nearly as well-known as two of his opponents, 12-term Rep. Cliff Stearns and state Sen. Steve Oelrich of Gainesville. Stearns, 71, had a huge cash advantage and had not been considered in jeopardy, but redistricting gave him a district that was more conservative. He committed a few errors, including focusing more of his attention on Oelrich. With just one paid employee—his 24-year-old campaign manager—Yoho stumped aggressively as a Christian (Roman Catholic) and a conservative. He embraced his tea party backing, and railed against "career politicians." He emphasized to voters his first-hand perspectives in running a successful small business and being on the receiving end of regulations and "garbage legislation" from Washington. Yoho promised that his "moral compass" wouldn't let him be beholden to anyone. He opposed raising taxes, but refused to sign lobbyist and conservative activist Grover Norquist's no-tax pledge on the grounds that a war or other events may leave few alternatives. He said he would serve no more than eight years in the House.

During the primary race, Yoho used humor to show voters that he was a different kind of politician, including a campaign ad showing suited "politicians" feeding from a pig trough and a video about an upcoming fundraiser with a President George W. Bush impersonator. Using $50,000 of his own money, he edged out Stearns by just 875 votes, with 34%; Oelrich trailed with 19%. Moments after Stearns conceded, Yoho celebrated for cheering supporters by emulating the practice of former University of Florida quarterback Tim Tebow of bending on one knee to say a prayer after a big play. He had no trouble in the general election against Democratic businessman J.R. Gaillot, taking 65% of the vote.

On his first day in office in January 2013, Yoho joined a protest by a small group of conservatives who refused to back a second term as House speaker for John Boehner of Ohio. Instead, Yoho cast his vote for Majority Leader Eric Cantor of Virginia. During his first term, he continued to style himself as a tea party leader who was eager to stand up to the political establishment. He advocated the impeachment of President Barack Obama, and said that voting rights should be limited to property owners. When House Republicans were seething after Obama's November 2014 executive order on immigration, Yoho introduced a bill to rescind the president's authority to stop deportations; the president's action, he later said, would open the door to "chain migration" into the United States. When Boehner suggested that the House vote on Yoho's bill as a step to keep the government open, conservative Republicans objected that the speaker's package was not sufficient. As a result, GOP leaders were forced to make additional concessions to scramble for Democratic votes on the omnibus spending bill. In the revision of House rules for the new Congress in January 2015, party leaders rejected Yoho's proposal to require that lawmakers have 72 hours to read a bill prior to its vote. "The American people expect and deserve better from us," he responded.

When a floating group of House conservatives, spurred by outside groups, said they would not vote to give Boehner a third term as speaker, Yoho was the first to volunteer as a candidate. He issued a statement, "Enough of career politicians, enough of political gamesmanship, and enough of the lack of leadership in Washington." But he failed to galvanize the opponents to Boehner. Rep. Daniel Webster, another Florida Republican, later emerged and attracted 12 votes as the leading GOP alternative to Boehner. In addition to his own vote, the other Yoho supporter was Rep. Thomas Massie of Kentucky. In January 2015, *GQ* magazine listed Yoho among "America's 20 craziest politicians." Tea party advocates continued to embrace him. He appeared secure in his district, at least until he honors his term-limit pledge.

FOURTH DISTRICT

Ander Crenshaw (R)

Elected 2000, 8th term; b. Sept. 1, 1944, Jacksonville; U. of GA, B.A. 1966, U. of FL, J.D. 1969; Episcopalian; married (Kitty); 2 children.

Elected Office: FL House, 1972-78; FL Senate, 1986-94.

Professional Career: Investment banker, 1980-2000.

DC Office: 2161 RHOB, 20515, 202-225-2501; Fax: 202-225-2504; Website: crenshaw.house.gov.

State Offices: Jacksonville, 904-598-0481.

Committees: *Appropriations:* Defense; Financial Services & General Government (Chmn); State, Foreign Operations & Related Programs.

Group Ratings

	ADA	ACLU	AFL-CIO	LCV	ITI	COC	HAFA	ACU	CFG	FRC
2014	0%	0%	–	3%	100%	93%	43%	56%	49%	88%
2013	0%	C	21%	0%	C	85%	C	52%	52%	C

National Journal Ratings

	2013 LIB	—	2013 CONS
Economic	44%	—	56%
Social	27%	—	71%
Foreign	24%	—	68%
Composite	33%	—	67%

Key Votes of the 113th Congress

1. Sandy storm spending	NV	5. Medical Marijuana	N	9. Syrian Rebels Training Y
2. Violence Against Women Act	Y	6. Farm Bill	Y	10. Keystone pipeline Y
3. Guantanamo Bay Detainees	N	7. Afghanistan Combat	N	11. Immigration Exec. Action Y
4. Abortion 20-week ban	Y	8. NSA Phone Data Collection	N	12. Bipartisan budget deal Y

Election Results

2014 general	Ander Crenshaw (R)	177,887	(78%)	$1,642,951	$2,162
	Paula Moser-Bartlett (I)	35,663	(16%)	$20,637	
	Gary Koniz (I)	13,690	(6%)	$15,000	
2014 primary	Ander Crenshaw (R)	38,613	(71%)		
	Ryman Shoaf (R)	15,817	(29%)		

Prior winning percentages: 2012 (76%), 2010 (77%), 2008 (65%), 2006 (70%), 2004 (100%), 2002 (100%), 2000 (67%)

Population		Race and Ethnicity		Income	
Total:	705,007	White	71.6%	Median income:	$55,461
Urban:	76.6%	Black	13.2%		*(161 of 435)*
Suburban:	17.8%	Latino	8.0%	Under $50,000	44.6%
Rural:	5.6%	Asian	4.5%	$50,000-$99,999:	32.9%
Land area:	1,344	Two races	2.3%	$100,000-$199,999:	17.7%
Pop/sq. mi.:	524.7	White Ethnic	24.8%	$200,000 or more:	4.8%
Born in state:	46.4%			Poverty Rate	12.2%
		Education			
Age Groups		H.S. grad or less:	35.7%	**Work**	
Under 18:	21.0%	Some college:	33.9%	White collar:	39.4%
18 to 34:	24.7%	College degree, 4 yr.:	20.7%	Blue collar:	43.3%
35 to 64:	40.5%	Post-grad study:	9.8%	Sales and service:	17.3%
Over 64:	13.8%				
		Military		Govt. workers:	11.9%
		Veterans/active duty:	13.6%		

Jacksonville Suburbs

With a metropolitan area of 1.3 million people, Jacksonville has outgrown its reputation as Florida's overlooked city. Not long ago, it was considered a backwater, dominated by insurance companies and smelly paper mills. Probably its biggest claim to fame was producing Southern rock band Lynyrd

Voter Turnout	
2013 Total Citizen 18+	528,498
2014 House Turnout	227,253
2014 Turnout as % CVAP	43.0%
2012 Turnout as % CVAP	64.8%

Skynyrd, named for the high school gym teacher (Leonard Skinner) in charge of enforcing the school policy against boys wearing their hair long. Jacksonville is now the largest city by land area in the contiguous 48 states, boasting a National Football League franchise, bold new skyscrapers looming above the St. Johns River, and a shopping mall that overshadows tiny shotgun houses. Wide freeways sidestep primeval wetlands on their way to huge beach-front subdivisions.

Jacksonville's harbor has grown as a destination for cargo and passenger operations. With Naval Station Mayport and Naval Air Station Jacksonville—two of the three largest metro-area employers—the city has a significant military employment base. Shipbuilding and repair provides more than 10,000 jobs in the area. Shrewd marketing has lured big-name private-sector companies as well. The city is the headquarters of railway giant CSX and also hosts major operations such as UPS and Bank of America. Residents held their breath when supermarket giant Winn-Dixie was purchased by Bi-Lo in 2012, but exhaled when Bi-Lo announced the combined headquarters would remain in Jacksonville. Business leaders are working to make the area into the "Silicon Valley of Logistics"—building on its land, air, and sea

2012 Presidential Vote		
Mitt Romney (R)................225,500	(66%)
Barack Obama (D) 111,079	(33%)
2008 Presidential Vote		
John McCain (R)................221,720	(66%)
Barack Obama (D) 114,412	(34%)
Cook Partisan Voting Index: R+19		

transportation facilities—and they have dredged the port for larger ships, which is crucial to the city's long-term growth. Jacksonville ended 2014 with unemployment slightly below the state and national rates. Job growth was especially strong in construction. Mayport is scheduled to receive in 2016 a new class of littoral combat ships, which will be faster and carry more weapons but with a smaller crew. In addition, Navy pilots are planning to fly overseas unmanned Triton drone systems from their computers at the naval air station. The air station has plans to expand several of its facilities in Jacksonville.

The 2012 redistricting excised almost all of the rural counties from the 4th District. Today, it includes most of Jacksonville, minus its African-American neighborhoods, which are in the 5th District. Overall, 86% of the district's population is in Duval County, although it also includes all of rapidly growing Nassau County to the north, where a massive 24,000-acre planned community in Yulee is scheduled between I-95 and state road A1A. The boosterish Jacksonville civic culture and significant military presence make the 4th a pro-business, pro-military, and pro-Republican district. Both John McCain and Mitt Romney received 66%, the second-best GOP district in Florida.

Ander Crenshaw (R)

Ander Crenshaw, a Republican first elected in 2000, is a low-profile conservative who works quietly on behalf of his district as a senior member of the Appropriations Committee and an ally of GOP leaders. When *The Hill* newspaper once asked him what he considered his biggest political achievement, he answered wryly: "Having several little political achievements."

Crenshaw grew up in Jacksonville, where his family roots date to the early 20th century. The son of a lawyer, he attended the University of Georgia on a basketball scholarship, then graduated from the University of Florida law school. His wife's father, Claude Kirk, was a one-term Republican governor of Florida in the 1960s. He has been in and out of government for more than four decades, including three unsuccessful runs for state-wide office. Crenshaw was elected to the state House in 1972 and served for six years, before running unsuccessfully for secretary of state. He then became an investment banker. In 1980, he ran for the Senate and finished third of six in the 1980 Republican primary, which was won by Paula Hawkins. From 1986 until 1993 he served in the state Senate and in 1992 became the first Republican state Senate president in 118 years. He ran for governor in 1994 but finished fourth in the primary, far behind Jeb Bush, who narrowly lost to Lawton Chiles in November. Crenshaw's opportunity to run for the House came in 2000, when Republican Rep. Tillie Fowler announced that she would honor her promise to serve only four terms. Crenshaw was promptly endorsed by local Republican leaders, which discouraged several potential candidates. He won the primary 70%-30% and the general election 67%-31%. He has won reelection easily since, though he drew some flak from local Republicans for supporting the 2008 financial industry rescue.

In the House, Crenshaw is a reliable conservative who was among the first to join the Tea Party Caucus in 2010. His service on Appropriations has made him a bit more centrist on foreign policy issues, particularly foreign aid. He and Washington state Democrat Adam Smith in 2011 launched the Congressional Caucus on Effective Foreign Assistance to make the case that such aid is highly useful and needs to be spared deep cuts. He chaired the Legislative Branch Appropriations Subcommittee in 2011-12, and held fast against repeated Democratic pleas to find $61 million to fix the aging Capitol dome, citing budget constraints. In 2013, he took over as chairman of the Financial Services and General Government Subcommittee at Appropriations. His annual spending bill enacted in December 2014 made cuts in Internal Revenue Service funding.

On Appropriations, his top priorities are the district's large military and veterans' facilities. In 2008, he slipped a provision into the military construction spending bill telling the

Navy to start work on converting Mayport to a nuclear base. The Navy announced in February 2012 that it was suspending plans to move a Norfolk-based aircraft carrier to Mayport, but promised to shift a three-ship amphibious group to the area. Crenshaw also pushed successfully for new veterans' cemeteries in Jacksonville and Sarasota, and he fought for expanded disability coverage for Gulf War veterans. After eight years of work, the House in December 2014 passed Crenshaw's bill to provide savings accounts for people caring for family members with disabilities. He came up with the idea after discussions with family friends who have a son with Down syndrome.

Crenshaw made a bid for the senior Republican seat on the Budget Committee, contributing nearly $1 million to other Republicans in the 2006 election to pay his dues. But the slot went to Paul Ryan of Wisconsin. He was not helped by his role in an earlier lobbying scandal that targeted Majority Leader Tom DeLay of Texas: Crenshaw had traveled with DeLay on a trip to South Korea in 2001, which had been paid for by lobbyists close to DeLay. Crenshaw also was on the wrong side of the pitched battle for DeLay's successor; he backed then-Rep. Roy Blunt of Missouri for the job, but John Boehner of Ohio emerged the winner. Still, Crenshaw has remained in the good graces of leadership as he has exercised growing influence as an appropriator.

FIFTH DISTRICT

Corrine Brown (D)

Elected 1992, 12th term; b. Nov. 11, 1946, Jacksonville; FL A&M, B.S. 1969, M.S. 1971, U. of FL, Ed.S. 1974; Baptist; divorced; 1 child.

Elected Office: FL House, 1982-92.

Professional Career: Prof., Edward Waters Col., FL Comm. Col., U. of FL, 1977-82; Guidance counselor, 1982-92.

DC Office: 2111 RHOB, 20515, 202-225-0123; Fax: 202-225-2256; Website: corrinebrown.house.gov.

State Offices: Gainesville, 352-376-6476; Jacksonville, 904-354-1652; Orlando, 407-872-2208.

Committees: *Transportation & Infrastructure:* Coast Guard & Maritime Transportation; Highways & Transit; Railroads, Pipelines & Hazardous Materials. *Veterans' Affairs* (RMM).

Group Ratings

	ADA	ACLU	AFL-CIO	LCV	ITI	COC	HAFA	ACU	CFG	FRC
2014	80%	77%	–	89%	80%	46%	11%	8%	6%	0%
2013	75%	C	100%	93%	C	38%	C	21%	11%	C

National Journal Ratings

	2013 LIB	—	2013 CONS
Economic	85%	—	14%
Social	85%	—	13%
Foreign	68%	—	31%
Composite	80%	—	20%

Key Votes of the 113th Congress

1. Sandy storm spending	Y	5. Medical Marijuana	Y
2. Violence Against Women Act	Y	6. Farm Bill	N
3. Guantanamo Bay Detainees	Y	7. Afghanistan Combat	N
4. Abortion 20-week ban	N	8. NSA Phone Data Collection	N

9. Syrian Rebels Training	Y
10. Keystone pipeline	N
11. Immigration Exec. Action	N
12. Bipartisan budget deal	NV

Election Results

2014 general	Corrine Brown (D) 112,340	(65%)	$607,418
	Glo Smith (R) 59,237	(35%)	$134,123
2014 primary	Corrine Brown (D) ....unopposed		

Prior winning percentages: 2012 (71%), 2010 (63%), 2008 (100%), 2006 (100%), 2004 (100%), 2002 (59%), 2000 (58%), 1998 (55%), 1996 (61%), 1994 (58%), 1992 (59%)

Population		Race and Ethnicity		Income	
Total:	729,368	Black	51.8%	Median income:	$33,024
Urban:	73.2%	White	31.1%		*(426 of 435)*
Suburban:	21.5%	Latino	12.3%	Under $50,000	67.9%
Rural:	5.2%	Asian	2.1%	$50,000-$99,999:	23.4%
Land area:	1,327	Two races	1.8%	$100,000-$199,999:	7.9%
Pop/sq. mi.:	549.7	White Ethnic	11.8%	$200,000 or more:	0.9%
Born in state:	55.7%			Poverty Rate	28.0%
		Education			
Age Groups		H.S. grad or less:	52.8%	**Work**	
Under 18:	25.3%	Some college:	30.3%	White collar:	25.6%
18 to 34:	25.9%	College degree, 4 yr.:	11.7%	Blue collar:	53.1%
35 to 64:	37.0%	Post-grad study:	5.2%	Sales and service:	21.3%
Over 64:	11.8%				
		Military		Govt. workers:	11.7%
		Veterans/active duty:	9.9%		

Northern Florida metro areas: Downtown Jacksonville and Orlando

Before the Civil War, most of Florida was still an uncharted watery wilderness, festooned with exotic greenery, inhabited by unusual animals, a part of the United States so far out of the experience of most Americans as to seem foreign. As late as 1940, Florida had the smallest population of any

Voter Turnout	
2013 Total Citizen 18+	503,577
2014 House Turnout	171,577
2014 Turnout as % CVAP	34.1%
2012 Turnout as % CVAP	59.7%

Southern state, and most of the people here lived in classic Dixie rural counties with small courthouse towns, where civic affairs were run by the richest white men, and African Americans lived in poorly constructed, unpainted shotgun shacks propped up on blocks, with little money and no vote. This was a land of swamps, lakes and orange groves, and of author Marjorie Kinnan Rawlings' Cross Creek, where she wrote the great children's classic *The Yearling*. The broad St. Johns River, one of the few North American rivers that flows (if only sluggishly) north, meanders through orange-grove country to the port of Jacksonville, which was for many years Florida's largest city. Proposals to deepen the shipping channel in the river to permit larger ships into the port of Jacksonville have drawn opposition, including from groups concerned about environmental damage. But in January 2015, the St. Johns Riverkeeper group dropped its opposition, and joined with the port community and the city to support the dredging, with agreement by all groups to abandon a dam on a tributary in nearby Putnam County.

The 5th Congressional District is a lengthy ribbon that stretches more than 140 miles from Jacksonville to Orlando, and cuts across much of this swampy terrain to connect various African-American enclaves throughout north and central Florida. The district follows the St. Johns River upstream from Jacksonville's city center to Palatka, originally founded as a (failed) utopian experiment in rehabilitating petty criminals, before jogging over to the African-American precincts in Gainesville and then down to Orlando. Along the way it crosses the I-4 "Dead Zone," known for its high number of automobile accidents and believed to have been built over a cemetery for victims of yellow fever in the 1800s. It reaches out to pluck additional minority and Democratic voters from parts of Sanford.

While roughly 79 percent of the district's residents are located in either Duval or Orange counties, its population is not wholly urban. The 5th takes in smaller black settlements, such as lettuce-producing Zellwood, and Eatonville, a town depicted in the stories of Zora Neale Hurston, a preeminent novelist and folklorist. In time, the relatively unpopulated, lake-filled portions of the district may become Florida's next development

2012 Presidential Vote		
Barack Obama (D)	210,615	(73%)
Mitt Romney (R)	74,805	(26%)
2008 Presidential Vote		
Barack Obama (D)	213,779	(73%)
John McCain (R)	77,017	(26%)
Cook Partisan Voting Index: D+21		

frontier. But in recent years it has struggled along with the rest of Florida: Orlando went from being the 13th strongest economy among U.S. metropolitan areas in 2007 to 52nd in 2012, according to Policom Corp. The Gallup-Healthways Well-Being Index in 2011 rated the 5th District 434 out of 436 for the overall well-being of its residents. The district was only tweaked during the 2012 redistricting. But the redistricting order by the Florida Supreme Court could result in the complete dismantling of the black-majority district, which in turn would have far-reaching consequences for six Republican-held districts, plus the predominantly Hispanic 9th District in the Orlando area, all of which border the 5th. It is solidly Democratic.

Corrine Brown (D)

Corrine Brown, a Democrat first elected in 1992, focuses on constituents in her committee work, and uses the slogan "Corrine Delivers" in her reelection campaigns. Her ability to provide money and other help to her financially ailing district has kept her in office, despite a string of controversial comments and ethics issues.

She grew up in Jacksonville, taught at a community college, was a guidance counselor, and in 1982, was elected to the Florida House. When she ran for the newly created black-majority district in the 1992 Democratic primary, she faced white talk-radio host Andy Johnson, who called himself "the blackest candidate in the race." But her political base in Jacksonville carried Brown to a lead of 43%-31% in the first round of balloting, and 64%-36% in the runoff. She easily prevailed in the general election 59%-41%.

Brown has compiled a liberal record on most issues. In her district, many voters work at military bases. She tends to support high defense spending and argues that the military can be a source of opportunity. She added an amendment to the fiscal year 2013 defense authorization bill to have the Army Corps of Engineers improve a section of the Port of Jacksonville to bolster ship navigation there. On the Veterans' Affairs Committee, she has sought additional veterans' cemeteries for Florida, which is the home to more veterans than any other state except California.

In 2013, Brown was eligible to become the Veterans' Affairs' Committee's top Democrat, but opted to let Representative Mike Michaud of Maine take the job so she could keep her chairmanship of the Transportation and Infrastructure Railroads Subcommittee. When Michaud left Congress to run unsuccessfully for governor, she sought the post two years later with the respect for seniority that the Congressional Black Caucus traditionally has shown. But her ascension was controversial. Veterans groups preferred Rep. Tim Walz of Minnesota, who served 24 years in a senior position in the Army National Guard. They pointed to Brown's record of missing hearings as evidence she was not committed to addressing problems that landed the Veterans Affairs Department in the national spotlight in 2014. At a January 2014 committee hearing, she described the VA system as "one of the best systems in the United States," which generated extensive criticism. "The fact that they're appointing Corrine Brown shows the House Democratic leadership is not serious about reforming and fixing the VA," said Dan Caldwell, CEO of Concerned Veterans for America, according to the *Washington Times*. "If they were, they would've put stronger members in leadership positions on that committee, but they didn't." In taking the job, Brown promised to work to implement the sweeping overhaul that became law in 2014, with a special emphasis on the nation's aging female veteran population.

On Transportation and Infrastructure, Brown worked on legislation to strengthen security at ports. Her long-standing project has been a high-speed rail line from Tampa to Orlando and Miami. In 2012, she accused her Florida GOP neighbor John Mica, the panel's chairman, of being on "a holy jihad" to "destroy" Amtrak. In 2014, she praised the opening of the first train station in downtown Orlando.

Brown's outspoken, partisan views have caused her problems at times. In 2004, she criticized Bush administration representatives at a briefing on the Haiti crisis, saying that they were "a bunch of white men" who "all look alike to me." After Republican Henry Bonilla of Texas called her on her remarks, Brown apologized, but she continued to say she thought White House policy on Haiti was racist. In a dispute in 2008 over the seating of convention delegates from Florida, Brown, who had endorsed Hillary Rodham Clinton for president, said, "If we are not seated, then nobody is going to be seated." The problem was resolved after Barack Obama became the certain nominee. In 2015, she criticized as "hidden racism" the large opposition in the Senate to the confirmation of Loretta Lynch as attorney general. In *Washingtonian* magazine's surveys of Capitol Hill staffers, she has twice been named the "least eloquent" House member.

Brown has survived spirited campaign opposition, resulting largely from personal issues. Her most difficult contests came amid charges of questionable ethical conduct. In June of 1998, *The St. Petersburg Times* reported that Brown's daughter had been given a $50,000 Lexus by agents of African millionaire Foutanga Sissoko. He had been imprisoned in Miami on federal charges of paying an illegal gratuity to a Customs Service officer, and Brown worked furiously to get him released, lobbying Attorney General Janet Reno to have him deported to Africa to continue his humanitarian work. The newspaper also reported that Brown kept a jazz singer on her payroll as a "congressional outreach specialist." Brown reacted with fury, filing a criminal contempt charge against the *Times* reporters with the Capitol Police, claiming they "accosted" her and their questions made her cry. The charges went nowhere. A subsequent investigation into the Sissoko matter by the House Ethics Committee found that Brown "demonstrated, at the least, poor judgment and created substantial concerns regarding both the appearance of impropriety and the reputation of the House." The panel dropped the case because, committee members said, they were unable to question key witnesses, including Sissoko.

But the story had political repercussions for Brown. The Republicans in 1998 found a credible challenger in Bill Randall, an African American and a former General Motors manager who had become a minister. He opposed abortion rights and favored local control of schools and government vouchers for private school tuition. He held Brown to a 55%-45% win.

Two years later, she faced a vigorous reelection challenge from Republican Jennifer Carroll, a retired 20-year Navy officer who criticized Brown for an inability to work with people. She outspent Brown. The incumbent called Carroll "a zero" and "a Republican puppet." With a strong grass-roots organization, Brown won 58%-42%. In 2002, Carroll again challenged Brown. But local Republicans were not enthusiastic about her candidacy in the heavily Democratic district and Brown prevailed, 59%-41%, again with huge leads in Jacksonville and Orlando. She has been unopposed or won with ease since. In 2010, former Florida GOP Chairman Tom Slade shared with *The Florida Times-Union* his advice for any would-be challengers: "Don't do it. Go find a tree and beat your head against it. You may find the result more pleasurable." Brown's problems have extended beyond the GOP: A Washington-based fundraising firm filed suit against her in 2011, claiming she owed $45,000 in unpaid bills.

Despite the ease with which she has been reelected, Brown in 2011 joined Florida Republican Mario Diaz-Balart in filing a legal challenge to the state's voter-approved Fair District amendment. That amendment to the Florida constitution, approved in a 2010 referendum, called for congressional districts to be drawn more compactly and to be impartial with regard to political party. The lawmakers said it would have a negative impact on minority voters and the Voting Rights Act guarantee to maximize minority districts. The suit angered Brown's Florida Democratic colleagues and longtime allies such as the NAACP who backed the referendum and called her challenge selfish.

In a separate state-court challenge to Florida's redrawn districts, Circuit Court judge Terry Lewis agreed that two districts were problematic: Brown's and the 10th District represented by Republican Daniel Webster. State lawmakers tinkered with the districts prior to the 2014 election; voting rights groups complained the changes were superficial. Lewis disagreed, saying that Brown's new district was "less serpentine and visually more compact." The new map, which removes Sanford from the district, was scheduled to become effective in 2016. In November 2014, Brown defeated Glo Smith, a female African-American conservative and social services organizer, with 65 percent of the vote. In July 2015, the state Supreme Court ordered major changes in the district extending it east-west from Jacksonville to Tallahassee instead of north-south to Orlando. Brown strongly objected, and filed court challenges. She faced the prospect of a serious primary challenge.

SIXTH DISTRICT

Ron DeSantis (R)

Elected 2012, 2nd term; b. Sept. 14, 1978, Jacksonville; Yale U., B.A. 2001, Harvard U., J.D. 2004; Catholic; married (Casey Black DeSantis).

Military Career: Navy, 2004-10; Navy Reserves, 2010-present.

Professional Career: Practicing atty. 2004-present.

DC Office: 308 CHOB, 20515, 202-225-2706; Fax: 202-226-6299; Website: desantis.house.gov.

State Offices: Port Orange, 386-756-9798; St. Augustine, 904-827-1101.

Committees: *Foreign Affairs:* Middle East & North Africa; Western Hemisphere. *Judiciary:* Constitution & Civil Justice (VChmn); Courts, Intellectual Property & the Internet. *Oversight & Government Reform:* Health Care, Benefits & Administrative Rules; National Security (Chmn).

Group Ratings

	ADA	ACLU	AFL-CIO	LCV	ITI	COC	HAFA	ACU	CFG	FRC
2014	5%	11%	–	0%	80%	64%	89%	100%	90%	88%
2013	5%	C	10%	7%	C	77%	C	100%	99%	C

National Journal Ratings

	2013 LIB	—	2013 CONS
Economic	0%	—	98%
Social	16%	—	74%
Foreign	24%	—	68%
Composite	17%	—	83%

Key Votes of the 113th Congress

1. Sandy storm spending	N	5. Medical Marijuana	Y	9. Syrian Rebels Training	N
2. Violence Against Women Act	N	6. Farm Bill	N	10. Keystone pipeline	Y
3. Guantanamo Bay Detainees	N	7. Afghanistan Combat	N	11. Immigration Exec. Action	Y
4. Abortion 20-week ban	Y	8. NSA Phone Data Collection	Y	12. Bipartisan budget deal	N

Election Results

2014 general	Ron DeSantis (R)	166,254	(63%)	$429,688	$1,296
	David Cox (D)	99,563	(37%)	$37,892	
2014 primary	Ron DeSantis (R)	unopposed			

Prior winning percentage: 2012 (57%)

Population		Race and Ethnicity		Income	
Total:	722,788	White	80.3%	Median income:	$44,505
Urban:	27.4%	Black	8.9%		*(327 of 435)*
Suburban:	62.2%	Latino	7.1%	Under $50,000	54.8%
Rural:	10.4%	Asian	1.6%	$50,000-$99,999:	27.7%
Land area:	2,509	Two races	1.4%	$100,000-$199,999:	13.3%
Pop/sq. mi.:	288.1	White Ethnic	30.1%	$200,000 or more:	4.2%
Born in state:	35.9%			Poverty Rate	15.0%
		Education			
Age Groups		H.S. grad or less:	39.7%	**Work**	
Under 18:	18.8%	Some college:	33.2%	White collar:	35.9%
18 to 34:	18.3%	College degree, 4 yr.:	17.1%	Blue collar:	45.4%
35 to 64:	39.8%	Post-grad study:	10.0%	Sales and service:	18.7%
Over 64:	23.1%				
		Military		Govt. workers:	11.2%
		Veterans/active duty:	12.9%		

Northeast Florida: Daytona Beach

In 1513, Spanish explorer Juan Ponce de León headed to the New World, hoping to discover the Fountain of Youth. Instead, he found Ponte Vedra Beach, located just south of modern day Jacksonville. A few decades later, Spanish colonists founded St. Augustine, the oldest permanent European settlement in North America—42 years older than Jamestown

Virginia, and 55 years older than the Plymouth colony in Massachusetts. New Smyrna Beach was established in 1768 in an attempt by the British to colonize Florida with Greek settlers, whom they believed to be ideally suited to the warm climate. They were not, however, well suited for the brutal

Voter Turnout	
2013 Total Citizen 18+	569,844
2014 House Turnout	265,817
2014 Turnout as % CVAP	46.6%
2012 Turnout as % CVAP	65.4%

wilderness conditions, and by 1777, many had abandoned the colony, walking and swimming the 75 miles north to St. Augustine. The area was a popular hideout for rum-runners during Prohibition, and today has become a popular vacation spot. Daytona's beaches have been attracting sun-seekers for decades, although the city is best known for the Daytona 500 held each February at Daytona International Speedway.

Further inland, northeast Florida still retains a taste of "Old Florida." DeLand has a small-town atmosphere centered on Stetson University, whose mascot is, appropriately, the Hatters, after the famous hat-maker who helped build the school that bears his name. Still further from the ocean is orange-growing territory, dotted with small towns like Interlachen and Crescent City. In tiny Pierson, known as the "Fern Capital of the World," 54 percent of the population was Latino, according to the 2010 census; many perform the labor-intensive work of trimming the fern fronds.

St. Johns and Flagler counties, the two coastal counties between Jacksonville and Daytona Beach, were filled with cattle ranches a few decades ago. But St. Johns grew by 54% between 2000 and 2010, while Flagler County nearly doubled. These growth rates slowed dramatically during the recession, when Flagler's unemployment hit 16%. In 2012, the Deltona-Daytona-Ormond Beach metropolitan area's economy was ranked 311th strongest out of 366 metro areas nationwide by Policom Corp. Since then, there have been signs of a rebound: Northrop Grumman and German-based 2G Cenergy Powers built new plants in the area, and tourists returned to the beaches. In 2014, St. Johns was the second fastest-growing county in the state and the wealthiest, according to the Census Bureau. Housing permits are ticking up, foreclosure rates are dropping, and there are serious attempts to develop a 150-acre international spaceport north of Cape Canaveral. For the 450th anniversary of St. Augustine in 2015, King Felipe of Spain scheduled a visit.

The 6th District covers the Atlantic coast for more than 100 miles, more than any other district in Florida, from Ponte Vedra Beach to the Canaveral National Seashore, and it takes in beachfront communities like Port Orange, New Smyrna Beach, and Edgewater. About 52% of the population is concentrated in Volusia County, 42% in the northern beach-

2012 Presidential Vote		
Mitt Romney (R)................209,140	(58%)
Barack Obama (D) 149,955	(41%)
2008 Presidential Vote		
John McCain (R)................192,811	(54%)
Barack Obama (D) 163,657	(46%)
Cook Partisan Voting Index:　R+9		

front communities, with the balance in the rural, inland areas. This area leans strongly Republican; in the past two presidential elections, GOP nominees John McCain and Mitt Romney won easily here.

Ron DeSantis (R)

Republican Ron DeSantis, who was first elected in 2012, embraces the tea party and has sought to reduce the federal government's "size, scope, and influence." He has managed to find a balance between collaborating with the most conservative Republicans and winning committee leadership assignments from the party establishment.

DeSantis grew up in northeast Florida, where his father installed television ratings devices for Nielsen. A talented baseball player, DeSantis played on a team from Dunedin that made the final four of the Little League World Series in 1991. He went on to captain the squad at Yale, where he majored in history. To help pay for his studies, he held a variety of jobs, including collecting trash, moving furniture, and coaching baseball clinics. He earned his law degree at Harvard, and became a judge advocate general in the Navy. His military service helped shape his views on national security, including his skepticism of nation-building. While there are a lot of "good people" in Iraq, he said "getting involved in guerilla war doesn't play to our strengths." He has remained a lieutenant commander in the Naval Reserve.

DeSantis ran for office when the new 6th District unexpectedly had no incumbent following the 2012 redistricting. Instead, veteran Rep. John Mica, who had represented much of the area, ran and won against freshman Rep. Sandy Adams in the new 7th District. DeSantis had written a book, *Dreams From Our Founding Fathers*, whose title is a play on the title President Barack Obama chose for his memoir, *Dreams From My Father*. He argued in the book that Obama and like-minded Democrats "have charted a course that is alien to our Republic's philosophical foundations."

Touting his military experience and strong conservative views, DeSantis easily led his six rivals in the August primary, with 39 percent of the vote. He credited old-fashioned retail politics for the win. "I started in February with zero percent name ID, and we'd go door-to-door on a Saturday and Sunday," he said. He also won endorsements from such tea party favorites as former U.N. Ambassador John Bolton and Sen. Mike Lee of Utah, and had a pronounced fundraising advantage.

In the general election, Democrat Heather Beaven, a fellow Navy veteran who had lost two years earlier to Mica, focused on fixing Florida's hard-hit economy by embracing entrepreneurship and renewable energy. In this Republican district. DeSantis won, 57%-43%.

DeSantis did not specify his term limits, but said he needed only a few—six terms, at most—to reach his goals. "I want to go and make it more of a citizen-leader body, rather than professionals who are there for years," he said. To cut back on career politicians, DeSantis said that lawmakers must be willing to eliminate incentives, such as pensions.

In the House, DeSantis bonded with conservative Republicans. Unlike several other junior Republicans from Florida, he voted in January 2015 to give John Boehner another term as Speaker, despite pressure from constituents to oppose him. "You've got to have pieces in place and you've got to have good candidates step forward," he responded. He was one of nine founding members of the Freedom Caucus to promote "liberty, safety and prosperity." He was awarded with positions of responsibility. DeSantis became chairman of the National Security Subcommittee of the Oversight and Government Reform Committee, where he pledged to "hold our national security agencies accountable on behalf of the American people." He also took over as vice chairman of the House Judiciary Subcommittee on the Constitution and Civil Justice. But facing pressure to toe the line for the party by Majority Whip Steve Scalise, he quit as a member of the Republican Whip team. In 2014, he was reelected with 63 percent of the vote against lightly funded Democrat David Cox.

After Marco Rubio said that he would not seek reelection to the Senate in 2016, DeSantis became the first significant Republican candidate to step forward. "I look forward to offering reforms based on limited government principles that will make our country stronger and more prosperous," he said in announcing his candidacy in May 2015. His initial plan was to run as the conservative alternative, with extensive support from national advocacy groups, such as the Club for Growth and Senate Conservatives Fund. He faced potentially steep challenges in what was expected to be a wide-open GOP primary, including his low name ID outside of his district, and that Florida Republicans were far more diverse than his constituency. Republicans should have no trouble holding his House seat.

SEVENTH DISTRICT

John Mica (R)

Elected 1992, 12th term; b. Jan. 27, 1943, Binghamton, NY; Miami-Dade Comm. Col., A.A. 1965, U. of FL, B.A. 1967; Episcopalian; married (Patricia); 2 children.

Elected Office: FL House, 1976-80.

Professional Career: Exec. dir., Palm Beach & Orange Cnty. Govt. Charter Study Commissions, 1970-74; Pres., MK Development, 1975-92; A.A., U.S. Sen. Paula Hawkins, 1981-85; Partner, Mica, Dudinsky & Assoc., 1985-92.

DC Office: 2187 RHOB, 20515, 202-225-4035; Fax: 202-226-0821; Website: mica.house.gov.

State Offices: Deltona, 386-860-1499; Maitland, 407-657-8080; Oviedo, 407-366-0833.

Committees: *Oversight & Government Reform:* National Security; Transportation & Public Assets (Chmn). *Transportation & Infrastructure:* Economic Development, Public Buildings & Emergency Management; Highways & Transit; Railroads, Pipelines & Hazardous Materials.

Group Ratings

	ADA	ACLU	AFL-CIO	LCV	ITI	COC	HAFA	ACU	CFG	FRC
2014	5%	0%	–	3%	100%	86%	72%	80%	75%	100%
2013	5%	C	10%	0%	C	77%	C	92%	71%	C

National Journal Ratings

	2013 LIB	—	2013 CONS
Economic	10%	—	88%
Social	13%	—	84%
Foreign	48%	—	51%
Composite	25%	—	75%

Key Votes of the 113th Congress

1. Sandy storm spending	N	5. Medical Marijuana	N	9. Syrian Rebels Training	Y
2. Violence Against Women Act	N	6. Farm Bill	Y	10. Keystone pipeline	Y
3. Guantanamo Bay Detainees	N	7. Afghanistan Combat	N	11. Immigration Exec. Action	Y
4. Abortion 20-week ban	Y	8. NSA Phone Data Collection	Y	12. Bipartisan budget deal	Y

Election Results

2014 general	John Mica (R)	144,474	(64%)	$727,556
	Wesley Neuman (D)	73,011	(32%)	$52,375
	Al Krulick (I)	9,679	(4%)	$15,955
2014 primary	John Mica (R)	32,084	(72%)	
	David Smith (R)	8,316	(19%)	
	Don Oehlrich (R)	2,285	(5%)	

Prior winning percentages: 2012 (59%), 2010 (69%), 2008 (62%), 2006 (63%), 2004 (100%), 2002 (60%), 2000 (63%), 1998 (100%), 1996 (62%), 1994 (73%), 1992 (56%)

Population		Race and Ethnicity		Income	
Total:	716,811	White	66.0%	Median income:	$52,197
Urban:	28.6%	Latino	19.2%		(202 of 435)
Suburban:	69.5%	Black	9.4%	Under $50,000	47.4%
Rural:	1.9%	Asian	3.6%	$50,000-$99,999:	32.3%
Land area:	855	Two races	1.5%	$100,000-$199,999:	16.3%
Pop/sq. mi.:	838.2	White Ethnic	25.9%	$200,000 or more:	4.0%
Born in state:	37.1%			Poverty Rate	13.7%
		Education			
Age Groups		H.S. grad or less:	32.8%	Work	
Under 18:	21.0%	Some college:	32.2%	White collar:	39.8%
18 to 34:	25.9%	College degree, 4 yr.:	24.0%	Blue collar:	46.2%
35 to 64:	39.0%	Post-grad study:	11.0%	Sales and service:	14.0%
Over 64:	14.1%				
		Military		Govt. workers:	12.1%
		Veterans/active duty:	8.8%		

Northern Orlando Suburbs: Seminole, Orange

For much of the 19th century, central Florida was a sparsely populated region at the southern frontier of the state. The native Timucua tribe had been driven to extinction as the result of war and disease, and only a few towns of any size dotted the state's interior. Steamboats traveled up and down the St.

Voter Turnout	
2013 Total Citizen 18+	537,259
2014 House Turnout	227,164
2014 Turnout as % CVAP	42.3%
2012 Turnout as % CVAP	61.5%

Johns River to supply small trading centers that sprang up at the end of the navigable portions of that waterway on Lake Monroe and Lake Jesup (known for its many alligators) in what is now Seminole County. This state of affairs largely persisted until 1971, when Walt Disney opened Disney World in neighboring Orange County, setting off startling growth and development in the region. Other theme parks followed, tourism flourished, and Seminole County became one of the primary beneficiaries of that explosive development. Its population shot up from 55,000 in 1960 to 422,718 in 2010. The once-quiet county became a collection of largely high-end suburbs with a median income of $59,000, the third-highest in the state. Like much of Florida, the area was hit hard by the housing collapse and the recession. But it has been rebounding. Unemployment fell to 4.5 percent in December 2014. In February 2015, work began on a $2.3 billion reconstruction of a 21-mile stretch of Interstate 4 in Seminole and Orange counties, which will add express lanes through Orlando.

2012 Presidential Vote		
Mitt Romney (R).................172,542	(52%)
Barack Obama (D) 155,489	(47%)

2008 Presidential Vote		
John McCain (R).................167,059	(50%)
Barack Obama (D) 164,563	(49%)

Cook Partisan Voting Index:　R+4

The 7th Congressional District of Florida was formed in 2012 by combining the inland portions of the former 7th and 24th districts. The 7th is anchored in Seminole County, which supplies about 60 percent of the population. There, the district takes in tony suburbs such as Winter Springs, Forest City, and Longwood, which briefly made national news in 1982 when an unusually rainy winter resulted in a sudden, unexplained invasion of small toads. Longwood's other major claim to fame, a 3,500-year-old pond cypress named "The Senator," the oldest in the world, was tragically burned down in 2012 by a methamphetamine user who was doing drugs near the tree. The district takes in the gated neighborhood where Hispanic crime-watch volunteer George Zimmerman touched off a national outcry in early 2012 after he fatally shot Trayvon Martin, an unarmed black teenager who was walking home from a convenience store. A jury found Zimmerman not guilty of second degree murder, and the Justice Department in February 2015 found insufficient evidence that he had violated Martin's civil rights.

The 7th crosses over into Volusia County to the northeast to take in the city of Deltona and surrounding areas. Deltona grew rapidly until the collapse of the housing market brought on a raft of foreclosures and slowed its growth to near zero in 2010. The remainder of the district comes from the northern edge of Orange County, including towns such as Maitland, Lockhart, and Winter Park. This is Republican territory, though not overwhelmingly so; presidential nominee Mitt Romney received 52 percent of the vote here in 2012, and John McCain led Barack Obama by 1 percentage point in 2008.

John Mica (R)

John Mica, a Republican first elected in 1992, is a colorful conservative who is unafraid of confrontation. As chairman of the Transportation and Infrastructure Committee, he battled the Obama administration to a partial shutdown of the Federal Aviation Administration and failed to persuade House Republican leaders to spend extra money on a major highway bill. After failing to get a waiver of term limits to continue as chairman, he now chairs an oversight subcommittee that deals with transportation issues.

Mica grew up in south Florida, in a bipartisan political family originally from upstate New York. His younger brother, Dan Mica, was a Democratic congressman from Palm Beach County from 1979 to 1988, when he lost a primary for the Senate, and another brother, David Mica, worked for Democratic Gov. Lawton Chiles. John Mica made a small fortune in real estate by developing the New Smyrna beachfront. He was elected to the state House in 1976 and served four years. He worked on the staff of Sen. Paula Hawkins, a Republican, from 1981 to 1985, then became a lobbyist. He ran for the House when the district was created after the 1990 census. In the GOP primary, his opponents attacked him as an insider representing special interests, to which Mica responded, "some of the finest folks I've met are lobbyists." (His daughter D'Anne eventually became one, taking over as director of government and political affairs at the National Ocean Industries Association in 2011.) He won the primary 53%-34%. In the general election, against a liberal Democrat, he won 56%-44%.

Mica has been a consistent conservative but also a brash reformer. After taking office, he led the charge to abolish House select committees, which was approved in 1995 when Republicans won House control. In 1995, Mica became chairman of Government Reform's Civil Service Subcommittee, and in that role helped pass the White House Accountability Act of 1996, imposing on the White House the laws that restrict the private sector. Mica's chief legislative front has been at Transportation and Infrastructure, where he has long advocated greater private-sector investment in transportation. He has been a passionate critic of Amtrak and the Transportation Security Administration, the latter of which he has described as a "Soviet-style bureaucracy."

Mica worked to build more airplane runways across the nation and to improve security in the post-September 11 era. When the Senate passed a bill that federalized airport screeners, Mica and other House Republicans sought to preserve some role for the private sector. They reached a deal to allow airports to opt out of the federal system after three years if they met certain standards. In March 2015, the Orlando airport board rejected a proposal to privatize its passenger security. Mica's bill to permit commercial airline pilots to carry guns in the cockpit was initially opposed by the Bush administration, and airlines worried about the risks. But the House voted 310-113 to allow pilots to carry guns. The Senate agreed 87-6, and President George W. Bush bowed to popular will.

At home, Mica has begun to see the fulfillment of his long-time dream of a commuter rail system in central Florida. The SunRail project will extend 61 miles north-south through Orlando. The first half of the system opened in May 2014, and initially averaged about 3,200 daily passengers once the introductory free service was abandoned. *The New York Times* said the federal government ranked the project as "one of the least cost-effective mass transit efforts in the nation." Critics contended that the chief beneficiary has been the CSX rail system, which has used the line for its freight service. Mica insists that SunRail has been far more cost-effective than expanding current highways. As of February 2015, the federal government had spent $230 million on the project.

In 2011, Mica turned his attention to the Federal Aviation Administration. The Obama administration and labor groups reacted angrily to a provision Mica added to the agency's authorization bill making it harder for unions to become certified as official representatives of aviation and rail workers. Then, in what he called "a tool to try to motivate some action" on the labor issue, Mica attached a provision to a routine FAA funding bill that would cut subsidies for airline service to 13 rural airports, including one in then-Senate Majority Leader Harry Reid's home state of Nevada. The resulting standoff led to a nearly two-week shutdown of the agency, furloughing thousands of federal employees and bringing construction projects to a halt. A chastened Mica told *The Washington Post* he was stunned at the vehemence of the Democrats' counterattack. "Quite honestly, we did not expect that," he said.

Mica then prepared for renewal of the surface transportation bill. He predicted that the measure would go beyond highways and transit programs to make "significant reforms" in rail and maritime programs that he said were not performing well. But House Democrats accused him of shutting them out of talks, and he wrangled with Democratic Sen. Barbara Boxer, who chaired the Senate Environment and Public Works Committee. Despite his efforts to expand funding, House members failed to agree, which weakened the chamber in negotiations with the Senate, whose bill had higher spending levels. The two chambers agreed in 2012 on a two-year bill, which Mica had earlier criticized as too short.

Mica was term-limited as chairman in 2012 under House Republican rules, but he sought a waiver. He dropped his bid when it became clear the GOP leadership would not support him. He failed in 2015 to become chairman of the Oversight and Government Reform Committee. Instead, he was tapped to chair that panel's Subcommittee on Transportation and Public Assets, the fifth subcommittee that he chaired in two decades.

Mica has been a sharp critic of the Obama administration. In 2010, he pinned the BP oil spill in the Gulf of Mexico on federal regulators. "I'm not going to point fingers at BP, the private industry, when it's the government's responsibility to set standards to do the inspections," he said. The same year, he blasted Obama's call for investing $50 billion in infrastructure projects, saying it was no substitute for not enacting a full, six-year transportation bill.

At home, Mica faced what appeared to be a serious challenge in 2002 from Democrat Wayne Hogan, a Jacksonville trial lawyer who spent $4.4 million of his own money on his campaign. Hogan, part of the legal team that won Florida's settlement with the tobacco industry, said he would fight for "ordinary families against powerful interests." Mica responded that Hogan was trying to buy the seat and that his pledge not to take contributions from political action committees was like "Rockefeller saying he won't take food stamps." Mica won comfortably, 60%-40%. Since then, he has not faced a serious Democratic challenge.

In 2012, Mica waged a member-on-member primary against Republican freshman Rep. Sandy Adams, rather than run in the new 6th District, which included much of his previous district. Mica had more money and won the often nasty contest, 61%-39%. His influence probably has peaked, but Mica still seemed to enjoy the stage.

EIGHTH DISTRICT

Bill Posey (R)

Elected 2008, 4th term; b. Dec. 18, 1947, Washington, D.C.; Brevard Comm. Col., A.A. 1969; Methodist; married (Katie Ingram); 2 children.

Elected Office: Rockledge City Cncl., 1976-86; FL House, 1992-2000; FL Senate, 2000-08.

Professional Career: McDonnell Douglas Astronautics Co., 1966-69; Crawford & Co./Gay & Taylor, 1970-74; Founder, Posey & Co. Realtors, 1974-present.

DC Office: 120 CHOB, 20515, 202-225-3671; Fax: 202-225-3516; Website: posey.house.gov.

State Offices: Melbourne, 321-632-1776.

Committees: *Financial Services:* Financial Institutions & Consumer Credit; Monetary Policy & Trade. *Science, Space, & Technology:* Oversight; Space.

Group Ratings

	ADA	ACLU	AFL-CIO	LCV	ITI	COC	HAFA	ACU	CFG	FRC
2014	15%	11%	–	0%	60%	64%	68%	92%	86%	100%
2013	10%	C	14%	4%	C	54%	C	88%	86%	C

National Journal Ratings

	2013 LIB	—	2013 CONS
Economic	18%	—	80%
Social	0%	—	87%
Foreign	51%	—	49%
Composite	26%	—	75%

Key Votes of the 113th Congress

1. Sandy storm spending	N	5. Medical Marijuana	N	9. Syrian Rebels Training	N
2. Violence Against Women Act	N	6. Farm Bill	N	10. Keystone pipeline	Y
3. Guantanamo Bay Detainees	N	7. Afghanistan Combat	Y	11. Immigration Exec. Action	Y
4. Abortion 20-week ban	Y	8. NSA Phone Data Collection	Y	12. Bipartisan budget deal	N

Election Results

2014 general	Bill Posey (R)	180,728	(66%)	$1,042,652	$1,023
	Gabriel Rothblatt (D)	93,724	(34%)	$106,402	$204,096
2014 primary	Bill Posey (R)	unopposed			

Prior winning percentages: 2012 (59%), 2010 (65%), 2008 (53%)

Population		Race and Ethnicity		Income	
Total:	704,053	White	76.8%	Median income:	$45,570
Urban:	65.0%	Latino	9.5%		*(308 of 435)*
Suburban:	30.6%	Black	9.4%	Under $50,000	53.9%
Rural:	4.4%	Asian	1.6%	$50,000-$99,999:	29.8%
Land area:	1,402	Two races	2.4%	$100,000-$199,999:	13.2%
Pop/sq. mi.:	502.3	White Ethnic	33.7%	$200,000 or more:	3.1%
Born in state:	33.8%			Poverty Rate	14.8%
		Education			
Age Groups		H.S. grad or less:	38.6%	**Work**	
Under 18:	18.7%	Some college:	35.0%	White collar:	34.3%
18 to 34:	17.6%	College degree, 4 yr.:	16.6%	Blue collar:	46.6%
35 to 64:	40.3%	Post-grad study:	9.8%	Sales and service:	19.0%
Over 64:	23.5%			Govt. workers:	13.4%
		Military			
		Veterans/active duty:	13.9%		

Space Coast/Northern Treasure Coast: Melbourne

When Cape Canaveral was chosen in the 1940s as the nation's rocket testing site, only 20,000 people lived in all of Brevard County, which stretches along 63 miles of the coast north and south of the cape. It was a quiet, winter-vacation spot that relied on fishing and citrus and its location on the sunny Atlantic Coast. Rockets could be launched eastward so that spent parts fell into the ocean. In 1948, the Brooklyn Dodgers established their spring training home in Vero Beach, 60 miles south of Canaveral in Indian River County. Brevard County had 557,000 people

Voter Turnout	
2013 Total Citizen 18+	552,300
2014 House Turnout	274,513
2014 Turnout as % CVAP	49.7%
2012 Turnout as % CVAP	66.6%

in 2014, although the Dodgers have moved their spring home to Arizona. The Kennedy Space Center attracts 1.5 million visitors annually, which is fewer than in the days when space flights captured the public's imagination. The county is mostly coastal communities and has no major city center. But it has plenty of strip shopping centers along highways, with a white-collar, service economy, knitted together by interest in the space program.

Uncertainty has grown since the retirement of the space shuttle fleet, a move that has slashed thousands of aerospace jobs. Local officials have sought alternatives. The high concentration of individuals affiliated with the space program has led to a spurt in technological entrepreneurship in sectors as varied as aviation, synthetic materials, and clean energy. The high-tech Harris Corp.—the only Fortune 500 company based in Brevard—has more than 6,600 employees, including scientists and engineers. Northrup Grumman has expanded its Manned Aircraft Design Center of Excellence in Melbourne. Proximity to Disney World has spawned growth in the cruise line business, and Port Canaveral in 2014 was the third-largest passenger port in the world, with its 3.9 million annual cruisers trailing only Miami and Port Everglades in south Florida. Eco-tourism is another promising avenue for growth. The Merritt Island National Wildlife Refuge and Canaveral National Seashore increasingly draw wildlife aficionados to view their vast array of flora and fauna. Further inland is the 6,194-acre St. Johns National Wildlife Refuge, established in 1971 to protect the dusky seaside sparrow, now extinct. At Jungle Adventures Nature Animal Park, near the town of Christmas, visitors can hold baby alligators and gawk at "Swampy," the 200-foot-long concrete alligator that guards the park. All of these divergent efforts seem to have paid off. Unemployment on the Space Coast was close to the national rate in 2014.

The 8th Congressional District of Florida starts at the northern edge of Brevard County, just north of the county seat of Titusville. It continues along the Atlantic Coast, encompassing all of Brevard and Indian River counties, and makes a nip in the east-

2012 Presidential Vote
Mitt Romney (R)................206,074   (57%)
Barack Obama (D) 153,138   (42%)

2008 Presidential Vote
John McCain (R)................200,870   (55%)
Barack Obama (D) 160,150   (44%)

Cook Partisan Voting Index: R+9

ern end of Orange County. About 80 percent of the population resides in Brevard. Among the bigger towns are Cocoa Beach, Melbourne, Palm Bay, and Vero Beach. The district has become safely Republican. John McCain won 55% of the vote here in 2008, while Mitt Romney captured 57% in 2012.

Bill Posey (R)

Bill Posey, a Republican first elected in 2008, has taken on serious work in Congress, despite some early splashes of publicity. *Florida Today* columnist Matt Reed wrote in 2011 that Posey "does his homework and seems motivated by an almost wonkish devotion to fiscal responsibility."

Posey was born in Washington, D.C., and moved several times because of his father's work in the aircraft business. His family landed in Brevard County in 1956, and after graduating from high school, Posey took a job with McDonnell Douglas Astronautics at the Kennedy Space Center. He worked on the Apollo 11 Launch Team that in 1969 sent the first men to the moon, and he attended Brevard Community College at night. After Apollo 11, Posey was laid off and went into real estate. He founded and remained president of Posey & Co. Realtors in 1974. Posey has been an accomplished stock car racer. He said he first got behind the wheel at the track at age 14. But he has taken a break from racing since an accident at an Orlando speedway in 2004 left him with spinal fractures.

Posey was the first member of his family to register as a Republican, a decision inadvertently inspired by a college professor who lauded the Democratic Party's championing of inflation and deficit spending. "He literally was trying to convince the class that inflation was good because you could buy the things you wanted now and finance them later with cheaper money," Posey recalled. He was elected to the Rockledge City Council in 1976 and served until 1986. Six years later, he won a seat in the Florida House of Representatives, where he authored legislation that set new standards for state government accountability. He wrote a book entitled *Activity Based Total Accountability* detailing his work on the issue. He served in the state House until 2000, when term limits forced him to move on. He then won a close state Senate race.

After seven-term GOP Rep. Dave Weldon announced his retirement in early 2008, Posey ran for the seat. He got Weldon's endorsement and that of Florida GOP Chairman Jim Greer, who called for the party to unite behind Posey. Veteran state Rep. Stan Mayfield, who had also announced his candidacy, fell in line, withdrew from the race, and endorsed Posey. Florida Democrats were unable to find a strong candidate, and Posey became the clear favorite to win the general election. He won the GOP primary with 77% of the vote and faced Democrat Stephen Blythe, a Melbourne family physician, in the general. Posey made government accountability and immigration reform the central themes of his campaign. It was an amiable contest. The candidates expressed mutual admiration and said they would vote for each other if they could not vote for themselves. Posey outspent Blythe by almost 9-to-1 and won 53%-42%.

Once in Washington, Posey quickly attracted attention when he filed a bill requiring future presidential candidates to file a birth certificate. That came at the height of the 2009 "birther" flap over whether President Barack Obama was born overseas, and it made Posey the target of considerable venom in the liberal blogosphere. He contended his bill had nothing to do with Obama, but even some of his GOP colleagues publicly expressed their distaste for the proposal. He joined Republicans in opposing Obama's major legislative initiatives, but subsequently showed a willingness to break with his party. He voted with Democrats on extending unemployment benefits and joined a bipartisan bill to double the one-year waiting period before lawmakers who leave their seats can lobby ex-colleagues. His skepticism about the war in Afghanistan made him practically a centrist on foreign policy: In 2011, he was among 16 House Republicans to vote in support of a phased withdrawal of troops. He also could be a hard-liner, as when he joined fellow Florida Republican Jeff Miller in opposing a 2010 resolution to wish Iranians a prosperous new year.

Posey has continued his quest for more accountability in government. On the Financial Services Committee, he got the results of every committee vote posted on its website within two days. He also pushed a proposal to require a 72-hour waiting period before legislation can be brought to the House floor, and he introduced another measure to require state governments to submit fiscal accounting reports as a condition of getting federal money. But he drew scorn in 2012 when he grilled a Centers for Disease Control and Prevention official at a hearing to determine if vaccines cause autism—an issue that the scientific community has said has no merit.

In 2013, he was appointed to the Space, Science, and Technology Committee, giving him a more prominent post from which to work on behalf of the Kennedy Space Center and a Space Coast still figuring out how to live with NASA cutbacks. He won praise from the local *Sunshine State News* for using that seat "as a bully pulpit to push private space flight and jab the Obama administration for retreating from space exploration." At a March 2015 committee hearing with Obama's science adviser, John Holdren, Posey noted that the earth warmed during the Ice Age to voice his doubts about the prevalence of climate change. "Just because we're alive now," he said, "the tectonic plate shifts aren't going to stop, the hurricanes [and] tsunamis aren't going to stop, the asteroid strikes aren't going to stop."

Democrats in 2014 thought that they had a credible challenger with Corry Westbrook, who was the legislative director for the National Wildlife Federation. But she was rocked by accusations that she plagiarized Florida Democratic Rep. Patrick Murphy's campaign website. Westbrook withdrew from the campaign and was replaced by weakly funded Gabriel Rothblatt. Posey won, 66%-34%. When the House convened in January 2015, he revived his maverick spirit by voting for fellow Florida Rep. Daniel Webster for speaker, instead of John Boehner.

NINTH DISTRICT

Alan Grayson (D)

Elected 2012, 3rd term; b. March 13, 1958, New York, NY; Harvard U., A.B. 1978, J.D. M.P.P. Ph.D. 1983; Jewish; married (Lolita); 5 children.

Elected Office: U.S. House, 2008-10.

Professional Career: Law clerk, CO Supreme Court, 1983, D.C. Court of Appeals, 1984-85; Practicing atty. 1985-90; Pres., IDT Corp., 1990-91; Partner, Grayson & Kubli, 1991-2008; Writer, commentator, 2011-present.

DC Office: 303 CHOB, 20515, 202-225-9889; Fax: 202-225-9742; Website: grayson.house.gov.

State Offices: Kissimmee, 407-518-4983; Orlando, 407-615-8889.

Committees: *Foreign Affairs:* Middle East & North Africa; Western Hemisphere. *Science, Space, & Technology:* Energy (RMM); Environment; Oversight.

Group Ratings

	ADA	ACLU	AFL-CIO	LCV	ITI	COC	HAFA	ACU	CFG	FRC
2014	90%	72%	–	91%	40%	43%	15%	13%	11%	0%
2013	85%	C	95%	96%	C	25%	C	12%	15%	C

National Journal Ratings

	2013 LIB	—	2013 CONS
Economic	86%	—	14%
Social	69%	—	28%
Foreign	81%	—	18%
Composite	79%	—	21%

Key Votes of the 113th Congress

1. Sandy storm spending	Y	5. Medical Marijuana	Y	9. Syrian Rebels Training	N
2. Violence Against Women Act	Y	6. Farm Bill	N	10. Keystone pipeline	N
3. Guantanamo Bay Detainees	Y	7. Afghanistan Combat	Y	11. Immigration Exec. Action	N
4. Abortion 20-week ban	N	8. NSA Phone Data Collection	Y	12. Bipartisan budget deal	Y

Election Results

2014 general	Alan Grayson (D)	93,850	(54%)	$3,102,601	
	Carol Platt (R)	74,963	(43%)	$439,306	$1,200
	Marko Milakovich (I)	5,060	(3%)		
2014 primary	Alan Grayson (D)	18,641	(74%)		
	Nick Ruiz (D)	6,441	(26%)		

Prior winning percentages: 2012 (63%), 2008 (52%)

Population		Race and Ethnicity		Income	
Total:	768,459	Latino	45.7%	Median income:	$44,995
Urban:	81.4%	White	38.9%		*(321 of 435)*
Suburban:	17.1%	Black	9.4%	Under $50,000	55.5%
Rural:	1.5%	Asian	3.6%	$50,000-$99,999:	31.0%
Land area:	1,875	Two races	1.7%	$100,000-$199,999:	11.5%
Pop/sq. mi.:	409.9	White Ethnic	14.0%	$200,000 or more:	2.0%
Born in state:	28.0%			Poverty Rate	20.6%
		Education			
Age Groups		H.S. grad or less:	45.5%	**Work**	
Under 18:	24.2%	Some college:	30.7%	White collar:	27.6%
18 to 34:	25.8%	College degree, 4 yr.:	16.9%	Blue collar:	52.1%
35 to 64:	38.7%	Post-grad study:	6.8%	Sales and service:	20.3%
Over 64:	11.3%				
		Military		Govt. workers:	9.9%
		Veterans/active duty:	6.8%		

Central Florida: Orlando, Kissimmee

In the earliest editions of *The Almanac of American Politics*, Orange County Florida was typically compared to Orange County California. Both were fast-growing counties located in fast-growing Sunbelt states. Both contained a Walt Disney theme park. Perhaps most importantly for followers of politics,

Voter Turnout	
2013 Total Citizen 18+	438,312
2014 House Turnout	121,204
2014 Turnout as % CVAP	27.7%
2012 Turnout as % CVAP	50.4%

both anchored the emerging conservative Republican politics of their respective states. In every election from 1948 to 1988, the Florida Orange went for the GOP presidential candidate, and in every one of those elections except for three—1948, 1964, and 1976—the margin was at least 25 percentage points. But things began to change here in 1996, when Republican presidential nominee Bob Dole barely won. In the past two elections, the Democrats have been winning the county by around 20 points. The general movement of transplanted suburbanites from the North toward Democrats has played a role. But changing ethnic demographics are driving the shift as well. In the 1980 census, Orlando was 4% Hispanic. By 2010, Hispanics had increased to over 25% of its population. These new arrivals were often of Puerto Rican ancestry and frequently arrived from New York City. The reasons for the migration? The same ones that brought the children of European immigrants out of crowded U.S. cities and into the suburbs in the 1940s and 1950s: A growing economy, better schools, low cost of living, and an escape from urban crime.

Orlando is now the city with the fastest-growing Puerto Rican population in the United States. Places like Meadow Woods and Azalea Park in Orange County, as well as Buenaventura Lakes (known as "BVL" to locals) in neighboring Osceola County, have populations that are upwards of 39% Puerto Rican. One local realtor who specializes in the Puerto Rican home market called BVL "a Puerto Rican Levittown," referring to the developments that sprung up after World War II near New York City and Philadelphia, where the children of turn-of-the-century immigrants made their first moves into suburban life and the American middle class. Businesses increasingly cater to this emerging "Little Puerto Rico." Banco Popular, a Puerto Rico-based bank, opened branches here in 1997. Goya foods located its central Florida distribution center near Meadow Woods. Non-Hispanic companies such as the supermarket chain Publix have also sought to adapt, opening Sabor (Spanish for "taste") stores here, for example. Countless small businesses appealing to the burgeoning Hispanic population line streets as well; small markets move thousands of chickens and plantains a month, and there are car-repair shops, dance clubs, churches, even funeral homes catering to Hispanics.

The 9th Congressional District of Florida represents a bow by Florida Republicans to the emerging political realities of central Florida. Democratic areas were excised from four neighboring districts to create the new 9th, which is 24.7% Puerto Rican and 46% Hispanic overall. Black neighborhoods in Orlando are mostly in the adjoining 5th District that sweeps up to Jacksonville. About half of the population lives in Orange County, another 40% in fast-growing, heavily Hispanic Osceola County, which has quintupled in size since 1980. The balance of the district is in eastern Polk County, where development from the Orlando area is beginning to spill over. The 9th leans strongly Democratic; it gave Barack Obama 60% of the vote in 2008 and 61% in 2012. The planned community of Destiny, which was designed as America's first "eco-sustainable community" with up to 300,000 residents in

2012 Presidential Vote		
Barack Obama (D)	168,348	(61%)
Mitt Romney (R)	103,730	(38%)
2008 Presidential Vote		
Barack Obama (D)	158,329	(60%)
John McCain (R)	102,838	(39%)
Cook Partisan Voting Index:	D+8	

rural areas of Osceola County, was officially declared dead in 2013. The Florida Department of Economic Opportunity identified concerns with "possible urban sprawl, energy inefficient land use patterns, the endangerment of natural resources, and the undermining of agriculture."

Alan Grayson (D)

Democrat Alan Grayson, elected in 2012, rejoined the House the way he left it two years earlier, as one of its most controversial figures. For many in his party, he's an outspoken progressive hero. To conservatives, he's a loud-mouthed demagogue. In either case, he gets attention.

Grayson grew up in the projects in the Bronx borough of New York City. He became interested in politics at an early age. "We had *The New York Times* and the *New York Post* at our doorstep each day," he told *National Journal*. While an undergraduate at Harvard, Grayson took odd jobs as a janitor and a night watchman. He ultimately left Harvard with a bachelor's degree, law degree and a master's in public policy. He worked as a law clerk in Colorado and for the Court of Appeals for the District of Columbia Circuit. At the D.C. court, he dealt with two future Supreme Court justices, Antonin Scalia and Ruth Bader Ginsburg, whose husband Martin Ginsburg asked Grayson to join his law firm. Grayson eventually started a telecommunications firm and became wealthy. He earned notoriety for his legal work during the second Iraq War, taking private defense contractors to court for providing faulty equipment to U.S. soldiers.

He made his first bid for Congress in 2006 but lost in the Democratic primary. In his 2008 run against Republican Rep. Ric Keller, he emphasized his work fighting corrupt contractors. Grayson accused Keller of being the deciding "no" vote on a bill that would have supplied returning war veterans with replacement limbs. One of his ads featured Grayson holding up an artificial leg. With the election of President Barack Obama, 2008 was a strong year for Democrats, and Grayson bested Keller, 52%-48%.

In the House, the pugnacious Grayson called conservative radio host Rush Limbaugh a "has-been hypocrite loser." He became one of the Federal Reserve Board's staunchest critics and joined with GOP Rep. Ron Paul of Texas to get the "Audit the Fed" bill passed. But he overstepped when in a radio interview he referred to a Fed senior adviser as a "K Street whore." Grayson apologized for the remark. During a floor speech on health care, he made the now-infamous comment: "If you get sick, America, the Republican health care plan is this: Die quickly." In 2010, Republican Daniel Webster ousted him 56%-38% in a highly negative campaign, in which Grayson had more than a 3-to-1 spending advantage.

In 2012, Grayson hoped that a more favorable climate for Democrats would help him make a comeback. The Orlando-based 9th District was redrawn to include a larger Hispanic constituency, with Webster's district pushed to the suburbs and made much more Republican. Grayson ran unopposed in the primary. Republicans nominated personal-injury lawyer Todd Long, who had several run-ins with the law and appeared to be an easy opponent for Grayson. Long, who called himself a "constitutional conservative," cast the race in David-versus-Goliath terms and referred to Grayson as a "big bully." Grayson ran an ad saying that Long wanted to dismantle Social Security, and Long appeared at a local Social Security office to dispute the claim. Long called for a 23% national sales tax to replace the income tax, while Grayson promised to protect entitlements. Grayson won handily, 63%-37%.

On his return to the House, Grayson enjoyed raising hell in his own party. He sided with many Republicans in opposing renewal of the Export-Import Bank for "subsidizing foreigners," in making loans to overseas businesses buying U.S. products. In February 2015, he criticized Obama for requesting a "blank check" for the use of military force against the Islamic State in the Mideast. He said that the president's plan to retain troops in Afghanistan "adopted the policy that we are the world's police officer." In his 2014 reelection, he was held to 54% of the vote against real estate agent Carol Platt in his heavily Democratic district, despite outspending his challenger 7-to-1. When centrist Democratic Rep. Patrick Murphy was embraced by many in the party establishment to run for Marco Rubio's Senate seat, Grayson said that he found those reports "annoying." In July 2015, to the dismay of Democratic officials, he launched his challenge against the younger Murphy. He hoped to attract support and funding from liberal groups.

TENTH DISTRICT

Daniel Webster (R)

Elected 2010, 3rd term; b. April 27, 1949, Charleston, WV; GA Inst. of Tech., B.S. 1971; Baptist; married (Sandra Jordan); 6 children.

Elected Office: FL House, 1980-98, speaker, 1996-98; FL Senate, 1998-2008.

Professional Career: Owner, Webster Air Conditioning & Heating.

DC Office: 1039 LHOB, 20515, 202-225-2176; Fax: 202-225-0999; Website: webster.house.gov.

State Offices: Clermont, 352-383-3552; Tavares, 352-383-3552; Winter Garden, 407-654-5705; Winter Haven, 863-453-0273.

Committees: *Transportation & Infrastructure:* Highways & Transit; Railroads, Pipelines & Hazardous Materials; Water Resources & Environment.

Group Ratings

	ADA	ACLU	AFL-CIO	LCV	ITI	COC	HAFA	ACU	CFG	FRC
2014	0%	0%	–	3%	80%	79%	56%	72%	66%	75%
2013	0%	C	20%	4%	C	85%	C	72%	67%	C

National Journal Ratings

	2013 LIB	—	2013 CONS
Economic	27%	—	72%
Social	27%	—	71%
Foreign	43%	—	57%
Composite	33%	—	67%

Key Votes of the 113th Congress

1. Sandy storm spending	N	5. Medical Marijuana	N	9. Syrian Rebels Training	Y
2. Violence Against Women Act	Y	6. Farm Bill	Y	10. Keystone pipeline	Y
3. Guantanamo Bay Detainees	N	7. Afghanistan Combat	N	11. Immigration Exec. Action	Y
4. Abortion 20-week ban	Y	8. NSA Phone Data Collection	N	12. Bipartisan budget deal	N

Election Results

2014 general	Daniel Webster (R)	143,128	(62%)	$941,147
	Michael Patrick McKenna (D)	89,426	(38%)	$33,623
2014 primary	Daniel Webster (R)	unopposed		

Prior winning percentages: 2012 (52%), 2010 (56%)

Population		Race and Ethnicity		Income	
Total:	732,296	White	64.7%	Median income:	$49,060
Urban:	41.0%	Latino	16.2%		*(254 of 435)*
Suburban:	57.6%	Black	11.7%	Under $50,000	50.7%
Rural:	1.4%	Asian	4.9%	$50,000-$99,999:	31.2%
Land area:	991	Two races	1.8%	$100,000-$199,999:	14.0%
Pop/sq. mi.:	739.3	White Ethnic	24.3%	$200,000 or more:	4.0%
Born in state:	36.4%			Poverty Rate	13.5%
		Education			
Age Groups		H.S. grad or less:	39.9%	**Work**	
Under 18:	21.4%	Some college:	29.8%	White collar:	35.9%
18 to 34:	20.9%	College degree, 4 yr.:	21.5%	Blue collar:	48.4%
35 to 64:	40.2%	Post-grad study:	8.8%	Sales and service:	15.7%
Over 64:	17.6%				
		Military		Govt. workers:	9.1%
		Veterans/active duty:	9.2%		

Central Florida: Lake, Downtown Orlando

Who would have supposed 40 years ago that the most popular tourist destination in the world would rise amid the swamps and orange groves of central Florida? The answer: Walt Disney, and just about no one else. In the mid-1960s, Disney looked at the map and decided that the intersection of Interstate 4 and Florida's Turnpike, the "crossroads of Florida," just a few miles southwest of Orlando, was the perfect place for the vast theme park he was planning. The spirit of the place was established by a man who never lived there but created something now taken for granted. Disney conceived the first theme park in Orange County, Calif., in 1955, but he perfected

Voter Turnout	
2013 Total Citizen 18+	531,100
2014 House Turnout	232,574
2014 Turnout as % CVAP	43.8%
2012 Turnout as % CVAP	61.9%

it in the 17,000 acres of Florida swamp that his associates stealthily snapped up and where Walt Disney World opened in 1971. With the invention of the theme park, Disney also pioneered sophisticated communications, utility, and waste-disposal methods—all out of sight and underground. Disney World is not just an engineering marvel. It required close to 60,000 "cast members" (employees) with know-how and earnest cheerfulness to entertain its 18.5 million visitors in 2013, a six percent annual increase. The number of workers is believed to be the largest in the world for a company at a single site.

Disney is hardly the only site that has made Orlando one of the world's great tourist destinations. Other popular theme parks here include Sea World and Universal Studios; Cape Canaveral is less than 40 miles away. The high-tech economy also has moved into Greater Orlando. Defense contractor Lockheed Martin has a "mission system and training" facility southwest of the city, with nearly 7,000 employees. Continuing growth—of the downtown skyline and in the expanding metropolitan region—has spurred what may be uphill efforts to control the sprawl and congestion in one of the nation's booming areas. Amid the growth, Orlando has been the least economically segregated major metro area in the nation.

In the 10th Congressional District of Florida, the most populous jurisdiction is Orange County, with much of southeastern and southwestern Orlando and most of the enormous Disney complex. Another quarter of the district lives past Lake Apopka, in northern Lake County, mostly in little market towns like Mount Dora and Eustis. Around here, turtles, alligators, and river otters go about their lives underneath cypress trees draped with Spanish moss, and life seems still untouched by the booming metro area. Nearby is Leesburg, where rock star Ozzy Osbourne's guitarist Randy Rhoads was killed in a plane crash in 1982 following a botched stunt. The remainder of the district is in northern Polk County

and southern Lake County, one of the newest frontiers in the urbanization of interior Florida. Economic growth and the housing market in Lake County suffered in the recession and bottomed out in 2012, with modest recent improvement in housing starts. Saudi Arabian investors have financed a huge new community called Villa City.

2012 Presidential Vote		
Mitt Romney (R)................175,112		(54%)
Barack Obama (D) 148,899		(46%)
2008 Presidential Vote		
John McCain (R)................164,732		(52%)
Barack Obama (D) 148,928		(47%)
Cook Partisan Voting Index: R+6		

Prior to the latest redistricting changes, Barack Obama carried the Orlando-based district by 5 percentage points. But under the lines for the new 10th District, he lost by 5 points to Republican nominee John McCain. In 2012, Mitt Romney enlarged this margin to 8 points.

Daniel Webster (R)

Republican Daniel Webster, a staunch conservative, prevailed in two of the most vitriolic elections in 2010 and 2012. He settled into the House with an insider's demeanor, but then unexpectedly became the chief GOP challenger to Speaker John Boehner in the last-minute bid by conservatives to register their unhappiness. Webster subsequently was stripped of his prime committee assignment, but he may have gained a niche among conservatives for his House leadership potential.

Webster was born in Charleston, West Virginia, and is distantly related to his 19th century namesake, considered one of the greatest senators and orators in history. His family moved to Florida when he was 7 years old because a doctor told them the climate would help cure young Daniel's sinus problems. He graduated from the Georgia Institute of Technology in 1971 with a degree in electrical engineering and began working in his family's heating and air conditioning business in Orlando. Webster eventually took over the family business. He became politically active in 1979, when he led his church's effort to turn a house into a Sunday school, only to be refused a zoning exemption by the county commission.

Webster won a seat in the state House in 1996 and later became the first Republican speaker of the Florida House in 122 years. He sponsored a bill to ban nude performances in bars and another that would have required the legislature to study the impact of proposed laws on families. In 1998, Webster moved on to the state Senate, where he pushed to ease gun regulations and to restrict abortion rights. He led legislative efforts to prolong the life of Terri Schiavo, a woman in a persistent vegetative state who became a national cause for conservatives. In 2008, he sponsored a bill requiring women to get an ultrasound test and view the results before getting an abortion.

With the backing of national Republicans, he challenged controversial Democratic Rep. Alan Grayson in 2010. Grayson had become a lightning rod for conservatives because of his harsh rhetoric during his two years in Congress. He once called Republicans "knuckle-dragging Neanderthals," and on another occasion charged that the GOP solution to the health care crisis was for people to "die quickly." His unapologetic liberalism made him a hero to the left, but Webster and Republicans believed that Grayson was a poor fit for the more tempered politics of the district. Webster easily won a crowded primary with 40% of the vote. In the fall, the contest heated up quickly. One of Grayson's television ads dubbed Webster "Taliban Dan," and accused him of proposing to make divorce illegal and of believing that women should submit to their husbands. A video clip of Webster in the ad, however, was taken out of context; Webster was asserting the opposite, according to the *Orlando Sentinel,* which endorsed Webster in part because of Grayson's negative campaigning. Webster refused to debate Grayson, and to return his attacks in kind, saying, "We're taking the high road. I'm not getting down in the dirt with him." He focused his campaign on the size of the federal government and the passage of President Barack Obama's health care law. Grayson's strategy energized liberals nationally, and he raked in $6 million for his campaign, far outspending Webster, who raised just $1.8 million. The voters turned out Grayson decisively, 56%-38%.

In the newly Republican-controlled House, Webster won a seat on the Rules Committee, a coveted position usually reserved for members whom leaders can trust to hew to the party line. He became the first GOP freshman to get a substantive bill through the House, with a measure aimed at limiting executive bonuses at companies that received financial industry bailout funds. He expressed support for House Budget Committee Chairman Paul Ryan's attempts to rein in spending and overhaul Medicare, a position that earned him national publicity in April 2011 after a hostile crowd at a town hall meeting in his district jeered him. He drew heavy flak in newspaper editorials in May 2012 when he proposed an amendment to the Commerce Department's spending bill ending the American Community Survey, a demographic study for tracking neighborhoods' social and economic changes. Webster called the survey "intrusive" and "unconstitutional," but his amendment failed. He voiced support in August 2013 for a plan that would give illegal immigrants a pathway to citizenship.

In 2012, Grayson talked about a rematch with Webster, but instead ran for—and won– the seat in the solidly Democratic 9th District. Webster was initially considered a reelection shoo-in against Val Demings, the former Orlando police chief, but she outworked and outraised the congressman, whose fundraising had been among the weakest of the GOP freshmen. The Democrat pulled ahead in the polls and got more than $2 million from New York Mayor Michael Bloomberg's political committee to assist candidates who supported gun control, with the Democratic Congressional Campaign Committee spending another $1.5 million. She repeatedly accused Webster of using taxpayer money to create a "lobbyists' lounge" when he served in the legislature, a reference to his decision to spend about $100,000 for renovations to the speaker's office suite. He adamantly denied that the remodeling was done to serve lobbyists. The GOP tilt of the district proved decisive and Webster won 52%-48%. In 2014, he had an uncompetitive campaign and won 62% of the vote.

As Congress prepared to convene in January 2015, Webster surprised many on Capitol Hill by speaking out against Speaker John Boehner and the Republican leadership's management of the House. In previous weeks, he had quietly circulated to other Republicans a white paper that was titled "Widgets, Principles and Republicans." It concluded that "Congress is broken, the Republican brand is in trouble, and nothing can change unless congressional processes become less power- and self-preservation driven, and more open to rank-and-file members," the *Orlando Sentinel* reported. "A lot of people liked it," Webster later said. A few lawmakers initially told him that he should run for speaker. When that number grew as others learned of his interest, Webster agreed to enter his name two hours before the vote. He was supported by 12 Republican lawmakers, which was fewer than the number who had told him they would support him, he said. A total of 25 House Republicans did not vote for Boehner. But he won a bare majority of the vote and avoided what could have been a catastrophic second ballot.

With Boehner's allies outraged by Webster's candidacy and urging retribution, the speaker did not include him and fellow Florida Republican Rick Nugent, who had voted for Webster, with the members he appointed to the Rules Committee. Following the vote, Webster issued a conciliatory statement that "my candidacy and vote was not a vote against personalities, policies or even John Boehner" and affirmed his friendship for Boehner. "It was a vote for initiating a process that I know can produce sound public policy for the people who sent us to Washington on their behalf." Boehner took no immediate action to start such a process. But he surely was watching Webster more closely. In August 2015, Webster encountered stormy waves at home when the Legislature's initial plan for redistricting turned his district into one that he said would be "impossible" for him to win.

ELEVENTH DISTRICT

Richard Nugent (R)

Elected 2010, 3rd term; b. May 26, 1951, Evergreen Park, IL; Saint Leo Col., B.A. 1990, Troy St. U., M.P.A. 1995; Methodist; married (Wendy); 3 children.

Military Career: IL Air Natl. Guard, 1969-75.

Elected Office: Sheriff, Hernando Cnty., 2000-10.

Professional Career: Police officer, Romeoville, IL, 1972-84; Operations bureau commander, Hernando Cnty. Sheriff's Office, 1984-2000.

DC Office: 1727 LHOB, 20515, 202-225-1002; Fax: 202-226-6559; Website: nugent.house.gov.

State Offices: Inverness, 352-341-2354; Ocala, 352-351-1670; Spring Hill, 352-684-4446; The Village, 352-689-4684.

Committees: *Armed Services:* Emerging Threats & Capabilities; Readiness. *House Administration. Joint Committee on Printing.*

Group Ratings

	ADA	ACLU	AFL-CIO	LCV	ITI	COC	HAFA	ACU	CFG	FRC
2014	0%	0%	–	3%	80%	79%	67%	80%	62%	88%
2013	5%	C	5%	4%	C	73%	C	76%	76%	C

National Journal Ratings

	2013 LIB	—	2013 CONS
Economic	21%	—	77%
Social	16%	—	74%
Foreign	48%	—	51%
Composite	31%	—	70%

Key Votes of the 113th Congress

1. Sandy storm spending	N	5. Medical Marijuana	N	9. Syrian Rebels Training	N
2. Violence Against Women Act	Y	6. Farm Bill	Y	10. Keystone pipeline	Y
3. Guantanamo Bay Detainees	N	7. Afghanistan Combat	N	11. Immigration Exec. Action	Y
4. Abortion 20-week ban	Y	8. NSA Phone Data Collection	Y	12. Bipartisan budget deal	N

Election Results

2014 general	Richard Nugent (R)	181,508	(67%)	$317,246
	David Koller (D)	90,786	(33%)	$67,137
2014 primary	Richard Nugent (R)	unopposed		

Prior winning percentages: 2012 (64%), 2010 (67%)

Population		Race and Ethnicity		Income	
Total:	715,956	White	80.0%	Median income:	$41,275
Urban:	32.7%	Black	8.8%		*(372 of 435)*
Suburban:	62.5%	Latino	8.8%	Under $50,000	58.8%
Rural:	4.9%	Asian	1.0%	$50,000-$99,999:	29.8%
Land area:	2,682	Two races	1.2%	$100,000-$199,999:	9.6%
Pop/sq. mi.:	266.9	White Ethnic	34.6%	$200,000 or more:	1.7%
Born in state:	30.0%			Poverty Rate	16.2%
		Education			
Age Groups		H.S. grad or less:	48.1%	**Work**	
Under 18:	16.6%	Some college:	32.1%	White collar:	28.0%
18 to 34:	15.4%	College degree, 4 yr.:	13.0%	Blue collar:	52.2%
35 to 64:	35.9%	Post-grad study:	6.9%	Sales and service:	19.8%
Over 64:	32.1%				
		Military		Govt. workers:	13.4%
		Veterans/active duty:	15.1%		

Northwest Florida: Ocala, Tampa suburbs

Over the past quarter-century, Florida's urban areas have grown in almost every direction, occupying the high ground between the swamps that still take up much of the state's peninsula. The pattern of development is evident in counties to the north and east of St. Petersburg and Tampa, where subdi-

Voter Turnout	
2013 Total Citizen 18+	582,340
2014 House Turnout	272,294
2014 Turnout as % CVAP	46.8%
2012 Turnout as % CVAP	62.3%

visions, trailer parks, and shopping centers with Eckerd drugstores (which were purchased by Rite-Aid in 2007) and Winn-Dixie supermarkets sprang up in what had been farms and sleepy little towns, with low brick buildings baking in the Florida sun. Drawn by the many inland lakes, greenery, and the pleasant climate, retirees from Michigan, Indiana, and Ohio flocked to Citrus and Hernando counties by traveling south on Interstate 75—a pattern distinct from the retirees who drove Interstate 95 from the Boston-Washington corridor to such destinations as Palm Beach, Fort Lauderdale, and Miami. The development here has been nothing short of astonishing; the population in Hernando County increased tenfold since 1970, while Citrus County increased at a similar rate, though the growth in both counties has slowed since 2010. As is often the case, rapid development exists in an uneasy tension with environmental concerns. The area is a haven for manatees, and the federal government declared the Crystal River National Wildlife Refuge a restricted manatee refuge after tourists were observed chasing, riding, and poking the gentle sea cows.

The 11th Congressional District of Florida occupies much of this rapidly growing area. To the east are Sumter and Marion counties, which contain some of the few areas on the Florida peninsula with large tracts of open land. The numbers here offer insight into changing retirement patterns. Sumter County's population is growing rapidly—by 22 percent from 2010 to 2014—in part due to a massive retirement community known as The Villages, with more than 100 miles of golf cart paths and a population that passed 100,000 in 2013. It has been the fastest growing metro area in the nation for the past two years. The average age in Sumter is 65.5 years, which makes it the oldest county in the nation. Further north, near Ocala, is Silver Springs, where tourists can view the world's largest formation of artesian springs from glass-bottomed boats, although water pollution and drought increas-

ingly threaten what is essentially a theme park dating from the early 1900s. Ocala was hard hit by the recession, with an unemployment rate spiking to over 14% in 2010, but it dropped to 5.8% in December 2014, in line with the Florida average. The area around Ocala is one of America's prime horse-breeding grounds. Marion County has the largest population in the district.

In coastal Citrus and Hernando counties,

2012 Presidential Vote		
Mitt Romney (R)................209,720	(59%)
Barack Obama (D) 143,380	(40%)
2008 Presidential Vote		
John McCain (R).................196,950	(56%)
Barack Obama (D) 152,040	(43%)
Cook Partisan Voting Index: R+11		

the beach areas are largely undeveloped. The bulk of the population lives inland, in places like Citrus Springs, Spring Hill, and Brooksville. In addition to Sumter and Marion counties, the district has a sliver of Lake County. While this was once politically marginal territory, it has become more Republican of late. Republicans have an 8% voter registration edge here, and Mitt Romney won almost 60% of the vote in 2012.

Richard Nugent (R)

Republican Richard Nugent, first elected in 2010, is a rock-solid fiscal conservative who gained unexpected attention when he supported fellow Republican Rep. Daniel Webster for speaker, which sufficiently dismayed John Boehner that he removed Nugent from the leadership-controlled House Rules Committee. He also has been known for his bill to allow members of Congress to opt out of the federal pension system.

Nugent was born in Evergreen Park Illinois, a Chicago suburb, the youngest of three children. His father worked in a steel mill and his mother was a homemaker. After high school, Nugent served in the Illinois Air National Guard for six years and became a police officer, working his way up to sergeant in the Romeoville department. Nugent joined the Hernando County Sheriff's Office in 1984; he was elected to his first term as sheriff in 2000, and was reelected in 2004 and 2008. Over the years, Nugent presided over a drop in violent crime and imposed new fiscal constraints. His office took control of operations of the Hernando County Jail, which had been privately run and had been criticized for being soft on prisoners. Nugent told the *St. Petersburg Times*, "There's a new sheriff in town. It's not going to be a relaxed, Club Med atmosphere." In his adopted home state of Florida, he got his bachelor's degree from Saint Leo University, a Catholic liberal arts college, and a master's in public administration from Troy State University. He and his wife, Wendy Nugent, have two sons who have been officers in the Army and a third in the Army Reserve.

In April 2010, Republican Rep. Ginny Brown-Waite announced she would not seek reelection to a fifth term because of health problems. She made the announcement on candidate filing day in Florida, which allowed Nugent to file the necessary legal papers by the deadline. Brown-Waite also issued a statement strongly endorsing Nugent. The arrangement sparked bitter complaints from other Republicans who had been waiting for the opportunity to run for a House seat. Nugent drew a primary challenge from Jason Sager, who was backed by tea party activists. But the upstart campaign never gained traction, and Nugent won the primary, 62%-38%.

In the general election, he faced Democrat Jim Piccillo, a business consultant and a former Republican. Piccillo cast himself as a pragmatist who would work to reduce federal spending and regulation on businesses, and he reprised the issue of Nugent's anointment by Brown-Waite. For his part, Nugent proposed a freeze in government spending and campaigned against the Democrats' $787 billion economic stimulus bill. He portrayed Piccillo as the "hand-picked candidate" of liberal House Speaker Nancy Pelosi, prompting Piccillo to call him a "flat out liar." Nugent outraised his opponent, $518,000 to $147,000, and won easily, 67%-33%.

As a freshman, Nugent took seats on the House Administration and Rules committees, positions given to leadership loyalists. He was less confrontational than many of his fellow GOP freshmen, but just as conservative. His first bill in March 2011 allowed lawmakers to opt out of their congressional pensions, as well as the federal match to their deferred compensation plan. Though the measure drew considerable publicity, it attracted just three cosponsors and no legislative action. Nugent has received a $72,000 annual pension for his work in Florida. He introduced a subsequent bill requiring federally elected officials to place their stocks, bonds, and other forms of assets in a blind trust. Nugent offered an amendment to the 2013 defense authorization bill permitting soldiers who served before Sept. 11, 2001, to qualify for the Army's Combat Action Badge, which was established in 2005 to honor members of units who would not normally qualify for other decorations. It made it into the House version, but the Senate dropped it.

Nugent got his moment in the congressional spotlight when he was one of 12 Republicans to support Webster for speaker during the organizational vote for Congress in January 2015. In addition to holding neighboring districts in central Florida, each also had a seat on the Rules Committee, which also is known as the "speaker's committee." Boehner removed both from the panel later that day. Although he left the door open for each to return to the committee, their seats subsequently were reassigned to two first-term members. Nugent, showing no regrets, responded in a newsletter that cited the speaker's failure to lead, and wrote "I don't believe that John Boehner is the best man for the job." Nugent retained his assignments on the Armed Services and House Administration panels, and probably did not miss the unpredictable schedule and often tedious demands that Rules Committee members handle.

At home, Nugent was challenged in 2012 by Democrat David Werder, a perennial candidate who called himself "the flagpole sitter" in recognition of his record-setting 439 days atop a flagpole in Clearwater in the 1980s to protest high gasoline prices. Werder raised no money for his campaign, and got 36% of the vote. David Koller, who challenged Nugent in 2014, was less celebrated and spent $67,000, but he got only 33%.

TWELFTH DISTRICT

Gus Bilirakis (R)

Elected 2006, 5th term; b. Feb. 8, 1963, Gainesville; St. Petersburg Jr. Col., attended 1981-83, U. of FL, B.A. 1986, Stetson U., J.D. 1989; Greek Orthodox; married (Eva Lialios); 4 children.

Elected Office: FL House, 1998-2006.

Professional Career: Intern, U.S. Pres. Ronald Reagan, 1983; Intern, NRCC, 1984; Aide, U.S. Rep. Don Sundquist, 1985; Teacher, St. Petersburg Col., 1997-2001; Practicing atty., 1989-2006.

DC Office: 2112 RHOB, 20515, 202-225-5755; Fax: 202-225-4085; Website: bilirakis.house.gov.

State Offices: New Port Richey, 727-232-2921; Tarpon Springs, 727-940-5860; Wesley Chapel, 813-501-4942.

Committees: *Energy & Commerce:* Commerce, Manufacturing & Trade; Communications & Technology; Health. *Veterans' Affairs* (VChmn): Health.

Group Ratings

	ADA	ACLU	AFL-CIO	LCV	ITI	COC	HAFA	ACU	CFG	FRC
2014	5%	0%	–	0%	100%	93%	59%	78%	60%	100%
2013	0%	C	14%	4%	C	85%	C	88%	72%	C

National Journal Ratings

	2013 LIB	—	2013 CONS
Economic	31%	—	69%
Social	0%	—	87%
Foreign	44%	—	54%
Composite	28%	—	73%

Key Votes of the 113th Congress

1. Sandy storm spending	N	5. Medical Marijuana	N
2. Violence Against Women Act	N	6. Farm Bill	N
3. Guantanamo Bay Detainees	N	7. Afghanistan Combat	N
4. Abortion 20-week ban	Y	8. NSA Phone Data Collection	N

9. Syrian Rebels Training	Y
10. Keystone pipeline	Y
11. Immigration Exec. Action	Y
12. Bipartisan budget deal	Y

Election Results

2014 general	Gus Bilirakis (R)..........................unopposed	$700,434
2014 primary	Gus Bilirakis (R)..........................unopposed	

Prior winning percentages: 2012 (63%), 2010 (71%), 2008 (62%), 2006 (56%)

Population		Race and Ethnicity		Income	
Total:	719,044	White	79.1%	Median income:	$50,115
Urban:	15.8%	Latino	11.6%		*(240 of 435)*
Suburban:	83.8%	Black	4.3%	Under $50,000	49.9%
Rural:	0.5%	Asian	2.8%	$50,000-$99,999:	29.4%
Land area:	771	Two races	1.8%	$100,000-$199,999:	16.4%
Pop/sq. mi.:	932.7	White Ethnic	35.7%	$200,000 or more:	4.4%
Born in state:	32.5%			Poverty Rate	11.6%
		Education			
Age Groups		H.S. grad or less:	39.5%	**Work**	
Under 18:	20.6%	Some college:	32.1%	White collar:	41.7%
18 to 34:	17.7%	College degree, 4 yr.:	18.6%	Blue collar:	45.0%
35 to 64:	40.9%	Post-grad study:	9.8%	Sales and service:	13.3%
Over 64:	20.8%			Govt. workers:	12.3%
		Military			
		Veterans/active duty:	12.2%		

Northern Tampa Suburbs: Pasco, Pinellas

In 1873, turtle hunters discovered a large sponge bed off the coast of the Pinellas Peninsula. Soon, boats from Key West began harvesting the sponges, and shortly thereafter, trading outposts were set up at sites that grew into Tarpon Springs and Anclote.

Voter Turnout	
2013 Total Citizen 18+	547,298
2014 House Turnout	0
2014 Turnout as % CVAP	0.0%
2012 Turnout as % CVAP	64.7%

Anclote is now just a speck on the map, but Tarpon Springs is a busy city of 24,000. With more than 10 percent of the population, it boasts the highest share of Greek-Americans of any place in the United States—descendants of the Greek sponge fishermen who began arriving in the early 1900s. Over the years, development has moved up the once-empty coast of Pasco County and inland via the major highways. Today, Pasco has become a classic bedroom community, with nearly half its workers commuting to jobs in other counties. But population density remains low compared to other parts of Florida. It has been possible to step out of a Dillard's department store and pet a cow grazing in a nearby field.

There have been plans to change this. Two big financial companies—St. Petersburg's Raymond James Financial and Baltimore's T. Rowe Price—had purchased land in Pasco County and each planned to build large campuses for thousands of employees. But officials of each company abandoned their plans in 2014, at least for some time. Still, the construction boom revived after the recession, and plenty of new communities and shopping malls have been built. Medical tourism has become a growing industry for patients who travel for treatment they cannot receive in their home states or other nations. In December 2014, MTV aired a reality television show, "Growing Up Greek," about life in Tarpon Springs. Some Greek nationality groups objected to the stereotypes.

The 12th Congressional District covers an area north and east of Tampa and St. Petersburg. In Pinellas County, the 12th includes Tarpon Springs, and the upscale residential community of Palm Harbor. The district also takes in many suburbs northwest of Tampa in Hillsborough County. But nearly two-thirds of the residents of the district live in Pasco County. Coastal Pasco was largely undeveloped until the 1950s, but now hosts a string of towns along the Gulf of Mexico like Holiday, New Port Richey, Bayonet Point, and Hudson. Further inland, the district covers older settlements like Land O'Lakes, Dade City, and Zephyrhills, established in 1911 as a retirement center for veterans of the Union Army. San Antonio, established as a colony for Catholics in 1881, is home to the annual Rattlesnake Festival; the accompanying Miss Rattler Pageant was discontinued in 2012.

In the 1950s and 1960s, only white-collar retirees could afford to buy new places in Florida, and they were heavily Republican. As Florida retirements became more feasible for people with modest incomes in the 1970s and 1980s, the partisan balance shifted toward Democrats. In the 1990s, young arrivals with professional and technical backgrounds and

2012 Presidential Vote		
Mitt Romney (R)	185,157	(54%)
Barack Obama (D)	153,386	(45%)
2008 Presidential Vote		
John McCain (R)	178,007	(52%)
Barack Obama (D)	159,371	(47%)
Cook Partisan Voting Index: R+7		

partisan independence turned this into a politically marginal area. But Republican-drawn redistricting and the modest minority populations have made the 12th District more Republican for presidential and congressional votes.

Gus Bilirakis (R)

Gus Bilirakis, a Republican first elected in 2006 to succeed his father, 12-term Republican Rep. Michael Bilirakis, came into office distancing himself from partisan fights and focusing on his legislative agenda. But in 2010 he joined the Tea Party Caucus, and since then has displayed a sharper rhetorical edge in criticizing Democratic initiatives.

Bilirakis remembers stuffing envelopes at age 7 for Republican Louis "Skip" Bafalis, who lost his 1970 bid for governor but was elected to five terms in Congress. During college, Bilirakis interned in the Reagan White House and went on to earn a law degree from Stetson University. He worked for former Rep. Don Sundquist, a Republican who became governor of Tennessee, and later was a probate lawyer and estate planner. In 1998, he was elected to the first of four terms in the Florida House. Bilirakis' career has been closely tied to his father's. When Michael Bilirakis decided not to seek a 13th term, his son drew only nominal opposition for the Republican nomination. Gus Bilirakis was not shy about running on the family name and his Greek heritage. He touted the relationship on his website, appeared on the ballot as Gus Michael Bilirakis and raised money from many political action committees that supported his father, who had had a seat on the powerful Energy and Commerce Committee.

Democrats recruited Phyllis Busansky, a former member of the Hillsborough County Commission and the first executive director of the state's welfare-to-work program. Both candidates were responsive to the district's large population of senior citizens. Busansky played up her background in health care and seniors' issues. Bilirakis pointed to his credentials as a lawyer who specialized in elder law. Bilirakis' soft-spoken style contrasted with Busansky's assertive personality. She ran television ads portraying Bilirakis as a follower and accused him of relying on his father's reputation. She trailed in the polls for much of the campaign, but gained some momentum in October after criticizing Bilirakis for his "deep and lucrative ties" to GOP leaders who had failed to act on knowledge of sexually explicit emails that Republican Rep. Mark Foley of Florida had sent to congressional pages. The national Republican Party did not leave this race to chance. President George W. Bush, Vice President Dick Cheney, and Speaker Dennis Hastert all stumped for Bilirakis and helped him raise money. In a strongly Democratic year, he outspent Busansky $2.6 million to $1.4 million, and won 56%-44%.

In the House, Bilirakis showed signs of centrism. Soon after taking office, he voted to increase the minimum wage. In 2008, he worked with Rep. Lloyd Doggett, a Texas Democrat, to win House passage of a "silver alert" bill to assist states in finding senior citizens who disappear. He was one of just 10 Republicans in 2009 to support a bill to limit executive bonuses in financial companies receiving government bailout money. But his politics shifted, as did those of his party. In 2010, he took the House floor on several occasions to denounce the Democrats' health care overhaul as a "government takeover." He denounced the law's Independent Payment Advisory Board, a cost-cutting panel charged with slowing the growth in Medicare spending, as an "unelected bureaucracy" that would trample on Congress' oversight authority.

After the 2012 elections, Bilirakis filled a vacancy on the Energy and Commerce Committee, where he came under attack from left-leaning groups for earlier signing a pledge that "opposes any legislation relating to climate change that includes a net increase in government revenue." The pledge was circulated by Americans for Prosperity, a group run by conservative activist brothers David and Charles Koch. Earlier on the Foreign Affairs Committee, he followed his father's footsteps in standing up for Greek causes. He also pursued some bipartisan cooperation. In February 2014, he worked with Democrats to oppose soaring premium hikes for flood insurance coverage. That resulted in the decision by then-Majority Whip Kevin McCarthy to bounce Bilirakis from his whip team. In response, he told the *Tampa Bay Times*, "I have no hard feelings at all, but I had to do what I had to do." In December 2014, President Barack Obama signed a bill sponsored by Bilirakis to promote travel by reauthorizing Brand USA, a public-private partnership that encourages tourists to visit the United States. Some conservatives had opposed the bill as excessive spending. As vice chairman of the Veterans' Affairs Committee, he worked on the 2014 law to overhaul the VA hospital system. That resulted, he said, in the opening of an out-patient clinic in New Port Richey.

Bilirakis has not faced a serious reelection challenge. In 2014, he ran without opposition in the primary and general elections.

THIRTEENTH DISTRICT

David Jolly (R)

Elected March 2014, 1st full term; b. Oct. 31, 1972, Dunedin; Emory U., B.A. 1994, George Mason U., J.D. 2001; Baptist; married (Laura Donahoe).

Professional Career: Office of Rep. Bill Young, 1994-2006; Associate, Fried, Frank, Harris, Shriver & Jacobson, 2001; Owner, Three Bridges Advisors, Three Bridges Law and 1924 Communications, 2008-present; VP, Boston Finance Group, 2012-present; CEO, Olympus Foundation Management, 2013-present.

DC Office: 1728 LHOB, 20515, 202-225-5961; Fax: 202-225-9764; Website: jolly.house.gov.

State Offices: Clearwater, 727-781-4400; Seminole, 727-392-4100; St. Petersburg, 727-823-8900.

Committees: *Appropriations:* Commerce, Justice, Science & Related Agencies; Military Construction, Veterans Affairs & Related Agencies; Transportation, Housing & Urban Development & Related Agencies.

Election Results

2014 general	David Jolly (R)	168,172	(75%)	$1,810,874*	$1,256,381*	$3,536,068*
	Lucas Overby (Lib)	55,318	(25%)	$55,143		
2014 primary	David Jolly (R)	unopposed*				

Prior winning percentage: 2014 special (49%)

* Includes special election

Population		Race and Ethnicity		Income	
Total:	699,288	White	79.8%	Median income:	$44,118
Urban:	68.9%	Latino	9.3%		*(334 of 435)*
Suburban:	31.1%	Black	5.3%	Under $50,000	55.2%
Rural:	0.0%	Asian	3.4%	$50,000-$99,999:	29.0%
Land area:	178	Two races	1.5%	$100,000-$199,999:	12.7%
Pop/sq. mi.:	3,925.6	White Ethnic	34.6%	$200,000 or more:	3.1%
Born in state:	30.0%			Poverty Rate	14.8%
		Education			
Age Groups		H.S. grad or less:	40.8%	**Work**	
Under 18:	16.8%	Some college:	31.4%	White collar:	35.9%
18 to 34:	18.4%	College degree, 4 yr.:	18.0%	Blue collar:	47.1%
35 to 64:	41.4%	Post-grad study:	9.8%	Sales and service:	17.1%
Over 64:	23.5%				
		Military		Govt. workers:	10.0%
		Veterans/active duty:	11.6%		

St. Petersburg, Clearwater

When Spanish explorers arrived in what is now St. Petersburg some 500 years ago, they discovered an area covered by a primeval pine forest and teeming with bears, panthers, turkeys, and bald eagles. They named the area "Punta Pinal" ("point of pines"), a name that has since been Anglicized

Voter Turnout	
2013 Total Citizen 18+	548,327
2014 House Turnout	223,576
2014 Turnout as % CVAP	40.8%
2012 Turnout as % CVAP	62.6%

into the Pinellas Peninsula. The area remained under-populated—only 50 families lived here when the Civil War broke out—until two things conspired to change the course of its development. First, the Orange Belt Railway connected the region to national markets in the 1880s. Second, Dr. W.C. Van Bibber, addressing the American Medical Society convention in 1885, named the peninsula the healthiest place on earth, setting off a stampede of interest. By 1897, the Belleview Hotel was built in Clearwater, and the area's transition to a major tourist destination—and, later, a retirement community—was underway.

The population of Pinellas County more than doubled in the 1920s, and did so once more in the 1950s. Mostly from the North and modestly affluent, the newcomers adapted easily to a place whose civic tone was set by the *St. Petersburg Times* (now the *Tampa Bay Times*) and its longtime owners, Nelson and Henrietta Poynter: sober, good-humored, and supportive of clean government and civil rights. They also brought with them Republican voting habits, and presaged the revolution in Florida politics that would take place as Northern immigrants spread down the coastlines. Democrats had a 56-point registration edge over Republicans here in 1940. By 1950,

2012 Presidential Vote		
Barack Obama (D) 171,102	(50%)
Mitt Romney (R)................166,087	(49%)

2008 Presidential Vote		
Barack Obama (D) 177,758	(51%)
John McCain (R)................164,644	(48%)

Cook Partisan Voting Index: R+1

that edge was only 6 points. In 1954, Pinellas County Republicans elected William Cramer to Congress, the first Republican representative from Florida since 1882 when Horatio Bisbee Jr. was elected in a district that spanned the eastern half of the peninsula. The Republican tilt faded over time, however, and Pinellas County is now a swing area of the state. But the House seat has remained in GOP hands.

The 13th Congressional District is located entirely within Pinellas County. It includes about half the population of St. Petersburg, exclusive of the heavily African-American and Democratic precincts in south St. Petersburg that are part of the Tampa-based 14th District. Working its way up the peninsula, it includes beach communities on the barrier islands facing the Gulf of Mexico, from Belleair Beach to Honeymoon Island State Park. Inland, it incorporates the new subdivisions of Largo in the center of the peninsula. Near the top end is Clearwater, where resorts have grown more upscale and where the Church of Scientology and several buildings of its religious center are headquartered. A widely viewed March 2015 HBO documentary "Going Clean," described how the church fought for decades with lobbying and lawsuits to get its tax-exempt status; the church dismissed the film as "bigoted propaganda." Almost 20 percent of Clearwater's population is over the age of 65; it once claimed the highest percentage of senior citizens in the nation but has since been eclipsed by other locales in Florida and Arizona.

According to a January 2015 survey by a credit-card firm, St. Petersburg appeals to millennials as the number-one place to settle in Florida. But there are less favorable perspectives: At the January 2015 Sundance Film Festival, European producers won a prize for "Pinellas Park," which depicts registered sex offenders living in a Pinellas County mobile home park. In 2008, this competitive district voted 51% for Barack Obama for president, a share that fell modestly to 50% in 2012.

David Jolly (R)

David Jolly, a former congressional aide and lobbyist, surprised many observers when he won a special election in March 2014 to succeed his late boss, Rep. C.W. "Bill" Young, the former chairman of the Appropriations Committee.

Jolly, a fifth-generation Floridian, was born in Dunedin and graduated from Pasco High School in Dade City. From there, he enrolled at Emory University in Atlanta, earning a bachelor's degree in history. Following his graduation, Jolly joined Young's staff, eventually becoming his general counsel. While he worked for Young on Capitol Hill, Jolly got his law degree at George Mason University. Jolly joined the Washington, D.C., law firm of Fried, Frank, Harris, Shriver & Jacobson after finishing school. In 2008, he founded his own communications and law firm before becoming vice president of the Clearwater, Fla.-based Boston Finance Group four years later.

In October 2013, Young announced he would not seek re-election after serving for 42 years. Less than two weeks later, Young passed away at the age of 82. Young's son and wife were both rumored as possible candidates for the seat, but Jolly entered the race, with the backing of Young's widow, Beverly Young. It marked his first bid for elected office. Initially, it looked like he would have an easy path to the Republican nomination, but state GOP Rep. Kathleen Peters entered just ahead of the filing deadline. The Young family's private disputes spilled into public view when Bill Young II, the son of the late congressman, endorsed Peters. His mother, who appeared in Jolly's first television ad, said that in her husband's final days, he wanted Jolly to succeed him in Congress. At a candidate forum, she confronted her son, telling him, "you have hurt me beyond belief," according to the *Tampa Bay Times*. Jolly later received the backing of former Price is Right host Bob Barker, a longtime supporter of Young. Barker made a cameo in one of Jolly's campaign ads, saying "with Jolly, the choice is right." Jolly won the Republican primary with 45% to 31% for Peters and 24% for retired Marine Mark Bircher.

Jolly was initially the underdog in the general election against former state Chief Financial Officer Alex Sink, who got the Democratic nomination without opposition. Sink was well-known after having barely lost to Florida Republican Gov. Rick Scott in the 2010 gubernatorial race. Shortly after the primary, Jolly ended his 15-year marriage, divorcing his wife, Carrie. Partisan groups quickly flooded the airwaves in the St. Petersburg-area district, in what became a bellwether for the 2014 midterm elections. Republican attacks on Sink largely focused on her support for the Affordable Care Act. Some GOP ads also raised ethical questions about Sink's tenure as state CFO. Democrats repeatedly criticized Jolly for lobbying on behalf of special interests. Two environmental groups teamed up to run ads hitting Jolly for his views on climate change. Sink handily outspent Jolly, but Republican-aligned outside groups helped level the financial playing field. Of the $12.7 million spent on the race, more than two-thirds of it came from outside groups. Jolly prevailed with 48.5% of the vote. Sink finished with 46.6%, while Libertarian candidate Lucas Overby took 4.9%. Republicans argued his election in the swing district was a sign of a promising 2014 election environment. They proved to be correct.

With his Capitol Hill experience, Jolly dove into his work with a mix of coalition-building and independence. In 2015, he got a seat on the Appropriations Committee, which was central to his predecessor's influence. He was one of the few House Republicans to voice support for same-sex marriage. In March 2015, he was one of 15 House Republicans to vote against the party's budget blueprint. He claimed that it failed to reduce the national debt. The *Tampa Bay Times* praised Jolly for his "pragmatism" as one of 75 House Republicans voting for a spending bill for the Homeland Security Department for the remainder of the fiscal year. He was among eight House members who announced creation of the bipartisan Congressional Coastal Communities Caucus, to work on issues ranging from flood insurance and disasters to marine habitats and tourism.

Jolly won an unexpectedly easy election for his first full term. After several other Democratic prospects turned down the opportunity, and with the local party dispirited over its failure to defeat Jolly in the special election, retired Marine Colonel Ed Jany planned to run but changed his mind at the filing deadline. Jolly got 75 percent of the vote against a Libertarian Party candidate. His brief career took a new twist when the initial plans for redistricting added black-majority neighborhoods to his district. Fearing an uphill battle for reelection, Jolly announced in July 2015 his candidacy for the open Senate seat.

FOURTEENTH DISTRICT

Kathy Castor (D)

Elected 2006, 5th term; b. Aug. 20, 1966, Miami; Emory U., B.A. 1988, FL St. U., J.D. 1991; Presbyterian; married (William Lewis); 2 children.

Elected Office: Hillsborough Cnty. Comm., 2002-06.

Professional Career: Asst. gen. counsel, FL Dept. of Community Affairs, 1991-94; Practicing atty., 1994-2000.

DC Office: 205 CHOB, 20515, 202-225-3376; Fax: 202-225-5652; Website: castor.house.gov.

State Offices: St. Petersburg, 727-873-2817; Tampa, 813-871-2817.

Committees: *Budget. Energy & Commerce:* Energy & Power; Health; Oversight & Investigations.

Group Ratings

	ADA	ACLU	AFL-CIO	LCV	ITI	COC	HAFA	ACU	CFG	FRC
2014	85%	77%	–	91%	60%	46%	11%	4%	4%	0%
2013	85%	C	100%	89%	C	33%	C	13%	16%	C

National Journal Ratings

	2013 LIB	—	2013 CONS
Economic	81%	—	19%
Social	61%	—	39%
Foreign	89%	—	10%
Composite	77%	—	23%

Key Votes of the 113th Congress

1. Sandy storm spending	Y	5. Medical Marijuana	Y	9. Syrian Rebels Training	Y
2. Violence Against Women Act	Y	6. Farm Bill	N	10. Keystone pipeline	N
3. Guantanamo Bay Detainees	Y	7. Afghanistan Combat	Y	11. Immigration Exec. Action	N
4. Abortion 20-week ban	N	8. NSA Phone Data Collection	N	12. Bipartisan budget deal	Y

Election Results

2014 general   Kathy Castor (D)...................unopposed $472,948 $1,101
2014 primary   Kathy Castor (D)...................unopposed

Prior winning percentages: 2012 (70%), 2010 (60%), 2008 (72%), 2006 (70%)

Population		Race and Ethnicity		Income	
Total:	733,381	White	42.4%	Median income:	$40,362
Urban:	86.1%	Latino	27.0%		*(388 of 435)*
Suburban:	13.9%	Black	25.7%	Under $50,000	58.6%
Rural:	0.0%	Asian	2.9%	$50,000-$99,999:	26.1%
Land area:	266	Two races	1.6%	$100,000-$199,999:	11.6%
Pop/sq. mi.:	2,754.1	White Ethnic	19.1%	$200,000 or more:	3.7%
Born in state:	40.7%			Poverty Rate	21.8%
		Education			
Age Groups		H.S. grad or less:	44.8%	**Work**	
Under 18:	22.4%	Some college:	27.5%	White collar:	34.4%
18 to 34:	26.5%	College degree, 4 yr.:	18.0%	Blue collar:	48.5%
35 to 64:	38.6%	Post-grad study:	9.6%	Sales and service:	17.0%
Over 64:	12.5%				
		Military		Govt. workers:	11.6%
		Veterans/active duty:	9.1%		

Tampa Bay: Tampa, Downtown St. Petersburg

Tampa's history goes back not much more than a century. Its industrial past can be traced to 1886, when Cuban cigar-makers from Key West settled in the city's Latin Quarter, called Ybor City. The city developed along the waterfront, with distinctive architectural touches like the 13 minarets on

Voter Turnout	
2013 Total Citizen 18+	510,373
2014 House Turnout	0
2014 Turnout as % CVAP	0.0%
2012 Turnout as % CVAP	58.8%

the Arabian-style Tampa Bay Hotel, built by railroad and real estate tycoon Henry B. Plant in the 1890s and now part of the University of Tampa. For a time, Tampa was Florida's only true industrial city, with a working-class, white population base. Today it has a diverse economy: a service sector, two universities, and tourism, led by the Busch Gardens theme park. Tampa's subdivisions and condominiums, office towers, and low-rise commercial buildings have spread inland across swamps and lowlands. Like most of Florida, it was hit hard by the recession. In 2010, the Tampa Bay area's unemployment rate topped 12%, the fifth highest among the largest U.S. metropolitan areas. Unemployment dropped to about 6% in 2014, and there was progress in completing housing foreclosures. Other economic data have been stagnant: The credit-counseling agency CredAbility in 2013 rated Tampa the third most financially distressed metropolitan area in the country, and the metro area in 2014 had the lowest median household income. There may be some positive signals. In November 2014, the international airport began work on a $1 billion upgrade. Other businesses planned $1 billion in developments projects along the waterfront.

Through its history, Tampa has remained a city of families and young people. Senior citizens account for only about 11% of the residents here, an unusually low percentage for Florida. It has been an important military center for much of its existence. During the Spanish-American War, when railroads were just making their way down Florida's Atlantic Coast, Tampa was a major embarkation point for U.S. troops. MacDill Air Force Base, on the south side of the city and jutting into Tampa Bay, is the headquarters of Central Command, which ran the Persian Gulf War and the campaigns in Afghanistan and Iraq. It is also headquarters for Special Operations Command, and in 2013 it gained a new assignment as coordinating center for international special operations forces. The city has been home to socialite Jill Kelley, who was caught up in an e-mail scandal related to the extramarital affair between

General David Petraeus and his biographer Paula Broadwell that ultimately forced his resignation as CIA director and a guilty plea for disclosing classified information.

2012 Presidential Vote		
Barack Obama (D) 191,255	(65%)
Mitt Romney (R)...................99,834	(34%)
2008 Presidential Vote		
Barack Obama (D) 182,595	(65%)
John McCain (R)...................95,075	(34%)
Cook Partisan Voting Index: D+13		

The 14th Congressional District is centered on Tampa. With about half of Hillsborough County, it includes most of the city of Tampa and its close-in suburbs, such as Town 'n' Country. The Port of Tampa handles 40% of all the cargo moving in and out of Florida ports. The district stretches down the lightly populated east shore of Tampa Bay before crossing over the water to incorporate heavily African-American and lower-income neighborhoods in St. Petersburg. It is a minority-majority district, with a population that is 25% black and 28% Hispanic. Democrat Barack Obama won the district with 65% of the vote in both 2008 and 2012, while winning Hillsborough County by only 7% both times.

Kathy Castor (D)

Kathy Castor, a Democrat first elected in 2006, uses her background as an environmental lawyer to staunchly uphold Democratic positions in energy debates. At the same time, Castor often works closely with Republicans to protect her district's sprawling MacDill Air Force Base.

Castor studied political science at Emory University, earned her law degree from Florida State University, and worked as a land-use attorney. Her parents were heavily involved in public service. Her father, Don Castor, sat on the Hillsborough County court for two decades. Her mother, Betty Castor, served in the state Senate, as state education commissioner and as president of the University of South Florida. In 2004, Betty Castor was the Democratic nominee for Senate, but lost 49%-48% to Republican Mel Martinez. Kathy Castor ran unsuccessfully for the state Senate in 2000, but two years later won a four-year term on the Hillsborough County Commission.

When Democratic Rep. Jim Davis ran for governor in 2006, Kathy Castor entered the contest, benefiting from the Castor name ID. In a district where Democrats enjoyed a nearly 2-to-1 advantage over Republicans, Castor faced four opponents in the primary. The most formidable was state Senate Minority Leader Les Miller, a veteran African-American legislator. Although Miller was familiar to voters, he failed to keep pace with Castor's prolific fundraising. With the support of EMILY's List, Castor raised nearly $1 million before the primary and outspent Miller 3-to-1. Castor trailed Miller in the heavily African-American portion of the Pinellas County, but she defeated him by more than 8,600 votes in Tampa's Hillsborough County. She won 54%-34%. The outcome of the general election was never in doubt. Castor campaigned for expanded health care for low-income families and stronger ethics and lobbying rules, and advocated a rapid withdrawal of U.S. troops from Iraq. She won the general election 70%-30%.

In the House, Castor established a liberal voting record. From her early days in Congress, she positioned herself for future roles in the Democratic leadership. She asked then- Speaker Nancy Pelosi to be appointed as the freshman representative to the Democratic Steering and Policy Committee, which determines committee assignments. Pelosi, surprised because no one had asked for the position before, promptly gave it to Castor. In 2007, she got choice seats on the Rules and Armed Services committees. Two years later, she agreed to serve on the House Ethics Committee, and subsequently became chair of the subcommittee looking into California Democrat Maxine Waters' alleged efforts to help get federal bailout money for a bank in which her husband owned stock. Waters was cleared of wrongdoing in 2012.

For her service on the Ethics panel, considered an undesirable posting, Castor was rewarded in 2009 with a seat on the Energy and Commerce Committee. She joined a group of liberals who insisted that any savings from a government-run public insurance option in the health care overhaul be used to increase subsidies to low-income people to purchase insurance. She also added an amendment to the energy and climate-change bill to allow states to set rates for electricity generated from renewable energy under state incentive programs.

Typically a party loyalist, Castor is among the lawmakers who have introduced a balanced budget constitutional amendment, normally a GOP priority, and in 2007 was one of only eight House Democrats to oppose the expansion of the State Children's Health

Insurance Program, complaining that Senate revisions to the bill made its benefits less favorable for Florida. She has avidly looked out for MacDill, headquarters of the U.S. Central Command and Special Operations Command, and worked in 2012 on an effort to bring the Air Force's next-generation aerial refueling jet, the KC-46, to the base.

She became a major player on offshore drilling following the BP oil spill in the Gulf of Mexico in 2010, prodding the company and the Obama administration for more research on the impact of the spill. She worked in 2012 to get a provision added to the transportation reauthorization bill directing that the bulk of fines under the Clean Water Act be devoted to the Gulf instead of going to the general treasury. When the Obama administration embraced increased trade and travel to Cuba, which she had long supported, she was the first member of Florida's House delegation to sign on to a bill in 2010 lifting travel restrictions and she successfully sought to add Tampa to the list of airports approved to host charter flights to Havana. She praised Obama's decision to reopen diplomatic relations with Cuba, and said it was long past time for the two nations to respect the concerns of their own people. When local officials in Miami objected to suggestions that they could host a Cuban chancery, Castor quickly volunteered Tampa as the site.

In the Republican year of 2010, Castor faced a tougher reelection challenge from Republican Mike Prendergast, a retired Army colonel. She narrowly outraised him and won, but with only 60 percent of the vote, the lowest of her career. In 2014, she was reelected without opposition. Her outspoken criticism of Florida Republicans' handling of issues such as Medicaid, transit funding and voting rights has fueled speculation that she might run for governor in 2018.

FIFTEENTH DISTRICT

Dennis Ross (R)

Elected 2010, 3rd term; b. Oct. 18, 1959, Lakeland; Auburn U., B.S. 1981, Samford U., J.D. 1987; Presbyterian; married (Cindy); 2 children.

Elected Office: FL House, 2000-08.

Professional Career: Practicing atty., 1987-89; Counsel, Walt Disney World, 1989; Founder, partner, Ross Vecchio P.A., 1989; Pres., Greater Lakeland Young Republicans, 1990; Chair, Polk County Republican Executive Committee, 1992-95.

DC Office: 229 CHOB, 20515, 202-225-1252; Fax: 202-226-0585; Website: dennisross.house.gov.

State Offices: Lakeland, 863-644-8215; Plant City, 813-752-4790.

Committees: *Financial Services:* Capital Markets and Government Sponsored Enterprises; Housing & Insurance.

Group Ratings

	ADA	ACLU	AFL-CIO	LCV	ITI	COC	HAFA	ACU	CFG	FRC
2014	0%	0%	–	3%	100%	93%	61%	76%	56%	100%
2013	5%	C	5%	7%	C	77%	C	84%	75%	C

National Journal Ratings

	2013 LIB	—	2013 CONS
Economic	7%	—	92%
Social	0%	—	87%
Foreign	24%	—	68%
Composite	14%	—	86%

Key Votes of the 113th Congress

1. Sandy storm spending	N	5. Medical Marijuana	N	9. Syrian Rebels Training	Y
2. Violence Against Women Act	N	6. Farm Bill	Y	10. Keystone pipeline	Y
3. Guantanamo Bay Detainees	N	7. Afghanistan Combat	N	11. Immigration Exec. Action	Y
4. Abortion 20-week ban	Y	8. NSA Phone Data Collection	Y	12. Bipartisan budget deal	Y

Election Results

2014 general	Dennis Ross (R)	128,750	(60%)	$1,436,048	$26,358
	Alan Cohn (D)	84,832	(40%)	$429,906	
2014 primary	Dennis Ross (R)	unopposed			

Prior winning percentages: 2012 (unopposed), 2010 (48%)

Population		Race and Ethnicity		Income	
Total:	718,325	White	63.9%	Median income:	$50,941
Urban:	54.2%	Latino	17.4%		*(222 of 435)*
Suburban:	44.9%	Black	13.2%	Under $50,000	48.9%
Rural:	0.9%	Asian	2.4%	$50,000-$99,999:	31.6%
Land area:	966	Two races	2.4%	$100,000-$199,999:	15.7%
Pop/sq. mi.:	743.8	White Ethnic	20.9%	$200,000 or more:	3.8%
Born in state:	45.8%			Poverty Rate	14.9%
		Education:			
Age Groups		H.S. grad or less:	44.2%	**Work**	
Under 18:	23.6%	Some college:	28.8%	White collar:	35.5%
18 to 34:	23.1%	College degree, 4 yr.:	17.0%	Blue collar:	43.7%
35 to 64:	39.2%	Post-grad study:	10.0%	Sales and service:	20.8%
Over 64:	14.1%				
		Military		Govt. workers:	12.9%
		Veterans/active duty:	10.0%		

Central Florida: Tampa Suburbs, Lakeland

The heart of central Florida is Polk County, filled with lakes and small-to-medium-sized cities. Lakeland, with a population of just over 100,000, is the biggest city here and home to the corporate headquarters of the Publix chain of grocery stores, the largest employee-owned supermarket chain in the

Voter Turnout	
2013 Total Citizen 18+	509, 612
2014 House Turnout	213,582
2014 Turnout as % CVAP	41.9%
2012 Turnout as % CVAP	59.7%

nation; Publix is rated the second-best chain in the nation, according to *Consumer Reports*. Lakeland-area home prices in 2014 remained below $100,000, making it one of the most affordable areas in the Sunshine State. But it also was among the top five counties nationwide in the share of home purchases that were distressed or short-sales. Historic Bartow, the county seat, is known for phosphate mining.

This is the part of Florida most dependent on agriculture. Strawberries, cattle, and citrus are economic mainstays, although periodic freezes in recent years have persuaded some orange growers to move south or to switch to tomatoes. Polk has had a double-digit percentage drop in the number of farms and acreage since 2001. Still, the county in 2013 had the most citrus acreage and trees, and had a sizable edge over DeSoto County as Florida's largest citrus producer. Proportionately, there are more manufacturing jobs here than almost anywhere else in Florida (though still not very many). Some new businesses, including distribution centers, have taken advantage of cheap property values to build new plants in Lakeland. One of the few remnants of old Florida, this area has not become a major retiree haven. In November 2014, *USA Today* listed Lakeland as one of six former "boomtowns" that had not yet recovered from the recession.

2012 Presidential Vote		
Mitt Romney (R)................160,920		(53%)
Barack Obama (D) 139,356		(46%)
2008 Presidential Vote		
John McCain (R)................158,042		(53%)
Barack Obama (D) 137,327		(46%)
Cook Partisan Voting Index: R+6		

The 15th Congressional District is a rural and suburban combo; 40% of the district's population lives in agricultural Polk County, and much of the rest is in the rapidly growing suburbs east of Tampa. Brandon is a place of strip malls and younger, pro-business families, while the Plant City area produces 90% of Florida's strawberry yield and nearly 11% of the nation's. At its annual strawberry festival, patrons consume 250,000 shortcakes. The Tampa-based University of South Florida is included in the 15th as well. Overall, the district is becoming reliably Republican. It voted 53% for John McCain in 2008 and gave Mitt Romney a similar victory in 2012.

Dennis Ross (R)

Republican Dennis Ross shares the solid conservative views of his GOP colleagues in the Class of 2010, but shuns incendiary rhetoric or media attention and is a bit of a loner, rarely attending group events. "I think the image of a conservative is stodgy and holier-than-thou and without a sense of humor," he told *National Journal* before inviting a reporter to go boar hunting with him. "I really like to enjoy life."

Ross grew up in Lakeland Florida, the youngest of five children. He remembers his mother, Loyola Ross, as a strict parent who preached the virtues of hard work. "She made us self-sufficient and believed in us working to earn our own spending money," Ross told the Lakeland *Ledger* after his mother died in 2006. "In the eighth grade, she had me mowing lawns and she was my accountant." He attended the University of Florida for a year before transferring to Auburn University and graduating in 1981 with a degree in organizational management. He spent a year working as a legislative aide to then-state Rep. Dennis Jones, installed and sold computers for a short time, then enrolled in law school at Samford University in Birmingham Alabama. He returned to Lakeland and became an in-house counsel for Walt Disney World, handling workers' compensation claims for the company. With $10,000 borrowed from a neighbor for less than a year, he opened a law firm that grew to seven lawyers and 27 employees. Ross spent three years as chairman of Polk County's Republican Executive Committee. In 2000, he won a seat in the Florida House, where he developed a reputation as a faithful, but not automatic, GOP vote.

When GOP Rep. Adam Putnam ran successfully for agriculture commissioner, Ross jumped into the race for his seat. In the August primary, he trounced fellow Republican John Lindsey, a businessman and political neophyte, winning 69% of the vote. In the general election, he faced Democrat Lori Edwards, the Polk County supervisor of elections, and tea party nominee Randy Wilkinson, a former Polk County commissioner. Edwards campaigned as a moderate, saying she would fit in with the Blue Dog Coalition of fiscally conservative Democrats. But Ross ran ads tying Edwards to President Barack Obama and liberal House Speaker Nancy Pelosi, while embracing Putnam's conservatism. Ross also had a big financial advantage, raising more than $1 million to Edwards' $657,000. Ross won convincingly, 48%-41%, with 11% of the vote going to Wilkinson.

In his first year in the House, Ross was among those tied for most-conservative member, according to *National Journal's* ratings. He was unapologetic about his wholehearted opposition to Obama's legislative agenda and his unwillingness to give Republican House Speaker John Boehner much leeway to negotiate a deal to raise the nation's debt ceiling in 2011. "I don't view this as clashing," he said. "It's more about slowing down the ship and working to put it in another direction." He joined the Tea Party Caucus and rejected accusations from members of the Congressional Black Caucus that the movement is racist, telling them to "get a grip."

As a member of the Oversight and Government Reform Committee for his first two years, Ross chaired the subcommittee overseeing federal workforce issues and proved himself a faithful ally of Chairman Darrell Issa. Ross was highly vocal about reports showing federal employees using increasing amounts of official time to participate in union activities. He, Issa, and Jason Chaffetz of Utah, unveiled a proposal that was designed to achieve a 10 percent federal workforce reduction within four years. That same month, he was among the conservatives backing a failed resolution from antiwar Democratic Rep. Dennis Kucinich of Ohio that would have urged Obama to remove U.S. forces from Libya within 15 days.

In 2013, Ross gained a seat on the Financial Services Committee and exited Issa's panel. He has filed legislation to create zero-based budgeting for the government, to shift the burden to federal agency heads to justify their spending. In June 2014, new House Majority Whip Steve Scalise of Louisiana named Ross as one of his five senior whips. After the Republican leadership experienced some legislative failures, Ross offered to resign, especially when he could not support the bill to extend spending for the Homeland Security Department because it failed to block Obama's executive order on immigration. Scalise refused to accept the resignation.

After running unopposed in 2012, Ross two years later faced Democrat Alan Cohn, a former local television reporter. Cohn said that his views on immigration, taxes and working families were consistent with those of the voters, provided he had enough campaign money to communicate. He had strong backing from organized labor, and criticized Ross' links to big banks and Wall Street. Ross largely ignored Cohn, and benefited from his big campaign spending advantage, $1.4 million to $430,000. Ross won 60%-40%, a clear improvement over his competitive contest in 2010. With his ambition, he might seek an opportunity to move up the House leadership ladder, or to run statewide.

SIXTEENTH DISTRICT

Vern Buchanan (R)

Elected 2006, 5th term; b. May 8, 1951, Detroit, MI; Cleary U., B.B.A. 1975, U. of Detroit, M.B.A. 1986; Baptist; married (Sandy); 2 children.

Military Career: MI Air Natl. Guard, 1970-76.

Professional Career: Taekwondo instructor, 1971-74; Marketing rep., Burroughs Corp., 1975-76; Founder, Vern Buchanan & Assoc., 1976-78; Founder & CEO, American Speedy Printing Centers, 1976-92; Founder & chmn., Buchanan Automotive Group, 1992-2007; Founder & chmn., Buchanan Enterprises, 1992-2007.

DC Office: 2104 RHOB, 20515, 202-225-5015; Fax: 202-226-0828; Website: buchanan.house.gov.

State Offices: Bradenton, 941-747-9081; Sarasota, 941-951-6643.

Committees: *Budget. Ways & Means:* Health; Trade.

Group Ratings

	ADA	ACLU	AFL-CIO	LCV	ITI	COC	HAFA	ACU	CFG	FRC
2014	0%	0%	–	9%	80%	86%	46%	71%	51%	88%
2013	5%	C	14%	0%	C	85%	C	80%	58%	C

National Journal Ratings

	2013 LIB	—	2013 CONS
Economic	35%	—	65%
Social	16%	—	74%
Foreign	48%	—	51%
Composite	35%	—	65%

Key Votes of the 113th Congress

1. Sandy storm spending	N	5. Medical Marijuana	N	9. Syrian Rebels Training	Y
2. Violence Against Women Act	Y	6. Farm Bill	Y	10. Keystone pipeline	Y
3. Guantanamo Bay Detainees	N	7. Afghanistan Combat	N	11. Immigration Exec. Action	Y
4. Abortion 20-week ban	Y	8. NSA Phone Data Collection	Y	12. Bipartisan budget deal	Y

Election Results

2014 general	Vern Buchanan (R)	169,126	(62%)	$851,628	$1,599
	Henry Lawrence (D)	105,483	(38%)	$60,744	
2014 primary	Vern Buchanan (R) ....unopposed				

Prior winning percentages: 2012 (54%), 2010 (69%), 2008 (56%), 2006 (50%)

Population		Race and Ethnicity		Income	
Total:	727,073	White	79.3%	Median income:	$48,202
Urban:	70.2%	Latino	11.2%		*(266 of 435)*
Suburban:	28.0%	Black	6.5%	Under $50,000	51.5%
Rural:	1.9%	Asian	1.4%	$50,000-$99,999:	29.8%
Land area:	1,554	Two races	1.3%	$100,000-$199,999:	14.2%
Pop/sq. mi.:	468.0	White Ethnic	31.9%	$200,000 or more:	4.5%
Born in state:	27.1%			Poverty Rate	14.4%
		Education			
Age Groups		H.S. grad or less:	40.0%	**Work**	
Under 18:	17.5%	Some college:	29.2%	White collar:	31.5%
18 to 34:	15.7%	College degree, 4 yr.:	18.6%	Blue collar:	50.7%
35 to 64:	37.1%	Post-grad study:	12.2%	Sales and service:	17.8%
Over 64:	29.6%			Govt. workers:	11.5%
		Military			
		Veterans/active duty:	12.2%		

Central Gulf Coast: Sarasota, Bradenton

When the Ringling Brothers made a success of the circus they founded in the 1880s, they needed a place for performers and animals to rest during the winter months. They settled on Sarasota: just far enough north to be reachable by railroad and just far enough south to be semitropical so the elephants would stay healthy. John Ringling established the Ringling Museum of Art and a huge sculpture garden, and built his own Venetian palace, the Ca' d'Zan. Next door, his brother, Charles, built a pair of neoclassical revival mansions in pink Georgia marble, which are now

Voter Turnout	
2013 Total Citizen 18+	555,841
2014 House Turnout	274,829
2014 Turnout as % CVAP	49.4%
2012 Turnout as % CVAP	65.4%

part of New College of Florida. But this was still a sparsely populated area until just after World War II, when the balmy Gulf Coast attracted new settlers—affluent, well-educated Republicans from upper-crust suburbs in the North. The population exploded. Manatee and Sarasota counties grew from a combined 64,000 people in 1950 to 702,000 in 2010. Like many Florida cities experiencing boom times, Sarasota was hit hard by the collapse of the housing market. In 2009, one of every 19 homeowners in Manatee and Sarasota counties received a foreclosure notice. As evidence of the local revival, the 2014 Sarasota opening of the $315 million luxury indoor Mall at University Town Center included new retail formats and technology. Feld Entertainment, the owners of the circus, in 2014 opened its new home in Ellenton in Manatee County.

The 16th Congressional District of Florida runs from the mouth of Tampa Bay to Lemon Bay, just north of Charlotte Harbor. It includes all of Sarasota County, which accounts for just over half the district's population. The remainder live in Manatee County to the north; the district takes in most of Manatee save for a small sliver in the east. It includes the idyllic beachfronts from sleepy Anna Maria to pricey Longboat Key and Lido Key and the more casual Siesta Key. Three of the wealthiest census tracts in all of Florida are located on these barrier islands.

The bayfront area along the Intracoastal Waterway is lined with high-rises and is often clogged with traffic from Bradenton to Sarasota. Below that, Venice—established in 1920 as a speculative land venture by the Brotherhood of Locomotive Engineers and known today as the "Shark Tooth Capital of the World"—sits directly on the Gulf of Mexico. Though some high-tech firms diversify the economy, the district as a whole remains reliant on tourists and well-off retirees: One-third of its population is 65 and older. Without a big increase in retirees since 2010, Sarasota would have lost population during that period. Bradenton, which styles itself as a center for sports tourism, has a rowing facility that has become a model for planners of the 2020 Olympic Games in Tokyo. The area ranks number-one nationwide in its Well-Being Index score. For many years, the 16th District was heavily Republican, and it remains that way in party registration. But like the affluent Northern suburbs from which so many of its voters came, it trended toward the Democrats in

2012 Presidential Vote		
Mitt Romney (R)	194,501	(54%)
Barack Obama (D)	161,100	(45%)

2008 Presidential Vote		
John McCain (R)	181,956	(51%)
Barack Obama (D)	172,028	(48%)

Cook Partisan Voting Index: R+6

the 1990s. The post-2010 redistricting made it a touch more Democratic, with working-class neighborhoods in Memphis, Palmetto, and Bradenton. In 2008, Republican John McCain won only 51% of the vote here, although Mitt Romney improved on that performance by more than 3 points.

Vern Buchanan (R)

Vern Buchanan, a Republican first elected in 2006, is the survivor of unusually tough election campaigns, but much of the pain has been self-inflicted. His business dealings and campaign finances have attracted the notice of both federal investigators and Democratic challengers.

Buchanan grew up outside of Detroit, the eldest of six children and the son of a factory foreman. He joined the Michigan Air National Guard and worked his way through college as a tae kwon do instructor. He earned a business degree at Cleary University and later an M.B.A. at the University of Detroit. Buchanan founded American Speedy Printing Centers and made his fortune by selling 700 quick-printing franchises before his 40th birthday. In 1990, he moved his family to Florida, where he found new success as an automobile dealer with franchises throughout the Southeast. Buchanan became active in Republican politics, serving as a top fundraiser for Gov. Jeb Bush and Sen. Mel Martinez. In 2002, he wanted to run for the 13th District House seat, but stepped aside for then-Florida Secretary of State

Katherine Harris, who had become a national figure for her role in the 2000 presidential vote recount.

Buchanan got his chance in 2006, when Harris ran for the Senate. His party connections and personal wealth made him the front-runner. In the primary, he stressed his conservative credentials and challenged his chief rival, former Sarasota Republican Party Chairman Tramm Hudson, for his positions on abortion rights and immigration. Hudson claimed that Buchanan resigned from his printing company just days before it declared bankruptcy. But Hudson stumbled when, in telling a story about his Army days, he asserted that black soldiers were poor swimmers. After spending more than $2 million of his own money, Buchanan won 32 percent of the vote in the five-way primary. But the bruising fight left Buchanan little time to recover before the general election.

The Democratic nominee was Christine Jennings, who like Buchanan was a transplanted Midwesterner and a self-made business success, as a bank owner. National Democrats pummeled Buchanan through the fall for his business dealings. Buchanan characterized Jennings as a pro-tax liberal, a charge that was tough to stick on the former Republican with a banking background. Despite the Republican advantage in the district, Buchanan was hurt by the attacks and the poor political environment for the GOP. This was the most expensive House race in 2006. Buchanan spent more than $8 million, including $5.5 million of his own money. Jennings spent $3 million, with about $2 million from her own pocket. Buchanan narrowly prevailed on Election Day, but Democrats disputed the results for another year. After a recount, Republican election officials certified Buchanan the winner by 369 votes out of nearly 240,000 cast. Jennings filed a lawsuit alleging voting machine malfunction, but several rounds of testing were inconclusive and she dropped her lawsuit.

In the House, Buchanan softened his ideological positions. He was one of 19 Republicans who supported most of the Democrats' early legislative agenda when they took control of the House in 2007. He voted for raising the minimum wage, cutting subsidies to industries, and allowing the federal government to negotiate lower drug prices with pharmaceutical companies. "I ran as a conservative, but I also ran as someone who is going to be independent," Buchanan told the *Sarasota Herald-Tribune*. After the BP oil spill in 2010, he pushed for a moratorium on all deep-water drilling permits in the Gulf of Mexico. He took stances further to the right on immigration and terrorism, calling for an English official-language law and using military tribunals instead of civilian courts to try terrorist suspects. The former car dealer voted against the bailout of Detroit automakers in 2008 because, he said, the companies "failed to develop viable restructuring proposals." The industry problems led him to sell several of his dealerships. On the Ways and Means Committee, he has been an advocate of corporate tax reform, and joined the bipartisan deal in March 2015 to adjust Medicare payments to doctors, and extend the Children's Health Insurance Program.

During the summer of 2011, Buchanan attracted unwanted attention. The *Sarasota Herald-Tribune* reported that during the past year Buchanan had spent almost $1 million in campaign contributions on himself, companies he owned, or family members. Most of the money reportedly was used to repay campaign checks he wrote to himself in 2006. Buchanan had previously faced allegations that business partners and employees of his car dealerships made contributions to his 2006 and 2008 congressional campaigns, and were then reimbursed by Buchanan's companies. He steadfastly denied any wrongdoing, and maintained that the Federal Elections Commission had exonerated him. But in December 2011, the *Herald-Tribune* unearthed FEC documents that attorneys investigating the matter found Buchanan to be "less than forthright and at times unbelievable." By 2012, both the Justice Department and the House Ethics Committee were looking into Buchanan's campaign activities. *Roll Call* newspaper has listed him high in its annual ratings of the wealthiest members of Congress. In January 2015, he ranked 11th, with a net worth of $37 million.

Buchanan has had campaign ups and downs, as well. He beat Jennings in a rematch in 2008 that, although less costly than the 2006 race, was similarly bitter, with accusations of business fraud, slander, and campaign finance violations. Buchanan emphasized his bipartisanship, and won 56%-37%. With ethics questions swirling in 2012, his House seat looked to be in jeopardy. His Democratic opponent, former state legislator Keith Fitzgerald, made Buchanan's integrity the main focus of his campaign and launched a website called the *Buchanan Files*, with links to news stories on the investigations. Then over the summer, the Ethics Committee cleared Buchanan of wrongdoing, and in September his office announced that the Justice Department had concluded its probe without charging him. Later that month, two of his associates pled guilty to illegally reimbursing employees who had made contributions to Buchanan. But the congressman said he had no knowledge of the reimbursements. Buchanan outraised Fitzgerald, $2.2 million to $1.4 million. He also attacked his opponent for helping direct $6 million to New College, where Fitzgerald taught. He prevailed, 54%-46%.

In the 2014 midterm election, as in 2010, Buchanan breezed to reelection against weakly funded opposition. He eyed other political opportunities, especially after Sen. Marco Rubio announced in April 2015 that he would not seek reelection. One downside of a Senate bid is that he has moved close to gaining a subcommittee chairmanship on Ways and Means.

SEVENTEENTH DISTRICT

Tom Rooney (R)

Elected 2008, 4th term; b. Nov. 21, 1970, Philadelphia, PA; Washington & Jefferson Col., B.A. 1993, U. of FL, M.A. 1996, U. of Miami, J.D. 1999; Catholic; married (Tara); 3 children.

Military Career: Army JAG, 2000-04; Army Reserves, 2004-07.

Professional Career: FL asst. atty. gen., 2004-05; CEO, Children's Place at HomeSafe, 2005-06; Practicing atty., 2006-08.

DC Office: 2160 RHOB, 20515, 202-225-5792; Fax: 202-225-3132; Website: rooney.house.gov.

State Offices: Punta Gorda, 941-575-9101; Riverview, 813-677-8646; Sebring, 863-402-9082.

Committees: *Appropriations:* Agriculture, Rural Development, FDA & Related Agencies; Military Construction, Veterans Affairs & Related Agencies; State, Foreign Operations & Related Programs. *Intelligence (Select):* Emerging Threats (Chmn); CIA.

Group Ratings

	ADA	ACLU	AFL-CIO	LCV	ITI	COC	HAFA	ACU	CFG	FRC
2014	0%	0%	–	3%	100%	86%	61%	76%	60%	100%
2013	0%	C	10%	0%	C	77%	C	76%	61%	C

National Journal Ratings

	2013 LIB	—	2013 CONS
Economic	39%	—	60%
Social	42%	—	57%
Foreign	47%	—	52%
Composite	43%	—	57%

Key Votes of the 113th Congress

1. Sandy storm spending	N	5. Medical Marijuana	N	9. Syrian Rebels Training	N
2. Violence Against Women Act	N	6. Farm Bill	Y	10. Keystone pipeline	Y
3. Guantanamo Bay Detainees	N	7. Afghanistan Combat	N	11. Immigration Exec. Action	Y
4. Abortion 20-week ban	Y	8. NSA Phone Data Collection	N	12. Bipartisan budget deal	Y

Election Results

2014 general	Thomas Rooney (R)	141,493	(63%)	$669,304
	William Bronson (D)	82,263	(37%)	$24,607
2014 primary	Tom Rooney (R)	unopposed		

Prior winning percentages: 2012 (59%), 2010 (67%), 2008 (60%)

Population		Race and Ethnicity		Income	
Total:	721,297	White	69.6%	Median income:	$41,798
Urban:	22.9%	Latino	18.9%		*(361 of 435)*
Suburban:	57.8%	Black	8.4%	Under $50,000	58.0%
Rural:	19.3%	Asian	1.2%	$50,000-$99,999:	29.0%
Land area:	4,451	Two races	1.6%	$100,000-$199,999:	11.0%
Pop/sq. mi.:	162.1	White Ethnic	23.9%	$200,000 or more:	2.0%
Born in state:	36.0%			Poverty Rate	18.1%
		Education			
Age Groups		H.S. grad or less:	52.1%	**Work**	
Under 18:	20.2%	Some college:	29.8%	White collar:	28.6%
18 to 34:	17.2%	College degree, 4 yr.:	11.9%	Blue collar:	47.2%
35 to 64:	36.4%	Post-grad study:	6.3%	Sales and service:	24.1%
Over 64:	26.3%				
		Military		Govt. workers:	13.7%
		Veterans/active duty:	13.4%		

South Central Florida: Charlotte, Polk

The population of Charlotte County, Fla., didn't reach 10,000 until the 1950s. But local histories, such as the definitive *Punta Gorda: In the Beginning, 1865-1900*, assure us that the region was anything but quiet before then. In 1886, when railroads reached the convergence of the Peace River and

Voter Turnout	
2013 Total Citizen 18+	533,642
2014 House Turnout	223,756
2014 Turnout as % CVAP	41.9%
2012 Turnout as % CVAP	56.5%

Charlotte Harbor, the area was home to a small fishing center, a port that mostly shipped phosphate, and a few cattle ranches. But the exotic locale—at that point it was the farthest south one could travel on the rail lines—pleasant climate, and emerging sport of tarpon fishing encouraged developers to turn it into a destination for the wealthy. Elizabeth Colt, widow of gun-manufacturer Samuel Colt; John Wanamaker, of the eponymous Philadelphia department store; and other wealthy individuals began making annual sojourns southward to winter in the semitropical paradise. But these riches existed uneasily alongside what was still a frontier-like culture. Violence among cattlemen was common in the 1890s, and a city marshal was assassinated in 1904 for enforcing the local liquor law.

Today, Charlotte County is a very different place. The advent of Social Security, the invention of air conditioning, and advances in transportation all conspired to drive rapid growth in the latter half of the 20th century: The county's population doubled in the 1950s, 1960s, and 1970s, and nearly did so again in the 1980s. Since then, the gains have been smaller. The population is now over 168,000, and Port Charlotte, developed in the 1950s, is now the most populous locale. The unemployment rate peaked here at almost 13% in 2010, but fell to 5.1% at the end of 2014. Punta Gorda itself maintains a small-town and small-business feel: Its more than 100 restaurants include hardly any national chains, and in 2015 it was named by *Kiplinger* as one of the top 10 most affordable places in the United States to retire.

The 17th Congressional District of Florida is based in Charlotte County, to the extent it is based anywhere. Charlotte County contributes 23% of the sprawling district's population, which is the largest of the 10 counties within its borders. About 16% of the population resides at the other end of the district, in southeastern Hillsborough County, while another 18% reside in southern Polk County. The remainder of the population is spread over the largely rural area north and west of Lake Okeechobee, a landscape still dominated by cattle farms and others that produce citrus, tomatoes, and vegetables. There

2012 Presidential Vote		
Mitt Romney (R)	170,573	(58%)
Barack Obama (D)	123,579	(42%)
2008 Presidential Vote		
John McCain (R)	166,643	(56%)
Barack Obama (D)	128,537	(43%)
Cook Partisan Voting Index:	R+10	

is at least one minor celebrity here: Bubbles, Michael Jackson's former pet chimpanzee, lives at the Center for Great Apes in rural Hardee County. Republicans maintain a 5-point registration advantage in the district, but in practice their edge is much larger; Mitt Romney carried the district easily in 2012.

Tom Rooney (R)

Tom Rooney, a Republican elected in 2008, is a former military prosecutor and West Point instructor who holds the firmly conservative views that such a background suggests. But in a highly polarized House, Rooney has been unusually adept in working with Democrats on issues of common interest.

The grandson of Pittsburgh Steelers founding owner Art Rooney, he was born in Philadelphia and was a water boy for the team. (Steelers employees were his largest single campaign contributor between 2008 and 2012.) When he was 14, his father moved to Palm Beach Gardens where his family owned the Palm Beach Kennel Club, a racetrack and gambling business. Rooney briefly attended Syracuse University, where he earned a spot as a tight end and deep snapper for the Orangemen. But with no desire for a professional football career, Rooney transferred to the smaller Washington and Jefferson College just outside Pittsburgh, where he played both football and golf. He was a staff assistant for Republican Sen. Connie Mack of Florida for a brief period, then got a law degree from the University of Miami, where he met his wife, Tara. After graduation, Rooney was a special assistant U.S. attorney at Fort Hood in Texas, and later taught constitutional and criminal law at the U.S. Military Academy at West Point. When then-Republican Charlie Crist became Florida attorney general, he hired Rooney as an assistant attorney general in 2004. Next, he headed a home for abused children and, in 2006, entered private law practice in Stuart.

Rooney ran for the House in 2008, with endorsements from Mack and Crist, who had since become governor. He won the primary by only 1,011 votes over state Rep. Gayle Harrell, 36.7%-34.9%. In the general election, Rooney challenged freshman Democrat Tim Mahoney, who seemed to be preparing for an easy reelection. Mahoney outpaced Rooney in fundraising and had a solid lead in most pre-election polls. But on Oct. 13, ABC News broke the story that Mahoney had paid a former aide $121,000 to keep quiet about their affair after he ended the relationship and fired her. The incumbent admitted to having "multiple affairs" while in Congress, but asserted he had done nothing to violate his oath of office. Rooney shot up nearly 25 points in the polls. Still, Mahoney declined to end his campaign, even after Democratic House Speaker Nancy Pelosi called for an Ethics Committee investigation into the payment. Mahoney's financial contributions quickly dried up. Rooney won easily with 60 percent of the vote.

In the House, he joined the Republican whip team and was given a seat on the Intelligence Committee. But he has shown independence and a repeated willingness to challenge GOP leaders. He sponsored a controversial House-passed resolution in February 2011 to cut $450 million in Pentagon spending, including a project to build a second engine for the F-35 jet fighter that was based near Republican Speaker John Boehner's Ohio district. Rooney worked with Florida Democrat Ted Deutch—with whom he occasionally plays in a rock band—on a 2011 measure that became law to help homeless veterans. And he was the lead sponsor of a bipartisan measure that passed the Judiciary Committee in February 2012 to ban the import or interstate trade of Burmese pythons and eight other species of snakes that have decimated native animal populations in the Everglades.

But Rooney's bipartisanship has its limits. After joining the Agriculture Committee in mid-2010, he became an outspoken critic of efforts to lift the ban on travel and food sales to Cuba. He has taken a strong stand against illegal immigration, introducing a bill in 2010 to require incarcerated illegal immigrants to be deported as soon as they are released from jail. He pushed a measure in 2011 to deny the Environmental Protection Agency the authority to enforce water pollution rules that agricultural interests deemed overly harsh. "I want to be the environmental congressman for my district," Rooney told EPA Administrator Lisa Jackson at a hearing. "But I also represent a lot of farmers." He was one of five House Republicans in July 2012 who called for an investigation into whether State Department aide Huma Abedin tried to improperly influence U.S. policy in favor of the Muslim Brotherhood—an accusation that drew strong criticism from Boehner and Sen. John McCain of Arizona. He supported six-year term limits for House members, but added that he would abide by them only if they were required for all House members. He joined the Appropriations Committee in 2013. Two years later, he became chairman of the Intelligence Subcommittee on Emerging Threats, which is an influential position but one that discourages public discussion.

Redistricting in 2012 moved him from a district that dipped down into Martin and Palm Beach Counties to the new, more rural 17th District. He has not been seriously challenged. In January 2015, he voted to give Boehner another term as speaker, unlike several other

Florida Republicans. When Sen. Marco Rubio announced that he will not seek a second term in 2016, Rooney seriously explored running for the Senate. His national security and National Football League backgrounds, plus his conservative base, would be a useful start for his candidacy in what looked to be a close contest.

EIGHTEENTH DISTRICT

Patrick Murphy (D)

Elected 2012, 2nd term; b. March 30, 1983, Miami; U. of Miami, B.S. 2006; Catholic; single.

Professional Career: Project mgr., engineer, Coastal Construction Group, 2001-06; Accountant, Coastal Construction Group, 2006-07; Auditor, Deloitte & Touche, 2007-10; V.P., Coastal Environmental Services, 2010-present.

DC Office: 211 CHOB, 20515, 202-225-3026; Fax: 202-225-8398; Website: patrickmurphy.house.gov.

State Offices: Fort Pierce, 772-489-0736; Palm Beach Gardens, 561-253-8433; Port St. Lucie, 772-336-2877; Stuart, 772-781-3266.

Committees: *Financial Services:* Capital Markets & Government-Sponsored Enterprises; Monetary Policy & Trade. *Intelligence (Select):* Department of Defense Intelligence & Overhead Architecture; NSA & Cybersecurity.

Group Ratings

	ADA	ACLU	AFL-CIO	LCV	ITI	COC	HAFA	ACU	CFG	FRC
2014	50%	66%	–	71%	80%	86%	12%	4%	19%	13%
2013	45%	C	86%	82%	C	77%	C	20%	11%	C

National Journal Ratings

	2013 LIB	—	2013 CONS
Economic	56%	—	43%
Social	55%	—	45%
Foreign	58%	—	42%
Composite	57%	—	44%

Key Votes of the 113th Congress

1. Sandy storm spending	Y	5. Medical Marijuana	Y	9. Syrian Rebels Training	Y
2. Violence Against Women Act	Y	6. Farm Bill	Y	10. Keystone pipeline	Y
3. Guantanamo Bay Detainees	N	7. Afghanistan Combat	Y	11. Immigration Exec. Action	N
4. Abortion 20-week ban	N	8. NSA Phone Data Collection	N	12. Bipartisan budget deal	Y

Election Results

2014 general	Patrick Murphy (D) 151,478	(60%)	$4,924,668	$1,276,236	
	Carl Domino (R) 101,896	(40%)	$1,498,450	$8,978	$155,079
2014 primary	Patrick Murphy (D) ....unopposed				

Prior winning percentage: 2012 (50%)

Population		Race and Ethnicity		Income	
Total:	705,469	White	70.6%	Median income:	$51,068
Urban:	40.5%	Latino	14.1%		*(220 of 435)*
Suburban:	54.3%	Black	11.4%	Under $50,000	49.1%
Rural:	5.2%	Asian	1.9%	$50,000-$99,999:	28.8%
Land area:	1,979	Two races	1.6%	$100,000-$199,999:	16.2%
Pop/sq. mi.:	356.5	White Ethnic	34.1%	$200,000 or more:	5.9%
Born in state:	32.8%			Poverty Rate	13.6%
		Education			
Age Groups		H.S. grad or less:	39.6%	**Work**	
Under 18:	19.2%	Some college:	31.4%	White collar:	35.0%
18 to 34:	17.6%	College degree, 4 yr.:	18.4%	Blue collar:	46.9%
35 to 64:	39.2%	Post-grad study:	10.6%	Sales and service:	18.0%
Over 64:	24.0%				
		Military		Govt. workers:	12.0%
		Veterans/active duty:	10.4%		

Palm Beach, Treasure Coast

Urban Florida has fanned far across the swamplands from its original nuclei in beachfront resort communities. Once, metro Palm Beach was a narrow stretch along Lake Worth; now it runs inland almost halfway to Lake Okeechobee, spreading out from its original locus around the posh Breakers Hotel. Old

Voter Turnout	
2013 Total Citizen 18+	534,172
2014 House Turnout	253,374
2014 Turnout as % CVAP	47.4%
2012 Turnout as % CVAP	64.9%

beach towns such as Hobe Sound have become the hub of affluent developments that stretch all the way to Stuart in Martin County. Farther north, near the old town of Fort Pierce, are larger but more modest developments like Port St. Lucie, which had a population of only 330 in 1970. Today it is the ninth largest city in Florida, with a population of over 171,000. Port St. Lucie was hit hard during the 2008 mortgage meltdown, resulting in more than 10,000 properties in foreclosure and an unemployment rate that surpassed 13% the following year. Recovery came slowly; unemployment was still above 10% in late 2012, and about 1 in every 200 homes in St. Lucie County was in some state of foreclosure that year, the third highest rate in the state. But by the end of 2014, the rate was down to a more mainstream 6.2%. Farther south, northern Palm Beach County is changing as well. The county, along with the state of Florida, subsidized the Scripps Research Institute's new center in Jupiter, in hopes of attracting biotechnology businesses. A German research group, the Max Planck Society, also opened a branch in Jupiter and has collaborated with two local universities. In 2014, the $150 million Harbourside Place entertainment complex opened in Jupiter, including a restaurant owned by golfer Tiger Woods.

The 18th Congressional District includes all of Martin County, with its affluent towns of Stuart and Hobe Sound, as well as all of more modest St. Lucie County. The 2012 election returns here reflect the counties' socioeconomic profiles: Republican Mitt Romney in 2012 received 61% of the vote in Martin County, but only 46% in more-populous St.

2012 Presidential Vote		
Mitt Romney (R)	177,300	(52%)
Barack Obama (D)	163,067	(48%)
2008 Presidential Vote		
Barack Obama (D)	172,218	(51%)
John McCain (R)	162,205	(48%)
Cook Partisan Voting Index: R+3		

Lucie. To the south, about 40% of the district's population resides in the northern precincts of Palm Beach County, including Palm Beach Gardens, an area filled with gated communities and home to the Professional Golfers' Association of America. Barack Obama carried the district with 51% of the vote in 2008, but it swung almost 4 points toward Romney in 2012.

Patrick Murphy (D)

Democrat Patrick Murphy, elected in 2012, became the youngest member of the new Congress. Having narrowly defeated tea party favorite Rep. Allen West in the cycle's most expensive and contentious House race, he laid the groundwork for an even more daunting campaign for the Senate in 2016.

Murphy was born in Miami but grew up in the Florida Keys. He is the youngest son of the founder of Florida-based Coastal Construction Group. The family relocated to Westin when Murphy was 12, but he recalls moving constantly to follow the construction business. The industry has been a part of his family history for five generations, tracing its origins to Ireland, where an ancestor was a shipbuilder. During his high school years, Murphy was class president and captain of the football and baseball teams. He also began working for the family business as a laborer, digging holes. A series of injuries made him reconsider his dream of playing sports in college. "I realized my body is not cut out for this," Murphy said.

He studied business administration at the University of Miami while continuing to work for Coastal. Murphy says he never felt pressured to join the family business after graduation. "My dad said from early on, 'Do what makes you happy. ... If you want to join the family business, we'd love to have you,'" he recalled. Murphy became a certified public accountant, eventually joining the consulting firm Deloitte Touche. In 2010, he returned to the family business. After the BP oil spill off the coast of Louisiana, Murphy decided to form a spinoff, Coastal Environmental Services, which allowed the company to branch out into disaster relief and cleanup. As the affiliate's vice president, Murphy traveled to affected areas and promoted a line of oil-skimming boats used to clean the water.

Murphy, originally a Republican, grew disillusioned over the Iraq War. He switched his party affiliation in January 2011. Two months later, he announced his bid to run against the outspoken West in the Democratic-leaning 22nd District. In early 2012, West announced he would run in the more GOP-friendly 18th District, and Murphy decided to challenge him there. "There is no safe district he can run to," he said.

After easily securing the Democratic nomination, Murphy was added to the Democratic Congressional Campaign Committee's "Red to Blue" program. The committee spent heavily on Palm Beach media. West trounced him in the money race, raising $18.5 million to Murphy's $4.5 million. Democratic Party groups spent more than $3 million for Murphy. He campaigned on his support for renewable energy technologies and on his background as a businessman. But a large part of his success was selling himself as the non-West. The incumbent attracted notoriety when he said a large number of House members are communists, and ran tough ads spotlighting Murphy's arrest in his freshman year in college for disorderly intoxication and possessing a fake driver's license. The charges had been subsequently dismissed.

Election Night returns showed Murphy with a small lead. West initially refused to concede, challenging the accuracy of St. Lucie County's elections supervisor. After two weeks, however, Murphy remained ahead by .58%, which was more than the .5% margin required under Florida law to trigger a full recount. West eventually conceded, with the final result showing a 50.3%-49.7% win for Murphy, a difference of 1,904 votes.

In the House, Murphy initially did not seek media attention. He devoted much of his focus to working with Republicans to gain support for bipartisan legislation. He and Kevin Brady of Texas won House passage in April 2015 of their bill to make permanent the deductibility of state and local sales taxes on federal tax returns. With Luke Messer of Indiana, Murphy filed a proposal for the post-9/11 GI bill to cover application fees for college, graduate and vocational students. He sought other ways to distance himself from the Democratic establishment in the House. In May 2014, he was one of seven Democrats to vote to create a committee to investigate the attacks on the American consulate in Benghazi, Libya. After the election, he told reporters that Democrats should consider other candidates for their party leader in addition to Nancy Pelosi. In early 2015, *The New York Times* listed Murphy among 10 House Democrats who crossed the aisle most often to vote with Republicans. Still, he got a leadership selection to the Intelligence Committee in January 2015.

In 2014, Murphy had a relatively easy reelection against Carl Domino, a former state legislator. He outspent the challenger $5 million to $1.5 million, and won 60%-40%. Murphy spent more money than any House Democrat seeking reelection in 2014.

He moved into the national spotlight in March 2015, when he announced that he would run for the Senate seat held by Marco Rubio, regardless of whether Rubio sought a second term. Rubio was "a career politician who has shown time and time again that he does not represent Florida's middle class," Murphy said. "Rubio denies climate change is real and wants to privatize Social Security. It's clear, it's time for Marco Rubio to go." Even after Rubio decided against reelection, Murphy remained the favorite of Senate Democratic campaign officials who liked his moderate stripes. That dismayed some progressive groups who were not enthusiastic about Murphy's record, and led Rep. Alan Grayson to declare his candidacy for the Democratic nomination.

NINETEENTH DISTRICT

Curt Clawson (R)

Elected 2014, 1st full term; b. Sept. 30, 1959, Tacoma, WA; Purdue U., B.A. B.S. 1984; Harvard U., M.B.A. 1990; Mormon; divorced.

Professional Career: Arvin Industries, 1986-95; Honeywell Corp (Allied Signal), 1995-98; Pres. and COO, American National Can 1998-2000; CEO, Hayes Lemmerz International, 2001-12.

DC Office: 228 CHOB, 20515, 202-225-2536; Fax: 202-226-0439; Website: clawson.house.gov.

State Offices: Cape Coral, 239-573-5837; Naples, 239-252-6225.

Committees: *Foreign Affairs:* Africa, Global Health, Global Human Rights & International Organizations; Middle East & North Africa. *Homeland Security:* Cybersecurity, Infrastructure Protection & Security Technologies; Oversight, Investigations & Management.

Election Results

2014 general	Curt Clawson (R)	159,354	(65%)	$4,824,230*	$107,202*	$864,361*
	April Freeman (D)	80,824	(33%)	$231,798		
	Ray Netherwood (Lib)	6,671	(3%)	$39,880		
2014 primary	Curt Clawson (R)	unopposed *				

Prior winning percentage: 2014 special (67%)
* Includes special election

Population		Race and Ethnicity		Income	
Total:	738,554	White	72.9%	Median income:	$49,135
Urban:	74.9%	Latino	16.9%		*(252 of 435)*
Suburban:	25.1%	Black	7.3%	Under $50,000	50.7%
Rural:	0.0%	Asian	1.4%	$50,000-$99,999:	27.7%
Land area:	782	Two races	1.1%	$100,000-$199,999:	15.3%
Pop/sq. mi.:	944.4	White Ethnic	31.1%	$200,000 or more:	6.3%
Born in state:	23.0%			Poverty Rate	15.0%
		Education			
Age Groups		H.S. grad or less:	40.6%	**Work**	
Under 18:	17.7%	Some college:	28.6%	White collar:	31.9%
18 to 34:	17.2%	College degree, 4 yr.:	19.1%	Blue collar:	50.2%
35 to 64:	36.3%	Post-grad study:	11.6%	Sales and service:	18.0%
Over 64:	28.8%			Govt. workers:	10.1%
		Military			
		Veterans/active duty:	11.5%		

Southern Gulf Coast: Fort Myers, Naples

Florida's Gulf Coast is at the edge of the tropics, a physical environment once teeming with disease and inhospitable to advanced civilization, but now evolved into a model for retirement living. One of the earliest white settlements here was Fort Myers, built in 1850 as an Army post to pursue the Semi-

Voter Turnout	
2013 Total Citizen 18+	546,444
2014 House Turnout	246,861
2014 Turnout as % CVAP	45.2%
2012 Turnout as % CVAP	60.7%

nole Indians; in 1858, the last of the natives were driven out. For a century after that, this corner of Florida was mostly deserted, save for some small resort communities developed around wide, white-sand beaches with gentle breakers. The inlets and broad estuaries are perfect for boating, and the wetlands are graced with exotic birds. Thomas Edison had his winter home in Fort Myers, Henry Ford used to visit here, and tourists were drawn to beaches thick with seashells on nearby Sanibel and Captiva islands. But the local economy could not support many permanent residents, and at the beginning of World War II, there were only 68,000 people living on the Gulf Coast from Bradenton south to Naples.

The climate and environment, and the fact that Florida has no state income or inheritance tax, soon attracted waves of affluent postwar suburbanites from the Midwest and Northeast. Developers such as Barron Collier, who financed the building of the Tamiami Trail across the soggy Everglades and designed Naples with the wealthy in mind, were determined to avoid the high-rise canyons that line the Atlantic from Palm Beach to Miami. Their alternative was to construct low-rise, city-style developments such as the retirement community of Cape Coral, located where the Caloosahatchee River completes its journey from Lake Okeechobee to San Carlos Bay.

Much of this area has been damaged by hurricanes in recent years, but there was no appreciable slowdown in development until the recession took hold in 2008. That year, land values sank and a large inventory of housing went unsold. The area had the nation's largest number of housing foreclosures, which accounted for nearly half of the home sales. In Lee County, the share of students taking free and reduced-cost meals climbed to 70 percent in 2012, a higher percentage than more urbanized school districts around Miami and Fort Lauderdale. Local officials' predictions of a slow recovery were borne out: The Cape Coral-Fort Myers area lost more jobs than any other metropolitan area in the state in 2012. Two years later, business conditions had improved notably. A January 2015 business forecast projected Collier as the fastest-growing county in the state, with Lee close behind. Also at that time, the unemployment rates for each county were below the national and state rates, and their rapid population growth had resumed. In a cautionary note, the income gap had grown wider than ever.

The 19th Congressional District occupies the southern half of the habitable Gulf Coast below Tampa Bay. Nearly 30% of the residents here are over the age of 65. The 19th includes almost all of Lee County and about half of the population of Collier County, including Naples and Marco Island. Over

2012 Presidential Vote		
Mitt Romney (R)................195,051	(61%)
Barack Obama (D) 124,784	(39%)
2008 Presidential Vote		
John McCain (R)................181,386	(57%)
Barack Obama (D) 135,070	(42%)
Cook Partisan Voting Index: R+12		

three-quarters of the district's residents live in Lee County, in Fort Myers, Cape Coral, and Bonita Springs and on Sanibel and Captiva islands. In a state where Republican registration rates often understate GOP voting strength, just 28% were registered Democrats, the lowest share of any Florida congressional district.

Curt Clawson (R)

Republican Curt Clawson won a June 2014 special election to replace first-term GOP Rep. Trey Radel, who bowed to calls from Florida Republicans to resign after his 2013 arrest on cocaine possession charges. Clawson, a college basketball player and wealthy former automotive CEO, won his seat with backing from tea party groups.

Clawson was born in Tacoma Washington and grew up in North Carolina, where he was an avid basketball player. He became good enough to play at Purdue University, where he was team captain for the squad that won the 1984 Big Ten championship. He also was a two-time All-Academic Big Ten selection. After obtaining his master's in business administration from Harvard, Clawson worked for several companies, most in the automotive industry. In 2001, he took over as CEO of Hayes Lemmerz, an international manufacturer of aluminum wheels. He steered the company out of bankruptcy. When it was sold to a Brazilian wheel company in 2012, he moved to Bonita Springs, where his parents had settled.

Radel had been elected in 2012 to the seat given up by GOP Rep. Connie Mack, who ran unsuccessfully for the Senate. A former radio talk-show host, the media-savvy Radel achieved prominence with his frequent use of social media, often posting video feeds on Twitter. After his arrest for buying cocaine from an undercover District of Columbia police officer, he took a self-imposed leave of absence and subsequently resigned his seat. Subsequently, he served probation, the cocaine charges were dropped, and Radel opened a media-consulting business. Clawson contacted him for occasional advice.

Despite never having sought elected office, Clawson believed that his extensive business background would play well with the district's mostly conservative voters, who gave Mitt Romney 61% of the presidential vote in 2012. "I got into this race because I felt like we needed more outsiders in Congress," he said in a tweet. "The career politicians aren't getting the job done." The local GOP establishment backed Lizbeth Benacquisto, who had risen swiftly as a state senator. Clawson poured $2 million into television ads—including one memorable spot in which he challenged President Barack Obama, another hoops enthusiast, to a three-point shooting contest. As he rose in the polls, he won the backing of Mack, GOP Sen. Rand Paul of Kentucky and national tea party groups such as the Tea Party Express. In the four-candidate field, he won the April primary with 38% percent of the vote to 26% for Benacquisto.

His Democratic opponent in the June special election was April Freeman, a TV and film production executive. She tried to seize on the Radel scandal by challenging Clawson to take a drug test, a challenge that Clawson—a Mormon who does not drink or smoke—gladly accepted. (Both of their results came back clean.) But Freeman struggled to raise money against Clawson, who continued to pour his own cash into the race. Clawson focused much of his campaign on restoring U.S. economic competitiveness. He said he thinks the tea party could win more elections and improve its reputation among voters if it combined that issue with its traditional focus on shrinking government. "The two walk hand in hand, and oppose that idea about tea party candidates being the unsophisticated people who are angry but just sit around not doing anything about it," he said. In the June special election, he defeated Freeman, 67%-29%.

In the House, Clawson received seats on the Homeland Security and Foreign Affairs committees. At a July hearing to welcome him to the Foreign Affairs Subcommittee on Asia, panel Chairman Steve Chabot of Ohio touted Clawson's business acumen and knowledge of four languages. But the freshman congressman proceeded to make a rookie mistake that cascaded across social media and the blogosphere: He incorrectly mistook two U.S. officials as representatives of India's government. "I'm familiar with your country; I love your country," he told the two officials, who worked for the State and Commerce departments.

Clawson made his mark on Opening Day of Congress in January 2015, when he was among the 25 Republicans who chose not to vote for John Boehner for speaker. Making it more painful for Boehner was that he owned a condo on Marco Island in Clawson's district. The newcomer, who voted for Sen. Rand Paul for speaker, rejected accusations that he was disloyal. "I think disagreement is good because it causes learning and progress," he told the *News-Press* of Fort Myers. Later that month, he gave the tea party response to Obama's State of the Union address. Largely ignoring the president's speech, Clawson offered his own vision of personal liberty and wealth creation. "We want opportunity for all, but favoritism for none," Clawson emphasized. But he had relatively few moments in the sun during his first year in Congress. Likewise, his November 2014 victory for a full term attracted little attention. In a near rerun of the special election, he defeated Freeman 65%-33%. His independence has raised eyebrows at home, and he could be vulnerable to a primary challenge from the GOP establishment.

TWENTIETH DISTRICT

Alcee Hastings (D)

Elected 1992, 12th term; b. Sept. 5, 1936, Altamonte Springs; Fisk U., B.A. 1958, Howard U., 1958-60, FL A&M, J.D. 1963; Methodist; divorced; 3 children.

Elected Office: Broward Cnty. Circuit Court judge, 1977-79.

Professional Career: Practicing atty., 1964-77, 1989-92; Federal judge, U.S. Dist. Court, 1979-89.

DC Office: 2353 RHOB, 20515, 202-225-1313; Fax: 202-225-1171; Website: alceehastings.house.gov.

State Offices: Ft. Lauderdale, 954-733-2800; Mangonia Park, 561-469-7048.

Committees: *Rules:* Legislative & Budget Process (RMM).

Group Ratings

	ADA	ACLU	AFL-CIO	LCV	ITI	COC	HAFA	ACU	CFG	FRC
2014	75%	83%	–	89%	80%	36%	9%	5%	7%	0%
2013	90%	C	100%	93%	C	42%	C	4%	13%	C

National Journal Ratings

	2013 LIB	—	2013 CONS
Economic	89%	—	11%
Social	93%	—	0%
Foreign	94%	—	0%
Composite	94%	—	6%

Key Votes of the 113th Congress

1. Sandy storm spending	Y	5. Medical Marijuana	NV	9. Syrian Rebels Training	N
2. Violence Against Women Act	Y	6. Farm Bill	N	10. Keystone pipeline	N
3. Guantanamo Bay Detainees	Y	7. Afghanistan Combat	Y	11. Immigration Exec. Action	N
4. Abortion 20-week ban	N	8. NSA Phone Data Collection	Y	12. Bipartisan budget deal	Y

Election Results

2014 general	Alcee Hastings (D)	128,498	(82%)	$811,995
	Jay Bonner (R)	28,968	(18%)	$25,609
2014 primary	Alcee Hastings (D)	29,236	(79%)	
	Jean Enright	5,256	(14%)	
	Jameel McCline	2,424	(7%)	

Prior winning percentages: 2012 (88%), 2010 (79%), 2008 (82%), 2006 (100%), 2004 (100%), 2002 (77%), 2000 (76%), 1998 (100%), 1996 (73%), 1994 (100%), 1992 (59%)

Population		Race and Ethnicity		Income	
Total:	728,883	Black	51.9%	Median income:	$37,105
Urban:	75.4%	White	23.6%		*(408 of 435)*
Suburban:	22.3%	Latino	20.9%	Under $50,000	63.6%
Rural:	2.3%	Asian	1.7%	$50,000-$99,999:	26.7%
Land area:	855	Two races	1.4%	$100,000-$199,999:	8.7%
Pop/sq. mi.:	852.4	White Ethnic	12.6%	$200,000 or more:	1.0%
Born in state:	41.0%			Poverty Rate	23.9%
		Education			
Age Groups		H.S. grad or less:	53.4%	**Work**	
Under 18:	24.0%	Some college:	27.9%	White collar:	23.8%
18 to 34:	23.5%	College degree, 4 yr.:	12.9%	Blue collar:	57.1%
35 to 64:	38.5%	Post-grad study:	5.8%	Sales and service:	19.2%
Over 64:	13.9%				
		Military		Govt. workers:	13.0%
		Veterans/active duty:	5.3%		

Parts of Fort Lauderdale and West Palm Beach

In the morning shadow of the high-rise condominiums that line the Atlantic Ocean, beyond the quiet waters that separate the barrier islands from the mainland, and a few blocks off old U.S. 1, are the African-American neighborhoods of South Florida's Gold Coast. They are clusters of older stucco homes

Voter Turnout	
2013 Total Citizen 18+	449,562
2014 House Turnout	157,466
2014 Turnout as % CVAP	35.0%
2012 Turnout as % CVAP	59.3%

and commercial storefronts, ranging from upper-middle-class enclaves to rundown slums. These neighborhoods, largely populated by the working poor and with relatively few seniors, are bypassed by most tourists.

The 20th Congressional District of Florida gathers together many of South Florida's black neighborhoods in a geographically contrived, but demographically coherent, constituency. It resembles a giant manta ray (or perhaps a flying Superman, with a billowing cape and outstretched arms). The body of the district is in the Everglades. This is a land of swamps and drainage canals, with some farms and citrus groves. Some people live in migrant worker camps, while others live in small towns around Lake Okeechobee such as Clewiston, the nation's largest sugar producer, nicknamed "America's sweetest town." Sugar is a big industry throughout this part of Florida. But in 2008, the South Florida Water Management District approved Republican Gov. Charlie Crist's proposal to buy much of the land owned by U.S. Sugar Corp. around Lake Okeechobee for $1.35 billion, with most farming to be phased out within seven years. That would allow water to pass over land from the lake, through the Everglades, to the Gulf of Mexico. The recession forced the plan to be delayed and scaled back to $197 million, and sugar farmers continued to battle against it, while environmentalists sought its revival.

The sugar industry faces other problems. The declining economy resulted in a decline in migrant workers, leaving some farmers worried about the availability of labor in the future. Lately, however, there simply have not been enough jobs. In July 2014, with unemployment at 12.5 percent, rural Hendry was the only Florida county that had double-digit joblessness. Businesses in Hendry are placing their hopes on AirGlades Airport, which the Federal Aviation Administration has certified as the only privately owned international airport in the nation. They viewed the facility, with a planned 12,000 foot runway, as a potential hub for commercial cargo, including flowers and fish from South America.

The bulk of the district's population resides in the two arms that extend east from the Everglades and get close to, but never quite reach, the Atlantic Ocean. One arm moves through northern Palm Beach County, past high-income Wellington and into West Palm Beach, and then continues south along Interstate 95 and U.S. 1 to take in heavily minority areas of Lake Worth and Boynton Beach. The second, and most populated, arm of the district reaches east into Broward County to take in African-American areas in Fort Lauderdale, Lauderhill, North Lauderdale, Pompano Beach, and Deerfield Beach. Lauderdale Lakes was slow to adjust spending levels following the financial collapse and was brought to the brink of insolvency amid charges that officials grossly mismanaged city funds. The city finally hiked taxes, cut 10% of its employees, and worked out a payment plan for its debt.

Overall, the population is 52% black and 21% Hispanic. This is the second-most heavily Democratic district in Florida, with incoming Cubans providing the only minor countertrend for the GOP. But it is not uniformly liberal on all issues. In 2008, African-American voters backed a state constitutional amendment banning same-sex marriage by about 2-to-1, enabling the measure to carry Broward County despite the county's large gay population.

2012 Presidential Vote		
Barack Obama (D) 216,496	(83%)
Mitt Romney (R)...................44,469	(17%)

2008 Presidential Vote		
Barack Obama (D) 205,844	(81%)
John McCain (R)...................47,128	(19%)

Cook Partisan Voting Index: D+29

Alcee Hastings (D)

Alcee Hastings, a personable Democrat first elected in 1992, has shrugged off an assortment of scandals, including his impeachment for bribery and perjury when he was a federal judge in the 1980s. Today he is an enduringly popular figure with Democratic colleagues in the House and South Florida constituents.

Hastings had a relatively wide-ranging upbringing in the segregated America of the post-World War II decades. He grew up in a black suburb of Orlando and moved as a child to Jersey City and New York, where his parents worked as domestic servants for a rich Jewish family. He attended a Rosenwald school in Altamonte Springs, one of hundreds established for Southern blacks by Sears executive Julius Rosenwald. He graduated from Fisk University in Nashville and from Florida A&M law school in Tallahassee. From those beginnings, he made a rapid ascent, practicing law in Fort Lauderdale and finishing fourth in the five-candidate Democratic primary when he ran for the U.S. Senate in 1970, at age 34. He became a state judge in Broward County in 1977 and was confirmed as a federal judge in 1979.

Then his career took a sharp turn downward. He was charged with conspiring with a friend to take a $150,000 bribe and give two convicted swindlers light sentences. A Miami jury acquitted Hastings in 1983, but the friend was convicted. The 11th Circuit Court of Appeals called for impeachment in 1987 and referred the case to Congress. Hastings was impeached by the House on a vote of 413-3 and convicted by the Senate 69-26. In the House, Democratic Rep. John Conyers of Michigan, a senior member of the Congressional Black Caucus, made the case for impeachment. As a footnote, during a 1997 investigation into the Federal Bureau of Investigation crime lab, the Department of Justice found that an agent falsely testified against Hastings. He and Conyers moved to reopen the case, but nothing came of it.

After his removal from the bench, Hastings in 1990 ran an abortive campaign for governor, then lost in a primary for secretary of state. When the 23rd District was created in 1992, he led in the primary 28%-27%. In the October runoff, he faced Palm Beach County legislator Lois Frankel, who blasted Hastings for his record. He responded, "The bitch is a racist." Hastings was helped by a ruling from federal Judge Stanley Sporkin that his removal from office was invalid because the full Senate did not hear the charges. The Supreme Court later ruled to the contrary in a case of another convicted federal judge in 1993, but by that time Hastings was in Congress. He won the runoff 58%-42%, with voting closely following racial lines. He won the general election 59%-31%. (Twenty years later, when Frankel ran successfully in the adjacent 22nd District, Hastings endorsed her and offered praise.) Since then, he has not had a serious primary or general election challenge. A 2012 write-in campaign waged by anti-abortion activist and Operation Rescue founder Randall Terry went nowhere.

In the House, Hastings' voting record has been mostly liberal, and his rhetoric has been proudly so. He blasted a GOP-passed defense authorization bill in 2011 for going too far in the name of fighting terrorism. "It commits us to seeing a 'terrorist' in anyone who ever criticizes the United States in any country, including this one," he said. Declining to attend a tea party event in September 2010, he wrote to the organizer, "You represent the 'party of me' while Democrats and I represent the 'party of we.'" Pro-Israel groups are among his most prominent campaign contributors, and he has been a strong supporter of Israel. In contrast to many House Democrats who boycotted the March 2015 appearance before Congress of Israeli Prime Minister Benjamin Netanyahu, Hastings said he agreed with Netanyahu that Europe had become increasingly dangerous for Jews.

In 2004, with the support of Republican Speaker Dennis Hastert, Hastings was elected president of the Organization for Security and Cooperation in the pan-European Parliamentary Assembly and served two one-year terms. In 2007, he became chairman of the counterpart U.S. commission. In 2006, the House passed his resolution condemning Iran for hosting a conference on Holocaust denial. The next year, Hastings pressed for the opening of Holocaust archives in Bad Arolsen, Germany, and three weeks later, the archives were opened. However, he drew the attention of ethics investigators in 2010 over whether he exceeded foreign travel stipends. He told the *Wall Street Journal* that he was generous in giving money to people he encountered and said: "You are all concerned about nickels and dimes, and I'm not. You know, in a taxicab in Kazakhstan, I don't have time to get a receipt—I don't speak Kazakh." The investigation was dropped in 2011. In September 2014, *Roll Call* listed Hastings as the second poorest member of Congress. His negative net worth of more than $2 million included many unpaid bills from his impeachment expenses.

After the 2006 election, he was seriously considered for chairman of the House Intelligence Committee. He had support from the Congressional Black Caucus but was opposed by the Blue Dog Democrats and others who maintained that his controversial past disqualified him. Hastings attacked his critics as "misinformed fools," but House Speaker Nancy Pelosi nevertheless selected Texas Democrat Silvestre Reyes. However, Hastings retains a seat on the Rules Committee, an influential post that gives him a hand in discussing the terms for bringing bills to the floor. He irked conservatives in 2010 for his defense of a controversial "deem and pass" strategy for the health care overhaul that was briefly considered. He paraphrased an expression of Thomas Edison's: "There ain't no rule around here; we're trying to accomplish something."

Taking an original stand, Hastings in June 2008 called for a commission to consider expanding the size of the House beyond 435 members. That number, he pointed out, was established by statute in 1929 and can be changed by an act of Congress. He said there were too many constituents in each district for lawmakers to serve them adequately. In a perhaps less original stand, he noted during a Rules Committee hearing in February 2015 that Texas was "a crazy state to begin with." When the Texas Republican delegation demanded an apology, he refused. With Republicans in control of the House, Hastings has been limited in what he can accomplish. And he has continued to draw—and survive—attention for issues apart from legislating. In July 2012, one of his former aides was sentenced to 42 months in prison for conspiracy, money laundering, wire fraud, and mail fraud. In December 2014, the House Ethics Committee dismissed charges of sexual harassment against Hastings that had been brought by a Republican congressional aide, but added that his behavior had been "less than professional." Hastings has opened the door to retirement. Following his reelection in 2014, he said that he will seek at least one more term and then will assess the prospects for Democrats regaining control of the House.

TWENTY-FIRST DISTRICT

Ted Deutch (D)

Elected April 2010, 3rd full term; b. May 7, 1966, Bethlehem, PA; U of MI, B.A. 1988, J.D. 1990; Jewish; married (Jill); 3 children.

Elected Office: FL Senate, 2006-10.

Professional Career: Practicing atty., 1991-2010.

DC Office: 2447 RHOB, 20515, 202-225-3001; Fax: 202-225-5974; Website: teddeutch.house.gov.

State Offices: Boca Raton, 561-470-5440; Coral Springs, 954-255-8336; Margate, 954-972-6454.

Committees: *Ethics. Foreign Affairs:* Europe, Eurasia & Emerging Threats; Middle East & North Africa (RMM). *Judiciary:* Constitution & Civil Justice; Courts, Intellectual Property & the Internet.

Group Ratings

	ADA	ACLU	AFL-CIO	LCV	ITI	COC	HAFA	ACU	CFG	FRC
2014	85%	77%	–	97%	80%	43%	10%	8%	13%	0%
2013	90%	C	90%	96%	C	54%	C	8%	12%	C

National Journal Ratings

	2013 LIB	—	2013 CONS
Economic	76%	—	22%
Social	69%	—	28%
Foreign	86%	—	13%
Composite	78%	—	22%

Key Votes of the 113th Congress

1. Sandy storm spending	Y	5. Medical Marijuana	Y	9. Syrian Rebels Training	Y
2. Violence Against Women Act	Y	6. Farm Bill	N	10. Keystone pipeline	N
3. Guantanamo Bay Detainees	Y	7. Afghanistan Combat	Y	11. Immigration Exec. Action	N
4. Abortion 20-week ban	N	8. NSA Phone Data Collection	Y	12. Bipartisan budget deal	Y

Election Results

2014 general	Ted Deutch (D)............................ 153,395	(100%)	$1,006,801
2014 primary	Ted Deutch (D)............................ 31,080	(92%)	
	Emmanuel Morel (D).................... 2,845	(8%)	

Prior winning percentages: 2012 (78%), 2010 (63%)

Population		Race and Ethnicity		Income	
Total:	738,875	White	63.1%	Median income:	$54,696
Urban:	37.6%	Latino	19.6%		(170 of 435)
Suburban:	62.4%	Black	11.9%	Under $50,000	45.5%
Rural:	0.0%	Asian	3.2%	$50,000-$99,999:	30.4%
Land area:	287	Two races	1.6%	$100,000-$199,999:	18.4%
Pop/sq. mi.:	2,572.4	White Ethnic	32.5%	$200,000 or more:	5.7%
Born in state:	27.5%			Poverty Rate	11.2%
		Education			
Age Groups		H.S. grad or less:	35.1%	**Work**	
Under 18:	21.7%	Some college:	31.4%	White collar:	37.2%
18 to 34:	18.2%	College degree, 4 yr.:	21.0%	Blue collar:	47.3%
35 to 64:	37.8%	Post-grad study:	12.4%	Sales and service:	15.5%
Over 64:	22.3%				
		Military		Govt. workers:	10.4%
		Veterans/active duty:	7.9%		

Inland Palm Beach and Broward

Voter Turnout	
2013 Total Citizen 18+	506,224
2014 House Turnout	153,970
2014 Turnout as % CVAP	30.4%
2012 Turnout as % CVAP	65.4%

When the first millionaires came to Palm Beach in the 1920s to winter in their new mansions, there was virtually nothing man-made between Palm Beach and Miami. In 1920, Dade, Broward, and Palm Beach counties boasted a mere 66,000 residents. By 1950, the combined population of the three counties had jumped to almost 700,000, and the beachfront areas had largely been incorporated and developed. But the interior regions of the counties, near where Florida's turnpike would soon be laid out, remained marshy, sparsely inhabited, and ripe for development. As the coastal areas were filling up, the inland swamps were being drained, abetted by a sequence of canals and levees built by the state in response to flooding from a series of hurricanes in 1947. The towns and cities that now populate the western portions of Broward County were generally incorporated in a relatively brief spurt during the late 1950s and early 1960s. This helped fuel yet another boom in Florida real estate, as people flocked to the new developments. It wasn't just retirees and developers who took an interest in the region either. Westinghouse Electric Corp. initially invested in Coral Springs in the 1960s as a sort of "urban laboratory" for products such as central air conditioning, motion detecting lights, security systems, and fully electric kitchens.

Today, more than 3 million people inhabit Broward and Palm Beach counties alone. The 21st District, with mostly regularly-shaped lines, does not touch the ocean at all, kept inland by the 20th and 22nd districts. About two-fifths of the district's population lives in Broward County, where the district includes the cities of Coral Springs—now the fourth-most populous city in the county, with continued growth and plans for a $56 million medical facility—Parkland, Margate, and the western part of Deerfield Beach (named for the numerous deer that once roamed the banks of the Hillsborough River). Wellington has become an international site for equestrian events, including polo.

The remainder of the district winds through a series of largely unincorporated residential communities to the west of Inter-state 95 in Palm Beach County. The district's Jewish percentage is one of the largest in the nation. Democrats maintain a 21% registra-tion advantage over Republicans. Barack Obama got 61% in the 2012 presidential contest, down from 64% in 2008. That is only a problem for Democrats if they need to roll up their vote in south Florida to balance setbacks elsewhere in the state.

2012 Presidential Vote		
Barack Obama (D) 196,266	(61%)
Mitt Romney (R).................125,833	(39%)

2008 Presidential Vote		
Barack Obama (D) 203,701	(64%)
John McCain (R).................115,178	(36%)

Cook Partisan Voting Index: D+10

Ted Deutch (D)

Democrat Ted Deutch, who won a special election in April 2010, is a liberal with a staunchly pro-Israel posture on foreign policy and a relatively easy-going style. He has become an active legislator, with a knack for making bipartisan deals.

Deutch has working-class roots in Bethlehem, Pa., where his father ran a small painting contracting company and his mother kept the books. His parents did not go to college and were determined that their five children would. He excelled in high school and was class president for four years. During that period, his father was forced into early retirement by heart disease and he spent a lot of time watching CNN. Deutch said that sitting next to his dad on the couch discussing events unfolding on the news channel fueled his budding interest in current events. At the University of Michigan, Deutch got a bachelor's degree in political science and then a law degree. He volunteered in political campaigns during sum-mers, including working for unsuccessful Democratic presidential candidate Joe Biden in 1987. He caught the eye of an academic advisor who encouraged him to apply for a Harry S. Truman Scholarship, which recognizes students such as Deutch with potential for public service careers.

After law school, Deutch specialized in real estate law. That provided his initial entry to Washington, at a firm hired to sell off government assets from the savings and loan cri-sis. He married Jill Weinstock and the couple moved to Cleveland, to be closer to his wife's family. Eventually, they moved with their three children to Boca Raton, Fla., where Ted's older brother, also a lawyer, hired him to handle his law firm's real estate business. Deutch got active in Florida politics. He worked on issues and raised money in the state for Bill Clinton's two presidential campaigns. He also lobbied for pro-Israel causes. In 2006, he was elected to the Florida Senate. During three years in the legislature, Deutch authored two signature measures: a bill putting a surcharge on tobacco products to help pay for smok-ing prevention programs and cancer research, and a bill barring the state from investing pension funds in any enterprise that aided Iran's effort to attain nuclear weapons or that indirectly abetted genocide in the Darfur region of Sudan.

When Democratic Rep. Robert Wexler resigned to head a Middle East think tank, Deutch announced for the seat the next day, and seemed a natural successor. His liberal, pro-Israel politics appealed to the region's many Jewish retirees and his state Senate seat included half of the congressional district. Deutch faced minimal opposition in the Demo-cratic primary, which was tantamount to election in a district where Democrats outnum-bered Republicans 2-to-1. In the general election, his Republican opponent was West Palm Beach business consultant Ed Lynch, who tried to make the race a referendum on the Obama administration and its health care bill. Lynch joined national Republican leaders in calling for repeal. Deutch maintained that the changes would improve access to health care for people without insurance, for those who had been denied insurance because of pre-existing medical problems, and for seniors who rely on Medicare for their prescription drugs. Deutch won 62%-35%, outspending his opponent $1.7 million to $117,000. He easily won a full term in November 2010.

In the House, Deutch got seats on the Foreign Affairs and Judiciary committees, where he displayed a savvy legislative instinct, even after Republicans won House control in 2010. He got a provision in the 2012 Iran sanctions law that required companies to disclose to the Securities and Exchange Commission their business dealings with Iran. He worked across the aisle with fellow Floridian Tom Rooney on a bill that was enacted to help homeless veterans, and with Scott Rigell of Virginia on a House-passed bill to protect consumers from contaminated drywall. He has drawn attention for sponsoring some innovative legislation. One was a constitutional amendment in 2011 to ban all corporate money in politics. That later evolved to his Democracy for All Amendment, which would overturn recent Supreme Court rulings that reduced restrictions on money in politics. When a bipartisan group of congressional leaders quietly added a provision to the December 2014 omnibus spending bill that removed some restrictions on campaign contributions to political parties, Deutch sought unsuccessfully to force a House vote. In 2012, he proposed a measure that would allow companies to apply to the government to allow their products to carry a "cancer-free" label.

As ranking Democrat on the Middle East and North Africa Subcommittee, where he often cooperates with Republican Chairwoman Ileana Ros-Lehtinen of South Florida, Deutch became a go-to guy for his many Jewish constituents and the broader pro-Israel lobby in Washington. In 2014, he helped to write the Iran Threat Reduction Act, which imposed additional transparency and human rights requirements on Iran. When many Democrats protested the March 2015 speech to Congress by Israeli Prime Minister Benjamin Netanyahu, Deutch welcomed him and was on the formal committee that escorted him into the House chamber. But Deutch joined Democratic Reps. Steve Israel and Nita Lowey, both of New York, in a letter to Speaker John Boehner that criticized him for an "attempt to politicize support for Israel."

Some Florida Democrats have speculated about Deutch as a potential statewide candidate. But that is unlikely in 2016. He quickly endorsed Democratic Rep. Patrick Murphy for the seat of retiring Republican Sen. Marco Rubio.

TWENTY-SECOND DISTRICT

Lois Frankel (D)

Elected 2012, 2nd term; b. May 16, 1948, New York, NY; Boston U., B.A. 1970, Georgetown U., J.D. 1973; Jewish; divorced; 1 child.

Elected Office: FL House, 1986-92, 1994-2002; Mayor, West Palm Beach, 2003-11.

Professional Career: Law clerk, Hon. Judge David Norman, 1973-74; Asst. public defender, West Palm Beach, 1974-78; Practicing lawyer, 1978-2003.

DC Office: 1037 LHOB, 20515, 202-225-9890; Website: frankel.house. gov.

State Offices: Boca Raton, 561-998-9045.

Committees: *Foreign Affairs:* Europe, Eurasia & Emerging Threats; Middle East & North Africa. *Transportation & Infrastructure:* Coast Guard & Maritime Transportation; Highways & Transit; Water Resources & Environment.

Group Ratings

	ADA	ACLU	AFL-CIO	LCV	ITI	COC	HAFA	ACU	CFG	FRC
2014	70%	77%	–	97%	40%	36%	12%	4%	4%	0%
2013	75%	C	95%	96%	C	31%	C	16%	19%	C

National Journal Ratings

	2013 LIB	—	2013 CONS
Economic	76%	—	22%
Social	79%	—	16%
Foreign	81%	—	18%
Composite	80%	—	20%

Key Votes of the 113th Congress

1. Sandy storm spending	Y	5. Medical Marijuana	Y
2. Violence Against Women Act	Y	6. Farm Bill	N
3. Guantanamo Bay Detainees	Y	7. Afghanistan Combat	Y
4. Abortion 20-week ban	N	8. NSA Phone Data Collection	N

9. Syrian Rebels Training	N
10. Keystone pipeline	N
11. Immigration Exec. Action	N
12. Bipartisan budget deal	N

Election Results

2014 general	Lois Frankel (D)	125,404	(58%)	$1,334,369
	Paul Spain (R)	90,685	(42%)	$145,297
2014 primary	Lois Frankel (D)	unopposed		

Prior winning percentage: 2012 (55%)

Population		Race and Ethnicity		Income	
Total:	734,319	White	64.7%	Median income:	$53,679
Urban:	60.5%	Latino	20.9%		(180 of 435)
Suburban:	39.5%	Black	10.5%	Under $50,000	47.0%
Rural:	0.0%	Asian	2.1%	$50,000-$99,999:	28.9%
Land area:	165	Two races	1.4%	$100,000-$199,999:	16.4%
Pop/sq. mi.:	4,456.0	White Ethnic	32.6%	$200,000 or more:	7.7%
Born in state:	27.0%			Poverty Rate	15.2%
		Education			
Age Groups		H.S. grad or less:	35.4%	**Work**	
Under 18:	16.4%	Some college:	28.8%	White collar:	36.2%
18 to 34:	20.8%	College degree, 4 yr.:	22.7%	Blue collar:	48.0%
35 to 64:	41.5%	Post-grad study:	13.0%	Sales and service:	15.9%
Over 64:	21.4%				
		Military		Govt. workers:	9.0%
		Veterans/active duty:	7.6%		

Coastal Palm Beach and Broward

The barrier islands of Florida's Gold Coast have been developed in spasms of land speculation, not just as vacation places and retirement homes but as embodiments of dreams and fantasies. Consider Palm Beach, the great beach resort of the 1920s, where rich WASPs bought Addison Mizner's

Voter Turnout	
2013 Total Citizen 18+	518,846
2014 House Turnout	216,095
2014 Turnout as % CVAP	41.6%
2012 Turnout as % CVAP	66%

pseudo-Mediterranean confections as a change of pace from their snow-covered Tudor and Georgian mansions. Mizner also built the Boca Raton Resort and Club in 1926. And Clyde Beatty brought his circus to winter in tiny Fort Lauderdale in the 1930s (locals complained about the roaring lions). Back in the 1950s, many of these beachfront communities were "restricted," which meant no Jews were allowed. Today, they are home to many Jewish retirees from New York and the Northeast generally. But there are also working-age people here and plans to attract more.

The Palm Beach area remains, as it has been since the 1920s, the precinct of the very rich. It was the favorite playground of high-stakes swindler Bernard Madoff—and many of his now unhappy former clients. Boca Raton sports the stylish Mizner Park, a collection of upscale stores. The top Rolls Royce dealer in the world is in Palm Beach, with a doubling of sales in 2014. Downtown Fort Lauderdale, separated from the beach by miles of canals, is the site of the Museum of Art Fort Lauderdale, the Broward Center for the Performing Arts, and the International Swimming Hall of Fame. It, along with neighboring Wilton Manors, became the home of choice for many gay people. In 2014, metro Fort Lauderdale had a higher percentage of same-sex couples than any other mid-size metropolitan area in the nation, including for retirees; with 12.5 percent same-sex households, Wilton Manors led the small cities. The housing market collapse hit the area hard and home prices initially were slow to recover. But an April 2015 listing of top five markets for housing growth included Fort Lauderdale. An earlier forecast that the recovery would take until 2030 was accelerated by a decade. In 2014, Port Everglades ranked second in the world for the number of passengers, behind only the port of Miami. It plans to double its capacity for container cargo.

The 22nd Congressional District of Florida covers much of the Gold Coast. The district begins just to the north of West Palm Beach, and proceeds down the Atlantic Coast. It includes part of Palm Springs, and it takes in Delray Beach, which was the site in 1956 of a civil rights showdown over access to the beaches and now has a large Haitian community. It also includes Boca Raton, where the azure fountains and red-tiled roofs of the Boca

Raton Resort & Club bespeak a vision of a holiday Florida, a bit mannered and antique to today's eye, but still exuberant and benefiting from tasteful refurbishing. After moving through coastal parts of Pompano Beach and Fort Lauderdale, the district includes parts of upscale Plantation but loops around African-American precincts, placed in the 20th District. By hewing to the coastline, the

2012 Presidential Vote		
Barack Obama (D) 178,331	(55%)
Mitt Romney (R).................147,290	(45%)
2008 Presidential Vote		
Barack Obama (D) 182,430	(57%)
John McCain (R).................137,096	(43%)
Cook Partisan Voting Index: D+3		

district takes in the more Republican areas of the two counties. But what was a Republican enclave in the past decade has become a Democratic-leaning district. Democrats have a 9% registration advantage, and President Barack Obama led Mitt Romney here in 2012, 55%-45%.

Lois Frankel (D)

Democrat Lois Frankel won election in 2012 in the 22nd District to succeed Republican firebrand Allen West, who ran and lost in what he thought was the more hospitable 18th District. In the minority party, Frankel has made efforts to reach across the aisle.

Frankel was born in New York City and raised in Great Neck on Long Island. Her father was in manufacturing, and her mother was a homemaker. Frankel was a tomboy growing up and enjoyed playing sports, especially basketball. She studied psychology at Boston University with the intent of becoming a psychiatrist, but her career plans changed when she became involved in the social movements of the late 1960s. "I was a student activist, and I was involved in antiwar protesting and the women's liberation movement," Frankel told *National Journal.* "There were so many movements … it was all bubbling." She has joked that she "majored in protests."

Hoping to be "a change agent from the inside," Frankel went to law school. After getting her degree from Georgetown University, she spent a year as a law clerk and then moved to West Palm Beach. She became a public defender and advocate for numerous social causes. In 1986, she won an open state House seat. She rose to become the first woman minority leader in Florida. She also wrote the state's first AIDS law, which among other things ensured confidentiality in testing. She ran unsuccessfully against Alcee Hastings for an open seat in 1992, losing 57%-43% in a runoff.

After term limits forced Frankel to leave the Florida House, she spent some time in 2002 as a candidate for governor against incumbent Jeb Bush, but withdrew before the primary. She ran for mayor of West Palm Beach in 2003 and defeated incumbent Joel Daves. Though she compiled what the *South Florida Sun-Sentinel* described as an "impressive" record, she angered several labor unions when the city laid off workers, and she developed a reputation for being abrasive.

In March 2011, Frankel announced she would challenge West, a freshman who was one of the tea party movement's most outspoken adherents. For nearly a year, Frankel and another Democrat, political newcomer Patrick Murphy, struggled to remain financially competitive with West. In February 2012, West announced he would run in the neighboring 18th District, made more GOP-friendly by redistricting. Democrats avoided a bruising primary when Murphy announced he would challenge West in the Treasure Coast district.

Democratic Broward County Commissioner Kristin Jacobs got into the primary contest. Frankel and Jacobs had nearly identical stances on issues, but Frankel had the backing of national leaders. She was endorsed by Hastings and got a rare visit from House Minority Leader Nancy Pelosi eight days before the primary. She coasted to a 61%-39% win.

Former state Rep. Republican Adam Hasner decided to end his failing Senate campaign and run as the Republican candidate in the 22nd District. In the general election campaign, Frankel attacked Hasner's support of Wisconsin Rep. Paul Ryan's budget plan, which introduced vouchers into the Medicare program, and his stance against abortion rights. An ad by the House Republican "Young Guns" program, later pulled because of inaccuracy, accused Frankel of frivolous spending while mayor. Frankel emphasized her work with small businesses to create incentives for more jobs.

Both she and Hasner tried to avoid sounding extreme, and the *Sun-Sentinel* remarked that each had "shed their past personas like pythons in the Everglades." *The Miami Herald* endorsed Frankel, citing her "longer familiarity" with the district, and its Democratic lean helped her pull out a 55%-45% win. Each candidate spent $3.4 million.

In the House, Frankel made some unusual alliances with conservative Republicans. With Rep. Tom Rice of South Carolina, she worked on port issues. During the 2014 State of the Union speech by President Barack Obama, she sought to make a statement of civility by sitting next to Republican Rep. Ileana Ros-Lehtinen of Florida, with whom Frankel served on the Foreign Affairs Subcommittee on the Middle East and North Africa. On the Transportation and Infrastructure Committee, she served on the House-Senate conference committee that reached a final agreement on a water resources bill, which included additional dredging for expansion of Port Everglades, plus water conservation and supply in the Everglades swamps.

Frankel ran in 2014 against Paul Spain, a retired financial adviser who promised to work for bipartisanship. Frankel outspent him $1.3 million to $145,000. She won 58%-42%, with a slightly better performance in Palm Beach than in Broward County. In 2015, Frankel became vice chairwoman of the bipartisan Congressional Women's Caucus, and vice chairwoman of the "Red to Blue" program of the Democratic Congressional Campaign Committee. In August 2015, the state Supreme Court redistricting order posed the risk that she would be thrown into the same district with Democratic Rep. Ted Deutch. Each pledged to avoid such a showdown.

TWENTY-THIRD DISTRICT

Debbie Wasserman Schultz (D)

Elected 2004, 6th term; b. Sept. 27, 1966, Forest Hills, NY; U. of FL, B.A. 1988, M.A. 1990; Jewish; married (Steve); 3 children.

Elected Office: FL House, 1992-2000, min. ldr. pro tem., 1999-2000; FL Senate, 2000-04.

Professional Career: Legis. aide, 1989-92.

DC Office: 1114 LHOB, 20515, 202-225-7931; Fax: 202-226-2052; Website: wassermanschultz.house.gov.

State Offices: Aventura, 305-936-5724; Pembroke Pines, 954-437-3936.

Committees: *Appropriations:* Legislative Branch (RMM); State, Foreign Operations & Related Programs.

Group Ratings

	ADA	ACLU	AFL-CIO	LCV	ITI	COC	HAFA	ACU	CFG	FRC
2014	70%	83%	–	94%	40%	50%	9%	0%	0%	25%
2013	65%	C	95%	75%	C	36%	C	9%	13%	C

National Journal Ratings

	2013 LIB	—	2013 CONS
Economic	81%	—	19%
Social	69%	—	28%
Foreign	69%	—	29%
Composite	74%	—	26%

Key Votes of the 113th Congress

1. Sandy storm spending	Y	5. Medical Marijuana	Y	9. Syrian Rebels Training	Y
2. Violence Against Women Act	Y	6. Farm Bill	N	10. Keystone pipeline	N
3. Guantanamo Bay Detainees	Y	7. Afghanistan Combat	N	11. Immigration Exec. Action	N
4. Abortion 20-week ban	N	8. NSA Phone Data Collection	N	12. Bipartisan budget deal	Y

Election Results

2014 general	Debbie Wasserman Schultz (D)	103,269	(63%)	$2,744,976	$6,000
	Joe Kaufman (R)	61,519	(37%)	$517,856	$9,785
2014 primary	Debbie Wasserman Schultz (D)	unopposed			

Prior winning percentages: 2012 (63%), 2010 (60%), 2008 (77%), 2006 (100%), 2004 (70%)

Population		Race and Ethnicity		Income	
Total:	719,732	White	46.2%	Median income:	$52,013
Urban:	87.3%	Latino	38.1%		(208 of 435)
Suburban:	12.7%	Black	10.4%	Under $50,000	47.6%
Rural:	0.0%	Asian	3.4%	$50,000-$99,999:	27.8%
Land area:	167	Two races	1.1%	$100,000-$199,999:	17.6%
Pop/sq. mi.:	4,320.8	White Ethnic	26.7%	$200,000 or more:	6.9%
Born in state:	30.4%			Poverty Rate	13.8%
		Education			
Age Groups		H.S. grad or less:	33.2%	**Work**	
Under 18:	20.7%	Some college:	29.4%	White collar:	39.9%
18 to 34:	21.2%	College degree, 4 yr.:	23.1%	Blue collar:	45.7%
35 to 64:	42.2%	Post-grad study:	14.4%	Sales and service:	14.3%
Over 64:	15.8%			Govt. workers:	9.4%
		Military			
		Veterans/active duty:	5.0%		

Southern Broward, Coastal Dade

When Broward County was created in 1915, its name was to be "Everglades County," reflecting its largely agricultural character, save for a few fledgling beachfront communities like Fort Lauderdale. Development proceeded slowly. Joseph Wesley

Voter Turnout	
2013 Total Citizen 18+	463,028
2014 House Turnout	164,788
2014 Turnout as % CVAP	35.6%
2012 Turnout as % CVAP	61.7%

Young dreamed of building a resort community by the sea and founded Hollywood in 1925. But a hurricane the following year devastated the infant town, people fled in droves, and Young's holdings were eventually auctioned off in 1930. But this prime beachfront real estate could not remain undeveloped for long, and by 1980, the population was exploding. At first, the newcomers were like those who had populated places such as St. Petersburg and Orlando, hailing from Midwestern states and bringing with them a Republican lean. But over time, these new South Florida residents increasingly came from the Northeast, and brought with them Northern Democratic politics. They were instrumental in transforming the state's Democratic Party from a rural, Southern party run by the so-called "Pork Chop Gang" of conservative senators into one more closely resembling its Northern counterparts, and eventually helped turn Florida into a swing state.

Today, Broward County is in the midst of another transformation. It is now a minority-majority county, the third largest in the nation (behind Riverside in California and Clark in Nevada), with the non-Hispanic white share of the 1.8 million population dropping to 41% in 2013. Blacks are 28% and Latinos are 26%; each is a big increase since 2000. These newcomers are by-and-large not the Cuban Americans who fueled much of South Florida's Republicanism in recent decades. Instead, the most common countries of origin are Haiti, Jamaica, and Colombia; almost one in three residents are foreign-born, but many of them are undocumented. While Broward gave Richard Nixon 72% of the vote in 1972, four decades later it was Barack Obama's second strongest county in the state, giving him over two-thirds of the vote. The county is developing its own economy. Port Everglades hosts nearly 4 million passengers a year and has annual revenue of about $143 million.

The 23rd District of Florida includes much of southern Broward County. The district is anchored by coastal Hollywood, where huge high-rises now house large numbers of retirees from New York and other Northeastern cities, plush new resorts attract vacationers, and a homeless shelter was bought out for $5 million. From there, the district moves inland, with a slight northwestern trajectory. It includes Davie, a former ranching town where the businesses lining downtown all have an "Old Western" motif. The western end of the district is new-growth suburbs, such as Southwest Ranches, where residents

2012 Presidential Vote		
Barack Obama (D)	178,314	(62%)
Mitt Romney (R)	109,959	(38%)

2008 Presidential Vote		
Barack Obama (D)	170,466	(61%)
John McCain (R)	108,497	(39%)

Cook Partisan Voting Index: D+9

have opposed roads and street lights, and Weston, which has a large concentration of Venezuelan Americans. About four-fifths of the district's residents live in Broward, with the remainder occupying a string of barrier islands in Miami-Dade County wedged between the

African-American majority 24th District and the Atlantic Ocean. Located here is the famous South Beach, which celebrated its 100th anniversary in March 2015, where old art-deco hotels attract the glitziest celebrities of North America, Latin America, and Europe. It also takes in the high-rises along Collins Avenue facing the ocean and the Latino neighborhoods north of 63rd Street.

The district's voting age population is 49% non-Hispanic white. There are patches of Republican voting in the western portions of Broward County and in South Beach, but the district overall leans substantially Democratic. Democrats enjoy a 22-point registration advantage, and Barack Obama topped 60% of the vote here in 2008 and 2012.

Debbie Wasserman Schultz (D)

Debbie Wasserman Schultz, a hard-charging Democrat elected in 2004, became chairman of the Democratic National Committee in 2011 in acknowledgment of her skills as a media messenger and fundraiser. After helping President Barack Obama carry her home state while her party picked up seats in the House and Senate, she stayed on for a second term at the DNC. Meanwhile, she has pursued her interest in a top leadership post in the House when vacancies open.

Like many of her constituents, Wasserman Schultz was born in Queens. She grew up on Long Island, where she ran for student council every year and always lost. She got bachelor's and master's degrees from the University of Florida. In her last year at school, she sent out 180 resumes to legislators in Florida and New York and got five interviews. Florida State Rep. Peter Deutsch, a Democrat and former New Yorker from Broward County, gave her a summer job and then appointed her as his legislative aide. In 1992, he ran for the House and urged Wasserman Schultz to run for his seat in the legislature. She did, knocking on doors for six months and finishing far ahead of four opponents in the Democratic primary. At age 26, she became the youngest woman ever elected to the state House. She served eight years there, including two as minority leader, followed by four in the state Senate. She called herself "a pragmatic liberal," and she sponsored a controversial law to require an equal number of men and women on state boards and a bill that failed to pass requiring that dry cleaners and some other businesses charge the same prices for women as for men.

When Deutsch ran in 2004 for the Democratic nomination for an open Senate seat, Wasserman Schultz again moved to replace him. By February 2004, she had lined up endorsements from Minority Leader Nancy Pelosi and six of Florida's seven House Democrats. Wasserman Schultz ultimately collected more than $1 million for what turned out to be an uncompetitive race, since no one else filed to run in the decisive Democratic primary. Wasserman Schultz called for repeal of the Bush-era tax cuts, a reduction in the budget deficit, greater use of diplomacy overseas, improved prescription drug coverage, gay civil rights, and abortion rights. Against a Republican who attacked the "homosexual agenda" in the public schools, she won 70%-30%. She has not faced a serious challenge since, allowing her to channel campaign contributions from a wide spectrum of Democratic interests to her colleagues.

In the House, Wasserman Schultz has a mostly liberal voting record, although she has been more centrist on foreign policy. She helped found the Cuba Democracy Caucus, a bipartisan group that works to thwart efforts to loosen the U.S. trade embargo with the island nation. She has been one of the Florida delegation's most ardent opponents of offshore oil drilling, declaring after the 2010 BP oil spill disaster in the Gulf of Mexico that "our country needs to run on something other than oil." In 2012, she worked with then-Judiciary Committee Chairman Lamar Smith of Texas to enact a bill giving law enforcement additional authority to combat child pornography while imposing tougher penalties on offenders. The House also passed her bill in August 2012 to curb tax-return identity theft.

Her blazing ascension up the leadership ladder began in 2006 when she was appointed co-chairwoman of the Democratic Congressional Campaign Committee's "Red to Blue" program. Working closely with then-Chairman Rahm Emanuel, now Chicago mayor, she became a party spokeswoman and a mentor to Democratic recruits. When Democrats won House control that year, Majority Whip James Clyburn tapped her as a chief deputy whip. She also snagged a seat on the Appropriations Committee, and immediately became a "cardinal" as chairwoman of the Legislative Branch Subcommittee. She took charge of the Capitol Visitors Center project, which was plagued by cost overruns, and extracted commitments on costs and completion dates. She pushed successfully for a unionization vote at the Government Accountability Office. She has remained the subcommittee ranking minority member with Republicans in control.

In the 2008 election season, Wasserman Schultz was criticized by liberal bloggers when she refused to campaign against the three Cuban-American House Republicans from South Florida as part of her DCCC duties. They were facing unusually strong Democratic challenges, and ultimately all three were reelected. Also in 2008, Wasserman Schultz was cochair of Hillary Rodham Clinton's presidential effort in Florida and nationally, and she was vice chair of the DCCC's incumbent retention program. A *National Journal* poll of party insiders in 2009 predicted she had the brightest political future of anyone on Capitol Hill.

Her success seemed all the more impressive when she announced in March 2009 that for much of the previous year she had been battling breast cancer. Although her tumor was in the early stages, which would typically require only surgery and radiation, she said that she elected to have a double mastectomy after learning that as an Ashkenazi Jew, she had a greater predisposition to recurrence. The mother of three school-aged children, Wasserman Schultz was diagnosed just after turning 40. "I didn't want it to define me," she told *The New York Times* of her illness. "I didn't want my name to be 'Debbie Wasserman Schultz, who is currently battling breast cancer.'"

In 2011, Wasserman Schultz beat out former Ohio Gov. Ted Strickland to take the helm of the DNC, with Vice President Joe Biden citing "her tenacity, her strength, her fighting spirit, and her ability to overcome adversity." Vowing that the party would be "laser-focused on the economy" as it sought to reelect Obama, she was a ferocious Republican critic. Having once declared that the country needed to run on something other than oil, she blamed the GOP for soaring gasoline prices in May 2011, citing "ridiculous, unacceptable subsidies to oil companies and massive tax breaks that even they have said they don't need." Later, she blasted House Budget Committee Chairman Paul Ryan's budget blueprint because it would "allow insurance companies to deny you coverage and drop you for pre-existing conditions"—a claim that the fact-checking website *PolitiFact* judged to be false. Republicans were outraged in September 2012 when she contended that Israel's U.S. ambassador had said that "what the Republicans are doing is dangerous for Israel," then accused the conservative-leaning *Washington Examiner* newspaper of "deliberately" misquoting her, even though her statement was captured on video.

Wasserman Schultz was frequently deployed in 2012 as a campaign surrogate for Obama, attending hundreds of events across the nation. But she developed a strained relationship with Obama campaign officials, who privately accused her of coming across as too partisan on television. They also reportedly wondered if Obama had made the right decision in selecting her for the DNC. Election Night's results served as her vindication: Not only did Obama win with substantial support from women and Jewish voters, two constituencies that Wasserman Schultz cultivated, but he captured Florida, a state where Republican Mitt Romney enjoyed a sizable lead in pre-election polls. With Pelosi staying on as minority leader, Wasserman Schultz had no apparent promotion in store in the House, and Obama's aides saw little political benefit in dumping a loyal soldier.

After the election, Wasserman Schultz continued her tough talk. As she told *Politico* in 2013: "I don't really do anything halfway." She helped lead the charge that the Republican Party was engaging in a "war on women," an expression meant to highlight the gender gap between the parties. She fiercely challenged attacks on the Affordable Care Act and predicted on CNN in November 2013: "I think actually that Democrats will be able to run on Obamacare as an advantage" in the future. Her comments occasionally landed her in hot water. In a visit to Wisconsin in September 2014, she said GOP Gov. Scott Walker "has given women the back of his hand. ... What Republican tea party extremists like Scott Walker are doing is, they are grabbing us by the hair and pulling us back." After causing a firestorm, she said, "I shouldn't have used the words I used."

Wasserman Schultz also rankled some Democrats. After being reelected as DNC chair in 2013, she ousted the organization's long-time secretary, Alice Germond. When that caused turmoil, she named Germond a "secretary emeritus." The next year, Orlando attorney John Morgan—a major Democratic donor—voiced frustration over her concerns about a medical marijuana proposal that he had worked to put on Florida's ballot. "I know personally the most powerful players in Washington, D.C. And I can tell you that Debbie Wasserman Schultz isn't just disliked. She's despised. She's an irritant," Morgan told the *Miami Herald*. She rejected Morgan's claims.

Obama's foreign policy pursuits have forced Wasserman Schultz to navigate tricky terrain. As a long-time critic of the Cuban regime, she offered only limited and murky support when the president in December 2014 announced breakthrough initiatives to Cuba. "While I have always been opposed to unearned changes in the status of our relationship with

Cuba, I will continue to work with the administration ... to support policies that benefit the Cuban people and do not further entrench the Castro regime," she said. When many House Democrats, including some Jewish members, protested the March 2015 speech to Congress by Israeli Prime Minister Benjamin Netanyahu, she carefully said, "Israel is an issue that should not be made partisan."

Her political options have long been a matter of great intrigue. In March 2015, Wasserman Schultz ruled out a race for Marco Rubio's Senate seat. That seemed to confirm that her future is in the House, and with a leadership bid. With the decision by Democratic Rep. Chris Van Hollen of Maryland to run for the Senate, she likely would be a front-runner when a top opening occurs. She would offer strong networking among colleagues, years of political favors, policy gravitas, media savvy, and a relentlessness that exceeds even most of her type-A colleagues. That helps to explain why Wasserman Schultz has been the target of usually unattributed criticism—and, no doubt, jealousy—from would-be rivals. The enmity of Obama aides and allies would have little impact, and might even be a plus for her, in a House leadership contest. Meanwhile, her past support for Hillary Rodham Clinton plus the prominence of Republicans Jeb Bush and Marco Rubio, with whom she had a long and adversarial history in Tallahassee, has increased her value as a Democratic spokeswoman. In short, she appeared to hold a lot of cards.

TWENTY-FOURTH DISTRICT

Frederica Wilson (D)

Elected 2010, 3rd term; b. Nov. 5, 1942, Miami; Fisk U., B.S. 1963, U. of Miami, M.S. 1972; Episcopalian; widowed; 3 children.

Elected Office: FL House, 1998-2002; FL Senate, 2002-10.

Professional Career: Teacher; principal; asst. principal.

DC Office: 208 CHOB, 20515, 202-225-4506; Fax: 202-226-0777; Website: wilson.house.gov.

State Offices: Miami Gardens, 305-690-5905; Miramar, 954-602-4357; Pembroke Pines, 954-450-6767; West Park, 954-989-2688.

Committees: *Education & the Workforce:* Health, Employment, Labor & Pensions; Workforce Protections (RMM).

Group Ratings

	ADA	ACLU	AFL-CIO	LCV	ITI	COC	HAFA	ACU	CFG	FRC
2014	90%	83%	–	89%	40%	43%	10%	8%	13%	13%
2013	80%	C	95%	96%	C	23%	C	8%	12%	C

National Journal Ratings

	2013 LIB	—	2013 CONS
Economic	83%	—	17%
Social	87%	—	7%
Foreign	89%	—	10%
Composite	88%	—	13%

Key Votes of the 113th Congress

1. Sandy storm spending	Y	5. Medical Marijuana	N	9. Syrian Rebels Training	Y
2. Violence Against Women Act	Y	6. Farm Bill	N	10. Keystone pipeline	N
3. Guantanamo Bay Detainees	Y	7. Afghanistan Combat	Y	11. Immigration Exec. Action	N
4. Abortion 20-week ban	N	8. NSA Phone Data Collection	N	12. Bipartisan budget deal	Y

Election Results

2014 general	Frederica Wilson (D)	129,192	(86%)	$234,359
	Dufirstson Julio Neree (R)	15,239	(10%)	$12,040
	Luis Fernandez (I)	5,487	(4%)	$13,344
2014 primary	Frederica Wilson (D)	35,456	(80%)	
	Michael Etienne (D)	8,628	(20%)	

Prior winning percentages: 2012 (unopposed), 2010 (86%)

Population		Race and Ethnicity:		Income	
Total:	725,282	Black	53.6%	Median income:	$36,748
Urban:	95.6%	Latino	29.5%		*(411 of 435)*
Suburban:	4.4%	White	13.8%	Under $50,000	63.3%
Rural:	0.0%	Asian	1.9%	$50,000-$99,999:	23.8%
Land area:	95	Two races	1.0%	$100,000-$199,999:	10.1%
Pop/sq. mi.:	7,619.5	White Ethnic	5.8%	$200,000 or more:	2.8%
Born in state:	42.6%			Poverty Rate	24.8%
		Education			
Age Groups		H.S. grad or less:	52.1%	**Work**	
Under 18:	23.1%	Some college:	26.8%	White collar:	28.4%
18 to 34:	26.0%	College degree, 4 yr.:	14.0%	Blue collar:	53.0%
35 to 64:	39.0%	Post-grad study:	7.1%	Sales and service:	18.6%
Over 64:	11.9%				
		Military		Govt. workers:	13.1%
		Veterans/active duty:	3.2%		

Northern Dade, Southern Broward

North from downtown, alongside Interstate 95, Miami's main north-south artery, is the city's largest African-American community. It stretches from the American Airlines Arena northwest to Overtown—originally called "Colored Town"—where racially restrictive covenants in the rest of Miami

Voter Turnout	
2013 Total Citizen 18+	430,249
2014 House Turnout	149,918
2014 Turnout as % CVAP	34.8%
2012 Turnout as % CVAP	60.3%

forced the city's original African-American laborers to reside. From there the community has spread through Allapattah and Liberty City to the brightly painted minarets and Moorish arches of the city of Opa-Locka, whose name is a shortened version of the Seminole name for the area: Opa-tisha-worka-locka. This has been a kind of frontierland in Miami, where hostilities between the city's blacks and its Cuban-American majority have played out. Many of Miami's African Americans have resented the economic upward mobility and political strength of the Cubans. There is also tension between the Cubans and the Haitians in Little Haiti as a result of federal policies that give Cubans who reach U.S. shores refugee status, while Haitians are treated as any other immigrant group with the potential for deportation. This animosity is reflected in partisan politics. Cuban Americans have been solidly Republican over the years, though somewhat less so recently. South Florida African Americans have remained largely Democratic, as has the growing Haitian-American community.

The 24th Congressional District covers the historic heart of Miami's black community. Located here are much of northeast Miami-Dade County, including Liberty City and Overtown, Opa-Locka, and Miami Gardens, the home of Trayvon Martin, the black teenager whose shooting death near Orlando in 2012 sparked a national debate about racial profiling. Miami Gardens, the third-largest city in Miami-Dade, has suffered from gang violence and drug crime, and numerous incidents of alleged police abuses, especially against blacks. In January 2015, after years of local controversy, the city of Miami reached an agreement with the Justice Department to give the Florida Department of Law Enforcement the authority to investigate police shootings and in-custody deaths.

At the far southern tip of the district is downtown Miami, and farther north are heavily Haitian-American towns like Golden Glades, El Portal, Ives Estates, and North Miami Beach. About 19% of the district resides in Broward County, in places like fast-growing Miramar and Pembroke Pines. The district does not include the beach towns north of Miami Beach or the heavily Latino Hialeah to the west. Some 55% of the district's residents are black, the highest percentage of any Florida district; 33% are non-black Hispanics. The district ranks among the top 10 in the nation in its minority share of the

2012 Presidential Vote
Barack Obama (D) 227,167   (88%)
Mitt Romney (R)...................31,651   (12%)

2008 Presidential Vote
Barack Obama (D) 207,630   (86%)
John McCain (R)...................33,669   (14%)

Cook Partisan Voting Index: D+34

population. It is also the most Democratic district in Florida, and among the top 10 in the nation; the party has a whopping 58-point registration advantage over Republicans.

Frederica Wilson (D)

Frederica Wilson, who was among the few Democrats elected to the House in 2010, is best known for her hundreds of brightly colored, often rhinestone-studded hats. She has compiled a solidly liberal voting record while speaking out on behalf of her low-income constituents, particularly Haitian Americans. She calls herself "a voice for the voiceless."

Wilson's politics were inspired by her father, Thirlee Smith, a native of Timpson, Texas, a town that in his day had an active chapter of the Ku Klux Klan. "He would sit me on his knee and tell me stories of what happened to him in Texas and how people were lynched," she recalled. During a visit to Miami, Smith met Frederica's mother, Beulah Finley; the two wed and settled in South Florida. In Miami, Smith ran a restaurant and a billiard hall, and became active in the civil rights movement, registering voters and pushing for sanitation workers' rights. The couple's three children were sensitized to acts of injustice at a young age. Once, in high school, Wilson spied a new kid in school being teased for wearing torn clothes. Wilson, who weighed about 70 pounds at the time, stepped into the circle of bullies and ordered them to leave the boy alone. She went on to pursue a career in education and eventually politics. Her brother, the late Thirlee Smith Jr., became the first African-American full-time reporter at *The Miami Herald*.

In 1963, Wilson graduated from Fisk University with a bachelor's degree in elementary education, and got her master's from the University of Miami. She worked as a teacher for a time and then became an assistant educational coordinator for a Head Start program. After taking a leave of absence to raise her three children, she returned to the field as an assistant principal and eventually became principal of a Miami elementary school. She also served on the Miami-Dade County School Board. During that period, she became more politically active. In 1984, she got involved in a campaign to lobby Congress to remove Haitian refugees from a local detention center. The Haitian women in particular, she said, "had no privacy at all, from guards, from visitors, from INS, from no one. When they would take a shower, they had no curtains. They were treating them like animals." The women were eventually released and allowed to remain in Miami.

Wilson first won a seat in the Florida House in 1998, serving two terms before being elected to the state Senate. In each chamber, she served as minority whip. She worked on immigrants' rights issues, proposing a bill in 2007 banning the term "illegal alien" from state documents. She also focused on education. In 2004, she led a sometimes bitter fight against then-Gov. Jeb Bush to scale back the use of standardized testing in schools, which she claimed had a negative impact on children. Wilson was known in the legislature for her trademark headgear, which was inspired by her grandmother, who wore similar hats as a cultural tradition in her native Bahamas.

When Democratic Rep. Kendrick Meek ran unsuccessfully for the Senate, Wilson decided to run for his House seat, continuing a pattern of succession: Wilson took Meek's seat when he left the Florida House and his place in the state Senate in 2002 when he ran for Congress. Eight other Democrats got into the August 2010 primary. Wilson won with 35% of the vote, helped by the district's sizable Haitian population splitting its support among the four Haitian-American candidates. Rudy Moise, a Haitian-American lawyer and doctor, came in second. In the fall, her only competition was lawyer Roderick Vereen, an underdog independent. She won with 86% of the vote.

In the House, Wilson drew immediate publicity when she was barred from wearing her hats on the floor of the chamber. She established herself as one of the body's most liberal members and became active in the Congressional Black Caucus. She delivered a series of impassioned speeches following the death of black teenager Trayvon Martin, who was shot in February 2012 in Sanford, Fla., by neighborhood watch volunteer George Zimmerman. Wilson said she was "tired of burying young black boys." Earlier, she called for a civil rights probe into the early 2011 spate of shootings by Miami police, involving seven black men over an eight-month period. Wilson founded the 5000 Role Models of Excellence Project, a local version of My Brother's Keeper, to assist at-risk young males. "There is this tension that never goes away between the police and especially black boys," she said. President Barack Obama praised her efforts during a White House event in February 2014. As part of the program, Jahvaris Fulton, the brother of Trayvon Martin, interned in her office.

She held forums in her district on enforcing the rights of Haiti's "poor majority." In October 2014, the Obama administration adopted her proposal for a family reunification program for Haitian immigrants who had become separated from their families. The action was part of the U.S. response to a devastating earthquake in Haiti in 2010 that left 1.5 million homeless. After several violent hazing incidents at colleges, Wilson proposed denying federal aid to students who are punished by colleges or convicted for hazing. The North American Interfraternity Conference backed her effort.

Moise returned for a rematch in the 2012 Democratic primary, and this time snagged a rare endorsement from a foreign leader, Haitian President Michel Martelly. But Wilson countered with one from Obama and won easily with 66%; she was unopposed in the general election. In April 2015, she endorsed Rep. Patrick Murphy in the contest to succeed retiring Sen. Marco Rubio.

TWENTY-FIFTH DISTRICT

Mario Diaz-Balart (R)

Elected 2002, 7th term; b. Sept. 25, 1961, Ft. Lauderdale; U. of S. FL, attended; Catholic; married (Tia); 1 child.

Elected Office: FL House, 1988-92, 2000-02; FL Senate, 1992-2000.

Professional Career: A.A., Miami Mayor Xavier Suarez, 1985-88; Public relations executive.

DC Office: 440 CHOB, 20515, 202-225-4211; Fax: 202-225-8576; Website: mariodiazbalart.house.gov.

State Offices: Doral, 305-470-8555; Naples, 239-348-1620.

Committees: *Appropriations:* Defense; State, Foreign Operations & Related Programs; Transportation, Housing & Urban Development & Related Agencies (Chmn). *Budget.*

Group Ratings

	ADA	ACLU	AFL-CIO	LCV	ITI	COC	HAFA	ACU	CFG	FRC
2014	5%	16%	–	3%	60%	93%	32%	44%	39%	88%
2013	0%	C	32%	4%	C	83%	C	52%	38%	C

National Journal Ratings

	2013 LIB	—	2013 CONS
Economic	48%	—	51%
Social	47%	—	53%
Foreign	40%	—	59%
Composite	45%	—	55%

Key Votes of the 113th Congress

1. Sandy storm spending	Y	5. Medical Marijuana	N	9. Syrian Rebels Training	Y
2. Violence Against Women Act	Y	6. Farm Bill	Y	10. Keystone pipeline	Y
3. Guantanamo Bay Detainees	N	7. Afghanistan Combat	N	11. Immigration Exec. Action	N
4. Abortion 20-week ban	Y	8. NSA Phone Data Collection	N	12. Bipartisan budget deal	Y

Election Results

2014 general   Mario Diaz-Balart (R)............unopposed $605,137
2014 primary Mario Diaz-Balart (R)............unopposed

Prior winning percentages: 2012 (76%), 2010 (67%), 2008 (72%), 2006 (80%), 2004 (73%), 2002 (66%), 2000 (69%), 1998 (67%), 1996 (57%)

Population		Race and Ethnicity		Income	
Total:	740,305	Latino	70.4%	Median income:	$45,697
Urban:	79.6%	White	20.6%		*(305 of 435)*
Suburban:	15.9%	Black	6.1%	Under $50,000	53.3%
Rural:	4.5%	Asian	2.0%	$50,000-$99,999:	29.6%
Land area:	2,389	Two races	0.8%	$100,000-$199,999:	13.7%
Pop/sq. mi.:	309.8	White Ethnic	7.8%	$200,000 or more:	3.3%
Born in state:	28.5%			Poverty Rate	18.4%
		Education			
Age Groups		H.S. grad or less:	50.1%	**Work**	
Under 18:	21.3%	Some college:	26.2%	White collar:	27.8%
18 to 34:	22.9%	College degree, 4 yr.:	14.9%	Blue collar:	48.9%
35 to 64:	40.3%	Post-grad study:	8.8%	Sales and service:	23.3%
Over 64:	15.5%				
		Military		Govt. workers:	9.1%
		Veterans/active duty:	3.3%		

Southern Florida: Hialeah, Other Miami Suburbs

Miami's Cuban-American community was a mere footnote in the inaugural edition of *The Almanac of American Politics*, published in 1971, which specu-lated that these residents of what was then Demo-cratic Rep. Claude Pepper's congressional district might end up being more conservative than the

Voter Turnout	
2013 Total Citizen 18+	421,695
2014 House Turnout	0
2014 Turnout as % CVAP	0.0%
2012 Turnout as % CVAP	58.5%

Jewish and African-American voters who then dominated Dade County. That turned out to be an understatement. Cuban Americans have proved to be one of America's most dynamic immigrant groups over the past half-century, growing from 50,000 in 1960, the year after Fidel Castro took over Cuba, to well over 1 million today. They almost singlehandedly trans-formed Dade County from a place that John Kennedy won by 15% in 1960 to one that George H.W. Bush won by 11% in 1988. Over time, the Cuban-American neighborhoods centered along S.W. 8th Street—Calle Ocho—expanded west to the Florida Turnpike Extension in Fountainebleau and Sweetwater, and northwest to Hialeah. Starting in the 1980s, there was an influx of other Latinos, from Nicaragua, El Salvador, Venezuela, and Colombia. In the process, new communities were built and old ones transformed. Built on swampland, Sweet-water is now probably more Cuban than the old Little Havana on Calle Ocho, although Nicaraguans make up a substantial minority in Sweetwater. In 2014, Ikea opened a huge store in Sweetwater, with Florida's largest non-utility solar-power system.

The 25th Congressional District remains very much a creature of Miami-Dade, where nearly two-thirds of its residents live. It includes many of the heavily Cuban neighborhoods west and northwest of Miami. To the west it takes in Fountainebleau, Sweetwater, and Doral, home to one of the nation's highest concentration of Venezuelan Americans. Some refer to Doral and its rapidly growing business center just beyond the Miami International Airport as "Doralzuela." Farther north it includes parts of raffish Hialeah and nearby Miami Lakes, a planned town developed in the 1960s. With 91 percent Spanish-speaking, Hialeah has the largest such concentration in the nation, and the smallest share of English-speaking resi-dents; about 53 percent were foreign-born. In April 2015, Hialeah officials and developers announced plans for a $4 billion American Dream Miami mega-mall and theme park. A small portion of the district is in Broward County, including the western extremes of Miramar and Pembroke Pines. Another sliver of population is in Hendry County, including the county seat of LaBelle, which holds an annual Swamp Cabbage Festival, featuring a

2012 Presidential Vote		
Mitt Romney (R)	117,925	(51%)
Barack Obama (D)	112,830	(49%)

2008 Presidential Vote		
John McCain (R)	121,469	(52%)
Barack Obama (D)	109,129	(47%)

Cook Partisan Voting Index: R+5

parade and crowning of the Swamp Cabbage Queen and Princess. The district also sprawls across the Everglades to the edge of fast-growing Naples in Collier County. Residents of

Collier County comprise about a fifth of the district's population; most of these live in heavily Republican suburbs and exurbs of Naples a few miles from the Gulf of Mexico.

The district's population is 70% Hispanic, 37% of whom report Cuban origins. Cuban voters continue to identify as heavily Republican, although Barack Obama may have narrowly carried them in 2012, with many younger Cubans less supportive of the embargo. Overall, this is the most Republican of the three districts held by GOP members in South Florida, but not overwhelmingly so. The GOP has a 6-point registration advantage, and Obama nearly carried the district in 2012.

Mario Diaz-Balart (R)

Mario Diaz-Balart, a Republican first elected in 2002, has become a pragmatic legislator who has been among the handful of GOP Latinos seeking to nudge their party closer to the political middle on immigration issues. He has been an unswerving hard-liner against Cuba's Castro regime, but has joined Democrats on some national and local issues.

The Diaz-Balart family history is intertwined with that of Fidel Castro and the rise of communism on the island nation of Cuba. Mario's father, Rafael Lincoln Diaz-Balart, was the majority leader in pre-revolution Cuba's House of Representatives. His uncle and grandfather also served in the Cuban House. The Diaz-Balarts fled Cuba in 1959, shortly after Castro took over and after their house was looted and burned while they were vacationing in Paris. His aunt was briefly Castro's wife and is the mother of the dictator's only recognized child. One of Mario's three older brothers is Lincoln Diaz-Balart, who served in the House from 1992 to 2010, then set up a consulting firm. Another brother Jose is an anchorman with MSNBC and Spanish-language Telemundo, and Rafa is an investment banker in Miami.

Mario Diaz-Balart was born in the United States after the family had resettled. He dropped out of the University of South Florida at age 24 to work for former Miami Mayor Xavier Suarez, a Republican. In 1988, he was elected to the Florida House; four years later, at age 31, he became the youngest person ever elected to the state Senate. Diaz-Balart was chairman of the Senate Ways and Means Committee, where he was a budget hawk. His 1995 call for state agencies to cut spending by 25% earned him the nickname "The Slasher"—a moniker he wore with pride. The eight-year term limit forced him from the Senate in 2000, so he again ran for the Florida House and was elected. No ordinary freshman, Diaz-Balart requested and received the chairmanship of the congressional redistricting committee. The resulting plan included a western Miami-Dade district that he tailored for himself. He coasted to victory over largely unknown Democratic state Rep. Annie Betancourt, a former social worker and the widow of a Bay of Pigs veteran. With support from teachers and other unions, Diaz-Balart won 65%-35%.

In the House, his voting record has generally been conservative on economic and foreign policy and more moderate on cultural issues. Republican leaders, eager to diversify their caucus, made him an assistant whip and gave him a coveted seat on the Appropriations Committee. He repeatedly has opposed oil drilling off Florida's coast in the Gulf of Mexico and used his Appropriations seat to secure funding for the Everglades, local transit and widening of Interstate 75. He moved up the seniority ladder at the committee, and took over in 2015 as chairman of its subcommittee on Transportation, Housing and Urban Development.

Diaz-Balart organized the Congressional Hispanic Conference, a Republican alternative to the Democrats' Congressional Hispanic Caucus, and he has often engaged with immigration issues. With GOP Rep. Ileana Ros-Lehtinen, also of South Florida, he supported a bill to allow children of illegal immigrants to qualify for college aid. After Republican Mitt Romney overwhelmingly lost the Hispanic vote to President Barack Obama in 2012, Diaz-Balart was among those vocally touting a House-passed bill to provide visas for foreign graduates of U.S. universities with advanced math and science degrees, as an initial step toward re-establishing GOP credibility on immigration. But he added that it was no substitute for a broader bill, which he has called the "800-pound gorilla." Republicans "cannot pretend there are not millions of people in an underground society," he told the *Orlando Sentinel*. "We can no longer pretend that it's not affecting our ability to be competitive." Since 2012, he has participated in private discussions with many members of each party in an effort to find common ground on immigration issues. When House Republican leaders said in July 2014 that the issue was dead until the next Congress, Diaz-Balart called the action "disappointing and highly unfortunate" and that it was "highly irresponsible not to deal with the issue." He has said that a major setback was the unexpected Republican primary defeat a month earlier of Majority Leader Eric Cantor, who had been spearheading efforts for an immigration bill.

Diaz-Balart strongly opposed the Obama administration's push to loosen travel to Cuba, saying that tourist travel was an important revenue source for Castro's government, and he adamantly opposed Obama's moves to resume diplomatic relations with Cuba. "President Obama is the appeaser-in-chief who is willing to provide unprecedented concessions to a brutal dictatorship that opposes U.S. interests at every opportunity," he said in response to Obama's December 2014 actions. Diaz-Balart said that Cuba had not met the terms set by Congress before the embargo could be lifted. With his Appropriations seat, he was well-placed to shape a GOP legislative response.

In 2008, he faced a serious challenge from Joe Garcia, the Miami-Dade County Democratic chairman and former executive director of the Cuban American National Foundation. Garcia opposed the restrictions on travel and remittances to Cuba and criticized the incumbent for focusing on Cuba rather than on gas prices and the crisis in housing foreclosures. Diaz-Balart won by a narrow 53%-47%. (Four years later, Garcia defeated Republican Rep. David Rivera in the 26th District, then lost his seat in 2014 after one term.)

After his close call, Diaz-Balart in 2010 sought and won his brother Lincoln's seat in a more Republican District when Lincoln retired from the House. Diaz-Balart ended up running unopposed. Then, after redistricting, he returned to the new 25th district that extended across the Everglades, and he was reelected with more than three-quarters of the vote: three different districts in three cycles. He has not faced a major-party opponent since 2008. That didn't stop him, though, from joining Democratic Florida Rep. Corrine Brown in a lawsuit challenging the state's Fair Districts reforms; they claimed the anti-gerrymandering law unfairly hurt minority voters. For the 2016 Republican presidential nomination, he has said that he's "all in" for Jeb Bush, but he has praised the "vast talent" of Sen. Marco Rubio. Diaz-Balart served with each in Tallahassee. Bush praised him as "a connector."

TWENTY-SIXTH DISTRICT

Carlos Curbelo (R)

Elected 2014, 1st term; b. March 1, 1980, Miami; U. Miami, B.A. 2002, M.A. 2011; Catholic; married (Cecilia); 2 children.

Elected Office: Miami Dade Cnty. School Board, 2010.

Professional Career: Founder, Public & media relations company, 2002-14; State director, U.S. Sen. George LeMieux, 2009-11.

DC Office: 1429 LHOB, 20515, 202-225-2778; Website: curbelo.house. gov.

State Offices: Florida City, 305-247-1234; Key West, 305-292-4485; Miami, 305-222-0160.

Committees: *Education & the Workforce:* Early Childhood, Elementary & Secondary Education; Higher Education & Workforce Training. *Small Business:* Agriculture, Energy & Trade (Chmn). *Transportation & Infrastructure:* Aviation; Coast Guard & Maritime Transportation (VChmn); Economic Development, Public Buildings & Emergency Management.

Election Results

2014 general	Carlos Curbelo (R)	83,031	(51%)	$2,347,633	$748,713	$2,484,612
	Joe Garcia (D)	78,306	(49%)	$3,787,930	$389,477	$5,553,442
	Angel Fernandez (I)	5,726	(2%)			
2014 primary	Carlos Curbelo (R)	13,861	(47%)			
	Ed MacDougall (R)	7,455	(25%)			
	Joe Martinez (R)	5,136	(17%)			
	David Rivera (R)	2,209	(8%)			

Population		Race and Ethnicity		Income	
Total:	741,247	Latino	69.5%	Median income:	$50,582
Urban:	68.9%	White	19.7%		*(232 of 435)*
Suburban:	15.4%	Black	8.4%	Under $50,000	49.3%
Rural:	15.6%	Asian	1.4%	$50,000-$99,999:	29.8%
Land area:	1,512	Two races	0.7%	$100,000-$199,999:	17.6%
Pop/sq. mi.:	490.1	White Ethnic	8.0%	$200,000 or more:	3.3%
Born in state:	34.1%			Poverty Rate	18.0%
		Education			
Age Groups		H.S. grad or less:	46.4%	**Work**	
Under 18:	20.2%	Some college:	25.6%	White collar:	32.5%
18 to 34:	23.1%	College degree, 4 yr.:	19.2%	Blue collar:	49.2%
35 to 64:	41.9%	Post-grad study:	8.8%	Sales and service:	18.2%
Over 64:	14.8%				
		Military		Govt. workers:	11.3%
		Veterans/active duty:	3.7%		

Southern Florida: Inland Dade, the Keys

At the tip of the Florida Keys, a string of islands connected to each other and to mainland Florida by U.S. 1, is Key West, the southernmost city in the continental United States. Over the years, Key West has attracted famous residents—Ernest Hemingway, Tennessee Williams, Jimmy Buf-

Voter Turnout	
2013 Total Citizen 18+	456,562
2014 House Turnout	161,337
2014 Turnout as % CVAP	35.3%
2012 Turnout as % CVAP	58.9%

fett—and a large gay population, many living in quaint clapboard bungalows called "conch houses." Along the way down U.S. 1, gawkers still stop to stare at "Betsy," a three-story tall, detailed sculpture of a spiny lobster that bespeaks the kitschy, tourist-trap laden Florida of yesteryear.

An influx of immigrants, first from Cuba and then from other Caribbean nations as well as Central and South America, has filled in the landscape of southern Miami-Dade County. This immigration surge has created a multicultural pastiche of ethnicities. Tamiami is majority Cuban, but now boasts sizable Nicaraguan, Colombian, Dominican, and Venezuelan communities. To the south is The Hammocks, a planned community dominated by non-Cuban Hispanics. Further south along U.S. 1 are a collection of agricultural towns such as Princeton, and a few older tourist attractions like the Metrozoo and the Monkey Jungle. Homestead, which was leveled by Hurricane Andrew in 1992 but has since been redeveloped, and neighboring Florida City have sizable African-American populations. Fun fact: Key West in 1982 voted to secede from the United States and declared itself the Conch Republic, after U.S. officials tightened security on the keys as part of their war on drugs. The secession has not been rescinded, but it has been celebrated annually with parades, parties, and a drag race.

The 26th Congressional District combines Monroe County with much of southern Miami-Dade County. The large majority of the district's residents live on the western and southern edges of metropolitan Miami, close to the swamps. Here one can drive out on roads past the subdivisions and find strawberry, tomato, and citrus farms. The trees thin out, and then the road just ends at the Everglades—an interconnected sea of wetlands that once covered 8.9 million acres of southern Florida, stretching from Orlando to the peninsula's southern tip. Then, it was a coherent ecosystem, a "river of grass" in which water moved slowly down a gentle slope to the ocean. But the state's white settlers were intent on making it more useful, and in 1948, Congress approved the construction of 1,720 miles of canals and levees to channel and drain the Everglades, making it possible to use the land for agri-

2012 Presidential Vote		
Barack Obama (D) 141,776	(53%)
Mitt Romney (R).................123,313	(46%)

2008 Presidential Vote		
Barack Obama (D) 133,875	(50%)
John McCain (R).................131,630	(49%)

Cook Partisan Voting Index: R+1

culture and housing. The Tamiami Trail, one of only two roads that cross swampy southern Florida from coast-to-coast, and which took three attempts to build, forms the northern boundary of the district in the eastern half.

In recent years, Floridians have had second thoughts about taming the Everglades. Since 2000, Congress, with the encouragement of President George W. Bush and his brother, then-Florida Gov. Jeb Bush, has approved billions of dollars for Everglades restoration. In 2008, the state proposed buying much of the land owned by U.S. Sugar Corp. around Lake Okeechobee for $1.35 billion, with farming to be phased out in seven years. That would allow water to pass over land from the lake, through the Everglades, to the Gulf of Mexico. The recession forced Gov. Charlie Crist to scale back the project by more than half. Overall the district is 75% Hispanic, but only 42% Cuban American. This is marginal political territory; Democrats hold the slightest of registration advantages here, and President Barack Obama carried the district 53%-46% in 2012.

Carlos Curbelo (R)

Republican Carlos Curbelo won a face-off in 2014 between two Cuban-Americans to regain the Miami-area 26th District for the GOP, using ethical issues to tarnish an incumbent who had won in 2012 by exploiting the ethics troubles of his predecessor. Democratic Rep. Joe Garcia held the seat only one term after losing twice before.

Curbelo was born in Miami to two Cuban exiles who fled the Castro regime in the 1960s. He earned degrees in business administration and public administration from the University of Miami. In 2002, Curbelo founded Capital Gains, a consulting firm, and worked as a lobbyist and campaign adviser. In 2009, Curbelo was state director for then-Sen. George LeMieux of Florida, advising the GOP lawmaker on Latin American policy and Hispanic issues. In 2010, he was elected to the Miami-Dade County School Board, a job he said he was inspired to seek after the birth of his first child.

Curbelo faced a primary challenge from former Rep. David Rivera, who had lost his seat to Garcia in 2012 amid a scandal over a complicated campaign financing scheme. The Republican establishment, seeing a strong opportunity to take the seat away from Garcia, rallied around Curbelo. Rivera (who had defeated Curbelo by a single vote for the Miami-Dade Republican chairmanship in 2008) temporarily suspended his campaign in July. Curbelo won a four-way primary with 47% of the vote to 25% for runner-up Ed MacDougall. Rivera got less than 8%.

The general election pitted two men with similar views on the central issue of immigration and different troubles with their comments on Florida-centric issues. Curbelo was roundly criticized for calling Social Security and Medicare a "Ponzi scheme"—not a vote-getter line in a state with many retirees. And Garcia was denounced for saying, in what appeared to be an ironic comment, that "communism works"—not the sort of characterization that played well in a district with Cuban refugees and their descendants. Garcia went after Curbelo for his lobbying activity, accusing him of not disclosing his clients. Meanwhile, Garcia had been linked to a voter-fraud scandal, with two former staffers accused of impropriety, though Garcia denied involvement. Curbelo broke with many in his party on immigration reform by supporting the "Dream Act" to allow certain children brought to the country illegally by their parents to remain in America. Curbelo pledged to work to pass an immigration-reform package, reduce the national debt, and create a "consumer-driven" health care system.

This was one of the most costly House races in 2014. Garcia outspent Curbelo $3.8 million to $2.3 million, but the national Republican Party spent about $5 million compared to a bit more than $2 million by Democrats. Curbelo won with 51.5% of the vote. He took 52.2% in Miami-Dade, but only 48.2% in less populous Monroe County, which encompasses the Florida Keys.

In the House, Curbelo got off to a quick start. In January, he gave the Spanish-language response to the State of the Union message by President Barack Obama. He announced his support for comprehensive immigration reform, and created a political action committee to support other Republicans who share that goal. He was the first Southern Republican to join mostly Democrats in cosponsoring a bill to restore a key part of the Voting Rights Act that the Supreme Court had found unconstitutional. An early challenge for 2016 came from Democrat Annette Taddeo, who was Charlie Crist's running mate in 2014 when he ran for governor. In July 2015, the state Supreme Court-ordered redistricting plan raised additional potential problems for Curbelo.

TWENTY-SEVENTH DISTRICT

Ileana Ros-Lehtinen (R)

Elected Aug. 1989, 13th full term; b. July 15, 1952, Havana, Cuba; Miami-Dade Comm. Col., A.A. 1972, FL Intl. U., B.A. 1975, M.S. 1986, U. of Miami, Ed.D. 2004; Episcopalian; married (Dexter); 4 children.

Elected Office: FL House, 1982-86; FL Senate, 1986-89.

Professional Career: Teacher, principal, & owner, Eastern Acad. Elem. Schl., 1978-85.

DC Office: 2206 RHOB, 20515, 202-225-3931; Fax: 202-225-5620; Website: ros-lehtinen.house.gov.

State Offices: Miami, 305-668-2285.

Committees: *Foreign Affairs*: Middle East & North Africa (Chmn); Western Hemisphere. *Intelligence (Select)*: Department of Defense Intelligence & Overhead Architecture; NSA & Cybersecurity.

Group Ratings

	ADA	ACLU	AFL-CIO	LCV	ITI	COC	HAFA	ACU	CFG	FRC
2014	5%	16%	–	3%	80%	92%	31%	50%	40%	85%
2013	0%	C	37%	7%	C	83%	C	61%	37%	C

National Journal Ratings

	2013 LIB	—	2013 CONS
Economic	48%	—	52%
Social	48%	—	52%
Foreign	43%	—	57%
Composite	46%	—	54%

Key Votes of the 113th Congress

1. Sandy storm spending	Y	5. Medical Marijuana	NV
2. Violence Against Women Act	Y	6. Farm Bill	Y
3. Guantanamo Bay Detainees	N	7. Afghanistan Combat	N
4. Abortion 20-week ban	Y	8. NSA Phone Data Collection	N

9. Syrian Rebels Training	Y
10. Keystone pipeline	NV
11. Immigration Exec. Action	N
12. Bipartisan budget deal	Y

Election Results

2014 general	Ileana Ros-Lehtinen (R)........unopposed	$850,120 $49,170
2014 primary	Ileana Ros-Lehtinen (R)........unopposed	

Prior winning percentages: 2012 (60%), 2010 (69%), 2008 (58%), 2006 (62%), 2004 (65%), 2002 (69%), 2000 (100%), 1998 (100%), 1996 (100%), 1994 (100%), 1992 (67%), 1990 (60%), 1989 special (53%)

Population		Race and Ethnicity		Income	
Total:	719,632	Latino	72.7%	Median income:	$42,262
Urban:	84.4%	White	18.3%		*(353 of 435)*
Suburban:	15.6%	Black	6.6%	Under $50,000	56.0%
Rural:	0.0%	Asian	1.7%	$50,000-$99,999:	23.4%
Land area:	151	Two races	0.5%	$100,000-$199,999:	13.7%
Pop/sq. mi.:	4,765.4	White Ethnic	7.0%	$200,000 or more:	6.9%
Born in state:	30.4%			Poverty Rate	20.1%
		Education			
Age Groups		H.S. grad or less:	47.1%	**Work**	
Under 18:	20.8%	Some college:	23.9%	White collar:	33.2%
18 to 34:	22.3%	College degree, 4 yr.:	17.5%	Blue collar:	48.2%
35 to 64:	40.6%	Post-grad study:	11.6%	Sales and service:	18.6%
Over 64:	16.4%				
		Military		Govt. workers:	9.7%
		Veterans/active duty:	2.8%		

Southern and Western Dade

A century ago, Miami was a tiny tropical village where the Miami River empties into Biscayne Bay. Today it is a world-class city. The surrealistic high-rises of Brickell Boulevard, the winding lanes of Coral Gables, and the shimmer of orange and pink neon signs in the hot night air: This is Miami today.

Voter Turnout	
2013 Total Citizen 18+	407,403
2014 House Turnout	0
2014 Turnout as % CVAP	0.0%
2012 Turnout as % CVAP	59.5%

It lives on the cusp of two civilizations, North America and Latin America, with different traditions, styles, and sensibilities converging in this one place, with the strengths of each despite some friction. From Miami, it is easy to fly directly to any part of Latin America where top business and banking services are available to a sophisticated, Spanish-speaking, and usually also English-speaking, clientele.

Miami for decades has also been the locus of Cuban America, ever since the first refugees fled Fidel Castro in 1959. In the 1960s, the tone of Miami civic life was set by the large Jewish community and the liberal voice of *The Miami Herald*. But increasing numbers of Cuban immigrants, implacably opposed to the totalitarian Castro, entered the voting stream as Republicans. Then, Cubans were a noisy minority in the Miami area. Now, they are a dominant voice in a Latino majority in Miami-Dade County (as Dade County was renamed in 1997). In 2010, the population of Miami-Dade was 65% Hispanic and 19% black, leaving Anglo whites a fading but still elite minority, with educational backgrounds and incomes well above the national average. Miami ranks high among cities with income inequality between lower and upper classes. In 2014, it was second to New York City with home sales listings of more than $1 million. But the Latino population grew more diverse: Little Havana, centered on Calle Ocho (S.W. 8th Street), is now home to many Nicaraguans, Hondurans, and Peruvians. Many of these Latino immigrants rose in their adoptive society by going to school at Miami Dade College, the nation's largest community college, or to Florida International University, and then starting businesses or joining professions in Miami's vibrant economy.

Politically, Miami-Dade County is sharply divided, with black neighborhoods north of downtown and the remaining heavily Jewish condominium developments in the northeast heavily Democratic, and the Latino districts in the west and south mostly Republican. At the southern end of the county, the neighborhoods again become more Democratic as the Cuban-American population gives way to a more heavily African-American and non-Cuban Hispanic population. Today, Cuban Americans are less monolithically Republican than in the past. Younger Cubans are less focused on overthrowing the Castro regime, and many oppose the U.S. government's restrictions on travel and diplomatic dealings with Cuba while still favoring the trade embargo. The county's voting patterns have reflected this. After giving narrow wins to Democrats Al Gore and John Kerry in their presidential contests, Barack Obama won the county twice by hefty margins.

The 27th Congressional District of Florida is one of Miami-Dade's three Hispanic-majority districts. It is 75% Hispanic and 8% non-Hispanic black. The district follows Calle Ocho from Little Havana west to heavily Hispanic West Miami and Westchester. North of Miami International Airport, which surpassed Orlando as Florida's busiest airport in 2009, the district includes Miami Springs and parts of Hialeah. To the south, it sweeps up many of metro Miami's high-income residential areas: Coral Gables, with luxurious streets laid out in the 1920s; Cocoplum, a gated community of huge houses and boat docks for rich Cuban Americans; and Key Biscayne, with its high-rise apartments owned mostly by Latino immigrants and their second-generation offspring. Kendall is the site of the upscale Dadeland Mall, where Spanish is heard more often than English. Further signs of the income inequality in this area: The street in America with the highest median home value ($21.5 million) is on the private island of Indian Creek in Biscayne Bay. At the far end of the district are low-income areas along U.S. 1, like Naranja and Homestead, which was leveled by Hur-

2012 Presidential Vote		
Barack Obama (D) 130,020	(53%)
Mitt Romney (R)................114,096	(47%)

2008 Presidential Vote		
John McCain (R)................123,543	(51%)
Barack Obama (D) 120,028	(49%)

Cook Partisan Voting Index: R+2

ricane Andrew in 1992 but has since been redeveloped. Here's an indicator of the area's low income: Of the 10 zip codes in the nation with the highest enrollment under the Affordable

Care Act, all are in the Miami-Fort Lauderdale area, *The New York Times* reported. For years, the district voted Republican, but there have been shifts here. Obama carried the district 53%-47% in 2012, and Democrats are even with Republicans in voter registration.

Ileana Ros-Lehtinen (R)

Republican Ileana Ros-Lehtinen in 1989 became the first Cuban American and the first Hispanic woman elected to Congress. Since then, she has blazed an unusual political trail—generally conservative on fiscal and foreign policy matters with moderate-to-liberal stances on gay rights, immigration, and other social issues that have kept her popular at home. Her fervent hostility toward the Cuban regime has not diminished.

Ros-Lehtinen was born in Havana. She came to Miami at the age of 8 not knowing English, and graduated from Miami Dade Community College and Florida International University. She became a teacher and then was the owner of a private school. In 2004, she got her doctorate in education from the University of Miami—a rare member of Congress who earned a degree while a lawmaker, rather than receiving an honorary degree. Her dissertation was on U.S. House members' views on national testing for high school students. She was elected to the Florida House in 1982, at age 30, and to the state Senate in 1986. While there, she met her husband, Dexter Lehtinen, who also served in both houses of the legislature and as U.S. attorney in Miami during the first Bush administration. She authored Florida's Prepaid College Plan, which has become the largest such tuition program in the nation. In 1989, Ros-Lehtinen ran for the House after the death of Democrat Claude Pepper, one of the most enduring liberals in American politics and a staunch opponent of Castro. At that time, no Republican and no Cuban American represented Miami or Dade County. Democratic nominee Gerald Richman played on suspicions of Cubans and won the votes of 96% of blacks and 88% of non-Hispanic whites. But 99% of Hispanics, almost all of them Cuban, voted for Ros-Lehtinen. That was enough to give her a 53%-47% victory. In the years afterward, the district became more Hispanic, and she had no serious challenge until 2008.

Ros-Lehtinen's voting patterns became more centrist as the House GOP veered to the right. She is a longtime supporter of gay rights, backing same-sex marriage and serving as one of the first GOP members of the Congressional LGBT Equality Caucus. LGBT issues are personal to her; her daughter Amanda is now a transgender man named Rodrigo Lehtinen. In an interview with CBS, she had advice for parents of transgenders: "Don't freak out, stay calm and don't be afraid." She was one of just 23 House Republicans to oppose a reauthorization of the Violence Against Women Act in June 2012 that Democrats called insufficient, and she abandoned the majority of her party in voting to support an increase in the minimum wage; raising automobiles' fuel-economy standards; tightening food safety; and giving the Food and Drug Administration authority to regulate some tobacco products.

When Republicans won a House majority in 1995, she refused to sign the party's Contract with America policy manifesto and was a harsh critic of Republican attempts to pass English-only legislation, to cut off welfare benefits for legal immigrants—she voted against the 1996 welfare bills—and to reduce the immigration quota for relatives of U.S. citizens. In the 2007 debate over immigration, she pleaded with Republicans not to alienate the growing Hispanic voting bloc. Ros-Lehtinen backed Republican Mitt Romney's presidential bids despite his hard-line immigration stance, saying his position on economic issues mattered far more to her.

When Republicans reclaimed control of the House in 2011, Ros-Lehtinen took over as chair of the Foreign Affairs Committee. She developed a tight relationship with the panel's ranking Democrat, Howard Berman of California, and they worked closely on enacting economic sanctions on Iran to discourage its nuclear program. In 2012, she introduced a bill with Iowa Democrat Bruce Braley to compensate the U.S. hostages who were held in Iran for 444 days starting in 1979. (The legislation did not move, but the movie *Argo* about the hostage crisis gave it some attention.) Ros-Lehtinen has been a strong supporter of Israel and a fierce critic of Middle East regimes such as Syria that are accused of sponsoring terrorism. During the "Arab spring" revolutions throughout the Middle East in 2011, Ros-Lehtinen kept close tabs on President Barack Obama and his top advisers. She criticized their failure to press quickly for reform in Egypt, and she chastised the administration for waffling on how to handle the Muslim Brotherhood. In 2015, she worked with Democrat Ted Deutch of Florida to launch the bipartisan task force for combating anti-Semitism.

Ros-Lehtinen strongly backed the 1996 Helms-Burton law that tightened sanctions against Fidel Castro's Cuba, and she has opposed farm-state Republicans who have sought to relax the trade embargo in effect since 1961. In February 2008, after Castro stepped down as head of state, she called for his indictment for shooting down two Brothers to the Rescue planes in 1996. Cuba's state-run newspaper, *Gramma*, once called her "a ferocious wolf disguised as a woman," which she shortened in Spanish to "LOBA FRZ" and proudly put on her license plate. She remained steadfast when Obama opened the door to Cuba. "Raul Castro can continue his dictatorial ways without giving in an inch while the White House gave Mr. Castro all the concessions he wanted," she wrote in a December 2014 op-ed. "Typical of the administration, the desire for a deal—any deal—was stronger than the interest in its contents." Republican term limits forced her to yield the Foreign Affairs gavel in 2013. But GOP leaders might give her another committee—not least because in 2017 all of their chairmen otherwise might be men.

In 2008, national Democrats thought Ros-Lehtinen was vulnerable. Democrat Annette Taddeo, owner of the LanguageSpeak translation service, launched a challenge and financed it with $400,000 of her own money. Colombian-born Taddeo favored the embargo on Cuba but wanted to ease travel restrictions. The Democratic Congressional Campaign Committee poured $1.4 million into television ads. Ros-Lehtinen won 58%-42%, even though the district voted 51%-49% for Obama. "If I can make it in this election, I can make it in any election," she told *The Miami Herald*. She won her next two with little effort, and ran unopposed in 2014. In early 2015, she endorsed Jeb Bush for President, even though two other candidates— Sens. Marco Rubio and Ted Cruz—shared her Cuban roots.

★ GEORGIA ★

Until recently, Georgia has not been one of the nation's most prominent states. It was the last of the 13 colonies to be founded, by British Gen. James Oglethorpe in 1733, as an "asylum of the unfortunate," reserved for debtors and other outcasts from England. Oglethorpe, a humanitarian, forbade slavery, but the settlers rebelled and repealed his ban in 1750. In 1790, the first census showed Georgia with the smallest population of any of the original 13 states except tiny Delaware and Rhode Island. It was only the fifth largest slave state when the Civil War began. Early in the 20th century, Georgia was still largely agrarian and sparsely populated. Then, beginning in the 1970s, the state shared in the growth explosion taking place in the South. By 2000, it was ranked in the top 10 most populous states, and by 2012, it was the eighth largest state. This is the result mainly of the stunning growth in metro Atlanta, which spreads out over the red clay hills of 29 of Georgia's 159 counties and which grew from 3.1 million people in 1990 to 4.2 million in 2000 and 5.3 million in 2010. Growth slowed in the 2007-09 recession, and foreclosures became frequent. Unemployment was in the double digits for over two years—from May 2009 to September 2011—and, despite falling to 6.3 percent by March 2015, remained above the national average. Still, the impact of decades of rapid growth remains pervasive.

Even before this demographic surge, Atlanta has been in many ways the center of the South. Before the Civil War, Atlanta, located at the south end of the Appalachian chain, was a railroad junction. Its capture by Gen. William Tecumseh Sherman in September 1864 and his scorched-earth March to the Sea did much to produce President Abraham Lincoln's reelection victory in November 1864 and the Union victory over the Confederacy seven months later. Neither Atlanta's rise to world eminence nor its role as the "capital" of the South was inevitable. A century ago, Richmond, Charleston and New Orleans all had stronger claims to being the cultural focus of the South. But in the 20th century, two figures imprinted Atlanta on the national imagination. One was Margaret Mitchell, whose 1936 novel *Gone With the Wind* inspired the 1939 movie of the same name. The other was Martin Luther King, Jr., who was based in Atlanta for most of his career and who, with other Atlanta-based organizations, ultimately led the civil rights revolution that changed the South and the nation. Linking the two was Atlanta's business community, notably Robert Woodruff, who headed Coca-Cola from 1923 to 1955 and made Coke—invented locally by John Stith Pemberton—a worldwide enterprise. Perhaps aware that a global company could not afford to be associated with racial segregation, Woodruff and William Hartsfield, the city's mayor from 1937 to 1961, cooperated with black leaders and promoted Atlanta as "the city too busy to hate." Hartsfield's successor, Ivan Allen, Jr., elected in 1961 and 1965, supported the Civil Rights Act of 1964, as Peachtree Center and the first Hyatt Regency were going up in downtown Atlanta. And if geography made Atlanta, like Chicago, a natural rail hub in the mid-19th century, it was their mayors—Hartsfield in Atlanta, Richard J. Daley in Chicago—who built major airports that made their cities major transportation hubs in the mid-20th century. Today, Georgia is the nation's fifth-largest logistics employer.

The new Atlanta grew up amid a mostly rural, deeply segregationist Georgia that, still angry at Sherman's march 96 years before, cast the second-highest Democratic percentage for president in 1960. In the next two elections, Georgia voters swung sharply, voting for Barry Goldwater in 1964 and George Wallace in 1968. Statewide election contests were typically fought out in Democratic primaries that pitted Atlanta-supported moderates against rural-supported segregationists or conservatives, and the latter usually won. Then came change, in the person of Jimmy Carter, a former two-term state senator who was elected governor in 1970 with a rural base. After taking office, Carter proclaimed racial reconciliation and installed a portrait of King in the state Capitol. Carter thus became one of the first politicians from the rural South to celebrate and honor the civil rights movement, and in the process, set himself on the road to being elected president in 1976. Carter was followed by a series of Democratic governors with mostly rural roots—George Busbee, Joe Frank Harris, Zell Miller and Roy Barnes.

In 1976, when every one of Georgia's 159 counties voted for Carter, 44 percent of the state's votes were cast in the 28 counties currently classified as metro Atlanta. In 2008 and 2012, 57 percent of the votes were cast in metro Atlanta. In the intervening years, Georgia has attracted thousands of in-migrants from other states while retaining most of its natives:

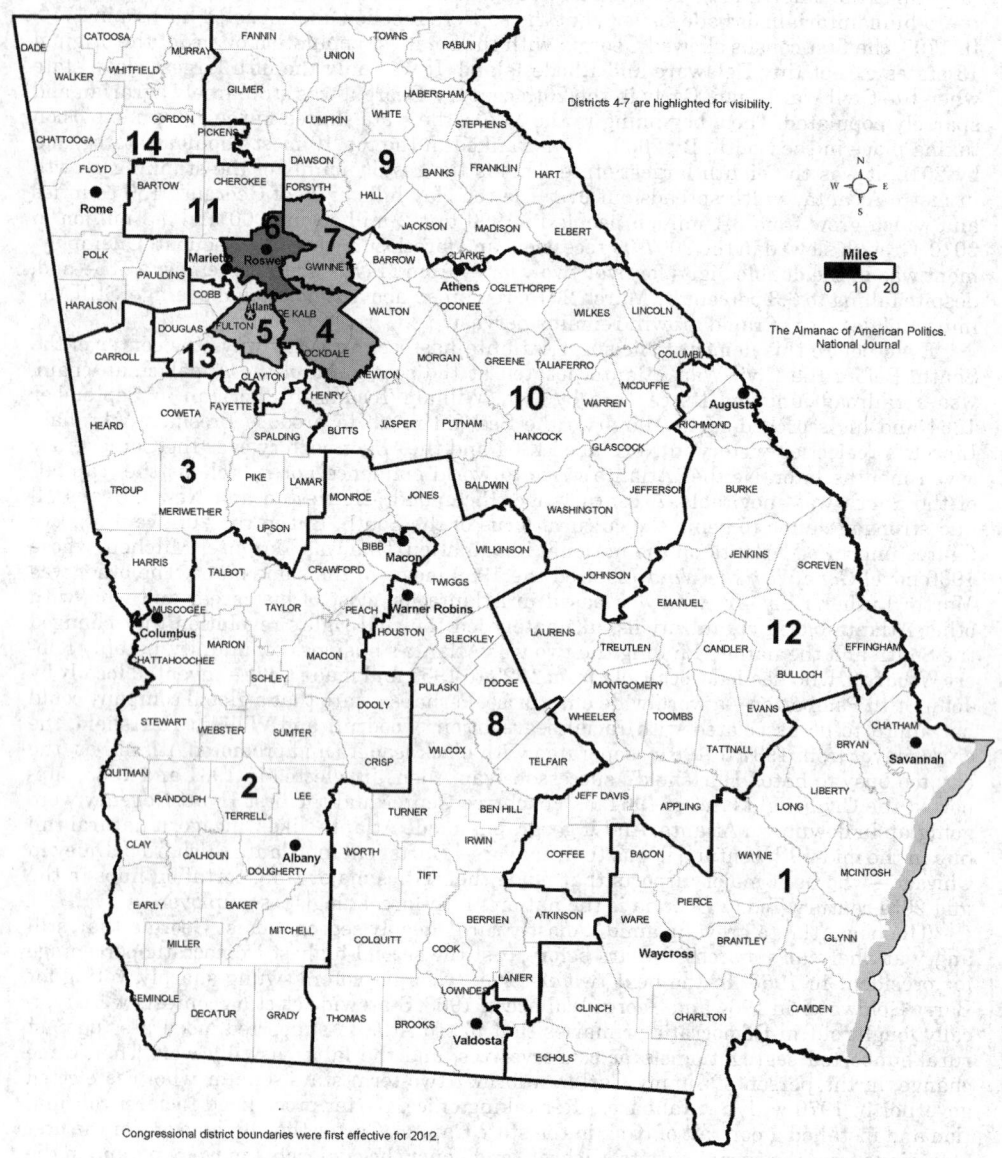

Districts 4-7 are highlighted for visibility.

The Almanac of American Politics.
National Journal

Congressional district boundaries were first effective for 2012.

The proportion of people born in the state who still live there is higher than in any other state except North Carolina and Texas. At the same time, countervailing political trends have transformed Georgia from a mostly Democratic state—Bill Clinton carried it narrowly in 1992 and lost it narrowly in 1996—to a mostly Republican one. Affluent voters in metro Atlanta have become generally Republican, while white voters outside metro Atlanta have seemingly forgotten about Sherman and Carter and, as in most of the non-metropolitan South, become Republican stalwarts.

Working in the other direction has been a substantial in-migration of African-Americans from the big cities of California, the Northeast and the industrial Midwest to metro Atlanta, attracted by its congenial Southern culture, inexpensive housing, and fast-growing suburbs. Georgia's black percentage rose from 26 percent in 2000 to 30 percent in 2010, higher than in any other state except Mississippi and Louisiana. Georgia's population in 2010 was 9 percent Hispanic and 3 percent Asian. That's the highest proportion of Hispanics in any southern state except for Florida, and it is up dramatically from 1.7 percent in 1990. Meanwhile, nearly one of every 10 Georgians is foreign-born, up from 2.7 percent in 1990. The result has been a Democratic trend in parts of metro Atlanta: Blacks have been moving to middle-class, suburban counties west and southeast of the city, and Hispanics have been clustering along Interstate 85 in Gwinnett County and Interstate 75 in Cobb County to the north. That movement enabled Barack Obama to carry metro Atlanta narrowly in the presidential elections of 2008 and 2012 while losing Georgia outside metro Atlanta by roughly 3-to-2.

The upshot is that Georgia swung heavily to the Republicans in the 21st century. George W. Bush carried the state 55%-42% in 2000 and Republican presidential nominees have carried it with between 52 and 58 percent of the vote ever since. In 2002, incumbent Democratic Gov. Roy Barnes, with a $19 million campaign chest, lost to Republican Sonny Perdue, 51%-46%. And incumbent Democratic Sen. Max Cleland, a wounded Vietnam veteran, who had won by one percent six years earlier, lost to Republican Rep. Saxby Chambliss 53%-46%. The Republican trend continued in 2004, as Democratic Sen. Zell Miller, about to retire from office, denounced his party in his book *A National Party No More*. He endorsed Bush for reelection and gave a rip-roaring speech at the Republican National Convention. With help from party switchers, Republicans captured the state Senate in 2002 and the state House in 2004. The Republican legislature passed a tough law on illegal immigration, requiring employers to consult a federal database when hiring and required welfare recipients to prove their legal status. They cut income, corporate and property taxes. And they passed a partisan redistricting plan for Georgia's 13 congressional districts. Perdue was reelected 58%-38% in 2006 and in 2010, Rep. Nathan Deal, like Perdue a former Democrat, was elected governor, 53%-43%.

The 2008 election saw sharply increased black turnout, and the Obama campaign toyed with targeting Georgia's 15 electoral votes. But Republican nominee John McCain carried the state 52%-47%; Obama won 98 percent among African-Americans and McCain 76 percent among whites. Chambliss, forced into a December 2008 runoff by Georgia's requirement that a candidate get 50 percent, won that contest 57%-43%—a margin similar to that won by his Senate colleague and friend from college days, Johnny Isakson, running in the more Republican years of 2004 and 2010. Running for governor in 2010, Deal beat Barnes,

Population		Race and Ethnicity		Income	
Total:	9,992,167	White	55.4%	Median income:	$47,439
Urban:	26.4%	Black	30.3%		*(36 of 50)*
Suburban:	51.5%	Latino	9.0%	Under $50,000	51.5%
Rural:	22.1%	Asian	3.3%	$50,000-$99,999:	29.2%
Land area:	57,513	Two races	1.6%	$100,000-$199,999:	15.3%
Pop/sq. mi.:	173.7	White Ethnic	14.5%	$200,000 or more:	3.9%
Born in state:	55.1%			Poverty Rate	14.4%
		Education			
Age Groups		H.S. grad or less:	43.1%	**Work**	
Under 18:	24.9%	Some college:	28.6%	White collar:	35.6%
18 to 34:	23.8%	College degree, 4 yr.:	17.8%	Blue collar:	42.4%
35 to 64:	39.4%	Post-grad study:	10.6%	Sales and service:	22.1%
Over 64:	11.9%				
		Military		Govt. workers:	15.1%
		Veterans/active duty:	8.9%		

the former governor, and Republicans won all of the other eight statewide offices for the first time, with margins ranging from 52%-44% to 56%-40%. They increased their majorities in the legislature.

The Republicans cut spending in 2011 and passed a controversial bill cracking down on illegal immigration. They set stricter conditions on the HOPE college

Voter Turnout		
2013 Total Citizen 18+		6,959,500
2014 Highest Statewide Turnout		2,567,761
2014 Turnout as % CVAP		36.9%
2012 Turnout as % CVAP		56.6%
Legislature		
Senate:	38R	18D
House:	114R	59D	1I, 6V

scholarship program initiated by Zell Miller in the 1990s. But not all issues in Georgia split voters along racial and partisan lines. Water is one example. Atlanta's water supply comes from federal dams that formed Lakes Lanier and Allatoona, and, since the 1990s, Florida and Alabama have charged that Georgia is diverting too much water from the Chattahoochee River. The issue sharpened when low rainfall in 2006-07 threatened to dry up the lakes. The state banned outdoor watering, mandated high-efficiency fixtures, and set aside $46 million in bonds for new reservoirs. However, water use declined and in June 2011, the federal appeals court overturned the trial judge's decision. Atlanta will not be parched. In 2008, the Georgia legislature called for restoring the border specified in the 1796 act of Congress admitting Tennessee to the Union, which surveyors in 1818 erroneously placed several miles to the south. That would give Georgia access to the waters of the Tennessee River. But as might be expected, Tennessee stoutly resisted the proposal.

The other issue that spanned partisan and racial lines was a November 2012 referendum to authorize more charter schools. The state NAACP and the Republican education superintendent followed the teachers' union in opposing the measure. But Deal favored it, and Atlanta Mayor Kasim Reed stayed neutral, while two young organizers mounted a campaign on black radio for the measure, citing Barack Obama's endorsement of charter schools. The measure passed two-to-one in metro Atlanta, with strong support from both heavily black and heavily Republican counties, but won by only 51%-49% in the rest of the state. The coalition was enough to win 59%-41% statewide.

Democratic hopes for a rebound were dashed in 2014, as Republicans defeated highly touted Democrats up and down the ticket by larger-than-predicted margins. Despite some stumbles, including blame for responding ineffectively to a January 2014 winter storm, Deal won reelection over state Sen. Jason Carter, grandson of the former president, by 53%-45%. In an open-seat Senate race, Republican David Perdue defeated Michelle Nunn, daughter of former Democratic Sen. Sam Nunn, by a similar margin. Other statewide Republican candidates won with 55 to 58 percent of the vote, and five-term Rep. John Barrow, the delegation's last white Democrat, was ousted, further underscoring how, in Georgia as in other southern states, the two parties have sorted racially. The lesson of 2014 was that, despite demographic changes, a Democratic comeback in Georgia will likely need to wait for at least a few more election cycles.

Presidential Politics Georgia has become a reliably Republican state in presidential elections, a far cry from the time when native son Jimmy Carter carried all 159 of its counties in 1976 and all but 13 in the 1980, when Ronald Reagan won a national landslide. In 2012, it voted for GOP nominee Mitt Romney by a comfortable 53%-45% margin. It was Romney's second-narrowest winning margin in the country after North Carolina, and closer than Arizona, Missouri, or Indiana. In 2012, Romney ran slightly ahead of 2008 nominee John McCain

2012 Presidential Vote		
Mitt Romney (R)	2,078,688	(53%)
Barack Obama (D)	1,773,827	(46%)
2012 Presidential Primary		
Newt Gingrich (R)	425,395	(47%)
Mitt Romney (R)	233,611	(26%)
Rick Santorum (R)	176,259	(20%)
Ron Paul (R)	59,100	(7%)
2008 Presidential Vote		
John McCain (R)	2,048,759	(52%)
Barack Obama (D)	1,844,123	(47%)

in metro Atlanta and the northern part of the state, and about the same in central and southern Georgia. For Democrats, the challenge is how to build upon their base in urban Atlanta, Savannah, Augusta, Columbus and Macon, and the declining rural counties in central Georgia that were once home to cotton plantations. Barack Obama has had success in reducing the GOP presidential margins in some of the Atlanta suburban counties such as Gwinnett and Cobb, but faster growing counties such as Forsyth and Cherokee north of Atlanta are producing more GOP votes to offset those Democratic gains.

Georgians like their presidential primary to play an important role in presidential politics. In 1992, Gov. Zell Miller had it scheduled one week before Super Tuesday in order to help Democratic nominee Bill Clinton, and it did: Clinton won solidly to balance losses in Maryland and Colorado the same day. The Dixie victory gave him critical momentum going into the large batch of southern primaries one week later, including the contests in delegate-rich states like Texas and Florida. Clinton swept those contests, and Miller was rewarded with a keynoter slot at the Democratic convention in New York's Madison Square Garden. (Miller would gain additional notoriety 12 years later in the same spot delivering the keynote address to the Republican convention, eviscerating Democratic standard-bearer John Kerry.) In 1996 and 2000, Georgia was of little consequence. In 2004, North Carolina's Sen. John Edwards had hoped to score a victory there, but Kerry beat Edwards 47%-41%, forcing him out of the race.

For 2008, Georgia moved up its primary to February 5, Super Tuesday. On the Democratic side, it was no contest once black voters swung behind Obama. He beat Hillary Clinton 66%-31%, as turnout rose sharply to over 1 million, by far the highest ever. Turnout was almost as high, 964,000, in the Republican primary which produced a near three-way tie. Mike Huckabee won with 34 percent, followed by John McCain, 32 percent, and Romney, 30 percent. Huckabee carried most of the rural counties while staying competitive with Romney and McCain in the Atlanta suburbs and exurbs. McCain won the Savannah River valley and the southwest corner of the state, both areas with big military bases. Romney won the top-four vote producing Atlanta metro counties; Cobb, Gwinnett, Fulton and DeKalb, although McCain ran a close second in the latter two. In 2012, Newt Gingrich, though not a Georgia resident since his resignation as speaker of the House in 1998, capitalized on his ties and won with 47 percent of the vote to 26 percent for Romney and 20 percent for Rick Santorum. Romney carried the two innermost metro Atlanta counties, Fulton and DeKalb, plus Savannah's Chatham County; Gingrich carried the other 156 counties. Georgia Secretary of State Brian Kemp has been a leader in organizing a 2016 regional presidential "SEC primary," named after the South's college football powerhouse Southeastern Conference. By mid-2015, four other states besides Georgia—Alabama, Arkansas, Tennessee and Texas—had March 1 tagged as their presidential primary date.

Congressional Districts   Georgia gained one seat from the reapportionment following the 2010 census, giving it a total of 14; only seven states have more. And unlike in 1991 and 2001, when Democrats drew some of the most convoluted lines in the country, Republicans were firmly in control of redistricting this time.

114th Congress Lineup	
10 R	4 D
113th Congress Lineup	
9 R	5 D

The legislature's threefold goals in the remap have proved successful. First, Republicans were able to add a new safe seat thanks to rapid growth along North Georgia's I-85 corridor, taking in much of the new 9th District. Second, they shored up Austin Scott in south Georgia's 8th District by removing downtown Macon and thereby giving nearby Democrat Sanford Bishop's 2nd District an African-American majority. Third, as their top priority, Republicans sought to target Augusta Democrat John Barrow, the only remaining white Democrat from the Deep South, by cutting Savannah's black neighborhoods out of his 12th District.

Republicans needed a second election cycle before they succeeded on the last count. After having dropped the black share of Barrow's seat from 43% to 34%, they nominated in 2014 businessman Rick Allen, a more credible challenger than the unpolished farmer who lost the GOP's challenge in 2012. Reality finally hit Barrow, whose seven-point survival in 2012 became a 10-point setback two years later. For now, Republicans appear secure with their 10-4 advantage in the delegation—a dramatic shift from the Democrats' 9-1 during most of the 1980s, when backbench Republican Newt Gingrich was plotting historic shifts. In reality, the true partisan balance in Georgia is somewhere between those two ratios. The new map has become so uncompetitive and the state so polarized that, of its 14 House members, seven were reelected in 2014 without major-party opposition—four Republicans and three Democrats.

Governor

Nathan Deal (R)

Elected 2010, term expires Jan. 2019, 2nd term; b. Aug. 25, 1942, Millen; Mercer U., B.A. 1964, J.D. 1966; Baptist; married (Sandra); 4 children.

Military Career: U.S. Army, 1966-68.

Elected Office: Hall Cnty. Juvenile Court judge, 1971-72; GA Senate, 1981-93, pres. pro tem, 1989-90, 1991-92; U.S. House, 1993-2010.

Professional Career: Asst. dist. atty., NE Judicial Circuit, 1970-71; Practicing atty., 1969-92.

Office: 206 Washington St., 111 State Capitol, Atlanta, 30334, 404-656-1776; Fax: 404-657-7332; Website: gov.georgia.gov.

Election Results

2014 general	Nathan Deal (R)	1,345,237	(53%)
	Jason Carter (D)	1,144,794	(45%)
	Andrew Hunt (L)	60,185	(2%)
2014 primary	Nathan Deal (R)	430,170	(72%)
	David Pennington (R)	99,548	(17%)
	John Barge (R)	66,500	(11%)

Prior winning percentages: 2010 (53%); House: 2008 (76%), 2006 (77%), 2004 (100%), 2002 (100%), 2000 (75%), 1998 (100%), 1996 (66%), 1994 (58%), 1992 (59%)

Nathan Deal, a Republican, was elected governor of Georgia in 2010 and reelected in 2014. He grew up in Gainesville, graduated from Mercer University, and then served in the Army from 1966 to 1968. He returned home to practice "street-level law," always choosing offices located on a ground floor. He was an assistant district attorney, a juvenile court judge, and a county attorney. In 1980, at age 38, he was elected to the state Senate as a Democrat; Jimmy Carter was still president, and the legislature was overwhelmingly Democratic. A capable legislator, Deal was elected Senate president pro tem twice. In 1992, when "Boll Weevil" Democrat Ed Jenkins retired from the House, Deal ran for his seat and defeated a Republican by winning 59 percent of the vote. Deal opposed Clinton policies and was seen as a potential party-switcher, but while campaigning in 1994 he said, "If I choose to switch during the term, I think the honest thing to do is resign and have a special election."

In early 1995, he worked with other Democrats to offer an alternative to the Republicans' welfare reform package. He expressed unhappiness with his party's opposition to tax cuts and with senior Democrats' criticism of Clean Water Act revisions that he had won on a bipartisan committee vote. In April 1995, back home in Gainesville, Deal announced that he was switching to the Republican Party—but he did not resign and run in a special election. He said the national Democratic Party was unwilling to admit it was "out of touch with mainstream America." Democrats were stunned, and Republican House Speaker Newt Gingrich of Georgia was delighted. Deal's reward was a seat on the powerful Energy and Commerce Committee.

Deal became chairman of the panel's Health subcommittee and, after Democrats took control of the House in 2007, he was the ranking Republican. In March 2010, with incumbent Republican Gov. Sonny Perdue term-limited, Deal announced he was running for governor. He resigned his seat immediately, possibly motivated by the fact that he faced an ethics probe into a 20-year business tie with the Georgia state government. The Office of Congressional Ethics (OCE) found in February 2010 that Deal intervened with state officials to preserve a state program that earned $300,000 a year for the salvaged vehicle business he ran with a business partner. Under the state program, Deal's firm dominated the vehicle inspection business in the Gainesville region. State Revenue Commissioner Bart Graham had proposed opening the program to competition beyond the handful of businesses already doing inspections, which would have threatened Deal's regional monopoly. In a series of meetings, Deal and his chief of staff discouraged the change, and Graham later told ethics investigators that one meeting grew "contentious." The OCE recommended that the House Ethics Committee open an investigation, but Deal left Congress before the panel could act to campaign for governor.

He called the charges a "political witch hunt," and said the business arrangement with the state had been pre-approved by the Ethics Committee. He delayed his resignation from the House from March 8 to March 21, so he could vote against the Democrats' health care bill, after which he promptly resigned. At that point, the House lost jurisdiction over any ethics complaint against him. This was not the only cloud over Deal's campaign concerning his personal finances. It was revealed that he was rendered insolvent by a $2.3 million debt for which he was liable after co-signing a loan for his daughter and son-in-law to start a sporting goods store. The store failed and they went bankrupt, leaving Deal in the position of having to sell his house to pay the debt.

His financial dealings were an issue in the Republican primary. In a seven-way contest, former Georgia Secretary of State Karen Handel, based in metro Atlanta, finished first with 34%, while Deal managed to win second place with 23%, edging out state Senate President Eric Johnson, with 20%, for a spot in the August runoff. The runoff campaign between Handel and Deal was highly negative. Gingrich endorsed Deal, saying he stood for "conservative Georgia values," while former Alaska Gov. Sarah Palin campaigned for Handel and dubbed her one of her "mama grizzlies" of 2010. Deal narrowly defeated Handel in the runoff, 50.2% to 49.8%, 2,519 out of 579,551 votes cast. The Democratic primary was a much quieter affair; former Gov. Roy Barnes won with 66% of the vote to 22% for Attorney General Thurbert Baker.

Barnes criticized Deal for voting against an increase in the minimum wage, which Deal called a "state's rights" issue. Deal emphasized his longtime opposition to birthright citizenship for the children of illegal immigrants. After remaining mum on birthright citizenship for many weeks, Barnes said he, too, opposed it but would not support changing the Constitution. In October, WAGA-TV in Atlanta reported that Deal's former chief of staff had used his congressional email to lobby Hall County to take over a private road next to Deal's salvage business. The Barnes campaign dubbed him "one of the most corrupt members of Congress." The Barnes campaign also circulated copies of a lien for $4,000 in taxes Deal had failed to pay the city of Gainesville. Deal won convincingly in a strong Republican year, 53%-43%. He did not run much ahead in metro Atlanta—50%-46%—but carried the rest of the state by an overwhelming 58%-39%.

When Deal took office, Georgia, like many states, faced serious fiscal problems. It faced an expected budget shortfall of as much as $1.8 billion, an especially challenging environment for Deal, who promised during his campaign to invest more in public education and cut taxes. He signed reductions in how much the HOPE Scholarship Program would cover for students; it had been under fiscal strain due to a failure of lottery funds to keep pace with rising tuition costs and enrollment levels. He approved a spate of bills that appealed to the conservative base. He signed a hotly debated bill that allowed law enforcement to check and detain those suspected of being in the country illegally; the bill also set penalties for transporting or harboring undocumented immigrants and made it a felony to apply for a job with false documents. Deal turned down Medicaid expansion under the Affordable Care Act and signed a bill to block an insurance-navigator program at the University of Georgia. He signed legislation to test food-stamp applicants suspected of taking drugs (which was opposed by the federal government) and signed one of the nation's strongest measures to expand gun rights, easing laws on the carrying of weapons into churches, bars and some government buildings.

During his 2014 reelection bid, ethics concerns resurfaced. State ethics commission director Holly LaBerge charged that Deal's office had pressured her in 2012 to make ethics complaints against the governor "go away," the *Atlanta Journal-Constitution* reported. In the GOP primary, Deal faced state school superintendent John Barge and former Dalton Mayor David Pennington, who had tea party backing, but the incumbent prevailed with 72 percent of the vote. In the general, he faced Democratic state Sen. Jason Carter, the grandson of the former president, and Libertarian Andrew Hunt. Carter was about as strong a challenger as Democrats could have mustered in the increasingly conservative state—he had name recognition, legislative experience and some votes with cross-party appeal, such as a vote for the gun bill. Carter led in some pre-election polls, but on a strongly Republican Election Day, Deal won by a larger-than-expected margin of 53%-45%. After his reelection, Deal won bipartisan passage of one of his legislative priorities—a $1 billion transportation bill, funded by a mix of tax cuts and increases and focused on delayed maintenance projects. He also signed a measure to allow certain patients to use cannabis oil, and he narrowly won the right to ask voters to approve a November 2016 referendum on his proposal to allow the state to take over failing schools. Deal also attracted notice for leading a bipartisan effort to reform the state's criminal-justice system, including greater judicial discretion in sentencing, and he added educational opportunities for inmates. The liberal *New Republic* said Georgia under Deal was "doing more to reform its criminal justice system than any other state in the country."

Senior Senator

Johnny Isakson (R)

Elected 2004, term expires Jan. 2017, 2nd term; b. Dec. 28, 1944, Atlanta; U. of GA, B.B.A. 1966; Methodist; married (Dianne); 3 children.

Military Career: GA Air Natl. Guard, 1966-72.

Elected Office: GA House, 1976-90, Repub. ldr., 1983-90; GA Senate, 1993-96; U.S. House, 1999-2004.

Professional Career: Northside Realty, 1967-99, pres., 1979-99; Co-chair, Dole GA presidential campaign, 1988, 1996; Chmn., GA Bd. of Ed., 1996-97.

DC Office: 131 RSOB, 20510, 202-224-3643; Fax: 202-228-0724; Website: isakson.senate.gov.

State Offices: Atlanta, 770-661-0999.

Committees: *Ethics (Select)* (Chmn); *Finance:* Int'l Trade, Customs & Global Competitiveness; Social Security, Pensions & Family Policy. Taxation & IRS Oversight. *Foreign Relations:* Africa & Global Health Policy; East Asia, the Pacific, & Int'l Cybersecurity Policy; State Dept. & USAID Mgmt., Int'l Operations, & Bilateral Int'l Development; Western Hemisphere, Transnational Crime, Civilian Security, Democracy, Human Rights, & Global Women's Issues. *Health, Education, Labor & Pensions:* Employment & Workplace Safety (Chmn). *Veterans' Affairs* (Chmn).

Group Ratings

	ADA	ACLU	AFL-CIO	LCV	ITI	COC	HAFA	ACU	CFG	FRC
2014	10%	0%	–	0%	33%	100%	49%	68%	53%	86%
2013	10%	C	33%	23%	C	63%	C	54%	59%	C

National Journal Ratings

	2013 LIB	—	2013 CONS
Economic	40%	—	58%
Social	30%	—	68%
Foreign	33%	—	66%
Composite	35%	—	65%

Key Votes of the 113th Congress

1. Sandy storm spending	N	5. Student Loan Rates	Y	9. Bipartisan Budget Deal	Y
2. Chuck Hagel Confirmation	N	6. Employee Non-Discrim'n Act	N	10. Farm Bill Conference Rept.	Y
3. Gun Background Checks	N	7. Senate Vote on Judgeships	Y	11. Unempl. Comp. Extension	N
4. Immigration Reform	N	8. Defense Dept. Spending	N	12. Keystone Pipeline	Y

Election Results

2010 general	Johnny Isakson (R)	1,489,904	(58%)	$8,954,540	$751,627
	Michael Thurmond (D)	996,516	(39%)	$336,174	$95,488
2010 primary	Johnny Isakson (R)	unopposed			

Prior winning percentages: 2004 (58%); House: 2002 (80%), 2000 (75%), 1999 special (65%)

Johnny Isakson, a Republican elected in 2004, is Georgia's senior senator. He is as staunchly conservative as other Georgia Republicans on most issues but exudes a Southern charm and a willingness to work across the aisle on occasion that makes him less off-putting to his liberal colleagues than others in the state's congressional delegation. The GOP takeover in 2015 handed him the chairmanship of the Veterans' Affairs and Ethics committees, making him the only senator to chair two committees.

Isakson grew up outside Atlanta, in south Fulton County. His father drove a Greyhound bus, and his parents bought old houses, renovated them, and sold them for a profit. Isakson graduated from the University of Georgia and served in the Air National Guard. He went to work for Northside Realty in 1967 and eventually became president of the firm. He volunteered for Republican Barry Goldwater's presidential campaign in 1964 and for President Richard Nixon's in 1972. In 1974, he ran for the state House and lost. In 1976, he ran again and won, and in 1983 became minority leader. He ran for governor in 1990, losing 53 percent to 45 percent to Democrat Zell Miller. Two years later, he was elected to the state Senate. In 1996, he ran statewide again and lost the Republican runoff for senator to self-financing businessman Guy Millner, who lost in November to Democrat Max Cleland, 49 percent to 48 percent. In December 1996, Gov. Miller appointed Isakson head of the state board of education. His partisan political career seemed over, but it was revived by two timely retirements.

In November 1998, Newt Gingrich announced that he was stepping down as speaker of the House and that he would resign his seat in Congress. That opened a vacancy in the state's heavily Republican 6th District, which included much of Atlanta's northern suburbs. Isakson was by far the best-known of the six candidates in the February 1999 nonpartisan election. He raised $1 million and spent $500,000 of his own money. He won the seat with 65 percent of the vote. In the House, Isakson served on the Transportation and Infrastructure Committee, where he pushed for a rapid transit line for the overburdened Georgia 400 corridor. On the Education and the Workforce Committee, he took a leading role in negotiations on President George W. Bush's signature education law, the No Child Left Behind Act, which tied federal funds for schools to test performance. He added a provision requiring that 25 percent of technology funds be used for teacher classroom training.

Isakson passed up a chance to run against Cleland in 2002. But the state's other Senate seat came open in 2004 when Zell Miller, who by then had moved from governor to senator, announced he would retire after just one term. Isakson had two serious competitors in the Republican primary: Herman Cain, who grew up in a black neighborhood in Atlanta and, starting from low-level jobs, became the owner of Omaha-based Godfather's Pizza (and later ran for president); and Rep. Mac Collins, whose district included the southern edge of metro Atlanta. Cain and Collins were both solid conservatives and abortion rights opponents, and they made abortion a major issue.

Isakson also was an opponent of abortion, but he had voted against a law preventing the use of foreign aid money to fund abortions overseas and had voted for allowing servicewomen to have abortions at their own expense in military hospitals. In the 1996 Senate primary, he had irked religious conservatives by running an ad saying, "I will not vote to amend the Constitution to make criminals of women and their doctors. I trust my wife, my daughter, and the women of Georgia to make the right choices." Collins called him "a certified moderate."

Cain also backed a consumption tax and private investment accounts in Social Security; Collins criticized Isakson for favoring an extension of the date for the turnover of sovereignty in Iraq. Isakson called for staying the course in Iraq and for tax reform. With his business contacts, Isakson raised $5.5 million for the primary; Cain spent $3 million, much of it his own money, and Collins spent $1.9 million. Many observers thought the race would end with a runoff. But Isakson got 53 percent of the vote to 26 percent for Cain and 21 percent for Collins.

In the general election campaign, Isakson faced 4th District Rep. Denise Majette, who had served just one term in the House after her upset victory over Cynthia McKinney in the 2002 primary. He attacked Majette's liberal voting record, including her vote against an $87 billion spending bill for Iraq. Majette criticized Isakson for undercutting Bush's education reforms by not voting to fully fund them. Isakson won 58 percent to 40 percent, almost the same margin by which Bush beat John Kerry in the state. carrying 140 of 159 counties.

Isakson has a conservative voting record in the Senate, though with a folksy demeanor and pragmatic streak. He said his experience selling homes taught him the virtues of negotiation and compromise. "If you want to ever learn how to accept rejection, sell real estate for a few years," he told the Associated Press in 2010. In 2013, President Obama asked him to plan a dinner with a dozen GOP senators to discuss ways they could work together on deficit reduction. Isakson described the ensuing dinner as "very meaningful."

As chairman of Veterans' Affairs, Isakson's agenda included overseeing the implementation of bipartisan bill signed into law in 2014 in response to reports of mistreatment at VA facilities. Isakson had been among those sounding early alarms about veterans' treatment, holding a committee field hearing at Atlanta's VA Medical Center in August 2013. But he did not join three other Senate Republicans in October 2014 in publicly blasting VA Secretary

Robert McDonald just a few months after McDonald was unanimously confirmed as the person to try to fix the agency. In 2015, he helped pass a bipartisan bill aimed at preventing military veteran suicides. President Obama signed the bill into law that February, at a ceremony with Isakson present.

Isakson also has a seat on the Finance Committee, where he looks out for Georgia's cotton growers. He questioned U.S. Trade Representative Michael Froman in January 2015 about the steep decline in the trading price of cotton and China's stockpiling enabling that country to subsidize its producers at twice the world market price. He and Delaware Democratic Sen. Chris Coons founded the Senate Chicken Caucus in 2013, and in 2015 Isakson complained to Froman about South Africa's duties imposed on U.S. chicken imports. In 2013 he backed a bipartisan budget deal negotiated by conservative Rep. Paul Ryan of Wisconsin and Washington Democratic Sen. Patty Murray, and in 2015 he introduced a bill to pass two-year, rather than one-year budgets.

On the Health, Education, Labor, and Pensions Committee, Isakson worked actively on pension reform, with the chief goal of advocating the interests of Delta Airlines, which was bankrupt and had huge pension obligations to its workers. In 2005, the Senate passed a pension reform measure that included Isakson's amendment to give airlines 20 additional years to meet their obligations. A version of the bill eventually passed Congress the next year.

Before Georgia Sen. Saxby Chambliss retired in 2014, he and Isakson often worked closely together. Although Isakson opposed the McCain-Kennedy immigration bill in 2006, he and Chambliss worked with a bipartisan group of senators in 2007 on a bill including a path to legalization for illegal workers, a guest worker program, and tougher enforcement. He and Chambliss were booed by anti-illegal-immigration hardliners at the May 2007 Republican state convention for their work. In June, when Democratic Majority Leader Harry Reid brought the bill to the floor, Isakson and Chambliss said they would vote against allowing it to go forward unless a separate appropriation boosting border security was passed. He similarly voted against the Senate's 2013 bipartisan immigration reform bill.

Isakson has been willing to compromise during high-stakes fiscal battles. The real estate specialist voted for the Troubled Asset Relief Program (TARP) and to bail out Fannie Mae and Freddie Mac during the 2008-2009 financial crisis. In August 2011, he broke with Chambliss on a key deficit reduction deal that raised the debt ceiling. After a tense standoff between Republican leaders and President Barack Obama, the Senate passed a compromise plan, 74-26. Isakson notably supported the Senate Republican leadership by voting for more modest cost-cutting measures, while Chambliss dissented and pushed for larger cuts. During negotiations over the "fiscal cliff"—when a combination of tax increases and spending cuts were scheduled to kick in on January 1, 2013—Isakson publicly pushed Senate leaders to broker a deal with the White House and keep Bush-era tax cuts for all but the wealthiest Americans. "No one wants taxes to go up on the middle class. I don't want them to go up on anybody, but I'm not in the majority in the United States Senate," Isakson said in late December 2012. Isakson later voted for the bill that extended tax cuts for those making less than $400,000 and postponing spending cuts.

In February 2009, the Senate unanimously passed Isakson's $15,000 tax credit for home-buyers as part of the economic stimulus bill, and later that year concurred with his argument that further extension of the credit was needed to boost the weak economy.

Isakson severely rebuked Republican National Committee Chairman Michael Steele in 2010 when Steele described the Afghanistan conflict as "a war of Obama's choosing." The same year, he joined Democrats on the Foreign Relations Committee in supporting the New START arms-reduction pact with Russia. He and Chambliss stood together in September 2008 in supporting the "Gang of 10" bipartisan energy bill that was opposed by many conservatives. He became entangled in a brief controversy during the 2009 health care debate when conservatives seized on end-of-life counseling provisions, which former Alaska Gov. Sarah Palin derided as "death panels." Obama responded that one of the leading sponsors of the effort was Isakson, a longtime advocate for end-of-life counseling and assistance in drafting living wills. But Isakson rebutted Obama, claiming that he backed a much different policy. The provisions ultimately were dropped from the bill. The flap came several months after Isakson had his own experience with the health care system: He was rushed to the hospital after having a toxic reaction to bacteria in his bloodstream and was diagnosed with an irregular heartbeat. More recently, Isakson disclosed in June 2015 that he had Parkinson's Disease, but said the illness will have no impact on his ability to carry out his Senate duties or on his decision to run for another term.

Isakson got involved in the fallout over the 2009 death of 24-year-old Peace Corps volunteer Kate Puzey, a Georgia native living in Benin. ABC News reported that Puzey was killed after telling her supervisors that a fellow Peace Corps worker was molesting female students. Isakson sponsored a bill to protect Peace Corps whistleblowers and help victims of sexual assault. The bill passed both houses and Obama signed it into law in November 2011.

On the Ethics Committee, Isakson has maintained a solid working relationship with California's Barbara Boxer, the panel's top Democrat. "Ethics is not fun ... you're sitting in judgment on your peers," Isakson told *The Atlanta Journal-Constitution* in April 2012. "And I've been impressed with her ability to look through an unfettered lens, and I do the same thing." The committee investigated former Republican Sen. John Ensign of Nevada, for trying to cover up an extramarital affair with a campaign aide and wife of one of his top staffers. In May 2011, the committee announced that it had uncovered evidence that Ensign broke the law, and the information was given to the Justice Department.

Outside watchdog groups are unhappy at the panel's record in meting out punishment in recent years; apart from the Ensign case, they noted that it dismissed every other case that came before it in 2012 and every new complaint filed in 2013. Boxer and Isakson issued a joint statement in October 2014 that the panel "has significantly increased its efforts to educate and train the Senate community to prevent misconduct and ensure that senators and staff live up to the highest ethical standards." Statistics showed Ethics conducted more ethics seminars in 2013 for new members and congressional offices than it had in recent years.

In 2010, Isakson breezed to reelection against Democrat Michael Thurmond, Georgia's labor commissioner, who in July had managed to raise just $117,000 compared to Isakson's $7.5 million. He kicked off his 2016 reelection campaign in November 2014, immediately beginning his fundraising push to scare off rivals in both parties and holding an event attended by dozens of Georgia elected officials including many conservative rising stars. "Two years sounds like a long time, but it's not. If you know that you're going to run, you ought to go ahead and let it be known," he told *The Hill* that month. "That gives you the time to lay the groundwork to build a campaign and deal with whatever comes." He was considered a likely bet to win a third term, especially after the Democrats' most-desired candidate, Atlanta Mayor Kasim Reed, took a pass. "I think 2016 will be very difficult to attract one of the leading Democrats to take on Sen. Isakson because of the reputation that he has in the state and the affection folks have for him," Reed told the Associated Press.

Junior Senator

David Perdue (R)

Elected 2014, term expires Jan. 2021, 1st term; b. Dec. 10, 1949, Macon; GA Inst. of Technology, B.S. 1972, M.S. 1976; Methodist; married (Bonnie); 2 children.

Professional Career: Mgmt. consultant, Kurt Salmon Associates; Sr. VP of Asia operations, Sara Lee; Pres. & CEO, Reebok; Chmn. & CEO, Dollar General; Co-founder, Perdue Partners.

DC Office: 383 RSOB, 20510, 202-224-3521; Fax: 202-228-1031; Website: perdue.senate.gov.

State Offices: Atlanta, 404-865-0087.

Committees: *Aging (Special). Agriculture, Nutrition, & Forestry:* Commodities, Risk Mgmt. & Trade. Conservation, Forestry & Natural Resources (Chmn); Rural Development & Energy. *Budget. Foreign Relations:* Multilateral Int'l Development, Multilateral Institutions, & Int'l Economic, Energy, & Environmental Policy; Near East, South Asia, Central Asia, & Counterterrorism; State Dept. & USAID Mgmt., Int'l Operations, & Bilateral Int'l Development (Chmn); Western Hemisphere, Transnational Crime, Civilian Security, Democracy, Human Rights, & Global Women's Issues. *Judiciary:* Antitrust, Competition Policy & Consumer Rights; Immigration & the National Interest; Privacy, Technology, & the Law.

Election Results

2014 general	David Perdue (R)	1,358,088	(53%)	$13,796,681	$3,875,475	$5,137,744
	Michelle Nunn (D)	1,160,811	(45%)	$16,063,248	$2,000,453	$12,871,729
2014 primary runoff	David Perdue (R)	245,725	(51%)			
	Jack Kingston	237,193	(49%)			
2014 primary	David Perdue (R)	185,466	(31%)			
	Jack Kingston (R)	156,157	(26%)			
	Karen Handel (R)	132,944	(22%)			
	Phil Gingrey (R)	60,735	(10%)			
	Paul Broun (R)	58,297	(10%)			

Republican David Perdue is Georgia's junior senator. He defeated Democrat Michelle Nunn in 2014 to succeed retiring Sen. Saxby Chambliss, edging out a surprise win in a contest that had been expected to go to a runoff. His win came on the heels of a tough primary in which he faced four other Republicans, and it marks his first post in an elected office following a career running some of the country's largest companies.

Perdue was born in Macon and grew up in Warner Robins in a family of schoolteachers. After studying industrial engineering and operations research, he launched a career in management consulting, followed by senior roles at Sara Lee, Haggar Clothing, Reebok, and Pillowtex. In 2003, he took over as CEO of Dollar General, where he streamlined operations and closed stores before selling the chain in 2007. After a stint with an Indian chemicals company, he started an Atlanta-based trading firm in 2011. Over the years, he established a reputation as a turnaround expert for troubled companies, though some of the methods he used—layoffs and outsourcing—became campaign issues.

Touting his business credentials, Perdue plunged into the race when Chambliss announced his retirement in 2013, hoping that he would get a boost from the family name—his cousin, Sonny Perdue, is a former governor. But the field to replace him quickly became crowded, with three Republican House members as well as well as a former Georgia secretary of state throwing their hats in the primary ring and all but guaranteeing a second-round primary runoff since no candidate was likely to get to the 50 percent threshold needed to get an outright win.

Perdue spent heavily in the first round of the primary, running clever ads painting himself as the only political outsider in the race and depicting his opponents as literal crybabies. He and Congressman Jack Kingston appeared to be the two early favorites—Kingston had the support of much of the Washington, D.C. establishment, including the U.S. Chamber of Commerce, and Perdue had the personal wealth and family name. Conservative congressman Phil Gingrey and Paul Broun ran weak campaigns with little strategy. But despite abysmal fundraising, former Secretary of State Karen Handel caught fire in the closing weeks of the campaign after a video emerged of Perdue mocking her for not having a college degree and a late endorsement from former GOP vice mocidinal nominee Sarah Palin. The final results in May were closer than initially expected, with Perdue pulling 31 percent, Kington getting the second runoff slot with 26 percent support, and Handel falling short with 22 percent.

Kingston led in early polling during the six-week runoff and he quickly locked in endorsements from both establishment and Tea Party leaders—Gingrey and Handel, former House Speaker Newt Gingrich, and RedState.com's Erick Erickson, a leading tea party voice in the state. He hammered Perdue on his business career, slamming him for ties to a national group that supported "amnesty" for undocumented immigrants and for outsourcing jobs while he was at Haggar. and making millions while shuttering Pillowtex. But Perdue spent heavily on ads portraying Kingston as a Washington insider, a dangerous thing to be, and playing up his independence. Perdue off a tight 51%-49% win, buoyed by a strong performance in the greater Atlanta media market.

Perdue advanced to face a top Democratic recruit in Nunn, the daughter of popular centrist former Sen. Sam Nunn and CEO of the Points of Light Foundation, a well-known Atlanta-based charity. Democrats were bullish about her chances despite the state's conservative lean and what was shaping up to be a rough year for the party nationally.

Nunn and Democrats hammered Perdue on his business career, slamming him for American jobs lost at various companies he worked for and portraying him as a heartless corporate raider. Nunn got a boost when it was revealed Perdue said he "spent most of my career" outsourcing during a legal deposition following Pillowtex's collapse. For a time Nunn led in public polling and it appeared that the race was likely headed to a runoff, as a libertarian candidate was siphoning enough of the vote to keep both candidates under 50 percent. Because of that there was surprisingly little outside spending by either party on the race. But Perdue dipped into his fortune once again to run ads relentlessly tying Nunn to President Obama, who was deeply unpopular in the state. He ended up winning on election night by a surprisingly strong 53%-45%.

Perdue received a seat on the Agriculture Committee, maintaining a decades-long Georgia tradition. He also was given slots on Budget, Foreign Relations, Judiciary and Special Aging. In his first months in the Senate he compiled a record as conservative as he promised on the campaign trail, introducing legislation to replace the federal income tax with a national sales tax on all goods and services, and to "rein in" the Consumer Financial Protection Bureau. He slammed Obama's executive actions on immigration, voted against a compromise bill to extend the Patriot Act while limiting some of its surveillance mechanisms, and criticized the Obama Administration's policy shift on Cuba and negotiations with Iran aimed at keeping it from a nuclear weapon.

FIRST DISTRICT

Buddy Carter (R)

Elected 2014, 1st term; b. Sept. 6, 1957, Port Wentworth; U. of GA., B.S. 1980; Methodist; married (Amy); 3 children.

Elected Office: Pooler City Cncl., 1994-95; Pooler mayor, 1996-2004; GA House, 2005-09; GA Senate, 2009-14.

Professional Career: Pharmacist; Owner, Carter's Pharmacy Inc..

DC Office: 432 CHOB, 20515, 202-225-5831; Fax: 202-226-2269; Website: buddycarter.house.gov.

State Offices: Brunswick, 912-265-9010; Savannah, 912-352-0101.

Committees: *Education & the Workforce:* Early Childhood, Elementary, & Secondary Education; Health, Employment, Labor, & Pensions. *Homeland Security:* Oversight & Mgmt. Efficiency; Transportation Security. *Oversight & Gov't Reform:* Gov't Operations; Health Care, Benefits, & Administrative Rules.

Election Results

2014 general	Buddy Carter (R)	95,337	(61%)	$1,606,049	$78,498	$397,795
	Brian Reese (D)	61,175	(39%)	$46,858		
2014 primary runoff	Buddy Carter (R)	22,861	(54%)			
	Bob Johnson (R)	19,621	(46%)			
2014 primary	Buddy Carter (R)	18,971	(36%)			
	Bob Johnson (R)	11,890	(23%)			
	John McCallum (R)	10,715	(21%)			
	Jeff Chapman (R)	6,918	(13%)			
	Darwin Carter (R)	2,819	(5%)			

Population		Race and Ethnicity		Income	
Total:	721,388	White	61.1%	Median income:	$43,270
Urban:	48.1%	Black	28.8%		*(341 of 435)*
Suburban:	18.2%	Latino	6.4%	Under $50,000	56.1%
Rural:	33.8%	Asian	1.8%	$50,000-$99,999:	28.0%
Land area:	6,473	Two races	1.4%	$100,000-$199,999:	12.8%
Pop/sq. mi.:	111.4	White Ethnic	18.7%	$200,000 or more:	3.1%
Born in state:	56.8%			Poverty Rate	19.4%
		Education			
Age Groups		H.S. grad or less:	43.4%	**Work**	
Under 18:	24.7%	Some college:	31.3%	White collar:	32.4%
18 to 34:	25.7%	College degree, 4 yr.:	15.8%	Blue collar:	42.7%
35 to 64:	36.9%	Post-grad study:	9.5%	Sales and service:	24.9%
Over 64:	12.7%			Govt. workers:	19.2%
		Military			
		Veterans/active duty:	15.7%		

Southeast Georgia: Savannah, Brunswick

In Georgia, the focus is usually on Atlanta, but the state also has some urbane smaller cities with deep roots in the past. One is Savannah, the state's first capital, which by the 1830s was one of America's booming cotton ports. It languished after the Civil War and lived off paper mills and chemical plants

Voter Turnout	
2013 Total Citizen 18+	524,935
2014 House Turnout	156,512
2014 Turnout as % CVAP	29.8%
2012 Turnout as % CVAP	50.2%

in the 20th century, while impoverished blacks on the islands a few miles offshore still spoke Gullah dialects. Then, a few decades ago, preservationists started restoring houses and churches on a street grid laid out more than 200 years before. Today, Savannah is one of the most graciously preserved cities in the country and a major tourist destination that has bolstered the local economy. The population of the city is 55 percent African American.

There have been efforts to keep the region vibrant as a center for overseas trade. State and local officials have been deepening the port of Savannah to 47 feet and extending the channel of the Savannah River by seven miles to attract the next generation of large container ships. The city actively competes with neighboring and equally well-preserved Charleston, South Carolina not only for tourists but for shipping. Savannah has the busiest single terminal for container cargo in North America, which expedites fast distribution to customers. Most local officials have supported President Barack Obama's decision to open the south Atlantic coast to off-shore oil drilling.

The 1st Congressional District of Georgia covers the state's coast, including all of Savannah. Also in the 1st are the Sea Islands, with a prospering resort economy and efforts to preserve the African-American Gullah culture and its eponymous West African-originated Creole language. Along the coast south of Savannah is the tiny, historic black settlement of Pin Point. Its citizens are mostly descendants of the first slaves in the area, and its most famous son is U.S. Supreme Court Justice Clarence Thomas. The Pin Point Heritage Museum and the restoration of a seafood factory where his mother once worked were a tribute to him. The district also has small cities like Brunswick, a World War II shipbuilding center that has been revitalized as the gateway to the Sea Islands, and isolated Waycross, a railroad junction and gateway to the Okefenokee Swamp, the largest swamp in North America. Many popular films about the South have been produced in the region, including *Glory* and *Forrest Gump*.

This was Democratic country for a century after Gen. William Tecumseh Sherman's troops marched through Georgia, but voters

2012 Presidential Vote		
Mitt Romney (R)................145,525	(56%)
Barack Obama (D) 111,903	(43%)
2008 Presidential Vote		
John McCain (R)................143,783	(55%)
Barack Obama (D) 116,218	(44%)
Cook Partisan Voting Index: R+9		

here are solidly conservative on most issues. For two decades, this part of south Georgia voted for national Republicans but Georgia Democrats. Today it leans strongly Republican, giving John McCain and Mitt Romney 56% and 55%, respectively.

Buddy Carter (R)

After surviving a fierce battle with a tea party candidate in 2014, Republican Earl "Buddy" Carter crushed his Democratic rival. Carter, who fits comfortably in the Main Street wing of the GOP, succeeded former Rep. Jack Kingston, who made an unsuccessful Senate bid.

A successful pharmacy owner, his campaign photo featured him in a pharmacist's uniform behind the counter of his drug store. Carter was spurred by his interest in local business issues to run for mayor of Pooler in 1996; he served eight years. He then won election to the state House in 2004 and moved to the state Senate in 2008, securing seats on the appropriations and health panels and eventually rising to deputy whip.

The 1st District is solidly Republican, but not as deep-red as other parts of Georgia, thanks in part to northern transplants who have settled there. That may have helped Carter in the primary, when he faced off against a well-funded challenger, surgeon Bob Johnson, who tried to outgun Carter from the right. Carter underscored his legislative and private-sector record, highlighting endorsements from the Chamber of Commerce and local business groups while diving into the wonky details of issues such as flood insurance and port dredging. He tried to shore up his right flank by calling for the repeal of the Affordable Care Act and highlighting his endorsement from the National Rifle Association.

Johnson blasted Carter as a political insider and pledged to adhere to term limits if elected. He took aim at Carter's ties to pharmacy groups, implying that Carter deliberately delayed the reporting of Medicaid reimbursements to his pharmacies. And he attacked Carter's willingness in 2012 to consider a sales tax for transportation projects. These positions helped Johnson win the backing of the Club for Growth, and he came close in the money race. Carter's more pragmatic message in the May primary secured him a comfortable lead over Johnson, 36%-23%.

In the July runoff, Carter tied himself closely to Kingston who also was on the runoff ballot, and he took aim at inflammatory comments that Johnson had made. Each candidate spent more than $200,000 of his own funds. The Club for Growth spent nearly $400,000 against Carter. He prevailed, 54%-46%. Carter took about 60% in Savannah-based Chatham County. Johnson led in his base of Glynn and Camden counties.

Democratic nominee Brian Reese was a supervisor for the United Parcel Service. He spent $47,000 against Carter and did not seriously challenge him. Carter won 61%-39%. Reese took 51% in Chatham County, with its large African-American population. Carter rolled up the vote in the rural counties.

In the House, Carter got seats on the Education and the Workforce, Homeland Security and Oversight and Government Reform committees. The first two bills he introduced were designed to limit intimidating practices of labor unions, with what he termed the "Union Boss Loophole" in stalking and identity-theft laws.

SECOND DISTRICT

Sanford Bishop (D)

Elected 1992, 12th term; b. Feb. 4, 1947, Mobile, AL; Morehouse Col., B.A. 1968, Emory U., J.D. 1971; Baptist; married (Vivian Creighton Bishop); 1 child.

Military Career: U.S. Army, 1969-71.

Elected Office: GA House, 1977-90; GA Senate, 1991-92.

Professional Career: Primary partner atty., Bishop & Buckner, P.C., 1972-92.

DC Office: 2407 RHOB, 20515, 202-225-3631; Fax: 202-225-2203; Website: bishop.house.gov.

State Offices: Albany, 229-439-8067; Columbus, 706-320-9477; Macon, 478-803-2631.

Committees: *Appropriations:* Agriculture, Rural Development, FDA and Related Agencies; Financial Services and General Government; Military Construction, Veterans Affairs and Related Agencies. (RMM).

Group Ratings

	ADA	ACLU	AFL-CIO	LCV	ITI	COC	HAFA	ACU	CFG	FRC
2014	35%	77%	–	43%	60%	92%	20%	8%	13%	0%
2013	55%	C	90%	39%	C	58%	C	21%	26%	C

National Journal Ratings

	2013 LIB	—	2013 CONS
Economic	57%	—	43%
Social	69%	—	28%
Foreign	60%	—	40%
Composite	63%	—	38%

Key Votes of the 113th Congress

1. Sandy storm spending	Y	5. Medical Marijuana	Y	9. Syrian Rebels Training	Y
2. Violence Against Women Act	Y	6. Farm Bill	N	10. Keystone pipeline	Y
3. Guantanamo Bay Detainees	Y	7. Afghanistan Combat	N	11. Immigration Exec. Action	N
4. Abortion 20-week ban	N	8. NSA Phone Data Collection	N	12. Bipartisan budget deal	NV

Election Results

2014 general	Sanford Bishop (D)	96,363	(59%)	$1,050,925 $1,388
	Greg Duke (R)	66,573	(41%)	$17,384
2014 primary	Sanford Bishop (D)	unopposed		

Prior winning percentages: 2012 (64%), 2010 (51%), 2008 (69%), 2006 (68%), 2004 (67%), 2002 (100%), 2000 (54%), 1998 (57%), 1996 (54%), 1994 (66%), 1992 (64%)

Population		Race and Ethnicity		Income	
Total:	696,006	Black	49.9%	Median income:	$32,787
Urban:	48.1%	White	41.9%		*(429 of 435)*
Suburban:	11.0%	Latino	4.9%	Under $50,000	65.9%
Rural:	40.9%	Asian	1.2%	$50,000-$99,999:	24.7%
Land area:	8,851	Two races	1.8%	$100,000-$199,999:	8.2%
Pop/sq. mi.:	78.6	White Ethnic	8.6%	$200,000 or more:	1.2%
Born in state:	71.0%			Poverty Rate	27.2%
		Education			
Age Groups		H.S. grad or less:	53.3%	**Work**	
Under 18:	24.4%	Some college:	30.0%	White collar:	27.7%
18 to 34:	25.1%	College degree, 4 yr.:	10.1%	Blue collar:	47.1%
35 to 64:	37.0%	Post-grad study:	6.6%	Sales and service:	25.2%
Over 64:	13.4%				
		Military		Govt. workers:	20.6%
		Veterans/active duty:	12.0%		

Southwest Georgia: Columbus, Macon

The hub of central Georgia, Macon is a city proud of its restored houses and its Japanese cherry trees, which it shows off during its annual International Cherry Blossom Festival. It has been the home of music legends Otis Redding, James Brown, Little Richard, and the Allman Brothers, and of the Harriet Tubman African-American Museum.

Voter Turnout	
2013 Total Citizen 18+	508,405
2014 House Turnout	162,900
2014 Turnout as % CVAP	32%
2012 Turnout as % CVAP	51.6%

The long shadow of history is felt here. Before the Civil War, the southwest corner of Georgia was mostly plantation country. This is where the Confederate Army ran the Andersonville military prison. About 13,000 of the 45,000 Union soldiers confined there died, and they are remembered at the National Prisoner of War Museum at Andersonville. Today, the U.S. military is a strong presence, and bases in the area have been largely unscathed by several rounds of base closings. Fort Benning, which spreads into Alabama, is the nation's fifth-largest military installation, home of the Army Infantry School and of the Army Armor School. Benning, which provided basic training to 95,000 in World War II, can now train as many as 16,000 soldiers at a time. In recent years, nearly $7 billion has been spent on improvements at the post. In 2015, a Defense Department budget proposal to cut 11,000 jobs at Benning produced a private-sector estimate of a $1 billion hit to the regional economy.

Much of the rest of this region is farmland. Cotton and peanuts are major crops, and pecans are also grown here. Near the Florida border is Cairo, the birthplace of baseball's black pioneer Jackie Robinson. Albany, with several factories, also has a civil rights museum and was the site of some of Martin Luther King Jr.'s civil rights protests in the 1960s. Not far from Albany, between upland pine stands and bottomland habitats, is the Chickasawhatchee Swamp, one of the Southeast's largest freshwater swamps and home to rare plant species such as the green fly orchid. Plains is the childhood home of President Jimmy Carter, who has said he wants to be buried in his front yard. Plains now has a major biofuels factory. But this is still hardscrabble country that struggles economically. Unemployment in Macon remained at 8.1% in December 2014, compared with the state average of 6.6%.

The 2nd Congressional District of Georgia covers the southwestern part of the state. It includes the cities of Columbus, Macon, and Albany, as well as Grady and Decatur

2012 Presidential Vote		
Barack Obama (D) 153,998	(59%)
Mitt Romney (R)................107,242	(41%)

2008 Presidential Vote		
Barack Obama (D) 153,890	(58%)
John McCain (R)................111,166	(42%)

Cook Partisan Voting Index: D+6

counties on the Florida border and the counties along the Chattahoochee River border with Alabama. The 2nd District is a black-majority district and has a Democratic lean, though not nearly as strong as the three black-majority districts in the Atlanta area.

Sanford Bishop (D)

Sanford Bishop, a Democrat first elected in 1992, calls himself a "traditionalist" on cultural issues, and his voting record is among the most conservative in the Congressional Black Caucus. His office web site touts his support for the Second Amendment and his A+ score from the National Rifle Association. On the Appropriations Committee, he has been an advocate for his district.

Bishop grew up in Mobile Alabama, where his father was a college president. He went to Morehouse College in Atlanta, where he was student body president in 1968 and sang at Martin Luther King Jr.'s funeral. "I resolved, after his death, that I would try to follow in his footsteps," he told the Columbus *Ledger-Enquirer* years later. He went to Emory Law School then served in the Army. After a year in New York, he settled in Columbus to practice law. He was elected to the state legislature in 1976 at age 29. He served there until 1990, when he was elected to the Georgia Senate. In 1992, he ran for the House against Democratic Rep. Charles Hatcher, who, with more than 800 check overdrafts, was damaged by the House bank scandal that year. Bishop defeated Hatcher in the runoff 53%-47% and won the general election 64%-36%.

Bishop joined the conservative Blue Dog Democrats and over the years has supported a balanced budget, school prayer, a ban on flag burning and a proposed constitutional amendment to prohibit same-sex marriage. He unsuccessfully sought the chairmanship of the Intelligence Committee after the 2006 election. He refused to back Rep. Nancy Pelosi for Democratic leader after their party lost control of the House in 2010, saying that having her at the helm would make it difficult to recruit candidates in the South and Republican-leaning states. But he strongly backed the Affordable Care Act, which she and President Barack Obama pushed through Congress, describing it in 2012 as "a piece of legislation whose time has come. People should not have to choose between going to the grocery store and getting their medicine." In 2013, Bishop joined the "Problem Solvers" coalition of lawmakers who agreed to meet monthly to promote bipartisanship. He has filed bipartisan legislation to repeal the federal estate tax.

With a seat on the Appropriations Committee since 2003, Bishop has worked to safeguard and deliver funds to the district's military facilities. In 2008, he won passage of an amendment to the defense spending bill that provided 180 days of health care for military members who transition from active to reserve status. In 2013, he became ranking Democrat on the Military Construction, Veterans Affairs and Related Agencies Subcommittee. Following a January 2015 meeting with Veterans Affairs Secretary Robert McDonald, Bishop said he was "hopeful that we can turn over a new leaf and strengthen the VA for the future."

Bishop also looks out for Georgia's peanut farmers. He worked with Republicans on the Freedom to Farm Act to fashion a "market-oriented, no-net cost" program for peanuts. In 2002, he helped to craft the scaled-back program for peanut support, which was designed to phase out quotas and price guarantees. On the 2008 farm bill, he helped design the peanut-rotation program, which he said encourages "a cleaner, greener method of planting while ensuring an affordable and accessible supply to the markets that rely on U.S.-grown peanuts."

Bishop faced serious reelection competition in 2000 from Republican Dylan Glenn, a former aide to President George H.W. Bush. The contest between two African-Americans in a rural, then majority-white district was unprecedented, but race was not an issue in the campaign. Bishop largely ignored the challenger and ran on his record, while Glenn offered the perspective of a new generation focusing on economic growth. Bishop won 54%-46%. Bishop contemplated a run in 2008 against GOP Sen. Saxby Chambliss but decided to stay in the House.

Then in 2010, Bishop found himself in the race of his life when Republicans targeted him for what they called excessive fealty to Pelosi. His opponent was Mike Keown, a white state representative who highlighted Bishop's support of the Democrats' health care overhaul. In the year's anti-incumbent climate, Keown also got a strong boost from news reports that Black Caucus Foundation scholarships had gone to Bishop's stepdaughter and his wife's niece. Bishop said the scholarships were awarded before rules barring such awards were enacted.

He attacked Keown for lacking much of a political record and got a break when a strategist for Keown was indicted in a vote-buying case in Alabama. Their battle went down to the wire, and Bishop prevailed 51%-49%. Republican-led redistricting in 2012 strengthened

Bishop and turned his seat into an African-American majority district, while reinforcing neighboring GOP Rep. Austin Scott. Bishop has not faced a serious challenge since then. In 2014, against Republican Greg Duke, who spent $17,000, Bishop lost several small rural counties. But he led by more than 2-to-1 in the counties with the three population centers: Macon, Columbus and Albany.

THIRD DISTRICT

Lynn Westmoreland (R)

Elected 2004, 6th term; b. April 2, 1950, Atlanta; GA St. U., attended 1969-71; Baptist; married (Joan); 3 children.

Elected Office: GA House, 1993-2004, min. ldr., 2000-03.

Professional Career: Real estate developer; Owner, L.A.W. Builders, 1982-present.

DC Office: 2202 RHOB, 20515, 202-225-5901; Fax: 202-225-2515; Website: westmoreland.house.gov.

State Offices: Newnan, 770-683-2033.

Committees: *Financial Services:* Financial Institutions & Consumer Credit; Housing & Insurance (VChmn); Monetary Policy & Trade. *Intelligence (Select):* CIA; NSA & Cybersecurity (Chmn); *Select Benghazi Committee.*

Group Ratings

	ADA	ACLU	AFL-CIO	LCV	ITI	COC	HAFA	ACU	CFG	FRC
2014	0%	0%	–	3%	100%	71%	78%	87%	87%	86%
2013	0%	C	19%	4%	C	83%	C	76%	79%	C

National Journal Ratings

	2013 LIB	—	2013 CONS
Economic	9%	—	90%
Social	27%	—	71%
Foreign	14%	—	85%
Composite	17%	—	83%

Key Votes of the 113th Congress

1. Sandy storm spending	N	5. Medical Marijuana	Y	9. Syrian Rebels Training	N
2. Violence Against Women Act	N	6. Farm Bill	Y	10. Keystone pipeline	Y
3. Guantanamo Bay Detainees	N	7. Afghanistan Combat	N	11. Immigration Exec. Action	Y
4. Abortion 20-week ban	Y	8. NSA Phone Data Collection	N	12. Bipartisan budget deal	Y

Election Results

2014 general	Lynn Westmoreland (R).........unopposed	
2014 primary	Lynn Westmoreland (R)..............37,106	(69%)
	Chip Flanagan (R) 16,294	(31%)

Prior winning percentages: 2012 (unopposed), 2010 (70%), 2008 (66%), 2006 (68%), 2004 (76%)

Population		Race and Ethnicity		Income	
Total:	713,143	White	67.5%	Median income:	$51,673
Urban:	7.4%	Black	23.4%		*(211 of 435)*
Suburban:	67.4%	Latino	5.6%	Under $50,000	48.2%
Rural:	25.2%	Asian	1.5%	$50,000-$99,999:	30.9%
Land area:	3,289	Two races	1.7%	$100,000-$199,999:	17.8%
Pop/sq. mi.:	216.8	White Ethnic	14.3%	$200,000 or more:	3.1%
Born in state:	62.6%			Poverty Rate	16.3%
		Education			
Age Groups		H.S. grad or less:	45.8%	**Work**	
Under 18:	25.4%	Some college:	29.8%	White collar:	32.5%
18 to 34:	22.0%	College degree, 4 yr.:	15.3%	Blue collar:	39.7%
35 to 64:	39.5%	Post-grad study:	9.1%	Sales and service:	27.7%
Over 64:	13.1%				
		Military		Govt. workers:	17.3%
		Veterans/active duty:	10.9%		

West-Central Georgia

South of Atlanta, Henry County is among the fastest growing areas in the United States, with a leap in population of 71 percent from 2000 to 2010. The county's flourishing residential, commercial and industrial development, which has become part of Atlanta's exurbs, took root near its Interstate 75

Voter Turnout	
2013 Total Citizen 18+	514,004
2014 House Turnout	156,277
2014 Turnout as % CVAP	30.4%
2012 Turnout as % CVAP	58.1%

interchanges. West of Henry County is the old courthouse town of Fayetteville, whose Holliday-Dorsey-Fife House is thought to have inspired the columned architecture of Tara in author Margaret Mitchell's classic *Gone With the Wind*. The town is now engulfed by subdivisions spreading out from Atlanta. Sprawl has reached Newnan and Carrollton and spreads farther south to Thomaston. In the old textile town of West Point in Troup County, along the Alabama border, South Korean automaker Kia built a $1.2 billion plant and, with its supplier companies, the company says that it brought 10,000 jobs to the region in addition to the 3,000 at West Point. In 2012, Kia had a record sales year in the U.S., with the popular Optima and Sorento CUV models from that plant, where the assembly line has three shifts during the week. But not all parts of this area are booming. In March 2015, NBC News reported that the most of the two-block business area of Grantville, a largely abandoned textile town south of Newnan, had been put up for sale.

Much of this territory is in the 3rd Congressional District of Georgia. It takes in part of the Atlanta metro area, including southwest and central Henry County and Peachtree City, where many airline pilots live and use the city's famous golf cart paths. Newnan is home of the African-American Museum and the adjacent Farmer Street Cemetery, believed to be the largest slave cemetery in the South. Carrollton made headlines in 2011 when its mayor cancelled a local production of the musical *The Rocky Horror Picture Show*, deeming it too risqué. The district stretches south to include LaGrange and

2012 Presidential Vote		
Mitt Romney (R)	195,075	(66%)
Barack Obama (D)	97,748	(33%)
2008 Presidential Vote		
John McCain (R)	195,440	(65%)
Barack Obama (D)	103,026	(34%)
Cook Partisan Voting Index: R+19		

part of Columbus. This is conservative country, with a large share of military and tradition-minded families. The ancestral politics of this area was Democratic, but that is as much a part of history now as Tara. The 3rd is a solidly Republican district. Mitt Romney got 66 percent of the vote against President Barack Obama in 2012.

Lynn Westmoreland (R)

Lynn Westmoreland, a Republican first elected in 2004, has played an important behind-the-scenes role for House Republicans, serving as their point person for redistricting efforts in 2012 and providing a conservative ally to GOP leaders.

Westmoreland grew up in the Atlanta area, left Georgia State University after two years, and became a real estate broker and homebuilder in Fayette County. After losing two races for the state Senate, Westmoreland was elected in 1992 to the Georgia House, where he founded the Conservative Policy Caucus, a group of fiscally conservative, anti-tax lawmakers. He got under the skin of the Democratic establishment to say the least; longtime Democratic House Speaker Tom Murphy once called him "a braying jackass." In 2000, he was elected House minority leader and in that position refused to agree to tax increases, even when it meant defying newly elected Republican Gov. Sonny Perdue.

In 2004, Republican Rep. Mac Collins ran for the Senate, and Westmoreland faced a choice between staying in the Georgia legislature, where he stood to become speaker when Republicans won a majority in the state House, or running for a safe Republican seat in the House. He chose the latter and ran on an anti-spending platform.

The primary race was a contest between Westmoreland and Dylan Glenn, a former staffer for Perdue and George H.W. Bush. Glenn, an African American from Columbus, was endorsed by former House Speaker Newt Gingrich of Georgia, who argued that a Glenn victory would help the party appeal to black voters. Republican Sen. Saxby Chambliss endorsed Westmoreland. In the primary, he led Glenn, 46%-38%. During the three weeks between the primary and the August runoff, Glenn accused Westmoreland of taking gifts from lobbyists, and Westmoreland labeled Glenn a "Washington insider." Westmoreland won 55%-45%. He has won reelection with token opposition.

In the House, Westmoreland has a solid conservative voting record and was among the first members to join the Tea Party Caucus in 2010. He repeatedly stresses the need for free-market solutions over government regulation. In early 2013, he became the Financial Services Committee's "whip," a mostly informal vote-counting role that makes him a lieutenant of committee Chairman Jeb Hensarling of Texas.

House Republican leaders put Westmoreland in charge of monitoring the states' redistricting efforts following the 2010 census. The National Republican Congressional Committee said in a post-election memo that the party's strength in redistricting ultimately made 17 "endangered" GOP-held seats safer. Westmoreland also has served as an NRCC vice chair, helping to recruit and raise money for candidates in the South.

In public, Westmoreland has shown a hard edge that has sometimes drawn controversy. He was one of five House Republicans in June 2012 who called for an investigation into whether Huma Abedin, an aide to Secretary of State Hillary Clinton, tried to improperly influence U.S. policy in favor of the Muslim Brotherhood, an accusation that drew strong criticism from Arizona Sen. McCain and House Speaker John Boehner. But Westmoreland has been sufficiently trustworthy that Boehner gave him a seat on the Intelligence Committee, where he chairs the NSA and Cybersecurity Subcommittee. He has become a prominent GOP spokesman on national security issues and congressional investigations. On his office website, he publishes Capitol Corner, a short weekly column that helps to disseminate his talking points.

Westmoreland was outspoken in his opposition to the extension of the Voting Rights Act, citing the "great progress" Georgia has made since enactment of the law in 1965. When the House debated the bill in 2006, he offered an amendment to make it easier for states to opt out of the law's requirements, but lost. But Westmoreland ultimately prevailed on that issue, when the Supreme Court, in its 2013 ruling in *Shelby County v. Holder*, threw out the required pre-review of voting rights changes in mostly Southern states. His views have led to rocky relationships with leading African-American politicians. During the 2008 presidential campaign, he called Democratic candidate Obama "uppity," and when he was criticized for the remark, said he was surprised to learn it was a racially loaded term.

FOURTH DISTRICT

Hank Johnson (D)

Elected 2006, 5th term; b. Oct. 2, 1954, Washington, D.C.; Clark Atlanta U., B.A. 1976, TX S. U., J.D. 1979; Buddhist; married (Mereda Davis); 2 children.

Elected Office: DeKalb Cnty. comm., 2001-06.

Professional Career: Practicing atty., 1980-2006; Assoc. judge, DeKalb Cnty. magistrate court, 1989-2001.

DC Office: 2240 RHOB, 20515, 202-225-1605; Fax: 202-226-0691; Website: hankjohnson.house.gov.

State Offices: Conyers, 770-987-8721; Lithonia, 770-987-2291.

Committees: *Armed Services:* Oversight & Investigations; Seapower & Projection Forces; Tactical Air & Land Forces. *Judiciary:* Courts, Intellectual Property & the Internet; Regulatory Reform, Commercial & Antitrust Law (RMM).

Group Ratings

	ADA	ACLU	AFL-CIO	LCV	ITI	COC	HAFA	ACU	CFG	FRC
2014	90%	88%	–	91%	40%	43%	8%	4%	4%	13%
2013	75%	C	100%	96%	C	31%	C	13%	14%	C

National Journal Ratings

	2013 LIB	—	2013 CONS
Economic	76%	—	22%
Social	60%	—	39%
Foreign	69%	—	31%
Composite	69%	—	31%

Key Votes of the 113th Congress

1. Sandy storm spending	Y	5. Medical Marijuana	Y	9. Syrian Rebels Training	Y	
2. Violence Against Women Act	Y	6. Farm Bill	Y	10. Keystone pipeline	N	
3. Guantanamo Bay Detainees	Y	7. Afghanistan Combat	Y	11. Immigration Exec. Action	N	
4. Abortion 20-week ban	N	8. NSA Phone Data Collection	N	12. Bipartisan budget deal	Y	

Election Results

2014 general	Hank Johnson (D)..................unopposed		$640,573	$1,398
2014 primary	Hank Johnson (D)....................... 26,514	(55%)		
	Thomas Brown............................ 21,909	(45%)		

Prior winning percentages: 2012 (74%), 2010 (75%), 2008 (100%), 2006 (75%)

Population		Race and Ethnicity		Income	
Total:	721,682	Black	56.2%	Median income:	$49,125
Urban:	6.1%	White	26.9%		*(253 of 435)*
Suburban:	93.9%	Latino	10.5%	Under $50,000	50.7%
Rural:	0.0%	Asian	4.4%	$50,000-$99,999:	31.9%
Land area:	591	Two races	1.5%	$100,000-$199,999:	14.9%
Pop/sq. mi.:	1,220.6	White Ethnic	7.4%	$200,000 or more:	2.4%
Born in state:	44.6%			Poverty Rate	18.2%
		Education			
Age Groups		H.S. grad or less:	39.1%	**Work**	
Under 18:	25.4%	Some college:	31.5%	White collar:	33.8%
18 to 34:	23.5%	College degree, 4 yr.:	18.7%	Blue collar:	45.3%
35 to 64:	41.4%	Post-grad study:	10.6%	Sales and service:	20.9%
Over 64:	9.7%				
		Military		Govt. workers:	15.5%
		Veterans/active duty:	8.7%		

Eastern Atlanta Suburbs: DeKalb

In 1920, when Gutzon Borglum began sculpting Jefferson Davis, Robert E. Lee and Stonewall Jackson into the side of Stone Mountain, the huge outcropping of granite—the largest single piece of sculpture in the world—was a day's drive into the country from central Atlanta and was soon to become a rallying point for the Ku Klux Klan. Even when the memorial was completed in 1972, suburban development barely reached that far. But today, after three decades of some of the most explosive metropolitan growth in the country, DeKalb (pronounced *duh-KAB* by locals) County is at the heart of the Atlanta metropolitan area. And this monument to the Confederacy—located along the Stone Mountain Freeway a few miles from the Interstate 285 Perimeter surrounding Atlanta—incongruously sits amid one of the most cosmopolitan and liberal constituencies in the South.

Voter Turnout	
2013 Total Citizen 18+	478,178
2014 House Turnout	161,211
2014 Turnout as % CVAP	33.7%
2012 Turnout as % CVAP	63.6%

South DeKalb County has been transformed from mostly rural territory in the 1970s into one of the nation's largest collections of affluent African-American neighborhoods, rivaled only by Prince George's County in Maryland. The county was a prime destination for evacuees from New Orleans following Hurricane Katrina in 2005. DeKalb's population grew by 22% in the 1990s, and by 4% from 2000 to 2010. It is now about 54% African American and 10% Latino. The county is culturally diverse, with more than 64 languages spoken.

The demographic changes have moved its politics to the left. DeKalb was a Republican county in the 1960s. Now it is the most heavily Democratic major county in Georgia. In 2004, DeKalb voted 73%-27% for Democrat

2012 Presidential Vote		
Barack Obama (D) 218,428	(74%)
Mitt Romney (R)...................76,016	(26%)

2008 Presidential Vote		
Barack Obama (D) 222,868	(73%)
John McCain (R)...................81,782	(27%)

Cook Partisan Voting Index: D+21

John Kerry, his best percentage in the state, except for one tiny rural county. Barack Obama raised that margin to 79%-20% in 2008 and 78%-21% in 2012. Despite its growing population, *The Atlanta Journal-Constitution* reported in 2012 that the county has been slow to attract new businesses.

The 4th Congressional District includes most of DeKalb County, though northern and western parts of DeKalb spill into the neighboring 5th and 6th districts. The district takes in a small part of Gwinnett County to the north, all of Rockdale County, and close to half of Newton County. In 2008, Rockdale elected its first black county commission chairman. Following revelations of police malpractice in Ferguson Missouri, the police department in Conyers—the only city in Rockdale County—announced in April 2015 that it would release race-specific arrest data to encourage fair police behavior. The 4th is a black-majority district and heavily Democratic, though the neighboring 5th District is more urban and even more Democratic.

Hank Johnson (D)

Hank Johnson, a Democrat who won the seat in 2006, has a solidly liberal voting record and a reputation as a thoughtful lawmaker, although he has made unusual verbal gaffes and occasional blunt attacks. He has faced competitive Democratic primary challenges.

Johnson was born in Washington, D.C., where his father was director of classifications and paroles for the Bureau of Prisons and his mother was a schoolteacher. He practiced law as a civil and criminal litigator and served 12 years as a magistrate judge in DeKalb County and then five years on the DeKalb County Commission. He resigned from the commission to run for Congress. Although his immediate family members are Presbyterians, he has been a Buddhist since the 1970s; he and Sen. Mazie Hirono, D-Hawaii, are the first practicing Buddhists in Congress. "If you could say what drives me, it's the middle ground, the middle way," he told *The Atlanta Journal-Constitution* in 2009, invoking a Buddhist principle.

In 2006, Johnson ousted Democratic Rep. Cynthia McKinney in the primary. McKinney was a controversial incumbent, once suggesting that President George W. Bush might have had prior knowledge of the September 11 terrorist attacks but did not act on it because a war on terrorism would boost defense stocks held by his father's friends. Her own party lost patience with her after she struck a Capitol police officer who had stopped her at a security checkpoint. In the July primary, McKinney led Johnson, 47%-44%, but her failure to break the 50% threshold in the three-candidate field forced a runoff. His fundraising suddenly picked up, as donors, including former Democratic Gov. Roy Barnes, weighed in against McKinney. She responded by criticizing Johnson's past financial troubles, which included declaring bankruptcy in the late 1980s. But in the runoff, turnout was up and Johnson easily won, 59%-41%. He breezed to victory in the general election.

In the House, Johnson has made several eyebrow-raising statements that have landed him atop liberal as well as conservative blogs. After South Carolina Republican Rep. Joe Wilson shouted, "You lie!" at President Barack Obama in 2009 when he unveiled his health care plan to Congress, Johnson suggested that if the House took no disciplinary action against Wilson, "We'll have folks putting on white hoods and white uniforms again." In 2012, Johnson gave a speech attacking Michigan's new right-to-work law and said, "What happens when you put, in a cage fight, a giant in with a midget? Well, the midget will not win the fight, I am going to tell you that."

On the Judiciary Committee, he is the ranking Democrat on the Regulatory Reform, Commercial and Antitrust Law Subcommittee, a good niche for a lawyer even though Johnson had less experience with business law in private practice. He said he would pursue his proposed Arbitration Fairness Act, to increase consumer protections in arbitration cases. In response to urban crime problems, he reintroduced in March 2015 a bill he filed with conservative Republican Raul Labrador of Idaho to restrict free Defense Department transfers of surplus military equipment to state and local law enforcement agencies. "Militarizing America's main streets won't make us any safer, just more fearful and more reticent," Johnson said. In response to police malpractice, he introduced in December 2014 a bill to reform grand jury procedures, including the appointment of special prosecutors in the investigations of police officers for the killing of civilians. That bill would apply to local law enforcement agencies that receive federal funding. His proposals may have dim prospects in the current Congress, but they could spark broader debates.

Johnson also has served on the Armed Services Committee, where he has challenged Republican provisions that have sought to hamstring the Obama administration, such as basing tactical nuclear weapons in South Korea to counter North Korea.

In 2009, Johnson announced that he had battled hepatitis C, an incurable blood-borne liver disease, for more than a decade. Two Democrats lined up to challenge him in the 2010 primary, and one of them, former DeKalb County CEO Vernon Jones, openly questioned his missing a series of debates. Johnson, however, insisted his health was fine and unveiled an endorsement from Obama, who said the congressman "has done an outstanding job." He won the July primary with 55% to Jones' 26% and former DeKalb County Commissioner Connie Stokes' 18%. He was challenged in 2014 by well-known DeKalb County Sheriff Tom Brown, who criticized Johnson's lack of accomplishments and mocked his 2010 comment that the island of Guam "will become so overly populated that it will tip over and capsize." With another Obama endorsement, Johnson won 55%-45%. He got 55% of the vote in DeKalb, which cast 74% of the total vote, and also led in the three other counties. The close contest could encourage future primary challengers.

FIFTH DISTRICT

John Lewis (D)

Elected 1986, 15th term; b. Feb. 21, 1940, Troy, AL; American Baptist Theol. Seminary, B.A. 1961, Fisk U., B.A. 1967; Baptist; widowed; 1 child.

Elected Office: Atlanta City Cncl., 1982-86.

Professional Career: Chmn., Student Nonviolent Coord. Cmte., 1963-66; Field Foundation, 1966-67; Community org. dir., Southern Regional Cncl., 1967-70; Exec. dir., Voter Ed. Project, 1970-76; Dir., ACTION, 1977-80; Community affairs dir., Natl. Consumer Coop. Bank, 1980-86.

DC Office: 343 CHOB, 20515, 202-225-3801; Fax: 202-225-0351; Website: johnlewis.house.gov.

State Offices: Atlanta, 404-659-0116.

Committees: *Ways & Means:* Human Resources; Oversight (RMM).

Group Ratings

	ADA	ACLU	AFL-CIO	LCV	ITI	COC	HAFA	ACU	CFG	FRC
2014	85%	72%	–	91%	40%	25%	13%	11%	15%	0%
2013	85%	C	95%	89%	C	33%	C	4%	11%	C

National Journal Ratings

	2013 LIB	—	2013 CONS
Economic	89%	—	11%
Social	72%	—	27%
Foreign	90%	—	10%
Composite	84%	—	16%

Key Votes of the 113th Congress

1. Sandy storm spending	Y	5. Medical Marijuana	NV	9. Syrian Rebels Training	N
2. Violence Against Women Act	Y	6. Farm Bill	N	10. Keystone pipeline	N
3. Guantanamo Bay Detainees	NV	7. Afghanistan Combat	Y	11. Immigration Exec. Action	N
4. Abortion 20-week ban	N	8. NSA Phone Data Collection	Y	12. Bipartisan budget deal	Y

Election Results

2014 general	John Lewis (D)..........................	170,326	(100%)	$745,566	$1,398
2014 primary	John Lewis (D)......................unopposed				

Prior winning percentages: 2012 (84%), 2010 (74%), 2008 (100%), 2006 (100%), 2004 (100%), 2002 (100%), 2000 (77%), 1998 (79%), 1996 (100%), 1994 (69%), 1992 (72%), 1990 (76%), 1988 (78%), 1986 (75%)

Population		Race and Ethnicity		Income	
Total:	719,920	Black	57.0%	Median income:	$42,597
Urban:	71.5%	White	28.3%		*(349 of 435)*
Suburban:	28.4%	Latino	9.2%	Under $50,000	56.2%
Rural:	0.1%	Asian	3.7%	$50,000-$99,999:	25.4%
Land area:	317	Two races	1.5%	$100,000-$199,999:	12.8%
Pop/sq. mi.:	2,270.6	White Ethnic	9.6%	$200,000 or more:	5.6%
Born in state:	52.9%			Poverty Rate	25.2%
		Education			
Age Groups		H.S. grad or less:	35.1%	**Work**	
Under 18:	21.6%	Some college:	23.9%	White collar:	42.6%
18 to 34:	31.9%	College degree, 4 yr.:	23.9%	Blue collar:	43.4%
35 to 64:	36.7%	Post-grad study:	17.0%	Sales and service:	14.0%
Over 64:	9.9%				
		Military		Govt. workers:	13.2%
		Veterans/active duty:	6.8%		

Atlanta Metro

Venture out of the quiet of the Ebenezer Baptist Church or the shade of the Rev. Martin Luther King Jr.'s boyhood home two blocks away and into the steamy heat of the Georgia sun, and one can see, a mile away, downtown Atlanta's atrium skyscrapers. They are evidence of the wealth and vibrant growth

Voter Turnout	
2013 Total Citizen 18+	521,905
2014 House Turnout	170,326
2014 Turnout as % CVAP	32.6%
2012 Turnout as % CVAP	54.4%

of the commercial capital of the South, the metropolis that has grown up where there was little more than a railroad junction at the time of the Civil War. But the human achievement that is downtown Atlanta is overshadowed by the revolution started in large part by a man who grew up on Auburn Avenue. Atlanta's white establishment during King's time, led by Mayors William Hartsfield and Ivan Allen and Coca-Cola's Robert Woodruff, deserve credit for abandoning segregation, but it was King and other civil rights leaders who took the risks that led them to do so. Atlanta's city fathers acted out of goodwill, but also with an eye for the economic growth of the city, having seen the damage that resulted in other Southern cities harmed by violent resistance.

Today, Atlanta is the center of the nation's ninth-largest metropolitan area. From Auburn Avenue, it spreads into two dozen counties of northern Georgia. Its Hartsfield-Jackson Atlanta International Airport is the busiest in the world, with 96 million passengers in 2014. That was a big lead over O'Hare, which was the U.S. runner-up with 70 million, though the Chicago airport led Atlanta in the number of flights. Business conventions and the airport helped bolster the city's $12 billion hospitality industry, although hotels struggled during the recession. Atlanta's occupancy rates reached 68% in 2014, with the fastest annual growth rate in the nation. Unemployment in metropolitan Atlanta climbed above 10% in 2010, but had dropped to 6.1% by February 2015. The new transportation of choice for local residents may be the three-mile electric streetcar route in downtown, which opened in December 2014 and is part of a broader plan for light rail lines.

Atlanta also has vibrant office centers, in downtown, Midtown, and Buckhead to the north. Modern stadiums and sports facilities were built for the 1996 Summer Olympics. Coca-Cola's skyscraper headquarters stands as a symbol of Atlanta's most successful worldwide business, and the company also donated a $10 million parcel of land near Centennial Olympic Park for a $100 million civil rights museum to house King's papers.

2012 Presidential Vote		
Barack Obama (D)	241,280	(83%)
Mitt Romney (R)	45,828	(16%)

2008 Presidential Vote		
Barack Obama (D)	255,683	(84%)
John McCain (R)	45,247	(15%)

Cook Partisan Voting Index: D+32

Atlanta's music scene has flourished in recent years, and *The Guardian* reported that the city remained in 2015 the world capital of hip hop. Hip hop and R&B acts such as Cee Lo Green, Young Jeezy, OutKast, and T.I. got their start in Atlanta.

The 5th Congressional District of Georgia includes much of the city of Atlanta and also Forest Park and the smaller communities of Lake City and Morrow in Clayton County. It includes most of the posh and Republican Buckhead. But the small population of Buckhead has more financial than political influence in this overwhelmingly Democratic district.

John Lewis (D)

John Lewis, a Democrat first elected in 1986, made history a half-century ago as a leader of the civil rights movement. That experience informs his work as a legislator on voting rights and poverty, and makes him an iconic figure in American politics. After three decades in the House, he carries great moral authority, but less legislative influence with Democrats in the minority.

A sharecropper's son from Troy Alabama, Lewis was seized by religious fervor as a child, preaching in the barnyard, determined to be a minister. Lewis was the first in his family to finish high school. He wrote to Rev. Ralph Abernathy for help in suing for the right to enter Troy State College, and he met Rev. Martin Luther King Jr. when he was 18. In 1959, at age 19, he helped organize the first lunch counter sit-in, which was received with open hostility. In 1960, the day after John F. Kennedy was elected president, Lewis sat in the Krystal Diner in Nashville, where a waitress poured cleansing powder down his back and water over his food to get him to leave. The restaurant manager then turned a fumigating machine on him.

In May 1961, he was on the first of the Freedom Rides, in which protesters rode buses through the South to challenge segregation, and were attacked as they went. Lewis was viciously beaten in Rock Hill, South Carolina, and Montgomery Alabama. He spoke at the 1963 March on Washington, criticizing Kennedy liberals for inaction on civil rights and calling for massive help for the poor. In 1964, he helped coordinate the Mississippi Freedom Project. And in March 1965, he led the Selma-to-Montgomery march to petition for voting rights. During that historic event, he was beaten by policemen, who fractured his skull. Quietly maintaining his poise and sound judgment under harsh circumstances, Lewis was one of the people who risked their lives to make the civil rights revolution happen. He worked for Robert Kennedy's campaign for president in 1968 and was with him in Indianapolis when they heard King had been shot. He recounted his experiences in his 1998 autobiography, *Walking with the Wind,* and in another book published in 2012, *Across That Bridge: Life Lessons and a Vision for Change*, in which he describes what he learned in his early years.

In Lewis' first foray into electoral politics in 1977, he was defeated by Democrat Wyche Fowler in a special election to succeed Democratic Rep. Andrew Young. After winning a seat on the Atlanta City Council in 1981, Lewis ran again for Congress in 1986. He trailed Julian Bond 47%-35% in the primary, but Lewis won the runoff by assembling a coalition of poor blacks and nearly 90% of the whites. "Vote for the tugboat, not the showboat" was his slogan, stressing his work on local issues. He has been reelected easily ever since.

Lewis has been a strong partisan, with a staunchly liberal voting record. Usually quiet, he can speak in the forceful cadences reminiscent of black civil rights-era preachers, as he did in opposition to the Gulf War resolution in January 1991 and to the impeachment of President Bill Clinton in December 1998. At the dramatic finale of the health care legislation in March 2010, Lewis linked arms with House Speaker Nancy Pelosi and walked to the Capitol through a gauntlet of taunting anti-health care reform protestors. "I think I will remember the walk across the street with John Lewis for the rest of my life," Rep. Brad Miller of North Carolina said later. In a September 2012 speech marking the 150th anniversary of the Emancipation Proclamation, Lewis said, "We're one people, one family, the American family. We live in the same house, the American house, the world house."

A decade earlier, when Pelosi became Democratic Whip, Lewis initially challenged her, then switched his support to Steny Hoyer of Maryland. Lewis is the senior chief deputy whip in the Democratic leadership, and also the ranking Democrat on the Ways and Means Oversight Subcommittee. Only occasionally does he defect from his party, as when he opposed the 1994 crime bill because of his disapproval of capital punishment, and when he voted against the Iraq supplemental spending bill in 2007 because it contained funds for continued military action. He has not been strongly identified with any issues of taxes or spending at Ways and Means.

Lewis has worked to commemorate the civil rights revolution in which he played such a large part. He got a federal building in Atlanta named for King and won historic trail designation for the demonstrators' route from Selma to Montgomery. During the 50th anniversary of the 1965 march, he reminisced that the Edmund Pettus Bridge was "almost a sacred site" because of the police attacks that took place there. "That's where some of us gave a little blood and where some people almost died." Since 1998, he has led members of Congress on pilgrimages to civil rights sites. Lewis has stoutly defended racial quotas and preferences. He strongly championed the reauthorization of the Voting Rights Act in 2006 when Republicans were the House majority, and his support helped ensure it carried by a large majority over the objections of critics who claimed it was no longer necessary. After the Supreme Court in 2013 limited Justice Department review of voting-law changes in the South, he built bipartisan support to reverse that ruling. But he failed to get a vote in the House or Senate before the 2014 election.

The 2008 presidential campaign was a difficult experience for Lewis. Following extensive pressure from various camps, he endorsed Hillary Clinton in 2007 as "a strong leader," and he defended her from attacks by other civil rights leaders. When Barack Obama won the Georgia primary, Lewis came under local and national pressure to switch to his camp. Some of the pressure came from two challengers in the July primary, which Lewis won, with 69 percent of the vote. In late February, he endorsed Obama "following a long, hard, difficult struggle" and spoke of Obama's candidacy as a transformational moment. "Something's happening in America, something some of us did not see coming," Lewis said. "It's a movement. It's a spiritual event."

Obama welcomed the switch, and Lewis became an outspoken advocate, perhaps excessively so, as in an October statement when he compared the campaign rhetoric of Republican nominee John McCain to that of former segregationist presidential candidate George Wallace of Alabama. McCain called the comparison "beyond the pale." At the Democratic convention in August, where he was treated as a hero, Lewis broke down in tears as he spoke of Obama's historic candidacy and the 45th anniversary of King's "I Have a Dream" speech. In a dramatic epilogue in February 2009, Elwin Wilson of Rock Hill apologized on national television for slugging Lewis in the Freedom Ride attack, saying, "I am ashamed." Seated next to him, Lewis embraced the 68-year-old man, and said, "I forgive you." Lewis called the apology "amazing, unreal, unbelievable" and said that it showed the "power of reconciliation."

Four years later, Lewis campaigned vigorously for Obama's reelection. During a speech in Florida, he said that Democrats needed to respond to criticism that Obama's supporters are "lost in a sea of despair, that we're disappointed. That's not the way I feel." He complained that voter identification laws and other measures passed by GOP-led state legislatures "constitute the most concerted effort to restrict the right to vote since before the Voting Rights Act."

SIXTH DISTRICT

Tom Price (R)

Elected 2004, 6th term; b. Oct. 8, 1954, Lansing, MI; U. of MI, B.A. 1976, M.D. 1979; Presbyterian; married (Elizabeth); 1 child.

Elected Office: GA Senate, 1997-2004, maj. ldr., 2002-03.

Professional Career: Practicing orthopaedic surgeon, 1979-2002; Asst. prof., Emory U., 2002-present.

DC Office: 100 CHOB, 20515, 202-225-4501; Fax: 202-225-4656; Website: tomprice.house.gov.

State Offices: Roswell, 770-998-0049.

Committees: *Budget*: (Chmn). *Ways & Means*: Health.

Group Ratings

	ADA	ACLU	AFL-CIO	LCV	ITI	COC	HAFA	ACU	CFG	FRC
2014	5%	0%	–	3%	100%	79%	78%	92%	83%	100%
2013	5%	C	14%	7%	C	85%	C	92%	88%	C

National Journal Ratings

	2013 LIB	—	2013 CONS
Economic	5%	—	94%
Social	0%	—	87%
Foreign	24%	—	68%
Composite	13%	—	87%

Key Votes of the 113th Congress

1. Sandy storm spending	N	5. Medical Marijuana	N	9. Syrian Rebels Training	N
2. Violence Against Women Act	N	6. Farm Bill	N	10. Keystone pipeline	Y
3. Guantanamo Bay Detainees	N	7. Afghanistan Combat	N	11. Immigration Exec. Action	Y
4. Abortion 20-week ban	Y	8. NSA Phone Data Collection	Y	12. Bipartisan budget deal	Y

Election Results

2014 general	Thomas Price (R)	139,018	(66%)	$1,724,935
	Robert Montigel (D)	71,486	(34%)	$14,573
2014 primary	Tom Price (R)	unopposed		

Prior winning percentages: 2012 (65%), 2010 (unopposed), 2008 (68%), 2006 (72%), 2004 (100%)

Population		Race and Ethnicity		Income	
Total:	726,129	White	64.1%	Median income:	$76,308
Urban:	43.6%	Black	12.9%		(39 of 435)
Suburban:	56.4%	Latino	11.8%	Under $50,000	33.2%
Rural:	0.0%	Asian	9.2%	$50,000-$99,999:	27.9%
Land area:	319	Two races	1.8%	$100,000-$199,999:	25.9%
Pop/sq. mi.:	2,273.5	White Ethnic	21.8%	$200,000 or more:	13.0%
Born in state:	32.3%			Poverty Rate	10.7%
		Education			
Age Groups		H.S. grad or less:	20.6%	**Work**	
Under 18:	24.4%	Some college:	22.4%	White collar:	51.6%
18 to 34:	21.4%	College degree, 4 yr.:	35.4%	Blue collar:	38.1%
35 to 64:	43.2%	Post-grad study:	21.6%	Sales and service:	10.3%
Over 64:	10.9%				
		Military		Govt. workers:	7.7%
		Veterans/active duty:	6.1%		

Northern Atlanta Suburbs: Fulton, Cobb

In the red clay north of Atlanta, an almost wholly new metropolitan quarter has grown up over the past four decades. Affluent Atlanta has spread out past the Perimeter, the local name for Interstate 285, into territory that was once farms, small towns, and modest factory cities. Where there were perhaps 100,000 people in the 1950s, there are more than 1 million today. No longer is downtown Atlanta the only focus. The edge city of Perimeter Center is not just for shopping: It is a major office center, exceeding downtown Atlanta in square footage. Along the usually jammed Georgia 400 highway, in the fast-growing northern part of Fulton County, are the affluent suburbs of Sandy Springs, Roswell and Alpharetta.

Voter Turnout	
2013 Total Citizen 18+	463,960
2014 House Turnout	210,504
2014 Turnout as % CVAP	45.4%
2012 Turnout as % CVAP	66.9%

Home Depot, the nation's second-largest retailer, is based in Sandy Springs. In 2012, Home Depot lobbied Georgia lawmakers for Internet sales taxes, arguing that tax loopholes for web retailers put on-the-ground companies at a competitive disadvantage. Georgia Gov. Nathan Deal later signed into law a bill requiring Internet retailers to collect sales taxes. Sandy Springs has been an innovator in outsourcing basic government services to private industry. In June 2012, *The New York Times* reported that the city "does not have a fleet of vehicles for road repair, or a yard where the fleet is parked. It does not have long-term debt. It has no pension obligations. It does not have a city hall, for that matter, if your idea of a city hall is a building owned

2012 Presidential Vote		
Mitt Romney (R)	186,998	(61%)
Barack Obama (D)	114,796	(37%)

2008 Presidential Vote		
John McCain (R)	182,881	(59%)
Barack Obama (D)	122,235	(40%)

Cook Partisan Voting Index: R+14

by the city. Sandy Springs rents." The Atlanta Braves plan to complete in 2017 their new baseball stadium in Cobb County, and will move there from downtown. Over the objections of some citizens groups, the county is paying nearly half the cost.

The 6th Congressional District is based in the northern Atlanta suburbs. It includes the northern sections of DeKalb and Fulton counties and the eastern part of Cobb County, where the Weather Channel is headquartered. Nearly half of the population is in Fulton. All parts of the district are safe Republican.

Tom Price (R)

Tom Price, a Republican first elected in 2004, has become a leading creator of and advocate for his party's conservative message. He fell short in a bid to move up the leadership ladder. But in 2015 he succeeded Paul Ryan as Budget Committee chairman, having decided a year earlier not to seek another leadership post or a Senate seat. Not a bad consolation prize.

Price grew up in Michigan and graduated from the University of Michigan and its medical school. His father and grandfather were both physicians. He did his residency in orthopedic surgery at Emory Medical School and then moved to Roswell, where he participated in civic affairs and was president of the Rotary Club. Working with the Medical Association of Georgia in the early 1990s, he campaigned locally against President Bill Clinton's health care plan. When a seat opened in the state Senate in 1996, he was elected and quickly moved up the leadership ranks. He became majority leader as Republicans captured the Senate in 2002 for the first time since Reconstruction.

When Republican Rep. Johnny Isakson ran for the Senate, the contest for this heavily Republican seat was hard-fought and big-spending. Three state senators ran—Price from Fulton County, and Robert Lamutt and Chuck Clay from Cobb County. Price spent $499,000 of his own money and contrasted his work in medicine with the legal and business careers of his two chief opponents. He highlighted his fiscal conservatism and strong support for limiting jury awards in malpractice suits, a position that won him considerable support from the medical community. Calling the federal income tax "broken," he supported a national retail sales tax. He said he had "a surgeon's mentality. ... I get things done."

Price led the first round of the primary with 35% of the vote; Lamutt made it into the runoff with 28%. Lamutt, who gave $1.5 million to his campaign, criticized Price as a "special interest" candidate because he raised large sums from fellow doctors. He also attacked Price's 2003 support for a 25-cent state tax increase on cigarettes. Price defended his vote as a tool to reduce property taxes. In the runoff, Price won 54%-46%.

In the House, Price was an original member of the Tea Party Caucus. On the tax-writing Ways and Means Committee, he has advocated the abolition of the Internal Revenue Service and replacing almost all taxes with a national sales tax. He told Fox News after President Barack Obama was reelected in 2012 that he disagreed with Speaker John Boehner's position to abandon efforts to repeal Obama's health care reform law. He introduced his own legislation to create tax incentives for consumers to purchase insurance on the individual insurance market.

In 2010, Price was elected chairman of the House Republican Policy Committee, the party's in-house idea factory. He focused on health care and energy policy, repeatedly calling for more domestic oil and gas production. During negotiations over raising the federal debt limit in 2011, he said on CNN that a default represented no large risk because debt-holders could still be paid, an assertion that the fact-checking website *PolitiFact* found to be false. When Democrats sought to extend unemployment benefits in 2010, Price cited economists who warned of a "moral hazard" in doing so. His enthusiasm for playing political hardball impressed his GOP colleagues, as did his energy for the fight. He told *The Atlanta Journal-Constitution* that he gets to his office before 7:30 a.m. and leaves at 10:30 or 11 p.m.

Price hoped to parlay his hard work into a higher leadership post. In late 2012, he sought the chairmanship of the Republican Conference, the No. 4-ranking job. He had the backing of Ryan, the GOP's 2012 vice presidential nominee. But Boehner favored Washington state's Cathy McMorris Rodgers, the conference vice chair. Boehner reportedly offered Price a ceremonial leadership posting to drop out and publicly pledge his loyalty to Boehner. Price declined the offer and lost to McMorris Rodgers in a closed-door vote.

Instead, Ryan named Price as Budget's vice chairman in 2013. He became a key House critic of the Obama administration's implementation of the Affordable Care Act, and sponsored a bill barring the Internal Revenue Service from enforcing or implementing the law. It passed the House, but went nowhere in the Democratic-controlled Senate. The House also passed, on a largely party-line vote in April 2014, his bill to require the Congressional Budget Office to assess the broad economic impact of major legislation beyond the simple fiscal cost.

Taking the Budget hat in 2015 when Ryan became Ways and Means chairman, Price said he hoped to tackle reforms to Social Security, an area that Ryan—and most politicians—have studiously avoided for fear of alienating senior citizens. Price said in a January speech: "All the kinds of things, you know about, whether it's means testing, whether it's increasing the age of eligibility ... all those things ought to be on the table and discussed." He also said he would continue to seek to repeal of the Affordable Care Act, but said that budget procedures to avoid a Senate filibuster were not a "silver bullet." The budget plan approved by the committee and passed by the House in March 2015 did not include Social Security changes. Impressively for Price, he kept most conservatives on board with the budget, even though 17 Republicans voted against the plan, which the House approved 228-199.

Though he called Obama's fiscal 2016 budget blueprint "reckless," he said that he agreed with parts of it, including a proposal to use taxes on profits that U.S. companies reap overseas to help fund a massive public works program. He said that he wasn't fazed by the president's veto threats. "If we're able to put pieces of legislation on the president's desk ... if he signs it, then from our perspective, we get a win because it's good public policy," Price said. "If he vetoes it, which is his right to be able to do, it provides the nation with a contrast, the difference between the two visions, and it's important for the nation to appreciate that vision."

Price has been reelected with only minor opposition. He got some negative attention in 2010 when it was revealed he was among eight lawmakers under investigation by the Office of Congressional Ethics for holding fundraisers or receiving donations from businesses shortly before voting on a Wall Street regulation bill. The House Ethics Committee subsequently dropped the charges.

Journal-Constitution columnist Jim Galloway in January 2013 described Price as "undoubtedly the most ambitious member of the Georgia delegation." News reports at the time indicated Price was mulling a primary challenge to Georgia Sen. Saxby Chambliss, who drew fire from conservatives for his willingness to work with Democrats and eventually retired. Price ultimately decided against running in 2014. He was unlikely to get much help from Georgia's Republican establishment: He originally backed fellow Rep. Nathan Deal for governor in 2010, then switched his allegiance to ex-Georgia Secretary of State Karen Handel while the rest of the state's delegation stuck with Deal. After Deal won the election, Price reportedly was all but shut out of a role in the redistricting process. In the House, the door remains open for Price to seek a leadership position, or more influence at Ways and Means, though several younger members have more seniority.

SEVENTH DISTRICT

Rob Woodall (R)

Elected 2010, 3rd term; b. Feb. 11, 1970, Athens; Furman U., B.A. 1992, U. of GA, J.D. 1998; Methodist; single.

Professional Career: Clerk, private firm, 1993-94; Chief of staff, legis. aide, Rep. John Linder, 1994-2010.

DC Office: 1724 LHOB, 20515, 202-225-4272; Fax: 202-225-4696; Website: woodall.house.gov.

State Offices: Lawrenceville, 770-232-3005.

Committees: *Budget. Rules. Transportation & Infrastructure:* Aviation; Highways & Transit.

Group Ratings

	ADA	ACLU	AFL-CIO	LCV	ITI	COC	HAFA	ACU	CFG	FRC
2014	0%	11%	–	0%	100%	79%	71%	88%	72%	75%
2013	5%	C	10%	4%	C	85%	C	80%	82%	C

National Journal Ratings

	2013 LIB	—	2013 CONS
Economic	5%	—	94%
Social	42%	—	57%
Foreign	47%	—	52%
Composite	32%	—	68%

Key Votes of the 113th Congress

1. Sandy storm spending	N	5. Medical Marijuana	Y	9. Syrian Rebels Training	Y
2. Violence Against Women Act	N	6. Farm Bill	Y	10. Keystone pipeline	Y
3. Guantanamo Bay Detainees	N	7. Afghanistan Combat	N	11. Immigration Exec. Action	Y
4. Abortion 20-week ban	N	8. NSA Phone Data Collection	N	12. Bipartisan budget deal	Y

Election Results

2014 general	Rob Woodall (R)........................ 113,557	(65%)	$500,041	$3,673
	Thomas Wight (D)...................... 60,112	(35%)	$19,471	
2014 primary	Rob Woodall (R).....................unopposed			

Prior winning percentages: 2012 (62%), 2010 (67%)

Population		Race and Ethnicity		Income	
Total:	735,051	White	49.5%	Median income:	$62,156
Urban:	3.9%	Black	18.3%		(98 of 435)
Suburban:	96.1%	Latino	17.6%	Under $50,000	39.7%
Rural:	0.0%	Asian	11.7%	$50,000-$99,999:	31.6%
Land area:	468	Two races	2.3%	$100,000-$199,999:	22.8%
Pop/sq. mi.:	1,571.7	White Ethnic	16.2%	$200,000 or more:	5.9%
Born in state:	36.1%			Poverty Rate	12.2%
		Education			
Age Groups		H.S. grad or less:	33.6%	**Work**	
Under 18:	28.4%	Some college:	29.3%	White collar:	40.5%
18 to 34:	21.4%	College degree, 4 yr.:	25.2%	Blue collar:	42.5%
35 to 64:	41.5%	Post-grad study:	11.9%	Sales and service:	17.0%
Over 64:	8.7%				
		Military		Govt. workers:	9.5%
		Veterans/active duty:	6.4%		

Northeastern Atlanta Suburbs: Gwinnett, Forsyth

In the past two decades, greater Atlanta has grown out in every direction: south past the airport, west over the Chattahoochee River, north past Perimeter Center, and east and northeast past Stone Mountain. The outer suburbs north of Atlanta have grown fastest of all. Gwinnett County features

Voter Turnout	
2013 Total Citizen 18+	438,345
2014 House Turnout	173,669
2014 Turnout as % CVAP	39.6%
2012 Turnout as % CVAP	61.8%

mature neighborhoods of affluent professionals and entrepreneurs and closer-in communities near Interstate 85 that have been attracting Georgia's largest concentration of Hispanics along with middle-class blacks. The county's rapidly growing school system boasts that its students speak more than 100 languages. Farther out in Lawrenceville, Duluth and Buford, downtown Atlanta seems very far away, both physically—it is 20 to 40 miles, and more than an hour of clogged rush-hour driving, to Peachtree Street—and in state of mind. For many, Atlanta is something off the highway on the way to Hartsfield-Jackson Atlanta International Airport.

2012 Presidential Vote		
Mitt Romney (R)................158,741	(60%)
Barack Obama (D) 101,169	(38%)

2008 Presidential Vote		
John McCain (R)................152,391	(60%)
Barack Obama (D) 99,388	(39%)

Cook Partisan Voting Index: R+14

The growth here and its diversity are hard to overstate. Gwinnett County's population grew 37% from 2000 to 2010, to more than 805,000; in the next four years, it grew to 878,000, despite the slowdown during the recession. Gwinnett was one of the metro Atlanta counties that benefited from $68 million in federal Neighborhood Stabilization Program funds from 2009 to 2012, and rather than tear down properties, it used the money to rehab abandoned houses, *The Atlanta Journal-Constitution* reported. Like other metro Atlanta counties, the non-Hispanic white population has been dropping in Gwinnett schools, while the overall student numbers soar. There are Mexicans in Norcross, Koreans in Duluth and Bosnians in Lawrenceville.

The 7th Congressional District of Georgia comprises most of Gwinnett County and a sizable portion of Forsyth County to its north, which is the fastest growing county in metro Atlanta. Gwinnett voted 54%-45% for Mitt Romney over President Barack Obama in the 2012 presidential race, but Forsyth went for Romney 81%-18%.

Rob Woodall (R)

Republican Rob Woodall was elected in 2010 to succeed his boss for 16 years, the retiring Rep. John Linder. His Capitol Hill experience makes him more savvy about how Congress works and less inclined to bash government than his GOP colleagues who entered with him, but he matches them in his avid fiscal conservatism.

Woodall was born in Athens, where his parents were finishing their studies at the University of Georgia. His father was an entomologist who would take Rob and his older sister on expeditions to collect bugs in swampy areas. The family was of modest means, shopped at Goodwill stores, and drove used cars. "Nobody squeezes a nickel harder than I do," Woodall said. He went to college on an ROTC scholarship and worked summers to pay his expenses, including a stint on the assembly line at an RC Cola bottling plant. While in law school, he worked for a firm in Washington on issues related to President Bill Clinton's energy policy and then-first lady Hillary Rodham Clinton's health care initiative. He loved being on the frontlines of national policymaking and worked out a deal with the dean of the University of Georgia School of Law to finish his degree in Washington. In 1994, Woodall took a 50% pay cut to start work as a legislative aide to Linder. He rose to chief of staff in 2000.

He became a candidate for the House after 18-year House veteran Linder announced his retirement. Eight candidates entered the GOP primary in July. Woodall and radio talk-show host Jody Hice received the most votes, but neither attained the 50% threshold necessary to avoid a runoff.

Hice self-funded his runoff campaign and had more money to spend than Woodall. Both candidates courted support from tea party groups. Woodall embraced the movement's principles of limited government, strict constitutional construction and fiscal responsibility. He also advocated shifting some of the federal government's powers to the states, repealing the Democratic health care overhaul, and creating tougher measures to deal with immigration. Yet, most local tea party groups backed Hice, especially after he bought billboards sporting a Soviet-era hammer and sickle and depicting Obama as a socialist. Woodall was endorsed by Linder and former Arkansas Gov. Mike Huckabee. He won the August runoff, 56%-44%. In the general election, he easily dispatched his Democratic opponent. In 2014, Hice was elected to the neighboring 10th District seat.

Like Linder, Woodall lists his main issue as the federal tax code, which he calls "a monstrosity" that should be replaced with a national sales tax. Woodall contributed to the book that Linder and nationally syndicated radio talk-show Neal Boortz published called *The FairTax Book*, which was a best seller in 2005. Woodall says that the tax code punishes productivity and encourages debt, and that a national sales tax would boost the rate of personal savings. A Fair Tax bill he introduced in 2011 drew 70 cosponsors but did not advance; he reintroduced it in 2013 and 2015. Woodall said after the 2012 election that Republican presidential candidate Mitt Romney was correct in saying that 47% of Americans don't pay income taxes.

In the House, Woodall got seats on the Rules and Budget committees in recognition of his familiarity with those panels' procedural issues as an ex-staffer. He joined most other GOP freshmen in opposing the New Year's Day 2013 deal on tax and spending cuts, aimed at averting the so-called fiscal cliff, calling it "all dessert and no vegetables. ... Spending is the problem in Washington, not tax revenue."

Woodall has shown signs of independence. He tackled the typically Democratic issue of campaign finance reform, introducing a bill in 2011 to bar incumbents from holding onto their campaign money between elections. Politicians' war chests discouraged many would-be challengers, he said. Also in 2011, he was one of just seven Republicans who refused to bar federal funding for National Public Radio and one of seven who opposed a measure allowing permit holders to carry concealed weapons across state lines. "If the Second Amendment protects my rights to carry my concealed weapon from state to state to state, I don't need another federal law," he said.

Woodall became chairman of the Republican Study Committee's budget and spending task force. When Louisiana's Steve Scalise stepped down as RSC chairman to become majority whip following Eric Cantor's unexpected primary defeat in June 2014, Woodall was appointed to serve as interim chairman. After the 2014 election, he ran for chairman of the Republican Policy Committee, but finished third behind Tom Reed of New York and the winner, Luke Messer of Indiana.

Woodall's vote in 2011 to raise the federal debt limit sparked a GOP primary challenge in 2012 from software engineer David Hancock, a tea party supporter. Woodall won easily with 72% of the vote. He faced no primary opposition in 2014.

EIGHTH DISTRICT

Austin Scott (R)

Elected 2010, 3rd term; b. Dec. 10, 1969, Augusta; U. of GA, B.B.A. 1993; Baptist; married (Vivien); 2 children.

Elected Office: GA House, 1997-2010.

Professional Career: Owner, Southern Group; Agent, Principal Financial Group, 1993-2010.

DC Office: 2417 RHOB, 20515, 202-225-6531; Fax: 202-225-3013; Website: austinscott.house.gov.

State Offices: Tifton, 229-396-5175; Warner Robins, 478-971-1776.

Committees: *Agriculture*: Biotechnology, Horticulture, & Research; Commodity Exchanges, Energy, & Credit (Chmn); General Farm Commodities & Risk Mgmt. *Armed Services*: Oversight & Investigations; Readiness.

Group Ratings

	ADA	ACLU	AFL-CIO	LCV	ITI	COC	HAFA	ACU	CFG	FRC
2014	0%	0%	–	6%	100%	57%	76%	92%	91%	100%
2013	0%	C	19%	4%	C	77%	C	80%	70%	C

National Journal Ratings

	2013 LIB	—	2013 CONS
Economic	30%	—	70%
Social	0%	—	87%
Foreign	15%	—	77%
Composite	19%	—	82%

Key Votes of the 113th Congress

1. Sandy storm spending	N	5. Medical Marijuana	N
2. Violence Against Women Act	N	6. Farm Bill	Y
3. Guantanamo Bay Detainees	N	7. Afghanistan Combat	N
4. Abortion 20-week ban	Y	8. NSA Phone Data Collection	N

9. Syrian Rebels Training	N
10. Keystone pipeline	Y
11. Immigration Exec. Action	Y
12. Bipartisan budget deal	Y

Election Results

2014 general   Austin Scott (R) ....unopposed
2014 primary Austin Scott (R) ....unopposed

Prior winning percentages: 2012 (unopposed), 2010 (53%)

Population		Race and Ethnicity		Income	
Total:	696,584	White	60.4%	Median income:	$38,714
Urban:	35.7%	Black	30.8%		*(400 of 435)*
Suburban:	11.0%	Latino	5.7%	Under $50,000	59.8%
Rural:	53.3%	Asian	1.3%	$50,000-$99,999:	27.9%
Land area:	8,573	Two races	1.6%	$100,000-$199,999:	10.6%
Pop/sq. mi.:	81.3	White Ethnic	12.2%	$200,000 or more:	1.7%
Born in state:	70.1%			Poverty Rate	21.6%
		Education			
Age Groups		H.S. grad or less:	52.5%	**Work**	
Under 18:	24.5%	Some college:	29.3%	White collar:	32.0%
18 to 34:	24.2%	College degree, 4 yr.:	11.0%	Blue collar:	43.7%
35 to 64:	37.7%	Post-grad study:	7.1%	Sales and service:	24.3%
Over 64:	13.6%			Govt. workers:	22.3%
		Military			
		Veterans/active duty:	10.7%		

South-Central Georgia

Central Georgia is a region of farm and forest lands and a collection of small, and some tiny, towns. Twiggs and Wilkinson counties have been among the world's major sources of kaolin, a clay used for china and ceramics. Juliette, along Interstate 75, is an old mill town that's too small for most maps.

Voter Turnout	
2013 Total Citizen 18+	504,358
2014 House Turnout	129,938
2014 Turnout as % CVAP	25.8%
2012 Turnout as % CVAP	51.9%

Scenes from *Fried Green Tomatoes* were filmed in Juliette—an old former hardware store there became the film's Whistle Stop Café. With its Air Logistics Center and testing and repair site for the F-22 Raptor, Robins Air Force Base and the surrounding city of Warner Robins have grown significantly in recent years. The sprawling base employed 22,000 people and had an economic impact of $2.7 billion in 2014.

In Pulaski County is Hawkinsville, founded on the banks of the Ocmulgee River and a winter home for harness horse training. Nearby is Tifton, home to the Georgia Museum of Agriculture. Farther south along Interstate 75 is Valdosta, a black-majority city of 55,500 that has the most successful high school football program in the country. No program in the nation has won more games than the Wild-cats, which have a win-loss record of 891-216-34 since 1913. Valdosta is also where Doc Holliday, made famous by the gunfight at the O.K. Corral, spent much of his youth. The city still has a bit of a wild side: Residents of dry towns in northern Florida frequently cross the Georgia border to buy liquor in Valdosta.

2012 Presidential Vote		
Mitt Romney (R)	163,908	(62%)
Barack Obama (D)	99,676	(38%)
2008 Presidential Vote		
John McCain (R)	163,390	(61%)
Barack Obama (D)	100,722	(38%)
Cook Partisan Voting Index:	R+15	

The 8th Congressional District includes all of Monroe and Jones counties north of Macon in central Georgia and stretches all the way south to the Florida border. It covers Berrien County, known for its turpentine and bell peppers, and it takes in most of Lowndes County, where Valdosta is located. The district is solidly Republican.

Austin Scott (R)

Republican Austin Scott defeated a veteran incumbent Democrat in 2010, an outcome that symbolized the disappearance of Blue Dog Democrats in the South, and he became a leader of his large freshman class. He has been active on military issues.

Scott was born in Augusta. His father was an orthopedic surgeon, and his mother was a teacher. He graduated from the University of Georgia with a degree in risk management and insurance in 1992. After college, Scott opened an insurance brokerage firm, which he continues to operate. Scott first won election to the state House at 26. He sponsored a bill to provide better funding for the state's trauma-care system. He championed the expansion of charter schools and supported the right of students to express their religious beliefs in schools. In January 2009, Scott got into the Georgia governor's race. To boost awareness of his campaign, he went on a 1,000-mile walk around the state, talking to voters. He made his 64-day journey in the height of summer, losing 7 pounds in the process. But his campaign failed to gain traction, and he decided to challenge four-term Democratic Rep. Jim Marshall.

Marshall ranked as one of the most conservative Democrats in Congress and voted against President Barack Obama's health care bill, but he was vulnerable in 2010 simply because he was a Democrat. In his campaign, Scott promised to reduce the deficit, and he attacked the incumbent for voting for Obama's $787 billion economic stimulus bill. Marshall, unlike most Democrats, was endorsed by the U.S. Chamber of Commerce and the National Rifle Association. In one ad, Marshall showed his driver's license to prove that he wasn't House Speaker Nancy Pelosi, who became a Republican symbol of the reviled Democratic agenda in Congress. Still, he lost the seat to Scott, who got 53% of the vote to 47% for Marshall. Since then, Scott has twice run for reelection without major-party opposition.

In the House, Scott was elected freshman class president and was regularly asked to explain his boisterous classmates' actions to the news media. He said in November 2011 that they never intended to speak with one voice: "I think of us as a group of independent thinkers." Though the group came in with lofty aims of reshaping Washington, he contended a year later that its main job was "to play defense against what [Obama] was going to do. I think we were pretty effective at doing that." Scott has taken a notably low profile.

He was given a seat on the Armed Services Committee, fulfilling a campaign promise from then-Minority Leader John Boehner. Unlike many of the military's boosters on the panel, he has maintained that defense spending must also be examined for budget cuts. But he hasn't been reluctant to advocate on behalf of his district. In March 2015, Scott collaborated with neighboring 1st District Republican Rep. Buddy Carter to urge support of the A10-C Warthog, which provides support for larger aircraft in low-visibility and low-altitude combat and has two squadrons at Moody Air Force Base in Valdosta. He has opposed the Obama administration's request for another round of base closings, which could jeopardize Warner-Robins and Moody.

On the Agriculture Committee, Scott became chairman in 2015 of the Commodity Exchanges, Energy, and Credit Subcommittee. In his work to reauthorize the Commodity Futures Trading Commission, he took on the financially complex and often risky derivatives markets, and said he was looking for "a bipartisan solution that strikes a balance between market integrity and market access." Elsewhere, Scott introduced a bill to abolish the Legal Services Corporation in August 2011—three days after it became public that its lawyers had won an action against a company in his district that had fired U.S. workers in favor of less-expensive immigrants with visas. In 2012, he sponsored a bill to limit the use of government-operated drone aircraft domestically, which he said stemmed in part from news reports that the Environmental Protection Agency was using drones to spy on cattle ranchers in Nebraska.

NINTH DISTRICT

Doug Collins (R)

Elected 2012, 2nd term; b. Aug. 16, 1966, Gainesville; N. GA Col., B.A. 1988, New Orleans Baptist Theological Seminary, M.Div. 1996, John Marshall Law Schl., J.D. 2008; Baptist; married (Lisa); 3 children.

Military Career: U.S. Air Force Reserve, 2007-present.

Elected Office: GA House, 2007-12.

Professional Career: Practicing atty., 2008-12; Pastor, Chicopee Baptist Church, 1994-2005.

DC Office: 1504 LHOB, 20515, 202-225-9893; Website: dougcollins. house.gov.

State Offices: Gainesville, 770-297-3388.

Committees: *Judiciary:* Courts, Intellectual Property & the Internet (VChmn); Regulatory Reform, Commercial and Antitrust Law. *Rules.* Legislative and Budget Process; Rules and Organization of the House.

Group Ratings

	ADA	ACLU	AFL-CIO	LCV	ITI	COC	HAFA	ACU	CFG	FRC
2014	5%	0%	–	3%	100%	71%	81%	84%	89%	100%
2013	0%	C	15%	7%	C	77%	C	88%	89%	C

National Journal Ratings

	2013 LIB	—	2013 CONS
Economic	4%	—	96%
Social	0%	—	87%
Foreign	15%	—	77%
Composite	10%	—	90%

Key Votes of the 113th Congress

1. Sandy storm spending	N	5. Medical Marijuana	N	9. Syrian Rebels Training	Y
2. Violence Against Women Act	N	6. Farm Bill	N	10. Keystone pipeline	Y
3. Guantanamo Bay Detainees	N	7. Afghanistan Combat	N	11. Immigration Exec. Action	Y
4. Abortion 20-week ban	Y	8. NSA Phone Data Collection	N	12. Bipartisan budget deal	Y

Election Results

2014 general	Doug Collins (R)	146,059	(81%)	$664,455
	David Vogel (D)	34,988	(19%)	$27,968
2014 primary	Doug Collins (R)	49,951	(80%)	
	Bernard Fontaine	12,315	(20%)	

Prior winning percentage: 2012 (76%)

Population		Race and Ethnicity		Income	
Total:	711,655	White	77.9%	Median income:	$43,657
Urban:	21.0%	Latino	12.3%		(338 of 435)
Suburban:	29.8%	Black	7.9%	Under $50,000	55.7%
Rural:	49.1%	Asian	1.0%	$50,000-$99,999:	28.3%
Land area:	4,030	Two races	0.8%	$100,000-$199,999:	13.4%
Pop/sq. mi.:	176.6	White Ethnic	17.0%	$200,000 or more:	2.6%
Born in state:	61.1%			Poverty Rate	20.1%
		Education			
Age Groups		H.S. grad or less:	52.3%	**Work**	
Under 18:	23.8%	Some college:	27.3%	White collar:	29.3%
18 to 34:	20.4%	College degree, 4 yr.:	13.0%	Blue collar:	41.2%
35 to 64:	39.4%	Post-grad study:	7.4%	Sales and service:	29.5%
Over 64:	16.4%				
		Military		Govt. workers:	13.5%
		Veterans/active duty:	8.7%		

Northeast Georgia

Northeast Georgia is a land where the coastal plains and cotton fields yield to gently rolling hills and, near the North Carolina border, to the Appalachian Mountains. For most of its history, this was quiet, rural country, with courthouse towns and a few small cities, mostly forgotten by national elites,

Voter Turnout	
2013 Total Citizen 18+	504,298
2014 House Turnout	181,047
2014 Turnout as % CVAP	35.9%
2012 Turnout as % CVAP	53.0%

bypassed even by Union soldiers on their march to the sea. These largely rural areas have been an occasional source of derision and curiosity. James Dickey's 1970 novel *Deliverance* is a thinly disguised portrait of life along the Coosawattee River in Gilmer and Murray counties (although the movie was filmed on the Chattooga River in Rabun County).

Though the area was traditionally agrarian, the northern part of Georgia has undergone a rush of change over two decades. Interstate highways have brought it within easy range of Atlanta. Vacation and retirement communities have sprung up in the mountains and around the lakes. Agribusiness remains important, with huge poultry processors in Hall County around Gainesville. The area around Lake Sidney Lanier, named for the 19th century poet who wrote "The Song of the Chattahoochee," is filled with vacation houses and second homes. Thousands of Latinos from Mexico and other countries came to the Gainesville area to snap up jobs before the 2007-09 recession, and the county is more than 26 percent Hispanic.

The agricultural town of Jefferson transitioned to textiles, and eventually manufacturing. Today the town of Elberton is a large producer of granite monuments, and Royston employs people in the metal and plastics industries. Baseball great Ty Cobb, nicknamed "The Georgia Peach," was born in tiny Narrows in Banks County and played semi-pro ball in Royston, which now houses the Ty Cobb Museum.

The 9th Congressional District of Georgia covers the northeast corner of the state. The district is anchored by Gainesville's Hall County, and includes part of Athens. Current Georgia Gov. Nathan Deal and Lt. Gov. Casey Cagle launched their careers in Gainesville. The 9th is rural and mostly white. It is the most Republican district in the state and the third most Republican in the country, according to *The Cook Political Report*. Mitt Romney got 78 percent of the vote here in 2012, which was surpassed only by two districts in west Texas.

2012 Presidential Vote		
Mitt Romney (R)	207,581	(78%)
Barack Obama (D)	54,310	(21%)
2008 Presidential Vote		
John McCain (R)	197,659	(75%)
Barack Obama (D)	63,694	(24%)
Cook Partisan Voting Index: R+30		

Doug Collins (R)

Republican Doug Collins is a Baptist minister who beat a tea party-backed candidate in 2012 to claim the newly drawn 9th District seat. He also is a lawyer who has shown sound legislative skills and has taken on House leadership assignments.

Collins was born in Gainesville and grew up in Hall County. His father was a state trooper, and his mother worked a variety of jobs in town. In 1988, Collins graduated from North Georgia College & State University, where he studied political science and business. The same year, he met his wife, Lisa, at church. He worked in several jobs in the hazardous materials industry but then felt a calling to the ministry. After spending some time volunteering as a youth minister, he entered the New Orleans Baptist Theological Seminary. He returned to Gainesville, serving as pastor of Chicopee Baptist Church. In 2002, Collins joined the Air Force Reserve and, in 2008, did a tour in Iraq as a chaplain, an experience that he says gave him "a whole different perspective of what freedom is like and what the lack of it is like." Later, he got a law degree in Atlanta and opened his own practice in Gainesville. He served six years in the state House, including one term as the floor leader for Republican Gov. Nathan Deal, whom he had known since high school.

When Georgia got a 14th district following the 2010 reapportionment, Republicans at the State House conveniently drew the new 9th District without an incumbent, where they could easily elect one of their own. When Collins decided to run for the seat, his chief primary opponent was Gainesville talk-show host Martha Zoller, a tea party favorite who campaigned as a political outsider. She criticized Collins' role in devising the referendum to raise the sales tax by a penny to address traffic congestion, which was widely rejected in most of the state. Collins touted his legislative experience crafting budgets and his service in Iraq. He also likened her status as a well-known radio host to an "Obama-style celebrity" and hammered her for having once admitted that President Barack Obama was "a nice guy."

The two fought to a near-draw in July's primary, with Collins coming out on top, 42%-41%, a difference of just 734 votes. In the runoff, Zoller was endorsed by national figures such as former Alaska Gov. Sarah Palin and 2012 presidential candidates Herman Cain, Newt Gingrich, and Rick Santorum. In the final days before the election, Deal recorded a robo-call for Collins, and he also had the backing of Georgia House Speaker David Ralston and Zell Miller, a former Georgia governor and senator. Collins played on the local roots of his major endorsers and gathered support with the slogan "We are the 9th District." In the end, Collins outspent Zoller by 3-to-2 and prevailed in the runoff, 55%-45%. In this overwhelmingly Republican district, Collins coasted to victory in the general election in 2012 and 2014.

In the House, Collins got seats on the Judiciary and Rules committees—good posts for a lawyerly mind. In April 2015, Judiciary Chairman Bob Goodlatte endorsed a resolution filed by Collins to express congressional disapproval of the net neutrality rules that had been approved by the Federal Communications Commission. Collins criticized those rules as "heavy-handed agency regulations that would slow Internet speeds, increase consumer prices and hamper infrastructure development," and said that he preferred the alternative of a free and open Internet. In March 2015, the Judiciary Committee approved his proposal to give more authority to state and local governments to enforce national immigration laws. At the start of the new Congress in 2015, Speaker John Boehner tapped Collins for a seat on the Rules Committee, which schedules legislation for the House and typically acts as an arm of the House leadership. The assignment signaled that Collins had become a legislative insider among House Republicans.

Environmental opponents feared damage to local forests and streams.

Collins broke a two-decade deadlock in his district by adding a provision to the defense spending bill in 2013 that transferred 282 acres of local land from the Forest Service to the U.S. Army, which has used the area for training of Army Rangers. The location in Lumpkin County is near the Military College of Georgia. The Army welcomed the freedom to alter the landscape without the approval of the Forest Service.

TENTH DISTRICT

Jody Hice (R)

Elected 2014, 1st term; b. April 22, 1960, Atlanta; Ashbury Col., B.A. 1982, Southwestern Baptist Theological Seminary, M. Div. 1986, Luther Rice U., D. Min. 1988; Baptist; married (Dee Dee); 2 children.

Professional Career: Adjunct faculty, Luther Rice U.; Pastor; Talk radio host, *The Jody Hice Show.*

DC Office: 1516 LHOB, 20515, 202-225-4101; Fax: 202-226-0776; Website: hice.house.gov.

State Offices: Milledgeville, 478-457-0007; Monroe, 770-207-1776; Thomson, 770-207-1776.

Committees: *Natural Resources:* Energy & Mineral Resources; Federal Lands; Oversight & Investigations. *Oversight & Gov't Reform:* Health Care, Benefits, & Administrative Rules; National Security.

Election Results

2014 general	Jody Hice (R)	130,703	(67%)	$949,720	$7,600
	Ken Dious (D)	65,777	(33%)	$35,774	
2014 primary	Jody Hice (R)	26,961	(54%)		
runoff	Mike Collins	22,673	(46%)		
2014 primary	Jody Hice (R)	17,408	(34%)		
	Mike Collins (R)	17,143	(33%)		
	Donna Sheldon (R)	7,972	(15%)		
	Gary Gerrard (R)	3,830	(7%)		

Population		Race and Ethnicity		Income	
Total:	699,534	White	66.1%	Median income:	$46,584
Urban:	11.3%	Black	24.3%		*(292 of 435)*
Suburban:	54.9%	Latino	5.2%	Under $50,000	52.4%
Rural:	33.8%	Asian	2.1%	$50,000-$99,999:	30.1%
Land area:	5,086	Two races	2.1%	$100,000-$199,999:	15.1%
Pop/sq. mi.:	137.6	White Ethnic	15.2%	$200,000 or more:	2.4%
Born in state:	66.2%			Poverty Rate	19.5%
		Education			
Age Groups		H.S. grad or less:	48.7%	**Work**	
Under 18:	24.1%	Some college:	28.0%	White collar:	32.6%
18 to 34:	23.8%	College degree, 4 yr.:	14.1%	Blue collar:	42.9%
35 to 64:	39.1%	Post-grad study:	9.1%	Sales and service:	24.4%
Over 64:	13.1%			Govt. workers:	18.8%
		Military			
		Veterans/active duty:	8.2%		

East-Central Georgia

The north and south wings of General William Tecumseh Sherman's Union Army converged at Milledgeville, wrote author E.L. Doctorow in his novel *The March:* "And then the town of Milledgeville, empty and quiet, sat in its dishevelment, gusts of wind flying paper and brush against the

Voter Turnout	
2013 Total Citizen 18+	512,789
2014 House Turnout	196,480
2014 Turnout as % CVAP	38.3%
2012 Turnout as % CVAP	57.3%

sides of buildings and the leavings of coal fires scuttering in the street." The ghosts of the Civil War never left this region. Baldwin County's Milledgeville was the capital of Georgia

from 1804 to 1868, and it is where Georgia
legislators decided in 1861 to secede from
the Union. Sherman's Army occupied the
town and burned the state penitentiary, and
the state capital was eventually moved to
Atlanta. In nearby Butts County, Sherman's
Army burned the courthouse in the county
seat of Jackson.

2012 Presidential Vote		
Mitt Romney (R)................184,162	(63%)
Barack Obama (D) 107,040	(36%)
2008 Presidential Vote		
John McCain (R)................172,128	(58%)
Barack Obama (D) 119,963	(41%)
Cook Partisan Voting Index: R+14		

It's no wonder that central Georgia and
its tragedies have served as inspiration for several great Southern writers. Alice Walker,
author of *The Color Purple*, was born in Eatonton, and her writing draws on family oral
histories of life in rural Georgia. Southern Gothic writer Flannery O'Connor lived in Milledgeville. Jean Toomer, a writer associated with the Harlem Renaissance, based his classic
work *Cane* on his experiences in Hancock County. And Erskine Caldwell's scandalous best-
seller, *Tobacco Road*, about an illiterate, Depression-racked farm family, was said to be influenced by his time living in the small town of Wrens in Jefferson County.

Today, the region's economy is dominated by small, high-tech manufacturing, Atlanta's
urban sprawl, and the long reach of the University of Georgia in Athens, a campus filled
with graceful Greek Revival mansions, boxwood gardens, and magnolias. In Walton County,
a locally based business that serves more than 100,000 accounts between Atlanta and Athens plans a one-megawatt community solar electricity generation farm, which would be the
largest in the eastern half of the United States. Sandersville is the site of General Biofuels
Georgia's new $60 million wood-pellet manufacturing plant. Pharmaceutical company Bax-
ter International is expected to open a $1 billion plasma products manufacturing facility
near Covington by 2018, creating 1,500 jobs.

The 10th Congressional District runs from Barrow, Oglethorpe, and Wilkes counties
in the north to Baldwin, Washington, and Jefferson counties in the south. Rapidly growing
and affluent Columbia County is divided between this district and the 12th. The district
also takes in some of fast-growing Henry County and the well-to-do county of Oconee. The
Lake Oconee area has more than 100 subdivisions, including gated communities and golf
courses that beckon second-home buyers and retirees. Despite the overall economic growth
in Georgia, some of the rural counties have been lagging. This district is solidly Republican.

Jody Hice (R)

Republican Jody Hice, who in 2014 won the open seat in the 10th District, had been a prominent talk-show host who made a career at the forefront of the culture wars. Hice may be an
apt successor to Republican Rep. Paul Broun, a self-styled "constitutional conservative" who
ran unsuccessfully for the Senate.

Hice was born in Atlanta and grew up in Tucker Georgia. He graduated from Asbury
College, earned his master's degree from Southwestern Seminary and his doctorate from
Luther Rice University, a Christian college and seminary in Lithonia. He was the founder
of The Culture and Values Network and the host of The Jody Hice Show, a conservative talk
radio program.

A Baptist minister who served several churches in the metro Atlanta area, he argued
in his 2012 book, *It's Now or Never: A Call to Reclaim America,* that supporters of abortion
rights are worse than Hitler and that homosexuality causes shorter life spans as well as
depression. He got his first taste of political battle in 2003 when he helped lead a campaign
against a lawsuit by the American Civil Liberties Union seeking to remove a Ten Commandments display at the Barrow County courthouse. Five years later, he waged a successful
effort against the Internal Revenue Service over whether politically active clergy can keep
their tax-exempt status. He has been a leader of the annual Pulpit Freedom Sunday movement sponsored by the Alliance Defending Freedom, which challenges what the group contends is a provision in the income tax code that censors what pastors can say from the pulpit.

After Broun announced his Senate candidacy, Hice jumped in and was among the best-
known names in a GOP primary field of seven. The initial favorite was trucking company
executive Mike Collins, who played up his success in business and the achievements of his
father, former Rep. Mac Collins. Hice slammed Collins as an insider who was too close to
Washington because of his father, whom he attacked as well.

Collins struck back, painting Hice as an extremist. He cited passages from Hice's book that argued against blanket First Amendment protections for Muslims. And Collins brought up comments Hice made in 2004, when he said women running for office should first consult their husbands. But Collins opened up a window of vulnerability in an interview with the newspaper *Roll Call* when he equivocated on the issue of Congress raising the debt ceiling. Hice used that to hammer Collins as a closet moderate.

Hice led the May primary by a hair, at 33.5%, with Collins 265 votes behind. That forced a July runoff, where Hice had the advantage because he could unify the conservative vote. Hice defeated Collins in the runoff, 54%-46%, then coasted to an easy general election victory. Immediately after the election, the liberal website Salon declared him "America's worst new congressman."

In the House, Hice's early focus was on social issues. In January 2015, he introduced the Sanctity of Human Life Act, stating that human life begins with "fertilization, cloning, or its functional equivalent," and the Nuclear Family Priority Act, addressing what he calls the problem of chain migration, by limiting the assurance that legal status will be granted to extended family members of legal immigrants. After he was assigned to the Healthcare Subcommittee of the Oversight and Government Reform Committee, he said he would use the position to "look out for the small businesses in my district, whose expansion and growth has been stifled by Obamacare."

During his campaign, Hice had said that he would support "new leadership with a backbone." In explaining his opening-day vote for John Boehner for speaker, Hice said he had voted against Boehner in the earlier organizational meetings of the Republican Conference, but was "extremely disappointed" that few conservatives joined him. When candidates did emerge shortly before the vote for speaker, but with little debate, Hice concluded that there was no "pathway to victory." Consequently, he said, "I had to convey my principles directly to the speaker while receiving his assurance that he would use the strength of our majority to advance conservative solutions." Hice could face a Republican primary reelection challenge, depending on how he handles the balance between his conservative advocacy and working with other House Republicans.

ELEVENTH DISTRICT

Barry Loudermilk (R)

Elected 2014, 1st term; b. Dec. 22, 1963, Riverdale; Wayland Baptist U., B.S. 1992; Baptist; married (Desiree); 3 children.

Military Career: U.S. Air Force, 1984-92.

Elected Office: GA House, 2005-10; GA Senate, 2011-13.

Professional Career: Chmn., GA Republican party, 2001-04; Business owner.

DC Office: 238 CHOB, 20515, 202-225-2931; Fax: 202-225-2944; Website: loudermilk.house.gov.

State Offices: Cartersville, 770-429-1776; Woodstock, 770-429-1776.

Committees: *Homeland Security:* Emergency Preparedness, Response, & Communications; Oversight & Mgmt Efficiency. *Science, Space, & Technology:* Energy; Oversight (Chmn).

Election Results

2014 general	Barry Loudermilk (R)	unopposed		$1,034,392	$70,323
2014 primary	Barry Loudermilk (R)	34,641	(66%)		
runoff	Bob Barr (R)	17,794	(34%)		
2014 primary	Barry Loudermilk (R)	20,862	(37%)		
	Bob Barr (R)	14,704	(26%)		
	Tricia Pridemore (R)	9,745	(17%)		
	Edward Lindsey (R)	8,448	(15%)		

Population		Race and Ethnicity		Income	
Total:	730,150	White	68.7%	Median income:	$60,434
Urban:	13.3%	Black	15.3%		*(123 of 435)*
Suburban:	85.3%	Latino	11.1%	Under $50,000	41.6%
Rural:	1.3%	Asian	2.8%	$50,000-$99,999:	31.4%
Land area:	1,111	Two races	1.5%	$100,000-$199,999:	20.3%
Pop/sq. mi.:	657.3	White Ethnic	20.0%	$200,000 or more:	6.7%
Born in state:	43.9%			Poverty Rate	14.0%
		Education			
Age Groups		H.S. grad or less:	35.0%	**Work**	
Under 18:	25.0%	Some college:	27.6%	White collar:	41.8%
18 to 34:	24.2%	College degree, 4 yr.:	25.2%	Blue collar:	40.9%
35 to 64:	40.0%	Post-grad study:	12.2%	Sales and service:	17.3%
Over 64:	10.7%				
		Military		Govt. workers:	10.6%
		Veterans/active duty:	7.6%		

Northwestern Atlanta Suburbs: Cobb, Cherokee

Marietta is one of Atlanta's largest suburbs. Its economic mainstay for many years was defense contractor Lockheed Martin, which built the F-22 jet fighter and the C-130 cargo plane. Then in 2009, the F-22 became the first casualty of the Obama administration's decision to cut what it considered

Voter Turnout	
2013 Total Citizen 18+	498,656
2014 House Turnout	161,532
2014 Turnout as % CVAP	32.4%
2012 Turnout as % CVAP	62.7%

unnecessary weapons programs. The final F-22 left the assembly line in December 2011. Fewer C-130 planes have been produced, resulting in 400 layoffs in 2012. The company also has moved jobs to other facilities and cut several thousand more jobs nationwide in 2014 and 2015. But the local plant was largely spared, chiefly because the Pentagon had ordered additional F-35 fighter jets, parts of which are built in Marietta. The WellStar Kennestone Regional Medical Center, a sprawling, 57-acre campus, is a major employer in Marietta. The city's population peaked in 2009 at 67,000, plunged below 57,000 in the next year, and recovered modestly to 59,000 in 2013. It retains far more racial and ethnic diversity than

nearby counties: 32% of Marietta is African-American, and 21% is Hispanic. Fast-growing Bartow County, to the northwest of Marietta, grew 32% from 2000 to 2010. The county seat of Cartersville hosts the Smithsonian-affiliated Booth Western Art Museum in Cartersville, which has a large collection of Western American and Civil War-era art.

2012 Presidential Vote		
Mitt Romney (R)................200,863	(67%)
Barack Obama (D) 94,634	(32%)
2008 Presidential Vote		
John McCain (R)................192,618	(65%)
Barack Obama (D) 102,471	(34%)
Cook Partisan Voting Index:	R+19	

The 11th Congressional District of Georgia is anchored by Marietta and takes in all of Bartow and Cherokee counties and part of close-in Cobb, where Marietta is the county seat and the largest city. It also includes the northern tip of Fulton County, including part of Buckhead, with the governor's mansion. It is a solidly Republican district.

Barry Loudermilk (R)

Republican Barry Loudermilk sailed to victory in 2014 without a Democratic challenger in the open 11th District. Tea party groups counted Loudermilk as one of their own and backed him in a lively primary against former Rep. Bob Barr, who sought another revival of his political career.

Loudermilk was born in Riverdale, and got an associate degree in telecommunications technology from the Air Force Community College and a bachelor of science in occupational education and information systems technology from Wayland Baptist University. He served in the Air Force from 1984 to 1992. After a stint in business, he turned to politics, winning a seat in the state House in 2004. He was elected in 2010 to the state Senate, where he chaired the science and technology panel. He authored a book, *And Then They Prayed*, which features inspirational stories from American history.

The GOP primary in May drew six candidates after Rep. Phil Gingrey announced he would make an ultimately unsuccessful primary bid for the Senate. Loudermilk and Barr were the top two vote-getters with 37% and 26% respectively, which forced a runoff in July. Barr, a former federal prosecutor, four-term House member, civil libertarian and Libertarian presidential candidate in 2008, played up his conservative bona fides, including his role in the 1998 impeachment proceedings against President Bill Clinton. Loudermilk, taking a sharp antiestablishment turn, cited Barr's Washington experience as a liability. He also called Barr too soft on immigration and criticized him for backing Attorney General Eric Holder's nomination in 2009.

Barr counterattacked by pointing out he later called for Holder to step down. He also took some personal swipes at Loudermilk, suggesting that he had embellished his Air Force record and that he was involved in an $80,500 settlement the state Legislature had reached in a racial discrimination suit involving a former Loudermilk staffer. Loudermilk denied both claims. Loudermilk drew criticism from some liberal groups outside the state and the blogosphere for his association with self-described historian David Barton. Barton has argued that the framers of the U.S. Constitution intended to establish a conservative Christian government and that the First Amendment applies only to Christians.

In the end, the attacks did little to slow Loudermilk's march to the runoff, where he trounced Barr 66%-34%. Loudermilk's biggest margins were in the outlying counties. He got 78% in Barton and 71% in Cherokee. The 11th District gave Mitt Romney 67% of the vote in 2012 and is so reliably Republican that no Democrat considered running for Congress. Loudermilk was one of seven members of the Georgia delegation who won without opposition in November, but the only freshman—which once was a rare accomplishment for a newcomer.

When the House Republican Conference met in November to organize for the new Congress and selected John Boehner in a voice vote for another term as speaker, Loudermilk was one of three Republicans (including fellow Georgia freshman Jodi Hice) who cast what he called a "principled vote" against Boehner. Like Hice, Loudermilk then voted for Boehner in the roll call House vote in January, on the grounds that November was "the time to have that fight," he told the *Cherokee Tribune*. He contended that the GOP opposition to Boehner in January was poorly organized. He added that he was "probably punished" by his failure to get the committee assignment he had sought. Instead, he got on Homeland Security and Oversight and Government Reform.

Congress operates in "a perpetual state of chaos," Loudermilk wrote in a review of his first three months in office that he posted on his official website. The "true problem in Washington is its tendency to govern by crisis," he perceptively observed. Inevitably, he added, "Congress would do what Congress does best—kick the can down the road to the next Congress." In contrast, he added, conservatives were working on a long-term vision of where to take the country.

TWELFTH DISTRICT

Rick Allen (R)

Elected 2014, 1st term; b. Nov. 7, 1951, Augusta; Auburn U., B.S. 1973; Methodist; married (Robin); 4 children.

Professional Career: Founder, R.W. Allen & Associates, 1976.

DC Office: 513 CHOB, 20515, 202-225-2823; Fax: 202-225-3377; Website: allen.house.gov.

State Offices: Augusta, 706-228-1980; Dublin, 478-272-4030; Statesboro, 912-243-9452; Vidalia, 912-403-3311.

Committees: *Agriculture:* Conservation & Forestry; General Farm Commodities & Risk Mgmt. *Education & the Workforce:* Health, Employment, Labor, & Pensions; Higher Education & Workforce Training.

Election Results

2014 general	Rick Allen (R)	91,336	(55%)	$2,488,060	$107,679	$2,792,502
	John Barrow (D)	75,377	(45%)	$3,536,271	$612,094	$3,849,471
2014 primary	Rick Allen (R)	25,093	(54%)			
	Eugene Yu (R)	7,677	(17%)			
	Delvis Dutton (R)	6,644	(14%)			
	John Stone (R)	5,826	(13%)			

Population		Race and Ethnicity		Income	
Total:	706,182	White	56.5%	Median income:	$39,779
Urban:	30.6%	Black	34.7%		*(393 of 435)*
Suburban:	18.3%	Latino	5.4%	Under $50,000	59.5%
Rural:	51.1%	Asian	1.6%	$50,000-$99,999:	26.3%
Land area:	9,180	Two races	1.3%	$100,000-$199,999:	11.8%
Pop/sq. mi.:	76.9	White Ethnic	12.8%	$200,000 or more:	2.4%
Born in state:	67.2%			Poverty Rate	24.9%
		Education			
Age Groups		H.S. grad or less:	49.9%	**Work**	
Under 18:	24.2%	Some college:	29.2%	White collar:	32.5%
18 to 34:	25.7%	College degree, 4 yr.:	12.5%	Blue collar:	42.9%
35 to 64:	37.5%	Post-grad study:	8.3%	Sales and service:	24.6%
Over 64:	12.6%				
		Military		Govt. workers:	20.9%
		Veterans/active duty:	11.1%		

East Georgia: Augusta

Upriver from Savannah is the city of Augusta. Founded in 1735 as a fur-trading post, it has been home since 1835 to the Medical College of Georgia, now part of Georgia Regents University, a public academic health center. It has become a manufac-

Voter Turnout	
2013 Total Citizen 18+	519,198
2014 House Turnout	166,814
2014 Turnout as % CVAP	32.1%
2012 Turnout as % CVAP	52.0%

turing hub for big companies like Procter & Gamble, International Paper, and Dart Container (formerly Solo Cup). It weathered the recession better than most Georgia cities, and was the only metropolitan area adding jobs in 2010, according to a Georgia State University report. Its jobless rate hovered around 9 percent in 2012. Many know the city best as the site of Augusta National Golf Club, a private club where

the Masters Tournament is held every April, amid reverence for its traditions by both players and spectators. It is the first of golf's four major annual tournaments and the only one played on the same course every year.

The 12th Congressional District takes in Augusta's Richmond County and part of neighboring Columbia County. The district has a military presence with the Fort Gordon

2012 Presidential Vote		
Mitt Romney (R)	148,622	(55%)
Barack Obama (D)	117,131	(44%)
2008 Presidential Vote		
John McCain (R)	146,559	(56%)
Barack Obama (D)	116,152	(44%)
Cook Partisan Voting Index:	R+9	

Army base, with 13,800 troops. And it includes the college town of Statesboro, where Georgia Southern University is located, and Vidalia, home of the famous sweet onion.

Rick Allen (R)

Republican Rick Allen claimed this increasingly red district for the GOP in 2014 by ousting five-term incumbent John Barrow, the only remaining white Democrat in the House representing a state in the Deep South. Allen's surprisingly comfortable victory highlighted the uphill challenge facing Democrats in the rural South.

A native of Augusta who still resides there, Allen graduated from Auburn University with a bachelor of science degree in building construction. After spending three years as a project manager with a local construction business, he founded R.W. Allen & Associates, a construction company that he has operated since 1976 in the Augusta and Athens areas. His experience as a small business owner and job creator formed the centerpiece of his congressional campaign.

Allen had sought the Republican nomination in 2012, but finished second in the primary to state Rep. Lee Anderson, who lost to Barrow 54%-46%. This time around, Allen spent nearly a million dollars of his own money. He won the five-way May primary with 54% of the vote, avoiding a runoff. In the general election, Allen criticized Barrow—one of the last fiscally conservative Blue Dog Democrats in the House—for hewing too closely to President Barack Obama's agenda, while touting his own conservative credentials. Allen advocated greater fiscal discipline and reductions in government spending, and blasted excessive taxation and regulation as barriers to job creation. Unlike Anderson, who drew criticism in 2012 from local newspapers for his refusal to debate Barrow, Allen debated the congressman, though he drew attention for refusing to do so at an Islamic community center. He called it a "suspect venue," and the location was changed to a government complex.

Allen touted his support for the Second Amendment, but Barrow boasted an A+ rating and an endorsement from the National Rifle Association. Allen won the backing of other traditionally Republican groups, such as the U.S. Chamber of Commerce. With little daylight between the candidates on many issues, the Republican strategy focused instead on the national Democratic Party. The National Republican Congressional Committee bolstered Allen's campaign with ads linking the congressman to Obama. Barrow outspent Allen $3.5 million to $2.5 million, but the nearly $4 million in national GOP assistance more than made up the difference. Allen won handily, 55%-45%. Barrow won Richmond (Augusta), the largest county, with 66% of the vote. But Allen won 71% in adjacent Columbia, the next-largest county, and all but two of the remaining 19 counties. In a post-election analysis, *Roll Call* credited Allen's success in defeating "the ultimate political survivor" Barrow to early commercials on his behalf by the NRCC, the GOP success in making the contest a national battleground campaign, and Allen's late loan of more than $900,000 to his own campaign.

Allen entered the House with more mainstream Republican views and style than other Georgia GOP freshmen elected in 2014, and was awarded with assignments to substantive committees: Agriculture and Education and the Workforce. Allen cited agriculture as Georgia's number-one industry, and said that he would work to "strengthen local control of our nation's schools ... and foster innovation and entrepreneurship in today's workforce." It seemed unlikely that Democrats would regain this district any time soon.

THIRTEENTH DISTRICT

David Scott (D)

Elected 2002, 7th term; b. June 27, 1945, Aynor, SC; FL A&M U., B.A. 1967, U. of PA, M.B.A. 1969; Baptist; married (Alfredia Aaron); 2 children.

Elected Office: GA House, 1975-82; GA Senate, 1983-2002.

Professional Career: Founder & pres., Dayn-Mark Advertising, 1979-2002.

DC Office: 225 CHOB, 20515, 202-225-2939; Fax: 202-225-4628; Website: davidscott.house.gov.

State Offices: Jonesboro, 770-210-5073; Smyrna, 770-432-5405.

Committees: *Agriculture:* Commodity Exchanges, Energy, & Credit (RMM); General Farm Commodities & Risk Management. *Financial Services:* Capital Markets & Gov't Sponsored Enterprises; Financial Institutions & Consumer Credit.

Group Ratings

	ADA	ACLU	AFL-CIO	LCV	ITI	COC	HAFA	ACU	CFG	FRC
2014	75%	72%	–	89%	80%	67%	13%	4%	3%	13%
2013	80%	C	95%	89%	C	54%	C	12%	16%	C

National Journal Ratings

	2013 LIB	—	2013 CONS
Economic	67%	—	33%
Social	73%	—	24%
Foreign	63%	—	36%
Composite	68%	—	32%

Key Votes of the 113th Congress

1. Sandy storm spending	Y	5. Medical Marijuana	Y	9. Syrian Rebels Training	Y
2. Violence Against Women Act	Y	6. Farm Bill	N	10. Keystone pipeline	Y
3. Guantanamo Bay Detainees	N	7. Afghanistan Combat	Y	11. Immigration Exec. Action	N
4. Abortion 20-week ban	N	8. NSA Phone Data Collection	N	12. Bipartisan budget deal	Y

Election Results

2014 general	David Scott (D).......................unopposed		$1,146,654 $1,398
2014 primary	David Scott (D)............................ 29,486	(82%)	
	Michael Owens (D) 6,367	(18%)	

Prior winning percentages: 2012 (72%), 2010 (69%), 2008 (69%), 2006 (69%), 2004 (100%), 2002 (60%)

Population		Race and Ethnicity		Income	
Total:	718,624	Black	53.3%	Median income:	$51,298
Urban:	12.3%	White	31.1%		*(213 of 435)*
Suburban:	87.4%	Latino	9.8%	Under $50,000	48.4%
Rural:	0.3%	Asian	2.9%	$50,000-$99,999:	34.6%
Land area:	723	Two races	2.1%	$100,000-$199,999:	15.0%
Pop/sq. mi.:	993.3	White Ethnic	8.8%	$200,000 or more:	2.0%
Born in state:	50.9%			Poverty Rate	18.4%
		Education			
Age Groups		H.S. grad or less:	41.5%	**Work**	
Under 18:	27.5%	Some college:	33.2%	White collar:	32.1%
18 to 34:	22.3%	College degree, 4 yr.:	15.8%	Blue collar:	43.7%
35 to 64:	41.0%	Post-grad study:	9.5%	Sales and service:	24.2%
Over 64:	9.2%				
		Military		Govt. workers:	14.3%
		Veterans/active duty:	8.9%		

Southwestern Atlanta Exurbs: Clayton, Cobb

Many of the great landmarks of the civil rights movement, and the headquarters of many of its leading organizations, are in the central city of Atlanta. In the 1960s, Atlanta's blacks were clustered in ghetto neighborhoods on the south and west sides of the city. The north side and the suburbs in every direction were heavily or entirely white. Today, metro Atlanta's thriving black middle class has moved outward in almost every direction

Voter Turnout	
2013 Total Citizen 18+	480,886
2014 House Turnout	159,445
2014 Turnout as % CVAP	33.2%
2012 Turnout as % CVAP	63.2%

in one of the nation's fastest-growing metro areas—to southern DeKalb County to the east, to Clayton County directly south of the city, to southwest Fulton County, to eastern and southern Cobb and Douglas counties to the west.

Cobb County has made news for its aggressive approach to immigration. It was the first county in the state to be certified for a federal program giving state and local law enforcement the authority to arrest illegal immigrants. The program has been hailed as effective, but it also has driven away immigrants seeking friendlier territory. In early 2013, Cobb County commissioners considered going even further: requiring local companies to partner with Immigration and Customs Enforcement to check on the immigration status of employees. Fast-food chain Chick-fil-A, headquartered in the Atlanta suburb of College Park, served up political controversy on a different social issue when chief executive Dan Cathy, a Christian conservative, spoke out against same-sex marriage. Gay rights groups protested nationwide, while conservative politicians stood in line to order waffle fries on an unofficial "Chick-fil-A Appreciation Day." In Cobb County, Austell is the home of Six Flags over Georgia, which opened in 1967 as the second franchise of the company. With the Six Flags White Water in Marietta, the facilities generated a $194 million economic impact for Cobb County in 2014.

The 13th Congressional District of Georgia is a collection of suburban areas that have attracted Atlanta's African-American middle class. It includes most of Clayton County, which is heavily dependent economically on the airport and is 66% African American and 14% Latino. It takes in all of Douglas County, and parts of Cobb, Fulton, Fayette and Henry counties. It is a black-majority district and solidly Democratic.

2012 Presidential Vote		
Barack Obama (D)	202,828	(69%)
Mitt Romney (R)	87,742	(30%)
2008 Presidential Vote		
Barack Obama (D)	201,058	(68%)
John McCain (R)	93,288	(32%)
Cook Partisan Voting Index: D+16		

David Scott (D)

Democrat David Scott, first elected in 2002, is distinctly more of a centrist than most of his fellow members of the Congressional Black Caucus. He usually gets along well with GOP colleagues, some of whom he knew in the Georgia legislature, and he avoids publicly criticizing them. He often works on issues that go beyond race.

Born in rural South Carolina, Scott is the son of a minister and grandson of a deacon. During his middle school years, his family moved to tony Scarsdale New York, where his parents took jobs as a chauffeur and housekeeper for a wealthy family. Scott was the only African American in his otherwise all-white school. He later graduated from Florida A&M University, then did an internship at the Labor Department in Washington. There he met George Taylor, an authority in labor-management relations who encouraged the bright young man to apply to the prestigious Wharton School at the University of Pennsylvania, which Scott did, eventually earning his MBA. He moved to Atlanta, and in 1974 was elected to the Georgia House. In 1982, he won election to the state Senate, where he chaired the Rules Committee. From 1979 to 2002, he owned Dayn-Mark Advertising, which creates and places radio, television and print ads. The firm has been operated by his wife and two daughters.

In 2002, Scott made a bid for the newly created 13th District seat, which was heavily Democratic. Four other Democrats ran, the best known of whom was former state party Chairman David Worley, who had nearly defeated Republican Rep. Newt Gingrich in 1990. Scott was familiar to many voters after more than a quarter-century in the state legislature. And if they didn't know Scott, they certainly knew of his campaign co-chairman: Hank Aaron, the Hall of Fame slugger and Atlanta-area icon, who is Scott's brother-in-law. Scott brought his advertising expertise to the campaign, plastering the interstate highways with eye-catching billboards. His chief competitors, Worley and state Sen. Greg Hecht of Clayton County, both white, ran ads attacking each other. Scott won the primary with 54% of the vote. He won the general election 60%-40%.

In the House, Scott has introduced relatively few bills. As a freshman, Scott was one of seven House Democrats to vote for final passage of President George W. Bush's tax cut and one of 16 to vote for the prescription drug benefit under Medicare. He split with most of his party by voting for a constitutional amendment to ban same-sex marriage. He has become a more reliable party vote in recent years but has had no reluctance to go his own way. He joined most Republicans in calling for an audit of the Federal Reserve in 2012. In 2014, he embraced a bipartisan approach to the mounting controversy at the Veterans Affairs Department, whose huge hospital in Atlanta encountered major problems.

On the Financial Services Committee, Scott criticized predatory lenders that exploit would-be homeowners in poor communities. He initially opposed the bailout of the financial markets, but after chairman Barney Frank of Massachusetts promised to address the Black Caucus' call for additional protections for homeowners facing foreclosure, Scott switched his vote in support of a revised version. On the Agriculture Committee, he has been the top Democrat on multiple subcommittees—currently at the Commodity Exchanges, Energy and Credit Subcommittee, which is chaired by fellow Georgia Rep. Austin Scott, a Republican. Scott joined Republicans in December 2011 in criticizing Commodity Futures Trading Commission Chairman Gary Gensler for not showing up at a hearing on MF Global, the commodities brokerage firm headed by former Democratic Sen. Jon Corzine of New Jersey that had collapsed several months earlier. "It's an example of why the American people are rapidly losing faith in Washington," Scott said.

In an unusual partisan clash for Scott in 2014, he urged President Barack Obama to withdraw his nominations of two federal judgeship nominees for district court seats in Alabama. Those two, Michael Boggs and Mark Cohen, had been recommended by the state's two Republican senators, Saxby Chambliss and Johnny Isakson, and were submitted by Obama after lengthy White House review as a matter of senatorial courtesy. Noting that both nominees were social conservatives, Scott said in an interview on NewsOne Radio, "what your audience needs to understand is the level of disrespect that this president has done to this nation on these appointments." Referring to his pride and love for Obama, Scott added, "But when you are hurt by the one you love, there's no greater pain than that." The Senate confirmed Cohen after the election with a group of other nominations, but did not act on Boggs because of objections to various rulings that he had issued as a state court judge, including on the state's old flag with its Confederate emblem.

At home, Scott has been an active presence in his district, sponsoring health and job fairs as well as "help for homeowners" events giving constituents the ability to ask questions of federal housing officials. Scott has been the subject of several unflattering stories about back taxes he owed on his home and business, and about payments out of his campaign fund to family members and Dayn-Mark Advertising. An attorney for Scott said that the transactions were legal under campaign finance law. He attracted both primary and general election challenges in 2008 and 2010. But none of his opponents held Scott below 60% of the vote. In 2014, Scott got 82% in the Democratic primary and faced no Republican opposition.

FOURTEENTH DISTRICT

Tom Graves (R)

Elected 2010, 3rd full term; b. Feb. 3, 1970, St. Petersburg, FL; U. of GA, B.B.A. 1993; Baptist; married (Julie); 3 children.

Elected Office: GA House, 2003-10.

Professional Career: Founder, Tough Turf Land Sculpting; Owner, Southern Vision; Real estate developer.

DC Office: 2442 RHOB, 20515, 202-225-5211; Fax: 202-225-8272; Website: tomgraves.house.gov.

State Offices: Dalton, 706-226-5320; Rome, 706-290-1776.

Committees: *Appropriations:* Defense; Financial Services and General Government; Legislative Branch (Chmn); *Library (Joint).*

Group Ratings

	ADA	ACLU	AFL-CIO	LCV	ITI	COC	HAFA	ACU	CFG	FRC
2014	5%	0%	–	3%	100%	79%	80%	92%	86%	75%
2013	5%	C	14%	7%	C	85%	C	92%	88%	C

National Journal Ratings

	2013 LIB	—	2013 CONS
Economic	10%	—	88%
Social	16%	—	74%
Foreign	24%	—	68%
Composite	20%	—	80%

Key Votes of the 113th Congress

1. Sandy storm spending	N	5. Medical Marijuana	Y	9. Syrian Rebels Training	Y
2. Violence Against Women Act	N	6. Farm Bill	N	10. Keystone pipeline	Y
3. Guantanamo Bay Detainees	N	7. Afghanistan Combat	N	11. Immigration Exec. Action	Y
4. Abortion 20-week ban	Y	8. NSA Phone Data Collection	Y	12. Bipartisan budget deal	Y

Election Results

2014 general	Tom Graves (R)	unopposed	$736,722
2014 primary	Tom Graves (R)	32,343	(74%)
	Kenneth Herron (R)	11,324	(26%)

Prior winning percentages: 2012 (73%), 2010 (unopposed), 2010 special (56%)

Population		Race and Ethnicity		Income	
Total:	696,119	White	78.1%	Median income:	$43,084
Urban:	17.6%	Latino	10.1%		*(343 of 435)*
Suburban:	58.1%	Black	9.7%	Under $50,000	55.8%
Rural:	24.3%	Asian	0.6%	$50,000-$99,999:	31.0%
Land area:	3,242	Two races	1.0%	$100,000-$199,999:	11.8%
Pop/sq. mi.:	214.7	White Ethnic	16.0%	$200,000 or more:	1.4%
Born in state:	59.1%			Poverty Rate	19.3%
		Education			
Age Groups		H.S. grad or less:	55.6%	**Work**	
Under 18:	**25.5%**	Some college:	27.7%	White collar:	28.1%
18 to 34:	21.2%	College degree, 4 yr.:	10.3%	Blue collar:	40.7%
35 to 64:	40.2%	Post-grad study:	6.4%	Sales and service:	31.2%
Over 64:	13.1%				
		Military		Govt. workers:	13.8%
		Veterans/active duty:	8.2%		

Northwest Georgia: Dalton

Northwest Georgia was long the home of the Cherokee Nation before the tribe was sent west in the
1830s on the Trail of Tears. It has been manufacturing country for the last century. Hundreds of
textile mills and dozens of carpet mills once clustered near the supply of natural cotton and along

Voter Turnout	
2013 Total Citizen 18+	489,583
2014 House Turnout	118,782
2014 Turnout as % CVAP	24.3%
2012 Turnout as % CVAP	48.3%

the railroad lines heading southwest at the base of the southern Appalachian chain. The late
19th-century boosters of the New South hailed factories as the vanguard of technological
progress, and in fact the plants produced a higher standard of living than did the farms on
this stubborn land. But the mills put scant premium on education or the cultivation of civic
virtues and did little to bring in higher-skilled work. All-white hiring practices maintained
racial segregation in mostly white north Georgia.

Today, this area is developing a different kind of economy, as metro Atlanta spreads out
along highways to the north and west. There are sprawling subdivisions in what once were
mill towns. Floyd County is home to an auto parts manufacturing cluster. To the north in
Dalton, the traditional craft of tufted bedspread handiwork was transformed into a carpet
industry so large that at its height it produced 60% of the world's tufted carpet. The carpet industry, more high-tech now than before, still plays a key economic role, although the
recession had a notable impact. The Dalton area lost 20% of its workforce soon after 2007.
Unemployment remained high at 8.4% in December 2014, but economic experts predicted an
acceleration in growth. The immigration debate also has moved front and center in Dalton.
Local businessmen who opposed the policies of President Barack Obama nonetheless welcomed the money that the illegal immigrants have brought to town, *The Wall Street Journal*
reported in December 2014. "If these people make more money and feel stability, it will help
my business," said a furniture store owner in Dalton. Immigrant advocates said that some
employers had been exploiting their workers.
More than half of the population of Dalton
was Hispanic.

The 14th Congressional District covers
the northwest corner of Georgia, including
all of Whitfield County and the city of Dalton. Chattanooga Tennessee's metro area has
expanded across the state line into places
like Chickamauga and LaFayette in Walker
and Catoosa counties. It takes in Floyd

2012 Presidential Vote		
Mitt Romney (R)	170,385	(73%)
Barack Obama (D)	58,886	(25%)
2008 Presidential Vote		
John McCain (R)	170,349	(71%)
Barack Obama (D)	66,722	(28%)
Cook Partisan Voting Index: R+26		

County and its largest city, Rome, as well as Paulding County, which extends beyond Cobb
County in exurban Atlanta. Politically, it is safe GOP territory. It ranked as the 12th most
Republican district in the nation, according to the Cook Partisan Vote Index.

Tom Graves (R)

Republican Tom Graves was elected in a June 2010 special election to replace 17-year
incumbent Nathan Deal, also a Republican, who resigned to run for governor. Well-regarded
by his fellow conservatives but a periodic annoyance to House GOP leaders, Graves lost a bid
in November 2012 to chair the conservative Republican Study Committee. But he has found
other routes to House influence.

Graves is from the small town of Ranger, with fewer than 100 people, where he still lives
with his wife, Julie Graves, and their three children on a farm. Growing up, he lived in a
single-wide trailer on a tar and gravel road, the son of a Georgia Power laborer who told him
to "dream big and then work hard." In high school, he wasn't a top student, but he excelled in
math and played both offensive guard and defensive linebacker on the football team. Graves
took out loans and worked to pay for college, becoming the first in his family to earn his
degree in business administration from the University of Georgia. After graduation, Graves
worked for Federated Department Stores, now Macy's, as an asset recovery specialist. He
saved his money and, in 1995, bought a small landscaping business. Graves eventually sold
off portions of the company to begin investing in real estate.

He met his future wife at Roswell Street Baptist Church, and she was instrumental in
getting him involved in the anti-abortion movement. He says he opposes abortion "without

exception," including cases in which the mother's life is at stake. In 2001, he and Julie, the founding president of the Gordon County Right to Life chapter, successfully opposed the construction of an abortion clinic in the area. The campaign propelled Graves to a seat on the county board and later in the Georgia House, where he served more than seven years. While a state legislator, he supported abortion restrictions and lower taxes, including a 2009 business tax cut. Of his political philosophy, he says, "there is a spectrum of conservatism from fiscal to social ... and I'm a conservative all the way across the board." He said former President Ronald Reagan is the figure he most admires in politics.

In the special election runoff to succeed Deal, Graves bested Republican state Sen. Lee Hawkins, 56%-44%, in a June 2010 runoff for the remainder of Deal's term. The two clashed again in the primary for a full term. Graves called for abolition of the departments of Education and Energy and the Environmental Protection Agency. He supported constitutional amendments to balance the budget and to give the president line-item veto power over spending bills. He opposed amnesty for illegal immigrants and advocated stricter enforcement of immigration laws. Both Graves and Hawkins supported a conservative proposal to replace the income tax with a national sales tax. Hawkins cast Graves as "out of touch" and attacked him for a bank loan that had gone into default. But he could not overcome Graves' backing by national Republican organizations, House Minority Leader John Boehner and local tea party groups. Graves outraised Hawkins, $1.3 million to $1 million and won the August runoff, 55%-45%, earning a full term without Democratic opposition.

In Washington, Graves joined the Tea Party Caucus. He got a slot on the Appropriations Committee, normally a coveted seat for members who want to help their districts. In an unusual move for an appropriator, Graves consistently voted to buck the leadership on spending bills. One of them was a failed September 2011 resolution to fund the government through mid-November; he was one of 48 Republicans who voted down the measure to protest the addition of $1 billion in disaster relief funds in the wake of Hurricane Irene and other weather disasters. Senior House Republicans, including some in leadership, reportedly urged that Graves be singled out for punishment on that vote, ideally by being stripped of his Appropriations seat. But Boehner declined to do so—a favor that Graves repaid with another bout of principled obstinacy.

In 2013, Graves led a rebellion against Boehner's strategy in that year's battle over a bill to fund government operations. With the clock ticking toward an Oct. 1 deadline to pass the measure, Graves proposed an amendment to stop funding for Obama's health care law, which was in the early stages of implementation. Boehner and other senior leaders opposed tying the two into one take-it-or-leave-it bill, but Graves drummed up support from 60 fellow conservatives; under pressure, Boehner backed down. As expected, the Democratic-controlled Senate voted 54-44 to strip the health care provision from the government funding bill. The subsequent stalemate led to the first partial government shutdown in 17 years, which exposed Republicans to a public backlash.

"You don't have to threaten to blow the whole thing up if you don't get your way," Obama said as the shutdown began. Even prominent Republicans such as Sen. John McCain of Arizona condemned the strategy as likely to fail. A Quinnipiac University poll showed that voters opposed closing the government to block implementation of the health care law by 72%-22%. The potential fallout for Graves was serious: If the shutdown proved politically damaging for his party, he would surely shoulder much of the blame, stunting further advancement in the Republican caucus. Graves replied to critics that his constituents supported him, and that the administration continued to botch implementation of the new law.

Graves has also drawn some negative headlines at home. He was accused of hypocrisy in March 2012 when *The Atlanta Journal-Constitution* reported that the Federal Deposit Insurance Corporation bailed out Graves and Georgia Senate Majority Leader Chip Rogers for about half of a $2.3 million loan the two men had received five years earlier to rehabilitate a North Georgia hotel. The dispute was settled privately out of court.

After his easy reelection in 2012, he sought to head the Republican Study Committee and won the endorsement of the group's founders, normally considered key to getting the nod. But the slightly more senior Steve Scalise of Louisiana also sought the job, citing his ability to work with the leadership and his success in passing bills. Scalise petitioned for the right to have the full membership hold a vote and, in doing so, pulled off an upset. For Scalise, that was a big step in his move toward majority whip in 2014.

Graves finally played his cards right and gained a different sort of insider position: chairman of the Legislative Branch Subcommittee on Appropriations, where congressional officials approach him and plead for funds. On accepting the position, Graves welcomed the honor and pledged to use it as "a prime opportunity to walk the conservative talk." It's all the more unusual for him to get the position at the start of his third full term. He would not be the first lawmaker to enter as a revolutionary and eventually become House-broken.

Graves won the 2014 Republican primary with 74 percent of the vote against Kenneth Herron, who spent a mere $13,000. He had no Democratic challenger in this GOP bastion.

★ HAWAII ★

America's state in the Pacific is geographically the most remote archipelago in the world, but it is hardly isolated. Thrust up from the ocean by volcanoes, it is geologically some of the youngest land on earth and continues to undergo transformations. Polynesians sailing double-hulled canoes from the Marquesas Islands nearly 2,000 miles away were the first humans to inhabit Hawaii roughly 1,600 years ago. Over time, several small kingdoms developed across the Islands, each ruled by an *ali'i nui* (a grand or great chief). The Islands' insulation from the Western world ended when British Captain James Cook, on an exploration to find the Northwest Passage, landed on Kauai in 1778. He would also die in Hawaii on a return visit a year later after a confrontation with natives. Towards the end of the century the most powerful *ali'i nui*, Kamehameha, began a campaign of conquest and by 1810, all the Islands were united into one kingdom under his rule. With unification came foreign trade: Pacific fur traders who stopped off in the Islands recognized that Hawaiian sandalwood would be popular in the markets of the Far East where it was prized for ornamental use and burning as incense. As king, Kamehameha controlled the harvesting of sandalwood, and by 1811 he was reaching deals with Boston maritime merchants whereby he would receive a hefty share of the profits from their sales. He died in 1819 and his memory is honored by a state holiday—King Kamehameha Day—every June 11.

One year later, two events occurred that would come to define the culture and economy of Hawaii. The first whaling ship arrived in 1820, and so did missionaries, led by a New England Congregationalist, Reverend Hiram Bingham. Within a decade, more than a hundred ships were making annual stops in Honolulu, which quickly became a thriving port. By 1850, the number of ships making Honolulu a port of call had increased fourfold. With the Gold Rush and California's admission to the union, shipping between San Francisco and Honolulu grew, strengthening ties to the United States. Mining companies in northern California began importing Hawaiian food and other supplies over the Pacific rather than wait for them to make the difficult trip across the American interior. Meanwhile, the missionaries were converting native Hawaiians to Protestant Christianity. That was steady work after King Kamehameha's successor, Liholiho, abandoned the *kapu* system, the religiously inspired code of taboos that was used to guide and regulate people's lives. But the missionaries' greatest impact on the Islands may not have been spiritual, but economic. When they left their religious duties, they took up other avocations and some went into the sugar business. In 1851, after being released from their missionary work, Samuel Northrup Castle and Amos Starr Cooke formed a partnership, Castle & Cooke, which ended up investing heavily in sugar plantations that sprung up on the Islands. Samuel Alexander and Henry Baldwin, both sons of missionaries, started the Haiku Sugar Company, which later become Alexander & Baldwin. Both of these partnerships expanded into other commercial enterprises and both were members of the "Big Five" companies that built the sugar industry and associated businesses like real estate, and dominated Hawaii's economy for generations. The boom in sugar required the importation of labor because a series of epidemics and other maladies ranging from measles and influenza to venereal disease devastated the native population as it came into more contact with Westerners. Soon, contract workers from China and Japan were coming to Hawaii. American sugar interests helped elect King Kalakaua to the Hawaiian throne over the British-leaning Queen Emma in 1874. Kalakaua returned the favor to his patrons and sought a trade agreement with the United States that was agreed to in 1876, allowing the duty-free sale of Hawaiian sugar in the states. But American planters and businessmen tired of the caprices of the royal family and, in January 1893, with the help of the Marines, ousted Queen Liliuokalani from the Iolani Palace and called on the United States to annex Hawaii. President Grover Cleveland demurred, and Hawaii for five years was a republic until President William McKinley annexed it. This history is a source of regret for some. An *Onipa'a* ceremony remembering Liliuokalani's overthrow was staged by John Waihee, the first governor of Native Hawaiian descent, in January 1993, with the American flag conspicuously absent. Later that year, Congress passed and President Bill Clinton signed an apology for the overthrow of Liliuokalani 100 years before. In 2009, Hawaii staged a commemoration, not a celebration, of the 50th anniversary of statehood.

The Japanese attack on Pearl Harbor led the United States to enter World War II, which brought a massive influx of U.S. armed forces to Hawaii. Military construction boomed. The

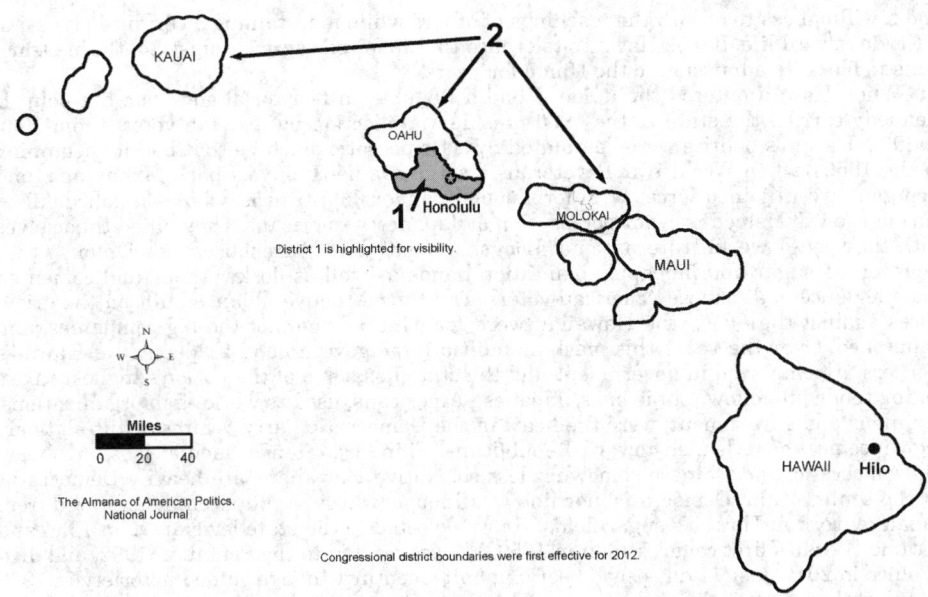

KAUAI

OAHU

Honolulu
1

District 1 is highlighted for visibility.

MOLOKAI

MAUI

N
W · E
S

Miles
0   20   40

HAWAII   Hilo

The Almanac of American Politics.
National Journal

Congressional district boundaries were first effective for 2012.

overall population of the Islands doubled to 858,000 in 1944, spurring greater demand for retail services and consumer products. After the war, the economy cooled as the nation demobilized, but with the Korean conflict in the early 1950s, there was another military build-up. The many sailors and troops that transited Hawaii on their way to the front lines, or who were stationed there, brought great exposure to the Islands and their charms that were invariably shared with family and friends by those military personnel when they returned home. Not surprisingly, Hawaii became a vacation destination aided by the development of turbo-propeller commercial airliners in the 1950s, followed shortly thereafter by the first jet airliners. By the 1960s, tourism had displaced sugar, pineapples and other agricultural products as Hawaii's leading industry. From statehood in 1959 to 1990, Hawaii's economic engine roared and the state's real gross domestic product increased at an annual average rate of 4.4 percent, easily eclipsing the national average. Then Hawaii ran into a trifecta of economic problems. The end of the Cold War brought a decline in military spending and work at the shipyard at Pearl Harbor slowed significantly. (In 2005, the Base Realignment and Closure Commission considered putting the shipyard, which has been less efficient than others, on the chopping block.) But it was Hawaii's traditional bonds across the Pacific that really brought economic woes to the Islands. The early 1990s recession in the United States was particularly severe in California and that reverberated in Hawaii with fewer investments and visitors coming from the Golden State. And ever since King Kamehameha exploited the sandalwood trade with the Far East, other than during World War II, Hawaii has always counted on Asian markets to help boost its bottom line. During Japan's "lost decade," its vacationers cut back their trips to Hawaii and Japanese real estate investors stopped bidding up and buying up properties in Oahu. Indeed, the 1990s were a decade of economic blues in Hawaii where growth declined on average about one percent a year while it grew by more than three percent in real terms across the nation.

For many years, Hawaii created a better life for its citizens than almost any other Pacific islands. Its people did not wall themselves off in ethnic blocs and have been mixing for the last century. Each group has made worthy contributions. The Asian migrant laborers brought traditions of hard work, family loyalty and group solidarity that found expression most vividly in the performance of the 442nd "Go for Broke" Regimental Combat Team, which was made up mostly of sons of Japanese immigrants and became the most decorated unit in U.S. military history. The Yankee spirit has been evident in Hawaii's commercial success and in its attachment to the rule of Anglo-American law. The Hawaiian spirit is apparent in the vitality of the *aloha* ambience, the welcoming of others despite their differences, and a willingness to absorb the teachings of others while maintaining a certain Polynesian attitude toward life. It was Hawaii's tolerance that inspired segregationist Southern Democrats to block its admission to the Union for years.

When Hawaii entered the union it had a Republican territorial governor, but John F. Kennedy carried the state in the 1960 presidential election by just 115 votes. From 1962 to 2002, Hawaii's politics were dominated by a Democratic machine that had its beginning in the 1950s, when World War II veterans such as Daniel Inouye, Spark Matsunaga, and George Ariyoshi joined forces with former mainlander John Burns, who as a police officer during the war helped prevent persecution of Japanese-Americans. They allied themselves with the then-powerful International Longshoremen's and Warehousemen's Union, which represented sugar and pineapple plantation hands as well as dockworkers, and cemented the allegiance of Japanese-American voters. The Burns-Inouye alliance built on the grievances against the *haole* (the Hawaiian word for white) owners of the big companies, and triumphed. Over the years this machine built a large government: 21 percent of Hawaii's workers are employed in government and the state has some of the nation's highest taxes. Voting tended to follow ethnic lines. Japanese-Americans, used to working in organizations, in unions and government, were the heart of the Democratic Party. Whites, with relatively high incomes, have leaned toward Republicans. Filipinos, often in menial jobs, are heavily Democratic, and Chinese somewhat less so. Native Hawaiians are heavily Democratic. At the center of the Democratic machine was Inouye, whose grandparents emigrated from Japan to work in Hawaii's sugar fields. He was elected to the state legislature in 1954 and became Hawaii's first congressman in 1959. He was elected to the Senate in 1962, and died in office in 2012, just 17 days shy of serving half a century. Inouye gained notoriety in 1973 as one of the questioners on the Senate Watergate Committee, but he was most comfortable operating behind the scenes. He was a veteran on the Appropriations Committee—the ultimate insiders' committee—who worked closely with his Republican colleague and friend Ted Stevens of Alaska to bring federal projects to both their states. He was "king of Hawaii" (*The Washington Post*'s term), and he kept close tabs on the state's politics. Those who crossed him incurred his anger. Inouye's deathbed wish was that his protégé, Rep. Colleen Hanabusa, succeed him in the Senate. Hawaii's Democratic machine has faced a few challenges over the years in divisive primaries and from third-party candidacies, and from Republican Linda Lingle, the mayor of Maui who was elected governor in 2002 and 2006 and ran unsuccessfully for the Senate in 2012. Lingle was unable, however, to persuade the heavily Democratic legislature to pass many of her policies. It even passed a tax increase over her veto, creating a top income tax rate of 11 percent. Her acrimonious fights with public employee unions resulted in spending cuts, furloughs and delayed tax refunds when the state faced huge deficits in 2009 and 2010. Democrats regained control of the governorship after Lingle was term-limited in 2010.

Hawaii has seen the demise of its plantation agriculture: Del Monte picked its last pineapples on the Islands in 2008 and Maui Land & Pineapple shut down its operations a year later. The state's last commercial grower is the Haliimaile Pineapple Co., which cultivates some 1,500 acres on Maui. The Hawaiian Commercial and Sugar Company is the last cane harvester on the Islands. Its plantation on Maui spreads over more than 35,000 acres and its parent company, real estate giant Alexander & Baldwin, an original Big Five member, remains one of the largest landowners in the state. Hawaii's agriculture today is dedicated to specialty crops like papayas, macadamia nuts, Kona coffee and genetically engineered seeds, but it contributes less than one-half of one percent to the state GDP. The Great Recession took its toll on the Islands. Real estate in Hawaii experienced a more severe downturn than in the country as a whole. Employment in that sector (which includes rentals and leasing) tumbled 32 percent between 2007 and 2012, compared to falling 12 percent nationally over that time period. Hawaii's tourism trade slumped and hit bottom in 2009, but it has since recovered, and then some. In 2014, Hawaii had a record 8.3 million visitors who spent a record $14.7 billion. Japan continues to account for almost one-fifth of the state's tourists and at 1.5 million in 2014, by far the most from any foreign country. But other nations are seeing much more rapid growth in travelers to the Islands. Between 2006 and 2013, visitors from Canada were up by more than 80 percent, while China saw a 142 percent rise, Australia's numbers jumped 161 percent, and Koreans soared 352 percent. Economic indicators point to modest growth for Hawaii over at least the next few years. The state's Department of Business, Economic Development & Tourism projected in 2015 that the state's real

Population		Race and Ethnicity		Income	
Total:	1,404,054	Asian	37.2%	Median income:	$61,408
Urban:	38.3%	White	22.9%		(9 of 50)
Suburban:	47.9%	Latino	9.2%	Under $50,000	36.1%
Rural:	13.8%	Pac. Island	8.9%	$50,000-$99,999:	32.2%
Land area:	6,423	Two races	19.7%	$100,000-$199,999:	25.1%
Pop/sq. mi.:	218.6	White Ethnic	14.1%	$200,000 or more:	6.6%
Born in state:	54.2%			Poverty Rate	8.6%
		Education			
Age Groups		H.S. grad or less:	36.4%	**Work**	
Under 18:	21.9%	Some college:	32.4%	White collar:	34.2%
18 to 34:	24.3%	College degree, 4 yr.:	20.8%	Blue collar:	47.5%
35 to 64:	38.1%	Post-grad study:	10.4%	Sales and service:	18.3%
Over 64:	15.7%				
		Military		Govt. workers:	21.0%
		Veterans/active duty:	13.6%		

GDP would grow about 2.5 percent that year, as well as in 2016, and that unemployment would stay below 4.0 percent.

So far removed from any other land, Hawaii has a particularly fragile ecology, with a profusion of bird and plant species that are vulnerable to invasive predators. Airliners' wheel housings are routinely inspected for the brown tree snakes that have killed off

Voter Turnout	
2013 Total Citizen 18+	1,000,863
2014 Highest Statewide Turnout	366,125
2014 Turnout as % CVAP	36.6%
2012 Turnout as % CVAP	43.9%

Legislature		
Senate:	24D	1R
House:	44D	7R

most of the birds in Guam. The oceans around the islands are vulnerable too, and a source of controversy. In 2006, President George W. Bush issued an order dedicating the Northwestern Hawaiian Islands Marine National Monument, which covers an expanse of ocean plus a few uninhabited islands that is 1,400 miles long and 100 miles wide. The area contains 70 percent of the nation's tropical, shallow-water coral reefs, some 7,000 marine species (one-quarter found nowhere else), the endangered Hawaiian monk seal population and threatened species of predatory fish (sharks, groupers, and jacks). Hawaii has great potential for wind and geothermal energy and the federal waters off Oahu are the site of a $1.6 billion offshore wind energy project that could be operational in about five years. That could come in handy. According to the U.S. Energy Information Association, in 2012, Hawaii imported 93 percent of the energy it consumed and state law mandates achieving 30 percent renewable energy by 2020 and 70 percent by 2040. Hawaii also had the highest electricity prices in the nation in 2013. But transmitting energy through the turbulent channels between the Neighbor Islands to Oahu, where 70 percent of Hawaiians live, poses severe difficulties. And nature is not always benign. The Kilauea volcano on the Big Island started erupting in 1983 and hasn't stopped. Its slow moving lava flow has consumed a cemetery and houses, and geologists closely monitor Kilauea for signs of a potential larger seismic event.

It wasn't an earthquake, but in 2015, Hawaii shut down its state-run health insurance exchange and transitioned to the federal system because of insufficient enrollment. The state spent at least $130 million on the project, but it may have been a victim of its own success: Hawaii has one of the lowest uninsured populations in the country and its citizens lead the nation in terms of life expectancy. It also has a 1974 law that requires employers to provide health insurance to employees who work more than 20 hours a week and caps employee contributions at 1.5 percent of their salary. According to Kaiser Health News, the Hawaii Health Connector was the nation's most expensive exchange costing $23,899 per 2014 enrollee. In 2015, Hawaii also became the first state to raise the legal age of smoking to 21, reflecting its health-conscious mores and an unusual faith that government knows what's best for its citizens. While wellness is not a big problem, homelessness is. With its tight and very expensive housing market, Hawaii has the highest per capita number of homeless people of any state in the country according to a 2015 report by the National Alliance to End Homelessness. Honolulu spends up to $15,000 a week cleaning out tent cities that have sprung up around Oahu, and it has passed an ordinance prohibiting people from sitting or lying down on sidewalks in Waikiki. The city converted old transit buses into mobile homeless shelters to help cope with the crisis. And Hawaii is losing much of its famed beachfront, which has drawn tourists from around the world. The U.S. Geological Survey estimates that chronic erosion is affecting 70 percent of the beaches on Oahu, Kauai and Maui, and a 2015 study by the University of Hawaii found that if current trends continue, the shoreline could recede by an average of 20 feet by 2050. Parts of Waikiki Beach, the birthplace of modern surfing where Olympic athlete Duke Kahanamoku introduced the longboard more than a century ago, are barely ribbons of carbonate sand today. Even in paradise there are problems.

Presidential Politics Hawaii's presidential voting over the years has been the product of two sometimes countervailing forces. One is the Islands' historic preference for the Democratic Party. The other is an inclination to support incumbents in a state where many of its citizens were once unjustly questioned and there is a large military presence. Unusually, it supported Ronald Reagan solidly in 1984, although it wasn't enough to help George H.W. Bush in 1992; Democrat Bill Clinton carried Hawaii 48%-37%. In

2012 Presidential Vote		
Barack Obama (D) 306,658	(71%)
Mitt Romney (R).................121,015	(28%)
2012 Presidential Caucus		
Mitt Romney (R)....................4,548	(44%)
Rick Santorum (R) 2,589	(25%)
Ron Paul (R) 1,975	(19%)
Newt Gingrich (R).................1,116	(11%)
2008 Presidential Vote		
Barack Obama (D) 325,871	(72%)
John McCain (R).................120,566	(27%)

1996 and 2000, Hawaii voted 57%-32% for Clinton and 56%-37% for Al Gore. In 2004, October polls showed a close race, and Dick Cheney flew 8,270 miles to appear in Honolulu at 10 p.m. on the Sunday night before the election and left two hours later. Hawaii's Democratic preference prevailed, and John Kerry won 54%-45%. Almost 70 percent of Hawaii's votes come from Oahu; the rest are cast on the other Islands, which are even more Democratic-leaning than the most urban island in the archipelago. The only time in recent memory that a major Republican candidate swept all the Islands was Gov. Linda Lingle's reelection victory in 2006. A GOP White House hopeful would have to carry Honolulu County (Oahu) by at least five-to-six percentage points to offset the Democratic vote on the outer Islands.

In 2008, the Democratic presidential candidate was for the first time a native of Hawaii. Barack Obama vacationed in Hawaii for a week before the Democratic National Convention, and he returned to the state just before the election to see his ailing grandmother, who died two days before the election. He carried Hawaii 72%-27%, winning in almost every precinct, his best showing in any state. As president, Obama has taken his Christmas vacations in Hawaii, and he had no trouble winning, 71%-28%, in 2012.

Hawaii chooses presidential delegates by caucus. In 2008, Hawaii Democrats gathered on February 19, and more than 37,000 voters turned out, compared with just 4,000 in 2004. The Obama campaign stressed the candidate's Hawaiian heritage, and his 76%-24% win was one of a string of victories in February that stretched his pledged delegate lead over Hillary Clinton and propelled him to the nomination. The Republican caucuses took place on May 17, long after Arizona's John McCain had clinched the party's nomination. In 2012, 10,228 Republicans caucused on March 13, and Mitt Romney led with 45 percent of the votes to 25 percent for Rick Santorum, 19 percent for Ron Paul and 11 percent for Newt Gingrich.

Congressional Districts Hawaii has two congressional districts: The 1st includes urban Honolulu and extends westward to Pearl Harbor and the rural area beyond. The 2nd includes the rest of Oahu and the Neighbor Islands. The 1st District, the only Asian-majority district in the country, is the slightly less

114th Congress Lineup	
0 R	2 D
113th Congress Lineup	
0 R	2 D

Democratic of the two and elected a Republican in 1986, 1988, and briefly in 2010, when Honolulu Councilman Charles Djou won an unusual special election against split Democratic opposition. The lower-income 2nd District has elected only Democrats since it was created in 1971.

Timing and ambition tend to overstep boundaries in Hawaii: In November 2010, Democrat Colleen Hanabusa unseated Djou in the 1st District although she lived in the 2nd; in 2012, both major candidates for the open 2nd District lived in the 1st. In 2014, Hanabusa gave up the seat in her unsuccessful primary challenge to Sen. Brian Schatz. Djou made another bid for the open 1st District, but fell narrowly short against Mark Takai—another military veteran who also had lengthy political experience.

Governor

David Ige (D)

Elected 2014, term expires 2018, 1st term; b. January 15, 1957, Honolulu; U of HI-Manoa, B.A., 1979; M.A., 1985; Buddhist; married (Dawn); 3 children.

Elected Office: HI Senate, District 16, 1994-2014; U.S. House, 1985 (appointed by gov. Ariyoshi to fill vacant seat).

Professional Career: Electronics engineer, Pacific Analysis Corp.; senior administrator, General Telephone & Electronics Hawaiian Telephone, 1981-99; project manager, Pihana Pacific, LLC., 1999-2001; vice president of Engineering for Net Enterprise, Inc., 2001-2002; project manager, R.A. Ige and Associates, Inc., 2003.

Office: Executive Chambers State Capitol, Honolulu, 96813, 808-586-0034; Fax: 808-586-0006; Website: governor.hawaii.gov.

Election Results

2014 general	David Ige (D)	181,065	(50%)
	J. "Duke" Aiona (R)	135,742	(37%)
	Mufi Hannemann (I)	42,925	(12%)
2014 primary	David Ige (D)	157,050	(67%)
	Neil Abercrombie (D)	73,507	(32%)

Democrat David Ige defeated Republican J. "Duke" Aiona and independent Mufi Hannemann in November 2014 to become Hawaii's eighth governor, after a dramatic primary upset of incumbent Gov. Neil Abercrombie. He took the office vowing to improve transparency and communication in government, standards he won acclaim for as a state legislator, displayed as a candidate, but didn't always maintain as governor.

Born and raised in Pearl City, Ige is the fifth of six boys of Japanese-American parents who settled in Hawaii a generation earlier. His father, Tokio, won a Purple Heart and a Bronze Star serving in the famous 100th Battalion, 442nd Regimental Combat Team of the U.S. Army during World War II, which was made up mostly of sons of Japanese immigrants. After studying engineering and business, his son launched a successful career as an electrical engineer and project manager, working on information technology and telecommunications. Ige wasn't even planning to enter politics in 1985, when Democratic Gov. George Ariyoshi, who was looking for smart young professionals to appoint to vacant seats in the legislature, tapped Ige, who had been recommended by local activists in Pearl City. Ige wasn't even a member of the Democratic Party when Ariyoshi reached out to him. He went on to win reelection four times before advancing to the state Senate in 1994, all while continuing his regular employment.

He brought a novice's sensitivities to his new job and recoiled when he quickly came to understand that the legislative process is often an inside game where knowledge is not always shared and the public is often excluded from decision making. That led to Ige's focus on improving communication with voters (and among his own colleagues) and their access to information. He also joined a faction of lawmakers who were policy oriented and committed to reform called the "Chess Club," and he set about ways to increase citizen-involvement with the legislature. Drawing on his experience in the private sector, he often applied technology to the tasks of meeting his goals. Ige took the lead in moving the Senate towards using less paper, and perhaps more importantly, posting draft legislation, hearing notices, and budget documents online. To help promote greater awareness of the legislature, he set up an electronic network to involve hundreds of high school students in the legislative process through a primitive form of videoconferencing. Ige wanted to take politics out of the backroom, and he is credited by colleagues with the now common practice in the legislature of holding committee votes in public, not in a closed session.

Ige built a reputation as a well-studied policy expert, working on issues ranging from education reform to auto insurance to land conservation. His years of committee work paid off when he rose to chair the state Senate Ways and Means Committee in 2009. In addition to helping guide Hawaii's recent fiscal turnaround—thanks to a tourism surge combined with budget cuts—Ige introduced legislation to shore up pension and health care plans for state retirees so that Hawaii would not run into a Detroit-style crunch.

When Ige announced his gubernatorial bid in 2013, it was widely seen as a David and Goliath contest. Abercrombie had presided over the state's economic revival, with unemployment dropping to 4.4 percent and the state budget swinging into the black by more than $800 million in 2013. Abercrombie outspent Ige by more than 10-to-1, and President Barack Obama, along with most other prominent Hawaii Democrats, endorsed him. What Abercrombie didn't expect was the voters' pushback against his personal style, which was widely viewed as confrontational. And in his quest to fix the state's budget shortfall, he seemed to antagonize everyone in the state, including some of his own supporters. Many Asian Americans also remained unhappy with his decision to appoint Lt. Gov. Brian Schatz, rather than Rep. Colleen Hanabusa, to fill the late Sen. Daniel Inouye's seat in 2012. To address the state's budget crisis, Abercrombie initially proposed taxing pension income, as most other states do, with exemptions for less well-off retirees. The legislature rejected that idea, but Abercrombie enraged Hawaii's powerful public sector unions when he proposed ending state reimbursements for federal Medicare Part B premiums for retired public workers that had been part of the benefits plan the state had established to try to hold down retiree healthcare costs. Asked by reporters if he anticipated and understood the critical reaction from union leaders, Abercrombie responded: "I am the governor. I'm not your pal. I'm not your counselor. I am the governor." Abercrombie also alienated teachers when he imposed a five percent pay cut on teachers after contract talks broke down. They would later get a raise, but Abercrombie infuriated them again when he called for a constitutional amendment to allow public funds to be spent on private preschool. It was little surprise when the Hawaii State Teachers Association, which had backed Abercrombie in his primary in 2010, decided to endorse Ige in 2014. And then, Abercrombie questioned the authenticity of the letter that Inouye wrote to the governor from his deathbed requesting that Abercrombie appoint Hanabusa. He quickly apologized for his comments, saying he regretted causing any disrespect to the Inouye family. Ige played up his image of quiet competence and argued in an understated manner that Abercrombie wasn't leading effectively and didn't have the confidence of legislators or the people to govern well. His low-key manner and the reputation for collaboration and openness in the legislature convinced Hawaii Democrats to give him that trust and he won a shocker, defeating Abercrombie in the August primary by a staggering 35 percentage points—the first time that a sitting Hawaii governor had lost a primary since 1962. Ige's next challenge was making sure that Hannemann didn't draw away too many centrist voters who would otherwise vote Democratic. Projecting his image for openness and communication, Ige participated in 15 debates with his Republican opponent, Aiona, when he might have been tempted to let the state's strong Democratic leanings carry him to victory. Ige, Aiona, and independent Hannemann, jousted over how to deal with Hawaii's homeless population, the state's troubled health exchange, the environment and economic growth. In the late summer and early fall, polls showed a fairly tight race. This wasn't surprising, given that Aiona had more name recognition than typical Republican nominees, having served as Gov. Linda Lingle's lieutenant governor and run for the state's top job before, albeit unsuccessfully, against Abercrombie in 2010. But by the closing weeks of the campaign, Ige consolidated his lead and ended up beating Aiona about a dozen percentage points.

Once in office, Ige broke with the tendency of most of his predecessors to govern as the *ali'i nui* (the term for a great or grand chief from Hawaii's early days) and began meeting every other week with the leaders of the state House of Representatives and Senate. Ige said he felt that was important because he could remember from his days in the legislature that he was often disappointed in how the governor would implement the measures passed by the lawmakers. But his ties to legislators didn't save his nomination of Carleton Ching to lead the Department of Land and Natural Resources, the state agency charged with protecting Hawaii's wondrous and delicate habitat. Ching was a controversial choice because he had spent 12 prior years as the chief lobbyist for Castle & Cooke, an original Big Five member that was still one of the state's biggest developers. Critics said that given his background, Ching would face numerous conflicts of interest if approved. But even after the Senate's Water and Land Committee voted 5-2 against Ching, Ige pressed ahead. Only minutes before the full Senate was to vote on the nomination did Ige pull it to avoid what appeared to be a likely narrow defeat. The governor said he didn't want to put Ching and his family through a potentially embarrassing floor vote. Some of Ige's closest former allies in the Senate and the "Chess Club" who, with Ige, had always maintained that votes should not be decided by friendship were among those who said they couldn't support Ching. Others never understood why Ige pushed the nomination forward after it was rejected in committee.

During the biennial budget process, Ige and the leaders in the legislature decided with little fanfare or public discussion to allow the temporary hike in the state's top income tax rate to expire. It had been passed to help balance the state's books at the depths of the Great Recession. The move represented as much as a 2.75 percentage point drop in the top rate for Hawaii's joint filers who made more than $400,000 a year. There was some irony in this move since it was the Democratic-controlled legislature in 2009 that overrode then GOP Gov. Lingle's veto of the bill that originally imposed the temporary tax increase. Ige secured a $26 billion biennial budget that generally conformed to his spending proposals. The most far-reaching measure he approved early in his first term was legislation that sets the most ambitious clean energy goal in the country: to make Hawaii self-sufficient in energy and meet 100 percent of its needs with renewable sources. For a state that imports roughly $5 billion of oil that could have enormous consequences. In signing the legislation Ige declared: "Making the transition to renewable, indigenous resources for power generation will allow us to keep more of that money at home, thereby improving our economy, environment and energy security."

Senior Senator

Brian Schatz (D)

Appointed Dec. 2012, term expires 2017, 1st term; b. Oct. 20, 1972, Ann Arbor, MI; Pomona Col., B.A. 1994; Jewish; married (Linda); 2 children.

Elected Office: HI House, 1998-2006; HI lt. gov., 2010-12.

Professional Career: CEO, Helping Hands HI, 2004-10; Chmn., HI Democratic Party, 2008-10.

DC Office: 722 HSOB, 20510, 202-224-3934; Fax: 202-228-1153; Website: schatz.senate.gov.

State Offices: Honolulu, 808-523-2061.

Committees: *Appropriations:* Defense; Labor, HHS; Education, & Related Agencies; Legislative Branch (RMM); Military Construction, Veterans Affairs, & Related Agencies; Transportation, Housing & Urban Development, & Related Agencies; *Commerce, Science & Transportation:* Aviation Operations, Safety & Security; Communications, Technology & the Internet; Oceans, Atmosphere, Fisheries, & Coast Guard; Space, Science, & Competitiveness; Surface Transportation & Merchant Marine Infrastructure, Safety, & Security. *Ethics. Indian Affairs.*

Group Ratings

	ADA	ACLU	AFL-CIO	LCV	ITI	COC	HAFA	ACU	CFG	FRC
2014	60%	93%	–	60%	100%	50%	0%	0%	0%	0%
2013	100%	C	100%	100%	C	38%	C	4%	0%	C

National Journal Ratings

	2013 LIB	—	2013 CONS
Economic	93%	—	0%
Social	73%	—	0%
Foreign	71%	—	0%
Composite	90%	—	11%

Key Votes of the 113th Congress

1. Sandy storm spending	Y	5. Student Loan Rates	Y	9. Bipartisan Budget Deal	Y
2. Chuck Hagel Confirmation	Y	6. Employee Non-Discrim'n Act	Y	10. Farm Bill Conference Rept.	Y
3. Gun Background Checks	Y	7. Senate Vote on Judgeships	N	11. Unempl. Comp. Extension	Y
4. Immigration Reform	Y	8. Defense Dept. Spending	Y	12. Keystone Pipeline	N

Election Results

2014 general	Brian Schatz (D)	246,770	(67%)	$5,156,058	$673,150
	Cam Cavasso (R)	97,983	(27%)	$539,273	
	Michael Kokoski (Lib)	8,936	(2%)		
2014 primary	Brian Schatz (D)	115,445	(49%)		
	Colleen Hanabusa (D)	113,663	(49%)		

Democrat Brian Schatz, the Senate's fourth-youngest member, was appointed on Dec. 26, 2012 to fill the unexpired term of Democrat Daniel Inouye, who died nine days earlier, despite Inouye's deathbed wish that then-Rep. Colleen Hanabusa replace him. He then won reelection to a full term in 2014, narrowly defeating Hanabusa in the Democratic primary. An ardent liberal with a particular interest in environmental issues, Schatz had been Hawaii's lieutenant governor, Democratic Party chair, and a state House member.

Schatz was born in Ann Arbor Michigan, one of two identical-twin sons of a cardiologist who worked at the University of Michigan hospital. (His brother, Steve, runs the Hawaii Department of Education's Office of Strategic Reform.) When he was 2 years old, his father accepted a job at the University of Hawaii and the family moved to the state. After high school, Schatz went to Pomona College and received a degree in philosophy. He returned to Hawaii after college and worked for a nonprofit organization.

In 1998, Schatz was elected at age 26 to represent urban Honolulu in the 25th District in the state legislature. He rose to chair the Economic Development Committee and was appointed majority whip. When Rep. Ed Case decided to challenge Democrat Daniel Akaka for the Senate in 2006, Schatz became one of 10 candidates in the Democratic primary for Case's seat. He lost to Mazie Hirono, who at the time was lieutenant governor and who is now his Senate colleague. Schatz got just 7 percent of the vote and finished sixth.

He then turned his attention to helping Barack Obama, another young politician who grew up in Hawaii and who shared Schatz's high school alma mater, the prestigious Punahou School. Schatz joined other Democrats in 2006 in founding a group urging Obama, then a senator from Illinois, to run for president. "For the last six years we've been governed by fear—fear of terrorists, fear of other countries, even fear of the other party ... Everyone is governing by fear, and Barack Obama changes all of that," Schatz told the Associated Press. "He wants to govern the United States by hope." Schatz ran for and won the state Democratic Party chairmanship in 2008, and served as Obama's Hawaii campaign spokesman that year.

Schatz announced his candidacy for lieutenant governor in January 2010 and ran with Neil Abercrombie, who had served 10 terms in the House before seeking the governorship. The campaign outraised GOP rival, Lt. Gov. James "Duke" Aiona, by a 2-to-1 margin and won by 17 percentage points. As lieutenant governor, Schatz worked on energy and climate issues and helped pass same-sex civil unions in the state.

After the November 2012 election, the 88-year-old Sen. Inouye fell ill, and just before he died, he urged Abercrombie to appoint Colleen Hanabusa as his replacement. But Abercrombie, who had a well-publicized rift with Inouye and much of the state's Democratic establishment, instead chose his ally Schatz. In announcing his selection, he said Schatz "has demonstrated all of the qualities Hawaii could ask for in a senator: respect for our traditions and a strong sense of values, remarkably strong character and problem-solving capacities, and above all an abiding love for and commitment to the people of our state." Schatz traveled to Washington on Air Force One with Obama, who had been spending his Christmas vacation in Hawaii.

Schatz's appointment made him the state's senior senator by just a few days. He was appointed in late December 2012, and began his service immediately. The state's other senator, Hirono, was first elected in November 2012 to replace the retiring Sen. Daniel Akaka, but her service did not begin until January 2013, giving Schatz a small head start.

In the Senate, Schatz was tied with New York's Chuck Schumer and Connecticut's Chris Murphy as the Senate's most-liberal member in 2013, according to *National Journal* rankings. He became especially involved on climate change, joining a group of House and Senate liberals in 2013 on a draft carbon-pricing bill. In March 2014 he also helped organize an all-night "talkathon" to try to draw more attention to the dangers of climate change, and as a member of the Energy and Natural Resources Committee introduced a number of bills relating to energy efficiency and green technologies. He also worked on bills to give federal civilian workers a raise and to improve street design to reduce traffic accidents.

Schatz also tended to a variety of Hawaii-related issues. On the Commerce, Science and Transportation Committee, he was involved in creating a new subcommittee on tourism policy, which he chaired. He also introduced a measure to study the creation of more national parks in the state. The Energy Committee in June 2014 passed his bill to increase grant funding for water conservation and drought projects that would make Hawaii projects eligible for the Bureau of Reclamation's WaterSMART grants.

Hanabusa, after weighing a run against Abercrombie, challenged Schatz in the Democratic primary, seeking to depict him as inexperienced. She was backed by the Inouye and Akaka political network and EMILY's List, which backs female Democrats who support abortion rights. Schatz lined up support from the Democratic establishment, including Obama, then-Senate Majority Leader Harry Reid, and progressive and environmental groups. And he out-raised Hanabusa, collecting $4.9 million to her $2.9 million.

The race broke along ethnic lines, as Hawaii's primaries often do, with the white Schatz winning with liberal white voters and the Japanese-American Hanabusa performing well with ethnic Hawaiians and Asian-Americans.

Most polling showed Schatz with a lead, but as often happens in Hawaii's difficult-to-forecast environment, most polls proved themselves wildly off the mark. After the August 9 election, which came on the heels of a tropical storm that damaged parts of Hawaii and prevented two precincts from voting, Schatz held a tenuous 1,635 vote lead. State election officials said that a make-up election would be held there the following Friday; Hanabusa filed a legal challenge contending those areas were insufficiently recovered to have voters cast ballots, but a judge struck her challenge. After those precincts voted Schatz's lead stood at 1,769 votes out of a statewide total of more than 237,000 ballots cast. After that, his election in November was a cakewalk.

Since winning a term in his own right Schatz has continued to focus on environmental issues, liberal causes and Hawaii's parochial concerns, using his perch on the Appropriations Committee to fight for money for the state and becoming the ranking Democrat on the Senate Commerce subcommittee on Communications, Technology and the Internet. In January 2015, his amendment to the Keystone XL oil pipeline bill put lawmakers on record on whether they believe "climate change is real and human activity significantly contributes" to it. The amendment, the first Senate vote on climate change in eight years, got 50 votes for it including five from Republicans. He also backed debt-free college and net neutrality legislation, causes popular with progressives.

Junior Senator

Mazie Hirono (D)

Elected 2012, term expires 2019, 1st term; b. Nov. 3, 1947, Fukushima, Japan; U. of HI, B.A. 1970, Georgetown U., J.D. 1978; Buddhist; married (Leighton Kim Oshima); 1 child.

Elected Office: U.S. House, 2006-12; HI lt.gov., 1994-2002; HI House, 1980-94.

Professional Career: Deputy HI atty. gen., 1978-80; Practicing lawyer, 1984-88.

DC Office: 330 HSOB, 20510, 202-224-6361; Website: hirono.senate.gov.

State Offices: Honolulu, 808-522-8970.

Committees: *Armed Services:* Airland; Readiness & Management Support; Seapower (RMM); *Energy & Natural Resources:* Energy; Public Lands, Forest, & Mining (RMM). *Intelligence. Small Business & Entrepreneurship. Veterans' Affairs.*

Group Ratings

	ADA	ACLU	AFL-CIO	LCV	ITI	COC	HAFA	ACU	CFG	FRC
2014	90%	100%	–	80%	100%	38%	0%	4%	7%	0%
2013	100%	C	100%	100%	C	38%	C	0%	0%	C

National Journal Ratings

	2013 LIB	—	2013 CONS
Economic	92%	—	7%
Social	73%	—	0%
Foreign	71%	—	0%
Composite	88%	—	12%

Key Votes of the 113th Congress

1. Sandy storm spending	Y	5. Student Loan Rates	N	9. Bipartisan Budget Deal	Y
2. Chuck Hagel Confirmation	Y	6. Employee Non-Discrim'n Act	Y	10. Farm Bill Conference Rept.	Y
3. Gun Background Checks	Y	7. Senate Vote on Judgeships	N	11. Unempl. Comp. Extension	Y
4. Immigration Reform	Y	8. Defense Dept. Spending	Y	12. Keystone Pipeline	N

Election Results

2012 general	Mazie Hirono (D) 269,489	(63%)	$5,644,499	$232,692	$585,000
	Linda Lingle (R)....................... 160,994	(37%)	$5,839,282	$1,031,875	$548,596
2012 primary	Mazie Hirono (D) 134,745	(58%)			
	Ed Case (D) 95,553	(41%)			

Prior winning percentages: House: 2010 (72%), 2008 (76%), 2006 (61%)

Democrat Mazie Hirono, the first Buddhist ever to serve in the Senate, won her seat in the 2012 elections and is Hawaii's junior senator by a few days. She succeeded Sen. Daniel Akaka, who retired after serving three full terms.

Hirono was born in Fukushima, Japan, and immigrated to Hawaii just before her eighth birthday with her mother, who fled an abusive husband with alcohol and gambling problems. As a child, she shared a single bed in a boardinghouse room with her mother and older brother, and at age 10 went to work to support the family. She mastered English in public schools and became a naturalized citizen in 1959, the year that Hawaii became a state. She's long emphasized her personal story on the campaign trail, arguing that her family's hardships made her realize the importance of government help. "I never forget where I came from or who I fight for and why," she says in her Senate website's autobiography.

After graduating from the University of Hawaii, Hirono got involved in politics by working on state House campaigns. She then earned a law degree from Georgetown University and worked in the Hawaii attorney general's office. She ran for the state House in 1980 and won, holding the seat for 14 years. In 1994, she was elected to the first of two terms as lieutenant governor. She ran against Republican Linda Lingle for governor in 2002, but her campaign was poorly organized and was undermined by Democratic corruption scandals and other problems. She lost, 52 percent to 47 percent.

Hirono formed a political action committee to assist state-level Democratic women supporting abortion rights. She got her chance to become an elected official again in 2006, when Rep. Ed Case challenged Akaka in the Democratic primary. She ran for Case's House seat, and emerged atop a 10-candidate Democratic primary field. She then easily beat GOP state Sen. Bob Hogue in a district that had never elected a Republican, becoming the first Asian immigrant woman to serve in Congress.

She had a solidly liberal voting record and a relatively low profile in the House. Her enthusiastic support of the Democratic agenda led the Hawaii *Tribune-Herald* to say, in endorsing her in 2008, "We wish she'd be a little more independent and less partisan." Like the late Sen. Daniel Inouye of Hawaii, she was a staunch defender of earmarking to benefit the state, and in fiscal 2010, she ranked third among all House members in accumulating special-request spending items, according to Taxpayers for Common Sense. She has said that each of the projects she requests has "an intrinsic value" and can often yield benefits far beyond their local scope.

When Akaka announced his retirement, Hirono was considered the early Democratic favorite. Republicans landed their best possible candidate as well when Lingle, after months of deliberation, agreed to run. She initially made the race competitive, campaigning on her successful record as a moderate governor and stressing that she wouldn't be beholden to Senate GOP leaders. She ran an ad criticizing Hirono for not getting any of her own bills signed into law. But Democrats eviscerated Lingle for her praise of then-Alaska Gov. Sarah Palin during her speech introducing her as the 2008 GOP vice presidential nominee at the Republican National Convention. Lingle said she would vote for Republican presidential nominee Mitt Romney, which Hawaii political analysts said didn't play well in Obama's home state.

Hirono argued that Lingle would vote with Republicans and that a vote for Lingle potentially could put the GOP in the majority, which she claimed would lead to the repeal of Obama's health care reform law, provide more tax cuts for the wealthy, and threaten Social Security and Medicare. Bringing the argument closer to home, she also asserted that a Republican majority would threaten the influence of Inouye, the Appropriations Committee's top Democrat and a beloved icon to Hawaiians. Hirono opened a double-digit lead by early October and went on to win, 63 percent to 37 percent.

She is Hawaii's junior senator. Senior Sen. Inouye died in office shortly after the November election, on December 17, 2012. Democratic Gov. Neil Abercrombie appointed his lieutenant governor, Brian Schatz, as Inouye's immediate replacement. Schatz started his service in the Senate in late December, and so surpassed Hirono in seniority by a few days because her Senate term did not begin until early January 2013, when the new Congress was sworn in.

In the Senate Hirono has kept up her low profile, spending much of her time on issues that directly impact Hawaii, as well as national security and veterans' issues. She serves on the Armed Services, Energy, Intelligence and Veterans' Affairs Committees, is the Democratic ranking member on the Senate Armed Service Committee's Seapower subcommittee, and has led the push to give Filipinos whose parents fought for the U.S. during World War II an easier path to citizenship. She's also sponsored patent reform legislation.

FIRST DISTRICT

Mark Takai (D)

Elected 2014, 1st term; b. July 1, 1967, Honolulu; U of HI, B.A., 1990; U of HI, M.P.H., 1993; Protestant; married (Sami); 2 children.

Military Career: HI Army Natl. Guard, 1999-present.

Elected Office: HI House (District 34), 1994-2012; HI House (District 33), 2012-2014.

Professional Career: Publications Coordinator, U of HI; Health Educator, Dept. of Health; Deputy Surgeon, HI Army Natl. Guard; Business Owner, Pacific First Health Solutions.

DC Office: 422 CHOB, 20515, 202-225-2726, Fax: 202-225-0688; Website: takai.house.gov.

State Offices: Honolulu, 808-533-0133.

Committees: *Armed Services:* Strategic Forces; *Natural Resources:* Energy & Mineral Resources; Federal Lands.

Election Results

2014 general	Mark Takai (D)	93,360	(52%)	$1,771,572	$454,409	$278,160
	Charles Djou (R)	86,419	(48%)	$1,013,176		$293,604
2014 primary	Mark Takai (D)	52,736	(45%)			
	Donna Kim (D)	33,678	(28%)			
	Stanley Chang (D)	12,135	(10%)			
	Ikaika Anderson (D)	7,937	(7%)			

Population		Race and Ethnicity		Income	
Total:	702,026	Asian	50.0%	Median income:	$72,302
Urban:	62.6%	White	15.9%		*(56 of 435)*
Suburban:	37.4%	Latino	7.8%	Under $50,000	32.5%
Rural:	0.0%	Pac. Island	7.3%	$50,000-$99,999:	33.2%
Land area:	249	Two races	16.6%	$100,000-$199,999:	26.8%
Pop/sq. mi.:	2,818.2	White Ethnic	10.9%	$200,000 or more:	7.5%
Born in state:	53.3%			Poverty Rate	8.9%
		Education			
Age Groups		H.S. grad or less:	34.5%	**Work**	
Under 18:	20.4%	Some college:	30.6%	White collar:	36.0%
18 to 34:	24.7%	College degree, 4 yr.:	22.9%	Blue collar:	46.7%
35 to 64:	38.1%	Post-grad study:	11.9%	Sales and service:	17.4%
Over 64:	16.8%			Govt. workers:	22.6%
		Military			
		Veterans/active duty:	14.7%		

Honolulu Metro

The landmarks for visitors to Honolulu are the Joint Base Pearl Harbor-Hickam military facility, the USS *Arizona* monument in Pearl Harbor, the downtown area, with its wondrously Victorian Iolani Palace, and, of course, Waikiki, with its 40-story hotels rising within a few feet of each other. This part of Hawaii is tightly packed with people living between the 3,000-foot Koolau Range and the beaches and harbor, where tropical bungalows and garden apartments house Hawaiians of all incomes. Behind New York, San Francisco and Los

Angeles, Honolulu is the densest metropolitan area in the nation. Hawaii's largest shopping centers and its state university are located here. Neighborhoods where the rich overlook the ocean are wedged next to poor enclaves where residents are crammed onto clogged streets. Hawaii's topography jams cars onto just a few freeways and avenues, where traffic slows during rush hour and the *aloha* spirit is sorely tested. But hope may be on the way for relief of traffic congestion. The Honolulu Authority for Rapid Transportation is working on a 20-mile elevated rail line—a first for the islands—that will serve downtown and outlying communities. The four-car trains will include racks for bicycles and surfboards. As of March 2015, costs had increased to $6 billion, and service for the first 10 miles was scheduled for 2018.

High taxes plus high land and utility costs have limited growth. The recession hit here early, resulting in declining hotel occupancy. Homelessness grew, and Aloha Airlines went bankrupt, ending its passenger service in 2008. But the Honolulu area weathered the recession better than most U.S. cities. Its unemployment rate in March 2010 was only 5.6%, below the 9-10% common in many cities at that time, and it fell to 3.4% in December 2014. The military remains an important presence on Oahu, even as the Naval Base at Pearl Harbor and Hickam Air Force Base merged in 2010. The base still operates Boeing's C-17 Globemaster III cargo jets. Honolulu is also key to Hawaii's roaring tourism industry. In 2014, Hawaii attracted an all-time record of 8.3 million visitors. Hawaiian Airlines has non-stop flights from Honolulu to several cities on the mainland. In another significant step, a local business plans completion in 2017 of the Seawater Air Conditioning project, which is designed to produce enough chilled fresh water to supply roughly half of downtown Honolulu's cooling needs.

Honolulu anchors the 1st Congressional District of Hawaii. It is an area of well-established neighborhoods. With little land left to develop on the southern part of Oahu, it is growing less rapidly than the rest of the state. Politically, the neighborhoods around Honolulu's downtown and the university campus are middle and lower-income and usually Democratic. To the west, around the harbor, are many military families in modest neighborhoods who vote for candidates from both parties. To the east, around Diamond Head and the Kahala and Koko Head beach areas, is higher-income territory that often votes Republican. Developers have explored plans to combat beach erosion at Waikiki, which is mostly man-made. For the less fortunate, the city has planned a new homeless site on Sand Island off the southern shore of Oahu near the international airport. The island was used as an internment camp for Japanese during World War II.

Asians are 55% of the population in Honolulu. Favorite-son Barack Obama, who was photographed bodysurfing at Sandy Beach during his first presidential campaign, got 70% of the vote in Honolulu County in 2008 and 69% in 2012. Otherwise, the district has become competitive.

Mark Takai (D)

Mark Takai, an Iraq War veteran, defeated a veteran of the Afghanistan war to keep the 1st District in Democratic hands following the move by Rep. Colleen Hanabusa to run unsuccessfully for the Senate. Takai won an unexpectedly close race for a seat in the Hawaiian delegation, which has experienced upheaval in the past few years.

Voter Turnout	
2013 Total Citizen 18+	498,520
2014 House Turnout	179,844
2014 Turnout as % CVAP	36.1%
2012 Turnout as % CVAP	44.1%

Takai was born in Honolulu and excelled at Pearl City High School as an All-American swimmer. He earned both his bachelor's degree in political science and a master's in public health from the University of Hawaii (Manoa), where he was a Western Athletic Conference champion swimmer. He was elected to the state House in 1994 and has served in the Hawaii Army National Guard since 1999, most recently as a lieutenant colonel. Takai took part in Operation Iraqi Freedom in 2009.

His experience in the military led Takai to focus heavily on veterans' issues, including the education of military children and homelessness among his fellow vets. In the legislature, he helped win approval of the Veterans Court, which combined the efforts of state courts with federal Veterans Affairs social services. He created the Hawaii Medal of Honor to recognize the state's fallen military personnel and their families. He was president of the Hawaii Army National Guard in 2012-13.

Takai sought the seat when Hanabusa challenged Sen. Brian Schatz. He won a seven-candidate primary in August over Senate President Donna Mercado Kim 43%-27%, and headed into the general election against Republican Charles Djou. A major in the Army Reserve, Djou had briefly served in Congress, winning a 2010 special election to fill the House seat of Democrat Neil Abercrombie, who had resigned to run for governor. Hanabusa won that general election 53%-47%. Djou challenged her again in 2012, interrupting his campaign for six months to deploy to Afghanistan, but lost 55%-45%.

Both Takai and Djou stressed their respective military experiences on the campaign trail. Although they disagreed on many policy issues, each styled himself as a centrist. In a debate, Djou said that while he felt President Barack Obama took too long to develop a strategy to deal with the Islamic State terrorist group, he favored the president's request to train and arm Syrian rebels and Iraqi forces. Takai said he would have voted no, adding, "the war in the Middle East, from my perspective, is really not our war." On domestic issues, Djou argued for lower taxes and less bureaucracy; Takai said that government is "a facilitator … that provides that necessary infrastructure."

Takai had a fundraising advantage of $1.8 million to $1.1 million. But he spent about one-third of his funds in the competitive Democratic primary, while Djou did not face a GOP contest. Neither national party directed much money to its nominee. That may have been a mistake by the Republicans. Takai won 51.9%-48.1% for Djou.

In the House, Takai joined the Armed Services and Natural Resources committees. He stated his objective that Hawaii should stay at the center of Obama's planned "defense rebalance." In a March 2015 hearing with Secretary of Defense Ashton Carter, he asked for more specifics on the administration's request to authorize the use of military force against the Islamic State. "I have serious questions regarding the scope of operations that we are getting into with the vague terms contained in the proposal," he said. Takai's first bill was designed to help the aging Filipino veterans from World War II unite with their families. He also called for an increase to $115 million in the support for Hawaii to serve as a host for regional immigrants.

2012 Presidential Vote		
Barack Obama (D) 151,023	(70%)
Mitt Romney (R)...................62,875	(29%)
2008 Presidential Vote		
Barack Obama (D) 156,580	(70%)
John McCain (R)...................63,035	(28%)
Cook Partisan Voting Index: D+18		

In the suddenly very junior all-Democratic Hawaii delegation, Takai and the others faced the challenge of establishing new working relationships.

SECOND DISTRICT

Tulsi Gabbard (D)

Elected 2012, 2nd term; b. April 12, 1981, Leloaloa, Am. Sam.; HI Pacific U., B.S. 2009; Hindu; married (Abraham).

Military Career: HI Army Natl. Guard, 2003-present (Iraq, Kuwait).

Elected Office: HI House, 2002-04; Honolulu City Cncl., 2010-12.

Professional Career: Founder, Kanu Productions, 2011-present; Co-founder, Healthy Hawaii Coalition, 2000-present; Legis. aide, Sen. Daniel Akaka, 2006-07.

DC Office: 1609 LHOB, 20515, 202-225-4906; Fax: 202-225-4987; Website: gabbard.house.gov.

State Offices: Honolulu, 808-541-1986.

Committees: *Armed Services:* Readiness; Seapower & Projection Forces; *Foreign Affairs:* Asia & the Pacific; Europe, Eurasia, & Emerging Threats.

Group Ratings

	ADA	ACLU	AFL-CIO	LCV	ITI	COC	HAFA	ACU	CFG	FRC
2014	65%	77%	–	94%	60%	43%	11%	8%	6%	0%
2013	80%	C	100%	96%	C	31%	C	16%	13%	C

National Journal Ratings

	2013 LIB	—	2013 CONS
Economic	69%	—	30%
Social	63%	—	36%
Foreign	60%	—	40%
Composite	64%	—	36%

Key Votes of the 113th Congress

1. Sandy storm spending	Y	5. Student Loan Rates	Y	9. Bipartisan Budget Deal	N
2. Chuck Hagel Confirmation	Y	6. Employee Non-Discrim'n Act	N	10. Farm Bill Conference Rept.	N
3. Gun Background Checks	Y	7. Senate Vote on Judgeships	N	11. Unempl. Comp. Extension	N
4. Immigration Reform	N	8. Defense Dept. Spending	Y	12. Keystone Pipeline	Y

Election Results

2014 general	Tulsi Gabbard (D).....................142,010	(79%)	$857,985
	Kawika Crowley (R)....................33,630	(19%)	
	Joe Kent (Lib) 4,693	(2%)	
2014 primary	Tulsi Gabbard.......................unopposed		

Prior winning percentage: 2012 (81%)

Population		Race and Ethnicity		Income	
Total:	702,028	White	29.9%	Median income:	$63,176
Urban:	14.0%	Asian	24.4%		(92 of 435)
Suburban:	58.3%	Latino	10.6%	Under $50,000	39.8%
Rural:	27.6%	Pac. Island	10.5%	$50,000-$99,999:	31.2%
Land area:	5,413	Two races	22.9%	$100,000-$199,999:	23.4%
Pop/sq. mi.:	129.7	White Ethnic	16.8%	$200,000 or more:	5.6%
Born in state:	55.1%			Poverty Rate	12.8%
		Education			
Age Groups		H.S. grad or less:	38.4%	**Work**	
Under 18:	23.4%	Some college:	34.3%	White collar:	32.4%
18 to 34:	23.9%	College degree, 4 yr.:	18.5%	Blue collar:	48.4%
35 to 64:	38.2%	Post-grad study:	8.8%	Sales and service:	19.2%
Over 64:	14.5%				
		Military		Govt. workers:	19.4%
		Veterans/active duty:	13.9%		

Outer Oahu, Other Islands

The 2nd Congressional District encompasses all of the islands in the Hawaii archipelago, including most of Oahu's acreage beyond Honolulu, which belongs to the state's other congressional district. It takes in Wheeler Army Airfield and some farmlands north of Pearl Harbor, between two jagged chains of

Voter Turnout	
2013 Total Citizen 18+	502,343
2014 House Turnout	180,333
2014 Turnout as % CVAP	35.9%
2012 Turnout as % CVAP	43.8%

mountains that lift the island out of the sea. Over the mountains to the west on Oahu is the Leeward Coast—calm, sultry, and lightly populated. Over the mountains to the northeast is the Windward Coast, with many prosperous subdivisions in and around Kaneohe and Kailua. After winning reelection in 2012, President Barack Obama and the first family vacationed at a beachside compound in Kailua.

The 137 islands have distinct personalities. Hawaii, the Big Island, is the size of Connecticut and boasts huge cattle ranches; the active volcano Kilauea, which started erupting in 1983 and has not stopped since; and Mauna Kea, the highest mountain in the world if the count begins at its base far under the ocean. Tourists are told that it is bad luck to take pieces of lava home. On the north shore, with heavy rainfall and tropical foliage, is the old port of Hilo and Hawaii's macadamia nut industry; this is a blue-collar Democratic area in a natural wonderland. On the Kona Coast, where there is little rainfall and the landscape is dominated by lava flows, there are retirement condominiums, resorts and a higher-income population. In November 2014, Obama declared the lava flow a "major disaster," as it threatened to destroy the major road in the town of Pahoa. There have been suggestions to attempt to divert the flow, but such options would be costly and risky. Scientists are more concerned about the long-term prospects for the volcano.

The island of Maui, favored more by North American than Asian tourists, has dozens of luxury condominiums and upscale resorts. In 2007, a new ferry service between the islands went into operation. Residents on Maui and Kauai feared it would bring heavy traffic and despoil fish stocks and habitats. In 2009, the private company was ordered to stop service by the Hawaii Supreme Court,

2012 Presidential Vote		
Barack Obama (D) 155,635	(71%)	
Mitt Romney (R)..................58,140	(27%)	
2008 Presidential Vote		
Barack Obama (D) 169,291	(73%)	
John McCain (R)..................57,531	(25%)	
Cook Partisan Voting Index: D+21		

which ruled that the legislature erred in exempting the firm from an environmental impact statement. The company went bankrupt, and the islands were again ferry-less. Short airplane flights are the best option between the islands.

Despite strong tourism, the local housing market has remained volatile. In 2012, Hawaii had the eighth highest foreclosure rate among the 50 states. The expense of transporting fuel from the mainland contributes to some of the highest energy prices in the nation. Maui has set a goal of 100 percent renewable energy, with a target date of 2040. As of 2013, about 24 percent of electricity came from solar and wind power. A large sugar plantation has explored plans to produce biofuels. Workers on the islands are employed chiefly in tourism, the military, social services and agriculture. In recent years, there has been a push to grow crops and algae for use as biofuels. Kauai, much of which was devastated by Hurricane Iniki in 1992, is the least developed and most agricultural of the main islands. Parts of it have the nation's highest rainfall, while others seldom get wet. Its large farm workforce—a reminder of what most of Hawaii was like a century ago—makes it highly Democratic.

Overall, the district is solidly Democratic.

Tulsi Gabbard (D)

Democrat Tulsi Gabbard, first elected in 2012 after surviving a hard-fought primary, is part of a recent wave of activist young women from both parties in the House. She is one of the first two female combat veterans and the first Hindu in the House.

The fourth of five children, Gabbard was born in American Samoa and moved with her family to Hawaii at a young age. Her father, Mike Gabbard, was the Republican candidate in 2004 for the 2nd District and currently serves in the Hawaii Senate; he switched parties in 2007 because he said he would have more influence as a Democrat. Her mother, Carol Gabbard, formerly served on the state Board of Education. Both made names in Hawaii politics as strong opponents of gay marriage, a position their daughter rejects. Gabbard was home-schooled, and along with her brothers and sister, helped run a family restaurant. She graduated from Hawaii Pacific University with a bachelor's degree in business administration.

At age 19, Gabbard and her father cofounded the Healthy Hawaii Coalition, an environmental-education nonprofit that teaches elementary students about the ways humans can positively and negatively affect the environment. In 2002, Gabbard won a seat representing West Oahu in the state House. At 21, she was the youngest woman ever elected to a legislature. "A lot of people told me I was crazy and too young, but I really felt the need and passion to do more with my life and be able to make a positive impact for others," she told *National Journal*.

While serving in the legislature, she enlisted in the Hawaii Army National Guard in 2003 as a private and completed her basic training in South Carolina between legislative sessions. In 2004, while campaigning for reelection, her unit was activated for Iraq, but Gabbard was not given orders to deploy. Declaring, "no way would I stay home and watch 3,000 of my brothers and sisters deploy without me," she withdrew from the campaign and voluntarily deployed with the medical unit for 18 months.

In 2007, she went to Fort McClellan's Officer Candidate School in Alabama, becoming the first woman to graduate at the top of her class. She deployed again in 2008, to Kuwait as a military police platoon leader training counterterrorism units. Gabbard has continued to serve as a captain in the National Guard. In between tours of duty, she worked as a legislative aide to Democratic Sen. Daniel Akaka. She also indulged her longtime interest in film and television by starting her own film production company, Kanu Productions. Gabbard was elected to the Honolulu City Council in 2010. She said that her proudest accomplishments in office include helping to legalize food trucks and organizing an environmental cleanup following a landfill overflow.

When Rep. Mazie Hirono announced her run for the retiring Akaka's seat, Gabbard was the first of six Democrats to jump into the race, touting herself as a fresh voice for Washington. Her main primary opponent, who led for most of the race, was former Honolulu Mayor Mufi Hannemann, who had run for governor in 2010. She ran on investing in alternative energy as a way of diversifying Hawaii's tourism-dependent economy, as well as making the state's energy supply more secure. Hannemann held a 3-to-1 lead in a February 2012 poll, but Gabbard steadily closed the gap. Still, her 55%-34% victory over the experienced Hannemann surprised observers. In the general, she got 81% against Kawika Crowley, a Republican handyman who was living out of his car and whose longtime issue has been the repeal of smoking bans in public places.

In the House, Gabbard got a seat on the Armed Services Committee, a useful assignment for a lawmaker from Hawaii. She often collaborated with Republicans, and grew increasingly critical of President Barack Obama's foreign policy. One of her main priorities has been to bring all troops home from Afghanistan. In June 2014, she said that it "makes no sense" to pursue military action against the Islamic State, and she added that summer that the mission was "lost." She criticized the administration for failing to "recognize that this is about radical Islam." Also in June, she told Defense Secretary Chuck Hagel that she opposed the swap of Taliban prisoners in exchange for Army Sgt. Bowe Bergdahl, who had abandoned his unit in Afghanistan. In September, she was one of 22 House Democrats who voted with all Republicans to condemn the administration for failing to notify Congress of the Bergdahl exchange. With Republican Rep. Martha Roby of Alabama, Gabbard wrote a letter to other House members in February 2015, warning that Pentagon spending cuts scheduled to take effect later that year would "undermin[e] our national security, local economies and the livelihoods of military families."

Elsewhere, Gabbard praised the election of Prime Minister Narenda Modi of India, and attended a speech he delivered in New York that she called "electric, inspiring, positive." She met personally with Modi in New York and then in New Delhi. On the House Foreign Affairs Committee, she worked with Republicans in 2015 on legislation to toughen economic sanctions against North Korea. On domestic issues, Gabbard joined a bipartisan "No Labels" group of about 70 House members seeking common ground on fiscal policies. "Millennials care less about party labels and blind partisanship, and care more about getting things done," she said. Gabbard also gained attention for joining some Republicans in the House gym for regular sessions of "CrossFit" and circuit training. In April 2015, she married Abraham Williams, a Hawaii-based cinematographer whom she first met when he assisted her 2012 campaign.

Gabbard coasted to reelection in 2014 with 76 percent of the vote in a rematch with Crowley. Although her criticism of Obama caused some grumbling among Hawaii Democrats, Gabbard increasingly has been described as a "rising star," both at home and in Washington.

★ IDAHO ★

Y ou may have seen the TV spot: A huge potato on an enormous flatbed truck is driving around the country to promote the consumption of Idaho potatoes. Now that Hawaii has quit producing pineapples in any quantity, no other state is associated so closely with a particular crop. But potatoes are not the only product of Idaho. Between 1990 and 2010, the population of this state, tucked off near the northwest edge of the continental United States, far from any major metro area, grew by 57 percent, the fourth-highest rate in the nation, trailing only Nevada, Arizona and Utah. Technology has played a role. Back in 1953, an eighth-grade dropout named J. R. Simplot patented the process of freezing French fries; with a handshake, he sealed a contract with a little restaurant chain called McDonald's and was on his way to becoming the biggest potato processor in the world and a billionaire. In the 1970s, Simplot put up $1 million to finance Micron Technology, which spawned a booming high-tech sector including Hewlett-Packard's laser-jet printers. Micron grew to a peak Idaho workforce of 9,000 by 2008, although it slid to 5,600 after the recession. A decade ago, Idaho produced more patents per worker than any other state, and in 2011, it was No. 6, far above average in per-capita research and development and initial public offerings. At the depth of the recession in June 2009, Idaho's unemployment rate was 9.7 percent, slightly higher than the national average, but joblessness fell faster in Idaho. By March 2015, Idaho's rate was down to 3.8 percent, compared to 5.5 percent for the nation as a whole. As in other states in America's broad middle, a strong market for agriculture was one reason. The value of Idaho's electronic-component exports now exceeds the value of its potato exports, trading one type of chip for another.

Idaho is big: The town of Montpelier in the southeast is closer to Farmington, New Mexico, than to Bonner Springs in the northern panhandle. And the wilderness is never far away. Towering over the state Capitol in Boise is the vast peak of Shafer Butte. Not far away are the sharp peaks and broad valleys of the Sawtooth range; the impassable mountains of the Frank Church-River of No Return Wilderness, the largest U.S. wilderness area outside Alaska; and the Salmon River, at 425 miles the longest undammed river in the lower 48 states. Idaho was the last North American area on which European fur traders set eyes. In the 1840s, New England Yankees led by ministers made their way west on the Oregon Trail through southern Idaho. Idaho's northern panhandle, an extension of Washington's Columbia River Valley, was first settled by miners seeking gold and silver, then by loggers seeking timber. Mormons moving north from Utah settled in the eastern part of the state, while Basque immigrants and their descendants have made a significant impact on Idaho and its politics.

Federal water reclamation projects first authorized in 1894 attracted the most settlers; they transformed the barren Snake River Valley into some of the nation's best volcanic, soil-enriched farmland, which along with warm days and cool nights, proved ideal for the Burbank russet potato and, more recently, for a fledgling wine industry. Still fresh in family lore are the people who pioneered this state, built the first towns and farms, established the first churches and schools and became its community leaders. Some major businesses got their start in Idaho—not just Simplot and Micron but also the Albertsons supermarket chain and the construction giant Morrison-Knudsen. And the Idaho National Laboratory in the eastern part of the state is one of the nation's major nuclear and cybersecurity outfits.

Idaho's economic vitality has attracted many newcomers in the past two decades. A few highly publicized entertainment personalities and investment bankers have moved to Sun Valley or over the state line from Jackson Hole, Wyoming, and professionals have cropped up in a fertile technology scene in Boise. But a much larger number of more conservative-leaning engineers and entrepreneurs have come, from California and all over, for a fresh environment and a fresh start, clean air and sparse crowds—and few cumbersome or expensive regulations. (The one exception to laissez-faire government: a tightly regulated water-rights regime.) As Gov. James Risch said in 2006, "People are coming not because they want to change Idaho, but because they like what they see."

As a result, Idaho has been transformed from a state of farms and small towns, where Boise, the pleasant state capital, was just the largest of them. Today, nearly 60 percent of its people live in just five counties in and around Boise, Idaho Falls, Coeur d'Alene, and Pocatello, and all but the last are growing rapidly. About 40 percent of Idahoans live in Treasure

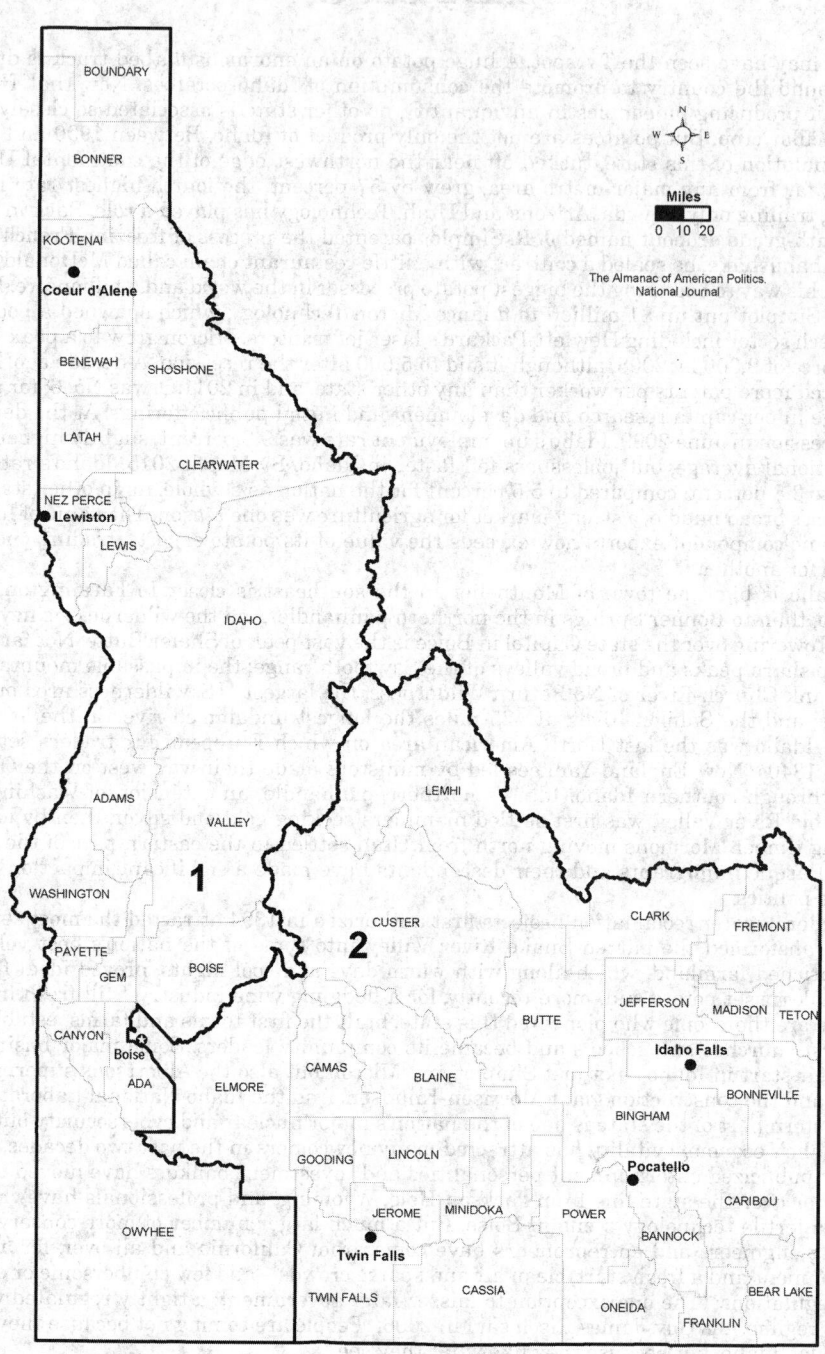

Congressional district boundaries were first effective for 2012.

Valley around Boise, which accounts for most of the state's recent population growth. Idaho has welcomed foreign investment and retirees from the rest of the United States; large influxes have come from California and from Mexico and other parts of Latin America. The state's Hispanic population increased by 73 percent between 2000 and 2010 and now accounts for about 11 percent of Idaho residents, the highest percentage of any state west of Illinois, east of the Pacific Coast and north of Colorado. African-Americans, at about 1 percent, are outnumbered by American Indians, 1.7 percent, and Asians, 1.3 percent. The state gives driver's license exams in English, Spanish, Serbo-Croatian, Russian, Arabic, and Vietnamese.

Voter Turnout	
2013 Total Citizen 18+	1,133,095
2014 Highest Statewide Turnout	439,830
2014 Turnout as % CVAP	38.8%
2012 Turnout as % CVAP	58.4%

Legislature		
Senate:	28R	7D
House:	57R	13D

In its early years as a silver-producing state, Idaho backed populism and opposed the gold standard; from 1900 to 1960, it was politically marginal. It used to elect prominent national Democrats such as Sen. Frank Church, an intelligence watchdog and 1976 presidential candidate, and Gov. Cecil Andrus, Jimmy Carter's Interior secretary. But Idaho has become staunchly Republican. Since 1964, no Democratic presidential nominee has won more than 37 percent of the vote here. Idahoans in small counties and in the Treasure Valley see themselves as pioneering entrepreneurs who, rather than seek federal help, want to get a bloated, bossy federal government off their backs. The U.S. government owns 63 percent of Idaho's land, and most Idahoans strongly oppose federal policies that block road-building on one-third of national forestland, limit grazing on public lands, and breach Snake River dams to protect salmon (in the process, depriving potato farmers of water). In 2004, Democratic presidential nominee John Kerry carried only one county, the richest by far in the state, where his wife, Teresa Heinz, owns a house. In 2008, Barack Obama carried that county and two others, one that includes Moscow, home of the University of Idaho, and another next to Jackson Hole. In 2012, he carried only the first two.

Idaho has elected only Republicans to the governorship starting in 1994 and to the Senate starting in 1978. Mike Crapo, the senior senator, was first elected in 1998. He carried every county that year, was unopposed in 2004, and carried all but three counties in 2010. The junior senator, James Risch, was elected lieutenant governor in 2002 and moved up to governor in May 2006, when Dirk Kempthorne resigned to become President George W. Bush's Interior secretary. When Rep. Butch Otter announced he would run for governor that fall, Risch ran for lieutenant governor again. That left him positioned to run successfully for the Senate in 2008, when Larry Craig, arrested on suspicion of soliciting sex in a men's room in the Minneapolis-St. Paul airport, did not seek reelection; Risch carried all but four counties. Otter won his third term as governor in 2014. Republicans have won every election in Idaho's two congressional districts since 1994, except in 2008, when Democrat Walt Minnick beat a fiery freshman in the western 1st District.

Population		Race and Ethnicity		Income	
Total:	1,612,136	White	83.5%	Median income:	$51,767
Urban:	32.7%	Latino	11.5%		(28 of 50)
Suburban:	29.5%	Asian	1.3%	Under $50,000	53.2%
Rural:	37.8%	Amer. Indian	1.1%	$50,000-$99,999:	32.4%
Land area:	82,643	Two races	2.0%	$100,000-$199,999:	11.9%
Pop/sq. mi.:	19.5	White Ethnic	19.3%	$200,000 or more:	2.5%
Born in state:	47.1%			Poverty Rate	9.9%
		Education			
Age Groups		H.S. grad or less:	38.0%	Work	
Under 18:	26.5%	Some college:	35.7%	White collar:	33.0%
18 to 34:	22.7%	College degree, 4 yr.:	18.0%	Blue collar:	42.3%
35 to 64:	37.0%	Post-grad study:	8.2%	Sales and service:	24.7%
Over 64:	13.8%			Govt. workers:	15.8%
		Military			
		Veterans/active duty:	9.9%		

Presidential Politics Idaho is one of the most Republican states in presidential politics. No Democratic nominee has come close to carrying it since the 1964 LBJ landslide, and Bill Clinton came within 1 percent of finishing third behind Ross Perot and George H.W. Bush in 1992. Despite his victories in both caucuses and primary here, Barack Obama was never in contention in Idaho. John McCain carried the state 62%-36% in 2008, and Mitt Romney carried it 65%-33% in 2012. Romney was especially

2012 Presidential Vote		
Mitt Romney (R)..................420,911	(65%)
Barack Obama (D) 212,787	(33%)
2012 Presidential Caucus		
Mitt Romney (R)...................27,514	(62%)
Rick Santorum (R) 8,115	(18%)
Ron Paul (R) 8,086	(18%)
2008 Presidential Vote		
John McCain (R).................403,012	(62%)
Barack Obama (D) 236,440	(36%)

strong in eastern Idaho with its large Mormon population; he carried Madison County 93%-6%. The only relative pocket of Democratic strength is Ada County, home to the state capital and Idaho's largest city, Boise. But even in Ada, Democrats regularly get beat. The rest of the state from the panhandle in the north to the industrial farms and ski resorts in its southern territory is solidly Republican.

Idaho holds its presidential primary in late May, long after the action in most recent presidential contests. But in 2008, Democrats there decided to select their delegates in caucuses, with the first round held on Super Tuesday, February 5. The Obama campaign organized supporters around the state and with 21,224 Idahoans participating, Obama beat Hillary Clinton, 80%-17%. This was a far bigger victory than the 56%-38% Obama win in the May 27 non-binding primary, in which some 42,800 Idahoans voted. Obama's success in this and other caucus states, mostly in the Midwest and West, provided his margin of victory over Clinton. After he had wrapped up the GOP nomination, McCain won the May 27 primary 70%-22% over Ron Paul.

In 2012, 44,672 Republicans caucused on March 6, and Romney won with 62 percent, with 18 percent each for Rick Santorum and Ron Paul. Romney lost in the sparsely attended caucuses in the northern Panhandle but won solidly in the Treasure Valley and by huge margins in eastern Idaho.

Congressional Districts Idaho has two congressional districts, which split Boise between them. It also has a six-member bipartisan reapportionment commission, which probably gives Democrats more of a role in the process than they deserve in a state where roughly four-fifths of state legislators are Republi-

114th Congress Lineup
2 R   0 D
113th Congress Lineup
2 R   0 D

cans. Still, drawing a seat friendly to Democrats is a near-impossible task in Idaho and the commission's tradition has been to simply shift the Boise dividing line between the 1st and 2nd districts slightly west every 10 years to accommodate the 1st District's stronger growth.

In 2011, strong growth in Northern Idaho and Boise's western suburbs forced the 1st District to shed about 58,000 residents. Democrats on the commission sought to unite Boise and its small but active liberal community. After a three-month stalemate, one Democratic commissioner folded and agreed to merely move the boundary three miles west. The shift subtly made the 1st District about a point more Republican, shoring up Republican freshman Raul Labrador and perhaps giving 2nd District Republican Mike Simpson a few more moderate primary voters. That might prove useful for Simpson, though he easily survived a conservative challenge in the 2014 primary.

Governor

Butch Otter (R)

Elected 2006, term expires Jan. 2019, 3rd term; b. May 3, 1942, Caldwell; Col. of ID, B.A. 1967; Catholic; married (Lori); 4 children.

Military Career: ID Natl. Guard, 1968-73.

Elected Office: ID House, 1973-76; ID lt. gov., 1986-2000; U.S. House, 2001-07.

Professional Career: Rancher; Chmn., Canyon Cnty. Republican Party; Dir., Food Products Div., Pres., Simplot Livestock, Pres., Simplot Intl., 1963-93.

Office: State Capitol, P.O. Box 83720, Boise, 83720, 208-334-2100; Fax: 208-334-3454; Website: gov.idaho.gov.

Election Results

2014 general	Butch Otter (R)	235,405	(54%)
	A.J. Balukoff (D)	169,556	(39%)
	John T. Bujak (Lib)	17,884	(4%)
	Jill Humble (I)	8,801	(2%)
2014 primary	Butch Otter (R)	79,779	(51%)
	Russell Fulcher (R)	67,694	(44%)

Prior winning percentages: 2010 (59%), 2006 (53%); House: 2004 (70%), 2002 (59%), 2000 (65%)

Republican Clement Leroy "Butch" Otter was elected Idaho governor in 2006 and reelected in 2010 and 2014. Though he presides over a deeply Republican state and has shown a flair for attracting media attention, he hasn't always been able to translate his goals into legislative success.

Otter was the sixth of nine children and the first in his family to get a college degree. His father was a journeyman electrician and carpenter and a lifelong Democrat. After high school, Otter entered an abbey to pursue the religious life, but quickly decided that was not his calling. In 1967, at the age of 25, he graduated from the College of Idaho. He went to work for his then-father-in-law, billionaire J.R. Simplot, at the J.R. Simplot Company, one of the largest potato processors in the world and owner of the largest feedlot in the nation. In 1972, Otter, a credentialed cowboy, won the first of two terms in the state House. He ran for governor in 1978, finishing third in the Republican primary, and in 1986, he was elected lieutenant governor.

His career was put at risk by a drunk-driving arrest. Otter unsuccessfully tried to talk the police officer out of charging him by explaining that he had not been drinking, but chewing tobacco soaked in Jack Daniel's whiskey. The officer didn't buy it. Otter was convicted in 1993 of drunk driving, dashing his hopes of running for governor the following year. Still, he went on to be re-elected lieutenant governor and held the post longer than anyone in Idaho history. He served under three governors before he was elected to Congress in 2000.

Otter has been a big supporter of gun ownership and property rights, but his libertarian political philosophy has at times taken him on a different path than that of social conservatives. In 1992, he won the "Mr. Tight Jeans" contest at the Rockin' Rodeo bar in Boise, and during his tenure in the state legislature, Otter voted against an anti-pornography bill by responding "Hell no!" during the roll call. He also questioned the government's right to restrict marijuana use, though in more recent years, neighboring Washington and Oregon have gone much further in that regard. Having become a ranch owner after his 1993 divorce, he was acquainted with the government's reach. The Environmental Protection Agency had charged him three times with violating the Clean Water Act. In 2001, after fighting the agency for two years, he paid a fine of $50,000 for dredging and filling wetlands without a permit.

When he was in Congress, Otter was one of three House Republicans to vote against the USA Patriot Act, a tough anti-terrorism enforcement law, because of potential intrusions on privacy and civil liberties. In 2004, he sponsored an amendment with independent Bernie Sanders of Vermont to prevent authorities from using the act to demand information on book buyers or library users. He lost on a tie vote after Republican leaders held the roll call open for 23 extra minutes to turn the outcome their way.

Otter announced his intention in December 2004 to run for governor, giving him an organizational and fundraising head start over then-Lt. Gov. James Risch, a Republican who was also considering running. In November 2005, Risch decided to run for reelection as lieutenant governor and Otter easily outdistanced three opponents in the May 2006 primary, winning with 70 percent. Otter then faced Democrat Jerry Brady, a former publisher of the Idaho Falls *Post Register* who was making his second consecutive bid for governor.

In heavily Republican Idaho, which hadn't elected a Democratic governor since 1990, Otter began as the front-runner. But Brady gained momentum by criticizing Otter's cosponsorship of a bill that would have sold millions of acres of federal land in Idaho and the western United States to raise money for Hurricane Katrina relief. Otter eventually rescinded his support for the bill. Brady also attacked Otter for accepting $6,000 from a company attempting to build a coal-fired power plant in Idaho. Otter countered by highlighting controversial editorials written by Brady's newspaper, including one that called for breaching Snake River dams to protect endangered salmon. Otter took a brief respite from campaigning in August to get married to a former Miss Idaho, whom he had first met at a Fourth of July parade in 1991.

Despite national discontent with the Republican Party, a lackluster campaign and the spirited challenge by Brady, Otter won, 53%-44%. In heavily Mormon eastern Idaho, where Otter's libertarian stands and lifestyle had hurt him in prior statewide elections, he lost just two counties: Bannock, home to Pocatello and Idaho State University, and Teton County, which shares a border with Wyoming's tony Jackson Hole.

Soon after taking office, Otter caused a minor controversy by halting construction on a $130 million statehouse expansion that the Republican-controlled legislature had approved the previous year. He objected to the project's cost and the fact that it represented an expansion of government. Negotiations with the legislature produced a compromise. That issue was one of many on which Otter has tangled with lawmakers despite working with a strong Republican majority; other issues early in his tenure included proposed changes to the state's grocery tax credit and a highway funding bill. In 2008, Otter proposed an 11 percent increase in the state's budget, a 5 percent pay raise for state employees, and an increase in vehicle registration fees to fund road repairs, all of which the legislature either modified or rejected outright. As the session came to a close, he criticized legislators publicly for rejecting his proposals, and they in turn accused him of refusing to compromise.

Otter's priority for the 2009 session was providing money for road and bridge construction and maintenance. Despite reservations about increased government spending, he decided to accept $1.2 billion in economic stimulus money from the federal government. Over the course of what became the second-longest legislative session in state history, he and Republican legislators hammered out a deal. Otter had sought a 6-cent increase in Idaho's gasoline tax, but lawmakers adamantly ruled it out. The governor had asked for $174.5 million, but eventually had to settle for $54 million.

Otter drew a challenge to his reelection in 2010 from Keith Allred, a professional mediator and founder of a bipartisan citizens' group called The Common Interest. During the legislative session, Allred frequently showed up at the Capitol to criticize Otter's "irrational pessimism" on low-balling the budget, something he said hurt public schools. He decided to run on the Democratic ballot line, though he had a well-earned reputation for being nonpartisan and he put some distance between himself and the Democratic Party. Allred proposed restoring education funding, eliminating tax exemptions to reduce the overall tax rate and starting a scholarship program for at-risk youths. Allred outraised Otter during the early months of 2010, and steadily chipped away at the governor's lead. But Idaho's staunch Republicanism enabled Otter to win, 59%-33%.

After President Barack Obama's 2012 reelection made it clear that his signature health care law would not be repealed by a Republican president, Otter declared he would support setting up a health insurance exchange in Idaho as part of the law. "Obamacare" was exceedingly unpopular in the state, but Otter cast his decision as a states' rights issue, calling an exchange the only alternative to being "at the federal government's mercy" for insurance. Otter faced resistance in the legislature, but he cobbled together enough Democrats and Republicans to enact a state-based marketplace, signing the law in March 2013.

Otter, by then 72, sought a third term in 2014. He attracted a primary challenge— from the right, state Sen. Russ Fulcher, and two others from off the charts—leather clad biker Harley Brown and Walt Bayes, a homeschooling activist with a prodigious beard and "77 descendants." After a colorful and sometimes baffling debate among the four candidates went viral nationally (to the embarrassment of some state Republicans), Otter prevailed in the primary with 51 percent of the vote. In the general election, he faced Democrat A.J. Balukoff. Once again, the state's Republican tilt carried Otter to victory, 54%-39%.

During his third term, Otter faced friction for negotiating an arrangement with the U.S. Energy Department to accept a modest amount of commercial spent nuclear fuel; two former governors, Democrat Cecil Andrus and Republican Phil Batt, came out publicly against the plan, citing contamination risks that could threaten the state's agriculture industry. Otter also tangled with environmentalists for his aggressive effort to kill wolves that threatened livestock and wildlife. Otter called a special legislative session to pass a bill that earlier had been expected to pass easily—for Idaho to join an agreement on collection of child support payments—but the bill was killed by a House committee after talk that foreign courts and Sharia law might trump Idaho rules. The bill then passed in the special. Otter has also exhibited a knack for publicity. When *The New England Journal of Medicine* concluded that regularly eating potatoes contributes to obesity, Otter took umbrage at what he considered the maligning of the state's signature crop. He quickly put out a statement: "News flash: Regularly eating ANYTHING in an irresponsible way contributes to weight gain and other health concerns!"

Senior Senator

Mike Crapo (R)

Elected 1998, term expires 2016, 3rd term; b. May 20, 1951, Idaho Falls; Brigham Young U., B.A. 1973, Harvard U., J.D. 1977; Mormon; married (Susan); 5 children.

Elected Office: ID Senate, 1985-92, ldr., 1988-92; U.S. House, 1993-98.

Professional Career: Clerk, Judge James M. Carter, 1977-78; Vice chmn., Bonneville Cnty. Republican Comm., 1979-81; Vice chmn., ID district 29 Republican Comm., 1982-84; Practicing atty., 1978-92.

DC Office: 239 DSOB, 20510, 202-224-6142; Fax: 202-228-1375; Website: crapo.senate.gov.

State Offices: Boise, 208-334-1776; Coeur D'Alene, 208-664-5490; Idaho Falls, 208-522-9779; Lewiston, 208-743-1492; Pocatello, 208-236-6775; Twin Falls, 208-734-2515.

Committees: *Banking, Housing & Urban Affairs:* Financial Institutions & Consumer Protection; Housing, Transportation, & Community Development; Securities, Insurance, & Investment (Chmn). *Budget. Environment & Public Works:* Clean Air & Nuclear Safety; Superfund, Waste Mgmt., & Regulatory Oversight; Transportation & Infrastructure. *Finance:* Energy, Natural Resources & Infrastructure; Fiscal Responsibility & Economic Growth; Taxation & IRS Oversight (Chmn). *Indian Affairs. Taxation (Joint).*

Group Ratings

	ADA	ACLU	AFL-CIO	LCV	ITI	COC	HAFA	ACU	CFG	FRC
2014	15%	6%	–	20%	33%	63%	81%	92%	85%	86%
2013	0%	C	6%	8%	C	63%	C	88%	92%	C

National Journal Ratings

	2013 LIB	—	2013 CONS
Economic	5%	—	93%
Social	21%	—	77%
Foreign	4%	—	95%
Composite	11%	—	89%

Key Votes of the 113th Congress

1. Sandy storm spending	N	5. Student Loan Rates	Y	9. Bipartisan Budget Deal	N
2. Chuck Hagel Confirmation	N	6. Employee Non-Discrim'n Act	N	10. Farm Bill Conference Rept.	Y
3. Gun Background Checks	N	7. Senate Vote on Judgeships	Y	11. Unempl. Comp. Extension	N
4. Immigration Reform	N	8. Defense Dept. Spending	N	12. Keystone Pipeline	Y

Election Results

2010 general	Mike Crapo (R)............................ 319,953	(71%)	$3,366,313	$21,873
	P. Tom Sullivan (D).................... 112,057	(25%)	$96,218	
	Randy Bergquist (CNP).............. 17,429	(4%)		
2010 primary	Mike Crapo (R)............................ 127,332	(79%)		
	Claude Davis (R)......................... 33,150	(21%)		

Prior winning percentages: 2004 (99%), 1998 (70%); House: 1996 (69%), 1994 (75%), 1992 (61%)

Republican Mike Crapo was first elected to the House in 1992 and to the Senate in 1998. He is known as a conservative and a loyal party member, yet is also well-regarded among Democrats.

Crapo grew up in Idaho Falls. His father ran the local post office, and his mother stayed home to care for their six children. The couple also farmed on 200 acres, growing potatoes and grain. He graduated from Brigham Young University and Harvard Law School. A devout Mormon, he was named a bishop in the church at age 31. A former congressional intern, he was elected to the state Senate at 33 in 1984, two years after leukemia took his older brother Terry's life. Terry Crapo had been state House majority leader and a rising star in state politics. The two brothers were close, and Mike Crapo decided to follow his brother's path to the legislature. He became state Senate leader in 1988. Four years later, he ran for Congress, campaigning against tax increases and in favor of spending cuts, a balanced-budget amendment, and the line-item veto. He won the primary, 68 percent to 32 percent. "Cowboy Democrat" J.D. Williams, the state controller, ran on a "Put America First" platform on industrial policy and trade. Crapo won, 61 percent to 35 percent.

With a self-professed "passion for reform," Crapo became a Republican freshman class leader and championed institutional reforms, advocating more power for rank-and-file members to bring bills to the floor and calling for more open voting. Like many Republicans then, Crapo favored hard-and-fast rules in the budget process to force tough decisions: he supported a balanced budget and across-the-board discretionary spending cuts, excluding Social Security. This approach persisted; in March 2015, Crapo joined other Senate Republicans in opposing a House GOP plan to boost defense spending by sidestepping spending caps. He blasted the maneuver as a "gimmick."

Crapo's overall voting record in the House was very conservative, with some exceptions on economics. He opposed the North American Free Trade Agreement in 1993 but supported normalizing trade relations with China in 2000. He criticized some trade agreements for accepting limits on U.S. agricultural exports as leverage for opening up access for other products.

Crapo, who prides himself on returning to Idaho Falls to be with his family every weekend, faced a career choice in 1997. Republican Gov. Phil Batt announced his retirement, and GOP Sen. Dirk Kempthorne said he would run for governor. Within days, Crapo announced he would run for the Senate seat the following year, and he was unopposed in the Republican primary. His opponent in the fall was Bill Mauk, a former Democratic state chairman and Boise trial lawyer. Idaho, one-quarter Mormon, had never elected a Mormon to the Senate, but this time it did. Crapo led in polls by a wide margin and won, 70 percent to 28 percent, carrying every county. Though he expressed interest in a federal District Court judgeship, Crapo sought reelection in 2004. He had no Democratic opponent. In 2010, he won handily against Democratic financial consultant Tom Sullivan, 71 percent to 25 percent.

From his seat on the powerful Senate Finance Committee, which he secured in 2005, Crapo has worked quietly and productively. He secured a permanent tax break for state colleges by attaching it to a pension bill, while separately heading off a proposed cut in food stamps. Crapo also urged the Internal Revenue Service to implement a tax break that would help the country's short-line railroads, one of the largest of which is used by Idaho farmers to move crops and equipment. Crapo and Montana Democrat Max Baucus, the Finance Committee's chairman, cosponsored bills to relax restrictions on agricultural sales to Cuba. During the 2009 health care debate, Crapo sought to amend the bill to prevent individuals making $200,000 annually and families earning $250,000 a year or less from being taxed to pay for the policy changes in the bill; it was defeated after Baucus called it a "killer amendment" that would deprive the legislation of needed revenue.

After the 2012 election, the unassuming Crapo got some unwanted national attention when he pleaded guilty to drunken driving and received a suspended sentence of 180 days in jail. He acknowledged having had several vodka tonics at his Capitol Hill apartment on December 22, and then driving into suburban Alexandria Virginia, where he scored a 0.11 blood-alcohol level on a breath test after running a red light. The legal limit in Virginia is .08. He asked for Idaho voters' forgiveness. "It was a poor choice to use alcohol to relieve stress—and one at odds with my personally held religious beliefs." Colleagues said he had been feeling overburdened by his responsibilities. The development bewildered Idahoans; an editorial in *The Lewiston Morning Tribune* was headlined, "Is This Mike Crapo the Same Guy We Knew?" Crapo sought to move past the incident, announcing several days later that he would serve as the chief deputy to new Minority Whip, John Cornyn of Texas. He was a logical choice: He was the third most-conservative in *National Journal's* 2011 rankings, and he chaired a panel tasked with assigning Republican senators to committees.

In 2013, Crapo became the ranking Republican on the Banking, Housing, and Urban Affairs Committee, succeeding the term-limited Richard Shelby of Alabama. Earlier on the committee, in 2006, he had won passage of a bill to ease regulation of the banking industry. Four years later, he worked on the Dodd-Frank financial industry overhaul legislation but said he was disappointed with the result, citing its creation of a new consumer protection bureau and its requirement for commercial banks to spin off most of their derivatives-trading operations. He also expressed frustration that the bill would not revamp troubled mortgage giants Fannie Mae and Freddie Mac. When President Obama's 2012 reelection dashed Republican hopes that Dodd-Frank could be repealed, Crapo expressed a desire to reshape parts of it, specifically a provision that was intended to shield most companies outside the financial sector from derivatives regulations. He said Congress intended the rules to apply to financial firms trading derivatives in search of a profit, but that regulators could mistakenly apply it to utilities and other industries that dabble in the derivatives market. In 2015, Crapo offered a bill to make the Consumer Financial Protection Bureau subject to a 10-year regulatory review from which it would have otherwise been exempt. He also worked with Democratic Sen. Mark Warner of Virginia to try to prevent the government from using funds raised from Fannie and Freddie to support federal spending; Crapo called it a hidden tax on homeowners.

He pursued some issues of interest to conservatives. In 2015, Crapo joined GOP Sens. James Inhofe and James Lankford of Oklahoma to introduce a bill to prevent the Education Department from setting policies that conflicted with those of local education authorities. He also used a budget maneuver in an attempt to starve funding for a Justice Department program known as Operation Choke Point—an effort to curb fraud by companies through scrutiny of their "third-party payment processors." Gun-rights advocates said the program was focusing too heavily on firearms sellers.

But Crapo hasn't let ideology get in the way of consensus-seeking. In 2010 he served on the bipartisan Simpson-Bowles debt reduction commission. He and fellow Republicans Tom Coburn of Oklahoma and Judd Gregg of New Hampshire endorsed the commission's final plan, putting them at odds with other GOP panelists, including House Budget Committee Chairman Paul Ryan of Wisconsin. Despite calling the plan "flawed and incomplete," Crapo and Coburn said in a joint statement that "the time for action is now." He served on the bipartisan "Gang of Six" that repeatedly tried to forge a budget compromise in 2011 and 2012. Though he backed the subsequent New Year's Day 2013 budget deal aimed at averting the so-called fiscal cliff, he called it a "missed opportunity to comprehensively address our nation's economic crisis," highlighting its lack of tax reform.

Oregon Democrat Ron Wyden, a frequent legislative partner, has said, "He is not a showboat. He is somebody who, day in and day out, is always a constructive force for sensible public policy." Reid in 2005 named Crapo as one of three GOP senators who would make "outstanding" Supreme Court justices. As a prostate cancer survivor, Crapo has been active in promoting screening for prostate and breast cancer; he introduced a bill in 2007 to create a new federal Office of Men's Health.

Junior Senator

James Risch (R)

Elected 2008, term expires Jan. 2021, 2nd term; b. May 3, 1943, Milwaukee, WI; U. of ID, B.S. 1965, J.D. 1968; Catholic; married (Vicki); 3 children

Elected Office: Ada Cnty. prosecuting atty., 1970-74; ID Senate, 1974-89, 1995-2003, maj. ldr., 1976-82, pres. pro temp., 1982-89; ID lt. gov., 2003-06, 2007-09; ID gov., 2006-08.

Professional Career: Rancher; Sr. partner, Risch Goss Insinger Gustavel, 1975-08.

DC Office: 483 RSOB, 20510, 202-224-2752; Fax: 202-224-2573; Website: risch.senate.gov

State Offices: Boise, 208-342-7985; Coeur d'Alene, 208-667-6130; Idaho Falls, 208-523-5541; Lewiston, 208-743-0792; Pocatello, 208-236-6817; Twin Falls, 208-734-6780.

Committees: *Energy & Natural Resources:* Energy (Chmn); Public Lands, Forests, & Mining; Water & Power. *Ethics (Select). Foreign Relations:* Europe & Regional Security Cooperation; Multilateral Int'l Development, Multilateral Institutions, & Int'l Economic, Energy, & Environmental Policy; Near East, South Asia, Central Asia, & Counterterrorism (Chmn); State Dept. & USAID Mgmt., Int'l Operations, & Bilateral Int'l Development. *Intelligence (Select). Small Business & Entrepreneurship.*

Group Ratings

	ADA	ACLU	AFL-CIO	LCV	ITI	COC	HAFA	ACU	CFG	FRC
2014	15%	0%	–	20%	33%	63%	84%	92%	85%	100%
2013	0%	C	6%	8%	C	63%	C	92%	94%	C

National Journal Ratings

	2013 LIB	—	2013 CONS
Economic	0%	—	95%
Social	0%	—	92%
Foreign	2%	—	96%
Composite	3%	—	97%

Key Votes of the 113th Congress

1. Sandy storm spending	N	5. Student Loan Rates	Y	9. Bipartisan Budget Deal	N
2. Chuck Hagel Confirmation	N	6. Employee Non-Discrim'n Act	N	10. Farm Bill Conference Rept.	Y
3. Gun Background Checks	N	7. Senate Vote on Judgeships	Y	11. Unempl. Comp. Extension	N
4. Immigration Reform	N	8. Defense Dept. Spending	N	12. Keystone Pipeline	Y

Election Results

2014 general	James Risch (R)	285,596	(65%)	$1,761,223
	Nels Mitchell (D)	151,574	(35%)	$357,052
2014 primary	James Risch (R)	119,209	(80%)	
	Jeremy Anderson (R)	29,939	(20%)	

Prior winning percentage: 2008 (58%)

Republican James Risch was elected to the Senate in 2008 after serving as Idaho's lieutenant governor and governor. He has been active on the Foreign Relations and Intelligence committees, establishing himself as a conservative counterweight to the Obama administration's foreign policy.

Risch grew up in Wisconsin and moved west to study forestry. He earned a law degree at the University of Idaho. In 1970, at age 27, Risch was elected Ada County prosecutor—a high-profile position in the state's capital and largest city, Boise. He went after the illicit drug trade so aggressively that his enemies tried to plant a bomb in his car. After that incident, Risch and his wife and political confidant, Vicki, put a piece of tape on the hood of their car every night so they could detect any tampering.

In 1974, Risch was elected to the state Senate, where he served longer than anyone else in Idaho history. He earned a reputation as an ambitious and determined legislator. He always carried an index card in his back pocket, one side listing bills that he wanted to pass and the other listing bills he was determined to kill. Immediately gunning for a leadership position, he became majority leader after the 1976 election, defeating a young colleague named Larry Craig for the position. Although popular with some of his colleagues, Risch was seen by some younger senators as a bully who pressured them to vote his way.

He was brought back to earth by a Democratic challenger who beat him in 1988. He ran again in 1990, but this time he was defeated in the GOP primary. Five years later, he was appointed to fill a state Senate vacancy. Less confrontational this time around, Risch moved back into the ranks of leadership as assistant Republican floor leader. He became one of the driving forces in the Idaho Republican Party, and in 2002, he ran for lieutenant governor, winning comfortably. For three years he served in the shadow of Republican Gov. Dirk Kempthorne, assuming the top job when President George W. Bush's tapped Kempthorne to be Interior secretary.

Risch had just seven months in what he considered his dream job, and he was determined to make the most of it. Within two weeks of taking office, Gov. Risch ordered a reorganization of Idaho's Health and Welfare Department. He created the position of state drug czar to counter the growth in the illicit methamphetamine market in the state. Displeased that the legislature failed to provide property tax relief during its regular session, he called the first special session in 14 years. One day in August, the heavily Republican legislature obediently passed bills cutting local property taxes by $260 million, raising the sales tax from 5 percent to 6 percent, and cutting state spending by $50 million. The voters approved the tax changes, 72 percent to 28 percent. After wide consultation, he prepared a roadless-areas plan for 9 million acres of national forest that was approved by U.S. Agriculture Secretary Mike Johanns and was generally accepted by environmental groups.

In an odd twist, Risch returned to the lieutenant governorship after his stint as governor, because then-Rep. Butch Otter had a head start on the 2006 gubernatorial campaign. In November, Risch defeated former Democratic Rep. Larry LaRocco for lieutenant governor, 58 percent to 39 percent. But another office soon revealed itself: the Senate seat first won by Craig, his old rival, in 1990. Craig was arrested in a Minneapolis airport men's room in 2007 for soliciting sex from an undercover police officer and pleaded guilty to disorderly conduct. He resisted immense pressure from his Senate colleagues to resign immediately, but he then decided against seeking reelection in 2008. Risch announced his intention to run.

Risch had little competition for the Republican nomination. His Democratic opponent was, once again, LaRocco, who had been elected to the House in 1990 and 1992, but was defeated in the Republican sweep of 1994. Another opponent was Democrat Rex Rammell, a rancher who ran as an independent. Risch raised more than twice as much money as LaRocco, and the national Democratic Party never targeted the race. He won the election, 58 percent to 34 percent, with 5 percent for Rammell.

Risch entered the Senate at age 65, following an extensive political career as well as years in business as owner of a trailer company and property management firm, which made him one of the Senate's wealthiest members. He has been an aggressive conservative ally of his more mild-mannered Idaho Senate colleague Mike Crapo. He and Crapo were among 16 senators to back Kentucky GOP Sen. Rand Paul's unsuccessful and ambitious amendment in March 2012 to dramatically slash federal spending. Risch has opposed most of President Barack Obama's spending initiatives. "I ran for this office as a deficit hawk, and now that I am here, I have moved even further in that direction," he told *The Idaho Statesman*.

On the Energy and Natural Resources Committee, Risch worked to add provisions increasing the roles for biomass and geothermal energy in the 2009 energy bill. He wound up voting against the final bill because, he said, it didn't go far enough to reduce U.S. dependence on foreign oil and did too little to encourage expansion of nuclear power. He told the *Twin Falls Times-News* in August 2011 he thought it was possible to have clean air and water "without sending out the Gestapo to enforce the thing." In subsequent years he has kept trying to pass a bill focused on geothermal energy, joining forces with Democrats Ron Wyden and Jeff Merkley of Oregon and Republicans Crapo and Lisa Murkowski of Alaska.

Risch has made his biggest splash as a critic of Obama's foreign policy, leveraging his perches on the Foreign Relations and Intelligence panels. He said in August 2012 that the Law of the Sea Treaty defining nations' ocean usage and another administration-backed effort to conclude a United Nations treaty on reducing firearms "would push the U.S. away from our constitutional foundations and supplement its authority with judgments from international courts and U.N. bureaucracies." When Foreign Relations sought to take up the New START arms control treaty with Russia in September 2010, Risch tried to stop the vote, citing new intelligence that he said he couldn't reveal in open session that led him to question Russia's intentions. And when the full Senate took up the pact in December 2010, he unsuccessfully demanded a delay, noting that Russian troops reportedly had stolen five U.S. Humvees used in military exercises.

After the Russian military began working to support rebels in eastern Ukraine in 2014, Risch urged the U.S. government to provide lethal weapons to the Ukrainian government. In a 2014 appearance to testify on Capitol Hill by Secretary of State John Kerry, Risch told him, "I tell you, you can't help but get the impression our foreign policy is just spinning out of control. And we are losing control in virtually every area we are trying to do something in." Idaho journalist Chuck Malloy noted that Risch had become a frequent guest of Wolf Blitzer on CNN, and for good reason. "What will keep Risch as a go-to source for Blitzer, and possibly others, is that he's a great interview," Malloy wrote. While Risch is "fair" as a public speaker, Malloy wrote, "he knocks out the television interviews. Risch is knowledgeable, engaging, quick on his feet and easy to understand."

In 2014, Risch easily won a second term in the Senate, defeating Boise attorney Nels Mitchell, a Democrat, 65 percent to 35 percent.

FIRST DISTRICT

Raúl Labrador (R)

Elected 2010, 3rd term; b. Dec. 8, 1967, Carolina, PR; Brigham Young U., B.A. 1992; U. of WA, J.D. 1995; Mormon; married (Rebecca Johnson); 5 children.

Elected Office: ID House, 2007-10.

Professional Career: Clerk, U.S. atty., WA St., 1994; Practicing atty., 1994-96; Law clerk, U.S. Dist. Court, Dist. of ID, 1996-98; Practicing atty., 1998-2010.

DC Office: 1523 LHOB, 20515, 202-225-6611; Fax: 202-225-3029; Website: labrador.house.gov.

State Offices: Coeur d'Alene, 208-667-0127; Lewiston, 208-743-1388; Meridian, 208-888-3188.

Committees: *Judiciary:* Crime, Terrorism, Homeland Security, & Investigations; Immigration & Border Security (VChmn). *Natural Resources:* Energy & Mineral Resources; Federal Lands; Oversight & Investigations.

Group Ratings

	ADA	ACLU	AFL-CIO	LCV	ITI	COC	HAFA	ACU	CFG	FRC
2014	10%	27%	–	3%	80%	43%	82%	84%	90%	100%
2013	10%	C	10%	7%	C	69%	C	100%	86%	C

National Journal Ratings

	2013 LIB	—	2013 CONS
Economic	13%	—	87%
Social	31%	—	67%
Foreign	51%	—	49%
Composite	32%	—	68%

Key Votes of the 113th Congress

1. Sandy storm spending		N	5. Medical Marijuana	N	9. Syrian Rebels Training	N
2. Violence Against Women Act	N	6. Farm Bill	N	10. Keystone pipeline	Y
3. Guantanamo Bay Detainees	N	7. Afghanistan Combat	Y	11. Immigration Exec. Action	P
4. Abortion 20-week ban	Y	8. NSA Phone Data Collection	Y	12. Bipartisan budget deal	N

Election Results

2014 general	Raúl Labrador (R)...................... 143,580	(65%)	$425,011	$1,040
	Shirley RIngo (D)........................ 77,277	(35%)	$225,144	
2014 primary	Raúl Labrador (R)........................ 56,206	(79%)		
	Lisa Marie (R) 5,164	(7%)		

Prior winning percentages: 2012 (63%), 2010 (51%)

Population		Race and Ethnicity		Income	
Total:	812,462	White	85.2%	Median income:	$48,053
Urban:	20.8%	Latino	9.8%		*(267 of 435)*
Suburban:	52.5%	Amer. Indian	1.3%	Under $50,000	52.0%
Rural:	26.7%	Asian	1.2%	$50,000-$99,999:	33.8%
Land area:	26,929	Two races	1.9%	$100,000-$199,999:	12.0%
Pop/sq. mi.:	30.2	White Ethnic	20.4%	$200,000 or more:	2.3%
Born in state:	42.4%			Poverty Rate	15.6%
		Education			
Age Groups		H.S. grad or less:	38.4%	**Work**	
Under 18:	26.0%	Some college:	36.9%	White collar:	32.5%
18 to 34:	20.9%	College degree, 4 yr.:	17.0%	Blue collar:	43.2%
35 to 64:	38.0%	Post-grad study:	7.7%	Sales and service:	24.3%
Over 64:	15.1%				
		Military		Govt. workers:	15.3%
		Veterans/active duty:	11.1%		

Western Idaho: Western Boise, Coeur D'Alene

The 1st District of Idaho stretches 479 miles from the Nevada border to Canada and includes some of Boise and all of the panhandle. It encompasses two high-growth areas: the western suburbs of Boise and the Coeur d'Alene area in Kootenai County. In Nampa—whose population nearly doubled in the

Voter Turnout	
2013 Total Citizen 18+	581,193
2014 House Turnout	220,864
2014 Turnout as % CVAP	38%
2012 Turnout as % CVAP	57.4%

1990s, and became Idaho's second-largest city—commercial developers have taken over land that not long ago grew wheat and alfalfa. Subdivisions are being constructed in nearby Meridian, the fastest-growing city in Idaho, with more than 50,000 new residents since 2000; it is among the 10 fastest-growing cities in the nation. The once sleepy Harrison has had a pump of adrenaline with invasions of bicycle enthusiasts seeking to experience a 72-mile trail that was created by converting old Union Pacific railroad lines.

Unemployment throughout Idaho has been below the national average. The median wage here is the lowest in the nation, though the cheap cost of living has mitigated the problem. Still, many Idahoans have received some form of cash assistance, with the highest rate of food stamp, child care and Medicaid assistance in Canyon County. About 26 percent of Canyon County residents had no health insurance in 2012, prior to the implementation of the Affordable Care Act. The University of Idaho is located in Moscow, and local officials have asked students to take jobs in the region after graduation. The university currently has about 12,000 students.

The growth is turning these once-rural areas into urban centers. But that has reinforced, rather than altered, the political landscape. Newcomers routinely say they moved to conservative Idaho to escape from city life, although some old-timers still worry that their communities may become new versions of San Jose or Orange County. Politically, the 1st District of Idaho is overwhelmingly Republican. Kootenai County, once a Democratic stronghold, is now likely to cast as many Republican votes as conservative Canyon County. In the 2012 presidential race, Republican Mitt Romney got 65% of the vote in Kootenai and 66% in Canyon. Northern mining counties were once the district's Democratic base; now that base is the university town of Moscow

2012 Presidential Vote		
Mitt Romney (R)................213,080	(65%)
Barack Obama (D) 105,645	(32%)

2008 Presidential Vote		
John McCain (R).................205,913	(63%)
Barack Obama (D) 115,667	(35%)

Cook Partisan Voting Index: R+18

in Latah County, one of only two in Idaho to vote against a 2006 state constitutional amendment outlawing same-sex marriage. In 2012, Latah was one of only two counties to vote for President Barack Obama. Bonners Ferry on the Canadian border was listed in March 2015 as a target on the Islamic State's hit list.

Ada County is split between the state's two districts, with most of Boise in the 2nd Congressional District. Both districts are heavily Republican. Barack Obama got 35% in the 1st District in 2008, and 32% in 2012.

Raúl Labrador (R)

Republican Raúl Labrador, elected in the GOP tidal wave of 2010, has been among the young conservatives disaffected with the House GOP leadership, and reportedly has been active in discussions to unseat John Boehner as speaker. He made a futile bid to challenge Rep. Kevin McCarthy for majority leader in June 2014.

Labrador was born in Puerto Rico and raised by his mother, Ana Pastor, who was unmarried. His father, who was married and had five other children, saw Raúl once a year on his birthday, according to *The Idaho Statesman*. Pastor, a sales representative for the Mars candy company in Puerto Rico, moved to Las Vegas for a new start when Raúl was a young teenager, taking a job as a change girl in a casino. She joined the city's Mormon Church, which provided help during lean times. A church official became a surrogate father for Labrador, helping pay his way to Brigham Young University, where he earned a bachelor's degree in Spanish and philosophy. He got a law degree from the University of Washington. Labrador spent most of his career in private practice. Before he came to Washington, he was the managing partner of Labrador Law Offices in Nampa, Idaho, which specializes in immigration law.

Labrador entered the political arena in 2006 when he won a seat in the state House. He quickly made a name for himself as a steadfast conservative, standing up to GOP Gov. Butch Otter on his plan to raise fuel taxes to pay for new roads. Labrador had a hand in legislation to restore gun rights to those deemed mentally defective by the courts and to exempt Idaho from the federal health care law.

He sought the Republican nomination to challenge conservative Democratic Rep. Walt Minnick in 2010 after Ken Roberts, the Republican caucus chairman in the Idaho House, withdrew for health reasons. In the primary, Marine Maj. Vaughn Ward, a decorated Iraq war veteran, had a 3-to-1 fundraising advantage and the backing of the state and national party establishment. Former Alaska Gov. Sarah Palin campaigned for Ward, who had been the Nevada director for John McCain and Palin in the 2008 presidential contest. But Ward made a series of gaffes that left him vulnerable, including violation of Pentagon rules prohibiting the use of military uniforms in campaign ads, and failure to disclose his wife's financial assets. Labrador beat Ward in the May primary, 48%-39%.

In the general election, Labrador targeted Minnick's vote to elect California liberal Nancy Pelosi as speaker of the House in 2009. He called for large cuts in federal spending and repeal of the Democratic health care law. Minnick, with $2.5 million in the bank and a 5-to-1 money edge, let loose a barrage of attacks, including one that showed a former U.S. marshal criticizing Labrador for running a website that "offers advice to illegal immigrants seeking amnesty." Labrador responded that he in fact advises illegal immigrants to return to their home countries and reapply for admission to the United States through proper channels. The attack ads were not enough to save Minnick in this Republican bastion. Labrador defeated Minnick, 51%-41%.

In the House, Labrador pushed for his freshman class to put its stamp on Washington but often fell short. "Why don't we pass the most conservative piece of legislation we can in the House?" he asked at a 2012 news conference. "Instead, we are always passing legislation we know was tacitly approved by [Democratic Senate Majority Leader] Harry Reid."

He and 46 other freshmen in February 2011 helped reject a controversial second engine for the F-35 Joint Strike Fighter that was manufactured at a plant in Boehner's Ohio district. During negotiations over raising the federal debt limit a few months later, Labrador said he would support an increase as long as Congress passed a balanced budget amendment to the Constitution. His stance led Boehner to add a planned balanced budget vote to the deal, which passed the House without Labrador's vote; he didn't think that it cut spending enough.

Labrador joined the call for Attorney General Eric Holder's resignation over the botched "Fast and Furious" gun-tracing program. He raised eyebrows in Idaho in June 2012 when he supported California Republican Tom McClintock's failed amendment to a spending bill to cut funding for the Energy Department's Office of Nuclear Energy, a key funding source for the Idaho National Laboratory. Upset with the news media's portrayal of him and other tea party freshmen, Labrador organized a group called "Conversations with Conservatives," which featured panels of lawmakers taking questions while sandwiches were served.

In 2013, he was among the unhappy Republicans looking to replace Boehner. Their effort stalled when they determined they could not get the 25 GOP votes they wanted. When the time came to elect a speaker, he and South Carolina Rep. Mick Mulvaney, another reported ringleader, declined to cast votes. He later complained to *The New Yorker* that senior House members "want our numbers, but they don't want our input, and they don't want our opinions." Despite his insurgency, he joined the Judiciary Committee because of his familiarity with immigration issues.

Labrador considered running for Idaho governor in 2014. He told the *Statesman* that his decision would hinge in part on the fate of immigration reform. "Whether we can get something done or not is going to be instrumental in helping me make my decision," he said. But he eventually decided against challenging incumbent Republican Butch Otter, telling an August 2013 news conference: "I do not feel that I have yet completed the mission you sent me to Congress to do."

In the subsequent battle over the budget that led to the October partial government shutdown, he expressed rare satisfaction with Boehner's management. But in April 2014, he again attacked the speaker, with a statement declaring he was "disappointed" that Boehner criticized his colleagues for dragging their feet on pursuing immigration reform. Labrador had worked with a bipartisan group of lawmakers that quietly met to seek a deal, but abandoned the effort amid disagreements about legalizing undocumented immigrants. After Obama in November 2014 issued his executive order on immigration, Labrador called it "illegal" and said that Congress should block related presidential requests.

When Majority Leader Eric Cantor unexpectedly lost his primary in June 2014, forcing a leadership scramble, Labrador entered the race less than a week before the vote on a new leader. By that point, McCarthy, the majority whip, appeared to have sewn up the support of a majority of Republicans. "What we've had is kind of a top-down approach where you talk to members of Congress and they feel like they're totally irrelevant," Labrador told Fox News. He lost to McCarthy, but the experience bolstered his stature as a conservative leader. "At the very least, he's shown his party something of what its future might look like," the *American Conservative* wrote of Labrador.

In Idaho, Labrador has been reelected easily. He remained interested in statewide office. He has clashed frequently with Mike Simpson, the veteran representative of Idaho's 2nd District. In a March 2015 column, Simpson wrote that the House GOP renegades were an "irresponsible, unrealistic, ineffective segment of the Republican Caucus." Simpson also criticized those Republicans who had abandoned immigration reform. The column did not explicitly cite Labrador, but many Idaho Republicans understood that he was the target.

SECOND DISTRICT

Mike Simpson (R)

Elected 1998, 9th term; b. Sept. 8, 1950, Burley; UT St. U., 1972, Washington U., D.MD. 1978; Mormon; married (Kathy).

Elected Office: Blackfoot City Cncl., 1980-84; ID House, 1984-98, speaker, 1993-98.

Professional Career: Practicing dentist, 1977-98.

DC Office: 2312 RHOB, 20515, 202-225-5531; Fax: 202-225-8216; Website: simpson.house.gov.

State Offices: Boise, 208-334-1953; Idaho Falls, 208-523-6701; Pocatello, 208-233-2222; Twin Falls, 208-734-7219.

Committees: *Appropriations:* Energy & Water Development & Related Agencies (Chmn); Interior, Environment & Related Agencies (VChmn); Labor, HHS, Education & Related Agencies.

Group Ratings

	ADA	ACLU	AFL-CIO	LCV	ITI	COC	HAFA	ACU	CFG	FRC
2014	0%	5%	–	3%	100%	93%	43%	68%	46%	88%
2013	0%	C	19%	0%	C	85%	C	46%	47%	C

National Journal Ratings

	2013 LIB	—	2013 CONS
Economic	44%	—	56%
Social	34%	—	62%
Foreign	34%	—	60%
Composite	39%	—	61%

Key Votes of the 113th Congress

1. Sandy storm spending	N	5. Medical Marijuana	N	9. Syrian Rebels Training	N
2. Violence Against Women Act	Y	6. Farm Bill	Y	10. Keystone pipeline	Y
3. Guantanamo Bay Detainees	N	7. Afghanistan Combat	N	11. Immigration Exec. Action	Y
4. Abortion 20-week ban	Y	8. NSA Phone Data Collection	N	12. Bipartisan budget deal	Y

Election Results

2014 general	Mike Simpson (R)	131,492	(61%)	$2,462,428	$2,298,755	$523,751
	Richard Stallings (D)	82,801	(39%)	$113,774		
2014 primary	Mike Simpson (R)	48,632	(62%)			
	Bryan Smith (R)	30,263	(38%)			

Prior winning percentages: 2012 (65%), (69%), 2008 (71%), 2006 (62%), 2004 (71%), 2002 (68%), 2000 (71%), 1998 (53%)

Population		Race and Ethnicity		Income	
Total:	799,674	White	81.8%	Median income:	$45,327
Urban:	44.9%	Latino	13.1%		*(314 of 435)*
Suburban:	6.0%	Asian	1.4%	Under $50,000	54.4%
Rural:	49.1%	Amer. Indian	0.9%	$50,000-$99,999:	31.1%
Land area:	33,808	Two races	2.0%	$100,000-$199,999:	11.9%
Pop/sq. mi.:	23.7	White Ethnic	15.6%	$200,000 or more:	2.6%
Born in state:	51.7%			Poverty Rate	15.6%
		Education			
Age Groups		H.S. grad or less:	37.7%	**Work**	
Under 18:	26.9%	Some college:	34.5%	White collar:	33.6%
18 to 34:	24.5%	College degree, 4 yr.:	19.2%	Blue collar:	41.4%
35 to 64:	35.9%	Post-grad study:	8.7%	Sales and service:	25.0%
Over 64:	12.6%			Govt. workers:	16.2%
		Military			
		Veterans/active duty:	9.5%		

Eastern Idaho: Eastern Boise, Idaho Falls

The 2nd District of Idaho, from Boise east to the Wyoming border, is one of America's most pictur-esque, with thick forests, mountain ranges, broad river valleys, and vacant expanses. It was settled from the east by overland pioneers who stopped in Idaho to establish farms, and from the south by Mor-

Voter Turnout	
2013 Total Citizen 18+	551,902
2014 House Turnout	214,293
2014 Turnout as % CVAP	38.8%
2012 Turnout as % CVAP	59.4%

mons moving up from Utah to Franklin, Bear Lake, and Caribou counties. It has one of the largest concentrations of Mormons among congressional districts.

Pocatello began as a railroad town, with unionized railroad workers. Fifty miles north on Interstate 15, Idaho Falls serves as the metropolis for a vast region stretching from West Yellowstone, Montana to the Salmon River Mountains. Near Idaho Falls, on a windswept, desolate range is Idaho National Laboratory, known locally as "The Site." The Energy Department's leading laboratory for civilian nuclear energy research, development and demonstra-tion, the facility covers 890 square miles and employs several thousand workers. It has kept the area's economy fairly stable, thanks in part to its work cleaning up Cold War-era nuclear plants. In both 2012 and 2013, however, the lab announced layoffs of about 300 people. The

French nuclear company Areva in 2010 won a $2 billion loan guarantee from the Energy Department to build a uranium enrichment plant nearby, but the company was deeply indebted and the project never broke ground. In December 2012, Greek yogurt maker Chobani opened a factory in Twin Falls that has employed about 400 people.

2012 Presidential Vote		
Mitt Romney (R)................207,831	(64%)
Barack Obama (D) 107,142	(33%)
2008 Presidential Vote		
John McCain (R)................197,099	(61%)
Barack Obama (D) 120,773	(37%)
Cook Partisan Voting Index: R+17		

West of the INL laboratory campus, amid the mountains, are Sun Valley and the nearby town of Ketchum. Sun Valley was established as a ski resort in 1936 by business mogul Averell Harriman before he began his political career. Ketchum attracted writer Ernest Hemingway in 1939, and various movie stars followed. In recent years, Blaine County, which includes both Sun Valley and Ketchum, has attracted rich expatriates from the East and West coasts, who have made it the most Democratic county in Idaho. In the 2012 presidential election, Blaine was one of only two counties in the state to vote for President Barack Obama. It stands in vivid contrast to the Idaho Falls area, the Mormon country, and the farmland along the Snake River, which are among the most Republican areas in the nation.

The 2nd District of Idaho includes most of Boise, where high-tech businesses and tourism have fueled the economy. Boise is home to Micron Technology, which is a leading patent holder and employs about 6,000 people. The Hewlett-Packard campus is also in the district. In 2012, *Forbes* magazine named Boise the second-best city in the country for raising a family, citing low crime rates and cheap living costs. The east side of Boise leans Republican but has some Democratic precincts. The district, like the state as a whole, is solidly Republican.

Mike Simpson (R)

Mike Simpson, an independent-minded Republican first elected in 1998, would be unusual even if he wasn't an influential lawmaker and didn't represent one of the nation's most right-leaning states. He often reaches out to Democrats on economic and social issues. He easily defeated a primary challenge from the right in 2014.

Simpson grew up in Blackfoot, became a dentist, and joined his father's dental practice. He was elected to the city council in 1980 and to the state House in 1984. In 1993, he became speaker of the Idaho House, but he maintained his dental practice. In the legislature, he was known as a moderate in a predominately conservative chamber, affable and able to get differing sides together. When Republican Gov. Phil Batt announced he would retire in 1998, Simpson wanted to run, but GOP Sen. Dirk Kempthorne's decision to seek the office closed that option. When GOP Rep. Mike Crapo ran for Kempthorne's Senate seat, that opened the House seat for Simpson.

The election was hotly contested. In the Republican primary, state Rep. Mark Stubbs called for lower payroll taxes. He had opposed nuclear programs at the Idaho National Laboratory, while Simpson wanted more work at the facility. Term limits were the big issue. Simpson refused to take a pledge to serve only three terms, while the other candidates agreed to it. Term-limit advocates spent large sums against Simpson. Angry at the ads, Batt endorsed Simpson five days before the election. Simpson ran ads against "out-of-state folk" interfering with Idaho's elections. He beat Stubbs 47%-41%.

The Democratic nominee was Richard Stallings, a former history professor who was elected to the House in 1984 and served four terms. In 1992, he ran against Kempthorne for the Senate and lost 57%-43%. Stallings emphasized his conservative voting record in the House, called for more education spending, and said he would act to fix falling farm commodity prices. Simpson won 53%-45%, losing Pocatello, Sun Valley and Boise, but carrying just about everywhere else.

In the House, Simpson's open-mindedness led *Esquire* magazine in 2008 to call him one of the 10 best members of Congress, saying he "lives by the philosophy that democratic representation is a matter of finding not advantageous positions but common ground." He was one of just 16 House Republicans in March 2012 to back a budget plan along the lines of the bipartisan commission chaired by Alan Simpson (not related) and Erskine Bowles, and he led a bipartisan group of legislators urging budget negotiators to "go big" and look at raising taxes as well as cutting spending. During subsequent negotiations on spending and taxes aimed at averting a so-called fiscal cliff, he told *The Wall Street Journal* that many Republicans likely would accept raising tax rates on households earning more than $500,000 or $1 million as long as Democrats backed substantial entitlement cuts. That proved too ambitious.

When President Barack Obama took office, Simpson supported Democratic bills to rein in credit card companies and predatory housing lenders, and opposed GOP bills to eliminate the Legal Services Corporation as well as reduce funding for the National Endowment for the Arts. He has had a contentious relationship with his Idaho GOP colleague Raul Labrador, a hero of the tea party movement. When Labrador reportedly was involved in plotting to oust John Boehner as speaker, Simpson told *The Idaho Statesman* that his actions were "irresponsible." Labrador responded by calling Simpson "a bully" as well as "an old-school legislator that went to Washington, D.C., to compromise."

Simpson has used his seat on the Appropriations Committee to secure funding for the national laboratory in the district, the Bureau of Reclamation, and the Army Corps of Engineers. Simpson became a leading defender of appropriations earmarks. He disagreed with his friend Boehner on restricting earmarks but supported greater transparency in the process. As chairman of the Interior Subcommittee in 2011, he successfully fought a Senate Democratic proposal to cut $150 million from the nuclear energy budget. In 2013, he took over as chairman of the Energy and Water Development Subcommittee, where he promoted the interests of the Idaho National Laboratory and other efforts to promote energy independence for the United States. In March 2015, he played a key parliamentary role on the House floor in successfully breaking the deadlock on funding the Homeland Security Department, even though he did not serve on the subcommittee responsible for that bill.

Simpson has said he would "die trying" to create a Boulder-White Cloud Management Area designating 330,000 acres in central Idaho as wilderness. He has spent years negotiating the plan with opposing constituencies, only to run into opposition from fellow Idaho Republicans. He filed a scaled-down version in January 2015 in a further move to find common ground, and to pre-empt a potential effort by Obama to take unilateral action to declare the area a national monument. "Congressman Simpson would rather have an Idaho solution than have the Obama administration impose a solution," his spokeswoman said.

After easily winning reelection, he encountered problems in 2010, when his support for the Wall Street bailout and his other independent stances drew two primary opponents, state Rep. Russ Mathews and tea party-backed Chick Heileson, a retired heating contractor. They held Simpson to 58%, his worst primary showing since 1998. By 2014, Simpson's legislative rating from the conservative group Heritage Action was 45%—17 percentage points below the House GOP average and far below the ratings of his Idaho colleagues. The anti-tax group Club for Growth made him one of its chief targets and spent more than $500,000 on behalf of Bryan Smith, who sought to portray Simpson as a Washington insider who was a captive of special interests. But the U.S. Chamber of Commerce, the National Rifle Association, the National Association of Realtors and other groups responded by pouring in about $4 million on Simpson's behalf, and 2012 presidential nominee Mitt Romney appeared in a Simpson ad. Smith ran ads criticizing Simpson as a "supporter of earmarks" and complaining that he "supports a scheme to give amnesty to illegal aliens." In the May primary, Simpson coasted to an easy 62%-38% victory against the overwhelmed Smith. In November, Stallings, making another attempt to return to office, lost 61%-39%. Despite his idiosyncratic style, Simpson appears to be more influential than ever.

★ ILLINOIS ★

Illinois and the giant city that dominates it, Chicago, have been experiencing the best and the worst of times. The best of times came in November 2008, when a crowd of one million people thronged to Chicago's lakefront Grant Park to cheer Barack Obama on Election Night. Downtown Chicago was festooned with posters hailing the election of Chicago's own as president of the United States. Then only a month later, the public had a chance to listen to tape recordings of Gov. Rod Blagojevich demanding recompense for nominating Obama's successor as senator, for which he was impeached and removed from office by the Illinois legislature in January 2009. But for the state and its leading metropolis, the worst kept coming. In 2015, Illinois had the lowest credit score of any state in the union and Chicago securities were given junk bond ratings. And the corrupt politicians for which the state is renowned added another member to its dishonor roll when Dennis Hastert, the former Speaker of the House of Representatives who had represented a district about 30 miles from Chicago's Loop, was indicted on a scheme to conceal payments to someone who was blackmailing him.

Illinois has come a long way since May 1860, when Abraham Lincoln was nominated at the Republican National Convention in the 10,000-seat Wigwam convention center in Chicago, less than a mile from Grant Park. That year, it was the nation's ninth largest city, with 112,000 people. Over the next three decades, it grew so rapidly that it became the second largest city with 1.4 million people by the time it hosted the Columbian Exposition in 1893. "Make no little plans," Chicago architect Daniel Burnham exhorted. And the city made enormous plans, building grand parks on the lakefront, erecting America's first downtown of skyscrapers, lining its boulevards with retail palaces, creating a great university from scratch on the Exposition's Midway Plaisance and housing union agitators as well as corporate leaders. Chicago started with the advantage of a great location, where the Great Lakes meet the prairies of the vast Mississippi Valley, and the city's entrepreneurs made it the hub of the nation's railroad network and the center of trade in lumber, grain, and meat. Today, Chicago is the nation's third-largest metropolis, a creative, world-class city, the center of a metropolitan area of 9.5 million people. In commerce, Chicago has been a prime producer and processor of food products, a major manufacturing center and the strongest service economy between the coasts. In finance, it is the home of the world's greatest commodities exchanges and futures markets. O'Hare International Airport, promoted and nurtured for half a century by both Mayors Daley—father and son served for 43 of the 56 years from 1955 to 2011—is one of the world's great hubs of commerce.

But Chicago is also in a severe slump. The years since 2000 have seen only minimal job growth. Manufacturing has declined, and while some factory sites have been gracefully gentrified, others lay fallow and underused. Data from the Federal Reserve showed that since 2010, Chicago has lost more than 100,000 mid-skilled jobs, the kind that built the city's bungalow belt and once sustained its middle class. Finance and commodities were hit by the economic collapse of 2008, and unemployment shot up above the national average in 2009 and 2010. Illinois has raised taxes while nearby states move in the other direction, making it more difficult for Chicago to keep its competitive edge with its neighbors, much less with its rivals on the coasts. In 2015, an analysis by the personal finance website WalletHub found that Illinois places a greater tax burden on the poor and middle class than any other state in the union. Illinois was judged to have the nation's second-worst tax system for low-income workers, who on average pay 12.1 percent of their wages in taxes (including property, income and sales taxes) and the worst tax code for middle-income workers, taking 11.3 percent of their earnings. In another 2015 study, the Institute on Taxation and Economic Policy reported that Illinois has the fifth most regressive state tax system in the nation due to its flat income tax and relatively high reliance on sales and property taxes.

The Illinois state government's financial woes stem from its habit of covering shortfalls in its annual budget with asset sales and other one-time revenue gimmicks or mostly some form of borrowing. The state also developed a tendency to just sit on its bills, and by the end of 2014 it had $6.5 billion in unpaid invoices for services that had already been rendered. A study by the University of Illinois Fiscal Futures Project found that by the end of 2014 fiscal year, the state's five retirement systems had enough assets to cover just 43 percent of their obligations, leaving an unfunded liability of $105 billion. Combined with past borrowing,

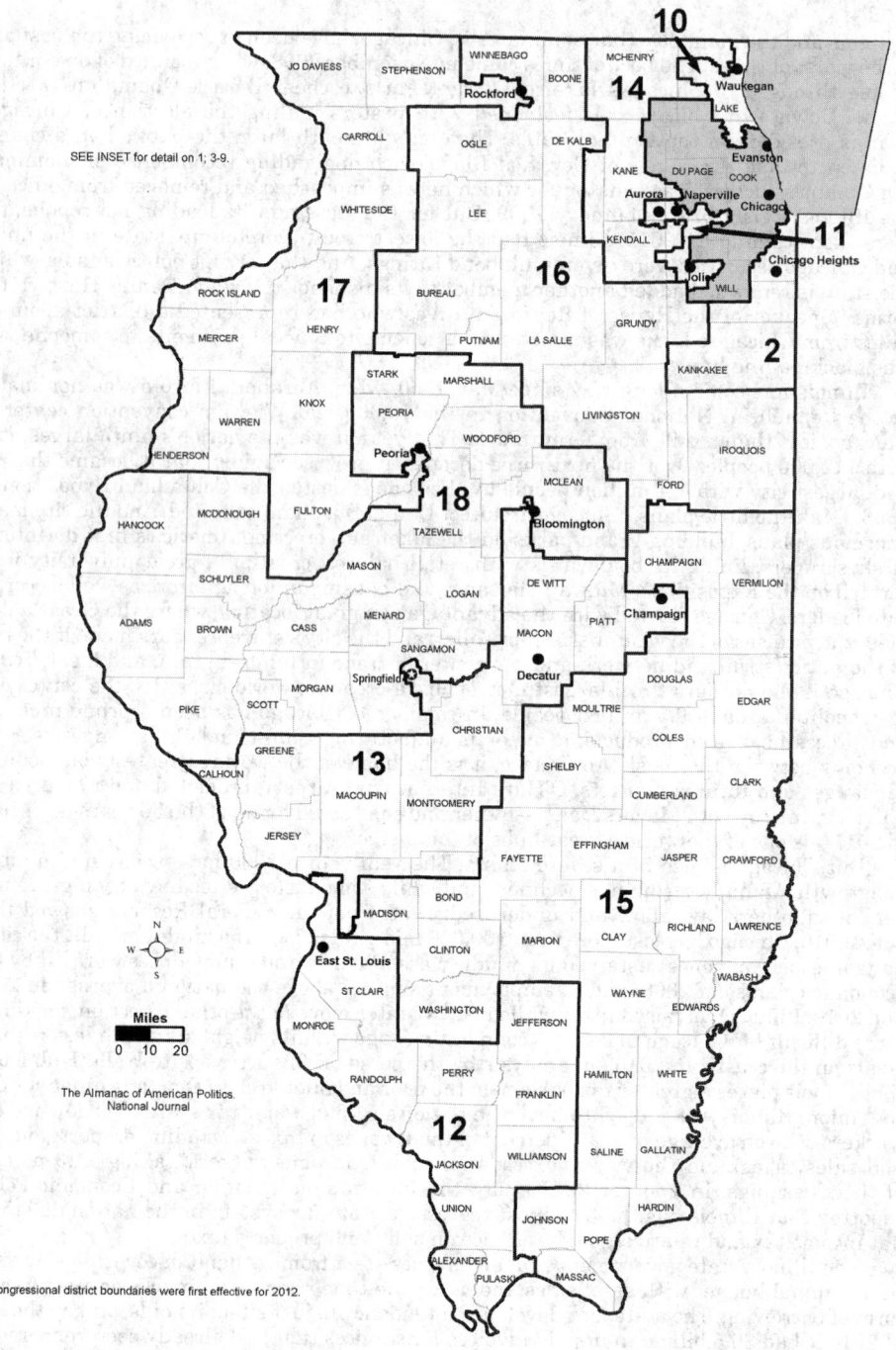

SEE INSET for detail on 1; 3-9.

The Almanac of American Politics.
National Journal

Miles
0   10   20

Congressional district boundaries were first effective for 2012.

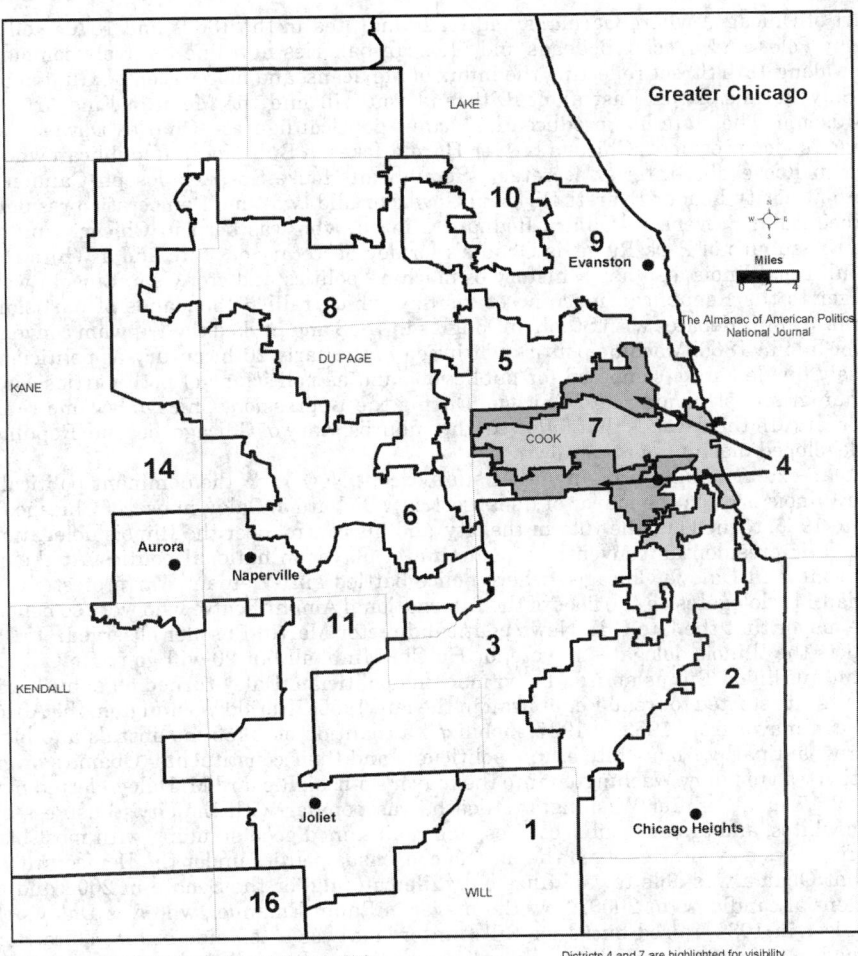

Congressional district boundaries were first effective for 2012.

Districts 4 and 7 are highlighted for visibility.

health care costs for retired state workers that have not been budgeted for, and unpaid bills, the study found the state had nearly $160 billion in unfunded obligations. The state's finances got another blow in 2015 when the Illinois Supreme Court ruled unanimously that the pension overhaul that lawmakers enacted at the end of 2013 violated the state constitution, which explicitly safeguards benefits for public employees. That plan would have reduced cost-of-living adjustments for public employees, raised the retirement age for some and means tested pensions for the highest salaried workers. The court acknowledged the state was in dire financial straits, but it also observed that lawmakers in Springfield had for decades evaded their duty to fund pensions adequately. It is a crisis for which the General Assembly itself is "largely responsible," wrote Justice Lloyd A. Karmeier.

Politically, Illinois emerged from the Civil War as a solidly Republican state, with fast-growing Chicago and the northern counties settled by Yankees decisively outvoting the Southern folk from Springfield south to Cairo, which is closer to Mississippi than to Chicago. Waves of immigrants moved to Chicago—first Irish and German, then Polish, Italian and Jewish in the Ellis Island years. In the quarter century from 1940 to 1965, Chicago attracted thousands of blacks from the South, and in the quarter century from 1982 to 2007, it attracted hundreds of thousands of Hispanics, primarily from Mexico to the point that in 2013, Illinois' population was 14% African-American and 16% Hispanic; in Chicago's Cook County, the population was 25% African-American and 25% Hispanic. A microcosm of that change can be seen in the Chicago neighborhood of Pilsen, also known as the

"Heart of Chicago," where Germans and Irish migrated in the 1860s and 1870s, followed later by Poles and Czechs. Bodegas and Mexican bakeries now line its lively commercial center along 18th Street reflecting the influx of Mexicans, and more recently, Guatemalans and Salvadorans. Stroll East along 18th and you will find the Mexican Fine Arts Center Museum. The state has produced important political figures—Charles Dawes, Calvin Coolidge's vice president; Chicago lawyer Harold Ickes, a Bull Moose Republican who was Franklin Roosevelt's Interior secretary; Republican House Speaker Joseph Cannon and Senate Minority Leader Everett Dirksen; Governor and two-time Democratic presidential nominee Adlai Stevenson. Hillary Rodham Clinton, who was born in Chicago and grew up in the suburb of Park Ridge, is Obama's former Secretary of State and a White House hopeful. But Illinois also has a history of machine politics and cronyism. Lincoln was no stranger to the Republican machine of his day, which rallied thousands of partisans to cheer him at his debates with Stephen Douglas in 1858 and packed the Wigwam convention hall for him in 1860. Machine politics continued in the early 20th century, as politicians in a closely divided state competed for public jobs and as politicians of both parties courted the immigrants streaming into Chicago. During the Depression, Chicago became reliably Democratic. In the decades that followed, the suburbs, wary of Chicago, became Republican and developed machines of their own.

To an extent unknown in any other state except New York, the dominant political figure in Illinois is often the mayor of its largest city. Richard J. Daley, mayor of Chicago from 1955 to 1976, turned out the vote in the city, and his control over the Illinois delegation at Democratic presidential conventions made him a player in national politics. At the 1968 party confab in Daley's Chicago—where police battled anti-Vietnam War protesters—Illinois had 118 delegates on the floor of the International Amphitheatre who were so beholden to the mayor that the late CBS News political director Martin Plissner observed, "If Daley instructs the Illinois delegates to vote for Ho Chi Minh, all but 20 will go to Ho Chi Minh without question." But as an iron-fisted machine politician, Daley turned off suburbanites, and the state started to trend Republican in the late 1960s. Harold Washington, the African-American mayor from 1983 to 1987, mobilized a coalition of lakefront liberals and blacks, but drew antipathy from white ethnic politicians and their constituents (Obama's original ambition was to follow Washington into the mayor's office). Richard M. Daley, elected mayor in 1989 17 months after Washington's death, was popular with the city's business elite, ethnic whites, and affluent suburbanites, and maintained good standing with most blacks and Hispanics as well. He forged the kind of consensus politics under the Democratic banner that Obama was able to capitalize on while running for the Senate in 2004 and as a presidential candidate in 2008. Now the mayor is Rahm Emanuel, who was Daley's chief fundraiser in 1989, raised bucks for Bill Clinton and was a top aide in his White House, returned to Chicago for a few years as an investment banker and then was elected to Congress in 2002. He engineered the Democrats' House takeover in 2006 and served as Obama's chief of staff until he resigned to run for mayor in 2011. In office he has had to deal with revenue shortfalls, insolvent pensions, recalcitrant public employee unions, and an under-performing school system. He's faced an epidemic of gang violence—more than 500 people were slain in Chicago in 2012, the most of any U.S. city—and there are dozens of impoverished blocks on the city's South Side that are known as the "Wild Hundreds." His attempt to

Population		Race and Ethnicity		Income	
Total:	12,882,135	White	63.1%	Median income:	$57,196
Urban:	39.8%	Latino	16.1%		(15 of 50)
Suburban:	45.3%	Black	14.3%	Under $50,000	45.0%
Rural:	14.9%	Asian	4.6%	$50,000-$99,999:	30.3%
Land area:	55,519	Two races	1.5%	$100,000-$199,999:	19.1%
Pop/sq. mi.:	232.0	White Ethnic	31.4%	$200,000 or more:	5.6%
Born in state:	67.2%			Poverty Rate	11.5%
		Education			
Age Groups		H.S. grad or less:	39.2%	Work	
Under 18:	23.5%	Some college:	28.7%	White collar:	36.6%
18 to 34:	23.6%	College degree, 4 yr.:	19.8%	Blue collar:	42.2%
35 to 64:	39.4%	Post-grad study:	12.4%	Sales and service:	21.2%
Over 64:	13.5%				
		Military		Govt. workers:	12.3%
		Veterans/active duty:	6.6%		

end a 2012 teachers' strike through a court injunction and his 2013 efforts to close 50 dilapidated schools—many of which were in black neighborhoods—antagonized the powerful Chicago Teachers Union. A catalogue of challenges like that would erode any politician's popularity, but Emanuel's hard-nosed manner in dealing with them only alienated some voters even more, and

Voter Turnout		
2013 Total Citizen 18+		8,979,422
2014 Highest Statewide Turnout		3,627,690
2014 Turnout as % CVAP		40.4%
2012 Turnout as % CVAP		58.7%
Legislature		
Senate:	39D	20R
House:	71D	47R

in 2015 he had to survive a fight to win a second term.

When Emanuel was forced into a run-off by former Chicago alderman Jesus "Chuy" Garcia, something he had avoided in 2011, his campaign cut a TV spot where Emanuel wore a V-neck sweater and apologized for his faults, admitting, "I can rub people the wrong way, or talk when I should listen." The humility tactic and a campaign warchest flush with contributions from Chicago's business establishment—GOP billionaire investor Kenneth Griffin kicked in $1.3 million to the effort—helped Emanuel prevail in the run-off, 56%-44%. Garcia, who was seeking to become the city's first Hispanic mayor and was endorsed by black leaders like Jesse Jackson, was unable to assemble the kind of multi-racial coalition that Harold Washington had. Many whites apparently felt that while Emanuel could have sharp elbows, perhaps he needed them to grapple the Chicago's many problems. In the white-majority wards Emanuel won almost two-thirds of votes cast and their turnout jumped about 20 percent above the level of the primary. Garcia easily carried Hispanic wards, where turnout also shot up, but there Emanuel managed to retain more than a third of the vote. In the black-majority wards turnout rose as well and Garcia won more votes than he had in the initial primary (when an additional white and two black candidates were on the ballot), but Emanuel still won a solid majority of the ballots cast in those precincts. In his second term, Emanuel has continued the difficult task of running his toddling town. The mayor's skill as a consummate political conjurer was evident when he persuaded the National Football League to pick Chicago for its annual player draft in 2015, the first time that glitz-filled event was held outside of New York since 1964. But he could not make the city's financial troubles go away. Emmanuel called Moody's Investors Service "irresponsible" for downgrading Chicago bonds to junk-level status, but that didn't change the Moody's assessment that the city's unfunded pension liabilities and debt adds up to roughly $26,000 for every one of its residents, the highest amount for any of the 7,000 local government and taxing entities across the county that the ratings agency reviews.

The hard-ball politics and the legend of political corruption in the Windy City inspired the 2011 Starz cable television series "Boss," which featured Kelsey Grammer as Chicago Mayor Tom Kane, a modern-day Richard J. Daley who ruthlessly cut deals with little concern for good government and destroyed the lives of those who got in his way. The show ran for two seasons. More successful has been the long-running CBS drama, "The Good Wife," which is also set in Chicago and stars Julianna Margulies as the attorney-wife of the governor of Illinois who must navigate the city's ethically challenged political and legal circles. In one episode, presidential confidant and Chicago denizen Valarie Jarrett, Obama's senior White House adviser, played herself. Democratic strategist Donna Brazile has had three cameos. But the caricature of Chicago's crookedness on these programs is all too real. Political corruption is endemic in Chicago and Illinois. Former Chicago alderman Dick Simpson and freelance writer Thomas J. Gradel have written a compelling book on the subject. "We do not have a few 'rotten apples'," write Simpson and Gradel in *Corrupt Illinois*. "We have a rotten apple barrel and a pervasive culture of corruption." When four Illinois governors in past 50 years have gone to the pokey (Blagojevich is due to be released in 2024), it's hard to argue with them. And the venality is pervasive: 1,913 individuals were convicted of public corruption in Illinois between 1976 and 2012, practically one a week. The nonchalant attitude that many Illinoisans have had over the years towards their self-dealing politicians didn't make lawmakers in Springfield any more diligent in handling the state's purse strings.

Illinois politics tends to be dominated by figures from Chicago, even though the city casts only 19 percent of the state's votes, and by particular families. The prime example is the Mayors Daley, but the list also includes Speaker Michael Madigan and his daughter, Attorney General Lisa Madigan; and Rep. Dan Lipinski, who took his father Bill Lipinski's seat in Congress. Longtime Chicago Council Finance Chairman Edward Burke succeeded his father in that post, and his wife, Anne Burke, is a justice on the Illinois Supreme Court.

And John Cullerton, the president of the Illinois Senate, comes from an entrenched Irish political clan in Chicago. His cousin Tim, who retired from the City Council in 2015, was the fourth Cullerton to serve as alderman for Chicago's 38th Ward since 1935. Tim's brother-in-law, Thomas Allen, also held the seat for some 18 years.

Presidential Politics   For a century, Illinois was a political bellwether, voting only twice for losing presidential candidates between 1896 and 1996—in 1916 and 1976, when it went Republican while the nation went Democratic. But starting in the 1990s, Illinois has become significantly more Democratic than the nation. It voted 55 percent for Al Gore and John Kerry in 2000 and 2004 and gave home-towner Obama 62 percent in 2008 and 58 percent in 2012. In that year, Obama won 84 percent in Chicago, 64 percent in the Cook County suburbs, and

2012 Presidential Vote		
Barack Obama (D)	3,019,512	(58%)
Mitt Romney (R)	2,135,216	(41%)
2012 Presidential Primary		
Mitt Romney (R)	435,859	(47%)
Rick Santorum (R)	326,778	(35%)
Ron Paul (R)	87,044	(9%)
Newt Gingrich (R)	74,482	(8%)
2008 Presidential Vote		
Barack Obama (D)	3,419,348	(62%)
John McCain (R)	2,031,179	(37%)

43 percent downstate (the other 96 counties). Obama's 2012 performance was only 3 percentage points ahead of Kerry's and Gore's showing, suggesting that there may be a something of a natural ceiling on Democratic strength in the state in presidential elections, but that is still a very high threshold for a Republican candidate to overcome. The ballots that Democratic candidates scoop up in the Chicago suburbs and the collar counties used to go to GOP White House hopefuls, but the demography of that turf has changed: Hispanic and black populations have risen notably in the near Chicago suburbs and farther out in the collar counties, and many whites are put off by the cultural conservatism of national Republicans. As GOP margins in Chicago's collar counties dwindled and disappeared, Illinois became a solidly Democratic state, and it has given Democratic presidential nominees double-digit percentage margins starting in 1992.

The Illinois primary was once a pivotal moment presidential nominating contests, but as more states have moved their primaries to earlier dates, Illinois has voted too late to decide a nomination. In 2007, the legislature moved the primary to February 5 to help Obama. Some 2 million people turned out to vote in the Democratic primary, many more than the 1.1 million who voted in 2004 or the record 1.66 million in 1984. Obama beat Hillary Clinton 65%-33%, losing only a few downstate counties. There was little campaigning on the Republican side, and only 893,000 Republican votes were cast, well below the record 1.1 million in 1980, when Illinois native Ronald Reagan and Illinois Reps. John Anderson and Phil Crane were on the ballot. In 2008, John McCain beat Mitt Romney 47%-29%, with his strongest margins in Chicago and its suburbs. Mike Huckabee, who ran third overall with 16 percent, performed best in the region south of Springfield. Those counties have a history of voting for Democratic candidates from the South including Jimmy Carter in 1976 and Bill Clinton in 1992 and 1996. For 2012, Illinois switched its primary back to March, when Republican turnout in the one contested primary race was 933,000. This time, it was Romney who ran strongest in the suburbs, and he beat Rick Santorum 47%-35%.

Congressional Districts   Illinois, with its sluggish population growth, lost its 20th House seat in the 2000 census and its 19th in the 2010 census; its peak was 27 seats in the 1930s. After the 2000 census, control of redistricting was split between the Democratic state house and the Republican state Senate

114th Congress Lineup	
8 R	10 D
113th Congress Lineup	
6 R	12 D

and governor. So in 2001, a bipartisan plan protected every incumbent except one unlucky junior Democrat in far downstate Illinois. Still, the map produced a fair share of competition: Democrats, who held 12 of 19 seats after 2008, fell to just eight after 2010.

In 2011, the tables turned dramatically. Democrats had hung onto the Illinois legislature and governor's office in 2010, awarding them their only free hand in the country to give a large state's existing map a total makeover. Under heavy pressure from party leaders desperate to offset Republican gains in other states, Democrats released a map designed to eliminate up to six Republican seats. The state's Republican delegation immediately put out a joint statement calling it "little more than an attempt to undo the results of the elections held just six months ago," and they were largely right. In the Chicago suburbs, Republicans lost three incumbents. The bloodbath also extended downstate.

Illinois Republicans sued to block the map in federal court, alleging Democrats had failed to draw an additional Latino majority seat in Chicago. Democrats mocked Republicans' sudden interest in Latino representation and pointed out that minority-rights groups such as MALDEF had not objected to keeping Chicago's two disparate Latino communities together in the earmuff-shaped 4th District. In December 2011, a three judge panel upheld the congressional map. In November 2012, Democrats swept four of five targets for a 12-6 edge. Their strategy largely paid off and generated a rare triumph in an otherwise wrenching redistricting year for the party.

But their over-reach backfired when 2014 became a Republican year—in Illinois and across the nation. Their redistricting shifts did not prove strong enough in the "swing" 10th District on Chicago's North Shore and in the long-time Democratic 12th District in the southern part of the state. That narrowed Democratic control of the delegation to 10-8, with all but one of their seats based in Chicago or its near-by suburbs.

The next redistricting cycle raises potential alarms for Democrats. Illinois likely will lose one seat, which might prove challenging for some Democratic-held seats based in Chicago that have stretched farther into the suburbs to gain sufficient population. If Republican Governor Bruce Rauner is reelected in 2018, his leverage could restore the kind of bipartisan deal-making that was familiar in past redistricting.

Governor

Bruce Rauner (R)

Elected 2014, term expires 2019, 1st full term; b. Feb., 18, 1957, Chicago; Dartmouth B.A.; Harvard U., MBA; married (Diana), 6 children.

Professional Career: Partner, Golder, Thomas, Cressey (GTCR), 1981-2012; ; Philanthropist, New Schools for Chicago; Chairman, Chicago Public Education Fund; the Noble Network of Charter Schools; Chicago Communities in Schools; the ACT Charter School.

State Offices: Springfield, 217-782-0244; Chicago, 312-814-2121.

Election Results

2014 general	Bruce Rauner (R)	1,823,627	(50%)
	Pat Quinn (D)	1,681,343	(46%)
	Chad Grimm (Lib)	121,534	(3%)
2014 primary	Bruce Rauner (R)	328,934	(40%)
	Kirk Dillard (R)	305,120	(37%)
	Bill Brady (R)	123,708	(15%)
	Dan Rutherford (R)	61,948	(8%)

Republican Bruce Rauner is a man taking on a machine. The first-time candidate for elective office captured the Illinois governorship in 2014 running on a platform of economic reform and challenging the hidebound political culture of the state dominated by Chicago Democrats. The battle for governor was bound to be a street fight—six former statehouse chiefs, after all, were charged with malfeasance during or after their terms, with four of them convicted—and Rauner's victory over incumbent Democrat Pat Quinn was no exception. After a brutal campaign in which Rauner accused Quinn of being part of a tradition of cronyism and corruption, the political novice became the first Republican to win the governorship since 1998.

Rauner was born in Chicago and grew up in the suburb of Deerfield. He graduated from Dartmouth College with a degree in economics, and got his M.B.A. from Harvard University. After leaving Harvard, Rauner went to work for the private-equity firm GTCR, rising to the post of chairman. He left in 2012 to open a self-financed venture-capital firm,

R8 Capital Partners. In so doing, he amassed a fortune, much of it from managing public employee pension funds. He has been active in educational issues and chaired the education panel of the venerable Civic Committee of the Commercial Club of Chicago. He supported and underwrote Chicago's ACT charter secondary school, but the Winnetka venture capitalist also applied the tools of his trade to overhaul it; shuttering the underperforming school, firing its leadership, and eventually merging it with the KIPP Charter Schools in Chicago, which Rauner has also supported. Rauner told the *Chicago Sun-Times* that he regretted how things played out, but said he had to make a "tough decision" on how to revive the school, which now teaches elementary students. He backs nonunion charter schools and favors instituting merit pay for principals in Chicago. Rauner has also has served as an adviser to Democratic Chicago Mayor Rahm Emanuel, and the two are on close terms. In the late 1990s, Rauner suggested Emanuel become an investment banker and subsequently hired him on a deal to help GTCR make an acquisition. Emanuel and his family have vacationed at Rauner's exclusive ranch in Montana where the two went fly-fishing.

Rauner dumped $6 million of his own money—a record for an Illinois governor's race—to secure the GOP nomination in a four-way primary where his main opposition was Kirk Dillard, a veteran GOP state senator from a suburban Chicago district. Dillard took several not-so-veiled shots at his opponent's wealth and inexperience, saying no one "should be able to buy a political office," but those tactics were unsuccessful and Rauner defeated him 40%-37%. Rauner also won more votes than incumbent Quinn got in the Democratic primary, foreshadowing the hard-fought general-election race. The two men engaged in a brutal, multimillion dollar air war, with Quinn casting Rauner as a Scrooge-like character who would cut education and other services to pay for tax cuts. Rauner described Quinn in a debate as having governed "one of the worst-run states in America." Rauner cast himself as a regular Joe with an $18 watch and a 20-year-old Volkswagen who would bring his business experience to Springfield. During the campaign, Rauner, who disclosed he'd earned $100 million in the three years prior to running for governor, resisted revealing his total net worth although he did tell a reporter from the *Sun-Times* who asked whether he was in the "1 percent" of wealthy Americans, "Oh, I'm probably .01 percent." Quinn and the Democrats tried to make an issue of Rauner's wealth noting that he was on record saying he would lower the state's $8.25-an-hour minimum wage to the federal standard of $7.25 an hour (a position he later retracted). It was also disclosed during the campaign that Rauner belongs to a wine club that charges a $140,000 initiation fee. But Rauner's wealth was more an asset than a liability in the campaign, and he defeated Quinn, 50%-46%.

As Tom Bevan, one of the founders of RealClearPolitics.com, wryly observed, the Illinois governor's race was a rerun of the 2012 presidential election, in which Democrats depicted the GOP candidate as a "vulture capitalist," while Republicans portrayed the Democrat as a career politician who had "no clue how to create jobs except by feeding the maw of Big Government." Only this time the contest had a different outcome, in no small part because Rauner challenged the bedrock belief of many GOP strategists that elections are won by mobilizing the conservative base of the party. Rauner tacked against that conventional wisdom and spent many hours campaigning in neighborhoods on Chicago's South Side, wooing the support of black voters. The attention paid off, and he won some endorsements from black business leaders and prominent pastors including the early backing of James Meeks, pastor of Salem Baptist Church on the Far South Side, who is also a former Democratic state senator. (Meeks has since been named by Ruaner to chair the State Board of Education.) On Election Day, African-Americans voted faithfully Democratic, and the exit poll indicated Rauner actually won fewer black votes statewide than Republican Bill Brady had four years earlier when he narrowly lost governor's race to Quinn. But turnout held steady and Rauner out-performed Brady by five percentage points in suburban Cook County and seven points in the five collar counties: Lake, McHenry, Kane, DuPage and Will. While it may not have garnered Rauner extra black votes in Chicago, his outreach efforts to minorities probably reassured white swing-voting Chicago suburbanites—who can be easily alienated by dogmatic conservative GOP candidates—that Rauner was a more modern Republican.

In his inaugural address, Rauner took dead aim at the state's political culture. "To the people of Illinois, and the people outside our state who have been reluctant to invest in Illinois because of the insider deals and cronyism," Rauner vowed, "I say this; I'm nobody that nobody sent, and I've come to work for you." It was clever play off the famous political phrase uttered by a Chicago Ward boss, "We don't want nobody, nobody sent," to a young

Abner Mikva—later a Chicago-area congressman and federal judge—who had just moved to the city and wanted to volunteer in the 1948 campaign. Rauner's message was unmistakable; he was going to challenge the old ways of lawmaking and conducting political business in Illinois, and he was prepared to take on the Democratic establishment in Springfield and Chicago to accomplish his goals. When Rauner introduced his "turnaround budget" that included sweeping spending cuts in safety net programs, government worker pensions, state universities and aid to mass transit, the long-time Illinois Democratic House Speaker Michael Madigan called the plan "reckless." Mayor Emanuel called Rauner's proposed cut to the Chicago Transit Authority "bad economics," adding, "I won't stand for it." During the budget deadlock in Springfield, Rauner, with a political action committee he controls, launched an unprecedented TV ad campaign attacking House Speaker Madigan by name and accusing him "and the politicians he controls" of blocking spending cuts and economic reforms in favor of tax increases. The ad blitz wasn't designed to defeat Madigan at the polls: he, and his fellow Democrat John Cullerton, the state Senate President, are secure in their Chicago fiefdoms. But the ads reflected a potential new era in Illinois politics, when a Republican governor with deep pockets might arouse public sentiment in the state enough to force an insular Democratic legislature in Springfield to bend to his pressure. Madigan has resisted efforts at public suasion before. In 2014, he won a legal battle against a term- limits group led by Rauner that sought to place that issue and redistricting reform before the voters as ballot initiatives. The test of wills between Rauner and Madigan, the multimillionaire Ivy League rookie pol versus the cagey Irish clan politician, each very successful in his own way, was likely to define the governor's first term in office.

Senior Senator

Richard Durbin (D)

Elected 1996, term expires 2021, 4th term; b. Nov. 21, 1944, E. St. Louis; Georgetown U., B.S. 1966, J.D. 1969; Catholic; married (Loretta); 3 children (1 deceased).

Elected Office: U.S. House, 1983-97.

Professional Career: Staff, Lt. Gov. Paul Simon, 1969-72; Legal counsel, IL Sen. Judiciary Cmte., 1972-82; Prof., S. IL Schl. of Med., 1978-82.

DC Office: 711 HSOB, 20510, 202-224-2152; Fax: 202-228-0400; Website: durbin.senate.gov.

State Offices: Carbondale, 618-351-1122; Chicago, 312-353-4952; Rock Island, 309-786-5173; Springfield, 217-492-4062.

Committees: *Appropriations:* Defense (RMM); Energy & Water Development; Financial Services & General Government; Labor, Health & Human Services, Education & Related Agencies; State, Foreign Operations & Related Programs; Transportation, HUD & Related Agencies. *Judiciary:* Constitution (RMM); Immigration & the National Interest; Oversight, Federal Rights & Agency Action; *Rules & Administration; Library.*

Group Ratings

	ADA	ACLU	AFL-CIO	LCV	ITI	COC	HAFA	ACU	CFG	FRC
2014	90%	100%	–	80%	100%	50%	2%	0%	0%	0%
2013	95%	C	100%	100%	C	50%	C	4%	2%	C

National Journal Ratings

	2013 LIB	—	2013 CONS
Economic	72%	—	27%
Social	73%	—	0%
Foreign	71%	—	0%
Composite	82%	—	19%

Key Votes of the 113th Congress

1. Sandy storm spending	Y	5. Student Loan Rates	Y	9. Bipartisan Budget Deal	Y
2. Chuck Hagel Confirmation	Y	6. Employee Non-Discrim'n Act	Y	10. Farm Bill Conference Rept.	Y
3. Gun Background Checks	Y	7. Senate Vote on Judgeships	N	11. Unempl. Comp. Extension	Y
4. Immigration Reform	Y	8. Defense Dept. Spending	Y	12. Keystone Pipeline	N

Election Results

2014 general	Richard Durbin (D) 1,929,637	(54%)	$12,614,224	$22,998	$717,746
	Jim Oberweis (R) 1,538,522	(43%)	$2,416,926	$5,353	$690,250
	Sharon Hansen (Lib) 135,316	(4%)	$2,367		
2014 primary	Richard Durbin (D)...............unopposed				

Prior winning percentages: 2008 (68%), 2002 (60%), 1996 (56%); House: 1994 (55%), 1992 (57%), 1990 (66%), 1988 (69%), 1986 (68%), 1984 (61%), 1982 (50%)

It was a source of bemusement and continuing chatter among congressional insiders, and ultimately inspired the satirical TV series *Alpha House*: The living arrangements of a rotating cast of influential Democratic legislators rooming together in a town house blocks from the U.S. Capitol. The landlord, former California Rep. George Miller, sold the residence in late 2014 when he retired from Congress after a 40-year tenure—following decades of renting out rooms to his one-time House colleagues, Dick Durbin of Illinois and Charles Schumer of New York. When Durbin moved into the residence in the early 1990s, Schumer had already been there for 10 years; both were House members at the time. That soon changed, with Durbin winning election to the Senate in 1996, followed by Schumer two years later. By the middle of the next decade, the two roommates had advanced to the top rungs of Senate leadership. And that's when the sitcom aspects of the real-life version of *Alpha House* acquired an element of melodrama.

In 2010, Senate Majority Leader Harry Reid was in deep reelection trouble in Nevada, sparking Hill chatter about a possible Durbin vs. Schumer competition to succeed him as leader. Reid pulled out a win back home and kept his leadership post. But the speculation about an eventual Durbin-Schumer confrontation continued, and, by all accounts, created strains in what had been a close friendship between Durbin, the Senate Democratic whip, and Schumer, who ranked just behind him in the leadership as chairman of the Democratic Policy and Communications Committee. The talk simmered as 2016 approached, and Reid faced another tough re-election bid. Then, in late March 2015, the 75-year old Reid reversed course—announcing his retirement, while seeking to put an end to the succession speculation by endorsing Schumer as his successor. While Durbin had served as Reid's No. 2 for a decade, the hard-charging Schumer was perceived as closer in style to the tough-talking Reid, a one-time amateur boxer. Durbin, by comparison, was widely seen as more diplomatic and less prone to partisan outbursts than the departing Senate leader.

What immediately followed Reid's decision was a late-night conversation on the Senate floor between Durbin and Schumer, whose week-day roommate arrangement had ended just months earlier. Seeking to put an end to years of behind-the-scenes jockeying, Durbin— according to an account he gave the *Washington Post*—told Schumer, "We've had a lot of good times together. We've had some differences, but I think you've earned this." In response, Schumer is reported to have wept. But what was—or wasn't said—next has conspired to keep the Durbin-Schumer plot line going. Durbin contended that, during their conversation, Schumer agreed to support Durbin staying on as whip. Schumer and his aides denied that any such deals were made. Durbin later claimed the votes to remain whip, but Washington Sen. Patty Murray, another member of the Democrats' leadership team, did not rule out a challenge to Durbin.

One way or another, it's a bumpy phase for Illinois' senior senator in a Capitol Hill career that dates back to the early 1980s. Durbin grew up in modest circumstances in East St. Louis, the youngest of three brothers. His father, a railroad night watchman, died of lung cancer when Durbin was 14—an event that later prompted Durbin to push for what became one of his signature legislative achievements. Graduating from Georgetown University and its law school, he returned to Illinois to join Democrat Paul Simon's staff when Simon was the lieutenant governor from 1969-73. Durbin was a state Senate staff member for much of the 1970s, serving for a time as that chamber's parliamentarian—valuable early training for someone who later gained a reputation for his expertise in Senate procedures. Durbin lost a race for a state Senate in 1976, and in 1978 was the lieutenant gubernatorial nominee on a losing Democratic ticket. But in 1982, he won the nomination to oppose Republican U.S. Rep. Paul Findley, then was among the few members of Congress to criticize Israel publicly and call for a more even-handed policy towards the Palestinians. Durbin had no trouble raising money from well-heeled Israel supporters, and narrowly ousted Findley from the central Illinois district.

In the House, Durbin won a seat on the Appropriations Committee, eventually becoming a member of Capitol Hill's version of the "college of cardinals"—the powerful chairmen of that panel's subcommittees. In 1993, Durbin took over the subcommittee with jurisdiction over agriculture programs as well as the Food and Drug Administration. Years later, in the Senate, he was able to enact major reforms in FDA's food safety inspection powers—but his centerpiece legislative accomplishment in the House was the ban on smoking on domestic airline flights, enacted in 1988. It was an effort inspired by the death of his chain-smoking father. At the time the law was passed, Durbin said he had no idea of the kind of the broad societal impact it would have. "I didn't realize that would make a difference in terms of whether you could smoke on a train, on a bus, in a building, in a restaurant, in a hospital," he said in a 2015 radio interview. He followed by pushing to limit tobacco subsidies and to give the FDA authority to regulate tobacco as a health hazard—both accomplished after years of effort.

Finding himself in the minority party in the House for the first time following the 1994 election, Durbin announced he would seek the Senate seat being relinquished in 1996 by Simon, his former boss and mentor. Durbin defeated former state treasurer (and future governor) Pat Quinn by better than 2-1 in the primary, and comfortably won the general election with 56 percent. He has not been seriously challenged since: He won re-election in 2002 and 2008 by 60 percent or more, and while held to 54 percent during a difficult year for Democrats in 2014, still defeated Republican businessman Jim Oberweis by a double-digit margin. (Leaving nothing to chance, Durbin outspent Oberweis by a better than 5-1 margin.)

Durbin has compiled a largely liberal voting record on Capitol Hill: In 2006, *National Journal*'s annual vote rankings pegged him as the most liberal senator, and his scores since then have continued to place him solidly in the ranks of the Senate's left wing. "He's able to pull off the style of sounding like a moderate or compromiser when he often doesn't act like one," University of Illinois political scientist Brian Gaines said. During negotiations on taxes and spending aimed at averting the so-called fiscal cliff in late 2012, Durbin did exhort Democrats to support a deal that included cuts to entitlement programs. "My liberal friends who say don't touch it (Medicare), they're crazy," Durbin said at the time. Earlier, he served on the bipartisan Simpson-Bowles deficit reduction commission that recommended raising the Medicare eligibility age, and was part of an informal group of senators that sought to reach agreement on long-term spending.

On social issues, Durbin has been a death penalty supporter, and, while in the House, favored restrictions on abortion. But Durbin, a Catholic, has opposed most legislation to restrict abortion since coming to the Senate. In 2004, the priest at his home church in Springfield said that he wouldn't give Durbin communion as a consequence of his position. Durbin responded by telling a local newspaper: "Is that all this church is about, is one issue? For bishops to announce that they are going to penalize Catholics on certain votes I think is … reaching too far."

Following the re-election defeat of then-South Dakota Sen. Tom Daschle in 2004, Reid was elevated to succeed Daschle as minority leader. Durbin, who had been named assistant floor leader by Daschle in 2001, moved quickly to secure election to Reid's old job as minority whip. He won by acclamation after one potential opponent counted heads and decided not to challenge him. Durbin became majority whip in 2007, and again assumed the minority whip title in 2015 following the Republicans' recapture of the Senate majority. Respected among colleagues for his willingness to work hard and an ability to articulate his party's themes in everyday language, Durbin is "one of the most skilled debaters we have," a Senate aide said. Others offer a more mixed assessment of his strengths. "He's a great guy," one long-time Democratic staffer told *Politico*, referring to Durbin. "But he thinks with his heart, not his head. He's great at communicating ideas, but not at thinking strategically."

Durbin's election as whip was but one significant development for him arising out of the 2004 election: He acquired a new junior colleague from Illinois, a former state senator named Barack Obama. In an institution of sizable egos, many senators have tense relationships with home-state colleagues—particularly when the two belong to the same party. It was little secret that Schumer was unhappy at the spotlight continually afforded his junior New York colleague, Hillary Clinton, during her Senate tenure. But Durbin enjoyed a warm relationship with Obama. Rather than chafing at Obama's quick rise and celebrity, Durbin in 2006 urged him to run for president. He endorsed Obama when the latter announced his candidacy in February 2007 and introduced him before his acceptance speech at the Democratic National Convention. Durbin did not join Obama at the massive 2008 Election Night celebration in Chicago's Grant Park because his 40-year-old daughter had died three days before, but again introduced Obama at the 2012 party convention.

When Obama was elected, Durbin declared, "To have a president of the United States who is a close, personal friend and has the opportunity to lead this nation and change the world is a dream come true for me in public life." Often described as Obama's top ally in the Senate, Durbin frequently has appeared on cable talk shows in support of Obama's major legislative achievement, the Affordable Care Act, regularly accusing Republicans of mis-statements and distortions; he performed the same task during the bruising 2011 debate over raising the federal debt limit. Even before Obama became president and sought to advance immigration reform, Durbin was the chief sponsor of the DREAM Act, a bill provid-ing a path to citizenship for children of illegal immigrants provisional on completing college or military service. He went to the floor regularly to highlight the stories of the DREAM Act-eligible children, and praised Obama in June 2012 for issuing an executive order addressing the issue when it became clear Congress would not act.

A rare difference between the two has been on trade policy. Despite a strongly pro-union voting record, Durbin split with organized labor early in his congressional career to support the North American Free Trade Agreement and normal trade relations with China during the Clinton administration. In part, his stance reflected Illinois' status as a major exporter. But in 2006, Durbin said he felt "betrayed" by the results of NAFTA and has opposed more recent trade agreements. In 2015 Durbin joined most Democratic senators in voicing opposi-tion to Obama's request that Congress grant him expedited authority to negotiate a major trade agreement with Asia.

In 2011, Obama signed a major food safety bill crafted by Durbin which, among other things, allowed the FDA to initiate a mandatory recall of a food product. He followed this up in early 2015 with legislation to centralize federal responsibility for food safety, complaining that it is now split among 15 agencies in three Cabinet departments. But perhaps Durbin's most high-profile legislative battle of recent years came in mid-2010, as Congress was con-sidering legislation to overhaul the federal government's financial regulatory structure. He engineered passage of what is widely referred to as the "Durbin amendment," giving the Fed-eral Reserve authority to reduce the "swipe fees" that banks charge merchants for processing debit card transactions. It made Durbin a scourge of the nation's banking industry, which later mounted an extensive lobbying effort to repeal the Durbin amendment. It failed, but the Federal Reserve reduced the fees by less than expected, leaving the retail industry unhappy.

During a legislative battle that stretched out over more than a year, Durbin often deliv-ered lengthy floor speeches criticizing the nation's leading banks. "...The banks—hard to believe in a time when we're facing a banking crisis that many of the banks created—are still the most powerful lobby on Capitol Hill. And they frankly own the place," Durbin fumed in an interview with an Illinois radio station at the time. At the same time, Durbin has not been hesitant to use his clout as a member of the Senate Appropriations Committee to keep an eye out for another major player in the nation's financial marketplace: the Chicago-based commodities exchanges. He has opposed new fees on the exchanges and in 2008, worked behind the scenes to soften the impact of proposed controls on speculators in the oil futures market as gas prices soared. It is emblematic of how Durbin has utilized his leadership posi-tion to look out vigorously for the interests of his home state.

"Illinois will always be at the table for any discussion of legislation involving the leader-ship," he has vowed. In 2010, when the House crafted a multi-year transportation bill whose modified funding formulas would have cost Illinois almost $120 million. Durbin was credited with heading off it off when it reached the Senate. In late 2012, Durbin helped prod the Jus-tice Department to assist his financially strapped state by buying the former state prison in Thomson, despite the objections of then-Virginia GOP Rep. Frank Wolf, a senior member of the House Appropriations Committee who feared it would be used to house inmates from Guantanamo Bay. In January 2013, Durbin picked up the prized chairmanship of Senate Appropriations' defense subcommittee, continuing as its top Democrat in 2015. He has used the position to benefit the Rock Island Arsenal and fund production of electronic warfare planes for the Navy manufactured at Boeing's St. Louis plant, just across the Mississippi River from Illinois.

If leading banks are no fan of Durbin's, neither are groups pushing for legal tort reform: They have long accused him of aggressively defending the interests of the nation's trial lawyers, and point to $3.4 million in contributions (according to the Center for Respon-sive Politics) that Durbin has received from lawyers and law firms in his last two bids for re-election. Durbin, a member of the Judiciary Committee, was particularly active on such issues in his first decade in the Senate. In 2003, serving as the Democrats' point man, he successfully blocked action on a bill to limit damages in medical malpractice suits. In 2006, he helped to defeat a proposal that would have replaced a multitude of lawsuits against the asbestos industry with a $140 billion fund to compensate victims of asbestos exposure. Durbin strongly opposed taking the matter out of the courts, although he conceded the need for "significant changes in the existing tort system."

In early 2015, Durbin introduced legislation to create an online database in which companies manufacturing and handling asbestos would have to file annual reports submitted to the EPA, while also listing publicly accessible locations where products with asbestos had been reported in the past year. The bill was sharply criticized by a spokesman for the American Tort Reform Association, who called it an attempt to increase the number of "phony" asbestos lawsuits "by clients of the plaintiffs' bar that haven't even necessarily been exposed to asbestos."

Durbin underwent surgery in 2010 for the removal of a small gastrointestinal tumor, later found to be benign. He subsequently dropped 20 pounds after reading a book on how to overcome the effects of aging. In June 2012, he was telling colleagues that he might retire in 2014, when he turned 70, according to the Chicago *Sun-Times*. He announced in early 2013 that he would seek another term after all, but recent actions seem to point to the prospect that Durbin will decide to call it quits in 2020—even as Capitol Hill, in the interim, awaits future episodes in the tale of the former roommates whose competing ambitions caused their friendship to be tested.

Junior Senator

Mark Kirk (R)

Elected Nov. 2010, term expires 2017, 2nd term; b. Sept. 15, 1959, Champaign; Universidad Nacional Autónoma de México, 1977-78, Cornell U., B.A. 1981, London Schl. of Econ., M.Sc. 1982, Georgetown U., J.D. 1992; Congregationalist; divorced.

Military Career: U.S. Naval Reserves, 1989-2013.

Elected Office: U.S. House, 2001-10.

Professional Career: Parliamentary aide, British House of Commons, 1981-83; A.A., U.S. Rep. John E. Porter, 1984-89; Staffer, World Bank, 1990-91; Special asst., U.S. Dept. of State, 1991-93; Practicing atty., 1993-95; Counsel, U.S. House Cmte. on Intl. Relations, 1995-2000.

DC Office: 524 HSOB, 20510, 202-224-2854; Fax: 202-228-4611; Website: kirk.senate.gov.

State Offices: Chicago, 312-886-3506; Springfield, 217-492-5089.

Committees: *Aging (Special)*. *Appropriations:* Commerce, Justice, Science & Related Agencies; Labor, Health & Human Services, Education & Related Agencies; Military Construction, Veterans Affairs & Related Agencies (Chmn); Legislative Branch; State, Foreign Operations & Related Programs; Transportation, HUD & Related Agencies. *Banking, Housing & Urban Affairs:* Financial Institutions & Consumer Protection; National Security & International Trade & Finance (Chmn); Securities, Insurance & Investment; *Health, Education, Labor & Pensions:* Children & Families; Primary Health & Retirement Security; Employment & Workplace Safety.

Group Ratings

	ADA	ACLU	AFL-CIO	LCV	ITI	COC	HAFA	ACU	CFG	FRC
2014	25%	40%	–	20%	66%	100%	37%	64%	36%	64%
2013	40%	C	38%	23%	C	88%	C	44%	74%	C

National Journal Ratings

	2013 LIB	—	2013 CONS
Economic	31%	—	68%
Social	42%	—	57%
Foreign	27%	—	72%
Composite	34%	—	66%

Key Votes of the 113th Congress

1. Sandy storm spending	N	5. Student Loan Rates	Y	9. Bipartisan Budget Deal	N
2. Chuck Hagel Confirmation	N	6. Employee Non-Discrim'n Act	Y	10. Farm Bill Conference Rept.	Y
3. Gun Background Checks	Y	7. Senate Vote on Judgeships	Y	11. Unempl. Comp. Extension	Y
4. Immigration Reform	Y	8. Defense Dept. Spending	N	12. Keystone Pipeline	Y

Election Results

2010 general	Mark Kirk (R)	1,778,698	(48%)	$14,079,356	$4,317,880	$7,778,048
	Alexi Giannoulias (D)	1,719,478	(46%)	$9,902,006	$4,341,384	$12,459,663
	LeAlan Jones (Green)	117,914	(3%)			
	Mike Labno (Lib)	87,247	(2%)			
2010 primary	Mark Kirk (R)	420,373	(57%)			
	Patrick Hughes (R)	142,928	(19%)			
	Donald Lowery (R)	66,357	(9%)			
	Kathleen Thomas (R)	54,038	(7%)			
	Andy Martin (R)	37,480	(5%)			

Prior winning percentages: 2010 special (47%); House: 2008 (53%), 2006 (53%), 2004 (64%), 2002 (69%), 2000 (51%)

For President Barack Obama, it was a case of insult added to injury: In the 2010 midterm election, as the Democrats lost control of the House and saw their majority shrink significantly in the Senate, the Senate seat held by Obama until his 2008 elevation to the White House also fell into Republican hands. In that contest, GOP moderate Mark Kirk won narrowly over a Democratic opponent with baggage, and was boosted by the blowback of a pay-to-play scandal—in which Illinois' Democratic governor ultimately went to prison for seeking to profit financially from his authority to make an appointment to fill out the balance of Obama's Senate term.

As he prepared to defend his seat in 2016, Kirk, a five-term House member prior to becoming the state's junior senator, could not count on the political fates being as kind this time around. While the state's GOP establishment has rallied around him, he will be running in a presidential election year—in a state that has not cast its Electoral College votes for a Republican in nearly three decades. Combine that with a more formidable group of Democratic opponents than in 2010, and Kirk has become the early pick of political handicappers as the most endangered Senate incumbent nationwide in the 2016 election.

But, to even get this far, Kirk has had to overcome a daunting personal challenge: Barely a year into his Senate term, he suffered a major stroke that limited movement on his body's left side. Three rounds of surgery and a protracted rehabilitation sidelined him for most of 2012. He returned on opening day of the 113th Congress in 2013, climbing the Capitol steps as hundreds applauded. He was assisted by Vice President Joe Biden and West Virginia Democratic Sen. Joe Manchin, his best friend in the Senate. Biden, who missed extended time as a senator in 1988 because of surgeries for brain aneurysms, reassured Kirk: "You got all day, pal. It took me seven months to make these steps." While he now needs a wheelchair and cane to make his way around the Senate, Kirk quickly made clear he had no intention of stepping aside after one term, and suggested his personal ordeal could turn out to be a political plus. "Now I'm definitely a disabled American with a wheelchair," Kirk told the *New York Times*. "That makes me not quite the demonizable Republican candidate that you would think." He could end up facing a Democratic challenger, Rep. Tammy Duckworth, with her own set of physical challenges: She is a military veteran who lost her legs when her helicopter was shot down during the Iraq war.

Kirk grew up in Kenilworth, a wealthy suburb north of Chicago. The son of a telephone company executive, he graduated from Cornell University and the London School of Economics and Political Science. He got a job in the Washington office of GOP Rep. John Porter of Illinois, and rose to chief of staff in three years. Kirk left Capitol Hill in 1989 but stayed in Washington, doing stints at the World Bank and then as a State Department aide while earning a law degree. After two years of international law practice, he returned to the Hill, where he spent five years as counsel to the House International Relations Committee. In 1999, when Porter announced his retirement, Kirk returned home to the Chicago suburbs, where he was one of 11 candidates in the GOP primary. This contest included six multi-millionaires who spent nearly $4 million of their personal fortunes. Kirk did not spend nearly as much, but had several advantages—the endorsement of the popular Porter and greater experience in government, along with being the only candidate with moderate views on cultural issues. He won with 31 percent, twice as much as the second place finisher—an heiress to the R.R. Donnelley & Sons printing company fortune. Democrats nominated state Rep. Lauren Beth Gash who, like Kirk, campaigned in the Porter mold of being fiscally conservative and socially moderate. Kirk won narrowly, 51 percent to 49 percent.

In the House, Kirk compiled a voting record that leaned liberal on social issues and conservative on foreign policy. He supported abortion rights, and while he voted against ending the "don't ask, don't tell" policy that barred gays and lesbians from serving openly in the military, he was generally supportive of gay rights. He received good marks from environmental groups, and was one of only eight Republicans to vote for the 2009 energy bill putting limits on industrial carbon emissions. He later found himself on the defensive over this legislation, and renounced support for it during the 2010 Senate campaign—saying he had concluded it was bad for Illinois businesses. In his last two congressional campaigns, 2006 and 2008, Kirk faced tough challenges from Democrat Dan Seals, a marketing specialist who built well-financed grassroots efforts. In both instances, Kirk survived, 53 percent to 47 percent. In 2006, the war in Iraq was a central issue. Kirk, while largely maintaining his support for the war, distanced himself from President George W. Bush and his handling of the conflict. In 2008, a tough year for Republicans—especially those from the home state of Democratic presidential nominee Obama—Kirk kept his distance from the national GOP, slamming John McCain's choice of Alaska Gov. Sarah Palin as a running mate.

Kirk decided to run for the Senate, months after then-Democratic Gov. Rod Blagojevich had been removed by the Illinois General Assembly amid allegations that he attempted to profit financially from his power to fill Obama's Senate seat until the 2010 election. Blagojevich, ultimately convicted of 18 counts of trying to trade or sell the appointment, was arrested on these charges just weeks after Obama's 2008 presidential victory. That did not stop Blagojevich from appointing Democrat Roland Burris, a former state attorney general and comptroller. Burris, the first African-American ever elected to statewide office in Illinois, had been a respected public official—but soon found his reputation badly damaged by the pay-to-play scandal. Burris' swearing-in was delayed by the Senate for more than a week amid litigation over the legitimacy of his appointment, and Burris later provided conflicting accounts of his conversations with Blagojevich's associates while the appointment was pending. In mid-2009, around the same time as Kirk was announcing plans to run, Burris bowed to political reality and said he would not be a candidate for a full term.

As a fiscal conservative and foreign policy hawk, Kirk was the only socially moderate Republican with a chance of winning a Senate seat in 2010, the year of the tea party; he avoided a tough challenge in the February primary. Meanwhile, Illinois Treasurer Alexi Giannoulias emerged from the Democratic primary bloodied, facing questions about his role in his family bank's loans to criminals and high-risk decisions that had put the bank in trouble. Federal regulators seized the bank in April 2010 after it became financially insolvent, and Giannoulias—who was a vice president of the bank before becoming state treasurer—was unable to escape questions about his role in its failure. Kirk faced his own character issue. During the campaign, he was caught telling voters he had been previously named the Navy's intelligence officer of the year, which wasn't true. He also exaggerated other aspects of his military record. He also was put on the defensive for some of his votes, including his support of the 2008 Wall Street bailout.

National Democrats pulled out all the stops for Giannoulias, including two appearances by Obama, a friend who included Giannoulias in pickup basketball games. This helped Giannoulias raise nearly $10 million, but Kirk still managed to top that with $14 million. Television ads from both sides reflected the battle over character. Democrats' spots called Kirk a liar, while Republicans highlighted Giannoulias' connection to reputed organized crime figures. In a state with a significant Democratic registration edge, polls in the final weeks showed a large segment of the electorate, roughly 15 percent, still undecided. On Election Day, Kirk eked out a 48-percent to 46-percent victory.

In the Senate, Kirk was given a seat on the Appropriations Committee as a reward for scoring a GOP pickup. His voting record put him firmly at the middle of the chamber. He generally sided with the GOP on major issues, but broke from most of his party on supporting repeal of the military's "don't ask, don't tell" policy—a shift from his House position—and on repealing ethanol subsidies. He also joined most Democrats in refusing to bar the use of federal funds for Planned Parenthood and in declining to limit the application of the Davis-Bacon Act, which sets prevailing wage rates. This pattern continued after Kirk's return to Capitol Hill after his stroke: A strong backer of sanctions against Iran, he was sharply critical in early 2015 of the Obama White House's efforts to limit that country's nuclear weapons capabilities through negotiation. But, little more than weeks earlier, he was the lone Republican to vote to confirm Obama's choice for surgeon general, a gun control supporter strongly opposed by the National Rifle Association. Kirk was among the first Republican senators to support same-sex marriage and, in early 2015, he blasted Indiana Gov. Mike Pence, a Republican, for signing a religious-freedom measure the LGBT community feared would result in discrimination against them.

"When I climbed the Capitol steps in January, I promised myself that I would return to the Senate with an open mind and greater respect for others," Kirk told the *Chicago Sun-Times* shortly after his return to his congressional duties. But if the stroke has left his speech somewhat impaired, he continues to exhibit a penchant for a sharp tongue and blunt talk. When a deal in the nuclear talks with Iran was announced, Kirk likened it to British Prime Minister Neville Chamberlain's pre-World War II appeasement of the Nazis: He told *Politico* "that Neville Chamberlain got a lot of more out of Hitler than Wendy Sherman got out of Iran," a reference to a top State Department negotiator on the agreement. But, just a month earlier, Kirk had publicly lectured the House Republicans' tea-party wing over holding up funding for the Department of Homeland Security in an effort to block Obama's executive action on immigration. "I think this is a battle that Republicans should have never fought—junking up a DHS bill, especially when we get a threat against the Mall of America," Kirk told *The Hill*. "We really, as a governing party, we've got to fund DHS and say to the House, 'Here's a straw so you can suck it up.'"

FIRST DISTRICT

Bobby Rush (D)

Elected 1992, 12th term; b. Nov. 23, 1946, Albany, GA; Roosevelt U., B.A. 1973, U. of IL, M.A. 1994, McCormick Seminary, M.A. 1998; Pentecostal; married (Carolyn); 7 children (1 deceased).

Military Career: Army, 1963-68.

Elected Office: Chicago city alderman, 1983-92; 2nd ward committeeman, 1984.

Professional Career: Member, Student Non-Violent Coord. Cmte., 1966-68; Co-founder, IL Black Panther Party, 1968; Med. clinic dir., 1970-73; Ins. agent, 1978-83.

DC Office: 2188 RHOB, 20515, 202-225-4372; Fax: 202-226-0333; Website: rush.house.gov.

State Offices: Chicago, 773-224-6500; Midlothian, 708-385-9550.

Committees: *Energy & Commerce:* Commerce, Manufacturing & Trade; Communications & Technology; Energy & Power (RMM).

Group Ratings

	ADA	ACLU	AFL-CIO	LCV	ITI	COC	HAFA	ACU	CFG	FRC
2014	40%	50%	–	66%	20%	33%	17%	8%	–	0%
2013	60%	C	92%	68%	C	33%	C	5%	22%	C

National Journal Ratings

	2013 LIB	—	2013 CONS
Economic	91%	—	0%
Social	87%	—	7%
Foreign	86%	—	13%
Composite	91%	—	9%

Key Votes of the 113th Congress

1. Sandy storm spending	Y	5. Medical Marijuana	Y	9. Syrian Rebels Training	N
2. Violence Against Women Act	Y	6. Farm Bill	N	10. Keystone pipeline	N
3. Guantanamo Bay Detainees	Y	7. Afghanistan Combat	NV	11. Immigration Exec. Action	N
4. Abortion 20-week ban	N	8. NSA Phone Data Collection	Y	12. Bipartisan budget deal	NV

Election Results

2014 general   Bobby Rush (D).........................162,268   (73%) $344,604
                Jimmy Lee Tilman (R)................59,748   (27%)
2014 primary   Bobby Rush (D).....................unopposed

Prior winning percentages: 2012 (74%), 2010 (80%), 2008 (86%), 2006 (84%), 2004 (85%), 2002 (81%), 2000 (88%), 1998 (87%), 1996 (86%), 1994 (76%), 1992 (83%)

Population		Race and Ethnicity		Income	
Total:	718,967	Black	51.1%	Median income:	$47,745
Urban:	63.5%	White	35.8%		*(271 of 435)*
Suburban:	35.9%	Latino	9.8%	Under $50,000	51.9%
Rural:	0.6%	Asian	2.0%	$50,000-$99,999:	27.9%
Land area:	281	Two races	1.1%	$100,000-$199,999:	17.0%
Pop/sq. mi.:	2,563.1	White Ethnic	26.8%	$200,000 or more:	3.2%
Born in state:	76.1%			Poverty Rate	20.2%
		Education			
Age Groups		H.S. grad or less:	40.7%	**Work**	
Under 18:	22.6%	Some college:	33.4%	White collar:	32.7%
18 to 34:	22.7%	College degree, 4 yr.:	15.8%	Blue collar:	48.4%
35 to 64:	40.0%	Post-grad study:	10.0%	Sales and service:	18.9%
Over 64:	14.6%				
		Military		Govt. workers:	17.7%
		Veterans/active duty:	6.3%		

Chicago: South Side, Southwest Suburbs

The South Side of Chicago has been home to a large urban black community for nearly a century, which is one of the reasons why the city has the third largest African-American population in the nation, after New York and Atlanta. A hundred years ago, there were just a few blocks where black families

Voter Turnout	
2013 Total Citizen 18+	531,498
2014 House Turnout	222,017
2014 Turnout as % CVAP	41.8%
2012 Turnout as % CVAP	64.7%

from the South could settle. But the ghetto grew rapidly with the first influx of blacks from the Mississippi Delta in the 1910s. By the 1920s, the South Side was well established, a center of black-owned businesses and of music, from blues to jazz. Politically, the South Side was a heavily Republican constituency throughout those years. The comfortable, white Protestants who settled in solid brick houses here believed in the party of Yankee propriety, while the African-Americans had faith in the party of Lincoln. This Republican Party heartland was represented in the House in the 1920s by Appropriations Chairman Martin Madden. After Madden died in the Appropriations Committee room in 1928, the 1st District elected Republican Oscar De Priest, the first African-American elected to the House in the 20th century. Blacks remained faithful to the party of Lincoln even during the Depression, voting for Herbert Hoover and De Priest in 1932.

The New Deal and the racial liberalism of New Dealers like Eleanor Roosevelt and Interior Secretary Harold Ickes, both former Republicans themselves, attracted blacks to the Democratic Party, and black Democrat Arthur Mitchell beat De Priest in 1934. The South Side has been Democratic ever since. For 40 years, it was a cooperative part of Chicago's Democratic machine. Then, after the death of longtime Rep. William Dawson, it rebelled against Mayor Richard J. Daley. The South Side seemed to take over the city when Rep. Harold Washington was elected mayor in 1983 and 1987. After he died in November 1987, other black South Side politicians were bogged down by infighting, though Chicago's black electorate peaked at about 40%.

The 1st Congressional District of Illinois includes about half of Chicago's African-American community on the South Side. It also takes in several black Cook County suburbs and extends about 40 miles (depending on your highway) into conservative-leaning rural parts of the Will County suburbs well beyond the city boundaries. Overall, its gerrymandered voting population is about half black. The 1st has a northern salient that includes the Gothic spires of the University of Chicago and the mansions of Kenwood, once the home of Chicago's Jewish aristocracy and now a more eclectic and racially integrated mix of well-to-do inhabitants. Kenwood, considered part of the greater Hyde Park community, is home to President Barack

Obama and first lady Michelle Obama. Before running for president, Obama was a regular at the local food co-op and frequent customer at 57th Street Books. After a lengthy competition and review, this area was chosen for his presidential library.

Several miles to the south, the Woodlawn neighborhood served as the setting for Lorraine Hansberry's 1959 play *A Raisin in the Sun* chronicling a black family's challenges moving into what was then a largely white neighborhood. In Englewood, once the city's second busiest shopping district before losing half of its population after 1970, thousands of homes have been built with federal support in recent years in hopes of creating a new black middle-class community. Some have gone up on vacant land or replaced abandoned buildings that had housed gangs.

Chicago has experienced a gang-fueled crime wave. Violent crime in 2012 spiked over 25%, and the problem was especially acute on the South Side, where the homicide rate jumped 90%. Although incidents of reported crime dropped during the following two years, some experts said that Mayor Rahm Emanuel had manipulated the data so that he could claim credit. In a lengthy report in April 2014, *Chicago* magazine found widespread evidence of "crimes, including serious felonies such as robberies, burglaries, and assaults, that were misclassified, downgraded to wrist-slap offenses, or made to vanish altogether." In March 2015, the University of Chicago announced that it was expanding its labs to explore the causes and possible solutions to local crime.

2012 Presidential Vote		
Barack Obama (D) 262,936	(79%)
Mitt Romney (R)...................67,557	(20%)
2008 Presidential Vote		
Barack Obama (D) 287,240	(81%)
John McCain (R)...................66,840	(19%)
Cook Partisan Voting Index: D+28		

The 1st District is overwhelmingly Democratic. Obama beat John McCain here in 2008, 81% to 19%. He slipped to 79%-20% against Mitt Romney in 2012.

Bobby Rush (D)

Once a Black Panther and prison inmate, Democrat Bobby Rush was elected in 1992 and is now an elder liberal statesman of Congress and Chicago's sharp-edged political scene. He also likely will go down in history as the only politician ever to beat Barack Obama in an election.

Rush grew up on the North Side, a Boy Scout whose mother was a Republican precinct captain. While in the Army, he became involved in the Student Nonviolent Coordinating Committee in the South, then became disillusioned with the military and went AWOL in 1968. That year, he founded the Illinois Black Panthers, with its "Power to the People" slogan, and recruited Fred Hampton, who became chairman of the organization but was later killed by police in a 1969 raid. The next day, police raided Rush's family's apartment, but he wasn't there. Rush served six months in prison for illegal possession of firearms. During his time with the Black Panthers, he ran a program providing free breakfasts to children and a medical clinic that developed the nation's first mass sickle-cell-anemia testing program. "I don't repudiate any of my involvement in the Panther party. It was part of my maturing," Rush later said. Ordained as a Baptist minister, Rush founded a church in 2002 in the depressed Englewood community, but it struggled financially.

In 1983, he was elected the 2nd Ward alderman on the Chicago City Council and was a strong supporter of Harold Washington, who became the city's first black mayor. As he built a career in politics, Rush went back to school and earned master's degrees in political science and theological studies. In 1992, he challenged Democratic Rep. Charles Hayes, an older-generation politician with a union background. Just before the primary, it was revealed that Hayes had 716 overdrafts at the House bank, a practice among lawmakers that blossomed into a national scandal. Rush won 42%-39%.

In the House, Rush has a liberal voting record. His rhetoric has softened over the years, and his more deliberate style contrasts sharply with his days as a Panther. But he sometimes chafes at legislative compromises. He backed the 2010 health care overhaul law, but only after sending mixed signals because of his unhappiness over the removal of a provision that reimburses hospitals for indigent care.

Gun violence caused great pain to Rush in 1999, when his son, Huey Rich, was murdered by a man wielding a handgun as he returned to his South Side home with his fiancée. After

17-year-old Trayvon Martin was shot dead in Florida in February 2012 in an incident that set off a national debate about race, Rush took to the House floor wearing a gray hooded sweatshirt—Martin's garb at the time of his death—in protest. "Just because someone is a young black male and wears a hoodie does not make them a hoodlum," he said.

He has devoted much of his time to the Energy and Commerce Committee, where he chaired the Commerce, Trade and Consumer Protection Subcommittee until Democrats lost control of the House in 2011. Since then, he has been the ranking Democrat on the Energy and Power Subcommittee. When gasoline prices soared in early 2012, he called for an investigation into the potential role of Wall Street speculators. After Henry Waxman retired in 2014 as the committee's top Democrat, Rush stepped aside during the intense competition for a successor between Frank Pallone of New Jersey (who was senior to Rush) and Anna Eshoo of California (who was slightly junior to him). In November 2014, the House Ethics Committee announced that it had decided not to investigate claims that Rush for many years had received free office space in Chicago for his campaign committee.

Rush waged a quixotic campaign in 1999 against Richard M. Daley's iron grip on the mayor's office. He was a frequent Daley critic, and during the campaign he attacked the mayor for tolerating police brutality, inadequate mass transit service, and cronyism in city government. Only three of the 50 aldermen endorsed him, and although Rush tried to build a multiracial coalition, his only chance was with black voters. Daley was popular, and his financial advantage overwhelming. The incumbent won the primary 72%-28%, with nearly 45% of the African-American vote and the support of many prominent black ministers.

After that pounding, Rush found himself challenged in his own primary in 2000 by two state senators—Donne Trotter and the then little-known Barack Obama. Obama waged an aggressive campaign, saying at the time that Rush "exemplifies a politics that is reactive, that waits for crises to happen, then holds a press conference, and hasn't been particularly effective at building broad-based coalitions." But Obama came under attack for being absent from the state legislature for two months and missing a vote on a gun control bill while on a family trip to Hawaii, where he was raised. "It was a race in which everything that could go wrong did go wrong," Obama later wrote in his book, *The Audacity of Hope*. Rush was also helped by an endorsement from President Bill Clinton. He beat Obama 61%-30%.

Not surprisingly, redistricting in 2002 shifted Obama's Hyde Park home two blocks outside the new lines. Rush has been routinely reelected since then. The *Chicago Tribune*, in endorsing his Republican opponent Donald Peloquin in 2012, complained he had become complacent and doesn't return calls from mayors in some of his district's small towns. When Obama ran for the Senate in 2004, Rush backed Democrat Blair Hull, who finished third in the primary. Afterward, he endorsed Obama. During Obama's pitched battle with Hillary Clinton in the presidential primary four years later, Rush endorsed Obama, calling it "one of the most difficult decisions I've had to make in politics."

In other political machinations, Rush in 2008 pushed to ensure that President-elect Obama's vacant Senate seat went to an African-American. He applauded Illinois Gov. Rod Blagojevich's appointment of Roland Burris, and then, when Burris declined to run for reelection in 2010, he backed former Chicago Urban League President Cheryle Robinson Jackson. After Jackson finished third in the Senate primary, Rush declined for months to endorse the winner, state Treasurer Alexi Giannoulias, who is white. He finally did so in October. After Daley announced he wouldn't run for reelection as mayor, Rush in early 2011 joined other black Democratic leaders in backing former Sen. Carol Moseley Braun. The voters gave the job to former Obama White House Chief of Staff Rahm Emanuel. In the 2015 mayoral election, Rush unexpectedly endorsed Emanuel, and criticized challenger Chuy Garcia for having "cheapened" the legacy of Harold Washington with his claims of building a Latino-Black coalition.

In the otherwise uneventful November 2014 election that Rush won with 73% of the vote, his African-American Republican challenger Jimmy Tillman took 72% in Will County. That suburban area cast only 15% of the total vote. But those numbers are a warning of the potential risk that continuing population changes could jeopardize one of the three African-American districts in Chicago in the 2021 redistricting.

Rush had a brush with cancer in 2008. He spent much of the year recovering from salivary gland cancer and surgery to remove a tumor near his jaw. Doctors later declared him cancer-free.

SECOND DISTRICT

Robin Kelly (D)

Elected April 2013, 1st full term; b. Apr. 30, 1956, New York, NY; Bradley U., B.A. 1977, Bradley U., M.A. 1982, N IL U., Ph.D. 2004; Christian; married (Nathaniel Horn); 2 children.

Elected Office: IL House, 2002-07.

Professional Career: Dir., minority student services and professional counselor, Bradley U., 1990-92; Dir., community affairs, Village of Matteson, IL, 1992-2006; Chief of staff, IL Treas., 2007-10; Chief admin. officer, Cook County Board pres., 2010-12.

DC Office: 1239 LHOB, 20515, 202-225-0773; Fax: 202-225-4583; Website: robinkelly.house.gov.

State Offices: Matteson, 708-679-0078; Kankakee, 708-679-0078.

Committees: *Foreign Affairs:* Terrorism, Nonproliferation, & Trade; Western Hemisphere; *Oversight & Government Reform:* Information Technology (RMM); National Security.

Group Ratings

	ADA	ACLU	AFL-CIO	LCV	ITI	COC	HAFA	ACU	CFG	FRC
2014	90%	72%	–	94%	80%	50%	14%	4%	6%	13%
2013	70%	C	100%	96%	C	55%	C	16%	17%	C

National Journal Ratings

	2013 LIB	—	2013 CONS
Economic	69%	—	31%
Social	72%	—	28%
Foreign	86%	—	13%
Composite	76%	—	24%

Key Votes of the 113th Congress

1. Guantanamo Bay Detainees	Y	5. Afghanistan Combat	Y	9. Immigration Exec. Action	N
2. Abortion 20-week ban	N	6. NSA Phone Data Collection	N	10. Bipartisan budget deal	Y
3. Medical Marijuana	Y	7. Syrian Rebels Training	N		
4. Farm Bill	N	8. Keystone pipeline	N		

Election Results

2014 general	Robin Kelly (D)	160,337	(79%)	$1,414,097	$911,020
	Eric Wallace (R)	43,799	(21%)	$21,789	
2014 primary	Robin Kelly (D)	unopposed			

Prior winning percentage: 2013 special (71%)

Population		Race and Ethnicity		Income	
Total:	699,363	Black	55.1%	Median income:	$41,708
Urban:	34.6%	White	28.9%		*(364 of 435)*
Suburban:	62.2%	Latino	13.3%	Under $50,000	56.3%
Rural:	3.2%	Asian	0.8%	$50,000-$99,999:	28.5%
Land area:	1,051	Two races	1.8%	$100,000-$199,999:	13.5%
Pop/sq. mi.:	665.7	White Ethnic	17.5%	$200,000 or more:	1.7%
Born in state:	75.7%			Poverty Rate	22.7%
		Education			
Age Groups		H.S. grad or less:	42.4%	**Work**	
Under 18:	24.5%	Some college:	35.8%	White collar:	29.4%
18 to 34:	21.4%	College degree, 4 yr.:	13.7%	Blue collar:	46.8%
35 to 64:	39.0%	Post-grad study:	8.1%	Sales and service:	23.8%
Over 64:	15.0%				
		Military		Govt. workers:	15.5%
		Veterans/active duty:	7.7%		

Southeast Chicago, Kankakee

Chicago is a great center of both commerce and industry, and if the city's white-collar offices are heavily concentrated in the Loop, its blue-collar heavy industries are most visible on the far South Side. This part of Chicago, diminished in economic importance today, is historically significant and,

Voter Turnout	
2013 Total Citizen 18+	506,061
2014 House Turnout	204,266
2014 Turnout as % CVAP	40.4%
2012 Turnout as % CVAP	60.6%

with the remnants of its great, hulking factories around Lake Calumet and the nearby rail yards, has a certain, undeniable majesty. Thomas Geoghegan wrote in his book, *Which Side Are You On?*, of the fights to win benefits for the workers of shuttered steel mills and of the decline of the labor movement in a place where it got much of its inspiration. This is where the Pullman strike of 1894 was broken by federal troops and where policemen killed 10 union supporters in the Little Steel strike of 1937.

Over the years, Chicago grew around the tight ethnic neighborhoods where workers went home at shift break each afternoon or midnight. Today, those workplaces are mostly empty buildings that suburbanites speed past on the Calumet and Dan Ryan expressways. Roseland, once a prosperous home to thousands of mostly white blue-collar workers, now has some of the highest murder and unemployment rates in the city. An August 2012 *New York Times* magazine story described President Barack Obama's work in Roseland as a young community organizer in the mid-1980s, before attending Harvard Law School. But as his presidency of hope neared its end, the crime statistics and fear seemed worse than ever in Roseland.

The 2nd Congressional District of Illinois is a mix of the urban, majority African-American landscape of Chicago's old South Side industrial area and several Cook County suburbs to the south. In the city, the district includes Jackson Park, where the Columbian Exposition of 1893 was held; South Shore, a once heavily Jewish neighborhood and now home to middle-class blacks; and the old industrial area around Lake Calumet. From its northern tip, the 2nd District extends more than 60 miles through eastern Will County and all of Kankakee County. It takes in Peotone where, with the reelection defeat of Gov. Pat Quinn, residents may have successfully resisted for now a proposal to build a third Chicago-area airport there. The district is one of the most Democratic in the nation.

The Chicago portion of the 2nd is overwhelmingly black, though many African-Americans, especially young parents fleeing Chicago public schools, are moving into suburbs directly to the south—Harvey, Dolton, Markham, Hazel Crest, and Lynwood. Farther south are economically revitalized Homewood and Flossmoor, with significant Jewish populations; high-income

2012 Presidential Vote		
Barack Obama (D)	250,777	(81%)
Mitt Romney (R)	57,692	(19%)
2008 Presidential Vote		
Barack Obama (D)	270,029	(81%)
John McCain (R)	60,104	(18%)
Cook Partisan Voting Index:	D+29	

Olympia Fields; and the still vibrant Park Forest, the post-war planned town where William H. Whyte's *The Organization Man* was set. At the southern edge of the Cook County suburbs is struggling Ford Heights, one of the poorest suburbs in the nation, where a quarter of the households are single women with children, many of whom live in public housing.

Robin Kelly (D)

Democrat Robin Kelly won an April 2013 special election to replace Rep. Jesse Jackson Jr., who resigned amid a criminal investigation and scandal over his conversion of campaign contributions to personal use. With her clean-government appeal and ardent support for stronger gun-control laws, she quickly gained positive response in Democratic circles.

Kelly grew up in New York and moved to Illinois to attend Bradley University in Peoria, where she graduated with a bachelor's degree in psychology and a master's degree in counseling and human development services. She earned a Ph.D. in political science from Northern Illinois University. After working at a youth shelter and a counseling center, she returned to Bradley to become director of minority student services. She then spent 14 years as director of community affairs in Matteson, a village on Chicago's South Side.

In 2002, Kelly won a seat in the Illinois House, where she served three terms. She concentrated on protecting victims of consumer fraud and also worked on extending voter registration, protecting victims of domestic violence, and improving public safety in the Chicago area. She resigned her seat in 2007 to become chief of staff to state Treasurer Alexi Giannoulias, who ran unsuccessfully in 2010 for an open Senate seat. Kelly sought to reduce staffing levels in the office as well as return greater amounts of lost cash and assets to Illinois residents and businesses. She ran to replace Giannoulias as treasurer, but lost to GOP state Sen. Dan Rutherford, 50% to 45%. She then became chief administrative officer to Cook County Board President Toni Preckwinkle.

Jackson, the son of civil rights leader Jesse Jackson, had been a popular figure in his district since his election in 1995. In 2012, he became the subject of a federal investigation into possible misuse of campaign funds. He took a medical leave of absence from the House in June, and received treatment for bipolar disorder. Jackson easily won reelection in November, but submitted his resignation two weeks later, citing mental and physical health problems. Three months later, he pleaded guilty to wire and mail fraud after prosecutors said he used about $750,000 in campaign money for personal expenses, including purchasing a fedora worn by singer Michael Jackson.

Amid considerable jostling for the seat among Illinois Democrats, Kelly stepped forward, and won newspaper endorsements and the backing of local Democratic power brokers. "She is not a showboat," the *Chicago Tribune* said in supporting her candidacy. "She won't dazzle you with ebullience. She doesn't grandstand. She just works hard." Kelly's biggest endorsement came from New York Mayor Michael Bloomberg, who created a super PAC to support politicians advocating tougher gun laws. His PAC broadcast ads lauding Kelly for backing universal background checks and a ban on military-style assault weapons, while criticizing former Democratic Rep. Debbie Halvorson, who had the National Rifle Association's endorsement when she represented a suburban district based in Will County. The issue took on special resonance in a city drawing national attention for gun violence.

Kelly faced criticism after a state inspector general's report and an internal audit alleged she violated timekeeping rules during her failed campaign for state treasurer. "I'm not going to tell you I didn't make a mistake, but I did not do anything wrong," she told the *Tribune*. But it mattered little. She easily won the February special election primary with 50% of the vote to Halvorson's 24%. Chicago Alderman Anthony Beale received 11%, and 13 other candidates split the remainder. April's general election was largely a formality, with Kelly trouncing Republican Paul McKinley, an ex-convict and unemployed political activist. "We not only won an election," Kelly said in her victory speech. "We took on the NRA, we gave a voice to the voiceless, and we put our communities on a brand new path to a brighter day."

In the House, Kelly gained positions as senior Democrat on the Oversight and Government Reform Subcommittee on Information Technology, and chairwoman of the Congressional Black Caucus's Health Braintrust. She advocated a third airport for Chicago in the south suburban area, and said that it would "create jobs for Illinois and cement Chicago's role as America's premier aviation hub." Her chief legislative focus was tighter gun control. Her several bills included a requirement that the Surgeon General issue an annual report on the effects of gun violence on public health, and a grant of authority to the Consumer Product Safety Commission to regulate pistols, revolvers and other firearms as consumer products. When the National Rifle Association harshly attacked her as "Assault Gun Kelly," she responded in January 2015 that she was not "anti-gun," but that she favored common-sense gun reform that respected "the right of every American to live free from the threat of gun violence."

Probably not coincidentally, the NRA attacks came as Kelly was giving serious consideration to challenging the 2016 reelection of Republican Sen. Mark Kirk, who narrowly defeated Giannoulias in 2010. In January 2015, she stated publicly that she was doing her "due diligence" to see if she had a pathway to victory. She criticized Kirk for taking conservative positions contrary to his earlier promises to be a moderate. Before she could challenge Kirk, she faced the prospect of a difficult Democratic primary. Rep. Tammy Duckworth, after declaring her candidacy in March, generated enthusiasm from many Democratic leaders and received the endorsement of EMILY's List, which supports Democratic women candidates who favor abortion rights. Having advised Illinois and Cook County officials and run statewide in her whirlwind political career, Kelly said that she had deeper experience. Even before deciding on her candidacy, Kelly reached out to potential voters beyond her district to show her interest in farm issues. In June 2015, she said that she will seek reelection to her House seat to work on the "unfulfilled promise" of her district.

THIRD DISTRICT

Daniel Lipinski (D)

Elected 2004, 6th term; b. July 15, 1966, Chicago; Northwestern U., B.S. 1988, Stanford U., M.A. 1989, Duke U., Ph.D. 1998; Catholic; married (Judy).

Professional Career: Asst. prof., U. of TN, 2001-04.

DC Office: 2346 RHOB, 20515, 202-225-5701; Fax: 202-225-1012; Website: lipinski.house.gov.

State Offices: Chicago, 312-886-0481; Lockport, 815-838-1990; Oak Lawn, 708-424-0853; Orland Park, 708-403-4379.

Committees: *Science, Space, & Technology:* Energy; Research (RMM). *Transportation & Infrastructure:* Aviation; Highways & Transit; Railroads, Pipelines & Hazardous Materials.

Group Ratings

	ADA	ACLU	AFL-CIO	LCV	ITI	COC	HAFA	ACU	CFG	FRC
2014	65%	16%	–	86%	60%	64%	15%	17%	2%	75%
2013	40%	C	90%	89%	C	62%	C	33%	16%	C

National Journal Ratings

	2013 LIB	—	2013 CONS
Economic	63%	—	36%
Social	56%	—	44%
Foreign	56%	—	44%
Composite	59%	—	42%

Key Votes of the 113th Congress

1. Sandy storm spending	Y	5. Medical Marijuana	N	9. Syrian Rebels Training	Y
2. Violence Against Women Act	Y	6. Farm Bill	N	10. Keystone pipeline	Y
3. Guantanamo Bay Detainees	N	7. Afghanistan Combat	N	11. Immigration Exec. Action	N
4. Abortion 20-week ban	Y	8. NSA Phone Data Collection	N	12. Bipartisan budget deal	Y

Election Results

2014 general	Daniel Lipinski (D)	116,764	(65%)	$618,212	$1,805
	Sharon Brannigan (R)	64,091	(35%)	$32,937	
2014 primary	Daniel Lipinski (D)	unopposed			

Prior winning percentages: 2012 (68%), 2010 (70%), 2008 (73%), 2006 (77%), 2004 (73%)

Population		Race and Ethnicity		Income	
Total:	737,806	White	62.4%	Median income:	$60,644
Urban:	53.3%	Latino	29.4%		*(120 of 435)*
Suburban:	46.7%	Black	3.7%	Under $50,000	41.1%
Rural:	0.0%	Asian	3.3%	$50,000-$99,999:	32.9%
Land area:	197	Two races	1.1%	$100,000-$199,999:	21.4%
Pop/sq. mi.:	3,743.0	White Ethnic	46.5%	$200,000 or more:	4.6%
Born in state:	69.3%			Poverty Rate	13.1%
		Education			
Age Groups		H.S. grad or less:	47.1%	**Work**	
Under 18:	25.0%	Some college:	27.6%	White collar:	30.5%
18 to 34:	22.8%	College degree, 4 yr.:	15.5%	Blue collar:	43.6%
35 to 64:	39.4%	Post-grad study:	9.8%	Sales and service:	25.9%
Over 64:	12.8%			Govt. workers:	12.4%
		Military			
		Veterans/active duty:	5.6%		

Chicago: Southwest Side, West Suburbs

A century ago, humorist Finley Peter Dunne's fictional Mr. Dooley pontificated on matters political in a saloon on Archery Road. This was Archer Avenue on the South Side of Chicago, one of the radial streets that cut across what was once open prairie near the Loop and along the Chicago River. Archer Avenue was one of the paths of outward migration and upward mobility for the children and grandchildren of Chicago's ethnic and cultural groups, and still is. Italians from the river wards along the Chicago and Sanitary and Ship Canal moved west, the South Side Irish moved west and south along Cicero Avenue toward Oak Lawn, and the Bohemians (as they

Voter Turnout	
2013 Total Citizen 18+	472,898
2014 House Turnout	180,855
2014 Turnout as % CVAP	38.2%
2012 Turnout as % CVAP	55.1%

were called then; now Czechs) were heavily concentrated in the neat bungalows of industrial suburbs like Berwyn. Today, Latinos are driving these same avenues, up before dawn to arrive at factory jobs, or taking Chicago Transit Authority "El" trains to the Loop or to "edge city" jobs along the expressways. Midway International Airport, Chicago's main airport from 1927 until O'Hare International Airport opened in 1955, is now a busy discount airline hub. In recent years, it renovated and expanded its congested terminals and parking lots, all squeezed into the heart of a busy commercial area on the Southwest Side.

The 3rd Congressional District of Illinois consists of much of this territory, crisscrossed by grid-pattern streets, the canal, the railroad lines, and the switching yards so common in this, the center of the nation's rail network. It is part of Chicago's bungalow belt, with one after another of the ubiquitous peaked brick houses neatly lining every street like Monopoly pieces, the handiwork of Swedish, Italian, and Polish masons. In the Archer Avenue neighborhoods, Poles cling to their heritage, with many weekend schools teaching Polish to local kids and adults. A narrow corridor on the near South Side extends to the Bridgeport neighborhood, the lifetime home of the late Mayor Richard J. Daley, father of former Mayor Richard M. Daley, and the storied Irish stronghold that produced four other Chicago mayors. In April 2005, Patrick Daley Thompson, the grandson and nephew of former mayors, won a runoff for election as Alderman from Bridgeport. The ballpark for the Chicago White Sox, U.S. Cellular Field, is a brisk walk away. In recent years, Bridgeport has diversified, as Hispanics and Asians have moved in along with artists taking studio space in old warehouses. The neighborhood has "reinvented itself as a happening commercial, entertainment, and arts destination," the *Chicago Advocate* reported in September 2014. But it attracts few African-American families, wary of Bridgeport's history of racial hostility and violence.

The 3rd also includes the far southwest edge of Chicago, with its early 20th century, prairie style houses; a few older, affluent suburbs like Western Springs; and middle-income towns like Oak Lawn and Palos Hills. An eastern slice of Will County includes the towns of Orland Park, Lockport, and Lemont, home to Argonne National Laboratory, which conducts basic and applied research in high energy physics and other disciplines; its presence has sparked numerous private research firms in the area.

The Hispanic voting-age population is about 24%, deliberately low to limit the influence of that community in a potential primary. But the district has the second largest Hispanic constituency in the state. It has become decidedly more suburban than urban: In 2010, 39% of its votes were cast in the city; in 2012, the rate was 29%. Politically, this area is ancestrally Democratic, culturally conservative, multiethnic and viscerally

2012 Presidential Vote
Barack Obama (D) 143,910   (56%)
Mitt Romney (R).................109,212   (43%)

2008 Presidential Vote
Barack Obama (D) 158,459   (58%)
John McCain (R).................110,044   (41%)

Cook Partisan Voting Index: D+5

patriotic. Of the seven congressional districts that include parts of Chicago, the 3rd has cast the highest percentages for Republican presidential candidates, although the GOP vote has fallen well short of a majority. It remains solidly Democratic, but worth monitoring for future political change. President Barack Obama won 58% and 56% of the vote here in his two presidential campaigns.

Daniel Lipinski (D)

Democrat Daniel Lipinski was first elected in 2004 to replace his father, Bill Lipinski, who represented the district for 22 years. Like his father, the younger Lipinski has focused on transportation and manufacturing, but he puts his engineering background to work on cyber security and other technology issues.

Daniel Lipinski grew up in Chicago, in the city's 23rd Ward, and first served as a campaign volunteer for his father in 1979. He got engineering degrees from Northwestern and

Stanford universities before switching to political science for his doctorate at Duke. He worked on the staffs of four House Democrats from Illinois, though not on his father's, and was an American Political Science Association congressional fellow for the House Democratic Policy Committee. He wrote his doctoral thesis on the topic of congressional newsletters (*Congressional Communication,* published by the University of Michigan Press). At the beginning of 2004, he was an assistant professor of political science at the University of Tennessee in Knoxville.

Lipinski's nomination to run for his father's seat is a case study in Chicago's still-thriving backroom politics. In the summer of 2004, Bill Lipinski denied widespread rumors that he would give up his seat. Then on August 13, he abruptly announced he would not seek reelection in November because he wanted to return to Chicago and "spend more time with my wife." (Not *that* much time, as it turns out, because he later became a transportation lobbyist.) A meeting was scheduled for August 17 for the 19 ward and township Democratic committeemen in the 3rd District. The group consisted of a *Who's Who* of connected Chicago politicians, including Bill Lipinski, the 23rd Ward committeeman. At the meeting, Lipinski proposed the most qualified person he could think of, his son, Daniel, and shortly afterward, he was nominated without opposition.

The nominee was not briefed quite as well as he perhaps should have been. At his first press conference, Lipinski, who had not lived in Illinois for 15 years, made the politically unconscionable assertion that he had for many years been a fan of the Chicago Cubs, Chicago's North Side baseball team. The White Sox are the hands-down favorite team of the 3rd District's Southwest Side neighborhoods and suburbs. Luckily for Lipinski, a Democratic nomination, even one decided by a group of longtime political bosses and pals, is tantamount to election in the 3rd District, and he sailed to victory in November.

In the House, Daniel Lipinski has kept his pledge to be "not really that different from my father," who was the most conservative Democrat in the Illinois delegation. He opposes same-sex marriage and abortion rights except when the mother's life is at stake. He was among the Democrats who has declined to vote for Nancy Pelosi as their party's leader in the House. In 2011, he cast his vote for Rep. Marcy Kaptur of Ohio, who is the House's most senior woman. Two years later, he backed Rep. Jim Cooper of Tennessee, an outspoken Pelosi critic. In 2015, he voted for Rep. Peter DeFazio of Oregon, the senior Democrat on the Transportation and Infrastructure Committee, where Lipinski serves. He declined to support the Democrats' health care overhaul, saying that its provision banning federal funds for abortions wasn't strong enough even as other anti-abortion Democrats expressed satisfaction with it. Of the 34 House Democrats who voted against the Affordable Care Act in 2010, he is 1 of only 3 who remain in the House. He has continued to press for changes in the law.

As a member of the Science, Space, and Technology Committee, where he is senior Democrat on the Research and Technology Subcommittee, Lipinski worked with Republican Michael McCaul of Texas to win House passage of a cyber-security bill in April 2012. In 2013-14, he took credit for bipartisan enactment of two bills designed to boost the economy: The American Manufacturing Competitiveness Act, which requires a National Strategic Plan for Manufacturing every four years; and the Cybersecurity Enhancement Act, to protect Americans from cybercrimes.

Lipinski always has an eye on Midway International Airport, which generates the most jobs of any employer in the district. After the Department of Transportation found that Midway had the worst on-time performance among the 29 largest U.S. airports through November 2010, he complained to Southwest Airlines about the tardiness of its Midway flights. The airline agreed to do better. He also devotes attention to rail infrastructure and has been a vocal advocate for CREATE, a public-private partnership to improve the Chicago area's passenger and freight rail. In March 2015, he and Rep. Mike Quigley of Chicago's North Side filed a bill to provide $1 billion over the next five years for rail-safety improvement projects. He noted that his district is home to four commuter rail lines, Amtrak, and six of the nation's seven Class I freight railroads. He teamed with Republican Rep. Joe Heck of Nevada to re-launch that same month the Congressional Unmanned Systems Caucus. They defined its objectives as educating other lawmaker on commercial applications of unmanned systems, and current industry trends with air, land, and sea-based autonomous systems.

Lipinski has drawn significant primary opposition in his reelection bids. In 2006, John Sullivan, an assistant Cook County state's attorney, made an issue of Lipinski getting the seat in "a backroom deal." Financial planner John Kelly used "no tricks, no fix" as a campaign slogan. Lipinski won with 54%, to 26% for Kelly and 20% for Sullivan. In the 2008 primary, Lipinski faced Cook County Assistant State's Attorney Mark Pera, an abortion rights supporter who criticized Lipinski's support for the war in Iraq and questioned his campaign payments to his father. Liberal interest groups, local reformers, and others contributed to Pera, who spent $770,000. Lipinski prevailed, 54%-25%. Redistricting did him two big favors in 2012: It removed much of the 3rd District's Hispanic population, and it shifted the home of wealthy Democratic businessman John Atkinson, who had planned for a primary challenge. He has easily won reelection since then against under-funded GOP challengers and little Democratic opposition.

FOURTH DISTRICT

Luis Gutierrez (D)

Elected 1992, 12th term; b. Dec. 10, 1953, Chicago; NE IL U., B.A. 1975; Catholic; married (Soraida); 2 children.

Elected Office: Chicago city alderman, 1986-92, pres. pro tem, 1989-92.

Professional Career: Teacher, Puerto Rico, 1977-78; Social worker, Chicago Dept. of Children & Family Services, 1979-83; Advisor, Chicago Mayor Harold Washington, 1984-86.

DC Office: 2408 RHOB, 20515, 202-225-8203; Fax: 202-225-7810; Website: gutierrez.house.gov.

State Offices: Chicago, 773-342-0774.

Committees: *Judiciary:* Crime, Terrorism, Homeland Security & Investigations; Immigration & Border Security. *Intelligence (Select).*

Group Ratings

	ADA	ACLU	AFL-CIO	LCV	ITI	COC	HAFA	ACU	CFG	FRC
2014	95%	77%	–	94%	80%	33%	17%	9%	15%	0%
2013	80%	C	95%	89%	C	46%	C	4%	16%	C

National Journal Ratings

	2013 LIB	—	2013 CONS
Economic	84%	—	15%
Social	84%	—	16%
Foreign	94%	—	0%
Composite	89%	—	12%

Key Votes of the 113th Congress

1. Sandy storm spending	Y	5. Medical Marijuana	Y
2. Violence Against Women Act	Y	6. Farm Bill	N
3. Guantanamo Bay Detainees	NV	7. Afghanistan Combat	NV
4. Abortion 20-week ban	N	8. NSA Phone Data Collection	N

9. Syrian Rebels Training	N
10. Keystone pipeline	N
11. Immigration Exec. Action	N
12. Bipartisan budget deal	Y

Election Results

2014 general	Luis Gutierrez (D)	79,666	(78%)	$408,968
	Hector Concepcion (R)	22,278	(22%)	
2014 primary	Luis Gutierrez (D)	21,625	(74%)	
	Alexandra Eidenberg (D)	4,796	(17%)	
	Jorge G. Zavala (D)	2,670	(9%)	

Prior winning percentages: 2012 (83%), 2010 (77%), 2008 (81%), 2006 (86%), 2004 (84%), 2002 (80%), 2000 (89%), 1998 (82%), 1996 (94%), 1994 (75%), 1992 (78%)

Population		Race and Ethnicity		Income	
Total:	712,077	Latino	71.8%	Median income:	$41,686
Urban:	90.8%	White	21.1%		*(365 of 435)*
Suburban:	9.2%	Black	3.5%	Under $50,000	56.9%
Rural:	0.0%	Asian	2.3%	$50,000-$99,999:	28.7%
Land area:	74	Two races	1.1%	$100,000-$199,999:	12.2%
Pop/sq. mi.:	9,651.9	White Ethnic	16.4%	$200,000 or more:	2.2%
Born in state:	52.9%			Poverty Rate	22.6%
		Education			
Age Groups		H.S. grad or less:	59.1%	**Work**	
Under 18:	27.6%	Some college:	21.1%	White collar:	23.1%
18 to 34:	28.6%	College degree, 4 yr.:	13.0%	Blue collar:	44.9%
35 to 64:	36.1%	Post-grad study:	6.8%	Sales and service:	32.0%
Over 64:	7.7%				
		Military		Govt. workers:	7.7%
		Veterans/active duty:	2.3%		

Chicago: Parts of North and Southwest Sides

Just west of the Loop, the Chicago River splits into the North and South Branches, both penetrating the heart of old neighborhoods where immigrants got their start. The South Branch is the guts of Chicago, the site of one of Western civilization's astonishing engineering feats. In 1900, the course of the

Voter Turnout	
2013 Total Citizen 18+	358,719
2014 House Turnout	101,944
2014 Turnout as % CVAP	28.4%
2012 Turnout as % CVAP	47.8%

river was reversed so that sewage flowed downstate through a canal rather than out into Lake Michigan. Just blocks away was Maxwell Street, then thronged with market stalls and long the arrival point for Chicago-bound Jews. Not far away in an Italian-American neighborhood on Halsted Street was Jane Addams' Hull House, the original settlement house, where social workers instructed new immigrants on adapting to American life. To the south were Pilsen, arrival neighborhood for the Bohemians (Czechs), and the Irish neighborhoods along Archer Avenue. To the north was Milwaukee Avenue, the main street of Polish-Americans and Ukrainian-Americans.

Today, many of these places are arrival neighborhoods again, mostly for Chicago's wide variety of Hispanic immigrants. On the South Side, in the old river wards, is Chicago's Mexican-American community, extending west into Pilsen and into the once Bohemian suburb of Cicero, famous as a haven for Al Capone's mobsters in the 1920s. Times have changed: Beginning in the 1980s, Cicero became a transit point for Mexican immigrants, many of whom then made their permanent residences elsewhere in Chicago. Its official census population is 84,000, but town officials believe the actual number is significantly higher because of the influx of undocumented residents. This is by far the largest Latino concentration north of Texas and Florida and between the two coasts; in Cicero, not long ago, Hispanics made up 93% of all children under the age of 5.

The 4th Congressional District of Illinois remains the only majority-Hispanic district in the Midwest. Latinos comprise 66% of the voting age population. With the South Side Mexican-American areas and the smaller North Side Puerto Rican communities separated by the West Side black ghetto, the solution was the creation of one of the most bizarrely shaped congressional

2012 Presidential Vote		
Barack Obama (D)	137,326	(81%)
Mitt Romney (R)	28,955	(17%)
2008 Presidential Vote		
Barack Obama (D)	145,019	(81%)
John McCain (R)	32,827	(18%)
Cook Partisan Voting Index:	D+29	

districts in the country, shaped like a pair of earmuffs. Essentially these two Latino communities, defined by careful boundaries to maximize the district's Hispanic percentage, are connected by a thin line of territory stretching around the black-majority 7th District to meet at the Cook-DuPage County line. Nearly fourth-fifths of the district votes are cast in Chicago or Cicero.

The district also contains the rapidly gentrifying Northwest Side neighborhoods of Logan Square, famous for its boulevards and spacious mansions, and Humboldt Park. There, young professionals are moving in, with trendy restaurants, new condominiums and boutique shops locating alongside traditional Latin American *taquerias* and Hispanic churches. The *Chicago Advocate* referred to the area as the "Hipster Mecca of the Midwest. The chief downside is for the long-time tenants who have been forced out by higher housing prices.

Luis Gutierrez (D)

Luis Gutierrez, a Democrat elected in 1992 and the only Hispanic to serve from Illinois, has been for years the House's most vocal advocate of comprehensive immigration reform, which he likens to the civil rights struggle. After President Barack Obama's resounding electoral support among Latinos in 2012 led many members of both parties to agree that the issue should be addressed, Chicago Mayor Rahm Emanuel joked that "the rest of America has caught up with Luis Gutierrez."

Gutierrez is of Puerto Rican descent and grew up in Chicago. As a student at Northeastern Illinois University in the 1970s, he joined a protest over the lack of basic English classes for students from other countries. Gutierrez after college worked as a teacher for two years in Puerto Rico. When he returned to Chicago, he worked as a cab driver and social worker. In 1983, he ran for 32nd Ward committeeman against Democratic Rep. Dan Rostenkowski and lost decisively. Then he became a staffer for Mayor Harold Washington, the city's first black mayor. He ran for alderman in 1984 and lost. In 1986, he ran again and won in a new Hispanic-majority ward. After Washington died, Gutierrez backed Richard M. Daley in the 1989 election. Backing winners is a formula that works in Chicago politics. In the 1992 primary, for the new House seat, rival and former Alderman Juan Soliz called Gutierrez a machine candidate. Gutierrez won, 60%-40%. Since easily winning a rematch in 1994, he has not had serious competition.

In the House, Gutierrez has staked out liberal positions, and is known for his feisty, blunt style. As a freshman, his outspoken opposition to congressional pay raises, including labeling the House "the belly of the beast" in a television interview, got him into hot water with Democratic leaders. "I've gotten my rear end kicked around here," Gutierrez told *The Washington Post.* But he later mended fences with party leaders, and in 2011 was appointed to the Intelligence Committee.

As a member of the Financial Services Committee, from which he has taken a leave of absence, he proposed higher FDIC charges for big banks and lower fees for community banks in 2009. He sponsored the $200 billion receivership fund (later reduced to $150 billion) for banks, which was included in the financial regulation bill of 2010. He called in March 2012 for the resignation of the Federal Home Financing Agency's acting Director Edward DeMarco for not doing enough to help those facing foreclosure. "We are facing serious problems in the housing market, and we simply can't use someone at FHFA who plugs his ears and refuses (to) try for workable solutions," he said.

Gutierrez has traveled the country appearing at rallies and other events—occasionally getting arrested—for a bill that gives illegal immigrants a potential path to citizenship. Over the years, he has pushed to restore food stamp eligibility to legal immigrants, to grant automatic citizenship to immigrants in military combat, and legal status to immigrants without documentation who make major contributions in the United States. "I want to be a spokesperson for people that are new to this country," he has said. In 2005, he was the lead Democratic sponsor of the House version of an overhaul in immigration policy, which passed the Senate in 2006 but died in the Republican-controlled House. After an appearance on MSNBC to debate the immigration issue, Gutierrez got into a shoving match with then-Rep. Tom Tancredo of Colorado, a Republican known for his tough, anti-illegal immigrant positions. Gutierrez said afterward, "It wasn't my best moment."

In March 2010, Gutierrez said he would vote against the Democrats' sweeping health care bill because it barred illegal immigrants from the proposed insurance exchanges; two days before the vote, he switched and said he would vote yes. During the first two years of President Barack Obama, he pressed the White House and House Democratic leaders to advance comprehensive immigration legislation, to no avail, leading him to regularly rebuke the president. He was quick to praise Obama in June 2012 for issuing an executive order allowing people who entered the United States illegally as children to remain and work without fear of deportation for at least two years. "With one swoop of the pen, he has mended a relationship with the Latino community that has been frayed," he told the *Chicago*

Sun-Times. He blasted Obama's rival, Mitt Romney, an immigration hard-liner, as someone who wanted to turn young children's dreams into "nightmares."

In recent years, Gutierrez has been part of a bipartisan group of House members that quietly met, off and on, to draft a proposal on immigration. He began as an optimist, hoping that a friendship he struck with 2012 GOP vice-presidential nominee Paul Ryan—the two worked out together at the House gym—would prove useful. He repeatedly called for action, warning Republicans in May 2014 that if they didn't act, George W. Bush will be "the last Republican president in American history." But Senate passage of a bipartisan bill did nothing to move legislation through the House, and by the following month Gutierrez urged Obama to act unilaterally. "Your chance to play a role in how immigration and deportation policies are carried out this year are over," he told colleagues in an angry floor speech. "Having given ample time to craft legislation, you failed." When Republicans complained about Obama's unilateral executive action on immigration in November 2014, Gutierrez told ABC, "Millions of American families are depending on the president fixing a broken immigration system because…my colleagues are tired of seeing U.S. servicemen being called to be deployed in defense of our nation and at the same time when they receive that deployment notice, they are receiving a notice that their wife should be deported."

Gutierrez has weighed in on Puerto Rican issues. He stoutly opposed the Democratic leadership's bill mandating a referendum on the island's commonwealth status and, if that were rejected, giving Puerto Rican voters a choice between the current status and independence. "This bill is not the product of consensus. It does not provide for true self-determination. The two-step process in the bill is designed to craft an artificial majority for statehood," he argued. The House passed the bill 223-169 in April 2010, but it died in the Senate.

In 2008, Gutierrez was the subject of unflattering news coverage about his dealings with local developers. The *Chicago Tribune* reported that, starting in 2002, he had made about $421,000 by investing in half a dozen real estate deals with campaign supporters and then exiting a short time later. Gutierrez told the newspaper that he had made a profit in five of the deals but lost money on the sixth. Developer Calvin Boender, who loaned him $200,000 in a 2004 deal, was convicted of bribery in March 2010. During the trial, there was testimony that Gutierrez helped Boender get a zoning change for a development on the West Side of Chicago.

Gutierrez faced another ethics controversy in 2013, when *USA Today* reported that he had made payments for a decade from his official House account to a lobbying firm run by his former chief of staff. Members are barred from hiring consultants on short-term contracts for "general, non-legislative" purposes. Gutierrez denied any wrongdoing, and the House Ethics Committee declined in May 2014 to launch a full-scale investigation into the matter.

Though he often plays the rebel, Gutierrez has sometimes built bridges among Chicago's fractious Democratic politicians to maximize Latino influence. He considered running for mayor of Chicago, but decided against challenging Mayor Daley after Democrats regained the House majority in 2006. More than once, he has announced he would retire from Congress, only to reverse that plan before the filing deadline.

FIFTH DISTRICT

Mike Quigley (D)

Elected April 2009, 4th full term; b. Oct. 17, 1958, Indianapolis, IN; Roosevelt U., B.A. 1981, U. of Chicago, M.P.P. 1985, Loyola U., J.D. 1989; married (Barbara); 2 children.

Elected Office: Cook Cnty. commissioner, 1998-2009.

Professional Career: Cook Cnty. aldermanic aide, 1983-89; Adjunct prof., Roosevelt U., 2006-07; Adjunct prof. in political science, Loyola U. Chicago, 2002-09; Practicing atty., 1990-present.

DC Office: 2458 RHOB, 20515, 202-225-4061; Fax: 202-225-5603; Website: quigley.house.gov.

State Offices: Chicago, 773-267-5926.

Committees: *Appropriations:* Financial Services & General Government; Transpiration, Housing & Urban Development, & Related Agencies; *Intelligence (Select):* Emerging Threats (RMM); NSA and Cybersecurity.

Group Ratings

	ADA	ACLU	AFL-CIO	LCV	ITI	COC	HAFA	ACU	CFG	FRC
2014	80%	77%	–	97%	80%	57%	10%	4%	9%	0%
2013	75%	C	89%	96%	C	54%	C	8%	14%	C

National Journal Ratings

	2013 LIB	—	2013 CONS
Economic	66%	—	34%
Social	63%	—	36%
Foreign	90%	—	6%
Composite	74%	—	26%

Key Votes of the 113th Congress

1. Sandy storm spending	Y 5. Medical Marijuana	Y 9. Syrian Rebels Training	Y
2. Violence Against Women Act	Y 6. Farm Bill	N 10. Keystone pipeline	N
3. Guantanamo Bay Detainees	Y 7. Afghanistan Combat	Y 11. Immigration Exec. Action	N
4. Abortion 20-week ban	N 8. NSA Phone Data Collection	N 12. Bipartisan budget deal	Y

Election Results

2014 general	Mike Quigley (D)...................... 116,364	(63%)	$779,868
	Vince Kolber (R)........................... 56,350	(31%)	$345,811
	Nancy Wade (G) 11,305	(6%)	
2014 primary	Mike Quigley (D)..................unopposed		

Prior winning percentages: 2012 (66%), 2010 (71%), 2009 special (69%)

Population		Race and Ethnicity		Income	
Total:	734,664	White	71.1%	Median income:	$68,792
Urban:	72.9%	Latino	17.9%		(65 of 435)
Suburban:	27.1%	Asian	6.8%	Under $50,000	36.6%
Rural:	0.0%	Black	2.3%	$50,000-$99,999:	30.3%
Land area:	105	Two races	1.6%	$100,000-$199,999:	23.2%
Pop/sq. mi.:	6,966.6	White Ethnic	47.6%	$200,000 or more:	9.9%
Born in state:	55.6%			Poverty Rate	10.7%
		Education			
Age Groups		H.S. grad or less:	28.2%	**Work**	
Under 18:	18.6%	Some college:	21.1%	White collar:	48.3%
18 to 34:	31.9%	College degree, 4 yr.:	31.2%	Blue collar:	39.1%
35 to 64:	37.7%	Post-grad study:	19.6%	Sales and service:	12.7%
Over 64:	11.9%				
		Military		Govt. workers:	9.3%
		Veterans/active duty:	3.9%		

Chicago: North Side, Central Cook

Few places in America today have more ethnic and cultural variety than the North Side of Chicago. This has been the destination of one immigrant group after another. Its neighborhoods harbor all manner of successful, middle-class people. Wooden workingmen's cottages from the late 19th century

Voter Turnout	
2013 Total Citizen 18+	531,902
2014 House Turnout	184,019
2014 Turnout as % CVAP	34.6%
2012 Turnout as % CVAP	54.9%

give way to sturdy brick houses from the early 1900s, and then to the prairie bungalows of the 1920s and the white-shuttered, orange-brick colonials of the 1950s. Chicago was America's top immigrant destination for Poles, Lithuanians, Czechs, Slovaks, Ukrainians, and Romanians. Something about the heavy, dull clouds of the long winters, the short, hot summers, and a climate suited to potatoes and cabbage and other hardy vegetables, may have reminded them of Central and Eastern Europe, with the addition of the bustling Loop.

By the late 1980s, upwardly mobile immigrants from Mexico and Guatemala, Korea, and the Philippines were moving in. The 1990s witnessed new rounds of immigrants from Poland and Ukraine, and also from Pakistan, India, and Bosnia. Family ties, webs of acquaintances that reach back to ancestral villages, have made the North Side of Chicago a natural port of entry for Eastern bloc migrants, even as other newcomers arrive with relationships extending to Latin America and Southeast Asia. A couple of blocks from the Chicago River and the Kennedy Expressway is the grand, old St. Stanislaus Kostka

Church, a traditional center of the Polish community since the 19th century that now conducts Masses in Spanish.

The 5th Congressional District covers an oddly shaped swath across Chicago's North Side and the city's western suburbs, running from the lakefront to, and including, O'Hare International Airport on the north end of the city, and dipping into western suburbs like Elmhurst and affluent Hinsdale. It takes in the old Polish-American and Ukrainian-American neighborhoods and shops around Milwaukee Avenue, and the Italian neighborhoods running west on Grand Avenue. But it also includes the gentrified Chicago neighborhoods of Old Town, where Crate & Barrel was founded in 1962, and where old houses and factories are being converted into upscale condominiums, often over the objections of preservationists. Nearby Lincoln Park is the second-richest neighborhood in Chicago (after the Gold Coast); it abounds with boutiques, clubs, and restaurants and contains DePaul University, the nation's largest Roman Catholic university. Those commercial activities have substantially reduced the residential population. Chicago Mayor Rahm Emanuel lives in trendy Ravenswood in the district, and he received strong support on the North Side in his 2015 reelection.

The district is home to baseball's famed Wrigley Field, which opened in 1914 and is a protected landmark that has defied the teardown trend in ballparks and endured the heartbreak of the Cubs. After taking over as the Cubs' new owner in 2009, businessman Tom Ricketts unveiled a renovation plan costing upward of $200 million to remodel and update the ballpark, but negotiations between the city and the Cubs were delayed. Work finally started during the winter of 2015, disrupted some early games that season, and is scheduled for completion in 2018. Just east of Wrigleyville is Boystown, the epicenter of Chicago's gay community; rainbow flags are present on most businesses

2012 Presidential Vote		
Barack Obama (D) 188,166	(66%)
Mitt Romney (R)...................90,715	(32%)
2008 Presidential Vote		
Barack Obama (D) 214,862	(70%)
John McCain (R)...................88,434	(29%)
Cook Partisan Voting Index: D+16		

in the neighborhood. The 5th District contains the largest white population of the seven districts based in Chicago: Only 16% of its voting age population is Hispanic. A scant 3% is African-American. While the 5th now has some Republican-leaning western suburbs, it remains a solidly Democratic district.

Mike Quigley (D)

Mike Quigley is a reform-minded Democrat who won a special election in April 2009 to succeed Democratic Rep. Rahm Emanuel, who later became mayor of Chicago. He is both an avid hockey player—he's had more than 300 stitches to prove it—and an ex-political science professor whom *The New York Times* once called "the king of Chicago's public-policy nerds."

Quigley grew up in the working-class suburb of Carol Stream in DuPage County. He graduated from Roosevelt University, got his law degree from Loyola University in Chicago, and practiced criminal law. He taught political science part-time at Loyola. He started his career in politics as an aide to Alderman Bernard Hansen while studying for a master's degree in public policy at the University of Chicago. He got involved in a community battle to stop the addition of lights for night games at Wrigley Field, which is in the heart of an old, gentrified neighborhood. In 1998, Quigley was elected to the Cook County Board of Commissioners, where he became an independent voice and a frequent nemesis of board President John Stroger. He pushed reforms such as ending patronage jobs at the Cook County Forest Preserve District, promoted environmental action, and sponsored a proposal to allow gay couples to register as domestic partners. In 2005, Quigley decided to challenge Stroger for board president, but later dropped out and backed Forrest Claypool, saying the two would have split the anti-incumbent vote if they had both remained in the race. Claypool repaid the favor by endorsing Quigley for the House seat.

After President Barack Obama plucked Emanuel from the House to serve as his chief of staff, many candidates jumped into the wide-open Democratic primary. State Rep. Sara Feigenholtz was endorsed by EMILY's List, which supports abortion rights. Alderman Patrick O'Connor and state Rep. John Fritchey had local party machine support. The appointment of Roland Burris to the Senate by impeached Democratic Gov. Rod Blagojevich became a campaign issue, with candidates seeking to burnish their credentials as reformers and attacking their opponents for having been associated with the disgraced governor. Fritchey suffered from having defended Burris at a legislative hearing in January 2009. Quigley ran a late ad comparing Feigenholtz to President Richard Nixon, saying she had resorted to unfair campaign charges. That may have extinguished any lingering friendship between Quigley and Feigenholtz, who had dated briefly years earlier.

Quigley received key newspaper endorsements from the *Chicago Sun-Times* and the *Chicago Tribune,* the latter praising him for an "outstanding record of independent, reform-minded performance in office." In a low-turnout event, Quigley won the primary with 20% of the vote to 17% for Fritchey and 15% for Feigenholtz. Quigley then breezed to victory in the general election against Republican Rosanna Pulido.

In the House, Quigley has been a consistent Democratic vote but one who is unafraid to ruffle feathers. He was among the first Democrats in 2010 to call on Rep. Charles Rangel of New York to give up his Ways and Means Committee chairmanship while battling ethics problems. Shortly after taking office, he supported Arizona Republican Rep. Jeff Flake's push for an ethics investigation of then-Rep. John Murtha of Pennsylvania and other senior appropriators. He cofounded the Congressional Transparency Caucus and introduced legislation requiring lobbyists to disclose the name of each affected executive branch official and each member of Congress and staff with whom they meet. In 2014, he wrote that Supreme Court Justices should comply with the same financial disclosure rules that apply to members of Congress and top officials of the Executive Branch. He sponsored a bill in 2012 requiring Congressional Research Service reports to be made public. The same year, he worked with other Illinois lawmakers to get a provision into a bill to block former congressmen convicted of corruption from collecting their public pensions. That responded to the conviction of Illinois Gov. Rod Blagojevich, an ex-Representative. He moved into the House hierarchy with a seat on the Appropriations Committee, where he was the only Illinois member from either party.

Quigley has been active in calling for tighter gun control laws. On two issues of importance to his constituents, he has pushed for an extension of the visa waiver program to Poland, and review of the policy that bans gay and bisexual men from donating blood. To learn more about what his constituents' lives are like, he took a series of temporary workday jobs ranging from collecting garbage to delivering pizza.

Quigley has coasted to reelection. He toyed with the idea of running in 2011 to succeed retiring Chicago Mayor Richard M. Daley but decided not to join the crowded field that included Emanuel, who went on to be elected mayor.

SIXTH DISTRICT

Peter Roskam (R)

Elected 2006, 5th term; b. Sept. 13, 1961, Hinsdale; U. of IL, B.A. 1983, Chicago-Kent Col. of Law, J.D. 1989; Anglican; married (Elizabeth); 4 children.

Elected Office: IL House, 1992-98; IL Senate, 2000-06, min. whip, 2003-06.

Professional Career: Aide, U.S. Rep. Tom DeLay, 1985-86; U.S. Rep. Henry Hyde, 1986-87; H.S. teacher, 1983-85; Exec. dir., Educational Assistance Ltd., 1987-93; Practicing atty., 1994-2006.

DC Office: 2246 RHOB, 20024, 202-225-4561; Fax: 202-225-1166; Website: roskam.house.gov.

State Offices: West Chicago, 630-232-0006; Barrington, 847-656-6354.

Committees: *Ways & Means:* Health; Oversight (Chmn). *Select Benghazi Committee.*

Group Ratings

	ADA	ACLU	AFL-CIO	LCV	ITI	COC	HAFA	ACU	CFG	FRC
2014	0%	0%	–	6%	100%	100%	50%	72%	46%	100%
2013	0%	C	24%	4%	C	85%	C	76%	61%	C

National Journal Ratings

	2013 LIB	—	2013 CONS
Economic	29%	—	70%
Social	38%	—	59%
Foreign	24%	—	68%
Composite	32%	—	68%

Key Votes of the 113th Congress

1. Sandy storm spending	N	5. Medical Marijuana	N
2. Violence Against Women Act	N	6. Farm Bill	Y
3. Guantanamo Bay Detainees	N	7. Afghanistan Combat	N
4. Abortion 20-week ban	Y	8. NSA Phone Data Collection	N

9. Syrian Rebels Training	Y
10. Keystone pipeline	Y
11. Immigration Exec. Action	Y
12. Bipartisan budget deal	Y

Election Results

2014 general	Peter Roskam (R)...................... 160,278	(67%)	$4,079,870	$3,115
	Michael Mason (D)...................... 78,465	(33%)		
2014 primary	Peter Roskam (R)...................unopposed			

Prior winning percentages: 2012 (59%), 2010 (64%), 2008 (58%), 2006 (51%)

Population		Race and Ethnicity		Income	
Total:	727,718	White	79.7%	Median income:	$89,683
Urban:	22.8%	Latino	7.9%		*(13 of 435)*
Suburban:	77.2%	Asian	7.9%	Under $50,000	25.9%
Rural:	0.0%	Black	2.8%	$50,000-$99,999:	28.9%
Land area:	357	Two races	1.5%	$100,000-$199,999:	30.5%
Pop/sq. mi.:	2,038.1	White Ethnic	48.4%	$200,000 or more:	14.8%
Born in state:	65.8%			Poverty Rate	5.2%
		Education			
Age Groups		H.S. grad or less:	23.6%	**Work**	
Under 18:	24.8%	Some college:	26.3%	White collar:	47.4%
18 to 34:	19.2%	College degree, 4 yr.:	30.3%	Blue collar:	39.0%
35 to 64:	43.1%	Post-grad study:	19.9%	Sales and service:	13.7%
Over 64:	13.0%				
		Military		Govt. workers:	10.4%
		Veterans/active duty:	5.4%		

West-Central Chicagoland: DuPage, Kane

Most residents of Chicagoland now live in the sub-urbs, and increasingly not even in Cook County, but in the collar counties surrounding Cook. DuPage County, straight west of Chicago, had 103,000 residents in 1940; in 2013, there were 932,000, with new subdivisions still springing up at the western

Voter Turnout	
2013 Total Citizen 18+	508,879
2014 House Turnout	238,752
2014 Turnout as % CVAP	46.9%
2012 Turnout as % CVAP	66%

edges. This is no longer a one-trick county of bedroom suburbs. It has become an engine of economic growth, containing the Illinois Technology and Research Corridor, one of suburban Chicago's biggest employment hubs. In Oak Brook are the headquarters of Ace Hardware, Federal Signal, and most famously, McDonald's and its Hamburger University, an 80-acre campus where more than 80,000 trainees have received bachelor of hamburgerology degrees since 1961, and which 7,500 attend each year. In early 2015, that campus suffered 120 layoffs.

Nearby are graceful, old railroad-commuter towns like Hinsdale and Downers Grove, plus Barrington Hills, known for its country manors and large open areas protected by preservationists. Naperville, once a country village, is now an edge city, with a school district that is top-ranked in science. Wheaton is home to the Illinois landmark Cantigny, a 500-acre public park and recreation area that was once the estate of Col. Robert McCormick, longtime publisher of the *Chicago Tribune*. Wheaton College, known as the "evangelical Harvard," boasts Reverend Billy Graham among its alumni.

Politically, these suburbs were once rock-ribbed Republican, convinced that civic virtues could best be realized by opposing the party of City Hall in Chicago. But in the 1990s, they became less Republican, as voters recoiled from the national party's cultural conservatism. After voting for Republicans in every presidential election in the 20th century, DuPage County voted for President Barack Obama twice, giving him a narrow 49.7% plurality of the vote in 2012. The once rural county has also become more diverse; foreign-born residents now make up over 17% of the county-wide population.

The 6th Congressional District of Illinois encompasses parts of Cook County and the Chicago collar counties of Kane, McHenry, and Lake; a bit more than half of the population lives in DuPage. It takes in towns including Barrington, Wheaton, Winfield, Downers

Grove, and parts of Naperville. The 6th was designed in redistricting as a Republican bastion, with the solidly GOP Palatine in Cook, St. Charles in Kane, and Crystal Lake in McHenry. It voted for Obama in 2008, but in 2012 flipped to Mitt Romney, whose business background matched the district's fiscal conservatism. It is one of six districts in Illinois that voted for Romney, but the only one in Chicagoland.

2012 Presidential Vote		
Mitt Romney (R)..................179,607	(53%)
Barack Obama (D) 151,760	(45%)
2008 Presidential Vote		
Barack Obama (D) 178,574	(51%)
John McCain (R)..................165,814	(48%)
Cook Partisan Voting Index: R+4		

Peter Roskam (R)

Peter Roskam, a Republican elected in 2006, is well-regarded among his GOP colleagues as smart, hard-working and fair-minded. He served as chief deputy whip until July 2014, when he sought the whip's job only to lose to the more-conservative Steve Scalise of Louisiana, who had the advantages of hailing from a red state and the South. Roskam remained a go-to player in the House.

A native of DuPage County, Roskam was a varsity gymnast in high school, graduated from the University of Illinois, and got his law degree while directing a charitable organization started by his father that used corporate resources to fund college scholarships. During law school, he was part of a team that won a national mock trial competition. As a young man, he worked as an aide to Republican Rep. Henry Hyde, his predecessor. Roskam served six years in the state House, and six years in the state Senate, where he was the Republican whip and floor leader. (He is the only current member of Congress who served with Barack Obama in the state Senate.)

Between those legislative stints, he ran unsuccessfully in 1998 for an open congressional seat, losing 45%-40% to state House colleague Judy Biggert in the Republican primary. In 2006, Hyde, one of the most widely respected conservatives on Capitol Hill, stepped down. Roskam raised nearly $400,000 in two months, and managed to scare off challengers for the GOP nomination, conserving his money for the general election.

In the fall, his Democratic opponent was Tammy Duckworth, a former manager for Rotary International and an Iraq war veteran. She was well-known as a Black Hawk helicopter pilot who served with the Illinois National Guard and lost both legs in Iraq after her helicopter was hit by a rocket-propelled grenade and crashed. She had won a highly competitive primary to get the Democratic nomination.

The two nominees sparred over tax cuts, spending earmarks, the Iraq war, and immigration policy. They also clashed over abortion rights, federal funding for embryonic stem cell research, and expansion of O'Hare International Airport, all of which Roskam opposed. Duckworth criticized Roskam as "a rubber stamp" for the Bush administration, and referred to the scandal-plagued House GOP Leader Tom DeLay of Texas as Roskam's "mentor." She benefited from favorable news coverage of her compelling personal story.

Roskam disparaged Duckworth as the "candidate from the Chicago Democratic machine" because of her ties to Rahm Emanuel, then a House member from a neighboring district. In one of the few Republican successes in a competitive House contest that year, Roskam won 51%-49%. (Duckworth was elected to the 8th District seat in 2012.)

In the House, Roskam opposed Democrats' economic proposals. He accused Obama, his one-time colleague in Springfield, of being unwilling to deal with Republicans. "You know, in the legislature, Barack Obama was somebody you could sit down and negotiate with. ... Now I think the problem is that the president has not shown any bipartisanship," he told *The Daily Beast* website in December 2012.

Early in his House career, Roskam was more moderate, casting votes in 2009 to tighten food safety, impose more stringent regulations on credit card companies, and give the Food and Drug Administration authority to regulate some tobacco products. He has styled himself as less centrist since his party regained House control in 2011.

As chief deputy whip, he won praise from colleagues. "People like him, he's smart, he's savvy, he understands the policy end and how it relates to the political end," Majority Leader Eric Cantor told the suburban Chicago *Daily Herald* in March 2012. It helped that he has been a skilled fundraiser, often not just donating money to Republican candidates but going to their districts to assist them. In the 2012 and 2014 election season, he took in more than

$8 million through his campaign and political action committees, according to the Center for Responsive Politics.

His friendship with party leaders got Roskam a seat in 2009 on the powerful Ways and Means Committee. When the panel approved a $15 billion package of small-business tax breaks in 2010, he unsuccessfully sought to index individual tax rates to reflect not only inflation but increases in federal spending. He said the change would enable household income to grow with federal spending without incurring a tax increase. More recently, he has made a priority of reforming the tax code, describing the current code as "a mess of loopholes, carve outs, and crony capitalism" that has hindered job growth. In 2015, he helped to prepare a package of bills designed to crack down on allegations of political bias at the Internal Revenue Service

When Cantor unexpectedly lost his primary in June 2014, Majority Whip Kevin McCarthy of California moved into the majority leader's slot. That left the whip's job open, and Roskam—who had been meeting with colleagues to discuss his future even before Cantor lost—threw his hat in the ring. He met resistance from some Republicans who questioned his conservatism. It didn't help him when the conservative website Breitbart.com reported that he had boasted of receiving praise from Obama on an "Obama Voters for Roskam" website in 2008. Despite his promise to appoint a deputy from a red state, he lost to Scalise. Rep. Marlin Stutzman of Indiana also ran and diluted the Midwest vote. Since then, Roskam has been given leadership assignments, including as leader of the House Democracy Partnership that assists legislatures in emerging democracies, and a member of the Benghazi investigating committee, where he criticized Hillary Clinton's failure to turn over emails from when she was secretary of State.

Illinois Sen. Dick Durbin vowed that Democrats would give Roskam a strong challenge in 2008. But in July 2007 Duckworth, the party's top prospect, decided to stay as head of the Illinois Veterans' Affairs Department. Instead, Democrats nominated another Iraq war veteran, retired Army Col. Jill Morgenthaler, who was the Army spokeswoman during the Abu Ghraib prison scandal. She campaigned on her support for President George W. Bush's troop surge in Iraq, and accused Roskam of having "extreme" views on abortion rights, health care, and the economy. Despite early Democratic hopes that Obama's coattails would reach across Illinois, the national party gave little help to Morgenthaler. Roskam handily won a second term, 58%-42%. After Illinois Democrats decided to pack as many Republicans as possible into his district to create two new neighboring Democratic seats, he has easily won reelection since 2012.

SEVENTH DISTRICT

Danny Davis (D)

Elected 1996, 10th term; b. Sept. 6, 1941, Parkdale, AR; AR AM&N Col., B.A. 1961, Chicago St. U., M.S. 1968, Union Inst., Ph.D. 1977; Baptist; married (Vera); 2 children.

Elected Office: Chicago city alderman, 1979-90; Cook Cnty. commissioner, 1990-96.

Professional Career: Teacher, Chicago Public Schls., 1962-69; Health care planner, 1969-79.

DC Office: 2159 RHOB, 20515, 202-225-5006; Fax: 202-225-5641; Website: davis.house.gov.

State Offices: Chicago, 773-533-7520.

Committees: *Ways & Means:* Human Resources; Health.

Group Ratings

	ADA	ACLU	AFL-CIO	LCV	ITI	COC	HAFA	ACU	CFG	FRC
2014	95%	83%	–	91%	40%	25%	15%	13%	15%	13%
2013	85%	C	94%	86%	C	25%	C	9%	16%	C

National Journal Ratings

	2013 LIB	—	2013 CONS
Economic	81%	—	19%
Social	65%	—	35%
Foreign	79%	—	20%
Composite	75%	—	25%

Key Votes of the 113th Congress

1. Sandy storm spending	Y 5. Medical Marijuana	Y 9. Syrian Rebels Training N
2. Violence Against Women Act	Y 6. Farm Bill	N 10. Keystone pipeline N
3. Guantanamo Bay Detainees	Y 7. Afghanistan Combat	NV 11. Immigration Exec. Action N
4. Abortion 20-week ban	N 8. NSA Phone Data Collection	Y 12. Bipartisan budget deal NV

Election Results

2014 general	Danny K. Davis (D)..................155,110	(85%)	$469,170
	Robert Bumpers (R)...................27,168	(15%)	
2014 primary	Danny Davis (D)...................unopposed		

Prior winning percentages: 2012 (85%), 2010 (82%), 2008 (85%), 2006 (87%), 2004 (86%), 2002 (83%), 2000 (86%), 1998 (93%), 1996 (83%)

Population		Race And Ethnicity		Income	
Total:	720,325	Black	54.1%	Median income:	$48,841
Urban:	95.6%	White	25.9%		*(258 of 435)*
Suburban:	4.4%	Latino	13.2%	Under $50,000	50.7%
Rural:	0.0%	Asian	5.2%	$50,000-$99,999:	24.3%
Land area:	70	Two races	1.2%	$100,000-$199,999:	16.4%
Pop/sq. mi.:	10,267.6	White Ethnic	17.9%	$200,000 or more:	8.7%
Born in state:	64.0%			Poverty Rate	25.7%
		Education			
Age Groups		H.S. grad or less:	38.0%	**Work**	
Under 18:	21.6%	Some college:	23.1%	White collar:	45.4%
18 to 34:	30.5%	College degree, 4 yr.:	20.0%	Blue collar:	40.6%
35 to 64:	36.9%	Post-grad study:	18.8%	Sales and service:	13.9%
Over 64:	11.0%			Govt. workers:	11.8%
		Military			
		Veterans/active duty:	4.0%		

Chicago: Downtown, West Side, Central Cook

An airplane passenger on a cloudless day can get a clear view of the biggest man-made cityscape between the Atlantic and Pacific oceans: Chicago's Loop. Its high rises and parks along Lake Michigan were built a century ago, and the downtown district was named in 1897 for the quadrilateral shape the

Voter Turnout	
2013 Total Citizen 18+	517,524
2014 House Turnout	182,278
2014 Turnout as % CVAP	35.2%
2012 Turnout as % CVAP	58.8%

elevated train forms around the city's center. International School modernists built their most impressive collection of buildings here and along Lake Shore Drive in the years after World War II. The Loop now spreads beyond the elevated train, or the "El" as it's known locally. It reaches west beyond the financial exchanges to the 110-story Willis (formerly Sears) Tower—once the world's tallest building, now twelfth and second in the United States behind One World Trade Center in New York—situated near the Chicago River. The Loop reaches north and stops at the Gold Coast, the wondrous shopping district along North Michigan Avenue. West of the Gold Coast is the River North neighborhood, which has become one of the city's most vibrant. Leases for businesses in this area are very high, and there are few vacancies.

This is the face Chicago likes to present to the world: giant structures rising where the prairies meet the great lake, a vast concentration of brains and muscle, the nerve center of the nation's commodities markets, and, most recently, a hive of political activity. President Barack Obama's high rise headquarters in 2012 filled a 50,000 square foot floor at One Prudential Plaza. The 2008 campaign office, by comparison, was a 33,000 square foot start-up a few blocks away on Michigan Avenue. South of the Loop sits McCormick Place, the largest convention center in North America, where Obama held his reelection rally. At Grant Park, the president delivered his historic 2008 victory speech in front of 240,000 onlookers cheering the election of the nation's first African-American president. The 319-acre park includes several of the city's civic treasures, including the Art Institute, Millennium Park, and Buckingham Fountain.

Not far west from the luxurious lakefront neighborhoods are the muscle and sinew, gristle and fat of the city. The West Side of Chicago, the vast acres directly west of the Loop, for years was a grimy and dangerous slum, with some areas almost completely abandoned. The decay spread west almost to the city border with upper-income and racially integrated

Oak Park. Many factories that made Chicago the chocolate and candy center of the nation were shuttered, and production went mostly overseas. The West Side began to revive in the 1990s. The United Center, the erstwhile home court of Michael Jordan, sparked commercial development, lower crime rates, and higher land values. Former meatpacking buildings have been turned into art galleries. A massive new downtown dormitory houses students from nearby DePaul University, Roosevelt University, and Columbia College.

The 7th Congressional District of Illinois contains the Loop, most of the North Michigan corridor, the Near North Side, and a few South Side neighborhoods. Its heart, demographically and spiritually, is the predominantly African-American West Side, which is more depopulated and socially disorganized than the predominantly black South Side. To preserve the district's shrinking African-American majority, Democratic redistricters drew in additional South Side precincts.

Just outside the city limits to the west, but in the district, is Oak Park, the boyhood home of writer Ernest Hemingway and the location of architect Frank Lloyd Wright's home and museum and many of his prairie-style houses. There is also well-heeled River Forest; more modest Maywood, which is a black-majority suburb; Broadview and Hillside. African-Americans now make up half of

2012 Presidential Vote		
Barack Obama (D) 263,928	(87%)
Mitt Romney (R)..................35,595	(12%)
2008 Presidential Vote		
Barack Obama (D) 283,996	(90%)
John McCain (R)..................31,475	(10%)
Cook Partisan Voting Index: D+36		

the district's voting-age population. It is the most heavily Democratic district in the state and in the top five nationwide. Obama got 90% here in 2008 and 87% in 2012.

Danny Davis (D)

Danny Davis, a Democrat first elected in 1996, is a liberal who has been eager for political advancement. He waged two unsuccessful campaigns for Chicago mayor and twice flirted with running for president of the Cook County Board of Commissioners. He sought the Senate seat vacated by President Barack Obama before changing his mind.

Davis grew up on a cotton farm in Arkansas, graduated from college in that state, then moved to Chicago and worked as a teacher, assistant principal, and guidance counselor in Chicago public schools. For 10 years, he ran a community health project on the West Side. He was elected alderman in the 29th Ward in 1979, and supported Mayor Harold Washington, the city's first black mayor, in his notorious 1980s battles with white machine aldermen dubbed the "Council Wars." In 1990, Davis was elected a Cook County commissioner.

In 1996, when Democratic Rep. Cardiss Collins retired after nearly 24 years in the House, Davis ran for the seat. His major opponents were 3rd Ward Alderman Dorothy Tillman, an ally of Chicago Mayor Richard M. Daley, and 28th Ward Alderman Ed Smith. Davis campaigned as a big government liberal, calling for a $7.60 minimum wage, affirmative action programs, and a nationalized health care plan. Davis won with 33%. He went on to win the general election with ease and has not faced a serious challenge since. However, he lost his 29th Ward committeeman post to a Daley-backed challenger in 2000.

In the House, Davis has a liberal voting record. He has pushed for tax incentives for businesses that create jobs in inner-city communities and distressed rural areas. He has opposed income tax cuts, even when advocated by Democratic President Bill Clinton. On the Oversight and Government Reform Committee, he was a champion of organized labor as he worked with a bipartisan coalition that in 2006 enacted major changes in the Postal Service. He criticized a new Postal Service overhaul bill that passed the committee under Republican control in September 2011, calling it "a glass half-empty approach that creates new bureaucracies, diminished congressional oversight, and continues to attack the worker rights of postal employees."

His devotion to issues affecting the poor has won him respect even among Republicans. With his wife, Vera Davis, Davis in the mid-2000s supported a local program to increase the low share of black home ownership in his district by offering credit counseling and innovative forms of mortgage financing. With the view that everybody deserves a second chance, Davis has taken a deep interest in the problems of former convicts seeking to transition to the mainstream. He teamed with then-Rep. Mark Souder, a conservative Republican from Indiana, on a bill creating tax credits to encourage transitional housing and job training for former prisoners. It evolved into his Second Chance Act, which President George W. Bush signed into law in 2008. He offered an amendment in May 2012 to increase Second Chance program funding by $10 million, but it failed overwhelmingly in a floor vote.

In 2006, Davis sought to become Cook County Board president when incumbent John Stroger suffered a serious stroke. But Democratic committeemen overwhelmingly supported Stroger's son, Todd, for the nomination. After the 2008 election, Davis campaigned publicly for the support of Democratic Gov. Rod Blagojevich to fill Obama's Senate seat. Blagojevich called Davis his top choice, but Davis turned down what was bound to be a tainted appointment after Blagojevich was criminally charged with trying to gain politically and personally from his power to make the appointment.

As a consolation prize, House Democratic leaders gave Davis a seat on the Ways and Means Committee. He was an outspoken defender of the committee's chairman, New York Democrat Charles B. Rangel, during his ethics scandal, and called the health care overhaul "good for black America."

In 2009, Davis weighed another bid for the Cook County board but ultimately did not run. After Daley announced in 2010 he would not seek reelection as mayor, Davis jumped into the race, collecting endorsements from 15 African-American aldermen. But with pressure mounting to settle on a single black candidate in early January, he endorsed former Sen. Carol Moseley Braun, who had stressed her fundraising advantage over Davis. She lost to Rahm Emanuel. In 2015, Davis again was on the losing side when he endorsed Chuy Garcia, who challenged Emanuel for reelection.

EIGHTH DISTRICT

Tammy Duckworth (D)

Elected 2012, 2nd term; b. March 12, 1968, Bangkok, Thailand; U. of HI, B.A. 1989, George Washington U., M.A. 1992, Capella U. PhD 2015.; deist; married (Bryan Bowlsbey) 1 child.

Military Career: Army Natl. Guard, 1992-2014.

Professional Career: Asst. secy., U.S. Veterans Affairs Dept., 2009-11; Dir., IL Veterans Affairs Dept., 2006-09; Mngr., Rotary Intl., 2003-04.

DC Office: 104 CHOB, 20515, 202-225-3711; Website: duckworth. house.gov.

State Offices: Schaumburg, 847-413-1959.

Committees: *Armed Services:* Readiness; *Oversight & Government Reform:* Information Technology; Transportation & Public Assets (RMM). *Select Benghazi Committee.*

Group Ratings

	ADA	ACLU	AFL-CIO	LCV	ITI	COC	HAFA	ACU	CFG	FRC
2014	70%	83%	–	80%	80%	45%	6%	4%	2%	0%
2013	55%	C	95%	86%	C	50%	C	16%	11%	C

National Journal Ratings

	2013 LIB	—	2013 CONS
Economic	64%	—	36%
Social	66%	—	32%
Foreign	71%	—	27%
Composite	68%	—	32%

Key Votes of the 113th Congress

1. Sandy storm spending	Y	5. Medical Marijuana	Y	9. Syrian Rebels Training	N
2. Violence Against Women Act	Y	6. Farm Bill	N	10. Keystone pipeline	NV
3. Guantanamo Bay Detainees	Y	7. Afghanistan Combat	N	11. Immigration Exec. Action	NV
4. Abortion 20-week ban	N	8. NSA Phone Data Collection	N	12. Bipartisan budget deal	Y

Election Results

2014 general	Tammy Duckworth (D)	84,178	(56%)	$2,289,837		
	Lawrence Kaifesh (R)	66,878	(44%)	$331,673	$5,237	$7,697
2014 primary	Tammy Duckworth (D)	unopposed				

Prior winning percentage: 2012 (55%)

Population		Race and Ethnicity		Income	
Total:	715,255	White	54.6%	Median income:	$62,705
Urban:	23.9%	Latino	26.3%		*(94 of 435)*
Suburban:	76.1%	Asian	12.7%	Under $50,000	39.6%
Rural:	0.0%	Black	5.0%	$50,000-$99,999:	34.7%
Land area:	244	Two races	1.3%	$100,000-$199,999:	21.8%
Pop/sq. mi.:	2,928.9	White Ethnic	38.4%	$200,000 or more:	3.9%
Born in state:	59.4%			Poverty Rate	11.1%
		Education			
Age Groups		H.S. grad or less:	39.1%	**Work**	
Under 18:	24.4%	Some college:	28.6%	White collar:	32.4%
18 to 34:	24.3%	College degree, 4 yr.:	21.1%	Blue collar:	43.0%
35 to 64:	40.1%	Post-grad study:	11.2%	Sales and service:	24.6%
Over 64:	11.2%				
		Military		Govt. workers:	7.9%
		Veterans/active duty:	4.7%		

Chicago's Northwest Suburbs, DuPage

Schaumburg may not be nationally known, but it has a long tradition as one of America's major corporate headquarters cities. Sixty years ago, this suburb northwest of Chicago was farmland. Today, Schaumburg—near the intersection of the North-

Voter Turnout	
2013 Total Citizen 18+	441,282
2014 House Turnout	151,056
2014 Turnout as % CVAP	34.2%
2012 Turnout as % CVAP	52.7%

west Tollway and Interstate 290, and a few miles beyond O'Hare International Airport—is the headquarters of Motorola Solutions and Zurich North American insurance. Nearby are the headquarters of Sears, as well as the Woodfield Mall with 300-plus shops and restaurants, and subdivisions as far as the eye can see. Schaumburg has built a performing arts center, formed an orchestra for young people, and built from scratch a traditional downtown district.

Despite those attractions, the area recently has faced challenges. Some large companies are abandoning their suburban mindset, finding that large, isolated corporate campuses breed insularity and make it harder to recruit talent. Roosevelt University in August 2014 said that it would abandon its academic campus and move downtown. Chicago Mayor Rahm Emanuel has capitalized on the trend by luring suburban businesses to relocate downtown with financial incentives. Motorola's mobile handset division, after being bought by Google, moved to downtown Chicago's Merchandise Mart. Sara Lee's meat business moved downtown from Downers Grove, while changing its name to Hillshire Brands. AT&T decided to leave its suburban Hoffman Estates office, and moved 500 employees to downtown Chicago, and another 2,500 to nearby suburbs. Sears stayed in Hoffman Estates, though it cut 100 jobs in January 2015. In late 2014, the vacancy rate for suburban Chicago offices dropped slightly to 23%. "Really, the only thing that's growing is tech, and most of that is downtown. There's not a lot of tech in the suburbs anymore," a suburban real-estate broker told Chicagolandcommercial.com.

The 8th Congressional District of Illinois is made up of Schaumburg and the more Democratic communities in Chicago's northwest suburbs, including Carol Stream in DuPage County and nearly majority Hispanic Elgin and Carpentersville in Kane County. About half of the population of the 8th resides in the northwest corner of Cook County; most of the remainder are within jagged lines of northern DuPage, plus a few are in a small slice of Kane. It is one of the most Asian-American districts in the Midwest, with a

2012 Presidential Vote		
Barack Obama (D) 133,208		(58%)
Mitt Romney (R)..................94,944		(41%)

2008 Presidential Vote		
Barack Obama (D) 150,911		(62%)
John McCain (R)..................90,219		(37%)

Cook Partisan Voting Index: D+8

13% Asian-American voting population. Schaumburg has one of the nation's largest concentrations of Indian-Americans, at 11%. Once-homogeneous DuPage County has seen an influx of immigrants, and more than a quarter of its residents now speak a first language other than English at home. The area lacks a regional identity, other than the "Northwest Suburbs." The local newspaper, the *Daily Herald* based in Arlington Heights, tried valiantly for a few years to give it a sense of place with a billboard campaign that dubbed it "Herald City." It didn't stick, and the paper abandoned the slogan.

In the past decade, like other parts of the Chicago suburbs, this area has moved toward the Democrats. Under its new lines, President Barack Obama carried the district with 62% in 2008 and 58% in 2012. But it retains its suburban sensibilities, voting for moderate Republican Mark Kirk in the closely contested 2010 Senate race.

Tammy Duckworth (D)

Democrat Tammy Duckworth was elected in 2012. A double-amputee veteran of the Iraq war, she was given prominent speaking slots at the Democratic National Convention in 2008 and 2012 to tell her unusual life story. She entered the 2016 Senate race to share her saga more broadly and with higher stakes. Meantime, she has become a veteran of rough-and-tumble Illinois and Democratic politics.

The daughter of a Vietnam War veteran father and a Thai mother, Duckworth spent much of her early life abroad, moving with her father's jobs at the United Nations and, later, at international companies. Born in Bangkok, she lived with her family in Singapore and Indonesia before settling in Hawaii when she was 16. "Thank God for the food stamps, public education, and Pell Grants that helped me finish high school and college," she said in her 2012 convention speech. Duckworth studied marine biology at the University of Hawaii. After graduation, she pursued a master's degree at George Washington University and worked at the Smithsonian's National Museum of Natural History. Her interest in Southeast Asian history, culture, and politics led her to doctoral work at Northern Illinois University.

In 1990, Duckworth joined the Army Reserve Officers' Training Corps at George Washington. Two years later, she became a commissioned officer. During her training she met her future husband, Bryan Bowlsbey, who has become a major in the National Guard. Although she later said she opposed President George W. Bush's decision to invade Iraq, she felt it was her duty to complete her military service. Duckworth became one of the first Army women to fly combat missions in Iraq. She was copiloting a Black Hawk helicopter when a rocket-propelled grenade struck the lower half of her body; she lost both legs and suffered serious damage to her right arm. "They should have left me behind," she recalled. She received a Purple Heart. While recovering at Walter Reed Army Medical Center, she met then-Sen. Barack Obama of Illinois, who eventually called her to testify in front of his Senate committee.

Senate Democratic Whip Dick Durbin urged Duckworth to run for the House in 2006. She narrowly lost to Republican Peter Roskam in the 6th District race. She later said she wasn't fully recovered from her injuries at the time. She then spent five years as a state and federal executive before giving elected office another try. In 2011, she left her post as assistant secretary of public and intergovernmental affairs in the Veterans Affairs Department to run again for Congress. The 8th District was redrawn by Democrats to make it more favorable for their party. With another endorsement from Durbin, Duckworth coasted to the March primary victory over New Delhi-born former Illinois Deputy Treasurer Raja Krishnamoorthi, 66%-34%.

Her general election opponent was incumbent GOP Rep. Joe Walsh, elected to the House in 2010 on the national tea party wave. He had a reputation for outspokenness but also for damaging political moments, such as when it became public that he failed to make child support payments to his ex-wife and when he engaged in a tirade at a constituent meeting. Walsh criticized Duckworth for using her military service as a political tool. "She is a hero, and that demands our respect, but it doesn't demand our vote," he told CNN. Redistricting left Walsh with only a small piece of his old district in the new 8th. Duckworth outspent him $5.2 million to $2 million, though Walsh benefited from several million dollars of spending by outside groups. Democrats enlisted rock singer Joe Walsh to denounce his political namesake, and Duckworth won with 55% of the vote. Demonstrating the skill of both Duckworth and the redistricters, she had comparable leads in each of the three counties.

In the House, Duckworth joined the Armed Services Committee, where she filed a bill to extend maternity leave for women serving in the military. She also proposed legislation to assist veterans, including their transition to the private sector and removal of abuses in the veterans benefit system. In February 2015, Obama signed a suicide-prevention bill that she co-authored with Democratic Rep. Tim Walz of Minnesota, which was designed to assist veterans struggling with mental health. When the Iraqi military abandoned positions under pressure from Islamic State forces, Duckworth said that she was "appalled," after the training and arms that they had received from the U.S. military. "This is also a tragedy for the

American people with all of the resources we put into that nation, as well as all the men and women who served in uniform there," she added.

Two weeks after her re-election in 2014, Duckworth announced the birth of her daughter Abigail. Days earlier, she created an unexpected furor among House Democrats, when Minority Leader Nancy Pelosi in December denied a request from Duckworth to vote by proxy in a House Democratic contest to select the senior Democrat on the Energy and Commerce Committee. Duckworth was supporting Frank Pallone of New Jersey, who ultimately prevailed over Anna Eshoo of California, a close ally of Pelosi. Pelosi lieutenants said that they did not want to create such a precedent.

Duckworth announced in March 2015 her challenge to Republican Sen. Mark Kirk in the 2016 campaign. "I view my time now as a bonus and that has allowed me to speak up without fear," she said in her announcement video. She showed her independence soon after when she said that she would hold Hillary Clinton "accountable" for erasing emails from her personal server that deal with murder of U.S. officials in Benghazi Libya. With Kirk not fully recovered from a stroke, their campaign would be unusual in that both candidates use a wheelchair and face significant limitations in their mobility. Whether that would improve the civility of such a contest remained to be seen. Before then, Duckworth faced the prospect of a competitive Democratic primary.

Democrats were well-positioned to hold the Duckworth seat in the House. Raja Krishnamoorthi, who lost to her in the 2012 primary, quickly announced his candidacy. He praised Duckworth and said that he had learned from their contest, "It always helps not to run against an American war hero."

NINTH DISTRICT

Jan Schakowsky (D)

Elected 1998, 9th term; b. May 26, 1944, Chicago; U. of IL, B.S. 1965; Jewish; married (Robert Creamer); 3 children.

Elected Office: IL House, 1990-98.

Professional Career: Founder, Natl. Consumers Unite, 1969-73; Prog. dir., IL Public Action, 1976-85; Exec. dir., IL St. Cncl. of Sr. Citizens, 1985-90.

DC Office: 2367 RHOB, 20515, 202-225-2111; Fax: 202-226-6890; Website: schakowsky.house.gov.

State Offices: Chicago, 773-506-7100; Evanston, 847-328-3409.

Committees: *Energy & Commerce:* Commerce, Manufacturing & Trade (RMM); Health; Oversight & Investigations.

Group Ratings

	ADA	ACLU	AFL-CIO	LCV	ITI	COC	HAFA	ACU	CFG	FRC
2014	95%	88%	–	97%	40%	36%	14%	8%	13%	0%
2013	95%	C	95%	96%	C	31%	C	16%	19%	C

National Journal Ratings

	2013 LIB	—	2013 CONS
Economic	91%	—	0%
Social	93%	—	0%
Foreign	94%	—	0%
Composite	96%	—	4%

Key Votes of the 113th Congress

1. Sandy storm spending	Y	5. Medical Marijuana	Y	9. Syrian Rebels Training	Y
2. Violence Against Women Act	Y	6. Farm Bill	N	10. Keystone pipeline	N
3. Guantanamo Bay Detainees	Y	7. Afghanistan Combat	Y	11. Immigration Exec. Action	N
4. Abortion 20-week ban	N	8. NSA Phone Data Collection	N	12. Bipartisan budget deal	N

Election Results

2014 general	Jan Schakowsky (D)	141,000	(66%)	$1,327,081
	Susanne Atanus (R)	72,384	(34%)	
2014 primary	Jan Schakowsky (D)	unopposed		

Prior winning percentages: 2012 (66%), 2010 (66%), 2008 (75%), 2006 (75%), 2004 (76%), 2002 (70%), 2000 (76%), 1998 (75%)

Population		Race and Ethnicity		Income	
Total:	709,590	White	65.4%	Median income:	$63,039
Urban:	74.4%	Asian	12.5%		*(93 of 435)*
Suburban:	25.6%	Latino	10.8%	Under $50,000	40.5%
Rural:	0.0%	Black	8.9%	$50,000-$99,999:	27.9%
Land area:	115	Two races	2.3%	$100,000-$199,999:	21.6%
Pop/sq. mi.:	6,182.5	White Ethnic	37.5%	$200,000 or more:	9.9%
Born in state:	53.1%			Poverty Rate	12.8%
		Education			
Age Groups		H.S. grad or less:	26.6%	**Work**	
Under 18:	20.3%	Some college:	21.4%	White collar:	48.9%
18 to 34:	23.4%	College degree, 4 yr.:	30.0%	Blue collar:	38.5%
35 to 64:	40.6%	Post-grad study:	22.0%	Sales and service:	12.6%
Over 64:	15.8%				
		Military		Govt. workers:	9.1%
		Veterans/active duty:	4.7%		

Chicago: North Side, Northern Cook

"Make no little plans," architect Daniel Burnham once said, and he made no small plans for the Chicago lakefront. The glorious parks he designed are among America's urban jewels, and the row of high-rise apartment buildings—some austere works of masters of the International style, some in tradi-

Voter Turnout	
2013 Total Citizen 18+	487,037
2014 House Turnout	213,450
2014 Turnout as % CVAP	43.8%
2012 Turnout as % CVAP	63.1%

tional styles evocative of some other place and time, some sleek Art Deco works of the 1920s and 1930s—is a splendid accompaniment. Beyond the lakefront is all the diversity of Chicago. In sturdy brick houses, with scarcely a shoehorn's space between them, or in stubby apartment buildings, are ethnic and racial groups of every sort, from Argentinians to Slavs, from Poles to Plains Indians. In the 1970s, the neighborhoods behind the lakefront seemed to be getting seedier and tipping downhill. But since the late 1980s, they have been gentrifying, as young couples and gays, professionals and entrepreneurs renovate old houses and open new businesses. Today, this part of Chicago has as much urban energy and lively diversity as any place in America.

The lakefront has long been the most heavily Jewish part of Chicago. The local Jewish community, prominent for more than a century, has never been as much of a political force as it is in New York, or connected to a glamorous industry as in Los Angeles. Yet these Jewish voters' liberal impulses have been strong: the 19th century impulse to resist state authority and the imposition of cultural uniformity, and the 20th century impulse to strive for social fairness. Chicago's North Side Jews have been a solidly Democratic voting bloc, involved with—but always keeping at arm's length—the old Democratic machine. In city politics since the 1980s, Jewish voters and lakefront liberals of all backgrounds have been a key swing group.

The 9th Congressional District of Illinois covers the north end of Chicago's lakefront, from just north of Diversey Harbor and the Lincoln Park Zoo past the thriving Asian and Orthodox Jewish communities in West Rogers Park and on to the suburb of Evanston, founded by Methodists to promote temperance (a cause that never prospered in Chicago). The home of Northwestern University, Evanston, which has moved from historic Yankee Republicanism to trendy postgraduate Democratic, rejected in November 2013 a 35-story condominium tower as not meshing with local style. From Evanston and upscale Wilmette, where the only Bahai Temple in the country often clogs local streets, the 9th presses inland through heavily Jewish Skokie to Morton Grove and Niles and

2012 Presidential Vote		
Barack Obama (D) 200,686	(65%)
Mitt Romney (R)................102,728	(33%)
2008 Presidential Vote	
Barack Obama (D) 222,304	(69%)
John McCain (R)..................98,150	(30%)
Cook Partisan Voting Index: D+15	

includes most of Des Plaines. Skokie made national headlines when Nazi sympathizers got court permission to march there in 1977. Skokie's residents settled the score with the opening in 2009 of the Illinois Holocaust Museum and Education Center; former President Bill Clinton and Nobel Prize-winning author Elie Wiesel attended.

The district reaches west to incorporate once rock-solid Republican territory—Park Ridge, where Hillary Rodham grew up at 235 Wisner; the cluster of office buildings and interchanges in Rosemont, next to O'Hare International Airport; and parts of Arlington Heights, developed in the 1950s and 1960s on the Chicago & Northwestern commuter rail line. The 9th's voting age population is 9% black, 10% Hispanic, and 13% Asian, and is solidly Democratic, though less so than most of the districts based in Chicago.

Jan Schakowsky (D)

Jan Schakowsky, a Democrat elected in 1998, is an outspoken progressive. *The Nation* magazine once called her "the truest heir to Paul Wellstone," the late Minnesota senator and champion of the left, while the more conservative *Chicago Tribune's* editorial page derided her as "one of the most partisan, liberal members of the House."

Schakowsky grew up in Rogers Park and worked for two years as a teacher. In 1969, she formed National Consumers Unite to fight for date-of-freshness labels on dairy products and other food. Later she joined Illinois Public Action, a consumer group. In 1985, she became executive director of the Illinois State Council of Senior Citizens, where she organized the pivotal 1989 protest of Democratic Ways and Means chairman Dan Rostenkowski's Medicare catastrophic health care law for seniors. Television news images of the powerful Rostenkowski fleeing an angry crowd of old people led Congress to repeal the benefit, which many said did not provide adequate coverage. In 1990, Schakowsky was elected to the state House from Evanston and Skokie, and later became Democratic floor leader.

In 1998, Schakowsky was selected in the Democratic primary to replace Sidney Yates, a liberal Democrat who had represented the lakefront in Congress for 48 years. Her strategy was to run from the left—"I don't think I can be defined as too far left in a district like this," she said—and to build a volunteer organization. With ads in college papers, she hired young field organizers to set about identifying Schakowsky voters. She raised $1.4 million, with help from the women's abortion rights group EMILY's List. Her opponent was state Sen. Howard Carroll, who had the support of most Democratic ward committeemen and attacked Schakowsky for her opposition to the death penalty. Schakowsky's 1,500 workers, 250 of them from labor unions, helped her to a 45%-34% win. She easily won the general election and has been reelected without difficulty.

Schakowsky has one of the most liberal voting records in the House and regularly scores perfect ratings from liberal interest groups. She irked conservatives in September 2012 when she accused Republicans of engaging in "daily sabotage against anything that would have made our economy better." A close ally of Democratic Leader Nancy Pelosi, Schakowsky has worked with Democratic leaders on electoral strategy, including heading a training program for political organizers and encouraging participation by women. She was an early supporter when Pelosi was getting her start in leadership, and Pelosi rewarded her with a chief deputy whip post. Her contacts with national liberal groups have helped Schakowsky become a major party fundraiser, drawing heavily from the traditional Democratic constituencies of lawyers, women's interest groups, and unions.

In early 2006, she ran for vice chairman of the Democratic Caucus. With support from Pelosi, Schakowsky was the early front-runner against New York's Joe Crowley and Connecticut's John Larson. But on the first ballot, she finished third. Schakowsky threw her support to Larson, another Pelosi ally. With Schakowsky's former supporters on board, Larson prevailed. Some Democrats speculated that Schakowsky was hurt by the timing of the contest, which occurred soon after her husband, Robert Creamer, the longtime head of Illinois Public Action Fund, pleaded guilty to bank fraud in a check-kiting scheme. Schakowsky said that her husband had "made mistakes," but that she was unaware of his financial problems and that she stood by him.

Schakowsky briefly considered a run for the Senate in 2004 but decided against it. Later, in 2008, she voiced interest in appointment to the remainder of President-elect Barack Obama's Senate term. She was an early backer of Obama for president, giving cover to other prominent Democratic women who may have wanted to back him but felt obliged to support then-New York Sen. Hillary Clinton.

As chairwoman of the Intelligence Oversight Subcommittee, Schakowsky tried to get spy agencies to be more forthcoming in briefing members of Congress about their actions. In July 2009, she backed Pelosi when Pelosi claimed that she had not been informed of the use by U.S. interrogators of water boarding. Schakowsky was the only committee member in December 2011 to oppose cyber security legislation, saying that the measure didn't do enough to safeguard civil liberties. In what she called an "anguished" decision, she boycotted the March 2015 speech to Congress by Israeli prime minister Benjamin Netanyahu on the grounds that his actions might jeopardize both nuclear talks with Iran and bipartisan support for Israel.

On the Energy and Commerce Committee, Schakowsky helped to enact in 2008 the child product safety bill, which toughened regulations, and she has remained active on consumer issues. In 2009, she was a strong supporter of legislation creating a federally-run insurance option in the Democrats' health care bill. The public option provision ultimately was dropped because of opposition from party moderates. In 2013, she became the senior Democrat on the Commerce, Manufacturing and Trade Subcommittee, which handles many consumer issues. She has filed legislation to establish minimum numbers of nurses in hospitals, and increase funds to train and retain nurses to address the nationwide shortage.

Pelosi appointed Schakowsky to the Simpson-Bowles commission on the national debt in 2010, where she opposed ending federal economic stimulus and argued that safety net spending should be exempt from budget cuts. She argued that any debt reduction options should include income distribution tables to show who would be hit hardest.

TENTH DISTRICT

Bob Dold (R)

Elected 2014, 2nd term; b. June 23, 1969, Evanston, IL; Denison U., B.A., 1991; Indiana U., J.D., 1996; Northwestern U., MBA, 2000; Christian; married. 3 children.

Elected Office: U.S. House, 2011-2013.

Professional Career: Staff, U.S. House, Committee on Reform & Oversight, 1997-1999; Company Owner, Rose Pest Solutions.

DC Office: 221 CHOB, 20515; 202-225-4835; Website: web.archive. org/web/20150109235250/https://dold.house.gov.

State Offices: Lincolnshire, 847-793-8400; Round Lake, 847-309-6627.

Committees: *Ways and Means:* Human Resources, Social Security.

Election Results

2014 general	Bob Dold Jr. (R)............................	95,992	(51%)	$3,648,085	$3,131,820	$3,252,218
	Brad Schneider (D)......................	91,136	(49%)	$4,754,838	$103,095	$3,870,783
2014 primary	Bob Dold Jr. (R)......................unopposed				

Prior winning percentage: 2010 (51%)

Population		Race and Ethnicity		Income	
Total:	716,308	White	60.5%	Median income:	$68,184
Urban:	10.7%	Latino	21.6%		*(68 of 435)*
Suburban:	89.3%	Asian	9.5%	Under $50,000	35.9%
Rural:	0.0%	Black	6.7%	$50,000-$99,999:	30.2%
Land area:	340	Two races	1.5%	$100,000-$199,999:	22.4%
Pop/sq. mi.:	2,107.8	White Ethnic	33.7%	$200,000 or more:	11.5%
Born in state:	55.8%			Poverty Rate	9.9%
		Education			
Age Groups		H.S. grad or less:	32.6%	**Work**	
Under 18:	25.6%	Some college:	24.5%	White collar:	41.3%
18 to 34:	21.3%	College degree, 4 yr.:	25.2%	Blue collar:	40.4%
35 to 64:	40.3%	Post-grad study:	17.7%	Sales and service:	18.3%
Over 64:	12.8%				
		Military		Govt. workers:	9.7%
		Veterans/active duty:	7.4%		

Northern Chicagoland: Lake, Northern Cook

Since 1855, when the Chicago & North Western opened the railroad line from downtown Chicago north along the lakeshore, the North Shore suburbs along Lake Michigan have been home to Chicago's elite. The North Shore starts in Evanston, goes north through Wilmette, Winnetka, and

Voter Turnout	
2013 Total Citizen 18+	451,973
2014 House Turnout	187,128
2014 Turnout as % CVAP	41.4%
2012 Turnout as % CVAP	61.1%

Glencoe, and then leaves Cook County and crosses into the eastern Lake County towns of Highland Park and Lake Forest. Each burg has a slightly different personality, each is long established and mightily prosperous, and each exudes a patina of age. These are communities of affluent, well-educated people living in an environment whose natural beauty—the vistas over Lake Michigan, the gentle rolling terrain, and the old trees—is carefully disciplined. Corporate headquarters fit comfortably here, including Baxter Healthcare, Abbott Laboratories, and Allstate Insurance. The North Shore suburbs were the setting for the 1980s films *Risky Business, Sixteen Candles,* and *Ferris Bueller's Day Off,* which depicted teen angst and lust for adventure among the pampered offspring of the rich. The one exception to the atmosphere of gracious high living is the area around the Great Lakes Naval Training Center, where the median income is dramatically lower.

The 10th Congressional District of Illinois is the North Shore district. The district starts on the lakefront in Glencoe and runs north all the way to the blue-collar, majority-Hispanic city of Waukegan and on to the Wisconsin border. It moves inland to include blue-collar territory in Lake County and some Cook County suburbs west to Wheeling and parts of Mount Prospect. Social disparity ranges from tony Northbrook and Deerfield to working-class Niles, a suburb featuring the "Leaning Tower of Niles," a half-size replica of Italy's Leaning Tower of Pisa (the landmark was featured in the opening montage of the popular teen movie *Wayne's World*). The district includes Libertyville, near where the Adlai Stevensons, the governor and three-time presidential candidate and his son the former senator,

2012 Presidential Vote		
Barack Obama (D) 157,400		(58%)
Mitt Romney (R)................112,552		(41%)
2008 Presidential Vote		
Barack Obama (D) 180,732		(63%)
John McCain (R)................103,170		(36%)
Cook Partisan Voting Index: D+8		

owned a farm. After the family home on the property was donated to Lake County, it was restored in 2008 as the Adlai Stevenson Center on Democracy. Politically, the 10th leans sufficiently Democratic that Barack Obama won 63% of the district vote in 2008 and 58% in 2012, but it is more competitive locally.

Bob Dold (R)

Republican Rep. Robert Dold is serving his second term in the 10th District. He regained the seat from Democrat Brad Schneider in a 2014 rematch after losing the seat to him two years earlier. Dold overcame his rival's criticisms that he was too far to the right of voters in the wealthy suburban Chicago district. He holds the most Democratic-leaning district of any Republican in the nation, and the local partisan mix will be very demanding for Dold to secure this swing and very wealthy district.

Dold grew up in Winnetka and earned a political science degree from Denison University. Later, he received a law degree from Indiana University and a master's in business administration from Northwestern. He got a job in President George H.W. Bush's White House, and then spent two years on the staff of the House Government Reform Committee, where he was on the team of GOP aides who investigated President Bill Clinton's fundraising practices during the 1996 campaign. He worked for an Internet service provider before returning to his family business, Rose Pest Solutions, which Dold describes as the oldest pest management company in the nation, and where he served as president.

When Rep. Mark Kirk, a friend of Dold, ran for the Senate in 2010, Dold entered the race and easily fended off four GOP primary opponents. He faced a tougher battle against Democratic business consultant Dan Seals, who had twice run for the seat. Dold campaigned on his business experience and moderate policy positions, and he eked out a 51.1%-48.9% win in one of the country's tightest races. During his first term in the House, he was an active member of the Financial Services Committee.

In 2012, first-time candidate Schneider followed Dold's example and campaigned on his business experience, portraying himself as a moderate. He accused Dold of voting in lockstep with GOP leaders on major issues, including women's health and the right to an abortion. Dold called the charge misleading and cited his dissents with the leadership on such issues as the environment, education, and gun control. But the Democratic tide in Illinois proved too much for him to overcome, and Dold was on the losing side of a 50.6%-49.4% contest. During his one term, Schneider served on the Foreign Affairs Committee and joined the business-friendly New Democrat Coalition. He joined President Barack Obama in calling for legislative solutions to gun violence, including universal background checks, and limits on high-capacity magazines and military-style assault weapons.

Without Obama, an Illinoisan, on the ticket in 2014, Republicans were enthusiastic about Dold's chances. He continued to stress his moderate credentials while depicting Schneider as ineffective; Schneider emphasized Dold's past votes in which he sided with the majority, including his support for House Budget Committee Chairman Paul Ryan's blueprint that sharply cut spending. This was the most expensive of Dold's three contests and one of the most expensive in the nation in 2014. Schneider outspent him $4.8 million to $3.6 million, while national parties and outside groups spent a total of roughly $10 million more in the contest. This time, Dold ended up winning in a comparative landslide of 51.3%-48.7%.

During his second tour in the House, Dold got a break when the unexpected resignation of Republican Rep. Aaron Schock of Illinois opened a seat on the powerful Ways and Means, which GOP leaders assigned to Dold in April 2015. With Democratic Rep. Loretta Sanchez of California, he filed a bill in February that was designed to foster job creation and innovation in America's economy through reforms to immigration policy and the tax code. Its provisions included a new visa program for up to 50,000 foreign graduate students in science, technology, engineering and math; 75,000 additional visas for immigrant entrepreneurs; and a limited research and development tax credit for startup companies that report less than $5 million in annual earnings.

Dold is virtually guaranteed another tough campaign in 2016. Schneider announced that he will seek his old seat. Highland Park Mayor Nancy Rotering, a Democrat, also said that she will run.

ELEVENTH DISTRICT

Bill Foster (D)

Elected 2012, 3rd full term; b. Oct. 7, 1955, Madison, WI; U. of WI, B.A. 1976, Harvard U., Ph.D. 1983; no religious affiliation; married (Aesook Byon); 2 children.

Elected Office: U.S. House, 2008-10.

Professional Career: Scientist, Fermi Natl. Accelerator Lab., 1990-2006; Co-founder, Electronic Theatre Controls, 1975-2007.

DC Office: 1224 LHOB, 20515, 202-225-3515; fax, 202-225-9420; Website: foster.house.gov.

State Offices: Aurora, 630-585-7672; Joliet, 815-280-5876.

Committees: *Financial Services:* Capital Markets & Government Sponsored Enterprises; Monetary Policy & Trade.

Group Ratings

	ADA	ACLU	AFL-CIO	LCV	ITI	COC	HAFA	ACU	CFG	FRC
2014	70%	77%	–	97%	60%	57%	6%	0%	13%	0%
2013	55%	C	79%	89%	C	62%	C	12%	13%	C

National Journal Ratings

	2013 LIB	—	2013 CONS
Economic	60%	—	39%
Social	79%	—	16%
Foreign	62%	—	37%
Composite	68%	—	32%

Key Votes of the 113th Congress

1. Sandy storm spending	Y	5. Medical Marijuana	
2. Violence Against Women Act	Y	6. Farm Bill	N
3. Guantanamo Bay Detainees	Y	7. Afghanistan Combat	N
4. Abortion 20-week ban	N	8. NSA Phone Data Collection	N

9. Syrian Rebels Training	Y
10. Keystone pipeline	N
11. Immigration Exec. Action	N
12. Bipartisan budget deal	Y

Election Results

2014 general	Bill Foster (D)	93,436	(53%)	$1,812,623	$13,348	
	Darlene Senger (R)	81,335	(47%)	$763,134	$88,691	$4,982
2014 primary	Bill Foster (D)	unopposed				

Prior winning percentages: 2012 (59%), 2008 (58%), 2008 special (53%)

Population		Race and Ethnicity		Income	
Total:	709,493	White	52.9%	Median income:	$66,747
Urban:	20.2%	Latino	26.6%		(75 of 435)
Suburban:	79.6%	Black	10.7%	Under $50,000	36.3%
Rural:	0.2%	Asian	6.9%	$50,000-$99,999:	33.4%
Land area:	482	Two races	2.3%	$100,000-$199,999:	24.8%
Pop/sq. mi.:	1,472.4	White Ethnic	35.8%	$200,000 or more:	5.5%
Born in state:	64.4%			Poverty Rate	10.3%
		Education			
Age Groups		H.S. grad or less:	37.4%	**Work**	
Under 18:	27.1%	Some college:	27.2%	White collar:	36.6%
18 to 34:	23.1%	College degree, 4 yr.:	22.8%	Blue collar:	42.2%
35 to 64:	39.7%	Post-grad study:	12.6%	Sales and service:	21.1%
Over 64:	10.1%			Govt. workers:	9.9%
		Military			
		Veterans/active duty:	5.6%		

Southwestern Chicagoland: Aurora, Joliet

Joliet, known as the city of steel and stone, got its start in the mid-19th century as a melting pot of Irish, German, Slovakian, Slovenian, Polish, Croatian and Hungarian immigrants who built the canals and railroads that con-

Voter Turnout	
2013 Total Citizen 18+	443,272
2014 House Turnout	174,772
2014 Turnout as % CVAP	39.4%
2012 Turnout as % CVAP	57.5%

nected the city with the rest of the state, from the Great Lakes to the Mississippi River. It emerged as the state's largest transportation hub outside Chicago. Workers labored in the stone quarries and steel mill, which by the turn of the century became the economic engine of the manufacturing city. The rails remain relevant to daily life, with officials working to upgrade the safety of the several trains that cross through Aurora each day with at least 100 cars filled with crude oil from North Dakota.

Joliet has become a fast-growing city in the otherwise declining Illinois, but has evolved to an entertainment destination. The landmark Rialto Square Theater, a 1920s-era vaudeville establishment that was a favorite of gangster Al Capone's, underwent a restoration and now is an arts center featuring plays, musicals, and comedy in a downtown that has been revitalized but has continued to struggle in some areas. Two riverboat casinos are among the top 10 employers in the city, although they have experienced steep drops in revenue since the Rivers Casino opened in 2011 in Des Plaines, which is closer to Chicago. In March 2015, 230 workers lost their jobs when the Caterpillar plant in Joliet shifted two production lines to Mexico "to remain cost competitive," the company said. Joliet was famously home to the Joliet Correctional Center, the prison featured in the movie *The Blues Brothers*, until it closed in 2002. Joliet is also the site of the 75,000-seat Chicagoland Speedway NASCAR racetrack.

The 11th Congressional District includes Joliet in Will County, parts of Naperville in southern DuPage County, and Aurora in Kane County. About 27% of the district is Hispanic, with 11% black and 7% Asian. Will County is the fastest-growing of the large suburban Chicago counties, jumping from a population of 502,000 in 2000 to 683,000 in 2013, as its Hispanic residents more than doubled and the number of Asian-Americans nearly tripled. But its growth spurt was interrupted by the collapse of the housing finance market and a spike in unemployment. Aurora, the state's second most populous city with a long history of manufacturing, saw its population grow 38% from 2000 to 2013, also thanks to a large influx of Hispanics.

The district's boundaries run along the technology corridor in DuPage County, and straddle some large engineering facilities. The Argonne National Laboratory, which conducts basic and applied research in disciplines that range from high energy physics to biotechnology, is establishing a research hub for batteries and energy storage, nicknamed by the lab's director as "Lithium Valley." In May 2014, the Lab announced that it had found new methods to use high-energy Lithium batteries for electric vehicles. The Lab plans to start operations in 2018 on a new $200 million super-computer that is 17 times faster than recent versions. Fermilab, another national laboratory, is just outside the district lines. This redrawn district gave President Barack Obama double-digit victory margins in 2008 and 2012. Its growing Hispanic population likely will keep it in the Democratic column with the current district lines.

2012 Presidential Vote		
Barack Obama (D) 151,825	(58%)
Mitt Romney (R).................106,532	(41%)
2008 Presidential Vote		
Barack Obama (D) 170,803	(62%)
John McCain (R).................100,755	(37%)
Cook Partisan Voting Index: D+8		

Bill Foster (D)

Democrat Bill Foster won a return to the House in 2012, with a big boost from redistricting. Foster, a scientist, initially won a special election following the resignation of former House Speaker Dennis Hastert, only to lose in 2010 to Republican Randy Hultgren.

Foster began life as a Washington insider. His parents met on Capitol Hill, where each worked for a senator. His father became a law professor at the University of Wisconsin, and Foster grew up in Madison, graduated from the university, and got his Ph.D. in physics from Harvard University. He was a physicist for 16 years at Fermilab, just outside the 11th District, where he pursued groundbreaking research in elementary particle physics. Foster also ran a theater lighting business with his younger brother that made them both multimillionaires.

He had not sought public office before volunteering in the 2006 campaign of Patrick Murphy, a Pennsylvania Democrat who ousted a House Republican incumbent. At age 51, Foster then spent five months working on Murphy's Capitol Hill staff. After Hastert resigned in 2007, Foster ran in the Democratic primary against the more liberal Jonathan Laesch, who had lost to Hastert in 2006. Foster won, 50% to 43%. In the March 2008 general election, he faced Republican Jim Oberweis, a successful dairy owner who had lost numerous statewide campaigns. Amid the clutter of negative charges and countercharges, Foster got a boost from a 30-second endorsement from the Barack Obama presidential campaign. He won, 53% to 47%, and defeated Oberweis again to win a full term in November. Foster was the first Democrat to represent the north-central Illinois district since the Great Depression.

In the House, Foster got a seat on the Financial Services Committee, where he supported the bailout of the financial markets. He helped to restore $62.5 million in funding for Fermilab. He voted for the $787 billion economic stimulus legislation and the 2010 health care overhaul. In the 2010 election, Foster did not mention his party affiliation and out-spent Hultgren, $3.7 million to $1.6 million. But Hultgren won, 51% to 45%.

Foster soon got another chance. During 2011 redistricting, Democrats carved out a new, Democratic-leaning district that covers Joliet and Aurora. Foster moved from Batavia to Naperville to run in the new district and easily beat two Democratic primary rivals. He then faced veteran Republican Rep. Judy Biggert, a moderate who received financial backing from a Republican gay rights group. Foster accused Biggert of supporting Social Security privatization, although her campaign maintained that she always opposed full privatization. At a face-to-face meeting with the *Chicago Tribune* editorial board, Foster tried to tie Biggert to President George W. Bush's economic policies that "eviscerated U.S. manufacturing." Biggert snapped back, "You Democrats have never talked about anything that you're going to do. It's always what we did wrong." At the same forum, Foster mentioned three areas he would cut in the federal budget, starting with military aircraft and crop insurance subsidies. Foster blanked on the third program he planned to cut and said, "I'll go back to it." The race wasn't always pretty, but Foster won convincingly with 59%.

In the House, Foster regained his seat on the Financial Services Committee. He warned that Republican bills to strip regulatory authority from the Securities and Exchange Commission would divert resources from investor protections. He filed a bill with Republican Rep. Scott Garrett of New Jersey to require more information from the federal government on "payer states" like Illinois that send more money to Washington than they receive in return. In January 2015, he joined the Science, Space and Technology Committee. As the only remaining Ph.D. scientist in Congress, he said, he wanted to counter the "attacks" on science, including the National Science Foundation, that have come from that committee and elsewhere.

Back home, Foster won reelection in 2014 with 53% of the vote against state Rep. Darlene Senger, whom he outspent by more than 2-to-1. The Republican had small leads in DuPage and Cook counties, but Foster rolled up big margins in Will and Kane counties. He considered running against Sen. Mark Kirk in 2016, and criticized Kirk's "incredibly irresponsible" decision to join a letter on nuclear-arms talks to the leaders of Iran that most Republican Senators signed. In April 2015, he decided not to run against Kirk and he endorsed Democratic Rep. Tammy Duckworth to avoid a costly primary.

TWELFTH DISTRICT

Mike Bost (R)

Elected 2014, 1st term; b. Dec. 30, 1960, Murphysboro, IL; U., of IL Firefighter Academy, Cert., 1993; Baptist; married (Tracy); 3 children.

Military Career: U.S. Marine Corps., 1979-1982.

Elected Office: IL State House of Reps., (District 115) 1995-2015; Trustee, Murphysboro Township, 1993-1995; Treasurer, Murphysboro Township, 1989-1992; Jackson County Board, 1984-1988.

Professional Career: Cert., Firefighter II Academy, U., of IL, 1993.

DC Office: 1440 LHOB, 20515; 202-225-5661; fax, 202-225-0285; website: bost.house.gov.

State Offices: Alton, 618-233-8026; Belleville, 618-233-8026; Carbondale, 618-457-5787; Granite City, 618-233-8026; Mt. Vernon, 618-513-5294.

Committees: *Agriculture:* Conservation and Forestry; General Farms Commodities and Risk Management. *Small Business:* Health and Technology; Investigations, Oversight and Regulations; *Veterans Affairs:* Disability Assistance and Memorial Affairs; Economic Opportunity.

Election Results

2014 general	Mike Bost (R)	110,038	(52%)	$1,291,883	$1,529,938	$3,174,727
	Bill Enyart (D)	87,860	(42%)	$1,968,427	$1,182,080	$3,057,566
	Paula Bradshaw (G)	11,840	(6%)			
2014 primary	Mike Bost (R)	unopposed				

Population		Race and Ethnicity		Income	
Total:	702,625	White	76.6%	Median income:	$44,133
Urban:	7.7%	Black	17.0%		*(333 of 435)*
Suburban:	65.0%	Latino	3.0%	Under $50,000	55.2%
Rural:	27.4%	Asian	1.1%	$50,000-$99,999:	29.1%
Land area:	5,180	Two races	2.0%	$100,000-$199,999:	13.4%
Pop/sq. mi.:	135.6	White Ethnic	23.4%	$200,000 or more:	2.3%
Born in state:	69.3%			Poverty Rate	18.4%
		Education			
Age Groups		H.S. grad or less:	42.9%	**Work**	
Under 18:	22.1%	Some college:	35.1%	White collar:	30.4%
18 to 34:	23.0%	College degree, 4 yr.:	13.5%	Blue collar:	46.1%
35 to 64:	40.0%	Post-grad study:	8.5%	Sales and service:	23.5%
Over 64:	14.9%			Govt. workers:	17.4%
		Military			
		Veterans/active duty:	12.3%		

Southwest Illinois: East St. Louis, Carbondale

Their waters roiling together, the nation's two mightiest rivers, the Mississippi and Missouri, join just a few miles below Alton Illinois. Its 19th-century buildings recall its turbulent history, when it was the home of antislavery agitator Elijah Lovejoy, who was murdered by a mob. Nearby in

Voter Turnout	
2013 Total Citizen 18+	539,669
2014 House Turnout	209,738
2014 Turnout as % CVAP	38.9%
2012 Turnout as % CVAP	57.6%

Hartford, explorers Lewis and Clark spent five months preparing their team and collecting supplies for their journey westward. More recently, it was the home of conservative crusader and columnist Phyllis Schlafly. Farther south along the Mississippi is East St. Louis, situated on the Illinois side of the river, with a view of the Gateway Arch in the larger St. Louis on the Missouri side. It is a terminus for dozens of rail lines and highways that funnel into bridges over the river.

Once a rail and stockyard center second only to Chicago, East St. Louis is now one of America's poorest and most troubled cities, a half-abandoned slum with one of the nation's highest crime rates and a rapidly declining tax base. The city's homicide rate of 102 per 100,000 residents is among the highest in the nation and rivals that of lawless third-world countries. It is dependent on a riverboat casino and an adjacent waterfront hotel for local revenue, but casino taxes have increased and revenues have dipped. After peaking at 82,000 in 1960, its population is now below 27,000 and almost entirely African-American. East St. Louis is in St. Clair County, long heavily Democratic. In February 2015, the jobless rate in the county was 6.7 percent.

South of East St. Louis and the industrial area around Belleville, the river counties are lightly inhabited. This was the site of the French Kaskaskia settlement that became Illinois's first capital in 1818, but repeated flooding turned it into an island and reduced its population to nine people and many more egrets. Farther south, the river abuts coal country and is not far from Carbondale, once a coal center but now, as the home of Southern Illinois University, bustling with students.

The southern end of Illinois is sometimes known as Little Egypt, where the Ohio River meets the Mississippi: flat, fertile farmland, protected by giant constructed levees because it is susceptible to yearly floods. The marshy landscape has created the Sinkhole Plain, with more than 10,000 sinkholes. There is more than a touch of Dixie here: The unofficial capital of Little Egypt, Cairo (pronounced *KAY-roh*), is a declining town closer to Memphis than to Chicago. A more enticing locale not far from Cairo is the Shawnee National Forest, which has preserved Native American sites that are 10,000 years old.

The 12th District of Illinois covers all of this Mississippi riverfront from Alton south to Cairo, with some inland territory as well. Most of its population is in the Metro East area in St. Clair and Madison counties. The largest employer in Southern Illinois is Scott Air Force Base near Belleville, which has a workforce of 14,200 and is home of the 375th Airlift Wing. The private sector continues to struggle. In March 2015, US Steel announced the temporary closing of its Granite City plant, with the loss of about 2,000 jobs. President Barack Obama barely won his home-state district in 2012 with

2012 Presidential Vote		
Barack Obama (D)	153,718	(50%)
Mitt Romney (R)	149,165	(48%)
2008 Presidential Vote		
Barack Obama (D)	179,180	(55%)
John McCain (R)	142,723	(44%)
Cook Partisan Voting Index:	EVEN	

50% of the vote against Mitt Romney, struggling with the socially conservative, blue-collar workers here. It was a steep drop from 2008, when Obama carried 55% of the vote against John McCain.

Mike Bost (R)

Republican Mike Bost convincingly defeated first-term Democratic Rep. Bill Enyart in 2014, handing the GOP one of its most hotly contested and expensive pickups in what was until recently a safe Democratic seat. Democrats can be expected to make a big effort to reclaim it in 2016.

Bost was born and raised in Murphysboro and enlisted in the Marines upon graduating from high school. After receiving an honorable discharge in 1982, he became a firefighter while working in the family trucking business. In 1989, he and his wife opened a beauty shop, the White House Salon, which they run to this day. In his advocacy of smaller government and lower taxes, Bost often cited his experience as a small-business owner as the formative experience that drove him into politics. After several stints in local office, Bost successfully ran for the Illinois House in 1994, and later became Republican Caucus chairman. His work focused on sectors important to the region—especially coal and agriculture—and he became known for tangling with Democrats, who have controlled that chamber since 1996. He won national attention with an outburst on the House floor in 2012 as he protested the rules for a pension bill. After he tossed papers into the air and punched them, he cried out, "Let my people go!" Video of his tirade wound up on YouTube and went viral, attracting more than 430,000 views.

Armed with name recognition—"Meltdown Mike"—that he tried to spin to his advantage, Bost announced in 2013 that he would challenge Enyart, one of two remaining Illinois Democrats in the House from outside the Chicago metro area. The district's growing divide over coal politics made it a top pick-up priority for the GOP. With neither man facing a primary, the contest soon escalated into one of the most expensive House races in the country. In his work on the Armed Services, Enyart cited the fact that he was the only retired two-star general in Congress. Bost tried to make the best of his outspoken reputation. "If you want a person who goes and sits and does nothing and not argue on your behalf, then I'm not your guy," he told voters. Each party spent more than $4 million on the contest, an extraordinary amount considering the relatively inexpensive media markets. Enyart out-spent Bost, $1.9 million to $1.2 million. Democrats played up the risk of Bost's temper, while the GOP attacked Enyart as a loyal ally of President Barack Obama, Minority Leader Nancy Pelosi, and beleaguered Gov. Pat Quinn.

In the end, Quinn's sagging popularity kept many Democrats at home, while the ad blitz for Bost did enough to motivate GOP voters. Bost won by a surprisingly comfortable 52%-42%, the first Republican to represent St. Clair County since 1942. Enyart took the two largest counties, St. Clair and nearby Madison, but by relatively small margins. Bost won 9 of the remaining 10 counties, with margins that exceeded 2-to-1 in some cases, including Carbondale-based Williamson County.

In the House, he placed his chief priority on increasing local jobs. In response to the March 2015 closing of a U.S. Steel plant, he urged the Obama administration to enforce international trade laws against unfair practices of other nations. Democrats quickly listed him as one of their top targets in 2016. Some talked up former Lt. Gov. Sheila Simon, the daughter of the late Sen. Paul Simon, as a potential challenger.

THIRTEENTH DISTRICT

Rodney Davis (R)

Elected 2012, 2nd term; b. Jan. 5, 1970, Des Moines, IA; Milliken U., B.A. 1992; Catholic; married (Shannon); 3 children.

Professional Career: Staff assistant, IL Sec. of State, 1992-96; Projects dir., Rep. John Shimkus, 1997-2012; Exec. dir., IL Republican Party, 2011.

DC Office: 1740 LHOB, 20515, 202-225-2371; Website: rodneydavis. house.gov.

State Offices: Champaign, 217-403-4690; Decatur, 217-791-6224; Taylorville, 217-824-5117; Springfield, 217-791-6224; Normal, 309-252-8834; Glen Carbon, 618-205-8660.

Committees: *Agriculture:* Biotechnology, Horticulture and Research (Chmn); Commodity Exchanges, Energy and Credit; Nutrition. *Transportation & Infrastructure:* Aviation; Highways & Transit; Water Resources & Environment. *House Administration.*

Group Ratings

	ADA	ACLU	AFL-CIO	LCV	ITI	COC	HAFA	ACU	CFG	FRC
2014	0%	5%	–	9%	80%	83%	42%	50%	48%	63%
2013	5%	C	38%	4%	C	77%	C	56%	48%	C

National Journal Ratings

	2013 LIB	—	2013 CONS
Economic	43%	—	57%
Social	50%	—	50%
Foreign	41%	—	57%
Composite	45%	—	55%

Key Votes of the 113th Congress

1. Sandy storm spending	Y	5. Medical Marijuana	Y	9. Syrian Rebels Training	Y
2. Violence Against Women Act	Y	6. Farm Bill	Y	10. Keystone pipeline	Y
3. Guantanamo Bay Detainees	N	7. Afghanistan Combat	N	11. Immigration Exec. Action	Y
4. Abortion 20-week ban	Y	8. NSA Phone Data Collection	Y	12. Bipartisan budget deal	Y

Election Results

2014 general	Rodney Davis (R)	123,337	(59%)	$3,382,441	$482,590	$926,684
	Ann Callis (D)	86,935	(41%)	$1,936,927		$103,648
2014 primary	Rodney Davis (R)	27,816	(55%)			
	Erika Harold (R)	20,951	(41%)			

Population		Race and Ethnicity		Income	
Total:	715,907	White	80.4%	Median income:	$47,130
Urban:	48.1%	Black	11.1%		(278 of 435)
Suburban:	25.6%	Asian	3.5%	Under $50,000	52.1%
Rural:	26.3%	Latino	3.1%	$50,000-$99,999:	29.8%
Land area:	5,662	Two races	1.7%	$100,000-$199,999:	14.5%
Pop/sq. mi.:	126.4	White Ethnic	24.7%	$200,000 or more:	3.5%
Born in state:	75.3%			Poverty Rate	18.9%
		Education			
Age Groups		H.S. grad or less:	40.5%	**Work**	
Under 18:	21.3%	Some college:	29.8%	White collar:	37.0%
18 to 34:	29.0%	College degree, 4 yr.:	18.0%	Blue collar:	43.5%
35 to 64:	35.7%	Post-grad study:	11.7%	Sales and service:	19.5%
Over 64:	14.0%				
		Military		Govt. workers:	20.0%
		Veterans/active duty:	9.0%		

West-Central Illinois: St. Louis exurbs, Champaign

Springfield, the capital of Illinois, has changed rather little since its great moment in history—when it was the home to Abraham Lincoln, railroad lawyer, elected to the House as a Whig opponent of the Mexican War and later, the 16th president of the United States. Today, beyond the suburban fringe, the prairie countryside outside of Springfield is still mostly farmland with few towns, filled with large industrial farms producing soybeans and corn. Farming technology has

Voter Turnout	
2013 Total Citizen 18+	543,712
2014 House Turnout	210,272
2014 Turnout as % CVAP	38.7%
2012 Turnout as % CVAP	55.2%

changed vastly, but the patterns of cultivation, the contours of the land, even the shape of the ribbons of back country roads, cannot be entirely different from what Lincoln saw as a lawyer making his way from one county seat to another on the circuit. Nor has downtown Springfield changed all that much, at least compared with booming Midwestern capitals, like Columbus, Indianapolis, or even Des Moines. Springfield has suffered from continuing job losses on the public payroll under governors of both parties.

If most of the office fronts and houses captured in old photographs are gone, some remain; and the scale has not changed. Lincoln's clapboard house is still in Springfield, and so is the courtroom where he argued cases before federal judges. The Greek revival downtown block where Lincoln and his partner William Herndon kept their law offices is open for inspection, as is the state Capitol building built here in 1839. The governor's mansion downtown, built in 1855, is the third oldest, continuously occupied residence in the country. In April 2015, on the 150th anniversary of Lincoln's assassination, the state used bad timing to reduce funding and staffing for his tomb. Today, Springfield is known more for its dysfunction; four of the state's last 10 governors were sentenced to jail time on corruption charges.

The 13th Congressional District contains rural, prairie lands from Collinsville, just outside St. Louis, to Champaign-Urbana, a three-hour drive northeast. It includes much of

Bloomington, birthplace of former Vice President Adlai Stevenson, who served under Democrat Grover Cleveland, and the hometown of his grandson, Governor Adlai Stevenson II, nominated by Democrats for president in 1952 and 1956. The largest of the towns in the district are anchored by the state's universities: The University of Illinois in Champaign-Urbana, Illinois State University in Bloomington-Normal, and Illinois Wesleyan University, also in Bloomington. In 2015, public university officials worried about the impact of Gov. Bruce Rauner's proposed budget cuts. Decatur is home to politically influential Archer Daniels Midland, one of the world's largest agricultural processors and a major champion of ethanol. The district also includes Panama, the Illinois coal town where John L. Lewis started his path upward in the United Mine Workers.

Politically, the district is one of the most closely divided in the country, with the cultural conservatism of the prairie meshing with the liberal academic population centers and government capital in Springfield. Barack Obama won the district easily in 2008, with 55 percent of the vote. But like the neighboring 12th District, the 2012 contest was much closer, when Mitt Romney took it by a grand total of 372 votes. The

2012 Presidential Vote		
Mitt Romney (R)	147,104	(49%)
Barack Obama (D)	146,732	(49%)
2008 Presidential Vote		
Barack Obama (D)	174,982	(55%)
John McCain (R)	139,445	(44%)
Cook Partisan Voting Index:	EVEN	

28,000-vote drop for Obama between the two elections can be explained, in part, by a lighter turnout operation in Illinois. But it also revealed, especially in rural areas, the diminished enthusiasm for Obama.

Rodney Davis (R)

Republican Rodney Davis, first elected in a tight 2012 contest to replace a veteran GOP incumbent, had an easier time than expected two years later when he was one of the most heavily targeted Republicans in the cycle. He may entrench in this seat for a lengthy tenure.

Davis was born in Des Moines, Iowa, but moved to Taylorville Illinois, when he was 7 years old, and has never left the area. His parents opened a McDonald's franchise, where Davis pitched in to work before going to college. He said that the experience taught him about the challenges facing small business owners. His political science courses at Millikin University spurred an interest in holding public office. After graduating in 1992, Davis joined Illinois Secretary of State George Ryan's staff. At the time, Ryan's office was engaged in what was later exposed as massive fraud, illegally selling government licenses. But Davis denied knowing of the scheme. "I doubt (Ryan) would even know who I was," he told *The State Journal-Register* of Springfield.

Davis moved on after four years with Ryan, and got his first campaign experience at 25, running for the Illinois legislature in 1996. He lost, but returned to the fray quickly, managing Rep. John Shimkus' first reelection bid in 1998. With time off to run unsuccessfully for mayor of his hometown in 2000, Davis stayed on Shimkus' district office staff until May 2012. During those years, he was the lawmaker's project coordinator, securing local, federal, and private funding for public works projects. "He's great at finding the right mix of funding to move a project forward," Shimkus told the Springfield weekly *Illinois Times*.

When Rep. Tim Johnson announced he was retiring from Congress shortly after winning his primary for reelection, a small group of Illinois GOP leaders chose Davis in May to replace him on the ballot. They were impressed by his fundraising acumen. In 2011, he served as the executive director of the Illinois Republican Party and managed to pay off the organization's $300,000 debt. Democrats were suspicious: A billionaire couple had given a number of $10,000-or-less donations to various county GOP organizers, totaling $200,000, and the organizations later transferred $120,000 to the Illinois GOP. The Democratic National Committee charged that Davis organized a money-laundering scheme to circumvent federal donation limits, which he denied. No charges were filed.

In the general election, Davis faced Democrat David Gill, an emergency room physician and a perennial candidate. Davis promoted his work on the board of education for his local church and as the athletic director of the school his three children attend. He stressed the need to repeal President Barack Obama's health care reform law and to cut government spending, though he made an exception for federal Pell Grants (the district has several colleges and universities). Both men—and their parties—waged fierce negative attacks over the airwaves, prompting Johnson at one point to tell both of them to stop it. Davis outspent Gill $1.4 million to $1.3 million, and he eked out a victory by a margin of 1,002 votes—46.5%-46.2%. The national parties spent more than $6 million on the contest.

In the House, Davis in some ways benefited from his experience as the unassuming staffer who did his work without making waves. He stayed busy with assignments to two committees: Agriculture, and Transportation and Infrastructure. Unusual for a freshman, he served on House-Senate conference committees handling two major pieces of legislation and he helped to shape each measure. On the farm bill, he added restrictions that the Environmental Protection Administration give farmers a seat at the table when the agency considered new regulations that affect their industry. On the water resources bill, he helped craft language that permits the Army Corp of Engineers to cooperate with private businesses to complete projects needed to improve the nation's waterways. Congress also enacted his bill, the Hire More Heroes Act, to assist small businesses hire more veterans. In 2015, he became chairman of the Agriculture Subcommittee on Biotechnology, Horticulture, and Research.

In 2014, Davis survived two significant challenges to his reelection. In the Republican primary, his challenger was Erika Harold, a Harvard Law School graduate and the 2003 Miss America who had tea party support and encouragement from national conservative organizations. *The Weekly Standard* described her as "smart" and "engaging." In her campaign, she said that she represented "the next generation of Republican leadership," and that the GOP needed to reach out to a broader constituency. She ran a credible campaign. But Davis, who largely focused on his record as a freshman, won, 55%-41%.

In the general election, Democrats initially were enthusiastic about their candidate Ann Callis, a former chief justice of the Madison County court. Callis took relatively conservative views for a Democrat, including her description of the Affordable Care Act as "a disaster." She referred to Davis as "a Washington politician." On energy issues, Callis won the support of the Sierra Club, while Davis was backed by the United Mine Workers and the coal industry, both of which were unhappy with the Obama administration's hostility to coal. Callis spent a credible $1.9 million, compared to $3.4 million for Davis. But her national party assistance diminished when House Democrats in 2014 became more concerned with salvaging their incumbents, including two who were defeated in Illinois. Davis won by a robust 59%-41%, and took all of the 14 counties except for university-based Champaign.

FOURTEENTH DISTRICT

Randy Hultgren (R)

Elected 2010, 3rd term; b. March 1, 1966, Park Ridge; Bethel U., B.A. 1988; Chicago-Kent Col. of Law, J.D. 1993; Christian; married (Christy); 4 children.

Elected Office: DuPage Cnty. Bd., 1994-98; IL House, 1998-2006; IL Senate, 2006-10.

Professional Career: Office mgr., Rep. Dennis Hastert, 1988-90; V.P., Trust Investment Advisors, 1995-2010; Practicing atty., 1993-2010.

DC Office: 2455 RHOB, 20515, 202-225-2976; Fax: 202-225-0697; Website: hultgren.house.gov.

State Offices: Campton Hills, 630-584-2734.

Committees: *Financial Services:* Capital Markets and Government Sponsored Enterprises; Oversight & Investigations. *Science, Space, & Technology:* Energy; Research & Technology.

Group Ratings

	ADA	ACLU	AFL-CIO	LCV	ITI	COC	HAFA	ACU	CFG	FRC
2014	0%	0%	–	6%	80%	79%	71%	76%	67%	100%
2013	5%	C	14%	4%	C	85%	C	84%	80%	C

National Journal Ratings

	2013 LIB	—	2013 CONS
Economic	2%	—	97%
Social	31%	—	67%
Foreign	41%	—	57%
Composite	26%	—	75%

Key Votes of the 113th Congress

1. Sandy storm spending	N	5. Medical Marijuana	N	9. Syrian Rebels Training	Y
2. Violence Against Women Act	N	6. Farm Bill	Y	10. Keystone pipeline	Y
3. Guantanamo Bay Detainees	N	7. Afghanistan Combat	N	11. Immigration Exec. Action	Y
4. Abortion 20-week ban	Y	8. NSA Phone Data Collection	Y	12. Bipartisan budget deal	Y

Election Results

2014 general	Randy Hultgren (R)	145,369	(65%)	$957,245
	Dennis Anderson (D)	76,861	(35%)	$55,202
2014 primary	Randy Hultgren (R)	unopposed		

Prior winning percentages: 2012 (59%), 2010 (51%)

Population		Race and Ethnicity		Income	
Total:	729,162	White	79.4%	Median income:	$80,726
Urban:	6.9%	Latino	12.2%		*(30 of 435)*
Suburban:	91.8%	Asian	3.8%	Under $50,000	28.9%
Rural:	1.3%	Black	2.8%	$50,000-$99,999:	32.8%
Land area:	1,073	Two races	1.7%	$100,000-$199,999:	29.9%
Pop/sq. mi.:	679.3	White Ethnic	46.5%	$200,000 or more:	8.4%
Born in state:	70.8%			Poverty Rate	6.4%
		EDUCATION:			
Age Groups		H.S. grad or less:	31.1%	**Work**	
Under 18:	26.8%	Some college:	31.2%	White collar:	39.8%
18 to 34:	19.1%	College degree, 4 yr.:	23.8%	Blue collar:	41.7%
35 to 64:	42.1%	Post-grad study:	13.9%	Sales and service:	18.4%
Over 64:	12.0%			Govt. workers:	11.4%
		Military			
		Veterans/active duty:	6.5%		

Northwestern Chicagoland: McHenry, Kane

At the peak of the housing boom, exurban Kendall County southwest of Chicago looked like the city's new suburban frontier. It was rated the fastest-growing large county in the nation by the Census Bureau in 2010. Its population more than doubled in the decade after 2000, as urban flight brought in families attracted by its affordable housing, good schools, and low crime rates, all located near job centers in suburban DuPage and Kane counties. Farmland quickly transformed into new housing subdivisions. In effect, Kendall became a suburb of the suburbs. But the downside of the rapid growth became evident during the collapse of the housing finance market, when Kendall posted the highest foreclosure rate in the state. Several newer developments in towns like Yorkville became ghost towns after a sudden halt to building. Kendall County grew only 3.6% from 2010 to 2013, barely above the national average. In the exurbs northwest of Chicago, the experience was similar: McHenry County's population dropped by 0.5% during that same period, after the population boomed by 19% in the previous decade. The housing market has started to rebound, but not nearly at the rate of the past. The area does not depend entirely on residential growth. In May 2014, the Wrigley Company, now owned by the giant Mars Inc., announced the expansion of its plant at Yorkville that manufactures Skittles, a popular candy.

Voter Turnout	
2013 Total Citizen 18+	504,429
2014 House Turnout	222,230
2014 Turnout as % CVAP	44.1%
2012 Turnout as % CVAP	65%

The 14th District of Illinois arcs through seven of the Chicago collar counties, including most of solidly-Republican Kendall and McHenry and also Republican-leaning chunks of Kane and western Lake County, where little lake communities are surrounded by new suburbs like Wauconda, Deer Park, and Volo. It also contains smaller parts of Will, DeKalb, and DuPage counties. Also here are parts of the Fox River Valley, including Batavia and the urbane town of St. Charles, which is filled with antique stores and restaurants and sponsors the well-attended Scarecrow

2012 Presidential Vote

Mitt Romney (R)	172,162	(54%)
Barack Obama (D)	140,495	(44%)

2008 Presidential Vote

Barack Obama (D)	163,745	(50%)
John McCain (R)	158,818	(49%)

Cook Partisan Voting Index: R+5

Festival. Of all the suburban Chicago districts, the 14th is the least ethnically diverse, with an 84% white voting-age population.

Not surprisingly, it is the most Republican district in the suburbs, with nearby Democratic cities Aurora and Elgin carved out and placed elsewhere. Still, in a good year, Democrats can run competitively here. President Barack Obama narrowly carried it, under the present lines, with 50% of the vote in 2008. But Mitt Romney got 54% in 2012.

Randy Hultgren (R)

Randy Hultgren, a Republican who ousted Democratic Rep. Bill Foster in 2010, represents a swath of Chicago's northern and western exurbs that includes Fermi National Laboratory, making him a big advocate for more mass transit and scientific research money even as he echoes traditional GOP calls for reining in spending.

Hultgren was raised in Wheaton, a suburb west of Chicago. He was the youngest of three children who lived above their family's funeral home. His penchant for politics developed early. In the eighth grade, Hultgren found he liked his government class, especially when the teacher organized the students into a mini model Congress. In high school, he got involved in student government, as well as in choir and musical theater. The grandson of a Baptist pastor, Hultgren became the third generation in his family to attend Bethel College (now Bethel University) in Minnesota. After graduation, he headed to Washington, and in 1988, was hired on the staff of Rep. Dennis Hastert of Illinois, who later became House speaker. Hultgren progressed quickly from intern to office manager for Hastert, and the work persuaded him to return to his hometown to pursue a degree from Chicago-Kent College of Law.

After graduation, Hultgren practiced law with a local firm, and in the mid-1990s, opened his own firm. During that time, he got a stock broker's license so that he could serve as an investment adviser, a practice he continued until his election to Congress. This period also shaped his political career. In 1990, he was elected as a Republican precinct committee member for Milton Township, and, four years later, Hultgren won a seat on the DuPage County Board, a governing body for several densely populated western suburbs. In 1998, when Hultgren caught wind that a personal friend, state Rep. Peter Roskam, was planning a bid for Congress, he ran for Roskam's Illinois House seat, which he won. Following that pattern in 2006, he was elected to succeed Roskam in the state Senate after Roskam ran for Congress.

As the 2010 election approached, Hultgren decided to take on Foster, who had won Hastert's former seat in a March 2008 special election. Hultgren wasn't the only one who sensed possibilities in a district that, before Foster came along, had been in GOP hands since the Great Depression. Hultgren competed for the nomination with Ethan Hastert, the son of his former political mentor. In an upset, Hultgren overcame Hastert's high name recognition and political pedigree to win the primary by a comfortable 10 percentage points.

During the general election, Hultgren portrayed Foster as a liberal out of touch with the exurban district, and he made frequent references to liberal House Speaker Nancy Pelosi of California. A Harvard-trained physicist, Foster decreed Hultgren to be too "far right" for the district. He raised significantly more money than Hultgren, and conspicuously did not mention his party affiliation. On Election Day, Hultgren won with 51% of the vote to Foster's 45%. Foster won only one population center—DeKalb County, home to the liberal-leaning academic community of Northern Illinois University. Hultgren won the largest county, Kane, 51%-46%; and he won Kendall County, 53% to 44%. (Foster subsequently won election in 2012 in the 11th District. The district that each now serves differs substantially from the district where they competed in 2010.)

In the House, the soft-spoken Hultgren generally avoided hard-right views and he didn't make waves like many of his freshman colleagues. "I'm never going to be the national media guy," he told *Roll Call* in November 2011. Like many other GOP freshmen, he voted against the final bill to raise the federal debt limit in 2011. But he showed his independence by opposing a move by Western conservatives to block the designation of national monuments and another proposal to bar money for government projects that require a union agreement. A member of the conservative Republican Study Committee, he refused to back its aggressive 2011 budget plan, citing its large cuts to Medicare and Medicaid.

Hultgren sought tax breaks for transit commuters as part of the surface transportation reauthorization bill in 2012, and helped form a bipartisan Science and National Labs Caucus that year to raise awareness of Fermilab's physics research. With Foster, he led an effort to increase funding for the labs. Hultgren also joined the Science, Space and Technology Committee to promote his objectives. In July 2014, the House passed his bill, the Department of Energy Laboratory Modernization and Technology Transfer Act of 2014 to modernize the national lab system, including a pilot program for cooperation between companies and the labs to develop new technology. In March 2015, he proposed renewal of an expired tax credit for short-line railroads that make track improvements.

Following redistricting changes that made the district safely Republican, Hultgren has managed to avoid primary opposition and he twice had an easy time in the general election against weakly-financed Democrat Dennis Anderson. For now, Illinois Democrats have higher priorities. Hultgren retained his focus on local problems. When Bruce Rauner was inaugurated as governor in January 2015, Hultgren said, "It's time to put Illinois back on solid fiscal footing and restore its credibility among its neighbors."

FIFTEENTH DISTRICT

John Shimkus (R)

Elected 1996, 10th term; b. Feb. 21, 1958, E. St. Louis; West Point Military Acad., B.S. 1980, Christ Col., teaching cert. 1990, Southern IL U., M.B.A. 1997; Lutheran; married (Karen); 3 children.

Military Career: Army, 1980-85; Army Reserves, 1985-2008.

Elected Office: Collinsville Township trustee, 1989-93; Madison Cnty. treas., 1990-96.

Professional Career: H.S. teacher, 1986-90.

DC Office: 2217 RHOB, 20515, 202-225-5271; Fax: 202-225-5880; Website: shimkus.house.gov.

State Offices: Danville, 217-446-0664; Effingham, 217-347-7947; Harrisburg, 618-252-8271; Maryville, 618-288-7190.

Committees: *Energy & Commerce:* Communication & Technology; Energy & Power; Environment & Economy (Chmn); Health.

Group Ratings

	ADA	ACLU	AFL-CIO	LCV	ITI	COC	HAFA	ACU	CFG	FRC
2014	0%	5%	–	6%	60%	93%	40%	60%	34%	88%
2013	5%	C	33%	7%	C	83%	C	46%	51%	C

National Journal Ratings

	2013 LIB	—	2013 CONS
Economic	46%	—	53%
Social	48%	—	50%
Foreign	46%	—	53%
Composite	47%	—	53%

Key Votes of the 113th Congress

1. Sandy storm spending	Y	5. Medical Marijuana		9. Syrian Rebels Training	Y
2. Violence Against Women Act	Y	6. Farm Bill	Y	10. Keystone pipeline	Y
3. Guantanamo Bay Detainees	N	7. Afghanistan Combat	N	11. Immigration Exec. Action	Y
4. Abortion 20-week ban	Y	8. NSA Phone Data Collection	N	12. Bipartisan budget deal	Y

Election Results

2014 general	John Shimkus (R)	166,274	(75%)	$1,816,163
	Eric Thorsland (D)	55,652	(25%)	$24,243
2014 primary	John Shimkus (R)	unopposed		

Prior winning percentages: 2012 (69%), 2010 (71%), 2008 (64%), 2006 (61%), 2004 (69%), 2002 (55%), 2000 (63%), 1998 (61%), 1996 (50%)

Population		Race and Ethnicity		Income	
Total:	705,563	White	90.9%	Median income:	$46,832
Urban:	8.9%	Black	4.6%		*(286 of 435)*
Suburban:	15.0%	Latino	2.4%	Under $50,000	52.7%
Rural:	76.1%	Asian	0.5%	$50,000-$99,999:	31.7%
Land area:	14,367	Two races	1.4%	$100,000-$199,999:	13.4%
Pop/sq. mi.:	49.1	White Ethnic	19.7%	$200,000 or more:	2.2%
Born in state:	75.0%			Poverty Rate	15.1%
		Education			
Age Groups		H.S. grad or less:	47.8%	**Work**	
Under 18:	22.3%	Some college:	34.3%	White collar:	29.1%
18 to 34:	20.5%	College degree, 4 yr.:	11.9%	Blue collar:	40.9%
35 to 64:	39.7%	Post-grad study:	6.0%	Sales and service:	30.0%
Over 64:	17.5%			Govt. workers:	13.5%
		Military			
		Veterans/active duty:	9.7%		

South-Central Illinois

Much of Southern Illinois is a land of prairies, of flat, treeless land sloping imperceptibly down to the Ohio and Mississippi rivers. It was settled almost entirely from the south by farmers coming overland from Kentucky, such as Abraham Lincoln's family, which settled in what was then the

Voter Turnout	
2013 Total Citizen 18+	542,256
2014 House Turnout	221,926
2014 Turnout as % CVAP	40.9%
2012 Turnout as % CVAP	56.9%

state capital of Vandalia. Just beyond the Ohio River, they found hilly terrain, some of which turned out to have vast coal deposits. As they traveled farther north, they must have been astonished, after miles of thick forest, to see the great American prairie stretch before them, a vast sea of empty land extending past the horizon. The prairie lands proved wondrously rich and were soon crisscrossed by rail lines taking their produce away and bringing in industrial products from St. Louis, Chicago, and points east. About the same time, several mining towns sprouted in Southern Illinois. This was the home turf of John L. Lewis, the imperious leader of the United Mine Workers for half a century and, in the late 1930s and early 1940s, one of the most powerful and eloquent figures in American public life.

The 15th Congressional District of Illinois, the largest geographically in the state, extends more than 250 miles up and down, and 150 miles across. Vermilion County and northern Champaign County represent the northern border of the district, which extends along the state's eastern and southeastern borders and along a jagged line that ends with Collinsville in Madison County. It covers all or part of 33 counties in the rich heartland of Southern Illinois. The old National Road (paralleled by Interstate 70), the traditional boundary between the part of downstate Illinois settled by Southerners and the part settled by Yankees, traverses the district. The city of Effingham, which straddles that line, is where corn and soybean fields give way to hills and valleys with orchards and woodlands. Racial diversity is limited here; in 2012, the district was 92 percent white.

The biggest voting blocs in the 15th are in Madison and Clinton counties (parts of the St. Louis metropolitan area), Coles County (home to Eastern Illinois University), plus Champaign and adjacent Vermilion County on the Indiana border. The district includes sparsely settled areas along the Ohio River, and some prairie counties along U.S. 40. Some of those towns recently have suffered

2012 Presidential Vote		
Mitt Romney (R)	197,262	(64%)
Barack Obama (D)	105,015	(34%)
2008 Presidential Vote		
John McCain (R)	180,711	(55%)
Barack Obama (D)	139,551	(43%)
Cook Partisan Voting Index: R+14		

from the closing of their final small grocery store. Politically, these prairie lands incline much more to the party of former House Speaker Joseph Cannon, a Republican from the manufacturing city of Danville (population, 32,977), which is the largest city in the district. Traditional Democrats have become hard to find here. In 2012, Mitt Romney won 32 of the 33 counties in the district. But despite his general election success, the culturally-conservative district more closely matches Rick Santorum's brand of Republicanism, with evangelical Christians making up a significant share of the GOP vote in Southern Illinois. In the 2012 Republican primary, Santorum defeated Romney in 30 of the 33 counties. This is the most Republican district in Illinois.

John Shimkus (R)

John Shimkus, a Republican first elected in 1996, has been an aggressive supporter of business and a fierce critic of regulations he considers overly burdensome. As a senior member of the Energy and Commerce Committee, he has shown interest in becoming chairman. He is a devout Christian, who uses his official Facebook and Twitter accounts to post daily Bible passages.

Shimkus grew up in Collinsville, in Madison County. His father was an installer for Illinois Bell, and his mother a township trustee. He is of Lithuanian descent, as is his predecessor in the seat, Democratic Sen. Dick Durbin. Shimkus graduated from West Point, trained in the Army as a Ranger and paratrooper, went to college in California, then came back to Collinsville to teach high school. Almost immediately, he began running for local office. In 1988, he ran for the Madison County Board and lost. The very next year, however, he was elected a Collinsville Township trustee. In 1990, at age 32, he beat a 12-year incumbent to become Madison County treasurer. He challenged then-Rep. Durbin in 1992 and lost 57%-43%, a closer margin than in Durbin's previous campaigns.

In 1996, when Durbin ran for the Senate, Shimkus easily won the Republican primary, with 51% against seven other candidates. In the general election, he faced state Rep. Jay Hoffman. Both were anti-abortion rights, anti-gun control, and pro-balanced budget amendment. Hoffman raised more money and had the support of the AFL-CIO, but Shimkus won, 50.3% to 49.7%.

In the House, Shimkus' voting record is generally conservative. He told *Esquire* magazine in 2010 that he believes President Barack Obama's world view "is of government control, of government solving the inequities of society. And that means big government and higher taxes. ... It's just not what makes this country great." In his Facebook and Twitter postings, his favorite verse is Ephesians 2:8-9: "For by grace are ye saved through faith; and that not of yourselves: it is the gift of God: Not of works, lest any man should boast."

Shimkus can show a centrist streak. After Republicans took control of the House in 2011, he voted against the GOP majority on eliminating funding for the Legal Services Corp., reducing funding for the National Endowment for the Arts, and cutting the Food and Drug Administration's tobacco regulation budget. He was one of only 16 House Republicans in March 2012 to back a budget plan along the lines of the bipartisan Simpson-Bowles commission.

On the Energy and Commerce Committee, Shimkus' ardor can sometimes give way to hyperbole that triggers criticism on the left. When Democrats issued a draft plan to regulate greenhouse gas emissions in April 2009, he called it the "largest assault on democracy and freedom in this country that I've ever witnessed." Around the same time, he drew attention for arguing that carbon dioxide—the leading greenhouse gas—is valuable "plant food" that did not need to be controlled. The floods that scientists warn could result from a rapidly changing climate won't happen, Shimkus said, because God promised the Earth would not be destroyed by a flood. During a December 2013 hearing with Health and Human Services Secretary Kathleen Sebelius to discuss the Affordable Care Act, he compared her responses to those of an official from North Korea.

He has been especially vocal about energy production: supporting nuclear power, extending tax credits for ethanol, and giving incentives to coal-to-liquid refineries to help coal-producing areas. In 2005, he helped to pass the law that gasoline must contain a minimum volume of renewable fuels, such as biodiesel and ethanol; that has resulted in what has become known as the Renewable Fuel Standard. After the 2010 election, he vied to become Energy and Commerce chairman, but lost out to the more senior Fred Upton of Michigan. Shimkus was named chairman of a new subcommittee on environment and the economy, where he closely monitors the Obama administration's regulatory activities. He regularly has challenged the Obama administration for its decision to abandon storing waste from commercial nuclear power plants at Yucca Mountain in Nevada. In 2011 and 2012, Shimkus amended spending bills to encourage the Nuclear Regulatory Commission to license the site. He also has sought revisions in chemical-safety laws.

As a former high school teacher, Shimkus took what seemed to be a routine assignment as chairman of the House page board. But five weeks before the 2006 election, revelations that Republican Rep. Mark Foley had sent inappropriate and sexually explicit e-mails to former male pages was a political bombshell for the party, including for Shimkus and then-GOP Speaker Dennis Hastert of Illinois. Both men had known of questionable contacts Foley had with pages and failed to investigate. The House Ethics Committee later found that Shimkus should have shared the information with other House members on the page board, but called for no sanctions against him.

In 2002, Shimkus had a redistricting-forced contest against Rep. David Phelps, a conservative Democrat. After a spirited contest, in which organized labor spent more than $1.5 million trying to dislodge him, Shimkus won 55%-45%. Since then, he has been reelected easily. When he first ran for the seat, Shimkus said he would limit himself to six terms. But in September 2005, he called his pledge "a mistake," and said, "Unless everyone plays by the same rules, term limits don't make sense." He has not faced a serious challenge since then. With Upton term-limited at the end of 2016, Shimkus will have another opportunity to become chairman of Energy and Commerce. But the more senior Ed Whitfield of Kentucky ranks one slot above him.

SIXTEENTH DISTRICT

Adam Kinzinger (R)

Elected 2010, 3rd term; b. Feb. 27, 1978, Kankakee; IL St. U., B.S. 2000; Protestant; single.

Military Career: Air Natl. Guard, 2003-present (Iraq, Afghanistan).

Elected Office: McLean Cnty. Bd., 1998-2003.

Professional Career: Partner, sales rep., STL Technology, 2000-03.

DC Office: 1221 LHOB, 20515, 202-225-3635; Fax: 202-225-3521; Website: kinzinger.house.gov.

State Offices: Ottawa, 815-431-9271; Watseka, 815-432-0580; Rockford, 815-708-8032.

Committees: *Energy & Commerce:* Commerce, Manufacturing & Trade; Communications & Technology; Energy & Power.

Group Ratings

	ADA	ACLU	AFL-CIO	LCV	ITI	COC	HAFA	ACU	CFG	FRC
2014	5%	5%	–	3%	100%	93%	42%	52%	39%	88%
2013	0%	C	19%	4%	C	85%	C	52%	49%	C

National Journal Ratings

	2013 LIB	—	2013 CONS
Economic	44%	—	56%
Social	43%	—	54%
Foreign	24%	—	68%
Composite	39%	—	61%

Key Votes of the 113th Congress

1. Sandy storm spending	N 5. Medical Marijuana	N 9. Syrian Rebels Training	Y
2. Violence Against Women Act	Y 6. Farm Bill	Y 10. Keystone pipeline	Y
3. Guantanamo Bay Detainees	N 7. Afghanistan Combat	N 11. Immigration Exec. Action	Y
4. Abortion 20-week ban	Y 8. NSA Phone Data Collection	N 12. Bipartisan budget deal	Y

Election Results

2014 general	Adam Kinzinger (R)	153,388	(71%)	$1,377,467	$20,559
	Randall Olsen (D)	63,810	(29%)	$11,506	
2014 primary	Adam Kinzinger (R)	56,593	(78%)		
	David Hale (R)	15,558	(22%)		

Prior winning percentages: 2012 (62%), 2010 (57%)

Population		Race and Ethnicity		Income	
Total:	697,856	White	84.7%	Median income:	$52,561
Urban:	14.6%	Latino	8.7%		*(191 of 435)*
Suburban:	39.0%	Black	4.1%	Under $50,000	47.4%
Rural:	46.3%	Asian	1.2%	$50,000-$99,999:	32.7%
Land area:	7,468	Two races	1.1%	$100,000-$199,999:	16.9%
Pop/sq. mi.:	93.4	White Ethnic	36.1%	$200,000 or more:	3.0%
Born in state:	77.4%			Poverty Rate	13.0%
		Education			
Age Groups		H.S. grad or less:	44.6%	**Work**	
Under 18:	22.6%	Some college:	33.9%	White collar:	30.9%
18 to 34:	21.7%	College degree, 4 yr.:	14.0%	Blue collar:	41.2%
35 to 64:	39.7%	Post-grad study:	7.6%	Sales and service:	27.9%
Over 64:	16.0%				
		Military		Govt. workers:	14.0%
		Veterans/active duty:	9.3%		

North-Central Illinois: Rockford, Ottawa

The third largest city in Illinois is Rockford, on the Rock River, settled by Swedes as well as Yankees, and once a leading furniture and machine tool manufacturer. Rockford's manufacturing base steadily declined after World War II, and by the 1980s, it had a serious unemployment problem. It

Voter Turnout	
2013 Total Citizen 18+	525,080
2014 House Turnout	217,198
2014 Turnout as % CVAP	41.4%
2012 Turnout as % CVAP	58.3%

temporarily rebounded as it moved toward becoming a center for professional services and high technology, but then the recession hit hard. The area's unemployment rate was the state's highest during much of 2009 and climbed to nearly 20% in early 2010 before creeping downward to 14% in early 2013 and finally dropping below 8% in February 2015.

Growth has become stagnant in DeKalb County, which had been booming with relatively cheap housing before the recession. In neighboring Boone County, the farming village of Poplar Grove saw its population triple between 2000 and 2010, but growth went flat and it now faces thousands of undeveloped lots left barren after the recession. The Obama administration's auto bailout provided a small jump start to the area's economy. There is a big Chrysler plant on 280 acres a few miles east of Rockford in Belvidere, where employment has boomed thanks to the bailout. The workforce at the factory was down to 200 in 2009, but it now employs 4,400 workers on three shifts, with additional workers at nearby suppliers.

The 16th Congressional District is where downstate Illinois begins, at least where it begins west of Chicago. It includes parts of Rockford, the population base of the district, after Democratic redistricters split the city for the first time since 1850 to maximize their House delegation. Farther south, on bluffs above the Illinois River, are the factory towns of Ottawa, LaSalle, and Streator. On the eastern side of the district is DeKalb County, long the world's leading manufacturer of barbed wire. Dixon, to the west, is where Ronald Reagan grew up. Farther south, the elongated district hooks to the Indiana border, forming a crescent with the Wisconsin border on the north.

2012 Presidential Vote		
Mitt Romney (R)	160,435	(53%)
Barack Obama (D)	137,749	(45%)
2008 Presidential Vote		
Barack Obama (D)	160,925	(50%)
John McCain (R)	154,801	(48%)
Cook Partisan Voting Index: R+4		

These rural areas surrounding Chicago traditionally were some of the most heavily Republican territory in the country, but they have become more competitive. After the 2010 census, Democrats drew the district to favor Republicans, although in a wave election, Democrats have an opportunity. Barack Obama carried it with 50% in 2008, but Mitt Romney won the district in 2012 with 53%, carrying 10 of its 14 counties.

Adam Kinzinger (R)

Republican Adam Kinzinger, elected in 2010, is a telegenic conservative in his 30s who has racked up considerable experience in the military and political worlds. A former Air Force pilot, he dispatched first-term Democratic Rep. Debbie Halvorson, and two years later, knocked off 10-term Republican Don Manzullo in a brutal Republican primary in 2012. He can be a savvy policy wonk.

Kinzinger was born in Kankakee, but spent the majority of his life in Bloomington. He attributes his interest in public service to his father, who ran a nonprofit homeless shelter, and his mother, a public school teacher. He says that growing up in a middle-class family with two siblings taught him to spend money prudently. Wanting to stay near home, he attended Illinois State University and graduated with a bachelor's degree in political science in 2000. His first foray into politics came before that: In 1998, as a college sophomore, he took seriously a joking suggestion that he run for the McLean County Board. He did, defeating an incumbent and serving until 2003. When the September 11 terrorist attacks occurred, "that's when I basically woke up," he recalled. A month later, he joined the Air Force. He worked in the private sector for STL Technology Partners until he could begin officer and pilot training. He served three tours in Iraq from 2007 to 2009 and a tour in Afghanistan.

In the summer of 2006, Kinzinger was returning from the border of Mexico as part of his mission when he saw an attempted murder. Seeing a woman whose throat had been slashed running from her knife-wielding aggressor, he wrestled the man to the ground until police arrived. As a result, he was awarded the National Guard's Valley Forge Cross for heroism. "During that whole thing, I thought I was going to die," he said. "It really was a life-changing moment about sacrificing yourself for others."

In May 2009, following his final tour in Iraq, Kinzinger campaigned for the district based in Will County. Touting his military service, he beat four opponents in the 2010 Republican primary, getting 64% of the vote. In the fall, he faced Halvorson, who had racked up an impressive 58% of the vote in 2008. Kinzinger had important backing from local tea party activists. Halvorson attacked Kinzinger's stance on free trade and depicted him as inexperienced. She ran a campaign ad with a senior citizen scolding, "Young man, you have no idea what you're doing." Kinzinger countered with endorsements from former governors and GOP leaders Mitt Romney and Sarah Palin. He won the support of the Chamber of Commerce and the National Federation of Independent Business over Halvorson, who had highlighted her advocacy of small business. He also picked up an endorsement from the *Chicago Sun-Times*, which often backs Democrats. Halvorson outspent him $2.5 million to $1.8 million, but Kinzinger won convincingly, 57%-43%.

When he got to Washington, *The New York Times* took him to task in a December 2010 editorial after Kinzinger held a $5,000-a-head breakfast at the Capitol Hill Club to raise money for his campaign debt. The editorial said it smacked of "business as usual" for a lawmaker who had promised to be different. But he became a favorite of House GOP leaders, who put him on the whip team and gave him a choice seat on the Energy and Commerce Committee, where he has generally upheld business' interests. He has called for dramatically overhauling the tax code to make it more friendly to companies. The House in September 2012 passed his bill aimed at helping states streamline certification requirements for veterans with emergency medical technician training who want to continue as civilian EMTs. *Time* named him as one of its "40 Under 40" young leaders.

For 2012, Democratic-engineered redistricting put Kinzinger in the same district as Manzullo, who was twice his age. The race upended the traditional rules of seniority: Kinzinger won the endorsement of top House GOP leaders, including Majority Leader Eric Cantor and Whip Kevin McCarthy, while Manzullo played up his tea party support and a nod from Freedom-Works PAC, an important financial backer of that movement. Kinzinger touted his combat tours and hit Manzullo for voting to raise the debt limit 12 times in his career. But Manzullo fired back, boasting in an ad that he had voted to cut $209 billion more in spending than Kinzinger in the current session of Congress. Primary voters decided to go with youth and the future over experience and the past, and Kinzinger won 54%-46%. In the fall, he had no trouble, winning with 62% over Democrat Wanda Rohl. For the first time, he won in a breeze in 2014.

Seemingly entrenched at home and with growing seniority, Kinzinger became more activist in the GOP's establishment wing. In October 2014, he criticized the Pentagon budget-cutting plan of Kentucky Sen. Rand Paul as "devastating for our party." In February 2015, he filed a resolution that would grant the president full authority to wage war against the threat posed by the Islamic State. His alternative, Kinzinger said, "removes the restrictions [President Barack Obama's] current proposal places on his and future presidents' ability to execute their role as Commander-in-Chief." Kinzinger, who remains a pilot in the Air National Guard, has filed a bill that would streamline certification for emergency medical technicians. On Energy and Commerce, he has been a major booster of nuclear energy that, he said, "will sustain our economic expansion and keep the lights on while we work to catch up with our international competition." With Democrat Dan Lipinski of Illinois, he won enactment of the American Manufacturing Competitiveness Act, which requires a national strategy to create U.S. manufacturing competitiveness.

SEVENTEENTH DISTRICT

Cheri Bustos (D)

Elected 2012, 2nd term; b. Oct. 17, 1961, Springfield; IL Col., U. of MD, B.S. 1983; U. of IL Springfield, M.A. 1985; Catholic; married (Gerry); 3 children.

Elected Office: East Moline City Cncl., 2007-11.

Professional Career: V.P., Iowa Health Systems, 2008-12; Sr. dir., Trinity Regional Health System, 2002-08; Reporter, Quad-City Times, 1985-2002.

DC Office: 1009 LHOB, 20515, 202-225-5905; Website: bustos.house .gov.

State Offices: Peoria, 309-966-1813; Rock Island, 309-786-3406; Rockford, 815-968-8011.

Committees: *Agriculture:* General Farm Commodities & Risk Management; Livestock, Rural Development, and Credit. *Transportation & Infrastructure:* Aviation; Highways & Transit.

Group Ratings

	ADA	ACLU	AFL-CIO	LCV	ITI	COC	HAFA	ACU	CFG	FRC
2014	50%	77%	–	80%	100%	77%	8%	8%	11%	13%
2013	50%	C	90%	79%	C	69%	C	8%	5%	C

National Journal Ratings

	2013 LIB	—	2013 CONS
Economic	58%	—	41%
Social	59%	—	41%
Foreign	58%	—	42%
Com	59%	—	42%

Key Votes of the 113th Congress

1. Sandy storm spending	Y	5. Medical Marijuana	Y	9. Syrian Rebels Training	Y
2. Violence Against Women Act	Y	6. Farm Bill	Y	10. Keystone pipeline	NV
3. Guantanamo Bay Detainees	Y	7. Afghanistan Combat	N	11. Immigration Exec. Action	N
4. Abortion 20-week ban	N	8. NSA Phone Data Collection	NV	12. Bipartisan budget deal	Y

Election Results

2014 general	Cheri Bustos (D) 110,560	(55%)	$3,089,768	$219,138	$225,914
	Bobby Schilling (R) 88,785	(45%)	$1,144,069	$23,890	$1,262,761
2014 primary	Cheri Bustos (D) ....unopposed				

Prior winning percentage: 2012 (53%)

Population		Race and Ethnicity		Income	
Total:	710,667	White	77.6%	Median income:	$42,349
Urban:	39.1%	Black	11.3%		*(351 of 435)*
Suburban:	18.2%	Latino	8.0%	Under $50,000	57.0%
Rural:	42.7%	Asian	1.0%	$50,000-$99,999:	29.3%
Land area:	6,716	Two races	1.7%	$100,000-$199,999:	12.2%
Pop/sq. mi.:	105.8	White Ethnic	21.7%	$200,000 or more:	1.5%
Born in state:	72.1%			Poverty Rate	18.3%
		Education			
Age Groups		H.S. grad or less:	49.1%	**Work**	
Under 18:	23.3%	Some college:	32.6%	White collar:	28.2%
18 to 34:	21.4%	College degree, 4 yr.:	12.7%	Blue collar:	43.2%
35 to 64:	38.7%	Post-grad study:	5.6%	Sales and service:	28.7%
Over 64:	16.5%				
		Military		Govt. workers:	12.0%
		Veterans/active duty:	9.2%		

Northwest Illinois: Moline, Rock Island

Illinois' western prairies are some of America's richest agricultural land. They were first settled by Yankees coming overland from northern Indiana and Ohio and upstate New York. After 1848, Germans left their homeland in search of better opportunities and settled in a place that in many

Voter Turnout	
2013 Total Citizen 18+	527,133
2014 House Turnout	199,361
2014 Turnout as % CVAP	37.8%
2012 Turnout as % CVAP	55.8%

ways resembled the flat, orderly plains of northern Germany. These migrants farmed quarter-sections and built small towns, with banks and stores, community churches, and libraries. As farming expanded, so did the need for agricultural equipment. Entrepreneurs and investors built farm-machinery factories, and the Quad Cities of the Mississippi—Davenport and Bettendorf in Iowa, and Rock Island and Moline in Illinois—became one of the nation's biggest agricultural equipment-manufacturing centers. John Deere, a blacksmith from Vermont, set up a "self-polishing plow" shop in 1837 in the small Rock River town of Grand Detour, Illinois. His company, now headquartered in Moline, is ranked 80th on the 2014 Fortune 500 list of largest American corporations. Caterpillar, ranked 42nd on that list, is another iconic local brand. The earth-moving company operates around the world. That helps to explain why its local payroll has shrunk to less than 16,000 from 35,000 jobs in the 1970s: 95 percent of its potential customers live outside the United States, and the company feels a need to manufacture where it sells.

The plants were unionized in the 1930s and 1940s, and in post-World War II America wages went up as the demand increased for more sophisticated machines on Midwest farms. In the early 1980s, as farm profits vanished and land values declined, orders for new machinery and equipment dried up. The result was a depression in western Illinois and neighboring Iowa, and a political swing toward the Democrats and away from the Republicans, who had been the ancestral party in most of this area.

A quarter century later, President Barack Obama sought to create jobs in the region and deal with a broader national-security problem when he ordered the purchase of a state-owned prison in Thomson, as part of a plan to move terrorist detainees out of the Guantanamo Bay, Cuba facility. The move to the northwest Illinois facility became bogged down in politics and the proposal was shelved. The Justice Department purchased the dormant prison site for $165 million in October 2012, and said it would house only inmates in the U.S. prison system. In August 2014, Rockford got good news when AAR, the largest aircraft maintenance company in North America, announced plans for a facility at the local airport that would service wide-body planes and create 500 jobs. Local officials said that the area already had 6,500 aerospace production workers.

The 17th Congressional District links the Illinois portion of the Quad Cities with arms extending to the Democratic-leaning parts of Peoria to the east and Rockford to the north. It takes in the hilly, almost mountainous country in the northwest corner of the state. The district is steeped in political history: Some 30 miles west of Rockford is Freeport, whose town square hosted 15,000 people coming to hear Abraham Lincoln and

2012 Presidential Vote

Barack Obama (D)	168,796	(57%)
Mitt Romney (R)	119,789	(41%)

2008 Presidential Vote

Barack Obama (D)	185,641	(60%)
John McCain (R)	119,033	(39%)

Cook Partisan Voting Index: D+7

Stephen Douglas in one of their seven debates in 1858. Not far away, on a little river once navigable by Mississippi River steamboats, is Galena, the home of Ulysses S. Grant.

The district contains some of the few parts of rural America carried by Obama. Granted, this is his home state. But his performance here in 2012 was better than his vote in rural southern Illinois.

Cheri Bustos (D)

Democrat Cheri Bustos, first elected in 2012, took advantage of her roots in Illinois politics— her father was a chief of staff for the late Democratic Sen. Alan Dixon—and the district's Democratic leanings. She has sought to assert influence as part of the few remaining House Democrats who represent large rural areas.

Bustos grew up in the state capital of Springfield. Her mother was a social worker and preschool teacher, and her father was a journalist before entering government. Her first paid job was selling tacos and lemonade at the Illinois State Fair. As a 10-year-old, she met future Democratic Sens. Paul Simon and Dick Durbin, who at the time was a staffer for then-Lt. Gov. Simon. After attending Illinois College, where she excelled at basketball and volleyball, Bustos graduated from the University of Maryland in 1983 with a bachelor's degree in political science and history. She earned a master's degree in journalism at the University of Illinois two years later, and moved to the Quad Cities area to become a reporter with the *Quad-City Times*, where she covered city government, corruption, crime, health care, and other issues over a 17-year career. Her husband, Gerry, has been a captain in the Rock Island Police Department and commander of the Quad City Bomb Squad.

After leaving journalism, Bustos went into public relations for regional health care providers, most recently as the vice president of public relations and communications for Iowa Health System. Health-related issues are a key concern for her: She lost her uninsured sister-in-law to cancer a few years ago, and her brother to cancer months later, after his insurance refused to cover the medication he needed. President Barack Obama's Affordable Care Act, she said, is "at least in the right direction," but Bustos insists that more needs to be done to improve what she calls a "broken" system.

She entered politics with a run for the City Council in East Moline, and served from 2007 to 2011. Emphasizing economic development, she founded and chaired the East Moline Downtown Revitalization Committee. As the 2012 election approached, Democrats in Springfield had used redistricting to make the House district more Democratic for a challenge to freshman Republican Bobby Schilling. When Bustos entered the race, her friendship with Durbin paid off. He provided a rare primary endorsement in January 2012 and urged other Democrats to exit the race. She went on to win the primary over two other candidates with 54% of the vote.

Her race in the fall against pizzeria owner Schilling attracted more than $3 million each from Democratic and Republican party groups, in addition to the more than $2 million that each candidate spent. Bustos received an early endorsement from abortion rights group EMILY's List and was backed by several labor unions. Schilling aligned himself with tea party activists. The race was negative. Bustos called her opponent "extreme" on abortion rights and suggested he didn't care about women's health. National Republicans ran an ad accusing Bustos of voting to spend $625,000 on improvements to the road "connecting her street to her local country club." The ad was debunked—repairs began before Bustos served on the council, and she simply joined other members in approving the project's second phase. And she never belonged to the country club. She won, 53%-47%.

In the House, Bustos enjoyed serving as a deal-cutter. On the Agriculture Committee, she joined the bipartisan coalition that approved a five-year farm bill in January 2014. She won approval of a provision that would quantify the impact on local agriculture from upgrading the aging locks and dams along the Mississippi and Illinois Rivers. On the Transportation and Infrastructure Committee, she worked on the bipartisan deal for a water resources bill. The final agreement included her public-private partnership provision that was designed to provide additional financing options to improve the locks and dams. She sided with local farmers and biofuel advocates who opposed a proposal by the Environmental Protection Administration to lower the level of biofuel blended into the nation's fuel supply. She also called for replacing what she called the "functionally obsolete" I-74 bridge in the Quad Cities.

In the 2014 election, Bustos had a rematch with Schilling. But it proved less competitive than their initial contest. This time, she outspent her opponent $3.1 million to $1.1 million, and Schilling had scant GOP financial support. In an otherwise Republican year in Illinois and elsewhere, Bustos rolled to a 55%-45% win, with 2-to-1 leads in Peoria and Rockford, and 54% of the vote in Rock Island County. After the election, she considered a challenge to Republican Sen. Mark Kirk in 2016, but said that she did not want to face Democratic Rep. Tammy Duckworth in a primary.

EIGHTEENTH DISTRICT
Vacant

Population		Race and Ethnicity		Income	
Total:	718,789	White	89.8%	Median income:	$58,030
Urban:	25.5%	Black	3.8%		(142 of 435)
Suburban:	27.3%	Asian	2.4%	Under $50,000	43.0%
Rural:	47.1%	Latino	2.3%	$50,000-$99,999:	33.3%
Land area:	9,089	Two races	1.3%	$100,000-$199,999:	19.8%
Pop/sq. mi.:	79.1	White Ethnic	25.1%	$200,000 or more:	3.8%
Born in state:	77.5%			Poverty Rate	10.8%
		Education			
Age Groups		H.S. grad or less:	38.0%	**Work**	
Under 18:	22.0%	Some college:	30.7%	White collar:	38.8%
18 to 34:	21.6%	College degree, 4 yr.:	20.7%	Blue collar:	40.2%
35 to 64:	39.9%	Post-grad study:	10.6%	Sales and service:	21.0%
Over 64:	16.5%				
		Military		Govt. workers:	14.9%
		Veterans/active duty:	9.2%		

West-Central Illinois: Parts of Peoria and Springfield

Old vaudeville bookers, presented with a new act, used to ask, "Will it play in Peoria?" The implication was that if an act went over in this small city on the bluffs above the Illinois River, 154 miles from Chicago and 171 miles from St. Louis, it would go over just about anywhere. In the first half of the 20th century, Peoria seemed pretty typical of America. If its citizens were mostly of British or German descent, with a small percentage of African-Americans, that was the image of ordinary America that prevailed through the 1960s. But Peoria's economy has changed, much as America's has changed. This is still a heavy manufacturing town, dominated by big plants that produce farm machinery and earth-moving equipment. Its biggest employer is Caterpillar, which was founded in 1910 with 12 employees, and a century later was the world's leading producer of earth-moving and construction equipment, and one of America's major exporters. There are more than just memories here of the sharp divide between blue collar and white collar, union and management, Democrat and Republican—the basis of the class warfare politics that was the norm in heavy industrial metropolises of the Great Lakes region.

Voter Turnout	
2013 Total Citizen 18+	546,098
2014 House Turnout	246,740
2014 Turnout as % CVAP	45.2%
2012 Turnout as % CVAP	61.2%

But the blue-collar workers now are not as numerous and the unions not as strong. The Peoria area went through terrible times in the 1980s, as big farm machinery plants laid off workers and even closed down. Memories of those hard times were revived by the 2007-09 recession. Caterpillar had laid off 22,000 employees by February 2009, when Obama came to Peoria to stump for his economic stimulus bill. But lately, there have been signs of hope for the manufacturing giant. As China and other countries rebounded economically, Caterpillar's sales revived and workers were rehired. Because Caterpillar operates around the world, that helps to explain why its local payroll has shrunk to less than 16,000 from 35,000 jobs in the 1970s: 95 percent of its potential customers live outside the United States, and the company feels a need to manufacture where it sells.

Peoria isn't the only industrial engine of the district. Beardstown, a small river town 200 miles southwest of Chicago, is home to a 430,000 square-foot slaughterhouse run by Cargill, the third-largest meatpacker in the country. Latino and African immigrants have flocked into rural Illinois towns like Beardstown looking for entry-level jobs in

2012 Presidential Vote		
Mitt Romney (R)	203,198	(61%)
Barack Obama (D)	125,079	(37%)

2008 Presidential Vote		
John McCain (R)	187,804	(54%)
Barack Obama (D)	152,369	(44%)

Cook Partisan Voting Index: R+11

manufacturing. Cargill's pork plant employs more than 900 people from at least 34 countries. Overall, the district is still ethnically homogeneous, with a 91 percent white voting-age population.

The 18th Congressional District of Illinois, variously configured, has been the Peoria district since the 1940s, though it now includes only part of the city and its suburbs, and doesn't take in the downtown area. The 18th begins at the Iowa border along the Mississippi River, includes Quincy, and then runs east through rich farmland to the suburbs of Peoria, Bloomington, and Springfield. It includes 10 of the 11 counties that President Abraham Lincoln represented during his one term in Congress, 1847-49. It has been represented by two national Republican leaders: Everett McKinley Dirksen, who was the Senate Republican leader from 1959-69, and Robert Michel, House Republican leader from 1981-95. It is the home of Eureka College, which dedicated the Ronald Reagan Peace Garden in honor of its 1932 graduate and the end of the Cold War that he helped to achieve. It is a heavily Republican district, one of only two statewide that voted for John McCain in 2008. In the past 10 congressional races here, the best Democratic performance was 41 percent.

Vacant

Following the resignation in March 2015 of ethics-tarred Republican Aaron Schock, Republicans nominated Darin LaHood as their candidate in the scheduled September 10 special election. LaHood became the virtually certain winner in this strongly Republican district. Democrats quickly conceded that they faced an uphill challenge, and made little effort to find or support a competitive contender in the home state of President Barack Obama.

Schock, who was elected in 2008, drew more notice for his youth and buff physique until the focus shifted to his office-decorating tastes and lifestyle. He had succeeded GOP Rep. Ray LaHood, who retired and became Secretary of Transportation in Obama's first term. The father of Darin LaHood, the senior LaHood served seven terms following the retirement of Robert Michel, the long-time House Minority Leader for whom Ray LaHood served as a top aide.

Schock, who never faced a serious election challenge, gained little attention for his legislative work, though he sought to make a name for himself on trade and tax reform issues at the Ways and Means Committee. An accumulation of well-publicized controversies involving his use of taxpayer money led him to announce his resignation.

In early 2015, he drew significant attention for multiple activities for which he would have preferred to remain out of the spotlight. First came a *Washington Post* article about the lavish redecoration of his House office in the style of the popular television series Downton Abbey. Although the decorator told the newspaper that she had offered her services for free, Schock later repaid the government $35,000 from his personal funds to cover the costs. *USA Today* reported that Schock had spent more than $100,000 of his taxpayer-funded account on renovations in earlier years.

Then Schock's communications director, Benjamin Cole—who had gotten into a tiff with the *Post* over the redecorating story—resigned after it was discovered that he had made racially insensitive comments on Facebook. Schock's problems continued to pile up: A liberal blog reported that Schock sold his Peoria home to an executive of the Caterpillar construction-vehicle company for more than three times the property's assessed value. Several news outlets delved into his overseas travel and found that he may have improperly used political and taxpayer funds to fly on private planes, leading the watchdog Citizens for Responsibility and Ethics in Washington to file a complaint.

The bad news didn't end. Various national and local news outlets found a pattern of eyebrow-raising activity. After *Politico* published a report raising questions about whether he was improperly reimbursed for thousands of dollars in mileage on his personal vehicle, Schock threw in the towel, effective March 31. "The constant questions over the last six weeks have proven a great distraction that has made it too difficult for me to serve the people of the 18th District with the high standards that they deserve and which I have set for myself," he said in a statement. Following his resignation, a grand jury continued to investigate his activities.

Darin LaHood, a conservative state senator, announced his candidacy the following day. *National Journal* profiled him as "a media-shy, ethics-focused political scion," a welcome antithesis to Schock. Several other prominent local Republicans considered entering the contest. But they all stepped aside, in apparent recognition of LaHood's strength and the desire of local Republicans to avoid more controversy. His only primary opponent was little-known

Mike Flynn, a libertarian Republican political operative and a former editor of the Breitbart News conservative website. He criticized the LaHoods as career politicians out of touch with the real world, and noted that Ray LaHood had become an ally of the Democratic president.

With support from the district's GOP establishment, Darin LaHood won the July 7 Republican primary, 69%-28%. The Democratic nominee Rob Mellon, a high school history teacher and captain in the Army Reserve, had raised little money or attention.

★ INDIANA ★

"**I**ndiana is a various state, in a sense the U.S. in little, the U.S. with all its faults and its virtues," wrote Indiana-raised journalist John Bartlow Martin in the 1940s. "Here is the flowering glory of native American capitalism; here are some aspects of its decay. Here is the frost on the pumpkin; here is the cocktail lounge." The imagery may be dated, but Martin was on to something when he called Indiana "the central place, the crossroads, the mean that is sometimes golden, sometimes only mean." Look no further than the map, with Indianapolis in the center and highways radiating at regular angles to all corners of the state. Indiana's name recalls its frontier past, when William Henry Harrison defeated Tecumseh's Indians at Tippecanoe in 1811. Its most famous venue opened a century later, in 1909—the Indianapolis Speedway where the Indy 500 is still held every Memorial Day weekend. (The original bricks have been replaced by asphalt, except for one yard at the start and finish lines.) Today, Indianapolis—the capital of the state that gave America such basketball icons as Larry Bird, Bobby Knight and the movie "Hoosiers"—has refashioned itself as a national sports center, with the football Colts' Lucas Oil Stadium, the basketball Pacers' Bankers Life Fieldhouse, and the NCAA headquarters. Indianapolis was happy to host the 2012 Super Bowl despite the cost. Indianapolis has non-sports attractions as well including the Indiana State Museum and the headquarters of the American Legion. It is home to one of the nation's largest foundations, the Lilly Endowment, which gives much of its money locally and has a knack for innovation. Back in the 1980s, it took the lead in pushing Indianapolis to become a national sports center.

The central economic force in the Hoosier State remains manufacturing. Geographically, Indiana sits at the center of American manufacturing: Almost half the nation's manufacturing jobs are east of Indiana and the other half are west, almost half are north and half are south. About 30 percent of the gross state product comes from manufacturing, about twice the share nationally, and Indiana has the nation's highest percentage of workers in manufacturing jobs. Its manufacturing productivity outranks its immediate neighbors, and it is the No. 1 steel producer in the country, with giant, heavily automated steel mills on the south shore of Lake Michigan and mini-mills scattered across the state. It is a leading producer of elevators, refrigerators, engines, engine electrical equipment, recreational vehicles, mobile homes and truck and bus bodies. It gives the world canned pork and beans, tomato juice, Coca-Cola bottles, Coffee-Mate, and Alka-Seltzer. American and Japanese auto companies—General Motors, Chrysler, Toyota, Subaru, Honda—have big auto plants in the state, as do many auto suppliers. Leveraging its central location, Indiana has also seen a boom in logistics, warehousing in particular.

The downside of a manufacturing economy, apparent in the 2007-09 recession, is that it is prone to sharp contraction when the economy is in decline. Indiana's economy did relatively well before the recession, increasing its manufacturing output 20 percent in the decade up to 2008 while, by contrast, Michigan's went down 12 percent. Growth was especially strong in metro Indianapolis, which produced most of the state's population growth between 2000 and 2010. But manufacturing is increasingly capital-intensive. Indiana continues to churn out huge tonnages of steel, but with less than 20,000 workers. The recession hit especially hard in a state that ranks third nationally in auto-related manufacturing. Unemployment skyrocketed from 4.5 percent in spring 2007 to 11 percent in spring 2009, as General Motors and Chrysler underwent bankruptcy, and Elkhart, which bills itself as the RV capital of the world, posted the nation's highest unemployment. But as it has in previous downturns, Indiana is bouncing back, with an unemployment rate under 6 percent by early 2015. The state regained about three-quarters of the manufacturing jobs it had lost during the recession by late 2014, a respectable showing considering the long-term decline of manufacturing jobs nationally. There were big job gains not only in autos and auto suppliers but also in life sciences, in which Indiana has been a leader. Eli Lilly, founded in Indianapolis in 1876, spends $5 billion annually on research and development. Other big life-science companies in the state are Roche Diagnostics, Dow AgroSciences, and Beckman Coulter. And Indiana from Bloomington to Warsaw is peppered with medical-device makers. Still, economic dislocation has dropped median income in the state by 12 percent and pushed up poverty by 29 percent since 2007.

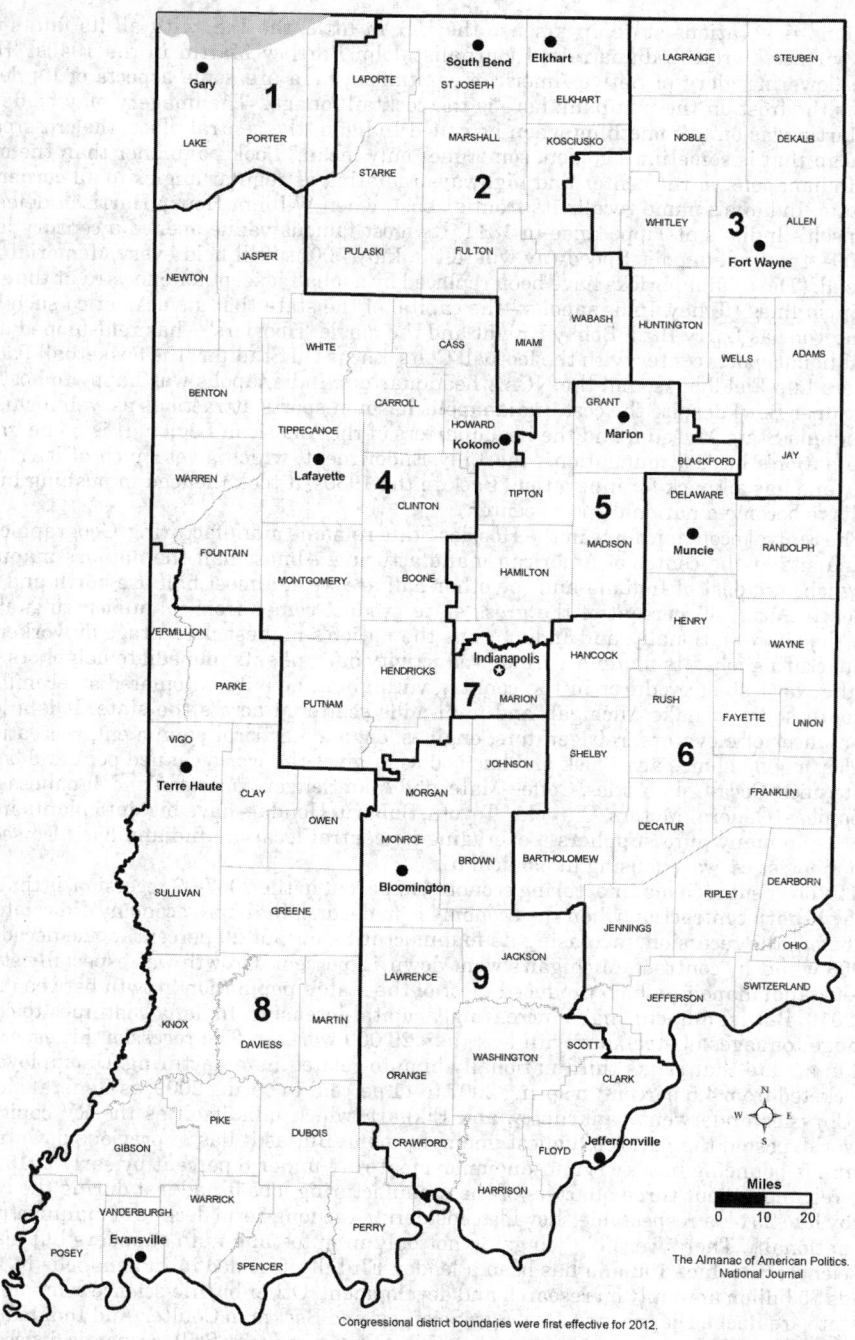

Culturally, Indiana is a lot like an earlier America. It retains some of the old norms that in the 1920s and 1930s attracted sociologists Robert and Helen Lynd to "Middletown," a fictional "typical" American place (Middletown was actually Muncie). Agriculture remains a significant business, particularly corn, soybeans and hogs. (Orville Redenbacher of popcorn fame hailed from Indiana.) Ethnically, Indiana seems like an earlier America, too. Except for the steel area around Gary—really an extension of the Chicago metropolitan area—Indiana has relatively few descendants from the 1840-1924 wave of immigration. In 2010, its population was 9 percent black, 6 percent Hispanic, and 2 percent Asian. It does have religious diversity, with 109 denominations; according to the Glenmary Research Center, only six states have more. In early 2015, Indiana played host to a high-profile, if brief, national battle between two big, longstanding constituencies within the state—its Christian conservatives and its pragmatic business class. These two camps battled over a religious-freedom law that critics said would make it possible for businesses to discriminate against gays and lesbians. After Republican Gov. Mike Pence signed the law, it drew fire not only from liberals but also from much of the state's business establishment, including such athletic mainstays as NASCAR, the NCAA and the NBA. The backlash pushed Pence and legislative leaders to scale back the measure.

The partisan patterns in Indiana state politics sometimes seem typical of an older America, with roots in the Civil War era and the union-organizing days of the 1930s. It was a crucial target state from the Civil War to the New Deal in the struggles between Republicans and Democrats, which is one reason why there were Hoosiers on 11 Republican and Democratic national tickets in the 16 elections between 1868 and 1928—more than any other state except New York. Party identification was handed down like religious affiliation—the Lynd research team noted that Presbyterians had little to do with Methodists, but that was nothing next to divisions between Republicans and Democrats. The people of Indiana, by and large, are descendants of its original settlers: Yankees from Ohio and New England, and "Butternuts," as they were called in the Civil War years, from Kentucky and the South. Most Yankees became Republicans, and most Butternuts became Democrats, a split that has persisted over generations and has been a factor in elections for state office from New Deal times until today. Those enduring traditions enabled Democrats to hold the governorship from 1988 to 2004 and to be competitive in state legislative elections. Democrat Evan Bayh, a former governor and senator, tended to run ahead in Butternut Indiana, whereas Republican former Gov. Mitch Daniels fared well in Yankee Indiana. Two of the three House seats that Democrats captured in 2006 and held in 2008 were in the Butternut south end of the state.

At the presidential level, Indiana's cultural conservatism and lack of a dovish tradition kept it in the Republican column for two generations, ever since it voted 56%-43% for Lyndon Johnson in 1964. In the next 10 elections, it was so resolutely Republican that it was never a target state for the Democrats, and only one Hoosier, Dan Quayle, was on a national ticket. A main reason was that Indianapolis and the smaller factory towns were not

Population		Race and Ethnicity		Income	
Total:	6,570,902	White	81.3%	Median income:	$50,553
Urban:	42.0%	Black	8.9%		*(31 of 50)*
Suburban:	30.0%	Latino	6.1%	Under $50,000	52.2%
Rural:	28.0%	Asian	1.6%	$50,000-$99,999:	31.3%
Land area:	35,826	Two races	1.9%	$100,000-$199,999:	13.8%
Pop/sq. mi.:	183.4	White Ethnic	22.7%	$200,000 or more:	2.6%
Born in state:	68.5%			Poverty Rate	12.6%
		Education			
Age Groups		H.S. grad or less:	46.7%	**Work**	
Under 18:	24.2%	Some college:	29.5%	White collar:	32.1%
18 to 34:	23.0%	College degree, 4 yr.:	15.2%	Blue collar:	40.4%
35 to 64:	38.9%	Post-grad study:	8.6%	Sales and service:	27.5%
Over 64:	13.9%				
		Military		Govt. workers:	11.5%
		Veterans/active duty:	8.2%		

as heavily Democratic as Chicago, Detroit or Cleveland (a trend only reinforced by 1970 consolidation of the city of Indianapolis and Marion County, which brought urban and suburban areas under the same jurisdictional umbrella). In the 1920s, the Lynds, liberal academics influenced by Marx's idea that political beliefs were determined by economic interests, were puzzled about why the

Voter Turnout	
2013 Total Citizen 18+	4,799,979
2014 Highest Statewide Turnout	1,341,814
2014 Turnout as % CVAP	28.0%
2012 Turnout as % CVAP	55.0%
Legislature	
Senate:	40R 10D
House:	71R 29D

factory workers in Muncie didn't vote against the bosses. One reason may be that cultural identity and personal values tend to be long-lasting and so have usually been the critical determinants of political allegiance, especially in the United States, where economic status can often be changeable. Another factor may be that the economic interests of Indiana's highly-skilled workers and its small and large factory owners may not be as adversarial as the academics supposed.

In 2008, for the first time in nearly 45 years, Indiana voted Democratic for president. A state that went 60%-39% for George W. Bush in 2004 voted 50%-49% for Barack Obama four years later. This was the biggest swing in any of the 50 states and was the product of many factors. The Obama campaign targeted Indiana early, vastly outspent the opposition, registered new and young voters, and made inroads in the ailing industrial towns that had resisted Democratic nominees for many years. Metro Indianapolis, like metro Columbus, Ohio—which has a similar economic base and Republican past—moved sharply to the Democrats, particularly affluent and better-educated voters.

But this did not hold true all the way down the ballot. Indeed, Indiana voted Republican for president and Democratic for governor in 1988, 1992, 1996, and 2000—and then Republican for governor and a Democrat for president in 2008. Daniels, elected governor by 53%-45% in 2004 after a stint as President Bush's first-term budget director, was reelected by a solid 58%-40% even as Obama was carrying the state. The victory was all the more remarkable because two of the governor's policies were hugely controversial: the leasing for 75 years of the Indiana Toll Road to an Australian-Spanish consortium (which would hit a major pothole in 2014 when the lease operator declared bankruptcy) and the adoption of Daylight Saving Time (a touchy issue, since Indiana straddles the Eastern and Central time zones). Daniels' popularity increased as he emphasized his Indiana Economic Development Corp., which committed $700 million in incentives to bring 75,000 jobs to the state; he had some big wins, but also some disappointments such as an effort to make Indiana a hub for new-generation battery production. He also pushed through a cut in the corporate tax, a 1 percent increase in the sales tax to pay for local property tax relief, and reductions in red tape. Beyond Indiana, he attracted attention as a possible 2012 presidential candidate and, in speeches and in a book, insisted that rising entitlement costs meant permanent budget deficits or economically disastrous tax increases. Then in May 2011, he announced he would not run, and after leaving office, he became president of Purdue University (and was named No. 41 on Fortune magazine's "World's Greatest Leaders" list).

Obama's 2008 win has seemed to be an exception rather than the rule in Indiana politics. In 2010, Democrat Evan Bayh retired from the Senate and left the way open for his predecessor, Republican Dan Coats, to win back the seat handily, while Republicans also picked up the 8th and 9th district House seats and won majorities in both houses of the legislature. In 2012, Indiana was not a target state for the Obama campaign, and it voted 54%-44% for Republican nominee Mitt Romney, while Pence was elected governor over Democrat John Gregg, 49%-47%. Republicans increased their lead in the House delegation to seven to two with the help of a favorable redistricting plan. But Democrats won a big consolation prize. Democratic Rep. Joe Donnelly ran for the Senate and got a break when six-term incumbent Richard Lugar, long beloved in Indiana, lost the Republican primary 61%-39% to state Treasurer Richard Mourdock. Lugar's refusal to endorse Mourdock—and Mourdock's politically devastating comment that pregnancy resulting from rape is part of God's plan—resulted in a 50%-44% Donnelly victory. In 2014, Republicans increased their legislative majorities to 70 percent in the House and 80 percent in the Senate, with little expectation that Democrats would be able to do more than nibble around the edges of those margins for the rest of the decade.

Presidential Politics Indiana saw little presidential campaigning between 1968—when Democrats Robert Kennedy and Eugene McCarthy battled in the May primary against Lyndon Johnson's stand-in, Gov. Roger Branigin—and 2008, when Barack Obama contested the state in both the primary and general election. Hillary Clinton, after solid victories in Ohio and Pennsylvania, hoped that a May 6 win in Indiana would balance an expected loss in North Carolina on the same day. But Indiana does not have party registration. Inde-

2012 Presidential Vote		
Mitt Romney (R)..............1,420,543	(54%)
Barack Obama (D) 1,152,887	(44%)

2012 Presidential Primary		
Mitt Romney (R).................410,635	(65%)
Ron Paul (R) 98,487	(16%)
Rick Santorum (R) 85,332	(13%)
Newt Gingrich (R)................41,135	(6%)

2008 Presidential Vote		
Barack Obama (D) 1,374,039	(50%)
John McCain (R)..............1,345,648	(49%)

pendents and Republicans could, and did, vote in the Democratic primary. Only 412,000 people cast ballots in the GOP primary, while nearly 1.3 million voted in the Democratic primary, four times as many as the 317,000 who voted in the 2004 Democratic contest. Obama won by huge margins among black and young voters. Clinton carried women, the elderly and blue-collar voters, but by much smaller margins. Indianapolis and its suburbs voted heavily for Obama, who also carried the counties that included Gary, South Bend, Elkhart and Fort Wayne, and the university towns of Lafayette and Bloomington. While Clinton won 51%-49%, she was denied the satisfaction of announcing her victory that night on prime-time television because Lake County authorities held back their results, and network analysts, knowing there were many black voters there, refrained from calling her the winner.

The Obama campaign's organizational work in the primary paid off in the general election. In a state that had seen no intensive presidential campaigning since the 1940s, the campaign opened 44 offices and attracted 80,000 volunteers. The Obama team outspent John McCain's campaign 5-to-1 in the state. Obama carried only 15 of Indiana's 92 counties, but he got a big vote out of Gary and Indianapolis, cut into traditional GOP margins in the Indianapolis suburbs and exurbs, won blue-collar counties such as Delaware (Muncie) and Madison (Anderson) and swept college towns to win 50%-49% over McCain. That is the basic equation for a Democrat to win Indiana and its electoral votes. One of the challenges is that Marion and the counties in the northwest corner of the state around Gary contribute less than a third of the statewide vote.

In 2012, the Republican race was already decided when Indiana voted May 8, and polling indicated that Obama had little chance to carry Indiana, so his campaign did not target the state. Mitt Romney won 64 percent of the votes in the primary and beat Obama 54%-44% in November. Voters under 30, 63%-35% for Obama in 2008, this time voted 49%-46% for Romney. Whites, who voted 54%-45% for McCain in 2008, voted 60%-38% for Romney. Metro Indianapolis, which voted 51%-48% for Obama in 2008, voted 53%-45% for Romney in 2012.

Congressional Districts Indiana law provides that if the House and Senate cannot agree on congressional redistricting, the decision goes to a five-member commission, with the tie-breaking member appointed by the governor. In 2011, Repub-

114th Congress Lineup	
7 R	2 D
113th Congress Lineup	
7 R	2 D

licans, with majorities in the legislature and Mitch Daniels as governor, had control of the process. It weakened the 2nd District for the Democrats. When incumbent Democrat Joe Donnelly in 2012 ran for the Senate, Republican Jackie Walorski took his House seat. That gave the GOP a 7-2 majority in the delegation, with Democrats retaining two heavily urban and minority districts centered on Gary and Indianapolis.

For now, Republicans seem entrenched in their seven seats. In recent decades, the delegation has been more evenly balanced and some of its seats often shifted parties. Partisan control of the redistricting map has not always assured success. In 2001, the commission adopted a largely Democratic plan. They hoped to retain the four seats they held and to improve their chances in at least one more. As often happens with redistricting, the results did not work out as intended. Both parties carried the 2nd, 8th, and 9th districts at different points in the ensuing six elections. Although Republicans have gained the upper hand in Indiana, Democrats hope to restore its competitiveness. Those same three districts, with revised lines, are the most likely to be in play.

Governor

Mike Pence (R)

Elected 2012, term expires Jan. 2017, 1st term; b. June 7, 1959, Columbus; Hanover Col., B.A. 1981, IN U., J.D. 1986; Protestant; married (Karen); 3 children.

Elected Office: U.S. House, 2000-12.

Professional Career: Practicing atty., 1986-91; Pres., IN Policy Review Foundation, 1991-93; Radio broadcaster, *The Mike Pence Show*, Network Indiana, 1992-99; Host, public affairs TV, UPN-23, 1995-99.

Office: Office of the Governor, 200 W. Washington St., Rm. 206, Indianapolis, 46204-2797, 317-232-4567; Website: in.gov/gov.

Election Results

2012 general	Mike Pence (R)	1,275,424	(49%)
	John Gregg (D)	1,200,016	(47%)
	Rupert Boneham (Lib)	101,868	(4%)
2012 primary	Mike Pence (R)	unopposed	

Prior winning percentages: House: 2010 (67%), 2008 (64%), 2006 (60%), 2004 (67%), 2002 (64%), 2000 (51%)

Mike Pence was elected governor in 2012 to succeed fellow Republican Mitch Daniels, who was term-limited. An articulate former six-term House member who rose to chair the House Republican Conference, Pence has called himself "a Christian, a conservative, and a Republican, in that order."

Pence grew up in Columbus, Indiana, as a John F. Kennedy-admiring Catholic and graduated from Hanover College as a Republican and evangelical Christian. He got his law degree from Indiana University and then went into practice, and within two years, he ran for Congress. He was the Republican nominee in 1988 and 1990 against longtime incumbent Philip Sharp. Afterward, he wrote "Confessions of a Negative Campaigner," an article in which he apologized for running negative ads. He was president of the conservative Indiana Policy Review Foundation, a think tank based in Fort Wayne, and then in 1994 began broadcasting *The Mike Pence Show*, a conservative talk-radio program that was syndicated statewide.

In 2000, when Republican 2nd District Rep. David McIntosh retired from Congress to run for governor, Pence ran for the House again. He won a six-candidate Republican primary, then won 51 percent of the vote in a three-way race. After that, he won reelection easily every two years. In Congress, Pence was one of the most outspoken conservatives, taking heat for stances that ran counter to his party's leadership, including President George W. Bush, but that proved to be adopted in due course by the GOP. As the only House member to become a plaintiff in the lawsuit challenging the constitutionality of the McCain-Feingold campaign finance law, Pence said that Arizona Republican Sen. John McCain was "so deep in bed with the Democrats that his feet are coming out of the bottom of the sheets." He was one of 34 House Republicans to vote against Bush's "No Child Left Behind" education bill in 2001 and one of just 19 to oppose Republicans' Medicare prescription drug bill in 2003, calling it too costly. He did vote for the big-spending farm bill in 2002, conceding, "I don't have clean hands," and later voiced regret about his vote.

Pence became chairman in 2005 of the Republican Study Committee, a group of conservative House Republicans, providing a platform to become "Rush Limbaugh on decaf," as he put it. Republicans suffered big losses in the 2006 election, prompting Pence to challenge John Boehner of Ohio for the party's top leadership job in the House. Pence won just 27 votes to Boehner's 168. After the 2008 election, when Republicans lost more seats, Pence was elected chairman of the Republican Conference with support from Boehner.

Pence launched a bid for governor in May 2011 after making trips to Indiana and South Carolina that triggered speculation that he might seek to run for president. He vowed to "build an even better Indiana on the solid foundation that Gov. Daniels has poured," in part by slashing the state's individual and corporate income taxes and eliminating the estate tax.

He also emphasized education, particularly his support of parental choice, but his campaign was largely devoid of specifics. Though he initially drew a primary challenge from businessman Jim Wallace, the state Election Commission voted to take Wallace's name off the ballot after it was found he was 14 signatures short of the number required.

Pence's Democratic opponent in the general election, former Indiana House Speaker John Gregg, stressed his moderate stands on issues while painting his rival as an "elite attack dog" of the far right. Gregg pointed to Pence's long-standing opposition to Planned Parenthood as well as a book of essays published by a group Pence once headed that called for repealing the Americans with Disabilities Act. Although Pence tried to keep the focus on jobs and education, he did sometimes stray into social conservative territory, such as when he promised to ask state regulators to assess how rules and regulations affect families via "family impact statements" that consider whether policies promote or discourage marriage. He had gaffes, too, such as comparing the Supreme Court's decision to uphold President Barack Obama's health care law to the September 11 terrorist attacks; he later apologized.

Despite Pence's massive financial advantage over Gregg, the Republican chose not to run negative advertisements that could have helped him rebut Gregg's criticisms. He also found himself hurt by fallout from the collapse of Republican Richard Mourdock's Senate campaign after Mourdock declared that pregnancy resulting from rape "is something that God intended to happen." Pence eked out a win, with 49 percent to Gregg's 47 percent and Libertarian Rupert Boneham's 4 percent—the closest margin of any Indiana gubernatorial race since 1960. Gregg decisively won most of the urban areas, getting 59 percent in Indianapolis' Marion County, 60 percent in Bloomington's Monroe County, and 67 percent in Gary's Lake County. But Pence dominated rural regions and won larger, conservative-leaning places such as Fort Wayne-based Allen County.

As governor, Pence concentrated on jobs and education. He pushed a 10 percent personal income tax cut, which the Legislature cut in half. Pence signed a bill to allow terminally ill patients to use drugs not yet approved by the Food and Drug Administration, joining such states as Michigan, Missouri, Colorado, Louisiana and Arizona that had already passed such a measure. He also signed an overhaul of sentencing, requiring most inmates to serve at least three-quarters of their sentences, a higher minimum than previously allowed inmates with good behavior. He also authorized a temporary exception to the state's anti-needle-exchange program amid a fast-spreading, drug-related HIV cluster in Scott County, a rural area adjoining I-65 north of Louisville Kentucky.

Pence has taken some bold stances, some with aspects that broke the political mold. On Pence's watch, Indiana became the first state in the nation to drop out of Common Core, the national K-12 standards that had become particularly unpopular among conservatives. Some Common Core opponents on the right, however, complained that he hadn't made a clean enough break, merely rebranding key aspects of the system under another name.

And when it came to expanding Medicaid under the Affordable Care Act, a contentious issue among many GOP governors, Pence did something more nuanced than his peers. He announced in January 2015 that he had won approval for his Healthy Indiana Plan 2.0, which expanded insurance for the poor while also containing some provisions that conservatives cheered. One was requiring participants to contribute to a health savings account, and penalizing non-payers by cutting off their coverage for six months.

The Medicaid proposal won plaudits, including from Democrats, but it was overshadowed by a self-inflicted controversy that month—the news that Pence planned to launch a state-run news outlet using taxpayer money to compete against for-profit media entities. He scrapped the plan after bipartisan opposition within the state and ridicule elsewhere. But even this setback paled in comparison to his signing of a religious-freedom law that critics said would enable businesses to discriminate against gay and lesbian customers. Criticism came not only from liberal activists but also much of the state's business establishment, which felt the law was terrible for the state's image. After several days of outcry and a poorly reviewed appearance on national television, Pence and leaders of the Republican-dominated state House and Senate agreed to a legislative fix that clarified that the state will not permit discrimination based on sexual orientation or gender identity; the change seemed to ease much of the outcry.

Still, the controversies cast doubt on Pence's future as a national candidate. "Pence was never meant to be a governor," wrote Matthew Tully in the *Indianapolis Star*. "A partisan and dysfunctional Congress that lives on bright-line divisions was his home for 12 years, and that's where he belongs." In June 2015, he announced his intention to run for a second term as governor in 2016, ruling out the possibility of a presidential bid that cycle. But he could run in the future. He's traveled to Israel—a favorite destination of many GOP candidates—and he has well-reported close ties to the billionaire Koch brothers. If he can recover from the PR hits, Pence could potentially bridge the tea party/establishment divide at some point, some Republicans say. "If you were going to design a perfect candidate, it would be a governor who's an economic conservative, a pro-life reformer, a strong communicator a la Ronald Reagan—and Pence would have to be at the top of your list," strategist Scott Reed told the *Washington Post.*

Senior Senator

Dan Coats (R)

Elected 2010, term expires 2016, 2nd full term; b. May 16, 1943, Jackson, MI; Wheaton Col., B.A. 1965; IN U., J.D. 1971; Presbyterian; married (Marsha); 3 children.

Military Career: U.S. Army Corps of Engineers, 1966-68.

Elected Office: U.S. House, 1981-89; U.S. Senate, 1989-99.

Professional Career: Asst. v.p. Mutual Security Life Ins., 1972-76; Staffer, Rep. Dan Quayle, 1976-80; Special counsel, Verner, Liipfert, Bernhard, McPherson & Hand, 2000-01; U.S. ambassador to Germany, 2001-05; Lobbyist, King & Spalding, 2005-10.

DC Office: 93 RSOB, 20510, 202-224-5623; Fax: 202-228-1820; Website: coats.senate.gov.

State Offices: Crown Point, 219-663-2595; Evansville, 812-465-6500; Fort Wayne, 260-426-3151; Indianapolis, 317-554-0750; Scottsburg, 812-754-0520.

Committees: *Intelligence (Select). Finance:* Energy, Natural Resources, & Infrastructure (Chmn); Health Care; Taxation & IRS Oversight. *Joint Economic Committee* (Chmn).

Group Ratings

	ADA	ACLU	AFL-CIO	LCV	ITI	COC	HAFA	ACU	CFG	FRC
2014	10%	0%	–	0%	33%	88%	59%	76%	63%	85%
2013	10%	C	22%	15%	C	88%	C	83%	75%	C

National Journal Ratings

	2013 LIB	—	2013 CONS
Economic	22%	—	77%
Social	14%	—	84%
Foreign	24%	—	73%
Composite	21%	—	79%

Key Votes of the 113th Congress

1. Sandy storm spending	N	5. Student Loan Rates	Y	9. Bipartisan Budget Deal	N
2. Chuck Hagel Confirmation	N	6. Employee Non-Discrim'n Act	N	10. Farm Bill Conference Rept.	Y
3. Gun Background Checks	N	7. Senate Vote on Judgeships	Y	11. Unempl. Comp. Extension	N
4. Immigration Reform	N	8. Defense Dept. Spending	N	12. Keystone Pipeline	Y

Election Results

2010 general	Dan Coats (R)	952,116	(55%)	$4,619,405	$83,145	$52,902
	Brad Ellsworth (D)	697,775	(40%)	$2,589,967	$1,025,316	$79,581
	Rebecca Sink-Burris (Lib)	94,330	(5%)	$16,879		
2010 primary	Dan Coats (R)	217,225	(39%)			
	Marlin Stutzman (R)	160,981	(29%)			
	John Hostettler (R)	124,494	(23%)			

Prior winning percentages: 1992 (57%), 1990 special (54%); House: 1988 (62%), 1986 (70%), 1984 (61%), 1982 (64%), 1980 (61%)

For the past quarter of a century, possession of this Senate seat has shifted between two men who are the political and personal heirs, respectively, of two other Hoosiers who held the seat for the previous quarter-century—and achieved national political prominence in the process. The present occupant, Republican Dan Coats—coming to the end of his second stint on Capitol Hill—in early 2015 announced plans to retire when his terms ends in 2016. With his departure, it appears likely that, for the first time since 1962, someone not named Bayh, Quayle or Coats will be chosen to fill the seat.

If Coats, now Indiana's senior senator, considers Dwight Eisenhower—whom he met briefly while growing up in neighboring Michigan—and Winston Churchill as his political idols, it is Dan Quayle to whom he owes his start in politics, along with a good measure of his advancement. After serving in the Army, graduating from law school and spending four years working for an insurance company, Coats turned down a job offer in 1976 from a bank to become a staffer for Quayle, then a newly elected member of the U.S. House from northeastern Indiana. In 1980, the boyishly handsome Quayle narrowly toppled another boyishly handsome Hoosier, three-term Democrat Birch Bayh—a prominent Senate liberal who had pursued his party's presidential nomination four years earlier. Both Quayle and Coats, who was running to succeed Quayle in the House, rode that year's Reagan presidential landslide to victory.

In 1988, Coats again followed closely in Quayle's political footsteps: He was appointed to succeed him in the Senate when Quayle was elected vice president. Coats was elected in 1990 to serve the remaining two years of Quayle's term with 54 percent, and was elected to a full term in 1992 by an even more comfortable margin. While championing the line-item veto, which he said would help curb federal spending, Coats compiled a largely conservative voting record during his tenure. He strongly opposed abortion rights and was a leader on banning research using fetal tissue. Coats did occasionally buck his party, voting for the assault weapons ban and the Family and Medical Leave Act.

In December 1996, Coats announced he would not seek reelection in 1998 after a decade in the Senate. At the time, most polls showed him trailing outgoing Democratic Gov. Evan Bayh—Birch Bayh's son, and a highly popular figure in his two terms as the state's chief executive. Coats signed on with a major Washington law/lobbying firm. In 2001, President George W. Bush considered him for Defense secretary before choosing Donald Rumsfeld, but appointed Coats as U.S. ambassador to Germany. Disagreement over the Iraq war strained U.S.-German relations during Coats' tenure. He left that post in 2005 and rejoined the Washington lobbying world, while taking on part-time tasks for the Bush administration. He tried to help drum up Senate support for Supreme Court nominee Harriet Miers—Bush's White House counsel—although she withdrew amid questions regarding her qualifications.

Meanwhile, the younger Bayh never appeared fully comfortable in the Senate during two terms there. He considered running for his old job as governor in 2004 before deciding to seek re-election, and, in 2008 created an exploratory committee for a presidential run, only to shut it down weeks later. Always considered more of a centrist than his avowedly liberal father, Bayh appeared to shift leftward as he positioned himself for a presidential run. In early 2010, with public opinion turning against the Democratic-controlled Congress, Bayh appeared vulnerable back home, and Republicans were searching for a top-tier candidate. Just two weeks after Coats announced his candidacy, Bayh declared he would not seek reelection.

Coats faced a crowded GOP primary field that included former Rep. John Hostettler and state Sen. Marlin Stutzman, both of whom appealed to tea party groups. Backed by the national GOP, Coats won the primary with 39 percent, as he benefitted from tea party Republicans splitting their votes between Stutzman and Hostettler. In the general election, Coats honed a message that he had returned to electoral politics to combat President Barack Obama's agenda. His opponent, Democratic Rep. Brad Ellsworth, was a former sheriff regarded as part of the centrist wing of his party—but Republicans blasted him for his votes in favor of the Obama administration's $787 billion stimulus package as well as the health care overhaul, while portraying him as a rubber stamp for House Speaker Nancy Pelosi. Democrats, in turn, hammered Coats for his lucrative career as a lobbyist employed by special interests, while seeking to attach the "Washington insider" label to him. In the final weeks before Election Day, Coats maintained a double-digit lead over Ellsworth, but took no chances. With his coffers running low after an expensive primary, he put $200,000 of his own money into the campaign. Overall, Coats outspent Ellsworth by about $2 million, and won, 55 percent to 40 percent.

An *Indianapolis Star* columnist once observed that Coats is part of an older school of Washington officeholders, noting that he generally avoids provocative sound bites and "seems more comfortable in serious Senate hearings than on the campaign trail." Regarded as a business-friendly conservative, Coats' first major speech upon returning to the Senate picked up where he had left off more than a decade earlier: He called for reform of the federal government's major entitlement programs—Social Security, Medicare, and Medicaid. Coats proposed increasing the age of Medicare eligibility from 65 to 67, an adjustment he advocated back in 1997. But this time around, austerity was more in vogue, and even Obama tacitly supported raising the Medicare eligibility age. Coats also pushed for tax reform, and voted against the 2011 deal to raise the debt limit and cut $2.4 trillion in spending because he said the spending cuts didn't go far enough. Notwithstanding his opposition, the bill cleared the Senate by a bipartisan 3-1 margin.

But, breaking from conservative orthodoxy, Coats said a year later that he was open to new taxes to avert the so-called fiscal cliff of automatic tax hikes and spending cuts. "I'm willing to raise revenues," he told *The Indianapolis Star.* "There's a way to do that that doesn't injure the economy and actually gives us a chance of a better recovery and getting people back to work." He favored closing tax "loopholes" and eliminating many of the tax subsidies now contained in law. Coats later voted for the Senate deal that allowed taxes to go up on households earning more than $450,000. The bill passed the Senate overwhelmingly before facing more substantial opposition from House Republicans. The Republican takeover of the Senate following the 2014 election elevated Coats to the chairmanship of the bicameral Joint Economic Committee.

As a member of the Senate Intelligence Committee, Coats has weighed in frequently on foreign policy and defense issues during his second Hill stint. In early 2014, his sharp criticism of Russia's annexation of the Crimean region of the Ukraine landed him on a list of a half-dozen members of Congress barred by the Russian government from visiting that nation. Early in the 114th Congress, he joined Florida Sen. Marco Rubio in a letter challenging Obama's power to unilaterally lift economic sanctions on Cuba. But, despite criticism of Obama's nuclear negotiations with Iran and an insistence that any deal reached be approved by Congress, former ambassador Coats was among only seven Senate Republicans to refrain from signing in March 2015 a controversial open letter to Iran during the talks. The letter was blasted by the White House as an unprecedented effort to undermine the president's ability to negotiate with foreign nations.

Announcing his decision not to run again in late March 2015, Coats—who will be 73 at the end of his term—declared, "While I believe I am well-positioned to run a successful campaign for another six-year term, I have concluded that the time has come to pass this demanding job to the next generation of leaders." Coats' decision immediately turned Indiana into a possible battleground Senate race in 2016, with the Democrats talking up none other than Evan Bayh—who was sitting on a leftover campaign treasury of almost $10 million, and, approaching 60, did not rule out a return to public life. But Bayh sent out word through intermediaries that he had no plans to seek to prolong the political game of round robin that has surrounded the seat in recent years. Absent Bayh, Indiana Democrats were left with a relatively thin bench. Former Rep. Baron Hill announced his intention to seek the Democratic nomination, but he is likely to get some competition for the nod. On the Republican side, Stutzman, Coats' leading primary foe in 2010 and now a member of the House, wasted little time in announcing his Senate candidacy, joining Coats aide and former state GOP chairman Eric Holcomb, who had Coats' endorsement. In July 2015, GOP Rep. Todd Young entered the contest with a fundraising advantage over his two primary opponents.

Junior Senator

Joe Donnelly (D)

Elected 2012, term expires Jan. 2019, 1st term; b. Sept. 29, 1955, Queens, NY; U. of Notre Dame, B.A. 1977, J.D. 1981; Catholic; married (Jill); 2 children.

Elected Office: Mishawaka Marian H.S. Bd., 1997-2001, pres., 2000-01; U.S. House, 2007-12.

Professional Career: Practicing atty., 1981-96; IN State Election Bd., 1988-89; Owner, Marking Solutions, 1996-2006.

DC Office: 720 HSOB, 20510, 202-224-4814; Fax: 202-224-5011; Website: donnelly.senate.gov.

State Offices: Evansville, 812-425-5862; Fort Wayne, 260-420-4955; Hammond, 219-852-0089; Indianapolis, 317-226-5555; Jeffersonville, 812-284-2027; South Bend, 574-288-2780.

Committees: *Aging (Special). Agriculture, Nutrition & Forestry:* Commodities, Risk Mgmt & Trade (RMM); Livestock, Marketing & Ag Security; Rural Development & Energy. *Armed Services:* Airland; Emerging Threats & Capabilities; Strategic Forces (RMM). *Banking, Housing, & Urban Affairs:* Financial Institutions & Consumer Protection; Housing, Transportation, & Community Development; Securities, Insurance, & Investment.

Group Ratings

	ADA	ACLU	AFL-CIO	LCV	ITI	COC	HAFA	ACU	CFG	FRC
2014	80%	86%	–	60%	100%	57%	2%	12%	10%	7%
2013	50%	C	94%	69%	C	38%	C	16%	6%	C

National Journal Ratings

	2013 LIB	—	2013 CONS
Economic	49%	—	49%
Social	47%	—	52%
Foreign	45%	—	53%
Composite	48%	—	52%

Key Votes of the 113th Congress

1. Sandy storm spending	Y	5. Student Loan Rates	Y	9. Bipartisan Budget Deal	Y
2. Chuck Hagel Confirmation	Y	6. Employee Non-Discrim'n Act	Y	10. Farm Bill Conference Rept.	Y
3. Gun Background Checks	Y	7. Senate Vote on Judgeships	N	11. Unempl. Comp. Extension	Y
4. Immigration Reform	Y	8. Defense Dept. Spending	Y	12. Keystone Pipeline	Y

Election Results

2012 general	Joe Donnelly (D)	1,281,181	(50%)	$5,579,171	$1,250,751	$12,320,701
	Richard Mourdock (R)	1,133,621	(44%)	$8,807,000	$5,098,505	$11,653,132
	Andrew Horning (Lib)	145,282	(6%)	$2,923		
2012 primary	Joe Donnelly (D)	unopposed				

Prior winning percentages: House: 2010 (48%), 2008 (67%), 2006 (54%)

If the tea party emerged as a major force in recent years by excoriating what it regards as the national Democratic Party's big brother approach to government, it also on occasion has served as the Democrats' unwitting political accomplice—by upending Republican primaries and foisting on the general electorate candidates with controversial pasts and/or prone to making controversial statements. Indiana's junior senator, Democrat Joe Donnelly, in 2012 was a poster child for the benefits of tea party fallout. After three terms in the House, Donnelly started that year as a longshot to reach the Senate. But the seat became very much in play after tea party-backed state Treasurer Richard Mourdock toppled six-term Sen. Dick Lugar in the May Republican primary. If the 80-year old Lugar's defeat was attributed more to his having lost touch with GOP voters than to the appeal of Mourdock's hard-line conservatism, it was Mourdock's incendiary comments on rape and abortion during the general election that helped put Donnelly over the top.

For Donnelly, it was a major stroke of luck in a political career that got off to a less than successful start. Raised in New York City's Long Island suburbs, he was the youngest of five children; a brother, two years older, was the first one in the family to attend college. Donnelly followed in those footsteps when he was accepted at the University Of Notre Dame in South

Bend, Ind., where he earned an undergraduate degree in government and later a law degree. He practiced law in the area until 1996, when he opened a printing and rubber stamp company. Donnelly served on the state election board in 1988 and 1989 after a stint as a recount attorney in a close 1986 congressional race. But early efforts to run for office himself were disappointing, to say the least. He ran unsuccessfully for the Democratic nomination for state attorney general in 1988, and then fell short in a bid for the state Senate in 1990. He also lost his first campaign for Congress in 2004, but held Republican Rep. Chris Chocola to 54 percent. The year 2006 was much more difficult for Republicans nationally, and Donnelly made President George W. Bush's handling of the Iraq war an issue. Although Chocola outspent him 2-to-1, this time Donnelly came out on top, 54 percent to 46 percent, in the north central Indiana-based 2nd District.

Elected from what had become something of a swing district over the prior three decades, Donnelly blended a centrist voting record with a low-key style. "In an era of screamers and cable-TV rock stars filling congressional seats, Donnelly has spent his time on Capitol Hill calmly and quietly working on the issues of the day," the *Indianapolis Star* observed. An opponent of abortion rights, Donnelly urged Democratic leaders to advance a moderate agenda in Congress, and also joined the fiscally conservative Blue Dog Coalition. Donnelly opposed the 2009 bill seeking to create a cap-and-trade system for reducing greenhouse gas emissions, but did support another major priority of national Democrats: the overhaul of the nation's health insurance system. However, he was among the anti-abortion Democrats who withheld their support of the final version until President Barack Obama agreed to issue an executive order reaffirming the government's ban on funding abortion-related services. On the Financial Services Committee, Donnelly backed the 2008 bailout for financial institutions that also covered the nation's automobile companies: Chrysler, whose transmission plants now employ about 7,000 workers in the 2nd District, took a major hit during the Great Recession.

After the Democrats lost the House majority in 2010, Donnelly refused to support the avowedly liberal former House Speaker, Nancy Pelosi of California, for minority leader. In a difficult year for Democrats, Donnelly barely won reelection, surviving by 48 percent to 47 percent. Indiana Republicans then successfully crafted a redistricting plan to tilt the 2nd District more toward the GOP, prompting Donnelly to announce a run for Senate in May 2011 rather than seek reelection. When Mourdock ousted Lugar in the primary a year later, comments made just hours after the polls closed provided Donnelly with a major opening. In several appearances on cable and broadcast television shows, Mourdock suggested he didn't believe in compromise. "I have a mind-set that says bipartisanship ought to consist of Democrats coming to the Republican point of view," Mourdock told the Fox News Channel. The remark allowed Donnelly and fellow Democrats to paint Mourdock as an extremist.

Mourdock worked to tie Donnelly to Obama, calling him "Obama Joe" in TV ads. But in October, Mourdock uttered what may be remembered—along with Missouri Senate candidate Todd Akin's comment about "legitimate rape"—as the most explosive remark of the 2012 campaign. Asked about the right to abortion in cases of rape, Mourdock said: "Life is that gift from God. And I think even when life begins in that horrible situation of rape, that it is something that God intended to happen." Donnelly, while a long-time abortion opponent, took the position that it should be permitted in cases of rape and incest as well as to save the life of the mother. The state's dominant newspaper endorsed Donnelly, and a Democratic poll gave him a 7-point lead. That was about how it came down on Election Day: Donnelly won, 50 percent to 44 percent.

In his victory speech, Donnelly sought to identify with Lugar, a pragmatic centrist with a reputation for bipartisanship. "I'm not going there as one party's senator or the other party's senator," he declared. He has since found himself at odds with the Obama White House on several occasions. In 2015, he sponsored legislation—with his senior Indiana colleague, Republican Dan Coats—to revise "Obamacare" by repealing the tax on medical manufacturers, which are a significant source of employment in Indiana. Donnelly also lined up with business groups pushing for a change in the law's definition of full-time workers. Both were moves the president opposed and threatened to veto if they reached his desk.

Donnelly also was among the handful of Democrats supporting legislation to build the controversial Keystone XL oil sands pipeline—running from Canada to the Gulf of Mexico—which Obama vetoed. And, while voting for a major 2013 immigration reform bill that cleared the Senate on a bipartisan vote, Donnelly later joined three fellow moderate Democrats in supporting a Republican move to roll back Obama's 2014 executive order on immigration policy. "I am as frustrated as anyone that Congress is not doing its job, but the president shouldn't make such significant policy changes on his own," Donnelly declared. However, in one of his first major votes after coming to the Senate, Donnelly—who ran with National Rifle Association support in his House campaigns—supported an unsuccessful effort by gun control advocates to expand background checks on those purchasing firearms. It was proposed in response to the 2012 shooting at a Connecticut elementary school that killed 26, most of them children. "My kids are a little older now, but I think of when they were six and seven years old, and I think we have a responsibility to make sure this never happens again," Donnelly told CNN.

Despite periodic Democratic electoral successes, Indiana remains the most reliably Republican state in the Northeast-Midwest "Rust Belt." Donnelly is likely to be high on GOP target lists in 2018, when he turns 61—particularly given the circumstances of his ascension to the Senate. "For a Democrat to win in Indiana, you have to catch a couple of breaks, but you also have to run a flawless campaign," Dan Parker, then chairman of the state Democratic Party, told *The New York Times* the night of Donnelly's 2012 victory, while adding. "Richard Mourdock brought all of this on himself."

FIRST DISTRICT

Peter Visclosky (D)

Elected 1984, 16th term; b. Aug. 13, 1949, Gary; IN U. Northwest, B.S. 1970, U. of Notre Dame, J.D. 1973, Georgetown U., LL.M. 1982; Catholic; married (Joanne Royce); 2 children.

Professional Career: Practicing atty., 1973-76, 1983-84; Aide, U.S. Rep. Adam Benjamin, 1977-82.

DC Office: 2328 RHOB, 20515, 202-225-2461; Fax: 202-225-2493; Website: visclosky.house.gov.

State Offices: Merrillville, 219-795-1844.

Committees: *Appropriations:* Defense (RMM); Energy & Water Development, & Related Agencies.

Group Ratings

	ADA	ACLU	AFL-CIO	LCV	ITI	COC	HAFA	ACU	CFG	FRC
2014	85%	88%	—	91%	20%	36%	18%	8%	15%	0%
2013	70%	C	95%	89%	C	38%	C	12%	19%	C

National Journal Ratings

	2013 LIB	—	2013 CONS
Economic	69%	—	31%
Social	87%	—	7%
Foreign	64%	—	36%
Composite	74%	—	26%

Key Votes of the 113th Congress

1. Sandy storm spending	Y	5. Medical Marijuana	Y	9. Syrian Rebels Training	N
2. Violence Against Women Act	Y	6. Farm Bill	N	10. Keystone pipeline	N
3. Guantanamo Bay Detainees	Y	7. Afghanistan Combat	N	11. Immigration Exec. Action	N
4. Abortion 20-week ban	N	8. NSA Phone Data Collection	N	12. Bipartisan budget deal	N

Election Results

2014 general	Peter Visclosky (D)	86,579	(61%)	$892,913
	Mark Leyva (R)	51,000	(36%)	$11,942
	Donna Dunn (L)	4,714	(3%)	
2014 primary	Peter Visclosky (D)	unopposed		

Prior winning percentages: 2012 (67%), 2010 (59%), 2008 (71%), 2006 (70%), 2004 (68%), 2002 (67%), 2000 (72%), 1998 (73%), 1996 (69%), 1994 (56%), 1992 (69%), 1990 (66%), 1988 (77%), 1986 (73%), 1984 (71%)

Population		Race and Ethnicity		Income	
Total:	719,164	White	63.8%	Median income:	$50,862
Urban:	12.3%	Black	19.5%		*(223 of 435)*
Suburban:	86.7%	Latino	14.1%	Under $50,000	49.1%
Rural:	1.0%	Asian	1.0%	$50,000-$99,999:	31.8%
Land area:	1,293	Two races	1.4%	$100,000-$199,999:	16.5%
Pop/sq. mi.:	556.3	White Ethnic	36.0%	$200,000 or more:	2.6%
Born in state:	58.8%			Poverty Rate	16.6%
		Education			
Age Groups		H.S. grad or less:	47.5%	**Work**	
Under 18:	24.0%	Some college:	32.0%	White collar:	30.3%
18 to 34:	22.0%	College degree, 4 yr.:	13.3%	Blue collar:	42.3%
35 to 64:	40.0%	Post-grad study:	7.2%	Sales and service:	27.5%
Over 64:	14.0%				
		Military		Govt. workers:	11.7%
		Veterans/active duty:	8.6%		

Northwest Indiana: Gary, Hammond

At the southernmost shore of Lake Michigan is a part of America made by steel. In the northwest corner of Indiana, where the water highway of the Great Lakes comes closest to the rail highway of the transcontinental railroads, America's leading capitalists of a century ago identified an ideal site for manufacturing steel. On

Voter Turnout	
2013 Total Citizen 18+	529,615
2014 House Turnout	142,293
2014 Turnout as % CVAP	26.9%
2012 Turnout as % CVAP	56.7%

empty sand dunes, United States Steel, then the nation's largest corporation, founded the city of Gary in 1906 and named it for the company's chairman, Chicago Judge Elbert Gary. For nearly 70 years, the steel mills attracted a diverse workforce, more like Chicago than the rest of Indiana: Irish, Poles, Czechs, Ukrainians and blacks from the South.

Politics here has always been turbulent, from the long and unsuccessful steel strike of 1919 to the racially polarized politics of the 1960s and 1970s. The tone of public life—the clash between union stewards and management foremen, between African Americans and Eastern European ethnics, between the stalwarts of different factions vying for control of Gary's massive City Hall—was a clash of steel on steel. Steel brought sudden growth and sudden depression to northwest Indiana. The massive storefronts built on Gary's aptly named Broadway bear witness to the confidence and exuberance of the 1920s. The steel mills went cold during the Depression but were again thronged with workers during World War II. In the years afterward, their massiveness helped create the illusion that a robust economic life in the steel towns of Gary, Hammond and East Chicago would last forever. Today they stand vacant—vandalized, whole blocks burned down—witness to steel layoffs, crime waves and an acute sense of loss. Technological advances replaced increasingly expensive workers with increasingly efficient machines. And the efforts to seal off the U.S. steel market from the world inevitably failed. Unemployment in northwest Indiana was 7.7 percent in March 2015, but Gary remained at 10.8 percent.

The oil crunch of 1979 was the catalyst for change, reducing the demand for large-sized autos, the biggest customer for steel. Steel employed 70,000 workers in northwest Indiana in 1979, but recent employment has dropped by more than three-fourths. Obsolete mills were closed, old mills modernized, and new ones built that cut the number of man hours needed by two-thirds. Just-in-time methods were introduced, and management and highly skilled workers cooperated to engineer higher-quality, less-expensive steel to meet market demands. In the shrinking market, Indiana remained the No. 1 steel-producing state in 2013, as it has been since 1980. The average pay-and-benefits package for U.S. Steel workers averaged about $55,000 a year, lower than at the company's plants in other states. Still, the industry remains vital to the local economy.

The dramatic decline of the industry left Gary in ruins. A 2012 Federal Reserve Bank of Chicago study categorized Gary as "overwhelmed" by the decline of manufacturing. Nobel Prize-winning economist Joseph Stiglitz in 2006 said the city was saddled with "the same problems facing less-developed countries." White flight to the suburbs has reduced the city's population from a peak of 178,000 in 1960 to below 79,000 in 2013. With the increased taxes in Illinois, Gary and Indiana officials have offered incentives to companies to move to their side of the state line in an intensifying competition. In November 2011, Gary elected its first female mayor, Karen Freeman-Wilson. The city is the birthplace of the late pop star Michael Jackson, and Gary also lent its name to a famous tune in the Broadway musical *The Music Man*.

Indiana's 1st Congressional District stretches from Gary and Hammond along the Lake Michigan shoreline east to Michigan City. In majority-white Hammond, the population loss has not been as dramatic as Gary's, and it has had an influx of Hispanic immigrants. The 1st includes Lake and Porter counties, and LaPorte County is divided between it and the neighboring 2nd District.

2012 Presidential Vote		
Barack Obama (D) 182,021	(61%)
Mitt Romney (R).................111,217	(37%)
2008 Presidential Vote		
Barack Obama (D) 194,540	(63%)
John McCain (R).................109,969	(36%)
Cook Partisan Voting Index: D+10		

In Porter County is the city of Valparaiso, notable for its annual Popcorn Festival honoring the late resident Orville Redenbacher. Nearly two-thirds of the vote is in Lake County. Like neighboring Chicago, the district is solidly Democratic. Unlike Illinois, Indiana has only two such districts.

Peter Visclosky (D)

Peter Visclosky, a Democrat first elected in 1984, is a former congressional aide who has found his niche in the House. "I'm an appropriator," he once said. "Money makes policy." In recent years, though, life on the spending side has become more complicated.

Visclosky grew up in Lake County. His father was mayor of Gary in the early 1960s, and Visclosky went to college there and to law school at the University of Notre Dame. He practiced law and then worked for six years in Washington for 1st District Rep. Adam Benjamin, a Democrat. Benjamin died of a heart ailment in 1982, and Visclosky returned to Indiana.

In 1984, he ran for the House seat in the Democratic primary against Katie Hall, a black state senator who had been given the 1982 nomination—and thus the election, in this Democratic district—by Gary Mayor Richard Hatcher, who was also the district's party chairman. In the 1984 contest, she faced a determined Visclosky, who pulled out all the stops to connect with voters since he couldn't rely on the local Democratic establishment, which was backing Hall. He called himself the "Slovak Kid" to connect with the district's many European ethnic groups, and he held hot dog dinners to attract young people and others not usually involved in local politics. Visclosky narrowly prevailed over Hall with 34% of the vote to her 33%. He easily won the general election with 71% of the vote.

Visclosky, now the dean of Indiana's congressional delegation, has trended moderate in his voting record, and he occasionally has shown independence. He broke Democratic ranks in opposing the New Year's Day 2013 budget deal aimed at averting the so-called fiscal cliff, saying that it left too many tax and spending issues unresolved. In 2008, he opposed creation of the Troubled Asset Relief Plan for the ailing financial services industry, although he did back a subsequent proposal to bail out major automakers.

Visclosky has concentrated much of his effort on projects to help the local economy, especially the steel industry. He has a solidly pro-union voting record. He is a leader of the Congressional Steel Caucus and has been vigilant in monitoring surges in steel imports. He urged the International Trade Commission in January 2013 to maintain trade protections against corrosion-resistant steel from Germany and South Korea and has repeatedly introduced bills requiring that federally funded projects use only American-made steel. In a July 2014 appearance before the ITC he said "there is no higher priority for our domestic steel industry today than the enforcement of our trade laws," and that it was time to take a stand that "we do not allow steel to be dumped here." When George W. Bush was elected president in 2000 with critical help from steel-producing areas, Visclosky had greater leverage, and Bush imposed steel import quotas. But when the quotas were removed, Visclosky protested that Bush "stabbed the American steelworkers in the back." He opposed the House-passed bill in 2009 establishing a cap-and-trade system to curb greenhouse gas emissions because it "leaves no margin of error as it relates to jobs in the domestic steel industry."

The retirement of veteran appropriator Norm Dicks of Washington enabled Visclosky to grab the coveted ranking Democrat slot on the Appropriations Defense Subcommittee in 2013. When Democrats were in the majority, he was chairman of the Energy and Water Development Subcommittee, making him one of the powerful "cardinals" of the House. But he was forced to step aside temporarily in June 2009 after he was subpoenaed as part of a grand jury investigation into possible corruption. In 2007, *The Indianapolis Star* reported that Visclosky had steered more than $12 million to out-of-state defense companies that contributed to his campaign. Much of that money had been secured through the efforts of a lobbying firm, PMA Group, that hired a former top Visclosky aide, Richard Kaelin, the newspaper reported. Visclosky said, "I have always abided by the law and adhered to the rules and code of ethics of the House." The House Ethics Committee formally cleared Visclosky and six other Appropriations members in February 2010. He has not challenged the decision of Democratic leaders to place Nita Lowey of New York as the top Democrat on the full committee, even though she has less seniority than Visclosky.

Visclosky had been adept at securing federal funding for projects in his district and at doling out such projects to other lawmakers. But those so-called earmarks have been prohibited since John Boehner became speaker in 2011. In recent years, he has echoed President Barack Obama's call for increased federal spending on infrastructure, which he said would help revitalize his district's economy. "I am very big on transformational projects," he told the *Northwest Indiana Times* in November 2012. "This area was transformed 100 years ago when somebody came in and built that first rail mill and built that first refinery. ... So we need to do some transformational things."

At home, Visclosky appeared secure politically until he became a target in the corruption probe. But Republicans had trouble finding a candidate who could compete in the costly Chicago media market, and challenge the Democratic performance in the 1st District. In 2010, the GOP nomination fell to Mark Leyva, a carpenter who had lost four previous races to Visclosky. All Leyva could do was narrow the margin of victory for Visclosky, who won with 59% of the vote. He elevated his winning total to 67% in 2012 against Joel Phelps, and 61% in a 2014 rematch with the perennial Leyva, indications that the scandal was behind him.

SECOND DISTRICT

Jackie Walorski (R)

Elected 2012, 2nd term; b. Aug. 17, 1963, South Bend; Taylor U., B.A. 1985; Christian; married (Dean Swihart).

Elected Office: IN House, 2004-10.

Professional Career: TV reporter, WSBT-TV, 1985-89; Exec. dir., St. Joseph Cnty. Humane Society, 1989-91; Dir. of institutional advancement, Ancilla Col., 1991-96; Dir. of annual giving, IN U., 1997-98; Founder, Impact Intl., 1999-2003.

DC Office: 419 CHOB, 20515, 202-225-3915; Fax: 202-225-6798; Website: walorski.house.gov.

State Offices: Mishawaka, 574-204-2645; Rochester, 574-223-4373.

Committees: *Agriculture:* General Farm Commodities & Risk Mgmt.; Nutrition (Chmn). *Armed Services:* Seapower & Projection Forces; Tactical Air & Land Forces. *Veterans' Affairs:* Oversight & Investigations.

Group Ratings

	ADA	ACLU	AFL-CIO	LCV	ITI	COC	HAFA	ACU	CFG	FRC
2014	0%	0%	–	3%	80%	86%	56%	64%	62%	88%
2013	0%	C	10%	0%	C	85%	C	68%	62%	C

National Journal Ratings

	2013 LIB	—	2013 CONS
Economic	33%	—	66%
Social	16%	—	74%
Foreign	34%	—	60%
Composite	31%	—	70%

Key Votes of the 113th Congress

1. Sandy storm spending	N	5. Medical Marijuana	N	9. Syrian Rebels Training	Y
2. Violence Against Women Act	Y	6. Farm Bill	Y	10. Keystone pipeline	Y
3. Guantanamo Bay Detainees	N	7. Afghanistan Combat	N	11. Immigration Exec. Action	Y
4. Abortion 20-week ban	Y	8. NSA Phone Data Collection	N	12. Bipartisan budget deal	Y

Election Results

2014 general	Jackie Walorski (R)	85,583	(59%)	$1,836,516	$13,116
	Joe Bock (D)	55,590	(38%)	$804,787	$5,642
	Jeff Petermamm (Lib)	4,027	(3%)		
2014 primary	Jackie Walorski (R)	unopposed			

Prior winning percentage: 2012 (49%)

Population		Race and Ethnicity		Income	
Total:	719,730	White	81.5%	Median income:	$42,611
Urban:	57.8%	Latino	8.4%		*(348 of 435)*
Suburban:	10.6%	Black	7.0%	Under $50,000	57.2%
Rural:	31.6%	Asian	1.0%	$50,000-$99,999:	29.8%
Land area:	4,163	Two races	1.7%	$100,000-$199,999:	10.9%
Pop/sq. mi.:	172.9	White Ethnic	27.6%	$200,000 or more:	2.1%
Born in state:	70.2%			Poverty Rate	18.3%
		Education			
Age Groups		H.S. grad or less:	51.5%	**Work**	
Under 18:	25.5%	Some college:	28.3%	White collar:	28.0%
18 to 34:	21.4%	College degree, 4 yr.:	13.0%	Blue collar:	39.6%
35 to 64:	38.5%	Post-grad study:	7.2%	Sales and service:	32.4%
Over 64:	14.6%			Govt. workers:	10.2%
		Military			
		Veterans/active duty:	8.5%		

North-Central Indiana: South Bend, Elkhart

When the University of Notre Dame was founded in 1842, Catholics were still a rarity in most of America and certainly rare on the limestone-bottomed plains of northern Indiana. This was still farm country and South Bend no more than a crossroads on the banks of the St. Joseph River. But by the 1920s, both the

Voter Turnout	
2013 Total Citizen 18+	511,958
2014 House Turnout	145,200
2014 Turnout as % CVAP	28.4%
2012 Turnout as % CVAP	53.7%

school and the town had grown. Notre Dame, thanks to its football team, the Fighting Irish, was the most famous Catholic university in the land, and South Bend was a significant industrial city, home of Studebaker, Bendix and dozens of other factories. In the past 50 years, Notre Dame has grown in size and reputation, but South Bend, like many Rust Belt cities, diminished in size and reputation. In the 1960s, Studebaker went out of business. In the early 1980s, there were massive factory layoffs.

But these high-visibility job losses were accompanied by the much less visible creation of jobs in small factories throughout the region. The work in those facilities required more skill than did the old assembly lines, and the products had to be more responsive to just-in-time prime contractors or computer-inventory retailers. In recent years, many employers have had trouble filling job openings, and the economic base is more secure than when it depended on the fate of two or three big companies. Today, Notre Dame is leading another transition, to a more high technology-focused economy. After acquiring the Midwest Institute for Nanoelectronics Discovery, it has researched the building blocks of the next generation of computers. A more recent focus of the university's more than $80 million in research projects has been its Environmental Change Initiative, which has explored the related problems of invasive species, land use and climate change, and their synergistic impact on water resources. On its better-known front, the school's reputation was dinged in 2012 after reports that university officials were slow to respond to rape and assault charges against student-athletes.

Elkhart County is a manufacturing hub that has found creative ways to turn a profit. Local companies there make everything from pharmaceuticals to musical instruments—oboes, bassoons and piccolos. The county is best known as the nation's manufacturing center for recreational vehicles, and it doesn't much care what the greenies think of that. The ups and down in gasoline prices, like those in recent years, can have a big impact in Elkhart. The onset of recession strangled demand for big-ticket goods like RVs. In 2008, Elkhart's unemployment jumped to 15%, the largest increase of any other metropolitan area in the nation, prompting *The New York Times* to call it "the white-hot center of the meltdown of the American economy." Nearly 18,000 jobs disappeared after the RV industry collapsed. The city council passed a law limiting residents to one garage sale per month. Even President Barack Obama dropped in for a visit in February 2009, to tout his economic recovery plan. Elkhart County got an infusion of federal dollars. "You can't drive anywhere in Elkhart and not see the stimulus," Democratic Mayor Dick Moore told *The Indianapolis Star* in 2010. With the lower cost of driving, the local economy made an impressive turn-around, as joblessness in Elkhart dropped to 4.8% in February 2015, and job growth was a robust 4%. One of every two RVs on the road today was manufactured in Elkhart. Shipments from

Elkhart were 321,000 in 2013, nearly double the total in 2009. Manufacturing employment rebounded from 28,000 to 38,000.

The 2nd Congressional District of Indiana is centered on South Bend. This is an industrial and ethnic city, with one of the nation's largest percentage of Hungarian Americans, plus a growing community of Mexican Americans. The latest redistricting plan increased its Republican base by about four percentage points. Wabash and Miami counties, plus rural and conservative parts of Kosciusko County, were added to the 2nd District, and it lost parts of Porter and LaPorte in the urban northwest corner of Indiana. Overall, it leans Republican.

2012 Presidential Vote		
Mitt Romney (R)	154,837	(56%)
Barack Obama (D)	116,320	(42%)
2008 Presidential Vote		
Barack Obama (D)	145,620	(50%)
John McCain (R)	144,921	(49%)
Cook Partisan Voting Index: R+6		

Jackie Walorski (R)

Republican Jackie Walorski wrested the redrawn 2nd District from the Democrats in 2012, winning the seat held by now-Democratic Sen. Joe Donnelly, who narrowly defeated her in 2010. After two close campaigns, she settled into her legislative work and was reelected comfortably.

Walorski grew up in a working-class family in South Bend, the granddaughter of Polish and German immigrants. Her father was a firefighter, and her mother worked at a hospital. She was the first in her family to attend college, graduating from Taylor University with a bachelor's degree in communications. She didn't become passionate about politics until she heard presidential candidate Ronald Reagan speak, recalling that he said Republicans "believed in smaller government and the power of individuals controlling their own destiny."

Walorski spent her first few years out of college working as a television reporter, and then became an administrator for Ancilla College and Indiana University. In 1999, Walorski and her husband, Dean Swihart, volunteered as Christian missionaries in Romania. The couple eventually set up their own nonprofit organization, Impact International. They were in Romania at the time of the September 11th terrorist attacks, an experience that she said was life-changing. "We sat and watched on the only television we had in Romania. The airspace was closed, we couldn't get back to our country," she said. "We really did not know if we'd ever see our country or family again."

When the couple returned to Indiana, Walorski won a seat in the state House in 2004. She cosponsored the state's voter identification law, which withstood a challenge in the Supreme Court, and worked to establish the Indiana Economic Development Corporation as a public and private cooperative venture.

In what has long been a swing district, Walorski has campaigned in tight races. In 2010, she challenged Donnelly and had high-profile endorsements from Sarah Palin and Newt Gingrich. The National Republican Congressional Committee placed this contest on its priority list, and Walorski got more than $1 million in national party aid. But Donnelly outspent her, $2 million to $1.3 million, and she lost 48%-47%, a margin of 2,538 votes. She remained active with the intention of challenging him again in 2012. When Donnelly ran for the Senate, Walorski was the early frontrunner. In the GOP primary, she had little trouble dispatching physician Greg Andrews. She faced off in the general against Democrat Brendan Mullen, an Army veteran of the Iraq war who campaigned as a pro-gun, anti-abortion rights moderate. Walorski went on the attack, running an ad that accused him of having three homes in Washington, D.C. Mullen said the homes were rental properties, and he criticized Walorski's vote for leasing operations of the Indiana Toll Road as a state lawmaker in 2006. Walorski outspent Mullen, $1.9 million to $1.2 million. The redrawn district's Republican tilt helped Walorski to a win, albeit still a close one, 49%-48%, a margin this time of 3,920 votes. Even with Donnelly's successful Senate campaign, he kept his distance from national Democrats. Walorski was boosted by the strong local performance of Mitt Romney's presidential bid and Mike Pence's campaign for governor.

In the House, Walorski scored some accomplishments, focused on local issues and avoided the leadership clashes and electoral ambitions of the several other junior Republicans in the delegation. As a member of the Agriculture Committee, she became chairwoman in 2015 of the Nutrition Subcommittee, and planned hearings for two years on how federal programs can better serve families and taxpayers to ensure that no child goes hungry. She toured her district's many farm communities and offered assistance in dealing with Washington. She also served on the Armed Services and Veterans' Affairs committees, and has worked with veterans' groups to encourage local business opportunities. She won enactment in the 2013 defense spending bill of her proposal to provide whistleblower protections for the victims of sexual assault in the military and create a safe environment for reporting attacks. That legislation was sponsored in the Senate by Democrats Amy Klobuchar of Minnesota and Claire McCaskill of Missouri.

In 2014, Walorski had grown more comfortable as the incumbent. Her challenger was Joe Bock, a global health professor at Notre Dame. Walorski attacked him for his votes to increase his own pay as a member of the Missouri legislature in the 1980s, and suggested that he was a carpetbagger. Bock criticized her as a career politician and for her role in the government shutdown in October 2013. Bock spent more than $800,000 to $1.8 million for Walorski, but this was a bad year for Democrats. The incumbent won 59%-38%, an indication that she was growing entrenched.

THIRD DISTRICT

Marlin Stutzman (R)

Elected Nov. 2010, 3rd full term; b. Aug. 31, 1976, Sturgis, MI; Trine St. U., attended; Baptist; married (Christy); 2 children.

Elected Office: IN House, 2002-08; IN Senate, 2008-10.

Professional Career: Co-owner, Stutzman Farms; Owner, Stutzman Farms Trucking.

DC Office: 2418 RHOB, 20515, 202-225-4436; Fax: 202-226-9870; Website: stutzman.house.gov.

State Offices: Bluffton, 260-824-1900; Fort Wayne, 260-424-3041; Winona Lake, 574-269-1940.

Committees: *Budget. Financial Services:* Financial Institutions & Consumer Credit; Monetary Policy & Trade.

Group Ratings

	ADA	ACLU	AFL-CIO	LCV	ITI	COC	HAFA	ACU	CFG	FRC
2014	5%	11%	–	3%	100%	64%	83%	96%	93%	100%
2013	0%	C	14%	7%	C	85%	C	96%	91%	C

National Journal Ratings

	2013 LIB	—	2013 CONS
Economic	8%	—	92%
Social	38%	—	62%
Foreign	44%	—	56%
Composite	30%	—	70%

Key Votes of the 113th Congress

1. Sandy storm spending	N	5. Medical Marijuana	N	9. Syrian Rebels Training	N
2. Violence Against Women Act	N	6. Farm Bill	N	10. Keystone pipeline	Y
3. Guantanamo Bay Detainees	N	7. Afghanistan Combat	N	11. Immigration Exec. Action	N
4. Abortion 20-week ban	Y	8. NSA Phone Data Collection	N	12. Bipartisan budget deal	Y

Election Results

2014 general	Marlin Stutzman (R)	97,892	(66%)	$1,061,404	$1,621
	Justin Kuhnle (D)	39,771	(27%)		
	Scott Wise (Lib)	11,130	(7%)		
2014 primary	Marlin Stutzman (R)	48,837	(82%)		
	Mark Baringer (R)	5,868	(10%)		
	James Mahoney (R)	5,094	(8%)		

Prior winning percentages: 2012 (67%), 2010 (63%), 2010 special (63%)

Population		Race and Ethnicity		Income	
Total:	729,747	White	84.6%	Median income:	$46,697
Urban:	43.1%	Black	6.1%		*(288 of 435)*
Suburban:	12.5%	Latino	5.5%	Under $50,000	53.3%
Rural:	44.4%	Asian	1.6%	$50,000-$99,999:	31.6%
Land area:	4,526	Two races	1.8%	$100,000-$199,999:	12.9%
Pop/sq. mi.:	161.2	White Ethnic	17.8%	$200,000 or more:	2.1%
Born in state:	73.0%			Poverty Rate	15.3%
		Education			
Age Groups		H.S. grad or less:	48.5%	**Work**	
Under 18:	25.8%	Some college:	30.4%	White collar:	29.0%
18 to 34:	21.8%	College degree, 4 yr.:	13.5%	Blue collar:	37.2%
35 to 64:	38.5%	Post-grad study:	7.6%	Sales and service:	33.8%
Over 64:	13.8%				
		Military		Govt. workers:	9.5%
		Veterans/active duty:	8.1%		

Northeast Indiana: Fort Wayne

The flat northeast corner of Indiana was first settled by people of New England Yankee stock, establishing orderly communities with public schools and even colleges. They were joined by German immigrants, who built tidy farms and their own civic institutions.

Voter Turnout	
2013 Total Citizen 18+	525,567
2014 House Turnout	148,793
2014 Turnout as % CVAP	28.3%
2012 Turnout as % CVAP	55.6%

In the northern part of the state, there are hills, lakes, and the strange swamp that is the central focus of Gene Stratton-Porter's children's classic, *A Girl of the Limberlost.* The one large city here, Fort Wayne, was built on the flat terrain along the Maumee River that flows to Toledo, Ohio. It grew as a factory town, surging ahead and then falling back as large factories, often tied to the auto industry, opened and closed over the years.

Manufacturing jobs in the Fort Wayne area dropped significantly in the 2000s, but the local economy started to revive after Claypool opened a $150-million biodiesel complex, including a soybean processing plant capable of producing 88 million gallons of fuel annually. A General Mills distribution center recently moved here. Fort Wayne's unemployment rate dropped to 4.9%, lower than the national rate, in 2014. Kosciusko County, named for the Polish general who served during the Revolutionary War, is renowned for medical supplies. In the town of Warsaw (yes, named for the Polish capital), residents have been making orthopedic devices for more than a century, and the demand keeps growing as Baby Boomers age. The head of the local Chamber of Commerce expects a big increase in demand for artificial knees, which is good news for Warsaw.

The 3rd Congressional District covers the northeastern part of the state and is centered on Fort Wayne. It is a surprisingly diverse area, with a mix that includes a concentration of Amish, plus Central Americans, Bosnians, Somalis and the nation's largest number of Burmese refugees. In the Fort Wayne metro area, only 3.3% of the total population is Hispanic, but of the population under 18, 33.6% is Hispanic. This part of Indiana has been heavily Republican since the Civil War, though it has sometimes veered Democratic in times of economic distress.

2012 Presidential Vote		
Mitt Romney (R)	179,629	(63%)
Barack Obama (D)	102,536	(36%)
2008 Presidential Vote		
John McCain (R)	164,922	(56%)
Barack Obama (D)	126,668	(43%)
Cook Partisan Voting Index:	R+13	

The seat sends its representatives on to higher positions: Dan Quayle, elected here in 1976, was later a senator and vice president. Dan Coats, who succeeded Quayle in the Senate, was ambassador to Germany before winning a second term in the Senate in 2010. Overall, this is the most Republican district in the state.

Marlin Stutzman (R)

Marlin Stutzman, a Republican elected in 2010, is a deeply conservative fourth-generation farmer. He favors creating a "market-friendly" environment for businesses and slashing government spending. He has shown his political ambition, notably with his run in 2016 for the Senate seat of retiring Sen. Dan Coats.

Stutzman grew up in Howe Indiana. His parents were Mennonites, a denomination of Anabaptists that shares historical roots with the Amish. When he was 14, Stutzman started raising his own livestock herd, which reached almost 100 animals before he sold them. He attended Tri-State University (now Trine University) for two years to study accounting, but he dropped out to focus on farming. He married a teacher when he was 23 and converted to her Baptist religion. He co-owned Stutzman Farms with his father and also was the sole owner of a trucking company before his election to Congress.

In 2002, when no one registered to challenge a longtime incumbent Democrat in the Indiana House, Stutzman filed papers to run on the last possible day. He won by 249 votes, becoming the youngest member of the House at age 26. In three terms, he helped to pass a tax credit for ethanol producers and authored Indiana's lifetime handgun permit law, which frees gun owners from having to renew their licenses. He pushed a bill that created tougher regulations for abortion providers. From 2005 to 2008, while a state representative, Stutzman worked as a special assistant in Rep. Mark Souder's district office. Stutzman won a seat in the state Senate in 2008.

The following year, he challenged Democratic Sen. Evan Bayh. Then in February 2010, Bayh said he would not seek reelection, creating an open seat opportunity that generated interest among other Republicans. In the primary, Stutzman faced former Sen. Dan Coats and former Rep. John Hostettler. Although national Republicans recruited Coats for the race, Stutzman had the support of tea party activists and conservative Sen. Jim DeMint of South Carolina, who was attempting to boost the number of like-minded candidates around the country. Coats ultimately won the nomination with 39% of the vote, and Stutzman came in second with 29%.

The results raised Stutzman's political profile and helped him win the support of Republican officials when Souder ran into political trouble in the spring of 2010. The incumbent was on his way to securing a ninth term when he revealed in May that he had engaged in an extramarital affair with one of his aides. Because Souder had already won the GOP primary, party officials chose Stutzman as their new nominee at their June caucus.

In the general election, he was the heavy favorite over former Fort Wayne City Council member Tom Hayhurst in the heavily Republican district. Although Hayhurst outraised Stutzman, $730,000 to $600,000, the Republican won with ease, with 63% of the vote to Hayhurst's 33%. At the same time, he was elected to fill the final weeks of Souder's term. That gave him slightly more seniority with which to leverage committee assignments. By January 2013, he was dean of the seven Indiana Republicans in the House.

Stutzman has been an unwavering conservative and one of the class of 2010 Republicans often chafing at Speaker John Boehner's willingness to make concessions to Democrats. "He needs to be clear in what our strategy is," Stutzman told *The New York Times* in January 2012, after the speaker struck a last-minute deal extending the payroll tax cut for two months. "I got chewed out by folks who said, 'Why did you fold?' I got scolded back home, and I don't really like it."

But he was named a deputy whip and, in 2013 got a seat on the Financial Services Committee, where he is an ally of Chairman Jeb Hensarling of Texas. He cosponsored Georgia GOP Rep. Rob Woodall's bill to replace the federal income tax with a national sales tax. He was highly critical of President Barack Obama's proposals to curb gun violence, calling on Obama to condemn "Hollywood's irresponsible glorification of violence." As chairman of the Second Amendment Caucus, he filed a bill that would allow anyone with a permit to carry concealed handguns in their home state to carry them in all other states that allow concealed carry. When Stutzman said that Republicans would not be "disrespected" and needed to "get something" to reopen the government following the shutdown in October 2013, Obama mocked him publicly, and cited "that attitude that you've got that you deserve to get something for doing your job." Stutzman has favored phasing out farm subsidies, even though his family received $179,000 in federal farm subsidies from 1995 through 2009. The subsidies, he says, are an unnecessary government interference in the free market and increase the federal debt.

Stutzman has sought leadership opportunities. When Kevin McCarthy moved up to majority leader in June 2014, Stutzman was a late entry in the contest to succeed him as whip. But Steve Scalise of Louisiana had a head start and a regional advantage because the top leadership team did not have a Southerner. The victory by Scalise created an opening at the conservative Republican Study Committee. Stutzman considered a bid for that post, but decided not to run. In January 2015, he was among 25 GOP renegades who did not vote for Boehner for speaker. Instead, he supported Republican Rep. Dan Webster of Florida.

In his heavily Republican district, Stutzman has twice won reelection with more than two-thirds of the vote. Given his previous run for the Senate and his leadership bid in the House, it was no surprise that he launched in May 2015 a campaign to succeed Republican Coats in the Senate. He said that he would provide "proven conservative leadership," including a balanced budget in six years and a simplified tax code. Stutzman gained early support from national conservative groups and faced the challenge of avoiding a repeat of his 2010 primary loss to Coats. The entry of Rep. Todd Young and former Coats aide Eric Holcomb into the GOP primary raised the possibility that Stutzman would benefit from a split in the GOP establishment.

FOURTH DISTRICT

Todd Rokita (R)

Elected 2010, 3rd term; b. Feb. 9, 1970, Chicago, IL; Wabash Col., B.A. 1992, IN U. Indianapolis, J.D. 1995; Catholic; married (Kathy); 2 children.

Elected Office: IN secy. of st., 2003-10.

Professional Career: Practicing atty., 1995-97; Gen. counsel, Office of IN Secy. of St., 1997-2000; IN deputy secy. of st. 2000-02.

DC Office: 1717 LHOB, 20515, 202-225-5037; Fax: 202-226-0544; Website: rokita.house.gov.

State Offices: Danville, 317-718-0404; Lafayette, 765-838-3930.

Committees: *Budget* (VChmn). *Education & the Workforce:* Early Childhood, Elementary & Secondary Education (Chmn); Workforce Protections. *Transportation & Infrastructure:* Aviation; Railroads, Pipelines, & Hazardous Materials; Water Resources & Environment.

Group Ratings

	ADA	ACLU	AFL-CIO	LCV	ITI	COC	HAFA	ACU	CFG	FRC
2014	0%	0%	–	6%	100%	93%	71%	88%	73%	88%
2013	0%	C	10%	4%	C	85%	C	82%	83%	C

National Journal Ratings

	2013 LIB	—	2013 CONS
Economic	7%	—	93%
Social	46%	—	54%
Foreign	0%	—	95%
Composite	19%	—	82%

Key Votes of the 113th Congress

1. Sandy storm spending	N	5. Medical Marijuana	N	9. Syrian Rebels Training	Y
2. Violence Against Women Act	Y	6. Farm Bill	Y	10. Keystone pipeline	Y
3. Guantanamo Bay Detainees	N	7. Afghanistan Combat	N	11. Immigration Exec. Action	Y
4. Abortion 20-week ban	Y	8. NSA Phone Data Collection	NV	12. Bipartisan budget deal	Y

Election Results

2014 general	Todd Rokita (R)	94,998	(67%)	$1,157,769 $1,773
	John Dale (D)	47,056	(33%)	$40,477
	Benjamin Gehlhausen (Lib)	10,565	(4%)	
2014 primary	Todd Rokita (D)	43,179	(71%)	
	Kevin Grant	17,472	(29%)	

Prior winning percentages: 2012 (62%), 2010 (69%)

Population		Race and Ethnicity		Income	
Total:	738,647	White	87.5%	Median income:	$52,486
Urban:	31.1%	Latino	5.3%		*(195 of 435)*
Suburban:	28.4%	Black	3.2%	Under $50,000	47.5%
Rural:	40.5%	Asian	2.4%	$50,000-$99,999:	35.2%
Land area:	6,646	Two races	1.2%	$100,000-$199,999:	15.2%
Pop/sq. mi.:	111.1	White Ethnic	23.4%	$200,000 or more:	2.1%
Born in state:	70.1%			Poverty Rate	12.6%
		Education			
Age Groups		H.S. grad or less:	46.7%	**Work**	
Under 18:	23.6%	Some college:	29.6%	White collar:	31.3%
18 to 34:	24.7%	College degree, 4 yr.:	15.0%	Blue collar:	39.6%
35 to 64:	37.7%	Post-grad study:	8.7%	Sales and service:	29.1%
Over 64:	14.0%				
		Military		Govt. workers:	13.3%
		Veterans/active duty:	8.3%		

West-Central Indiana: Indianapolis Suburbs, Lafayette

The landscape of central and western Indiana is some of the most prosaic in the United States. It is mostly flat, with neat farms and towns of frame bungalows, looking mostly unchanged from many years ago. Across this landscape run some of the nation's

Voter Turnout	
2013 Total Citizen 18+	540,339
2014 House Turnout	142,054
2014 Turnout as % CVAP	26.3%
2012 Turnout as % CVAP	52.3%

chief transportation arteries. The earliest was the old National Road, from Baltimore to St. Louis, which was paralleled by U.S. 40 in the 1930s. The region was also crisscrossed by the great east-west rail lines carrying famed passenger trains like the *Wabash Cannonball*. There is no *Cannonball* today. People bounce around the Midwest on commuter airlines from small city to hub, and U.S. 40 has been superseded by Interstate 70. The landscape still looks rural, and there are some large farms. But the economy is more industrial, with small factories in crossroads and courthouse towns. Manufacturing in Lafayette accounted for roughly 16,000 workers. This is a slice of the country that is 91 percent white, with little heritage from the early waves of immigration, relatively few African Americans, and only modest numbers of Latino and Asian immigrants.

Tippecanoe County's Lafayette, where the main employer is Purdue University, has been growing and prosperous. It has benefited from a partnership between Toyota and longtime local manufacturer Subaru that helped the Lafayette plant's workforce grow to 3,500 people by the end of 2012. Subaru has begun a $400 million expansion of its plant, which is scheduled to be completed in 2017 and will increase its assembly line to 450,000 vehicles annually. The city ranked sixth on *Forbes* magazine's 2009 list of "smartest small towns in America," and Lumosity, a neuroscience research company, ranked Lafayette the nation's second "brainiest" metro area in 2012.

Much of the farming territory around Lafayette and west-central Indiana was hurt by a severe drought in the summer of 2012.

2012 Presidential Vote		
Mitt Romney (R)	170,244	(61%)
Barack Obama (D)	103,103	(37%)
2008 Presidential Vote		
John McCain (R)	162,898	(54%)
Barack Obama (D)	133,960	(45%)
Cook Partisan Voting Index:	R+11	

Tippecanoe County was categorized with "extreme drought" by the U.S. Drought Monitor. But conditions improved so much a year later that some local farmers were forced to deal with flooding.

The 4th Congressional District covers much of west-central Indiana, as well as parts of suburban Indianapolis. It is solidly Republican.

Todd Rokita (R)

Republican Todd Rokita, elected in 2010, is a former Indiana secretary of state and devout conservative who has become an energetic partisan.

Rokita grew up in Munster, which is part of Lake County. His father was a dentist who owned his own practice, and his mother was a dental hygienist. Rokita was president of his high school student body and won a full scholarship to Wabash College. He majored in political science, focusing on political philosophy, and studied for a semester at the University of Essex in England. His semester in Europe reinforced Rokita's already conservative political beliefs. Fellow students told him about long lines and poor service in government-run hospitals, and he noticed the high cost of goods because of a value-added tax, which is collected in Europe. His experience abroad was "a good glimpse into what the future of America would and could be with liberalism on the march here," he said.

After earning his law degree at Indiana University, Rokita worked in private practice for several years. A licensed pilot, Rokita focused on aviation law, among other fields. He also was a volunteer pilot, flying people in need of non-emergency medical care to hospitals and clinics throughout the Midwest. While working on local and state campaigns, he met Indiana's then-Secretary of State Sue Anne Gilroy, who hired him as her general counsel and later made him deputy secretary of state. Rokita worked for George W. Bush's presidential campaign in 2000, training workers to challenge ballots during the historic Florida recount.

In 2002, Gilroy was term-limited out of office, and Rokita ran for the Republican nomination to succeed her. Rokita took a leave of absence from his job, bought a surplus police car, and drove across the state, meeting at their homes with delegates who would make the selection at a party convention. He won the Republican nomination on the third ballot and went on to win the general election.

In office, he fulfilled a campaign pledge to get a bill through the legislature requiring a photo ID at polling places to combat voter fraud. Critics of the 2005 law argued that it disenfranchised poor voters who are less likely to have driver's licenses (and are more likely to vote Democratic). A lawsuit challenging the constitutionality of the law was heard by the Supreme Court, which upheld it in 2008.

Rokita was embroiled in another controversy with civil rights undercurrents. In a 2007 speech, he questioned why 90% of blacks vote for Democrats. "How can that be?" Rokita said, according to the Associated Press. "Ninety to 10. Who's the master and who's the slave in that relationship? How can that be healthy?" After African-American leaders condemned his remarks, Rokita apologized. In 2009, he infuriated members of both political parties when he proposed making it a felony for lawmakers to draw legislative districts based on political data such as party registration and where incumbents live.

Rokita considered challenging Democratic Sen. Evan Bayh in 2010 but jumped into the congressional race instead when GOP Rep. Steve Buyer announced his retirement. His main primary opponent was state Sen. Brandt Hershman, Buyer's district director. With high name recognition and solid fundraising, Rokita won 42% of the vote to Hershman's 17%, while 11 other candidates split the rest. Rokita went on to easily win in November against Purdue University professor David Sanders, the Democratic candidate, 69%-26%.

In the House, Rokita was one of three GOP freshmen who were named to the Republican Steering Committee, which makes committee assignments. He recruited fellow freshmen to donate at fundraising events and took in nearly $200,000 through his leadership political action committee for the 2012 election. But he remained willing to break ranks with Republican leaders. He voted against the New Year's Day 2013 budget deal on taxes and spending aimed at averting the so-called fiscal cliff, and he was one of 67 Republicans to oppose Hurricane Sandy relief for the Northeast, saying, "Just as normal American families do, we have to be willing to cut spending on less important things if we want to pay for emergency expenses."

On the Education and the Workforce Committee, he became chairman of the Early Childhood, Elementary and Secondary Education Subcommittee. The panel planned to rewrite in 2015 the controversial No Child Left Behind Act, with Rokita's goal to return more school choices to local control. President Barack Obama has said that he would veto the Student Success Act, a companion measure that Rokita prepared in 2013. No fan of labor unions, Rokita successfully attached an amendment to a House-passed omnibus spending bill in June 2011 barring the Transportation Security Administration from using money for collective bargaining. He also came up with a "Red Tape Rollback" initiative that aims to change or delay implementation of regulations he deemed harmful to business.

He hasn't had to break a sweat in winning reelection. Although he deferred on running for the seat of retiring Sen. Dan Coats, he will have other statewide opportunities.

FIFTH DISTRICT

Susan Brooks (R)

Elected 2012, 2nd term; b. Aug. 25, 1960, Auburn; Miami U., OH, B.A. 1982, IN U., J.D. 1985; Catholic; married (David); 2 children.

Professional Career: Deputy mayor of Indianapolis, 1998-99; Practicing atty., 2000-01; U.S. atty., S. Dist. of IN, 2001-07; Sr. V.P., gen. counsel, Ivy Tech Comm. Col., 2007-12.

DC Office: 1505 LHOB, 20515, 202-225-2276; Fax: 202-225-0016; Website: susanwbrooks.house.gov.

State Offices: Anderson, 765-640-5115; Carmel, 317-848-0201.

Committees: *Energy & Commerce:* Commerce, Manufacturing, & Trade; Health; Oversight & Investigations. *Ethics. Select Benghazi Committee.*

Group Ratings

	ADA	ACLU	AFL-CIO	LCV	ITI	COC	HAFA	ACU	CFG	FRC
2014	0%	0%	—	3%	100%	93%	51%	68%	53%	88%
2013	0%	C	14%	0%	C	92%	C	80%	63%	C

National Journal Ratings

	2013 LIB	—	2013 CONS
Economic	26%	—	73%
Social	16%	—	74%
Foreign	15%	—	77%
Composite	22%	—	78%

Key Votes of the 113th Congress

1. Sandy storm spending	N	5. Medical Marijuana	N	9. Syrian Rebels Training	Y
2. Violence Against Women Act	Y	6. Farm Bill	Y	10. Keystone pipeline	Y
3. Guantanamo Bay Detainees	N	7. Afghanistan Combat	N	11. Immigration Exec. Action	Y
4. Abortion 20-week ban	Y	8. NSA Phone Data Collection	N	12. Bipartisan budget deal	Y

Election Results

2014 general	Susan Brooks (R)	105,277	(65%)	$1,018,137	$1,573
	Shawn Denney (D)	49,756	(31%)	$3,987	
	John Krom (Lib)	6,407	(4%)	$6,948	
2014 primary	Susan Brooks (R)	34,996	(73%)		
	David Stockdale (R)	7,327	(15%)		
	David Campbell (R)	5,790	(12%)		

Prior winning percentage: 2012 (58%)

Population		Race and Ethnicity		Income	
Total:	743,062	White	82.2%	Median income:	$61,285
Urban:	52.2%	Black	7.7%		*(109 of 435)*
Suburban:	35.8%	Latino	4.6%	Under $50,000	41.8%
Rural:	12.0%	Asian	2.7%	$50,000-$99,999:	30.7%
Land area:	1,776	Two races	2.6%	$100,000-$199,999:	20.5%
Pop/sq. mi.:	418.4	White Ethnic	23.9%	$200,000 or more:	7.0%
Born in state:	65.8%			Poverty Rate	11.1%
		Education			
Age Groups		H.S. grad or less:	31.0%	**Work**	
Under 18:	24.9%	Some college:	26.7%	White collar:	45.0%
18 to 34:	21.2%	College degree, 4 yr.:	26.3%	Blue collar:	38.5%
35 to 64:	40.9%	Post-grad study:	16.0%	Sales and service:	16.6%
Over 64:	13.0%				
		Military		Govt. workers:	10.4%
		Veterans/active duty:	7.6%		

Northern Indianapolis Metro

Indiana's most rapid growth has taken place in the suburban ring counties around Indianapolis, especially in Hamilton County, directly north of the city. This is affluent suburbia, with subdivisions full of spacious houses, shopping centers, and office developments in what were not too long ago farm fields. Ham-

Voter Turnout	
2013 Total Citizen 18+	536,608
2014 House Turnout	161,440
2014 Turnout as % CVAP	30.1%
2012 Turnout as % CVAP	64.3%

ilton County's population increased from 82,000 in 1980 to 182,000 in 2000 and to 275,000 in 2010—a 50% jump in a decade, making it one of the fastest growing counties in the Midwest. The growth continued, and exceeded 300,000 in 2014. A group of business and civic leaders has developed a mass transit plan that could spur even greater growth.

Hamilton County has drawn many wealthy people from Indianapolis, where they had been concentrated on the north side of the city. Now, they're more likely to be in the former farm communities of Carmel, Fishers and Noblesville. Hamilton has the highest median household income in Indiana and is the 35th richest county in the nation. Hamilton is the most Republican of the large counties in Indiana and is one of the most Republican in the nation. It voted 61%-38% for John McCain in 2008 and 66%-32% for Mitt Romney in 2012.

2012 Presidential Vote		
Mitt Romney (R)..................196,743	(58%)
Barack Obama (D) 139,300	(41%)
2008 Presidential Vote		
John McCain (R)..................180,360	(53%)
Barack Obama (D) 159,549	(47%)
Cook Partisan Voting Index: R+9		

The 5th Congressional District is located in the center of the state and includes the northern Indianapolis suburbs. In addition to Hamilton County, which is the core of the district, the 5th takes in Republican-leaning Grant and Tipton counties. In Marion, the largest city in Grant County, a black granite monument has been planned to honor James Dean, an actor with a large cult following who was born in Marion and died in 1955 at age 24 in an automobile accident. The district also includes the politically marginal Madison County, with its county seat in Anderson, a manufacturing town. The overall makeup of this district is Republican.

Susan Brooks (R)

Republican Susan Brooks, first elected in 2012, channels the understated conservatism of the Indianapolis political establishment. Having eked out a narrow victory over former Rep. David McIntosh in the Republican primary, she moved quickly to build on her impressive experience and assert herself in the House.

Brooks was born in Auburn Indiana and raised in Fort Wayne. At Homestead High School, she played basketball, volleyball, and tennis—and was a member of the cheerleading squad. Her mother and father both worked at Homestead High School, which made for an adolescence that was "wonderful and miserable at the same time," she told *National Journal*. "It was somewhat like growing up in a fishbowl."

Brooks attended Miami University in Oxford, Ohio, where she pursued a joint degree in political science and sociology and was president of her sorority. She earned a law degree from Indiana University and joined an Indianapolis-based criminal defense practice. That exposed her to what she calls the "root causes" of crime, such as domestic strife and mental health problems.

In 1998, Brooks was named deputy mayor of Indianapolis under Republican Mayor Stephen Goldsmith. At his behest, Brooks established the Indianapolis Violence Reduction Partnership, a multiagency collaboration designed to curb homicide, gun assaults and armed robberies. In October 2001, Brooks was appointed U.S. attorney for the Southern District of Indiana by President George W. Bush. Over the next six years, she prosecuted drug kingpins, helped consolidate the Southern District's counter terrorism apparatus, and drew attention to human trafficking, "something we really weren't talking about in Indianapolis," she said. In 2007, Brooks was appointed senior vice president and general counsel for Ivy Tech Community College, a statewide institution.

In the 2012 House race, Brooks and her chief GOP rival, McIntosh, entered the race before Burton announced his retirement, which may have contributed to the congressman's decision to endorse another candidate, Marion Mayor Wayne Seybold. Burton's endorsement had no discernible impact on the race, however, and in the months leading up to the primary,

Brooks and McIntosh each raised more than $500,000. McIntosh, who served in the House from 1995 to 2001, received endorsements from Republican power brokers, including former Vice President Dan Quayle, former Sen. Fred Thompson of Tennessee, anti-tax activist Grover Norquist, and the National Rifle Association.

McIntosh's campaign was undone by questions about his residential status. After relinquishing his seat in Congress to run for governor of Indiana, he moved his family to the Washington area to work as a lobbyist in a large Washington law firm. At the same time, he continued to vote in Indiana, renting area properties to maintain his residency. McIntosh was later absolved of any wrongdoing by a local election board, but not before he had lost the Republican primary. In a crowded field, Brooks prevailed with 30% of the vote to 29% for McIntosh, a difference of 1,010 votes. Seybold finished fourth with 11%. Brooks' opponent in the fall was Democrat Scott Reske, a state legislator and former Marine Corps officer. He had a hard time getting traction in the Republican district, and Brooks won 58%-38%.

In the House, Brooks co-chaired the Congressional High-Tech Women's Caucus, with an objective to encourage more women to enter the tech industry. The House passed her Social Media Working Group Act, which would codify the Homeland Security Department's social media techniques. She received leadership assignments to the Ethics Committee and the Select Committee to Investigate Benghazi. She was one of 87 Republicans who voted to end the partial government shutdown in October 2013, which she termed "very much a low point in governing for me."

Brooks was part of a bipartisan House group that successfully pushed in March 2015 for extension of the Children's Health Insurance Program, along with changes in Medicare payments to doctors. In January 2015, she got a seat on the influential Energy and Commerce Committee. For that panel, she set as a top priority repeal of the medical device tax in the Affordable Care Act.

Following the retirement announcement of Sen. Dan Coats, Brooks considered running for the seat. She said she concluded that she can achieve more positive impact for Indiana by staying in the House.

SIXTH DISTRICT

Luke Messer (R)

Elected 2012, 2nd term; b. Feb. 27, 1969, Evansville; Wabash Col., B.A. 1991, Vanderbilt U., J.D. 1994; Presbyterian; married (Jennifer); 3 children.

Elected Office: IN House, 2003-06.

Professional Career: Legal counsel, Koch Industries, 1995-96; Staff, Rep. John Duncan Jr., 1997; Press secy., Rep. Ed Bryant, 1998; Legal counsel, Reps. Dan Burton & David McIntosh, 1998-99; Legal counsel, House Government Reform & Oversight Committee, 1999; Exec. dir., IN Republican Party, 2001-05; Practicing atty., 2006-present; Pres., Hoosiers for Economic Growth Network, 2010-12.

DC Office: 508 CHOB, 20515, 202-225-3021; Website: messer.house.gov.

State Offices: Muncie, 765-747-5566; Richmond, 765-962-2883; Shelbyville, 317-421-0704.

Committees: *Education & the Workforce:* Health, Employment, Labor & Pensions; Higher Education & Workforce Training. *Financial Services:* Capital Markets & Gov't Sponsored Enterprises; Monetary Policy & Trade.

Group Ratings

	ADA	ACLU	AFL-CIO	LCV	ITI	COC	HAFA	ACU	CFG	FRC
2014	0%	0%	–	0%	100%	85%	68%	80%	66%	88%
2013	0%	C	10%	4%	C	85%	C	88%	81%	C

National Journal Ratings

	2013 LIB	—	2013 CONS
Economic	10%	—	88%
Social	31%	—	67%
Foreign	0%	—	95%
Composite	15%	—	85%

Key Votes of the 113th Congress

1. Sandy storm spending	N 5. Medical Marijuana	N 9. Syrian Rebels Training Y
2. Violence Against Women Act	Y 6. Farm Bill	Y 10. Keystone pipeline Y
3. Guantanamo Bay Detainees	N 7. Afghanistan Combat	N 11. Immigration Exec. Action Y
4. Abortion 20-week ban	Y 8. NSA Phone Data Collection	N 12. Bipartisan budget deal Y

Election Results

2014 general	Luke Messer (R)...................... 102,187	(66%)	$841,608	$3,604
	Susan Hall Heitzman (D).......... 45,509	(29%)	$8,149	
	Eric Miller (Lib) 7,375	(5%)		
2014 primary	Luke Messer (R)...................unopposed			

Prior winning percentage: 2012 (59%)

Population		Race and Ethnicity		Income	
Total:	724,638	White	92.6%	Median income:	$45,691
Urban:	23.8%	Latino	2.3%		*(306 of 435)*
Suburban:	24.2%	Black	2.1%	Under $50,000	54.5%
Rural:	52.0%	Asian	1.0%	$50,000-$99,999:	31.9%
Land area:	5,712	Two races	1.9%	$100,000-$199,999:	12.1%
Pop/sq. mi.:	126.9	White Ethnic	18.9%	$200,000 or more:	1.5%
Born in state:	70.7%			Poverty Rate	15.3%
		Education			
Age Groups		H.S. grad or less:	51.6%	**Work**	
Under 18:	22.8%	Some college:	28.5%	White collar:	30.5%
18 to 34:	21.4%	College degree, 4 yr.:	12.5%	Blue collar:	40.4%
35 to 64:	39.9%	Post-grad study:	7.4%	Sales and service:	29.2%
Over 64:	15.8%			Govt. workers:	11.9%
		Military			
		Veterans/active duty:	9.2%		

Southeast Indiana: Muncie

Muncie became famous as the "Middletown" where sociologists Robert and Helen Lynd lived and did research for their landmark report in 1924 and 1925. The Lynds were attracted to Muncie because it was typical of "every small city from Maine to California," as *Life* magazine put it. But it wasn't exactly. Muncie

Voter Turnout	
2013 Total Citizen 18+	549,250
2014 House Turnout	155,071
2014 Turnout as % CVAP	28.2%
2012 Turnout as % CVAP	52.4%

was a factory town in a country still almost 50 percent rural in the 1920s, and it was almost entirely Protestant and Northern in a country that was one-fifth Catholic and one-third Southern. Muncie was more typical in that it was culturally homogeneous but economically riven. In the 1920s, when General Motors opened a plant in Muncie, the city celebrated its common values and was loath to admit its economic disparities. In the 1930s, those differences were exposed when Muncie, like much of the industrial Midwest, was unionized, a process that sometimes led to violent clashes. Workers who were joining CIO unions and voting for Democrats fiercely opposed the business elite—local bankers, merchants, GM executives, and the Ball family's glass company. Partisan politics took on the sharp, bitter tone of a struggle for wealth between two rival classes whose claims seemed irreconcilable.

Today, the region is still a story of both sides of the American economic coin. "Local auto parts plants were in many ways the engine that drove the Muncie economy. At its peak in the 1950s, Warner Gear (later BorgWarner Automotive) employed more than 5,000 workers," the Muncie *Star-Press* wrote in a profile of its hometown when it celebrated its 150th anniversary in 2015. It was devastated by the loss in 2006 of a General Motors manual transmission plant, but it regained some of its manufacturing heft with the arrival of a foreign-owned automaker: Honda opened a plant in Greensburg that employs 2,300 people engaged in making Civics and Acuras. The GM plant was unionized; the Honda plant is not. Yet Muncie has been unable to entirely reinvent itself, plagued by the economic insecurities playing out in many formerly industrial towns.

There is one constant in Muncie and the surrounding environs: basketball. It is the civic religion here. Most of the nation's largest high school gyms are in Indiana. The Fieldhouse, in New Castle, near the Indiana Basketball Hall of Fame, is the largest of them all. Milan

High School's 1954 state championship victory over Muncie Central was the basis for the 1986 movie *Hoosiers*.

The 6th Congressional District of Indiana covers most of the east-central and southeast parts of the state. It includes Muncie in the north as well as Richmond, founded by a major branch of American Quakers and home to their Earlham College. Richmond is also the site of Tom Raper Inc., the largest RV dealer in the Midwest. Batesville, to the south, is the site of the Batesville Casket Co., which makes the coffins for U.S. military personnel who die in the line of duty. This is a comfortably Republican district.

2012 Presidential Vote		
Mitt Romney (R)	172,452	(60%)
Barack Obama (D)	106,365	(37%)

2008 Presidential Vote		
John McCain (R)	167,843	(55%)
Barack Obama (D)	133,164	(44%)

Cook Partisan Voting Index: R+12

Luke Messer (R)

Republican Luke Messer in 2012 took the seat of Mike Pence, the prominent conservative who ran successfully for governor. After having lost in the GOP primary in two runs for Congress during the previous decade, he took only two years to be elected chairman of the House Republican Policy Committee, the No. 5 GOP leadership post.

Messer was born in Evansville, and the family moved to Greensburg when he was 4 years old. A sixth-generation Hoosier, Messer traces his Republican ideology and interest in politics to his family roots. Messer's grandmother, Helen Rotzien, was a ward chairman and secretary of the Marion County Republican Central Committee in the 1960s. His "personal hero," Messer told *National Journal*, is his mother, a 40-year employee of Delta Faucet who raised him as a single mother. He said she exemplifies hard-working values and taught him that "anyone can come from humble beginnings." Messer attended Wabash College, paying his tuition by working as a waiter and telemarketer and graduating in 1991 with a major in speech.

Messer earned a law degree from Vanderbilt University in 1994 and went on to jobs on Capitol Hill with three members of Congress, including Republican Rep. Dan Burton. In 2000, Messer ran for an open House seat against Pence and lost in the GOP primary. He became executive director of the Indiana Republican Party in 2004 and had a role in the successful gubernatorial campaign of Republican Mitch Daniels.

Messer was appointed to a vacancy in the Indiana House, and represented Shelby and Bartholomew counties. His signature issue was education. His legislation aimed at curbing high school drop-out rates received national attention after Shelbyville High School became a symbol of a national dropout crisis. As highlighted in a *Time* magazine cover story and a special on *The Oprah Winfrey Show*, Messer's 2005 bill made Indiana raise its minimum dropout age from 16 to 18. After the legislation was implemented, Shelbyville High School's graduation rate increased from 75% to 90%. Messer was inspired to write a children's book called *Hoosier Heart*. The book, illustrated by his wife, Jennifer, follows the journey of Emma and Ava (named after his daughters) and their friend, Ben, as they discover what it means to be a Hoosier.

In 2010, Messer challenged longtime incumbent Burton, his former boss, in the Republican primary and lost 30%-28%. Republicans in charge of redistricting the following year thoughtfully put his home of Shelbyville in the adjacent district, solid GOP turf perfect for Messer. He publicly aligned himself with Pence's policies. His top competitor was real estate investor Travis Hankins. Messer vastly outraised him, but Hankins ran a competitive grassroots campaign, personally calling more than 19,000 voters and spending the majority of his funds on yard signs to cover the 19-county district. Messer remained the choice of the GOP establishment and benefited from a timely endorsement from the popular Daniels days before the primary. Messer defeated Hankins 40%-29%. His $1.1 million overall spending and the Republican lean of the district virtually assured him a victory over Democrat Bradley Bookout, a former Delaware County Council member; Messer won, 59%-35%.

In the House, Messer has been a loyal conservative. He immediately impressed his like-minded colleagues, and was a Republican freshman class president. Kentucky GOP Rep. Thomas Massie told *The Indianapolis Star* that Messer was "probably the best listener I have met here in Congress" and that he is "always able to articulate what I think better than what I can." He has been a vigorous champion of school choice, drawing on his earlier work in Indiana. He formed the Congressional School Choice Caucus in 2014, and has filed legislation to allow states to use federal education funds to expand school choice programs. "The simple truth is too many kids in America have their destiny determined by zip codes," he wrote in an op-ed column. "That's because too many families live in neighborhoods with bad schools, and they can't afford to do anything about it." On another issue facing education, he introduced with Democratic Rep. Jared Polis of Colorado the Student Digital Privacy and Parental Rights Act, which was designed to protect the information that computer programs gather on students. The bill was drafted with assistance from White House officials and education leaders.

In November 2014, Messer ran for Policy Committee chairman after James Lankford of Oklahoma moved to the Senate. Playing up support from Pence, who was highly respected among conservatives, Messer donated money to numerous candidates and promised to expand the Policy Committee's staff to help all GOP members. Messer beat New York's Tom Reed 137-90 after Rob Woodall of Georgia was eliminated on the first ballot. "We need a positive agenda, so we're not defined by just what we oppose," Messer said after he was selected. After a long struggle to get to Congress, he may have other opportunities to move up the leadership ladder.

SEVENTH DISTRICT

André Carson (D)

Elected March 2008, 4th full term; b. Oct. 16, 1974, Indianapolis; Concordia U., B.A. 2003, IN Wesleyan U., M.S. 2005; Muslim; married (Mariama); 1 child.

Elected Office: Indianapolis/Marion City-Cnty. Cncl., 2007-08.

Professional Career: Investigator, IN St. Excise Police, 1996-2005; Investigator, IN Dept. of Homeland Security, 2006-08.

DC Office: 2453 RHOB, 20515, 202-225-4011; Fax: 202-225-5633; Website: carson.house.gov.

State Offices: Indianapolis, 317-283-6516.

Committees: *Intelligence (Permanent):* CIA; Emerging Threats. *Transportation & Infrastructure:* Aviation; Economic Development, Public Buildings, & Emergency Mgmt (RMM).

Group Ratings

	ADA	ACLU	AFL-CIO	LCV	ITI	COC	HAFA	ACU	CFG	FRC
2014	85%	88%	–	94%	40%	50%	6%	4%	6%	0%
2013	85%	C	95%	93%	C	23%	C	20%	12%	C

National Journal Ratings

	2013 LIB	—	2013 CONS
Economic	83%	—	16%
Social	93%	—	0%
Foreign	74%	—	25%
Composite	85%	—	15%

Key Votes of the 113th Congress

1. Sandy storm spending		5. Medical Marijuana	Y
2. Violence Against Women Act	Y	6. Farm Bill	N
3. Guantanamo Bay Detainees	Y	7. Afghanistan Combat	N
4. Abortion 20-week ban	N	8. NSA Phone Data Collection	Y

9. Syrian Rebels Training   Y
10. Keystone pipeline   N
11. Immigration Exec. Action   N
12. Bipartisan budget deal   Y

Election Results

2014 general	Andre Carson (D)	61,443	(55%)	$782,921
	Catherine Ping (R)	46,887	(42%)	$10,917
	Chris Mayo (Lib)	3,931	(4%)	
2014 primary	Andre Carson (D)	19,446	(89%)	
	Curtis Godfrey	1,209	(6%)	

Prior winning percentages: 2012 (63%), 2010 (59%), 2008 (65%), 2008 special (54%)

Population		Race and Ethnicity		Income	
Total:	743,136	White	57.3%	Median income:	$37,453
Urban:	97.4%	Black	28.1%		*(406 of 435)*
Suburban:	2.6%	Latino	10.0%	Under $50,000	62.8%
Rural:	0.0%	Asian	1.7%	$50,000-$99,999:	26.9%
Land area:	332	Two races	2.5%	$100,000-$199,999:	8.8%
Pop/sq. mi.:	2,237.4	White Ethnic	15.3%	$200,000 or more:	1.4%
Born in state:	67.7%			Poverty Rate	24.1%
		Education			
Age Groups		H.S. grad or less:	48.8%	**Work**	
Under 18:	25.8%	Some college:	30.2%	White collar:	29.6%
18 to 34:	26.7%	College degree, 4 yr.:	14.0%	Blue collar:	44.4%
35 to 64:	36.8%	Post-grad study:	7.0%	Sales and service:	26.0%
Over 64:	10.7%				
		Military		Govt. workers:	10.6%
		Veterans/active duty:	7.5%		

Indianapolis

Indianapolis, radiating outward from the soldiers and sailors statue in Monument Circle, is precisely at the center of Indiana and is the largest, and most dominant, city in the state. What residents once disparaged as "Nap Town" has become a thriving metropolis, including the downtown district. The city

Voter Turnout	
2013 Total Citizen 18+	506,076
2014 House Turnout	112,261
2014 Turnout as % CVAP	22.2%
2012 Turnout as % CVAP	52.1%

is the political and governmental capital, industrial and financial center, and the intellectual center of Indiana as well. It is symmetrically laid out: Just to the west of the circle is the state Capitol, to the north is the American Legion headquarters, to the east is the City-County building, and to the south is the Circle Centre mall and Lucas Oil Stadium, home of the NFL's Indianapolis Colts. In 2012, Lucas Oil was the site of the state's first-ever Super Bowl, an event that caused grumbling about the weather but brought the city favorable notice.

Farther out are some classic and some new Indianapolis institutions: the Indiana University Medical Center; the Convention Center; the Eiteljorg Museum of American Indians and Western Art; Bankers Life Fieldhouse, where the NBA's Indiana Pacers play; and the headquarters of the NCAA. Home of the iconic Indianapolis 500, the motorsports industry contributes some 23,000 jobs for the entire state. Indianapolis has fostered its niche as the nation's amateur sports capital, especially for basketball, and it is a popular place for religious conventions.

With its strong service economy, Indianapolis did better than most cities during the recession, with its downtown experiencing a multibillion-dollar construction boom. Pharmaceutical giant Eli Lilly & Co. has spent $400 million to expand by 2016 its insulin manufacturing operations, including two insulin cartridge filling lines. After reports in 2012 that the Indianapolis Airport's dwindling number of nonstop flights had hurt the local convention business, the airport highlighted nonstop service to 37 airports.

Indiana's 7th Congressional District takes in most of Indianapolis. In the past, Indianapolis had robust political competition in local and national races. Republicans held the mayor's office from 1967, when Richard Lugar won it, until 1999. Lugar, who later became a six-term senator, expanded Indianapolis' city limits to include all of Marion County in a new entity called UniGov, which made it a solidly Republican constituency. More recently, affluent young people have been moving to counties farther out, and Marion County has become solidly Democratic, though its population remains more

2012 Presidential Vote		
Barack Obama (D)	164,902	(63%)
Mitt Romney (R)	92,674	(35%)

2008 Presidential Vote		
Barack Obama (D)	185,573	(66%)
John McCain (R)	91,874	(33%)

Cook Partisan Voting Index: D+13

than 60% white. Barack Obama won Marion 64%-35% in 2008 and 60%-38% in 2012. The 7th is one of only two Democratic districts in the state; the other is the Gary-based 1st.

André Carson (D)

Democrat André Carson won his seat in a March 2008 special election to succeed his grandmother, Julia Carson, who died in office after representing the district for nearly 11 years. A hard-working and occasionally outspoken liberal, Carson is active in the Congressional Black Caucus and has expanded his portfolio beyond civil rights.

As a child, Carson studied religion. Originally interested in the priesthood, he later converted to Islam and became the second Muslim elected to Congress, following Minnesota Democratic Rep. Keith Ellison. Carson also had an artistic side. He wrote poetry as a young man and performed as a rap artist under the name "Juggernaut." But his career took him into law enforcement. He got a bachelor's degree in criminal justice management from Concordia University and a master's degree in business management from Indiana Wesleyan. Carson spent nine years as a plainclothes officer of the Indiana Excise Police, which enforces alcohol and tobacco laws. "I loved law enforcement," he told *Esquire* magazine in 2010. "But this job sure beats sitting and waiting for something bad to go down at three in the morning."

He recalled that his political interest began in 1984, at age 10, when he attended the Democratic convention in San Francisco and heard civil rights leader Jesse Jackson speak. Carson said that his thinking was transformed by reading *The Autobiography of Malcolm X,* and he attended Louis Farrakhan's Million Man March in 1995. In 2007, at age 32, he won a seat on the Indianapolis City-County Council, his first elected office.

After Julia Carson died in December 2007, her grandson faced significant opposition for the Democratic nomination in the special election to fill the remainder of her term. At the January 2008 Democratic caucus, he won a bare majority with 223 of the 439 votes; state Rep. David Orentlicher, a lawyer and doctor, got 123 votes, and Marion County Treasurer Michael Rodman came in third with 27 votes.

Against Republican state Rep. Jon Elrod, a young lawyer, Carson received extensive assistance from the Democratic Congressional Campaign Committee. On issues, he called for withdrawing U.S. troops from Iraq, endorsed tax cuts for working families, and said that companies should have incentives to keep them from sending jobs overseas. Elrod emphasized aid to small businesses and tougher enforcement of immigration laws, and he called for an end to federal spending earmarks. Carson won, 54%-43%.

Meanwhile, Carson continued campaigning in the May primary for a full term. Running as the incumbent this time and with an endorsement from presidential candidate Barack Obama, Carson won the primary with 47% of the vote to 24% for former state Health Commissioner Woodrow Myers. Elrod won the GOP nomination, but he soon withdrew and failed to retain his seat in the state House. Carson has faced minimal opposition since.

In the House, Carson has established a liberal voting record. He was named a senior whip on Minority Whip Steny Hoyer's team in 2013. Two years later, he became the first Muslim to get a seat on the Intelligence Committee. He also was part of the Black Caucus leadership team. His biting rhetoric has sometimes gotten him in trouble. At a town hall meeting in August 2011, Carson said that some members of the tea party movement in Congress would love to see blacks "hanging on a tree." A year later, he caused another uproar on the right when he advised at an Islamic convention: "America will never tap into educational innovation and ingenuity without looking at the model that we have in our madrassas, in our schools, where innovation is encouraged, where the foundation is the Koran." He later clarified his remarks by saying that faith-based schools of all religions were models for public education to follow. Before the final vote on the health care overhaul in March 2010, he drew national attention by contending that angry protesters outside the Capitol hurled racial epithets at him and Rep. John Lewis of Georgia, a leader of the civil rights movement.

Legislatively, Carson has served on the Transportation and Infrastructure Committee, where he is the ranking Democrat on the Economic Development, Public Buildings, and Emergency Management Subcommittee. He added language to defense spending bills to provide military service members an evaluation of mental health assessments before and after deployment, and to offer service members and their spouses with financial counseling before leaving the military. As a member of the Financial Services Committee, he initially opposed the $700 billion bailout of the financial markets in 2008 but switched his position after Obama encouraged him to support it.

EIGHTH DISTRICT

Larry Bucshon (R)

Elected 2010, 3rd term; b. May 31, 1962, Taylorville, IL; U. of IL Urbana-Champaign, B.S. 1984, U. of IL Chicago, M.D. 1988; Lutheran; married (Kathryn); 4 children.

Military Career: U.S. Navy Reserve, 1989-98.

Professional Career: Practicing cardiothoracic surgeon, 1995-98; Ohio Valley HeartCare, 1998-2010, pres., 2003-10; Chief & Medical Dir., St. Mary's Hospital.

DC Office: 1005 LHOB, 20515, 202-225-4636; Fax: 202-225-3284; Website: bucshon.house.gov.

State Offices: Evansville, 812-465-6484; Jasper, 812-482-4255; Terre Haute, 812-232-0523; Vincennes, 855-519-1629.

Committees: *Energy & Commerce:* Environment & the Economy; Health; Oversight & Investigations.

Group Ratings

	ADA	ACLU	AFSCME	LCV	ITIC	NTU	COC	ACU	CFG	FRC
2014	0%	0%	–	3%	100%	93%	58%	72%	46%	75%
2013	0%	C	14%	4%	C	85%	C	84%	71%	C

National Journal Ratings

	2013 LIB — 2013 CONS		
Economic	13%	—	85%
Social	16%	—	74%
Foreign	5%	—	86%
Composite	15%	—	85%

Key Votes of the 113th Congress

1. Sandy storm spending	N	5. Medical Marijuana	N	9. Syrian Rebels Training	Y
2. Violence Against Women Act	Y	6. Farm Bill	Y	10. Keystone pipeline	Y
3. Guantanamo Bay Detainees	N	7. Afghanistan Combat	N	11. Immigration Exec. Action	Y
4. Abortion 20-week ban	Y	8. NSA Phone Data Collection	N	12. Bipartisan budget deal	Y

Election Results

2014 general	Larry Bucshon (R)	103,344	(60%)	$820,413	$1,755	$17,615
	Tom Spangler (D)	61,384	(36%)	$32,276		
	Andrew Horning (Lib)	6,587	(4%)	$2,511		
2014 primary	Larry Bucshon (R)	30,967	(75%)			
	Andrew McNeil	10,405	(25%)			

Prior winning percentages: 2012 (53%), 2010 (57%)

Population		Race and Ethnicity		Income	
Total:	720,976	White	91.4%	Median income:	$45,999
Urban:	41.6%	Black	3.9%		*(299 of 435)*
Suburban:	13.0%	Latino	2.0%	Under $50,000	54.3%
Rural:	45.4%	Asian	0.9%	$50,000-$99,999:	30.7%
Land area:	7,429	Two races	1.6%	$100,000-$199,999:	12.9%
Pop/sq. mi.:	97.0	White Ethnic	17.6%	$200,000 or more:	2.0%
Born in state:	75.2%			Poverty Rate	15.1%
		Education			
Age Groups		H.S. grad or less:	48.8%	**Work**	
Under 18:	22.6%	Some college:	30.9%	White collar:	30.7%
18 to 34:	22.5%	College degree, 4 yr.:	13.4%	Blue collar:	40.8%
35 to 64:	39.4%	Post-grad study:	6.9%	Sales and service:	28.5%
Over 64:	15.5%			Govt. workers:	12.3%
		Military			
		Veterans/active duty:	8.9%		

Southwest Indiana: Evansville, Terre Haute

"Evansville," wrote John Bartlow Martin in 1947, "is the capital of a tri-state area comprising the neglected tag ends of Indiana, Kentucky, and Illinois." It was a factory town then, making car parts and refrigerators, drawing workers from Kentucky, Tennessee, and the picturesque but not very fertile hills of Southern Indiana. Today, Evansville has become the headquarters for a number of midsized companies that offer high-paying, skilled jobs. Car parts still get made here, though it is auto assembly that helps anchor the local manufacturing economy. Toyota in 1998

Voter Turnout	
2013 Total Citizen 18+	549,638
2014 House Turnout	171,315
2014 Turnout as % CVAP	31.2%
2012 Turnout as % CVAP	52.4%

opened a plant in nearby Princeton that builds SUVs and minivans. With another addition scheduled for completion in 2016, employment will total 5,000 workers, with an overall investment of $4 billion. The auto industry helped Evansville weather the recession; its unemployment rate was 8% in 2010 and 5.4% at the end of 2014, among the lowest in Indiana and not bad for an economy reliant on manufacturing. But the local Whirlpool refrigerator production plant closed in 2010, followed by the shuttering of its refrigeration product design center. Much of that production shifted to Mexico. Only a few years earlier, Whirlpool employed about 1,500 in the Evansville area.

In Vanderburgh County, Evansville is one of two major population centers of the 8th Congressional District, which covers Southwest Indiana. The other, in Vigo County, is Terre Haute, an old manufacturing town and the boyhood home of socialist Eugene Debs. It hosts a maximum-security penitentiary, which includes the only federal death chamber; Oklahoma City bomber Timothy McVeigh was executed there in 2001. The district also takes in Vincennes, now a small town on the banks of the Wabash River but important in Indiana history. Downstream is New Harmony, established by Welsh philanthropist and visionary Robert Owen.

Southern Indiana is ancestrally Democratic, just as northern Indiana is ancestrally Republican. The southern counties were hostile to the Union during the Civil War, and then in New Deal times, workers in Evansville moved toward the Democrats. The result has been a very close political balance, and this district has become known as the "Bloody 8th" for its tight congressional races. At one point in the 1970s, it sent four different members to the House in four successive elections. In 1984, the state certified the Republican the winner by exactly 34 votes. The Democratic majority in the House overturned the result, however, in a fight that left many Republican members bitter. Since then, the district has

2012 Presidential Vote		
Mitt Romney (R)	169,317	(58%)
Barack Obama (D)	114,907	(40%)
2008 Presidential Vote		
John McCain (R)	156,723	(51%)
Barack Obama (D)	149,099	(48%)
Cook Partisan Voting Index:	R+8	

flipped between the two parties. The trend in its presidential politics, however, is away from national Democrats. The district leans Republican, but could be competitive with the right kind of Democrat.

Larry Bucshon (R)

Republican Larry Bucshon, elected in 2010, is among the physicians from his party who is outspokenly critical of Democrats on health care. With his seat on the Energy and Commerce Committee, he was positioned to craft GOP alternatives and to seek opportunities for consensus.

Bucshon was raised in the rural town of Kincaid Illinois, southeast of Springfield. His mother was a nurse and his father a coal miner; both tended to vote Democratic. Bucshon developed his own ideology as an undergraduate at the University of Illinois, and his rightward shift was solidified when he became enamored of President Ronald Reagan. While still in high school, Bucshon decided on a career in medicine, inspired by the surgeons he met at the hospital where his mother worked. After college, he enrolled in medical school at the University of Illinois at Chicago. He completed a residency at the Medical College of Wisconsin and landed a fellowship there specializing in cardiothoracic surgery. Bucshon then enlisted with the Naval Reserve, serving for nearly a decade. After three years in private practice in Wichita, Kan., in 1998 he joined Ohio Valley HeartCare, a large cardiology and cardiovascular surgery practice in Evansville. Five years later, he became its president.

With a long-time interest in national office, Bucshon ran when Democratic Rep. Brad Ellsworth sought the Senate in 2010. With help from the National Republican Congressional Committee, Bucshon prevailed over seven other candidates in the May GOP primary with 33% of the vote, edging out second-place finisher Kristi Risk, a tea party-backed candidate, by 4 percentage points.

In the general election, he faced Democratic state Rep. Trent Van Haaften, who fit the centrist mold of Ellsworth. Van Haaften was a prosecutor in rural Posey County and was praised there for his work fighting a regional methamphetamine epidemic. In the campaign, he emphasized his law-and-order background, while Bucshon campaigned on curbing spending and repeal of the Democrats' health care overhaul. Democrats accused Bucshon of favoring the privatization of Social Security. Bucshon raised and spent $1.1 million, compared to $762,000 for Van Haaften. He won with 57% of the vote to Van Haaften's 38%.

In the House, Bucshon got a bill into law in 2012 allowing active-duty military to get commercial driver's licenses in states where they serve or receive military training. He voted a solidly conservative line, boasting in a report at the end of his freshman term that he had voted to cut more than $1.8 trillion "in unnecessary, frivolous spending." He strongly opposed an excise tax on medical device equipment, as well as a Medicare cost control board included in the health care law. "I have been a practicing physician for over 15 years, and I don't think I have seen anything potentially more detrimental to seniors' health care than the Independent Payment Advisory Board," he said. But he opened himself up to conservatives' criticism for backing the August 2011 increase in the debt limit, unlike other Indiana GOP freshmen. He also broke with them by opposing the Republican Study Committee's fiscal 2012 budget proposal that slashed more in spending than House Budget Committee Chairman Paul Ryan's blueprint.

As a new member of the Energy and Commerce Committee in 2015, he joined in bipartisan support for the new law making a permanent fix in Medicare reimbursement of doctor fees. Bucshon cited his cooperation with another doctor, Democratic Rep. Ami Bera of California, on a successful amendment to repeal a complex billing procedure imposed by Medicare officials. With committee Democrats Frank Pallone of New Jersey and Joe Kennedy of Massachusetts and Republican Ed Whitfield of Kentucky, Bucshon filed a bill to encourage monitoring programs for prescription drug addiction. His new committee assignment also gave him opportunities to work on energy legislation to promote his district's large coal resources, and telecommunications topics such as expanded broadband access.

In the 2012 GOP primary, Risk, the tea party candidate, mounted another challenge to Bucshon but could not come close to competing financially, and the incumbent won with 58% of the vote. His Democratic challenger in the general election was broadcaster and former state Rep. Dave Crooks, who ran an effective campaign and raised a respectable $980,000. He sought to portray Bucshon as out of touch with regular voters and touted his own culturally and fiscally conservative views. *The Tribune-Star* of Terre Haute endorsed Crooks, saying Bucshon hadn't shown enough willingness to compromise with Democrats on key issues. Bucshon, meanwhile, castigated Crooks as being in lockstep with President Barack Obama. He raised $1.4 million and got help from conservative super PACs that ran ads on his behalf in the campaign's closing weeks, eventually notching a solid but hardly overwhelming 53%-43% victory. Crooks led in Vigo County, 51%-45%, but Bucshon took 15 of the other 18 counties, including Vermillion. In 2014, he had an easier time against Democrat Tom Spangler, who spent only $32,000; Bucshon won 60%-36%.

NINTH DISTRICT

Todd Young (R)

Elected 2010, 3rd term; b. Aug. 24, 1972, Lancaster, PA; U.S. Naval Acad., B.S. 1995, U. of Chicago, M.B.A. 2000, U. of London, M.A. 2001, IN U., J.D. 2006; Christian; married (Jenny); 4 children.

Military Career: U.S. Navy, 1990-91; U.S. Marine Corps, 1995-2000.

Professional Career: Staff, Heritage Foundation, 2001; Legis. asst., Sen. Richard Lugar, 2001-03; Adviser, Gov. Mitch Daniels, 2004; Mgmt. consultant, 2004-06; Deputy prosecutor, Orange Cnty., 2007-10.

DC Office: 1007 LHOB, 20515, 202-225-5315; Fax: 202-226-6866; Website: toddyoung.house.gov.

State Offices: Bloomington, 812-336-3000; Greenwood, 317-661-0696; Jeffersonville, 812-288-3999.

Committees: *Ways & Means:* Human Resources; Select Revenue Measures; Social Security.

Group Ratings

	ADA	ACLU	AFL-CIO	LCV	ITI	COC	HAFA	ACU	CFG	FRC
2014	0%	0%	–	6%	80%	93%	52%	76%	59%	63%
2013	0%	C	19%	0%	C	92%	C	84%	66%	C

National Journal Ratings

	2013 LIB	—	2013 CONS
Economic	30%	—	69%
Social	42%	—	57%
Foreign	15%	—	77%
Composite	31%	—	69%

Key Votes of the 113th Congress

1. Sandy storm spending	Y	5. Medical Marijuana	Y	9. Syrian Rebels Training	N
2. Violence Against Women Act	Y	6. Farm Bill	Y	10. Keystone pipeline	Y
3. Guantanamo Bay Detainees	N	7. Afghanistan Combat	N	11. Immigration Exec. Action	N
4. Abortion 20-week ban	Y	8. NSA Phone Data Collection	N	12. Bipartisan budget deal	Y

Election Results

2014 general	Todd Young (R)	101,594	(62%)	$1,405,165	$7,622
	Bill Bailey (D)	55,016	(34%)	$112,786	
	Mike Frey (Lib)	6,777	(4%)		
2014 primary	Todd Young (R)	30,402	(79%)		
	Kathy Lowe-Heil (R)	4,607	(12%)		
	Mark Jones (R)	3,293	(9%)		

Prior winning percentages: 2012 (55%), 2010 (52%)

Population		Race and Ethnicity		Income	
Total:	731,802	White	90.6%	Median income:	$50,346
Urban:	17.4%	Latino	2.9%		(237 of 435)
Suburban:	56.9%	Black	2.6%	Under $50,000	49.6%
Rural:	25.6%	Asian	1.7%	$50,000-$99,999:	33.1%
Land area:	4,573	Two races	1.9%	$100,000-$199,999:	14.6%
Pop/sq. mi.:	160.0	White Ethnic	20.4%	$200,000 or more:	2.7%
Born in state:	65.6%			Poverty Rate	15.0%
		Education			
Age Groups		H.S. grad or less:	46.6%	**Work**	
Under 18:	22.5%	Some college:	28.9%	White collar:	32.8%
18 to 34:	25.0%	College degree, 4 yr.:	15.3%	Blue collar:	41.4%
35 to 64:	38.5%	Post-grad study:	9.2%	Sales and service:	25.8%
Over 64:	14.0%				
		Military		Govt. workers:	13.4%
		Veterans/active duty:	9.7%		

South-Central Indiana: Louisville Suburbs, Indianapolis Suburbs

The immense Ohio River is the largest tributary of the Mississippi. In Southern Indiana, it runs along the Indiana-Kentucky border and is an artery of commerce. Utilitarian barges have replaced the old steamers, except for riverboat casinos. Along the river are towns like Corydon, which was the state

Voter Turnout	
2013 Total Citizen 18+	550,928
2014 House Turnout	163,387
2014 Turnout as % CVAP	29.7%
2012 Turnout as % CVAP	55.6%

capital from 1816 to 1825. Charlestown was settled on a hill two miles from the Ohio in 1808. An early visitor to Charlestown was Jonathan Jennings, who moved to the area from Pennsylvania to launch his political career and became Indiana's first governor in 1816. French Lick, a former resort town, is well-known to basketball fans as the hometown of former Boston Celtics star Larry Bird. Salem was the home of John Milton Hay, personal secretary to President Abraham Lincoln and later secretary of State in the William McKinley and Theodore Roosevelt administrations. In rural Scott County, where many residents continue to live in poverty, Governor Mike Pence in March 2015 declared a health emergency following an HIV outbreak that was linked to the use of contaminated syringes. He authorized a short-term exchange program for clean needles.

The people who live in the hills along the Ohio River in Indiana's 9th Congressional District have typically voted Democratic, but the Louisville, Ky., suburbs in Clark and Floyd counties have trended Republican. The largest city in the 9th is Bloomington, where Indiana University and its 46,000 students are based. In April 2015, the university announced a new health campus and hospital. Bloomington, which is a highly rated small-city locale for high-tech employment, has been seeking a high-profile corporate partner for its tech park. This is a Democratic stronghold, but its vote usually is overwhelmed—especially by nearby Johnson and Morgan Counties, which are growing Republican bastions in the suburbs of Indianapolis.

With the 2011 redistricting shift to the neighboring 8th of other Democratic-leaning counties along the Ohio River, the 9th District

2012 Presidential Vote		
Mitt Romney (R)	173,433	(57%)
Barack Obama (D)	123,436	(41%)
2008 Presidential Vote		
John McCain (R)	166,057	(53%)
Barack Obama (D)	145,767	(46%)
Cook Partisan Voting Index: R+9		

leans comfortably Republican. For 34 years, until his retirement in 1998, the district was represented by Democrat Lee Hamilton, who chaired the House Intelligence and Foreign Affairs committees.

Todd Young (R)

Republican Todd Young, who unseated Democratic Rep. Baron Hill in 2010, shares some similarities with his Ways and Means Committee Chairman, Paul Ryan: Both are telegenic Midwesterners and deficit-conscious policy wonks who cut their teeth on Capitol Hill and at conservative think tanks. And both are well-regarded within their party, with ambitions and opportunities to move up the ladder of influence.

Born in Lancaster Pennsylvania, Young spent the first 13 years of his life outside Indiana, but his family has deep ties to the Hoosier State stretching back five generations. His father is a small business owner who sells heating, ventilation and air-conditioning equipment. His mother is a registered nurse. He went to high school in Hamilton County Indiana where his prowess on the soccer field helped his team win a state championship. When he graduated in 1990, he enlisted in the Navy and a year later received an appointment to the U.S. Naval Academy, where he played on the soccer team. When he graduated, he joined the Marine Corps because of its reputation for toughness. "If I was going to be in the military, I wanted to be in the warrior class," he told *National Journal*. In the Marines, he worked with unmanned aerial vehicles doing reconnaissance work, which included a stint aiding government anti-narcotics efforts in the Caribbean. In 1998, he was transferred to Chicago, where he managed Marine recruiting in the area.

Young attended the University of Chicago's business school at night, became a fan of free-market economist Friedrich von Hayek, and got an M.B.A. Young went to the University of London's Institute of United States Studies, where he got another master's degree and wrote a thesis on the economic history of Midwestern agriculture. Shortly after graduating,

Young moved to Washington, where he worked at the conservative Heritage Foundation and later for GOP Indiana Sen. Richard Lugar as his legislative assistant for energy policy. In 2004, Young returned to Indiana to help craft energy and veterans' policies for the gubernatorial campaign of Republican Mitch Daniels. He also earned a law degree at Indiana University.

In the GOP primary for the right to challenge Hill, Young narrowly won a tight three-way contest with Travis Hankins and former Rep. Mike Sodrel, a trucking company owner who held the House seat from 2004 to 2006. (Hill first won the seat in 1998, held it until he was defeated in 2004 by Sodrel, then won it back in the pro-Democratic year of 2006.)

In the fall campaign, Young portrayed Hill as a rubber stamp for the Obama administration and the Democratic congressional leadership, hammering Hill for his votes in favor of the $787 billion economic stimulus bill, the health care overhaul, and an energy bill setting limits on carbon emissions. Hill emphasized his Hoosier roots as a former high school basketball star, while characterizing Young as a wealthy, out-of-touch lawyer who had spent much of his career outside the state. Hill also slammed Young for comments at a town hall meeting referring to Social Security as a "Ponzi scheme." Young said that his comments were taken out of context and that he did not endorse privatizing the program.

The candidates raised and spent about the same amount of money, Hill with $2.2 million and Young with $2 million. Young was also the beneficiary of $437,000 in independent expenditures from the National Republican Congressional Committee and more than $250,000 from the conservative American Future Fund. He won with 52% of the vote to 42% for Hill. Libertarian candidate Greg Knott got 5%.

As a House freshman, Young concentrated on military and economic issues as a member of the Armed Services and Budget committees. Unlike some of his Class of 2010 colleagues, he supported the 2011 compromise to raise the debt limit, saying he wanted deeper spending cuts but that the measure "moves us in the right direction." But he blasted the New Year's Day 2013 deal on taxes and spending aimed at averting the so-called fiscal cliff deal, because he said it "does very little to restore a degree of certainty to our economy." Despite his avowed desire to work with Democrats, Young once called Senate Democratic Leader Harry Reid "useless" and his House counterpart Nancy Pelosi "an irrelevant cheerleader for lost-cause liberalism" at a local GOP event.

In 2013, Young got his seat on Ways and Means. He took over as the lead sponsor of the REINS Act requiring congressional approval of federal regulations with an economic impact exceeding $100 million. With Democratic Rep. Dan Lipinski of Illinois, Young filed a bill to revise the Affordable Care Act by setting the traditional definition that a work week is 40 hours. For local interest, he got a provision in the 2013 defense spending bill to help old military installations get liability protection when businesses redevelop the sites, which will help the former Indiana Army Ammunition Plant.

Like the neighboring "Bloody 8th," voters in the 9th District have alternated their allegiances between the two parties since veteran Democrat Lee Hamilton's retirement in 1998. Young's 2012 Democratic opponent was Shelli Yoder, a former Miss Indiana who easily won a five-way primary in May. Yoder called for turning the region into a leader in clean energy technologies while increasing funding to retrain unemployed workers. She criticized Young for supporting the cuts in Ryan's budget blueprint and seeking to repeal the health care law. But the incumbent outraised her by 4-to-1 and won 55%-45%. In 2014, he had an easy run against Democrat William Bailey, a former mayor of Seymour, who had little funding and lost 62%-34%.

When Sen. Dan Coats in March 2015 announced his retirement, Young said that he was "very serious" about running to succeed him, and he stepped up his fundraising. He is aware of the challenges in running a modern campaign. In an October 2014 speech to Republicans at Indiana University, he said that Democrats in 2012 were more skillful with new technologies. "We were out-flanked, frankly, by the Democratic Party in terms of the social media and really adopting a 21st century campaign platform," Young said, the *Indiana Daily Student* reported. "I'm not talking about the issues, but I'm talking about the infrastructure." In July, Young declared his candidacy with support from many leading Indiana Republicans. With Hill the chief Democratic contender, they could be facing each other again.

★ IOWA ★

The early settlers who founded Iowa could hardly have imagined that their state would one day have more people living in the big city than the small towns. In the 1840s, young Yankee and German farmers streamed across the Mississippi River into the fertile rolling land beyond. Wagon trains headed to the Oregon Trail, and the thousands of Mormons mustered by Brigham Young traveled across Iowa's rolling hills to Council Bluffs on the Missouri River, and then to points further west. Iowa was young and proud of its hundreds of schools and dozens of colleges, sending more than its share of young men back East to fight for the Union. After the Civil War, Iowans built a solid civilization based on farming, farm-machine manufacturing, and meat processing that resisted the blandishments of William Jennings Bryan's populism and cheap money. Politically, Iowa became one of the most solidly Republican states in the nation.

Starting around 1900, Iowa's model society stopped attracting new transplants. "If you build it, they will come" was the theme from the movie *Field of Dreams*, set in Iowa. Yet during much of the 20th century very few people came. The region's commercial and financial center remained the railroad hub of Chicago, Iowa's economy failed to diversify and develop the dense manufacturing base of the Great Lakes states, and its young people started to move east or west to make their fortunes. The state's population, which increased from 674,000 in 1860 to 2.2 million in 1900, did not reach 3 million until 2008. In 1900, Iowa had 11 congressional districts and California had seven. Today, Iowa has four and California 53. Iowa's solid Capitol, a memorial to its Civil War dead, its stately courthouses, and its sturdy but mostly old housing stock give testimony to Iowa's strengths but also suggest a lack of dynamism. Its great economic achievement has been the development of ever more productive, but also less labor-intensive, agriculture. Iowa is the nation's leading producer of pork, corn, and soybeans. It had a particularly tough time in the 1980s, when the number of farmers and farmland values dropped precipitously and the state's population shrank by 4.7% between 1980 and 1990, down to the 1960 level.

Ethanol provided a significant boost to the Iowa economy starting in 1998, when Republican Sen. Charles Grassley got the ethanol tax credit extended. In 2007, a law required a steady increase over time in the amount of renewable fuels such as ethanol blended into gasoline to help address global warming and boost rural economies. In 2014, Iowa produced 27 percent of the nation's ethanol, and the renewable fuels industry supports 47,000 jobs in the state, some of which are high-skilled positions required to operate sophisticated ethanol plants. But ethanol may have peaked. Increased demand for corn has raised meat prices in the United States and tortilla prices in Mexico; the federal ethanol blenders tax credit has expired; and the amount of ethanol legally required in gasoline has reached its maximum. In 2015, the Environmental Protection Agency proposed slowing the increase in the amount of ethanol in the nation's gasoline supply, cutting the amount required under the 2007 law by more than 4 billion gallons in 2015 and by more than 3 billion gallons in 2016. That reduction, though less than what the Obama administration initially proposed in 2013, was met by stiff resistance from agricultural and renewable fuels interests. Iowa also has a thriving wind energy industry that supplies it with almost 29 percent of its power needs, the highest level of any state in the nation, according to the American Wind Energy Association.

In ethanol's wake, farmland prices hit their high in 2012, and fell about 15 percent by 2015, due to lower corn and soybean prices. Iowa's high level of literacy and midwestern industriousness produced white-collar and high-tech growth in and around Des Moines, Cedar Rapids, and Iowa City. Even as many old factories closed, some Iowa emigrants to big cities like Chicago were persuaded to come home, and Mexican immigrants moved to smaller cities with meatpacking plants. Jobs and small-town life attracted Bosnians and Liberians as well as Congolese, Sudanese and Somali refugees. But this is still a mostly white state: In 2014, Iowa's population was 3% black, 5% Hispanic and 2% Asian. Iowa lost far fewer jobs in the 2007-09 recession than in the 1980s. Unemployment rose to 6.6 percent in mid-2009 and fell to a seasonally adjusted 3.8 percent in May 2015. Researchers at the Iowa Data Center reported that year that the state has been experiencing it longest run of sustained population growth since 1900. But those gains have occurred almost entirely in metropolitan areas, and more than half of the state's population today is concentrated in just 10 of its 99 counties. From 2010 to 2014, the state's metro counties grew by 4.3 percent, while non-metro

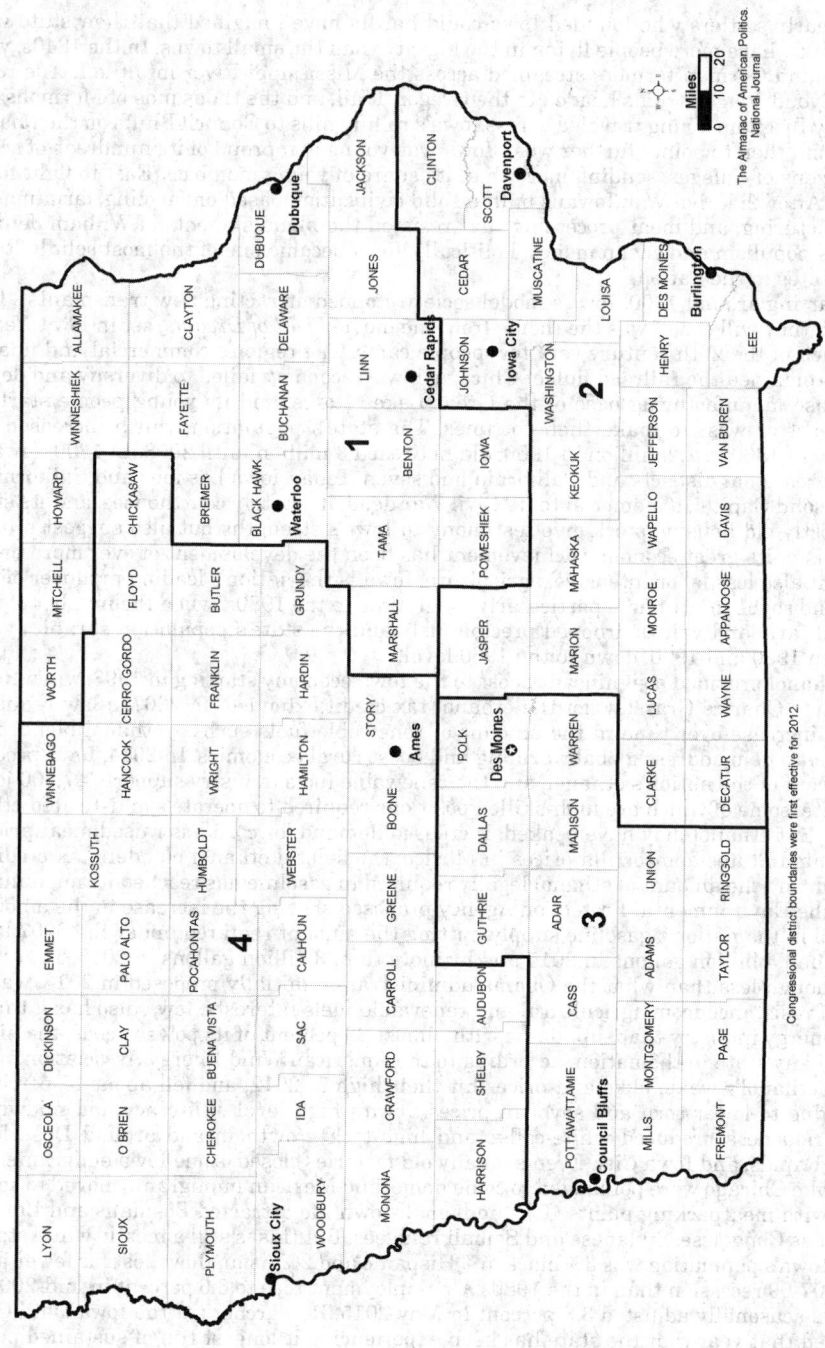

The Almanac of American Politics.
National Journal

Congressional district boundaries were first effective for 2012.

counties dropped by 1.1 percent. That change is evident around Des Moines, where cornfields are giving way to exurban development. West of the capital city, Clive, Johnston, Waukee and West Des Moines all saw double-digit population growth from 2010 to 2014. To the north, Ankeny, Altoona and Bondurant have been booming. The state's two major college towns, Iowa City (University of Iowa) and Ames (Iowa

Voter Turnout	
2013 Total Citizen 18+	2,284,244
2014 Highest Statewide Turnout	1,129,700
2014 Turnout as % CVAP	49.5%
2012 Turnout as % CVAP	69.5%
Legislature		
Senate:	26D	24R
House:	57R	43D

State) are also seeing significant population gains. Impeding growth in many rural areas of the state is insufficient high-speed Internet that can support multiple devices or run a business.

For much of the 20th century, Iowa was a culturally and politically counter-cyclical state, headed in the opposite direction of the rest of the nation—determinedly with confidence in its own chipper rectitude and unabashedly out of step. In the industrial New Deal era, it stayed mostly agricultural and Republican, even as Davenport and Des Moines radio announcer Ronald Reagan became an enthusiastic Roosevelt Democrat and headed to Hollywood. In the 1980s, when Reagan, by then a conservative Republican, was president and Iowa's economy was hit hard, anxiety became the dominant note of Iowa's politics, as voters sought protection from the vagaries of the market. In the 1988 caucuses, Iowa Republicans voted against Reagan's vice president, George H.W. Bush, and Iowa Democrats voted for populist Dick Gephardt. That fall, Iowa gave Democratic presidential nominee Michael Dukakis his second highest vote percentage of any state. Since then, Iowa and the nation have converged politically. It voted twice for Democrat Bill Clinton and went for Democrat Al Gore by 4,144 votes in 2000 and for Republican George W. Bush by 10,059 votes in 2004. Iowa gave Democrat Barack Obama a critical boost in its 2008 precinct caucuses and then gave him its Electoral College votes in 2008 and 2012.

After 30 years of Republican governors, Iowa elected Democrats three times, starting in 1998, and then in 2010 and 2014 voted for Republican Terry Branstad as it had in 1982, 1986, 1990 and 1994 when Branstad also ran. Iowans can get comfortable with their elected officials; Democrat Tom Miller is currently serving his ninth term as the state's attorney general, and Michael Fitzgerald, the Democratic state treasurer, has been on the job since 1983. Republicans won majorities in the legislature in the 1990s, lost them in 2004, and regained a state House majority in 2010. The state Senate remained in Democratic hands. Collectively, these results indicate a sort of steady moderation. Iowa remains quirky in some respects. It is still probably one of the most dovish, isolationist-prone states, and at the same time, very much aware of its role as an international exporter. Its delegation voted for the 1993 North American Free Trade Agreement and for normalizing trade relations with China in 1999 (Mexicans eat lots of corn and the Chinese like pork). Iowa's entire congressional delegation voted in 2015 to give Trade Promotion Authority to President Obama.

Iowans like to think of themselves as tolerant and in April 2009, the state Supreme Court unanimously ruled that the state's limitation of marriage to opposite-sex couples

Population		Race and Ethnicity		Income	
Total:	3,090,416	White	88.4%	Median income:	$54,855
Urban:	34.9%	Latino	5.0%		(19 of 50)
Suburban:	14.3%	Black	2.8%	Under $50,000	47.6%
Rural:	50.9%	Asian	1.8%	$50,000-$99,999:	33.3%
Land area:	55,857	Two races	1.6%	$100,000-$199,999:	15.9%
Pop/sq. mi.:	55.3	White Ethnic	22.7%	$200,000 or more:	3.2%
Born in state:	71.2%			Poverty Rate	11.3%
		Education			
Age Groups		H.S. grad or less:	41.1%	**Work**	
Under 18:	23.4%	Some college:	32.4%	White collar:	34.3%
18 to 34:	22.9%	College degree, 4 yr.:	18.1%	Blue collar:	40.4%
35 to 64:	38.1%	Post-grad study:	8.4%	Sales and service:	25.3%
Over 64:	15.5%				
		Military		Govt. workers:	13.5%
		Veterans/active duty:	8.6%		

violated the state constitution. Many in Iowa applauded the decision, but others called it judicial overreach. In November 2010, voters had their say when three of the Supreme Court justices came up for retention (jurists are selected by a commission and the governor, but then face the voters to stay on the bench). Ordinarily, approval is routine, but all three were defeated. But in 2012, aided by higher turnout and many gay weddings in the state, opinion shifted and the one justice up for retention who had participated in the marriage case prevailed, evidence of the trend seen in national polls indicating increased support for same-sex marriage. The state's high court took another liberal stand in 2015, unanimously striking down a rule by the Iowa Board of Medicine that would have prohibited Iowa doctors from using telemedicine to provide abortion-inducing drugs to rural women. Ironically, three of the justices in the abortion case were tapped by Branstad in 2011 to replace the three who were defeated for retention in 2010 after ruling in favor of gay marriage. This decision will test the strength of the state's substantial anti-abortion movement.

Iowa has its distinctive political rituals, notably its first-in-the-nation presidential caucuses. But one, two, even three years prior, White House hopefuls journey to the Iowa State Fair, held every August on the east side of Des Moines, to shake hands, eat a pork chop on a stick, and marvel at the famed butter cow sculpted out of 600 pounds of churned whole milk. The would-be presidents are there to identify with and pay homage to the state's farming traditions. The 11-day event routinely draws roughly one million visitors each year, quite a feat for a state with a total population of just over three million. Those crowds are on a par with the attendance at the 10-day annual Smithsonian Folk Life Festival held on the National Mall, a major tourist destination in the midst of a metropolitan area with nearly six million people. So while most now live in urban centers, Iowans and their folkways remain firmly attached to the state's agrarian roots.

Presidential Politics Every four years, in the dead of winter, tens of thousands of Iowans troop to caucuses in nearly 2,000 precincts to begin the formal process of electing a president. The caucuses were scheduled early in the 1972 cycle by liberal Democrats who wanted more leverage for their views, and that year they started George McGovern on his way to the Democratic nomination. But the caucuses have had other, unanticipated consequences. In 1976, Jimmy Carter's chief strategist, Hamilton Jordan, determined that intensive campaigning could produce a surprise victory that could make a little-

2012 Presidential Vote		
Barack Obama (D) 822,544	(52%)
Mitt Romney (R).................730,617	(46%)

2012 Presidential Caucus		
Rick Santorum (R) 29,839	(25%)
Mitt Romney (R)...................29,805	(25%)
Ron Paul (R) 26,036	(21%)
Newt Gingrich (R)................16,163	(13%)
Rick Perry (R)......................12,557	(10%)

2008 Presidential Vote		
Barack Obama (D) 828,940	(54%)
John McCain (R).................682,379	(44%)

known candidate a national contender. About 50,000 Iowa Democrats caucused and Carter got the boost Jordan anticipated, finishing second to an "uncommitted" slate but winning more votes than any other actual candidate, almost 28 percent. With momentum from Iowa, Carter won the subsequent New Hampshire primary and was on his way. Without Iowa, the former Georgia governor may well not have become president.

Over the next 20 years, the Iowa caucuses were less influential, but they almost always drew a crowd of White House hopefuls. In 1980, George H.W. Bush's intensive campaigning gave him a victory among Republicans and the "Big Mo," while Carter, profiting from incumbency and connections he made in the state four years earlier, trounced Edward Kennedy on the Democratic side. But Bush lost the nomination to Ronald Reagan, and Carter lost in November to Reagan. In 1984, Democratic favorite Walter Mondale won 49% of the "delegate equivalents" (Democrats don't tally the actual votes cast at a caucus and instead compute a projected number of state and national convention delegates each candidate would be entitled to), but the momentum went to the 17% second-place finisher Gary Hart, though Mondale did win the nomination. In 1988, Iowa failed to pick the winners on either side. Dick Gephardt capitalized on Iowa's economic woes to win among Democrats; Republicans voted for Kansas' Bob Dole and televangelist Pat Robertson—a sign of the strength of Christian conservatives in the party—ahead of George H.W. Bush, the eventual nominee. Gephardt and Dole lost in New Hampshire and neither was nominated. In 1992 Iowa went dark. No Democrat challenged Iowa's Tom Harkin and Pat Buchanan began his campaign against Bush in New Hampshire. In 1996, Dole had the support of leading Republicans, led by GOP

Gov. Terry Branstad and Sen. Charles Grassley, and farm-state roots as well. Dole's very narrow victory was an omen of the weakness of his candidacy. Democrats, happy with Bill Clinton in the White House, did not hold a presidential caucus.

In 2000, the Iowa caucuses became decisive again for both parties, and remained so for Democrats in 2004 and 2008. Heading to 2000, George W. Bush won the 25,000-strong August 1999 Republican straw poll at Ames, after which Dan Quayle, Lamar Alexander and Elizabeth Dole dropped out, unable to win over enough GOP donors who flocked to Bush. John McCain avoided that embarrassment by skipping the straw poll and the caucuses and staked his candidacy on winning the New Hampshire primary. Bush continued to build his organizational strength and won the straw poll with 41% of the vote to Steve Forbes' 31%. Alan Keyes was third with 14%. On the Democratic side, the race was between Al Gore and Bill Bradley. In his 1988 campaign, Gore had skipped what he called the "madness" in "the small state of Iowa," but a decade later, he was proclaiming, "I love Iowa." With the help of Iowa's labor unions, Gore won in "delegate strength" with 63% to Bradley's 37%. That gave Gore momentum in New Hampshire, which he won eight days later, although by only 50%-46%. With five weeks to the next Democratic contest, Bradley dropped out, and Gore became the nominee.

Iowa was critical in 2004, as well. With George W. Bush unopposed for re-nomination, this was the Democrats' show. The leader in Iowa polls in late 2003 and early 2004 was Howard Dean. His opposition to the war in Iraq was popular among the overwhelmingly dovish caucus-goers. His thousands of out-of-state volunteers built the best turnout organization. But as the year opened, Democrats suddenly confronted the possibility that they could actually defeat Bush. The question for many became not who could most stridently criticize the president and his policies, but who could defeat him. Dean's comment that the Dec. 13 capture of Iraqi Leader Saddam Hussein "has not made America safer" raised doubts about his electability. His irritated out-shouting of a 68-year-old Republican questioner in Oelwein on Jan. 11 was seen as a breach of Iowa manners. His poll numbers fell. Gephardt, supported by labor unions and veterans of his campaign 16 years earlier, failed to gather new adherents. John Edwards, endorsed by the *Des Moines Register*, had only a few chipper out-of-staters organizing things. John Kerry, who mortgaged his Boston house for $6.4 million and put all of his effort into Iowa, had the superior organization, the endorsement of Christie Vilsack, the wife of the technically neutral Democratic Gov. Tom Vilsack, and a strong message. Joined in Iowa by a Green Beret he had rescued in the waters of Vietnam, Kerry proclaimed that he could stand up to Bush on Iraq. On caucus night, Dean's 3,500 orange-stocking-capped volunteers were swarming in the streets of Des Moines, but Kerry got the votes. The final results in "delegate equivalents" were Kerry 37%, Edwards 33%, Dean 17%, and Gephardt 11%. Gephardt soon left the race. Dean was effectively finished even before he emitted his famous scream that night. Kerry clinched the nomination six weeks and one day later. But it was Iowa Democrats—some 122,000 of them—who gave him his head start.

In 2008, both parties had candidates competing in the Iowa caucuses, but the Democratic contest was more vigorous. By the end of the year, Democratic candidates had at least 500 paid staffers in Iowa, while Republicans had fewer than 100. John Edwards had never really stopped visiting Iowa after the 2004 campaign and by November 2007, he had made appearances in all 99 counties. Barack Obama, taking advantage of the propinquity of his home in Chicago, was often in the state. Joe Biden and Christopher Dodd took time off from their duties as chairmen of the Senate Foreign Relations and Banking committees, respectively, to campaign frequently in the state. And in November, Dodd moved his family to Iowa and enrolled his daughter in a Des Moines kindergarten. Hillary Clinton visited less often, and in the spring, a staffer's memo that recommended she skip Iowa leaked to the press. She led in initial polls, but her vote for the 2002 Iraq war resolution and her refusal to apologize for it (as Edwards had in 2005) hurt her with dovish Iowa Democrats. But in the fall, she stepped up her Iowa campaign. The chief event of the Democratic race was the Jefferson-Jackson Day Dinner on Nov. 10. All of the candidates had fans in the crowd, but the highlight was an electrifying speech by Obama. His campaign shrewdly distributed tapes of the almost entirely white crowd cheering their candidate to African-American Democrats in South Carolina and other states.

Republican candidates attracted less attention. Mitt Romney outspent all the other Republicans combined and had many more staffers in the state. He started running television ads in the spring and leapt to a lead in the polls. But Mike Huckabee built a network made up largely of evangelical Christians and home-schooling parents, and on the stump, the former Baptist minister displayed an appealing sense of humor and a folksy manner. At the Ames straw poll in August 2007, Romney finished first and Huckabee an impressive second. But turnout was only 14,300. Fred Thompson trailed. Rudy Giuliani and John McCain, with unpopular positions on abortion and immigration, respectively, did not show up.

About 239,000 people participated in the Democratic caucuses, nearly double the record set in 2004. Obama won 38% of "delegate strength," a clear lead. He had big leads in the counties with universities: Johnson (Iowa City), Story (Ames), Polk (Des Moines), Linn (Cedar Rapids), and Scott (Davenport). He won especially large margins among independents, liberals, unmarried voters and affluent voters. Edwards, carrying mainly small, rural counties, finished second with 30% "delegate strength," just ahead of Clinton, with 29%. She carried western Iowa, the most conservative part of the state, but did not roll up big numbers in industrial counties as Gore had done in 2000. The 15% threshold essentially eliminated the rest of the field from the race: Bill Richardson, Biden, and Dodd.

Obama's victory in a state with a 3% black population was pivotal. Through December 2007, polls showed that he had been splitting the black vote with Clinton in South Carolina and in other states. After Iowa, his support from black voters skyrocketed. Had Clinton won, she might have clinched the nomination on or before Super Tuesday. Her victory in the New Hampshire primary five days later was the beginning of a long, close race. In retrospect, it's hard to see how Obama could have become president without winning the Iowa caucuses.

The result on the Republican side was important. Caucus turnout was 119,000, about half the level of the Democrats. Three out of five caucus attendees told entrance poll-takers that they were evangelical or born-again Christians; and nearly half of them voted for Huckabee, who won with 34% of the vote. Romney, for all his campaigning and spending, finished second with 25%. Trailing were Thompson (13%), McCain (13%), Ron Paul (10%) and Giuliani (4%). Romney carried the eastern and western ends of the state and Huckabee won pretty much everything in between, including vote-rich Polk County (Des Moines). But in the primaries to come, Huckabee was unable to expand his appeal much beyond evangelical and born-again Christians, who made up a larger percentage of Iowa caucus-goers than of primary voters in almost any other state. Romney's defeat, after once having been the frontrunner in Iowa, eroded his support in New Hampshire, which enabled McCain to revive his candidacy with a victory there and go on to clinch the GOP nomination on Super Tuesday. The Arizonan was the first Republican presidential nominee to have finished lower than third in Iowa.

In 2012, Obama was running for reelection and only Republicans had a contest. Romney eschewed any extensive campaigning and didn't participate in the Ames straw poll, although he made an appearance at the State Fair shortly beforehand. Tim Pawlenty, from neighboring Minnesota, regarded Iowa as a must-win state and worked to bring voters to the straw poll. But Michele Bachmann, also from Minnesota, attracted support from Tea Party Republicans. Also campaigning hard, and with determined supporters, was libertarian Paul. Bachmann finished first with 29%, and Paul second with 28%. Pawlenty, running third with 14%, withdrew the next morning. Little noticed was the fourth-place finish, with 10%, of Rick Santorum, the only candidate to make appearances in all 99 counties.

In the final weeks before the caucuses, Romney stepped up his efforts in the state. Turnout was 121,000, just a bit higher than in 2008. Romney and Santorum both won 25% of the votes and Paul, 21%. Bachmann finished sixth, with only 6,046 votes, not much more than the 4,823 she had won at the straw poll, and she dropped out of the race the next day. But there was ambiguity about who actually won. The counting is done by the Iowa GOP, not state officials, and initial reports showed Romney ahead of Santorum by a handful of votes; counting continued and 16 days later, Santorum was announced the winner by 34 votes, but results from eight precincts were missing.

In 2000 and 2004, Iowa was one of the closest states in presidential elections. It was one of only three that switched between the two elections, giving Gore a narrow victory in 2000 but voting for Bush in 2004. In 2008 and 2012, it was again a target state, but the results were not so close. The balance of enthusiasm, as demonstrated in caucus turnout, was on Obama's side and he carried Iowa 54%-44%, winning four of the five congressional districts except Republican Steve King's western district. Obama was especially strong in eastern Iowa. He won 61%-36% among young voters. White evangelical Protestants voted 65%-33% for McCain, but Catholics, traditionally Democratic in Iowa, voted 59%-41% for Obama.

In 2012, the race was a bit closer. This time Obama won 52%-46%, but his support was down among young voters and Romney narrowly carried Catholics. White evangelical Protestants voted 64%-35% for Romney, slightly less than for McCain and well below his margin among that group in many other states.

Iowa's caucuses have come under attack, but they have survived efforts in both parties to take away the state's kick-off role in the presidential nominating contests. As David Yepsen, the longtime dean of Iowa political reporters, wrote in September 2008, "Defending the caucuses is a never-ending battle and a never-ending responsibility of political leaders in both parties in Iowa." Prompted by complaints that Iowa and New Hampshire lack racial diversity, Democrats staged a second early caucus in Nevada and, after the New Hampshire primary, a second early primary in South Carolina, which the GOP adopted years ago. After the botched vote count in 2012, some Republicans talked of dumping Iowa, but to no avail. To help fend off that criticism, the 16-member central committee of the Iowa Republican Party voted unanimously in June 2015 to cancel its straw poll, which began in 1979.

Congressional Districts Iowa's congressional district lines are drawn by the nonpartisan Legislative Services Bureau and then approved by the governor and legislature. But it is not entirely apolitical. The bureau is not supposed to take past voting patterns or a legislator's place of residence into account,

114th Congress Lineup	
3 R	1 D
113th Congress Lineup	
2 R	2 D

and in good Iowa fashion they don't. But the governor and legislators can and do. The plan approved in 2001 produced more strenuous competition, at least in non-presidential years, than has been seen in most states.

Iowa lost a House seat in the reapportionment following the 2010 census. The Legislative Services Bureau's plan announced in March 2011 placed two sets of incumbents—Republicans Tom Latham and Steve King, and Democrats Bruce Braley and Dave Loebsack—in the same district. The plan was nevertheless approved by near-unanimous votes in the Democratic Senate and Republican House and by Republican Gov. Terry Branstad. Loebsack moved a few miles into another district, and Latham moved 40 miles from Ames to Clive and defeated Democratic incumbent Leonard Boswell in the 3rd district. In 2014, three of the four districts were competitive, including two open seats. The winners were held to 53 percent of the vote or less. Although additional factors help to account for the close races, the redistricting process is key.

Governor

Terry Branstad (R)

Elected 2010, term expires Jan. 2019, 6th term; b. Nov. 17, 1946, Leland; U. of IA, B.A. 1969, Drake U., J.D. 1974; Catholic; married (Chris); 3 children.

Military Career: U.S. Army, 1969-71.

Elected Office: IA House, 1972-78; IA lt. gov., 1978-82; IA gov., 1983-98.

Professional Career: Practicing atty. & farmer, 1974-82; Pres., Des Moines U., 2003-09.

Office: State Capitol, 1007 E. Grand Ave., Des Moines, 50319, 515-281-5211; Website: governor.iowa.gov.

Election Results

2014 general	Terry Branstad (R)	666,023	(59%)
	Jack Hatch (D)	420,778	(37%)
2014 primary	Terry Branstad (R)	129,752	(83%)
	Tom Hoefling (R)	26,299	(17%)

Prior winning percentages: 2010 (53%), 1994 (57%), 1990 (61%), 1986 (52%), 1982 (53%)

Republican Terry Branstad was elected Iowa's governor for the sixth time in 2014 and is on track to become the longest-serving governor in the country's history once he breaks the 21-year record tenure of George Clinton, New York's first governor, in December 2015. Not bad for a guy who, after his first election in 1982, was called "one-term Terry" by his skeptics as he grappled with a farm crisis in the state.

Branstad was born on a farm in Northern Iowa. He calls himself "a country kid" who learned hard work through farming and has never claimed to be an intellectual. But he likes to note that he has been running for office, and winning, since the eighth grade. He grew up in a Democratic family but was converted by reading Barry Goldwater's *Conscience of a Conservative*. He was a conservative at the left-leaning University of Iowa in the late 1960s and then spent two years in the Army in the military police. He returned to his Lake Mills farm, started a family, and graduated from law school. Branstad was elected to the state House in 1972, at age 25, and served three terms. In 1978, he was elected Iowa lieutenant governor, winning the primary with conservative support and coasting into office on the ticket with moderate Republican Bob Ray, who had been in office for a decade. In 1982, when Ray retired as governor, Branstad ran and defeated a Democrat who had legally avoided paying state taxes.

Des Moines-based journalist Thomas Fogarty once wrote that Branstad has a "total absence of flashiness in a state where most voters seem to think that bland is beautiful." While Branstad can be stolid and his instincts are certainly conservative, he's demonstrated a willingness to set ideology aside in governing. During his first terms as governor in the 1980s, despite his aversion to taxes and gambling, Branstad increased the state sales tax by one cent in 1983, approved a state lottery in 1985, raised gas taxes in 1989 and went along with legalizing riverboat casinos that same year. In 1985 he declared a state economic emergency that triggered a moratorium on farm foreclosures and he blamed the downturn in the state's farm economy in part on policies of GOP President Ronald Reagan's administration. He signed onto to some activist government initiatives, a groundwater preservation law in 1987 and state regulations for Iowa's feedlots in 1995. In 1992, he approved another penny state sales tax increase, but income taxes were lowered during his tenure.

Branstad retired from office in 1998 and, living on 17 acres in Boone, Iowa, became a consultant and joined a law firm. From 2003 to 2009, he was president of Des Moines University, an osteopathic medical school. But he never completely turned his back on state politics and in 2009, encouraged by some of this long-time allies, Branstad decided to make a comeback. His fifth campaign for governor resembled his earlier efforts in which he focused on jobs and the economy. During his first tour as governor he had notched several victories on social issues, including parental notification for abortion for minors, legalizing home schooling, and a state defense of marriage law, but on the stump, he preferred to focus on pocketbook issues. Before Branstad could take on Democratic incumbent Chet Culver, the son of former Sen. John Culver who was struggling with budget woes exacerbated by the recession, he had to dispatch Sioux City business consultant Bob Vander Plaats. The 2006 Republican nominee for lieutenant governor, Vander Platts was the darling of Iowa's conservative evangelicals in the GOP primary. Branstad substantially outspent his opponent and had wide support across the state. He went on a charm offensive, deploying his gift for remembering names and faces, and won the primary 50%-41%. He declined to name Vander Plaats as his running mate, as 2006 GOP gubernatorial nominee Jim Nussle had, and Vander Plaats refused to endorse Branstad. The nominee's choice for lieutenant governor, state Sen. Kim Reynolds, was approved by just 56% of the delegates at the GOP state convention over the opposition of Vander Plaats and his conservative supporters. Branstad raised more money than Culver and attacked the incumbent for using federal economic stimulus dollars to increase spending. The Republican pledged to join other states in lawsuits challenging the constitutionality of the national Democrats' health care law, and he voiced support for Arizona's law letting police check the immigration status of people stopped for other reasons. Culver responded by pointing to Branstad's record of raising taxes after promising not to. The election wasn't close. Branstad beat Culver 53%-43%, carrying 90 of 99 counties. It was the first time an Iowa governor had been defeated for reelection since 1962. Republicans made significant gains in the state legislature, winning a solid majority in the House and falling just short of a majority in the Senate. And as Branstad had urged, voters denied three of the seven members of the Supreme Court new terms, two by margins of 54%-46%, and one, 55%-45%, signaling disapproval of the court's same-sex marriage ruling.

Like other Republican governors, Branstad debated joining the new state exchanges established by the 2010 Affordable Care Act. He ultimately decided to partner with the federal government in lieu of the state running its own exchange system or the federal government running it entirely. He initially rejected the ACA's offer to states to expand state Medicaid programs, fearing the federal government wouldn't come through with the necessary funding to include coverage for childless adults. But Branstad changed his mind and the state legislature passed a compromise using federal expansion dollars to pay for managed-care policies that the working poor would buy from the federal exchange. At the end of 2013, Iowa received federal waivers to use Medicaid funds as premium assistance. Branstad signed on to the 2011 legal challenge to the ACA that the Supreme Court ultimately rejected. However, he declined to join other Republican governors who filed amicus briefs in the *King v. Burwell* lawsuit seeking to deny public subsidies for health insurance purchased on the federal exchange. As state surpluses grew with an improving economy, Branstad and the legislature were able to agree in 2013 on a compromise for sweeping reductions in residential, business and agricultural property taxes—a $4 billion cut over 10 years. It was the largest tax reduction in the state's history. But Branstad's goals for personal and corporate tax reductions were more elusive, in part because of his sometime rocky relations with state lawmakers. He drew criticism for vetoing the legislature's decision in 2012 to spend $500,000 to help the state's food banks, saying private donations were a better source. He eliminated a provision in a 2011 bill that required the state to spend money to keep unemployment offices open. The Iowa Supreme Court subsequently ruled that his move was unconstitutional. And Branstad wasn't reluctant to chastise his party's 2012 presidential nominee, Mitt Romney, who opposed extending the wind energy tax credit—an initiative supported by the Obama administration. Branstad referred to the Romney team as "a bunch of East Coast people that need to get out here in the real world to find out what's really going on." What was going on in Iowa is that wind energy was providing jobs. By 2014, some 6,000 people were employed in the state's wind energy industry, according to the American Wind Energy Association.

Branstad's 2014 reelection campaign was not much of battle with veteran Democratic legislator Jack Hatch, the assistant majority leader in the Iowa state Senate. Branstad was able to brush off some minor personnel scandals, including the firing of state officials, some of whom were paid settlements not to discuss their dismissals. Although his job approval ratings had dipped since he began his fifth term, they were still positive and a majority of Iowans felt the state was heading in the right direction. Branstad cruised to a 59%-37% victory and carried every county in the state except for Johnson, home to the University of Iowa. Branstad began what is likely to be his final term as governor with relatively modest goals and focused on increasing state transportation funding. He worked with Democrats in the legislature and in February 2015 signed a bipartisan agreement that raised gasoline and diesel taxes 10 cents a gallon to help fund a $700 million state road maintenance and highway construction program. The legislature also agreed to a rural broadband expansion plan that Branstad had pushed and approved a status quo budget. Asked about his limited agenda at the outset of 2015, Branstad told the annual Associated Press Iowa legislative seminar, "I would rather under-promise and over-deliver." Maybe that's how you win six terms in the statehouse.

Senior Senator

Charles Grassley (R)

Elected 1980, term expires 2016, 6th term; b. Sept. 17, 1933, New Hartford; U. of N. IA, B.A. 1955, M.A. 1956; Baptist; married (Barbara); 5 children.

Elected Office: IA House, 1959-74; U.S. House, 1975-81.

Professional Career: Farmer; Sheet metal shearer, 1959-61; Assembly line worker, 1961-71.

DC Office: 135 HSOB, 20510, 202-224-3744; Fax: 202-224-6020; Website: grassley.senate.gov.

State Offices: Des Moines, 515-288-1145.

Committees: *Agriculture, Nutrition & Forestry:* Commodities, Risk Mgmt. & Trade; Conservation, Forestry, & Natural Resources; Livestock, Marketing, & Ag Security. *Budget. Finance:* Energy, Natural Resources & Infrastructure; Health Care; Int'l Trade, Customs & Global Competitiveness. *Judiciary* (Chmn): Antitrust, Competition Policy & Consumer Rights; Immigration & the National Interest; Oversight, Agency Action, Federal Rights & Federal Courts. *Joint Committee on Taxation.*

Group Ratings

	ADA	ACLU	AFL-CIO	LCV	ITI	COC	HAFA	ACU	CFG	FRC
2014	5%	6%	–	0%	33%	88%	73%	92%	91%	93%
2013	0%	C	11%	23%	C	75%	C	88%	86%	C

National Journal Ratings

	2013 LIB	—	2013 CONS
Economic	10%	—	87%
Social	0%	—	92%
Foreign	18%	—	80%
Composite	12%	—	89%

Key Votes of the 113th Congress

1. Sandy storm spending	N	5. Student Loan Rates	Y	9. Bipartisan Budget Deal	N
2. Chuck Hagel Confirmation	N	6. Employee Non-Discrim'n Act	N	10. Farm Bill Conference Rept.	N
3. Gun Background Checks	N	7. Senate Vote on Judgeships	Y	11. Unempl. Comp. Extension	N
4. Immigration Reform	N	8. Defense Dept. Spending	N	12. Keystone Pipeline	Y

Election Results

2010 general	Charles Grassley (R)................ 718,215	(64%)	$7,797,516	$192,763	$21,768
	Roxanne Conlin (D) 371,686	(33%)	$3,123,307	$94,098	
	John Heiderscheit (Lib) 25,290	(2%)			
2010 primary	Charles Grassley (R)............unopposed				

Prior winning percentages: 2004 (70%), 1998 (68%), 1992 (70%), 1986 (66%), 1980 (54%); House: 1978 (75%), 1976 (57%), 1974 (51%)

Republican Chuck Grassley, Iowa's senior senator, self-effacingly describes himself as "just a farmer from Butler County," and still climbs aboard his tractor to till land on his family-owned farm. In fact, Grassley has spent a lot more of his career brokering legislative deals and barking at recalcitrant committee witnesses than busting sod: His tenure in elected office goes back almost six decades, including more than 40 years in Congress and stints as chairman of two powerful Senate committees. His time on the tractor on weekends and during congressional recesses is often punctuated by legislative business, courtesy of a cell-phone he keeps tucked under his cap. Nonetheless, Grassley's "aw shucks" charm—along with a reputation for accessibility and straight talk—has made him Iowa's most popular politician. A fellow Iowa politician, former Democratic Rep. Bruce Braley, learned this lesson the hard way in 2014. Seeking the state's other Senate seat, Braley—alluding to the prospect of Grassley chairing the Judiciary Committee if the Republicans regained the Senate majority—dismissed Grassley as "a farmer from Iowa who never went to law school." It turned into a highly damaging political gaffe that contributed to Braley's loss to Republican Joni Ernst.

"I commune with Iowans on a regular basis, and I think they know that. They appreciate it, and they don't feel like Washington has gone to my head. I suppose if I don't get smug and overconfident, I'll be reelected," Grassley observed in 2004, shortly before winning a fifth Senate term with 70 percent of the vote. Grassley has held meetings in each of Iowa's 99 counties every year he has been in the Senate, and has complemented this by becoming a regular user of Twitter at age 80-plus. Although he is now the Senate's second oldest member (California Democrat Dianne Feinstein is just three months his senior), Grassley—as of mid-2015—was giving every indication that he planned to seek a seventh term in 2016, when he will be 83. Unless he has a change of heart, few in either Washington or Iowa are betting that he won't be back for another six years: In his prior reelection bids, he has regularly won by margins at or exceeding 2-1.

As his popularity has climbed at home, perceptions of Grassley on Capitol Hill have evolved significantly since his arrival in the Senate in 1980. His election that year was facilitated by the Reagan presidential landslide, which brought a wave of reliable, often hardline conservatives into that chamber. But virtually all of the Senate Republican class of 1980 was gone within a term or two, with several retired involuntarily by an electorate inevitably swinging back toward the political center. Grassley is the one of that group who has not only survived, but thrived. He has transcended an initial image as a one-dimensional conservative, and has been seen increasingly over the years as a dogged overseer of federal agencies and a hero to government whistleblowers, as well as an independent-minded deal-maker.

Grassley grew up on a farm in Butler County in northeastern Iowa. His parents were Democrats who switched to the Republican Party when Franklin Roosevelt ran for a third term in 1940. Grassley received his bachelor's degree from the University of Northern Iowa, and while still in graduate school, ran for the Iowa House in 1956, losing by only 70-some votes. Two years later, he ran again and was elected at age 25. While in the state legislature, he worked as a sheet metal shearer and on an assembly line to make ends meet. He won an open U.S. House seat in 1974, the hugely successful post-Watergate year for the Democrats: Grassley squeaked in with 51 percent of the vote. Six years later, Grassley garnered 54 percent of the vote in ousting Democratic Sen. John Culver, who had come under fire from religious conservatives. Culver, a classmate of the late Massachusetts Sen. Edward Kennedy at Harvard, was among the group of influential liberals—notably George McGovern of South Dakota, Birch Bayh of Indiana, and Frank Church of Idaho—who dominated the Senate during the 1960s and 1970s, but were swept out of office in the 1980 election.

Grassley was, and remains, a committed fiscal conservative; he was among just eight senators to oppose the 2013 tax and spending deal aimed at averting the so-called fiscal cliff because, he declared, "Washington has a spending problem, not a taxing problem, and this deal doesn't do anything about the spending problem." He also is a steady conservative on social issues: He opposes abortion and most gun control initiatives. In 2013, he voted to block a compromise measure to expand background checks for gun owners in the wake of the mass shooting at a Connecticut elementary school, in which 26 were killed. Grassley voted against the confirmation of President Barack Obama's two nominees to the Supreme Court, Sonia Sotomayor and Elena Kagan—marking the first time he had opposed high court nominees. He singled out Sotomayor's views on gun rights as well as property rights. In 2015, Grassley sought support to block federal funding for the so-called Common Core, a set of math and English language standards adopted by most states—but a subject of intense controversy among GOP conservatives.

But Grassley is also a populist in the Midwestern agrarian tradition, suspicious of concentrations of both public and private power. He has made oversight of bloated, indifferent, or corrupt government agencies a focal point of his Senate career, conducting intensive oversight of the FBI, the Homeland Security Department, the Centers for Medicare and Medicaid Services, and the Food and Drug Administration. In the mid-1980s, Grassley's first major legislative achievement was passage of the Federal False Claims Act, which authorized lawsuits for fraud on behalf of the government; he says it has since returned more than $17 billion to the federal treasury. More recently, in early 2015, Grassley chaired a hearing at which he sharply criticized the Justice Department over its administration of civil asset forfeiture laws, a position that put him in league with the American Civil Liberties Union. Grassley complained that these forfeiture statutes, as now written, have created a "perverse incentive" for police to seize and sell property without clear evidence that a crime has been committed.

To the chagrin of his party, Grassley also has taken on well-heeled political contributors, as many a pharmaceutical executive can attest. Throughout the George W. Bush presidency, he repeatedly went after FDA officials whom he thought were too cozy with the industries they were supposed to regulate. Grassley also has shown an inclination to challenge Wall Street. He attacked the Securities and Exchange Commission in 2011 for failing to detail how it handled nearly 20 referrals of suspicious trading at a major hedge fund. A year earlier, he was one of only four Republicans who voted for the Senate version of the Dodd-Frank bill overhauling regulation of the nation's financial markets, although he voted against the final version of the legislation that cleared Congress. The same year, he was the only Republican to vote with Democrats on the Senate Agriculture Committee for sweeping reform of the derivatives market. He did, however, support the government rescue of the financial industry during the final months of the Bush administration in 2008, a vote for which he faced criticism from Iowa conservatives.

Grassley took the helm of the Judiciary Committee in 2015, after serving as the committee's ranking Republican during the prior two Congresses while the Democrats controlled the Senate majority. Early in Obama's second term, before becoming chairman, Grassley exhibited his partisan side: He came under sharp criticism from Democrats and others for seeking to block votes on many of the president's federal judgeship nominees. At the same time, Grassley has long enjoyed a good relationship with Vermont's Patrick

Leahy, the panel's top Democrat. "When he's wanted to open an investigation during the time I've been chairman, I just say, 'Fine'," Leahy once said. "He has that kind of credibility."

Grassley and Leahy have worked together on such matters as satellite television access, cellphone unlocking legislation and patent reform. In April 2015, Grassley and Leahy unveiled legislation, co-sponsored by a bipartisan group of five other Judiciary Committee members, addressing the perennial legislative issue of how best to address abuses in the current patent system. Immigration policy also is within the purview of the Judiciary panel, and Grassley has been among the Senate's sharpest critics of the so-called H-1B visa program, which enables the U.S. technology industry to bring in highly skilled labor from overseas. On the committee, Grassley has teamed up with a leading Senate Democrat, Minority Whip Dick Durbin of Illinois, to seek to curb the program—which Grassley contends is being used to replace U.S. workers and reduce wages.

Previously, Grassley also enjoyed a warm relationship with then-Montana Democratic Sen. Max Baucus when the two men took turns chairing the powerful Finance Committee. Grassley was chairman in the first half of 2001 and from 2003 to the end of 2006. When Democrats took control of the Senate following the 2006 election, Baucus became chairman and Grassley the panel's ranking Republican until 2010. Grassley held weekly meetings and worked closely with Baucus, often to the dismay of conservative Republicans who thought Grassley was too accommodating. But their relationship was crucial to several successful initiatives during the early part of the George W. Bush presidency. Baucus helped Grassley to round up bipartisan support for Bush's income tax cuts early on, and later supported the Republican-sponsored Medicare prescription drug program legislation that Grassley was a leader in crafting. By the same token, when Obama became president in 2009 and proposed his signature bill to bring more people into the health insurance market, Grassley was one of the Senate negotiators trying to broker a deal, despite pressure from within his party. In the end, Grassley voted against the legislation, complaining it would cut funding for Medicare and would neither hold down taxes nor contain health care costs.

With his populist bent, Grassley has long pursued "fairness" in the tax code. At one point, he convinced the Finance Committee to tighten the rules on partial gifts of art, which allowed donors to retain possession while receiving tax deductions. Snapped Grassley: "Call it what it is, a subsidy for millionaires to buy art. Where I come from, the word 'giving' doesn't mean 'keeping.'" Amid talk that Congress might take up a major overhaul of the tax code, Grassley publicly mused about trying to reclaim the chairmanship of the Finance panel when it appeared the Republicans were poised to retake the Senate majority following the 2014 election. Under internal party rules, Grassley was compelled to step down as ranking member of the Finance Committee at the end of 2010, prompting him to move to the top slot at the Judiciary panel. However, those same rules made him eligible for one last two-year term as chairman of Finance. But trying to reclaim that post would have likely have created a messy battle within the Republican ranks against Utah Sen. Orrin Hatch, who had taken over as ranking member of Finance in 2010 from Grassley and was eagerly eyeing the chairmanship. Grassley sidestepped the fight by opting to chair the Judiciary Committee, making him the first non-lawyer ever to head that panel.

Protection of government whistleblowers also has been a continuing legislative passion for Grassley. "Whistleblowers are often treated like skunks at a picnic. It takes guts to put your career on the line to expose waste and fraud, and whistleblowers need senators who will listen and advocate for them," Grassley declared in 2014 in announcing creation of the Senate Whistleblower Protection Caucus. The announcement came on the 25th anniversary of passage of the 1989 Whistleblower Protection Act—which he co-authored. He also helped pass, in late 2012, an update of the whistleblower law that, among other things, created ombudsmen to educate federal agency managers about whistleblower rights.

Former FBI agent Jane Turner said the senator has led many frustrated federal workers to turn to his office instead of the media. One whistleblower, John Dodson, worked with Grassley's staff in exposing the "Operation Fast and Furious" scandal at the Bureau of Alcohol, Tobacco and Firearms, in which the agency lost track of hundreds of firearms sold to straw purchasers for Mexican drug cartels. Turner worked with Grassley on controversies such as bureau staffers' thefts of artifacts from Ground Zero after the 9/11 attacks. "Without Grassley, you would have tenfold more [Edward] Snowdens [and] Wikileaks, because he's the only true hope that whistleblowers have," Turner told the *Des Moines Register*. However, Grassley has kept his distance—rhetorically and otherwise—from Snowden, whose disclosures of National Security Agency telephone and data mining programs data have made him the most visible government whistleblower of recent times. In the wake of that episode, Grassley told *The Hill* that Snowden "surely isn't a hero" and should be prosecuted for what many intelligence experts characterized as one of the most serious information leaks in U.S. history.

In his career as a part-time farmer, Grassley took an 80-acre farm in New Hartford, Iowa that he inherited in 1960 and added to it over the years; it is now a 710-acre concern producing corn and soybeans that is managed by Grassley's son. In his career as a full-time legislator, Grassley has exhibited his populist skepticism in debates over farm subsidies. He has consistently argued that high payments to individual farmers put the entire agriculture program in political jeopardy, and added an amendment to a 2012 Senate version of the farm bill that would cap payments to farmers along with closing loopholes allowing non-farmers to qualify for payments. When the House and Senate were working on a compromise farm bill a year later, Grassley, writing in an op-ed in *Politico*, declared: "It seems some members want to reduce food stamps while reopening loopholes for multi-million-dollar farming entities. There's bipartisan agreement that the food-stamp program needs reform, but how can we save money in one program and at the same time turn a blind eye to the loopholes that millionaires exploit?"

Grassley utilized his perch at the Finance Committee to look out for the interests of fellow farmers in particular and his home state in general. Corn-based ethanol is an important product of Iowa's agribusiness, and Grassley has used his influence to win advantageous tax treatment of ethanol. He has also sought tax incentives for biodiesel, made with soybean oil or recycled cooking oil. The United States is a major exporter of agricultural products, and Grassley has been a consistent supporter of free trade agreements. On another issue important to his state, Grassley in 2012 publicly tangled with GOP presidential candidate Mitt Romney over tax credits for wind energy production; he called Romney's opposition "a knife in my back."

Grassley cited the interests of his home state, when, in September 2013, he announced plans to seek reelection in 2016, Noting the impending retirement of his veteran Democratic colleague, Tom Harkin, he told reporters that "if Iowa had to start over two years from now with two very junior senators, it would hurt Iowans' opportunities to get anything done in the Senate." As of mid-2015, he was actively raising money for a campaign, his approval ratings stood at 67 percent in an independent poll, and no top-tier Democratic challengers had emerged. As for his age—if reelected, he would be 89 when his next term ended—Grassley told the *Associated Press*, "I think that age isn't a factor or I wouldn't be running for office—or I wouldn't be running this morning." It was a reference to his regular jogging sessions; he runs three miles four times a week.

As he again prepares to face Iowa voters, Twitter has given Grassley a national following, and over 87,000 followers. He posts his own updates on the social media platform from his iPhone and is known for his typos, misspellings, and abbreviations. Ever direct—online as well as in person—Grassley takes regular aim at Obama, once calling the president "stupid" (which led Obama senior adviser David Axelrod to tweet back, "I think a 6-year-old hijacked your account and is sending out foolish Tweets just to embarrass you!"). One of his best-known offerings came in October 2012 after he struck a deer with a car and reported to his followers: "Assume deer dead." It was retweeted more than 2,300 times, and a parody account on the animal's behalf was launched.

Junior Senator

Joni Ernst (R)

Elected 2014, term expires Jan. 2021, 1st term; b. July 1, 1970, Red Oak; IA St. U., B.A. 1992, Columbus St. U., M.P.A. 1995; Lutheran; married (Gail); 1 child.

Military Career: U.S. Army Reserves, 1993-2001; IA National Guard, 2001-present.

Elected Office: IA Senate, 2011-14.

Professional Career: Auditor, Montgomery Cnty. IA, 2005-11.

DC Office: 111 RSOB, 20510, 202-224-3254; Fax: 202-224-9369; Website: ernst.senate.gov.

State Offices: Cedar Rapids, 319-365-4504; Council Bluffs, 712-352-1167; Davenport, 563-322-0677, Des Moines, 515-284-4574; Sioux City, 712-252-1550.

Committees: *Agriculture, Nutrition & Forestry:* Livestock, Marketing, & Ag Security; Nutrition, Specialty Crops, & Ag Research; Rural Development & Energy (Chmn). *Armed Services:* Airland; Emerging Threats & Capabilities; Readiness & Mgmt. Support. *Homeland Security & Gov't Affairs:* Federal Spending Oversight & Emergency Mgmt.; Regulatory Affairs & Federal Mgmt. *Small Business & Entrepreneurship.*

Election Results

2014 general	Joni Ernst (R).......................... 588,575	(52%)	$11,913,212	$12,247,026	$25,196,618
	Bruce Braley (D)..................... 494,370	(44%)	$12,068,095	$4,225,010	$18,841,528
	Douglas Butzier (Lib) 26,815	(2%)			
2014 primary	Joni Ernst (R).......................... 88,535	(56%)			
	Sam Clovis (R) 28,418	(18%)			
	Mark Jacobs (R) 26,523	(17%)			
	Matt Whitaker (R) 11,884	(8%)			

When veteran Sen. Tom Harkin announced his retirement from the Senate in early 2013, his fellow Democrats felt good about their chances for holding the seat—notwithstanding the storm clouds gathering over the party's national prospects in the 2014 election. Four-term Democratic Rep. Bruce Braley quickly announced his candidacy to succeed Harkin, while the Republicans struggled for months as several top-tier contenders declined to step up. Consequently, it ranked as one of the one of the biggest—if not the biggest—upset of the election cycle when Republican state Sen. Joni Ernst ended up defeating Braley to become the state's new junior senator, as well as the first woman ever to represent Iowa in Congress. Ernst's folksy manner on the campaign trail—she highlighted her family's roots in farming, most memorably in a TV that mentioned her experience castrating hogs—helped her prevail amid a fusillade of Democratic attacks on several hard-line conservative positions she had taken. But, even in a swing state that had twice voted for Barack Obama, Democrats were unable to overcome the political damage done by Braley's gaffe-prone candidacy, which several political publications and handicappers later anointed as the worst campaign of 2014.

Born and raised on a farm in Montgomery County (pop. 10,740) in southwest Iowa, Ernst won scholarships to attend Iowa State University, where she majored in psychology, while later earning a master's degree in public administration from Georgia's Columbus State University. She joined the National Guard in 1993 and was deployed to Kuwait during Operation Iraqi Freedom a decade later; she highlighted her status as a veteran and her current rank as a lieutenant colonel in the Guard throughout the 2014 campaign, during which national security was high on the list of voter concerns. Ernst was elected Montgomery County auditor in 2004, serving two terms before winning election to the state Senate in 2010.

When a number of better known Republicans wooed by the party strategists—notably then-Rep. Tom Latham—opted against running for Harkin's seat, Ernst became part of a five-way primary. Some establishment Republicans swung behind wealthy businessman Mark Jacobs, after he indicated a willingness to pump several million dollars of his personal fortune into the race. But the "hogs" ad pushed Ernst to front of the pack. "I grew up castrating hogs on an Iowa farm, so when I get to Washington, I'll know how to cut pork.... Washington's full of big spenders, let's make them squeal," she declares in the ad. It was followed by an edgy paid spot showing Ernst, in a black leather jacket, stepping off her Harley-Davidson and firing shots at a shooting-range target as a narrator intones, "Joni Ernst will take aim at wasteful spending, and once she sets her sights on Obamacare, Joni's gonna unload." If the ads caused some controversy, they delivered by painting Ernst as a political outsider, even as she demonstrated an ability to attract support from the party's establishment as well as the tea party wing: Both 2012 presidential nominee Mitt Romney and 2008 vice-presidential candidate Sarah Palin endorsed her. In the June primary, Ernst easily won with 56 percent.

Meanwhile, Braley, a former trial lawyer first elected to the U.S. House in 2006, was beset by a series of self-inflicted wounds. In a radio interview during the federal government shutdown in late 2013, he complained about the impact on the House gym. "There's hardly anybody working down there. There's no towel service, we're doing our own laundry...," he griped. Voter perceptions of aloofness intensified several months later, when a dispute erupted over a neighbor's chickens wandering onto Braley's vacation home property. Braley denied he had threatened to sue the neighbor, but a memo from an attorney for the local community association quotes Braley as hinting at legal action. It didn't sit well in a rural state where folkways dictate that disputes between neighbors are best handled through face-to-face discussion. But Braley's biggest gaffe occurred at a private fundraiser of trial lawyers in Texas, when he was caught on tape deriding the prospect of six-term Sen. Chuck Grassley chairing the Judiciary Committee if the Republicans regained a Senate majority—characterizing Grassley as "a farmer from Iowa who never went to law school, never practiced law." As *Washington Post* politics blogger Chris Cillizza put it: "In the space of two sentences, Braley managed to: (1) insult popular Sen. Chuck Grassley (2) insult farmers and (3) sound as super-arrogant as humanly possible."

Democrats counterattacked by seeking to portray Ernst in the tea party mold of Palin and former Minnesota Rep. Michele Bachmann: Democratic National Committee Chairwoman Debbie Wasserman Schultz called Ernst "an onion of crazy." Braley and Democratic allies hammered away at Ernst's calls to abolish the Education Department and the Environmental Protection Agency, as well as her opposition to federal minimum wage laws and her support for a "personhood" constitutional amendment to ban all abortions. And a recording of an Ernst appearance at a 2012 National Rifle Association rally in Iowa surfaced, during which she boasted of owning "a beautiful little Smith & Wesson, 9 millimeter, and it goes with me virtually everywhere." Ernst continued. "...I believe in the right to defend myself and my family—whether it's from an intruder, or whether it's from the government, should they decide that my rights are no longer important." The comments came shortly after 12 people were killed and 58 others wounded in a shooting rampage in an Aurora Colorado movie theater. Democrats griped about Ernst being the Teflon candidate of 2014.

A star-crossed year for Braley was capped when First Lady Michelle Obama appeared in Iowa on his behalf, only to refer several times to "Bruce Bailey" and erroneously noting that he was a Marine Corps veteran. Ernst pulled in $6 million in the third quarter of the year alone, double what Braley raised during that period. On Election Day, Ernst won easily, 52%-44%.

Republican leaders immediately moved to capitalize on a new female face in their ranks: Less than a month after being sworn in, Ernst was tapped to give the GOP response to Obama's State of the Union address. She delivered a speech that was heavy on personal retrospective; i.e. "...Growing up, I had only one good pair of shoes. So on rainy school days, my mom would slip plastic bread bags over them to keep them dry." One of her first pieces of legislation was to expand mental health services for veterans, even as the left-leaning *Huffington Post* questioned her claim to being the first female combat veteran elected to serve in the Senate—pointing out that she had commanded a transportation company that never came under fire during her service in Iraq. "It was only by luck and the blessings of God that my soldiers did not encounter an assault," Ernst shot back.

But, in the mold of past senators who have arrived on Capitol Hill with a measure of celebrity but strived to demonstrate a seriousness of purpose, Ernst placed her early attention on state and local media and getting around her home state, while avoiding the national cable TV circuit. "There will be plenty of opportunities for that in the future," she told the *Des Moines Register*. "What we really want to do is focus on Iowa." Nonetheless, her desire to be a power broker in the state that selects the first delegates to the quadrennial political conventions was apparent. Early on, she scheduled the first annual "Roast & Ride" fundraising event for the summer prior to the Iowa caucuses—a Republican counterpart to the Harkin Steak Fry hosted by her predecessor, which presidential wannabes long considered a must-show.

FIRST DISTRICT

Rod Blum (R)

Elected 2014, 1st term; b. April 26, 1955, Dubuque; Loras Col., B.A. 1977, U. of Dubuque, M.B.A. 1989; Episcopalian; married (Karen); 5 children.

Professional Career: Boys basketball coach, Dubuque Senior HS; Columnist, Telegraph Herald; Real estate developer; Owner, Digital Canal Software.

DC Office: 213 CHOB, 20515, 202-225-2911; Website: blum.house.gov.

State Offices: Cedar Falls, 319-266-6925; Cedar Rapids, 319-364-2288; Dubuque, 563-557-7789.

Committees: *Budget. Oversight & Gov't Reform:* Information Technology.

Election Results

2014 general	Rod Blum (R)	147,762	(51%)	$1,031,470	$181,857	$1,339,184
	Pat Murphy (D)	141,145	(49%)	$1,416,830	$125,926	$871,463
2014 primary	Rod Blum (R)	16,886	(55%)			
	Steve Rathje (R)	11,420	(37%)			
	Gail Boliver	2,413	(8%)			

Population		Race and Ethnicity		Income	
Total:	766,821	White	90.3%	Median income:	$52,237
Urban:	42.7%	Latino	3.2%		(200 of 435)
Suburban:	9.6%	Black	3.1%	Under $50,000	47.6%
Rural:	47.7%	Asian	1.1%	$50,000-$99,999:	34.2%
Land area:	14,303	Two races	1.7%	$100,000-$199,999:	15.8%
Pop/sq. mi.:	53.6	White Ethnic	24.2%	$200,000 or more:	2.4%
Born in state:	76.5%			Poverty Rate	11.8%
		Education			
Age Groups		H.S. grad or less:	43.6%	**Work**	
Under 18:	23.1%	Some college:	32.6%	White collar:	32.6%
18 to 34:	22.7%	College degree, 4 yr.:	15.9%	Blue collar:	40.9%
35 to 64:	38.1%	Post-grad study:	7.9%	Sales and service:	26.5%
Over 64:	16.1%				
		Military		Govt. workers:	11.8%
		Veterans/active duty:	8.9%		

Northeast Iowa: Cedar Rapids, Waterloo

Northeast Iowa, along the Mississippi River and westward, has some of the loveliest landscape in America. Here the Mississippi flows past green bluffs, then broadens out in great quiet pools alongside picturesque towns. A century and a half ago, as settlers surged west of the Mississippi, Ger-

Voter Turnout	
2013 Total Citizen 18+	574,295
2014 House Turnout	289,306
2014 Turnout as % CVAP	50.4%
2012 Turnout as % CVAP	69.9%

mans stopped at the river bluffs reminiscent of their native land and built neat farmhouses and substantial towns. Inland, on the rolling hills portrayed with surprisingly little exaggeration in the paintings of Iowa's Grant Wood, and in the more open territory to the west, New England Yankees and Midwesterners built their characteristic farmhouses, barns, town halls, church spires, and small colleges. Railroad companies, headquartered in Chicago, extended their networks of steel rails over the plains and rivers. German Catholics settled Dubuque, whose giant Victorian courthouse looks down on the river. In 1996, the city replaced the courthouse's old boiler with a new geothermal heating system.

Dubuque is a self-styled green city that has some large factories but is also proud of its waterfront-generated tourism. *Forbes* magazine in 2010 named Dubuque the best small city in America for families, and the city received All America City awards in 2012 and 2013. Local leaders cite their vision of a "Sustainable Dubuque," which allowed them to transform a rusting city in the 1980s into a successful "Envision 2010" that rejuvenated urban life. Among the long-standing employers is John Deere tractor, which employs 2,500 people and has boosted its output of crawler products (a type of tractor). The company reports that its 1050K Crawler Dozer, which is "the largest, most powerful dozer" that it has ever built, has added hundreds to its Dubuque payroll.

2012 Presidential Vote		
Barack Obama (D) 225,585	(56%)
Mitt Romney (R)................170,753	(42%)

2008 Presidential Vote		
Barack Obama (D) 227,310	(58%)
John McCain (R)................156,980	(40%)

Cook Partisan Voting Index: D+5

Southwest of Dubuque is Cedar Rapids, Iowa's second-largest city. It sports high-tech employers and contemporary office buildings. Unlike most of Iowa, its population boomed in the past decade, and its per capita income rose. Both Cedar Rapids and Waterloo "built an Internet infrastructure in the mid-1990s to draw technology companies to the area," and then nurtured small technology companies, the *Des Moines Register* reported. The production of ethanol and other biofuels in Cedar Rapids contributed to its economic health, although ethanol in recent years has slumped with the decline in demand for gasoline blends and with the expiration of the federal tax credit for ethanol in 2012. Yet traditional industries are still a mainstay: Go down by the river, and you can't miss the smell of cooking oats coming from the Quaker Oats and General Mills factories. Anamosa, in Jones County just east of Cedar Rapids, was the home of Wood, best known for his famous *American Gothic* painting—the models for the two figures were his dentist and Wood's own sister, who died in 1990.

The 1st Congressional District covers much of northeast Iowa, including the Mississippi riverfront and Cedar Rapids, Dubuque, and Waterloo. Politically, this area leans Democratic. Dubuque, heavily German Catholic, was for years Iowa's most Democratic city and still is, unless abortion rights are the issue. Waterloo and nearby Cedar Falls, once Republican, trended Democratic in the 1980s. In the 2012 presidential election, President Barack Obama got 56 percent of the vote and won 17 of 20 counties here, losing only Benton, Delaware, and Iowa counties.

Rod Blum (R)

Republican businessman Rod Blum, elected in 2014 to represent the Democratic-leaning 1st District, scored one of the most surprising upsets that election night. He successfully characterized his opponent as a "career politician" and escaped the Democrats' depiction of him as a "millionaire candidate" by emphasizing his working-class roots.

A Dubuque native, Blum highlighted his background during the campaign. His father quit school in 10th grade to enlist in the Navy during World War II and later worked as a foreman at Dubuque Packing Co., while his mother earned extra income cleaning houses. Blum, one of four children, worked his way through college, earning a finance degree at the local Loras College and later an M.B.A. at the University of Dubuque. He worked in the software business, rising to president and CEO of Eagle Point Software before launching his own company. He was a basketball coach at Dubuque Senior High School and has worked as a real estate developer.

Blum had dipped a toe into politics in the 1990s, serving two years as the Dubuque County GOP chairman. In 2012 he made a brief bid against Democratic Rep. Bruce Braley— who ran unsuccessfully for the Senate in 2014—but lost in the GOP primary. This time around, he relied on a more professional staff and repeatedly declared, "I'm not a career politician." He won a three-way primary with 51 percent of the vote.

His race against former House speaker Pat Murphy, who had spent 25 years in the Legislature, tightened as November neared. Blum advocated lower taxes on businesses, reduced federal spending and repeal of the Affordable Care Act in favor of a free-market approach. He opposed same-sex marriage and supported protection of gun owners' rights. His campaign ran ads featuring footage of "angry career politician" Murphy screaming on the state House floor, followed by a narrator saying that Murphy lied about creating jobs in Iowa. And when Murphy blamed congressional Republicans for the government's handling of Ebola because they had not provided enough funding for the Centers for Disease Control and Prevention, Blum responded: "Spoken like a career politician. We never have enough funding in government."

House Speaker John Boehner appeared in Hiawatha to campaign for Blum, and Blum picked up endorsements from the Dubuque *Telegraph Herald*, for which he previously was a political columnist, and the Cedar Rapids *Gazette*. National Democrats at the end of the race poured $600,000 into an ad campaign. One ad targeted "millionaire Rod Blum," saying he had made a career of putting profits ahead of Iowa workers. But the Republican tide proved too much for Murphy to overcome. "As Braley tanked in the closing weeks to Joni Ernst, he brought Murphy down with him in his own backyard," said David Wasserman of the *Cook Political Report*. Blum was outspent $1.4 million to $1 million, and Murphy had a big advantage with party funds. Blum surprised them all with a victory of 51.1%-48.9%, a margin of 6,617 votes, and took 15 of 20 counties. He narrowly lost the three population centers (Dubuque, Cedar Rapids, Waterloo), but rolled up big margins in the rural areas.

On Blum's first day in office, he was one of 25 House Republicans to oppose Boehner's nomination for speaker, casting his vote instead for Florida GOP Rep. Dan Webster. Although he respected Boehner as "a good man," he said that his vote was a statement on behalf of Iowans to "stand up to the status quo in Washington, D.C." He spent his early months trying to change how Congress works. With Democratic Rep. Beto O'Rourke of Texas, he created the Congressional Term-Limits Caucus, with the hope that frequent turnover would stimulate fresh and innovative thinking. He filed a bill that would impose a lifetime ban on former members of Congress lobbying their ex-colleagues. In analyzing prospects for the proposal, *Vox* approvingly wrote that although "Blum's idea may face long odds at the moment, if he and other reformers keep pressing, its moment may one day come." He was quickly in demand among GOP presidential candidates seeking insight on winning support in the first presidential caucus state. "I always tell them I thought it was my charm and good looks that won and they laugh. I'm kidding obviously," he told the *Wall Street Journal*.

Not surprisingly, Blum became an early Democratic target for 2016. Among the initial contenders were Cedar Rapids councilwoman Monica Vernon, who lost the primary to Murphy in 2014, and Gary Kroeger, who was a performer on "Saturday Night Live" in the mid-1980s and has been working at an advertising agency in Waterloo.

SECOND DISTRICT

Dave Loebsack (D)

Elected 2006, 5th term; b. Dec. 23, 1952, Sioux City; IA St. U., B.S. 1974, M.A. 1976, U. of CA Davis, Ph.D. 1985; Methodist; married (Terry); 4 children.

Professional Career: Prof., Cornell Col., 1982-2006.

DC Office: 1527 LHOB, 20515, 202-225-6576; Fax: 202-226-0757; Website: loebsack.house.gov.

State Offices: Davenport, 563-323-5988; Iowa City, 319-351-0789.

Committees: *Energy & Commerce:* Communications & Technology; Energy & Power.

Group Ratings

	ADA	ACLU	AFL-CIO	LCV	ITI	COC	HAFA	ACU	CFG	FRC
2014	55%	83%	–	86%	60%	64%	8%	4%	17%	0%
2013	70%	C	95%	82%	C	31%	C	8%	4%	C

National Journal Ratings

	2013 LIB —	2013 CONS
Economic	63% —	37%
Social	66% —	32%
Foreign	71% —	27%
Composite	67% —	33%

Key Votes of the 113th Congress

1. Sandy storm spending	Y	5. Medical Marijuana	Y	9. Syrian Rebels Training	Y
2. Violence Against Women Act	Y	6. Farm Bill	Y	10. Keystone pipeline	Y
3. Guantanamo Bay Detainees	Y	7. Afghanistan Combat	Y	11. Immigration Exec. Action	N
4. Abortion 20-week ban	N	8. NSA Phone Data Collection	Y	12. Bipartisan budget deal	Y

Election Results

2014 general	Dave Loebsack (D)..................... 143,431	(53%)	$1,721,736	$90,707	$948,183
	Marianette Miller-Meeks (R) 129,455	(47%)	$940,493	$115,433	$508,442
2014 primary	Dave Loebsack (D)................unopposed				

Prior winning percentages: 2012 (56%), 2010 (51%), 2008 (57%), 2006 (51%)

Population		Race and Ethnicity		Income	
Total:	774,072	White	87.9%	Median income:	$50,855
Urban:	26.4%	Latino	4.8%		*(224 of 435)*
Suburban:	12.9%	Black	3.4%	Under $50,000	49.2%
Rural:	60.7%	Asian	2.0%	$50,000-$99,999:	32.0%
Land area:	13,171	Two races	1.7%	$100,000-$199,999:	15.7%
Pop/sq. mi.:	58.8	White Ethnic	23.3%	$200,000 or more:	3.1%
Born in state:	68.2%			Poverty Rate	13.9%
		Education			
Age Groups		H.S. grad or less:	40.6%	**Work**	
Under 18:	22.8%	Some college:	31.5%	White collar:	34.8%
18 to 34:	23.7%	College degree, 4 yr.:	17.9%	Blue collar:	39.7%
35 to 64:	38.1%	Post-grad study:	10.0%	Sales and service:	25.5%
Over 64:	15.4%				
		Military		Govt. workers:	15.5%
		Veterans/active duty:	9.0%		

Southeast Iowa: Davenport, Iowa City

Southeast Iowa is little-known to outsiders. It is a land of rolling hills and deep river valleys, of undulant farm fields and big skies, of prosperous small towns and grain elevators and factories. Even political writers, who come to Iowa by the thousands for the quadrennial presidential caucuses, tend to

Voter Turnout	
2013 Total Citizen 18+	579,442
2014 House Turnout	273,329
2014 Turnout as % CVAP	47.2%
2012 Turnout as % CVAP	69.0%

hang out in Des Moines and do their reporting there or in the counties within an hour's drive of the city. In the southeastern part of the state, one can find Iowa's contributions to the Quad Cities: Davenport and Bettendorf. The Quad Cities—despite the name, there are actually five cities—sit along the Mississippi River and the Iowa-Illinois border. Davenport, on the hills over the Mississippi, still has the look of the city where Ronald Reagan got his first radio job. Bettendorf is where riverboat gambling was launched in the U.S. in 1991.

West of Davenport is Iowa City, a university town dotted with trendy bookstores and vegetarian eateries. The University of Iowa is known for its Writers' Workshop, which produced the nation's first creative writing degree program and some of its most gifted young authors, including John Irving and Ann Patchett. Iowa City has been ranked among the most gay-friendly cities by various publications. Iowa City resident Zach Wahls cofounded the group Scouts for Equality in 2012 to push the Boy Scouts of America to accept gays. Muscatine County, near the Mississippi River, had the first two towns in Iowa with a Hispanic majority, a legacy of abundant farm work in the area and, more recently, jobs at the Tyson Foods pork processing plant in nearby Columbus Junction. Tyson reports that hundreds of workers who perform grueling jobs at the plant are Burmese refugees. Since a 2008 raid of an Iowa slaughterhouse, where nearly 400 immigrants were arrested, companies report that they have become more careful to hire only employees with legal papers. Employers are eager for workers. In January 2015, Iowa City reported its unemployment rate was 2.8 percent, among the 10 lowest cities in the nation.

The 2nd Congressional District covers the southeast quadrant of the state. Its population centers are Davenport and Iowa City, but it also offers up some offbeat claims to fame. Bentonsport, in Van Buren County

2012 Presidential Vote

Barack Obama (D) 219,946	(56%)
Mitt Romney (R)................168,534	(43%)

2008 Presidential Vote

Barack Obama (D) 219,565	(57%)
John McCain (R)................159,959	(41%)

Cook Partisan Voting Index: D+4

near the Missouri border, is an artists' and craftsmen's colony. Iowa's newest city, incorporated in 2001, is Maharishi Vedic City, in Jefferson County, where followers of the Maharishi Mahesh Yogi built Maharishi University in 1973 and made the town a magnet for believers in transcendental meditation. Politically, the district supports Democrats, thanks in large part to big Democratic majorities in Iowa City and Johnson County. Overall, the 2nd leans Democratic. But, like the rest of the state, its voters don't like to be taken for granted.

Dave Loebsack (D)

Democrat Dave Loebsack, elected in 2006, is a retired college professor who offsets his liberal leanings by seeking out similarly pragmatic Republicans. Stunningly, he has become the only Democrat in the six-member Iowa delegation. He too has had close races.

A native of Sioux City, Loebsack lived as a child in poverty with his mother, grandmother, and three siblings in a two-bedroom house and worked as a high school janitor to pay for college. He got a master's degree at Iowa State University and went on to the University of California, Davis, to earn a Ph.D. in political science. From 1982 until his election to Congress, he was a professor of international relations at Cornell College in Mount Vernon, a few miles from Cedar Rapids. He had been active in local politics for several years, including a stint as fundraising chairman for Linn County Democrats.

When Loebsack decided to challenge 15-term GOP Rep. Jim Leach in 2006, he insisted that his campaign was not an attack on Leach's three decades in Congress but rather on the GOP leadership in Congress; he called the popular Leach, a moderate and cerebral Republican, an "enabler" for his party leaders. The war in Iraq was a pivotal issue then. Leach was the only member of the Iowa delegation to oppose the war, but Loebsack sought to tie him to President George W. Bush's Defense secretary, Donald Rumsfeld, on the basis that Leach had been an aide to Rumsfeld when he was a House member from Illinois in the late 1960s. Leach refused to disparage his former boss, calling him a friend and insisting that Rumsfeld's ouster would not change the administration's policy in Iraq.

Loebsack raised $522,000, which ordinarily would not have been nearly enough for a competitive House race, and he had little support from the Democratic Congressional Campaign Committee. But Leach unwittingly helped Loebsack overcome those obstacles. Leach eschewed modern campaign practices, particularly negative campaigning, and was a notoriously reluctant fundraiser. When the Iowa Republican Party sent out negative mailers targeting Loebsack, Leach told them to stop. He refused to accept contributions from political action committees or from sources outside the district and raised only $491,000. Leach was endorsed by the district's major newspapers, but that wasn't enough. Loebsack won, 51%-49%.

In Washington, Loebsack has had a lower profile than most other members of Iowa's congressional delegation. House Minority Whip Steny Hoyer told the *Iowa City Press-Citizen* that he considered him "one of the more thoughtful members" of Congress. One of his first official actions was to sponsor a measure to name the federal building in Davenport, Iowa, the James A. Leach Federal Building; it passed the House in 2007.

He has compiled a liberal voting record, although he moved slightly to the center on fiscal issues after Republicans regained control of the House in 2011. He has been among the Democrats joining Republicans in calling for the comptroller general to audit the Federal Reserve, and he joined GOP lawmakers in supporting an end to public subsidies of the national party conventions. He joined the Center Aisle Caucus, an informal group of around 40 House members seeking to establish greater civility between the parties, and a subsequent bipartisan group of "Problem Solvers" headed by West Virginia Democratic Sen. Joe Manchin and former Utah GOP Gov. Jon Huntsman. He has sought to retain his outsider status, with proposals to cut salaries for members of Congress and require broader disclosure of their travel.

On the Armed Services Committee, Loebsack added a provision to the 2012 defense authorization bill to have behavioral health specialists embedded with National Guard and Reserve units during training. He drew praise at home for protecting the Rock Island Arsenal from cutbacks. In January 2015, he made an unusual mid-career switch of committee assignments to Energy and Commerce. He said that he hoped to have more impact on job creation and alternative energy development.

Loebsack has faced some competitive campaigns. He won a comfortable reelection, 57%-39%, in 2008 against political neophyte Mariannette Miller-Meeks, a Republican ophthalmologist. Miller-Meeks returned for a rematch in 2010, hoping the national political climate favoring her party would give her a boost. She criticized Loebsack's support for the health care overhaul and called for reforming the tax code. She remained roughly even with Loebsack on fundraising, and some polls showed her ahead in the closing weeks. But his work on behalf of flood-stricken communities in the district helped offset his support of Obama's policies, and he won, 51%-46%.

When redistricting left Loebsack with nearly half of his voters who were new, GOP strategists hoped his professorial style might alienate some rural voters and they put up John Archer, a conservative attorney for farm equipment maker John Deere, an iconic company in Iowa. The National Republican Congressional Committee spent more than $760,000 to boost Archer's chances, but Loebsack spent plenty of time back home—he estimated attending 400 events during the first nine months of 2012—and won handily, 56%-43%. In 2014, he was a national Republican target. His opponent again was Miller-Meeks. She spent $1 million from her own campaign and another million from the NRCC. Loebsack spent $1.7 million, and survived the Iowa Democratic massacre that year, with 52.6% of the vote. His 19,600-vote margin in Johnson County exceeded his 14,000-vote overall lead in the district, which should be a warning signal. Loebsack also took the other relatively urban counties with Davenport, Burlington and Ottumwa, but trailed badly in rural areas.

THIRD DISTRICT

David Young (R)

Elected 2014, 1st term; b. May 11, 1968, Van Meter; Drake U., B.A. 1991; Lutheran; single.

Professional Career: Staff, U.S. Sen. Hank Brown, 1993-96; Staff, U.S. Sen. James Bunning, 1998-2006; Chief of staff, U.S. Sen. Charles Grassley, 2006-13.

DC Office: 515 CHOB, 20515, 202-225-5476; Website: davidyoung. house.gov.

State Offices: Council Bluffs, 712-325-1404; Creston, 641-782-2495; Des Moines, 515-282-1909.

Committees: *Appropriations:* Agriculture; Homeland Security; Transportation.

Election Results

2014 general	David Young (R)	148,814	(53%)	$1,967,925	$1,012,449	$4,317,688
	Staci Appel (D)	119,109	(42%)	$2,162,366	$129,932	$3,026,351
	Ed Wright (Lib)	9,054	(3%)	$17,723		
2014 primary	Brad Zaun (R)	10,522	(25%)			
	Robert Cramer (R)	9,032	(21%)			
	Matt Schultz (R)	8,464	(20%)			
	Monte Shaw (R)	7,220	(17%)			
	David Young (R)	6,604	(16%)			

Population		Race and Ethnicity		Income	
Total:	788,588	White	85.6%	Median income:	$57,593
Urban:	46.2%	Latino	6.3%		*(145 of 435)*
Suburban:	32.8%	Black	3.6%	Under $50,000	43.1%
Rural:	21.1%	Asian	2.6%	$50,000-$99,999:	34.0%
Land area:	9,887	Two races	1.6%	$100,000-$199,999:	18.2%
Pop/sq. mi.:	79.8	White Ethnic	22.0%	$200,000 or more:	4.6%
Born in state:	67.5%			Poverty Rate	11.6%
		Education			
Age Groups		H.S. grad or less:	36.8%	**Work**	
Under 18:	24.9%	Some college:	31.9%	White collar:	37.3%
18 to 34:	22.8%	College degree, 4 yr.:	22.5%	Blue collar:	42.2%
35 to 64:	38.9%	Post-grad study:	8.8%	Sales and service:	20.5%
Over 64:	13.4%			Govt. workers:	12.8%
		Military			
		Veterans/active duty:	8.3%		

Des Moines, Council Bluffs

Iowa, which today seems very much in the middle of the country, was once part of the West. It was not only the home of sober farmers and pious burghers, but also the eastern terminus of the first transcontinental railroad, a way station for people in a hurry to get across the Great Plains to the

Voter Turnout	
2013 Total Citizen 18+	564,381
2014 House Turnout	282,066
2014 Turnout as % CVAP	50.0%
2012 Turnout as % CVAP	71.1%

Rockies and the Pacific Northwest. Those who stayed behind used the wealth accumulated by methodical husbandry of their fertile farmlands to implant firmly the glories of Western civilization. One can feel that impulse today in Des Moines, looking across the river from downtown to the Victorian capitol, its gold dome above a Corinthian pediment. Terrace Hill, the beautifully restored governor's mansion, sits atop a hill overlooking the Raccoon River.

The city of Des Moines remains classically Middle American, even as it gains a livelier downtown and spreads into the countryside. *Forbes* in 2011 named Des Moines the top spot in the country for young professionals. The area has become a sanctuary for people from outside of Iowa looking for a family-friendly urban lifestyle. More than 12,000 Bosnians have settled in Des Moines, many of whom work at meat-packing. Insurance, agricultural supply, and printing and service businesses are expanding in office centers downtown and at freeway interchanges. In July 2014, Kemin Industries, which makes nutritional ingredients, announced that it was tripling a planned $40 million expansion that it had announced in 2010. The plant specializes in food science to improve food freshness and extend its shelf life. Principal Financial Group employs more than 6,000 people in the area, and the company also has naming rights to Principal Park, where the city's Iowa Cubs minor league baseball team plays. The city was dealt a financial blow in late 2012, when the annual defense spending bill removed 21 F-16 fighter jets from the Des Moines Air National Guard Base. But overall, the city's economy is stable, with steady job growth since the recession ended.

Des Moines and the southwest corner of Iowa make up the 3rd Congressional District. The second-most populous city here is Council Bluffs, home to the mansion of General Grenville Dodge, who in 1859 lobbied Illinois lawyer Abraham Lincoln on the need for a transcontinental railroad. Lincoln got it through Congress in 1863, Dodge became its chief engineer, and Council Bluffs became its eastern terminus when it was completed in 1869. Surrounded by beef grazing territory, Council Bluffs looks west across the Missouri River to Omaha, taking on the culturally more conservative tone of Nebraska and the

2012 Presidential Vote		
Barack Obama (D)	203,622	(51%)
Mitt Romney (R)	186,645	(47%)
2008 Presidential Vote		
Barack Obama (D)	197,112	(52%)
John McCain (R)	173,967	(46%)
Cook Partisan Voting Index: EVEN		

conservative politics of the *Omaha World-Herald*. The area has developed an economically hip side with separate data centers owned by Microsoft, Facebook and Google. In April 2015,

Google announced plans to spend another $1 billion to expand its center in Council Bluffs. Also in the district is Madison County, famous for the wooden covered bridges that gave their name to a best-selling novel and film.

President Barack Obama narrowly won the district in each of his campaigns.

David Young (R)

Former Senate aide David Young held the 3rd District for the GOP in 2014 by defeating Democrat Staci Appel, a former state senator. His surprisingly comfortable general election win capped an improbable rise from near-defeat in the GOP primary for Young.

A native of Des Moines, Young attended Drake University and worked as a consumer-loan trainee after graduating. He served on the legislative staffs of then-GOP Sens. Hank Brown of Colorado and Jim Bunning of Kentucky. Most recently, he spent several years as chief of staff to Sen. Chuck Grassley of Iowa, which can be a productive way to learn about a state and its politics. His pitch to voters relied heavily on his experience, as he vowed to hit the ground running as soon as he was sworn into office. Democrats castigated him as a Beltway insider.

In a 2012 post-redistricting battle of veteran incumbents after Iowa had lost a House district, which became a prelude to the success for Young, Republican Tom Latham in 2012 defeated Democrat Leonard Boswell, 52%-44%. That made Latham one of just 17 House Republicans sitting in districts carried by President Barack Obama that year. When Latham decided to retire in 2014, Young ran and placed fifth in a six-way Republican primary. But after nobody received the requisite 35 percent of the vote, he emerged victorious from a special nominating convention that went five ballots, allaying the fears of the establishment and drawing the ire of conservative and libertarian activists.

Against Appel, Young won an endorsement from *The Des Moines Register*, which empha-sized his experience on Capitol Hill. Both candidates threw everything they had into the contest, and made a priority of job creation and economic growth. Appel emphasized wom-en's health and Young focused on government reform. Gun control also emerged as an issue in the campaign: Americans for Responsible Solutions PAC, the political arm of the anti-gun-violence group started by former Rep. Gabby Giffords of Arizona, launched a six-figure ad buy in October criticizing Young, while the National Rifle Association sought to link Appel with former New York City Mayor Michael Bloomberg, a leading NRA critic. Appel outspent Young $2.2 million to $2 million, and they roughly split about $7 million in national party aid. Appel proved to be a weak candidate. Young won with unexpected ease, 52.9%-42.3%, better than Latham's margin two years earlier. Appel won 48.4%-47.3% in Polk County, which cast a bit more than half of the district vote. But Young won every other county, sev-eral by more than 2-to-1 margins.

In the House, he kept a low profile and made few waves during his first months in office. Young again displayed his insider skill, when he was one of two freshmen Republicans to get a seat on the Appropriations Committee. He said that he was helped because he knew committee Chairman Hal Rogers of Kentucky from his earlier work with Bunning. Plus, his predecessor Latham was a veteran member of Appropriations. Unlike fellow Iowa GOP freshman Rod Blum, Young voted for John Boehner for speaker. Having those connections was helpful. More important was Young's ability to utilize them. He spent time with GOP presidential candidates at early Iowa caucus events.

State senator Brad Zaun, who led the first round of the GOP primary vote, proposed to rewrite Iowa election law to require that the top two candidates in the primary have a runoff if no one wins more than 35 percent of the vote. Not coincidentally, Zaun voiced interest in challenging Young in the 2016 primary. Appel also discussed a potential re-match. Young likely will spend considerable time getting to know his constituents.

FOURTH DISTRICT

Steve King (R)

Elected 2002, 7th term; b. May 28, 1949, Storm Lake; NW MO St. U., 1967-70, attended; Catholic; married (Marilyn); 3 children.

Elected Office: IA Senate, 1996-2002.

Professional Career: Owner, King Construction Co., 1975-2002.

DC Office: 2210 RHOB, 20515, 202-225-4426; Fax: 202-225-3193; Website: steveking.house.gov.

State Offices: Ames, 515-232-2885; Fort Dodge, 515-573-2738; Mason City, 641-201-1624; Sioux City, 712-224-4692; Spencer, 712-580-7754.

Committees: *Agriculture:* Conservation & Forestry; Livestock & Foreign Agriculture. *Judiciary:* Constitution & Civil Justice; Immigration & Border Security. *Small Business:* Agriculture, Energy & Trade; Contracting & Workforce.

Group Ratings

	ADA	ACLU	AFL-CIO	LCV	ITI	COC	HAFA	ACU	CFG	FRC
2014	0%	0%	–	6%	100%	69%	72%	84%	78%	100%
2013	0%	C	14%	0%	C	77%	C	88%	71%	C

National Journal Ratings

	2013 LIB	—	2013 CONS
Economic	25%	—	74%
Social	0%	—	87%
Foreign	15%	—	77%
Composite	17%	—	83%

Key Votes of the 113th Congress

1. Sandy storm spending	N	5. Medical Marijuana	N	9. Syrian Rebels Training	Y
2. Violence Against Women Act	N	6. Farm Bill	Y	10. Keystone pipeline	Y
3. Guantanamo Bay Detainees	N	7. Afghanistan Combat	N	11. Immigration Exec. Action	P
4. Abortion 20-week ban	Y	8. NSA Phone Data Collection	N	12. Bipartisan budget deal	N

Election Results

2014 general	Steve King (R)	169,834	(62%)	$1,983,501	$53,950	$79,993
	Jim Mowrer (D)	105,504	(38%)	$2,167,517	$5,411	
2014 primary	Steve King (R)	unopposed			

Prior winning percentages: 2012 (53%), 2010 (66%), 2008 (60%), 2006 (59%), 2004 (63%), 2002 (62%)

Population		Race and Ethnicity		Income	
Total:	760,935	White	89.7%	Median income:	$49,497
Urban:	23.8%	Latino	5.8%		*(248 of 435)*
Suburban:	1.3%	Asian	1.6%	Under $50,000	50.4%
Rural:	74.9%	Black	1.1%	$50,000-$99,999:	33.0%
Land area:	24,901	Two races	1.4%	$100,000-$199,999:	14.0%
Pop/sq. mi.:	30.6	White Ethnic	19.1%	$200,000 or more:	2.5%
Born in state:	72.9%			Poverty Rate	13.4%
		Education			
Age Groups		H.S. grad or less:	43.7%	**Work**	
Under 18:	22.7%	Some college:	33.8%	White collar:	32.3%
18 to 34:	22.4%	College degree, 4 yr.:	15.8%	Blue collar:	38.8%
35 to 64:	37.6%	Post-grad study:	6.7%	Sales and service:	28.9%
Over 64:	17.3%				
		Military		Govt. workers:	14.1%
		Veterans/active duty:	9.3%		

Northwest and Central Iowa: Sioux City, Ames

Sioux City, one of the oldest market towns on the Great Plains, is nestled in the loess bluffs above the Missouri River. Sioux City has not grown much in the past half century. Its original economic base has become obsolete: The waterfront, once raucous with boatmen and stockyard workers, is now quiet. Downtown stores have been replaced by shopping malls at the edge of town, where people spend a day doing a season's shopping and then drive for hours to get home. The stockyards, which employed thousands and slaughtered millions of hogs during their peak years in the 1920s, are shuttered.

Voter Turnout	
2013 Total Citizen 18+	566,126
2014 House Turnout	275,633
2014 Turnout as % CVAP	48.7%
2012 Turnout as % CVAP	68.1%

But there are still plenty of hogs in western Iowa. Instead of meeting sellers in the markets in Sioux City, packers now contract directly with large farms and have built modern slaughterhouses nearby. Tyson Foods has facilities in Buena Vista and Crawford counties. Meanwhile, 27% of Iowa's energy is based on wind farming and it is second only to Texas in the amount of electricity generated by wind, despite objections from some farmers to the noise and the hazard to birds. Mid-America, which is owned by Warren Buffett's Berkshire Hathaway, recently built the state's largest wind farm, with 218 wind turbines, near Primghar. All of this helped Sioux City rank 13th on Forbes' 2014 list of best places for doing business. Its jobless rate was just 4% in late 2014. In April 2015, 5 million laying hens were destroyed in Osceola County because of an outbreak of avian influenza.

Western Iowa is small-town territory, and has some of the world's most productive soil and some of its most creative agricultural scientists and farmers. Ames, in Story County, is home of Iowa State University. That site had been the host of the Iowa Republican straw poll, which has launched several nomination contests. But it initially was moved for 2015 to nearby Boone and its Central State Expo, reportedly because its rental fee was much lower. But Iowa GOP leaders decided in June to cancel the straw poll as a nationally monitored political event. Iowa Republican Gov. Terry Branstad remarked in November 2012 that the straw poll had "outlived its usefulness." That still may be true, but the state party and travel industry have found the financial windfall enticing. Ames is part of the growth zone around

Des Moines. Its unemployment rate was a microscopic 2.3% in February 2015, one of the lowest in the nation. In Winnebago County is Winnebago Industries, which manufactures motor homes and recreational vehicles on computer-controlled assembly lines with robotic equipment. It employed about 2,700 people in 2013, with its main factory in Forest City. Mason City is the boyhood home of *The Music Man* author Meredith Wilson.

2012 Presidential Vote
Mitt Romney (R).................204,685   (53%)
Barack Obama (D) 173,391   (45%)

2008 Presidential Vote
John McCain (R).................191,473   (50%)
Barack Obama (D) 184,953   (48%)
Cook Partisan Voting Index: R+5

The 4th Congressional District is Iowa's largest geographically, stretching from the northwest corner through the middle of the state to include Ames. The 4th District leans Republican, but it could be competitive.

Steve King (R)

Republican Steve King, who first won his seat in 2002, practices a brand of incendiary, in-your-face conservatism that is shared by tea party-friendly House colleagues but increasingly hostile to party leaders. He generates lots of attention with his strongly stated views, but his influence has been limited, even when Republicans control the House.

King was born in Storm Lake and attended Northwest Missouri State University, though he didn't graduate. In 1975, he founded the King Construction Co. After building up his business, he launched his political career in 1996, with his election to the state Senate, where he quickly gained a reputation as a strong conservative. He opposed abortion rights, racial quotas and preferences, and same-sex marriage. He sponsored Iowa's "God and Country" bill, which required Iowa schools to recognize that the United States "has derived its strength from biblical values," and he was a driving force behind the state's English-only law. On economic matters, King supported repeal of the state's inheritance tax, and backed a 15% state income tax cut and a national right-to-work law.

When the House seat came open in 2002, there were four main contenders in the Republican primary. King ran as a full-spectrum conservative and as the only rural candidate, and called for limiting federal control of local schools. He led in the June primary with 30% of the vote. Because no candidate received the required 35% of the vote, the nomination was determined by a special party convention three weeks later. The 533 voting delegates needed three ballots to select a winner. King led on each ballot and defeated House Speaker Brent Siegrist of Council Bluffs, 272-253, in the final round. The general election outcome was never in doubt.

In the House, King has not been shy about sharing his hyper-partisan views, and he gets national press coverage for controversial remarks. He is known for his sometimes outrageous rhetoric. King has compared the process of awarding visas to immigrants to choosing a dog; speculated that President Barack Obama's family could have conspired to fake his U.S. citizenship with a "telegram from Kenya"; and accused Hurricane Katrina victims of spending federal money on "Gucci bags and massage parlors." During the January 2015 State of the Union message, he complained on Twitter that an undocumented immigrant seated with first lady Michelle Obama was "deportable." After King filed a bill that intended to keep the courts from ruling on gay-marriage cases, Democratic Rep. Jared Polis of Colorado joked in April 2015 that he planned to file the "Restrain Steve King from Legislating Act." A Carroll, Iowa, *Daily Times Herald* columnist who assembled some of King's quotes into a book, *King Kong Krazy,* calls him "maniacally nationalistic."

The conservative super PAC American Crossroads, backed by top GOP political strategist Karl Rove, announced an effort in 2013 to discourage what it considers fringe candidates like King from running in primaries against more electable Republicans. The group's president, Steven Law, cited King's potential interest in running in the 2014 Senate race to succeed retiring Democrat Tom Harkin. "We're concerned about Steve King's Todd Akin problem," Law told *The New York Times*, referring to the Missouri conservative whose 2012 Senate campaign self-destructed with his comment that pregnancy cannot result from "legitimate rape."

King makes no apologies for his style. "We've got to shoot from the hip sometimes," he said. "It's not always 'Ready, aim, fire.' Sometimes it's just time to fire." He told *The Council Bluffs Daily Nonpareil* in October 2012, "to the common-sense world, I'm exactly in the center." Of the American Crossroads effort, King said it made him more inclined to seek the Senate seat. "If I would back up in front of Karl Rove's initiative, that would just empower him, and he would go on state after state, candidate after candidate."

King has been an outspoken proponent of tougher immigration laws. He advocates English as the official language of the United States. In April 2008, an Iowa district court judge ruled in favor of King's challenge to state officials who had placed bilingual voting forms on state websites. In 2007, King, as the ranking Republican on the Judiciary Immigration Subcommittee, built a model fence on the House floor to show how simple it would be to construct a 2,000-mile fence on the border with Mexico.

When Republicans took control of the House in 2011, King introduced a bill to end birthright citizenship, a controversial idea that had gained currency in conservative circles the previous year but was widely unpopular among Hispanics. "Steve King is positioning our party for disaster," the Latino group Somos Republicans said in a statement. The measure went nowhere. With Republicans in the majority, King was positioned to rise to chairman of the Immigration Subcommittee, but the gavel went instead to the less bombastic Elton Gallegly of California. King blamed Speaker John Boehner, whom he said "isn't very aggressive on immigration." When Democratic Sen. Charles Schumer of New York blamed "the Steve Kings of the world" for the unwillingness of the House to consider immigration legislation in 2014, King challenged Senate Democratic leaders to a firearms duel, and said that with their approach to immigration legislation, "America would be wiped out from a perspective of the rule of law." In a December 2014 interview with *The New York Times*, he said that Congress should take the initial steps of an impeachment inquiry against Obama, and that Republicans suffered no political harm from the government shutdown in October 2013. Referring to the 2014 election results, he added, "We picked up 15 seats in the House and maybe nine in the Senate. That's the kind of punishment I can handle."

After endorsing Republican Fred Thompson for president in 2008, he said that March that "radical Islamists and their supporters will be dancing in the streets" if Obama won. John McCain's campaign condemned those remarks, but King declined to apologize. He briefly considered a bid for Iowa governor in 2010. GOP presidential hopefuls in 2012, courting tea party voters, actively sought King's endorsement in the Iowa caucuses. Texas Gov. Rick Perry and former Sen. Rick Santorum of Pennsylvania went on pheasant hunts with King. In the end, King did not make an endorsement.

He had his own reelection troubles that year. His Democratic opponent was Christie Vilsack; her husband, Tom Vilsack, was Iowa governor and later became Obama's secretary of Agriculture. Christie Vilsack scored points by blasting King for failing to sign a Democratic measure to force a vote on the stalled 2012 farm bill. But popular Gov. Terry Branstad helped him, and he escaped with a 53%-45% victory. That was an expensive contest, with King outspending Vilsack $3.8 million to $3.5 million, plus a few million more dollars spent on behalf of the candidates by national parties and groups. In the strongly Republican 2014 campaign in Iowa, King breezed with 62% of the vote against Jim Mowrer, an Iraq war veteran, who outspent King $2.2 million to $2 million and described him as ineffective and embarrassing. King criticized Democrats for their lack of cooperation in Congress, though he mentioned his support for the bipartisan farm bill that was enacted in 2014.

In January 2015, King took a leading role in opposing the selection of Boehner for another term as House speaker. "We need a speaker of the House who carries in his bones the conviction of our oath," he wrote for Breitbart.com. When King in March 2015 voted against the spending bill for the Homeland Security Department, King said the speaker was "throwing tantrums" and denying him a seat on a House overseas delegation. The intraparty conflicts help to explain why King again was denied the Immigration subcommittee chairmanship.

★ KANSAS ★

Kansas is usually depicted as flat, average, and uninteresting: Contrast the black and white Kansas scenes of the classic movie *Wonderful Wizard of Oz* with the richly colored scenes of Oz. But there is more to Kansas than that. The state's flatness—flatter than an IHOP pancake, reported some geographers in 2003—is not unrelieved. The Flint Hills between Kansas City and Wichita are irregular uplands, with the Tallgrass Prairie National Preserve hosting bus trips where bison still range. The Kansas City Symphony holds a concert every June in the Flint Hills, and concertgoers sometimes get pelted with rain, a reminder of the imaginary tornado that swept Dorothy and Toto out of Kansas and of the very real 205-mile-per-hour tornado that destroyed the town of Greensburg on the plains in 2007. Kansas can also be afflicted by drought, with seasonal rainfall measured in tenths of inches: The 2011 drought, the worst since the dust storms of the 1930s, lowered the water table while livestock and wildlife died from thirst and reservoirs were drained to keep barges afloat on the Missouri River. In 2014, all but 7 percent of the state was facing severe drought, and the Kansas Water Office noted that the Ogallala Aquifer—the Great Plains' vast underground reservoir—is declining faster than it is recharging and could be 70 percent gone within a half-century.

Kansas history has been punctuated by episodes of anger and rage sweeping through the tall sheaves like a tornado. Indeed, the state was born in a moment of violence: the Bleeding Kansas of the 1850s that led proximately to the war that divided the nation. The trigger was the Kansas-Nebraska Act of 1854, which left to local settlers the question of whether the new Kansas Territory would be a free or slave state. Pro-slavery "bushwhackers" rode over the line from Missouri, stealing elections and writing a pro-slavery constitution. But much larger numbers of free-soil "jayhawkers," from New England and the New England-Yankee-settled Great Lakes states, put down roots and, despite the massacres of the mad John Brown, prevailed and established their own law and order. This was a civil war before the Civil War. Later, Kansas became the birthplace of the Buffalo Soldiers, the African-American units that fought in the Indian Wars; their home base, Fort Leavenworth, is the oldest continuously active military reservation west of the Mississippi River and remains a key facility today.

The ultimate effect of the battle over slavery was calming for Kansas: The anti-slavery majority bent the soil to the plow and built small towns with sturdy networks of schools, churches, and colleges. But the rebellious impulse did not entirely die out. Kansans' livelihoods were always at risk: Hailstorms, grasshopper invasions, dry seasons, or a drop in world farm prices could mean disaster for thousands of families. The high rainfall of the 1880s attracted hundreds of thousands of new settlers to Kansas. The low rainfall of the 1890s produced a bust and a populist rebellion. "What you farmers should do," Kansas orator Mary Ellen Lease said, "is to raise less corn and more hell." For a few years in the Populist era of the 1890s and then in the farm rebellions of the 1930s, 1950s and 1970s, Kansans did, but afterwards, the state always returned to jayhawker Republicanism.

Kansas was, and remains, a farm state, but it has growing metropolitan pockets. The 2010 census showed that 52 percent of its people live in metro Kansas City and in the counties containing Lawrence, Topeka and Wichita. Nearly half the state's population growth from 2010 to 2011, according to Census Bureau estimates, occurred in affluent, suburban Johnson County, just south of Kansas City, Kansas and southwest of its Missouri eponym. A majority of Kansans live in or within easy reach of metropolitan Kansas City, the nation's second largest railroad hub, which has a diverse economy that is by no means dependent on farming (though it does produce some of the nation's best barbecue). Wichita is the home base of Koch Industries, a conglomerate that started as an oil refining company and which recently has become a major force in politics, spending lavishly to promote the free-market credo of its owners, Charles and David Koch. But Kansas' trademark industry is aircraft. Beechcraft, Cessna, Lear, and Spirit have plants there and Wichita factories produce 40 percent of the world's general aviation planes, though Wichita was hit hard when Boeing announced in January 2012 that it was closing its 97-building operation after 80 years. Kansas' rural counties have lost population during recent decades (putting a new spin on the phrase, "Get the hell out of Dodge," which refers to the frontier town Dodge City in southwestern Kansas), though the trend seems to be at least partially reversing. The 2010-11

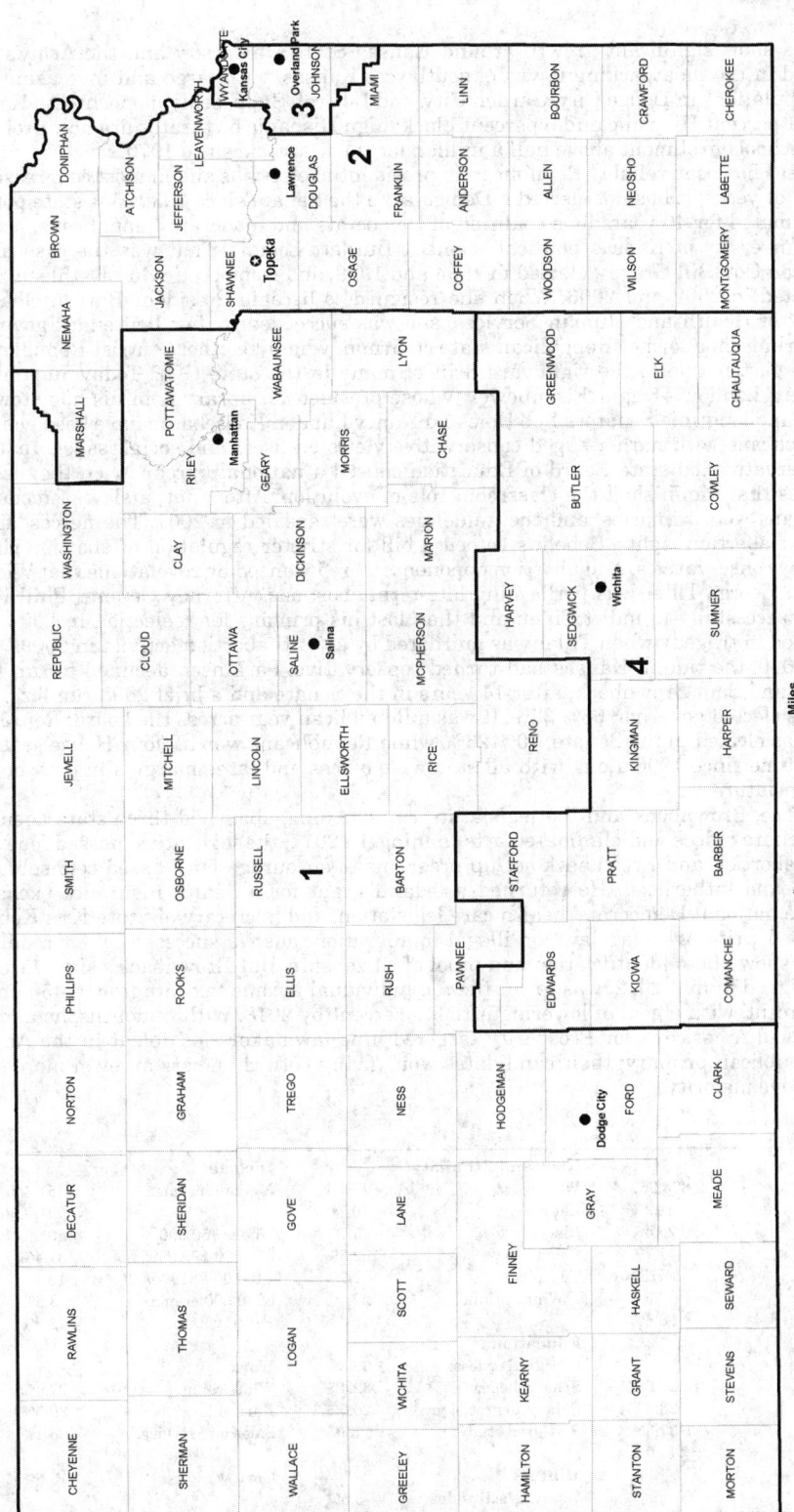

The Almanac of American Politics,
National Journal

Congressional district boundaries were first effective for 2012.

estimates show significant growth around Kansas State University and the Army's Fort Riley and in the meatpacking towns of southwest Kansas, with large and increasing Hispanic populations in Dodge City, Garden City, and Liberal. Supposedly monochrome Kansas is now 11 percent Hispanic and 6 percent black; high Hispanic birthrates are now projected to push school enrollment above half a million for the first time since 1970.

Kansas has been reliably Republican in presidential elections and in most congressional contests for years; it has not elected a Democrat to the Senate since 1932. But state politics was dominated for 40 years by a coalition of Democrats and moderate Republicans, according to University of Kansas political scientist Burdett Loomis. That was the case under Republican Gov. Bill Graves, elected in 1994 and 1998, and Democratic Gov. Kathleen Sebelius, elected in 2002 and 2006. When she resigned to become President Barack Obama's secretary of Health and Human Services, she was succeeded by her lieutenant governor, Mark Parkinson, a former Republican state chairman who (like other centrist Republicans) switched parties due to the rightward drift of many in the state GOP. Today, Republican heirs of Alf Landon, Dwight Eisenhower (whose presidential library is in his hometown of Abilene) and longtime Senators Bob Dole and Nancy Landon Kassebaum have been eclipsed by Republicans with harder-edged conservative views on fiscal and social issues. In 1999, the conservative-led state Board of Education caused a national uproar when they issued guidelines that diminished the classroom role of evolution. After that, a slew of moderate Republicans won primaries, and the guidelines were repealed in 2007. The fiercest fights came over abortion rights. Sebelius vetoed a bill for stricter regulation of abortion clinics favored by conservatives. And abortion opponents were incensed by revelations that Wichita physician George Tiller was performing late-term abortions. Attorney General Phill Kline tried unsuccessfully to indict Tiller, and then lost his primary for reelection in 2006. The fight ended in tragedy when Tiller was murdered by an anti-abortion activist in 2009.

By 2010, the tide in Kansas had turned conservative. Parkinson declined to run for a full term and Sam Brownback, after 14 years in the Senate and a brief 2008 run for president, was elected governor, 63%-32%. It was a Republican year across the board: Rep. Jerry Moran was elected to the Senate, 70%-26%, while Republicans won all four House seats for the first time since 1996 along with all statewide offices and large margins in both houses of the legislature.

In office, Brownback and the legislature cut spending, abolished three state agencies, closed welfare offices and eliminated arts funding. In 2011, the legislature passed four bills limiting abortion and Brownback set up programs to encourage faith-based counseling on marriage and fatherhood. He returned a federal grant for a health insurance exchange under the national Democrats' health care legislation, and Secretary of State Kris Kobach, who helped write Arizona's laws on illegal immigration, pushed successfully for requiring voters to show photo identification and proof of citizenship. But Brownback's signature initiative, signed in mid-2012, was to cut the top individual income tax rate from 6.45 percent to 4.9 percent, with a goal of lowering it to 3.9 percent by 2018. Within months, he and the Koch-backed Americans for Prosperity targeted nine lawmakers for defeat in the August 2012 Republican primary; their candidates won, giving both chambers an even more solid conservative majority.

Population		Race and Ethnicity		Income	
Total:	2,893,957	White	77.7%	Median income:	$51,485
Urban:	31.9%	Latino	10.7%		(29 of 50)
Suburban:	26.4%	Black	5.7%	Under $50,000	49.0%
Rural:	41.7%	Asian	2.3%	$50,000-$99,999:	31.4%
Land area:	81,759	Two races	2.7%	$100,000-$199,999:	16.1%
Pop/sq. mi.:	35.4	White Ethnic	22.4%	$200,000 or more:	3.5%
Born in state:	58.8%			Poverty Rate	12.5%
		Education			
Age Groups		H.S. grad or less:	36.6%	**Work**	
Under 18:	24.9%	Some college:	32.4%	White collar:	37.4%
18 to 34:	23.8%	College degree, 4 yr.:	20.0%	Blue collar:	39.5%
35 to 64:	37.3%	Post-grad study:	11.1%	Sales and service:	23.1%
Over 64:	14.0%			Govt. workers:	15.6%
		Military			
		Veterans/active duty:	9.5%		

But the early economic returns from the tax cuts were underwhelming. Despite the national recovery, state revenue declined, producing large budget deficits and prompting Standard & Poor's and Moody's to slash the state's credit rating. Throughout 2014, Brownback's approval ratings lagged, giving a surprising opening to his Democratic challenger, Paul Davis. Adding to the volatility was a wild Senate race between incumbent Republican Pat Roberts, who had been weakened during the GOP primary, and Independent Greg Orman, who received the support of most Democrats in the state. But in a solidly Republican mid-term election, both incumbents prevailed—Brownback by four points, Roberts by double digits—and the polarizing Kobach won reelection as well, cementing the state's increasingly red hue.

Voter Turnout	
2013 Total Citizen 18+	2,056,785
2014 Highest Statewide Turnout	869,502
2014 Turnout as % CVAP	42.3%
2012 Turnout as % CVAP	56.4%
Legislature	
Senate:	32R 8D
House:	97R 28D

Presidential Politics Except for 1964, when it narrowly favored Lyndon Johnson over Barry Goldwater, Kansas has voted Republican for president for three-quarters of a century. Of the 105 counties, George W. Bush and Mitt Romney lost only two: Wyandotte, which has a majority-minority population; and Douglas, which is home to the University of Kansas in Lawrence. John McCain in 2008 lost one more, by just over 200 votes, Crawford County, home to Pittsburg State University. In 1996, the state legislature voted to cancel the April presidential primary and none has been held since. In 2008, Barack Obama overwhelmed Hillary Clinton in the Feb. 5 Democratic caucuses by a nearly 3-1 margin. He had been endorsed by then Gov. Kathleen Sebelius. Mike Huckabee beat McCain in the GOP caucuses by more than a 2-1 margin. In 2012, the March 10 GOP caucuses drew almost 30,000 and Rick Santorum beat Romney, 51%-21%.

2012 Presidential Vote		
Mitt Romney (R)	692,634	(60%)
Barack Obama (D)	440,726	(38%)
2012 Presidential Caucus		
Rick Santorum (R)	15,290	(51%)
Mitt Romney (R)	6,250	(21%)
Newt Gingrich (R)	4,298	(14%)
Ron Paul (R)	3,767	(13%)
2008 Presidential Vote		
John McCain (R)	699,655	(57%)
Barack Obama (D)	514,765	(42%)

Congressional Districts In 2002, Republicans had full control of redistricting in Kansas for the first time since the 1960s, but did not use it to partisan advantage. At the request of the University of Kansas, they kept the Democratic college town of Lawrence in the 3rd District, which also included Johnson County and Kansas City. That helped reelect Democrat Dennis Moore, until he retired in the Republican surge of 2010.

114th Congress Lineup	
4 R	0 D
113th Congress Lineup	
4 R	0 D

In the spring of 2012, a coalition of Democrats and moderate Republicans in the state Senate passed one redistricting plan and the conservative-dominated House passed another; they adjourned in May without reaching agreement. A three-judge federal court took the case in June, and approved a map that took Lawrence out of the 3rd District, and put Manhattan, home of Kansas State University, and Fort Riley in the western and central 1st district. With the growing Republican dominance of Kansas, including all four seats in its House delegation, redistricting seems less relevant in partisan terms and more important for regional and business interests.

Governor

Sam Brownback (R)

Elected 2010, term expires Jan. 2019, 2nd term; b. Sept. 12, 1956, Garnett; KS St. U., B.S. 1978, U. of KS, J.D. 1982; Catholic; married (Mary); 5 children.

Elected Office: U.S. House, 1995-96; U.S. Senate, 1996-2011.

Professional Career: Radio broadcaster, KKSU, 1978-79; Practicing atty., 1982-86, 1993; Prof., KS St. U. Law Schl., 1982-86; Ogden & Leonardville city atty., 1983-86; KS secy. of ag., 1986-93; Fellow, White House Office of USTR, 1990-91.

Office: Capitol, 300 S.W. 10th Ave., Suite 241S, Topeka, 66612-1590, 785-296-3232; Fax: 785-368-8788; Website: governor.ks.gov.

Election Results

2014 general	Sam Brownback (R)	433,196	(50%)
	Paul Davis (D)	401,100	(46%)
	Keen Umbehr (Lib)	35,206	(4%)
2014 primary	Sam Brownback (R)	166,687	(63%)
	Jennifer Winn (R)	96,907	(37%)

Prior winning percentages: Governor: 2010 (63%); Senate: 2004 (69%), 1998 (65%), 1996 special (54%); House: 1994 (66%)

Kansas Republican Gov. Sam Brownback was elected in 2010 after spending two years in the House and 14 in the Senate. Then he was reelected in 2014. A social conservative who made a short-lived stab at the presidency in 2008, his aggressive exercise of power has put him at the vanguard of activist conservative governors and dismayed the state's Democrats and moderate Republicans, almost leading to his defeat in 2014. He won a second term by just four points, aided by running in a strongly Republican midterm election.

Brownback grew up on a farm in Anderson County, some 50 miles south of Kansas City; he has family roots in Osawatomie, a center of evangelical abolitionism in Kansas in the 1850s. He was state president of Future Farmers of America while in high school and student body president at Kansas State University. He worked briefly as a farm broadcaster before graduating from law school at the University of Kansas. He practiced law for four years in Manhattan, Kansas, and then he was appointed secretary of the state Board of Agriculture in 1986, serving until it was abolished in 1993. Brownback was a White House Fellow, working from 1990 to 1991 for Special Trade Representative Carla Hills.

Brownback's path to Congress began in March 1994, when 2nd District Rep. Jim Slattery, a Democrat, ran for governor. Brownback announced his candidacy for the seat, condemning "a welfare system that discourages the work ethic and encourages the disintegration of families, and a government that can't say no to spending or yes to reform." In the general election, Brownback defeated John Carlin, who was governor from 1978 to 1986, by carrying every county in a 66%-34% win. Brownback was among the "revolutionary" Republican freshmen in 1995 who tried to shake up Congress. He headed a group called the "New Federalists" that sought to abolish three Cabinet departments, and he denounced influence peddling in Washington. His legislative director was an ambitious young conservative named Paul Ryan, later to become a House member and the GOP's 2012 vice presidential nominee. As the immigration issue heated up, Brownback played a key role in passage of a bill cracking down on illegal immigration.

In 1995, he had a melanoma removed, and this brush with a fatal disease led him toward a deeper faith. An evangelical Christian, Brownback converted to Catholicism, with Sen. Rick Santorum of Pennsylvania as his sponsor. On Sundays in Topeka he attends both Catholic mass and a service at the Topeka Bible Church. At a prayer breakfast, he apologized to then-Sen. Hillary Clinton of New York for having despised her and her husband years earlier when President Bill Clinton was in office. He also described washing the feet of a staffer at a farewell party to demonstrate respect and humility.

In May 1996, Republican Bob Dole of Kansas, in the midst of his presidential campaign, announced that he would resign from the Senate that June. Two days later, Brownback said he would seek the seat. But Republican Gov. Bill Graves chose a fellow moderate, Lt. Gov. Sheila Frahm, to fill the vacancy until the election, setting up a primary contest between Frahm and conservative Brownback. She favored abortion rights; he did not. Brownback won the August primary, 55%-42%.

In the fall race for the remaining two years of Dole's term, Brownback faced Democrat Jill Docking, a Wichita stockbroker and the wife of a former lieutenant governor whose father and grandfather both served as governor. Docking promised "Kansas common sense" while Brownback campaigned on reducing the size of the federal government, reforming Congress, and returning to the basic values that built the country: "Work and family and the recognition of a higher moral authority." He promised to serve only two terms. Brownback won convincingly, 54%-43%.

In the Senate, Brownback had a mostly conservative voting record. He sponsored bills to require doctors to tell women seeking abortions that fetuses can feel pain and to bar doctors from prescribing controlled drugs for use in assisted suicides. With Democratic Rep. John Lewis of Georgia, he worked to authorize the African-American museum on the National Mall, and with Democratic Sen. Byron Dorgan of North Dakota, he sponsored a resolution apologizing to American Indians for past government misdeeds. To the dismay of many conservatives, Brownback was a leading co-sponsor of the immigration bill that passed in the Senate in 2006 and established a guest worker program.

Brownback was elected to a full, six-year term in 1998 after well-known Democrats declined to run. In 2004, Democrats again had a hard time finding a candidate to run against him, and he was reelected, carrying 104 of Kansas's 105 counties.

After that election, conservatives encouraged Brownback to run for president. He made several trips to Iowa, where, he hoped, his background in agriculture and his strong religious convictions would resonate with Republican caucus-goers. He touted Social Security privatization, but lagging in the polls and in fundraising, he was unable to break out of the pack. At the Iowa straw poll in August 2007, he finished third with 15 percent and soon after withdrew.

By early 2009, Brownback began seeking a different higher office: the governorship. No prominent Democrat rose to the challenge, leaving Brownback to face state Sen. Tom Holland, an information-technology consultant, in the general election. Brownback campaigned on a platform of economic growth, with fewer regulations and lower taxes. Holland sought to portray Brownback as a "career Washington politician" with ties to the energy conglomerate Koch Industries of Wichita, a leading financial backer of conservative candidates and causes. But in a Republican wave year, Brownback won 63%-32%, becoming the state's first conservative governor in half a century.

Early on, Brownback referred to his tenure as a "real live experiment" in right-wing governance, a characterization he said later that he regretted. He signed a bill banning late-term abortions and another to strip Planned Parenthood of federal family-planning grants. He appointed a secretary of social and rehabilitation services, Robert Siedlecki, who rewrote state contracts to encourage providers of state services to promote fatherhood and pro-family ideals. He drew national attention when he vetoed funding for the Kansas Arts Commission, making the state the only one in the country without an arts agency. He caused further consternation among Democrats, and even some Republicans, when he subsequently announced that he would return a $31.5 million federal grant aimed at helping the state set up health insurance exchanges under Obama's new health care law.

In 2012, Brownback—advised by supply-side guru Arthur Laffer and opposed by Democrats and moderate Republicans—enacted the largest tax cut in Kansas history, trimming more than $1 billion in state revenue. Brownback's ambitions were boosted further that August, when a number of moderate GOP lawmakers were ousted in primary elections and conservatives won control of the Senate.

In the run-up to his 2014 reelection bid, Brownback's approval numbers were weak, weighted down not just by controversies surrounding his policy agenda but also by the state's floundering economy. Amid a budget gap of hundreds of millions of dollars and slower growth rates than those of its neighbors, the credit agencies downgraded the state's rating, and the poverty rate rose. At the same time, some of Brownback's advisers came under investigation for influence peddling. Brownback won his primary, but his little-known challenger, Jennifer Winn, won a surprisingly large 37 percent of the vote. The state House minority leader, Paul Davis, mounted a challenge and charted the type of moderate course that had succeeded for Democrats in the past, picking up endorsements from more than 100 current and former Republican officials from the party's out-of-favor moderate wing.

Polls in mid-2014 showed Davis with a lead, and some forecasters labeled the contest a toss-up. But Brownback eked out a 50%-46% victory, aided by Republican efforts to save embattled GOP Sen. Pat Roberts. Exit polls showed Davis was able to attract just 19 percent of Republicans' votes to Brownback's 80 percent. He became just the second Republican in Kansas to win re-election to the governorship in half a century. Despite the narrow win, Brownback proceeded to move the state in a staunchly conservative direction. He signed a measure to limit what welfare recipients can spend money on (from movies and swimming pools to, somewhat inexplicably, cruise ships), and he overturned a 2007 executive order by the former Democratic governor Kathleen Sebelius that had provided protection against job discrimination due to sexual orientation. He also signed a bill authorizing the concealed carry of handguns without a permit. But the main question mark concerned how to make up the budget gap.

Senior Senator

Pat Roberts (R)

Elected 1996, term expires 2021, 4th term; b. April 20, 1936, Topeka; KS St. U., B.A. 1958; United Methodist; married (Franki); 3 children.

Military Career: Marine Corps, 1958-62.

Elected Office: U.S. House, 1981-97.

Professional Career: Co-owner & editor, *The Westsider*, 1962-67; A.A., U.S. Sen. Frank Carlson, 1967-68; A.A., U.S. Rep. Keith Sebelius, 1968-80.

DC Office: 109 HSOB, 20510, 202-224-4774; Fax: 202-224-3514; Website: roberts.senate.gov.

State Offices: Dodge City, 620-227-2244; Overland Park, 913-451-9343; Topeka, 785-295-2745; Wichita, 316-263-0416.

Committees: *Agriculture, Nutrition & Forestry* (Chmn: ex officio member of each subcommittee). *Ethics (Select). Finance:* Health Care; International Trade, Customs & Global Competitiveness; Taxation & IRS Oversight. *Health, Education, Labor & Pensions:* Children & Families; Employment & Workplace Safety; Primary Health & Retirement Security. *Rules & Administration. Joint Committee on the Library. Joint Committee on Printing.*

Group Ratings

	ADA	ACLU	AFL-CIO	LCV	ITI	COC	HAFA	ACU	CFG	FRC
2014	5%	0%	-	20%	33%	67%	90%	86%	90%	93%
2013	0%	C	11%	8%	C	75%	C	84%	84%	C

National Journal Ratings

	2012 LIB	—	2012 CONS
Economic	15%	—	80%
Social	0%	—	92%
Foreign	8%	—	90%
Composite	10%	—	90%

Key Votes of the 113th Congress

1. Sandy storm spending	N	5. Student Loan Rates	Y	9. Bipartisan Budget Deal	N
2. Chuck Hagel Confirmation	N	6. Employee Non-Discrim'n Act	N	10. Farm Bill Conference Rept.	N
3. Gun Background Checks	N	7. Senate Vote on Judgeships	Y	11. Unempl. Comp. Extension	N
4. Immigration Reform	N	8. Defense Dept. Spending	N	12. Keystone Pipeline	Y

Election Results

2014 general	Pat Roberts (R)	460,350	(53%)	$8,113,419	$3,380,996	$5,794,771
	Greg Orman (I)	368,372	(43%)	$5,702,323	$1,016,961	$7,230,146
	Randall Batson (Lib)	37,469	(4%)			
2014 primary	Pat Roberts (R)	127,089	(48%)			
	Milton Wolf (R)	107,799	(41%)			
	D.J. Smith (R)	15,288	(6%)			
	Alvin Zahnter (R)	14,164	(5%)			

Prior winning percentages: 2008 (60%), 2002 (83%), 1996 (62%); House: 1994 (77%), 1992 (68%), 1990 (63%), 1988 (100%), 1986 (75%), 1984 (76%), 1982 (68%), 1980 (62%)

Republican Pat Roberts, Kansas' senior senator, was first elected to his current seat in 1996—just months after the most prominent Kansas politician of recent decades, Bob Dole, resigned from the Senate to pursue an ultimately unsuccessful run for the presidency. Stylistically, Roberts is Dole's political heir: Both gained a reputation on Capitol Hill for blunt plain-spokenness and acerbic wit. In substance, there are differences. Dole moved toward the political center as he ascended through the Senate leadership; conversely, Roberts has shifted rightward in the latter part of his career, in apparent response to a changing political landscape in his home state. (He was the eighth most conservative member of the Senate in 2013, according to *National Journal* vote rankings.) And, unlike Dole, Roberts has shunned the leadership ranks to make his mark on agricultural and national security issues. In 2015, Roberts became chairman of the Senate Agriculture Committee, after chairing the House Agriculture panel two decades earlier.

But, besides a sharp tongue, Dole and Roberts also share a history as natives of an overwhelmingly rural state in the nation's geographical center who went on to spend most of their adult years working and living in the nation's capital. For Roberts, a perception among many home state voters that he had become more a creature of Washington than of Kansas came close to ending his Senate career in 2014, at the age of 78.

His abolitionist great-grandfather, Roberts likes to say, "arrived in Kansas with a flat-bed press, a six-gun, and a Bible" and founded the state's second-oldest newspaper, the *Oskaloosa Independent*. His father was briefly Republican National Committee chairman during the years when perhaps Kansas' most famous son, Dwight Eisenhower, was president. Born in the state capital of Topeka, Roberts graduated from Kansas State University with a journalism degree. He served four years in the Marine Corps, and then spent five years running a weekly newspaper in the suburbs of Phoenix. In 1967, Roberts arrived on Capitol Hill as an aide to Republican Sen. Frank Carlson of Kansas. He then served for 12 years as chief aide to Republican Keith Sebelius, who represented Kansas' 1st District and was the father-in-law of future Gov. Kathleen Sebelius. The relationship between Roberts and Kathleen Sebelius, once friendly, would years later become severely strained amid partisan warfare over President Barack Obama's signature health insurance overhaul.

Keith Sebelius had succeeded Dole in the 1st District in 1968 when the latter was elected to the Senate. When Sebelius retired in 1980, Roberts won the make-or-break GOP primary with 56 percent of the vote in a three-way contest, and went on to easily win the general election. For 14 years, he was in the minority party in the House. Roberts concentrated on farm issues, learning their intricacies and minutiae, and traveling in a van to keep in touch with constituents in the "Big First"—a district that sprawls across central and western Kansas, covering an area so large that it took two weeks to visit every county seat. His voting record was regarded as moderate. In 1996, when Republican Sen. Nancy Landon Kassebaum retired, Roberts ran for her seat, easily defeating his Democratic opponent, 62%-34%.

Roberts had no Democratic challenger in 2002. In 2008, former Rep. Jim Slattery, who had been working in Washington as a lawyer and lobbyist since losing a race for governor in 1994, returned to the state to challenge Roberts. Slattery ran a vigorous campaign, but Roberts, who routinely visited all 105 Kansas counties, spent nearly $7 million and won, 60%-36%, in a campaign in which he derided Slattery as a lobbyist, "Gucci loafers and all." Six years later, the tables would be turned, and Roberts had to defend himself against efforts to portray him as a captive of the Capital Beltway.

Initially, Roberts was considered a safe bet for a fourth term in 2014, especially with home-state colleague, Sen. Jerry Moran, running the Senate GOP campaign committee. But Roberts almost fell victim to anti-incumbency sentiment and a novice opponent in Milton Wolf, a radiologist who had the strong support of tea-party groups ascendant in Kansas Republican politics. Wolf—a second cousin to Obama—frequently noted that Roberts had been in Washington as either an aide or legislator for half a century. He based his campaign around his opposition to his second cousin's Affordable Care Act. "My mission is to save the Republican Party and save the republic," Wolf told ABC News.

Roberts was hardly a fan of the Affordable Care Act: A member of the Senate Finance Committee that shared jurisdiction over the legislation prior to its 2010 passage, Roberts declared at the time, "All indications are that this bill will be pulled increasingly toward more cost, more regulations, and more rationing as it continues through this process." When his old friend, HHS Secretary Sebelius, said she would have "zero tolerance" for insurers claiming costs were increased by the bill, Roberts was livid. "She is threatening to shut down private companies for exercising their First Amendment right to free speech," he charged. In October 2013, Roberts went so far as to call for Sebelius' resignation, accusing her of "gross incompetence" in conjunction with the problem-plagued rollout of the Web site for enrolling in "Obamacare." Coincidentally or not, Roberts call for Sebelius' resignation came three days after Wolf announced his primary challenge.

Wolf appeared to gain traction in February 2014, when news outlets reported Roberts did not have a home of his own in Kansas, listing as his voting address a Dodge City home belonging to longtime supporters. Roberts' aides responded by noting the senator—who owns a home in Washington's Virginia suburbs—also owned a house in Dodge City, but that it had been rented out to tenants. Roberts, seeking to defuse the controversy, did himself little good when he told a local radio station, "Every time I get an opponent—I mean, every time I get a chance, I'm home." It evoked memories of the 2012 campaign when a veteran colleague, Indiana Sen. Richard Lugar, was ousted by a tea party opponent after it was disclosed Lugar was using the address of a house he had sold in 1976 to vote in the state. But Wolf found himself dealing with an embarrassing controversy of his own: He was discovered to have posted patient X-rays on his Facebook page, accompanying some of them with jokes that many found distasteful. Though polls showed Roberts up by wide margins, he managed only a 48%-41% August primary win, getting help from two other candidates who split the remaining vote.

Unlike other incumbent Republicans in 2014 who emerged victorious in primaries, Roberts' troubles didn't end there. His Democratic opponent, Chad Taylor, dropped out of the race in September. The move was seen as elevating the chances of Greg Orman, a well-funded independent candidate. Orman, seeking to show just how much he disdained both parties, said he would not decide which party he would caucus with until it was certain which one held the majority. Republicans blasted Orman's past support for Obama and other prominent Democrats (in 2008, he filed an exploratory committee as a Democrat to challenge Roberts, but ultimately decided against a bid) as well as his positions on issues such as abortion and immigration. They also raised questions about lawsuits and past business deals.

Polls late in the race showed it to be a toss-up, placing Roberts in danger of becoming the first Kansas Republican to lose a Senate race in more than 80 years. It didn't help Roberts that his former Senate colleague, Sam Brownback, was encountering considerable trouble in his bid for re-election as governor. Nor did it help when media outlets reported in October that the senator had missed two-thirds of the Agriculture Committee meetings since 2000, feeding critics' arguments that he was out of touch. The National Republican Senatorial Committee sought to take control of Roberts' race by sending Chris LaCivita, a veteran party operative, to Kansas. Republicans also were forced to pour money—more than $10 million—into what a race they had thought was over once the primary ended. A barrage of last-minute ads and campaign appearances helped pull in independent voters, and Roberts ended up beating Orman by nearly 11 points.

Since his re-election, Roberts has pushed to prohibit the federal government from pressuring states to develop national education guidelines such as the so-called Common Core standards for math and language arts. The latter, while adopted by the overwhelmingly majority of states, have nonetheless become anathema to conservatives and a frequent punching bag for 2016 GOP presidential contenders. Meanwhile, with Roberts poised to become chairman of the Agriculture Committee as a result of the Republican takeover of the Senate in the 2014 election, some Democrats—remembering his red-meat rhetoric about food stamps during his bruising reelection bid—worried that Roberts might seek to reopen the 2014 farm bill reauthorizing agriculture and nutrition programs, which he had opposed. But Roberts sought to dampen such speculation, and stressed his desire to talk to panel members of both parties. "No committee chairman will go into the wilderness with a machete and chop left and right," he told *National Journal.* "You've got to check with the committee and calm the waters."

"When you're from Kansas, you're not appointed to [the Agriculture Committee], you're sentenced to it," Roberts once quipped, displaying his trademark humor. In 2011-12, Roberts was the Senate Agriculture panel's ranking Republican, and used his acumen to shape an earlier version of the farm bill. The Senate-passed version in 2012 called for ending a system of target prices as part of a larger shift away from fixed prices and payments for farmers. Roberts joined Democrats, and many Northern Republicans, in arguing that the farm bill shouldn't be about making sure certain groups get the same amount of federal aid they received in the past. But House Republicans and many Southern growers fought the idea: Those farmers contended the private crop insurance called for in the Senate proposal did not work well for crops such as rice and peanuts. Leaders of the House Agriculture Committee, whose membership is more oriented toward the South, reportedly found Roberts difficult to deal with. It was left to Senate Minority Leader Mitch McConnell of Kentucky to negotiate a nine-month farm bill extension as part of the larger New Year's Day 2013 budget deal aimed at averting the so-called "fiscal cliff."

Mississippi Republican Thad Cochran, term-limited in the ranking spot on the Appropriations Committee, then exercised his seniority to become Agriculture's new ranking member when the new Congress opened in early 2013. Roberts briefly considered challenging Cochran, who had opposed the 2012 farm bill proposal. Roberts ultimately decided against challenging Cochran, but remained on the panel.

Roberts' experience with the 2012 farm bill in some ways was reminiscent of a battle waged nearly two decades earlier. In 1995, after Republicans won majority control of Congress for the first time in 40 years, Roberts became chairman of the House Agriculture Committee. He had long believed that the huge subsidies of the early 1980s would never return. Faced with tight Republican budget parameters, Roberts drafted the so-called Freedom to Farm bill designed to phase out subsidies over seven years. In September 1995, his bill failed in committee when Southern Republicans, eager to protect cotton, rice and peanut subsidies, voted against it. Two months later, Roberts persuaded Agriculture conferees to include most of his bill in the 1996 budget reconciliation bill, which President Bill Clinton vetoed. To attract more support, Roberts agreed to changes, including maintaining cotton and rice marketing loans. Still, his legislation was the biggest change in agriculture policy since the New Deal of 1933. Roberts' revised bill became law in April—just months before his election to the Senate.

The Freedom to Farm Act worked well in 1997, and farmers seemed to do fine with a diminished government role in their businesses. But in 1998, crop prices plunged and some farmers demanded a return to the old system. From his new seat in the Senate, Roberts resisted, and bills were passed to accelerate payments and to give farmers an extra $4 billion in disaster aid. In 2000, the pattern continued. Roberts argued that limiting production would not raise prices because the U.S. accounts for less than one-fifth of world production. The problem seemed intractable. The number of family farmers continued to decline in places like western Kansas, yet prices were not sufficient to maintain many operations.

Freedom to Farm came up for reauthorization in 2002, when Democrats were in control of the Senate. Roberts acknowledged the Freedom to Farm Act "didn't work out as anybody would have hoped" and, with Cochran, pushed for farm savings accounts. But their proposal was rejected in favor of the Democrats' approach of reviving countercyclical subsidies when crop prices are low, plus a larger Conservation Reserve Program, which paid farmers to leave land fallow to protect environmentally sensitive areas. Roberts argued the legislation that ultimately passed would provide no aid when production was low and crop prices rose, which is what happened when drought struck the Great Plains in the summer of 2002.

Roberts has tried to encourage farm exports in a number of ways: He was a lead sponsor of the 2000 law signed by Clinton that relaxed the embargo on export of food and medicine to Cuba for humanitarian reasons. Roberts was joined by his 1st District successor and now-junior Senate colleague, Moran, in contending that such a move would benefit Kansas farmers, even though moves to normalize relations with Cuba were fought by many of their Republican colleagues.

Roberts' other major sphere of influence has been national security. In 1999, as the new chairman of the Emerging Threats and Capabilities Subcommittee on Armed Services, he held hearings probing the nation's vulnerability to terrorists and—two years prior to 9/11—presciently asserted that targets would be "selected for their symbolic value, like the World Trade Center in the heart of Manhattan."

He was particularly immersed in the issue of intelligence gathering as the Intelligence Committee chairman in 2003-2007. Over time, members of both parties on the committee arrived at the conclusion that intelligence prior to the 2003 start of the Iraq war was deeply flawed. In the summer of 2004, committee members led by Roberts unanimously criticized intelligence-gathering on Iraq and concluded that the Central Intelligence Agency had not seriously considered the possibility that Iraqi leader Saddam Hussein had no weapons of mass destruction. Roberts proposed that the Intelligence panel take over from the Armed Services Committee oversight of Defense Department intelligence operations, but the proposal met with predictable resistance on turf-conscious Capitol Hill.

The New York Times touched off another partisan battle in the committee when it reported in December 2005 that the National Security Agency was secretly monitoring contacts between al-Qaida suspects abroad and individuals in the United States. Democrats led by Sen. Jay Rockefeller of West Virginia sought a committee investigation, while Roberts insisted that the program was not only within the president's constitutional powers, but "legal, necessary, and reasonable." In March 2006, the committee voted along party lines not to conduct an investigation into the domestic surveillance program but to establish a seven-member panel charged with that responsibility.

Roberts complained that some Democrats "believe the gravest threat we face is not Osama bin Laden and al-Qaida, but rather the president of the United States," referring to President George W. Bush. Roberts rotated off the committee in early 2007, but, after Obama took office, Roberts staunchly opposed sending detainees at Guantanamo Bay, Cuba to Fort Leavenworth in Kansas. "Not in our backyard. Not in Kansas. Not on my watch," he declared. He and Brownback placed holds on executive branch appointees to the Defense and Justice departments to pressure the Pentagon to block the proposed transfers, and the idea eventually died.

Given that he will be 84 when his current Senate term ends in 2020 and his close call politically in 2014, speculation in Kansas is that Roberts' long political career is entering its final phase. While not tipping his hand as to his political future, Roberts has compiled a "bucket list" of things to do before he dies. So far, he has succeeded in conducting the Kansas symphony orchestra, and riding, very briefly, a rodeo bull. He also jokingly complains of not being satisfied with frequently being named "funniest senator" in *Washingtonian* magazine's anonymous survey of congressional staff. "I was lobbying for the 'hottie of the year,' but I can't even get to lukewarm," deadpanned the utterly bald septuagenarian.

Junior Senator

Jerry Moran (R)

Elected 2010, term expires 2017, 1st term; b. May 29, 1954, Great Bend; U. of KS, B.S. 1976, J.D. 1981; Methodist; married (Robba); 2 children.

Elected Office: KS Senate, 1989-97, maj. ldr., 1995-96; U.S. House, 1997-2011.

Professional Career: Operations officer, Consolidated State Bank, 1975-77; Mgr., Farmers State Bank & Trust Co., 1977-78; Practicing atty., 1981-96; Instructor, Ft. Hays St. U., 1986.

DC Office: 521 DSOB, 20510, 202-224-6521; Fax: 202-228-6966; Website: moran.senate.gov.

State Offices: Hays, 785-628-6401; Manhattan, 785-539-8973; Olathe, 913-393-0711; Pittsburg, 620-232-2286; Wichita, 316-631-1410.

Committees: *Appropriations:* Agriculture, Rural Development, Food and Drug Administration & Related Agencies (Chmn); Department of Defense; Departments of Labor, Health & Human Services, Education & Related Agencies; Financial Services & General Government; Legislative Branch; State, Foreign Operations & Related Programs. *Banking, Housing & Urban Affairs:* Economic Policy; Housing, Transportation & Community Development; Securities, Insurance & Investment. *Commerce, Science & Transportation:* Aviation Operations, Safety & Security; Communications, Technology & the Internet; Consumer Protection, Product Safety & Insurance (Chmn); Space, Science & Competitiveness; Surface Transportation & Merchant Marine Infrastructure, Safety & Security. *Indian Affairs. Veterans' Affairs.*

Group Ratings

	ADA	ACLU	AFL-CIO	LCV	ITI	COC	HAFA	ACU	CFG	FRC
2014	5%	20%	–	0%	33%	71%	67%	75%	69%	83%
2013	0%	C	19%	15%	C	75%	C	80%	75%	C

National Journal Ratings

	2013 LIB	—	2013 CONS
Economic	14%	—	85%
Social	28%	—	71%
Foreign	8%	—	90%
Composite	17%	—	83%

Key Votes of the 113th Congress

1. Sandy storm spending	N	5. Student Loan Rates	Y
2. Chuck Hagel Confirmation	N	6. Employee Non-Discrim'n Act	N
3. Gun Background Checks	N	7. Senate Vote on Judgeships	Y
4. Immigration Reform	N	8. Defense Dept. Spending	N

9. Bipartisan Budget Deal	N
10. Farm Bill Conference Rept.	Y
11. Unempl. Comp. Extension	N
12. Keystone Pipeline	Y

Election Results

2010 general	Jerry Moran (R)	587,175	(70%)	$6,525,438	$7,148
	Lisa Johnston (D)	220,971	(26%)	$31,235	
2010 primary	Jerry Moran (R)	163,483	(50%)		
	Todd Tiahrt (R)	146,702	(45%)		

Prior winning percentages: House: 2008 (82%), 2006 (79%), 2004 (91%), 2002 (91%), 2000 (89%), 1998 (81%), 1996 (73%)

In late 2012, as Republicans were looking for someone to lead their effort to regain the Senate majority in the 2014 election, Kansas's junior senator, Jerry Moran—by his own acknowledgment—did not immediately jump to mind. Throughout his tenure on Capitol Hill—14 years in the House prior to election to the Senate in 2010—Moran had established a reputation as a low-key legislator focused on the needs of his constituents. "Most people looking at my time in politics would not think this was a job that I would be willing to do or would pursue," Moran later told the *Wichita Eagle*. Some GOP senators initially hoped the chairmanship of the National Republican Senatorial Committee would be of interest to the higher-profile Rob Portman of Ohio, a vice presidential contender in 2012. But Portman said he preferred to concentrate on legislating, and Moran pursued and won the NRSC post. He ultimately succeeded in realizing a party goal that had proven elusive during the two prior election cycles—returning the Senate to Republican control.

Moran started the election cycle with the numbers in his favor: Of the 36 Senate seats up in 2014, the Democrats had to defend 21 of them. But Moran also worked to avoid mistakes that had tripped up his party in the prior two cycles—nomination of poorly vetted, ideologically rigid candidates whose missteps had allowed several imperiled Democrats to survive. "We tried to get all aspects of our party—from tea party to the Chamber of Commerce—to sit in a room and decide on a candidate they could all agree on," he later recalled. Moran reached out to Portman, a member of the GOP's establishment wing, who agreed to serve as the NRSC's vice chairman for finance—while tea party favorite Texas Sen. Ted Cruz was appointed vice chairman for grassroots and political outreach.

In the Senate, success in chairing a party's in-house campaign committee has frequently translated into ascending the leadership ladder. But Moran, a onetime majority leader of the Kansas Senate, has downplayed any leadership aspirations on Capitol Hill. His reward from the 2014 election, he insists, is that a GOP majority would make it easier to advance the legislative agenda his heavily Republican state elected him to pursue. "I like my independence. The more that you are part of the leadership, the less flexibility you sometimes have in the positions you take. I want to make sure my focus is on Kansas, not trying to ingratiate myself to Washington," he told the *Eagle*. Moran has demonstrated an independent streak during his years in Congress while accumulating a generally conservative voting record. In recent years, he has found himself under pressure due to the increasing role of the tea party within the Kansas Republican Party.

Moran grew up in the tiny town of Plainville on the western plains of Kansas, the son of an oil-field worker. In college, he worked as a summer intern for then-GOP Rep. Keith Sebelius of Kansas, father-in-law of future Democratic Gov. Kathleen Sebelius. The job gave Moran a close-up view of the 1974 impeachment hearings of President Richard Nixon. After graduating with a degree in economics from the University of Kansas, Moran worked as a banker before earning a law degree. In 1988, he won election to the state Senate, becoming majority leader in his last term. When Republican Rep. Pat Roberts ran for the Senate in 1996, Moran sought the open 1st District House seat. He won the primary with 76 percent, tantamount to election in a sprawling rural district as big as the state of Illinois. Moran had no trouble winning reelection a half-dozen times in Kansas' "Big First," where he annually held town hall meetings in each of the district's 69 counties.

Since 2000, Moran has cited Kansas farmers in pushing to reopen trade with Cuba, a position that put him at odds with many in his party. In 2007, he won House approval of an amendment to ease restrictions on shipments of food and medicine to Cuba, only to see it removed from the final legislation to avoid a veto by President George W. Bush. In the Senate, Moran inserted a provision into a 2012 appropriations bill to ease agricultural trade by allowing direct cash payments from Cuban buyers to U.S. institutions. Again, it was stripped out of the final legislation. In 2015, after President Barack Obama moved to normalize relations with Cuba, Moran declared in a speech: "…What we have been doing has not worked… because it's a unilateral sanction. When wheat, for example, is not sold to Cuba, it's not that they're not buying wheat, it's that wheat's being purchased from some other place: our competitors."

Moran's independence also showed up on other issues during his House tenure. To the dismay of Speaker Dennis Hastert, he was one of 25 House Republicans who opposed the 2003 Republican-sponsored Medicare prescription drug bill. Moran said the bill did not do enough to lower prescription drug prices, and favored a Democratic proposal to give federal officials negotiating authority to lower drug costs. He later joined Democrats in backing an expansion of the Children's Health Insurance Program.

Moran resisted GOP leaders' pressure to challenge popular Gov. Sebelius in 2006. But he decided to run for the Senate in 2010 when Republican Sam Brownback announced he would step aside to run for governor, after Sebelius resigned to become Obama's secretary of Health and Human Services. Moran first had to get by fellow GOP Rep. Todd Tiahrt, who preceded him in the House by two years. The two waged a nasty and expensive primary race, costing nearly $7 million combined. Tiahrt sought to turn the contest into a referendum on who was more conservative, and the candidates battled over endorsements. Former Alaska Gov. Sarah Palin and former Pennsylvania Sen. Rick Santorum were in Tiahrt's camp, while Moran secured the backing of two outspoken Senate conservatives—Tom Coburn of Oklahoma and Jim DeMint of South Carolina—along with the more pragmatic John McCain of Arizona. With the endorsement of most of the state's leading newspapers, Moran won by 50%-45% over Tiahrt, prevailing on the strength of his base in the state's most Republican district. He won the general election with 70 percent.

One of Moran's first moves was to join the Senate Tea Party Caucus, a group formed to capitalize on the momentum of tea party activists during the 2010 off-year election. He sounded very much the tea party advocate in lashing out at big government when, in 2012, he slammed the Labor Department for a proposal to prevent children under age 16 from working in dangerous farm jobs. "If the federal government can regulate the kind of relationship between parents and their children on their own family's farm, there is almost nothing off-limits in which we see the federal government intruding in a way of life," he declared. But, notwithstanding the tea party's anti-immigration bent, Moran crossed party lines to work with Democratic Sen. Mark Warner of Virginia on a highly publicized bill that would create a new visa for foreign students receiving graduate degrees from U.S. schools.

Moran found himself in a particularly awkward situation when a frail, 89-year old former Republican Sen. Bob Dole—who for three decades had occupied the seat Moran now holds—showed up on the Senate floor in December 2012 in a wheelchair. Dole, who has had limited use of his right arm since being wounded in World War II, in 1990 had engineered passage of the Americans with Disabilities Act; he went to the Senate floor in 2012 to lobby for an international treaty designed to encourage other countries to follow suit. But Moran, after earlier declaring he supported the treaty and would be "standing up for the rights of those with disabilities," cast a key vote to block treaty ratification. In a statement afterward, Moran declared "foreign officials should not be put in a position to interfere with U.S. policymaking." The statement embraced an argument made by hardline conservatives but adamantly disputed by the treaty's proponents—that the treaty could be used by the United Nations to dictate U.S. policy. Pressed later in an interview with the *Boston Globe,* Moran contended: "I'm saying I tried to help [the treaty] come to the floor, and had never made a conclusion as to whether I was for or against it, and concluded that it was a bad idea to have the United Nations involved in this."

Moran was given a seat on the Appropriations Committee following the 2010 election, while committing to efforts to ban controversial "earmarks"—funds directed to a legislator's pet projects. Moran sought earmarked funding while in the House, and took heat for it during the primary against Tiahrt. He defended himself by noting he also had sought earmark restrictions while still in the House. In August 2011, he was one of 26 senators to oppose a bipartisan deal to raise the nation's debt limit, noting that the $21 billion in deficit reduction over the first year of the agreement would cover less than a week's worth of borrowing. In

December 2014, Moran found himself among a group of 11 Republicans aligned with Cruz—and at odds with his party's Senate leadership—on a series of votes to stall or derail a $1.1 trillion measure funding federal department and agencies.

The speculation in home-state media was that Moran had cast these votes with an eye to 2016, when he is expected to seek a second term. Moran appears in little peril in a general election; Kansas has not elected a Democratic senator since 1932. But conservative activists remained upset at Moran's efforts to help his senior colleague, Roberts, withstand a primary challenge in 2014 from Milton Wolf, a tea party-backed physician, and were hoping to find a candidate to take on Moran. Wolf, who came within 7 points of ousting Roberts, was a possibility. Rep. Tim Huelskamp, a tea party favorite who now holds the "Big First" seat formerly occupied by Moran, considered a primary challenge—but told *CQ Roll Call* in early 2015 that his wife had vetoed the idea.

One issue that Moran may find himself answering for in 2016 is his attendance record: Data from www.govtrack.us show him missing 8 percent of all floor votes since he took office in 2011, more than any other senator except Florida Republican Marco Rubio. In response, his office told the *Kansas City Star:* "Sen. Moran best serves our state's interests in Washington through direct and consistent communication with Kansans and his travel schedule occasionally conflicts with votes."

FIRST DISTRICT

Tim Huelskamp (R)

Elected 2010, 3rd term; b. Nov. 11, 1968, Fowler; Col. of Santa Fe, B.A. 1991, American U., Ph.D. 1995; Catholic; married (Angela); 4 children.

Elected Office: KS Senate, 1997-2011.

Professional Career: Farmer, rancher.

DC Office: 1110 LHOB, 20515, 202-225-2715; Fax: 202-225-5124; Website: huelskamp.house.gov.

State Offices: Dodge City, 620-225-0172; Hutchinson, 620-665-6138; Manhattan, 785-309-0572; Salina, 785-309-0572.

Committees: *Small Business:* Agriculture, Energy & Trade; Economic Growth, Tax & Capital Access. *Veterans' Affairs:* Health; Oversight & Investigations.

Group Ratings

	ADA	ACLU	AFL-CIO	LCV	ITI	COC	HAFA	ACU	CFG	FRC
2014	15%	27%	–	3%	60%	43%	92%	96%	100%	100%
2013	10%	C	10%	7%	C	62%	C	96%	98%	C

National Journal Ratings

	2013 LIB	—	2013 CONS
Economic	18%	—	80%
Social	31%	—	67%
Foreign	51%	—	49%
Composite	34%	—	66%

Key Votes of the 113th Congress

1. Sandy storm spending	N	5. Medical Marijuana	N	9. Syrian Rebels Training	N
2. Violence Against Women Act	N	6. Farm Bill	N	10. Keystone pipeline	Y
3. Guantanamo Bay Detainees	N	7. Afghanistan Combat	Y	11. Immigration Exec. Action	Y
4. Abortion 20-week ban	Y	8. NSA Phone Data Collection	Y	12. Bipartisan budget deal	N

Election Results

2014 general	Tim Huelskamp (R)	138,764	(68%)	$878,253 $233,945
	Jim Sherow (D)	65,397	(32%)	$170,569
2014 primary	Tim Huelskamp (R)	42,847	(55%)	
	Alan LaPolice (R)	35,108	(45%)	

Prior winning percentages: 2012 (unopposed), 2010 (74%)

Population		Race and Ethnicity		Income	
Total:	722,463	White	78.8%	Median income:	$45,273
Urban:	11.5%	Latino	14.1%		*(315 of 435)*
Suburban:	0.3%	Black	3.2%	Under $50,000	54.6%
Rural:	88.2%	Asian	1.5%	$50,000-$99,999:	32.0%
Land area:	55,244	Two races	1.9%	$100,000-$199,999:	11.1%
Pop/sq. mi.:	13.1	White Ethnic	20.7%	$200,000 or more:	2.3%
Born in state:	63.2%			Poverty Rate	15.5%
		Education			
Age Groups		H.S. grad or less:	41.9%	Work	
Under 18:	24.2%	Some college:	34.2%	White collar:	32.5%
18 to 34:	25.8%	College degree, 4 yr.:	15.9%	Blue collar:	38.7%
35 to 64:	34.8%	Post-grad study:	7.9%	Sales and service:	28.8%
Over 64:	15.3%				
		Military		Govt. workers:	18.3%
		Veterans/active duty:	11.4%		

Central and Western Kansas

"A prairie is not any old piece of flatland in the Midwest," wrote Kansas-born reporter Dennis Farney. "No, a prairie is wine-colored grass, dancing in the wind. A prairie is a sun-splashed hillside, bright with wild flowers. A prairie is a fleeting cloud shadow, the song of the meadowlark. It is the wild

Voter Turnout	
2013 Total Citizen 18+	512,629
2014 House Turnout	204,161
2014 Turnout as % CVAP	39.8%
2012 Turnout as % CVAP	50.9%

land that has never felt the slash of the plow." The prairie Farney described once covered almost all of Kansas. Now only a little virgin prairie can still be found, in the Flint Hills region west and south of Topeka, where you can see 30 miles on a clear day and a waist-deep sea of grass waves in the wind as it did when pioneers on the Santa Fe Trail passed through some 150 years ago.

Farther west, near the 100th meridian, begins a region where the Rocky Mountains block moisture from reaching the land, and the prairie gives way to plains. The landscape becomes what Major Stephen Long in 1823 called the "Great American Desert." Much of this western area was grazing land, first for buffalo, and then for the cattle driven to Kansas railheads like Abilene and Dodge City in the 1870s and 1880s. This brief moment in history has been recaptured in the Boot Hill Museum of kitschy Dodge, where Main Street is called Wyatt Earp Boulevard. That they divided the land into so many counties, many with towns sporting grandiose names

2012 Presidential Vote		
Mitt Romney (R)	184,232	(70%)
Barack Obama (D)	72,668	(28%)
2008 Presidential Vote		
John McCain (R)	189,895	(67%)
Barack Obama (D)	87,641	(31%)
Cook Partisan Voting Index:	R+23	

like Montezuma, Garden City, and Syracuse, is a testament to the big dreams these settlers brought with them. Today, the area's farm-dependent economy is changing. Big meatpacking plants in Dodge City, Garden City and Liberal (the "Golden Triangle of meatpacking") have attracted large numbers of Hispanic immigrants; Seward and Ford counties have become majority-Hispanic. The dairy industry has made something of a comeback, enticed by inexpensive land and labor and abundant feed stocks. In far western counties like Finney, housing growth has resulted from young people taking advantage of tax incentives.

The 1st Congressional District covers all of western and north-central Kansas. It extends more than 300 miles from the Colorado border to the outskirts of Topeka. While the area today is solidly Republican, it was not always so. Farmer uprisings handed the area to the Populists for much of the late 1800s, a Democrat represented southwest Kansas during the farm depression of the 1920s and 1930s, and one did so again in the late 1950s. Republican Bob Dole represented western Kansas from 1960 to 1968. The 1st is now one of the most reliably Republican districts in the country: Ellis County, settled by German Catholics and home to the Cathedral of the Plains, is the only county here to have voted for a Democratic presidential candidate since 1976 (it did so in 1988 and 1992). The district takes in almost everything west of the Flint Hills and Abilene, the boyhood home of President Dwight Eisenhower. Just south of Salina, near the center of the state, is Lindsborg, which has one of the highest concentrations of Swedish Americans in the country, and where the biennial Svensk Hyllningsfest celebrates the area's early settlers. It also includes Emporia, where progressive newspaper editor William Allen White published the once-famous *Emporia Gazette*; the paper is still run by the White family.

The district contains 61 full counties and parts of two others; only Nebraska's 3rd District and South Dakota's at-large seat have more counties. Their average population is about 12,000 people. Mitt Romney won more than 70% of the vote here in 2012.

Tim Huelskamp (R)

Tim Huelskamp, a Republican first elected in 2010, has maintained the no-holds-barred conservatism for which he was known as a state legislator. Perhaps the most outspoken internal critic of his party's leadership, he was stripped of his seats on the Budget and Agriculture committees after the 2012 election and seemed to make little effort to win them back, but he raised his profile among adherents on the far right.

Huelskamp was born in Fowler Kansas and from an early age worked on the farm that his grandparents founded in 1925. He was valedictorian of his high school graduating class and was active in 4-H and Future Farmers of America. He said that his "first political realization" was President Jimmy Carter's imposition of a grain embargo against the Soviet Union in January 1980, when Huelskamp was 11 years old. He became enamored of Carter's successor, Ronald Reagan. "He had a way of communicating basic American principles and concerns in a way that people really got it," Huelskamp said. He briefly attended a seminary in Santa Fe, New Mexico, and later graduated from the College of Santa Fe, working part-time as a budget and legislative analyst for the state government. He got a doctorate in political science, specializing in agricultural policy from American University in Washington. He then went back to Fowler to work on the family farm.

In 1996, Huelskamp won a seat in the state Senate, becoming the youngest member there in 20 years. He authored the state's anti-gay marriage amendment that voters passed in 2005 and was active on anti-abortion issues. In 2009, Huelskamp called for legislation to deny federal funding used by Planned Parenthood for family planning programs in Kansas. His maverick ways got him in hot water with the GOP leadership, and in 2003, he lost his seat on the Ways and Means Committee. Huelskamp said it was because he opposed wasteful spending, but two state Republican leaders told *The Topeka Capital-Journal* in 2010 he was booted off because he would not work with the leadership. That pattern later became more familiar.

He considered running for the 1st District seat for years. He finally got his chance in 2010, when Jerry Moran left the House seat and ran successfully for the Senate. He faced five other candidates. Huelskamp distinguished himself by picking up endorsements from the National Rifle Association and former Arkansas Gov. Mike Huckabee. One of his television ads boasted, "He's not one of those weak-kneed Republicans." Huelskamp won with 35% of the vote. His general election opponent was Democrat Alan Jilka, a former Salina mayor who campaigned as a pragmatic problem-solver. With a commanding lead in fundraising—he took in more than $1.2 million compared to Jilka's $162,000—and the district's heavily Republican lean, Huelskamp won an easy 74%-23% victory.

In Washington, Huelskamp joined the Tea Party Caucus and landed a seat on the Budget Committee, a good platform for his strong views on the need to slash federal spending. "The debt crisis cannot be overstated," he said at a February 2011 town hall meeting." He was 1 of 53 Republicans who voted against a short-term resolution to fund the government in March 2011, while Democrats and Republicans sought to negotiate a budget deal for the rest of the fiscal year. That early vote marked the start of Huelskamp's apostasy. He and fellow freshman Justin Amash of Michigan in 2012 opposed Budget Committee Chairman Paul Ryan's budget blueprint, which they said didn't cut spending enough even as it drew Democratic criticism for doing just the opposite; he was one of 10 Republicans who opposed the plan during the House vote. He blasted GOP leaders for seeking to pass a reauthorization of surface transportation programs without offsetting spending cuts. In July 2011, he was one of 22 House GOP members who refused to back the deal to raise the debt limit that Speaker John Boehner, struck with President Barack Obama.

On the Agriculture panel, he opposed continuing the practice of direct federal payments to farmers, a leading concern for tea party voters. While other Kansas Republicans worked for an extension of the wind energy tax credit, he dismissed it as corporate welfare. After the

2012 election, when he faced no opposition from either party, he learned of his removal from the Budget and Agriculture panels, a decision he told reporters was "petty and vindictive." But it did nothing to curb his iconoclasm; he voted against the New Year's Day 2013 budget deal aimed at averting the so-called "fiscal cliff," and cast his vote for outgoing GOP Study Committee Chairman Jim Jordan of Ohio for speaker over Boehner. There were signs that he tried to organize a wider rebellion against Boehner, too. News outlets reported that he sat on the House floor during the vote with an iPad showing a list of members he hoped would join him in opposing the speaker. He declined to comment on the list, but later told *National Journal,* "I think it was the least I could do to the speaker to return the favor. We wanted to send a message that we are frustrated, all across the conference."

Back home, he faced a serious challenger in the 2014 Republican primary. Former school superintendent Alan LaPolice said that Huelskamp had failed to work for his constituents, or to find solutions to problems. Because he had voted against the farm bill that year and no longer had a seat on the Agriculture Committee, the Kansas Farm Bureau and the Livestock Federation refused to endorse him. These were clear signs of unhappiness by the party faithful. Huelskamp won 55%-45%, a margin of 7,739 votes. He won the general election with 68% of the vote against Democrat Jim Sherow, a Kansas State University history professor and a former Manhattan mayor. But other Republicans, who saw the blood in the water, made plans for a primary challenge in 2016. Huelskamp quickly ruled out the option that he might challenge Moran in the Republican primary for Senate. In January 2015, he continued to show his party independence by voting for Florida Rep. Dan Webster for speaker.

SECOND DISTRICT

Lynn Jenkins (R)

Elected 2008, 4th term; b. June 10, 1963, Topeka; KS St. U., A.S. 1985, Weber St. U., B.S. 1985; Methodist; divorced; 2 children.

Elected Office: KS House, 1999-2001; KS Senate, 2001-03; KS treas., 2003-08.

Professional Career: C.P.A., 1984-98.

DC Office: 1526 LHOB, 20515, 202-225-6601; Fax: 202-225-7986; Website: lynnjenkins.house.gov.

State Offices: Independence, 620-231-5966; Pittsburg, 620-231-5966; Topeka, 785-234-5966.

Committees: *Ways & Means:* Health; Trade.

Group Ratings

	ADA	ACLU	AFL-CIO	LCV	ITI	COC	HAFA	ACU	CFG	FRC
2014	5%	5%	–	3%	100%	93%	66%	84%	77%	88%
2013	5%	C	19%	4%	C	92%	C	80%	74%	C

National Journal Ratings

	2013 LIB	—	2013 CONS
Economic	18%	—	80%
Social	16%	—	74%
Foreign	24%	—	68%
Composite	23%	—	77%

Key Votes of the 113th Congress

1. Sandy storm spending	N	5. Medical Marijuana	N	9. Syrian Rebels Training	Y
2. Violence Against Women Act	Y	6. Farm Bill	Y	10. Keystone pipeline	Y
3. Guantanamo Bay Detainees	N	7. Afghanistan Combat	N	11. Immigration Exec. Action	Y
4. Abortion 20-week ban	Y	8. NSA Phone Data Collection	Y	12. Bipartisan budget deal	Y

Election Results

2014 general	Lynn Jenkins (R)	128,742	(57%)	$3,122,372	$165,383
	Margie Wakefield (D)	87,153	(39%)	$777,141	
	Chris Clemmons (Lib)	9,791	(4%)		
2014 primary	Lynn Jenkins (R)	41,850	(69%)		
	Joshua Joel Tucker (R)	18,680	(31%)		

Prior winning percentages: 2012 (57%), 2010 (63%), 2008 (51%)

Population		Race and Ethnicity		Income	
Total:	715,785	White	83.5%	Median income:	$48,926
Urban:	37.3%	Latino	5.9%		*(256 of 435)*
Suburban:	10.8%	Black	4.8%	Under $50,000	50.9%
Rural:	51.9%	Asian	1.3%	$50,000-$99,999:	32.3%
Land area:	15,085	Two races	3.1%	$100,000-$199,999:	14.6%
Pop/sq. mi.:	47.4	White Ethnic	23.1%	$200,000 or more:	2.2%
Born in state:	63.7%			Poverty Rate	15.4%
		Education			
Age Groups		H.S. grad or less:	40.3%	**Work**	
Under 18:	23.3%	Some college:	32.6%	White collar:	35.8%
18 to 34:	24.1%	College degree, 4 yr.:	16.3%	Blue collar:	41.0%
35 to 64:	37.5%	Post-grad study:	10.8%	Sales and service:	23.2%
Over 64:	15.2%				
		Military		Govt. workers:	19.9%
		Veterans/active duty:	10.2%		

Eastern Kansas: Topeka, Kansas City Suburbs

The green plains of eastern Kansas have seen more than their share of American history. In 1827, on bluffs above the Missouri River, the Army built Fort Leavenworth, famous in later years for its war college and military prison and now the oldest U.S. fort west of the Mississippi River. In the 1850s,

Voter Turnout	
2013 Total Citizen 18+	535,164
2014 House Turnout	225,686
2014 Turnout as % CVAP	42.2%
2012 Turnout as % CVAP	55.2%

newly founded towns along the Kansas River and along the Missouri border were the centers of Bleeding Kansas, the name the state took after pro-slavery bushwhackers set up a state capital in tiny Lecompton and anti-slavery New Englanders established their stronghold down the river at Lawrence. These tensions bled into the Civil War; William Quantrill's infamous nighttime raid on pro-Union Lawrence in 1863 resulted in the burning of all but two businesses to the ground and the death of around 200 inhabitants.

Today's Kansas is a much more staid place. The sole capital, Topeka, sits on a low bluff above the Kansas River 23 miles west of Lawrence. Topeka's system of legal segregation prompted the 1954 landmark case *Brown v. Board of Education*, that concluded "separate but equal" is not equal. In 2004, the city council appointed James McClinton as its first African-American mayor, although he declined to run for a full term. Topeka has had some success attracting corporate headquarters, including Hill's Pet Nutrition and Payless Shoe Source (which later was sold for $2 billion to another group of buyers). Population loss is not as great here as in western Kansas.

The area around Lawrence, where the University of Kansas is based, has grown steadily. Farther south of the cities, on the Missouri border, are the hills called "the Balkans," where Eastern European coal miners settled in towns such as Pittsburg and Girard. This area was once a center of American socialism: Clarence Darrow and Upton Sinclair made pilgrimages, and the local paper, *Appeal to Reason*, had a national circulation of 750,000. There are still remnants of this left-leaning tradition; Crawford County was the only county outside of the Kansas City

2012 Presidential Vote
Mitt Romney (R).................163,138   (55%)
Barack Obama (D) 124,401   (42%)

2008 Presidential Vote
John McCain (R).................170,029   (53%)
Barack Obama (D) 145,729   (45%)

Cook Partisan Voting Index: R+8

area to support Barack Obama in 2008. But Crawford returned to the Republicans in 2012. Recently, coal-bed methane gas wells have provided an economic boost to southeast Kansas. Although its production has declined slightly, oil production has increased.

These disparate areas, Topeka and Lawrence, Fort Leavenworth, the wheat-growing counties, and the Balkans—most of eastern Kansas except the Kansas City metropolitan area—make up the 2nd Congressional District. In recent decades, Democrats have been competitive in state races here, especially in Topeka. For 20 of the years from 1970 to 1994, Democrats held the 2nd District seat. Republicans have since held it for all but two of the 20 years. The district leans substantially Republican.

Lynn Jenkins (R)

Republican Lynn Jenkins, who has served her district since 2008, was elected vice chair of the House Republican Conference in 2013—one of three women in the GOP leadership. She has at least as much clout on the Ways and Means Committee, where she is a reliable conservative vote who has an accountant's familiarity with the tax code. But she has sometimes struggled to bridge the divide with the GOP's tea party wing.

Jenkins was born in Topeka and grew up in the rural town of Holton on a dairy farm. After graduating from college, she worked for nearly 15 years as an accountant. She was elected to the state House in 1998 for one term, and then one in the state Senate. In 2002, Jenkins was elected Kansas treasurer and was reelected four years later. She next set her sights on the 2nd District seat. In 2006, Democrat Nancy Boyda had pulled off a big upset by unseating Republican Jim Ryun.

Jenkins needed to win two competitive contests. In the GOP primary, she faced Ryun, the former Olympics medalist runner, who had held the seat for five terms and wanted it back. The contest was a clash between the two long-warring wings of the state Republican Party. Ryun was a staunch conservative, while Jenkins had a profile as a pro-business and pro-abortion-rights moderate. Although heavily outspent by Ryun, Jenkins eked out a win by just over 1,300 votes. Eager to quash any bitterness from the contest, Ryun heartily endorsed her. Jenkins still faced an uphill battle. Boyda had carefully crafted a voting record mostly in line with her constituents' views, and sought to distance herself from her party by publicly renouncing support from the Democratic Congressional Campaign Committee. Jenkins tied Boyda to liberal House Speaker Nancy Pelosi every chance she got and accused her of supporting tax increases by voting for Democratic budgets that phased out the Bush-era tax cuts for high-income earners. The strategy paid off. Jenkins won 51%-46%.

Jenkins had a bumpy first term. After criticizing spending earmarks during the campaign, Jenkins in 2009 submitted requests for 23 earmarked projects totaling $68 million to the Appropriations Committee. The conservative group Club for Growth removed her from its "Sworn off Earmarks" list. She responded that her pledge "only set rigorous standards for how a congressional member must go about requesting those earmarks." She got more negative publicity at a town hall meeting in Hiawatha. Discussing possible Republican candidates' future prospects, Jenkins said, "Republicans are struggling right now to find the great white hope." She later apologized and said she did not realize the phrase had a negative connotation and that she was referring to GOP House leaders, not the Republican field of challengers to President Barack Obama in 2012.

Although she was among the Tea Party Caucus' initial members in 2010, Jenkins had second thoughts. She told a Kansas group in 2011 that members of the movement "don't even like the term compromise. They don't even like the term common ground. ... I have always been willing to work with everyone," according to the *Lawrence Journal-World*. In 2013, she joined the "Problem Solvers" coalition of lawmakers who agreed to meet monthly to foster bipartisanship in Congress.

When she joined Ways and Means in 2011, Jenkins was part of a Republican effort to overhaul the tax code. As a tax practitioner, she told the *Washington Examiner* in November 2014, tax reform was "something near and dear to my heart." But while awaiting that long-term goal, she proposed her own tax preferences with their complexities. She introduced a bill to extend tax credits to small businesses that hire National Guard members. She sponsored the "Kelsey Smith Act," to require wireless communication providers to turn over cell phone call-location data to police after a Kansas girl's killer was identified with the help of cell phone data; it did not become law. When Republicans organized for the new Congress after the 2012 election, Jenkins defeated Martha Roby of Alabama for her leadership post. She was a big supporter of giving trade-negotiating authority to President Barack Obama, and cited that one in five Kansas jobs results from international trade. Jenkins occasionally cooperated across the aisle. With Democratic Rep. Jim McGovern of Massachusetts, she re-launched the Hunger Caucus in March 2015, with their joint appearance at the D.C. Central Kitchen.

Back home, some conservatives have been unhappy with Jenkins' record. State Sen. Dennis Pyle challenged her in the 2010 primary. Without spending much money, he held Jenkins to a 57%-43% win. In 2014, both parties believed that Jenkins might be facing a legitimate threat from Margie Wakefield, a Democratic attorney. But Jenkins won easily, 57%-39%, with assistance from her campaign spending of $3.1 million to $800,000 for Wakefield. Jenkins may have suffered a bit because Republican voters were unhappy with GOP statewide incumbents. During an April 2015 speech in Lawrence, she welcomed that Congress had become less partisan and more productive.

THIRD DISTRICT

Kevin Yoder (R)

Elected 2010, 3rd term; b. Jan. 8, 1976, Hutchinson; U. of KS, B.A. 1999, J.D. 2002; Methodist; married (Brooke); 1 child.

Elected Office: KS House, 2002-10.

Professional Career: Practicing atty., 2002-10.

DC Office: 215 CHOB, 20515, 202-225-2865; Fax: 202-225-2807; Website: yoder.house.gov.

State Offices: Overland Park, 913-621-0832.

Committees: *Appropriations:* Agriculture, Rural Development, FDA & Related Agencies (VChmn); Financial Services & General Government; Transportation, Housing & Urban Development.

Group Ratings

	ADA	ACLU	AFL-CIO	LCV	ITI	COC	HAFA	ACU	CFG	FRC
2014	5%	0%	–	6%	100%	86%	68%	80%	77%	88%
2013	5%	C	14%	4%	C	85%	C	84%	74%	C

National Journal Ratings

	2013 LIB	—	2013 CONS
Economic	29%	—	70%
Social	16%	—	74%
Foreign	0%	—	95%
Composite	18%	—	82%

Key Votes of the 113th Congress

1. Sandy storm spending	N 5. Medical Marijuana	N 9. Syrian Rebels Training Y
2. Violence Against Women Act	Y 6. Farm Bill	Y 10. Keystone pipeline Y
3. Guantanamo Bay Detainees	N 7. Afghanistan Combat	N 11. Immigration Exec. Action Y
4. Abortion 20-week ban	Y 8. NSA Phone Data Collection	Y 12. Bipartisan budget deal Y

Election Results

2014 general	Kevin Yoder (R)......................... 134,493	(60%)	$1,971,402		
	Kelly Kultala (D) 89,584	(40%)	$376,690	$10,929	
2014 primary	Kevin Yoder (R).....................unopposed				

Prior winning percentages: 2012 (68%), 2010 (58%)

Population		Race and Ethnicity		Income	
Total:	738,508	White	73.4%	Median income:	$64,266
Urban:	19.6%	Latino	11.5%		*(83 of 435)*
Suburban:	78.6%	Black	8.6%	Under $50,000	39.1%
Rural:	1.8%	Asian	3.7%	$50,000-$99,999:	30.9%
Land area:	1,071	Two races	2.4%	$100,000-$199,999:	23.3%
Pop/sq. mi.:	689.3	White Ethnic	24.7%	$200,000 or more:	6.7%
Born in state:	43.6%			Poverty Rate	10.1%
		Education			
Age Groups		H.S. grad or less:	27.0%	**Work**	
Under 18:	26.2%	Some college:	28.3%	White collar:	45.4%
18 to 34:	22.4%	College degree, 4 yr.:	28.2%	Blue collar:	38.9%
35 to 64:	39.4%	Post-grad study:	16.5%	Sales and service:	15.6%
Over 64:	12.0%			Govt. workers:	10.7%
		Military			
		Veterans/active duty:	7.7%		

Kansas City Metro

Though its central core is in Missouri, about 40% of metropolitan Kansas City's residents live west of the state line in Kansas. Some are in Kansas City, Kan., or KCK as it is sometimes called, where the low-lying land near the Missouri River used to house one of the nation's largest stockyards. This is still a working-class town with lots of modest frame houses, new Latino neighborhoods, a large African-American community, and a Catholic ethnic neighborhood. Kansas City's Wyandotte County has lost 29,000 people since the 1970s, and is now majority-minority: 25% black and 27% Hispanic. It is one of only four such counties in the state; the other three are in the southwestern corner, where farms and meatpacking plants have attracted immigrants from Mexico.

Voter Turnout	
2013 Total Citizen 18+	503,190
2014 House Turnout	224,280
2014 Turnout as % CVAP	44.6%
2012 Turnout as % CVAP	65.9%

South of Kansas City and Wyandotte County is Johnson County, which is much more affluent and more than three times the size of Wyandotte. The newer neighborhoods are arrayed along the interstates, as subdivisions have replaced croplands. They have grown to the point that Overland Park, Olathe, Shawnee and Lenexa are among the largest cities in the state. Like many suburbs, these towns became more than just residential neighborhoods over the past few decades. Sprint Nextel is headquartered in Overland Park, which is now the largest city in the metropolitan area on the Kansas side of the border. Applebee's left Lenexa for Kansas City, Mo., in 2011, but city officials responded by convincing SelectQuote Senior Insurance Services to move from the Missouri side two years later. This swap is emblematic of an emerging problem for the region: Tax incentives are used by states to lure businesses across the state borders, producing a net wash in job creation, but a decrease in overall revenues.

2012 Presidential Vote		
Mitt Romney (R)	177,886	(54%)
Barack Obama (D)	146,406	(44%)
2008 Presidential Vote		
John McCain (R)	172,856	(50%)
Barack Obama (D)	168,922	(49%)
Cook Partisan Voting Index:	R+6	

Johnson County has been diversifying demographically. In 1980, the county was 97% white, but the share of non-Hispanic whites has dropped to 82% of the population. Politically, Wyandotte County has an old Democratic machine style of politics, though its influence has been tempered by the consolidation of city and county governments. Johnson County has long been heavily Republican, but with plenty of moderate and even liberal voters on cultural issues. It has been a battleground for the fierce fights between moderate and conservative wings of the Kansas Republican Party, which sometimes benefit the Democrats.

The 3rd Congressional District consists of all of Johnson and Wyandotte counties, and a part of rural Miami County. The 3rd is comfortably Republican, though President Barack Obama had his best Kansas performance in this district in each of his two campaigns.

Kevin Yoder (R)

Republican Kevin Yoder, who won his seat in 2010, has been an energetic star of his large freshman class. His image took a serious hit after it emerged in 2012 that he took a nude swim in the Sea of Galilee during a trip with other House members. But a back-room deal that weakened a major banking law may be a more significant part of his public record.

Yoder grew up on a farm in the aptly named town of Yoder, founded in 1907 by an Amish settler. His family has been there since the 1880s, and hundreds of Yoders live in the area. His father's farm produces grains, soybeans, corn, and meat. His maternal grandfather, William Alexander, who grew up as a poor farmer, was the Republican mayor of Wilmette Illinois, and president of the Chicago Bar Association. As a child, Yoder recalls visits to his grandfather in downtown Chicago, drawing inspiration from him. Yoder studied English and political science at the University of Kansas, where he was student body president.

He was a registered Democrat before undergoing what he calls his own "personal maturation and growth" and switching to become a Republican. During his senior year in college and into law school, he volunteered in campaigns and interned at the state legislature. He worked as a law clerk at the Pentagon in Washington doing counter-narcotics work. He left a month before the Sept. 11, 2001, terrorist attacks, an event that inspired him to get more involved with politics. Yoder was elected to the Kansas House in 2002 at age 26, and got a seat on the Appropriations Committee, where he had interned in college. He eventually chaired the committee.

When Democratic Rep. Dennis Moore announced he would not seek another term, Yoder jumped into the race. His state legislative district, which includes some of Overland Park and the headquarters of Sprint, gave him access to a large donor base, and his acumen at fundraising forced the early GOP front-runner, state Sen. Nick Jordan, out of the race. Yoder's primary opponents pointed to his party switch as evidence of flip-flopping on issues. But Yoder managed to win the nine-person contest with 44 percent of the vote.

In the fall, his Democratic opponent was Stephene Moore, the wife of the retiring incumbent and a nurse by trade. She supported President Barack Obama's health care bill while Yoder opposed it. He also came out against reinstating the estate tax, which affects many family farms and was about to expire, while Moore favored keeping the tax but at lower rates.

Moore seized on a *Topeka Capital-Journal* report that Yoder refused to take a preliminary breath test during a 2009 traffic stop. Yoder pleaded guilty to refusing a law enforcement officer's request and was fined $165. His campaign said that he wasn't drunk and that he refused the test because he had passed a field sobriety test. Moore was criticized for going too far in running an ad comparing Yoder to celebrities Lindsay Lohan and Mel Gibson. *The Kansas City Star* endorsed Yoder, calling him "quick-witted and thoughtful," and saying he "could be a force in Congress." He won 58%-39%.

In the House, Yoder was given a seat on the Appropriations Committee. Though he voted a strongly conservative line, he avoided the anti-government rhetoric of his fellow freshmen and joined Rhode Island Democrat David Cicilline's Common Ground Caucus. He was among the few Republicans to refuse to sign activist Grover Norquist's pledge never to raise taxes, saying no one can predict the future. In August 2011, Yoder introduced a bill to ban the issuing of $1 coins for 15 years as a way of saving money; the Treasury Department later suspended the coins' production.

In 2014, Yoder used his seat on Appropriations to work with a bipartisan group of lawmakers who cut a deal that rolled back a controversial provision in the Dodd-Frank banking law of 2010. He told *Roll Call* that the result was "a minor fix." But critics said that the removal of restrictions on the ability of banks to trade in certain commodities created a major loophole, which was pushed actively by big Wall Street banks and was strongly opposed by Sen. Elizabeth Warren of Massachusetts.

In August 2012, news accounts reported that during a fact-finding trip to Israel the previous summer, several House freshmen took a late-night swim in the Sea of Galilee, a pilgrimage site for Christians. The other members remained clothed, but Yoder shed his clothing, prompting a rebuke from Majority Leader Eric Cantor and an avalanche of negative publicity. GOP presidential candidate Mitt Romney called the incident "reprehensible," while comic David Letterman turned it into a list of "Top 10 Congressman Kevin Yoder Excuses." A chastened Yoder apologized. In November, he was reelected without major-party opposition, but libertarian Joel Balam, a college professor who raised less than $3,200 to Yoder's $1.7 million, received an unusually large 32% of the vote. Yoder's indiscretion continued as an issue during the 2014 campaign when his Democratic opponent, Kelly Kultala, ran an ad that featured a group of nudists talking about Yoder's behavior. Yoder won 60%-40%, which was close to his margin in 2010 and suggested that the Galilee swim after three years had likely run its course.

FOURTH DISTRICT

Mike Pompeo (R)

Elected 2010, 3rd term; b. Dec. 30, 1963, Orange, CA; U.S. Military Acad., B.S. 1986, Harvard U., J.D. 1994; Presbyterian; married (Susan); 1 child.

Military Career: Army, 1986-91.

Professional Career: Practicing atty., 1994-96; CEO, Thayer Aerospace, 1996-2006; Pres., Sentry Intl., 2006-10.

DC Office: 436 CHOB, 20515, 202-225-6216; Fax: 202-225-3489; Website: pompeo.house.gov.

State Offices: Wichita, 316-262-8992.

Committees: *Energy & Commerce:* Commerce, Manufacturing & Trade; Communications & Technology; Energy & Power. *Intelligence (Select):* CIA Members; NSA & Cybersecurity. *Select Benghazi Committee.*

Group Ratings

	ADA	ACLU	AFL-CIO	LCV	ITI	COC	HAFA	ACU	CFG	FRC
2014	5%	11%	–	3%	100%	55%	87%	100%	100%	100%
2013	0%	C	10%	7%	C	85%	C	100%	96%	C

National Journal Ratings

	2013 LIB	—	2013 CONS
Economic	3%	—	96%
Social	0%	—	87%
Foreign	34%	—	60%
Composite	16%	—	84%

Key Votes of the 113th Congress

1. Sandy storm spending	N	5. Medical Marijuana	N	9. Syrian Rebels Training	Y
2. Violence Against Women Act	N	6. Farm Bill	N	10. Keystone pipeline	Y
3. Guantanamo Bay Detainees	N	7. Afghanistan Combat	N	11. Immigration Exec. Action	Y
4. Abortion 20-week ban	Y	8. NSA Phone Data Collection	N	12. Bipartisan budget deal	N

Election Results

2014 general	Mike Pompeo (R)...................... 138,757	(67%)	$2,673,678	$179,983	$363,445
	Perry Schuckman (D) 69,396	(33%)	$12,196		
2014 primary	Mike Pompeo (R)......................... 43,564	(63%)			
	Todd Tiahrt (R) 25,977	(37%)			

Prior winning percentages: 2012 (62%), 2010 (59%)

Population		Race and Ethnicity		Income	
Total:	717,201	White	75.2%	Median income:	$48,560
Urban:	59.9%	Latino	11.2%		(263 of 435)
Suburban:	14.5%	Black	6.2%	Under $50,000	51.4%
Rural:	25.7%	Asian	2.8%	$50,000-$99,999:	30.5%
Land area:	16,238	Two races	3.6%	$100,000-$199,999:	15.3%
Pop/sq. mi.;	44.2	White Ethnic	18.5%	$200,000 or more:	2.9%
Born in state:	65.3%			Poverty Rate	15.2%
		Education			
Age Groups		H.S. grad or less:	37.6%	**Work**	
Under 18:	25.9%	Some college:	34.6%	White collar:	34.9%
18 to 34:	23.0%	College degree, 4 yr.:	19.2%	Blue collar:	39.3%
35 to 64:	37.3%	Post-grad study:	8.7%	Sales and service:	25.8%
Over 64:	13.8%				
		Military		Govt. workers:	13.9%
		Veterans/active duty:	10.0%		

South Central Kansas: Wichita

With about 386,000 people, Wichita is smaller than the 2-million-plus metro Kansas City, but it is a Great Plains metropolis of the magnitude of Omaha or Tulsa and still growing. It began as a farm market town and grew with local oil and gas discoveries in the 1920s. Its real impetus came dur-

Voter Turnout	
2013 Total Citizen 18+	505,802
2014 House Turnout	208,153
2014 Turnout as % CVAP	41.2%
2012 Turnout as % CVAP	53.1%

ing World War II and the years just afterward, when aircraft factories sprouted up on the Kansas plains, and Wichita suddenly became the nation's major producer of small aircraft. Workers poured in, many from neighboring Arkansas and Oklahoma, giving the city a taste of Southern culture. The September 11 attacks were a severe blow to the airline industry, with the loss of some 15,000 jobs in Wichita. The Navy gave the area a boost in 2004 with a contract for 100 modified 737s to be used to hunt submarines. Then, the 2007-09 recession sparked another wave of layoffs, with Cessna and Hawker Beechcraft idling more than 1,000 workers; the latter filed for bankruptcy in 2012. Boeing, once the area's largest employer, shut down its local facilities in 2014; company officials cited cuts in the Pentagon budget and high overhead costs. Its 413-acre site was bought by developers, who planned to lease most of its office buildings. The four hangars included one that can house three 747 jetliners.

The aviation industry is just one facet of the local economy, which maintains slow but steady growth. Wichita has become a regional health care center in the Plains. Cargill Meat

Solutions, one of 75 businesses under Cargill Inc., the largest privately held corporation in the United States, is based in Wichita, as is Koch Industries, owned by the politically active and conservative Koch brothers. It ranked second to Cargill as the nation's largest privately held company in 2014, and employs about 60,000 in the United States. At a time when the Kochs were battered

2012 Presidential Vote		
Mitt Romney (R)................164,553	(62%)
Barack Obama (D) 96,433	(36%)
2008 Presidential Vote		
John McCain (R).................166,875	(59%)
Barack Obama (D) 112,473	(40%)
Cook Partisan Voting Index: R+14		

politically for their well-financed conservative activism, their company was beloved at home as an employer and philanthropist. By 2015, business leaders were discussing the need for innovation and growth in the local economy, with aerospace, health, and oil and gas remaining as key components.

Kansas' 4th Congressional District is centered on Wichita, covering wheat-growing areas to the east and west, but with most of its people in Wichita and Sedgwick County. Politically, it is solidly Republican in federal elections. It occasionally votes Democratic in local and state contests, and the city elected its first African-American mayor, Democrat Carl Brewer, in 2007. He served two terms and was hailed as a consensus-builder when he stepped down in April 2015.

Mike Pompeo (R)

Republican Mike Pompeo was elected in 2010 to succeed Rep. Todd Tiahrt, who ran for the Senate. On the Energy and Commerce Committee, Pompeo worked against what he considers the excessive regulation of business, particularly Koch Industries, a generous donor to Pompeo and other conservatives. He easily turned back an unusual primary bid by Tiahrt to re-capture his seat in 2014.

Pompeo's mother met his father over the phone while she was working as a purchasing clerk for Boeing in Wichita, and he was selling parts to the company from Southern California. They married in Wichita and moved to Santa Ana, in the heart of conservative Orange County, where Pompeo was born, raised, and attended high school. He graduated first in his class from West Point, and served as a tank platoon leader, cavalry troop executive officer, and squadron maintenance officer in Germany. Pompeo left the Army with the rank of captain. He graduated from Harvard Law School, and joined the Washington, D.C., law firm of Williams & Connolly, specializing in tax law. He did volunteer work on behalf of Arkansas residents who brought an ultimately unsuccessful lawsuit to defend term limits for members of Congress.

Pompeo moved to Kansas in 1996 to start the company Thayer Aerospace, which provided components for aircraft. The company later opened a factory in Mexicali, Mexico, which became an issue in his first political campaign. Opponents argued that he was willing to outsource jobs from Kansas. Pompeo responded that he won a contract for the factory that created 40 jobs at his Kansas site. Pompeo became active in Republican politics, ultimately serving as a GOP national committeeman.

When Tiahrt decided to seek the Senate seat that Sam Brownback vacated to run for governor, Pompeo jumped into the Republican primary for the House seat. His chief opponents were state Sen. Jean Schodorf and businessmen Wink Hartman, who spent more than $1.6 million on the race. Hartman ran into trouble after Pompeo's campaign charged that he had taken up residency in Florida for tax purposes. The moderate Schodorf, meanwhile, faced a series of negative ads from outside groups supporting Pompeo, one of which featured a man seeking a hunting license to "bag a RINO"—a reference to "Republican in Name Only," a pejorative term conservatives use to describe moderates in their party. Pompeo won the primary with 39% of the vote, to 24% for Schodorf, and 23% for Hartman. The losing candidates later complained to the *Wichita Eagle* about Pompeo's negative campaigning.

Pompeo's Democratic opponent in the general election, state Rep. Raj Goyle, emphasized his commitment to helping laid-off aircraft workers in the district, and he was financially competitive, raising $1.9 million to Pompeo's $2.2 million. Goyle objected to a billboard ad by a Pompeo supporter that read, "Vote American. Vote for Pompeo." Goyle, whose parents are from India, called the ad "bigoted," and it came down. In a strongly Republican year and district, Pompeo won, 59%-36%.

In the House, Pompeo established himself as a leading conservative in his freshman class. He focused more on policy than on butting heads with party leaders. He introduced a resolution in 2011 calling for the elimination of all energy subsidies, a measure that drew criticism from energy investor T. Boone Pickens. In the debate over raising the nation's debt limit, Pompeo blasted President Barack Obama as "irresponsible and reckless." But he backed the subsequent deal, drawing criticism from some tea party activists. He was one of four freshmen whom the National Republican Congressional Committee tapped as regional representatives. On an important matter locally, he led congressional criticism of a 2012 Pentagon decision to award a $355 million contract to supply attack aircraft to the Afghan air force. Wichita's Hawker Beechcraft sued the Air Force after its bid was disqualified. With Democratic Rep. G.K. Butterfield of North Carolina, Pompeo generated controversy in 2015 with a bipartisan bill to create a voluntary federal labeling standard for genetically modified foods. The measure, backed by food and agriculture industries, sought to block state efforts to require mandatory labeling. Pompeo described the bill as an attempt to set a framework for the increased role of biotechnology in growing crops.

Pompeo gained attention for his relationship with Koch Industries, owned by conservative brothers Charles and David Koch. Pompeo in 2010 received $80,000 in campaign donations from Koch Industries and its employees, more than any other candidate. He hired a former Koch lawyer as his chief of staff, and quickly jumped on some of the brothers' top legislative priorities, including trying to eliminate funding for a database of consumer complaints about unsafe products and for an Environmental Protection Agency registry of global-warming polluters. "I'm sure he would vigorously dispute this, but it's hard not to characterize him as the congressman from Koch," University of Kansas political scientist Burdett Loomis told *The Washington Post* in 2011. Pompeo contended that he shared the company's belief in limited government, and that that view is widespread in his district. He wrote a February 2012 op-ed column for *Politico* in which he defended the company against criticism by House Democrats. "Given that many Americans are now desperate for jobs, we should be begging entrepreneurs to look for new opportunities—not attacking them because their companies might make a profit," he wrote.

Pompeo won leadership assignments to deal with national security issues on the Intelligence and Benghazi committees. He drew headlines when former National Security Agency contractor Edward Snowden spoke via video from Russia at the South by Southwest festival in Austin Texas in March 2014. Pompeo wrote an open letter arguing that Snowden's appearance condoned "lawlessness" and perpetuated an "ongoing intentional distortion of truth that he and his media enablers have engaged in."

Pompeo has been easily reelected. His chief bump in the road came in the August 2014 primary challenge by Tiahrt. He sought to cast Pompeo as a supporter of the Affordable Care Act, purportedly based on his votes on several bills that financed the health care law. Pompeo fought back, with considerable financial help from Koch Industries plus the anti-tax Club for Growth, which usually supports challengers. He led in every county, and notched a blowout 63%-37% victory. In November, he scored a 2-to-1 win.

★ KENTUCKY ★

Kentucky's image remains very much what it was at its beginnings, a Jeffersonian commonwealth built on an agrarian culture: growing tobacco, horses (nine out of 10 Kentucky taxpayers in 1800 owned at least one) and brewing whiskey. Later, coal and its extraction became a pillar of the state. Some of those traditions remain, and have thrived, but others have been displaced by societal change and the modern economy. Now Amazon is one of the biggest employers in the state.

When Thomas Jefferson was writing his *Notes on the State of Virginia* and early settlers were coming through the Cumberland Gap, Kentucky was part of Virginia. When it was split off from Virginia and admitted to the union in 1792, it was the first state west of the Appalachian chain. In 1798, Thomas Jefferson, aroused by the Federalists' anti-sedition acts, ghostwrote the Kentucky Resolutions, a defense of self-governance by the states. Kentucky's largest county is named for Jefferson, and its largest city for the monarch to whom he was credentialed as ambassador to France, Louis XVI. Kentucky has a constitution informed by a Jeffersonian suspicion of concentrating power. Its one-term limit on governors was raised to two only in 1992, when voters amended the state constitution (only after then Gov. Brereton Jones vowed not to seek a second term for himself). Until 2001, it limited its state legislature to one 60-day session every two years and much important business was done in special sessions.

Just as the Cumberland Gap, the pass through the Appalachian Mountains where Virginia meets Kentucky and Tennessee, was America's first gateway for westward expansion, Kentucky today is logistical hub for much of the nation. The state is within a day's drive of more than half of the U.S. population and its large air-freight shipping terminals at the Louisville and Cincinnati-Northern Kentucky airports offer access to customers around the world. That was a big reason why Amazon.com opened a fulfillment center in Campbellsville, Kentucky in 2000. Now the nation's largest online retailer has 11 fulfillment, return and customer service centers in the state employing some 7,000 full time workers and the company plans to invest $25 million in the commonwealth for workforce development. But before Amazon came to Kentucky, the automobile industry arrived, seeking some of the same logistical advantages the state had to offer, as well as a business-friendly environment. According to an analysis by the University of Louisville's Urban Studies Institute, Kentucky has benefited handsomely from the migration of automakers to the South. The state is at the center of "auto alley," which runs from the Great Lakes to the Gulf of Mexico, a corridor that includes 29 vehicle assembly plants. On average, Kentucky is closer to those plants than any other state, which offers transportation cost savings for suppliers shipping auto parts to those assembly lines. And while the nation saw a 30 percent decline in auto parts manufacturing jobs from 1990 to 2013, Kentucky saw an 87 percent increase in employment in that sector, which includes metal stamping and the manufacturing of engine parts, steering and suspension components, brake systems and seating. Kentucky is also home to four car and truck assembly lines: two Ford plants in Louisville, a Toyota plant in Georgetown, and a General Motors plant in Bowling Green. The state produced 1.3 million vehicles in 2014, roughly one out of every nine built in the U.S., and the auto and auto parts industries employed some 85,000 Kentuckians.

Three of those plants, the two in Louisville and the one in Georgetown, which is just north of Lexington, are located in the portion of Kentucky known as the "Golden Triangle," the most productive and populous part of the state. The Golden Triangle extends from Jefferson County (Louisville) east to Fayette County (Lexington) and then north to Boone and Kenton Counties (suburban Cincinnati), the state's four largest counties by population. They are faster growing and have higher median household incomes than Kentucky as a whole, and several of their adjacent counties are wealthier still and seeing more rapid population growth. Scott County, near Lexington, grew more than 40 percent, from 2000 to 2010, and between 2010 and 2014, it's grown another 9 percent, more than five times faster than the state. Oldham County, next door to Louisville, grew three times faster than the state from 2010 to 2014, and it has a median household income of more than $83,0000, almost double the state average.

The territory includes the state's famed Bluegrass region, where its prized Thoroughbred industry is centered. And the Golden Triangle even includes Bourbon County, where

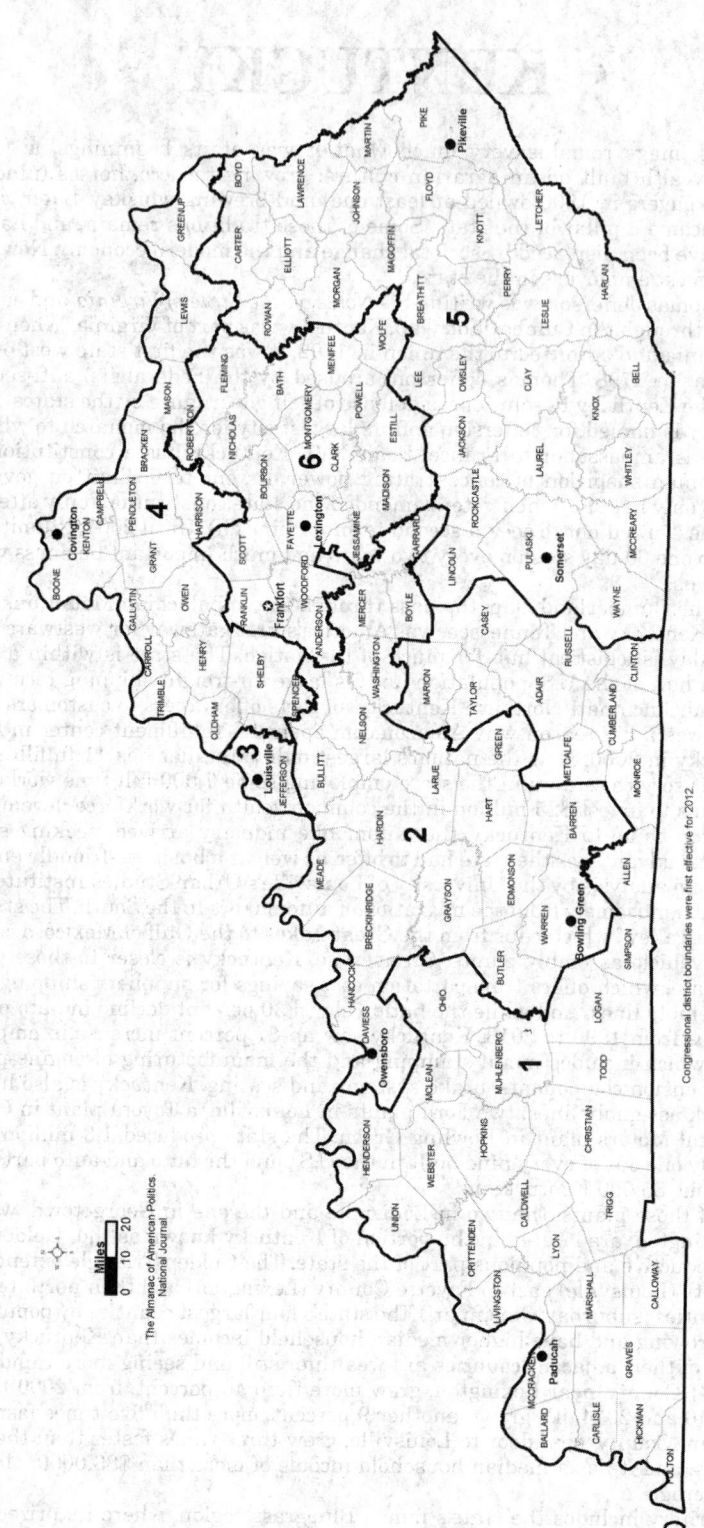

The Almanac of American Politics.
National Journal

Miles
0 10 20

Congressional district boundaries were first effective for 2012.

the sweet brown liquor was first distilled in the 18th century. A 2012 University of Kentucky Ag Equine survey reported that the state's horse breeding and racing industry generated more than 40,000 jobs that year and a total economic impact of almost $3 billion. And a 2014 study by the University of Louisville's Urban Studies Institute found that Kentucky produces as much 95 percent of all the Bourbon on the planet, generating some 15,400 jobs in distilleries and corporate offices—up from 8,690 jobs in 2012—and an annual payroll of more than $700 million. But most of Kentucky is not doing as well. According to an analysis by the Kentucky Center for Economic Policy, a research group that focuses on state budget issues and their impact on low-to-moderate-income families, only 28 of the state's 120 counties had more people employed in March 2015 than in March 2007, before the recession began. The counties where the job growth has been strongest are mostly clustered in central and northern Kentucky. Major job gains, in both percentage terms and raw numbers, have occurred in Scott, Oldham, Woodford, Jessamine, Campbell, Fayette and Jefferson—all in the Golden Triangle. Counties close to major highways have seen their auto, transportation and logistics industries rebound. In these places, the problem is the lack of skilled labor. But rural Kentucky counties have seen their economies suffer as manufacturing and coal production decline.

The increasing popularity of hydraulic fracturing for low-cost natural gas has contributed significantly to the national slowdown in coal production. Tougher federal regulations to protect water quality around mines and higher Environmental Protection Agency emissions standards on coal-burning power plants have exacerbated the downturn. In Kentucky coal counties, you won't find a lot of fans of the Obama administration, especially in the eastern part of the state: Once the state's center of coal mining, production and jobs there have been slashed in half over five years. The Kentucky Energy and Environment Cabinet reported that in 2009, coal-industry employment in Eastern Kentucky averaged 14,100 people, who extracted 75.3 million tons of coal from its hillsides. In 2014, employment at the region's mines averaged 7,288, and production totaled just 37.5 million tons. In Western Kentucky, production was not nearly as hard hit. Ironically, the higher sulfur content coal from this part of the state once had difficulty coping with clean-air rules, but the installation of scrubbers at many power plants has helped sustain the region's mines. At the end of 2014, an estimated 11,574 people were working in Kentucky's coal industry, the fewest statewide since the state began keeping records in the 1920s. Once the state's cash crop, tobacco farming has also seen a decline. For most of the last century nearly every Kentucky farmer grew at least a small crop of tobacco, but health concerns and more recently social mores gradually took their toll. According to William Snell, a professor of agricultural economics at the University of Kentucky and a leading expert on the burley leaf, horses overtook tobacco as the state's leading farm product by 1999. But tobacco's fall has picked up speed since then. In 2002, before the federal buyout program to ease the transition for tobacco growers began in 2005, there were 29,237 tobacco farms in Kentucky. In 2012, according the Agriculture Census, there were just 4,537, an 85 percent tumble in ten years. The cash payments to farmers who had previously owned tobacco quotas ended in 2014. Corn and soybeans have replaced tobacco for many Kentucky farmers and some are anticipating their first hemp

Population		Race and Ethnicity		Income	
Total:	4,395,295	White	86.1%	Median income:	$42,158
Urban:	33.1%	Black	7.9%		(43 of 50)
Suburban:	20.0%	Latino	3.0%	Under $50,000	55.9%
Rural:	46.9%	Asian	1.1%	$50,000-$99,999:	28.9%
Land area:	39,486	Two races	1.6%	$100,000-$199,999:	12.5%
Pop/sq. mi.:	111.3	White Ethnic	18.4%	$200,000 or more:	2.7%
Born in state:	70.1%			Poverty Rate	14.8%
		Education			
Age Groups		H.S. grad or less:	49.1%	**Work**	
Under 18:	23.1%	Some college:	28.4%	White collar:	32.7%
18 to 34:	22.6%	College degree, 4 yr.:	13.3%	Blue collar:	40.7%
35 to 64:	39.9%	Post-grad study:	9.3%	Sales and service:	26.5%
Over 64:	14.5%			Govt. workers:	15.1%
		Military			
		Veterans/active duty:	8.8%		

crops in 2016. Still, the leafy product has not completely shriveled: dark tobacco, used in smokeless consumption, has seen its production grow.

Kentucky long favored the Democratic Party, which can trace its ancestry at least tenuously back to Jefferson. But here, too, there has been change recently. Democrats have maintained a hold on the governorship, losing it only three times—in 1943, 1967, and 2003—in the last eight decades. But Kentucky has gone solidly Republican in the last four presidential elections, both of its Senators and five of its six House members are Republicans, and the party has held a majority in the state Senate since 2000. Democrats continue their narrow grip on the state House. Over the years, Kentucky has seen hearty if usually lopsided political competition, with most of the 120 counties usually voting as they did in the Civil War era. The Bluegrass region and the western end of the state were slaveholding territory and voted Democratic. Louisville, with many German immigrants, was an anti-slavery town, and for years flirted with Republicans, but the city and surrounding Jefferson County has been conspicuously more Democratic than the state in this century. The eastern mountains were pro-Union and remain Republican, except for some counties where the United Mine Workers organized coal miners in the 1930s. But coal country has been swinging Republican: Al Gore carried the eastern and western counties with active coal mines, but in 2008 they voted 58%-40% for John McCain and in 2012, 68%-27% for Mitt Romney, even as the two parties' shares in the rest of the state varied by only three percentage points in the elections between 2000 and 2012.

Voter Turnout	
2013 Total Citizen 18+	3,299,161
2014 Highest Statewide Turnout	1,435,868
2014 Turnout as % CVAP	43.5%
2012 Turnout as % CVAP	54.7%

Legislature		
Senate:	27R	11D
House:	54D	46R

Presidential Politics For many years, Kentucky was a competitive state when Democrats ran a Southerner or two on their ticket, as in such widely separated years as 1952, 1976, 1980, 1992, and 1996. In 2000, Al Gore initially targeted Kentucky, which had voted for the Clinton-Gore ticket and was just north of his home state of Tennessee. But Kentucky was trending away from Clinton Democrats in the 1990s, and Gore had taken stands seen as hostile to tobacco, coal, and automobiles. George W. Bush carried the state 57%-41% that year, and

2012 Presidential Vote		
Mitt Romney (R)	1,087,190	(61%)
Barack Obama (D)	679,370	(38%)

2012 Presidential Primary		
Mitt Romney (R)	117,621	(67%)
Ron Paul (R)	22,074	(13%)
Rick Santorum (R)	15,629	(9%)
Newt Gingrich (R)	10,479	(6%)

2008 Presidential Vote		
John McCain (R)	1,048,462	(57%)
Barack Obama (D)	751,985	(41%)

Republicans have won by similar margins ever since. In 2012, Barack Obama carried only four of Kentucky's 120 counties, including those containing the state's two largest cities, Louisville and Lexington, and the state capital of Frankfort. He carried only one historically Democratic county in the eastern mountains. By way of comparison, even when losing by landslide margins, George McGovern carried seven mountain counties in 1972 and Walter Mondale carried 12 mountain counties and seven historically Democratic counties in the west in 1984.

This was not Obama's first weak showing in Kentucky. The state's presidential primary is held in May, by which time both parties' nominees were effectively chosen in every year from 1980 to 2004. But in May 2008, Hillary Clinton was still struggling to overcome Obama's narrow lead in delegates and she campaigned hard in Kentucky as a fighter for working people. Obama made only one appearance after August 2007, and ran a few ads stressing his Christian faith. Clinton won 65%-30%, more than in any other state except Arkansas and West Virginia. Obama carried the counties containing Louisville and Lexington and lost the other 118; in 19 counties, he got less than 10% of the vote. In the general election, only 69% of self-identified Democrats and 54% of Clinton primary voters voted for Obama—unusually low figures. When he ran for reelection in 2012, Obama did win the May Democratic primary, but 42% of the votes were cast for the only alternative, "Uncommitted," which carried 67 counties and tied in one. The late May primary had no impact on the Republican nominating contests in 2008 or 2012: John McCain won the former with 72% and Mitt Romney won the latter with 67%.

Congressional Districts   Republicans controlled the state Senate and Democrats the state House after the 2000 and 2010 censuses. House Democrats presented plans that would have weakened Republican incumbents, but acceded to compromise plans that made few shifts in congressional district lines each time. Democrats have an edge in party registration in all six current districts, but five of them have elected Republicans since 2012. John Yarmuth, the only Democrat, has become entrenched in the formerly marginal 3rd District in Louisville's Jefferson County.

114th Congress Lineup	
5 R	1 D
113th Congress Lineup	
5 R	1 D

Governor

Steve Beshear (D)

Elected 2007, term expires Dec. 2015, 2nd term; b. Sept. 21, 1944, Dawson Springs; U. of KY, B.A. 1966, U. of KY, J.D. 1968; Baptist; married (Jane); 2 children.

Military Career: U.S. Army Reserve, 1969-75.

Elected Office: KY House, 1974-79; KY atty. gen., 1980-84; KY lt. gov., 1984-88.

Professional Career: Practicing atty., 1968-71, 1989-2006.

Office: State Capitol, 700 Capitol Ave., Suite 100, Frankfort, 40601, 502-564-2611; Fax: 502-564-2517; Website: governor.ky.gov.

Election Results

2011 general	Steve Beshear (D)	464,245	(56%)
	David Williams (R)	294,034	(35%)
	Gatewood Galbraith (I)	74,860	(9%)
2011 primary	Steve Beshear (D)	unopposed	

Prior winning percentage: 2007 (59%)

Although formerly limited to just one term in office, the governor of Kentucky is often the state's most influential politician with broad authority over the state budgets, appointments and administration. Steve Beshear has not been shy about seeking that power or exercising it.

The son and grandson of Baptist ministers, Beshear grew up in Dawson Springs, a small western Kentucky town with a population of less than 3,000. His family had strong ties to the community; his father was also a funeral director and served as mayor. Perhaps Beshear got the political bug as a young boy in the early 1950s, when he would spend time with his great uncle, a four-term state legislator, as he campaigned from town to town. Valedictorian of his high school class, Beshear went on to the University of Kentucky, was elected student body president in his junior year, and later earned a law degree from the school, graduating with honors. In a moot court national competition in New York City, Beshear impressed the judges with a skillful performance, and he was invited to interview with two international law firms. Offered a job by both, Beshear accepted a position with the Wall Street firm White & Case, and during that time, he joined an Army Reserve unit in the Bronx, serving as an intelligence analyst. After three years in the Big Apple, Beshear was ready to return home. He and his wife, Jane, whom he had met in college, settled in Lexington, where he took a job with a smaller firm.

In 1973, he launched his first campaign for state representative to succeed a retiring member. Winning easily, Beshear went on to serve three terms in Frankfort, where he gained a reputation for supporting proposals to stimulate job growth and attract businesses to the state. One of his early accomplishments was leading a successful effort to improve neonatal care at the University of Kentucky Medical Center. In 1979, Beshear made his first successful bid for statewide office, winning a race for attorney general at age 35. During his term, he readily took stands that were unpopular in the conservative state. In 1982, he declared that a state law restricting abortion was unconstitutional. Then, he issued an opinion based on a U.S. Supreme Court decision that required copies of the Ten Commandments to be removed from Kentucky classrooms. His decision prompted thousands of calls to the governor's office.

A billboard that said, "Keep the 10 Commandments, Remove Steve Beshear" went up in Lexington.

In 1983, then-Lt. Gov. Martha Layne Collins captured the Democratic nomination for governor and selected Beshear as her running mate. The two defeated the Republican challenger, Jim Bunning (later a senator), by 10 percentage points, making Collins the first and only female governor in the commonwealth's history. Beshear sought his party's nomination for governor in 1987. The primary drew two other high-profile choices: KFC millionaire and former Gov. John Brown and wealthy bookstore businessman Wallace Wilkinson, who ended up winning. Beshear finished a distant third. After his defeat, Beshear joined the Lexington law firm Stites & Harbison, where he specialized in business litigation and was involved in some high-profile cases including the Bluegrass bankruptcy of the famed Calumet horse farm. In 1996, Beshear challenged Republican Sen. Mitch McConnell, who was seeking a third term. Beshear knew the odds of defeating McConnell were long, but he felt that the Kentucky Democratic Party needed to put up a credible candidate and that with President Bill Clinton, who was fairly popular in Kentucky, at the head of the ticket, he might get lucky. Beshear's critics have viewed him more as a serial office seeker: "Typical politician running for everything," is how former Gov. Brown once described Beshear. In 1996 election, Clinton carried Kentucky by less than one percent and that was not nearly enough to overcome McConnell who had better than a 2-1 fundraising advantage and won handily, 55%-43%. Following his second loss, Beshear went back to his law practice in Lexington. While Democrats had once been dominant in the state, by the mid-1990s, the congressional delegation and state offices were shifting toward Republicans, aided by the aggressive efforts of McConnell, who helped engineer the party switches that gave Republicans a majority in the state Senate in 1999.

But in 2006, Democratic fortunes were on the rise everywhere, including in Kentucky. In the race for governor in 2007, the time seemed ripe for Democrats to oust embattled GOP Gov. Ernie Fletcher, who was indicted on minor charges after a 15-month investigation into political patronage. Ultimately, the case was settled, and Fletcher was cleared of the charges. Despite calls for his resignation, Fletcher ran again and beat back primary challenges from former Rep. Anne Northup and his former finance chairman, Billy Harper. In seeking the Democratic nomination to take on Fletcher, Beshear called for expanded gambling in the state. Citing the huge sums Kentuckians were already spending at casinos across the border in Illinois, Indiana, and West Virginia, Beshear argued that legalized gambling could provide money for education reform and expanded health care. He won the May 2007 primary relatively easily, 41%-21%, beating hospital executive Bruce Lunsford and narrowly avoiding a runoff. In the general election campaign, Fletcher condemned Beshear's gambling proposal in an attempt to rally social conservatives to his side. He also emphasized Beshear's past support of abortion rights and his position on the Ten Commandments display. But the indictment and investigation had taken a toll. Beshear won, 59%-41%.

As soon as Beshear came into office in early 2008, he exercised his sweeping authority over the state budget and chopped about $78 million from previously approved spending to address an anticipated shortfall. He also ordered the state to use another $190 million in left-over or unbudgeted funds from the previous fiscal year to cover the gap. In 2009, Beshear and state lawmakers struggled to come up with ways to deal with the faltering economy, as the state's unemployment rate climbed past 9%, its highest level in 25 years. But the session ended with lawmakers spurning his request to take up several high profile measures, including tax credits to lure a NASCAR race to the Kentucky Speedway. He also sought approval of a measure allowing Kentucky's horse racing tracks to operate video slot casinos, but it failed to get out of committee. Senate President David Williams, a Republican, declared the idea dead for the 2010 session as well, angering Beshear. The governor's troubles didn't end there: A recording of Lt. Gov. Daniel Mongiardo criticizing his boss in a profanity-laced tirade as the state's "worst" governor surfaced on the Internet. After Mongiardo unsuccessfully sought the Democratic nomination for the Senate in 2010, Beshear announced Louisville Mayor Jerry Abramson would be his running mate in 2011.

When Beshear was up for reelection in 2011, Williams challenged him, easily securing the GOP nomination. He pushed for comprehensive tax reform and attacked Beshear over his handling of the state's budget. Williams also tried to tie Beshear to President Barack Obama, who was unpopular in the state. Beshear sought to portray himself as a budget-cutter who had reduced his own salary and sold state airplanes. He kept his distance from the national Democratic Party and Washington, running an ad in August showing photos of Obama, House Speaker John Boehner, House Minority Leader Nancy Pelosi and Senate Majority Leader Harry Reid, with an announcer saying that "the mess in Washington has disappointed us all." He also touted his "A" rating from the National Rifle Association, although he remained supportive of abortion rights. Beshear raised significantly more money than Williams—some $10 million by October—and led in the polls. In an attempt to rally support among the state's many devout Christians, Williams criticized Beshear for participating in a Hindu prayer ceremony, while the governor's supporters ridiculed the complaint as an act of desperation. Beshear won with 56% to 35% for Williams, with 9% going to independent Gatewood Galbraith.

Williams exacted revenge in February 2012, when the state Senate voted down, 21-16, Beshear's latest proposal to allow casino gambling. An angry governor accused his rival of "sabotage" for scheduling the vote when he knew one of its supporters would be out of town, and later signed a two-year plan for Kentucky's roads after vetoing about $50 million for road projects in or near Williams' district. But after the U.S. Supreme Court ruled to uphold the Affordable Care Act, Beshear took a much bolder move in July and issued an executive order establishing the Kentucky Health Benefit Exchange to extend health coverage throughout the state. Some 400,000 additional Kentuckians were enrolled in Medicaid through the state exchange, Kynect, numbers that alarmed Republican legislators who worried about the additional costs the state would eventually bear for the added coverage beginning in 2017. But only about 76,000 Kentuckians purchased private plans that offered subsidies to families earning between 138 and 400 percent of the poverty level. The relatively high proportion of new Medicaid enrollees was not unexpected given the number of rural poor people in the state who had gone without health care. At the same time, private insurance companies that offer coverage plans on the state exchange need a lot of younger, healthier customers to offset the cost of covering more people with pre-conditions and those who are simply older. Beshear continued his health promotion efforts in 2014, signing an executive order prohibiting the use of all tobacco products and e-cigarettes on state-owned property and in state-owned vehicles.

In 2015 Beshear signed comprehensive legislation to combat the heroin epidemic that has killed hundreds of Kentuckians every year. The bi-partisan measure includes new treatment programs, needle exchanges and tougher penalties for possessing relatively large amounts of heroin. He also issued an executive order raising the minimum wage for employees of the executive branch of state government from $7.25 an hour to $10.10. The move would only affect the wages of about 800 state workers. The order would eventually require companies with state contracts to pay at least $10.10 per hour to their employees working on those contracts. Beshear's surprise announcement was seen as a prelude to the race to succeed him: Democratic gubernatorial nominee and state Attorney General Jack Conway has called for raising the minimum wage.

Beshear shook up state politics in November 2014, when he announced that Lt. Gov. Abramson was resigning to become Director of Intergovernmental Affairs in the Obama White House and that he would be replaced by Crit Luallen, former state auditor. Luallen, who was generally well regarded for her past efforts to root out government waste and fraud, was the first appointed lieutenant governor since the current state constitution was adopted in 1891. Legal experts said that while the state constitution was unclear on how to fill the vacancy created by Abramson's departure, most agreed that the document also gave Kentucky's governor broad appointment powers. Republicans in the legislature didn't challenge Luallen's appointment or Beshear's authority to make it and she was sworn in a week after she was named to the post. Long before her appointment, Luallen had forsworn any interest in running for governor in 2015, and she seemed prepared for life after politics before Beshear cut short her retirement. But she has avoided ruling out whether she might run for the seat of GOP Sen. Rand Paul in 2016.

Two candidates set to run for governor in 2015 were Attorney General Conway, who waltzed to the Democratic nomination, defeating Geoff Young by more than 100,000 votes in the primary, and wealthy Louisville businessman Matt Bevin, who managed to eek out an 83-vote victory over state Agriculture Commissioner Jamie Comer in a contentious Republican primary. Bevin was a tea party favorite when he unsuccessfully challenged McConnell in the 2014 Republican Senate primary, and that contest was bruising with McConnell running ads that calling Bevin an "East Coast Con Man," and "Bailout Bevin," because his company in Connecticut received state subsidies. Bevin refused to endorse McConnell after the Senate primary, but the Senate majority leader promptly endorsed Bevin once a re-canvass of votes in the gubernatorial primary confirmed that he was the victor. Bevin, who has largely self-funded his campaign, will face the challenge of becoming a more polished candidate in the general election and uniting the Kentucky Republicans, including those in the party establishment who view the outsider with suspicion. Conway was relatively well-positioned going into the fall campaign: For the first time in four decades Kentucky Democrats did not have a competitive primary for governor, enabling the attorney general to build up his war chest for the general election and remain above the political fray. Conway has won two elections for attorney general, in 2007 and 2011, but he knew what it's like to lose: In 2002, Rep. Anne Northup defeated him 52%-48% in a race for her Louisville-based seat, and as the 2010 Democratic Senate nominee he was defeated by Paul, 56%-44%, for that open seat.

Senior Senator

Mitch McConnell (R)

Elected 1984, term expires Jan. 2021, 6th term; b. Feb. 20, 1942, Tuscumbia, AL; U. of Louisville, B.A. 1964, U. of KY, J.D. 1967; Baptist; married (Elaine Chao); 3 children.

Elected Office: Jefferson Cnty. judge exec., 1978-85.

Professional Career: Chief legis. asst., U.S. Sen. Marlow Cook, 1968-70; Deputy asst. U.S. atty. gen., 1974-75.

DC Office: 317 RSOB, 20510, 202-224-2541; Fax: 202-224-2499; Website: mcconnell.senate.gov.

State Offices: Bowling Green, 270-781-1673; Ft. Wright, 859-578-0188; Lexington, 859-224-8286; London, 606-864-2026; Louisville, 502-582-6304; Paducah, 270-442-4554.

Committees: Senate Majority Leader. *Agriculture, Nutrition & Forestry:* Conservation, Forestry & Natural Resources; Livestock, Dairy, Poultry, Marketing & Ag Security; Nutrition, Specialty Crops, Food & Ag Research. *Appropriations:* Agriculture, Rural Development, FDA, & Related Agencies; Defense; Energy & Water Development; Interior, Environment, & Related Agencies; Military Construction, Veterans Affairs & Related Agencies; State, Foreign Operations & Related Programs. *Intelligence (Select):* Ex-officio. *Rules & Administration.*

Group Ratings

	ADA	ACLU	AFL-CIO	LCV	ITI	COC	HAFA	ACU	CFG	FRC
2014	5%	6%	–	20%	33%	100%	67%	84%	55%	100%
2013	0%	C	17%	0%	C	88%	C	92%	87%	C

National Journal Ratings

	2013 LIB	—	2013 CONS
Economic	15%	—	80%
Social	23%	—	75%
Foreign	24%	—	73%
Composite	22%	—	78%

Key Votes of the 113th Congress

1. Sandy storm spending	N	5. Student Loan Rates	Y	9. Bipartisan Budget Deal	N
2. Chuck Hagel Confirmation	N	6. Employee Non-Discrim'n Act	N	10. Farm Bill Conference Rept.	Y
3. Gun Background Checks	N	7. Senate Vote on Judgeships	Y	11. Unempl. Comp. Extension	N
4. Immigration Reform	N	8. Defense Dept. Spending	N	12. Keystone Pipeline	Y

Election Results

2014 general	Mitch McConnell (R)	806,787	(56%)	$30,435,557	$5,855,598	$10,552,995
	Alison Lundergan Grimes (D)	584,698	(41%)	$18,829,908	$1,481,186	$17,092,419
	David Patterson (Lib)	44,240	(3%)			
2014 primary	Mitch McConnell (R)	213,753	(60%)			
	Matt Bevin (R)	125,787	(35%)			

Prior winning percentages: 2008 (53%), 2002 (65%), 1996 (55%), 1990 (52%), 1984 (50%)

If many politicians look in the mirror and see a presidential candidate, Republican Mitch McConnell always aspired to be Senate majority leader—and, at the outset of the 114th Congress, the senior senator from Kentucky finally realized that ambition after two decades of climbing the leadership ladder. McConnell has not sought to be a household name; he is a dour presence on Sunday TV news shows, with *New York Times* columnist Gail Collins once observing that McConnell has "the natural charisma of an oyster." Rather, his power is derived from his mastery of the Senate's arcane procedures and his close-to-the-vest strategizing, bringing to mind the Capitol Hill power brokers of an era prior to advent of mass media. As minority leader for eight years before the Republicans captured the Senate majority in 2014, he made it his quest to lead the opposition to President Barack Obama, who McConnell—in a *Times* interview in early 2015—characterized as "the most left-wing president since Woodrow Wilson, who believed the Founding Fathers kind of got it wrong when they made Congress as strong as it is." But McConnell also has proven to be a skillful and pragmatic negotiator at times of crisis, when partisanship has threatened the ability of the government to function.

During his stint as minority leader, McConnell stressed cohesion to his GOP colleagues, as he preached how sticking together and playing what he calls "team ball" would give them greater leverage with the Democratic White House; it was a strategy that ended up working for Senate Republicans in many instances. In stark contrast to his blunt-spoken Democratic counterpart, Minority Leader Harry Reid of Nevada—who dueled with McConnell for eight years as majority leader—McConnell is a cautious and highly disciplined speaker. "The idea of an off-the-cuff comment is anathema to him," wrote Louisville *Courier-Journal* columnist John David Dyche in a 2009 biography. And while McConnell has focused most of his energy on thwarting Democrats, fellow Republican know that they cross him at their peril. "There are few things more daunting in politics than the determined opposition of McConnell," Arizona GOP Sen. John McCain once said, perhaps recalling McConnell's ongoing effort to derail the McCain-Feingold campaign law that passed Congress in 2002.

The determined Republican partisan who now controls the Senate agenda began his career on the left wing of his party. Another biographer, *New Republic* writer Alec MacGillis, noted in his 2014 volume that McConnell was both pro-abortion rights and pro-labor—favoring collective bargaining for public employees—in the years prior to his election to the Senate, later moving rightward as the GOP did. McConnell grew up in Alabama, where he overcame polio, and at age 13, moved to Louisville. He has been in politics for virtually all of his adult life. Between college and law school at the University of Louisville, he was an intern for Kentucky Republican Sen. John Sherman Cooper, then a member of what has become a nearly extinct bloc in the Senate: moderate Republicans. McConnell later said he admired Cooper for carrying out "his best judgment instead of pandering to the popular view." The young McConnell watched as Cooper helped round up the votes to break the Senate filibuster of the 1964 Civil Rights Act, and accompanied Cooper to the White House when President Lyndon Johnson signed the measure.

Soon after graduating from law school, McConnell became chief legislative assistant to Kentucky Sen. Marlow Cook. He served in the Ford administration's Justice Department and then moved back to Louisville. In 1977, at age 35, McConnell won the office that had been Cook's political stepping-stone, Jefferson County judge-executive. He was reelected in 1981, and in 1984, took on Democratic Sen. Walter (Dee) Huddleston. McConnell ran a clever ad that has become a something of a classic in political advertising circles: It showed bloodhounds sniffing for Huddleston in vacation locales where Huddleston had collected fees for speeches while the Senate was in session. McConnell won by a little more than 5,000 out of 1.2 million cast.

In 1990, after winning a second term, McConnell sought to get on the leadership ladder by running for the chairmanship of the National Republican Senatorial Committee, the Senate GOP's campaign arm. He lost, but tried again in 1996 and won, serving in the post for the 1998 and 2000 election cycles. McConnell's skills as a campaign strategist have been on frequent display in the years since. In a prescient 2009 speech to the Republican National Committee, he warned the GOP to expand its base beyond the South and parts of the Midwest or risk being seen as a "regional party." And he often seeks to shape the party's overall message, repeating poll-tested phrases intended to sway public opinion. After Obama signed his health care legislation into law in 2010, McConnell launched Republicans on the campaign to "repeal and replace" it, which became the byword of the GOP opposition to the measure.

Home in Kentucky, as the state trended increasingly red, McConnell established himself as the behind-the-scenes power in the state Republican Party. But his grip has been loosened in recent years with the rise of the GOP's tea party wing. After helping Republican Jim Bunning win in 1998, McConnell lost faith in Bunning's political skills—and, going into the

2010 election, made it clear he felt that Bunning should not run again. Bunning was livid, calling McConnell a "control freak," but he bowed out. The choice of McConnell and other state Republicans to replace Bunning was Kentucky Secretary of State Trey Grayson. But also running was Rand Paul, the son of one-time Libertarian Party presidential candidate Ron Paul, a Republican House member from Texas.

Bunning and influential conservative Sen. Jim DeMint of South Carolina endorsed Paul, who also had support from tea party groups. In the May 2010 primary, Paul trounced Grayson, and went on to win in November. Since then, the McConnell-Paul relationship has made for one of the more interesting subplots on Capitol Hill. Facing his own difficult re-election bid in 2014, McConnell sought to reach out to Paul; to make inroads among tea party groups, he hired as his campaign manager Jesse Benton, who had worked for both Rand and Ron Paul. McConnell endorsed Paul for president, even likening him to McConnell's political hero: Kentucky's Henry Clay, the Great Compromiser. "To sum up his significance not only for our state but for our country, in a very short period of time, I can say without fear of contradiction that Sen. Rand Paul is, if he chooses to do this, [our] most credible candidate for president of the United States since Henry Clay," McConnell enthusiastically told a gathering of Kentucky Republicans during the 2014 campaign, before Paul jumped into the 2016 presidential race.

However, the relationship was noticeably strained five months into McConnell's tenure as majority leader, as McConnell reacted with visible agitation while Paul repeatedly invoked Senate procedures to stall a reauthorization of the USA Patriot Act over the National Security Agency's bulk collection of telephone data from millions of Americans. Paul had made opposition to this controversial practice a major issue in his presidential campaign, and his tactics highlighted a broader challenge for McConnell in his managing the Senate: the presence of four Republicans seeking to promote their own agendas as they seek the presidency, as well as the large contingent of hardline conservatives elected in recent years with tea party support.

Opposition Democrats pounced on McConnell for waiting until the 11th hour to bring up the Patriot Act authorization, ultimately causing a brief lapse in the government's post-9/11 surveillance powers before a new bill was signed into law. McConnell had gambled—and lost—on senators fearing the political fallout from such a lapse. "Everyone has always assumed Sen. McConnell has an ace up his sleeve, but Sen. Paul called his bluff," declared New York Sen. Charles Schumer, Reid's designated successor as Democratic leader. "You don't leave yourself in that position." Meanwhile, McConnell, who had vigorously opposed a House-passed version of the bill that turned the NSA's storage of phone data over to private companies, ended up having to accept the House bill as the only alternative to continued stalemate.

For his part, McConnell said he was seeking a return to the elusive goal of "regular order," including a more free-flowing Senate floor debate frequently absent during the Democrats' eight-year majority. "We need to get committees working again. We need to recommit to a rational, functioning appropriations process," McConnell said on the Senate floor during the first full day of 2015. "We need to open up ... the legislative process in a way that allows more amendments from both sides." In his first major bill as majority leader, McConnell chose a measure to clear the way for the controversial Keystone XL pipeline running from Canada to the Gulf of Mexico through the Midwest. During the Keystone debate, Republicans crowed that they had voted on more amendments on one bill that on all the bills on the floor during 2014, when the Democrats were still in control. Democratic critics shrugged that it was a hollow gesture, since Obama had vowed to veto the Keystone bill—and there were not sufficient votes to override the veto and have the bill actually become law.

In October 2010, just days before the off-year elections, McConnell—in an interview with *National Journal*—memorably declared: "The single most important thing we want to achieve is for President Obama to be a one-term president." Coming two years prior to Obama standing for a second term, the quote came to exemplify the impede-at-all costs philosophy that critics saw as McConnell's true colors. McConnell subsequently complained those critics had overlooked a second quote in the interview that quickly followed the first, in which he had said of Obama, "...If he's willing to meet us halfway on some of the biggest issues, it's not inappropriate for us to do business with him." (McConnell was somewhat less conciliatory a couple of months earlier when, after having his first one-on-one meeting with the Obama, he expressed limited interest in finding common ground. Asked whether there was too much obstruction in the Senate, he replied, "I think the Senate is operating largely like our founding fathers anticipated it would.")

A rare instance of a bipartisan push for a major piece of legislation occurred four and a half years later, in May 2015, when McConnell—in what he later jokingly referred to as an "out of body experience" in an interview with *The New York Times*—worked with the Obama White House to pass so-called "fast track" trade negotiating authority. The administration was seeking the latter to expedite negotiation and ultimate approval of a 12-nation Asian trade deal that McConnell strongly supported. After top Senate Democratic leaders opposed to fast track, including Reid and Schumer, dealt the White House an initial defeat, McConnell helped to bring around wavering Democratic senators by promising a series of stand-alone floor votes on several trade-related issues. McConnell and other Senate Republican leaders initially tried to maneuver around Reid and Schumer and cut deals with Democrats supportive of the trade bill. But after Reid and Schumer—borrowing a page from McConnell's old playbook—demonstrated their muscle by holding the Democrats in line and temporarily blocking the fast track bill, McConnell was forced to deal with his counterparts in the Democratic leadership.

Earlier in the year, McConnell was also forced to relent when the Democrats hung tough over moving a nearly $40 billion measure to fund operations for the Department of Homeland Security. McConnell initially tried to move a House-passed DHS funding bill with provisions aimed at blocking Obama's controversial executive order on immigration—which the president had issued in late 2014 after blaming congressional Republicans for failing to act on the matter. Senate Democrats successfully blocked the bill passed by the Republican-controlled House on four occasions, leading to an agreement between McConnell and Reid to move a "clean bill." Faced with a choice of capitulating to the White House or risking blame for a shutdown of homeland security programs, McConnell opted for the former.

McConnell entered the 114th Congress with a Republican caucus of 54, a far better position than he had started the 111th Congress at the outset of Obama's first term. Democrats emerged from the 2008 election with a larger majority in the House and with 58 seats in the Senate, leaving them just short of the 60 votes needed to overcome a filibuster. McConnell was not entirely successful at first in holding Republicans together: In February 2009, the Senate approved Obama's $787 billion economic stimulus bill by 61-37, with three Republican defecting to join the Democrats. Then he got more bad news. Arlen Specter of Pennsylvania, trailing his 2004 Republican primary opponent Pat Toomey in the polls, switched parties and joined the Democrats. In July, when Democrat Al Franken was seated in Minnesota after a protracted recount, the Democrats got to the magic 60.

During the 2009 debate on Obama's signature health care insurance overhaul, with his Republicans united and Democrats divided, McConnell took aim at the option in the bill for a federally run insurance provider, and the so-called public option was eventually dropped. McConnell tried in the spring of 2010 to stop the Dodd-Frank financial regulation bill—a response to the Wall Street financial crash of 2008—but, like health care, it ultimately passed. However, McConnell's ability to hold his caucus together paid off at some critical moments. After the 2010 election, Obama hoped to strike a deal with congressional Republicans to extend the Bush-era tax cuts for two more years for all households except those earning over $200,000 a year. But Senate Republicans, led by McConnell, rejected any proposal that did not extend the tax cuts for everyone, and Obama was forced to go along. The Senate also stopped in its tracks the bill passed by the House, then still under Democratic control, to impose a cap-and-trade system of emission limits on polluters.

Republicans gained six Senate seats in the November 2010 election, leaving McConnell with 47 GOP votes and Democrats far short of a filibuster-proof majority. Among the new arrivals were independent-minded conservatives who were plugged into the tea party movement and who had beat establishment-backed candidates, including McConnell's new Kentucky colleague, Paul. McConnell indulged the Republican newcomers' appetite for confrontation. He followed the lead of the House, back under GOP control following the election, and brought up repeal of the health care law in February, knowing it would not pass the Senate. Aware of the need to show unity, he ceded to the House on other matters, including a ban on budget earmarks. He did reach agreement with Reid on modest changes to Senate rules, including an informal pact to reduce the number of filibusters in exchange for allowing more amendments from the minority side. But McConnell discouraged individual Republican senators from making deals with Democrats. And he blocked the appointment of the director of the new Consumer Financial Protection Bureau created under Dodd-Frank, saying the confirmation process was "the only tool we have against the most stridently left-wing administration we've seen in this country."

Next came the drawn-out duel over raising the federal debt ceiling in 2011. McConnell at first sounded an ambitious tone: "Divided government is the best time—and some would argue the only time—where you can do really big stuff," he said in May. When negotiations with the White House over the debt limit stalled, McConnell espoused a more incremental approach in the form of a last-ditch "backup" that would permit a series of debt increases, putting the onus on Democrats to vote for additional borrowing. Members of both parties denounced it as a political solution to a policy problem, while—as the clock ticked toward an economically damaging default—McConnell began warning about the political consequences of failing to act.

He met with his old Senate colleague, Vice President Joe Biden—known in the White House as "the McConnell Whisperer," according to Bob Woodward's book *The Price of Politics*—to strike a deal. The final agreement denied Obama any increases in taxes or revenue and foisted the hard budget choices on a bipartisan "super committee." The protracted process over increasing the debt limit, a move made necessary by earlier spending decisions by Congress, greatly disturbed many both on and off Capitol Hill, but McConnell said the debt ceiling had become a highly useful GOP bargaining chip. "I think some of our members may have thought the default issue was a hostage you might take a chance at shooting," he told *The Washington Post*. "Most of us didn't think that. What we did learn is this: It's a hostage that's worth ransoming."

The debt ceiling talks served as a prelude to the "fiscal cliff" negotiations in late 2012, aimed at averting automatic budget cuts and tax hikes that could impair the nation's economic recovery. By then, the super committee had become gridlocked, Obama had won a second term, and Senate Democrats added two seats to their majority. Once again, talks between Obama and congressional Republicans proved fruitless, and again, McConnell reached out to Biden. "Does anyone down there know how to make a deal?" McConnell reportedly asked the vice president, setting in motion more than a dozen conversations that culminated in a New Year's Day 2013 agreement. The Senate overwhelmingly approved their handiwork, 89-8, and despite conservatives' opposition, it drew sufficient votes to pass in the House as well.

McConnell called the measure "an imperfect solution," but said it was preferable to the large spending cuts that would have immediately kicked in—while vowing not to accept any new revenue in future dealings with Democrats. Still, activists on the right were outraged that it gave Obama his long-desired tax increase on the wealthy. ForAmerica Chairman Brent Bozell, in an ad targeting McConnell, charged, "His role as President Obama's bag man in the latest fiscal cliff disaster clearly demonstrates that Sen. McConnell is more interested in the art of the bad deal than standing up and fighting for conservative principles."

Despite the acrimony from the right, political experts said the bipartisanship evident in the agreement probably enhanced McConnell's stature among Kentucky's moderate voters. But the gathering political forces against McConnell in the lead-up to the 2014 election made it far more difficult for him to play the role of dealmaker when yet another budget standoff unfolded in October 2013. House Republicans effectively shut down the government by demanding a rollback of the Obama health care law in return for their votes funding routine government operations. The president refused, and unlike the earlier budget battles, there seemed to be little potential for the White House to open quiet, back-channel negotiations with McConnell.

Facing his fifth race for re-election, McConnell took the challenge seriously given approval ratings in Kentucky at or below the 50 percent mark. By the fall of 2013, he had raised more than $13 million. He drew a potentially serious threat in the GOP primary from Matt Bevin, a wealthy businessman favored by the state's potent tea party forces. Two national conservative groups with deep pockets took an interest in Bevin's candidacy: the Madison Project, which helped Republican Ted Cruz's insurgent and ultimately successful Senate bid in Texas, and the Senate Conservatives Fund, a political action committee allied with former South Carolina Sen. Jim DeMint, president of the Heritage Foundation and a leader of the no-compromise conservative faction. But Bevin was an inexperienced candidate who made numerous errors—he attended a cock-fighting rally and claimed it was a "state's rights" event—and McConnell crushed him, 60%-35%. (Bevin made a comeback a year later, narrowly capturing the GOP gubernatorial nomination.)

In the general election, McConnell faced Democrat Alison Lundergan Grimes, Kentucky's 34-year-old secretary of state. Lundergan Grimes initially was seen as a very credible opponent, but she committed several errors, notably refusing to answer a question about whether she had voted for Obama in 2012. It was widely viewed as an opportunistic effort to keep the president, highly unpopular in Kentucky, at a distance. Democrats thought the race would be about which candidate voters liked better, a fight they thought they could win given McConnell's weak approval numbers at the start of the race. Instead, the race became about who voters trusted, and McConnell relentlessly tied Grimes to Obama at every turn. McConnell ended up capturing 56 percent of the vote.

McConnell has seldom had an easy time of it in his reelection bids. He had spirited competition from former Louisville Mayor Harvey Sloane in 1990, future Gov. Steve Beshear in 1996, and Lois Combs Weinberg, daughter of a former governor, in 2002. Sloane and Beshear held McConnell to 52 percent and 55 percent, respectively. He did much better against Weinberg, winning with 65 percent. In 2008, Democrats, still smarting from former Majority Leader Tom Daschle's defeat for re-election in South Dakota in 2004, were determined to put up a tough opponent against McConnell. They found Bruce Lunsford, a multimillionaire hospital and nursing home operator.

Lunsford spent nearly $11 million, more than $7 million of it his own money, and ran a string of negative ads against McConnell, including one showing dogs chasing the senator—a takeoff on McConnell's 1984 bloodhound ads—and another criticizing McConnell for supporting the financial industry bailout legislation in 2008. McConnell raised $21 million, and ultimately spent it all. His ads compared himself to Kentucky's long-serving Democratic Sen. Alben Barkley, who was the Senate majority leader and later Harry Truman's vice president, and reminded voters of the money and projects he had brought home. McConnell won with 53 percent, running behind GOP presidential candidate John McCain's 57 percent in Kentucky. That victory made McConnell the longest-serving senator in Kentucky history.

McConnell became Republican whip just after his third re-election victory in 2002. He campaigned for months among his colleagues when the job came open, and his only opponent, Larry Craig of Idaho, dropped out several days before the contest. Then, in December 2002, Republican Leader Trent Lott of Mississippi came under a storm of criticism when he spoke favorably of Strom Thurmond's segregationist campaign for president in 1948 at an event honoring Thurmond on his 100th birthday. McConnell was Lott's strongest public defender, threatening retaliation against Democrats if they moved to censure him. But, as the controversy showed no sign of abating, he privately recommended to Lott that he "step down as soon as possible." Ordinarily, McConnell might have been in line for the leader's position, but he did not challenge Tennessee's Bill Frist when Frist—urged on by the Bush White House—ran for Lott's post. (Interestingly enough, McConnell's wife, Elaine Chao, whom he married in 1993, was labor secretary throughout the Bush administration.) Frist became Senate majority leader and McConnell majority whip and a key adviser to Frist, who was relatively unversed in Senate procedures. When Frist retired in 2006, McConnell ran for leader. Republicans ended up losing their majority in 2006, so McConnell became minority leader instead.

In February 2007, Reid introduced a resolution, supported by some Republicans, opposing President George W. Bush's strategy for a troop surge in Iraq. McConnell said he would block debate on Reid's resolution unless Republicans got votes on their resolutions setting 11 goals for the Iraqi government. On this, as on other issues over the next two years, McConnell was able to hold 41 or more Republicans together to get Reid to meet his demands, as Republicans conducted a record number of filibusters. McConnell observed that he lived by "an 80/20 rule": He spent 80 percent of his time trying to coax 20 percent of Republican senators to stick with the party.

As a freshman senator, McConnell became heavily involved in the debate over campaign finance reform, ultimately emerging as the Senate's leading opponent of efforts to curb political action committees and soft money—large, unregulated contributions to political parties. He argued such restrictions were unconstitutional infringements of free speech. In late 1999, with more than 40 senators on his side, he killed a version of the McCain-Feingold campaign finance bill. In early 2001, McCain brought the bill forward again, and despite McConnell's efforts, it became law in 2002. "There won't be any less speech or money spent. Dramatically more will be spent, just in a different way," McConnell predicted. He warned that unregulated fundraising groups known as 527s would raise and spend huge amounts of money—as has indeed occurred. When he was challenged about the potential inconsistency between his opposition to campaign finance regulation and his vote for amending the Constitution to allow the banning of flag-burning, another form of free expression, McConnell switched his position—and became one of the few Republicans to consistently vote against measures to ban the burning of the American flag.

Junior Senator

Rand Paul (R)

Elected 2010, term expires Jan. 2017, 1st term; b. Jan. 7, 1963, Pittsburgh, PA; Baylor U., attended 1981-84, Duke U., M.D. 1988; Presbyterian; married (Kelley Ashby); 3 children.

Professional Career: Ophthalmologist, 1993-2010; Founder, S. KY Lions Eye Clinic, 1995.

DC Office: 167 RSOB, 20510, 202-224-4343; Website: paul.senate.gov.

State Offices: Bowling Green, 270-782-8303; Crescent Springs, 859-426-0165; Hopkinsville, 270-885-1212; Lexington, 859-219-2239; Louisville, 502-582-5341; Owensboro, 270-689-9085.

Committees: *Foreign Relations:* African & Global Health Policy; Europe & Regional Security Cooperation; Near East, South Asia, Central Asia, & Counterterrorism; State Dept. & USAID Mgmt., Int'l Operations, & Bilateral Int'l Development. *Health, Education, Labor & Pensions:* Children & Families (Chmn); Employment & Workplace Safety. *Homeland Security & Governmental Affairs:* Investigations; Federal Spending Oversight & Emergency Mgmt. (Chmn). *Small Business & Entrepreneurship.*

Group Ratings

	ADA	ACLU	AFL-CIO	LCV	ITI	COC	HAFA	ACU	CFG	FRC
2014	5%	26%	–	0%	33%	75%	93%	96%	95%	100%
2013	0%	C	0%	15%	C	75%	C	96%	97%	C

National Journal Ratings

	2013 LIB	—	2013 CONS
Economic	13%	—	86%
Social	19%	—	79%
Foreign	20%	—	79%
Composite	18%	—	82%

Key Votes of the 113th Congress

1. Sandy storm spending	N	5. Student Loan Rates	Y	9. Bipartisan Budget Deal	N
2. Chuck Hagel Confirmation	Y	6. Employee Non-Discrim'n Act	N	10. Farm Bill Conference Rept.	N
3. Gun Background Checks	N	7. Senate Vote on Judgeships	Y	11. Unempl. Comp. Extension	N
4. Immigration Reform	N	8. Defense Dept. Spending	N	12. Keystone Pipeline	Y

Election Results

2010 general	Rand Paul (R)	755,411	(56%)	$7,675,875	$771,433	$2,862,846
	Jack Conway (D)	599,843	(44%)	$5,913,193	$511,483	$4,632,823
2010 primary	Rand Paul (R)	206,986	(59%)			
	C. M. 'Trey' Grayson (R)	124,864	(35%)			

In announcing for the 2016 Republican presidential nomination, Rand Paul, Kentucky's junior senator, followed in the footsteps of his father, former Texas Rep. Ron Paul, who sought the party's presidential nod in 2008 and 2012. The younger Paul shares many aspects of his father's political philosophy—Ron Paul temporarily left the GOP to run as the Libertarian Party's presidential nominee in 1988—and is now in a position to inherit the elder Paul's devoted following among strict adherents of limited government. But Ron Paul, during two stints on Capitol Hill totaling nearly 25 years, was a limited political presence in the 435-member House. In contrast, Rand Paul, since first being elected to the Senate in 2010, has aggressively—and deftly—utilized the chamber as a platform to promote both his ideas and his presidential aspirations. It has not endeared him to many of his Senate Republican colleagues.

In May 2015, Paul conducted an 11-hour filibuster to delay reauthorization of the USA Patriot Act, while objecting to the government's bulk collection of phone records under the statute. His procedural tactics not only led to a brief lapse in some government surveillance powers granted under the law, passed in the wake of the 9/11 attacks, but helped to force Majority Leader Mitch McConnell, Paul's senior Kentucky colleague, to swallow House-passed changes in the statute that McConnell at first vigorously opposed. McConnell, who had worked to build a relationship with Paul—going so far as to embrace his presidential bid—was visibly irritated. A rival for the 2016 nomination, South Carolina Sen. Lindsay Graham, rolled his eyes as Paul spoke to the Senate. And the party's 2008 presidential nominee, Arizona Sen. John McCain—who two years earlier had labeled Paul a "wacko bird"—angrily suggested Paul was simply using the issue to help fund his presidential bid. "He obviously has a higher priority for his fundraising and political ambitions than for the security of the nation," McCain told *Politico,* as Paul's campaign Web site contained pitches such as "Get your Rand Paul filibuster starter pack!"

The combative Paul—he has acknowledged a need to work "at holding my tongue and holding my temper"—was unapologetic about his actions during that debate. "I'm always concerned about our country's safety and I think that the Constitution is a great and powerful tool for collecting records on people you have suspicion of," he told reporters. "And so I think we should collect more records on terrorists. I just don't want to collect them on innocent Americans." He added, "I've been fighting this battle since I came here." Indeed, he sought to block the extension of the Patriot Act when it was previously up for renewal in May 2011. And in 2013 he filibustered for nearly 13 hours to protest the administration's use of lethal drone strikes; the move delayed confirmation of John Brennan as director of the CIA. Paul later told a student audience in the liberal bastion of Berkeley California that the intelligence community was "drunk with power. Such episodes highlight the philosophical divide—if not chasm—that separates Paul from many other Republicans, particularly concerning the United States' role abroad.

Born in Pittsburgh, Paul was raised in Lake Jackson, Texas, where his father relocated to set up a practice in obstetrics. While stories have circulated that he was named for the iconic Ayn Rand—the writer whose advocacy of laissez-faire capitalism makes her highly popular in libertarian circles—both Paul and his father have denied this. The third of five children, Paul was named Randall at birth and known as Randy while growing up, switching to Rand as an adult. He attended Baylor University, where he was an active member of the Young Conservatives of Texas. Although he failed to get an undergraduate degree at Baylor, Paul chose to follow in his father's footsteps and become a physician. He got a high score on the medical entrance exam and was admitted to Duke University, where he received his medical degree. Paul subsequently moved to Bowling Green, Kentucky, near his wife's home town, and opened an ophthalmology practice, while establishing an eye clinic to treat low-income patients.

He mulled entering politics for some time, writing newspaper columns, helping with his father's campaigns, and founding an anti-tax watchdog group called Kentucky Taxpayers United. When he gave a speech on April 15, 2009—Tax Day—to a tea party group, the energy of the crowd persuaded him that "something enormous was going on," as he later told the *Bowling Green Daily News,* and he decided to run for the Senate. The seat was held by two-term Republican Jim Bunning, who had a solid conservative record but had been only barely reelected in 2004 and was being pressed by McConnell, the *de facto* boss of the Kentucky GOP, to step down. In July 2009, Bunning announced he would retire. The favorite for the nomination was Kentucky Secretary of State Trey Grayson, who won the backing of McConnell and much of the state Republican establishment. But Paul had his father's name and access to his network of contributors. Backers eagerly embraced his outspoken views that government should stick to the functions outlined in the Constitution, agencies such as the Environmental Protection Agency and the Education Department should be abolished, and the powers of the Federal Reserve should be drastically curbed.

McConnell appeared in television ads for Grayson, and—foreshadowing criticism that would later confront Paul's presidential bid—Grayson ran spots charging Paul was weak on national security. But Paul ended up winning the primary in a rout, 59%-35%. McConnell made a point of appearing at a victory rally for Paul, who decided to vote for McConnell for Senate Republican leader after previously declining to say whether he would. However, Paul's decisive upset was quickly overshadowed by an appearance on MSNBC's *Rachel Maddow Show.* Displaying his libertarian leanings, Paul voiced his opposition in principle to the 1964 Civil Rights Act, arguing that the federal government shouldn't interfere with private businesses. The remarks caused a furor, even after Paul issued a statement saying he did not support repealing the landmark law. After that, he limited his media appearances.

On the Democratic side, Attorney General Jack Conway narrowly defeated Lt. Gov. Dan Mongiardo, 44%-43%, for the Senate nomination. Conway hammered Paul over the comments on the Civil Rights Act, and also seized on Paul's support for raising the Social Security retirement age and opposing federal involvement in drug enforcement. Paul had plenty of material to work with, however, in his attempt to paint Conway as too liberal. In contrast to the anti-abortion Paul, Conway supported abortion rights and also backed the Democrats' health care insurance overhaul, repeal of the ban on being openly gay in the military, and a pro-union bill effectively abolishing the secret ballot in unionization elections. Conway may also have hurt himself with an ad that political insiders considered over the top. In it, the narrator asks, "Why was Rand Paul a member of a secret society that called the Holy Bible a 'hoax'?...Why did Rand Paul once tie a woman up, tell her to bow down before a false idol, and say ... god was Aqua Buddha?" The charges mostly referred to pranks during Paul's college years. *GQ* magazine had reported Paul once belonged to a secret society called the NoZe Brotherhood, which often taunted the school's administration; he and a friend were once accused of blindfolding a female acquaintance and trying to get her to smoke marijuana.

Paul defeated Conway, 56%-44%, with his victory counted among the major triumphs of 2010 for the emerging tea party movement. Upon arriving in the Senate, Paul established a Tea Party Caucus, and quickly sought to use his power to block anything he viewed as government overreach. In September 2011, he used Senate procedures to slap a "hold" on a bill to strengthen safety regulations for oil and gas pipelines in the wake of a deadly pipeline rupture near San Francisco the year before. His opposition came despite the fact that the legislation was even supported by pipeline trade associations and the natural gas industry. Paul later dropped his hold on the bill, and it eventually became law.

As the Patriot Act came up for renewal in 2011, Paul offered an amendment to restrict the government's power to obtain gun records, but the measure was overwhelmingly defeated. Paul made national news in January 2012 when he refused a pat-down from the Transportation Security Administration at a Tennessee airport. Five months later, he wanted to relax tough gun control laws adopted by the District of Columbia in exchange for giving the city more budget autonomy—leading Democrats to accuse him of hypocrisy, in light of his hands-off philosophy of government. The following year, he was one of the loudest objectors to President Barack Obama's proposed anti-gun violence proposals unveiled after the December 2012 school shooting in Newtown Connecticut in which two dozen were killed. "I'm afraid that President Obama may have this 'king complex' sort of developing," Paul complained.

But there also were instances that illustrated the occasional ideological intersection between Republican libertarians and left-wing Democrats. During a November 2011 debate over a defense authorization bill, Paul was a vocal opponent of a provision to allow the military to detain terrorism suspects indefinitely. In 2013, he teamed up on legislation with Judiciary Committee Chairman Patrick Leahy, a Vermont Democrat, to give federal judges greater flexibility on imposing mandatory minimum sentences, while pledging to work with Leahy to eliminate mandatory minimum sentences for marijuana possession. When a budget blueprint from House Budget Committee Chairman Paul Ryan, which included a controversial plan to revamp Medicare, came to a vote in the Senate in May 2011, Paul was one of five Republicans who joined Democrats in successfully voting it down. But, in this case, Paul's motivations were starkly different than the others—who opposed Ryan's plan because of its deep cuts to Medicare. Paul opposed the plan because he felt the reductions didn't go far enough.

When it comes to foreign policy and national security issues, it often seems Paul—both as a senator and a presidential candidate—has been as much, if not more, at odds with fellow Republicans as he is with Democrats. "The people who argue that the world will end and we will be overrun by jihadists are trying to use fear," Mr. Paul contended during the Patriot Act debate of May 2015. "Little by little, we've allowed our freedom to slip away." Several days earlier, he sought to put the blame for the growth of the radical Islamic State—ISIS—squarely on others in the GOP. "ISIS exists and grew stronger because of the hawks in our party, who gave arms indiscriminately, and most of those arms were snatched up by ISIS," he said during an appearance on MSNBC. His comments were widely criticized by leading Republicans.

Earlier in the year, Paul's hands-off stance on Iraq's civil war led Texas Gov. Rick Perry, another potential 2016 presidential aspirant, to write a *Washington Post* op-ed column headlined "Why Rand Paul Is Wrong on Iraq." Similarly, Paul's old hawkish nemesis, McCain, charged Paul's reluctance to back a U.S. intervention was a step toward a "fortress America." The presence of such a mentality among many in Paul's base may help to explain why he was among just five Republican senators in 2015 to oppose granting Obama so-called fast track authority to expedite negotiation of a 12-nation Asian trade deal. A *Wall Street Journal/NBC News* poll earlier in the spring found a plurality of Paul supporters believed free trade had hurt the United States.

Paul's stance on Israel also has been fodder for critics within the party. In 2012, Paul forced a vote on his proposal to limit aid to Pakistan, Libya, and Egypt. But McCain and Graham forcefully opposed it, saying it could limit aid to Israel and other countries as well, and it was resoundingly rejected. In 2014, Paul sought to combat perceptions that he was not sufficiently pro-Israel by introducing a bill to bar the Palestinian government from receiving foreign aid unless it recognized Israel as a state. A libertarian Capitol Hill staffer described the measure to *The New York Times Magazine* as "complete pandering." But a Paul spokesman said the senator never specifically targeted Israel in his calls to cut foreign aid and maintained, "Sen. Paul's position was exactly what Prime Minister [Benjamin] Netanyahu said to Congress on July 10, 1996 and May 24, 2011—Israel will be better off when it does not have to count on anyone else for its protection."

As he has courted those on Wall Street and in Silicon Valley who had financially backed George W. Bush and Mitt Romney, Paul also sought to reach out to constituencies outside the traditional Republican base—albeit with uneven results. He appeared at the National Urban League conference in July 2014 and pronounced his unequivocal support for the Civil Rights Act. When Ferguson Missouri was swept by rioting that summer after a black teenager was killed by a white police officer, Paul argued for overhauling police departments, writing in *Time* magazine: "If I had been told to get out of the street as a teenager, there would have been a distinct possibility that I might have smarted off. But, I wouldn't have expected to be shot." But, during the April 2015 riots in Baltimore that followed the death of a black man in police custody, Paul adopted a different tone in speaking to conservative radio talk show host Laura Ingraham. "I am very sympathetic to the plight of the police in this," he said, while noting he had just come through Baltimore by train. "I'm glad it didn't stop," he added, in a wisecrack that raised some eyebrows.

Paul also has sought to broaden Republican support among Latinos, floating a plan to enable the nation's 12 million illegal immigrants to seek legal status while clamping down on immigration in the interim. (His support of the Obama administration initiative to restore diplomatic relations with Cuba is another issue that separates him from many of his Republican presidential rivals.) But Paul was ridiculed within the Democratic blogosphere as well as on comedy shows when, during a tour of Iowa in mid-2014, he was captured on video leaving a restaurant table in mid-mouthful after an angry immigration activist approached him. Satirist Stephen Colbert dubbed the maneuver "the Rand Paul-eo Diet." Paul defended himself by saying he had no time for what he called a "kamikaze interview," but the incident raised questions—even among some Republicans—about whether it reinforced their party's political weaknesses among Hispanics.

In addition to his presidential bid, Paul has indicated plans to run for a second Senate term in 2016—notwithstanding Kentucky, unlike several other states, prohibits candidates from appearing on the ballot for two offices. To get around this, the state GOP in early 2015 agreed to hold a presidential caucus rather than a primary, avoiding the prospect of Paul appearing on the primary ballot for both president and senator. What remains unclear is what happens if Paul wins the nomination for both offices: Kentucky Secretary of State Alison Lundergan Grimes has said she would take Paul to court if he tried to run for both during the general election. Complicating the situation is that Grimes, the unsuccessful challenger to McConnell in 2014, could be a leading contender for Paul's Senate seat if it comes open.

FIRST DISTRICT

Ed Whitfield (R)

Elected 1994, 11th term; b. May 25, 1943, Hopkinsville; U. of KY, B.S. 1965, J.D. 1969; Methodist; married (Connie); 1 child.

Military Career: U.S. Army Reserve, 1967-73.

Elected Office: KY House, 1974-75.

Professional Career: Practicing atty., 1969-79; Owner, Rhodes Oil Co., 1975-79; Counsel, Seaboard System Railroad, 1979-83; V.P., CSX, 1983-91; Counsel, Interstate Commerce Comm., 1991-93.

DC Office: 2184 RHOB, 20515, 202-225-3115; Fax: 202-225-3547; Website: whitfield.house.gov.

State Offices: Henderson, 270-826-4180; Hopkinsville, 270-885-8079; Paducah, 270-442-6901; Tompkinsville, 270-487-9509.

Committees: *Energy & Commerce:* Commerce, Manufacturing, & Trade; Energy & Power (Chmn); Environment & the Economy; Health.

Group Ratings

	ADA	ACLU	AFL-CIO	LCV	ITI	COC	HAFA	ACU	CFG	FRC
2014	0%	0%	–	9%	80%	77%	43%	52%	47%	100%
2013	0%	C	30%	7%	C	85%	C	60%	54%	C

National Journal Ratings

	2012 LIB	—	2012 CONS
Economic	44%	—	56%
Social	30%	—	70%
Foreign	24%	—	68%
Composite	34%	—	66%

Key Votes of the 113th Congress

1. Sandy storm spending	Y	5. Medical Marijuana	N	9. Syrian Rebels Training	N
2. Violence Against Women Act	N	6. Farm Bill	Y	10. Keystone pipeline	Y
3. Guantanamo Bay Detainees	NV	7. Afghanistan Combat	N	11. Immigration Exec. Action	Y
4. Abortion 20-week ban	Y	8. NSA Phone Data Collection	N	12. Bipartisan budget deal	Y

Election Results

2014 general	Ed Whitfield (R)	173,022	(73%)	$1,447,566
	Charles Hatchett (D)	63,596	(27%)	
2014 primary	Ed Whitfield (R)	unopposed		

Prior winning percentages: 2012 (70%), 2010 (71%), 2008 (64%), 2006 (60%), 2004 (67%), 2002 (65%), 2000 (58%), 1998 (55%), 1996 (54%), 1994 (51%)

Population		Race and Ethnicity		Income	
Total:	723,347	White	88.2%	Median income:	$38,369
Urban:	5.1%	Black	7.2%		(402 of 435)
Suburban:	13.7%	Latino	2.5%	Under $50,000	62.0%
Rural:	81.2%	Asian	0.6%	$50,000-$99,999:	26.4%
Land area:	11,485	Two races	1.3%	$100,000-$199,999:	10.2%
Pop/sq. mi.:	63.0	White Ethnic	15.0%	$200,000 or more:	1.4%
Born in state:	70.3%			Poverty Rate	20.2%
		Education			
Age Groups		H.S. grad or less:	55.4%	**Work**	
Under 18:	22.9%	Some college:	29.0%	White collar:	27.8%
18 to 34:	21.7%	College degree, 4 yr.:	9.0%	Blue collar:	38.8%
35 to 64:	38.6%	Post-grad study:	6.5%	Sales and service:	33.4%
Over 64:	16.8%			Govt. workers:	16.2%
		Military			
		Veterans/active duty:	10.3%		

Western Kentucky

The point where the Ohio River flows into the Mississippi—the intersection Huckleberry Finn and Jim missed in the fog—must have struck early settlers as a site for a great city. But no Pittsburgh or St. Louis grew up on the fertile black soil. Instead, the Kentucky land west of the dammed-up Tennes-

Voter Turnout	
2013 Total Citizen 18+	552,084
2014 House Turnout	236,618
2014 Turnout as % CVAP	42.9%
2012 Turnout as % CVAP	53.6%

see and Cumberland rivers, bought from the Chickasaw Indians by Gen. Andrew Jackson and Gov. Isaac Shelby in 1818—the Jackson Purchase—was settled by farmers, mostly from the South. This was one area of Kentucky where public sentiment clearly favored the Confederacy during the Civil War. A group of delegates from western Kentucky and western Tennessee gathered in Mayfield in 1861 and are believed to have voted to join together into a single state in the Confederacy (most of the papers have been destroyed and the record is unclear). The movement was stopped by Tennessee's eventual decision to secede from the Union. Jefferson Davis, the president of the Confederacy, was born in western Kentucky's Christian County, near Hopkinsville.

To the east of the Jackson Purchase are coalfields and the Pennyrile (after pennyroyal, a common variety of local wild mint), a land of low hills and small farms. There is Lyon County, founded by Matthew "Spitting" Lyon, who represented western Kentucky in the House from 1803 to 1811 and earned his epithet for spitting on a fellow member of Congress, prompting a brawl on the floor of the House; Lyon also once bit off a voter's thumb during a fight.

The 1st Congressional District of Kentucky is made up of the Jackson Purchase and much of the Pennyrile. There is a distinctive Southern atmosphere here—in the crops that are grown, in the historically low wages, and in the fact that the big city with the most influence locally is Nashville, not Louisville.

2012 Presidential Vote		
Mitt Romney (R)	197,074	(66%)
Barack Obama (D)	95,273	(32%)

2008 Presidential Vote		
John McCain (R)	185,540	(62%)
Barack Obama (D)	111,047	(37%)

Cook Partisan Voting Index: R+18

Paducah, on the Ohio River, has reinvented a large area with an artist relocation program that has boosted development in the Lowertown Arts District. The city spent $9 million in the past decade, and leveraged that into more than $40 million in private investment and a vibrant community. Turkey-hunting also has become a draw for outsiders. The large Army base at Fort Campbell is home to the 101st Airborne Division, which deployed multiple times during the Iraq and Afghanistan conflicts.

The Jackson Purchase and the Pennyrile are ancestrally Democratic. Paducah produced one of the most enduring Democratic politicians of the 20th century: Alben Barkley, whose career from 1912 to 1956 included 14 years in the House, 23 in the Senate and four as vice president. Even today, there are more registered Democrats than Republicans here. But the Republican voting pattern has been firmly established in the 1st District in national elections. John McCain and Mitt Romney won with huge majorities in 2008 and 2012, respectively.

Ed Whitfield (R)

Ed Whitfield, a Republican elected in 1994, is more moderate than his Kentucky GOP colleagues. But as the influential chairman of the Energy and Commerce Subcommittee on Energy and Power, and next in line to chair the full committee, he shares their ardent devotion to the coal industry and their skepticism of federal regulations.

Whitfield grew up in Hopkinsville and Madisonville, in a family with Pennyrile roots going back to the 18th century. He served in the Army Reserve, practiced law in Hopkinsville, and was elected to the state legislature in 1973 as a Democrat. After one term in Frankfort, Whitfield ran an oil distributorship in the west Kentucky coalfields, and then in 1979, moved to Washington, D.C., to become an executive for the Seaboard and CSX railroads. He was legal counsel to the chairman of the Interstate Commerce Commission from 1991 to 1993, then returned to west Kentucky to run for Congress.

The district had been represented by quiet, long-serving, conservative Democrats. But in 1994, the first-term incumbent, Tom Barlow, was a free-spirited supporter of the Clinton administration. Encouraged by Sen. Mitch McConnell, Whitfield ran as a Republican, turned aside criticism that he was a carpetbagger, and attacked Barlow's vote for Clinton's budget and tax increase. With help from the mountain counties and running strongly in the Pennyrile, Whitfield won 51%-49% in that year's big Republican sweep.

In the House, the usually soft-spoken Whitfield has a moderate-to-conservative voting record. He generally takes his party's side on major votes, but occasionally shows his independence. He was one of just 10 Republicans in March 2012 to oppose Budget Committee Chairman Paul Ryan's fiscal 2013 spending blueprint, saying: "I am not going to vote for a budget that takes more than 20 years to be in balance." In 2009, Whitfield supported the Lilly Ledbetter Fair Pay Act extending the statute of limitations in equal pay lawsuits. He voted for the minimum wage hike two years earlier—both Democratic priorities.

Whitfield's subcommittee chairmanship puts him at the helm of Republican efforts to fight President Barack Obama on his environmental policies, including rules rolled out in 2014 aimed at slashing smog and soot pollution from power plants. In response to the rules proposed by the Environmental Protection Agency, he prepared legislation to allow judicial review of any final rule before requiring states to comply. He cited testimony from Harvard Law professor Laurence Tribe, once an Obama mentor, who has called the proposed EPA rule unconstitutional.

He has been a strong proponent of "clean coal" technology as well as sequestration research that experts say could someday lead to ways to store underground carbon captured in the atmosphere. He has shrugged off environmentalists' concerns about preparing for a fossil fuel-free world. "We've got a 250-year reserve of coal in this country, and my understanding is that we have about the same length of time in oil and maybe even more in natural gas," Whitfield told *National Journal*. He also has called on the Environmental Protection Agency to examine the economic impact of all its pending regulations before issuing them, citing their potential negative impact on businesses and job creation. He has filed a bill that would make major changes in improvements to deteriorating river locks and dams. It won him a "Golden Fleece" award from the watchdog group Taxpayers for Common Sense, which said it would further subsidize an already heavily subsidized barge industry. In April 2015, he spearheaded House passage of energy efficiency legislation that was signed by Obama.

On health issues before the committee, Whitfield authored a 2005 law to discourage "doctor shopping" by prescription drug addicts. It established an electronic database that states can use to monitor people who cross state lines to buy pharmaceuticals. Whitfield has also used his seat to tend to local concerns. He worked to secure agreement on federal aid for workers exposed to radiation at the Energy Department uranium plant in Paducah, and won bipartisan support for a site clean-up, which is projected to cost more than $3 billion and last until around 2030.

A thoroughbred owner, Whitfield cosponsored legislation in 2006 to ban the killing of horses for meat. The House overwhelmingly passed the bill, but it died in the Senate. He also has worked with the Humane Society on bills to restrict performance-enhancing drugs given to racehorses. In March 2015, the House Ethics Committee announced that it was investigating Whitfield on whether his office had "dispensed special favors or privileges" to his wife Connie Harriman-Whitfield, a senior policy adviser for the Humane Society Legislative Fund.

When he ran for reelection in 1996, Whitfield drew Democratic opposition from lawyer Dennis Null, and won, 54%-46%, carrying 18 of the district's 31 counties. Two years later, he faced former Rep. Barlow and won 55%-45%. Since then, he has won easily. Despite token reelection opposition, he has received $1.1 million in campaign contributions from energy interests since he became Energy and Power chairman, according to the Center for Responsive Politics. A spokesman responded that Whitfield had raised the money because of his leadership responsibilities, and that he had given much of it to Republican organizations. As the next-senior eligible Republican on Energy and Commerce, he has an opportunity to become chairman when Rep. Fred Upton of Michigan is term-limited after the 2016 election. Rep. John Shimkus of Illinois has sought the chairmanship in the past.

SECOND DISTRICT

Brett Guthrie (R)

Elected 2008, 4th term; b. Feb. 18, 1964, Florence, AL; U.S. Military Acad., B.S. 1987, Yale U., M.P.P.M. 1997; Restorationist; married (Beth); 3 children.

Military Career: U.S. Army, 1987-90; U.S. Army Reserve, 1990-2002.

Elected Office: KY Senate, 1998-2008.

Professional Career: V.P., Trace Die Cast, 2001-08.

DC Office: 2434 RHOB, 20515, 202-225-3501; Fax: 202-226-2019; Website: guthrie.house.gov.

State Offices: Bowling Green, 270-842-9896.

Committees: *Education & the Workforce:* Health, Employment, Labor & Pensions; Higher Education & Workforce Training. *Energy & Commerce:* Communications & Technology; Health (VChmn).

Group Ratings

	ADA	ACLU	AFL-CIO	LCV	ITI	COC	HAFA	ACU	CFG	FRC
2014	0%	0%	–	3%	100%	86%	60%	64%	61%	100%
2013	0%	C	14%	4%	C	92%	C	72%	69%	C

National Journal Ratings

	2013 LIB	—	2013 CONS
Economic	36%	—	64%
Social	16%	—	74%
Foreign	5%	—	86%
Composite	22%	—	78%

Key Votes of the 113th Congress

1. Sandy storm spending	N	5. Medical Marijuana	N	9. Syrian Rebels Training	Y
2. Violence Against Women Act	N	6. Farm Bill	Y	10. Keystone pipeline	Y
3. Guantanamo Bay Detainees	N	7. Afghanistan Combat	N	11. Immigration Exec. Action	Y
4. Abortion 20-week ban	Y	8. NSA Phone Data Collection	N	12. Bipartisan budget deal	Y

Election Results

2014 general	Brett Guthrie (R) 156,936	(69%)	$1,292,843	
	Ron Leach (D) 69,898	(31%)	$144,599	$2,759
2014 primary	Brett Guthrie (R) ....unopposed			

Prior winning percentages: 2012 (64%), 2010 (68%), 2008 (53%)

Population		Race and Ethnicity		Income	
Total:	737,296	White	88.3%	Median income:	$46,471
Urban:	34.4%	Black	5.4%		*(295 of 435)*
Suburban:	22.1%	Latino	3.0%	Under $50,000	53.4%
Rural:	43.5%	Asian	1.0%	$50,000-$99,999:	32.2%
Land area:	6,594	Two races	1.9%	$100,000-$199,999:	12.2%
Pop/sq. mi.:	111.8	White Ethnic	18.2%	$200,000 or more:	2.3%
Born in state:	70.6%			Poverty Rate	17.1%
		Education			
Age Groups		H.S. grad or less:	51.5%	**Work**	
Under 18:	23.6%	Some college:	28.7%	White collar:	29.6%
18 to 34:	22.5%	College degree, 4 yr.:	11.5%	Blue collar:	40.7%
35 to 64:	39.5%	Post-grad study:	8.3%	Sales and service:	29.7%
Over 64:	14.4%			Govt. workers:	15.3%
		Military			
		Veterans/active duty:	11.7%		

Central Kentucky: Elizabethtown, Louisville Suburbs, Bowling Green

In the 1770s and 1780s, Americans began settling the limestone-soil country of central Kentucky, staking out towns like Bardstown and Elizabethtown and starting academies and colleges. They were well-settled when Stephen Foster wrote "My Old Kentucky Home" just before the Civil War. The

Voter Turnout	
2013 Total Citizen 18+	552,454
2014 House Turnout	226,834
2014 Turnout as % CVAP	41.1%
2012 Turnout as % CVAP	53.8%

war tore deeply here. This part of Kentucky gave birth to Abraham Lincoln, and during the conflict, it lost thousands of soldiers, both Union and Confederate. The Lincoln family was not immune to this division; Mary Todd Lincoln's brother-in-law, Benjamin Hardin Helm, fought on the side of the Confederacy and rose to the rank of general before dying at the Battle of Chickamauga. Lincoln himself was never particularly popular here prior to his death. Kentucky's most famous son won only 1% of the vote in the state in 1860; his home county gave him just three votes. Today, the area hosts several Kentucky landmarks—Fort Knox, the nation's gold depository; some of the nation's largest bourbon distilleries; and Mammoth Cave, the world's largest accessible cavern, which is near Bowling Green.

2012 Presidential Vote		
Mitt Romney (R)..................186,231	(63%)
Barack Obama (D) 103,410	(35%)

2008 Presidential Vote		
John McCain (R)..................183,789	(62%)
Barack Obama (D) 111,111	(37%)

Cook Partisan Voting Index: R+16

The 2nd Congressional District of Kentucky consists of much of the territory south and southwest of Louisville, starting with Spencer County and heading south to Bowling Green. That city is the headquarters of apparel giant Fruit of the Loom, and it has a bustling General Motors Corvette assembly plant, the only place in the world where the classic sports cars have been produced since 1981. *Forbes* has listed Bowling Green among its "best places to retire." The district jogs west along the Ohio River to Owensboro, a port with warehouses that receive aluminum alloys to make lightweight engine parts. The city has successfully courted new economic development, including the headquarters of U.S. Bank, the fifth-largest commercial bank in the United States, with 1,900 employees locally. *Area Development* magazine has rated it the 25th best metropolitan area for growth. Yet Owensboro still tries to preserve the feeling of

"Old Kentucky," and hosts an annual international barbecue festival where mutton, a throwback to Welsh shepherds who settled in western Kentucky, remains a favorite.

The district also reaches into the Lexington suburbs, including Lancaster, home of Kentucky's first Republican governor, William O'Connell Bradley, who successfully shepherded an anti-lynching law in 1897. Centre College is located here, in picturesque Danville, where the 2012 vice presidential debate was held. Much of the district is rural and small-town country. For many years, it favored the Democrats, but in the 1990s, voters moved to the Republican Party, which better matched their conservative cultural leanings. Neither John McCain nor Mitt Romney had any trouble carrying the district.

Brett Guthrie (R)

Republican Brett Guthrie, elected in 2008, has a military and business background that plays well with constituents, plus a reputation as a loyal party vote that endears him to GOP leaders. He holds a plum seat on the Energy and Commerce Committee, enabling him to work with neighboring Kentucky Republican Ed Whitfield on protecting the state's coal and oil industries.

A graduate of West Point, Guthrie served 14 years in the Army, first in the Reserve, then as a field artillery officer with the 101st Airborne division at Fort Campbell. After his discharge, Guthrie joined the family business in Bowling Green, Trace Die Cast Inc., a leading supplier of aluminum castings for the automobile industry. His father started the business with his savings and just five employees in the 1980s. Guthrie eventually became vice president. In 1998, he was elected to the state Senate, where he became chairman of the Transportation Committee, helping the state develop its highway budget. Republicans expected him to join their leadership, but Guthrie set his sights on Congress.

After GOP Rep. Ron Lewis announced his retirement, his longtime chief of staff, Daniel London, jumped into the race to succeed him. Leading local Republicans complained that the two had rigged a succession plan: Lewis had waited until just before the filing deadline to announce his retirement, leaving little time for candidates other than London to file. London apologized and withdrew from the race. Guthrie avoided a contested primary and marshaled his resources for the general election.

The Democratic nominee was state Sen. David Boswell, a 30-year veteran of Kentucky politics. He ran as a conservative Democrat, and the two contenders were virtually indistinguishable on the issues. Both opposed abortion rights and supported gun ownership, and both spoke out against the massive bailout for the financial industry that Congress passed in the fall of 2008. National Democrats made the contest one of their top priorities. Guthrie ran ads tying Boswell to liberal Democrats and their opposition to offshore drilling. And he emphasized his military background to the district's large active and retired military population. The Democratic Congressional Campaign Committee ran an ad claiming that Trace Die Cast had sent jobs to Mexico. Former President Bill Clinton stumped for Boswell in the district; first lady Laura Bush put in an appearance for Guthrie. Guthrie proved more adept at fundraising, with a war chest of nearly $1.3 million compared with Boswell's $917,000. He won 53%-47%.

Once in the House, Guthrie proved to be a dependable Republican. The House in 2011 passed his bill to water down the Democrats' Affordable Care Act by converting mandatory funding for teaching health centers to annual congressional spending. Guthrie took a softer line in criticizing the Environmental Protection Agency than other Republicans on Energy and Commerce, telling the *Owensboro Messenger-Inquirer* that the agency needed to strike a better balance between regulation and the economy. "I've been to Mexico City and Beijing," he said. "I don't want to have to wear a mask when I go outside. But I want regulations that don't put companies out of business and cost my district $60,000-a-year jobs." On Energy and Commerce, he was a leader in 2012 of a bipartisan working group on how the federal government could more efficiently use wireless spectrum. In 2013, the House enacted his bill to reauthorize the National Center for Missing and Exploited Children. Guthrie became vice chairman in 2015 of the Health Subcommittee on Energy and Commerce, and he promised new steps to hold the Obama administration accountable. He and Kentucky Democrat John Yarmuth have led the Congressional Bourbon Caucus. "I have Heaven Hill and Jim Beam in my district," Guthrie told *The Washington Post* in 2012. "I lost Maker's Mark in redistricting."

Guthrie has sailed to reelection. When Kentucky Sen. Rand Paul declared his presidential candidacy in April 2015, Guthrie said that he liked that the Bowling Green resident "doesn't blow with the wind," and Guthrie embraced the senator's views on free enterprise, freedom and opportunity.

THIRD DISTRICT

John Yarmuth (D)

Elected 2006, 5th term; b. Nov. 4, 1947, Louisville; Yale U., B.A. 1969; Jewish; married (Catherine); 1 child.

Professional Career: Stockbroker, 1969-71; Sr. aide, U.S. Sen. Marlow Cook, 1971-75; Publisher, *Louisville Today* magazine, 1976-82; Asst. V.P. of university relations, U. of Louisville, 1983-86; V.P., Caretenders, 1986-90; Owner, columnist, & exec. editor, *Louisville Eccentric Observer*, 1990-2002; Co-host, Yarmuth & Ziegler, 2003; Commentator, Hot Button, 2004-05.

DC Office: 403 CHOB, 20515, 202-225-5401; Fax: 202-225-5776; Website: yarmuth.house.gov.

State Offices: Louisville, 502-582-5129 or 502-933-5863.

Committees: *Budget. Energy & Commerce:* Communications & Technology; Energy & Power; Oversight & Investigations.

Group Ratings

	ADA	ACLU	AFL-CIO	LCV	ITI	COC	HAFA	ACU	CFG	FRC
2014	95%	77%	–	94%	60%	43%	12%	12%	13%	13%
2013	85%	C	90%	89%	C	38%	C	8%	12%	C

National Journal Ratings

	2013 LIB	—	2013 CONS
Economic	82%	—	17%
Social	85%	—	13%
Foreign	89%	—	10%
Composite	86%	—	14%

Key Votes of the 113th Congress

1. Sandy storm spending	Y	5. Medical Marijuana	Y	9. Syrian Rebels Training	Y
2. Violence Against Women Act	Y	6. Farm Bill		N	10. Keystone pipeline	N
3. Guantanamo Bay Detainees	Y	7. Afghanistan Combat	Y	11. Immigration Exec. Action	N
4. Abortion 20-week ban	NV	8. NSA Phone Data Collection	Y	12. Bipartisan budget deal	Y

Election Results

2014 general	John Yarmuth (D)	157,056	(64%)	$833,527	$4,377
	Michael Macfarlane (R)	87,981	(36%)	$176,004	
2014 primary	John Yarmuth (D)	52,026	(87%)		
	Ray Pierce (D)	7,747	(13%)		

Prior winning percentages: 2012 (64%), 2010 (55%), 2008 (59%), 2006 (51%)

Population		Race and Ethnicity		Income	
Total:	739,047	White	70.0%	Median income:	$46,918
Urban:	97.0%	Black	20.5%		*(282 of 435)*
Suburban:	3.0%	Latino	4.6%	Under $50,000	52.5%
Rural:	0.0%	Asian	2.3%	$50,000-$99,999:	29.4%
Land area:	384	Two races	2.4%	$100,000-$199,999:	14.4%
Pop/sq. mi.:	1,926.5	White Ethnic	18.8%	$200,000 or more:	3.7%
Born in state:	69.3%			Poverty Rate	16.1%
		Education			
Age Groups		H.S. grad or less:	39.4%	**Work**	
Under 18:	22.7%	Some college:	30.2%	White collar:	35.8%
18 to 34:	23.5%	College degree, 4 yr.:	17.5%	Blue collar:	41.6%
35 to 64:	39.6%	Post-grad study:	12.8%	Sales and service:	22.6%
Over 64:	14.2%				
		Military		Govt. workers:	12.0%
		Veterans/active duty:	8.8%		

Louisville Metro

At the falls of the Ohio River, George Rogers Clark founded one of America's first inland metropolises in 1778: the river port and industrial city of Louisville. It is heavily influenced by the Cavalier culture that the second sons of big landowners from England brought to Virginia in the 17th century—and

Voter Turnout	
2013 Total Citizen 18+	543,828
2014 House Turnout	247,355
2014 Turnout as % CVAP	45.5%
2012 Turnout as % CVAP	60.1%

their heirs brought over the Appalachians to the valleys of Kentucky in the 18th century. When Kentucky decided not to secede from the union in 1861, the decision was not unanimous, and the culture of tidewater Virginia is still evident in the Louisville lawn party. Mint juleps are served on the verandas of mansions, especially (but not only) during Kentucky Derby week in May; horse racing is a preoccupation throughout the year. The last president who owned slaves while in office, Zachary Taylor, is interred at Zachary Taylor National Cemetery. The obscure antebellum president briefly made headlines in 1991, when a professor at the University of Florida convinced Taylor's surviving descendants to authorize the exhumation of the body to test for arsenic poisoning; the tests were negative.

With 757,000 persons in 2013, Louisville is Kentucky's largest city, surpassing Lexington in 2003 after voters decided to consolidate the city and surrounding Jefferson County. Its economy is in many ways "pre-postindustrial:" It produces cigarettes and whiskey, GE appliances and Ford automobiles. Louisville is also the headquarters of Humana health services, the long-term health care facility operator Signature HealthCARE, and several fast food companies, including Yum! Brands, which owns KFC, Pizza Hut and Taco Bell; Papa John's pizza; and A Great American Brand, which operates Long John Silver's. The unemployment rate here peaked past 12% in 2010 before declining to 4.9% in early 2015, a sign of robust business activity. The real estate market tightened and rents climbed an average of 9% in 2014. In March 2015, a landmark disappeared when Hillerich and Bradsby sold its Louisville Slugger baseball bat brand to Wilson Sporting Goods.

The 3rd Congressional District of Kentucky includes all but a handful of precincts in Louisville-Jefferson County. The large African-American population, which is 21% of the overall district, resides chiefly in the West End of Louisville. A low-income white population is along the strip highway that leads to Fort Knox. West Buechel, southeast of the city, has one of the highest concentrations of Yugoslavian Americans in the United States, many of whom were Bosnian refugees relocated by the government. The suburbs to the east tend to be affluent. Small, elite neighborhoods—Mockingbird Valley, Glenview and Ten Broeck—are nestled in the hills above the Ohio River.

The district, like Louisville, has long been an odd duck in Kentucky politics. If its elite were Virginia Cavaliers, many of its burghers were Germans and Pennsylvanians who made the river town a Republican and anti-slavery island in a secessionist and pro-slavery sea. That tradition helps explain how Republican Mitch McConnell won election as

2012 Presidential Vote		
Barack Obama (D)	183,015	(56%)
Mitt Romney (R)	140,539	(43%)
2008 Presidential Vote		
Barack Obama (D)	193,320	(56%)
John McCain (R)	147,224	(43%)
Cook Partisan Voting Index: D+4		

Jefferson County judge-executive in 1977 and 1981, when the state was electing Democrats to most other offices. As recently as 2006, the district was held by a Republican. Since the 1990s, Louisville has trended toward the Democrats, even as the rest of Kentucky trended Republican. The Democrats' voter registration advantage over the Republicans has been similar to that in the 1st and 6th districts, but the Democrats here have become much more reliable supporters of Andrew Jackson's party than those in the other two. Jefferson County was one of only four Kentucky counties to vote for President Barack Obama in 2012.

John Yarmuth (D)

Democrat John Yarmuth, who was first elected in 2006, is a former journalist whose candor and independence sometimes lead him to go off-message in discussing his party's shortcomings. But he also enjoys rebuking Republicans, especially home-state colleague Mitch McConnell, the Senate majority leader.

Yarmuth hails from a wealthy family. His father, Stanley Yarmuth, founded National Industries, a conglomerate that started as a used car business; his maternal grandfather,

Samuel Klein, ran the Bank of Louisville. John Yarmuth grew up in Louisville and went to Atherton High School, where he was elected student government president. After graduating from Yale University, he worked briefly as a stockbroker and then as an aide to Republican Sen. Marlow Cook. Yarmuth attended two years of law school but didn't finish his degree.

In 1976, he founded *Louisville Today* magazine, and served as publisher until 1982. He ran unsuccessfully for Louisville alderman in 1975, and for county commissioner in 1981. He worked in public relations from 1983 to 1990 for the University of Louisville and for a health care company. Unhappy with the policies of President Ronald Reagan, Yarmuth switched his party affiliation to Democrat in 1985. (He says he first registered as a Republican as a favor to his father, who was a fundraiser for President Richard Nixon.) In 1990, Yarmuth founded the *Louisville Eccentric Observer*, a free newsweekly popularly known as LEO, and for the next 15 years penned a column called "Hot Coals" that promoted his mostly liberal views. He sold the publication in 2003, but continued his column and did televised political commentary.

In 2006, five-term Republican Rep. Anne Northup was vulnerable in the district. The Democratic Congressional Campaign Committee touted attorney Andrew Horne, an Iraq war veteran and first-time candidate. But Yarmuth raised more money and proved a more formidable candidate than Horne, winning the four-way primary 54%-32%. He called for an immediate pullout of troops from Iraq and referred to Northup as a "rubber stamp" for President George W. Bush. Northup campaigned on the Republican tax cuts and her work for the district.

The mother of six children, Northup suffered a wrenching personal tragedy during the campaign when her son died of an undiagnosed heart condition. She suspended her campaign for six weeks before returning to campaigning at the end of the summer. Then she unleashed a radio, television, and Internet offensive that blasted Yarmuth for his liberal writings, saying he supported removing the phrase "under God" from the Pledge of Allegiance and legalizing marijuana. Northup raised nearly $3.4 million to Yarmuth's $2.3 million, which included $700,000 of his own money. Northup could not overcome a national tide against Republicans that year, an environment made worse locally by a patronage scandal surrounding Republican Gov. Ernie Fletcher. Yarmuth won 51%-48%.

In the House, Yarmuth told *Esquire* magazine in 2010 that he had trouble adjusting to elected office: "I never had to compromise on my opinion in the column. Suddenly you have to swallow all sorts of compromises, and that's not easy at all." With his journalism background, he joined a "messaging" group that advised Speaker Nancy Pelosi and other Democratic leaders on media strategy. He snared a seat on the Ways and Means Committee in 2009, but lost it after Republicans regained control of the House in 2011. He has pursued occasional bipartisan opportunities. In April 2015, he proposed with Republican Rep. Dave Reichert of Washington the Runaway and Homeless Youth and Trafficking Prevention Act. He also filed his "Keeping Our Campaigns Honest Act," which would require disclosure of the donors behind Super PACs and tax-exempt organizations that flood the airwaves with anonymous ads.

He moved over to the Budget and Energy and Commerce committees, where he frequently jabs at McConnell. After McConnell wrote an op-ed in April 2012 blasting President Barack Obama's health care law, Yarmuth fired off a lengthy response that accused him of "misrepresentations." During the subsequent budget showdown aimed at averting the so-called fiscal cliff, Yarmuth told MSNBC that the minority leader was keeping an eye on possible 2014 GOP primary challengers in his negotiations with Democrats. "Mitch McConnell will always do what's in Mitch McConnell's best interest," he said. Yarmuth sparked widespread attention for talking up actress and Kentucky native—and recently a Tennessee resident and political activist—Ashley Judd as a possible McConnell challenger. "The money would pour in here as soon as she entered the race," Yarmuth said. After Judd decided not to run, Yarmuth talked up Democratic nominee Alison Lundergan Grimes in her failed challenge to McConnell.

Yarmuth goes places rhetorically where most Democrats won't venture. After the House passed the fiscal-cliff budget compromise, he praised House Speaker John Boehner for being "courageous" in sending the Senate-passed deal to the House floor. He earlier told *Roll Call* newspaper that the health care law was the right thing to do policy-wise, but "big picture, politically, it probably wasn't worth it." He told a Louisville radio station after the Senate made changes to the bill, "We couldn't really go to the average American citizen and say, 'Here's what it means to you.'"

He has become entrenched in his seat. In 2008, Northup returned for a rematch, after losing a primary contest for governor. She criticized Yarmuth for supporting the $700 billion bailout for the financial markets, and attacked his "present" vote on a resolution honoring Christmas, asserting he had lost touch with his constituents. (Yarmuth is Jewish.) Even though Northup raised more money, Yarmuth won much more easily than their first contest, 59%-41%.

Yarmuth finished first among members of the House—and 14th overall—in *Golf Digest*'s most recent ranking of the 150 best golfers in Washington's political world. He says that the demands of serving in Congress prompted him to scale back his plans to spend a month every year at a home he built near a golf course in Ireland.

FOURTH DISTRICT

Thomas Massie (R)

Elected Nov. 2012, 2nd full term; b. Jan. 13, 1971, Huntington, WV; MA Inst. of Tech., B.S. 1993, M.S. 1996; Methodist; married (Rhonda); 4 children.

Professional Career: Founder, chmn., & chief tech. officer, SensAble Technologies, 1993-2003; Judge exec., Lewis Cnty. KY, 2010-12; Farmer, 2003-present.

DC Office: 314 CHOB, 20515, 202-225-3465; Fax: 202-225-0003; Website: massie.house.gov.

State Offices: Ashland, 606-324-9898; Crescent Springs, 859-426-0080; LaGrange, 502-265-9119.

Committees: *Oversight & Govt. Reform:* Gov't Operations; Transportation & Public Assets. *Science, Space, & Technology:* Energy; Oversight. *Transportation & Infrastructure:* Economic Development, Public Buildings, & Emergency Mgmt.; Highways & Transit; Water Resources & Environment.

Group Ratings

	ADA	ACLU	AFL-CIO	LCV	ITI	COC	HAFA	ACU	CFG	FRC
2014	10%	44%	–	11%	60%	57%	76%	80%	86%	63%
2013	30%	C	29%	14%	C	62%	C	88%	93%	C

National Journal Ratings

	2013 LIB	—	2013 CONS
Economic	37%	—	63%
Social	50%	—	49%
Foreign	55%	—	45%
Composite	48%	—	53%

Key Votes of the 113th Congress

1. Sandy storm spending	N	5. Medical Marijuana	Y	9. Syrian Rebels Training	N
2. Violence Against Women Act	N	6. Farm Bill	N	10. Keystone pipeline	Y
3. Guantanamo Bay Detainees	N	7. Afghanistan Combat	Y	11. Immigration Exec. Action	Y
4. Abortion 20-week ban	Y	8. NSA Phone Data Collection	Y	12. Bipartisan budget deal	N

Election Results

2014 general	Thomas Massie (R)	150,464	(68%)	$478,876
	Peter Newberry (D)	71,694	(32%)	
2014 primary	Thomas Massie (R)	unopposed		

Prior winning percentages: 2012 (62%), 2012 special (60%)

Population		Race and Ethnicity		Income	
Total:	736,293	White	90.6%	Median income:	$54,683
Urban:	13.4%	Black	3.6%		*(171 of 435)*
Suburban:	62.6%	Latino	3.0%	**Under $50,000**	45.7%
Rural:	24.0%	Asian	1.0%	$50,000-$99,999:	32.3%
Land area:	4,321	Two races	1.1%	$100,000-$199,999:	17.2%
Pop/sq. mi.:	170.4	White Ethnic	24.0%	$200,000 or more:	4.8%
Born in state:	62.2%			Poverty Rate	14.1%
		Education			
Age Groups		H.S. grad or less:	43.3%	**Work**	
Under 18:	24.7%	Some college:	30.4%	White collar:	34.9%
18 to 34:	21.0%	College degree, 4 yr.:	16.7%	Blue collar:	41.3%
35 to 64:	41.1%	Post-grad study:	9.6%	Sales and service:	23.8%
Over 64:	13.2%				
		Military		Govt. workers:	12.1%
		Veterans/active duty:	8.8%		

Northern Kentucky: Cincinnati and Louisville Suburbs

Along the Ohio River are some very different parts of Kentucky. Ashland, near the West Virginia border, is industrial, the former home of Ashland Inc.; the river here is bound in by tight hills that hold smoke and soot in the air. Farther down the river, the country is more bucolic. This is where Eliza fled

Voter Turnout	
2013 Total Citizen 18+	544,195
2014 House Turnout	222,158
2014 Turnout as % CVAP	40.8%
2012 Turnout as % CVAP	57.4%

across the ice floes in Harriet Beecher Stowe's *Uncle Tom's Cabin*. Farther west, between Louisville and Cincinnati, are counties that look like they're still in the 19th century. But metropolitan growth obtrudes. Oldham County, just upriver from Louisville, has some of Kentucky's oldest homes, and is by far the most affluent county in the state. The three Northern Kentucky counties across the river from Cincinnati—Campbell, Kenton and fast-growing Boone—are urban and suburban. Overlooking the suspension bridge built by John Roebling are new buildings on the Covington waterfront, and new subdivisions are rising on the hills in Boone County, above the river, near the Cincinnati/Northern Kentucky International Airport. Newport, with its panoramic view of the Cincinnati skyline plus its nightlife, has become a regional hot spot. In the Cincinnati metro area, there have been some encouraging signs: Housing sales are up (although prices are down). By early 2015, the unemployment rate in the area declined to 4.8%; it remained at 6% in the Ashland area.

The 4th Congressional District of Kentucky is the northernmost district in the state, and much of it has a closer kinship to Cincinnati than to Lexington. It covers 12 counties and 280 miles along the Ohio River and also lightly populated counties just inland. Economically, it runs the gamut from coal mining towns to rich suburbs. Oldham County gave Mitt Romney more than

2012 Presidential Vote		
Mitt Romney (R)	.197,098	(63%)
Barack Obama (D)	.108,348	(35%)
2008 Presidential Vote		
John McCain (R)	.191,812	(62%)
Barack Obama (D)	.115,480	(37%)
Cook Partisan Voting Index:	R+16	

two-thirds of the vote, while the three northern Kentucky counties across the river from Cincinnati, which cast nearly half the district's votes, are also heavily Republican. This is now one of two districts in the state where Republicans' registration approaches that of the Democrats; the other is the 5th. It is solidly Republican in national elections.

Thomas Massie (R)

Republican Thomas Massie, first elected in 2012 as a political outsider, has featured his rebellious stripes in Congress and has been a constant thorn to Speaker John Boehner, whose district is a short drive away on the other side of the Ohio River.

Massie has an impressive scientific background. He was raised in Vanceburg Kentucky, and attended the Massachusetts Institute of Technology. While at MIT, Massie was part of a group that invented the Phantom, a device enabling users to interact with objects in cyberspace through touch. To market the product, he and his wife, Rhonda (his high school sweetheart and also an MIT student), started the firm SensAble Technologies in 1993. He won a $30,000 Lemelson-MIT Student Prize for his work in technology. After earning his master's degree in engineering, Massie continued to raise venture capital to expand the company.

Massie eventually left SensAble Technologies in 2003, and returned to Kentucky with his family to run a farm, where he built a timber-frame house that runs on solar energy. He got interested in politics after learning about a proposed tax in rural Lewis County that would fund a building for a local conservation office. After writing a letter to the editor objecting to the tax, "It was probably at that point there was no turning back from my involvement in politics," he later told a gathering in Newport, according to *The Cincinnati Enquirer*. In 2010, he entered politics by winning a campaign for Lewis County judge-executive. In that position, Massie boasted that he eliminated enough wasteful spending in his first nine months to pay three years of his salary.

Massie launched his campaign to replace retiring Republican Rep. Geoff Davis in January 2012. A self-described "conservative with conviction and common sense," Massie campaigned on his business background and budget-cutting experience as a county official. In an early speech, Massie harkened to his time with SensAble: "For me, the government was one of those entities that was putting land mines in the field that I had to navigate when we started the company." In a seven-candidate field, Massie's two closest competitors were establishment favorites: Republican state Rep. Alecia Webb-Edgington and Boone County Judge-Executive Gary Moore. Webb-Edgington, a former state trooper and narcotics detective, was endorsed by Davis.

The all-important support of tea party activists went to Massie. He had supported tea party favorite Rand Paul in his 2010 Senate race, and Massie named former Paul aide Ryan Hogan as his campaign manager. Paul appeared in a TV ad for Massie. Webb-Edgington and Moore attacked Massie for benefiting from the largesse of Liberty for All, a Texas-based super PAC that reportedly was bankrolled primarily by James Ramsey, a 21-year-old Texas college student with a hefty inheritance. He provided the group with more than $500,000 to spend on behalf of Massie.

Massie effectively portrayed himself as the outsider, as Webb-Edgington and Moore split the establishment vote. Massie won the primary handily, with 45% of the vote to Webb-Edgington's 29% and Moore's 15%. In this solidly Republican district, Massie easily won in November against Grant County lawyer Bill Adkins.

In the House, he showed his rebellious streak on his first House vote in January 2013, when he opposed Boehner for a new term as House speaker, instead voting for Rep. Justin Amash of Michigan, who had no chance of winning. Massie occasionally crossed the aisle to work with Democrats on civil liberties issues, on which the wings of both parties came together in opposition to Big Government. In May 2015, he cosponsored a bill with Democratic Rep. Zoe Lofgren of California to require that the National Security Agency seek a judicial warrant before it could spy on U.S. citizens in its on-line surveillance. With Democratic Rep. Marc Pocan of Wisconsin, he filed a bill to repeal the Patriot Act, which was enacted after the 2001 terror attacks and has provided broad authority to security agencies. *Buzzfeed* profiled Massie as "Democrats' new go-to Republican." But on most social issues, he remained a solid conservative vote. "Here's the difference between a partisan and an ideologue: An ideologue reads the bill, every word, period and section; a partisan reads the whip recommendation," he told *Buzzfeed*.

Massie has worked with other conservatives to channel their opposition to GOP leaders. He again voted against Boehner for speaker in 2015. The House leadership, he said, had become "a significant source of the dysfunction" in the House. He worked with other members in the conservative Freedom Caucus, who sought to strengthen their legislative leverage. In January 2015, Massie used parliamentary tactics to delay the bill funding the Homeland Security Department. Boehner and House appropriators ultimately circumvented him and cooperated with Democrats to pass the bill. During his first term, Massie chaired the Technology Subcommittee, a logical assignment for his background. In his second term, he no longer chaired that subcommittee, or any other. That seemed a clear message from Boehner and his team.

FIFTH DISTRICT

Harold Rogers (R)

Elected 1980, 18th term; b. Dec. 31, 1937, Barrier; U. of KY, B.A. 1962, LL.B. 1964; Baptist; married (Cynthia); 3 children.

Military Career: KY & NC Army Natl. Guard, 1957-64.

Professional Career: Practicing atty., 1964-69; Pulaski-Rockcastle Commonwealth's atty., 1969-80.

DC Office: 2406 RHOB, 20515, 202-225-4601; Fax: 202-225-0940; Website: halrogers.house.gov.

State Offices: Hazard, 606-439-0794; Prestonsburg, 606-886-0844; Somerset, 800-632-8588.

Committees: *Appropriations* (Chmn).

Group Ratings

	ADA	ACLU	AFL-CIO	LCV	ITI	COC	HAFA	ACU	CFG	FRC
2014	0%	0%	–	3%	100%	93%	42%	60%	41%	100%
2013	0%	C	20%	4%	C	85%	C	65%	47%	C

National Journal Ratings

	2012 LIB	—	2012 CONS
Economic	46%	—	54%
Social	27%	—	71%
Foreign	34%	—	60%
Composite	37%	—	63%

Key Votes of the 113th Congress

1. Sandy storm spending	Y	5. Medical Marijuana	N	9. Syrian Rebels Training	Y
2. Violence Against Women Act	N	6. Farm Bill	Y	10. Keystone pipeline	Y
3. Guantanamo Bay Detainees	N	7. Afghanistan Combat	N	11. Immigration Exec. Action	Y
4. Abortion 20-week ban	NV	8. NSA Phone Data Collection	N	12. Bipartisan budget deal	Y

Election Results

2014 general	Hal Rogers (R)	171,350	(78%)	$1,125,832
	Kenneth Stepp (D)	47,617	(22%)	$6,253
2014 primary	Hal Rogers (R)	unopposed		

Prior winning percentages: 2012 (78%), 2010 (77%), 2008 (84%), 2006 (74%), 2004 (100%), 2002 (78%), 2000 (74%), 1998 (78%), 1996 (100%), 1994 (79%), 1992 (55%), 1990 (100%), 1988 (100%), 1986 (100%), 1984 (76%), 1982 (65%), 1980 (67%)

Population		Race and Ethnicity		Income	
Total:	714,729	White	96.2%	Median income:	$31,348
Urban:	1.6%	Black	1.3%		*(432 of 435)*
Suburban:	0.8%	Latino	0.9%	Under $50,000	68.9%
Rural:	97.6%	Asian	0.3%	$50,000-$99,999:	23.1%
Land area:	12,151	Two races	1.0%	$100,000-$199,999:	7.2%
Pop/sq. mi.:	58.8	White Ethnic	12.3%	$200,000 or more:	0.8%
Born in state:	79.8%			Poverty Rate	26.7%
		Education			
Age Groups		H.S. grad or less:	62.9%	**Work**	
Under 18:	22.0%	Some college:	23.7%	White collar:	28.9%
18 to 34:	20.8%	College degree, 4 yr.:	7.3%	Blue collar:	43.1%
35 to 64:	41.8%	Post-grad study:	6.1%	Sales and service:	28.0%
Over 64:	15.5%			Govt. workers:	19.7%
		Military			
		Veterans/active duty:	7.1%		

Eastern Kentucky

Mountainous eastern Kentucky has been a unique place since Daniel Boone came through the Cumberland Gap in 1775. Scots-Irish pioneers soon followed him, bringing their assertive egalitarianism, loyalty to family and community, and passionate willingness to defend

honor by feuds or violence. Most inhabitants
of the mountains today are descendants of the
Ulster Protestant and Border Scot families
who settled there in the two or three generations after Boone. In the 2010 census, 0% of
the population of Elliott, Magoffin and Menifee

Voter Turnout	
2013 Total Citizen 18+	554,790
2014 House Turnout	218,967
2014 Turnout as % CVAP	39.5%
2012 Turnout as % CVAP	47.2%

counties reported being foreign-born. Handed down were living memories of the old ways of
doing things from an era when there was little contact with the outside world. Even if the
demographics have been stable, the politics of the area have gone through much change.
The first agent of change here was the Civil War. This was never slave territory—hardly any
blacks have ever lived in these mountains, and even today Leslie County is the whitest in
the state. The settlers had little use for the party of slavery, and still don't. The mountains
and the Cumberland Plateau became a Republican stronghold. Today, the counties around
Somerset and Corbin in south central Kentucky cast some of the highest Republican percentages in the nation, election after election; President Barack Obama won 12% of the vote
in nearby Jackson County in 2012, a slight decline from his 14% in 2008 and Bill Clinton's
22% in 1996. But this is a very different economic base and culture than the new Republican heartland in places like suburban Georgia and rural Texas. Much of the area is socially
conservative. When Kentucky voters in 2004 approved a constitutional amendment banning
gay marriage, Magoffin, with 94 percent, was the county with the strongest support.

Early in the 20th century, vast seams of coal were discovered under the Kentucky mountains, and a new economy sprang up, bringing a new politics. Coal mining was harsh and
deadly work, as described in countless country and western songs with titles like "You'll
Never Leave Harlan Alive" and "Miner's Prayer." Mine accidents, black lung disease, and
simple exhaustion killed tens of thousands of miners, while low wages and company stores
kept them poor. Then, John L. Lewis's United Mine Workers came in, and open warfare followed, with both mine operators and union organizers willing to use violence. The union
mostly won in eastern Kentucky and brought Democratic politics to these counties. In his
War on Poverty, President Lyndon Johnson brought attention to this and other parts of
Appalachia. He launched his "war" from the front porch of a cabin in the town of Inez in these
mountains. A half-century later, high-school graduation rates and life expectancy remained
low. In some of these areas, the coal mines have closed, and people have left. For years,
the political geography was determined in large part by the extent of unionization; heavily
Democratic areas existed just a mountain ridge away from heavily Republicans ones. But
as the Democratic Party has increasingly become an urban coalition of upscale whites and
minorities, eastern Kentucky may be undergoing a third political revolution. Knott County
gave Clinton 73% of the vote in 1996, but Obama managed only 25% there in 2012.

The 5th Congressional District of Kentucky includes much of the territory east of
the Pottsville Escarpment, which separates
the Cumberland Plateau and most of the
eastern mountains from the rest of the state.
It includes a few counties in the eastern Pennyrile region: small towns like Somerset,
Monticello and Mount Vernon. And it takes
in Republican areas of the mountains to the

2012 Presidential Vote		
Mitt Romney (R)	196,192	(75%)
Barack Obama (D)	60,760	(23%)
2008 Presidential Vote		
John McCain (R)	174,245	(67%)
Barack Obama (D)	82,582	(32%)
Cook Partisan Voting Index:	R+25	

east, including Corbin, where Colonel Harland Sanders first served his fried chicken with
11 herbs and spices, birthing fast food franchise KFC. The northeast section of the district
is coal country. There are no major metropolitan areas in the district and few highways go
through the mountains; only a handful of towns have a population over 10,000. Overall this
is a heavily Republican district: Mitt Romney received 75% of the vote in the 5th in 2012.

Harold Rogers (R)

Harold Rogers, a Republican first elected in 1980, chairs the House Appropriations Committee. He is an old-school deal-maker who, in the days before the ban on earmarks, not only
defended them but boasted about the prodigious sums he steered back home. *The Lexington
Herald-Leader* dubbed him the "Prince of Pork," and he is beloved in his rural district: He
regularly is reelected with more than 75% of the vote.

Rogers grew up in Wayne County, graduated from the University of Kentucky, served in the National Guard, and then practiced law in Somerset before buying the Citizens National Bank in Somerset. In 1969, at age 34, he was elected Pulaski-Rockcastle Commonwealth attorney. In 1979, he was the Republican nominee for lieutenant governor. The following year, when the 5th District congressman retired, Rogers was one of 11 Republicans in the primary. He got the nomination with 23% of the vote (Kentucky has no runoff except in gubernatorial races) and then easily won in November.

His toughest race came in 1992, after redistricting. At first, his likely opponent was 7th District Rep. Chris Perkins, a Democrat and the son of longtime Rep. Carl Perkins. Together, they had held the seat for 44 years. But then Perkins suddenly retired from Congress, just before it was revealed that he had 514 overdrafts at the House bank when such overdrafts were developing into a major Washington scandal. Rogers faced state Sen. John Doug Hays of Pike County. Rogers won with 55% of the vote in a year many Southern Democrats were turning out to vote for Arkansas Gov. Bill Clinton for president.

His voting record is mostly, but not always, conservative. His district has long been hungry for federal aid, and Rogers often has found it difficult to maintain an impeccably conservative record on spending issues. He has defended the Appalachian Regional Commission, a perennial target of conservative groups, against amendments to slash its funding. He has argued that the federal/state partnership has successfully helped to close the gap between the impoverished area and the rest of the country.

During Republicans' initial 12 years in the House majority, Rogers chaired the Commerce, Justice, State Subcommittee starting in 1995, took over the Transportation Subcommittee in 2001, and became chairman in 2003 of the newly created Homeland Security Subcommittee. He helped to increase Kentucky to the fourth-highest state in transportation funding per capita. "The rate of return on highway spending far exceeds most other investments and is a proven engine," Rogers once wrote when he was criticized for his earmarked spending. The Daniel Boone Parkway, from London to Hazard, has been renamed the Hal Rogers Parkway.

In recent years, controversy over earmarks, the special provisions that lawmakers slip into spending bills for their districts and states, put an unaccustomed spotlight on Rogers and other powerful appropriators, who for years quietly went about their business. When he was criticized for fighting to keep the Transportation Worker Identification Credential program in Corbin, he replied that it was one of only three government facilities with sufficient security to produce the cards. Rogers has continued raising significant sums of political cash from firms that have won homeland security contracts. He responded, "I've had a lot of fundraisers. Campaign contributions mean nothing on my watch."

Rogers rose to chairman of Appropriations in 2011 after Republicans regained control of the House. He had first sought the post after the 2004 election, but the GOP leadership chose the more senior Jerry Lewis of California. After the 2010 election, Lewis sought a waiver of the Republicans' three-term limit on chairman and ranking member positions, but the Republican Steering Committee did not agree and named Rogers as chairman.

Rogers became committee chairman just as most House Republicans, especially the 87 freshmen elected in 2010, were determined to end the practice of earmarking. Despite his work over the years funding projects at home, he went along with incoming House Speaker John Boehner's moratorium on earmarks in November 2010. After winning reelection in 2012, Rogers touted his success in helping to cut wasteful spending. "We've cut the spending Congress does for three years now, which has not happened since World War II," he said. "We've cut $100 billion off the spending Congress appropriates." The earmark ban did not eliminate his influence entirely. *The New York Times* reported in April 2012 that an earmark he had added three years earlier was still in place to benefit a Kentucky company that manufactures drip pans to catch leaking transmission fluid on the Army's Black Hawk helicopters, even though there was a cheaper alternative.

Part of the reason for Rogers' continuing clout is his ability to work with Democrats. "He's very approachable," committee Democrat Marcy Kaptur of Ohio said. "He's a matter-of-fact sort of gentleman—I mean, he doesn't spend a lot of time on wasted words, he's terse—but I think very effective."

Another source of his influence has been the inability of recent congressional majorities to pass individual appropriations bills. That led to massive omnibus spending bills, something that enabled Republicans to make policy via "riders" on the omnibus legislation. The December 2011 final spending bill included the elimination of more than two dozen federal programs and imposed limits on several key provisions of the Dodd-Frank financial reform law. In 2014, Rogers encouraged rank-and-file Republicans to take an early part in the appropriations process to minimize attempts to add last-minute "poison pill" amendments on the floor.

Rogers worked well with Maryland's Democratic Sen. Barbara Mikulski, who in 2013 became his counterpart at the Senate Appropriations Committee. The pair achieved a significant goal in January 2014 when Congress approved an omnibus spending bill—the first time since 2009 that Congress completed appropriations bills that went beyond continuing resolutions. "Chairman Rogers and I work well together because we have the same goals," Mikulski told *FCW*.

Later in 2014, Rogers turned up his nose at President Barack Obama's request for $3.7 billion to deal with the refugee crisis at the Texas-Mexico border. "It's too much money; we don't need it," he told reporters. "Secondly, a lot of what he's requesting is being considered in the regular bill process." At the same time, he helped steer through the committee a natural resources funding bill that cut the Environmental Protection Agency's budget by 9 percent. He blasted the president for being "hell bent on adding layer after layer of regulatory red tape to the economy" and for trying to hurt coal miners.

When Obama in November issued an executive order protecting some illegal immigrants, many conservatives vowed to overturn it. But Rogers warned against using the issue to provoke another spending-bill confrontation. "I just don't think it's very smart, wise or prudent to talk about a shutdown scenario," he said. That enraged conservative activists. *National Review Online* ran an article headlined "Hal Rogers, Obama Republican," and talk show host Laura Ingraham demanded that Rogers draw a primary challenger in 2016. "Hal Rogers refuses to consider the sensible process of defunding Obama's executive amnesty and instead throws up all of these false roadblocks to defunding Obama's executive amnesty," she said.

When Republicans later sought to use the Homeland Security Department spending bill to try to block the move, Rogers joined his GOP colleagues in criticizing the resistance by Senate Democrats. "They should pass the bill, which funds a very vital national security agency but also turns back this blanket amnesty, which is illegal and unconstitutional," he said in February 2015. Rogers also was in line with his fellow Republicans in reacting negatively to Obama's fiscal 2016 proposed budget, which he complained asked "for billions in additional spending without any realistic way of paying for it."

Rogers over the years has focused on homeland security. Even before the September 11 attacks, he lamented that most airport screeners were not U.S. citizens, and after Congress voted to federalize screeners, he kept a close watch on the new agency. In 2010, he challenged the Obama administration's proposals for airport body scanners because he doubted that such a costly and manpower-intensive approach would get results. Rogers also questioned the Immigration and Customs Enforcement agency's policy of giving work permits to apprehended illegal immigrants who testify against their employers. The Obama administration, he complained, had practically given up deporting illegal immigrants arrested at work sites in favor of what he derisively called "virtual amnesty."

Drug abuse is another Rogers priority. Since 2000, his office boasts, he helped obtain more than $35 million to help the Kentucky National Guard and U.S. Forest Service get rid of marijuana growing in the Daniel Boone National Forest. He and Democrat Stephen Lynch of Massachusetts launched a caucus on prescription drug abuse.

Rogers is term-limited as committee chairman after the November 2016 election. He is unlikely to get a waiver. At age 78, he could retire or become chairman of another Appropriation subcommittee. In any case, he would not need to worry about winning reelection, and Republicans would not need to worry about keeping his seat.

SIXTH DISTRICT

Andy Barr (R)

Elected 2012, 2nd term; b. July 24, 1973, Lexington; U. of VA, B.A. 1996, U. of KY, J.D. 2001; Episcopalian; married (Carol); 2 children.

Professional Career: Legis. asst., U.S. Rep. Jim Talent, 1996-98; Instructor, Morehead St. U.; Atty., KY gov.'s office, 2004-07; Practicing atty., 2008-12.

DC Office: 1432 LHOB, 20515, 202-225-4706; Website: barr.house .gov.

State Offices: Lexington, 859-219-1366.

Committees: *Financial Services:* Financial Institutions & Consumer Credit; Housing & Insurance; Task Force to Investigate Terrorism Financing.

Group Ratings

	ADA	ACLU	AFL-CIO	LCV	ITI	COC	HAFA	ACU	CFG	FRC
2014	0%	0%	–	6%	100%	86%	59%	64%	54%	88%
2013	0%	C	10%	4%	C	85%	C	76%	76%	C

National Journal Ratings

	2013 LIB	—	2013 CONS
Economic	21%	—	79%
Social	34%	—	62%
Foreign	0%	—	95%
Composite	20%	—	80%

Key Votes of the 113th Congress

1. Sandy storm spending	N	5. Medical Marijuana	N
2. Violence Against Women Act	Y	6. Farm Bill	Y
3. Guantanamo Bay Detainees	N	7. Afghanistan Combat	N
4. Abortion 20-week ban	Y	8. NSA Phone Data Collection	N

9. Syrian Rebels Training	Y
10. Keystone pipeline	Y
11. Immigration Exec. Action	Y
12. Bipartisan budget deal	Y

Election Results

2014 general	Andy Barr (R)	147,404	(60%)	$2,295,731	$257,419	$20,601
	Elisabeth Jensen (D)	98,290	(40%)	$886,670	$18,645	
2014 primary	Andy Barr (R)	unopposed				

Prior winning percentage: 2012 (51%)

Population		Race and Ethnicity		Income	
Total:	744,583	White	83.2%	Median income:	$46,167
Urban:	45.2%	Black	9.0%		*(296 of 435)*
Suburban:	17.3%	Latino	4.0%	Under $50,000	53.0%
Rural:	37.5%	Asian	1.7%	$50,000-$99,999:	30.0%
Land area:	4,897	Two races	1.9%	$100,000-$199,999:	13.9%
Pop/sq. mi.:	152.1	White Ethnic	19.1%	$200,000 or more:	3.1%
Born in state:	68.6%			Poverty Rate	18.8%
		Education			
Age Groups		H.S. grad or less:	41.8%	**Work**	
Under 18:	22.6%	Some college:	28.1%	White collar:	36.9%
18 to 34:	25.8%	College degree, 4 yr.:	17.7%	Blue collar:	39.4%
35 to 64:	38.8%	Post-grad study:	12.4%	Sales and service:	23.7%
Over 64:	12.8%				
		Military		Govt. workers:	16.9%
		Veterans/active duty:	7.8%		

Bluegrass Country: Lexington

With its white picket fences, horse farms and small towns, the rolling plateau of Bluegrass in central Kentucky is the part of interior America longest settled by English speakers: Lexington was founded in 1775. Tobacco farming started here in the 1770s, horse racing in 1787, and the Reverend Elijah Craig is often credited with inventing bourbon distilling in 1789 (though many rivals have also affixed stakes to that claim). Tobacco, whiskey and racehorses remained the staples of the Bluegrass economy for six generations, until 1956, when IBM built its typewriter plant in Lexington. The personal computer eventually outclassed the typewriter, and the IBM plant was put on the block. The big employer here became Lexmark International, an IBM spi-

Voter Turnout	
2013 Total Citizen 18+	551,810
2014 House Turnout	245,694
2014 Turnout as % CVAP	44.5%
2012 Turnout as % CVAP	55.4%

noff. Another mainstay is the Toyota plant in Georgetown, a town with early-19th-century houses and lush countryside just one county north of the city. This is the largest Toyota plant in the nation, with more than 7,000 workers; by late 2015, it planned to start production of the first U.S.-assembled Lexus, which would increase the plant's annual production to 550,000 vehicles. In April 2014, environmental activists succeeded in halting plans for the proposed Bluegrass natural gas pipeline in Franklin County.

Lexington, which includes all of Fayette County, steadily grew by a sprightly 36% between 1990 and 2013, as its well-educated, young populace—it has the highest percentage of college graduates in the state and Scott County to the north has the youngest population—continued to attract business. Lexington voters in 2014 elected construction executive Jim Gray to a second term as mayor, making it the third-largest U.S. city with an openly gay chief executive. His sexual orientation was not an issue in his campaigns. It is the second-largest metropolitan area in the state, after Louisville-Jefferson County.

The 6th Congressional District of Kentucky includes Lexington and the surrounding counties. Lexington casts about 40% of its votes. It is the only district in Kentucky that does not border another state. To the northwest is the state capital of Frankfort, platted during the War for Independence by

2012 Presidential Vote		
Mitt Romney (R)	170,056	(56%)
Barack Obama (D)	128,564	(42%)
2008 Presidential Vote		
John McCain (R)	165,833	(54%)
Barack Obama (D)	138,456	(45%)
Cook Partisan Voting Index: R+9		

Gen. James Wilkinson, who was also secretly a paid agent of the Spanish Crown and who worked to cede various portions of the United States, including Kentucky, to Spain. This was traditionally a swing area of the state, but it has become more Republican. Mitt Romney carried the district with 56% of the vote in 2012, a clear indication that the 6th has joined the GOP heartland.

Andy Barr (R)

Persistence has paid off for Republican attorney Andy Barr. Two years after losing to Democratic Rep. Ben Chandler by just 647 votes, he got his revenge in 2012 by winning by nearly 11,800 votes in Kentucky's 6th District. In 2014, he was reelected with 60 percent of the vote. He seems well-placed for a successful political career, perhaps with an eventual statewide bid.

Barr grew up in Lexington and graduated from the University of Virginia with a bachelor's degree in government and philosophy. After two years as a legislative assistant for Republican Rep. Jim Talent of Missouri, Barr returned home to earn a law degree from the University of Kentucky. He practiced law, and taught constitutional and administrative law as a part-time instructor at Morehead State University.

Barr served as a deputy general counsel to former Kentucky Gov. Ernie Fletcher, whose tenure was marred by a scandal over the hiring, promoting, and firing of state employees based on their political loyalties. In his 2010 challenge to Chandler, Barr distanced himself from Fletcher, while Chandler and his backers sought to play up those ties plus Barr's membership in a country club that until 2009 had never admitted an African American. The race went down to the wire. Barr decided against a recount and conceded to Chandler 10 days after the election.

Barr got an earlier start in his 2012 rematch. But Chandler got help from redistricting, thanks to a last-minute deal in the legislature that excised from the 6th District some southern counties that voted heavily for Barr in 2010 and added traditionally Democratic-leaning counties to the east. Barr attacked President Barack Obama's policies—especially on coal, an important issue to the district—and aggressively went after his rival, using a picture of his own baby daughter on a campaign mailer that called Chandler a "pro-abortion extremist."

Going on the attack, Chandler brought up Barr's guilty plea to possession of a fake ID when he was 19, claiming that Barr lied on a job application because he failed to mention the arrest when applying for the position with Fletcher's administration. Barr responded with an ad calling the incident as a teenager a "dumb mistake" and blasting his rival as a "desperate politician scared of losing."

Chandler's campaign attacked one of Barr's ads in which a coal executive was shown as a coal miner, releasing a spot accusing the Republican of playing fast and loose with the truth. But Chandler's move proved premature when it was revealed that the executive was a registered miner who was wearing his own hard hat in the spot. This may have been Barr's biggest break in the campaign. Even though Chandler slightly outspent him, Barr got fundraising help from GOP Sen. Rand Paul of Kentucky and outside Republican groups that helped put him over the top. He won, 51%-47%.

In the House, Barr joined the Financial Services Committee. In March 2015, he filed legislation that would streamline financial regulations, especially affecting community banks and credit unions, which often are important in rural communities. The House passed in 2014 his bill that addressed a similar target and had a clever acronym, the Helping Expand Lending Practices in Rural Communities Act. Barr spoke out against what he called President Barack Obama's "radical energy-rationing agenda" that would kill the coal industry. He chaired the Congressional Horse Caucus, and has filed bills that would strengthen the area's equine, bourbon, energy, agriculture and manufacturing industries.

In his 2014 reelection, Barr was challenged by Elizabeth Jensen, an education advocate and Democratic activist, whom he outspent $2.2 million to nearly $900,000. He coasted to victory with 60% of the vote and won all 19 counties. His closest margin was 53%-47% in Fayette County.

★ LOUISIANA ★

"There is on the globe one single spot, the possessor of which is our natural and habitual enemy," wrote Thomas Jefferson. "It is New Orleans, through which the produce of three-eighths of our territory must pass to market." He was writing as Americans were streaming through the narrow gaps of the Appalachian chain, settling land drained by the fast-flowing Ohio and Mississippi rivers. In 1718, the French founded New Orleans on a ridge formed by deposits of silt and declared the Mississippi Valley the colony of Louisiana. It was transferred to Spain in 1763, and after France took possession again, Jefferson sought to buy the city in 1802. When Napoleon offered to sell the entire Louisiana Territory, Jefferson's envoys quickly and eagerly agreed to purchase it—almost doubling the land area of the young republic. Its large French and small Spanish population had been ruled under European civil law rather than English common law. When Louisiana was admitted as a state in 1812, it included territory well to the north of the city that would soon be overrun by Americans heading west. The state's boundaries were rounded out with the acquisition of West Florida, the land north of Lake Pontchartrain heading west to Baton Rouge. With its large sugar and cotton slave plantations, Louisiana boomed, and by the outbreak of the Civil War, New Orleans was the nation's sixth largest city—the only substantial city in the Confederate South.

Louisiana has remained distinctive and exotic ever since. It is divided between a Catholic Cajun south, a Baptist Protestant north, and idiosyncratic New Orleans. Its population is 33 percent black, the second-highest percentage of any state; it was black Louisianans who developed American jazz. The state's economy has always been based on the export of raw materials—sugar, rice, and cotton in the 19th century; oil and gas in the 20th and 21st centuries. Its most talented politician was Huey Long, who as a young Public Service Commission chairman championed a severance tax on oil, and who, in less than a single term each as governor (1928-32) and as a senator (1932-35), left an imprint on the state's public life and imposed an organization on its politics that faded into history only a generation ago. Long's genius was not that he promised to tax the rich to help the poor—hundreds of idealists and demagogues in America have done that—but that to an amazing extent he delivered. He dominated the legislature so thoroughly that, as governor, he roamed the floors of both chambers at will, bringing to the podium bills he insisted lawmakers pass without changing a comma—and they did. He was ready to use bribery, intimidation and physical violence. He built a new skyscraper Capitol, a new Louisiana State University, a Mississippi River bridge in New Orleans, and more miles of roads than any other state but rich New York and huge Texas. He also built a national following and, by 1935, was planning to run for president on a platform of "Share the wealth, every man a king." That year, Long was assassinated at age 42 in the hallway of the Capitol he built. The bullet holes can still be seen in the marble walls.

Long's impact was lasting, and not just in the literary character he inspired—Willie Stark of Robert Penn Warren's *All the King's Men*. The Long threat may have moved President Franklin D. Roosevelt to embrace the liberal programs—the Wagner Labor Act, Social Security, and steeply graduated taxes—of the Second New Deal. For Louisiana, Long delivered a political structure that revolved around him even after he was dead—and a class of political leaders who, lacking his talents, treated the state as Long's incompetent doctors had treated his fatal wound, leaving Louisiana with neither a fully developed economy nor a fully competent public sector. For 50 years, until Huey's son, Sen. Russell Long, retired in 1986, Longs and Long protégés held high political office in Louisiana and elections were run along pro- and anti-Long lines. The Long experience strengthened Louisiana's already strong predispositions—tolerance of corruption, disinterest in abstract reform, and a taste for colorful extremists regardless of their short-term means or long-term ends.

This has not helped to create a vibrant economy. Louisiana has chronically suffered low incomes, low workforce participation, and low levels of education, with income disparities greater than almost anywhere else in the United States. Louisiana has the nation's highest incarceration rate, the second-biggest gender pay gap in the nation and the lowest share of female legislators at 12.5 percent. New Orleans' elite class has been notoriously tight-knit, not venturesome, and determined to hold on to its wealth against the grasp of the impecunious and unlearned masses. Louisiana momentarily prospered when oil prices spiked

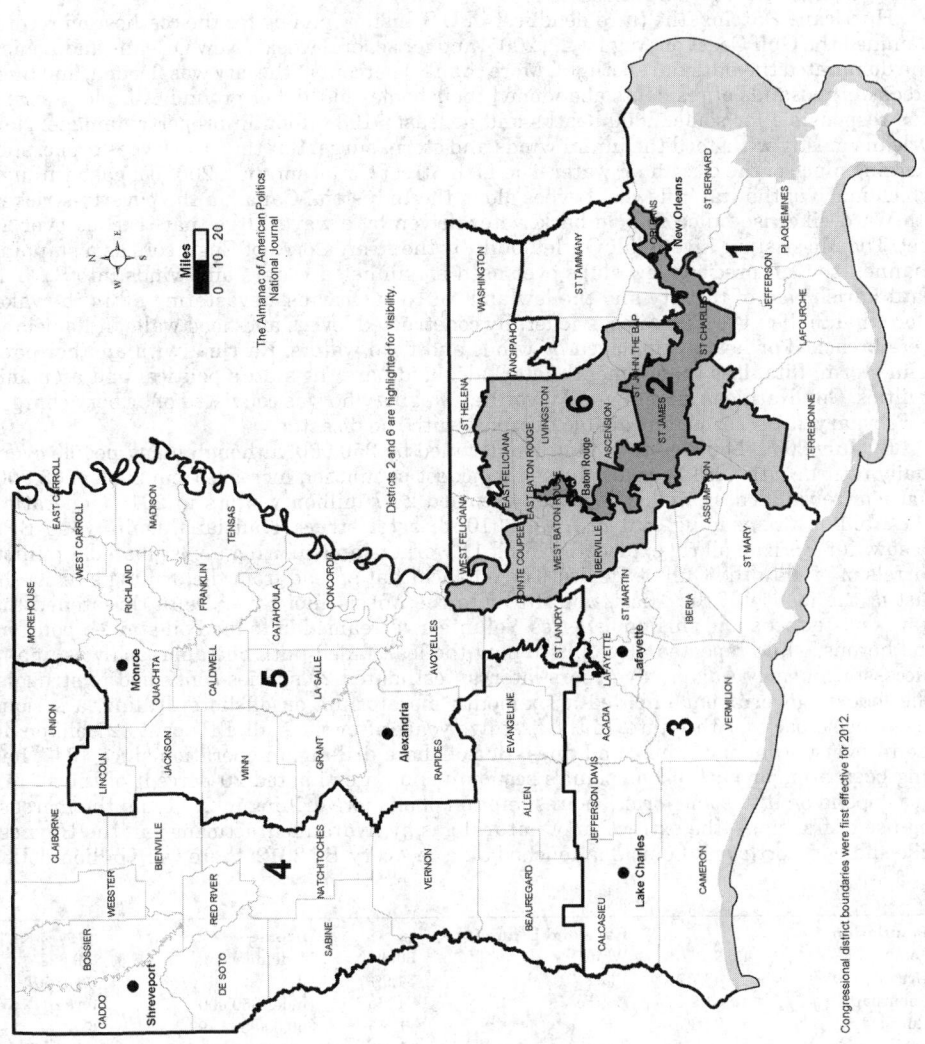

The Almanac of American Politics
National Journal

Districts 2 and 6 are highlighted for visibility.

Congressional district boundaries were first effective for 2012.

upwards in 1973 and 1979, but then jobs and people flowed out in the 1980s as it failed to develop a diverse economy similar to that of its similarly oil-rich neighbor, Texas. This has made a huge difference over time. Metro New Orleans in 1940 had a population of 564,000; it was about the same size then as metro Houston (610,000) and metro Dallas (624,000). But in 2004, just before Hurricane Katrina struck, metro Houston had 5.1 million people, metro Dallas 5.8 million, and New Orleans just 1.3 million. From 1980 to 2005, Louisiana increased in population only 7 percent, far less than any other Southern state and less than any state nationally except two in the Great Plains and the industrial triangle of Ohio, Pennsylvania and West Virginia.

Hurricane Katrina, the third deadliest in U.S. history and by far the costliest on record, slammed the Gulf Coast on August 29, 2005, and for several weeks, New Orleans and Louisiana dominated the national spotlight. More than 80 percent of the city was flooded, and hundreds of thousands of residents abandoned their homes for higher ground. All told, Katrina was responsible for some 1,800 deaths and at least $108 billion in property damage. New Orleans mostly withstood the initial winds and storm surge. But then the levees broke, submerging much of the city under water. The 17th Street Canal sprang a 200-foot gash through which much of the water flowed. Levees along the Industrial Canal, in the poverty-stricken 9th Ward, likewise failed to hold back water driven by a wave surge that reached over 20 feet. The Mississippi River Gulf Outlet, built by the Army Corps of Engineers as a shipping channel (though precious few ships ever used it), funneled waters and winds into St. Bernard Parish east of the city and the lowlands of New Orleans, devastating all in its wake. More than half of the 270 miles of federally constructed levees and flood walls in Louisiana were breached or heavily damaged by winds and flood waters. Katrina (with another powerful storm, Rita, less than a month later) also laid bare the state's political and economic frailties. Gov. Kathleen Blanco and Mayor Ray Nagin (who was convicted of bribery charges in February 2014) seemed incapable of coping with the disaster.

By July 2006, Louisiana's population declined by 250,000, although many people eventually returned; the 2010 census showed a modest population increase from 2005 of 38,000. Tourism rebounded as well: The state welcomed 28.7 million visitors in 2014, generating $11.2 billion in spending. But in April 2010, disaster struck Louisiana again when BP's Deepwater Horizon oil rig exploded, killing 11 workers and spewing an estimated 4 million barrels of oil into the Gulf of Mexico. The oil slick that spread from the drilling site southeast of the mouth of the Mississippi River to the Mississippi River Delta threatened the state's oyster beds and shrimp fisheries. Volunteers streamed in to tend oil-stained pelicans and herons, while repeated attempts to plug the leak failed until one approach was finally successful in early August; five years later, an estimated 20 species continued to struggle. The federal government imposed a six-month moratorium on offshore drilling, a serious economic setback for the state. In the first five years after the spill, BP spent $27 billion on the recovery, economic claims and fines. But offshore drilling, in operation since 1947, has long been a major part of Louisiana's economy and an estimated 20 percent of the state's jobs depend on it in some form. The resumption of offshore drilling in 2011 and the increasing use of fracking—the extraction of natural gas by hydraulic fracturing—in the Haynesville shale in northwest Louisiana touched off a recovery. By 2012, there were billion-dollar

Population		Race and Ethnicity		Income	
Total:	4,625,470	White	60.0%	Median income:	$39,622
Urban:	43.7%	Black	31.9%		(50 of 50)
Suburban:	31.5%	Latino	4.3%	Under $50,000	54.4%
Rural:	24.8%	Asian	1.6%	$50,000-$99,999:	27.3%
Land area:	43,204	Two races	1.4%	$100,000-$199,999:	14.7%
Pop/sq. mi.:	107.1	White Ethnic	29.6%	$200,000 or more:	3.6%
Born in state:	77.9%			Poverty Rate	18.3%
		Education			
Age Groups		H.S. grad or less:	50.5%	Work	
Under 18:	24.1%	Some college:	27.0%	White collar:	32.1%
18 to 34:	24.6%	College degree, 4 yr.:	14.9%	Blue collar:	43.1%
35 to 64:	38.2%	Post-grad study:	7.6%	Sales and service:	24.8%
Over 64:	13.1%			Govt. workers:	15.1%
		Military			
		Veterans/active duty:	7.8%		

investments in refineries, gas-to-liquid facilities, and liquefied natural gas export terminals. Petroleum and coal products were Louisiana's top export in 2014 at $25.7 billion, chemicals were second at $8.6 billion. Unemployment in Louisiana has had an unusual track, peaking at 8.3 percent in the fall of 2010, when the national rate was more than a full point higher, but since then improving more slowly than the national average—6.6 percent in March 2015 when the national rate had plunged more than one point lower.

Louisiana's politics have changed. For years after the Civil War, the state was solidly Democratic, with political divides expressed in Democratic primaries. There were splits between the Cajun Catholic parishes, which cast about 30 percent of the state's votes, and Protestant parishes north of Baton Rouge, which cast about 45 percent. Another division was by income. Low-income voters of both races tended to support Huey Long and his populist successors; higher-income voters often opposed them. So for a long time, Louisiana politics were a struggle between reformist and conservative forces on one side and roguish populists on the other, a struggle waged in lavishly financed campaigns with grandiloquent rhetoric. For more than two decades the lead role in state politics was played by Edwin Edwards, a colorful Cajun populist who was elected governor in 1972 and 1975, sat out 1979 because he was ineligible to run, and then in 1983 won a third term. While in office, he faced corruption charges and was acquitted by a jury in 1986. He lost a bid for reelection in 1987 but ran again in 1991. In Louisiana's (since altered) all-party system, he won 34 percent of the vote to 32 percent for David Duke, a onetime Nazi sympathizer and Klansman who had won a special election to the legislature as a Republican in 1989. Duke was repudiated by Republican National Committee Chairman Lee Atwater and President George H.W. Bush as well as Louisiana Republicans. Bumper stickers read, "Vote for the crook—it's important," and a majority of voters listened; Edwards won the runoff, 61%-39%. He was convicted on corruption charges in May 2000 and went to prison. (Attempting a post-prison comeback in 2014 by running for Congress, Edwards lost the runoff, 62%-38%.)

In the years since, Louisiana has become increasingly Republican. It voted for Bill Clinton in 1992 and 1996 (the only deep-South state to do so), but it cast increasing percentages for Republican candidates in the four presidential elections from 1996 to 2008. In 2008, blacks voted 94 percent for Barack Obama and whites voted 84 percent for John McCain. There was no exit poll in the state in 2012, but the statewide and parish percentages were very much the same, except for an apparent increase in black turnout in New Orleans, which cut the Republican margin by 1 percent, to 58%-41%. Democratic Sen. Mary Landrieu was elected to three terms starting in 1996, but never with more than 52 percent of the vote, and in 2014, she lost her seat to Republican Bill Cassidy. Republican Sen. David Vitter was elected in 2004 with 51 percent under Louisiana's system of multiparty primaries, and despite scandal in his personal life, was reelected 57%-38% in 2010. Republican Bobby Jindal, defeated for governor 52%-48% by Democrat Blanco in 2003, came back in 2007 and won the multiparty primary with 54% of the vote. The congressional delegation now has five Republicans and one Democrat; the legislature, Democratic since Reconstruction, changed hands as party switchers brought about Republican majorities in the state House in 2010 and the state Senate in 2011. Overall, Louisiana is now, for the first time since blacks briefly voted during Reconstruction, a Republican state.

In recent years, Louisiana has seen the seniority of its Washington representatives fall precipitously, after decades in which long-tenured members were able to cobble together federal funds to aid constituents. In the process, Louisiana politics has also, perhaps, become less distinctive and more nationalized. "The greatest expressions of Louisiana's particularity have been its politics: populist, locally attuned, based on personality rather than party, fond of deal-cutting, often ethically dubious, but, above all, interesting. Or, at least, that used to be the case," the *New York Times* wrote in 2014. "Over the past decade, the bungled government responses to a series of hurricanes, including Katrina, and to the BP oil spill have drained the appeal of entertaining politicians; an aversion to taxes has rendered the old populism model unsustainable; and, perhaps most of all, the effects of 24-hour news channels, national political debates on television, and the Internet have left hyperlocal politicking a mostly fading memory."

Jindal, a political wunderkind, came into the governorship as a policy wonk, but he has governed more as ideologue than pragmatist—beneficial, perhaps, for his presidential aspirations but a drag on his approval ratings back home, which fell to the low 30s and even to the high 20s, which was worse than Obama in the state. In 2012, Jindal called for phasing out the state income tax as a way of attracting business investment, but he scrapped the plan in early 2013 in the face of widespread opposition. In 2013, he signed a law that, he acknowledged, allows teachers to "teach our kids about creationism." His administration stiffened Louisiana's regulations on abortion clinics, and he has clashed with his own state schools superintendent, John White, over the fate of the Common Core school standards. Louisiana, with Jindal's support, had adopted

Voter Turnout	
2013 Total Citizen 18+	3,415,068
2014 Highest Statewide Turnout	1,472,039
2014 Turnout as % CVAP	43.1%
2012 Turnout as % CVAP	58.8%

Legislature			
Senate:	26R	13D	
House:	58R	44D	2I

Common Core in 2010, but amid rising national Republican opposition, Jindal became one of the program's most outspoken opponents in the nation. Most urgently, Louisiana on his watch was hammered by lower oil prices, leading to a projected budget shortfall of $1.6 billion, including the potential for big cuts at LSU.

Meanwhile, on climate change, Jindal has acknowledged that humans are having some impact, but "the real question is how much." He has also called climate change "a Trojan horse" for more government regulation. That makes sense for the governor of an oil-dependent state, but low-lying Louisiana is also uniquely at risk from rising sea levels. Brett Anderson of the New Orleans *Times-Picayune* has written that if maps of the state rendered wetlands as water and counted only solid "walkable" ground as land, then the very shape of Louisiana—its iconic "boot"—would appear "as if it came out on the wrong side of a battle with a lawnmower's blades." Now, as ever, Louisiana's fate is intricately linked with water, from the meandering Mississippi River to the Gulf of Mexico.

Presidential Politics   Democrat Bill Clinton carried Louisiana twice in the 1990s, and Republican George W. Bush won here by only 53%-45% in 2000. But no general election presidential campaign ads are going to be taped in Cajun any time soon. Louisiana voted for Republican nominees by 57%, 59%, and 58% in the last three presidential races. Democrat Barack Obama swept Orleans Parish by a margin of roughly 4-1 in both 2008 and 2012, and he ran even with Mitt Romney in 2012 in the Baton Rouge area and lost it narrowly to John McCain in 2008. But those two parts of the state account for only about a quarter of the statewide vote. The rest of the state, which casts about three-fourths of the vote, is routinely carried by Republicans with little difficulty.

2012 Presidential Vote		
Mitt Romney (R)	1,152,262	(58%)
Barack Obama (D)	809,141	(41%)

2012 Presidential Primary		
Barack Obama (D)	115,150	(76%)
John Wolfe (D)	17,804	(12%)
Bob Ely (D)	9,897	(7%)
Darcy Richardson (D)	7,750	(5%)

2012 Presidential Primary		
Rick Santorum (R)	91,321	(49%)
Mitt Romney (R)	49,758	(27%)
Newt Gingrich (R)	29,656	(16%)
Ron Paul (R)	11,467	(6%)

2008 Presidential Vote		
John McCain (R)	1,148,275	(59%)
Barack Obama (D)	782,989	(40%)

Louisiana has seldom played a significant role in presidential primaries and caucuses, with one odd exception. That was 1996, when GOP allies of candidate Phil Gramm of Texas set up a pre-Iowa caucus in Louisiana on Feb. 6. The aim was to jump-start Gramm's campaign. Instead, the caucuses killed it. Only 65,000 Republicans showed up at 42 voting sites (compared with almost 100,000 at 2,000 sites later in Iowa), and conservative commentator Pat Buchanan won more votes than Gramm and took 13 of the 21 delegates. Gramm's candidacy never recovered and he left the race after a dismal fifth-place showing in the Iowa caucuses. The 2000 and 2004 primaries were held in March, after both parties' nominees had effectively been chosen.

As recently as 2000, the body of registered Democrats in Louisiana was 58% white and 40% African-American, but in 2008, after a big rush in registration, blacks made up nearly half of the state's registered Democrats. Democratic turnout in the Feb. 9 primary—scheduled to avoid a conflict with Mardi Gras—was 384,000, roughly double what it had been in 2004 and 2000. Obama won 57% of the vote (and about four out of five black votes), and Hillary Clinton got 36%. There was less enthusiasm on the Republican side in 2008 because it was pretty clear after Super Tuesday that McCain would be nominated. Nonetheless, evangelical Christians and others set up telephone networks for Mike Huckabee. With a turnout of 161,000 voters, half the Democratic level but the highest Republican turnout ever in Louisiana, Huckabee won 43% of the vote to 42% for McCain. But it didn't matter. Candidates were required to win at least 50% of the vote in Louisiana's Republican primary to win any delegates. A few days later, party insiders awarded 44 of the 47 delegates to McCain. In the March 2012 Republican primary, Romney spent precious little time campaigning and Rick Santorum beat him 49%-27%, with186,000 votes cast. Romney carried New Orleans, while Santorum carried every other parish.

Congressional Districts During the 2002 redistricting in Louisiana, six of the seven House incumbents (one was running for the Senate) submitted a plan to the legislature. The legislators made minor tweaks in the incumbents' plan. It was opposed by the Black Legislative Caucus, which drew up a plan

114th Congress Lineup	
5 R	1 D
113th Congress Lineup	
5 R	1 D

with a second black-majority district stretching from Lafayette and Baton Rouge along the Mississippi River to the Arkansas border. The legislature rejected it. Instead, the new map favored Republicans. But five of the seven districts elected members of both parties in the elections from 2002 to 2010.

Those politics have changed. The exodus from Louisiana after Hurricane Katrina led to the drop to six House seats after the 2010 census. As recently as 1980, the state had eight seats. Demographically, the 2nd District, centered in New Orleans, suffered the greatest population loss by far. Its black-majority district now extends to parts of Baton Rouge. The latest round of redistricting eliminated a district in Cajun country. With Republican population centers in the New Orleans suburbs, Baton Rouge, the Bayous, Shreveport and the northeast corner, creating a second black-majority district would require creative gerrymandering. The adjacent 4th and 5th Districts in northern Louisiana have 34% and 36% black population, respectively.

Governor

Bobby Jindal (R)

Elected 2007, term expires Jan. 2016, 2nd term; b. June 10, 1971, Baton Rouge; Brown U., B.A. 1991, Oxford U., M.Lit. 1994; Catholic; married (Supriya); 3 children.

Elected Office: U.S. House, 2004-07.

Professional Career: Consultant, McKinsey & Co., 1994-95; Secy., LA Dept. of Health & Hospitals, 1996-98; Exec. dir., Natl. Bipartisan Comm. on the Future of Medicare, 1998-99; Pres., U. of LA System, 1999-2001; Asst. secy., U.S. Dept. of HHS, 2001-03.

Office: Office of the Governor, P.O. Box 94004, Baton Rouge, 70804-9004, 225-342-7015; Fax: 225-342-7099; Website: gov.state.la.us.

Election Results

2011 general	Bobby Jindal (R)	673,239	(66%)
	Tara Hollis (D)	182,925	(18%)

Prior winning percentages: 2007 (54%); House: 2006 (88%), 2004 (78%)

Republican Bobby Jindal, first elected in October 2007, grew up in Baton Rouge, the son of immigrants from India who came to the United States so his mother could do graduate work at Louisiana State University. His given name is Piyush, but as a boy he insisted on being called Bobby, after his favorite character in the television series *The Brady Bunch*. As a teenager, he converted from Hinduism to Catholicism. He was an honors student at Baton Rouge High School, went on to graduate from Brown University with degrees in biology and public policy, then studied at Oxford as a Rhodes Scholar.

After college, Jindal worked briefly for McKinsey & Co. in Washington, D.C., and then landed his first job in politics as an intern for Rep. Jim McCrery, a Louisiana Republican. He quickly built an impressive resume. When McCrery assigned him to work on health policy, Jindal holed himself up in the Library of Congress for two weeks to master the complexities of the Medicare program. He eventually plopped on McCrery's desk a thick report spelling out possible solutions to the financial problems confounding the gigantic government-run medical program for the elderly.

A few years later, Jindal, at age 24, set his sights on becoming the new head of Louisiana's Department of Health and Hospitals and asked McCrery to introduce him to the governor, Republican Mike Foster. "Bobby knocked their socks off," McCrery told the Baton Rouge *Advocate*. Foster gave Jindal the job of running a 13,000-employee agency that accounted for about 40 percent of the state budget. Jindal managed to erase a $400 million deficit within two years. He returned to Washington and, at age 27, became executive director of the National Bipartisan Commission on the Future of Medicare. In 2001, he became assistant secretary for planning and evaluation at the Health and Human Services Department.

In 2003, Jindal ran for governor, his first race for elective office. He campaigned as a policy expert with ideas for restructuring government. He attracted national attention, and his candidacy was front-page news in India. In the October 2003 primary, he came in first, with 33 percent of the vote, ahead of three Democrats: Lt. Gov. Kathleen Blanco, with 18 percent; Attorney General Richard Ieyoub, with 16 percent; and former Rep. Buddy Leach, with 14 percent. Between the primary and the runoff, Blanco ran ads raising doubts about Jindal's success running the state health department, to which Jindal failed to respond forcefully. In the November runoff, he lost to Blanco 52%-48%, but he carried the New Orleans, Baton Rouge, Shreveport and Monroe metro areas. Blanco carried her home area, the Cajun country, by a wide margin. Jindal carried only three of the northern parishes that most Republicans have won in other statewide races.

When Rep. David Vitter decided in 2004 to run for the Senate seat of retiring Democrat John Breaux, Jindal ran for Vitter's House seat, ideally situated in a congressional district where Jindal's wife's family lived and where he had won 68 percent of the vote in his campaign for governor. Republican state Rep. Steve Scalise (a decade before he became the House Majority Whip in Congress) abandoned his campaign in August after trailing badly in fundraising and the polls, and Jindal was endorsed by state GOP leaders. He won 78 percent of the vote in November and was elected without a runoff. He was the first Indian-American elected to Congress since Democrat Dalip Saund won in the 29th District of California in 1956. Jindal was elected president of the Republican freshman class and spoke out early for the GOP proposal to create private retirement accounts in the Social Security program. He helped enact a bill that opened more than 8 million acres in the Gulf of Mexico to offshore drilling and mandated that a substantial portion of the revenues go to Louisiana and other Gulf states with Hurricane Katrina damage.

Jindal never stopped thinking about running again for governor. He kept a campaign-style schedule during congressional recesses, traveling around the state to give speeches and hold fundraisers. Blanco had been widely criticized for her response to Katrina, and in March 2007, when she announced she would not seek another term, Jindal was ready. He had three serious opponents. Democratic state Sen. Walter Boasso spent personal money liberally and argued that he had worked to reduce patronage politics at levee boards. Businessman John Georges also spent millions and ran as a nonpartisan political unifier. Public Service Commissioner Foster Campbell, a Democrat, ran on a proposal to replace the state income tax with a levy on oil and gas producers. Jindal stressed his work in Congress on post-Katrina aid and promised to clean up the state's famously corrupt politics and rejuvenate Louisiana's economy; he won 54 percent, enough to avoid a runoff.

Taking office, Jindal called a special session of the legislature in February 2008 and won passage, with only minor changes, of ethics bills requiring elected and appointed officials to disclose their personal finances and banning them from doing business with the state. He called a second special session in March to "eliminate unorthodox business taxes that are holding Louisiana's economy back." The legislature voted to accelerate $367 million in tax phase-outs on utilities, machinery purchases, and corporate debt and to pass $20 million in tuition and home schooling tax credits. In addition, he persuaded the legislature to spend much of the $1.1 billion budget surplus on repairs to public university buildings and on infrastructure—roads, bridges, ports and hurricane protection.

In the regular session that followed, the legislature did not always ratify Jindal's initiatives. The state House cut health and education funds in his budget and declined to pass his proposal for merit pay for teachers. He was dogged as well by his campaign's failure to report $100,000 in financial help from the state Republican Party. But his biggest misstep involved a raise in legislators' pay, which had not gone up in years. During his campaign, he had pledged to oppose a pay increase. In June 2008, after the legislature passed a pay raise, he said he would allow it to become law without his signature. There was widespread protest, and on June 27, papers were filed for a recall petition. Jindal responded by vetoing the pay raise.

When Hurricane Gustav bore down on New Orleans in September, he was determined to do a better job than Blanco had during Katrina. He canceled a speaking date at the Republican National Convention and ordered the evacuation of 1.9 million people from coastal parishes. Jindal gave frequent press conferences, seemingly in total command. He began to get national attention. GOP leaders in Washington chose him to deliver the rebuttal to President Barack Obama's address to Congress in February 2009. In a speech he wrote himself, he talked about his immigrant heritage and attacked high government spending. But his delivery was uninspiring, and the critical postgame analysis was almost entirely negative.

In 2010, the devastating BP oil spill in the Gulf further elevated Jindal's national profile. Unlike most governors in the region, he was fiercely and openly critical of the Obama administration's handling of the issue. He made repeated visits to afflicted areas and proposed building a protective line of sand booms, or islands, using mud dredged from the Gulf. In the months after the oil company capped the damaged well, he proceeded with plans to build the sand barriers, aided by the Obama administration agreements that BP should foot the $260 million cost. The National Oil Spill Commission later said the barriers captured only a small fraction of the escaped oil.

In the 2010 legislative session, Jindal got much of his education plan into law, including a controversial change to let local schools seek waivers from a variety of state rules and regulations. Another controversial bill he signed into law, allowing guns to be carried into churches, drew nationwide criticism from gun control advocates. In 2011, he signed 420 bills and used his veto pen on 18 occasions. He signed bills increasing penalties for human trafficking and sex crimes, barring contractors from public projects for three years if they fail to verify the legal status of their workers, making death and disability benefits available retroactively for National Guard troops who fought in Afghanistan and Iraq, and allowing a deceased Guard member's surviving child or spouse to attend state college for free. Facing nine challengers in his October 2011 reelection bid, he won 66 percent of the vote.

In 2012, Jindal, despite some chatter, was passed over as a vice presidential candidate. He used Mitt Romney's loss and the GOP's failure to regain control of the Senate as a platform to unleash scathing criticism on his party. He said Republicans should "stop being the stupid party," citing the explosive statements on rape made by failed Senate candidates Richard Mourdock of Indiana and Todd Akin in Missouri. Jindal attacked "dumbed-down conservatism" and said, "We need to stop being simplistic, we need to trust the intelligence of the American people, and we need to stop insulting the intelligence of the voters."

As the 2016 presidential season kicked into gear, though, Jindal turned to the right. He declared that he would opt out of two main components of President Obama's health care law: setting up a health insurance exchange and expanding Medicaid to cover greater numbers of low-income residents. Heading into the 2013 legislative session, Jindal set his sights on replacing the state's personal income and corporate taxes with sales taxes, though this initiative didn't fare as well: He scrapped the plan in April after it encountered considerable opposition from politicians and the public. His approval rating, already dropping, plummeted down to the 30s.

Jindal was once a proponent of Common Core, which seeks to establish consistent benchmarks for elementary-school students. But as national conservative opposition mounted against the initiative in 2014, he joined the fray. He sought to end the standards in his state, contending that Common Core "involves the federal government in local decisions where the federal government has no business being." He filed suit against the Obama administration, arguing that it violated the Constitution in forcing the standards on the states in return for education funding.

And he tossed rhetorical red meat to the conservative base. During a January 2015 visit to London, Jindal warned of Muslim "no-go zones" in the West in which "non-assimilationist Muslims establish enclaves and carry out as much of Sharia law as they can." Though numerous media outlets disputed the assertion, Jindal continued to express it. He also said on a U.S. radio appearance that if Muslims "want to come here and they want to set up their own culture and values, that's not immigration. That's really invasion, if you're honest about it." He called Obama "unfit to be commander-in-chief" and he energetically supported a letter signed by 47 Senate Republicans to the government of Iran that sought to prevent a nuclear deal.

As Jindal was focusing his attentions nationally—he spent 165 days outside Louisiana in 2014, including four trips to New Hampshire and five to Iowa, according to the *Advocate* newspaper—his state was facing increasing strain. Louisiana faced a projected $1.6 billion deficit, a far cry from the roughly $1 billion surplus Jindal inherited in 2008. He proposed eliminating $526 million in tax rebates for businesses and cutting higher education, which had already suffered significantly reduced budgets. But the wunderkind was finding his approval at home dropping, to as low as 27 percent—even as other Republicans in the presidential field made a bigger impact.

Senior Senator

David Vitter (R)

Elected 2004, term expires Jan. 2017, 2nd term; b. May 3, 1961, New Orleans; Harvard U., B.A. 1983, Rhodes Scholar, Oxford U., B.A. 1985, Tulane Law Schl., J.D. 1988; Catholic; married (Wendy); 4 children.

Elected Office: LA House, 1992-99; U.S. House, 1999-2005.

Professional Career: Practicing atty., 1988-99; Adjunct law prof., Tulane U. & Loyola U., 1995-98.

DC Office: 516 HSOB, 20510, 202-224-4623; Fax: 202-228-5061; Website: vitter.senate.gov.

State Offices: Alexandria, 318-448-0169; Baton Rouge, 225-383-0331; Lafayette, 337-993-9502; Lake Charles, 337-436-0453; Metairie, 504-589-2753; Monroe, 318-325-8120; Shreveport, 318-861-0437.

Committees: *Banking, Housing & Urban Affairs:* Financial Institutions & Consumer Protection; Housing, Transportation, & Community Development; Securities, Insurance & Investment. *Environment & Public Works:* Clean Air & Nuclear Safety; Superfund, Waste Mgmt., & Regulatory Oversight; Transportation & Infrastructure (Chmn). *Judiciary:* Crime & Terrorism; Immigration & the Nat'l Interest; Oversight, Agency Action, Federal Rights & Federal Courts; the Constitution. *Small Business & Entrepreneurship* (Chmn).

Group Ratings

	ADA	ACLU	AFL-CIO	LCV	ITI	COC	HAFA	ACU	CFG	FRC
2014	5%	6%	–	0%	33%	88%	70%	86%	60%	93%
2013	5%	C	18%	15%	C	50%	C	79%	78%	C

National Journal Ratings

	2013 LIB	—	2013 CONS
Economic	15%	—	80%
Social	13%	—	86%
Foreign	11%	—	88%
Composite	14%	—	86%

Key Votes of the 113th Congress

1. Sandy storm spending	Y	5. Student Loan Rates	Y
2. Chuck Hagel Confirmation	N	6. Employee Non-Discrim'n Act	N
3. Gun Background Checks	N	7. Senate Vote on Judgeships	Y
4. Immigration Reform	N	8. Defense Dept. Spending	N

9. Bipartisan Budget Deal	N
10. Farm Bill Conference Rept.	Y
11. Unempl. Comp. Extension	N
12. Keystone Pipeline	Y

Election Results

2010 general	David Vitter (R)	715,415	(57%)	$12,787,261	$587,527	$15,302
	Charlie Melancon (D)	476,572	(38%)	$4,718,938	$588,104	
2010 primary	David Vitter (R)	85,225	(88%)			
	Chet Traylor (R)	6,841	(7%)			
	Nick Accardo (R)	5,232	(5%)			

Prior winning percentages: 2004 (51%); House: 2002 (81%), 2000 (80%), 1999 special (51%)

Republican David Vitter, elected in 2004 and now Louisiana's senior senator, is a confrontational conservative with an appetite for hardball tactics, such as holding up presidential appointments and forcing floor votes on bills. His disdain for President Barack Obama has made him popular among Louisiana voters, who have forgiven him for a 2007 prostitution scandal. In June 2014, he announced that he would run for governor in 2015.

Vitter grew up in the New Orleans area, the son of a Chevron petroleum engineer. He graduated from Harvard University and Tulane University's law school and was a Rhodes Scholar. He was a business attorney and taught law at Tulane and Loyola. In 1991, Vitter was elected to the state House from the district that had been represented by former Ku Klux Klansman David Duke. There he passed a term-limits bill through a reluctant state legislature and was noted for his ability to irritate other politicians. Many of them held grudges because of his crusade for term limits; others were put off by his crusades for ethics in government. Vitter led the effort to recall Democratic Gov. Edwin Edwards, who ultimately went to prison for racketeering. A popular sheriff sued Vitter three times after Vitter criticized his ethics.

Vitter ran for Congress and won in a May 1999 special election to replace Republican Rep. Bob Livingston, the speaker-designate who announced in late 1998 that he would resign after confessing that he had had extramarital affairs. Several Republicans jumped into the race, including Duke. The establishment choice was David Treen, 70, who had served four terms in the House starting in 1972 and had been elected governor in 1979. Vitter argued, in effect, that Treen was too old, saying, "We need a younger congressman like me, so we can start building up the seniority we lost when Bob Livingston resigned." The top two vote-getters in the initial balloting were Treen, with 25 percent, and Vitter, with 22 percent. The two advanced to the runoff under the system then in use. Duke, unnervingly close to making the runoff, finished third with 19 percent. Vitter went on to win the runoff, 51%-49%.

Vitter had one of the most conservative voting records in the House and the most conservative in the Louisiana delegation. He twice won reelection in his heavily Republican, suburban New Orleans district with at least 80 percent of the vote.

In December 2003, Democratic Sen. John Breaux announced that he would not seek a fourth term, and two days later, Vitter jumped into the contest. Wooden in manner, a self-described loner, and highly conservative, Vitter was the stylistic opposite of Breaux, a gregarious dealmaker and respected centrist from Cajun country who had been a major force for reform of federal entitlements and health care. But the state party and national Republicans worked hard to clear the field for Vitter, viewing him as the strongest candidate, thanks to his suburban political base and his habit of traveling the state to announce projects secured from his perch on the House Appropriations Committee. He was also familiar in Cajun country after his well-publicized opposition to an Indian casino in southwestern Louisiana.

On the Democratic side, three serious candidates joined the race: Rep. Chris John; two-term state Treasurer John Kennedy; and state Rep. Arthur Morrell, an African-American from New Orleans. There was little doubt that Vitter would win the state's unique Election Day primary against a divided Democratic field; the real issue for Democrats was holding him below the 50 percent-plus-one threshold necessary to avoid a December runoff. Vitter ran as a strong supporter of President George W. Bush and called for making Bush's tax cuts permanent; he opposed abortion rights, same-sex marriage, and gun-ownership restrictions. He said he best represented "mainstream Louisiana values" and painted John as an out-of-touch Washington liberal who was close to John Kerry, the 2004 Democratic presidential nominee.

Sugar was an important issue. Louisiana is the prime cane sugar-producing state, and producers worry about being undercut by cheap imports. Vitter broke with the Bush administration over the Central American Free Trade Agreement, opposing it because it did not exempt sugar imports from the deal. Vitter ran some of the most creative television ads of the election cycle, making light of his image as a stiff politician with humorous commercials featuring his daughter's home movies. Meanwhile, John failed to gain momentum and was caught in the crossfire between Vitter on the right and Kennedy and Morrell on the left.

Vitter led going into November and won the race outright with 51 percent, becoming the first Republican in 121 years to represent Louisiana in the Senate. John got 29 percent, Kennedy 15 percent and Morrell 3 percent. Vitter won Mississippi River parishes that Bush lost, carried nearly all of Louisiana north of Baton Rouge, and posted large margins in the New Orleans suburbs. His 60,000-vote margin in populous St. Tammany Parish, which he had represented in Congress, was more than enough to erase John's 25,000-vote advantage in New Orleans.

In the Senate, Vitter has been one of the chamber's most conservative members, and he's been prickly. He called Senate Majority Leader Harry Reid "an idiot" in January 2013 for saying that Hurricane Sandy, which hit the East Coast, was worse than Hurricane Katrina, which hit the Gulf Coast. Vitter cast one of the two votes against confirming Hillary Clinton as Secretary of State. Before his Democratic Louisiana colleague Mary Landrieu lost her re-election bid in 2014, she and Vitter made little secret of their contempt for each other, although they grudgingly worked together on state-specific matters. Vitter's enmity hasn't been confined to Democrats. He has been at odds with Louisiana GOP Gov. Bobby Jindal on state budget issues and other matters, a feud that was punctuated by Jindal's lack of interest in defending Vitter during his prostitution scandal and his decision not to endorse Vitter during his 2010 reelection bid.

But at times Vitter has worked effectively with Democrats. As the ranking Republican on the Environment and Public Works Committee, he worked with Democratic Chairman Barbara Boxer of California—who is as liberal as he is conservative—to pass the first reauthorization of the Water Resources Development Act since 2007. It took the pair more than a year, but in June 2014, Obama signed the $12.3 billion measure into law. It authorized seven coastal restoration projects in Louisiana while streamlining the review process for some Army Corps of Engineers projects. Vitter also worked with the late Sen. Frank Lautenberg of New Jersey to overhaul the 1976 Toxic Substances Control Act so the chemical industry had greater assurance that new regulations wouldn't pose a threat to its bottom line. Their bill picked up support from more than 20 other lawmakers in both parties, but it did not move. Vitter continued working on a similar measure with Democratic Sen. Tom Udall of New Mexico. In another odd-couple pairing, he and liberal Democrat Sherrod Brown of Ohio worked on a measure to make banks considered "too big to fail" set aside more capital reserves.

At least as common, though, was partisan combat, particularly when Vitter targeted Obama's nominees. He attached an amendment to a September 2009 Interior appropriations bill that would have blocked funds for any policy initiated by Carol Browner, the White House climate change and energy adviser; his amendment was defeated. On the Banking, Housing, and Urban Affairs Committee, Vitter opposed Ben Bernanke's second term as Federal Reserve chairman in early 2010, complaining that the Fed had doled out trillions of dollars and "worsened our economic crisis by making 'too big to fail' a permanent government policy." He formed an unlikely alliance with socialist Sen. Bernie Sanders of Vermont, who is an independent but caucuses with Democrats., in placing a hold on Bernanke's nomination, and Vitter ultimately voted against confirmation. In 2012, seeking a vote on an extension of the National Flood Insurance Program, Vitter blocked two nominees to the Federal Reserve Board; he later reached an agreement with then-Senate Majority Leader Harry Reid of Nevada.

Then, when the Affordable Care Act was being implemented in September 2013, Vitter demanded a vote for his proposal to repeal federal dollars that could pay coverage for lawmakers and their aides under the law. Angry Democrats reportedly fired back by floating a plan to deny lawmakers those contributions if there was "probable cause" that they had solicited prostitutes—a direct slap at Vitter. The senator responded by filing ethics complaints against Boxer, Reid and others. Vitter also opposed Obama's pick for attorney general, Loretta Lynch.

Some of his legislative guerrilla tactics have enjoyed success. When Obama sought to raise Interior Secretary Ken Salazar's pay to the same level as other Cabinet secretaries in 2011, Vitter vowed in a news release to keep his "boot on the neck" of the Interior Department until it approved more drilling permits. Salazar eventually asked that the legislation be withdrawn. The Senate Ethics Committee, chaired by Boxer, looked into the matter but took no action because no existing rule dealt with the issue. But the committee said in a 2012 letter, "It is inappropriate to condition support for a secretary's personal salary increase directly on his or her performance of a specific official act."

Vitter's political career was dealt a major blow in July 2007, when it was revealed that between 1999 and 2001 his phone number appeared on the call list of "D.C. Madam" Deborah Jeane Palfrey. A week later, he appeared with his wife, Wendy, at his side and issued a public apology, saying he had committed "a very serious sin." The same year, the Senate Ethics Committee debated whether to punish Vitter but ruled that the conduct in question had occurred before he got to the Senate. Vitter tried to use his campaign funds to pay $160,000 in legal fees in the case, but the Federal Election Commission would not permit it. In another round of negative publicity, in March 2009, the Transportation Security Administration looked into an incident in which Vitter allegedly opened a security gate to try to board a flight at Dulles Airport after the flight had been boarded and the doors locked. The attempt set off alarms. Vitter later claimed he had mistakenly gone through the wrong door at the gate, and the TSA ruled that he had not posed a security threat.

Trouble for Vitter continued with an ABC News report in 2010 that a longtime Vitter aide had had repeated brushes with the law, including a knife-wielding incident with an ex-girlfriend. The staff member was kept on board two years after the episode, during which he worked on women's issues for the senator. The aide resigned in late June. Then, the Federal Election Commission fined a Louisiana businessman $170,000 in 2012 for using corporate funds to funnel illegal contributions to the campaigns of both Vitter and Landrieu. A year earlier, the FEC deadlocked 3-3 along partisan lines over whether a California dry cleaning corporation made illegal campaign contributions to Vitter's 2010 reelection campaign. Still, the prostitution issue remained the most explosive, leading "to several years of what other senators and top aides described as a sort of ostracism," wrote the *Washington Post*'s Paul Kane. "Senators didn't necessarily avoid Vitter, but they didn't seek him out."

Vitter has taken an interest in law-and-order issues. In February 2010, he cosponsored with Democratic Sen. Amy Klobuchar of MInnesota a bill giving administrative subpoena authority to the Marshals Service, the Bureau of Immigration and Customs Enforcement, and the Postal Inspection Service in cases of child exploitation. He also sponsored a bill to require the states to collect DNA samples from convicted felons. In 2015, he introduced bills to repeal birthright citizenship; to require the Census Bureau to ask respondents about their immigration status, something not allowed today; and to block undocumented immigrants from getting federal student aid or credit cards.

The deadly April 2010 explosion of the BP-operated Deepwater Horizon oilrig off the coast of Louisiana sparked outrage from fisherman and residents throughout the Bayou State. BP became the focus of considerable public criticism. Vitter's campaigns had received more than $450,000 from the oil and gas industry in the preceding five years, putting him in tough political terrain. After the administration announced a six-month moratorium on deep-water drilling in the Gulf of Mexico, Vitter wrote to Obama warning that the moratorium would result in the loss of 20,000 jobs in the state. He advocated that drilling operations be shut down only if specific safety problems were identified during rig inspections, and he opposed Democratic efforts to eliminate the cap on liability for oil companies after a spill.

Considering his run of well-publicized scandals, Vitter did remarkably well in his bid for a second term in 2010 over Democratic Rep. Charlie Melancon. In anticipation of a tough contest and a rehash of the prostitution story, Vitter raised $12.6 million to Melancon's $4 million. Indeed, Melancon made an issue of Vitter's "sin," but in running a predominately anti-Vitter campaign, he failed to define himself. Vitter did that for him by portraying Melancon as an Obama administration yes-man, slamming him for his vote for the president's $787 billion economic stimulus bill. To counter the attacks about his use of prostitutes, Vitter ran a negative ad critical of overseas trips Melancon took at taxpayers' expense, including one to Paris with his wife, which Melancon called a fact-finding mission to learn about the energy policies of U.S. NATO allies. But Vitter also came under fire for an ad that depicted illegal Mexican immigrants sneaking through a fence. The Hispanic Chamber of Commerce denounced the ad as racist. Vitter accused his critics of "ridiculous political correctness," saying the ad revealed "a fact and not a stereotype." Making the most of his three and a half years to repair his image, Vitter won another term, 57%-38%.

In 2015, Vitter became chairman of the Small Business & Entrepreneurship Committee, and he proposed a flurry of legislation on a variety of topics favored by conservatives. But as the end of Jindal's second term approached, Vitter shifted his focus to the governorship, a powerful post in Louisiana. In January 2014, Vitter confirmed that he would run in the state's off-year 2015 gubernatorial election. By the summer of 2015, the crowded field included Republican Public Service Commissioner Scott Angelle, Republican Lt. Gov. Jay Dardenne and Democratic state Rep. John Bel Edwards, but Vitter enjoyed strong fundraising and was generally considered the frontrunner. He spent time creating space between himself and Jindal, who had become unpopular back home. Vitter's message did hit something of a bump in December 2014 when he came out against the Common Core education standards that conservatives have vilified, four months after he had publicly backed them; he even introduced a bill in 2015 to prevent the Education Department from encouraging states to adopt the standards. Nevertheless, a poll that month showed him with 36 percent support, 10 percentage points ahead of his closest rival.

Junior Senator

Bill Cassidy (R)

Elected 2014, term expires Jan. 2021, 1st term; b. Sept. 28, 1957, Highland Park, IL; LA St. U., B.S. 1979, MD. 1983; Protestant; married (Laura); 3 children.

Elected Office: LA Senate, 2006-08; U.S. House, 2009-2015.

Professional Career: Physician; Co-founder, Greater Baton Rouge Community Clinic; Assoc. prof., LSU Medical Schl., 1990-present.

DC Office: 703 HSOB, 20510, 202-224-5824; Fax: 202-224-9735; Website: cassidy.senate.gov.

State Offices: Baton Rouge, 225-929-7711; Lafayette, 337-261-1400; Metairie, 504-838-0130.

Committees: *Appropriations:* Homeland Security; Interior, Environment, & Related Agencies; Dept. of Labor, HHS, & Education, & Related Agencies; Military Construction & Veterans Affairs, & Related Agencies; State, Foreign Operations, & Related Programs; Transportation, HUD, & Related Agencies. *Energy & Natural Resources:* Energy; Nat'l Parks (Chmn); Public Lands, Forests, & Mining. *Health, Education, Labor, & Pensions:* Children & Families; Employment & Workplace Safety; Primary Health & Retirement Security. *Veterans' Affairs. Joint Economic Committee.*

Group Ratings (House)

	ADA	ACLU	AFL-CIO	LCV	ITI	COC	HAFA	ACU	CFG	FRC
2014	5%	0%	–	0%	80%	92%	58%	75%	54%	100%
2013	5%	C	10%	0%	C	77%	C	80%	64%	C

National Journal Ratings (House)

	2013 LIB	—	2013 CONS
Economic	21%	—	77%
Social	0%	—	87%
Foreign	15%	—	77%
Composite	16%	—	84%

Key Votes of the 113th Congress (House)

1. Sandy storm spending	N	5. Medical Marijuana	N
2. Violence Against Women Act	N	6. Farm Bill	Y
3. Guantanamo Bay Detainees	N	7. Afghanistan Combat	N
4. Abortion 20-week ban	Y	8. NSA Phone Data Collection	Y

9. Syrian Rebels Training	Y
10. Keystone pipeline	Y
11. Immigration Exec. Action	Y
12. Bipartisan budget deal	Y

Election Results

2014 general	Bill Cassidy (R)	712,379	(56%)	$14,655,887	$2,345,107	$11,190,682
	Mary Landrieu (D)	561,210	(44%)	$19,969,352	$824,174	$12,479,854
2014 primary	Mary Landrieu (D)	619,402	(42%)			
	Bill Cassidy (R)	603,084	(41%)			
	Rob Maness (R)	202,556	(14%)			

Prior winning percentages: House: 2012 (79%), 2010 (66%), 2008 (48%)

Smart and telegenic, if low-key by Louisiana standards, three-term Republican Rep. Bill Cassidy easily defeated Democratic Sen. Mary Landrieu in a December 2014 runoff election. Cassidy, who had been one of only five Republicans to defeat a House Democratic incumbent in 2008, managed six years later to avoid the mistakes that had doomed Landrieu's previous opponents. He relentlessly tied her to President Obama, a widely disliked figure in Louisiana, as well as his health care law, which Landrieu had voted for.

The son of a life-insurance salesman, Cassidy grew up in Baton Rouge and went to college at Louisiana State University. He went on to graduate from LSU's medical school. Cassidy was an associate professor of medicine at LSU and taught at the same hospital. He went on to co-found the Greater Baton Rouge Community Clinic, which provides free dental and health care to the working uninsured. He developed a school-based hepatitis B vaccination program that has immunized more than 36,000 public and private schoolchildren at no cost to parents or schools. During his medical training, Cassidy met his wife, Laura, who also is a physician and was formerly the chief of surgery at Earl K. Long Hospital. The *Times-Picayune* has called Laura his "most trusted political adviser." She founded Louisiana Key

Academy, a public charter school specializing in children with dyslexic symptoms, after their daughter was diagnosed with dyslexia.

Cassidy had a defining moment when Hurricane Katrina hit in 2005. He created a make-shift field hospital with the help of several other physicians in an abandoned Kmart store. In a PBS documentary, he recalled entering the store after the storm to discover grease covering the floor, no electricity, and no working phone lines. In two days, he and the others transformed the space to be ready to receive patients. He won a December 2006 special election to the state Senate and was reelected in 2007. He sponsored several bills to improve health standards in Louisiana, including one to overhaul the children's mental health system and another to expand Medicaid coverage to patients at new organ-transplant centers.

When GOP Rep. Richard Baker resigned his seat to head a Washington trade group, Cassidy passed up the opportunity to compete in the May 2008 special election. But after state Rep. Don Cazayoux defeated social conservative Woody Jenkins 49 percent to 46 percent, with a big boost from the Democratic Congressional Campaign Committee, to win the seat in the special election, Cassidy vowed to take the district back for the Republicans in the regularly scheduled November congressional election.

In that campaign, Cassidy described himself as a "pro-life, pro-gun-rights" social conservative in favor of free enterprise, limited government, and lower taxes. He made the economy his focus, highlighting his record in the state Senate of voting against spending bills and cutting taxes for businesses and for parents with children in private schools. He also criticized Cazayoux for supporting Democratic presidential nominee Barack Obama's tax plan. Cazayoux ran an ad criticizing Cassidy for supporting the creation of private savings accounts in the Social Security program. State Rep. Michael Jackson, who is African-American, ran as an independent, due partly to his unhappiness over the national Democrats' early support for Cazayoux in the special election. Cassidy won comfortably, with 48 percent to 40 percent for Cazayoux and 12 percent for Jackson. He twice coasted to reelection.

In the House, Cassidy was a reliable conservative vote and was made a part of the GOP leadership's whip team. He was given a plum seat on the Energy and Commerce Committee and was called on to publicly criticize the Obama administration on health care. Cassidy said the government should step out of the way of patients, and he supports providing incentives for preventive care along with creating health savings accounts. He introduced a bill in November 2012 intended to increase access to life-saving prescription drugs by seeking to more accurately match Medicare reimbursement rates for those drugs in the hope of encouraging manufacturers to increase production.

Like the rest of his state's delegation, Cassidy has been an ardent advocate for the oil and gas industry. When the Natural Resources Committee approved a 2010 measure to overhaul federal management of energy as a response to the BP oil spill in the Gulf of Mexico, Cassidy unsuccessfully tried to amend the bill to push back the effective date of most of the legislation until the Interior secretary certified it would not result in higher energy costs or increased unemployment. He introduced a bill a year later aimed at encouraging independent natural-gas producers to create more filling stations and other infrastructure.

When Democrats controlled the House, Cassidy in 2010 was one of four Republicans on the Agriculture Committee to vote to end the ban on American travel to Cuba and ease regulations on sales of U.S. agricultural exports to the island nation. He backed Democratic bills to extend unemployment benefits and praised the Teach for America program that has established a post-Katrina presence in Louisiana.

Cassidy's impressive reelection margins and his legislative work led Louisiana Republicans and political pundits to deem him the most formidable potential challenger to Landrieu, the last remaining Senate Democrat from the Deep South. Landrieu had been elected with 50 percent of the vote in 1996 and beat two flawed challengers in 2002 and 2008 with 52 percent each time. But over the course of her career, Louisiana slipped politically and demographically away from the Democrats, accelerated by the departure of an estimated 125,000 Democratic voters after Katrina.

Cassidy began holding public events in cities outside his district in January 2013 and he formally jumped into the race a few months later. His candidacy initially aroused suspicions among conservative groups about whether he truly was one of them; the Senate Conservatives Fund endorsed tea-party-aligned Rob Maness, a retired Air Force colonel. Cassidy responded by making some moves to the right. He repudiated his earlier support of the Troubled Asset Relief Program created to assist Wall Street in 2008, and he accepted the backing of Americans for Prosperity, the conservative group affiliated with Kansas's Koch brothers, which spent more than $3 million on ads attacking Landrieu. By mid-2014, polls showed the race a dead heat. Cassidy had to deal with a distraction when he disclosed that his unmarried 17-year-old daughter was pregnant. Still, Landrieu drew just 42 percent of the vote in the eight-candidate election—eight points short of what she needed to avoid a runoff. Cassidy finished second with just under 41 percent.

With the GOP already having won enough seats to take over the Senate, much of the national import of the Landrieu-Cassidy race dissipated. But with the chance to expand the new GOP majority's edge by a seat, conservative groups poured an estimated $5.65 million in ads on his behalf during the runoff. National Democrats, by contrast, "just walked away from this race," as Landrieu put it. In a last-ditch attempt to keep her seat, Landrieu played up her status as the top Democrat on the Energy and Natural Resources Committee and worked to push through a vote on the controversial Keystone XL pipeline, which she ardently supported but which had been opposed by many in her party. The measure fell short in the Senate by one vote. With Obama's job-approval rating in the state just 39 percent in November, TV ads backing Cassidy "came down to four words: *Mary Landrieu, Barack Obama*," as Jason Berry, a New Orleans writer, put it. Cassidy rolled to an easy victory, 56%-44%, with exit polls showing that only 18 percent of whites backed Landrieu. His victory left Louisiana without a Democrat elected statewide for the first time since 1876.

As promised during the campaign, Cassidy was given a seat on Energy and Natural Resources, where Landrieu had been the chair before her loss, along with seats on Appropriations; Health, Education, Labor and Pensions; and Veterans Affairs. He urged Republicans to offer a viable alternative to the Affordable Care Act. "It's actually in our nation's interest for people to have insurance," he said, but the law should be voluntary, using tax credits and auto-enrollment with opt-outs. Cassidy also worked with Democratic Sen. Chris Murphy of Connecticut to produce a bill that would overhaul the country's mental-health system. Amid growing concern about parents opting not to vaccinate their children—an issue he had worked to reverse for years—Cassidy proposed heightened disclosure for parents about the vaccination status of their children's classmates. Cassidy joined Democratic Sens. Tammy Baldwin of Wisconsin and Al Franken of Minnesota to offer amendments related to testing on an education bill. And Cassidy introduced in the Senate—as he had in the House—legislation that would bar the use of taxpayer money on oil paintings of government leaders.

FIRST DISTRICT

Steve Scalise (R)

Elected May 2008, 4th full term; b. Oct. 6, 1965, New Orleans; LA St. U., B.S. 1989; Catholic; married (Jennifer); 2 children.

Elected Office: LA House, 1996-2007, LA Senate, 2008.

Professional Career: Systems engineer, Diamond Data Systems, eVenture Technologies.

DC Office: 2338 RHOB, 20515, 202-225-3015; Website: scalise.house .gov.

State Offices: Hammond, 985-340-2185; Houma, 985-879-2300; Mandeville, 985-893-9064; Metairie, 504-837-1259.

Committees: House Majority Whip. *Energy & Commerce:* Communications & Technology.

Group Ratings

	ADA	ACLU	AFL-CIO	LCV	ITI	COC	HAFA	ACU	CFG	FRC
2014	5%	0%	–	0%	100%	86%	76%	96%	82%	100%
2013	5%	C	14%	4%	C	77%	C	100%	84%	C

National Journal Ratings

	2013 LIB	—	2013 CONS
Economic	8%	—	91%
Social	0%	—	87%
Foreign	0%	—	95%
Composite	6%	—	94%

Key Votes of the 113th Congress

1. Sandy storm spending	N	5. Medical Marijuana	N	9. Syrian Rebels Training	Y
2. Violence Against Women Act	N	6. Farm Bill	N	10. Keystone pipeline	Y
3. Guantanamo Bay Detainees	N	7. Afghanistan Combat	N	11. Immigration Exec. Action	Y
4. Abortion 20-week ban	Y	8. NSA Phone Data Collection	Y	12. Bipartisan budget deal	N

Election Results

2014 general	Steve Scalise (R) 189,250	(78%)	$2,735,431	$1,425
	Vinny Mendoza (D)...................... 24,761	(10%)		
	Lee Dugas (D) 21,286	(9%)		
	Jeff Sanford (Lib)......................... 8,707	(4%)		

Prior winning percentages: 2012 (67%), 2010 (79%), 2008 (66%), 2008 special (75%)

Population		Race and Ethnicity		Income	
Total:	781,134	White	74.9%	Median income:	$54,521
Urban:	45.2%	Black	12.6%		(172 of 435)
Suburban:	46.4%	Latino	7.7%	Under $50,000	45.5%
Rural:	8.4%	Asian	1.9%	$50,000-$99,999:	30.9%
Land area:	2,225	Two races	1.5%	$100,000-$199,999:	17.5%
Pop/sq. mi.:	351.1	White Ethnic	47.1%	$200,000 or more:	6.2%
Born in state:	74.3%			Poverty Rate	13.5%
		Education			
Age Groups		H.S. grad or less:	44.4%	**Work**	
Under 18:	22.9%	Some college:	28.0%	White collar:	34.3%
18 to 34:	23.3%	College degree, 4 yr.:	17.4%	Blue collar:	42.3%
35 to 64:	39.3%	Post-grad study:	10.1%	Sales and service:	23.4%
Over 64:	14.5%				
		Military		Govt. workers:	12.2%
		Veterans/active duty:	7.5%		

New Orleans Suburbs, Southeast Louisiana

Founded in 1718 and the nation's sixth-largest city at the outbreak of the Civil War, New Orleans is ancient for an American metropolis. It is still closely girded by the peculiar wilderness of the mushy Delta lands of the sluggish Mississippi River. For decades, you could climb a levee overlooking the

Voter Turnout	
2013 Total Citizen 18+	578,704
2014 House Turnout	244,004
2014 Turnout as % CVAP	42.2%
2012 Turnout as % CVAP	58.7%

Mississippi and see an expanse of water with untidy clumps of trees and disorganized-looking, seemingly abandoned docks—what Mark Twain had in his mind's eye while writing *Life on the Mississippi* in the 1870s. For years, the river funneled the products of half a continent down to a single port with an international heritage and flair. The New Orleans metropolitan area has lived off that geography and history, with an inward-looking elite preoccupied with who is in which Mardi Gras krewe and interested more in the genealogy of old families than in the geography of the Oil Patch.

The old buildings of New Orleans are finely proportioned and its old neighborhoods charming, like those in France. Its early-20th century improvements, like City Park and Frederick Law Olmsted's Audubon Park, were grand. But its late-20th century streetscapes and subdivisions were without ornament or charm, utilitarian works that were part of an attempt to master the below-sea-level environment. After Hurricane Katrina struck with Category 3 force on August 29, 2005, many of those details changed dramatically. The city's population plummeted, housing stock was destroyed, some levees were breached, and others were no longer reliable. The last act of nature to have wreaked so much damage on an American city was the San Francisco earthquake of 1906. Plaquemines and St. Bernard parishes were ravaged by high winds and floodwaters, and many people fled and did not return. By 2013, St. Bernard's population of 43,000 was down about one-third from what it was in 2000. In Plaquemines, the restaurant business still had not recovered as of December 2014.

Louisiana's southern coast experienced yet more turmoil with the man-made disaster known as the BP Deepwater Horizon oil spill. The rig exploded on April 20, 2010, and spewed more than 200 million gallons of crude oil into the Gulf of Mexico over three months. Shrimp fishermen, whose profits were already under pressure from aquaculture-raised Asian and

Latin American shrimp, were idled as BP and the federal government struggled to seal off the underwater leak. Once the well was finally stemmed in July, the hardest part was yet to come: Cleaning up from the largest marine oil spill in U.S. history, one that caused extensive damage to wildlife and habitats, not to mention Louisiana's coastal economy. About 600 miles of shoreline were

2012 Presidential Vote		
Mitt Romney (R)	235,799	(71%)
Barack Obama (D)	89,430	(27%)
2008 Presidential Vote		
John McCain (R)	239,802	(73%)
Barack Obama (D)	82,965	(25%)
Cook Partisan Voting Index: R+26		

affected. Grand Isle, a large commercial fishing area, finally reopened in December 2014. Coastal erosion is another concern in these parts; every hour, an area of wetlands about the size of a football field is lost.

The 1st Congressional District of Louisiana stretches from suburban St. Tammany Parish north of New Orleans to Houma in Terrebonne Parish. The district takes in the vast suburb of Metairie in Jefferson Parish as well as part of western New Orleans. Metairie has remained an attractive place for new businesses, with growth in commercial real estate and a building occupancy rate of 94% in July 2014. The jobless rate in New Orleans-Metairie-Kenner, which was just 4.7% in late 2012, jumped back to 6.2% in early 2015. The uncertainties reflect the unique mix of the local recovery, with its new and younger citizenry, plus depopulation.

Most people in the 1st District live in Jefferson and St. Tammany parishes. Jefferson, which is split between the 1st and the 2nd districts, had almost 435,000 residents in 2013—down 20,000 from 2000—but it's still one of the state's most populous. In November 2013, the Federal Emergency Management Agency agreed to local requests that it forgive the final $54.8 million that Jefferson Parish still owed in loans. Nearly 75% of the homes in St. Tammany were damaged by Katrina, but much of the parish, with the notable exception of Slidell, was spared from the worst effects. As a result, St. Tammany neighborhoods recovered more quickly, and in the first year after Katrina, the local real estate market surged and the population grew by about 22%. Weeks after the billion dollar Fremaux Town Center in Slidell opened in February 2014, developers began work on Phase Two, which was scheduled for completion in late 2015.

The percentage of African Americans in the 1st (13%) is the lowest of any Louisiana district. It is a mostly upscale, affluent, highly-educated—and heavily Republican—district. John McCain and Mitt Romney, respectively, won 73% and 71% of the vote in the 2008 and 2012 presidential elections.

Steve Scalise (R)

Republican Steve Scalise won a special election in May 2008 to succeed GOP Rep. Bobby Jindal, who became governor. Six years later, he vaulted to House majority whip through a blend of staunch conservatism, Cajun charm and an unexpected opportunity. As the third-ranking House Republican leader, and the only Southerner, he was at the center of many conflicts and tensions within the GOP.

A native of New Orleans, Scalise grew up in Metairie. When his parents gave their son a battery-powered microphone, he played town crier on his neighborhood street, decorating his bicycle in red, white and blue and calling people to the polls—the start of a political career. He majored in computer science at Louisiana State University, where he was twice elected speaker of the student assembly. After college, he settled in Jefferson Parish as a systems engineer. In 1995, when he was 30, he was elected to the state House, where he served 12 years before winning a state Senate seat in 2007. He pushed legislation to give incentives to the motion picture industry to produce films in Louisiana, and he helped pass a bill that made it the first state to bar cities from suing gun manufacturers for the actions of criminals. Scalise had considered running for the open seat in the 1st District in 1999 and 2004 but deferred first to David Vitter, now a senator, and then reluctantly to Jindal.

In the special election to replace Jindal, the key contest was the Republican runoff between Scalise and state Rep. Tim Burns of Mandeville in St. Tammany. Burns cited Scalise's opposition to a bill banning smoking in restaurants and tried to tie him to special interests. Scalise called for limits on "out-of-control spending" and said he had "the experience to hit the ground running from Day One." Scalise won 58%-42%, capturing 83% of the

Jefferson Parish vote. The final contest against Democrat Gilda Reed, a college instructor and political neophyte, was never in doubt in this lopsidedly Republican district. Scalise won 75%-23%.

The following November, when Scalise ran for his first full term, he faced a bigger challenge. Democrat Jim Harlan, a venture capitalist, sank $1.8 million of his own money into the race and was not shy about throwing mud. In one television ad, he tried to tie Scalise to a local scandal involving a federal investigation of the abuse of tax credits by the Louisiana Institute of Film Technology; Scalise had sponsored the tax credit program in the legislature. Scalise cited his opponent's support of presidential candidate Barack Obama as evidence that Harlan was too liberal for the district. Scalise coasted to a 66%-34% win, taking 71% in Jefferson Parish and 68% in St. Tammany, which together accounted for 71% of the total vote. Since then, he has coasted to reelection.

Scalise is a down-the-line Republican whose rhetorical edge is sharper than that of his influential predecessors—Jindal, Vitter and former Appropriations Committee Chairman Bob Livingston. He has railed against what he calls Obama's "radical agenda" and backed Texas Gov. Rick Perry's short-lived 2012 presidential bid.

In 2009, Scalise joined the powerful Energy and Commerce Committee, a useful assignment for this district. He called for more energy production, including offshore drilling. After the massive BP oil spill in the Gulf in 2010, he shepherded colleagues to the region to see the disaster for themselves and was incensed by Obama's moratorium on offshore drilling, calling it "reckless." He later guided through the House and into law the 2012 RESTORE Act, which calls for at least 80 percent of fines collected from BP and other parties to be sent directly to areas affected by the disaster, including some of the bayous and wetlands that he gained in the 2012 redistricting.

A fierce skeptic of human-caused climate change, he succeeded in amending the House's fiscal 2012 agriculture bill to bar the Agriculture Department from implementing its climate protection plan. He was a vocal opponent in 2009 of the Democrats' cap-and-trade bill to allow industries to trade emissions credits in an effort to reduce greenhouse gas emissions.

Before joining the leadership, he showed an occasional willingness to cross it. But he also paid his dues as a rank-and-file member. He opposed the 2011 compromise on raising the debt limit, and he joined most other Louisiana Republicans in refusing to support a relief bill for Hurricane Sandy in January 2013 because it didn't have offsetting cuts in spending. The House in September 2012 passed his bill allowing people to pay extra at tax time to help reduce the deficit. In a dig at billionaire investor Warren Buffett, whose call for having the wealthy pay more in taxes became a Democratic rallying cry, Scalise called his bill the "Buffett Rule Act." And he joined 80 other like-minded conservatives in signing a 2013 letter that urged defunding the Affordable Care Act in appropriations bills. Scalise served as the chief recruiter for the National Republican Congressional Committee during the 2012 election cycle.

Scalise was the House's fourth most-conservative member in 2013, according to *National Journal* rankings. But he also has been known for his sense of humor and is friendly with many Democrats. He plays basketball with 2nd District Democrat Cedric Richmond, an old friend from their days in Baton Rouge. After the House Appropriations Committee stripped out $17 million in Louisiana coastal restoration funds from the fiscal 2013 energy and water spending bill, Scalise and Richmond won bipartisan House approval of an amendment restoring $10 million. "Steve is an example of how things used to work in Congress," Republican Rep. Patrick McHenry of North Carolina, a close Scalise ally, told *The Times-Picayune*. "You'd battle it out and afterwards you can sit down and be friendly with one another."

When Ohio Republican Jim Jordan stepped down as chairman of the Republican Study Committee following the 2012 election, Georgia Republican Tom Graves was set to take his place, winning the endorsement of the group's founders and past chairmen, which is the traditional means of ascent. But Scalise, who had been managing communications for the group, jumped in and demanded a more democratic method of choosing the leader. "From the beginning, I felt like this ought to be a member-driven organization, and the members should decide who's the next chairman," he told *National Journal*. He touted his record of "getting things done," including enactment of his bill limiting the ability of a president to appoint "czars" without Senate approval. Scalise said he won the secret ballot "with votes to spare." That was a vital step in his move up the House GOP leadership ladder.

Within hours of Virginia Republican Eric Cantor's shocking primary defeat in June 2014, Scalise mobilized his bid to join the leadership. Kevin McCarthy of California, who had been whip, faced token opposition to replacing Cantor as majority leader. It helped that as RSC chairman, Scalise had a built-in base of support; it also helped that many Southern Republicans were anxious to see one of their own in a high-ranking post. Another benefit is that he and McCarthy had been friends since long before either was elected to Congress; that stemmed from McCarthy's national leadership of Young Republicans. But Scalise left nothing to chance, lobbying many colleagues personally to eventually beat Illinois' Peter Roskam and Indiana's Marlin Stutzman for the job. "He's ... open and direct and he likes it when you're open and direct back to him," Rep. Kevin Brady of Texas, with whom Scalise shares housing on Capitol Hill, told *The Times-Picayune.* "But he doesn't take stuff personally. He's friendly, engaging with everyone."

Yet Scalise also can be tough. At the Republican Study Committee, he threw representatives of the prominent Heritage Foundation think tank out of meetings in 2013 after the group caused an internal furor with its advocacy of splitting the farm bill into two parts: one dealing specifically with agriculture policy (called a "farm-only bill") and another legislating the Supplemental Nutrition Assistance Program, the food-stamp program whose budget conservatives have desperately sought to cut.

When House Financial Services Committee Chairman Jeb Hensarling of Texas balked at passing a flood insurance bill in March 2014, an undaunted Scalise helped engineer enough GOP support for the measure to pass the House on a bipartisan basis—an accomplishment that became a tryout for the whip's job. "We had to build a coalition, and we had to overcome a lot of obstacles," he told *The Advocate* of Baton Rouge. For Scalise, it helped that he was well-versed on the program, which is vital to his district.

In the days before he was formally sworn in as whip, Scalise promised that Republicans would avoid a repeat of 2013's government shutdown and would fund the government at current levels. But he refused to rule out the possibility of impeaching Obama, a controversial idea that had galvanized some elements of the far right but one that Boehner had resolutely rejected. In his first week on the job, he was faced with the task of attracting supporters for a bill to address the Central American refugee crisis at the U.S.-Mexico border. He and other House leaders had to pull their initial bill because of a lack of support, leading former Republican National Committee Chairman Michael Steele to declare on MSNBC that Scalise and McCarthy "can't count." His abrupt entry into the leadership posed challenges. Both he and McCarthy lacked Cantor's legislative experience. At a personal level, Scalise had not been close to Boehner, though the speaker needed allies given the hostility that he faced from many conservatives. Plus, Scalise needed to reassure the Southern base whose support was essential to his victory in the contest for whip. By the spring of 2015, Scalise and the revamped GOP leadership team appeared to have successfully passed its initial training period, though plenty of challenges remained.

His early work as whip was overshadowed in December 2014 when a Louisiana liberal blogger reported that Scalise had spoken to a group of white supremacists and neo-Nazis in 2002, six years before he was elected to Congress. When the story first broke, Scalise didn't fully explain how he had been picked as a keynote speaker at the meeting of the European-American Unity and American Rights Organization. Two days later, after a storm of criticism, he expressed his regrets about the appearance and said he had been there to seek support for a tax proposal. He distanced himself from the group, saying he "wholeheartedly condemned" its views, and House GOP leaders as well as other Republicans backed him. A key—and credible—defender was his friend Richmond, the African-American colleague from New Orleans. As part of a damage-control effort, he spent the early months of 2015 meeting with the Congressional Black Caucus and civil rights leaders. Other liberal groups seized on the opportunity to try to depict Republicans as racists. Scalise later called it "a painful time" and "the ugly side of politics," and told *Politico* that he would be "forever grateful" to Richmond for coming to his defense.

Not everyone welcomed Scalise's denials of decade-old connections to the right-wing group. Former Ku Klux Klan leader David Duke, who ran for the 1st District seat in 1999, called Scalise a "sell-out." Duke threatened to challenge him in the 2016 election. If he is serious, such a contest likely would be uncomfortable for Scalise. But it could provide an opportunity to demonstrate that his credentials are mainstream.

SECOND DISTRICT

Cedric Richmond (D)

Elected 2010, 3rd term; b. Sept. 13, 1973, New Orleans; Morehouse Col., B.A. 1995, Tulane U., J.D. 1998; Baptist; married (Raquel); 1 child.

Elected Office: LA House, 2000-08.

Professional Career: Practicing atty., 1998-2010.

DC Office: 240 CHOB, 20515, 202-225-6636; Fax: 202-225-1988; Website: richmond.house.gov.

State Offices: Baton Rouge, 225-636-5600; Gretna, 504-365-0390; New Orleans, 504-288-3777.

Committees: *Homeland Security:* Cybersecurity, Infrastructure Protection, & Security Technologies (RMM); Oversight & Mgmt. Efficiency. *Judiciary:* Courts, Intellectual Property & the Internet; Crime, Terrorism, Homeland Security & Investigations.

Group Ratings

	ADA	ACLU	AFL-CIO	LCV	ITI	COC	HAFA	ACU	CFG	FRC
2014	75%	66%	–	63%	60%	75%	16%	0%	0%	0%
2013	80%	C	100%	64%	C	46%	C	17%	20%	C

National Journal Ratings

	2013 LIB	—	2013 CONS
Economic	63%	—	37%
Social	64%	—	35%
Foreign	59%	—	41%
Composite	62%	—	38%

Key Votes of the 113th Congress

1. Sandy storm spending	Y	5. Medical Marijuana	Y
2. Violence Against Women Act	Y	6. Farm Bill	N
3. Guantanamo Bay Detainees	NV	7. Afghanistan Combat	NV
4. Abortion 20-week ban	N	8. NSA Phone Data Collection	Y

9. Syrian Rebels Training	Y
10. Keystone pipeline	Y
11. Immigration Exec. Action	N
12. Bipartisan budget deal	N

Election Results

2014 general	Cedric Richmond (D)	152,201	(69%)	$1,133,989	$99,008
	Gary Landrieu (D)	37,805	(17%)		
	Samuel Davenport (Lib)	15,237	(7%)		
	David Brooks (I)	16,327	(7%)	$13,717	

Prior winning percentages: 2012 (55%), 2010 (65%)

Population		Race and Ethnicity		Income	
Total:	784,928	Black	62.3%	Median income:	$36,032
Urban:	65.9%	White	27.3%		*(415 of 435)*
Suburban:	31.9%	Latino	5.9%	Under $50,000	62.7%
Rural:	2.2%	Asian	2.8%	$50,000-$99,999:	23.9%
Land area:	1,275	Two races	1.4%	$100,000-$199,999:	11.1%
Pop/sq. mi.:	615.5	White Ethnic	16.7%	$200,000 or more:	2.2%
Born in state:	78.4%			Poverty Rate	26.5%
		Education			
Age Groups		H.S. grad or less:	50.8%	**Work**	
Under 18:	23.1%	Some college:	27.4%	White collar:	29.7%
18 to 34:	26.5%	College degree, 4 yr.:	13.7%	Blue collar:	45.6%
35 to 64:	38.8%	Post-grad study:	8.1%	Sales and service:	24.7%
Over 64:	11.6%				
		Military		Govt. workers:	14.6%
		Veterans/active duty:	6.4%		

New Orleans Metro, Parts of Baton Rouge

Established by the French and ruled by the Spanish from 1763 for almost 40 years, New Orleans was a Creole city—part French, a bit Spanish, more than a touch Caribbean—when the American flag was raised over what is now Jackson Square in 1803. The statue of Andrew

Jackson still seems an intrusion in a square set off by the French Market, the Cabildo, the Presbytere, the Pontalba apartments, and St. Louis Cathedral. New Orleans was one of the six largest American cities from 1820 until the Civil War and the only sizable city in the South. It was urbanized, yet poor,

Voter Turnout	
2013 Total Citizen 18+	577,182
2014 House Turnout	221,564
2014 Turnout as % CVAP	38.4%
2012 Turnout as % CVAP	58.4%

with yellow fever epidemics late in the 19th century, even as it was installing electric lights. It had a riot in which Italian immigrants were massacred, even as it was laying streetcar tracks and telephone lines. It also was one of the most corrupt American cities during Reconstruction and the Gilded Age, when its votes were regularly bid for and bought. Like other Southern cities, it became rigidly segregated after 1890.

For a time during the 1970s oil boom, New Orleans seemed to be a fast-growing Sun Belt city. It suffered economically through the 1980s, when it lost substantial port business—oil to Houston and Latin American trade to Miami. By the 1990s, New Orleans was humming again. Crime rates fell and no longer depressed tourism. Incomes went up, and home ownership increased, among African-Americans as well as whites. The downtown Superdome was the friendly host of the August 1988 Republican convention.

Then, Hurricane Katrina made landfall early on a Monday morning, August 29, 2005. A nightmarish scene unfolded at the Superdome, the shelter of last resort for more than 20,000 people, many of whom had fled the rising water without food, water, or medicine. Conditions worsened when the storm ripped two holes in the roof. A few days later, city officials began to load people on buses for transport to cities better positioned to provide services. The breach of the city's levees led to a surge that churned through the low-income 9th Ward, while the French Quarter, on higher ground, was largely untouched by the floodwaters. Still, 80% of New Orleans flooded.

New Orleans was in for a very long recovery. Thousands of government trailers became semi-permanent homes. City residents who had fled the floodwaters only slowly trickled back. It took years to restore regular utility service. Expectations repeatedly were downsized. Then in 2008, the last government trailer parks closed, and the restaurants in the French Quarter were back in business. By 2014, the city's population was 384,000, 20% smaller than it was in 2000, but more than 80% larger than in 2006, indicating an impressive recovery from the storm in many—but not all—parts of the city. Post-recession wages and median household income in the city and suburbs were also on the rise (although New Orleans was a relatively poor city before the hurricane and remains so; more than one-quarter of its residents live below the poverty line). "It's very clear we're going to have a much smaller, very different New Orleans," retired Brown University geographer Robert Kates told *USA Today*.

The city's post-hurricane recovery lost some momentum when a second disaster struck in April 2010. BP's Deepwater Horizon offshore rig exploded and spewed oil into the Gulf of Mexico at an estimated rate of 60,000 barrels a day. Despite efforts to contain it, the oil slick spread from the drilling site southeast of the mouth of the Mississippi River to the Mississippi River Delta, posing a major threat to the area's oyster beds and fisheries. A federally mandated moratorium on offshore drilling put thousands of oil industry jobs in the region at risk as well, although it was lifted in October 2010 under pressure from local and state officials and the Louisiana congressional delegation. The fragile regional economy took another serious blow when the 5,000 jobs at the Avondale shipyard in 2010 were all but eliminated, leaving only 200 workers at a research and teaching lab. This eliminated 1% of the 520,000 jobs in the greater New Orleans area.

Still, New Orleans, with its unique character and characters, remains a popular tourist destination. In the French Quarter—the *Vieux Carré* as it was originally called—are the 19th-century row houses decked out in their island pastels and ornate wrought-iron railings. At street level are restaurants, art galleries, and jazz and blues clubs, and the narrow sidewalks fill up nightly with diners,

2012 Presidential Vote
Barack Obama (D)	248,947	(76%)
Mitt Romney (R)	74,987	(23%)

2008 Presidential Vote
Barack Obama (D)	235,276	(74%)
John McCain (R)	82,242	(26%)

Cook Partisan Voting Index: D+23

revelers, and patrons of the tiny voodoo establishments found only in New Orleans. Its storied restaurants serve a cuisine all New Orleans' own—spicy, rich, and unaffected by trends in low-fat food.

Upriver from the Quarter is the Central Business District, with its skyscrapers and the Superdome, and the Garden District, with the graceful intact homes of the rich early American settlers lining St. Charles Avenue. (The Garden District is where former New Orleans Saints quarterback Archie Manning raised his two quarterback sons, Peyton and Eli Manning.) A total of 9.5 million tourists visited New Orleans in 2014 and they spent a record-breaking $6.8 billion. A 2013 University of New Orleans study found that job losses in construction and manufacturing had been offset by gains in educational services, leisure and hospitality. The jobless rate in New Orleans was 6.6% in February 2015, down from a recession peak of 10.9%. Much to the relief of locals, when Hurricane Isaac hit the Gulf Coast in August 2012, the city's revamped $14.5 billion flood control system worked. By the fall of 2014, there were no more neighborhood schools, and more than nine in 10 students were attending charter schools.

The 2nd Congressional District of Louisiana includes much of the city of New Orleans. It contains nearly half of Jefferson Parish, most of Orleans Parish, and all or part of seven other parishes between New Orleans and Baton Rouge. It includes more than 100,000 residents in largely black neighborhoods on Baton Rouge's north side. Most of the voters reside in the New Orleans area, and nearly half of them are in Orleans Parish. The 2nd is 63% African American and one of the most Democratic districts in the South.

Cedric Richmond (D)

Democrat Cedric Richmond, elected in 2010, has formed tight alliances with key senior Congressional Black Caucus members and worked successfully with Louisiana Republicans on obtaining money for the state. He's also become known for his peerless pitching in the annual congressional charity baseball game.

Richmond grew up in eastern New Orleans. His father died when he was 7 years old, and he was raised by his mother, a public school teacher. In his youth, life revolved around an urban park where he loved to play sports and later, while in high school, coached teams of younger boys. He graduated from Atlanta's Morehouse College, the nation's only all-male historically black college, and returned to his hometown to earn a law degree from Tulane University.

Richmond was elected in 2000 to the state House at age 26, becoming the youngest lawmaker in Baton Rouge. He pushed initiatives such as a redevelopment tax credit for weather-damaged areas, funding for playgrounds, and a ban on certain types of semi-automatic rifles. He also strongly opposed a proposed legislative pay raise in 2008. Richmond ran for the New Orleans City Council in 2005 but was ejected from the race for falsifying his qualifying papers when it was determined in court that he didn't meet the residency requirement to represent the district as he had attested. His law license was later briefly suspended as a result. Despite the controversy, Richmond was reelected to the legislature in 2007.

He ran for Congress in 2008, as New Orleans only slowly recovered from Hurricane Katrina and was represented by a scandal-plagued incumbent, Rep. William Jefferson, a Democrat who had been stripped of his committee assignments after being indicted on federal corruption charges. Richmond was one of six Democrats in the contest, and the divided field split the anti-Jefferson vote. Finishing third, Richmond failed to qualify for the runoff. Republican Anh "Joseph" Cao then eked out a 50%-47% general election victory over Jefferson, who was subsequently sentenced to 13 years in jail for bribery.

In the midterm election, despite having established one of the most independent voting records among House Republicans, Cao was viewed as extremely vulnerable given the heavily Democratic makeup of the district. Richmond won the August 2010 primary over three other Democrats, taking 61% of the vote. He garnered two-thirds of the ballots cast in heavily black precincts as well as nearly half of those in heavily white areas. On the campaign trail, he reminded voters of Cao's votes against the stimulus and the final version of the health care bill in 2010. His central message was that he would be a more dependable supporter of Obama's agenda than Cao. He was bolstered when Obama endorsed him, and called him "a leader on hurricane recovery and a fighter for the people of New Orleans." The Democratic Congressional Campaign Committee helped Richmond tap campaign funds, though Cao outspent him, $2.1 million to $1.1 million.

Richmond had several problems of his own. In addition to the fallout from his 2005 City Council filing offense, a political group called Louisiana Truth PAC launched a website that highlighted a misdemeanor charge stemming from a 2007 bar fight. Richmond's response was that he was only trying to defend himself. Richmond won easily, 65%-33%. Cao held the challenger's vote down in Jefferson Parish, but got wiped out in Orleans. Richmond has not been seriously challenged since.

In the House, Richmond has been a loyal Democrat, on rare occasions departing from the party line in deference to his state's needs. He belongs to the business-friendly New Democrat Coalition. He supported a transportation bill in April 2012 that a majority of Democrats opposed because it included the controversial Keystone XL pipeline. Richmond has argued that more oil royalty payments go to Louisiana and other energy-producing states. He has worked extensively on curbing youth violence and in 2013 was given a seat on the Judiciary Committee. In *Washingtonian*'s 2012 survey of Capitol Hill aides, he tied for second (with Oklahoma Republican James Lankford) in the "surprise standout" category.

When the House is in session, he regularly eats dinner with fellow black Democrats James Clyburn of South Carolina, the assistant minority leader, and Bennie Thompson of Mississippi, the Homeland Security Committee's top Democrat. With Clyburn, Richmond took on voter-mobilization responsibilities for House Democrats in the 2016 campaign. He also is a friend of his Bayou State Republican colleague Steve Scalise, with whom he has worked on obtaining more disaster-recovery money and other issues. Scalise, now majority whip, said he would be "forever grateful" to Richmond for coming to his defense in December 2014 when a website raised questions about a speech that Scalise had given to a group of white supremacists in 2002. "I don't think Steve Scalise has a racist bone in his body," Richmond said.

In the 2011 congressional baseball game, Richmond, who played at Morehouse, threw a one-hitter and struck out 13, prompting Republican Rep. Joe Barton of Texas to joke on the House floor: "I do want to point out to Mr. Richmond that the congressional salary is $175,000. The major league minimum salary is $350,000, and I know the owner of the [Houston] Astros and the Texas Rangers." The following year, Richmond led his party to an 18-5 romp, banging out several hits for good measure and being named the game's most valuable player. In that game, Scalise got a run-scoring hit off Richmond, who previously hadn't allowed any hits. Following another complete-game victory in 2014, Richmond had shoulder surgery later in the year. That jeopardized one of the few House contests in which Democrats have been favored to win.

THIRD DISTRICT

Charles Boustany (R)

Elected 2004, 6th term; b. Feb. 21, 1956, New Orleans; U. of SW LA, B.S. 1978, LA St. U., M.D. 1982; Episcopalian; married (Bridget); 2 children.

Professional Career: Practicing surgeon, 1982-2004.

DC Office: 1431 LHOB, 20515, 202-225-2031; Fax: 202-225-5724; Website: boustany.house.gov.

State Offices: Lafayette, 337-235-6322; Lake Charles, 337-433-1747.

Committees: *Ways & Means:* Human Resources (Chmn); Trade.

Group Ratings

	ADA	ACLU	AFL-CIO	LCV	ITI	COC	HAFA	ACU	CFG	FRC
2014	0%	0%	–	0%	100%	93%	46%	68%	60%	88%
2013	0%	C	29%	4%	C	85%	C	64%	50%	C

National Journal Ratings

	2013 LIB	—	2013 CONS
Economic	36%	—	64%
Social	31%	—	67%
Foreign	24%	—	68%
Composite	32%	—	68%

Key Votes of the 113th Congress

1. Sandy storm spending	Y	5. Medical Marijuana		9. Syrian Rebels Training	Y
2. Violence Against Women Act	Y	6. Farm Bill	Y	10. Keystone pipeline	Y
3. Guantanamo Bay Detainees	N	7. Afghanistan Combat	N	11. Immigration Exec. Action	Y
4. Abortion 20-week ban	Y	8. NSA Phone Data Collection	N	12. Bipartisan budget deal	Y

Election Results

2014 general	Charles Boustany (R)	185,867	(79%)	$2,118,901 $30,148
	Russell Richard (I)	28,342	(12%)	
	Bryan Barrilleaux (R)	22,059	(9%)	

Prior winning percentages: 2012 (61%), 2010 (unopposed), 2008 (62%), 2006 (71%), 2004 (55%)

Population		Race and Ethnicity		Income	
Total:	769,331	White	68.7%	Median income:	$45,858
Urban:	38.7%	Black	24.7%		*(304 of 435)*
Suburban:	40.9%	Latino	3.0%	Under $50,000	53.3%
Rural:	20.4%	Asian	1.4%	$50,000-$99,999:	27.5%
Land area:	6,269	Two races	1.4%	$100,000-$199,999:	15.6%
Pop/sq. mi.:	122.7	White Ethnic	35.0%	$200,000 or more:	3.7%
Born in state:	83.0%			Poverty Rate	16.7%
		Education			
		H.S. grad or less:	53.3%	**Work**	
Age Groups		Some college:	26.7%	White collar:	29.9%
Under 18:	25.0%	College degree, 4 yr.:	13.5%	Blue collar:	43.4%
18 to 34:	24.1%	Post-grad study:	6.5%	Sales and service:	26.7%
35 to 64:	38.5%			Govt. workers:	12.8%
Over 64:	12.5%	**Military**			
		Veterans/active duty:	7.9%		

Southwest Louisiana: Lafayette, Lake Charles

More than 200 years ago, French-speaking settlers in Canada were forced to leave their land of Acadie, which the British had taken over and renamed Nova Scotia. They made their way to the wetlands of southern Louisiana, called Acadiana. Here, with-

Voter Turnout	
2013 Total Citizen 18+	565,423
2014 House Turnout	236,268
2014 Turnout as % CVAP	41.8%
2012 Turnout as % CVAP	60.1%

out much notice, they built steep-roofed houses to slough off nonexistent snow and adapted French cuisine to the crawfish and muskrats they found in abundance in the pelican-tended swamps. They are the Cajuns, and the heart of their adopted homeland is around Lafayette, just west of the Atchafalaya Basin, where Mississippi River waters pour through bayous and canals. An 18-mile section of Interstate 10 was built here on elevated stilts. Cajun country has thrived, thanks to the oil and gas that are plentiful on land and just offshore in the Gulf of Mexico. Oil rigs are common, and every once in a while, the swampy foliage parts to reveal a giant refinery or petrochemical plant.

Cajun French has survived decades of efforts to eliminate it. Cajun music—and its black-influenced variant, zydeco—are popular here and nationally; spicy Cajun cooking attracts food lovers, who learn its secrets and then carry them home, in understated form. It's estimated that as many as 200,000 Louisianans speak French as a second language. Lafayette, with its Acadian Village and plethora of oil exploration firms, features an annual *Festivals Acadiens* to celebrate music, food and crafts. Mardi Gras is not just a great party but great for local business—it contributes an estimated $110 million annually to the economy in Lafayette Parish. Louisiana was the only state that still permitted cockfighting until it was

finally banned in 2008, but remnants of it can still be found here. A number of Lafayette residents were arrested during a police crackdown in 2011.

In 2005, Hurricane Rita, not Katrina, was the natural disaster with the most devastating local impact. With winds of 120 miles per hour and a storm surge of 15 feet, Rita left a path of destruction 200 miles west of New

2012 Presidential Vote		
Mitt Romney (R)	220,490	(66%)
Barack Obama (D)	107,613	(32%)

2008 Presidential Vote		
John McCain (R)	210,959	(64%)
Barack Obama (D)	111,829	(34%)

Cook Partisan Voting Index: R+19

Orleans. It virtually erased some coastal communities, especially in Cameron Parish. While the nation was spellbound by every development in New Orleans, local residents complained that they were victims of "Rita amnesia." Lafayette's unemployment rate of 5.1 percent was the lowest among metropolitan areas in Louisiana in early 2015, and its growth became an exception as more than half of the state's parishes had lost population since 2010. The city ranked 19th nationally on the Milken Institute's Best Performing Cities Index for creating and sustaining jobs in 2014. That year, three high-tech companies announced plans to move to Lafayette, each with hundreds of jobs. That became a welcome development when the price of oil plunged and many area rigs shut down. The Lafayette area also diversified culturally, as workers were imported for tourism and seafood processing plants. Spanish replaced French as the second language, but Cajun food grew even more popular nationally.

The 3rd Congressional District was enlarged during 2011 redistricting. When Louisiana was forced to give up a House seat after the 2010 census, the GOP-controlled legislature merged parts of the two former Bayou districts. The new district, which covers most of the southern coast and much of Cajun country, previously stopped in Lafayette Parish. Now, it extends east to Iberia, St. Martin, and St. Mary parishes. The new 3rd District, like most of southern Louisiana, remains very conservative. Republican Mitt Romney got 66 percent of the vote here in the 2012 presidential race.

Charles Boustany (R)

Charles Boustany in 2004 became the first Republican elected from southwest Louisiana since 1884. He is a heart surgeon with a prized seat on the Ways and Means Committee and has been active on health care, mostly upholding the GOP line but sometimes willing to explore common ground with pragmatic Democrats.

Of Lebanese ancestry, Boustany grew up in Lafayette, where his father was parish coroner. He was one of 10 children and told *Roll Call* in 2012: "If you didn't show up on time for dinner, guess what? You didn't get anything to eat." He graduated from the University of Southwestern Louisiana and from Louisiana State University's medical school.

When Democrat Chris John ran for the Senate in 2004, Boustany was one of five candidates running to succeed him. The other Republican was David Thibodaux of Lafayette, who had run unsuccessfully for the seat three times. He raised little money, some party leaders viewed him as too conservative, and Boustany quickly became the GOP favorite. Democratic front-runners were state Sen. Don Cravins, who was seeking to become the first African American to hold this seat, and state Sen. Willie Mount.

Boustany raised plenty of money early and campaigned on his "prescription for prosperity"— expansion of health savings accounts, high-speed Internet access for small businesses, and opposition to the Central America Free Trade Agreement. Boustany led the November primary with 39% of the vote, to 25% for Mount, 24.6% for Cravins, and 10% for Thibodaux. In the December runoff, Cravins refused to endorse Mount, still angry over the state Democratic Party's "unity ballot" sent to black voters, which included Mount's name and not his. Cravins' neutrality hurt Mount in the Lafayette area. She pointed to her legislative experience, while Boustany emphasized his "values" agenda. Boustany won 55%-45%.

In the House, Boustany's voting record has been relatively moderate for a Southern Republican. He has become more of a loyalist since his party reclaimed the House majority in 2011. He initially opposed the $700 billion Wall Street rescue in 2008 but later switched to "yes." He has a close relationship with House Speaker John Boehner, which proved helpful in 2009, when he secured a seat on Ways and Means.

As the only physician on the committee in 2009, Boustany took a prominent role during the health care debate. With his soft-spoken yet authoritative manner, he became a popular television news guest. He gave the Republican response to President Barack Obama's September 2009 address to Congress on health care and used the opportunity to talk up GOP ideas such as allowing people to cross state lines to buy insurance. He initially expressed hope that any overhaul could be bipartisan. His approach emphasized patient-centered health care solutions, such as increased access to tax-free health savings accounts. He advised other Republican physicians seeking House seats in 2010, appearing at some of their campaign events. The House in February 2012 passed his bill aimed at keeping welfare recipients from spending government-assistance checks at liquor stores, casinos, or strip clubs. He won committee approval that year of his bill changing a regulation that forced workers to forfeit unused flexible spending account funds at the end of the year.

At Ways and Means, he chaired from 2011 to 2014 the Oversight Subcommittee, which investigated improper targeting by the IRS of conservative groups seeking tax-exempt status. He pressed for recovery of emails that former IRS official Lois Lerner claimed to have lost. In 2015, he became chairman of the Human Resources Subcommittee, where he examined ways to make welfare programs work more efficiently as a step out of poverty. He also worked on trade issues, and filed legislation to protect seafood companies against ineligible imports. Boustany has shifted positions on trade issues depending on how he perceives their impact on his state. In January 2015, he added a rider to a House-passed appropriation bill demanding that the Customs Bureau reimburse the crawfish industry for duties that were owed from Chinese interests that had illegally dumped their products. With Democratic Rep. Joe Crowley of New York, he filed a bill to increase the number of residency slots for doctors, with an emphasis on teaching hospitals.

After the 2010 BP oil spill in the Gulf of Mexico, Boustany and Rep. Gene Green of Texas pressed for allowing new drilling in shallower Gulf waters. His local priorities included more federal funding to restore Louisiana's eroding coastline and to complete Interstate 49 from Lafayette through Houma to New Orleans. After Hurricanes Katrina and Rita, he enacted special rules for disaster relief employment for individuals displaced by the storms and to assist the disabled.

The Democratic Congressional Campaign Committee tried to recruit Chris John to run for his old seat in 2006 but he declined. With John out of the running, Boustany got 71% of the vote. In 2008, he won 62%-34% against state Sen. Don Cravins Jr., the son of Boustany's 2004 opponent.

In 2012, he was dragged into Louisiana's messy redistricting when the state lost one congressional seat. Fellow GOP Rep. John Fleming accused Boustany of backing a plan that could enhance his own district while handing Fleming's seat to a Democrat. Freshman Republican Jeff Landry's coastal district ultimately was eliminated, throwing him into Boustany's and setting up an establishment-versus-tea party fight. Landry attacked Boustany as a moderate in thrall to the Washington establishment, while the better-funded Boustany portrayed his rival as ineffectual and prone to missing votes. In the November primary, Boustany got 45% of the vote to Landry's 30%. In the December runoff, Boustany coasted to a win with 61%, after outspending Landry $4.9 million to $2.2 million. With the ancestral Democratic base having shrunk, he was entrenched.

Continuing tensions within the Louisiana delegation became apparent in June 2014 when Boustany supported Ways and Means colleague Peter Roskam of Illinois for majority whip over home-state Rep. Steve Scalise, who prevailed. Boustany maneuvered for support from David Vitter to replace him in the Senate if Vitter was elected governor in November 2015. Boustany said publicly that he would run if Vitter's seat became open.

FOURTH DISTRICT

John Fleming (R)

Elected 2008, 4th term; b. July 5, 1951, Meridian, MS; U. of MS, B.S. 1973, M.D. 1976; Baptist; married (Cindy); 4 children.

Military Career: U.S. Navy, 1976-82.

Elected Office: Webster Parish coroner, 1996-2000.

Professional Career: Businessman; Physician.

DC Office: 2182 RHOB, 20515, 202-225-2777; Fax: 202-225-8039; Website: fleming.house.gov.

State Offices: Bossier City, 318-549-1924; Leesville, 337-238-0778; Shreveport, 318-798-2254.

Committees: *Armed Services:* Strategic Forces; Tactical Air & Land Forces. *Natural Resources:* Energy & Mineral Resources; Water, Power & Oceans (Chmn).

Group Ratings

	ADA	ACLU	AFL-CIO	LCV	ITI	COC	HAFA	ACU	CFG	FRC
2014	5%	5%	–	0%	80%	57%	76%	96%	85%	100%
2013	5%	C	14%	4%	C	69%	C	88%	83%	C

National Journal Ratings

	2013 LIB	—	2013 CONS
Economic	13%	—	85%
Social	13%	—	84%
Foreign	5%	—	86%
Composite	13%	—	87%

Key Votes of the 113th Congress

1. Sandy storm spending	N	5. Medical Marijuana	N	9. Syrian Rebels Training	N
2. Violence Against Women Act	N	6. Farm Bill	N	10. Keystone pipeline	Y
3. Guantanamo Bay Detainees	N	7. Afghanistan Combat	N	11. Immigration Exec. Action	Y
4. Abortion 20-week ban	Y	8. NSA Phone Data Collection	Y	12. Bipartisan budget deal	Y

Election Results

2014 general	John Fleming (R)	152,683	(73%)	$803,078
	Randall Lord (Lib)	55,236	(27%)	

Prior winning percentages: 2012 (75%), 2010 (62%), 2008 (48%)

Population		Race and Ethnicity		Income	
Total:	762,517	White	59.4%	Median income:	$40,403
Urban:	41.5%	Black	33.8%		*(384 of 435)*
Suburban:	9.2%	Latino	3.3%	Under $50,000	58.7%
Rural:	49.3%	Amer. Indian	0.8%	$50,000-$99,999:	26.8%
Land area:	12,662	Two races	1.6%	$100,000-$199,999:	11.9%
Pop/sq. mi.:	60.2	White Ethnic	20.1%	$200,000 or more:	2.7%
Born in state:	74.1%			Poverty Rate	21.3%
		Education			
Age Groups		H.S. grad or less:	52.1%	**Work**	
Under 18:	24.7%	Some college:	27.5%	White collar:	30.7%
18 to 34:	23.9%	College degree, 4 yr.:	13.9%	Blue collar:	43.0%
35 to 64:	37.2%	Post-grad study:	6.5%	Sales and service:	26.3%
Over 64:	14.1%			Govt. workers:	17.8%
		Military			
		Veterans/active duty:	11.8%		

Northwest Louisiana: Shreveport, Bossier City

Northwestern Louisiana, south of Arkansas and just east of Texas, is part of the Deep South. The overwhelming majority of people here are Protestants, not Catholics, and they are often tradition-minded, with names that are English or Scottish, not French. The tone is set not by wide-open New

Voter Turnout	
2013 Total Citizen 18+	563,038
2014 House Turnout	207,919
2014 Turnout as % CVAP	36.9%
2012 Turnout as % CVAP	57.5%

Orleans—which was not easily accessible by interstate until 1996, when the last chunk of Interstate 49 was completed—but by the smaller Shreveport, which could be just another East Texas oil-patch town, albeit one that has its own, comparatively sedate, Mardi Gras. In 2014, developers had plans to upgrade the downtown area, which includes entertainment and residential spaces. The countryside is agricultural, though there are some vestiges of large riverfront plantations. Roots here go back a long way. Natchitoches is the oldest town in Louisiana, founded by Louis Antoine Juchereau de St. Denis in 1714, and Shreveport was founded in the 1830s.

Oil provided the basis for much of the region's economic growth in the 20th century, but natural gas took off in the 21st, helping to sustain it during the recession. Gas was discovered in 1870, and the nation's first gas pipeline was built from Caddo Field to Shreveport in 1908. However, it wasn't economical to drill until gas prices soared in 2000. In addition to natural gas, riverboat gambling and the Port of Caddo-Bossier supplement the local economy. A billion-dollar steel mill, under construction at the port, was scheduled for opening in late 2015.

2012 Presidential Vote		
Mitt Romney (R)	191,417	(59%)
Barack Obama (D)	128,659	(40%)

2008 Presidential Vote		
John McCain (R)	187,020	(59%)
Barack Obama (D)	126,885	(40%)

Cook Partisan Voting Index: R+13

Barksdale Air Force Base in Bossier City, one of the nation's largest airfields, is where President George W. Bush landed on Sept. 11, 2001, and spoke briefly to the nation. In 2009, the Air Force chose Barksdale as home of the Global Strike Command, which combined the nation's land-based nuclear missiles and long-range nuclear bombers under single leadership. The new command created about 1,000 jobs in the region.

The 4th Congressional District of Louisiana drops down the western side of the state to the Bayous. Nearly half of the population is in Caddo Parish and suburban Bossier Parish around Shreveport. The rest is scattered in rural areas. The district overall is about 34 percent African American and the least partisan of Louisiana's five GOP-held districts, but nonetheless solidly Republican.

John Fleming (R)

Republican John Fleming, elected in 2008, is a physician, a multi-millionaire owner of business franchises, and an ardent conservative who has taken up rhetorical arms against the Obama administration on issues affecting businesses.

Fleming grew up in Meridian Mississippi, the son of a utility substation operator who worked two or three jobs to make ends meet. His father died of a heart attack just before Fleming finished high school. His mother was disabled and relied on Social Security to support Fleming and two younger siblings. After undergraduate and medical school at the University of Mississippi, he spent six years in the Navy, where he did his medical residency. He later opened a family medical practice in Minden Louisiana and served as coroner of Webster Parish in the 1990s. He had other sidelines: Fleming operated 30 Subway restaurants in the state and had a stake in 130 UPS stores, from Mississippi to Texas. He also wrote a book called *Preventing Addiction: What Parents Must Know to Immunize Their Kids Against Drug and Alcohol Addiction*.

The House seat opened when influential Rep. Jim McCrery, ranking Republican on the Ways and Means Committee, announced his retirement. The early front-runners for the GOP nomination were trucking-company executive Chris Gorman and Bossier Chamber of Commerce President Jeff Thompson, whom McCrery and the National Republican Congressional Committee supported. In the first round of voting, Fleming led with 35%, to 34% for Gorman and 31% for Thompson. In the runoff campaign, both men held similar views, emphasizing the need to reduce federal spending and taxes, and both spent heavily. Fleming captured the nomination 56%-44%.

Meanwhile, Democrats lined up behind Paul Carmouche, a 30-year Caddo Parish district attorney who styled himself as a centrist Blue Dog Democrat and campaigned against abortion rights and crime. Fleming emphasized his conservative credentials, calling himself a Ronald Reagan Republican. He called for abolishing the Internal Revenue Service and replacing the current income tax with a national sales tax. He favored tough measures against illegal immigrants, decrying an "invasion by illegal aliens." Fleming out-raised Carmouche $1.4 million to $1.2 million and got a big helping hand from the NRCC. The election was held on December 6, 2008, after being delayed a month by the threat from Hurricane Gustav. Fleming won by 350 votes.

In the House, Fleming has a seat on the Armed Services Committee to protect Barksdale Air Force Base outside Shreveport. He endorsed the decision to create the Global Strike Command at the base as "the voice needed to fully support the long-range strike mission." He chairs the Natural Resources Subcommittee on Water, Power and Oceans. He has co-chaired the House GOP's Doctors Caucus, and has advocated conscience protections for medical personnel who choose not to participate in abortion practices. He strongly opposed legalization of marijuana, including voter approval of its use in the District of Columbia. Claims of its medicinal benefit were "complete rubbish," he said.

Fleming's fondness for fiery rhetoric has drawn admiration from the far right, but even some members of his party have viewed him as a loose cannon. He drew widespread publicity in February 2012 when his office posted on his Facebook page—and later quickly deleted— an article from the satirical newspaper *The Onion* about Planned Parenthood's development of an $8 billion "abortionplex" that his staff mistook as factual. One of the first Republicans to join the Tea Party Caucus, Fleming regularly makes House floor speeches bashing President Barack Obama. In a newspaper column, he accused the president of "undermining this country's national defense on purpose." Fleming drew scorn from progressives when he publicly supported a Florida urologist's decision to deny care to patients who supported Obama, saying it was the doctor's "First Amendment right."

During a vote in 2011 on a spending resolution aimed at averting a government shutdown, Fleming was one of 48 Republicans who defied the GOP leadership by voting no, saying the measure did not cut spending enough. Fleming came under fire for comments he made on MSNBC after being asked about a *Wall Street Journal* report that he had a gross income of some $6.3 million. "The amount that I have to invest in my business and feed my family is more like $600,000 of that $6.3 million," he said. "So by the time I feed my family I have, maybe, $400,000 left over to invest." Fleming was criticized by blogosphere and cable TV liberals for being insensitive to the plight of workers with far less disposable income. But Fleming was unapologetic, explaining later on Fox News that higher taxes mean business owners have less money to hire new workers.

Democrats have failed to field a serious challenger to Fleming since he was first elected. In 2011, Fleming lashed out at fellow Louisiana GOP Rep. Charles Boustany for backing a redistricting plan that Fleming said could have undermined his prospects in 2012, but his district's partisan makeup was only modestly changed. Fleming spoke openly about his plan to seek the potentially open Senate seat held by David Vitter, who was running for governor in 2015. "There are more tools available to a senator to make changes to reform government and reform policy than there are for a House member," he told the *Shreveport Times* in January 2015.

FIFTH DISTRICT

Ralph Abraham (R)

Elected 2014, 1st term; b. Sept. 16, 1954, Alto; LA St. U., B.A. 1980, D.V.M. 1980, M.D. 1994; Baptist; married (Dianne); 3 children.

Military Career: U.S. Army Reserves; MS Nat'l Guard Special Forces, 1986-89; Coast Guard Auxiliary, present.

Professional Career: Flight instructor; General family practitioner; Aviation medical examiner.

DC Office: 417 CHOB, 20515, 202-225-8490; Fax: 202-225-5639; Website: abraham.house.gov.

State Offices: Alexandria, 318-445-0818; Monroe, 318-322-3500.

Committees: *Agriculture:* General Farm Commodities & Risk Mgmt; Nutrition. *Veterans' Affairs:* Disability Assistance & Memorial Affairs (Chmn); Health.

Election Results

2014 general	Ralph Abraham (R)	134,616	(64%)	$784,868	$2,974	
	Jamie Mayo (D)	75,004	(36%)	$196,199		$89,614
2014 primary	Jamie Mayo (D)	67,611	(28%)			
	Ralph Abraham (R)	55,489	(23%)			
	Zach Dasher (R)	53,628	(22%)			
	Vance McAllister (R)	26,606	(11%)			
	Clyde Holloway (R)	17,877	(7%)			

Population		Race and Ethnicity		Income	
Total:	754,131	White	60.0%	Median income:	$34,243
Urban:	22.8%	Black	35.9%		*(423 of 435)*
Suburban:	17.6%	Latino	1.8%	Under $50,000	62.2%
Rural:	59.6%	Asian	0.5%	$50,000-$99,999:	24.7%
Land area:	15,248	Two races	1.5%	$100,000-$199,999:	10.7%
Pop/sq. mi.:	49.5	White Ethnic	20.7%	$200,000 or more:	2.5%
Born in state:	80.7%			Poverty Rate	24.8%
		Education			
Age Groups		H.S. grad or less:	58.3%	**Work**	
Under 18:	24.5%	Some college:	25.2%	White collar:	30.0%
18 to 34:	24.0%	College degree, 4 yr.:	11.5%	Blue collar:	44.4%
35 to 64:	37.5%	Post-grad study:	5.1%	Sales and service:	25.6%
Over 64:	14.0%			Govt. workers:	18.6%
		Military			
		Veterans/active duty:	8.0%		

Northeast Louisiana: Monroe, Alexandria

Northeast Louisiana is perhaps the least known part of the state. Along the Mississippi River and the Red River and their dozens of tributaries, it was plantation country before the Civil War, and there are African-American majorities today in many parishes. Away from the rivers, in the hill country,

Voter Turnout	
2013 Total Citizen 18+	562,798
2014 House Turnout	239,551
2014 Turnout as % CVAP	42.6%
2012 Turnout as % CVAP	58.4%

small farmers scratched out a living on land connected to parish courthouses by dusty lanes. Such was Winn Parish, where Huey P. Long, the transformative figure in modern Louisiana politics, was born in 1893 and from which he began his meteoric political career. Elected governor in 1928 and senator in 1930, he was a national figure when he was assassinated in 1935 in the new high-rise Capitol he built in Baton Rouge.

The 5th Congressional District of Louisiana contains much of this country, from the hills of Winn Parish to the several small black-majority parishes along the Mississippi. About 36 percent of the population is African American. The biggest urban areas here, with slightly less than 50,000 people each, are Monroe in the north and Alexandria in the south. Monroe, in Ouachita Parish, is heavily Protestant. Alexandria, in Rapides Parish, sits at the northern extension of Cajun, Catholic Louisiana and is majority black. After the federal government stunned local officials in 2010 by determining that the Red River's levees were no longer certified, which would put much of the area in a flood zone, officials in Rapides Parish used federal disaster relief funds and had repaired about two-thirds of the levees by early 2015. The district also includes a few parishes east of the Mississippi River and on the outskirts of Baton Rouge. This is one of

2012 Presidential Vote		
Mitt Romney (R)	201,058	(61%)
Barack Obama (D)	124,054	(38%)
2008 Presidential Vote		
John McCain (R)	203,250	(62%)
Barack Obama (D)	122,577	(37%)
Cook Partisan Voting Index: R+15		

the largest row-crop farming districts in the nation, including cotton, rice, corn and soybeans. A biofuels plant in Alexandria was scheduled to start operations in early 2016. This remains a very Republican district.

Ralph Abraham (R)

Republican Ralph Abraham, a rural doctor and humanitarian pilot, elected in 2014, has a lower profile than his predecessor, Vance McAllister, who had a brief and rocky tenure. He also was less known than the Republican he defeated in November to advance to the runoff—Zach Dasher, nephew of TV's *"Duck Dynasty"* star Phil Robertson. Voters preferred Abraham's emphasis of his life experiences to Dasher's ardent tea party views.

Abraham grew up in rural Richland Parish, which remains his home. He trained to be a veterinarian at the LSU School of Veterinary Medicine and practiced for 10 years. But he changed careers in his late 30s, and earned his medical degree at the LSU School of Medicine in Shreveport. He likes to boast he "can treat anything that walks on two or four legs." He was a 1st Lieutenant in the Army and remains an Aircraft Commander in the Coast Guard Auxiliary. He worked as a volunteer pilot with Pilots for Patients, a Monroe group that provides free air transportation to people who need medical assistance and live far from hospitals or doctors.

Abraham was the third Republican elected to this seat in two years. Rodney Alexander took office in January 2013 for his sixth term, and served on the Appropriations Committee, where he chaired the Legislative Branch Subcommittee. He resigned in August 2013 to become head of the Louisiana Department of Veterans Affairs. In the special election, state senator Neil Riser, the initial favorite of the Republican establishment, spent the most money and led the first round of voting with 32% of the vote to 18% for runner-up McAllister, a political novice who had made money in the oil exploration and production business. McAllister benefited in the runoff from his outsider status and his endorsement by the reality television show family in "Duck Dynasty."

McAllister won the runoff for the special election, 60%-40%, and appeared to be politically untouchable in a district that gave Mitt Romney 61% of the vote in 2012. But in April 2014, a local newspaper published a surveillance video showing the married congressman passionately kissing his office's scheduler. Following the widespread airing of the videotaped embrace with an aide that led him to be dubbed "the Kissing Congressman," McAllister issued a statement saying he had "fallen short," and asked for forgiveness. He rejected leadership suggestions that he should resign. After initially declining to seek reelection, he changed his mind and filed to run.

Abraham, who had never held political office, said he had been considering a run for Congress for several years and felt that the time was ripe. He loaned his campaign $200,000 of his own money in September, and repaid half of that in December. "It's not the America in which we grew up," he told Gannett Newspapers. "Somebody has to step up and change it." He played up his 39-year marriage, pilot experiences and "family values." Dasher drew attention when he argued that atheism has led to moral decay in society, which he said played a part in the 2012 school massacre in Newtown Connecticut. McAllister, an energy businessman who self-financed much of his campaign, claimed that voters were not concerned about his widely publicized kissing incident. The conservative Club for Growth political action committee backed Dasher with $250,000 in advertising that attacked McAllister for his personal issues.

In the November all-party election, Abraham ran a low-profile, grass-roots campaign and finished first among Republicans with 23% of the vote, just 1,861 votes ahead of Dasher's 22% and well ahead of McAllister's 11%. Abraham ran strongly in Monroe and the northern parishes. Dasher ran strongly in Alexandria and the southern parishes. Abraham had a runoff with the leading vote-getter in the nine-candidate race—Democrat Jamie Mayo, the mayor of Monroe, who got 30% of the vote in the first round. That proved to be a no-contest. Mayo sought to make an issue of Abraham's assertion that he would retain his medical practice as a congressman, saying it would diminish his opponent's effectiveness. Abraham outspent Mayo 4-to-1 for the entire campaign, and easily won the runoff, 64%-36%. Of the 24 parishes, Mayo won five; each was on or close to the Mississippi River. Mayo lost his home parish of Ouachita by nearly 2-to-1.

In the House, Abraham seemed to fit comfortably in the GOP establishment wing. He was rewarded with seats on the Agriculture and Veterans' Affairs committees, and chaired the latter's Subcommittee on Disability Assistance and Memorial Affairs—one of the few freshmen to get a gavel. He complained when VA officials said they wanted to take money from the 2014 law designed to improve benefits and use it to cover nearly $1 billion in cost overruns at their Denver medical center. "That money was designated for those veterans," Abraham told the Monroe *News-Star*. "We need it in Louisiana. We need it all over the nation."

Abraham said he planned to focus on reducing poverty and working with Democrats. Mostly, he said, he wanted to be "steadfast" with his constituents. Given the recent turmoil in the district, they might welcome that.

SIXTH DISTRICT

Garret Graves (R)

Elected 2014, 1st term; b. Jan. 31, 1972, Baton Rouge; U. of AL, LA Tech U., American U., attended; Catholic; married (Carissa); 3 children.

Professional Career: Staff, U.S. Sen. John Breaux; Staff, U.S. Rep. Billy Tauzin; Staff, U.S. Sen. David Vitter; Chmn., Coastal Protection & Restoration Authority of LA; Vice chmn., Gulf Coast Ecosystem Restoration Task Force, U.S. EPA.

DC Office: 204 CHOB, 20515, 202-225-3901; Fax: 202-225-7313; Website: garretgraves.house.gov.

State Offices: Baton Rouge, 225-442-1731; Livingston, 225-686-4413; Thibodaux, 985-448-4103.

Committees: *Natural Resources:* Energy & Mineral Resources; Water, Power & Oceans. *Transportation & Infrastructure:* Coast Guard & Maritime Transportation; Water Resources & Environment (VChmn).

Election Results

2014 general	Garret Graves (R)	139,209	(62%)	$1,527,595	$139,197
	Edwin Edwards (D)	83,781	(38%)	$432,873	
2014 primary	Edwin Edwards (D)	77,866	(30%)		
	Garret Graves (R)	70,715	(27%)		
	Paul Dietzel (R)	35,024	(14%)		
	Dan Claitor (R)	26,524	(10%)		
	Lenar Whitney (R)	19,151	(7%)		

Population		Race and Ethnicity		Income	
Total:	773,429	White	69.8%	Median income:	$57,033
Urban:	47.0%	Black	22.0%		*(150 of 435)*
Suburban:	42.2%	Latino	4.2%	Under $50,000	44.3%
Rural:	10.8%	Asian	2.1%	$50,000-$99,999:	30.2%
Land area:	3,534	Two races	1.1%	$100,000-$199,999:	21.2%
Pop/sq. mi.:	218.8	White Ethnic	36.3%	$200,000 or more:	4.3%
Born in state:	77.1%			Poverty Rate	16.1%
		Education			
Age Groups		H.S. grad or less:	44.6%	**Work**	
Under 18:	24.2%	Some college:	26.9%	White collar:	37.0%
18 to 34:	25.6%	College degree, 4 yr.:	19.4%	Blue collar:	40.4%
35 to 64:	38.1%	Post-grad study:	9.2%	Sales and service:	22.5%
Over 64:	12.0%				
		Military		Govt. workers:	15.6%
		Veterans/active duty:	7.0%		

Baton Rouge

Baton Rouge sits on a cultural fault line in Louisiana, the boundary between the French-speaking, Catholic Cajun country and the heavily Baptist region to the north. Historically, it was part of the Florida Parishes, the territory east of the Mississippi River and north of Lake Pontchartrain that

Voter Turnout	
2013 Total Citizen 18+	567,923
2014 House Turnout	258,479
2014 Turnout as % CVAP	45.5%
2012 Turnout as % CVAP	59.7%

was not included in the Louisiana Purchase in 1803. It still belonged to Spain, until the locals rebelled and declared their own Republic of West Florida in 1810. Then it quickly became part of Louisiana and the United States.

Today, Baton Rouge is the center of a metropolitan area of 800,000 people, an increase from 700,000 in 2000. It sits on the east bank of the Mississippi and reaches inland to Livingston Parish. It is the largest inland deep-water port located on the river. This is one of the faster-growing parts of Louisiana and did well in coping with the recession. The Milken Institute Best-Performing Cities report ranked Baton Rouge 21st among the fastest growing cities in the nation in 2014, based on economic growth and its ability to sustain jobs. It has been called the "Creative Capital of the South," because of its success in creating public-private partnerships in high-growth sectors, including a new IBM technology center in downtown. New Orleans was long the state's largest city, but Baton Rouge, with 230,000 people, has grown closer to post-Katrina New Orleans in size. In 2014, its newspaper, *The Advocate*, surpassed the circulation of the *Times Picayune* of New Orleans. In the district are the old Gothic-style capitol, where Huey Long took office, and the 34-story Art Deco capi-

tol, which he built and where he later died at the hands of an assassin in 1935. Also here is Louisiana State University, another Long legacy. The region benefits from the research productivity of LSU's main campus and the Pennington Biomedical Research Center.

The 6th Congressional District of Louisiana includes the majority of residents in East and West Baton Rouge parishes. Redistricting in 2012 moved Baton Rouge's black

2012 Presidential Vote		
Mitt Romney (R)	228,507	(66%)
Barack Obama (D)	110,430	(32%)
2008 Presidential Vote		
John McCain (R)	224,642	(68%)
Barack Obama (D)	103,383	(31%)
Cook Partisan Voting Index: R+21		

neighborhoods into the New Orleans-based 2nd District, reducing the 6th's black population from 35% to 24%. As a result, the district moved solidly into the GOP camp. The 6th runs south into the bayous and to Thibodaux, which *Smithsonian* magazine ranked as one of the 20 best small towns in the nation to visit in 2015.

Garret Graves (R)

Republican Garret Graves was elected in a December 2014 runoff to take the open 6th District seat. Although the national news media focused on the Democratic candidate, the 87-year-old former governor and ex-federal convict Edwin Edwards, the real battle here was for the Republican nomination. Graves won each round handily.

Graves, a native of Baton Rouge, is an experienced politician and policy wonk. He had been familiar with Washington as a congressional aide and known statewide as Gov. Bobby Jindal's adviser on coastal restoration. He left home for Washington in his early 20s and began his political career as an intern for Democratic then-Sen. John Breaux. After a couple of months, he joined the office of GOP Rep. Billy Tauzin and worked his way up the ladder. He also worked for the House Energy and Commerce Committee, which Tauzin chaired, and later for Louisiana Sen. David Vitter. In 2008, the newly elected Jindal selected Graves to chair the Louisiana Coastal Protection and Restoration Authority and serve as his coastal adviser. Graves earned praise for a $50 billion, 50-year master plan to promote coastal restoration and improve hurricane protection, as well as for coordinating the state's response to the 2010 Deepwater Horizon oil spill in the Gulf of Mexico. He was Jindal's point man in a Southeast Louisiana Flood Protection Authority-East lawsuit against more than 100 oil and gas companies, which alleged that decades of drilling and extraction had contributed to wetlands destruction. He said that he was responsible for $18 billion in projects to improve the economic, environmental and community resilience of the state.

After Republican Rep. Bill Cassidy challenged Democratic Sen. Mary Landrieu, Graves stepped down from his state job and dove into the open-seat contest. In the all-party primary, he faced 11 other candidates, including eight Republicans. His best-known opponent was Democrat Edwin Edwards, who had been governor for 16 years and served eight years in federal prison on corruption charges. In the first round of voting in November, Edwards took 30% of the vote and Graves had 27%. Running third was Paul Dietzel II, with 14%.

Edwards, whose colorful past exploits vastly increased national attention to the contest though he had been out of public office since 1996, became increasingly combative as the election drew near. He ran as a self-described New Deal Democrat and "old relic" who unabashedly favored government spending to help the district. Graves, for his part, repeatedly voiced surprise at the voters' selection of his runoff opponent. "This was the guy that was a legend or a folklore when I was a kid," he told National Public Radio. "And the fact that he's still around and we were just standing here debating him is really just a surreal experience."

At a final debate before the runoff, Graves mockingly said that he hadn't done anything "illegal, immoral, or unethical." He supported free-market principles and reduced government, and called for a halt to welfare in favor of incentivized hard work. "Our future is bright here. But we've got to get the federal government out of the way." He worked to convince voters that his familiarity with Washington would be a benefit but that he was not a "Washington insider." He outspent Edwards, $1.5 million to $400,000. A major factor was that the district is overwhelmingly Republican. In 2012, 66% voted for presidential candidate Mitt Romney. No surprise, Graves won 62%-38%. In East Baton Rouge Parish, which cast nearly one-half of the vote, Graves took 59%. Edwards won three small rural parishes. Following the election, Edwards said that his next project would be a coffee-table photo book of his public life.

Even before he was formally elected, House Republican leaders assigned seats to Graves on the Natural Resources, and Transportation and Infrastructure committees, both of which are important to his district. He became vice chairman of the Water Resources and Environment Subcommittee. He brought to his new job unusually broad experience in dealing with energy and environmental issues, especially in a state at the center of many of those conflicts. His willingness to address climate change and its potential problems could make him an influential player among House Republicans. "We have measured sea rise in south Louisiana. For us to stick our heads in the sand and pretend it's not happening is idiotic, and it puts the lives of 2 million people who live in south Louisiana in jeopardy," he told *Bloomberg News* following his election. Later, he criticized the Obama administration for not issuing enough leases for oil and gas drilling in the Gulf of Mexico.

At 42, when he took office, Graves had the potential for a long and productive career in Congress.

★ MAINE ★

The phrase "up in Maine" conveys some of the state's distinctive personality—ornery, contrary-minded, almost bullheaded, and rough-hewn. In the far northeast corner of the United States, Maine is the state geographically closest to Europe, but it was not heavily settled until the mid-19th century, by people from the South and the West—not the usual direction of American migrations. Maine grew in a rush, and then mostly stopped. There were 600,000 people there in 1860, but the population dipped after the Civil War—many soldiers did not return—and it did not top 1 million until the 1970s. In the urbanizing and rapidly changing country of the early 20th century, Maine was famous for its pointed firs and steady habits, with a few dozen small factory towns and paper-mill towns but nothing like a major metropolis.

Over the past 30 years, Maine has lost jobs in shoe manufacturing, chicken processing, papermaking, leather processing, and timber, but gained them in tourism, call centers and health care to serve its aging population. The Grand Banks have been overfished and fishing seasons shortened, but the lobster industry has been thriving with the harvest rising from 39 million in 1994 to 124 million in 2014. That year, according to the Maine Department of Marine Resources, the value of the crop was more than $450 million. And prices are up, in part because of the high demand for Maine lobsters in China where a growing middle class views the crustacean as a dining status symbol. But there are signs that the state's signature product could be facing difficult times: The waters in the Gulf of Maine are heating up faster than almost any other part of the world's oceans. Species that have been the staple of commercial fishing, like cod, herring and northern shrimp, are leaving for colder waters. And a study of multiple locations in the gulf by researchers at the Department of Marine Resources found that the population of young lobsters has declined by 50 percent from 2007 levels. Young lobsters can be quite sensitive to changes in temperature and take about eight years to reach the legal size for harvest. The researchers attributed the decline to warmer ocean temperatures, pollution and other changes in atmospheric conditions, not overfishing. Scratching small Maine boiling potatoes out of the soil of Aroostook County has gotten harder, although high schools in northern Maine still shut down at the end of September for "harvest break" for a couple of weeks so farmers can pull their dwindling crop from the ground before it freezes. The nation's top potato producer 50 years ago, Maine sat in ninth place in 2013. Tourism continues to be the biggest business. And though it has a long-term contract to build 21 *Arleigh Burke* Class Naval destroyers, Bath Iron Works, once the state's largest private employer, now trails Hannaford supermarkets, Walmart, L.L. Bean and Maine Medical Center.

Despite the Yankee work ethic of its citizens, Maine has repeatedly found itself at the bottom of various assessments of business climates in the states. In 2014, Maine was ranked No. 49 on the *Forbes* "Best States for Business" list, which was up from dead last, where the state had been ranked for the previous four years. Part of the negative critiques stem from the state's archaic tax code and relatively high corporate tax rates, but a bigger challenge the state is facing is a demographic one—it's old. Maine is like Western Europe, with an aging population that's probably closer to the neighboring Canadian territory of New Brunswick than the rest of the United States. The Census reported that in 2013, Maine's population had the highest median age—43.9 years—of any state in the country. It was tied with Vermont for having the lowest percentage of total population under age 5—4.9 percent—indicating that the state had relatively few young families who were growing "up in Maine." From 2013 to 2014, the Census estimates that Maine's overall population grew a paltry 0.1 percent, among the lowest rates in the nation. Although that was an improvement over previous years, when the state's population actually declined, businesses aren't likely to expand or locate in Maine if they don't think there will be a growing number of customers for their products and services. Likewise, employers will have more difficulty finding and attracting employees if the pool of working age people is stagnant or actually shrinks.

Maine's innkeepers and restaurant owners survived a scare in early 2015, when the U.S. Department of Labor briefly stopped issuing temporary work permits known as H-2B visas because of a court case. As a result, the federal government couldn't process applications from businesses looking to hire foreign workers for seasonal jobs. Because there aren't enough local workers to meet the increased need for waiters, waitresses, cooks and

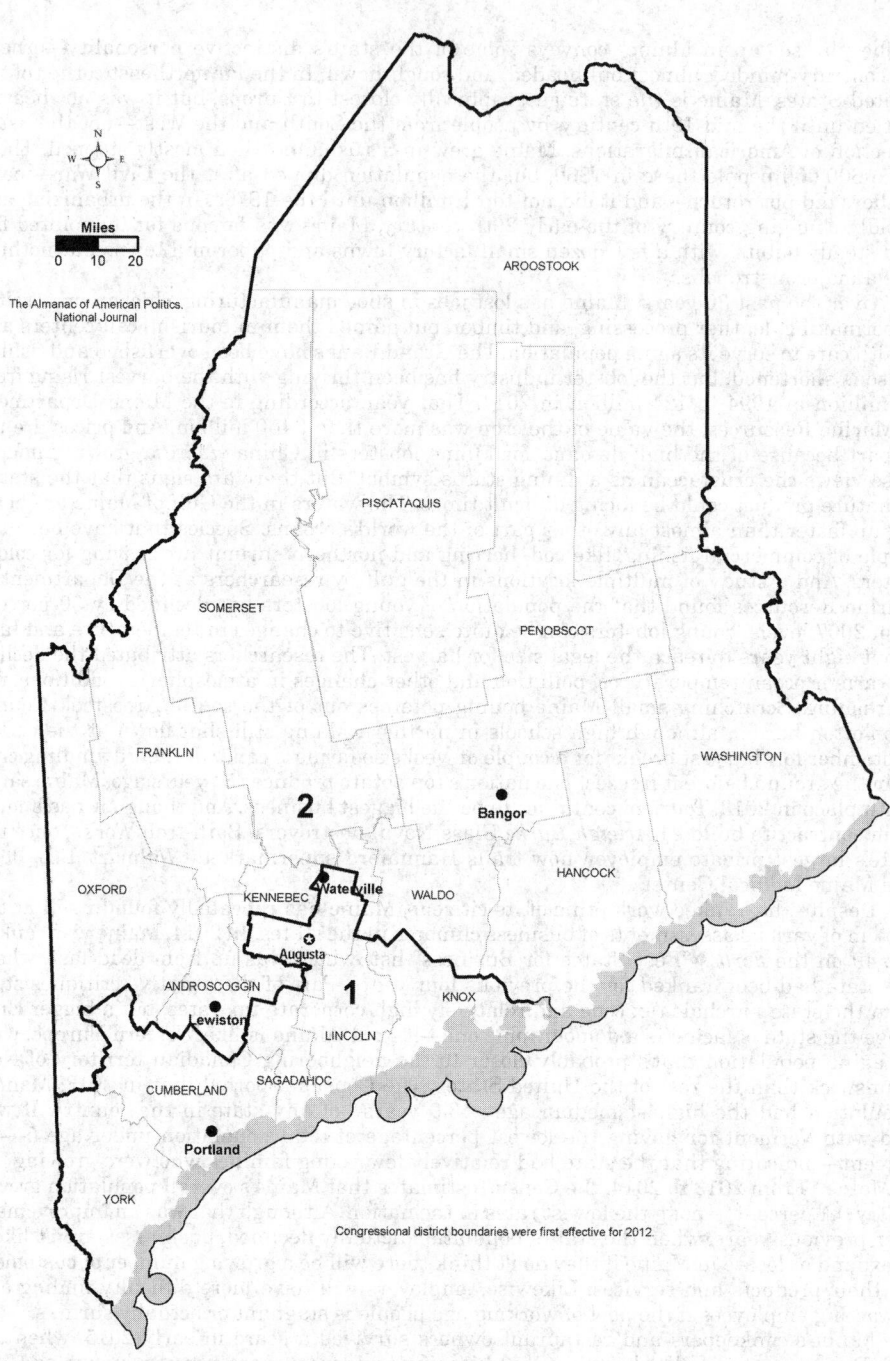

The Almanac of American Politics.
National Journal

Congressional district boundaries were first effective for 2012.

housecleaning personnel during the summer tourist season, Maine business owners typically hire 1,000 to 1,300 temporary seasonal workers each year under the H-2B program. Overall, the U.S. Bureau of Economic Analysis found that Maine's total economic output was almost flat from 2013 to 2014, rising an estimated 0.2 percent, well behind the growth rates for the nation (2.2 percent) and New England (1.6 percent) during that same period. What growth there was came primarily from an increase in output in the health care, social assistance and management sectors. In effect, there are two Maines—moderately humming coastal Maine and declining interior Maine, one symbolized by the lobster and the other by the moose.

In politics, Maine is contrary. Until 1958, it held state elections in September, a date originally chosen because it followed the state's early harvest. Starting in 1840, long before the advent of public opinion polls, the election results were taken as a gauge of national sentiment—hence the saying, "As Maine goes, so goes the nation." Actually, Maine didn't vote like the rest of the country most of the time. In September 1936, Maine voted 56% for a Republican for governor (Lewis Barrows), but in November, only Maine and Vermont voted for Republican Alf Landon over Democrat Franklin D. Roosevelt, prompting Roosevelt's campaign manager to observe, "As Maine goes, so goes Vermont." Maine was known for its flinty Yankee Republicanism and for Prohibition; it banned liquor in 1851, after which other states enacted "Maine laws." Since voting four times against FDR, it has voted for the loser in the close presidential elections of 1948, 1960, 1968, 1976, 2000, and 2004—a record equaled by no other state. Maine cast the nation's highest percentages for third-party presidential candidate Ross Perot—30% in 1992 and 14% in 1996. In 1974, it elected independent James Longley, a former Republican, as governor; in 1994 and 1998, it elected independent Angus King, a former Democrat, as governor. In 2010, it came close to electing as governor independent Eliot Cutler, who might have won except that early voting allowed many ballots to be cast before it was apparent that support for the Democratic nominee was plummeting. The beneficiary was Republican Paul LePage, who eked out a victory with 38% to Cutler's 36%. In the past ten gubernatorial elections, Maine voted four times for Republicans, four times for Democrats, and twice for independents. In 2012, after Sen. Olympia Snowe retired, King ran for the Senate as an independent. Local and national Democrats, mindful of how LePage won in a split contest, effectively abandoned the Democratic nominee and King beat Republican Charlie Summers by a 53%-31% margin. As expected, in the Senate, King caucused with the Democrats.

In state politics, Maine has been a muddle. In 2009, the legislature approved by solid margins a bill sanctioning same-sex marriage. But opponents put the issue on the November 2009 ballot where, despite favorable poll results, the same-sex marriage law was rejected 53%-47%. Counties on the coast supported same-sex marriage 53%-47%; those in the interior opposed it 61%-39%. In 2012, advocates put it on the November ballot, and this time, Maine voters approved same-sex marriage by 53%-47%. It won 59%-41% in the coastal counties and lost by only 55%-45% in interior counties. Higher turnout in the presidential year may have made a difference, but this shift towards gay marriage is in line with national attitudes. In 2010, in addition to Republican LePage's victory as governor, Republicans gained majorities in both houses of the legislature. Two years later, Democrats

Population		Race and Ethnicity		Income	
Total:	1,328,302	White	94.3%	Median income:	$50,121
Urban:	15.4%	Latino	1.3%		(33 of 50)
Suburban:	35.3%	Asian	1.0%	Under $50,000	52.6%
Rural:	49.3%	Black	1.0%	$50,000-$99,999:	31.0%
Land area:	30,843	Two races	1.8%	$100,000-$199,999:	13.4%
Pop/sq. mi.:	43.1	White Ethnic	53.6%	$200,000 or more:	3.0%
Born in state:	63.7%			Poverty Rate	12.6%
		Education			
Age Groups		H.S. grad or less:	42.0%	**Work**	
Under 18:	19.6%	Some college:	29.8%	White collar:	34.6%
18 to 34:	19.9%	College degree, 4 yr.:	18.1%	Blue collar:	42.5%
35 to 64:	42.7%	Post-grad study:	10.1%	Sales and service:	22.9%
Over 64:	17.8%				
		Military		Govt. workers:	14.1%
		Veterans/active duty:	11.0%		

recaptured majorities in both houses. When
LePage was reelected in 2014, Republicans
regained control of the state Senate, but not
the House. Maine has more partisan turnover
in its legislature than just about any other
state. It has small legislative districts—the
average population of a state House district is
8,800. Mainers apparently often vote for the
person, not the party. Vestiges of Maine's eth-

Voter Turnout	
2013 Total Citizen 18+	1,050,835
2014 Highest Statewide Turnout	611,255
2014 Turnout as % CVAP	58.2%
2012 Turnout as % CVAP	68.3%
Legislature	
Senate:	20R 15D
House:	79D 68R 4I

nic divides remain: Protestants have voted more Republican than Catholics in the last three
presidential elections.

Presidential Politics   From 1972 to 1988,
Republicans carried Maine in presidential
elections. Since 1992, Maine has voted for
a Democratic presidential candidate six
straight times. In 2000, Republican George
W. Bush, despite his family's Kennebunkport
summer home, lost 49%-44% to Democrat
Al Gore. In 2004, John Kerry beat Bush
54%-45%. Maine is one of two states
(Nebraska is the other) that gives two electors to the statewide winner and one elector
to the winner in each congressional district.
That earned it campaign visits from GOP

2012 Presidential Vote		
Barack Obama (D) 401,306		(56%)
Mitt Romney (R).................292,276		(41%)
2012 Presidential Caucus		
Mitt Romney (R)....................2,373		(38%)
Ron Paul (R) 2,258		(36%)
Rick Santorum (R) 1,136		(18%)
Newt Gingrich (R) 405		(6%)
2008 Presidential Vote		
Barack Obama (D) 421,923		(58%)
John McCain (R).................295,273		(40%)

vice presidential nominee Sarah Palin in 2008, but Democrat Barack Obama's lead widened
even while Palin was on the stump, and John McCain lost the more rural 2nd District 55%-
43% and the state 58%-40%. McCain did carry Piscataquis County, deep in the woods, the
only county he carried in New England. In 2012, Maine was not at all a target state. Obama
carried it by the reduced margin of 56%-41%.

Maine held its first-ever presidential primary on March 5, 1996, in an attempt to attract
the candidates' early attention. But the tactic didn't work, and the state abolished its presidential primary for 2004. In 2008, the parties held caucuses on different dates in early February. When Republicans voted on the first three days in February, some 5,000 people turned
out. Republican Sens. Olympia Snowe and Susan Collins endorsed McCain early on, but that
didn't make much difference. Mitt Romney won 52% of the Republican caucus vote, just days
before his campaign was ended by the Super Tuesday results. McCain got 21% and Ron Paul
got 18%. Democrats voted on February 10, when their race was still very much contested.
Gov. John Baldacci endorsed Hillary Clinton, and in the week after Super Tuesday, she campaigned in the mill town of Lewiston and at the University of Maine in Orono, while Obama
campaigned in Bangor. Caucus turnout was only 3,500 people, and Obama won 59%-40%.
Clinton carried Lewiston and three northern counties. Obama was strongest along the coast.
In 2012, Republicans caucused on February 11. This was a heated contest between Romney
and Paul, with a turnout of about 5,800. Romney won 39% of the votes and Paul 36%.

Congressional Districts   Maine has a bipartisan advisory
commission that draws up a redistricting plan, which the legislature and governor can consider, but a state statute has stipu-
lated that redistricting must be approved by a two-thirds vote
in the legislature and delayed until the third year after the cen-

114th Congress Lineup	
1 R	1 D
113th Congress Lineup	
0 R	2 D

sus. In practice, this has not made much difference. Since Maine lost its third congressional
district in the reapportionment following the 1960 census, the lines between the largely
rural northern district and the Portland-based southern district have shifted only slightly.

In March 2011, two citizens brought a lawsuit in federal court arguing that the timetable violated the Constitution since it left in place for one election districts that were not
of equal population. Although the census showed the two districts' populations differed by
only 8,669 people, the court in June ruled for the plaintiffs and ordered a new plan be
adopted by January 2012. The advisory commission met in July and the two political parties submitted plans in August, while Republican Gov. Paul LePage called a special session
of the legislature for late September. The Democrats' plan shifted the lines just a bit. The

Republicans' plan would have moved six of the 16 counties to a different district and placed the two Democratic incumbents in the same district. The advisory commission voted 8-7 to submit the Democratic plan to the legislature. Harsh words were exchanged, amid threats of a lawsuit if the Republican legislators adopted their plan with less than the two-thirds required by state statute. But when the legislature met, it adopted the Democratic plan with only three dissenting votes and LePage signed it into law. Perhaps the Republicans knew what they were doing. In 2014, the 2nd District elected the state's first Republican to the House in 20 years.

Governor

Paul LePage (R)

Elected 2010, term expires Jan. 2019, 2nd term; b. Oct. 9, 1948, Lewiston; Husson U., B.S. 1971, U. of ME, M.B.A. 1975; Catholic; married (Ann); 4 children.

Elected Office: Waterville mayor, 2003-11.

Professional Career: CEO, LePage & Kasevich Consulting, 1983-96; Gen. mgr., Marden's Surplus & Salvage, 1996-2011.

Office: #1 State House Station, Augusta, 04333-0001, 207-287-3531; Fax: 207-287-1034; Website: maine.gov/governor/lepage.

Election Results

2014 general	Paul LePage (R)	294,533	(48%)
	Mike Michaud (D)	265,125	(43%)
	Eliot Cutler (I)	51,518	(8%)
2014 primary	Paul LePage (R)	unopposed	

Prior winning percentage: 2010 (38%)

"Actions speak louder than words," was one of the 2014-reelection slogans of Maine's notoriously blunt-spoken and imprudent Republican Gov. Paul LePage, who began the political year as one of the most vulnerable incumbents in the country. To the astonishment of many pundits, Maine's laconic voters agreed with the slogan and gave their conservative and combative governor a bigger victory than they had four years prior.

LePage has a compelling rags-to-riches story. He was the oldest son of 18 children in a poverty-stricken, dysfunctional family. One night in a crowded dark tenement, he stumbled over the body of his 4-year-old brother, who had fallen and died. After numerous beatings from his alcoholic father, at age 11 LePage ran away and spent two years living on the streets of Lewiston, supporting himself by shining shoes and cleaning horse stables. He slept in hallways, cars, and even a strip joint. "Some of those strippers were like surrogate moms," he told *Forbes* magazine in 2010. When he was 13, two families jointly adopted him, and he earned money hauling boxes and washing dishes. He eventually befriended Peter Snowe, a state legislator who later married future Maine Republican Sen. Olympia Snowe. Peter Snowe persuaded officials at Husson University to let LePage take the SAT test in French after LePage, who had been raised speaking French in Lewiston's "Little Canada," struggled with the verbal section of the test. LePage was admitted and went on to earn a degree in business administration, followed by an MBA from the University of Maine. He worked in forestry and as a consultant before becoming general manager of Marden's Surplus and Salvage, a Maine-based discount store chain, in 1996.

LePage entered politics in 1998, when he ran for the City Council in Waterville, a town of about 15,000 between Augusta and Bangor in the middle of the state. He served two terms, then ran for mayor in 2003 and won. During his gubernatorial race, he boasted that he lowered taxes 13 percent in six years, improved the city's credit rating, and increased its rainy day fund from $1 million to $10 million—all without cutting services and while working with a solidly Democratic council. When he couldn't get Democrats to agree to his ideas, he would make his case to the people through the news media, which earned him the nickname "Front Page LePage."

When LePage entered the 2010 governor's race, he was part of a crowded, seven-candidate Republican field. He cast himself as a solid fiscal and social conservative who agreed with the principles of the Tea Party, which was ascendant in Maine in 2010. He promised to cut every dollar of state spending he considered wasteful and used his life story to illustrate how that approach could succeed in a Democratic-leaning state. "All my life, I've been told what I can't do," he said at the state Republican convention. "They were wrong every single time, and they'll be wrong again in November." He was the surprise winner of the June GOP primary with 37% of the vote, even though he spent less money than all but one other candidate. His victory set up a battle with Democratic state Senate president Libby Mitchell and attorney Eliot Cutler, a former associate director of the Office of Management and Budget under President Jimmy Carter who was running as an independent. Though LePage started out with a lead, his campaign ran into obstacles that stemmed in part from his blunt, take-no-prisoners style. He proposed a five-year limit on welfare benefits and said, "At the end of five years, if you still need welfare, I will personally buy (you) a ticket to Massachusetts so (you) can start over." He also drew criticism when he said at a September forum, "As your governor, you're going to be seeing a lot of me on the front page saying, 'Governor LePage tells [President Barack] Obama to go to hell.' " Cutler picked up several newspaper endorsements, and narrowed LePage's lead, but he ran out of time and LePage eked out a victory, 38%-36%. Mitchell finished a distant third with 19%.

LePage vowed to rectify the state's budget problems, which included a revenue shortfall estimated at $1 billion. Fulfilling a campaign pledge, he unveiled a budget revision that paid down a portion of the state's debt to hospitals. But he continued to show a penchant for controversial remarks. When the NAACP criticized him for declining to take part in Martin Luther King Day events, he said: "Tell them to kiss my butt." In the legislature, LePage enjoyed the luxury of both a Republican-controlled House and Senate. In his first year, he was able to pass a 2011 biennial budget that featured the state's largest-ever tax cut, lowering the top income tax rate from 8.5 percent to 7.95 percent and doubling the estate tax exemption from $1 million to $2 million. He also won legislation overhauling the health insurance market for about 40,000 residents who bought independently or through employers with 50 or fewer workers. The legislation's effect was more widespread, because it imposed a tax on premiums of up to $4 per person per month to help cover people with high medical costs. In 2013 and 2014, LePage vetoed bills the legislature sent him to expand Medicaid; he favored tightening eligibility restrictions, eliminating services, and repealing coverage for thousands of recipients. LePage set a record for vetoes in his first term, 179. He imposed that five-year limit on welfare benefits, and pushed for investigations of fraud and abuse to prevent Maine from being a "destination state" for welfare seekers.

But LePage's pugnaciousness grated on lawmakers. Senate Republicans told him in a closed-door caucus that his bullish style was interfering with legislating. And the *Portland Press Herald* said in an editorial, "The governor has recklessly established a culture of so-called 'straight talk' that more often than not manifests itself in outrageous pronouncements and hurtful wisecracks that leave many Mainers at least shaking their heads and sometimes shaking their fists." As Obama swept all but one of Maine's 16 counties in the 2012 election, state Democrats used LePage and his record as a foil and picked up six seats in the Senate and 15 in the House to regain control of both chambers. Two embarrassed GOP lawmakers were anonymously quoted by the *Press Herald* as saying that at a 2013 GOP fundraiser they attended with LePage, he said Obama "hates white people." LePage denied he made disparaging comments about the president. It seemed as though Mainers might be growing weary of LePage's no-holds-barred approach, and in 2013 polls found a majority disapproved of how the governor was handling his job.

In his reelection campaign, LePage faced two opponents, Democratic Rep. Mike Michaud and independent Cutler. Both Michaud and LePage had similar backgrounds: Franco-Americans who came from working class backgrounds. But after he got into the race, Michaud disclosed in a *Bangor Daily News* article that he was gay. That was not made an issue in the campaign and Michaud stressed his ability to work across the aisle in contrast to the governor's confrontational style. LePage emphasized his first-term tax cuts and efforts to rein in state spending, and largely stayed on that message, asking voters to look at his deeds, not his words. He avoided the kind of verbal lunges he was known for, but right before the election, LePage jumped back into the headlines during the Ebola scare. When a nurse returned to Maine after treating Ebola victims in West Africa and tested negative for the virus, she refused the request of state health officials to remain in her home until the 21-day incubation period for the virus expired. LePage told ABC News that the town where the nurse lived was "scared to death" and state police were stationed outside her home to monitor her movements. State officials sought a court order for a 21-day quarantine, but a Maine judge turned down the request. LePage acquiesced to the ruling, but called it "unfortunate." The voters didn't rebuke LePage for his latest actions and he defeated Michaud, 48%-43%. Cutler won only 8%. LePage carried every Maine county except for two: Cumberland with the state's major metro, Portland, and Knox County, where Rockland is a popular seacoast tourist destination. Neither of these counties is part of Michaud's former northern Maine congressional district where he was for the most part, soundly beaten. An initiative banning bear baiting was also on the ballot and rural Maine voters came out in droves to defeat it, which probably helped LePage.

LePage started off his second term vetoing scores of bills passed by the legislature because it wouldn't agree to his tax code reforms that include a ballot initiative in 2016 to amend the Maine constitution and repeal the state income tax. Winning reelection also did nothing to tame LePage's shoot-from-the-hip style. In a radio address he implied that the state's most famous resident, author Stephen King, had headed off to Florida to avoid paying Maine's state income tax (Florida has no state income tax). King, who owns a winter home in the Sunshine State, denied that allegation and said he and his wife paid $1.3 million in Maine income tax in 2013 and probably a similar amount in 2014. LePage's office amended the governor's remarks, but LePage declined to apologize to King and said the best-selling writer should "just make me the villain of your next book and I won't charge you royalties."

Senior Senator

Susan Collins (R)

Elected 1996, term expires 2021, 4th term; b. Dec. 7, 1952, Caribou; St. Lawrence U., B.A. 1975; Catholic; married (Thomas Daffron).

Professional Career: Legis. aide, U.S. Sen. Bill Cohen, 1975-87, Staff dir., Oversight of Gov. Mgmt. Subcmte., 1981-87; Professional & Financial Regulation Comm., 1987-92; New England regional dir., U.S. Small Business Admin., 1992; ME deputy treas., 1993; Exec. dir., Ctr. for Family Business, Husson Col., 1994-96.

DC Office: 413 DSOB, 20510, 202-224-2523; Fax: 202-224-2693; Website: collins.senate.gov.

State Offices: Augusta, 207-622-8414; Bangor, 207-945-0417; Biddeford, 207-283-1101; Caribou, 207-493-7873; Lewiston, 207-784-6969; Portland, 207-780-3575.

Committees: *Aging (Special)* (Chmn). *Appropriations:* Agriculture, Rural Development, Food and Drug Administration & Related Agencies; Commerce, Justice, Science & Related Agencies; Defense; Energy & Water Development; Military Construction, Veterans Affairs & Related Agencies; Transportation, HUD & Related Agencies (Chmn). *Health, Education, Labor & Pensions:* Primary Health & Retirement Security. *Intelligence (Select).*

Group Ratings

	ADA	ACLU	AFL-CIO	LCV	ITI	COC	HAFA	ACU	CFG	FRC
2014	35%	60%	–	0%	66%	88%	22%	44%	34%	36%
2013	50%	C	56%	69%	C	75%	C	28%	39%	C

National Journal Ratings

	2013 LIB	—	2013 CONS
Economic	44%	—	55%
Social	45%	—	54%
Foreign	44%	—	55%
Composite	45%	—	55%

Key Votes of the 113th Congress

1. Sandy storm spending	Y	5. Student Loan Rates	Y	9. Bipartisan Budget Deal	Y
2. Chuck Hagel Confirmation	N	6. Employee Non-Discrim'n Act	Y	10. Farm Bill Conference Rept.	N
3. Gun Background Checks	Y	7. Senate Vote on Judgeships	Y	11. Unempl. Comp. Extension	Y
4. Immigration Reform	Y	8. Defense Dept. Spending	N	12. Keystone Pipeline	Y

Election Results

2014 general	Susan Collins (R)......................413,505	(68%)	$5,563,101	$1,157,937	$51,797
	Shenna Bellows (D)..................190,254	(32%)	$2,335,587	$180,057	
2014 primary	Susan Collins (R)..................unopposed				

Prior winning percentages: 2008 (61%), 2002 (58%), 1996 (49%)

Susan Collins, Maine's senior senator, is among the last vestiges of a political breed that, until recent decades, inhabited Capitol Hill in significant numbers: the Northeastern moderate Republican. In 2012, with the retirement of her fellow Maine GOP moderate, Olympia Snowe, and the ouster of Scott Brown of Massachusetts, Collins was left very much on her own regionally. The subsequent 2014 election served to underscore her status as one of the few remaining centrists from either party in the Senate nationally. But she has been a pivotal swing vote on numerous issues since her initial election in 1996, and, with seniority, has increasingly emerged as a leading deal-maker and consensus seeker.

At the outset of the administration of President Barack Obama, Collins was among the very few Senate Republicans to back two of his signature initiatives: a $787 billion economic stimulus package and legislation overhauling regulation of the nation's financial markets. By the same token, Collins has generally sided with her fellow Republicans on national security, along with some fiscal matters. This has tended to keep Senate Republican leaders at bay—as has the political reality that Collins' independence has been integral to her winning reelection handily in a state that has tilted increasingly Democratic in recent years.

Notwithstanding her frequent differences with many in today's GOP, Collins insisted in a 2012 interview with *BU Washington News Service* that she "would never be anything but a Republican." Chuckling, she added: "It's in my DNA. It really is. I come from a part of the country where you're expected to apply independent judgment and that's what I've always tried to do." However, Washington gridlock and her increasingly isolated position as a Senate centrist has fueled widespread speculation in Maine that Collins might seek to become the state's first woman governor in 2018 when the incumbent, Paul LePage, is barred from seeking a third term. Collins, who unsuccessfully ran for governor more than two decades ago before winning her Senate seat, has stopped well short of slamming the door on this option. "I can tell you I am not at all focused on my re-election or future campaigns or what I might run for," she told the *Bangor Daily News* in the early spring of 2015. "It's just way too early to be thinking about that."

Collins grew up in Caribou, in potato-growing Aroostook County, about as far northeast as you can get in the United States—and closer to the capitals of the Canadian provinces of New Brunswick and Quebec than to the Maine capital of Augusta. Collins' family has been in the lumber business since 1844 and also has long been involved in politics: Her father was a state senator, her mother was mayor of Caribou and chairwoman of the board of trustees of the University of Maine System. Her introduction to Washington was as a high school senior, when she visited as part of a Senate youth program; in what Collins has termed the "highlight of that week," Sen. Margaret Chase Smith, then the Senate's only woman, spent nearly two hours talking with her in Smith's office. Collins today occupies the Senate seat Smith once held, sitting at desk on the Senate floor that Smith used.

Another role model was Republican William Cohen, her predecessor in the Senate and, before that, her boss for more than a decade. The lesson that both Cohen and Smith imparted to her, Collins said, is "do what you think is right, no matter the consequences." She interned for Cohen during the summer of 1974, when, as a freshman member of the Judiciary Committee, Cohen joined several other Republicans in voting to impeach President Richard Nixon. Upon her graduation from St. Lawrence University a year later, Cohen hired Collins, and she remained on his staff for 12 years. Cohen moved to the Senate in 1978, and Collins spent six years as staff director for the Governmental Affairs Subcommittee on Oversight of Government Management, which Cohen chaired. Two decades later, Collins would find herself chairing the full committee.

After Republicans lost the Senate majority in 1986, Collins returned to Maine to work for GOP Gov. John McKernan and then to serve as regional administrator of the Small Business Administration. In 1994, after winning the Republican nomination for governor, she ran third in a three-way general election contest won by independent Angus King—now her Senate colleague. Two years later, Cohen announced his retirement. There was a precedent in Maine for a third-place gubernatorial finisher to be elected senator: Democrat George Mitchell was similarly humiliated in 1974, and then, after being appointed senator in 1980, won big victories in 1982 and 1988. In the Senate primary, Collins played up her similarities to fellow moderates Cohen and Snowe, while calling for a balanced budget amendment, the presidential line item veto, and term limits. She pledged to serve no more than two terms—broken when she successfully sought a third term in 2008.

Collins was opposed in the general election by former Democratic Gov. Joseph Brennan. He attacked Collins on economic issues and gun control, criticizing Collins for supporting a repeal of the assault weapons ban that had cleared Congress a couple of years earlier. At the time, there were more gun owners per capita in Maine than any state except Alaska, and gun control was anathema in much of the state's rural 2nd Congressional District, where Collins had grown up. But restrictions on firearms were a more popular cause in the state's more densely populated 1st District, which Brennan had represented in Congress. Brennan cut into Collins' lead with his attacks on her gun stance—but she outraised him significantly, and ended up winning, 49%-44%. Years later, in 2013, Collins voted against an assault weapons ban when it was brought before the Senate. But, at the same time, she became one of only four Republicans to break with her party and support a compromise measure to expand background checks on firearms purchases, following the Newtown Connecticut school shooting in which 26 died.

The gun control issue is emblematic of a broader evolution for Collins: While a committed centrist throughout her Senate career, she was at first more conservative than her now-departed Maine colleague, Snowe. But she eventually eclipsed Snowe in the frequency with which she broke with the party. In 2012, their last year in the Senate together, Collins was the second most liberal Republican in the Senate, according to *National Journal*'s annual vote ratings, with Snowe a couple of points behind in fourth place. Collins' lifetime score from the conservative Club for Growth through 2014 was 37 percent, by far the lowest of any current GOP senator. Collins has utilized her status as a swing vote to win concessions: In 2009, she and a moderate Democrat, Nebraska Sen. Ben Nelson, insisted that the price tag of Obama's stimulus package be reduced from $900 billion to $787 billion before providing votes crucial to its passage. Collins told *Maine Today*, "I knew that those provisions, that funding, would translate into real jobs for real people in Maine." But Obama's attempts to win Collins' support for the 2010 health care bill proved fruitless despite months of wooing. She expressed disdain for what she saw as a token effort to include a few Republican ideas in a predominantly Democratic-written measure.

Collins has joined the Democrats on other issues, ranging from changes in the tax code to gay rights. In May 2010, she was the only Republican on the Armed Services Committee to vote to repeal the ban on openly gay people in the military. At a news conference a year later, she held up a postcard she received from an anonymous Army soldier thanking her for her vote. "...I felt so strongly it was the right thing to do," Collins said later, adding that getting the policy repealed "was pretty tough, because even though we ultimately got eight Republican votes [on the Senate floor], I was going up against a person I admire greatly"—Arizona Republican Sen. John McCain, whom Collins calls "a friend and a hero." In 2014, Collins became the fourth Republican senator to publicly support same-sex marriage.

During the 2011-12 debate over avoiding the so-called "fiscal cliff" of tax increases and spending cuts that threatened to throw the U.S. economy back into recession, Collins also found herself at odds with fellow Republicans: She supported a surtax on millionaires to compensate for extending the middle-income tax cuts passed early in the administration of President George W. Bush. "They can afford to pay more to help with our deficit, and that's an area where I differ with many in our party," said Collins, the only Senate Republican to vote in favor of implementing the White House's so-called Buffett rule. Inspired by comments from billionaire Warren Buffett, the proposal called for those taking in $2 million or more annually to pay at least 30 percent in taxes. In earlier legislative battles, Collins advocated reducing the size of the Bush tax cuts and for applying pay-as-you-go rules to tax cuts as well as to spending increases.

Similarly in late 2013, Collins led a group of 14 senators—seven Republicans, six Democrats and King, her Maine colleague and a political independent—in an effort to find a bipartisan solution to a budget crisis that shut down the federal government for 16 days. The crisis was instigated by conservatives in the House, who demanded rollbacks in Obama's health care law in return for their votes on a bill to fund government operations. Collins tried to forge a compromise that called for a two-year delay in the health care law's medical device tax, extended government funding for six months, and raised the debt ceiling through the end of January 2014. But Senate Democrats objected to the continuation of automatic spending cuts that were part of the deal, and it failed to advance.

Nevertheless, Collins' efforts were praised for defusing some of the partisan tension that had prevented movement toward a compromise. Days later, Majority Leader Harry Reid and Minority Leader Mitch McConnell were able to come to an agreement that reopened the government, although it was a fairly limited, short-term measure. Shortly after that, Collins was among the Republicans involved in a bipartisan deal in March 2014 to extend expired long-term unemployment benefits. And a few months later, she threw herself into an unsuccessful attempt to find a compromise over Democratic demands to raise the minimum wage. But she opposed the Democratic calls for it to be set at $10.10 an hour, saying it was "too much and will cost jobs."

Some of Collins' clout comes from her status on the Appropriations Committee, where— thanks to her party's recapturing the Senate majority—she took over the chairmanship of Transportation Housing and Urban Development Subcommittee at the beginning of 2015. Just prior to that, in December 2014, she got a controversial transportation provision attached to a bill funding the government for the balance of the 2015 fiscal year: It eliminated the requirement that truck drivers would have to get two nights' sleep in a row before starting work. Transportation Secretary Anthony Foxx warned the measure would "put lives at risk" because of driver fatigue, but Collins contended the rule "presented some unintended and unanticipated consequences" needing more study.

Before stepping down in 2013 due to internal Senate Republican rules, Collins was for a decade chairwoman or ranking Republican on the Homeland Security and Governmental Affairs Committee, where she had once been a staffer. There, she worked closely with another party outlier, Connecticut Sen. Joe Lieberman, prior to his 2012 retirement. Collins chaired the panel from 2003-2007 until turning the gavel over to Lieberman when the Democrats gained Senate control in the 2006 election. In the wake of 9/11, with Collins in the chair, they collaborated on a reorganization of the intelligence community, creating the Office of the Director of National Intelligence and a new counter-terrorism center. Later, with Lieberman as chairman, they sought to move a cybersecurity bill to allow the Department of Homeland Security to share information on vulnerabilities with private companies. But the measure ran into resistance from some Republicans, who said it gave the department too much control. Their friendship extended to the campaign trail: Collins in 2006 endorsed Lieberman when the latter lost the Connecticut Democratic primary and successfully sought reelection as an independent. Lieberman, while still nominally a Democrat, returned the favor in 2008 when Collins faced a competitive challenge.

In recent years, Collins has been active on energy policy. Teaming with Democrat Maria Cantwell of Washington State, she introduced a "cap-and-dividend" bill at the end of 2009 to address carbon emissions. Companies would buy carbon shares in auctions, passing on costs to consumers, with 75 percent of the fund paid as dividends to citizens and 25 percent devoted to clean energy research and development. They pressed their bill as an alternative to the Democrats' cap-and-trade legislation, to no avail. But, seeking a fourth term in 2014, Collins gained the support of several leading environmental groups, who cited her belief in human-caused climate change and her support of rollbacks in allowable levels of carbon emissions. In 2011, Collins was the only Senate Republican to vote against an amendment that would have barred the EPA from regulating greenhouse gases tied to climate change. While some environmental advocates took issue with several of Collins' other votes, she won reelection with 68 percent of the vote against her underfunded Democratic opponent, Shenna Bellows, a former director of the Maine chapter of the American Civil Liberties Union.

Collins had more formidable opposition in her prior two reelection bids, but won comfortably. In 2002, she was challenged by former state Senate Majority Leader Chellie Pingree, sponsor of the state law allowing government negotiations with pharmaceutical companies as a way of lowering prescription drug costs. Pingree ran ads saying Collins was "siding with the big drug companies." But Collins cited an amendment she sponsored successfully to make prescription drugs cheaper. Collins won with 58 percent of the vote, and, six years later, Pingree was elected to the 1st District House seat vacated by Democrat Tom Allen, who decided to take on Collins in 2008. Allen made the Iraq war a central issue; Collins voted for the 2002 resolution authorizing the war, and later opposed a Democratic attempt to set a timetable for troop withdrawal. The war became a less salient issue as the success of Bush's troop surge strategy became evident. Collins maintained double-digit leads in the polls throughout the campaign and won with 61 percent in the face of a banner year for the Democrats nationwide.

As of mid-2015, Collins had cast more than 5,900 consecutive floor votes, extending a streak dating to her arrival in the Senate more than 18 years earlier. Collins, who once twisted an ankle while racing to a roll call, has said that the streak was inspired by Margaret Chase Smith, who maintained a similar streak for 13 years until surgery forced her to break it. In 2012, Collins married for the first time, at 59. Her husband, government consulting executive Thomas Daffron, then 73, was, like Collins, once a staffer to Cohen, and is also a former chief operating officer of the Baltimore Orioles. The wedding took place in Caribou, and Collins and her husband are said to be spending increasing amounts of time in Maine— fueling speculation among insiders that Collins may be looking to finish her political career in Augusta rather than inside the Beltway.

Junior Senator

Angus King (I)

Elected 2012, term expires 2019, 1st term; b. March 31, 1944, Alexandria, VA; Dartmouth Col., B.A. 1966, U. of VA, J.D. 1969; Episcopalian; married (Mary Herman); 5 children.

Elected Office: ME gov., 1995-2003

Professional Career: Practicing atty., 1969-83, 2003-present; Chief counsel, Sen. William Hathaway, U.S. Senate Subcommittee on Alcoholism & Narcotics, 1972-75; Host, ME Public Television's MaineWatch, 1975-93; V.P., gen. counsel, Swift River/Hafslund, 1983-89; Founder, pres., Northeast Energy Mgmt., 1989-94; Partner, Independence Wind, 2007-12.

DC Office: 133 HSOB, 20510, 202-224-5344; Website: king.senate .gov.

State Offices: Augusta, 207-622-8292; Presque Isle, 207-764-5124; Scarborough, 207-883-1588.

Committees: *Armed Services:* Personnel; Seapower; Strategic Forces. *Budget. Energy & Natural Resources:* Energy; National Parks; Water & Power. *Intelligence (Select). Rules & Administration.*

Group Ratings

	ADA	ACLU	AFL-CIO	LCV	ITI	COC	HAFA	ACU	CFG	FRC
2014	85%	86%	–	80%	100%	63%	0%	4%	0%	0%
2013	85%	C	100%	92%	C	38%	C	13%	4%	C

National Journal Ratings

	2013 LIB	—	2013 CONS
Economic	57%	—	42%
Social	57%	—	41%
Foreign	58%	—	36%
Composite	59%	—	41%

Key Votes of the 113th Congress

1. Sandy storm spending	NV	5. Student Loan Rates	Y	9. Bipartisan Budget Deal	Y
2. Chuck Hagel Confirmation	Y	6. Employee Non-Discrim'n Act	Y	10. Farm Bill Conference Rept.	Y
3. Gun Background Checks	Y	7. Senate Vote on Judgeships	N	11. Unempl. Comp. Extension	Y
4. Immigration Reform	Y	8. Defense Dept. Spending	Y	12. Keystone Pipeline	N

Election Results

2012 general	Angus King (I)	370,580	(53%)	$2,850,780	$1,314,443	$3,354,401
	Charles Summers (R)	215,399	(31%)	$1,225,838	$345,360	$1,778,522
	Cynthia Ann Dill (D)	92,900	(13%)	$190,528	$204,806	$186,434

Prior winning percentages: Governor: 1998 (59%), 1994 (35%)

Residents of this state in the nation's Northeast tip, with its rocky and sometimes remote terrain, have often demonstrated an independent streak—and, when it comes to politics, Angus King, Maine's junior senator, is Exhibit No. 1. Originally a Democrat, King came to believe that "sometimes the best thing the government can do is get out of the way;" he entered the 1994 governor's race as an independent, attacking government meddling in business. After serving two terms as Maine's chief executive, King left politics for a decade, only to emerge as a candidate for an open Senate seat in 2012, decrying the legislative gridlock in Congress. He again ran as independent, refusing to say during the campaign with which party he would caucus if elected. When he won the seat, King announced he would join the Senate Democratic caucus, a choice that did not surprise those who had watched his political progression in recent years. He proceeded to vote consistently with the Democrats in the first years of his Senate term.

However, in the spring of 2014, with the Republicans given a good chance of retaking the Senate majority in that fall's election, King created a stir when he said he might be willing to caucus with the GOP if he felt the interests of his constituents would be served. But, when the Republicans regained Senate control, King announced the day after the election that he would remain aligned with the Democrats. (Independents are compelled to join one of the two caucuses to secure seats on Senate committees.) "I think it is in Maine's interest to have a senator in each camp," King said, alluding to his senior colleague, Republican Susan Collins. "The reality of the current Senate, whether it is controlled by Democrats or Republicans, is that nothing can or will happen without bipartisan support."

King was raised in the Washington, D.C. suburb of Alexandria Virginia but has spent most of his adult life "Down East." After attending Dartmouth College and the University of Virginia law school, he moved to Maine to work for a legal assistance organization and then became an aide to Maine Sen. William Hathaway, a Democrat. When King was 29, physicians discovered he had cancer during a routine checkup, which he said he would not have scheduled if it weren't free through his insurance. Years later, as a senator, he reacted angrily to a report that opponents of the Obama administration's health insurance overhaul were urging college students not to sign up under the Affordable Care Act, suggesting those dispensing such advice were "guilty of murder." King told the *Bangor Daily News:* "I think the reason I feel so strongly about this is that if someone had given me that advice when I was 25, I wouldn't be here. I'd be dead."

After leaving Hathaway's office, King returned to Maine to practice law and start an energy conservation business. He sold the latter for $20 million in 1994, just prior to running for governor—a race in which he invested $750,000 of his own money. For 18 years, he had hosted Maine Public Television's *MaineWatch*, making him a well-known figure in the state. King ran a campaign in which he criticized high taxes and called for specific spending cuts; on Election Day, he edged out former Democratic Gov. Joseph Brennan, 35%-34%. Running a distant third was the Republican nominee, now-Sen. Collins.

As governor, King cut the state budget and workforce. He shortened environmental permit delays from nine months to 45 days, helping to attract employers like National Semiconductor, and opposed the ban on timber clear-cutting. But he signed a bill imposing tight controls on paper mills' dioxin discharges into rivers—celebrating afterward by jumping fully clothed into the Kennebec River. In 1998, with a soaring job approval rating, King won a second term with 59 percent. He then signed legislation to have the state leverage its buying clout to negotiate lower prices for prescription drugs for those without Medicaid or private health insurance. The law was overturned by a federal judge in 2000, but the state won on appeal. Perhaps his best known initiative was to provide middle school students with laptop computers—then a precedent-setting idea. He convinced the legislature to provide $30 million for the effort.

Barred by law from seeking a third term in 2002, there was speculation about King running for Senate, but he opted to leave politics. His first move after departing the governorship was to embark on a six-month, 15,000-mile road trip through 33 states, as he, his wife and two children lived in a 40-foot recreational vehicle. It produced a book: *Governor's Travels: How I Left Politics, Learned to Back Up a Bus, and Found America.* Later, King lectured at a couple of the state's colleges, worked for a law firm and a mergers-and-acquisitions advisory firm, and formed a wind energy company.

King's reentry into politics, at the age of 68, was almost by accident: Republican Olympia Snowe had been raising money and was expected to seek a fourth term. But, in February 2012, Snowe, a leading Senate moderate, announced her retirement, expressing fatigue over a partisan climate that made passing legislation increasingly daunting. King stepped in, vowing to continue where Snowe had left off. "I can be a broker for common sense. I can speak from the middle," he declared in announcing for the seat. His campaign headquarters prominently featured two photographs side by side: one of Ronald Reagan and the other of Robert Kennedy. "My desire is to be as independent as I can be, as long as I can be, subject to being effective," King told *The Washington Post*. "I'm not going just for symbolism. I want to do something."

However, the widespread speculation was that King was aligned with Democrats, having revealed he would support President Barack Obama for reelection. He also had backed Obama in 2008 and Democratic presidential nominee John Kerry in 2004, although he endorsed the Republican nominee, George W. Bush, while governor in 2000. National Democrats did little to support their official nominee in the Senate contest, state Sen. Cynthia Dill, figuring that King—who started the race a heavy favorite—would win and end up in their camp. A super PAC with Republican ties ran ads to boost Dill, hoping to siphon enough Democratic votes from King to allow the Republican nominee, Maine Secretary of State Charlie Summers, to win a plurality. The conservative nonprofit Crossroads GPS ran ads blasting King's support of tax hikes as governor, and the National Republican Senatorial Committee broadcast an ad accusing King of using political connections to win a "sketchy" federal loan guarantee for his wind energy firm—of which he had divested himself before the election—to build an industrial wind farm. While the ad barrage caused some tightening in the polls, King won handily on Election Day with 53 percent, to 31 percent for Summers and Dill at 13 percent.

Upon his decision to join the Democratic caucus, King was given a seat on the Armed Services Committee, important to Maine given the economic impact of the Portsmouth Naval Shipyard and the Bath Iron Works in the southern part of the state. And, notwithstanding his election as a political independent, King voted with a majority of Senate Democrats 94 percent of the time in 2013-2014, according to a *Washington Post* congressional voting database. In response, King has argued that it was not him, but rather the political landscape, that had shifted since his days in the statehouse. "I've agreed more with the Democrats in part because the Republican Party has moved so far to the right," King said during an interview in late 2013 with *BU Washington News Service*. "When I was an independent in Maine 20 years ago as governor, the Republican Party was a different party."

Others contended that King's floor vote record told only part of the story. "...If you look at who is working behind the scenes trying to find compromise, I think he is much more in that bipartisan school than are most of the Democrats and the Republicans," said Colby College government professor Sandy Maisel. A notable instance of King parting company with Democrats came when he helped to craft a Republican-backed student loan deal approved in August 2013. The plan linked loan rates more closely to the financial markets, which a number of Democrats contended could create larger long-term financial burdens for borrowers. King was also an active participant in a bipartisan group of 14 Republicans and Democrats that Collins brought together in October 2013 in an effort to end the government shutdown. In 2014, around the time he was suggesting he might switch to the Republican caucus, King joined the Republicans in voting to block one of the Democrats' showcase bills, the Paycheck Fairness Act—designed to force employers to prove that salary gaps between men and women employees were based on factors other than gender.

Early in his tenure, King hosted a dinner for the Senate's informal former governors' caucus, comprised of former state chief executives now on Capitol Hill, and pledged to continue such gatherings. "I think former governors of both parties are a good place to start to find practical non-partisan solutions. Governors tend to be people that want to get things done, and they're impatient with the process," he said, jokingly adding, "Some have said it could be the former governors' caucus—or the extremely frustrated caucus."

King, who overcame an aggressive form of skin cancer when he was barely 30, disclosed in June 2015 that he had been diagnosed with prostate cancer in its early stages. He said it would not affect his plans to seek reelection in 2018, when he turns 74. Maine Gov. Paul LePage, a Republican, suggested on a Boston radio show in early 2015 that he might challenge King, but the mercurial LePage said a day later he had been joking. LePage, a conservative, won two terms as governor with a plurality due to a split in the opposing vote, and cannot succeed himself in 2018. It is unclear whether GOP Rep. Bruce Poliquin might be interested in a Senate race. But Poliquin, first elected in 2014, would first have to overcome what is expected to be a major Democratic effort to oust him in 2016 from northern Maine's 2nd District. If King, as a member of the Senate Democratic Caucus, were to retire, a short list of possible Democrats for the seat would likely start with former Gov. John Baldacci, now an adviser to a Portland-based law firm, and 1st District Rep. Chellie Pingree, who ran for Senate in 2002 and also considered a Senate bid in 2012 when King first ran. Former Rep. Mike Michaud, who lost narrowly to LePage in 2014, is considered more likely to try again for governor if he seeks office in 2018.

FIRST DISTRICT

Chellie Pingree (D)

Elected 2008, 4th term; b. April 2, 1955, Minneapolis, MN; Col. of the Atlantic, B.A. 1979; Lutheran; married (Donald Sussman); 3 children.

Elected Office: ME Senate, 1992-2000, maj. ldr., 1996-2000.

Professional Career: Farmer, 1977-80; Founder & pres., N. Island Designs Co., 1981-92; Pres. & CEO, Common Cause, 2003-07.

DC Office: 2162 RHOB, 20515, 202-225-6116; Fax: 202-225-5590; Website: pingree.house.gov.

State Offices: Portland, 207-774-5019; Waterville, 207-873-5713.

Committees: *Appropriations:* Agriculture, Rural Development, FDA & Related Agencies; Interior, Environment & Related Agencies.

Group Ratings

	ADA	ACLU	AFL-CIO	LCV	ITI	COC	HAFA	ACU	CFG	FRC
2014	85%	83%	–	94%	60%	36%	17%	8%	11%	0%
2013	100%	C	95%	96%	C	23%	C	17%	18%	C

National Journal Ratings

	2013 LIB	—	2013 CONS
Economic	91%	—	0%
Social	87%	—	70%
Foreign	83%	—	15%
Composite	90%	—	10%

Key Votes of the 113th Congress

1. Sandy storm spending	Y	5. Medical Marijuana	Y	9. Syrian Rebels Training	N
2. Violence Against Women Act	Y	6. Farm Bill	N	10. Keystone pipeline	N
3. Guantanamo Bay Detainees	Y	7. Afghanistan Combat	Y	11. Immigration Exec. Action	N
4. Abortion 20-week ban	N	8. NSA Phone Data Collection	Y	12. Bipartisan budget deal	N

Election Results

2014 general	Chellie Pingree (D) 186,674	(60%)	$381,502	$2,405
	Isaac James Misiuk (R) 94,751	(31%)	$20,788	
	Richard Paul Murphy (I) 27,410	(9%)	$8,759	
2014 primary	Chellie Pingree (D) ....unopposed			

Prior winning percentages: 2012 (65%), 2010 (57%), 2008 (55%)

Population		Race and Ethnicity		Income	
Total:	670,714	White	93.8%	Median income:	$52,680
Urban:	14.0%	Latino	1.6%		*(189 of 435)*
Suburban:	58.8%	Asian	1.3%	Under $50,000	47.5%
Rural:	27.2%	Black	1.3%	$50,000-$99,999:	31.5%
Land area:	3,480	Two races	1.6%	$100,000-$199,999:	16.9%
Pop/sq. mi.:	192.8	White Ethnic	55.3%	$200,000 or more:	4.1%
Born in state:	57.4%			Poverty Rate	12.0%
		Education			
Age Groups		H.S. grad or less:	35.9%	**Work**	
Under 18:	19.4%	Some college:	29.6%	White collar:	38.1%
18 to 34:	20.1%	College degree, 4 yr.:	22.1%	Blue collar:	41.7%
35 to 64:	43.1%	Post-grad study:	12.4%	Sales and service:	20.2%
Over 64:	17.4%			Govt. workers:	13.3%
		Military			
		Veterans/active duty:	10.8%		

Southern Maine: Portland

The 1st District of Maine stretches from southernmost Kittery and nearby Kennebunkport to the craggy-shored, ancestrally Republican counties to the east. The historic center is Portland, Maine's largest city, home to the yuppies and lawyers who have revived and renovated its downtown landmarks. Portland's antique charm, mostly booming economy, and tolerant lifestyle have made it a haven for singles and gays. In 2012, a ballot initiative to legalize gay marriage passed with 53% of the vote. In a November 2013 referendum, Portland voters approved recreational use of marijuana. The more than 100-year-old L.L.Bean is not far away in Freeport. Former farm

Voter Turnout	
2013 Total Citizen 18+	531,627
2014 House Turnout	308,898
2014 Turnout as % CVAP	58.1%
2012 Turnout as % CVAP	71.9%

towns have been transformed into suburbia, and old mill towns like Biddeford and Sanford have been redeveloped.

The area also has a strong defense presence. Various base-closing rounds have spared the Portsmouth Naval Shipyard at Kittery, the nation's oldest continually operating naval shipyard. In December 2014, Portsmouth said that it would hire 715 more civilian workers, which would create a total of more than 5,000. Still, the shipyard's future is always a topic of worried discussion for locals. "Portsmouth's days are probably numbered if there is a rigorous and comprehensive review of bases," defense expert Loren Thompson told the *Kennebec Journal* in 2012. Brunswick Naval Air Station closed in 2011, costing the area more than $200 million in annual wages and military contracts. In 2014, large parts of the area's shopping centers remained vacant, as local officers reviewed options for the 3,200 acres of real estate available for commercial use. The good shipyard news locally was that Bath Iron Works began work on a fifth destroyer that the Navy approved in March 2014.

Portland and several other coastal towns in southern Maine are in the 1st Congressional District. The 1st also takes in several remote islands off the coast, where people enjoy a lifestyle more reminiscent of the Alaska wilderness, shuttling to the mainland on ferries and Cessna aircraft. In the summer, the air traffic includes the families of *Fortune* 500 executives traveling to their estates. In the winter, lobstermen and local business owners board most flights. Lobsters are not just a tradition here but also an economic resource. In 2014, about 5,900 licensed lobstermen in the state hauled in an estimated 120 million pounds, with a recovery from what had been virtually giveaway prices. But local scientists have sounded the alarm that climate change and warmer temperatures in the Gulf of Maine could hurt the lobster population in the future.

2012 Presidential Vote		
Barack Obama (D)	223,040	(59%)
Mitt Romney (R)	143,024	(38%)
2008 Presidential Vote		
Barack Obama (D)	231,351	(61%)
John McCain (R)	141,445	(37%)
Cook Partisan Voting Index:	D+9	

Politically, the 1st District votes very much like the state as a whole: quirkily, often for independents, and splitting tickets with abandon. In 2008, every county voted for Republican Sen. Susan Collins, and all but one voted for Democratic presidential nominee Barack Obama. The 1st remains the more comfortably Democratic district in Maine.

Chellie Pingree (D)

Chellie Pingree, elected in 2008, was the first Democratic woman from Maine elected to Congress, even though the state has a long history of electing women. A blunt-talking liberal, Pingree has maintained her popularity by paying close attention to state issues, from ships to seafood.

Pingree grew up in Minnesota, the granddaughter of Scandinavian immigrants who worked as dairy farmers. Her parents moved to Minneapolis, where her father was an accountant and her mother a nurse. The city's anti-war activism during the Vietnam era had a profound influence on Pingree, and she left high school early for alternative education programs on the East Coast. At one program in Worcester Massachusetts, she met her future husband and followed him to Maine, where they settled on remote North Haven Island in Penobscot Bay. As disciples of the "back to the land" movement, they lived for years in a cabin without running water or electricity and made their living as organic farmers. Although the couple later divorced, Pingree thrived on the island, both politically and professionally. In 1981, she started her own business selling knitting kits. At its peak, the business, the North Island Designs Co., distributed 100,000 mail-order catalogs. She started her political career in local offices on the island, including serving as tax assessor and on the planning and school boards.

In 1991, Pingree attended a speech by then-Rep. Patricia Schroeder of Colorado, who briefly sought the Democratic presidential nomination in 1988, which inspired her to take her friends' advice and run for an open seat in the state Senate. She went door-to-door in the traditionally Republican district in Knox County and won. Pingree rose to majority leader in 1996. As leader, she fought a challenge from pharmaceutical companies and persuaded reluctant players to agree to a law allowing the state to negotiate prescription drug prices, the first such law in the country.

In 2002, Pingree ran unsuccessfully against Sen. Susan Collins, a Republican moderate, who won 58%-42%. Shortly after her loss, she became president of Common Cause, the Washington, D.C., government and campaign watchdog group. She took the reins of the nonprofit organization just as it had been thrust into the national spotlight by the successful push to overhaul the nation's campaign finance laws. That fight was not easy. She recalls an often strained relationship with Sen. John McCain of Arizona, the Republican cosponsor of the law, who accused her of injecting partisanship into her work. As president, Pingree also directed Common Cause to lobby against media consolidation in the hands of a few powerful companies.

She left Common Cause in 2007 to run for the House seat that Democrat Tom Allen gave up to run another sacrificial campaign against Collins. Although she had worked for years to limit the influence of money in politics, Pingree had no trouble raising far more of it than any of her five rivals for the Democratic nomination. She mostly eschewed money from political action committees but enjoyed the backing of EMILY's List, which funds women candidates who support abortion rights. Pingree won the primary with 44% of the vote. In the general election, she had a decisive fundraising advantage, bringing in $2.2 million compared with her Republican opponent, state Sen. Charles Summers, who raised about $645,000. Pingree won 55%-45%.

In the House, Pingree has been a consistently loyal Democrat. In 2013, she was awarded a plum seat on the Appropriations Committee, where she looked after her region's defense interests. She has been successful with the Portsmouth Naval Shipyard that virtually straddles the Maine border, and the Pratt & Whitney plant a few miles away that in March 2014 got a $1 billion contract to manufacture engines for the F-35 fighter jet. In 2012, when an excess supply of lobsters drove down prices precipitously, Pingree contacted cruise ship companies that dock vessels in Maine and successfully urged them to buy thousands of pounds' worth of the crustaceans. She takes a strong interest in environmental issues, helping to form the House Sustainable Energy and Environmental Coalition and introducing a bill to force BP to pay royalties on the oil from its massive spill in the Gulf of Mexico in 2010.

In her 2010 reelection campaign, Pingree's opponent was alternative energy company owner Dean Scontras, who got support from tea party activists. The Maine Republican Party ran ads accusing Pingree of taking trips on the corporate jet of her fiancée, hedge-fund billionaire Donald Sussman. (Pingree and Sussman married in 2011.) Scontras also sought to tie her to liberal House Speaker Nancy Pelosi. The nation's anti-incumbent sentiment helped him close the gap, even with far less money than Pingree. But her familiarity with the voters gave her a 57%-43% win. She has handily won reelection since. She has considered running for both the Senate and governor, and has clashed with Republican Gov. Paul LePage on his call for cuts in the state's Medicaid spending.

In 2012, Sussman, who has been a major donor to Democratic super PACs, bought a controlling interest in two prominent newspapers, the *Portland Press Herald* and the *Kennebec Journal*, in Pingree's district. She said that her husband had no influence over her job. With her wealth, Pingree—with her husband—has become by far the biggest contributor among members of Congress to their colleagues: a total of $3.1 million since she took office, according to the Center for Responsive Politics. Runner-up was Sen. Dianne Feinstein of California, with $1.9 million. Pingree is young enough and the state is unpredictable enough that she still has an opportunity for statewide office.

SECOND DISTRICT

Bruce Poliquin (R)

Elected 2014, 1st term; b. Nov. 1, 1953, Waterville; Harvard U., A.B. 1976; Catholic; widowed; 1 child.

Elected Office: ME Treas., 2011-13.

Professional Career: Bank employee, 1976; Investment consulting firm, 1978; Business owner & manager; Investor company principal, 1981-96.

DC Office: 426 CHOB, 20515, 202-225-6306; Fax: 202-225-2943; Website: poliquin.house.gov.

State Offices: Bangor, 207-942-0583; Lewiston, 207-784-0768; Presque Isle, 207-764-1968.

Committees: *Financial Services:* Capital Markets & Government Sponsored Enterprises; Oversight & Investigations.

Election Results

2014 general	Bruce Poliquin (R)	133,320	(47%)	$1,710,616	$211,469	
	Emily Cain (D)	118,568	(42%)	$1,969,517	$335,188	$8,750
	Blaine Richardson (I)	31,337	(11%)	$7,772		
2014 primary	Bruce Poliquin (R)	19,736	(57%)			
	Kevin Raye	14,987	(43%)			

Population		Race and Ethnicity		Income	
Total:	657,588	White	94.7%	Median income:	$41,499
Urban:	16.7%	Latino	1.1%		*(367 of 435)*
Suburban:	11.3%	Amer. Indian	1.0%	Under $50,000	58.0%
Rural:	71.9%	Asian	0.6%	$50,000-$99,999:	30.4%
Land area:	22,670	Two races	1.9%	$100,000-$199,999:	9.8%
Pop/sq. mi.:	29.0	White Ethnic	50.7%	$200,000 or more:	1.9%
Born in state:	70.2%			Poverty Rate	16.0%
		Education			
Age Groups		H.S. grad or less:	48.3%	**Work**	
Under 18:	19.8%	Some college:	30.0%	White collar:	30.7%
18 to 34:	19.7%	College degree, 4 yr.:	13.9%	Blue collar:	43.3%
35 to 64:	42.4%	Post-grad study:	7.8%	Sales and service:	26.0%
Over 64:	18.1%				
		Military		Govt. workers:	15.1%
		Veterans/active duty:	11.9%		

Northern and Central Maine, Lewiston, Bangor

The 2nd District of Maine is heavily forested, rough-hewn, and enormous. Covering the northern three-quarters of the state, it is larger than the states of New Hampshire, Vermont and Massachusetts combined. The population is not evenly distributed. The district includes the heavily Democratic mill town of Lewiston and also Eastport. At Belfast on Penobscot Bay, art galleries and boutiques have replaced fish-processing plants. There are several different Maines represented here: The bays of coastal Maine, with their small fishing towns; the potato fields of far northern Aroostook County; and the mill towns on the fast-running streams of western Maine. Some valleys have more moose than people. This was one of America's frontiers in the 1850s, when Bangor, on the Penobscot River, was the lumber capital of the world. Today, tiny Bangor is the second-largest city in the district after Lewiston, which was the site a half-century ago of the famous boxing fight in which Muhammad Ali knocked out Sonny Liston for the heavy-weight championship with what many claimed was a "phantom punch."

Voter Turnout	
2013 Total Citizen 18+	519,208
2014 House Turnout	283,473
2014 Turnout as % CVAP	54.6%
2012 Turnout as % CVAP	64.7%

These parts of Maine have had economic troubles, losing 22,000 jobs to neighboring Canada and other foreign markets with the free-trade agreements in the 1990s. Potato production is less than half what it was in 1960. A once-thriving sardine-canning industry ended with the closing of the last cannery in 2010. Logging, long the largest industry in Maine, has suffered job cutbacks as big paper

2012 Presidential Vote		
Barack Obama (D) 178,266	(53%)
Mitt Romney (R).................149,252	(44%)
2008 Presidential Vote		
Barack Obama (D) 190,572	(54%)
John McCain (R).................153,828	(44%)
Cook Partisan Voting Index: D+2		

companies sell off acreage and shut down mills. A movement to set aside yet more acreage in a Maine North Woods National Park, which would be larger than the Yellowstone and Yosemite parks combined, has sparked protests. The proposed park would cover 15 percent of Maine, mostly forests but also including 32,000 miles of rivers and streams. Bumper stickers around the state read: "If you don't like cutting trees, try using plastic toilet paper."

There have been signs of economic life. Washington County's sandy soil plains produce more than 90% of the nation's wild blueberry crop. In the past decade, potato acreage has fluctuated slightly, but yield has increased by 10% and prices have jumped by 40%. Bangor's unemployment rate dropped from 8.5% in early 2011 to 5.1% in early 2015.

Politically, the district is iconoclastic and permanently enamored of neither major political party. The old 2nd was presidential candidate Ross Perot's strongest district in the nation, with 33% in 1992 and 16% in1996. The district leans Democratic, but it is less liberal and more competitive than the neighboring 1st District.

Bruce Poliquin (R)

Republican Bruce Poliquin was elected in 2014 to an open seat that Democrats had controlled for 20 years. His victory, which doubled the number of House Republicans from New England, required the Republican to strike a delicate ideological balance in independent Maine.

Poliquin was born and raised in Waterville and studied at Phillips Exeter Academy and Harvard. After college, he launched a lucrative business career that took him to Chicago and New York, including a stint managing $5 billion in worker pension funds for Bath Iron Works and International Paper, both major Maine employers at the time. He made his first political bid in 2010 when he ran for governor, spending more than $700,000 of his own money. He was trounced in the six-person field but he mended fences with the winner, GOP Gov. Paul LePage, and was elected state treasurer by the Maine Legislature.

Poliquin's tenure hit a few bumps, including criticism that he had used the office for personal gain in his various holdings and properties. In one case, Democrats charged that he had exploited a tax preference program for forested land to reduce his own property taxes. After striking a deal on the land, he was not charged with wrongdoing. But ethics questions lingered. When he ran in 2012 for the Senate seat of retiring Republican Olympia Snowe, he was second in the five-candidate primary to Charles Summers, 28%-22%.

Poliquin saw his next opening in 2013, when Rep. Michael Michaud left his House seat to launch an unsuccessful challenge for governor against LePage. In the primary, he won, 57%-43% over state Sen. Kevin Raye, who had lost two races against Michaud. He faced a strong Democratic challenger in Emily Cain, a 34-year-old rising star who had compiled a long political record, including as state House minority leader, where she had worked across the aisle to cut deals. Despite his positive comments about the tea party during earlier campaigns, Poliquin distanced himself from its supporters. House Speaker John Boehner stumped on Poliquin's behalf in September, tying Cain to President Barack Obama and taking aim at the Affordable Care Act.

The National Republican Congressional Committee spent $1.3 million to help him, while the Democrats' House Majority PAC countered with a $600,000 ad buy tying Poliquin to Wall Street. Poliquin made his case more personal by discussing his wife's tragic death and his life as a single father, which was effective in neutralizing Democratic criticism of him as a Wall Street robber baron. He also benefited from a bear-baiting referendum that energized turnout among gun owners. For her part, Cain played up Poliquin's ties to LePage, who has been a polarizing figure in the state. The Democratic Congressional Campaign Committee spent less than $100,000 for Cain. She slightly outspent Poliquin, but ran into headwinds on two fronts. One was Obama's unpopularity, which dragged down Democrats.

The other was independent Blaine Richardson, a former Republican and self-styled conservative who played outside the partisan lines and drew 11% of voters. Poliquin eked out a plurality, 47%-42%. He was the first Republican to win the seat since Snowe moved to the Senate in 1994.

In the House, Poliquin parlayed his background in banking issues into a seat on the Financial Services Committee. He said that he planned to use the assignment to reduce government red tape and create a better business climate. On the panel's task force on terrorism financing, he said it was imperative to investigate how terrorists were receiving funds to carry out their attacks. In his first speech to the House, he called for a constitutional amendment to balance the budget, a proposal that had received scant attention in recent years. He said that if federal regulators did not act on natural gas pipeline requests within a year, the projects should be automatically approved. "I'm someone who does not sit back and watch things," he told the *Portland Press-Herald*. "I get involved."

Several Democrats were mentioned as potential challenges to Poliquin in 2016, including Cain and Bangor city councilor Joe Baldacci, brother of former Gov. John Baldacci, who earlier represented the 2nd District for eight years.

★ MARYLAND ★

Just south of the Mason-Dixon line and north of the Union-Confederate lines during most of the Civil War (and the scene of its bloodiest battle, Antietam), Maryland is a crossroads state, with both Northern and Southern influences and with both industrial and rural economies. This was the only one of the 13 colonies founded by Roman Catholics—the Calvert family—and its embrace of religious tolerance came less from high-minded ideals than from the Calverts' desire to protect their property from religious attacks. Similarly, although hot-blooded Baltimoreans wanted to secede from the Union in 1861 (the state song, "Maryland, My Maryland," is based on a poem condemning Abraham Lincoln's suppression of pro-Confederate rioters), cooler heads prevailed.

The Puritan impulse was never lively here. Prohibition was enforced only laxly in Baltimore, to the delight of its great journalist-cum-lexicographer H.L. Mencken, who called it Charm City. Slot machines were legal for years in the rural counties of the Eastern Shore, and, after years of controversy and over the pleas of racetrack owners, were legalized statewide in 2007; voters approved table games in 2012. An old state law guaranteeing blacks equal access to public accommodations specifically excluded the Eastern Shore. By not pursuing any one course rigorously, Maryland could be many things at once—Northern as well as Southern, moralistic as well as libertine, citified but also reliant on nature—mostly leaving people to their own devices. Perhaps as a result, much of Maryland's political history reads like a chronicle of rogues. Maryland's genial tolerance may have given it a little too savory a history, but this state cherishes its uniqueness.

The Chesapeake Bay is the nation's largest estuary, with water saltier than a river but fresher than the ocean, and with unique watermen and shellfish. Pollution and years of overharvesting drastically reduced its yield, and the terrapin and Chesapeake oyster are rare today. But an ongoing statewide Save-the-Bay movement is having an impact. The Chesapeake blue crab population was higher in 2012 than in any year since 1993, and the oozing of sediment on the Conowingo Dam that feeds the Bay has lessened. But the state's program to seed oyster beds hasn't revived that population.

Maryland has reason to be proud of the economy, or economies, it has built over the years. During and after World War II, half the state's population lived in the city of Baltimore and only one-fifth in the suburbs. Then—in a pattern documented in Barry Levinson's Baltimore movie trilogy of *Diner*, *Tin Men* and *Avalon*—the proportions reversed, and then some. Now, 11 percent live in Baltimore, and 76 percent in counties classified as suburbs. Population sank from about 1 million in the early 1950s to 623,000 in 2014. With its large suburban population, Maryland is at or near the top of most rankings for median household income. The median income for four-person households is a rather remarkable $106,452, though the high cost of living cuts into that (and leaves Maryland residents with the fourth-highest credit-card debt loads in the nation). The Census Bureau defines Washington-Baltimore as a combined statistical area, the nation's fourth largest, with 8 million people. But Baltimore and Washington are not fraternal twins like Dallas and Fort Worth or Minneapolis and St. Paul; they have different histories, economic bases and attitudes.

Washington is a one-industry, white-collar capital city, dependent on the federal government that kept it economically vibrant while the rest of the country endured recession and a sluggish recovery. The massive National Institutes of Health complex in Bethesda has generated many health-related and biotech jobs in Montgomery County. Baltimore, by contrast, started off as a port and industrial city and managed to stay diversified and largely successful as it spread out into the countryside from its new central core at the Inner Harbor and the solidly built edifices of its downtown streets. It is home of the popular Oriole Park at Camden Yards (the first of the new-old ballparks of the 1990s) and to Johns Hopkins University, with its Georgian buildings along the affluent corridor that runs directly north from downtown all the way to the developing edge city of Hunt Valley.

Nearly half of Marylanders live in the Baltimore metropolitan area, and its influence is far greater than Washington's on the Eastern Shore and in western Maryland. For years, most of Maryland's successful statewide politicians came from Baltimore, including two mayors who won the governorship, William Donald Schaefer and Martin O'Malley. For three decades, Maryland's senators have lived in Baltimore and commuted to Washington. Baltimore has a long Democratic tradition and most of its voters are registered Democrats.

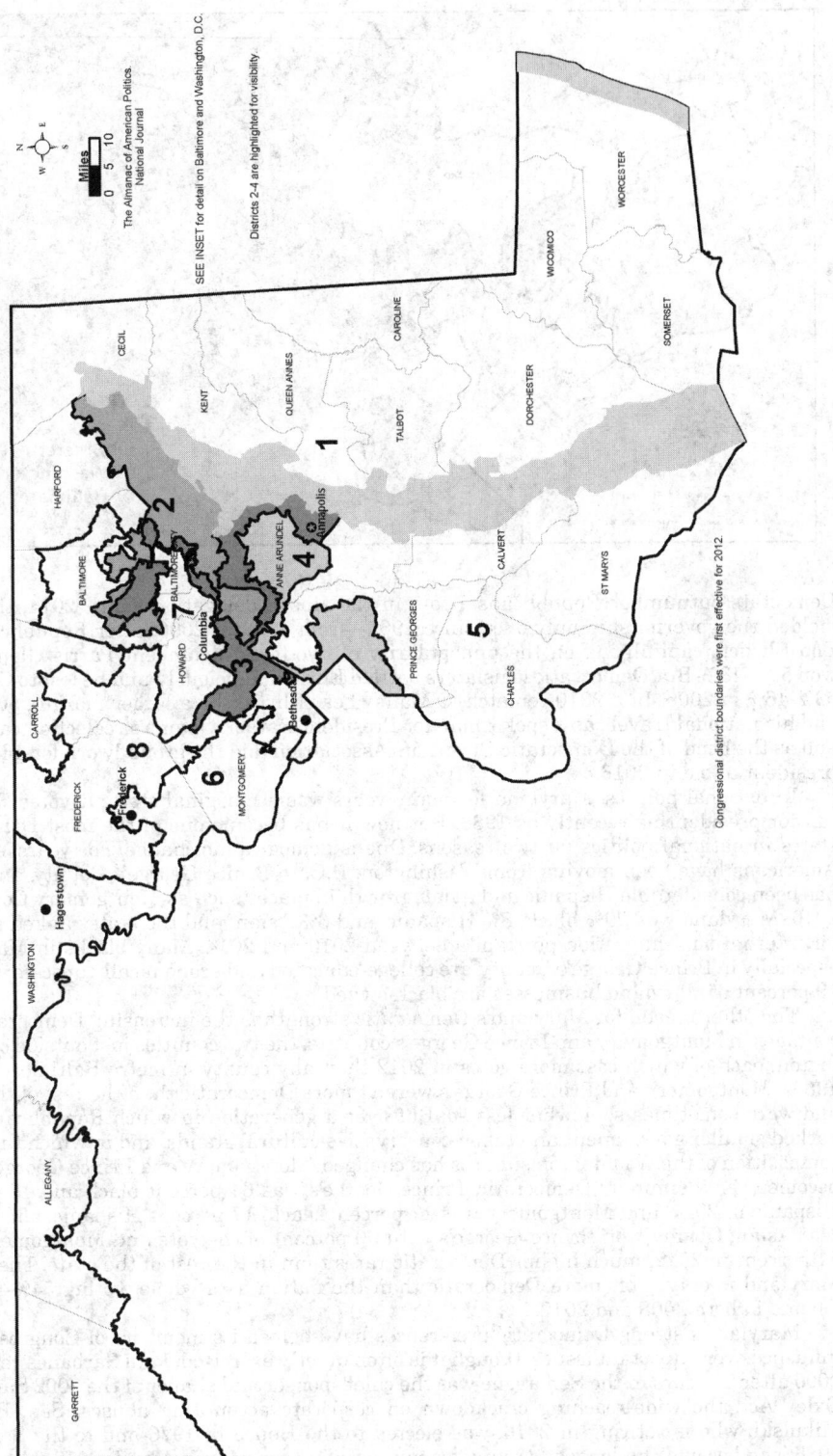

The Almanac of American Politics.
National Journal

SEE INSET for detail on Baltimore and Washington, D.C.

Districts 2-4 are highlighted for visibility

Congressional district boundaries were first effective for 2012.

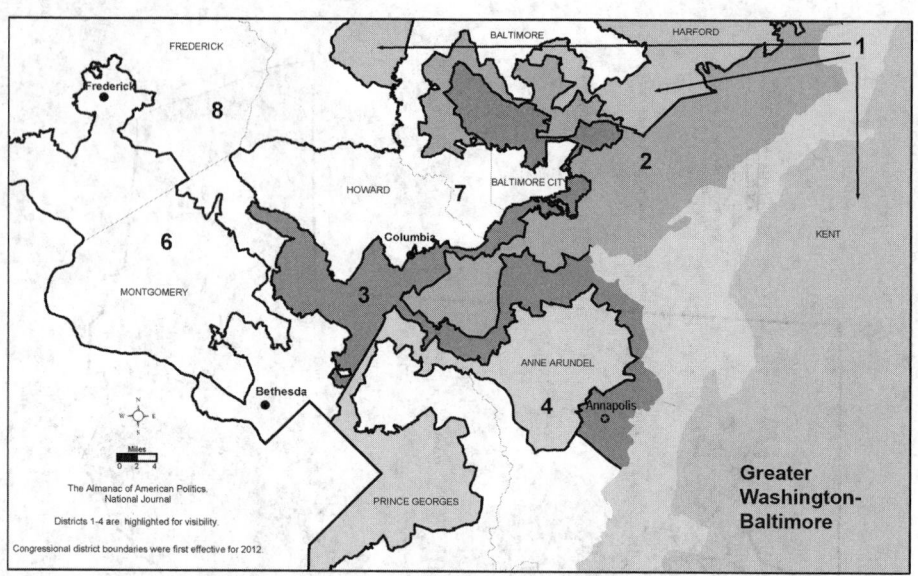

Democrats outnumber Republicans 7-to-1 in the House delegation. Until 2014, they had yielded the governorship only once since 1966—from 2002 to 2006, after Republican Rep. Bob Ehrlich, capitalizing on the unpopularity of two-term incumbent Parris Glendening, won 52%-48%. But Democratic legislators battled Ehrlich ferociously, and he lost to O'Malley 53%-46% in 2006. In a 2010 rematch, O'Malley beat Ehrlich by a larger margin, 56%-42%, and his national travels as a spokesman for President Barack Obama's reelection campaign and as the head of the Democratic Governors Association laid the groundwork for a longshot presidential bid in 2016.

In national politics, Maryland for many years was a marginal state. It voted Republican for president as recently as 1988. But now it has become one of the most Democratic states in national politics for two reasons. One is demographic change. For years, African-Americans have been moving from Washington, D.C. to Prince George's County, and there has been considerable Hispanic and Asian growth in places such as Montgomery County. In 2010, Maryland was 29% black, 8% Hispanic, and 6% Asian, and the state ranked seventh for international migration per capita between 2010 and 2014. Many blacks in Maryland, especially in Prince George's County, are college-educated and economically upscale; roughly 19 percent of Maryland businesses are black-owned.

The other reason for Maryland's Democratic strength is the increasing Democratic percentages in Montgomery and Prince George's counties, the two counties just outside of Washington, each of which cast more votes in 2012 than any county in metro Baltimore. In the 1980s, Montgomery and Prince George's weren't more Democratic than the rest of the state and were sometimes somewhat less so. But over a generation in which Republicans have backed smaller government and taken conservative cultural stands, and in which the racial composition of the Washington suburbs has changed, Montgomery and Prince George's have become overwhelmingly Democratic. Prince George's was 64 percent black and 15 percent Hispanic in 2010, and Montgomery was 17 percent black, 17 percent Hispanic, and 14 percent Asian; Obama won Prince George's with 90 percent of the vote and Montgomery with 71 percent in 2012, much higher Democratic rates than in the rest of the state. The rest of Maryland is only a bit more Democratic than the nation as a whole, voting 54%-44% for Obama in both 2008 and 2012.

Maryland's strong Democratic preferences have helped its members of Congress wield influence over important issues, though it is often quietly exercised. Paul Sarbanes retired in 2006 after 30 years in the Senate; he was the chief sponsor and shaper of the 2002 Sarbanes-Oxley Act, the wide-reaching crackdown on corporate accounting abuses. Sen. Barbara Mikulski, who is retiring in 2016, was elected to the House in 1976 and to the Senate in 1986; she became the longest-serving woman ever in Congress in March 2012. Maryland's

Population		Race and Ethnicity		Income	
Total:	5,928,814	White	54.2%	Median income:	$65,262
Urban:	30.7%	Black	29.1%		*(4 of 50)*
Suburban:	65.1%	Latino	8.4%	Under $50,000	33.9%
Rural:	4.2%	Asian	5.6%	$50,000-$99,999:	31.0%
Land area:	9,707	Two races	2.1%	$100,000-$199,999:	26.2%
Pop/sq. mi.:	610.8	White Ethnic	25.0%	$200,000 or more:	8.9%
Born in state:	47.6%			Poverty Rate	9.7%
		Education			
Age Groups		H.S. grad or less:	36.5%	**Work**	
Under 18:	22.7%	Some college:	26.1%	White collar:	44.5%
18 to 34:	23.3%	College degree, 4 yr.:	20.3%	Blue collar:	40.1%
35 to 64:	40.6%	Post-grad study:	17.1%	Sales and service:	15.4%
Over 64:	13.4%				
		Military		Govt. workers:	22.2%
		Veterans/active duty:	9.0%		

other senator, Ben Cardin, served 20 years in the House before winning a Senate seat. Meanwhile, two of Maryland's House members are influential in the Democratic leadership. One is Steny Hoyer, the former House majority leader and now the minority whip. (Hoyer's chief competition in moving up the ladder has been San Francisco's Nancy Pelosi, whose father, Thomas D'Alesandro, was a congressman and mayor of

Voter Turnout	
2013 Total Citizen 18+	4,204,096
2014 Highest Statewide Turnout	1,733,177
2014 Turnout as % CVAP	41.2%
2012 Turnout as % CVAP	65.4%
Legislature	
Senate:	33D 14R
House:	91D 50R

Baltimore. The two rivals once served together as interns in the office of Sen. Daniel Brewster of Maryland.) The other House leader from Maryland is Chris Van Hollen, who headed the House Democrats' campaign committee in 2008 and 2010, and became the ranking minority member on the Budget Committee in 2011. He is one of several Democrats seeking to succeed Mikulski in a free-for-all primary.

In 2012, Maryland voters approved a Democratic engineered congressional redistricting map—criticized by good-government advocates as one of the nation's most convoluted—as well as in-state college tuition for children of illegal immigrants. They also approved ballot measures in favor of same-sex marriage and for allowing table games in Maryland casinos. Both passed 52%-48%, though with different coalitions. Casino gambling won in metro Washington and western Maryland and lost in metro Baltimore and on the Eastern Shore. Montgomery County voted 66 percent for same-sex marriage, Prince George's 50.4 percent against it. Metro Baltimore voted 53 percent for same-sex marriage, the Eastern Shore and western Maryland 58 percent and 56 percent against it, respectively.

In 2014, though, voters fired a warning shot at Democratic complacency. In the gubernatorial primary, Democrats had to choose from several flawed candidates, including Lt. Gov. Anthony Brown, whose portfolio included overseeing a botched state health-insurance exchange under the Affordable Care Act; Attorney General Doug Gansler, who attracted negative notice for allegedly pressuring state troopers to drive him in an unsafe manner and for his brief presence at a Beach Week party attended by his son; and state Del. Heather Mizeur, whose stances put her to the left even of many Maryland Democrats. Brown prevailed with 51 percent, but he never sparked much affection among voters. In the general, Brown faced a little-known Republican activist, Larry Hogan, who slowly but surely snuck up on Brown and, in one of election night 2014's biggest surprises, beat Brown, 51%-47%, on the strength of much improved GOP performance in swingy suburban Baltimore County and weak turnout in traditionally Democratic areas. The GOP also gained seats in the legislature, though the party remains a distinct minority.

Hogan faced his first crisis within months, after Baltimore resident Freddie Gray, 25, died of spinal injuries after being taken into police custody. Though initially slow to ignite, the incident brought to a head long-simmering tensions between poor black residents of Baltimore and the police force, ones that had been painstakingly (and prophetically) chronicled by the celebrated HBO dramatic series *The Wire*. In a 2014 article, *The Baltimore Sun* had revealed that the city paid the staggering sum of $5.7 million for harms inflicted by police between 2011 and 2014, with more than 100 victims winning court judgments. After Gray's death, rioting, particularly in the Sandtown-Winchester neighborhood, resulted in the burn-ing of a $16 million, partially built senior-citizens' housing project as well as the looting of Mondawmin Mall, a CVS and a number of small retail businesses. A curfew was imposed, and eventually charges were filed against six police officers.

In Sandtown-Winchester, a majority of households earned less than $25,000 a year in 2011, while unemployment in the neighborhood was double the city average, domestic vio-lence was 50 percent higher and bachelor's degrees were one-quarter as common as the city as a whole. "It was only a matter of time before Baltimore exploded," journalist Michael A. Fletcher wrote in the *Washington Post*. "In the more than three decades I have called this city home, Baltimore has been a combustible mix of poverty, crime, and hopelessness, uncomfortably juxtaposed against rich history, friendly people, venerable institutions and pockets of old-money affluence." Complicating matters, Fletcher noted, the "mayor, city coun-cil president, police chief, top prosecutor, and many other city leaders are black, as is half of Baltimore's 3,000-person police force."

Presidential Politics Maryland has become one of the most Democratic states in the race for the presidency. In the six presidential elections from 1992 to 2012, its Democratic percentages have ranked high among the states—second in 1992, sixth in 1996, fourth in 2000 and 2004, and fifth in 2008 and 2012. Barack Obama got 62% of the vote in both 2008 and 2012. He carried 94% of African-Americans and 47% of whites in 2008, and 97% of African-Americans and 43% of whites in 2012.

2012 Presidential Vote		
Barack Obama (D) 1,677,844		(62%)
Mitt Romney (R)................971,869		(36%)
2012 Presidential Caucus		
Mitt Romney (R)................122,400		(49%)
Rick Santorum (R) 71,349		(29%)
Newt Gingrich (R)................27,240		(11%)
Ron Paul (R) 23,609		(10%)
2008 Presidential Vote		
Barack Obama (D) 1,629,467		(62%)
John McCain (R)................959,862		(36%)

From 1992 to 2004, Maryland held its presidential primaries a week before Super Tuesday to try to get noticed, with limited suc-cess. The one significant result was in 1992, when, in the Democratic primary, Paul Tson-gas beat Bill Clinton 41%-33%, with big margins in suburban Montgomery and Baltimore counties. In 2008, the primary was held on February 12, the same day that Virginia and the District of Columbia held primaries. This was the single best day in the nomination contest for Obama. He won Virginia 64%-35%, D.C. 75%-24%, and Maryland 61%-36%. He won 79% in Prince George's County and 74% in Baltimore City and carried all of Maryland's major suburban counties as well. In 2012, Mitt Romney won the Republican primary over Rick Santorum 49%-29%, with Santorum carrying one small county in the lower Eastern Shore and another in the far west. In 2008, John McCain defeated Mike Huckabee 55%-29%, and won every county.

Congressional Districts Democrats controlled the redis-tricting process after both the 2000 and 2010 censuses and used their power to maximum advantage. Going into the 2002 election, the delegation was divided 4-4 between the two major parties. After the boundaries were changed, the suburban

114th Congress Lineup	
1 R	7 D
113th Congress Lineup	
1 R	7 D

Baltimore 2nd District became inhospitable to Republican Bob Ehrlich, and he decided to run for governor instead, successfully in 2002. Heavily minority areas were added to the Montgomery County-centered 8th district, and Connie Morella, a moderate Republican, lost her reelection bid. Those two districts produced Democrats who became key players on important committees, Dutch Ruppersberger on Intelligence and Chris Van Hollen on Budget.

That left only two Republican districts, the 1st and the 6th. In 2011, Gov. Martin O'Malley and Democratic legislators decided to finish one of them off. They made the 1st District more Republican by adding GOP precincts in suburban Baltimore and heavily Republican areas in Carroll County, which had been in the 6th. Republican Andy Harris ended up with a very safe seat, which also covered the Eastern Shore. At the same time, they made the 6th Dis-trict in western Maryland far less Republican, especially after they added a large chunk of heavily Democratic Montgomery County and subtracted much of Frederick County. These moves made the adjacent 8th District less Democratic, but not enough to put Van Hollen in peril. As intended, Republican Roscoe Bartlett lost in the newly drawn 6th.

In order to maintain two black-majority districts—the 4th in metro Washington and the 7th in metro Baltimore—the redistricters had to draw some very convoluted lines that have been prominently featured among the nation's most gerrymandered districts. Although 6th District Democratic Rep. John Delaney had a scare in 2014, that map has been one of the national Democrats' few success stories from the latest redistricting.

Governor

Larry Hogan (R)

Elected 2014, term expires Jan. 2019, 1st term; b. May 25, 1956, Landover; FL St. U., B.A. 1978; Catholic; married (Yumi); 3 children.

Professional Career: Founder, pres., Hogan Companies, 1985-present; Realtor, Murphy Hogan Commercial Real Estate Services, 1999-2003; MD Secy. of Appointments, Office of Governor, 2003-07; Founder, chmn., Change Maryland, 2011-present.

Office: 100 State Circle, Annapolis, 21401, 410-974-3901; Fax: 410-974-3275; Website: governor.maryland.gov.

Election Results

2014 general	Larry Hogan (R)	884,400	(51%)
	Anthony Brown (D)	818,890	(47%)
2014 primary	Larry Hogan (R)	92,376	(43%)
	David Craig (R)	62,639	(29%)
	Charles Lollar (R)	33,292	(16%)
	Ron George (R)	26,628	(12%)

After barely five months in office, Republican Gov. Larry Hogan called a press conference on a hot summer afternoon to share the disturbing news that he had just been diagnosed with "a very advanced and very aggressive" form of cancer: lymphoma. Seeking to lighten the mood in the room, the affable Hogan wisecracked, "The best news is that my odds of getting through this and beating this are much, much better than the odds I had of beating Anthony Brown," as the audience laughed and aides applauded.

The quip underscored that Hogan's surprise victory in deep-blue Maryland over Brown—lieutenant governor under two-term Democratic Gov. Martin O'Malley—ranked as one of the major upsets nationwide in 2014. It came in a deep-blue state where Democrats enjoy a 2-1 registration edge and which has been on the cutting edge of progressive initiatives—ranging from gun control to same-sex marriage to repeal of the death penalty—in recent years. But Hogan's campaign focused tightly on voters' economic unease amid a period of wage stagnation, as Hogan pointed a finger at the state's tax structure and repeatedly accused O'Malley and Brown of seeking and imposing "40 consecutive tax increases" (including tolls and fees as well as taxes) over eight years. He was aided by a Brown campaign that, in the view of Democratic insiders, made several strategic blunders.

In the early months of his tenure, Hogan faced a series of political challenges, as he dueled with a state legislature dominated by Democrats and was forced to respond to riots in Baltimore, the state's largest city, in the wake of the death of a black man, Freddie Gray, in police custody. But these momentarily paled in late June, as he described the personal challenge of battling what he described as "an aggressive B-cell, non-Hodgkin's lymphoma" in late stage 3—and facing an 18-week course of chemotherapy. Hogan vowed to remain in office, and physicians not connected to his case indicated five-year survival rates for the type of cancer he has are now running at 70 percent. But Hogan's disclosure also focused closer attention on his lieutenant governor, Boyd Rutherford, who previously served with Hogan in state government before becoming an assistant agriculture secretary in the administration of President George W. Bush. Hogan said he planned to rely on Rutherford to fill in for him on state business and make decisions as necessary; under the Maryland constitution, Rutherford could be designated as acting governor if Hogan is temporarily unable to perform the duties of office.

As he sought to portray himself as the outsider during his uphill bid for governor, Hogan often boasted he wasn't a career politician and had never held elective office. Nonetheless, he grew up immersed in politics. As a teenager in the Washington D.C. suburb of Landover Maryland, Hogan often spent weekends on Capitol Hill where his father, Republican Larry Hogan Sr., served in the House from 1969-1975. The elder Hogan achieved national attention in 1974 as the only Republican on the House Judiciary Committee to vote for all three articles of impeachment against President Richard Nixon, and his son still speaks admiringly of the integrity and political courage his father displayed. By that time, the younger Hogan was in Florida, where he had moved with his mother following his parents' divorce. He graduated from Florida State University before returning to the Washington area to work briefly as a congressional aide, and then for his father: The elder Hogan was elected Prince George's County executive in 1978, and the younger Hogan served as his intergovernmental liaison aide.

The fact that Hogan did not hold elected office until being sworn in as governor in January 2015 was not for lack of trying. He took time out from his duties in the Prince George's County executive's office to run in a 1981 special election when his father's former congressional seat came open, finishing second in a 12-way Republican primary race. The seat was ultimately won by Democrat Steny Hoyer, now the House minority whip. The elder Hogan's political career ended in 1982 with an unsuccessful bid for Senate in which his son also worked, and the younger Hogan went into the real estate business. In 1992, he made a second bid for Congress, challenging Hoyer after the latter's district was redrawn to extend beyond Prince George's County. Hoyer came out on top, but by the narrowest margin of his career, 53%-44%.

Hogan vowed to try again in 1994, but was forced to forgo the race when his real estate business foundered in the wake of a series of bank failures in the early 1990s. After declaring personal bankruptcy in 1994, Hogan rebuilt the business, now a success and based in Annapolis. In 2002, Hogan helped Rep. Robert Ehrlich, whom he had known for more than two decades, become the first Republican elected governor of Maryland since Spiro Agnew in 1966. Hogan took a leave from the real estate business to serve as Ehrlich's secretary of appointments, a post that involved overseeing filling vacancies in the executive, legislative, and judicial branches.

Ehrlich was ousted by O'Malley in 2006, later making an unsuccessful comeback bid in 2010. Hogan initially contemplated running in 2010, but stepped aside for Ehrlich. A year later, he began laying the foundation for a 2014 run by founding Change Maryland, an anti-tax group that scrutinized the economic impact of the O'Malley administration's actions. By the time Hogan won the 2014 Republican primary—winning 43 percent of the vote against three opponents—Change Maryland's Facebook page had more than 100,000 followers. Research funded by the organization helped build the foundation of Hogan's fall campaign against Brown, during which Hogan ran ads complaining that O'Malley and Brown "never met a tax that they didn't like or at least one they didn't hike." At a time when several indicators showed the state's economy to be struggling, with federal spending cutbacks having an adverse effect, Hogan pledged to move as quickly as possible to roll back tax hikes implemented under O'Malley, while carefully avoiding being pinned down on precisely which taxes he would cut.

Brown, the son of a Jamaican father and a Swiss mother, easily won a three-way Democratic primary thanks to the backing of much of the state's Democratic establishment and the size of the African-American vote; by some estimates, blacks comprise as much as 40 percent of Democratic registration in the state. In the wake of the June primary, polls showed Brown with a large lead, and he outspent Hogan—who opted to take public financing—by 3-1 during the campaign. However, by the fall, it was clear that Hogan was closing the gap. While some blamed a nationwide wave for the GOP, President Barack Obama—a classmate of Brown's at Harvard Law School—was more popular in Maryland than many other places, and was brought in to campaign for his former classmate. Rather, along with the resonance of Hogan's anti-tax message, Brown's collapse was largely attributed to what was seen in Democratic Party circles as one of the most poorly run campaigns in recent state history.

Brown remained largely unknown after eight years of serving in O'Malley's shadow. He did little to introduce himself to the general electorate—and almost immediately began running attack ads characterizing Hogan as a "dangerous conservative" whose election would endanger many of the progressive reforms enacted under the O'Malley administration. But Hogan, while disagreeing with some of these measures while they were being debated, shrewdly sidestepped them—declaring them to be closed matters already decided by the state legislature of the voters. Many Democratic insiders felt the Brown attack ads over-reached by seeking to paint Hogan, with his guy-next-door persona, as a scary right-winger. In contrast, a former Army officer who seemed anything but at ease on the campaign trail, kept a low personal profile, relying on the state's large Democratic base to show up at the polls and put him over the top. It didn't work: On Election Day, Hogan won, 51%-47%. Of the state's 24 major jurisdictions, Hogan won 20. And turnout in Democratic bastions such as the city of Baltimore and suburban Montgomery County was not enough for Brown to make up for landslide Hogan margins elsewhere in the state.

The post-mortem was that Brown never clearly spelled out where he wanted to take Maryland. "He never created the Brown vision for the state," Maryland Democratic strategist Mike Morrill told the *Washington Post.*. "He made the major front-runner's mistake, trying to protect his lead instead of building his lead. As his lead eroded, he ran a negative campaign. He was trying to stop the erosion rather than giving people a reason to vote for him." It allowed Hogan to paint a Brown governorship as little more than a third term for O'Malley. O'Malley, getting ready to launch a bid for the Democratic presidential nomination, later complained publicly that Brown's campaign had made little effort to educate voters of the benefits to state services that had been yielded by the tax increases under his watch.

The early months of the Hogan administration had some Democrats grumbling about a sometimes confrontational style by the new governor that they said evoked memories of Hogan's former boss, Ehrlich—who had lost a bid for reelection after several years of legislative stalemate. Hogan delivered an inaugural speech in January widely praised for its appeal for bipartisanship and consensus. But the mood in Annapolis went downhill a couple of weeks later, with Democrats complaining that Hogan's "State of the State" address before the Maryland General Assembly—normally a blueprint for governing in the year ahead—sounded much like a stump speech from the 2014 campaign. Hogan and Democratic legislative leaders tussled over spending priorities, with Hogan ultimately refusing to spend nearly $70 million allocated by the General Assembly to aid school budgets in high cost areas. Hogan charged the legislature was seeking to divert money needed to shore up the state's pension fund, but critics saw a political motivation—since much of the withheld funding would have gone to heavily Democratic jurisdictions that had not voted for the new governor.

After campaigning for office pledging to roll back taxes, Hogan made little headway on this front in his first session of the General Assembly, but claimed a modicum of victory in the fact that the legislature's work product did not contain any additional tax increases. In one small victory, Hogan signed a bill rolling back a requirement passed during O'Malley's watch that Maryland's 10 most populous jurisdictions collect a storm-water mitigation fee to fund programs to reduce Chesapeake Bay pollution. Republicans derided the fee as the "rain tax," and it became a frequent applause line during Hogan's campaign. Hogan continued to tread carefully around social issues: He allowed two measures sought by the gay and transgender communities to become law without his signature. And he took the same approach on legislation imposing a two-year ban on so-called natural gas fracking, even though he supported fracking during the campaign. A majority of the state's large independent bloc of voters backed Hogan, and polling has shown this group, while often fiscally conservative, has tended to be more liberal on social and environmental issues.

In late April 2015, Hogan faced the first major crisis of his administration when rioting broke out in Baltimore on the day of Freddie Gray's funeral. Some referred to it as Hogan's potential "Chris Christie moment"—an opportunity to demonstrate decisive leadership, much as Christie had benefited politically from his performance in the wake of the 2012 destruction wreaked by Hurricane Sandy. (Christie made multiple appearances for Hogan in Maryland in 2014.) Hogan initially griped that Baltimore Mayor Stephanie Rawlings-Blake, a Democrat, failed to return his phone calls for two hours as the rioting spread, causing a delay in sending in the National Guard. But he later sought to downplay differences with the mayor, while relocating his base of operations to Baltimore for a week and appearing around the city. Democratic strategist Morrill gave Hogan high marks, telling *The Baltimore Sun:* "He's been in the city; he's done what a governor should have done…His operating refrain of sort of being in charge and taking charge was good on that one day of the crisis." By comparison, Rawlings-Blake, who had been talked up as a possible Democratic challenger to Hogan before the riots, saw her political stock take a major hit, as she was criticized for not being sufficiently visible or proactive.

Just three days after disclosing his cancer diagnosis, Hogan announced a long-awaited, politically delicate decision: He gave a tentative go-ahead for construction of a light rail project, the Purple Line, in the state's Washington suburbs, after criticizing both the cost and viability of the mass transit line during the 2014 campaign. The project was supported by a broad coalition in Montgomery and Prince George's counties, the state's two largest jurisdictions— both of which had voted against him. But killing the project ran the risk of intensifying future opposition to him in the fast-growing region, while also offending the influential Washington area business community—which backed the Purple Line as a major opportunity for economic development, a priority issue for Hogan during the campaign and in his first months in office. Hogan exhibited political deftness in unveiling the Purple Line decision: Hours before a scheduled press conference, his allies leaked the news that he would also be announcing nearly $850 million in new road building projects around the state. This move appeared likely to assuage his political base in Maryland's more rural areas, where local leaders had complained of cutbacks in road funding and an overemphasis on mass transit under O'Malley.

The last Maryland Republican governor to win reelection to a second term was former Baltimore Mayor Theodore McKeldin in the 1950s, and Hogan was starting to schedule fundraisers to build up a campaign war-chest in advance of 2018. His health issues now raise questions about his political future. If he is unable to complete his first term, Rutherford would succeed him. If so, Rutherford—an attorney who is also a former chief administrative officer of the Republican National Committee—would become only the fourth African-American since Reconstruction to become governor of a state. He would also become Maryland's first black governor, a distinction many thought would go to Anthony Brown until Hogan's upset win. With Rawlings-Blake's political future also in question, the leading African-American contender in the potential Democratic gubernatorial field for 2018 appears to be term-limited Prince George's County Executive Rushern Baker. But most speculation on possible Democratic candidates has centered on 6th District Rep. John Delaney, a multimillionaire financial business owner, and Obama's Labor Secretary Tom Perez, who began his political career by winning election to the Montgomery County Council.

Senior Senator

Barbara Mikulski (D)

Elected 1986, term expires Jan. 2017, 5th term; b. July 20, 1936, Baltimore; Mt. St. Agnes Col., B.A. 1958, U. of MD, M.S.W. 1965; Catholic; single.

Elected Office: Baltimore City Cncl., 1971-76; U.S. House, 1977-87.

Professional Career: Social worker, Baltimore Dept. of Social Services, 1965-70; Chmn., DNC Delegate Selection Comm., 1972; Adjunct prof., Loyola Col., 1972-76.

DC Office: 503 HSOB, 20510, 202-224-4654; Website: mikulski.senate .gov.

State Offices: Annapolis, 410-263-1805; Baltimore, 410-962-4510; Greenbelt, 301-345-5517; Hagerstown, 301-797-2826; Salisbury, 410-546-7711.

Committees: *Appropriations* (RMM): Commerce, Justice, Science & Related Agencies (RMM); Defense; Labor, HHS, Education, & Related Agencies; State, Foreign Operations, & Related Programs; Transportation, HUD, & Related Agencies; ex officio on remaining subcommittees. *Health, Education, Labor & Pensions:* Children & Families; Primary Health & Retirement Security. *Intelligence (Select).*

Group Ratings

	ADA	ACLU	AFL-CIO	LCV	ITI	COC	HAFA	ACU	CFG	FRC
2014	90%	93%	–	80%	100%	50%	0%	0%	0%	0%
2013	95%	C	100%	92%	C	38%	C	4%	0%	C

National Journal Ratings

	2013 LIB	—	2013 CONS
Economic	82%	—	8%
Social	73%	—	0%
Foreign	71%	—	0%
Composite	86%	—	14%

Key Votes of the 113th Congress

1. Sandy storm spending	Y	5. Student Loan Rates	Y	9. Bipartisan Budget Deal	Y
2. Chuck Hagel Confirmation	Y	6. Employee Non-Discrim'n Act	Y	10. Farm Bill Conference Rept.	Y
3. Gun Background Checks	Y	7. Senate Vote on Judgeships	N	11. Unempl. Comp. Extension	Y
4. Immigration Reform	Y	8. Defense Dept. Spending	Y	12. Keystone Pipeline	N

Election Results

2010 general	Barbara Mikulski (D) 1,140,531	(62%)	$4,891,554	$154,513
	Eric Wargotz (R)........................ 655,666	(36%)	$932,330	
2010 primary	Barbara Mikulski (D) 396,252	(82%)		
	Christopher Garner (D) 36,194	(8%)		

Prior winning percentages: 2004 (65%), 1998 (71%), 1992 (71%), 1986 (61%); House: 1984 (68%), 1982 (74%), 1980 (76%), 1978 (100%), 1976 (75%)

Democrat Barbara Mikulski, Maryland's senior senator, hardly looks or sounds like the traditional politician: She is just shy of 5 feet tall, with a manner charitably described as gruff and unvarnished. But in her 40 years on Capitol Hill—10 in the House, followed by 30 in the Senate—she has emerged as a savvy insider. And she will retire at the end of 2016, at the age of 80, with her place in congressional history secure. In 2012, she became the longest serving woman in the history of Congress (surpassing the late Republican Rep. Edith Nourse Rogers of Massachusetts)—the same year that she became the first woman to chair one of the Senate's most influential panels, the Appropriations Committee. She is also only the second woman—and first Democratic woman—elected to the Senate whose husband or father did not serve in high office.

Mikulski's modest roots are in East Baltimore, where her Polish immigrant grandparents ran a bakery, and her father had a grocery store. She attended the Institute of Notre Dame—the same high school that produced former House Speaker Nancy Pelosi—and later earned a social work degree at the University of Maryland. She got a job as a social worker, helping at-risk children and educating seniors about Medicare. In her current role on Capitol Hill, she likes to characterize herself as a "social worker with power." Mikulski still lives in Baltimore and commutes to Washington, nearly 40 miles to the south. Her Baltimore office is in Fells Point, the city's original port area, where she lived for many years. She moved to a more secure condominium building two decades ago after being mugged near her Fells Point townhouse.

Mikulski first got involved in politics when she organized a grassroots effort to stop a highway from going through Baltimore's Highlandtown area, where she grew up. She won, saving several neighborhoods whose subsequent revitalization has been a bright spot for a city besieged by numerous urban ills in recent years. Mikulski drew national attention for a 1970 speech in which she urged more respect for "ethnic Americans"—working-class whites whose families had emigrated from Europe—and called for an alliance of whites and blacks against "those who have power." A year later, she won a seat on the Baltimore City Council. In 1974, she was the Democrats' longshot nominee against Republican incumbent Charles Mathias, and garnered a respectable 43 percent of the vote. It paved the way for her move to Capitol Hill two years later.

In 1976, when Democratic Rep. Paul Sarbanes ran for the state's other Senate seat, Mikulski made a successful bid for his 3rd District House seat. Ten years later, when Mathias retired, she gave up her safe seat in the House for what seemed like a chancy Senate race. But she won the primary handily, with 50 percent, to 31 percent for Rep. Michael Barnes, who represented a district in the Washington D.C. suburbs, and 14 percent for Gov. Harry Hughes, then in his second and final term in Annapolis. In the general election, Mikulski beat Republican Linda Chavez, a Civil Rights Commission official under President Reagan, 61%-39%. In four subsequent re-election bids, she has never won with less than 62 percent of the vote, and occasionally has garnered in excess of 70 percent. When she departs Capitol Hill at the end of her current term, Mikulski will share with Sarbanes the title of longest serving senator in Maryland history.

"People identify with her, I think," Sarbanes said in a 2011 interview with the *Baltimore Sun*, as he assessed Mikulski's appeal among voters. "They see her as a fighter. They appreciate that." To be sure, Mikulski has evinced little interest in the usual niceties of politics. She will snap at reporters whom she feels don't get to the point quickly enough, and at committee hearings she is a self-described "table-pounder" who will rebuke witnesses with whom she disagrees. In *Washingtonian* magazine's annual survey of congressional staffers, she has been routinely named as "meanest senator." But her admirers say they appreciate both her energy and her forthrightness. "You never say anything you don't mean," Vice President Joe Biden, a Senate colleague for more than two decades, told Mikulski at a reception honoring her longevity. And the female senators who arrived in the years following Mikulski's initial election view her with affection. "For the women of the Senate, she will always be our dean— the woman who opened up the doors of the Senate wide enough to let the women of America walk in," declared Democrat Barbara Boxer of California, who is also retiring in 2016.

In Mikulski's early years, the only other woman in the chamber was Republican Nancy Kassebaum of Kansas, daughter of a former governor, Alf Landon, who was the 1936 Republican presidential nominee. In 1993, Mikulski and Kassebaum appeared on the Senate floor wearing pants, in defiance of a rule requiring women to wear skirts or dresses. The rule was soon changed. That incident occurred just months after the 1992 election, which increased the number of women in the Senate to six, then a record. It was heralded by pundits as "the year of the woman," prompting Mikulski—with characteristic irascibility—to snap at the time: "Calling 1992 the year of the woman makes it sound like the year of the caribou or the year of the asparagus. We're not a fad, fancy or a year." But she has taken her role as dean of Senate women seriously: Every two years since 1992, Mikulski has held workshops for incoming women senators to help them learn the ropes in what is still a male-dominated realm, although the number of women in the chamber had swelled to 20 in January 2015. And, for the past couple of decades, she has hosted regular dinners for her female colleagues, now held every other month. The rules: "No staff, no memos, no leaks."

Mikulski's policy agenda has included numerous initiatives aimed at women, even though she has regularly contended that all issues are women's issues, whether they relate to the economy, health care, or national security. She has pushed to create Individual Retirement Accounts for homemakers, to ensure that women are included in clinical trials and to establish mammography clinic standards. She got an amendment added to the health care overhaul in 2010 requiring mammograms and other preventative services for women with no copayment—a swipe at a Republican argument that restricting mammograms would be the first step in the Democrats' plan to ration health care. Among her best-known legislative accomplishments is the Lily Ledbetter Fair Pay Act, which extended the amount of time that workers had to file wage discrimination complaints: It was the first law signed by President Barack Obama after he took office. As a follow-on, Mikulski in 2015 introduced the Paycheck Fairness Act, requiring employers to demonstrate that pay differences were not related to gender; a similar measure was blocked by Senate Republicans a year earlier.

However, while a solid liberal and strong abortion rights advocate, much of Mikulski's focus has been on using her seat on the Appropriations Committee—to which she was appointed during her first term—to bring home the bacon to her constituents. Endorsing her for reelection in 2010, her hometown newspaper, the *Sun,* noted that she could "bark like a vicious terrier," but added, "She's our terrier. And…she's delivered, big time." Her efforts have included funding to ensure that the Port of Baltimore remains competitive, to clean up the Chesapeake Bay, and to continue efforts on reseeding the bay's once plentiful oyster beds—an issue of crucial economic importance to a number of struggling communities along the Chesapeake. Most notably, she has been one of the Senate's chief advocates of the space program, which includes the Goddard Space Flight Center in Maryland's Washington, D.C. suburbs, and the Wallops Flight Facility in Virginia, just across the border from Maryland along the Chesapeake.

When she became chair of the full Appropriations Committee in December 2012 upon the death of Hawaii Democrat Daniel Inouye, Mikulski already had chaired the panel's Commerce, Justice, Science, and Related Agencies Subcommittee—which includes jurisdiction over the National Aeronautics and Space Administration—for nearly six years. Even before she took over the subcommittee, she won a big victory when, in 2006, NASA announced the agency could repair and upgrade the Hubble telescope safely and within budget. Since then, she has pressed NASA to move more quickly and cheaply in proceeding with the James Webb Space Telescope, Hubble's more powerful but over-budget successor, planned for launch in 2018. Grateful astronomers using the Hubble announced in April 2012 that they had named an exploding star "Supernova Mikulski" in her honor. When Obama sought to cut NASA's fiscal year 2015 by about $190 million over the previous year, Mikulski was uncharacteristically restrained, telling a gathering of aerospace professionals the proposal "was well intentioned, but I considered it advisory." She went to work, and NASA instead received a $350 million increase for 2015.

A national co-chair of Hillary Clinton's 2008 presidential campaign, Mikulski's relations with Obama have been lukewarm. In March 2014, when Obama came forward with an election year budget proposal for additional spending and a tax hike, Mikulski flatly indicated she wasn't interested. "We have a budget agreement for fiscal year 2015, and the Senate Appropriations Committee will adhere to the spending caps in that deal," she declared. When Mikulski had assumed the chairmanship of the full committee more than a year earlier, the panel, while still a coveted assignment, had lost some of its former luster. One reason was that the Senate, following the House's example, had banned earmarks that allowed members to steer funds directly to favored projects. Another was that annual spending bills had become routinely lumped together in stopgap continuing resolutions, due to Congress' increasing polarization. But Mikulski vowed to preside over the panel's reinvigoration. Working closely with her House counterpart, Kentucky Republican Harold Rogers, she was able to get Congress in January 2014 to adopt an omnibus spending bill; it was the first time since 2009 that lawmakers didn't settle for a continuing resolution. Rogers praised his counterpart's "open-minded approach to negotiations."

On a more parochial front, Mikulski wielded her clout to hamstring Maryland Gov. Martin O'Malley, a fellow Democrat who was once an aide to her. Mikulski added language to the fiscal 2015 defense spending bill to block the Navy from finalizing an agreement with developers of a wind farm on Maryland's Eastern Shore until researchers studied how to mitigate the effects of the wind turbines. O'Malley had vetoed legislation in Maryland's General Assembly that imposed a delay, saying further study was unnecessary. But opponents of the wind farm contended it could disrupt operations at the Patuxent River Naval Air Station, just across the Chesapeake Bay in southern Maryland—and ultimately threaten the future of the facility. (O'Malley declared for the Democratic presidential nomination in May 2015, but Mikulski made clear she was once again in the Hillary Clinton camp when it came to 2016.)

When Mikulski ran for and won reelection in 2010 after some retirement speculation, many saw that as her last term—until her unexpected elevation to the Appropriations chairmanship. (Some political luck came into play in the latter promotion: Vermont Democrat Patrick Leahy was ahead of Mikulski in seniority on Appropriations, but chose to forsake the gavel in favor of retaining his chairmanship of the Senate Judiciary Committee.) Mikulski had to give up the chair in January 2015, becoming the committee's ranking Democrat, after the Democrats lost the Senate majority in the 2014 election. But many thought she would still seek another term: She moved to assert herself as the titular head of the Maryland Democratic Party after the term-limited O'Malley left office and Republican Larry Hogan became governor in early 2015, and she started her annual tour of the state's 23 counties.

So her retirement announcement in March 2015 came as something of a surprise in state political circles. Asserting that she was in good health, Mikulski added that, at 78, she wanted to change her focus. "Do I spend my time raising money? Or do I spend my time raising hell?" she asked. Unlike some colleagues, she insisted she was not leaving in frustration over the increasing gridlock on Capitol Hill. "There's nothing gloomy about this announcement," she declared. "I'm not frustrated with the Senate." Her retirement may give her more time to devote to her sideline of writing mystery novels. She has coauthored two, *Capitol Offense* and *Capitol Venture*, featuring the fictional character Eleanor "Norie" Gorzack, a freshman senator from Pennsylvania.

Mikulski's retirement marks only the fourth time in more than 50 years that a Maryland Senate seat has come open, and it set off an immediate scramble: Every member of the eight-person Maryland congressional delegation, save for House Democratic Whip Steny Hoyer, declined to rule out running. Two quickly jumped into the Senate Democratic primary contest: Reps. Donna Edwards and Chris Van Hollen. Van Hollen had been regarded as a possible successor to Pelosi as House Democratic leader, and his decision to run for Senate without much hesitation was widely seen as an indication that the Democrats have little hope of regaining House control in the foreseeable future. He was immediately endorsed by Senate Democratic Leader Harry Reid, while Edwards picked up the backing of EMILY's List—the potent campaign finance group devoted to electing Democratic women who are pro-abortion rights, and which had helped to send Mikulski to the Senate shortly after its 1985 formation. The Democratic Senatorial Campaign Committee stayed neutral in the primary.

Both are solidly in the liberal camp, although Edwards—tied with six other legislators as the most liberal House member in *National Journal*'s 2013 vote ratings—is generally perceived as being to Van Hollen's left. Van Hollen is the political insider who has held several House leadership posts, and who has touted that experience in arguing he would be the more effective senator. Edwards is the outsider—she has been at odds with organizations ranging from the Congressional Black Caucus to the Maryland Democratic Party—and has sought to mobilize supporters by suggesting that Van Hollen is willing to compromise on key issues important to the Democratic base. Either Edwards or Van Hollen, if elected, would be the first senator from the state's Washington, D.C. suburbs in a century. A third potential candidate, Baltimore-based Rep. Elijah Cummings, could scramble the Democratic contest. Like Edwards, Cummings is African-American, but could have the advantage of a unified geographic base; a poll he commissioned in early 2015 reportedly showed him with a narrow lead. Cummings represents a district that includes the site of the April 2015 Baltimore riots, and emerged from that episode with both increased statewide visibility and high marks for efforts to maintain calm in his troubled city.

Junior Senator

Ben Cardin (D)

Elected 2006, term expires Jan. 2019, 2nd term; b. Oct. 5, 1943, Baltimore; U. of Pittsburgh, B.A. 1964, U. of MD, LL.B. J.D. 1967; Jewish; married (Myrna Edelman); 2 children (1 deceased).

Elected Office: MD House, 1966-86, speaker, 1979-86; U.S. House, 1987-2006.

Professional Career: Practicing atty., 1967-86; Ways & Means Committee, MD, 1974-79; Chmn., MD Legal Services Corp., 1988-95.

DC Office: 509 HSOB, 20510, 202-224-4524; Fax: 202-224-1651; Website: cardin.senate.gov.

State Offices: Baltimore, 410-962-4436; Bowie, 301-860-0414; Cumberland, 301-777-2957; Rockville, 301-762-2974; Salisbury, 410-546-4250.

Committees: *Environment & Public Works:* Clean Air & Nuclear Safety; Fisheries, Water, & Wildlife; Transportation & Infrastructure. *Finance:* Health Care; Taxation & IRS Oversight. *Foreign Relations* (RMM): Africa & Global Health Policy; East Asia, the Pacific, & Int'l Cybersecurity Policy (RMM); Near East, South Asia, Central Asia, & Counterterrorism; ex officio on remaining subcommittees. *Small Business & Entrepreneurship.*

Group Ratings

	ADA	ACLU	AFL-CIO	LCV	ITI	COC	HAFA	ACU	CFG	FRC
2014	90%	100%	–	80%	100%	50%	0%	0%	0%	0%
2013	100%	C	100%	100%	C	38%	C	4%	0%	C

National Journal Ratings

	2013 LIB	—	2013 CONS
Economic	82%	—	8%
Social	73%	—	0%
Foreign	71%	—	0%
Composite	86%	—	14%

Key Votes of the 113th Congress

1. Sandy storm spending	Y	5. Student Loan Rates	N	9. Bipartisan Budget Deal	Y
2. Chuck Hagel Confirmation	Y	6. Employee Non-Discrim'n Act	Y	10. Farm Bill Conference Rept.	Y
3. Gun Background Checks	Y	7. Senate Vote on Judgeships	N	11. Unempl. Comp. Extension	Y
4. Immigration Reform	Y	8. Defense Dept. Spending	Y	12. Keystone Pipeline	N

Election Results

2012 general	Ben Cardin (D)........................ 1,474,028	(56%)	$6,281,916	$32,091
	Daniel John Bongino (R) 693,291	(26%)	$1,767,837	$168,845
	S. Rob Sobhani (I) 430,934	(16%)	$8,078,928	
2012 primary	Ben Cardin (D)......................... 240,704	(74%)		
	C. Anthony Muse (D) 50,807	(16%)		

Prior winning percentages: 2006 (55%); House: 2004 (63%), 2002 (66%), 2000 (76%), 1998 (78%), 1996 (67%), 1994 (71%), 1992 (74%), 1990 (70%), 1988 (73%), 1986 (79%)

Newspaper coverage in the home state of Democrat Ben Cardin, Maryland's junior senator, frequently has referred to him as a centrist or moderate. In fact, according to *National Journal*'s vote rankings, Cardin has regularly ranked among the top 10 most liberal senators since being elected to that body a decade ago. The gap between perception and reality does not arise from any marked ideological shift during Cardin's nearly half-century in elected office, but rather appears to be a function of his low-key style. Throughout his career, Cardin has been an unabashed policy wonk with an agreeable personality, able to work effectively with Republicans because he shuns partisan sound bites and has a sincere interest in the nitty-gritty of crafting legislation.

Events in early 2015 conspired to give Cardin an unaccustomed share of the national limelight. In the wake of an indictment on corruption charges, New Jersey Sen. Robert Menendez stepped down as the ranking Democrat on the Foreign Relations Committee, with Cardin inheriting the ranking member's slot. The Menendez indictment came as the outlines of a deal intended to block Iran from developing nuclear weapons were emerging, and Cardin immediately found himself thrust into the center of a fractious debate over Congress' response. The Republican majority on Capitol Hill was pushing for review power over the deal, embodied in legislation that President Barack Obama was vowing to veto. Cardin's fellow Democrats were sharply split over the matter, with some lining up with the White House and others with Israel—which was deeply skeptical of the emerging accord.

At the direction of Senate Democratic Leader Harry Reid, Cardin negotiated with the chairman of the Foreign Relations panel, Tennessee Sen. Bob Corker, and won plaudits for coming up with a compromise that satisfied the White House and cleared the Senate on a 98-1 vote. "We have sent a clear message today that on this most vital national security issue—keeping Iran from obtaining nuclear weapons—the Senate can find common ground and speak with one voice," Cardin declared after the vote, while noting, "Such bipartisanship has eluded the Senate of late..." Depending on the outcome of the legal proceedings against Menendez and Democratic efforts to regain the majority in coming elections, Cardin could find himself capping off his congressional career in other high visibility situations—possibly from a perch as chairman of the Foreign Relations Committee.

While he was 63 years old when he reached the Senate in 2006, Cardin was once a boy wonder of Maryland politics. Elected to the Maryland House of Delegates at the age of 23—six months prior to earning his law degree—he was House speaker by the time he was 35. Just as he later operated in Washington, Cardin gained a reputation in Annapolis as a consensus builder who reached across the political aisle. The son and nephew of state legislators, Cardin grew up in the Jewish neighborhoods of northwest Baltimore: The area and the era were later depicted in Barry Levinson's 1982 movie "Diner." After achieving the top job in the House of Delegates, Cardin's ambitions seemed aimed at moving from the first to the second floor of the Maryland State House—where the governor's office is located. But, when Democrat Barbara Mikulski left her 3rd District House seat to run for the Senate in 1986, Cardin jumped into the congressional race and was easily elected.

In his second term in the House, Cardin obtained a seat on the tax-writing Ways and Means Committee, where he was able to be a productive legislator—even after the Democrats were relegated to the minority after the 1994 elections, and many of his party colleagues lacked the independence or shrewdness to deal with their diminished circumstances. Along with then-Republican Rep. Rob Portman of Ohio, Cardin cosponsored the 1998 Internal Revenue Service reform law and the 2000 bipartisan legislation to expand 401(k) savings and other retirement plans. In 2001, when Congress enacted the Bush tax cut, it included Cardin's provision to increase the limits for maximum IRA and 401(k) contributions. Cardin's hometown newspaper, the *Baltimore Sun* called him a "master of bipartisan lawmaking." But he continued to eye the governorship, and seriously considered giving up his House seat to run in both 1994 and 1998.

Open Senate seats in the state don't come around often in Maryland—and so when Democrat Paul Sarbanes decided to retire in 2006 after three decades in office, Cardin didn't hesitate. He began as the front-runner even though his earnest, somewhat bland demeanor raised questions about his viability as a statewide candidate. Cardin's leading primary opponent was former Democratic Rep. Kweisi Mfume, who resigned his House seat in 1996 to head the NAACP. Mfume and Cardin were friends—both were elected to Congress in 1986—but Mfume and other black leaders warned that the state Democratic establishment's support for Cardin could breed resentment among African-American voters, who by some estimates comprise 40 percent of registered Maryland Democrats. Mfume also had a compelling life story and an abundance of charisma. But Cardin outspent Mfume by 4-1, and won narrowly, 44%-41%. The vote broke down heavily along racial lines: Mfume overwhelmingly carried the majority-black jurisdictions of Baltimore city and Prince George's County, while Cardin won 21 of the 22 remaining counties in the state.

The Republican nominee was Lt. Gov. Michael Steele, the first African-American statewide officeholder in Maryland. Steele ran quirky, unconventional ads highlighting his outsider status while Democrats, including Mfume, coalesced around Cardin and portrayed Steele as an inexperienced lightweight. Without a legislative record, Steele made for an elusive target, so Cardin sought to link him to President George W. Bush and criticized Steele for his support for the Iraq war. Cardin won 54%-44%, in a tough year for Republicans nationwide. In contrast to the primary, African-Americans voted overwhelmingly for Cardin. In early 2009, Steele became the first African-American chairman of the Republican National Committee, where he became known for several well-publicized gaffes until his ouster in 2011.

The elevation of Cardin to the role of the Senate Democrats' leading spokesman on foreign policy gives that portfolio to someone who has been more supportive of the Obama administration's overseas initiatives than his predecessor, Menendez. When Obama announced in December 2014 that he was moving to restore diplomatic ties with Cuba, Cardin voiced support, declaring at a committee hearing: "It goes without saying that our previous policy did not achieve the progress that we wanted to see, and so a new approach is needed." In contrast, Menendez, a Cuban-American, continued to resist any engagement with the Castro regime. Asked his opinion of Obama's shift in strategy on the day it was announced, Menendez bluntly told reporters, "I think it stinks."

Obama's new approach was unveiled in conjunction with Cuba's freeing of U.S. government contractor Alan Gross, a Maryland resident, after a five-year imprisonment. Cardin had pressed the State Department to make Gross' freedom a top priority, and condemned his detention as a major human rights violation. As a former co-chair of the U.S. arm of the Commission on Security and Cooperation in Europe, which monitors international human rights issues, Cardin has long been focused on such matters. "My name is well-known in Russia, some places better than in Maryland," he wryly observed. One of his major legislative successes came with the December 2012 passage of a bill that normalized trade relations with Russia after nearly 40 years—but which also required the United States to freeze the assets of, and deny visas to, Russians implicated in human rights abuses. The roster of sanctioned individuals became known in some quarters as the "Cardin List." The provision so angered Russian President Vladimir Putin that he retaliated by moving to end U.S. adoptions of Russian children, a response Cardin called "embarrassing."

Closer to home, Cardin spent his first four years in the Senate on the Judiciary Committee, and remains involved in a number of issues that fall within that committee's jurisdiction. Two years before rioting broke out in his hometown of Baltimore in April 2015—when the death of a black man in custody brought police-community relations to the boiling point—Cardin introduced legislation to end racial profiling. The legislation would provide training for law enforcement officials in the differences between suspect descriptions and racial profiling. "We can begin to reduce the racial disparities that plague our justice system," Cardin said in 2014, a month after an unarmed black teenager, Michael Brown, was shot and killed by a police officer in Ferguson, Missouri. Brown "did not need to die," Cardin asserted.

Cardin left the Judiciary Committee in 2011 when he won a seat on the influential Finance Committee, a logical segue to his 18 years on the House Ways and Means panel. In late 2014, Cardin exhibited his policy wonk side by introducing a comprehensive overhaul of the nation's tax code. While certain to face daunting political hurdles, the plan garnered attention amid increasing calls on Capitol Hill for tax reform. Cardin's plan would eliminate income taxation—and filing—for households earning less than $100,000, while lowering rates but eliminating many deductions for those above that level. Notably, it would shift the focus of the tax system to a 10-percent levy on consumption, while seeking to encourage exports by rebating that tax on sales of products or services to foreign markets.

Upon his joining the Finance Committee, Senate Democratic leaders put Cardin and Ohio's Sherrod Brown in charge of an effort to shape the party's message on the newly passed health care reform law. But Cardin also successfully sponsored a 2011 bill with the Finance Committee chairman, Montana Democrat Max Baucus, to repeal a much-criticized provision in the health care law that called for businesses to submit forms to the Internal Revenue Service for all purchases above $600. Before joining the committee, Cardin led the fight to include pediatric dental care as an essential benefit under the Affordable Care Act—an effort prompted by the death of a 12 year-old Maryland boy who suffered a brain infection that started as untreated tooth decay. It was the basis of a campaign ad that ran in the weeks leading up to the April 2012 primary as Cardin was seeking a second term; a young girl recounts the episode and praises Cardin, ending with the tag line, "He's my friend Ben—I hope he's your friend, too."

Other ads in the much-noticed "My Friend Ben" series showed the then 69-year old incumbent helping to load bags onto an airplane and hauling in oysters with Maryland watermen, as narrators highlighted his efforts to land funds for expansion of Baltimore-Washington International Airport as well as restoration of the Chesapeake Bay. To an extent, the ads were an effort to compensate for Cardin's low-key modus operandi, which appeared to have left many Maryland voters with a hazy image of who he was and what he had accomplished in his first term.

In the end, Cardin had little to worry about: He turned back a primary challenge from an African-American state senator by nearly 5-1, and, in the general election, he won 56 percent, with the opposition split between the Republican nominee and a wealthy businessman running as a self-financed independent. If there was any question as to the draw of the Cardin name in the state, it was answered during the 2014 campaign—when a state delegate named Jon Cardin sought the Democratic nomination for state attorney general. He ultimately fell short, but led in the polls for much of the contest: Pundits concluded that many rank-and-file voters had initially thought they were voting not for Jon Cardin, but rather his uncle, Ben.

FIRST DISTRICT

Andy Harris (R)

Elected 2010, 3rd term; b. Jan. 25, 1957, Brooklyn, NY; Johns Hopkins U., B.S. 1977, M.D. 1980, M.H.S. 1995; Catholic; widowed; 5 children.

Military Career: U.S. Naval Reserve, 1988-2010.

Elected Office: MD Senate, 1998-2010, min. whip.

Professional Career: Anesthesiologist, Johns Hopkins Hosp., 1980-2010; Assoc. prof., Johns Hopkins Med. Schl., 1984-2010.

DC Office: 1533 LHOB, 20515, 202-225-5311; Fax: 202-225-0254; Website: harris.house.gov.

State Offices: Bel Air, 410-588-5670; Kent Island, 410-643-5425; Salisbury, 443-944-8624.

Committees: *Appropriations:* Agriculture, Rural Development, FDA, & Related Agencies; Homeland Security; Labor, HHS, Education & Related Agencies.

Group Ratings

	ADA	ACLU	AFL-CIO	LCV	ITI	COC	HAFA	ACU	CFG	FRC
2014	10%	0%	–	0%	80%	57%	77%	88%	75%	100%
2013	5%	C	14%	0%	C	77%	C	92%	82%	C

National Journal Ratings

	2013 LIB	—	2013 CONS
Economic	10%	—	88%
Social	16%	—	74%
Foreign	5%	—	86%
Composite	14%	—	86%

Key Votes of the 113th Congress

1. Sandy storm spending	N	5. Medical Marijuana	N	9. Syrian Rebels Training	N
2. Violence Against Women Act	N	6. Farm Bill	Y	10. Keystone pipeline	Y
3. Guantanamo Bay Detainees	N	7. Afghanistan Combat	N	11. Immigration Exec. Action	N
4. Abortion 20-week ban	Y	8. NSA Phone Data Collection	Y	12. Bipartisan budget deal	N

Election Results

2014 general	Andy Harris (R)	176,342	(70%)	$1,169,106	$1,308
	Bill Tilghman (D)	73,843	(30%)	$573,289	
2014 primary	Andy Harris (R)	45,477	(78%)		
	Jonathan Goff (R)	12,913	(22%)		

Prior winning percentages: 2012 (64%), 2010 (54%)

Population		Race and Ethnicity		Income	
Total:	723,716	White	80.5%	Median income:	$66,538
Urban:	12.6%	Black	12.2%		*(76 of 435)*
Suburban:	63.3%	Latino	3.3%	Under $50,000	37.0%
Rural:	24.1%	Asian	1.9%	$50,000-$99,999:	32.2%
Land area:	2,914	Two races	1.8%	$100,000-$199,999:	24.4%
Pop/sq. mi.:	248.3	White Ethnic	33.7%	$200,000 or more:	6.5%
Born in state:	62.7%			Poverty Rate	10.7%
		Education			
Age Groups		H.S. grad or less:	41.9%	**Work**	
Under 18:	21.7%	Some college:	27.8%	White Collar:	39.7%
18 to 34:	20.2%	College degree, 4 yr.:	18.1%	Blue Collar:	41.0%
35 to 64:	41.2%	Post-grad study:	12.2%	Sales and service:	19.3%
Over 64:	16.9%				
		Military		Govt. workers:	18.4%
		Veterans/active duty:	9.8%		

Northern Baltimore Suburbs, Eastern Shore

Chesapeake Bay is technically not a bay but an estuary. It was the central focus of the most thickly settled of the 13 colonies and today remains a central focus for much of modern Maryland. The first British here were amazed at the Chesapeake's oysters and terrapin turtles and crabs and rockfish.

Voter Turnout	
2013 Total Citizen 18+	552,347
2014 House Turnout	250,418
2014 Turnout as % CVAP	45.3%
2012 Turnout as % CVAP	64%

This was an estuary civilization in colonial days, with every little hamlet tied together by the highways of bays and creeks and inlets off the Chesapeake. The streets and docks of Chestertown, Oxford, St. Michaels and Cambridge still look something like they did when George Washington slept there.

In post-colonial times, when most Americans were caught up in the romance of westward movement, these estuaries and peninsulas were mostly forgotten, located too far off the main lines of railroads and highways. In the 160 years between 1790 and 1950, the Eastern Shore counties of Maryland only doubled in population. Over the past six decades, much of the Chesapeake has changed beyond recognition, the area has grown vigorously, with second-home buyers, retirees and commuters crossing the Chesapeake Bay Bridge. Now, this is a land of genteel estates fronting the water and of Frank Perdue's thriving chicken empire around Salisbury. Easton has a Waterfowl Festival and quaint St. Michaels has an Oyster-Fest, as do other towns on that part of the three-state DelMarVa peninsula. This growth has forced people along the Bay to confront issues that once would have been unimaginable here, such as high-rise condominiums obscuring the sunrise in an old fishing village like Crisfield. Away from the shore, in Harford County, where the population had more than tripled since 1960, the rate has almost flattened since 2010, partly due to job losses, especially among federal contractors.

Even more threatening is pollution. Agricultural and suburban runoff have vastly depleted marine populations, and only a few watermen still make their living bringing crabs and oysters to shore. Since 1990, the blue crab harvest has dropped by two-thirds. In 2014, the number of spawning females dropped by more than half to about 70 million, which experts said was unsustainable. But those numbers can change quickly, and early reports in 2015 were more positive. The bay's oyster harvest in 2014 was the largest in 30 years. Various attempts at cleanup by governmental agencies over the years have been helpful but not entirely successful. In early 2009, the Chesapeake Bay Foundation filed a lawsuit seeking to force the Environmental Protection Agency to enforce limits on pollution entering the bay, settling 15 months later

2012 Presidential Vote		
Mitt Romney (R)................214,988		(61%)
Barack Obama (D) 132,286		(37%)
2008 Presidential Vote		
John McCain (R).................208,977		(60%)
Barack Obama (D) 134,621		(39%)
Cook Partisan Voting Index: R+14		

after the agency agreed to step up enforcement of regulations on developers and farmers. The EPA had originally committed to getting the bay off the nation's list of dirtiest bodies of water by 2010, but that has been extended to 2025. As of 2015, scientists reported that some progress had been made. Good news for yacht owners: In 2015, the Legislature passed a bill that permits pleasure boats up to 200 feet long to navigate state waters without a licensed bay pilot. Previously, the law required vessels longer than 79 feet to hire a pilot.

The 1st Congressional District of Maryland includes all nine counties of the Eastern Shore. At the top of the bay, it takes in parts of the northern Baltimore suburbs of Harford, Baltimore and Carroll counties; Carroll and Harford are the most solidly Republican suburbs of Maryland. Although most people think of this as the Eastern Shore district, nearly half of the votes are cast on the west side of the bay. The district also has some Republican precincts in the outer Baltimore suburbs to maximize Democratic performance in neighboring districts. This is now the only district in the state where Republicans hold a voter registration edge, and the only one that presidential nominee Mitt Romney carried in 2012—with 61 percent of the vote, no less.

Andy Harris (R)

Andy Harris, elected in 2010, is the lone Republican in Maryland's congressional delegation. He juggles working with his Terrapin State colleagues on local matters with agitating for his fervently conservative views. At least until the next redistricting, he has no reason to worry about reelection. He has considered running statewide.

Harris, a Johns Hopkins University anesthesiologist and professor, was born in Brooklyn New York, to immigrants from Eastern Europe. His father, a Hungarian anti-communist activist, had been jailed in a Siberian gulag for over a year for his political views before meeting Harris' mother, who had fled Ukraine, at a displaced persons camp in Austria. Harris credits his parents' escape from communism and the spirited dinner-table conversations they encouraged among their four sons with fostering his fiercely held beliefs in the ills of big government and the sanctity of the private sector. After Harris completed his medical studies at Johns Hopkins, he began to practice and teach there, and lived in a suburb north of Baltimore.

Harris was elected to the state Senate to represent Baltimore County in 1998. In Annapolis, he was one of the most conservative members, and he served as the chamber's minority whip from 2003 to 2007. He gained a reputation for his artful filibusters—during a fight against a stem cell research bill, he read from a biology textbook on DNA.

In 2008, Harris challenged Rep. Wayne Gilchrest, a moderate Republican, in a bloody primary. When Harris defeated him, Gilchrest refused to concede and then endorsed Frank Kratovil, the Democratic nominee. Kratovil continued Gilchrest's strategy of portraying Harris as too far right for the district and won by fewer than 3,000 votes.

Harris returned for a rematch in 2010. He cast Kratovil as a puppet for President Barack Obama in a year when anti-incumbent anger was rampant and voters were deeply divided over the president's overhaul of the health insurance system. Pledging not to raise taxes and to repeal the health care overhaul, Harris connected with Republicans in a district that gave Sen. John McCain nearly 60 percent of the vote in the presidential race. Harris raised almost $2.4 million while Kratovil brought in $2.6 million. Since he first ran in 2008, Harris began to practice medicine a few days a week on the Eastern Shore, which helped deflect the criticism that he was running in an area where he had spent little time.

Kratovil attacked Harris for his support of a conservative proposal to replace the income tax with a national sales tax. At the same time, Kratovil highlighted his differences with Obama over the expiring Bush-era tax cuts, saying he favored an across-the-board extension. The freshman Kratovil was swept away by the Republican tide, losing to Harris, 54%-42%.

Harris said the "proudest moment" of his first few months in office was voting for the House-passed omnibus spending bill that cut $61 billion for fiscal 2011. In 2013, Harris infuriated Maryland Democrats by joining 66 Republicans in voting against $9.7 billion in relief from Hurricane Sandy, which had battered parts of the Eastern Shore. He explained he wanted the bill to strengthen the National Flood Insurance Program instead of writing "another blank check." In September 2014, he dropped his bid to be chairman of the Republican Study Committee following the recent sudden death of his wife Sylvia. Although he voted for John Boehner for speaker in January 2015, Harris heatedly objected when a Boehner aide was quoted in *Politico* that the 25 Republicans voting against Boehner were "fringe guys." He demanded that Boehner deliver on his promises to conservatives. In an unusual incident, C-SPAN captured Harris winking several times to the camera while he was seated on the House floor. The explanation, an aide told *National Journal*: "His mother watches C-SPAN, and it makes her day to see him."

Harris sought to help the Eastern Shore by introducing a bill in 2011 authorizing federal money to study oxygen-starved "dead zones" in the Chesapeake Bay and the Gulf of Mexico that drive away fish. Some environmentalists criticized the measure, saying it emphasized research instead of action. In February 2014, he spurred an investigation by the Health and Human Services Department of how the state had mishandled implementation of the health care law. Harris infuriated residents of the District of Columbia when he sought to use congressional authority to stifle Washington's November 2014 referendum legalizing sales of marijuana. Some suggested a boycott of the Eastern Shore, which would be a major sacrifice in lifestyle for many. "The fact is the Constitution gives Congress the ultimate oversight about what happens in the federal district," Harris responded.

In his 2012 reelection bid, Harris got several breaks. First, Kratovil decided against another rematch. Then, Maryland's Democratic redistricters decided to focus on ousting 6th District Republican Roscoe Bartlett. They ended up adding more Republicans from Baltimore's northern suburbs to Harris' district. Finally, his Democratic rival, businesswoman Wendy Rosen, unexpectedly dropped out of the race in September after the state party said she had voted in both Maryland and Florida in two earlier elections. Democrats quickly got physician John LaFerla to run as a write-in candidate, but Harris coasted to a win with 63% of the vote. In 2014, Harris got 70% of the vote against Democrat Bill Tilghman, a retired lawyer from a longtime Eastern Shore family. Tilghman spent $573,000, but he was outspent 2-to-1 and failed to get much traction. In 2015, Harris was the only significant Republican who voiced interest in running for the Senate seat of retiring Democrat Barbara Mikulski. But multiple factors seemed to tilt against making a move, including: the Republican lean of his district; the Democratic lean of the state; and his membership on the House Appropriations Committee. In his district, former state delegate Michael Smigiel threatened to challenge Harris in the 2016 GOP primary because of opposition by Harris to marijuana in D.C.

SECOND DISTRICT

Dutch Ruppersberger (D)

Elected 2002, 7th term; b. Jan. 31, 1946, Baltimore; Baltimore City Col., U. of Baltimore, J.D. 1970; Methodist; married (Kay); 2 children.

Elected Office: Baltimore Cnty. Cncl., 1986-94; Baltimore Cnty. exec., 1994-2002.

Professional Career: Clerk, Judge Kenneth C. Proctor, 1970-72; Asst. state atty., Baltimore Cnty., 1972-80; Partner, Ruppersberger, Clark & Mister, 1980-94.

DC Office: 2416 RHOB, 20515, 202-225-3061; Fax: 202-225-3094; Website: ruppersberger.house.gov.

State Offices: Timonium, 410-628-2701.

Committees: *Appropriations:* Defense; State, Foreign Operations, & Related Programs.

Group Ratings

	ADA	ACLU	AFL-CIO	LCV	ITI	COC	HAFA	ACU	CFG	FRC
2014	60%	55%	–	91%	80%	64%	17%	9%	2%	0%
2013	65%	C	95%	89%	C	54%	C	17%	13%	C

National Journal Ratings

	2013 LIB	—	2013 CONS
Economic	71%	—	29%
Social	66%	—	32%
Foreign	58%	—	42%
Composite	65%	—	35%

Key Votes of the 113th Congress

1. Sandy storm spending	Y	5. Medical Marijuana	Y	9. Syrian Rebels Training	Y
2. Violence Against Women Act	Y	6. Farm Bill	N	10. Keystone pipeline	N
3. Guantanamo Bay Detainees	N	7. Afghanistan Combat	N	11. Immigration Exec. Action	N
4. Abortion 20-week ban	N	8. NSA Phone Data Collection	N	12. Bipartisan budget deal	Y

Election Results

2014 general	Dutch Ruppersberger (D)	120,412	(61%)	$893,339	$9,135
	David Banach (R)	70,411	(36%)		
	Ian Schlakman (G)	5,326	(3%)	$2,787	
2014 primary	Dutch Ruppersberger (D)	43,614	(78%)		
	Paul Rundquist (D)	6,450	(11%)		
	Blaine Taylor (D)	6,164	(11%)		

Prior winning percentages: 2012 (66%), 2010 (64%), 2008 (72%), 2006 (69%), 2004 (67%), 2002 (54%)

Population		Race and Ethnicity		Income	
Total:	745,135	White	54.8%	Median income:	$60,376
Urban:	31.5%	Black	31.0%		(125 of 435)
Suburban:	68.5%	Latino	6.5%	Under $50,000	40.5%
Rural:	0.0%	Asian	4.7%	$50,000-$99,999:	33.9%
Land area:	355	Two races	2.5%	$100,000-$199,999:	21.4%
Pop/sq. mi.:	2,100.1	White Ethnic	26.9%	$200,000 or more:	4.2%
Born in state:	62.4%			Poverty Rate	12.0%
		Education			
Age Groups		H.S. grad or less:	42.1%	**Work**	
Under 18:	22.4%	Some college:	28.5%	White collar:	39.1%
18 to 34:	25.3%	College degree, 4 yr.:	17.4%	Blue collar:	43.7%
35 to 64:	40.0%	Post-grad study:	12.0%	Sales and service:	17.3%
Over 64:	12.4%				
		Military		Govt. workers:	20.4%
		Veterans/active duty:	10.4%		

Baltimore Metro: Parts of Baltimore County

The spokes of Baltimore's avenues spread out in all directions from the Inner Harbor, connecting the central city with the suburbs, where most residents of metropolitan Baltimore live. The streets reach east to Dundalk and Essex, industrial suburbs where the tone of life was set for years by the

Voter Turnout	
2013 Total Citizen 18+	543,276
2014 House Turnout	196,354
2014 Turnout as % CVAP	36.1%
2012 Turnout as % CVAP	59%

giant Sparrows Point steel mill, long the biggest in the country, but which was shuttered in 2012. Northeastward, they extend to charming Havre de Grace and the oldest lighthouse in continuous use on the East Coast, as well as to modest working-class suburbs in Harford County. Aberdeen has generated military and civilian job growth, but the locale is now better known for its Ripken Stadium, home of the Aberdeen IronBirds, a Class A baseball team owned by hometown hero Cal Ripken, the Hall of Fame legend who played 2,632 consecutive games for the Baltimore Orioles. In an arc north of downtown are middle-income towns from Randallstown to Owings Mills. A couple of miles northwest of the Baltimore County seat of Towson is Timonium, the site of the annual Maryland State Fair.

The 2nd Congressional District of Maryland is an irregularly shaped hodgepodge that includes much of this territory. Most of the district is not far from the Chesapeake Bay, including the terminal for the bustling Port of Baltimore. The port of Baltimore employs 14,600 workers, and is ranked 13th in the nation for its volume of cargo, including 800,000 automobiles in 2014. With the widening of the Panama Canal, Baltimore and Norfolk Virginia are the only East Coast ports wide and deep enough for post-Panamax cargo ships.

The Aberdeen Proving Ground, which tests a wide variety of military weapons, in 2014 awarded about $12 billion in contracts, including $1.3 billion in Maryland. Down the Baltimore-Washington Parkway is Fort Meade, the large Army post that houses the National Security Agency and gained more than 20,000 jobs during the latest realignment of military bases. It has evolved from

2012 Presidential Vote		
Barack Obama (D) 193,834	(63%)
Mitt Romney (R)................107,890	(35%)
2008 Presidential Vote		
Barack Obama (D) 185,470	(61%)
John McCain (R)................114,875	(38%)
Cook Partisan Voting Index: D+10		

an army base to a cybersecurity center, which now houses the nation's cyber defense operations and the Defense Information Systems Agency.

Like the arms of a Maryland crab, the district angles inland to include some Baltimore County suburbs, residential neighborhoods in northeast Baltimore, and an industrial pocket in far southeast Baltimore. At that point, the district crosses the Harbor Tunnel to capture the row houses of Brooklyn and Curtis Bay, whose residents are mainly descendants of German and East European immigrants who moved there to work on the docks and in the factories along the Patapsco River and the harbor. About 60% of the district's population is in Baltimore County, with 13% in Baltimore city, and the remainder divided among Anne Arundel, Howard and Harford counties. About one-third of its population is African American. This is a comfortably Democratic district, with some Republican enclaves. In 2014, working-class Dundalk voted Republican in down-ballot contests for the first time in many decades.

Dutch Ruppersberger (D)

Dutch Ruppersberger, elected in 2002 in a district drawn for him, stepped down in 2015 as the House Intelligence Committee's ranking Democrat, where he had a close relationship with the committee's then-chairman, Michigan Republican Mike Rogers. But he retained his focus on national security issues.

Charles Albert Ruppersberger grew up in Baltimore, attended the University of Maryland, and graduated from the University of Baltimore School of Law. Working as a Baltimore County assistant state's attorney, Ruppersberger had a near-fatal car accident in 1975 while investigating a drug-trafficking case. When he asked his doctors at the University of Maryland's Shock Trauma Center how he could thank them, he said, they urged him to run for office so he could fund their facility. In 1986, he won a seat on the Baltimore County Council and made good on his promise to help the hospital. In 1994, he was elected Baltimore County executive, a position held in the 1960s by future Republican Vice President Spiro Agnew.

Barred from seeking a third term in 2002, Ruppersberger seriously considered running for governor. But he was dissuaded by state party leaders who felt he was politically vulnerable at the time. In 2000, he had backed a plan to give him the power of eminent domain to redevelop large pieces of the county, but voters rebuked him and rejected it 2-to-1 in a referendum. Compounding the situation for Ruppersberger was a damaging story in *The Baltimore Sun* saying that he had given county work to a firm to which he had financial ties. Kathleen Kennedy Townsend, the daughter of the late Robert F. Kennedy, became the gubernatorial candidate. She lost, but Ruppersberger took advantage of a favorable House district when Democrats redrew the congressional map.

Because he considered his last name to be too long for a bumper sticker, Ruppersberger used his lifelong nickname of "Dutch" in his political campaign. His little-known primary opponent, investment banker Osman Bengur, spent more than $500,000 of his own money. Ruppersberger was backed by the state's Democratic establishment, and he won 50%-36%. In the fall, he faced former Republican Rep. Helen Delich Bentley, who served in the House for a decade until she ran, unsuccessfully, for governor in 1994. She had a strong record of constituent service and cross-party popularity. Both candidates supported additional dredging of shipping channels in the Chesapeake Bay and increased port security. Ruppersberger won, 54%-46%. His popular-vote margin was more than 13,000 in the small part of the district in Baltimore city, which he carried 79%-21%, and only 3,000 in the rest of the district.

In the House, Ruppersberger has had the least liberal voting record among Maryland Democrats. Though he generally sticks with his party on major legislation, he supported an extension of several key provisions of the Patriot Act in 2011. With the help of Baltimore native and Democratic leader Nancy Pelosi, he was appointed to the Intelligence Committee, where he called for expanded oversight of the intelligence agencies and for shifting resources from the Iraq war to terrorist "safe havens" in Afghanistan.

Ruppersberger and Rogers, a former FBI agent, repaired the panel's reputation for partisan infighting. "We both focus more on the teamwork," Ruppersberger told *The Washington Post*. The two men traveled together to foreign hot spots, and sat together at classified White House briefings. Ruppersberger did not hesitate to criticize President Barack Obama and his administration. In April 2009, he said that he had not been adequately consulted on its ambitious plan to buy and launch spy satellites. He added a provision to the 2010 intelligence authorization bill to ensure better oversight of satellite programs. In June 2014, he criticized as a "dangerous precedent" the decision by Obama to release five Taliban prisoners of war in exchange for U.S. prisoner of war Bowe Bergdahl. With Rogers, he signed a report in December 2014 that defended the Pentagon and the Central Intelligence Agency for their handling of the attacks on the U.S. diplomatic compound in Benghazi, Libya. He was an early drafter and advocate of the House-passed bill in May 2015 to end the National Security Agency's bulk collection of telephone and email data.

In early 2010, Ruppersberger backed a House-passed bill to strengthen cybersecurity, an area he said had been neglected under Obama. He said in May 2012 that administration leaks of highly classified information—which Republicans sought at the time to turn into an election-year campaign issue—were "about the worst that I've seen." Concerned about the potential sale of shipping operations at the Port of Baltimore to the United Arab Emirates, Ruppersberger helped to enact port-security legislation. After anti-gay rights groups conducted a series of highly controversial protests at the funerals of U.S. soldiers, he introduced a bill in 2011 barring such demonstrations at cemeteries during the five hours before and after a memorial service. After his departure from the Intelligence Committee, where Pelosi had twice extended his term limits, he returned to the Appropriations Committee and focused there on national security funding.

Ruppersberger has been reelected easily. His statewide ambitions have dimmed with the election of other Baltimore-area Democrats to vacant seats for governor and the Senate. He thought about running for the open seat for governor in 2014, but other Democrats made a quicker start. A similar situation ensued after he voiced interest in running for the Senate in 2016.

THIRD DISTRICT

John Sarbanes (D)

Elected 2006, 5th term; b. May 22, 1962, Baltimore; Princeton U., B.A. 1984, Harvard U., J.D. 1988; Greek Orthodox; married (Dina); 3 children.

Professional Career: Clerk, Judge Fred Motz, 1988-89; Practicing atty., Venable LLP, 1989-2006; Special asst. MD Schls. Superintendent, 1998-2005.

DC Office: 2444 RHOB, 20515, 202-225-4016; Fax: 202-225-9219; Website: sarbanes.house.gov.

State Offices: Annapolis, 410-295-1679; Burtonsville, 301-421-4078; Towson, 410-832-8890.

Committees: *Energy & Commerce:* Energy & Power; Health.

Group Ratings

	ADA	ACLU	AFL-CIO	LCV	ITI	COC	HAFA	ACU	CFG	FRC
2014	95%	83%	–	97%	20%	43%	10%	8%	13%	0%
2013	95%	C	95%	93%	C	25%	C	4%	10%	C

National Journal Ratings

	2013 LIB	—	2013 CONS
Economic	91%	—	0%
Social	79%	—	16%
Foreign	94%	—	0%
Composite	91%	—	9%

Key Votes of the 113th Congress

1. Sandy storm spending	Y	5. Medical Marijuana	Y	9. Syrian Rebels Training	Y
2. Violence Against Women Act	Y	6. Farm Bill	N	10. Keystone pipeline	N
3. Guantanamo Bay Detainees	Y	7. Afghanistan Combat	Y	11. Immigration Exec. Action	N
4. Abortion 20-week ban	N	8. NSA Phone Data Collection	Y	12. Bipartisan budget deal	Y

Election Results

2014 general	John Sarbanes (D)	128,594	(60%)	$756,851
	Charles Long (R)	87,029	(40%)	$3,715
2014 primary	John Sarbanes (D)	54,926	(85%)	
	Matthew Molyett (D)	9,564	(15%)	

Prior winning percentages: 2012 (67%), 2010 (61%), 2008 (70%), 2006 (64%)

Population		Race and Ethnicity		Income	
Total:	740,451	White	62.0%	Median income:	$75,431
Urban:	46.8%	Black	20.6%		*(43 of 435)*
Suburban:	53.2%	Asian	7.7%	Under $50,000	32.3%
Rural:	0.0%	Latino	6.8%	$50,000-$99,999:	31.6%
Land area:	271	Two races	2.2%	$100,000-$199,999:	26.3%
Pop/sq. mi.:	2,737.0	White Ethnic	30.9%	$200,000 or more:	9.8%
Born in state:	48.0%			Poverty Rate	7.9%
		Education			
Age Groups		H.S. grad or less:	30.1%	**Work**	
Under 18:	21.7%	Some college:	24.0%	White collar:	50.7%
18 to 34:	25.5%	College degree, 4 yr.:	24.7%	Blue collar:	36.8%
35 to 64:	39.0%	Post-grad study:	21.2%	Sales and service:	12.5%
Over 64:	13.8%			Govt. workers:	21.0%
		Military			
		Veterans/active duty:	10.0%		

Baltimore Metro, Annapolis

Downtown Baltimore, one of America's major urban centers since the Revolution, has been viewed as one of America's star cities. Its Inner Harbor redevelopment, with a spectacular, multilevel aquarium on the water, and its ballpark at Camden Yards are national models. The local cuisine—crab cakes and

Voter Turnout	
2013 Total Citizen 18+	535,877
2014 House Turnout	215,946
2014 Turnout as % CVAP	40.3%
2012 Turnout as % CVAP	64.3%

steamed crabs spiced a certain way—is known well beyond the watershed of the Chesapeake Bay. In 2009, about half of the city became a National Heritage Area, a designation that boosted tourism and economic development. The minority neighborhoods of Baltimore have had terrible urban problems—high crime, controversial policing, abandoned neighborhoods, poor schools—but the greater Baltimore area that has grown far beyond the city and county lines has fared better and retains a distinctive character. To the south, Annapolis was laid out as a capital in 1694, and the marble-halled Statehouse, built in 1772, is where the Continental Congress ratified the Treaty of Paris and is the oldest state capitol in continuous use. Annapolis is also the home of the U.S. Naval Academy, and the city's gentrified waterfront is both a waterman's and yachter's port.

The 3rd District of Maryland consists of three oddly disjointed pieces of geography that extend from the Inner Harbor area. As it scoops up parts of Baltimore City, Baltimore County, Anne Arundel County, Howard County, and a small slice of Montgomery County, the 3rd is a leading contender for the most-gerrymandered district in the nation, and was named the ugliest-drawn congressional district by Comedy Central's *The Daily Show with Jon Stewart*. From a distance, it seems like an ink spot. But there is a rationale to what some might consider its absurdity. Its boundaries were designed by Democrats with politics in mind: The 3rd borders the majority-black 7th

2012 Presidential Vote		
Barack Obama (D)	205,929	(61%)
Mitt Romney (R)	122,604	(37%)

2008 Presidential Vote		
Barack Obama (D)	196,970	(60%)
John McCain (R)	124,446	(38%)

Cook Partisan Voting Index: D+9

District on three sides. One spoke extends northeast and takes in black city neighborhoods; another extends north and west from the city to the Baltimore County seat of Towson and the heavily Jewish suburbs of Pikesville and Owings Mills. The last crooked spoke extends south to Glen Burnie and the Baltimore-Washington International Thurgood Marshall Airport, a major hub for low-cost airlines, where it splits into two tangents: one goes south to growing Anne Arundel County and all of Annapolis, and the other heads west to Columbia in Howard County, plus rural Olney and Calverton in Montgomery County. About a third of the district's population resides in Anne Arundel, and another quarter is in Baltimore city.

In Baltimore's revived Locust Point industrial neighborhood on the waterfront is the iconic orange Domino Sugars sign glowing from the refinery plant's rooftop—now powered by solar panels. The plant is still refining 6.6 million pounds of raw sugar a day, but other industrial land along the water is being redeveloped into upscale residential and commercial properties. The district also includes such neighborhoods as Roland Park, and the fabled restaurants and bars of Little Italy and Fell's Point. A water wheel, with solar and water power, periodically removes tons of trash and debris from the Inner Harbor. These sites are close to the troubled neighborhoods of the Baltimore riots that broke out in the spring of 2015 after a black man, Freddie Gray, died in police custody, but those areas are in the 7th District. The Baltimore Orioles postponed two of their baseball games and played a third before no spectators at Camden Yards, which was about five miles east of the center of the disturbances. The 3rd is solidly Democratic.

John Sarbanes (D)

Democrat John Sarbanes, elected in 2006, is the son of a former longtime senator from Maryland. He has a coveted seat on the Energy and Commerce Committee, where he works on issues ranging from campaign finance reform to the cleanup of Chesapeake Bay. His ambition has been to follow his father's path from the House to the Senate.

Sarbanes graduated from Princeton University and Harvard Law School, following the academic route taken by his dad, Paul Sarbanes, who retired in 2006 after 36 years in Congress. The younger Sarbanes returned to Baltimore to clerk for a federal District Court judge, then joined the Venable law firm, where he chaired the health care practice and represented nonprofit hospitals and senior-living providers. He also spent seven years as special assistant to the Maryland superintendent of schools, serving as the liaison to the Baltimore schools.

Though his 2006 campaign was his first bid for public office, Sarbanes enjoyed a considerable advantage because of his name recognition. But the primary race was no cakewalk. Openings in the Maryland congressional delegation are rare, so when Democratic Rep. Ben Cardin announced he was giving up his seat to run for the Senate seat of the senior Sarbanes, eight candidates filed for the September primary. Contenders included veteran state Sen. Paula Hollinger and former Baltimore Health Commissioner Peter Beilenson, the son of former Democratic Rep. Anthony Beilenson of California.

Sarbanes issued lengthy, detailed proposals on health care and education, which he called his top two legislative priorities. Beilenson emphasized his experience managing a large government budget. Hollinger was endorsed by the teachers union, and had been an active state lawmaker. Sarbanes, who had a small fundraising advantage, won the Democratic primary with 32% to 25% for runner-up Beilenson and 21% for Hollinger. In the general election, Republican nominee John White, the founder and CEO of a marketing company, spent nearly a half-million dollars, most of it from his own pocket, but got little attention in a Democratic year and lost the general election to Sarbanes, 64%-34%.

In the House, Sarbanes has a solidly liberal voting record. He has promoted a novel 'Government by the People" campaign finance plan that would give contributors tax credits for donations and create a fund to match donations to "grassroots" candidates who refuse political action committee money. Although he concedes that its congressional prospects are slim for now, he has been encouraged that some local governments have approved the model. He urged the Federal Trade Commission in November 2011 to take action against Pfizer for what he described as its attempts to keep consumers away from generic versions of its successful anti-cholesterol drug Lipitor. When House Republicans shot down a proposal to create a national climate change service, he attacked them for their "reckless political stunt of climate change denial." In 2010, Sarbanes got a provision in an auto safety bill to fund research into new technologies to prevent drunk-driving accidents. Mothers Against Drunk Driving strongly backed the idea, but the American Beverage Institute and some Republicans complained it went too far.

Earlier, when he served on the House education panel, Sarbanes won approval of amendments to bolster school instruction on protecting the environment. He also got a bill signed into law enabling college graduates to erase student loan debts after 10 years of work in public service or the non-profit sector. He has advocated legislative solutions to clean up pollution in the Chesapeake. He unsuccessfully sought in committee in February 2012 to prevent offshore drilling near the bay. Like his father, he has been an outspoken advocate of Greece and its Hellenic values. Sarbanes has been reelected easily. He says that he drives home to Towson every night. When Sen. Barbara Mikulski announced her retirement in March 2015, Sarbanes initially kept his cards close to his vest. But he soon ruled out a bid for her seat.

FOURTH DISTRICT

Donna Edwards (D)

Elected June 2008, 4th full term; b. June 28, 1958, Yanceyville, NC; Wake Forest U., B.A. 1980, Franklin Pierce Law Center, J.D. 1989; Baptist; divorced; 1 child.

Professional Career: Asst. dir., UN Development Program, 1980-82; Project engineer, Lockheed Corp., 1982-86; Clerk, Superior Ct. Judge Stephen Eilperin, 1989-90; Lobbyist, Public Citizen & Congress Watch, 1992-94; Exec. dir., Ctr. for a New Democracy, 1994-96; Co-founder & exec. dir., Natl. Network to End Domestic Violence, 1996-99; Exec. dir., The Arca Foundation, 2000-08.

DC Office: 2445 RHOB, 20515, 202-225-8699; Fax: 202-225-8714; Website: donnaedwards.house.gov.

State Offices: Severna Park, 410-421-8061; Suitland, 301-516-7601.

Committees: *Science, Space, & Technology:* Environment; Space (RMM). *Transportation & Infrastructure:* Economic Development, Public Buildings & Emergency Mgmt.; Highways & Transit; Water Resources & Environment.

Group Ratings

	ADA	ACLU	AFL-CIO	LCV	ITI	COC	HAFA	ACU	CFG	FRC
2014	85%	77%	–	94%	40%	46%	8%	8%	4%	0%
2013	95%	C	95%	96%	C	23%	C	13%	11%	C

National Journal Ratings

	2013 LIB	—	2013 CONS
Economic	91%	—	0%
Social	93%	—	0%
Foreign	94%	—	0%
Composite	96%	—	4%

Key Votes of the 113th Congress

1. Sandy storm spending	Y	5. Medical Marijuana	Y	9. Syrian Rebels Training	N
2. Violence Against Women Act	Y	6. Farm Bill	N	10. Keystone pipeline	N
3. Guantanamo Bay Detainees	Y	7. Afghanistan Combat	Y	11. Immigration Exec. Action	N
4. Abortion 20-week ban	N	8. NSA Phone Data Collection	Y	12. Bipartisan budget deal	Y

Election Results

2014 general	Donna Edwards (D)	134,628	(70%)	$564,094
	Nancy Hoyt (R)	54,217	(28%)	$39,688
2014 primary	Donna Edwards (D)	53,648	(87%)	
	Warren Christopher (D)	8,021	(13%)	

Prior winning percentages: 2012 (71%), 2010 (83%), 2008 (86%), 2008 special (81%)

Population		Race and Ethnicity		Income	
Total:	739,293	Black	53.1%	Median income:	$72,281
Urban:	21.9%	White	26.0%		*(57 of 435)*
Suburban:	78.1%	Latino	15.6%	Under $50,000	32.4%
Rural:	0.0%	Asian	3.3%	$50,000-$99,999:	33.4%
Land area:	335	Two races	1.6%	$100,000-$199,999:	26.9%
Pop/sq. mi.:	2,206.8	White Ethnic	13.7%	$200,000 or more:	7.3%
Born in state:	30.2%			Poverty Rate	9.1%
		Education			
Age Groups		H.S. grad or less:	41.3%	**Work**	
Under 18:	23.5%	Some college:	28.3%	White collar:	36.8%
18 to 34:	24.5%	College degree, 4 yr.:	17.8%	Blue collar:	44.6%
35 to 64:	40.5%	Post-grad study:	12.6%	Sales and service:	18.6%
Over 64:	11.6%			Govt. workers:	23.5%
		Military			
		Veterans/active duty:	9.5%		

Eastern D.C. Suburbs: Prince George's County

In 1696, the proprietors of the colony of Maryland created a new county between the Potomac and Patuxent rivers and named it after the husband of the heir to the throne, Prince George of Denmark. During its 300 years, Prince George's County has not often won national fame—maybe

VoterTurnout	
2013 Total Citizen 18+	487,688
2014 House Turnout	191,837
2014 Turnout as % CVAP	39.3%
2012 Turnout as % CVAP	68.8%

briefly when investigators chased the plotters of Abraham Lincoln's murder here— but it might now. With a population that is nearly two-thirds African American, Prince George's is the home of America's largest black middle class. It is also the wealthiest county with a majority black population. Historically, Prince George's was tobacco country, dotted by slave plantations and pretty much controlled by its white property owners. A hundred years after the Civil War, the population grew as middle-class blacks moved out of neighboring Washington, D.C., into modest suburbs at the county's edge and affluent subdivisions farther to the east. Its African-American population increased from 14% in 1970, to 37% in 1980, to 65% in 2013, the highest in the state. The county continues to grow, with working-class black and Hispanic residents leaving gentrified Washington for more affordable housing and better schools across the border. With Hispanic population climbing above 15%, there has been some pushback from black groups over jobs, plus new schools and public facilities in immigrant neighborhoods, including Largo and Langley Park.

With office and shopping mall development, Prince George's County has become more commercially vibrant than adjacent parts of the District of Columbia. Commuters travel into the county across the Potomac River on the 12-lane Woodrow Wilson Bridge. Just over the bridge is the National Harbor development area, where a $1.2 billion MGM casino is scheduled to open in 2016 with nearly 4,000 employees, after Maryland voters approved a hotly contested referendum in 2012. The Washington Redskins play at FedEx Field in nearby Landover, with occasional protests over the franchise's name.

Prince George's County is affluent by national standards, and ranks as the 69th wealthiest county in the nation. The county's median household income of $73,447 easily tops the national median of about $50,502 and is more than double the $32,229 national median for black households. Nearly 30% of the county population over 25 holds an undergraduate degree, which is slightly higher than the overall national average. Yet amid this success, considerable problems remain: Prince George's homicide rates are high for a suburban county. The recession hit hard at over-extended local homeowners with a disproportionate share of sub-prime mortgages.

2012 Presidential Vote
Barack Obama (D) 255,226   (78%)
Mitt Romney (R)..................69,323   (21%)

2008 Presidential Vote
Barack Obama (D) 247,535   (77%)
John McCain (R)..................69,767   (22%)

Cook Partisan Voting Index: D+26

In 2009, the median value of a home in the county dropped from $343,000 to $245,000. Housing finance continues to plague Prince George's. In 2014, there was a 50% increase in foreclosures compared to 2013, *American Prospect* reported.

The 4th Congressional District of Maryland includes most of Prince George's County inside the Capital Beltway that rings Washington, and a GOP-leaning eastern salient into relatively rural central Anne Arundel County, including Severna Park. This is still a safely Democratic seat; President Barack Obama carried Prince George's by an extraordinary 90%-9% in 2012, his fourth-best countywide showing. On certain social issues, however, the district is more conservative: While a 2012 referendum legalizing same-sex marriage in Maryland passed statewide with 52% of the vote, it narrowly failed in Prince George's County. The district's biggest employer is the federal government. Suitland, just across the D.C. border, is the home of the Census Bureau, and local and state officials are trying to lure the FBI, which plans to move its longtime headquarters from downtown Washington.

Donna Edwards (D)

Democrat Donna Edwards, who won a special election in 2008, is the first black woman to represent Maryland in Congress. A staunch liberal, she is known for her drive and ambition as well as her occasional tendency to rile the state's Democratic establishment. After the 2014 election, she became co-chair of the Democratic Steering and Policy Committee. When Sen. Barbara Mikulski announced her retirement in March 2015, Edwards quickly declared her candidacy, with a claim on the progressive mantle.

Edwards was born in North Carolina, the second of six children. The family moved frequently as a result of her father's career in the Air Force. Edwards says she learned adaptability from her mother, and, as she told *The Washington Post*, "There's not a room I go in where I feel like a stranger." She was president of her high school class in New Mexico, and returned to her home state for college at Wake Forest University, where she was one of six African-American women in her class.

She went to work for Lockheed at the Goddard Space Flight Center in Greenbelt, Md., and after the 1986 explosion of the space shuttle *Challenger,* she decided to attend law school. At Franklin Pierce University in New Hampshire, she focused on public-interest law. She returned to Maryland and settled in Fort Washington, and clerked for a District of Columbia Superior Court judge. Later, she co-founded and was the first executive director of the National Network to End Domestic Violence. Edwards earned national recognition for her work on behalf of battered women. She was also executive director of the Center for a New Democracy, where she focused on campaign finance reform. In 2000, she became executive director of The Arca Foundation in Washington, which focuses on social equity and justice.

After separating from her husband, Edwards briefly was homeless and then lived with her young son in a room in her mother's home. In voicing support for President Barack Obama at the 2012 Democratic convention, she talked of her experience battling pneumonia and being forced to go to a food bank. "He knows that no one should end up in an emergency room, facing financial ruin and the loss of a middle-class life, just because they can't afford a doctor's visit and $20 of antibiotics," she said.

In 2006, Edwards challenged seven-term Rep. Albert Wynn in the Democratic primary and surprised him with a late-blossoming but well-funded campaign. She ran to his left ideologically, benefited from strong local opposition to the Iraq war, which Wynn backed, and attacked the incumbent's close ties to business interests. Wynn accused Edwards of distorting his record. He won, but by a hair, 49.7%-46.4%. Wynn took his home Prince George's County, 57%-40%. In Montgomery, which cast 32% of the vote, Edwards led 60%-35%. Edwards almost immediately began preparing for a rematch.

In the 2008 primary, she benefitted from the support of MoveOn.org, the liberal grassroots group, and EMILY's List, the abortion-rights fundraising powerhouse for women, while criticizing Wynn for his reliance on special interest money (Edwards did not take political action committee contributions.) Still, she spent $1 million to get her message to voters. The outcome this time was not close. Boosted by heavy turnout from the presidential primary, Edwards won, 59%-37%. She led 55%-41% in Prince George's, and 67%-27% in Montgomery County.

Six weeks later, Wynn unexpectedly announced that he was quitting Congress to join the Washington law firm of Dickstein Shapiro. That decision gave Edwards a chance to take the seat early. Gov. Martin O'Malley scheduled a special election for June 17; Edwards won 81%-18% over Republican Peter James, a technology developer, in a low-turnout event.

In the House, Edwards was tied for most-liberal member in *National Journal's* 2011 and 2013 rankings. She occasionally has brought unwanted attention to herself. At a Washington Press Club Foundation dinner in 2014, her joking criticisms of Republicans were viewed as going too far over the line; at one point, she compared working with the GOP to a commercial for the erectile-dysfunction drug Cialis. "Rep. Donna Edwards Weirds Out Washington," read a headline in *U.S. News & World Report.*

Edwards has been ardent in her liberal views. She criticized the Obama administration's efforts in Afghanistan and cosponsored Democratic Rep. Dennis Kucinich's failed proposal in March 2010 to withdraw U.S. forces there. In December 2014, she voted against the House-Senate conference report on the defense spending bill because, she said, it included funding to train rebels in Syria and to oppose the Islamic State, "absent a full debate and vote by Congress—that is our constitutional responsibility." On the Science, Space, and Technology Committee, she has worked for greater tracking of minorities' participation in science and math programs. As ranking Democrat on the Space Subcommittee, she has sought to increase the budget for NASA, which has a large workforce in her district. She filed a bill to establish a national park on the moon to commemorate NASA's Apollo moon-landing program.

When state's attorney Marilyn Mosby brought an indictment against six Baltimore police officers in the death of Freddie Gray during the April 2015 riots, Edwards commended Mosby "for moving forward in a thorough and expeditious manner." In an op-ed piece in *The Washington Post*, Edwards wrote, "Today, far too many black people believe the police stand against them, and far too many police officers look the other way or deny the existence of any problem at all. It's time for good police officers to stand with good citizens to change the culture."

She has kept her independence from party leaders. She was alone among Maryland's House Democrats in expressing opposition to a 2012 referendum to expand gambling in the state, saying there were better means of economic development. *The Post* reported that she had alienated colleagues who said she needed to forge better relationships within the state party. Earlier that year, Edwards refused to back Rob Garagiola, the state Senate majority leader and an ally of House Minority Whip Steny Hoyer, in a primary to challenge GOP Rep. Roscoe Bartlett. She endorsed businessman John Delaney, who ended up winning the seat.

Edwards reportedly mulled a bid for House Democratic Caucus vice chair in November 2012, but opted not to run. In some areas, she has sought to mend fences with party leaders. She served as co-chair of the Democratic Congressional Campaign Committee's candidate-recruitment in 2012, and in 2014 took full charge of the effort. She often turned up on talk shows to give the party line, and helped organize a national bus tour in which she and Minority Leader Nancy Pelosi appealed to women voters.

After the Democrats' drubbing at the polls in 2014, the influential liberal website Daily Kos touted Edwards as a potential DCCC chair, saying, "If you're a longtime Daily Kos reader, you will remember that Donna Edwards is one of us." Instead, Pelosi named Edwards co-chair of the Steering and Policy Committee, a powerful group that makes committee assignments and other internal decisions.

Edwards has been politically untouchable since her 2008 election. But the 2014 results suggested the limits of her support beyond her home base. Against Republican Nancy Hoyt, who spent about $40,000, Edwards won 70%-28%. Although Edwards took a robust 92% of the vote in her Prince George's base, she got only 32% in Anne Arundel, which cast 36% of the total vote.

In March 2015, Edwards announced that she would seek the Democratic nomination for the seat of retiring Sen. Barbara Mikulski. She unveiled a two-minute video with her firm pledge to maintain Social Security and Medicare with "no ifs, ands, buts or willing to considers," a pointed jab at declared Democratic candidate Rep. Chris Van Hollen, who has emphasized his work on the House Budget Committee in search of a "grand bargain." She promised to be a voice for "the middle-class American dream." EMILY's List and some national progressive groups quickly lined up behind Edwards. But it remained to be seen whether she could be financially competitive with Van Hollen, a proven fundraiser who was endorsed by Senate Minority Leader Harry Reid of Nevada. There also were questions about the extent of her support from members of the Congressional Black Caucus, where her ambition has "ruffled feathers," *National Journal* reported.

FIFTH DISTRICT

Steny Hoyer (D)

Elected May 1981, 17th full term; b. June 14, 1939, New York, NY; U. of MD, B.S. 1963, Georgetown U., J.D. 1966; Baptist; widowed; 3 children.

Elected Office: MD Senate, 1966-79, pres., 1975-78.

Professional Career: Practicing atty., 1966-80; MD Bd. of Higher Ed., 1978-81.

DC Office: 1705 LHOB, 20515, 202-225-4131; Fax: 202-225-4300; Website: hoyer.house.gov.

State Offices: Greenbelt, 301-474-0119; Waldorf, 301-843-1577.

Committees: House Minority Whip.

Group Ratings

	ADA	ACLU	AFL-CIO	LCV	ITI	COC	HAFA	ACU	CFG	FRC
2014	70%	77%	–	91%	80%	50%	13%	0%	2%	0%
2013	75%	C	90%	82%	C	42%	C	12%	19%	C

National Journal Ratings

	2013 LIB	—	2013 CONS
Economic	76%	—	24%
Social	79%	—	16%
Foreign	77%	—	23%
Composite	78%	—	22%

Key Votes of the 113th Congress

1. Sandy storm spending	Y	5. Medical Marijuana	Y	9. Syrian Rebels Training	Y
2. Violence Against Women Act	Y	6. Farm Bill	N	10. Keystone pipeline	N
3. Guantanamo Bay Detainees	Y	7. Afghanistan Combat	N	11. Immigration Exec. Action	N
4. Abortion 20-week ban	N	8. NSA Phone Data Collection	N	12. Bipartisan budget deal	N

Election Results

2014 general	Steny Hoyer (D)	144,725	(64%)	$3,843,176	$30,259
	Chris Chaffee (R)	80,752	(36%)	$26,577	
2014 primary	Steny Hoyer (D)	unopposed			

Prior winning percentages: 2012 (69%), 2010 (64%), 2008 (74%), 2006 (83%), 2004 (69%), 2002 (69%), 2000 (65%), 1998 (65%), 1996 (57%), 1994 (59%), 1992 (53%), 1990 (81%), 1988 (79%), 1986 (82%), 1984 (72%), 1982 (80%), 1981 special (55%)

Population		Race and Ethnicity		Income	
Total:	752,393	White	50.6%	Median income:	$88,481
Urban:	13.7%	Black	37.0%		(15 of 435)
Suburban:	84.8%	Latino	5.7%	Under $50,000	25.4%
Rural:	1.5%	Asian	3.7%	$50,000-$99,999:	31.8%
Land area:	1,053	Two races	2.3%	$100,000-$199,999:	33.3%
Pop/sq. mi.:	714.5	White Ethnic	21.7%	$200,000 or more:	9.5%
Born in state:	39.1%			Poverty Rate	7.6%
		Education			
Age Groups		H.S. grad or less:	36.6%	**Work**	
Under 18:	23.3%	Some college:	30.5%	White collar:	42.7%
18 to 34:	23.3%	College degree, 4 yr.:	19.7%	Blue collar:	41.7%
35 to 64:	42.2%	Post-grad study:	13.3%	Sales and service:	15.7%
Over 64:	11.2%				
		Military		Govt. workers:	30.9%
		Veterans/active duty:	12.9%		

Southern Maryland, D.C. Suburbs: Prince George's County

Southern Maryland was established as a colony of the British Lords Baltimore, who were seeking a refuge for English Catholics in the New World. The Lords Baltimore, first George and then Cecil Calvert, founded St. Mary's in 1634, not long after the founding of Jamestown and Plymouth Rock.

Voter Turnout	
2013 Total Citizen 18+	543,686
2014 House Turnout	226,040
2014 Turnout as % CVAP	41.6%
2012 Turnout as % CVAP	67.3%

Maryland became one of the two great Chesapeake tobacco colonies, with plantation houses on every inlet off the broad Potomac and Patuxent rivers. For years, the towns of southern Maryland grew slowly, and even today, many of their residents are directly descended from the old families. The region was never Puritan country. Liquor flowed even during Prohibition, and for years, Maryland law specifically allowed slot machines. But tobacco farming is nearing an end, even if the area hasn't completely renounced its tobacco heritage. The highlight of the annual Charles County Fair remains the crowning of Queen Nicotina, who must be a local high school senior.

The area's economic base has owed much to government installations: the Civil War Point Lookout prisoner-of-war camp; the Navy's Patuxent River complex, where many astronauts began their training; and the Naval Air Warfare Center. Today, metro Washington and Baltimore are spreading into southern Maryland, with rapid growth in Calvert, Charles and St. Mary's counties. Charles County has become the new home of many African-American families fleeing crime and troubled schools in Prince George's County. Today, most of Charles County's schoolchildren are black. Its median household income rose to $93,160 in 2013, thanks in part to many two-government-employee families.

2012 Presidential Vote		
Barack Obama (D)	234,859	(66%)
Mitt Romney (R)	114,536	(32%)
2008 Presidential Vote		
Barack Obama (D)	221,877	(65%)
John McCain (R)	114,624	(34%)
Cook Partisan Voting Index:	D+14	

The 5th Congressional District of Maryland comprises all of Calvert, Charles, and St. Mary's counties, plus most of Prince George's County outside of the Capital Beltway and a small part of southern Anne Arundel County. Prince George's, with about 40% of the population, and Charles, with 20%, are the largest and most Democratic counties in the district. The three smaller ones lean Republican. The district takes in College Park, home of the University of Maryland, and nearby Hyattsville, Greenbelt, Beltsville and Bowie. Whites in the rural areas have trended Republican, but African Americans—both new suburbanites and descendants of old Southern Maryland families—make up 37% of the district's population. The district has been a Democratic stronghold for decades.

Steny Hoyer (D)

Democrat Steny Hoyer, elected in 1981, is the longest-serving House member from Maryland. He is the minority whip and the de facto leader of his party's shrinking moderate wing in the House, and he is at heart a bipartisan deal-cutter despite his role as a public critic of Republicans.

Hoyer is of Danish descent. His first name, he says, was his parents' adaptation of the Danish name Steen. He grew up in New York City, but moved from place to place with his mother and stepfather, who was in the Air Force and, when Steny was in high school, was transferred from Florida to Andrews Air Force Base in Maryland. Hoyer graduated from the University of Maryland, where in 1959 he listened to Democratic presidential candidate John F. Kennedy deliver a campaign speech that inspired him to switch his major from public relations to political science. While working on his law degree at Georgetown University in Washington, Hoyer interned one summer with Maryland Sen. Daniel Brewster. Another intern in Brewster's office that summer was Nancy D'Alesandro, daughter of the former mayor of Baltimore and now House Minority Leader Nancy Pelosi.

In 1966, just after graduating from law school, Hoyer was elected to the Maryland Senate at age 27. He was Senate president from 1975 to 1978, the youngest person to hold that post in Maryland history. In 1978, he ran for lieutenant governor on a losing ticket. In 1981, after incumbent Gladys Spellman was incapacitated by a heart attack, the 5th District seat was declared vacant. Hoyer won the special election, edging out Spellman's husband and several other Democrats in the primary and beating a well-financed Republican in the general. The district then was entirely in Prince George's County.

A fast riser in Maryland politics, Hoyer was also a fast riser in Congress. He excelled at constituent service and won a seat on the Appropriations Committee, where he worked with Republicans and became a champion for the Washington metro area. He has been an advocate of more spending for education and other social programs, and better pay and benefits for federal workers. He was the chief House sponsor of the Americans with Disabilities Act of 1990, which outlawed discrimination against people with disabilities. He counts that as his greatest legislative achievement, along with the 2002 federal election reform known as the Help America Vote Act that President George W. Bush signed into law. Hoyer also took the lead in crafting bipartisan election reform legislation and in enhancing security in the Capitol complex. When the political parties in the House became more polarized in the late 1990s, Hoyer initiated monthly lunches with Roy Blunt of Missouri, who was then the chief deputy whip for the Republican majority. On Sept. 11, 2001, it was Hoyer's idea to have lawmakers gather in front of the Capitol in a show of unity. The group spontaneously sang "God Bless America," an image captured vividly on television on a dark day in U.S. history.

His voting record is relatively moderate among Democrats, especially on foreign policy issues. He broke with the party by supporting the balanced budget amendment in 1995; he backed many of the free-trade initiatives of recent years that organized labor opposed, including the 1993 North American Free Trade Agreement. In 2002, he voted to authorize military action in Iraq and later complained that President Bush "under resourced" the war. He is a former chairman of the Helsinki Commission, and has remained a champion of human rights around the world.

Hoyer won his first leadership post in 1989 as chairman of the Democratic Caucus. When he tried to move up to the job of majority whip in 1991, he lost, 160-109, to David Bonior of Michigan, who had the support of liberals and the committee chairmen. In 2001, Bonior, faced with unfavorable redistricting changes at home, decided to run for governor. Both Hoyer and Pelosi sought to replace him as minority whip. Hoyer argued that he had greater experience in leadership positions and could do a better job of unifying the caucus. Pelosi had more publicly committed votes going into the October 2001 Democratic Caucus election, and she won 118-95. (Both did less well than predicted, as usually happens in secret-ballot leadership contests.)

Although he was a two-time loser of leadership contests, Hoyer was undeterred when Dick Gephardt stepped down as minority leader in 2002. With Pelosi running to succeed Gephardt, Hoyer ran for minority whip, the No. 2 position in the Democratic hierarchy. He collected commitments for months and was elected unanimously. In that position, it was his job to be partisan, and he often was. In the majority, both House Democrats and Republicans have taken a dim view of members of their party who buck their leadership on procedural issues. As Hoyer said in 2010, as he was being criticized by Republicans, "I think both parties have acted defensively in some respects when they were in the majority."

In the pivotal 2006 campaign, Hoyer worked closely with Illinois Rep. Rahm Emanuel, who chaired the effort to elect a Democratic majority. His September prediction that Democrats would gain 30 seats turned out to be right on the money. Many of the freshmen subsequently credited the help that Hoyer provided, especially those from swing districts where liberal Democratic leaders were not always welcome.

Even so, when it came time to elect leaders to the new Democratic House in late 2006, Hoyer had to fight for the position of majority leader against Pennsylvania Rep. John Murtha, who had the backing of incoming House Speaker Pelosi. In spite of their years working together in the leadership, Pelosi and Hoyer still viewed each other with suspicion. A defense hawk, Murtha had become an outspoken opponent of the Iraq war, while Hoyer supported the war effort. Murtha contended that he could work better with Pelosi. Hoyer had little choice but to speak positively about his long-standing relationship with her—he called her a "favorite daughter" of Maryland—and their success in largely unifying an often-unruly party. But he left no doubt about his dismay over her arm-twisting on Murtha's behalf.

In spite of Pelosi's efforts for Murtha, Hoyer prevailed 149-86, a powerful endorsement of him for majority leader. Democrats responded to his "ability, patience, know-how, and experience," said a Democratic lobbyist. Even more impressive, Hoyer won the support of many California Democrats who previously had been unified behind Pelosi and of numerous prospective committee chairmen who doubted Murtha's ability to do the job. "Nancy thought she could put these people away because of pressure," former California Rep. Tony Coelho told *The New York Times*. Hoyer "has a tremendous capacity for friendship, and when you have that, people don't flake off on you," Coelho said.

As majority leader, Hoyer assumed responsibility for determining the floor schedule, helping guide Democratic initiatives to passage, and holding weekly press briefings. He described his recipe for holding together what had historically been a fractious caucus this way: "First of all, work very hard on communications, find out what people can do and can't do. Secondly, put together a consensus that, while it may not be the first choice of every-body, it is a choice they can live with." And for the most part, the record justifies his boast that House Democrats, in their first two years in the majority, were "the most unified the Democratic Party has been in over half a century." Hoyer kept communications open with the opposition. He stayed in close touch with Blunt, and they maintained one of the best cross-party relationships on Capitol Hill. When Democrats lost their majority in 2010, Hoyer returned to Democratic whip and Pelosi took the top slot as minority leader.

In recent years, Hoyer has found himself at odds with the majority of Democrats on some issues. He voted for military funding in Iraq and consistently against linking war funding to a timetable for withdrawing U.S. troops, earning him criticism from the liberal MoveOn.org. He worked on the changes in the Foreign Intelligence Surveillance Act, which is a law enforcement tool in catching terrorists, and he backed the version of the legislation releasing telecommunications companies from legal liability for complying with government requests for warrantless surveillance of U.S. citizens' communications. Many Democrats did not want to let the companies off the hook.

On domestic issues, Hoyer came out in favor of same-sex marriage in May 2012, shortly before his daughter, Stefany Hoyer Hemmer, announced publicly that she is a lesbian. He actively pushed a "Make It in America" package of Democratic bills to boost U.S. manufac-turers, with several becoming law. In early 2009, working with Pelosi, Hoyer steered to pas-sage the $787 billion economic stimulus legislation, the first major initiative of the Obama administration. Only 11 House Democrats voted against it, and all of the Republicans opposed it. Weeks earlier, Hoyer strongly supported the bailout bill for the financial services industry, although he expressed misgivings about the legislation. He also had a hand in the Democrats' successful efforts to increase the hourly minimum wage and in the adoption of most of the 9/11 commission's homeland security and intelligence-reform recommendations.

More inclined to defer to committee chairs and hew to regular order than Pelosi, he sup-ported doing away with term limits for committee leaders, which the Republicans imposed when they were in the majority. Pelosi left term limits in place during the first two years of Democratic rule. (Term limits work to the advantage of the leadership because they make committee chairs less autonomous and therefore less powerful.) At Hoyer's urging, Pelosi agreed to repeal term limits in late 2008. "I am not for term limits for chairmen," Hoyer said. "It puts intellect on hold."

Hoyer has fine political instincts, works hard, and can speak in an old-fashioned, patriotic style that can be genuinely moving. With Democrats in the minority, he spends much of his time dueling on the House floor. He drew criticism from some conservatives for his rhetoric on the GOP's hardline stance on "fiscal cliff" budget negotiations shortly after the December 2012 school massacre in Newtown Connecticut. "It's somewhat like taking your child hostage and saying to somebody else, 'I'm going to shoot my child if you don't do what I want done,'" Hoyer said of Republicans. Behind the scenes, though, Hoyer tried to work out a deal, just as he had done on earlier bills. Then-Majority Whip Kevin McCarthy of California approached Hoyer in April 2011 seeking help on a spending resolution that was expected to be a close vote; the measure passed easily, with 81 Democrats offsetting the 59 Republican "no" votes.

Over the years, Hoyer has remained unable to edge out Pelosi in the leadership of House Democrats. After it became clear in October 2012 that the Democrats would not achieve majority control, speculation swirled that Pelosi would give up her party post, which would have allowed Hoyer to ascend to the top spot. He told *The Washington Post*, however, that he wasn't fixated on his future. "I'm very comfortable with what I do, very comfortable with the role I play. ... I'm not very anxious about the next step. It'll take care of itself." Pelosi eventually decided to stay on. She and Hoyer have put aside their differences to form a good working relationship.

Hoyer again got the better of Pelosi in November 2014 in the internal jockeying among House Democrats to succeed California's Henry Waxman as ranking member on the Energy and Commerce Committee. Pelosi advocated on behalf of her close friend, fellow Californian Anna Eshoo, while Hoyer backed New Jersey's Frank Pallone. Hoyer was able to mobilize members of the Congressional Black Caucus on Pallone's behalf; caucus members worried that Eshoo's ascension would disrupt the tradition of seniority. Hoyer's ability to count votes is "unmatched," a grateful Pallone said. "Hoyer, he's a shark who never sleeps.... He's a shark with a killer disposition," Missouri Democrat Emanuel Cleaver, a senior Black Caucus member, told *Politico*.

A month later, Hoyer worked with the unlikely team of Senate Majority Harry Reid of Nevada and House Speaker John Boehner to help President Barack Obama get a massive so-called "cromnibus" spending bill into law. Pelosi and other liberals, including Massachusetts Sen. Elizabeth Warren, objected to the measure, in large part because it loosened regulations on Wall Street banks. Hoyer worked to get 57 Democrats to vote for the measure, joining 162 Republicans. Occasionally, he parted company with Obama, including the "sequestration" of defense spending, which he called "totally unacceptable and irresponsible." After fellow Marylander—and Pelosi favorite—Chris Van Hollen decided in early 2015 to run for the Senate, questions remained whether Hoyer would have the leverage to replace Pelosi if she stepped down.

In his district, Hoyer has pushed for funding for Chesapeake Bay cleanup. He has worked shrewdly to maintain and increase the number of jobs at the Goddard Space Flight Center in Greenbelt, at Naval Air Station Patuxent River, and at the Naval Surface Warfare Center at Indian Head. In 2014, he successfully took the side of the air station against a wind energy farm on the other side of the Bay that he said "would constitute an unacceptable risk to the security of the United States" and potentially a local loss of Pentagon jobs. Another of his projects was getting the National Center for Weather and Climate Prediction based in College Park. In earlier years, he worked with Republican Rep. Tom Davis of Virginia and D.C. Democratic Delegate Eleanor Holmes Norton to pass a bill giving the District of Columbia a vote in the House. He sponsored bills allowing more government employees to work four-day weeks, granting eight weeks of paid parental leave, and raising the government contribution to federal employees' health care premiums. Following the April 2015 riots in Baltimore, Hoyer suggested reforms in police practices. He kept his hand in other Maryland political campaigns, and usually but not always prevailed.

The last time Hoyer had serious competition in a general election was 1992, the first election after the district was reconfigured to extend beyond Prince George's County. He has won easily since then, and he has won the loyalty of African-American voters in Democratic primaries.

SIXTH DISTRICT

John Delaney (D)

Elected 2012, 2nd term; b. April 16, 1963, Wood-Ridge, NJ; Columbia U., B.S. 1985, Georgetown U., J.D. 1988; Catholic; married (April McClain-Delaney); 4 children.

Professional Career: Founder, CEO, Health Care Financial Partners, 1993-99; Founder, Chmn., Capital Source, 2000-12; Founder, Blueprint MD, 2011-present.

DC Office: 1632 LHOB, 20515, 202-225-2721; Website: delaney.house .gov.

State Offices: Gaithersburg, 301-926-0300; Hagerstown, 301-733-2900.

Committees: *Financial Services:* Financial Institutions & Consumer Credit; Oversight & Investigations.

Group Ratings

	ADA	ACLU	AFL-CIO	LCV	ITI	COC	HAFA	ACU	CFG	FRC
2014	60%	83%	–	91%	80%	57%	12%	0%	2%	0%
2013	70%	C	86%	89%	C	62%	C	20%	18%	C

National Journal Ratings

	2013 LIB	—	2013 CONS
Economic	64%	—	36%
Social	79%	—	16%
Foreign	66%	—	32%
Composite	71%	—	29%

Key Votes of the 113th Congress

1. Sandy storm spending	Y	5. Medical Marijuana	Y	9. Syrian Rebels Training	Y
2. Violence Against Women Act	Y	6. Farm Bill	N	10. Keystone pipeline	N
3. Guantanamo Bay Detainees	Y	7. Afghanistan Combat	N	11. Immigration Exec. Action	N
4. Abortion 20-week ban	N	8. NSA Phone Data Collection	N	12. Bipartisan budget deal	Y

Election Results

2014 general	John Delaney (D)	94,704	(50%)	$2,586,097	$4,526
	Dan Bongino (R)	91,930	(48%)	$1,465,984	$10,606
	George Gluck (G)	3,762	(2%)		
2014 primary	John Delaney (D)	unopposed			

Prior winning percentage: 2012 (59%)

Population		Race and Ethnicity		Income	
Total:	747,058	White	61.9%	Median income:	$73,832
Urban:	31.8%	Black	13.7%		*(48 of 435)*
Suburban:	60.8%	Latino	11.2%	Under $50,000	33.5%
Rural:	7.4%	Asian	10.4%	$50,000-$99,999:	30.2%
Land area:	1,707	Two races	2.2%	$100,000-$199,999:	26.2%
Pop/sq. mi.:	437.6	White Ethnic	23.8%	$200,000 or more:	10.1%
Born in state:	44.2%			Poverty Rate	9.7%
		Education			
		H.S. grad or less:	34.1%		
Age Groups		Some college:	24.8%	**Work**	
Under 18:	23.6%	College degree, 4 yr.:	21.8%	White collar:	45.7%
18 to 34:	21.8%	Post-grad study:	19.2%	Blue collar:	39.4%
35 to 64:	41.5%			Sales and service:	14.8%
Over 64:	13.1%				
		Military		Govt. workers:	19.8%
		Veterans/active duty:	8.0%		

D.C. Exurbs, Western Maryland: Montgomery County

One of America's first frontiers was Western Maryland, where the Appalachian ridges that cross the state diagonally from northeast to southwest cut through long sloping fields. The land was settled by Pennsylvania Dutch and Scots-Irish hill people, not Chesapeake Bay tobacco growers. Maryland is

Voter Turnout	
2013 Total Citizen 18+	506,708
2014 House Turnout	190,536
2014 Turnout as % CVAP	37.6%
2012 Turnout as % CVAP	64.9%

where the 19th century's great paths to the interior were staked out: The National Road; the nation's first combined freight and passenger railroad, the Baltimore & Ohio, which crossed the wide valleys of bounteous farms and climbed over the Catoctin Mountains; and the Chesapeake and Ohio Canal, which began operating in 1828, primarily to haul coal from Western Maryland to the port of Georgetown in Washington. Towns grew up with narrow streets of row houses that today are overhung with telephone wires. They planted themselves among cornfields, pastureland and ancient mountains.

Across this placid land moved vast armies during the Civil War. In Frederick, city officials paid the Confederates $200,000 not to burn the town, and near Sharpsburg, blue- and-gray-clad soldiers fought the Battle of Antietam on the bloodiest day in American military history. A century later, President Lyndon Johnson unveiled his War on Poverty on the steps of City Hall in Cumberland, near the coal-laced hills of Appalachia. Poverty fell here in the 1970s, but conditions worsened in the 1980s with the closure of several large factories. The 2007-09 recession hit the region hard: Small Washington County (Hagerstown) accounted for 15 percent of the manufacturing jobs lost in the state after 2006. Hard-pressed as it is, Western Maryland is trying to preserve its natural wonders of small mountains and thick, deciduous forests. Cumberland has attempted to refashion itself as an arts community, with dozens of studios cropping up. Frederick and Washington counties have seen large increases in Hispanics since 2000.

2012 Presidential Vote		
Barack Obama (D)	176,364	(55%)
Mitt Romney (R)	138,539	(43%)

2008 Presidential Vote		
Barack Obama (D)	176,039	(56%)
John McCain (R)	131,343	(42%)

Cook Partisan Voting Index: D+4

The quickly diversifying population has created tensions: Frederick County became the first in Maryland to declare English its official language, and county officials struggling to deal with a rise in illegal immigration have sought to deport some immigrants. In Montgomery County, by contrast, officials have said that they will not honor federal requests to detain immigrants. In the five western counties of the states, small secessionist groups have sprung up, chiefly to voice their unhappiness with leaders in Annapolis. The focus of their unhappiness includes new gun control laws for the state.

The 6th Congressional District now stretches nearly 200 miles from the West Virginia border to the Washington, D.C., suburbs. Instead of heading east to Harford County as in the past, redistricters in 2011 gave the district a major drop south into Montgomery County. Republican-leaning Western Maryland remains, including Frederick, but it also scoops up heavily Democratic Washington suburbs in Montgomery County, including most of affluent Potomac (home of the 29th richest zip code in the nation), multicultural Gaithersburg, and fast-growing Germantown, whose population increased from about 9,700 in 1980 to 90,700 in 2013. Nearly half of the district's population lies in suburban Washington. Montgomery County has added diversity: The district has the highest concentration of Asian Americans in the state (10%), and Hispanics make up 11% of its population. With the district transformed into a Democratic-leaning bellwether, President Barack Obama carried it 55%-43% in 2012.

John Delaney (D)

Wealthy financier John Delaney was elected in 2012 when he ousted 10-term Republican Rep. Roscoe Bartlett, with a big boost from redistricting. Delaney styled himself as a consensus-builder seeking to restore the nation's competitiveness, and added that he was the only former CEO of a publicly traded company who is serving in the House.

A native of New Jersey, Delaney was raised by a homemaker mother and an electrician father, who was a member of the International Brotherhood of Electrical Workers. His father had never attended college, but other union members pooled their money for a scholarship fund for his son, allowing Delaney to pursue a degree in biology at Columbia University. He was planning to become a doctor, but eventually switched to business. He received his law degree from Georgetown University.

Delaney founded his first business, HealthCare Financial Partners, in 1993 and served as its chairman for seven years before starting CapitalSource, a Montgomery County-based investment company that lends money to small- and mid-sized businesses. *The Baltimore Sun* reported in 2012 that Delaney's wealth made him the fourth-richest member of Congress, with a net worth between $52 million and $232 million. (Candidates and lawmakers are not required to report exact income figures, only ranges of income.)

In the Democratic primary, state Senate Majority Leader Rob Garagiola was considered the front-runner. Yet Delaney benefited from some high-powered connections. He is a friend of both former President Bill Clinton and former Secretary of State Hillary Clinton, and donated and bundled contributions to her 2008 presidential campaign. Bill Clinton endorsed Delaney in the primary over Garagiola, a decisive moment in the campaign.

Garagiola opted not to pursue an aggressive broadcast advertising strategy, and Delaney suddenly had the airwaves to himself. Delaney, a Catholic and lifelong Democrat, campaigned as a social liberal, championing same-sex marriage and women's issues while comparing himself to more centrist-leaning, business-minded Democrats like Bill Clinton and Sen. Mark Warner of Virginia, on fiscal issues. Delaney won a resounding, 52%-29% victory in April.

Delaney had a considerable advantage in the 2012 general election. Besides the redistricting changes that created a more Democrat-friendly territory, the moderate Bartlett was idiosyncratic and not an easy politician to define. A physiologist by training, he chastised conservative Republicans for not accepting the science of climate change. But he was in his mid-80s, and many observers thought he would retire, a suspicion bolstered by the fact that he raised almost no money in the early months. Bartlett picked up the pace a bit, but it didn't change the perception that Republicans were ceding the seat. By the end of September, Delaney had raised $3.5 million (with $2.4 million from his own pocket) to Bartlett's $1 million. Delaney won 59%-38%. Bartlett took the three small western counties, but Delaney won Frederick 58%-38% and took Montgomery by an overwhelming 68%-29%.

In the House, Democratic leaders rewarded Delaney with a seat on the Financial Services Committee. His biggest initiative was a proposal to create a national infrastructure fund that would be financed by private companies that bring home the cash that they have been keeping overseas; Republican Rep. Mike Fitzpatrick of Pennsylvania was his chief cosponsor. Delaney criticized both parties for their handling of health care, and was harsh on Maryland Democratic officials for the state's bumbling implementation of the Affordable Care Act. In April 2015, Delaney wrote in *The Huffington Post* that Republicans were wrong to seek to eliminate federal estate taxes on the wealthy. The GOP proposal, he said, "will simply add to the debt, hurt our ability to build a stronger economy and worsen economic inequality."

Delaney denied that he was interested in running for the open seat for governor in 2014, and prepared for what seemed likely to be an easy reelection. Republicans nominated Dan Bongino, a former Secret Service agent with strong conservative roots that helped him to raise $1.5 million. It turned out to be an unexpectedly close contest, despite Delaney including $938,000 of his own money in the $2.6 million that he spent. Bongino ran ads that Delaney was not friendly to business. After two additional days to count the votes, Bongino conceded to Delaney for his 49.7%-48.2% win. As in his first election, Delaney had a big lead in Montgomery, though this time he got only 61% of the county vote. Still, this outcome made clear that the redistricting had been vital to the outcome.

Delaney left open the possibility of running for the Senate seat of retiring Barbara Mikulski. But Maryland political insiders speculated that he was more likely to run for governor in 2018.

SEVENTH DISTRICT

Elijah Cummings (D)

Elected April 1996, 10th full term; b. Jan. 18, 1951, Baltimore; Howard U., B.S. 1973, U. of MD, J.D. 1976; Baptist; married (Maya Rockeymoore); 3 children.

Elected Office: MD House, 1983-96, speaker pro tem, 1995-96.

Professional Career: Practicing atty., 1976-96; Chief judge, MD Moot Ct. Bd.

DC Office: 2230 RHOB, 20515, 202-225-4741; Fax: 202-225-3178; Website: cummings.house.gov.

State Offices: Baltimore, 410-685-9199; Catonsville, 410-719-8777; Ellicott City, 410-465-8259.

Committees: *Oversight & Gov't Reform* (RMM). *Transportation & Infrastructure:* Coast Guard & Maritime Transportation; Railroads, Pipelines & Hazardous Materials. *Select Benghazi Committee* (RMM).

Group Ratings

	ADA	ACLU	AFL-CIO	LCV	ITI	COC	HAFA	ACU	CFG	FRC
2014	95%	83%	–	97%	40%	43%	13%	8%	11%	0%
2013	90%	C	100%	96%	C	23%	C	12%	11%	C

National Journal Ratings

	2013 LIB	—	2013 CONS
Economic	86%	—	14%
Social	87%	—	7%
Foreign	89%	—	10%
Composite	89%	—	12%

Key Votes of the 113th Congress

1. Sandy storm spending	Y	5. Medical Marijuana	Y	9. Syrian Rebels Training	N
2. Violence Against Women Act	Y	6. Farm Bill	N	10. Keystone pipeline	N
3. Guantanamo Bay Detainees	Y	7. Afghanistan Combat	Y	11. Immigration Exec. Action	N
4. Abortion 20-week ban	N	8. NSA Phone Data Collection	Y	12. Bipartisan budget deal	Y

Election Results

2014 general	Elijah Cummings (D)	144,639	(70%)	$787,933	$10,187
	Corrogan Vaughn (R)	55,860	(27%)		
	Scott Soffen (Lib)	6,103	(3%)		
2014 primary	Elijah Cummings (D)	48,564	(87%)		
	Bryant Alexander (D)	4,786	(9%)		

Prior winning percentages: 2012 (77%), 2010 (75%), 2008 (80%), 2006 (100%), 2004 (73%), 2002 (74%), 2000 (87%), 1998 (86%), 1996 (83%), 1996 special (81%)

Population		Race and Ethnicity		Income	
Total:	724,692	Black	54.2%	Median income:	$54,943
Urban:	46.9%	White	34.5%		*(166 of 435)*
Suburban:	53.1%	Asian	4.8%	Under $50,000	45.8%
Rural:	0.0%	Latino	3.5%	$50,000-$99,999:	27.8%
Land area:	526	Two races	2.4%	$100,000-$199,999:	18.7%
Pop/sq. mi.:	1,377.9	White Ethnic	17.2%	$200,000 or more:	7.7%
Born in state:	63.1%			Poverty Rate	17.6%
		Education			
Age Groups		H.S. grad or less:	39.3%	**Work**	
Under 18:	22.4%	Some college:	24.6%	White collar:	46.6%
18 to 34:	24.9%	College degree, 4 yr.:	18.8%	Blue collar:	40.3%
35 to 64:	39.2%	Post-grad study:	17.3%	Sales and service:	13.1%
Over 64:	13.4%				
		Military		Govt. workers:	21.6%
		Veterans/active duty:	7.1%		

Baltimore Metro: Western and Northern Baltimore

At the junction of North and South, Baltimore is a product of both European immigration and the migration of African Americans from the South. Its black community has a rich history. The *Afro-American* newspaper has been published there for more than 100 years, and there was once a black

Voter Turnout	
2013 Total Citizen 18+	528,303
2014 House Turnout	206,809
2014 Turnout as % CVAP	39.1%
2012 Turnout as % CVAP	62.2%

symphony orchestra. Eubie Blake, one of the founders of ragtime music, grew up in Baltimore and now has a museum in his honor on Charles Street. Jazz great Billie Holiday, Cab Calloway, the 1930s and 1940s big band leader, and Thurgood Marshall, the country's first African-American Supreme Court justice, all had roots in Baltimore. Near downtown on the west side is the childhood home of slugger Babe Ruth and the home of writer H.L. Mencken. For years, this side of town had a biracial, bipartisan politics in which Democrats like Gov. Albert Ritchie and Republicans like Gov. Theodore McKeldin competed zestfully for black and white votes. Baltimore overall has been a black majority city since the late 1970s.

In the 1990s, the city was hit by a crime wave, with open drug markets on both the west and east sides. The city's gritty side was vividly depicted in HBO's acclaimed crime drama *The Wire*. In recent years, crime had declined but remained at intolerable levels. The city reported the fifth-highest murder rate among large cities in 2014, and more than 60% of the state's prisoners were from Baltimore. Democratic Mayor Stephanie Rawlings-Blake made curtailing gun crime a top priority of her administration. Meanwhile, Baltimore has lost 4% of its population since 2000, and is down more than a third from its peak in 1950.

Community anger exploded in April 2015, following the death of Freddie Gray, a young black man who had suffered serious injuries in a police wagon after he had been arrested. The initial response was a series of marches and peaceful protests throughout the west side of the city, especially the Sandtown-Winchester neighborhood. That turned violent as demonstrators smashed storefront windows, and threw rocks at police and damaged their cruisers as officers made dozens of arrests. The looting intensified after Gray's funeral. Rawlings-Blake cited the difficult "balancing act" that she faced and was slow to increase security before she imposed a curfew on the city for several nights. Gov. Larry Hogan declared a state of emergency and sent in 3,000 National Guard troops following a request from the mayor. Their presence generally restored order. But the larger questions endured about social conditions, police dealings with the neighborhoods, and the bleak nexus of poverty, race and class that continued to roil many urban centers across the nation. "Baltimore has been a combustible mix of poverty, crime and hopelessness, uncomfortably juxtaposed against rich history, friendly people, venerable institutions and pockets of old-money affluence," wrote Michael Fletcher, a reporter for *The Washington Post,* a Baltimore resident for more than 30 years. "The violence

2012 Presidential Vote
Barack Obama (D) 257,222   (76%)
Mitt Romney (R)..................76,446   (23%)

2008 Presidential Vote
Barack Obama (D) 251,564   (77%)
John McCain (R)..................73,830   (23%)

Cook Partisan Voting Index: D+24

that followed Freddie Gray's funeral Monday, with roaming gangs looting stores and igniting fires, demands that something be done. But what to do?"

Maryland's 7th Congressional District includes most of Baltimore's west side, plus the heavily African-American suburbs west of the city and extending to Catonsville along the old Baltimore National Pike. It includes much of suburban Howard County. About 40% of the district's votes are cast in Baltimore city's precincts, largely north of Pratt Street and including Charles Village, which is home to Johns Hopkins University. Baltimore County and Howard County each cast about 30%. Howard County is quite a different area. It grew 32% in the 1990s, and another 22% since then. Its largest community, Columbia, is a planned town that attracts a culturally liberal population that tends to vote Democratic. There is a sharp socioeconomic contrast between these two parts of the district. Howard County is predominately white and affluent, with the fifth-highest median household income of all counties in the nation. In Baltimore city, only 7% of households earn more than $100,000, and almost one-quarter of residents have incomes below the national poverty level.

Elijah Cummings (D)

Democrat Elijah Cummings, who came to Congress in a 1996 special election, is a liberal who can be blunt in defending his party. As the ranking Democrat on the Oversight and Government Reform Committee, he has parried with Republicans on investigations of the Obama administration that Cummings regularly dismisses as "witch hunts." In 2015, he initially sought a positive relationship with the new chairman, Jason Chaffetz of Utah.

Cummings is the son of sharecroppers from South Carolina who moved north for a better life for their seven children. He grew up in Baltimore, where as an 11-year-old he was one of the first children to integrate a park's swimming pool. "People were throwing bottles, rocks, and screaming, calling us everything but a child of God," he recalled to *Baltimore* magazine. He graduated Phi Beta Kappa from Howard University, and got a law degree from the University of Maryland. He practiced law in Baltimore, and then in 1982, at age 31, he ran successfully for the House of Delegates, where he served 14 years and rose through the ranks to become speaker pro tem.

He ran for the House after Kweisi Mfume resigned to become president of the NAACP. Cummings' main competition was the Rev. Frank Reid III, stepbrother of Baltimore Mayor Kurt Schmoke, who raised $255,000. Cummings had support from local businesses and community-development organizations, and raised $450,000. He won with 37% of the vote to 24% for Reid. He has not been seriously challenged in a primary or general election since.

Cummings lives in troubled west Baltimore, and he is a crusader against drug abuse, for stricter gun control, and for help for low-income homeowners. When Democrats won the majority in 2006, he became chairman of the Coast Guard and Maritime Transportation Subcommittee at Transportation and Infrastructure, a useful niche for his port-dependent district. The House unanimously passed his bill in July 2009 to reform Coast Guard acquisition practices, and a year later he helped get an authorization bill for the agency into law that included some acquisition reforms as well as other changes. In January 2015, he urged support for the proposed Red Line cross-town light rail project in Baltimore.

He is close to President Barack Obama, having bucked most of the Maryland Democratic establishment in 2007 by announcing his early support for the then-Illinois senator in the Democratic primary. He called Obama "absolutely brilliant" in an August 2011 speech, and regularly took to cable TV to rip Republican Mitt Romney during the 2012 presidential race. After Romney's July trip to Europe in which he committed several widely publicized gaffes, Cummings declared Romney "not ready for prime time." But Cummings hasn't spared Obama in his committee work. He took part in several bipartisan investigations in which he rebuked the administration for management deficiencies that led to Secret Service scandals and a lavish General Services Administration conference in Las Vegas.

Cummings got the Oversight ranking member slot in 2010 after the Republicans gained control of the House. Many Democrats worried that the top Democrat at the time, Edolphus Towns of New York, would not be a tough enough foil to the energetic and partisan chairman, Californian Darrell Issa. Towns agreed to step aside, and Cummings took over the job after beating New York's Carolyn Maloney by a 119-61 vote. Two years earlier, when California's Henry Waxman was chosen to chair the Energy and Commerce Committee, some Democrats urged Cummings to challenge Towns to replace Waxman as chairman of Oversight. But Cummings did not run, partly to avoid conflict within the seniority-sensitive Congressional Black Caucus, an influential group that Cummings chaired in 2003 and 2004.

Cummings publicly battled in 2011 and 2012 with Edward DeMarco, overseer of government-backed mortgage giants Fannie Mae and Freddie Mac, over debt reduction for homeowners struggling to pay mortgages. He is a staunch defender of labor unions, which have been his top source of campaign funds throughout his career. In the 2010 campaign, when some Democrats were de-emphasizing their support of the health care overhaul, Cummings was doing just the opposite. "I know the media wants us to apologize for being Democrats," he said at one rally. "They want us to apologize for health care. Why? Because the Democratic Party is the humane party."

On the Oversight panel, Cummings has forcefully pushed back against the GOP on subpoena powers, Democrats' access to records, and numerous other matters. But he has won respect from Republicans. "It's not about politics to him; he says what he believes," South Carolina's Trey Gowdy told *The Hill* newspaper. "And you can tell the ones who are saying it because it was in the memo they got that morning and you can tell the ones who it's coming from their soul. And with Mr. Cummings, it's coming from his soul."

One of the biggest flare-ups on the committee came when GOP lawmakers voted in 2012 to hold Attorney General Eric Holder in contempt of Congress for refusing to provide information relating to "Operation Fast and Furious," a botched effort to trace guns to drug cartels and smugglers that instead allowed firearms to cross the border into their hands. Cummings was among Holder's chief defenders, saying the attorney general "acted honorably." When a draft of the contempt citation was leaked to the news media, Cummings sent Issa an angry letter saying the move "suggests that you are more interested in perpetuating your partisan political feud in the press than in obtaining any specific substantive information."

When Republicans subsequently went after the Internal Revenue Service for allegedly targeting conservative groups, Cummings found himself the subject of unwanted attention. Activist Catherine Engelbrecht, founder of the organizations True the Vote and the King Street Patriots, accused the congressman in February 2014 of seeking to intimidate her by asking questions that subjected her to repeated scrutiny from federal agencies. Cummings denied the allegations, saying he was just trying to determine if voting rights had been infringed.

A month later, when Cummings spoke at an IRS hearing, Issa abruptly adjourned the session, ordering staffers to cut off the Democrat's microphone. The Congressional Black Caucus rose to Cummings' defense to demand that Issa be stripped of his chairmanship and publicly apologize. Issa did apologize to Cummings, who later compared Issa's tactics to those used in the 1950s by Communist-hunting Sen. Joseph McCarthy. In a sign of the high regard in which he is held by Democrats, including party leaders, Cummings was named in May 2014 as senior Democrat on the House select committee investigating the administration's handling of the murders of U.S. officials at the diplomatic compound in Benghazi, Libya.

For all of his partisan rhetoric, Cummings also has a pragmatic streak that occasionally allows him to work with Republicans in legislative coalitions. He helped secure enactment in 2014 of the DATA Act, which requires federal agencies to publish spending information online in a searchable format. Cummings worked with Indiana conservative Republican Mark Souder to reauthorize the White House drug control office and to establish federal policy to combat rapidly multiplying methamphetamine labs.

When Chaffetz took over as committee chairman in January 2015, he promised that he would work with Democrats more cooperatively than his predecessor. Chaffetz earlier spent a day with Cummings in his Baltimore district to get to know him better. "Chaffetz is a good guy," he told local residents. But at the panel's first meeting, Chaffetz pushed through a rules package that Cummings complained was "worse than the rules we had under Chairman Issa." Cummings and other Democrats tried and failed to roll back the chairman's ability to subpoena witnesses or documents without obtaining the prior consent of the ranking member, or putting the subpoena request to a vote of the full committee.

In February 2015, he teamed with Massachusetts Sen. Elizabeth Warren on a "Middle Class Prosperity Project," a series of public events aimed at trying to bolster the image of their party and Obama with the middle class. "Families might have survived as their incomes flattened, except for one hard fact: the costs of basic needs like housing, education and child care exploded," the lawmakers wrote in a *USA Today* op-ed.

The April 2015 death of Freddie Gray and subsequent riots in his home town raised the local and state profile of Cummings and increased pressure on him to help resolve conflicts, both immediate and more deep-seated. He joined marches and engaged with protesters, many of whom were his neighbors. "I am telling you we will not rest until we address this and see that justice is done," he said during an emotional speech at Gray's funeral.

Cummings usually wins reelection by landslide margins. He backed Mfume in the Democratic primary for the open Senate seat in 2006, and then played a constructive role in coalescing Democrats behind the successful nominee, Ben Cardin. A decade later, he was viewed as having considerable influence in the Democratic primary to succeed the retiring Senator Barbara Mikulski, either as a potential candidate or as a king-maker. In the spring of 2015, he said that he was too focused on the unrest in Baltimore to turn his attention to the Senate contest.

EIGHTH DISTRICT

Chris Van Hollen (D)

Elected 2002, 7th term; b. Jan. 10, 1959, Karachi, Pakistan; Swarthmore Col., B.A. 1982, Harvard U., M.P.P. 1985, Georgetown U., J.D. 1990; Episcopalian; married (Katherine); 3 children.

Elected Office: MD House, 1991-95; MD Senate, 1995-2003.

Professional Career: Practicing atty.; Legis. asst., U.S. Sen. Charles McC. Mathias, 1985-87; Staff, U.S. Senate Foreign Relations Comm., 1987-89; Sr. legis. advisor, Gov. William Donald Schaefer, 1989-91.

DC Office: 1707 LHOB, 20515, 202-225-5341; Fax: 202-225-0375; Website: vanhollen.house.gov.

State Offices: Mt. Airy, 301-829-2181; Rockville, 301-424-3501.

Committees: *Budget* (RMM).

Group Ratings

	ADA	ACLU	AFL-CIO	LCV	ITL	COC	HAFA	ACU	CFG	FRC
2014	90%	83%	–	97%	60%	43%	12%	8%	13%	0%
2013	80%	C	90%	96%	C	38%	C	24%	15%	C

National Journal Ratings

	2013 LIB	—	2013 CONS
Economic	83%	—	16%
Social	79%	—	16%
Foreign	83%	—	15%
Composite	83%	—	17%

Key Votes of the 113th Congress

1. Sandy storm spending	Y	5. Medical Marijuana	Y	9. Syrian Rebels Training	N
2. Violence Against Women Act	Y	6. Farm Bill	N	10. Keystone pipeline	N
3. Guantanamo Bay Detainees	Y	7. Afghanistan Combat	Y	11. Immigration Exec. Action	N
4. Abortion 20-week ban	N	8. NSA Phone Data Collection	N	12. Bipartisan budget deal	Y

Election Results

2014 general	Chris Van Hollen (D)	127,260	(60%)	$1,357,453
	Dave Wallace (R)	83,711	(40%)	$15,818
2014 primary	Chris Van Hollen (D)	60,556	(91%)	
	George English (D)	3,834	(6%)	

Prior winning percentages: 2012 (63%), 2010 (73%), 2008 (75%), 2006 (77%), 2004 (75%), 2002 (52%)

Population		Race and Ethnicity		Income	
Total:	756,076	White	63.5%	Median income:	$97,192
Urban:	40.4%	Latino	14.2%		(9 of 435)
Suburban:	58.8%	Black	11.6%	Under $50,000	24.0%
Rural:	0.8%	Asian	8.2%	$50,000-$99,999:	27.4%
Land area:	898	Two races	2.1%	$100,000-$199,999:	32.8%
Pop/sq. mi.:	841.6	White Ethnic	29.8%	$200,000 or more:	15.8%
Born in state:	32.4%			Poverty Rate	6.7%
		Education			
Age Groups		H.S. grad or less:	27.3%	**Work**	
Under 18:	22.8%	Some college:	20.5%	White collar:	53.9%
18 to 34:	20.8%	College degree, 4 yr.:	23.6%	Blue collar:	34.2%
35 to 64:	41.5%	Post-grad study:	28.6%	Sales and service:	12.0%
Over 64:	14.8%				
		Military		Govt. workers:	21.4%
		Veterans/active duty:	7.3%		

Northern D.C. Suburbs: Montgomery, Frederick

Colonial farmers once rolled barrels of tobacco to the port of Georgetown in Maryland, along an old road that is today the commercial spine of one of America's most affluent and best-educated areas. Wisconsin Avenue begins at the Potomac River in Washington, D.C., traverses the city, and then

Voter Turnout	
2013 Total Citizen 18+	506,211
2014 House Turnout	225,097
2014 Turnout as % CVAP	44.5%
2012 Turnout as % CVAP	72.4%

becomes Rockville Pike after it passes under the Capital Beltway in Montgomery County. The foundation of the economy here is the federal government, with its huge facilities—Bethesda Naval Hospital (now merged with the Army's Walter Reed), the National Institutes of Health, and the Food and Drug Administration. Montgomery is one of the centers of America's biotech industry, the home of firms such as Human Genome Sciences which, in parallel with the Human Genome Project, pioneered the study of the human genetic code. Defense contractor Lockheed Martin, with 5,200 employees, is the only manufacturing company among the county's top 10 employers.

From the 1960s through the 1980s, Montgomery County ranked at or near the top among counties nationwide in income and education. Downtown Bethesda is a glitzy and popular entertainment and dining destination, with expanding high-rise apartment buildings. But Montgomery changed gradually as it became a magnet for legal immigrants attracted by the region's strong and stable economy. Today, Montgomery has a diverse population and has been overtaken in affluence regionally by other suburban counties in the metropolitan areas. Along with its very upscale neighborhoods, Montgomery now has large Latino communities in neighborhoods from Wheaton northwest to Rockville. The county's population in 2013 was 19% African American, 18% Hispanic, and 15% Asian. In 2013, *Forbes* ranked Bethesda as the best city in the nation to find a job. Average pay for scientists and engineers was higher than in Silicon Valley. A more pessimistic note: In March 2015, Marriott announced that it will move its huge corporate headquarters from Bethesda to another site in the Washington area, chiefly due to what company officials described as a business climate that has not been good for Maryland companies.

Still, the county has the nation's second highest percentage of adults with graduate school degrees, and it is thoroughly liberal on cultural issues and loyal to the Democratic Party. Montgomery County provided the margin of victory to the 2012 referendum legalizing same-sex marriage in Maryland; it narrowly passed with 52% of the statewide vote, but garnered an overwhelming 66% in the state's largest county. In 2014, the county passed legislation creating partial public financing of local elections.

The 8th Congressional District of Maryland includes much of the heavily populated parts of Montgomery County (Bethesda, Rockville, and Silver Spring). To assist Democrats in the 6th District, it now extends beyond the Washington suburbs to include rural Republican precincts from Frederick and Carroll counties. The presidential retreat of Camp David, where Jimmy Carter brokered the Israeli-Egyptian peace accords, is within the district, outside the small town of Thurmont. The district is reliably Democratic but it's not as overwhelmingly liberal as before. For President Barack Obama, his share of the

2012 Presidential Vote		
Barack Obama (D)	222,125	(62%)
Mitt Romney (R)	127,542	(36%)
2008 Presidential Vote		
Barack Obama (D)	215,394	(63%)
John McCain (R)	121,976	(36%)
Cook Partisan Voting Index:	D+11	

2008 vote was 74% under the old map, and a still substantial 63% with the new map. Perhaps its most unique precinct is Leisure World in Silver Spring, with its 8,500-plus senior citizens and an extraordinarily high voter-turnout rate, mostly Democrats.

Chris Van Hollen (D)

Chris Van Hollen, first elected in 2002, has been among the most influential Democrats in the House and was often mentioned as a future Democratic leader before announcing in March 2015 that he would seek the Senate seat held by the retiring Barbara Mikulski. Wonky, self-assured, and with an unusual mix of policy and political skills, Van Hollen became a top lieutenant to Speaker Nancy Pelosi after helping the party take control in 2006.

The son of a Foreign Service officer, Van Hollen was born in Pakistan, and grew up around the globe, living in several countries, including Sri Lanka, where his father was the U.S. ambassador. He graduated from Swarthmore College, and got a master's degree in public policy from Harvard University and a law degree from Georgetown University. In the 1980s, he worked for the Senate Foreign Relations Committee, where he co-authored a report on Iraq's use of chemical weapons. In 1990, he was elected to the Maryland House of Delegates and in 1994 to the state Senate.

In 2002, Van Hollen challenged liberal Republican Connie Morella, an eight-term veteran. Maryland's Democratic legislature had changed the district, removing affluent Republican precincts in Potomac and adding heavily Democratic territory to the east. His chief opponent in the Democratic primary was state Del. Mark Shriver, son of Sargent and Eunice Kennedy Shriver, who had extensive labor and party establishment support. Bolstered by the endorsement of *The Washington Post*, Van Hollen defeated Shriver 43%-41%, with former trade official Ira Shapiro getting 13%.

Van Hollen had only eight weeks to campaign against Morella, a hard-working and congenial Republican with a voting record suited to the district's many Democrats. Van Hollen did not directly attack Morella, but argued that she was an enabler of the Republican majority, and that her vote to organize the House with Republicans kept in power conservatives who were out of sync with most district voters. Morella criticized Van Hollen's record in Annapolis, including his decision to quit a Senate subcommittee over proposed budget cuts. In a race in which the two candidates together spent nearly $6 million, Van Hollen won 52%-47%.

Van Hollen's early years in Congress portended a swift rise. He won an early legislative victory when he got a majority, including 26 Republicans, to approve his amendment to limit a plan to outsource federal jobs. In 2005, he was appointed by then-Rep. Rahm Emanuel of Illinois, chairman of the Democratic Congressional Campaign Committee, to manage candidate recruitment and its "Red to Blue" campaign plan. Working closely with the hard-driving Emanuel, the low-key and genial Van Hollen traveled to many battleground districts for hands-on candidate mentoring.

When Democrats won a majority in 2006, Van Hollen was rewarded with a seat on the Ways and Means Committee. He focused on revisions to the alternative minimum tax, which threatened many of his affluent constituents, changes to make prescription drugs more affordable for low-income consumers, and legislation to curb speculation and manipulation in oil markets. On other issues, he worked with Emanuel to require lobbyists to make additional disclosure of campaign contributions. He sought more money for the region's Metro transit system and for initiatives to clean up Chesapeake Bay.

Pelosi showed her confidence in Van Hollen by appointing him to head the DCCC after Emanuel stepped down. He worked closely with her on campaign strategy in both the 2008 and 2010 political seasons. His goal was to try to reverse historical forces that generally produced losses for a winning party after a wave election like the one in 2006. He helped Democrats win special elections in unlikely territory—downstate Illinois; Baton Rouge Louisiana; and northeast Mississippi. He ran a skillful in-house research operation and expanded the field program. He also performed well in the most important function for any DCCC chairman—raising money. The committee took in $176 million in the 2008 election cycle, compared with $118 million for its counterpart NRCC. Overall, Democrats gained 21 seats in November 2008, many in traditionally Republican areas, and Van Hollen and the DCCC got much of the credit. Only four freshman Democrats, all in Republican-leaning areas, were defeated out of a class of 33. *The Washington Post* dubbed Van Hollen the party's "Mr. Fix-It." No doubt, he was helped by unpopular Republicans and the cratering economy at the time.

After his 2008 electoral success, Van Hollen contemplated a challenge to Caucus Chairman John Larson of Connecticut, a step up the leadership ladder. But Pelosi persuaded him to stay on as DCCC chairman and gave him a new leadership post, assistant to the speaker. He remained active on substantive issues. In April 2009, he introduced a cap-and-dividend bill, an alternative to the Democrats' cap-and-trade legislation that would impose a carbon tax on coal, oil and gas producers and distribute the proceeds as dividends to citizens. He was concerned about the effect the stricter cap-and-trade bill would have on members in coal states. The energy bill ultimately died in the Senate. In 2015, he replaced the retired Henry Waxman as co-chair of the bicameral task force on climate change. During debate on health care reform, Van Hollen cosponsored a successful amendment allowing dependents up to age 26 to stay on their parents' health insurance—a major talking point for Democrats defending the bill in the 2010 campaign.

When the U.S. Supreme Court in January 2010 overturned many restrictions on corporate involvement in campaign advertising, Van Hollen filed a bill to increase disclosure requirements for corporations; the House passed a modified version, 219-206. Van Hollen also has a strong interest in foreign policy. He sponsored a successful amendment to a Pakistan aid bill in June 2009 with a provision providing for duty-free entry to goods produced in reconstruction zones in Afghanistan and Pakistan.

Much of Van Hollen's time was necessarily spent on the DCCC's mandate to protect its majority in 2010. Sensing the national mood turning against incumbents, he said in February 2009 that his job was to "hold the line" and that there would be no "third wave." He worked to give freshman Democrats the lead role on popular amendments. He identified 41 "endangered species" members and worked to give those with conservative districts leeway to vote against the leadership on the budget.

When poll results showed many Democratic incumbents trailing little-known Republican challengers, he warned in August 2010 that Democrats were in for "a very tough campaign season." He contributed $1.6 million of his own campaign money to others, but he admitted after the election that he had cut off from further DCCC funding nine incumbents who could not be saved, sending $12 million to districts where Democrats might win in the final days. "Just on the triage side, we believe we saved 15-20 seats," he later told *The New York Times*. Even so, Democrats lost 63 seats—more than either party had lost since 1948.

When his party returned to the minority in 2011, Van Hollen gained the plum assignment as the ranking Democrat on the Budget Committee. He established a cordial working relationship with Chairman Paul Ryan of Wisconsin, one of the GOP's intellectual leaders. "He's probably one of the best articulators of the Democrats' position ... but he does it without being too partisan," Ryan told *The Baltimore Sun*. Van Hollen remained a vocal critic of Republican spending plans. He gave speeches and appeared on talk shows, seeking to frame the debate over Ryan's proposals. He argued they would undermine Medicare and that they relied too heavily on spending cuts and not enough on tax hikes on high-earners.

In 2011, Van Hollen served as the House Democrats' point man in bicameral negotiations over raising the nation's debt limit and was also named to the bipartisan "super committee" that unsuccessfully sought to craft a long-term deficit deal. In 2012, after Republican presidential nominee Mitt Romney tapped Ryan as his running mate, Van Hollen became the de facto explainer of his party's objections to Ryan's budget policies. President Barack Obama's reelection team tapped him to help prepare Vice President Joe Biden for his debate with Ryan. Van Hollen also crisscrossed the country to campaign for candidates and was a ubiquitous TV presence during the party conventions. "There are few better at explaining the choice we face in this election," Obama's deputy campaign manager, Stephanie Cutter, told *The Sun*.

Ryan was replaced in 2015 as Budget Committee chairman by Georgia's Tom Price, who was more of a hard-liner. On opening day in January, the House on a largely party-line vote approved the controversial practice of "dynamic scoring," which takes the economic effects of legislation into account for budget cost estimates. "It's absolutely astounding that within minutes—minutes—of us being sworn in, our Republican colleagues want to pass a rule that will stack the deck in favor of trying to give another big tax cut, not to the middle class, but to millionaires," Van Hollen said.

Van Hollen showed he could turn on Obama's budget, too. He helped to persuade the president to drop from his proposed budget a move to tax college savings accounts known as "529 Plans." The plans are popular with middle-class parents, including many constituents of Van Hollen. After he reportedly telephoned Minority Leader Nancy Pelosi as she flew with Obama on Air Force One in India, the idea was jettisoned.

At home, Van Hollen has been almost invulnerable to challenge. One potential warning signal was his poor showing in 2014 in the rural additions to his district. Against a weak challenger, Van Hollen got a scant 30% of the vote in Carroll County and 38% in Frederick County, while he won an impressive 76% in Montgomery County.

When Maryland Sen. Paul Sarbanes announced his retirement in early 2005, Van Hollen gave serious thought to entering the multicandidate Democratic primary. He backed down, under pressure from some party leaders. But after Mikulski's announcement that she would not seek another term, Van Hollen barely missed a beat as he was the first to enter the contest and quickly picked up support from his state's Democratic leadership. "People have confidence in him," Montgomery County Executive Isaiah "Ike" Leggett told *The Sun*. "He has a solid record to run on." Two days after his announcement, Senate Minority Leader Harry Reid endorsed Van Hollen as "the best and most effective person for the job." Among those unhappy with his move was Pelosi, who viewed him as a prospective successor as House leader. In his House district, several Democratic officials and past candidates voiced interest in seeking to replace Van Hollen. The contest should be a lock for whoever wins the primary.

★ MASSACHUSETTS ★

It would be a city upon a hill, John Winthrop wrote of the Massachusetts Bay Colony that he and his fellow Puritans were building, an example to the entire world. And in the nearly four centuries since, Massachusetts has always assumed that it has a lot to teach others. The Puritans' austere creed taught that only the elect would be saved and that they must extirpate the forces of Satan—Indians, Papists and tolerationists. For 150 years, New England was partial to learning, but it also was insular, hostile to outsiders, sending merchants and fishing boats out to sea but keeping the world at bay. Then, after the American Revolution, the wars between royal Britain and revolutionary and Napoleonic France allowed New England ship owners to cross enemy lines to become the world's leading merchants. They made vast profits and invested the money in textile mills, then railroads, then coal mines and steel mills, providing much of the capital that made industrial America.

Massachusetts remade the country in other ways. Intellectually, New England flowered in the 19th century, more than 200 years after Plymouth Rock. Writers from Boston and Cambridge, Concord and Salem—Ralph Waldo Emerson, Henry Wadsworth Longfellow, Henry David Thoreau, John Greenleaf Whittier and Nathaniel Hawthorne—created an American literature and popularized an American philosophy. There was a surge of New England Yankee influence across the continent, and beyond. By the 1820s, Boston whaling merchants and New England missionaries were planting their flag in the Sandwich Islands (Hawaii). By the 1850s, Yankees were in Iowa, Kansas, and Oregon's Willamette Valley, and by the 1870s, in Los Angeles. They helped found the Republican Party and did much to start—and win—the Civil War. They planted their economic system and their values, articulated in the *McGuffey Readers*, across the continent.

In the meantime, Massachusetts itself and Boston, the "Hub of the Universe," were being remade. The Irish potato famine of the 1840s and an imploding economy sent Irish immigrants across the Atlantic, and many came to Boston, looking for work in the mills, docks, and factories of Massachusetts. Yankee Protestants had seen Catholics as their great political and cultural enemy since the 17th century and many felt that their commonwealth was under siege. As Catholics became a majority, first in Boston and then statewide, Protestants feared that the Irish would use their political clout to ladle out government jobs and benefits to their own—and the Irish had a much better flair for politics than instinct for commerce. But they encountered such bigotry and rejection by the Yankees that even as successful an Irish Catholic as Joseph Kennedy abandoned Boston for New York in 1927. Politics in Massachusetts for years was a kind of culture war between Yankee Republicans and Irish Democrats, an argument not so much over the distribution of income or the provision of services as over whose vision of Massachusetts should be honored, and whose version of history should be taught—an argument not unlike the battles being fought between cultural liberals and conservatives today.

Sometimes the stakes were concrete—control of patronage, command of the Boston Police Department—but more often they were symbolic. Yankee Republicans tended to back activist government programs: public works and protective tariffs to help business; the Civil War and Reconstruction to help suitably distant oppressed people such as Southern blacks; uplifting (and productivity-enhancing) social movements such as temperance. The Irish found the 19th-century Democratic Party and its philosophy of laissez-faire more congenial. The Irish had come from a place where the government was the enemy, and they didn't want government spending money to help the rich or to stimulate commerce. They also didn't want government to restrict immigration, to advance blacks (potential competitors in the labor market), or to ban alcohol.

Massachusetts' Irish and Catholic percentages rose slowly over the years. Yankees had smaller families, moved west, intermarried with people of immigrant stock, and lost their Yankee identity. The Irish mostly stayed put, raised large families, and maintained their identity. Slowly but surely, Massachusetts moved from being one of the most Republican states to one of the most Democratic. Economically, early-20th century Massachusetts progressed little. The descendants of the Yankees who had been so venturesome in the early 19th century became cautious investors in the early 20th. The predominance of the textile mills meant that for a century beginning in the 1820s, Massachusetts imported low-skill labor and exported high-skill people. As textile mills started moving south in the 1920s,

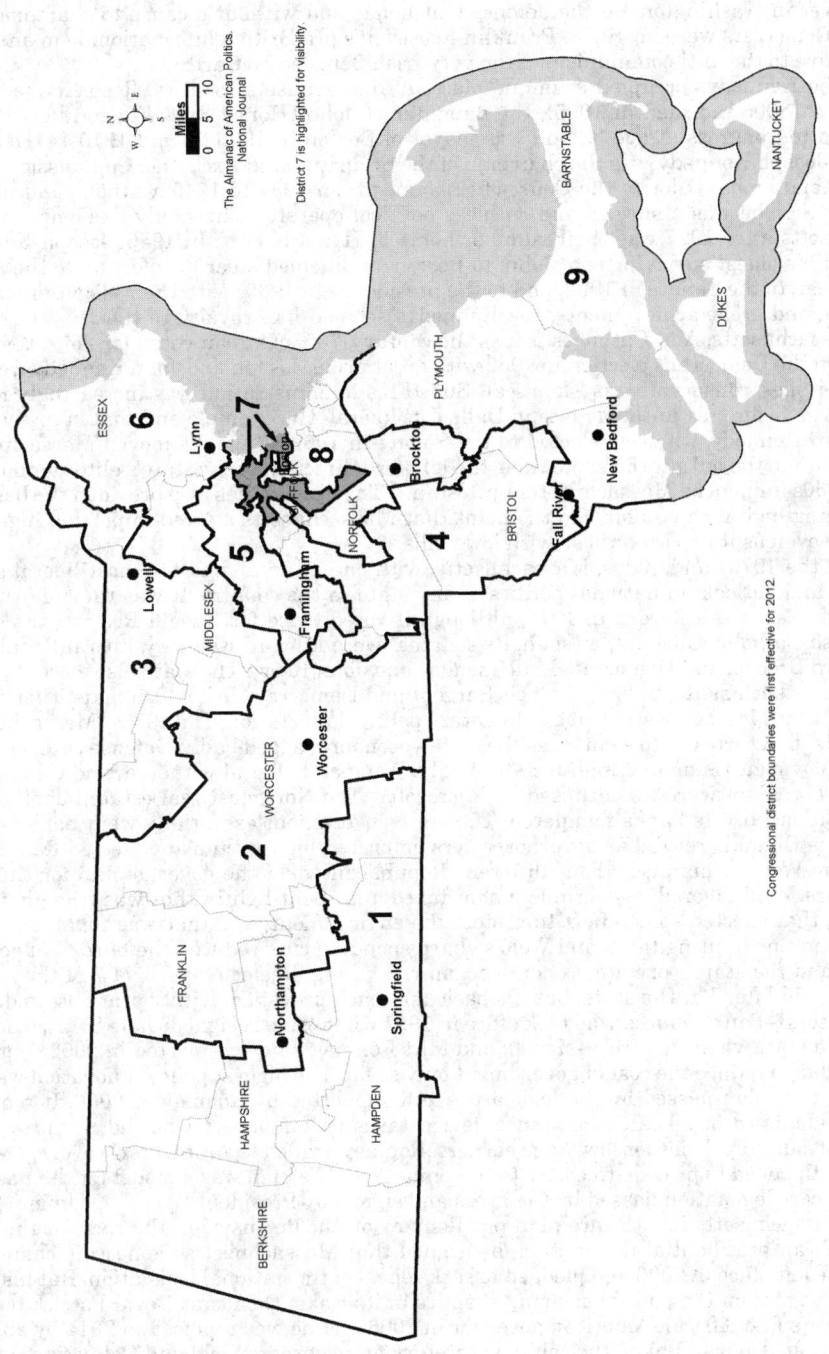

The Almanac of American Politics.
National Journal

District 7 is highlighted for visibility

Congressional district boundaries were first effective for 2012

Massachusetts started exporting low-skill people as well. From the waning of Yankee authority until the national rise of the Kennedys, Massachusetts seemed to run out of things to teach the rest of the nation. The state's Yankee Republicans were backward looking, out of power in Washington, on the defensive at home, and without a cause to champion. The Irish Democrats were hostile to Franklin Roosevelt's pro-British internationalism and were receptive to the anti-communism of the very Irish Sen. Joe McCarthy.

The Kennedys occupied a unique place in Massachusetts politics. Rose Kennedy was born in 1890 (and died in 1995), the daughter of John "Honey Fitz" Fitzgerald, who was elected to Congress at age 32 and was mayor of Boston in 1906-07 and 1910-14. Her husband, Joseph Kennedy, was the chairman of the Securities and Exchange Commission in the 1930s and ambassador to the Court of St. James from 1937 to 1940. Catholic and uncommonly rich, he was a shrewd and ruthless political operator. Their only residence in Massachusetts after 1927 was their summer home in Hyannis Port. In 1946, Joseph Kennedy moved his oldest surviving son, John, to Boston, and helped steer his election to the House that year, to the Senate in 1952, and to the presidency in 1960. With their elegant manners, charm, and great achievements, the Kennedys seemed like royalty to the Irish Catholics of Massachusetts. And Catholics across the country, 78% of whom voted for John Kennedy, greeted the Democrat's election in 1960 with great pride. Joseph and John Kennedy were, on many issues, conservative or skeptical. But JFK's administration was increasingly identified, even before his untimely fate in Dallas, as liberal. His example and that of his brother, Edward Kennedy, who was elected to the Senate in 1962 at age 30, moved Massachusetts Catholics to the left. At the same time, the leftward direction of the state's elite campuses in the 1960s influenced Massachusetts Protestants. The universities also provided the basis for a surging high-tech economy, to the point that Massachusetts started importing high-skill people even as it exported those with low skills.

In the 1970s and 1980s, Massachusetts, with one interval, had the most liberal governance and outlook on national politics of any state in the country. It was the only state to vote for George McGovern in 1972, although it voted twice for Ronald Reagan, the son of an Irish Catholic. During that span, its senators were Edward Kennedy, liberal Republican Edward Brooke, and Democrats Paul Tsongas and John Kerry. The state also elected liberal governors such as Republican Francis Sargent and Democrat Michael Dukakis. Then in the early1990s, Massachusetts had a momentary political revolution. The 1980s "Massachusetts Miracle" had turned into a curse, as the state's economy sagged badly. Defense cutbacks sent unemployment rising and high-tech firms like Wang and Digital withered, and Cambridge-based Lotus' software was eclipsed by Microsoft's. The Northeast real estate bubble burst, and Massachusetts banks foundered. The state government essentially went bankrupt. In 1990, as Dukakis retired as governor, voters embraced big tax cuts and elected Republican William Weld in his place. Four different Republicans held the governorship for the next 16 years. Weld favored a government that taxed and spent lightly, that was friendly to gay rights, that exerted some effort to protect the environment, and that was tough on crime. Referendums limiting taxes and Weld's sharp spending cuts reduced the burden of government and the state's private economy began recovering. Reelected with 71% of the vote in 1994, Weld later left the state, but his basic approach prevailed, with variations, under his successors—Paul Cellucci, who took office in 1997 when Weld resigned; Jane Swift, who took office in 2001 when Cellucci resigned; and Mitt Romney, who was elected in 2002. But they were able to reduce the cost of government only so far. The biggest policy innovation was the health care plan passed by the legislature and supported by Romney in 2006. It required all residents to buy health insurance, levied taxes on employers who did not provide it, and subsidized policies for low-wage earners. Romney argued that universal coverage would reduce the need to provide free care to the uninsured. His plan was a model for the national health care legislation passed by Congress and signed by President Barack Obama in 2010. The Massachusetts health care plan put Romney on the defensive in the race for the 2012 Republican presidential nomination; he argued that Massachusetts Democrats changed it after he left office in 2006 and pledged to seek repeal of the national legislation. But his radical about-face on the policy left many skeptics in its wake. Democrat Deval Patrick became the state's first African-American governor in 2006 and he was replaced in 2014 by another Republican, Charlie Baker, the cabinet secretary for governors Weld and Cellucci.

Massachusetts saw a slowdown in the mid-2000s, but its high-tech and defense industries prospered. The towns along the circumferential Route 128, once the center of the mainframe computer industry now became a biotech center—a natural evolution with metro

Boston's massive university hospital systems. With taxes lowered, Massachusetts stopped losing high earners to New Hampshire, though downscale outmigration continued. Its education reforms and increasingly upscale population helped it achieve the highest test scores in the nation. There has been significant immigration, some from Ireland but also from Brazil; Massachusetts has many descendants of Portuguese and Azorean immigrants, and the Brazilians have evidently been attracted to the most lusophone part of the United States. Overall, the population of Massachusetts has remained fairly stable over the past couple of decades, but it has seen significant growth in residents between the ages of 20 and 44 since 1980. This rise in the working-age population has contributed to the state's economic vitality and the steady rise in income levels in Massachusetts, which have outpaced the national as a whole. State unemployment rates have typically remained below the national average and peaked at 8.8 percent in 2009 during the Great Recession. And with economic recovery, unemployment in Massachusetts in May 2015 stood at 4.6 percent. Manufacturing jobs have steadily shrunk as part of the Bay State's economic base over the last two decades, replaced by employment growth in business, education, health, hospitality and professional services. These sectors now account for almost half of total payroll employment in the state, according to an analysis by the University of Massachusetts Donahue Institute Economic and Public Policy Research group. Technology remains a key component of Massachusetts's economic success, and the availability of a skilled and well-educated population is an important economic driver for the Commonwealth. It had the highest percentage of any state of adults with a bachelor's degree or higher in 2013, according to the Census Bureau American Community Survey. Researchers from several Boston hospitals and universities, including Harvard University, Massachusetts General Hospital, MIT, Boston Children's Hospital, Boston University, Brigham and Women's Hospital, and Tufts University, were named to the Thomson Reuter's 2014 list of the "World's Most Influential Scientific Minds." An Innovation District has sprung up along the South Boston waterfront, an area that not long ago was marked by parking lots and abandoned warehouses. Despite the home-grown talent at local universities, the challenge for both established technology firms and start-ups in the Boston area remains attracting and retaining the skilled engineers and next generation of software developers. These highly prized employees can opt to work in Silicon Valley, North Carolina's Research Triangle or even the great nemesis to the south, New York City, which is nurturing a growing number of tech startups with venture capital deals and building a technology campus that could rival MIT's.

With an educated electorate, strong Democratic leanings in national politics, and mostly moderate Republicans in the governor's office, cultural liberalism gradually prevailed over conservative Catholic social views in the state. Gov. Weld was one of America's first politicians to endorse gay rights, and he appointed Supreme Judicial Court Chief Justice Margaret Marshall, who pushed through the 4-3 decisions in November 2003 requiring the

Voter Turnout

2013 Total Citizen 18+	4,846,112
2014 Highest Statewide Turnout	2,158,326
2014 Turnout as % CVAP	44.5%
2012 Turnout as % CVAP	66%

Legislature

Senate:	34D	6R
House:	125D	35R

Population		Race and Ethnicity		Income	
Total:	6,692,824	White	75.8%	Median income:	$62,963
Urban:	33.5%	Latino	9.9%		(7 of 50)
Suburban:	64.3%	Black	6.2%	Under $50,000	38.6%
Rural:	2.1%	Asian	5.5%	$50,000-$99,999:	28.9%
Land area:	7,800	Two races	1.8%	$100,000-$199,999:	24.2%
Pop/sq. mi.:	858.1	White Ethnic	59.0%	$200,000 or more:	8.3%
Born in state:	62.1%			Poverty Rate	10.1%
		Education			
Age Groups		H.S. grad or less:	36.0%	**Work**	
Under 18:	20.8%	Some college:	23.7%	White collar:	44.0%
18 to 34:	24.0%	College degree, 4 yr.:	22.5%	Blue collar:	40.4%
35 to 64:	40.4%	Post-grad study:	17.8%	Sales and service:	15.6%
Over 64:	14.8%			Govt. workers:	12.3%
		Military			
		Veterans/active duty:	6.3%		

legislature to give gays equal marriage rights. When the legislature declined, the judge in 2004 declared that same-sex couples have the right to marry. Romney opposed the decision and urged the legislature to send to the voters a constitutional amendment banning same-sex marriage and endorsing civil unions. Democrats in the state House resisted, and over the next two years, public opinion seemed to accept a change that was already occurring without notable disruption. In 2007, the state House voted 151-45 against the amendment, five votes shy of the 50 needed to place the measure on the ballot. Soon, courts and legislatures across the country were legalizing same-sex marriage. In November 2012, voters in Maine, Maryland, and Washington explicitly approved it, while in Minnesota voters rejected a constitutional amendment forbidding same-sex marriage. It was another lesson from the Massachusetts experience and Winthrop's vision of the Bay Colony's elect providing inspiration to the world.

Presidential Politics   Over the last five presidential elections, Massachusetts has been the third most Democratic state. Its average Democratic percentage has been 61.13%, just behind Rhode Island's 61.14% and Hawaii's 61.8%. It was Bill Clinton's best state in 1996, Al Gore's second best state in 2000, John Kerry's best in 2004. It was Barack Obama's seventh best in 2008 and sixth best in 2012. It has voted almost precisely the same in the last three presidential elections: 62%-37%, 62%-36%, and 61%-38

2012 Presidential Vote		
Barack Obama (D) 1,921,290		(61%)
Mitt Romney (R)..............1,188,314		(38%)
2012 Presidential Primary		
Mitt Romney (R)................266,313		(72%)
Rick Santorum (R) 44,564		(12%)
Ron Paul (R) 35,219		(10%)
2008 Presidential Vote		
Barack Obama (D) 1,904,097		(62%)
John McCain (R)..............1,108,854		(36%)

Democratic, with Massachusetts' own Kerry and Mitt Romney getting the highest percentage for their parties in the three races. What is also striking about Massachusetts is how many serious presidential candidates it has produced over the last three decades: Edward Kennedy in 1980, Michael Dukakis in 1988, Paul Tsongas in 1992, Kerry in 2004, and Romney in 2008 and 2012. Only mega-states California and Texas have produced more serious candidates over that period. Some credit must be given to New Hampshire, which holds the nation's first primary, where most of its residents receive Boston television stations. But even more credit must go to the hyper- political culture of Boston. Only Chicago seems as preoccupied by its political figures.

In 2012, Obama ran just a little behind his 2008 showing. He did particularly well among young voters (73% in the 2012 exit poll) and women (65%; Massachusetts has a big gender gap). There's evidence in the exit poll of the split between the university elite and the private-sector affluent, which proved decisive in the January 2010 special Senate election, when Republican Scott Brown upset Democrat Martha Coakley. Obama carried those earning more than $100,000 by only 54%-45%, while he won those with postgraduate degrees 65%-33%.

Massachusetts' presidential primary has long been held in early March and was once the scene of great commotion. It produced victories for Bay Staters Dukakis, Tsongas, Kerry, and Romney. In 2000, it voted solidly for Democrat Gore and Republican John McCain, as many independents reregistered as Republicans. In 2008, Massachusetts voted on Super Tuesday, February 5, and it was one of the few states where polls showed close races in both parties. Obama was endorsed by then Gov. Deval Patrick and Kerry. Edward Kennedy gave a rousing welcome to Obama at a rally the night before the primary in Boston's Faneuil Hall. But Hillary Clinton also had her Massachusetts supporters, including Boston Mayor Thomas Menino and Reps. Richard Neal and Jim McGovern. And, as in New Hampshire, she had the support of downscale Democrats. While Obama carried the university towns, she carried the mill towns and won 56%-41% in a statewide turnout of 1.2 million voters.

Far fewer people, 500,000, voted in the 2008 Republican primary. Many Massachusetts Republicans are liberal on cultural issues, and Romney's turn to the right in that area early in the election season may have produced a backlash. His two predecessors as governor, Paul Cellucci and Jane Swift, endorsed McCain. Romney won by just 51%-41%. And because Massachusetts Republicans, unlike those in many other states, didn't have a winner-take-all rule, his delegate edge was minimal, while McCain on the same day was harvesting delegates in winner-take-all states such as New York, New Jersey, Missouri, and California. In 2012, Massachusetts voted on March 6. This time, Romney had no significant competition and won 72% of the vote.

Congressional Districts For many years, Massachusetts has had some of the most convoluted congressional district boundaries in the nation. It also had a habit of electing moderate Republicans from suburban enclaves. But that practice has disappeared, and the number of House seats fell from 14 in

114th Congress Lineup	
0 R	9 D
113th Congress Lineup	
0 R	9 D

1960. The 2010 census reduced the count to nine, and gave the state legislature a chance to smooth the lines. Since all of the seats were held by Democrats, it would mean a Democratic loss. Any suspense about which district would disappear vanished when the 1st District's John Olver announced he would retire. That was the westernmost district, and its elimination meant that Springfield-based Richard Neal could absorb the heavily Democratic Berkshires and that Worcester-based Jim McGovern would have a district that did not extend all the way east to Fall River. The other districts did not present incumbents with vast swaths of new territory.

In 2012 and 2014, Republican Richard Tisei ran in the 6th District, narrowly losing to ethically scarred incumbent John Tierney and then falling far short against Seth Moulton, who defeated Tierney in the Democratic primary. That continued the state's streak of not having elected a Republican to Congress since 1994. The GOP's best opportunity, though still a long shot, probably is the 9th District, which covers Cape Cod and the South Shore.

Governor

Charlie Baker (R)

Elected 2014, term expires 2019, 1st term; b. Nov. 13, 1956, Elmira, NY; Harvard U., B.A. 1979, Northwestern U., M.B.A. 1986; Protestant; married (Lauren); 3 children.

Elected Office: Swampscott Board of Selectmen, 2004-09.

Professional Career: Founder, Pioneer Institute for Public Policy Research, 1988-91; State Health Undersecretary, 1991-92; State Health & Human Svcs. Secretary, 1992-94; State Administrations & Finance Secretary, 1994-98; CEO, Harvard Vanguard Medical Associates, 1998-99; Entrepreneur, 2011-14.

Office: State House, Rm 280, Boston, 02133, 617-725-4005; Fax: 617-727-9725; Website: mass.gov/governor.

Election Results

2014 general	Charles D. Baker (R)	1,044,573	(48%)
	Martha Coakley (D)	1,004,408	(47%)
	Evan Falchuk (I)	71,814	(3%)
2014 primary	Charles D. Baker (R)	116,004	(74%)
	Mark Fisher (R)	40,240	(26%)

Charlie Baker won the Massachusetts governorship in 2014 by tapping two inherent advantages: He's a moderate Republican in a blue state with a history of electing socially liberal, fiscally conservative Republicans to the post. And he was running against Democrat Martha Coakley, the state attorney general still smarting from her upset loss to Scott Brown in the 2010 election to fill the seat of the late Sen. Edward Kennedy.

Baker was born in Elmira New York to a family steeped in politics and public service: His great-grandfather was a federal prosecutor and state assemblyman; his grandfather was a prominent Newburyport politician; his father Charles was a well-connected conservative Republican who had worked for Republican presidents Richard Nixon and Ronald Reagan. His mother was a liberal Democrat, leading to political arguments at the dinner table in Needham, where Baker mostly grew up and went to public schools. He earned a bachelor's degree in English from Harvard University and an MBA from the Kellogg Graduate School of Management at Northwestern University. He married the daughter of a Fortune 500 CEO, and delved in policy work as the first executive director of the Pioneer Institute, a conservative think tank in Boston, created in part by Baker's dad. At 36, Baker began his career in public service in 1992 when GOP Gov. Bill Weld appointed him secretary of Health and Human Services to head up the largest department in state government. Baker, efficient and diligent in his work, was elevated by Weld in 1994 to be secretary of Administration and Finance, putting him in charge of at the state's budget. Weld's successor, Paul Cellucci, kept Baker on in that post, where, among other things, he was the original architect of the financial plan for the Big Dig, the Boston tunnel project plagued by delays and cost overruns. When Baker left government, he went to become the CEO of Harvard Pilgrim Health Care, a nonprofit health benefits organization, from 1999 to 2009. In 2004, Baker was elected to the Board of Selectmen in his home town of Swampscott, an old fishing town on the North Shore of Boston whose skyline can be seen in the distance. Despite his high-profile pedigree in state government, Baker was described in a *Boston* magazine story as someone who preferred working in the background on the details of the town budget.

In his first run for governor, Baker took on Gov. Deval Patrick, who was seeking a second term in 2010. Baker's campaign was occasionally hampered by what some considered an arrogant and distant personal style as well as some stances that put him at odds with the state's Democratic electorate. He echoed the pledge on taxes of George H. W. Bush saying, "Read my lips, no new taxes," a position that even the 41st president had to abandon once in office. He came out in opposition to the Cape Wind energy farm and was agnostic on global warming, views that offended many Massachusetts environmentalists. Baker's task in the election was complicated by the presence of a third candidate, former state Treasurer Tim Cahill, who left the Democratic Party to run as an independent. This effectively split the base of the state's fiscally conservative and moderate voters that Baker needed to rally to have any hopes of winning. On Election Day, Patrick defeated Baker, 48%-42% while Cahill captured 8%.

But when he mounted a second campaign for governor in 2014, Baker was a changed candidate, softening his image from the brash campaigner of 2010 to a more genial—and female-voter-friendly—contender against Martha Coakley, the Democratic nominee. Baker cast himself as a fiscally responsible businessman, able to use his private-sector fiscal skills to heal what he called a poorly run Democratic administration. He emphasized his liberal take on social issues such as abortion and gay marriage. After stumbling with female voters in 2010, Baker picked a woman, Karyn Polito, as his running mate. The new Baker tweeted out messages on Twitter from Boston Red Sox games and spoke easily about his openly gay brother. While Coakley accused Baker of being weak on gender issues (he downplayed the Supreme Court's *Hobby Lobby* decision on birth control, a statement he later clarified, and called a female reporter "sweetheart," for which he apologized), the strategy did not stick. The Baker of 2014 succeeded where the Baker of 2010 could not. The staid *CommonWealth* magazine declared: "This is the new Charlie Baker. He's relaxed, he's likable, he's fun to drink beer with." Massachusetts voters liked the second-time gubernatorial hopeful as well. In the election, Coakley swept deeply Democratic Suffolk County (Boston) and Berkshire, Hampshire, and Franklin Counties in Western Massachusetts, with its college towns and resort communities full of liberal artists and former hippies. She also carried Middlesex County, with its mix of wealthy Boston suburbs like Cambridge, Belmont and Newton, heavily ethnic, heavily blue collar towns like Malden and Watertown, and Boston's I-495 exurban ring. But she only did so by a narrow 50%-46% margin. Baker won the rest of the state including Worcester County, with its classic New England small towns; Essex County, with its Merrimack Valley mill towns and North Shore affluent Boston exurbs; and Norfolk County, with its mix of upper income Boston exurbs and coastal towns of the South Shore populated by upper middle class Irish Catholics.

Baker's choices for his cabinet were eclectic. Coupling traditional pro-business Republicans with a mix of Democrats, he tapped some individuals who disagreed with positions he had taken while running for governor. He appointed Stephanie Pollack, the associate director for research at Northeastern University who had once advised Democratic Gov. Patrick, as secretary of Transportation. She is a strong advocate for public transportation who opposed the repeal of gas-tax indexing that Baker had supported in the campaign. He named Ronald Walker, a Democratic banker who was co-founder and president of Roxbury's Next Street, "a merchant bank for the urban enterprise," as secretary of Labor and Workforce Development. And Baker selected Democratic state Rep. Carlo Basile of East Boston to be his chief secretary and patronage dispenser in charge of appointments to state boards and commissions. To the positions in state government that he had previously held, Baker appointed two women. His budget chief and secretary of Administration and Finance is Kristen Lepore, a Republican regular who worked with Baker in the Cellucci administration. She had previously been a registered lobbyist for the Associated Industries of Massachusetts, where she opposed a bill that required insurance companies to cover up to 14 days of in-patient care for substance abuse, a position Baker supports. For secretary of Health and Human Services he named

Marylou Sudders, a veteran advocate for children and the former commissioner of the state's Department of Mental Health whose appointment was praised by Baker's defeated Democratic rival, Coakley. True to his roots as a budgeter, in early 2015 Baker signed a plan offering early retirement to state employees in order to reduce the workforce by up to 5,000 jobs. The Massachusetts General Court gave bipartisan approval to the proposal, a down payment on Baker's efforts to close the state's gaping budget deficit.

Senior Senator

Elizabeth Warren (D)

Elected 2012, term expires Jan. 2019, 1st term; b. June 22, 1949, Oklahoma City, OK; U. of Houston, B.S. 1970, Rutgers Schl. of Law, J.D. 1976; Methodist; married (Bruce Mann); 2 children.

Professional Career: Prof., U. of TX, 1981-87; Prof., U. of PA Law Schl., 1987-95; Prof., Harvard Law Schl., 1992-2013; Chair, Congressional Oversight Panel for the Troubled Asset Relief Program, 2008-10; Asst. to the pres. & special adviser to treas. secy., 2010-11.

DC Office: 317 HSOB, 20510, 202-224-4543; Website: warren.senate .gov.

State Offices: Boston, 617-565-3170; Springfield, 413-788-2690.

Committees: *Aging (Special). Banking, Housing & Urban Affairs:* Economic Policy (RMM); Financial Institutions & Consumer Protection; Housing, Transportation & Community Development; Securities, Insurance & Investment. *Energy & Natural Resources:* Energy; National Parks; Public Lands, Forests & Mining. *Health, Education, Labor & Pensions:* Children & Families; Primary Health & Aging.

Group Ratings

	ADA	ACLU	AFL-CIO	LCV	ITI	COC	HAFA	ACU	CFG	FRC
2014	100%	100%	–	80%	100%	13%	7%	8%	19%	0%
2013	90%	C	100%	100%	C	57%	C	4%	2%	C

National Journal Ratings

	2013 LIB	—	2013 CONS
Economic	75%	—	19%
Social	73%	—	0%
Foreign	54%	—	44%
Composite	73%	—	27%

Key Votes of the 113th Congress

1. Sandy storm spending	Y	5. Student Loan Rates	N	9. Bipartisan Budget Deal	Y
2. Chuck Hagel Confirmation	Y	6. Employee Non-Discrim'n Act	Y	10. Farm Bill Conference Rept.	N
3. Gun Background Checks	Y	7. Senate Vote on Judgeships	N	11. Unempl. Comp. Extension	Y
4. Immigration Reform	Y	8. Defense Dept. Spending	Y	12. Keystone Pipeline	N

Election Results

2012 general	Elizabeth Warren (D).............	1,696,346	(54%)	$42,211,677	$2,108,019	$2,192,513
	Scott Brown (R).......................	1,458,048	(46%)	$35,058,354	$687,364	$3,096,795
2012 primary	Elizabeth Warren (D)............unopposed					

Democrat Elizabeth Warren, Massachusetts' senior senator, occupies the seat held for nearly half a century by the late Sen. Edward Kennedy. Just as the traditional liberal wing of the Democratic Party long looked to Kennedy for leadership and inspiration, Warren is now viewed in much the same manner by progressive activists working to push the party to the left. Since her election to the Senate in 2012—and even prior to that—the former Harvard Law School professor has been the subject of seemingly non-stop speculation as a potential presidential candidate, despite her repeated disavowals of interest in the White House.

Such disavowals notwithstanding, Warren's career track has been reminiscent of another former law school professor, Barack Obama—who also was touted as presidential timber even before his 2004 election to the Senate. During his first term in the White House, Obama helped to launch Warren's political career when he named her a special adviser to the Treasury Department in 2010, tasking her with setting up the Consumer Financial Protection

Bureau created by that year's landmark Dodd-Frank financial regulatory bill. But, nearly midway through her first Senate term, Warren was to find herself in testy public exchanges with Obama. The immediate issue was a sweeping trade bill that Obama hoped would be one of his legacy achievements. More broadly, it was a debate fueled by longstanding tensions between the Obama White House and a Democratic left wing that believes Obama has spent insufficient political capital on the income equality issues to which Warren has given voice.

"Working families have been getting slammed. Washington has been rigged to work for those who can hire an army of lawyers and an army of lobbyists," Warren declared in an interview with *National Journal*. While she was growing up, she added, the United States was "a country of expanding opportunities. ... Now we talk much more about protecting those who have already made it." If such populist-sounding assertions aren't usually associated with members of the Harvard Law School faculty, Warren traces her political convictions to hardscrabble origins as well as academic research. She grew up in Oklahoma City where her teen years were marred when her father, a maintenance man, suffered a heart attack. His lost pay and medical bills imperiled the family's finances; Warren and her mother went to work, with Warren, then 13, waiting tables at her aunt's Mexican restaurant. Betsy, as she was then known, also developed into a champion high school debater; her skills enabled her to win a scholarship and become the first in her family to receive a college diploma.

Warren married a high school sweetheart at 19, had two children, taught elementary school, picked up a law degree from Rutgers University in 1976, and went through a divorce—earning an appreciation for working mothers. She developed a specialty in bankruptcy law as a member of the law faculty at three universities before arriving at Harvard in 1992. Along the way, she remarried, to Bruce Mann, who remains a Harvard law professor. As recently as 1996, Warren was a registered Republican. But she said the families she met in her research into bankruptcy changed her. "These were hard-working, middle-class families who by and large had lost jobs, gotten sick, had family breakups, and that's what was driving them over the edge financially. It changed my vision," Warren said during a 2007 appearance at the University of California.

Warren combined her academic expertise with an ability to translate complicated policy issues into terms that could frame the broader political debate, enabling her to emerge as a leading advocate for consumer financial interests. In 1995, she became chief adviser to the National Bankruptcy Review Commission and unsuccessfully led the fight against legislation to make it harder for consumers to file for bankruptcy. In the process, she made appearances on the TV talk show circuit—including *The Daily Show with Jon Stewart*—and, with her daughter, Amelia Warren Tyagi, co-authored a couple of books on consumer finance aimed at a general audience. The second, *All Your Worth: The Ultimate Lifetime Money Plan*, made *The New York Times* best-seller list after its 2005 publication. In 2008, in the wake of the financial crash, Senate Majority Leader Harry Reid named Warren to chair the congressional oversight panel for the $700 billion Troubled Asset Relief Program enacted that year.

A year earlier, Warren had written an article in which she proposed a "Financial Product Safety Commission" modeled on the Consumer Product Safety Commission created in the early 1970s. "...It is time for a new model of financial regulation, one focused primarily on consumer safety rather than corporate profitability," she wrote. "Financial products should be subject to the same routine safety screening that now governs the sale of every toaster, washing machine, and child's car seat sold on the American market." Her idea was incorporated into the 2010 Dodd-Frank law as a new agency within the Treasury Department, and Warren was hired by the White House to design and launch the Consumer Financial Protection Bureau. But her barbed criticisms over the years had made her a *bete noire* to many sectors of the nation's financial industry. With Senate Republicans vowing to block her appointment, Obama instead nominated former Ohio Attorney General Richard Cordray as the bureau's first director.

But the visibility that Warren achieved during her year in the Obama administration prompted many Massachusetts Democrats, searching for a high-profile candidate to challenge Republican Sen. Scott Brown, to encourage her to run. Not long after leaving her post as a special adviser to the Treasury secretary in late 2011, Warren announced her candidacy. She became a national sensation when a speech she gave, exhorting wealthy Americans to recognize the debt they owe to the community and "pay forward for the next kid who comes along," went viral. Warren became a "Doonesbury" cartoon heroine and got a prime-time speaking slot at the 2012 Democratic convention—fueling talk of a future presidential bid even before she had captured a Senate seat.

Brown had shocked Democrats when he won a January 2010 special election to succeed Kennedy. He received substantial support from tea party interests upset about Obama's health care overhaul, but generally steered clear of the tea party in compiling a centrist voting record. Brown's everyman persona—he drove a pickup truck—made him well-liked among voters, and Warren initially struggled to put a dent in his support. He pointedly referred to her as "Professor Warren", seeking to drive a wedge between her background at an elite university and the rank-and-file electorate. However, in the last months of the campaign, she frequently asserted a vote for Brown was a vote for a Republican Senate majority, a sentiment that resonated with voters. Brown, recognizing he was vulnerable, repeatedly attacked Warren for claiming she had Cherokee ancestry, an assertion not uncommon among Oklahoma natives. But Brown's backers charged it was a ruse by Warren used to exploit affirmative action plans at schools where she had been hired, an allegation she denied. Warren won, 54%-46%. Both candidates agreed to seek to ban outside spending, but it still ended up as one of the most expensive Senate races ever: Brown raised $28 million (and spent $35 million), Warren raised and spent more than $42 million.

Warren's victory made her a colleague of many of the same Republicans who had vowed never to allow her nomination as director of the Consumer Finance Protection Bureau to be approved. But if she was occasionally compared to another senator first elected in 2012, Texas Republican Ted Cruz—whose fervent following among tea party hardliners mirrored Warren's enthusiastic reception by Democratic left-wingers—Warren avoided Cruz's take-no-prisoners legislative style. While Cruz alienated colleagues by blocking votes and sending the Senate into overtime sessions, Warren reached across the political aisle to find occasional common ground. One of her legislative achievements was the late 2014 passage of the Smart Savings Act, which altered federal worker retirement accounts to provide greater returns on their investments. The House sponsor of the measure, California Rep. Darrell Issa, is among that chamber's more partisan Republicans.

Warren was hardly the most liberal member of the Senate in her first year. She broke with Obama in voting to repeal the Affordable Care Act's medical device tax—a core element to funding the health insurance overhaul. It was an instance of her choosing constituency over party: Many medical device manufacturers are based in Massachusetts. She also joined with most Republicans—and at odds with a number of the Senate's leading liberals—in supporting an amendment to the annual budget resolution to "repeal or reduce the estate tax, but only if done in a fiscally responsible way. " Still, much of her early focus in the Senate has dovetailed with the issues and causes that brought her to prominence.

Before being sworn in, Warren sought a seat on the Banking Committee. Financial industry executives openly crusaded against the idea, but her liberal allies pushed back and she was named to the panel. In 2013, Warren pushed to reinstitute some of the separation between banks and other financial institutions swept away when the Glass-Steagall Act was repealed in the late 1990s; she introduced a bill to separate traditional banks that offer checking and savings accounts from riskier financial services. The measure picked up the support of Arizona Republican John McCain, but other GOP lawmakers wouldn't touch it and it languished. At the end of 2014, Warren organized an unsuccessful effort to kill a massive spending bill designed to keep the government running into 2015: She objected to its softening of provisions in the Dodd-Frank law. Several months earlier, Warren fell a handful of votes short in trying to move legislation to allow those holding student loans to refinance them at current rates, in the manner one can now do with a home mortgage or car loan as rates fall. She reintroduced it at the outset of the 114th Congress.

Her jawboning of federal regulators achieved greater success. During her first hearing as a Banking Committee member in early 2013, Warren pressured federal regulators to take legal action against more of the nation's largest financial institutions. "They can break the law and drag in billions in profits and then turn around and settle, paying out of those profits. They don't have much incentive to follow the law," she complained. She later pressed the Securities and Exchange Commission to seek admission of guilt from corporations found to have violated the law rather than allowing them to pay a fine without admitting or denying guilt—and claimed part of the credit when the policy was changed to do so. Her pointed grilling of top Treasury Department and Federal Reserve officials won her more admiration from the left; *The New Republic* in April 2013 dubbed her a "Regulatory Rock Star."

These highly visible, adversarial encounters, readily available via YouTube, served to nourish the Warren for President talk, as did the spring 2014 publication of another best-selling book, *A Fighting Chance*—part autobiography, part a packaging of her philosophy.

At the liberal Netroots Nation conference that summer, Warren supporters handed out hats, signs and bumper stickers urging a run for the White House, and she brought the crowd to its feet with her angry denunciations of big business. A draft-Warren movement quickly ramped up; by January 2015, MoveOn.org and Democracy for America collected nearly 250,000 signatures in an online petition urging her to run.

The only problem was that the potential candidate wasn't biting. "I had to work really hard to get here [to Congress]," she told *Esquire*. "I said, 'If I get to the United States Senate, I'm going to use that opportunity to work for the middle class and for working families every chance I get.'" In interviews, she repeatedly batted away questions about her presidential future by answering, "I am not running for president." When questioners noted that such verbal constructions did not foreclose her running in the future, Warren began employing the future tense. "I am not running and I am not going to run," she declared in March 2015. By summer, MoveOn.org and Democracy for America announced they were folding their draft-Warren group, "Run, Warren, Run".

At that point, non-candidate Warren already had succeeded in defining the battle lines of the 2016 contest for the Democratic presidential nomination—perhaps as much, if not more so, than if she had run. Her influence was formally recognized when, following the November 2014 election, Senate Minority Leader Harry Reid named her as a member of the Senate Democratic leadership. In her newly created post, "strategic policy adviser" to the Democratic Policy and Communications Committee, she was charged with being an envoy to liberal groups and helping to shape the party's message. Hillary Clinton, preparing to launch her second presidential bid, privately solicited ideas from Warren in a meeting held at Clinton's request at the end of 2014. Clinton's subsequent rhetoric often made her sound much like Warren.

An illustration of Warren's use of her Senate seat to influence the broader debate within the party came in early 2015, when Antonio Weiss, nominated by Obama as Treasury undersecretary for domestic finance, withdrew his name. He had drawn Warren's fierce opposition: She felt his role as a Wall Street investment banker made him unsuited for a post that involved implementation of the Dodd-Frank law. Warren's allies said the episode typified how she intended to use her clout—by reminding presidential candidates of both parties, including Clinton, of the public's disgust with Wall Street having its way in Washington. "The worst case for us is that [Clinton] gives a feisty speech now and then, but surrounds herself with the same old" economic advisers with close ties to the financial world, a Warren adviser told *The Washington Post*.

The Weiss episode turned out to be a relative skirmish in advance of the battle over the Obama's pursuit of a 12-nation Asian trade deal. In an op-ed article in February 2015, Warren contended the Trans-Pacific Partnership agreement, by setting up international arbitration panels, would "undermine U.S. sovereignty" and "allow foreign companies to challenge U.S. laws—and potentially to pick up huge payouts from taxpayers—without ever stepping foot in a U.S. court." The White House quickly issued a response disputing Warren's arguments in detail, but she turned up the heat a couple of months later—just as the Senate was about to vote on a related measure giving Obama "fast track" authority to expedite negotiation of the Asian trade accord. Once again, the issue was the future of the Dodd-Frank financial regulatory legislation.

While declaring that "I very much hope" the Democrats retain the White House in 2016 and 2020, Warren contended "a Republican president could easily use a future trade deal to override our domestic financial rules … A six-year fast-track bill is the missing link they need to make that happen." White House officials again disputed that such a scenario could occur under the terms of the legislation. But, this time, it was clear that Warren had gotten under the skin of the president himself.

In an interview aired by *Yahoo*'s news site, an uncharacteristically blunt Obama called Warren "absolutely wrong" and seemed to question her motives. "The truth of the matter is that Elizabeth is, you know, a politician like everybody else," he declared. "And you know, she's got a voice that she wants to get out there. And I understand that. And on most issues, she and I deeply agree. On this one, though, her arguments don't stand the test of fact and scrutiny." To some, it was a president who had taken office vowing to change the ways of Washington but who ultimately had to bow to political reality venting frustration—at an adversary who continued to be perceived by many as more a consumer advocate and crusading populist than a politician. "I'll always be an outsider," Warren told the *Washington Post* at the outset of 2015. "That's how I understand the world."

Junior Senator

Edward Markey (D)

Elected June 2013, 1st full term; b. July 11, 1946, Malden; Boston Col., B.A. 1968, J.D. 1972; Catholic; married (Susan Blumenthal).

Military Career: Army Reserves, 1968-73.

Elected Office: MA House, 1973-76; U.S. House, 1976-2013.

DC Office: 255 DSOB, 20510, 202-224-2742; Website: markey.senate .gov.

State Offices: Boston, 617-565-8519; Fall River, 508-677-0523; Springfield, 413-785-4610.

Committees: *Commerce, Science & Transportation:* Aviation Operations, Safety & Security; Communications, Technology, Innovation & the Internet; Consumer Protection, Product Safety, Insurance & Data Security; Oceans, Atmosphere, Fisheries & Coast Guard; Space, Science & Competitiveness; Surface Transportation & Merchant Marines Infrastructure, Safety & Security. *Environment & Public Works:* Superfund, Waste Management & Regulatory Oversight (RMM); Clean Air & Nuclear Safety; Fisheries, Water & Wildlife. *Foreign Relations:* Africa & Global Health Policy (RMM); Europe & Regional Security Cooperation; Multilateral International Development, Multilateral Institutions & International Economic, Energy & Environmental Policy; Western Hemisphere, Transnational Crime, Civilian Security, Democracy, Human Rights & Global Women's Issues. *Small Business & Entrepreneurship.*

Group Ratings

	ADA	ACLU	AFL-CIO	LCV	ITI	COC	HAFA	ACU	CFG	FRC
2014	90%	46%	–	80%	100%	25%	7%	8%	17%	0%
2013	–	C	100%	100%	C	67%	C	0%	0%	C

Key Votes of the 113th Congress

1. Student Loan Rates   N
2. Employee Non-Discrim'n Act   Y
3. Senate Vote on Judgeships   N
4. Defense Dept. Spending   NV
5. Bipartisan Budget Deal   Y
6. Farm Bill Conference Rept. N
7. Unempl. Comp. Extension   Y
8. Keystone Pipeline   N

Election Results

2014 general	Ed Markey (D)	1,289,944	(62%)	$17,857,729	$3,214,292	$724,589
	Brian Herr (R)	791,950	(38%)	$118,532		
2014 primary	Ed Markey (D)	unopposed				

Prior winning percentages: 2013 special (55%); House: 2012 (76%), 2010 (66%), 2008 (76%), 2006 (100%), 2004 (74%), 2002 (100%), 2000 (100%), 1998 (71%), 1996 (70%), 1994 (64%), 1992 (62%), 1990 (100%), 1988 (100%), 1986 (100%), 1984 (71%), 1982 (78%), 1980 (100%), 1978 (85%), 1976 special/ general combined (77%)

When Democrat Edward Markey, now Massachusetts' junior senator, arrived in the Senate after winning a June 2013 special election, it was the culmination of a nearly 30-year wait. Back in 1984, Markey, then a four-term House member, had jumped into the Democratic primary for an opening created by the retirement of Sen. Paul Tsongas. But, amid a bumpy reception to his candidacy, Markey soon reassessed his position, withdrew from the Senate contest and successfully sought re-election to the House. The ultimate winner of the Senate seat that year was then-Lt. Gov. John Kerry, who held onto it until President Barack Obama nominated him as Secretary of State at the end of 2012. Even as he accumulated seniority and influence in the House, Markey continued to eye the seat—hoping that it might come open in 2004 if Kerry, then the Democratic presidential nominee, had won the White House. Finally, with Kerry poised to move to the Cabinet, Markey, at age 66, saw his opportunity and grabbed it.

Markey was only 30 when he was first elected to the House in 1976, and, over the years, became a key player on environmental and technology issues—topics on which he has continued to focus as a senator, while displaying the barbed wit that has long endeared him to consumer advocates and environmentalists. But what makes his move from one side of the U.S. Capitol to the other extraordinary is that there has never before been a House member with Markey's seniority—nearly 37 years—who opted to trade that in to become a freshman senator. In fact, in September 2009, when the death of Democrat Ted Kennedy opened the seat

Kennedy had held for nearly five decades, Markey passed: The Democrats then held the House majority, and Markey, in addition to being in third in line for the chairmanship of the powerful Energy and Commerce Committee, was also chairing a special panel tasked with laying the groundwork for legislation to curb global warming. That changed a year later: House Democrats lost their majority in the 2010 election, with no clear prospect of regaining it in the near future, and a high visibility, if junior, Senate slot became significantly more appealing.

Markey grew up in the Boston suburb of Malden, where his father was a milkman. He graduated from Boston College, and was elected to the state House, at age 26, soon after graduating from Boston College's law school. He moved to an open House seat four years later, winning a 12-candidate primary with 22 percent. Markey broke out of the crowded field with a TV ad that remains a classic in Bay State political circles: It played off an episode in which state House leaders removed the furniture from Markey's office to retaliate for a court reform bill he had pushed over their objections. The ad shows a desk in the hallway of the Massachusetts State House, as Markey declares: "The bosses may tell me where to sit, nobody tells me where to stand."

Throughout most of his long career on Capitol Hill, Markey has ranked among the most liberal members of Congress. But, in winning in 1976, Markey favored school prayer and advocated constitutional amendments to end school busing and ban abortion—positions geared to a conservative Catholic population in his home base. He subsequently disavowed all of these positions prior to his brief Senate bid in 1984, but the timing of these reversals became a liability during that short-lived campaign. In recent decades, he has sidestepped questions about the change of position on these issues early in his career, telling the *Boston Globe* in 2013: "For 30 years, I have taken the progressive position, the liberal position, on each and every issue. I just evolved."

In the 2013 special Senate election, Markey was the establishment favorite and the more traditional liberal Democrat against Rep. Stephen Lynch, whose district includes working class neighborhoods in and around south Boston. Lynch was generally regarded as the most conservative of the Massachusetts Democratic congressional delegation, although he sought to moderate his anti-abortion stance early in the Senate campaign. As a onetime iron worker, he enjoyed substantial labor union support. But, with Markey's 3-1 cash advantage at the start of the primary, Lynch was unable to get traction and Markey won, 57%-43%. Markey had expected his fiercest competition to come in the special general election—from former Republican Sen. Scott Brown, who had lost the state's other seat to Democrat Elizabeth Warren in one of the nation's highest-profile Senate contests of 2012. But Brown opted not to run in the special election, instead waiting and ultimately mounting a competitive but unsuccessful Senate bid in neighboring New Hampshire in 2014.

Instead, Markey faced businessman Gabriel Gomez. A former Navy Seal and a bilingual son of Colombian immigrants, Gomez was no easy target. Markey attacked him on gun control. "Gomez is against banning high-capacity magazines, like the ones used in the Newtown School shooting," one ad charged, referring to the mass shooting at a Connecticut elementary school in December 2012 in which 26 were killed. In response, Gomez mocked the Democratic attack ads, with one Gomez ad sarcastically declaring: "Gabriel Gomez is a very bad man. He kills old people. He hates women. He even leaves the toilet seat up," The ad continued: "This is ridiculous … Markey is everything that's wrong with Congress: 37 years of pay raises, bounced checks, taking millions from people he regulates." But Markey had amassed a large campaign treasury, thanks in large part to being a veteran member of a House committee with jurisdiction over a host of heavily lobbied issues. He outspent Gomez by a margin approaching 4-1, and won, 55%-45%. Sixteen months later, Markey was easily elected to a full six-year term in the 2014 general election, defeating his little-known opponent, businessman and local selectman Brian Herr, 59%-36%.

As a senator, Markey has comfortably fit in with the chamber's other left-leaning members from the Northeast, including his higher-profile Massachusetts colleague, Warren. But he drew unwanted attention for a political stumble not long after being sworn in. When the Foreign Relations Committee voted in September 2013 to authorize President Obama's use of force against Syria, Markey voted "present" while most other committee Democrats voted in support. Markey said he was concerned about the "unintended consequences" of a U.S. military attack, which never ended up occurring—but critics saw it as an attempt to sidestep a tough issue. In particular, Markey's vote was regarded as a swipe at his predecessor, Kerry, who had worked to clear the way for Markey to succeed him. *Boston Magazine* afterward captured the widespread reaction in a headline that read, "Ed Markey Annoys Literally

Everyone by Voting 'Present' on Syrian Resolution." Markey's straddling of the issue may have been related to his vote a decade earlier in favor of the 2002 resolution authorizing the war in Iraq, a vote about which he later expressed strong regret.

As a member of the Senate Commerce Committee, Markey has been a leader on "net neutrality," which would prohibit Internet carriers from selectively charging higher fees to certain content providers in return for faster delivery speeds. When a U.S. District Court ruling in January 2014 opened the door for service providers to engage in such practices, Markey introduced a bill to keep the open-Internet rule until the Federal Communications Commission adopted new rules that could hold up in court. "Without a truly open Internet, America will be closed to innovation," he said in July.

During his House years, Markey left his most lasting impact on telecommunications policy, where he often worked with Republicans to come up with innovative initiatives. His proposals were often inclined toward deregulation, but consumer advocates regarded him as a friend—blaming the skyrocketing cable TV bills of recent years not on Markey's legislation, but on the failure of the industry to produce the level of competition originally promised. Markey's Massachusetts colleague, House Speaker Tip O'Neill, early on put him in a position to be a serious legislator, with a seat on the Energy and Commerce Committee. Impressed by the high-tech boom around Route 128, Markey joined the panel's Telecommunications Subcommittee. In early 1987, after a decade in the House, Markey became chairman of the panel. This was a couple of years after a court ordered the breakup of the old "Ma Bell" monopoly, which put a transformation of the nation's telecommunications industry into motion.

In 1992, Markey crafted a cable television regulation bill with enough support that Congress was able to override President George H.W. Bush's veto—the only bill passed over his veto. The measure helped to establish today's satellite TV industry. Markey lost the gavel of the Telecommunications Subcommittee when the Republicans captured the House majority in 1994, but remained as ranking minority member and continued to exert influence: Telecommunications policy has been an area where bills are hard to pass in the absence of bipartisan consensus. He was a major player in the passage of the landmark Telecommunications Act of 1996. The legislation, co-authored with Texas Republican Rep. Jack Fields, helped to prod cable companies to build the broadband networks integral to the flow of information and images over today's Internet. "Google, Hulu, YouTube—none of it was possible before the 1996 Telecom Act," Markey told the *Globe* years later. "It required broadband in order to make the business models possible."

When the Democrats regained control of the House in the 2006 election, Markey's other major legislative interest—energy and environmental issues—became his focus. House Speaker Nancy Pelosi chose Markey in 2007 to be chairman of a Select Committee on Energy Independence and Global Warming. This was an attempt to get around Michigan Rep. John Dingell, who as chairman of the Energy and Commerce Committee and representative of a district in suburban Detroit, had resisted efforts to toughen auto emissions standards. When Dingell strenuously objected, she announced the select committee would not have authority to propose legislation, but she gave Markey free rein to hold hearings and make the case for a far-reaching bill to curb global warming. After the 2008 election, California Democrat Henry Waxman defeated Dingell for the chairmanship of the full Energy and Commerce Committee, and Markey became chairman of the Energy and Environment Subcommittee while retaining the select committee gavel. It gave Pelosi the players she needed to achieve the Democrats' goal of an 85 percent cut in greenhouse gas emissions by 2050, along with a cap-and-trade program that would compel companies to buy and sell emissions credits with the overall goal of reducing emissions.

Markey worked with oil and gas interests, with the auto industry, and with manufacturers in general, to gain their support—or at least to reduce their level of opposition. The Congressional Budget Office said the bill would cost average households less than $200 a year, which helped blunt Republicans' characterization of the bill as "cap-and-tax." (When an iceberg four times the size of Manhattan broke off Greenland in 2010, Markey—exhibiting his trademark sarcastic wit—observed that the development created "plenty of room for global-warming deniers to start their own country.") After fierce negotiations, the bill came to the floor in June 2009, and passed 219-212. Markey hailed House passage of the bill as demonstrating the advantages of business and consumer interests cooperating "to create a pathway that works for both." But the Senate never took up the bill, and House Republicans used it as a political club in 2010 campaigns.

Markey was more successful in toughening automobile fuel efficiency standards. In 2007, working closely with Pelosi, Markey proposed an increase in fuel efficiency standards to 35 miles per gallon by 2018. The domestic auto industry and the United Auto Workers union criticized the plan as extreme and said that it would impose a far lower burden on foreign companies. Their allies backed a 2022 deadline and more flexible terms. The bill that was passed into law maintained the 35 miles per gallon standard but pushed the deadline back to 2020. It marked the first increase in the fuel efficiency standards since 1975. In his first bill introduced after his election to the Senate, Markey in October 2013 took aim at electric utilities—proposing a requirement that 25 percent of the power they distribute come from renewable energy sources by 2025. Noting that 30 states had taken similar steps on their own, Markey declared: "There is real bipartisan support for energy efficiency here in the Senate. These are policies that should be embraced and not blocked."

In substance, it's not far from where Markey began his career more than one-third of a century earlier—as a strong foe of nuclear power. At the 1980 Democratic National Convention in New York, anti-nuclear activists threatened to collect enough signatures to put Markey onto the ballot for the vice presidential nomination if convention organizers did not grant him a prime-time speaking slot. The ploy gave the 34-year old Markey 10 minutes to make the case to a national audience to shut down its nuclear reactors and increase solar energy. But today, Markey is pursuing increased production of "green" energy as gray-haired congressional insider who methodically seeks to create bipartisan alliances and pass legislation. In a 2013 interview with the *Globe*, Pelosi, upon her arrival on Capitol Hill in the mid-1980s, said she counted Markey among the "disrupters." Her perspective today? "He's operational," she said, intending it as compliment, while adding that Markey knows "how to get the job done."

FIRST DISTRICT

Richard Neal (D)

Elected 1988, 14th term; b. Feb. 14, 1949, Worcester; American Intl. Col., B.A. 1972, U. of Hartford, M.A. 1976; Catholic; married (Maureen); 4 children.

Elected Office: Springfield City Cncl., 1978-83; Springfield mayor, 1984-88.

Professional Career: Staff asst., Springfield Mayor William C. Sullivan, 1973-78; H.S. & college teacher, 1978-83.

DC Office: 341 CHOB, 20515, 202-225-5601; Fax: 202-225-8112; Website: neal.house.gov.

State Offices: Pittsfield, 413-442-0946; Springfield, 413-785-0325.

Committees: *Ways & Means:* Select Revenue Measures (RMM); Trade.

Group Ratings

	ADA	ACLU	AFL-CIO	LCV	ITI	COC	HAFA	ACU	CFG	FRC
2014	80%	61%	—	94%	60%	50%	9%	8%	12%	0%
2013	85%	C	100%	96%	C	42%	C	9%	13%	C

National Journal Ratings

	2013 LIB	—	2013 CONS
Economic	86%	—	13%
Social	93%	—	0%
Foreign	94%	—	0%
Composite	93%	—	7%

Key Votes of the 113th Congress

1. Sandy storm spending	Y	5. Medical Marijuana	Y	9. Syrian Rebels Training	Y
2. Violence Against Women Act	Y	6. Farm Bill	N	10. Keystone pipeline	N
3. Guantanamo Bay Detainees	Y	7. Afghanistan Combat	N	11. Immigration Exec. Action	N
4. Abortion 20-week ban	N	8. NSA Phone Data Collection	Y	12. Bipartisan budget deal	Y

Election Results

2014 general	Richard Neal (D)	167,612 (98%)	$1,241,117
2014 primary	Richard Neal (D)	unopposed	

Prior winning percentages: 2012 (unopposed), 2010 (57%), 2008 (98%), 2006 (100%), 2004 (100%), 2002 (100%), 2000 (100%), 1998 (100%), 1996 (72%), 1994 (59%), 1992 (53%), 1990 (100%), 1988 (80%)

Population		Race and Ethnicity		Income	
Total:	729,965	White	75.0%	Median income:	$52,300
Urban:	27.5%	Latino	15.3%		*(199 of 435)*
Suburban:	64.9%	Black	5.7%	Under $50,000	47.9%
Rural:	7.6%	Asian	1.9%	$50,000-$99,999:	29.6%
Land area:	2,455	Two races	1.6%	$100,000-$199,999:	19.3%
Pop/sq. mi.:	297.3	White Ethnic	65.5%	$200,000 or more:	3.2%
Born in state:	66.1%			Poverty Rate	15.7%
		Education			
Age Groups		H.S. grad or less:	44.5%	**Work**	
Under 18:	21.2%	Some college:	27.7%	White collar:	36.3%
18 to 34:	22.3%	College degree, 4 yr.:	16.0%	Blue collar:	43.5%
35 to 64:	40.5%	Post-grad study:	11.8%	Sales and service:	20.1%
Over 64:	16.0%				
		Military		Govt. workers:	15.5%
		Veterans/active duty:	8.8%		

Western Massachusetts: Springfield, Pittsfield

The stony hills and green mountains of western Massachusetts, which so inspired Henry David Thoreau in the 1840s, look a lot like they did 300 years ago. This was the frontier in the 17th century, where Puritan preachers founded towns in the wilderness, farmed the rocky soil and preached against

Voter Turnout	
2013 Total Citizen 18+	554,214
2014 House Turnout	171,110
2014 Turnout as % CVAP	30.9%
2012 Turnout as % CVAP	61.4%

declension. It remained Yankee New England's western frontier for nearly 200 years. In the 19th century, the area was the home of writers and artists. Edith Wharton lived grandly on her estate in Lenox. Herman Melville struck up a friendship with Nathaniel Hawthorne after purchasing a farm near Hawthorne's Pittsfield home, not far from where the Boston Symphony plays at the Tanglewood Festival each summer. As the 20th century progressed, and trees grew on stony land in the Berkshire mountains that were once farmed, western Massachusetts came to look less settled. The exceptions were areas near giant factories like the Crane & Co. paper mill along the Housatonic River in Dalton, which since 1879 has been the only company to print money for the U.S. Treasury. Armed guards protect the facility's secret plating process, which is the benchmark for producing currency and preventing counterfeiting. In 2012, Crane expanded and consolidated its stationery operations at its North Adams plant. But there no longer are any family members in management.

Springfield is the largest city in western Massachusetts and the third-largest in the Bay State, far from Boston but with its own historical cachet. It is the site of the armory where unhappy soldiers mounted the Shays' Rebellion in 1786-87. It is where basketball was invented and where the Webster's unabridged dictionaries (2nd and 3rd editions) were edited and published. Founded by Puritans in the 17th century, Springfield has become home to immigrants from a dozen countries who have worked their way up here. African Americans and Hispanics today account for more than half the population.

Like other New England city centers, Springfield's downtown has emptied, and its tax base has shrunk in recent decades. Business leaders have tried to revive it, in part with the expansion of the Basketball Hall of Fame. The firearms manufacturer Smith & Wesson is headquartered in Springfield. But the once-robust city has suffered from corruption and serious crime, and in 2004 was

2012 Presidential Vote		
Barack Obama (D)	213,423	(64%)
Mitt Romney (R)................	114,339	(34%)
2008 Presidential Vote		
Barack Obama (D)	212,498	(64%)
John McCain (R)................	111,583	(34%)
Cook Partisan Voting Index: D+13		

forced to submit to state control in a financial bailout. Until June 2009, the state board reorganized city government. Springfield had more foreclosures than any other city in Massachusetts in 2010. In 2013, that total declined by half, but remained higher than in Boston, which is four times larger. Groundbreaking in March 2015 for an MGM casino in the South End of Springfield created rare hope for the future of the city. In April 2015, the state took control of "chronically underperforming" schools in Holyoke.

For many years, western Massachusetts was a heartland of the Republican Party—flinty, thrifty and chilly, just like the area's most famous politician, Calvin Coolidge. House Speaker Frederick Gillett overlapped with President Coolidge for part of his six years as speaker. The area now contains some of the most liberal parts of the United States. Progressive MSNBC host Rachel Maddow has a home here with her partner, Susan Mikula. "We kind of forget we're gay," Mikula told *New York* magazine in 2008. "We live in western Mass and New York, and it's very accommodating." Alice's Restaurant in Great Barrington was immortalized by folk singer Arlo Guthrie in his anti-war song of the same name.

The 1st District in western Massachusetts includes Springfield and the old mill towns Chicopee and Holyoke along the wide Connecticut River, plus Dalton and Pittsfield in the Berkshires. It stretches east to take in some Worcester County towns such as Charlton and Southbridge. There are year-round, weekend, and vacation homes throughout the Berkshires. The district now votes overwhelmingly Democratic, with scant Republicans.

Richard Neal (D)

Democrat Richard Neal, first elected in 1988, has established himself as one of his party's pro-business leaders on economic policy. He holds a senior position on the powerful Ways and Means Committee and has close ties to the insurance and investment industries, which are his leading sources of campaign funds.

Neal grew up in Springfield amid the racial tensions of the 1960s. His parents died when he was a teenager, and Neal and his younger sisters received monthly Social Security survivor benefits while being raised by their grandmother and aunt. He graduated from American International College and earned a master's degree in public administration from the University of Hartford. In Springfield, he worked for the mayor; and in 1978, while teaching high school and college history, he was elected to the City Council. As mayor from 1984 to 1988, Neal worked to rehabilitate the downtown area and revitalize neighborhoods.

His congressional predecessor, 36-year incumbent Edward Boland, a senior House appropriator and longtime pal of Democratic Speaker Tip O'Neill, essentially bequeathed him the House seat. Boland announced his retirement just before the filing deadline—and after Neal had traveled the district for a year. Unopposed in the Democratic primary, Neal won the general election with 80 percent of the vote.

Neal has a generally liberal voting record, especially since Democrats were consigned to the minority in 2011, but has favored enough moderate initiatives to separate himself from more-liberal Massachusetts colleagues. He voted for the 1996 welfare overhaul and supported both the North American Free Trade Agreement and normalization of trade relations with China, although organized labor opposed the pacts. He is active in the Democratic Congressional Campaign Committee's Business Council, with its outreach to industry.

Neal is the ranking Democrat on the Select Revenue Measures Subcommittee of Ways and Means, which handles many tax and tariff bills and which he chaired when Democrats were in the majority. He crusaded for repeal of the alternative minimum tax, which was designed to ensure that the highest earners pay some tax even if they have offsetting deductions, but which has been increasingly ensnaring middle-income taxpayers. After years of trying, he succeeded in early 2013 in passing a permanent "patch" on the tax to keep pace with inflation. He took the lead for House Democrats on a popular proposal to clamp down on companies that incorporate in Bermuda and other offshore havens to avoid U.S. taxes. Neal worked with the Obama administration on a bill to require employers who do not sponsor retirement plans for their workers to automatically enroll them in individual retirement accounts funded by payroll deductions, unless an employee opts out. In February 2015, with two Republican members of Ways and Means, he filed a proposal to make permanent the "new markets" tax credit that is designed to spur private investment in low-income neighborhoods where access to capital is often limited. Neal also has sought to reform the tax code, which he has said is "creaking under its own weight."

Neal is the Democratic leader of the Friends of Ireland Caucus. In September 2014, he was one of two Democrats in the nine-member Massachusetts delegation who voted for the House-passed bill to give President Barack Obama the authority to train and arm Syrian rebels.

When Democrat Charles Rangel of New York was forced to step down as Ways and Means chairman in March 2010 while battling ethics problems, Neal was mentioned as a possible successor, but the gavel went to the more senior Sander Levin of Michigan. Neal vigorously pushed for the job, arguing that the party needed to shelve its seniority tradition in favor of having a better spokesman in the role. He contended he would be a more business-friendly alternative to Levin, who is strongly pro-labor, and could work more closely with Republicans to get bills passed. Neal raised substantial sums for endangered Democratic incumbents in the 2010 election—always a good way to get the leadership to take notice. After the election, he won a 23-22 vote of the Democratic Steering Committee. But he lost to Levin in a vote of the full caucus, 109-78, with many Democrats saying they were not ready to upend seniority. Now the dean of the New England House delegation, he is positioned to eventually get the top Ways and Means slot, though Levin and three other Democrats remained senior to him—and many years older.

On local issues, Neal has focused on the economic problems of Springfield. He was instrumental in securing a $22 million grant for renovation of its Union Station in 2007, as well as $121 million in 2010 for high-speed rail service in the region. To help the growing number of craft-beer brewers in his district and elsewhere, he introduced a bipartisan bill in 2013 to cut excise taxes on beer in half.

Neal had serious primary challenges in 1990 and 1992, but won reelection by healthy margins. He ran unopposed in four successive elections before facing a challenge in 2010 from Republican business executive Thomas Wesley, who spent only $144,000 to $2.2 million for the incumbent. Neal campaigned aggressively, getting Education Secretary Arne Duncan to appear with him on opening day of school in Springfield, but was held to 57 percent of the vote. Since then, Neal has not had major-party opposition.

SECOND DISTRICT

James McGovern (D)

Elected 1996, 10th term; b. Nov. 20, 1959, Worcester; American U., B.A. 1981, M.P.A. 1984; Catholic; married (Lisa); 2 children.

Professional Career: Aide, U.S. Sen. George McGovern, 1981-84; Sr. aide, U.S. Rep. Joseph Moakley, 1982-96.

DC Office: 438 CHOB, 20515, 202-225-6101; Fax: 202-225-5759; Website: mcgovern.house.gov.

State Offices: Leominster, 978-466-3552; Northampton, 413-341-8700; Worcester, 508-831-7356.

Committees: *Agriculture:* Biotechnology, Horticulture & Research; Nutrition (RMM). *Rules:* Rules and Organization of the House.

Group Ratings

	ADA	ACLU	AFL-CIO	LCV	ITI	COC	HAFA	ACU	CFG	FRC
2014	100%	83%	–	94%	60%	38%	12%	8%	11%	0%
2013	100%	C	95%	96%	C	33%	C	8%	10%	C

National Journal Ratings

	2013 LIB	—	2013 CONS
Economic	91%	—	0%
Social	93%	—	0%
Foreign	90%	—	6%
Composite	95%	—	5%

Key Votes of the 113th Congress

1. Sandy storm spending	Y	5. Medical Marijuana	Y	9. Syrian Rebels Training	N
2. Violence Against Women Act	Y	6. Farm Bill	N	10. Keystone pipeline	NV
3. Guantanamo Bay Detainees	Y	7. Afghanistan Combat	Y	11. Immigration Exec. Action	N
4. Abortion 20-week ban	N	8. NSA Phone Data Collection	Y	12. Bipartisan budget deal	Y

Election Results

2014 general	Jim McGovern (D)	169,640	(98%)	$855,087
2014 primary	Jim McGovern (D)	unopposed		

Prior winning percentages: 2012 (unopposed), 2010 (56%), 2008 (98%), 2006 (100%), 2004 (71%), 2002 (100%), 2000 (100%), 1998 (57%), 1996 (53%)

Population		Race and Ethnicity		Income	
Total:	738,642	White	81.2%	Median income:	$61,313
Urban:	24.8%	Latino	8.3%		*(108 of 435)*
Suburban:	66.9%	Asian	4.6%	Under $50,000	41.4%
Rural:	8.4%	Black	3.9%	$50,000-$99,999:	30.7%
Land area:	1,658	Two races	1.7%	$100,000-$199,999:	22.5%
Pop/sq. mi.:	445.6	White Ethnic	61.3%	$200,000 or more:	5.4%
Born in state:	64.9%			Poverty Rate	14.0%
		Education			
Age Groups		H.S. grad or less:	37.3%	**Work**	
Under 18:	21.2%	Some college:	25.7%	White collar:	42.3%
18 to 34:	25.0%	College degree, 4 yr.:	20.7%	Blue collar:	40.7%
35 to 64:	40.3%	Post-grad study:	16.3%	Sales and service:	17.0%
Over 64:	13.6%				
		Military		Govt. workers:	14.4%
		Veterans/active duty:	7.0%		

West Central Massachusetts: Worcester

For more than 200 years, Worcester has been one of the nation's centers of tinkering, contriving, and inventing, even though it is one of the few active industrial cities not located on a river, lake or seacoast. In the past, its biggest industries were valentine-making, wire-making, textiles, grinding wheels,

Voter Turnout	
2013 Total Citizen 18+	539,510
2014 House Turnout	172,745
2014 Turnout as % CVAP	32%
2012 Turnout as % CVAP	62.5%

and envelopes. It is where the birth control pill was invented and where Worcester native and Clark University professor Robert Goddard shot off experimental rockets before relieved locals saw him off to New Mexico.

In the 1970s and 1980s, electronics and computer firms sprouted along Interstate 495—the circumferential highway 20 miles east of Worcester—just as they had earlier around Route 128, closer to Boston. The high-tech boom brought prosperity, labor shortages, new residents, and higher housing prices to central Massachusetts. Then, in the early 1990s, the minicomputer industry slumped, bringing a recession. But Worcester's ingenious entrepreneurs and skilled labor force hustled. Local leaders set up a Biotechnology Research Institute to draw on the city's nine colleges and higher learning institutions to steer the city back on course.

Just as Worcester's economy has changed, so has its face, with steep increases in Asians and Hispanics, mainly from Puerto Rico. The area has also attracted Hmong, Albanians, and Africans, many of whom had fled the civil war in Liberia. The second-largest city in New England, after Boston, Worcester's population increased 5 percent from 2000 to 2010. Since 2000, Worcester County has led the state in growth, which is expected to continue.

2012 Presidential Vote		
Barack Obama (D)	199,549	(59%)
Mitt Romney (R)	133,195	(39%)
2008 Presidential Vote		
Barack Obama (D)	202,394	(60%)
John McCain (R)	124,947	(37%)
Cook Partisan Voting Index:	D+8	

The concentration of colleges and universities in the Pioneer Valley west of Worcester brings together a critical mass of scholars and graduate students. The University of Massachusetts in Amherst is the largest of these, and it has continued to expand on former farmland. Also nearby are Amherst College, Hampshire College and Smith College in Northampton. Noted abolitionist Thomas Wentworth Higginson was the pastor of the Free Church in Worcester during the 1850s. He also became a literary mentor to a young Emily Dickinson, who lived quietly most of her life in Amherst. In 2014, several incidents of racist and anti-Semitic graffiti and related actions in the area led to community discussions. Elsewhere, the area recently has become the site of filming for major Hollywood productions, including "The Judge" with Robert Downey and Robert Duvall.

The 2nd Congressional District includes Worcester and part of Pioneer Valley. Its Asian population slightly exceeds its blacks, with each at 5 percent. To the north, it takes in Connecticut River towns such as Deerfield. To the west, it covers Northampton ("Hamp" to locals;

"NoHo" to the younger, artsy crowd). To the south, it includes Oxford, birthplace of American Red Cross founder Clara Barton; the Blackstone River Valley town of Millbury; and the mostly rural Sutton. This district extends east to Leominster (pronounced *LEMON-stir*), a western outpost of the Boston suburbs. After the 2010 census, redistricters patterned the new 2nd District after the old 3rd, with its base in Worcester. But it is now stretched north to the Vermont border, rather than south and east to Fall River. It leans strongly Democratic.

James McGovern (D)

Jim McGovern, a liberal Democrat first elected in 1996, is not related to George McGovern, but once worked for the 1972 presidential nominee and called him "my inspiration, my mentor, my dearest friend" after the former senator's death in 2012. Massachusetts' McGovern is active on such international causes as human rights and ending hunger while urging President Barack Obama to embrace a more progressive agenda at home. He also holds an important legislative niche in the House.

McGovern grew up in Worcester, where his parents owned a liquor store. He attended American University in Washington and, while in graduate school, he worked in South Dakota Sen. McGovern's office. He ran McGovern's 1984 campaign in the Massachusetts presidential primary, where the senator finished third with 21% of the vote, and nominated him that year at the Democratic convention in San Francisco. He went to work as an aide in Boston-area Rep. Joe Moakley's office and became chief of staff just as Moakley ascended to chairman of the Rules Committee. McGovern got into the spotlight, leading a 1989 investigation of the murders of six Jesuits and two lay women in El Salvador, which led to a cutoff of U.S. aid to the country.

In 1994, McGovern ran for the House and lost in the Democratic primary, 38%-30%. In 1996, he ran again, this time with no primary opposition. In the general election, two-term Republican Rep. Peter Blute stressed his independence from then-Speaker Newt Gingrich and attacked McGovern for liberal stands on abortion rights and Cuba. McGovern ran a humorous spot that asked, "If you wouldn't vote for Newt, why would you ever vote for Blute?" At age 36, McGovern won, 53%-45%.

With deft maneuvers reflecting his Capitol Hill experience, McGovern positioned himself as a power broker in the Democratic caucus. In 2001, the dying Moakley personally asked Democratic Leader Dick Gephardt to help McGovern get a seat on Rules, which schedules most legislation for the House floor. As it turned out, the next seat went to Florida's Alcee Hastings, but McGovern got a commitment for the next available Democratic seat, with seniority over Hastings. And, it seems, McGovern is a good boss. A 2013 *Washington Times* study found that he had the lowest turnover among staff of any member of Congress in the previous decade.

On Rules, McGovern started with the advantage of being well-versed in House procedures. With GOP lawmakers dominating the panel, he has shown a sharp partisan edge as he pursued parliamentary maneuvers that led to cries of outrage from House Republicans. When Louise Slaughter of New York, now in her mid-80s, retires, McGovern likely will replace her in the top Democratic post on Rules. With his leverage, he became a party leader on Iraq war policy, though his influence has been more rhetorical than in changing policy. He sponsored an unsuccessful 2007 bill to withdraw U.S. troops from Iraq in six months. Later that year, he proposed a war surtax, but Democratic leaders rejected it. He turned his attention to Afghanistan, and in May 2011 nearly succeeded in getting the House to pass a resolution aimed at accelerating troop withdrawals.

McGovern has been outspoken on other overseas issues. He is a member of the Cuba Working Group, which has called for easing sanctions against the Castro regime. He contends that the U.S. embargo has not achieved its goal of improving human rights in the island nation. He welcomed the December 2014 announcement by President Barack Obama to open the diplomatic door to Cuba as "a historic, long-overdue day." McGovern was the House sponsor of a measure signed into law in 2012 that imposed a visa ban and asset freeze on suspected Russian human rights abusers. Russian President Vladimir Putin protested it was an intrusion into his country's affairs and retaliated by halting U.S. adoptions of Russian children, prompting McGovern to call Putin a "bully." McGovern has gotten to know George Clooney through the actor's work on human rights in the Sudan, and told *The Sun-Chronicle* of Attleboro in 2012: "Most celebrities are prima donnas. He's the opposite."

On domestic issues, McGovern has been among the most-liberal House members. He pushed for a government-run public option in the 2010 health care overhaul bill, but he backed the bill anyway when the public option was dropped under pressure from Democratic moderates. Since the Supreme Court's 2010 *Citizens United* decision, he has introduced bills aimed at diminishing the influence of money in politics.

As chairman of the Congressional Hunger Center, McGovern has pushed for more spending on international nutrition and for less support of biofuels, which he says have driven up food costs. He schedules regular events to publicize his cause, sometimes with Republican allies, including a series of "End Hunger Now" speeches. He branded House GOP efforts to cut domestic funding for food stamps "unconscionable" and "immoral." He has become the ranking Democrat on the House Agriculture Subcommittee on Nutrition. "We know how to end hunger. It's not that hard," he says.

Although Republicans held this seat not long ago, they have all but given up on it. McGovern has been unopposed in six of the past eight elections, though he was held to 57 percent in the anti-Democratic environment of 2010. Less than a week later, he was treated for thyroid cancer and given a promising prognosis. Like other old-school Democrats, he is comfortable in setting long-term strategies and pressing until their time returns.

THIRD DISTRICT

Niki Tsongas (D)

Elected Oct. 2007, 4th full term; b. April 26, 1946, Chico, CA; MI St. U., attended, Smith Col., B.A. 1968, Boston U., J.D. 1988; Episcopalian; widowed; 3 children.

Professional Career: Social worker; Practicing atty.; Dean of external affairs, Middlesex Comm. Col., 1997-2007.

DC Office: 1714 LHOB, 20515, 202-225-3411; Fax: 202-226-0771; Website: tsongas.house.gov.

State Offices: Fitchburg, 978-459-0101; Haverhill, 978-459-0101; Lawrence, 978-459-0101; Lowell, 978-459-0101; Marlborough, 978-459-0101.

Committees: *Armed Services:* Military Personnel; Tactical Air & Land Forces *Natural Resources:* Energy & Mineral Resources; Federal Lands (RMM).

Group Ratings

	ADA	ACLU	AFL-CIO	LCV	ITI	COC	HAFA	ACU	CFG	FRC
2014	85%	88%	–	97%	40%	31%	17%	8%	11%	0%
2013	90%	C	95%	96%	C	42%	C	12%	13%	C

National Journal Ratings

	2013 LIB	—	2013 CONS
Economic	87%	—	13%
Social	69%	—	28%
Foreign	78%	—	22%
Composite	79%	—	22%

Key Votes of the 113th Congress

1. Sandy storm spending	Y	5. Medical Marijuana	Y	9. Syrian Rebels Training	N
2. Violence Against Women Act	Y	6. Farm Bill	N	10. Keystone pipeline	N
3. Guantanamo Bay Detainees	Y	7. Afghanistan Combat	Y	11. Immigration Exec. Action	N
4. Abortion 20-week ban	N	8. NSA Phone Data Collection	Y	12. Bipartisan budget deal	Y

Election Results

2014 general	Niki Tsongas (D)	139,140	(63%)	$958,140
	Ann Wofford (R)	81,638	(37%)	$29,646
2014 primary	Niki Tsongas (D)	unopposed		

Prior winning percentages: 2012 (66%), 2010 (55%), 2008 (99%), 2007 special (51%)

Population		Race and Ethnicity		Income	
Total:	742,932	White	72.8%	Median income:	$67,009
Urban:	25.4%	Latino	16.0%		*(74 of 435)*
Suburban:	74.5%	Asian	6.3%	Under $50,000	38.9%
Rural:	0.1%	Black	2.6%	$50,000-$99,999:	29.5%
Land area:	786	Two races	1.6%	$100,000-$199,999:	24.0%
Pop/sq. mi.:	944.8	White Ethnic	56.5%	$200,000 or more:	7.7%
Born in state:	62.3%			Poverty Rate	12.2%
		Education			
Age Groups		H.S. grad or less:	39.5%	**Work**	
Under 18:	23.0%	Some college:	24.4%	White collar:	41.2%
18 to 34:	21.7%	College degree, 4 yr.:	21.0%	Blue collar:	38.9%
35 to 64:	41.8%	Post-grad study:	15.1%	Sales and service:	19.9%
Over 64:	13.5%				
		Military		Govt. workers:	12.1%
		Veterans/active duty:	6.5%		

North Central Massachusetts: Lowell, Lawrence

When Massachusetts was a kind of maritime republic in the 19th century, with its farmers struggling to scratch out a living from the stony soil, a few clever Yankees used their profits from the sea trade to try to tame the rapidly flowing Merrimack River and build cotton-spinning mills. Creating the

Voter Turnout	
2013 Total Citizen 18+	520,369
2014 House Turnout	220,946
2014 Turnout as % CVAP	42.5%
2012 Turnout as % CVAP	64.5%

cities of Lowell and Lawrence, they built model dormitories and recreation programs for their female workers. This was the center of America's textile industry for more than a century, long after the maritime industry faded. But in the 1920s, the price of labor rose and newly built mills in the Carolinas, much closer to the cotton supply, decimated the local industry that Lawrence and Lowell built. Many residents waited forlornly for an upturn in the local economy.

It came eventually, from an unexpected source. The high-technology industry drove the growth, beginning in the 1960s around the Massachusetts Institute of Technology, and then moving out to the Route 128 ring road and eventually to Interstate 495, which passes through once-distant Lowell and Lawrence. Wang, headquartered in Lowell, grew spectacularly, and Democratic Sen. Paul Tsongas—the local kid who made it big before his early death to cancer—spearheaded a historic restoration of the old mill area. This was the Massachusetts miracle of the 1980s. Then came the bust: Sales of Wang's word processors and minicomputers slumped as businesses purchased personal computers and linked them together in networks.

But Lowell revived again. New immigrants provided vitality and entrepreneurial creativity. Cambodians own many small businesses and are nearly one-quarter of the local population, making Lowell second only to Long Beach, California as a U.S. home for transplanted Cambodians. Although they have been slow to gain political influence, their experience in Lowell has helped to preserve Cambodian heritage and culture. The old Wang buildings have been replaced with health care, banking, telecommunications and Internet companies, plus fledgling

2012 Presidential Vote		
Barack Obama (D)	189,461	(57%)
Mitt Romney (R)	137,869	(41%)
2008 Presidential Vote		
Barack Obama (D)	188,098	(58%)
John McCain (R)	126,781	(39%)
Cook Partisan Voting Index: D+6		

renewable energy firms. Old mills have been converted to artists' lofts and upscale condos. Lowell-born boxer "Irish" Micky Ward was immortalized in the 2010 film *The Fighter*, and fight scenes in the movie were shot at the Tsongas Center. The recession took its toll. Unemployment in Lowell climbed above 12% in 2009, though job growth in the information technology and financial sectors brought it down to 6.7% in early 2015. The economic slump has remained much more severe in Lawrence. Its unemployment at that time hovered at 10%, twice the statewide rate.

The 3rd Congressional District of Massachusetts includes Lowell, Lawrence and the high-tech corridor along I-495. The district also includes tony suburbs near the Revolutionary

War battleground of Concord, where the Minutemen stood their ground in 1775; rural and old mill towns that never revived to the west in mountains along the New Hampshire state line; and the small towns west of Lowell. Except for Lowell and Lawrence, the district is ancestrally Yankee Republican. It is culturally liberal, with pockets of big wealth, and it trended Democratic in the early 1970s. Back then, this area produced two Democratic candidates who would later run for president: Tsongas and John Kerry. In the 1980s and early 1990s, amid the high-tech boom, it went Republican in national and some statewide elections. The district as a whole leans to the Democrats.

Niki Tsongas (D)

Democrat Niki Tsongas, who won the seat in a 2007 special election, is the widow of Paul Tsongas and now a political force in her own right. She has had less of a media presence than many of her Massachusetts colleagues, but has gained increasing recognition for her work on behalf of women in the military.

Growing up in an Air Force family, Tsongas never had a place to call home thanks to her father's frequent moves. While interning at the Pentagon as an undergraduate at Smith College, she was invited to a party where she met her future husband, who was an intern for 5th District Republican Rep. Brad Morse. On one of their early dates, he told her of his plans to get involved in electoral politics by running for the Lowell City Council. Niki followed him to Lowell in 1968 to help with his successful campaign for city councilor. They were married soon after. Tsongas often stumped for her husband during his various campaigns for office. "I couldn't have run for office if I hadn't spent time campaigning on my own," she said.

Paul Tsongas was first elected to the U.S. House in 1974 and to the U.S. Senate four years later. After retiring in 1984 with non-Hodgkin's lymphoma, he regained his health and launched a campaign for the 1992 Democratic presidential nomination. Although he won the New Hampshire primary, then-Arkansas Gov. Bill Clinton's surprise second-place finish in the Granite State gave him the momentum to overtake Tsongas, who withdrew in March. The Tsongases moved back to Lowell, and soon thereafter Paul's cancer returned. He succumbed to the disease in 1997.

After graduating from Boston University law school, and while acting as a political adviser to her husband, Tsongas started the first all-woman law firm in Lowell, raised their three daughters, and eventually took a job at Middlesex Community College as the dean of external affairs. When Democratic Rep. Marty Meehan retired in 2007 to become chancellor of the University of Massachusetts at Lowell, Tsongas decided to run for the seat. Noting that Massachusetts had not had a female House member in 25 years, Tsongas was also motivated by what she saw as the need for change in Washington and her strong disagreement with the Bush administration on the Iraq war.

Facing four other Democrats in a September primary, she was the early favorite. Her most formidable challenge came from former Lowell Mayor Eileen Donoghue. Tsongas drew heavily on her ties to Lowell and emphasized her husband's years representing the district. But she erred during a debate in saying she spent 10 years in Washington representing the 5th District, a statement that actually described her husband's career. Tsongas' opponents seized on the comment to highlight her lack of elective experience and criticized her for moving from Lowell to nearby Charlestown. Tsongas said she moved to be closer to her daughters, who were attending college in Boston. Tsongas edged out Donoghue, 36%-31%. Tsongas lost nearly 2-to-1 in Lowell but won most of the other towns.

In the general election, Tsongas faced a Republican with an intensely personal story and a recognizable name in the district. Retired Air Force Lt. Col. Jim Ogonowski's brother, John, was the pilot of the first plane to hit the World Trade Center on Sept. 11, 2001. Each candidate sought to wrap the George W. Bush administration around the other. Ogonowski criticized Tsongas for supporting a path to citizenship for illegal immigrants, which Bush favored. Tsongas attacked Ogonowski for not supporting the expansion of the Children's Health Insurance Program, then up for renewal in Congress. Both national parties spent heavily on the race, and EMILY's List worked for Tsongas. Her victory was surprisingly close, 51%-45%. Ogonowski won 11 towns. Tsongas handily took Lowell and Lawrence, plus the area closer to Boston.

In the House, Tsongas has been a reliable liberal who has backed her party on major votes. But she occasionally goes her own way, including support for pay-as-you-go legislation requiring new spending to be offset, calling it a "critical first step" toward addressing the deficit. She reduced the amount of an excise tax on medical device manufacturers that was included in the health care overhaul law, and later joined Republicans in an effort to repeal it. She said the tax hurts small Massachusetts companies.

On the Armed Services Committee, Tsongas was the ranking Democrat on the Oversight and Investigations Subcommittee in 2013-14. She has pushed for reductions of U.S. forces in Iraq and demanded a more defined strategy for Afghanistan. She enacted provisions in defense spending bills speeding up development of lightweight body armor and protecting the legal rights of sexual assault victims. She helped persuade the Pentagon in 2012 to have assault cases reviewed by colonels rather than by company commanders, who often know the alleged assailants. Her efforts were featured in the documentary *The Invisible War*, which was nominated for an Academy Award in 2013. In the fiscal 2016 defense bill, she got committee approval of her provision that the Army should develop a comprehensive policy of breastfeeding for female soldiers. "It's only when you have women at the table, and women as part of the military, that you force change," Tsongas has said.

She also has been an active member of the Natural Resources Committee. In 2015, she became ranking Democrat on its Federal Lands Subcommittee, whose jurisdiction includes national parks and forests. She planned to expand to other communities the concept of urban national parks, which Lowell pioneered. She worries that climate change can have a disastrous impact on traditional national parks, and has advocated more aggressive environmental stewardship of the sites.

After her tough contests a year earlier, Tsongas was reelected in 2008 without opposition. The 2010 election was a far different story. She drew seven Republican and four independent challengers. The GOP nominee was Jon Golnik, a former Wall Street currency trader who enjoyed tea party backing. He invoked standard tea party themes of individual power over government control while blasting Tsongas' votes on President Barack Obama's health care bill and other legislation. But he had to compete with a higher-profile gubernatorial election as well as the incumbent's overwhelming financial advantage—Tsongas raised more than $1.9 million to his $400,000. She won with 55% of the vote. Golnik returned for a rematch in 2012. But in a year in which Obama easily carried Massachusetts, Tsongas coasted with 66%. She considered, but ultimately decided against, running for the open Senate seat vacated in 2013 when Democrat John Kerry became secretary of State. She is the most senior of the three women in the Massachusetts congressional delegation.

FOURTH DISTRICT

Joe Kennedy (D)

Elected 2012, 2nd term; b. Oct. 4, 1980, Brighton; Stanford U., B.S. 2003, Harvard U., J.D. 2009; Catholic; married (Lauren Birchfield).

Professional Career: Peace Corps, 2004-06; Asst. dist. atty., Cape & Islands, 2009-11; Asst. dist. atty., Middlesex Cnty., 2011-12.

DC Office: 306 CHOB, 20515, 202-225-5931; Fax: 202-225-0182; Website: kennedy.house.gov.

State Offices: Attleboro, 508-431-1110; Newton, 617-332-3333.

Committees: *Energy & Commerce:* Commerce, Manufacturing & Trade; Health; Oversight & Investigations.

Group Ratings

	ADA	ACLU	AFL-CIO	LCV	ITI	COC	HAFA	ACU	CFG	FRC
2014	85%	77%	–	97%	80%	36%	13%	8%	11%	25%
2013	90%	C	95%	96%	C	33%	C	8%	10%	C

National Journal Ratings

	2013 LIB	—	2013 CONS
Economic	88%	—	11%
Social	87%	—	7%
Foreign	89%	—	10%
Composite	89%	—	11%

Key Votes of the 113th Congress

1. Sandy storm spending	Y	5. Medical Marijuana	N	9. Syrian Rebels Training	N
2. Violence Against Women Act	Y	6. Farm Bill	N	10. Keystone pipeline	N
3. Guantanamo Bay Detainees	Y	7. Afghanistan Combat	N	11. Immigration Exec. Action	N
4. Abortion 20-week ban	N	8. NSA Phone Data Collection	N	12. Bipartisan budget deal	Y

Election Results

2014 general Joe Kennedy (D)......................... 184,158 (98%) $1,629,037
2014 primary Joe Kennedy (D).....................unopposed

Prior winning percentage: 2012 (61%)

Population		Race and Ethnicity		Income	
Total:	746,358	White	86.5%	Median income:	$85,262
Urban:	18.5%	Asian	5.5%		*(23 of 435)*
Suburban:	81.5%	Latino	4.2%	Under $50,000	30.1%
Rural:	0.0%	Black	1.9%	$50,000-$99,999:	26.6%
Land area:	663	Two races	1.4%	$100,000-$199,999:	28.8%
Pop/sq. mi.:	1,125.5	White Ethnic	68.5%	$200,000 or more:	14.5%
Born in state:	61.1%			Poverty Rate	7.4%
		Education			
Age Groups		H.S. grad or less:	28.9%	**Work**	
Under 18:	23.1%	Some college:	22.7%	White collar:	49.6%
18 to 34:	20.2%	College degree, 4 yr.:	24.9%	Blue collar:	36.1%
35 to 64:	42.4%	Post-grad study:	23.5%	Sales and service:	14.3%
Over 64:	14.3%				
		Military		Govt. workers:	11.2%
		Veterans/active duty:	6.4%		

Western Boston Suburbs, Southern Massachusetts

The political transformation of Massachusetts is nowhere better illustrated than in the Boston suburbs of Newton and Brookline. These were Yankee enclaves a century ago, with avenues built to resemble the sweep of Haussmann's Grand Boulevards in Paris.

Voter Turnout	
2013 Total Citizen 18+	539,885
2014 House Turnout	188,098
2014 Turnout as % CVAP	34.8%
2012 Turnout as % CVAP	69.8%

Brookline was where the country club (the very first one) was established in 1882, and where Joseph Kennedy, an Irish Catholic, 20-something banker seeking respectability, moved his family in 1914. Brookline and Newton then were solidly Republican in politics, the base of such leading politicians as Christian Herter, the governor of Massachusetts and U.S. secretary of State in the 1950s. As late as 1960, Brookline, Newton and adjacent wards of Boston were electing a Republican to Congress.

Then came the transformation, personified by the election in 1962 of Michael Dukakis at age 29 to the General Court (the legislature). As Massachusetts' university-educated classes became more liberal, as Jewish populations of Brookline and Newton grew, and as young, liberal-minded families refurbished the graceful old houses, these towns became Democratic bastions. Now there are growing numbers of Russian Jews and Orthodox and Hasidic synagogues. The towns continue to diversify. Brookline is now 16% Asian, and nearly half of its school students are non-white. A local public school teaches Mandarin in kindergarten. In 2014, Newton was 13th and Brookline 21st when *Money* magazine ranked the "Best Places to Live in America." But local real estate prices are steep. In Newton, the median sales price of single-family homes in 2013 was $889,000.

The 4th Congressional District of Massachusetts starts with Brookline and Newton at its northern tip. Anchoring the district, they account for about a fifth of its population. About 40 miles away at the southern end of this district are the Bristol County cities of Freetown, Somerset and part of Fall River. The northern and southern ends of the

2012 Presidential Vote		
Barack Obama (D) 211,423	(57%)
Mitt Romney (R).................152,699	(41%)
2008 Presidential Vote		
Barack Obama (D) 212,409	(58%)
John McCain (R).................143,740	(39%)
Cook Partisan Voting Index: D+6		

districts are very different sociologically and economically—affluent Boston suburbs suffered relatively little in the 2007-09 recession, the old textile-mill town of Fall River, quite a lot.

Connecting them is a corridor with a considerable variety of towns—Foxborough with its Patriots football stadium; Wellesley with its college and high-income residents; Dover, the home of some old-time Boston Brahmins; and Sharon with its Orthodox Jews. Politically, these areas were historically mostly Republican but in recent decades they have been, like most of middle-income Massachusetts, Democratic.

Joe Kennedy (D)

The election to the House in 2012 of Democrat Joseph (Joe) Kennedy III, the grandson of the late Sen. Robert F. Kennedy, restores a Kennedy to Congress after the long tradition was briefly suspended when Rhode Island Rep. Patrick Kennedy retired in 2010. The third-generation Kennedy kept a low profile as he learned his way. He seemed to be making the right moves.

The son of former Rep. Joe Kennedy II, who represented the Cambridge-based district from 1987 to 1999, Kennedy was born in Brighton, attended the elite Buckingham, Browne and Nichols School and shuffled between his divorced parents' homes in Cambridge and Brighton with his fraternal twin, Matt. Both he and Matt majored in management science and engineering at Stanford University, where Kennedy was also a starting lacrosse goalie and team co-captain with Matt. His teammates knew him as a committed teetotaler, reportedly ordering milk when they went to bars and nicknaming him "Milkman." After graduating in 2003, Kennedy embarked on two years in the Peace Corps. While serving in the Dominican Republic, he helped to implement an economic development project. Fluent in Spanish, he's still in touch with people he met there and returns frequently.

Kennedy helped Matt manage their great-uncle Edward Kennedy's 2006 Senate reelection campaign, and he went on to study law at Harvard, where he was active in the Legal Aid Bureau, working as an advocate for tenants facing eviction from foreclosed properties. He also worked on the Human Rights Journal and started an after-school program for at-risk youth in Boston. After graduating, Kennedy became an assistant prosecutor in the Cape and Islands District Attorney's Office and moved up to assistant district attorney in Middlesex County in 2011.

For as long as Kennedy has been alive, Democratic Rep. Barney Frank had represented Massachusetts' 4th District. When Frank decided to retire, Kennedy moved to Brookline to run for the seat. The AFL-CIO quickly endorsed him, and other potential candidates decided not to challenge the family name and money. Kennedy easily secured the nomination in a September primary with 90% of the vote. He made economic fairness the central theme of his fall campaign, talking often about the need to create equal opportunity for education and jobs. He also championed abortion rights. Kennedy got help from his family, with grandmother Ethel Kennedy and both of his parents standing on street corners for him. Matt remained his most trusted confidant. "A day doesn't go by when I don't talk to my twin brother," Kennedy told *National Journal.*

Kennedy's Republican opponent, Marine reservist Sean Bielat, argued that Kennedy was running on his name. An October *Boston Globe* editorial echoed Bielat's criticism of Kennedy for not agreeing to more debates. Kennedy characterized Bielat as a rubber stamp for the budget proposals of Republican Rep. Paul Ryan of Wisconsin, including a plan to introduce vouchers into the Medicare program. Bielat joined Republican presidential nominee Mitt Romney in supporting across-the-board tax cuts. But he was outspent by Kennedy, $3.9 million to $1.1 million. Kennedy defeated Bielat in November, 61%-36%. Kennedy won by margins of 3-to-1 in Newton, and 4-to-1 in Brookline and Fall River. Bielat took four small towns.

During his first term, Kennedy identified his chief priority as boosting economic opportunities in his district through improved education and job training. He was one of several chief sponsors of the Revitalize American Manufacturing Act, which called for a national manufacturing strategic plan and was enacted in 2014. He marched in a gay pride parade in Boston, and ran the Boston Marathon in 2014. He emphasized that he was building his own record and not relying on his famous name, though it was unlikely that he would have made it to Congress at his age without those connections. In 2015, he got a coveted seat on the Energy and Commerce Committee, where he said that his priorities include combating drug abuse and reducing energy prices.

Kennedy demonstrated impressive fund-raising skills. Even though he did not face major-party opposition in his 2014 reelection, he raised nearly $7 million for his first two campaigns, and began 2015 with a $1.4 million surplus. He was one of several contenders whom Democratic Leader Nancy Pelosi considered for chairman of the Democratic Congressional Campaign Committee before selecting Ben Ray Lujan of New Mexico.

FIFTH DISTRICT

Katherine Clark (D)

Elected 2013, 1st full term; b. July 17, 1963, New Haven, CT; St. Lawrence U., B.A. 1985, Cornell U., J.D. 1989; Harvard U., M.P.A. 1997; Protestant; married (Rodney Dowell); 3 children.

Elected Office: MA House, 2008-2011; MA Senate, 2011-2013.

Professional Career: Clerk, Hon. Alfred Arraj, 1990-91; Prosecutor, Colorado Atty. Gen. office, 1991-93; Gen. counsel, MA Office of Child Care Svcs.; Policy Division Chief, MA Atty. General.

DC Office: 1721 LHOB, 20515, 202-225-2836; Website: katherine-clark.house.gov.

State Offices: Framingham, 508-319-9757; Medford, 781-396-2900.

Committees: *Education & the Workforce:* Early Childhood, Elementary & Secondary Education; Workforce Protections. *Science, Space & Technology:* Energy; Research & Technology.

Group Ratings

	ADA	ACLU	AFL-CIO	LCV	ITI	COC	HAFA	ACU	CFG	FRC
2014	100%	44%	–	94%	100%	38%	15%	8%	11%	0%
2013	–	C	–	–	C	–	C	0%	–	C

Key Votes of the 113th Congress

1. Guantanamo Bay Detainees	Y	4. Syrian Rebels Training	N	7. Bipartisan budget deal	Y
2. Medical Marijuana	Y	5. Keystone Pipeline	N		
3. Afghanistan Combat	Y	6. Immigration Exec. Action	N		

Election Results

2014 general	Katherine Clark (D)	182,100	(98%)	$1,943,089	$87,243
2014 primary	Katherine Clark (D)	57,014	(81%)		
	Sheldon Schwartz (D)	13,070	(19%)		

Prior winning percentage: 2013 special (66%)

Population		Race and Ethnicity		Income	
Total:	754,065	White	75.6%	Median income:	$83,430
Urban:	48.7%	Asian	9.9%		(25 of 435)
Suburban:	51.3%	Latino	7.4%	Under $50,000	31.0%
Rural:	0.0%	Black	4.1%	$50,000-$99,999:	26.7%
Land area:	272	Two races	2.5%	$100,000-$199,999:	28.5%
Pop/sq. mi.:	2,770.6	White Ethnic	54.1%	$200,000 or more:	13.8%
Born in state:	54.5%			Poverty Rate	8.2%
		Education			
Age Groups		H.S. grad or less:	27.5%	**Work**	
Under 18:	20.2%	Some college:	18.0%	White collar:	53.2%
18 to 34:	25.8%	College degree, 4 yr.:	27.5%	Blue collar:	35.9%
35 to 64:	39.8%	Post-grad study:	27.0%	Sales and service:	10.9%
Over 64:	14.2%				
		Military		Govt. workers:	10.3%
		Veterans/active duty:	4.9%		

Northern and Western Boston Suburbs

The Yankee Protestants and Irish Catholics who settled Massachusetts arrived by boat, the Yankees to a cold, stony land with a few Indians, the Irish to a crowded city with Yankees who seemed no more welcoming. The Yankees whose ancestors once farmed the soil had, by the early 20th century,

Voter Turnout	
2013 Total Citizen 18+	522,404
2014 House Turnout	185,260
2014 Turnout as % CVAP	35.5%
2012 Turnout as % CVAP	70.2%

founded suburbs filled with solid brick and white frame houses. As the years went on, their local public schools emptied as young people with children moved out, and attendance at Protestant churches fell. The Irish, for decades heavily concentrated in the crowded wards of Boston, started moving out to the suburbs after World War II. There were other ethnic groups here and there (Jews, Italians, French Canadians), but the major conflict—fought out in neighborhood playgrounds, in school committee meetings, and not least in political campaigns—was between Protestant Yankee Republicans and Catholic Irish Democrats.

2012 Presidential Vote		
Barack Obama (D) 235,984	(65%)
Mitt Romney (R)................119,934	(33%)

2008 Presidential Vote		
Barack Obama (D) 231,423	(66%)
John McCain (R)................110,618	(32%)

Cook Partisan Voting Index: D+14

The 5th Congressional District of Massachusetts is made up of northern and western Boston suburbs, where vestiges of this conflict can still be seen. Geographically, the district forms an arc around Boston, starting with the clapboard beach towns of Winthrop and Revere just beyond Logan Airport, going north as far as working-class Woburn (where Charles Goodyear developed the art of vulcanizing rubber) and encompassing Natick and Framingham, the headquarters town of Staples and TJX (T.J. Maxx, Marshalls, HomeGoods). The local Framingham economy has been healthy. In February 2015, the city's unemployment rate was just 3.8 percent, the lowest among Massachusetts' metropolitan areas. In 2014, MassBay Community College made plans for a new $60 million campus in downtown Framingham.

The 5th extends south to take in Ashland, Holliston and Sherborn, and west to take in most of Sudbury and Wayland. Sudbury is home to the historic Longfellow's Wayside Inn, which was renamed after Henry Wadsworth Longfellow's 1863 book *Tales of a Wayside Inn* made it a sight-seeing attraction. In Lexington, minutemen fired the shots heard 'round the world in 1775. The district also includes university towns—part of Cambridge and the epicenter of Harvard University, including Harvard Yard; Medford, home of Tufts University; and Waltham, home of Brandeis University. With the university presence, high technology and biotechnology have become driving forces of economic growth in the area. In April 2015, the Cambridge City Council made life more challenging for shoppers: It passed an ordinance that imposed a fee on paper bags and banned single-use plastic bags. The record-setting 111 inches of snow in 2014-15, more than half of it in February, was a character-builder for the local psyche and economy.

Politically, the district is solidly Democratic.

Katherine Clark (D)

Democrat Katherine Clark got her House seat in a December 2013 special election that resulted, in turn, when previous Rep. Edward Markey won a special election six months earlier to fill the Senate seat of John Kerry, who had resigned to become secretary of State.

Clark was born and raised in New Haven Connecticut and graduated from St. Lawrence University, where she majored in history. She attended law school at Cornell University in New York before moving to Chicago and California to practice law. In 1995, Clark relocated to Massachusetts to earn a master's in public administration from Harvard's Kennedy School of Government. She then worked as general counsel for the Massachusetts Office of Child Care Services and as policy chief for Attorney General Martha Coakley. She was elected to the state House in 2008 and two years later to the state Senate, where she chaired the Judiciary Committee.

Markey had represented the 5th District since 1976, and his promotion set off a scramble for the safe Democratic seat among Democrats with years of pent-up political ambition. Clark's biggest hurdle was the crowded Democratic primary in October. She competed against six candidates, including Middlesex County Sheriff Peter Koutoujin, and three other state lawmakers. Clark was one of the first candidates to announce her candidacy in February, which gave her an edge financially and in the polls.

The state senator focused her campaign on issues that appealed to her party's base, including equal pay for women and abortion rights. She vowed to fight "extremist Republicans" in Congress who she said opposed pay equity and access to women's health care. Clark wove the stories of her grandmother, a machinist during World War II, and her mother, who was discouraged from pursuing engineering as a young girl, into her TV ads. And she discussed her husband and three young sons to repeatedly make the point that "women's issues are family issues." Clark won the endorsement of Coakley in the primary and received a fundraising boost from the abortion-rights group EMILY's List, which proved a boon in a race where progressive and labor endorsements were fractured.

Clark prevailed in the primary with 32% of the vote, to 22% for Koutoujin. The sheriff and the other state legislators each won in isolated areas. Only Clark showed strength across the district. She went on to win easily in the December general election, defeating perennial Republican candidate Frank Addivinola with 66% of the vote.

In the House, Clark serves on two committees: Education and the Workforce, and Science, Space and Technology. She has given particular attention to problems facing very young children. Reviewing her first year in Congress, she said that a highlight was the enactment, as the result of Senate action, of her proposal to add infant and toddler care improvement to child care block grants to the states. In April 2015, she filed a bill to improve education for children up to age 5 who experience higher barriers to learning because of chronic stress or trauma outside of school. With Republican Rep. Steve Stivers of Ohio, she filed a bill to assist hospitals to diagnose and treat the large increase in the number of babies who are born with drug withdrawal, which is referred to as neonatal abstinence syndrome.

At home, Clark was reelected without opposition and seems entrenched in her new seat.

SIXTH DISTRICT

Seth Moulton (D)

Elected 2014, 1st term; b. Oct. 24, 1978, Salem; Harvard U., B.S. 2001, M.B.A., M.P.A., 2011; Protestant; single.

Military Career: Marine Corps, 2002-08.

Professional Career: Railway managing director, 2011-12; Health care company president, 2012-13.

DC Office: 1408 LHOB, 20515, 202-225-8020; Fax: 202-225-5915; Website: moulton.house.gov.

State Offices: Peabody, 978-531-1669.

Committees: *Armed Services:* Seapower & Projection Forces; Tactical Air & Land Forces. *Budget. Small Business:* Health & Technology (RMM).

Election Results

2014 general	Seth Moulton (D)	149,638	(55%)	$3,326,394	$1,529,184	$535,070
	Richard Tisei (R)	111,989	(41%)	$2,008,059	$2,235,513	$19,981
	Chris Stockwell (I)	10,373	(4%)			
2014 primary	Seth Moulton (D)	36,575	(51%)			
	John Tierney (D)	28,915	(40%)			
	Marisa DeFranco (D)	4,293	(6%)			

Population		Race and Ethnicity		Income	
Total:	750,623	White	84.1%	Median income:	$76,182
Urban:	9.3%	Latino	8.1%		*(40 of 435)*
Suburban:	90.7%	Asian	3.7%	Under $50,000	33.3%
Rural:	0.0%	Black	2.6%	$50,000-$99,999:	29.6%
Land area:	528	Two races	1.3%	$100,000-$199,999:	27.8%
Pop/sq. mi.:	1,420.6	White Ethnic	66.1%	$200,000 or more:	9.3%
Born in state:	70.2%			Poverty Rate	8.8%
		Education			
Age Groups		H.S. grad or less:	32.5%	**Work**	
Under 18:	21.4%	Some college:	25.3%	White collar:	44.6%
18 to 34:	19.6%	College degree, 4 yr.:	25.6%	Blue collar:	40.3%
35 to 64:	42.8%	Post-grad study:	16.6%	Sales and service:	15.1%
Over 64:	16.2%				
		Military		Govt. workers:	11.9%
		Veterans/active duty:	7.1%		

North Shore

The North Shore of Massachusetts Bay has often been at the leading edge of the nation's economy. In 1640, the Saugus Iron Works was built here—the beginning of American heavy

industry. When Europe's great powers were con-
vulsed in international war from 1792 to 1815,
American shipowners suddenly became the richest
in the world, and traders from Boston and Salem
accumulated the capital needed to build textile
mills and railroads and to finance much of the

Voter Turnout	
2013 Total Citizen 18+	552,159
2014 House Turnout	272,219
2014 Turnout as % CVAP	49.3%
2012 Turnout as % CVAP	70.9%

American Industrial Revolution. From the small port of Salem, ships left for China, bringing
back porcelain and artifacts. Salem had the nation's first millionaire, Elias Hasket Derby,
and in 1900, it was the richest city per capita in the nation.

Today, the North Shore is a quiet place. From Boston Harbor north to the mouth of the
Merrimack River, it is a collection of ethnic factory towns from Lynn to Peabody (once one
of the world's great leather producers, with more than 100 tanneries) to the former shipbuilding Newburyport. There are a few high-income enclaves, such as Marblehead with its
yachts. Eastern coastal towns include artsy Rockport and the fishing center of Gloucester.
Salem's House of the Seven Gables is a popular tourist site. Built in 1668, it inspired the
novel by Nathaniel Hawthorne and is the oldest surviving wooden mansion in New England.
The Salem witch trials are probably the town's most famous legacy, and local officials have
capitalized on the fact with Halloween festivities that contribute to Salem's $100 million
annual tourism industry.

The 6th Congressional District includes the North Shore from Saugus and Lynn northward to the New Hampshire line, plus towns and cities inland west to Tewksbury and Bedford. The district is mostly based in Essex County, but includes part of Middlesex County
as well. Lynn is the district's largest city, and local leaders have sought to revitalize its
downtown area. The General Electric jet engine plant, its largest employer, has seen its
payroll drop from a peak of 13,000 in 1985 to a recent total of 3,100 jobs. It produces helicopter engines for the Black Hawk troop transport and jet engines for the F-18 Super Hornet
fighter.

The district's high-income Yankee towns
historically were liberal Republican, while
the old mill towns of Lynn, Salem, Peabody
and Merrimac were Irish working-class
Democratic. The 6th has been a Democratic
district since the 1960s, although only marginally so in the 1980s and early 1990s. While
the district is the site of the original gerrymander—named after Elbridge Gerry—the

2012 Presidential Vote
Barack Obama (D) 212,003   (55%)
Mitt Romney (R).................169,966   (44%)

2008 Presidential Vote
Barack Obama (D) 210,170   (56%)
John McCain (R).................155,308   (42%)

Cook Partisan Voting Index: D+4

current boundaries are hardly grotesque by contemporary standards. The 6th leans Democratic, but it is marginally the least liberal district in the Bay State.

Seth Moulton (D)

Democrat Seth Moulton, a former Marine captain and Iraq War veteran, was elected in 2014.
Massachusetts came within a hair's breadth in 2012 of electing the first Republican to its
House delegation since 1996, when Republican Richard Tisei lost to embattled Democratic
Rep. John Tierney by 4,330 votes. Two year later, Tisei lost his chief rationale as the alterna-
tive to the incumbent when Moulton ousted Tierney in the primary.

Moulton was born in Salem and grew up in Marblehead, the eldest of three siblings. He
attended Phillips Academy Andover, an elite boarding school. He got his bachelor's degree
in physics from Harvard University, delivering the Undergraduate English Oration at his
commencement in which he focused on the importance of service. After graduation, he joined
the Marine Corps, attending Officer Candidate School in Quantico, Va. He graduated in 2002
with the rank of second lieutenant and was among the first soldiers to enter Baghdad at
the beginning of the Iraq War. He served four tours of duty from 2004 to 2008, and in 2008
he was a special liaison with tribal leaders in southern Iraq at the request of Gen. David
Petraeus. He left the Marines with the rank of captain. He later earned his M.B.A. and
master's in public policy from Harvard.

Moulton decided to get involved in politics while still in the Marines. "I actually remember the moment," he told *The Atlantic*. "It was after a difficult day in Najaf in 2004. A young

marine in my platoon said, 'Sir, you should run for Congress someday. So this s—doesn't happen again.'" He considered running as an independent candidate in 2012 against Tierney (Moulton said he would have caucused with Democrats), but decided against it. Tierney was under fire because his wife, Patrice, had pleaded guilty to helping her brother file false tax returns, and Republicans charged that the congressman must have been aware of the activity. He eked out a 48%-47% victory against Tisei, whose résumé—he is gay and a fiscal conservative who vocally opposed the social policy of his party—made him just the sort of Republican who can win in a part of deep-blue Massachusetts. Tisei ran again in 2014 and appeared well-positioned to take Tierney out.

Moulton foiled those plans when he challenged Tierney in the Democratic primary, secured *The Boston Globe*'s endorsement, and won the nomination by 51%-41%. Without the baggage of the Tierney campaign, Moulton ran as a progressive Democrat and cast Tisei, a Realtor who was first elected to the state Legislature in 1984, as a political insider. "We won't get fresh thinking and new leadership by sending someone to Washington who was first elected to office when I was just 6 years old," Moulton said after winning the primary.

Tisei offered himself up as an independent thinker who favored limited government and would be a Bay State ambassador to the GOP majority in the House. Moulton won endorsements from Petraeus, retired Army Gen. Stanley McChrystal, and former New York City Mayor Michael Bloomberg. He outspent Tisei $3.3 million to $2 million. The outcome wasn't close. Moulton won 55%-41%. Each candidate was aided by millions of dollars from national parties and outside groups. Moulton was the biggest draw, with $2.3 million from the Washington-based votevets.org Action Fund. Tellingly, the National Republican Congressional Committee spent only $96,000 on behalf of Tisei in 2014, after it had spent $1.6 million in his challenge to Tierney. (Who said that politics isn't a tough business?)

Moulton immediately began drawing attention for his unusual-for-a-Democrat resume. He vowed not to be a typical congressman, saying he told his former Marine buddies to watch him closely. "It's very important when you go to Washington to try and keep yourself grounded," he told *Politico*. "I've asked a few guys in particular to in fact speak up and call me out if I become quote-unquote 'one of them.'" House campaigns expert David Wasserman wrote that "Moulton underplayed his military service during the campaign by hiding the fact that he earned a Bronze Star. Then the *Globe* discovered it, and gave him great press in the closing weeks of the race."

In the House, he had a bumpy transition when Tierney refused to talk to him. Moulton got an opportunity to show his expertise with a seat on the Armed Services Committee and he pledged to focus on improving veterans' health care. In February 2015, after joining a House delegation to Iraq and Afghanistan, he said that defeating the Islamic State was vital, and that key to success would be "to provide the Iraqi government with diplomatic and political support, and empower Iraqi leaders to take on this fight." He became the top Democrat on the Small Business Subcommittee on Health and Technology, where he planned to examine how health care policies promote job creation.

SEVENTH DISTRICT

Michael Capuano (D)

Elected 1998, 9th term; b. Jan. 9, 1952, Somerville; Dartmouth Col., B.A. 1973, Boston Col., J.D. 1977; Catholic; married (Barbara); 2 children.

Elected Office: Somerville alderman, Ward 5, 1977-79; Somerville alderman-at-large, 1985-89; Somerville mayor, 1990-98.

Professional Career: Chief legal counsel, MA Legislature Taxation Cmte., 1978-84; Practicing atty., 1984-90.

DC Office: 1414 LHOB, 20515, 202-225-5111; Fax: 202-225-9322; Website: capuano.house.gov.

State Offices: Cambridge, 617-621-6208.

Committees: *Ethics. Financial Services:* Financial Institutions & Consumer Credit; Housing & Insurance; Oversight & Investigations. *Transportation & Infrastructure:* Aviation; Highways & Transit; Railroads, Pipelines & Hazardous Materials (RMM).

Group Ratings

	ADA	ACLU	AFL-CIO	LCV	ITI	COC	HAFA	ACU	CFG	FRC
2014	100%	77%	–	97%	20%	33%	9%	4%	7%	0%
2013	95%	C	100%	96%	C	25%	C	12%	12%	C

National Journal Ratings

	2013 LIB	—	2013 CONS
Economic	83%	—	16%
Social	73%	—	24%
Foreign	90%	—	6%
Composite	83%	—	17%

Key Votes of the 113th Congress

1. Sandy storm spending	Y	5. Medical Marijuana	Y	9. Syrian Rebels Training	N
2. Violence Against Women Act	Y	6. Farm Bill	N	10. Keystone pipeline	N
3. Guantanamo Bay Detainees	Y	7. Afghanistan Combat	Y	11. Immigration Exec. Action	NV
4. Abortion 20-week ban	N	8. NSA Phone Data Collection	Y	12. Bipartisan budget deal	Y

Election Results

2014 general   Mike Capuano (D).....................142,133   (98%) $653,147
2014 primary   Mike Capuano (D).................unopposed

Prior winning percentages: 2012 (84%), 2010 (98%), 2008 (99%), 2006 (91%), 2004 (100%), 2002 (100%), 2000 (100%), 1998 (82%)

Population		Race and Ethnicity		Income	
Total:	751,062	White	42.5%	Median income:	$52,036
Urban:	94.9%	Black	23.6%		*(207 of 435)*
Suburban:	5.1%	Latino	19.9%	Under $50,000	47.8%
Rural:	0.0%	Asian	10.0%	$50,000-$99,999:	27.4%
Land area:	79	Two races	2.4%	$100,000-$199,999:	19.0%
Pop/sq. mi.:	9,451.5	White Ethnic	30.9%	$200,000 or more:	5.8%
Born in state:	44.1%			Poverty Rate	21.0%
		Education			
Age Groups		H.S. grad or less:	41.1%	**Work**	
Under 18:	17.3%	Some college:	18.6%	White collar:	43.1%
18 to 34:	38.0%	College degree, 4 yr.:	21.3%	Blue collar:	44.8%
35 to 64:	33.8%	Post-grad study:	19.0%	Sales and service:	12.1%
Over 64:	10.9%				
		Military		Govt. workers:	9.6%
		Veterans/active duty:	2.9%		

Boston, Somerville, Cambridge

Boston, the most political of cities, has often been the focal point of essential moments in American history. On its streets, originally laid out as 17th century cowpaths with many that still survive, Samuel Adams and Paul Revere plotted revolution, the abolitionist movement helped ignite the Civil

Voter Turnout	
2013 Total Citizen 18+	503,632
2014 House Turnout	144,546
2014 Turnout as % CVAP	28.7%
2012 Turnout as % CVAP	57.6%

War, and various Kennedys opened their campaign headquarters. Today's Boston is different from the Boston of John F. Kennedy's era. Then it was a gray city with no new buildings and dust on every windowsill. The sky was dark with pollution, and the air was thick with ancient Yankee and Irish animosity. The old office buildings were full of Brahmins seeking safe investments for their antique family fortunes. The government was full of Irishmen, scampering after good patronage jobs and regaling one another with political war stories. These days, that Boston is mostly gone.

The new skyscrapers are full of well-educated venture capitalists, lawyers and management consultants, many working for high-tech companies radiating from Cambridge out into the countryside. Boston-Cambridge-Quincy ranks fourth among large U.S. metropolitan areas in the share of residents with college degrees, according to the Brookings Institution. Greater Boston may well have a larger concentration of graduate students and post-graduate hangers-on than any other major American city, and this graduate student community's world is centered in Cambridge, home of Harvard University. Boston's neighborhoods, full of large Irish families—and 95 percent white—when the city reached its peak population of 801,000 in 1950, are now different, with young singles in roughhouse apartments, professionals in waterfront apartment towers and African Americans in old triple-deckers. Today, Boston has had a recent growth spurt to 646,000 people, and it is 24% African American and almost 18% Hispanic.

2012 Presidential Vote		
Barack Obama (D) 233,382	(82%)
Mitt Romney (R)...................44,275	(16%)
2008 Presidential Vote		
Barack Obama (D) 220,368	(82%)
John McCain (R)...................41,680	(16%)
Cook Partisan Voting Index: D+31		

One of its premier civic events, the fabled Boston Marathon, was the scene of a national tragedy in April 2013 when terrorists detonated two bombs that exploded 12 seconds apart near the finish line, killing three people and injuring more than 170 others. President Barack Obama, who went to Boston soon after the attack and spent three years locally at Harvard Law School, said "Boston is a tough and resilient town. So are its people. I'm supremely confident that Bostonians will pull together, take care of each other and move forward as one proud city." The May 2015 jury verdict that convicted killer Dzhokhar Tsarnaev and gave him the death penalty riveted the city. The U.S. Olympic Committee in January 2015 unexpectedly selected Boston to bid for the 2024 Olympic site, but reversed itself in July amid doubts in the business community and quickly organized opposition.

The 7th Congressional District includes most of Boston, although the State House and many of the historic sites in the North End are in the neighboring 8th District. Much of Cambridge is in the 5th district, but the Massachusetts Institute of Technology is in the district, helping to make it an important high-tech center. The new Cambridge-based "big data" computing center, where computer engineers are looking for ways to handle enormous volumes and variety of data with high velocity, announced in its 2014 report that it had assembled a Foundation for Global Leadership.

The 7th takes in Somerville, economically revived Chelsea, and many Boston neighborhoods—newly upscale and diverse East Boston around Logan Airport, Brighton and the Back Bay, Fenway, Mattapan, Mission Hill and the South End. It also includes Randolph, where minorities are a majority; and Dorchester, a neighborhood with large numbers of working-class black, Latino, Caribbean Americans and Asian Americans. The Rev. Martin Luther King Jr. lived in Dorchester while he was earning his doctorate at Boston University. The district has become the state's first minority-majority district. Even by Massachusetts' standards, the 7th is overwhelmingly Democratic and among the most Democratic districts in the nation. Obama twice won here with 82 percent of the vote.

Michael E. Capuano (D)

Blunt-talking liberal Michael Capuano won a 10-candidate brawl in the 1998 Democratic primary and has been safe ever since. His early days as a loyal soldier for Democratic Leader Nancy Pelosi have evolved, as he has failed in his hopes to move to the Senate and voiced doubts that she could lead a Democratic return to the House majority.

Capuano was born and raised in Somerville. His paternal grandfather emigrated from Italy, and his father was the first Italian-American elected official in Somerville. His mother is the granddaughter of Irish immigrants. Capuano graduated from Dartmouth and Boston College Law School. He returned to Somerville to raise his family, practice law and enter politics. By day, he worked for the legislature's Joint Committee on Taxation and practiced law. In off-hours, he served as alderman of the 5th Ward, as his father had. He won election five times as Somerville mayor. For decades an Irish and Italian town, Somerville has become dominated by graduate students and young couples. Capuano seems to have been the right politician for this mix, with deep Somerville roots and a penchant for innovation and reform.

He had a solid base of support to run for the House seat when Joe Kennedy declined to seek reelection. In a 10-candidate field, Capuano led with 23%, with former Boston Mayor Ray Flynn the runner-up at 17%. He has not faced a serious challenge since.

In the House, Capuano is among the most liberal Democrats. He harshly criticized the Bush administration's handling of the war in Iraq, and questioned President Barack Obama's decision in 2011 to order air strikes against Libya without congressional approval. On the Financial Services Committee, he worked closely with Massachusetts neighbor

Rep. Barney Frank, proposing in 2012 to merge the Securities and Exchange Commission with the Commodities Futures Trading Commission to try to prevent financial disasters like the $1.2 billion loss at derivatives broker MF Global. On the Transportation and Infrastructure Committee, Capuano unsuccessfully sought in 2011 to amend a Federal Aviation Administration reauthorization bill to require greater disclosure of a passenger's baggage fees when a fare is quoted. After years of effort, he got final approval in January 2015 of the Green Line rapid-transit extension from Cambridge to Somerville and Medford. He is the ranking Democrat on the Railroads, Pipelines and Hazardous Materials Subcommittee.

Capuano has been close to Pelosi, who shares with Capuano an urban, ethnic political background. After Democrats won the majority in 2006, Pelosi put Capuano in charge of the transition, and gave him other institutional responsibilities. Tasked with helping to revise party caucus rules and ethics guidelines, Capuano emphasized inclusion and reform. In March 2008, the House passed his chief proposal, creating an Office of Congressional Ethics, an independent board that for the first time allowed non-lawmakers to review possible ethics violations by House members. He also chaired the House Administration Committee's Capitol Security Subcommittee, in charge of the Capitol Police force and other internal operations of Congress, and the Commission on Mailing Standards, which supervises franked mail, another sensitive insider task that requires the trust of House leaders. Republicans groused about possible free speech violations in a Capuano proposal to require House approval of members' postings on outside websites, but he responded that the criticism was "laughably inaccurate."

Despite his close dealings with the Democratic leadership, Capuano has a penchant for taking on the political elite. The *Boston Herald* observed in an August 2012 editorial that he "has this unorthodox (for a politician) habit of telling the unvarnished truth." His tongue got him into trouble in February 2011 when he addressed a Boston group protesting Wisconsin Gov. Scott Walker's anti-union policies. "Every once in a while, you need to get out on the streets and get a little bloody when necessary," Capuano said. He later said his choice of words was inappropriate. Two years earlier, he told the leaders of eight banks that took a government bailout, "All or most of you engaged in all or some of the activities that created this crisis. You come here today on your bicycles after buying Girl Scout cookies and helping out Mother Teresa. You're saying, 'We're sorry. We didn't mean it. We won't do it again. Trust us.' America doesn't trust you anymore."

In September 2010, before Democrats were swamped in the election, Capuano complained about Obama and his top advisers to *The Daily Beast* website: "They're too disconnected from the grass roots and members of the House close to the grass roots," he said. After Democrats lost their House majority in the election, despite his alliance with Pelosi, he said that the entire leadership team should step down, and told *Politico*, "If the Red Sox came in and lost every game of the year and they kept the manager at the end of the year, that's a problem. That's what we seem to be on the verge of doing." But he nonetheless supported Pelosi for minority leader when she sought the post. His candid advice that she should step down intensified in April 2015. With Democrats' hopes for the majority having faded, he told a Boston public television station, "I think we need leadership that understands that, if something you're doing is not working, change what you're doing."

After Democratic Sen. Edward Kennedy died in 2009, Capuano entered the special election contest for the remainder of his term. Pelosi endorsed him and came to his defense when Democratic candidate Martha Coakley, the state attorney general, criticized his vote in 2009 for the health care overhaul that included an amendment banning coverage for abortions in insurance plans receiving federal funds. He emphasized his vote against the Patriot Act and its provision authorizing roving wiretaps. But Coakley had superior name recognition and won the December primary 47%-28%, though she lost the general election to Republican Scott Brown.

Capuano considered running against Brown in 2012, but deferred to national progressive folk hero Elizabeth Warren and became an enthusiastic surrogate in her successful challenge. After the election, when Obama named Massachusetts Sen. John Kerry as his secretary of State, Capuano considered running for Kerry's seat but again deferred, this time to fellow Democratic Rep. Ed Markey.

EIGHTH DISTRICT

Stephen Lynch (D)

Elected Oct. 2001, 7th full term; b. March 31, 1955, Boston; Wentworth Inst., B.S. 1988, Boston Col. Schl. of Law, J.D. 1991, Harvard U. JFK Schl. of Gov., M.A. 1998; Catholic; married (Margaret); 1 child.

Elected Office: MA House, 1995-96; MA Senate, 1997-2001.

Professional Career: Structural ironworker, 1973-91; Practicing atty., 1991-2001.

DC Office: 2369 RHOB, 20515, 202-225-8273; Fax: 202-225-3984; Website: lynch.house.gov.

State Offices: Boston, 617-428-2000; Brockton, 508-586-5555; Quincy, 617-657-6305.

Committees: *Financial Services:* Capital Markets & Government Sponsored Enterprises; Financial Institutions & Consumer Credit. *Oversight & Government Reform:* Government Operations; National Security (RMM).

Group Ratings

	ADA	ACLU	AFL-CIO	LCV	ITI	COC	HAFA	ACU	CFG	FRC
2014	75%	77%	–	97%	40%	46%	11%	8%	6%	0%
2013	80%	C	100%	96%	C	33%	C	17%	12%	C

National Journal Ratings

	2013 LIB	—	2013 CONS
Economic	90%	—	10%
Social	62%	—	37%
Foreign	68%	—	31%
Composite	74%	—	26%

Key Votes of the 113th Congress

1. Sandy storm spending	Y	5. Medical Marijuana	Y	9. Syrian Rebels Training	Y
2. Violence Against Women Act	Y	6. Farm Bill	N	10. Keystone pipeline	N
3. Guantanamo Bay Detainees	Y	7. Afghanistan Combat	N	11. Immigration Exec. Action	N
4. Abortion 20-week ban	N	8. NSA Phone Data Collection	Y	12. Bipartisan budget deal	Y

Election Results

2014 general	Stephen Lynch (D).....................200,644	(99%)	$2,542,068	$293,379	$452,574
2014 primary	Stephen Lynch (D)................unopposed				

Prior winning percentages: 2012 (76%), 2010 (68%), 2008 (99%), 2006 (78%), 2004 (100%), 2002 (100%), 2001 special (66%)

Population		Race and Ethnicity		Income	
Total:	759,336	White	76.5%	Median income:	$75,359
Urban:	33.9%	Black	8.3%		(44 of 435)
Suburban:	66.1%	Asian	6.5%	Under $50,000	33.9%
Rural:	0.0%	Latino	5.3%	$50,000-$99,999:	28.8%
Land area:	306	Two races	1.8%	$100,000-$199,999:	27.8%
Pop/sq. mi.:	2,477.7	White Ethnic	59.7%	$200,000 or more:	9.6%
Born in state:	66.6%			Poverty Rate	9.2%
		Education			
Age Groups		H.S. grad or less:	33.7%	**Work**	
Under 18:	20.6%	Some college:	23.0%	White collar:	47.1%
18 to 34:	24.0%	College degree, 4 yr.:	25.6%	Blue collar:	40.0%
35 to 64:	40.8%	Post-grad study:	17.8%	Sales and service:	12.9%
Over 64:	14.6%				
		Military		Govt. workers:	12.2%
		Veterans/active duty:	6.6%		

Downtown Boston, Quincy, Brockton

The Irish remain the dominant political tribe in Boston, even as parts of South Boston, long the center of Irish Boston, have gentrified. Southie's influence endures in the memory of two Irish Democrats who represented the area for all but two years from the Great Depression to the start of the 21st century. The first was John McCormack, an old style, backroom deal-maker who served as House speaker during the 1960s; the second was Joe Moakley, a close pal of Speaker

Voter Turnout	
2013 Total Citizen 18+	559,550
2014 House Turnout	203,351
2014 Turnout as % CVAP	36.3%
2012 Turnout as % CVAP	67.8%

Tip O'Neill, who chaired the influential Rules Committee before Democrats lost the House majority in 1994.

The 8th Congressional District of Massachusetts is the most blue-collar district in the Boston suburbs. It takes in South Boston as well as Beacon Hill, the Massachusetts State House, and is a living museum with many of the historic sites in downtown Boston. They include the Paul Revere House; Faneuil Hall and a statue of revolutionary patriot Samuel Adams; the Old State House and the site of the Boston Massacre; the John F. Kennedy Presidential Library and Museum plus the new Edward M. Kennedy Institute for the United States Senate at Columbia Point.

Completion of the transformational and high-dollar Big Dig highway project, with a tunnel under Boston Harbor, spurred economic development along the waterfront, including office buildings, hotels, condominiums, the John Joseph Moakley Courthouse, and a huge convention center. The movie business has followed as well; in recent years, the crime dramas *The Town*, *Gone Baby Gone* and *The Departed* were filmed in South Boston. The extensive development has reduced some of the parochialism but has increased complaints about pricing the working class out of old neighborhoods.

The district also takes in Brockton, a once-bustling shoe manufacturing town that is now lined with stretches of empty buildings. In 2014, it suffered from crime and extensive gun violence. It had Massachusetts' highest foreclosure rate, though the number had been reduced by half from the previous year. One-third of Brockton home mortgages were underwater. Blacks and Latinos are close to a majority of the city. Also in the district is Braintree, where a 1920 armed robbery and slaying of a shoe factory paymaster and his guard led to the trial and execution of two

2012 Presidential Vote		
Barack Obama (D)	213,364	(58%)
Mitt Romney (R)	150,825	(41%)

2008 Presidential Vote		
Barack Obama (D)	208,779	(59%)
John McCain (R)	140,293	(39%)

Cook Partisan Voting Index: D+6

Italian immigrants blamed for the killings, Nicola Sacco and Bartolomeo Vanzetti, which became one of the most controversial legal disputes in American history.

Ethnically, the 8th remains a heavily Irish congressional district, and also a Democratic one. The annual St. Patrick's Day parade in Southie is preceded by a political breakfast and roast that is a must-attend for state politicians.

Stephen Lynch (D)

Democrat Stephen Lynch, who won a special election in 2001 to succeed the late Joe Moakley, is an ironworker-turned-lawyer who is popular with both blue-collar and white-collar constituents. He is less liberal than his Massachusetts Democratic colleagues, but no less ambitious—he jumped into the 2013 special election for the Senate seat vacated by John Kerry's confirmation as Secretary of State.

Lynch grew up in Boston's housing projects and took pride in making good by following the old ethnic precepts of hard work, family loyalty and personal determination. After graduating from South Boston High School, he joined his father as a full-time ironworker while attending the Wentworth Institute of Technology, where he got a bachelor's degree in construction management. Eventually, he became the youngest president of the 2,000-member Local 7 of the Ironworkers union. After a fall on the job cut short that career, he graduated from Boston College Law School and opened a legal practice representing working people. As an iron worker, he worked at several large plants that he later said suffered job losses as a result of unfair foreign trade practices. In 1994, he was elected to the state House. Fourteen months later, he won a special election for a seat in the state Senate.

Lynch built a political base in South Boston and had strong union ties, advantages when he pursued the seat after Moakley announced in February 2001 that he would not seek reelection. The ailing Moakley, who was beloved by many House Democrats as a link between the party's old and new generations, died that May. Max Kennedy, son of Robert and Ethel Kennedy, expressed interest in the race but his campaign never gained traction. Lynch became the front-runner. He stumbled after *The Boston Globe* revealed his student loan defaults years earlier, plus a tax lien that was resolved in 1998. He had been arrested twice two decades earlier, for striking an anti-America student demonstrator and for smoking marijuana at a concert.

Three other state senators opposed Lynch, and the strongest among them was Cheryl Jacques, who was openly gay and had support from EMILY's List and other national feminist groups that criticized Lynch's opposition to abortion rights. Her switch in opposition to capital punishment stirred controversy. Moakley's two brothers, who wielded much influence, endorsed Lynch. Primary Election Day was Sept. 11, 2001, but Republican Gov. Jane Swift decided not to postpone the vote despite the terrorist attacks. Lynch bested Jacques, 39%-29%. In the anti-climactic general election, he defeated another state senator, Jo Ann Sprague, 66%-33%.

In the House, Lynch's views have been right of center in the Democratic Caucus, and he has had the most conservative voting record in the Massachusetts delegation, especially on cultural issues. "That's like being called the slowest of the Kenyans in the marathon," he quipped to the *Boston Herald*. He backed building a fence on the U.S.-Mexico border and was one of three Massachusetts House members to vote for the Iraq war resolution. He moderated his stance on abortion in February 2013, saying he believes it is a constitutionally protected right and that as a senator he would oppose anti-abortion Supreme Court nominees. He showed unexpected support for gay rights causes, developing a political alliance with home-state colleague Barney Frank, an openly gay Democrat.

Lynch's mother was a postal clerk, and he has taken an interest in helping the financially strapped Postal Service. To address its overpaying tens of billions of dollars into the Civil Service Retirement System, he sponsored a plan to recalculate the retirement system obligations. He praised a wide-ranging Postal Service overhaul that the Senate passed in 2012 but that House Republicans condemned as too costly. In 2015, he became the top Democrat on the Oversight and Government Reform Subcommittee on National Security, where he said his priority was "defending against threats to America." He also took the top Democratic slot on a Financial Services Committee task force on terrorism financing, where he explored the challenges facing counterterrorism officials and possible new steps.

Lynch joined the congressional investigation into steroid use in professional baseball. When former Red Sox star pitcher Roger Clemens testified in February 2008 that he had not used steroids, Lynch said he doubted that Clemens was telling the truth and called for prosecuting players who use steroids. After questioning the extent of the FBI's involvement with infamous South Boston mobster James "Whitey" Bulger, Lynch called for more congressional oversight of law enforcement agencies' use of confidential informants.

His occasional departures from the party line have been tolerated by the leadership, but Lynch went too far for them in opposing the final health care overhaul bill in 2010. He was one of five Democrats to switch their votes after having backed the initial House version. Not even a last-minute appeal from Sen. Edward Kennedy's widow, Victoria Reggie Kennedy, changed his mind. He cited the Senate's decision to strip an antitrust exemption for insurance companies and the elimination of the government-run public option to compete with insurers. "In the end, we allowed the insurance companies to prevail," he said. But he has opposed House Republican proposals to repeal the law. During an April 2015 broadcast interview in Boston, he said that Nancy Pelosi should step aside as House Democratic leader. "Nancy Pelosi is not going to lead the Democrats back into the majority," he said.

Lynch has been reelected without great difficulty. His opposition to the health care bill prompted a primary challenge from the left in 2010 from Mac D'Alessandro, a former regional political director for the Service Employees International Union. D'Alessandro drew support from MoveOn.org and other progressive groups. But Lynch stressed his independence to voters, outraised his opponent by more than 2-to-1, and won handily, 66%-34%. In early 2013, Lynch entered the contest for Kerry's seat, a race that also drew his Democratic colleague, Ed Markey. Lynch said, "I think what the Senate could use—it's such an elite club—is someone to bring the concerns of the average American people to the U.S. Senate, so they're not so insulated." Markey won the primary, 57%-42%. Lynch led with 56% in Norfolk and 62% in Plymouth counties, which are part of his district, but he trailed by more than 2-to-1 in Middlesex and the western part of the state.

NINTH DISTRICT

William Keating (D)

Elected 2010, 3rd term; b. Sept. 6, 1952, Norwood; Boston Col., B.A. 1974, M.B.A. 1982, Suffolk U., J.D. 1985; Catholic; married (Tevis); 2 children.

Elected Office: MA House, 1977-84; MA Senate, 1985-98; Norfolk Cnty. dist. atty., 1999-2010.

Professional Career: Practicing atty., 1999-2010.

DC Office: 315 CHOB, 20515, 202-225-3111; Fax: 202-225-5658; Website: keating.house.gov.

State Offices: Hyannis, 508-771-0666; New Bedford, 508-999-6462; Plymouth, 508-746-9000.

Committees: *Foreign Affairs:* Europe, Eurasia & Emerging Threats; Terrorism, Nonproliferation & Trade (RMM). *Homeland Security:* Counterterrorism & Intelligence; Transportation Security.

Group Ratings

	ADA	ACLU	AFL-CIO	LCV	ITI	COC	HAFA	ACU	CFG	FRC
2014	80%	83%	–	97%	40%	43%	12%	8%	11%	25%
2013	85%	C	100%	96%	C	33%	C	16%	12%	C

National Journal Ratings

	2013 LIB	—	2013 CONS
Economic	80%	—	20%
Social	65%	—	35%
Foreign	86%	—	14%
Composite	77%	—	23%

Key Votes of the 113th Congress

1. Sandy storm spending	Y	5. Medical Marijuana	N	9. Syrian Rebels Training	N
2. Violence Against Women Act	Y	6. Farm Bill	N	10. Keystone pipeline	N
3. Guantanamo Bay Detainees	Y	7. Afghanistan Combat	Y	11. Immigration Exec. Action	N
4. Abortion 20-week ban	N	8. NSA Phone Data Collection	Y	12. Bipartisan budget deal	Y

Election Results

2014 general	William Keating (D) 140,413	(55%)	$1,387,397	$4,717	
	John Chapman (R) 114,971	(45%)	$1,016,238	$56,781	
2014 primary	William Keating (D) ....unopposed				

Prior winning percentages: 2012 (59%), 2010 (46%)

Population		Race and Ethnicity		Income	
Total:	719,841	White	88.4%	Median income:	$59,245
Urban:	17.6%	Latino	4.2%		*(133 of 435)*
Suburban:	78.9%	Black	2.9%	Under $50,000	42.9%
Rural:	3.5%	Other	1.3%	$50,000-$99,999:	31.2%
Land area:	1,164	Two races	1.8%	$100,000-$199,999:	20.5%
Pop/sq. mi.:	618.4	White Ethnic	69.0%	$200,000 or more:	5.3%
Born in state:	69.4%			Poverty Rate	11.4%
		Education			
Age Groups		H.S. grad or less:	39.5%	**Work**	
Under 18:	19.2%	Some college:	28.4%	White collar:	35.7%
18 to 34:	18.8%	College degree, 4 yr.:	19.5%	Blue collar:	44.2%
35 to 64:	41.7%	Post-grad study:	12.6%	Sales and service:	20.1%
Over 64:	20.2%			Govt. workers:	13.9%
		Military:			
		Veterans/active duty:	8.8%		

Southeast Massachusetts: Cape Cod, Fall River

The South Shore of Massachusetts Bay, from Boston southward to Plymouth and then down Cape Cod (there is a lot of dispute about which way is up and down on the Cape), is Massachusetts's oldest settled territory. The Pilgrims landed here at Plymouth Rock in 1620. This stony land was farmed by John Adams' father, who was anything but the aristocrat some later members of the Adams family would have had you believe. Daniel Webster lived in the South Shore town of Marshfield, today a high-income suburb of Boston far out on the usually clogged Southeast Expressway.

Voter Turnout	
2013 Total Citizen 18+	554,389
2014 House Turnout	255,541
2014 Turnout as % CVAP	46.1%
2012 Turnout as % CVAP	68.1%

The Kennedys spent their summers at Hyannis Port on the Cape. Provincetown, at the tip of the Cape, is still a fishing port and also one of the major gay vacation areas in the country. Famed writers Norman Mailer, Eugene O'Neill and Tennessee Williams all spent time in Provincetown. The islands of Martha's Vineyard and Nantucket, rich whaling ports in the early 19th century, are favored summer resorts for the liberal rich of Boston, New York and Washington. The Cape is also filled with retirees who enjoy the beauty and quiet pace. Cape Cod Bay is filled with cranberry growers, who brought in $100 million in crops in 2014 from more than 14,000 acres of bogs.

The 9th Congressional District of Massachusetts follows the South Shore from Rockland to the Cape and extends west to the famous whaling seaport of New Bedford and to coastal Fall River, both of which have large Hispanic populations. It includes the two tony islands, where the glitterati generated a "not in my backyard" fury over a proposed windmill farm in the nearby channel waters. In April 2015, Sen. Edward Markey voiced concern that the Pilgrim nuclear power plant in Plymouth contained nearly four times more nuclear waste than it was designed to hold. With the loss of blue-collar jobs, busi-

2012 Presidential Vote
Barack Obama (D) 212,701   (55%)
Mitt Romney (R)................165,212   (43%)

2008 Presidential Vote
Barack Obama (D) 217,957   (58%)
John McCain (R)................153,905   (41%)

Cook Partisan Voting Index: D+5

ness growth in the South Shore has been slower than elsewhere in the Boston area. The South Shore and the Cape were once exclusively Protestant and Yankee, but in the Massachusetts way, they have changed over the years, with Irish and Italian surnames as common as Yankee ones.

Politically, this district leans Democratic. But it can be competitive in some circumstances.

William Keating (D)

Democrat William Keating, elected in 2010, is a former prosecutor who has put his experience to work on homeland security and terrorism issues. He also has sought to expand maritime-related economic development in Massachusetts' coastal areas.

Keating's father was a police officer and later a veterans' services agent who assisted former soldiers with service-related disabilities. Keating put himself through Boston College by working at a post office. In 1977, at the age of 24, he was elected to the Massachusetts House. One of the first things Keating did was work on a law requiring smoke detectors in houses, after a fire in a nearby town killed a family living in a house without detectors. In 1985, Keating was elected to the state Senate, eventually becoming chairman of the Judiciary Committee and then the Committee on Taxation. He also worked on environmental issues, sponsoring a bill to safeguard lakes and streams from pollutants by banning phosphates in household cleaners.

In 1998, Keating was elected district attorney for Norfolk County. Four years later, his office became the first in the state to win a murder conviction in the absence of a victim's body. In that case, DNA evidence taken from a saw helped to convict Joseph D. Romano Jr. of murdering and dismembering his wife. Keating also worked to curb bullying in schools, a hot-button issue in the state after a teenage girl in western Massachusetts committed suicide after being bullied. He set up facilities for veterans suffering from post-traumatic stress disorder. And he helped create the Norfolk Advocates for Children, an organization for children who have been victimized by sexual assault.

Keating ran for Congress in a district that had been in Democratic hands for more than 30 years, but it is relatively marginal for Massachusetts. It gave Republican Scott Brown 60 percent of the vote in his upset victory in the 2010 special election to fill the late Democratic

Sen. Edward Kennedy's seat. After actively supporting the Democrats' health care overhaul, Keating got help from Kennedy's widow, Victoria Reggie Kennedy, who said that Keating shared her husband's commitment to universal health care. Keating was generally supportive of President Barack Obama's $787 billion economic stimulus bill, although he said he would have done it differently, doling out money "more slowly" and in a "more targeted" way.

In contrast, tea party-backed Republican Jeff Perry, a member of the state House, campaigned for smaller government and less spending. Keating's campaign strategy sought to paint Perry, a police officer, as having a "troubled relationship with the truth," pointing to a case in the 1990s in which an officer under Perry's command was involved in illegal strip searches of teenage girls. Perry said he did not know about the searches at the time. Keating had a slight edge in both candidate spending, $1.5 million to $1.2 million, and spending by outside groups, including $1.5 million from the Democratic Congressional Campaign Committee. He provided Democrats a rare, though unimpressive, triumph on an otherwise dismal Election Night for the party in 2010. He won with 45.6% of the vote to Perry's 41.3%. Three other candidates divided the remaining votes.

In the House, Keating became a persistent inquisitor of Homeland Security officials, with an early interest in failings in perimeter safety at airports. He challenged the Transportation Security Administration on its overly aggressive searches of passengers, and compared the two situations to "locking all the doors on your house but leaving the windows open." With Republican Michael McCaul of Texas, he passed a bill in the House in November 2012 that created an independent review of how the Homeland Security Department was ferreting out waste and abuse. He urged the Nuclear Regulatory Commission to delay relicensing of the Pilgrim nuclear power plant in Plymouth until safety issues were addressed. To promote his vision for the South Shore and South Coast as a major maritime industry center, he filed a bill calling for fines from New England fishermen to be sent to the New England Fishery Management Council. In 2015, he became the top Democrat on the Foreign Affairs Subcommittee on Terrorism, Non-proliferation, and Trade,

At home, Keating amassed an overwhelming financial advantage over his two rivals in the 2012 election and won comfortably with 59% of the vote. But his 2014 contest was tighter. GOP attorney John Chapman, a first-time candidate, raised $1 million, to $1.4 million for the incumbent. Keating won 55%-45%, with the benefit of big margins in New Bedford and Fall River. The candidates split many of the small towns on the Cape and South Shore. The outcome might encourage other potential Republican challengers.

★ MICHIGAN ★

Nearly 200 years ago, when the French aristocrat Alexis de Tocqueville wanted to visit the American frontier, he boarded a boat and steamed across Lake Erie to visit the Michigan Territory. Tocqueville was not the first Frenchman to travel there. In the 17th century, French explorers and missionaries sailed the Great Lakes and slapped their version of Indian names on the landscape, which is why Michigan's *ch* is pronounced like *sh* and why Mackinac is pronounced with a silent final *c*. (But Michiganders don't carry it to extremes: Detroit ends with a robust English *oit*.) Michigan was not effectively occupied by the United States until 1796 and was bypassed in the initial westward rush into Ohio, Indiana and Illinois. In 1831, Tocqueville was still able to travel through virgin woods occupied by Indian tribes. But later in that decade, Michigan was settled in a rush by Yankee migrants from upstate New York and New England, who cut down trees and built farms and orderly towns complete with schools and colleges. Politically, Michigan was full of Yankee reformers who hated slavery, manned the Underground Railroad, promoted temperance and in 1855 gave Michigan a constitution that banned (as its successors have done to this day) capital punishment. Michigan was one of the birthplaces of the Republican Party, which held its first official meeting in Jackson in 1854, and up through the 1920s, Michigan was one of the most Republican states in the nation.

After the Civil War, Michigan developed an industrial economy. Its Lower Peninsula was mostly covered with trees, and lumber was the first boom industry on which Michigan relied too much. Forests were clear-cut or swept by blazes such as the 1881 fire that burned out half of Michigan's "Thumb." In the late 1800s, huge copper deposits were discovered on the Keweenaw Peninsula, which juts from the Upper Peninsula into icy Lake Superior. Immigrants from Italy and Finland, Cornwall and Croatia found work in the mines. Then came the auto industry. A combination of accident and shrewdness—the prickly genius of Henry Ford and the willingness of local bankers to finance auto start-ups—ensured that America's fastest-growing industry for the first 30 years of the 20th century was centered in Michigan. Detroit became a boomtown, the nation's fastest-growing major metropolitan area after Los Angeles, which was then much smaller. The three-county Detroit metro area zoomed from a population of 426,000 in 1900 to 2.2 million in 1930, more than half the 4 million it has today. The auto industry drew labor from outside Michigan, from southern Ontario, and from the farms of Ohio and Indiana. It attracted Poles and Italians, Hungarians and Belgians, Greeks and Jews. During World War II and the two following decades, it attracted whites from the Kentucky and Tennessee mountains and blacks from the cotton lands of Alabama and Mississippi.

This influx of a polyglot proletariat eventually changed Michigan's politics. The catalyst was the Great Depression of the 1930s and company managers' desire to use machines efficiently, treating employees as extensions of machines and with great distrust. That culminated in the 1937 sit-down strikes organized by the new United Auto Workers (UAW). Management and labor fought, sometimes literally, for pieces of what both sides feared was a shrinking pie. The UAW won and organized most of the companies after Democratic Gov. Frank Murphy refused to send in troops to break the illegal strikes. In the years that followed, autoworkers became a heavily Democratic voting bloc.

Michigan politics became a kind of class warfare, conducted with a bitterness that split families and neighbors. The union mostly won, because demographics benefited the Democrats: Autoworkers and post-1900 immigrants were larger in number and produced more children than did outstate Yankees or management. After Walter Reuther's election as UAW president in 1946, voters elected young, liberal G. Mennen Williams as governor in 1948. By 1954, the Democrats, closely tied to the UAW, seemed to have become the natural majority in the state. As growth continued, economic issues became less bitter. By the early 1960s, class warfare had dissipated; in 1964, Henry Ford II joined Reuther in backing Democrat Lyndon Johnson for president. Republican George Romney, the former American Motors president elected governor in 1962, and his successor, William Milliken, accepted the social welfare policies endorsed by the UAW leadership and the Democrats. The state government was one of the nation's most generous, and not just to the poor and the unemployed. It supported one of the nation's most distinguished and extensive higher-education systems, built state parks and recreation areas, and pioneered efforts to end racial discrimination.

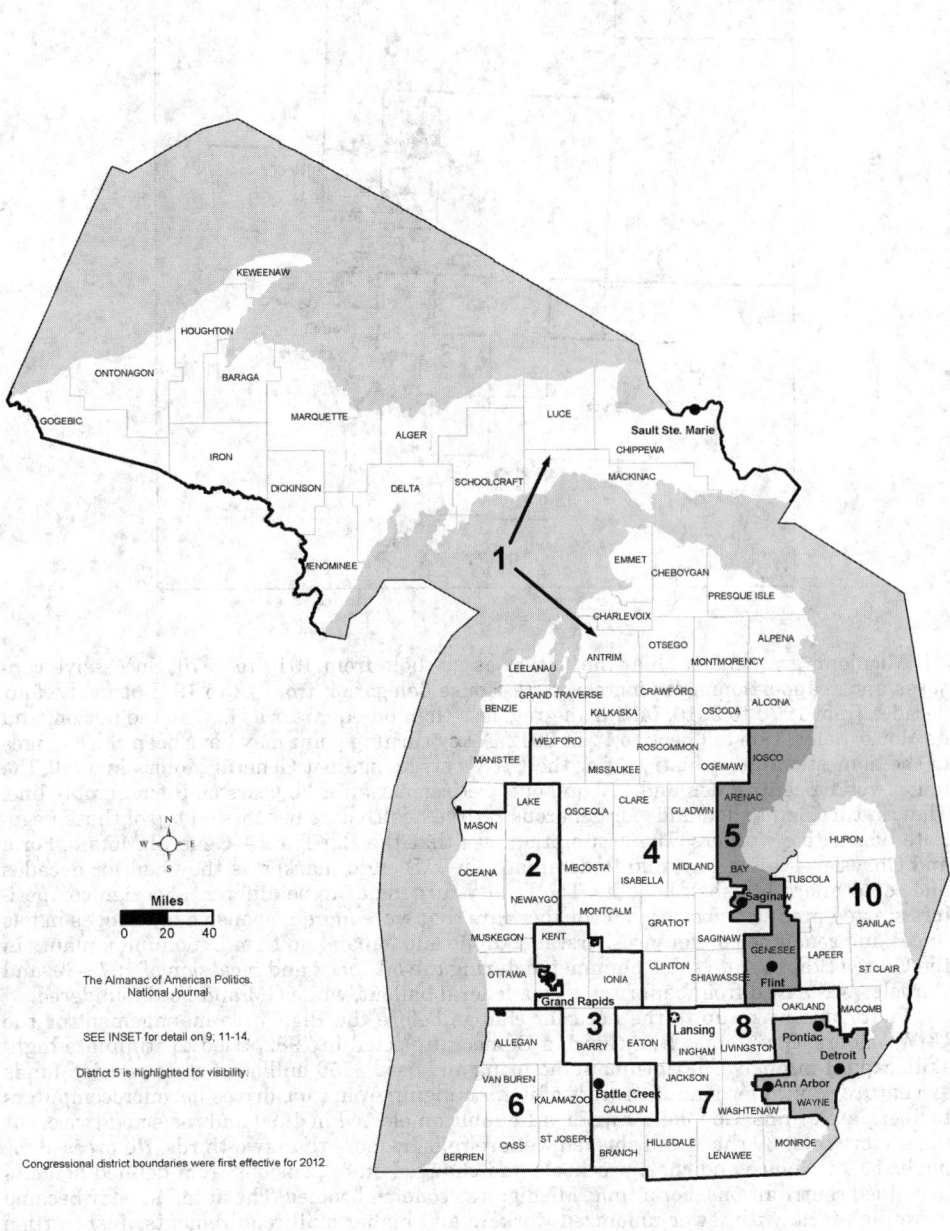

KEWEENAW

HOUGHTON

ONTONAGON

BARAGA

GOGEBIC

MARQUETTE

IRON

DICKINSON

DELTA

ALGER

SCHOOLCRAFT

LUCE

Sault Ste. Marie

CHIPPEWA

MACKINAC

MENOMINEE

EMMET

CHEBOYGAN

PRESQUE ISLE

CHARLEVOIX

1

ANTRIM

OTSEGO

MONTMORENCY

ALPENA

LEELANAU

GRAND TRAVERSE

CRAWFORD

OSCODA

ALCONA

BENZIE

KALKASKA

MANISTEE

WEXFORD

MISSAUKEE

ROSCOMMON

OGEMAW

IOSCO

MASON

LAKE

OSCEOLA

CLARE

GLADWIN

ARENAC

HURON

2

MECOSTA

ISABELLA

MIDLAND

5

BAY

TUSCOLA

10

OCEANA

NEWAYGO

MONTCALM

GRATIOT

Saginaw

SANILAC

MUSKEGON

KENT

IONIA

SAGINAW

GENESEE

LAPEER

ST CLAIR

OTTAWA

CLINTON

SHIAWASSEE

Flint

Grand Rapids

ALLEGAN

3

BARRY

EATON

Lansing

INGHAM

8

LIVINGSTON

OAKLAND

Pontiac

MACOMB

Detroit

VAN BUREN

JACKSON

Ann Arbor

6

KALAMAZOO

Battle Creek

CALHOUN

7

WASHTENAW

WAYNE

BERRIEN

CASS

ST JOSEPH

BRANCH

HILLSDALE

LENAWEE

MONROE

Miles

0   20   40

The Almanac of American Politics.
National Journal

SEE INSET for detail on 9; 11-14.

District 5 is highlighted for visibility.

Congressional district boundaries were first effective for 2012.

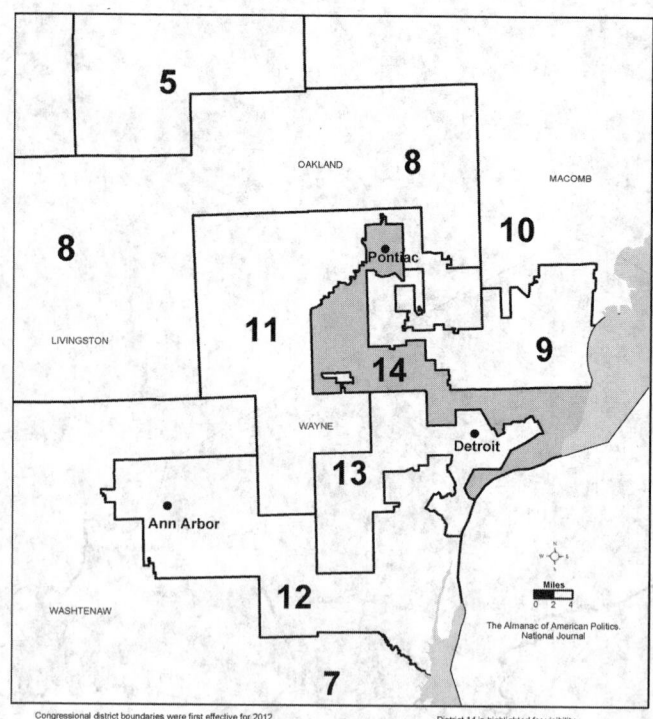

Congressional district boundaries were first effective for 2012.

District 14 is highlighted for visibility.

Michigan grew faster than the nation as a whole from 1910 to 1970. Successive censuses and reapportionments increased its House delegation from 12 to 19. But in the four decades from 1970 to 2010, Michigan grew less than one-quarter as fast as the nation, and its House delegation fell back to 14 in 2012. A key turning point may have been the changes in the domestic auto industry. After the UAW's strike against General Motors in 1970, the union won its central demand: "30 and out," retirement after 30 years on the assembly line. That, in turn, led to demands for generous retiree health care benefits on top of those negotiated for active workers. The assumption was that the Big Three—General Motors, Ford, and Chrysler—would continue to dominate the U.S. auto market as they had for decades and could afford top-shelf benefits. The reality turned out to be different. Foreign competitors started producing better and cheaper cars that were more responsive to changes in gas prices and consumer preferences, first in Europe and Japan and then in nonunion plants in the United States. Auto sales plummeted during the oil shock and recession of 1979-82, and Chrysler was saved from bankruptcy by a federal bailout, while GM and Ford foundered.

Politicians woke up to the need for change before the Big Three management or the UAW leaders. Gov. James Blanchard, a Democrat elected in 1982, tried to stimulate high-skill, capital-intensive, flexible manufacturing and used $750 million of state pension funds as venture capital for manufacturers of items ranging from tape drives for microcomputers to fiberglass coffins. Gov. John Engler, a Republican elected in 1990 and reelected twice, cut taxes more than 30 times and slashed welfare rolls by more than two-thirds. He pressed for public school choice and charter schools and changed state pensions from defined benefits to defined contributions. For a time, Michigan's economy boomed. The auto industry became more high-tech, with fewer unionized workers and higher skill requirements. Just-in-time production methods encouraged subcontractors to stay in Michigan near big assembly plants, and the state boasted the nation's highest per capita concentration of engineers. Michigan's population grew 7 percent in the 1990s, and unemployment stayed below the national average. Grand Rapids, Traverse City, and the northern and western Detroit suburbs seemed to be booming. The great exception was the city of Detroit, whose population fell from 1.8 million in 1950 to 713,000 in 2010. Starting with the 1967 rioting, crime rates in Detroit remained intolerably high for 25 years, and much of the city simply vanished—houses were abandoned or burned down, commercial frontage had nearly 100 percent vacancy rates, and the downtown was a beleaguered fortress surrounded by vacant square miles. Detroit's crumbling architecture helped give birth to a subgenre of photography called "ruin porn."

Detroit began rebounding in the 1990s; crime and welfare rolls were down, new sports stadiums, and even some new housing, were built downtown, and old theaters were refurbished. But the 2000-10 decade halted Michigan's economic progress. The Big Three, desperate to generate cash to pay huge costs for workers' and retirees' benefits, squeezed their subcontractors into bankruptcy, and GM and Chrysler followed in 2009; Ford managed to stay afloat only by mortgaging almost all its assets in 2007.

All told, Michigan lost 631,000 jobs between from 2002 to 2009, and in June 2009, unemployment peaked at 14.9 percent, the highest of any state. And in this recession, workers tended to remain unemployed for much longer periods than in the past; median household incomes declined 21 percent in the decade, and net outmigration was higher than from any state except for New York. Even before this grim decade, immigration to Michigan was minimal: its population in 2010 was 14 percent black but only 4 percent Hispanic and 2 percent Asian; while it has the nation's largest Arab-American population, their numbers amount to less than 2 percent of the population. The number of K-12 students plunged by 200,000, and state funding of public colleges and universities was cut by one-third while tuition nearly doubled. Gov. Jennifer Granholm, a Democrat elected in 2002 and 2006, encouraged redevelopment, arranged for tax breaks for new facilities for the automakers and provided tax breaks to filmmakers who made movies in the state. But any positive effect was overwhelmed by the woes of the Detroit auto companies, with General Motors and Chrysler undergoing arranged bankruptcies in 2009 that protected the benefits of current UAW members even as non-union employees suffered layoffs and pay and benefit cuts.

Michigan did recover along with the rest of the nation. By March 2015, unemployment had fallen to 5.6 percent, or roughly the national average. The state's population even grew slightly in 2012 and 2013 after seven straight years of contraction. The Big Three started making profits, and GM and Chrysler began buying back government-owned stock. But while manufacturing remained the state's predominant industry, the scars were lasting: The manufacturing workforce plunged from 894,082 to 554,327 between 2000 and 2013, a 38 percent drop. The state's most persistent albatross was Detroit, where a severe fiscal crisis led to years of governmental and judicial *sturm und drang* before the city emerged from a 17-month bankruptcy in 2014 after striking deals with key creditors. "We still have enormous challenges delivering services in the city every day, but at least now we are no longer a city that's in bankruptcy," said Mayor Mike Duggan, whose path to becoming mayor began by winning the 2013 primary as a write-in candidate.

Politically, Michigan was heavily Republican from the 1850s through the 1920s, then developed a partisan equipoise during the 1930s Depression and has mostly maintained it since. A typical result in the class-warfare era was John F. Kennedy's 51%-49% victory in 1960—Kennedy carried metro Detroit, 62%-38%, while Richard Nixon carried outstate Michigan, 60%-39%. Since then, outstate Michigan has become more Democratic, while whites in metro Detroit have become more Republican. The Grand Rapids area, with its large Dutch-American population and many Christian conservatives, is usually the most Republican

Population		Race and Ethnicity		Income	
Total:	9,895,622	White	76.3%	Median income:	$48,801
Urban:	31.6%	Black	13.9%		*(34 of 50)*
Suburban:	46.8%	Latino	4.5%	Under $50,000	51.5%
Rural:	21.6%	Asian	2.4%	$50,000-$99,999:	30.2%
Land area:	56,539	Two races	2.2%	$100,000-$199,999:	15.1%
Pop/sq. mi.:	175.0	White Ethnic	33.6%	$200,000 or more:	3.2%
Born in state:	76.9%			Poverty Rate	12.0%
		Education			
Age Groups		H.S. grad or less:	40.2%	**Work**	
Under 18:	22.7%	Some college:	32.9%	White collar:	34.4%
18 to 34:	22.1%	College degree, 4 yr.:	16.4%	Blue collar:	42.5%
35 to 64:	40.2%	Post-grad study:	10.5%	Sales and service:	23.1%
Over 64:	15.0%			Govt. workers:	11.1%
		Military			
		Veterans/active duty:	7.9%		

part of the state. Industrial Flint, Saginaw and the Bay City corridor, with their union heritage, tend to be heavily Democratic, as do the areas around Lansing, the state capital, and Ann Arbor, home of the University of Michigan. The Upper Peninsula, historically Democratic, followed the patterns of rural America, voting for Republicans George W. Bush in 2000 and 2004 and Mitt Romney in 2012.

Voter Turnout	
2013 Total Citizen 18+	7,386,520
2014 Highest Statewide Turnout	3,156,531
2014 Turnout as % CVAP	42.7%
2012 Turnout as % CVAP	64.4%

Legislature		
Senate:	27R	11D
House:	63R	43D

In the relatively prosperous 1990s, Michigan leaned toward Republicans in statewide contests. Engler won three elections for governor, and in 1994, Spencer Abraham became the first Republican to win a Senate seat in Michigan since 1972. In the 2000s, the state moved toward the Democrats. Debbie Stabenow narrowly ousted Abraham in 2000, and Granholm won a close governor's race in 2002. Both were reelected in 2006 with 57 percent and 56 percent of the vote, respectively, while Sen. Carl Levin was reelected with 63 percent in 2008. Democratic presidential nominee Barack Obama won Michigan 57%-41% in 2008, carrying suburban Oakland and Macomb Counties and Grand Rapids' Kent County as well. Democrats won the state House in 2006 and 2008, but Republicans held onto their majority in the state Senate.

Then, in 2010, Michigan swung to the Republicans. Businessman Rick Snyder won the Republican primary as a self-styled "one tough nerd" and in the general election, he overwhelmed Lansing Mayor Virg Bernero, 58%-40%. Republicans expanded their margin in the state Senate to 26-12 and won a 63-47 majority in the House. Snyder campaigned as a moderate, shunned divisive cultural issues, and called for a sweeping restructuring of state government. He won a tighter reelection in 2014, but that same year the state's congressional delegation suffered major blows, headlined by the retirements of Democratic Rep. John Dingell, first elected in 1955 to succeed his father and in turn succeeded by his wife, Debbie; Democratic Sen. Carl Levin, elected in 1978; and House Republican committee chairmen Dave Camp and Mike Rogers. In one fell swoop, the tenuously recovering state lost more than a century of congressional seniority.

Presidential Politics   For a time, Michigan was a bellwether state. In three elections in a row—1984, 1988 and 1992—it voted within 1% of the national average for all major presidential candidates. Starting in 1996, it has voted 3%-to-4% more Democratic in presidential contests. It was still seen as up for grabs in 2000 and 2004, but not in 2008 or 2012. Contributing to that was the change in affluent suburban Oakland County, where whites shifted to the Democrats on cultural issues even as many African-Americans moved north beyond

2012 Presidential Vote		
Barack Obama (D)	2,564,569	(54%)
Mitt Romney (R)	2,115,256	(45%)

2012 Presidential Primary		
Mitt Romney (R)	409,522	(41%)
Rick Santorum (R)	377,372	(38%)
Ron Paul (R)	115,911	(12%)
Newt Gingrich (R)	65,027	(7%)

2008 Presidential Vote		
Barack Obama (D)	2,872,579	(57%)
John McCain (R)	2,048,639	(41%)

Detroit's Eight Mile Road city limit. So Michigan, which voted Republican in five presidential elections from 1972 to 1988, has voted Democratic in all six presidential elections since 1992, when Bill Clinton came close to carrying Oakland county in that year's three-way presidential contest. But starting in 1996, Oakland voted Democratic in the presidential race and it hasn't deviated from that course since.

Michigan has had problems getting influence in the presidential selection process. Michigan Democrats, led by former Sen. Carl Levin and Rep. Debbie Dingell, worked to make their state one of the early primary contests. They have argued, not unreasonably, that there is nothing sacred about Iowa and New Hampshire voting first. In 2003, they scheduled the Michigan Democratic caucus for the same day as the New Hampshire primary, but the Democratic National Committee threatened not to recognize the results. They backed down after getting a pledge that a new commission would reexamine the delegate selection process after the 2004 election. It was duly appointed, and the DNC voted to allow two new early contests, a Nevada caucus and a South Carolina primary, not the result Michigan Democrats had hoped for.

In 2006, the two state parties agreed to hold their 2008 presidential primaries on January 15, the earliest in state history. The DNC objected and asked presidential candidates to withdraw their names from the ballot. Barack Obama, John Edwards, Joe Biden, and Bill Richardson did so in October; Hillary Clinton and Christopher Dodd did not. The state Supreme Court reversed lower courts and upheld the primary on November 21 and on December 1, the DNC voted to strip Michigan of all of its delegates as punishment for holding its primary too early. The Republican National Committee, in contrast, stripped Michigan of only half its delegates, and Republican candidates did campaign in the state. Only 600,000 people voted in the Democratic primary, compared with 869,000 in the Republican primary, and Clinton ran ahead of "uncommitted" 55%-40%. "Uncommitted" ran ahead in heavily black precincts and in the university towns; these were obviously mostly votes for Obama, who had won the Iowa caucuses 12 days earlier. On the Republican side, Mitt Romney beat John McCain 39%-30%, with 16% for Mike Huckabee. McCain had hoped to duplicate his Michigan victory in 2000, when he won among self-identified Democrats and independents and lost to George W. Bush among self-identified Republicans. But with at least a semblance of a contest on the Democratic side, there were fewer crossover voters this time. Romney grew up in Michigan, and his father, George Romney, was elected governor three times in the 1960s. He promised to restore the American auto industry, while McCain said that some jobs that had been lost would never be recovered. Romney ran strongest in metro Detroit and in affluent areas like the Traverse Bay region. McCain ran strongest in small-town, western Michigan and in the Upper Peninsula. The Michigan results were accepted by national Republicans, and no one was much troubled by the state's losing half its delegates, as McCain essentially clinched the nomination on Super Tuesday, February 5. But the Democratic contest continued until June, and controversy continued over whether the delegates from Michigan and Florida, which held its primary January 29, should be disqualified. Dingell and other Michigan Democratic leaders tried to schedule a rerun primary but got no cooperation from the Republican-controlled state Senate. Pundits argued whether the Michigan and Florida numbers should be included wholly or partially when calculating which candidate had won the most popular votes. On May 31, the DNC voted to seat half the Michigan delegates, allocating 69 delegates to Clinton and 59 to Obama—a ratio more favorable to Obama than the election results.

In 2012, the Michigan primary was held on February 28, a date allowed under both parties' rules. It turned out to be a close contest between Romney and Rick Santorum. Despite his Michigan roots, Romney won by only 41%-38%. As in 2008, Romney's strongest area was his native Oakland County, which he carried by 31,671 votes; he carried the other 82 counties by only 479 votes. Santorum won western Michigan.

Congressional Districts   In 1980, Michigan had 19 House seats and Georgia had 10. Now, each has 14. In 1950, the city of Detroit had five entire congressional districts; today, it has barely enough population for one. But the loss of clout isn't exclusive to Detroit. In 1960, the Upper Peninsula had suffi-

114th Congress Lineup	
9 R	5 D
113th Congress Lineup	
9 R	5 D

cient residents for 74% of a district; today, it's just 44% of a district. Republicans controlled redistricting in 2011 and were tasked with eliminating one seat. Importantly, they had also won control of the Michigan Supreme Court, a key arbiter in determining what Republicans could and could not draw. So far, they have been successful in protecting their control of the delegation.

Republicans held a 9-6 delegation edge going into 2011. Eager to shore up their own seats, two of which had voted for Democrats earlier in the decade, GOP Gov. Rick Snyder and the Republican-controlled legislature set out to axe one Democrat. With two untouchable African-American-majority districts and iconic veteran Democrats John Dingell, Sander Levin, and Dale Kildee representing safe Democratic seats, the logical target was sophomore Democrat Gary Peters' Oakland County-based 9th District, coincidentally the most compact in the state. So Republicans attached Pontiac, the Democratic heart of the 9th, to the Detroit-based 14th District and used more Republican parts of the 9th to shore up Republican Thad McCotter's nearby 11th District.

The result is a bow-legged 14th District that awkwardly meanders from Detroit's waterfront through stately Grosse Pointe to the black-majority suburb of Southfield and industrial Pontiac. Peters, a solid fundraiser with plenty of ambition, shrewdly chose not to run in the new 9th but to wage a primary challenge to ill-prepared freshman Democrat Hansen

Clarke in the 14th District. Although running as a white candidate in a majority black district, Peters prevailed. The map has held up in Republican districts—including in 2014, when they retained three open seats in competitive battlegrounds that Barack Obama had won in 2008. It's not impossible to imagine Democrats making a gain or two in Michigan before the next reapportionment, in which the state is now forecast to lose yet another seat.

Governor

Rick Snyder (R)

Elected 2010, term expires Jan. 2019, 2nd term; b. Aug. 19, 1958, Battle Creek; U. of MI, B.A. 1977, M.B.A. 1979, J.D. 1982; Presbyterian; married (Sue); 3 children.

Professional Career: Adjunct asst. prof., U. of MI, 1982-84; Employee & partner, Coopers & Lybrand, 1982-91; Exec. V.P., Gateway Inc., 1991-96; Pres. & COO, Gateway Inc., 1996-97; Founder & pres., Avalon Investments Inc., 1997-2000; Founder, chmn., & CEO, Ardesta, 2000-10.

Office: P.O. Box 30013, Lansing, 48909, 517-373-3400; Fax: 517-335-6863; Website: michigan.gov/snyder.

Election Results

2014 general	Rick Snyder (R)	1,607,399	(51%)
	Mark Schauer (D)	1,479,057	(47%)
2014 primary	Rick Snyder (R)	unopposed	

Republican Rick Snyder was elected governor of Michigan in 2010 in his first foray into electoral politics, styling himself as "one tough nerd" able to rise above political gridlock. Like better-known Wisconsin GOP Gov. Scott Walker, Snyder has been at the center of several intense partisan storms over his policies, most prominently in 2012 for making Michigan a right-to-work state that bans unions from requiring members to pay dues. Still, he weathered the controversies with greater cross-party appeal than Walker, winning reelection in 201, though he showed no interest in running for president.

Snyder grew up in Battle Creek and graduated from the University of Michigan and both its law and business schools. He went to work for the accounting firm of Coopers & Lybrand, first in Detroit and then in Chicago. In 1991, he joined Gateway, the direct-sales personal computer firm. Gateway was wildly successful in the 1990s, rising to No. 194 on the *Fortune* 500 list. Snyder became president and chief operating officer in 1996; in 1997, he left active management but remained on the board of directors. Exercising options on 2 million shares of stock made him, by age 40, a very rich man.

In 1997, Snyder moved to Ann Arbor and, with $100 million of his own and investors' money, established Avalon Investments. This venture-capital fund had some successes: Esperion Therapeutics in Plymouth, Michigan., and HealthMedia in Ann Arbor. In 2000, he started another $100 million venture-capital firm, Ardesta, to invest in micromechanical technologies and microsystems. Its one great success, HandyLab, produced molecular diagnostic testing products, and it eventually sold for $275 million. Gateway fared less well. It struggled to diversify its product line and sent most of its workforce offshore. Snyder came back as CEO in 2006, and in 2007, it was sold to a Taiwanese firm for $1.90 a share.

In 1999, Republican Gov. John Engler named him the first head of the Michigan Economic Development Corporation. But Snyder had higher ambitions: He used to tell friends his plan was to be elected governor or U.S. senator by the time he was 50. So in July 2009, to little acclaim, Snyder announced his candidacy for governor—at 51, a year behind schedule. As the election approached, Democratic Gov. Jennifer Granholm was term-limited, and her job approval ratings were foundering amid the state's deep recession and her job approval was foundering amid the state's deep recession. In 2009, a *Detroit News* poll of the GOP primary field showed Snyder with 2 percent, far behind bigger names such as Attorney General Mike Cox and Rep. Pete Hoekstra, who had chaired the House Intelligence Committee. In February 2010, Snyder ran a 60-second spot during the Super Bowl that unveiled the "one tough nerd" brand, pitching the candidate as a practical man who could turn Michigan's economy around. The ad broke Snyder out of the pack. He took some positions that appealed to core Republican core voters—he opposes abortion in almost all cases—but he had some that made them uneasy, such as supporting embryonic stem cell research. "Social issues are not on my agenda. If you look at where we're at in Michigan today, it's about our economy, it's about jobs and young people," Snyder told the *Detroit Free Press*.

A shaky campaigner at first, Snyder ducked debates and refused to respond to interest group questionnaires. He put $5.9 million of his own money into his campaign, enabling him to dominate television advertising. He was endorsed by Michigan Right to Life, the state Chamber of Commerce, and Amway scion Dick DeVos, who had challenged Granholm in 2006. But he also won the endorsement of William Milliken, the liberal Republican governor from 1969 to 1983, and he courted crossover votes (Michigan does not have party registration). In August 2010, over 1 million people voted in the Republican primary—almost double the number in recent GOP primaries—and Snyder won with 36 percent of the vote. Virg Bernero—the Lansing mayor and former state lawmaker known for his spirited advocacy of bailouts for General Motors and Chrysler and his denunciations of Wall Street financiers and free traders—won the Democratic primary. Snyder called for replacing the Michigan business tax with a 6 percent corporate profits tax and said he would streamline regulation and switch teachers to defined contribution pensions. He took divisive cultural issues off the table by proclaiming he would not press for a right-to-work law, for anti-abortion rights measures, or for the reversal of referenda favoring medical marijuana and rejecting same-sex marriage. Bernero called for a state-run bank to lend money to small businesses and for universal preschool and all-day kindergarten. Snyder won 58%-40%, carrying 79 of 83 counties. Snyder made only minor inroads among blacks and college-town voters but major gains among just about every other demographic group.

Snyder surprised insiders by appointing Democrat Andy Dillon, who had been House Speaker and who had lost to Bernero in the primary, to be state treasurer. In the budget he unveiled in February 2011, he followed through on his promise to replace the business tax with a 6 percent corporate profits tax. He proposed eliminating the earned income tax credit for low-wage earners, while also calling for a freeze of the state income tax at 4.25 percent. He renounced legislators' efforts to pass a right-to-work law and declined to challenge public employee unions' bargaining privileges. But Snyder quickly found himself in fights on fiscal matters. The legislature passed his unorthodox bill to enhance a provision for governors to name emergency financial managers with broad powers to take over financially troubled cities and school districts. (It was later repealed by the voters, but then largely reinstated by the legislature.) He also called for an income tax on pensions. Thousands of people took to the streets around the Capitol in Lansing in March 2011 to protest the new budget proposals, and even some Republican lawmakers expressed doubts about taxing pensions. Snyder also signed a bill into law reducing from 26 to 20 weeks the maximum time in which a person could receive state unemployment benefits—the fewest of any state, despite persistently high unemployment.

Snyder's poll numbers turned downward, but as Michigan's economy brightened, he exuded optimism. He called for $1.4 billion a year to improve roads as well as progress on a new international bridge between Detroit and Windsor, Ontario. He also asked the legislature to set up an insurance exchange under the Affordable Care Act instead of giving the federal government control, but the legislature refused. To help Detroit's ailing finances, he proposed a consent agreement that gave the state sweeping power to manage the city; Detroit officials balked. After weeks of intense debate, the City Council agreed to a deal that handed financial oversight to an advisory board, partly appointed by the state. By June, Snyder's political fortunes had improved to the point that an activist group seeking to recall the governor said it had fallen short in its signature-collecting. The same month, Snyder signed a bridge deal with Canadian Prime Minister Stephen Harper.

Depending on the issue, Snyder veered left and right. Snyder surprised his party in July 2012 by siding with Democrats in refusing to sign bills that would have required photo identification for absentee voting, restricted voter registration drives, and mandated a ballot-box affirmation of citizenship. Later that year, just days after the school massacre in Newtown Connecticut, Snyder vetoed legislation to allow concealed weapons inside public schools, day care centers, and hospitals. And with much effort, he successfully expanded Medicaid under the Affordable Care Act, enraging many conservatives but winning him points with Democrats. On the other hand, when the legislature in December passed a right-to-work bill, Snyder swiftly signed it, contradicting his promise from the 2010 campaign. Unions and their Democratic allies were outraged at this turn of events in a state with strong historic ties to the labor movement; President Barack Obama joined in the criticism. Meanwhile, in March 2013, Snyder disappointed Democrats by appointing an emergency financial manager for Detroit, which had a deficit of topping $325 million. Snyder touted his pragmatism. "I'm a proud Republican—there's no issue with that at all, so why can't I be a proud Republican and just try to solve problems?" Snyder told the *New York Times*. "I feel a lot of this is just common sense. If you dropped all the rhetoric, all the fighting, in a lot of ways people could come up with solutions they could all agree on."

In 2014, Snyder faced a competitive race against former Democratic Rep. Mark Schauer, who charged the incumbent with favoring the affluent and insufficiently funding education. But on a strongly Republican Election Day nationally, Snyder prevailed, 51%-47%, even as Democrat Gary Peters was easily defeating Republican Terri Lynn Land in an open-seat Senate race. In his second term, Snyder pushed hard for a May 2015 ballot measure to raise sales taxes by nearly $2 billion—about two-thirds for roads and one-third for other forms of transportation, schools, local governments and tax cuts for lower-income residents. But voters rejected it by a resounding 4-to-1 margin—the worst outcome for a Michigan constitutional amendment in half a century. Snyder vowed to find a way to enact a transportation package, but the results left him with little room to maneuver, especially with many fellow Republicans unhappy with the idea of raising taxes. The ballot measure's loss convinced Snyder to turn away from flirting with a 2016 presidential bid and focus fully on state issues; a bid in any case would have faced major obstacles in early primary and caucus states, which are dominated by the party's right flank.

Senior Senator

Debbie Stabenow (D)

Elected 2000, term expires Jan. 2019, 3rd term; b. April 29, 1950, Gladwin; MI St. U., B.A. 1972, M.S.W. 1975; United Methodist; divorced; 2 children.

Elected Office: Ingham Cnty. comm., 1975-78, chair, 1976-78; MI House, 1979-91; MI Senate, 1991-94; U.S. House, 1997-2001.

Professional Career: Social worker; Consultant & co-founder, MI Leadership Inst., 1995-96.

DC Office: 731 HSOB, 20510, 202-224-4822; Website: stabenow.senate.gov.

State Offices: Detroit, 313-961-4330; East Lansing, 517-203-1760; Flint, 810-720-4172; Grand Rapids, 616-975-0052; Marquette, 906-228-8756; Traverse City, 231-929-1031.

Committees: *Agriculture, Nutrition & Forestry* (RMM; ex officio member of each subcommittee). *Budget. Energy & Natural Resources:* Energy; National Parks; Public Lands, Forests, & Mining. *Finance:* Health Care (RMM); Int'l Trade, Customs & Global Competitiveness. *Joint Committee on Taxation.*

Group Ratings

	ADA	ACLU	AFL-CIO	LCV	ITI	COC	HAFA	ACU	CFG	FRC
2014	90%	100%	–	80%	100%	50%	0%	0%	0%	0%
2013	95%	C	100%	100%	C	38%	C	0%	0%	C

National Journal Ratings

	2013 LIB	—	2013 CONS
Economic	75%	—	19%
Social	73%	—	0%
Foreign	71%	—	0%
Composite	83%	—	17%

Key Votes of the 113th Congress

1. Sandy storm spending	Y	5. Student Loan Rates	N	9. Bipartisan Budget Deal	Y
2. Chuck Hagel Confirmation	Y	6. Employee Non-Discrim'n Act	Y	10. Farm Bill Conference Rept.	Y
3. Gun Background Checks	Y	7. Senate Vote on Judgeships	N	11. Unempl. Comp. Extension	Y
4. Immigration Reform	Y	8. Defense Dept. Spending	Y	12. Keystone Pipeline	N

Election Results

2012 general	Debbie Stabenow (D) 2,735,826	(59%)	$13,434,824	$402,183	$1,156,926
	Pete Hoekstra (R) 1,767,386	(38%)	$5,646,406	$330,393	$2,350
2012 primary	Debbie Stabenow (D) .... unopposed				

Prior winning percentages: 2006 (57%), 2000 (49%); House: 1998 (57%), 1996 (54%)

When Democrat Debbie Stabenow, Michigan's senior senator, found herself in line to chair the Agriculture Committee in early 2011, alarm bells went off among leaders of the nation's farm industry—many of whom viewed Stabenow as an urban liberal interested mainly in two of her state's best-known products: automobiles and cherries. With work about to get underway on a new farm bill reauthorizing the federal government's agriculture and nutrition programs, some were so nervous that they begged then-North Dakota Sen. Kent Conrad to leave his post at the helm of the Senate Budget Committee and use his seniority to take over the Agriculture panel. Conrad advised the farm leaders to keep their powder dry, according to the *Hagstrom Report*, a Washington-based publication that covers agriculture policy. He assured them that Stabenow, also a Budget Committee member, had been a low-key, mainstream presence in previous budget negotiations, and would do fine. Indeed, by the time a new farm bill had been enacted into law in early 2014, much of the leadership of the agriculture industry had done a political U-turn on Stabenow.

Signing the farm bill in a ceremony at Michigan State University, Stabenow's alma mater, President Barack Obama noted that Stabenow had been "a huge champion of American manufacturing but really shepherded through this farm bill, which was a very challenging piece of business." These sentiments were privately echoed by many in the nation's leading agricultural groups, who agreed the final bill was very much Stabenow's product— and praised her work, during a process that stretched over two Congresses, for deftly balancing competing interests in what is invariably one of the most heavily lobbied pieces of legislation to come before Capitol Hill. Stabenow was reported to be so persistent that her colleagues began to fear her approach on the Senate floor. "Past farm bills pit regions against regions. I said that we were going to support all of agriculture," Stabenow told *The New York Times* following passage of the bill. That included some enhanced benefits for producers in her home state, best known for so-called specialty crops—such as apples and blueberries in addition to cherries.

Stabenow has held elected office in Michigan for 40 years, making her one of the more enduring figures in state politics. She has a warm, personable demeanor that often causes opponents to underestimate her political toughness. "For nearly four decades, Republicans have sneered at Debbie Stabenow ... then she beats them, every time," Detroit *Metro Times* columnist Jack Lessenberry observed in 2012. Stabenow grew up in the small northern Michigan town of Clare, where her father was an auto dealer (Oldsmobiles) and her mother was a nurse. But her base has long been Lansing and surrounding Ingham County, where Michigan State University is located. She holds a B.A. as well as a master's degree in social work from the latter; she counseled students in public schools and made extra money singing folk songs in coffeehouses. She was politically active, marching in anti-Vietnam War rallies and volunteering for George McGovern's anti-war presidential bid in 1972. Stabenow was first elected to office at the age of 24: Angered when the Ingham County Commission closed a nursing home, she ran for the commission in 1974 and beat an incumbent who had referred to her as "that young broad."

Stabenow was elected to the Michigan House in 1978 when she was just 28, and moved to the state Senate in 1990. Four years later, while running for governor, she was at the center of a storm in state politics. In response to Republican Gov. John Engler's call for changes in financing education, she proposed to zero out the property tax and start over, apparently calculating he would reject such a drastic tax cut. Instead, he accepted her proposal and passed a plan reducing property taxes vastly and increasing the sales tax, which was approved by voters 70%-30% in 1994. But, in that year's primary, the state Democratic establishment—including the Michigan Education Association, the United Auto Workers and the AFL-CIO—opposed Stabenow. She won 30 percent of the vote, behind former Rep. Howard Wolpe's 35 percent. She was chosen as Wolpe's lieutenant gubernatorial running mate for the general election, but the ticket lost to Engler by a 3-2 margin.

Undaunted, Stabenow almost immediately began running for Congress, in a district that included Democratic Ingham County and heavily Republican Livingston County to the east. Stabenow raised more than $1 million in individual contributions, and won 54 percent of the vote in 1996 in ousting freshman Republican Rep. Dick Chrysler. In 2000, she challenged first-term Republican Sen. Spencer Abraham, in what turned out to be one of that year's critical Senate races. In the summer, Abraham used his money advantage—he ultimately spent $13 million to Stabenow's nearly $8 million—to run ads spotlighting his own program for prescription drugs for senior citizens, and attacking Stabenow as a free-spending liberal favoring increased bureaucracy and higher taxes, opposing welfare reform, and supporting lenient sentences for criminals. Stabenow hoarded her money for an October ad buy, which turned out to be a wise strategy. She was down by 17 points in polls in mid-October, but answered charges that she was a liberal by citing her House votes for a balanced budget and ending the marriage penalty in the tax code. She attacked Abraham as beholden to corporations and special interests. On Election Day, Stabenow won 49%-48%, helping the Democrats to gain a 50-50 split of the Senate.

Soon after she was sworn in, Senate Democrats moved to help her strengthen her grip on the seat: Capitalizing on a central issue of her election campaign, they named Stabenow head of a task force on prescription drugs, the cost of which was then among the country's hottest issues. She organized bus trips of seniors to Canada, and pressed for measures allowing the importation of U.S. drugs from that country. Stabenow has been among the most loyal of Democrats, particularly on economic and social issues. But she has joined a number of other leading Democrats in challenging the international trade agenda put forth by Obama as well as his Republican predecessor, George W. Bush. In early 2015, when Obama was seeking so-called "fast track" authority to facilitate the negotiation of a 12-nation Asian trade deal, Stabenow not only voted against it—but, in the Senate Finance Committee, unsuccessfully proposed an amendment requiring the administration to seek enforceable currency manipulation standards in such a deal. When White House officials called the amendment a "poison pill" that would derail the talks, Stabenow shot back that, if including currency meant that a free trade deal might die, it was worth the price. "Then it shouldn't go through," she told the *Detroit News*.

The currency manipulation amendment was heavily lobbied for by the Big Three domestic automakers, particularly Ford Motor Co., who contended that, without such a provision in a trade agreement, Japanese auto manufacturers could get a big boost from unfair currency intervention. Like other Michigan lawmakers, a significant focus for Stabenow on Capitol Hill has involved pushing the interests of her state's most visible industry. She strongly supported loan guarantees for the automakers and the government acquisition of General Motors and Chrysler in the wake of the 2008 financial crash, and has worked to get the automakers federal assistance to better compete, developing a program to authorize loans to re-equip and expand factories to produce advanced technology vehicles and components. She also worked on a plan that led to the Energy Department announcing two new advanced battery research facilities in Michigan in November 2012, part of a five-year partnership with private companies. Earlier, when the Senate passed the "Cash for Clunkers" program providing government reimbursements for trading in old cars for more fuel-efficient models in 2009, Stabenow successfully fended off a proposal by California Democrat Dianne Feinstein for higher mileage standards.

Late in her first term, Stabenow decided to try to gain a toehold in Senate leadership. In November 2004, when Barbara Mikulski stepped down as secretary of the Democratic caucus, Stabenow called Mikulski to ask for her support, and the two worked the phones. Stabenow got the job, the No. 4 position in the Democratic leadership. It gave her a voice at leadership meetings, though her impact was limited. Other senior Senate Democrats quietly discussed replacing her after the 2006 election—during which Stabenow won a second Senate term by easily defeating her Republican opponent, Oakland County Sheriff Michael Bouchard, with 57 percent. (Two higher visibility Republicans, Reps. Candice Miller and Mike Rogers, declined to take her on.) Following her re-election, an agreement was reached in which Stabenow got a seat on the influential Finance Committee and became chair of the Democratic Steering and Outreach Committee, while Washington Sen. Patty Murray replaced her as caucus secretary. In 2011, Stabenow returned to the Senate leadership as vice chair of the Democratic Policy Committee, now the Democratic Policy and Communications Committee.

At the same time, Stabenow inherited the Agriculture Committee gavel, becoming the second woman ever to chair the panel, after the first—Arkansas Sen. Blanche Lincoln—was defeated for re-election in 2010. (Stabenow became ranking member in 2015, following the Republican takeover of the Senate in the 2014 election.) Traditionally, farm bills have favored crops such as corn and wheat that receive big subsidies of various kinds, and such crops continue to benefit heavily in the new farm bill. Nonetheless, subsidies for these commodities were cut by about 30 percent over 10 years. Meanwhile, funding for specialty crops—fruits, vegetables and nuts—as well as organic farming, although still a relatively small part of the overall legislation, were increased sharply in the bill that Stabenow shepherded to passage. Producers of specialty crops were also given enhanced access to crop insurance programs long utilized by corn and wheat growers. "This is not your father's farm bill," Stabenow repeatedly boasted, as she pointed to savings—notably elimination of a $5 billion a year, much-criticized subsidy that paid farmers whether they grew crops or not.

The House-Senate conference report on the bill contained some concessions to Southern growers from the House version, but most provisions originated in the Senate, making it very much Stabenow's handiwork. It took her close to three years of patient work to pull off. She had to navigate differences between Northern and Midwestern legislators—notably Kansas Republican Pat Roberts, who succeeded her as Agriculture Committee chairman in 2015—and Southern lawmakers. Roberts contended that federal target prices for crops were an out-of-date mechanism to aid farmers, but Southern growers had little experience with the private crop insurance programs envisioned as a replacement. The farm bill version that Stabenow produced in 2012, with Roberts as ranking member of the Agriculture Committee, had no target prices. The issue helped to stall final passage of a new farm bill until 2013, when Mississippi Republican Thad Cochran became ranking member, and insisted on target prices—which were inserted in a new version of the bill. Throughout the jockeying, Stabenow was credited with dealing with such conflicts without allowing them spill out into public view.

On the nutrition titles of the farm bill—which comprise about 80 percent of the funding in the measure—Stabenow asserted herself against House conservatives who wanted to cut $39 billion over 10 years from the Supplemental Nutrition Assistance Program, formerly known as food stamps. This move would have cut several million individuals from SNAP assistance. The initial Senate version of the bill had a far more modest $4 billion cut. In the final agreement, Stabenow refused to go any further than tightening a loophole that some states used to trigger SNAP aid, increasing the estimated savings to $8.6 billion. At one point, House conservatives demanded drug testing for SNAP recipients. According to *The New York Times*, Stabenow told them she would agree only if those receiving farm subsidies were also tested.

Anti-hunger advocates remained unhappy, saying the SNAP reductions could reduce benefits an average of $90 per month for hundreds of thousands of households. Conservatives felt that, despite total budget savings estimated at $17 billion over 10 years, that the latest farm bill remained overly costly, and yet others complained about subsidies to interests ranging from crop insurers to sugar producers—whom they said were doing just fine without federal aid. But the final legislation crafted by Stabenow overwhelmingly cleared the Senate on a bipartisan vote, 68-32.

The new farm bill became law a little over a year after Stabenow had won a third term in 2012 against former Rep. Pete Hoekstra, a onetime House Intelligence Committee chairman who had made an unsuccessful stab at Michigan's governorship two years earlier. Early on, Stabenow was targeted by what was arguably the most controversial—and ill-advised—TV ad of the election cycle. It ran during the Super Bowl in February 2012, featuring an Asian woman bicycling through a rice paddy and thanking "Sen. Debbie Spend-It-Now" in broken English for sending U.S. jobs to China. The spot caused an uproar, but not in the way Hoekstra intended. Republicans and Democrats alike attacked him for playing on racial stereotypes; prominent GOP consultant Mike Murphy tweeted that the ad was "…really, really dumb. I mean really." Even the actress in the ad apologized. Hoekstra never recovered, and Stabenow—with a boost once again from a Democratic trend that helped Obama beat Republican Mitt Romney in Romney's home state—bettered her 2006 performance, winning re-election with 59 percent.

Junior Senator

Gary Peters (D)

Elected 2014, term expires Jan. 2021, 1st term; b. Dec. 1, 1958, Pontiac; Alma Col., B.A. 1980, U. of Detroit, M.B.A. 1984, Wayne St. U., J.D. 1989, MI St. U., M.A. 2007; Episcopalian; married (Colleen); 3 children.

Military Career: U.S. Naval Reserve, 1993-2000, 2001-05.

Elected Office: Rochester Hills City Cncl., 1991-93; MI Senate, 1995-2002; U.S. House, 2009-15.

Professional Career: Asst. V.P., Merril Lynch, 1980-89; V.P., UBS/Paine Webber, 1989-2003; Chief admin. officer, MI bureau of investments, 2003; Commissioner, MI Lottery Bureau, 2003-07; Prof., Central MI U., 2007-08.

DC Office: 724 HSOB, 20510, 202-224-6221; Website: peters.senate.gov.

State Offices: Detroit, 313-226-6020; Lansing, 517-377-1508.

Committees: *Commerce, Science, & Transportation:* Aviation Operations, Safety, & Security; Communications, Technology, Innovation, & the Internet; Oceans, Atmosphere, Fisheries, & Coast Guard; Space, Science, & Competitiveness (RMM). *Homeland Security & Governmental Affairs:* Federal Spending Oversight & Emergency Mgmt.; Regulatory Affairs & Federal Mgmt. *Small Business & Entrepreneurship. Joint Economic Committee.*

Group Ratings (House)

	ADA	ACLU	AFL-CIO	LCV	ITI	COC	HAFA	ACU	CFG	FRC
2014	60%	66%	–	91%	80%	69%	8%	8%	14%	0%
2013	60%	C	90%	93%	C	46%	C	16%	3%	C

National Journal Ratings (House)

	2013 LIB	—	2013 CONS
Economic	63%	—	37%
Social	61%	—	39%
Foreign	59%	—	41%
Composite	61%	—	39%

Key Votes of the 113th Congress (House)

1. Sandy storm spending	Y	5. Medical Marijuana	Y	9. Syrian Rebels Training	Y
2. Violence Against Women Act	Y	6. Farm Bill	Y	10. Keystone pipeline	N
3. Guantanamo Bay Detainees	N	7. Afghanistan Combat	Y	11. Immigration Exec. Action	N
4. Abortion 20-week ban	N	8. NSA Phone Data Collection	N	12. Bipartisan budget deal	Y

Election Results

2014 general	Gary Peters (D)	1,704,936	(55%)	$10,289,555	$5,970,696	$8,040,765
	Terri Lynn Land (R)	1,290,199	(41%)	$12,270,048	$1,960,159	$14,712,548
	Jim Fulner (L)	62,897	(2%)			
2014 primary	Gary Peters (D)	unopposed				

Prior winning percentages: House: 2012 (82%), 2010 (50%), 2008 (52%)

As Michigan's junior senator, Gary Peters *is* the Democratic freshman class of 2014—the sole Democrat to win an open Senate seat in an election that held few bright spots for his party. While he spent part of the campaign touring the state on a Harley-Davidson Dyna Super Glide, Peters is frequently referred to as wonky; he boasts degrees from four different colleges and universities in his home state. Less charitably, he has been described as lacking in charisma, or even a bit stodgy, by those questioning his political appeal. But Peters has had success at the polls going back more than two decades, including three tough races for the House before moving to the Senate. "Peters does get called wonky a lot, because admittedly, he is," Democratic T.J. Bucholz told the *MLive Media Group* during the 2014 campaign. "He's a smart guy, cerebral and thoughtful. But to be fair, this is the race to replace Carl Levin, who is no firebrand either." Levin, another wonky politician, held the seat for more than one-third of a century, ultimately rising to chair the Senate Armed Services Committee.

To be sure, Peters benefited from political serendipity in 2014: In a year in which little went wrong for the Republicans in most battleground races, little went right for them in

Michigan. Levin, first elected during the Carter administration, announced his retirement in March 2013, and Peters immediately expressed interest. He had the Democratic nomination all but locked up in weeks, as other potential Democratic contenders took themselves out of the running. When the eventual Republican nominee, former Michigan Secretary of State Terri Lynn Land, announced in late spring, her candidacy was met with something short of enthusiasm among party leaders, and Republicans spent months trying to recruit another candidate. When that failed, Land proceeded to run a campaign that alternated between bumbling and bizarre—causing national Republicans to put distance between themselves and the Land effort toward the end of the campaign.

Once Democrats re-engineered Peters' campaign in the spring of 2014, replacing senior staff and consultants, he ran a solid if unspectacular campaign with ads emphasizing his family history and his military service. His family has lived in Oakland County outside Detroit for five generations, and Peters grew up in Pontiac, the son of a public school teacher and a nursing home aide. After college, he spent more than two decades working as a financial advisor for a couple of large investment firms, while earning a law degree and an M.B.A. He enlisted in the U.S. Navy Reserve, becoming a lieutenant commander and serving in the Persian Gulf as part of the military operation enforcing a no-fly zone following the 1991 Gulf War. He left the Navy Reserve in 2000, but re-enlisted following 9/11, and served for another four years.

Peter's political career began with his election to the Rochester Hills City Council in 1991, followed by winning a seat in the Michigan Senate in 1994, where he led an effort to ban oil drilling in the Great Lakes. Forced by term limits to give up his Senate seat, Peters mounted a short-lived candidacy for governor before shifting to the state attorney general's race. He lost narrowly in the 2002 election, his only electoral defeat. He then spent nearly five years as the state's lottery commissioner, earning another degree on the side at Michigan State University—an M.A. in philosophy, with a focus on the ethics of development. Peters challenged eight-term Republican Rep. Joe Knollenberg in 2008, and received help from the national Democratic Party and the United Auto Workers. Jack Kevorkian, a physician who garnered national attention as an assisted suicide advocate, was among three other candidates. Peters won with 52 percent, becoming the first Democrat since 1893 to represent the district.

Peters has described himself as a centrist who is pro-business and socially liberal. As a House member, he backed his party on major votes, but showed independence at times. He voted against the 2011 bill to raise the nation's debt limit, saying the measure didn't close tax loopholes. In his freshman term, he was put on the 2010 conference committee that drafted the final version of the landmark Dodd-Frank financial regulatory overhaul; Peters added a provision intended to boost the financing businesses of the nation's automakers. His investment background made him a logical choice for the Dodd-Frank conference committee, although his appointment also appeared designed to bolster him in his first re-election race.

Running for a second term in the traditionally Republican district in 2010, Peters won, 50%-47%, in a year less hospitable to Democrats. In 2012, Michigan lost a congressional seat through reapportionment, and the new map carved up Peters' district. He faced two tough options: challenge long-time Democratic Rep. Sander Levin in another Detroit suburban district, or go up against freshman Rep. Hansen Clarke, an African-American, in a majority-black district encompassing a portion of the city. Peters had some ties to the latter district from his state Senate days, and he courted labor unions and church leaders. He won 47 percent of the vote to Clarke's 35 percent, with another African-American candidate, Southfield Mayor Brenda Lawrence (who captured the seat in 2014) getting 13 percent. Peters went on to easily prevail in the general election.

Entering the Senate race in early 2013, Peters—dubbed "the congressman from Chrysler" in the House for his stalwart defense of the auto industry—sought to emphasize job creation and other middle-class concerns. "I've always believed that the things middle-class families struggle with around their kitchen tables should define my work in Washington," he said when announcing his candidacy. Both Levin and Democratic Sen. Debbie Stabenow endorsed Peters in the late spring of 2013, more than 14 months prior to the primary—in which he ran unopposed. His Republican opponent, Land, also ended up unopposed in the primary, but only after GOP strategists failed to convince a couple of high-profile House members, Rep. Dave Camp (outgoing chairman of the powerful Ways and Means Committee) and Rep. Mike Rogers, to run.

Polls in early 2014 gave Land a lead, as her campaign benefited from her family's wealth (she ultimately donated $3.35 million in personal funds to a campaign that spent a total of about $12.3 million). But she made a couple of early missteps, and never managed to regain her footing. First, she launched her TV campaign with what may have been the oddest ad of the election cycle. In it, Land declares: "Congressman Gary Peters and his buddies want you to believe I'm waging a war on women. Really? Think about that for a moment." The rest of the ad involves 12 seconds of silence as Land sips from a coffee mug, shakes her head, and looks at her watch. The ad was criticized in Republican circles.

Several weeks later, Land put on what was viewed as a lackluster performance before the Detroit Regional Chamber of Commerce, and then all but froze when facing questions from the press. "I can't do this," she declared, as she pushed away a cluster of microphones and departed. The gaffe was compounded by efforts to avoid the media for much of the rest of the campaign, as her organization was often criticized for failing to disclose in advance where she would be appearing. She sought to use TV advertising to get her message out, but, when the National Republican Senatorial Committee canceled a $1 million TV buy in the closing weeks, it was seen as tantamount to a concession. All told, the NRSC spent about $1.5 million on Land's behalf, while the Democratic Senatorial Campaign Committee poured in more than $4.9 million on behalf of Peter—who trounced Land, 55%-41% on Election Day.

Three days before the voters went to the polls, Peters became the only 2014 Senate candidate for whom President Barack Obama made an appearance. Obama's unpopularity had prompted most candidates in battleground states to shun him, and Peters beforehand seemed diffident about the president showing up. "The president will come to Michigan to campaign, and I'm going to stand next to the president," he told *Atlantic.com*. But, when Obama appeared at the rally at Detroit's Wayne State University, Peters stressed the bailout of the auto industry, declaring to the crowd, "Thank God, our president stood up for American workers." After being sworn into the Senate, Peters assumed a seat on the Commerce Committee, which has jurisdiction over the nation's automakers.

FIRST DISTRICT

Dan Benishek (R)

Elected 2010, 3rd term; b. April 20, 1952, Iron River; U. of MI, B.S. 1974, Wayne St. U., M.D. 1978; Catholic; married (Judy); 5 children.

Professional Career: Gen. surgeon, Dickinson Cnty. Memorial Hosp., 1983-2010; Gen. surgeon, V.A. Med. Ctr., 1990-2010.

DC Office: 514 CHOB, 20515, 202-225-4735; Fax: 202-225-4710; Website: benishek.house.gov.

State Offices: Alpena, 989-340-1634; Iron Mountain, 906-828-2114; Marquette, 906-273-2074; Traverse City, 231-421-5599.

Committees: *Agriculture:* Conservation & Forestry; Nutrition. *Natural Resources:* Energy & Mineral Resources; Indian, Insular & AK Native Affairs. *Veterans' Affairs:* Health (Chmn); Oversight & Investigations.

Group Ratings

	ADA	ACLU	AFL-CIO	LCV	ITI	COC	HAFA	ACU	CFG	FRC
2014	5%	0%	–	6%	100%	86%	49%	68%	62%	57%
2013	0%	C	19%	4%	C	85%	C	68%	61%	C

National Journal Ratings

	2013 LIB	—	2013 CONS
Economic	31%	—	68%
Social	38%	—	59%
Foreign	50%	—	50%
Composite	40%	—	60%

Key Votes of the 113th Congress

1. Sandy storm spending	N	5. Medical Marijuana	NV
2. Violence Against Women Act	Y	6. Farm Bill	Y
3. Guantanamo Bay Detainees	N	7. Afghanistan Combat	Y
4. Abortion 20-week ban	Y	8. NSA Phone Data Collection	N

9. Syrian Rebels Training	Y
10. Keystone pipeline	Y
11. Immigration Exec. Action	Y
12. Bipartisan budget deal	Y

Election Results

2014 general	Dan Benishek (R)	130,414	(52%)	$2,158,322	$907,515	$616,527
	Jerry Cannon (D)	113,263	(45%)	$1,002,506	$8,010	$430,739
2014 primary	Dan Benishek (R)	49,540	(70%)			
	Alan Arcand (R)	21,497	(30%)			

Prior winning percentages: 2012 (48%), 2010 (52%)

Population		Race and Ethnicity		Income	
Total:	704,991	White	91.8%	Median income:	$41,971
Urban:	0.0%	Amer. Indian	2.6%		(357 of 435)
Suburban:	0.0%	Black	1.6%	Under $50,000	58.4%
Rural:	100.0%	Latino	1.5%	$50,000-$99,999:	30.4%
Land area:	25,224	Two races	1.9%	$100,000-$199,999:	9.1%
Pop/sq. mi.:	27.9	White Ethnic	39.1%	$200,000 or more:	2.1%
Born in state:	80.2%			Poverty Rate	15.6%
		Education			
Age Groups		H.S. grad or less:	44.6%	**Work**	
Under 18:	19.2%	Some college:	32.4%	White collar:	29.0%
18 to 34:	19.0%	College degree, 4 yr.:	14.6%	Blue collar:	46.2%
35 to 64:	41.2%	Post-grad study:	8.3%	Sales and service:	24.8%
Over 64:	20.6%			Govt. workers:	13.7%
		Military			
		Veterans/active duty:	11.9%		

Northern Michigan: Upper Peninsula

Michigan's Upper Peninsula, commonly known as the U.P., is a land apart. Surrounded on three sides by frigid Lakes Superior, Huron and Michigan, the U.P. is no farther north than Montreal or Seattle, but there are places here that have some of the coldest climates in settled parts of North America.

Voter Turnout	
2013 Total Citizen 18+	564,294
2014 House Turnout	250,131
2014 Turnout as % CVAP	44.3%
2012 Turnout as % CVAP	62.8%

The winter storms can be legendary: The area surrounding Keweenaw County, which juts into Lake Superior, often ranks high in the nation's heaviest snowfall. These storms can also be cruel. The "gales of November" have caught hundreds of vessels by surprise and sent them to the bottom of the lake, including the SS *Edmund Fitzgerald*, whose loss was memorialized in a Gordon Lightfoot ballad.

With ground too frozen and stony and a growing season too short for most crops, the peninsula was considered a poor consolation prize when much of it was appended to the Michigan Territory in 1836 in exchange for the incipient state giving up its claim to Toledo and its surrounding areas. This ended an occasionally violent feud with Ohio known as the Toledo War. Views on the fairness of the exchange likely shifted when prospectors found rich veins of ore up north.

2012 Presidential Vote		
Mitt Romney (R)	189,387	(54%)
Barack Obama (D)	160,231	(45%)
2008 Presidential Vote		
Barack Obama (D)	183,283	(50%)
John McCain (R)	178,548	(48%)
Cook Partisan Voting Index:	R+5	

The mineral veins of the Keweenaw Peninsula eventually produced more than 13 billion pounds of copper, while the Marquette, Menominee and Gogebic iron ranges produced more than 1 billion tons of iron ore. Immigrants flocked here to work the mines: Irish, Italians, Swedes, Norwegians, miners' sons from Wales and Cornwall—stands selling pasties (pronounced with a short "a"), a Cornish pastry filled with meat and vegetables, still dot the countryside—and most prominently, Finns, who must have found this cold land with its lakes and hills much like home. The western counties of the U.P. remain the only ones in the United States with a plurality of residents of Finnish ancestry. By the early 1900s, the U.P. had become a northern industrial belt with a workforce disposed to radical ideas and union movements.

A major strike in 1913-14 and falling ore prices after World War I—events that would be long forgotten elsewhere—are recalled in the U.P. as accelerating the copper decline. But the accessible copper veins were mostly depleted by then, mining iron ore became less labor intensive, and lumber and farming provided only a few thousand jobs. As extraction methods have improved, companies have taken a second look at abandoned mines, and some locals are cheered that there may yet be more minerals in the area. But the trend is unmistakable. The Empire Mine in Marquette County has cut back or temporarily laid off hundreds of workers (including in the summer of 2015) because of limited supply and demand. Other industries have taken root. The region's natural beauty—90% of the U.P. is forested—has made tourism a leading economic driver. Skiers can take advantage of the average 200 inches of annual snowfall at several mountain resorts. Marinette Marine, which builds Coast Guard cutters and military ships just across the state border in Wisconsin, is important to Menominee County. Population of the U.P. peaked at 332,000 in 1920. In 2014, there were 310,000 "Yoopers," as the locals call themselves, many of whom harbor a strong sense of place.

The 1st Congressional District of Michigan includes the Upper Peninsula and 16 1/2 northern counties in the Lower Peninsula. Almost half the people live in the U.P. Often-snowbound Marquette, with 21,500 people, is the largest city in the district. Mackinac Island, home to a resort area where almost all cars are banned (even UPS delivers packages by bicycle), lies just east of the breathtaking Mackinac Bridge, which connects the two peninsulas. State officials created in April 2015 the Superior Trade Zone to encourage economic cooperation between the two largest cities, Marquette and Escanaba. On the Lower Peninsula, along Lake Michigan, are affluent resort areas around Petoskey and Charlevoix, long summer places for people from Chicago (this is Ernest Hemingway's "Up in Michigan"). There is some agriculture on the district's southern end; the Traverse City area accounts for nearly 50% of the tart cherry production in the United States.

Politically, the U.P. has a lengthy Democratic tradition, but it can be contrarian. This is one part of Michigan that has opposed many Democratic environmental and gun control stands. The Lower Peninsula is more reliably Republican, creating a competitive district. Mitt Romney won the district 54%-45% over President Barack Obama in 2012, a six-point increase over the GOP vote in 2008. That was common in GOP-leaning districts in Michigan, and likely resulted in part from affection for Romney in his home state.

Dan Benishek (R)

Republican Dan Benishek, first elected in 2010 on a wave of tea party support to replace retiring Democratic Rep. Bart Stupak, has twice been narrowly reelected. Democrats have complained that he hadn't done enough to help his swing district, but haven't been able to convince the district's voters.

Benishek was born in Stambaugh, on the rural Upper Peninsula. He and his brother, Tim, were raised by their mother and grandparents after their father died in a mining accident when Dan was 5 years old. As a teenager, he made beds, cooked, cleaned, and hauled beer at his grandparents' hotel and bar, earning $10 a week—money that helped get him through college. In 1970, Benishek took a bus to Ann Arbor to enroll as a freshman at the University of Michigan, the first time he had crossed the Mackinac Bridge that separates the U.P. from the rest of the state. He studied first to be an engineer, but took an uncle's suggestion and switched to medicine on the assumption that a medical degree would allow him to work wherever he wanted. After medical school at Wayne State University, he was a family medicine resident in Flint and then became a surgeon. He returned to the U.P., joined a private practice in Iron Mountain and worked part-time at the local V.A. medical center.

Benishek and his friends were discussing their unhappiness with Democratic policies in Washington during an ice-fishing excursion; one of them suggested that Benishek seek to unseat Stupak. At the time, Stupak was at the center of the national health care debate and insisting on an amendment to prevent federal funding for abortions. Stupak backed off and voted for the legislation, angering anti-abortion Republicans, who began donating money to Benishek. "The phone didn't stop ringing for a week," he said. Stupak announced in April 2010 that he would not seek reelection. In the GOP primary in August, Benishek faced state Sen. Jason Allen. With tea party support, Benishek edged out Allen by just 15 votes out of nearly 99,000 cast.

In the general election campaign, Benishek's competition was Democratic state Rep. Gary McDowell, a Teamsters Union member who drove a UPS truck for over 30 years, was a county commissioner and then a member of the Michigan House. He sought to paint Benishek as an extremist by highlighting his comments in favor of privatizing Social Security. McDowell supported the Democrats' health care overhaul and called for withholding tax breaks from companies that send jobs offshore. Benishek wooed voters with tea party themes of less spending and lower taxes, and he got national attention when he slammed President Barack Obama's "socialist agenda." Benishek outspent McDowell $1,343,000 to $838,000, and GOP groups surpassed their Democratic rivals. He won 52%-41%, breaking the Democrats' two-decade hold on the seat.

In the House, Benishek joined with Democratic Rep. Joseph Crowley of New York in urging colleagues to allocate money in 2012 that would have been spent on the wars in Iraq and Afghanistan to reimburse doctors scheduled to get a cut in Medicare payments. But he was more predictably Republican about the health care law, declaring, "There is no way to 'fix' this law. It needs to be fully repealed." He was assigned to the Natural Resources Committee and got a bill through the panel in 2011 to require the Interior Department to prioritize the use of public lands for hunting and fishing. Benishek had to fight the perception that his commitment to cutting spending interfered with his ability to help the district, such as his support for ending the Essential Air Service program, which supports rural airports like those in his district.

As chairman of the Veterans Affairs Subcommittee on Health, Benishek gained a useful niche that combined his experience as a physician with the large number of veterans in his district. He helped to craft the 2014 bipartisan deal to overhaul the problem-ridden VA hospital system, and called that measure a first step that will "begin to make access to care easier." He also enacted a bill that gave local veterans' groups greater access to surplus federal property, such as spare vehicles and equipment. In April 2015, Benishek filed a bipartisan bill that called for a VA study of health conditions affecting children and grandchildren of veterans exposed to toxic chemicals during their military service.

In 2012, he had a rematch with McDowell, who this time got more than $3 million from super PACs, plus labor and environmental groups that helped to offset Benishek's fundraising advantage. Benishek touted his fiscal responsibility, but McDowell hammered away at his rival's support for GOP Rep. Paul Ryan's budget blueprint calling for changes in Medicare and accused him of not helping the region's farmers cope with drought and a spring freeze. *The Traverse City Record-Eagle,* in endorsing McDowell, said the congressman "has done virtually nothing to earn reelection." Benishek pulled out a narrow 48.1%-47.6% victory, a margin of 1,881 votes.

Benishek had a more comfortable reelection in the Republican-leaning 2014 campaign. After winning the GOP primary with 70% of the vote against Air Force veteran Alan Arcand, he faced Jerry Cannon, a former Kalkaska County sheriff and a retired Army National Guard general. Benishek outspent Cannon, $2.2 million to $1 million. Cannon had early national Democratic support, but that funding dried up several weeks before the election as the party focused on better opportunities in Michigan and elsewhere. Benishek won 52%-45%. In 2015, he broke an earlier pledge to limit himself to three terms in the House. Both parties prepared for another competitive contest in 2016.

SECOND DISTRICT

Bill Huizenga (R)

Elected 2010, 3rd term; b. Jan. 31, 1969, Zeeland; Calvin Col., B.A. 1991; Christian Reformed; married (Natalie); 5 children.

Elected Office: MI House, 2003-08.

Professional Career: Realtor, 1991-96; Aide, Rep. Pete Hoekstra, 1997-2002; Admin., Zeeland Christian Schls., 2009-10; Co-owner, Huizenga Gravel, 1999-present.

DC Office: 1217 LHOB, 20515, 202-225-4401; Fax: 202-226-0779; Website: huizenga.house.gov.

State Offices: Grand Haven, 616-414-5516; Grandville, 616-570-0917.

Committees: *Financial Services:* Capital Markets & Gov't Sponsored Enterprises; Monetary Policy & Trade (Chmn)

Group Ratings

	ADA	ACLU	AFL-CIO	LCV	ITI	COC	HAFA	ACU	CFG	FRC
2014	0%	0%	–	3%	80%	93%	67%	88%	73%	100%
2013	5%	C	10%	4%	C	69%	C	80%	75%	C

National Journal Ratings

	2013 LIB	—	2013 CONS
Economic	10%	—	88%
Social	0%	—	87%
Foreign	24%	—	68%
Composite	15%	—	85%

Key Votes of the 113th Congress

1. Sandy storm spending	N 5. Medical Marijuana	N 9. Syrian Rebels Training N
2. Violence Against Women Act	N 6. Farm Bill	Y 10. Keystone pipeline Y
3. Guantanamo Bay Detainees	N 7. Afghanistan Combat	N 11. Immigration Exec. Action Y
4. Abortion 20-week ban	Y 8. NSA Phone Data Collection	Y 12. Bipartisan budget deal Y

Election Results

2014 general	Bill Huizenga (R) 135,568	(64%)	$1,105,248
	Dean Vanderstelt (D) 70,851	(33%)	$53,345
2014 primary	Bill Huizenga (R) ....unopposed		

Prior winning percentages: 2012 (61%), 2010 (65%)

Population		Race and Ethnicity		Income	
Total:	717,114	White	80.8%	Median income:	$48,717
Urban:	41.0%	Latino	8.7%		*(261 of 435)*
Suburban:	31.9%	Black	5.9%	Under $50,000	51.1%
Rural:	27.1%	Asian	2.1%	$50,000-$99,999:	33.0%
Land area:	3,011	Two races	2.1%	$100,000-$199,999:	14.0%
Pop/sq. mi.:	238.2	White Ethnic	27.6%	$200,000 or more:	1.9%
Born in state:	79.9%			Poverty Rate	15.6%
		Education			
Age Groups		H.S. grad or less:	42.5%	**Work**	
Under 18:	24.3%	Some college:	33.5%	White collar:	29.9%
18 to 34:	23.9%	College degree, 4 yr.:	16.8%	Blue collar:	41.2%
35 to 64:	37.9%	Post-grad study:	7.2%	Sales and service:	28.9%
Over 64:	13.9%				
		Military		Govt. workers:	8.8%
		Veterans/active duty:	8.0%		

West-Central Michigan: Grand Rapids Suburbs

When the glaciers receded from Michigan some 16,000 years ago, they left behind piles of boulders, sand and clay. Over time, the lake winds eroded the boulders, while waves ground up glacial drift deposited in the lake and washed it ashore. The end result is a lakeshore that today is home to the largest collection of freshwater dunes in the world, located along the western rim of the state.

Voter Turnout	
2013 Total Citizen 18+	527,888
2014 House Turnout	213,072
2014 Turnout as % CVAP	40.4%
2012 Turnout as % CVAP	64.1%

In the late 19th century, the river ports on this shoreline were choked with logs and full of lumbermen from Norway and Sweden, Ireland and Scotland, Quebec and New England. During the timber boom, the shoreline was the locus of the country's largest migration from the Netherlands and today still has the nation's largest concentration of Dutch-Americans. Wooden shoes are now seen only at the Tulip Festival in the town of Holland, but conscientious Dutch work habits have produced many highly skilled workers. This is a busy manufacturing area, with products

2012 Presidential Vote		
Mitt Romney (R) 184,732	(56%)
Barack Obama (D) 142,077	(43%)
2008 Presidential Vote		
John McCain (R) 175,945	(50%)
Barack Obama (D) 168,007	(48%)
Cook Partisan Voting Index: R+7		

ranging from baby food at Gerber in Fremont to office furniture at Herman Miller in Zeeland and Haworth in Holland.

The 2007-09 recession hit this area hard, with unemployment rates getting close to 20% and recovery coming slowly. Job growth has sputtered in Muskegon County, but the unemployment rate dropped to 6% in February 2015. Holland's recovery, though also fitful, has strengthened, with the jobless rate at 4.3%. Away from the shore is fruit-growing country, with some of the nation's largest cherry orchards to the north and blueberry patches to the south.

The 2nd Congressional District of Michigan occupies the Lake Michigan shoreline counties, plus a tier of inland counties. It stretches from the old lumber port of Ludington south to Holland. For years, Dutch-American voters have been strongly Republican, and fast-growing. Heavily Dutch Ottawa County, which is the most populous county in the district, gave Mitt Romney 67% of the vote in 2012. About a fifth of the district's residents now live in an arc of suburbs surrounding Grand Rapids in Kent County; these aren't as Republican as other parts of the district, but still tilt toward the party of Lincoln. The chief exception to Republican voting patterns comes from the old industrial centers in Muskegon County. Overall, this is the most Republican district in the state.

Bill Huizenga (R)

Republican Bill Huizenga was elected in 2010 to succeed his friend and former boss, Rep. Pete Hoekstra. He upholds the rock-solid conservatism of his western Michigan district and has moved even further to the right on banking and fiscal issues than Hoekstra.

Huizenga grew up in Zeeland, and minus a few short absences, he has lived there all of his life. His grandparents were farmers who started a gravel business by selling the leftover sand and stone that was lying around the farm. In high school, Huizenga was an inattentive student who ultimately transferred to vocational school. His instructors told him he had academic potential and advised him to go to college. Huizenga studied political science at Calvin College. Between his freshman and sophomore years, he made his first real estate investment: With money saved from working in his father's gravel pit, he became the junior stakeholder in a 19-unit housing development. As a young adult, Huizenga indulged his love of travel, taking trips around the world. During anti-government unrest just before the fall of the Berlin Wall, he was chased by riot police and dogs at a pro-democracy rally in Prague.

After college, he worked for a local real estate firm and took over as co-owner in the family business, Huizenga Gravel. Hoekstra offered him a job in his district office, and he later became Hoekstra's director of public policy. After six years, he decided to run for office, winning a seat in the Michigan House in 2002. He was reelected twice and was chairman of the Commerce Committee.

When Hoekstra ran for Michigan governor in 2010, the real contest for his heavily Republican district was the GOP primary. In the seven-way race, former pro-football tight end Jay Riemersma, also of Zeeland, raised $850,000 to Huizenga's $553,000. Huizenga touted his conservative credentials, saying he supported a flat tax, which would replace the income tax with a 23% sales tax, and private Social Security accounts. He also opposed abortion rights. Riemersma, the former regional director for the Family Research Council, also ran as an anti-abortion and fiscal conservative. He attacked Huizenga for voting for a state business tax in 2007. Huizenga eked out a victory with a better political organization, built largely on the many contacts he had made among local political and business leaders while on Hoekstra's staff. He prevailed by just 663 votes out of about 106,000 cast. In the general election, he faced nominal Democratic opposition from history professor Fred Johnson.

In the House, Huizenga won notice for his facility with the inner workings of Congress, in contrast to other freshmen. *Washington Post* conservative blogger Jennifer Rubin said admiringly in January 2011 that he "seems to understand how to advance aggressive goals without being aggressive or off-putting." After opposing the New Year's Day 2013 budget deal aimed at averting the so-called "fiscal cliff" of tax hikes and deep spending cuts, he called for providing block grants for Medicare and Medicaid to states while re-examining who qualifies for Social Security. In addition to sharing many fiscal views with Ways and Means Committee Chairman Paul Ryan, Huizenga has joined Ryan in grueling P90X fitness workouts.

Huizenga took up Hoekstra's longtime crusade against Federal Prison Industries, contending that their access to cheap labor takes work from small businesses. On the Financial Services Committee, he explored ways to reduce the impact on businesses of the Dodd-Frank financial regulation law. He enacted a bill in December 2012 giving taxpayers and businesses who submit information to the Consumer Financial Protection Bureau the same confidentiality protection that other financial regulators are required to provide.

In 2015, Huizenga became chairman of the Subcommittee on Monetary Policy and Trade, which gave him oversight authority over the Federal Reserve Board. He pledged more transparent discussion of monetary policy. He raised questions about the extension of the Export-Import Bank, including its cost to the taxpayer and its track record of "corruption, bribery, and fraud." In April 2015, the House passed his Mortgage Choice Act, which he said was designed to remove "technicalities" in qualification requirements for lower and middle-income homeowners.

In contrast to his earlier race, Huizenga has had no trouble winning reelection and seems entrenched in this Republican bastion.

THIRD DISTRICT

Justin Amash (R)

Elected 2010, 3rd term; b. April 18, 1980, Grand Rapids; U. of MI, B.A. 2002, J.D. 2005; Orthodox Christian; married (Kara); 3 children.

Elected Office: MI House, 2008-10.

Professional Career: Practicing atty., 2006-07; Consultant, MI Industrial Tools, 2005-10.

DC Office: 114 CHOB, 20515, 202-225-3831; Fax: 202-225-5144; Website: amash.house.gov.

State Offices: Battle Creek, 269-205-3823; Grand Rapids, 616-451-8383.

Committees: *Oversight & Gov't Reform:* Transportation & Public Assets. *Joint Economic Committee*

Group Ratings

	ADA	ACLU	AFL-CIO	LCV	ITI	COC	HAFA	ACU	CFG	FRC
2014	15%	55%	–	11%	60%	38%	88%	84%	100%	50%
2013	25%	C	24%	18%	C	58%	C	92%	99%	C

National Journal Ratings

	2013 LIB	—	2013 CONS
Economic	28%	—	72%
Social	52%	—	47%
Foreign	58%	—	41%
Composite	46%	—	54%

Key Votes of the 113th Congress

1. Sandy storm spending	N	5. Medical Marijuana	Y
2. Violence Against Women Act	N	6. Farm Bill	N
3. Guantanamo Bay Detainees	Y	7. Afghanistan Combat	Y
4. Abortion 20-week ban	Y	8. NSA Phone Data Collection	Y

9. Syrian Rebels Training	N
10. Keystone pipeline	P
11. Immigration Exec. Action	Y
12. Bipartisan budget deal	N

Election Results

2014 general	Justin Amash (R)	125,754	(58%)	$1,454,134	$114,557
	Bob Goodrich (D)	84,720	(39%)	$317,529	
	Tonya Duncan (G)	6,691	(3%)		
2014 primary	Justin Amash (R)	39,706	(57%)		
	Brian Ellis (R)	29,422	(43%)		

Prior winning percentages: 2012 (53%), 2010 (60%)

Population		Race and Ethnicity		Income	
Total:	720,731	White	80.0%	Median income:	$51,202
Urban:	49.4%	Black	8.8%		(216 of 435)
Suburban:	35.2%	Latino	6.9%	Under $50,000	48.7%
Rural:	15.5%	Asian	1.3%	$50,000-$99,999:	32.9%
Land area:	2,752	Two races	2.5%	$100,000-$199,999:	15.1%
Pop/sq. mi.:	261.9	White Ethnic	29.9%	$200,000 or more:	3.3%
Born in state:	78.2%			Poverty Rate	14.9%
		Education			
Age Groups		H.S. grad or less:	37.6%	**Work**	
Under 18:	24.9%	Some college:	32.5%	White collar:	35.1%
18 to 34:	22.3%	College degree, 4 yr.:	18.7%	Blue collar:	41.1%
35 to 64:	39.3%	Post-grad study:	11.2%	Sales and service:	23.8%
Over 64:	13.4%				
		Military		Govt. workers:	8.9%
		Veterans/active duty:	8.4%		

West-Central Michigan: Grand Rapids Metro

Grand Rapids is Michigan's second-largest city and the center of its most prosperous metropolitan area. It grew as a center for turning the hardwood forests of northern Michigan into furniture. By the early 20th century, Grand Rapids was the leading furniture manufacturer in the nation. The Depression

Voter Turnout	
2013 Total Citizen 18+	521,118
2014 House Turnout	217,165
2014 Turnout as % CVAP	41.7%
2012 Turnout as % CVAP	65.4%

knocked the bottom out of the residential furniture market, and many manufacturers moved to North Carolina, where labor was cheaper. So Grand Rapids reinvented itself. It went into office furniture, and today three of the nation's largest office furniture manufacturers—Steelcase, Haworth and Herman Miller—are located in its metropolitan area.

It also capitalized on a knack for sales. Rich DeVos and Jay Van Andel started Amway, the direct sales empire, which now has about 90 percent of its sales abroad. In 2012, Amway surpassed Avon Products as the largest direct-selling company in the world, including strong sales in China. Frederik and Hendrik Meijer started Meijer's Thrifty Acres, combining supermarkets with discount stores. The Grand Rapids area is a center for machine tools, Hush Puppies shoes, and Bissell carpet sweepers. Fifty years ago,

2012 Presidential Vote		
Mitt Romney (R)	177,772	(53%)
Barack Obama (D)	153,052	(46%)

2008 Presidential Vote		
Barack Obama (D)	174,352	(50%)
John McCain (R)	170,665	(49%)

| **Cook Partisan Voting Index:** R+4 |

Grand Rapids and its up-and-coming businesses were outshone by Detroit and the auto industry. Today, while Detroit struggles to stay afloat, more diversified Grand Rapids chugs along. The metropolitan area had the nation's ninth-fastest growing economy in 2014. The local unemployment rate was 3.8% in February 2015.

Politically, the Grand Rapids area has been the center of Michigan Republicanism for much of the last century; cultural conservatism and a belief in market economics run deep among the descendants of the pious Dutch immigrants who settled in western Michigan in the 1870s. It has also produced national Republican leaders. The conversion of Sen. Arthur Vandenberg (1928-1951) from isolationism to internationalism during World War II provided key support for the foreign policies of Franklin D. Roosevelt and Harry Truman. Another was Gerald Ford, who rose to House Republican leader in 1965, vice president in 1973, and then president after Richard Nixon resigned in 1974. A Democratic win in the special election to replace Ford—the first for a Democrat here since 1910—was part of a string of five special election pickups for the Democrats in early 1974 that helped convince Republicans that Nixon needed to resign, and which presaged the Democratic landslide later that year. The election of the local Democrat did not last long.

The 3rd Congressional District of Michigan can be thought of in three distinct parts. The first is the city of Grand Rapids itself, which constitutes about 25% of the population and has become heavily Democratic; Barack Obama won 65% of the vote there in 2008. The second includes most of the remainder of Kent, Ionia and Barry counties, and a small portion of Montcalm County. This part of the district, which includes a majority of its residents, is heavily Republican. The third part of the district is Calhoun County, which tends to vote close to the national average and is centered on Battle Creek, where sanitarium operator W.K. Kellogg invented corn flakes as a health food and where the Air National Guard base has become a prominent site for the Defense Department's cybersecurity operations. The net result is a district that leans Republican; Mitt Romney won 53% of the vote here in 2012.

Justin Amash (R)

Justin Amash, a Republican elected in 2010, has been perhaps the most iconoclastic member of his iconoclastic class. A persistent thorn in the side of House GOP leaders with his libertarian views, he lost his seat on the Budget Committee in 2012 for his refusal to toe the party line, and reportedly has been active in abortive efforts to depose John Boehner as speaker.

Amash was born in Grand Rapids, the son of a wealthy Palestinian tool importer who immigrated to the United States with the sponsorship of a Christian church. He began high school at the time of the Republican tidal wave of 1994 and graduated as class valedictorian. He majored in economics and graduated magna cum laude at the University of Michigan, and earned a degree from its law school. He counts himself as an admirer of both the 19th-century author Frederic Bastiat, who argued against taxing people to pay for schools or roads, and the 20th-century writer Friedrich Hayek, a favorite of the tea party movement who strongly opposed government intervention in the economy. Amash kept Hayek's portrait on the wall of his congressional campaign offices.

He has been a consultant to his family's tool-import business, and served as a corporate lawyer for a year before he was elected to the Michigan House in 2008. He fought to eliminate state taxes on businesses. A proponent of states' rights, he proposed an amendment to the state constitution that would prevent the implementation of President Barack Obama's health care law. *The Grand Rapids Press* reported in July 2010 that Amash was the only "no" vote on 59 bills in his first term, including measures toughening penalties for human trafficking and allowing military members to get out of cell phone contracts if deployed overseas.

Amash entered the 3rd District race, he said, because he was fed up with the moderate voting record of eight-term GOP incumbent Vern Ehlers. When Ehlers announced his retirement, that opened the door for other Republican candidates, including former Kent County Commissioner Steve Heacock, whom Ehlers personally asked to run. In the primary race, Amash outraised both Heacock and state Sen. Bill Hardiman, and he was endorsed by the anti-tax group Club for Growth. He won the August primary, getting 40% of the vote to Heacock's 26% and Hardiman's 24%.

His victory set up a general election race against Democratic lawyer Pat Miles, a former Harvard Law School classmate of Obama. Miles accused Amash of exporting jobs to China through his ownership of Dynamic Source International, a Chinese company that supplies industrial tools to his father's tool-import business. In his ads, Amash accused Miles of supporting taxpayer-funded abortions because he backed the Democrats' health care overhaul. Amash got a boost when *Time* magazine named him to its "40 under 40" list of civic leaders. He won 60%-37%.

In the House, Amash immediately displayed his independence by refusing to vote in favor of legislation he believed either was unconstitutional or not given adequate time for consideration, voting "present" on numerous bills. Fox News host Greta Van Susteren called him a "coward" for doing so. He was one of just 22 Republicans in July 2011 to oppose Boehner's bill to raise the federal debt limit, later telling a local audience that the leadership urged him to back it because Obama disliked it. "Is this really the standard by which we should base our votes?" he asked. He explained to *The New York Times* how he votes: "I follow a set of principles, I follow the Constitution. And that's what I base my votes on. Limited government, economic freedom and individual liberty."

Amash introduced a balanced budget amendment that that would limit spending to the federal government's average annual revenues for the previous three years. He deployed his Facebook page to detail his reasons for all of his actions and got into a "Facebook feud" with the National Rifle Association for opposing legislation that granted reciprocity for concealed weapons permits. He said the measure subverted states' rights.

In 2012, Democrats thought they had a chance to defeat Amash by drawing alienated GOP moderates from him, and nominated Steve Pestka, a former state representative, prosecutor and judge. He criticized Amash for his contrarian votes and began climbing in the polls after loaning his campaign more than $1 million. Amash beat Pestka by a not overwhelming 53%-44%. Pestka edged out Amash in Calhoun County, but Kent County hewed to its historic Republican tendency.

Returning to Washington for a lame-duck session, Amash learned that the Boehner-controlled Republican Steering Committee had taken him off the Budget Committee, making him one of four Republicans to receive such punishment. He called it "a slap in the face" to the GOP's expanding libertarian faction. News accounts named him as a central figure in an attempt to persuade fellow Republicans to vote against Boehner for speaker in January 2013, but the effort collapsed shortly before the vote when the group could not secure the 25 votes they believed were needed to withstand expected defections. Amash got a vote from Kentucky freshman Thomas Massie.

Amash was mentioned as a contender for the seat of retiring Democratic Sen. Carl Levin, but said in September 2013 that he wouldn't seek the job. He became one of the House's leading champions of former National Security Agency contractor Edward Snowden after Snowden leaked details of the agency's domestic surveillance efforts. He managed to unite the Republican leadership and the White House against him when he proposed an amendment in July to strip funding for an NSA phone-surveillance program; it fell short by just 12 votes. In May 2015, when the House overwhelmingly voted to end the meta-data phone collection program, Amash voted against it because he said "it actually expands the statutory basis for the large-scale collection of most data." In 2015, he chaired the newly formed Liberty Caucus, a small group of libertarian-minded conservatives who have sought to affect policy decisions in the House.

Establishment Republicans challenged Amash in the 2014 primary. Their candidate was Brian Ellis, who served on the East Grand Rapids school board and drew support from local and national Chamber of Commerce-types. Ellis criticized what he called Amash's "bizarre" voting record. Amash's allies in the Club for Growth ran ads bashing Ellis for "leaving massive deficits" on the school board and serving on a panel appointed by Democratic Gov. Jennifer Granholm that "wasted taxpayer dollars on a golf resort." Amash and his allies cried foul at an attack ad calling the congressman "al-Qaida's best friend in Congress." Citing his Palestinian-American heritage, Amash called the ad "disgusting." He prevailed in the August primary, 57%-43%, and lashed out at former Michigan Rep. Pete Hoekstra, who supported the challenger. "I want to say to lobbyist Pete Hoekstra, you're a disgrace," Amash said. "I'm glad we can hand you one more loss before you fade into total obscurity and irrelevance." He easily defeated Democrat Bob Goodrich in November, 58%-39%. In May 2015, Amash joined Rand Paul at a campaign event in Grand Rapids.

FOURTH DISTRICT

John Moolenaar (R)

Elected 2014, 1st term; b. May 8, 1961, Midland; Hope Col., B.S. 1983, Harvard U., M.P.A. 1989; Christian; married (Amy); 6 children.

Elected Office: Midland MI City Cncl., 1997-2000; MI House, 2003-08; MI Senate, 2011-14.

Professional Career: Chemist, Dow Chemical; Dir., Middle MI Development Corp. Small Business Cntr.; Schl. admin., Midland Academy of Ad-vanced & Creative Studies.

DC Office: 117 CHOB, 20515, 202-225-3561; Fax: 202-225-9679; Website: moolenaar.house.gov.

State Offices: Midland, 989-631-2552.

Committees: *Agriculture:* Biotechnology, Horticulture, & Research; Nutrition. *Budget. Science, Space, & Technology:* Environment; Research & Technology (VChmn).

Election Results

2014 general	John Moolenaar (R)	123,962	(57%)	$1,128,662	$596,204
	Jeff Holmes (D)	85,777	(39%)	$133,563	
	Georgia M. Zimmer (UST)	4,990	(2%)		
	Will Tyler White (Lib)	4,694	(2%)		
2014 primary	John Moolenaar (R)	34,399	(52%)		
	Paul Mitchell (R)	23,844	(36%)		
	Peter Konetchy (R)	7,408	(11%)		

Population		Race and Ethnicity		Income	
Total:	709,423	White	92.0%	Median income:	$42,813
Urban:	18.4%	Latino	2.8%		*(347 of 435)*
Suburban:	15.3%	Black	2.0%	Under $50,000	57.5%
Rural:	66.3%	Asian	0.9%	$50,000-$99,999:	29.4%
Land area:	7,301	Two races	1.5%	$100,000-$199,999:	11.2%
Pop/sq. mi.:	97.2	White Ethnic	32.3%	$200,000 or more:	1.9%
Born in state:	85.7%			Poverty Rate	18.4%
		Education			
Age Groups		H.S. grad or less:	45.6%	**Work**	
Under 18:	21.2%	Some college:	34.2%	White collar:	29.8%
18 to 34:	22.7%	College degree, 4 yr.:	13.1%	Blue collar:	42.8%
35 to 64:	39.3%	Post-grad study:	7.2%	Sales and service:	27.5%
Over 64:	16.8%			Govt. workers:	13.2%
		Military			
		Veterans/active duty:	9.3%		

Central Michigan: Lansing

Flat and treeless for miles, the central reaches of Michigan's Lower Peninsula are farm country, exposed to bitter winds and snowdrifts in winter and shining sun for precious weeks in summer. Like the steppes of Eastern Europe, these are farmlands that produce hearty crops: potatoes, navy beans,

Voter Turnout	
2013 Total Citizen 18+	551,393
2014 House Turnout	219,423
2014 Turnout as % CVAP	39.8%
2012 Turnout as % CVAP	59.1%

sugar beets. The cities here are often small factory towns, with neat, tree-lined streets that end at bare fields. Midland in 1891 was a declining lumber town when Herbert Dow perfected an electrolytic process to extract chemicals from northern Michigan's extensive brine wells. That was the start of Dow Chemical, still headquartered in this now upscale town and today a large producer of pesticides and agricultural biotech products. Owosso was the birthplace of Thomas E. Dewey, later New York governor and Republican nominee for president in 1944 and 1948. It was also the home of novelist James Oliver Curwood and the location of his Curwood Castle writing studio. Mount Pleasant, to the north, is

2012 Presidential Vote		
Mitt Romney (R)................171,862	(53%)
Barack Obama (D) 146,088	(45%)

2008 Presidential Vote

Barack Obama (D) 170,697	(50%)
John McCain (R)................167,011	(49%)

Cook Partisan Voting Index: R+5

the home of Central Michigan University, the third largest public university in the state, which opened a medical school in 2013. The economy recently has been steady: Better than Detroit, but not as strong as Grand Rapids.

The 4th Congressional District of Michigan, geographically the state's second-largest, includes much of this territory north of Lansing and Grand Rapids and west of Flint and Saginaw. Much of its populace lives in rural areas, but redistricting has moved it closer to Flint and Lansing. It stretches north up the freeways, rarely venturing outside U.S. 131 to the west and Interstate 75 to the east. The rolling country around Houghton Lake was once lumber country and is now a retirement and resort area, with condominiums and knotty-pine cottages clustered around icy green lakes. This is historically Republican territory, having sent only one Democrat to Congress since it was created in 1912. It remains so today, but not overwhelmingly. Mitt Romney carried it with 53% of the vote in 2012, but Barack Obama led John McCain in 2008, 50%-49%.

John Moolenaar (R)

Republican John Moolenaar was elected in 2014 after winning a spirited three-way primary, with outspoken views on the economy. Conservative credentials and endorsements trumped cash in the contest. Moolenaar succeeded the retiring Dave Camp, who chaired the Ways and Means Committee. He got the incumbent's district, but not his gavel.

Born in Midland, Moolenaar earned his bachelor's in chemistry from Hope College, a liberal arts school in Holland Michigan. He got his master's in public administration from Harvard. He was a chemist and director of business development for MITECH+ and Dow Chemical, where he helped develop new product markets. In 2002, he was elected to the state House, and he was elected to the Senate in 2010. In the Senate, he chaired the Veterans, Military Affairs and Homeland Security Committee. A Democratic foe sought to recall Moolenaar in 2011 because he voted for a bill allowing taxation of public employee pensions. The effort failed when the petition did not attract enough signatures.

Camp's retirement led to a battle among three GOP primary contenders: Moolenaar, businessman Paul Mitchell, and software consultant Peter Konetchy. Mitchell vastly outspent his opponents, dumping $2 million of his own money—several times what Moolenaar and Konetchy had raised, combined—into his campaign to finance an aggressive TV ad blitz. He attacked Moolenaar as insufficiently conservative, accusing the state lawmaker in an ad of enabling the Affordable Care Act by voting to expand Medicaid. Moolenaar, who signed a pledge to repeal the health care law, had voted for an overall state health agency budget that included federal dollars for Medicaid expansion.

Moolenaar turned Mitchell's campaign cash advantage against him, saying in a GOP primary debate that "quite frankly, I don't think this seat is up for sale." He had key Republican endorsements, including those of Camp and former Sen. Rick Santorum of Pennsylvania.

Moolenaar also questioned Mitchell's conservative credentials, including his contribution to the 2006 campaign of Democratic Sen. Debbie Stabenow. Moolenaar won the nomination with 52% of the vote, to 36% for Mitchell and 11% for Holmes. He scored especially well in his base of Midland, where he got 67%.

Democrat John Holmes waged an uphill battle to turn the longtime Republican seat blue. Holmes said he did not want to repeal the health care law, which he argued was helping many people, including young adults who could remain on their parents' insurance policies. Instead, Holmes preferred to improve the law. But Moolenaar's more conservative views played far better in the GOP-friendly district. He won 57%-39%, and led in 14 of the 15 counties.

In the House, Moolenar was named vice chair of the Science, Space and Technology Subcommittee on Research and Technology. He also got seats on the Agriculture and Budget Committees. In an early sign that he would be a team player, he was one of five House Republicans named to the House-Senate conference committee that resolved differences on the annual budget resolution.

FIFTH DISTRICT

Dan Kildee (D)

Elected 2012, 2nd term; b. Aug. 11, 1958, Flint; Central MI U., B.S. 2011; Catholic; married (Jennifer); 3 children.

Elected Office: Flint MI Bd. of Ed., 1977-85; Genesee Cnty. Bd. of Comm., 1985-97; Genesee Cnty. treas., 1997-2009.

Professional Career: Youth specialist, Whaley Children's Ctr., 1976-85; Founder, Genesee Cnty. Land Bank; Co-founder & CEO, Ctr. for Comm. Progress, 2009-12.

DC Office: 227 CHOB, 20515, 202-225-3611; Website: dankildee. house.gov.

State Offices: Flint, 810-238-8627.

Committees: *Financial Services:* Monetary Policy & Trade; Task Force to Investigate Terrorism Financing.

Group Ratings

	ADA	ACLU	AFL-CIO	LCV	ITI	COC	HAFA	ACU	CFG	FRC
2014	75%	83%	–	97%	60%	43%	6%	4%	4%	0%
2013	85%	C	100%	96%	C	31%	C	8%	10%	C

National Journal Ratings

	2013 LIB	—	2013 CONS
Economic	78%	—	22%
Social	87%	—	7%
Foreign	75%	—	23%
Composite	81%	—	19%

Key Votes of the 113th Congress

1. Sandy storm spending	Y	5. Medical Marijuana	Y	9. Syrian Rebels Training	Y
2. Violence Against Women Act	Y	6. Farm Bill	N	10. Keystone pipeline	N
3. Guantanamo Bay Detainees	Y	7. Afghanistan Combat	Y	11. Immigration Exec. Action	N
4. Abortion 20-week ban	N	8. NSA Phone Data Collection	Y	12. Bipartisan budget deal	Y

Election Results

2014 general	Dan Kildee (D)	148,182	(67%)	$938,757
	Allen Hardwick (R)	69,222	(31%)	
	Hal Jones (Lib)	4,734	(2%)	
2014 primary	Dan Kildee (D)	unopposed		

Prior winning percentage: 2012 (65%)

Population		Race and Ethnicity		Income	
Total:	682,848	White	74.4%	Median income:	$39,662
Urban:	51.3%	Black	17.4%		*(394 of 435)*
Suburban:	37.4%	Latino	4.6%	Under $50,000	60.4%
Rural:	11.3%	Asian	0.8%	$50,000-$99,999:	27.6%
Land area:	2,737	Two races	2.3%	$100,000-$199,999:	10.3%
Pop/sq. mi.:	249.5	White Ethnic	32.1%	$200,000 or more:	1.7%
Born in state:	84.3%			Poverty Rate	21.4%
		Education			
Age Groups		H.S. grad or less:	45.4%	**Work**	
Under 18:	22.7%	Some college:	36.0%	White collar:	29.5%
18 to 34:	20.8%	College degree, 4 yr.:	11.4%	Blue collar:	46.4%
35 to 64:	40.1%	Post-grad study:	7.2%	Sales and service:	24.0%
Over 64:	16.4%			Govt. workers:	11.1%
		Military			
		Veterans/active duty:	9.1%		

East-Central Michigan: Flint, Bay City

The flat plains south of Saginaw Bay, the inlet of Lake Huron that separates Michigan's Thumb (people really call it that) from the mitten of the Lower Peninsula, was once one of America's top industrial areas. Some 130 years ago, it was the nation's pre-

Voter Turnout	
2013 Total Citizen 18+	523,994
2014 House Turnout	222,138
2014 Turnout as % CVAP	42.4%
2012 Turnout as % CVAP	64.4%

mier lumber country, with huge stands of virgin trees feeding 36 sawmills in Bay City. When the trees were gone, farmers took over, and the land was sown with beans and sugar beets. Then, a century ago, came the automobile. Flint, a small town on a minor branch of the Saginaw River, was the home base of W.C. Durant, the investor who merged several young auto firms to form General Motors in 1908. GM put its Chevrolet and Buick factories in Flint and its power steering facility in Saginaw, chosen because it was already a center of precision machinery manufacturing.

From 1910 through the 1950s, Flint grew lustily as it built Chevys and Buicks. U.S. Highway 23, which brushes along Flint's outskirts, passes through the east Kentucky coal fields and provided a direct artery for coal miners seeking a better life in the North, a migration memorialized by country music singer Dwight Yoakum's "Readin', Rightin', Rt. 23." Mountain folk from eastern Tennessee and farmers from the Black Belt of Alabama also found their way to Flint, and before long, Southern accents were common in an area settled by New England Yankees. Labor strife followed industrialization. In

2012 Presidential Vote		
Barack Obama (D)	205,804	(61%)
Mitt Romney (R)	129,896	(38%)
2008 Presidential Vote		
Barack Obama (D)	230,776	(63%)
John McCain (R)	129,513	(35%)
Cook Partisan Voting Index:	D+10	

January 1937, Flint was the scene of the great sit-down strike that began when workers noticed GM preparing to move the dies that were used to stamp cars out of its plant—a potential prelude to a move to the South—and ended with GM recognizing the United Auto Workers as the bargaining agent for its workers.

Economic disaster struck with the energy crisis of the 1970s. Imports, especially from Japan, that were higher quality and lower priced than American cars, took an increasing share of the market. In 1979, GM employed more than 70,000 workers in its Flint plants, a huge share of the labor force in a metropolitan area of 430,000 people. Eventually, GM closed 13 of its 15 factories, and by the late 2000s, the GM payroll had fallen below 12,000. In June 2009, the company filed for bankruptcy.

By 2010, over 40 percent of Flint households were in poverty, and many skilled workers had fled what *Forbes* magazine called one of "America's fastest-dying cities." Only two other U.S. cities—Cleveland and Detroit—lost more people in 2009. Michael Moore, the liberal filmmaker, has used his hometown of Flint as the locale for much of his work about rust-belt hardships. There have been some flickering signs of hope: Since General Motors emerged from bankruptcy in 2010, it has kept open a Flint engine plant and added a third shift at its truck assembly facility, which is the oldest GM factory in the nation. Other plants remained empty on nearby property. In April 2015, GM announced that its old Chevrolet plant, where Chevrolet Avenue crosses the Flint River, will be turned into an automotive research area with the local Kettering University. Local unemployment remained at 11.2 percent in February 2015, still painfully high but down from 27.2 percent in June 2009.

In April 2015, Gov. Rick Snyder announced the end of the 41-month "financial emergency" in Flint, and the restoration of authority to the mayor and city council. In the meantime, $30 million in official deficits had been eliminated, and new management systems had been put in place. Some restaurants and other businesses have taken advantage of city loan programs to open downtown, while industrial space has been turned into lofts. Allison Krusky, a researcher at the University of Michigan School of Public Health, found in a 2015 study about Flint that residents who maintained produce gardens at their residence were much more likely to maintain their property than those who kept their lot vacant or overgrown.

The 5th Congressional District includes Flint and surrounding Genesee County—which are about 60 percent of the district—Saginaw and eastern Saginaw County, Bay City and Bay County, rural Arenac and Iosco counties, and a strip of rural Tuscola County. Flint, evenly divided between the parties during the sit-down strikes, is now heavily Democratic, Saginaw and Bay City somewhat less so. The district overall is strongly Democratic, and is the only Democratic district in the state that is not located at least partly in Wayne or Oakland counties.

Dan Kildee (D)

Democrat Dan Kildee, elected in 2012, has followed in the footsteps of his uncle Dale Kildee, who retired after 36 years in the House: a quiet and usual reliable soldier for the team, who focuses chiefly on local issues.

The younger Kildee grew up in a close-knit neighborhood in Flint. There were six children in his family, and so many in the neighborhood—48 elementary school-aged kids lived on Kildee's West Genesee Street—that they formed their own football team, the Genesee Jets. He carried that athleticism into high school and became captain of the hockey team, but says he never really fit in with the jocks. "Some kids hang out at the gym or at the ballpark or at the pool, and I would every two years hang out at the campaign headquarters," he told *National Journal*. He worked on his uncle's campaigns for the state legislature and for Congress, distributing yard signs and doing other tasks.

After high school, Kildee enrolled at the University of Michigan's Flint campus and worked part-time at a treatment facility for emotionally disturbed children. That job became full-time, and Kildee dropped out of college, although he returned to Central Michigan University in 2007 to earn a bachelor's degree in administration. Kildee was elected to the Flint Board of Education as a college freshman. "I'd go to visit the schools and I'd quite literally get asked for a hall pass," he said. During his more than seven years on the board, he fought unsuccessfully for a ban on corporal punishment, which the state legislature outlawed soon after he left the post.

Sticking with local politics, Kildee served as a commissioner in Genesee County from 1985 to 1997 before becoming county treasurer and founding a local land bank. His method for tackling abandoned properties—getting rid of them—brought him national attention. Though he saw the idea as "a common-sense approach to urban planning in an age of decline," others viewed it as "a radically un-American idea that embraces defeat and limited horizons," according to a 2010 profile of Kildee in *Slate*. That year, he entered the Michigan governor's race but dropped out after less than a month, saying he wanted to avoid a fractious primary fight.

He stayed in the public policy realm as cofounder of the Center for Community Progress, a nonprofit organization that recommends policy solutions to cities and towns across the country. In May 2012, he took a leave of absence to run for the House seat and was instantly a strong contender, given his family name and his years of public service. Several prominent Democrats, including former Rep. James Barcia, considered a challenge, but Kildee won the primary unopposed. He had little trouble dispatching Republican former state Rep. Jim Slezak in the general election, 65%-31%.

In the House, Kildee got a seat on the Financial Services Committee. His first bill focused on cleaning up blight in Flint. He eventually got $100 million in federal funds for local demolition. He pushed for the renewal of extended unemployment benefits. With a bipartisan group of House members, he filed a resolution seeking to prevent any threat to the Great Lakes from a proposed Canadian nuclear waste site.

Kildee was reelected by a 67%-31% margin against political newcomer Allen Hardwick. In 2015, he became chairman of the Frontline program of the Democratic Congressional Campaign Committee, which assists vulnerable incumbents.

SIXTH DISTRICT

Fred Upton (R)

Elected 1986, 15th term; b. April 23, 1953, St. Joseph; U. of MI, B.A. 1975; Protestant; married (Amey); 2 children.

Professional Career: Project coord., U.S. Rep. David Stockman, 1975-80; Legis. affairs, O.M.B., 1981-83, dir., 1984-85.

DC Office: 2183 RHOB, 20515, 202-225-3761; Fax: 202-225-4986; Website: upton.house.gov.

State Offices: Kalamazoo, 269-385-0039; St. Joseph, 269-982-1986.

Committees: *Energy & Commerce* (Chmn: ex officio member of each subcommittee).

Group Ratings

	ADA	ACLU	AFL-CIO	LCV	ITI	COC	HAFA	ACU	CFG	FRC
2014	5%	5%	–	6%	100%	93%	46%	56%	39%	50%
2013	0%	C	24%	4%	C	92%	C	72%	64%	C

National Journal Ratings

	2013 LIB	—	2013 CONS
Economic	29%	—	70%
Social	38%	—	59%
Foreign	24%	—	68%
Composite	32%	—	68%

Key Votes of the 113th Congress

1. Sandy storm spending	N	5. Medical Marijuana	Y	9. Syrian Rebels Training	Y
2. Violence Against Women Act	Y	6. Farm Bill	Y	10. Keystone pipeline	Y
3. Guantanamo Bay Detainees	N	7. Afghanistan Combat	N	11. Immigration Exec. Action	Y
4. Abortion 20-week ban	Y	8. NSA Phone Data Collection	N	12. Bipartisan budget deal	Y

Election Results

2014 general	Fred Upton (R)	116,801	(56%)	$3,941,684	$634,086	$1,701,246
	Paul Clements (D)	84,391	(40%)	$793,362	$410,631	
	Erwin Haas (Lib)	5,530	(3%)			
2014 primary	Fred Upton (R)	37,731	(71%)			
	Jim Bussler (R)	15,283	(29%)			

Prior winning percentages: 2012 (55%), 2010 (62%), 2008 (59%), 2006 (61%), 2004 (65%), 2002 (69%), 2000 (68%), 1998 (70%), 1996 (68%), 1994 (73%), 1992 (62%), 1990 (58%), 1988 (71%), 1986 (62%)

Population		Race and Ethnicity		Income	
Total:	709,976	White	81.8%	Median income:	$46,738
Urban:	36.1%	Black	8.5%		(287 of 435)
Suburban:	34.2%	Latino	5.5%	Under $50,000	52.8%
Rural:	29.6%	Asian	1.3%	$50,000-$99,999:	31.7%
Land area:	3,193	Two races	2.4%	$100,000-$199,999:	13.3%
Pop/sq. mi.:	222.3	White Ethnic	27.4%	$200,000 or more:	2.2%
Born in state:	70.2%			Poverty Rate	16.8%
		Education			
Age Groups		H.S. grad or less:	41.4%	**Work**	
Under 18:	23.2%	Some college:	32.9%	White collar:	33.2%
18 to 34:	22.7%	College degree, 4 yr.:	15.8%	Blue collar:	41.0%
35 to 64:	39.0%	Post-grad study:	9.8%	Sales and service:	25.8%
Over 64:	15.1%				
		Military		Govt. workers:	10.5%
		Veterans/active duty:	8.8%		

Southwest Michigan: Kalamazoo

The southwest corner of Michigan was settled by New England Yankees and Upstate New Yorkers in the 1830s and 1840s. They built small towns with schools, churches and colleges; supported temperance; and opposed capital punishment. And in 1854, they joined the newly formed Republican Party.

Voter Turnout	
2013 Total Citizen 18+	528,095
2014 House Turnout	208,976
2014 Turnout as % CVAP	39.6%
2012 Turnout as % CVAP	61.9%

There are towns in southwest Michigan that still recall proudly their past as termini of the Underground Railroad, and there are black families whose ancestors made their way north out of slavery to freedom; Cass County has a sizable rural black population dating back to those days.

Later, big industries transformed some of the small towns into significant cities. Kalamazoo, started by Dutch Americans who introduced celery to this country, became the home of Upjohn pharmaceuticals, which is now part of Pfizer. Predominantly black and struggling Benton Harbor and predominantly white and prosperous St. Joseph sit just across from each other where the St. Joseph River empties into Lake Michigan. In April 2015, a columnist for the local newspaper described the contrasts in their school systems as a "sad tale of educational apartheid."

Benton Harbor has been best known as the headquarters for Whirlpool. But Whirlpool closed its plant in 2010, and many other local companies and famous industrial names such as Gibson Guitars have moved out of the area, taking their thousands of jobs. Some of their downtown properties have become a championship golf course. Kalamazoo has had some success keeping its young people in school with the Kalamazoo Promise program, funded by anonymous philanthropists, that pays college tuition for all public high school students who graduate; it has stabi-

2012 Presidential Vote		
Mitt Romney (R)	163,306	(50%)
Barack Obama (D)	158,963	(49%)
2008 Presidential Vote		
Barack Obama (D)	184,186	(53%)
John McCain (R)	156,835	(45%)
Cook Partisan Voting Index: R+1		

lized enrollment and racial balance and has resulted in higher test scores. The recession hit this area hard, with damages compounded by an oil spill that polluted the Kalamazoo River. Michigan's southwest corner is also heavily influenced by Chicago, which is much closer than is Detroit; people here watch Chicago television and root for the Cubs or White Sox rather than the Detroit Tigers.

The 6th Congressional District occupies the southwest corner of Michigan, with Kalamazoo and Benton Harbor-St. Joseph its two major urban areas. It takes in five counties and most of a sixth. The counties in the far southwest of the state—Cass, Berrien, and Van Buren—are part of the so-called "cabinet counties," named, respectively, for Andrew Jackson's secretary of War, attorney general, and vice president.

The 6th was for many years arch-Republican territory; the district and its predecessors have sent only three Democrats to Congress since the 1890s. Its tradition was to elect conservative congressmen who deplored federal spending and welfare-state measures: New Deal opponent Clare Hoffman (1935-63), Nixon defender Edward Hutchinson (1963-77), and Reagan-era Office of Management and Budget Director David Stockman (1977-81). But over the past two decades, while continuing with Republican representation, the district, in particular Kalamazoo, has trended toward the Democrats, and today it is nearly evenly divided between the two parties.

Fred Upton (R)

Fred Upton, an affable Republican first elected in 1986, chairs the House Energy and Commerce Committee. He has an unusually moderate voting record for a Republican committee chairman, but he offsets his centrism by regularly aligning with the interests of business against what he considers excessive government regulation.

The grandson of one of the founders of Whirlpool, Upton grew up in St. Joseph. He attended the University of Michigan and worked for David Stockman, first on Stockman's congressional staff, then at the White House in the Office of Management and Budget from 1981 to 1985. Upton returned home and ran in the 1986 Republican primary against Rep.

Mark Siljander, a conservative and evangelical Christian, and won 55%-45%, going on to win the seat handily in the general election.

Upton's family fortune puts him in the upper echelon among members of Congress in wealth, but he has a regular-guy image. He is well known for insisting that everyone, from reporters to staffers to fellow lawmakers, call him "Fred," and says he personally reads and signs all of his legislative mail. He is a devout Chicago Cubs fan, rarely missing an Opening Day at Wrigley Field, and has a bat from Cubs slugger Sammy Sosa in his office. His niece, Kate Upton, is a supermodel who graced the covers of *Sports Illustrated*'s 2012 and 2013 swimsuit issues. After the initial issue appeared, Upton said colleagues jokingly asked him, "Fred, are you adopted?"

Early in his House career, Upton was known for his amendments to force across-the-board cuts in appropriations. As a leader of the moderate Republicans' Tuesday Group, he also was outspoken about the need to find middle ground. He freely exercised his independence when his party controlled the House from 1995 to 2006, and he occasionally caused heartburn for GOP leaders. He sought, with limited success, to reduce the tax cuts of the Bush era. He backed increases in the minimum wage, increased funding for Amtrak, and Democratic measures to expand medical insurance for poor children. He also voted with Democrats to preserve the Endangered Species Act.

On Energy and Commerce, Upton was more of a party regular when he chaired the Telecommunications Subcommittee for six years. He supported a bill to allow regional telephone companies to provide broadband service more easily, and he pushed for larger fines against broadcasters for indecent programming. President George W. Bush signed his bill to create a "safe playground for kids" on the Internet, free of pornography and other inappropriate material.

Upton sought and was awarded the Energy and Commerce gavel after the 2010 election despite pleas from GOP Rep. Joe Barton of Texas to waive term limits so he could regain the job. But Barton had opposed incoming Speaker John Boehner in the race for Republican leader in 2006, and his public apology to BP during the June 2010 hearings on the massive oil spill in the Gulf of Mexico made him a political liability. Two less-senior members of the committee, Cliff Stearns of Florida and John Shimkus of Illinois, also ran for the post in the hope that Upton would be rejected as too moderate. Upton launched an aggressive bid for the chairmanship, contributing thousands of dollars to Republican challengers. The contest heated up when conservative talk radio host Rush Limbaugh came out against Upton, and pundit Glenn Beck called him "all socialist." Nevertheless, the GOP Steering Committee, heavily influenced by fellow Midwesterner Boehner, chose Upton. Boehner has been consistent in complying with the GOP rule on six-year term limits for chairmen.

In his voting patterns, Upton became more conservative as he was courting Republican leaders for the chairmanship in 2010. That year, his American Conservative Union rating was 92. Since then, he has returned to the range of his lifetime rating of 73.

Taking the helm of Energy and Commerce in 2011, he was under pressure to show fellow Republicans that he was more than the squishy moderate that had been emblematic of his career. He confidently predicted that "a significant number of Democrats" would join his party's efforts to overturn President Barack Obama's 2010 health care law, which he dismissed as "a massive new government program that does real and lasting damage to our current system and all those covered under it." It turned out, though, that the repeated repeal votes never drew more than a handful of Democrats in support.

Then in the fall of 2013, Upton successfully got through the House a bill to allow policyholders to keep their health insurance for a year even if it failed to meet the standards set out in the law. Upton's bill passed 261-157 over the objections of Obama and with the help of 39 Democrats, many of whom were worried about being punished at the ballot box for the president's broken promise that people who liked their policies could keep them. Upton's legislation never moved in the Democratically controlled Senate.

Many of Upton's other initiatives in his first four years as chairman got through the House on largely party-line votes and were left for dead in the Senate. They included legislation to overturn the Environmental Protection Agency's authority to regulate greenhouse gas emissions blamed for global warming. Another bill overturned Federal Communications Commission's net neutrality rules designed to prevent Internet providers from creating tiered pricing structures. He and other Republicans, with support from the cable television industry, said net neutrality rules are unnecessary and were enacted without the proper authority. On the investigative front, his panel dug into the Obama administration's loan guarantees to the failed solar company Solyndra Corp., which became a prominent GOP campaign issue in 2012.

Upton's efforts delighted fellow Republicans, who once had derided him as "Red Fred" for his bipartisan tendencies. But the Sierra Club and other environmental groups began running ads against him at home. And some Michiganders wondered what had happened to the politician who had championed a bill to ban incandescent light bulbs as part of the 2007 energy bill, and then voted four years later to undo the measure. "The old Upton who five, six, eight years ago would have been more moderate on votes and parted company with his party, that old Upton is gone," Bill Ballenger, editor of the newsletter *Inside Michigan Politics* told *The Chicago Tribune*.

With Republicans in control of the Senate in 2015, Upton expressed hope that some of his efforts to block federal environmental regulations could at least clear Congress, if not get signed into law. He released an outline of potential energy legislation that, while containing few specifics, appeared to be geared toward pragmatism. His agenda promised to address "permitting challenges" that thwart development of infrastructure to modernize electricity systems and make them more secure, as well as develop an energy workforce that could address "21st century challenges" and include more minority and low-income workers, along with provisions on energy exports and energy efficiency. He worked with Democratic Rep. Diana DeGette to accelerate innovative medical treatments and devices. In July 2015, the House passed their 21st Century Cures Act on a 344-77 vote.

Upton has been an election target from both the left and right. In 2010, former state Rep. Jack Hoogendyk ran against him in the GOP primary, criticizing Upton for voting for the $787 billion bailout of the financial industry and for the Republicans' Medicare prescription drug bill in 2003. Upton vastly outspent Hoogendyk and won 57%-43%, not a robust outcome for a longtime incumbent. He went on to win 62%-34% in the general election.

Hoogendyk came back for another challenge in 2012. But Upton took him more seriously this time, conducting outreach to tea party groups and winning with ease, 67%-33%. His Democratic opponent that year was Mike O'Brien, a former Marine and office furniture company manager making his first run for elective office. He blasted Upton's support of Budget Committee Chairman Paul Ryan's spending plan. Though he was lauded for running a good campaign, the $294,000 that O'Brien raised was no match for Upton's $4.7 million, contributions that are readily available to the Energy and Commerce chairman. Upton won, 55%-43%, the smallest margin in his career. He took every county, though the race in Kalamazoo County, the district's largest, was a virtual tie.

In 2014, Upton drew a better-funded Democratic challenger—Paul Clements, a Western Michigan University political scientist who decided to run after becoming dismayed by Upton's reversal on climate change. Clements received help from Harvard law professor Lawrence Lessig's Mayday political action committee, which spent more than $2 million to portray Upton as a captive of oil and drug companies. Lessig cultivated and received extensive media attention, but it wasn't clear how much influence he had on voters. Upton denied the allegations from Lessig, and responded that he continued to work on a bipartisan basis to steer clear of the Washington dysfunction. One week before the election, a poll showed Clements within the margin of error, but Upton spent $3.9 million to $800,000 for Clements and won with 56%.

His term as Energy and Commerce chair ends in 2016, and there has been speculation Upton could retire. Within the Michigan delegation, recent term-limited committee chairmen have decided to retire. On the other hand, Barton of Texas is among several senior House Republicans who have maintained a post-chairmanship career. An open seat in this district likely would be competitive, and could prompt the fierce challenges in each party that recently have been lodged against Upton.

SEVENTH DISTRICT

Tim Walberg (R)

Elected 2010, 4th term; b. April 12, 1951, Chicago, IL; Fort Wayne Bible Col., B.S. 1975, Wheaton Col., M.A. 1978; Christian; married (Sue); 3 children.

Elected Office: MI House, 1983-98; U.S. House, 2007-09.

Professional Career: Minister, 1973-82; Pres., Warren Reuther Ctr., 1999-2000; Div. mgr., Moody Bible Inst., 2000-05.

DC Office: 2436 RHOB, 20515, 202-225-6276; Fax: 202-225-6281; Website: walberg.house.gov.

State Offices: Jackson, 517-780-9075.

Committees: *Education & the Workforce:* Health, Employment, Labor, & Pensions; Workforce Protections (Chmn). *Oversight & Gov't Reform:* Gov't Operations; Health Care, Benefits, & Administrative Rules (VChmn).

Group Ratings

	ADA	ACLU	AFL-CIO	LCV	ITI	COC	HAFA	ACU	CFG	FRC
2014	0%	0%	–	0%	100%	93%	63%	88%	66%	100%
2013	0%	C	10%	7%	C	85%	C	84%	79%	C

National Journal Ratings

	2013 LIB	—	2013 CONS
Economic	23%	—	77%
Social	0%	—	87%
Foreign	5%	—	86%
Composite	13%	—	87%

Key Votes of the 113th Congress

1. Sandy storm spending	N	5. Medical Marijuana	N	9. Syrian Rebels Training	Y
2. Violence Against Women Act	N	6. Farm Bill	Y	10. Keystone pipeline	Y
3. Guantanamo Bay Detainees	N	7. Afghanistan Combat	N	11. Immigration Exec. Action	Y
4. Abortion 20-week ban	Y	8. NSA Phone Data Collection	N	12. Bipartisan budget deal	Y

Election Results

2014 general	Tim Walberg (R)	119,564	(54%)	$1,784,291	$21,412	
	Pam Byrnes (D)	92,083	(41%)	$1,372,605	$7,010	$4,300
	Ken Procter (Lib)	4,530	(2%)			
	David Swartout (I)	4,369	(2%)	$4,892		
2014 primary	Tim Walberg (R)	38,046	(79%)			
	Douglas Radcliffe North (R)	9,934	(21%)			

Prior winning percentages: 2012 (53%), 2010 (50%), 2006 (50%)

Population		Race and Ethnicity		Income	
Total:	703,537	White	89.0%	Median income:	$50,462
Urban:	30.9%	Black	4.0%		*(233 of 435)*
Suburban:	39.5%	Latino	4.0%	Under $50,000	49.6%
Rural:	29.6%	Asian	0.8%	$50,000-$99,999:	32.1%
Land area:	3,167	Two races	1.8%	$100,000-$199,999:	15.6%
Pop/sq. mi.:	222.1	White Ethnic	33.6%	$200,000 or more:	2.7%
Born in state:	74.9%			Poverty Rate	14.6%
		Education			
Age Groups		H.S. grad or less:	42.0%	**Work**	
Under 18:	22.8%	Some college:	34.8%	White collar:	30.7%
18 to 34:	20.3%	College degree, 4 yr.:	14.9%	Blue collar:	42.2%
35 to 64:	41.5%	Post-grad study:	8.3%	Sales and service:	27.1%
Over 64:	15.4%			Govt. workers:	12.7%
		Military			
		Veterans/active duty:	8.8%		

Southern Michigan: Jackson, Monroe

The small cities and towns nestled in and around southern Michigan's Irish Hills, near where the major glaciers stopped their southward crawl in the last ice age, have been incubators of innovation since they were settled by Yankees from New England 150 years ago. Hillsdale, a picture book old

town south of Jackson, is home to Hillsdale College, founded about the same time as the Republican Party, by likeminded people. It has been proudly admitting African Americans and women since the 1850s while refusing all forms of federal aid.

Southern Michigan mostly rejected New Deal tinkering and was hostile to the United Auto Workers union. But the people here were receptive to moral claims made by later 20th-century reformers challenging racial segregation, the Vietnam War, and the Watergate cover-up. In the past 100 years, the congressional district for the region has tended to elect Democrats only in wave years: in 1912, 1932, 1964, and 2008.

Jackson, an old industrial town named for a founder of the Democratic Party and site of Michigan's first prison, is one of five towns that claim to have been the birthplace of the Republican Party in 1854. Today, Jackson is a city in decline. It ranked 324th out of 381 cities in economic health in 2015, according to *Policom*. It has lost 2,900 residents since 2000—nearly 8% of its total population—and its population is down almost 40% from its peak in 1930.

The district has had some positive developments. General Motors announced in April 2015 that it planned to spend $520 million at its Lansing Delta Township factory for tooling and equipment of future new vehicle programs. That assembly plant already had

2012 Presidential Vote
Mitt Romney (R)..............169,310 (51%)
Barack Obama (D) 158,963 (48%)

2008 Presidential Vote
Barack Obama (D) 177,638 (51%)
John McCain (R)...............165,747 (47%)

Cook Partisan Voting Index: R+3

3,500 workers. Another piece of good news was the decision by Clemens Food Group to build a $255 million pork processing plant in Branch County, which will employ more than 800. In May 2015, the federal Nuclear Regulatory Commission approved a construction license for a nuclear reactor near Monroe, though prospects were unclear whether the facility would be built.

The 7th Congressional District takes in all of six counties in southern Michigan plus parts of another. The district includes three of the so-called "cabinet counties," named for members of President Andrew Jackson's administration (Jackson presided over Michigan's admission to the Union): Branch County, named for Jackson's secretary of the Navy; Eaton County, for his first secretary of War; and Jackson County, for the president himself. The city of Jackson votes Democratic, as do the parts of Lansing in Eaton County. But the district also includes the outer townships of Washtenaw County, which lean Republican. The district overall leans Republican, though not overwhelmingly so; Mitt Romney won here 51%-48% in 2012.

Tim Walberg (R)

Republican Tim Walberg is an ardent social and fiscal conservative who was first elected in 2006. He lost narrowly two years later to Democrat Mark Schauer and then reclaimed the seat in 2010 in a continuing series of close elections. For now, Walberg has shown that he can rely on his conservative base.

Walberg was born in Chicago, growing up on the city's South Side. He worked in a steel mill to get through college and got his bachelor's degree from Fort Wayne Bible College and a master's from Wheaton College. He was a minister for 10 years before running for office. In 1982, he won a seat in the Michigan House by beating a moderate GOP incumbent. In his 16 years as a state legislator, Walberg had a reputation as a tireless advocate for gun rights, an opponent of abortion rights, and a foe of reckless government spending. He belonged to a group dubbed the "No" caucus for its unflinching opposition to tax hikes and increased spending. Term limits put an end to his tenure, and from 1998 to 2005, he was president of a conservative education foundation and a division manager for the Moody Bible Institute of Chicago.

Walberg made a bid for the 7th District seat in 2004 when Republican Rep. Nick Smith retired after 12 years. He came in third in a GOP primary field crowded with other conservatives; moderate Joe Schwarz won the primary with 28 percent of the vote and went on to win the general election. Two years later, Walberg tried again. In a primary challenge reminiscent of 2010's tea party fueled campaigns, he ran on a record of having never once voted for a tax increase in the legislature. The well-funded anti-tax Club for Growth took notice and poured $500,000 into television ads attacking Schwarz. The national GOP backed the incumbent, and Schwarz had a spending advantage of 2-to-1. Walberg nevertheless prevailed 53%-47%, and went on to defeat a weak Democratic opponent, 50%-46%. He became a prime target for Democrats in 2008.

That year, Democrats nominated Schauer, the Michigan Senate's minority leader and a former community organizer. With unemployment rising, Schauer focused on the economy and secured an endorsement from Republican Schwarz. Schauer benefited from the favorable national environment for Democrats and the enthusiasm generated by Barack Obama's campaign for president. The Club for Growth again spent heavily for Walberg, but Schauer had strong union support and won narrowly, 49%-46%.

Walberg came back for a rematch in 2010 in a much more favorable climate for his party. In August, he won a three-way Republican primary with 57% of the vote. In the general election, Walberg and his allies attacked Schauer for his vote for Obama's $787 billion economic stimulus, saying that he was part of the problem of deficit spending in Washington. Schauer and his backers portrayed Walberg as too far right for the district, highlighting his support for privatizing Social Security. They also spotlighted a September radio interview in which Walberg said he didn't know whether Obama is an American citizen. "We don't have enough information about this president," he said. By day's end, he reversed course and acknowledged that Obama is "certainly an American citizen." Schauer outspent Walberg, $3.3 million to $1.6 million, and outside groups and national parties showered more than $7 million on the race. Walberg won the seat back, 50%-45%.

In the House, Walberg has had one of the most conservative voting records among the Michigan delegation's Republicans. His amendment proposing to cut National Endowment for the Arts funding by more than $20 million narrowly passed the House in 2011 but went nowhere in the Democratic-controlled Senate. He introduced a resolution expressing support for prayer at school board meetings. On the Oversight and Government Reform Committee, Walberg expressed the view of many conservative activists that the botched "Operation Fast and Furious" operation intending to trace guns actually was designed to take away gun owners' rights.

As chairman of the Education and the Workforce's Subcommittee on Workforce Protections, Walberg joined panel chairman John Kline of Minnesota in arguing that the Obama administration's proposal giving home-care workers minimum wage and overtime protections would result in reduced hours for workers and higher costs for taxpayers. He later helped block a Labor Department proposal to ban youths younger than 16 from working on family farms. At a June 2014 hearing of his subcommittee, Walberg voiced concern that the Equal Employment Opportunity Commission had been overstepping its authority. In September 2014, the House passed Walberg's Senior Executive Service Accountability Act, which makes it easier for federal agencies to suspend or fire their top managers, for sufficient cause.

Schauer declined a rematch in 2012 after Michigan's GOP redistricters moved his Battle Creek home into the 3rd District. In the GOP primary, Walberg easily beat former police officer Dan Davis, setting up a general election matchup against Democratic attorney Kurt Haskell. Walberg refused to debate Haskell, citing Haskell's claim that the federal government was involved in supplying a faulty explosive to the so-called "underwear bomber" who tried to set off a bomb aboard a Detroit-bound airplane in 2009. Despite raising $1.5 million to Haskell's $101,000, Walberg won with just 54% of the vote. In Republican-leaning 2014, against Democrat Pam Byrnes who spent $1.4 million but had little outside assistance, Walberg again got 53% of the vote. The pattern indicates that this remains a swing district, with a slight Republican lean.

EIGHTH DISTRICT

Mike Bishop (R)

Elected 2014, 1st term; b. March 18, 1967, Almont; U. of MI, B.A. 1989, Detroit Col., J.D. 1993; Congregationalist; married (Cristina); 3 children.

Elected Office: MI House, 1999-2003; MI Senate, 2003-11, maj. ldr., 2007-11.

Professional Career: Practicing atty.; Chief legal officer, Int'l Bancard Corp.; Instructor, Thomas M. Cooley Law Schl.

DC Office: 428 CHOB, 20515, 202-225-4872; Fax: 202-225-5820; Website: mikebishop.house.gov.

State Offices: Brighton, 810-227-8600.

Committees: *Education & the Workforce:* Early Childhood, Elementary, & Secondary Education; Workforce Protections. *Judiciary:* Crime, Terrorism, Homeland Security, & Investigations; Regulatory Reform, Commercial & Antitrust Law

Election Results

2014 general	Mike Bishop (R)	132,739	(55%)	$1,015,365	$7,582
	Eric Schertzing (D)	102,269	(42%)	$503,638	
2014 primary	Mike Bishop (R)	35,422	(60%)		
	Tom McMillin (R)	23,358	(40%)		

Population		Race and Ethnicity		Income	
Total:	713,867	White	83.4%	Median income:	$61,456
Urban:	20.2%	Black	5.5%		*(106 of 435)*
Suburban:	77.6%	Latino	4.6%	Under $50,000	41.0%
Rural:	2.2%	Asian	3.7%	$50,000-$99,999:	31.6%
Land area:	1,475	Two races	2.5%	$100,000-$199,999:	21.8%
Pop/sq. mi.:	483.9	White Ethnic	38.8%	$200,000 or more:	5.6%
Born in state:	75.9%			Poverty Rate	12.1%
		Education			
Age Groups		H.S. grad or less:	27.8%	**Work**	
Under 18:	22.4%	Some college:	33.6%	White collar:	42.2%
18 to 34:	24.0%	College degree, 4 yr.:	22.7%	Blue collar:	41.0%
35 to 64:	40.6%	Post-grad study:	15.8%	Sales and service:	16.8%
Over 64:	13.0%				
		Military		Govt. workers:	13.4%
		Veterans/active duty:	7.2%		

Central Michigan: Detroit Exurbs, Lansing

Lansing is Michigan's state capital, chosen in 1847 because of its geographic position halfway between Lake Huron and Lake Michigan—and away from the border with Canada and the threat of invasion by British forces. The only drawback was fewer days with sunshine than anywhere else in the state. But

Voter Turnout	
2013 Total Citizen 18+	531,948
2014 House Turnout	243,125
2014 Turnout as % CVAP	45.7%
2012 Turnout as % CVAP	68.5%

it is a tidy and pleasant city with more than its share of amenities. It has a beautifully restored Capitol, a fine state history museum, and is neighbor to Michigan State University in East Lansing, founded in 1855 as America's first land grant college.

Its Oldsmobile plant stimulated growth in the first half of the 20th century, and state government did the same in the second half. GM closed its Olds line and two other Lansing plants in 2004, but two highly efficient GM assembly plants have been constructed in the Lansing area. The Oldsmobile name also remains alive at two local museums, but the baseball stadium where the Lansing Lugnuts play, formerly Oldsmobile Park, has been renamed the Cooley Law School Stadium. The Lansing area voted Republican up through the 1960s, but as public employee unions have grown in membership and strength, Lansing, like other state capitals, has become heavily Democratic, as is East Lansing. Unlike other state capitals, the population has been slowly declining, down 13% from its 1970s peak. In a May 2015 referendum, East Lansing voters approved the legalization of marijuana—for the possession, use or transfer of up to one ounce for people over 21 on private property.

Just east of Lansing's Ingham County is quite another part of Michigan, Livingston County. (Most of the counties in these parts

2012 Presidential Vote		
Mitt Romney (R)................183,510	(51%)
Barack Obama (D) 172,131	(48%)
2008 Presidential Vote		
Barack Obama (D) 195,798	(52%)
John McCain (R)................174,506	(46%)
Cook Partisan Voting Index: R+2		

were named for members of President Andrew Jackson's Cabinet: Livingston was secretary of State and Ingham secretary of the Treasury.) Forty years ago, Livingston County was mostly rural, known mainly for its many lakes. But over the years, thousands of Detroit area commuters have driven out Interstate 96 to Brighton, Howell and other Livingston townships. Subdivisions, schools and shopping malls sprouted up. (The community of Hell, Mich. is located here, too; the average high temperature in the area is below 32 degrees Fahrenheit in January, so one assumes it freezes over regularly.) Most of these people are conservatives, happy to leave the urban problems of Detroit behind, unhappy about high taxes, and hewing to traditional religious faiths. They have made Livingston one of Michigan's fastest-growing counties—its population rose 59% from 1990 to 2013—and one of its most Republican.

The 8th Congressional District of Michigan includes all of Ingham and Livingston counties. With the two counties more-or-less canceling each other out politically (combined they gave President Barack Obama about 52% of the vote in 2012), the tie-breaker in the district is in northern Oakland County, in places like Republican-leaning Rochester and Rochester Hills, and farther out in Springfield and Oxford. The Oakland County portion of the district has about as many residents as Ingham County and went for Republican John McCain by 10 percentage points in 2008. The district leans Republican overall, but not dramatically so.

Mike Bishop (R)

Republican Mike Bishop, elected in 2014, was the party establishment favorite to succeed retiring GOP Rep. Mike Rogers. He got the nod over a tea party challenger in the primary, and had a relatively easy time against his Democrat opponent.

Bishop, a life-long resident of Oakland County, got his bachelor's degree at the University of Michigan and his law degree from Michigan State. He had his own Oakland County law firm. A licensed real estate broker, he also worked as chief legal officer for International Bancard and as an adjunct professor at Thomas M. Cooley Law School.

Bishop was elected to the Michigan House in 1998, and served four years there before he was elected to the state Senate in 2002, filling a seat previously held by his father, Donald Bishop, and rising to majority leader. As a state senator, Bishop sponsored legislation to create the Michigan Child Protection Registry to shield children from receiving pornography, tobacco and other unsuitable materials. He also authored the Michigan Identify Theft Protection Act, which established identity theft as a felony. Term limited in 2010, he ran for and lost the Republican nomination for attorney general that year.

In the abbreviated campaign following the retirement announcement by Rogers, Bishop presented himself as the classic conservative option, pledging to secure the border, promote a strong military and reform Social Security. He describes himself as an avid fisherman and hunter, strongly supporting gun rights. He was challenged by state Rep. Tom McMillin, who was a more active social conservative and known for his outspoken opposition to gay rights as well as for graphic images of late-term abortions in his campaign literature.

Bishop became the preferred candidate of the GOP establishment, and quickly won the endorsement of Rogers. "I'm here supporting Mike Bishop because I think he will not embarrass this district," Rogers said succinctly. Speaker John Boehner, a friend of Rogers, gave Bishop a pre-primary contribution. Bishop won the primary 60%-40%.

In the general election, Democratic nominee Eric Schertzing, the treasurer of Ingham County, faced an uphill battle for the seat, especially after the Democratic Congressional Campaign Committee in early October canceled ads that it had planned to run on his behalf. Schertzing criticized his opponent for participating in two government shutdowns in Michigan while he served in the Senate, and for comments about not supporting the federal bailout of the auto industry. Bishop outspent Schertzing 2-to-1, and was elected, 55%-42%.

Bishop was held to 35% of the vote in Ingham, but he took 65% in Livingston and 67% in his base of Oakland.

In the House, Bishop got seats on the Judiciary Committee, plus Education and the Workforce, where he discussed the need to reduce the debt on student loans and to loosen restrictions on local government in the No Child Left Behind Act. He was a freshman representative on the Boehner-controlled Republican Steering Committee, which makes committee assignments.

NINTH DISTRICT

Sander Levin (D)

Elected 1982, 17th term; b. Sept. 6, 1931, Detroit; U. of Chicago, B.A. 1952, Columbia U., M.A. 1954, Harvard U., LL.B. 1957; Jewish; married (Pamela Cole); 4 children.

Elected Office: Oakland Bd. of Supervisors, 1961-64; MI Senate, 1965-70, min. ldr., 1969-70.

Professional Career: Practicing atty., 1957-64, 1970-76; Fellow, Harvard JFK Schl. of Govt., 1975; Asst. admin., U.S. Agency for Intl. Devel., 1977-81.

DC Office: 1236 LHOB, 20515, 888-810-3880; Fax: 202-226-1033; Website: levin.house.gov.

State Offices: Roseville, 586-498-7122.

Committees: *Ways & Means* (RMM). *Joint Committee on Taxation.*

Group Ratings

	ADA	ACLU	AFL-CIO	LCV	ITI	COC	HAFA	ACU	CFG	FRC
2014	90%	72%	–	97%	60%	43%	16%	12%	11%	25%
2013	80%	C	100%	96%	C	31%	C	12%	17%	C

National Journal Ratings

	2013 LIB	—	2013 CONS
Economic	80%	—	19%
Social	69%	—	28%
Foreign	71%	—	27%
Composite	74%	—	26%

Key Votes of the 113th Congress

1. Sandy storm spending	Y	5. Medical Marijuana	N
2. Violence Against Women Act	Y	6. Farm Bill	N
3. Guantanamo Bay Detainees	Y	7. Afghanistan Combat	Y
4. Abortion 20-week ban	N	8. NSA Phone Data Collection	N

9. Syrian Rebels Training	Y
10. Keystone pipeline	N
11. Immigration Exec. Action	N
12. Bipartisan budget deal	N

Election Results

2014 general	Sander Levin (D)	136,342	(60%)	$1,491,687	$2,529
	George Brikho (R)	81,470	(36%)	$42,050	
	Gregory Creswell (Lib)	4,792	(2%)		
2014 primary	Sander Levin (D)	unopposed			

Prior winning percentages: 2012 (62%), 2010 (61%), 2008 (72%), 2006 (70%), 2004 (69%), 2002 (68%), 2000 (64%), 1998 (56%), 1996 (57%), 1994 (52%), 1992 (53%), 1990 (70%), 1988 (70%), 1986 (76%), 1984 (100%), 1982 (67%)

Population		Race and Ethnicity		Income	
Total:	713,212	White	81.1%	Median income:	$51,154
Urban:	48.6%	Black	10.9%		*(217 of 435)*
Suburban:	51.4%	Asian	3.7%	Under $50,000	48.9%
Rural:	0.0%	Latino	1.6%	$50,000-$99,999:	31.2%
Land area:	196	Two races	1.9%	$100,000-$199,999:	16.5%
Pop/sq. mi.:	3,632.0	White Ethnic	45.8%	$200,000 or more:	3.5%
Born in state:	76.6%			Poverty Rate	14.8%
		Education			
Age Groups		H.S. grad or less:	39.7%	**Work**	
Under 18:	21.2%	Some college:	31.4%	White collar:	36.4%
18 to 34:	22.6%	College degree, 4 yr.:	17.8%	Blue collar:	43.9%
35 to 64:	40.5%	Post-grad study:	11.0%	Sales and service:	19.7%
Over 64:	15.7%				
		Military		Govt. workers:	8.6%
		Veterans/active duty:	6.9%		

Northern Detroit Suburbs: Southern Macomb, Eastern Oakland

The flat expanse of land just north of Eight Mile Road, Detroit's northern city limit, was mostly vacant in the years just after World War II. A string of suburbs in Oakland County ran along Woodward Avenue from the Detroit city limits to the National Shrine of the Little Flower Catholic Church in

Voter Turnout	
2013 Total Citizen 18+	530,672
2014 House Turnout	225,757
2014 Turnout as % CVAP	42.5%
2012 Turnout as % CVAP	64.8%

Royal Oak, where Father Charles Coughlin in the 1930s made his radio broadcasts opposing Franklin D. Roosevelt and denouncing bankers and Jews. In the 1950s and 1960s, Woodward was one of America's greatest cruising highways, where teenagers drove big Detroit cars up and down the eight lanes and where the lights were timed at 42 miles per hour. (Since 1994, the Woodward Dream Cruise of old cars has commemorated that era with a celebration drawing more than 1 million spectators.) To the east, in Macomb County, was some industrial development along rail lines, but this was mostly empty land, too.

Then Polish Americans began migrating out Van Dyke Avenue from Hamtramck to Warren. Italian Americans headed out Gratiot Avenue from Detroit's east side to Roseville and Clinton Township. Belgian

2012 Presidential Vote		
Barack Obama (D) 199,625	(57%)
Mitt Romney (R)...............146,185	(42%)
2008 Presidential Vote		
Barack Obama (D) 213,968	(58%)
John McCain (R)...............148,234	(40%)
Cook Partisan Voting Index: D+6		

Americans from the Mack corridor moved out farther to St. Clair Shores. Today, these areas are well-settled suburbs, long since built up; a few neighborhoods are edging toward seediness, while many others are continually renovated. Today, half of metro Detroit's population is north of Eight Mile, as African Americans have joined whites in moving to the suburbs. In 2013, 14% of Oakland County residents and 11% of Macomb County residents were black. Freddie Kennedy, who moved to Macomb County a few years earlier, summed up his reasons for *The Detroit News*: "Everything's better in Warren. You call the police, and they respond."

The 9th Congressional District covers this suburban territory, with about two-thirds of its population in Macomb County. On the Oakland County side are Royal Oak and Ferndale, which have been economically revitalized, attracting singles and gays as well as traditional families. The Macomb side includes the more Democratic neighborhoods in the southern part of the county: Warren and much of Sterling Heights, site of the General Motors Technical Center, a big Chrysler plant, and the M-1 tank plant, which helps make metro Detroit a major defense manufacturer. Warren's Tank-Automotive and Armaments Command (TACOM) has become one of the Army's largest weapon systems research organizations and employs 7,500. In April 2015, GM announced a $419 million expansion of its Tech Center, which could create 2,600 jobs. Also that month, University of Michigan economist Donald Grimes said that Oakland County had reached full employment and might soon experience shortages of high-tech workers.

Farther east are the blue-collar communities of Macomb: Eastpointe (formerly known as East Detroit, it voted to change its name to make it sound less like Detroit and more like tony Grosse Pointe); Roseville; St. Clair Shores; Clinton Township; and Mount Clemens.

Overall, the district is Democratic, although not overwhelmingly so, the least partisan of the four Democratic-held district in metro Detroit.

Sander Levin (D)

Sander Levin, first elected in 1982, is the ranking Democrat on the Ways and Means Committee, having briefly served as its chairman before Republicans regained the majority in 2011. Like his younger brother, retired Sen. Carl Levin, he is an old-school liberal and one of his party's most respected voices on tax and trade matters. Former Ways and Means Republican member Jim McCrery of Louisiana described him as "a Democrat's Democrat—he defends Democratic positions with vigor and substance."

Sander Levin grew up in Detroit and got degrees from the University of Chicago, Columbia University and Harvard Law School. In college, Levin sat at a lunch counter in protest with black students as they were denied service together. He later studied village democracy in India. "I was essentially trained by World War II vets who combined a progressive view of life with a deep distrust of anything authoritarian," he told *National Journal.*

He settled in the suburb of Berkley after school and was elected state senator in 1964. In 1970 and 1974, he ran for governor and lost narrowly each time to Republican William Milliken. During the Carter administration, he was a top appointee at the Agency for International Development.

In 1982, a House seat opened after redistricting when two incumbents retired. Levin won a spirited primary and has held the seat since, with shifts of geography. The 1992 redistricting moved him east, into Macomb County, and placed him in the same district with Democratic Rep. Dennis Hertel, who retired. Levin had serious competition in the next two elections from Republican retired Army Col. John Pappageorge and won by just 53%-46% in 1992 and 52%-47% in 1994. Since then, he has won easily.

Levin is a hard worker and a details man, willing to spend endless hours with others working out solutions. He got into a tense exchange with fellow Michigander Dave Camp, then Ways and Means chairman, at a December 2011 Rules Committee meeting, arguing over whether the 2009 economic stimulus law had reduced unemployment. "Your policies certainly haven't worked very well," said Camp, prompting the normally even-keeled Levin to retort, "Let's not argue about the policies, because I think you're wrong!"

In earlier years, Levin played an important role on significant issues. On welfare reform, Levin helped to shape the 1996 overhaul that introduced more work requirements for welfare beneficiaries. In 2005, as the ranking Democrat on the Social Security Subcommittee, his outspoken opposition to personal retirement accounts put Republicans on the defensive and helped stop the proposal. "He led us in the winning strategy, which was an inside-outside strategy, that we would mobilize people around the country, and two, that we would not offer an alternative—that was absolutely key," said Rep. Jan Schakowsky of Illinois, a fellow liberal.

For years, he has been at the center of trade debates, seeking ways, as he has put it, to shape globalization. He favored the 1980s free trade agreement with Canada, which helped the auto industry. He was a strong opponent of the North American Free Trade Agreement in 1993, but supported normal trade relations with China, playing an instrumental role in crafting details with the Clinton administration. With many union leaders, Levin has pushed for trade agreements to contain provisions on workers' rights, ways of settling workers' disagreements and environmental protection. He insisted on changes in provisions on workers' rights and environmental protections in the agreements that the Bush administration negotiated with Peru, South Korea Colombia, and Panama.

In March 2011, Levin defended the Obama administration's insistence on taking more time to complete deals with Colombia and Panama, while simultaneously seeking quick congressional approval of a newly negotiated agreement with South Korea. "The old conventional wisdom about trade policy is outdated, and there is a new model, exemplified by changes to the Peru and Korea agreements, waiting to be seized," he said in a speech to trade experts. In early 2015, he demanded more transparency and voiced strong objections to emerging details of the Trans-Pacific Partnership as Congress began consideration of the prospective package.

During her four years as House Speaker, Nancy Pelosi tended to defer to Levin as support for free trade pacts in the Democratic Caucus declined dramatically. Levin has pressed hard for China to allow its currency to rise in value and introduced a bill to authorize the Commerce Department to decide whether an undervalued currency is an export subsidy. On the House Democrats' cap-and-trade energy bill to reduce carbon emissions, Levin reached agreement with supporters on requiring taxes in 2020 on China, India and other developing countries if they failed to similarly curb carbon emissions, but the bill ultimately died in the Senate. He also worked with Senate Finance Committee Chairman Max Baucus of Montana on multiple issues in a 2010 tax bill to extend unemployment benefits, boost oil company payments for spills, and create a tax credit for electric vehicle technology development. Levin's customary standard is that taxes should be "fair and progressive."

While Democrats were still in power, Levin got the gavel at Ways and Means after Chairman Charles Rangel became mired in an ethics scandal. In March 2010, Rangel, facing charges he had failed to pay taxes, resigned the chairmanship. For a day, Pelosi installed the next most senior Democrat, her neighbor Pete Stark of northern California, in the post. But prominent Democrats privately expressed concerns about the flamboyant Stark, given his propensity for controversial remarks. Moreover, Stark had voted no on the cap-and-trade bill and so was not in favor with Democratic leaders. Next in line in seniority after Stark was the level-headed Levin, who was deemed an acceptable replacement. But he managed to rankle committee Republicans during his brief tenure. "You can just kind of keep your mouth shut because everyone knows what your style was, and it wasn't an inclusive style," said Ohio Republican Pat Tiberi, referring to Levin. "It wasn't a bipartisan style. It was very dictatorial."

After the 2010 election, Levin was challenged for the ranking minority position by Richard Neal of Massachusetts. The Democratic Steering Committee voted 23-22 for Neal. Levin, having gained some chits by giving $570,000 to other Democrats during the election season, took his case to the full Democratic Caucus and prevailed over Neal on a 109-78 vote.

After more redistricting shuffles in 2012, Levin had little trouble dispatching Republican Don Volaric, whom he had beaten two years earlier. The win came three months after Levin, whose wife Vicki died in 2008 after 50 years of marriage, was remarried to Pamela Cole, a Penn State psychology professor. He told Michigan Radio in January 2013 that, even in the minority at 81, he felt energized. "Do I have fire in my belly? In a sense, more than ever," he said. Besides, he remained junior within the Detroit-area delegation to John Conyers, and John Dingell did not retire until he was 88.

TENTH DISTRICT

Candice Miller (R)

Elected 2002, 7th term; b. May 7, 1954, Detroit; attended, Macomb Cnty. Comm. Col., 1973-74, Northwood Inst.; Presbyterian; married (Donald); 1 child.

Elected Office: Harrison Twnshp. Bd., 1979-80; Harrison Twnshp. supervisor, 1980-92; Macomb Cnty. treas., 1992-94; MI secy. of st., 1994-2002.

Professional Career: Secy. treas., D.B. Snider Inc. marina, 1972-79.

DC Office: 320 CHOB, 20515, 202-225-2106; Fax: 202-226-1169; Website: candicemiller.house.gov.

State Offices: Shelby Township, 586-997-5010.

Committees: *Homeland Security:* Border & Maritime Security (Chmn); Counterterrorism & Intelligence. *House Administration* (Chmn). *Transportation & Infrastructure:* Aviation; Railroads, Pipelines & Hazardous Materials; Water Resources & Environment. *Joint Committee on the Library.*

Group Ratings

	ADA	ACLU	AFL-CIO	LCV	ITI	COC	HAFA	ACU	CFG	FRC
2014	0%	5%	–	6%	80%	86%	64%	72%	74%	75%
2013	0%	C	14%	4%	C	77%	C	76%	71%	C

National Journal Ratings

	2013 LIB	—	2013 CONS
Economic	10%	—	88%
Social	16%	—	74%
Foreign	24%	—	68%
Composite	20%	—	80%

Key Votes of the 113th Congress

1. Sandy storm spending	N	5. Medical Marijuana	N	9. Syrian Rebels Training	Y
2. Violence Against Women Act	Y	6. Farm Bill	Y	10. Keystone pipeline	Y
3. Guantanamo Bay Detainees	N	7. Afghanistan Combat	N	11. Immigration Exec. Action	Y
4. Abortion 20-week ban	Y	8. NSA Phone Data Collection	N	12. Bipartisan budget deal	Y

Election Results

2014 general	Candice Miller (R)......................	157,069	(69%)	$795,742
	Chuck Stadler (D)........................	67,143	(29%)	
	Harley Mikkelson (G)....................	4,480	(2%)	
2014 primary	Candice Miller (R)..................unopposed			

Prior winning percentages: 2012 (69%), 2010 (61%), 2008 (66%), 2006 (66%), 2004 (69%), 2002 (63%)

Population		Race and Ethnicity		Income	
Total:	711,342	White	90.9%	Median income:	$55,027
Urban:	2.8%	Latino	3.5%		*(165 of 435)*
Suburban:	77.3%	Black	2.5%	Under $50,000	45.5%
Rural:	19.9%	Asian	1.5%	$50,000-$99,999:	33.4%
Land area:	3,382	Two races	1.5%	$100,000-$199,999:	18.0%
Pop/sq. mi.:	210.3	White Ethnic	45.9%	$200,000 or more:	3.2%
Born in state:	83.4%			Poverty Rate	11.6%
		Education			
Age Groups		H.S. grad or less:	42.8%	**Work**	
Under 18:	22.6%	Some college:	35.1%	White collar:	32.9%
18 to 34:	18.6%	College degree, 4 yr.:	14.4%	Blue collar:	40.6%
35 to 64:	43.2%	Post-grad study:	7.8%	Sales and service:	26.5%
Over 64:	15.6%				
		Military		Govt. workers:	10.7%
		Veterans/active duty:	9.0%		

Detroit Suburbs, "The Thumb": Macomb, St. Clair

Macomb County, just northeast of Detroit, has been one of the nation's most closely watched political battlegrounds, a place where it once seemed the electoral fate of Michigan and even the entire country might be determined. It owes much of that to

Voter Turnout	
2013 Total Citizen 18+	534,347
2014 House Turnout	228,692
2014 Turnout as % CVAP	42.8%
2012 Turnout as % CVAP	64.6%

its reputation as blue-collar suburbia, but that is no longer accurate: More people hold white-collar jobs than blue-collar jobs these days, and there is far less work in auto plants than during earlier generations. In 2013, Macomb had 855,000 people, compared with 185,000 residents in 1950. It continues to grow, as farms continue to convert to subdivisions. New business development in 2014 was the highest since 2007.

These suburbanites were often from the east side of Detroit and were typically Catholic, at least modestly well-off, and ancestrally Democratic. They accepted the New Deal as part of their natural heritage. In 1960, Macomb County was the most Democratic major suburban county in the nation, voting 63% for the first Catholic president, John F. Kennedy. But these Democrats resented the efforts of Detroit politicians to tax them to pay for welfare programs and were fearful of the city's crime problem. Over the next three decades, Macomb moved away from national Democrats. From 1980 to 1992, no Democratic

2012 Presidential Vote		
Mitt Romney (R)................	187,660	(55%)
Barack Obama (D)	148,425	(44%)

2008 Presidential Vote		
John McCain (R)................	177,218	(50%)
Barack Obama (D)	170,050	(48%)

Cook Partisan Voting Index: R+6

presidential candidate got more than 40% of the vote here. In 1996, after great effort and with the advice of pollster Stan Greenberg, who had studied Macomb closely, Bill Clinton carried the county by a solid 50%-39%.

Lately, central and northern Macomb County have been filling up with fast-growing and expensive subdivisions that are not as culturally liberal as the affluent parts of Oakland County, and Macomb is best characterized as a swing county. Republican George W. Bush carried it 50%-49% in 2004. Democrat Barack Obama defeated John McCain handily in Macomb in 2008, 53%-45%, and he beat Mitt Romney in 2012, 51%-47%. But in between the Democratic victories, GOP gubernatorial candidate Rick Snyder racked up a big win in Macomb, getting 61% of the vote. In his tighter 2014 reelection, Snyder got 54% in Macomb.

The recent recession hit Macomb every bit as hard as Detroit—between 2007 and 2009, the number of people in poverty jumped nearly a third in the county, while median income dropped from $68,000 in 1999 to $49,000 in 2010, though it rose above $53,000 in 2013 (in inflation-adjusted dollars). In response, local officials visited China to try to lure students and manufacturing firms.

The 10th Congressional District of Michigan centers on the northern two-thirds of Macomb County. It also includes Lapeer County and most of Michigan's "Thumb," where population declined over the past decade. The second-largest county is St. Clair, with Port Huron and its Blue Water Bridge to Canada; Students for a Democratic Society drafted its famous Port Huron Statement just north of here in Lakeport in 1962, setting the stage for the counterculture movement. Northern Macomb has become increasingly Republican, Lapeer and St. Clair have long been fairly Republican, and the Thumb has long been very Republican. Half of the voters are in Macomb. Overall, the district has voted Republican in recent presidential elections, including a double-digit win for Romney in 2012.

Candice Miller (R)

Candice Miller, a Republican elected in 2002, is a mostly loyal vote for her party, but she sometimes strays on fiscal issues. Known for her tough stance against illegal immigration, she lost a bid to chair the Homeland Security Committee in 2012 and instead was given the leadership of House Administration, enabling the GOP to award at least one woman a full committee gavel. In March 2015, she announced that she will not seek reelection, adding another senior retiree from the Michigan delegation.

Miller grew up in Macomb County. Her family ran a marina, and Miller enjoyed life on the water from an early age. She was on the crew team in high school and later was a member of the first all-women team to sail the prestigious Bayview Mackinac Boat Race, one of the longest fresh water regattas. In 1979, at age 25, she was elected Harrison Township trustee. A year later, she was elected as the youngest and first woman supervisor of the township. She won an upset bid in 1992 to become Macomb County treasurer. Two years later, she defeated 24-year incumbent Richard Austin to become Michigan secretary of state, the first woman to hold the post.

Term limited in 2002, Miller was the favorite to succeed Democratic Rep. David Bonior, who ran for governor, in a district that had been redrawn to make it lean Republican. Democrats were enthusiastic about Macomb County Prosecutor Carl Marlinga, who had held the office for 20 years. But Marlinga could not keep pace with Miller's fundraising. He also called himself a "Hubert Humphrey Democrat"—not a big advantage in the 10th—while Miller called herself a "George W. Bush Republican."

She opposed abortion rights, supported free trade agreements, and favored making the Bush-era tax cuts permanent—all contrary to Marlinga's positions. Both candidates supported gun rights. Citing her daughter's membership in the United Auto Workers, Miller reached out to unions and was endorsed by the Teamsters, though not the AFL-CIO. She won handily, 63%-36%, carrying Macomb County 61%-37%.

In the House, Miller has a moderate-to-conservative voting record, but occasionally has been a maverick. She has opposed the majority of her party on funding for Amtrak, and for nutrition programs for women and children, and in allowing new species to be listed under the Endangered Species Act. She supported the 2007 minimum wage increase and the 2009 expansion of the Children's Health Insurance Program. She cosponsored the bipartisan bill creating the 2009 "Cash for Clunkers" program in which the government gave people money for trading in old cars for new fuel-efficient models.

Miller became chairman in 2011 of the Homeland Security Subcommittee on Border and Maritime Security, giving her a platform for her tough illegal immigration views. The House in May 2012 passed, by voice vote, her bill requiring the Homeland Security Department to develop a plan to control the Southwest border in five years. She proposed a constitutional amendment to exclude illegal aliens from the congressional reapportionment process, calling it "absolutely outrageous" that non-citizens have "a profound impact on our political system."

After President Barack Obama won reelection in 2012 with overwhelming Latino support, she was among the few Republicans who no longer opposed the DREAM Act aimed at aiding children who came to the country illegally with their parents. But she remained resolutely opposed to Obama's 2014 executive order allowing certain categories of illegal immigrants to remain in the country. Months before the order was issued, she wrote in a *Detroit News* op-ed: "Middle- and working-class Americans cannot survive and thrive in a labor marketplace skewed by unskilled, low-wage workers who are here illegally. And our taxpayers cannot bear the burden of providing services—education, health and welfare—to millions of illegals." During that year's Central American refugee crisis on the Mexican border, she called for using free trade agreements with the refugees' home nations as leverage. "We need to whack them, our neighbors, to understand that they are just not going to keep taking our money and we are just going to be sitting here like this," she said at a hearing. Another option, she said, would be to suspend foreign aid to Central American nations.

Miller sought to replace the term-limited Peter King of New York as chairman of the full Homeland Security panel, but lost to the more conservative and deep-pocketed Michael McCaul of Texas. Partly to assure that at least one woman chaired a committee, House Republican leaders gave her a consolation prize of sorts as chairwoman of House Administration, which oversees the chamber's internal workings. Some of her tasks, including administration of election rules, were comparable to her work as secretary of state in Michigan. She played a role in the congressional decision to end taxpayer subsidies for national political conventions.

As chairman, one of Miller's jobs is setting the budget for each House committee. At a February 2015 hearing, she said she was "very appreciative" of chairmen who asked for no increases at a time of tight budgets. Earlier, she formally hired lawyer David Rivkin to pursue House Republicans' contention that Obama was guilty of abusing his executive authority on immigration. "No president is above nor should operate beyond the limits of the Constitution," she said. In 2013, she overturned a policy that prevented holiday greetings in lawmakers' communications to constituents. "I feel it is entirely appropriate for members of Congress to include a simple holiday salutation, whether it is Merry Christmas, Happy Hanukkah, and so on," she said.

Miller has been preoccupied with issues that affect auto manufacturing, which is vital to her state's economy. She has criticized advocates of tougher fuel-efficiency standards for seeking "to bankrupt Detroit." Miller takes seriously her district's nexus to the natural assets of the Great Lakes and has warned that the lakes cannot be relied on "to solve the nation's water problems." Speaking to the House in support of a Great Lakes restoration bill in December 2014, she said: "God gave us these magnificent lakes that have provided us with so much, but we need to be better stewards of them and have a lot of making up to do to Mother Nature."

Miller had an unusual encounter with the Ethics Committee. The panel admonished her for attempting to influence the vote of Republican Rep. Nick Smith of Michigan in 2003, when he opposed the Republican bill to create a prescription drug benefit in Medicare. The committee concluded that Miller tried to intimidate Smith to vote for the legislation. Miller dismissively told the *Detroit Free Press:* "If a black belt can be intimidated by an overweight, middle-age woman, that's too bad."

Miller has been reelected easily. When Democratic Sen. Carl Levin announced his retirement in 2013, Michigan Republicans considered Miller their best candidate. Despite her previous success as a statewide candidate, she decided not to seek the position. In hindsight, that may have been a tip-off that she was preparing to end her career in Congress. Following that announcement, she indicated possible interest in running for governor in 2018. Republicans are favored to keep her House seat, but Democrats could be competitive.

ELEVENTH DISTRICT

Dave Trott (R)

Elected 2014, 1st term; b. Oct. 16, 1960, Birmingham; U. of MI, B.A. 1981, Duke U., J.D. 1985; Catholic; married (Kappy); 3 children.

Elected Office: Bingham Farms Village Cncl., 1989-91.

Professional Career: Practicing atty., Trott & Trott, P.C.; MI St. Building Authority Bd. of Trustees, 2011-15.

DC Office: 1722 LHOB, 20515, 202-225-8171; Fax: 202-225-2667; Website: trott.house.gov.

State Offices: Troy, 248-528-0711.

Committees: *Foreign Affairs:* Europe, Eurasia, & Emerging Threats; Middle East & North Africa. *Judiciary:* Immigration & Border Security; Regulatory Reform, Commercial & Antitrust Law.

Election Results

2014 general	Dave Trott (R)	140,435	(56%)	$4,958,200	$177,702
	Bobby McKenzie (D)	101,681	(41%)	$815,445	
	John Tatar (Lib)	7,711	(3%)		
2014 primary	David Trott (R)	42,008	(66%)		
	Kerry Bentivolio (R)	21,254	(34%)		

Population		Race and Ethnicity		Income	
Total:	717,393	White	82.0%	Median income:	$73,294
Urban:	0.9%	Asian	7.3%		(53 of 435)
Suburban:	99.1%	Black	4.7%	Under $50,000	33.1%
Rural:	0.0%	Latino	3.6%	$50,000-$99,999:	32.4%
Land area:	487	Two races	2.1%	$100,000-$199,999:	26.7%
Pop/sq. mi.:	1,473.6	White Ethnic	43.2%	$200,000 or more:	7.9%
Born in state:	71.2%			Poverty Rate	6.7%
		Education			
Age Groups		H.S. grad or less:	25.8%	**Work**	
Under 18:	22.9%	Some college:	28.8%	White collar:	47.8%
18 to 34:	19.3%	College degree, 4 yr.:	26.6%	Blue collar:	37.3%
35 to 64:	43.6%	Post-grad study:	18.9%	Sales and service:	15.0%
Over 64:	14.2%				
		Military		Govt. workers:	9.4%
		Veterans/active duty:	6.6%		

Central Detroit Suburbs: Central Oakland, Northern Wayne

While Detroit struggles with seemingly endemic urban decay, many of its suburbs have shown more resilience than the city that spawned them—and a more youthful adaptability to economic change. In affluent subdivisions like Northville, median household income far exceeds the state's as a whole. North-

Voter Turnout	
2013 Total Citizen 18+	515,048
2014 House Turnout	251,238
2014 Turnout as % CVAP	48.8%
2012 Turnout as % CVAP	73.8%

ville's median income was $104,000 in 2011, compared to $49,000 for Michigan. Sixty years ago, Livonia had 18,000 people. By 2013, it had 95,000. Although General Motors closed an engine plant in the area in 2010, other businesses have thrived. Battery maker A123 Systems opened a large lithium ion factory in Livonia in 2010, and Ford is producing its all-electric Transit Connect van there as well. A University of Michigan-Dearborn study ranked the city among the state's top communities for fostering business development and local entrepreneurship. Tying Livonia and nearby suburbs together is Interstate 275, which runs along its western edge and provides easy access to Metro Airport.

Bloomfield Hills, where 2012 GOP presidential nominee Mitt Romney grew up, is metro Detroit's wealthiest community (the median income in 2013 was $132,000, a drop from recent years), and there are large corporate office centers plus a professional basketball arena in Auburn Hills. Novi, in Oakland County, is a high-income suburb that grew 22% between 2000 and 2013. Its Asian-American population was 16% in 2010, and it is now nicknamed "Little Tokyo." Many of these newcomers have work visas and participate in research and development, as Japanese automotive suppliers increasingly build their products in the United States; the city has adapted by offering multilingual instruction in its hospitals, workplaces and schools.

The 11th Congressional District of Michigan covers several suburbs west and northwest of Detroit. About three-fifths of the district is in southern Oakland County,

2012 Presidential Vote		
Mitt Romney (R)..............199,308	(52%)
Barack Obama (D) 178,768	(47%)
2008 Presidential Vote		
Barack Obama (D) 194,092	(50%)
John McCain (R)................186,010	(48%)
Cook Partisan Voting Index: R+4		

including Troy, Birmingham and Novi, plus Bloomfield Hills and Waterford to the north; the remainder are in western Wayne County, with Northville and Plymouth plus Livonia. The district has more Asians than African Americans or Latinos, but the 83 percent white population leaves relatively few of any minority group. Livonia was long closely divided between the two major parties, but the recent affluent influx into this part of Wayne County locale has made it more Republican. The district has taken on a distinct Republican lean since the 2012 redistricting. Those shifts reduced the 2008 performance by Barack Obama in this district from 54% to 50%. Romney won the 11th by 5 points in 2012.

Dave Trott (R)

Businessman and foreclosure lawyer Dave Trott in 2014 became the third Republican elected during the past three elections in this suburban district west and northwest of Detroit. Trott and the voters likely hope for a return to normalcy following the cartoonish behavior of his two predecessors.

Trott, who was born in Birmingham, got his bachelor's from the University of Michigan and his law degree from Duke. He returned home to the family law firm, which he later chaired. In a campaign ad, he said that he expanded the company from six people to 1,200. The business became the largest foreclosure law firm in Michigan and one of the largest in the country, and not surprisingly became an issue in his campaign.

Trott initially challenged first-term Republican Rep. Kerry Bentivolio—a part-time reindeer rancher and Santa Claus impersonator in a traveling Christmas show before coming to Congress. Bentivolo had become the accidental congressman in 2012 when the district's seemingly entrenched five-term GOP congressman, Thaddeus McCotter, was found not to have enough valid signatures on his nominating petitions to qualify for the ballot. McCotter, a former House Republican leader who ran a baffling presidential campaign in 2011, resigned amid a broader investigation of the signature-gathering process conducted by his campaign.

To the embarrassment of local Republicans, that left Bentivolo as the only Republican on the primary ballot after the filing deadline. With support from some of the GOP establishment, former state Sen. Nancy Cassis spent nearly $500,000 on a write-in campaign. But that proved to be too little and too late. With tea party support, Bentivolo got the nomination with 66% of the vote. He won the general election that year against Democratic physician Syed Taj, 51%-44%. Adding to the merriment, the 2012 election also featured the victory of Democrat David Curson in a special election for the final two months of McCotter's term. Curson was the drive-by congressman between the baffling and accidental congressmen.

Trott styled himself as an innovative and problem-solving businessman who had lived the American Dream. His background with the economic woes of Michigan left him uniquely prepared to provide job-creating measures in Congress, he said. For the most part, he avoided discussion of the work of his law firm. Bentivolio launched a negative campaign, calling Trott the "Foreclosure King." A real-life campaign ad featured a 101-year-old Detroit woman who had lived in the family home for 65 years and lost it to a foreclosure handled by Trott's firm. The woman's son, without her knowledge, had taken out a reverse mortgage and hidden eviction notices from her. That saga resulted in a media outcry, and the woman soon returned to her home. "While I served my country in two wars, he was serving foreclosure notices," Bentivolio said of Trott. In an interview with the *Detroit Free Press*, Trott defended his business, saying, "I'm just doing my job for my clients." In a contest that *Mother Jones* headlined "Santa vs. Scrooge," voters apparently agreed with Trott. The outcome was not close. Trott won 66%-34%.

Perhaps missing another opportunity to run an experienced local political figure, Democrats nominated Bobby McKenzie, a former counterterrorism adviser to the State Department.

He also attacked Trott for his foreclosure practice, but Trott's solid conservatism—he pledged to repeal the Affordable Care Act, secure the border, and defend gun rights—played well with voters. "What you see is what you get," he promised on his campaign website. "I will not tell you one thing and do another." National Democratic and liberal groups stayed away from this contest. Trott overwhelmed McKenzie, as he did Bentivolo, with his free-spending $5 million budget, of which $3.3 million came from his own deep pocket. He won the general election 56%-40%. A limited and late-starting write-in campaign on behalf of Bentivolo yielded an inconsequential 1,411 votes. McKenzie spent a total of $815,000, and Bentivolo spent $747,000.

Trott got seats on the Foreign Affairs and Judiciary committees. In April 2015, he joined a presidential delegation to Armenia for the centennial observance of the Armenian genocide. Michigan has 15,000 residents of Armenian descent. During an interview, Trott described a social encounter at the White House for new members of Congress. With his wife Kappy, Trott said that he spoke with President Barack Obama and they chiefly discussed their golf games. "At one point, the president looked at my wife and asked, 'Do you play?' My wife is a good golfer, better than me, and before she could answer, I said, 'Mr. President, she's a very good golfer ...' and then out of nowhere my wife points at me and said, 'He's got a horrible reverse pivot!' Mr. Obama then looked at me and said, 'I'd rather play with you then,'" he told the *Free-Press*.

TWELFTH DISTRICT

Debbie Dingell (D)

Elected 2014, 1st term; b. Nov. 23, 1953, Detroit; Georgetown U., B.S.F.S. 1975, M.S. 1996; Catholic; married (John David); 4 children.

Elected Office: Wayne St. U. Bd. of Governors, 2007-14.

Professional Career: Pres., sr. exec. public affairs, GM Foundation; Founder, chmn., Nat'l Women's Health Resource Cntr. & the Children's Inn, Nat'l Inst. of Health; Co-host, Detroit public TV show "Am I Right."

DC Office: 116 CHOB, 20515, 202-225-4071; Fax: 202-226-0371; Website: debbiedingell.house.gov.

State Offices: Dearborn, 313-278-2936; Ypsilanti, 734-481-1100.

Committees: *Budget. Natural Resources:* Federal Lands; Oversight & Investigations (RMM); Water, Power & Oceans

Election Results

2014 general	Debbie Dingell (D)	134,346	(65%)	$1,272,508	
	Terry Bowman (R)	64,716	(31%)	$47,906	$15,444
	Gary Walkowicz (I)	5,039	(2%)		
2014 primary	Debbie Dingell (D)	45,162	(71%)		
	Raymond Mullins (D)	18,793	(29%)		

Population		Race and Ethnicity		Income	
Total:	711,313	White	76.3%	Median income:	$52,193
Urban:	34.2%	Black	10.2%		*(204 of 435)*
Suburban:	65.8%	Latino	5.2%	Under $50,000	48.2%
Rural:	0.0%	Asian	4.5%	$50,000-$99,999:	29.3%
Land area:	538	Two races	3.3%	$100,000-$199,999:	18.3%
Pop/sq. mi.:	1,321.0	White Ethnic	39.5%	$200,000 or more:	4.2%
Born in state:	68.1%			Poverty Rate	17.9%
		Education			
Age Groups		H.S. grad or less:	36.8%	**Work**	
Under 18:	22.2%	Some college:	30.5%	White collar:	39.3%
18 to 34:	26.7%	College degree, 4 yr.:	17.2%	Blue collar:	39.7%
35 to 64:	38.4%	Post-grad study:	15.5%	Sales and service:	21.0%
Over 64:	12.8%			Govt. workers:	14.9%
		Military			
		Veterans/active duty:	7.1%		

Southern Detroit Suburbs, Ann Arbor

The American-made automobile may be a vanishing breed elsewhere, but it still reigns supreme in Dearborn, the home of Ford Motor Co.'s headquarters. At the far eastern edge of Dearborn is Ford's famous River Rouge complex, which initially produced anti-submarine ships for use in World War

Voter Turnout	
2013 Total Citizen 18+	520,447
2014 House Turnout	206,660
2014 Turnout as % CVAP	39.7%
2012 Turnout as % CVAP	63.2%

I and which at one point contained almost all of the equipment needed to manufacture an automobile from raw materials through finished product.

The 12th Congressional District of Michigan covers southern and central Wayne County and is a predominantly white, blue-collar district centered on Dearborn. South of Dearborn, the district swings around heavily African-American Romulus and Inkster, taking in several working-class Detroit suburbs known collectively as the "Downriver" area: Taylor; Southgate; Woodhaven, the site of another big Ford plant; and Flat Rock, home to a joint Ford-Mazda auto plant, one of the few Japanese plants in Michigan. The district also takes in Ypsilanti, where GM closed a facility in 2010 and where housing foreclosures remain a major problem. Despite some economic improvement, Wayne County continues to lose population—a drop from1.95 million in 2008 to 1.78 million in 2013. Most of that downsizing has been in Detroit.

2012 Presidential Vote		
Barack Obama (D)	217,542	(66%)
Mitt Romney (R)	107,632	(33%)

2008 Presidential Vote

Barack Obama (D)	234,573	(67%)
John McCain (R)	110,099	(31%)

Cook Partisan Voting Index: D+15

Also in the 12th is the University of Michigan and Ann Arbor, one of the nation's largest university towns and part of Washtenaw County. It is oriented to the university but also home to auto executives and young families who like a town with plenty of bookstores, coffeehouses and liberal neighbors. In 2004, the city voted 74% to legalize medical marijuana. In 2006, it landed the headquarters of Google's AdWords unit, which operates the company's "pay-per-click" advertising method, Google's main revenue source. The recession postponed the initial plan for Google to have a workforce of 1,000 in Ann Arbor. In May 2015, company officials said they would double their office space and move to a new corporate campus near the university, and expand their payroll of more than 400.

The district is Democratic territory, and President Barack Obama won it with 66% of the vote in 2012. The Washtenaw County portion includes about 40% of the district and is its biggest center of Democratic strength, where Obama won almost 80% in 2008.

Debbie Dingell (D)

Democrat Debbie Dingell, a longtime power player and the wife of former Rep. John Dingell, easily won her first election in 2014. Her victory constituted a historic level of political continuity: With her husband and his father John Dingell Sr., the seat has now been held by the Dingell family since 1933. And she became the first wife of a sitting member to take a seat while the spouse remained alive.

During the long era that her husband was a powerful member of Congress, Debbie Dingell was a well-known figure in her own right following their marriage in 1981, the year he became chairman of the Energy and Commerce Committee. She grew up in a Catholic family with close ties to General Motors. Her grandfather cofounded Fisher Body, an early and important GM acquisition. After completing college at Georgetown, she joined GM as a lobbyist in 1977. That year she also met her future husband. After they married, she formally gave up her lobbying role but remained a senior GM executive until 2009, managing its public-affairs operation and heading the GM Foundation.

As an influential operative, Dingell developed an extensive network that opened the door to high-profile political activities. A member of the Democratic National Committee, she ran Al Gore's Michigan campaign in 2000 and took on the same role for John Kerry four years later. She won election to the Wayne State University Board of Governors in 2006 and promoted women's health issues and Michigan economic development through her work with foundations.

Dingell considered a run for the Senate when Democratic Sen. Carl Levin, announced he would retire in 2014. But she decided against it and Rep. Gary Peters ran instead. When her husband announced in February 2014 that he would end his tenure as Congress' longest-serving member, she became his likely successor. Not only is the district solidly blue, encompassing liberal Ann Arbor as well as working-class Detroit suburbs, but it's also a place where close ties to GM help rather than hurt. Dingell shares her husband's more centrist views on environmental regulation and gun control, which are in line with the electorate.

Dingell faced only token opposition in the August primary, which she won with 78% of the vote. Against Republican Terry Bowman, a Ford autoworker whom she outspent 38-to-1, Dingell coasted to a 65%-31% victory in November, roughly the margin of her husband's recent victories. After her win, she said, "I am more interested in finding solutions than looking for fights."

As a lowly freshman in the minority party, Dingell had few tools of influence. She got seats on the Budget and Natural Resources committees, and was ranking Democrat on the latter's Oversight and Investigations Subcommittee. Dingell showed nuances in her support for gun rights when she praised Michigan Gov. Rick Snyder for vetoing a bill that would have permitted concealed-weapon permits for individuals with a history of domestic violence. She was named a senior whip by Minority Whip Steny Hoyer, who was a long-time ally of her husband. She also became co-chair of a Democratic Congressional Campaign Committee project to recruit more women candidates for Congress.

THIRTEENTH DISTRICT

John Conyers (D)

Elected 1964, 26th term; b. May 16, 1929, Detroit; Wayne St. U., B.A. 1957, LL.B. 1958; Baptist; married (Monica); 2 children.

Military Career: MI Natl. Guard, 1948-50; U.S. Army, 1950-54 (Korea); U.S. Army Reserve, 1954-57.

Professional Career: Legis. asst., U.S. Rep. John Dingell, 1958-61; Practicing atty., 1959-64; Referee, MI Workmen's Comp. Dept., 1961-63; Exec. bd., Detroit NAACP, 1963-present; Exec. bd., Detroit ACLU, 1964-present.

DC Office: 2426 RHOB, 20515, 202-225-5126; Fax: 202-225-0072; Website: conyers.house.gov.

State Offices: Detroit, 313-961-5670; Westland, 734-675-4084.

Committees: *Judiciary* (RMM).

Group Ratings

	ADA	ACLU	AFL-CIO	LCV	ITI	COC	HAFA	ACU	CFG	FRC
2014	100%	88%	–	94%	40%	43%	13%	8%	11%	0%
2013	100%	C	95%	93%	C	23%	C	13%	16%	C

National Journal Ratings

	2013 LIB	—	2013 CONS
Economic	91%	—	0%
Social	84%	—	15%
Foreign	94%	—	0%
Composite	92%	—	8%

Key Votes of the 113th Congress

1. Sandy storm spending	Y	5. Medical Marijuana		9. Syrian Rebels Training	Y
2. Violence Against Women Act	Y	6. Farm Bill	Y	10. Keystone pipeline	N
3. Guantanamo Bay Detainees	Y	7. Afghanistan Combat	Y	11. Immigration Exec. Action	N
4. Abortion 20-week ban	N	8. NSA Phone Data Collection	Y	12. Bipartisan budget deal	N

Election Results

2014 general	John Conyers, Jr. (D)	132,710	(80%)	$833,999	$22,010
	Jeff Gorman (R)	27,234	(16%)		
	Chris Sharer (Lib)	3,537	(2%)		
	Sam Johnson (I)	3,466	(2%)		
2014 primary	John Conyers, Jr. (D)	42,005	(86%)		
	Horace Sheffield (D)	6,696	(14%)		

Prior winning percentages: 2012 (83%), 2010 (77%), 2008 (92%), 2006 (85%), 2004 (84%), 2002 (83%), 2000 (89%), 1998 (87%), 1996 (86%), 1994 (82%), 1992 (82%), 1990 (89%), 1988 (91%), 1986 (89%), 1984 (89%), 1982 (97%), 1980 (95%), 1978 (93%), 1976 (92%), 1974 (91%), 1972 (88%), 1970 (88%), 1968 (100%), 1966 (84%), 1964 (84%)

Population		Race and Ethnicity		Income	
Total:	673,446	Black	56.2%	Median income:	$30,706
Urban:	59.0%	White	33.6%		*(433 of 435)*
Suburban:	41.0%	Latino	6.5%	Under $50,000	69.9%
Rural:	0.0%	Asian	1.2%	$50,000-$99,999:	23.0%
Land area:	176	Two races	2.1%	$100,000-$199,999:	6.3%
Pop/sq. mi.:	3,827.8	White Ethnic	17.0%	$200,000 or more:	0.7%
Born in state:	76.6%			Poverty Rate	32.9%
		Education			
Age Groups		H.S. grad or less:	51.7%	**Work**	
Under 18:	24.8%	Some college:	34.0%	White collar:	23.7%
18 to 34:	23.6%	College degree, 4 yr.:	8.8%	Blue collar:	49.4%
35 to 64:	39.0%	Post-grad study:	5.5%	Sales and service:	26.9%
Over 64:	12.7%				
		Military		Govt. workers:	9.8%
		Veterans/active duty:	6.7%		

Detroit Metro West

Detroit's early auto factories—Packard, Hudson, Ford Highland Park, Dodge Main, Briggs, Ford Rouge, Cadillac, Kelsey-Hayes, Chrysler, Plymouth, DeSoto—were built between 1905 and 1925 about five miles from the city's center and at what was then the edge of urban development. Almost

Voter Turnout	
2013 Total Citizen 18+	484,976
2014 House Turnout	166,947
2014 Turnout as % CVAP	34.4%
2012 Turnout as % CVAP	59%

instantly, the flat farmlands all around were platted in streets arranged in a grid and built up with wooden bungalows and brick prairie-style houses. Detroit's neighborhoods filled up with factory workers and civil servants, professionals and maintenance men, corner-store owners and management personnel, Catholics and Protestants and Jews: a middle-class melting pot. With one exception—Detroit in those days had few blacks, who did not begin their great migration from Alabama and the rest of the South in earnest until around 1940, when defense plants began hiring African Americans in large numbers. In 1910, blacks made up 1% of Detroit's population; in 1970, the share had risen to 43.7%. Today, Detroit is 83% black.

The history of the city is one of conflict and uplift, inspiration and tragedy. The wartime mixture of Appalachian whites and Deep South blacks proved volatile. During the war years, blacks were pent up in a few severely overcrowded neighborhoods like the Black Bottom, most of it now covered by the Chrysler Freeway; whites opposed any attempt to expand black neighborhoods, sometimes with violent measures. This tinderbox erupted in June 1943 after a fight started on a beach on Belle Isle; rumors spread among blacks that a white man had thrown a black woman and

2012 Presidential Vote
Barack Obama (D) 249,656   (85%)
Mitt Romney (R)..................41,911   (14%)

2008 Presidential Vote
Barack Obama (D) 273,824   (86%)
John McCain (R)..................40,628   (13%)

Cook Partisan Voting Index: D+34

her baby off a bridge, while a competing rumor spread among whites that a white woman had been raped and murdered on the bridge. The ensuing race riot lasted three days and resulted in 34 deaths.

After 1945, when African Americans began moving outward, real estate agents played on racial fears, and in the 1950s whole square miles of Detroit changed racial composition in a matter of months. In the 1960s, there was hope that the civil rights movement, encouraged by Walter Reuther's United Auto Workers union, would improve matters, and in fact many black Detroiters found good jobs and made good incomes. Then came the riots of July 1967, followed by extensive white flight and steep increases in crime. Detroit's first African-American mayor, Democrat Coleman Young, elected in 1973, pressured major employers like the Big Three auto companies to build facilities in Detroit and raised taxes to support expanded city services. But economic conditions continued to deteriorate and violent crime became a part of everyday life.

Detroit took on a garrison atmosphere. Crime reduced the value of much residential real estate to near zero, and the city's population dropped from 1.7 million in 1960 to 689,000 in 2013. Local demographers estimate that the continuing decline will bottom out at about 609,000 in 2030 before it slowly begins to rise. The public sector took a larger share of residents' income than almost anywhere else in the country and served citizens poorly. Turnaround came agonizingly late in the 1990s, when Democratic Mayor Dennis Archer, elected in 1993, worked to fight crime and encourage private sector growth. Incomes rose, as did median housing value, from $32,000 to $71,000. The city made some small progress under Mayor Dave Bing, a former NBA star with the Detroit Pistons. The downtown and midtown areas are increasingly attracting young professionals, students, and empty nesters; the occupancy rates for rentals here approach 100%; a Whole Foods grocery market opened in June 2013, and a second was scheduled to follow soon. The Detroit City Planning Commission recently approved an ordinance expanding community gardens, urban farming, and even fish farming on vacant lots.

The auto industry's fortunes have also brightened since the government takeover of General Motors and Chrysler in 2009. Violent crime in the city fell nearly 8% during the first six months of 2010, while homicides dropped 28% during that period. But despite these salutary trends, the city remains largely blighted. In 2012, Detroit confronted its severe fiscal crisis. It had $14 billion in liabilities, near-zero cash flow, and a budget deficit of more than $325 million. In March 2013, Gov. Rick Snyder declared the city in a state of financial emergency and he appointed Kevin Orr as emergency manager to try to steer the city to fiscal stability. In December 2014, Detroit emerged from bankruptcy and Orr gave up his responsibilities. But that transition marked only the start of the long-term revival of the city, under Mayor Mike Duggan (who was elected as the city's first white mayor in a half-century) and a rapidly changed population. Local finances would remain subject to oversight by a commission with a majority of its members appointed by the state.

The 13th Congressional District of Michigan, which covers much of the western half of the city, was radically altered by Republican redistricters. Their dual objectives were to maintain two black majority districts even though there are barely enough blacks to achieve those numbers, and to maximize Republican strength in the neighboring suburban districts. The 13th, based entirely in Wayne County, covers an area stretching from Highland Park to the east side of downtown Detroit. One salient to the southwest takes in parts of "Mexicantown," with its growing Hispanic population, as well as the cities of Ecorse, River Rouge and Melvindale. Another swings south through some white-majority neighborhoods, such as Dearborn Heights, Garden City and Westland, to take in heavily African-American Inkster and Romulus, which plans a $100 million luxury Outlets of Michigan mall and is the home of Detroit's Metro Airport. Overall the district is about 56% African American and is one of the most strongly Democratic districts in the country. Barack Obama got 86% of the vote in 2008, and 85% in 2012.

John Conyers (D)

John Conyers is the ranking Democrat on the Judiciary Committee and is now the longest-serving current member of Congress. He was the first African American to chair the committee and remains a soft-spoken yet stubborn counterweight to the panel's numerous conservatives. First elected in 1964, on the eve of the Voting Rights Act, Conyers was a founder of the Congressional Black Caucus and has been among the most liberal members of the House.

The son of a UAW operative, Conyers grew up in Detroit. He played cornet at Northwestern and Cass Technical High Schools and watched jazz greats at Baker's Keyboard Lounge. He served in the Army in Korea, got his bachelor's and law degrees from Wayne State University, practiced law, then worked on the staff of a young Rep. John Dingell, the longest-serving member of Congress before his 2015 retirement.

Conyers was one of six African Americans in the House when he was first elected. Conyers won his primary, in which 60,000 votes were cast, by 108 votes. Civil rights heroine Rosa Parks, who by then had moved to Detroit, worked on his 1964 campaign and then in his Detroit office until her retirement in 1988. When she died, Conyers sponsored the resolution paving the way for her to lie in state in the Capitol Rotunda, the first woman so honored. He sponsored the original Martin Luther King Jr., holiday bill just days after the civil rights leader was assassinated in 1968 and he persevered until it passed in 1983. Since 1989, he has sponsored legislation to establish a commission to examine slavery and its lingering effects and to consider whether reparations should be paid to descendants of slaves. He has been wary of crime legislation that strengthens the power of law enforcement and he opposed the welfare changes of the 1990s. "Through the course of my career, I've had a straightforward aim—to live out Martin Luther King Jr.'s vision of a society oriented toward jobs, justice and peace," he told the *Michigan Chronicle* in January 2015.

Gun control has long been one of Conyers' chief causes. He supports banning high-capacity ammunition magazines, requiring background checks for all gun sales, and toughening penalties for the transfer of multiple firearms to anyone forbidden to own guns, such as convicted felons. On immigration, he railed against the Republicans' emphasis on enforcement, calling it "a race to the bottom," and has compared the issue to the struggle for civil rights. "Like the civil rights movement, the journey may be long and the path uneven, but the result will be a stronger and more just America," he wrote in a June 2012 op-ed column.

But it is questionable just how much influence Conyers carries with a second-term President Barack Obama. He was an early supporter of Obama's, but has had differences with him since then. He accused the president in a November 2009 radio interview of "bowing down" to "nutty right-wing" proposals on the health care overhaul and also said that the president was "getting bad advice from … clowns" on Afghanistan. More recently, he has been critical of the administration's use of unmanned drone aircraft both at home and overseas.

Conyers has shown he is capable of bipartisanship. In the tense weeks after the September 11 attacks, Conyers, as Judiciary's ranking member, worked hand-in-hand with the Republican chairman, conservative Jim Sensenbrenner of Wisconsin, on anti-terrorism legislation. They agreed that the government could detain immigrants suspected of terrorism without bringing charges, but only for seven days, and they introduced the anti-terrorism bill together. Over time, Conyers worked with Sensenbrenner on other issues, despite the broad ideological differences between the two. Conyers did not enjoy the same close relationship with Sensenbrenner's successor, Judiciary Chairman Lamar Smith of Texas, though they did work together on patent overhaul legislation in 2009 and 2010.

He has had his differences with current chairman Bob Goodlatte of Virginia, though they agreed in early 2015 to seek common ground on legislation to address police practices. "Our country has been plagued by unrest due to a series of tragic incidents related to police-involved violence. In far too many cases, we have experienced situations that are further dividing communities and law enforcement," Conyers said at a May 2015 hearing, where he voiced appreciation to Goodlatte for his willingness to work on the issue. Earlier, he reintroduced with Democratic Sen. Ben Cardin of Maryland his bill to prohibit racial profiling by law-enforcement officers. He voiced hope that "it's a different scene" because the public had become more attuned to abusive police tactics, especially against young men in minority communities.

Conyers ascended to Judiciary chairman in 2007 after Democrats won control of the House. He favored bringing a censure motion against President George W. Bush and Vice President Dick Cheney for allegedly misleading Congress and the American people on the rationale for invading Iraq in 2003. He called for creation of a special committee to investigate. But House Speaker Nancy Pelosi, in an effort to calm partisan tensions after the 2006 elections, ruled out an investigation. Still, Conyers examined the Bush presidency, including the use of presidential signing statements that went beyond the terms of the legislation. He pushed contempt charges against Bush White House Chief of Staff Joshua Bolten and former counsel Harriet Miers after they refused to give sworn testimony about the firings of U.S. attorneys across the country.

Taking a hand in the huge government bailout of the financial sector in 2008, Conyers pushed to allow bankruptcy judges to lower mortgage rates or the principal for homeowners who go bankrupt. He achieved one of his longtime goals in 2010 when he won enactment of a law reducing the sentencing disparities between crack and powder cocaine, something he and other civil rights activists had argued for years was unfair to African Americans. But he has been unable to advance another priority, requiring radio stations to pay performers a fee for playing their music on air.

In recent years, Conyers has been the subject of negative news stories at home. In 2003, the *Detroit Free Press* reported that Conyers assigned his congressional staff to work on his political campaigns and also made them run personal errands and babysit his two children. In 2006, the House Ethics Committee concluded an investigation of the allegations by saying Conyers must take "a number of additional, significant steps to ensure that his office complies with all rules and standards regarding campaign and personal work by congressional staff." Then in June 2009, his wife, Detroit City Council President Pro Tem Monica Conyers, pleaded guilty to taking bribes for helping a company called Synagro Technologies get a sludge-hauling contract with the city. She was released in 2013 following her three-year sentence, and got a job in neighborhood legal services.

Nevertheless, Conyers—described by *The Detroit News* as "part showman, part junkyard dog, part evangelist"—has been reelected mostly without difficulty, relying on his longevity to cover other political weaknesses. "He's a terrible campaigner and doesn't raise much money, but he's an institution," Bill Ballenger, editor of *Inside Michigan Politics* newsletter, told the *Free Press* in 2012. He made two runs for mayor of Detroit, in 1989 and 1993. But he waged desultory campaigns, and trailed far behind in each.

Some political observers thought Conyers might be vulnerable in 2012 with significantly redrawn lines that included Downriver and western Wayne County. He drew four Democratic primary challengers: state senators Bert Johnson and Glenn Anderson, state Rep. Shanelle Jackson, and Wayne-Westland school board member John Goci. All of them castigated Conyers for being out of touch and unresponsive to constituents, but none of them had much money. Conyers won with 55% of the vote, thus ensuring his reelection in November.

Conyers faced more drama in 2014, when the county clerk and secretary of state ruled that hundreds of signatures that his reelection campaign had gathered were invalid. He was struck from the ballot, and his aides discussed the possibility of a write-in campaign. But a federal judge subsequently ordered him on the ballot after the congressman's lawyers joined civil rights activists in contending the law setting requirements for people gathering signatures was itself unconstitutional.

Before the judge's ruling, Detroit's *Metro Times* columnist Jack Lessenberry suggested that Conyers gracefully retire. "When the votes are cast, when it comes to anything that matters, he is nearly always on the side of the angels," Lessenberry wrote. "But here's something else you should know about John Conyers: Increasingly, he isn't the man he once was." Rev. Horace Sheffield, his opponent in the primary, questioned "whether or not he's capable at this point." Still, his constituents remained supportive, and he won the primary 74%-26%. By virtue of his long tenure and his committee position, he carries authority, even though he may be a voice from another era. As the new House dean, he said that his priorities remained "justice and peace," including a $15 hourly minimum wage. That goal is unlikely to be enacted in a House with John Boehner as speaker, but Conyers and his allies have been successful with their goal in other forums.

FOURTEENTH DISTRICT

Brenda Lawrence (D)

Elected 2014, 1st term; b. Oct. 18, 1954, Detroit; Central MI U., B.A. 2005; Christian; married (McArthur Lawrence); 2 children.

Elected Office: Southfield Bd. of Ed., 1992-96; Southfield City Cncl., 1997-2001, pres., 1999; Southfield mayor, 2002-15.

Professional Career: Mgr., USPS.

DC Office: 1237 LHOB, 20515, 202-225-5802; Fax: 202-226-2356; Website: lawrence.house.gov.

State Offices: Detroit, 313-423-6183; Southfield, 248-356-2052.

Committees: *Oversight & Gov't Reform:* Interior (RMM); Nat'l Security. *Small Business.*

Election Results

2014 general	Brenda Lawrence (D)	165,272	(78%)	$660,743	$166,173
	Christina Barr (R)	41,801	(20%)		
2014 primary	Brenda Lawrence (D)	26,387	(36%)		
	Rudy Hobbs (D)	23,996	(32%)		
	Hansen Clarke (D)	22,866	(31%)		

Population		Race and Ethnicity		Income	
Total:	706,429	Black	56.8%	Median income:	$41,588
Urban:	52.0%	White	30.9%		*(366 of 435)*
Suburban:	48.0%	Latino	4.6%	Under $50,000	56.9%
Rural:	0.0%	Asian	4.3%	$50,000-$99,999:	24.4%
Land area:	210	Two races	3.1%	$100,000-$199,999:	14.3%
Pop/sq. mi.:	3,360.3	White Ethnic	16.2%	$200,000 or more:	4.4%
Born in state:	72.3%			Poverty Rate	26.4%
		Education			
Age Groups		H.S. grad or less:	40.9%	**Work**	
Under 18:	23.1%	Some college:	30.6%	White collar:	35.1%
18 to 34:	23.0%	College degree, 4 yr.:	15.7%	Blue collar:	45.9%
35 to 64:	39.2%	Post-grad study:	12.8%	Sales and service:	19.1%
Over 64:	14.8%			Govt. workers:	10.5%
		Military			
		Veterans/active duty:	5.9%		

Detroit Metro North and East

Few central cities in America were as vibrant in the 20th century as Detroit, the nation's fourth-largest city during the middle decades-, then in a class shared or surpassed only by New York, Chicago Philadelphia and Los Angeles. Few have been as diminished as Detroit, which now stands as the

Voter Turnout	
2013 Total Citizen 18+	516,432
2014 House Turnout	212,468
2014 Turnout as % CVAP	41.1%
2012 Turnout as % CVAP	67.1%

nation's 18th-largest city, behind Fort Worth and just ahead of El Paso, both of which continue to grow. This was America's first automobile city, not just because it manufactured so many cars but also because it was built to automobile scale. Detroit started the 20th century about the size of Milwaukee, with fewer than half a million people and extending no farther than four or five miles from the site where the French built Fort Pontchartrain on the Detroit River in 1701. As the Motor City boomed, it grew outward along wide avenues and, starting in the 1950s, along freeways. Metro Detroit eventually expanded to 4 million people, each generation moving out in all directions, leaving behind the previous generation's neighborhoods and civic institutions.

Today, large parts of Detroit are literally empty. Formerly iconic buildings in the downtown area have been demolished, and others are all but vacant, while officials struggle to create new population centers and reestablish a business district. Crime is a major problem. The murder rate in Detroit has long been higher than in its suburbs, and those who could afford to leave have done so. On the positive side, GM bought, for $72 million, the 70-story Renaissance Center, built in the 1970s for $350 million, and the company moved several thousand employees there.

2012 Presidential Vote		
Barack Obama (D)	273,273	(81%)
Mitt Romney (R)	62,794	(19%)
2008 Presidential Vote		
Barack Obama (D)	301,342	(81%)
John McCain (R)	67,646	(18%)
Cook Partisan Voting Index:	D+29	

Quicken agreed to move in from the suburbs, and there has been some urban revitalization near Comerica Park (the ballpark itself is in the 13th District). But beyond these well-policed enclaves lie acres of vacant lots and half-empty blocks where there were once five-story apartment buildings and brick houses.

Former steel supply executive and professional basketball star Dave Bing took over as mayor with a promise to lift the city from despair. He slashed $180 million from a $330 million budget while also managing to make a dent in violent crime. "We are a work in progress," Bing said in early 2011. "Detroit is at a crossroads." But the city's finances remained in dire shape, and in March 2013 Gov. Rick Snyder declared the city in a state of financial emergency and appointed an emergency manager to try to steer the city into the black. When that control ended nearly two years later, Detroit's finances were nominally in better shape. But both the city and its nearby suburbs, plus state officials in Lansing, faced continuing crises about the direction of the metropolitan area. That future likely would be nothing like the good times—or the bad—of the past half-century.

The 14th Congressional District of Michigan is a serpentine amalgamation of heavily minority areas in metro Detroit. Its bizarre shape offers testimony to the difficulty of maintaining majority-minority districts as African Americans increasingly move out of compact neighborhoods in inner cities. The district takes in Hamtramck and the Grosse Pointes, both white majority areas, and also the northern neighborhoods of Wayne County, which became heavily African American following the flight of whites in the 1970s and 1980s. It includes the newest frontiers in African-American migration in southern Oakland County; Southfield was 0.1% black in the 1970 census and 70% black in the 2010 census, while Oak Park went from being 0.2% black to 57% in the same period. To the north and east, the district takes in majority-black Pontiac, where the police department was disbanded in 2010 during a fiscal emergency. The state police filled in, and brought a return of trooper patrol cars in November 2013. The resulting district is about 57% African American and is overwhelmingly Democratic. It is split almost evenly between Wayne and Oakland counties, with their separate political networks.

Brenda Lawrence (D)

Democrat Brenda Lawrence was elected in 2014, chiefly in a competitive three-way primary, in the diversifying 14th District. She succeeded Democrat Gary Peters, who ran successfully for the Senate.

Lawrence was born and raised in Detroit, earned a bachelor's degree in public administration from Central Michigan University, and started her career in the U.S. Postal Service. As her children went through the public school system in Southfield, a suburb bordering Detroit, she became drawn to education issues and ran successfully for the local school board in 1992. Four years later, she won a seat on the City Council, followed by a successful mayoral bid in 2001. As the first African-American woman to hold that post, she was reelected three times. She has underscored Southfield's resilience as a corporate hub that held up relatively well despite the economic collapse of Detroit.

Lawrence's long tenure as mayor helped to solidify her name recognition, although it didn't always translate into political victories. She ran unsuccessfully for Oakland County executive in 2008, then for lieutenant governor in 2010, when her ticket with gubernatorial candidate Virg Bernero fell far short in the face of the GOP momentum that year.

In 2012, Lawrence made her first bid for the House after the lines for the 14th were redrawn, running against Peters as well as Rep. Hansen Clarke, who had been elected in 2010. That primary became a contentious debate over race. Clarke, a biracial candidate who claimed African American ancestry, came under criticism (as well as aggressive robo-calling) amid questions over whether he was truly "black." Later, a local media outlet, with an assist from Lawrence's campaign, reported that the death certificate of Clarke's mother actually listed her as white. That skirmishing gave the unmistakably white Peters a chance to stay above the fray, and he won the primary handily, with 47% of the vote to 35% for Clarke and 13% for Lawrence. Clarke dominated the vote in Wayne County, but Peters did even better in his base of Oakland County. Throughout those campaigns, she remained mayor of Southfield.

Lawrence got another chance when Peters announced his Senate bid. State Rep. Rudy Hobbs, who was endorsed by Detroit Mayor Mike Duggan, was seen as the early Democratic front-runner. But Lawrence gained an edge with key Democratic endorsements, including that of Bernero, the mayor of Lansing, as well as support from unions and local business groups. Clarke jumped into the race, hoping to win back his seat. But Lawrence made the best of her ground operation, claiming a narrow victory by just a few thousand votes in the August primary. This time, Lawrence got 36% to 32% for Hobbs and 31% for Clarke. She got 41% of the vote in Oakland County but only 32% in Wayne, a sign that she may have some work to do.

She initially prepared to face Republican Christina Conyers, a cousin of Democratic Rep. John Conyers. But Conyers withdrew from the race in September after she moved to Maryland, and Republicans substituted Christina Barr. It made no difference. Lawrence won 77% of the vote and ended her losing streak.

In the House, Lawrence wanted to start a caucus of the more than 20 former mayors now serving. "Mayors, we think differently. A pothole doesn't have an R or D on it," she said. She got seats on the Small Business and Oversight and Government Reform committees, including as ranking member of the Interior Subcommittee. She planned to be a strong advocate for improved roads, bridges and regional transit, but failed to get a seat on the Transportation and Infrastructure Committees, as she had hoped. "My goal is to help make 8 Mile a major thoroughfare that is the 50-yard line of the congressional district that I represent, not a line that demarcates the haves and the have-nots," she wrote in the *Detroit Free-Press*. With Rep. Alan Lowenthal of California, she filed a bill that provides dedicated funding to upgrade freight-related railroad infrastructure. Minority Whip Steny Hoyer named Lawrence as a senior whip.

★ MINNESOTA ★

Minnesota is, in a word, nice. Not always nice in the sense of being polite—there have been some hot political controversies in the frozen North—but nice in that some of the most recognizable aspects of the upside of American culture were spawned there. It is the birthplace of Scotch tape, Betty Crocker, Target and the Mall of America, and it's the home of dyspeptic chroniclers of small town America from Sinclair Lewis to Garrison Keillor. The Twin Cities boast of having more museums than any other city but Chicago and Washington; the Minnesota Historical Society was founded in 1849, nine years before statehood (when there wasn't much Minnesota history yet). Beyond the Twin Cities, you can visit the Spam Museum in Austin, the Judy Garland Museum in Grand Rapids, and the Laura Ingalls Wilder Museum in Walnut Grove near the banks of Plum Creek. Politically, Minnesota for much of the 20th century provided the nation with some of its most articulate and honorable leaders—Harold Stassen, Hubert Humphrey, Eugene McCarthy, Walter Mondale—and with traditions of probity, civic-mindedness, and innovation that are second to none.

Minnesota began as the node of the transcontinental railroads that linked the winter wheat fields of the northern prairies to the great grain-milling center of Minneapolis to the bustling Pacific ports of Puget Sound. The far northern states were ignored by most Yankee migrants, who headed straight west into Iowa, Nebraska, and Kansas. But others saw opportunity in Minnesota's icy lakes and ferocious winters. James J. Hill, the builder of the Great Northern Railroad, once said, "You can't interest me in any proposition in any place where it doesn't snow." He and other entrepreneurs, operating out of Minneapolis and St. Paul—already twin cities by 1860—worked to attract Norwegian, Swedish, and German migrants who would find the terrain and climate congenial. (One can get lutefisk—smelly, lye-soaked cod—around Christmastime in Minneapolis restaurants.) By 1890, the Twin Cities were the nerve center of a sprawling and rich agricultural empire stretching west from Minnesota through the Dakotas into Montana and beyond. Minneapolis and St. Paul became the termini of its rail lines and the site of its grain-milling companies. The Twin Cities also became the center of a three-party politics and an economic radicalism reminiscent of Scandinavia. In politics, these Upper Midwestern commonwealths pioneered this continent's welfare states and shaped national public policy far out of proportion to their numbers. Alarmed by the unprecedented concentration of economic power and wealth in the hands of a few identifiable millionaires who lived on St. Paul's Summit Avenue or on the hill above Minneapolis's Hennepin Avenue, the immigrants from Scandinavia drew on their native traditions of cooperative activity and bureaucratic socialism.

As in Wisconsin and North Dakota, a strong third political party developed here in the years after the Populist era. This Farmer-Labor Party elected senators in the 1920s and came to dominate state politics when Floyd B. Olson was elected to three two-year terms as governor beginning in 1930. Prior to that, Republicans had held the Minnesota governorship for 63 of the 73 years that the state had been in the union. Olson transformed state governance and midway through his tenure he had secured a lengthy list of reforms that would become the foundation for modern and progressive Minnesota, including: the state's first income tax, municipally owned liquor stores, ratification of the federal amendment prohibiting child labor, large appropriations for relief, a two-year moratorium on farm foreclosures, a ban on injunctions in labor disputes and a limit on hours worked by women in industrial jobs to 54 per week. "This boy Olson is, in my opinion, about the smartest 'Red' in the country," wrote journalist Lorena Hickok. When Olson, who had supported Franklin Roosevelt, was asked about possibly leading a third party in a presidential campaign, he averred, "I think I'm a little too radical." Hurt by their ties to communists, the Farmer-Laborites were beaten by Gov. Harold Stassen's Republicans in 1938. But this was still a New Deal state, and by 1944, the bedraggled local Democrats were merged with the anti-communist faction of Farmer-Laborites to form the Democratic-Farmer-Labor Party. Hubert Humphrey, the mayor of Minneapolis in 1945 and the dazzling advocate of the civil rights plank at the 1948 Democratic National Convention, played a key role in this progression. Humphrey's DFL—clean, idealistic, closely tied to labor unions, backed by many farmers—attracted dozens of talented politicians, including Eugene McCarthy, Orville Freeman, and Walter Mondale. Humphrey's convention speech helped put the Democrats on record in favor of civil rights, and he was elected to the Senate at age 37.

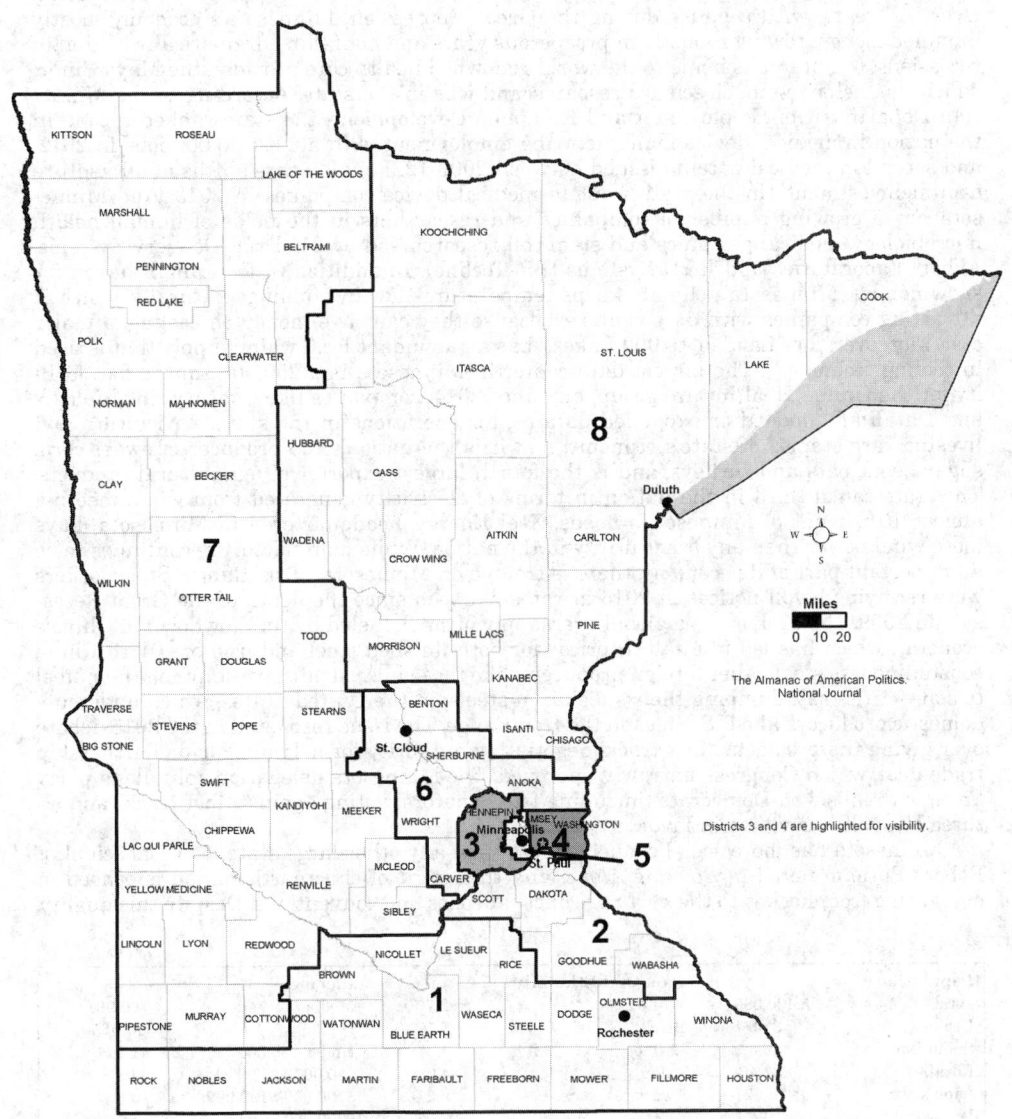

KITTSON
ROSEAU
LAKE OF THE WOODS
MARSHALL
BELTRAMI
KOOCHICHING
PENNINGTON
RED LAKE
COOK
POLK
CLEARWATER
ITASCA
ST. LOUIS
LAKE
NORMAN
MAHNOMEN
HUBBARD
CLAY
BECKER
CASS
8
WADENA
AITKIN
CARLTON
Duluth
7
OTTER TAIL
CROW WING
WILKIN
MILLE LACS
PINE
GRANT
DOUGLAS
TODD
MORRISON
KANABEC
TRAVERSE
STEVENS
POPE
STEARNS
BENTON
BIG STONE
ISANTI
CHISAGO
SWIFT
St. Cloud
SHERBURNE
KANDIYOHI
MEEKER
ANOKA
6
CHIPPEWA
WRIGHT
HENNEPIN
RAMSEY
LAC QUI PARLE
Minneapolis
WASHINGTON
3
4
YELLOW MEDICINE
MCLEOD
St. Paul
5
RENVILLE
CARVER
LINCOLN
LYON
REDWOOD
SIBLEY
SCOTT
DAKOTA
BROWN
NICOLLET
LE SUEUR
2
RICE
GOODHUE
WABASHA
1
WASECA
DODGE
OLMSTED
PIPESTONE
MURRAY
COTTONWOOD
WATONWAN
BLUE EARTH
STEELE
Rochester
WINONA
ROCK
NOBLES
JACKSON
MARTIN
FARIBAULT
FREEBORN
MOWER
FILLMORE
HOUSTON

Miles
0 10 20

The Almanac of American Politics.
National Journal

Districts 3 and 4 are highlighted for visibility.

Congressional district boundaries were first effective for 2012.

In the years that followed, the DFL dominated Minnesota politics while a series of progressive businesses led the development of a strong diversified economy. The DFL stood for a generous, compassionate government, for strong labor unions and high wages, for an expansionist fiscal policy to encourage consumer-led economic growth, for civil rights, and for an anti-communist, but not bombastic, foreign policy. Its base was among blue-collar workers in the Twin Cities, in Duluth and the Iron Range, and among farmers of Scandinavian origin. Minnesota's business leaders were politically conservative and professionally innovative. Over the years, with a pause during the Great Depression, Minnesota's economy mostly hummed along, growing robustly in prosperous years and not falling dramatically behind in recessions. Minnesota is home to the world-renowned health care provider, the Mayo Clinic, which has helped spur bioscience research and jobs in the state. According to the Minnesota Department of Employment and Economic Development, the state ranked second in the nation in medical device manufacturing employment with almost 30,000 jobs in 2012, and second in medical patents issued between 2008-12. Roughly three-fifths of all venture capital investments in the state went to medical device companies in 2013. And Minnesota has a growing number of companies and researchers in the fields of human health microbiology, medical genomics and stem-cell research, led by 3M Drug Delivery Systems, Abbott Laboratories and R&D Systems (Bio-Techne). In addition to fostering a haven for snowmobiles, Minnesota's climate keeps temperatures low in buildings naturally, which is attracting companies with data centers, because they can save money on cooling, a major cost. Moreover, the "Land of 10,000 Lakes," has an abundant local water supply that is used in cooling technology. The largest data center in Minnesota is a 250,000 square foot facility for the United Health Care group, but since 2014, companies like CenturyLink, Cologix and DataBank, opened or expanded data center operations in the state. Agriculture and livestock are staples of state's economy, and it is the nation's top producer of sweet corn, sugar beets, oats and turkeys, and is the fourth largest exporter of agricultural products. The state ranks third in the nation in terms of electricity generated from wind, meeting almost 10 percent of Minnesota's needs. Xcel Energy, headquartered in Minnesota, buys more wind power than any other utility in the nation. While manufacturing continues to be an important part of its economy, there is trouble on Minnesota's Iron Range: Steelworkers were receiving layoff notices in 2015 at rates not seen since the depth of the Great Recession in 2009. The problem is a global oversupply of steel, fueled by the slowdown in China's economy, which has led to a fall in prices for both finished steel and iron ore. With China consuming less steel, other foreign producers, like those in Australia are shipping their steel to sell—critics say, dumping their subsidized steel—in the United States, which undercuts domestic producers like U.S. Steel on the Iron Range. The issue resonated in the 2015 debate over giving the president "fast track' negotiating authority for a Trans-Pacific Partnership trade deal, which Congress narrowly approved: The Minnesota delegation split along party lines, with all seven Democrats (including two Senators) voting against "fast track" and all three Republicans voting in favor.

Minnesota has more social connectedness than any other large state, political scientist Robert Putnam noted in *Bowling Alone,* and this spirit of civic participation is echoed in everything from hockey to the party precinct caucuses and conventions. Despite this quality,

Population		Race and Ethnicity		Income	
Total:	5,420,380	White	82.7%	Median income:	$60,907
Urban:	31.9%	Black	5.1%		(11 of 50)
Suburban:	36.8%	Latino	4.8%	Under $50,000	41.2%
Rural:	31.4%	Asian	4.0%	$50,000-$99,999:	33.3%
Land area:	79,627	Two races	2.2%	$100,000-$199,999:	20.6%
Pop/sq. mi.:	68.1	White Ethnic	26.0%	$200,000 or more:	4.9%
Born in state:	68.1%			Poverty Rate	8.1%
		Education			
Age Groups		H.S. grad or less:	33.9%	**Work**	
Under 18:	23.7%	Some college:	32.6%	White collar:	38.8%
18 to 34:	23.0%	College degree, 4 yr.:	22.4%	Blue collar:	40.5%
35 to 64:	39.4%	Post-grad study:	11.1%	Sales and service:	20.7%
Over 64:	13.9%				
		Military		Govt. workers:	11.8%
		Veterans/active duty:	7.9%		

the state faces a serious challenge in maintaining its workforce and coping with an exodus of young adults. On balance, about 9,300 18- to 24-year-olds depart the state annually, according to the Minnesota State Demographic Center. Combine that trend with declining birthrates and an aging population—more Minnesotans are expected to retire in the next 15 years than in the previous six decades—and

Voter Turnout	
2013 Total Citizen 18+	3,964,732
2014 Highest Statewide Turnout	1,981,511
2014 Turnout as % CVAP	50%
2012 Turnout as % CVAP	74.9%

Legislature		
Senate:	39D	28R
House:	72R	62D

by 2020, the state is forecast to have a shortage of more than 100,000 workers. The state's population problems have been tempered, because it has attracted an interesting array of immigrants: Hmong and Vietnamese in the 1980s and 1990s, and Somalis since 2000. Once pretty much all white, its population is now 5% African-American, 5% Hispanic, 4% Asian. Yet not all is harmonious. In 2010 in Minneapolis, the Justice Department indicted Somali immigrants for allegedly raising money for the Islamist militant group Al-Shabaab. And while the economy has gained, there are still not enough economic options for Somalis. Figures for 2013, put Somalis' unemployment at 21 percent in Minnesota, about three times the state average over the same period of time. Somali community leaders say the lack of opportunity can lead to despair, especially among young people who are then drawn to Islamic extremism.

After the Humphrey breakthrough in 1948, the Republican Party in Minnesota was barely an afterthought and practically wiped out in the 1974 Watergate mid-term elections. Addressing Minnesota's GOP State Central Committee one month later, Rep. Bill Frenzel declared the party had "lost everything but our underwear." As part of its rehabilitation effort, the Republican Party of Minnesota became the Independent-Republican Party. But the DFL had slowly begun to weaken as well. The skillful politicians who had led the party followed Humphrey to Washington: Freeman became secretary of agriculture for Presidents Kennedy and Johnson, and after that went to New York to head a business consulting firm; Mondale was appointed to the Senate in 1964, elected in 1966, reelected in 1972 and started to have White House ambitions. In 1978, after DFL Gov. Wendell Anderson appointed himself to the Senate, voters who viewed his move as self-serving reacted by electing Republicans to the two U.S. Senate seats and the governorship. Liberal domination of DFL nominating conventions elevated some weak statewide candidates, and, in 1998, three contenders in the Democratic "my three sons" primary were Hubert Humphrey III, Mike Freeman and Ted Mondale. Freeman had been endorsed by the DFL convention and was particularly miffed that Humphrey didn't stand down. Minnesota "nice" was frayed a bit when Freemen attacked Humphrey during a break in a debate, saying, "Skip Humphrey is going to destroy the party." Humphrey won the primary to face St. Paul GOP mayor Norm Coleman, but former professional wrestler and suburban mayor Jesse Ventura ran as an independent and won the election. Ventura's candidacy sparked a huge rise in turnout, especially in the Minneapolis-St. Paul media market beyond the Twin Cities core of Hennepin and Ramsey counties.

In 2002, when Ventura did not run for reelection, the Twin Cities exurbs—the area just outside the Hennepin and Ramsey core—went heavily Republican, helping Tim Pawlenty win the governorship in another three-way race in which former Democratic Rep. Tim Penny ran as an independent. In the Senate race that year, Coleman defeated Walter Mondale, whom Democrats turned to and placed on the ballot after two-term DFL incumbent Sen. Paul Wellstone died in a plane crash. In 2004, heavy Democratic turnout in Hennepin and Ramsey counties enabled Democratic presidential nominee John Kerry to win. In 2006, the DFL had the upper hand. Pawlenty was reelected by only 47%-46%, and the DFL's Amy Klobuchar won an open Senate seat by a huge margin. In 2008, Democrat Barack Obama won comfortably in the presidential contest, and DFL nominee Al Franken held Coleman to a 42%-42% tie; after eight months of contentious ballot recounts and court challenges, Franken was certified as the winner in July 2009. After the 2010 election, every statewide elected post was in DFL hands.

Presidential Politics Minnesota has the longest consecutive streak of voting Democratic for president of any state. The last time Minnesota voted Republican was in 1972, and even then it gave Richard Nixon his lowest percentage margin over George McGovern. Before 1932 and the New Deal, it had voted Republican in every presidential race except 1912, when it went for Teddy Roosevelt. In 2000 and 2004, both parties vigorously contested

Minnesota, and voters gave Democrats Al Gore and John Kerry victories of only 48%-46% and 51%-48%, respectively. In 2008, Barack Obama won 54%-44%. In 2012, the result was almost the same—53%-45% in Obama's favor. In both elections, Obama ran way ahead among young voters, and the Hubert Humphrey generation narrowly went for him too. The Democratic-Farmer-Labor Party base, formerly blue-collar workers from industrial communities and the Iron Range, is now more likely to be the cultural liberals who cluster in comfortable neighborhoods in Minneapolis and St. Paul.

2012 Presidential Vote		
Barack Obama (D) 1,546,167	(53%)	
Mitt Romney (R)..............1,320,225	(45%)	
2012 Presidential Caucus		
Rick Santorum (R) 21,988	(45%)	
Ron Paul (R) 13,282	(27%)	
Mitt Romney (R).....................8,240	(17%)	
Newt Gingrich (R) 5,263	(11%)	
2008 Presidential Vote		
Barack Obama (D) 1,573,354	(54%)	
John McCain (R)..............1,275,409	(44%)	

Minnesota has a tradition of selecting national convention delegates in caucuses. The DFL tried to attract more voters to its March 2000 caucuses by moving them from Tuesday night to Saturday and holding a presidential preference vote, with national convention delegates assigned proportionately. But by the time Minnesotans caucused, Gore had already clinched the nomination. Republican Gov. Tim Pawlenty tried but failed in 2003 to move the caucus date to February. In 2004, Minnesota was one of 10 states holding contests on March 2. In the Democratic contest, John Kerry carried 51% of the 55,000 votes cast in the presidential preference vote, John Edwards took 27%, and Dennis Kucinich finished third with 17%. In 2008, the caucuses were held on Feb. 5, Super Tuesday, and DFL turnout was a thumping 214,000. Obama beat Hillary Clinton 66%-32% in a contest in which more than half the votes were cast in Hennepin and Ramsey counties. Republican turnout was much lower, at 62,000. Despite Pawlenty's early endorsement of John McCain, Mitt Romney beat him 41%-22%, with 20% going to Mike Huckabee and 16% to Ron Paul.

In 2012, after Pawlenty ended his presidential campaign as a consequence of losing the Iowa straw poll to fellow Minnesotan Michele Bachmann in August 2011, Republican turnout on February 7 fell to 48,000, and Rick Santorum, with help from the state's large right-to-life constituency, carried 82 of the state's 87 counties, winning 45% of the vote, to 27% for Paul, 17% for Romney, and 11% for Newt Gingrich. The Paul forces remained active, securing the Republican Senate nomination for Kurt Bills. But Bills lost to Democratic incumbent Amy Klobuchar by 65%-31%, the widest Senate margin in Minnesota history except for Humphrey's last race in 1976.

Congressional Districts   Minnesota was on the cusp of losing a House seat in the reapportionment following the 2010 census. But under the statutory formula, it qualified for the 435th House seat by a margin of about 9,000 people, narrowly edging out North Carolina, which missed gaining a 14th seat. As

114th Congress Lineup	
3 R	5 D
113th Congress Lineup	
3 R	5 D

a result, Minnesota kept its eight House seats. In 2011, a Republican-led legislature voted for major changes to the map along party lines. But Democratic Gov. Mark Dayton followed through on his promise to veto any map that lacked broad bipartisan support, and a five-judge special judicial panel took over the process.

The Republican proposal stacked Northern Minnesota's 7th and 8th districts horizontally rather than vertically; by attaching Democrat Collin Peterson's base in the far northwest to the heavily Democratic Iron Range in the far northeast, freshman Republican Chip Cravaack would have gotten a more reliably Republican seat to the south, stretching from the Dakotas to Wisconsin. Instead, Democrats proposed a map that would have extended suburban Minneapolis Republican Erik Paulsen's 3rd District into more Democratic suburbs south of the Twin Cities, putting his seat into play.

In February 2012, the judges made only minor changes to the congressional layout. Tea party Republican Michele Bachmann lambasted the "activist judges" in fundraising emails, but kept running in the exurban 6th District to the north, which actually got a point more Republican by shedding Stillwater. As it turned out, the judges' minor moves may have saved Bachmann. But Cravaack lost handily in the Iron Range 8th District. The Democrats' gain gave them a 5-3 edge in the delegation—not quite the bipartisan outcome that Dayton had supposedly endorsed. But both the 7th and 8th Districts remain Republican opportunities. In the next reapportionment, Minnesota likely will lose one of its districts.

Governor

Mark Dayton (D)

Elected 2010, term expires Jan. 2019, 2nd term; b. Jan. 26, 1947, Minneapolis; Yale U., B.A. 1969; Presbyterian; divorced; 2 children.

Elected Office: MN auditor, 1990-94; U.S. Senate, 2001-07.

Professional Career: Teacher, N.Y. City public schl., 1969-71; Counselor & admin., social service agency, Boston, MA, 1971-75; Legis. asst., U.S. Sen. Walter Mondale, 1975-76; Aide, MN Gov. Rudy Perpich, 1977-78; MN Comm. of Econ. Devel., 1978-82; MN Comm. of Energy & Econ. Devel., 1983-86; Founder & pres., Vermillion Investment Co., 1987-90, 1995-97.

Office: 116 Veterans Service Bldg., 20 W 12th Street, St. Paul, 55155; 651-201-3400; Fax: 651-797-1850; Website: mn.gov/governor.

Election Results

2014 general	Mark Dayton (D)	989,113	(50%)
	Jeff Johnson (R)	879,257	(45%)
	Hannah Nicollet (I)	56,900	(3%)
2014 primary	Mark Dayton (D)	177,849	(93%)

Prior winning percentages: 2010 (44%); Senate: 2000 (49%)

As a candidate, Mark Dayton has freely spent his personal wealth to win elections. But once in high office, he often becomes a beleaguered politician. In 2010, he reclaimed the Minnesota governorship for the Democratic-Farmer-Labor Party for the first time since the mid-1980s, and retained it for the DFL in 2014.

Dayton grew up in Minnesota, the son of Bruce Dayton, longtime head of the department store chain Dayton Hudson (now Target). Mark Dayton graduated from Yale University in 1969—he was a fraternity brother at Delta Kappa Epsilon of future President George W. Bush—and taught ninth grade science in a New York school in the Bowery for two years. He next worked as a counselor and administrator for a Boston crisis center for teenage runaways. He was a conscientious objector and was active in the anti-Vietnam war movement and his name found its way—presumably because of the prominence of his family and that of his then-wife, a Rockefeller—onto President Richard Nixon's enemies list. In 1975 and 1976, he worked for Democratic Sen. Walter Mondale. Dayton then returned to Minnesota to work for DFL Gov. Rudy Perpich. In 1979, after Perpich lost, Dayton spent $400,000 funding a nonprofit agency to spur development in rural Minnesota.

Dayton's first run for elected office was in 1982, when he spent $7 million of his own money against former Sen. Eugene McCarthy, and won 69%-24% in the DFL primary to run for the Senate. He lost the general election, 53%-47%, to Republican incumbent David Durenberger. In 1990, he was elected state auditor. In 1998, he ran in the DFL primary for governor, spending $2 million of his own money, but he finished fourth, far behind the winner, Skip Humphrey, with 18% of the vote. In 2000, Dayton challenged Sen. Rod Grams, the most vulnerable Republican senator up that year. Grams' very conservative voting record was out of line with Minnesota opinion on many issues, and he had no signal legislative accomplishments. To call attention to the issue of high prescription drug prices, Dayton accompanied busloads of senior citizens to Canada to buy medicine at lower prices than in the United States. His "Rx Express" got plenty of media attention. Dayton spent his own money liberally and won the primary with 41% of the vote. Dayton presented voters with a clear contrast to Grams. He favored universal government-run health insurance, called for the federal government to lower prescription drug prices, and advocated doubling the $500 per child tax credit. He spent $11.6 million, almost all of it his own money, doubling the previous Minnesota record, set by him 18 years earlier. Grams raised $6 million. Dayton won 49%-43%, with 6% for Jim Gibson, the candidate of Gov. Jesse Ventura's Independence Party.

The prime legislative achievement of Dayton's first two years in the Senate was the passage of an amendment giving Congress the right to a separate vote on any trade agreement provision weakening U.S. anti-dumping laws, a priority on the state's Iron Range. In October 2004, after Congress had recessed for the election, Dayton attracted national attention when he announced that he was closing his Washington office because of security threats. No other member took such action, and The Minneapolis *Star Tribune* ran a critical editorial that said, "In staking out this Cassandra position, Dayton has added considerably to unfortunate aspects of his reputation: loner, loose cannon, flake." Dayton responded, "I still believe in my soul I made the necessary and wise decision to protect my staff and constituents who might visit my office." Dayton's action resulted in low poll showings and raised doubts about his ability to win reelection in 2006, and he announced he would not seek a second term. Four years after leaving the Senate, Dayton ran for governor, aware that he would have to answer for some personal baggage. He told the *Star Tribune* in December 2009 that he was a recovering alcoholic who had a lapse late in his term as a senator and that he had entered a treatment program in February 2007, a month after his Senate term expired. In addition, he said that he had been treated for mild depression during most of his adult life, but was able to control it with diet, exercise, and medication. Dayton promised to reverse the policies of two-term Republican Gov. Tim Pawlenty, who had fought with considerable success against the DFL legislators who controlled one house during his first term and both houses during his second. Pawlenty blocked DFL plans for tax increases, except on cigarettes, and tried to advance his conservative cultural views. By 2010, Pawlenty was focused on a budding but ultimately unsuccessful campaign for the presidency in 2012.

Dayton declined to compete in the DFL precinct caucuses or state convention, making it clear that he would run in the primary against the party-endorsed candidate. In May 2010, he signaled his strategy by naming as his candidate for lieutenant governor state Sen. Yvonne Prettner Solon, who represented a blue-collar Duluth and Iron Range district. In the August primary, his opponents were House Speaker Margaret Anderson Kelliher, who was endorsed by the DFL convention, and former House Minority Leader Matt Entenza, who spent $5 million of his family money on his campaign and cast himself as a centrist. Investing $3 million of his own money in his campaign, Dayton targeted Duluth and the Iron Range, rural areas generally, and elderly voters. He was endorsed by the United Steelworkers and by Minnesota teacher unions. Dayton beat Kelliher by just 41%-40%, with 18% of the vote going to Entenza. Kelliher carried the Twin Cities metro area by wide margins, but Dayton ran well over 50% in Duluth and the Iron Range, and he carried many rural counties and places with large numbers of elderly voters. The Republican nominee was state Rep. Tom Emmer, a conservative. State Republicans immediately ran an ad that said, "Dayton is too risky for Minnesota." The contrast was sharp. Dayton called for higher taxes on the wealthy and more spending on education. Emmer called for lower taxes, less regulation, and reducing the size of state government. Polls showed a close race right into Election Day. Drawing heavily on his personal money, Dayton outspent Emmer by nearly 2-1. When the results came in, Dayton led Emmer by 8,770 votes, 43.6% to 43.2%, with 12% for Independence Party candidate Tom Horner. The recount process concluded on December 7, and Emmer conceded. Dayton became the first DFL governor elected since 1986.

Dayton faced a legislature with unexpectedly solid Republican margins—37-30 in the Senate, 72-62 in the House. They closed ranks in opposition to Dayton's tax increases. He vetoed the first budget sent to him in February 2011, and lashed out at Republicans a month later for proposing budget cuts that he said would close state parks and end meat and restaurant inspections while offering income tax cuts to the wealthy. He and GOP lawmakers remained deadlocked for months, and by July 1, Minnesota became the only state that year to experience a government shutdown. After two weeks and considerable national publicity, the two sides struck a compromise to raise $1.4 billion in revenue. The budget battle served as a prelude to other struggles for Dayton. The Minnesota Vikings wanted the state's help in building a new football stadium, but some lawmakers said the public had no business taking on most of the costs of a new facility for a profitable sports team. Dayton played up the job-creation potential, and after a hard-fought battle, he signed an agreement in May 2012 to build the Vikings a $975 million stadium at the downtown Minneapolis site of the team's current home, the Metrodome. On another front, he sought $775 million for school and transportation construction projects, but GOP lawmakers balked at the price tag and he eventually signed a bill providing $496 million, saying that it was better than nothing.

With a popular Democratic president on the ballot, Minnesota's political winds in 2012 shifted, and the state Senate and House DFL caucuses reestablished their solid majority in both legislative chambers. With unified Democratic control in St. Paul, Dayton scored some notable victories: To help close a budget shortfall in 2013, Minnesota lawmakers approved his request raise to raise the state's top income tax rate to 9.85 percent, two percentage points above the prior top rate. In 2014, Dayton won an increase in the state's minimum wage from $6.15 per hour to $9.50 by 2016, which is then indexed to inflation. It passed the legislature with just Democratic votes. With those accomplishments in hand, as well as falling unemployment rates and a recovering economy, Minnesota's Democrats headed into the 2014 elections confident about their prospects. Dayton faced off against Republican Jeff Johnson, the Hennepin County commissioner, and Independent Hannah Nicollet in what many observers felt was an underwhelming campaign. Dayton said he would push for increases in education spending in his second term, but he declined to say whether he would raise taxes to help pay for them. He adopted a conventional campaign for an incumbent whose state was on the rebound and said he would focus on jobs and the economy in a second term. Johnson pledged he would push for reforming the state's tax code and would also consider expanding the sales tax. Late in the campaign, the state GOP ran a radio ad claiming that Dayton hadn't done enough to prepare for an Ebola outbreak in the state and criticized him for not supporting a travel ban from West African countries. On Election Day, Minnesotans trudged off to the polls uninspired by the campaign and gave Dayton a 50%-45% victory, recording their lowest turnout since 1986. Dayton won the way Democrats normally prevail in Minnesota, rolling up healthy majorities in the Twin Cities' Hennepin and Ramsey Counties and sweeping the counties on the Iron Range. Johnson carried every one of the suburban and exurban counties that ring the Twin Cities, and much of the rest of the state. But Republicans were able to retake control of the state House, making most of their gains in rural and outstate Minnesota outside of the Democratic turf on the Iron Range.

Dayton began his second term with a $1 billion state budget surplus, a far cry from the nearly $6 billion budget deficit in 2011 that resulted in a standoff with Republican lawmakers, leading to a 21-day government shutdown. He announced that he would not seek elective office again and told the Minneapolis *Star Tribune* that in dealing with issues facing the state he was going to "call them as I see them," freed from the political constraints of another campaign. His priorities were a $10 billion transportation plan that includes a gas-tax hike, and state-funded universal, all-day Pre-K programs for 4-year-olds, which would apply to some 57,000 children. But, after two years of Democrats running state government, Dayton faced a new GOP House majority with very different goals. The governor didn't help his legislative prospects when his relations with the DFL-run Senate were frayed after he called Senate Majority Leader Tom Bakk a "back stabber," for freezing pay hikes Dayton had approved for state commissioners. Asked if he was surprised by the governor's comments, Bakk blandly replied, "Well, I thought he overreacted." Bakk then worked with the Republican House to pass a state budget. Dayton failed to secure his transportation plan or universal pre-K, although he did win a significant funding increase for existing education programs. Asked about his initial legislative disappointments in 2015, Dayton told a reporter, "I won some and I lost some. When you get to the point where leaders in both sides, House and Senate, conspire against me, it's hard." Not a great foundation for his remaining three years in office.

Senior Senator

Amy Klobuchar (D)

Elected 2006, term expires 2019, 2nd term; b. May 25, 1960, Plymouth; Yale U., B.A. 1982, U. of Chicago, J.D. 1985; Protestant; married (John Bessler); 1 child.

Elected Office: Hennepin Cnty. atty., 1998-2006.

Professional Career: Practicing atty., 1985-98.

DC Office: 302 HSOB, 20510, 202-224-3244; Fax: 202-228-2186; Website: klobuchar.senate.gov.

State Offices: Minneapolis, 612-727-5220; Moorhead, 218-287-2219; Rochester, 507-288-5321; Virginia, 218-741-9690.

Committees: *Agriculture, Nutrition & Forestry:* Conservation, Forestry & Natural Resources; Rural Economic Growth & Energy Innovation; Livestock, Marketing & Ag Security. *Commerce, Science & Transportation:* Communications, Technology & the Internet; Consumer Protection, Product Safety & Insurance; Surface Transportation & Merchant Marine Infrastructure, Safety & Security. *Joint Economic Committee. Judiciary:* Antitrust, Competition Policy & Consumer Rights (RMM); Crime & Terrorism; Immigration & the National Interest, Oversight, Agency Actions, Federal Rights & Federal Courts. *Rules & Administration.*

Group Ratings

	ADA	ACLU	AFL-CIO	LCV	ITI	COC	HAFA	ACU	CFG	FRC
2014	90%	93%	–	80%	100%	38%	0%	4%	13%	0%
2013	85%	C	100%	100%	C	38%	C	4%	1%	C

National Journal Ratings

	2013 LIB	—	2013 CONS
Economic	67%	—	31%
Social	68%	—	29%
Foreign	71%	—	0%
Composite	74%	—	26%

Key Votes of the 113th Congress

1. Sandy storm spending	Y	5. Student Loan Rates	Y	9. Bipartisan Budget Deal	Y
2. Chuck Hagel Confirmation	Y	6. Employee Non-Discrim'n Act	Y	10. Farm Bill Conference Rept.	Y
3. Gun Background Checks	Y	7. Senate Vote on Judgeships	N	11. Unempl. Comp. Extension	Y
4. Immigration Reform	Y	8. Defense Dept. Spending	Y	12. Keystone Pipeline	N

Election Results

2012 general	Amy Klobuchar (DFL)	1,854,595	(65%)	$8,532,377	$31,565
	Kurt Bills (R)	867,974	(31%)	$955,342	$24,162
	Stephen Williams (Ind)	73,539	(3%)		
2012 primary	Amy Klobuchar (DFL)	183,766	(91%)		

Prior winning percentage: 2006 (58%)

Although she has not attracted the national media attention of some of her female colleagues—notably Massachusetts' Elizabeth Warren and New York's Kirsten Gillibrand—Democrat Amy Klobuchar, Minnesota's senior senator, is widely seen as aiming for bigger things. First elected in 2006, Klobuchar—who turned 55 in 2015—has been variously mentioned as a potential Cabinet appointee or Supreme Court nominee, to say nothing of a future presidential candidate. Following the 2014 election, she won a post in the Senate Democratic leadership as chair of the Steering and Outreach Committee, tasked with keeping in touch with key party constituencies and developing a policy agenda for Senate Democrats. And, if she is sometimes dinged by critics for not taking on the difficult, controversial issues associated with her Minnesota Senate forebears—ranging from Hubert Humphrey to Eugene McCarthy to Paul Wellstone—she can claim a solid record of legislative accomplishment. "I just keep working on what we can get done, and I've had a pretty pragmatic approach to that," she told the Minneapolis *Star Tribune* in late 2014.

Klobuchar has utilized the traditional political sidestep when asked about her future, smiling and saying she is committed to her Gopher State constituency. But she has done the kinds of things future presidential contenders do: During the 2013-2014 election cycle, she traveled to a dozen states, delivering keynote speeches and raising campaign funds for fellow Democrats. During that period, she made four trips to Iowa—Minnesota's neighbor to the south, but also where the first delegates to presidential nominating conventions are chosen. "I feel at home here. Maybe people from other states don't feel at home here. I feel at home here," Klobuchar gushed during an Iowa Jefferson-Jackson Day dinner speech in the fall of 2014. And, literally borrowing a page from other presidential wannabes, Klobuchar was slated to release her autobiography in the summer of 2015, entitled *The Senator Next Door: A Memoir from the Heartland*. Klobuchar has said on numerous occasions that she backs Hillary Rodham Clinton in 2016, and so has been seen as positioning herself for 2020 or 2024—or, perhaps, as a running mate if Clinton is nominated and were to opt for an all-woman ticket.

Unlike the other Democratic women senators mentioned as presidential contenders, Klobuchar represents a state that has become a political battleground in recent years. While she has been a fairly reliable Democratic vote in the Senate, she has exhibited centrist tendencies; the 2013 *National Journal* vote rankings put her as the 29th most liberal senator, placing her squarely in the middle of the Senate Democratic caucus. She has sought to reach across the political aisle; on Election Day 2014, Klobuchar spent much of the day calling colleagues who were on the ballot, including several Republicans with whom she had sponsored bills, "There seems to be a genuine interest to move forward," she later told the *Washington Post,* adding, "We can't handle another year of partisan sniping and the Ted Cruz view of the world"—a reference to the Texas Republican whose procedural tactics have at times brought the Senate to a standstill. Known for her sharp wit, Klobuchar later joked she and North Dakota Republican Sen. John Hoeven, a good friend, could easily step in as majority and minority leaders, since they get along far better than the current Senate leaders: Kentucky Republican Mitch McConnell and Nevada Democrat Harry Reid.

But the early months of 2015 were hardly a barrel of laughs for Klobuchar: A seemingly noncontroversial human trafficking bill she co-authored ended up creating a six week-long controversy that stalled the confirmation of President Barack Obama's nomination of Loretta Lynch as attorney general. The trafficking bill had sailed through the Judiciary Committee, on which Klobuchar serves, in February. But, it was only when the measure was poised to be taken up on the floor that several Democrats noticed a provision expanding the scope of the so-called Hyde Amendment, which bars federal dollars from being spent on abortions. Until a deal was ultimately reached in late April, the abortion language prompted the Democrats to repeatedly block the bill from advancing—with McConnell, under heat from conservatives over the Lynch nomination, refusing to move on Lynch until the human trafficking bill passed. It caused strains among Senate Democrats. During a closed-door Senate luncheon, there was reportedly a suggestion that Klobuchar was being unfairly blamed by male senators for the error, while Klobuchar, in turn, raised eyebrows among some colleagues by seeking to shift blame to a staff aide for failing to alert her to the anti-abortion provision. Asked later about the personal toll of the episode, Klobuchar told *Politico:* "Not the most pleasant."

Klobuchar was born in the Minneapolis suburb of Plymouth, the daughter of longtime *Star Tribune* columnist Jim Klobuchar. On her father's side, Klobuchar is the descendant of Slovenian immigrants who settled in northern Minnesota's Iron Range; her grandfather worked in the iron mines along with many others of Eastern European ancestry. Today, Klobuchar serves *potica*, a traditional Slovenian holiday nut roll, at the weekly Thursday meetings she holds for visiting Minnesota constituents when the Senate is in session. Growing up, Klobuchar helped her father recover from alcoholism, a battle that he later documented in a book—and that she also discusses in her new memoir. She graduated from Yale, where she wrote a paper on the machinations behind the building of Minneapolis' Hubert H. Humphrey Metrodome. She earned a law degree from the University of Chicago, and returned home to work as a lawyer and a lobbyist. In 1998, Klobuchar ran successfully for Hennepin County prosecuting attorney, serving two terms. She spearheaded a crackdown on gun crimes and was credited with securing nearly 300 homicide convictions.

Hennepin County is the center of a media market that includes much of the state's population, providing Klobuchar an excellent springboard when Democrat Mark Dayton (now the state's governor) announced he would not seek reelection to the Senate in 2006. Republican Rep. Mark Kennedy, victorious in three consecutive highly competitive House races, made it clear he was running for Senate. While the GOP establishment quickly united behind him, it took the Democratic-Farmer-Labor Party field time to shake out. Klobuchar declared her candidacy in April, as several prominent DFLers subsequently announced they would not run. Minneapolis Heart Institute Foundation President Ford Bell did run, but dropped out after Klobuchar received the DFL endorsement at the state convention in June.

In the general election, Kennedy sought to distance himself from the Iraq war and President George W. Bush, but it did little good in what turned out to be a heavily Democratic year. Klobuchar slammed Kennedy as a "rubber stamp" for Bush while advocating middle-class tax relief and a minimum wage increase. She touted her record as a prosecutor, even as Kennedy sought to highlight the increasing rate of violent crime in Minneapolis. Klobuchar consistently led in polls and easily won, 58%-38%.

Klobuchar serves on the Commerce Committee, and a primary focus of her work has been consumer protection. She got a number of provisions to toughen airline safety into the Federal Aviation Administration reauthorization that became law in February 2012. She also has pushed for several measures aimed at giving cell phone users more clout in dealing with telecommunications companies. Shortly after her election, in 2007, when a six-year-old sustained serious injuries from a swimming pool drain in a Minneapolis suburb, Klobuchar and Minnesota Republican Rep. Jim Ramstad sponsored a bill, ultimately signed into law, banning swimming pool covers that fail to meet entrapment safety standards and requiring automatic drain shutoffs. The next year, after news stories described the discovery of lead in children's toys made in China, Klobuchar sponsored provisions in a child safety bill that banned lead in children's products and required that toys contain batch numbers to make recalls easier. She served on the conference committee that negotiated the final version of the legislation, which became law. As an Agriculture Committee member, she has advocated strong country-of-origin labeling for imported food.

In 2012, Klobuchar and Republican Sen. Roy Blunt of Missouri won passage of a measure eliminating redundant baggage screening for travelers arriving from airports that participate in the United States' preclearance program. (Klobuchar and Blunt share more than legislation in common: They were tied for first place as the Senate's best cooks in the 2014 version of the annual survey of congressional staffers conducted by *Washingtonian* magazine.) That legislation is among several bipartisan bills and initiatives in which Klobuchar has been involved during the course of her Senate tenure. After gasoline prices spiked in the summer of 2008, she joined a bipartisan group pushing coastal states to allow offshore drilling—although she coupled that with support for a windfall profits tax on oil companies. When the financial industry regulation overhaul passed in 2010, Klobuchar and Texas Republican Kay Bailey Hutchison won a provision to maintain regional Federal Reserve banks' supervision of community banks.

More recently, Klobuchar was part of the bipartisan group organized by Maine moderate Republican Susan Collins—seven Republicans, six Democrats and an independent—that helped pave the way for an end to the stalemate that caused a 16-day government shutdown in late 2013. Speaking to a political event in early 2015, Klobuchar noted that half of that 2013 bipartisan group were women, notwithstanding that women comprised only 20 percent of the overall Senate. "Women have gotten things done," she declared.

Klobuchar's fans among Republicans include *New York Times* columnist David Brooks, who wrote in 2012: "She represents the modern senator to me. Not some big-hair blowhard, but a happy regular person with an independent streak." But others have suggested she has concentrated on popular, easy-to-support legislative matters while avoiding the tougher ones; former Minnesota GOP Gov. Arne Carlson once called her "the great avoider." Klobuchar told the *Star Tribune* in 2012 that the criticism is unwarranted. "I've worked on things that have actually passed and gotten done, that have helped people," she said, while noting the present-day partisan divisions that have intensified the difficulty of moving legislation on many controversial issues.

Klobuchar's centrist tendencies have prompted occasional griping from the left as well. The *Star Tribune* reported that gay activists said she should have been quicker to support ending the military's "don't ask, don't tell" ban on openly gay service members, and that environmentalists were angry at her efforts to remove Minnesota wolves from the federal endangered species list and her support for a new bridge over the St. Croix River. Outside of Minnesota, Klobuchar ran afoul of teen-pop sensation Justin Bieber in 2011 when she introduced a bill making it a felony to profit from streaming unlicensed content online. "She needs to be locked up, put away in cuffs," asserted Bieber, who gained fame when his music got exposure on YouTube. Bieber and other critics notwithstanding, polls at home have regularly put Klobuchar's approval rating at 60 percent or above. Seeking a second term in 2012, she crushed her Republican opponent, state Rep. Kurt Bills, by 65% to 31%, after several better-known Republicans passed on challenging her.

If she lacks the professional experience of her Minnesota Senate colleague, former "Saturday Night Live" regular Al Franken, Klobuchar had developed a reputation as a resident wit before Franken joined her on Capitol Hill in 2009. She was a hit as a speaker at a national press dinner in 2009, joking that while she held the Senate record for raising money from ex-boyfriends, the House record belonged to then-Rep. Barney Frank, the openly gay Massachusetts Democrat. At an Iowa delegation breakfast at the 2012 Democratic National Convention, she tweaked former Alaska Gov. Sarah Palin's infamous statement about her state's proximity to Russia, exclaiming, "I can see Iowa from my porch!" And, at the Iowa Jefferson-Jackson Day dinner in 2014, she had a jab for New Jersey Gov. Chris Christie—also visiting Iowa at the time, amid seeking to untangle his candidacy from the controversy back home over politically motivated lane closures on the George Washington Bridge. Christie "is actually here to film a movie sequel—the 'Closed Bridges of Madison County,'" Klobuchar declared to laughter and applause, alluding to a onetime best-selling book set in the Hawkeye State.

Junior Senator

Al Franken (D)

Elected 2008, term expires 2021, 2nd term; b. May 21, 1951, New York City, NY; Harvard U., B.A. 1973; Jewish; married (Franni); 2 children.

Professional Career: Writer, network comedy show; Radio talk show host.

DC Office: 309 HSOB, 20510, 202-224-5641; Fax: 202-224-0044; Website: franken.senate.gov.

State Offices: Duluth, 218-722-2390; Rochester, 507-288-2003; St. Cloud, 320-251-2721; NW Mobile Office, 218-230-9487; St. Paul, 651-221-1016.

Committees: *Energy & Natural Resources:* Energy; Public Lands, Forests, and Mining; Water & Power. *Health, Education, Labor & Pensions:* Children & Families; Employment & Workplace Safety (RMM). *Indian Affairs. Judiciary:* Antitrust, Competition Policy & Consumer Rights; Crime & Terrorism; Immigration & the National Interest; Privacy, Technology & the Law (RMM); Constitution.

Group Ratings

	ADA	ACLU	AFL-CIO	LCV	ITI	COC	HAFA	ACU	CFG	FRC
2014	95%	100%	–	80%	100%	38%	2%	4%	13%	0%
2013	90%	C	100%	100%	C	38%	C	4%	0%	C

National Journal Ratings

	2013 LIB	—	2013 CONS
Economic	82%	—	8%
Social	73%	—	0%
Foreign	71%	—	0%
Composite	86%	—	14%

Key Votes of the 113th Congress

1. Sandy storm spending	Y	5. Student Loan Rates	Y	9. Bipartisan Budget Deal	Y
2. Chuck Hagel Confirmation	Y	6. Employee Non-Discrim'n Act	Y	10. Farm Bill Conference Rept.	Y
3. Gun Background Checks	Y	7. Senate Vote on Judgeships	N	11. Unempl. Comp. Extension	Y
4. Immigration Reform	Y	8. Defense Dept. Spending	Y	12. Keystone Pipeline	N

Election Results

2014 general	Al Franken (D)	1,053,205	(53%)	$31,908,222	$867,752	$471,547
	Mike McFadden (R)	850,227	(43%)	$7,026,515	$23,620	$1,215,810
	Steve Carlson (I)	47,530	(2%)			
2014 primary	Al Franken (D)	182,720	(95%)			
	Sandra Henningsgard (D)	10,627	(5%)			

Prior winning percentage: 2008 (42%)

When Democrat Al Franken was sworn in as Minnesota's junior senator in 2009, he did a couple of things unusual for most politicians: He studiously avoided the spotlight and did his best not to exhibit a sense of humor in public. He declined to talk to the national media, and members of the Capitol Hill press corps recounted stories of Franken telling a joke to his colleagues, only to stop in mid-sentence when a reporter got within earshot. Meanwhile, Franken dived into issues ranging from health care to consumer privacy to the reauthorization of federal farm programs. It was all part of a conscious strategy by Franken—previously known not for his policy-making skills, but for his comedic talent during years as a fixture on NBC's "Saturday Night Live"—to demonstrate he could be serious as well as funny. The gambit appears to have worked, much as it did for other new senators in the past—ranging from Bill Bradley to Hillary Rodham Clinton—who had initially gained celebrity in another role.

"People have seen that I did what I said I would do. I came to Washington, I put my shoulder to the wheel and I did the work," Franken said in a June 2013 interview with the *Associated Press,* as he was ramping up to run for a second term. He punted on whether he would seek a more prominent national voice in a second term, insisting, "I'm more worried about what I'm working on tomorrow." But, having gone on to win re-election in 2014 by a comfortable margin, there are increasing signs Franken is coming out of the self-imposed shell of his first six years. It was nearly five years into his first term before he agreed to appear on a Sunday news show, but he now increasingly cracks jokes on the Senate floor as well as on national television. "You know, sometimes students ask me 'How do you become a U.S. senator?'" Franken related during an appearance on "CBS This Morning" in the spring of 2015. He went on to wisecrack, "And I say 'Do comedy for about 35 years and then run for the Senate. It works every time'."

Nonetheless, the Harvard-educated Franken remains attuned to public perceptions of his persona. "It's something I'm conscious of," he told *Politico* in May 2014. "There's this false dichotomy: If you're a comedian, you can't be serious, and if you're serious, you can't be funny. If you look at satirists like Jon Stewart and Stephen Colbert, you know that they're very serious people." Not only did Franken find it necessary to prove he was serious once he arrived on Capitol Hill; he faced a tortuous path to get there. He was not sworn into office until six months after the opening of the 111th Congress, when a protracted court battle ended with him being declared the victor by 312 votes out of more than 2.86 million cast. Born in New York City, Franken moved when he was four to St. Louis Park, a heavily Jewish suburb of Minneapolis, where his father was a printing salesman and his mother a real estate agent. From a young age, Franken reconciled competing political and comedic impulses by combining them. As a seventh grader, he ran for class president as "Honest Al" and hung posters in the hallways picturing himself with a fake beard and a stovepipe hat.

After graduating from Harvard in 1973, Franken took a writing job in New York for "Saturday Night Live" when it was launched in 1975. For most of the next 20 years, Franken helped to define the program's sense of humor, as it evolved from a fledgling variety show into a pop culture mainstay. He also frequently appeared on the program, most memorably as Stuart Smalley, an obnoxious self-help guru. Franken left the show in 1995 and began working as a political commentator while writing four books, including "Rush Limbaugh Is a Big Fat Idiot". In 2004, he joined the new liberal Air America Radio network with a daily, three-hour show that ran in the same time slot as Limbaugh's program. Franken spent the next three years excoriating conservatives of every stripe, from Bush administration officials to Fox News personality Bill O'Reilly, whom Franken singled out in his 2003 book *"Lies and the Lying Liars Who Tell Them: A Fair and Balanced Look at the Right"*. Fox sued Franken over use of "fair and balanced" in the title, but a judge denied its request for an injunction, and the network dropped the suit.

Franken began thinking about returning to Minnesota to run for the Senate after Democratic Sen. Paul Wellstone, a hero to many liberals, died in a plane crash in October 2002 while running for a third term against former St. Paul Mayor Norm Coleman. Democrats chose former Vice President Walter Mondale to replace Wellstone on the ballot, at the 11th hour, but, despite Mondale's prominence and long political history in the state, Coleman won, 50%-47%. Franken moved his radio talk show in 2006 from New York to Minneapolis, and in February 2007, he announced he would seek the Democratic-Farmer-Labor nomination to take on Coleman. For a time, Franken appeared to have a clear shot at the party nod, but damaging revelations on the eve of the DFL convention in June threatened to derail him. A sexually explicit satirical article he wrote for *Playboy* in 2000 about a virtual sex institute diminished enthusiasm for him among feminist groups. Franken apologized for the article and won the DFL endorsement, but polling showed him looking increasingly weak against Coleman.

Franken slowly won over skeptical Democrats and kept pace with Coleman in fundraising; Franken and Coleman each ended up sending more than $19 million. The dynamics of the race shifted considerably in July, when former Sen. Dean Barkley—appointed to fill the few months remaining in Wellstone's term in 2002—entered the race as the Independence Party candidate. Franken attacked Coleman for reportedly receiving free suits and below-market rent in Washington from political benefactors. But Franken was embarrassed by disclosures that he owed $70,000 in back taxes, and he paid a $25,000 fine to New York State for failing to carry workmen's compensation insurance for his employees. As the returns came in on Election Night, the race was exceedingly tight, with 42 percent for both Coleman and Franken and 15 percent for Barkley.

On Nov. 18, the Minnesota Canvassing Board showed Coleman with a 206-vote lead. A recount began the next day, and the board ultimately concluded Franken was 225 votes ahead. Coleman went to court to contest the results. On March 31, a three-judge court issued an order designating 400 absentee ballots for review; 351 were opened and counted. Finally, on April 13, the judges ruled Franken had received the highest number of votes by a margin of 312. Coleman appealed to the state's highest court, and conceded the contest after it ruled in Franken's favor. Each side ended up spending $6 million on the recount process. Franken was sworn into the Senate on July 7, 2009.

With Franken's arrival in the Senate, Democrats had the 60 votes they needed to prevent Republicans from using the filibuster to block bills, notably with regard to President Barack Obama's signature health insurance overhaul. Franken may have had the greatest legislative impact of his first term on the Affordable Care Act. In September 2009, he introduced a bill requiring that at least 90 percent of health insurance premiums be spent directly on improving the quality of health care. The percentage ultimately was lowered to 85 percent, but the idea was incorporated as a provision of the new law.

In *National Journal*'s annual vote ratings, Franken tied with Illinois' Richard Durbin, the Senate majority whip, as the third most-liberal senator in 2012. He was tied with three other senators as the fifth most liberal in 2013. But, while he has supported the Obama administration on most issues—his 2014 Republican opponent accused Franken of voting with Obama more than 97 percent of the time—Franken sometimes did so reluctantly. In January 2010, after a trip to Afghanistan (where he did exhibit his comic side to entertain the troops) Franken told the *St. Paul Pioneer Press* that Obama's plan for a temporary surge in U.S. troops was "probably the best of a series of options that weren't so great." After Obama agreed in December 2010 to extend the Bush-era tax cuts for everyone, not just lower- and middle-class taxpayers as Democrats preferred, Franken said he would vote for it reluctantly. And the newly minted senator showed little reluctance to take on top White House aides: At a White House meeting in February 2010, he excoriated Obama adviser David Axelrod for failing to set a clear course on health care legislation, and later reportedly got into a profanity-laden exchange with economic adviser Gene Sperling about taxes.

Franken is among the few non-lawyers on the Judiciary Committee, and, as a veteran of television, has taken a particular interest in mergers and acquisitions in that industry and their impact on the distribution of entertainment. He was an early critic of the plan by Comcast to acquire Time Warner Cable, and some analysts said his outspoken opposition helped lead to the collapse of the deal in early 2015. He also opposed the planned AT&T takeover of T-Mobile, breaking with organized labor to do so. Franken said the deal would mean higher consumer prices, while the Communications Workers of America supported the merger because it could add some 20,000 new union members; the $39 billion takeover collapsed in late 2011. Franken chaired the Judiciary Privacy, Technology and the Law Subcommittee, and remains its ranking member with the Republicans in majority. He has used the panel as a platform to go after Uber, the ride-sharing app, over allegations it was misusing data collected on where customers travel—and has questioned major TV manufacturers, such as Samsung and LG, on reports that televisions manufactured by those firms could record personal conversations.

As he sought to demonstrate his seriousness of purpose as a legislator, Franken moved quickly to reach across the political aisle. His first bill, to provide 200 service dogs for wounded veterans, was co-sponsored by three Republicans and became law. He worked with

Maine GOP moderate Olympia Snowe to let women in the military have access to emergency contraception. And he joined Indiana Republican Richard Lugar on funding for diabetes prevention, Arkansas Republican John Boozman on rural veterans' health care, and Iowa Republican Chuck Grassley on improving student loan forms. "He's surprised me," Grassley told *Politico*. "He's taken very seriously doing the work of a senator…I think he's shown he's a senator and not a comedian." But another Republican senator was more skeptical, anonymously telling the publication: "There is no way ever, ever, you could work with Al Franken on a major, serious bipartisan issue. He's a partisan."

Notwithstanding that reputation, Franken has tried some lighthearted gestures to foster better relations between the two parties. He set up a "Hotdish Off" competition within the Minnesota delegation, which attracted TV cameras looking for images of a tea party favorite, Republican Rep. Michele Bachmann, and Franken cooking side-by-side. Franken also organized a "Secret Santa" gift exchange among Democrats and Republicans. When Senate Democratic leaders asked Franken, a magnet for donors, to chair the Democratic Senatorial Campaign Committee for the 2011-2012 election, he declined—saying he needed to stay focused on Minnesota issues. Even so, he frequently traveled to stump for Senate candidates that year, such as Massachusetts' Elizabeth Warren (a frequent guest on his old radio talk show), along with Montana's Jon Tester and Ohio's Sherrod Brown. In his appearances, he often auctioned off hand-drawn U.S. maps while exhorting audiences to avoid complacency.

Given his narrow margin of victory in 2008, Franken was an early GOP target in 2014, with Republican strategists hoping Obama's unpopularity in the state would have a negative effect on his candidacy. But Coleman declined to seek a rematch, and at least two Republican members of the Minnesota House delegation opted not to run. Without a top-tier GOP candidate in the race, Franken became the clear favorite. His eventual opponent, businessman Mike McFadden, defeated four other contenders in the August GOP primary. While McFadden sought to tie Franken closely to Obama, Franken focused as much as possible on Minnesota and as little as possible on the president. Franken spent nearly $32 million, four times as much as McFadden—while sharply attacking McFadden's business record. He charged the Republican was behind business deals resulting in large layoffs and relocation of corporations overseas to avoid taxes. Although McFadden was gaining in the polls late in the campaign amid a nationwide Republican wave, Franken won comfortably, 53%-43%.

The nationwide results on Election Night 2014 put Franken in the Senate minority for the first time in his short career. In comments to the *St. Paul Pioneer Press*, one Franken watcher, Washington University political science Steve Smith, asked: "Is he the kind of senator who could work with a Republican majority? And, the truth is, that's a big unknown." And some speculated about the role that Franken, an acerbic critic of President George W. Bush during his days as a liberal talk show host, might take on if the 2016 election puts another Republican in the White House.

FIRST DISTRICT

Tim Walz (D)

Elected 2006, 5th term; b. April 6, 1964, West Point, NE; Chadron St. Col., B.S. 1989, MN St. U., M.S. 2001; Lutheran; married (Gwen); 2 children.

Military Career: Army Natl. Guard, 1981-2005.

Professional Career: Teacher, Pine Ridge Indian Reservation, SD, 1984; Teacher, People's Republic of China, 1989-90; Founder, Educational Travel Adventures, 1991-2006; H.S. teacher, 1989-2006.

DC Office: 1034 LHOB, 20515, 202-225-2472; Website: walz.house.gov.

State Offices: Mankato, 507-388-2149; Rochester, 507-388-2149.

Committees: *Agriculture:* General Farm Commodities and Risk Management (RMM). *Armed Services:* Tactical Air and Land Forces; Military Personnel. *Veterans' Affairs:* Oversight and Investigations.

Group Ratings

	ADA	ACLU	AFL-CIO	LCV	ITI	COC	HAFA	ACU	CFG	FRC
2014	45%	88%	–	77%	80%	64%	8%	17%	17%	0%
2013	70%	C	90%	86%	C	38%	C	12%	8%	C

National Journal Ratings

	2013 LIB	—	2013 CONS
Economic	61%	—	39%
Social	73%	—	24%
Foreign	71%	—	27%
Composite	69%	—	31%

Key Votes of the 113th Congress

1. Sandy storm spending	Y	5. Medical Marijuana	Y	9. Syrian Rebels Training	Y
2. Violence Against Women Act	Y	6. Farm Bill	Y	10. Keystone pipeline	Y
3. Guantanamo Bay Detainees	Y	7. Afghanistan Combat	NV	11. Immigration Exec. Action	N
4. Abortion 20-week ban	N	8. NSA Phone Data Collection	Y	12. Bipartisan budget deal	Y

Election Results

2014 general	Tim Walz (D)	122,851	(54%)	$1,559,503	$3,858
	Jim Hagedorn (R)	103,536	(46%)	$238,634	
2014 primary	Jim Hagedorn (R)	12,748	(54%)		
	Aaron Miller (R)	10,870	(46%)		

Prior winning percentages: 2012 (58%), 2010 (49%), 2008 (63%), 2006 (53%)

Population		Race and Ethnicity		Income	
Total:	668,726	White	87.9%	Median income:	$55,397
Urban:	28.1%	Latino	5.8%		*(162 of 435)*
Suburban:	3.9%	Black	2.4%	Under $50,000	45.0%
Rural:	68.0%	Asian	2.1%	$50,000-$99,999:	34.4%
Land area:	13,179	Two races	1.5%	$100,000-$199,999:	16.8%
Pop/sq. mi.:	50.7	White Ethnic	21.8%	$200,000 or more:	3.8%
Born in state:	69.6%			Poverty Rate	11.5%
		Education			
Age Groups		H.S. grad or less:	39.5%	**Work**	
Under 18:	23.4%	Some college:	34.2%	White collar:	34.1%
18 to 34:	23.0%	College degree, 4 yr.:	17.7%	Blue collar:	40.1%
35 to 64:	37.8%	Post-grad study:	8.6%	Sales and service:	25.8%
Over 64:	15.8%			Govt. workers:	10.7%
		Military			
		Veterans/active duty:	8.4%		

South Minnesota: Rochester

The Mississippi River flows majestically southeast from Minneapolis and St. Paul, cutting through rolling hills and, where it widens, forming calm lakes. This far north, the westward tide of Yankee migrants thinned out; most settlers following the railroads on the flood plains west of the river after

Voter Turnout	
2013 Total Citizen 18+	494,427
2014 House Turnout	226,695
2014 Turnout as % CVAP	45.9%
2012 Turnout as % CVAP	70.2%

the Civil War were Germans and Scandinavians, bringing their families to a terrain much like the Rhineland and to the rolling uplands beyond, which resemble the northern European plain.

Along the Mississippi River, tourism spiked upward after the old St. Paul and Milwaukee Railroad was converted to a hiker-biker nature trail in the 1990s. A little to the west is Rochester, home to the renowned Mayo Clinic, founded in 1863 when English-born physician William Mayo set up a practice to examine inductees into the Union Army. Today, 135,000 people annually visit the clinic for cancer treatment. With more than 33,000 people employed at Mayo, Rochester is prosperous and was the fastest-growing metropolitan area in Minnesota in 2014. That growth will continue, with Mayo's plan for a new $6 billion high-tech medical center. A Medicare review of the nation's hospitals in April 2015 gave the clinic four stars out of five; only 7 percent of hospitals got five stars. A large IBM manufacturing facility in Rochester suffered some job losses early that year. In March 2015, state officials announced their review of several options for a high-speed link to Minneapolis-St. Paul.

In Mower County, Austin is the headquarters of the Hormel meatpacking firm, which produces "miracle meat" Spam, Hormel chili and Dinty Moore stew. Farther west is flat farmland. This was the southern locus of the 1862 Dakota Uprising, which resulted in the simultaneous hangings of 38 Dakota warriors at Mankato. Many of the bodies were dug up at night by doctors—including William Mayo—for use in medical study. To the north is Le Sueur, where Minnesota Valley Canning Co., later renamed Green Giant, was founded; a 55-foot statue of the iconic giant was erected in 1978 in Blue Earth. The farther west you go, the more frequently you find communities with a German heritage, like New Ulm, where the "Hermann the German" monument guards the town. Many small towns in Southern Minnesota are now filling up with Hispanic farmworkers. Somalis have established a growing presence in Rochester and Austin.

2012 Presidential Vote		
Barack Obama (D) 170,377	(49%)
Mitt Romney (R)................165,720	(48%)
2008 Presidential Vote		
Barack Obama (D) 177,494	(51%)
John McCain (R)................162,737	(47%)
Cook Partisan Voting Index: R+1		

The 1st Congressional District of Minnesota includes most of the state's two southern tiers of counties. It stretches over 250 miles, from the South Dakota border to the Wisconsin border. This historically was a political borderland, with Civil War Republicans in the east and Farmer-Laborites more common in the west, but the traditions have been upended. Rochester had long been a Republican stronghold, but like many Northern white-collar areas, it has trended Democratic. With its working-class tradition, Austin has remained solidly Democratic-Farmer-Labor. To the west, the population-losing farm counties between Mankato and the South Dakota border now vote solidly Republican. A February 2015 study showed that the 1st ranked ninth in the nation in farm production. This is one of three adjacent districts in Minnesota that are competitive at the presidential level. Barack Obama won here with 51% in 2008, and 49% in 2012.

Tim Walz (D)

Tim Walz, a Democrat first elected in 2006, has survived competitive elections in his rural district by balancing strong support for farmers, military veterans and gun owners with a commitment to the main economic planks of his party's agenda.

Walz grew up in Nebraska and joined the Army National Guard when he was 17. When he retired from the Guard 24 years later, in 2005, he held the rank of command sergeant major. Walz earned his teaching degree in Nebraska, taught school in China for a year through a Harvard University program, and later established an educational travel company that helped high school students study in China. He and his wife moved to Minnesota in 1996 to take teaching jobs in Mankato. There, he taught high school geography and coached the football team to two state championships.

Walz got into politics relatively late in life—he was 42 when he ran for Congress. In 2004, President George W. Bush made an appearance in the area as part of his reelection campaign. Walz took two students to the event, where Bush campaign staffers demanded to know whether he supported the president and barred the students from entering after discovering one had a sticker for Democratic candidate John Kerry. Walz suggested that it might be bad PR for the Bush campaign to arrest an Army veteran, and he and the students were allowed in. Walz said the experience sparked his interest in politics, first as a volunteer for the Kerry campaign and then as a congressional candidate. "I don't know if I'd necessarily call it an epiphany, but it was definitely one of those things that pushed me into" politics, Walz said.

In 2006, Walz challenged six-term Republican Rep. Gil Gutknecht, an affable conservative who was not considered especially vulnerable. The district had sent Republicans to Washington for 100 of the previous 114 years. Walz was not a polished campaigner. His speaking style was didactic compared to the ease with which Gutknecht, a former auctioneer, handled a crowd. But he struck a chord with his message of declining middle-class wages, tax cuts for high earners and Congress' failure to hold Bush accountable on the Iraq war. He ran as a political outsider and painted Gutknecht as too closely tied to Bush. Walz supported abortion rights and opposed a ban on same-sex marriage. His military experience and football coaching gave an aura of authenticity to his campaign that made him harder to attack. On Election Day, Walz defeated Gutknecht 53%-47%. He became the highest-ranking enlisted soldier ever to serve in Congress.

In the House, Walz has established a mostly centrist voting record. He was one of just 17 Democrats to vote to hold Attorney General Eric Holder in contempt of Congress for allegedly withholding information relating to the "Fast and Furious" gun-tracing operation. He opposed the creation of the Troubled Asset Relief Program to assist the financial services industry because he said it didn't do enough to protect homeowners from foreclosure. His championing of gun owners' rights has earned him the National Rifle Association's endorsement. In February 2015, he voted for the Keystone XL pipeline, to the dismay of environmental groups. But he has backed most of President Barack Obama's major initiatives, including health care reform and the 2009 cap-and-trade bill to reduce carbon emissions. In calling for more domestic renewable energy to replace oil imports from countries hostile to the United States, Walz likes to say, "We export $1 billion a day to countries who hate us. They'll hate us for free."

Walz has introduced a number of good-government bills. He scored his highest-profile legislative victory in February 2012 when the House passed a version of his bill barring the use of inside information by lawmakers to make financial trades and requiring members to disclose their investments. The measure had languished for five years, but picked up momentum after it was featured in a *60 Minutes* story. That year, another Walz bill, which he cosponsored with Republican Rep. Jeff Denham of California, also became law. It sought to make it easier for veterans to find jobs using skills acquired through military training. Walz has worked on other veterans issues, including suicide prevention and improving the treatment of traumatic brain injuries.

With a seat on the Agriculture Committee, Walz secured increased access to credit and conservation opportunities for farmers in the 2008 farm bill. In the debate over the 2012 farm bill, he urged House Republicans to take up the committee-passed version instead of seeking a better bill. "Perfect is what you get in heaven," he said. "The U.S. House of Representatives is closer to hell." In 2015, he became the ranking Democrat on the General Farm Commodities and Risk Management Subcommittee. He had sought the top Democratic slot on the Veterans Affairs Committee and had support from several veterans organizations. But he lost to Corrine Brown of Florida, who benefited from seniority and the support of Democratic leaders. Instead, Pelosi tapped Walz to chair her quarterly roundtables on veterans' issues. Also in 2015, Walz gave up his seat on the Transportation and Infrastructure Committee to join Armed Services, where he sought changes in retirement and pension benefits.

He has faced some competitive reelections. In 2010, his Republican opponent was state Rep. Randy Demmer, a farmer who slammed Walz's support of the Democratic agenda and drew financial help from outside Republican groups. Walz enjoyed a huge financial advantage, thanks in part to money raised from Mayo Clinic employees. He highlighted a video of his opponent seeming receptive to the idea of partially privatizing Social Security. Demmer denied the charge, but had trouble persuading voters that Walz was too liberal. Walz won 49%-44%. His reelection in 2012 was far easier. His Republican opponent was former state Rep. Allen Quist, who didn't help himself when he told an audience that radical liberals were a bigger threat to the country than terrorism. Walz won with 58% of the vote. In 2014, pro-business Republican Tim Hagedorn, whose father Tom Hagedorn represented the district in the 1970s, won the primary 54%-46% over convention-endorsed Aaron Miller, a social conservative. The National Republican Congressional Committee stayed out of the race, and Walz outspent Hagedorn in the general $1.6 million to $239,000. The challenger took six counties in the western part of the district. Walz took Rochester-based Olmsted County 54%-46%, and won the district by the same margin. Republican State Rep. Tony Cornish voiced early interest in a 2016 bid. He shared Walz's approach as a pragmatist, with support from veterans and gun-rights groups.

SECOND DISTRICT

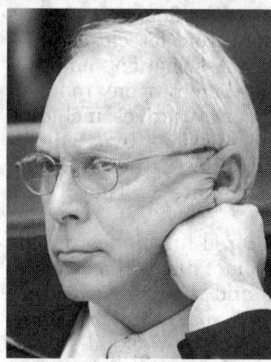

John Kline (R)

Elected 2002, 7th term; b. Sept. 6, 1947, Allentown, PA; Rice U., B.A. 1969, Shippensburg U., M.P.A. 1988; Methodist; married (Vicky); 2 children.

Military Career: Marine Corps, 1969-94 (Vietnam).

Professional Career: V.P., Ctr. of the American Experiment, 2001-02.

DC Office: 2439 RHOB, 20515, 202-225-2271; Fax: 202-225-2595; Website: kline.house.gov.

State Offices: Burnsville, 952-808-1213.

Committees: *Armed Services:* Military Personnel; Emerging Threats & Capabilities; *Education & the Workforce* (Chmn).

Group Ratings

	ADA	ACLU	AFL-CIO	LCV	ITI	COC	HAFA	ACU	CFG	FRC
2014	0%	0%	–	6%	100%	93%	50%	80%	68%	88%
2013	0%	C	19%	0%	C	85%	C	72%	58%	C

National Journal Ratings

	2013 LIB	—	2013 CONS
Economic	31%	—	68%
Social	34%	—	62%
Foreign	24%	—	68%
Composite	32%	—	68%

Key Votes of the 113th Congress

1. Sandy storm spending	N	5. Medical Marijuana	N	9. Syrian Rebels Training	Y
2. Violence Against Women Act	Y	6. Farm Bill	Y	10. Keystone pipeline	Y
3. Guantanamo Bay Detainees	N	7. Afghanistan Combat	N	11. Immigration Exec. Action	Y
4. Abortion 20-week ban	Y	8. NSA Phone Data Collection	N	12. Bipartisan budget deal	Y

Election Results

2014 general	John Kline (R)	137,778	(56%)	$3,226,367	$6,367	$51,420
	Mike Obermueller (D)	95,565	(39%)	$933,332		
	Paula Overby (I)	12,319	(5%)	$8,472		
2014 primary	John Kline (R)	unopposed				

Prior winning percentages: 2012 (54%), 2010 (63%), 2008 (57%), 2006 (56%), 2004 (56%), 2002 (53%)

Population		Race and Ethnicity		Income	
Total:	681,195	White	84.2%	Median income:	$73,381
Urban:	1.4%	Latino	5.2%		*(52 of 435)*
Suburban:	83.9%	Asian	4.0%	Under $50,000	31.5%
Rural:	14.8%	Black	3.6%	$50,000-$99,999:	35.1%
Land area:	2,814	Two races	2.5%	$100,000-$199,999:	27.2%
Pop/sq. mi.:	242.1	White Ethnic	29.6%	$200,000 or more:	6.2%
Born in state:	67.5%			Poverty Rate	8.4%
		Education			
Age Groups		H.S. grad or less:	29.7%	**Work**	
Under 18:	25.7%	Some college:	32.8%	White collar:	41.5%
18 to 34:	21.3%	College degree, 4 yr.:	25.5%	Blue collar:	39.9%
35 to 64:	41.3%	Post-grad study:	12.0%	Sales and service:	18.6%
Over 64:	11.7%			Govt. workers:	11.5%
		Military			
		Veterans/active duty:	8.0%		

Twin Cities' South Suburbs

Drive south from the Twin Cities and one encounters big-box stores, catering to the youngish families that live nearby in new housing developments
and who work in managerial, business and technical careers. Many come from elsewhere, attracted

Voter Turnout	
2013 Total Citizen 18+	485,136
2014 House Turnout	245,848
2014 Turnout as % CVAP	50.7%
2012 Turnout as % CVAP	79%

by Minnesota's strong economy and pleasant living
(provided they can tolerate its cold winters). They have turned places such as Eagan,
Lakeville, Apple Valley, Mendota Heights and Burnsville in Dakota County into fast-growing suburbs. The upscale suburbs of Scott County grew by an impressive 51 percent since
2000. In recent years, these suburban areas have begun to see an influx of lower-income
residents, attracted by the good schools and low crime rates. Northfield, with its boutique
economy and arts scene, was ranked second nationally among small towns by Livability.
com. *Money* magazine listed it as the nation's best place to retire. In his book *Shot All to
Hell*, Mark Gardner wrote about Northfield's previous claim to fame, when it was the site
in 1876 of the final bank robbery attempt of Jesse James and his gang.

The local economy was dealt a blow when Lockheed Martin closed its Eagan plant in
2013, with a loss of 1,000 jobs. Two years later, developers announced plans to build a shopping district in its place. Delta Air Lines has steadily cut jobs in the area following its merger
with Northwest Airlines. But unemployment has stayed relatively low, as employers like
Ecolab and UPS continue major operations, and a $100 million outlet mall opened in 2014.
Tech support company Stream Global Services relocated its headquarters from Boston in
2012, and was purchased in 2014 by Cincinnati-based Convergys, a corporate rival. Drive
farther south on Interstate 35 and U.S. 52—a little farther every year—and suddenly you
are in farm country. There are also modest-sized towns here such as Northfield, the idyllic
home of Carleton College and its late profes-
sor-turned-liberal-senator, Paul Wellstone.

These suburbs and hamlets make up
the 2nd Congressional District of Minnesota.
Dakota County, just south of St. Paul, casts
over half the votes in the district and historically was marginally Democratic, although
today it is more of a swing county. Neighboring Scott County has the highest median
income in the state, and is heavily Republican, though it casts about one-third as many

2012 Presidential Vote
Barack Obama (D) 184,802   (49%)
Mitt Romney (R).................184,576   (49%)

2008 Presidential Vote
Barack Obama (D) 184,918   (50%)
John McCain (R).................174,721   (48%)

Cook Partisan Voting Index: R+2

votes as Dakota. The redistricting shift of heavily Republican Carver County to the 6th
District has made the 2nd a more competitive district.

John Kline (R)

Republican John Kline, first elected in 2002, is a no-nonsense conservative ally of House
Speaker John Boehner. He chairs the House Education and the Workforce Committee, a
panel that Boehner himself once headed, and he retains interest in national security from
his previous career as a well-connected Marine.

Kline grew up in Corpus Christi, Texas, where his father owned a small hometown
newspaper and his mother managed the Corpus Christi Symphony Orchestra. After graduating from Rice University, he served for 25 years in the Marine Corps, during which he
served in Vietnam, commanded Marine aviation forces in Somalia, and oversaw the Corps'
$50 billion program-objective memorandum, a budget and planning analysis. He also was
assigned to the White House and carried the so-called "football"—the package containing
the nuclear launch codes—for presidents Jimmy Carter and Ronald Reagan; he surely has
had more face time with presidents than most other members of Congress. "It's not something I expected to do when I completed my four years with Marine One," he told Townhall
magazine in 2014. "I thought it was time to get back to day-to-day flying, Marine Corps
missions and living in tents and things like that, but it was suggested to me that the White
House needed another military aide." When he retired in 1994, he settled in Lakeville, in
Dakota County, where he managed his wife's family farm.

Kline challenged Democratic Rep. Bill Luther in 1998, after Luther had had several expensive and fierce campaigns to keep the seat. Kline favored tax cuts, more military spending, and the resignation of President Bill Clinton in that year's impeachment proceedings. He also opposed abortion rights. He spent only $283,000; Luther, who raised $1 million, spent only $412,000. That might have been a mistake. Luther won by only 50%-46%. Kline hardly stopped running. More experienced and better financed in 2000, he made his rematch with Luther one of the nation's high-profile House contests. The result was closer, but Luther survived 50%-48%, and Kline said he was unlikely to run again.

Then the unexpected happened. The redistricting plan that the state Supreme Court ordered in March 2002 placed Kline's home in a new 2nd District where there was no incumbent. State GOP leaders urged Kline to run again. Luther's home was in the new 6th District, which was considerably more Republican after the redistricting. So he decided to take on Kline in the 2nd District. The acrimonious campaign resumed. Luther called Kline an extremist who held "Texas values." This time, Kline won 53%-42%.

In the House, Kline's voting record has been solidly conservative. He proposed legislation to replace Ulysses S. Grant with former President Ronald Reagan on the $50 bill. He became a trusted deputy of Boehner and gained responsibilities at the National Republican Congressional Committee. When the ranking Republican slot on Education and Labor came open in 2009, House Republicans wanted a tough counterweight to liberal panel chairman George Miller of California. Kline leapfrogged over several more senior Republicans while fending off a challenge from the more junior Rep. Cathy McMorris Rodgers, another Boehner loyalist. Kline has shown that he can be tough on conservatives, as when they pledged to abolish the Education Department to save money. "That's simply not going to get done," he responded.

As chairman, Kline has sought bipartisan backing on a rewrite of the No Child Left Behind education law, which expired in 2007 and which members of both parties have found severely wanting. After discussions with Miller, he released a bill in 2011 that essentially cut Democrats out of negotiations. The legislation ratcheted back the federal role in education and handed power back to states and local leaders, whom he said "are clamoring to ... revive innovation in our classrooms." Democrats excoriated his efforts, joining with business and civil rights groups in arguing that his proposed changes would unfairly impact minorities, low-income students and students with disabilities. The measure was adopted by the House on a party-line vote, and went nowhere in the Senate.

Kline worked with committee liberals to pass bipartisan bills aimed at modernizing benefits for federal workers and promoting the development of high-performing charter schools. But he turned back their efforts in 2012 to investigate mine safety, an area that Congress has not addressed despite several deadly mining accidents in recent years. He also introduced a bill in October 2011 to preempt a National Labor Relations Board plan to implement faster union elections, a move that he said would give businesses less time to make a case against unionization. Kline has been a staunch defender of for-profit higher education, repeatedly fighting the Obama administration's attempts to regulate those schools. Liberal interest groups have pointed to the sizable campaign donations he has received from the for-profit sector, but he denies they have influenced his thinking. Fearful of what he called a "ticking time bomb" if some plans fail, he has backed changes in underfunded pension plans to permit a reduction of payments to retirees.

Kline antagonized another largely Democratic constituency, LGBT activists, in December 2014. He and Michigan Republican Rep. Tim Walberg asked the Office of Federal Contract Compliance Programs to slow down its implementation of a new rule to bar federal contractors from discriminating against lesbian, gay, bisexual and transgender workers. "Everyone should have the right to work and make a living and be judged on their performance, not their orientation, so it's shameful that Congressman Kline wants to withdraw a rule supporting this basic idea of fairness in the workplace," the Human Rights Campaign's Fred Sainz said in a statement. Kline had little reaction to the criticism or to other initiatives by gay-rights activists.

With a Republican Senate in 2015, Kline returned his attention to No Child Left Behind. In a January op-ed, he promised to steer through legislation embodying four principles: restoring local control "by eliminating the federal accountability system and calling on states to develop a better approach"; eliminating bureaucratic waste and giving state and local leaders more spending flexibility; eliminating federal requirements on academic credentials; and giving parents more options by expanding access to charter schools. He ran into opposition from conservative advocacy groups. Early Senate moves toward bipartisanship were encouraging. In January 2015, Kline opposed as too ambitious the proposal by President Barack Obama to have the federal government pick up the tab for community college for some students. "Unless the president has a responsible plan to meet our existing commitments, he shouldn't be making new promises the American people can't afford," he responded.

GOP leaders chose Kline and two other committee chairmen to draft their alternative to the Affordable Care Act if the Supreme Court struck down the health care law. Though he provided few specifics, he suggested that the measure would cover people with preexisting health conditions as well as so-called "high risk pools" offering subsidized insurance for those who couldn't otherwise get coverage. Another potential option was to replace the benefits with tax credits. Facing term limits as committee chairman in 2016, he could shift his focus to his work on the Armed Services Committee.

In 2006, Democrats appeared to find a strong challenger to Kline in Coleen Rowley, a retired FBI agent who was lauded by *Time* magazine in 2002 for going public with the FBI's decision to ignore recommendations to investigate Zacarias Moussaoui, a figure in the September 11 attacks. As a first-time candidate, Rowley struggled to find her footing, and the party lost interest in her campaign. While other Republicans distanced themselves from Bush and the Iraq war, Kline voiced support for the war, emphasizing his background as a former Marine and as the father of a young Army Blackhawk helicopter pilot who did a tour of duty in Iraq. He defeated Rowley, 56%-40%.

After the 2012 redistricting made the district more competitive, he got a challenge from Mike Obermueller, a lawyer and former state representative who took moderate stances, such as cutting wasteful spending. Obermueller raised $700,000 and got limited help from national liberal groups. Kline outraised his rival by 3-to-1 and notched a 54%-46% win. Obermueller ran again in 2014, and each candidate spent a bit more money. Outside liberal groups attacked Kline for his bill to tie student loan interest rates to market rates, which they said could make college more burdensome for students. Left-wing talk show host Bill Maher targeted Kline in his "Flip a District" campaign, even making a personal stop in the district in October. He called Kline "just wrong about everything." In a Republican year, Kline improved his winning performance to 56%-39% in a rematch against Obermueller. Maher responded on Twitter, "Enjoy it John Kline, at least people are on to U now." Democratic challengers quickly stepped forward for 2016, including St. Jude Medical Foundation President Angie Craig, a lesbian with a wife and four children.

THIRD DISTRICT

Erik Paulsen (R)

Elected 2008, 4th term; b. May 14, 1965, Bakersfield, CA; St. Olaf Col., B.A. 1987; Lutheran; married (Kelly); 4 children.

Elected Office: MN House, 1995-2008, maj. ldr., 2002-06.

Professional Career: Marketing analyst, Target Corp.

DC Office: 127 CHOB, 20515, 202-225-2871; Fax: 202-225-6351; Website: paulsen.house.gov.

State Offices: Eden Prairie, 952-405-8510.

Committees: *Ways & Means:* Select Revenue Measures; Trade. *Joint Economic Committee.*

Group Ratings

	ADA	ACLU	AFL-CIO	LCV	ITI	COC	HAFA	ACU	CFG	FRC
2014	0%	0%	–	11%	100%	93%	56%	80%	68%	88%
2013	0%	C	14%	7%	C	85%	C	84%	70%	C

National Journal Ratings

	2013 LIB	—	2013 CONS
Economic	21%	—	77%
Social	34%	—	62%
Foreign	15%	—	77%
Composite	26%	—	74%

Key Votes of the 113th Congress

1. Sandy storm spending	N	5. Medical Marijuana	N	9. Syrian Rebels Training	Y
2. Violence Against Women Act	Y	6. Farm Bill	Y	10. Keystone pipeline	Y
3. Guantanamo Bay Detainees	N	7. Afghanistan Combat	N	11. Immigration Exec. Action	Y
4. Abortion 20-week ban	Y	8. NSA Phone Data Collection	N	12. Bipartisan budget deal	Y

Election Results

2014 general	Erik Paulsen (R)	167,515	(62%)	$2,695,111	$7,188
	Sharon Sund (D)	101,846	(38%)	$127,647	
2014 primary	Erik Paulsen (R)	unopposed			

Prior winning percentages: 2012 (58%), 2010 (59%), 2008 (48%)

Population		Race and Ethnicity		Income	
Total:	685,092	White	80.8%	Median income:	$77,647
Urban:	33.6%	Black	6.4%		(36 of 435)
Suburban:	66.4%	Asian	6.0%	Under $50,000	30.9%
Rural:	0.0%	Latino	3.7%	$50,000-$99,999:	31.5%
Land area:	554	Two races	2.5%	$100,000-$199,999:	27.8%
Pop/sq. mi.:	1,236.4	White Ethnic	26.9%	$200,000 or more:	9.8%
Born in state:	62.6%			Poverty Rate	6.4%
		Education			
Age Groups		H.S. grad or less:	23.2%	**Work**	
Under 18:	24.8%	Some college:	30.2%	White collar:	46.3%
18 to 34:	20.2%	College degree, 4 yr.:	31.6%	Blue collar:	39.0%
35 to 64:	41.9%	Post-grad study:	15.0%	Sales and service:	14.7%
Over 64:	13.1%			Govt. workers:	8.0%
		Military			
		Veterans/active duty:	7.5%		

Twin Cities' West Suburbs

Over the past half century, Minnesota's two-headed metropolis has spread out from the neat streets inside the city limits of Minneapolis and St. Paul into the countryside all around. People have sorted themselves out geographically. In the lower lands

Voter Turnout	
2013 Total Citizen 18+	489,030
2014 House Turnout	269,585
2014 Turnout as % CVAP	55.1%
2012 Turnout as % CVAP	83.1%

along the Mississippi and Minnesota rivers, where rail lines fan out from the Twin Cities, are the blue-collar suburbs, with modest houses and warehouses and factories near the tracks. Inland, around the lakes Minnesota is so proud of, in subdivisions with curved streets hugging the hills, are more affluent neighborhoods, quiet and unflashy in the Minnesota way but comfortable whether blanketed with snow or with a nearby lake glinting in the summer sun. At the edge of Lake Minnetonka is Wayzata, a moneyed suburb and a generous ZIP code for political donations.

In between are the freeway interchanges where some of the Twin Cities' innovations can be seen—Southdale shopping center in Edina, the first enclosed mall; huge indoor water parks; and the giant Mall of America in Bloomington, with its 4.9 million square feet, 520-plus stores, 85 eating options, 14 movie screens, 25 rides, and 11,000 year-round employees. Radisson opened in 2013 a 500-room luxury hotel, which is the only hotel connected directly to the mall. The mall attracts 42 million people annually. A planned expansion, which may double the size, calls for more facilities that appeal to upscale patrons who travel a greater distance. To the west is Eden Prairie, which *Money* magazine in 2010 named the best medium-sized U.S. city. For years, this was a high-growth area, but there are some signs that the trend has changed; 26 suburbs in the Twin Cities area lost population in the 2010 census, including many in the 3rd District: Coon Rapids, Corcoran, Dayton, Deephaven, Minnetonka, Orono and Shorewood.

The 3rd Congressional District of Minnesota consists mostly of the Hennepin County

2012 Presidential Vote		
Barack Obama (D)	199,093	(50%)
Mitt Romney (R)	195,802	(49%)

2008 Presidential Vote		
Barack Obama (D)	199,555	(51%)
John McCain (R)	185,396	(47%)

Cook Partisan Voting Index: R+2

suburbs of the Twin Cities. On the north side of the district is working-class Brooklyn Park, long a Democratic-Farmer-Labor Party stronghold, where professional wrestler-turned-governor Jesse Ventura began his political career as mayor. On the south is middle-income Bloomington. To the west are Edina, Plymouth, Wayzata and other towns around Lake Minnetonka, all traditionally Republican. The 3rd is the home of Minnesota's traditional Republican establishment, but like many Northern suburban districts, it has moved toward the Democrats in recent years. Overall, the district is close to evenly matched in presidential contests. Barack Obama twice won it narrowly: 51% in 2008, 50% in 2012.

Erik Paulsen (R)

Republican Erik Paulsen, first elected in 2008, is a serious-minded Republican who followed his former boss Jim Ramstad to the Ways and Means Committee and focuses on tax and trade issues that boost Minnesota businesses.

Raised in the Twin City suburbs, Paulsen was the oldest of four children. He attended nearby St. Olaf College, where he met his wife, Kelly, in a math class. After graduation, Paulsen followed a lifelong dream to work for a summer in Yellowstone National Park, then returned to the Twin Cities to begin a career in marketing. He later took a job in Ramstad's Washington office, where he worked for a year and a half before returning to Minnesota to manage the district office. In 1995, he was elected to the Minnesota House of Representatives, rising to majority leader in 2003. He was a leading supporter of Republican Gov. Tim Pawlenty's no-new-taxes policy. While in the legislature, Paulsen worked as a business analyst for the Minneapolis-based Target Corp.

In early 2008, when Ramstad retired, Paulsen faced no Republican competition and got an early fundraising lead. Democratic newcomer Ashwin Madia, an Iraq war veteran, was his opponent in the general election. Madia had upset better-known state Sen. Terri Bonoff to secure the Democratic-Farmer-Labor nomination, and he soon pulled even with Paulsen in the polls. Paulsen called himself "one of a new generation of Republican reformers." On the stump, he emphasized his differences with Madia on taxes, contrasting his support for making the Bush-era tax cuts permanent with Madia's position allowing them to expire for people with annual incomes over $250,000.

The campaign turned highly negative. The Democrats ran ads that attempted to link Paulsen to a Republican fundraiser at a Las Vegas strip club. Paulsen parried with ads accusing Madia of lying about his voting record. Republicans ran an ad in the final days of the campaign that the Madia camp said deliberately depicted Madia's skin tone as darker than it is. Madia is of Indian descent. The two candidates each spent about $2.7 million. A third candidate, businessman David Dillon, ran as an independent. In this competitive district, Paulsen withstood the national Democratic wave with 48% to Madia's 41%. Dillon picked up 11%, drawing support in areas where Madia should have been strong.

In the House, Paulsen usually has been a reliable Republican vote, which was essential to snag a prized seat on Ways and Means. He filed a bill to repeal the medical device tax that was included in the 2010 health care overhaul, calling it "a tax on innovation" that hurt several Minnesota companies. The measure passed the House in June 2012. It went nowhere in the Senate under Democratic control, but Paulsen relaunched his efforts in 2015. A devout free-trade enthusiast, he co-chaired an informal GOP working group on South Korea and said he was encouraged by the bipartisan votes on trade deals. "Our constituents expect us to be results-oriented," he told the Minneapolis *Star-Tribune*. He co-chairs the House Medical Technology Caucus, where he advocates on behalf of the industry's technologies and jobs. Paulsen opposed the New Year's Day 2013 bipartisan budget compromise aimed at averting the so-called "fiscal cliff," saying it failed to significantly rein in government spending.

During earlier service on the Financial Services Committee, Paulson tried without success in 2009 to strip the Treasury Department of the power to extend the Wall Street bailout program for another year. He showed independence by joining with Democrats on expanding the Children's Health Insurance Program, a credit card overhaul bill and a measure giving the Food and Drug Administration some authority to regulate tobacco products. He also showed his moderate credentials when he backed a measure adding sexual orientation and gender identity to federal hate crimes statutes. He has been a leading advocate of House-passed bills to limit child sex trafficking.

Since his first election, he has outraised his campaign opponents by several multiples and has not been seriously challenged for reelection.

FOURTH DISTRICT

Betty McCollum (D)

Elected 2000, 8th term; b. July 12, 1954, Minneapolis; Inver Hills Comm. Col., A.A. 1980, Col. of St. Catherine, B.A. 1987; Catholic; divorced; 2 children.

Elected Office: N. St. Paul City Cncl., 1986-92; MN House, 1992-2000.

Professional Career: Teacher; Retail sales & mgmt.

DC Office: 2256 RHOB, 20515, 202-225-6631; Fax: 202-225-1968; Website: mccollum.house.gov.

State Offices: St. Paul, 651-224-9191.

Committees: *Appropriations:* Defense; Interior, Environment & Related Agencies (RMM); *Legislative Branch.*

Group Ratings

	ADA	ACLU	AFL-CIO	LCV	ITI	COC	HAFA	ACU	CFG	FRC
2014	75%	88%	–	89%	60%	43%	9%	4%	4%	0%
2013	90%	C	95%	93%	C	31%	C	12%	10%	C

National Journal Ratings

	2013 LIB	—	2013 CONS
Economic	90%	—	9%
Social	93%	—	0%
Foreign	66%	—	32%
Composite	85%	—	15%

Key Votes of the 113th Congress

1. Sandy storm spending	Y	5. Medical Marijuana	Y
2. Violence Against Women Act	Y	6. Farm Bill	N
3. Guantanamo Bay Detainees	Y	7. Afghanistan Combat	Y
4. Abortion 20-week ban	N	8. NSA Phone Data Collection	Y

9. Syrian Rebels Training	N
10. Keystone pipeline	N
11. Immigration Exec. Action	N
12. Bipartisan budget deal	Y

Election Results

2014 general	Betty McCollum (D)	147,857	(61%)	$740,086	$3,803
	Sharna Wahlgren (R)	79,492	(33%)	$130,282	
	Dave Thomas (I)	14,059	(6%)		
2014 primary	Betty McCollum (D)	unopposed			

Prior winning percentages: 2012 (62%), 2010 (59%), 2008 (68%), 2006 (70%), 2004 (57%), 2002 (62%), 2000 (48%)

Population		Race and Ethnicity		Income	
Total:	686,098	White	70.7%	Median income:	$61,574
Urban:	70.3%	Asian	10.4%		*(104 of 435)*
Suburban:	29.7%	Black	9.0%	Under $50,000	41.3%
Rural:	0.0%	Latino	6.3%	$50,000-$99,999:	30.5%
Land area:	381	Two races	3.0%	$100,000-$199,999:	22.3%
Pop/sq. mi.:	1,799.5	White Ethnic	28.5%	$200,000 or more:	5.9%
Born in state:	60.6%			Poverty Rate	13.6%
		Education			
Age Groups		H.S. grad or less:	29.7%	**Work**	
Under 18:	23.7%	Some college:	28.0%	White collar:	43.6%
18 to 34:	25.4%	College degree, 4 yr.:	26.0%	Blue collar:	40.1%
35 to 64:	38.3%	Post-grad study:	16.3%	Sales and service:	16.3%
Over 64:	12.6%			Govt. workers:	13.8%
		Military			
		Veterans/active duty:	6.9%		

St. Paul Metro

Above the Mississippi River bluffs stand St. Paul's two most distinctive landmarks: the Minnesota State Capitol and Archbishop John Ireland's Cathedral of St. Paul. St. Paul's origins are actually quite a bit more colorful than its pious name and status as state capital might imply. Its original name was

Voter Turnout	
2013 Total Citizen 18+	488,256
2014 House Turnout	241,637
2014 Turnout as % CVAP	49.5%
2012 Turnout as % CVAP	77.3%

actually "Pig's Eye," after the tavern set up by the first European settler in the area, Pierre "Pig's Eye" Parrant. It almost wasn't the capital either; the territorial legislature in 1857 passed a bill moving the capital to St. Peter, near Mankato. But a legislator hid the physical bill, keeping the governor—who owned the land on which the new capitol building was slated to be built—from signing it, thus preventing the move. The area was settled mainly by Catholic Irish and German immigrants in the 1850s, as opposed to the Protestant Swedes and Yankees who settled Minneapolis.

St. Paul later became a major transportation hub, a railroad center and river port, while Minneapolis, farther upriver at the Falls of St. Anthony, became the nation's largest grain milling center. Both industries stoked the ire of farmers in the Dakotas who had no choice but to deal with them to make a living. With the large curve in the river, St. Paul borders a longer stretch of the Mississippi than any other city. Beneath the Capitol and the cathedral, the city's skywalk-linked downtown is home to the Ordway Center for the Performing Arts, the headquarters of Minnesota Public Radio and Garrison Keillor's "Prairie Home Companion," and an active pop music industry.

Beyond the cathedral is Summit Avenue, on which capitalists like the Great Northern Railway's James J. Hill built grandiose Romanesque houses. Along with Monument Avenue in Richmond and Meridian Street in Indianapolis, it remains one of America's grand 19th century residential boulevards. The parallel Grand Avenue is home to a pleasant commercial strip with a walkable, urban feel. The Minnesota state fairgrounds are in nearby Falcon Heights, where each year a new "Princess Kay of the Milky Way" is crowned; she and the other finalists sit in a walk-in cooler for six hours while their effigies are carved into 90-pound blocks of butter.

Businesses in the area range from multinational conglomerates like 3M, formerly known as Minnesota Mining and Manufacturing Co., to small enterprises like the William Marvy Co., the last makers of barber poles in the United States. Prospects for economic development got a boost with the June 2014 opening of the 11-mile Green Line light rail—previously referred to as the Central Corridor—that links the city with Minneapolis; its 18 stations include 5 stations that are shared with the Blue Line in downtown Minneapolis. The area has become home to more than 24,000 Hmong immigrants, some of whom were recruited by the Central Intelligence Agency during the Vietnam War and resettled here after Laos fell to the communists in 1975. A spacious indoor marketplace on St. Paul's east side called Hmong Village caters to their shopping preferences. The city and Ramsey County have identified seven large sites that are prime opportunities for redevelopment. Like much of the Twin Cities metro area, Ramsey County grew 5 percent from 2010 to 2014, a notable increase from the previous decade. The increase in Hmongs has had an unexpected consequence: Declining use of the 13 hockey rinks (most of them aging) in the county.

Minnesota's 4th Congressional District is based in St. Paul. Even before the Democratic-Farmer-Labor Party was formed in 1944, St. Paul was a firmly Democratic part of Minnesota. Ramsey County hasn't voted for a Republican presidential candidate since it narrowly went for Calvin Coolidge in 1924. Its congressional district has sent liberal standard-bearers such as Eugene McCarthy to Washington. Meeting at the Xcel Energy Center in St. Paul in September 2008, Republicans nominated John McCain for president. The 4th takes in suburbs to the north, which run the gamut from staunchly Democratic to

2012 Presidential Vote
Barack Obama (D) 231,511   (62%)
Mitt Romney (R)................131,521   (35%)

2008 Presidential Vote
Barack Obama (D) 229,353   (63%)
John McCain (R).................129,816   (36%)

Cook Partisan Voting Index: D+11

staunchly Republican. That includes about two-thirds of Washington County, which is more evenly balanced politically. To the east are Lake St. Croix and Wisconsin. Overall, the district is solidly Democratic.

Betty McCollum (D)

Democrat Betty McCollum, first elected in 2000, is an ally of Minority Leader Nancy Pelosi of California, whom she calls a mentor. With her partisanship and liberal views, McCollum can be an assertive voice in her party, though she sometimes works with Republicans.

McCollum grew up in North St. Paul and graduated from the College of St. Catherine. She was a substitute social studies teacher, while working as a retail sales manager at a Sears department store and raising two children. After her daughter suffered a fractured skull on a slide in a city park, McCollum worked with local officials to repair the slide. She ran for the North St. Paul City Council and lost. In 1986, she ran again and was elected. McCollum served until 1992, when she was elected to the state House after defeating incumbents in both the primary and general elections.

When the congressional seat opened, McCollum was endorsed by the Democratic-Farmer-Labor Party. She faced three opponents in the primary. With the DFL's backing, McCollum won easily, with 50% to 23% for state Sen. Steve Novak.

Republicans nominated state Sen. Linda Runbeck, a vigorously anti-abortion candidate. McCollum backed prescription drug coverage under Medicare and opposed tax cuts before Congress paid down the national debt. Runbeck, who opposed gun control and took conservative positions on health care and education, attacked McCollum and her Democratic allies for running "hateful, vicious attack ads." This was a three-way race, thanks to the candidacy of former Ramsey County prosecutor Tom Foley, a longtime DFLer who ran on the ticket of Gov. Jesse Ventura's Independence Party. Once again, McCollum won unexpectedly easily, 48%-31%, with 21% for Foley.

In the House, McCollum has a consistently liberal voting record. With Pelosi's help, she has secured some plums, including an Appropriations Committee seat. In 2015, she became the top Democrat on the Interior-Environment Subcommittee. That panel has jurisdiction over one of her long-time interests: funding for Indian tribes across the nation, especially for school construction. She has worked with Republicans to build support for that goal. On Appropriations, McCollum has advocated major changes in committee operations, which are not likely to gain the approval of majority Republicans but might help Democrats to define their own views. She wants to end the practice of adding policy-focused "riders" to spending bills. She would reinstate "earmarks" for specific projects rather than continue to yield control to the executive branch; Congress in 2011 banned the practice. She also would end the budget "sequestration" that has restrained discretionary spending.

McCollum raised her profile when she offered an unsuccessful amendment to a budget bill in February 2011 to end military sponsorships in sports—including NASCAR, a passion in the Republican-dominated South. She later told *The New York Times*, "The Defense Department said it didn't have anything that could be cut. Seven million dollars to sponsor a car and we're cutting cops, we're cutting teachers, we're cutting programs for homeless vets?" The move triggered hate mail and angry blog posts, but the Army joined the Navy and Marine Corps in 2013 in abandoning the sponsorships. McCollum drew attention when she tangled with her home-state GOP colleague Michele Bachmann, the doyenne of the tea party movement, over Bachmann's House-passed bill in March 2012 to build a $700 million bridge between Minnesota and Wisconsin. McCollum had backed a cheaper alternative. In April 2015, she highlighted new splits among Minnesotans when she proposed to restrict most copper-nickel mining in the national forest near Minnesota's Boundary Waters Canoe Area Wilderness.

Encouraging lawmakers to view the World Bank more positively, McCollum founded a caucus advocating more dialogue with the global financier. She has noted that Congress and the bank participate in many of the same overseas efforts, including fighting poverty and AIDS. She urged President Barack Obama in 2012 to nominate to head the World Bank an American with an understanding of helping women in Third World countries; she later said Obama "hit a home run" by nominating Jim Young Kim, a Korean-American physician with a background in health care overseas.

An important local project for McCollum has been the light-rail link between downtown St. Paul and Minneapolis, which finally was completed in 2014. She had secured an initial $2 million for the project and was incensed when conservative Republicans targeted proposed additional funding as pork barrel spending. She and Republican Gov. Tim Pawlenty clashed over her insistence that he sign a statement supporting congressional funding for the project. When Pawlenty vetoed a companion state funding plan in 2008, the project seemed dead. McCollum helped to keep it alive by securing $20 million in the omnibus fiscal 2009 spending bill to cover the final design work. The Green Line began operating in 2014.

McCollum has been reelected easily.

FIFTH DISTRICT

Keith Ellison (D)

Elected 2006, 5th term; b. Aug. 4, 1963, Detroit, MI; Wayne St. U., B.A. 1985, U. of MN, J.D. 1990; Muslim; divorced; 4 children.

Elected Office: MN House, 2002-06.

Professional Career: Practicing atty., 1990-2002.

DC Office: 2263 RHOB, 20515, 202-225-4755; Fax: 202-225-4886; Website: ellison.house.gov.

State Offices: Minneapolis, 612-522-1212.

Committees: *Financial Services*: Capital Markets & Government Sponsored Enterprises; Housing & Insurance; Oversight & Investigations.

Group Ratings

	ADA	ACLU	AFL-CIO	LCV	ITI	COC	HAFA	ACU	CFG	FRC
2014	95%	88%	–	89%	40%	36%	13%	8%	15%	0%
2013	100%	C	95%	96%	C	23%	C	20%	16%	C

National Journal Ratings

	2013 LIB	—	2013 CONS
Economic	91%	—	0%
Social	93%	—	0%
Foreign	94%	—	0%
Composite	96%	—	4%

Key Votes of the 113th Congress

1. Sandy storm spending	Y	5. Medical Marijuana	Y	9. Syrian Rebels Training	Y
2. Violence Against Women Act	Y	6. Farm Bill	N	10. Keystone pipeline	N
3. Guantanamo Bay Detainees	Y	7. Afghanistan Combat	Y	11. Immigration Exec. Action	N
4. Abortion 20-week ban	N	8. NSA Phone Data Collection	Y	12. Bipartisan budget deal	N

Election Results

2014 general	Keith Ellison (D)	167,079	(71%)	$1,984,754
	Doug Daggett (R)	56,577	(24%)	$39,019
	Lee Bauer (I)	12,001	(5%)	
2014 primary	Keith Ellison (D)	unopposed		

Prior winning percentages: 2012 (75%), 2010 (68%), 2008 (71%), 2006 (56%)

Population		Race and Ethnicity		Income	
Total:	697,725	White	64.7%	Median income:	$52,468
Urban:	88.3%	Black	15.5%		*(197 of 435)*
Suburban:	11.7%	Latino	9.7%	Under $50,000	47.1%
Rural:	0.0%	Asian	5.7%	$50,000-$99,999:	29.8%
Land area:	164	Two races	3.3%	$100,000-$199,999:	18.3%
Pop/sq. mi.:	4,255.5	White Ethnic	24.6%	$200,000 or more:	4.8%
Born in state:	55.0%			Poverty Rate	16.8%
		Education			
Age Groups		H.S. grad or less:	30.3%	**Work**	
Under 18:	20.5%	Some college:	26.7%	White collar:	45.0%
18 to 34:	31.0%	College degree, 4 yr.:	27.5%	Blue collar:	40.4%
35 to 64:	37.5%	Post-grad study:	15.4%	Sales and service:	14.7%
Over 64:	11.0%			Govt. workers:	10.7%
		Military			
		Veterans/active duty:	6.1%		

Minneapolis Metro

From almost nowhere in Minneapolis today can you see the geographic feature that created the city: the Falls of St. Anthony, where rapids still course beneath low downtown bridges. In olden days, every riverboat had to stop here—these are the only significant waterfalls on the

Voter Turnout	
2013 Total Citizen 18+	502,890
2014 House Turnout	236,009
2014 Turnout as % CVAP	46.9%
2012 Turnout as % CVAP	76.9%

upper Mississippi River—and the waterpower generated by the falls was the energy source first for the pioneers' grist mills and then for the giant grain mills that processed northern Great Plains wheat into food for the United States. By 1890, Minneapolis and St. Paul made up one of America's largest urban areas, living mainly off grain. Today, grain is still important to Minneapolis; after all, the headquarters for General Mills is located in nearby Golden Valley. But Minneapolis is also a center of high technology, banking and finance. It had one of the best-performing economies during the 2007-09 recession—sixth in the United States, according to the Brookings Institution. The unemployment rate in the Twin Cities metro area never exceeded 8.5%, and was among the lowest in the nation at 4% in March 2015. In a lengthy story in the March 2015 issue of *Atlantic*, headlined "The Miracle of Minneapolis," writer Derek Thompson argued that "fiscal equalization" accounts for the success. "By spreading the wealth to its poorest neighborhoods, the metro area provides more-equal services in low-income places, and keeps quality of life high just about everywhere."

The city of Minneapolis and a few of its older suburbs make up the 5th Congressional District. In the southwest corner are the affluent neighborhoods around Lake Calhoun and Lake Harriet—long built-up and proudly maintained, amid trees that turn golden in early autumn. Not far away are Minneapolis' skywalk-laced downtown skyscrapers, the museum quarter on the hill above Hennepin Avenue, and the Hubert H. Humphrey Metrodome, where the inflatable roof collapsed in December 2010 after a snowstorm, prompting a decision to build a new football stadium that will open in 2016. Its location in Downtown East has spurred more than a score of nearby residential and office tower projects. Straddling the Mississippi River is the University of Minnesota, which has fostered the area's cutting-edge biotechnology research and medical innovations, and nearby Dinkytown, a student area where Robert Zimmerman discovered folk music and reinvented himself as Bob Dylan. The Witch's Hat Water Tower in Prospect Park is believed to be the inspiration for Dylan's classic "All Along the Watchtower." Left-leaning in its politics, the area is a product of Minneapolis's unique brand of liberalism, which is drawn from the Yankee tradition of clean government, the Scandinavian tradition of cooperative enterprise, and the industrial-labor tradition of economic redistribution.

Most of the 5th District is low on the income scale. Many of the working-class neighborhoods of small frame houses and ample parks are now kept up by new immigrants, and over a third of the district is nonwhite, the highest percentage in the state. To the northeast, behind the railroad and warehouse district along the Mississippi, are many Hmong from Laos. Hennepin County is also home to the largest number of African immigrants in the state, and Brooklyn Center has a large concentration of Liberians. The Jewish community here also has increased with immigrants from the former Soviet Union. The resulting district is the most heavily Democratic in the state. Barack Obama won it each time with 73% of the vote.

2012 Presidential Vote
Barack Obama (D) 274,635 (73%)
Mitt Romney (R)..................89,643 (24%)

2008 Presidential Vote
Barack Obama (D) 270,310 (73%)
John McCain (R)..................90,500 (25%)

Cook Partisan Voting Index: D+22

Keith Ellison (D)

Keith Ellison, a Democrat first elected in 2006, is the first Muslim to serve in Congress and the first black representative from Minnesota. He has remained an outspoken liberal in the mold of the late Democratic Sen. Paul Wellstone, whom Ellison has called his inspiration in politics.

Ellison was raised Catholic in Detroit, the son of a psychiatrist and the third of five boys. (Four became lawyers and the fifth a doctor.) Ellison studied economics at Wayne State

University, and it was there that he converted to Sunni Islam. He moved to Minnesota in 1987 to study law at the University of Minnesota, worked in private practice, and ran a non-profit criminal defense firm while also hosting a public affairs radio show. Ellison won the first of two terms in the state House in 2002.

The retirement of veteran Democratic Rep. Martin Olav Sabo, which created an open seat for the first time since 1978, unleashed a torrent of pent-up political ambition. Nearly a dozen Democrats sought the party endorsement at the May 2006 Democratic-Farmer-Labor district convention. The main contenders were Ellison, longtime Sabo aide Mike Erlandson and former state Sen. Ember Reichgott Junge. Ellison attracted support from war opponents and backers of Wellstone, who died in the crash of a small airplane in the final days of his 2002 reelection campaign. "I have the passion of a Wellstone and the practicality of a Sabo," he told convention activists. Ellison easily won the DFL endorsement, but Erlandson and Reichgott Junge competed anyway for the Democratic nomination in the seven-way September primary.

Ellison campaigned on his opposition to the war in Iraq and support for government-funded universal health care. But he had to overcome several unhelpful personal revelations: Unpaid parking tickets and moving violations had led to multiple suspensions of his driver's license, and he once owed $25,000 in back taxes. Most damaging were his ties to the controversial Nation of Islam leader Louis Farrakhan, and Farrakhan's anti-Semitic pronouncements. Ellison said his association with the group was limited to the 18 months he spent helping organize the 1995 Million Man March in Washington, D.C., although his writings about Farrakhan were traced back to his law school days. Ellison reached out to local Jewish leaders, insisting that he'd been unaware of the group's anti-Semitic views. Despite the personal baggage, Ellison won the primary with 41%, followed by Erlandson with 31% and Reichgott Junge with 21%.

In the general election, Republican Alan Fine described Ellison as "an embarrassment to our district, our state, our country, and our world." But Ellison won with 56% of vote, while Fine and Independence Party candidate Tammy Lee each got 21%. He has not been seriously challenged since. Controversy followed Ellison after the election. A conservative commentator stirred up opposition to Ellison's plan to take the oath of office with the Quran, rather than the Bible. In a politically adept move, Ellison borrowed a Quran from the Library of Congress that was once owned by Thomas Jefferson.

Ellison quickly established a strongly liberal voting record; he was elected co-chair of the Congressional Progressive Caucus in 2010. He has led efforts to end racial profiling and voter ID laws that he and others say are thinly veiled attempts to suppress minority voting. He has continued to be a frequent target for conservatives. Judson Phillips, founder of the Tennessee-based Tea Party Nation, called for his defeat in 2010 because of his religious beliefs. Former Republican Rep. Allen West of Florida in 2011 called Ellison "the antithesis of the principles upon which this country was established." But Ellison has mostly ignored the patter of criticism, and has won recognition for his legislative work. In *Washingtonian* magazine's anonymous survey of Capitol Hill staffers in 2010, he placed third in the "surprise standout" category.

On the Financial Services Committee, Ellison has challenged predatory lending practices and foreclosures by credit card and mortgage companies, which he said "have torn holes in the fabric of neighborhoods" in Minneapolis and elsewhere. He introduced a bill in December 2012 to replace the mortgage interest tax deduction with a 20% flat rate tax credit, which he said would bring in $27 billion in new federal revenue while increasing the number of participants from 43 million to 60 million. A month later, he joined other Democrats in introducing a measure to abolish the federal debt ceiling. On the 2009 bill to overhaul credit card practices, he added a provision to stop companies from raising rates on people with unrelated debt problems. In March 2015, he introduced a bill that would raise billions of dollars for economic investment by taxing Wall Street financial transactions. His measure, which was described as modern-day Robin Hood by robbing the rich to give to the poor, spurred vigils across the country by community activists.

Ellison is frequently called on as a spokesman for his faith. (Indiana Democratic Rep. André Carson joined him in 2008 as another Muslim in Congress.) He has decried what he calls attempts by conservatives, including his former home-state GOP colleague Rep. Michele Bachmann, to demonize Muslims. Bachmann in July 2012 told radio host Glenn Beck that Ellison is associated with the Muslim Brotherhood, which has ties to the Palestinian terrorist group Hamas. He dismissed the charge. When Homeland Security Chairman Peter King of New York, called hearings to explore al-Qaida's attempts to radicalize American Muslims in 2011, Ellison offered examples of Muslims who had thwarted several plots by reporting them to law enforcement officials. In March 2011, he broke into tears as he testified before the King panel, recounting the death of a Muslim-American firefighter on September 11. "The best defense against extreme ideologies is social inclusion and civic engagement," Ellison said. "I fear these hearings may undermine our efforts in this direction."

Ellison was among a group of U.S. Muslims in 2011 who appealed to Hamas to release Gilad Shalit, an Israeli who had been abducted and held for five years. Shalit subsequently was released in a prisoner exchange. In December 2008, he became the first member of Congress to make the Hajj pilgrimage to the Muslim holy city of Mecca, later describing it as a "transformative" experience.

In a December 2014 interview with *New York* magazine, Ellison explained the significance of the broad opposition to the "cromnibus" spending bill that Congress narrowly approved that month. "The lesson is that there are at least 206 members of Congress and at least 40-some members of the Senate who have finally realized that a government of, by, and for the people should be on the side of the people," Ellison said. "You're seeing a realignment, an adjustment of substantial portions of the Congress in alignment with the American people. Congress is finally catching up on fighting for the interests of working people. We're going to dig in."

SIXTH DISTRICT

Tom Emmer (R)

Elected 2014, 1st term; b. March 3, 1961, South Bend, IN; U. of AK-Fairbanks, B.A. 1984; William Mitchell Col. of Law, J.D. 1988; Catholic; married (Jacquie), 7 children.

Elected Office: Independence City Council, 1995-2002; Delano City Council, 2003-2004; MN House, 2004-10 (Deputy Minority Leader, 2007-08).

Professional Career: Atty.; radio talk show host

DC Office: 503 CHOB, 20515; 202-225-2331; Fax: 202-225-6475; Website: emmer.house.gov.

State Office: Otsego, 763-241-6848.

Committees: *Agriculture:* Commodity Exchanges, Energy and Credit; Livestock and Foreign Agriculture. *Foreign Affairs:* Africa, Global Health, Global Human Rights, & International Organizations; Western Hemisphere.

Election Results

2014 general	Tom Emmer (R)......................... 133,328	(56%)	$2,030,950	$7,094	
	Joe Perske (D)............................. 90,926	(38%)	$221,219		
	John Denney (I) 12,457	(5%)	$6,220		$11,250
2014 primary	Tom Emmer (R)............................. 19,557	(73%)			
	Rhonda Sivarajah (R)................... 7,125	(27%)			

Population		Race and Ethnicity		Income	
Total:	675,687	White	90.6%	Median income:	$71,340
Urban:	15.5%	Latino	2.5%		(59 of 435)
Suburban:	72.0%	Asian	2.3%	Under $50,000	32.1%
Rural:	12.5%	Black	2.2%	$50,000-$99,999:	38.0%
Land area:	3,030	Two races	1.9%	$100,000-$199,999:	25.8%
Pop/sq. mi.:	223.0	White Ethnic	30.1%	$200,000 or more:	4.0%
Born in state:	78.5%			Poverty Rate	8.2%
		Education			
Age Groups		H.S. grad or less:	34.4%	**Work**	
Under 18:	26.1%	Some college:	37.6%	White collar:	34.8%
18 to 34:	22.4%	College degree, 4 yr.:	19.9%	Blue collar:	41.4%
35 to 64:	40.5%	Post-grad study:	8.0%	Sales and service:	23.8%
Over 64:	11.0%			Govt. workers:	11.6%
		Military			
		Veterans/active duty:	8.7%		

Twin Cities Exurbs, St. Cloud

The earliest settlers of Minneapolis and St. Paul lived within walking distance of the mills and factories and rail yards where they worked. As the first streetcars and then automobiles allowed them to live farther from their jobs, they spread out in the Twin Cities and then all around the

Voter Turnout	
2013 Total Citizen 18+	489,542
2014 House Turnout	236,846
2014 Turnout as % CVAP	48.4%
2012 Turnout as % CVAP	74.9%

lake-strewn countryside. The flatlands are bleak here when the winter sun struggles to pierce gray clouds, but even so, the creativity and productivity of Minnesotans have turned the countryside into some of the nation's most pleasant suburbs. Taking maximum advantage of their lakes, they refurbished old towns and farmhouses and built comfortable homes in new subdivisions.

The 6th Congressional District of Minnesota is a suburban and exurban area north of St. Paul and Minneapolis. It is a mix of upscale and working-class suburbs, based in Anoka County. To the northwest, along the Mississippi River, are Wright, Sherburne and Benton counties, which have grown rapidly from a combined total of 141,000 people in 1990 to more than 258,000 in 2013. Overall, these counties have accounted for much of the job growth in the metro area during that time. The district also includes the eastern half of St. Cloud-based Stearns County, a heavily German-Catholic area and a stronghold of anti-abortion rights sentiment. St. Cloud is 85% white, but its demographics are chang-

ing: The 1990s brought an influx of Vietnamese, Chinese and Japanese immigrants. Since 2000, several thousand Somalis have moved in and started businesses. Federal and local investigators have reviewed charges that Somalis in the public schools of St. Cloud have suffered civil rights violations, and there have been allegations of bullying of young Somalis. Business leaders have sought to educate local citizens about

2012 Presidential Vote		
Mitt Romney (R)	205,652	(56%)
Barack Obama (D)	151,238	(41%)

2008 Presidential Vote		
John McCain (R)	194,396	(55%)
Barack Obama (D)	153,633	(43%)

Cook Partisan Voting Index: R+10

the Somali culture. Six Somalis were arrested in April 2015 and charged with trying to travel to Somalia to join the al-Shabab terrorist group.

The district overall is solidly Republican. Mitt Romney took 56% of the vote in 2012, his largest Minnesota margin.

Tom Emmer (R)

Republican Tom Emmer, a former state representative and conservative talk-show host, scored a solid victory in 2014 to take over the seat vacated by Michele Bachmann, the one-time presidential contender. Emmer all but sealed his victory when he won the GOP primary in August. During his early months in the House, Emmer was less of a firebrand than his predecessor and occasionally cooperated with party leaders.

Like tea party icon Bachmann, Emmer has been an ardent conservative. His great-grandfather founded a lumber business in Minneapolis in 1907 that his family still runs, and is now known as Viking Forest Products. He was born in South Bend, Indiana, where his father was completing a degree at Notre Dame, and grew up in Edina. He majored in political science and got his bachelor's degree at the University of Alaska in Fairbanks, and his law degree from William Mitchell College. Emmer practiced law in his own firm, and served on the city councils of Independence and Delano before being elected to the state Assembly in 2004. During six years in office, he often took the lead in debates against the Democratic-Farmer-Labor majority. His GOP colleagues voted him deputy majority leader, despite his lack of seniority.

In 2010, he easily won the Republican nomination for governor and challenged Democrat Mark Dayton. Emmer staked out one of the most conservative platforms that this blue-leaning state had seen in decades. Along with calls to cut spending, slash taxes and promote socially conservative values, he proposed a constitutional amendment requiring a supermajority in the Legislature to approve any federal law before it could take effect in the state. The national Republican wave was not strong enough to lift him over Dayton. A recount determined that Dayton won by 8,770 votes out of the 2.1 million cast. Emmer subsequently launched a conservative AM radio talk show in the Twin Cities.

As soon as Bachmann announced her retirement in 2013, Emmer spotted the opportunity for a political rebound. He was the first Republican to declare, and he promptly gave up his radio slot to raise money and rack up endorsements, including from the local GOP. By the time of the primary, he had outraised his leading opponent, Anoka County Board Chair Rhonda Sivarajah, by a 20-to-1 ratio. He coasted to his primary victory with 73% of the vote in a low-turnout race. In the general election, which was not seriously contested, Emmer outspent DFL nominee Joe Perske $2 million to $221,000. He won, 56%-38%, and took all eight counties.

Emmer quickly showed that he intended to be a player in Congress. A week after the election, he said that he was impressed with the leadership style of Speaker John Boehner, at least at the start. "I am being very—and I will be very—deliberate," he told *USA Today*. "I'm here to accomplish something." He got seats on the Agriculture and Foreign Affairs Committees. With Democratic Rep. Grace Meng of New York, he filed a bill to accelerate the visa process for physicians from overseas to work in U.S. hospitals. He joined dozens of House colleagues who attended the commemoration of the 50th anniversary of the march in Selma Alabama and noted that all Americans deserve "equal protection under the law." With California Rep. Mimi Walters, he led an effort by freshmen House Republicans in March to send a letter to President Barack Obama with their support for approval of the Trans-Pacific Partnership. Following his trip in April on a House delegation to Ethiopia and Kenya, he said that it opened his eyes about the value of foreign aid.

Emmer disagreed with conservatives who opposed funding the Homeland Security Department because of the conflict over immigration policy, and warned that the threatened government shutdown was a bad idea. "Two wrongs don't make a right," he said. The leader of the Minnesota Tea Party Alliance responded that he was "very disappointed" by his early votes. But Emmer defended what he called his incremental approach, and seemed to make a pointed and informed jab at Bachmann, his erstwhile ally, about how to succeed in Congress. "If you want to go out there and make a lot of noise, maybe you're going to get people from all across the country to send you a lot of money, and that's great because then you can increase your own brand. But you'll never change the inside of the building," he told the *St. Cloud Times*.

The move by Emmer toward the more establishment wing of his party could position him for another run for statewide office, perhaps an eventual bid for the Senate.

SEVENTH DISTRICT

Collin Peterson (D)

Elected 1990, 13th term; b. June 29, 1944, Fargo, ND; Moorhead St. U., B.A. 1966; Lutheran; divorced; 3 children.

Military Career: Army Natl. Guard, 1963-69.

Elected Office: MN Senate, 1976-86.

Professional Career: Accountant, 1966-90.

DC Office: 2204 RHOB, 20515, 202-225-2165; Fax: 202-225-1593; Website: collinpeterson.house.gov.

State Offices: Detroit Lakes, 218-847-5056; Marshall, 507-537-2299; Montevideo, 320-235-1061; Red Lake Falls, 218-253-4356; Redwood Falls, 507-637-2270; Willmar, 320-235-1061.

Committees: *Agriculture* (RMM).

Group Ratings

	ADA	ACLU	AFL-CIO	LCV	ITI	COC	HAFA	ACU	CFG	FRC
2014	10%	38%	–	11%	100%	93%	27%	48%	33%	75%
2013	25%	C	67%	14%	C	77%	C	42%	15%	C

National Journal Ratings

	2013 LIB	—	2013 CONS
Economic	54%	—	46%
Social	56%	—	43%
Foreign	57%	—	43%
Composite	56%	—	44%

Key Votes of the 113th Congress

1. Sandy storm spending	Y	5. Medical Marijuana		9. Syrian Rebels Training	Y
2. Violence Against Women Act	Y	6. Farm Bill	Y	10. Keystone pipeline	Y
3. Guantanamo Bay Detainees	N	7. Afghanistan Combat	N	11. Immigration Exec. Action	Y
4. Abortion 20-week ban	Y	8. NSA Phone Data Collection	N	12. Bipartisan budget deal	Y

Election Results

2014 general	Collin Peterson (D)	130,546	(54%)	$1,569,350	$502,240	$4,834,653
	Torrey Westrom (R)....................	109,955	(46%)	$1,022,303	$89,633	$3,501,426
2014 primary	Collin Peterson (D) ....unopposed					

Prior winning percentages: 2012 (60%), 2010 (55%), 2008 (72%), 2006 (70%), 2004 (66%), 2002 (65%), 2000 (69%), 1998 (72%), 1996 (68%), 1994 (51%), 1992 (51%), 1990 (54%)

Population		Race and Ethnicity		Income	
Total:	662,860	White	90.4%	Median income:	$50,655
Urban:	0.0%	Latino	3.8%		*(231 of 435)*
Suburban:	7.1%	Amer. Indian	2.8%	Under $50,000	49.3%
Rural:	92.9%	Asian	0.9%	$50,000-$99,999:	34.5%
Land area:	34,049	Two races	1.3%	$100,000-$199,999:	13.7%
Pop/sq. mi.:	19.5	White Ethnic	18.3%	$200,000 or more:	2.5%
Born in state:	72.9%			Poverty Rate	11.9%
		Education			
Age Groups		H.S. grad or less:	42.9%	**Work**	
Under 18:	23.4%	Some college:	36.2%	White collar:	32.1%
18 to 34:	20.6%	College degree, 4 yr.:	15.1%	Blue collar:	38.8%
35 to 64:	37.7%	Post-grad study:	5.8%	Sales and service:	29.2%
Over 64:	18.2%			Govt. workers:	14.1%
		Military			
		Veterans/active duty:	9.2%		

West Minnesota

The fabled Mississippi River begins modestly in Minnesota's Itasca State Park, 2,552 miles from the Gulf of Mexico. At that point, it can be crossed by foot on stepping-stones. The lake-strewn country in which the river begins has made its own contributions to American literature. More than a century ago, Sinclair Lewis grew up in the town of Sauk

Voter Turnout	
2013 Total Citizen 18+	499,818
2014 House Turnout	240,835
2014 Turnout as % CVAP	48.2%
2012 Turnout as % CVAP	67.8%

Centre, which provided grist for his critical but affectionate portrayals of small-town America in *Main Street* and *Babbitt*. In those years, this seemingly placid country was seething with rage, as WASP nationalists banned German from schools, renamed sauerkraut "liberty cabbage," and boycotted German-American businesses. This was also once prime logging country. Although that industry is in long-term decline here, Bemidji is still home to giant statues of Paul Bunyan and Babe the Blue Ox; Earl Bucklen, then the mayor, was used as the model for Bunyan. In April 2015, the Bemidji city council agreed to new plaques that described the atrocities committed against local Indian tribes. To the west, on the North Dakota border, is Moorhead, the largest city in the district (pop. 39,000). Moorhead was the planned destination of Ritchie Valens, Buddy Holly and J.P. "The Big Bopper" Richardson when their airplane took off from Iowa in a snowstorm in 1959; the plane crashed, and February 3 would be committed to the ages by singer/songwriter Don McLean as "the day the music died."

Farther south, settled more than 100 years ago by Republican Norwegians, Democratic Swedes, and swing-voting Germans, is great farming country, the beginnings of the wheat fields that sweep across the Dakotas and into Montana. Even today, farmers toil against the elements to make a profitable living, although many acres have been taken out of production by the federal Conservation Reserve Program. Farmers have been increasingly turning to corn and soybeans, which have more markets and uses. This area is the nation's leading producer of sugar beets and a leading supplier of turkeys.

On the shores of Plum Creek, near Walnut Grove, is where Laura Ingalls Wilder's family came on the way west to South Dakota in the *Little House* books. After all their struggles, Wilder's family left the farm for town as soon as they could. Their pain would be all too familiar to contemporary residents along the Red River of the North, which overflowed its banks in 1997, inundating East Grand Forks and Grand Forks North Dakota, dislocating 50,000 people—America's largest mass evacuation between the Civil War and Hurricane Katrina. Southwest of Walnut Grove is Pipestone National Monument. Native Americans have used rocks collected from the quarries here to make ceremonial pipes for centuries; the lines of Longfellow's famous "The Song of Hiawatha"—"On the Mountains of the Prairie/On the great Red Pipe-stone Quarry..."—refer to this location. In 2015, Pipestone was scheduled to be a site for the largest solar project in Minnesota.

The 7th Congressional District of Minnesota covers almost all of the western part of the state. Its southeastern end is 30 miles from Minneapolis. From the Canadian border to the southern end of the district is roughly a 400-mile drive. It takes in the wheat-farming plains adjoining North Dakota as well as the German Catholic areas, with their farm villages named for saints. This is the fourth most productive farm district in the nation.

The 7th's political history could be a segment on Garrison Keillor's *Lake Wobegon Days*: In 1958, DFL Rep. Coya Knutson was defeated for reelection when her husband, Andy, issued a plaintive statement urging her to come home from Washington and make his breakfast again. She was the only incumbent Democrat to lose in that heavily Democratic year; they divorced shortly thereafter. For the next three decades, this was a prime marginal district. In 2000, the unpopularity of Clinton administration environmental and gun control policies produced a 54%-40% victory for George W. Bush. Mitt Romney in 2012 also won the district with 54%. The 7th is the second-most Republican district in the state, and it is the most Republican district in the nation that elected a Democrat in 2014.

2012 Presidential Vote		
Mitt Romney (R)	180,334	(54%)
Barack Obama (D)	147,750	(44%)
2008 Presidential Vote		
John McCain (R)	173,463	(50%)
Barack Obama (D)	162,218	(47%)
Cook Partisan Voting Index: R+6		

Collin Peterson (D)

Collin Peterson, first elected in 1990, is one of the few conservative "aggies" left in an increasingly liberal and metropolitan Democratic caucus. He has the dubious honor of holding the Democratic seat that leans most heavily Republican. He is the top Democrat on the Agriculture Committee, where he works well with like-minded lawmakers representing rural regions. "I am just a country boy, and I am doing the best I can," he once said.

Peterson grew up on a farm in Baker, just across the Red River of the North from Fargo North Dakota. He graduated from Moorhead State College and then started a certified public accounting business in Detroit Lakes. In 1976, he was elected to the state Senate. In 1982, he ran for the House but lost in the Democratic-Farmer-Labor Party caucus, then set out to prove that he's nothing if not persistent. He tried three more times, losing to Republican Arlan Stangeland in 1984 and 1986 (by only 121 votes that year) and losing a DFL primary in 1988. But in 1990, when the *St. Cloud Times* reported that Stangeland made 341 credit card calls to a woman who was not his wife, Peterson won with a robust 54 percent of the vote.

In office, Peterson has been known as a free spirit, wearing cowboy boots and playing guitar in a bipartisan rock band called the Second Amendments that covers Del Shannon and the Eagles. He has performed with Willie Nelson at Farm-Aid concerts. He is very candid with Capitol Hill reporters, sometimes revealing more about the thinking of Republicans than do GOP lawmakers themselves. He has acted as his own campaign consultant and pilot, flying his single-engine plane to stops around the district.

On environmental issues, Peterson takes the view of his constituents, who hunt and fish as a way of life and often see environmentalists' policies as hindrances. He has supported lifting trade restrictions on Cuba, a move favored by farmers eager for another export market. He also backs labor unions, a vital Democratic constituency. He has supported Minority Leader Nancy Pelosi on the theory, he said, that only a liberal can tell liberals what to do. Pelosi accepted Peterson's invitation to attend Farmfest in Redwood County in August 2006, where she ate pork chops on a stick and got a warm reception.

When Democrats controlled the House, Peterson chaired Agriculture. "There were people in my party who were skeptical of me taking that position. I was seen as a renegade, a maverick," he told *National Journal* in 2013. He had been a skeptic of the Republicans'

1996 Freedom to Farm Act and he joined the bipartisan majority that restored market controls when the farm program was renewed in 2002. In the mid-2000s, Peterson called for extending the Conservation Reserve Program to keep millions of additional acres of farmland idle to produce switch grass and plant waste that could be used to make ethanol. With a ready supply of raw material, Peterson predicted, cellulosic ethanol plants would prove to be profitable.

Peterson worked with Republicans to achieve many of his goals on the farm bill enacted in 2008. It was not easy. It took six short-term extensions of the bill and two votes to override President George W. Bush's veto. Peterson sought an income limit of $900,000 annually for subsidy payments, and the final deal set a ceiling of $750,000 for farmers receiving direct payments. It also barred payments to persons with more than $500,000 in nonfarm income. He finally got his permanent disaster fund so that farmers could get their aid more quickly following a drought or flood. Peterson boosted the subsidy for cellulosic ethanol to $1 per gallon, while reducing the subsidy for corn ethanol from 51 cents to 45 cents per gallon.

With demands for new acreage, especially from the large fruit and vegetable states of Florida and California, the committee reduced the Conservation Reserve Program from 39 million acres to 32 million acres. Peterson, the former accountant, proved adept at figuring the costs of commodity programs.

Many of Peterson's views are a throwback to earlier political times. A fiscal conservative and founding member of the Blue Dog Coalition, Peterson has shown a bit more loyalty to his party since it lost the majority in 2011. But in his Republican-leaning district, he has felt free to oppose many of President Barack Obama's major initiatives. He voted against the New Year's Day 2013 budget deal aimed at averting the so-called "fiscal cliff" and joined Republicans in 2012 in voting to hold Attorney General Eric Holder in contempt of Congress for withholding information relating to the botched "Fast and Furious" gun-tracing operation. He supports a balanced-budget constitutional amendment and opposes abortion rights and gun control. Peterson voted against the economic stimulus bill in 2009, explaining to *The Food & Fiber Letter* that he voted no "for the same reasons I voted against the initial bailout package for the banks, because I knew it would not work." Peterson also committed party apostasy by voting against the Affordable Care Act, and in favor of dozens of GOP attempts to repeal it.

Peterson has been cooperative on a few big issues, but generally only after extracting legislative concessions. He said in 2009 that the Democrats' cap-and-trade bill to limit carbon emissions was "an urban-dominated bill" that catered to the environmental lobby. As part of his support for the deal, Peterson insisted that the Agriculture Department, rather than the Environmental Protection Agency, oversee the carbon emissions offset program for farmers. The bill passed the House, but it died in the Senate. When the EPA announced it would move on its own to begin regulating carbon emissions under the Clean Air Act, Peterson cosponsored a bill to block the move.

In 2010, on a major financial industry regulatory bill, Peterson struck an agreement with Financial Services Chairman Barney Frank of Massachusetts that preserved for the Commodity Futures Trading Commission some oversight of agricultural commodities trading. The deal stopped Frank's committee from grabbing jurisdiction of the commission.

Peterson had hoped a five-year farm bill could be passed in 2012, but declared in March that House Budget Committee Chairman Paul Ryan's GOP budget blueprint made that task impossible because it called for unacceptably steep reductions while ending direct payments to farmers. "It is appalling that in an attempt to avoid defense cuts, the Republican leadership has elected to leave farmers and hungry families hurting," Peterson said. Another complication arose over Peterson's desire to come up with a new program for the dairy industry. His proposal would let the government manage the milk supply by setting production limits for farmers enrolling in a market-stabilization program. Republicans said his measure would only worsen what House Speaker John Boehner derided as "Soviet-style" management of the farm program. Work on the bill was halted by a months-long stalemate with Senate Democrats over cuts in food and nutrition programs.

House Republicans brought up a five-year bill in June 2013 that they hoped could win at least 40 Democratic votes with Peterson's help. But the White House, angered that the measure cut food-stamp programs by more than $20 billion, mobilized Democrats against it. Peterson could attract only 23 members of his party to back it. Boehner was enraged. "The Democrats walked away from this," he told *The Hill*. Republicans passed another bill in July that removed food stamps from the bill. It passed on a 216-208 without the backing of any

Democrats—including Peterson. In 2014, Congress cleared a bill with bipartisan support that cut about $9 billion.

Republicans have been eager for him to retire, which they believe is the best way to take his seat. He typically has won reelection easily. Despite the Republican wave in 2010, Peterson prevailed 55%-38%. Four years later, Republicans were confident they could finally beat him. The National Republican Congressional Committee recruited state Sen. Torrey Westrom, who is legally blind, and outside groups poured millions into ads depicting Peterson as out of touch for his use of a taxpayer-subsidized plane to get around his district. But Peterson touted his work on the farm bill and won easily, 54%-46%. He said in January 2015 that he was planning to run again in 2016. "They [Republicans] energized me last time, they got me fired up," he told the *Star Tribune*. Their threats to target him again make him less likely to retire, he said, showing his independent streak.

EIGHTH DISTRICT

Rick Nolan (D)

Elected 2012, 5th term; b. Dec. 17, 1943, Brainerd; U. of MN, B.A. 1966; Catholic; married (Mary); 4 children.

Elected Office: U.S. House, 1974-80; MN House, 1969-73.

Professional Career: Pres., Emily Forest Products, 1994-2011; Pres., MN World Trade Ctr. Corp., 1987-94; Pres., U.S. Export Corp., 1981-86; Teacher, 1968-69; Head Start ed. dir., 1968; Staff asst., Sen. Walter Mondale, 1966-68.

DC Office: 2366 RHOB, 20515, 202-225-6211; Fax: 202-225-0699; Website: nolan.house.gov.

State Offices: Brainerd, 218-454-4078; Center City, 218-491-3131; Duluth, 218-464-5095; Chisholm, 218-491-3114.

Committees: *Agriculture; Transportation & Infrastructure:* Aviation; Highways & Transit; Water Resources & Environment; Railroads, Pipelines & Hazardous Materials.

Group Ratings

	ADA	ACLU	AFL-CIO	LCV	ITI	COC	HAFA	ACU	CFG	FRC
2014	60%	88%	–	80%	60%	57%	8%	4%	6%	0%
2013	80%	C	100%	86%	C	40%	C	8%	12%	C

National Journal Ratings

	2013 LIB	—	2013 CONS
Economic	65%	—	35%
Social	73%	—	24%
Foreign	90%	—	6%
Composite	77%	—	23%

Key Votes of the 113th Congress

1. Sandy storm spending	Y	5. Medical Marijuana	Y	9. Syrian Rebels Training	N
2. Violence Against Women Act	Y	6. Farm Bill	Y	10. Keystone pipeline	Y
3. Guantanamo Bay Detainees	Y	7. Afghanistan Combat	Y	11. Immigration Exec. Action	N
4. Abortion 20-week ban	N	8. NSA Phone Data Collection	Y	12. Bipartisan budget deal	Y

Election Results

2014 general	Rick Nolan (D)	129,090	(49%)	$2,113,281	$753,048	$5,060,015
	Stewart Mills (R)	125,358	(47%)	$2,087,731	$1,015,200	$5,920,532
	Skip Sandman (G)	11,450	(4%)			$16,853
2014 primary	Rick Nolan (D)	unopposed				

Prior winning percentages: 2012 (54%), 1978 (55%), 1976 (60%), 1974 (55%)

Population		Race and Ethnicity		Income	
Total:	662,997	White	92.8%	Median income:	$49,860
Urban:	14.6%	Amer. Indian	2.5%		*(244 of 435)*
Suburban:	18.4%	Latino	1.3%	Under $50,000	50.1%
Rural:	67.0%	Black	1.0%	$50,000-$99,999:	33.8%
Land area:	25,796	Two races	1.6%	$100,000-$199,999:	14.2%
Pop/sq. mi.:	25.7	White Ethnic	27.2%	$200,000 or more:	1.9%
Born in state:	78.8%			Poverty Rate	12.9%
		Education			
Age Groups		H.S. grad or less:	42.1%	**Work**	
Under 18:	21.6%	Some college:	35.5%	White collar:	30.9%
18 to 34:	19.9%	College degree, 4 yr.:	15.2%	Blue collar:	44.7%
35 to 64:	40.3%	Post-grad study:	7.2%	Sales and service:	24.4%
Over 64:	18.2%				
		Military		Govt. workers:	15.0%
		Veterans/active duty:	10.8%		

Northeast Minnesota: Duluth, Northern Twin Cities

In the 1860s, prospectors in Minnesota's Arrowhead region, northwest of Lake Superior in the low hills of the Mesabi Range, happened upon one of the nation's largest veins of iron ore. They moved on, looking for gold. But in the 1880s, Duluth banker George Stone and Philadelphia financier

Voter Turnout	
2013 Total Citizen 18+	515,633
2014 House Turnout	266,083
2014 Turnout as % CVAP	51.6%
2012 Turnout as % CVAP	70.5%

Charlemagne Tower started mining the Iron Range. Rail lines were built from the Range south to the port of Duluth, where the average low temperature is below freezing six months of the year. Duluth, with its signature aerial lift bridge traversing its shipping channel, is nestled on dramatic bluffs over the always-cold and often frozen waters of Lake Superior— one of the most beautiful settings for a city in North America, though also one of the most isolated. Duluth was a grain shipping rival of Chicago and the premier iron ore port. Its city plan was drawn up by architect Daniel Burnham, who also planned Chicago, and its splendid turn-of-the-century buildings still celebrate the triumph of technology and civilization over wilderness and the elements. Millions of tons of ore have been dug out of the Range and loaded into railcars for the ride to Duluth, and into Great Lakes freighters for shipment to Chicago, Gary, Detroit, Cleveland, Pittsburgh and Buffalo.

For most of the 20th century, about 100,000 people lived on the Iron Range and another 100,000 in Duluth, most of them descendants of America's 1880-1924 wave of immigration: Italians, Poles, Serbs, Croats, Swedes Finns and Eastern European Jews. In this punishing environment, they built solid houses with staunch central heating, and wore layers of warm clothing to survive the brutal winter. The work was hard, the hours long and the pay low. The churches, a separate one for each ethnic group, were the main community institutions. Living conditions improved vastly in the booming growth after World War II. But periods of economic distress persisted. More efficient iron mines and steel mills needed fewer workers. Employment is well below its 1970s peak. But unemployment dropped to 4.5% in February 2015, a sign of sufficient jobs for the dwindling number of residents. Following the opening of a new airport terminal in Duluth in 2013, several economic development projects were underway, including resorts for adventure tourists.

Duluth's population of about 86,000 has been flat for the past quarter-century. The port still ships large quantities of grain, and in the late 1990s, a new taconite and steelmaking factory was built—the first big new plant in more than 20 years. Rising commodity prices brought new mining companies to the area to explore the possible extraction of copper, nickel and other nonferrous metals. Automakers test their new models' performance under extreme winter conditions at International Falls in Koochiching County. The region spawned a new sports competition—the winter ultra-marathon, a 135-mile endurance contest of walking, running, cycling or skiing from International Falls to Tower.

The 8th Congressional District of Minnesota includes Duluth and the Iron Range, plus much of the state's north woods and lake country to the west and south. It extends south to the boundaries of the Twin Cities metro area, to Isanti and Chisago counties, where young families are building new homes in pleasant old lakeside towns. In 1928, Duluth-based

St. Louis County gave Herbert Hoover 61% of the vote; no Republican has topped 40% here since. From 1946 through 2008, the district elected only two congressmen, both Democrats. The second one had worked for the first. But there are signs the politics here are changing. The fast-growing counties in the south and west have trended Republican. Although Duluth and the Iron Range remain

2012 Presidential Vote		
Barack Obama (D) 186,761	(52%)
Mitt Romney (R)................166,977	(46%)
2008 Presidential Vote		
Barack Obama (D) 195,862	(53%)
John McCain (R)................164,382	(45%)
Cook Partisan Voting Index: D+1		

Democratic, issues like gun control and environmental regulation have sometimes moved those areas toward the Republicans. The 8th leans Democratic, but only marginally.

Rick Nolan (D)

Democrat Rick Nolan returned to the House after a 32-year absence. When he quit in 1981, Nolan told *The Washington Post*, "Congress is relatively impotent to make the changes the country needs." But he returned, a full generation later, confident that he could get things done in a district that had limited overlap with his old one.

Nolan grew up as the middle of three children in the old railroad town of Brainerd, Minn. When he was a teenager, his aunt, Eleanor Nolan, was appointed Minnesota's first female district judge. He calls her his biggest political influence growing up. He got his bachelor's degree at the University of Minnesota, and did graduate study in public policy at the University of Maryland and later in education at St. Cloud State University. He campaigned for antiwar candidate Eugene McCarthy in the 1968 presidential race before serving two terms in the Minnesota House.

In 1974, Nolan was elected to the House from southwest Minnesota, and compiled a liberal voting record. He made his mark in 1979 when he traveled to Cuba to secure the release of American prisoners. Nolan and Cuban leader Fidel Castro bonded over fishing, and Castro—after agreeing to the prisoners' release—extended an invitation for him to return for some deep-sea angling. Nolan also battled what he saw as the federal government's favoritism of large farms and pushed legislation for education programs, equipment loans and tax-code changes to benefit small farmers.

Frustrated with his party's leadership, Nolan broke ranks and joined five House colleagues to lobby Sen. Edward Kennedy of Massachusetts to challenge Jimmy Carter for the 1980 Democratic nomination for president. He left Congress, calling himself a "liberal idealist unhappily turned wiser and more realistic," and returned to Minnesota.

When the Minnesota World Trade Center Corp., or WTC, launched in 1983, Nolan was appointed as an unpaid chairman by then-Democratic Gov. Rudy Perpich, and in 1987 he went on the payroll as the organization's president. Nolan claims to have created 326,000 Minnesota jobs through his work at the organization, a public-private initiative to help Minnesota businesses expand into international markets. But his Republican foes criticized his $70,000 salary, which they considered high for a civil servant at the time, and the budget deficits the company ran up. In 1994, Nolan became president of Emily Forest Products, a sawmill and pallet manufacturer. He is an avid hunter, fisherman and farmer; he harvests wild rice and makes his own maple syrup.

The lack of local jobs, he says, inspired him to return to Washington at age 69 to push for small business tax breaks and infrastructure investment. In 2012, national Democrats targeted tea party-backed freshman Republican Chip Cravaack, who scored a big upset in 2010 by beating 18-term Rep. Jim Oberstar, then chairman of the Transportation and Infrastructure Committee. Nolan, who first entered the House with Oberstar in the huge Democratic class of "Watergate babies," beat two other candidates in the Democratic primary with 38% of the vote, setting up a confrontation with Cravaack in the fall.

Cravaack dismissed Nolan as "a big-government, more-taxes, more-spending, more-regulation kind of guy." Nolan played up his support for small business and blasted Cravaack for backing House Budget Committee Chairman Paul Ryan's plans to introduce vouchers into Medicare. Cravaack outspent Nolan, $2.4 million to $1.2 million. Each benefited from more than $8 million in outside spending on the contest, which was closely divided between the two sides. Nolan won 54%-46%.

In the House, Nolan strongly opposed a bill filed by fellow Minnesota Democratic Rep. Betty McCollum that would limit mining in the watershed of the Boundary Waters, which is in Nolan's district. "This bill is a duplicative, overlapping regulatory scheme designed to prohibit mining on the Iron Range," he objected. On the Transportation and Infrastructure Committee, he advocated steps to promote tourism in the Duluth area, including additional airline service and highway improvements.

Reminiscing with constituents about how Congress had changed between his two stints, Nolan said he was frustrated by repeated votes to repeal the Affordable Care Act, without having the opportunity to discuss the law in more detail. A proponent of single-payer health care, he conceded that the 2010 law had "plenty of room for improvement." Republican attacks on environmental regulation were also frustrating, he said, because of the huge improvements during the previous 40 years in air pollution, water pollution and chemical waste. Nolan also found that the news media overstated the extent of gridlock in Congress. "I've had a Republican partner on everything I have done," he said, according to the *Chisago County Press*.

Some Democratic campaign insiders have criticized Nolan for his unwillingness to adjust to modern campaign realities, including the need for constant fundraising. "Rick is an old-school politician and doesn't believe in a lot of the things that members of Congress have to do in tight districts," a Minnesota Democratic strategist told *Roll Call*, a Capitol Hill newspaper, during the 2014 campaign. With his objections to modern campaign techniques, Nolan somewhat concedes the point. "Money has become a terribly corruptive influence in our politics," he said, while explaining his proposed "We The People" constitutional amendment that campaign speech is not protected by the First Amendment.

Nolan's reelection campaign in 2014 was very competitive. His Republican opponent was Stewart Mills, a wealthy heir and executive of his family's Mills Fleet Farms stores. With his good looks and long blond hair, Republicans called their candidate "Brad Pitt of the GOP." Each candidate spent about $2 million, and outside groups this time spent more than $10 million on the contest. Nolan won, 48.5%-47.1%. Nolan led by about 15,000 votes in St. Louis County, which cast about 30% of the votes, while Mills led in the remainder of the district by 11,500 votes. "The Democratic Congressional Campaign Committee bailed Nolan out in more ways than one," wrote David Wasserman of the Cook Political Report. "Not only did they spend enormously because Nolan refused to raise a lot of money, they also sent a tracker to take footage of Mills in a suit coiffing his hair outside a fundraiser, which was a killer in the blue-collar Iron Range. Democrats also cast Mills as an immature millionaire playboy—spreading Facebook pictures of Mills doing beer bongs, etc."

Nolan likely will remain high on the Republicans' target list.

★ MISSISSIPPI ★

Tragedy and pride: These are two strains that run through Mississippi's history and through Mississippi today. The state has long lagged behind almost all others in just about every leading indicator. But now, half a century after the success of the civil rights movement, it has in many ways entered the American mainstream while keeping some of the distinct regional character of which so many Mississippians are proud. This green land was settled in a rush in Jacksonian America, mostly by small farmers heading west from Georgia and south from Tennessee, and also by a few big planters who made, and sometimes lost, vast fortunes, built grand mansions, brought thousands of slaves in ship holds and coffles, and sent their sons to fight in the Civil War. For a century afterward, as planters and engineers drained the Delta lands, Mississippi, with its racial segregation, subsistence farmers and sharecroppers, and low wages, lived apart from most of America. William Faulkner's Mississippi never knew giant factories, the rushes of immigration, or the burgeoning of the suburbs that characterized much of 20th-century America. Mississippi never developed great cities: Its two commercial hubs, Memphis and New Orleans, are just outside its borders.

But if Mississippi did not thrive in commerce, it did produce great art. Mississippi gave us the blues (from the impoverished Mississippi Delta south of Memphis) and Elvis Presley William (who was born in Tupelo). It produced writers like William Faulkner, Eudora Welty, Walker Percy, and Shelby Foote. The state with the lowest literacy rate has also produced the most Pulitzer Prize winners for literature. Their work was informed by a sense of the tragic that is missing or forgotten in most of America, where life is a triumphant sales pitch or a labor-saving invention. For years, no other state had such a painful contrast between image and reality, between an ideal sincerely strived for and the tawdry facts of everyday life. Magnolia trees on the lawns of antebellum mansions and golden-haired women in white dresses on the veranda, alongside black servants and retainers: This was once the ideal. And behind it stood loose-jointed frame houses and unpainted back-country stores, shotgun shacks without plumbing, and poor white crossroads. As David Sansing wrote, "We at one time have the scent of magnolias and the smell of burning crosses."

Today, Mississippi still ranks low on many quality-of-life scales. It's rated the nation's worst-performing health care system by both the Commonwealth Fund and the United Health Foundation, and was ranked last among the 50 states by the Information Technology and Innovation Foundation for its strides towards creating a "new economy" focused on innovation, globalization and technology. Still, the gulf between this state and the rest of America has narrowed enormously. In 1940, Mississippi had an economy based on low-wage, subsistence, or sharecropper agriculture and a system of racial segregation often enforced by violence. Per capita income in Mississippi was 36% of the national average in 1940. It rose to 67% in 1990 and 73% in 2010, still well below average but, given its lower cost of living, a level recognizably American. Nearly every classroom in the state is air-conditioned and is being wired for the Internet.

An older generation would be astonished by relations between whites and blacks, who make up 37% of the population, the highest percentage in any state. Forty years ago, blacks held no public offices in Mississippi. Today, the state has more black elected officials than any other, and an African-American state senator from Tishomingo County, in the far northeast part of the state, was elected from a rural district that is 87% white in 2008. Voters have elected black mayors in Vicksburg, Jackson, Hattiesburg, Greenville, and Natchez.

That's not to say that race has disappeared as an issue; it still hovers over interactions in Mississippi to a degree it doesn't in most other places, and it remains uncomfortably present in some Mississippi elections. In 2000, voters approved a ballot measure to remove the ban on interracial marriage from the state constitution—but a full 41% of voters voted to keep the unenforced language on the books. A year later, 65% of voters chose to retain the Confederate battle cross—a symbol offensive to many—in the state flag. Yet Mississippi has also made efforts to salve some of its oldest racial wounds. After four decades, prosecutors hunted down and tried Ku Klux Klan members who had killed civil rights activists in the 1960s. Former Republican Gov. Haley Barbour signed bills authorizing a civil rights curriculum in public schools and a civil rights museum in Jackson. The Jackson airport is

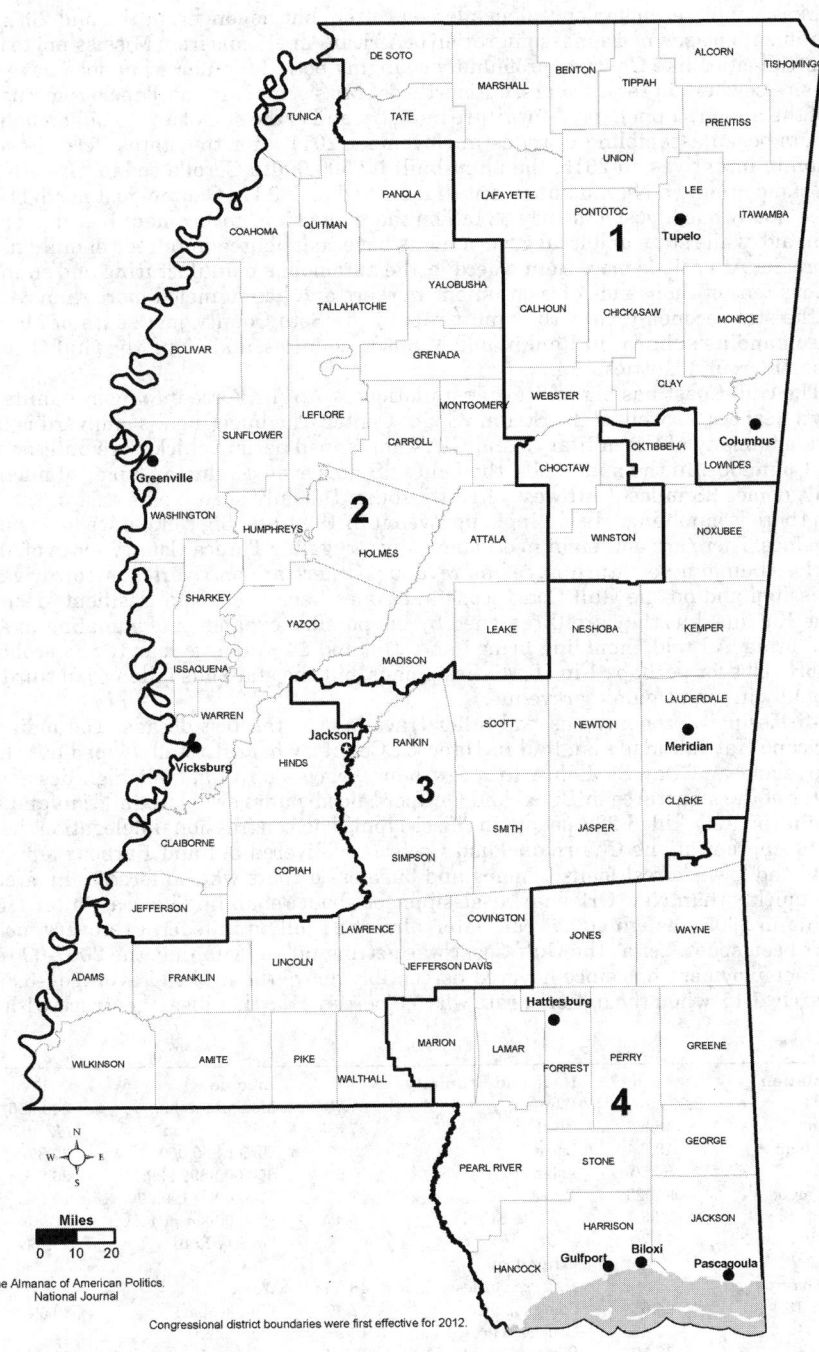

DE SOTO
ALCORN
TISHOMINGO
MARSHALL
BENTON
TIPPAH
TUNICA
TATE
PRENTISS
UNION
PANOLA
LAFAYETTE
LEE
PONTOTOC
ITAWAMBA
COAHOMA
QUITMAN
1
Tupelo
YALOBUSHA
TALLAHATCHIE
CALHOUN
CHICKASAW
MONROE
GRENADA
BOLIVAR
WEBSTER
CLAY
MONTGOMERY
LEFLORE
SUNFLOWER
CARROLL
OKTIBBEHA
Columbus
CHOCTAW
LOWNDES
Greenville
2
WASHINGTON
HUMPHREYS
HOLMES
ATTALA
WINSTON
NOXUBEE
SHARKEY
YAZOO
LEAKE
NESHOBA
KEMPER
ISSAQUENA
MADISON
WARREN
LAUDERDALE
Jackson
SCOTT
NEWTON
Meridian
Vicksburg
RANKIN
HINDS
3
CLARKE
CLAIBORNE
SMITH
JASPER
COPIAH
SIMPSON
JEFFERSON
LAWRENCE
COVINGTON
JONES
WAYNE
LINCOLN
JEFFERSON DAVIS
ADAMS
FRANKLIN
Hattiesburg
MARION
LAMAR
PERRY
GREENE
FORREST
WILKINSON
AMITE
PIKE
WALTHALL
4
GEORGE
STONE
PEARL RIVER
JACKSON
HARRISON
Biloxi
Gulfport
Pascagoula
HANCOCK

N
W   E
S

Miles
0   10   20

The Almanac of American Politics.
National Journal

Congressional district boundaries were first effective for 2012.

named for the assassinated civil rights leader Medgar Evers, and in 2013, Mississippi belatedly ratified the 13th amendment to the U.S. Constitution, which abolished slavery back in 1865.

Mississippi's economy once depended on cotton, but no longer; in the mid-20th century, mechanization spawned a mass migration of African Americans from Mississippi to northern industrial cities like Chicago, profoundly changing both. Manufacturing jobs have declined here as elsewhere in recent years, but northeast Mississippi around Tupelo remains the center of the nation's upholstered furniture industry and is the site of a $1.3 billion plant where workers began assembling Corollas in November 2011 after the state offered Toyota $296 million in incentives; in 2015, the plant built its 500,000th Corolla sedan. Growth has also been rapid around a Nissan auto plant that opened in 2003 in Canton, just north of Jackson. The company has invested nearly $3 billion there; the state government has given $378 million in aid, while state and local governments have contributed hundreds of millions more in tax breaks. After little more than a decade, the automobile manufacturing and supply sector employs tens of thousands of (non-union) workers and has funneled more than $4.1 billion into the state economy. Growth is most rapid in DeSoto County, just south of Memphis, in Jackson and its suburbs in Rankin and Madison counties, and along the Gulf Coast and to the north around Hattiesburg.

The Gulf Coast has big military installations, with Air Force intelligence units and the Navy's Seabees, as well as the Stennis Space Center. The huge Ingalls shipyard is in Pascagoula, and many of the military's and CIA's unmanned aerial vehicles are built on the Gulf or in Columbus. In the mid-1960s, the United States even conducted a pair of nuclear tests in salt domes 28 miles southwest of Hattiesburg, the only such blasts east of the Rockies. Then there is gambling. Mississippi approved it in 1990, and big companies have built some 30 casinos. There are now eight in economically struggling Tunica County south of Memphis; one closed amid a downturn in casino revenue. Others are on riverboats downriver on the Mississippi and on the Gulf Coast; coastal casinos have been more resilient, despite Hurricane Katrina, but they are threatened by the possible expansion of gambling in Alabama and Florida. All told, gambling brings an estimated $4 billion a year to the economy and supports jobs for perhaps 1 in 10 Mississippians, but the state has fallen from third to sixth nationally in casino gaming revenue.

Mississippi's economy has had other travails over the last decade. The main force of Hurricane Katrina made landfall in Hancock County, where it totally wiped out the towns of Waveland and Bay St. Louis. In a few hours, waves up to 55 feet high destroyed one-quarter of the structures in Biloxi and Gulfport; floodwaters swept 10 miles inland, and the storm ultimately killed 238 people in Mississippi. The congressional delegation, headed by Senate Appropriations Chairman Thad Cochran, delivered aid and Barbour administered grants and low-interest loans to home and business owners who suffered uninsured losses. More quickly than New Orleans, Mississippi set about rebuilding its coast after Hurricane Katrina in 2005, though eight years later, almost $1 billion in federal recovery money still hadn't been spent. Yet as the Gulf Coast was getting up and running, the 2007-09 recession hit. Unemployment has since hovered perceptibly above the national average—6.8 percent in March 2015, when the national rate was 5.5 percent. Further disaster struck with a major

Population		Race and Ethnicity		Income	
Total:	2,991,207	White	57.7%	Median income:	$40,850
Urban:	15.8%	Black	37.3%		*(47 of 50)*
Suburban:	19.8%	Latino	2.7%	Under $50,000	60.8%
Rural:	64.5%	Asian	0.9%	$50,000-$99,999:	26.7%
Land area:	46,923	Two races	1.0%	$100,000-$199,999:	10.6%
Pop/sq. mi.:	63.7	White Ethnic	13.4%	$200,000 or more:	1.9%
Born in state:	71.7%			Poverty Rate	20.1%
		Education			
Age Groups		H.S. grad or less:	48.3%	**Work**	
Under 18:	24.6%	Some college:	31.4%	White collar:	30.5%
18 to 34:	23.4%	College degree, 4 yr.:	12.9%	Blue collar:	42.5%
35 to 64:	38.1%	Post-grad study:	7.5%	Sales and service:	27.0%
Over 64:	13.9%				
		Military		Govt. workers:	18.0%
		Veterans/active duty:	8.2%		

flood in 2011 and a massive tornado outbreak in 2014 that killed 14 and destroyed hundreds of structures.

Voter Turnout	
2013 Total Citizen 18+	2,218,063
2014 Highest Statewide Turnout	631,858
2014 Turnout as % CVAP	28.5%
2012 Turnout as % CVAP	58.4%

Legislature			
Senate:	32R	20D	
House:	67R	54D	1V

Mississippi—once almost unanimously Democratic, but ready to support segregationist presidential candidates like Strom Thurmond in 1948 and George Wallace in 1968—is now reliably Republican. It was Richard Nixon's No. 1 state in 1972, Ronald Reagan gave a high-profile speech at the Neshoba County Fair in 1980, and it has been solidly Republican in presidential elections starting in 1980. Republicans have held both U.S. Senate seats since John Stennis retired in 1988. On the federal level, Democrats now have only the black-majority district they've held since 1986, which includes the Delta and much of metro Jackson; even Democrats as conservative Gene Taylor, who held the Gulf Coast House district from 1989 to 2010, have a hard time winning today. (In his latest race, he switched to the GOP and lost in the 2014 primary.) Among the 50 states, Gallup found, Mississippi is tilted most heavily conservative.

A turning point in the state's shift from Democratic to Republican leadership came in 2003, when Haley Barbour, emphasizing his Yazoo City roots over his decades as a Washington powerbroker, unseated Democratic Gov. Ronnie Musgrove. Barbour was re-elected 58%-42% in 2007, and by 2011, both chambers of the legislature had switched from Democratic to Republican control. That same year, Lt. Gov. Phil Bryant beat Hattiesburg Mayor Johnny DuPree, the first black Democratic gubernatorial nominee, 61%-39%, and Republicans won all statewide offices except attorney general. Such is the tide against Democrats that the party's remaining figures with statewide promise—Attorney General Jim Hood and Public Commissioner Brandon Presley—both turned down a chance to challenge Bryant for re-election in 2015.

Voting in Mississippi runs along racial lines, with whites heavily Republican in most contests and blacks heavily Democratic. (At 3 percent, Mississippi has the smallest percentage of Hispanics in the South.) Perhaps spurred by memories of the franchise denied, black turnout percentages in Mississippi have actually exceeded white turnout in some recent elections. Black voters also showed their muscle in the hard-fought Senate primary runoff contest between Cochran and tea party-aligned Chris McDaniel in 2014, arguably carrying the aging and comparatively moderate senator to a seventh term. And on some issues, there is consensus. In a state with the highest percentage of "very religious" residents—almost 61 percent—Mississippians in 2004 voted by 86% to ban same-sex marriage. Meanwhile, abortion is opposed by both blacks and whites; only one abortion clinic operates in the state, and its ability to continue is under judicial attack from opponents, including the state government itself.

Presidential Politics Mississippi voted for Jimmy Carter in 1976 and came within 12,000 votes of doing so again in 1980. But starting in 1984, Democratic presidential nominees have won only between 37% and 44% here. Presidential voting is heavily racially polarized. Mississippi voted 56%-43% for Republican John McCain in 2008, with whites voting 88%-11% for McCain and blacks 98%-2% for Democrat Barack Obama, the nation's first African-American president. In 2012, Obama's percentages went

2012 Presidential Vote		
Mitt Romney (R)...............710,746	(55%)
Barack Obama (D) 562,949	(44%)

2012 Presidential Primary		
Rick Santorum (R) 96,156	(33%)
Newt Gingrich (R) 91,499	(31%)
Mitt Romney (R)...................90,069	(31%)

2008 Presidential Vote		
John McCain (R)...............724,597	(56%)
Barack Obama (D) 554,662	(43%)

down 1% among whites and 2% among blacks, but his statewide percentage improved, and Republican Mitt Romney won the state by a reduced 55%-44%. Black turnout increased, from 33% in 2008 to 36% in 2012.

Mississippi has held a presidential primary in the second week of March since 1988, too late to make a difference in the nominating contests. That was certainly the case for Republicans in 2008, as Mike Huckabee withdrew from the contest the week before Mississippi voted. Only 145,000 people voted in the Republican primary—fewer than in 1988, 1992, and 1996—with 79% of voters supporting McCain. On the Democratic side, the race was still on, and turnout was 434,000, topping the record of 359,000 in 1988. With voting along racial lines, Obama beat Hillary Clinton 61%-37%, his biggest primary margin anywhere except in Virginia, Georgia, and the District of Columbia.

In 2012, Mississippi Republicans voted on March 13, the same day as Alabama. This was after Newt Gingrich had won in South Carolina and Georgia and Rick Santorum had nearly beaten Mitt Romney in Michigan. The race turned out to be almost a three-way tie: Santorum won 32.8% of the vote, Gingrich 31.2%, and Romney 30.6%. Romney ran best in metro Jackson and on the Gulf Coast, Santorum best in northeast Mississippi.

Congressional Districts Redistricting in Mississippi following the 2010 census was relatively simple, though with an unusual procedural twist. The state retained its four seats and after the 2010 wave election, Republicans held all three white-majority districts while Democrat Bennie Thompson held the

114th Congress Lineup	
3 R	1 D
113th Congress Lineup	
3 R	1 D

black-majority 2nd District. Republicans held the governorship and state Senate, but some were fearful that the Obama Justice Department would deny preclearance to any map that didn't create a second African-American seat. So they filed suit asking federal judges to step in, because any map drawn by a federal court doesn't need to win Justice Department pre-approval.

The end-around worked. A three-judge federal panel gave the legislature until December 2011 to draw its own map. When the legislature failed to meet its deadline, the court put its own proposal into place. The map made only minor changes, shifting racially mixed Grenada, Panola and Yalobusha counties from the northeastern 1st District, which contains fast-growing DeSoto County in the Memphis suburbs, to the 2nd District, which was under-populated by 73,000 residents. The African-American share of the Delta 2nd ticked down only 2%, from 66% to 64%, ensuring Thompson's continued safety. The three other districts range from 23% to 35% black. Elsewhere, the courts simply smoothed out existing boundaries, reducing the number of counties split from eight to four statewide.

Governor

Phil Bryant (R)

Elected 2011, term expires Jan. 2016, 1st term; b. Dec. 9, 1954, Moorhead; U. of Southern MS, B.S. 1977, MS Col., M.S. 1988; Methodist; married (Deborah); 2 children.

Elected Office: MS House, 1991-96; St. auditor, 1999-2008; MS lt. gov., 2008-11.

Professional Career: Jailer, deputy sheriff, Hinds Cnty; Sheriff's Office, 1976-81; Ins. investigator, 1981-91; St. auditor appointee, 1996-99.

Office: P.O. Box 139, Jackson, 39205, 601-359-3150; Fax: 601-359-3741; Website: governorbryant.com.

Election Results

2011 general	Phil Bryant (R)	544,787	(61%)
	Johnny DuPree (D)	348,417	(39%)
2011 primary	Phil Bryant (R)	172,300	(59%)
	Dave Dennis (R)	74,546	(26%)
	Ron Williams (R)	25,555	(9%)

Mississippi's Gov. Phil Bryant, elected in 2011, is a Republican who succeeded term-limited Haley Barbour. Bryant had served as lieutenant governor under Barbour, and while he lacks his predecessor's humor and common touch, he has pleased conservatives with his willingness to go even further to the right than Barbour on social issues.

Bryant was born in Moorhead in the Mississippi Delta. His father was a diesel mechanic and his mother a homemaker. His family eventually relocated to South Jackson, where Bryant finished high school. He worked in a tire store to earn extra money and decided that he needed more schooling. "Changing tires five-and-a-half days a week made me decide I would check out community college," Bryant told the Biloxi-based *Sun Herald*. He later earned a bachelor's degree in criminal justice from the University of Southern Mississippi. Bryant worked for the local police as a deputy sheriff and later spent time in the private sector as an insurance investigator.

Bryant first ran for office in 1991, winning a state House seat representing Rankin County. In 1996, he was appointed state auditor by Republican Gov. Kirk Fordice. Bryant was elected to two full terms as auditor in 1999 and 2003 before being elected on the Barbour ticket as lieutenant governor in 2007. He became a favorite of tea party groups for his tough stance on illegal immigration. Bryant presided over the state Senate, which put him in the middle of some heated legislative battles, including legislative redistricting in 2011. With Barbour term-limited, Bryant sought to succeed him. Despite his ties to the popular incumbent, Bryant had to fight off four other candidates in the Republican primary. He won with 59%, exuding more of a common touch than Barbour but less national influence.

In the general election, Bryant faced Democrat Johnny DuPree, the mayor of Hattiesburg and the state's first African-American gubernatorial nominee. The campaign was relatively low-key and congenial, with both candidates vowing to focus on issues and refrain from attacking each other personally. Despite his best efforts, DuPree remained an underdog in this conservative state. Bryant had far more campaign cash and maintained a sizable lead in the polls, and he won easily, 61% to 39%. The race was almost overshadowed by controversial ballot initiatives—an anti-abortion "personhood amendment" that both Bryant and DuPree supported but which failed, and a voter ID measure that Bryant favored and DuPree opposed, and which passed.

As governor, Bryant quickly distanced himself from Barbour's controversial decision, shortly before leaving office, to pardon more than 200 inmates, including more than 20 convicted of murder, manslaughter, or homicide. Bryant's state budget proposal called for cutting his own office expenses, and he later sold the state jet, which Barbour had used extensively, for $2 million (though he kept a prop plane). On social issues, he signed into law a bill requiring all physicians at abortion clinics to be board-certified gynecologists and to have admitting privileges at a local hospital, an effort widely perceived as being aimed at shutting down the state's only remaining clinic. Amid unemployment rates persistently above the national average, Bryant was a tireless promoter of economic development. He used conservative talk radio to promote his agenda.

On health care, Bryant squabbled for months with state Insurance Commissioner Mike Chaney over whether to establish an insurance exchange under the Affordable Care Act, but ultimately, Bryant's position—that the state not set up an exchange—won out, and the federal government set up one instead. Then, after the Supreme Court allowed states to opt out of the law's Medicaid expansion provision, Bryant pushed passionately against expanding Medicaid in Mississippi, despite the state's 50th-place ranking for health in several national studies and the possibility that 137,800 uninsured residents could have received Medicaid coverage, according to Kaiser Family Foundation estimates.

In 2014, Bryant signed three bills curbing organized labor, which was already rare in the state—only 3.7 percent of the workforce belonged to unions in 2013. "Just to be blunt about it: We just don't want unions involved in our businesses or our public sector," Bryant said upon signing the bills. He also signed a bill to allow residents to carry concealed guns without a license. On criminal justice, he signed a bill requiring convicts to serve at least 50 percent of their sentence, and at least 25 percent for those convicted of a nonviolent offense—a less stringent requirement than previously, and with added flexibility for judges to impose sentences that don't include incarceration. The aim was to reduce the cost of a corrections budget that had been rapidly expanding.

In 2015, Bryant proposed a $50 million boost to worker training over two years, supported by excess money from the unemployment trust fund, as well as a tax cut for working families earning less than $52,000, though neither was enacted. He also burnished his conservative credentials, criticizing the federal government for its "troubling" decision to send roughly 200 of the 30,000 unaccompanied children who crossed the U.S.-Mexico border to family members or guardians in Mississippi, and vetoing a bill critical of Common Core educational standards because it wasn't tough enough.

"We are not yet where we need to be to move to a new level, but we are moving ahead and should not be timid about recognizing the good in Mississippi," he said in his 2015 State of the State address. "Others will certainly revel in the bad. But as for me, I am proud of my Mississippi." Bryant headed into his 2015 reelection in good shape, with a 72 percent approval rating and a 61%-39% lead over potential Democratic challenger Vicki Slater in a Mason-Dixon poll.

Senior Senator

Thad Cochran (R)

Elected 1978, term expires 2021, 7th term; b. Dec. 7, 1937, Pontotoc; U. of MS, B.A. 1959, J.D. 1965, Rotary Fellow Trinity Col. U. of Dublin, Ireland, 1963-64; Baptist; married (Kay Webber); 2 children.

Military Career: U.S. Navy, 1959-61; U.S. Navy, summers 1962-64.

Elected Office: U.S. House, 1973-78.

Professional Career: Practicing atty., Watkins & Eager, 1965-72.

DC Office: 113 DSOB, 20510, 202-224-5054; Website: cochran.senate .gov.

State Offices: Gulfport, 228-867-9710; Jackson, 601-965-4459; Oxford, 662-236-1018.

Committees: *Agriculture, Nutrition & Forestry:* Commodities, Risk Mgmt. & Trade; Conservation, Forestry & Natural Resources; Rural Development & Energy. *Appropriations* (Chmn): Agriculture, Rural Development, FDA & Related Agencies; Defense (Chmn); Homeland Security; Interior, Environment & Related Agencies; Labor, HHS, Education & Related Agencies; Energy & Water Development; ex officio on all remaining subcommittees. *Rules & Administration.*

Group Ratings

	ADA	ACLU	AFL-CIO	LCV	ITI	COC	HAFA	ACU	CFG	FRC
2014	10%	0%	–	0%	33%	100%	51%	63%	44%	86%
2013	10%	C	28%	31%	C	63%	C	60%	56%	C

National Journal Ratings

	2013 LIB	—	2013 CONS
Economic	42%	—	57%
Social	12%	—	87%
Foreign	42%	—	57%
Composite	33%	—	68%

Key Votes of the 113th Congress

1. Sandy storm spending	Y	5. Student Loan Rates	Y
2. Chuck Hagel Confirmation	Y	6. Employee Non-Discrim'n Act	N
3. Gun Background Checks	N	7. Senate Vote on Judgeships	Y
4. Immigration Reform	N	8. Defense Dept. Spending	N

9. Bipartisan Budget Deal	N
10. Farm Bill Conference Rept.	Y
11. Unempl. Comp. Extension	N
12. Keystone Pipeline	Y

Election Results

2014 general	Thad Cochran (R)	378,481	(60%)	$7,868,305	$2,435,395	$3,779,663
	Travis Childers (D)	239,439	(38%)	$668,975	$20,305	
	Shawn O'Hara (REF)	13,938	(2%)			
Prim. run-off	Thad Cochran(R)	194,932	(51%)			
	Chris McDaniel (R)	187,265	(49%)			
2014 primary	Chris McDaniel (R)	157,733	(50%)			
	Thad Cochran(R)	156,315	(49%)			

Prior winning percentages: 2008 (61%), 2002 (85%), 1996 (71%), 1990 (100%), 1984 (61%), 1978 (45%); House: 1976 (76%), 1974 (70%), 1972 (48%)

Republican Thad Cochran, Mississippi's senior senator, was elected in 1972 to the House and in 1978 to the Senate, where he sits at Jefferson Davis's old desk. He personifies an all-but-vanished breed of Southern Republicans—amiable to all, conservative but not rigidly so, a devoted institutionalist, and a proficient procurer of funding for his poor, rural state. With the help of the national GOP establishment and his state's black voters, he escaped an embarrassing defeat in a June 2014 primary runoff. He returned in 2015 to chair the Appropriations Committee, a post he'd held a decade earlier.

Cochran grew up in small towns in northern Mississippi near Jackson, the son of a principal and a mathematics teacher. Cochran was athletic in high school, lettering in football, basketball, and baseball. He was also valedictorian of his senior class and a talented musician; he sometimes relaxes by playing a baby grand piano in his Senate office. Cochran excelled academically at Ole Miss; he was also a cheerleader, which was not uncommon for men at that time and was considered an honor. (Former Mississippi Sen. Trent Lott was one as well.) Cochran went on to get a law degree from Ole Miss, served in the Navy, spent a year abroad, and then practiced law in Jackson.

In 1968, he worked on the Nixon-Agnew presidential campaign in Mississippi, where Richard Nixon ran third. Four years later, when President Nixon was sweeping Mississippi, Cochran ran for Congress and was elected as a Republican from the Jackson-area district with a plurality against a white Democrat and a black independent. When segregationist Sen. James Eastland, a Democrat, retired, Cochran jumped into the race and once again won with a plurality over a white Democrat and a black independent.

In the House and in the Senate, Cochran managed for years to amass a generally conservative record with little controversy or acrimony. His courtly demeanor, his refusal to engage in racial politics, and his Republican Party label—in a state where most whites have been voting Republican for president for three decades—have made him acceptable to voters at home. Until 2014, his toughest race came in 1984, when he was opposed by popular former Democratic Gov. William Winter. Winter could make a case for himself, but not against Cochran. Cochran outraised him $2.7 million to $738,000, and won 61%-39%.

Cochran competed for years with Lott to climb the leadership ladder, and he usually wound up losing. In 1990, Cochran was elected to the chairmanship of the Senate Republican Conference, the No. 3 position. Although he had less seniority than Cochran, Lott set his sights higher. Rather than wait his turn to move up, Lott challenged Wyoming's Alan Simpson for majority whip, the No. 2 position. Cochran pointedly endorsed Simpson, but Lott won anyway, with the support of junior Senate conservatives, and leapfrogged over Cochran to the higher-ranking post of whip. Then in 1996, the top job of Senate majority leader came open when Kansas Republican Bob Dole ran for president. Cochran and Lott both entered the race. Lott was able to sew up a majority of votes quickly. Cochran stayed in the contest and lost, 44-8.

Cochran played an important role in shaping the very different 1996, 2002, and 2008 farm bills. In 1996, he supported the Republican initiative to phase out most crop subsidies, although he insisted on maintaining the cotton marketing loan plan that he largely wrote in 1985. In 2002, he supported the strategy of reviving annual crop payments and of vastly increasing the Conservation Reserve Program. In 2005, Cochran defeated on the Senate floor Iowa Republican Charles Grassley's move to cap subsidies to individual farmers at $250,000. In 2006, he opposed President George W. Bush's proposed 5 percent cut in farm subsidies. And in 2008, he supported the farm bill that passed over Bush's veto. The president said the bill was too costly and did not go far enough to curb subsidies.

But Cochran has made his biggest mark on the Appropriations Committee. He regularly incensed reformers with his additions to spending bills for Mississippi projects. He takes a particular interest in his state universities' research needs and casts a wide net—in the fiscal 2009 omnibus spending bill, he earmarked $3.5 million to the University of Mississippi's National Center for Natural Products Research, at the time the country's legal producer of marijuana for medical research. The *Washington Post* noted that four university buildings in the state bear his name, and it calculated that 112 news articles in Lexis-Nexis paired the terms "Thad Cochran" and "King of Pork." Between 2001 and 2012, almost half of the state's revenue came from federal sources.

Cochran chaired Appropriations from 2005 to 2007, when Republicans controlled the Senate. When he first became chairman, Cochran promised to get appropriations bills passed on time, rather than rolling multiple bills into large "omnibus" measures, which had become practice as Congress grew more partisan and unable to agree on individual spending bills. While Cochran said that he wouldn't have "runaway spending" on the committee, earmarks and discretionary spending became major issues.

Hurricane Katrina struck on August 29, 2005, causing massive damage in Mississippi, and suddenly keeping tight controls on spending was not the chairman's prime concern. Cochran viewed the devastation by helicopter on August 31, and then persuaded the Senate to immediately vote for $10.5 billion in disaster relief. A week later, he persuaded it to vote for $52 billion more. In late October, Bush called for an additional $17 billion. Cochran, working closely with Republican Gov. Haley Barbour and others in the Mississippi and Louisiana delegations, pushed for $35 billion, with community development block grants available for homeowners and business owners with uninsured losses. This was a new policy, and one not included in the administration request. On December 21, Congress passed a $29 billion bill, with $11.5 billion for community development block grants. Mississippi received $5 billion of the CDBG funds. In the meantime, work on the regular appropriations bills bogged down, and Cochran and House Appropriations Chairman Jerry Lewis of California, Republican, resigned themselves to a continuing resolution for nine appropriations bills they couldn't get passed.

The following year, 2006, brought more vagaries in the appropriations process in the form of the Bush administration's request for large amounts of additional money for the war in Iraq. The president asked for a supplemental Iraq funding bill, a proposal sweetened with nearly $20 billion in additional funds for hurricane recovery. Cochran drafted a bill that included some controversial provisions: $700 million for building a CSX rail line inland, to replace the line on the Gulf Coast; $500 million for Northrop Grumman, which was in litigation with the insurers of its Pascagoula shipyard; and $1 billion for Katrina housing. Speaker Dennis Hastert and House Majority Leader John Boehner called his bill a "special-interest shopping cart," and conservative Republican Sen. Tom Coburn of Oklahoma tried to kill it. But Cochran prevailed on the Senate floor, 50-47. Ultimately, Congress agreed to supplemental spending for Iraq and to $20 billion for Katrina recovery, although it rejected the railroad line.

As Cochran worked to pass the regular appropriations bills on time, earmarked spending came increasingly under fire as more conservatives took issue with Congress's long-standing practice of approving special projects for individual lawmakers, projects that often were not requested by any government agency. Cochran and Lewis managed to get through both chambers just two of the 12 spending bills in 2006, those for defense and homeland-security appropriations. Budget hawks raised objections to earmarks in the remaining 10 bills, and GOP Majority Leader Bill Frist declined to bring them to the floor before the November election. When Democrats won majorities in both houses, Congress passed a temporary measure to keep the government running, and work ceased on the remaining spending bills. Cochran lost his chairmanship. Cochran had the highest total of earmarks in fiscal years 2008, 2009, and 2010, with more than $497 million in fiscal 2010 alone, according to Taxpayers for Common Sense.

Cochran continued to defend earmarking, but when Republicans announced an earmark moratorium for 2011-12, which continued into the following years, he reluctantly went along. Despite the moratorium, he was still able to secure funding for many of his priorities, including his state's NASA Stennis Space Center and the Coast Guard. Cochran gave up his position as Appropriations' ranking Republican in January 2013 to take the same position on the Agriculture Committee, using his seniority to bump Pat Roberts of Kansas from the post. Roberts initially said he was ready to force a vote challenging Cochran before backing down. Cochran was expected to seek to overturn Roberts' work on the Senate's 2012 farm bill, which focused on insurance options to replace the traditional system of direct cash payments to growers. Southern rice, peanut, and wheat producers objected strenuously to the change. Cochran faced the added challenge of dealing with House members who sought to cut far more in spending on food stamp and nutrition programs than the Senate.

After the GOP took back the Senate in 2014, Cochran returned to the Appropriations gavel with the backing of Majority Leader Mitch McConnell, a fellow appropriator. Cochran has often has partnered with his Mississippi Senate colleague Roger Wicker, a Republican whose ascension in the Senate in 2007—to succeed Cochran's old rival, Lott—was a welcome change for Cochran. He also has a long relationship with Maryland's Barbara Mikulski, the panel's top Democrat, who assiduously sought his help on getting military and other spending for her state. One of Cochran's most notable habits in recent years has been a willingness to abandon his party on floor votes. He was one of just 11 Republicans to support a $17 billion Democratic jobs bill in 2010, and he joined Democrats that year in backing the New START arms reduction treaty with Russia. He teamed with Maryland Democrat Ben Cardin in 2012 on an amendment to the surface transportation bill that bypassed state transportation agencies and sent money for programs such as bicycle and walking paths directly to local agencies. He worked with Louisiana Democrat Mary Landrieu in January 2013 to expedite the disaster recovery process in the aftermath of Hurricane Sandy, and he was the first GOP senator to back President Barack Obama's choice of former Republican Sen. Chuck Hagel for secretary of Defense.

Cochran's 2008 reelection was his closest since 1984, but he still won comfortably, 61%-39%. Questions surfaced about whether he would run again in 2014, but Cochran ended months of speculation by announcing in December 2013 that he would make another bid. The ensuing primary—one of the bitterest in the nation in recent years—unexpectedly launched Cochran into the national spotlight. He drew a challenge from outspoken state Sen. Chris McDaniel, who with the support of tea party groups, the Club for Growth and the Senate Conservatives Fund, mounted a full-throttle assault on Cochran as insufficiently conservative for the deeply red state. McDaniel succeeded in holding Cochran barely below the 50-percent mark in a June 3 primary, forcing a runoff, which the challenger entered as a modest favorite. The race's ugliest moment came when a McDaniel supporter took photos of Cochran's long-ailing wife Rose—who would pass away in December 2014—in bed at a nursing home and posted them online without her consent. McDaniel denied any connection with the incident, in which four men were arrested. One of the men committed suicide; another pleaded guilty to conspiracy.

In the three-week runoff, Cochran staged a remarkable political comeback. He reintroduced himself to voters via advertisements, running one spot that listed 20 institutions or companies he had helped by procuring funds. The Republican establishment, led by McConnell and business groups, leapt into action by writing checks and providing other assistance. Most strikingly, Cochran's campaign took a calculated risk by seeking to reach out to Democrats—particularly African Americans—who were eligible to vote in the runoff. The strategy paid off: Amid unexpectedly high turnout, Cochran eked out a victory in the runoff, 51%-49%. Harry Enten of fivethirtyeight.com concluded that, based on county-level results, "traditionally Democratic voters provided Cochran with his margin of victory." A furious McDaniel filed a formal challenge alleging thousands of voting irregularities; a judge dismissed it. Undeterred, he appealed to the Mississippi Supreme Court, which dismissed it just before the November election. Not that Cochran was in any trouble in the general: He beat former Democratic Rep. Travis Childers, likely the strongest candidate Democrats could have run, by 23 points.

After Cochran's victory, members of the Congressional Black Caucus said he owed them one. "Absolutely we have expectations," Democratic Rep. Marcia Fudge of Ohio told *Politico*. And in his new term, Cochran did continue displaying a moderate streak. He declined to join most of his caucus in signing a letter to Iran's leaders critical of Obama's nuclear negotiations, and he was one of just 10 Republicans who voted to confirm Obama's pick for attorney general, Loretta Lynch. In May 2015, Cochran quietly married Kay Webber, a longtime aide who was 77, like the senator.

Junior Senator

Roger Wicker (R)

Appointed Dec. 2007, term expires Jan. 2019, 1st full term; b. July 5, 1951, Pontotoc; U. of MS, B.A. 1973, J.D. 1975; Baptist; married (Gayle); 3 children.

Military Career: U.S. Air Force, 1976-80; U.S. Air Force Reserve, 1980-2004.

Elected Office: Tupelo city judge pro tem, 1986-87; MS Senate, 1988-94; U.S. House, 1995-2007.

Professional Career: Staff, U.S. House Rules Cmte., 1980-82; Practicing atty., 1982-94; Lee Cnty. public defender, 1984-87; Bd. of Visitors, U.S. Naval Acad., 2005.

DC Office: 555 DSOB, 20515, 202-224-6253; Fax: 202-228-0378; Website: wicker.senate.gov.

State Offices: Gulfport, 228-871-7017; Hernando, 662-429-1002; Jackson, 601-965-4644; Tupelo, 662-844-5010.

Committees: *Armed Services:* Airland; Personnel; Seapower (Chmn). *Budget. Commerce, Science & Transportation:* Aviation Operations, Safety & Security; Communications, Technology, Innovation & the Internet (Chmn); Oceans, Atmosphere, Fisheries & Coast Guard; Surface Transportation & Merchant Marine Infrastructure, Safety & Security. *Environment & Public Works:* Clean Air & Nuclear Safety; Fisheries, Water, & Wildlife; Transportation & Infrastructure. *Rules & Administration.*

Group Ratings

	ADA	ACLU	AFL-CIO	LCV	ITI	COC	HAFA	ACU	CFG	FRC
2014	15%	0%	–	0%	33%	100%	45%	68%	47%	86%
2013	10%	C	28%	31%	C	63%	C	60%	68%	C

National Journal Ratings

	2013 LIB	—	2013 CONS
Economic	34%	—	65%
Social	33%	—	66%
Foreign	28%	—	70%
Composite	32%	—	68%

Key Votes of the 113th Congress

1. Sandy storm spending	Y	5. Student Loan Rates	Y	9. Bipartisan Budget Deal	N
2. Chuck Hagel Confirmation	N	6. Employee Non-Discrim'n Act	N	10. Farm Bill Conference Rept.	Y
3. Gun Background Checks	N	7. Senate Vote on Judgeships	Y	11. Unempl. Comp. Extension	N
4. Immigration Reform	N	8. Defense Dept. Spending	N	12. Keystone Pipeline	Y

Election Results

2012 general	Roger Wicker (R)	709,626	(57%)	$8,646,288
	Albert Gore, Jr. (D)	503,467	(41%)	
2012 primary	Roger Wicker (R)	254,669	(89%)	
	Robert Maloney (R)	18,822	(7%)	

Prior winning percentages: 2008 special (55%); House: 2006 (66%), 2004 (79%), 2002 (71%), 2000 (70%), 1998 (67%), 1996 (68%), 1994 (63%)

Roger Wicker was appointed in late 2007 to serve as Mississippi's junior senator, filling the vacancy created by the resignation of Trent Lott, a powerful Mississippian who had served as both majority and minority leader. Wicker went on to win a special election for the seat in 2008 and was reelected four years later. He has been part of the core of Senate Republicans implacably opposed to most of President Barack Obama's initiatives, and in 2015 entered the GOP leadership ranks as chairman of the National Republican Senatorial Committee.

Wicker grew up in Pontotoc, the same north Mississippi town where his senior colleague in the Senate, Republican Thad Cochran, spent part of his childhood. Wicker's father was a conservative Democrat, a state senator, and a circuit judge. He attended public schools and as a teenager became interested in Republican politics. From then on, his career was intertwined with the two more senior and well-established Mississippians, Lott and Cochran. He was a page in the U.S. House—one of perhaps two dozen congressional pages who later served as members—and he campaigned door-to-door for Cochran in his first race for Congress, in 1972. At Ole Miss, where both Lott and Cochran had gone to school, Wicker served in student government and went on to get a law degree. He spent four years in the Air Force Judge Advocate General Corps and remained in the Reserve until 2004.

In 1980, Wicker went to work for Lott on the House Rules Committee. He returned to Mississippi in 1982, set up a law practice, and served as the county public defender in his wife's hometown of Tupelo. In 1987, at age 36, he was elected to the state Senate, the first Republican elected in northern Mississippi since Reconstruction. In the legislature, Wicker helped draft the state's strict abortion law and was also a leading advocate of government-sponsored vouchers for private school tuition.

In 1994, Rep. Jamie Whitten, a Democrat, momentously retired after becoming the longest-serving member of the House in history. The retirement of the powerful Whitten, the chairman of the Appropriations Committee, left big shoes to fill in Mississippi's 1st District. Pent-up demand produced crowded primaries; Mississippi was then more politically competitive, attracting six Republicans, including Wicker, and three Democrats. On the strength of support from his home base of Tupelo, Wicker finished first in the GOP primary, 27%-19%. He won the runoff against Grant Fox, a young former aide to Cochran, 53%-47%, then easily defeated Democratic state Rep. Bill Wheeler, 63%-37%, in the general election. A district that had been held for five decades by a leading Democrat thus shifted to the GOP.

Wicker compiled a solidly conservative voting record in the House. He got a seat on Appropriations, an unusual prize for a freshman. Appropriators tend to operate in an atmosphere of bipartisan cooperation, and Wicker worked quietly in subcommittees to get funding for Yalobusha River flood control and an interstate highway through DeSoto County. He delivered research dollars to Mississippi universities, and he worked with Lott, by then a senator, to attract defense technology firms to the state. Citizens Against Government Waste gave him the dubious distinction of No. 1 earmarker in the House for securing $176 million in projects, most of it for his district. "I am a fiscal conservative, and I believe in keeping spending low," Wicker said in 2008. "But once the national budget is set, I think it is only fair to fight for our fair share for Mississippi." (He did reluctantly support the GOP's earmark ban starting in 2011.)

In November 2007, Lott announced that he would retire from the Senate before the end of the year. Wicker wanted the seat, but so did 3rd District GOP Rep. Chip Pickering and Netscape founder and Mississippi native James Barksdale. On December 31, 2007, Gov. Haley Barbour appointed Wicker and announced that the election for the remainder of Lott's term would be held on Nov. 4, 2008; Democrats sought a quicker special election, but the state Supreme Court upheld the Barbour's date. Wicker spent his first year in the Senate focusing on the election. Mississippi Democrats had not seriously contested a Senate race in 20 years, but President Bush's low poll ratings, enthusiasm among African-American voters for Democratic presidential nominee Barack Obama, and a victory by Democrat Travis Childers in Wicker's old House district combined to give them hope. The Democratic nominee was better known in much of the state: former Gov. Ronnie Musgrove, who had been ousted by Barbour in 2003 and had good poll ratings. It was a battle between old friends: Wicker and Musgrove had both been elected to the state Senate for the first time in 1987 and had roomed together in an apartment in Jackson.

Musgrove criticized Wicker for his support of earmarks and called him a "poster child" for a moratorium on pork-barrel spending. Musgrove also criticized him for opposing increases in the minimum wage. Musgrove even hinted at ethical misconduct, criticizing Wicker for securing a $6 million earmark, not sought by the Pentagon, for Aurora Flight Sciences to build unmanned aerial vehicles in north Mississippi, as company executives were contributing $17,000 to his campaign and hiring Wicker's former chief of staff to lobby for the project. Wicker said the effort was all about bringing high-paying jobs to Mississippi. However, this was neutralized after the indictment of three executives of a Georgia company that had defaulted on a state government guaranteed loan of $54 million; they had contributed $59,000 to Musgrove's 2003 campaign. Wicker outspent Musgrove, $6.2 million to $5.3 million, though the Democratic Senatorial Campaign Committee pumped in more than enough money to compensate. Wicker ended up winning, 55%-45%, with 82 percent of whites backing Wicker and 92 percent of blacks supporting Musgrove.

In the Senate, Wicker has voted slightly to the right of Cochran, especially on social issues. Wicker has introduced legislation in successive congresses to give state officials "special standing" to challenge proposed regulations under the Tenth Amendment. He drew widespread attention in January 2015 when he cast the lone "no" vote against Democrat Sheldon Whitehouse's amendment to the Keystone XL pipeline bill attempting to get Republicans to acknowledge on record that climate-change is actually occurring. Because the amendment didn't specify whether humans were responsible, even such ardent climate skeptics as Oklahoma Republican Sen. James Inhofe, a colleague on the Environment and Public Works Committee, backed it. But not Wicker, who called it a "gag." Wicker said he agreed "with the more than 31,000 American scientists who do not believe the science on this matter is settled." *National Journal* reported that Wicker compared himself to Galileo and Copernicus, leading the magazine to place him in "the top tier of the Senate's Republican skeptics of climate change science, along with the likes of David Vitter and Ted Cruz."

Wicker has repeatedly introduced legislation to overturn *Roe v. Wade,* the Supreme Court decision legalizing abortion. He called the health care overhaul the "great fight for the rest of this term, maybe our lifetimes" and later introduced a bill to enable state officials to challenge the law. In the interest of protecting gun owners, he amended a fiscal 2010 transportation spending bill to allow Amtrak passengers to carry firearms and ammunition in checked baggage. After Congress voted in late 2010 to repeal the "don't ask, don't tell" ban on openly gay service members, Wicker and Inhofe introduced a bill forbidding same-sex marriages on military bases.

Wicker has worked closely with Cochran, who had often been at odds with Lott, in backing local projects and cosponsoring bills. Wicker has also worked with Democrats to protect Mississippi's interests. With then-Democratic Rep. Gene Taylor, Wicker pushed amendments allowing purchasers of federal flood insurance to add wind coverage to their policies, something helpful to a state battered by Hurricane Katrina. And as a member of the Helsinki Commission on human rights, Wicker worked closely with Maryland Democratic Sen. Ben Cardin to enact a law in late 2012 that imposed tough penalties on Russians accused of violating human rights. The measure led Russian President Vladimir Putin to announce a subsequent ban on U.S. adoptions of Russian-born children.

Wicker faced far fewer headwinds in winning a full six-year term in 2012, defeating Albert Gore, a retired United Methodist minister and distant relative of the former vice president who ran a bare-bones campaign. Wicker spent more than $8 million and won 57 percent of the vote; Gore reported no spending. Wicker poked fun at his fundraising chops during a fundraiser for the Shakespeare Theater Company; he played "Super PAC Man," using his checkbook to taunt others.

In 2013-14, most of Wicker's work was focused on Mississippi matters. Joining with Cochran, he offered a bill to extend Medicare reimbursements for telemedicine in rural and other areas without extensive health resources; the measure was reintroduced in 2015. In April 2014, the Environment and Public Works panel approved his bill to reauthorize a Safe Drinking Water Act program that aids rural communities, but it did not advance, and he reintroduced it in 2015 with Democratic Sen. Heidi Heitkamp of North Dakota. Wicker now chairs the Armed Services Committee's seapower subcommittee, an important panel for his state, and the Commerce, Science and Transportation Committee's subpanel on technology and the Internet. He has said his chief focus would be to secure more broadband access for rural areas.

Wicker drew unwanted attention in April 2013, when an envelope sent to his Washington office tested positive for ricin. A Mississippi man—an Elvis impersonator from the singer's birthplace of Tupelo—pleaded guilty in 2014 to sending letters with the toxic substance to Wicker, who had once hired him for a gig, as well as to Obama and other officials. He was sentenced to 25 years in prison.

In 2014, Wicker devoted considerable effort to helping Cochran survive a 2014 primary. Cochran, 76, hadn't had a tough race in years, but he faced an aggressive challenge from tea party-backed Chris McDaniel. Neither Cochran nor McDaniel reached 50 percent in the primary; in the runoff, Cochran narrowly edged McDaniel amid concerted support from establishment Republicans that included outreach to African-American voters, an unusual effort that may have put Cochran over the top. "I think we did the country a favor, and certainly the party a favor, because we got a good man back in office," Wicker said.

Wicker's role in returning Cochran to the Senate aided his bid for the NRSC chairmanship. When seeking the post, one of his first calls was to Lott, who told him, "Golly, Roger, why would you want that job? It's the toughest job in the Senate leadership," *CQ-Roll Call* reported. Wicker faced Nevada GOP Sen. Dean Heller, who said he was well-positioned to help take down his party's chief 2016 election target—Democratic leader Harry Reid. But Wicker prevailed in a secret ballot (and Reid later announced that he wouldn't seek another term). As NRSC chairman, Wicker faces a formidable task: His party has to defend 24 seats, compared to 10 for the Democrats. Several Republicans running are in blue and purple states, and the presidential race could divert money and attention. But at least outwardly, Wicker remained confident. "I think we can do this, but it's going to take resources. It's going to involve everybody helping," he said.

FIRST DISTRICT

Trent Kelly (R)

Elected June 2015, 1st term; b. March 1, 1966, Union; U. of MS, B.A. 1989, J.D. 1994, U.S. Army War Col., M.A. 2010; Methodist; married (Sheila); 3 children.

Military Career: MS Army Natl Guard, 1987-present (Gulf War, Iraq).

Elected Office: Tupelo City Prosecutor, 1999-2011; 1st Circuit Judicial District atty., 2012-15.

Professional Career: Practicing atty., 1995-99.

DC Office: 1427 LHOB, 20515, 202-225-4306; Fax: 202-225-3549; Website: trentkelly.house.gov.

State Offices: Columbus, 662-327-0748; Hernando, 662-449-3090; Tupelo, 662-841-8808.

Committees: *Agriculture:* Commodity Exchanges, Energy, & Credit; Livestock & Foreign Agriculture. *Small Business:* Contracting & Workforce; Economic Growth, Tax & Capital Access.

Election Results

2015 special general	Trent Kelly (R)	69,516	(70%)	$510,246	$370,334
	Walter Zinn Jr. (D)	29,831	(30%)	$27,841	$29,823
2015 special primary	Walter Zinn Jr. (D)	15,385	(17%)		
	Trent Kelly (R)	14,418	(16%)		
	Mike Tagert (R)	11,231	(13%)		
	Greg Pirkle (R)	7,142	(8%)		
	Starner Jones (R)	6,993	(8%)		
	Chip Mills (R)	6,929	(8%)		

Population		Race and Ethnicity		Income	
Total:	756,459	White	68.9%	Median income:	$40,887
Urban:	0.0%	Black	26.3%		*(378 of 435)*
Suburban:	21.4%	Latino	3.0%	Under $50,000	58.2%
Rural:	78.6%	Asian	0.5%	$50,000-$99,999:	29.4%
Land area:	11,093	Two races	1.2%	$100,000-$199,999:	11.0%
Pop/sq. mi.:	68.2	White Ethnic	13.1%	$200,000 or more:	1.5%
Born in state:	63.5%			Poverty Rate	20.7%
		Education			
Age Groups		H.S. grad or less:	50.3%	**Work**	
Under 18:	24.4%	Some college:	31.7%	White collar:	27.3%
18 to 34:	22.6%	College degree, 4 yr.:	11.8%	Blue collar:	41.5%
35 to 64:	39.0%	Post-grad study:	6.2%	Sales and service:	31.2%
Over 64:	14.0%			Govt. workers:	14.5%
		Military			
		Veterans/active duty:	7.7%		

Northeast Mississippi: Memphis area, Tupelo

Voter Turnout	
2013 Total Citizen 18+	561,936
2014 House Turnout	151,111
2014 Turnout as % CVAP	26.9%
2012 Turnout as % CVAP	57.5%

The university town of Oxford—the "Jefferson" of William Faulkner's fictional Yoknapatawpha County—sits on a divide between the hill country of Mississippi and the flat farmlands of the Mississippi Delta. Named for Oxford, England, it is home to the University of Mississippi, where violence broke out in 1962 when James Meredith became the school's first black student. Ole Miss, as it is known, now houses Meredith's papers in its library. Also in 1962, Republican Sen. Thad Cochran was a student at the Ole Miss law school, and former Senate Majority Leader Trent Lott of Mississippi was a senior. To the west is the Delta, with a large African-American majority, and DeSoto County, just south of Memphis and Mississippi's fastest-growing county and one of its most affluent. The county is becoming a magnet for Memphis commuters looking for affordable housing, better schools, and lower taxes across the border.

Southaven (population, 48,982) in DeSoto County is the fourth-biggest city in the state. In 2011, *CNNMoney* ranked it as the sixth-best place in the country to retire because of the "unique tax perks" for retirees. East of Oxford is the hill country, which stretches to where the Tennessee River nicks the northeast corner of Tishomingo County. This was traditional farming country, but it is now more engaged in small manufacturing. DeSoto has become very aggressive in economic development, and has taken business from Memphis.

The Golden Triangle in the Starkville area has become a center for aerospace research, including work on unmanned air vehicle designs for surveillance and communications. The biggest town in the area is Tupelo, home to an upholstered furniture industry that has survived more prosperously than furniture centers elsewhere, and continues to grow. Tupelo was also the birthplace of Elvis Presley in 1935, and the family's two-room house today is open to visitors. The town produces many Christian conservatives, the kind of townsfolk who were shocked by Presley's music and hip-swirling dance moves in the early days of rock 'n' roll. Donald Wildmon's American Family Association, a prominent Christian conservative organization, is based there. The Tupelo region got a big economic boost when Toyota in 2011 started operations at a new assembly plant, where it now boasts a workforce of 2,000 producing 189,000 of its signature Corollas a year. Several Toyota suppliers have sprung up nearby, with employment of another 2,000 people. Clay County has become a tire-manufacturing center.

The 1st Congressional District of Mississippi includes Southaven, the district's biggest city, Oxford, Tupelo and most of the hill country. It is the descendant of the district represented by Jamie Whitten, the longtime Democratic chairman of the Appropriations Committee and formerly the longest-serving House member. He held office 53 years and 62 days, ending in January 1995; Democratic

2012 Presidential Vote		
Mitt Romney (R)	197,980	(62%)
Barack Obama (D)	118,435	(37%)
2008 Presidential Vote		
John McCain (R)	202,734	(62%)
Barack Obama (D)	118,724	(37%)
Cook Partisan Voting Index:	R+16	

Rep. John Dingell of Michigan surpassed his mark in February 2009. This once-conservative Democratic territory has become solidly Republican in national politics, 62 percent each for John McCain in 2008 and Mitt Romney in 2012.

Trent Kelly (R)

Republican Trent Kelly won the June 2, 2015, special election in the 1st District. He succeeded Rep. Alan Nunnelee, who died in February after being ill for several months. In this heavily Republican district, the key event was Kelly's narrow victory in the 12-candidate Republican field in the May 12 primary.

Kelly graduated from the business school and law school at the University of Mississippi. He also got a master's degree in strategic studies from the U.S. Army War College in Carlisle Pennsylvania. Kelly has been in the National Guard since the mid-1980s as an engineer, and has achieved the rank of colonel. He served in Iraq during the Gulf War, then had two tours of duty during the Iraq War, where he commanded 670 troops. He received two Bronze Stars and numerous other military awards. He became city prosecutor in Tupelo in 1999, and held that position for 12 years before he was elected district attorney for seven rural counties in the northeast corner of the state.

After Nunnelee died, 13 candidates filed for the special election. Of the 12 Republicans, not one was from DeSoto County, which is the population center of the district. That led to a wide-open contest, with none of the candidates a big fundraiser. Mike Tagert, the northern Mississippi transportation commissioner, started with important political support as an ally of former Republican Gov. Haley Barbour, according to the *Cook Political Report* in an analysis two weeks before the vote. That report also cited Kelly; bank software executive Boyce Adams; plus Oxford attorney and lobbyist Quentin Whitwell, who also had served two terms on the city council of Jackson, which is outside the district. Kelly received contributions from Nunnelee's campaign fund, assistance from his former consultant and an aide, and what likely was an important endorsement, from his widow Tori, who said that nobody "respected the men and women who defend this country more than" her late husband.

In the "jungle primary," in which the top two candidates go to a runoff unless one of them gets 50 percent of the vote, Walter Zinn, the only Democrat, led with 17.4 percent, Kelly got 16.3 percent, and Tagert finished third with 12.7 percent. All other candidates had a single-digit share of the vote. Zinn, who also was the only African-American candidate in the field, had worked for two former mayors of Jackson and had been a Democratic campaign assistant in contests in the Midwest. Given the Republican tilt of the district, he was a distinct underdog in the primary. Kelly won with 70 percent of the vote, and took his oath of office on June 9.

Nunnelee, who had brain cancer, was a loyal Republican soldier who deliberately made fewer waves than his more boisterous colleagues from the freshman class of 2010. During a 16-year career in the state Senate, he chaired the Appropriations Committee. That experience, and his view that Congress had a responsibility to fund the government, led to his getting a seat on House Appropriations as a freshman. He typically was a leadership loyalist, and easily won reelection. Prior to the diagnosis of brain cancer, he had a series of health problems that caused absences from Congress.

SECOND DISTRICT

Bennie Thompson (D)

Elected April 1993, 11th full term; b. Jan. 28, 1948, Bolton; Tougaloo Col., B.A. 1968, Jackson St. U., M.S. 1972; Methodist; married (London); 1 child.

Elected Office: Bolton Bd. of Aldermen, 1968-72; Bolton mayor, 1973-80; Hinds Cnty. supervisor, 1980-93.

DC Office: 2466 RHOB, 20515, 202-225-5876; Fax: 202-225-5898; Website: benniethompson.house.gov.

State Offices: Bolton, 601-866-9003; Greenville, 662-335-9003; Greenwood, 662-455-9003; Jackson, 601-946-9003; Marks, 662-326-9003; Mound Bayou, 662-741-9003.

Committees: *Homeland Security* (RMM).

Group Ratings

	ADA	ACLU	AFL-CIO	LCV	ITI	COC	HAFA	ACU	CFG	FRC
2014	85%	77%	–	89%	80%	50%	15%	5%	6%	0%
2013	90%	C	100%	82%	C	38%	C	17%	20%	C

National Journal Ratings

	2013 LIB	—	2013 CONS
Economic	69%	—	31%
Social	73%	—	24%
Foreign	62%	—	37%
Composite	69%	—	31%

Key Votes of the 113th Congress

1. Sandy storm spending	Y	5. Medical Marijuana	Y
2. Violence Against Women Act	Y	6. Farm Bill	N
3. Guantanamo Bay Detainees	Y	7. Afghanistan Combat	Y
4. Abortion 20-week ban	N	8. NSA Phone Data Collection	Y

9. Syrian Rebels Training	N
10. Keystone pipeline	Y
11. Immigration Exec. Action	N
12. Bipartisan budget deal	N

Election Results

2014 general	Bennie Thompson (D)	100,688	(68%)	$1,138,674
	Troy Ray (I)	36,465	(25%)	
	Shelley Shoemake (REF)	11,493	(8%)	
2014 primary	Bennie Thompson (D)	41,618	(96%)	
	Damien Fairconetue (D)	1,860	(4%)	

Prior winning percentages: 2012 (67%), 2010 (61%), 2008 (69%), 2006 (64%), 2004 (58%), 2002 (55%), 2000 (65%), 1998 (71%), 1996 (60%), 1994 (54%), 1993 special (55%)

Population		Race and Ethnicity		Income	
Total:	726,159	Black	65.1%	Median income:	$30,582
Urban:	13.5%	White	31.9%		*(434 of 435)*
Suburban:	11.3%	Latino	1.8%	Under $50,000	67.9%
Rural:	75.3%	Asian	0.4%	$50,000-$99,999:	23.1%
Land area:	14,165	Two races	0.6%	$100,000-$199,999:	7.5%
Pop/sq. mi.:	51.3	White Ethnic	7.2%	$200,000 or more:	1.5%
Born in state:	83.0%			Poverty Rate	32.5%
		Education			
Age Groups		H.S. grad or less:	50.9%	**Work**	
Under 18:	25.6%	Some college:	30.2%	White collar:	29.5%
18 to 34:	23.9%	College degree, 4 yr.:	11.9%	Blue collar:	44.5%
35 to 64:	37.2%	Post-grad study:	7.0%	Sales and service:	25.9%
Over 64:	13.2%				
		Military		Govt. workers:	21.8%
		Veterans/active duty:	6.1%		

Mississippi Delta, Jackson

"The Mississippi Delta," wrote native David Cohn, "begins in the lobby of the Peabody Hotel in Memphis and ends on Catfish Row in Vicksburg." For centuries, the flooding Mississippi and Yazoo rivers left their sediments here, producing a fertile, dark soil. Ironically, what may well be America's richest

Voter Turnout	
2013 Total Citizen 18+	534,578
2014 House Turnout	148,646
2014 Turnout as % CVAP	27.8%
2012 Turnout as % CVAP	62.3%

agricultural land has been home for more than a century to many of its poorest people. Crisscrossed by rivers and famously disease-ridden, the Delta wasn't much settled until after the Civil War. Then, Reconstruction-era profit-seeking operators used late-19th-century technology to drain the land, line the river with levees and build railroads on tracks above the rise of the river. Black sharecroppers and field hands worked here in conditions little better than bondage. From this episode of industrial farming came both great misery and great art: Clarksdale in Coahoma County, where Martin Luther King in 1958 held the first meeting of the Southern Christian Leadership Conference, was the real birthplace of blues music, the home of W.C. Handy and Muddy Waters, John Lee Hooker, Ike Turner, and Sam Cooke. Greenville on the Mississippi has produced writers of the caliber of Walker Percy and Shelby Foote. Yazoo City produced author Willie Morris and bluesman Skip James. Today, Vicksburg's antebellum mansions and battlefield monuments attract about 1.5 million tourists annually.

Twentieth-century technology changed life in the Delta. The mechanical cotton-picking machine, invented in 1944, came along just as Northern factories were seeking low-wage workers. The great exodus to Chicago and other Northern cities accelerated, and the Delta's population has been declining ever since. Income levels remain very low, the teen pregnancy rate high and infant mortality at Third World levels. Yet there are signs of hope. Soybeans have become a big-dollar crop here and poultry farms have become a major enterprise. The Delta produces most of the nation's catfish, although excessive summer heat has recently driven up production costs. The Agriculture Department announced in 2012 it would buy an extra $10 million of catfish to help the distressed farmers. In 2015, the USDA took a more conventional approach to help the domestic industry. It slapped import limits on the soaring supplies of a catfish-like product from Vietnam.

In the decade ending in 2010, each of the 16 counties in the Delta suffered a double-digit population loss. In a lengthy article in January 2015, the *Atlantic* described how farms fared best when the white managers stayed on the land. Tunica County is one of the nation's poorest counties, its struggling economy dependent on the area's eight casinos, which help to generate 10 million visitors and 15,000 tour busses annually; Harrah's, a ninth casino, closed in June 2014 due to an apparent glut. The casinos have increased local per capita income, but there is still a gulf between rich and poor. One high-profile new business set up shop in 2013, though with only 100 employees: GreenTech Automotive, a clean energy startup chaired by Virginia Gov. Terry McAuliffe, opened in December 2014 a 300,000-square-foot plant, which produces its two-seat battery-powered MyCar electric vehicle for use chiefly at stadiums and on large campuses. Just north of the fast-growing and affluent suburbs of

Jackson, Nissan operates a 6,300-employee factory in Canton. In 2014, the plant announced its second large expansion in four years to add a third shift to its production line for Altima sedans, which is expected to result in annual production of 507,000 vehicles by 2017. The United Auto Workers has made several costly bids to unionize the plant, but all have failed, most recently in 2014.

The 2nd Congressional District of Mississippi includes the entire Delta, indeed the whole Mississippi riverfront from Tunica almost to Natchez. It includes most of heavily African-American Jackson and surrounding Hinds County except for the affluent Belhaven neighborhood. This is Mississippi's one black-majority district. It includes a few counties in the east that are majority white and vote Republican, but the political tone of the district is set by the African-American neighborhoods in Jackson and the Delta counties. In 1986, the district elected its first black congressman since Reconstruction, Democrat Mike Espy, whose grandfather and father were among the biggest landowners in the state. In 2012, the 2nd was the only Mississippi district to vote for President Barack Obama. It did so by a 2-to-1 margin.

2012 Presidential Vote		
Barack Obama (D)	219,273	(66%)
Mitt Romney (R)	109,180	(33%)
2008 Presidential Vote		
Barack Obama (D)	214,639	(64%)
John McCain (R)	117,427	(35%)
Cook Partisan Voting Index:	D+13	

Bennie Thompson (D)

Bennie Thompson, who was elected in April 1993, has established himself as a liberal Democratic fixture in an otherwise deeply conservative Republican state. His official bio says that he "has spent his entire life giving a voice to the voiceless." He looks out for the needs of his poor, rural district while serving as the top Democrat on the House Homeland Security Committee.

Thompson grew up in Bolton, in Hinds County outside Jackson, and graduated from Tougaloo College and got a master's degree from Jackson State University. He was elected alderman in Bolton in 1969, at age 21, and elected mayor four years later. A longtime volunteer firefighter, he got the first fire engine for Bolton and also a street named after the Rev. Martin Luther King Jr. In 1980, he became a Hinds County supervisor. A lifelong grass-roots activist and labor organizer, he led voter-registration drives and successfully encouraged other African Americans to run for office. He organized associations of Mississippi black mayors and supervisors.

After Democratic Rep. Mike Espy exited Congress to become President Bill Clinton's Agriculture secretary, Thompson ran for the seat in an all-party primary. He came out ahead of Henry Espy, Mike Espy's brother and mayor of Clarksdale, 28%-20%. Hayes Dent, an aide to Gov. Kirk Fordice, led Republicans with 34%. Voting in the runoff was largely along racial lines, and Thompson won 55%-45%, with his margin coming mostly from Hinds County.

Thompson has a staunchly liberal voting record. He initially made little attempt to win white votes in his district, making roughly as few concessions across the racial divide as white lawmakers had earlier made. In time, he moderated his votes and reached out to whites, including some of the district's large farmers. He backs expansion of Medicaid to assist millions of Americans who have problems paying their medical bills. He accused Republican Gov. Phil Bryant of refusing to go along with the plan of President Barack Obama "just because a black man created it," *Buzzfeed* reported. Thompson publicly supported GOP Sen. Thad Cochran in his successful June 2014 runoff against tea party favorite Chris McDaniel, then urged Cochran to expand efforts to assist the black community.

A few months earlier, Thompson drew widespread attention for comments in an interview with a New Nation of Islam radio show in which he called Supreme Court Justice Clarence Thomas an "Uncle Tom" and accused Senate Republican leader Mitch McConnell of being racist toward Obama. For years he has eaten dinner every night that Congress is in session with James Clyburn of South Carolina and Cedric Richmond of Louisiana, also black and the only Democrats in the House from their states. "It's tough being the lone voice of reason from your state," Thompson told *USA Today*. "You got to have some solace with talking to somebody."

The locus of his legislative activity is the Homeland Security Committee. As both chairman and ranking minority member, Thompson has focused on the needs of first responders. He has been increasingly vocal about the threat of computer-based attacks and pushed back in 2012 against Republican calls to scale back the Homeland Security Department's role in favor of defense and intelligence agencies. He also has criticized the GOP's desire to replace Transportation Security Administration (TSA) workers with private screeners at airports. "On September 11th, screeners at our airports were employed by private companies; a return to a pre-9/11 status for screeners would not improve aviation security or assist national security," he said in 2012.

Thompson has made sure that Tougaloo, his alma mater, has reaped benefits from his service on the committee. The tiny private college near Jackson offers academic programs in disaster management, cybersecurity and emergency preparedness, and has a National Transportation Center of Excellence sponsored by the TSA.

When he arrived on the committee in 2005, Thompson began a sometimes-productive working relationship with the top Republican, Peter King of New York. The two worked together to restructure the Federal Emergency Management Agency after FEMA's failures in the aftermath of Hurricane Katrina in 2005. House Republicans wanted it to become an independent agency. Thompson and King called for keeping it within the Homeland Security Department, but with the kind of autonomy the Coast Guard has. They came to an agreement, but when Thompson demanded an additional $3 billion to improve state and local communications capability, King declined and the deal foundered.

Taking over as chairman in 2007, Thompson shepherded through the House one of the new Democratic majority's "first 100 hours" bills, which was to adopt the unfinished recommendations of the 9/11 commission. It included a requirement to screen all passenger jet and ship cargo and became law in 2007. In 2009, Thompson unsuccessfully pushed to centralize House oversight of Homeland Security under his committee, seeking to end the spreading of jurisdiction across dozens of panels. He worked with King to pass Homeland Security authorization bills each year, only to have the Senate ignore them.

After Republicans regained control of the House in 2011 and Thompson returned to the minority side, he unsuccessfully sought to expand King's hearings on the radicalization of American Muslims to include neo-Nazis and other domestic extremist groups. He was named a vice chair of a House Democratic task force on gun violence formed after the December 2012 school massacre in Newtown, Conn. He regularly gets "F" ratings from the National Rifle Association, but Thompson is an avid hunter and says the ratings don't reflect sportsmen's views.

Thompson's confrontational politics have brought occasional campaign opposition. In 2002, he was reelected by a less than impressive 55%-43% against Republican challenger Clinton LeSueur, a consultant to the Yazoo Community Action Agency. In 2006, state Rep. Chuck Espy, nephew of the former representative, challenged him in the primary, but Thompson prevailed 64%-35%. He has faced no serious challengers since then.

In 2009, he came under fire from local Republicans after Jackson's *Clarion-Ledger* reported on trips he took to Las Vegas, Fort Lauderdale and St. Maarten Island at the expense of interest groups, including labor unions. Thompson defended the trips as necessary to learn firsthand about homeland security issues and said they were approved by the House Ethics Committee. Also that year, *The Washington Post* reported that Thompson used his committee's consideration of new rules for credit card companies to extract $15,000 in campaign donations from the companies. His staff denied the charge. In 2012, the *Post* reported that Thompson obtained a $900,000 earmark to resurface about two dozen Mississippi roads, including those in a neighborhood where he and his daughter owned two homes. He said it was up to the county to decide where the work should be done. "I didn't say, 'Do the street that I live on,'" he said. In February 2010, the Ethics Committee exonerated Thompson and several colleagues of wrongdoing.

THIRD DISTRICT

Gregg Harper (R)

Elected 2008, 4th term; b. June 1, 1956, Jackson; MS Col., B.S. 1978, U. of MS, J.D. 1981; Baptist; married (Sidney); 2 children.

Professional Career: Practicing atty., 1981-present; City prosecutor, Brandon, Richland; Chmn, Rankin Cnty. Republican Party, 2000-07.

DC Office: 307 CHOB, 20515, 202-225-5031; Fax: 202-225-5797; Website: harper.house.gov.

State Offices: Brookhaven, 601-823-3400; Meridian, 601-693-6681; Pearl, 601-932-2410; Starkville, 662-324-0007.

Committees: *Energy & Commerce:* Commerce, Manufacturing & Trade; Energy & Power; Environment & the Economy (VChmn). *House Administration. Joint Committee on the Library:* (VChmn).

Group Ratings

	ADA	ACLU	AFL-CIO	LCV	ITI	COC	HAFA	ACU	CFG	FRC
2014	0%	0%	–	3%	80%	93%	42%	76%	57%	86%
2013	0%	C	29%	4%	C	85%	C	52%	41%	C

National Journal Ratings

	2013 LIB	—	2013 CONS
Economic	47%	—	53%
Social	38%	—	59%
Foreign	34%	—	60%
Composite	41%	—	59%

Key Votes of the 113th Congress

1. Sandy storm spending	Y	5. Medical Marijuana	N	9. Syrian Rebels Training	Y
2. Violence Against Women Act	Y	6. Farm Bill	Y	10. Keystone pipeline	Y
3. Guantanamo Bay Detainees	NV	7. Afghanistan Combat	N	11. Immigration Exec. Action	Y
4. Abortion 20-week ban	Y	8. NSA Phone Data Collection	N	12. Bipartisan budget deal	Y

Election Results

2014 general	Gregg Harper (R)	117,771	(69%)	$770,336	$2,818
	Doug Magee (D)	47,744	(28%)		
	Barbara Washer (I)	3,890	(2%)		
2014 primary	Gregg Harper (R)	85,674	(92%)		
	Hardy Caraway (R)	7,258	(8%)		

Prior winning percentages: 2012 (80%), 2010 (68%), 2008 (63%)

Population		Race and Ethnicity		Income	
Total:	750,332	White	60.4%	Median income:	$39,890
Urban:	17.3%	Black	35.1%		*(391 of 435)*
Suburban:	22.3%	Latino	2.1%	Under $50,000	59.8%
Rural:	60.4%	Amer. Indian	0.9%	$50,000-$99,999:	24.9%
Land area:	10,944	Two races	0.7%	$100,000-$199,999:	12.1%
Pop/sq. mi.:	68.6	White Ethnic	12.5%	$200,000 or more:	3.1%
Born in state:	77.2%			Poverty Rate	22.3%
		Education			
Age Groups		H.S. grad or less:	45.5%	**Work**	
Under 18:	24.2%	Some college:	29.6%	White collar:	35.9%
18 to 34:	22.8%	College degree, 4 yr.:	15.4%	Blue collar:	39.7%
35 to 64:	38.6%	Post-grad study:	9.5%	Sales and service:	24.3%
Over 64:	14.4%				
		Military		Govt. workers:	19.3%
		Veterans/active duty:	7.4%		

South Central Mississippi: Jackson Suburbs

The Neshoba County fair has been held every August since 1889 in the town of Philadelphia. What started as a farmer's picnic has become the traditional place where Mississippi politicians announce their candidacies, with the crowds watching to take their measure. Devotees call it "Mississippi's Giant

Voter Turnout	
2013 Total Citizen 18+	557,608
2014 House Turnout	170,946
2014 Turnout as % CVAP	30.7%
2012 Turnout as % CVAP	60.9%

House Party," and many stay for the entire week. The crowds are also there to watch the races on the state's only legal horse track. But nationally, Philadelphia and Neshoba County are known for something less harmonious. There is no memorial, except engraved stones at two African-American churches, to mark the events of the summer of 1964, when three civil rights workers, two white and one black, were murdered for the crime of urging black American citizens to register to vote. It wasn't until June 2005 that a jury of nine whites and three blacks convicted Edgar Ray Killen, by then an 80-year-old preacher and sawmill operator, of manslaughter and sentenced him to three life sentences. In November 2014, President Barack Obama commemorated the 50th anniversary when he awarded the presidential Medal of Freedom to James Chaney, Andrew Goodman and Michael Schwerner.

The 3rd Congressional District of Mississippi has its population centers in the Jackson suburbs in Rankin County and south Madison County, plus the affluent neighborhoods of northeast Jackson in Hinds County. East and north of Jackson, subdivisions, shopping centers and office complexes have sprouted in the countryside. Even as other areas of the state continued to suffer from the nationwide recession, Rankin County has had an unemployment rate below that of the state and nation since before the recession, and was just 4 percent in February 2015. The state's first Whole Foods Market opened in February 2014 in wealthy northeast Jackson. Demographers predict big increases in Asian and Latino population in this area during the coming decades. A different kind of wealth opened along the southern border of the district in 2014, as oil gushers burst forth from fracked wells.

From the Jackson suburbs, the 3rd stretches north to Starkville, home of Mississippi State University, and south almost to Laurel. In the southwest, it includes Natchez, where 600 antebellum mansions and other properties with live oaks sit atop bluffs overlooking the Mississippi River. The small town of Macon was the scene in 2007 of a first-ever Justice Department lawsuit against a black Democratic Party official for discriminating against the voting rights of minority whites. In the middle of the district are Neshoba County and Meridian, home of Peavey Electronics Corp., whose electric guitars and powerful amplifiers are popular with rock stars, though the plant suffered layoffs in

2012 Presidential Vote
Mitt Romney (R)	204,232	(60%)
Barack Obama (D)	133,114	(39%)

2008 Presidential Vote
John McCain (R)	208,508	(61%)
Barack Obama (D)	131,676	(38%)

Cook Partisan Voting Index: R+14

early 2015. The district's political tradition remained Democratic for decades, but its preference now is strongly Republican, even with its 35% black population. In 2012, Mitt Romney had no problem winning the district, 60%-39%.

Gregg Harper (R)

Gregg Harper, a Republican elected in 2008, is a dependable conservative vote who has impressed his party's leaders, and he has shown a desire to join them in the leadership.

Harper was born in Jackson, where his father was a petroleum engineer and his mother was a homemaker. The family moved frequently because of his father's job, but always returned home to Mississippi. Harper became a Christian after attending a youth rally in high school, and later met his wife, Sidney, at a church function. Their adult son Livingston suffers from a developmental disorder called fragile X syndrome.

Harper graduated from Mississippi College and got his law degree from the University of Mississippi. He has long experience in politics. He was chairman of the Rankin County Republican Party and worked on several local and state campaigns. When the 2000 presidential election was in limbo and hinged on results in Florida, Harper volunteered as a legal observer for George W. Bush's recount efforts. Until 2008, he was the prosecuting attorney for the cities of Brandon and Richland.

He jumped into the primary contest for the House seat when GOP Rep. Chip Pickering announced his retirement. Harper's toughest Republican competitors were state Sen. Charlie Ross, considered the early favorite, and wealthy businessman David Landrum. Ross rolled up endorsements from local leaders and national groups such as the anti-tax Club for Growth, and both he and Landrum outspent Harper. Harper rallied a hardworking core of young volunteers and family members for door-to-door campaigning. He got a key endorsement from former Senate Majority Leader Trent Lott of Mississippi. In the March 2008 primary, Ross led with 33%, and Harper finished second with 28%. In the April runoff, Ross portrayed Harper as too inexperienced for the job, but Harper emphasized his conservative stances against abortion rights and same-sex marriage. He won the runoff 57%-43%. In the general election, Democrat Joel Gill, a rancher and a Pickens alderman, ran folksy ads that referred to him as "Joel the Cattleman." Still, a catchy ad was not enough in this GOP district, and Harper easily won with 63% of the vote. He has not been seriously challenged since.

In the House, Harper became the only freshman on the Republican Steering Committee, and he got a slot on the House Administration Committee, which oversees election laws and internal housekeeping tasks. He was next in line to become its chairman when Dan Lungren of California lost his reelection bid in 2012. At the time, Harper was running for House Republican Conference secretary. He dropped out of the race in expectation of getting the committee gavel, but GOP leaders instead gave it to Candice Miller of Michigan.

With his plum seat on the Energy and Commerce Committee, Harper frequently blasted the health care overhaul law and called for more domestic energy production while beseeching President Barack Obama to approve the Keystone XL pipeline from Canada. "If he cared about jobs and the energy independence in this country, it's a no-brainer," he told *The Meridian Star* in 2012. In May 2014, Obama had a White House signing ceremony for a bill introduced by Harper to increase funding for pediatric medical research, especially for cancer. With Mississippi playing a leadership role in the development of telemedicine, Harper has filed legislation to expand telemedicine payments. The House in 2011 passed his bill to eliminate the Election Assistance Commission, a group setting voluntary voting system guidelines for states. The bill died in the Democratic-controlled Senate, but Harper sought to revive it in 2015.

After the 2010 election, Harper joined the tight-spending Tea Party Caucus. But with his son in mind, he is bipartisan on governmental aid to children with special needs. Harper chairs the Fragile X Caucus, and he has worked with Democrats to secure $1.9 million for fragile X syndrome research at the Centers for Disease Control and Prevention, and he made the disorder eligible for Defense Department medical research. He included a provision in the bipartisan pharmaceutical user fee agreement that became law in 2012 to extend market exclusivity for drugs that treat fragile X syndrome, autism and other neurological disorders. He also has filed the "TEAM Act," designed to make it easier for people with intellectual disabilities to move into the workforce.

FOURTH DISTRICT

Steven Palazzo (R)

Elected 2010, 3rd term; b. Feb. 21, 1970, Gulfport; U. of Southern MS, B.S. 1994, M.A. 1996; Catholic; married (Lisa); 3 children.

Military Career: U.S. Marine Corps Reserve, 1988-96 (Persian Gulf); MS Army Natl. Guard, 1997-present.

Elected Office: MS House, 2007-10.

Professional Career: FO, Biloxi Housing Authority; Owner, Palazzo & Co. PLLC.

DC Office: 331 CHOB, 20515, 202-225-5772; Website: palazzo.house .gov.

State Offices: Biloxi, 228-864-7670; Hattiesburg, 601-582-3246; Pascagoula, 228-202-8104.

Committees: *Appropriations:* Agriculture, Rural Development, FDA, & Related Agencies; Commerce, Justice, Science, & Related Agencies; Legislative Branch.

Group Ratings

	ADA	ACLU	AFL-CIO	LCV	ITI	COC	HAFA	ACU	CFG	FRC
2014	0%	0%	–	0%	80%	86%	65%	86%	70%	100%
2013	0%	C	24%	4%	C	77%	C	80%	69%	C

National Journal Ratings

	2013 LIB	—	2013 CONS
Economic	23%	—	76%
Social	0%	—	87%
Foreign	0%	—	95%
Composite	11%	—	89%

Key Votes of the 113th Congress

1. Sandy storm spending	Y	5. Medical Marijuana	NV	9. Syrian Rebels Training	N
2. Violence Against Women Act	N	6. Farm Bill	Y	10. Keystone pipeline	Y
3. Guantanamo Bay Detainees	N	7. Afghanistan Combat	N	11. Immigration Exec. Action	Y
4. Abortion 20-week ban	Y	8. NSA Phone Data Collection	N	12. Bipartisan budget deal	Y

Election Results

2014 general	Steven Palazzo (R)	108,776	(70%)	$1,178,696
	Matt Moore (D)	37,869	(24%)	
	Cindy Burleson (I)	3,684	(2%)	
	Joey Robinson (L)	3,473	(2%)	$9,581
2014 primary	Steven Palazzo (R)	54,268	(51%)	
	Gene Taylor(R)	46,133	(43%)	

Prior winning percentages: 2012 (64%), 2010 (52%)

Population		Race and Ethnicity		Income	
Total:	758,257	White	69.5%	Median income:	$41,374
Urban:	32.1%	Black	22.8%		(370 of 435)
Suburban:	23.8%	Latino	4.0%	Under $50,000	58.1%
Rural:	44.1%	Asian	1.9%	$50,000-$99,999:	29.0%
Land area:	8,419	Two races	1.4%	$100,000-$199,999:	11.5%
Pop/sq. mi.:	90.1	White Ethnic	19.5%	$200,000 or more:	1.5%
Born in state:	63.6%			Poverty Rate	21.2%
		Education			
Age Groups		H.S. grad or less:	46.5%	**Work**	
Under 18:	24.3%	Some college:	33.9%	White collar:	29.3%
18 to 34:	24.1%	College degree, 4 yr.:	12.3%	Blue collar:	44.3%
35 to 64:	37.7%	Post-grad study:	7.3%	Sales and service:	26.4%
Over 64:	13.8%				
		Military		Govt. workers:	17.1%
		Veterans/active duty:	12.9%		

Southeast Mississippi: Gulfport/Biloxi, Hattiesburg

Coastal Mississippi has gone through several transformations in its history. French explorers founded Biloxi in 1699, before New Orleans or St. Louis, and made it the capital of an empire extending to what is now Yellowstone National Park. Two hundred years later, rich people from New Orleans came to

Voter Turnout	
2013 Total Citizen 18+	563,941
2014 House Turnout	155,576
2014 Turnout as % CVAP	27.6%
2012 Turnout as % CVAP	52.9%

this section of the Gulf Coast in the summer to get away from yellow fever and to rest on Victorian verandas. Six American presidents have vacationed here, and Pascagoula is the birthplace of the original beach bum, singer Jimmy Buffett. There is also a military flavor to the Gulf Coast. Biloxi's Keesler Air Force Base, one of the elite bases in the world, in 2013 employed nearly 12,000 and offers cyberspace training. Pascagoula, the largest manufacturing employer in the state, is home to 11,000 workers over 800 acres at Ingalls Shipyard, whose gray, hangar-like buildings and skeletons of ships under construction loom over the landscape.

The region's economic growth was put on hold for several years after these coastal communities took a direct hit from Hurricane Katrina on Aug. 29, 2005. From Waveland to Pascagoula, about 80 miles were obliterated: Beachfront cottages, fishing villages, hotel casinos, oil-drilling platforms, and refineries all were either cruelly swamped or swept away. Status meant nothing. The homes of Confederate President Jefferson Davis in Biloxi and former Senate Majority Leader Trent Lott in Pascagoula were destroyed. The eye of the monster storm passed over the region, and in an instant, countless livelihoods were gone and property losses reached tens of billions of dollars.

If there was a saving grace, many of the communities were left with a clean slate to start over, with more control over the building of high rises and strip malls that had started to overwhelm more distinctive properties. As the cleanup wore on, important decisions were made, especially in Biloxi. Condominium projects were more carefully managed, and shrimp boaters got docks for their boats and places to sell their catch. The state got $560 million in hurricane recovery money for a planned $1.6 billion expansion of the Port of Gulfport. Even after work began, questions remained about how many jobs an expanded port would create and whether elevating the port would be worth the cost. It seemed unlikely that the amount of cargo in the port would come close to competing with New Orleans or Mobile. Meanwhile, in the spring of 2010, the Gulf areas suffered another setback with the massive BP oil spill, although beach tourism had rebounded a year later. The huge fines from the recovery helped the state set more rigorous standards for the restoration of the coast and its facilities.

This is the heart of the 4th Congressional District. Despite Katrina and BP, the three Gulf Coast counties of Mississippi experienced net population growth from 2000 to 2010. The rest of the district's people live inland, in farm counties or around Hattiesburg and Laurel. It has long been Republican territory. A different configuration of the district gave President Richard Nixon his highest percentage of any congressional district in 1972, and it voted five times against fellow Southerners Jimmy Carter, Bill Clinton, and Al Gore. In 2012, the district gave 68% of the vote to Mitt Romney, his highest in the state and in the top 5% of districts nationwide.

2012 Presidential Vote		
Mitt Romney (R)	199,354	(68%)
Barack Obama (D)	92,127	(31%)
2008 Presidential Vote		
John McCain (R)	195,927	(68%)
Barack Obama (D)	89,622	(31%)
Cook Partisan Voting Index:	R+21	

Steven Palazzo (R)

Republican Steven Palazzo, who upset veteran Blue Dog Democrat Gene Taylor in 2010, is a fervent fiscal and social conservative representing an area where Hurricane Katrina caused severe damage and imposed huge costs. He drew considerable attention for voting against paying Hurricane Sandy claims on the East Coast without offsetting cuts. He struggles to satisfy what may be irreconcilable elements among local Republicans.

Palazzo was born and raised in Gulfport, where his family has deep roots: Five generations have called South Mississippi home. He described his community as filled with "God-fearing men and women" who believe in faith and personal responsibility. After graduating from high school and enrolling for a semester at his local community college, Palazzo enlisted in the Marines, inspired by his grandfather, who served in the Pacific during World War II. From 1988 to 1996, Palazzo was assigned to the 3rd Force Reconnaissance Company, gathering intelligence and taking tours of duty in Kuwait and Saudi Arabia during the Persian Gulf War. "The Marine Corps breaks you down and builds you back up," Palazzo told *National Journal*. "The traditions and the warrior spirit—those things are still instilled in me." He remained active in the military following his full-time service, joining the Mississippi Army National Guard in 1997 and spending a year supporting base operations at Camp Shelby for Operation Iraqi Freedom.

After he returned from the Persian Gulf War, Palazzo earned his bachelor's and master's degrees in accounting from the University of Southern Mississippi. He worked in accounting positions at various firms, primarily in the construction industry. In 2001, he and his wife, Lisa Belvin, started the accounting practice Palazzo & Co., which grew into an international firm specializing in individual income tax returns for expatriates.

In 2007, Palazzo was elected to the state House. Two years later, he decided to challenge Taylor, although the incumbent was almost a folk hero in Coastal Mississippi—Taylor lost his home to Katrina, was in good stead with the National Rifle Association, had one of the most conservative voting records among House Democrats, and had spoken out against many of his party's major initiatives, including health care reform.

But even Taylor, once viewed as a safe Democrat in the House, had reason to sweat in the anti-incumbent environment of 2010. Even though it was difficult to attack Taylor's conservative voting record, Palazzo portrayed him as an enabler of the Democratic agenda for his vote for Nancy Pelosi of California as House speaker, which he said showed Taylor's support for a "liberal socialist agenda." That vote was, implicitly at least, a trade-off for Taylor to chair an Armed Services subcommittee. Taylor couldn't count on much help from national Democrats, whom he had often bucked over the years. Taylor touted his conservative positions and even boasted to his local newspaper that he voted for Republican John McCain for president in 2008. It wasn't enough, not in 2010. Palazzo won 52%-47%.

In the House, Palazzo joined the Tea Party Caucus and followed his large freshman class in insisting that spending be sharply reduced. He opposed the New Year's Day 2013 budget deal aimed at averting the so-called "fiscal cliff," saying it failed to cut enough. A member of the Armed Services Committee, he added an amendment to the House-passed fiscal 2013 Pentagon spending bill to ban same-sex marriage ceremonies on military bases; it was dropped in the Senate.

Opposing a proposal in 2012 by Democratic Rep. Betty McCollum of Minnesota to end military sponsorships of NASCAR and other sports, he said there was "no reason Congress should be telling the Department of Defense where and how to spend money." A year earlier, however, he added money to a defense spending bill to buy land to expand a National Guard facility in his district, as well as for ship design and feasibility studies at Ingalls Shipbuilding in nearby Pascagoula. Recalling his attacks on Taylor for pork-barrel spending, Democrats and watchdog groups accused Palazzo of hypocrisy.

Palazzo has had occasional bouts of bad publicity. Some constituents publicly accused him of being inaccessible, in stark contrast to the gregarious Taylor, a charge that he denied. *Roll Call* newspaper reported in November 2011 that Palazzo's staffers threw a raucous weekend party in Annapolis that drew a police visit. That article and others prompted speculation that Palazzo would get a serious primary challenge. But he survived. He easily defeated two underfunded activists in the 2012 Republican primary. Taylor declined to run for his old seat, and Palazzo defeated Democrat Matt Moore, a 36-year-old community college student, with 64% of the vote.

Following the election, Palazzo drew the most attention of the 67 House Republicans who voted against the bill allowing $9.7 billion in government borrowing to pay claims from Sandy, which did considerable damage in the Northeast. He contended the measure should have made offsetting spending cuts. Most other GOP lawmakers from coastal areas backed the bill, prompting the *Sun Herald* of Biloxi to say of Palazzo, "Seldom has a single vote in Congress appeared as cold-blooded and hard-headed." Aware of the political damage, Palazzo toured Sandy-stricken areas and then co-signed a letter calling on colleagues to support a larger aid bill. GOP leaders tapped Palazzo in January 2013 to lead efforts to reform disaster relief programs. He joined in what he called a "team effort" to secure in the 2015 defense spending bill $1 billion for the Navy's LPD-28 amphibious assault ship, which would be built at Ingalls; he also got a provision to discourage downsizing at Keesler Air Force Base. With Democratic Rep. Tim Walz of Minnesota, he became co-chairman in 2015 of the National Guard and Reserve Components Caucus.

In 2014, Palazzo survived an unusual contest when Taylor changed parties and challenged him in the Republican primary. Having determined that it was "impossible" for a Democrat to win, Taylor offered himself as the candidate best-equipped to deliver for the 4th District. Palazzo barely avoided a run-off, with 50.5 percent of the vote to 43% for Taylor. In November, he easily beat Matt Moore again, 70%-24%.

But internal tensions remained. After more than one hour of a "man to man" conversation with John Boehner the evening before the vote, Palazzo decided that he was "willing to give the speaker and his team a last chance to put us back on a conservative path for America." Southern Mississippi Tea Party Chairman Barry Neyrey responded angrily that Palazzo was a "coward" and had "betrayed us;" Neyrey promised Palazzo to "work tirelessly to see that you don't get another term." Two months later, Palazzo got a coveted seat on the Appropriations Committee following the death of home-state Republican Alan Nunnelee. He styled himself as an insider. "Serving as an appropriator is a privilege and a tremendous responsibility that I don't take lightly," he said. It was highly unlikely that he would have won that seat if he had voted against Boehner. Time will tell whether support for a speaker leads to the downfall of another representative from this district.

★ MISSOURI ★

The Gateway Arch, rising gracefully over the Mississippi River, is a worthy tribute to St. Louis and Missouri as the gateway to the American West, but it is no longer a gleaming symbol of the state's vigor and prosperity. This land was part of France's thinly settled North American empire; St. Louis, just below the swirling confluence of the Missouri River and the Mississippi, was founded by Pierre Laclède and Auguste Chouteau in 1764, while further south in Missouri, the French began mining in the Old Lead Belt as early as 1720. All this and much more was acquired by the United States with the Louisiana Purchase of 1803, and on May 14, 1804, at Thomas Jefferson's direction, Meriwether Lewis, William Clark, and their party set out from St. Louis on their expedition to the Pacific. St. Louis was then the one well-established city in America's interior, with an aristocracy of French merchants, a brawling bourgeoisie of Yankee and Southern frontiersmen and fur traders, and a proletariat of black slaves. Statehood came in 1821, and for years thereafter, the frontier democracy was a passage for westward expansion, captured in the paintings of George Caleb Bingham. West of St. Louis, new areas were settled: St. Joseph was the eastern terminus of the Pony Express; Westport, now part of Kansas City, was the starting point of the Santa Fe Trail; Independence, identified by Joseph Smith as the site of the Second Coming, was settled by Mormons who left after Gov. Lilburn Boggs ordered them "exterminated"; and in Hannibal, on the Mississippi River, a boy named Sam Clemens engaged in pranks and watched the early steamboats that he would later chronicle as Mark Twain.

Missouri was also a focus of the furious battle over slavery. It was the northernmost slave state in 1850, and Missouri ruffians rode across the border and killed antislavery settlers in the Kansas Territory. The state had its own bloody civil war in the hilly counties along the Missouri River and in the southwest. After the war, in 1874, the Eads Bridge opened, one of the very few spans on the Mississippi; St. Louis' Cupples Station was then the largest rail hub in the world. At the turn of the 20th century, Missouri was the fifth-largest state, and St. Louis was the fourth-largest city, site of the 1904 World's Fair, and one of the few cities with two Major League Baseball teams, the Cardinals and the Browns. Missouri was also the national center of the mule trade (Harry Truman's father's line of work), an important business at a time when half of Americans lived on farms, and motorized tractors had not yet been invented. After the 1900 census, Missouri had 16 congressional districts, twice the number it has now. In the 20th century, Americans increasingly headed toward the coasts, to the big cities of the East and West, and eventually to Florida and Texas (as did the baseball Browns, who moved to Baltimore in 1954, and the football Cardinals, who moved to Phoenix in 1988). Missouri has had below-average population growth since 1900, and today it is the 18th-largest state. But Missouri was the geographic center of the nation's population in the 2010 census: An imaginary, flat map of the United States population, if everyone weighed the same, would balance in Texas County, Missouri.

Inside its narrow 19th century boundaries, the city of St. Louis had 622,000 people in 1970 and 317,000 in 2014. St. Louis County, which does not include the city's population, has been pretty stable: 952,000 people in 1970 and 1,002,000 in 2014. The three suburban-exurban counties around St. Louis County, Franklin, Jefferson and St. Charles, grew from 253,000 to 704,000. Trend data from just 2010 to 2014 show pretty much the same picture as the historical patterns: St. Louis city continued to shrink, St. Louis county grew marginally, and the adjacent suburban-exurban counties grew faster, led by St. Charles with a population jump almost 5 percent in those four years. Overall, the state grew by 1.2 percent from 2010 to 2014, while the nation grew 3.3 percent. Most recently, the state's population grew by only three-tenths of a percent from 2013 to 2014. Only eight of 114 counties grew by more than 1 percent and 67 mostly rural counties and the city of St. Louis all lost population. One bright spot, the Lake of the Ozarks region in central and southwest Missouri, around the country music center of Branson, has been attracting modest-income retirees looking for traditional lifestyles and inexpensive recreation.

Overall, the recovery from the Great Recession has been weak in Missouri and its economy grew just 0.9 percent in 2014, well below the national average of 2.2 percent, according to Commerce Department figures. That makes the fifth year in a row that the state's GDP has grown less than the national average. From 2011 to 2014, job growth in the state's two major metropolitan areas was anemic: in the Kansas City area, jobs were up 3.3 percent,

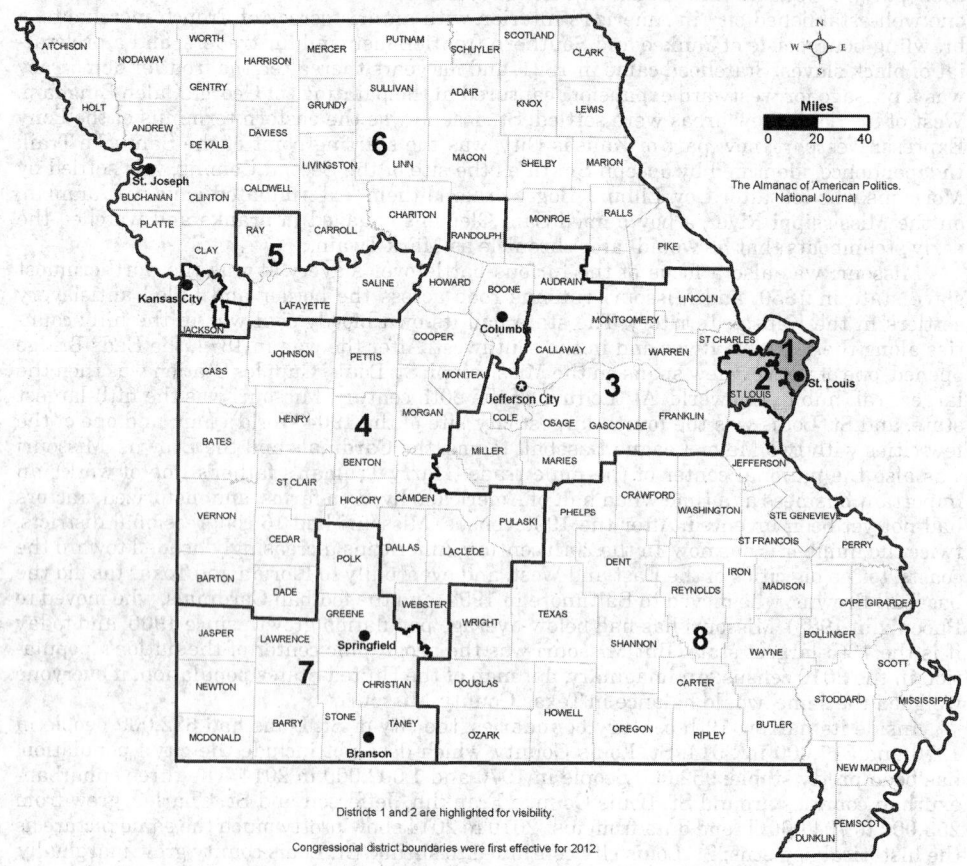

Districts 1 and 2 are highlighted for visibility.

Congressional district boundaries were first effective for 2012.

The Almanac of American Politics.
National Journal

while the St. Louis metro saw only a 2 percent gain. Transportation manufacturing remains an important component in the Missouri, employing more than 40,000 people in 2014 at plants for Boeing, Ford, General Motors and the auto supply firms Yanfeng USA and TG Missouri, among others. Missouri failed to woo Boeing with a reported $3 billion incentive package to locate a new assembly line for its 777X commercial aircraft next to Lambert-St. Louis International Airport, and the aerospace giant decided in early 2014 to build the airplane at an existing plant in Washington state. Far more jobs, 120,000, are found in the hospital industry, which includes some of the state's largest employers, BJC HealthCare and Mercy Health Systems. St. Louis is home to Express Scripts, the largest pharmacy benefit manager in the country. Major companies established there—McDonnell Douglas, TWA, Ralston Purina, May Department Stores, Monsanto, Anheuser-Busch—have been acquired by outside competitors and multinational corporations. Falling commodity prices have hurt the state's agricultural sector and farmers had to deal with severe flooding on the Missouri River in 2011 and drought conditions in 2012.

Culturally, Missouri remains more conservative than most of the larger states. Its relatively slow-growing metro areas have not overwhelmed the countryside, a land of farms and small towns thick with churches and modest shopping centers and laced with artificial lakes and boat launches. Only one city outside the two big metro areas, Springfield, has a population over 150,000, and in the state's rural heartland, life—and politics—seem not to have changed much over the past half-century. Missouri has some tough immigration laws, even though it has attracted relatively few immigrants. Local law enforcement agencies have cracked down on the scourge of methamphetamine: In 2014, for the first time in at least a decade, the state did not lead the nation in meth lab seizures, dropping to No. 3, behind Indiana and Tennessee, according to the National Clandestine Laboratory Seizure System. Stepped up law enforcement and new local ordinances controlling the over-the-counter sale of the decongestant pseudoephedrine, meth's main ingredient, have curbed illegal production. In southeastern Missouri, where such laws are now common, meth lab busts fell 80 percent between 2010 and 2013. While also falling, the actual number of lab seizures in 2015 was highest in suburban St. Louis. The state's urban-rural divide was in sharp relief in the August 2014 balloting when Missouri voters narrowly endorsed a "freedom to farm" state constitutional amendment. Although some proponents of family farms argued the measure would primarily benefit agribusinesses, the measure won easy approval in almost all of the state, while it was solidly rejected by voters in Boone County (Columbia/University of Missouri), Green County (Springfield), Kansas City, St. Louis County and St. Louis. Ferguson, a city of 21,000 in St. Louis County where two-thirds of the population is African American, was rocked by riots in 2014 after an unarmed black teenager, Michael Brown, was fatally shot in a confrontation with a white police officer who was later cleared of any criminality by a Justice Department investigation. A St. Louis County grand jury had previously declined to indict the officer. Brown's death became a symbol of what critics said was the nation's disregard for young black lives and it triggered protests and marches in cities across the country. A Justice Department probe did find that the Ferguson police department was infected with racism and engaged in abusive policing. The Missouri legislature responded in 2015 by enacting a law to curb the use of traffic fines as a revenue

Population		Race and Ethnicity		Income	
Total:	6,044,171	White	80.8%	Median income:	$50,311
Urban:	25.7%	Black	11.4%		(32 of 50)
Suburban:	40.6%	Latino	3.6%	Under $50,000	52.5%
Rural:	33.8%	Asian	1.6%	$50,000-$99,999:	30.5%
Land area:	68,742	Two races	2.1%	$100,000-$199,999:	14.0%
Pop/sq. mi.:	87.9	White Ethnic	24.0%	$200,000 or more:	3.0%
Born in state:	66.2%			Poverty Rate	11.6%
		Education			
Age Groups		H.S. grad or less:	42.8%	**Work**	
Under 18:	23.1%	Some college:	30.2%	White collar:	34.8%
18 to 34:	23.1%	College degree, 4 yr.:	16.9%	Blue collar:	43.2%
35 to 64:	38.8%	Post-grad study:	10.0%	Sales and service:	21.9%
Over 64:	15.0%			Govt. workers:	12.7%
		Military			
		Veterans/active duty:	9.5%		

stream to fill municipal coffers, a practice
that disproportionately affects the poor.
The law also ended jail time for people who
couldn't afford to pay traffic fines, a policy
that had been sharply criticized by many
Ferguson protesters. The state House also
passed a bill limiting the use of deadly force
by police, but the measure failed to come to
a vote in the Senate before the legislature's
regular session ended.

Voter Turnout	
2013 Total Citizen 18+	4,532,501
2014 Highest Statewide Turnout	1,426,303
2014 Turnout as % CVAP	31.5%
2012 Turnout as % CVAP	61.2%

Legislature			
Senate:	25R	9D	
House:	116R	44D	1I, 2V

For a century, Missouri was one of America's political bellwether states. It voted for
every presidential winner but one from 1904 to 2004; the exception was in 1956 when
it narrowly backed Adlai Stevenson. From the 1960s to the 1990s, it mirrored national
trends by moving its congressional politics from mostly Democratic to leaning Republican. Missouri was not only a mixture of urban and rural, but its Civil War political
divisions still held: Democrats dominated in Little Dixie in the northeast, first settled by
Virginians, and in the northwest, settled by southerners. Republicans held sway in the
Ozarks in the southwest, which was pro-Union, and the southeast was split, like next-
door downstate Illinois. But by 2000, those historic patterns were being overridden. The
large metro areas became even more Democratic and the remainder of the state turned
Republican as Civil War loyalties gave way to cultural conservatism—as it had done in
the 1980 and 1984 presidential wins by Ronald Reagan. The result was equipoise. In the
state's 10 contests for president, senator, and governor between 2000 and 2008, only two
were decided by wide margins: Republican Sen. Christopher Bond's reelection in 2004 and
Democratic Gov. Jay Nixon's election in 2008. In the eight other contests, Republicans got
between 47% and 53% of the vote, Democrats between 46% and 50%. In the 2008 presidential contest the state narrowly went for Republican John McCain. Democrat Barack
Obama won Jackson County (Kansas City), St. Louis, St. Louis County, Boone, and only
five of the other 111 counties. In 2012, Mitt Romney easily carried the state for the GOP
and Obama won just Boone, Jackson and St. Louis counties, and the city of St. Louis.
The great division in the state is between metropolitan and rural. And in one other way,
Missouri is uniquely divided: This is the only state whose name is pronounced two ways,
depending on where you're from. In metro St. Louis, they say "Mizuree." In the rest of the
state it's "Mizuruh."

Presidential Politics Before 1904, Democratic strength in Missouri outside of its
big cities made the state more Democratic
in presidential races than the nation. Since
2000, Republican strength outside the two
big metro areas has made it more Republican than the nation. Missouri was a toss-
up in 2008, and Republican John McCain's
3,903-vote margin might have sparked a
challenge but for the fact that it would not
affect the outcome of the presidential contest and the election of Democrat Barack

2012 Presidential Vote		
Mitt Romney (R)..............1,482,440	(54%)
Barack Obama (D) 1,223,796	(44%)

2012 Presidential Primary		
Rick Santorum (R) 139,272	(55%)
Mitt Romney (R)...................63,882	(25%)
Ron Paul (R) 30,647	(12%)

2008 Presidential Vote		
John McCain (R)..............1,445,814	(49%)
Barack Obama (D) 1,441,911	(49%)

Obama. In 2012, the Obama reelection campaign conceded Missouri and concentrated
its organizational efforts elsewhere. Turnout was down 6% statewide from 2008, and it
was down 10% in St. Louis and 13% in Kansas City, cities where about half the voters
are black.

Missouri joined the Super Tuesday multi-state primary for 1988, returned to multi-
tiered caucuses to elect delegates in 1992 and 1996, and then rejoined Super Tuesday in
2000. Expected victories for Missouri natives did not result. Both Bill Bradley (who grew up
in Jefferson County) in 2000 and Dick Gephardt (who grew up on the south side of St. Louis)
in 2004 were effectively out of the Democratic primary race before Missourians got to vote.
On Super Tuesday in February 2008, the stark political differences between metropolitan
and rural Missouri were apparent in both the Democratic and Republican presidential primaries. Obama beat Hillary Clinton by 49%-48%. But he carried only St. Louis City, which
was about half African-American, and five of the 114 counties. Two of those included many

blacks and many affluent whites: St. Louis County (23% black), which cast 23% of the state's votes, and Kansas City's Jackson County (24% black), which cast 14% of the state's votes. The others were the sites of the state capital, the University of Missouri, and Northwest Missouri State College.

McCain won a similarly close victory in the Republican primary, with 33% of the vote to 32% for Mike Huckabee and 29% for Mitt Romney. McCain carried metro St. Louis over Romney, while Romney carried metro Kansas City over McCain. In the largely rural rest of the state, where more than half of the votes were cast, Huckabee led overall, followed by McCain and then Romney. McCain's narrow victory gave him all 58 of Missouri's delegates thanks to the party's winner-take-all rules. That narrow victory played a key role in forcing Romney out of the Republican race two days later. In 2008, some 825,000 Missourians voted in the Democratic primary and 588,000 in the Republican primary. In 2012, only 252,000 voted in the non-binding February Republican primary; convention delegates were selected in a caucus process that began in March. Romney effectively conceded the state to Rick Santorum, who won 55% of the vote to 25% for Romney.

Congressional Districts Slow population growth cost Missouri its ninth seat in the 2010 census, and split redistricting authority only heightened the drama. Republicans held huge state legislative majorities and badly wanted to expand their 6-3 advantage into a 6-2 edge by eliminating Democrat

114th Congress Lineup	
6 R	2 D
113th Congress Lineup	
6 R	2 D

Russ Carnahan's 3rd District in the St. Louis suburbs. The sole Democratic obstacle was Gov. Jay Nixon. Republicans held a sufficient majority in the state Senate (26-8) but not quite in the state House (106-57) to override a veto. In April 2011, the Republican legislature passed a plan folding much of Carnahan's 3rd District into African-American Democrat William Lacy Clay's 1st District based in St. Louis.

As expected, Nixon vetoed the map, but did so seemingly halfheartedly. Some Democrats contended Nixon could have helped Carnahan more by delaying his veto and reducing Republicans' window to override. Nonetheless, it was up to Republicans to find the 109 votes to override, and in soap opera fashion, they did. Four African-American Democrats, under private pressure from Clay and Kansas City 5th District Democrat Emanuel Cleaver, then chairman of the Congressional Black Caucus, ultimately broke ranks to provide the decisive votes. One, Kansas City state Rep. Jonas Hughes, held his tearful face in his hand afterwards, explaining "[Cleaver] asked me to."

In this example of how underlying tension between black and white Democrats often helps Republicans on redistricting, Cleaver and Clay, eager to keep the strong African-American constituencies the Republican map offered them, didn't mind throwing Carnahan under the bus. Carnahan reacted by, reportedly, swearing at Clay on the floor of the House, then mounting a weak and uphill primary challenge to him in the 1st District. Cleaver's relatively narrow win in 2014 was evidence that he could have been in jeopardy with a different slice of the redistricting knife. Republicans easily retained their six districts, despite considerable geographic shifts. The state's once-influential centrist Democrats in the House have become a relic of the past.

Governor

Jay Nixon (D)

Elected 2008, term expires Jan. 2017, 2nd term; b. Feb. 13, 1956, DeSoto; U. of MO, B.A. 1978, J.D. 1981; Methodist; married (Georganne); 2 children.

Elected Office: MO Senate, 1986-92; MO atty. gen., 1992-2008.

Professional Career: Practicing atty., 1981-92.

Office: P.O. Box 720, Jefferson City, 65102, 573-751-3222; Fax: 573-751-1495; Website: gov.mo.gov.

Election Results

2012 general	Jay Nixon (D)	1,494,056	(55%)
	David "Dave" Spence (R)	1,160,265	(43%)
	Jim Higgins (Lib)	73,509	(3%)
2012 primary	Jay Nixon (D)	270,140	(86%)
	William Campbell (D)	25,775	(8%)
	Clay Thunderhawk (D)	18,243	(6%)

Prior winning percentage: 2008 (58%)

Jay Nixon was first elected governor in 2008 and became a prime example of how a centrist Democrat could succeed in a conservative state; his name was even bandied about as a possible presidential candidate. By 2015, Nixon was a besieged politician, undone by his clumsy handling of the racial unrest in Ferguson and restrained by a solidly Republican state legislature.

Nixon grew up in DeSoto, in Jefferson County, 47 miles southwest of St. Louis. His mother was a teacher and president of the DeSoto school board and his father, a lawyer, was mayor of DeSoto when *Look* magazine named it an "All-America City." Jay Nixon graduated from the University of Missouri and its law school and then practiced in Jefferson County. In 1986, when a local state senator retired, he ran for the seat and won. His views were in sync with most of the voters in his district: pro-gun, anti-abortion and opposed to busing to achieve school desegregation. In 1988, at age 32, he ran against Sen. John Danforth, a Republican who had held statewide office in Missouri for 20 years. It was not a deft campaign. His "Nixon '88" signs evoked memories of the disgraced former president, and his attacks on Danforth for running for a third term fell flat. He was trounced 68%-32%, winning St. Louis city proper and losing all 114 counties.

Nixon did not have to give up his state Senate seat, however, nor his ambition for statewide office. In 1992, he ran for attorney general, calling busing "a failed social experiment." He beat then state House Minority Leader David Steelman for the office Republicans had held for 24 straight years. In 1998, Nixon ran for the Senate again, against two-term incumbent Republican Christopher (Kit) Bond. But Nixon was criticized by many black leaders for his stands in the school desegregation cases and got lukewarm support from Kansas City Mayor Emanuel Cleaver, a prominent African-American who is now a House member. Bond, who courted African-American leaders and voters, ended up winning 53%-44%. Nixon, Missouri's longest serving attorney general, developed innovative programs such as No Call, which created a do-not-call list off limits to telemarketers. He established the Agriculture and Environment Division to enforce Missouri's environmental laws. In 2000, Nixon successfully argued before the U.S. Supreme Court to maintain Missouri's campaign contribution limits, a major victory. He eventually settled the protracted school desegregation cases in St. Louis and Kansas City.

Nixon challenged first-term Republican Gov. Matt Blunt when Blunt was up for reelection in 2008. He criticized Blunt for cuts in Medicaid that removed 100,000 people from the rolls and for the sale of assets of the Missouri Higher Education Loan Authority, and opposed the governor's limits on damages in lawsuits. In a surprise move, Blunt announced in January 2008 that he would not run for a second term, saying he had accomplished most of what he had set out to do. Republicans nominated Rep. Kenny Hulshof, who was friends with Nixon, having worked with him in the attorney general's office. Nixon called for rescinding Blunt's Medicaid cuts, for expanding college scholarships for families with incomes under $80,000, and for regulation of payday loans. He cast Hulshof as a Washington insider and attacked him for voting for tax breaks for oil companies. Hulshof characterized Nixon as "old way Jay" and criticized him for seeking a contribution from a utility while investigating the collapse of one of its reservoirs. Nixon was the front-runner throughout the campaign and won 58%-39%. He carried not only the cities but also 66 of the state's 114 counties.

When he came into office, Nixon faced declining state revenues and a legislature with significant Republican majorities in both houses. Nixon worked with Republicans to pass a comprehensive jobs bill as well as an initiative to get colleges to produce hundreds more graduates trained for high-demand health care fields. In 2009, he ran into budget problems as a result of the recession and cut $430 million in planned spending. In 2010, Nixon called for consolidating departments, cutting 1,000 jobs, slashing tax credits, and eliminating some holidays for state employees, including Harry Truman's birthday. The governor got some of what he wanted, including the reduction in jobs, but could not persuade lawmakers to cut the holidays or reduce tax credits. Among his first-term setbacks was a 2009 *Kansas City Star* story that said his Department of Natural Resources had withheld a report showing elevated E. coli bacteria in the Lake of the Ozarks in order to protect the lake's tourism season. Nixon contended that his office had nothing to do with the decision and was unaware of the report until late June. But the controversy continued to dog him, and in September he suspended Natural Resources Director Mark Templeton for two weeks without pay. In January 2011, Nixon stunned political observers when he commuted the sentence of a murderer on death row to life imprisonment, a decision that some called a dangerous move politically. He also found himself confronted by an assertive GOP state legislature and vetoed the redistricting map that Republicans sent him, as well as a bill that would have required voters to show government-issued photo identification. Lawmakers overrode his redistricting veto. In his desire to avoid picking too many battles, he signed a bill requiring some federal welfare recipients to be tested for drugs, a measure that enraged some Democrats. He also allowed to become law, without his signature, two other bills popular with conservatives: a measure imposing new restrictions on late-term abortions and another lowering the minimum age to get a concealed weapon permit. He made no apologies for his centrism. "I don't bring a highly partisan edge or a highly radical philosophical edge to things. I try to get things done," he told *The Kansas City Star*.

A high point of Nixon's first term came in 2011 when he skillfully and assuredly responded to the destruction in Joplin, a Southwest Missouri city of 50,000, which had been struck by a devastating tornado. Nixon was in Joplin the morning after the storm hit and ordered the Highway Patrol to help the city cope with the wreckage. He was a steady presence in Joplin, which he visited throughout that summer. The governor won wide bipartisan praise for his handling of the Joplin cleanup efforts as well as for his aggressive moves to provide relief to farmers whose wells ran dry during a prolonged 2012 drought. That provided a good backdrop for Nixon's reelection campaign. His Republican challenger was Dave Spence, a St. Louis business executive who was little known: his primary asset was his ability to self-fund his campaign with $4.5 million. Nixon ran on his mostly moderate record and aggressively took on Spence, running attack ads alleging that he mismanaged a St. Louis bank with bad investments and received an insider loan to buy a mansion. Spence denounced the ads as false. On top of his other difficulties, Spence, as a Republican, probably suffered from the fallout from Missouri GOP Senate candidate Todd Akin's explosive comments about pregnancy and "legitimate rape." Nixon won 55%-43%. But the 2012 elections also saw the GOP strengthen its grip on the legislature, netting two additional Senate seats and seven in the House. Republicans gained a Democratic state Senate seat and picked up three Democratic House seats in Nixon's own Jefferson County, which he carried by roughly 14 percentage points.

Following the election, Nixon started to adopt more conventional Democratic left-leaning positions. In 2013, he came out against arming teachers after the Newtown Connecticut school massacre and opposed the Republican legislature's proposal to cut state income taxes, successfully vetoing the bill. Nixon proposed expanding Medicaid coverage for the working poor, but the GOP legislature ignored him. He closed 2013 coming out in support of same-sex marriage. Nixon saw even more confrontation with legislature in 2014, but this time he was not so successful fending it off. He vetoed 33 pieces of legislation, the most in any year since he took office, and line-item vetoed some 160 provisions in the 2015 fiscal year budget. But GOP lawmakers overrode Nixon's vetoes on a number of important measures, including a 72-hour waiting period for a woman to undergo an abortion, one of the longest wait times in the country; the state's first major income tax cut in almost 90 years; a guns-right bill that lowered the minimum age for acquiring a concealed-carry permit to 19 and allowed permit holders to openly carry their firearms anywhere in the state. The legislature also overrode 47 of Nixon's line-item budget vetoes.

While he didn't hesitate to wield his veto pen, Nixon was sharply criticized for a lack of leadership in the wake of the fatal August 2014 shooting of unarmed black teenager Michael Brown by a white police officer in Ferguson, a predominantly black city of 21,000 in St. Louis County. He did not visit Ferguson until five days after the incident, by which time angry protests had erupted and the shooting prompted a national discussion about race and law enforcement. Nixon had the Highway Patrol take over security from local officials, but that did not stop the disturbances and Nixon later had to issue a state of emergency for the area and impose a curfew. Nixon declined to appoint a special prosecutor to investigate the shooting, leaving that responsibility to the local district attorney. After a St. Louis County grand jury declined to indict the police officer, rioting again broke out in Ferguson and Nixon was pilloried for not anticipating that reaction and not taking more forceful measures to prevent the looting and many fires that ensued.

The unrest in Ferguson and his inadequate handling of the situation stopped talk about Nixon's political future—he is limited to two terms as governor—and now speculation has turned to his potential successors. The GOP field could be crowded: former state House Speaker Catherine Hanaway, former state Rep. Randy Asbury, and state Sen. Mike Parson have all announced their candidacies. Businessman and 2012 Senate hopeful John Brunner (he lost the GOP primary to then-Rep. Todd Akin), retired Navy Seal and author Eric Greitens, and Lt. Gov. Peter Kinder have all considered the race. Republican state Auditor Tom Schweich was viewed as the potential frontrunner for the GOP nomination before he committed suicide in early 2015. Attorney General Chris Koster could have the Democratic field to himself, and he is arguably the party's strongest potential candidate. Meanwhile, Nixon kept on dueling with the GOP legislature, which overturned his veto and passed a law cutting 15 months from the previous five-year maximum for recipients of the state's Temporary Assistance for Needy Families program. When that law goes into effect in 2016, it will remove several thousand families from benefit rolls. The Republican legislative leadership also hit some turbulence in May 2015, when House Speaker John Diehl, one of Nixon's top adversaries in Jefferson City, resigned from office after admitting he had traded sexually charged text messages with a 19-year-old college intern at the Capitol. It was later revealed that Diehl had had an affair with a lobbyist for the governor. Diehl's successor, Todd Richardson, said it was important to clean up the "culture" of the isolated state capital, which has been likened to a rolling frat house party when the legislature is in session. That may be a bigger challenge for Missouri GOP lawmakers to overcome than Nixon.

Senior Senator

Claire McCaskill (D)

Elected 2006, term expires 2019, 2nd term; b. July 24, 1953, Rolla; U. of MO, B.S. 1975, J.D. 1978; Catholic; married (Joseph Shepard); 7 children.

Elected Office: MO House, 1982-88; Jackson Cnty. legislature, 1990-92; Jackson Cnty. prosecutor, 1992-98; MO auditor, 1998-2006.

Professional Career: Law clerk, MO Court of Appeals, 1978; Asst. Jackson Cnty. prosecutor, 1978-82; Practicing atty., 1983-92.

DC Office: 730 HSOB, 20510, 202-224-6154; Fax: 202-228-6326; Website: mccaskill.senate.gov.

State Offices: Cape Girardeau, 573-651-0964; Columbia, 573-442-7130; Kansas City, 816-421-1639; Springfield, 417-868-8745; St. Louis, 314-367-1364.

Committees: *Aging (Special)* (RMM). *Armed Services:* Airland; Personnel; Readiness & Management Support. *Commerce, Science & Transportation:* Communications, Technology & the Internet; Consumer Protection, Product Safety & Insurance; Surface Transportation & Merchant Marine Infrastructure, Safety & Security. *Homeland Security & Governmental Affairs:* Federal Spending Oversight & Emergency Management; Investigations (Permanent) (RMM).

Group Ratings

	ADA	ACLU	AFL-CIO	LCV	ITI	COC	HAFA	ACU	CFG	FRC
2014	80%	93%	–	40%	100%	38%	8%	9%	19%	0%
2013	65%	C	100%	77%	C	50%	C	4%	7%	C

National Journal Ratings

	2013 LIB	—	2013 CONS
Economic	46%	—	53%
Social	57%	—	41%
Foreign	53%	—	46%
Composite	53%	—	47%

Key Votes of the 113th Congress

1. Sandy storm spending	Y	5. Student Loan Rates	NV	9. Bipartisan Budget Deal	Y
2. Chuck Hagel Confirmation	Y	6. Employee Non-Discrim'n Act	Y	10. Farm Bill Conference Rept.	Y
3. Gun Background Checks	Y	7. Senate Vote on Judgeships	N	11. Unempl. Comp. Extension	NV
4. Immigration Reform	Y	8. Defense Dept. Spending	Y	12. Keystone Pipeline	Y

Election Results

2012 general	Claire McCaskill (D)................ 1,494,125	(55%)	$21,264,093	$2,384,795	$1,220,150
	Todd Akin (R)........................... 1,066,159	(39%)	$6,165,888	$2,626,339	$6,653,741
	Jonathan Dine (Lib)................... 165,468	(6%)			
2012 primary	Claire McCaskill (D)..............unopposed				

Prior winning percentage: 2006 (50%)

Democrat Claire McCaskill, Missouri's senior senator, was reelected to a second term in 2012—arguably the luckiest candidate of the election cycle. An early backer of Barack Obama's 2008 presidential candidacy—she and Obama were Senate colleagues from neighboring states during her first two years on Capitol Hill—McCaskill saw her approval ratings sink as her home state, which nearly voted for Obama during his first presidential bid, trended increasingly to the right. But she caught a big break when her general election opponent, Republican Rep. Todd Akin, proceeded to commit the most disastrous gaffe of the 2012 election cycle—his now infamous remark about "legitimate rape." It caused national Republicans to flee from his candidacy, and enabled the once politically endangered McCaskill to cruise to a 16-point win even as the GOP presidential nominee, Mitt Romney, was scoring a 9-point victory over Obama in the Show-Me State.

While Akin and other Republicans sought to hammer McCaskill as a liberal during the 2012 campaign, her Senate voting record has been decidedly centrist—even as the blunt-spoken former prosecutor has not hesitated to take on controversial issues and situations, on which she displayed her independence. Despite her friendship with Obama, vote ratings compiled by *CQ/Roll Call* for the early months of 2015 found McCaskill tied for last among 46 members of the Senate Democratic Caucus in terms of voting in tandem with President Obama's positions. Included in this analysis was the March 2015 vote in which McCaskill was among eight Democrats to join all Republican senators in a vote to override Obama's veto of legislation to move ahead on the Keystone XL Pipeline project; the veto was sustained. When McCaskill did side with the president on another major vote in 2015—giving Obama so-called fast track authority to expedite to expedite negotiation of a 12-nation Asian trade deal—it pitted her against the large majority of her Democratic colleagues.

After the Democrats lost the Senate majority in the 2014 election, McCaskill was among a handful of Democrats from Republican-leaning states to oppose Nevada Sen. Harry Reid remaining as Senate Democratic leader; McCaskill was the first senator to publicly announce her opposition to Reid. McCaskill told reporters she saw the loss of nine Senate seats as a message that change was needed at the top of the Senate leadership. Her comments brought speculation that McCaskill, like others in a diminishing band of Senate Democratic centrists, was growing frustrated on Capitol Hill and looking homeward to a possible run for governor. But in early 2015, to the relief of Senate Democrats, McCaskill said she would not run in 2016 to succeed term-limited Democratic Gov. Jay Nixon. "I look at the makeup of the current U.S. Senate and I see what might be possible in terms of me helping forge some… compromises, and at the end of the day the work is too important, the job is too rewarding and too fulfilling," she told KCUR Radio in Kansas City. She added she was "very likely" to seek reelection in 2018, and expected to soon start raising money for what is likely to be another tough political battle.

McCaskill had run for governor a decade earlier, ousting a sitting governor in the Democratic primary but narrowly losing the November election to the son of then-House Majority Whip Roy Blunt; the elder Blunt is now McCaskill's junior Senate colleague. It was not the first electoral encounter between the Blunt and McCaskill families: In 1978, McCaskill's mother, Betty, lost a race to Roy Blunt's father, Leroy, for a seat in the Missouri House.

Claire McCaskill was born in Rolla, about halfway between St. Louis and Springfield; the family was then living in the small town of Houston, about 50 miles to the south. Her father, William, later served as state insurance commissioner, and her mother became the first female city council member in the university town of Columbia after the family moved there. McCaskill earned degrees from the University of Missouri and its law school, and worked as an assistant prosecutor. In 1982, at 29, she was elected to the Missouri House, where she was the first woman member to have a baby while in office. Ten years later, she became Jackson County (Kansas City) prosecutor.

In 1998, she was elected state auditor, and halfway through her second term, in 2004, she challenged incumbent Democratic Gov. Bob Holden. Holden's administration had started off on the wrong foot, holding a $1 million inaugural that wound up $417,000 in debt. Things didn't get much better as a tough economic climate necessitated deep spending cuts, and Holden battled with the legislature. Many Democrats felt the party needed a stronger candidate to survive a Republican challenge, and McCaskill stepped in, defeating Holden in the primary, 52%-45%. In the general election, McCaskill sought to take advantage of the youth and relative inexperience in state government of her opponent, 33-year old Secretary of State Matt Blunt, boasting she would not need on the on-the-job training. But Blunt won, 51%-48%.

Despite that narrow loss, McCaskill, with three statewide races under her belt, was a prize Senate recruit for the national party in 2006. She would be running for a seat that had changed partisan hands in both 2000 and 2002. In 2000, term-limited Democratic Gov. Mel Carnahan took on Republican incumbent John Ashcroft and was elected, even though Carnahan was killed in a plane crash just days prior to the polls opening. Carnahan's widow, Jean, was appointed to fill the seat, and served until 2002, when former GOP Rep. Jim Talent was elected to fill the remaining four years of the term. McCaskill announced her candidacy against Talent on the steps of the Houston feed mill where her father once worked. It was a backdrop that telegraphed her focus on the rural counties, where her weak showing cost her the governor's election. She denounced tax breaks for oil companies, called for an increase in the minimum wage, and said she would push tax credits for first-time home purchases as well as for child care and college education.

McCaskill linked Talent to President George W. Bush, whose popularity was sinking. But the controversial issue of embryonic stem cell research generated the most attention. A proposed state constitutional amendment forced both candidates to address whether they supported more government funding for the research. McCaskill supported it, with Talent opposed. Missouri Republicans were split: State business leaders backed the proposal in hopes of attracting biomedical research, while religious conservatives opposed it, regarding use of surplus human embroyos as tantamount to abortion. In October, Talent targeted McCaskill's family's finances, demanding that her husband, Joseph Shepard, a developer of low income housing financed by government loans, release his tax returns—filed separately from his wife's. Talent also suggested the couple hadn't paid all of their taxes, and accused Shepard of owning an offshore tax shelter. On Election Day, McCaskill won 50%-47%, the third consecutive election for the seat decided by fewer than 50,000 votes. As in the governor's race, McCaskill won big margins in the Kansas City and St. Louis metro areas, but unlike 2004, she held her own in outstate Missouri and carried 11 rural counties she lost earlier.

In the Senate, McCaskill has emphasized her independence, with a voting record placing her among the half-dozen least liberal members of the Democratic majority. In the Senate overall, she has been smack in the middle: *National Journal's* 2011 and 2012 vote rankings put her as the 50th most liberal senator, followed by a 49th place ranking in 2013. McCaskill has departed from the Democratic line on a host of major issues. She did support Obama's signature health insurance overhaul, but later said she would consider changing its individual mandate requirement. In 2010, she joined other moderates in questioning the party's support for continual extensions of expanded unemployment benefits. "At some point, it starts to look like another entitlement program," she observed. In her first year in the Senate, she opposed a 2007 immigration bill that created a guest worker program and a path to citizenship for illegal immigrants. A year later, she declined to commit to California Democratic Sen. Barbara Boxer's bill tightening restrictions on greenhouse gases.

In 2010, after incumbent Democrats across the country were portrayed as pork-barrel spenders in the midterm elections, McCaskill joined with conservative Republican Sen. Tom Coburn of Oklahoma to push for a ban on so-called earmarks, historically used by influential members of Congress to direct money to favored projects back home. The move failed on a procedural vote. In early 2011, Appropriations Committee Chairman Daniel Inouye announced an earmark moratorium, which was extended a year later—even as McCaskill and Republican Sen. Pat Toomey of Pennsylvania failed in bid to make the earmark ban permanent. McCaskill and Toomey have since reintroduced the permanent ban, most recently in 2015, even as an informal ban on earmarks has remained in place, due in large measure to the opposition of both Obama and House Republicans to this procedure.

Earmark proponents have argued that banning them compromises Congress' constitutional "power of the purse", but McCaskill has countered that earmarking didn't begin in earnest until the 1970s. Consequently, arguments that a permanent ban would impede congressional power are "horseradish," McCaskill declared in the folksy vernacular that has become a trademark. Her blunt-spoken style has helped to win points with Democratic colleagues despite her parting of company with them on some key issues, such as when she declared in July 2011 that Minority Leader Mitch McConnell had "lost his mind" by allowing political considerations to take precedence over striking a deal to raise the federal debt limit.

The earmark battle has been consistent with her focus, as a former state auditor, on government reform. The crowning achievement of her first term was a bill included in the fiscal 2013 defense authorization law. It requires government agencies to prove that money will not be wasted on projects before they allocate funds, while at the same time strengthening the powers of inspectors general investigating fraud and abuse. The bill also established a clear chain of authority for contracting oversight in the Defense Department, State Department, and Agency for International Development. But McCaskill's image as a watchdog suffered a blow in 2011 with news reports that she had spent $76,000 in taxpayer funds to fly on a private plane she co-owned with her husband. She contended it was a minor oversight, and sought to extinguish the controversy by reimbursing the Treasury. But the situation—dubbed "Air Claire"—became more embarrassing when McCaskill acknowledged she had failed to pay more than $287,000 in personal property taxes on the plane. She later paid $88,000 to the government to cover all costs associated with the flights and sold the plane.

Amid the "Air Claire" flap and Missouri's increasingly conservative leanings, McCaskill headed into the 2012 election high on the list of Senate Democrats seen as vulnerable, with approval rating back home stuck just above 40 percent. By August of that year, groups such as Republican political strategist Karl Rove's American Crossroads had poured more than $15 million into attack ads against her. Besides Akin, who had developed a reputation in the House for vehement social conservatism, the primary field included more moderate Republicans such as former state Treasurer Sarah Steelman and St. Louis businessman John Brunner. McCaskill made no secret of her desire to take on Akin rather than a more centrist candidate. With the help of the Democratic Party and its allies, she sought to boost Akin's chances by airing an ad that branded Akin the "true conservative." The Democratic Senatorial Campaign Committee followed with ads that aired on conservative talk radio stations. The gambit worked: Akin won with 36 percent, with Brunner and Steelman running second and third in an eight-person Republican field. McCaskill's tactic has since been emulated by other Democratic campaigns without much success.

As she had in the prior campaign, McCaskill pressed for a minimum wage increase, while vowing to protect Social Security. But she also refused to cede rural areas, driving to small towns to highlight how often she had differed with her party. While early polls gave Akin a lead, the race abruptly changed two weeks after the August primary, when Akin appeared on St. Louis TV station KTVI. Asked if women who had been raped should be afforded the option of abortion, he dropped a bombshell: "If it's a legitimate rape, the female body has ways to try to shut that whole thing down." Realizing the disaster on their hands, Republicans from Romney on down called on Akin to withdraw from the race. National Republican Senatorial Committee Chairman John Cornyn of Texas said he would no longer provide Akin financial help (although it was later revealed the NRSC provided $760,000 in the race's closing days). Akin refused to get out, and on Election Day, it wasn't even close, with McCaskill winning, 55%-39%. Akin won most of the small rural counties, but McCaskill won several that she had lost in 2006, including St. Charles County in the St. Louis suburbs, which had been considered an Akin stronghold.

Back for a second term, McCaskill attracted media attention in 2013 as she and a Democratic colleague, New York Sen. Kirsten Gillibrand, aggressively lobbied their colleagues on behalf of rival proposals for dealing with an increasingly high-profile issue: Sexual assault in the military. Both women, members of the Armed Services Committee, sought to address complaints that the military was not dealing seriously enough with such transgressions. Gillibrand wanted to remove sexual assault cases from the military chain of command, while McCaskill advocated for a more incremental approach that limited the discretion of military commanders without removing court-martial proceedings from their jurisdiction.

As a former prosecutor, McCaskill reportedly spent hundreds of hours meeting with military and civilian prosecutors and others involved in the issue. Her approach was backed by the Defense Department, while victims' groups favored Gillibrand's alternative. The two women avoided public shots at one another, but McCaskill was said to be enraged when one victims' group took out newspaper ads in Missouri attacking her. In 2014, the Senate voted in favor of McCaskill's plan. McCaskill and Gillibrand subsequently put aside their differences to work together on combating a related problem: sexual assault on college campuses.

In August 2014, McCaskill was a high-profile presence in the wake of unrest in the St. Louis suburb of Ferguson following the shooting death of a black teenager, Michael Brown, by a white police officer. While suggesting much of the violence that followed Brown's death was the work of outsiders, McCaskill criticized the response of the Ferguson police to nightly demonstrations. "I think most Americans were uncomfortable watching a suburban street in St. Louis with vivid images of a war zone," McCaskill told a hearing of the Senate Homeland Security and Governmental Affairs Committee, on which she serves. "Those lawful, peaceful protesters did not deserve to be treated like enemy combatants." She was critical of a Defense Department program that provided surplus military equipment to local police forces, some of which was used in Ferguson, and advocated "demilitarization." She sponsored legislation to require local police be trained in the use of such equipment, along with providing federal grants to help municipalities equip police with body cameras.

Amid the unrest, McCaskill said via social media that she had made "dozens" of calls "to de-escalate the tense and unacceptable situation in Ferguson." It highlighted her status as one of Congress' most avid users of Twitter, where she has attracted more than 100,000 followers by regularly tweeting political and personal tidbits. After the National Rifle Association called for more armed guards in schools following the 2012 Newtown Connecticut school shooting in which two dozen died, she tweeted: "Conservatives preach no federal govt and local control of schools until the NRA wants the federal government to mandate guns in schools?" On a lighter note, as she geared up for reelection in November 2011, she tweeted her intention to lose weight: "I have divorced bread and pasta. I'm hoping someday we can be friends again." She ultimately shed 50 pounds.

Junior Senator

Roy Blunt (R)

Elected 2010, term expires 2017, 1st term; b. Jan. 10, 1950, Niangua; SW Baptist U., B.A. 1970, SW MO St. U., M.A. 1972; Baptist; married (Abigail); 4 children.

Elected Office: MO secy. of st., 1984-93; U.S. House, 1997-2011.

Professional Career: H.S. teacher, 1970-73; Greene Cnty. clerk, 1973-85; Adjunct instructor, Drury Col., 1976-82; Pres., SW Baptist U., 1993-96.

DC Office: 260 RSOB, 20510, 202-224-5721; Fax: 202-224-8149; Website: blunt.senate.gov.

State Offices: Cape Girardeau, 573-334-7044; Clayton, 314-725-4484; Columbia, 573-442-8151; Kansas City, 816-471-7141; Springfield, 417-877-7814.

Committees: *Appropriations:* Agriculture, Rural Development, Food and Drug Administration & Related Agencies; Defense; Interior, Environment & Related Agencies; Labor, Health and Human Services, and Education & Related Agencies (Chmn); State, Foreign Operations & Related Programs; Transportation, HUD & Related Agencies. *Commerce, Science & Transportation:* Aviation Operations, Safety & Security; Communications, Technology & the Internet; Consumer Protection, Product Safety & Insurance; Surface Transportation & Merchant Marine Infrastructure. *Intelligence* (Select). *Rules & Administration* (Chmn). *Joint Committee on the Library.*

Group Ratings

	ADA	ACLU	AFL-CIO	LCV	ITI	COC	HAFA	ACU	CFG	FRC
2014	5%	6%	–	0%	33%	100%	52%	76%	47%	100%
2013	10%	C	17%	23%	C	88%	C	71%	67%	C

National Journal Ratings

	2013 LIB	—	2013 CONS
Economic	35%	—	62%
Social	35%	—	64%
Foreign	35%	—	64%
Composite	36%	—	64%

Key Votes of the 113th Congress

1. Sandy storm spending	N	5. Student Loan Rates	Y	9. Bipartisan Budget Deal	N
2. Chuck Hagel Confirmation	N	6. Employee Non-Discrim'n Act	N	10. Farm Bill Conference Rept.	Y
3. Gun Background Checks	N	7. Senate Vote on Judgeships	Y	11. Unempl. Comp. Extension	N
4. Immigration Reform	N	8. Defense Dept. Spending	N	12. Keystone Pipeline	Y

Election Results

2010 general	Roy Blunt (R)	1,054,160	(54%)	$12,095,571	$2,349,670	$4,067,016
	Robin Carnahan (D)	789,736	(41%)	$10,311,557	$985,136	$4,172,808
	Jonathan Dine (Lib)	58,663	(3%)			
	Jerry Beck (CNP)	41,309	(2%)			
2010 primary	Roy Blunt (R)	411,040	(71%)			
	Chuck Purgason (R)	75,663	(13%)			
	Kristi Nichols (R)	40,744	(7%)			

Prior winning percentages: House: 2008 (68%), 2006 (67%), 2004 (70%), 2002 (75%), 2000 (74%), 1998 (73%), 1996 (65%)

Republican Roy Blunt, Missouri's junior senator, is among the handful of legislators to reach the ranks of the leadership of both houses of Congress. After serving in the House as both majority and minority whip—and, for several months in 2005, as acting House majority leader—Blunt, just a year after his 2010 election to the Senate, was chosen as vice chairman of the Republican Conference. The latter post is the No. 5 slot in the Senate GOP leadership, and Blunt added to his influence in 2015, when the Republicans gained the Senate majority, by assuming the chairmanship of the Rules and Administration Committee—whose jurisdiction includes the internal management of the Senate.

Blunt also presides over a family with a multitude of connections to the lobbying community, which have occasionally prompted public interest groups to raise conflict-of-interest questions. Blunt's second wife, Abigail, is now the head of governmental affairs for Kraft Foods, and was previously a lobbyist for the Altria Group, parent company of the Philip Morris tobacco giant. The Blunts insist they don't mix business with family matters: Abigail Blunt (nee Perlman) formally abstained from lobbying the House when her husband served there, and filed disclosure forms in 2011 saying she would not lobby the Senate. The family's lobbying connections also extend to a couple of sons from Blunt's first marriage. His oldest son, Matt, who was Missouri's governor from 2004-2008, is president of the American Automotive Policy Council, which represents the Big Three automakers. Another son, Andrew, runs a Missouri-based lobbying firm, whose clients have included AT&T, American Airlines, MillerCoors and Motorola. He also managed his father's 2010 Senate campaign and will reprise that role for Blunt's 2016 re-election bid.

Roy Blunt grew up on a farm in Niangua, near Springfield in southwest Missouri. His father, Leroy, was a dairy farmer who won election as a state representative in 1978 by defeating the mother of Democratic Sen. Claire McCaskill, now Roy Blunt's senior Missouri colleague. By then, the younger Blunt's political career was well underway. In 1970, he graduated from Southwest Baptist University, teaching high school classes in history and government while earning his master's degree in 1972. He got his start in politics the same year, volunteering in the unsuccessful congressional campaign of Republican John Ashcroft—who went on to become governor, senator, and U.S. attorney general. In 1973, then-GOP Gov. Christopher (Kit) Bond named the 23-year-old Blunt as Greene County clerk. In 1980, Republican Sen. John Danforth asked Blunt to run for lieutenant governor, but Blunt lost. Four years later, he was elected Missouri secretary of state, the first Republican to win that office in half a century, and served two terms. In 1992, he ran for governor and narrowly lost the Republican primary, and took a respite from politics to become president of Southwest Baptist University, his alma mater.

In 1996, when Republican Rep. Mel Hancock retired, Blunt ran for the open House seat in the Springfield area and won with two-thirds of the vote. The district had been traditionally Republican, and Blunt was reelected easily in his following six terms. In his 14 years in the House, Blunt had a solidly conservative voting record, with intermittent moves toward the center on social issues. In 2006, he won passage of his Combat Meth Act, the first comprehensive approach to fighting the supply of methamphetamine. He also sponsored a measure creating an Internet database of federal spending: The sponsor of the Senate companion bill: a young Illinois Democrat named Barack Obama. But Blunt's greater impact was in his leadership roles in the House, which gave him a say in shaping the major legislation produced by the Republican majority from 1995 to 2006.

In 1999, Blunt was one of 10 original members of then-Texas Gov. George W. Bush's presidential exploratory committee. Bush called him "a leader who knows how to raise his sights and lower his voice." Blunt's rise in leadership began in early 1999, when Majority Whip Tom Delay, a Texas Republican, plucked him from the ranks of deputy whips and made him chief deputy whip, an important leadership stepping stone. In contrast to DeLay, nicknamed "the Hammer," Blunt had a reputation as a good listener with a light touch. On numerous issues, Blunt's job was to make certain bills the leadership hoped to pass were palatable to conservatives. But he also paid attention to party moderates, then a larger share of the House GOP Conference. Blunt spent a good deal of time meeting with lobbyists and organizing groups around issues such as trade, taxes, and energy, while raising substantial sums for GOP candidates. When Majority Leader Dick Armey of Texas announced he would retire in 2002, DeLay moved up to replace him, which left the post of whip available for Blunt.

For the most part, Blunt was successful as whip. He met his toughest challenge in passing the 2003 bill to create a prescription drug benefit as part of the Medicare program. In a highly controversial vote in which the roll call was held open for three hours, he was able to persuade two Republicans to switch their votes. But there were also rocky moments. In 2003, the House leadership was embarrassed by disclosures in the *Washington Post* that Blunt, the previous fall, had quietly sought to insert into a homeland security bill a provision benefiting Philip Morris. At the time, Blunt was dating his future wife, then a Philip Morris lobbyist (the couple married in 2003) and Blunt's son, Andrew, was doing work for Philip Morris in Missouri. Blunt defended the provision, dropped after other House leaders objected to it, as "good policy" aimed at curbing bootlegged cigarette sales. He said it was a "serious homeland security issue" because such sales had become a source of terrorist financing. But the flap came on the heels of another episode for which Blunt took heat: According to the *Wall Street Journal*, he was behind a last-minute effort to block a German-owned competitor of United Parcel Service—another client of his son's—from expanding in the United States.

In 2005, Blunt temporarily held two leadership posts, as acting majority leader as well as whip—a situation created when DeLay was forced to step down as leader after being indicted by a Texas grand jury for election law violations. It was too heavy a burden for Blunt, particularly when the House was dealing with the devastating impact of Hurricane Katrina in the South. During the next three months, House Republicans struggled to pass bills. In January 2006, after DeLay announced he would permanently give up his post as leader, Blunt positioned himself to take over permanently and, after a week of lobbying his colleagues, claimed he had the votes to win. But John Boehner of Ohio was aggressively campaigning against him, and the multiple DeLay controversies involving well-heeled lobbyists indirectly hurt Blunt, himself viewed as being overly cozy with Washington's vaunted K Street. While Blunt led on the first ballot in the Republican Caucus, coming within a half-dozen votes of the needed majority, on the second ballot Boehner prevailed, 122-109, over Blunt—who suffered the double indignity of losing his bid and looking like a whip who couldn't count votes.

Blunt remained majority whip and developed a smooth working relationship with Boehner. When House Republicans lost their majority in November 2006, Blunt became minority whip. In September 2008, Boehner gave him the thankless task of negotiating the $700 billion financial bailout bill, which proved to be wildly unpopular with fellow Republicans. After the 2008 election, Blunt stepped down from the minority whip to make way for his chief deputy, Virginia Rep. Eric Cantor. "Ten years of asking people to do things they don't want to do is a long time," Blunt told reporters, adding he had promised himself—after the Republicans lost the House majority in 2006—that he would only serve two more years as whip unless the GOP recaptured the House. But, even with a majority, it was also clear Blunt's path to becoming House speaker had been permanently obstructed.

Barely three months later, in February 2009, Bond—who had helped to launch Blunt's political career almost four decades earlier—announced he would not seek reelection to a fifth Senate term, and Blunt began to focus on a campaign to succeed him. A couple of potentially competitive primary opponents opted out. State Sen. Chuck Purgason did run and tried to create momentum with an appeal to tea party activists, but Blunt easily prevailed in the August primary with 71 percent. The fall campaign was the real contest. Blunt faced Secretary of State Robin Carnahan, scion of a Missouri Democratic dynasty whose surname brought her instant name recognition. Blunt did his best to tie Carnahan to President Obama and Democratic policies unpopular with conservative voters. His opposition to the Obama-backed health care overhaul played well for him, and his ads featured images of Carnahan with Obama at a Kansas City fundraiser.

Carnahan tried to paint Blunt as the insider in the race. But her family ties made it a stretch for voters to see her as an outsider: Her father was a popular governor, her mother had served two years as an appointed senator, and both her grandfather and brother served in the House. Carnahan also sought to link Blunt to corruption, with one ad featuring a Fox News clip in which anchor Chris Wallace mentioned Blunt inserting the provision favorable to Philip Morris into the homeland security legislation. But it appears to have mattered little to Missouri voters in a year in which Obama's popularity sharply dropped. The race began as a close contest, but on Election Night, Blunt won 54%-41%. Blunt's margin of victory served as an early sign of the state's continued drift to the right.

Blunt moved into a suite of offices in the Senate Russell Building on Capitol Hill occupied by Harry Truman when the latter was a Democratic senator from Missouri. Blunt's voting record remains conservative, but he differs from the tea party-oriented Republicans who take a dim view of government spending. Just months after taking office, when a May 2011 tornado devastated the town of Joplin, and killed 159 people, Blunt pushed for a strong federal relief effort to help the battered community. (Blunt represented Joplin while in the House.) When Cantor, by then majority leader with Republicans back in House control, suggested that the disaster relief aid should be offset with other budget cuts, Blunt told *Politico*, "We need to prioritize spending, and this needs to be a priority."

A similar political dynamic was in play during a Senate leadership reshuffling in late 2011, as Blunt announced he would run for an open slot as the vice chairman of the Republican Conference. It set up a faceoff against Wisconsin Sen. Ron Johnson, another freshman, with the race portrayed as a battle of the establishment and tea party wings of the GOP. Despite Johnson's efforts to pitch himself as a fresh conservative face, Blunt prevailed in a secret ballot that reportedly went 25-22 in his favor. Blunt's return to a leadership position on Capitol Hill came shortly after Republican presidential aspirant Mitt Romney asked him in September 2011 to be his primary liaison to the House and Senate to win support from lawmakers. It was an encore of the job he had performed for George W. Bush a decade earlier as he was starting to climb in the House leadership. Blunt's wife, at that point a top lobbyist for Kraft Foods, became one of the Romney campaign's "bundlers" to gather checks from other supporters.

Upon his election to the Senate, Blunt was named to a seat on the Appropriations Committee, where, with the Republicans back in the majority following the 2014 election, he assumed the chairmanship of the subcommittee with jurisdiction over the Labor, Health and Human Services, and Education departments—giving him an influential voice in how a large portion of the federal government's domestic discretionary budget is allocated. Earlier, in 2013, he stirred controversy by attaching a rider to an agriculture spending bill in the committee's jurisdiction intended to protect St. Louis-based Monsanto's efforts to plant genetically modified crops against Agriculture Department court challenges. The Center for Food Safety decried the provision as "corporate welfare," and the liberal magazine *Mother Jones* dubbed Blunt "Monsanto's Man in Washington." In response, Blunt told *Politico* he had worked closely with Hawaii Democratic Sen. Daniel Inouye, who chaired the Appropriations panel before his death in late 2012, and who was concerned about protecting the company's operations in Hawaii.

But Blunt's most prominent legislative move during the first part of his Senate term was his February 2012 sponsorship of an amendment that would allow employers to exclude any insurance benefit they deemed immoral. His action came after Obama proposed a new contraception coverage rule in response to complaints from religious groups. Blunt and other supporters tried to frame the issue as one of religious freedom. But the move mobilized women's groups, who charged the amendment would allow employers to choose women's health care options based on an employer's moral beliefs. The amendment was narrowly defeated; with three Democrats joining Republicans in backing it and a GOP moderate, Maine's Olympia Snowe, siding with Democrats against it.

An issue later that year was a personal one for Blunt: When Russian President Vladimir Putin announced in December 2012 he would ban U.S. adoptions of Russian children in retaliation for a law enabling the Obama administration to target Russian human rights violators, Blunt led an effort to persuade Putin to allow adoptions that had been completed. He related the story of how he and his wife had adopted a son born in a Russian orphanage in late 2004.

At the outset of 2015, one of Blunt's priorities was to pay for deteriorating roads, bridges and other infrastructure without raising taxes. He joined a bipartisan group of lawmakers that looked to give corporations a tax break on profits earned overseas, with the resulting federal revenue replenishing the Highway Trust Fund and creating a new infrastructure fund. But much of Blunt's legislative effort in early 2015 seemed aimed at taking on Obama administration policy. He helped to lead an unsuccessful Senate fight to tie continued funding for the Homeland Security Department to a move to block implementation of Obama's 2014 executive order on immigration policy. He voted against the nomination of Loretta Lynch for attorney general, joining many of his GOP colleagues who opposed Lynch to protest what they saw as Obama's attempt to usurp Congress on immigration. Blunt was also among just five senators to oppose the nomination of Ashton Carter as defense secretary, going to the Senate floor to accuse Obama of micromanaging the Pentagon without laying out a clear national security strategy against the radical Islamic group known as ISIS. He also sponsored a couple of largely symbolic measures taking aim at Obama's climate change policies.

Facing reelection in 2016, Blunt seemed to be treading the same path as several other establishment Republican senators in recent years, who had veered to the right in the run-up to an election to pre-empt a tea party primary challenge. Former Republican Rep. Todd Akin, whose comments about "legitimate rape" in his 2012 campaign against McCaskill set off a national firestorm, briefly considered a challenge to Blunt in early 2015 before backing off. But Blunt continued to be the subject of grumbling among some conservative groups, with a spokesman for the Club to Growth telling *Roll Call* that Blunt's 47-percent conservative voting score in 2014 was "certainly not...outstanding" and "would raise concern." In a general election, Blunt is considered a strong favorite in a one-time bellwether state that has trended increasingly conservative. But Democrats are touting their likely nominee: Missouri Secretary of State Jason Kander, a former Army intelligence officer. Such a race would be a generational battle: Kander is barely half the age of Blunt, who turned 65 in January 2015.

FIRST DISTRICT

William Lacy Clay (D)

Elected 2000, 8th term; b. July 27, 1956, St. Louis; U. of MD, B.S. 1983; Catholic; divorced; 2 children.

Elected Office: MO House, 1983-90; MO Senate, 1991-2001.

Professional Career: Asst. doorkeeper, U.S. House, 1976-83; Paralegal, 1988-98; Real estate agent, 1986-2000.

DC Office: 2428 RHOB, 20515, 202-225-2406; Fax: 202-226-3717; Website: lacyclay.house.gov.

State Offices: Florissant, 314-383-5240; St. Louis, 314-367-1970; St. Louis City, 314-669-9393.

Committees: *Financial Services:* Financial Institutions & Consumer Credit (RMM); Housing & Insurance. *Oversight & Government Reform:* Government Operations.

Group Ratings

	ADA	ACLU	AFL-CIO	LCV	ITI	COC	HAFA	ACU	CFG	FRC
2014	80%	66%	–	86%	80%	46%	11%	0%	9%	0%
2013	95%	C	100%	93%	C	46%	C	8%	16%	C

National Journal Ratings

	2013 LIB	—	2013 CONS
Economic	75%	—	24%
Social	85%	—	13%
Foreign	74%	—	26%
Composite	79%	—	22%

Key Votes of the 113th Congress

1. Sandy storm spending	Y	5. Medical Marijuana	NV	9. Syrian Rebels Training	Y
2. Violence Against Women Act	Y	6. Farm Bill	N	10. Keystone pipeline	N
3. Guantanamo Bay Detainees	Y	7. Afghanistan Combat	Y	11. Immigration Exec. Action	N
4. Abortion 20-week ban	N	8. NSA Phone Data Collection	Y	12. Bipartisan budget deal	Y

Election Results

2014 general	William Lacy Clay (D)	119,315	(73%)	$384,887
	Daniel Elder (R)	35,273	(22%)	
	Robb Cunningham (Lib)	8,906	(5%)	
2014 primary	William Lacy Clay (D)	unopposed		

Prior winning percentages: 2012 (79%), 2010 (74%), 2008 (87%), 2006 (73%), 2004 (75%), 2002 (70%), 2000 (75%)

Population		Race and Ethnicity		Income	
Total:	737,033	Black	48.8%	Median income:	$40,372
Urban:	41.6%	White	42.9%		*(385 of 435)*
Suburban:	58.4%	Latino	3.2%	Under $50,000	59.5%
Rural:	0.0%	Asian	2.3%	$50,000-$99,999:	27.9%
Land area:	241	Two races	2.6%	$100,000-$199,999:	10.2%
Pop/sq. mi.:	3,058.2	White Ethnic	18.8%	$200,000 or more:	2.5%
Born in state:	69.5%			Poverty Rate	21.5%
		Education			
Age Groups		H.S. grad or less:	37.5%	**Work**	
Under 18:	22.1%	Some college:	32.7%	White collar:	35.4%
18 to 34:	27.3%	College degree, 4 yr.:	17.4%	Blue collar:	48.0%
35 to 64:	38.4%	Post-grad study:	12.4%	Sales and service:	16.6%
Over 64:	12.2%				
		Military		Govt. workers:	12.5%
		Veterans/active duty:	7.6%		

St. Louis and Suburbs

For a century or more, St. Louis seemed the center of America: the starting point for the Lewis and Clark expedition in 1804, the locus half a century later of the *Dred Scott* slavery case, and the site of the 1904 World's Fair, which introduced the hotdog and the ice cream cone and got 19 million people

Voter Turnout	
2013 Total Citizen 18+	552,938
2014 House Turnout	163,494
2014 Turnout as % CVAP	29.6%
2012 Turnout as % CVAP	64%

to *Meet Me in St. Louis*. Its 630-foot-high Gateway Arch is just below the point where the waters of the Missouri surge into the Mississippi, about halfway between New Orleans and Lake Superior, between the Atlantic and the Pacific. This was the first major American city west of the Mississippi River, the final resting place of Daniel Boone, and for many years, Chicago's rival as the transportation hub of America. It was a heavily German city, with a Teutonic solidity and orderliness that distinguished it from the surrounding Southern-accented rural terrain. And from *Mitteleuropa* came the founders of St. Louis's great businesses—the Anheuser-Busch brewery, May Company department stores, Joseph Pulitzer's *St. Louis Post-Dispatch*—and its first great politician, Carl Schurz, the senator and Interior secretary. There is almost a European aura to Forest Park, the site of the 1904 fair, and the dozen mansion-lined private streets nearby.

St. Louis is still one of the nation's 20 largest metro areas, but today it does not occupy as central a place in the national consciousness, and the central city itself has largely emptied out. The German order that made so many people comfortable living in close quarters and commuting by streetcar has yielded to an American desire for suburban spaces and the less restrictive automobile. St. Louis' population peaked at 856,000 in 1950; now it is at its lowest level since the late 19th century—318,416 in 2013, an 8% decrease from 2000. In recent years, downtown St. Louis has been spruced up: A new Busch Stadium opened in 2006 with a panoramic view of the Arch and downtown, part of more than $4.5 billion that has been spent on a variety of projects since 1999. In 2008, local icon Anheuser-Busch was taken over by Belgium-based InBev, raising fears locally that the famed headquarters could move out of St. Louis. The corporate offices and factory operations have remained, but employment has dropped by more than 20%.

About 10 miles up Interstate 70 from the Arch is the suburb of Ferguson, which became a center of riots and heated discussion of police practices following the shooting death in August 2014 of Michael Brown, an unarmed 18-year-old, by police officer Darren Wilson. A short time earlier, Brown and a friend had been videotaped in a local convenience store, apparently stealing cigars. The next day, the county police chief said that Brown had assaulted Wilson. Like other parts of St. Louis County, Ferguson (pop. 21,111) has a majority-black population, 67% in this case. But the minority white population had managed to keep control of the local government and the police department. As the details of Brown's death spread, there were growing protests and then riots in the streets of Ferguson, with police using tear gas and arresting dozens of persons. A week after the incident, Gov. Jay Nixon ordered a state of emergency and a curfew in Ferguson, then deployed the National Guard. A fragile calm eventually was restored until November, when the county prosecutor announced that a grand jury had decided not to indict Wilson, which resulted in additional protests.

News accounts described how several municipalities in St. Louis County, including Ferguson, had profited from poverty and from police and court actions that resulted from often petty offenses, which added to the economic and social dislocation. In a March 2015 report requested by President Barack Obama, a panel of outside experts working with the Justice Department concluded that there was persistent racial bias by Ferguson authorities, who had created a system of using arrest warrants to raise large sums for the operation of the city. Many of those officials in Ferguson resigned, and voters replaced two white members of the city council with African Americans, though more activist candidates were defeated. The protests, of course, created additional financial and social costs in Ferguson, St. Louis County and the metropolitan area.

The 1st District takes in all of St. Louis, plus 43% of the people in suburban St. Louis County. It includes all of the predominantly African-American suburbs north of the city, including Ferguson, plus Bellefontaine Neighbors, Spanish Lake and Black Jack. It also includes working-class St. Ann, part of Bridgeton and, west of the city, the affluent suburb of University City, which has a significant Jewish population. The district no longer has an outright black majority. African Americans are a 48.8% plurality, but they still account for far more than half the votes in Democratic primaries. Whites make up 44% of the district's population. It is heavily Democratic, although the party organization has been weakened by the loss of patronage and by state approval of term limits. Obama twice got 80% of the vote in this district.

2012 Presidential Vote		
Barack Obama (D) 280,194	(80%)
Mitt Romney (R)...................66,286	(19%)
2008 Presidential Vote		
Barack Obama (D) 308,944	(80%)
John McCain (R)...................71,776	(19%)
Cook Partisan Voting Index: D+28		

William Lacy Clay (D)

Democrat William Lacy Clay was first elected in 2000 to the seat that his father, Bill Clay, held for 32 years. In recent years, he has faced serious race-based conflicts in his district and in his political life.

Born in St. Louis, Clay, who goes by "Lacy," moved to the Washington area at age 12 after his father's election to the House. He attended public schools in suburban Silver Spring, Maryland and then the University of Maryland, studying by night for seven years while he worked as a House staffer by day. He had started law classes at Howard University when he returned to St. Louis for a special election to the state House in 1983. Party leaders appointed him the Democratic nominee. Eight years later, party leaders again chose him to run in a special election for a safely Democratic state Senate seat.

In 1999, his father announced that he would retire from Congress, after helping to enact many labor and education laws. Clay wanted to take his father's place, but he had a serious primary contest. St. Louis Councilman Charlie Dooley, an African American with a base of support in the mostly white suburbs of St. Louis County, raised nearly $400,000. Dooley said that the office should not be "inherited," and he attacked what he called Clay's old-style tactics of political threats and bossism. The St. Louis Labor Council and Missouri AFL-CIO, long allied with Bill Clay, declined to endorse his son, but more than 30 locals did. The candidate played up his father's name and revved up the still reliable machine. He won the primary 61%-28% over Dooley, winning St. Louis City 76%-12% and the county, where twice as many votes were cast, 49%-39%. In the general election, Clay won 75%-22%, and has won reelection since then by comparable margins.

In the House, Clay has had a mostly liberal voting record. He is a member of the House Democrats' whip organization, and is active in the Congressional Black Caucus, where his father had been a founding member. He can show his partisanship, as he did in 2012 when he denounced a House Republican vote to hold Attorney General Eric Holder in contempt of Congress as a "disgraceful political witch hunt." But Clay is usually low-key and can be diplomatic in resolving differences among other lawmakers. "He's a peacemaker," fellow Missouri Democratic Rep. Emanuel Cleaver told the *St. Louis Post-Dispatch*. "He has just the right personality to take the temperature up, or bring it down." Clay also can be a deal-maker. He agreed to support Nancy Pelosi over Steny Hoyer for Democratic whip in 2001 only after securing a promise of $5 million to clean up contaminants at an Army plant in his district.

Clay has worked to protect voting rights for blacks and is the main proponent of creating a national Civil Rights Trail, with markers linking important sites in the civil-rights movement, including those in St. Louis. He succeeded in pushing the Census Bureau in 2010 to stop automatically counting prison inmates—many of them urban African Americans and Latinos—as residents of the rural, mainly white communities that host prisons.

On the Financial Services Committee, Clay in 2011 became ranking Democrat on the Domestic Monetary Policy and Technology Subcommittee. With frequent absences by Chairman Ron Paul of Texas, who was campaigning for the 2012 Republican nomination for president, the panel accomplished little. In 2015, Clay became the ranking Democrat on the Financial Institutions and Consumer Credit Subcommittee. He was a leading advocate for continuing the authority of the Export-Import Bank, which supported $339 million in exports from his district, Clay said.

Nothing raised Clay's profile like the riots that followed the police shooting of an unarmed black man in Ferguson, a city in his district, in August 2014. He criticized police for a "heavy-handed" approach to peaceful demonstrations and said that law enforcement organizations needed more diversity in their ranks. He called on the federal government to take over the investigation into the shooting, which he called a "murder," saying in a radio interview: "I have absolutely no confidence in the Ferguson police, the county prosecutor. I know we won't get a fair shake there." Clay defended Missouri Gov. Jay Nixon for his handling of the emergency, and said on Twitter that Nixon was trying to protect civil rights and public safety. In May 2015, he filed legislation that called for more "sensitivity training" for local police, and threatened the loss of federal law-enforcement funds to cities that don't require independent investigations when police use deadly force. He also sought reforms in the police use of military equipment.

After Missouri lost a seat in the 2010 reapportionment, Republicans in Missouri eliminated the neighboring district of Democratic Rep. Russ Carnahan. He decided to challenge Clay, a move that was partly in retribution for Clay's tacit support of the GOP-engineered map. The newly drawn 1st District included 70% of Clay's old district and just 30% of Carnahan's.

Race became an issue in the campaign. Clay ran a radio ad featuring representatives of two prominent black churches urging listeners to stand behind "leaders like Lacy Clay and President Obama." The *Post-Dispatch* endorsed Carnahan, saying that Clay "has coasted on the organization that his father and predecessor built but without being as deeply and continuously involved in local issues as Bill Clay was." Clay won the primary overwhelmingly, 63%-34%. Reflecting the demographic shifts in the area, Clay ran more strongly in St. Louis County, where he got 66% of the vote, than in the city, where he had 60%. He has been easily reelected since.

SECOND DISTRICT

Ann Wagner (R)

Elected 2012, 2nd term; b. Sept. 13, 1962, St. Louis; U. of MO, B.S. 1984; Catholic; married (Raymond); 3 children.

Professional Career: Mgr., Hallmark Cards; Mgr. Ralston Purina; MO dir., George H. W. Bush reelection campaign, 1992; Chair, MO Republican Party, 1999-2005; Co-chair, Republican Natl. Committee, 2001-05; U.S. ambassador to Luxembourg, 2005-09; Chairwoman, Roy Blunt for Senate campaign, 2009-10.

DC Office: 435 CHOB, 20515, 202-225-1621; Website: wagner.house. gov.

State Offices: Ballwin, 636-779-5449.

Committees: *Financial Services:* Capital Markets and Government Sponsored Enterprises; Oversight & Investigations.

Group Ratings

	ADA	ACLU	AFL-CIO	LCV	ITI	COC	HAFA	ACU	CFG	FRC
2014	0%	0%	–	3%	100%	93%	57%	64%	49%	100%
2013	0%	C	15%	4%	C	85%	C	88%	71%	C

National Journal Ratings

	2013 LIB	—	2013 CONS
Economic	12%	—	87%
Social	0%	—	87%
Foreign	0%	—	95%
Composite	7%	—	93%

Key Votes of the 113th Congress

1. Sandy storm spending	N	5. Medical Marijuana	N	9. Syrian Rebels Training	Y
2. Violence Against Women Act	N	6. Farm Bill	Y	10. Keystone pipeline	Y
3. Guantanamo Bay	N	7. Afghanistan Combat	N	11. Immigration Exec. Action	Y
4. Abortion 20-week ban	Y	8. NSA Phone Data Collection	N	12. Bipartisan budget deal	Y

Election Results

2014 general	Ann Wagner (R)	148,191	(64%)	$1,165,959	$2,830
	Arthur Lieber (D)	75,384	(33%)	$56,306	
	Bill Slantz (Lib)	7,542	(3%)		
2014 primary	Ann Wagner (R)	unopposed			

Prior winning percentage: 2012 (60%)

Population		Race and Ethnicity		Income	
Total:	768,428	White	88.1%	Median income:	$72,888
Urban:	3.1%	Asian	3.9%		*(54 of 435)*
Suburban:	96.7%	Black	3.8%	Under $50,000	32.3%
Rural:	0.2%	Latino	2.4%	$50,000-$99,999:	32.5%
Land area:	603	Two races	1.6%	$100,000-$199,999:	26.1%
Pop/sq. mi.:	1,274.7	White Ethnic	34.5%	$200,000 or more:	9.1%
Born in state:	66.1%			Poverty Rate	5.9%
		Education			
Age Groups		H.S. grad or less:	24.4%	**Work**	
Under 18:	22.7%	Some college:	26.9%	White collar:	48.8%
18 to 34:	19.1%	College degree, 4 yr.:	30.0%	Blue collar:	38.5%
35 to 64:	41.3%	Post-grad study:	18.7%	Sales and service:	12.7%
Over 64:	16.9%			Govt. workers:	8.0%
		Military			
		Veterans/active duty:	8.4%		

St. Louis Suburbs

Just as the geographic center of the U.S. population has moved west from St. Louis to rural Texas County, so has the center of metropolitan St. Louis moved farther west from the Gateway Arch on the Mississippi River. Now the midpoint is suburban St. Louis County, established in 1876 when the

Voter Turnout	
2013 Total Citizen 18+	576,196
2014 House Turnout	231,117
2014 Turnout as % CVAP	40.1%
2012 Turnout as % CVAP	73.1%

city, tired of paying for dusty back roads, separated itself from the sticks. That year, there were 350,000 people in the city and 31,000 in the county. In 2014, there were 317,000 in the city and 1 million in St. Louis County. The area's office center is also fast moving out along the Daniel Boone Expressway (U.S. 40) to Chesterfield. Near the city-county border is Grant's Farm, where Ulysses S. Grant lived in the 1850s and where Anheuser-Busch bred the Budweiser Clydesdales.

The 2nd Congressional District of Missouri consists of central and western St. Louis County, part of St. Charles County across the Missouri River, and a small sliver of Jefferson County to the south. Along the expressway, in the center of St. Louis County, are long-settled suburbs: Kirkwood; most of high-income Town and Country and Ladue; Chesterfield, where Monsanto in 2010 acquired a sprawling research center from Pfizer and unveiled plans in 2013 for an expanded campus and a total of more than 5,000 jobs; and Sunset Hills. Chesterfield has the most expensive housing in the area, and upscale shopping. Ballwin is a growing center for immigrants with biotech and health care jobs. More than three-fourths of the population is in St. Louis County, which has had a big increase in racial minorities.

They are all Republican areas, more so in the newer family-oriented subdivisions than in the leafy precincts of the older enclaves. Fast-growing St. Charles County, where the supply of available land and affordable hous-

2012 Presidential Vote		
Mitt Romney (R)................235,374	(57%)	
Barack Obama (D) 170,786	(42%)	
2008 Presidential Vote		
John McCain (R).................225,408	(53%)	
Barack Obama (D) 199,105	(47%)	
Cook Partisan Voting Index: R+8		

ing is tight, now has more people and casts more votes than the city of St. Louis and is the most Republican suburban county in Missouri. From 2000 to 2010, it gained nearly 27,000 jobs, even as the number of jobs in St. Louis city dropped by 14%. This conservative district voted for Mitt Romney in 2012, 57%-42%, a four-point bump from John McCain's performance in 2008.

Ann Wagner (R)

A former Republican National Committee co-chair and fundraiser, Ann Wagner captured Missouri's 2nd District seat in 2012 by overpowering her opponents financially and with her political expertise. She quickly became a favorite of GOP leaders, and seemed to have a bright future.

Wagner grew up in the St. Louis suburbs, where her father ran a carpet store and her grandfather owned a paint business. At an all-girls Catholic school, she acted in musicals, playing the female roles at all-boys' schools. "Of all the things formative in my life," Wagner told *National Journal*, "I would go back to the music." She said she learned confidence, connecting with others, and conquering vulnerability—all useful political traits. Her father wanted to see his daughter get a business degree. She graduated with one from the University of Missouri, then went to work for Hallmark Cards and Ralston Purina. Her involvement in politics began in 1989 when her husband, Raymond, took a job with John Ashcroft, then governor of Missouri. She oversaw Missouri's redistricting after the 1990 census, and ran the Missouri campaign for President George H.W. Bush's failed reelection bid in 1992.

In 1999, Wagner became chairman of the Missouri GOP, just as the state was evolving from blue to red. In the 2002 elections, both chambers of the General Assembly went Republican for the first time in 54 years. She became a member of the RNC in 2001. President George W. Bush in 2005 named her ambassador to Luxembourg, and for four years she rotated her family between Missouri and the tiny European nation.

It wasn't until 2012—with two of her children out of the house, the third a high school senior, and a Democratic administration that she charged was "mortgaging" her children's future—that she decided it was time to run for office. After GOP Rep. Todd Akin announced his bid for the Senate, she jumped into the contest for his seat, quickly raising money, with substantial contributions coming from employees of St. Louis-based Enterprise Rent-A-Car, where her husband is an executive. Some Republicans accused Enterprise of essentially buying her the seat, but her campaign said the donations merely reflected the employees' trust in her.

Initially, Wagner seemed likely to have a fight on her hands. But Republican Ed Martin, who had unsuccessfully challenged Democratic Rep. Russ Carnahan in 2010, dropped out of the race. And Carnahan, whose district was eliminated in redistricting, decided to challenge fellow Democrat William Lacy Clay rather than run against Wagner. That left Democrat Glenn Koenen, a former food pantry executive director, who faced insurmountable odds. When Akin made his now-infamous comment that "legitimate rape" does not cause pregnancy, Missouri Republicans speculated about Wagner switching places with Akin and running for the Senate. But after Akin apologized for his remark, Wagner said she was committed to her own race. Wagner won, 60%-37%. She spent $2.5 million, compared to a paltry $60,000 by Koenen.

In the House, Wagner had one of the most conservative voting records. She became one of four House members from Missouri to serve on the Financial Services Committee, where they tend to their home state's large financial community. She filed a bill that would delay so-called "fiduciary standards," dealing with financial advisers, which were mandated by the 2010 Dodd-Frank banking law. She complained that the proposed rules would adversely affect access for low-income groups. Wagner worked with Democrats, including Rep. Debbie Wasserman Schultz, on the rights of victims of sexual assault. In May 2015, the House passed her bill to prevent advertisements that might be used for sexual trafficking.

Wagner also found roles within the House GOP. She was chosen leader of the freshman class, and played a prime role in the recruitment of candidates by the National Republican Congressional Committee. When Rep. Steve Scalise of Louisiana became whip in June 2014, he selected Wagner as one of five senior deputy whips. She had become politically close to Scalise since her 2012 campaign, when he subbed at a campaign appearance for her on the day after her father died. Wagner's diverse and extensive activities suggested that she had her own leadership ambitions.

At home, her 2014 victory performance increased to 64%-33% against lightly financed Democrat Arthur Lieber.

THIRD DISTRICT

Blaine Luetkemeyer (R)

Elected 2008, 4th term; b. May 7, 1952, Jefferson City; Lincoln U., B.A. 1974; Catholic; married (Jackie); 3 children.

Elected Office: MO House, 1999-2005.

Professional Career: Bank examiner, State of MO, 1974-76; Loan officer, Bank of St. Elizabeth, 1978-2008; Pres., Luetkemeyer Ins. Agency, 1978-2008; Dir., MO div. of tourism, 2007-08.

DC Office: 2440 RHOB, 20515, 202-225-2956; Fax: 202-225-5712; Website: luetkemeyer.house.gov.

State Offices: Jefferson City, 573-635-7232; Washington, 636-239-2276; Wentzville, 636-327-7055.

Committees: *Financial Services:* Financial Institutions & Consumer Credit; Housing & Insurance (Chmn). *Small Business* (VChmn): Agriculture, Energy & Trade; Health & Technology.

Group Ratings

	ADA	ACLU	AFL-CIO	LCV	ITI	COC	HAFA	ACU	CFG	FRC
2014	0%	0%	–	6%	100%	93%	53%	68%	52%	88%
2013	0%	C	15%	4%	C	77%	C	80%	69%	C

National Journal Ratings

	2013 LIB	—	2013 CONS
Economic	23%	—	76%
Social	0%	—	87%
Foreign	5%	—	86%
Composite	13%	—	87%

Key Votes of the 113th Congress

1. Sandy storm spending	N	5. Medical Marijuana	Y	9. Syrian Rebels Training Y
2. Violence Against Women Act	N	6. Farm Bill	Y	10. Keystone pipeline Y
3. Guantanamo Bay Detainees	N	7. Afghanistan Combat	N	11. Immigration Exec. Action Y
4. Abortion 20-week ban	Y	8. NSA Phone Data Collection	N	12. Bipartisan budget deal Y

Election Results

2014 general	Blaine Luetkemeyer (R)............ 130,940	(68%)	$800,888
	Courtney Denton (D).................. 52,021	(27%)	
	Steven Hedrick (Lib) 8,593	(5%)	
2014 primary	Blaine Luetkemeyer (R) 71,030	(80%)	
	John Morris (R)............................. 9,786	(11%)	
	Leonard Steinman (R).................. 8,580	(10%)	

Prior winning percentages: 2012 (63%), 2010 (77%), 2008 (50%)

Population		Race and Ethnicity		Income	
Total:	760,643	White	91.6%	Median income:	$53,371
Urban:	13.7%	Black	3.2%		*(182 of 435)*
Suburban:	58.1%	Latino	2.3%	Under $50,000	45.6%
Rural:	28.2%	Asian	0.9%	$50,000-$99,999:	34.7%
Land area:	6,026	Two races	1.6%	$100,000-$199,999:	17.1%
Pop/sq. mi.:	126.2	White Ethnic	26.8%	$200,000 or more:	2.6%
Born in state:	74.4%			Poverty Rate	11.2%
		Education			
Age Groups		H.S. grad or less:	44.4%	**Work**	
Under 18:	24.2%	Some college:	32.1%	White collar:	33.4%
18 to 34:	21.8%	College degree, 4 yr.:	16.3%	Blue collar:	42.5%
35 to 64:	39.9%	Post-grad study:	7.2%	Sales and service:	24.2%
Over 64:	14.1%				
		Military		Govt. workers:	11.9%
		Veterans/active duty:	9.8%		

East-central Missouri: St. Louis area

Missouri was the first state settled west of the Mississippi, and the folks who settled it were a picture of pioneer diversity. Virginians and other Southerners made their way to counties north of the Missouri River, while Germans settled around the small capital, Jefferson City. A taste of that diver-

Voter Turnout	
2013 Total Citizen 18+	568,224
2014 House Turnout	191,620
2014 Turnout as % CVAP	33.7%
2012 Turnout as % CVAP	62.4%

sity can be found in the Capitol, with its mural by Thomas Hart Benton, great-grandnephew of one of Missouri's first senators, who championed hard money and westward expansion for 30 years and lost his seat for opposing the expansion of slavery. The painting depicts dance hall girls, black coal miners, and a mother diapering an infant. In the small town of Washington, Meerschaum Co. remains the largest and oldest manufacturer of corn cob pipes in the world, having been in business since 1869.

The 3rd Congressional District covers central Missouri, stretching from Jefferson City to the western St. Louis exurbs of St. Charles and Jefferson counties, and extends like a claw both north and south of St. Louis County and city. Its population base is in the western parts of fast-growing St. Charles County. In early 2015, General Motors added a third shift and 750 employees, making a total 3,350 workers at its Wentzville plant, 40 miles west of St. Louis, where it produces the Chevy Express and GMC Savana vans, plus the new GMC Canyon midsize pickup. The GM expansion, which has been a boon to parts suppliers, was a welcome contrast to the recent closing of Ford and Chrysler plants in the area.

The economic growth in these exurbs has been noted as a sharp distinction from beleaguered St. Louis city and riot-scarred Ferguson. In December 2014, the National Association for the Advancement of Colored People took a 135-mile "Journey for Justice" walk from Ferguson to Jefferson City. Social reality also has hit St. Charles County. In 2014, local groups sponsored their first Gay

2012 Presidential Vote		
Mitt Romney (R)................218,926	(62%)
Barack Obama (D) 127,104	(36%)
2008 Presidential Vote		
John McCain (R)................205,593	(56%)
Barack Obama (D) 157,284	(43%)
Cook Partisan Voting Index: R+13		

Pride event, and a former Protestant minister pleaded guilty to spending church money on himself.

The district includes Fulton, home of Westminster College, where former Prime Minister Winston Churchill, accompanied by President Harry Truman, told the world in 1946: "From Stettin in the Baltic to Trieste in the Adriatic, an iron curtain has descended across the continent." The district is solidly Republican, with every county voting for Mitt Romney in the 2012 presidential race. Jefferson County backed Barack Obama in the 2008 election with 50% of the vote, but Romney won it by a 13-point margin in 2012.

Blaine Luetkemeyer (R)

Republican Blaine Luetkemeyer, first elected in 2008, has a firm political grip on a large swath of suburban and rural Missouri and has been mentioned as a possible candidate for statewide office. He once worked in the banking business and has been a conservative protector of the industry on the Financial Services Committee.

Luetkemeyer has Missouri roots that stretch back five generations. He grew up in St. Elizabeth, where his father worked as an insurance agent and then owned a bank. Luetkemeyer was a star high school baseball player, but his Major League tryouts were unsuccessful. He graduated from Lincoln University, a historically black college in Jefferson City, with a degree in political science. He and his wife settled on his great-grandfather's farm in St. Elizabeth. In addition to farming, he joined his family's banking operations and founded the Luetkemeyer Insurance Agency.

Luetkemeyer was elected in 1999 to the state House of Representatives, where he developed a reputation as a thoughtful legislator. He campaigned for Missouri treasurer in 2004 but lost in the Republican primary. In 2007, Luetkemeyer was appointed director of the Missouri Division of Tourism.

A year later, a House seat opened when Republican Rep. Kenny Hulshof ran unsuccessfully for governor. Luetkemeyer entered a five-way GOP primary and was the Republican favorite. The conservative anti-tax group Club for Growth endorsed GOP state Rep. Bob Onder, but Luetkemeyer gained a critical endorsement from Missouri Right to Life. Luetkemeyer trounced the competition with 40% of the vote.

In the general election, he faced state Rep. Judy Baker, a health care consultant from Columbia. Republicans did not think Baker's liberal message would play well in the district's conservative-leaning rural counties. Luetkemeyer ran as a social conservative opposed to abortion rights and same-sex marriage. He emphasized his farming background to the district's largely rural constituency. He raised $2.8 million, two-thirds of it his own money; Baker raised $1.7 million. In the election, Baker carried populous Boone County (Columbia), but Luetkemeyer prevailed in the rural counties and those west of St. Louis. In a Democratic year, he won 50%-47.5%.

In the House, Luetkemeyer joined the Tea Party Caucus and established himself as a devout social and fiscal conservative. He successfully amended a House-passed bill in February 2011 to bar the United States from contributing to the United Nation's Intergovernmental Panel on Climate Change, which he said engaged in "dubious science." Earlier, he told a tea party rally that most of conservative cable provocateur Glenn Beck's controversial assertions "must be true, because nobody's refuting" them. He dismissed President Barack Obama's economic stimulus as a "large-scale failure," but the liberal think tank Center for American Progress noted that he later called "critical" a grant from the program to Frankford and joined Missouri lawmakers in requesting $100 million in stimulus money for a road project.

Luetkemeyer introduced a bill in February 2012 barring the Health and Human Services Department from forcing organizations to provide contraceptive and sterilization coverage in violation of their religious beliefs. He blasted HHS six months later when it put a rule to the contrary into effect. "It is a sad day when our government completely disrespects Americans' religious freedoms and conscience rights," he said.

On the Financial Services Committee, he and Democratic Rep. David Scott of Georgia enacted a bill in 2012 eliminating the physical fee-warning notices on automatic-teller machines in favor of having them displayed on-screen. Luetkemeyer won House approval in April 2015 of his bill with Democratic Rep. Brad Sherman of California that eliminates the requirement that banks mail customers annual privacy notices even if their privacy policies have not changed. He organized conservative support for the reauthorization of the Export-Import Bank, which some on the right opposed as unnecessary government intervention. Earlier, he scorned the Democrats' Dodd-Frank Wall Street reform bill as detrimental to small banks, writing in a *Washington Times* op-ed, "People on Main Street understand that community banks did not cause the financial crisis and that they already carry daunting regulatory burdens."

In 2015, he became chairman of the Financial Services Subcommittee on Housing and Insurance. Following a February hearing with Housing and Urban Development Secretary Julian Castro, Luetkemeyer said HUD "suffers from not only misguided policy but also mismanagement." He was especially unhappy with the inadequate funding of the mutual mortgage insurance fund, which he said might require another bailout. In May, the committee approved his bill to reduce regulation of advisers of Small Business Investment Companies. He has sought repeatedly to end the Justice Department's Operation Choke Point, which is designed to attack consumer fraud but allegedly has terminated many legitimate banking accounts.

Luetkemeyer has breezed to reelection every two years. Redistricting in 2011 removed the liberal college town of Columbia and made his district more Republican, even though a Democratic district outside St. Louis also was eliminated. He kept the door open when Republicans encouraged him to run for governor in 2016.

FOURTH DISTRICT

Vicky Hartzler (R)

Elected 2010, 3rd term; b. Oct. 13, 1960, Archie; U. of MO, B.S. 1983; U. of Central MO, M.S. 1992; Christian; married (Lowell); 1 child.

Elected Office: MO House, 1995-2001.

Professional Career: Teacher, 1983-94; Spokeswoman, Coalition to Protect Marriage, 2004; Appointee, MO Women's Cncl., 2005-10; Owner, Hartzler Equipment Co.

DC Office: 2235 LHOB, 20515, 202-225-2876; Fax: 202-225-0148; Website: hartzler.house.gov.

State Offices: Columbia, 573-442-9311; Harrisonville, 816-884-3411; Lebanon, 417-532-5582.

Committees: *Agriculture:* Livestock & Foreign Agriculture; Nutrition. *Armed Services:* Oversight & Investigations (Chmn); Readiness; Seapower & Projection Forces. *Budget.*

Group Ratings

	ADA	ACLU	AFL-CIO	LCV	ITI	COC	HAFA	ACU	CFG	FRC
2014	0%	0%	–	0%	80%	93%	60%	68%	50%	100%
2013	0%	C	14%	4%	C	77%	C	72%	64%	C

National Journal Ratings

	2013 LIB	—	2013 CONS
Economic	21%	—	77%
Social	0%	—	87%
Foreign	34%	—	60%
Composite	22%	—	78%

Key Votes of the 113th Congress

1. Sandy storm spending	N	5. Medical Marijuana	NV	9. Syrian Rebels Training	Y
2. Violence Against Women Act	N	6. Farm Bill	Y	10. Keystone pipeline	Y
3. Guantanamo Bay Detainees	N	7. Afghanistan Combat	N	11. Immigration Exec. Action	Y
4. Abortion 20-week ban	Y	8. NSA Phone Data Collection	N	12. Bipartisan budget deal	Y

Election Results

2014 general	Vicky Hartzler (R)	120,014	(68%)	$707,937	$12,499
	Nate Irvin (D)	46,464	(26%)		
	Herschel Young (Lib)	9,793	(6%)		
2014 primary	Vicky Hartzler (R)	65,404	(75%)		
	John Webb (R)	22,131	(25%)		

Prior winning percentages: 2012 (60%), 2010 (50%)

Population		Race and Ethnicity		Income	
Total:	756,407	White	87.9%	Median income:	$43,857
Urban:	14.8%	Black	4.9%		*(335 of 435)*
Suburban:	14.6%	Latino	3.3%	Under $50,000	55.6%
Rural:	70.6%	Asian	1.3%	$50,000-$99,999:	30.6%
Land area:	14,908	Two races	2.1%	$100,000-$199,999:	11.6%
Pop/sq. mi.:	50.7	White Ethnic	22.3%	$200,000 or more:	2.2%
Born in state:	62.1%			Poverty Rate	19.6%
		Education			
Age Groups		H.S. grad or less:	46.3%	**Work**	
Under 18:	22.6%	Some college:	30.4%	White collar:	34.3%
18 to 34:	25.7%	College degree, 4 yr.:	14.3%	Blue collar:	41.7%
35 to 64:	36.6%	Post-grad study:	9.0%	Sales and service:	24.0%
Over 64:	15.1%				
		Military		Govt. workers:	18.5%
		Veterans/active duty:	13.6%		

West-central Missouri: Columbia

Roughly equidistant from St. Louis and Kansas City, Columbia in central Missouri has emerged as an economic hub in its own right. Nicknamed the Athens of Missouri, Columbia is now the fifth-largest city in the state, with a population that jumped 34% from 2000 to 2013. With a nearly 35,000-person student body, the University of Missouri is the biggest employer in the city and helped the town survive the recession. Columbia's 2.9% unemployment rate at the end of 2014 was far below the national average. A number of graduates stay in the city to work in the health care and insurance industries. It ranked ninth on *Forbes'* 2012 "Best Small Places for Businesses and Careers" list. But Columbia has limited air transportation; the one-gate Columbia Regional Airport flies only four round-trips a day, American Airlines flights to Chicago and Dallas.

Voter Turnout	
2013 Total Citizen 18+	572,509
2014 House Turnout	176,286
2014 Turnout as % CVAP	30.8%
2012 Turnout as % CVAP	57.8%

The 4th Congressional District occupies Columbia and rural west central Missouri. Columbia's Boone County was one of just four counties in the state to support President Barack Obama in 2012, but did so narrowly, 50-47%. South of Kansas City, the district includes fast-growing Belton and Raymore in Cass County, which have tended to vote Democratic.

But much of the rest of the district is Republican, and the district overall is safe. The southern portion, near Springfield, is predominately Republican. (President Harry S Truman was born in Barton County

2012 Presidential Vote		
Mitt Romney (R)	201,702	(61%)
Barack Obama (D)	119,932	(36%)

2008 Presidential Vote		
John McCain (R)	197,384	(57%)
Barack Obama (D)	146,233	(42%)

Cook Partisan Voting Index: R+13

and lived in Independence, a few miles from Blue Springs. He spent much of Election Night 1948, when just about everyone thought he would lose, in Excelsior Springs.) There are two big military bases here: Fort Leonard Wood in Pulaski County, where Marines, sailors, and airmen train in joint exercises with Army troops; and Whiteman Air Force Base, near Knob Noster in Johnson County, from which B-2 bombers flew to drop precision-targeted bombs in Afghanistan. In July 2014, the Air Force announced plans to upgrade its B-2 fleet. The Missouri State Fair in Sedalia got unusual attention in August 2013, when a rodeo clown mocked President Barack Obama. Many in the news media criticized the alleged slight to the president, and officials of both parties said that the incident was inappropriate. But conservative talk-radio hosts dismissed the critics as thin-skinned.

Vicky Hartzler (R)

Republican Vicky Hartzler was elected in 2010 when she defeated Democrat Ike Skelton, the powerful chairman of the Armed Services Committee. A former activist who led the movement to ban same-sex marriage in Missouri, she has been an energetic social and fiscal conservative.

Hartzler has spent her entire life in rural Cass County, where she grew up working alongside her parents and sister on the family farm. Faith was a cornerstone of the household. "As farmers, we prayed for rain, and when it rained too much, we relied on prayer to hope that we had a crop that year," she told *National Journal*. In high school, she excelled in athletics, captained the girls' volleyball and basketball teams, and was a member of the track team. She was also editor of the school yearbook and president of the Future Homemakers of America. After getting her bachelor's degree in education, she went to work as a high school home economics teacher. She remained in the classroom for 11 years. The trajectory of her career changed in 1994 when Hartzler got a phone call from a friend while she was grading papers, urging her to run for state representative. "He asked me to think about it and pray about it, and I did," she said. "After 30 days, I knew I was supposed to run."

Hartzler served three terms in Missouri's House and counts overhauling Missouri's outdated adoption statutes among her proudest accomplishments. In 2000, she decided not to run for reelection after her daughter, Tiffany, was born. Hartzler and her husband, Lowell, live on a 1,600-acre farm outside of Harrisonville, where they raise corn, soybeans and cattle and run the Hartzler Equipment Co., which sells farming equipment.

In 2004, Hartzler headed the Coalition to Protect Marriage in Missouri, a campaign to add an amendment to the state's constitution banning same-sex marriage. Despite being outspent 17-to-1 by opposition groups, the amendment passed with 71% of the vote. The liberal magazine *Mother Jones* headlined an article about her in October 2010, "Is Vicky Hartzler the Most Anti-Gay Candidate in America?" She wrote the book *Running God's Way: Step by Step to a Successful Political Campaign*, a detailed guide for Christian candidates.

Hartzler's bid to unseat Skelton in 2010 drew tea party interest. In the conservative district, Skelton had relied on crossover GOP voters in the past. But in an election year that went from bad to worse for Democrats, Hartzler's message resonated. She assailed Skelton on his votes with "the liberal leadership" for the $787 billion economic stimulus bill and an energy bill imposing caps on carbon emissions. "I don't have a 'To Do list,' I have an 'Undo list," she said. "We have to undo all these destructive policies." Hartzler tried to turn Skelton's image as a wise legislative elder into a negative, saying in her stump speech, "So many people in Washington [are] removed from rural America. Ike's lost touch." Skelton raised $3 million and outspent Hartzler 3-to-1. Hartzler prevailed, 50%-45%.

In the House, Republican leaders made good on their promise to give Hartzler a seat on Armed Services so she could continue Skelton's stewardship of the district's military bases. She added a provision to the House's fiscal 2012 defense bill defining marriage as a union between a man and a woman for the purpose of military benefits and policy. The provision was dropped in conference with the Senate. She introduced a bill preventing military veterans convicted of sexual abuse of children from being buried in Arlington National Cemetery. In 2015, she took over as chairwoman of the Oversight and Investigations Subcommittee at Armed Services, and pledged to ensure accountability by the Pentagon. In the annual defense spending bill, the House in May 2015 approved her provision for construction at Whiteman Air Force Base of a Consolidated Stealth Operations and Nuclear Alert Facility. She also took credit for approval of 12 additional F/A-18F Super Hornet aircraft, which she said would be built in Missouri.

After supporting Budget Committee Chairman Paul Ryan's budget-cutting efforts, Hartzler got a seat on the committee in 2013. She was among the Republicans who opposed the New Year's Day 2013 bipartisan deal aimed at averting the so-called "fiscal cliff." During debate on the budget in 2011, she invoked the phrase "absolute power corrupts absolutely" in comparing President Barack Obama to a tyrant. In 2015, with most Republicans, she supported the annual budget resolution. But she urged Congress to take further action to end the budget "sequestration" that makes automatic cuts in Defense Department spending, which threatened "impending devastation to our military," she warned. For defense hawks like Hartzler, the tight-budget demands of fiscal hawks can be objectionable.

Hartzler was forced to absorb Democratic-leaning Columbia in her district after the 2011 redistricting, which was done to make other Republican districts safer. But she was compensated with more of her home base in Cass County, and the 4th remained solidly conservative. She has not been seriously challenged for reelection. For the first time, she won Boone County in her 2014 contest.

FIFTH DISTRICT

Emanuel Cleaver (D)

Elected 2004, 6th term; b. Oct. 26, 1944, Waxahachie, TX; Prairie View A&M U., B.S. 1968, St. Paul Schl. of Theology, M.Div. 1974; Methodist; married (Dianne); 4 children.

Elected Office: Kansas City Cncl., 1979-91; Mayor, Kansas City, 1991-99.

Professional Career: Pastor, 1970-present; Radio talk-show host, 2002-04.

DC Office: 2335 RHOB, 20515, 202-225-4535; Fax: 202-225-4403; Website: cleaver.house.gov.

State Offices: Higginsville, 660-584-7373; Independence, 816-833-4545; Kansas City, 816-842-4545.

Committees: *Financial Services:* Housing & Insurance (RMM); Oversight & Investigations.

Group Ratings

	ADA	ACLU	AFL-CIO	LCV	ITI	COC	HAFA	ACU	CFG	FRC
2014	80%	77%	–	80%	80%	67%	5%	0%	0%	0%
2013	85%	C	100%	68%	C	38%	C	18%	14%	C

National Journal Ratings

	2013 LIB	—	2013 CONS
Economic	89%	—	11%
Social	68%	—	32%
Foreign	69%	—	29%
Composite	76%	—	24%

Key Votes of the 113th Congress

1. Sandy storm spending	NV	5. Medical Marijuana	NV	9. Syrian Rebels Training	N
2. Violence Against Women Act	Y	6. Farm Bill	N	10. Keystone pipeline	N
3. Guantanamo Bay Detainees	Y	7. Afghanistan Combat	Y	11. Immigration Exec. Action	N
4. Abortion 20-week ban	N	8. NSA Phone Data Collection	Y	12. Bipartisan budget deal	Y

Election Results

2014 general	Emanuel Cleaver (D)..................	79,256	(52%)	$1,015,923
	Jacob Turk (R)............................	69,071	(45%)	$142,593
	Rpy Welborn (Lib)........................	5,308	(4%)	
2014 primary	Emanuel Cleaver (D)	44,296	(82%)	
	Mark Memoly (D)..........................	2,988	(6%)	
	Charles Lindsey(D).......................	2,687	(5%)	

Prior winning percentages: 2012 (61%), 2010 (53%), 2008 (64%), 2006 (64%), 2004 (55%)

Population		Race and Ethnicity		Income	
Total:	758,911	White	65.2%	Median income:	$44,496
Urban:	55.1%	Black	21.1%		*(328 of 435)*
Suburban:	35.5%	Latino	8.7%	Under $50,000	54.7%
Rural:	9.4%	Asian	1.7%	$50,000-$99,999:	30.7%
Land area:	2,760	Two races	2.6%	$100,000-$199,999:	12.6%
Pop/sq. mi.:	274.9	White Ethnic	19.8%	$200,000 or more:	2.0%
Born in state:	61.1%			Poverty Rate	18.0%
		Education			
Age Groups		H.S. grad or less:	43.1%	Work	
Under 18:	23.3%	Some college:	31.6%	White collar:	32.6%
18 to 34:	24.3%	College degree, 4 yr.:	16.0%	Blue collar:	46.0%
35 to 64:	38.5%	Post-grad study:	9.3%	Sales and service:	21.4%
Over 64:	14.0%				
		Military		Govt. workers:	11.6%
		Veterans/active duty:	8.6%		

Kansas City Metro

Kansas City, named after a state it isn't in and a river it doesn't touch, is the center of one of America's largest metro areas, the biggest on the central Great Plains. The first settlers here started little towns on the bluffs above the Missouri River—Independence, Kansas City, Westport—that

Voter Turnout	
2013 Total Citizen 18+	558,330
2014 House Turnout	153,635
2014 Turnout as % CVAP	27.5%
2012 Turnout as % CVAP	60.5%

coalesced a few decades later. Here, traders on the Santa Fe Trail set out to cross the Sand Hills of Kansas to reach Mexican territory, and pioneers headed for Oregon and California. Kansas City was a rail center and, in the 1920s, had one of the largest stockyards in the country, a major commercial center with lean skyscrapers, and the Country Club Plaza, the first shopping center in America. Harry Truman grew up on a farm now in the suburb of Grandview and lived in his wife's family's house in Independence, the old county seat just to the east. The city is famous for its National Negro Leagues Baseball Museum, its historic jazz district that has been home to musicians like Scott Joplin, Charlie Parker and Count Basie, and for its much-praised barbecue. As part of redevelopment activity downtown, a new Kauffman Center for the Performing Arts opened in 2011. About 20,000 people now live downtown, most of them millennials.

Overall, Kansas City fared better than most cities during the recession. It was bolstered in part by the designation of a 150-block area as a Green Impact Zone in 2009. The idea was to use federal economic stimulus money and other public funds on infrastructure, along with other strategies, to transform the urban core into a national model of sustainable living. A two-mile downtown streetcar is scheduled to start service in early 2016. The initiative has had some success, but also has drawn criticism from conservatives who contend its benefits do not translate on a wide scale. In February 2014, *Time* magazine asked what had been the impact. "Less than folks had hoped," wrote David von Drehle. The stimulus program "pumped money into the Green Impact Zone as fast as local agencies could push it out the door—more than $1 million per city block on average. Perhaps this prevented things from getting worse. But it's not the transformation that was touted." Some development has been encouraging. As the launch city for Google Fiber, Kansas City had moved "to the front of the line in the innovation economy," the *Kansas City Star* reported in March 2015. The Green Impact Zone quietly closed its office in early 2014.

The 5th Congressional District of Missouri includes most of Kansas City, the largest city in Missouri, plus Grandview and the bulk of Independence. Most of the Kansas City area's landmarks, including the Truman home, are here, but much of the metropolitan area's growth has been across the state line in Kansas. More than 20% of the district's residents are African-American,

2012 Presidential Vote		
Barack Obama (D)	198,356	(59%)
Mitt Romney (R)	132,632	(39%)

2008 Presidential Vote		
Barack Obama (D)	228,766	(62%)
John McCain (R)	134,365	(37%)

Cook Partisan Voting Index: D+9

the second highest percentage among Missouri districts. Politically, the seat leans strongly Democratic, giving President Barack Obama 59% of the vote in 2012.

Emanuel Cleaver (D)

Democrat Emanuel Cleaver, first elected in 2004, is an ordained minister who is known for his leadership of the Congressional Black Caucus as well as his efforts to improve civility to Congress. "I am convinced, irreversibly, that the lack of civility is causing most of the problems we have in our government," he said in 2011.

Cleaver grew up in Waxahachie Texas, in a three-room shack with no plumbing or electricity. He graduated from Prairie View A&M University, moved to Kansas City and earned a divinity degree, and then became pastor of St. James United Methodist Church. He was elected to the city council in 1979 and as mayor in 1991. In city hall, s Cleaver voiced support for the Clinton administration's changes in welfare policy, which he described as "corrective surgery." He backed expansion of downtown's Bartle Hall Convention Center and supported renovation of the deteriorating Liberty Memorial, the country's largest World War I memorial. After leaving office, he hosted a radio talk show.

In December 2003, Democratic Rep. Karen McCarthy announced that she would not run for reelection, and Cleaver was widely expected to succeed her. His road to Congress was tougher than expected. In the primary, he faced former National Security Council aide Jamie Metzl, who raised substantial funds. Metzl hammered Cleaver on ethics issues, questioning the propriety of a loan that Cleaver took out to purchase a car wash and his failure to pay $36,000 in back taxes on the business. Cleaver won the primary by 60%-40%.

In the general election, Cleaver faced Republican businesswoman Jeanne Patterson, who had $3 million of her own money to spend. Like Metzl, she made an issue of Cleaver's ethics, emphasizing bribery and fraud convictions of his allies, though there was no evidence that he was involved in any crimes. He said that Patterson was politically inexperienced and was trying to buy the seat. Cleaver won 55%-42%.

In the House, Cleaver's voting record initially was near the center of the Democrats, but it has moved leftward in recent years, particularly on economic matters. Despite his religious background, he disdains injecting religion into politics. In his first term, he was one of 22 members, all Democrats, who opposed a Republican House-passed resolution expressing support for Christmas that he dismissed as a sop to social conservatives. He opposed the 2011 deal to raise the federal debt limit, describing it to an audience back home as a "sugar-coated Satan sandwich" that would cost jobs and hurt the poor. He later advocated means-testing of Medicare as part of a deficit reduction deal, calling it far preferable to across-the-board cuts. He has sponsored bills to promote financial literacy and to make it easier for students to vote. Speaker Nancy Pelosi designated Cleaver to act as a liaison with mayors and faith communities on those issues.

He proposed changing House rules to require members to lease energy efficient vehicles in their districts. "The public would rather see a sermon than hear one," said Cleaver, whose own taxpayer-leased car ran on used cooking grease. (He drew criticism in 2009 when it was revealed that the car's $2,900 monthly cost was higher than that of any other House member.) His idea to create a Green Impact Zone in Kansas City became a reality in 2009.

On the Financial Services Committee, Cleaver initially opposed the creation of the Troubled Assets Relief Program to bail out the financial industry, but backed a revised version in the face of constituents' anger. As ranking member of the Housing and Insurance Subcommittee in 2015, he pledged to work for affordable housing.

Cleaver chaired the Black Caucus in 2011-12 at a time when members often expressed dissatisfaction with President Barack Obama for failing to do more to help low-income minorities. Cleaver, who had backed Hillary Clinton over Obama for the 2008 nomination, tried to walk a fine line between joining in the criticism and working to ensure the reelection of the nation's first black president. "With 14% [black] unemployment, if we had a white president, we'd be marching around the White House. ... The president knows we are going to act in deference to him in a way we wouldn't to someone white," he told *The Root* in September 2012. He led a Black Caucus job creation initiative featuring public events in several cities that caucus members said led to as many as 2,000 people getting work. He called for dismissal of ethics charges against two Black Caucus members—Democrats Maxine Waters of California and Charles Rangel of New York—and questioned why blacks were predominately the targets of ethics investigations.

Cleaver periodically has remained in the spotlight on issues involving race. When Republican Sen. Rand Paul of Kentucky said in January 2014 that extending unemployment benefits discouraged people from looking for work, Cleaver told MSNBC that he was writing a song for Paul modeled after James Brown's "Say It Loud, I'm Black and Proud":

"Say it loud, I'm stingy and I'm stuck." And when then-House Budget Committee Chairman Paul Ryan of Wisconsin made comments about poverty in March 2014 that some African-American lawmakers said were highly offensive, Cleaver said Ryan ended up in "a mouth trap" because of his lack of experience with inner-city issues. After the August 2014 fatal police shooting of an unarmed black teenager in Fergusond Missouri touched off riots there, he defended Obama's decision not to visit the city, even as he told MSNBC that it "resembles Fallujah" because of the militarized law-enforcement presence, which he called "un-American." Cleaver filed a bill in March 2015 to make it a civil rights violation for police to set criminal or traffic violations for the purpose of raising local revenue, and he urged passage of police reform legislation.

Cleaver has tried, with varying success, not to come across as an angry partisan. He and West Virginia Republican Shelley Moore Capito in 2011 resurrected their idea for a "Civility Caucus," and Cleaver issued regular pronouncements to colleagues stressing the importance of collegiality. "Bees cannot sting and make honey at the same time; they have to make a choice," he said. He made an impassioned plea for togetherness in a speech at the 2012 Democratic National Convention, bringing attendees to their feet and drawing positive reviews. "There is more power in unity than division," he said.

Questions about his car wash have continued to hound him. Bank of America sued him and his wife in 2012 over outstanding debt, late fees and interest costs for a loan used to buy the business. The Small Business Administration guaranteed 75% of the loan, and local newspapers pointed out that if the Cleavers defaulted, taxpayers could be responsible. In February 2014, the Jackson County court clerk issued an order to withhold part of Cleaver's salary to repay more than $1.3 million that he and his wife owed the bank. News organizations have reported that he is one of the poorest members of Congress.

In the 2014 election, Cleaver faced Republican Jacob Turk for the fifth time, and led in campaign spending $1 million to $143,000. The outcome this time was their closest yet: a 52%-46% win for Cleaver. He won by nearly 3-to-1 in Kansas City, which cast about one-third of the vote. But Turk won each of the five counties in the district. Cleaver requires an increasingly strong turnout in Kansas City to keep his seat.

SIXTH DISTRICT

Sam Graves (R)

Elected 2000, 8th term; b. Nov. 7, 1963, Tarkio; U. of MO, B.S. 1986; Baptist; divorced; 3 children.

Elected Office: MO House, 1992-94; MO Senate, 1994-2000.

Professional Career: Farmer.

DC Office: 1415 LHOB, 20515, 202-225-7041; Fax: 202-225-8221; Website: graves.house.gov.

State Offices: Hannibal, 573-221-3400; Kansas City, 816-792-3976; St. Joseph, 816-749-0800.

Committees: *Armed Services:* Readiness; Tactical Air & Land Forces.*Transportation & Infrastructure:* Aviation; Highways & Transit (Chmn); Railroads, Pipelines & Hazardous Materials.

Group Ratings

	ADA	ACLU	AFL-CIO	LCV	ITI	COC	HAFA	ACU	CFG	FRC
2014	0%	0%	–	6%	100%	82%	60%	64%	56%	100%
2013	5%	C	19%	7%	C	85%	C	72%	71%	C

National Journal Ratings

	2013 LIB	—	2013 CONS
Economic	32%	—	67%
Social	0%	—	87%
Foreign	5%	—	86%
Composite	16%	—	84%

Key Votes of the 113th Congress

1. Sandy storm spending	N	5. Medical Marijuana	N	9. Syrian Rebels Training	Y
2. Violence Against Women Act	N	6. Farm Bill	Y	10. Keystone pipeline	Y
3. Guantanamo Bay Detainees	N	7. Afghanistan Combat	N	11. Immigration Exec. Action	Y
4. Abortion 20-week ban	Y	8. NSA Phone Data Collection	N	12. Bipartisan budget deal	Y

Election Results

2014 general	Sam Graves (R)	124,616	(67%)	$1,124,266
	Bill Hedge (D)	55,157	(30%)	$52,587
	Russ Monchil (Lib)	7,197	(4%)	
2014 primary	Sam Graves (R)	56,789	(77%)	
	Christopher Ryan (R)	8,745	(12%)	
	Kyle Reid (R)	4,598	(6%)	
	Brian Tharp (R)	4,244	(6%)	

Prior winning percentages: 2012 (65%), 2010 (69%), 2008 (59%), 2006 (62%), 2004 (64%), 2002 (63%), 2000 (51%)

Population		Race and Ethnicity		Income	
Total:	754,588	White	89.2%	Median income:	$51,219
Urban:	32.2%	Black	3.9%		*(215 of 435)*
Suburban:	23.3%	Latino	3.1%	Under $50,000	48.7%
Rural:	44.6%	Asian	1.2%	$50,000-$99,999:	32.3%
Land area:	14,810	Two races	1.9%	$100,000-$199,999:	16.5%
Pop/sq. mi.:	51.0	White Ethnic	22.4%	$200,000 or more:	2.5%
Born in state:	65.6%			Poverty Rate	13.3%
Age Groups		**Education**			
Under 18:	24.2%	H.S. grad or less:	45.1%	**Work**	
18 to 34:	21.9%	Some college:	29.1%	White collar:	33.7%
35 to 64:	39.0%	College degree, 4 yr.:	16.9%	Blue collar:	41.7%
Over 64:	14.9%	Post-grad study:	8.9%	Sales and service:	24.6%
		Military		Govt. workers:	13.4%
		Veterans/active duty:	9.9%		

Northern Missouri: Kansas City suburbs

The rolling fields along the Missouri River in northwest Missouri were settled in a rush in the late 19th century. These lands lost people for most of the 20th century as fewer hands were needed on farms. But increased efficiencies lately have led to resurgent production. In 1940, northern Missouri had one of

Voter Turnout	
2013 Total Citizen 18+	562,027
2014 House Turnout	186,970
2014 Turnout as % CVAP	33.3%
2012 Turnout as % CVAP	61.0%

the largest meatpacking operations in the world. In recent years, the business has expanded in St. Joseph and has drawn many Hispanics. Barge traffic on the Missouri reopened in late 2014, following an increase in water levels and record corn and soybean crops. Kansas City officials explored ways to extend rail service to the terminal. Twenty northern Missouri counties lost population in the past decade: Atchison County, in the northwest corner of the state, led the pack with a population decline of 12% from 2000 to 2010.

Little Dixie, the swath of Missouri along the Mississippi River, was settled by Southerners from Kentucky and Virginia. Its most famous native son is Mark Twain, born Samuel Langhorne Clemens in Hannibal, then as now a little town on bluffs overlooking the river. Hannibal was the thinly disguised St. Petersburg of Twain's classics, *The Adventures of Tom Sawyer* and *The Adventures of Huckleberry Finn*.

Hannibal is on the eastern edge of the 6th Congressional District, which takes in all or parts of 36 counties in northern Missouri, stretching more than 200 miles from Illinois to Nebraska. On the western edge is the river town of St. Joseph, which was the starting point for the Pony Express and its roughly 10-day transport of mail to Sacramento. St. Joseph is the biggest city north of Kansas City. In 2008, Rock Port in the northwest corner became the first town in the country to get all of its energy from wind power. Some farmers in northern

Missouri have objected that transmission lines for wind power interfere with their crops or reduce property values.

The 6th also takes in the Kansas City suburbs of Clay and Platte and a sliver of eastern Jackson County. That area casts about half of the district's vote. The historic political tradition here was mostly Democratic, but it has been tempered by dislike for national Democrats' cultural liberalism. The rural vote here, as across the nation, has moved solidly Republican. Barack Obama lost all the counties north of Kansas City except for Buchanan in 2008. The Kansas City suburb of Clay County traditionally has been a reliable national bellwether, but it's swinging the GOP's way, too: Democrat Al Gore won in 2000 by one vote, but Republican Mitt Romney carried Clay by nine percentage points in 2012, and the overall district, 60%-38%.

Sam Graves (R)

Republican Sam Graves, first elected in 2000, took over in 2015 as chairman of the influential Highways and Transit Subcommittee. He previously headed the Small Business Committee, which gave him a platform for battling Democrats over curbing federal regulations on business.

Graves is a lifelong resident of Tarkio in the northwest corner of the state. An Eagle Scout, he regularly played "Taps" on his bugle at local cemeteries, a practice he has continued in his district each Memorial Day. He graduated from the University of Missouri with a degree in agronomy, farmed with his father and brother, and joined the Farm Bureau. He ran for the state House in 1992 and beat a longtime Democratic incumbent. Two years later, he was elected to the state Senate. He attracted attention in 1998 with a five-hour filibuster against a school desegregation bill that he said put rural areas at a disadvantage, but the bill eventually passed.

Graves got his opportunity to run for the House when Democratic Rep. Pat Danner withdrew from her race for reelection just minutes before the filing deadline. Not by accident, the immediate favorite to succeed her was her son, state Sen. Steve Danner, also a Democrat. Graves entered the race within the short window provided by state law and drew support from national Republicans. Teresa Loar, a moderate Republican on the Kansas City Council, attacked Graves as the darling of extremist party leaders, but Graves beat her in the primary, 68%-17%.

In the general election, Danner billed himself as a conservative Democrat and switched from being pro-abortion rights to opposing abortion. In an editorial endorsing Graves, *The Kansas City Star* said that Danner's campaign switch on abortion showed that he "engaged in raw opportunism at the slightest opportunity." Graves won 51%-47%.

In the House, Graves has been a rock-solid fiscal conservative but has deviated on some social issues. He was one of just nine Republicans to vote in March 2011 against reinstituting a school voucher program for District of Columbia students. He was one of 54 to oppose barring the use of funds to administer the Davis-Bacon Act, which requires prevailing union wages on federal projects. But he remained a hard-liner on immigration. He amended a fiscal 2013 spending bill to effectively stop the Obama administration's family unity waiver system, which allows illegal immigrants who are married to U.S. citizens to remain with their spouses while their green-card status is reviewed. His measure died in the Democratic-controlled Senate.

On the Small Business Committee, he was a regular critic of the Obama administration's initiatives. He held hearings on the Environmental Protection Agency's failure to comply with a law requiring agencies to analyze the effects of regulations on small entities and to consider less burdensome alternatives. In July 2014, he filed a bill to stop all new regulations by the EPA. He has opposed an effort to make more businesses eligible for a tax credit under the 2010 health care law; the credit was designed to help businesses afford health insurance for their workers. Graves worked with Democrats to pass a series of bills in 2012 aimed at fixing small business contracting problems. In a December 2014 retrospective on his chairmanship, he told the Associated Press that he had made the committee "relevant," and forced the administration to analyze the burdens that regulations placed on small business. More changes are needed in federal contracting to encourage small businesses, he added.

With his new focus on transportation programs, he said that a long-term solution is needed for funding shortfalls in the highway trust funds. He has doubted that an increase in the gasoline tax would receive much support. Instead, he has backed a proposal to take a few billion dollars annually in royalties from new oil and gas exploration on public lands. Graves believes that public-private partnerships for new highways are worth exploring, but he objects to toll roads. An experienced private pilot, he co-chairs the House's General Aviation Caucus and contends that government needs to better understand the impact of its aircraft regulations. His work on highway issues could position Graves to seek the chairmanship of the parent Transportation and Infrastructure Committee.

On local issues, Graves has sought to compel the Army Corps of Engineers to emphasize flood control on the Missouri River, telling the *St. Joseph News-Press* that the agency's focus on environmental recovery over levee operations and maintenance was "out of whack." In 2005, the House passed his amendment to the transportation bill to preempt state laws governing liability for damages involving rental cars, a measure of interest to St. Louis-based Enterprise Rent-A-Car.

Graves was the subject of an ethics investigation for allegedly violating House rules for his role in arranging testimony before his committee by a family friend. The matter touched off a rare public squabble between the new Office of Congressional Ethics and the House Ethics Committee. OCE recommended that the case be investigated further, but the Ethics Committee found deficiencies in the office's handling of the matter and voted unanimously in October 2009 to clear Graves.

In 2008, national Democrats were excited when former Kansas City Mayor and St. Joseph native Kay Barnes announced she would challenge Graves. But Graves attacked Barnes for "San Francisco values" and supporting "a homosexual agenda" because her picture had appeared in a gay magazine; he won, 59%-37%. His recent victory margins have exceeded 2-to-1.

SEVENTH DISTRICT

Billy Long (R)

Elected 2010, 3rd term; b. Aug. 11, 1955, Springfield; U. of MO, attended; Presbyterian; married (Barbara); 2 children.

Professional Career: Talk show host, 1999-2006; Realtor, 1978-2010; Owner, Billy Long Auctions.

DC Office: 1541 LHOB, 20515, 202-225-6536; Fax: 202-225-5604; Website: long.house.gov.

State Offices: Joplin, 417-781-1041; Springfield, 417-889-1800.

Committees: *Energy & Commerce:* Communications & Technology; Energy & Power; Health.

Group Ratings

	ADA	ACLU	AFL-CIO	LCV	ITI	COC	HAFA	ACU	CFG	FRC
2014	0%	0%	–	0%	100%	93%	70%	88%	66%	100%
2013	0%	C	14%	4%	C	85%	C	88%	81%	C

National Journal Ratings

	2013 LIB	—	2013 CONS
Economic	18%	—	80%
Social	0%	—	87%
Foreign	5%	—	86%
Composite	12%	—	88%

Key Votes of the 113th Congress

1. Sandy storm spending	N	5. Medical Marijuana	N	9. Syrian Rebels Training	Y
2. Violence Against Women Act	N	6. Farm Bill	Y	10. Keystone pipeline	Y
3. Guantanamo Bay Detainees	N	7. Afghanistan Combat	N	11. Immigration Exec. Action	Y
4. Abortion 20-week ban	Y	8. NSA Phone Data Collection	N	12. Bipartisan budget deal	N

Election Results

2014 general	Billy Long (R)............................	104,054	(64%)	$952,827	$4,736
	Jim Evans (D)	47,282	(29%)	$78,335	
	Kevin Craig (Lib)	12,584	(8%)		
2014 primary	Billy Long (R).............................	55,505	(62%)		
	Marshall Works (R).....................	33,498	(38%)		

Prior winning percentages: 2012 (64%), 2010 (63%)

Population		Race and Ethnicity		Income	
Total:	759,566	White	89.7%	Median income:	$40,364
Urban:	39.2%	Latino	4.2%		*(387 of 435)*
Suburban:	24.7%	Black	1.6%	Under $50,000	60.2%
Rural:	36.1%	Asian	1.0%	$50,000-$99,999:	27.8%
Land area:	7,641	Two races	2.7%	$100,000-$199,999:	10.0%
Pop/sq. mi.:	99.4	White Ethnic	22.1%	$200,000 or more:	1.9%
Born in state:	57.3%			Poverty Rate	17.9%
		Education			
Age Groups		H.S. grad or less:	45.7%	**Work**	
Under 18:	23.1%	Some college:	31.6%	White collar:	31.2%
18 to 34:	23.8%	College degree, 4 yr.:	14.6%	Blue collar:	45.2%
35 to 64:	37.1%	Post-grad study:	8.1%	Sales and service:	23.6%
Over 64:	16.0%				
		Military		Govt. workers:	11.7%
		Veterans/active duty:	10.3%		

Western Ozarks: Springfield, Joplin

One of the biggest tourist destinations in America today is Branson Missouri something almost no one would have predicted 30 years ago. Branson has only 11,000 year-round residents, but it thrives thanks to the surging popularity of country and western music. It has more than 50 theaters and

Voter Turnout	
2013 Total Citizen 18+	571,869
2014 House Turnout	163,957
2014 Turnout as % CVAP	28.7%
2012 Turnout as % CVAP	57.6%

60,000 seats—more than Broadway and equaling Las Vegas—and has become a hub for nonstop, low-cost entertainment, attracting 8 million visitors a year. As *The Kansas City Star* put it, each attraction is "more church-loving, more family-friendly, more country than the next."

Nearby are fishing, boating and plenty of shopping. These diversions have made southwest Missouri the fastest-growing part of the state in the past 20 years, generating new businesses and attracting retirees as well as vacationers. Branson even got its own privately financed small airport in 2009, a new concept in the United States but more familiar elsewhere; some scheduled service is available. City officials voted approval in 2014 of a master plan for their Spirit of 76 upgrade of much of the commercial center, with investment by many businesses in the area and the prospect of more tourist attractions on the strip.

Springfield is the biggest city in southwest Missouri and the self-styled "buckle of the Bible Belt." It is home to more than 200 churches, including the headquarters of the Assemblies of God, one of the nation's largest and fastest-growing Protestant denominations. In April 2015, 51 percent of voters agreed in a referendum to repeal the city's prohibitions on LGBT discrimination. Advocates of the anti-discrimination provisions said they would seek action by the state. Southwest Missouri is also dairy country and home to a grow-

ing poultry industry; the state ranks fourth in the nation for turkey production. Latinos have been moving into McDonald County to work in chicken-processing plants; roughly 1,000 of the 1,600 employees at the Tyson Foods chicken plant in Noel are minorities. In a town of fewer than 2,000 residents that had been known as the "Canoe Capital of the Ozarks," the influx has diversified Noel,

2012 Presidential Vote		
Mitt Romney (R).................	220,146	(68%)
Barack Obama (D)	98,889	(30%)

2008 Presidential Vote		
John McCain (R).................	216,157	(63%)
Barack Obama (D)	121,048	(35%)

Cook Partisan Voting Index: R+19

including its cultural and dining opportunities, but housing and social services remain scarce.

In Jasper County, the city of Joplin (pop. 50,150) has been almost completely rebuilt following a devastating May 2011 tornado that killed 158 people and heavily damaged or destroyed 2,000 buildings, including a hospital and schools. By 2014, more businesses were operating locally than before the disaster.

The 7th Congressional District of Missouri includes Branson and Springfield. This area has been Republican territory since 1861, when it opposed secession. Pro-union Springfield changed hands several times as Missouri staged its own civil war. Its conservative response to the big-spending government of the 1960s and cultural liberalism of the 1970s reinforced its allegiance to the GOP, and now it is the most Republican part of Missouri. In 2012, Mitt Romney won all of the counties here, many by 2-to-1 margins.

Billy Long (R)

Republican Billy Long, elected in 2010, succeeded Roy Blunt when he was elected to the Senate. Long couldn't differ more stylistically from the polished Blunt. His orientation is tea party and rural rather than K Street, and his campaign motto was an anti-Beltway "Fed Up!" He has displayed an occasional willingness to forge alliances with Democrats.

Long grew up in Springfield, where he developed an interest in Republican politics at an early age. When he was 9 years old, he told the *Springfield News-Leader,* he would ride his bike to pass out bumper stickers for a Greene County sheriff's candidate who was the brother of a family friend. A few years later, he taught his dog a trick: He would ask, "Little Bear, would you rather be a Democrat or a dead dog?" The family pet responded by flopping over and sticking his feet in the air. While still a teenager, Long was given responsibility, along with his sister, for running his family's miniature golf course. After briefly attending the University of Missouri to study business, he became interested in real estate and attended auction school, eventually starting a company that would conduct as many as 200 auctions a year. He moved into radio in 1999, spending six years as a morning-drive talk show host for an AM station covering southwest Missouri.

When Blunt sought the Senate seat, Long ran as a plain-talking conservative who would clamp down on federal spending and set Congress straight. He billed his lack of experience in elected office as a plus. "We have enough political experience in Washington, D.C., to choke a horse," he told the Associated Press. "That's exactly the problem." He prevailed in the GOP primary over seven other candidates, including two veteran state senators, with more than 37% of the vote.

In the fall, Long's Democratic opponent was former gubernatorial aide Scott Eckersley, who sought to make an issue of racist remarks that Long was accused of making at a bar that featured strippers and illegal gambling tables—a claim that Long dismissed as a "flat-out lie." Long campaigned in support of a constitutional amendment to limit the federal government's taxation powers and for repeal of the Democrats' health care law. He said he would oppose all earmarks on spending bills. He wore a cowboy hat and inveighed against "elitist politicians." In this Republican bastion, Long won 63%-30%.

In the House, Long made good on his promise to try to change Washington's ways. He voted against several spending resolutions and for a conservative budget alternative with deeper cuts than the version by Budget Committee Chairman Paul Ryan. A Long bill that attracted widespread support, but did not move, called for ensuring that the Environmental Protection Agency does not impose regulations intended for hazardous-waste cleanups on livestock operations. He adamantly opposed President Barack Obama's January 2013 proposals intended to reduce gun violence, including limiting the sale of ammunition clips to those holding 10 rounds or fewer. "If you're lying in bed at 4 in the morning and four people kick your door in, would you like to be restricted to five shots or six shots?" he asked the *News-Leader*.

In 2013, GOP leaders gave Long a coveted seat on the Energy and Commerce Committee. In the 21st Century Cures bill, which the committee approved in May 2015, Long won bipartisan support for his amendment to improve information to consumers about new pharmaceuticals to treat illnesses. He generated conservative enthusiasm for his Taxpayer Transparency Act, which requires executive branch agencies to disclose when there are expenses in their advertising or promotional material. Similar disclosure requirements apply to congressional materials, such as newsletters.

Long's lack of polish showed at times. Not long after his arrival in Washington, he posed for a photo with Minority Leader Nancy Pelosi, a heretical act to conservatives. He drew widespread criticism in July 2011 for a tweet comparing the spending habits of Congress with singer Amy Winehouse, who died from drug and alcohol addictions. He later apologized for the comparison. But he won bipartisan praise for his role in the disaster response to the deadly Joplin tornado, working closely with the Obama administration to provide funding to the ravaged area. "It was a lot heaped onto a freshman," Missouri Democratic Rep. William Lacy Clay told the *News-Leader*. "But you could see him right before our eyes grow into the job and grow into his responsibility."

Some of Long's votes—such as supporting a raise in the federal debt limit and reauthorizing the Export-Import Bank—annoyed conservatives back home, and he drew a primary challenge in 2012. Republicans Mike Moon and Tom Stilson split the anti-Long vote, and the incumbent won easily with 60%. In a 2014 campaign ad, he spoke to the camera and said that he remained "fed up," especially with political ads. "I approve this message because I'm still fed up with Obama's agenda, and all these ads," he closed. He outspent Democratic challenger Jim Evans $953,000 to $78,000, and got his customary 64% of the vote.

EIGHTH DISTRICT

Jason Smith (R)

Elected 2013, 1st full term; b. June 16, 1980, St. Louis; U. of MO, B.S. 2001, OK City U. Schl. of Law, J.D. 2004; Pentecostal; single.

Elected Office: MO House, 2005-2013.

Professional Career: Farmer, practicing atty., 2004-2013.

DC Office: 1118 LHOB, 20515, 202-225-4404; Fax: 202-226-0326; Website: jasonsmith.house.gov.

State Offices: Cape Girardeau, 573-335-0101; Farmington, 573-756-9755; Rolla, 573-364-2455; West Plains, 417-255-1515.

Committees: *Ways & Means:* Human Resources; Oversight.

Group Ratings

	ADA	ACLU	AFL-CIO	LCV	ITI	COC	HAFA	ACU	CFG	FRC
2014	0%	0%	–	0%	100%	86%	67%	88%	72%	100%
2013	5%	C	20%	4%	C	78%	C	88%	82%	C

National Journal Ratings

	2013 LIB	—	2013 CONS
Economic	18%	—	82%
Social	0%	—	87%
Foreign	15%	—	85%
Composite	13%	—	87%

Key Votes of the 113th Congress

1. Guantanamo Bay Detainees	N	5. Afghanistan Combat	N	9. Immigration Exec. Action	Y
2. Abortion 20-week ban	Y	6. NSA Phone Data Collection	Y	10. Bipartisan budget deal	N
3. Medical Marijuana	N	7. Syrian Rebels Training	Y		
4. Farm Bill	Y	8. Keystone pipeline	Y		

Election Results

2014 general	Jason Smith (R)	106,124	(67%)	$1,589,517	$17,200
	Barbara Stocker (D)	38,721	(24%)	$181,810	
	Terry Hampton (I)	6,821	(4%)	$6,797	
	Doug Enyart (CNP)	3,799	(2%)	$34,271	
	Rick Vandeven (Lib)	3,759	(2%)		
2014 primary	Jason Smith (R)	unopposed			

Prior winning percentage: 2013 special election (67%)

Population		Race and Ethnicity		Income	
Total:	748,595	White	91.1%	Median income:	$37,617
Urban:	6.3%	Black	4.5%		*(405 of 435)*
Suburban:	12.4%	Latino	1.6%	Under $50,000	63.0%
Rural:	81.3%	Asian	0.5%	$50,000-$99,999:	27.7%
Land area:	20,296	Two races	1.8%	$100,000-$199,999:	8.3%
Pop/sq. mi.:	36.9	White Ethnic	20.8%	$200,000 or more:	1.1%
Born in state:	74.0%			Poverty Rate	20.2%
		Education			
Age Groups		H.S. grad or less:	57.5%	**Work**	
Under 18:	23.0%	Some college:	27.5%	White collar:	26.5%
18 to 34:	20.9%	College degree, 4 yr.:	9.2%	Blue collar:	42.6%
35 to 64:	39.1%	Post-grad study:	5.8%	Sales and service:	30.9%
Over 64:	17.0%				
		Military		Govt. workers:	15.2%
		Veterans/active duty:	10.6%		

Southeast Missouri

The southeast quadrant of Missouri is part river valley, part industrial mining, and part agriculture. For years, there has been a population outflow from the Missouri Bootheel, as machines replaced low-wage farm workers and crops shifted from cotton to rice, corn and soybeans. Dairy cattle,

Voter Turnout	
2013 Total Citizen 18+	570,408
2014 House Turnout	159,224
2014 Turnout as % CVAP	27.9%
2012 Turnout as % CVAP	53.5%

pigs, apples and berries, plus some timber, are among the area's other products. The area is also home to Missouri's Lead Belt, a mining region rich in ore minerals such as lead, zinc, copper, silver and cadmium. Reynolds and Iron counties alone produce about 70% of the nation's lead. Ste. Genevieve County has the nation's largest cement plant, which sparked a welcome mini-economic boom after it opened at a huge limestone quarry in 2009 and initially produced four million metric tons per year. An aluminum smelting plant in New Madrid has provided 900 jobs, but lower aluminum prices led Noranda Aluminum to cut 200 jobs and threaten a shutdown. The result in April 2015 was a 20% cut in its electricity bill. Doe Run Resources Corp., the largest lead producer in the country, closed its smelter in December 2013 following an agreement with Missouri and the Environmental Protection Agency, but continued to produce metal from recycled lead and to consider other options.

Carrying many of these industrial goods to market is the Mississippi River, which Mark Twain might not recognize today. The river is hidden behind levees, which ordinarily screen small towns and river roads from rows of barges tethered together, full of coal and corn and soybeans. The Mississippi today is an industrial waterway. But it was never really all that romantic. Twain's steamboats, as he was at pains to point out, were dangerous, noisy contraptions, forever blowing up or getting embedded in roots and branches in the river currents. This is one of the oldest settled parts of the United States. French pioneers founded such Missouri towns as Cape Girardeau in the late 1700s. The big growth here has been around the retail and medical hub of Cape Girardeau and along Interstate 44. The poverty rate in the Bootheel is the highest in the state. New Madrid has had some of the most powerful earthquakes in the nation; the most famous was in 1811-12.

The 8th District of Missouri covers the state's southeast corner, including rural Ste. Genevieve County, the site of Missouri's oldest permanent settlement, and also taking in southern Jefferson County. It includes Plato, the tiny Missouri village named the new population midpoint of the country based on 2010 census data. The district's political heritage is mixed. The Bootheel was once

2012 Presidential Vote		
Mitt Romney (R)	201,522	(66%)
Barack Obama (D)	97,982	(32%)
2008 Presidential Vote		
John McCain (R)	194,325	(60%)
Barack Obama (D)	124,383	(38%)
Cook Partisan Voting Index: R+17		

solidly Democratic, and some mining counties show traces of Democratic sentiment. Cape Girardeau is heavily Republican and the hometown of conservative commentator Rush Limbaugh. Once a safely Democratic district, it has been represented since 1980 by Republicans, and today the 8th is solidly in the GOP camp. President Barack Obama's vote in the district dropped from 38% in 2008 to 32% in 2008.

Jason Smith (R)

Republican Jason Smith won a special election in June 2013 to replace Republican Jo Ann Emerson, who had resigned to become president of the National Rural Electric Cooperative Association. Smith is a young, fervent advocate of limited government who is far more conservative than his predecessor. He moved quickly to show his influence.

Smith grew up as the son of a church pastor in Salem. Mo., and he still runs the family farm that his great-grandfather started. At the University of Missouri, he received degrees in agricultural economics and business administration. He earned his law degree from Oklahoma City University. After returning to run the family farm and practice law, he soon became alarmed by "the harm that the overbearing government was inflicting on Missourians and our economy," according to his campaign website. He won a seat in the state House in 2005 and rose to become majority whip and speaker pro tempore. In 2013, he sponsored a bill to amend the state constitution to protect farmers' rights, which he said was necessary to protect Missouri farmers from out-of-state animal rights groups and "environmental extremists." He also joined social conservatives on gun rights and abortion-related legislation.

A former co-chair of the House GOP's centrist Tuesday Group, Emerson had been elected to succeed her late husband Bill Emerson, served 16 years, and was a veteran of the Appropriations Committee and its Agriculture Subcommittee, where she fought to add money for food stamp programs. She and liberal Democratic Rep. Jim McGovern of Massachusetts once lived for a week on a $21 food budget to dramatize the plight of some of the program's recipients.

Smith, by contrast, ran a campaign that centered on his opposition to President Barack Obama's health care law and other issues of strong interest to the GOP's right-wing base. "Voters do not want Obamacare, they are tired of burdensome and costly regulations and they know our $16 trillion national debt is a ticking time bomb," Smith said. Contending that that they could win the special election, Democrats noted that their party's Sen. Claire McCaskill and Gov. Jay Nixon had come within hundreds of votes of taking the district on their way to getting reelected in November 2012, despite the drag Obama placed on the ticket in the state.

Steve Hodges, a state representative with pro-gun rights and anti-abortion views, won the Democratic nomination at a February convention on the sixth ballot over Lt. Gov. Peter Kinder, who could not overcome a string of controversial allegations involving his use of campaign funds and his connection with a stripper and former *Penthouse* Pet. Hodges sought to make an issue of Smith's missed state legislative votes during the special election campaign, and he tried to paint him as vulnerable over an unpopular state sales tax hike. But he got little help from national Democrats, and Smith countered with positive ads touting himself as a "common-sense conservative."

Smith raised just over $500,000, more than double what Hodges took in. Among his donors were banking and agricultural interests, including Emerson's rural electric group, which contributed $5,000. The result wasn't close. Smith won 67%-27%, and took all 30 counties except for two in the bootheel. In 2014, he took all of the counties and won his first full term in another landslide, 67%-24%, against Democrat Barbara Stocker.

At age 32 when he entered the House, Smith was its fifth-youngest member. He initially served on the Judiciary and Natural Resources committees. He sought to defend the interests of rural America: opposed to excessive regulations, in search of new markets for farmers and ranchers, and protecting his constituents' way of life. At a February 2014 hearing of the Natural Resources panel, Smith strongly objected to tentative plans by the National Park Service to restrict recreational use of the Ozarks National Scenic Riverways, and vowed to fight "tooth and nail" to resist any change. He filed the Searching for and Cutting Regulations that are Unnecessarily Burdensome (SCRUB) bill, which would create a nine-member presidential panel to review all federal regulations. The Judiciary Committee approved the measure in March 2015.

In January 2015, Smith took a step up the ladder of influence by getting a seat on the Ways and Means Committee. In a column that month for *The Hill*, he criticized the lack of clarity in the tax code, and said that Congress needed to move on tax reform, in part, "to provide our small-business owners, farmers and entrepreneurs with the assurances they need to grow the economy."

★ MONTANA ★

In April 1805, Meriwether Lewis, William Clark, and their pirogues wended up the Missouri River just past the Yellowstone River into what now is Montana. It was open country under a big sky—and most of it still is. To celebrate July 4, 1976, the historian Stephen E. Ambrose (who would retire to Helena and write the Lewis and Clark history *Undaunted Courage*) took his family to Lemhi Pass, where Lewis was the first U.S. citizen to cross the Continental Divide. Ambrose noted that the terrain was little changed from when Lewis and Clark passed through.

In recent years many have come to Montana, to see for themselves this vast expanse—buying up ranchlands and condominiums. Yet American civilization has only lightly encroached on Montana. It is still a land of great empty vistas, with mountains in the west and vast plateaus and plains in the east—the 4th largest state in area and the 44th in population. Eons ago, dinosaurs roamed, their remains scattered more densely and uncovered more frequently than in any other state. Almost nowhere is the wilderness out of sight. It has the Lower 48's largest population of grizzly bears and bison—the "department store of the plains" to the Native Americans who used every last part. Montana sits atop the spine of the continental United States, spanning the Rockies so that on Interstate 15 one can cross the Continental Divide three times. The first settlers here were itinerant trappers seeking fur and miners seeking gold, silver, and copper. They built ramshackle towns and in a few cases, gained sudden wealth, which made them kings not of their barren homestead but of the metropolises back East. Then came the workers who built and serviced the Northern Pacific and Great Northern railroads, followed by wheat farmers and ranchers.

Statehood arrived in 1889, less than a century after Lewis and Clark. The mining economy gave Montana a radical, class-warfare political tradition. On one side was the Anaconda Mining Co., which until 1959 owned five of Montana's six daily newspapers, the Montana Power Co., and many of the state's politicians. The company had strong allies in the Stockmen's Association and the Farm Bureau. On the other side were progressives like Sen. Thomas Walsh, who exposed the Teapot Dome scandal, and Sen. Burton Wheeler, a New Dealer who broke with President Franklin D. Roosevelt over court packing and isolationism. Allied with them were the labor unions (Montana has no right-to-work law and has been the most pro-union Rocky Mountain state) and pork-barrel beneficiaries (for a while in the 1930s, Montana received more federal money per capita than almost any other state). In 1912, Montana voters passed the Corrupt Practices Act to curb influence in elections, striking a major blow against the Copper Kings. The act stood for a century until plaintiffs cited the *Citizens United* decision in a successful U.S. Supreme Court challenge. But the impetus remained; in 2015, Gov. Steve Bullock signed a bipartisan law that requires "dark money" groups to disclose their spending in state races.

For years, the focus of the skirmishing was Butte, with its gold and copper mines on "The Richest Hill on Earth," with its gamblers, bootleggers, and millionaires; its company goons, union thugs, and IWW organizers. Butte and surrounding Silver Bow County had 60,000 people in 1920—the fourth highest in the Rocky Mountain states, behind only the counties containing Denver, Salt Lake City, and Phoenix—but only 33,000 in 2010. The mines are closed, their ore depleted; the stone temples of commerce are grim. Most spectacular is Butte's Berkeley Pit—a disused open copper mine more than a mile in diameter that's now filled with a toxic brew of contaminated groundwater.

As mines gradually closed after Butte's population peak in 1920, agriculture—wheat growing and cattle grazing—became the mainstay of Montana's economy. Class warfare died down. Other towns grew, although only Billings has ever topped 100,000. Other growth areas recently have been the university town of Missoula, Kalispell near Flathead Lake, the university and resort town of Bozeman, and the state capital of Helena. The lasting muscular tone of the state can be traced to the mountain men, miners, and cowboys who drove herds of Texas longhorns across the open range. And there is still the sense of space. Hunting and fishing opportunities abound; development in the small cities and resort areas has not been enough to drive the game away. Montana's libertarian streak persists: For a stretch in the 1990s, the state had no speed limit, and after one was reimposed by the courts, lawmakers raised it to 80 miles per hour in 2015, becoming only the fifth state with a limit that high. Montana has no state limits on texting while driving.

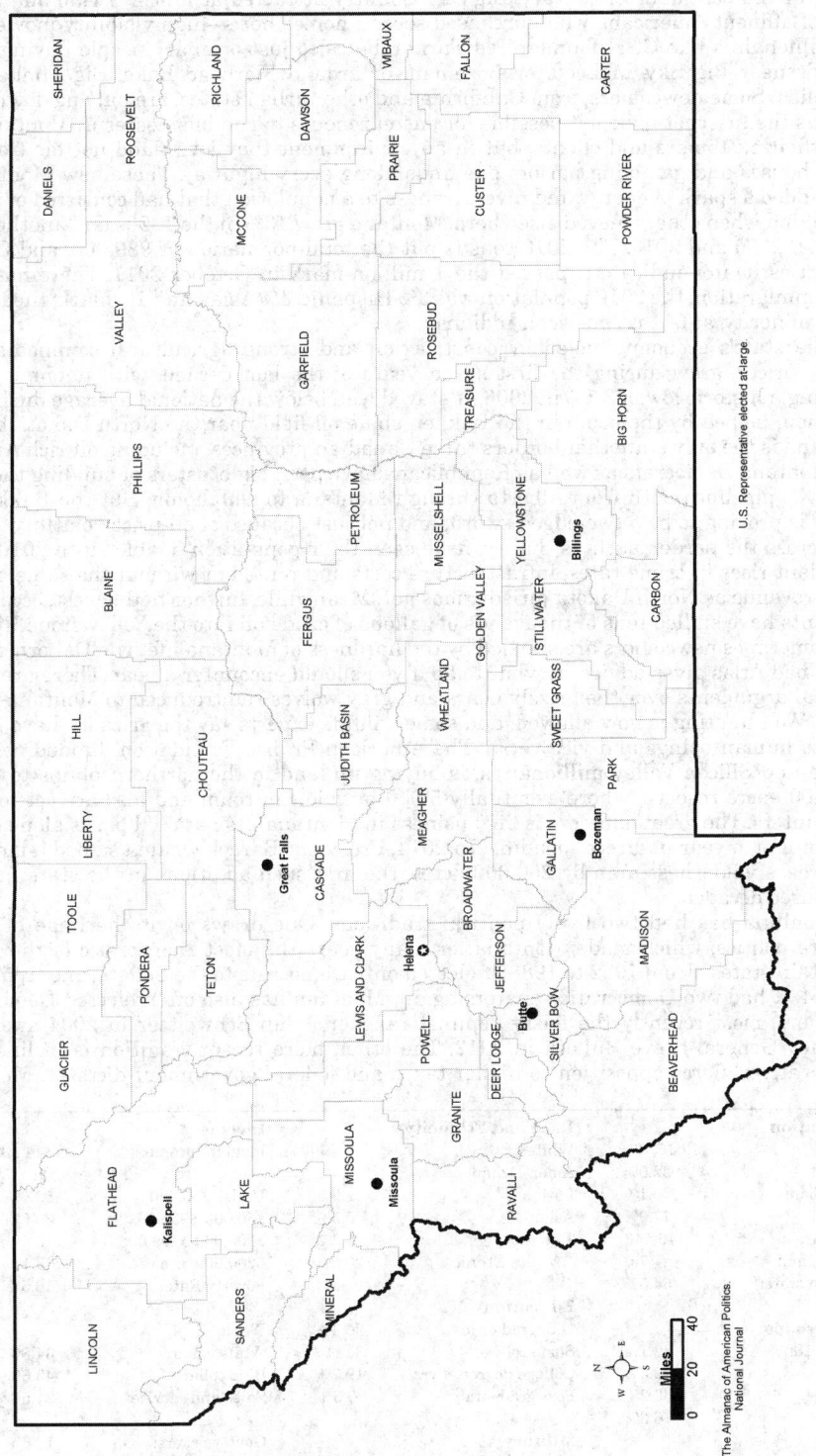

U.S. Representative elected at-large

The Almanac of American Politics
National Journal

Over the past quarter-century, Big Sky Country attracted at first a trickle and then a flood of affluent Americans who purchased second homes here—high-visibility movie stars and billionaires like CNN founder Ted Turner, but also just ordinary people buying small spreads near Big Sky, McLeod, or Bozeman, or around Flathead Lake, Big Timber, and Whitefish. Some newcomers, from California and other urban states, are putting down roots here, as the Internet makes it possible for entrepreneurs to run businesses in Montana, far from their customers and clients, but in an environment they love—and not far from the coffee houses and gambling parlors one finds along every highway. These new Montanans have added a spark of energy and inventiveness to a population that had consisted of people left behind when others moved elsewhere. Montana grew 13% in the 1990s and another 10% between 2000 and 2010. The 2010 census put the total population at 989,000, and Census Bureau estimates indicate it passed the 1 million-mark in October 2011. There has been little immigration; the 2010 population was 3% Hispanic, 1% Asian and 1% black; the largest racial minority, at 6%, is American Indians.

The state's economy, fueled by construction and strong agricultural commodity and energy prices, grew during the first seven years of the last decade, with unemployment reaching a historic low of 3.1% in 2006. It stayed well below the national average during the recession, helped by the boom in the Bakken shale oil field near the North Dakota border. Montana is the only state that borders three Canadian provinces, including oil-rich Alberta, and Montana Democrats as well as Republicans have been big boosters of building the Keystone XL pipeline south from Alberta through Montana to Oklahoma. But the Bakken oil frenzy is proving to be a two-edged sword, and not just because of oil-price volatility. Towns just across the border, such as Sidney, have seen their population double since 2010, with attendant rises in crime rates, infrastructure costs and rents but without the same gusher of tax revenue as North Dakota jurisdictions get. Meanwhile, further to the west, occasional accidents have spilled tens of thousands of gallons of crude oil into the Yellowstone River.

Sometimes newcomers are startled by the hardness of Montana life. The DeLorme Montana Road Atlas gives advice on what to do if you should encounter a bear. There are lively political arguments over the grizzly bears and gray wolves reintroduced to Montana in the 1990s. Wolf hunting is now allowed, and some wildlife experts say the grizzlies have gotten used to human beings and vice versa. The American Prairie Foundation, funded by Manhattan and Silicon Valley millionaires, is buying up land in the northern plains to create a 500,000-acre reserve, where eventually 5,000 buffalo can roam and also attract tourists and hunters. The great outdoors is big business in Montana: Its national parks alone create $400 million a year in direct spending. In 2014, President Barack Obama signed a measure to increase wilderness area by 250,000 acres, the first such additions in the state in more than three decades.

Montana has had two lively political traditions. One draws on its heritage of class-warfare politics, which made Montana for many years the most Democratic of the Rocky Mountain states. From 1952 to 1988, it elected only Democrats to the Senate, and from 2006 to 2014, it had two Democratic senators again. Montana has also often elected Democratic governors, most recently the feisty populist rancher Brian Schweitzer in 2004 and state Attorney General Steve Bullock in 2012. The other, more recent tradition is in line with conservatives' fierce opposition to higher taxes and federal government dictates. Montana

Population		Race and Ethnicity		Income	
Total:	1,015,165	White	87.4%	Median income:	$44,132
Urban:	22.9%	Amer. Indian	6.4%		(39 of 50)
Suburban:	0.1%	Latino	2.9%	Under $50,000	52.6%
Rural:	77.0%	Asian	0.5%	$50,000-$99,999:	30.6%
Land area:	145,546	Two races	2.2%	$100,000-$199,999:	13.6%
Pop/sq. mi.:	7.0	White Ethnic	26.6%	$200,000 or more:	3.1%
Born in state:	54.5%			Poverty Rate	16.5%
		Education			
Age Groups		H.S. grad or less:	36.4%	**Work**	
Under 18:	22.1%	Some college:	34.6%	White collar:	34.8%
18 to 34:	22.5%	College degree, 4 yr.:	19.7%	Blue collar:	43.6%
35 to 64:	39.2%	Post-grad study:	9.3%	Sales and service:	21.5%
Over 64:	16.3%			Govt. workers:	18.6%
		Military			
		Veterans/active duty:	10.6%		

has not elected a Democrat to the House since 1996, and Montana is usually a safe Republican state in presidential elections, although Bill Clinton carried it in 1992 and came close in 1996, and Barack Obama held John McCain to a 50%-47% margin in 2008. The Democratic tradition is strongest in the old mining towns like Butte and Anaconda, on Indian reservations, in old railroad towns like Great Falls and Havre, in university towns like Missoula and

Voter Turnout	
2013 Total Citizen 18+	783,143
2014 Highest Statewide Turnout	369,826
2014 Turnout as % CVAP	47.2%
2012 Turnout as % CVAP	62.2%
Legislature		
Senate:	29R	21D
House:	59R	41D

Bozeman, and in the state capital of Helena. The Republican tradition is strongest in the population-losing eastern plains counties (where a closely watched militia standoff occurred in 1996) and in fast-growing Flathead and Ravalli counties in the west.

Montana's senators have often had an impact in Washington far greater than the state's share of the national population, going back to the days of Walsh and Wheeler. Mike Mansfield, who was born to Irish immigrants in 1903 and became a Far Eastern history professor, was elected to the Senate in 1952. He rose to Senate majority leader in 1961 and held the job until his retirement in 1976, after which he was appointed ambassador to Japan by President Jimmy Carter. Max Baucus was scion of the family that owns the Sieben Ranch. He was elected to the House in 1974 at age 32 and to the Senate in 1978; in 2001, he became the ranking Democrat on the Senate Finance Committee and held that position or the chairmanship until his retirement in 2014. Montana lost its second House seat in the reapportionment following the 1990 census. Its population growth percentage in the 2000s was almost the same as the national average, but it still came up short in the reapportionment following the 2010 census. It continues to have just one at-large seat in the House, giving it the largest population of any House district in the country.

Presidential Politics Usually Montana, with its three electoral votes and remote location, doesn't see much of presidential candidates. But it was a close state in 1992, when Democrat Bill Clinton carried it by 3%, and in 1996, when he lost by 3%, and again in 2008. Montanans liked Republican John McCain's selection of Alaska Gov. Sarah Palin as his running mate, but after the financial crisis in mid-September, McCain's numbers fell, while the Obama team ran television ads and organized new voters. It was not quite enough, but still impressive. Montana, which had voted 59%-39% for President George W. Bush in 2004, voted

2012 Presidential Vote		
Mitt Romney (R)	267,928	(55%)
Barack Obama (D)	201,839	(42%)
Gary Johnson (Lib)	14,165	(3%)
2012 Presidential Primary		
Mitt Romney (R)	96,121	(68%)
Ron Paul (R)	20,227	(14%)
Rick Santorum (R)	12,546	(9%)
2008 Presidential Vote		
John McCain (R)	242,763	(50%)
Barack Obama (D)	231,667	(47%)
Ron Paul (CNP)	10,638	(2%)

only 49%-47% for McCain. Obama had big wins on the Indian reservations in Silver Bow (Butte) and Missoula counties. Montana was not vigorously contested in 2012 and Republican Mitt Romney carried it 55%-42%.

Montana holds its presidential primaries in June, at the end of the primary season when nominations have usually long since been decided. But 2008 was different. State Republicans, hoping to be relevant, opted for a February 5 caucus rather than a June primary. But only 1,630 party and local officials participated, giving a win to Romney, whose campaign was immediately ended by other Super Tuesday results. Democrats, pumped up after the successive victories of Gov. Brian Schweitzer in 2004 and Sen. Jon Tester in 2006, stuck with the June primary, by which time the nomination was still being contested. Obama's campaign targeted Montana, with its openness to new Democrats and its lack of racially polarized politics, as a state where he could have appeal. Obama won 57%-41%, balancing Hillary Clinton's simultaneous win in South Dakota. He scored heavily on the Sioux reservation; in Missoula and Gallatin counties, with their university communities; in relatively fast-growing Flathead County, with its affluent new migrants; and in Lewis and Clark County, with its government employees who work in the state capital of Helena. In 2012, Republicans opted to choose their delegates in the June primary. At that point, the race was all but over, and Romney won with 68% of the vote. Ron Paul was second at 14%.

Governor

Steve Bullock (D)

Elected 2012, term expires Jan. 2017, 1st term; b. April 11, 1966, Missoula; Claremont McKenna Col., B.A. 1988, Columbia U., J.D. 1994; Catholic; married (Lisa); 3 children.

Elected Office: MT atty. gen., 2008-12.

Professional Career: Chief legal counsel, MT secy. of st., 1996-97; Exec. asst. atty. gen., MT Dept. of Justice, 1997-2001; Practicing atty., 2001-04, 2005-08; Adjunct prof., George Washington U. Schl. of Law, 2001-04; Acting chief deputy, MT Dept. of Justice, 2001.

Office: P.O. Box 200801, Helena, 59620-0801, 406-444-3111; Fax: 406-444-5529; Website: governor.mt.gov.

Election Results

2012 general	Steve Bullock (D)	236,450	(49%)
	Rick Hill (R)	228,879	(47%)
	Ron Vandevender (Lib)	18,160	(4%)
2012 primary	Steve Bullock (D)	76,738	(87%)
	Heather Margolis (D)	11,823	(13%)

Democrat Steve Bullock was elected governor of Montana in 2012 to succeed term-limited Democrat Brian Schweitzer. A popular state attorney general, he beat former Congressman Rick Hill in a contest in which a Libertarian candidate was a spoiler.

Bullock, 47, was born in Missoula and raised in Helena, where his newspaper delivery route included the governor's mansion. He received his undergraduate degree from Claremont McKenna College and his law degree from Columbia University. After a brief stint at a law firm following his graduation from law school, Bullock returned to his home state in 1996 to be the chief legal counsel to Democratic Secretary of State Mike Cooney. A year later, he moved to the state Justice Department, where he held positions as executive assistant attorney general and then as acting chief deputy attorney general. He was also the attorney general's legislative director.

In 2000, Bullock made an unsuccessful bid for attorney general, losing the Democratic primary to Mike McGrath, 70% to 30%. McGrath won the general election and was re-elected in 2004 without opposition. After his 2000 loss, Bullock moved to Washington, D.C., to join the law firm of Steptoe & Johnson and to teach as an adjunct professor at George Washington University Law School. He returned to Montana in 2004 to work in private practice in Helena.

Bullock did better in his second try for attorney general in 2008. He won a three-way Democratic primary with 42% of the vote and took 53% in the general election. He created the state's prescription drug registry and its 24/7 Sobriety program, which holds repeat DUI offenders accountable by requiring them to submit to, and pay for, regular blood alcohol tests. He also developed a Children's Justice Center to improve law enforcement's ability to track down and prosecute child predators. He supported Montana's century-old ban on corporate campaign contributions, fighting for it until it was struck down by the U.S. Supreme Court. And he became known for teaming with Schweitzer's administration on public-lands access laws.

In 2012, Bullock ran for governor to succeed Schweitzer, who had developed a national reputation as a folksy, bolo-tie-wearing, maverick with a touch of populism and a flair for the dramatic. While Bullock had a more buttoned-down pedigree, he portrayed his candidacy as a continuation of Schweitzer's work. After the primary, he told the *Missoulian* that the race is about "what sort of progressive Montana we want this to be." After eight years of Democratic control of the governorship, Montana Republicans felt that they were in a solid position to pick up the governor's office, but they first had to get through an acrimonious seven-way primary. Hill won the nomination but had to work to unite the party behind his candidacy and to replenish his campaign coffers, and that gave Bullock a head start in the general election.

Both Hill and Bullock had to compete with the higher-profile Senate race between incumbent Democrat Jon Tester and GOP Rep. Denny Rehberg. Outside groups poured millions of dollars into the Senate contest, most of which were spent on television ads. But several outside Democratic groups focused their activities on voter registration to help Tester, and Bullock benefited. Hill was hurt late in the campaign when the courts disallowed his accepting a $500,000 contribution from the Republican Party during a period when the state's contribution limits had been struck down. Republicans faced another problem: the presence of a Libertarian candidate on the general election ballot. Libertarians have long been a presence on statewide ballots in Montana, but they generally get substantially less support than pre-election polls suggest and rarely affect the outcome of the race. This time, however, Libertarian candidate Ron Vandevender won 3.76% of the vote on Election Day, and his 18,160 votes may well have cost Hill the election. Bullock came out on top by 7,571 votes, or 48.9%, to Hill's 47.3%. If just half of Vandevender's votes had gone to Hill, the Republican would have won.

In his initial State of the State speech in January 2013, Bullock appealed to lawmakers for cooperation, saying, "We need each other if we are going to make progress." This olive branch stood in contrast to Schweitzer's antagonistic relationship with the GOP-led legislature, sometimes punctuated by his use of red-hot "veto" branding irons in front of the capitol. But Bullock ended up using the veto almost as much as his predecessor. He vetoed three tax-relief bills that were high on the GOP's agenda, arguing that they would put the state's $300 million surplus at risk. He also vetoed GOP-backed firearm bills, including a measure to allow most adults to carry a concealed weapon without a permit. Meanwhile, the GOP legislature worked to stymie many of Bullock's initiatives, including an expansion of Medicaid under the Affordable Care Act and a $37 million proposal for state-funded preschools. Bullock was unafraid to take a few liberal positions, including support for overturning the state's ban on same-sex marriage and for efforts to oppose a possible transfer of federal land to the state, which was seen by environmentalists and others as a way to turn over public resources to resource industry. Bullock could face continued leftward pressure as he takes the reins of the Democratic Governors Association for the 2015-2016 cycle.

One setback for Bullock was his selection of Lt. Gov. John Walsh as the temporary successor for the retiring Democratic Sen. Max Baucus in 2014. Walsh was the underdog in the race for a full-six year term later that year, but revelations about plagiarism in a paper he had written at the Army War College pushed him out of the race entirely. Bullock said he had no knowledge of this part of Walsh's background when he appointed him. Bullock's efforts on health care and campaign finance had happier endings, however. Just as happened in 2013, the legislature in 2015 tabled his Medicaid expansion proposal. But Bullock worked with moderate Republicans to draft a compromise expansion plan that won approval in the legislature. Meanwhile, after the Supreme Court put the kibosh on the state's century-old law, Bullock worked with Republican and Democratic lawmakers to craft a bill that required disclosure by "dark money" groups spending on state races. He signed it into law in 2015. Both victories burnished his chances going into his 2016 re-election bid.

Senior Senator

Jon Tester (D)

Elected 2006, term expires Jan. 2019, 2nd term; b. Aug. 21, 1956, Havre; Col. of Great Falls, B.S. 1978; Christian; married (Sharla); 2 children.

Elected Office: Big Sandy Schl. Bd., 1983-92, chmn., 1986-91; MT Senate, 1998-2006, min. ldr., 2003-05, pres., 2005-06.

Professional Career: Music teacher, F.E. Miley Elementary, 1978-80; Custom butcher, T-Bone Farms, 1978-98; Farmer, T-Bone Farms, 1978-present.

DC Office: 311 HSOB, 20510, 202-224-2644; Fax: 202-224-8594; Website: tester.senate.gov.

State Offices: Billings, 406-252-0550; Bozeman, 406-586-4450; Butte, 406-723-3277; Glendive, 406-365-2391; Great Falls, 406-452-9585; Helena, 406-449-5401; Kalispell, 406-257-3360; Missoula, 406-728-3003.

Committees: *Appropriations:* Agriculture, Rural Development, FDA & Related Agencies; Defense; Homeland Security; Energy & Water Development; Interior, Environment & Related Agencies; Military Construction, Veterans Affairs & Related Agencies (RMM). *Banking, Housing & Urban Affairs:* Economic Policy; Housing, Transportation, & Community Development; Securities, Insurance & Investment. *Homeland Security & Governmental Affairs:* Investigations; Regulatory Affairs & Federal Mgmt. Indian Affairs (Vice Chmn). *Veterans' Affairs.*

Group Ratings

	ADA	ACLU	AFL-CIO	LCV	ITI	COC	HAFA	ACU	CFG	FRC
2014	85%	93%	–	60%	100%	38%	5%	12%	17%	0%
2013	80%	C	94%	92%	C	38%	C	12%	3%	C

National Journal Ratings

	2013 LIB		2013 CONS
Economic	51%	—	48%
Social	54%	—	45%
Foreign	58%	—	36%
Composite	56%	—	44%

Key Votes of the 113th Congress

1. Sandy storm spending	Y	5. Student Loan Rates	Y	9. Bipartisan Budget Deal	Y
2. Chuck Hagel Confirmation	Y	6. Employee Non-Discrim'n Act	Y	10. Farm Bill Conference Rept.	Y
3. Gun Background Checks	Y	7. Senate Vote on Judgeships	N	11. Unempl. Comp. Extension	Y
4. Immigration Reform	Y	8. Defense Dept. Spending	Y	12. Keystone Pipeline	Y

Election Results

2012 general	Jon Tester (D)........................236,123	(49%)	$13,347,866	$1,683,327	$11,624,934
	Denny Rehberg (R)...................218,051	(45%)	$9,526,859	$575,574	$10,924,254
	Dan Cox (Lib)............................31,892	(7%)			
2012 primary	Jon Tester (D)........................unopposed				

Prior winning percentage: 2006 (49%)

Democrat Jon Tester was elected in 2006 and won a tough reelection fight in 2012. With his signature $8 flattop haircut and his plain-spoken Western manner inveighing against "D.C. politicians," he doesn't come across like a typical Democrat, but he takes his party's side on key votes often enough to satisfy party leaders. His campaign prowess landed him the chairmanship of the Democratic Senatorial Campaign Committee for the crucial 2016 cycle, when his party has a favorable map in its quest to retake the chamber.

Tester grew up in a farming family, on the same prairie land his grandparents homesteaded almost a century ago near the small town of Big Sandy, home of Big Bud 747, the largest farm tractor in the world. His family ran a custom butcher shop behind their barn; at the age of 9, Tester lost three fingers from his left hand in a meat grinder. The accident, he says, changed him from a saxophone player to a trumpet player. He earned a music degree from the University of Great Falls and later taught music at a local elementary school before devoting himself to farming. He has raised wheat, hay, alfalfa, barley, buckwheat, lentils, millet, and peas and also served on the local Soil Conservation Service Committee. He then switched to organic farming. He told *Esquire* magazine, "In the eighties, we realized we had to do something to add value to our product, to make it more marketable, to get a better price for it. That's when we made the conversion to organic. It's been a blessing for us. Before we converted, when we sprayed weeds, I just planned on being sick for about a week."

Tester's political career began on the Big Sandy school board, where he served for a decade. In 1998, when his neighbor, a Republican state senator, decided not to run for reelection, Tester ran for the seat and won. In 2002, he became minority leader, then Senate president in 2005 after Democrats won a majority. In that role, he helped pass a budget that cut taxes for small businesses and middle-class families while increasing funding for public education. When the 2005 legislative session adjourned, Tester announced he would challenge three-term Republican Sen. Conrad Burns.

He was one of five Democrats seeking the party nomination; his only significant opposition came from two-term state Auditor John Morrison, a former president of the Montana Trial Lawyers Association and the son of a state Supreme Court justice. Morrison outspent Tester nearly 2-to-1, but in a campaign that focused on Burns' ethics, Morrison was weakened by the disclosure that he had an extramarital affair in 1998 with the fiancée of a businessman who was later investigated by the auditor's office. Running as an unabashed populist, Tester gained support from Daily Kos and other progressive Internet activists, and in Montana he assembled a formidable grass-roots operation with hundreds of volunteers. He beat Morrison, 61%-35%.

Tester was taking on the only Republican senator Montana voters had ever reelected. But by 2006, the 71-year-old conservative incumbent had two serious problems. The first was his connection to disgraced and later convicted lobbyist Jack Abramoff. He was the largest congressional recipient of campaign donations from Abramoff's clients, and he faced campaign accusations that he "sold his vote" and betrayed Montana's American Indian population by earmarking funds for Abramoff's Indian clients in other states. Burns' second handicap was a gaffe-prone style, ill-suited for the *YouTube* era. In 2006, while discussing the war on terrorism, he spoke of enemies who "drive taxicabs in the daytime and kill at night."

It was a bare-knuckled campaign. Burns spent $9 million, $3.5 million more than Tester, and argued that Tester was too liberal for Montana because of his opposition to the Bush-era PATRIOT Act anti-terrorism law and his links to "radical environmentalists" and left-wing bloggers. But Tester was not so easily caricatured. His haircut, highlighted in a television ad filmed at the Riverview Barbershop in Great Falls, combined with his beefy farmer's build, his 3,000 acre farm, his size 12-C cowboy boots and his down-to-earth way (he's fond of saying, "You have two ears and one mouth; act accordingly.") worked to temper the criticism. The race was decided by just 3,562 votes. Burns carried 41 of 56 counties, including Yellowstone County, which includes Billings, the state's largest city. But Tester prevailed in several large counties including Cascade (Great Falls), Lewis and Clark (Helena), and Missoula (home of the University of Montana), carrying the latter nearly 2-to-1. In Washington, Democrats hailed Tester's victory as a signal of a new political direction in the Mountain West.

Arriving in Washington, he stressed the importance of transparency and accountability in government, distancing himself from the questionable practices that hurt his predecessor. Tester cosponsored a Republican bill to ban former members of Congress from ever lobbying, and he joined a group of senators seeking to ban secret holds on legislation and nominations, a longtime Senate practice. Tester drew notice for his practice of prominently posting his daily schedule on the Internet, a Senate first. He was distinctive in other ways, hauling in his luggage a supply of beef he'd butchered himself.

Tester supports abortion rights and same-sex marriage, but takes a Westerner's attitude on firearms. He cosponsored with Republican Sen. John McCain of Arizona an amendment to repeal the District of Columbia's gun control laws, which effectively stopped legislation to give D.C. a voting representative in Congress. Early in Barack Obama's presidency, Tester and fellow Montana Democratic Sen. Max Baucus also made it clear they would oppose any notion of reinstating the ban on military-style assault weapons. After the Newtown, Connecticut school massacre in 2012, though, Tester expressed a willingness to listen to proposals dealing with assault weapons, as long as other issues such as the mental health of gun purchasers were addressed.

Baucus' departure to become Ambassador to China in early 2014 opened other top Senate posts and gave him the chairmanship of the Indian Affairs Committee. In his first few months he impressed tribal observers with his energy, getting 15 bills through the panel dealing with housing, education, water rights and a legislative remedy for a 2009 Supreme Court decision that limited the Interior Department ability to take lands into trust for tribes. *Indian Country Today* praised Tester's "shoe leather diplomacy," including visits to Native American communities to gauge education, health and environmental programs. He called for protection of the Badger-Two Medicine area near Glacier National Park in Montana, a place sacred to the Blackfeet Tribe but long a bone of contention with oil and gas companies. Tester, along with Montana's junior senator, Republican Steve Daines, won committee-level approval of federal recognition for the Little Shell Tribe of Chippewa Indians.

On the Banking, Housing, and Urban Affairs Committee, Tester worked on the credit card regulation act signed into law in 2009, banning certain fees and deadlines and providing an extra week for paying bills. In May 2010, he sponsored a successful amendment requiring large banks to pay higher Federal Deposit Insurance Corporation fees. He and Tennessee Republican Sen. Bob Corker sought to block new limits on the "swipe fees" that banks and credit card companies charge stores for debit card transactions, arguing that the fee limits would hurt small rural banks. Their amendment in June 2011 drew 54 votes, six short of the 60 needed. Tester was named in 2013 to chair the Banking panel's Securities, Insurance, and Investment Subcommittee, which is responsible for overseeing computerized high-speed traders and efforts to rein in technological snafus that hurt investor confidence in the markets. Tester is also on the Homeland Security and Governmental Affairs Committee; in that capacity, he authored a bill, signed into law in December 2014, to simplify Customs and Border Protection's overtime pay practices. Tester also voiced criticism of how political scientists from Stanford and Dartmouth were able to send a "voter guide" to 100,000 Montanans to test theories about how voters respond to nonpartisan contests; Tester said that "using the people of Montana as their guinea pigs is bad enough, but the truth is that elections should not be a lab for political experiments."

At times, Tester tested the boundaries of party loyalty. He was one of only two Democrats in October 2011 to join Republicans in a filibuster of Obama's jobs bill, contending it contained "tax gimmicks" that did not address deficit reduction. He aroused the ire of left-wing bloggers in December 2010 when he voted against the DREAM Act, which would provide a path for citizenship for the children of illegal immigrants who attend college or serve in the military. Even though Montana has one of the lowest percentages of immigrants, legal or illegal, of any state, Tester said, "Illegal immigration is a critical problem facing our country, but amnesty is not the solution." The Daily Kos' Markos Moulitsas, a staunch Tester backer in 2006, said he would do whatever he could to defeat him in 2012. In 2015, Tester again raised liberals' ire with his complaint, on Montana Public Radio, that "every logging sale in Montana right now is under litigation." Under fire, his staff revised the claim not once but twice, but the *Washington Post* Fact Checker still gave Tester Four Pinocchios, its worst rating, saying he was "wildly off the mark."

Tester envisioned a tough reelection battle even before Republican Denny Rehberg, Montana's sole House member, announced in February 2011 that he would run for the seat in 2012. In 1996, Rehberg had given Baucus his closest race ever, losing by just 50%-45%. By October 2011, the nonpartisan Center for Responsive Politics found that Tester, despite running as an outsider, had accepted more campaign contributions from lobbyists than any other member of Congress. Republicans also pointed to Tester's financial support from large banks on the swipe-fee issue as evidence of his hypocrisy.

Rehberg relied on the familiar Republican strategy of attacking Tester as a liberal Obama ally, citing his vote in favor of the president's health care law. Tester replied that the law was "about being able to get health care without breaking the bank." He took a page from the national Democratic playbook in sowing doubt about Rehberg's support for Social Security and Medicare. Although Rehberg got outside GOP money, national Democratic interests from labor and women's groups came into the state to assist Tester, organizing a get-out-the-vote effort that proved effective. The senator also got help from an unlikely source, the Seattle grunge-rock group Pearl Jam. He used his friendship with bassist Jeff Ament, a Big Sandy native, to raffle off to campaign donors a prize of two onstage reclining concert seats, along with dinner with Tester and Ament.

Republican Mitt Romney had carried Montana with 55 percent of the vote, and election forecaster Nate Silver determined that Tester had just a 34 percent chance of winning. Yet Tester ended up winning, 49%-45%, with 7% for Libertarian Dan Cox. Tester improved on his earlier strong showing in Missoula County, got 52 percent in Bozeman-based Gallatin County, and narrowly eked out a win in Yellowstone County to offset Rehberg's strong showing elsewhere.

Tester's campaign-trail acumen helped him overcome his occasional breaks with Senate leadership to win him the DSCC job, where he will have to defend just 10 seats, compared to 24 for the GOP. Despite Tester's acknowledged misgivings about the job's intense fundraising demands, Montana State University political scientist David C.W. Parker called him an inspired choice, given his affinity to reach rural white voters who have escaped the party in droves. "People instinctively like him; he smiles and listens patiently when engaging with constituents and fellow politicians alike ... If Tester applies these lessons to his work at the DSCC, he'll recruit Senate candidates who fit the places they come from rather than imposing ideological litmus tests," Parker wrote in *The Washington Post*.

Junior Senator

Steve Daines (R)

Elected 2014, term expires Jan. 2021, 1st term; b. Aug. 20, 1962, Van Nuys, CA; MT St. U., B.S. 1984; Presbyterian; married (Cindy); 4 children.

Elected Office: U.S. House, 2013-15.

Professional Career: Operations mgmt., Procter & Gamble, 1984-97; V.P., Clair Daines Construction, 1997-2000; Gen. mgr./V.P., Right-Now Technologies, 2000-12.

DC Office: 320 HSOB, 20150, 202-224-2651; Website: daines.senate .gov.

State Offices: Billings, 406-245-6822; Bozeman, 406-587-3446; Great Falls, 406-453-0148; Helena, 406-443-3189; Missoula, 406-549-8198.

Committees: *Appropriations:* Agriculture, Rural Development, FDA, & Related Agencies; Defense; Interior, Environment & Related Agencies; State, Foreign Operations & Related Programs; Transportation, HUD, & Related Agencies. *Commerce, Science, & Transportation:* Communications, Technology, Innovation & the Internet; Consumer Protection, Product Safety, Insurance, & Data Security; Space, Science, & Competitiveness; Surface Transportation & Merchant Marine Infrastructure, Safety & Security. *Energy & Natural Resources:* Energy; Public Lands, Forests, & Mining; Water & Power. *Indian Affairs.*

Group Ratings (House)

	ADA	ACLU	AFL-CIO	LCV	ITI	COC	HAFA	ACU	CFG	FRC
2014	0%	5%	–	0%	100%	86%	58%	76%	73%	75%
2013	5%	C	14%	4%	C	85%	C	80%	77%	C

National Journal Ratings (House)

	2013 LIB	—	2013 CONS
Economic	30%	—	69%
Social	34%	—	62%
Foreign	5%	—	86%
Composite	25%	—	75%

Key Votes of the 113th Congress (House)

1. Sandy storm spending	N	5. Medical Marijuana Y	9. Syrian Rebels Training Y
2. Violence Against Women Act Y	6. Farm Bill Y	10. Keystone pipeline Y
3. Guantanamo Bay Detainees N	7. Afghanistan Combat N	11. Immigration Exec. Action Y
4. Abortion 20-week ban Y	8. NSA Phone Data Collection Y	12. Bipartisan budget deal N

Election Results

2014 general	Steve Daines (R)	213,709	(58%)	$6,668,759	$377,362	$303,790
	Amanda Curtis (D)	148,184	(40%)	$968,388	$39,751	$43,265
	Roger Roots (Lib)	7,933	(2%)			
2014 primary	Steve Daines (R)	110,565	(83%)			
	Susan Cundiff (R)	11,909	(9%)			
	Champ Edmunds (R)	10,151	(8%)			

Prior winning percentage: House: 2012 (53%)

Republican Steve Daines was elected Montana's junior senator in 2014. He was considered a strong favorite for the Senate well before the candidacy of his presumed opponent, appointed Democratic Sen. John Walsh, imploded over a plagiarism scandal. Daines had demonstrated his appeal statewide in winning election to Montana's at-large House seat in 2012, and Democrats did little to support state Rep. Amanda Curtis, a late ballot replacement for Walsh. Daines became the first Republican to hold the seat since Joseph M. Dixon in 1913, when senators were still appointed by state legislatures.

Daines grew up in Bozeman, where his father started a home-construction business. He went on to study chemical engineering at Montana State University, and during his senior year, he became one of the youngest delegates at the 1984 Republican National Convention. When he graduated, Daines spent 13 years with consumer goods giant Procter & Gamble. After seven years managing operations in the United States, he moved his young family overseas for a six-year stint with the company in Hong Kong and China. In 1997, Daines left P&G to join the family construction business in Bozeman. Three years later, he got a call from local entrepreneur Greg Gianforte, founder of RightNow Technologies, asking him to come on board as vice president of customer service.

He dipped into local politics in 2007 when he and his wife, Cindy, founded *Giveitback .com,* a nonprofit organization that pushed for the return of the state's $1 billion budget surplus to taxpayers. Not long after that, former Arkansas Gov. Mike Huckabee asked Daines to serve as Montana state chairman for his presidential campaign. Daines also chaired Montana's delegation to the 2008 Republican National Convention. That same year, he ran for lieutenant governor on a ticket with former state Sen. Roy Brown, but they failed to oust Democratic Gov. Brian Schweitzer.

Two years later, Daines announced his intention to challenge Democrat Jon Tester for his Senate seat. But when Rep. Denny Rehberg said in February 2011 that he would run against Tester, Daines dropped out of the Senate race to vie for Rehberg's vacated House seat instead. He ended up winning with 53 percent of the vote.

In the House, Daines compiled a conservative voting record, especially on foreign policy issues, but was not as far to the right as other recent GOP arrivals. Daines bucked some in his party by ultimately voting to end the government shutdown and to reauthorize the Violence Against Women Act. He also sponsored a bill to bar energy development on the North and Middle forks of the Flathead River. But he took a variety of conservative stands as well, supporting the budget crafted by Wisconsin Rep. Paul Ryan, and voting for a measure to make abortion illegal after 20 weeks. The House in December 2013 passed his bill to expand hydropower production in Montana, and he successfully amended several other bills to include provisions specific to his state's energy production.

Daines's rise to the Senate included some luck. Rehberg left politics after losing the 2012 race to Tester. The state's other Democratic senator, Max Baucus, announced his retirement and subsequently resigned his seat early when President Barack Obama named him Ambassador to China. Daines jumped into the race, just 14 months after election to the House. After former Gov. Brian Schweitzer declined to run, the Democrats turned to Walsh, who had been tapped by Democratic Gov. Steve Bullock to succeed Baucus. But in June, the *New York Times* published a bombshell story saying that Walsh had plagiarized large portions of his master's thesis at the U.S. Army War College. A muddled response by Walsh and his staff only made matters worse, and in August, shortly before the ballot deadline, Walsh exited the race. The party chose Curtis to take his place, but a race that had already favored the well-funded Daines increasingly looked like a rout in the making. On Election Day, Daines defeated Curtis, 58%-40%—making this one of the key races that helped the GOP take over the chamber.

Daines was given seats on two panels of special interest to Montana—Energy and Natural Resources and Indian Affairs—as well as Appropriations and Commerce, Science and Transportation. The first Senate bill he introduced was the Balanced Budget Accountability Act, which would force lawmakers to balance the budget or give up their salaries. He also urged approval of the Keystone XL pipeline and decried federal regulations that curbed timber harvests.

REPRESENTATIVE-AT-LARGE

Ryan Zinke (R)

Elected 2014, 1st term; b. Nov. 1, 1961, Bozeman; U. of OR, B.S. 1984, Natl U., M.B.A. 1991, U. of San Diego, M.S. 2003; Lutheran; married (Lolita); 3 children.

Military Career: U.S. Navy SEAL, 1985-2008.

Elected Office: MT Senate, 2009-12.

DC Office: 113 CHOB, 202-225-3211; Fax: 202-225-5687; Website: zinke.house.gov.

State Offices: Billings, 406-969-1736; Great Falls, 406-952-1210; Helena, 406-502-1435; Missoula, 406-540-4370.

Committees: *Armed Services:* Emerging Threats & Capabilities; Seapower & Projection Forces. *Natural Resources:* Energy & Mineral Resources; Federal Lands.

Election Results

2014 general	Ryan Zinke (R)	203,871	(55%)	$4,665,055	$359,826
	John Lewis (D)	148,690	(40%)	$1,703,086	$188,999
	Mike Fellows (Lib)	15,402	(4%)		
2014 primary	Ryan Zinke (R)	43,766	(33%)		
	Corey Stapleton (R)	38,591	(29%)		
	Matt Rosendale (R)	37,965	(29%)		
	Elsie Arntzen (R)	9,011	(7%)		

A former Navy SEAL, Republican Ryan Zinke won the Montana at-large seat in 2014 to replace Steve Daines, who moved to the Senate. To his intensive background in national security operations, Zinke has added practical political experience in his home state plus personal views on foreign policy to make a potentially compelling and timely profile.

Voter Turnout	
2013 Total Citizen 18+	783,143
2014 House Turnout	367,963
2014 Turnout as % CVAP	47.0%
2012 Turnout as % CVAP	62.2%

Zinke is a third-generation Montanan; he grew up in the small railroad and logging town of Whitefish. He played football at the University of Oregon and earned a degree in geology before joining the Navy and training for the SEALs. During 23 years with the elite force, he served as deputy and acting commander of Special Forces in Iraq, where he led 3,500 members of the Special Operations forces. He also served in Bosnia, Kosovo and the Pacific.

After leaving the military in 2008, Ryan was elected to the state Senate in Montana, chaired the Education Committee, and served one term. He founded and served as CEO of a consulting firm, Continental Divide, and sits on the board of directors of Save the World Air.

In 2012, Republican Neil Livingstone tapped Zinke to be his running mate in an unsuccessful campaign for governor. Zinke next turned his attention to the open Montana House seat vacated by Daines. His campaign focused on national security, as Zinke criticized the Obama administration for taking "an iffy policy" of the George W. Bush administration and making it "a real bad one." Ground troops ultimately would have to fight international terrorism, he added. He also focused on energy independence. "We can't power this nation and bring back manufacturing on pixie dust and hope," he said. Democrats demanded the release of his military records, probing for alleged letters of reprimand. Zinke admitted he was ordered in the mid-1990s to pay back $211 for a one-way plane ticket to Montana. Records he released commended his fitness levels and reported his two Bronze Stars for combat.

Early in his campaign, in January 2014, he gained national headlines when he called former Secretary of State Hillary Clinton the "Antichrist." He later admitted that the words were "perhaps a little harsh," but he explained that he knew two Navy SEALS who died at the U.S. diplomatic post in Benghazi, Libya, during the armed attack in September 2012. He has been equally unsparing in his comments about President Barack Obama. "This administration's inaction and lack of commitment and resolve" in fighting the Islamic State and other terrorist groups, he told the *Washington Free Beacon*, "provides fuel for terrorism. It gives them hope that they can win, and it has ramifications worldwide."

In the hard-fought June primary, he faced four other candidates, including two state senators. Zinke won with 33% of the vote to 29% for each of the senators, Matt Rosendale and Corey Stapleton. That contest nearly depleted his finances.

For the general election, Democrats nominated John Lewis, who had been an aide to former Montana Sen. Max Baucus. Zinke dismissed Lewis as "a D.C. staffer whose entire life has been in D.C." He quickly refilled his coffers—raising a total of $4.7 million, compared with $1.7 million for Lewis. Zinke also had support from the super PAC Special Operations for America, which he created in 2012 and handed over to a fellow former SEAL before running for Congress. He defeated Lewis, 55%-40%.

As a former SEAL elected to Congress, Zinke logically got a seat on the Armed Services Committee, plus Natural Resources. He describes himself as a "constitutional conservative," who believes strongly in the separation of power among the three branches of government, plus sovereignty of the states. He acknowledged that he has heard suggestions that he might run for the Senate, presumably against Democrat Jon Tester in 2018.

★ NEBRASKA ★

"The sea of Nebraska." That's how the first travelers on the Oregon Trail in the 1840s described what they saw when they crossed the Missouri River and moved west along the Platte River. For miles on end you can see nothing but rolling brown fields, sectioned off here and there by barbed wire fences, and in the distance, a grain elevator towering over a tiny town and its railroad depot. The Platte is not actually a single river, but a braid of streams that weaves a silver chain around sandbars and islands, flooding the level floor of the Nebraska plain—a mile wide, the saying goes, and six inches deep. Nebraska was mostly settled in a single rush in the 1880s, when its population increased from 452,000 to 1 million. In the 1880s, Omaha became a major railroad center, Lincoln the state capital, and farming and food products the main businesses. Czechs, Germans, and Danes came to work the factories in Omaha and farms on the Plains—Willa Cather tells the story beautifully in her novels. Then for about a century, Nebraska remained pretty much the same. From 1890 to 2010, its population rose from 1 million to just 1.8 million. This is not what its founders envisioned. They hoped that Nebraska would develop a diversified farming, industrial, and commercial economy like those of Illinois, Missouri, and Ohio. But climate is hard to predict. Rains were plentiful in the 1880s, but the 1890s were years of drought, and Nebraska abruptly stopped growing. Many rural counties, and even Omaha, lost population. Nebraska exported people for 100 years: 48% of Nebraskans in 1890 were children; in 2010 only 25% were. For a long time, the creative energies in the American economy seemed to have skipped over the Great Plains and moved west.

The sudden boom of the 1880s and the bust of the 1890s produced the most colorful—and atypical—politics of Nebraska's history: the populist movement and William Jennings Bryan, the "silver-tongued orator of the Platte." Bryan was only 36 when he delivered his Cross of Gold speech at the 1896 Democratic National Convention and was swept to the nomination. "From the first sentence, the audience was with me," recalled Bryan in his memoirs. But the country wasn't. Bryan was so radical that Democratic President Grover Cleveland wouldn't support him, although he still won 47% of the popular vote in the first of his three attempts at the presidency. Since Bryan's time, Nebraska's most notable politician has been George Norris, who led the House rebellion against Speaker Joseph Cannon in 1910. In 1934, Norris spurred adoption of the state's unicameral, nonpartisan legislature (in which every bill gets a public hearing where anyone can speak). In Washington, Norris sponsored the Norris-LaGuardia Anti-Injunction Act, the first federal pro-union legislation, and the Tennessee Valley Authority Act. But most Nebraskans were repelled by the New Deal, which seemed to threaten their way of life. Although it sometimes elects Democratic governors and senators, Nebraska over the past half-century has been strongly Republican in presidential elections.

Since 1990, Nebraska has been growing relatively robustly for the first time in decades. Its population grew 16 percent between 1990 and 2010—the total population increase in that 20-year span was greater than that in the 60 years between 1930 and 1990. But compared to the country as a whole, it is still growing at a slower pace. Farming has been profitable, with high demand for corn for ethanol, of which Nebraska is the largest producer after Iowa. Droughts, most recently in 2012, have been tough on ranchers, but Nebraskans cheered when Japan opened its market to U.S. beef in January 2013 and are now pushing for China to open up too. According to the Department of Agriculture Foreign Agricultural Service, Nebraska accounted for $6.6 billion in agricultural exports, led by soybeans, beef, animal feeds and corn. It ranked 5th among the states in the value of its agricultural exports, and helped support more than 50,000 Nebraska jobs on farms and in industries such as food processing, transportation, and manufacturing. Omaha has been thriving economically, and not just because America's second-richest man, Warren Buffett, lives there. (He can jet to either coast for lunch and be back in Omaha for his favorite steak and Cherry Coke dinner.) Omaha is home to five Fortune 500 companies: Buffett's Berkshire Hathaway, ConAgra Foods, Union Pacific, the construction, engineering and mining giant Kiewit, and Mutual of Omaha. The locals fret about what would happen to ConAgra if investors and hedge funds split up the agribusiness, which employs about 2,600 at its Omaha headquarters and at manufacturing facilities in Lincoln and Council Bluffs. But the Omaha metro area also harbors large companies like Green Plains Renewable Energy, TD Ameritrade and Valmont

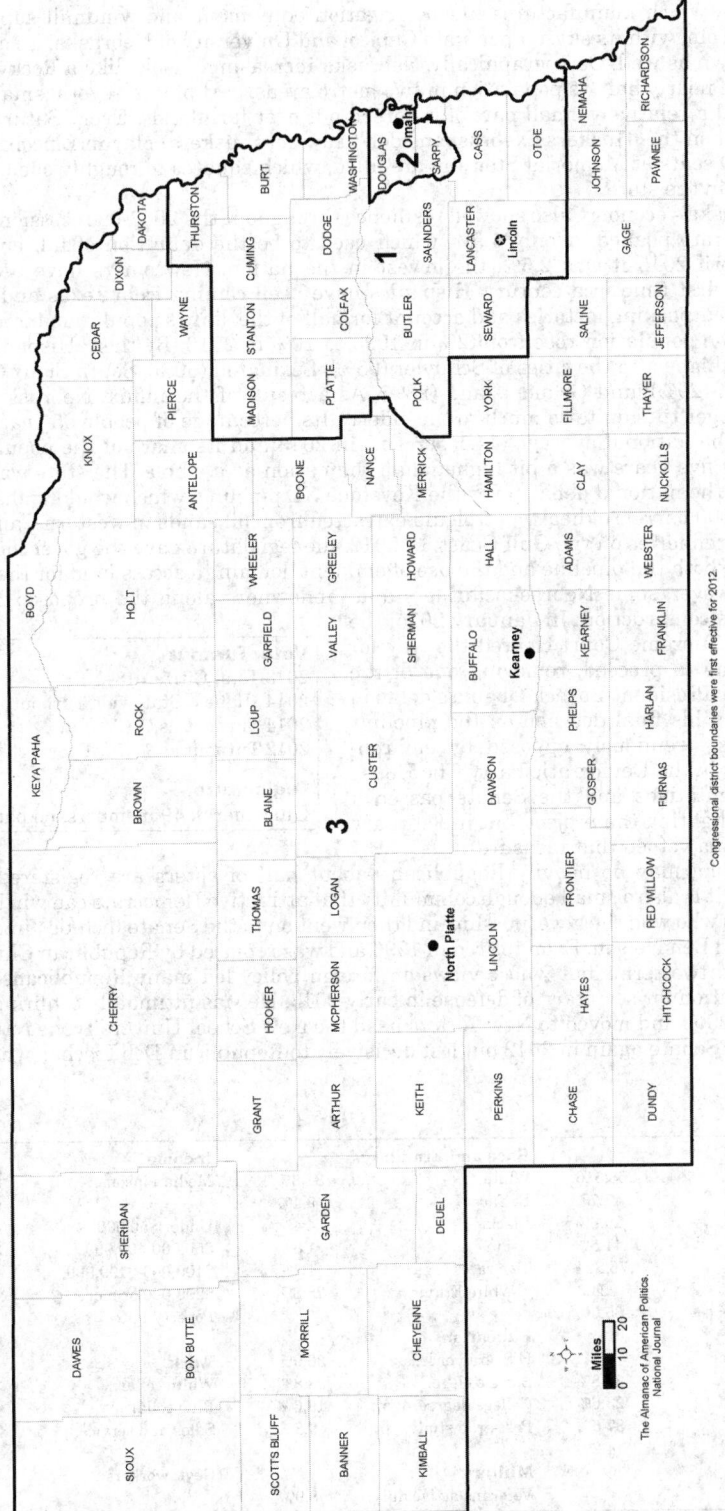

Congressional district boundaries were first effective for 2012.

The Almanac of American Politics,
National Journal

Miles
0 10 20

Industries, which manufactures linear irrigation equipment and windmill support structures. Lincoln, with its skyscraper state Capitol and University of Nebraska, is something of a boom town as well. Demographically, Nebraska increasingly looks like a Rocky Mountain state, with nearly half its population in two metro areas, part of it in several smaller factory towns, and a relatively small part of it spread out over farmlands. Every Saturday during the fall, when the 'Huskers (Nebraskans don't say Cornhuskers) play in Lincoln, nearly all the 92,000 seats at Memorial Stadium are filled, which equates to roughly one out of every 20 people in the state.

Nebraska's economy also showed resilience throughout the 2007-09 recession; its unemployment rate peaked at only 4.9%, which used to be the definition of full employment, and in April 2015 it was 2.5%, the lowest in the nation. Newcomers have been moving in for the first time in a century. Hispanics have been coming from Texas and Mexico to work in meatpacking factories and account for half of the state's population increase. Their share of the population rose from 2% in 1990 to 10% in 2010. By then, Hispanic percentages were highest in the cities of Schuyler (65%), Lexington (60%), South Sioux City (44%), Scottsbluff (29%), and Grand Island (28%). As a result of the influx, Nebraska's population no longer tilts quite so much to the elderly. Its percentage of people 65 years and over matched the national average (14.1 percent) in 2013 and its share of the population that was under five years was a bit higher than the nation as a whole. The state was a battleground in the national debate over the Keystone XL pipeline, which would transport more than 800,000 barrels of heavy petroleum extracted from oil sands in western Canada to the ports and refineries on the Gulf Coast. In 2012, the legislature gave the governor authority to approve both the pipeline and the use of eminent domain to access land for the pipeline's route. However, some Nebraska farmers and landowners along the proposed route sued to block its construction. In January 2015, the Nebraska Supreme Court cleared the way for the pipeline to proceed, removing one of the reasons for President Barack Obama's delay in announcing his final decision on the pipeline, which was strenuously opposed by environmentalists in the Democratic Party. The House of Representatives and the Senate passed a bill green-lighting the project, but in February 2015, Obama vetoed that measure.

Voter Turnout	
2013 Total Citizen 18+	1,330,474
2014 Highest Statewide Turnout	539,891
2014 Turnout as % CVAP	40.6%
2012 Turnout as % CVAP	59.9%
Legislature	
Unicameral: 49 members, no party labels	

Nebraska may be heavily Republican—about half of voters are registered with the GOP—but it is also a small enough community that attractive Democrats can win high office. Democrats who won the governorship and then went on to the Senate include Jim Exon, Bob Kerrey, and Ben Nelson. Exon retired in 1996 and was replaced by Republican Chuck Hagel, who served two terms but whose views on foreign policy led many Republicans to oppose his nomination for secretary of defense in early 2013. He was ultimately confirmed. Kerrey retired in 2000 and moved to New York to head the New School University; he returned and ran for the Senate again in 2012 but lost decisively to Republican Deb Fischer, who replaced

Population		Race and Ethnicity		Income	
Total:	1,868,516	White	81.8%	Median income:	$53,774
Urban:	47.7%	Latino	9.4%		(24 of 50)
Suburban:	10.8%	Black	4.4%	Under $50,000	48.2%
Rural:	41.5%	Asian	1.8%	$50,000-$99,999:	32.6%
Land area:	76,824	Two races	1.7%	$100,000-$199,999:	15.7%
Pop/sq. mi.:	24.3	White Ethnic	28.8%	$200,000 or more:	3.4%
Born in state:	65.0%			Poverty Rate	9.5%
		Education			
Age Groups		H.S. grad or less:	36.9%	**Work**	
Under 18:	24.8%	Some college:	33.8%	White collar:	35.7%
18 to 34:	23.6%	College degree, 4 yr.:	19.6%	Blue collar:	40.7%
35 to 64:	37.5%	Post-grad study:	9.8%	Sales and service:	23.6%
Over 64:	14.2%				
		Military		Govt. workers:	14.0%
		Veterans/active duty:	8.9%		

Nelson in the Senate. Starting in 1998, Nebraska has elected Republican governors—Mike Johanns in 1998 and 2002, before he became a one-term Senator, and Dave Heineman in 2006. Heineman beat Rep. Tom Osborne, a former Huskers football coach, by 50%-44% in the 2006 GOP primary. He was easily reelected in 2010. Pete Ricketts became the third Republican in row to win the governorship in 2014.

Presidential Politics Over the past 50 years, Nebraska has voted an average of 60% Republican in presidential elections, more than any other state except Utah, Idaho, and Wyoming. But 2008 was different. Nebraska Democrats decided to stir up interest by choosing their delegates in a February 9 caucus rather than in the traditional May primary, which hasn't had much significance since Robert Kennedy and Eugene McCarthy contested it in 1968 and Frank Church won a surprise victory in 1976. As in other caucus states, Obama's presidential campaign was

2012 Presidential Vote		
Mitt Romney (R)................475,064	(60%)
Barack Obama (D) 302,081	(38%)
2012 Presidential Primary		
Mitt Romney (R)................131,436	(71%)
Rick Santorum (R) 25,830	(14%)
Ron Paul (R) 18,508	(10%)
Newt Gingrich (R)..................9,628	(5%)
2008 Presidential Vote		
John McCain (R)................452,979	(57%)
Barack Obama (D) 333,319	(42%)

enthusiastic and well organized, while Hillary Clinton's was practically invisible. Obama carried the caucus vote 68%-32%, running up big margins in Lincoln and Omaha. Republicans held a meaningless caucus in July, long after John McCain had wrapped up the GOP nomination.

The strength of the Obama campaign organization was evident in the general election as well. Nebraska is one of two states (Maine is the other) that allocate two of its Electoral College votes to the statewide winner and the others to the winners in each of the congressional districts. In 2008, Obama's strategists targeted the 2nd District, which includes all of Omaha's Douglas County and most of its Sarpy County suburbs, opened three offices and enlisted some 1,500 volunteers. The work paid off and Obama won the 2nd Congressional District by 50%-49%, by just 3,370 votes out of 277,809 cast. McCain carried the state overall, 57%-42%. Thus, one electoral vote from Nebraska was cast for Obama, the first time a Democrat picked up one of the state's Electoral College votes since 1964. Some Nebraska Republicans have talked about revising the state's allocation scheme, but those efforts have failed to gain serious momentum in the state legislature.

In the 2012 Republican primary, Nebraska voted on May 15, too late to make a difference in the contest. Mitt Romney was well on his way to becoming the nominee and captured 71% to 14% for Rick Santorum. Romney swept the state in the fall, 61%-38%, and Obama carried only one small rural county out of the state's 93.

Congressional Districts Nebraska has had three congressional districts since the 1960 census. Its slow population growth may whittle it down to two in a not-so-distant decade. Boundaries can generate strong feelings in Nebraska if only because it has been one of just two states where Electoral Col-

114th Congress Lineup	
2 R	1 D
113th Congress Lineup	
3 R	0 D

lege votes are apportioned by congressional district. The unicameral legislature is technically nonpartisan, but in reality, Republicans have long controlled the process. In 2015, some Republicans sought to eliminate the Electoral College anomaly.

As the sparse western two-thirds of the state has shed residents, the western 3rd District has needed to expand, and the Lincoln-based 1st District and Omaha-based 2nd District have needed to shrink. This time they needed to reshuffle about 80,000 residents. Republicans' obvious top priority was to shore up the Omaha 2nd District, not only because President Barack Obama had narrowly carried it by 3,370 votes in 2008, but because Republican Lee Terry nearly lost it the same year. So, the legislature passed a map trading politically mixed Bellevue and Offutt Air Force Base south of Omaha to the 1st District in exchange for the deeply Republican western half of Sarpy County, making the 2nd about a percentage point safer overall. To give neighboring Republican Jeff Fortenberry extra insurance, legislators also shifted very conservative Platte County from the 3rd to the 1st. To offset the move, the "Big Third" now stretches from Wyoming to Missouri and Iowa and includes all or part of 75 counties, more than any other seat in the country. But that wasn't enough to protect Terry, whose maladroit rhetoric helped to make him one of only two congressional Republicans who lost their seats in 2014.

Governor

Pete Ricketts (R)

Elected 2014, term expires Jan. 2019, 1st term; b. Aug. 19, 1964, Nebraska City, U. of Chicago, B.A., M.A.; Catholic; married (Susanne), 3 children.

Professional Career: Customer Services, Senior VP Strategy & Business Devel., Senior VP of Product Devel., Senior VP of Marketing, COO at Ameritrade, 1993-2005; Founder, Drakon, LLC.

Office: P.O. Box 94848, Lincoln, 68509, 402-471-2244; Fax: 402-471-6031; Website: governor.nebraska.gov.

Election Results

2014 general	Pete Ricketts (R)	308,751	(57%)
	Chuck Hassebrook (D)	211,905	(39%)
	Mark G. Elworth Jr. (Lib)	19,001	(4%)
2014 primary	Pete Ricketts (R)	58,671	(27%)
	Jon Bruning (R)	56,324	(26%)
	Beau McCoy (R)	46,196	(21%)
	Mike Foley (R)	42,394	(19%)

When Republican Pete Ricketts was elected Nebraska governor in 2014, his family's wealth and influence helped pave the way for his political career. His last name was well known in Nebraska before he ever tried for public office; his father, Joe, founded the TD Ameritrade Holding Corp., based outside of Omaha and the family owns Major League Baseball's storied franchise, the Chicago Cubs. But Ricketts worked to burnish his image as more than a candidate with deep pockets, and to fend off constant criticism that he—and his politically engaged father—were trying to buy the governor's mansion.

Ricketts is one of four children (and the eldest son). On the campaign trail, he told voters that growing up in Omaha he and his siblings were latchkey kids in a middle-class home where both parents worked and his father built a financial empire. He graduated from Westside High School in Omaha and attended the University of Chicago, earning a bachelor's degree in biology and an MBA. After college, Ricketts joined the family business, rising to president and chief operating officer. He left TD Ameritrade in 2005 to run for the Senate against incumbent Democrat Ben Nelson in 2006. Republicans were not looking for a wealthy scion to be their standard-bearer against Nelson, who was a former two-term governor born in the small plains town of McCook that had also produced Nebraska icon George Norris. But after a number of other notable Republicans, including Gov. Dave Heineman, former Gov. Mike Johanns, and congressmen Lee Terry and Tom Osborne, all passed on the race, Republicans rallied around Ricketts who could self-fund his campaign. Running on a platform of tax cuts and smaller government, Ricketts sought to appeal to the conservative values of the state. He defeated former attorney general Don Steinberg in the GOP primary 48%-36%. In the general election, the political rookie supported a guest-worker program for immigrants, enabling Nelson to run to the right of Ricketts and call for securing the border. Ricketts, with his investment background, also came out in favor of private accounts invested in financial securities as a way to modernize Social Security. Nelson opposed the idea. Ricketts also supported a ban on congressional earmarks in the federal budget, which Nelson had directed to Nebraska communities for years. Ricketts plowed almost $12 million of his own money into the race and outspent Nelson by almost a 2-1 margin. But on Election Day, he lost overwhelmingly with 36% to Nelson's 64%.

For the next five years, Ricketts served on the Republican National Committee, building his connections to the party establishment, grassroots activists in Nebraska and GOP political players around the country. He also invested in startups, served on various boards, and developed philanthropic interests. He founded Drakon LLC, based in Omaha, a management firm that supports local entrepreneurs and new growth companies, and the Platte Institute for Economic Research, a conservative think tank in Omaha. "I was brand new to the political world and the thing about that is, you don't know what you don't know," Ricketts told *Omaha.com*, as he prepared for his 2014 campaign. He vowed that he was going "to do things differently" in this race and not rely on hired guns from Washington for advice. But Ricketts got a lot of outside help for his second run for high office. He won endorsements from Wisconsin Gov. Scott Walker, Indiana Gov. Mike Pence, 2012 vice presidential nominee Rep. Paul Ryan of Wisconsin, and Sen. Ted Cruz of Texas, among others. As White House hopefuls looking to woo Republican mega-donors, the 2014 governor's contest in Nebraska offered an opportunity to warm up to Ricketts' father, whose End Spending Super PAC has doled out or spent more than $25 million on behalf of GOP candidates across the country, including Walker, Cruz, and Mitt Romney's 2012 presidential campaign, since it was founded in 2010. Pete Ricketts's brothers Todd and Tom, who is chairman of the Cubs, have also given to GOP candidates. But Pete's sister, Laura Ricketts, was a major campaign fundraiser for President Barack Obama in 2012, tapping her network of wealthy friends and business associates to collect hundreds of thousands of dollars for his reelection bid. She was one of 27 high-profile gay and lesbian "bundlers" for Obama and is the first openly lesbian co-owner of a major sports franchise. She has also been an advocate for gay marriage.

During the GOP primary, Republican challengers criticized Ricketts for highlighting opposition to same-sex marriage and for distancing himself from the Cubs' sponsorship of gay-pride events. He frequently had to explain how he disagreed with Laura, but always added, "I love her." Ricketts' main rival for the GOP nod was Attorney General Jon Bruning, and the primary at times had the feel of a grudge match. In 2012, Bruning was the leading contender for Nebraska's open Senate seat that had been vacated by Democratic incumbent Nelson, and the choice of the party establishment. But he lost a bitter primary to long-shot Deb Fisher, who was aided by a last-minute TV ad blitz funded by Joe Ricketts and his End Spending Super PAC. Bruning repeatedly accused the Ricketts family of using its wealth to buy another victory and he gained the last-minute backing from outgoing GOP Gov. Heineman. But Ricketts countered by focusing his closing pitch on support he had from Nebraskans, not presidential wannabes, and one of his final TV ads featured the backing of former Nebraska GOP Gov. Kay Orr. It was a taut race, and in a field of six candidates-Ricketts narrowly beat Bruning 27%-26%. In the general election, Chuck Hassebrook, the executive director of the Center for Rural Affairs in Lyons, who had been unopposed for the Democratic nomination, took a few stabs at making the Ricketts' fortune an issue, but was unsuccessful. Ricketts emphasized his business experience and said he would focus on reducing state spending, taxes, and business regulations. Hassebrook favored allowing the children of undocumented immigrants brought to the country illegally to have access to driving licenses, while Ricketts opposed issuing licenses. Ricketts supported the Keystone XL pipeline, saying it would bring jobs to the state, while Hassebrook opposed the pipeline and said it would ultimately contribute to global warming. Ricketts' campaign suffered an embarrassing hitch in September when his running mate, then-Lt. Gov. Lavon Heidemann, resigned his office and withdrew from the campaign the day after a local judge issued a protection order to keep him away from his sister, who had leveled a domestic abuse allegation against him. Ricketts was able to get state Auditor Mike Foley to take Heidemann's spot on the ticket. But that ended up being just a hiccup and Ricketts overwhelmed Hassebrook, 57%-39%, carrying 89 of the state's 93 counties. Ricketts' campaign spent roughly $7 million, including almost $1 million from his personal checkbook and more than $1 million from his family members—more than twice what Hassebrook spent. The Democrat's largest contribution came from Berkshire Hathaway CEO Warren Buffet, $100,000.

Entering office, Ricketts enjoyed a state surplus and favorable economy, but that did not help him prevail in a number of tests with the state legislature in 2015. First, the Nebraska lawmakers overrode Ricketts's veto of a gas tax hike, which will increase one-and-a-half cents next year and continue at that rate each year through 2019. Ricketts said the jump in the gas tax would hurt "hard-working Nebraskans," but the legislature wanted the estimated $75 million generated annually by the tax increase for state road repair and maintenance. Then, despite Ricketts' firm opposition, the legislature overrode his veto of a bill to end the state's death penalty, becoming the first conservative state in more than four decades to abolish capital punishment. Lawmakers who backed doing away with the death penalty spanned the ideological and political spectrum. With the backing of local law enforcement officials, Ricketts had lobbied the legislature for months against banning the death penalty and repeatedly urged Nebraskans to tell their lawmakers to oppose ending it. In a statement after the vote, Ricketts declared, "While the legislature has lost touch with the citizens of Nebraska, I will continue to stand with Nebraskans and law enforcement on this important issue." The legislature also voted to override Ricketts' veto of a bill that would allow immigrants who were brought into the country illegally as children to get a driver's license. The governor called this "an inappropriate benefit to non-citizens."

At a press conference after the legislative session ended, Ricketts defended his record and pointed to his work with lawmakers to contain the growth in the state spending to 3.5 percent and the enactment of a major property tax relief program. The governor deflected questions about his administration's miscues saying, "Certainly we'll get together and talk about what we could have done better in the session and learn from those things and put those in place for the next session." Ricketts learned lessons after he lost the Senate race in 2006, but his family's name apparently won't help him win over lawmakers in Lincoln.

Senior Senator

Deb Fischer (R)

Elected 2012, term expires 2019, 1st term; b. March 1, 1951, Lincoln; U. of NE, Lincoln, B.S. 1988; Presbyterian; married (Bruce); 3 children.

Elected Office: NE Legislature, 2005-12; Valentine Rural High Schl. Bd. of Ed., 1990-2004.

Professional Career: Rancher, 1972-2012.

DC Office: 454 RSOB, 20510, 202-224-6551; Fax: 202-228-1325; Website: fischer.senate.gov.

State Offices: Kearney, 308-234-2361; Lincoln, 402-441-4600; Omaha, 402-391-3411; Scottsbluff, 308-636-6344.

Committees: *Armed Services:* Emerging Threats & Capabilities (Chmn); Readiness & Management Support; Strategic Forces. *Commerce, Science & Transportation:* Aviation Operations, Safety & Security; Communications, Technology & the Internet; Consumer Protection, Product Safety & Insurance; Surface Transportation & Merchant Marine Infrastructure, Safety & Security (Chmn). *Environment & Public Works:* Clean Air & Nuclear Safety; Transportation & Infrastructure; Fisheries, Water & Wildlife. *Small Business & Entrepreneurship.*

Group Ratings

	ADA	ACLU	AFL-CIO	LCV	ITI	COC	HAFA	ACU	CFG	FRC
2014	5%	6%	–	20%	33%	100%	65%	80%	76%	86%
2013	5%	C	17%	15%	C	75%	C	76%	74%	C

National Journal Ratings

	2013 LIB	—	2013 CONS
Economic	20%	—	78%
Social	25%	—	74%
Foreign	21%	—	76%
Composite	23%	—	77%

Key Votes of the 113th Congress

1. Sandy storm spending	N	5. Student Loan Rates	Y	9. Bipartisan Budget Deal	N
2. Chuck Hagel Confirmation	N	6. Employee Non-Discrim'n Act	N	10. Farm Bill Conference Rept.	Y
3. Gun Background Checks	N	7. Senate Vote on Judgeships	Y	11. Unempl. Comp. Extension	N
4. Immigration Reform	N	8. Defense Dept. Spending	N	12. Keystone Pipeline	Y

Election Results

2012 general	Deb Fischer (R)	455,593	(58%)	$5,146,461	$1,500,923	$1,806,421
	Bob Kerrey (D)	332,979	(42%)	$6,116,555	$257,359	$1,811,313
2012 primary	Deb Fischer (R)	79,941	(41%)			
	Jon Bruning (R)	70,067	(36%)			
	Don Stenberg (R)	36,727	(19%)			

As the only Republican in the country in 2012 to pick up a Senate seat that had previously been in Democratic hands, Deb Fischer, now Nebraska's senior senator, was one of the national GOP's bright spots in a year that saw President Barack Obama reelected and

Democrats increase their Senate majority. A state senator from a rural town who lacked a statewide profile when the contest began, Fischer stunned political observers when she beat two better-known Republicans in the May primary. She went on to defeat Democrat Bob Kerrey in the general election, derailing his bid to reclaim the Senate seat he gave up in 2000. Since arriving in Washington, Fischer has been a reliably conservative vote and voice on most matters, but has sought to reach out to Democrats on some issues—notably the expansion of the Internet and the development of related new technologies.

Fischer grew up in Lincoln, the state capital, where her mother, Florence Strobel, was an elementary school teacher and her father, Jerry Strobel, spent many years as an engineer in the Nebraska Department of Roads, finishing his career heading the department in the late 1980s. She attended the University of Nebraska, where she met her husband, Bruce Fischer. In 1972, she left school to marry him, and the couple settled on the Fischer family ranch in Valentine, in northern Nebraska. Despite growing up in what she described as the "big small town" of Lincoln, Fischer said that she had little trouble adjusting to ranching life. She honed one talent often associated with farm wives. "She's infamous for her pie-making," her husband told the *Omaha World Herald* shortly after Fischer was nominated for the Senate. "She doesn't do it very often, but it's a darn-sure treat when she does." But, as her three boys grew older, Fischer temporarily returned to the University of Nebraska in Lincoln to finish her work on her degree.

While she had no plans to teach, Fischer graduated with a degree in education in 1988. Fischer said she believed the degree would help her make decisions in the leadership roles in education she had assumed, which began with service on the school board for Valentine's small country school. Her first run for elected office was in 1990, when she won a seat on the Valentine Rural High School Board of Education. She later became president of the Nebraska Association of School Boards and served on the Nebraska Coordinating Commission for Postsecondary Education, the state's oversight agency for higher education institutions. In 2004, Fischer won a seat in Nebraska's unicameral state legislature, representing a district that sprawled across a dozen counties in northern Nebraska—a geographic area the size of the state of New Jersey. She was unopposed for a second term in 2008. During her first term, an upheaval in the legislature gave Fischer the chairmanship of the Transportation and Telecommunications Committee. Among her biggest achievements was helping to win passage of legislation to shift about $70 million of the state's sales tax revenues to road construction on an annual basis.

Fischer said she was initially drawn to the Republican Party by its focus on limited government, and this philosophy was evident as she placed her imprint on several issues. In 2007, she joined in a move to filibuster a bill to ban smoking statewide for indoor worksites and other public places. She was somewhat mollified when the bill was amended to allow cities and council to vote to opt out of the restrictions. A year earlier, responding to a 2005 U.S. Supreme Court decision, she won passage of legislation barring use of eminent domain for government-backed economic development projects. But some of Fischer's constituents were said to be less than happy with her support of the Keystone XL Pipeline, which cut across Nebraska in its route from Canada to the Gulf of Mexico. Some questioned how her support of the pipeline jibed with her criticism of eminent domain, a legal option being utilized by the company seeking to build the pipeline. (In 2015, Fischer joined all of her GOP Senate colleagues in an unsuccessful attempt to override an Obama veto of a bill to move ahead on the Keystone XL Pipeline.)

Barred by law from seeking a third term in the state legislature in 2012, Fischer waited until the end of the legislative session to enter the race to succeed retiring Democratic Sen. Ben Nelson. Nelson, like Kerrey, had served as governor before winning a Senate seat. While he had accumulated one of the most conservative voting records among members of his party, he took intense political heat for his crucial 2009 vote in favor of Obama's health insurance overhaul—particularly after it was disclosed he had cut a side deal with Senate Majority Leader Harry Reid to relieve his home state of millions in Medicaid payments required under the law. The deal backfired: Republicans derided it as "the Cornhusker Kickback," and Nelson ultimately renounced it as his approval ratings in Republican-dominated Nebraska hit the skids. Nelson's decision to retire came in the face of the political reality that a bid for a third term would have been an uphill battle.

Fischer began her Senate bid as the underdog in a primary against state Attorney General Jon Bruning and state Treasurer Don Stenberg. Bruning enjoyed the support of the GOP establishment, while tea party leaders, including Sen. Jim DeMint of South Carolina rallied behind Stenberg. Fischer, however, steadily gained traction as Stenberg and Bruning turned their fire against each other. She also benefitted from the endorsement of one tea party favorite, 2008 vice presidential nominee Sarah Palin, along with a last-minute television ad blitz funded by wealthy businessman Joe Ricketts, founder of the Omaha-based TD Ameritrade stock brokerage. Fischer won the primary with 41 percent, followed by Bruning with 36 percent and Stenberg with 19 percent.

In the general election, she faced Kerrey, who—having held office as governor and senator throughout the 1980s and 1990s—was considered the Democrats' best hope in a state where nearly half of voters identify as Republicans, while only about one-third register as Democrats. But, although Kerrey was a household name, many voters were turned off by the fact that he had been living out of state since leaving the Senate in 2000; he served as president of the New York City-based New School University from 2001-2010. Kerrey's long absence from the state made him a target of attacks from Republican-aligned independent expenditure groups even before he decided to mount a political comeback. He responded by pointing to his continuing Nebraska ties, including several businesses he owned in the state. After initially sending conflicting signals about whether he would get back into politics, Kerrey in early 2012 said he would run to reclaim the seat.

Fischer campaigned vowing not to serve more than two terms in the Senate, and backed a constitutional amendment to limit service to two terms in the Senate and three in the House. She stressed her family's ranching background and her work in the legislature on issues important to rural Nebraska. In light of her criticism of the scope of the federal government's reach, Kerrey tried to make an issue of her family's use of grazing rights on 11,000 federal land, calling her a "welfare rancher." He also dubbed her a "bad neighbor" for suing an elderly couple in the 1990s in a dispute over ownership of more than 100 acres along the scenic Snake River, and suggested Fischer had used her influence in the state legislature to try to bar the couple from later selling the land in question to the state. Fischer's campaign countered that such attacks were offensive to thousands of Nebraska farmers and a "transparent act of desperation" on Kerrey's part. The charges were contained in an ad that Kerrey launched in mid-October, as polls showed him trailing by double digits. On Election Day, Fischer came out ahead, 58%-42%. While Kerrey carried the state's two most populous counties around Omaha and Lincoln, Fischer won all but a handful of counties throughout the rest of the state.

One of Fischer's first votes upon arriving in the Senate in early 2013 was to join most of her Republican colleagues in voting against Obama's nomination of another former Nebraska senator, Republican Chuck Hagel, as secretary of defense. She cited what she termed Hagel's "confusing and contradictory" testimony before the Senate Armed Services Committee, of which she was then a newly appointed member. In voting against Hagel, Fischer parted company from Republican Mike Johanns, then Nebraska's senior senator, whom Fischer had called a role model. Few were particularly surprised by her vote since Hagel, who represented Nebraska in the Senate from 1996-2008, had backed Kerrey in the fall election.

Fischer's philosophy has put her in the conservative Republican mainstream on issues ranging from taxes to abortion rights (she is a strong abortion opponent, saying it should be allowed only in cases where necessary to save the life of the mother). In the Senate, she has used her seat on the Environment and Public Works Committee to excoriate the Environmental Protection Agency for regulatory overreach. And, having started her career as a school board member, Fischer has criticized the 2002 No Child Left Behind law for not providing flexibility to states. But she has shown a pragmatic streak, declining to go as far as other conservatives who have called for abolishing the EPA and the Education Department. "I've always said…that if I would stand up and say we should abolish the Department of Education, and we should abolish the EPA, many people in the crowd would stand up and applaud," Fischer said during the 2012 campaign. "Those of you who know me know that I have a more thoughtful approach. I believe we need to look at the programs that are involved in the department, and [ask] if they are effective, if they are meeting their purpose."

As 2015 got underway, Fischer, also a member of the Commerce Committee, reached out to Democratic colleagues on several technology-related proposals. She and Florida Democrat Bill Nelson sponsored legislation allowing manufacturers to put warranties online; it was a follow-on to a bill that Fischer got passed into law in late 2014 that allowed manufacturers of radio frequency equipment to utilize the option of electronic labeling in place of affixing physical labels to equipment. She combined with Massachusetts Democrat Edward Markey and Minnesota Democrat Amy Klobuchar on separate bills to provide incentives for federal agencies to relinquish underutilized spectrum for mobile broadband services, and to encourage wireless carriers to lease unused spectrum to expand wireless coverage in rural communities. Fischer also has joined a bipartisan group of senators seeking ways to promote the economic potential of the so-called "Internet of Things," an expanding market of consumer products in which information can be transmitted without the need to consult a computer.

Junior Senator

Ben Sasse (R)

Elected 2014, term expires 2021, 1st term; b. Feb. 22, 1972, Plainview; Harvard U., B.A. 1995, St. John's Col., M.A. 1998, Yale U., Ph.D. 2004; Lutheran; married (Melissa), 3 children.

Professional Career: Chief of Staff, U.S. Dept. of Justice Office of Legal Policy, 2004-05; Chief of Staff, U.S. Rep. Jeff Fortenberry, 2005; Asst. Prof., U. of TX-Austin 2005-06; Counselor to secretary, Health & Human Services; Assist. Assist. Sec. Health & Human Services, 2007-09;Pres., Prof. U. of TX-Austin, 2009; Midland U. 2010-14.

DC Office: 386A RSOB, 20510; 202-224-4224; Website: sasse.senate .gov.

State Offices: Kearney, 308-233-3677; Lincoln, 402-476-1400; Omaha, 402-550-8040; Scottsbluff, 308-632-6032.

Committees: *Aging (Special): Agriculture, Nutrition, & Forestry:* Conservation Forestry & Natural Resources; Nutrition, Specialty Crops & Agricultural Research; Livestock, Marketing & Agriculture Security (Chmn); *Banking, Housing, & Urban Affairs:* Economic Policy; National Security & International Trade & Finance; Securities, Insurance & Investment; *Homeland Security & Governmental Affairs:* Permanent Subcommittee on Investigations; Federal Spending Oversight & Emergency Management; Regulatory Affairs & Federal Management; *Joint Economic Committee.*

Election Results

2014 general	Ben Sasse (R)	347,636	(64%)	$5,864,653	$1,681,914	$297,050
	Dave Domina (D)	170,127	(32%)	$1,227,205		$18,597
	Jim Jenkins (I)	15,868	(3%)	$354,598		
2014 primary	Ben Sasse (R)	110,802	(49%)			
	Sid Dinsdale (R)	50,494	(23%)			
	Shane Osborn (R)	47,338	(21%)			
	Bart McLeay (R)	12,840	(6%)			

Republican Ben Sasse, Nebraska's junior senator, arrived on Capitol Hill following the 2014 election with an unusual political pedigree. He's a tea party-backed conservative, but with no less than four degrees from a couple of elite East Coast universities (Harvard and Yale), and considerable experience working inside the Beltway. In fact, his chief primary opponent, former state Treasurer Shane Osborn, sought to portray Sasse as a creature of Washington during the 2014 primary. But Sasse collected critical endorsements from numerous national conservative groups and significant financial support outside the state, allowing him to easily win the nomination and general election despite a run-in with Kentucky Sen. Mitch McConnell, now Senate majority leader.

Sasse is a fifth-generation Nebraskan who, growing up, spent summers working in soybean fields and cornfields. (He bears a scar on his forehead from a boyhood fall from a hayloft.) He was born in the small town of Plainview in northeastern Nebraska, and was raised and went to high school in the nearby city of Fremont. Sasse, who turned 43 in 2015, then spent nearly two decades away from the state before returning in 2009 to head a struggling university. Recruited for Harvard thanks to his prowess as a high school wrestler, he graduated in 1994, while spending a junior year abroad at the University of Oxford in England. Sasse spent a year at the Boston Consulting Group, the financial firm where Mitt Romney had earlier gotten his start, before returning to school. He collected a master's degree from St. John's College in Annapolis, Maryland (he tutored and proctored House pages on Capitol Hill during that time), followed by two more master's degrees from Yale University on his way to earning a Ph.D. in American history from Yale in 2004. That led to a teaching post at the University of Texas' Lyndon B. Johnson School of Public Affairs.

But Sasse spent most of the five years after earning his Ph.D. working in Washington, first for the Justice Department and then briefly as chief of staff to Nebraska Republican Rep. Jeff Fortenberry, followed by consulting for the Homeland Security Department. He was at the Health and Human Services Department the last two years of the administration of George W. Bush, first as a counselor to the secretary and later, following Senate confirmation, as HHS assistant secretary for planning and evaluation. At the end of the Bush administration, Sasse went back to Nebraska to become president of Midland University in Fremont, a 130-year-old school affiliated with the Evangelical Lutheran Church that had been beset by financial difficulties. At 37, he was among the youngest college presidents in the country; during the 2014 campaign, he boasted of successfully executing a "turnaround job" that has now made Midland University what he termed "one of the fastest growing in the Midwest." He ended lifetime tenure for professors, convinced some to take buyouts, and helped bring about a takeover of a rival school.

In early 2013, Republican Mike Johanns, a former Nebraska governor and U.S. secretary of agriculture, announced he would retire from the Senate after just one term. Sasse said in July 2013 he would run for the seat, about a month after Osborn had announced he would run. Before launching his political career, Osborn was a Navy pilot detained by the Chinese briefly in 2001 after a midair collision with a Chinese fighter jet forced him to make an emergency landing. In the primary, Osborn sought to cast Sasse as too close to Washington and insufficiently conservative: Sasse had penned a column in 2009 for *U.S. News and World Report* calling Medicare Part D, the prescription-drug benefit passed by a GOP-controlled Congress during the Bush administration, "enormously successful" and a "viable model for reform." But conservative groups rallied around Sasse as he headed to the top of the polls, and the Club for Growth and the Senate Conservatives Fund spent heavily on his behalf. Campaign visits by GOP crowd-pleasers, including Sen. Ted Cruz of Texas as well as former Alaska Gov. Sarah Palin, helped cement Sasse as the conservative choice in the primary. In January 2014, Sasse was featured on the cover of the conservative *National Review* as a "rising conservative star."

About three months earlier, Sasse had posted a video, complaining about federal taxpayers underwriting health care insurance premiums for members of Congress and their staffs, and taking particular aim at members of his own party. "It is time for every Republican in Washington, starting with Minority Leader Mitch McConnell, to show some actual leadership on this issue by voluntarily giving up their healthcare subsidy," Sasse declared in the video.

The video was said to have enraged McConnell, who was himself trying to turn back a conservative primary challenger in his own reelection bid in Kentucky. According to an account in *National Review*, Sasse visited McConnell in November 2013 in an effort to clear the air, and to deny rumors he had secretly vowed to oppose McConnell's election as leader if he won the Senate seat. But the session reportedly did little to assuage McConnell—who was upset not only about the video, but also by Sasse's support from the Senate Conservatives Fund and his interaction with leaders of that organization. McConnell had long been at odds with the group, which not surprisingly was supporting McConnell's conservative challenger, Matt Bevin, in the Kentucky primary. McConnell ultimately defeated Bevin on his way to reelection to a sixth term, and there is no indication McConnell sought to quietly work against Sasse in retaliation.

In the May Nebraska primary, a late surge by wealthy bank executive Sid Dinsdale, who ran a largely self-funded campaign, raised the prospect of an upset if the conservative vote divided between Sasse and Osborn. But Dinsdale met with attack ads from the Club for Growth and others hitting him as being too liberal. Sasse finished far ahead, with 49 percent, followed by 23 percent for Dinsdale and 21 percent for Osborn. National Democrats made no attempt to seriously contest the seat in the general election, in which Sasse defeated Democrat Dave Domina, an Omaha attorney who had last sought public office three decades earlier, by 64%-32%.

Sasse, whom *National Review* called "Obamacare's Nebraska nemesis," was sworn into office with the goal of undoing the Affordable Care Act atop his list of priorities. He introduced the "Winding Down Obama Care Act", which was seen as a potential Republican fallback position if the Supreme Court had failed to uphold a key provision of the ACA—subsidies to the federal health insurance exchange—in June 2015. Sasse's bill proposed to do away with the current subsidies under ACA, replacing them with general tax credits that would disappear within 18 months. He argued this would give the Republican-controlled Congress time to come up with an alternative to the ACA.

Beyond just Obamacare, however, Sasse—who is married with three young children, all of whom are being home-schooled—is clearly taking aim at the overall current scope and power of the federal government. When Richard Cordray, the director of the Treasury Department's Consumer Financial Protection Bureau (created by the 2010 Dodd-Frank financial regulatory overhaul law) visited Omaha in the summer of 2015, Sasse issued a press release disdainfully declaring: "Richard Cordray and the CFPB aren't accountable to Congress or the American people. With access to honest and accurate information, moms and dads can make financial decisions for themselves and for their families. I hope Mr. Cordray listens to Nebraskans, and recognizes that unlimited agency power cannot implement what hard work and honesty achieve."

While describing himself as a "market-oriented conservative who believes in decentralized solutions wherever possible," Sasse has shied away from the tea party label. "I don't exactly know what tea party means," he told Nebraska public television during the 2014 campaign, "because if you look at some of the polling, about 60 percent of Nebraska Republicans say they don't like the term tea party, but they identify with the tea party's stances on issues. That's another way of saying it's a pretty useless term mostly foisted by the media, and I think at the end of the day, what tea party means in Nebraska is mostly urgency. Nebraskans think there are big and broken problems, and they want Washington to move faster about the most urgent ones."

FIRST DISTRICT

Jeff Fortenberry (R)

Elected 2004, 6th term; b. Dec. 27, 1960, Baton Rouge, LA; LA St. U., 1982, Franciscan U. of Steubenville, M.A. 1985, Georgetown U., M.P.P. 1986; Catholic; married (Celeste); 5 children.

Elected Office: Lincoln City Cncl., 1997-2001.

Professional Career: Staffer, U.S. House Comm. on Ag., 1986; Research assoc., Gulf South Research Inst., 1987-89; Asst. dir., Baton Rouge Downtown Dev. Dist., 1989-92; Sales rep., Sandhills Publishing, 1995-2004.

DC Office: 1514 LHOB, 20515, 202-225-4806; Fax: 202-225-5686; Website: fortenberry.house.gov.

State Offices: Fremont, 402-727-0888; Lincoln, 402-438-1598; Norfolk, 402-379-2064.

Committees: *Appropriations:* Military Construction, Veterans Affairs & Related Agencies (VChmn); Energy & Water Development, & Related Agencies; State, Foreign Operations, & Related Programs.

Group Ratings

	ADA	ACLU	AFL-CIO	LCV	ITI	COC	HAFA	ACU	CFG	FRC
2014	5%	0%	–	6%	100%	93%	50%	56%	51%	100%
2013	5%	C	24%	4%	C	85%	C	63%	54%	C

National Journal Ratings

	2013 LIB —	2013 CONS
Economic	48% —	52%
Social	34% —	62%
Foreign	34% —	60%
Composite	40% —	60%

Key Votes of the 113th Congress

1. Sandy storm spending	N	5. Medical Marijuana	N	9. Syrian Rebels Training	Y
2. Violence Against Women Act	N	6. Farm Bill	Y	10. Keystone pipeline	Y
3. Guantanamo Bay Detainees	N	7. Afghanistan Combat	N	11. Immigration Exec. Action	Y
4. Abortion 20-week ban	Y	8. NSA Phone Data Collection	N	12. Bipartisan budget deal	Y

Election Results

2014 general	Jeff Fortenberry (R)................. 123,219	(69%)	$396,337	$2,563
	Dennis Crawford (D) 55,838	(31%)	$44,690	
2014 primary	Jeff Fortenberry (R).................... 63,673	(86%)		
	Jessica L. Turek (R)..................... 5,902	(8%)		
	Dennis Parker (R)........................ 4,407	(6%)		

Prior winning percentages: 2012 (68%), 2010 (71%), 2008 (70%), 2006 (58%), 2004 (54%)

Population		Race and Ethnicity		Income	
Total:	628,082	White	84.3%	Median income:	$52,195
Urban:	49.4%	Latino	7.9%		*(203 of 435)*
Suburban:	12.0%	Black	2.5%	Under $50,000	47.3%
Rural:	38.5%	Asian	2.1%	$50,000-$99,999:	33.2%
Land area:	9,898	Two races	2.0%	$100,000-$199,999:	16.5%
Pop/sq. mi.:	63.5	White Ethnic	27.9%	$200,000 or more:	3.1%
Born in state:	67.4%			Poverty Rate	12.9%
		Education:			
Age Groups		H.S. grad or less:	35.5%	**Work**	
Under 18:	24.4%	Some college:	34.5%	White collar:	34.6%
18 to 34:	25.4%	College degree, 4 yr.:	20.2%	Blue collar:	41.6%
35 to 64:	36.5%	Post-grad study:	9.9%	Sales and service:	23.8%
Over 64:	13.7%				
		Military:		Govt. workers:	16.3%
		Veterans/active duty:	9.9%		

Eastern Nebraska: Lincoln

The eastern half of Nebraska, between the Missouri River and the 98th parallel, was laid out in relentless Midwestern mile-square grids and became some of America's prime farmland during the 1880s. Here the Plains have completed most of their gentle decline from the Rockies to sea level, and the land

Voter Turnout	
2013 Total Citizen 18+	453,848
2014 House Turnout	179,057
2014 Turnout as % CVAP	39.5%
2012 Turnout as % CVAP	59.3%

has contours just regular enough, and weather just favorable enough, to make farming economically viable. The area was settled by Yankee-descended farmers from the Midwest and immigrants from Germany and other countries. Traces of the immigrant heritage can still be found. Many people from Luxembourg, for example, settled along the Platte River in Butler County, where St. Mary's Presentation Parish still has a statue of Our Lady of Luxembourg. Not far away are villages with names that recall other immigrant groups—Prague (Czechs), Malmo (Swedes), Aloys (Germans).

Today, a new wave of immigrants is coming to eastern Nebraska, including Latinos from Mexico and the southwest United States, to work in the region's meatpacking factories. Fremont, a town of 37,000 northwest of Omaha that is about 11% Hispanic, made national news in 2010 when voters overwhelmingly approved an ordinance mandating immigration background checks for anyone seeking to rent an apartment or house. A few thousand refugees from Vietnam settled in Lincoln, and organized community groups.

The 1st Congressional District of Nebraska comprises 16 counties and parts of two others in the eastern slice of the state. It surrounds but does not take in Omaha, which is in the 2nd District. By far the most populous county is Lancaster, home to the city of Lincoln and the main campus of the University of Nebraska, which has many scientific units that receive large research grants. Growing and affluent, Lincoln has above-national average income and its unemployment rate—2.3% in February 2015—has been among the lowest in the nation. The city is home to more than 100 companies and government agencies with 250 or more workers, including a strong manufacturing sector that makes up more than 13% of its economy. In the smaller towns, there are many farm equipment and meatpacking factories. A few miles from Omaha, the district includes the eastern part of fast-growing Sarpy County and the city of Bellevue, home of Offutt Air Force Base, headquarters of the Strategic Air Command. Bellevue is the more urban and less conservative part of Sarpy County.

Politically, Lincoln is fond of moderate Democrats but is still, on balance, Republican in national contests. Small Thurston County in the 1st had the distinction of being the only county in Nebraska won by President Barack Obama in 2012.

2012 Presidential Vote		
Mitt Romney (R)	152,021	(57%)
Barack Obama (D)	108,082	(41%)
2008 Presidential Vote		
John McCain (R)	143,124	(54%)
Barack Obama (D)	117,515	(44%)
Cook Partisan Voting Index:	R+10	

Jeff Fortenberry (R)

Republican Jeff Fortenberry, elected in 2004, has a reputation as a brainy policy expert who has evolved into a centrist. In the tradition of many Nebraskans (including former Senators Chuck Hagel and Bob Kerrey), Fortenberry takes a strong interest in foreign policy.

Fortenberry grew up in Baton Rouge Louisiana where his father was a life insurance salesman and his mother worked as a 4-H Club extension agent. When Fortenberry was 12, his father was killed in a car accident. "It taught me a hard lesson that you wouldn't want to wish on any other child—you have to figure out a lot of things on your own," he told *Esquire* magazine. Fortenberry got the political bug early as a page to a Democratic state senator, but switched to the Republican Party after he graduated from Louisiana State University. He earned one master's degree in theology from Franciscan University of Steubenville, Ohio, and another in public policy from Georgetown University. (For a time, he studied for the priesthood.)

In 1995, Fortenberry moved to Nebraska to take a public relations position with Sandhills Publishing, a publisher of trade magazines for the trucking, aircraft and computer industries. He later got into the sales end of the business. Fortenberry's first foray into politics came in 1997, when he won a seat on the Lincoln City Council. He served for four years, focusing on neighborhood concerns and on an increase in the police force.

When the seat opened in 2004, three candidates mounted competitive campaigns for the Republican nomination: Fortenberry; Curt Bromm, the speaker of the state's unicameral legislature; and Greg Ruehle, a former executive vice president of the Nebraska Cattlemen Association. The moderate Bromm began as the front-runner. But he lost momentum after a barrage of negative television ads financed by the Club for Growth, a national anti-tax group that supported Ruehle. Fortenberry, a social conservative, drew criticism from his opponents as a single-issue candidate, but his superior grassroots operation and fundraising carried him to victory. Fortenberry won with 39% of the vote, to 33% for Bromm and 21% for Ruehle. He won just seven of the 24 counties, but in Lincoln's Lancaster County, which cast 43% of the votes, he got 52%.

In November, Fortenberry faced state Sen. Matt Connealy, a farmer from Decatur who sought to exploit Republican divisions; Bromm refused to endorse Fortenberry after the primary. He characterized Fortenberry as a stranger to Nebraska farm issues, a potent charge in a state where one in four jobs is connected to agriculture. Fortenberry responded by promising to improve trade policies for farmers and to support ethanol development. His main message, however, focused on socially conservative themes: opposition to abortion rights, support of capital punishment, and a ban on same-sex marriage. Fortenberry won 54%-43%, losing only two American Indian reservation counties.

In the House, Fortenberry has moved over time to the ideological center. He was one of 37 House Republicans in 2011 to back a Democratic amendment allowing the Obama administration to list new species and habitats for protection under the Endangered Species Act, and he was one of 33 that year to support spending $10 million more for renewable energy and energy efficiency programs. He backed the 2011 compromise to raise the federal debt limit as well as the New Year's Day 2013 budget deal aimed at averting the so-called "fiscal cliff." He was one of a handful of Republicans who signed a Democratic "discharge petition" seeking to force a floor vote on the stalled farm bill. In May 2011, he praised President Barack Obama's speech outlining his approach in the Middle East and North Africa that conservatives panned. He noted that he and Obama both won Lincoln in 2008. "People here pride themselves on independence," he told *Esquire*. Earlier, he supported President George W. Bush on the war in Iraq, won House approval of an increase in visas for Iraqi translators, and got a bill into law barring U.S. assistance for governments using children as soldiers.

Fortenberry has remained a strong social conservative. He has filed a bill that would repeal the Obama administration's contraception coverage requirements and allow religious institutions and small businesses to refuse to provide services that violate their beliefs. It drew more than 220 cosponsors, and his visibility in opposition to the president was enough to earn him a seat on the Appropriations Committee in 2013. His subcommittee work focuses on foreign aid, military construction and veterans, plus energy and water projects. He supported extension of the Export-Import Bank of the United States on the basis that "we don't have a perfect world." As evidence of his on-going interests overseas, he co-chairs both the Caucus on Religious Minorities in the Middle East and the Congressional Study Group on Europe.

In 2006, Fortenberry's first reelection campaign was against former Democratic Lt. Gov. Maxine Moul, who made the Iraq war an issue. Even with ample fundraising, Moul's campaign did not catch fire in the district, which has not elected a Democrat since 1964. Fortenberry won 58%-42%. He hasn't been held below 68% since.

SECOND DISTRICT

Brad Ashford (D)

Elected 2014, 1st term; b. Nov. 10, 1949, Omaha; Colgate U., B.A. 1971; Creighton U., School of Law, J.D. 1974; Lutheran; married (Ann), 3 children.

Elected Office: NE State Senate, 1987-95; 2007-15 (District 20).

Professional Career: Staff, U.S. Senator Roman Hruska, NE, 1974-75; Atty., Fed. Hwy. Admin., 1974-75; Hearing Examiner, NE Dept. of Ed., 1983-84; Judge, NE Court of Industrial Relations, 1984-86. CEO, Omaha, NE Housing Authority, 1987-1994.

DC Office: 107 CHOB, 20515; 202-225-4155; Fax: 202-226-5452; Website: ashford.house.gov.

State Offices: Omaha, 402-916-5678.

Committees: *Agriculture:* General Farm Commodities & Risk Mgmt., Nutrition. *Agriculture; Armed Services:* Strategic Forces; Emerging Threats & Capabilities.

Election Results

2014 general	Brad Ashford (D)	83,872	(49%)	$1,216,468	$228,665	$1,003,241
	Lee Terry (R)	78,157	(46%)	$3,084,768	$237,980	$1,293,877
	Steven Laird (Lib)	9,021	(5%)			
2014 primary	Brad Ashford (D)	16,989	(81%)			
	Mark Aupperle (D)	3,872	(19%)			

Population		Race and Ethnicity		Income	
Total:	634,418	White	74.4%	Median income:	$54,879
Urban:	81.8%	Latino	10.3%		*(167 of 435)*
Suburban:	17.1%	Black	9.8%	Under $50,000	45.6%
Rural:	1.1%	Asian	2.8%	$50,000-$99,999:	31.3%
Land area:	525	Two races	2.1%	$100,000-$199,999:	18.4%
Pop/sq. mi.:	1,207.6	White Ethnic	33.1%	$200,000 or more:	4.7%
Born in state:	59.9%			Poverty Rate	13.6%
		Education			
Age Groups		H.S. grad or less:	31.2%	**Work**	
Under 18:	26.5%	Some college:	31.8%	White collar:	40.6%
18 to 34:	24.9%	College degree, 4 yr.:	23.8%	Blue collar:	41.4%
35 to 64:	37.7%	Post-grad study:	13.1%	Sales and service:	18.0%
Over 64:	10.9%				
		Military		Govt. workers:	10.3%
		Veterans/active duty:	8.1%		

Greater Omaha

Omaha is the commercial heart of Nebraska and the largest city on the Great Plains north of Kansas City and west of Minneapolis. It got its start from the government, when President Abraham Lincoln picked it as the eastern terminus of the Union Pacific railroad, from which emerged the stockyards

Voter Turnout	
2013 Total Citizen 18+	434,144
2014 House Turnout	171,050
2014 Turnout as % CVAP	39.4%
2012 Turnout as % CVAP	62.3%

and livestock exchange that made it a thriving town. Over the years, Omaha filled up with cattle hands and European immigrants, especially Germans and Czechs. It developed fine civic institutions, from the Joslyn Art Museum to Boys Town, an orphanage founded by the Rev. Edward Flanagan in 1917 and the subject of a 1938 movie. Today, the facility is a gender-neutral home for troubled youth. While Norfolk to the west became known for launching talk show host Johnny Carson, a number of Hollywood legends had roots in Omaha: Fred Astaire, Marlon Brando, Montgomery Clift and Henry Fonda.

Though a major city by the 1880s, Omaha has remained small enough to be intimate. One doesn't feel distant, physically or psychologically, from the other side of town. The older, less affluent part of Omaha is near Iowa and the Missouri River. Downtown and the riverfront have experienced substantial growth and development; the Tower at First National Center is the tallest structure between Minneapolis and Denver. To the west, the city has been quietly flourishing with the rise of upscale neighborhoods and shopping malls. Omaha has also entered the Wall Street vernacular as the place where investor Warren Buffett—ranked by *Forbes* in 2014 as the nation's second-richest person, with $70 billion in net worth—lives and works. Buffett is a high-profile supporter of President Barack Obama, and his so-called "Buffett Rule"—that wealthy people should pay a greater share of taxes—has become a frequent Democratic talking point.

Omaha was largely spared from the recession; unemployment in the metro area peaked at 6% in 2010 and dropped to under 4% in 2012. In recent years, it has experienced a construction boomlet, with a $370-million cancer center with more than 4,600 employees projected at the University of Nebraska Medical Center, a $2 billion sewer separation project, and expansions into new buildings of the headquarters of Omaha-based TD Ameritrade and Tenaska, an energy company. While Omaha's economy remains dependent on overseas sales of meat (ConAgra Foods and Omaha Steaks are based there), it has also become the nation's telecommunications hub, employing more than 30,000 people at more than three dozen telemarketing centers. In May 2015, Omaha-based Right at Home received an award at a White House ceremony for helping to expand U.S. exports. Millennials are 38% of this expanding workforce. The city is also becoming more ethnically diverse: It's about 13% Hispanic and 14% African American.

The 2nd Congressional District includes Omaha and all of Douglas County. Omaha has long had competitive politics, with Democrats strong on the south side around the stockyards and the northeast and Republicans strong on the west side. As Omaha and Nebraska have boomed, they have become more Republican, and increasingly it is the Republican primary that decides elections. But Obama scored an impressive achievement when he won the district in 2008 by 50%-49%, ensuring him one elector from Nebraska as a consequence of the state's proportional division of Electoral College votes.

2012 Presidential Vote		
Mitt Romney (R)...............140,976		(53%)
Barack Obama (D)............121,889		(46%)
2008 Presidential Vote		
Barack Obama (D)............133,018		(50%)
John McCain (R)...............131,223		(49%)
Cook Partisan Voting Index: R+4		

But four years later, Obama lost Douglas 35%-46% and came up empty handed. This is the least conservative district in Nebraska and Democrats can prevail in local elections under the right circumstances.

Brad Ashford (D)

Brad Ashford was one of two Democrats nationwide to oust a House Republican incumbent in 2014. The former state senator took advantage of his own non-partisan—or multipartisan—background, plus the occasional gaffes of Republican Rep. Lee Terry. With this district's slightly Republican lean, Ashford immediately became a top GOP target for 2016.

Ashford grew up in Omaha and moved east to attend Colgate University. His father received a Distinguished Flying Cross for his service as a B-26 pilot during World War II, and his mother's father had been a business owner and philanthropist in Omaha. A Republican during college, young Ashford interned for then-GOP Sen. Roman Hruska of Nebraska. He returned home to get his law degree at Creighton University, then worked briefly in the Federal Highway Administration's general counsel's office in Washington before joining an Omaha law firm. He switched political parties in the 1980s to support then-Democratic Gov. Bob Kerrey, who later became a senator.

Ashford was elected in 1986 to Nebraska's unicameral Legislature and served two terms. He ran for the 2nd District seat in 1994 after switching parties again to become a Republican but finished a distant second in the primary. He was an adviser on economic development to Republican Mayor Hal Daub of Omaha. After a 12-year absence, he returned to the Legislature in 2007 and rose to Judiciary Committee chairman. He worked on a justice reform package aimed at reducing prison overcrowding, enhancing substance-abuse treatment programs, and exploring alternatives to prison. He ran for Omaha mayor in 2013 as an independent but took fourth in the primary.

Terry had been a target of Democrats for several years. He drew headlines in 2010 when the *New York Post* reported that he flirtatiously asked a female lobbyist, "Why did you get me so drunk?" at a Capitol Hill club. And at the height of the October 2013 government shutdown, he told the *Omaha World-Herald* he would continue to take his paycheck because he had a "nice house and a kid in college." The first sign of trouble for Terry in 2014 was in the primary, when he took just 53 percent against a weak opponent, "a strong indication that even many Republicans personally disliked him," according to David Wasserman.

Ashford—who returned to the Democratic fold in 2013—decided to seek Terry's seat after Omaha City Council President Pete Festersen, a Democrat, determined that the race was more than he could handle and dropped out in December. Ashford portrayed himself as a nonpartisan consensus-builder: "I could care less what political party anyone is," he told the *World-Herald*.

Terry ran ads accusing Ashford of having a "dangerous" record on fighting crime, highlighting his rival's opposition to changing the state's "good time" law reducing inmates' sentences. The National Republican Congressional Committee also ran a spot featuring a man who killed four people after his release from prison, an ad that some observers compared to the 1988 Willie Horton ad against Massachusetts Gov. Michael Dukakis. Ashford highlighted Terry's paycheck statement and questioned whether the congressman had been effective. Ashford received $1.2 million in national party money, compared with $1.5 million for Terry, though the challenger was outspent from his own campaign funds, $3.1 million to $1.2 million. His 49%-45.7% victory provided one of the Democratic Party's few bright spots in the House on Election Night. In Douglas County, which cast 84% of the total vote, Ashford led 51%-44%.

In the House, Ashford got prime seats for a freshman on the Agriculture and Armed Services committees, and said that Offutt Air Force Base and the Strategic Air Command are vital to the nation's military infrastructure. He joined two bipartisan "problem-solver" caucuses. He was among the early House Democrats to announce support of the Trans-Pacific Partnership following an April 2015 meeting in which he and other centrist Democrats joined President Barack Obama at the White House. He kept a campaign promise to cut his congressional salary by 10 percent. Ashford received unusual publicity when he was struck by a purse in the House chamber during the March 2015 speech by Israeli Prime Minister Benjamin Netanyahu. The purse was owned by the wife of Sheldon Adelson, who was seated in the gallery and accidentally lost control of it. In a presumed coincidence, Adelson had spent $35,000 on behalf of Terry during the 2014 campaign. This probably was the closest that Ashford would get to the assets of the billionaire Republican campaign supporter.

He was pressured by Democratic campaign strategists—and some of his own staff resigned—over concerns that he was not focusing sufficiently on fundraising for reelection within weeks after taking office. "I think I'm not doing it the way it's normally done," he told a *World-Herald* reporter in March 2015. In a May speech to the Sarpy County Chamber of Commerce, Ashford said the political system is "wholly broken," and that he would not bow to internal pressure from other Democrats. Republicans were hopeful that he would become "one and done" in November 2016.

THIRD DISTRICT

Adrian Smith (R)

Elected 2006, 5th term; b. Dec. 19, 1970, Scottsbluff; U. of NE, B.S. 1993; Christian; married (Andrea).

Elected Office: Gering City Cncl., 1994-98; NE Legislature, 1998- 2006.

Professional Career: Realtor, Buyer Realty, 1997-2006; Owner, My Other Garage, 2003-06.

DC Office: 2241 RHOB, 20515, 202-225-6435; Fax: 202-225-0207; Website: adriansmith.house.gov.

State Offices: Grand Island, 308-384-3900; Scottsbluff, 308-633-6333.

Committees: *Ways & Means:* Health; Trade.

Group Ratings

	ADA	ACLU	AFL-CIO	LCV	ITI	COC	HAFA	ACU	CFG	FRC
2014	0%	0%	–	3%	100%	79%	59%	84%	70%	100%
2013	0%	C	19%	4%	C	85%	C	84%	65%	C

National Journal Ratings

	2013 LIB	—	2013 CONS
Economic	32%	—	68%
Social	0%	—	87%
Foreign	5%	—	86%
Composite	16%	—	84%

Key Votes of the 113th Congress

1. Sandy storm spending	N	5. Medical Marijuana	N	9. Syrian Rebels Training	Y
2. Violence Against Women Act	N	6. Farm Bill	Y	10. Keystone pipeline	Y
3. Guantanamo Bay Detainees	N	7. Afghanistan Combat	N	11. Immigration Exec. Action	Y
4. Abortion 20-week ban	Y	8. NSA Phone Data Collection	N	12. Bipartisan budget deal	N

Election Results

2014 general	Adrian Smith (R)	139,440	(75%)	$877,940
	Mark Sullivan (D)	45,524	(25%)	$57,041
2014 primary	Adrian Smith (R)	67,113	(68%)	
	Tom Brewer (R)	31,436	(32%)	

Prior winning percentages: 2012 (74%), 2010 (70%), 2008 (77%), 2006 (55%)

Population		Race and Ethnicity		Income	
Total:	606,016	White	86.6%	Median income:	$48,263
Urban:	10.2%	Latino	10.1%		*(265 of 435)*
Suburban:	3.0%	Black	1.0%	Under $50,000	51.8%
Rural:	86.8%	Amer. Indian	0.8%	$50,000-$99,999:	33.4%
Land area:	75,231	Two races	0.9%	$100,000-$199,999:	12.2%
Pop/sq. mi.:	8.1	White Ethnic	23.8%	$200,000 or more:	2.5%
Born in state:	67.9%			Poverty Rate	13.1%
		Education			
Age Groups		H.S. grad or less:	43.9%	**Work**	
Under 18:	23.6%	Some college:	35.0%	White collar:	31.4%
18 to 34:	20.2%	College degree, 4 yr.:	14.8%	Blue collar:	39.0%
35 to 64:	38.1%	Post-grad study:	6.3%	Sales and service:	29.5%
Over 64:	18.1%				
		Military		Govt. workers:	15.5%
		Veterans/active duty:	9.6%		

Central and Western Nebraska

West of Grand Island, Nebraska is wheat and livestock country. For miles on end there are rolling brown fields, only occasionally interrupted by barbed wire fences. The wind, rain and tornadoes that come suddenly remind you that the original settlers likened this part of the country to an ocean

Voter Turnout	
2013 Total Citizen 18+	442,482
2014 House Turnout	184,964
2014 Turnout as % CVAP	41.8%
2012 Turnout as % CVAP	58%

and thought themselves in their wooden wagons almost as helpless as passengers at sea in a rowboat. Settlers passed through here on the Oregon Trail in the 1840s, and then set down roots in the 1880s. But the rain they hoped for fell too unreliably, and wheat lands gave way to pasture and open range. It is a beautiful but hard land, exacting much from its people, as the novels of western Nebraska's Willa Cather make poignantly clear. Chimney Rock—a clay and sandstone spire that marked a good camping spot and offered reliable spring water for travelers and their animals—was the landmark that travelers on the Oregon Trail most frequently mentioned in their journals. This symbol of westward expansion now graces the Nebraska issue of the U.S. quarter.

Dozens of small counties in the region today have fewer people than they did in 1900. Severe droughts in recent years have seemed a kind of end point for some, as the grasslands turned dry and brown, reservoirs and aquifers began to run dry, and ranchers sold off their thinning herds. Still, many farmers have found ways to adapt. The $17.7 billion value of farm production sold in this large area was higher than any other congressional district in the nation, according to the Census of Agriculture in 2012. That total included $7.7 billion for cattle. Economic life also sets records in other industries. In North Platte, Bailey Yard is the world's largest railroad classification yard, covering 2,850 acres and handling 14,000 rail cars every 24 hours. The Union Pacific line from North Platte east to Gibbon is the busiest freight rail corridor in the world, with 139 trains a day passing through here. The railroads employ about 8,000 people in Nebraska. In early 2015, the booming economy in North Platte led to a shortage of housing.

The town of Sidney is home to Cabela's, a large mail order and Internet business for hunting, fishing and camping gear. The company and Sidney entered into a $400 million partnership in 2012 to build 800 new homes in the area. When the Keystone XL oil pipeline was proposed to go through the environmentally sensitive Sandhills area in north central Cornhusker politicians pushed to have the pipeline rerouted. President Barack Obama rejected the company's application in early 2012 in part, he said, because of concerns about this region. That set off a new round of review in Nebraska, with the state Supreme Court in January 2015 upholding the decision by Gov. Dave Heineman to approve the route.

2012 Presidential Vote		
Mitt Romney (R)	182,067	(70%)
Barack Obama (D)	72,110	(28%)
2008 Presidential Vote		
John McCain (R)	178,632	(67%)
Barack Obama (D)	82,786	(31%)
Cook Partisan Voting Index:	R+23	

The 3rd Congressional District is geographically massive, larger than the state of New York. The district takes in all or part of 75 counties, more than any other district in the nation. This is among the top five percent of the most conservative districts, and is solidly Republican.

Adrian Smith (R)

Republican Adrian Smith, elected in 2006, is an unwavering conservative who uses his seat on the Ways and Means Committee and his low-key style to focus intently on the rural issues important in his district.

Smith hails from a politically active family; his father is a former county Republican chairman, and his mother is the state GOP secretary. But the most significant political influence in Smith's life was President Ronald Reagan. When he was in fourth grade, Smith recalls, adults around him were weighing Reagan's attributes against that of Democrat Jimmy Carter's, and it sunk into the boy's head that Reagan favored a strong defense. "It just made sense to me that we needed a strong military," said Smith, whose congressional office is filled with portraits of the former president. In college, Smith served as an intern in the Nebraska governor's office and as a page in the state's unicameral legislature.

At 23, shortly after graduating from the University of Nebraska, he won election to the Gering City Council in his hometown. Four years later, he knocked off a Democratic incumbent to win the first of two terms in the legislature. There, Smith devoted his efforts to opposing abortion rights, protecting Nebraskans' right to bear arms, fighting tax increases and blocking efforts to expand casino gambling. He also worked as a real estate agent and owned a storage business.

In May 2005, Smith joined the race for the open seat. Leading the crowded Republican primary field were Grand Island Mayor Jay Vavricek and John Hanson, the former district director of retiring Rep. Tom Osborne. Smith championed tax incentives to attract new residents and encourage local investment. He promised to expand global markets for Nebraska farmers.

Still, his opponents charged that he betrayed rural Nebraska by accepting more than $300,000 in contributions from members of the Club for Growth, a national anti-tax group that opposes farm subsidies. Smith supports caps on subsidies, which many of his farming constituents do not. He parried by touting his support from the Nebraska Farm Bureau. Smith ultimately won the nomination with 39% of the vote. Hanson finished second with 29%, while Vavricek got 27%.

In the general election, the Democrats fielded an unusually strong nominee: Yale-educated cattle rancher Scott Kleeb, who called for changes in farm policy to emphasize niche markets, and accused Smith of "distorting the truth" about the Club for Growth's opposition to farm subsidies. Smith portrayed Kleeb as a political carpetbagger who grew up overseas on military bases and attended schools in Colorado and Connecticut before settling in Nebraska on a family-owned ranch. Kleeb was competitive financially and kept the race close in the polls. Still, Smith won 55%-45%. He has easily won reelection since.

In Washington, Smith has been more conservative than his Nebraska colleagues in the House. He is a member of the Tea Party Caucus, and he once answered a survey from the conservative Heritage Foundation about what makes him happy by responding, "Having the freedom to pursue opportunities relating to my faith while upholding the ideals of our Founding Fathers."

Smith was rewarded for his party loyalty with a coveted assignment on Ways and Means in 2011. With a focus on agriculture and trade issues, he sought to ensure that agriculture was part of the talks held by a U.S.-European Union working group that met to consider a free trade agreement. He was a leading voice in calling for repeal of the estate tax, which was eliminated for all but a few thousand wealthy taxpayers in the New Year's Day 2013 budget compromise. He has advocated lower corporate tax rates to keep the United States more competitive in the world economy, and he contends that free-trade agreements are good for the nation's overall economy, especially agriculture.

Smith stood by President George W. Bush as support for the war in Iraq waned, turning down the Democrats' offer of billions of dollars in drought relief if he joined them in pushing timetables for withdrawing troops. As co-chairman of the Congressional Rural Caucus, Smith pushed to preserve federal grants for tiny airports. He has urged President Barack Obama to create a new Office of Rural Affairs. In 2009, Smith got the House to pass his bill setting up a grant program to relieve veterinarian shortages. As founder and co-chairman in 2015 of the Modern Agriculture Caucus, Smith promoted scientifically based policies to move agriculture forward and to educate other lawmakers about the issues that farmers face.

★ NEVADA ★

Nevada has been a land of boom and bust from its very beginnings as a territory. The evidence of the latest boom is apparent as your plane descends for a landing at Las Vegas' McCarran International Airport. You see a pyramid rising from the desert; just across the street from the Sphinx-like lion are New York City-style skyscrapers. Nearby are a fair-sized Eiffel Tower, the gondolas of Venice, the mansard roofs of Paris, and a flaming pirate ship. But get around town and you see signs of bust—giant hotels and condominiums with no lights on at night, retail space up for rent, subdivisions where half the houses are unoccupied, and a seamy side of town expertly mined by *CSI,* the flagship of the long-running TV crime procedural. All this is set in one of North America's most forbidding landscapes, a bowl-shaped desert valley rimmed by barren peaks. "Geologically, Nevada is a gigantic, post-oceanic ditch between the Rockies and the Sierras, filled with rough, secondary mountain ranges that stack and twine across the naked landscape like ranks of FEMA house trailers in a storage lot," writes Las Vegas art critic Dave Hickey.

A similar description, minus the reference to government-issued trailers, might have been made by the prospectors who first came to mine silver and gold in Virginia City, on a mountain 6,700 feet above sea level, or by Mark Twain and Bret Harte, who documented the heyday of the Comstock Lode, discovered in 1859, which produced $500 million worth of silver in the next 20 years. President Abraham Lincoln's Republicans made Nevada a state in 1864, even though it did not meet the population requirement, in order to win three more electoral votes. But that boom went bust, and by 1900, Nevada had only 42,000 residents, down 68% from its 1880 peak. It seemed questionable whether this was a viable state. In the early 1930s, when there were still only 91,000 Nevadans, the state government was about to go bankrupt. So Nevada decided to roll the dice. It reduced its residency requirement for divorce to six weeks and legalized gambling. Catering to what most Americans considered sin—casinos, pawnshops, divorce mills, quick-wedding chapels, and even legal brothels—turned out to be good business. The 6.75% gambling receipts tax generated enough revenue to make it unnecessary for Nevada to impose income, corporate, or inheritance taxes.

From mining boom to gambling boom, Nevada has been a second-chance state, a place for outcasts to succeed and misfits to rebound. Like Alaska, it is one of the few states with more men than women. It has the highest per capita divorce rate of any state, 12.9 percent for men and 14.9 percent for women—though it is less of an outlier than it once was. Only 24% of Nevadans were born in-state, the lowest of any state; in Stateline on Lake Tahoe, just 5% were born in Nevada. The state has been an avenue of success for ethnic groups who faced roadblocks elsewhere. The four owners of the Comstock Lode—MacKay, Fair, Flood, and O'Brien—were Irishmen. The first big hotel on the Las Vegas strip, the Flamingo, was built in 1946 by the Jewish gangster Bugsy Siegel, who was later gunned down in his Beverly Hills home. Most of the big casinos were owned by mobsters until industrialist Howard Hughes—a different kind of outcast—bought them up in the late 1960s. The job market has attracted African-Americans and, since the 1980s, many Hispanics and even some Asians (especially from the Philippines). In 2011, Nevada's population was 28% Hispanic, 9% black, and 8% Asian. Nevadans tend to be nonreligious and not highly educated. In 2010, Gallup reported that 30% regularly attend church, the fifth lowest level of any state. Nevada ranked 45th in the nation in advanced degrees, and dead last in high-school graduation rates at 63%, at a time when the national rate was hitting a record high of 80%. Nevada was one of the lowest-ranked states for supporting advanced industry in 2015, according to a Brookings Institution study.

Gaming (the state's preferred term for gambling) has generated enormous growth: The 91,000 people in the state that legalized gambling had become a population of 2.7 million in 2010. Las Vegas was a dot on the map when gambling became legal, a one-traffic-light crossroads in Clark County with only 8,532 people county-wide. In 2010, Clark County had just a shade under 2 million and Las Vegas was one of America's 25 largest metropolitan areas. Las Vegas' 23,000 hotel rooms in 1973 mushroomed into 150,000 by 2011. Reno, once known as the "biggest little city in the world," now has 425,000 people in its metro area. Nevada was America's fastest-growing state in the 1960s, 1970s, 1980s, and 1990s and from 2000 to 2007. For a long time, gaming was a good economic bet. But in 2007, gaming revenues declined even before the national economy fell into recession. Nevada suddenly went

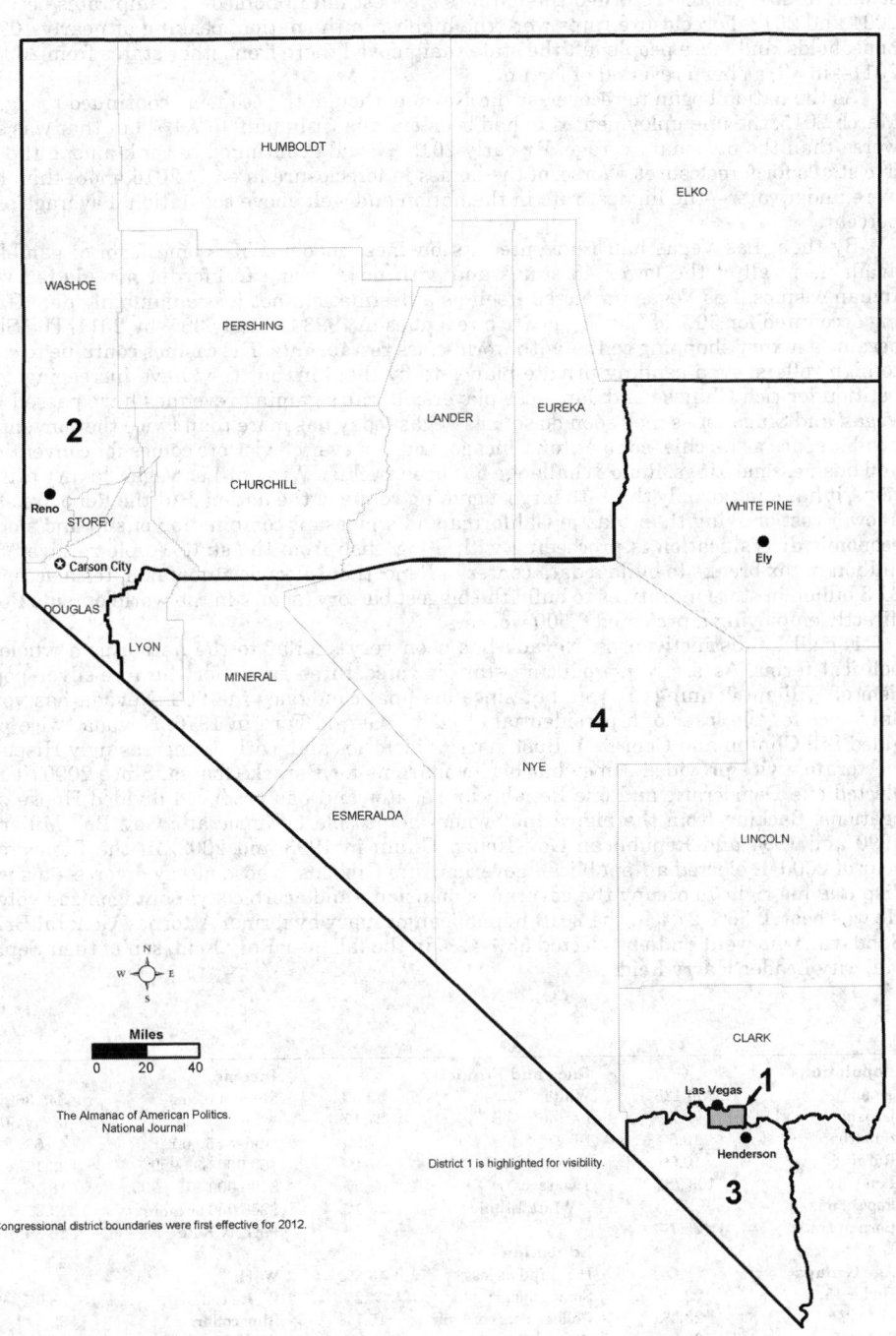

HUMBOLDT

ELKO

WASHOE

PERSHING

2

Reno

STOREY

LANDER

EUREKA

WHITE PINE

Ely

CHURCHILL

Carson City

DOUGLAS

LYON

MINERAL

4

NYE

ESMERALDA

LINCOLN

N
W E
S

Miles
0   20   40

CLARK

Las Vegas   **1**

District 1 is highlighted for visibility.

Henderson

3

The Almanac of American Politics.
National Journal

Congressional district boundaries were first effective for 2012.

bust, with the decline in gaming revenues cascading into a housing and construction crash. Nevada had the nation's highest unemployment rate, peaking at 13.7% in a three-month stretch in 2010; it also recorded the nation's steepest fall in homeownership rates between 2004 and 2012. Foreclosure rates were the highest in the nation, peaking at nearly 10% of households, and more people left the state than moved there from other states from 2008 to 2011—in all, a sharp reversal of fortune.

As the nation began to recover, so did Nevada, though the economy continued to lag. By March 2015, the unemployment rate had been cut almost in half, to 7.1%, but that was still worse than the national average. By early 2015, Nevada continued to rank among the top five states for foreclosures. Worse, of the homes in foreclosure in early 2015, more than half were underwater—the highest rate in the nation and well above the national average of 35 percent.

By then, Las Vegas had reinvented its business model. With some form of gambling available in all of the lower 48 states and with neighboring California now dotted with Indian casinos, Las Vegas promoted itself as a destination, not just a gambling den. Gaming accounted for 50% of Las Vegas Strip revenues in 1998 but only 38% by 2011. The Strip became a luxury shopping center with world-class restaurants. The casinos continue to cater to high rollers, even sending private planes to fly them in, but they have increasing competition for rich Chinese and Japanese players; Macau's gaming revenues have passed Las Vegas' and Singapore's may soon do so. Las Vegas today has more than twice the convention exhibit space as its chief competitor, Chicago, and 1 of every 8 visitors comes for conventions and business meetings. Reno's challenge has been trickier. Without Las Vegas' luxury attractions, it has sunk to only the 14th largest gaming venue in the nation. But the Reno area has a lower cost of living than coastal California and a pleasant combination of sun and slopes; economic diversification is proceeding with a big push from the state. Apple received $89 million in tax breaks to build a data center in Reno; then, electric automaker Tesla accepted $1.3 billion in state incentives to build the biggest battery factory in the world outside Reno, directly employing a projected 6,500 workers.

For all its distinctiveness, Nevada has been very similar to the nation as a whole in political terms. As a silver-producing state it voted three times for the free-silver populism of William Jennings Bryan, but since his final candidacy in 1908, Nevada has voted only once for the loser of a presidential election—Gerald Ford in 1976. Nevada twice provided Bill Clinton and George W. Bush narrow victories and, with its increasingly Hispanic electorate, twice provided somewhat bigger margins for Barack Obama. Since 2000, it has elected one Democratic and one Republican senator and has produced divided House delegations. Backing from the big casino owners helped elect Democratic Gov. Bob Miller in 1990 and 1994 and Republican Gov. Kenny Guinn in 1998 and 2002. In the Democratic year of 2006, it elected a Republican governor, Jim Gibbons, whose messy divorce—his wife disputed his right to occupy the governor's mansion—and acerbic style antagonized voters. He was beaten 56%-27% in the 2010 Republican primary by former Attorney General Brian Sandoval, who went on to be elected 53%-42% in the fall over Rory Reid, son of then-Senate Majority Leader Harry Reid.

Population		Race and Ethnicity		Income	
Total:	2,790,136	White	53.5%	Median income:	$45,369
Urban:	79.3%	Latino	27.1%		*(38 of 50)*
Suburban:	10.8%	Black	7.8%	Under $50,000	48.6%
Rural:	10.0%	Asian	7.1%	$50,000-$99,999:	32.1%
Land area:	109,781	Two races	2.9%	$100,000-$199,999:	16.1%
Pop/sq. mi.:	25.4	White Ethnic	23.1%	$200,000 or more:	3.2%
Born in state:	25.7%			Poverty Rate	10.6%
		Education			
Age Groups		H.S. grad or less:	43.3%	**Work**	
Under 18:	23.7%	Some college:	34.2%	White collar:	28.0%
18 to 34:	23.4%	College degree, 4 yr.:	15.1%	Blue collar:	53.0%
35 to 64:	39.2%	Post-grad study:	7.5%	Sales and service:	19.0%
Over 64:	13.6%				
		Military		Govt. workers:	12.2%
		Veterans/active duty:	10.1%		

For years, this sparsely populated desert sent politically shrewd Democrats to Washington and kept them there to protect the interests of a state heavily dependent on the federal government; for starters, nearly 87% of Nevada's land is federally owned. The most powerful were Key Pittman, chairman of the Senate Foreign Relations Committee, who backed President Franklin Roosevelt's foreign

Voter Turnout		
2013 Total Citizen 18+		1,871,443
2014 Highest Statewide Turnout		547,349
2014 Turnout as % CVAP		29.2%
2012 Turnout as % CVAP		55.9%
Legislature		
Senate:	11R	10D
House:	25R	17D

policy only after Roosevelt agreed to buy absurdly large amounts of Nevada silver; and Sen. Pat McCarran—author of the repressive McCarran Act on immigration—who shamelessly pushed aid for Reno and Las Vegas (where the airport is named for him) and became suddenly solicitous of civil liberties when mobsters and casino owners were called to testify before the Kefauver Committee investigating racketeering.

The most enduring figure in recent Nevada politics is Harry Reid. He was elected lieutenant governor as long ago as 1970, on a ticket with his former teacher and boxing coach Mike O'Callaghan. He headed the Nevada Gaming Commission from 1977 to 1981, overseeing an industry with organized crime involvement; his life was threatened and he indignantly turned down an offer of a bribe. In 1982, he won election to the House and in 1986, when Republican Sen. Paul Laxalt retired, Reid ran for the seat and won 50%-45%. He rose up the leadership ladder, becoming majority leader in 2007 after Democrats won control of the Senate. Keeping him in this position was of immense importance to the gaming industry and to the Culinary Union, which represents many casino employees and has a crackerjack political organization. When the federal government planned to build a national nuclear waste repository at Yucca Mountain, a scant 90 miles from Las Vegas, Reid fought it mightily—and successfully. The prickly Reid escaped defeat when his seat came up in the Republican year of 2010, beating back a challenge by Republican Sharron Angle, 50%-45%.

In the 2014 elections, Reid lost his Senate majority, suffered a serious accidental injury and decided to retire. The politician poised to inherit the mantle of leading politician in Nevada is Brian Sandoval, who's a Republican but one with enough maverick stances to generate crossover appeal, including among his fellow Hispanics. He favors abortion rights, promoted cooperation with the Affordable Care Act and, following a blowout re-election victory in 2014, has made improving education his signature issue, proposing tax increases totaling $1.1 billion to fund the effort. With Sandoval winning in a landslide atop the 2014 ballot, the Republicans swept to majorities in the legislature and in statewide offices, even ones with credible Democratic nominees. But Sandoval's moderation is already causing tensions with the GOP's tea party wing, and whether the GOP—which won amid record low turnout in 2014—can maintain its newfound dominance in a higher-turnout presidential year in 2016 remains to be seen. In June 2015, he announced that he would not seek Reid's Senate seat.

Presidential Politics After going heavily Republican in the 1980s, Nevada voted narrowly, by a margin of three-tenths-of-one percent, for Bill Clinton in 1992. Since then, it has been a battleground in every presidential election and has voted for the winner in each one. Clinton's and George W. Bush's victories all came by slim margins, with Las Vegas' Clark County voting Democratic, Reno's Washoe County voting Republican, and the cow counties—as Nevada's rural, cattle-grazing counties are known—voting heavily Republican (with lots of votes for Ross Perot in 1992).

2012 Presidential Vote		
Barack Obama (D)	531,373	(52%)
Mitt Romney (R)	463,567	(46%)
2012 Presidential Caucus		
Mitt Romney (R)	16,486	(50%)
Newt Gingrich (R)	6,956	(21%)
Ron Paul (R)	6,175	(19%)
Rick Santorum (R)	3,277	(10%)
2008 Presidential Vote		
Barack Obama (D)	533,736	(55%)
John McCain (R)	412,827	(43%)

The 2008 election was different. Democrats, drawing on the rapidly increasing number of Hispanics (mostly Mexican) and Asians (mostly Filipino) who are naturalized immigrants, increased their advantage in party registration from 12,000 in 2006 to 109,000 in 2008. The collapse of Nevada's economy and the rising tide of foreclosures put Republicans on the defensive, and the Barack Obama campaign was instrumental in getting more than half of the state's voters to cast their ballots early. Obama won 76% of the Hispanic vote (15% of the electorate), 94% of the African-American vote, and lost the white vote by only 51%-47%. Voters younger than 30 cast two-thirds of their ballots for Obama as did three-out-of-five voters aged 30 to 44. Obama carried Las Vegas' Clark County by a solid 59%-40%, and also won Reno's Washoe County 55%-43%, a real feat considering it had voted Republican for years. John McCain carried the rest of the state, 58%-38%, but that did not even make it close statewide. Obama carried this battleground by a comfortable 55%-43%. Central for any Democrat's success is winning Clark, which casts roughly two-thirds of the statewide vote. In 2012, with the economy still weak after four years of Democratic rule, the Obama tide fell back, but not enough to change the result: Obama prevailed over Mitt Romney by 52%-46%. Again, Democrats did a great job of turning out their voters. Obama's lead among Hispanics fell to 70%-25%, but they made up 18% of the electorate this time. Romney carried white voters, 57%-41%, but that was not enough to win.

Another change in Nevada politics took place in 2008: For the first time, it became an important part of the presidential nominating process. The Democratic National Committee, under heavy pressure from Senate Majority Leader Harry Reid, chose Reid's home state as one of four allowed to hold early contests, along with Iowa, New Hampshire, and South Carolina. Reid argued that overwhelmingly white Iowa and New Hampshire were not typical of an increasingly diverse nation and that Nevada—with its mix of Hispanics, African-Americans, and Asians—was. Labor leaders pointed out that Nevada, unlike the three other states, has a large number of union members working at the casinos. Other Democrats argued, presciently as it turned out, that Nevada was one of several Western states trending Democratic. So both parties held caucuses on Jan. 19, just 16 days after the Iowa caucuses. Hillary Clinton and Obama both organized in the state. Clinton came out the winner, 51%-45%, her only caucus victory all year; support from Hispanics enabled her to carry Clark County and the state. Some 44,000 Republicans turned out, including the state's many Mormons, who voted heavily for Mitt Romney. He won 51% of the vote, way ahead of the 14% for Ron Paul and 13% for John McCain. In 2012, the Republican turnout was lighter, 32,965. Mormons cast 25% of the votes and white evangelicals cast 24%; the former voted 88% for Romney and the latter 43%, and he won with 50%, to 21% for Newt Gingrich and 19% for Paul.

Congressional Districts Nevada's population surged 66% in the 1990s and 35% in the 2000s, leading the nation each time. The boom may finally be subsiding, but the state has rocketed from one district in 1980 to four in 2012. In 2011, partisan control was split and tension ran high. Democrats in charge of the

114th Congress Lineup	
3 R	1 D
113th Congress Lineup	
2 R	2 D

legislature, including several eyeing a promotion to Congress, passed maps creating one safely Republican seat in northern Nevada and three Democratic-leaning seats in Clark County. Republican Gov. Brian Sandoval vetoed the maps on the grounds that Latinos had accounted for 46% of the state's growth between 2000 and 2010 and deserved a majority Latino seat based in the northeast quadrant of metro Las Vegas. Democrats decried Sandoval's position as a veiled attempt to pack Democratic voters and create three Republican-leaning seats in the process. The debate fractured Latino advocacy groups, and the legislature adjourned in a stalemate.

Carson City District Judge James Todd Russell appointed three independent special masters—a county elections administrator, a former state legislative research director, and a lawyer—to draw a map. The trio submitted a diplomatic plan that created a safely Democratic, 43% Latino 1st District and preserved a Republican-leaning 2nd District in the north. They created a slightly more Republican 3rd District including Henderson to the south, and a new Democratic-leaning 4th District linking substantially Latino North Las Vegas with several rural counties to the north. The result in 2012 was an even 2-2 split. Republicans unexpectedly picked up the 4th District in 2014, giving a victory to Sandoval. But that district seems certain to remain competitive.

Governor

Brian Sandoval (R)

Elected 2010, term expires Jan. 2019, 2st term; b. Aug. 5, 1963, Redding, CA; U. of NV, Reno, B.A. 1986, OH St. U., J.D. 1989; Catholic; married (Kathleen); 3 children.

Elected Office: NV Assembly, 1994-98; Atty. gen., 2002-05.

Professional Career: NV Gaming Commission, 1998-2001; Tahoe Regional Planning Authority, 1998-2001; Judge, U.S. Dist. Court, 2005-09.

Office: 101 N. Carson St., Carson City, 89701, 775-684-5670; Fax: 775-684-5683; Website: gov.nv.gov

Election Results

2014 general	Brian Sandoval (R)	386,340	(71%)
	Robert Goodman (D)	130,722	(24%)
	None of these candidates	15,751	(3%)
	David Lory VanderBeek (I)	14,536	(3%)
2014 primary	Brian Sandoval (R)	105,857	(90%)

Prior winning percentage: 2010 (53%)

Republican Brian Sandoval was elected Nevada's first Latino governor in 2010. Handsome and telegenic, Sandoval has been heralded as a trailblazer in Republican circles, having previously been Nevada's first Hispanic elected to statewide office as attorney general and the first Hispanic to take the bench as a U.S. District Court judge.

Sandoval was born in Redding, Calif., and his family moved to Fallon, Nev., when he was five. He grew up in Sparks, just east of Reno. His mother worked as a legal secretary for the U.S. Attorney and for a magistrate judge; as a teenager, Sandoval worked at the cafeteria at Reno's federal courthouse. He attended the University of Nevada-Reno and went to law school at Ohio State University, then went into private practice. After five years, he ran for a seat in the state Assembly and won. He served two terms, developing a reputation as a moderate. He left office to take over the gaming commission, a powerful post that U.S. Senate Majority Leader Harry Reid once held. In three years in that job, the commission adopted regulations to limit neighborhood gambling, prohibited child-themed slot machines, and enhanced protections for problem gamblers.

Sandoval quit the commission to run for attorney general in 2002 and he won easily, 59%-34%. In the job, he was thrust into the ongoing legal fight over storing nuclear waste from commercial power plants at Yucca Mountain, which was a priority for the Bush administration. Sandoval also created the state's first public integrity unit to prosecute corrupt lawmakers. Midway through his term, in 2005, an opening came up on the U.S. District Court in Las Vegas. Reid reached out to Sandoval, and he accepted the offer to become, at 42, one of the youngest federal judges in the country. (The arrangement also removed Sandoval from contention as a potential Senate challenger to Reid in 2010.)

Meanwhile, Nevada GOP Gov. Jim Gibbons, a former House member, was elected in 2006 but was caught in a seemingly endless series of scandals. The collapse of the national housing market and the recession did him no favors, and by mid-2008, Gibbons had become highly vulnerable. When Sandoval decided to challenge Gibbons in the GOP primary in 2010, he had no trouble raising money, although with tea party activists gaining strength, Sandoval began shifting his emphasis from consensus-builder to that of a committed conservative. He backed neighboring Arizona's stringent new immigration law that allowed law enforcement officials to detain people suspected of being in the country illegally, a position that angered Hispanics. In the June 2010 primary, Sandoval defeated Gibbons, 56%-27%, setting up a fall matchup with Rory Reid, a Clark County commissioner and the son of Harry Reid. Sandoval tried to repair his image with Hispanic voters, going on Spanish-language

TV to remind them of the historic nature of his candidacy; he promised to maintain Nevada's low-tax climate, to add as much as $2 million in state spending on economic development, and to privatize some state services. He steered clear of divisive issues such as immigration, and Sandoval ended up winning by a comfortable 53%-42% margin, dominating rural counties while topping his opponent by 7,000 votes on his home turf in Clark County.

In marked contrast to Gibbons, Sandoval was active and engaged with legislators, meeting personally with all 63 during his first 100 days. He cheered fellow Republicans by hewing to his promise not to raise taxes under any circumstances and by appointing GOP Rep. Dean Heller in April to serve the unexpired U.S. Senate term of John Ensign, who had resigned amid a sex scandal. But Democrats were less impressed, and by May activists had set up "Sandoville," a tent encampment near the state Capitol in protest. To help balance the $6 billion budget, the governor borrowed a tactic from the previous administration and siphoned money from a local sewer district, a move that the Nevada Supreme Court said was improper. Calling the ruling a "game-changer," Sandoval reversed himself on his no-new-taxes pledge, prompting outrage from conservatives. But he managed to quiet the storm by scaling back his initial pronouncement and eventually reached agreement with lawmakers for temporarily reauthorizing $620 million in taxes that had been set to expire June 30.

Through his legislative battles, Sandoval remained relentlessly upbeat, earning the nickname "Governor Sunny," and he racked up some of the highest approval ratings of any governor in the country. Increasingly, he hewed to the center. He angered conservatives by agreeing to establish a state health-insurance exchange under the federal health care law and to expand Medicaid—two policies that other GOP governors resisted. (Technical problems eventually forced Nevada, along with a number of other states, to abandon their state exchanges for the federal marketplace.) He also expressed moderate-to-liberal views on abortion and same-sex marriage.

In his 2014 re-election bid, Sandoval was never in danger; his Democratic opponent, Bob Goodman, an octogenarian businessman who was so obscure that he won his party's nod only by finishing second to "none of the above"—a ballot line that is a quirk of Nevada's election law. Sandoval outspent Goodman, $3.7 million to a few thousand dollars; he won, 71%-24%. Bolstered by Sandoval's rout, Republicans rolled to victory up and down the ballot, sweeping statewide offices and taking control of the legislature—the GOP's first unified control of state governance since 1929.

In his 2015 State of the State address, Sandoval offered a bold agenda. He proposed hiking a range of taxes in order to provide an additional $1.1 billion for education—an area where the state fares poorly in national rankings. Veteran Nevada political commentator Jon Ralston called Sandoval's speech a "nearly perfect combination of rhetoric and substance" as well as "visionary and controversial." The plan drew immediate opposition from the tea party wing of the GOP, which had gained ground in the low-turnout 2014 vote. But in April, the Senate easily passed Sandoval's tax plan in a bipartisan vote. In May, the Assembly amended a new version of his plan into another tax bill and passed it. The Senate then voted for the new plan and sent it to the governor, who signed it. He also signed several other education measures that expanded programs on literacy, pre-kindergarten education and English as a second language, along with a more controversial school-choice bill that's among the nation's most far-reaching.

On immigration, Sandoval broke with others in his party; he opposed the decision by newly elected Republican attorney general Adam Laxalt to join the multi-state lawsuit against President Barack Obama's executive actions on immigration. And Sandoval made another daring move by shepherding $1.3 billion in incentives for Tesla Motors to build a "gigafactory" for electric car batteries near Reno. The plant would "change Nevada forever" by creating a projected 20,000 jobs and $100 billion in economic activity, Sandoval argued, but skeptics wondered whether subsidies of perhaps $190,000 per job were warranted. Such efforts raised Sandoval's national profile, and his resume and ethnic heritage would make him a strong national candidate. However, his departures from GOP orthodoxy were expected to pose significant complications within his own party. Meanwhile, in early 2015, Reid announced his retirement in 2016, but Sandoval showed little interest in seeking to replace him. In June, he announced that he would not run for the Senate. "My heart is in my responsibilities as Governor and continuing to build the New Nevada."

Senior Senator

Harry Reid (D)

Elected 1986, term expires Jan. 2017, 5th term; b. Dec. 2, 1939, Searchlight; S. UT St. Col., A.S. 1959, UT St. U., B.S. 1961, George Washington U., J.D. 1964, U. of NV, 1969-70; Mormon; married (Landra); 5 children.

Elected Office: NV Assembly, 1968-70; NV lt. gov., 1970-74; U.S. House, 1982-86.

Professional Career: Practicing atty., 1969-82; Henderson City atty., 1964-66; Chmn., NV Gaming Commission, 1977-81.

DC Office: 522 HSOB, 20510, 202-224-3542; Fax: 202-224-7327; Website: reid.senate.gov.

State Offices: Carson City, 775-882-7343; Las Vegas, 702-388-5020; Reno, 775-686-5750.

Committees: Senate Minority Leader. *Intelligence (Select)*.

Group Ratings

	ADA	ACLU	AFL-CIO	LCV	ITI	COC	HAFA	ACU	CFG	FRC
2014	60%	86%	–	80%	100%	63%	10%	24%	13%	29%
2013	90%	C	94%	100%	C	50%	C	16%	0%	C

National Journal Ratings

	2013 LIB	—	2013 CONS
Economic	93%	—	0%
Social	61%	—	38%
Foreign	71%	—	0%
Composite	81%	—	19%

Key Votes of the 113th Congress

1. Sandy storm spending	Y	5. Student Loan Rates	Y	9. Bipartisan Budget Deal	Y
2. Chuck Hagel Confirmation	Y	6. Employee Non-Discrim'n Act	Y	10. Farm Bill Conference Rept.	Y
3. Gun Background Checks	N	7. Senate Vote on Judgeships	N	11. Unempl. Comp. Extension	Y
4. Immigration Reform	Y	8. Defense Dept. Spending	N	12. Keystone Pipeline	N

Election Results

2010 general	Harry Reid (D)	362,785	(50%)	$25,975,547	$2,533,458	$7,892,151
	Sharron Angle (R)	321,361	(45%)	$28,262,487	$2,837,773	$3,936,959
	None of these candidates	16,197	(2%)			
2010 primary	Harry Reid (D)	87,366	(72%)			
	Alex Miller (D)	9,715	(8%)			

Prior winning percentages: 2004 (61%), 1998 (48%), 1992 (51%), 1986 (50%); House: 1984 (56%), 1982 (58%)

Harry Reid of Nevada, the Senate minority leader, is one of Washington's most accomplished deal-makers and masters of parliamentary procedure, yet also someone whose brusque manner has driven Republicans to distraction and has led to some torturous reelection races. Reid began 2015 diminished both by the Democrats' loss of the Senate in the 2014 election and a nasty fall that broke six of his ribs and badly damaged his right eye. In March 2015, Reid announced that he would not run for reelection, marking the end of an era both for the Senate Democratic Caucus and for Nevada. He came to the Senate in 1986, after serving two terms in the House.

Reid grew up in the tiny, gritty mining town of Searchlight, enduring a hard life. His father, a hard-rock miner, was an alcoholic who killed himself at age 58. His mother did laundry for a nearby bordello to keep the family afloat. Reid grew up in a small house without indoor plumbing, and hitchhiked 40 miles to high school in Henderson, where his civics teacher and boxing coach, Mike O'Callaghan, became his political mentor. As a young man, Reid was a middleweight boxer of some local renown, but he aspired to better himself through education. Henderson businessmen helped him pay for college, and he graduated from Southern Utah State, where he and his wife became Mormons. To put himself through law school at George Washington University, he worked nights as a U.S. Capitol Police officer.

Reid returned to Henderson to practice law, and at age 28, he was elected to the Nevada Assembly. In 1970, O'Callaghan won the governorship and Reid, running separately, was elected lieutenant governor. In 1974, Reid came within 624 votes of toppling Republican Sen. Paul Laxalt, and two years later, he failed in a run for mayor of Las Vegas. O'Callaghan named him to head the Nevada Gaming Commission from 1977 to 1981, a sensitive post overseeing the state's top industry at a time when it was controlled by organized crime. Reid later recounted that his life was threatened and his car wired with a bomb. He persevered; his slim frame and soft-spoken style has often led his rivals to underestimate his steeliness.

In 1982, when Nevada got two House seats for the first time and Rep. Jim Santini ran for the Senate, Reid ran in the Las Vegas-based 1st District and won. As Reid was completing his second term in the House, Laxalt retired and Reid tried again for the Senate seat. His opponent turned out to be Santini, who had switched parties at the last minute and ran as a Republican. Reid won, 50%-45%. This electoral pattern would be repeated: In only one of his five Senate elections (2004) did Reid exceed 51 percent of the vote. The closest was 1998, when GOP Rep. John Ensign ran a well-financed campaign. Both Reid and Ensign, whose stepfather was head of the Mandalay Resort Group, one of the big Las Vegas casinos, raised large amounts of money from the gambling industry. Reid spent $4.9 million and Ensign spent $3.5 million. After a nasty campaign, Reid prevailed by just 428 votes. (Two years later, Ensign was elected to Nevada's other Senate seat; the two men worked effectively and without rancor.)

Reid's rise to leader was set in motion when he supported Tom Daschle's leadership bid in 1994. This led Daschle to name Reid co-chair of the Senate Democratic Policy Committee, which was, and remains, a stepping stone to bigger posts in leadership. Reid's promotion of the party's interests in that position later gave him a leg up in a successful bid for the minority whip job in 1998. For the next six years, he was a constant presence on the floor, advancing his party's causes and maintaining civil relations with GOP leaders. He played a key role in persuading Vermont's Sen. Jim Jeffords to leave the Republican Party in May 2001 and become an independent who caucused with the Democrats; the move effectively put the Democrats in the majority. When Republicans held all-night sessions in November 2003 to protest Democratic filibusters of nominees for appellate court judgeships, Reid retaliated by speaking for nine hours, reading from his book about his upbringing in Searchlight. Later, in May 2005, he acquiesced to the agreement of the bipartisan "Gang of 14" to allow some of the nominees to come to a vote.

In 2004, Reid campaigned for fellow Democrats and contributed generously to their political treasuries. When Democratic Leader Tom Daschle of South Dakota lost his seat in a stunning upset that year, Reid had already lined up the votes needed to be elected Democratic leader, though the party was now back in the minority. Reid was hardly the Senate's best orator and not much of a policy visionary, but his colleagues knew him as a crafty parliamentarian and a scrappily effective defender of their interests. Reid worked deftly behind the scenes to block non-germane amendments from bills and bottle up portions of the Bush agenda that Democrats strongly opposed, such as individual retirement accounts in Social Security. But Reid sometimes undercut himself by letting slip indecorous comments and insults. He once called Bush a "loser" and a "liar," and Federal Reserve Board Chairman Alan Greenspan "a political hack." He was quoted in a book on the 2008 presidential race as saying he believed Obama could win because he was a "light-skinned" African-American "with no Negro dialect, unless he wanted to have one." Reid acknowledged making the remarks and apologized to Obama.

Reid also has been vulnerable on the ethics front, although he has maintained that none of the issues raised against him over the years have had merit. After a 2003 *Los Angeles Times* story pointed out that his son and a son-in-law were lobbying in Washington for Nevada companies, Reid banned relatives from lobbying his office. In October 2006, it was reported that Reid had not disclosed a transaction on a land deal that netted him more than $1 million in 2004. Reid said he had purchased the land in 1998 at market price, and then sold it to a friend's corporation in 2001 in return for a stake in the corporation. He got his share of the proceeds in 2004, he said, when the property was sold to a shopping center developer. The *Las Vegas Review-Journal* reported in April 2013 that two partners at a Las Vegas law firm made $150,000 in contributions to a super PAC associated with Reid as he considered a member of the firm for a federal judgeship.

In 2006, Democrats won the six seats they needed to regain the Senate majority, and Reid ascended to majority leader. He was often stymied by Republican filibusters, but in 2008, when the Democrats achieved a majority in Congress and control of the White House, Reid slipped into the role most comfortable for him—that of behind-the-scenes deal-maker.

Reid won bipartisan support for tough, new ethics and lobbying rules and expansion of the student loan program. In early 2009, he guided the new administration's $787 billion economic stimulus bill to passage (which also happened to include funding for a high-speed bullet train between Las Vegas and Anaheim, Calif.) When the $700 billion bailout for the financial industry was in trouble in the House, Reid made several changes to the Senate bill to attract additional votes, enabling its passage.

For Reid, the downside of Obama's rise to power was the expectation that he would carry water for the new administration even when its policies hurt him in his politically competitive state. By late 2009, when Senate committees had failed to come up with a health care overhaul that could attract the needed 60 votes, Reid stepped in to avoid being blamed for the death of Obama's signature domestic initiative. (The House had already passed a health care bill.) With the Senate's 40 Republicans united in opposition, Reid needed all 60 Democrats, including the two independents who caucused with them, a task that required significant horse-trading. Just before the year ended, Reid was able to pass a health care bill. It was a great victory for him on the national stage, but it set the stage for a dramatic reelection bid in 2010.

Republicans sought to topple Reid much as they had Daschle in 2004—at the pinnacle of power. Reid began the race with polls showing him trailing his would-be GOP challengers. Sharron Angle, a former state assemblywoman who drew spirited tea party support, won a messy Republican primary; her staunchly conservative stances and propensity for saying controversial things made her Reid's most advantageous opponent. Over the summer, Reid opened up a lead in the polls, but Angle kept the race close, in part because relentless mudslinging managed to tarnish both candidates. Reid raised $24.8 million, within range of Angle's $28.1 million. The key ended up being his masterful mobilization of Hispanics and the powerful culinary workers' union; despite the strongly Republican election year, Reid defeated Angle, 50%-45%. A large 2.25 percent of votes were cast for the state's quirky "none of the above" ballot line.

Meanwhile, back in Washington, the chamber that liked to call itself the world's greatest deliberative body was descending into increasing dysfunction and vitriol on Reid's watch. In truth, both parties were at fault: Republicans pushed the envelope on the use of the filibuster to block Obama's agenda, and Reid retaliated by preventing Republicans from offering amendments. The battles between Reid and Republican Leader Mitch McConnell of Kentucky "have sometimes reduced Senate debate to the level of divorce proceedings between a couple who loathe each other," wrote columnist Scot Lehigh in the *Boston Globe*. This pattern produced an unrelenting spiral of gridlock, punctuated by brief windows of legislative accomplishment, notably the lame-duck session after the 2012 election, when the chamber helped repeal the military's "don't ask, don't tell" policy barring openly gay service members and ratified the New START nuclear arms treaty with Russia.

Most of the time, though, tensions in the chamber were high during Reid's tenure. During negotiations with Republicans over an extension of the federal debt limit and a tax and spending bill to avoid the so-called "fiscal cliff," Reid said of House Speaker John Boehner of Ohio, "I don't understand his brain." At a subsequent meeting outside the Oval Office, Boehner snapped to Reid, "Go f—yourself." Reid stepped into the 2012 presidential election by charging, without detailing his sources, that GOP nominee Mitt Romney had paid no federal income taxes for 10 years. Republican National Committee Chairman Reince Priebus labeled Reid "a dirty liar," and neutral observers questioned the propriety of Reid's accusation.

When several of his younger Democratic colleagues sought to improve the chamber's functioning by dramatically overhauling the use of filibusters, Reid initially balked, instead endorsing a more modest compromise. But Reid eventually changed his stance, acting in November 2013 to use a controversial parliamentary maneuver known as the "nuclear option" to bar filibusters for most federal judgeships and executive-branch appointments. Republicans angrily decried the move as upsetting the chamber's longstanding traditions, though in reality the two parties had expressed opposite opinions of such a change a few years before, at a time when the majority and minority were controlled by the opposite party.

Early in his Senate career, Reid had a more moderate voting record than many Senate Democrats. He voted against resolutions endorsing *Roe v. Wade,* the Supreme Court ruling legalizing abortion, and he co-sponsored the constitutional amendment to outlaw flag-burning. Reid was one of the few Senate Democrats to vote for the Persian Gulf War resolution in 1991, and he voted for the Iraq war resolution in 2002. He has consistently opposed environmental groups on mining issues and blocked attempts to impose higher fees on hard-rock mining. He has opposed most gun control measures, although he supported a failed attempt to ban assault weapons in April 2013 because, he said, "saving the lives of young police officers and innocent civilians is more important than preventing imagined tyranny."

But as American politics became increasingly polarized, Reid's voting record took a more liberal turn, and his leadership style became more that of a partisan warrior. From the Senate floor, he repeatedly railed against the Koch brothers, libertarian billionaires who did much to finance Republican candidates during the 2014 election. He brought up bills designed to unify Democrats and embarrass Republicans, with their political impact typically outweighing their prospects for passage in the Senate (not to mention the House, which was controlled by a strongly conservative GOP majority that pushed its own bills that had zero chance of winning Senate approval). Still, not even this strategy helped the Democrats keep their majority; in November 2014, the Republicans won enough seats to seize the chamber and shunt Reid back into the minority.

Following the lead of House Democratic Leader Nancy Pelosi of California, Reid refused to fall on his sword after losing the majority in 2014; his caucus gave him another term as party leader, though with at least six dissenters, mainly moderates from red and purple states. Reid was facing another reelection bid in 2016, one that promised, as usual, to be tough. Then, in January 2015, Reid, 75, suffered a serious accident during one of his trademark exercise sessions at his home in Henderson, which were said to include 250 sit ups a day. After a period of recuperation, he returned to the Senate chamber wearing dark sunglasses to conceal his damaged right eye. But by March, Reid announced what many had speculated would be coming—that he would not seek another term. (He said he had made the decision before his injury.) In an equally stunning development, Reid sold his home and 110 acres of land in Searchlight—the bedrock of his political story—to a gold-mining firm for $1.75 million. (In addition to his home in Henderson, Reid and his wife Landra own a unit in the posh Ritz-Carlton in Washington, D.C.)

Reid quickly backed a longtime confidant, New York Sen. Charles Schumer to succeed him as party leader after his retirement, leapfrogging the caucus' No. 2, Dick Durbin of Illinois. Reid also worked to coalesce support for former Nevada attorney general Catherine Cortez Masto in the 2016 election to fill his Senate seat. The July 2015 candidacy of GOP Rep. Joe Heck made this a toss-up contest. The trickier task for Reid would be to preserve his legacy. "Reid's legacy to Nevada," wrote longtime Nevada journalist Jon Ralston, "will be of a man who ascended to the pinnacle and used every opportunity to turn potential power into kinetic power." Ralston quoted former Nevada Governor and Senator Richard Bryan saying that Reid "wanted to be feared, not loved. He liked power, he knew how to use it and he wasn't afraid to use it to advocate for the interests of the state."

Nowhere has this been clearer than with the Yucca Mountain nuclear-waste repository, located northwest of Las Vegas. In the late 1980s, the federal government named the site as the top candidate for a permanent home for waste from nuclear reactors that had been piling up at temporary sites in 39 states. Reid opposed the repository with every parliamentary and political tool at his command. Bill Clinton carried Nevada by narrow margins in 1992 and 1996 after promising to veto the establishment of even a temporary site at Yucca Mountain. Reid succeeded in corralling enough votes to prevent an override of Clinton's veto. In 2002, President George W. Bush designated Yucca Mountain as the permanent site. The law provided for a veto by the governor, which could be overridden by majorities in both chambers of Congress. In April 2002, Republican Gov. Kenny Guinn issued his veto. Reid tried, but failed, later that year to defeat the bill approving the site. But for Reid, the fight was not over. As the chairman of the Appropriations subcommittee with jurisdiction over the Energy Department, he was able to block funding for the repository year after year.

In November 2004, Reid, by then the Senate minority leader, negotiated with the Bush administration over judicial appointments and agreed to approve 175 Bush nominees in return for the appointment of his aide, Gregory Jaczko, to the Nuclear Regulatory Commission, which had to approve the site before it could go forward. He pushed to move up Nevada's presidential primary to January 2008, a move that ended up forcing candidates to take an early stand on waste storage. Then-Democratic candidate Barack Obama obliged by opposing the Yucca Mountain site and, after taking office, put the repository on hold. Now, with the looming prospect of a Senate without Reid, pro-Yucca Mountain forces are preparing for a new assault.

Junior Senator

Dean Heller (R)

Appointed May 2011, term expires Jan. 2019, 1st full term; b. May 10, 1960, Castro Valley, CA; U. of S. CA, B.A. 1985; Mormon; married (Lynne); 4 children.

Elected Office: NV Assembly, 1990-94; NV secy. of st., 1994-2006, U.S. House, 2007-11.

Professional Career: Stockbroker, 1983-88; Chief deputy st. treas., 1988-90; Public funds rep., Bank of America, 1990-95.

DC Office: 324 HSOB, 20510, 202-224-6244; Fax: 202-228-6753; Website: heller.senate.gov.

State Offices: Las Vegas, 702-388-6605; Reno, 775-686-5770.

Committees: *Banking, Housing & Urban Affairs:* Economic Policy (Chmn). Financial Institutions & Consumer Protection; Housing, Transportation & Community Development. *Commerce, Science & Transportation:* Aviation Operations, Safety & Security; Communications, Technology & the Internet; Consumer Protection, Product Safety & Insurance; Surface Transportation & Merchant Marine Infrastructure, Safety & Security. *Aging (Special). Finance:* Health Care; Taxation & IRS Oversight; Social Security, Pensions, & Family Policy (Chmn); *Veterans' Affairs.*

Group Ratings

	ADA	ACLU	AFL-CIO	LCV	ITI	COC	HAFA	ACU	CFG	FRC
2014	25%	26%	—	0%	66%	75%	63%	71%	70%	79%
2013	5%	C	22%	23%	C	88%	C	83%	89%	C

National Journal Ratings

	2013 LIB	—	2013 CONS
Economic	20%	—	78%
Social	29%	—	70%
Foreign	7%	—	92%
Composite	19%	—	81%

Key Votes of the 113th Congress

1. Sandy storm spending	Y	5. Student Loan Rates	Y	9. Bipartisan Budget Deal	N
2. Chuck Hagel Confirmation	N	6. Employee Non-Discrim'n Act	Y	10. Farm Bill Conference Rept.	N
3. Gun Background Checks	N	7. Senate Vote on Judgeships	Y	11. Unempl. Comp. Extension	Y
4. Immigration Reform	Y	8. Defense Dept. Spending	NV	12. Keystone Pipeline	Y

Election Results

2012 general	Dean Heller (R)	457,656	(46%)	$9,192,588	$1,234,469	$13,098,190
	Shelley Berkley (D)	446,080	(45%)	$11,624,756	$1,258,783	$12,389,046
	David Lory VanderBeek (IAP)	48,792	(5%)			
	None of these candidates	45,277	(5%)			
2012 primary	Dean Heller (R)	88,958	(89%)			
	Sherry Brooks (R)	5,356	(5%)			

Prior winning percentages: House: 2010 (63%), 2008 (52%), 2006 (50%)

Republican Dean Heller was appointed Nevada's junior senator in May 2011 after Republican Sen. John Ensign resigned amid a scandal involving an extramarital affair and allegations of a hush-money scheme. Heller went on to win the seat in the 2012 election even as Democratic President Barack Obama was carrying Nevada.

Heller was a political fixture in Carson City long before he won his first House contest in 2006. He got a taste of politics during childhood when his newspaper route included deliveries at the state capitol. He graduated from the University of Southern California in 1985 with a degree in business administration, and then worked as a stockbroker trading on the Pacific Stock Exchange. In 1990, he won the first of two terms in the Nevada House, and in 1994, he was elected to the first of three terms as Nevada secretary of state. During his 12-year tenure, Heller streamlined the corporation registration process, increasing revenues tenfold. He supported more public access to government records and greater transparency in the state campaign finance system. Nevada was seen as a national model in

2004, when it became the first state to create a paper trail for its electronic voting machines. Heller declined to use his office to boost his party during the razor-close 1998 Senate contest, affirming incumbent Democrat Harry Reid's defeat of Ensign, then a House member, by about 400 votes. At times, Democrats even hoped he might switch parties.

But Heller remained a Republican, and he made his move when five-term Republican Rep. Jim Gibbons gave up his 2nd District seat to run for governor. Heller faced competition for the Republican nomination from Assemblywoman Sharron Angle and former Assembly-woman Dawn Gibbons, the outgoing congressman's wife. Gibbons' underfunded candidacy never took off, but Angle, a Christian conservative, emerged as a serious primary rival after she picked up the endorsement and financial support of the deep-pocketed and fiscally con-servative Club for Growth. In the primary, Heller barely edged Angle by 421 votes. His campaign treasury depleted, Heller entered the general election campaign against Demo-crat Jill Derby, an 18-year veteran of the Nevada Board of Regents. While Republican can-didates elsewhere considered President George W. Bush a liability in 2006, Heller got Bush to stump twice for him, helping motivate the traditionally Republican-leaning rural vote. Heller defeated her, 50%-45%, and won reelection with ease in 2008 and 2010.

In the House, Heller was enough of a loyalist to land a coveted seat on Ways and Means in 2009, although he found little success securing passage of amendments. In early 2011, he was being mentioned as a candidate to succeed the fast-unraveling Ensign. In selecting Heller to replace Ensign, Republican Gov. Brian Sandoval cited the need for an "experienced voice" in Washington. Nevada was among the states hardest hit by the 2007-09 recession; by March 2011, unemployment had soared to 13.2 percent, the nation's highest.

Heller's electorate "shifted overnight from the domain of staunch, mostly white conser-vatives ... to an increasingly Democratic one that is projected to be majority-minority by 2030," Nevada journalist Steve Friess wrote. Perhaps as a result, Heller has taken some maverick stances for a Republican. On the Energy and Natural Resources Committee, he called for an end to some of the same subsidies to large oil companies that Democrats have sought to repeal. He was the only GOP senator to support a Democratic balanced-budget plan in December 2011, and one of just five Republicans in October 2011 to join Demo-crats in rejecting an amendment that would have limited the taxpayer liability for mortgage giants Fannie Mae and Freddie Mac. He was among the first in the party to publicly distance himself from 2012 GOP presidential nominee Mitt Romney's secretly recorded speech saying that 47 percent of voters wouldn't support him because they were reliant on the government. He was one of 12 GOP senators in January 2013 to support raising the federal debt limit. The latter measure incorporated his bill to cut off the salaries of House and Senate members in years they do not meet deadlines to pass a budget or individual spending bills. He also voted for the Senate immigration bill in 2013.

As majority leader, Reid tangled openly with Heller, even though he had avoided feuding with Ensign. Most prominently, Reid squawked about Heller's role in a bill legalizing online poker that both supported. Reid accused Heller in September 2012 of "a failure of leader-ship" for failing to round up the 15 Senate votes needed for passage; Heller responded that Reid deliberately waited until close to the Nov. 6 election to bring up a vote on Internet gam-ing, knowing that it would not pass. In Heller's bid for a full term in 2012, Democrats made the race a priority. His general election rival was Rep. Shelley Berkley, an outspoken Demo-crat who had served with him on Ways and Means. Berkley hitched her wagon to Obama's, aware that the president would make an all-out effort to win a state that he had captured in 2008. In one of the cycle's nastiest races, Berkley and other Democrats attacked Heller for his support of House Budget Committee Chairman Paul Ryan's budget plan. But Berkley had a significant piece of political baggage—she was the subject of a House ethics committee investigation into whether she had used her position to benefit the financial interests of her husband, a physician who operates dialysis centers in Nevada.

Heller also sought to raise broader questions about Berkley's ethics, running ads that questioned her real estate investments and a 2008 taxpayer-funded trip to Italy after attend-ing a conference in neighboring Slovenia. He got considerable financial help from conserva-tive casino mogul Sheldon Adelson, who had a history of feuding with Berkley. Heller eked out a 45.9%-44.7% victory, with Independent American Party candidate David VanderBeek drawing 5% and the state's "none of these candidates" option registering 4.5%. Heller won his native Washoe County, which includes Reno, with 51 percent, and he held Berkley to 50 percent in her stronghold of Las Vegas-based Clark County.

After his reelection, Heller considered siding with gun-control advocates but ultimately decided to join with almost all Republicans and some Democrats to vote against legislation that would have banned assault weapons, limited magazine capacity, and expanded background checks for gun sales. But on another issue, Heller bucked key players in his party—in the fall of 2013, he supported the Employment Non-Discrimination Act, which would bar discrimination against gays in the workplace. It had been stalled in the Senate for lack of a 60th vote to break a threatened filibuster. Heller, noting that Nevada already had a similar law, issued a statement saying he would vote for the bill, giving Democrats a sufficient number of Republican votes for passage. The federal bill passed, 64-32, with Heller joining 10 Republicans voting yes.

In 2014, Heller worked with Democratic Sen. Jack Reed of Rhode Island to push legislation to retroactively provide unemployment compensation. "I believe there ought to be a safety net," he said, "and that safety net needs to be solid." He joined Democratic Sens. Claire McCaskill of Missouri and Kirsten Gillibrand of New York in backing a measure to hold universities more accountable to students who are raped. In a rare misstep, Heller initially spoke favorably toward those who rallied to support Nevada rancher Cliven Bundy, who was in the midst of an armed standoff with federal law enforcement officers. "What Sen. Reid may call domestic terrorists, I call patriots," Heller said. But after Bundy was caught on video making racist comments, Heller backtracked, saying, "I am very quick in calling American citizens 'patriots,' maybe in this case, too quick."

With the GOP takeover in the November 2014 elections—and the demotion of Reid to minority leader—Heller saw his influence rise. He became the first Nevada senator to chair a subcommittee on the influential Finance Committee (Social Security, Pensions, and Family Policy), and he took the reins of a subcommittee on Banking, Housing, and Urban Affairs. He lost a closed-door election against Mississippi Sen. Roger Wicker to head the National Republican Senatorial Committee, perhaps because of his low-key role in Reid's tight 2010 reelection bid against Angle, but he did get the consolation prize of becoming one of three vice chairs. With Reid's days numbered, Heller took on growing responsibility for defending the state against activation of the planned, but long-delayed, Yucca Mountain nuclear waste site northwest of Las Vegas. In March 2015, Heller joined with several fellow Nevada lawmakers to introduce a bill to give the state veto power over Yucca. "We are still going to fight this thing tooth and nail," he promised.

As a member of the majority, Heller continued to take an eclectic mix of stances. He secured passage of an amendment that would require extra training for airport and border agents in detecting possible human trafficking. He signed on to a bipartisan measure to remove marijuana from Schedule I of the Controlled Substances Act, the most stringent level. And as "the senator from the only state where sports betting is legal," Heller urged a thorough investigation of the "deflate-gate" charges against the New England Patriots.

FIRST DISTRICT

Dina Titus (D)

Elected 2012, 3rd term; b. May 23, 1950, Thomasville, Ga.; Col. of William and Mary, B.A. 1970, U. of GA, M.A. 1973, FL St. U., Ph.D. 1976; Greek Orthodox; married (Tom Wright).

Elected Office: U.S. House, 2008-10; NV Senate, 1988-2008.

Professional Career: Prof., U. of NV, Las Vegas, 1977-2011; Prof., N. TX St. U., 1975-76.

DC Office: 401 CHOB, 20515, 202-225-5965; Website: titus.house.gov.

State Offices: Las Vegas, 702-220-9823.

Committees: *Transportation & Infrastructure:* Aviation; Economic Development, Public Buildings & Emergency Management; Highways & Transit; Water Resources & Environment; *Veterans' Affairs:* Disability Assistance & Memorial Affairs (RMM); Economic Opportunity.

Group Ratings

	ADA	ACLU	AFL-CIO	LCV	ITI	COC	HAFA	ACU	CFG	FRC
2014	65%	77%	–	97%	100%	50%	14%	8%	13%	0%
2013	70%	C	100%	93%	C	54%	C	12%	16%	C

National Journal Ratings

	2013 LIB	—	2013 CONS
Economic	66%	—	33%
Social	79%	—	16%
Foreign	71%	—	27%
Composite	73%	—	27%

Key Votes of the 113th Congress

1. Sandy storm spending	Y	5. Medical Marijuana	Y	9. Syrian Rebels Training	N
2. Violence Against Women Act	Y	6. Farm Bill	N	10. Keystone pipeline	N
3. Guantanamo Bay Detainees	Y	7. Afghanistan Combat	Y	11. Immigration Exec. Action	N
4. Abortion 20-week ban	N	8. NSA Phone Data Collection	N	12. Bipartisan budget deal	Y

Election Results

2014 general	Dina Titus (D)	45,643	(57%)	$1,012,672	$10,652
	Annette Teijeiro (R)	30,413	(38%)	$73,068	
	Richard Charles (Lib)	2,617	(3%)		
	Kamau Bakari (IAP)	1,626	(2%)		
2014 primary	Dina Titus (D)	12,966	(86%)		
	Herbert Peters (D)	2,106	(14%)		

Prior winning percentages: 2012 (64%), 2008 (47%)

Population		Race and Ethnicity		Income	
Total:	673,794	Latino	42.9%	Median income:	$39,265
Urban:	100.0%	White	36.0%		*(397 of 435)*
Suburban:	0.0%	Black	8.8%	Under $50,000	62.2%
Rural:	0.0%	Asian	8.5%	$50,000-$99,999:	26.9%
Land area:	159	Two races	2.7%	$100,000-$199,999:	9.2%
Pop/sq. mi.:	4,232.5	White Ethnic	15.8%	$200,000 or more:	1.7%
Born in state:	23.6%			Poverty Rate	22.6%
		Education			
Age Groups		H.S. grad or less:	57.5%	**Work**	
Under 18:	23.1%	Some college:	28.0%	White collar:	18.4%
18 to 34:	26.0%	College degree, 4 yr.:	10.2%	Blue collar:	61.8%
35 to 64:	39.1%	Post-grad study:	4.3%	Sales and service:	19.8%
Over 64:	11.9%				
		Military		Govt. workers:	6.4%
		Veterans/active duty:	7.9%		

Central Las Vegas area

Las Vegas, that garish and improbable city, had a fittingly colorful beginning. It began as a Paiute Indian settlement that in the late 1700s served as a watering stop for Spanish priests making the 1,200-mile trek between New Mexico and California. By the 1800s, the Old Spanish Trail, as it

Voter Turnout	
2013 Total Citizen 18+	403,964
2014 House Turnout	80,299
2014 Turnout as % CVAP	19.9%
2012 Turnout as % CVAP	48%

came to be known, was used by horse and mule smugglers, by explorers like John C. Fremont, and by Mormon emigrants heading west. Las Vegas was still a small crossroads when Nevada, its mining industry a shambles, legalized gambling in the 1930s. The WPA Guide to Nevada, published in 1940 when the city had 10,000 people, describes a prim Las Vegas: "Relatively little emphasis is placed on the gambling clubs and divorce facilities—though they are attractions to many visitors—and much effort is being made to build up cultural attractions."

All that changed big-time after World War II, when gangster Bugsy Siegel built the Flamingo hotel and casino on what became the Strip south of the city limits. Pseudo-romantic architectural themes became the order of the day (flamingos are found in the waters of Florida, not in the deserts of Nevada), and one casino followed another. Organized crime provided much of the money and muscle for Las Vegas, and investment capital came from Teamsters pension funds. In the late 1960s, eccentric billionaire Howard Hughes moved into the Desert Inn, bought most of the casinos, and hired Mormons to run them. After Hughes abruptly left town, most of his hotels eventually were torn down, and other operators built casinos like Caesars Palace, Circus Circus, the Mirage, Excalibur, the lavish Bellagio and the Venetian. In the 1970s, the casinos were the haven of flashy high rollers, of Frank Sinatra and showgirls. By the 1990s, diversification became the buzzword. Las Vegas began to produce more family-oriented entertainment, shopping, and even high art, with the Bellagio's museum-quality art collection on view. Las Vegas also built the biggest convention center in the country. But the city has not neglected its core clientele: people who fly in from elsewhere to be entertained, and to be, for a weekend, maybe even a little naughty. "What happens in Vegas stays in Vegas," has become the unofficial motto. Gambling now makes up less than half of casino revenue, with increasing amounts of money spent on food, beverages and all sorts of entertainment. The scent of the underworld has not entirely disappeared. The flashy Oscar Goodman, a former mob lawyer, was elected mayor and actively promoted the city. Barred from seeking a fourth term in 2011, his wife, Carolyn, succeeded him and was elected to a second term in April 2015. She continued his habit of taking scantily clad showgirls to events promoting the city.

Because of the city's dependence on leisure-time spending, the recession hit hard here and persisted long after other areas recovered, with gambling down, joblessness up, and many new homes unsold. The unemployment level climbed above 14% in 2010, higher than in any other metropolitan area; it slowly dropped to 7.4% in March 2015. Casinos on the Las Vegas Strip lost a net $1.7 billion in 2012. The recovery in the housing market remained very slow. In January 2015, the average home value had declined a staggering 39% since 2006, though that was an improvement from the low point of 58% in 2011. But there was good news on the Strip. In 2014, it broke an attendance record with more than 40 million visitors. Helped by a major marketing campaign, the average age of visitors dropped five years from 50 to 45. The downside for the gaming industry is that many of the new arrivals were more interested in shopping, concerts and nightlife. At Planet Hollywood, resident entertainer Britney Spears was grossing nearly $500,000 per show. Plans were underway for the construction of new resort complexes, with the implosion of outdated hotels to make available prime real estate.

The 1st Congressional District of Nevada consists of the inner core of Las Vegas that visitors are most likely to see. They cross into it as soon as they drive their rental cars out

2012 Presidential Vote		
Barack Obama (D) 123,205		(65%)
Mitt Romney (R)...................60,812		(32%)
2008 Presidential Vote		
Barack Obama (D) 121,329		(65%)
John McCain (R)...................62,107		(33%)
Cook Partisan Voting Index: D+14		

of the lot at McCarran International Airport. On the three-mile Strip are 14 of the nation's 15 largest hotels, each with thousands of rooms that extend far back on their properties. The District is 43% Hispanic, the highest proportion in the state, and is the only solidly Democratic district in Nevada.

Dina Titus (D)

Democrat Dina Titus was elected to Nevada's 1st District House seat in 2012 after losing reelection two years earlier to Republican Joe Heck. The game became more favorable for Titus when redistricting moved her home to the liberal, Las Vegas-based 1st, which had become an open seat. A political science professor, she has welcomed political challenges.

Raised in Tifton, Ga., Titus retains her thick Southern drawl. "I get teased a lot because I haven't lost the accent, but that's kind of become part of how people know me," she told *National Journal.* Her upbringing gave her a strong interest in politics. She recalls listening to local politicians talk shop at her grandfather's Greek restaurant across from the courthouse. Her father ran for city council, and her Republican "black sheep" uncle, as she puts it, served in the Georgia Legislature.

Titus attended the College of William and Mary, where she majored in political science; she later obtained a master's degree from the University of Georgia and a doctorate from Florida State University. After teaching at the University of North Texas, she joined the faculty at the University of Nevada, Las Vegas. She taught there for 34 years, until she retired in 2011. Titus has authored two nonfiction books, *Bombs in the Backyard: Atomic Testing and American Politics*, and *Battle Born: Federal-State Relations in Nevada During the Twentieth Century*. Her husband, Thomas Wright, is a Latin American history professor at UNLV. In 1988, Titus put her political knowledge to use and was elected to the Nevada Senate, where she was minority leader from 1993 to 2008. She became an advocate for people with disabilities and her work was recognized when a Las Vegas affordable-housing complex for the disabled was named after her. In 2006, she lost a run for governor to former Rep. Jim Gibbons, a Republican.

In 2008, Titus ran successfully for the House, defeating Republican incumbent Jon Porter. That first tour of duty was short-lived. She was swept out of office by the Republican wave in 2010, losing a bruising battle to Heck by 1,748 votes out of more than 314,000 cast.

In 2012, Titus ran in the 1st District, which has a 2-1 Democratic edge in voter registration. Democratic state Sen. Ruben Kihuen also got in the race but withdrew after Titus significantly outraised him. In November, she largely avoided engaging Republican Chris Edwards, a naval officer making his first foray into politics. Abortion rights groups NARAL Pro-Choice America PAC and EMILY's List endorsed Titus. She won, 64%-32%.

Since her return to the House, Titus has been the ranking Democrat on the Veterans' Affairs Subcommittee on Disability Assistance and Memorial Affairs. In February 2015, she filed a bill that would overturn the VA's prohibition on doctors signing off on marijuana for patients. She also has introduced legislation to permit same-sex couples to be eligible for veterans' benefits. On the Transportation and Infrastructure Committee, Titus is an enthusiastic advocate of reopening rail service from Las Vegas to Los Angeles, perhaps with a private partner. Amtrak shut down the line in 1997. She has strongly opposed creating a nuclear waste dump at Yucca Mountain, and is a staunch ally of the casinos—including their opposition to the .0025 percent tax on sports betting.

Titus voiced interest in a 2016 run for the Senate seat of retiring Majority Leader Harry Reid. But that would require her to defeat Reid's choice for Democratic nominee, former Attorney General Catherine Cortez-Masto. Titus and Reid have had a distant relationship. Having lost two elections in the past decade, she was circumspect about giving up her safe seat in the House.

SECOND DISTRICT

Mark Amodei (R)

Elected Sept. 2011, 2nd full term; b. June 12, 1958, Carson City; U. of NV Reno, B.A. 1980, U. of the Pacific, J.D. 1983; Christian; divorced; 2 children.

Military Career: U.S. Army, Judge Advocate Gen. Corps, 1983-87.

Elected Office: NV Assembly, 1997-98; NV Senate, 1999-2010.

Professional Career: Asst. U.S. atty. & asst. post judge advocate, 1984-87; Practicing atty., 1987-96.

DC Office: 322 CHOB, 20515, 202-225-6155; Fax: 202-225-5679; Website: amodei.house.gov.

State Offices: Elko, 775-777-7705; Reno, 775-686-5760.

Committees: *Appropriations:* Financial Services & General Government; Interior, Environment, & Related Agencies; Legislative Branch (VChmn).

Group Ratings

	ADA	ACLU	AFL-CIO	LCV	ITI	COC	HAFA	ACU	CFG	FRC
2014	5%	5%	–	3%	100%	100%	45%	64%	43%	63%
2013	5%	C	10%	4%	C	83%	C	75%	67%	C

National Journal Ratings

	2013 LIB	—	2013 CONS
Economic	24%	—	76%
Social	43%	—	54%
Foreign	24%	—	68%
Composite	32%	—	68%

Key Votes of the 113th Congress

1. Sandy storm spending	N	5. Medical Marijuana	Y	9. Syrian Rebels Training	N
2. Violence Against Women Act	Y	6. Farm Bill	Y	10. Keystone pipeline	Y
3. Guantanamo Bay Detainees	N	7. Afghanistan Combat	N	11. Immigration Exec. Action	Y
4. Abortion 20-week ban	Y	8. NSA Phone Data Collection	Y	12. Bipartisan budget deal	Y

Election Results

2014 general	Mark Amodei (R).......................	122,402	(66%)	$698,201
	Kristen Spees (D)........................	52,016	(28%)	$10,904
	Janine Hansen (IAP).................	11,792	(6%)	
2014 primary	Mark Amodei (R)...................unopposed			

Prior winning percentages: 2012 (58%), 2011 special (58%)

Population		Race and Ethnicity		Income	
Total:	690,786	White	68.5%	Median income:	$53,093
Urban:	49.7%	Latino	21.1%		*(184 of 435)*
Suburban:	21.6%	Asian	3.7%	Under $50,000	46.8%
Rural:	28.6%	Amer. Indian	2.2%	$50,000-$99,999:	31.1%
Land area:	34,300	Two races	2.2%	$100,000-$199,999:	18.1%
Pop/sq. mi.:	20.1	White Ethnic	25.7%	$200,000 or more:	4.0%
Born in state:	29.7%			Poverty Rate	14.3%
		Education			
		H.S. grad or less:	38.5%	**Work**	
Age Groups		Some college:	36.6%	White collar:	31.7%
Under 18:	22.8%	College degree, 4 yr.:	16.3%	Blue collar:	45.6%
18 to 34:	22.7%	Post-grad study:	8.5%	Sales and service:	22.7%
35 to 64:	39.5%			Govt. workers:	15.9%
Over 64:	15.0%	**Military**			
		Veterans/active duty:	11.0%		

Northern Nevada: Reno

Outside of metro Las Vegas, huge, empty, and mountainous Nevada has only one sizable population center, a cluster of small cities and towns near the border with California: the casino cities of Reno and Sparks, the small capital of Carson City, the restored Comstock Lode boomtown of Virginia City,

Voter Turnout	
2013 Total Citizen 18+	491,180
2014 House Turnout	186,210
2014 Turnout as % CVAP	37.9%
2012 Turnout as % CVAP	61.3%

and the resort areas that surround (and endanger) the deep, impossibly blue waters of Lake Tahoe. Reno is so remote from Las Vegas that the only quick way to get there is by air; it takes more than nine hours to drive. Ghost towns that once bustled with miners dot the parched, sand-swept deserts, and in some places the land is distinctly rutted from the wagon trains that crossed here more than 100 years ago. Today, Nevada's small towns survive on mining, ranching and, in some cases, servicing the human sins of greed and lust: Nevada's legal brothels are generally found in the small, desert counties. Another distinction is the Basque influence. Immigrant Basque shepherds once tended their flocks in remote portions of northern Nevada; Basque festivals, social clubs, and restaurants can still be found in Winnemucca and Elko.

The military has holdings in the Nevada interior, including the Fallon Naval Air Station, home to the Navy Fighter Weapons "Top Gun" School. Many places in Nevada are dependent on other federal government programs: The Newlands Irrigation Project near Fallon was among the first of its kind, and Nevada's gold-mining operations, booming since 2000, do not have to pay royalties to the government thanks to the Mining Act of 1872. The spread of legalized gambling throughout the country has hurt Reno, and it had dropped to the 16th largest gaming city in 2012, with only 10% of the revenues of Las Vegas. The recession hit here with great force—unemployment in the Reno-Sparks area and in Carson City remained at 11% in early 2013; but it improved to 6.9% in March 2015. Economic diversification is coming by way of budding solar- and wind-energy enterprises, bio-agriculture, and high-precision technologies. Apple opened a $1 billion data center in Reno in early 2013, then doubled its size a year later; the facility operates by solar power. Electric-car manufacturer Tesla Motors is building a huge factory near Sparks, where it plans to start lower-cost cell production for its batteries starting in 2017.

The 2nd Congressional District of Nevada takes in Reno and Carson City in territory that covers nearly the northern half of Nevada. It includes Churchill, Pershing, Humboldt and Elko counties. Washoe

2012 Presidential Vote		
Mitt Romney (R)	155,186	(53%)
Barack Obama (D)	131,540	(45%)
2008 Presidential Vote		
Barack Obama (D)	141,333	(49%)
John McCain (R)	137,854	(48%)
Cook Partisan Voting Index: R+5		

County, which includes Reno and Sparks, has nearly two-thirds of the district's population. The 2nd leans Republican, but barely. Washoe was an important swing county in the 2012 presidential election, and Democratic President Barack Obama won it with 51% of the vote. In the district, as a whole, Mitt Romney won 53%-45%. The GOP increased its voter-registration advantage in Washoe in the 2014 campaign.

Mark Amodei (R)

Republican Mark Amodei won a 2011 special election to fill the seat of now-GOP Sen. Dean Heller. A former state Senate president pro tempore and state party chairman, Amodei is a Western, small-government conservative who wants to open public lands to mining and other uses. His governing experience has surpassed his ideological stripes in allying him with the GOP establishment.

Amodei grew up in Carson City, Nevada's capital, the son of an Italian immigrant father who worked for the state Forestry Division and a mother who was a physician. He attended the University of Nevada at Reno, where he joined ROTC, and earned a law degree from the University of the Pacific's McGeorge School of Law. He joined the Army and became a prosecutor for the Judge Advocate General Corps, handling criminal matters.

After opening a law practice in his hometown, Amodei won a state Assembly seat in 1996. Two years later, he moved to the state Senate, chaired the Judiciary Committee, and took his leadership post in 2003. That year, Amodei worked on a comprehensive tax bill, which later drew criticism when he ran for Congress. The measure would have raised $900 million in taxes over two years. In 2007, Amodei became president of the Nevada Mining Association. He said that he saw no conflict of interest with his work as a senator, but a year and a half later he stepped down from the organization because he said he didn't want to have a "distracting" dual role during the legislative session.

In September 2009, Amodei announced a challenge to Senate Majority Leader Harry Reid, portraying himself as a common-sense conservative who could appeal to independent voters in his bid to oust the powerful Democrat. He dropped out of the contest six months later, explaining that he was able to raise only about $80,000, a pittance compared to Reid's multimillion-dollar war chest.

The state's other Senate seat came open after Republican John Ensign resigned amid a sex scandal with the wife of one of his former aides. Heller was appointed in May 2011 to replace Ensign, and Amodei announced his bid for Heller's seat. The next month, he won the GOP nomination with ease, taking 221 out of 323 ballots of the GOP state Central Committee members to defeat state Sen. Greg Brower, who received 56 votes. Amodei's victory set up a special-election matchup with Democratic state Treasurer Kate Marshall. Marshall boasted of support from the National Rifle Association and said she would have voted against increasing the federal debt ceiling, which Amodei also opposed. She joined other Democrats in attacking House Budget Committee Chairman Paul Ryan's proposal to restructure Medicare.

Amodei played up his conservative credentials, calling for tax cuts and passage of a balanced-budget amendment to the Constitution. He backed opening more public lands to domestic oil and gas production and protecting the Mining Act of 1872, which environmentalists consider antiquated but which Amodei said protected Nevada's standing as one of the world's largest gold producers. He used an ad with his mother to deflect the Medicare attacks. The National Republican Congressional Committee pumped in more than $600,000 to pummel Marshall, and the Democratic Congressional Campaign Committee never came to her rescue. Amodei won, 58%-36%.

In the House, Amodei has been an often pragmatic conservative vote who emphasizes spending discipline. He was the only Nevada lawmaker to oppose the New Year's Day 2013 budget compromise aimed at averting the so-called "fiscal cliff." "To go back to [constituents] and say, 'We have not taken this opportunity to do anything on spending or debt'—that is just at odds with what I represented to people I would try to do." On Appropriations, he became vice chairman of the Legislative Branch Subcommittee in 2015. In 2014, the Interior Subcommittee approved his provision to protect the water rights of private land-holders.

A vice chairman of the Western Caucus, Amodei has concentrated on natural resource issues. He got a bill through the House in 2012, and again in 2014, to allow the city of Yerington to buy 10,000 acres of federal land around a copper mine to help recharge the impoverished region, but the measure stalled each time in the Senate. He suggested that the locally unpopular Yucca Mountain proposed burial site for high-level nuclear waste storage be examined instead as a potential home for nuclear reprocessing and research.

He has brought a home-spun approach to his job, and believes that lawmakers need to talk more with each other. In a May 2015 interview with the *Sparks Tribune*, Amodei said that the problems of immigration are "eminently solvable," except that "everybody's got a political angle." In his view, "I'd rather be criticized for trying to do something because I'm tired of defending nothing." He reached across the aisle to Democrat Jared Polis of Colorado to seek common ground on the topic. He was 1 of only 11 Republicans to oppose the bill in 2014 to end President Barack Obama's executive actions to stop the deportation of some undocumented immigrants. Democratic Rep. John Garamendi of California told the *Reno Gazette-Journal* that Amodei "knows the legislative process," and they have worked together on issues related to Lake Tahoe. When Amodei is on the House floor, said Republican Rep. James Renacci of Ohio, "Everybody knows him and sees him as someone they can work with."

Amodei quickly ruled out running for Reid's Senate seat in 2016. But, citing his extensive experience in state government, he kept the door open to run for governor or attorney general in 2018.

THIRD DISTRICT

Joe Heck (R)

Elected 2010, 3rd term; b. Oct. 30, 1961, Queens, NY; PA St. U., B.S. 1984; Philadelphia Col. of Osteopathic Medicine, D.O. 1988, U.S. Army War Col., M.S.S. 2006; Catholic; married (Lisa); 3 children.

Military Career: Army Reserve, 1991-present (Iraq).

Elected Office: NV Senate, 2004-08.

Professional Career: Emergency physician, SW Emergency Assocs., 1992-98; Med. dir., Uniformed Services, U. of Health Sciences, 1998-2003; Emergency physician, U. Med. Ctr., 2002-10; Pres., Specialized Med. Ops. Inc., 2002-10.

DC Office: 132 CHOB, 20515, 202-225-3252; Fax: 202-225-2185; Website: heck.house.gov.

State Offices: Las Vegas, 702-387-4941.

Committees: *Armed Services:* Oversight & Investigations; Military Personnel (Chmn). *Education & the Workforce:* Health, Employment, Labor & Pensions; Higher Education & Workforce Training. *Intelligence (Select):* Department of Defense Intelligence & Overhead Architecture (Chmn); Emerging Threats.

Group Ratings

	ADA	ACLU	AFL-CIO	LCV	ITI	COC	HAFA	ACU	CFG	FRC
2014	5%	16%	–	6%	100%	93%	48%	56%	39%	50%
2013	0%	C	19%	14%	C	77%	C	72%	70%	C

National Journal Ratings

	2013 LIB — 2013 CONS	
Economic	39% —	60%
Social	43% —	54%
Foreign	47% —	52%
Composite	44% —	56%

Key Votes of the 113th Congress

1. Sandy storm spending	N	5. Medical Marijuana	Y	9. Syrian Rebels Training	N
2. Violence Against Women Act	Y	6. Farm Bill	N	10. Keystone pipeline	Y
3. Guantanamo Bay Detainees	N	7. Afghanistan Combat	N	11. Immigration Exec. Action	Y
4. Abortion 20-week ban	Y	8. NSA Phone Data Collection	N	12. Bipartisan budget deal	N

Election Results

2014 general	Joe Heck (R)	88,528	(61%)	$1,979,832	$1,721,619	$152,594
	Erin Bilbray (D)	52,644	(36%)	$1,156,610	$15,782	
2014 primary	Joe Heck (R)	unopposed				

Prior winning percentages: 2012 (50%), 2010 (48%)

Population		Race and Ethnicity		Income	
Total:	720,438	White	61.1%	Median income:	$61,217
Urban:	96.4%	Latino	15.4%		*(110 of 435)*
Suburban:	1.0%	Asian	11.7%	Under $50,000	38.7%
Rural:	2.6%	Black	7.2%	$50,000-$99,999:	35.8%
Land area:	2,700	Two races	3.4%	$100,000-$199,999:	20.6%
Pop/sq. mi.:	266.8	White Ethnic	27.7%	$200,000 or more:	4.9%
Born in state:	21.8%			Poverty Rate	9.7%
		Education			
Age Groups		H.S. grad or less:	31.9%	**Work**	
Under 18:	22.4%	Some college:	37.4%	White collar:	34.5%
18 to 34:	21.5%	College degree, 4 yr.:	20.3%	Blue collar:	51.6%
35 to 64:	41.0%	Post-grad study:	10.4%	Sales and service:	14.0%
Over 64:	15.1%				
		Military		Govt. workers:	11.0%
		Veterans/active duty:	10.0%		

Southern Las Vegas area: Henderson

Las Vegas, "The Meadows" in Spanish, began as a stop along the Old Spanish Trail trading route between Santa Fe and California in the 1830s. Water from artesian wells had created vast grasslands in the area and let traders replenish their supplies. In the early 20th century, Las Vegas was

Voter Turnout	
2013 Total Citizen 18+	516,538
2014 House Turnout	145,719
2014 Turnout as % CVAP	28.2%
2012 Turnout as % CVAP	57.2%

a terminus of the Las Vegas & Tonopah Railroad, a link to Nevada's silver mines. Even at the end of the 1930s, soon after gambling was legalized in Nevada, it was still a town of less than 10,000. Then came decades of amazing growth, as Las Vegas became America's destination for gambling and entertainment. From 2000 to 2008, the Las Vegas metropolitan area grew by 36%, to 1.9 million, making it one of the five fastest-growing metropolitan areas in America. It spread across the desert in every direction from the few blocks around Fremont Street that it occupied in the 1930s, and today it is an exuberant, undisciplined and chaotic city. Following the fast pace of building, Las Vegas was particularly hard hit by the crisis in the credit markets, and the red-hot real estate market tanked. The metro area had the highest foreclosure rate in the nation in 2010, according to *RealtyTrac*. In November 2014, the foreclosures remained high enough that Henderson created a registry to monitor abandoned properties.

The 3rd Congressional District covers the southern part of Clark County and several Las Vegas suburbs. It includes retiree communities, small blue-collar towns such as Blue Diamond, and a variety of planned, and often gated, areas like Summerlin South, where young families have sought job opportunities and retired baby boomers have purchased vacation homes. Southeast of Las Vegas, the district takes in the population hub of Henderson, and Boulder City, originally built for federal workers at Hoover Dam. (Under an old agreement with the federal government, Boulder City is the only place in Nevada where gambling and prostitution are prohibited.) After the dam was completed, many of the workers unexpectedly decided to stay in the hot desert locale. The sale of liquor was legalized in 1969. Fun fact: Henderson provides tours of its "Artisan Booze" district.

The 3rd includes the Nevada half of Lake Mohave on the Arizona border, plus the state's southernmost tip, including Searchlight, the hometown of Senate Majority Leader Harry Reid. Amid a local gold rush, Reid in 2014 sold his home and 110 acres of land, plus the water and mining rights, to a mining company for $1.75 million. The sale was "a very difficult decision," he said. The 3rd, about 15% Latino, is politically competitive. President Barack Obama won the district with 49% of the vote in 2012.

2012 Presidential Vote		
Barack Obama (D)	140,501	(49%)
Mitt Romney (R)	138,238	(49%)

2008 Presidential Vote		
Barack Obama (D)	140,472	(54%)
John McCain (R)	117,089	(45%)

Cook Partisan Voting Index: EVEN

Joe Heck (R)

Republican Joe Heck was known as a moderate in the Nevada legislature. When he was elected to the House in 2010, he defeated Democratic Rep. Dina Titus by embracing some tea party positions. He has since returned to his moderate ways and he strengthened himself politically prior to his announcement that he will run for the open Senate seat in 2016.

Heck was born in Queens New York and raised in Pennsylvania in a tight-knit family where he says he learned the values of service and giving back to the community. As a young man, he became a volunteer firefighter and ambulance attendant. After his undergraduate years at Pennsylvania State University in health education, he got a doctorate of osteopathy from the Philadelphia College of Osteopathic Medicine and completed a residency in emergency medicine at the Albert Einstein Medical Center. In 1992, his work took him to southern Nevada. Heck said that his career in emergency medicine put him on the "front lines of health care. … I get to see what works and what doesn't work," he told *National Journal*.

A member of the Army Reserve, Heck was called to active duty in 1996 during the Bosnian war and was deployed again in Iraq, where he ran an Army hospital in 2010. "I was militarily inclined as a kid," he said. "I thought about going into the service earlier, but I had decided I wanted to go into medicine and didn't want the military to dictate what my specialty would be." From 1998 to 2003, Heck was medical director of the casualty care research center of the Uniformed Services University of the Health Sciences in Bethesda Maryland. He provided medical support for federal law enforcement agencies, and the experience sparked his interest in politics. Returning to Nevada, he won a state Senate seat in 2004, and started a medical training and consulting business. In 2014, the Senate confirmed him as a brigadier general in the Army Reserves.

Heck considered running for governor in 2010, but instead challenged Titus, a former state Senate colleague. Excited by Sharron Angle's challenge to Senate Majority Leader Harry Reid of Nevada, Heck tacked to the right during the campaign, taking more tea party-style positions than he had as a state senator. He called for abolition of the Education Department and the addition of optional private accounts to Social Security. On the stump, Heck described himself as conservative but "a very pragmatic lawmaker, unafraid to cross party lines."

Titus accused him of using "the Republican talking points" and ran an ad calling Heck and Angle "two peas in a pod with the same bad ideas." She also characterized him as dangerous to women for voting against a bill that would have required insurance companies to cover a vaccine for the HPV virus, a precursor to cervical cancer. Heck had substantial help from outside groups, including Americans for Tax Reform, which spent $600,000 for him. Titus got help from AFSCME and the SEIU unions representing government workers and service industry employees. Heck spent $1.4 million, to $2.6 million for Titus. Heck won narrowly, 48.1%-47.5%. Heck's victory margin was 1,748 votes out of about 268,000 cast. (Titus won the neighboring 1st District seat in 2012).

In the House, Heck landed on good committees—Armed Services, Education and the Workforce, and Intelligence—as a reward for beating an incumbent Democrat. In 2015, he chaired Subcommittees on Military Personnel, and Department of Defense Intelligence and Overhead Architecture. He objected to attempts to reduce pay and benefits for service members. He proved to be far less conservative than most other GOP freshmen. He distanced himself in March 2012 from presidential candidate Mitt Romney's call to let the housing foreclosure process "hit bottom," saying in response, "We have been bouncing along the bottom for years." He introduced a bill that month creating a federal program to ensure fresh loans to foreclosed homeowners. His other legislative proposals included an attempt to streamline federal workforce training programs and to increase foreign tourism by speeding up travel visas for foreigners. In May 2015, the House passed his bill to permit low-income disabled veterans to qualify for housing assistance. The House-passed annual military spending bill in May 2015 included several measures pressed by Heck: steps to prevent retaliation against Armed Forces members who report sexual assault, the establishment of a unified medical command, and improvements in the pay and retirement system.

Hoping to snatch the seat back in 2012, Democrats nominated John Oceguera, the state Assembly speaker. Oceguera drew poor reviews for his evasive answers on a political talk show, and the *Las Vegas Review-Journal* reported that he collected $452,516 in salary and unused sick leave for working just five months in 2011 as an assistant fire chief in North Las Vegas. National Democrats turned their attention elsewhere. Meanwhile, Heck made regular visits to Hispanic chambers of commerce, Filipino businesses, and an out-of-district Chinatown where many of his constituents shop, to connect with minority voters. He outspent Oceguera, $2.3 million to $1.5 million, and won 50%-43%.

In 2014, Heck had what started as another competitive challenge from Erin Bilbray-Kohn, a political consultant and Democratic National Committeewoman, whose father Jim Bilbray served eight years in the House as a Nevada Democrat. Once again, Democrats abandoned this contest months before the election. Bilbray was outspent $2 million to $1.2 million. Heck won his first landslide, 61%-36%.

With the retirement of Reid, Heck said in April 2015 that he was doing his "due diligence" about a possible candidacy for the Senate. In July, he launched his bid in a video that focused on his life's experiences, including his military background. He became the Republican front-runner and was viewed as competitive in the likely tight general election.

FOURTH DISTRICT

Cresent Hardy (R)

Elected 2014, 1st term; b. June 23, 1957, Mesquite; attended Dixie State Col.; Mormon; married (Peri), 4 children.

Elected Office: Member, Mesquite City Council, 1997-2002; NV State Assembly, 2011-15.

Professional Career: Licensed Contractor, Dir., Mesquite Public Works, 1986-93.

DC Office: 430 CHOB, 20515; 202-225-9894; Fax: 202-225-9783; Website: hardy.house.gov.

State Offices: North Las Vegas, 702-912-1634.

Committees: *Natural Resources:* Energy & Mineral Resources; Federal Lands; *Small Business:* Investigations, Oversight, & Regulations (Chmn); Contracting & Workforce; *Transportation & Infrastructure:* Highways & Transit (Vice-Chmn); Railroads, Pipelines & Hazardous Materials; *Water Resources & Environment.*

Election Results

2014 general	Cresent Hardy (R) 63,466	(49%)	$382,088	$295,413	$481,069
	Steven Horsford (D).................... 59,844	(46%)	$1,934,822	$219,259	$869,438
	Steve Brown (Lib)........................ 4,119	(3%)			
	Russell Best (IAP)........................ 3,352	(3%)			
2014 primary	Cresent Hardy (R)....................... 10,398	(43%)			
	Niger Innis................................. 8,077	(33%)			
	Mike Monroe............................... 5,393	(22%)			

Population		Race and Ethnicity		Income	
Total:	705,118	White	47.5%	Median income:	$51,708
Urban:	70.8%	Latino	29.7%		*(210 of 435)*
Suburban:	20.5%	Black	13.6%	Under $50,000	48.3%
Rural:	8.7%	Asian	4.3%	$50,000-$99,999:	34.1%
Land area:	19,988	Two races	3.3%	$100,000-$199,999:	15.7%
Pop/sq. mi.:	35.3	White Ethnic	21.2%	$200,000 or more:	1.9%
Born in state:	27.8%			Poverty Rate	16.9%
		Education			
Age Groups		H.S. grad or less:	46.8%	**Work**	
Under 18:	26.6%	Some college:	34.3%	White collar:	26.2%
18 to 34:	23.6%	College degree, 4 yr.:	12.7%	Blue collar:	53.9%
35 to 64:	37.2%	Post-grad study:	6.2%	Sales and service:	19.9%
Over 64:	12.5%				
		Military		Govt. workers:	15.6%
		Veterans/active duty:	12.9%		

Central Nevada: Northern Las Vegas area

A vast majority of the land in Nevada is owned by the federal government—a constant source of tension with local officials, ranchers, loggers and miners. Their pursuits, frequently solitary and often ornery, shaped Nevada's culture from its earliest days.

Voter Turnout	
2013 Total Citizen 18+	459,761
2014 House Turnout	130,781
2014 Turnout as % CVAP	28.4%
2012 Turnout as % CVAP	56.4%

On the desolate frontier, speculation runs wild: Art Bell used to broadcast his popular radio show about the paranormal, aliens and other unexplained phenomena from tiny Pahrump. The federal government's top-secret aviation experiments at places like Area 51 on the Nellis Air Force Gunnery Range have stoked UFO lore to the point that adjoining Route 375 was rededicated as the Extraterrestrial Highway in 1996. Anti-establishment views also flourish here in more mainstream ways. Nevada residents have long opposed a nuclear waste repository 1,000 feet beneath Yucca Mountain, 90 miles northwest of Las Vegas. Congress finally approved the project in 2002. But President Barack Obama shelved it and a commission recommended alternative storage options.

The vast interior away from Las Vegas includes the 3-million-acre Nellis Air Force range. Also found here is the Energy Department's Nevada National Security Site, which was created by President Harry Truman. More than 800 underground tests of nuclear weapons were conducted here, as well as 100 above ground tests, before they ended in 1962. The explosions left the Rhode Island-sized facility pockmarked with unstable "subsidence craters" as far as the eye can see. In a potentially significant twist, Nye County officials in 2015 approved the shipment of uranium waste from the Oak Ridge National Lab in Tennessee to a landfill at the nuclear site. Yucca Mountain also is located in Nye County.

Due to the state's fast-growing population, Nevada gained a new rural and suburban district outside of central Las Vegas in the 2010 census. The new 4th District contains much of North Las Vegas and stretches north into the state's interior. The northern part of Clark County, as well as Esmeralda, Mineral, White Pine (and the city of Ely),

2012 Presidential Vote		
Barack Obama (D) 136,124	(54%)
Mitt Romney (R)................109,329	(44%)

2008 Presidential Vote		
Barack Obama (D) 130,602	(56%)
John McCain (R)..................95,777	(41%)

Cook Partisan Voting Index: D+4

Nye and Lincoln counties are in the district. Clark County, which dropped from 61% non-Hispanic white in 2000 to 46% in 2013, has become one of the largest majority-minority counties in the nation, with 30% Hispanic, 12% black and 10% Asian. About 85% of the district vote is cast in Clark. Democrats have a voter registration edge of 46%-33% and President Barack Obama took the 4th in 2012 by 54%-44%. But the district, which is 30% Hispanic and 14% black, is competitive.

Cresent Hardy (R)

In a huge surprise and blow to House Democrats, Republican state legislator Cresent Hardy in 2014 upset well-financed freshman Democratic Rep. Steven Horsford. Hardy, who described himself as a "constitutional conservative," took advantage of growing discontent with President Barack Obama. He became a top Democratic target for 2016.

A fifth-generation Nevadan, Hardy was raised in rural Mesquite, where he worked on his father's ranch. He attended Dixie State College in St. George, Utah, and returned home where he held several positions in the city and Clark County. He was director of public works in Mesquite for seven years and served on several boards overseeing the water district and regional flood-control district. For six years, he served on the Mesquite City Council. In the private sector, he was an engineering contractor. Hardy was elected to the state Assembly in 2010, campaigning against the "tax-and-spend" policies of the Democratic-controlled Legislature, and became assistant minority leader in 2013.

In the June GOP primary to challenge Horsford, Hardy defeated tea party activist Niger Innis. Early in the general election campaign against Horsford, he struggled to raise money. He suffered from a series of gaffes, including repeating Mitt Romney's unpopular comment that 47 percent of the country relied on government assistance. Earlier in the year, he said he opposed the Senate-passed Employment Non-Discrimination Act that would bar workplace discrimination on the basis of sexual orientation or gender identity. He said the measure amounted to a "segregation" law and "puts one class of person over another."

Hardy continued to speak about his support for a flat tax and comprehensive immigration reform as he campaigned against first-termer Horsford, an African American who won 50%-42% in 2012 and had been seen as a rising star by his party in this 14% black district. Crossroads Grassroots Policy Strategies, a super PAC with ties to conservative strategist Karl Rove, spent $1.1 million advertising against Horsford. Two weeks before Election Day, Republicans began early voting in large numbers. To close the campaign, Hardy sought to emphasize Horsford's ties to Obama. In his own campaign ad, Hardy featured audio from Horsford's radio ad in which Obama credits the Democrat's work on the Nevada economy. He aired it in rural areas of the district where he wanted to boost voter turnout. Labor unions hit the streets in the days leading up to the election to campaign on Horsford's behalf, and Hardy was out-spent $1.9 million to $382,000.

In the shocking outcome, Hardy won 48.5%-45.8%. "Democrats simply had no reason to show up and vote," according to David Wasserman. "Voter participation dropped a staggering 49.8% here from 2012, and that was mostly minority drop-off." Horsford led by 1,923 votes in vote-heavy Clark County. But Hardy rolled up 58% of the vote in the six other counties, compared with only 32% for Horsford, and won by 3,622 votes overall. "I'm about as far right as you can get on the issues," he told the *Las Vegas Sun* after the election. "But I'm a realist." He said that the federal government had overstepped its bounds on a wide range of issues, from health care to taxes. He added that he planned to reach out to voters across the diverse district.

In the House, Hardy got useful committee assignments from Republican leaders who were eager to help him establish a presence: Natural Resources, Transportation and Infrastructure, and Small Business, where he became chairman of the Investigations, Oversight and Regulations Subcommittee. In March 2015, he wrote an op-ed calling for an "honest discussion" of the future of the proposed nuclear-waste site at Yucca Mountain. For the most part, he had a low profile during his first few months in office. "Hardy has carefully kept out of the spotlight in Washington," the *Las Vegas Review-Journal* reported in May 2015. He responded, "There's nobody [who] can outwork me."

Hardy clashed with Obama on a controversial local issue when he spoke out strongly against administration plans to designate 704,000 acres in central Nevada as the nation's newest national monument, tentatively named the Basin and Range National Monument. The proposal, which was backed by Senate Majority Leader Harry Reid of Nevada and opposed by most Republicans, became a prominent item on Obama's agenda of executive actions. Hardy objected that the monument area is below the Air Force airspace of the nearby Nellis Test and Training Range. In May 2015, he added an amendment to the House-passed defense spending bill to protect national-security activities on or above land with a national monument that the president has established; it was approved on a voice vote. Hardy said his amendment "elevates national security above politics and legacy projects, and gives our military the certainty it needs to adequately train and prepare for current and future conflicts."

Hardy sided with Obama on another contentious issue when he was one of 26 Republicans who opposed in January 2015 an amendment to block funding for the president's Deferred Action for Childhood Arrivals executive order, which is known as the DREAMer program.

In March 2015, Horsford announced that he would not make another bid for the seat. That opened the door to several potential Democratic challengers to Hardy, who started the campaign as a significant underdog.

★ NEW HAMPSHIRE ★

In June 1788, New Hampshire voted to ratify the Constitution and, as the ninth state to do so, made it effective. But nowhere in the Constitution is there any provision that foreshadows New Hampshire's current prominence in American political life. For this small and scarcely typical state, with just .42 percent of the nation's population, every four years becomes the center of the political universe, the place where the contest for the American presidency is temporarily focused, where every vote is avidly sought—handshake by handshake. New Hampshire gave a huge boost to Dwight Eisenhower's candidacy in 1952 and prompted the retirement of Lyndon Johnson in 1968. It helped launch Jimmy Carter in 1976, Ronald Reagan in 1980, George H.W. Bush in 1988, and Bill Clinton in 1992, who had his "Comeback Kid" moment in the Granite State.

The lever with which this small state has sometimes moved the political world is its first-in-the-nation presidential primary, given that status by Democratic rules writers in the 1970s and exploited by Republicans in the 1980s. The state fiercely defends its first-in-the-nation prerogative, led for decades now by Secretary of State Bill Gardner, whose intense advocacy for keeping New Hampshire's primary the nation's earliest has made him arguably the safest incumbent in the nation, appointed by the legislature regardless of party since 1976. New Hampshire's disproportionate weight in presidential elections is even more impressive considering that its public policies are arguably atypical of the nation, and its political terrain is unusual to the point of eccentricity. This is one of the few states that over the past half-century has had more registered Republicans than Democrats, and it was for many years the state with the most antipathy toward taxes.

And New Hampshire has not always picked winners. The last three candidates to win the presidency did so after finishing second here. New Hampshire winners have won major party nominations in each of the last four elections, but Al Gore, John Kerry, John McCain, and Mitt Romney all lost in November. New Hampshire gave conservative commentator Patrick Buchanan a surprising 37% of the vote in 1992 and a 27% victory in 1996, but he never did as well elsewhere and wound up leaving the Republican Party in 1999. It gave McCain a thumping victory over George W. Bush in 2000, but that proved to be a harbinger for the Northeast and not for the rest of the country. It fooled the pollsters when it gave Hillary Clinton a surprise victory in 2008, but she still fell short of the nomination.

New Hampshire has been quirky from its beginnings. In a country that prides itself on its feistiness and freedom from outside direction, it has always been even feistier and more lightly fettered by authority. Before the Revolutionary War, New Hampshire was almost an outlaw colony, its great fortunes made by poachers in the king's forests and smugglers avoiding taxes. Boxed in by bossy Puritan Massachusetts on two sides (for Maine was part of that colony and state until 1820), New Hampshire embodied the spirit of Revolutionary War General John Stark's words, "Live free or die." New Hampshire was the first colony with an independent government and was fighting the British before the Minutemen stood at Lexington and Concord.

In the early republic, New England merchants turned inland and built textile mills along fast-flowing rivers. The Amoskeag Mills in Manchester, lining the Merrimack River for a mile, were once the largest cotton mills in the world, employing 17,000 people and producing enough cloth every two months to extend around the world. Around the mills grew a city of red-brick dormitories and three-family frame houses filled with immigrants from Quebec, Ireland, Poland and Greece, set down amid villages of dirt roads and flinty Yankee farmers and mechanics. New Hampshire held to its traditions of local government and little external control, and for years refused to join most other states in enacting an income or sales tax, or to provide statewide guidance of schools and social services. This stifled progress, many said.

Instead, low taxes proved to be New Hampshire's fortune. From 1960 to 1990, the state's population grew 83%, more than double the national rate of 39%. During that time and through the 1990s, it had the fastest growth in the Northeast, attracting businesses from Massachusetts and other high-tax states. It became a location of choice for entrepreneurs and high-tech innovators. The bedraggled New Hampshire of 50 years ago, of poor Yankee farmers and French Canadian mill hands, has been overtaken by one of the nation's most prosperous economic communities. The low taxes that spurred New Hampshire's growth

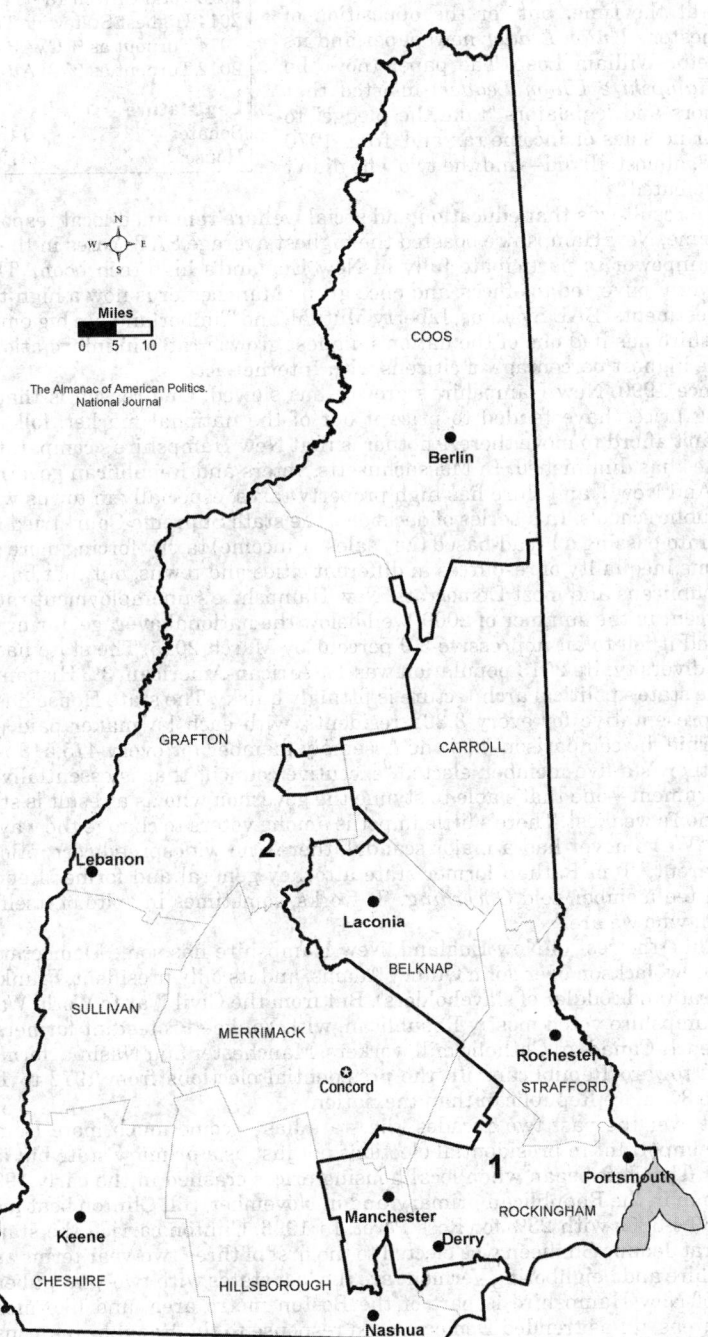

COOS

Berlin

GRAFTON

CARROLL

Lebanon

2

Laconia

BELKNAP

SULLIVAN

MERRIMACK

Rochester

Concord

STRAFFORD

1

Portsmouth

Keene

Manchester

Derry

ROCKINGHAM

CHESHIRE

HILLSBOROUGH

Nashua

N
W   E
S

Miles
0   5   10

The Almanac of American Politics.
National Journal

Congressional district boundaries were first effective for 2012.

would probably have been raised in the late 1960s or early 1970s, as they were in so many states at the time, but for the opposition of Manchester's *Union Leader* newspaper and its proprietor William Loeb. The paper (now the *New Hampshire Union Leader*) insisted that governors and legislators "take the pledge" to vote for no sales or income tax and, from 1970 to 1998, almost all did—and the two who didn't were defeated.

Voter Turnout			
2013 Total Citizen 18+			1,019,033
2014 Highest Statewide Turnout			488,159
2014 Turnout as % CVAP			47.9%
2012 Turnout as % CVAP			70.1%
Legislature			
Senate:	14R	10D	
House:	237R	160D	1I, 2V

The result was that education and social welfare remained local responsibilities. At the same time, New Hampshire boasted the highest average SAT scores in the country and had the brainpower to participate fully in New England's high-tech boom. The old Amoskeag Mills were converted to offices, and once-grimy Manchester is now a high-tech center. Fidelity Investments, BAE Systems, Liberty Mutual, and Timberland are big employers, and New Hampshire has had one of the nation's highest growth rates in information technology jobs and the highest percentage of citizens with Internet access.

Since 1990, New Hampshire's growth has slowed. One reason is that the state's high housing prices have tended to price it out of the national market; folks from the heartland can't afford to move there. Another is that New Hampshire's comparative advantage in tax rates has diminished. In Massachusetts, voters and Republican governors have cut tax rates. And New Hampshire has high property taxes, especially in towns where voters want good public schools. In a series of decisions, the state Supreme Court tried to push the legislature into passing a broad-based (i.e., sales or income) tax by forcing more state spending to overcome inequality of resources in different cities and towns, but that has been resisted by all Republicans and most Democrats. New Hampshire's unemployment rate peaked at only 6.6 percent in the summer of 2009, well below the national average during the recent recession, and it fell to an impressive 3.9 percent by March 2015. The state has suffered from a lack of diversity: Its 2013 population was 1% African-American, 3% Hispanic, and 2% Asian.

The state's political architecture is fittingly quirky. The state House has 400 members—one representative for every 3,302 residents, with each lawmaker paid just $100 a year. (California, by comparison, has one Assembly member for every 475,518 residents.) Meanwhile, there's a five-member, elected "executive council" that is essentially a fourth branch of government—one that's able to stymie the governor, who as a result is structurally one of the nation's weakest. There's little impetus among voters to change the way the government works. "We've never had a major scandal, there's no widespread corruption and it's pretty transparent," Tom Rath, a former state attorney general and former Republican National Committee member, told *Governing*. "It works, sometimes in spite of itself, but it works. It fits with who we are."

Unlike the rest of New England, New Hampshire has some Democratic roots: It voted for Andrew Jackson over John Quincy Adams, and its only president, Franklin Pierce, was a Democrat (and coddler of slaveholders). But from the Civil War to World War II and beyond, New Hampshire voted mostly Republican, with Yankee Protestant farmers outvoting Irish and French-Canadian Catholic mill workers. Manchester and Nashua, formerly Democratic, trended toward Republicans. In the presidential elections from 1972 to 1988, it voted on average 8% more Republican than the nation.

But over the past two decades, the state has become much more Democratic and has become important in presidential elections not just as a primary state but as a target in the general. The shift began when local housing prices crashed in the early 1990s. That helped Buchanan in the Republican primary, and in November, Bill Clinton beat incumbent George Bush, 39%-38%, with 23% for Ross Perot. In 1996, Clinton carried the state 49%-39%, and Democrat Jeanne Shaheen was elected to the first of three two-year terms as governor. (New Hampshire and neighboring Vermont are the last states with two-year gubernatorial terms.) Much of New Hampshire is part of the Boston metro area, and like most non-Southern metro areas, it has trended Democratic in response to the Republicans' conservative stands on cultural issues. And if New Hampshire voters don't like broad-based taxes, many don't much like religion either. In the 2012 exit poll, 30% said they never attend religious services, 18% said they belonged to no religion, and only 12% called themselves white born-again Christians.

Population		Race and Ethnicity		Income	
Total:	1,323,459	White	92.0%	Median income:	$71,322
Urban:	17.9%	Latino	2.9%		(1 of 50)
Suburban:	44.5%	Asian	2.2%	Under $50,000	38.7%
Rural:	37.6%	Black	1.1%	$50,000-$99,999:	33.5%
Land area:	8,953	Two races	1.6%	$100,000-$199,999:	22.5%
Pop/sq. mi.:	147.8	White Ethnic	65.1%	$200,000 or more:	5.3%
Born in state:	42.2%			Poverty Rate	5.6%
		Education			
Age Groups		H.S. grad or less:	36.5%	**Work**	
Under 18:	20.5%	Some college:	28.9%	White collar:	39.0%
18 to 34:	21.0%	College degree, 4 yr.:	21.9%	Blue collar:	40.2%
35 to 64:	43.2%	Post-grad study:	12.6%	Sales and service:	20.8%
Over 64:	15.3%				
		Military		Govt. workers:	13.3%
		Veterans/active duty:	9.9%		

New Hampshire went for George W. Bush in 2000 but for John Kerry in 2004 and Barack Obama in 2008 and 2012; the two George W. Bush elections were very close. Below the presidential level, the state has been one of the nation's swingiest. Republican Rep. John Sununu, whose father was governor in the 1980s, was elected to the Senate in 2002, but he lost to Shaheen in the Democratic year of 2008. Republican Craig Benson was elected governor in 2002, but in 2004 he lost to Democrat John Lynch, who took the no-taxes pledge and was widely popular. Lynch won four straight terms, including a narrow victory in 2010 when Republicans otherwise swept the state.

The GOP had a good year in 2010, as Attorney General Kelly Ayotte won a Senate seat and Republicans recaptured both House seats and won huge margins in the state legislature. But newly empowered Republican legislative leaders took a confrontational approach, alienating business leaders, and their attempts to repeal same-sex marriage failed. Two years later, New Hampshire went decisively Democratic. Barack Obama carried the state, 52%-46%, Democrats won back both House seats and a majority in the state House. In the governor's race, Democrat Maggie Hassan, who pledged to oppose a broad-based tax, beat conservative Republican Ovide Lamontagne by a 55%-43% margin. The state made history in 2012 when all five of its full-time politicians were women—Hassan, Shaheen, Ayotte, and Reps. Carol Shea-Porter and Ann Kuster. The 2014 election proved to be a split decision, with Republicans ousting Shea-Porter and winning back the state House, but failing to unseat Hassan, Shaheen or Kuster, even on a strongly Republican Election Night nationally—an indication that the state will continue to be an electoral battleground.

Presidential Politics Since 1920, New Hampshire has held the first-in-the-nation primary, and since 1952, when candidates' names were first put on the ballot, it has had extraordinary influence on the presidential selection process. There are arguments for having early contests in small states that provide a venue for retail politics, in which candidates meet voters in person, listen to them, share their vision for the country, and allow citizens to gauge their character. The arguments get weaker when you consider that Iowa holds its caucuses and New Hampshire its primary during the dead of winter and, in the last two cycles, within a week of the year-end holidays. These two states are not only visually white with snow, they are demographically white, with a distinct lack of minority presence.

2012 Presidential Vote
Barack Obama (D) 369,561 (52%)
Mitt Romney (R).................329,918 (46%)

2012 Presidential Primary
Mitt Romney (R)...................97,591 (39%)
Ron Paul (R) 56,872 (23%)
Jon Huntsman (R)................41,964 (17%)
Rick Santorum (R) 23,432 (9%)
Newt Gingrich (R) 23,421 (9%)

2008 Presidential Vote
Barack Obama (D) 384,826 (54%)
John McCain (R).................316,534 (45%)

New Hampshire is small enough physically that candidates can efficiently meet voters. Everything except the lightly populated North Country is within an hour's drive of Manchester, and for all the state's abstract dislike of government, New Hampshire does an excellent job of keeping its roads clear of snow. Like Iowa, New Hampshire's retail politics offers little-known candidates the ability to propel themselves into the national spotlight. In the 1970s, the national Democratic Party tried to confine primaries to a "window" period in which New Hampshire would have competition. But New Hampshire, with its don't-tread-on-me tradition, insisted it would hold its primary before the window if necessary, confident that candidates and reporters would pay it heed even if its tiny delegation was not seated at the national convention as punishment. In 1996, Iowa Gov. Terry Branstad and New Hampshire Gov. Steve Merrill, both Republicans, threatened voter retaliation against candidates who took part in caucuses or primaries held before those in their states.

In 2003, the Michigan Democratic Party, led by then-Sen. Carl Levin, attempted to challenge New Hampshire's first-in-the-nation status by moving the 2004 Michigan Democratic caucuses to the same January date as New Hampshire's primary. After a noisy debate, Michigan backed down. But Levin got the national party to promise to convene another commission in 2005 to study the nomination process. In the 2008 cycle, Michigan scheduled its primary on January 15 in an attempt to outflank New Hampshire, but in August 2007, the Democratic National Committee instructed Democratic candidates not to campaign there. In November, after the Michigan Supreme Court upheld the state's January primary date, New Hampshire Secretary of State William Gardner simply announced that his state's primary would be held on January 8. Gardner has been in his job since 1976 and has the unilateral authority to select a primary date, a power he has wielded effectively to thwart any state that might attempt to crowd New Hampshire on the primary starting line. Gardner's move led Iowa Democrats and Republicans to schedule their precinct caucuses on January 3. Democratic and Republican leaders in both states have developed a pact to work together to maintain their two states' unique political rituals at the beginning of the presidential nominating calendar.

New Hampshire has more registered Republicans than Democrats, but "undeclared" registrants are the largest bloc of voters in the state. They can vote in either party's presidential primary and on occasion they have provided the margin of victory for both Democratic and Republican winners. Once upon a time, the state's registered Democrats were mill workers in Manchester and other factory towns, ethnics who rejected the Yankee Republican consensus of the state. Those days are long gone. Democratic turnout is not concentrated in the two largest cities, Manchester and Nashua, which can vote Republican, but in the state capital of Concord and clusters of towns around universities—the area around Durham (University of New Hampshire) and Dover on the seacoast region, the area around Keene (Keene State College) in the southwest and the area around Hanover (Dartmouth College). The New Hampshire counties across the Connecticut River from Vermont are Democratic—a sort of East Vermont. In 2000, the upscale character of the electorate was already clear. With strong support from labor unions, Al Gore had won a wide victory in Iowa. But in New Hampshire, he was fortunate to squeeze out a 50%-46% victory against Bill Bradley, who ran to Gore's left on most issues.

In the 2004 election, former Vermont Gov. Howard Dean led in the New Hampshire polls in the run-up to the primary over Massachusetts Sen. John Kerry. Dean's appeal came from his harsh denunciations of President Bush and the war in Iraq. About half of Dean's support evaporated after his third-place showing in Iowa and his infamous caucus night cri de coeur, a.k.a., "the scream." Kerry argued, as he had in Iowa, that he was the Democrat best able to defeat Bush. New Hampshire gave him 38% of the vote, to 26% for Dean, 12.4% for Wesley Clark, who had skipped Iowa, 12% for John Edwards, and 9% for Joe Lieberman, who had also skipped Iowa.

In 2008, despite the Republican registration advantage, there was higher turnout on the Democratic side—a harbinger of the November results. Hillary Clinton, who had led in New Hampshire polls most of the year, trailed Obama after his win in the Iowa caucuses. But shortly before the primary, at a coffeehouse in Portsmouth, Clinton was asked how she was withstanding the rigors of campaigning, and in response she seemed to tear up as she talked about how the country needed to change. This was the one primary in 2008 in which the result differed from the late polls. Clinton stunned many Democrats inside the Beltway, who on the afternoon of the primary were anticipating her defeat and exit from the race, and she edged Obama 39%-36%; Edwards got 17%, Bill Richardson 5%. Turnout was 288,000 people, up 30% from 2004 and almost double that of 2000. Clinton carried Manchester, the southeast and the North Country. She won among women and downscale voters, much as Gore had in 2000. Obama carried Concord and towns in the west, and won among upscale and well-educated voters, much as Bradley had eight years earlier. Turnout on the Republican side was nearly 240,000, just above what it was in 2000. And the winner, as in 2000, was McCain. He edged Mitt Romney 37%-32%; 11% went for Mike Huckabee and 8% for Rudy Giuliani, who had abandoned serious efforts in the state. McCain carried western and northern New Hampshire and the seacoast. Romney carried the southeastern corner of the state, where he was well known from his four years as Massachusetts governor. The win injected life into the McCain candidacy, which had nearly collapsed just six months before.

In 2012, New Hampshire was the site of intensive campaigning. For Romney this was a must-win state: Voters knew him from his 2008 run, and he also owned a summer house in the Lake Country in Wolfeboro. Romney had far more volunteers, more road signs, and far more money than other candidates. But New Hampshire Republicans nevertheless flirted with Rick Perry, Herman Cain, and Newt Gingrich, who was endorsed by the *New Hampshire Union Leader*. Jon Huntsman stayed out of Iowa and staked his whole campaign on New Hampshire. Perhaps not surprisingly in a state with a penchant for minimalist government, Paul found many enthusiastic adherents in New Hampshire, very few of whom had been involved in standard Republican politics. Romney went into the primary as the declared winner in Iowa, although the results were later judged to be a draw with rival Rick Santorum. One of the lingering questions from the 2012 primary season is whether Santorum would have gotten more attention and fared better in New Hampshire had Romney not been declared the winner in Iowa the morning after the caucuses. Romney won the primary with 39% of the vote, running strongest in affluent towns near the Massachusetts border and in the Lake Country. Paul was second with 23%, running strongest in the North Country. Huntsman came in third with 17%, running strongest around Concord and the Connecticut River counties. Santorum and Gingrich each won 9%. Perry, after his terrible debate performance, skipped New Hampshire to campaign in South Carolina, and won just 1%.

Until the 1992 election, political reporters left New Hampshire the day after the primary and never returned in the fall, since it was assumed that the state would go Republican. But in five of the six elections between 1992 and 2012, New Hampshire has voted Democratic. It has often been close: Clinton in 1992, Bush in 2000, and Kerry in 2004 won the state by just 1%. But Clinton carried the state 49%-39% in 1996, and Obama carried it 54%-45% in 2008 and 52%-46% in 2012.

Congressional Districts New Hampshire's two congressional districts have had roughly the same boundaries since 1881, neatly separating the Merrimack River mill towns of Manchester and Nashua, the state's largest cities, along a mostly north-south line.

114th Congress Lineup	
1 R	1 D
113th Congress Lineup	
0 R	2 D

That was originally done to split the Catholic Democratic vote, and for years the arrangement helped Republicans hold both districts. But lately, New Hampshire's movement away from its Yankee Republican roots and its high share of independent voters have led to wild gyrations: both seats swung to Democrats in the wave of 2006, then to Republicans in 2010, and back to Democrats in 2012. At the presidential level, the flinty 2nd District along Vermont's border has crept more Democratic than the eastern 1st District, with its tax-averse Massachusetts exiles.

In 2011, 2nd District Republican Charlie Bass, cognizant of the Democratic trend in his district, pleaded with 1st District Republican Frank Guinta to trade him more Republican-leaning towns. Guinta refused, and Democratic Gov. John Lynch signed a bill moving six small towns around with negligible partisan implications. In 2012, both Bass and Guinta lost. But Guinta succeeded in his comeback two years later. His third consecutive contest with Democratic Rep. Carol Shea-Porter resulted in the district's third consecutive defeat of the incumbent. As the state's official motto commands, Live free or die!

Governor

Maggie Hassan (D)

Elected 2012, term expires 2017, 2nd term; b. Feb. 27, 1958, Boston, MA; Brown U., B.A. 1980, Northeastern Law Schl., J.D. 1985; Protestant; married (Tom); 2 children.

Elected Office: NH Senate, 2004-10.

Professional Career: Practicing atty., 1996-2009; Assoc. gen. counsel, Brigham & Women's Hosp., 1993-96; Practicing atty., 1985-92; Information officer, MA Dept. of Social Services, 1980-82.

Office: State House, 107 N. Main Street, Concord, 03301, 603-271-2121; Fax: 603-271-7640; Website: governor.nh.gov..

Election Results

2014 general	Maggie Hassan (D)	254,659	(53%)
	Walter Havenstein (R)	229,596	(47%)
2014 primary	Maggie Hassan (D)	39,185	(94%)

Democrat Maggie Hassan was elected governor in 2012 to succeed retiring Democrat John Lynch and was reelected two years later. Her election helped make New Hampshire the first state to have a female governor as well as an all-female congressional delegation.

Hassan grew up in the Boston area. Her mother was the head of the local chapter of the League of Women Voters, and her father, a World War II veteran, was involved in community matters. She attended Brown University and Northeastern University's law school, and then practiced law in Boston. Her husband, Tom Hassan, became principal of Phillips Exeter Academy, the elite college prep school. They have two children, one of whom, a son, has cerebral palsy. She credits him with inspiring her career in public service, which began in 1999 when then-Gov. (now Sen.) Jeanne Shaheen appointed her to be a citizen advisor on an education panel. "I had a moment when he was 3," she told NECN. "The school bus came to pick him up for the first day of pre-school, and it was a mainstream pre-school here in town ... and I found myself thinking, 'You know, he's going to school in his hometown and he's going to have a chance to make friends and a chance to learn.'"

Hassan ran for the New Hampshire Senate in 2002 but lost to incumbent Republican Russell Prescott. Two years later, she ran again and beat him, serving six years until he reclaimed his seat in 2010. During her three terms, she served as assistant Democratic whip, president pro tempore, and majority leader. As leader, she proposed a bill in 2010 to set up a government commission to regulate health care costs; Republicans dubbed the idea "Maggie Care" and it was unsuccessful. She also worked on decreasing mercury emissions from coal-fired electric power plants.

After Lynch announced in September 2011 that he would not seek a fifth term as governor, Hassan got into the race in October. She focused on boosting growth through investing in higher education while eliminating business tax breaks. She promised to restore $50 million in funding for the University System of New Hampshire that the Legislature had cut in exchange for a two-year tuition freeze. She also backed a proposed casino on the Massachusetts border as a way of raising state revenues. She easily defeated two Democratic primary rivals, former state Sen. Jackie Cilley and firefighter Bill Kennedy, with 54%.

Her Republican opponent in the general election was Ovide Lamontagne, a lawyer who had run unsuccessfully for governor in 1996 against Shaheen and who had lost to Kelly Ayotte in the 2010 Republican Senate primary. Hassan sought to portray Lamontagne as a rubber stamp for the GOP Legislature, saying that her "New Hampshire way" was preferable to his "tea party way." Lamontagne, meanwhile, branded her as a tax-and-spend liberal who lacked his "real world business experience." Polls in the campaign's final weeks showed a close race, but President Barack Obama's strong showing—he beat Republican Mitt Romney in the state even though the former Massachusetts governor has a vacation house there—helped her take 55% to Lamontagne's 43%, winning every county.

Taking office with a Democratic House and a Republican Senate, Hassan stressed the need for bipartisanship, with lawmakers from both parties agreeing with her that they needed to look past some of the bitter battles of recent years. In her first year, Hassan worked with Democrats and Republicans to restore some higher-education and mental-health funding, but she was unable to achieve one of her highest priorities, expanding gambling. In her second year in office, Hassan secured bipartisan support to expand Medicaid under the Affordable Care Act and signed the state's first gas-tax increase in more than two decades. She signed a bill to prevent employers from barring workers from talking about their compensation; the measure also extended the deadline for filing discrimination complaints from one to three years. She signed legislation to boost mental-health resources in the wake of a Department of Justice-backed class-action lawsuit, and she enacted a series of laws aimed at curbing domestic violence and human trafficking, preventing sexual abuse and limiting the parental rights of rapists. She vetoed a bill designed to protect public employees from on-the-job bullying, saying the language was too broad and subjective. Despite some belt-tightening amid concerns about interim revenue shortfalls, the state ended up with surpluses on her watch.

In the 2014 gubernatorial election, Hassan faced Republican Walt Havenstein, the former CEO of defense contractor BAE Systems, who had defeated Tea Party-backed small-businessman Andrew Hemingway in the primary. Havenstein proposed cutting the state's corporate tax from 8.5% to 7.4%, opposed Hassan's stand on gambling, backed a right-to-work law, and said that under Hassan the state's economic recovery had lagged that of its neighbors. He spent $2 million of his own money and received support on five separate visits by New Jersey Gov. Chris Christie, the chair of the Republican Governors Association. But many of Hassan's policy achievements had received bipartisan support, and she benefited from incumbency—it's rare for a one-term New Hampshire governor to be ousted. Havenstein managed to close the gap from 20 points in June to essentially a dead heat by Election Day, but Hassan prevailed, 53%-47%—one point better than Shaheen notched in her higher-profile Senate win that day.

As she began her second term, Hassan faced an all-Republican Legislature (the GOP had taken back the House) as well a GOP majority on the state's unusual Executive Council, which approves the governor's picks for agencies and judgeships as well as major state contracts. Hassan stood up to Republicans by vetoing a bill that would have curbed the Common Core education standards, and she threatened to veto a bill to restore unlicensed concealed-carry rules for guns. Meanwhile, a Senate committee rejected her proposal to spend $4 million to study a commuter rail line to Boston. She did sign the nation's first law banning sub-minimum wages for people with disabilities, as well as a bill to back $28 million in bonds to help redevelop the Balsams, a resort in Dixville Notch that had closed in 2011. (Dixville Notch is also known for its tradition of first-in-the-state midnight voting on election days.) By the spring of 2015, a WMUR poll showed Hassan with a 55% approval rating. A string of favorable poll results fueled speculation that Hassan would forgo another term as governor to challenge Ayotte for her Senate seat in 2016—a move that would give Democrats a boost in their bid to recapture the chamber and that would set up a competitive contest to succeed her as governor.

Senior Senator

Jeanne Shaheen (D)

Elected 2008, term expires 2021, 2nd term; b. Jan. 28, 1947, St. Charles, MO; Shippensburg Col., B.A. 1969, U. of MS, M.A. 1973; Protestant; married (William); 3 children.

Elected Office: NH Senate, 1990-96; NH gov., 1997-2003.

Professional Career: Teacher, 1969-71; A.A., U. of NH, 1973-74; Parents' Assoc. Program Coord., 1982-86; Mgr., seasonal retail business, 1973-76; Campaign mgr., Carter/Mondale NH pres. campaign, 1979-80; Hart, NH pres. campaign, 1983-84; McEachern, NH gov. campaign, 1986-88.

DC Office: 520 HSOB, 20510, 202-224-2841; Fax: 202-228-3194; Website: shaheen.senate.gov.

State Offices: Berlin, 603-752-6300; Claremont, 603-542-4872; Dover, 603-750-3004; Manchester, 603-647-7500; Nashua, 603-883-0196; Keene, 603-358-6604.

Committees: *Appropriations:* Commerce, Justice, Science & Related Agencies; Energy & Water Development; Homeland Security (RMM); Labor, Health & Human Services, Education & Related Agencies; State Foreign Operations & Related Programs; *Armed Services:* Emerging Threats & Capabilities; Readiness & Management Support; Seapower; *Foreign Relations:* Europe & Regional Security Cooperation (RMM); Multilateral Institutions & International Economic, Energy & Environmental Policy; Near East, South Asia, Central Asia, & Counterterrorism; *Small Business & Entrepreneurship* (RMM).

Group Ratings

	ADA	ACLU	AFL-CIO	LCV	ITI	COC	HAFA	ACU	CFG	FRC
2014	90%	100%	–	80%	100%	50%	5%	4%	0%	0%
2013	90%	C	94%	100%	C	50%	C	8%	3%	C

National Journal Ratings

	2013 LIB	—	2013 CONS
Economic	67%	—	31%
Social	63%	—	36%
Foreign	66%	—	29%
Composite	67%	—	33%

Key Votes of the 113th Congress

1. Sandy storm spending	Y	5. Student Loan Rates	Y	9. Bipartisan Budget Deal	Y
2. Chuck Hagel Confirmation	Y	6. Employee Non-Discrim'n Act	Y	10. Farm Bill Conference Rept.	Y
3. Gun Background Checks	Y	7. Senate Vote on Judgeships	N	11. Unempl. Comp. Extension	Y
4. Immigration Reform	Y	8. Defense Dept. Spending	Y	12. Keystone Pipeline	N

Election Results

2014 general	Jeanne Shaheen (D)	251,184	52%	$16,436,371	$1,402,045	$10,104,403
	Scott Brown (R)	235,347	48%	$9,163,652	$3,913,621	$13,027,425
2014 primary	Jeanne Shaheen (D)	unopposed				

Prior winning percentages: 2008 (52%); Governor: 2000 (49%), 1998 (66%), 1996 (57%)

Democrat Jeanne Shaheen, New Hampshire's senior senator, is the first woman in U.S. history to be elected both governor and senator, as well as the first woman in New Hampshire history who was elected to either of those offices. She has been a political fixture in the Granite State for four decades, first coming to notice not as a candidate but as a behind-the-scenes political operative—engineering victories for Jimmy Carter and Gary Hart in the state's first-in-the-nation presidential primary. In her current role, Shaheen has been a reliable Democratic vote: She was hammered during the 2014 campaign for voting with President Barack Obama 99 percent of the time. As a result, she came close to being upset by former Massachusetts Republican Sen. Scott Brown, who had moved across the border to take her on. But Shaheen, who spent much of the 2012 election season as a campaign surrogate for Obama, has been adept at balancing partisan loyalties with the political reality that she represents a state that has become a hypersensitive political bellwether. She once taught a university course on how elected officials can overcome partisanship, and she has sought to put those lessons into practice by reaching across the aisle to build coalitions.

In 2011, Shaheen teamed with Ohio Sen. Rob Portman, a Republican, on an energy effi-ciency bill, which sought to increase efficiency in buildings by offering mortgage incentives and getting the federal government more involved in working with manufacturers. Finally, after four years of effort by the bipartisan duo, a stripped-down version of the bill was passed and signed into law by Obama in the spring of 2015. Although a modest policy achievement, it was highlighted as a rare victory over the partisan gridlock that has plagued Capitol Hill. First, the bill failed in September 2013 after it became entangled in debates over two high-profile controversies: the Affordable Care Act and Keystone XL pipeline. It failed again in May 2014 after Republicans insisted on being able to offer amendments, including proposals to speed up natural gas exports and oppose Environmental Protection Agency regulations on future power plants. "On the bill's merits—creating jobs, saving consumers money and reducing pollution—it was never a hard sell," Shaheen told *The New York Times*. "The tough part was convincing Washington to not play politics with a good idea."

Shaheen grew up in the suburbs of St. Louis, where her father was in the shoe manu-facturing business and her mother was a secretary at their local church. She graduated from Shippensburg College in Pennsylvania with a degree in education; after teaching for a couple of years, she earned a master's degree in political science from the University of Mississippi. Shaheen was raised in a Republican family, and cast her first presidential vote for Richard Nixon in 1968. But she registered as a Democrat while still an undergraduate at Shippensburg, where her activities reflected the campus activism of the era: She success-fully challenged a campus curfew that applied to women but not to men. While in Missis-sippi, she came to admire Carter, then the governor of Georgia, for his efforts to foster racial integration.

She moved to New Hampshire in 1973, where she worked as a teacher and ran a sea-sonal silver and leather business with her husband, attorney William Shaheen, a New Hampshire native who himself has been a behind-the-scenes political power in the state. In December 2007, as Jeanne Shaheen was preparing to make a second bid for the Senate, William Shaheen—in his capacity as co-chairman of Hillary Clinton's national and New Hampshire presidential campaigns—told reporters that Republicans would attack one of Clinton's rivals, Obama, for admitting in his autobiography that he "got into drinking" and experimented with drugs. The next day, Clinton apologized, and William Shaheen resigned his position in the Clinton campaign.

Three decades earlier, William and Jeanne Shaheen were among Carter's earliest New Hampshire supporters when, in 1975, the former Georgia governor began laying the ground-work for his longshot bid for the presidency. Carter won the 1976 New Hampshire primary, and, with Carter in the White House, William Shaheen was appointed U.S. attorney for New Hampshire. In 1980, Jeanne Shaheen was named Carter's state director in New Hampshire, and guided the incumbent to a 10-point win in the presidential primary over the insurgent candidacy of Massachusetts Sen. Edward Kennedy. Four years later, another longshot presi-dential hopeful, Colorado Sen. Gary Hart, recruited Shaheen to manage his New Hampshire primary campaign. Hart defeated the Democratic frontrunner, Walter Mondale, by 9 points.

At the time, Democrats had limited success in winning statewide office in then-solidly Republican New Hampshire. Shaheen oversaw two unsuccessful efforts to elect Democrat Paul McEachern as governor. The first time, McEachern failed to oust incumbent John Sununu, later White House chief of staff for President George H.W. Bush; the second time, McEachern lost an open seat race to then-Republican Rep. Judd Gregg, who later went on to serve three Senate terms. Shaheen then became a candidate herself, and was elected in 1990 to the state Senate, where she supported expanded health care coverage and term limits on federal and state legislators. In 1996, she ran for governor. She had no serious pri-mary opposition, while the Republicans had a close race between Rep. Bill Zeliff and Board of Education Chairman Ovide Lamontagne, a strong conservative who won the nomination. Shaheen took what is referred to in New Hampshire as "The Pledge," to oppose an income or sales tax. Such a vow had long been politically sacrosanct in a jurisdiction that has prided itself as the only state in the nation not to impose a broad-based tax. Shaheen won, 57%-39%, carrying every county and becoming only the third Democrat in 70 years to serve as the Granite State's governor.

As governor, Shaheen won more funding from the legislature for kindergarten programs and signed a bill creating a needle exchange pilot program. She vetoed bills that would have abolished the estate tax and the death penalty. A 1997 state Supreme Court ruling that outlawed New Hampshire's system of local school financing provided a continual challenge.

Shaheen proposed increasing state revenues through slot machine gambling and a hike in the tobacco tax, but the court invalidated her plan in 1998. That year, when her two-year term was up, Shaheen was reelected by 66%-31%. But she then abandoned her pledge to oppose an income or sales tax and was reelected in 2000 by only 49%-44%. During that term, the controversy over school funding continued, and the GOP-controlled legislature refused to pass either an income or sales tax.

Shaheen ran for the Senate in 2002, as Republicans faced a seriously contested primary in which Rep. John Sununu, son of the former governor and White House chief of staff, defeated the incumbent, Robert Smith 53%-45%. (Smith had angered Republican leaders when, after an unsuccessful bid for the 2000 GOP presidential nomination, he temporarily left the party.) During the general election campaign, Shaheen supported President George W. Bush's tax cuts and the authorization of military force in Iraq passed by Congress in October 2002. But her abandonment of the tax pledge came back to haunt her, and Sununu won 51%-46%. In the 2004 election season, Shaheen served as the national chairman of Democrat John Kerry's presidential campaign and helped orchestrate his victory in the New Hampshire primary. After Kerry's loss in the general election, Shaheen became director of the Kennedy School of Government's Institute of Politics at Harvard, where she earlier taught education policy. (Earlier, at Tufts University, she taught a course in 2003 called "Governing in a Partisan Environment.")

Shaheen insisted she had no interest in running for office again. But after the 2006 election, which returned both houses of Congress to Democratic control, New Hampshire Democrats pressed her to seek a rematch with Sununu in 2008. A July 2007 poll showed Shaheen far ahead of Sununu in a theoretical matchup. In September, Shaheen quit her job at Harvard and announced that she was running again for Senate. Other Democrats already in the race, including Katrina Swett, wife of former Rep. Dick Swett and daughter of the late California Rep. Tom Lantos, dropped out to clear the field for her.

While the 2008 Senate campaign had the same candidates as six years earlier, it took place in a very different political atmosphere. In 2002, Shaheen had emphasized areas where she agreed with Bush and congressional Republicans; in 2008, she emphasized her disagreements with them. She attacked Sununu for votes against changing the tax treatment of oil companies and was supported by environmental groups. Shaheen led in polls throughout the campaign, but Sununu rebounded after gas prices reached $4 a gallon, and he criticized Shaheen's opposition to offshore oil drilling. He also attacked her for doubling state spending in her six years as governor. But he may have lost ground in October 2008, when he voted for a $700 billion government bailout for the financial industry, which Shaheen, like many challenger candidates in both parties, opposed. The outcome was a reversal of 2002. Shaheen won 52%-45%. It was the first Democratic Senate victory in New Hampshire since 1974.

In the Senate, Shaheen's loyalty to her party was rewarded with a seat on the Appropriations Committee in 2013. Though she is a disciplined politician who tends to stay on message and refrain from headline-grabbing sound bites, she did attract attention in January 2013 when she called the lack of women in Obama's second-term Cabinet up to that point "disappointing." Nine months later, as the Obama administration began experiencing problems with rolling out the Affordable Care Act, she became the first Senate Democrat to call for extending the open-enrollment period to obtain health insurance. During debate on the health insurance overhaul early in her first term, Shaheen got several provisions into the final bill, including one closing a loophole allowing drug companies to avoid competition with generic drugs. On another health issue, Shaheen's interest has been personal: Her granddaughter, Elle Shaheen, has Type 1 diabetes and participated in a medical trial for an artificial pancreas. The senator has been involved in numerous efforts to highlight the problems associated with juvenile diabetes, and has actively tried to persuade the Food and Drug Administration to issue "clear and reasonable guidance" on artificial pancreas devices.

Shaheen has sought ways to avoid the frustrations many former governors experience once in the Senate, and witness a slow pace and limited volume of accomplishment. Borrowing an idea from her days as a chief executive, she introduced a bill with Georgia Republican Johnny Isakson in 2011 to move to a two-year budget cycle. Along with the energy efficiency bill co-authored with Portman, it was another in a series of bipartisan efforts in which she has participated. Shaheen also worked with a bipartisan group that sought to enact many of the recommendations made by Obama's deficit commission in 2010, and, in 2013, was part of the group of 14 senators (seven Republicans, six Democrats and an independent) brought together by Maine Republican moderate Susan Collins to find a way out of the budget stalemate that had led to a government shutdown. In early 2015, she and Florida Sen. Marco Rubio, a Republican presidential hopeful, won Senate passage of their "Girls Count Act", which would set aside funds from foreign aid programs to create birth registries in underdeveloped countries. Shaheen and Rubio noted 51 million children around the world are not registered at birth, most of them girls, and that this often bars them from receiving vital services, while leaving them vulnerable to exploitation.

Despite representing a state where Republicans still hold a registration edge, Shaheen has not shied away from the culture wars. She has been a strong supporter of Planned Parenthood, often under fire from House Republicans who accuse the group of using federal dollars to fund abortions. In March 2011, more than four years before the U.S. Supreme Court paved the way for same-sex marriage across the country, Shaheen signed on to cosponsor a bill to repeal the Defense of Marriage Act and allow the federal government to provide benefits to same-sex married couples. She later introduced a bill that would ensure same-sex married couples receive military benefits such as spousal support upon death. As a member of the Senate Armed Services Committee, she got provisions into the fiscal year 2013 defense authorization bill to repeal a policy denying military women abortion coverage in cases of rape or incest.

Shaheen picked up the Armed Services seat in 2011, where—in tandem with her Republican New Hampshire colleague, Kelly Ayotte, also an Armed Service member—she keeps an eye on the Portsmouth Naval Shipyard, an important employer in eastern New Hampshire. On another local matter, Shaheen used her Appropriations perch to get funding for a new federal prison in upstate Berlin. Congress had tried to cut $276 million for the facility, but Shaheen argued it would supply 332 jobs and put $40 million annually into the economy of northern New Hampshire.

Shaheen was regarded as a favorite to win reelection in 2014. A WMUR Granite State Poll conducted for the University of New Hampshire in February 2013 found she was the state's most popular statewide elected official, with a 59-percent approval rating. But the dynamics of the race changed when Brown announced an exploratory committee in March 2014 and announced his candidacy a month later. In early 2010, Brown had capitalized on public unease over passage of the Affordable Care Act to win a special election to fill the Massachusetts Senate seat left vacant by Kennedy's death. His upset win in that solid-blue state foreshadowed the GOP's domination of the subsequent nationwide midterm elections. Despite receiving substantial tea party support in 2010, Brown compiled a moderate voting record. In 2012, he was soundly defeated 54%-46% by Democrat Elizabeth Warren, as the Bay State's Democratic voters came out in force to reelect Obama.

After his loss to Warren, Brown worked as a commentator for Fox News. He and his wife sold their residence in Massachusetts and moved to New Hampshire, where they long had owned a vacation home. His campaign got off to a rocky start, but picked up steam after he won the endorsement of part-time New Hampshire resident Mitt Romney and was joined on the campaign trail by Arizona Sen. John McCain, who twice won the New Hampshire presidential primary. Brown gained traction by relentlessly seeking to tie Shaheen, a co-chair of the 2012 Obama campaign, to the president, including continual use of the statistic that she had voted with Obama's position 99 percent of the time. (That figure came from a *CQ/Roll Call* analysis of Shaheen's voting record in 2013.) Obama, despite having won the state in both 2008 and 2012, had seen his popularity nosedive: Polls were showing fewer than 40 percent of New Hampshire voters approved of the job he was doing.

A University of New Hampshire/WMUR poll in August 2014 shocked political observers when it showed Shaheen with a 46%-44% lead, within the poll's margin of error. A month earlier, the same poll had Shaheen leading by 12 points. Shaheen's campaign professed itself to be unfazed, saying it had been prepared for a tough race. "…Sometimes there are factors beyond your control, and there are things happening in the country that affect a race," Shaheen observed during one debate. "I think we're seeing this now in this race." The two candidates together raised and spent more than $25 million: $16.4 million by Shaheen and more than $9 million by Brown, and outside groups tossed in nearly $30 million on efforts to influence the contest—for a $55 million total. Although polls showed Brown within a hair of the incumbent heading into Election Day, she managed to win with 52 percent—narrowly blocking Brown's bid to become the first person in 135 years to represent two different states in the Senate.

Junior Senator

Kelly Ayotte (R)

Elected 2010, term expires Jan. 2017, 1st term; b. June 27, 1968, Nashua; PA St. U., B.A. 1990, Villanova U., J.D. 1993; Catholic; married (Joe Daley); 2 children.

Professional Career: Law clerk, 1993-94; Practicing atty., 1994-98; Prosecutor, NH Atty. Gen. Office, 1998-2003; Legal counsel, Gov. Craig Benson, 2003; NH deputy atty. gen., 2003-04; NH atty. gen., 2004-09.

DC Office: 144 RSOB, 20510, 202-224-3324; Fax: 202-224-4952; Website: ayotte.senate.gov.

State Offices: Manchester, 603-622-7979; Nashua, 603-880-3335; Portsmouth, 603-436-7161; North Conway, 603-752-7702.

Committees: *Armed Services:* Emerging Threats & Capabilities; Readiness & Management Support (Chmn); Seapower; *Budget, Commerce, Science & Transportation:* Aviation Operations, Safety & Security (Chmn); Communications, Technology & the Internet; Oceans, Atmosphere, Fisheries & Coast Guard; Surface Transportation & Merchant Marine Infrastructure, Safety & Security. *Homeland Security & Governmental Affairs:* Investigations; Federal Spending Oversight & Emergency Management; *Small Business & Entrepreneurship.*

Group Ratings

	ADA	ACLU	AFL-CIO	LCV	ITI	COC	HAFA	ACU	CFG	FRC
2014	15%	20%	–	0%	66%	100%	48%	63%	60%	79%
2013	20%	C	17%	31%	C	100%	C	68%	79%	C

National Journal Ratings

	2013 LIB	—	2013 CONS
Economic	29%	—	69%
Social	38%	—	61%
Foreign	31%	—	68%
Composite	33%	—	67%

Key Votes of the 113th Congress

1. Sandy storm spending	N	5. Student Loan Rates	Y	9. Bipartisan Budget Deal	N
2. Chuck Hagel Confirmation	N	6. Employee Non-Discrim'n Act	Y	10. Farm Bill Conference Rept.	N
3. Gun Background Checks	N	7. Senate Vote on Judgeships	Y	11. Unempl. Comp. Extension	Y
4. Immigration Reform	Y	8. Defense Dept. Spending	N	12. Keystone Pipeline	Y

Election Results

2010 general	Kelly Ayotte (R)	273,218	(60%)	$5,041,009	$1,049,207	$20,715
	Paul Hodes (D)	167,545	(37%)	$4,912,819	$447,947	$953,982
	Chris Booth (I)	9,194	(2%)			
2010 primary	Kelly Ayotte (R)	53,056	(38%)			
	Ovide Lamontagne (R)	51,397	(37%)			
	Bill Binnie (R)	19,508	(14%)			
	Jim Bender (R)	12,611	(9%)			

Republican Kelly Ayotte, New Hampshire's junior senator, is the GOP's top elected official in the state with the nation's first presidential primary, giving her political prominence and clout beyond her years of public service. But, even as her potential endorsement is a prized commodity for her party's large field of 2016 White House contenders, Ayotte must also prepare for the challenge of the general election that will follow—when she faces reelection in a state that has been swamped by several national political waves in recent years. Once reliably Republican, New Hampshire has turned a distinct shade of purple over the past couple of decades. For the most part, Ayotte has been a reliably conservative vote since her first election in 2010, while demonstrating a pragmatism that has pulled her toward the center on several issues. In a state that has ended up in the Democratic column in five of the last six presidential elections, Ayotte is likely to find herself increasingly buffeted by the political currents as she seeks a second term in a presidential year.

Ayotte grew up in Nashua, and studied political science at Pennsylvania State University. She was active in her sorority, Delta Gamma, and skied competitively. She earned a law degree from Villanova University, where she was the editor of the *Environmental Law Journal. She clerked for a* state Supreme Court justice, and then spent several years in private law practice. In an early legal case, Ayotte was the court-appointed counsel for the defendants in a highly publicized murder of two guards in an armored car robbery in 1994. The experience gave her a taste of trial work, and in 1998 she sought a job as a prosecutor with the New Hampshire attorney general's office, eventually rising to become head of the homicide division. In a case that attracted national attention and that Ayotte has cited as her most challenging, she secured the convictions of two Vermont teenagers in the 2001 murders of Dartmouth College professors Half and Susanne Zantop.

In 2002, newly elected Republican Gov. Craig Benson interviewed her about being his legal counsel; Ayotte instead told him that she wanted to be his attorney general. "I liked her aggressiveness," Benson later told *The Boston Globe.* Ayotte spent a year as Benson's counsel, but then became deputy attorney general before Benson, in 2004, named her as New Hampshire's first female attorney general. In one of her most celebrated cases, she defended the state against numerous court challenges to a law requiring parental notification for minors seeking abortions. In 2005, newly elected Democratic Gov. John Lynch asked her to drop the case and file a brief opposing the law. Ayotte instead opted to defend the law all the way to the U.S. Supreme Court. The high court ruled unanimously that states may require parental notification as long as an exception is allowed for medical emergencies. New Hampshire, however, repealed the law in 2007.

Despite Ayotte's differences with Lynch over abortion rights, he nominated her for a second term as attorney general in 2009. Four months later, she resigned to make her first bid for elected office in the Senate race to succeed Republican Judd Gregg, a one-time governor who had announced his retirement following three terms as senator. In a crowded primary field, Ayotte campaigned as a fiscal and social conservative (she indicated she was opposed to abortion except in cases of rape, incest or medical emergency). But tea party activists and South Carolina Sen. Jim DeMint, a hard-line conservative who injected himself into several GOP primaries that year, supported 1996 gubernatorial nominee Ovide Lamontagne. Ayotte also had primary competition from a couple of wealthy businessmen, Bill Binnie and Jim Bender. However, she got a boost from a tea party favorite, former Alaska Gov. Sarah Palin, the former Republican governor of Alaska, who called Ayotte "one tough Granite Grizzly." Lamontagne enjoyed a late surge in the race, but Ayotte edged him out, 38%-37%, a margin of 1,660 votes out of 139,000 cast.

In the general election, Rep. Paul Hodes, first elected in 2006 to represent the state's 2nd District, had the field for the Democratic Senate nomination pretty largely to himself, allowing him to spend his resources getting acquainted with potential general election voters. In his first television ad, he accused Ayotte of failing to investigate a mortgage Ponzi scheme that cost New Hampshire investors $80 million. Ayotte countered with ads that portrayed her as a tough prosecutor, while hammering Hodes for his support of President Barack Obama's health care overhaul and vowing to vote to repeal it. In the end, it wasn't even close: Ayotte won, 60%-37%, carrying all 10 counties in the state. Gregg, who endorsed Ayotte, told *The Telegraph,* "Ninety percent of the fight is people liking you and agreeing with your philosophy, and she nailed that from the beginning." But Ayotte also benefitted from the latest national political wave, this one a Republican crest. Along with her victory, New Hampshire's two congressional seats and the state legislature, all of which had shifted from the Republicans to the Democrats four years earlier, swung back to the GOP.

Only 42 when she was sworn into the Senate in January 2011, Ayotte was named counsel to Minority Leader Mitch McConnell in 2013. It gave her a post once held by Gregg, and guaranteed her a seat at the leadership table. But she also appeared to become more independent of her GOP colleagues as her first term progressed. According to analyses by *CQ/ Roll Call*, Ayotte, after voting with the Republicans on partisan votes 97 percent of the time in 2011, had scores that dropped to 86, 82 and then 74 percent in the three years that followed. In *National Journal*'s annual vote ratings, Ayotte stood as the 35th most conservative senator, putting her 10 slots to the right of her Maine neighbor, Republican Susan Collins, the least conservative Senate Republican. But, in October 2013, Ayotte—a self-described budget hawk who supports a constitutional balanced budget amendment—joined a bipartisan group of senators organized by Collins seeking a compromise to a budget stalemate that caused a government shutdown. The group (seven Republicans, six Democrats and an independent) was credited with coming up with a plan that helped to bring an end to the 16-day standoff.

In early 2015, when a fight over Obama's controversial executive order on immigration became entangled with continued funding for the Department of Homeland Security, Ayotte—while terming Obama's immigration edict "illegal"—lined up behind a plan by McConnell, now the chamber's majority leader, to separate DHS funding from the immigration issue. McConnell's move came after Senate Democrats had repeatedly blocked GOP efforts to use the DHS bill as a vehicle to nullify the Obama edict. According to *Politico*, Ayotte faced down hard-line conservatives during a private luncheon, arguing McConnell's plan was the only option to not hamper law enforcement agencies relying on money from DHS. Her move came as she was taking heat from Democrats back home over the possibility of a cutoff of homeland security funds. Nearly four years earlier, in the summer of 2011, Ayotte took a less pragmatic approach during the standoff over raising the nation's debt limit. At that time, she held out for deeper cuts in government spending, and, when Obama and the Republican leadership finally reached a compromise in August 2011, she was one of 19 Senate Republicans who voted against it. An editorial in the conservative *New Hampshire Union Leader* criticized her for "holding out for a perfect option that didn't exist."

Other high profile votes during Ayotte's first term have attracted heat from both sides of the political spectrum in her home state. In April 2015, she was among just 10 Republicans to vote to confirm Obama's nomination of Loretta Lynch as attorney general. The large majority of Republicans voted against the Lynch nomination to protest Obama's executive order on immigration policy, and Ayotte's vote for Lynch was met with conservative backlash in New Hampshire. Two years earlier, in April 2013, she was subjected to complaints from the left when she voted against a compromise measure to expand background checks for gun owners in the wake of the Newtown, Conn., school shootings several months earlier in which two dozen were killed. It left the bill several votes short of the 60-vote supermajority needed to proceed under Senate rules. Ayotte, who earlier had voted to allow the legislation to come to the floor for debate, said she could not support it because it "would place unnecessary burdens on law-abiding gun owners and allow for potential overreach by the federal government into private gun sales."

Ayotte has been open to supporting some increased environmental regulation. She joined four other GOP senators in June 2012 in siding with Democrats to defeat a proposal that would have blocked the Environmental Protection Agency from promulgating the first federal standards to reduce toxic air pollution from power plants. While she joined all other Senate Republicans in early 2015 in an unsuccessful effort to override Obama's veto of the Keystone XL Pipeline, an analysis by the League of Conservation Voters found she had split with a majority of fellow Republicans a total of 10 times during the Keystone debate to support amendments the LCV said would bolster environmental safeguards, particularly with regard to climate change. The only Republican senator to vote more often with the Democrats was Collins, endorsed by the LCV when she sought reelection in 2014.

However, Ayotte's highest profile visibility has been on national security matters, as a member of the Armed Services Committee. In a sign of her growing influence, Ayotte was included in a December 2012 meeting between United Nations Ambassador Susan Rice and GOP Sens. John McCain of Arizona and Lindsey Graham of South Carolina, both of whom had joined Ayotte in expressing concerns about the possibility of Rice becoming secretary of state because of her handling of the response to the terrorist attack in Benghazi, Libya. The three senators' concerns led Obama to instead nominate Massachusetts Sen. John Kerry for the post. She also joined McCain and Graham in 2013 in questioning former Nebraska GOP Sen. Chuck Hagel's fitness to become defense secretary, and she joined most of her Republican colleagues in opposing Hagel's nomination. (Hagel and McCain, once close friends, had a falling out over Iraq policy in 2007, and Hagel did not endorse McCain's 2008 presidential candidacy.)

Ayotte has a parochial as well as global interest in defense policy: The Portsmouth Naval Shipyard, located along the Maine-New Hampshire border, employs about 3,900 civilians—many of them Ayotte's constituents—in the repair and overhaul of Navy's nuclear-powered submarine fleet. With McCain, Ayotte cosponsored a bill in October 2011 aimed at controlling costs in major defense acquisition programs, and she later added a provision to the fiscal 2013 defense bill calling for a full audit of the Pentagon by September 2014. Drawing on her experience as a former prosecutor, she fought efforts by the Obama administration to try terrorism suspects in civilian courts. She and Independent Sen. Joe Lieberman of Connecticut argued in a *Washington Post* op-ed in July 2011 that suspected terrorists should be kept at

U.S. detention facilities in Guantanamo Bay, Cuba. "When an enemy combatant is captured, the primary focus should be intelligence-gathering, not criminal prosecution," they wrote.

Given New Hampshire's first-in-the-nation primary status, Ayotte was courted by GOP presidential candidates in 2012, and ultimately endorsed Mitt Romney, the Republican front-runner and former governor of neighboring Massachusetts. Romney cited her as one of 15 Republicans who could end up as his or someone else's running mate. "That was a surprise," she told the *Union Leader*. Though she didn't get the nod—her regional proximity to Romney probably worked against her—she was an energetic surrogate as his campaign sought to reach out to suburban women voters. She is likely to figure into the vice-presidential speculation again in 2016, when the Republicans may find it desirable to put a woman on their ticket to balance the prospect of Hillary Clinton as the Democratic nominee.

Ayotte focused on what is likely to be one of the country's most competitive races of 2016. Much of the speculation about a possible Democratic opponent to Ayotte centered on current two-term Gov. Maggie Hassan, who was expected to make a decision by late summer 2015 on whether to run for Senate. In early 2015, outside Republican groups spent $1 million on anti-Hassan ads, hoping to either dissuade her from taking on Ayotte or to soften her approval ratings if she opted to run. Early polling showed an Ayotte-Hassan race to be close. "If you had a race between Maggie Hassan and Kelly Ayotte, you literally have a race between the two most popular political figures in the state," said former state Attorney General Tom Rath, a major player in state Republican politics. Ayotte appeared to have dodged a possible primary challenge: Lamontagne, who ran against Hassan in 2012 after nearly beating Ayotte in the 2010 primary, was reported by the *Globe* to have told associates he was not interested in a 2016 Senate race.

Since 2001, Ayotte has been married to Joseph Daley, a fellow Nashua native who flew combat missions during the Iraq war. Daley retired from the Air National Guard as a lieutenant colonel. In 2003, Ayotte helped him launch Daley's Outdoor Services, a landscape design and installation company that does snow removal during the state's often harsh winters. "I'm proud of the fact that in addition to being a United States senator, I'm also pretty good with a snow plow," Ayotte joked in 2012.

FIRST DISTRICT

Frank Guinta (R)

Elected 2014, 2nd term; b. Sept. 26, 1970, Edison, NJ; Assumption College, B.A, 1993.; Franklin Pierce Law, M.A 2000.; Catholic; married (Morgan), 2 children.

Elected Office: Elected Office: NH House, 2000-02; Manchester alderman, 2002-06; Staff, U.S. Rep. Jeb Bradley, 2003-04; Mayor of Manchester, 2006-10; U.S. Rep. NH-1, 2011-13.

Professional Career: Insurance Consultant.

DC Office: 326 CHOB, 20515; 202-225-5456; Fax: 202-225-5822; Website: guinta.house.gov.

State Office: Manchester, 603-641-9536.

Committees: *Financial Services:* Financial Institutions & Consumer Credit; Monetary Policy & Trade.

Election Results

2014 general	Frank Guinta (R)	125,508	(52%)	$1,221,539	$1,067,261	$3,089,610
	Carol Shea-Porter (D)	116,769	(48%)	$1,713,765	$393,672	$4,520,579
2014 primary	Frank Guinta (R)	29,246	(49%)			
	Dan Innis (R)	24,342	(41%)			
	Brendan Kelly (R)	4,999	(8%)			

Prior winning percentage: 2010 (54%)

Population		Race and Ethnicity		Income	
Total:	662,473	White	92.1%	Median income:	$64,681
Urban:	21.2%	Latino	3.1%		*(81 of 435)*
Suburban:	61.2%	Asian	2.0%	Under $50,000	37.9%
Rural:	17.6%	Black	1.2%	$50,000-$99,999:	34.1%
Land area:	2,595	Two races	1.4%	$100,000-$199,999:	22.8%
Pop/sq. mi.:	255.3	White Ethnic	67.7%	$200,000 or more:	5.2%
Born in state:	42.4%			Poverty Rate	7.9%
		Education			
Age Groups		H.S. grad or less:	34.8%	**Work**	
Under 18:	20.5%	Some college:	29.9%	White collar:	38.9%
18 to 34:	21.3%	College degree, 4 yr.:	22.8%	Blue collar:	41.4%
35 to 64:	43.3%	Post-grad study:	12.5%	Sales and service:	19.7%
Over 64:	15.0%			Govt. workers:	13.3%
		Military			
		Veterans/active duty:	10.1%		

Eastern New Hampshire: Manchester

The greatest growth in New Hampshire over the past two decades has been in the southeast and south-central parts of the state—the Seacoast and the Manchester area. Manchester was once famous for the Amoskeag Mills, the world's largest textile mill complex. In the first half of the 20th century, it

Voter Turnout	
2013 Total Citizen 18+	509,820
2014 House Turnout	242,736
2014 Turnout as % CVAP	47.6%
2012 Turnout as % CVAP	70.3%

was the quintessential mill town, with a few mansions for mill owners and managers and closely packed neighborhoods of frame houses for mill workers, many of them immigrants—from Quebec, Ireland and Greece. By the beginning of the 21st century, it was something quite different: a high-tech city, with big shopping malls at freeway interchanges, a spiffy new airport and downtown arena, spruced-up neighborhoods, and growth extending to the wooded suburbs all around. A quarter of New Hampshire residents claim French or French-Canadian ties, and racial minorities are sparse here. Manchester had participated in a State Department program to resettle refugees—more than 60 languages are spoken in the school system—but the city's Republican mayor halted the program, out of concern for the strain on public services.

The Seacoast, within easy commuting distance of Massachusetts, is a collection of towns of ancient pedigree and high-tech growth along the 18-mile coastline. The biggest city on the coast is Portsmouth, the colonial capital of New Hampshire, with its busy naval shipyard and old seaport with well-preserved houses and a solid local economy that includes many art galleries and bars. Pease Air Force Base, shuttered in 1991, has been successfully redeveloped as the Pease International Tradeport, with office buildings and an airplane runway, resulting in the addition of more than 160 businesses and nearly 10,000 jobs in the Seacoast. In Stratham, Swiss chocolate maker Lindt has a major facility, and Exeter is home to Phillips Exeter Academy, the elite boarding school.

The 1st Congressional District of New Hampshire includes the Manchester area and the Seacoast from Manchester and next-door Bedford, its most affluent suburb, east to Portsmouth. It also extends north to include Laconia and gentrifying Lake Winnipesaukee, studded with summer resorts and new mansions, including former Massachusetts Gov. Mitt Romney's $10 million vacation home in Wolfeboro. Robert Copeland, that town's 82-year-old police commissioner, resigned in May 2014 after he acknowledged using a racial slur in referring to President Barack Obama. Romney had called for his resignation and an apology; Copeland was silent on the latter. In May 2015, Portsmouth opened an African Burying Ground Memorial to commemorate slaves who arrived in New Hampshire in the 18th century. Politically, this is the slightly more Republican of New Hampshire's two congressional districts. It has been the destination of many people fleeing high taxes

2012 Presidential Vote
Barack Obama (D) 179,148   (50%)
Mitt Romney (R)................173,419   (48%)

2008 Presidential Vote
Barack Obama (D) 186,561   (53%)
John McCain (R)................163,941   (46%)

Cook Partisan Voting Index: R+1

in Massachusetts. Manchester, the largest city in the state, is a politically competitive bellwether.

Portsmouth, with its trendy coffee shops, is Democratic, as are Durham, home of the University of New Hampshire, and nearby Dover, once a mill town and now the fastest-growing city in the state. Most of the smaller towns in the Seacoast and to the north have been solidly Republican, though that is changing. Even though Romney has a residence here, he lost the swing district to Obama, 50%-48%, in 2012.

Frank Guinta (R)

In an ongoing seesaw battle, Republican Frank Guinta in 2014 reclaimed the seat he held before Rep. Carol Shea-Porter ousted him in 2012. They first met in 2010 when Guinta prevailed with 54 percent of the vote. As of mid-2015, another confrontation in 2016 appeared likely, assuming Guinta seeks and receives the GOP nomination for another term. With four switches in the past five elections, and another one looming, this district might earn an award for being a ping pong ball.

Guinta grew up in Montgomery New Jersey, one of three children in a house that served as a base for his parents' court-stenographer business. From them, he became a believer in limited government interference in the private sector. He went to Assumption College in Worcester, Massachusetts where he met his wife, Morgan. After graduation, the two moved to Boston, where Guinta became an insurance-claims adjuster and a consultant. He got a master's degree in intellectual property from Franklin Pierce Law Center in Concord, settled in New Hampshire and became active in local politics. He served in the state House, and as a Manchester alderman. As mayor, he cut taxes and spending, and lowered the crime rate. He won praise from the state's conservatives, not least for his ability to work with the heavily Democratic Board of Aldermen. Along the way, he developed a reputation as a pragmatic, bipartisan official.

In his first race against Shea-Porter, Guinta had to overcome a contentious GOP primary battle that sullied his reputation when he failed to disclose a bank account worth at least $250,000. He blamed a paperwork error for the lack of disclosure. He ran in the general election on a pledge to reduce the size of government, a popular theme for Republicans in 2010. Guinta called for government-hiring freezes and cast Shea-Porter as a big spender. He won the endorsements of several GOP presidential candidates stumping for votes in his state, including Mitt Romney and former House Speaker Newt Gingrich of Georgia. He won by an impressive 54%-42%.

In Congress, Guinta practiced fiscal conservatism, supporting the Republican Study Committee's failed budget plan in 2012 that contained steep spending reductions. In their 2012 rematch, the candidates debated entitlements and the effectiveness of the 2009 stimulus bill, which Shea-Porter supported. That was a stronger year for Democrats, and Shea-Porter took back the seat 50%-46%. Shea-Porter's total matched the vote share President Barack Obama received against Romney in the district.

Shea-Porter, who arrived in Congress amid widespread voter discontent with the Iraq War, moderated some of her liberal positions. In November 2013, she voted for GOP Rep. Fred Upton's bill to allow health insurance policyholders to keep their current plan even if it did not meet the Affordable Care Act's regulations.

In 2014, Guinta survived a tough primary challenge from University of New Hampshire administrator Dan Innis. Shea-Porter then attacked him for "being funded by the billionaire Koch brothers." But she could not turn around voters' discontent with Obama that ultimately contaminated her campaign and that of many other Democrats nationwide, though statewide Democrats in New Hampshire managed to survive the onslaught. Asked during a campaign debate about their proudest accomplishments in Washington, Shea-Porter cited the Affordable Care Act, while Guinta referred to a bill that he sponsored that restored a cemetery in the Philippines where thousands of Americans are buried.

This time, Guinta's victory margin was 51.7%-48.1%. Interestingly, Guinta as challenger was out-spent in his two successful runs. Shea-Porter spent about $1.7 million in each of her campaigns. Both candidates, especially Guinta, received extensive national party and interest-group assistance in each contest. In 2014, Guinta benefited from about $5.6 million, mostly from GOP groups.

In his second term, Guinta went through another round of freshman orientation and he upgraded his committee assignment to Financial Services, where he pledged to improve access to capital for families and businesses. As his service resumed, he emphasized the need for bipartisanship and for cooperation among the relatively few lawmakers in New Hampshire and New England to maximize their influence. With Democratic Rep. Ann McLane Kuster of New Hampshire, he announced in May their plans to file a bill to improve mental health services across the nation. "I know firsthand how our current system is failing those with these illnesses and also where there are opportunities to strengthen our system," Guinta said, while noting that a member of his family suffered from mental illness.

But he ran into a potentially career-ending incident in May 2015, when he agreed to a settlement of charges by the Federal Election Commission that he had accepted $355,000 in illegal campaign contributions from his parents, which Guinta had described as a loan in 2010. After the FEC required that he repay the money, which was the focus of charges during his initial campaign, Guinta agreed to resolve the charges that he said had become "distractions." Some New Hampshire Republicans viewed the action as a mortal wound to his incumbency and political future, and demanded that he resign immediately. That included Sen. Kelly Ayotte, who faced reelection in 2016. "Frank is dead politically," said Fergus Cullen, a former state GOP chairman. The conservative *Manchester Union-Leader* joined the call for his resignation. Guinta initially sought to ride out the storm, and to retain at least the neutrality of House GOP leaders. Shea-Porter increased the pressure on Guinta when she said that she was "ready to win" back the seat, though she said that she was hoping he would resign. Credible Republican candidates made moves to run in the primary. Federal prosecutors had earlier investigated the loan, and decided not to file charges.

SECOND DISTRICT

Ann McLane Kuster (D)

Elected 2012, 2nd term; b. Sept. 5, 1956, Concord; Dartmouth Col., B.A. 1978; Georgetown U., J.D. 1984; Episcopalian; married (Brad Kuster); 2 children.

Professional Career: Owner, Newfound Strategies, 2011-13; Practicing lawyer, 1984-2010; Legis. aide, U.S. Rep. Pete McCloskey, 1978-81.

DC Office: 137 CHOB, 20515, 202-225-5206; Fax: 202-225-2946; Website: kuster.house.gov.

State Offices: Concord, 603-226-1002; Nashua, 603-595-2006; North Conway, 603-444-7700.

Committees: *Agriculture; Veterans' Affairs;* Health; Oversight & Investigations (RMM).

Group Ratings

	ADA	ACLU	AFL-CIO	LCV	ITI	COC	HAFA	ACU	CFG	FRC
2014	60%	72%	–	94%	100%	64%	12%	0%	13%	0%
2013	65%	C	90%	26%	C	54%	C	12%	15%	C

National Journal Ratings

	2013 LIB	—	2013 CONS
Economic	62%	—	38%
Social	63%	—	36%
Foreign	80%	—	19%
Composite	69%	—	31%

Key Votes of the 113th Congress

1. Sandy storm spending	Y	5. Medical Marijuana	Y	9. Syrian Rebels Training	Y
2. Violence Against Women Act	Y	6. Farm Bill	N	10. Keystone pipeline	N
3. Guantanamo Bay Detainees	Y	7. Afghanistan Combat	Y	11. Immigration Exec. Action	N
4. Abortion 20-week ban	N	8. NSA Phone Data Collection	N	12. Bipartisan budget deal	Y

Election Results

2014 general	Ann McLane Kuster (D)	130,700	(55%)	$3,641,777	$87,381	$2,192,271
	Marilinda Garcia (R)	106,871	(45%)	$1,195,084	$512,527	$4,775,229
2014 primary	Ann McLane Kuster (D)	unopposed			

Prior winning percentage: 2012 (50%)

Population		Race and Ethnicity		Income	
Total:	660,986	White	91.9%	Median income:	$63,835
Urban:	14.6%	Latino	2.7%		*(85 of 435)*
Suburban:	27.7%	Asian	2.4%	Under $50,000	39.5%
Rural:	57.6%	Black	1.0%	$50,000-$99,999:	32.9%
Land area:	7,103	Two races	1.8%	$100,000-$199,999:	22.2%
Pop/sq. mi.:	93.1	White Ethnic	61.6%	$200,000 or more:	5.4%
Born in state:	42.0%			Poverty Rate	9.6%
		Education			
Age Groups		H.S. grad or less:	38.3%	**Work**	
Under 18:	20.4%	Some college:	28.0%	White collar:	39.1%
18 to 34:	20.7%	College degree, 4 yr.:	20.9%	Blue collar:	38.9%
35 to 64:	43.1%	Post-grad study:	12.8%	Sales and service:	22.0%
Over 64:	15.7%				
		Military		Govt. workers:	13.4%
		Veterans/active duty:	10.3%		

Western New Hampshire: Nashua, Concord

Political reporters covering New Hampshire's first-in-the-nation primary usually stay in Manchester, the state's largest city and within an hour's drive of the rest of the state except for the North Country.

Voter Turnout	
2013 Total Citizen 18+	509,213
2014 House Turnout	238,149
2014 Turnout as % CVAP	46.8%
2012 Turnout as % CVAP	69.9%

Yet there are other noteworthy cities and towns in New Hampshire. Concord, north of Manchester, is the state capital. On one side of Main Street is the handsome, small, granite Capitol, and on the other you can usually find the headquarters of the two political parties and many candidates: an entire state's politics within 100 yards. Nashua, south of Manchester and on the Massachusetts line, is the state's second-largest city, a high-technology and financial services center that has been mostly booming for three decades.

To the east is prosperous and growing Salem, first chartered in 1750 and the largest of the border suburbs. To the west of Nashua, past the pleasant country around Mount Monadnock, is Keene, the hub of southwest New Hampshire, and the largest city in the state north or west of Concord. To the north are towns along the Connecticut River; some are mill towns, and some are vacation enclaves. New Hampshire's prosperity has spread to most of them. Hanover, home of Dartmouth College, is a tiny, picturesque town set in the mountains. And every political reporter's itinerary has to include a trip, usually by plane, to the little lumber mill city of Berlin in the middle of the North Country, where the last paper mill has closed, and perhaps also to Dixville Notch in the White Mountains, where the town's 12 voters cast their ballots at a minute past midnight and provide the first reported returns in every presidential election. The vote split 5-5 in 2012 between President Barack Obama and Mitt Romney. (Hint for election night analysts: If Dixville Notch doesn't go heavily Republican, the Republicans are in trouble.)

2012 Presidential Vote		
Barack Obama (D)	190,413	(54%)
Mitt Romney (R)	156,499	(44%)

2008 Presidential Vote		
Barack Obama (D)	198,261	(56%)
John McCain (R)	152,591	(43%)

Cook Partisan Voting Index: D+3

The 2nd Congressional District of New Hampshire includes Concord, Nashua, Salem, Keene, the Connecticut River counties, Hanover, Berlin and Dixville Notch. It also includes Mount Washington, with its spectacularly violent weather and winds that have been measured up to 231 miles per hour; entrepreneurs have considered wind power plants, but the manager of its state park said the location was too windy and icy to be practical. The district also takes in the Bretton Woods resort, where the world monetary system was established at a conference in 1944.

Politically, this region is mixed, but it has become the more Democratic of New Hampshire's two congressional districts. Nashua is more Democratic than Manchester, Salem more Republican. The area between Mount Monadnock and Keene and the territory running north along the Connecticut River to Hanover and Dartmouth has become very Democratic, much like Vermont across the river. The district hasn't been carried by a Republican presidential candidate since 1988.

Ann McLane Kuster (D)

Democrat Ann McLane Kuster, elected in 2012, has had three hard-fought contests and won the last two. In doing so, she toppled veteran Rep. Charlie Bass, one of the House's few remaining GOP moderates, and she sought a longer-term claim on the district.

Kuster was born in Concord and is part of a prominent political family in the Granite State. Her great-grandfather John McLane served as governor of New Hampshire from 1905 to 1907, while her father, Malcolm McLane, was mayor of Concord and an unsuccessful gubernatorial candidate in 1972. Her mother, Susan McLane, was a Republican state legislator for 25 years. "Politics was sort of a way of life in our family," Kuster said.

When Kuster was 16, she worked on the 1972 presidential campaign of Republican Rep. Pete McCloskey of California, an anti-Vietnam War candidate who challenged President Richard Nixon. Kuster later graduated from Dartmouth College and worked in McCloskey's Washington office for three years. During that time, she specialized in foreign policy and traveled to South Africa, where the apartheid system was still in place, and to newly independent Zimbabwe.

Kuster earned her law degree from Georgetown University and returned to Manchester to practice law. She spent many years in Concord as a state-based lobbyist and adoption lawyer. "I represented women with unplanned pregnancies from age 14 to 40, and they ranged from living in their car to living in the nicest neighborhoods in town," she said of her adoption work. "Unplanned pregnancy is an equal-opportunity affliction."

She published a 2004 memoir based on interviews with her mother called *The Last Dance*. It dealt with Susan McLane's struggles with Alzheimer's disease before she died in 2005. Kuster also began to immerse herself in politics and served as a delegate at the 2004 Democratic National Convention. She got heavily involved in Barack Obama's 2008 presidential campaign, touring with him as he met New Hampshire's first-in-the-nation primary voters.

In 2010, Kuster faced off against Bass, and was the underdog in a strong year for Republicans. She criticized his role in securing tax rebates for wood-pellet stove buyers before investing in a wood-pellet stove company himself, New England Wood Pellet. Bass denied any wrongdoing, but the issue gave her momentum. Kuster came under fire over an anecdote she repeated on the campaign trail about a New Hampshire firm that lost 4,000 jobs to outsourcing; a local newspaper found that no such company existed. The incumbent Bass was outspent 2-to-1, but he eked out the victory 48%-47%.

In 2012, Kuster had a rematch with Bass and a more favorable political climate, as the strength of the anti-government tea party receded locally. The two candidates debated taxes, with Kuster calling for a return to the Clinton-era tax rate and Bass favoring an extension of the deeper Bush-era tax cuts. Kuster supported Obama's 2010 health care overhaul, and Bass called the law a "bureaucratic boondoggle." At a rally in Concord, Kuster grabbed a camera away from a Bass campaign staffer. The dustup was caught on video, and the National Republican Congressional Committee ran an ad criticizing her. Kuster countered that the Bass staffer was harassing her. Kuster again outspent Bass by more than a million dollars and had a comparable advantage in the outside money that was spent on the contest. This time she won, 50%-45%.

In the House, Kuster served on the Veterans' Affairs Committee and said that her biggest accomplishment during her first term was the passage of legislation to improve healthcare options for veterans. Her biggest disappointment, she said, was relentless partisanship and gridlock. She began to address that issue in 2015, when she cooperated with home-state Republican Rep. Frank Guinta on health issues, including veterans' access to care. As ranking Democrat on the Veterans Affairs' Oversight and Investigations Subcommittee, she gained additional opportunities to work on those issues, including cost overruns at VA facilities. Kuster took up the local causes of alternative-energy development and home-heating assistance.

In 2014, she faced a reelection challenge from state Rep. Marilinda Garcia, a young conservative activist. Kuster called her opponent "naïve," and won 55%-45%. Kuster outspent Garcia 3-to-1, and outside groups flooded the contest with more than $7.5 million. The contest was "much fiercer than the final margin would seem to suggest," according to House elections expert David Wasserman. "Given Garcia's status as a Latina millennial, she became a national conservative star and received heavy backing from the Club for Growth. But that also helped Kuster portray Garcia as out of touch with a district that is clearly becoming much more culturally liberal."

★ NEW JERSEY ★

From its notoriety as the setting for the mobster series *The Sopranos* to the grating stereotypes of its citizens on *Jersey Shore*, New Jersey gets a bad rap, and it has for a long time. During his two years as governor, Woodrow Wilson said, just a tad defensively, New Jersey is "a sort of laboratory in which the best blood is prepared for other communities to thrive on."

Its early settlers included Dutch in towns behind the Palisades on the Hudson and Quakers on Delaware River bottomlands opposite Philadelphia. From the start, New Jersey was plagued by rival claims from its neighbors and, still defensive in the 1980s, went to the U.S. Supreme Court to argue that it and not New York owns the Statue of Liberty and Ellis Island. New Jersey eventually got most of the islands' acreage, but New York got the immigrant museum and the Great Hall, which are built on fill land. For a century after the American Revolution, New Jersey was a modest, slow-growing, even backward state. It became known as the Garden State because of its vegetable farms, which supplied the tomatoes for Campbell's Soup, based in Camden. But its proximity to New York and Philadelphia brought into its empty spaces immigrants and inventors.

While New Jersey is caught between these two metropolises, Jersey City, Newark, and Camden grew to be significant cities in their own right. Thomas Edison churned out inventions in his laboratory at Menlo Park and gave birth to General Electric and Bell Labs. On open fields near large labor pools, U.S. automakers built assembly plants in the years after World War II, and the container port on the New Jersey side of New York harbor overshadowed the crumbling, racketeer-plagued docks of Manhattan and Brooklyn. Much of the pharmaceutical industry came to be concentrated in New Jersey, including the headquarters of Merck, Johnson & Johnson, Bristol-Myers Squibb, Novartis, and Schering-Plough. Connected to Wall Street by Hudson tubes and ferries, New Jersey became the home of finance professionals and lawyers. This economy gave the state a high median income, a well-educated workforce, and a prosperous middle class, with a high concentration of scientists and engineers. New Jersey has long had one of the highest median household incomes of any state—it's now fifth, behind Maryland, New Hampshire, Connecticut and Virginia. But it also has, by some measures, the eighth highest in income inequality in the nation, and New Jersey was one of just three states (with New Mexico and Washington) that saw the number of people living in poverty rise between 2012 and 2013.

Physically, New Jersey has been transformed in recent decades. The oil tank farms, concrete ribbons of turnpike and Meadowlands swamps—places where young people would "meet 'neath that giant Exxon sign / that brings this fair city light," in the words of native son Bruce Springsteen—are still there, but they have been joined by sports palaces and office complexes. The Singer factory in Elizabeth, the Western Electric factory in Kearny, and the Ford Motor plant in Mahwah are all gone, replaced by shopping centers and hotels. The intersection of Interstates 78 and 287 has become a major shopping and office edge city. U.S. 1 north from ivy-draped Princeton University to North Brunswick, home of the state university, Rutgers, has become one of the nation's high-tech centers. Casting off its suburban image, New Jersey has developed an identity of its own. It is the home of big-league football and hockey franchises and of the world's longest expanses of boardwalk, on the Jersey Shore from Cape May to Sandy Hook.

Within New Jersey's close boundaries is great diversity—geographically, from beaches to mountains; demographically, from old Quaker stock to new Hispanic arrivals; economically, from inner-city slums to hunt-country mansions. Although New York writers are inclined to look on New Jersey as a land of 1940s diners and 1970s shopping malls, the state much more closely resembles the rest of America than does Manhattan, although drivers will find some peculiarities, such as jug-handle intersections (to make a left turn, you exit to the right and then cross over after the light has changed), and a ban on self-service gas stations. The row houses one used to encounter upon emerging from the Holland Tunnel are now joined by office and apartment towers and, a few miles further out, the skyscrapers of Newark and its new performing arts center. Farther out are comfortably packed middle-income suburbs and the horse country around Far Hills, old industrial cities such as Paterson and Trenton (also the state capital), and dozens of suburban towns and small factory cities. Among them are commuter towns such as Middletown, whose commuter trails lead to Lower Manhattan. In South Jersey is the desolate expanse known as the pine barrens, where Christopher

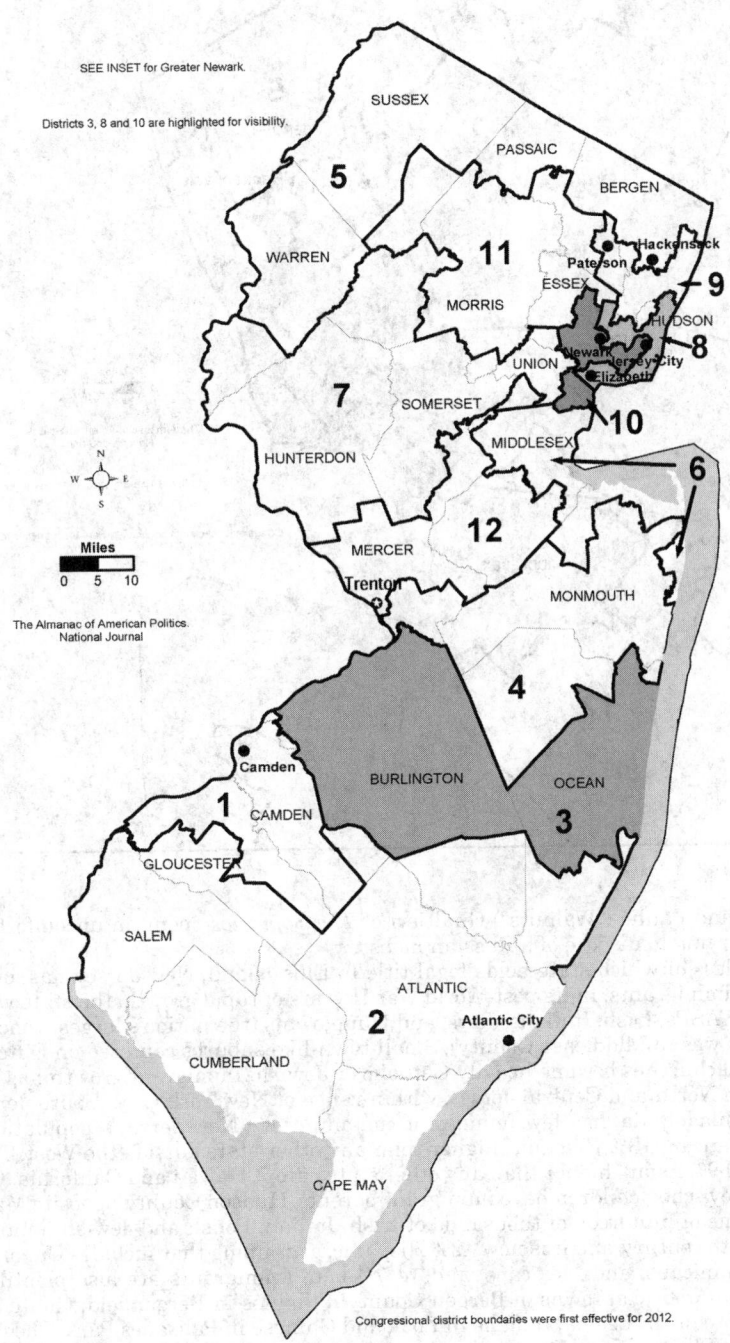

SEE INSET for Greater Newark.

Districts 3, 8 and 10 are highlighted for visibility.

The Almanac of American Politics.
National Journal

Congressional district boundaries were first effective for 2012.

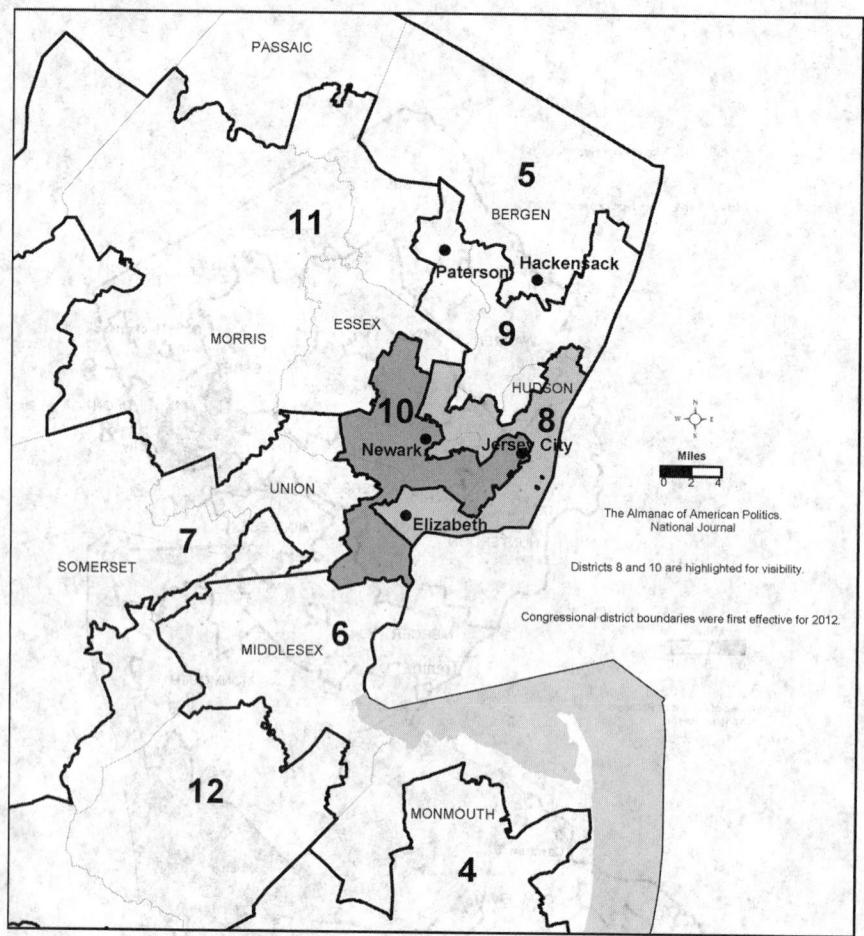

Moltisanti and Paulie ("Walnuts") Gualtieri of *The Sopranos* spent an uncomfortable winter's night trying to dispose of a Russian mobster.

Regardless of which state holds legal title to Ellis Island, New Jersey has long been a magnet for immigrants. In its post-World War II years of rapid growth, the state was a quilt pattern of WASPs, Irish, Italians, Jews, and Hungarians (the nation's largest concentration of the latter was in Middlesex County). Small-town-like suburbs centered on Dutch Reform or Episcopal churches became heavily Catholic or Jewish. Immigrant growth has been concentrated in North and Central Jersey, within range of New York City. (South Jersey, as in adjacent Philadelphia, has few immigrant communities.) New Jersey's population is 15% African-American; 18% Hispanic, higher than any other state outside the West, Texas, and Florida; and 9% Asian, higher than any other state except Hawaii and California. One-third of New Jersey schoolchildren have immigrant parents. Hudson County, opposite Manhattan, was the home of hundreds of thousands of Irish, Italian, Polish and Jewish immigrants in the early 20th century, and it is now 42% Hispanic, a grouping that includes Cubans, Puerto Ricans, Dominicans, and Mexicans, and 14% Asian. Immigrants are also plentiful in the small middle-American towns of Bergen County: Filipinos in Bergenfield, Guatemalans in Fairview, Koreans in Leonia, Indians in Lodi, and Chinese in Palisades Park. The old industrial cities of Elizabeth and Paterson are majority Hispanic, and Newark is majority black.

For all its strengths, New Jersey has faced difficulties in the new century. Population growth has slowed to a crawl, with only very small patches of suburban boom. United Van Lines reported that among its moves to and from New Jersey in 2014, about two-thirds were outbound, higher than any other state—evidence that people in New Jersey are indeed "Born to Run." Only Ocean County, with its retirement communities, and Gloucester County, on the New Jersey Turnpike outside of Philadelphia, have attracted significant numbers of non-immigrant new residents in recent years. There's evidence that the newest generation of workers are less keen on working in suburban office parks than their parents were, and would prefer walkable cities.

Economically, New Jersey was hit hard by the recession, and it hasn't fully recovered. Unemployment peaked at 9.8 percent in fall 2009, and by March 2015 it had fallen only to 6.5 percent, one of the nation's highest rates. By early 2015, the number of jobs was still 2.1 percent below the state's pre-recession peak, even though the nation as a whole was up by 2 percent over the same period. Foreclosure rates often ranked among the nation's highest. Households making at least $1 million were the only ones who saw income-adjusted income gains between 2010 and 2012, the *Asbury Park Press* calculated.

New Jersey's recovery was hampered by superstorm Sandy, which struck on October 29, 2012. A storm surge hit the whole Jersey Shore from Cape May to Sandy Hook and peaked at eight-and-a-half feet. Damage was substantial on barrier-island communities and in low-lying land next to New York Harbor and the Passaic and Hackensack rivers. Bridges were smashed, and the Holland Tunnel and much of the Garden State Parkway were shut down; utilities were not restored for many days and evacuation orders in some areas continued for two weeks. At least 72,000 homes and businesses were damaged.

Longer-term trends hurt the state's economy as well. Atlantic City's glittering casinos were hit by the recession and by the expansion of gambling to Pennsylvania, with revenues falling from $4.9 billion in 2006 to $2.9 billion in 2013; four of the city's 12 casinos closed by 2014. Meanwhile, the state's biomedical industry sustained a slower, but even more serious, hit—a combination of expiring drug patents, rampant mergers and the gravitation of research to university-based labs in places like Massachusetts and California. New Jersey's rank in receiving venture-capital funding fell from fourth in 2004 to 13th in 2013, and over the past two decades, the state's share of pharmaceutical jobs dropped from 20% to 10%. Telecommunications firms also suffered: Lucent, the successor to Bell Labs, was burned in the high-tech bust and was acquired in 2006 by the French firm Alcatel.

State government has helped build New Jersey's identity, but it also has placed heavy burdens on its private sector. In the 1970s, Democratic Gov. Brendan Byrne pushed through an income tax in a state that, until that point, had far lower taxes than New York. A revolt crested against Democratic Gov. Jim Florio's tax increase in 1990, and it took on national significance with his defeat by Republican Christine Todd Whitman in 1993. In the 1990s, crime and welfare rolls dropped, but auto insurance and property taxes remained the highest in the nation. Health insurance premiums skyrocketed, thanks to state mandates requiring all policies to cover all manner of treatments. Meanwhile, property taxes kept rising.

Politically, New Jersey leaned Republican from the 1940s through the 1980s. But in the last two decades, it has become a Democratic bastion because of its growing immigrant population and the presence of many affluent suburbanites who reject the GOP's conservative stands on cultural issues. Until Chris Christie's re-election in 2013, no Republican had won 50% of the state vote for president or governor since presidential candidate George

Population		Race and Ethnicity		Income	
Total:	8,899,339	White	58.6%	Median income:	$61,782
Urban:	36.9%	Latino	18.1%		(8 of 50)
Suburban:	62.8%	Black	12.7%	Under $50,000	36.7%
Rural:	0.3%	Asian	8.4%	$50,000-$99,999:	28.7%
Land area:	7,354	Two races	1.5%	$100,000-$199,999:	24.9%
Pop/sq. mi.:	1,210.1	White Ethnic	43.7%	$200,000 or more:	9.7%
Born in state:	52.6%			Poverty Rate	6.8%
		Education			
Age Groups		H.S. grad or less:	40.3%	**Work**	
Under 18:	22.7%	Some college:	23.2%	White collar:	40.4%
18 to 34:	21.7%	College degree, 4 yr.:	22.6%	Blue collar:	42.0%
35 to 64:	41.2%	Post-grad study:	14.0%	Sales and service:	17.6%
Over 64:	14.4%			Govt. workers:	13.8%
		Military			
		Veterans/active duty:	5.5%		

H.W. Bush in 1988 and Tom Kean in 1985. No Republican has won a Senate election since Clifford Case in 1972. On a map showing election results by city and township, Democrats have carried the spine of the state, on either side of the Amtrak Acela corridor and through the South Jersey suburbs of Philadelphia. Republicans have carried the outlying areas, most of the Jersey Shore on the east, and the affluent suburban and exurban areas on the northwest. The 2012 exit poll found that 18% of the voters are African-American, 10% are Latino and 3% Asian, meaning that Republicans need to get about two-thirds of the votes from whites to win.

Voter Turnout	
2013 Total Citizen 18+	6,054,175
2014 Highest Statewide Turnout	1,869,535
2014 Turnout as % CVAP	30.9%
2012 Turnout as % CVAP	60.6%

Legislature		
Senate:	24D	16R
House:	48D	32R

Other factors beyond demographics have helped Democrats. New Jersey's high-earning, relatively well-educated voters tend not to vote in often crucial primaries—nearly half are not registered in either party—and those who do vote tend to defer to the choices of county and city political machines, which possess varying degrees of competence and cronyism. For candidates in both parties, it is a great advantage to have the designation of the local county party on the primary ballot. Another factor has been Democrats' willingness to pitch losers aside, and the willingness of the legal and political establishments to go along. In September 2002, Sen. Robert Torricelli, plagued by scandal, was allowed by the state Supreme Court to drop out of his race for re-election and to be replaced by former Sen. Frank Lautenberg, who won in the fall. In August 2004, Gov. Jim McGreevey announced that he would resign amidst a gay sex scandal. Democratic Senate President Richard Codey stepped in as acting governor and considered running for a full term, but was elbowed aside by Sen. Jon Corzine. This tendency will be tested with the case of Democratic Sen. Robert Menendez, who was indicted in April 2015 on federal corruption charges. In the immediate aftermath, members of his party largely stood by him.

Christie won office in 2009. As U.S. attorney, Christie had secured the convictions of dozens of political figures from both parties. New Jersey government, he argued, was bloated and overly expensive, and he promised not to raise taxes. Corzine had a huge financial advantage, spending his own money while Christie was limited to the state's public financing. But Christie stuck to his themes and won 48%-45%. Christie's first term produced successes, including a bipartisan measure to require public employees to pay more for their pensions and health coverage. He also worked with Democrats to balance the budget, though at a cost—he did not fully fund the state's depleted pension funds, which eventually contributed to repeated downgrades to the state's bond rating. Having gained a national profile, presidential nominee Mitt Romney tapped him for the keynote speech at the 2012 Republican National Convention, and in 2013, Christie rolled to a second term. But his tendency to speak bluntly and act aggressively, often a positive in a state that champions the tough guy, was also polarizing, making it harder for him to inspire sympathy when his administration, shortly after he was re-elected, faced investigations into the closing of a lane on the George Washington Bridge, which some suspected was a way to punish Christie's political detractors. Sagging approval ratings put a big question mark over his 2016 presidential ambitions.

Presidential Politics In the second half of the 20th century, New Jersey was a close state in close presidential elections, giving small margins to winners in 1960 and 1968 and to losers in 1948 and 1976. In the 1980s, the vast suburban expanses of New Jersey leaned toward the Republicans. Since the middle 1990s, New Jersey has leaned decidedly Democratic. The suburbs, with many secular and Jewish voters and few Christian conservatives, reject Republican positions on cultural issues, and rising immigrant communities have generally voted Democratic. As a result, New Jersey, which had voted 56%-43% for George H. W. Bush in 1988 (a race where he carried 18 of the state's 21 counties), voted

2012 Presidential Vote		
Barack Obama (D)	2,125,101	(58%)
Mitt Romney (R)	1,477,568	(41%)

2012 Presidential Primary		
Mitt Romney (R)	188,121	(81%)
Ron Paul (R)	24,017	(10%)
Rick Santorum (R)	12,115	(5%)

2008 Presidential Vote		
Barack Obama (D)	2,215,422	(57%)
John McCain (R)	1,613,207	(42%)

54%-36% for Bill Clinton in 1996 (he won 16 counties) and 56%-40% for Al Gore in 2000. In 2004, George W. Bush's campaign strategists kept an eye on New Jersey's polls to see whether September 11 had had enough impact on voters to make the state worth contesting. It didn't and Democrat John Kerry won the state 53%-46%.

In 2008, Barack Obama carried the state 57%-42%, the best Democratic showing since 1964. In 2012, New Jersey was one of five states where Obama increased his percentage, to 58%-41%. This may have been the result of Hurricane Sandy: Turnout was down everywhere, but down most in Republican Ocean and Monmouth counties on the Jersey Shore. Obama visited the devastation before the election and GOP Gov. Chris Christie praised the president for his pledge to steer federal relief to the Garden State.

For years, New Jersey held its presidential primary in early June, but it was usually overshadowed by the California primary on the same day. In 1996, 2000, and 2004, both parties' nominations were sewn up long before New Jersey voted. In April 2007, the legislature rescheduled the primary for February 5, Super Tuesday. But New Jersey again got lost in the shuffle. Polls showed Hillary Clinton and John McCain with solid leads here and in New York, which also voted on Super Tuesday. So every campaign decided to save money by not buying New York television. Democratic turnout was 1.1 million, nearly double the previous record, and Clinton beat Obama 54%-44%. She carried Jewish and Latino voters, while Obama carried blacks and did well in high-income suburbs, except those with large Jewish populations. Turnout on the Republican side was only 566,000, more than ever before but only half the number of Democrats who voted. McCain defeated Romney by a surprisingly large 55%-28% margin. Romney was unable to duplicate here the appeal he demonstrated in high-income suburbs in several other states. McCain topped 50% in all but two counties. In 2012, New Jersey went back to the June primary. By then the race was over, and Romney won 81% with a very light turnout.

Congressional Districts Since 1991, New Jersey has employed a bipartisan redistricting commission, made up of 12 members—six Democrats and six Republicans—appointed by the party leaders in the legislature. The members pick a tie-breaking arbiter, and in both 1991 and 2001, they chose Rut-

114th Congress Lineup	
6 R	6 D
113th Congress Lineup	
6 R	6 D

gers University professor Alan Rosenthal. In 1991, Rosenthal picked the Republicans' plan, with grotesquely shaped districts, but New Jersey's trend towards Democrats in the 1990s reduced Republicans to six of the state's 13 seats by 2000. In 2001, the 13 incumbents agreed on a bipartisan, if contorted, map and submitted it to the commission. Rosenthal liked the incumbent-protection plan, and over the next 10 years, only the South Jersey 3rd District switched parties.

The 2010 census cost New Jersey a House seat, raising the stakes and rendering protection of all seven Democratic and six Republican incumbents impossible. In 2011, the commission appointed former state Attorney General John Farmer as its 13th member, and then the sides retreated to their war rooms. (Rosenthal died in 2013.) Democrats argued that the state's Democratic drift made a 7-5 partisan split logical, with the unwieldy Republican-held 7th District ripe for the chopping block. Republicans contended the urban northeastern corner of the state had grown the slowest, and while the black-majority 10th District and Hispanic-majority 13th District were sacrosanct, the nearby Democratic-held 8th and 9th districts were logical choices to merge.

Farmer let it be known that he preferred considering population over party breakdown. The commission's Democrats, who happened to include a former top aide to 8th District incumbent Bill Pascrell, proposed a "fair fight" Bergen County district combining Democrat Steve Rothman's 9th District with Republican Scott Garrett's 5th District, sparing Pascrell. Republicans proposed pitting Rothman against Garrett in a much more Republican seat. Farmer chose the Republican plan, which actually stuffed most of Rothman's political base into Pascrell's district. The Republican gambit succeeded: Rather than face Garrett, Rothman opted to primary Pascrell and was trounced. Since then, each party's seats have remained secure, though the Democrats overall have had larger victory margins.

Governor

Chris Christie (R)

Elected 2009, term expires Jan. 2018, 2nd term; b. Sept. 6, 1962, Newark; U. of DE, B.A. 1984, Seton Hall U., J.D. 1987; Catholic; married (Mary Pat); 4 children.

Elected Office: Morris Cnty. freeholder, 1994-98; Dir., Freeholder Bd., 1997.

Professional Career: Practicing atty., partner, Dughi Hewit & Palatucci, 1987-2001; U.S. atty. for NJ, 2002-08.

Office: The StateHouse, PO Box 001, Trenton, 08625, 609-292-6000; Fax: 609-777-2922; Website: state.nj.us/governor.

Election Results

2014 general	Chris Christie (R)	1,278,932	(60%)
	Barbara Buono (D)	809,978	(38%)
2014 primary	Chris Christie (R)	205,666	(92%)
	Seth Grossman (R)	18,095	(8%)

Prior winning percentage: 2009 (48%)

Chris Christie, a Republican, was elected governor of New Jersey in 2009 and quickly became lionized in his party as the archetypal "Jersey guy" for his confident, cut-the-crap persona. He was chosen to give the 2012 Republican National Convention's keynote address and became the subject of speculation about a future White House race, but a home-grown bridge-closing scandal and economic challenges for the state have cast a cloud over his presidential ambitions.

Christie grew up in Livingston, a comfortable suburb 10 miles west of Newark, the son of an accountant who was an ardent Republican, and a Sicilian-American mother who was a lifelong Democrat. He was president of his class throughout middle school and high school and was selected for student leadership programs in Washington. In 1977, when he was 15, he volunteered in Republican Thomas Kean's race for governor, and Kean became his role model. He graduated from the University of Delaware and Seton Hall Law School.

After law school, Christie joined a firm in Cranford, where he specialized in corporate securities law and appellate work, making partner in 1993. His wife, Mary Pat Christie, pursued a career in investment banking. One of Christie's law partners, Bill Palatucci, was state coordinator for George H.W. Bush's campaign in 1992 and the two together raised money in 2000 for his son, George W. Bush. In 1994, Christie was elected as a Republican to the Morris County Board of Chosen Freeholders. In 1995, he ran for the Assembly but lost to candidates favored by the county Republican organization. In 1997, he was defeated in the Republican primary for the freeholder position.

Christie's political work paid off when President George W. Bush appointed him U.S. attorney for New Jersey in 2002. This was a critical position in a state known for its corrupt politics; Supreme Court Justice Samuel Alito once held the post. Ordinarily, U.S. attorneys are chosen by a state's senators, but both were Democrats, and Bush evidently wanted to bypass the county Republican organizations and appoint someone who was not indebted to them. The selection was strongly criticized in the state's legal circles as political patronage; Christie had no experience in criminal law. But he ultimately silenced his critics with a string of successful cases against corrupt public officials, street gangs, child pornographers, and terrorists. He was best known for a crackdown on public corruption in the state that yielded 130 convictions of both Democrats and Republicans, including that of a former state Senate president and a former Newark mayor.

One aspect of his record that drew criticism was his practice of awarding contracts to law firms to monitor corporations. The companies could avoid indictment for fraud if they paid for a monitor to oversee their practices. One such contract went to former Attorney General John Ashcroft; another went to David Kelley, who as a federal prosecutor in Manhattan had declined to charge Christie's brother, Todd Christie, in a securities fraud investigation. Christie defended the program, saying the contracts were awarded on merit. In June 2009, he stormed out of a hearing of the House Judiciary Committee, which was examining the use of deferred prosecution. Christie said that as an Italian-American, he found offensive a comment from one committee Democrat that the companies were pressured to accept the monitoring fees as a result of Mafia-style offers that they "could not refuse."

In 2008, Christie resigned as U.S. attorney to run against Gov. Jon Corzine, a former senator and chief executive officer of Goldman Sachs. Republicans had not won a statewide race in New Jersey since 1997. Plus, Corzine had deep pockets, having spent more than $100 million of his own money on his 2000 and 2005 campaigns. But Corzine had problems. He had been unable to fulfill his campaign pledge of lowering property taxes in a state with the highest rates in the nation. And his proposal to increase the tolls on the New Jersey Turnpike to provide long-term financing for transportation was rejected by the Democratic legislature. State government faced dizzying budget shortfalls, and the legislature had passed a temporary "millionaire's tax" on people with incomes over $400,000.

Christie campaigned as a middle-class native of the state, a father of four children under the age of 15, and a Mets baseball fan. He said he played New Jersey native Bruce Springsteen's song "Prove It All Night" to get psyched before press conferences, and in 2003 he attended nine Springsteen concerts. (He has attended nearly 130 shows and finally met his idol, after a period of being rebuffed by the singer. "We hugged and he told me it's official: We're friends," the governor exulted to an audience.) Christie was endorsed by most Republican county organizations, but he had primary competition from the right from Steve Lonegan, former mayor of Bogota in Bergen County. Christie won the June primary, 55%-42%.

In the fall campaign, Christie said he would slash state spending down to essentials, take on powerful public employee unions and, finally, cut property tax rates. Corzine spent $27 million of his own money on the campaign, while Christie was limited by New Jersey's public financing law to spending $11 million. One ad depicted the corpulent Christie struggling to emerge from a car with the suggestion that as U.S. attorney, he had "thrown his weight around" during a traffic stop. By mid-October, Corzine and Christie were running about even, with Christopher Daggett, a former Republican running as an independent, getting as much as 20%, seemingly splitting the anti-Corzine vote. Despite a rally for Corzine headlined by President Barack Obama, Christie beat him, 48%-45%, with 6% for Daggett. Christie ran well in the central part of the state, with popular vote margins in Monmouth and Ocean counties on the Jersey Shore exceeding Corzine's margins in Hudson and Essex counties (Jersey City and Newark). He also carried normally Democratic Middlesex County.

When Christie settled into budget-making, the outlook was grim: State government faced a projected deficit of $11 billion. In March 2010, he unveiled a $29 billion budget plan that leaned heavily on spending cuts, including layoffs of 1,300 state workers, a $3 billion reduction in scheduled pension payments, and an $820 million cut in aid to schools. The proposal aimed to save on Medicaid costs by establishing a $350 deductible for beneficiaries. He reneged on a campaign promise to allow a popular property tax rebate scheduled for May 2010 to go through, announcing he was suspending it for a year. Although Democratic Speaker Sheila Oliver called the budget a "disaster for middle-class families," she said her party would be willing to work with Christie on a proposal to cap yearly property tax increases at 2.5%. He also took on New Jersey's state employee unions. In early 2010, he issued an executive order limiting their political spending, but it was overturned in court. He also charged that teachers' union members were "using the students like drug mules" to distribute propaganda to parents. In response to his urgings, twice as many voters came out in the April school elections and rejected proposed property tax increases.

Structurally, New Jersey's governor is one of the nation's most powerful, and Christie used his authority aggressively. He picked a fight with the judicial branch. In May 2010, he refused to reappoint Supreme Court Justice John Wallace, as previous governors had routinely done, because of what he called "out of control" activism on the court. Democratic Senate President Stephen Sweeney refused to let the Senate vote on Christie's nominee to fill the post. In October 2010, he canceled proposed rail tunnels to Manhattan, turning down $3 billion in federal money on the grounds that estimated costs for the project were rising to $14 billion and that the state would be stuck paying for the cost overruns. During the 2011 legislative session, Christie vetoed Democratic bills taxing millionaires to pay for schools and to provide tax relief for low-income workers. He also vetoed $7.5 million for family planning clinics, but redirected those dollars towards Federally Qualified Health Centers, which provide some of the same services for women minus the more controversial family planning. Christie used his line-item veto to cut $900 million from a Democratic spending plan and avert a government shutdown. He signed legislation allowing non-public schools to be converted into charter schools.

Yet Christie did not totally cut off relations with New Jersey Democrats, including Oliver, Newark Mayor (and later Sen.) Cory Booker and Essex County Executive Joseph DiVincenzo. Christie's most fruitful relationship was with Sweeney, a moderate with blue collar cred—he served as an organizer of the International Association of Ironworkers. Their relationship was stormy—Christie once enraged Sweeney so much that he called him a "rotten prick"—but together they produced important accomplishments, including legislation requiring that public employees pay more for their pensions and health insurance, in exchange for higher payments to pension funds to make up for past short contributions. Christie won bipartisan praise for his call for drug courts, which take a more treatment-oriented approach. A measure to cut business taxes passed both chambers unanimously, and lawmakers backed his controversial plan to hand control over most of New Jersey's University of Medicine and Dentistry to Rutgers University. "He knows all the tools and knows how to use them," Tom Wilson, a former state GOP chairman told *Governing*. "He has a deep appreciation that political capital does not have a long shelf life, and that it's best appreciated by spending it."

Christie's big personality helped make his achievements possible, but his tendency to shoot from the hip has also gotten him in trouble. Irritated by criticism from Assemblyman Reed Gusciora about Christie's opposition to gay marriage, he called the state's first openly gay lawmaker "numbnuts." Challenged at a town meeting by Rutgers law student Bill Brown, Christie called the former Navy SEAL an "idiot." He called a nonpartisan legislative analyst "a joke," a "handmaiden" for the majority and "the Dr. Kevorkian of numbers." In a video, Christie explained his confrontational style: "I have an Irish father and I had ... a Sicilian mother. For those of you who have been exposed to the combination of Irish and Sicilian, it has made me not unfamiliar with conflict."

On the national stage in 2012, Christie threw himself into campaigning for GOP presidential nominee Mitt Romney, though in his convention keynote, he focused on his own accomplishments, a decision that drew some criticism for seeming to place his own political career over Romney's. In the closing days of the 2012 campaign, Superstorm Sandy ravaged New Jersey's coastline. Christie accompanied Obama to damaged areas and heaped praise on the president's responsiveness. Asked about the wisdom of offering such accolades so close to the election, he was dismissive: "I've got a job to do here in New Jersey that's much bigger than presidential politics, and I could care less about any of that stuff." When House Speaker John Boehner, R-Ohio, subsequently delayed a vote on Sandy relief legislation, an apoplectic Christie called the decision "absolutely disgraceful. ... It's why the American people hate Congress." The bill eventually passed and became law, but Christie paid a political price among the GOP base. He further irked conservatives when he announced an expansion of the state's Medicaid program.

By 2013, Christie was stronger politically than ever (and personally slimmer, following weight-loss surgery). In February, a Quinnipiac University poll gave him an approval rating of 74%—the highest that poll had found in 17 years of testing New Jersey governors. Nearly half of Democrats surveyed—48%—felt that he deserved another term. He won the June GOP primary with 92% of the vote and was a heavy favorite against Democratic state Sen. Barbara Buono. The Democratic Governors Association spent less than $5,000 for her, compared to $6 million on a highly competitive Virginia gubernatorial election the same year. Christie won with 60%, impressive in a Democratic-leaning state.

The victory fueled speculation about Christie's chances for the White House. Then came "Bridgegate." In September 2013, two of the three toll lanes on the George Washington Bridge linking Fort Lee, N.J., to New York were closed to morning rush-hour traffic. Streets were backed up for several days until the Port Authority—citing a potential danger to lives—reopened the lanes. Christie adamantly denied knowing anything about the lane closures, joking at a news conference in December, "Unbeknownst to anyone, I was working the cones." But in January he apologized to Fort Lee, the people of the state and the Legislature for his staffers' actions; several Christie aides resigned, and the governor fired his deputy chief of staff after an email surfaced saying it was "time for some traffic problems in Fort Lee." There was considerable speculation that the move was made to retaliate against Fort Lee Mayor Mark Sokolich, a Democrat who had refused to endorse Christie's re-election. Christie was booed at a Super Bowl ceremony and even his beloved Springsteen mocked him in song alongside Jimmy Fallon on *The Tonight Show* ("highways jammed with pissed off drivers with no place left to go," went their parody of "Born to Run.") Christie hired a law firm, at upwards of $7 million in taxpayer money, and it issued a report clearing him of any wrongdoing. In May 2015, a former senior Christie appointee, David Wildstein, pleaded guilty to conspiracy in the Bridgegate matter, saying the closings were political punishment against Sokolich; the governor's former deputy chief of staff, Bridget Anne Kelly, and former Port Authority deputy executive director Bill Baroni were indicted. Christie himself was not implicated.

But Bridgegate was not Christie's only setback. He faced a $3 billion budget gap for fiscal 2015, and Moody's lowered the state's credit rating for the sixth time during his governorship. A gambling implosion in Atlantic City forced him to appoint an emergency manager for the city. And in February 2015, a state Superior Court judge threw a wrench into one of Christie's signature achievements, his 2011 pension overhaul. After the state found that it lacked the money to cover pension contributions—and after Christie vetoed a Legislature-passed budget that financed the contributions with tax increases, including one on incomes exceeding $1 million—Christie reduced new pension contributions to less than half of the targeted amount. When public-employee unions sued, the judge ruled that the unions had a constitutionally protected contractual right to the payments. His administration appealed and the state Supreme Court backed Christie.

Politically, Christie had some big wins in 2014. As chairman of the Republican Governors Association, he spearheaded an outstanding election night for GOP governors, flipping Democratic seats not just in red states like Arkansas but in blue ones like Illinois, Massachusetts and Maryland, while endangered GOP governors in Florida, Wisconsin, Kansas, Maine, Georgia and Michigan beat the odds to survive. Still, it wasn't clear that this near-sweep provided Christie with much of a boost for his 2016 presidential run. A May 2015 WMUR-TV poll in New Hampshire—a must-win state for the comparatively moderate Christie—showed him with the support of just 3% of Republican voters. And in a national Wall Street Journal/NBC News poll in March 2015, 57% of Republicans said they could not see themselves supporting Christie for the nomination—the second-highest percentage to Donald Trump. Meanwhile, Christie's positioning in the heavily conservative Republican field drove him to the right on some issues. On immigration, he supported a suit by other states against Obama's executive action on immigration, and he seemed to backtrack on his prior support for a path to citizenship for illegal immigrants. He said the Common Core school standards—which had become toxic among conservative Republicans—are "simply not working," even though he had helped implement them in 2010. And Christie continued to oppose same-sex marriage. By May 2015, just 35 percent of registered voters in the state approved of his job performance, his lowest-ever showing in a Monmouth University poll.

Senior Senator

Robert Menendez (D)

Appointed Jan. 2006, term expires Jan. 2019, 2nd full term; b. Jan. 1, 1954, New York, NY; St. Peter's Col., B.A. 1976, Rutgers U., J.D. 1979; Catholic; divorced; 2 children.

Elected Office: Union City Bd. of Ed., 1974-82, CFO, 1978-82; Union City mayor, 1986-92; NJ Assembly, 1987-91; NJ Senate, 1991-92; U.S. House, 1993-2006

Professional Career: Practicing atty., 1980-92.

DC Office: 528 HSOB, 20510, 202-224-4744; Fax: 202-228-2197; Website: menendez.senate.gov.

State Offices: Barrington, 856-757-5353; Newark, 973-645-3030.

Committees: *Banking, Housing & Urban Affairs:* Financial Institutions & Consumer Protection; Housing, Transportation & Community Development (RMM); Securities, Insurance & Investment. *Finance:* Health Care; Taxation & IRS Oversight. *Foreign Relations.*

Group Ratings

	ADA	ACLU	AFL-CIO	LCV	ITI	COC	HAFA	ACU	CFG	FRC
2014	90%	46%	–	80%	100%	38%	2%	4%	7%	0%
2013	95%	C	100%	100%	C	50%	C	4%	2%	C

National Journal Ratings

	2013 LIB	—	2013 CONS
Economic	81%	—	18%
Social	73%	—	0%
Foreign	71%	—	0%
Composite	85%	—	16%

Key Votes of the 113th Congress

1. Sandy storm spending	Y	5. Student Loan Rates	N
2. Chuck Hagel Confirmation	Y	6. Employee Non-Discrim'n Act	Y
3. Gun Background Checks	Y	7. Senate Vote on Judgeships	N
4. Immigration Reform	Y	8. Defense Dept. Spending	Y

9. Bipartisan Budget Deal	Y
10. Farm Bill Conference Rept.	Y
11. Unempl. Comp. Extension	Y
12. Keystone Pipeline	N

Election Results

2012 general	Robert Menendez (D).............	1,985,783	(59%)	$16,226,545	$1,053,060
	Joe Kyrillos (R)	1,329,405	(39%)	$4,559,919	$479,304
2012 primary	Robert Menendez (D)............unopposed				

Prior winning percentages: 2006 (53%); House: 2004 (76%), 2002 (78%), 2000 (79%), 1998 (80%), 1996 (79%), 1994 (71%), 1992 (64%)

For Robert Menendez, New Jersey's senior senator, it's been a political rollercoaster ride since his 2012 reelection. In February 2013, a month after he was sworn in for a second full term, Massachusetts Sen. John Kerry was confirmed as the Obama administration's secretary of state, enabling Menendez to succeed Kerry as chairman of the Foreign Relations Committee—and providing Menendez with a highly visible chairmanship despite only seven years of Senate seniority. But, after losing the gavel at the end of 2014 when Republicans gained control of the Senate, Menendez stepped down temporarily as the committee's ranking Democrat in the spring of 2015, when he became only the 12th sitting senator in history to be indicted for a crime.

The indictment—which charged both the senator and Salomon Melgen, a Florida eye surgeon whom Menendez has characterized as a friend and political supporter—followed allegations that first surfaced as Menendez was assuming the chairmanship of Foreign Relations. A Justice Department spokesman described it as "a bribery scheme in which Menendez allegedly accepted gifts from Melgen in exchange for using the power of his Senate office to benefit Melgen's financial and personal interests." The gifts that Menendez allegedly received include travel and more than $750,000 in campaign contributions. Menendez has asserted his innocence while vowing to fight the charges. And he has continued to speak out regularly on recent foreign policy issues on which he has had significant differences with President Barack Obama. But, as the legal proceedings against Menendez move ahead—his trial was tentatively scheduled to start in late 2015—it has raised questions about the future of a political career that dates back more than 40 years.

Ironically, Menendez first gained political prominence in the early 1980s when he agreed to testify at a corruption trial against Union City Mayor William Musto, a political mentor. Menendez, the child of Cuban immigrants who arrived in the United States prior to his birth, grew up in Union City and got into politics at an early age. He was elected to the school board in 1974, at age 20, and worked for Musto before quitting and testifying against the mayor; Menendez wore a bulletproof vest for protection during the trial because of death threats. Menendez himself went on to be elected in 1986 as mayor of Union City, located in an area that is home to the largest concentration of Cuban-Americans in the United States outside of Miami. He was also elected to the New Jersey Assembly in 1987 and later the state Senate in 1991; he served simultaneously as mayor and state legislator, which was common practice in New Jersey politics. As head of the Democratic Party organization in Hudson County, which has the third-highest number of registered Democrats of any county in the state, he was a major player in state politics well prior to winning a Senate seat.

In 1992, when new congressional district lines were drawn and incumbent Frank Guarini retired, Menendez was elected to Congress, winning both the primary and general election by 2-1 margins. He was the first Hispanic-American to represent New Jersey in the

House. By the late 1990s, he was on track for a possible Senate candidacy. When Democratic Sen. Frank Lautenberg announced his retirement in 1999, Menendez was widely expected to run for the seat. But support was not forthcoming from New Jersey Sen. Bob Torricelli, the Democratic Senatorial Campaign Committee chairman, who preferred Jon Corzine, a wealthy former investment banker who could self-finance his campaign. (Three years later, when Torricelli was forced to abandon a run for reelection amid controversy over his acceptance of gifts from a businessman who had pleaded guilty to violating federal election laws, Lautenberg stepped in to win a second Senate stint.) Minority Leader Dick Gephardt urged Menendez to stay in the House, arguing that as a leader of a Democratic majority—Democrats came within a few seats of winning a majority in November 2000—he would soon have more influence. Menendez busied himself raising more than $4 million for fellow Democrats and traveling around the country campaigning.

Ambitious and hard-driving, Menendez has been admired—if not always warmly regarded—for his prodigious fundraising as well as his strategic savvy. In 2002, when an opening arose for the House Democrats' No. 2 leadership job, party whip, California's Nancy Pelosi was chosen over Maryland's Steny Hoyer. Menendez announced he would run for caucus chairman, the No. 3 leadership position, against Rosa DeLauro of Connecticut. Pelosi endorsed DeLauro, and Hoyer endorsed Menendez. On a secret ballot, Menendez won 104-103. As caucus chairman, he continued to raise large sums for the party in the 2003-04 election season.

Later, following his election to the Senate, Menendez got some negative attention for blocking a promotion for a prosecutor investigating Puerto Rican Gov. Aníbal Acevedo Vilá, a friend of his, who, as the non-voting delegate from Puerto Rico in the House, had cast a decisive vote for Menendez in the caucus chairman race. The prosecutor was in line to become the U.S. attorney in Puerto Rico and, at the time, was investigating Acevedo Vilá's fundraising practices. The prosecutor got the appointment in the end, and Acevedo Vilá was indicted for violating campaign finance and tax laws in 2008.

When Corzine was elected New Jersey governor in 2005, Menendez made it known that he would run for Corzine's Senate seat. He had amassed more than $4 million for a statewide campaign, far more than two potential Democratic rivals—Reps. Robert Andrews and Frank Pallone. Democrats worried about Menendez's Hudson County political baggage, and had questions about his relationship with former aide Kay LiCausi and his efforts to steer lobbying and consulting work her way. Nonetheless, Corzine appointed Menendez to his Senate seat in January 2006. As an election for the seat loomed the following November, Andrews and Pallone each decided they probably couldn't compete with Menendez, and declined to challenge him in the primary, leaving Menendez free to focus on his Republican opponent: state Sen. Tom Kean Jr., son and namesake of popular former Republican Gov. Thomas Kean. Menendez campaigned against the Iraq war, while Kean said he would have voted for the Iraq war resolution, while opposing a timetable for withdrawing U.S. troops.

Kean also sought to call attention to Menendez's activities and influence in Hudson County. In September 2006, then-U.S. Attorney Chris Christie subpoenaed records from a lease arrangement between Menendez and an anti-poverty group for which Menendez had sought federal funding, and that paid him some $300,000 in rent on a building he owned in Union City. (A subsequent U.S. attorney closed the case in 2011 after Christie was elected governor.) Menendez counterattacked with an attack ad linking Kean to contributors with ethics problems. Then it was revealed that the Kean campaign's opposition researchers had contacted former Hudson County Executive Robert Janiszewski, who was serving time in federal prison on corruption charges. Menendez struck back with a television ad accusing Kean of a smear campaign: "Federal prisoner 25038-050. He's Tom Kean Jr.'s newest adviser." Polls late in the season showed Menendez with only a slight lead, but won by 53%-44%.

Menendez has a voting record consistent with most other Democrats from the Northeast; *National Journal*'s 2013 vote rankings rated him as the 12th most liberal senator, and his stance on several issues at one point prompted an effort by conservative tea party activists to recall him. However, on foreign policy issues ranging from Cuba to Iran to Russia and the Ukraine, he has had a scratchy relationship with the Obama White House. (Menendez supported Hillary Clinton for the 2008 Democratic presidential nomination.) These differences were accentuated when Menendez became chairman of the Foreign Relations panel in 2013.

Reflecting both his own background and his constituent base, Menendez has been a strong supporter of anti-Fidel Castro legislation since his election to the House. As a senator, in March 2009, he placed a hold on two of Obama's nominees to administration jobs to protest a provision easing travel restrictions to Cuba that was included in an appropriations bill. His refusal to vote for the spending bill prevented it from getting the needed 60 vote super-majority to move until he was offered assurances by the administration that the Cuba rider would have little impact. When the Obama administration moved in late 2014 to open diplomatic relations with Cuba, Menendez angrily charged that Obama's move had "vindicated the brutal behavior of the Cuban government."

He pressed for a more aggressive response to Russia's aggression in the Ukraine, urging increased sanctions on the former and increased military assistance for the latter. Meanwhile, in early 2015, as the administration negotiated with Iran in an effort to prevent that country from developing nuclear weapons, Menendez—as the Foreign Relations panel's ranking Democrat—said he would give Obama two months before defying a veto threat and voting for new sanctions against Iran. When asked by *The New York Times* whether the White House had lobbied him for the reprieve, Menendez responded, "I don't get calls from the White House," a seeming acknowledgment of his rift with Obama.

Under normal circumstances, Menendez would have relished the limelight that came with the Foreign Relations chairmanship, in order to detail his agenda on such issues. But, as Menendez was poised to take over the committee, news outlets reported in early 2013 that he had possibly violated Senate rules by accepting two round-trip flights to the Dominican Republic in 2010 from Melgen, whose Florida medical offices had been raided by the FBI. After a New Jersey Republican lawmaker filed a complaint with the Senate Ethics Committee, Menendez paid the estimated $58,500 cost of the flights and related expenses. He explained that the issue "unfortunately fell through the cracks."

Later news accounts said the senator's staff had thwarted U.S. donations of cargo-screening equipment to the Dominican government because the equipment could have jeopardized a port security contract benefiting Melgen. In addition, *The Washington Post* reported that Menendez spoke with top federal health officials in 2009 and 2012 about a finding that Melgen had overbilled Medicare by almost $9 million. The paper later reported that a federal grand jury in Miami was investigating the senator's dealings with Melgen. At the same time, conservative news websites trumpeted allegations, from an anonymous tipster, that Menendez had hired prostitutes in the Dominican Republic. The FBI said it could not substantiate the allegations, and Dominican police later said an attorney there paid three women to make up the stories.

The senator denied any wrongdoing, and later blamed the Castro government for orchestrating a smear campaign. However, both *The New York Times* and *The Star-Ledger* of Newark called for Menendez to relinquish his Foreign Relations chairmanship while the Ethics Committee addressed his dealings with Melgen, although the senator refused to do so. When he was indicted by the Justice Department two years later, some supporters in the New Jersey Cuban-American community suggested it was payback by the Obama administration for Menendez's hardline stances on Cuba and Iran—although Menendez himself publicly disavowed such suggestions.

Before claiming the Foreign Relations gavel, Menendez had spent his Senate career at the center of several major issues, notably immigration. He took part in bipartisan discussions on a comprehensive immigration bill, but walked out of the talks in May 2007, complaining that Massachusetts Democratic Sen. Edward Kennedy had made too many concessions to Republicans and that the bill would "tear at the fabric of family reunification." After that bill died, he defended tax rebates to illegal immigrants in the 2008 economic stimulus bill, and introduced comprehensive immigration legislation in September 2010. One of its components—the DREAM Act, offering children of illegal immigrants a path of citizenship in return for military service or college attendance—ran into Democratic as well as GOP opposition in the 2010 lame-duck session. But when immigration became a front-burner issue during the 2012 election season, Menendez was part of a bipartisan group of eight senators that secretly crafted a comprehensive reform proposal. Among the senators was Florida Republican Marco Rubio, another Cuban-American whom Menendez had gotten to know when the two served as chairman and ranking member of Foreign Relations' subcommittee on Latin America.

Menendez won a coveted slot on the Finance Committee in 2009. In that role, he backed two attempts in the committee to add a government-run "public option" to the health insurance overhaul legislation, but both failed. His stance on that issue, as well as on immigration and other Democratic priorities, incensed New Jersey tea party activists, and in early 2010, they launched a recall effort. Menendez dismissed the recall as a "political stunt" and in April appealed to the state Supreme Court to stop their actions, calling them an "attack on the Constitution" because the document forbids the recall of a sitting U.S. senator. Seven months after hearing arguments, the state court issued a 4-2 decision agreeing with him.

Menendez also raised his profile on energy and environment issues. When the Energy and Natural Resources Committee approved a bipartisan energy bill in 2009, Menendez refused to support it, saying its renewable energy mandate needed to be stronger and objecting to a provision allowing oil drilling within 45 miles of coastlines. A year later, following the BP oil spill disaster in the Gulf of Mexico, Menendez was a central figure on the contentious issue of liability caps on legal damages that companies would face for the BP and future spills. He introduced a bill to eliminate the $75 million cap, but the measure ran into strong opposition from Republicans as well as fellow oil-state Democrats. He tried in 2011 to eliminate $2 billion in tax breaks for the oil industry, which he said no longer needed them in light of massive profits. But his measure failed to clear the 60-vote procedural hurdle.

Menendez took over the chairmanship of the Democratic Senatorial Campaign Committee in the 2010 election cycle, giving him the fourth-ranking leadership position in the Senate Democratic majority. His low-key approach contrasted sharply with that of his frenetic and publicity-driven predecessor, New York Democrat Chuck Schumer. But the economic downturn and the public's discontent with the Democrats' health care bill worked heavily against him, and his party was shocked by Republican Scott Brown's upset win in Massachusetts in a January 2010 special election. An anonymous White House aide was quoted as blaming the loss on Menendez, adding to strains in the Obama-Menendez relationship.

Under Menendez, the DSCC outraised its Republican counterpart, $130 million to $115 million. Even though Democrats lost six Senate seats, many in the party were relieved the damage wasn't worse. Several vulnerable incumbents, including Majority Leader Harry Reid of Nevada and Colorado's Michael Bennet, hung on to win. And it marked the first time in 100 years that the party in power had held onto the Senate while losing control in the House. "The windstorm he was walking into, it wasn't just 30 miles per hour winds with gusts up to 40 miles per hour; it was a hurricane," Reid said of Menendez to *The Record* of Hackensack. Reid's victory was attributed partly to Hispanic voter turnout that Menendez helped to bolster.

Menendez declined to stay on as DSCC chairman for the 2012 cycle to concentrate on his own reelection. Republicans were targeting him, but finding a GOP candidate who could compete financially remained elusive. The task fell to state Sen. Joe Kyrillos, a good friend of Christie's whose best weapon became the governor accompanying him to campaign events. Kyrillos took in $4.6 million, but Menendez again demonstrated his fundraising prowess by bringing in more than $17 million. Menendez won, 59%-39%.

If Menendez's legal troubles force him from office before his term is up in 2018, a special election would be called to elect a successor. The potential field in such a race is currently unclear, particularly since an open gubernatorial contest in 2017 will attract prominent Democrats. Pallone, who has eyed a Senate seat for more than a decade, is now ranking Democrat on the powerful House Energy and Commerce Committee. But he could run in a special election without giving up his House seat. Other possible candidates on the Democratic side include former Rep. Rush Holt—who, like Pallone, ran unsuccessfully in the 2013 special primary won by now-Sen. Cory Booker—and state Sen. Richard Codey, who, as state Senate president, served two lengthy stints as acting governor. Torricelli, who has been in private business since leaving office in 2002 after being formally admonished by the Senate Ethics Committee over gifts he accepted, in mid-2015 gave an interview to *The Star Ledger* saying he would like to get back into politics. On Republican side, Kean and Kyrillos, Menendez's challengers in 2006 and 2012, respectively, are possibilities in a state that has not elected a GOP senator since 1972.

Democrats who express an interest in the seat ran the risk of offending the still influential Menendez, who continues to express confidence he will prevail in court, reassume his Foreign Relations Committee post, and remain New Jersey's senior senator for the foreseeable future. "Look, I have fought my entire life for what I believe in and for everything I have ever achieved—and most of the time, against some pretty tough odds," he told *The Washington Post* in June 2015. "So that's just who I am."

Junior Senator

Cory Booker (D)

Appointed Oct. 2013, term expires Jan. 2021, 1st full term; b. April 27, 1969, Washington, DC; Stanford U., B.A. 1991, M.A. 1992, Rhodes Scholar, U. of Oxford, 1994, Yale Law Schl., J.D. 1997; Baptist; single.

Elected Office: Newark City Cncl., 1998-2002; Newark mayor 2006-13.

Professional Career: Practicing atty.

DC Office: 59 DSOB, 20510, 202-224-3224; Fax: 202-224-8378; Website: booker.senate.gov.

State Offices: Camden, 856-338-8922; Newark, 973-639-8700.

Committees: *Commerce, Science, & Transportation:* Aviation Operations, Safety, & Security; Communications, Technology, Innovation & the Internet; Consumer Protection, Product Safety, Insurance, & Data Security; Oceans, Atmosphere, Fisheries, & Coast Guard (RMM); Space, Science, & Competitiveness; Surface Transportation & Merchant Marine Infrastructure, Safety & Security (RMM). *Environment & Public Works:* Fisheries, Water, & Wildlife; Superfund, Waste Mgmt., & Regulatory Oversight. *Homeland Security & Governmental Affairs:* Federal Spending Oversight & Emergency Mgmt.; Regulatory Affairs & Federal Mgmt. *Small Business & Entrepreneurship.*

Group Ratings

	ADA	ACLU	AFL-CIO	LCV	ITI	COC	HAFA	ACU	CFG	FRC
2014	90%	100%	–	80%	–	38%	0%	4%	17%	0%
2013	–	C	100%	–	C	–	C	0%	0%	C

Key Votes of the 113th Congress

1. Employee Non-Discrim'n Act	Y	5. Farm Bill Conference Rept.	N
2. Senate Vote on Judgeships	N	6. Unempl. Comp. Extension	Y
3. Defense Dept. Spending	Y	7. Keystone Pipeline	N
4. Bipartisan Budget Deal	Y		

Election Results

2014 general	Cory Booker (D) 1,043,866	(56%)	$16,871,163	$1,452,027	$534,109
	Jeff Bell (R) 791, 297	(42%)	$599,118	$86,711	
2014 primary	Cory Booker (D) ....unopposed				

Prior winning percentage: 2013 special (55%)

Even before he was sworn in as New Jersey's junior senator following an October 2013 special election, Cory Booker was a force in national Democratic politics. For the seven years prior to moving to Capitol Hill, the former Rhodes Scholar was the high-profile mayor of Newark, the state's largest municipality—and long a national poster child for the problems and challenges that confront urban America. ("Wherever the cities of America are going, Newark will get there first," one of Booker's mayoral predecessors, Kenneth Gibson, famously declared in the 1970s.) From his gritty political base, Booker built an impressive network of celebrity friends and acquaintances in the technology and entertainment sectors—contacts that yielded benefits to Newark and bountiful coverage of Booker in the national media. However, such star power at times has proven to be a double-edged sword: During both his mayoralty and his initial run for Senate, Booker often faced criticism for traveling the country to tend to his influential network, at the expense of dealing with the problems of his constituents back home.

Booker is not only New Jersey's first African-American senator; he is one of only five African-Americans elected to the Senate since Reconstruction, a group that also includes current Sen. Tim Scott, a South Carolina Republican, as well as former Illinois Sen. Barack Obama. (Two other African-Americans have been appointed to the Senate in recent years to fill unexpired terms, but did not stand for election.) Booker was born in Washington, D.C., but was raised in the affluent, predominantly white New York City suburb of Harrington

Park, New Jersey. It was less than a decade after the passage of the Civil Rights Act of 1964, and, according to Booker, housing rights activists helped the family buy their first home after they initially faced hurdles due to racial bias. His parents were IBM business executives active in the civil rights movement. Booker attended top schools, earning both a bachelor's and master's degree at Stanford University, where he played varsity football. He studied modern history at England's Oxford University as a Rhodes Scholar before attending Yale Law School, graduating in 1997.

A year later, in 1998, Booker ran successfully for the city council in Newark, about 25 miles to the south of where he had grown up. Booker made waves by moving into Brick Towers, one of the city's poorest and most violent housing projects, to call attention to the problems of drug-dealing and crime there, along with the lack of consistent utility service and a functioning elevator. He lived there until the Newark Housing Authority razed the building in 2006, the year he was elected mayor. He then bought a home in Newark's predominantly African-American Central Ward, where he now resides.

As a member of the city council, Booker recalls that he was regularly outvoted by margins of 8-1. In 2002, he challenged longtime Mayor Sharpe James, a fellow Democrat and also an African-American. On one level, it was a generational battle: The 33-year old Booker was half the age of his rival. The bitterly negative race increased tensions in the violence-prone city, and the federal government sent in observers on Election Day to prevent fraud. The campaign became the subject of a documentary film called *"Street Fight"* that portrayed Booker as an idealistic political newcomer taking on a ruthless establishment fighting to hang onto power. The film was nominated for an Oscar—and Booker, although defeated, was on his way to becoming a national political figure. After his narrow loss, 53%-47%, he practiced law and worked for nonprofit civic organizations, as he geared up for rematch against James in 2006. But, after serving five terms—and perhaps glimpsing what the future had in store for him—James declined to run again in 2006. He was indicted the following year on corruption charges. (When Booker was elected to the Senate, the city's newspaper, the *Star-Ledger*, wryly observed he deserved kudos for "being the first mayor in 45 years not to leave City Hall under the shadow of an indictment.")

Booker easily defeated a former James deputy with 72 percent of the vote, and his coattails helped to elect a slate of political allies to the city council. During the campaign, Booker promised nothing short of a renaissance of one of the most troubled cities in the United States. He succeeded on several fronts. The city achieved a balanced budget for the first time in a decade, opened new parks, and spent more money for mass transit. Two new office towers went up in the business district and a $150 million educational complex opened downtown. Booker raised $400 million for philanthropic efforts in the city, including $100 million for the public school system from a member of his celebrity network: Facebook co-founder Mark Zuckerberg. He persuaded electronics manufacturer Panasonic to relocate to Newark, and other companies opened offices. But the successes came with some noteworthy failures, topped by his inability to make a lasting dent in Newark's notorious crime problem. As Booker was poised to depart for Capitol Hill, a *Star-Ledger* story noted that the city had 83 homicides and about 2,850 other violent crimes in 2003 under James—as compared to 95 homicides and 3,220 violent crimes in 2012, the last full year of the Booker administration.

Still, Booker enjoyed approval ratings that routinely topped 60 percent, and he easily won re-election in 2010. His persona as the city's savior gained novel-like dimensions after she shoveled an elderly resident's walk when a city plow failed to show up, and when he rescued a neighbor from a burning house in April 2012. (Booker and his security detail got the woman out of the house before the fire department arrived, and Booker was treated for smoke inhalation.) Meanwhile, his national profile increased with positive coverage of Newark's accomplishments in the national media and his friendship with Obama as well as such entertainment luminaries as producer Jerry Weintraub, actors Ben Affleck and Matt Damon, and talk show impresario Oprah Winfrey. He was a featured speaker at the 2012 Democratic National Convention, where he drew large crowds.

But even some longtime political allies groused about the amount of time he spent on the road, while failing to follow up on important city projects. And Booker created a particularly embarrassing moment for Obama during the 2012 presidential campaign when, on a national news program, he criticized Democratic attacks on Republican opponent Mitt Romney's business dealings at Bain Capital as "crap" and "nauseating." Booker was less defending Romney than sticking up for the private equity industry, which is important to New Jersey. Still, he was roundly criticized within his party.

Booker was often mentioned as a possible candidate for higher office: The only question was when. In January 2013, he announced plans to seek the Senate seat held by Democrat Frank Lautenberg when it came open in 2014. The 89-year old Lautenberg had suffered from several health problems, and was seen as all but certain to retire. But, after a 30-year career on Capitol Hill, he bristled at what he regarded as a lack of deference by Booker, whom he publicly likened to a disrespectful child who needed to be spanked. While Lautenberg announced shortly thereafter that he would not seek reelection, Booker's eagerness created some political fallout when Lautenberg's death from viral pneumonia in June 2013 triggered a special election: Members of the Lautenberg family endorsed a Booker rival, Rep. Frank Pallone, in the Democratic primary. Alluding to the criticism occasionally aimed at Booker, the Lautenberg family issued a statement declaring, "Frank Pallone knows that gimmicks and celebrity status won't get you very far in the real battles that Democrats face in the future."

Republican Gov. Chris Christie appointed his attorney general, Jeffrey Chiesa, as a temporary senator, while scheduling an Oct. 13, 2013 special election to fill the seat. The special election could have as easily been held during New Jersey's regularly scheduled general election that November, at a savings to the state of $24 million. Politically, the move was viewed as Christie's way of avoiding having the popular Booker on the ballot when Christie himself was up for reelection. But first, Booker had to get through a relatively crowded August primary. Pallone, first elected to the House in 1988, had been eyeing a run for statewide office for a decade. He attracted labor backing, including from the state's teachers, who viewed Booker warily due to his backing of charter school expansion and an end to lifetime teacher tenure as Newark's chief executive. Also filing in the primary were Rep. Rush Holt, a former research physicist, and state Assembly Speaker Sheila Oliver.

With the aid of greater name recognition and a larger campaign treasury, Booker had little trouble winning the primary, garnering 59 percent—nearly three times the 20 percent captured by Pallone; Holt trailed with 17 percent, with Oliver at 4 percent. But Booker collected political dents along the way, notably a *New York Times* report disclosing that, while full-time mayor of a struggling city, he had founded an Internet start-up on the side—with money raised from friends such as Winfrey and Google executive Eric Schmidt. The site, Waywire, was designed to make it easier to collect and share Web videos. To put the controversy behind him, Booker stepped down from the company's board and donated his ownership interest to charity to "remove even the perception that the mayor's attention would be diverted from his job as senator or that he would stand to personally benefit in any way from his holdings in the company," a spokesman said.

Booker's general election opponent was Steve Lonegan, a former Republican mayor of Bogota, and state director of the tea party-affiliated Americans for Prosperity. Lonegan's right-wing profile made him a decided underdog in a state with 700,000 more registered Democrats than Republicans, and which had not elected a Republican to the Senate since 1972. Booker overwhelmed Lonegan in fundraising, taking in more than $11 million to $1.3 million for his opponent. But Lonegan managed to capitalize on Booker's vulnerabilities to make it a closer race than many had expected. He hammered at Newark's stubbornly high crime rate as well as Booker's ties to Obama, whose approval ratings in New Jersey were following a national downward trend. Lonegan also made some political headway with radio ads that highlighting Booker's post-primary trips to Los Angeles and Silicon Valley to raise money, as he sought to paint his rival as being more interested in boosting himself on a national stage than being around New Jersey voters.

Booker also created some problems on his own, with ill-conceived Twitter messages to a dancer at a strip club and questionable claims about his relationship with a drug dealer he called T-Bone, who turned out to be what Booker described as an "archetype" of Newark's many problems. But while Lonegan cut into Booker's lead in polls, the Democrat still pulled off a solid victory, 55%-44%.

Like other high-wattage figures who have been elected to the Senate—notably Democrat Bill Bradley, who in 1978 won the seat Booker now occupies following a professional basketball career—Booker initially sought to keep a low profile and focus on state-specific issues. "He represents a new type of Democrat—fiscally conservative, socially progressive," George Norcross, a southern New Jersey Democratic power broker who backed Booker in the primary, told the *Associated Press*. Striving to show his bipartisanship, he even sought to make friends with arch-conservative Texas Sen. Ted Cruz, meeting him for a three-hour dinner that Booker later described to a local Fox News station as "one of the best constitutional law discussions since I got out of law school." He joined with another tea party standard-bearer, Kentucky Sen. Rand Paul, on a bill to overhaul the criminal justice system, in part by encouraging states to change policies to steer children away from being tried as adults. As Booker later declared in a tweet: "I did not to go to Washington to be New Jersey's Democratic Senator, I went to be New Jersey's Senator."

In early 2015, Paul and Booker joined forces on another bill—this one designed to remove the threat of federal prosecution against patients who use medical marijuana in states where it is legal. The Booker-Paul relationship appears to have developed after a rocky start. Paul traveled to New Jersey to campaign for Lonegan in 2013, jabbing at Booker as having "an imaginary friend with imaginary problems"—an allusion to the T-Bone controversy. "If Cory will introduce me to T-Bone when I get there, I'd love to meet T-Bone. If T-Bone's not real, maybe we need to get Mr. Booker to talk about real problems," Paul told *Politico* in an interview. But Booker told ABC News in mid-2014 that the two had bonded via Twitter once Booker arrived in the Senate. The apparent starting point of their bond: an affinity for Festivus, the made-up holiday popularized on TV's long-running "Seinfeld." If Booker gave up his stake in an Internet start-up before winning the Senate seat, he has hardly given up his interest in social media. In the latest annual *Washingtonian* magazine survey of congressional staffers, Booker, who has more than 1.5 million Twitter followers, ranked No. 2 in the category of Senate tweet master.

Booker ran for a full term in 2014 against another Republican conservative: Jeffrey Bell, who won the GOP nomination with 30 percent of the vote in a five-way field. In 1978, when Booker was still in elementary school, Bell defeated moderate Republican Sen. Clifford Case in the primary, and then lost the general election to Democrat Bradley. For most of the intervening one-third of a century, Bell had lived in Virginia and worked as a public affairs consultant, returning to New Jersey at age 70 to take on Booker. Having virtually no money, Bell ran an unconventional populist campaign centered on monetary policy, in which he blamed a weak dollar for the problems afflicting middle-class families. Most polls gave Booker a double-digit lead, until a CBS News/*New York Times* poll in August raised eyebrows when it showed Bell trailing by just 7 points. Booker went on the attack, tearing into Bell for his support for returning to the gold standard, which he said would "go back to voodoo economics." And he contrasted his efforts at bipartisanship by noting Bell once wrote a book called *The Case for Polarized Politics*. Booker ended up winning by 56%-42%, similar to his margin a year earlier.

Just 44 years old when elected to the Senate, Booker immediately faced speculation about his future beyond Capitol Hill—similar to the speculation that accompanied Obama's arrival in Washington a decade earlier. Following the 2013 special election, Booker told reporters that he "absolutely... unequivocally" was not interested in running for president or vice president in 2016. Asked again after his 2014 election to a full term, he replied, "I'm focused on being New Jersey's United States senator for the next six years." When one reporter noted the statement was a shift in tone from what he said a year earlier, Booker picked up the reporter's voice recorder and spoke directly into it. "Absolutely, unequivocally not," he declared.

FIRST DISTRICT

Donald Norcross (D)

Elected 2014, 1st full term; b. Dec. 13, 1958, Camden; Camden Cnty. Col., A.S. 1979; Lutheran; married (Andrea); 3 children.

Elected Office: NJ Assembly, 2010; NJ Senate, 2010-14.

Professional Career: Electrician; Asst. business mgr., Local 351, Int'l Brotherhood of Electrical Workers; Pres., Southern NJ AFL-CIO.

DC Office: 1531 LHOB, 20515, 202-225-6501; Fax: 202-225-5683; Website: norcross.house.gov.

State Offices: Cherry Hill, 856-427-7000.

Committees: *Armed Services:* Emerging Threats & Capabilities; Tactical Air & Land Forces. *Budget.*

Election Results

2014 general	Donald Norcross (D) 93,315	(57%)	$2,075,838	$815,857
	Garry Cobb (R)........................... 64,073	(39%)	$108,464	$1,041
2014 primary	Donald Norcross (D) 18,504	(72%)		
	Frank Broomell, Jr. (D)................. 3,871	(15%)		
	Frank Minor (D) 3,303	(13%)		

Prior winning percentage: 2014 special (58%)

Population		Race and Ethnicity		Income	
Total:	730,895	White	65.7%	Median income:	$61,369
Urban:	19.7%	Black	15.4%		*(107 of 435)*
Suburban:	80.3%	Latino	11.6%	Under $50,000	41.4%
Rural:	0.0%	Asian	5.0%	$50,000-$99,999:	30.9%
Land area:	468	Two races	1.9%	$100,000-$199,999:	23.2%
Pop/sq. mi.:	1,562.8	White Ethnic	52.2%	$200,000 or more:	4.5%
Born in state:	55.3%			Poverty Rate	13.5%
		Education			
Age Groups		H.S. grad or less:	44.6%	**Work**	
Under 18:	23.1%	Some college:	26.9%	White collar:	37.3%
18 to 34:	22.6%	College degree, 4 yr.:	18.6%	Blue collar:	44.5%
35 to 64:	40.2%	Post-grad study:	9.9%	Sales and service:	18.2%
Over 64:	14.1%				
		Military		Govt. workers:	13.7%
		Veterans/active duty:	7.0%		

Philadelphia suburbs: Camden and Gloucester counties

The closely built streets of Camden, across the Delaware River from Philadelphia, have seen a fair amount of history. This was where the poet Walt Whitman lived when he wrote some of the versions of his *Leaves of Grass*. It was an immigrant-jammed industrial city then, with tinkerers and

Voter Turnout	
2013 Total Citizen 18+	534,198
2014 House Turnout	162,492
2014 Turnout as % CVAP	30.4%
2012 Turnout as % CVAP	60.5%

inventors. In 1894, a Camden machinist named Eldridge Johnson produced the Victor Talking Machine, the birth of the recorded music industry and a company that became RCA Victor in 1929. A few years later, the new Campbell Soup Co. began producing condensed soups. Camden remained for years a major industrial locus on the New Jersey side of the Delaware River, not the broadest and certainly not the most picturesque of Atlantic estuaries, but probably the East Coast's premier industrial waterway, with a concentration of steel mills, chemical plants, and oil tank farms equal to any in the country. The flatlands all around, mostly ignored in the 19th century, had easy access to cheap water transportation and plenty of skilled labor from the Philadelphia area. For a quarter-century starting in the 1940s, this was one of the country's fastest-growing industrial areas.

In the 1980s and 1990s, Camden emptied out. Many of its factories had closed, and fewer than 10,000 manufacturing jobs remained. Its neighborhoods were beset by crime, its mostly minority residents were heavily dependent on public assistance, and its mayor was convicted of doing favors for Philadelphia's organized crime leaders. Camden continues to struggle. Census figures released in 2012 showed Camden with a poverty rate of 42%, the highest in the nation. Its average household income of $26,000 compares to $71,000 for the state. From 2002 to 2010, the state controlled its finances and government. In 2011, the mayor laid off almost half of the police department, citing a $26.5 million deficit. The following year, a new county force took over police functions for the city. According to FBI data, Camden had the highest crime rate in the nation in 2012. Gov. Chris Christie and local officials cite a dramatic drop in violent crime since then, though it remains high.

Camden has had some recent bright spots: a redeveloped riverfront park, the New Jersey aquarium, and a state-of-the-art amphitheater. Campbell in 2010 opened an addition to its world headquarters, and in 2012, Rowan University opened a $139 million medical school in the city, the first new medical college in New Jersey in 35 years. The port of Camden rebounded from the recession, spurred by Del Monte's large fruit-processing plant and increased steel imports. In December 2014, *The New York Times* reported an "economic revival" from six major commercial development projects in the past six months, with companies such as Lockheed Martin and Subaru taking advantage of state tax incentives, plus a resurgence in housing for the growing medical community.

2012 Presidential Vote		
Barack Obama (D)	212,236	(66%)
Mitt Romney (R)	110,377	(34%)
2008 Presidential Vote		
Barack Obama (D)	219,570	(65%)
John McCain (R)	116,187	(34%)
Cook Partisan Voting Index:	D+13	

The 1st Congressional District is greater Camden, the Delaware riverfront from Palmyra south to a point across from the Delaware state line. The district is traversed by Black Horse Pike and White Horse Pike, which connect Philadelphia to its South Jersey suburbs. Many of the nearby boroughs and townships developed over the past half-century as a result of flight from Camden. Haddonfield, an old-fashioned community filled with galleries and shops, was once described by *The Philadelphia Inquirer* as "a Norman Rockwell picture come to life." The district includes a growing number of Hispanics, who make up 47 percent of Camden's population. Democratic-leaning Cherry Hill is more affluent. Politically, the district remains safe for Democrats. This is the only Democratic-held seat in New Jersey that does not reach into the New York City suburbs.

Donald Norcross (D)

Democrat Donald Norcross, who was first elected in November 2014, defeated his Republican opponent, former Philadelphia Eagles linebacker Garry Cobb. The brother of South Jersey's chief political boss, Norcross succeeded Democratic Rep. Robert Andrews, who resigned earlier in the year. He gave every reason to expect that he will be a reliable ally of Democratic leaders and organized labor.

Norcross graduated from Camden County College. He started his career as an electrician, who installed power lines in refineries and on the top of bridges. Later, he became a business manager for the International Brotherhood of Electrical Workers, and president of the Southern New Jersey AFL-CIO. Norcross jumped into politics in 2009, when he won election to the state Assembly. A year later, he was appointed to fill a state Senate seat. He was a leading backer of the state's constitutional amendment to raise the minimum wage as well as a bill providing tax incentives to businesses that operate in hard-hit areas. On some social issues—notably charter schools—Norcross has staked out more centrist positions.

Norcross got his opening when Andrews announced his resignation to take a job at a Philadelphia law firm. At the time, Andrews was facing an ethics probe into alleged misuse of campaign funds. Under congressional rules, such inquiries must end when a member retires. Andrews denied any connection between the probe and the decision to step away from his seniority and influence. Instead, he cited the need to provide for his children's education.

Norcross was primed to run from the start. With Andrews' backing, he lined up endorsements from key Democrats across South Jersey. Not only was he the favored Democrat in a blue district, but his brother, George Norcross III, has been a longtime power broker in the state and owned a majority stake in *The Philadelphia Inquirer*. (George Norcross divested his interest in the newspaper soon after his brother's campaign began.) Norcross's two primary opponents, Frank Minor and Frank Broomell, tried to play up his entrenched political ties as a liability. But he handily defeated them with 72% of the primary vote.

Republican Cobb, a local talk-radio personality, faced an uphill battle in a district where President Barack Obama won 66% of the vote in 2012. He emphasized that he was an outsider from the "Norcross machine" and that he wanted to clean up politics in South Jersey, but he was outspent $2.1 million to $108,000. Norcross won with a comfortable, though less than overwhelming, 57%-39%. He also won a special election the same day and filled the remaining seven weeks of his predecessor's term.

Norcross got plum seats on the Armed Services and Budget committees. He pledged support for the military installations based in New Jersey. His initial votes included approval of the Keystone XL pipeline, which has been strongly backed by many labor unions but opposed by most Democrats. The first bill he filed, the Toxics by Rail Accountability and Community Knowledge (TRACK) Act, would improve safety measures for rail shipments of hazardous materials, and was based on recommendations that followed a 2012 train derailment in Paulsboro. "I was an electrician for many, many years, and understanding some of the complex issues in trying to get the economy growing is something I deal with every day," Norcross said upon taking office. He was named the freshman representative on the House Democratic Steering and Policy Committee.

SECOND DISTRICT

Frank LoBiondo (R)

Elected 1994, 11th term; b. May 12, 1946, Bridgeton; St. Joseph's U., B.A. 1968; Catholic; married (Tina); 2 children.

Elected Office: Cumberland Cnty. Bd. of Chosen Freeholders, 1985-87; NJ Assembly, 1988-94.

Professional Career: Operations mgr., LoBiondo Bros. Motor Express Inc., 1968-94.

DC Office: 2427 RHOB, 20515, 202-225-6572; Fax: 202-225-3318; Website: lobiondo.house.gov.

State Offices: Mays Landing, 609-625-5008 or 800-471-4450.

Committees: *Armed Services:* Readiness; Tactical Air & Land Forces. *Intelligence (Select)* CIA (Chmn); Emerging Threats. *Transportation & Infrastructure:* Aviation (Chmn); Coast Guard & Maritime Transportation; Highways & Transit.

Group Ratings

	ADA	ACLU	AFL-CIO	LCV	ITI	COC	HAFA	ACU	CFG	FRC
2014	25%	5%	–	37%	80%	93%	42%	40%	29%	50%
2013	20%	C	62%	25%	C	100%	C	44%	57%	C

National Journal Ratings

	2013 LIB	—	2013 CONS
Economic	53%	—	47%
Social	51%	—	48%
Foreign	41%	—	57%
Composite	49%	—	51%

Key Votes of the 113th Congress

1. Sandy storm spending	Y	5. Medical Marijuana	Y	9. Syrian Rebels Training	Y
2. Violence Against Women Act	Y	6. Farm Bill		10. Keystone pipeline	Y
3. Guantanamo Bay Detainees	N	7. Afghanistan Combat	N	11. Immigration Exec. Action	Y
4. Abortion 20-week ban	Y	8. NSA Phone Data Collection	N	12. Bipartisan budget deal	Y

Election Results

2014 general	Frank LoBiondo (R)	108,875	(62%)	$2,425,940	$187,558	$11,100
	Bill Hughes, Jr. (D)	66,026	(37%)	$756,354		
2014 primary	Frank LoBiondo (R)	14,294	(83%)			
	Mike Assad (R)	3,037	(18%)			

Prior winning percentages: 2012 (58%), 2010 (65%), 2008 (59%), 2006 (62%), 2004 (65%), 2002 (69%), 2000 (66%), 1998 (66%), 1996 (60%), 1994 (65%)

Population		Race and Ethnicity		Income	
Total:	732,764	White	67.0%	Median income:	$56,532
Urban:	25.9%	Latino	15.0%		*(155 of 435)*
Suburban:	72.1%	Black	12.6%	Under $50,000	44.5%
Rural:	2.0%	Asian	3.6%	$50,000-$99,999:	31.0%
Land area:	1,704	Two races	1.3%	$100,000-$199,999:	20.1%
Pop/sq. mi.:	429.9	White Ethnic	49.6%	$200,000 or more:	4.4%
Born in state:	59.7%			Poverty Rate	15.6%
		Education			
Age Groups		H.S. grad or less:	50.4%	**Work**	
Under 18:	22.1%	Some college:	25.5%	White collar:	31.8%
18 to 34:	20.9%	College degree, 4 yr.:	16.4%	Blue collar:	48.3%
35 to 64:	40.7%	Post-grad study:	7.7%	Sales and service:	19.9%
Over 64:	16.3%				
		Military		Govt. workers:	17.1%
		Veterans/active duty:	8.4%		

South Jersey: Atlantic City, Philadelphia exurbs

The builders of the Camden & Atlantic Railroad in 1852 may not have known it, but when they extended their line to the little inlet town of Absecon, they were launching one of America's first beach resorts, Atlantic City. Like all resorts,

Voter Turnout	
2013 Total Citizen 18+	536,691
2014 House Turnout	177,148
2014 Turnout as % CVAP	33.0%
2012 Turnout as % CVAP	58.3%

it was a product of developments elsewhere—of industrialization and spreading affluence. In the years after the Civil War, Atlantic City and the Jersey Shore, from Brigantine to Cape May, became a seaside resort, and Atlantic City developed its characteristic features: the boardwalk in 1870, the amusement pier in 1882, the rolling chair in 1884, salt water taffy in the 1890s, and the Miss America pageant in 1921. In the book *Boardwalk Empire*, author Nelson Johnson argues that in order to attract tourists, a powerful alliance of local politicians and racketeers allowed gambling, prostitution and Sunday liquor laws to be flouted. "Nothing could interfere with the visitors' fun or they might stop coming," he writes. But a long period of decline came after World War II, and by the early 1970s Atlantic City was grim, featuring a bedraggled convention hall (site of the 1964 Democratic National Convention), empty hotels and bleak streets.

Then in 1977, New Jersey voters legalized casino gambling in Atlantic City, and gleaming new hotels sprang up, big-name entertainers came in, and the resort became more stylish than it had been in 90 years. But it hasn't been that way for everyone: Casino and hotel jobs tend to be low-wage, and decrepit neighborhoods begin just feet from the casinos' massive parking lots. For years, its dozen casinos had net annual revenues nearly as high as Las Vegas' casinos. Then, the recession hit the entertainment sector hard. From 2006 to 2012, the city's casino

2012 Presidential Vote		
Barack Obama (D)	166,908	(54%)
Mitt Romney (R)	141,480	(46%)
2008 Presidential Vote		
Barack Obama (D)	174,413	(53%)
John McCain (R)	148,485	(45%)
Cook Partisan Voting Index:	D+1	

revenues dropped 41 percent, to about $3 billion. Employment in the industry during that period plummeted from 50,000 to 33,000 jobs. The casinos also suffered from competition from slots parlors popping up in New York and Pennsylvania. To protect the region's economic engine, Republican Gov. Chris Christie in 2011 signed legislation easing regulatory oversight of the casinos, which angered watchdog groups that said it was unfair to single out gambling for special treatment. But four casinos closed in 2014 and others sought tax relief as gambling revenues continued to drop and the local economy struggled. In the first quarter of 2015, Atlantic County had the highest foreclosure rate of any metropolitan area in the nation.

Other beach resorts lie south of Atlantic City. There is the old Methodist town of Ocean City, where Gay Talese grew up the son of Italian immigrants, a story he told movingly in *Unto the Sons*. Commercial and residential properties in Ocean City and Sea Isle City suffered substantial damage from Hurricane Sandy in 2012. There is Wildwood, with its refurbished 1950s motels, and also Cape May, with its lovingly preserved Victorian houses. In 2015, Cape May was rated among the top 10 family beaches in the nation by a TripAdvisor site. West of the Jersey Shore are swamps and flatlands, the Pine Barrens and vegetable fields that gave New Jersey its "Garden State" nickname. Growth has been slow in these small towns and gas station intersections. The Northeast's high-tech and service economy boom has not reached this far south in Jersey.

The 2nd Congressional District covers the southern end of New Jersey. Politically, it has strong Democratic leanings in the chemical industry towns along the Delaware River and in Vineland and a strong Republican presence in Cape May County. Atlantic City often votes Democratic, but it has an antique Republican machine. The 2nd remains politically marginal, and is the least secure of the six Republican-held seats in the state.

Frank LoBiondo (R)

Republican Frank LoBiondo, first elected in 1994, is one of his party's most moderate members, especially on labor and environmental matters. "LoBo," as he is known to colleagues, keeps a low profile on Capitol Hill and has seemed content to climb the seniority ladder on the Transportation and Infrastructure Committee. But behind closed doors, he apparently speaks his mind.

LoBiondo grew up in Vineland, on the vegetable farm his grandparents established after leaving Sicily. His father started transporting his produce to market in a used truck, and as Atlantic City boomed in the early 20th century, he found that he could make a good living transporting the produce of other farmers as well. He created LoBiondo Brothers Motor Express, where his son worked when he was young. After getting his bachelor's degree in business administration from St. Joseph's University in Philadelphia, he joined the family business.

LoBiondo was first elected to public office in 1984 with the Cumberland County Board of Chosen Freeholders. In 1987, he was elected to the New Jersey Assembly; there, he stoutly opposed new taxes and gun control laws. He ran against veteran Rep. William Hughes, a Democrat, in 1992 and lost 56%-41%. After Hughes retired in 1994, LoBiondo ran again. In the primary, he competed with state Sen. William Gormley, whom LoBiondo portrayed as favoring tax increases and gun control. LoBiondo won 54%-35%, and easily won the general election, 65%-35%.

In the House, LoBiondo has retained his conservative stance on gun rights but has often bolted his party on other issues. In 2009, he was one of eight Republicans who joined Democrats on energy legislation creating a "cap and trade" system on greenhouse-gas emissions. He also backed an expansion of the Children's Health Insurance Program, and food safety legislation. He cosponsored the so-called "card check" bill aimed at making it easier to organize work sites by eliminating the secret ballot in union elections. In 2008, LoBiondo voted against the bailout of the financial markets because, he said, taxpayers were not sufficiently protected.

LoBiondo was among the New Jersey lawmakers incensed at Speaker John Boehner in January 2013 for initially delaying a vote on disaster relief following Hurricane Sandy. New Jersey news outlets reported that the two men got into an angry confrontation. "I've never been this angry. ... This could have been a poster child for bipartisanship; instead, this is what we have," LoBiondo told the website *PolitickerNJ*. He also took to the House floor to blast colleagues from disaster-prone areas for failing to be supportive. "Shame on you!" he said. "What does the misery index have to get to for our constituents?" In April 2015, he was one of only 14 House Republicans—and the only one from New Jersey—who voted against the final version of the GOP's budget plan for the next year. With Democratic Rep. Frank Pallone of New Jersey, he was the senior co-chairman of the newly created bipartisan Congressional Coastal Communities Caucus.

In 2013, LoBiondo took over as chairman of Transportation and Infrastructure Subcommittee on Aviation. That gave him an opportunity to help the William J. Hughes Technical Center near Atlantic City, the Federal Aviation Administration's national scientific testing base. "I've said repeatedly that our tech center is a premier site ... and for whatever reason, they've been under-recognized and under-appreciated," he told *The Press of Atlantic City*. He also faced the task of implementing the FAA's Next Generation Air Transportation System, commonly known as NextGen. It covers several initiatives aimed at making air travel more efficient as it moves from a radar-based to a satellite-based system. LoBiondo opposes oil drilling within 125 miles of the Jersey coast, and helped to enact the Delaware River Protection Act, increasing the liability for single-hull oil tankers that pollute.

On the Armed Services Committee, LoBiondo expressed reservations about the Iraq war, but he opposed efforts to set a timetable for troop withdrawals. He opposed trying terrorists in civilian courts, and lamented that homeland security has become "lost in the mix" of debates during the Obama administration. In 2013, he joined the Select Intelligence Committee, where he has concentrated on North Africa, considered a growing hotspot for terrorist activity. In 2015, he became chairman of the subcommittee with oversight of the CIA.

When he was first elected, LoBiondo promised to serve no more than 12 years, but has since broken that pledge. Still, he routinely wins reelection by comfortable margins. In 2014, he faced William Hughes Jr., a lawyer with an Atlantic City law firm and the son of the congressman to whom he initially lost. His $2.4 million more than tripled the spending of Hughes, who had little party assistance. What had been viewed as potentially a close contest turned out to be a surprisingly easy victory for the incumbent, 61%-37%. LoBiondo remains a good fit for his district. But local Democrats contend that state senator Jeff Van Drew would give him a serious challenge.

THIRD DISTRICT

Tom MacArthur (R)

Elected 2014, 1st term; b. Oct. 16, 1960, Hebron, CT; Hofstra U., B.A. 1982; Episcopalian; married (Debbie); 3 children (1 deceased).

Elected Office: Randolph City Cncl., 2011-13; deputy mayor, Randolph, 2012; Randolph mayor, 2013-14.

Professional Career: Insurance adjuster; Chmn & CEO, York Risk Services Group, 1999-2010.

DC Office: 506 CHOB, 20515, 202-225-4765; Fax: 202-225-0778; Website: macarthur.house.gov.

State Offices: Marlton, 856-267-5182; Toms River, 732-569-6495.

Committees: *Armed Services:* Military Personnel (VChmn); Tactical Air & Land Forces. *Natural Resources:* Federal Lands; Water, Power & Oceans.

Election Results

2014 general	Tom MacArthur (R)	100,471	(54%)	$5,648,742	$72,138	$1,771,677
	Aimee Belgard (D)	82,537	(44%)	$1,773,981	$87,532	$1,495,517
2014 primary	Tom MacArthur (R)	15,908	(60%)			
	Steve Lonegan (R)	10,643	(40%)			

Population		Race and Ethnicity		Income	
Total:	742,640	White	76.3%	Median income:	$72,798
Urban:	5.5%	Black	10.4%		*(55 of 435)*
Suburban:	94.4%	Latino	7.5%	Under $50,000	32.2%
Rural:	0.2%	Asian	3.4%	$50,000-$99,999:	34.2%
Land area:	778	Two races	2.0%	$100,000-$199,999:	26.8%
Pop/sq. mi.:	954.4	White Ethnic	61.0%	$200,000 or more:	6.8%
Born in state:	61.0%			Poverty Rate	5.4%
		Education			
Age Groups		H.S. grad or less:	41.5%	**Work**	
Under 18:	21.6%	Some college:	27.4%	White collar:	39.2%
18 to 34:	18.8%	College degree, 4 yr.:	20.4%	Blue collar:	43.7%
35 to 64:	41.5%	Post-grad study:	10.8%	Sales and service:	17.2%
Over 64:	18.0%			Govt. workers:	19.0%
		Military			
		Veterans/active duty:	10.3%		

South Central New Jersey

The Pine Barrens of New Jersey is one of the last
vacant spots on the eastern seaboard—not quite
terra incognita, but still not thickly populated.
Encroached on by the Philadelphia suburbs of
South Jersey on the west and burgeoning retirement developments of the Jersey Shore on the

Voter Turnout	
2013 Total Citizen 18+	564,131
2014 House Turnout	186,103
2014 Turnout as % CVAP	33%
2012 Turnout as % CVAP	61.2%

east, the 1 million acres of heavy forest and white sand, with their unusual plant life, are
crossed mostly by narrow two-lane roads. For years, the Pine Barrens was seen as a barrier to development. Only recently have environment-minded Jerseyites come to see the
relatively unspoiled area as a natural treasure. There are only a few small towns here, plus
Joint Base McGuire-Dix-Lakehurst, the giant amalgamation of an Air Force base, Army
military reservation, and Navy air station. The Joint Base was a finalist to host Boeing's
KC-46A air-refueling tankers in 2017. But some military analysts have contended that it is
in jeopardy of a shutdown before then, if Pentagon budget cuts continue, especially with the
base's older-model KC-10 refueling planes. Fort Dix had been a major training site for troops
heading to Afghanistan and Iraq. In November 2014, Lockheed Martin, a big employer with
its naval electronics and surveillance system plant, opened in Moorestown the Surface Navy
Innovation Center to develop new technologies.

East of the Pine Barrens is Ocean County, including the barrier islands from Mantolok-
ing south to Stafford, with older communities on the beachfront and larger clusters of new
subdivisions and condominiums inland. Here you can find the house in Seaside Heights
where several seasons of MTV's *Jersey Shore* were set. Ocean County has been the fastest-
growing part of New Jersey, a kind of Frost Belt Florida, with many retirees from New
York and North Jersey eager to leave urban
crime and high taxes. But it hasn't been
all paradise lately; Hurricane Sandy in
2012 damaged more than 40,000 buildings
in the county, its 20-foot waves smashing
boardwalks and flooding dunes. In Seaside Heights, a partially submerged roller
coaster off shore became a visual symbol of
the storm's intensity. In January 2013, the

2012 Presidential Vote
Barack Obama (D) 179,028   (52%)
Mitt Romney (R)................163,204   (48%)

2008 Presidential Vote
Barack Obama (D) 188,563   (51%)
John McCain (R)................176,237   (48%)

Cook Partisan Voting Index: R+1

federal government announced $348 million in emergency aid to Jersey communities; the
largest sum of $157 million went to Ocean County.

The 3rd Congressional District of New Jersey spans the Pine Barrens and thousands of
acres of farmland. It includes large parts of Burlington and Ocean counties. About 60% of
the population resides in Burlington. The largest city in the district is Toms River, which had
been home to a Ciba-Geigy Chemical plant before it closed while settling a $13.7 million law-
suit in 2001 without admitting responsibility for the air and water pollution that residents
claimed caused cancer. The district includes several suburban Philadelphia townships. This
is comfortable, but not affluent, suburban territory. President Barack Obama got 51% of the
vote in 2008, and 52% in 2012. This is likely to remain a swing district.

Tom MacArthur (R)

Tom MacArthur didn't shy away from a fight—or a lawsuit—as he battled his way through
a nasty primary and an equally bitter general election in 2014 to win the seat opened by the
retirement of Republican Jon Runyan. MacArthur's defeat of Democrat Aimee Belgard, a
Burlington County freeholder, marked the first time since the 1930s that a Republican has
replaced another Republican in the 3rd District.

MacArthur grew up in Hebron, Conn., and lives in Toms River, N.J., with other homes
in Randolph and Barnegat Light. He earned his bachelor's degree from Hofstra University,
spent 28 years working in the insurance industry, including 11 years as chairman and CEO
of York Risk Services Group. In 2011, he became a Randolph Township councilman, and was
deputy mayor and mayor of Randolph. He lived 90 miles away in Morris County before his
campaign in the south Jersey district.

MacArthur and his wife, Debbie, created and funded the St. Peter's Sandy Relief Fund to help victims of Superstorm Sandy. MacArthur's foundation, In God's Hands Charitable Foundation, has distributed 1,600 wheelchairs worldwide, the campaign said, in honor of the couple's special-needs daughter Grace, who died at age 11.

Both the primary and general campaigns were divisive, and in both cases MacArthur pushed back with a lawsuit or the threat of one. In the primary, MacArthur faced Steven Lonegan, a former Bogota mayor and conservative activist who in October 2013 lost the special-election Senate race to Democrat Cory Booker. Lonegan accused MacArthur's insurance firms of underpaying or denying payment to wildfire victims in California. MacArthur's campaign responded that the few claims were not only dismissed, but settled after MacArthur left the company. MacArthur sued the Lonegan campaign, naming the tea party-backed former mayor as well as six members of his staff for defamation. MacArthur was endorsed by the GOP organization in each county and took the primary, 60%-40%, with similar margins in both counties.

In the general election, MacArthur styled himself as a self-made businessman focused on job creation. He earned endorsements from both the United Brotherhood of Carpenters and the Laborers' International Union of North America. He favored replacing the Affordable Care Act with a system that limits malpractice suits and might provide an insurer of last resort for people without coverage.

MacArthur criticized Belgard (a lawyer who also had worked in the insurance industry) for failing to denounce an ad that MacArthur claimed was untrue. The Democratic Congressional Campaign Committee ad featured a firefighter who accused MacArthur's insurance company of denying injury claims from firefighters. MacArthur threatened to sue, noting he had sold the company a year before the claims mentioned in the ad, and the DCCC pulled the spot. MacArthur spent $5.6 million in the overall campaign, of which $5 million was a loan from himself, compared with $1.8 million for Belgard. The two candidates benefited from more than $3 million in additional spending by national party and interest groups. MacArthur won by an unexpectedly comfortable margin, 54%-44%. Belgard led by a few hundred votes in Burlington County, which was her base. MacArthur took a huge 63% in Ocean.

MacArthur was assigned to the Armed Services and Natural Resources committees, both good fits for his district. He had several early meetings at Joint Base McGuire and with Pentagon officials, in attempts to show his support and to understand its status and the risk of a potential shutdown. He attacked "outrageous" maneuvering by the Obama administration to seek ways to shut down military facilities if Congress did not agree to a base-closing review. "Shuttering our military installations devastates local economies and harms tight-knit communities, and I won't let that happen in South Jersey," MacArthur warned.

FOURTH DISTRICT

Chris Smith (R)

Elected 1980, 18th term; b. March 4, 1953, Rahway; Trenton St. Col., B.S. 1975; Catholic; married (Marie); 4 children.

Professional Career: Sales exec., family-owned sporting goods business, 1975-80; Exec. dir., NJ Right to Life, 1976-78.

DC Office: 2373 RHOB, 20515, 202-225-3765; Fax: 202-225-7768; Website: chrissmith.house.gov.

State Offices: Freehold, 732-780-3035; Hamilton, 609-585-7878; Plumstead, 609-286-2571.

Committees: *Foreign Affairs:* Africa, Global Health, Global Human Rights & Int'l Organizations (Chmn); Western Hemisphere.

Group Ratings

	ADA	ACLU	AFL-CIO	LCV	ITI	COC	HAFA	ACU	CFG	FRC
2014	10%	0%	–	29%	100%	79%	43%	56%	26%	100%
2013	20%	C	48%	29%	C	92%	C	54%	55%	C

National Journal Ratings

	2013 LIB	—	2013 CONS
Economic	53%	—	46%
Social	50%	—	50%
Foreign	44%	—	54%
Composite	50%	—	51%

Key Votes of the 113th Congress

1. Sandy storm spending	Y	5. Medical Marijuana	N	9. Syrian Rebels Training	N
2. Violence Against Women Act	N	6. Farm Bill	N	10. Keystone pipeline	Y
3. Guantanamo Bay Detainees	N	7. Afghanistan Combat	N	11. Immigration Exec. Action	Y
4. Abortion 20-week ban	Y	8. NSA Phone Data Collection	Y	12. Bipartisan budget deal	Y

Election Results

2014 general	Chris Smith (R)......................... 118,826	(68%)	$459,641	$1,349
	Ruben Scolavino (D) 54,415	(31%)	$8,038	
2014 primary	Chris Smith (R).....................unopposed			

Prior winning percentages: 2012 (64%), 2010 (69%), 2008 (66%), 2006 (66%), 2004 (67%), 2002 (66%), 2000 (63%), 1998 (62%), 1996 (64%), 1994 (68%), 1992 (62%), 1990 (63%), 1988 (66%), 1986 (61%), 1984 (61%), 1982 (53%), 1980 (57%)

Population		Race and Ethnicity		Income	
Total:	735,064	White	78.7%	Median income:	$73,710
Urban:	20.6%	Latino	9.3%		*(50 of 435)*
Suburban:	79.4%	Black	6.3%	Under $50,000	35.2%
Rural:	0.0%	Asian	4.0%	$50,000-$99,999:	28.1%
Land area:	531	Two races	1.4%	$100,000-$199,999:	26.8%
Pop/sq. mi.:	1,384.2	White Ethnic	61.5%	$200,000 or more:	9.9%
Born in state:	59.4%			Poverty Rate	9.6%
		Education			
Age Groups		H.S. grad or less:	37.8%	**Work**	
Under 18:	24.3%	Some college:	24.8%	White collar:	40.4%
18 to 34:	18.6%	College degree, 4 yr.:	23.5%	Blue collar:	43.5%
35 to 64:	39.2%	Post-grad study:	13.9%	Sales and service:	16.1%
Over 64:	18.0%			Govt. workers:	15.0%
		Military			
		Veterans/active duty:	7.5%		

Central New Jersey: Monmouth and Ocean Counties

Voter Turnout	
2013 Total Citizen 18+	518,547
2014 House Turnout	174,849
2014 Turnout as % CVAP	33.7%
2012 Turnout as % CVAP	63.6%

An invisible and not-well-defined line divides North Jersey and South Jersey. North of the line, people watch New York television stations, eat hero sandwiches, and root for the Yankees. South of the line, they watch Philadelphia television, eat hoagies, and root for the Phillies. The state capital of Trenton lies south of the line, which passes east somewhere around Six Flags Great Adventure in the Pine Barrens and heads southeast past Lakewood and Brick all the way to the Jersey Shore. But on both sides of the line, a stronger New Jersey identity has developed over the past two decades. The big cities—New York and Philadelphia—are not all that close, particularly when traffic is heavy, which is often. And the economy of central New Jersey has its own character, with big pharmaceutical companies and the consolidated Joint Base McGuire-Dix-Lakehurst. (The German zeppelin *Hindenburg* exploded while docking in 1937 at what was then called Lakehurst Naval Air Station.)

No less a true New Jersey persona than Bruce Springsteen was raised in Freehold Borough, the subject of his bleak portrayal in "My Hometown." Freehold Township, which grew 15 percent from 2000 to 2010, is now a city of 36,000. Nearby Ocean County was smashed by Hurricane Sandy in the fall of 2012; of the nearly 72,000 buildings damaged in the storm, more than half were in Ocean County. As of April 2015, the state housing agency had made $360 million in loan commitments for 18 affordable-housing projects in Ocean and Monmouth counties. Lakewood, the area's biggest town, is home to a large population of Orthodox Jews, and in 2011 it became a sister city of Bnei Brak, Israel. A sagging economy led to the creation of a Lakewood area "Tent City," filled with teepees and shanties for the homeless. In July 2014, it finally closed as county officials found temporary housing for those who remained and then destroyed the remaining structures. In May 2015, environmentalists sued Six Flags over its plan to level 90 acres of trees to support its planned solar-power facility.

2012 Presidential Vote		
Mitt Romney (R)	180,437	(55%)
Barack Obama (D)	148,621	(45%)
2008 Presidential Vote		
John McCain (R)	190,798	(54%)
Barack Obama (D)	160,955	(45%)
Cook Partisan Voting Index: R+7		

Fun fact: With more than 90,000 responses, the nj.com website in 2015 determined the boundary between North Jersey and South Jersey also included a swath called Central Jersey; its northern-most towns were Alexandria, Bridgewater, Edison and Hazlet, and its southern limits were Fort Dix, Lakehurst and Toms River.

The Fourth Congressional District of New Jersey is based in Monmouth County, which has about 55% of its population, with Mercer County and the fast-growing exurban Ocean County making up the rest. The district has become relatively safe for Republicans. Mitt Romney got 55% of the vote here in 2012, which was his best district in New Jersey.

Chris Smith (R)

Republican Chris Smith, first elected in 1980, combines outspoken opposition to abortion with an equally passionate commitment to human rights, whoever the perpetrator may be. Such independence does not always sit well with Republican leaders, but Smith's tenacity has made him one of the most successful legislators at guiding bills into law.

Smith grew up in the Trenton area, worked in his family's sporting goods business, and, after graduating from the College of New Jersey with a degree in business administration, he became executive director of the New Jersey Right to Life Committee in 1976. Four years later, he ran for the House in the Trenton-centered district and defeated 26-year Rep. Frank Thompson, a Democrat convicted in the Abscam bribery scandal. First elected at age 27, he has become the fourth most-senior Republican in the House.

He won passage of 30 bills from 1991 to 2008, the fifth-largest number for any member of Congress during that period. Even during the four years in which Democrats controlled the House from 2007 to 2010, Smith still managed to get 11 of his bills passed. Smith "has a gift for embracing issues that touch nerves and generate publicity," Bob Braun, a columnist for *The Star-Ledger* of Newark, once wrote. His recent successes include the Autism Collaboration, Accountability, Research and Education (CARES) Act of 2014, which provided $1.3 billion over five years for research into the causes of autism.

A devout Roman Catholic, Smith is best known for his unwavering fight against legalized abortion. He has worked to stop abortions in military hospitals, and he persuaded the George W. Bush administration to reinstate Reagan-era restrictions denying federal funds to family-planning organizations that promote abortions abroad. (In 2009, President Barack Obama rescinded the restrictions during his first week in office.) Smith was a prime mover of legislation to ban "partial birth" abortions. He has fought not only Democrats but also the House GOP leadership on the issue. In 2002, Smith rounded up like-minded Republicans to vote "no" on a major bankruptcy bill to protest a provision preventing abortion protestors from using bankruptcy to discharge civil disobedience fines. The abortion section was ultimately stripped out, and the bill passed the House.

After Republicans regained control of the House in 2011, Smith passed a bill taking away tax benefits from employee-sponsored health insurance plans that offer abortion coverage. Critics said his bill was a step toward outlawing abortions outright. He sought to add the word "forcible" to a long-standing exemption for rape, drawing angry criticism from abortion-rights advocates, who said the change could exclude statutory rape or rapes where the victim was drugged or unconscious. He later agreed to remove the word.

Smith has long crusaded for his Unborn Child Pain Awareness Act, which would require doctors to inform pregnant women that some experts say that a fetus can feel pain after 20 weeks of gestation. The House passed the bill in May 2015, after agreeing to limits to accommodate several House GOP women. He also has a bill to revoke the Food and Drug Administration's approval of the abortifacient RU-486, which Smith calls "baby pesticide." He has opposed federal funding for embryonic stem cell research, which uses excess embryos from in vitro fertilization, but he has been a champion of other stem cell research. In 2005, Congress enacted his Stem Cell Therapeutic and Research Act, which funds research and therapy using umbilical cord stem cells plus cells from bone marrow transplants. Disgusted by Obama's policies and appointments, Smith declared in January 2013 that Obama "is the abortion president."

Smith has brought his strong moral views to his work against human rights abuses abroad. He has sharply criticized China for its forced sterilizations and abortions, and its persecution of Christians and other religious minorities. As a result, he opposed normalizing trade relations with the country. Smith has condemned Russia for barring entry of foreign Catholic priests, and he criticized the Saudis for treating foreign servants as slaves. In 2000, Congress enacted his legislation to combat sex trafficking around the world, including requiring yearly reports on each nation's record. At one point, Smith learned of Ukrainian girls being held against their will in brothels in Montenegro; he personally called the country's prime minister, who ordered a raid on the operation.

He often has traveled great distances on behalf of his principles. On the eve of the Olympics in July 2008, Smith tried to meet human rights lawyers in Beijing, but they were placed under house arrest. He unsuccessfully urged President George W. Bush not to attend the Olympic opening ceremonies. In August 2008, he traveled to Tbilisi in the Georgia Republic and helped to rescue two young New Jersey girls who were at risk during the Russian invasion there. Less than a year later, he flew to Brazil to reunite a New Jersey man with his 8-year-old son whose Brazilian mother had taken him out of the United States in defiance of a court order.

Overall, Smith has been one of the most moderate members of the House GOP. In 2009, he was one of eight Republicans to support the Waxman-Markey energy bill imposing a cap-and-trade system to limit greenhouse gas emissions. He cosponsored the so-called "card check" bill aimed at making it easier for unions to organize work sites by eliminating secret ballot elections. In recent years, he has joined his party's side on major votes such as controversial budget blueprints.

He dramatized his willingness to buck his party for the sake of his beliefs and to accept the consequences when, as chairman of the Veterans' Affairs Committee, Smith angered budget conservatives by pushing generous benefits for veterans. In a major breach of party protocol, he voted for the Democratic spending plan because it contained more money for veterans. In early 2005, the Republican Steering Committee booted Smith from his committee chairmanship and gave it to Steve Buyer of Indiana. Veterans groups expressed outrage, to no avail. Smith's warnings that veterans' programs were underfinanced proved true that June, when Veterans Affairs Secretary Jim Nicholson announced that the department had underestimated the number of returning Iraq war veterans and needed an additional $2.6 billion. Smith's bid to chair the Foreign Affairs Committee in 2013 was thwarted when GOP leaders chose the more reliably conservative Ed Royce of California. Instead, Smith took the chairmanship of the tailor-made Subcommittee on Africa, Global Health, Global Human Rights and International Organizations.

Smith's devotion to principle and his reputation for tending to constituent problems have made him popular in the 4th District. He has been a prominent backer of Republican Gov. Chris Christie, helping to get him elected in 2009. Since 1984, Smith has received at least 61% of the vote. In 2008, Democratic challenger Joshua Zeitz, a first-time candidate, accused him of being a resident of Virginia because Smith owns a home there and his daughter paid in-state Virginia tuition. Smith rents a townhouse in Hamilton Township. He was reelected that year 66%-33%.

FIFTH DISTRICT

Scott Garrett (R)

Elected 2002, 7th term; b. July 9, 1959, Englewood; Montclair St. U., B.A. 1981, Rutgers U., J.D. 1984; Protestant; married (Mary Ellen); 2 children.

Elected Office: NJ Assembly, 1990-2002.

Professional Career: Practicing atty., 1984-2002.

DC Office: 2232 RHOB, 20515, 202-225-4465; Fax: 202-225-9048; Website: garrett.house.gov.

State Offices: Glen Rock, 201-444-5454; Newton, 973-300-2000.

Committees: *Budget. Financial Services:* Capital Markets & Gov't Sponsored Enterprises (Chmn); Housing & Insurance.

Group Ratings

	ADA	ACLU	AFL-CIO	LCV	ITI	COC	HAFA	ACU	CFG	FRC
2014	5%	11%	–	3%	80%	50%	86%	96%	100%	75%
2013	5%	C	19%	11%	C	77%	C	100%	89%	C

National Journal Ratings

	2013 LIB	—	2013 CONS
Economic	13%	—	85%
Social	16%	—	74%
Foreign	34%	—	60%
Composite	24%	—	76%

Key Votes of the 113th Congress

1. Sandy storm spending	Y	5. Medical Marijuana
2. Violence Against Women Act	N	6. Farm Bill
3. Guantanamo Bay Detainees	N	7. Afghanistan Combat
4. Abortion 20-week ban	Y	8. NSA Phone Data Collection

Y	9. Syrian Rebels Training	N
N	10. Keystone pipeline	Y
N	11. Immigration Exec. Action	Y
Y	12. Bipartisan budget deal	N

Election Results

2014 general	Scott Garrett (R)	104,678	(55%)	$2,245,456	$6,656	$5,002
	Roy Cho (D)	81,808	(43%)	$1,251,518		
2014 primary	Scott Garrett (R)	unopposed				

Prior winning percentages: 2012 (55%), 2010 (65%), 2008 (56%), 2006 (55%), 2004 (58%), 2002 (59%)

Population		Race and Ethnicity		Income	
Total:	733,032	White	72.8%	Median income:	$88,280
Urban:	28.8%	Latino	12.6%		*(16 of 435)*
Suburban:	70.1%	Asian	8.4%	Under $50,000	28.9%
Rural:	1.1%	Black	4.4%	$50,000-$99,999:	26.5%
Land area:	1,043	Two races	1.2%	$100,000-$199,999:	29.7%
Pop/sq. mi.:	702.7	White Ethnic	50.9%	$200,000 or more:	15.0%
Born in state:	52.6%			Poverty Rate	7.1%
		Education			
Age Groups		H.S. grad or less:	31.5%	**Work**	
Under 18:	22.8%	Some college:	22.7%	White collar:	46.9%
18 to 34:	17.6%	College degree, 4 yr.:	28.4%	Blue collar:	39.3%
35 to 64:	43.7%	Post-grad study:	17.4%	Sales and service:	13.8%
Over 64:	15.9%				
		Military		Govt. workers:	13.2%
		Veterans/active duty:	6.0%		

Northern New Jersey: Bergen County

The northern edge of New Jersey was settled three centuries ago by the Dutch, for whom this plateau of land behind the Hudson River Palisades seemed a natural part of Nieuw Amsterdam. The Dutch influence is seen in old, steep-roofed farmhouses and in many of the place names—Bergen County, Cresskill, Closter. But overall, northernmost New Jersey has

the well-settled look of so many northeastern suburbs, with touches of both affluence and small-town
hominess, crisscrossed at its edges with limited-
access highways and shopping centers. Since the
late 1950s, Paramus has been transformed from
celery farms to the site of three shopping malls and

Voter Turnout	
2013 Total Citizen 18+	519,939
2014 House Turnout	188,921
2014 Turnout as % CVAP	36.3%
2012 Turnout as % CVAP	63.7%

numerous shopping centers that do more than $5 billion a year in retail sales. Recently, some
local mall executives have begun to reconsider the most effective use of their space, with possibilities such as office, hotel or residential use, or sites for online deliveries. Bergen is one
of the last urban counties in the nation that widely complies with "Blue Law" limitations on
Sunday retailing. In 2014, an advocacy group, Modernize Bergen County, reviewed options
for a referendum to challenge the practice.

Not far away are Saddle River and Franklin Lakes, with million-dollar houses on multi-
acre lots, and Park Ridge, with office buildings and condominiums. This area may look like
WASP suburbia on the surface, but in fact it is home to successful people of all ethnic groups,
many of them descended from those who first saw the Statue of Liberty from steerage. Bergenfield has a sizable population of Filipino descent, and it's known locally as "Little Manila."

The 5th Congressional District of New Jersey comprises most of northern Bergen
County, plus a swath of North Jersey stretching west to the upper reaches of the Delaware
River. About 72% of its population is in Bergen County. Farther west are less rural, but
still heavily Republican, Sussex and Warren
counties. In recent years, the recession took
a toll on many of these suburban enclaves as
foreclosures and a large inventory of unsold
homes sent property values plummeting. But
it remains relatively affluent. In the fall of
2012, Hurricane Sandy brought 60 mile-per-
hour winds here, knocking down trees and
power lines. But Bergen County suffered far
less damage than the counties on the shore.

2012 Presidential Vote		
Mitt Romney (R)	172,451	(52%)
Barack Obama (D)	162,318	(49%)
2008 Presidential Vote		
John McCain (R)	183,827	(51%)
Barack Obama (D)	175,802	(48%)
Cook Partisan Voting Index: R+4		

Redistricting changes added more of Bergen County to the district and reduced John
McCain's local vote of 54% to 51%. Though the 5th District still favors Republicans, it could
become more competitive.

Scott Garrett (R)

Republican Scott Garrett, elected in 2002, is the most conservative member of New Jersey's
congressional delegation. His uncompromising views on reining in federal spending and the
regulation of the banking system set him apart from his Garden State colleagues, but make
him a player on the Budget and Financial Services committees.

Garrett grew up on a farm in Wantage, where his parents grew tomatoes and Christmas
trees. The family's main income came from his father's job as a salesman for Uniroyal. A
conservative from the start, Garrett questioned his high school administration's spending
practices and kept a picture of David Stockman, the father of Reaganomics, at his desk. He
graduated from Montclair State College and Rutgers law school, and became a trial lawyer
in Sussex County. He is a born-again Christian who meets most Saturday mornings for three
hours with a small group that calls itself Joshua Men.

In 1989, Garrett was elected to the New Jersey General Assembly, where he quickly
became one of the most conservative members. In 1998 and 2000, he challenged veteran Rep.
Marge Roukema, a moderate Republican, in the primary. He attacked Roukema for supporting abortion rights and gun control. She emphasized her conservative votes on economic
issues and was backed by the House Republican leadership. Each time, Garrett carried the
western part of the district, but Roukema ran strongly in her Bergen County base, winning
by 53%-47% in 1998 and 52%-48% in 2000.

When Roukema announced that she would not seek another term in 2002, Garrett ran
again. His challenge in the primary was to sell his views in Bergen County, where Sussex
County is viewed as a distant province somewhere near Idaho. Two well-known Republicans from Bergen entered the race: state Sen. Gerald Cardinale and Assemblyman David
Russo. They argued that nominating Garrett would put the seat at risk. But Garrett won

the primary with 41% to 26% for Russo and 25% for Cardinale. Garrett won 81% of the vote in Sussex and 68% in Warren, but only 25% in Bergen County, raising Democratic hopes.

The Democratic nominee was Anne Sumers, a former Republican who switched parties in early 2002 and stressed her agreement with Roukema on most issues. With help from national Democrats, Sumers attacked Garrett as "extremist," pointing to his call for limited federal aid to education. Garrett pounced on Sumers' failure to vote in local school board elections and her musings on a liberal website, where she characterized American patriotism as "jingoistic." Meanwhile, he soft-pedaled some of his more conservative views. Sumers outspent Garrett, $1.6 million to $1.3 million, including nearly $400,000 of her own money. National Republicans spent heavily on issue ads for Garrett. This turned out to be less of a contest than many people expected. Garrett won 59%-38%. In Bergen County, which cast 64% of the total vote, he led 55%-43%.

In the House, Garrett does not fit comfortably with the typically moderate New Jersey Republicans. "I believe Scott, with all due respect, is to the right of Attila the Hun," Democratic Rep. Bill Pascrell told *The Record* of Hackensack in September 2012. Garrett was the only New Jersey delegation member to oppose extending unemployment benefits, the only one to vote against making gasoline price gouging a crime, and the only one to vote for lifting a ban on oil and gas drilling off the coast of New Jersey. After Hurricane Sandy ravaged parts of New Jersey in October 2012, he was the only delegation member who initially refused to sign a letter asking for prompt action. He did, however, support the legislation that passed the House.

His vote against the Republicans' Medicare prescription drug bill in 2003 angered GOP leaders and limited his influence in the House for years. He has long pushed for a resolution that would require all legislation to cite an enumerated power in the Constitution, and he wants to require congressional staff to receive annual training on the document. He told a tea party audience in October 2012: "Government regulations dictate what kind of health insurance we have, what kind of light bulb we buy, what kind of soda we drink, what kind of car we drive. This is a dark time for our republic."

Even though many of his constituents work on Wall Street, Garrett opposed the bailout of the financial markets in 2008, saying he was "wary of using taxpayer dollars to prop up failing businesses." In 2009, he leapfrogged other members and became the ranking Republican on the Financial Services Committee's Subcommittee on Capital Markets, Insurance, and Government-Sponsored Enterprises. He became chairman after the Republican takeover of the House in 2011, and made clear his intention to slow down funding to agencies with responsibilities for implementing the sweeping Dodd-Frank financial services overhaul law passed a year earlier. But the Democratic-controlled Senate was disinclined to curb Dodd-Frank, and House Republican leaders were reluctant to swallow Garrett's idea to replace Fannie Mae and Freddie Mac, the housing mortgage giants, with a purely private mortgage market.

Garrett has overcome serious reelection challenges. In 2006, Paul Aronsohn, a former aide to Democratic Gov. Jim McGreevey, called Garrett "too extreme, too disconnected to the people he represents," raised nearly $600,000, and cut Garrett's margin in Bergen to 51%-48%. But with more than 60% of the vote in Sussex and Warren counties, Garrett won 55%-44%. He sailed to victory in 2010.

In 2012, Democrats had trouble attracting a high-profile challenger, and the job fell to Teaneck Deputy Mayor Adam Gussen. *The Record* endorsed Gussen and rebuked Garrett for failing to acknowledge "that America is a much more complicated place in 2012 than it was in 1787." Gussen raised a pitiable $51,000 while Garrett collected almost $2.4 million, and the incumbent won 55%-43%. In the Republican year of 2014, Democratic challenger Roy Cho raised $1.3 million and had support from the district's growing Korean community. Garrett spent heavily on radio and television advertising in the closing weeks, and attacked Cho as a carpetbagger. The outcome was a familiar 55%-43%.

His relatively tight reelections have not led Garrett to moderate his views. In early 2015, he was one of 25 Republicans who opposed the reelection of John Boehner as speaker. "A large number of my constituents have called on me to demand new leadership in the House," he said in a statement. He also joined the new Freedom Caucus that has pressed for a more conservative agenda, and was the only member of the New Jersey delegation in March 2015 to vote against continued funding for the Homeland Security Department to protest President Barack Obama's executive order on immigration. Garrett may be increasing his vulnerability to a skillful Democratic challenger.

SIXTH DISTRICT

Frank Pallone (D)

Elected Nov. 1988, 14th full term; b. Oct. 30, 1951, Long Branch; Middlebury Col., B.A. 1973, Tufts U., M.A. 1974, Rutgers U., J.D. 1978; Catholic; married (Sarah); 3 children.

Elected Office: Long Branch City Cncl., 1982-88; NJ Senate, 1983-88.

Professional Career: Asst. prof., Rutgers U., 1979-80; Practicing atty., 1981-83; Instructor, Monmouth Col., 1984-86.

DC Office: 237 CHOB, 20515, 202-225-4671; Fax: 202-225-9665; Website: pallone.house.gov.

State Offices: Long Branch, 732-571-1140; New Brunswick, 732-249-8892.

Committees: *Energy & Commerce* (RMM: ex officio member of each subcommittee).

Group Ratings

	ADA	ACLU	AFL-CIO	LCV	ITI	COC	HAFA	ACU	CFG	FRC
2014	95%	83%	–	97%	60%	29%	17%	8%	15%	0%
2013	80%	C	100%	75%	C	33%	C	11%	26%	C

National Journal Ratings

	2013 LIB	—	2013 CONS
Economic	91%	—	0%
Social	84%	—	15%
Foreign	94%	—	0%
Composite	92%	—	8%

Key Votes of the 113th Congress

1. Sandy storm spending	Y	5. Medical Marijuana	Y	9. Syrian Rebels Training	N
2. Violence Against Women Act	Y	6. Farm Bill	N	10. Keystone pipeline	N
3. Guantanamo Bay Detainees	Y	7. Afghanistan Combat	Y	11. Immigration Exec. Action	N
4. Abortion 20-week ban	N	8. NSA Phone Data Collection	NV	12. Bipartisan budget deal	N

Election Results

2014 general	Frank Pallone (D) 72,190	(60%)	$3,164,507	$1,316	$31,000
	Anthony Wilkinson (R) 46,891	(39%)	$134,057	$1,041	
2014 primary	Frank Pallone (D) .... unopposed				

Prior winning percentages: 2012 (63%), 2010 (55%), 2008 (67%), 2006 (69%), 2004 (67%), 2002 (66%), 2000 (68%), 1998 (57%), 1996 (61%), 1994 (60%), 1992 (52%), 1990 (49%), 1988 (52%), 1988 special (52%)

Population		Race and Ethnicity		Income	
Total:	738,398	White	50.8%	Median income:	$74,164
Urban:	26.5%	Latino	20.8%		*(46 of 435)*
Suburban:	73.5%	Asian	17.2%	Under $50,000	34.5%
Rural:	0.0%	Black	9.0%	$50,000-$99,999:	29.9%
Land area:	263	Two races	1.9%	$100,000-$199,999:	27.3%
Pop/sq. mi.:	2,812.0	White Ethnic	42.8%	$200,000 or more:	8.3%
Born in state:	49.4%			Poverty Rate	11.8%
		Education			
Age Groups		H.S. grad or less:	39.2%	**Work**	
Under 18:	22.5%	Some college:	22.8%	White collar:	40.8%
18 to 34:	24.5%	College degree, 4 yr.:	23.0%	Blue collar:	40.2%
35 to 64:	40.8%	Post-grad study:	15.0%	Sales and service:	19.0%
Over 64:	12.3%			Govt. workers:	13.1%
		Military			
		Veterans/active duty:	4.6%		

East-Central New Jersey: Middlesex and Northern Monmouth Counties

For generations, great transportation arteries have brought people out of the huge central cities of New York and Philadelphia and into the flatlands and hills of New Jersey—to vacation, to raise families, to work toward affluence, and to build communities. The railroads of the late 19th century created the towns of the Jersey shore. After 1874, when the first train from New York City reached Long Branch, the shore became the summer home of seven presidents from Grant to Wilson (James Garfield, convalescing after he was shot, died there in 1881), and of New York racehorse owners and socialites. But over time, the ambiance degraded, and the fishing pier

Voter Turnout	
2013 Total Citizen 18+	477,376
2014 House Turnout	120,457
2014 Turnout as % CVAP	25.2%
2012 Turnout as % CVAP	54.9%

and much of the boardwalk went up in flames in 1987. A shopping and dining complex took its place, though developers have explored a pier for elsewhere in Long Branch.

The freight rail lines in the New York-Philadelphia corridor sparked electrical and chemical industries here—many of them building on the inventions of Thomas Edison, produced in his Menlo Park laboratory just off the rail lines. Today, a 131-foot tower stands as a memorial to the inventor. The same corridor was the site of America's first cloverleaf intersection, at the junction of U.S. 1 and U.S. 9. The New Jersey Turnpike roars past oil tank farms and petrochemical plants, major rail lines, Newark Liberty International Airport, and the oily waters of Raritan Bay.

The 6th Congressional District inelegantly ties together these great transportation nodes, and the upward mobility that has taken place around them. The district is shaped like a backward capital F, with a string of towns running from Piscataway down the Atlantic coast to Long Branch and Asbury Park. Middlesex County accounts for 69% of the district's population, with the remainder in Monmouth County. It includes the central core of Middlesex: New Brunswick, Highland Park, Metuchen, Sayreville, Edison Township—an industrial area that has housed some of America's great research and development facilities, plus part of the sprawling campus of Rutgers, the state university of New Jersey. Asbury Park, which began as a Christian resort and was immortalized in the music of Bruce Springsteen, is plagued by a poverty rate of almost 34%.

With close proximity to Raritan Bay and the coastline, much of this area was devastated by Hurricane Sandy in 2012. More than 100 homes were destroyed in Union Beach; 14-foot waves flooded Sayreville; and the marina in the sailing town of Perth Amboy was ripped apart. "Many people who live along the Raritan Bay and in riverside communities throughout Middlesex County were left with nothing," *The Star-Ledger* newspaper reported in November 2012. Two years later and after spending more than $10 million, Perth Amboy reopened its marina and added

2012 Presidential Vote		
Barack Obama (D)	163,428	(62%)
Mitt Romney (R)	99,564	(38%)
2008 Presidential Vote		
Barack Obama (D)	170,981	(58%)
John McCain (R)	118,362	(41%)
Cook Partisan Voting Index:	D+8	

higher dock pilings. In April 2015, Gov. Chris Christie announced a $202 million flood-control project with new levees, floodwalls, tide gates and pump stations.

The two biggest cities in the 6th are Edison and Woodbridge. One of the 17th century founding fathers of Woodbridge was Jonathan Singletary Dunham, whose eighth-great-grandson is President Barack Obama. He got 62% of the vote here in 2012, but there were five districts in New Jersey where he fared better. The district is now 22% Latino and 10% black.

Frank Pallone (D)

Democrat Frank Pallone, elected in 1988, became the ranking Democrat on the Energy and Commerce Committee in 2015 after edging out Anna Eshoo, who was actively supported by her long-time friend, Minority Leader Nancy Pelosi. He has been one of his party's chief messengers on health care and environmental issues.

Pallone is the son of a disabled Long Branch policeman. He became an environmentalist in 1969, when as a Middlebury College freshman in Vermont he worked for that state's first-in-the-nation bottle deposit law. After getting a master's degree in international relations from Tufts University and a law degree from Rutgers, he was elected to the Long Branch City Council in 1982, at age 31, and to the New Jersey Senate a year later.

Pallone ran for an open seat that a Democrat had long held. The district leaned Republican, but residents were angry about untreated sludge, plastic containers, and medical waste washing up on the beach. Pallone's bumper sticker, which didn't mention party affiliation, said, "Stop Ocean Dumping." That, combined with his conservative views on taxes and crime, helped him to win 52% of the vote.

Pallone started as a political maverick, but he became more loyal to the Democratic Party as he rose in the hierarchy. He was tied for most liberal House member in *National Journal* rankings in 2011. His environmental focus has been on protecting the New Jersey shoreline. In 2006, he won passage of a bill to reduce and prevent debris in the marine environment. Two years later, he was the lead sponsor of a bipartisan bill to rebuild American fisheries, in part by requiring a review of factors that lead to over-fishing.

After the BP oil spill in the Gulf of Mexico in 2010, Pallone was among several New Jersey Democrats who unsuccessfully implored President Barack Obama to reverse his decision to open waters for drilling off the East Coast, from Virginia to Georgia. In 2015, he filed legislation to reverse that action. He criticized the administration's response to Hurricane Sandy, which damaged many of his district's coastal communities in 2012. He repeatedly demanded that the Federal Emergency Management Agency provide mobile homes for thousands of stranded residents, then criticized the agency when it came through with just 50 trailers.

As chairman of Energy and Commerce's Subcommittee on Health in 2009, Pallone helped steer to passage the Democrats' expansion of the Children's Health Insurance Program, which he called "a down payment to ensuring that all Americans have access to affordable health care." On the Democrats' economic stimulus bill, he backed an increase in the federal matching rate for Medicaid as a step to reduce the program's financial burden on states. During the health care overhaul debate, he shuttled among various factions of Blue Dogs and progressives to try to get them to be flexible. After the bill passed in 2010, and Republicans tried to repeal it, Pallone was among its most outspoken defenders. "The fact of the matter is, that if we pass these defunding amendments in the guise of budget austerity, (Republicans) are one step towards repealing the largest deficit-cutter passed in the last decade, and that's the Affordable Care Act," he said in February 2011. Pallone got a bill through the subcommittee that set guidelines for the time period student athletes must be benched after suffering concussions. Before the 2010 World Series, he called on baseball teams to stop using chewing tobacco, saying that it set a bad example for children.

On district issues, he worked with other Garden State lawmakers to prevent a National Oceanic and Atmospheric Administration research lab in his district from closing. In a bow to the many people of Armenian descent in the district, Pallone helped push congressional approval of normalizing trade relations with Armenia. He sponsored the controversial resolution that labeled the 1915 killing of Armenians by Ottoman Turks as genocide, which wasn't passed due to vehement opposition by Turkey. He has been active on issues involving India and has introduced a resolution condemning violence against the upper-caste Hindus known as Kashmiri Pandits. In April 2015, he criticized Gov. Chris Christie for his move to withdraw New Jersey from the regional Greenhouse Gas Initiative, which is designed to reduce carbon dioxide emissions from power plants, a decision that Pallone called "misguided."

Since 1994, Pallone has usually been reelected with at least 60% of the vote. In 1998, he faced a tough challenge from 28-year-old Republican Mike Ferguson, an ally of former GOP Gov. Thomas Kean. An insurance group unhappy with Pallone's support of President Bill Clinton's plan to regulate health maintenance organizations spent nearly $2 million on Ferguson's campaign. But Pallone won 57%-40%. Ferguson won a neighboring district two years later and served eight years. In 2010, Pallone drew another formidable opponent in Republican Anna Little, the mayor of Highlands. With strong tea party backing, Little took socially conservative positions and blasted Pallone's efforts to pass the health care bill. Pallone was bolstered by a series of newspaper endorsements and kept his seat, 55%-44%.

He has long wanted to run for the Senate. When Democratic Sen. Jon Corzine ran for governor in 2005, Pallone endorsed him. Corzine was elected, but he disappointed Pallone by appointing Rep. Robert Menendez to his Senate seat. During Corzine's reelection bid against Christie, Pallone became an attack dog for the governor, raising questions about Christie's work as U.S. attorney for New Jersey and burnishing his own reputation among state party leaders. After Democratic Sen. Frank Lautenberg died in June 2013, Pallone ran in the special election and entered the Democratic primary with an appeal to party regulars. Newark Mayor Cory Booker, a rising star in the party, easily prevailed with 59 percent to 20 percent for Pallone, the runner-up.

Eshoo had been Pelosi's choice to succeed retiring Rep. Henry Waxman as ranking Democrat on Energy and Commerce, but in November 2014, she was edged out by Pallone 100-90 in secret balloting by the entire Democratic Caucus. The Pelosi-controlled Democratic Steering and Policy Committee had endorsed Eshoo for the position, 30-19. Pallone highlighted the fact that he had four years more seniority than Eshoo, which appealed to many in the Congressional Black Caucus and other traditionalists. He acknowledged the big boost that he received from Minority Whip Steny Hoyer. He downplayed any lingering effects. "There's always going to be squabbles. It's a campaign," he said, describing the committee as a stage where Democrats can demonstrate that "we really are out there to try to protect the average person's interests."

In his early months in his new position, Pallone voiced continued differences with committee Republicans. But he made progress in reducing the fractiousness on the panel, and finding areas of common ground, including health care research and chemical safety. With Republican Chairman Fred Upton of Michigan, he filed a bill to prohibit the sale or distribution of personal care products that contain synthetic plastic microbeads, which can pollute waterways.

SEVENTH DISTRICT

Leonard Lance (R)

Elected 2008, 4th term; b. June 25, 1952, Easton, PA; Lehigh U., B.A. 1974, Vanderbilt U., J.D. 1977, Princeton U., M.P.A. 1982; Catholic; married (Heidi Rohrbach); 1 child.

Elected Office: NJ Assembly, 1991-2002; NJ Senate, 2002-08, min. ldr., 2002-08.

Professional Career: Clerk, Warren Cnty. Court, 1977-78; Asst. counsel, Gov. Thomas H. Kean, 1983-90.

DC Office: 2352 RHOB, 20515, 202-225-5361; Fax: 202-225-9460; Website: lance.house.gov.

State Offices: Flemington, 908-788-6900; Westfield, 908-518-7733.

Committees: *Energy & Commerce:* Commerce, Manufacturing & Trade (VChmn); Communications & Technology; Health.

Group Ratings

	ADA	ACLU	AFL-CIO	LCV	ITI	COC	HAFA	ACU	CFG	FRC
2014	10%	5%	–	6%	100%	86%	53%	72%	63%	75%
2013	0%	C	29%	21%	C	92%	C	64%	60%	C

National Journal Ratings

	2013 LIB	—	2013 CONS
Economic	51%	—	48%
Social	46%	—	53%
Foreign	41%	—	57%
Composite	47%	—	53%

Key Votes of the 113th Congress

1. Sandy storm spending	Y	5. Medical Marijuana	N	9. Syrian Rebels Training	Y
2. Violence Against Women Act	Y	6. Farm Bill	N	10. Keystone pipeline	Y
3. Guantanamo Bay Detainees	N	7. Afghanistan Combat	N	11. Immigration Exec. Action	Y
4. Abortion 20-week ban	Y	8. NSA Phone Data Collection	N	12. Bipartisan budget deal	Y

Election Results

2014 general	Leonard Lance (R)	104,287	(59%)	$1,031,920	$10,892
	Janice Kovach (D)	68,232	(39%)	$116,468	
	Jim Gawron (Lib)	3,478	(2%)		
2014 primary	Leonard Lance (R)	15,900	(54%)		
	David Larsen (R)	13,308	(46%)		

Prior winning percentages: 2012 (57%), 2010 (59%), 2008 (50%)

Population		Race and Ethnicity		Income	
Total:	748,580	White	74.1%	Median income:	$101,222
Urban:	7.8%	Latino	11.7%		*(5 of 435)*
Suburban:	92.2%	Asian	8.4%	Under $50,000	24.0%
Rural:	0.0%	Black	4.2%	$50,000-$99,999:	25.0%
Land area:	852	Two races	1.1%	$100,000-$199,999:	31.1%
Pop/sq. mi.:	878.5	White Ethnic	54.4%	$200,000 or more:	19.9%
Born in state:	56.6%			Poverty Rate	4.8%
		Education			
Age Groups		H.S. grad or less:	28.7%	**Work**	
Under 18:	23.5%	Some college:	21.0%	White collar:	49.6%
18 to 34:	17.2%	College degree, 4 yr.:	29.3%	Blue collar:	37.4%
35 to 64:	45.1%	Post-grad study:	21.0%	Sales and service:	13.0%
Over 64:	14.2%				
		Military		Govt. workers:	13.1%
		Veterans/active duty:	5.0%		

North-Central New Jersey: Somerset, Union and Hunterdon Counties

The transportation arteries beneath the First Watchung Mountain played a large role in New Jersey's development. The rail lines of the late 19th century opened up commuter suburbs. In the 1940s, the four lanes of U.S. 22 made those communities readily accessible by car. Next, Interstate

Voter Turnout	
2013 Total Citizen 18+	528,429
2014 House Turnout	175,997
2014 Turnout as % CVAP	33.3%
2012 Turnout as % CVAP	65.2%

78, completed in the mid-1980s, put Newark only an hour's distance from the Pennsylvania line. The interstate stimulated the development of an edge city called Bridgewater Commons halfway between Philadelphia and Manhattan. An enormous shopping mall and office development, which included the headquarters of AT&T, rose up in the horse country around Far Hills and Bernardsville, where the likes of Malcolm Forbes and Charles Engelhard owned huge estates. (New Jersey claims more horses per square mile than any other state.) These towns are in Somerset County, with a median household income in 2013 of $99,020, the sixth highest among U.S. counties. In Essex County, Short Hills has the third highest median income of any town in the nation, *Business Insider* reported in 2014.

Nearby, fast-growing Hunterdon County has the fourth highest median household income in the country. To the east, Diamond Nation in Flemington is a 35-acre baseball and softball complex and the site of many tournaments. Flemington was also the setting of the "trial of the century," in the kidnapping and murder of the 20-month-old son of aviator Charles Lindbergh.

The 7th Congressional District of New Jersey covers several generations of suburban development. It crosses the breadth of the state, from the edge of Pennsylvania's Lehigh Valley in the west to parts of Union County in the east. It is an agglomeration of

2012 Presidential Vote		
Mitt Romney (R)................178,318	(53%)
Barack Obama (D) 157,285	(47%)
2008 Presidential Vote		
John McCain (R)................188,348	(52%)
Barack Obama (D) 171,277	(47%)
Cook Partisan Voting Index: R+6	

places, and includes parts of six counties. The largest slice of population is the 32% in Somerset County, with 25% in Union County and about 18% in Hunterdon County. The district favors Republicans, but not overwhelmingly. John McCain got 52% here in 2008, and Mitt Romney took 53% in 2012.

Leonard Lance (R)

Leonard Lance is a wonky, self-styled "Eisenhower Republican" elected in 2008. His moderate stances have drawn primary challenges from the right, but his pragmatic fiscal conservatism and social liberalism have proven popular in a suburban district that, politically, still likes Ike.

Lance's English-German ancestors have lived in Hunterdon County for 300 years, and he and his twin brother, James, grew up there in the small town of Glen Gardner. Politics is in Lance's blood. His father, Wesley Lance, was a state senator and eventually rose to Senate president. The younger Lance went to Lehigh University to get his bachelor's degree, then headed south to Vanderbilt University for a law degree. He returned to New Jersey to pursue a master's from Princeton University. One of his early jobs was as Republican Gov. Thomas Kean's assistant counsel for county and municipal matters. In 1990, he was elected to the New Jersey legislature, where he made a name for himself as a budget hawk and independent thinker. He opposed a spending plan by GOP Gov. Christie Whitman, a move that cost him the Budget Committee chairmanship.

In 2008, GOP Rep. Mike Ferguson did not seek reelection after narrowly holding his seat two years earlier against Democratic Assemblywoman Linda Stender. Lance got into the primary race against six other candidates. He was the establishment Republicans' pick, but he faced tough competition from Whitman's daughter, Kate Whitman, who outraised him and questioned his fiscal bona fides. He spent nearly all of his funds early, yet he won the primary by a surprisingly large margin, 39%-20%, over Whitman.

Lance started the general election campaign seriously outmatched by Stender, who was running again and outspent him 2-to-1. She criticized Lance for opposing her legislation to make it mandatory for pharmacies to fill prescriptions for birth control pills, including emergency contraception. Lance said he voted against the bill because he believed that mom-and-pop pharmacies should have the right to decide whether to fill such prescriptions. Both political parties pulled out all the stops for this seat. President George W. Bush stumped for Lance, and Democratic House Speaker Nancy Pelosi and New York Sen. Hillary Clinton each came to the district to campaign for Stender. Lance did better than expected, winning by 50%-42%.

In his first term, Lance was one of just eight Republicans to support energy legislation that included a cap-and-trade program aimed at reducing greenhouse gas emissions, and one of just three to back the Lilly Ledbetter Fair Pay Act, which made it easier to sue over alleged wage discrimination. He held firm against most of President Barack Obama's economic agenda, voting against the stimulus bill even as he touted a flood control project in his district that was ready for stimulus money. A former member of the Financial Services Committee, he was a critic of the Dodd-Frank Wall Street reform law, saying he was especially troubled by its reliance on unused government bailout funds.

Lance's moderate stances have brought him primary challenges. In 2010, he defeated three tea party-backed challengers with 56% after winning the support of local Republican organizations. He then faced Democrat Ed Potosnak, who had been a staffer for Democratic Rep. Mike Honda of California and was openly gay. He criticized Lance's opposition to repealing the "don't ask, don't tell" policy barring openly gay military service members. But Lance outraised him by 4-to-1 and won easily, 59%-41%. After the election, he was rewarded with a plum spot on the Energy and Commerce Committee.

Lance increasingly has joined conservatives on major legislation. Despite his backing of abortion rights, he voted with Republicans in 2011 to cut off funding for Planned Parenthood; he said he had never supported public funding of abortions. He also voted in favor of New Jersey Republican Scott Garrett's budget proposal that year that cut spending even further than Budget Committee Chairman Paul Ryan's blueprint, and for a measure to repeal the ban on incandescent light bulbs established in the 2007 energy law. Lance resisted Republican attempts to eliminate or slash funding for such programs as the Foreign Agricultural Service and Legal Services Corporation. On opening day of the new Congress in January 2015, he introduced a constitutional amendment to require a balanced budget. In May, he was among nine members listed by the Ethics Committee in its investigation of a bipartisan delegation that received extensive gifts in Azerbaijan. The charges were dismissed in July.

Lance has drawn regular primary challenges from tea party-backed candidate David Larsen, who has called his rival "totally disconnected from the people." A lightly funded businessman in home improvement who has no experience in elected office and cites neighboring Rep. Scott Garrett as a model, Larsen has continued to narrow the gap. Lance won 61%-39% in 2012, and 54%-46% in 2014. In their most recent contest, Larsen led in Morris County and Lance narrowly took Somerset. Lance attributed that outcome to low turnout. In general elections, Lance has cited his bipartisan work on issues such as mental health and violence against women, and he has easily dispatched Democratic challengers. This district bears watching if conservatives intensify their challenge to Lance.

EIGHTH DISTRICT

Albio Sires (D)

Elected Nov. 2006, 5th full term; b. Jan. 26, 1951, Bejucal, Cuba; St. Peter's Col., B.A. 1974, Middlebury Col., M.A. 1985; Catholic; married (Adrienne); 1 child.

Elected Office: West New York mayor, 1995-2006; NJ Assembly, 2000-2006, speaker, 2002-06.

Professional Career: H.S. Spanish & ESL teacher, 1975-85; Special asst., NJ Dept. of Comm. Affairs, 1985; Part-owner, A.M. Title Agency, 1986-2006.

DC Office: 2342 RHOB, 20515, 202-225-7919; Fax: 202-226-0792; Website: sires.house.gov.

State Offices: Elizabeth, 908-820-0692; Jersey City, 201-309-0301; West New York, 201-558-0800.

Committees: *Foreign Affairs:* Europe, Eurasia, & Emerging Threats; Western Hemisphere (RMM). *Transportation & Infrastructure:* Economic Development, Public Buildings & Emergency Mgmt.; Highways & Transit; Railroads, Pipelines & Hazardous Materials.

Group Ratings

	ADA	ACLU	AFL-CIO	LCV	ITI	COC	HAFA	ACU	CFG	FRC
2014	70%	72%	–	94%	60%	64%	13%	4%	6%	0%
2013	65%	C	100%	89%	C	42%	C	16%	14%	C

National Journal Ratings

	2013 LIB	—	2013 CONS
Economic	85%	—	14%
Social	85%	—	13%
Foreign	74%	—	25%
Composite	82%	—	18%

Key Votes of the 113th Congress

1. Sandy storm spending	Y	5. Medical Marijuana	Y	9. Syrian Rebels Training	N
2. Violence Against Women Act	Y	6. Farm Bill	N	10. Keystone pipeline	Y
3. Guantanamo Bay Detainees	Y	7. Afghanistan Combat	Y	11. Immigration Exec. Action	N
4. Abortion 20-week ban	N	8. NSA Phone Data Collection	N	12. Bipartisan budget deal	Y

Election Results

2014 general	Albio Sires (D)	61,510	(77%)	$581,950
	Jude Anthony Tiscornia (R)	15,141	(19%)	
2014 primary	Albio Sires (D)	unopposed		

Prior winning percentages: 2012 (78%), 2010 (74%), 2008 (75%), 2006 (78%), 2006 special (97%)

Population		Race and Ethnicity		Income	
Total:	758,406	Latino	54.4%	Median income:	$52,524
Urban:	94.1%	White	27.1%		(193 of 435)
Suburban:	5.9%	Black	8.3%	Under $50,000	47.8%
Rural:	0.0%	Asian	7.7%	$50,000-$99,999:	28.6%
Land area:	66	Two races	1.0%	$100,000-$199,999:	17.4%
Pop/sq. mi.:	11,532.1	White Ethnic	19.5%	$200,000 or more:	6.2%
Born in state:	37.1%			Poverty Rate	19.2%
		Education			
Age Groups		H.S. grad or less:	52.0%	**Work**	
Under 18:	21.4%	Some college:	19.3%	White collar:	31.5%
18 to 34:	29.9%	College degree, 4 yr.:	17.3%	Blue collar:	42.8%
35 to 64:	38.8%	Post-grad study:	11.4%	Sales and service:	25.7%
Over 64:	9.9%				
		Military		Govt. workers:	9.1%
		Veterans/active duty:	2.2%		

Jersey City/Newark Area

Standing in New York Harbor since 1886, the Statue of Liberty has been the symbol of America's receptiveness to immigrants. Actually, the statue is on the New Jersey side of the harbor, and so is, as the U.S. Supreme Court ruled in 1998, most of Ellis Island, where immigrants once were processed. So

Voter Turnout	
2013 Total Citizen 18+	417,388
2014 House Turnout	79,518
2014 Turnout as % CVAP	19.1%
2012 Turnout as % CVAP	50.1%

it's natural that the towns atop the granite and gneiss ridge of Hudson County, overlooking the harbor, became immigrant territory. Many children and grandchildren of Irish and Italian immigrants stayed in Hudson County, living in the same neighborhoods, working on the same docks or in the factories, and voting the dictates of the same political machine. Hudson County was the setting of one of America's classic political machines, undisciplined by any metropolitan elite. From 1917 to 1949, the boss of Hudson County was Frank ("I am the law") Hague. His machine chose governors and U.S. senators, prosecutors and judges, and had influence in the White House of Franklin D. Roosevelt. Hague collected high taxes from industries clustered here, which then passed them on to consumers, and in return, he gave them an orderly city, free of most crime and vice, and a workforce insulated against racketeers and militant unions. Hague's successor, John V. Kenny, was boss from 1949 to 1971—continuous power for 54 years.

But Hudson County began changing. New immigrants were coming in—refugees from Fidel Castro's Cuba and other Latinos and Asians arrived. Union City became predominantly Cuban, and in recent years, it has gained a mix of Colombian, Ecuadoran, Peruvian, Dominican, and Filipino immigrants. Jersey City neighborhoods and Guttenberg became heavily Latino. Starting in the 1980s, huge new condominium and office developments went up in Jersey City, housing big banks, securities firms and, later, Internet businesses. Upscale young singles looking for lower rents moved into Hoboken's five-story Victorians; they were a quick commute through the PATH tubes to Wall Street or Greenwich Village. Recently, riders have asked to add the PATH routes to the New York City subway maps. In Hoboken, the home of Frank Sinatra and the Oreo cookie, shopping and apartment complexes have taken up the waterfront sites where factories were common (and where the classic movie *On the Waterfront* was filmed). Hoboken continues to attract urban professionals plus a growing number of families seeking affordable housing; the city grew by 36% from 2000 to 2013. In 2015, Jersey City officials reported an unprecedented amount of construction. Since 2010, the 5.5% population increase in Hudson has made it the fastest-growing county in the state.

Hudson County, which seemed to be dying a generation ago, is now more vibrant. But challenges remain: The county suffered double-digit unemployment well after the recession, but the jobless rate dropped to 6.4% in 2015, not far above the national rate. Hurricane Sandy in the fall of 2012 did

2012 Presidential Vote		
Barack Obama (D)	161,443	(79%)
Mitt Romney (R)	42,896	(21%)

2008 Presidential Vote		
Barack Obama (D)	160,903	(73%)
John McCain (R)	56,502	(26%)

Cook Partisan Voting Index: D+24

severe damage in Hoboken. Bayonne has become a cruise ship port, and work is underway to raise the 5,780-foot-long bridge, built in 1931, so it is tall enough for the latest super-sized container ships.

The 8th Congressional District includes much of Hudson County, plus most of the immigrant entry ports along the water and the bustling docks along the Hudson River and New York Bay. It takes in Hoboken and Elizabeth, now almost 60% Hispanic; nearly half of Newark; West New York and Weehawken; parts of Jersey City and Bayonne; working-class Harrison, an aging factory town where European immigrants have been replaced by Hispanic immigrants; and part of industrial Kearny. The district is 55% Hispanic, by far the largest percentage in the state. A bit more than 70% is in Hudson, as are sections of Essex and Union and a thin slice of Bergen County. Like all six of their districts in New Jersey, this is easy territory for Democrats to defend.

Albio Sires (D)

Democrat Albio Sires, who won a special election in 2006, is the only Cuban-American Democrat in the House. Like his predecessor, Sen. Robert Menendez, Sires has long been a political player in Hudson County, and he concentrates on local issues, as well as taking a tough stance against Cuba's Castro regime.

Sires, who was born in Cuba, remembers the book-burning following the Communist revolution there. His family fled Fidel Castro's regime in 1962 when he was 10. He attended St. Peter's College on a four-year basketball scholarship—he is 6-feet-4-inches—and then earned a master's degree from Middlebury College. He became a high school Spanish teacher.

On his fourth try, he was elected mayor of West New York as a Republican in 1995, and held that post until 2006. He focused on the creation of more affordable housing in the small but densely populated town and won praise for merging the fire department with three neighboring departments. He switched parties in 1999 and, with the support of party leaders, defeated a veteran Democratic incumbent in the primary to win a state House seat (until recently, dual office-holding was a common practice in New Jersey). With strong support from newly elected Democratic Gov. Jim McGreevey in 2002, he became speaker of the Assembly.

After newly elected Democratic Gov. Jon Corzine appointed Menendez to replace him in the Senate, Sires became the front-runner for the House seat. In the primary, he faced a fierce challenge from Joe Vas of Perth Amboy, who likewise was a state House member and a mayor. Vas assailed Sires as a puppet of the Hudson County Democratic machine. Sires responded by depicting Vas as soft on crime and won the support of most leading Democrats, except for his longtime rival Menendez, who remained neutral. Vas carried his home base of Middlesex County 76%-24%, but Sires crushed him 80%-20% in Hudson County, which cast 74% of the total vote. Overall, Sires won 72%-28%. In the general election, Republicans nominated John Guarini, who raised little money and posed no threat. Sires won 78%-19%. Sires has been reelected easily since.

In the House, Sires established a liberal voting record that has placed him in the middle of the pack among New Jersey's House Democrats. He allied himself in 2007 with South Florida members who wanted to keep U.S. sanctions on Cuba in place; he joined them again three years later in opposing the Obama administration's proposed loosening of restrictions on travel and economic aid. In 2013, he became ranking Democrat on the Foreign Affairs Committee's Western Hemisphere panel. In December 2014, he criticized President Barack Obama's increased dealings with Cuba as "naïve and disrespectful," and said that the effort to "encourage a form of Cuban glasnost is a dangerous miscalculation."

On the Transportation and Infrastructure Committee, he was successful in convincing the Army Corps of Engineers to raise the Bayonne Bridge's height to accommodate larger ships. As of early 2015, the new approach ramps had been completed and officials were proceeding with the more complex plans to replace the main span. The result will provide an additional 64 feet of clearance, and provide access for all container ships to the port, with completion scheduled for 2017. He also introduced legislation to revitalize urban parks, and to increase transit and help commuters find alternative ways to get to work. In January 2015, he was one of 28 House Democrats who sided with organized labor in support of the Keystone XL pipeline. He enacted a bill in January 2013 to combat fraud in international adoptions by requiring accreditation for all inter-country adoption service providers.

In the 2010 election, Sires was a vice chair of the Democratic Congressional Campaign Committee, in charge of member participation and outreach. After Democrats lost their majority, he called for Speaker Nancy Pelosi to step down, although he subsequently backed her bid to become minority leader. His comments didn't endear him to Democratic leaders, nor did the fact that he raised significantly less money than other DCCC leaders.

NINTH DISTRICT

Bill Pascrell (D)

Elected 1996, 10th term; b. Jan. 25, 1937, Paterson; Fordham U., B.A. 1959, M.A. 1961; Catholic; married (Elsie Marie); 3 children.

Military Career: Army, 1961-62; U.S. Army Reserves, 1962-67.

Elected Office: Pres., Paterson Bd. of Ed., 1979-82; NJ Assembly, 1988-97, min. ldr. pro tem; Paterson mayor, 1990-96.

Professional Career: H.S. teacher, 1960-74; Dir., Paterson Dept. of Public Works, 1974-77; Dir., Paterson Dept. of Policy, 1977-87.

DC Office: 2370 RHOB, 20515, 202-225-5751; Fax: 202-225-5782; Website: pascrell.house.gov.

State Offices: Englewood, 201-935-2248; Lyndhurst, 201-935-2248; Passaic, 973-472-4510; Paterson, 973-523-5152.

Committees: *Budget. Ways & Means:* Health; Trade.

Group Ratings

	ADA	ACLU	AFL-CIO	LCV	ITI	COC	HAFA	ACU	CFG	FRC
2014	90%	77%	–	97%	80%	36%	14%	8%	15%	0%
2013	80%	C	100%	96%	C	38%	C	16%	14%	C

National Journal Ratings

	2013 LIB	—	2013 CONS
Economic	87%	—	13%
Social	72%	—	27%
Foreign	83%	—	15%
Composite	81%	—	19%

Key Votes of the 113th Congress

1. Sandy storm spending	Y	5. Medical Marijuana	Y	9. Syrian Rebels Training	Y
2. Violence Against Women Act	Y	6. Farm Bill	N	10. Keystone pipeline	N
3. Guantanamo Bay Detainees	Y	7. Afghanistan Combat	Y	11. Immigration Exec. Action	N
4. Abortion 20-week ban	NV	8. NSA Phone Data Collection	Y	12. Bipartisan budget deal	Y

Election Results

2014 general	Bill Pascrell (D)	82,498	(69%)	$1,161,104	$4,881
	Dierdre Paul (R)	36,246	(30%)	$8,823	$1,041
2014 primary	Bill Pascrell (D)	................unopposed			

Prior winning percentages: 2012 (74%), 2010 (63%), 2008 (71%), 2006 (71%), 2004 (69%), 2002 (67%), 2000 (67%), 1998 (62%), 1996 (51%)

Population		Race and Ethnicity		Income	
Total:	760,064	White	41.7%	Median income:	$60,439
Urban:	81.2%	Latino	33.6%		*(122 of 435)*
Suburban:	18.8%	Asian	12.8%	Under $50,000	42.5%
Rural:	0.0%	Black	10.5%	$50,000-$99,999:	28.1%
Land area:	110	Two races	1.0%	$100,000-$199,999:	22.5%
Pop/sq. mi.:	6,940.3	White Ethnic	28.7%	$200,000 or more:	6.9%
Born in state:	43.6%			Poverty Rate	15.1%
		Education			
Age Groups		H.S. grad or less:	47.1%	**Work**	
Under 18:	23.0%	Some college:	20.8%	White collar:	36.1%
18 to 34:	23.6%	College degree, 4 yr.:	20.7%	Blue collar:	41.0%
35 to 64:	40.0%	Post-grad study:	11.4%	Sales and service:	22.9%
Over 64:	13.4%			Govt. workers:	10.2%
		Military			
		Veterans/active duty:	3.6%		

Northeast New Jersey: Southern Bergen County, Paterson

Paterson is one of the few American cities that has turned out pretty much as planned. It was the brainchild of Alexander Hamilton, who in the 1790s journeyed 20 miles from Manhattan to the Great Falls of the Passaic River in New Jersey. Watching the water surge down

72 feet—the highest falls along the East Coast—he predicted an industrial city would rise on the site. Hamilton formed the Society for Establishing Useful Manufactures, which opened a calico factory in 1794, and got Pierre L'Enfant, the designer of Washington, D.C., to design Paterson (named after

Voter Turnout	
2013 Total Citizen 18+	462,221
2014 House Turnout	120,459
2014 Turnout as % CVAP	26.1%
2012 Turnout as % CVAP	55.8%

then-Gov. William Paterson). In 1836, Samuel Colt began manufacturing revolvers there. One of the first American locomotives, the Sandusky, was built in Paterson in 1837. Paterson ultimately became America's "Silk City," employing 25,000 silk mill workers before the great strike of 1913 led by the radical Industrial Workers of the World. Throughout, Paterson attracted immigrants from England, Ireland and, after 1890, Italy and Poland.

The city continues to attract immigrants today, even if its economy produces more service jobs than manufacturing jobs. It has a lively artists' community in its postindustrial setting, and downtown's "Little Palestine" reflects the city's sizable Arab community—Palestinians, Lebanese, Jordanians, plus Syrian refugees escaping their civil war since 2011. Like Paterson, the surrounding area is a melting pot. Old towns like Rutherford have enclaves of Americans of Polish, German, and Italian descent. Blue-collar Palisades Park has a large concentration of Korean Americans. Englewood is home to middle-class blacks and Orthodox Jewish families.

The 9th Congressional District takes in the leafy suburbs of Englewood, Palisades Park and fast-growing Edgewater, where dwellers in luxury apartment houses brag about their views of New York City. The high-rise towers of Fort Lee became famous in 2013 when aides to Gov. Chris Christie decided to slow traffic to the George Washington Bridge. The district also takes in East Rutherford and the Meadowlands Sports Complex. Once 8,400 acres of wetlands and home to thousands of species of animals and plants, the Meadowlands was developed in the 1970s. A generation later, the state built a new $1.6 billion MetLife Stadium at that site for the National Football League's Giants and Jets that opened in 2010. The stadium hosted the Super Bowl in 2014 and shared many of the related events with New York City.

The district also includes Paterson, Clifton and Passaic. Nearly half the population resides in Bergen County and about 45% in Passaic County, though the election results have shown that more than 60% of the voters are in Bergen as the result of lower voting patterns among Hispanics. This was a growth area in the 1950s and 1960s, as New Yorkers moved out of the city. It lost population in the next two decades, as young people moved farther out. Now, the population is rising with the influx of new immigrants, many of them low-income. Home prices in blue-collar neighborhoods plunged during the recession, and sales figures in early 2015 showed that

2012 Presidential Vote
Barack Obama (D) 173,070 (69%)
Mitt Romney (R)...................77,988 (31%)

2008 Presidential Vote
Barack Obama (D) 171,658 (64%)
John McCain (R)...................94,237 (35%)

Cook Partisan Voting Index: D+14

they had not recovered. From 2000 to 2013, the number of Hispanics in Bergen County grew nearly 90% to 168,000 (now, 18% of 933,000), and in Passaic County, the Latino population grew to 39% of the 509,000 residents. The 9th is a rapidly changing but still solidly Democratic district.

Bill Pascrell (D)

Bill Pascrell, elected in 1996, is a kind of a Democratic version of Gov. Chris Christie: He shares Christie's feisty Jersey-guy demeanor as a local boss. And he can be candid about expressing his displeasure with his party on the national scene, where he often operates as an old-style, favor-trading pol.

He grew up in Paterson, the grandson of Italian immigrants. His father worked for the railroad, and Pascrell was the first one in his family to graduate from college. He worked his way through Fordham University, served in the Army, then taught high school for 14 years. From there Pascrell went into politics, first as director of Paterson's public works department, and then as school board president. In 1987, he was elected to the New Jersey Assembly. In 1990, Pascrell was elected mayor of Paterson but continued to serve in the Assembly—a common practice in New Jersey until the legislature voted in 2007 to stop the practice.

In 1996, Pascrell challenged first-term Rep. Bill Martini, a Republican, whom Pascrell portrayed as the tool of an "extremist" House leadership; his ads showed Martini's face on a puppet being manipulated by Republican House Speaker Newt Gingrich. Despite Martini's support from the Sierra Club and labor unions, Pascrell won 51%-48%.

In the House, Pascrell has compiled a liberal record on economics and a more moderate one on cultural and foreign issues. He has voted for some restrictions on abortion, including a parental notification requirement. In 2002, he voted to authorize the use of force in Iraq, and, on the Homeland Security Committee, he was a voice for improved communications among first responders. "How is it we can talk to people on the moon, but we can't talk one block away?" Pascrell asked. He authored the Firefighter Investment and Response Enhancement (FIRE) Act in 2001, and has fought regularly to increase grants to local fire departments. Pascrell is a big supporter of the Community Oriented Policing Services (COPS) office. After the program was targeted for budget cuts, Pascrell and Republican Rep. Dave Reichert of Washington in 2011 won House passage of a measure to restore $199 million to the office.

At home, Pascrell endeared himself to Bruce Springsteen fans when he joined their gripes against Ticketmaster after the ticket service advertised drastically marked-up seats through a subsidiary's website just minutes after several of the Jersey rocker's shows had sold out. When Russian businessman Mikhail Prokhorov sought to buy the New Jersey Nets basketball team in 2010 and then moved them to Brooklyn, Pascrell called for an investigation into Prokhorov's investment bank's ties with Zimbabwe for possible violations of U.S. sanctions. The National Basketball Association called his claims misinformed and approved the sale, a move Pascrell called "extremely short-sighted."

As a member of the powerful House Ways and Means Committee, Pascrell has worked with labor and consumer groups to promote "fair trade," and to expand the Trade Adjustment Assistance program for workers who have lost their jobs. Two of his pet projects were successful. A bill to designate Paterson's Great Falls as a 120-acre national park was enacted in 2009. The following year, the House passed his bill calling for development of a new set of concussion-management guidelines for student athletes. That bill has been part of his continuing focus on research for traumatic brain injuries, which he calls the "silent epidemic," especially among military members as well as athletes.

As his party's political fortunes declined in 2010, Pascrell was among the Democrats who were open in venting frustrations. When White House spokesman Robert Gibbs speculated that the Democrats' House majority was in doubt in the 2010 election, Pascrell told *The Washington Post*, "What the hell do they think we've been doing the last 12 months? We're the ones who have been taking the tough votes." During the debt ceiling standoff in the summer of 2011, Pascrell said his own party should shoulder some of the blame. He criticized House Minority Leader Nancy Pelosi, his one-time ally, for refusing to accept any deal with cuts to entitlement programs.

The 2011 round of redistricting put his comfortable House seat in jeopardy, and Pascrell survived two unusual contests. The new 9th District included his home base of Paterson, but it contained a large share of Democratic colleague Steve Rothman's former Bergen County-based district. Rothman moved to Englewood to run in the 9th, setting up a primary showdown against Pascrell.

Throughout the campaign, Pascrell hammered Rothman for running against him rather than taking on Republican Scott Garrett in the newly drawn 5th District. Rothman portrayed himself as the "Democrat's Democrat," although their voting records were quite similar. He also attacked Pascrell's record on abortion rights, while Pascrell touted his work on President Barack Obama's 2010 health care law. The race became a battle of turnout, with Pascrell's Passaic County machine up against the Rothman Bergen County team. Former President Bill Clinton endorsed Pascrell. Although Obama officially remained neutral, his top political adviser David Axelrod campaigned for Rothman. In the end, the race was not close. Pascrell turned out his voters, and won 61%-39%.

In the 2012 general election, he had an easy time against Republican Shmuley Boteach, a celebrity rabbi who wrote a best-selling book for couples entitled *Kosher Sex*. Billionaire casino magnate Sheldon Adelson seemed to waste $1 million on super PAC ads promoting Boteach. (Later, in 2014, there were news reports in New Jersey that Adelson was exploring options to build a casino in the Meadowlands, which might explain his local political interest.) Pascrell won 74%-25%. In 2014, his campaigns were uneventful. William Pascrell III, an attorney with a Passaic firm and also the counsel to Passaic County, reportedly has been groomed to succeed his father in the House.

TENTH DISTRICT

Donald Payne Jr. (D)

Elected Nov. 2012, 2nd full term; b. Dec. 17, 1958, Newark; Kean Col., attended; Baptist; married (Bea); 3 children.

Elected Office: Freeholder-at-large, Essex Cnty., 2005-2012; At-large rep., Newark City Cncl., 2006-2012, pres. 2010-12..

Professional Career: NJ highway authority, 1990-96; Dist. leader, Newark's South Ward, 1992-2013.

DC Office: 103 CHOB, 20515, 202-225-3436; Fax: 202-225-4160; Website: payne.house.gov.

State Offices: Jersey City, 201-369-0392; Newark, 973-645-3213.

Committees: *Homeland Security:* Emergency Preparedness, Response & Communications (RMM); Transportation Security. *Small Business.*

Group Ratings

	ADA	ACLU	AFL-CIO	LCV	ITI	COC	HAFA	ACU	CFG	FRC
2014	95%	83%	–	94%	60%	38%	17%	8%	13%	0%
2013	85%	C	95%	93%	C	42%	C	8%	15%	C

National Journal Ratings

	2013 LIB	—	2013 CONS
Economic	81%	—	18%
Social	73%	—	24%
Foreign	94%	—	0%
Composite	84%	—	16%

Election Results

2014 general	Donald Payne Jr. (D)...................95,734	(85%)	$552,332
	Yolanda Dentley (R)...................14,154	(13%)	
2014 primary	Donald Payne Jr. (D)...................24,490	(91%)	

Key Votes of the 113th Congress

1. Sandy storm spending	Y	5. Medical Marijuana	Y	9. Syrian Rebels Training	N
2. Violence Against Women Act	Y	6. Farm Bill	N	10. Keystone pipeline	NV
3. Guantanamo Bay Detainees	Y	7. Afghanistan Combat	NV	11. Immigration Exec. Action	N
4. Abortion 20-week ban	N	8. NSA Phone Data Collection	N	12. Bipartisan budget deal	Y

Prior winning percentages: 2012 (88%), 2012 special (97%)

Population		Race and Ethnicity		Income	
Total:	733,056	Black	51.9%	Median income:	$45,421
Urban:	93.2%	White	21.2%		*(311 of 435)*
Suburban:	6.8%	Latino	16.5%	Under $50,000	53.5%
Rural:	0.0%	Asian	6.9%	$50,000-$99,999:	26.1%
Land area:	83	Two races	1.9%	$100,000-$199,999:	15.8%
Pop/sq. mi.:	8,877.2	White Ethnic	13.9%	$200,000 or more:	4.6%
Born in state:	51.4%			Poverty Rate	20.8%
		Education			
Age Groups		H.S. grad or less:	46.0%	**Work**	
Under 18:	24.0%	Some college:	26.5%	White collar:	33.3%
18 to 34:	25.6%	College degree, 4 yr.:	18.0%	Blue collar:	47.5%
35 to 64:	39.2%	Post-grad study:	9.5%	Sales and service:	19.2%
Over 64:	11.2%				
		Military		Govt. workers:	16.5%
		Veterans/active duty:	4.1%		

Newark/Jersey City area

Newark was once the heart of New Jersey. All of the main transportation arteries led there, and its corporate headquarters buildings were the tallest in the state. In 1930, 442,000 people lived in Newark, one of every nine in New Jersey. The city fell on hard times in the latter half of the 20th century. Whole sections of the city were dominated by criminals and deserted by most law-abiding residents. By the year 2000, there were just 273,000 people left in Newark, representing one in every 30.

Voter Turnout	
2013 Total Citizen 18+	473,663
2014 House Turnout	112,123
2014 Turnout as % CVAP	23.7%
2012 Turnout as % CVAP	58%

In recent years, Newark has been attempting a turnaround. Population was up to 278,000 in 2013; new office buildings have joined the Prudential and Public Service Enterprise Group headquarters; and the New Jersey Performing Arts Center has been popular with city-dwellers seeking a less expensive experience than Manhattan. There are new restaurants and trendy bars, and a new downtown arena that houses the New Jersey Devils hockey team. The young and charismatic mayor, Democrat Cory Booker, brought energy to the city and declared war on street gangs before he was elected to the Senate in 2013. New Mayor, Ras Baraka, reached out to gang members in 2014 to try to reduce crime and he hired more police in 2015. In 2010, Facebook founder Mark Zuckerberg gave $100 million to Newark public schools—conditioned on matching grants; the program expected to employ 2,300 young people in the summer of 2015. But much remains to be done. Crime is still intolerably high and the Newark schools are under state control. Downtown office buildings had plenty of empty spaces, including plans by Prudential to vacate its office space at the end of 2015. In April 2015, a survey by WalletHub ranked Newark last among 150 cities as the best place to start a business.

There has been some industrial development around Newark Liberty International Airport, a glass and aluminum facility that has been greatly expanded for international carriers and is prospering as a hub for United Airlines. Port Newark-Elizabeth Marine Terminal is part of the larger Port of New York and New Jersey, the busiest container port on the East Coast. Old warehouses there have been cleared for more modern facilities.

2012 Presidential Vote		
Barack Obama (D) 240,052	(88%)
Mitt Romney (R)...................31,352	(12%)
2008 Presidential Vote		
Barack Obama (D) 241,834	(85%)
John McCain (R)...................42,288	(15%)
Cook Partisan Voting Index: D+34		

The 10th Congressional District of New Jersey is centered in Essex County and includes the majority of Newark. It takes in the predominantly African-American city of East Orange, where the late pop singer Whitney Houston grew up. Also in the district are parts of Bloomfield, West Orange, Jersey City and Bayonne. It is a black-majority district and one of the most heavily Democratic in the nation. President Barack Obama won 88% of the vote in 2012.

Donald Payne Jr. (D)

Donald Payne Jr., elected in 2012, succeeded his father, Rep. Donald Payne Sr., who died of colon cancer. He has been a reliable Democratic vote and initially made few waves as he focused on homeland security issues, which are vital to his metropolitan region.

A Newark native, Payne became involved in politics as a teenager when he founded and became president of the Newark South Ward Junior Democrats. He attended Kean College (now Kean University) and studied graphic arts, but did not graduate. At 21, he began working in the tolls division of the New Jersey Highway Authority, but a back injury prompted him to give up the job a few years later. In 1996, at the age of 27, he became a school bus monitor with the Essex County Educational Services Commission, and went on to become director of student transportation for the county.

In 1992, Payne was elected by local Democrats to the party position of South Ward leader in Newark. In 2006, Payne was elected to the Newark Municipal Council and was its president from 2010 to 2012. During his tenure, he co-founded Embracing Arms, a nonprofit youth-advancement organization that sponsors a book club, art programs, and public service projects for young people.

As council president, Payne also served on the board of the Newark Watershed Conservation Development Corporation, an independent and taxpayer-funded agency. Early in 2012, the finances of the corporation were called into question when *The Star-Ledger* of Newark reported on misuse of tax dollars there. Local activists demanded an investigation by the city council, resulting in a conflict of interest for Payne, so he stopped attending Watershed meetings.

Following his father's death, Payne entered the Democratic primary for the 10th District seat. His family pedigree made him a heavy favorite. Not only was his father the first

African-American member of Congress to represent New Jersey, but his uncle, William Payne, served in the New Jersey General Assembly for 10 years. Payne Jr. had the backing of the powerful Democratic Party machines in Essex, Hudson and Union counties.

Political opponents and journalists raised questions about his readiness for Congress. In an editorial board meeting with *The Star-Ledger* before the election, Payne named creating jobs as his chief priority, but declined to provide specific details. He was vague about how he would deal with several other issues, including ensuring the future of Medicare and Social Security and solving the Israeli-Palestinian conflict. On the latter issue, he said, "I have people in Congress that are looking forward to helping me understand." The newspaper editorialized, "The dispiriting truth is that his claim to the seat is based entirely on his last name. He has only the vaguest grip on key federal issues. He is simply not ready for the job, and hasn't done his homework."

Payne won the primary election with 60% of the vote, beating out fellow Newark Councilman Ron Rice and state Sen. Nia Gill, who got 19% and 17% of the vote, respectively. He got 88% in the general election in the solidly Democratic district, and appears to have become entrenched with little difficulty.

In the House, Payne got seats on Small Business and Homeland Security, where he is the ranking Democrat on the Emergency Preparedness, Response and Communications Subcommittee. In 2014, he won House passage of the bipartisan SMART Grid Study Act of 2014, which seeks to examine ways to upgrade and strengthen the nation's electric grid to protect critical infrastructure from natural disasters and cyberattacks. The House also passed his DHS Interoperable Communications Act of 2015, legislation from the Homeland Security Committee to improve emergency communications capabilities for first responders. He participated in House passage of the $51 billion Hurricane Sandy relief package, and has worked to assure the funds are delivered to the families and small business owners most in need. With Republican Rep. Markwayne Mullin of Oklahoma, he created in 2015 and co-chairs the Congressional Men's Health Caucus, which calls attention to the need for cancer screenings.

ELEVENTH DISTRICT

Rodney Frelinghuysen (R)

Elected 1994, 11th term; b. April 29, 1946, New York City, NY; Hobart Col., B.A. 1969; Episcopalian; married (Virginia); 2 children.

Military Career: U.S. Army, 1969-71 (Vietnam).

Elected Office: Morris Cnty. Bd. of Freeholders, 1974-83, dir., 1980; NJ Assembly, 1983-94.

Professional Career: Coordinator & admin. asst., Morris Cnty. Bd. of Freeholders, 1972-74.

DC Office: 2306 RHOB, 20515, 202-225-5034; Fax: 202-225-3186; Website: frelinghuysen.house.gov.

State Office: Morristown, 973-984-0711.

Committees: *Appropriations:* Defense (Chmn); Energy & Water Development, & Related Agencies; Homeland Security (VChmn).

Group Ratings

	ADA	ACLU	AFL-CIO	LCV	ITI	COC	HAFA	ACU	CFG	FRC
2014	10%	11%	–	9%	100%	93%	42%	64%	43%	75%
2013	5%	C	29%	11%	C	92%	C	54%	52%	C

National Journal Ratings

	2013 LIB	—	2013 CONS
Economic	50%	—	50%
Social	48%	—	50%
Foreign	44%	—	54%
Composite	48%	—	52%

Key Votes of the 113th Congress

1. Sandy storm spending	Y	5. Medical Marijuana	N	9. Syrian Rebels Training	Y
2. Violence Against Women Act	Y	6. Farm Bill	Y	10. Keystone pipeline	Y
3. Guantanamo Bay Detainees	N	7. Afghanistan Combat	N	11. Immigration Exec. Action	Y
4. Abortion 20-week ban	N	8. NSA Phone Data Collection	N	12. Bipartisan budget deal	Y

Election Results

2014 general	Rodney Frelinghuysen (R)......... 109,455	(63%)	$1,442,973	$6,607
	Mark Dunec (D) 65,477	(37%)	$173,617	
2014 primary	Rodney Frelinghuysen (R)........... 15,697	(67%)		
	Ricky Van Glahn (R) 7,828	(33%)		

Prior winning percentages: 2012 (59%), 2010 (67%), 2008 (62%), 2006 (62%), 2004 (68%), 2002 (72%), 2000 (68%), 1998 (68%), 1996 (66%), 1994 (71%)

Population		Race and Ethnicity		Income	
Total:	735,846	White	76.8%	Median income:	$100,143
Urban:	9.4%	Asian	9.2%		(7 of 435)
Suburban:	90.4%	Latino	8.8%	Under $50,000	22.9%
Rural:	0.3%	Black	3.5%	$50,000-$99,999:	27.0%
Land area:	529	Two races	1.7%	$100,000-$199,999:	31.9%
Pop/sq. mi.:	1,390.6	White Ethnic	59.9%	$200,000 or more:	18.3%
Born in state:	59.3%			Poverty Rate	4.7%
		Education			
Age Groups		H.S. grad or less:	28.5%	**Work**	
Under 18:	22.2%	Some college:	19.8%	White collar:	51.2%
18 to 34:	18.2%	College degree, 4 yr.:	30.8%	Blue collar:	38.1%
35 to 64:	43.1%	Post-grad study:	20.8%	Sales and service:	10.7%
Over 64:	16.5%			Govt. workers:	13.0%
		Military			
		Veterans/active duty:	5.3%		

North-Central New Jersey: Eastern Morris and Essex Counties

Morris County in New Jersey, west of the Watchung Mountains, was one of the first parts of the United States west of the seaboard to be settled. It has long been a place of comparative wealth, the home of skilled craftsmen working in the water mills and iron forges in the 19th century. But only in the late

Voter Turnout	
2013 Total Citizen 18+	529,652
2014 House Turnout	174,932
2014 Turnout as % CVAP	33%
2012 Turnout as % CVAP	65.4%

20th century did it come into its own, as one of the most affluent parts of the United States. Based on median household income, Morris County was the 10th-wealthiest county in the nation in 2014.

The very rich have lived here for many decades, connected to Manhattan by commuter rail. But starting in the 1970s, new residents rushed out through the newly completed interstates. Prompted by court-required zoning changes, old farms and woods were cleared to make way for new subdivisions. This is not just a bedroom community. New Jersey's economic energy, entrepreneurial creativity and research expertise are found in office complexes and corporate headquarters. Large forested areas of state parkland remain, and preservation of the state's Highlands region, a 1,000-square-mile forest- and lake-filled oasis, has been a priority. The Highlands Council, tasked with protecting the area from development, voted in 2012 to remove its executive director in favor of a pro-business ally of Republican Gov. Chris Christie, who is a resident of Morris County. Environmentalists blasted Christie, and the council endured turmoil as the next executive director departed after less than two years. In October 2012, Hurricane Sandy's winds knocked down utility poles and caused 171,000 people to lose power. Six

2012 Presidential Vote		
Mitt Romney (R)................183,427	(53%)	
Barack Obama (D) 163,183	(47%)	
2008 Presidential Vote		
John McCain (R)................194,639	(52%)	
Barack Obama (D) 175,560	(47%)	
Cook Partisan Voting Index: R+6		

Morris County buildings were damaged in the storm. But the county is far enough inland that the power of the storm had subsided from when it crossed the shore.

The 11th Congressional District of New Jersey takes in about three-fourths of Morris County, including the county seat of Morristown, Randolph and Rockaway. In 2014, *Money* magazine ranked Parsippany-Troy Hills 16th among the best places to live. Morris is about half of the district, which also includes slices of Essex, Passaic and Sussex counties. This area is family territory, with relatively few singles. It's not strongly culturally conservative, but not aggressively liberal, either. It is predominantly white, though Hispanics have grown to 9 percent of the population. The 11th still leans firmly Republican, with a moneyed caste.

Rodney Frelinghuysen (R)

Republican Rodney Frelinghuysen, first elected in 1994, has a record as a foreign policy conservative and a fiscal moderate. As chairman of the House Appropriations Subcommittee on Defense, he has faced major challenges in balancing a tight budget with the many demands that have been placed on it. As the second most-senior Republican on the full committee, he appears to be in line in 2017 to take that chairmanship, still one of the House's most powerful posts.

Frelinghuysen is the scion of one of New Jersey's most durable political families. The Frelinghuysens emigrated from Germany near the Dutch border in 1720 and settled in what is now the 11th District. Four Frelinghuysens served as senators from New Jersey, starting in 1793 and as recently as 1923. Theodore Frelinghuysen was the candidate for vice president in 1844 (spawning the memorable chant, "Hurrah! Hurrah! The country's risin',' for Henry Clay and Frelinghuysen"). Frederick Frelinghuysen was President Chester Arthur's secretary of state. Peter Frelinghuysen, Rodney's father, was elected to the House in 1952 and served until his retirement in 1974. "He was always my role model," he told *The Star-Ledger* of Newark after his father's death in 2011.

History tends to repeat itself, and Frelinghuysens have been involved in every presidential impeachment. Rodney Frelinghuysen's great-great-grandfather Frederick voted to convict Andrew Johnson in 1868, and his father, Peter, after the revelations of July 1974, would have voted to impeach Richard Nixon if the president had not resigned. The current-generation Frelinghuysen voted to impeach Bill Clinton in December 1998.

As a child, Rodney Frelinghuysen lived in the large brick house on Georgetown's N Street that was later owned by *Washington Post* Editor Ben Bradlee and his wife, Sally Quinn. He attended St. Albans preparatory school with the future Democratic vice president, Al Gore. After graduating from Hobart College, he completed Army basic training at Fort Dix and served in Vietnam, where he built roads in the Mekong Delta. In 1972, he was an aide to Morris County Freeholder Dean Gallo, who was later elected to Congress. Frelinghuysen was a freeholder himself from 1974 to 1983. He was elected to the state Assembly in 1983, and had two tours as chairman of the Appropriations Committee. He ran for Congress in 1990 in a nearby district, but lost the primary to Dick Zimmer. In August 1994, Gallo retired from Congress because of illness, and Frelinghuysen was chosen to be the Republican nominee at a September party convention. He was elected with 71% of the vote.

Frelinghuysen has taken moderate and even liberal stands on some social issues, though he generally aligns with his party on defense and foreign policy. He refused to join three fellow New Jersey Republican moderates who supported in 2009 the cap-and-trade bill aimed at reducing greenhouse gas emissions, calling it a "job-killer." But he was one of seven House Republicans that year who voted to protect federal funding for Planned Parenthood, which led to anti-abortion protests outside his New Jersey office. In 2012, he joined Democrats in opposing GOP measures to open the Arctic National Wildlife Refuge to oil drilling, to eliminate the Economic Development Administration and Legal Services Corporation, and to double the number of oil and gas drilling leases on federal land. In May 2015, he was one of four Republicans who voted against the House-passed bill that would ban abortions after 20 weeks of pregnancy. He has cited numerous objections to the Affordable Care Act, and has supported its repeal along with the chief Republican priorities in the House majority.

While still a freshman, he secured a seat on the Appropriations Committee. As Frelinghuysen has gained seniority, he claimed the gavel of the Energy and Water Development Subcommittee in 2011. He sounded an ominous note for Obama's clean energy research plans when he said that in theory, he supported the arm of the Energy Department that conducts such research, but that, "I'm not sure in these times I'd find that many members who would agree." The energy and water bill he got through the House in 2012 reduced energy efficiency and renewable energy programs by $886 million. Obama's Office of Management and Budget objected, saying that amount represented the largest cut in those areas since 2006 and would "leave U.S. competitiveness at risk in new markets and clean energy industries." The bill was eventually rolled into a continuing resolution that maintained funding at current levels.

Following the death of veteran Appropriations Republican Rep. Bill Young of Florida in October 2013, Frelinghuysen became chairman of the Defense Subcommittee. When he took the position, he described the responsibility to "provide for a strong national defense and support the men and women who provide for that defense each and every day." He has made numerous trips to Afghanistan and the Mideast to monitor how the military is spending its money. Following an April 2015 trip to that region in a delegation led by Speaker John Boehner, he reported "growing concern about Iran's aggressive behavior," and the need for a "clear comprehensive strategy" to take on the growing threat posed by the Islamic State. "The Middle East is truly on fire and the United States needs to demonstrate our clear support for our allies and partners," he concluded. In May 2015, *Politico* reported that Frelinghuysen's spending bill was on a "collision course" with Obama because of the budget gamesmanship on both sides. As approved by the committee, it included increased funding for air reconnaissance and surveillance operations for American combat commanders. In the final analysis, he predicted, "there will be some sort of grand bargain" that will include defense spending. In June, he lost a late-night House floor battle to the Armed Services Committee on budget control of the new *Ohio*-class submarine program.

As his official biography notes, Frelinghuysen "is well known for championing the important work being done at New Jersey's vital military installations," including McGuire Air Force Base and Fort Dix, whose future has become a concern to many officials in New Jersey. As Defense Subcommittee chairman, Frelinghuysen is positioned to be an influential booster of those facilities. His experience as a veteran also has made him a strong defender of Veterans Affairs medical centers, in New Jersey and elsewhere.

Appropriations chairman Hal Rogers of Kentucky is term-limited in that position after the 2016 election. With Frelinghuysen next in line in Republican seniority, that positions him to take over as committee chairman. He could face a challenge from within the ranks, which GOP leaders would need to resolve. As chairman, he would receive far more news-media attention, compared to the low profile that he has kept and received from reporters.

Because New Jersey currently has no senator on the Senate Appropriations Committee, and no Democrat on House Appropriations, Frelinghuysen has become the go-to guy for the entire delegation on projects benefiting New Jersey. In past years, he has concentrated on big projects: construction of the Hudson-Bergen light rail, dredging of channels in the Port of New York and New Jersey, and slowing erosion on the Jersey Shore.

On other issues, Frelinghuysen has been known nationally as the sponsor of the "Know Your Caller" law, which bars telemarketers from interfering with Caller ID systems of customers seeking to avoid such solicitations. Another of his pet projects has been environmental cleanup in his district, which has a large number of Superfund sites. He tours the sites annually with environmental and local officials to get updates on cleanup progress.

Frelinghuysen has not been seriously challenged for reelection. In 2012, Democrat John Arvanites held him to 59%, the lowest winning percentage of his career. Two years later, he faced a primary challenge from Rick von Glahn, a home-improvement contractor who wanted to rein in federal spending. Frelinghuysen won, 67%-33%. In November, he was reelected 63%-37% against Democrat Mark Dunec, a political newcomer and self-styled problem-solver, who was out-spent $1.4 million to $173,000. In January 2015, *Roll Call* newspaper reported that Frelinghuysen had slipped to 19th among the wealthiest members of Congress.

TWELFTH DISTRICT

Bonnie Watson Coleman (D)

Elected 2014, 1st term; b. Feb. 6, 1945, Camden; Thomas Edison St. Col., B.A. 1985; Baptist; married (William); 3 children.

Elected Office: NJ Assembly, 1998-2014, maj. ldr., 2006-09.

DC Office: 126 CHOB, 20515, 202-225-5801; Fax: 202-225-6025; Website: watsoncoleman.house.gov.

State Offices: Ewing, 609-883-0026.

Committees: *Homeland Security:* Emergency Preparedness, Response & Communications; Oversight & Mgmt. Efficiency (RMM). *Oversight & Gov't Reform:* Health Care, Benefits, & Administrative Rules; Transportation & Public Assets.

Election Results

2014 general	Bonnie Watson Coleman (D)	90,430	(61%)	$1,388,283	
	Alieta Eck (R)	54,168	(37%)	$223,879	$1,041
2014 primary	Bonnie Watson Coleman (D)	15,603	(43%)		
	Linda Greenstein (D)	10,089	(28%)		
	Upendra Chivukula (D)	7,890	(22%)		
	Andrew Zwicker (D)	2,668	(7%)		

Population		Race and Ethnicity		Income	
Total:	750,594	White	50.8%	Median income:	$75,927
Urban:	28.2%	Black	17.1%		*(41 of 435)*
Suburban:	71.8%	Latino	15.1%	Under $50,000	32.6%
Rural:	0.0%	Asian	14.6%	$50,000-$99,999:	29.1%
Land area:	395	Two races	1.2%	$100,000-$199,999:	26.5%
Pop/sq. mi.:	1,900.8	White Ethnic	35.5%	$200,000 or more:	11.7%
Born in state:	46.6%			Poverty Rate	9.6%
		Education			
Age Groups		H.S. grad or less:	36.0%	**Work**	
Under 18:	22.1%	Some college:	20.9%	White collar:	43.8%
18 to 34:	22.7%	College degree, 4 yr.:	24.3%	Blue collar:	40.1%
35 to 64:	41.6%	Post-grad study:	18.8%	Sales and service:	16.0%
Over 64:	13.6%			Govt. workers:	13.6%
		Military			
		Veterans/active duty:	4.6%		

Central New Jersey: Middlesex County, Trenton

New Jersey politics is centered in Trenton. The city has been a manufacturing mecca since the 19th century, when it was the setting for the Lenox and Boehm china factories and the old Roebling ironworks, which produced parts for many of the great American bridges. Its lifeline today is U.S. 1, on any

Voter Turnout	
2013 Total Citizen 18+	491,940
2014 House Turnout	148,366
2014 Turnout as % CVAP	30.2%
2012 Turnout as % CVAP	60.4%

day crowded with cars taking high-salaried workers and clerical help to one of the East Coast's thickest concentrations of office buildings. The highway also is now a locus of telecommunications and pharmaceutical research, and a vital artery to the brain centers of Princeton and Rutgers.

The 12th Congressional District includes Trenton, which is 52% African American and 34% Hispanic. It stretches east to East Brunswick, with a significant Asian population, and South River, a city that has attracted Polish, Russian and Portuguese immigrants. It is home to Princeton, with its distinguished universe of alumni that includes first lady Michelle Obama. Since 1865, the iconic "Dinky" train has connected the town of Princeton with nearby Princeton Junction, ferrying passengers such as Albert Einstein and Woodrow

Wilson. With roughly $2 billion in annual spending, Princeton has become a vital cog in the local economy. By contrast, the weak economy of Trenton has forced it to make continuing cutbacks in operations.

In the north, the district takes in Plainfield, Scotch Plains and modest-income suburbs such as Franklin, which made *Money* magazine's list of 50 best small cities to live in for 2014. Much of the district's population is in Middlesex and Mercer counties, which both voted heavily for President Barack Obama in the 2012 presidential race. Somerset and Union counties have small slices of the district. As recently as two decades ago, this was a highly competitive district that House Republicans frequently won. Back then, it had a small minority population, in contrast to the latest 17% African American and 15% Hispanic. The district as a whole is safe for Democrats.

2012 Presidential Vote		
Barack Obama (D)	198,155	(67%)
Mitt Romney (R)	96,520	(33%)
2008 Presidential Vote		
Barack Obama (D)	203,899	(66%)
John McCain (R)	103,322	(33%)
Cook Partisan Voting Index:	D+14	

Bonnie Watson Coleman (D)

Democrat Bonnie Watson Coleman was easily elected in 2014 to succeed retiring Democratic Rep. Rush Holt. A well-regarded state legislator and active partisan, she is the first African-American woman to represent New Jersey in Congress, and the first woman that her state has sent to Capitol Hill since 2002.

Watson Coleman grew up in a political family, with her father, a state assemblyman, often guiding debates at the dinner table. She graduated from Thomas Edison State College. Her public service began in 1966, when she went to work for the state public safety department's civil rights division. She later headed the civil rights office of the state's Department of Transportation before taking on senior roles at the Department of Community Affairs. In 1997, she was elected to the General Assembly, where she rose through the ranks to become majority leader. She was the first African-American woman to chair the State Democratic Committee.

In the Assembly, Watson Coleman promoted strongly liberal positions on issues such as gun safety, the minimum wage and women's health care funding, and worked to reduce recidivism among state prisoners. She took an active role in legislation on identity-theft protection and the expansion of urban enterprise zones. In 2014, she joined the panel investigating GOP Gov. Chris Christie's role in the 2013 George Washington Bridge closing, but stepped down after she came under fire for partiality; she had said earlier that Christie should resign.

When Holt, a nuclear physicist and a leading progressive in Congress, said that he would step down, Watson Coleman announced her bid. She got a boost from the Progressive Change Campaign Committee, major unions and women's groups such as EMILY's List. In the June primary, only state senator Linda Greenstein posed any real competition. Watson Coleman topped the field with 43% to 28% for Greenstein, who ran relatively close only in her Middlesex County base. She breezed in November with 61% against Republican Alieta Eck, who sought to become the first woman physician in Congress but was out-spent 6-to-1.

In the House, Watson Coleman joined the committees on Oversight and Government Reform, and Homeland Security, where she is ranking Democrat on the Homeland Oversight subcommittee. In May 2015, the House-passed Cybersecurity Protection Advancement Act included her amendment to encourage public awareness and education on personal cybersecurity issues. She also filed a bill to restrict online sales of ammunition.

★ NEW MEXICO ★

New Mexico has some of the oldest settlements in America and some of its newest technologies, often in surrealistic proximity to one another. The oldest permanently inhabited city in the United States is not Plymouth or Jamestown or St. Augustine; it is probably Acoma, which thrived in what is now New Mexico long before the Spanish conquistadors arrived in 1540, and has been continuously inhabited for more than 470 years since. While the settlers of Jamestown and Plymouth were building flimsy wood houses, the Indians in New Mexico were living in extensive dwellings hundreds of years old, made with the adobe that is still the characteristic building material here. They used small pebbles as mulch to retain scarce moisture on the rocky desert land.

Nearly five centuries later, much of what makes New Mexico distinctive derives from centuries of Indigenous architecture and artistic traditions. The cultures in other states are mostly an outgrowth of what early European settlers brought to the land. The number of Native American people sharply declined, either killed off by disease or maltreatment or driven onto reservations. History took a different course in New Mexico, the northernmost salient of the great Indian-Spanish civilizations of the Cordillera, the mountain chain that extends south to Mexico and through Central and South America to the southern end of Chile. The Spanish settled in Santa Fe in 1609 and although their hold on the town was often tenuous, their imprint remains. There are still 19 Indian pueblos in New Mexico today, plus the reservations of the Navajo and the Jicarilla Apache and the Mescalero Apache. A very substantial minority of today's New Mexicans are descendants of those Indians, or the Spanish, or both. New Mexico's population was 47% Hispanic in 2010, the highest percentage of any state, and 10% American Indian; only 40% are non-Hispanic whites. Few Hispanics are immigrants: Only 10% of the population is foreign born, but 36% speak a foreign language at home.

Modern New Mexico got a boost from science and technology. It was to a remote mesa called Los Alamos that Gen. Leslie Groves brought his Manhattan Project scientists during World War II to build a secret town and develop a secret weapon that would, in two explosions, end World War II and change the course of history. Los Alamos is still a government laboratory crucial to producing U.S. nuclear weapons, and it's still sometimes a source of controversy; in 2012, the Obama administration announced an indefinite delay of the $5.8 billion Chemistry Metallurgy Research Replacement Facility, but then Sen. Carl Levin of Michigan put it back in the 2012 defense bill. New Mexico has other high-tech sites as well: the White Sands Missile Range near Alamogordo, where the first atomic bomb was detonated in July 1945, and the Sandia National Laboratories, near Albuquerque, run by Lockheed Martin, a non-nuclear weapons research facility with one of the fastest computers in the world, used to simulate nuclear explosions. But science has limits. At the federal Waste Isolation Pilot Plant (WIPP) near Carlsbad, where the U.S. deposits transuranic radioactive waste, a 55-gallon drum of nuclear waste buried in a salt mine cavern burst apart in 2014, shutting down the nuclear waste disposal site. The incident gave more ammunition to critics who have questioned the Department of Energy's management of nuclear waste. A DOE report said workers at the Los Alamos National Laboratory improperly prepared the waste for disposal by mixing it with organic kitty litter as an absorbent, creating a reactive and ignitable waste. Inorganic material was called for. The Energy Department agreed to fund $73 million in road and water projects around New Mexico as part of a settlement with the state over the radiation leakage. Energy officials said it could cost roughly $500 million to make the facility fully operational by 2018. At the western edge of White Sands in Sierra County is Spaceport America, an 18,000-acre facility in the New Mexico desert built with more than $215 million in state and local tax dollars to support space tourism. The list of boosters included both former Democratic Gov. Bill Richardson and Republican Gov. Susana Martinez, and billionaire Richard Branson predicted his Virgin Galactic would be ferrying passengers on space tours by 2014 for up to $250,000 a ticket. The project was viewed as a potential source of private-sector jobs in a region that could use them. But those hopes were dashed in October 2014, when Virgin Galactic's SpaceShipTwo rocket plane broke up on a test flight and crashed in the Mojave Desert, killing a pilot. The crash renewed calls from some New Mexico lawmakers to sell the facility.

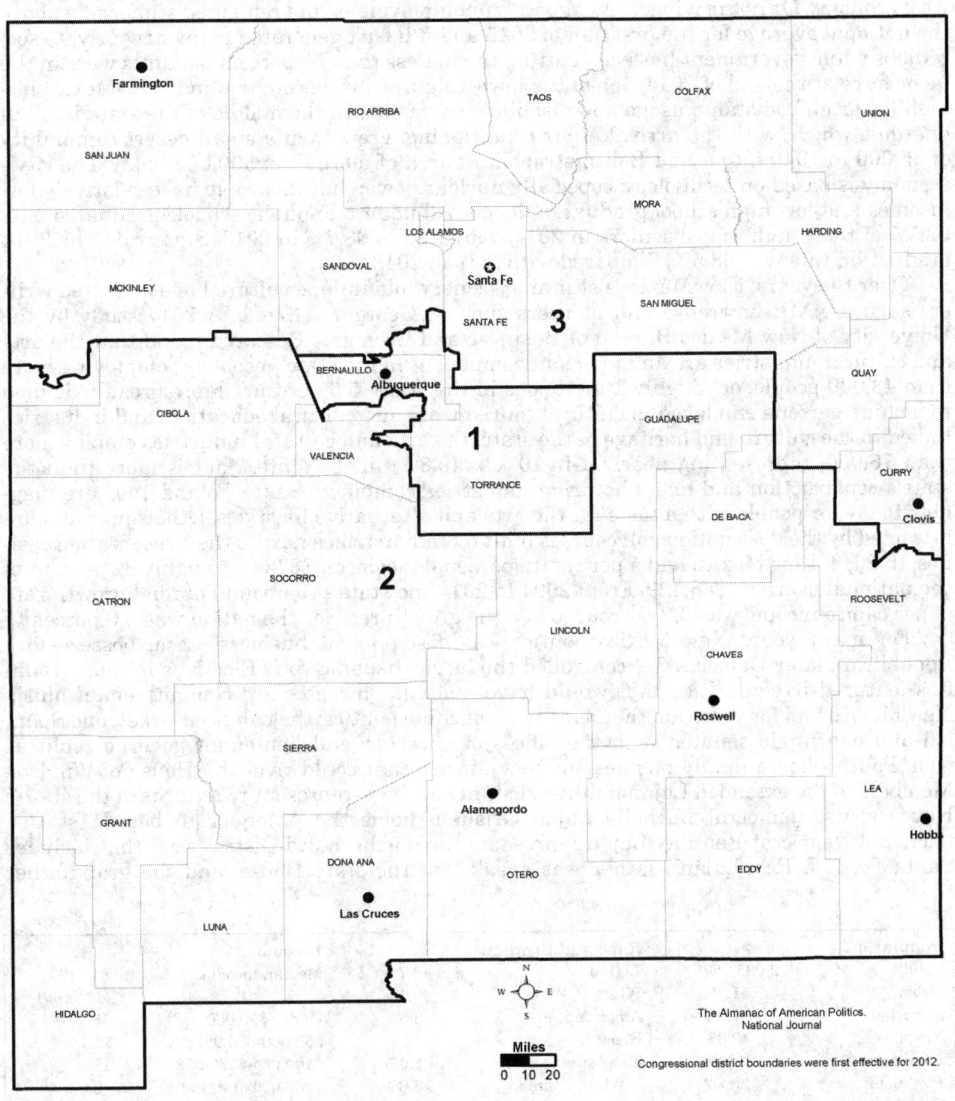

The Almanac of American Politics.
National Journal

Congressional district boundaries were first effective for 2012.

Miles
0 10 20

New and old New Mexico intermingle in varying proportions in this land of majestic vistas. Historic Acoma shares its nickname, "Sky City," with a nearby casino. The Hispanic and Indian cultures predominate north and west of Albuquerque, with picturesque old towns and active pueblos, low-income Indian reservations, and lavish gambling resorts. "Little Texas" in the south and east has small cities, plenty of oil wells, vast cattle ranches, and desolate military bases; the region resembles, economically and culturally, the adjacent West Texas high plains. Here, as everywhere in New Mexico, government is a prime employer, accounting for 24% of jobs, one of the highest figures in the country, and often the moving force in the local economy. Or not moving. New Mexico's unemployment rate remained stubbornly above the national average for the first half of 2015 and it hasn't generated many new private sector jobs while government has been cutting them. Less than 58 percent of adults were in the labor force at the end of 2014, one of the lowest figures in the country, and New Mexico has high levels of food stamp usage and disability payments. In the middle of the state is Albuquerque, which, with the arrival of air conditioning, grew from a small desert community of 35,000 in 1940 into a Sun Belt metropolitan area of more than 900,000 today. The city's economy is based on technology, especially nuclear power, but its people have relatively low incomes and low high school graduation levels. Albuquerque public schools graduated only 62.5% of their high school seniors in 2014 compared to 68.7% in 2013. Statewide, the 2014 graduation rate was 68.5%, compared with 70% in 2013.

Over the years, New Mexico's stunning scenery and unique culture have attracted writers such as D.H. Lawrence and painters such as Georgia O'Keeffe. A 2014 study by the University of New Mexico Bureau of Business and Economic Research found that the arts and cultural industries are an important component in the state's economy, employing more than 43,000 people, or roughly 1-in-18 jobs in the state (5.5 percent). More broadly defined to include persons employed in cultural tourism, art and cultural education, and industries linked to the culture and heritage of the state, the arts and cultural industries employ more than 76,000, representing nearly 1-in-10 jobs (9.8%) in the state. That is more than the state's construction and manufacturing industries combined. Santa Fe and Taos are magnets today for people with a taste for the arts and alternative lifestyles. Other migrants are attracted by the destination golf courses built by Indian tribes next to their reservation casinos. In 2014, New Mexico had a per capita personal income of $37,605, roughly 82 percent of the national average, $46,129. From 2004 to 2014 the state's compound annual growth rate of per capita income was 3.2 percent, while the growth rate for the nation was 3.0 percent.

For many years New Mexico politics was a somnolent business. Local bosses—first Republican, later Democratic—controlled the large Hispanic vote. Elections in many counties featured irregularities that would have made a Chicago ward committeeman blush. New Mexico had for years another feature of machine politics: the balanced ticket, one Spanish and one Anglo senator, with the offices of governor and lieutenant governor split as well. Politics has a family business in New Mexico that could rival the House of Windsor. Members of the extended Luján family—distant cousins—represent two-thirds of the state's House seats: Democrat Michelle Luján Grisham holds the Albuquerque-based 1st District, and Democrat Ben Ray Luján represents the northern 3rd District seat that includes Santa Fe. Ben Ray Luján's father was speaker of the state House, and the grandfather

Population		Race and Ethnicity		Income	
Total:	2,085,287	Latino	46.7%	Median income:	$42,127
Urban:	51.3%	White	40.1%		(44 of 50)
Suburban:	7.9%	Amer. Indian	8.5%	Under $50,000	55.1%
Rural:	40.8%	Black	1.7%	$50,000-$99,999:	28.2%
Land area:	121,298	Two races	1.6%	$100,000-$199,999:	13.8%
Pop/sq. mi.:	17.2	White Ethnic	13.6%	$200,000 or more:	2.8%
Born in state:	52.0%			Poverty Rate	17.9%
		Education			
Age Groups		H.S. grad or less:	42.3%	**Work**	
Under 18:	24.4%	Some college:	31.3%	White collar:	34.7%
18 to 34:	23.3%	College degree, 4 yr.:	15.0%	Blue collar:	43.5%
35 to 64:	37.6%	Post-grad study:	11.4%	Sales and service:	21.8%
Over 64:	14.7%				
		Military		Govt. workers:	22.7%
		Veterans/active duty:	10.3%		

of Michelle Luján Grisham was chief justice of the state Supreme Court. Her uncle, Manuel Luján Jr., was a longtime GOP congressman for the 1st district as well as secretary of interior for President George H.W. Bush. And Manuel Luján's father was mayor of Santa Fe. As former GOP Sen. Pete Domenici once joked, New Mexico has three political parties: Democrats, Republicans and the Lujáns.

Voter Turnout	
2013 Total Citizen 18+	1,451,562
2014 Highest Statewide Turnout	512,805
2014 Turnout as % CVAP	35.3%
2012 Turnout as % CVAP	53.8%

Legislature		
Senate:	24D	18R
House:	37R	33D

Presidential Politics New Mexico was a battleground state in the first two presidential elections in this century, but fell off the list in the third. In 2000, after some ragged vote counting, the state gave a 366-vote margin to Al Gore. In 2004, it reported a 5,988-vote margin for George W. Bush. Then-GOP Sen. Pete Domenici had worked the phones with television network news officials in the early morning hours after Election Day insisting that the state was going to tip into the GOP column. Voter rolls and turnout swelled that year, thanks to Gov. Bill Richardson's well-publicized efforts to register

2012 Presidential Vote		
Barack Obama (D)	415,335	(53%)
Mitt Romney (R)	335,788	(43%)
Gary Johnson (Lib)	27,788	(4%)

2012 Presidential Primary		
Mitt Romney (R)	65,935	(73%)
Rick Santorum (R)	9,517	(11%)
Ron Paul (R)	9,363	(10%)
Newt Gingrich (R)	5,298	(6%)

2008 Presidential Vote		
Barack Obama (D)	472,422	(57%)
John McCain (R)	346,832	(42%)

new Democrats and to the Bush campaign's less-noticed organizational efforts. Bush won 44% of the Hispanic vote, up from 32% in 2000.

The 2008 contest was another story, with Barack Obama beating John McCain 57%-42%. The Obama campaign opened 39 offices across the state and shrewdly concentrated its efforts where there were new Democrats. In most counties, turnout rose only 1% to 9%, and in 12 counties it actually dropped. But it rose 7% or more in metro Albuquerque, Santa Fe, and Taos, in heavily Hispanic Rio Arriba County, and in the two heavily Indian counties to the west, in and around Las Cruces. Obama won 74% of first-time voters, 71% of young voters, and 83% of young Latino voters. McCain won whites 56%-42%, almost identical to Bush's 56%-43% support among whites in 2004. But Obama carried Hispanics 69%-30%. The story was similar in 2012, except that former Republican Gov. Gary Johnson was running on the Libertarian ticket and won 4% in his home state. Obama's vote dipped in nearly every part of the state from its 2008 levels. Whites voted 56%-41% for Mitt Romney, and the exit poll showed Hispanics casting a lower percentage of the vote than in 2008, 37% versus 41%. But Obama's 65%-29% margin among them was enough for a solid 53%-43% victory.

New Mexico traditionally held its presidential primary in June; long after every major party nomination was clinched from 1984 to 2004. For 2008, with Richardson as a candidate, New Mexico scheduled its Democratic primary for February 5, Super Tuesday. By that time, Richardson had withdrawn, but the race between Obama and Hillary Clinton was so close it took nine days to count all the votes, including 17,000 provisional ballots. Clinton won 49%-48%, carrying heavily Hispanic counties and Little Texas. Obama carried metro Albuquerque, Santa Fe, Taos, and two rural counties. The Republicans did not hold their primary until June, when no one was paying attention. McCain won 86% of the vote. In 2012, the primary was again in June, and Romney won 73%.

Congressional Districts New Mexico's three congressional districts have been substantially the same since the state gained a third seat in 1982: one heavily Hispanic and Democratic district in Santa Fe and the north, one more rural and Republican district in the south, and a competitive Albuquerque seat in the

114th Congress Lineup	
1 R	2 D
113th Congress Lineup	
1 R	2 D

middle. Both parties have held all three seats at various points, but as Albuquerque's 1st District has moved away from Republicans, the prevailing balance has shifted from a 2-to-1 Republican edge to a 2-to-1 Democratic advantage. In 2001, Democrats in the legislature sought to make the 1st, then held by Republican Heather Wilson, more Democratic. But

Republican Gov. Gary Johnson vetoed their proposal, a court made only minimal changes, and Democrats didn't pick up the 1st until 2008.

New Mexico grew faster than the national average between 2000 and 2010, but fell far short of gaining a fourth seat. Control once again was split between a Democratic legislature and a Republican governor, and this time Democrats couldn't agree on an approach. Many preferred to shore up the 1st District because Democrat Martin Heinrich was running for Senate. Others sought to make the 2nd District more Hispanic. The state Supreme Court assigned the matter to retired Judge James Hall, who in December 2011 adopted a compromise plan supported by both Martinez and a band of Democratic legislators. The new map shifted part of Valencia County from the 1st District to the 2nd to balance population, but bore little partisan consequence.

Governor

Susana Martinez (R)

Elected 2010, term expires Jan. 2019, 2nd term; b. July 14, 1959, El Paso, TX; U. of TX, El Paso, B.A. 1981, U. of OK, J.D. 1986; Catholic; married (Chuck Franco); 1 child.

Elected Office: Dist. atty., Dona Ana Cnty., 1996-2010.

Professional Career: Prosecutor, Dona Ana Cnty., 1986-97.

Office: 490 Old Santa Fe Trail, Rm. 400, Santa Fe, 87501, 505-476-2200; Website: governor.state.nm.us.

Election Results

2014 general	Susana Martinez (R)	293,443	(57%)
	Gary King (D)	219,362	(43%)
2014 primary	Susana Martinez (R)	unopposed	

Prior winning percentage: 2010 (53%)

Republican Susana Martinez became the first Hispanic woman governor of a state when she was elected in 2010, and from that point on she's been seen as a rising GOP star. While she jousted with Democratic state legislators, and an occasional Republican, she easily won reelection in 2014 campaigning as a pragmatist with broad appeal, which is likely to keep her in the national limelight.

Martinez was born and raised in El Paso, Texas, the daughter of a sheriff's deputy who started a successful security business with his wife. She helped to care for her developmentally disabled older sister while working part-time as a security guard and going to school. After graduating from the University of Texas at El Paso, she went on to law school at the University of Oklahoma. Martinez joined the Dona Ana County district attorney's office in Las Cruces, an hour's drive north of El Paso, and mainly handled prosecution of crimes against children.

In 1996, she decided to run for district attorney. Although she was a registered Democrat, she agreed to meet with local Republicans who hoped to recruit her—an idea she said she initially disdained. "I remember telling my husband, 'We're going to be very polite. We're going to say thank you very much, and we're going to leave,'" she told the *Los Angeles Times*. But she said the meeting influenced her thinking, and recalled her reaction, "We got in the car, we looked at each other and said, 'Oh my God, we are Republicans! Now what do we do?'" Martinez switched parties and did not expect to win in an area where registered Democrats outnumber Republicans by about 3-to-1. But she managed to attract enough support from her old party to capture the office with nearly 60% of the vote. She went on to win reelection three times with ease. As district attorney, she gained a reputation for being driven and meticulous. She went after members of Mexico's drug cartels and prosecuted a number of high-profile child abuse cases herself. She also developed a habit of generously rewarding her staff; the *Albuquerque Journal* reported in August 2010 that she gave out around

$477,000 in bonuses from fiscal years 2006 to 2010, more than three times as much as any other district attorney in the state.

In July 2009, Martinez announced her candidacy for governor, vowing to "remove pay-to-play in this state." She drew the attention of the Republican Governors Association, which saw the merits of having a female Hispanic join its ranks. The organization steered money to her campaign and helped line up a coveted endorsement from former Alaska Gov. Sarah Palin. She won the June 1 GOP primary with 51% over four other candidates, including long-time New Mexico Sen. Pete Domenici's son, Pete Domenici Jr., and Allen Weh, a former state Republican chairman. Her victory set up a battle with Lt. Gov. Diane Denish, whom Martinez wasted no time linking with outgoing Democratic Gov. Bill Richardson whose image had been eroded by an unsuccessful 2008 presidential bid and a federal investigation into state billing practices (that didn't result in any charges against him). She even challenged the outgoing governor to a debate and promised to reverse Richardson's policies on climate change and water pollution, which she claimed had driven away industries. The national Republican tide was strong in 2010 and Martinez won 53%-47%. In addition to winning her home county of Dona Ana, she edged out Denish in Bernalillo County, the state's most populous, and dominated most of the state's rural areas.

Taking office, Martinez signed executive orders to enhance public access to state records, a sharp contrast to Richardson, whose administration was criticized for invoking executive privilege to deny records requests. She ordered the sale of the state's jet and terminated two personal chefs at the governor's residence. Her first, $5.4 billion budget provided more money for public school classrooms while cutting spending for colleges, universities, and local education administrators. She also pulled the state out of a federal program to reintroduce Mexican gray wolves into the Southwest, and tried to suspend regulations aimed at reducing greenhouse gas emissions blamed for global warming, before the state Supreme Court overruled her. She showed a populist streak that helped keep her approval rating at high levels. When record-low temperatures led to natural gas shortages, she dispatched National Guardsmen to help the gas company relight the pilot lights of freezing homeowners.

She occasionally rankled Democratic lawmakers by avoiding negotiations on many of her initiatives. She further angered them when her political action committee aggressively went after two of the legislature's top Democrats and helped to unseat one of them in the November 2012 elections—Senate President Pro Tem Tim Jennings, a veteran conservative Democrat popular among his GOP colleagues. Jennings later scoffed at the idea promoted by some national media outlets that Martinez was adept at reaching across the aisle. "It's her way or the highway," Jennings told *The New Mexican*. Democrats have also called her a "dictator." Former GOP state chairman Harvey Yates Jr. told an online publication that Martinez's administration had "too often been a divisive force rather than a uniting force" in its dealings with the legislature. But she has also broken with party orthodoxy on a number of fronts. Although she had opposed President Barack Obama's Affordable Care Act as a candidate for governor, in 2013, Martinez approved a state expansion of Medicaid under the law, which could cover up to 170,000 of the working poor. She told the state Legislature: "The election is over and the Supreme Court has ruled. My job is not to play party politics, but to implement this law in a way that best serves New Mexico." Unlike many of her GOP counterparts, Martinez has remained a defender of the Common Core public education standards believing that they are the best way to measure school achievement, which has lagged in the state. She also continues to support comprehensive immigration reform. And in 2012, she criticized the comments by the party's presidential standard bearer that undocumented immigrants should self-deport as well as his candid musings at a fundraising event that "47 percent" of Americans were dependent on the government and thus unlikely to vote for him.

Democrats were hopeful they might be able to derail Martinez's 2014 reelection bid and their standard bearer was an established political figure, Attorney General Gary King, who was elected in 2006 after serving a dozen years in the state House of Representatives. His father, Bruce King was the longest-serving governor in the state's history, winning three terms, 1971-75, 1979-1983 and 1991-1995. But the son lacked dad's talent as a folksy, glad-handing pol who maintained a cowboy image. Despite the state's lackluster economy, a poverty rate that was the second highest in the nation, and festering social ills, Martinez exuded her trademark charisma on the stump. Her campaign warchest overwhelmed King's, and the Republican Governors Association also spent heavily on her behalf, attacking the Democrat so Martinez could remain above the partisan fray. Touting her bi-partisan credentials, her campaign even ran an ad featuring praise from the liberal American Civil

Liberties Union for signing a law promoting equal pay for women, a rarity for Republican candidates. Despite the fact that Democrats hold roughly a three-to-two advantage in party registration, Martinez won easily, 57%-43%, carrying 28 of the state's 33 counties, except for the Democratic strongholds around Santa Fe and Taos in the north. She handily won Hispanic majority counties like Chavez and Guadalupe in rural New Mexico, and Valencia near Albuquerque. But her victory was magnified by the GOP takeover of the state House of Representatives, the first time that had happened in 60 years. Martinez had contributed to that effort and the party picked up three House seats in Las Cruces and Dona Ana County, her old political base.

As the nation's only GOP Latina governor, Martinez has been touted as a potential running mate for the 2016 Republican presidential nominee, but during her 2014 campaign she vowed to serve a full term if reelected. That circumspection didn't stop her from weighing in on the claims by 2016 GOP White House hopeful Donald Trump that Mexican immigrants brought drugs and crime to the U.S. and are rapists. "I think those are horrible things to say about anyone or any culture ... anyone of any ethnicity," said Martinez. "I mean, that is uncalled for ... completely." As her second term began, the governor signed a long-term gaming agreement between the state and five tribal governments, pending federal approval, that designated a portion of casino revenues for gambling addiction services, a $295 million capital infrastructure improvement bill, a modest package of tax incentives to stimulate economic growth targeting investors, high-tech employers and New Mexicans who incur major out-of-pocket medical expenses. She also approved a law sharply restricting the practice of civil forfeiture, a policy that critics, particularly libertarians, say denies citizens due process and gives a financial incentive to law enforcement to seize property. That combination reflects the broad political appeal Martinez has nurtured in the state.

Senior Senator

Tom Udall (D)

Elected 2008, term expires Jan. 2021, 2nd term; b. May 18, 1948, Tucson, AZ; Prescott Col., B.A. 1970, Cambridge U., B.L.L. 1975, U. of NM, J.D. 1977; Mormon; married (Jill Cooper); 1 child.

Elected Office: NM atty. gen., 1990-98; U.S. House, 1998-2008.

Professional Career: Clerk, 10th Circuit Court of Appeals, 1977; Asst. U.S. atty., Dist. of NM, 1978-81; Practicing atty., 1981-83, 1985-90; Chief counsel, NM Health & Environment Dept., 1983-84.

DC Office: 531 HSOB, 20510, 202-224-6621; Website: tomudall.senate .gov

State Offices: Albuquerque, 505-346-6791; Carlsbad, 575-234-0366; Las Cruces, 575-526-5475; Portales, 575-356-6811; Santa Fe, 505-988-6511.

Committees: *Appropriations:* Agriculture, Rural Development, FDA & Related Agencies; Defense; Energy & Water Development; Interior, Environment & Related Agencies (RMM); Military Construction, Veterans Affairs & Related Agencies. *Commerce, Science, & Transportation:* Aviation Operations, Safety, & Security; Communications, Technology, Innovation & the Internet; Consumer Protection, Product Safety, Insurance & Data Security; Space, Science, & Competitiveness; Surface Transportation & Merchant Marine Infrastructure, Safety & Security. *Foreign Relations:* Africa & Global Health Policy; East Asia, the Pacific & Int'l Cybsecurity Policy; Multilateral Int'l Development, Multilateral Institutions, & Int'l Economic, Energy, & Environmental Policy (RMM); Western Hemisphere, Transnational Crime, Civilian Security, Democracy, Human Rights, & Global Women's Issues. *Indian Affairs. Rules & Administration. Joint Committee on Printing.*

Group Ratings

	ADA	ACLU	AFL-CIO	LCV	ITI	COC	HAFA	ACU	CFG	FRC
2014	90%	100%	–	80%	100%	50%	0%	0%	0%	0%
2013	95%	C	100%	100%	C	38%	C	8%	0%	C

National Journal Ratings

	2013 LIB	—	2013 CONS
Economic	82%	—	8%
Social	59%	—	39%
Foreign	66%	—	29%
Composite	72%	—	28%

Key Votes of the 113th Congress

1. Sandy storm spending	Y	5. Student Loan Rates	N	9. Bipartisan Budget Deal	Y
2. Chuck Hagel Confirmation	Y	6. Employee Non-Discrim'n Act	Y	10. Farm Bill Conference Rept.	Y
3. Gun Background Checks	Y	7. Senate Vote on Judgeships	N	11. Unempl. Comp. Extension	Y
4. Immigration Reform	Y	8. Defense Dept. Spending	Y	12. Keystone Pipeline	N

Election Results

2014 general	Tom Udall (D)	286,409	(56%)	$8,736,822	$154,367	$173,814
	Allen Weh (R)	229,097	(44%)	$3,630,413	$70,867	
2014 primary	Tom Udall (D)	unopposed				

Prior winning percentages: 2008 (61%); House: 2006 (75%), 2004 (69%), 2002 (100%), 2000 (67%), 1998 (53%)

Democrat Tom Udall, New Mexico's senior senator, was elected to the House in 1998 and to the Senate in 2008. He belongs to a well-known political clan that is sometimes called the "Kennedys of the West." He is the son of Stewart Udall, the Arizona congressman (1955-61) and Interior secretary (1961-69), and the nephew of Morris "Mo" Udall, an Arizona congressman (1961-91). He is also the first cousin of Mark Udall of Colorado, who lost his Senate reelection bid in 2014.

Tom Udall grew up in Tucson and in McLean, Virginia, a well-to-do Washington, D.C., suburb. He went to Prescott College in Arizona, got a degree at Cambridge University in England, and graduated from the University of New Mexico Law School. He worked as a law clerk for a federal judge, then as a lawyer in the New Mexico state government before going into private law practice.

Politics was obviously on his mind. He ran for Congress in 1982, when the 3rd District was newly created, and finished last among four candidates, with 13 percent of the vote. The winner was Democrat Bill Richardson, who went on to become New Mexico's governor. In 1988, Udall ran in the open, Albuquerque-based 1st District and won the Democratic nomination, but he lost the general election to Republican Steven Schiff, 51%-47%. In 1990, he was elected state attorney general, and in that role, focused on the environment and consumer protection. He successfully sued the federal government to delay the planned opening of the Waste Isolation Pilot Plant, the nation's first deep underground nuclear waste burial site, located in far southeastern New Mexico.

In 1997, when Richardson resigned the 3rd District seat, Republican Bill Redmond, an independent Christian minister from Los Alamos, won it in an upset, assisted by a Green Party candidate nominee who won 17 percent of the vote. In 1998, Udall decided he had a shot at the seat, given the district's heavy ratio of Democrats to Republicans. Drawing on lawyers, the arts community and friends of the Udall family, he raised impressive sums. The Sierra Club and the League of Conservation Voters criticized Redmond and ran waves of ads against him. As for the third-party threat, Udall said, "I intend to make peace with the Greens." He won with 53 percent of the vote. Redmond got the same 43 percent he had won 18 months before, while Green Party nominee Carole Miller saw her 17 percent evaporate to 4 percent. Udall easily won reelection four times.

Udall had a seat on the House Resources Committee, on which his father had served and which his uncle had chaired. He helped to enact a bill to explore establishment of a national historical park at Los Alamos. Locally, he called for a ban on oil drilling in the Valle Vidal area of the Carson National Forest, which was passed in 2006. He sponsored an amendment to the 2007 energy bill requiring 15 percent of electricity to be generated from renewable sources other than nuclear power by 2020. The Democratic leadership supported this amendment, and the bill passed 220-190. But the Senate refused to accept Udall's proposal, and it was dropped from the final legislation.

With a largely liberal voting record, he voted against the Bush administration's USA Patriot Act, which gave law enforcement greatly expanded powers to investigate terrorists. He proposed revisions in the act to limit police authority to obtain search warrants and to restore civil liberty protections for libraries and bookstores. Udall opposed the 2002 Iraq war resolution and called "misguided" a bill to restrict illegal immigrants from obtaining driver's licenses. After Democrats took control of the House in 2007, Udall secured a seat on the powerful Appropriations Committee.

When Republican Sen. Pete Domenici announced he would not run for reelection in 2008, Republican Reps. Heather Wilson and Steve Pearce immediately jumped into the race;

several Democrats, including moderate Albuquerque Mayor Martin Chavez, considered it as well. But Udall was urged to run by Gov. Richardson and Democratic Senatorial Campaign Committee Chairman Charles Schumer of New York, and his entry into the race quickly cleared the Democratic field. Domenici endorsed Wilson over Pearce a few days before the June primary, but Pearce won, 51%-49%.

The primary depleted Pearce's war chest, and Udall was able to outspend him, $7.8 million to $4.6 million. Pearce painted Udall as captive to the liberal wing of the Democratic Party and its "hippie" traditions. A former oil executive, Pearce also hammered Udall for his opposition to new exploration in environmentally sensitive areas. Udall responded that he was for a "do-it-all" approach to energy. It was apparent long before November that this wasn't much of a contest. Udall won 61%-39%. Pearce carried only Little Texas in the southeast and the San Juan Basin in the far northwest corner.

In the Senate, Udall joined his cousin, Mark Udall, who had just won election to a Colorado Senate seat. They worked together closely, but tried to avoid serving on the same committees so they could "branch out" and cover a greater range of issues, Tom Udall said. He has been a more faithful Democrat than his cousin, and he and Connecticut Democrat Richard Blumenthal tied for most-liberal senator in *National Journal's* 2012 rankings. In a nod to his state's rural leanings, however, Udall has not supported all of the gun control measures backed by other liberals.

Udall is amiable and avoids fierce rhetoric, which enables him to work with senators on the other side of the ideological spectrum. He teamed in 2012 with conservative Republican Jon Kyl of Arizona on a measure to study the Energy Department's much-criticized National Nuclear Security Administration and with libertarian Rand Paul of Kentucky in 2011 in calling for a faster troop withdrawal from Afghanistan. A Udall amendment providing tax credits for employers hiring military veterans discharged after 2001 was included in the 2009 economic stimulus bill. He was given a seat on the Appropriations Committee in 2013, a vital position for a state as dependent on federal spending as New Mexico.

Udall's legislative interests have ranged widely. On the Environment and Public Works Committee, Udall has continued the push he began in the House for a national renewable energy standard, recently joined in his effort by his fellow New Mexico senator, Martin Heinrich. On the Foreign Relations Committee, Udall sponsored a bipartisan measure to boost agricultural sales to Cuba, and in November 2014, Udall and Republican Sen. Jeff Flake of Arizona met with Alan Gross, an American prisoner in Cuba; Gross was released a month later. Udall has also pushed for the closure of the U.S. detention facility at Guantanamo Bay, Cuba.

On the Commerce committee, Udall has focused on consumer issues. He asked the Federal Trade Commission in 2011 to investigate misleading safety claims in the sales of football helmets and introduced a 2010 bill requiring new cars to have "black box" data recorders to help investigate crashes. He also introduced a bill in 2011 to crack down on the use of painkillers and performance-enhancing drugs in horse racing. The legislation gained some attention following a *New York Times* exposé that showed rampant abuses at racetracks, but it did not advance.

Udall joined Sen. Bernie Sanders, an independent from Vermont who caucuses with Democrats, in introducing a long-shot constitutional amendment explicitly allowing Congress and the states to "set reasonable limits on the raising and spending of money by candidates and others to influence elections," including distinguishing between "natural persons and corporations." "Americans' right to free speech should not be proportionate to their bank accounts," they wrote in a *Politico* op-ed. Udall has also taken up issues of special interest back home. He and Heinrich introduced a bill to expand federal compensation for those in close proximity to above-ground nuclear tests, including some carried out decades ago in New Mexico, and they worked to insert land-preservation provisions in a defense authorization bill. With Pearce and Democratic Rep. Ben Ray Lujan, the two senators sponsored a bill to reauthorize a federal program to preserve Native American Languages. (Udall serves on the Indian Affairs Committee.)

Udall made waves by becoming the lead Democratic negotiator in bipartisan talks to update the nation's chemical-safety laws, picking up the mantle from the late New Jersey senator, Frank Lautenberg. In 2015, the industry-backed measure won approval from the Environment and Public Works Committee, 15-5. Still, the bill, and Udall's role in it, stoked the ire of some Democrats, notably California Sen. Barbara Boxer, a former chairwoman of the committee; she and some others favored a bill that took a tougher line on the industry, and she all but threatened a filibuster. Udall countered, "I am fighting for our children and trying to make sure they are not being pumped full of chemicals in the next generation. We can't do something that is pie in the sky; we have to deal with the reality."

But Udall may have drawn the most attention for a fight about procedure—his efforts to alter how the Senate conducts its business. Like many senators who come over from the House, he dislikes the frequent use of filibusters to delay or block pending legislation. In 2011, he offered a plan to bar the use of the filibuster on the initial motion to begin debate, but permit lawmakers to filibuster a final bill if they remained on the floor during debate. His plan also would eliminate secret "holds" used to delay nominations of executive branch officials. The Senate fell 16 votes short of the number needed to adopt Udall's proposed changes. Eventually, in 2013, Reid did push through a no-filibuster rule for most judicial and executive-branch appointments. But in 2015, Udall pointed to the long wait for President Barack Obama's attorney general appointee, Loretta Lynch, as evidence that additional changes were needed.

Udall is a popular figure in New Mexico, and—in marked contrast to his cousin—he won reelection easily in 2014 over Allen Weh, a retired Marine and self-funding businessman. He got fundraising help from, among others, George R.R. Martin, a longtime Santa Fe resident and author of the popular series of novels upon which the TV series *Game of Thrones* is based.

Junior Senator

Martin Heinrich (D)

Elected 2012, term expires Jan. 2019, 1st term; b. Oct. 17, 1971, Fallon, NV; U. of MO, B.S.E. 1995; Lutheran; married (Julie); 2 children.

Elected Office: Albuquerque City Cncl., 2003-07, pres. 2005-06; U.S. House, 2009-13.

Professional Career: Contractor, Phillips Laboratories; Exec. dir., Cottonwood Gulch Foundation, 1997-2002; NM natural resources trustee, 2006-08.

DC Office: 303 HSOB, 20510, 202-224-5521; Website: heinrich.senate.gov.

State Offices: Albuquerque, 505-346-6601; Farmington, 505-325-5030; Las Cruces, 575-523-6561; Roswell, 575-622-7113; Sante Fe, 505-988-6647.

Committees: *Armed Services:* Airland; Readiness & Mgmt. Support; Strategic Forces. *Energy & Natural Resources:* Energy; Nat'l Parks (RMM); Public Lands, Forests, & Mining. *Intelligence (Select). Joint Economic Committee..*

Group Ratings

	ADA	ACLU	AFL-CIO	LCV	ITI	COC	HAFA	ACU	CFG	FRC
2014	90%	100%	–	80%	100%	50%	0%	4%	0%	0%
2013	95%	C	100%	100%	C	38%	C	12%	0%	C

National Journal Ratings

	2013 LIB	—	2013 CONS
Economic	75%	—	19%
Social	56%	—	43%
Foreign	58%	—	36%
Composite	65%	—	35%

Key Votes of the 113th Congress

1. Sandy storm spending	Y	5. Student Loan Rates	Y	9. Bipartisan Budget Deal	Y
2. Chuck Hagel Confirmation	Y	6. Employee Non-Discrim'n Act	Y	10. Farm Bill Conference Rept.	Y
3. Gun Background Checks	Y	7. Senate Vote on Judgeships	N	11. Unempl. Comp. Extension	Y
4. Immigration Reform	Y	8. Defense Dept. Spending	Y	12. Keystone Pipeline	N

Election Results

2012 general	Martin Heinrich (D)	395,717	(51%)	$6,692,326	$937,245	$2,657,362
	Heather Wilson (R)	351,260	(45%)	$7,108,688	$771,629	$1,702,707
	Jon Ross Barrie (IAP)	28,199	(4%)	$26,483		
2012 primary	Martin Heinrich (D)	83,432	(59%)			
	Hector Balderas (D)	58,128	(41%)			

Prior winning percentages: House: 2010 (52%), 2008 (56%)

Democratic Rep. Martin Heinrich became New Mexico's junior senator after winning the seat of retiring five-term Sen. Jeff Bingaman in 2012. He defeated former Republican Rep. Heather Wilson by portraying himself as a younger version of Bingaman: a deliberate, if unflashy, thinker interested in science and devoted to protecting the federal government's large New Mexico presence.

Heinrich was born in Fallon Nevada, the son of an electrician and a factory worker. His parents moved to Missouri when he was a child, and he earned a bachelor's degree in engineering from the University of Missouri. He moved to New Mexico in 1995 to found a political consulting business and serve as executive director of The Cottonwood Gulch Foundation, which runs adventure programs in the Southwest. In 2003, he was elected to the Albuquerque City Council. His signature issue was increasing New Mexico's minimum wage in 2006. Heinrich worked with the city's business leaders and community activists to produce compromise legislation mandating a gradual increase. He also lobbied for federal protection of the Ojito Wilderness.

Encouraged by then-Democratic Gov. Bill Richardson, Heinrich announced that he would challenge Wilson for her House seat in 2008. National Democrats backed Heinrich's candidacy, and he defeated three other hopefuls in the primary. In October 2007, Wilson announced her intention to give up the seat to run for the Senate. (She lost in the primary.) Republicans fielded a strong replacement in Bernalillo County Sheriff Darren White. But Heinrich tied White to the unpopular incumbent president by reminding voters that White had served as President George W. Bush's Bernalillo County reelection chairman in 2004. White in turn questioned Heinrich's business practices, saying that although nonprofit groups paid him for advocacy work, he didn't register as a lobbyist. Heinrich maintained that the law had not required him to register when he was a political consultant for the Coalition for New Mexico Wilderness from 2002 to 2005. Thanks in part to that year's Democratic wave, Heinrich won easily, 56% to 44%.

Like Bingaman, Heinrich, during his two terms in the House, advocated expanding energy production through a broad range of sources. He also sought to avoid being a down-the-line Democrat. He supported many of President Barack Obama's major initiatives, including the 2010 health care overhaul, but he endorsed spending cuts in some appropriations bills and, like many Western lawmakers, backed gun owners' rights. As a member of the Natural Resources Committee, he introduced a bill in 2009 aimed at creating clean energy jobs by providing a dedicated funding stream for the Bureau of Land Management to process a backlog in clean energy project applications. To help his district's Sandia National Laboratories, Heinrich worked to raise the percentage of money spent on high-tech research and development at national labs. He also added a provision to the fiscal 2011 defense bill for a pilot program in which military bases and the labs work together on developing new electric power systems. He won reelection in 2010 over Republican Jon Barela, a former president of the Albuquerque Hispano Chamber of Commerce. Later that year, he did a solid favor for Tom Udall, his future Senate colleague, by sponsoring a measure to name the Interior Department building for Udall's father, Stewart, who was a former Interior Secretary. The measure was signed into law, and in the Senate, the two would collaborate frequently on issues.

New Mexico's Democratic establishment was eager for Heinrich to run for Bingaman's seat as soon as the senator announced his retirement. Heinrich drew a Democratic primary opponent in state Auditor Hector Balderas, who hoped to tap into the state's sizable Hispanic vote. But the party rallied around the more politically experienced Heinrich, and he won the primary with 59 percent of the vote. That set up a general election matchup against Wilson. This was a contest between two well-regarded candidates. A former Air Force officer and National Security Council staffer, Wilson was the political protégé of popular former GOP Sen. Pete Domenici. With the help of Domenici's network of supporters, she won several close reelection races in the House before losing to Steve Pearce in the 2008 GOP primary to succeed Domenici in the Senate.

In running against Heinrich, Wilson stressed her independence from her party, running a biographical ad that played up her military record without mentioning that she was a Republican. She got outside financial help from conservative groups, including Crossroads GPS, headed by Karl Rove, former George W. Bush White House strategist. (After leaving Congress, she served on Crossroads' board for six months.) Heinrich benefited from the Obama campaign's heavy presence in the state and touted his connection to the president. Wilson consistently trailed Heinrich in polls, eventually prompting national Republicans to turn their attention elsewhere, and the Democrat won, 51% to 45%. Heinrich won their mutual home base in Bernalillo County, 54%-43%, and did even better in southern New Mexico's rapidly growing Dona Ana County, winning 56%-39%. Santa Fe County was no contest; he trounced Wilson there 72%-26%.

In the Senate, Heinrich was assigned to the Armed Services, Energy and Intelligence Committees. He criticized the Obama administration for over-broad use of surveillance, arguing that the National Security Agency's bulk phone records program "is a major invasion of Americans privacy and has done little if anything to further the fight against terrorism." He also zeroed in on land issues, criticizing calls to transfer federal land to state-government control, pushing for two new wilderness areas, the Cerro del Yuta Wilderness and Rio San Antonio Wilderness, and working to ensure hunting and fishing access to lands owned by the federal government.

Despite his lack of seniority, Heinrich has attracted a measure of attention in the chamber. He won one dubious distinction from *Roll Call* (the poorest member of the Senate) and a more favorable one from *Washingtonian* magazine (runner-up for "hottest senator," behind South Dakota Republican John Thune). Heinrich twice took part in a 26.2-mile memorial marathon for veterans of the Bataan Death March held in New Mexico's rugged White Sands Missile Range. But his biggest splash came from a Discovery Channel reality show he starred in with Jeff Flake, his Arizona Republican colleague. *Rival Survival* featured the bipartisan duo spending six days with minimal supplies on the island of Eru, located in a shark sanctuary half-way between Hawaii and Australia. The pair later tried to adapt the bipartisan approach by holding a Senate lunch for members of both parties; typically, the parties hold their luncheons separately.

FIRST DISTRICT

Michelle Lujan Grisham (D)

Elected 2012, 2nd term; b. Oct. 24, 1959, Los Alamos; U. of NM, B.U.S. 1981, J.D. 1987; Catholic; widowed; 2 children.

Elected Office: Commissioner, Bernalillo Cnty., 2010-12.

Professional Career: Dir., NM St. Agency on Aging, 1991-2002; Secy., NM Aging & Long-Term Services Dept., 2002-04; Secy., NM Dept. of Health, 2004-07; Co-owner, Delta Consulting Group, 2008-present.

DC Office: 214 CHOB, 20515, 202-225-6316; Fax: 202-225-4975; Website: lujangrisham.house.gov.

State Offices: Albuquerque, 505-346-6781.

Committees: *Agriculture:* Conservation & Forestry (RMM); Nutrition. *Budget. Oversight & Government Reform:* Health Care, Benefits, & Administrative Rules.

Group Ratings

	ADA	ACLU	AFL-CIO	LCV	ITI	COC	HAFA	ACU	CFG	FRC
2014	70%	77%	–	86%	80%	43%	13%	9%	6%	0%
2013	80%	C	95%	89%	C	38%	C	12%	10%	C

National Journal Ratings

	2013 LIB	—	2013 CONS
Economic	78%	—	22%
Social	79%	—	16%
Foreign	63%	—	36%
Composite	74%	—	26%

Key Votes of the 113th Congress

1. Sandy storm spending	Y	5. Medical Marijuana	Y	9. Syrian Rebels Training	Y
2. Violence Against Women Act	Y	6. Farm Bill	N	10. Keystone pipeline	N
3. Guantanamo Bay Detainees	Y	7. Afghanistan Combat	NV	11. Immigration Exec. Action	N
4. Abortion 20-week ban	N	8. NSA Phone Data Collection	Y	12. Bipartisan budget deal	Y

Election Results

2014 general   Michelle Lujan Grisham (D) 105,474   (59%) $1,478,600
                 Mike Frese (R) 74,558   (41%) $331,910
2014 primary Michelle Lujan Grisham (D) ....unopposed

Prior winning percentage: 2012 (59%)

Population		Race and Ethnicity		Income	
Total:	694,442	Latino	48.1%	Median income:	$47,124
Urban:	88.8%	White	41.8%		(279 of 435)
Suburban:	4.7%	Amer. Indian	3.7%	Under $50,000	51.8%
Rural:	6.6%	Black	2.3%	$50,000-$99,999:	29.9%
Land area:	7,024	Two races	2.1%	$100,000-$199,999:	14.7%
Pop/sq. mi.:	98.9	White Ethnic	14.8%	$200,000 or more:	3.6%
Born in state:	51.7%			Poverty Rate	19.5%
		Education			
Age Groups		H.S. grad or less:	36.7%	**Work**	
Under 18:	23.0%	Some college:	31.0%	White collar:	38.3%
18 to 34:	24.7%	College degree, 4 yr.:	18.1%	Blue collar:	43.1%
35 to 64:	38.5%	Post-grad study:	14.1%	Sales and service:	18.5%
Over 64:	13.8%				
		Military		Govt. workers:	20.1%
		Veterans/active duty:	10.1%		

Albuquerque Area

New Mexico's past and future come together in its single metropolis, Albuquerque. The city's Spanish and Indian past is memorialized in its name (for a 17th-century Spanish nobleman), its age (founded in 1706) and its quaint Old Town. But Albuquerque's future is decidedly high-tech. For decades, the

Voter Turnout	
2013 Total Citizen 18+	487,410
2014 House Turnout	180,032
2014 Turnout as % CVAP	36.9%
2012 Turnout as % CVAP	57.6%

Sandia National Laboratories, Kirtland Air Force Base and the University of New Mexico have attracted scientists and engineers to Albuquerque and promoted private-sector technology growth. The city's minor-league baseball team is the Isotopes, named in part to honor the area's association with the Atomic Age. When rocket scientist Robert Goddard moved here in 1930 and nuclear scientist J. Robert Oppenheimer reconnoitered the site in 1940, Albuquerque was still a town of 35,000 at the junction of the Rio Grande River and old U.S. 66, which paralleled the Santa Fe Railroad. "A dirty, red sod-hut tortilla desert highway city," novelist Tom Wolfe wrote.

Now, metro Albuquerque, spreading out from Bernalillo County into Sandoval and Valencia counties, has more people—907,000 in 2015—than all of New Mexico did when the scientists first arrived. Bill Gates founded a little company called Microsoft here in 1975, although the software maker moved its 13 employees to Bellevue, Washington, in 1979. In late 2013, Intel employed 3,300 people at an advanced chip-making facility before it laid off 400 workers. The University of New Mexico is becoming a magnet for biotechnology, with more than a dozen local startups working to commercialize UNM's biomedical discoveries. The city's prosperous neighborhoods have climbed the gently rising heights to the east; poorer residents have spread north and south along the Rio Grande. Hemmed in by the Sandia Mountains and by federal installations, growth is moving west and north. Santolina, a planned 22 square mile development west of Albuquerque, drew opposition in May 2015 from community groups concerned about water resources.

In the Old Town centered on the plaza, some of the adobe buildings date to the 18th century. Albuquerque has seen some modest growth in tourism—every October, it hosts the International Balloon Fiesta, which features many resident balloonists. It has a large public sector—nearly 24% of its workforce is employed by government, but those numbers declined after 2007. Its recession was the mildest among cities in the mountain West region, but that doesn't mean it was spared hardship. The construction and financial services industries have struggled in the city. The AMC television series *Breaking Bad* was set and filmed here for five years and explored issues prevalent in the Southwest: drug trafficking, economic instability, immigration and porous borders. It was replaced by another well-received series, *Better Call Saul*.

The 1st Congressional District includes almost all of Albuquerque and some of its suburbs. It is 49% Hispanic and takes in most of Bernalillo County, all of sparsely populated Torrance County in the desert, and small slices of Sandoval, Santa Fe and

2012 Presidential Vote		
Barack Obama (D) 155,915	(55%)
Mitt Romney (R).................111,749	(40%)
2008 Presidential Vote		
Barack Obama (D) 177,494	(60%)
John McCain (R).................115,818	(39%)
Cook Partisan Voting Index: D+7		

Valencia counties. The district elected only Republicans to Congress for many years. But with an expanding number of Latino voters, it has grown increasingly Democratic. In 2010 in Bernalillo County, Republican Susana Martinez edged out Democratic Lt. Gov. Diane Denish 51%-49% in the race for governor. Two years later, President Barack Obama won the county with 55%. Still, Martinez upped her 2014 local win to 55%-45%.

Michelle Lujan Grisham (D)

With her election in New Mexico's 1st District in 2012, Democrat Michelle Lujan Grisham joined a state family dynasty. Her grandfather, Eugene Lujan, was the Supreme Court's first Latino chief justice; her uncle, Manuel Lujan Jr., was a GOP congressman and Interior secretary; her distant cousin, Rep. Ben Ray Luján, represents the 3rd District.

The daughter of a dentist, Lujan Grisham was born in Los Alamos and attended high school in Santa Fe. After earning bachelor's and law degrees from the University of New Mexico, she was named director of the State Bar of New Mexico's Lawyer Referral for the Elderly Program, which provides basic legal services to seniors. In 1991, then-Gov. Bruce King appointed Lujan Grisham director of the New Mexico State Agency on Aging. She remained in that position for the next 13 years, serving under a Republican as well as two Democratic governors—a point she stressed later in her House campaign to contend that she can be bipartisan.

In 2004, Lujan Grisham's college sweetheart and husband of 22 years, Gregory Alan Grisham, collapsed while jogging and died the next day from a ruptured cerebral aneurysm. Three years later, Lujan Grisham filed a wrongful death lawsuit, seeking damages from an Albuquerque physician who had misdiagnosed him with migraines, but the suit was dismissed.

After her husband's death, Lujan Grisham was named secretary of the New Mexico Department of Health, which had 3,800 employees and a $440 million budget. In that role, Lujan Grisham emphasized prophylactic care, or "precautionary principles." In 2007, the Justice Department filed a lawsuit against New Mexico in response to substandard conditions and practices at the state-run Fort Bayard Medical Center. A settlement was reached four days later, but Lujan Grisham resigned the next month, telling the *Albuquerque Journal* that overseeing the Department of Health was the "hardest job on the planet."

In 2008, Lujan Grisham made an unsuccessful run for the 1st District seat, placing third in the Democratic primary. Two years later, she was elected a commissioner of Bernalillo County and sought to increase ethical standards.

When Rep. Martin Heinrich, a Democrat, decided to run for the Senate, Lujan Grisham was a long-shot candidate to replace Heinrich. She maintained that her real-life hardships gave her insight into voters' problems. "As a widow and a caregiver and a single mother, I'm living the experience that New Mexicans are," she told the *Journal*.

She conserved cash while her rivals for the Democratic nomination, state Sen. Eric Griego and former Albuquerque Mayor Marty Chavez, attacked each other and did not take her seriously until it was too late. At the end, Lujan Grisham surged past her opponents and won the primary with 40% of the vote to 35% for Griego and 25% for Chavez. With that bruising battle over, Lujan Grisham cruised to victory over former Republican state Rep. Janice Arnold-Jones, 59%-41%. In 2014, she was reelected with the same share of the vote against Republican small business owner Michael Frese.

On the Agriculture Committee, Lujan Grisham became ranking Democrat on the Conservation and Forestry Subcommittee, where she planned to focus on healthier forest reserves and stronger watershed programs. Those issues are important to New Mexico, which has more than 9 million acres of Forest Service land. She filed a proposal in November 2014, which she reintroduced in 2015, to create a Care Corps, a national organization that would help seniors and people with disabilities continue to live independently and also provide support to family caregivers.

In January 2015, Lujan Grisham became vice chairwoman of the Hispanic Caucus. *The Washington Post* reported in May that she was part of a bipartisan delegation to Azerbaijan that received a large number of gifts and other expenses that they failed to disclose to the Ethics Committee. She responded that she did not believe that the rugs that she received were "particularly valuable." In July, the committee dismissed the case.

SECOND DISTRICT

Steve Pearce (R)

Elected 2010, 6th term; b. Aug. 24, 1947, Lamesa, TX; NM St. U., B.B.A. 1970, Eastern NM U., M.B.A. 1991; Baptist; married (Cynthia); 1 child.

Military Career: Air Force, 1970-76 (Vietnam).

Elected Office: NM House, 1997-2000; U.S. House, 2003-09.

Professional Career: Owner, Lea Fishing Tools.

DC Office: 2432 RHOB, 20515, 202-225-2365 or 855-4-PEARCE (855-473-2723); Website: pearce.house.gov..

State Offices: Alamogordo, Hobbs, Las Cruces, Los Lunas, Roswell, Socorro, 855-4-PEARCE (855-473-2723).

Committees: *Financial Services:* Financial Institutions & Consumer Credit (VChmn); Housing & Insurance; Monetary Policy & Trade.

Group Ratings

	ADA	ACLU	AFL-CIO	LCV	ITI	COC	HAFA	ACU	CFG	FRC
2014	0%	5%	–	6%	100%	86%	60%	67%	73%	88%
2013	5%	C	20%	4%	C	69%	C	76%	73%	C

National Journal Ratings

	2013 LIB	—	2013 CONS
Economic	35%	—	64%
Social	33%	—	66%
Foreign	5%	—	86%
Composite	26%	—	74%

Key Votes of the 113th Congress

1. Sandy storm spending	N	5. Medical Marijuana	N	9. Syrian Rebels Training	Y
2. Violence Against Women Act	Y	6. Farm Bill	Y	10. Keystone pipeline	Y
3. Guantanamo Bay Detainees	N	7. Afghanistan Combat	N	11. Immigration Exec. Action	Y
4. Abortion 20-week ban	Y	8. NSA Phone Data Collection	Y	12. Bipartisan budget deal	N

Election Results

2014 general	Steve Pearce (R)	95,209	(64%)	$2,282,213 $13,687
	Roxanne "Rocky" Lara (D)	52,499	(36%)	$1,415,027
2014 primary	Steve Pearce (R)	unopposed		

Prior winning percentages: 2012 (59%), 2010 (55%), 2006 (59%), 2004 (60%), 2002 (56%)

Population		Race and Ethnicity		Income	
Total:	697,027	Latino	52.1%	Median income:	$41,367
Urban:	24.2%	White	39.4%		*(371 of 435)*
Suburban:	2.7%	Amer. Indian	5.5%	Under $50,000	59.3%
Rural:	73.1%	Black	1.5%	$50,000-$99,999:	26.7%
Land area:	63,066	Two races	0.9%	$100,000-$199,999:	11.9%
Pop/sq. mi.:	11.1	White Ethnic	12.0%	$200,000 or more:	2.1%
Born in state:	48.4%			Poverty Rate	22.9%
		Education			
Age Groups		H.S. grad or less:	48.6%	**Work**	
Under 18:	25.3%	Some college:	31.0%	White collar:	28.7%
18 to 34:	23.8%	College degree, 4 yr.:	12.0%	Blue collar:	44.7%
35 to 64:	35.5%	Post-grad study:	8.3%	Sales and service:	26.6%
Over 64:	15.5%				
		Military		Govt. workers:	23.4%
		Veterans/active duty:	11.6%		

Southern New Mexico: Las Cruces

Southeastern New Mexico is a disparate landscape: endless sagebrush-strewn acreage and then, suddenly, 9,000-foot mountain peaks rising along the Continental Divide. (The Robledo Mountains, says the Smithsonian Institution, are the world's greatest repository of pre-dinosaur-era fossil tracks.) The

Voter Turnout	
2013 Total Citizen 18+	467,765
2014 House Turnout	147,777
2014 Turnout as % CVAP	31.6%
2012 Turnout as % CVAP	48.5%

eastern part of this region—places like Lovington and Hobbs—speaks with a Texas twang rather than a northern New Mexico lilt. In Little Texas, as southeastern New Mexico is known, oil has long been the economic mainstay. Cattle ranching is common, and cotton is grown on irrigated land. One of the larger towns is Roswell, site of a supposed flying saucer landing in 1947 and now home of the International UFO Museum and Research Center. Farther west is White Sands National Monument, with its immaculate gypsum dunes and specially evolved animals with white coloration that allows them to elude predators in the harsh environment. Virgin Galactic, a company started by billionaire Richard Branson, leased land near White Sands to build the nation's first commercial spaceport (called Spaceport America). By early 2011, more than 400 people had put down deposits to travel to the edge of space. But those plans have become dubious. The $218 million facility "sits largely vacant," *The Wall Street Journal* reported in December 2014. A few months later, state officials were trying to sell the facility. Close by is Alamogordo, not far from where the first atomic bomb was exploded in the empty land at 5:29:45 a.m. Mountain War Time on July 16, 1945.

Las Cruces, New Mexico's second-largest city, has grown at rates well above the state-wide average, thanks to migrants from Mexico coming up the Rio Grande. For decades, Anglo and Mexican ranchers across the border spoke "the common language of cattle," and communities frequently shared public services with their cross-border neighbors. But rapid development after the 1993 North American Free Trade Agreement, a surge in illegal immigration and a sharp uptick in drug trafficking altered that environment. Still, the New Mexico portion of the largely empty 150-mile U.S.-Mexico border remains sleepier than elsewhere. According to government figures, 7,983 people were apprehended near the New Mexico border in 2013, compared with 125,942 in Arizona.

As in many places on America's high plains, population here is thinning and old economic pillars are crumbling. Once reliant on potash mining, Carlsbad aggressively sought the Waste Isolation Pilot Plant, a nuclear waste repository that after 1999 buried shipments of plutonium-contaminated garbage from the nation's Energy Department weapons factories. Local officials, undaunted by opposition elsewhere in the state, lobbied for consideration as a storage site for additional toxic trash. But the repository shut down following a "radiation event" and fire in February 2014, and many top executive positions went unfilled. East of Carlsbad, a uranium enrichment plant was built in Eunice, the first such facility licensed by the Nuclear Regulatory Commission.

The 2nd Congressional District of New Mexico covers the southern part of the state, reaching to Albuquerque's southern suburbs. Demographically and politically, it is diverse. It includes most of Little Texas—majority Anglo and solidly conservative—but also politically marginal Las Cruces and the Indian country around the pueblos, which is

2012 Presidential Vote		
Mitt Romney (R)	119,168	(52%)
Barack Obama (D)	103,438	(45%)

2008 Presidential Vote		
John McCain (R)	122,892	(50%)
Barack Obama (D)	118,663	(48%)

Cook Partisan Voting Index: R+5

strongly Democratic. The district is 52% Hispanic and 5% Indian. This is a rare Republican-leaning district with a Hispanic majority. Many Latinos here are migrant workers and not part of an organized, Democratic voting bloc.

Steve Pearce (R)

Republican Steve Pearce first won the 3rd District seat in 2002, abandoned it for an unsuccessful Senate race in 2008, then reclaimed it two years later in the Republican landslide. He has moved further rightward since then, with occasional bipartisan moments.

Pearce grew up in Hobbs, near the Texas line, graduated from New Mexico State University and received an M.B.A. from Eastern New Mexico University. He served in the Air Force and was a combat pilot with 518 hours of missions during the Vietnam War. He returned to Hobbs and became wealthy after he started an oil-field service company. In 1996, he was elected to the state House, where he chaired the Republican Caucus. Pearce became the frontrunner when the House seat opened in 2002. After winning the primary over two competitors, he defeated Democratic state Sen. John Arthur Smith 56%-44%.

During Pearce's first stint in the House, he was chairman of the National Parks subcommittee and made park accessibility a priority. He proposed giving states and counties broad authority over rights of way on federal land, but made little progress on the measure before Democrats won majority control in 2006.

After he returned in 2011, Pearce voted increasingly with conservatives. On the Financial Services Committee, Pearce joined in GOP attacks on the Consumer Financial Protection Bureau, created under the 2010 Dodd-Frank financial services overhaul. He lambasted Federal Reserve Chairman Ben Bernanke in February 2013 for keeping interest rates low, depriving senior citizens of interest income. He invited Bernanke to attend a town meeting in his district "to get out among people who have manure on the bottom of their boots." Pearce was an enthusiastic supporter of hydraulic fracturing for oil and gas extraction, and said that federal and state regulators had not documented a single case of contaminated underground drinking water at such sites, a conclusion the EPA would also eventually reach.

In January 2013, he was one of nine Republicans to oppose John Boehner of Ohio for another term as speaker. Pearce's spokesman said the congressman was upset by Boehner's deal with President Barack Obama to avert the so-called "fiscal cliff," in part, by raising taxes on high-income earners. In January 2015, Pearce voted for Boehner for speaker. He issued a statement that day that said, somewhat elliptically, "I will fight the hard fight." The next step came in June when Majority Whip Steve Scalise removed Pearce and two other Republicans from the GOP whip team because they abandoned the party on a key procedural vote dealing with an international trade agreement. Pearce responded that he would continue to "vote on principle."

Pearce recently has made efforts to cross the aisle. In 2014 he joined with Democratic Rep. Beto O'Rourke of Texas on a bill to improve training for Border Patrol officers. An aide to Pearce, who represents an adjoining district along the border, reportedly said, "He trusts O'Rourke and O'Rourke trusts him." In 2015, he filed a bill with California Democratic Rep. Eric Swalwell of California to seek ways for House members, especially from the West, to limit their travel to Washington for committee hearings.

When Republican Sen. Pete Domenici retired in 2008, Pearce jumped into the race along with the more moderate GOP Rep. Heather Wilson. Pearce attacked Wilson for supporting the Democrats' expansion of the Children's Health Insurance Program, which he called "socialized medicine," and for voting to raise taxes. Domenici endorsed Wilson a few days before the June primary, but Pearce won, 51%-49%. The primary drained Pearce's war chest. Democratic Rep. Tom Udall outspent Pearce, $7.8 million to $4.6 million and won the seat, 61%-39%. Wilson likely would have made the contest closer, but her victory would have been a steep challenge given that Obama won the state in that election, 57%-42%.

Harry Teague took advantage of the national Democratic wave in 2008 to capture Pearce's House seat. In 2010, Pearce challenged Teague for his old job, attacking him for his vote in favor of the 2009 cap-and-trade bill to reduce carbon emissions, which Pearce argued would hurt the region's oil and gas industry. He ran ads calling Teague "one of the richest men in Congress," as a fellow owner of an oil-field service company, while neglecting to mention his own personal fortune.

Bolstered by the national Republican tide, Pearce won easily, 55%-45%. He turned down the opportunity to run for another open Senate seat in 2012. Since then, he has easily won reelection to the House.

THIRD DISTRICT

Ben Ray Luján (D)

Elected 2008, 4th term; b. June 7, 1972, Santa Fe; NM Highlands U., B.B.A. 2007; Catholic; single.

Elected Office: NM public reg. comm., 2004-08, chmn., 2005-07.

Professional Career: NM deputy state treas., 2002-03; Dir. admin. services, CFO, NM Cultural Affairs Dept., 2003-04.

DC Office: 2446 RHOB, 20515, 202-225-6190; Fax: 202-226-1528; Website: lujan.house.gov.

State Offices: Farmington, 505-324-1005; Gallup, 505-863-0582; Las Vegas, 505-454-3038; Rio Rancho, 505-994-0499; Santa Fe, 505-984-8950; Tucumcari, 575-461-3029.

Committees: *Energy & Commerce:* Communications & Technology; Health.

Group Ratings

	ADA	ACLU	AFL-CIO	LCV	ITI	COC	HAFA	ACU	CFG	FRC
2014	85%	77%	–	91%	80%	43%	14%	8%	6%	0%
2013	90%	C	95%	93%	C	38%	C	12%	12%	C

National Journal Ratings

	2013 LIB	—	2013 CONS
Economic	91%	—	0%
Social	87%	—	7%
Foreign	66%	—	32%
Composite	84%	—	16%

Key Votes of the 113th Congress

1. Sandy storm spending	Y	5. Medical Marijuana	Y	9. Syrian Rebels Training	N
2. Violence Against Women Act	Y	6. Farm Bill	N	10. Keystone pipeline	N
3. Guantanamo Bay Detainees	Y	7. Afghanistan Combat	Y	11. Immigration Exec. Action	N
4. Abortion 20-week ban	N	8. NSA Phone Data Collection	Y	12. Bipartisan budget deal	Y

Election Results

2014 general	Ben Ray Luján (D)	113,249	(62%)	$1,045,768
	Jefferson Byrd (R)	70,775	(38%)	$110,501
2014 primary	Ben Ray Luján (D)	50,709	(88%)	
	Robert Blanch (D)	7,207	(12%)	

Prior winning percentages: 2012 (63%), 2010 (57%), 2008 (57%)

Population		Race and Ethnicity		Income	
Total:	693,818	Latino	39.8%	Median income:	$44,400
Urban:	40.9%	White	38.9%		*(330 of 435)*
Suburban:	16.4%	Amer. Indian	16.6%	Under $50,000	54.5%
Rural:	42.7%	Black	1.4%	$50,000-$99,999:	28.0%
Land area:	41,876	Two races	1.9%	$100,000-$199,999:	14.7%
Pop/sq. mi.:	16.6	White Ethnic	13.1%	$200,000 or more:	2.8%
Born in state:	55.9%			Poverty Rate	23.4%
		Education			
Age Groups		H.S. grad or less:	41.8%	**Work**	
Under 18:	24.8%	Some college:	31.9%	White collar:	36.6%
18 to 34:	21.4%	College degree, 4 yr.:	14.7%	Blue collar:	42.8%
35 to 64:	38.9%	Post-grad study:	11.6%	Sales and service:	20.6%
Over 64:	14.9%			Govt. workers:	24.9%
		Military			
		Veterans/active duty:	10.4%		

Northern New Mexico: Santa Fe

"The dancing ground of the sun" is what the Pueblo Indians called the land of northern New Mexico, where the long vistas, dotted with low-lying scrub, are painted in pastel hues in the cold light and clear air. For 100 years, artists have been coming here, attracted by the scenery and by a unique

Voter Turnout	
2013 Total Citizen 18+	496,387
2014 House Turnout	184,076
2014 Turnout as % CVAP	37.1%
2012 Turnout as % CVAP	55.2%

civilization that is part Indian, part Anglo, part Spanish, and a little Mexican. (Northern New Mexico was under Mexican control from 1821-46.) The Indians were here first and built adobe pueblos, including some of the world's earliest apartment buildings. The Spanish conquistadors and priests brought the Catholic religion, the baroque architectural accents, and the Spanish language. The Palace of the Governors, built in Santa Fe in 1610, is now a museum on Santa Fe's Plaza and is the nation's oldest extant public building. Zoning laws vigorously enforce the height and adobe-like appearance of buildings in the historic district.

Along the back roads in Rio Arriba or Taos counties, one can find a religion that mixes Catholicism with adaptations of Indian festivals, buildings not that much different from the old pueblos, and a standard of living reminiscent of the Indian past, sometimes punctuated by high rates of drug abuse and alcoholism. It's quite a contrast with the ski lodges in the Taos Valley, the high-security research facilities of Los Alamos County—which has the third highest median income in the nation and has among the most PhDs per capita, thanks to Los Alamos National Laboratory—and the affluent, bohemian lifestyles of modern-day Santa Fe.

The 3rd Congressional District of New Mexico contains most of the state's historic Spanish-speaking and Indian regions. This district, similar in size to Pennsylvania, runs from the High Plains along the Texas border, past the haunting Sangre de Cristo Mountains, through the vast ridges and isolated buttes in the center, to the windy and dusty desert-like plains. With 92,000 residents, Rio Rancho is the district's most populous city, but the trendy state capital of Santa Fe, which has the most museums of any city in the nation except New York, remains its most lively and dominant. The district's Hispanic population is 40%, the lowest of the state's three districts. Another 16% of the population is Indian, the highest in the state. Concentrated in and around the Navajo reservation in the west, many of the district's Indians live in abject poverty.

The politics of northern New Mexico have been unique. For years, votes were bartered in Spanish by Republicans and Democrats, often cynically, sometimes corruptly. Loyalties ran to families and communities

2012 Presidential Vote		
Barack Obama (D)	155,983	(58%)
Mitt Romney (R)	104,871	(39%)

2008 Presidential Vote		
Barack Obama (D)	176,065	(61%)
John McCain (R)	108,045	(38%)

Cook Partisan Voting Index: D+8

more than to principles or parties. Those traditions evolved. Hispanics and Indians are solidly Democratic. In Santa Fe and Taos, the affluent and hippie migrants have produced a strong leftist tilt, and the 3rd District leans strongly Democratic.

Ben Ray Luján (D)

Democrat Ben Ray Luján, who was elected in 2008, has ascended in his party's ranks. In 2013, he became a chief deputy Democratic whip and was elected to the Hispanic Caucus's No. 2 post. Two years later, he entered the House leadership as chairman of the Democratic Congressional Campaign Committee.

A seventh-generation New Mexican, Luján is the son of Ben Luján, a former state House speaker and legendary figure in state politics. The younger Luján has sought to separate himself from his family connections by focusing on complex topics important to the state, especially energy and technology. He was born in Santa Fe and grew up on his family's farm, where he and his three siblings helped raise cattle, sheep and chickens. After graduating from high school, Luján worked as a card dealer in a casino while attending classes at New Mexico Highlands University; he graduated in 2007. He had several state jobs, including deputy treasurer, and chief financial officer and director of administrative services at the Department of Cultural Affairs.

Luján launched into electoral politics in 2004, when he was elected to the New Mexico Public Regulation Commission, which regulates utilities, telecommunications, insurance and transportation. His fellow commissioners elected him chairman. The most pressing issue was the failure of Qwest Communications to invest a promised $788 million in its New Mexico communications network. Under Luján's leadership, the PRC ordered Qwest to invest in infrastructure or refund the money to customers. Qwest refused, and Democratic Gov. Bill Richardson advocated a settlement. But Luján and the PRC steadfastly rejected Qwest's settlement offer, opting instead to take the company to the New Mexico Supreme Court. In 2006, the court sided with the commission, and Qwest finally agreed to spend $270 million in the state over three years. He worked with other regulatory commissioners from the West to create regional solutions to climate change.

When Rep. Tom Udall gave up his House seat to run for the Senate, Luján courted the local Democratic establishment. New Mexico developer Donald Wiviott also ran. At the Democratic convention, Luján got 40% of the vote and Wiviott 30%; since both passed the 20% threshold, their names were on the primary ballot. Also on the ballot was Benny Shendo, former head of the New Mexico Indian Affairs Department. The primary race quickly turned negative. Wiviott ran ads claiming Luján's father had helped him secure his job as deputy state treasurer. Luján responded with ads claiming that Wiviott's Texas trailer parts company had been charged by the Federal Trade Commission with price-fixing. Shendo caused the race's biggest controversy when he implied at a candidate forum that Luján was gay. Shendo drew criticism from local gay rights groups.

Luján picked up endorsements from Richardson, local labor unions and the Sierra Club. Wiviott spent almost $1.6 million of his own money in the campaign; Luján spent less than $800,000, and won with 42% of the vote to Wiviott's 26%; Shendo got 16%. The general election was a foregone conclusion. Luján won with 57% of the vote to 30% for Republican building contractor Daniel East and 13% for independent Carol Miller. He has not faced serious competition since.

Luján has a liberal voting record, but with some moderate strokes. He sided with northern New Mexico ranchers in 2011 in their fight against the U.S. Forest Service over reducing cattle-grazing allotments within the Santa Fe and Carson National Forests, a position that dismayed state environmental groups. Luján has pushed several bills aimed at preserving wilderness areas and settling some high-profile water rights disputes in his state. He has filed legislation to authorize additional money for victims of diseases caused by uranium mining and nuclear tests, many of whom are citizens of the Navajo nation. He supports the natural gas industry, which has a strong presence in the northwest Four Corners region.

He secured a seat on the Energy and Commerce Committee in 2013, giving him a more prominent perch from which to work on two of his pet causes: alternative energy and Los Alamos National Laboratory's non-nuclear weapons scientific research. He became an advocate for conservation and sustainability. He called for moving federal funding directly to the labs instead of through the Energy Department. In a February 2015 speech to the New Mexico Legislature, Luján urged creation of a public-private consortium for the state's two national labs to bid on federal contracts. Earlier, he organized the bipartisan Technology Transfer Caucus to funnel research from the labs to the private sector. He joined the Congressional Progressive Caucus, but has steered clear of partisan rhetoric and concentrated on state-specific matters. In the Hispanic Caucus, he has been close to California's Xavier Becerra in the Democratic leadership. Luján has combined his caucus and whip duties in joining the effort to pass comprehensive immigration reform.

After Democratic Sen. Jeff Bingaman announced in 2011 that he would retire, Luján expressed interest in running for the seat. National Democrats made it clear that Rep. Martin Heinrich was their preferred choice. Luján stepped aside. He was rewarded in November 2014 when, in a surprise move, Minority Leader Nancy Pelosi chose him to head the DCCC over other House Democrats who had publicly advocated their case. His selection highlighted Democrats' continued outreach to progressives and Hispanics, with the party anxious to make up ground for the numerous seats it had lost in recent elections. Pelosi described Luján as "a dynamic and forward looking leader with fresh energy and ideas." He promised to go "on the offensive to put the majority in play." But the early months of 2015 revealed little change in DCCC strategy or prospects to regain control from their smallest number of House seats since the 1928 elections. Democrats missed opportunities to compete in special elections, especially in the Staten Island district of New York.

★ NEW YORK ★

"**E**ven old New York was once *Nieuw Amsterdam*," the old song goes. Today's New York—America's largest city, financial capital, artistic and media center, and largest immigrant destination—seems far removed from once tiny, rough-hewn *Nieuw Amsterdam*. But this is a city with a certain enduring character that goes back to its birth as a 17th-century Dutch colony. Simon Schama's *The Embarrassment of Riches* paints a picture of the Old World Amsterdam that speaks to the character of the New World settlers. They came to America from "the richest city in the world; full of people who work hard all day and stay up late at night, smoke too much tobacco and drink too much coffee and gin, but are dazzlingly smart and shrewd; people who know their way around every corner of the globe and can make fine aesthetic discriminations, but are attached to their uncomfortable, crowded, bad-smelling city. They were merchants and manipulators with no aristocratic pedigree, welcoming any religious or ethnic group who can achieve and accumulate and show good taste, cherishing education and culture but indifferent to credentials."

Less than 2% of today's New Yorkers are descended from the Dutch of *Nieuw Amsterdam*, but the character of the place endures in daily life and in its great institutions and helps explain its miraculous growth. Combine Amsterdam and America, Dutch character with British-born political freedoms and American military strength, and you have the opportunity to build a city-state that can lead the world—and become the natural target of terrorists who hate that civilization.

New York was not always the nation's leader. In 1776, it was only the seventh most populous colony. Only in the 19th century did the descendants of Dutch patroons, Huguenot refugees, British West Indies traders, and Yankee farmers become the nation's most successful merchants and capitalists, forging the first routes to the great American interior through the valleys of the Hudson and the Mohawk rivers and building grand brownstone mansions on broad midtown Manhattan avenues. That early diversity provides one clue to New York's success. If New York has been cynical, ready to cooperate with Loyalists and Revolutionaries, it has also been tolerant, ready to accept anyone smart or rich enough to be counted a success. It has been propelled upward at each stage, forging ahead of London as a financial and manufacturing center by World War I and staying ahead of surging Chicago and Los Angeles by incorporating every immigrant wave and consistently rewarding intelligence and hard work, with no concern about preserving hierarchies.

New York state's success has been a product not only of market economics, but also of government and politics. The English saw New York as a pivotal point in North America, the connecter of its northern and southern colonies and an avenue to the interior. That is why the 30-year-old James, Duke of York, as Lord High Admiral, ordered the fleet to take Nieuw Amsterdam in 1664; the city and state are named for the man who was later King James II. The Iroquois, the most deeply rooted and militarily strong Native Americans, were kept in place for 100 years by an alliance with British troops and then were driven out of their homelands in Upstate New York after the Revolution.

New York led the nation in political innovation. Martin Van Buren's Albany Regency was the first state political machine, an ally of New York City's Tammany Hall. Van Buren invented or institutionalized the Democratic Party, the national convention, and the inaugural parade. His adversaries, Thurlow Weed and William Seward, formed the Whig Party and ultimately became Republicans. Noting that Van Buren's Democrats were winning large margins from Irish Catholics and other immigrants, the Whigs and Republicans also made bids for the newcomers' votes. Both parties served the function of mediating between the divergent interests of the New York City masses and Upstate New York's farmers and burghers, a conflict still evident in New York between city and country, immigrant and native, Catholic and Protestant, the Big Apple and the apple-knockers.

Both parties also worked to protect New Yorkers against the untrammeled workings of free economic and political markets. Tammany Democrats embarked on an unprecedented, labor-intensive campaign to build infrastructure—the bridges and tunnels that made Greater New York possible. The tradition carried on from the time of Mayor Abram Hewitt, elected in 1886 over the single-taxer Henry George and the 27-year-old Theodore Roosevelt, up through the time of Gov. Al Smith in the 1920s and his protégé Robert Moses, who built bridges, tunnels, highways, beaches, and the World's Fairs of 1939 and 1964, laying the

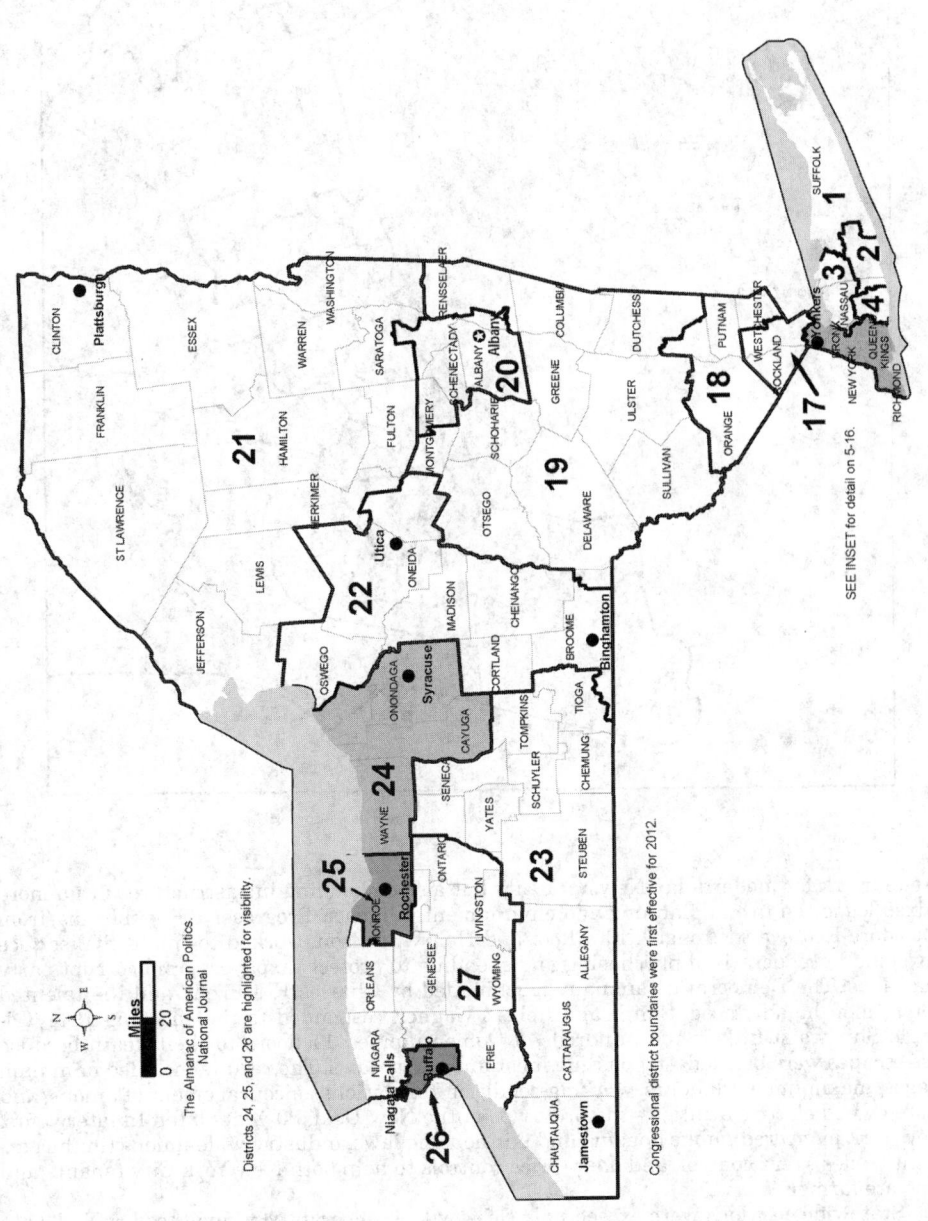

The Almanac of American Politics.
National Journal

Districts 24, 25, and 26 are highlighted for visibility.

Congressional district boundaries were first effective for 2012.

SEE INSET for detail on 5-16.

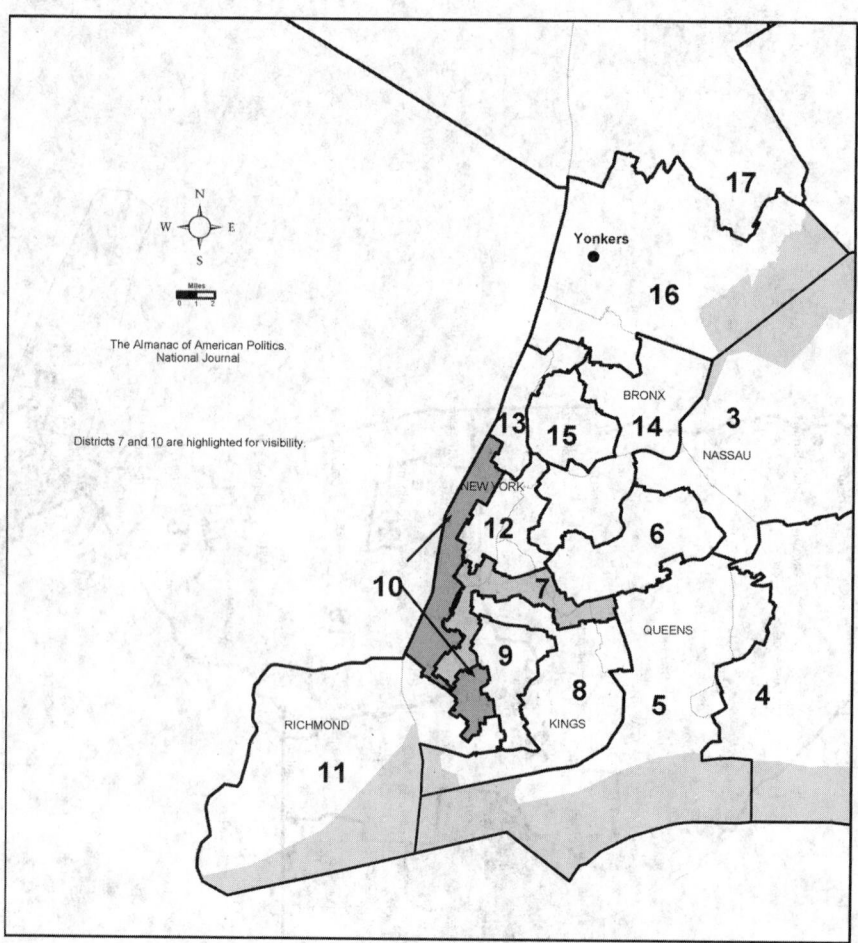

N

W ←⊕→ E

S

Miles
0 · 1 · 2

The Almanac of American Politics.
National Journal

Districts 7 and 10 are highlighted for visibility.

Yonkers

17

16

BRONX

13 15 14 3

NASSAU

NEW YORK

12 6

10 7 QUEENS

9 8 5 4

RICHMOND KINGS

11

Congressional district boundaries were first effective for 2012.

groundwork for modern-day New York City but also embedding infrastructure with a more mixed legacy on urban planning and environmental impact. Progressive Republicans, from Theodore Roosevelt through Elihu Root and Henry Stimson, worked to create civil service laws and bureaucratized purchasing and spending to protect taxpayers from corrupt party machines. The Democratic Tammany machine led by Charles F. Murphy and the talented young men he advanced, Smith and Robert Wagner, responded to the shocking 1911 Triangle Shirtwaist fire—when hundreds of women jumped 11 floors to their death because fire escapes were blocked—by passing labor and safety laws. The results included minimum wages, maximum work hours, working-condition regulations, encouragement of unions, and state-owned electric utilities—the prototype of the New Deal, 20 years later. In later years, New York pioneered public housing and fair housing laws, industry-wide unions (in the garment trades), rent control, and dairy price controls to help both New York City tenants and Upstate farmers.

Statewide elections were exceedingly close, with Democrats carrying the New York City Catholic vote and Republicans winning Upstate Protestants. Swing votes were cast by more than 1 million Jewish immigrants, who supported a generous welfare state but mistrusted the Tammany machine and valued civil rights. The politician who combined these appeals most cannily was Fiorello LaGuardia, a nominal Republican but almost a socialist, an Episcopalian who was half Jewish as well as Italian, and the man who, as mayor of New York City from 1933 to 1945, built much of the public housing and many of the civic monuments that still stand. Incensed that New York had no airport, he built what is now LaGuardia within a year. Both parties produced politicians whose positions appealed to these swing voters. At a time when the national media was much more concentrated in Manhattan than in Washington, D.C., many became nationally prominent and often presidential candidates: Democrats Smith, Wagner, Franklin D. Roosevelt, and Averell Harriman; Republicans Thomas Dewey, Wendell Willkie, and Nelson Rockefeller. Dwight Eisenhower, then president of Columbia University, was a New Yorker when elected president in 1952.

The polity that these men built was productive, generous, tolerant, and closely regulated. The country was becoming accustomed to working in big units—being employed by big corporations, represented by big unions, regulated by big government—and in this, New York was a natural leader. The financial dominance of Wall Street and the big banks was protected by federal regulation. The high technology thrust of America in the mid-20th century was directed by big companies headquartered in New York's suburbs or Upstate: General Electric and IBM, Eastman Kodak and Xerox. New York took for granted the productivity of its thousands of entrepreneurs and the high skills of its largely immigrant-born, public- and Catholic-school-educated workforce. It was blasé about its own miraculous infrastructure—the bridges and subways, electronic cables and wires connecting it better than anyplace else with every corner of the world.

But in the last quarter of the 20th century, New York's public strengths became weaknesses. The state that was clearly the national leader of a big-unit America—*Mad Men* America—lost the leadership role once growth had shifted to small economic units and where flexibility and adaptability had become more important than centralized planning. The institutions, practices, and infrastructure that had helped produce New York's successes became ossified. Welfare state benefits became too expensive; measures meant to protect against corruption stifled innovation. Payoffs and rackets were part of the everyday cost of doing business in New York as in no other place in the country. Rent control kept housing scarce, school bureaucracies and teacher unions stifled good teaching, and public hospitals rationed care. The government that intended to aid growth seemed to be cutting it off—not completely, but enough to explain why New York state, which grew 45% in population from 1930 to 1970, grew only 6% from 1970 to 2010, while California grew 87% and Texas 125%.

People and businesses started voting with their feet, especially during the terms of Mayor John Lindsay, a liberal Republican who caved to municipal unions' demands and borrowed against next year's revenues to pay this year's bills. Two years after he left office, that approach brought the city to the brink of bankruptcy in 1975—"Ford to City: Drop Dead," as the *Daily News* famously summarized the president's hardball tactics during the crisis. In the 1970s, the population of New York, city and state, dropped by 1 million, an unprecedented hemorrhage of talent and productivity. Retrenchment followed, and private financiers and the state government took control of city government, cut spending, and negotiated cutbacks in jobs and salaries with public employees' unions. In the 1980s, Wall Street boomed, and Manhattan once again brimmed with confidence. Taxes were cut further under Democratic Mayor Edward Koch (1978-89) and Democratic Gov. Mario Cuomo (1982-94), public employees' unions were for a time reined in, and Rational Management was installed. But institutional problems remained. New York's legislature remained tightly controlled by the two chambers' leaders—the Democratic Assembly speaker from New York City and the Republican state Senate president from Upstate or the suburbs—who engaged in classic political logrolling, lavishing taxpayers' dollars on each other's pet projects. Public employees' unions reestablished their stranglehold. The mild recession of the early 1990s struck New York with force. Big Upstate companies—Xerox, Kodak, IBM—suffered serious reverses, and a private sector that had grown little if at all outside Wall Street could no longer finance the growing demands of the state.

By the end of the 1990s, New York seemed to have gotten back on track. Republican Mayor Rudolph Giuliani, first elected in 1993, cut crime and welfare rolls in half and cut hard deals with the unions, though with a swagger that was polarizing. Republican Gov. George Pataki, first elected in 1994, imposed huge tax and spending cuts in 1995. Wall Street and the financial services industry boomed in the late 1990s, to the point that the jobs lost in the early-1990s recession were replaced. Then came September 11, 2001.

It was a beautiful late-summer morning, the sunshine lighting a blue sky above the skyscrapers of Manhattan, commuters hurrying through the streets and subways to work. At 8:46 a.m., the first plane hit the North Tower of the World Trade Center. When the second plane hit the South Tower 17 minutes later, it was clear that America was under attack, at war, even as office workers fled the burning buildings and New York firefighters streamed in. The terrorists had chosen to attack the seat of government in Washington—the Pentagon and a second target saved by the heroes of United Flight 93—and the seat of commerce in New York to inflict the maximum possible damage. The people of New York, like those at the Pentagon and on United 93, responded with courage and determination. Firefighters, police officers, and rescue workers risked death to help others. Strangers helped strangers. People who had no experience with disaster figured out how to cope and help others. Millions volunteered to give blood, send money, and provide food and supplies. In less than a week, the New York Stock Exchange reopened.

Giuliani and Pataki performed well in the national spotlight. But New York faced an economic downturn and a turn in the course of government. Despite heroic efforts at recovery, Manhattan and New York lost 200,000 jobs in 2001 and 2002. Downtown real estate values tumbled as financial services firms decentralized and sought office space elsewhere. Giuliani was term-limited, and all the leading contestants were well to his left. Media billionaire Michael Bloomberg, previously a Democrat, became a Republican and spent $70 million of his own money on the campaign; he beat city Public Advocate Mark Green, 50% to 48%. Faced with a fiscal crunch in 2002, Bloomberg increased property taxes 18% and raised other taxes as well. In his third term as governor, Pataki tried to hold down spending, but big tax increases, supported by Assembly Democrats and Senate Republicans, were passed over his veto. Nevertheless, the financial industry boomed as never before, generating revenues well beyond expectations—until the underlying driver of the boom, mortgage-backed securities and other toxic assets, imploded in September 2008, with repercussions internationally, nationally and locally.

In the first decade of the 21st century, when Bloomberg won a third term with a onetime change approved by the City Council, New York City's economy grew largely because of the boom in financial services, while its population growth was fueled almost entirely by immigration. The city's population grew 2% from 2000 to 2010, to nearly 8.2 million, and the four close-in suburban counties grew 3%. But this small change masked much greater movements. The elderly moved out, heading to Florida and other warmer climes, and middleincome workers and young blue-collar workers headed to lower-cost and lower-tax states like the Carolinas, Georgia, and Florida. Moving in, meanwhile, were immigrants who streamed into outer-borough neighborhoods and created new businesses, churches, and neighborhood institutions—Afro-Caribbeans in Flatbush; Chinese in Flushing, Borough Park, and on Staten Island; Colombians and Mexicans in Corona; Pakistanis and Bangladeshis in Jackson Heights; Greeks in Astoria; Russians in Brighton Beach; and Dominicans in Washington Heights and much of the Bronx. The 2010 census showed Hispanics' percentages as 54% in the Bronx, 28% in Queens, 25% in Manhattan, and 20% in Brooklyn. At the same time, the city's black population declined, and Hispanics now outnumber blacks in every borough except Brooklyn. The census also reported that 23% of the people in Queens are Asians, the highest percentage for any county east of the San Francisco Bay Area (though nearly equaled in Middlesex County, New Jersey).

Today's immigrants are arriving in a different sort of city. New York has long since lost most of its manufacturing jobs, and many corporate headquarters have moved elsewhere.

Population		Race and Ethnicity		Income	
Total:	19,651,127	White	57.8%	Median income:	$53,843
Urban:	62.2%	Latino	18.0%		(23 of 50)
Suburban:	28.5%	Black	14.4%	Under $50,000	44.4%
Rural:	9.2%	Asian	7.4%	$50,000-$99,999:	28.1%
Land area:	47,126	Two races	1.7%	$100,000-$199,999:	20.2%
Pop/sq. mi.:	417.0	White Ethnic	37.3%	$200,000 or more:	7.3%
Born in state:	63.6%			Poverty Rate	14.5%
		Education			
Age Groups		H.S. grad or less:	41.2%	**Work**	
Under 18:	21.6%	Some college:	24.7%	White collar:	39.2%
18 to 34:	24.4%	College degree, 4 yr.:	19.3%	Blue collar:	44.1%
35 to 64:	39.7%	Post-grad study:	14.8%	Sales and service:	16.6%
Over 64:	14.4%				
		Military		Govt. workers:	15.4%
		Veterans/active duty:	5.2%		

The financial-services industry pays enormous salaries and bonuses to those at the very top and generates service jobs for those who tend to the needs of the rich. But finance was sent reeling by the financial meltdown of 2008, and although it has rebounded, it's not clear whether the cornucopia will be as bounteous as before. As historian Fred Siegel points out, the

Voter Turnout		
2013 Total Citizen 18+		13,546,582
2014 Highest Statewide Turnout		3,819,010
2014 Turnout as % CVAP		28.2%
2012 Turnout as % CVAP		52.8%

Legislature			
Senate:		32R	31D
House:		105D	44R	1V

outer boroughs are increasingly dependent on public sector jobs, with one-third of jobs in Brooklyn and one-half in the Bronx directly dependent on the city or state governments. New York's Medicaid program, designed by Republican Gov. Nelson Rockefeller in 1966 to be far more generous than any other state's, provides a lot of jobs, including many for immigrants. That said, the outer boroughs, particularly Brooklyn, started to experience a revival during the Bloomberg years, as artisanal-minded, latte-swilling hipsters helped gentrify older neighborhoods; these areas became iconic through HBO's *Girls* and other depictions in the media. Hillary Clinton would eventually choose Brooklyn as the headquarters for her 2016 presidential campaign. The liberal drift was made clear by the 2013 mayoral victory of Bill de Blasio to succeed Bloomberg as mayor. It came amid slackening support for Bloomberg's anti-crime stop-and-frisk policy, particularly among minorities most at risk from the strategy. Questions about the death of Eric Garner, a black man in Staten Island, after being put in a police chokehold on July 17, 2014, raised tensions over policing; the tensions were only intensified after the claimed revenge killing of NYPD officers Wenjian Liu and Rafael Ramos later that year.

In the suburbs, the problems stemmed from having much higher property taxes than those in the city. The high property taxes are in effect tuition to good suburban school districts but become a heavy burden when the kids go off to college. The immigrant inflow in the four suburban counties of Nassau, Rockland, Suffolk, and Westchester was smaller, 3% from 2000 to 2009, with a domestic outflow of 7%. Places like Levittown, buzzing with young families moving from Brooklyn in the 1950s, aged and lost population. Immigrant communities coalesced in low-income suburbs whose first residents had departed. But with their high taxes and utility rates, the suburbs are not attractive to new businesses—the hedge-fund sector bloomed across the state line in Greenwich Connecticut.

Upstate New York has even greater problems. Burdened with a state tax system constructed to support New York City's needs, it has been at a substantial disadvantage compared with nearby northeastern states, not to mention the Sun Belt, when it comes to attracting jobs. Medicaid mandates have forced Upstate counties to drastically raise property taxes. Large, formerly paternalistic companies have been shedding jobs. IBM cut back heavily in the Hudson Valley and in Southern New York. Kodak, hard hit by competition from digital cameras, employed 60,000 people in the Rochester area in 1981 but by 2015 had cut its local workforce to 2,000 (out of 7,250 worldwide). Xerox jobs in the area fell from 16,000 to 8,000. Buffalo, once one of the nation's great steel producers, has become a center for the debt-collection industry. Overall, Upstate New York gained 2% in population from 2000 to 2010, but the only areas of robust growth were the mid-Hudson Valley, the capital area around Albany, and the Finger Lakes.

In this decade, both Upstate and the city have been dealt blows by the elements. In August 2011, Hurricane Irene came roaring through Upstate New York, causing record flooding and damage. And in late October 2012, superstorm Sandy—not technically a hurricane—struck the beaches of New Jersey, New York City, and Long Island. Sandy's winds came in just at high tide and funneled water from the ocean and New York Harbor into low-lying areas in all five boroughs. Houses were smashed and swept away on the Rockaway Peninsula, and subway tunnels were flooded. A major electric power station blew, leaving Manhattan below 34th Street without power for days. On Staten Island, thousands remained homeless for weeks. Sandy prompted a pause in the presidential campaign and gave President Barack Obama an opportunity to inspect the damage and promise recovery funds. The rebuilding effort has been problematic; after more than two years of work, the *New York Times* wrote, the hallmarks of the city's program to help people rebuild homes were "crushing uncertainty, postponed promises and hopeless bottlenecks." Other recent economic development efforts have also struggled. Start-Up New York, a program to provide tax advantages to companies relocating in the state, was begun in 2013 by Democratic Gov. Andrew Cuomo, but after spending tens of millions of dollars in its first year, the effort resulted in fewer than 100 new jobs, according to the *Times*.

In the first half of the 20th century, New York politics was a battle between the Democratic city, then with more than half the state's population, and the Republican Upstate. Jewish voters, concentrated in the city and moored to neither party, provided critical swing votes. In the post-World War II period, the suburbs grew and tended to produce small Republican majorities. Today the picture is different. The 2012 exit poll showed that only 23% of New York voters were white Protestants, 33% were white Catholics, and 6% were Jewish. By 2013, census data showed the state's population as 16% black, 18% Hispanic, and 7% Asian—all heavily Democratic constituencies which made up 16%, 13%, and 2%, respectively, of the electorate in the exit poll. New York City was 26% black, 29% Hispanic and 13% Asian.

In races for statewide office, New York has been voting heavily Democratic. It voted 58% for John Kerry in 2004 and 63% for Obama in 2008 and 2012. It voted 70% for Gov. Eliot Spitzer in 2006 and 63% for Gov. Andrew Cuomo in 2010 and 54% in 2014. In Senate races, it voted 71% and 66% for Charles Schumer in 2004 and 2010, 67% for Hillary Clinton in 2006, and 63% and 72% for Kirsten Gillibrand in 2010 and 2012. Most of these Democrats would have won if not a single vote had been cast in New York City; both the New York suburbs and Upstate New York have voted Democratic, though not always by very large margins. The Republican Party remains a factor only in the state Senate, which the GOP controlled from 1965 to 2008, in part because the heavily Democratic Assembly let the Senate Republicans draw their own chamber's district lines. Republicans won the majority back in 2010 and, have generally controlled the chamber through a shifting series of alliances with renegade Democrats.

Albany's long-festering problems with ethics and corruption have come to a head in recent years. Spitzer, elected in 2006, visited high-end prostitutes, got caught, and resigned; his successor, David Paterson, had such low job approval ratings that he decided not to seek a full term. During their tenures, the state Senate was often laid low by power plays and petty maneuverings, often by lawmakers just one step ahead of legal or ethics problems. Various observers called Albany the most dysfunctional state government in America.

The election of Cuomo in 2010 represented a turn toward improved political stability and stronger public support. Cuomo earned the gratitude of liberals by securing the legalization of same-sex marriage, including decisive votes from Republican state senators, while appealing to moderates with a more conservative approach on fiscal issues. But after Cuomo won a second term by a diminished margin in 2014, the longtime power players in both chambers—Assembly Speaker Sheldon Silver, a Democrat, and Senate Majority Leader Dean Skelos, a Republican—were both indicted on separate federal corruption charges, leaving Cuomo that last untainted man standing.

Presidential Politics   In the first half of the 20th century, New York was the dominant state in presidential politics. It had the most electoral votes, and of all the large states, it was usually the most evenly divided between the two parties. In the 21st century, New York—with 33 electoral votes in 2000, 31 in 2004 and 2008, and 29 in 2012—has come to be the most heavily Democratic large state. It's easy to forget that in 1976, Jimmy Carter only carried the state with 52% of the vote, winning just seven counties and only three outside

2012 Presidential Vote		
Barack Obama (D) 4,480,244		(63%)
Mitt Romney (R)..............2,489,569		(35%)
2012 Presidential Primary		
Mitt Romney (R).................118,912		(62%)
Ron Paul (R) 27,699		(15%)
Newt Gingrich (R) 23,990		(13%)
Rick Santorum (R) 18,997		(10%)
2008 Presidential Vote		
Barack Obama (D) 4,804,945		(63%)
John McCain (R)..............2,752,771		(36%)

New York City. But by 2008 and 2012, only the District of Columbia, Hawaii, and Vermont cast higher percentages for Barack Obama. How did this come to pass? One reason is that Jewish voters, who did not identify strongly with either major party in the first half of the 20th century, became strong Democrats in the second. Increases in the percentages of black and Hispanic voters raised the Democratic percentage. White Catholic voters took conservative positions on cultural issues like crime in the 1970s and 1980s, which was one reason that Sen. James Buckley was elected on the Conservative Party line in 1970, that Republican Ronald Reagan won New York's electoral votes narrowly in 1980 and 1984, and that Republican George H.W. Bush was beaten by only 52%-48% in 1988. But today, these voters, and their descendants, are more likely to take liberal stands on cultural issues such as gun control, abortion and gay rights. Republican allegiance in the New York City suburbs—on Long Island and in the upscale commuter towns of Rockland and Westchester counties—also faded away starting in 1992. Now the only county in the New York City metropolitan area that still cast its ballots for GOP presidential hopefuls is tiny Putnam. In the past five elections, Democratic presidential nominees have won 59%, 60%, 58%, 63%, and 63% of New York's votes. In 2008, Obama won 59% of Catholics and much higher percentages of Latinos and Jews. In 2012, he did even better, even with lower turnout driven by Hurricane Sandy. New York was one of five states (the others were New Jersey, Maryland, Mississippi, and Louisiana) in which Obama won a higher percentage of the votes in 2012 than in 2008.

For 2008, New York scheduled regular primaries for both parties on February 5, Super Tuesday. It was one of more than a dozen states voting that day and got little attention from candidates (except for holding Manhattan and Hamptons fundraisers) because New York's own, Hillary Clinton and Rudy Giuliani, were well ahead in the polls. When Giuliani dropped out after the Florida primary on January 29, he endorsed John McCain. Republican turnout was only 670,000 voters, far fewer than the 2 million who voted for delegate slates in 2000. McCain beat Mitt Romney 52%-28%, carrying every county and congressional district and, with the Republicans' winner-take-all rule, winning all the delegates. Only 12% of Republican primary votes were cast in New York City; 25% came from the suburbs, and 63% from Upstate. Turnout in the Democratic primary was high, 1.9 million voters, beating the record of 1.5 million set in 1988. In 2008, Clinton beat Obama 57%-40%, carrying 26 of the 29 congressional districts—all but three heavily black districts in Brooklyn and Queens—and 61 of 62 counties, the exception being Tompkins County, home of Cornell University and Ithaca College. Blacks favored Obama by 24%. Jews, Latinos, and white ethnics gave about two-thirds of their votes to Clinton. A little more than half of all Democratic primary votes were cast in New York City, 18% in the four suburban counties, and 30% Upstate.

In 2012, New York did not vote until May 24, when the Republican race was effectively over. Turnout was an exceptionally low 189,000, and Romney won with 63% of the vote. New York City cast just 13% of the votes, with 28% coming from the suburbs and 59% from Upstate. New York law allows third parties to cross-endorse major party candidates, and once upon a time, third parties played a serious role in the state's politics. The Liberal Party and its predecessor, the American Labor Party, were founded to give Jewish garment workers a ballot line on which to vote for Franklin D. Roosevelt for president but against local Tammany Hall candidates. The Liberal line was a help to Giuliani in the 1993 and 1997 mayoral elections. But in 2002, the Liberals lost their ballot position when their candidate for governor, Andrew Cuomo, received far fewer than the 50,000 votes required.

The Conservative Party was formed in the 1960s to oppose the liberal-leaning Rockefeller Republicans and provided a line on the ballot for William F. Buckley Jr.'s quixotic run for mayor in 1965 and for his brother James Buckley's successful race for the Senate in 1970. It endorsed Republicans Alfonse D'Amato for the Senate and George Pataki for governor but has had only occasional influence on local races since. The newest third party is the Working Families Party, which was formed in 1998 by public employee unions and usually endorses Democrats. The most successful recent third party-line effort was Mayor Michael Bloomberg's creation of an Independent line to support his reelection as mayor in 2009.

Congressional Districts When John F. Kennedy was elected president in 1960, New York elected 43 members, California 30, and Florida eight. In 2012, New York and Florida each elected 27 members and California 53. Reapportionment has been carnage time for New York: the state lost five districts

114th Congress Lineup	
9 R	18 D
113th Congress Lineup	
6 R	21 D

in the 1980 census, three in 1990, and two each in 2000 and 2010. New York has more than 200 state legislators, but legislative decisions have been made by three power brokers: the state Senate president, Assembly speaker, and a veto-wielding governor. Traditionally, the trio only starts crafting a redistricting deal when courts threaten to take over the process, and House incumbents have no choice but to hire expensive and well-wired Albany lobbyists to preserve their seats.

In 2002, faced with the loss of two seats and under heavy pressure from incumbents to avoid a court-drawn map, Democratic Assembly Speaker Sheldon Silver and Republican Senate President Joseph Bruno hatched a last-minute deal to merge two sets of districts in slow-growing Upstate New York. (Each party leader subsequently was indicted, on other grounds.) The plan, signed by Republican Gov. George Pataki, ultimately compelled one senior member from each party to reluctantly retire and spare their neighbors. Elsewhere, incumbents were protected, though Democrats' 19-10 edge ballooned to a 26-3 near-monopoly after 2008 and settled to a 22-7 advantage in 2011.

In 2012, Democrats held the governorship and state Assembly, but Republicans clung to a tiny majority in the state Senate. Once again, New York needed to trim two seats, and this time it was clear Upstate and Downstate would need to split the loss. But the "old way" of deal-cutting hit two snags. First, Democratic Gov. Andrew Cuomo, along with late New York City Mayor Ed Koch, had made major redistricting reform a signature issue. In 2010, Cuomo threatened to "veto any redistricting plan in 2012 that reflects partisan gerrymandering." Second, in January 2012, a federal court ruled New York would need to move up its federal primary from September to June to prevent disenfranchisement of overseas voters, further compressing the tortoise-like legislature's timeline.

Republican state Senate President Dean Skelos (who also was later indicted) cleverly responded to Cuomo and Koch's entreaties for a nonpartisan commission by gaining Senate passage of a constitutional amendment creating one—in time for 2020. As the partisan deadlock continued, a federal three-judge panel appointed U.S. Magistrate Judge Roanne Mann as special master in charge of implementing a map should the legislature fail. Frantically, three of the four legislative caucuses submitted their own proposals to Mann, each eliminating the Upstate seat of retiring Democrat Maurice Hinchey. But the prospects of a grand bargain dimmed with each passing day.

Mann released her own proposal, drawn up by hired consultant and law professor Nathaniel Persily, which morphed the state's 29 existing contorted districts into 27 geographically compact seats. In a past era, indignant House incumbents might have browbeaten the legislature into halting such a rearrangement. But in 2012, the court map was largely met with reluctant acceptance. The plan even-handedly eliminated retiring Democrat Hinchey's Upstate seat and the Queens seat of Republican special election winner Bob Turner, who hadn't expected to win reelection anyway. In November 2012, Democrats netted a single seat: Republican freshmen in Syracuse and the Hudson Valley lost their seats, but Democrat Kathy Hochul also lost after her Western New York district was made more Republican. Five other incumbents—three Republicans and two Democrats—survived by less than 6 percentage points.

Republicans had a notably better showing in 2014, when they turned back hyped Democratic challenges and took three Democratic seats: one on the eastern end of Long Island, and two in the northeast region Upstate. That left the delegation with an 18-9 Democratic edge; Republicans held six of the nine House seats north of the New York City suburbs and two of the four Long Island seats east of the City. Many of those districts are potentially competitive, which could turn New York into a regular battleground.

Governor

Andrew Cuomo (D)

Elected 2010, term expires Jan. 2019, 2nd term; b. Dec. 6, 1957, Queens; Fordham U., B.A. 1979, Albany Law Schl., J.D. 1982; Catholic; divorced; 3 children.

Elected Office: NY atty. gen., 2006-10.

Professional Career: Asst. dist. atty., Manhattan, 1984-85; Practicing atty., Blutrich Falcone & Miller, 1985-88; Founder, Housing Enterprise for the Less Privileged, 1988-93; Asst. secy., Dept. of Housing & Urban Development, 1993-97; Secy., HUD, 1997-2001.

Office: NYS St. Capitol Building, Albany, 12224, 518-474-8390; Website: governor.ny.gov.

Election Results

2014 general	Andrew Cuomo (D)	2,069,480	(54%)
	Rob Astorino (R)	1,536,879	(40%)
	Howie Hawkins (G)	184,419	(5%)
2014 primary	Andrew Cuomo (D)	361,380	(63%)
	Zephyr Teachout (D)	192,210	(34%)

Prior winning percentage: 2010 (63%)

Democrat Andrew Cuomo was elected governor in 2010 and rapidly piled up a record of accomplishments that, along with soaring approval ratings, led many to wonder if he would compete for the White House. Cuomo is a former state attorney general and secretary of the U.S. Department of Housing and Urban Development, and he is the son of the late three-term Gov. Mario Cuomo. Ultimately, he didn't jump in the 2016 race, and despite winning reelection in 2014, his star dimmed somewhat, especially among liberals, and amid a furor involving ethics reform and feuding with New York City Mayor Bill de Blasio.

Cuomo was born in Queens and grew up in the middle-class neighborhood of Hollis, the second of five siblings. At the time, his father was a lawyer in Brooklyn who assisted journalists such as Pete Hamill, Jimmy Breslin, and Jack Newfield in exposing and addressing injustices on city housing policy and other issues. The younger Cuomo showed an early aptitude for repairing and building automobiles. "If Andrew gets a car, it's about (him) making the car," his brother Chris Cuomo, a journalist for CNN, told *Esquire* in 2010. "It's really a metaphor for what he does in government—he does it himself, he fixes things." He graduated from Fordham University in 1979, one year after his father was elected lieutenant governor, and from Albany Law School in 1982.

He began working for his father's campaign for governor that year and received credit for masterminding his come-from-behind primary victory against popular New York City Mayor Ed Koch. However, some critics said the younger Cuomo was too willing to engage in dirty politics. "Andrew Cuomo was his father's id, aggressive where Mario was cerebral—the muscle that helped win Mario three terms as governor of New York," as *New York* magazine put it. He spent several years as an aide to his father, working for $1 a year, as the governor's national profile skyrocketed in the wake of his eloquent denunciation of President Ronald Reagan's policies as keynote speaker at the 1984 Democratic National Convention.

After a short stint in the Manhattan district attorney's office, Cuomo in 1986 founded the Housing Enterprise for the Less Privileged (HELP USA), a nonprofit organization dedicated to helping the homeless. He left his private law practice in 1989 to run the group, which became a national model for its formula of offering shelter but also job training, education, drug treatment, and other assistance. Two years later, he married Kerry Kennedy, the daughter of Robert F. Kennedy, in a widely-publicized union that was described as a merger of two Democratic political dynasties.

Cuomo's work at HELP caught the attention of Arkansas Gov. Bill Clinton, who asked Cuomo to serve on his transition team after being elected president in 1992 and then as assistant secretary of community planning and development at HUD. After Clinton's reelection in 1996, Cuomo took over as secretary of the department. He won praise for his energetic efforts to make housing more affordable, but he also adopted policies to broaden home ownership for low-income Americans that some later said contributed to the housing crisis a decade later. One of those policies was a dramatic rise in the number of loans that government-sponsored mortgage giants, Fannie Mae and Freddie Mac, were required to buy. HUD also produced rules that explicitly forbade imposing new reporting requirements on the two enterprises. Years later, when questions arose on the campaign trail, his aides blamed policies enacted under Republican President George W. Bush for the mortgage meltdown.

Cuomo returned to New York in 2001 with the intention of running for governor the following year. But he did himself in with some brash and ill-advised remarks. He said that Republican Gov. George Pataki had done little after 9/11 other than hold New York Mayor Rudy Giuliani's coat. He also angered African-Americans who had been looking to State Comptroller Carl McCall as their party's candidate. Cuomo dropped out of the race before the primary, and McCall lost to Pataki. Around the same time, Cuomo became engaged in a bitter public divorce and child custody battle with Kennedy.

Cuomo largely disappeared from the public eye for the next several years. In 2006, he came back to run for New York attorney general when the incumbent in that job, Eliot

Spitzer, ran for governor. He patched up his differences with Democrats and won the primary with ease, then easily beat the Republican nominee, former Westchester District Attorney Jeanine Pirro, 58%-40%. He conducted investigations into alleged misdeeds within the financial industry, something that had propelled Spitzer to the governorship. At the same time, he looked into the student loan industry's deceptive marketing practices, uncovered fraud among health insurers, and crusaded against online child pornography. He also ended up investigating Spitzer for using the state police to gather information about then-state Senate Majority Leader Joseph Bruno. Cuomo's popularity rose.

When Spitzer resigned in disgrace in 2008 over revelations that he had been the client of a prostitution ring, Lt. Gov. David Paterson took over, becoming the state's first African-American chief executive. But by March 2009, Paterson's job ratings were the lowest in state history. Suburbanites were angry about cuts in school funding, New York City residents were mad about cuts in city aid, and leaders of public employee unions were angry about proposed layoffs and revisions in fringe benefits. The muddy process for appointing Rep. Kirsten Gillibrand to the Senate seat vacated by Hillary Clinton did not help. Paterson eventually acceded to the demands of the Obama White House, which insisted he not run for a full term fearing that he would become a drag on the entire ticket in New York.

In May 2010, Cuomo announced his candidacy, declaring the state had slipped from being a "national model" under his father to a "national disgrace." He unveiled a long list of proposals, from creating more high-tech and energy jobs to a spending cap and salary freeze on state workers. Accompanying him at the announcement was his girlfriend Sandra Lee, host of a popular cooking show on the Food Network. The only question remaining was who would run against him as the Republican underdog. Former two-term Rep. Rick Lazio (who had lost a Senate race to Hillary Clinton) sought the GOP nomination but lost overwhelmingly in the September primary to Carl Paladino, a wealthy real estate executive who self-funded his campaign with support from Tea Party activists.

Paladino was known for his aggressive and prickly style, and some members of Cuomo's camp wondered if his unpredictability in an anti-establishment climate would work against them. But Paladino hurt no one more than himself, as New York tabloids dubbed him "Crazy Carl." He said that though he did not discriminate against gays, he did not want children "brainwashed into thinking that homosexuality" is acceptable. He accused Cuomo of being unfaithful to his ex-wife but offered no evidence. Cuomo had little trouble rolling to a landslide 63%-33% victory. Although Paladino won most western New York state counties, Cuomo received more than 75% of the vote in higher-turnout areas such as Queens and the Bronx.

Cuomo warned in his initial inaugural address that the state was spending too much and receiving too little in return. He promised that his fiscal plan would not involve new borrowing or higher taxes on the wealthy, a stand that irked some state lawmakers. The grumbling among those lawmakers increased dramatically when Cuomo seemed unwilling to produce specifics on how to balance the budget. His administration broke with usual practice in leaving others to fill in the details of almost half of the $8.9 billion in spending cuts it proposed. Just days before the March 31 deadline, he was able to strike a deal with the legislature's leaders on a $132.5 billion budget that reduced year-to-year spending by about 2% without imposing taxes. He agreed to add $250 million for schools, education, human services, and prescription drugs for the elderly. News of the deal outraged New York City Mayor Michael Bloomberg, who said the cuts would disproportionately affect the city even though it was responsible for generating much of the state's revenue. The two men later reportedly settled their differences during a phone call from Cuomo.

Another of Cuomo's proposals, to create an independent nonpartisan redistricting commission, met resistance and ultimately failed a year later. And his efforts to win cooperation from unions—a problem confronting governors in numerous other cash-strapped states—brought strong criticism from labor groups. The public, however, remained solidly in Cuomo's corner. In a February 2011 Siena College poll, he scored an impressive 77% favorability rating. He even won praise from Republicans. Senate Minority Leader Mitch McConnell of Kentucky publicly cited Cuomo and the more bombastic GOP Gov. Chris Christie of New Jersey as "two examples of gubernatorial leadership people ought to look to."

Cuomo decided to use his political capital on an ambitious undertaking: legalizing same-sex marriage, which the state Senate had defeated two years earlier. He met with wealthy Republican campaign donors, asking them to insulate GOP senators from conservative attacks. To avoid infighting among gay rights activists, he had them merge into a single coalition and hire a consultant with ties to his office. And he repeatedly assured wavering lawmakers that he had their back. "I can help you. I am more of an asset than the vote will be a liability," he reportedly assured them. At the same time, he successfully tamped down opposition from the Catholic Church.

In the end, six senators who had voted against the bill in 2009 voted for it in June 2011, including three Republicans, and New York became the largest state to permit such unions. Political commentators of all stripes said the governor's maneuvering was masterful, and national gay activists as well as prominent liberals began opening their wallets to him in gratitude. Other accomplishments followed, including the implementation of a 2% annual cap on property taxes and a rewrite of the state tax code in which the wealthy paid higher rates while middle-income earners saw theirs go down.

Cuomo entered 2012 with his highest job-approval rating as governor—62% in the Siena poll, along with a 73% favorability rating. He did not shirk from another confrontation with public employee unions, proposing a teacher evaluation system and limiting pension benefits for future government workers. He was able to strike a deal the next month on evaluations that blocked positive ratings for teachers who failed to at least minimally boost their students' performance. And he won a new fund fueled by $1.2 billion in additional state and federal spending for infrastructure.

His name began popping up on the early lists of 2016 presidential prospects. Even his father stoked the speculation: At a July party for his 80th birthday, Mario Cuomo reportedly called his son "the best governor in modern times" and said that he might someday "have an opportunity to serve at a higher level, to serve the people of the United States." Mindful of comparisons with his father's 1984 address, the governor stayed out of the spotlight at August 2012's Democratic National Convention.

In 2013, Cuomo called for raising New York's minimum wage, decriminalizing small amounts of marijuana, and a Women's Equality Act that would promote pay equity, stop pregnancy discrimination, and toughen human-trafficking laws. But the proposal that drew the most attention was his call for action on gun control in the wake of the Newtown Connecticut school massacre. He proposed tightening the definition of assault weapons and lowering the maximum magazine capacity. "We are a community based on progressive principles," he said in his annual State of the State speech. "We must remain that progressive capital of the nation." He quickly got the legislation into law, which caused his job-approval rating to dip below 60% in late January. While Democrats remained in his corner, his support among Republicans suffered.

Cuomo dealt with controversy over the Common Core educational standards in 2014. The standards, which were designed to improve classroom instruction, ran into substantial opposition from conservatives across the country—and from moderates in New York—who regarded them as being overly inflexible and intrusive. Cuomo acknowledged flaws in the implementation of Common Core and later struck a compromise with legislators to delay and restrict certain elements of the program, such as testing and teacher evaluations. Taxes remained another priority: He proposed a $2 billion tax-cut package that critics said largely rewarded the wealthy while hurting state services. At the same time, he scoffed at de Blasio's call to impose a city tax on the rich to finance universal pre-kindergarten. The mayor eventually received $300 million from the state for the program, less than the $340 million he had sought, and the state adopted a number of provisions dealing with charter schools that de Blasio opposed.

But those controversies were overshadowed by an even larger one. *The New York Times* reported in July that his administration had sought to thwart the progress of the independent commission he had established to investigate corruption after the panel began delving into issues that involved him and his political supporters. Cuomo said he disbanded the panel when an ethics law was passed in March that strengthened anti-bribery laws and achieved roughly nine of its 10 goals. But the unmet goal, a system of publicly financing campaigns that cut off unlimited donations, was seen by the governor's critics as the most important.

Cuomo drew a Democratic primary challenger from Zephyr Teachout, a Fordham University law professor who made fighting corruption the centerpiece of her campaign. *The Times* refused to endorse either candidate, calling Cuomo's failings and his rival's lack of experience equally dispiriting. "As he has repeatedly shown, Mr. Cuomo knows how to bend lawmakers to his will, especially when it serves his political interest," the newspaper said in an editorial. "But he has repeatedly failed to do so when it comes to cleaning up Albany." By the numbers, Cuomo prevailed easily, 63%-34%, but Teachout's showing was better than expected. In the general election against Westchester County Executive Rob Astorino, Cuomo used his 9-to-1 fundraising advantage to pull out a victory, but with just 54%, well below the 65% figure with which his father won a second term.

Observers saw a duality in Cuomo's first term: Substantive achievements, undercut by political mistakes that led to sinking popularity. As *New York* magazine noted, Cuomo's first term was strong on paper, including the gun restrictions and same-sex marriage law. "The state has gone from a $10 billion deficit in 2010 to a projected $6 billion surplus. He's restored functionality, if not total rationality, to a state government that had become a national embarrassment," including the passing of four on-time budgets and the state's highest credit rating in more than four decades. Yet Cuomo "underestimated the anger of the state's left wing" and, on the ethics issue, acted in ways that "fueled the perception that he views himself as above the democratic process."

In 2015, the legislative landscape experienced an earthquake, as Assembly Speaker Sheldon Silver, a Democrat, and Senate Majority Leader Dean Skelos, a Republican, were both arrested on federal corruption charges. Cuomo's on-time budget streak ended (technically—the bill passed only three hours late) but it included key education provisions he backed, including tougher personnel rules for teachers and consequences for low-performing schools, as well as enhanced disclosure rules for state lawmakers. The liberal wing of his party bemoaned that the budget deal didn't include a minimum wage hike (Cuomo supported a $10.50 rate, smaller than the $15 many liberals wanted) and critics called the ethics reforms insufficient. Within weeks, Cuomo did use his powers to go around the Legislature to set in motion a minimum wage boost for fast-food workers, and he traveled to Havana to promote engagement and trade with Cuba. He also promised to stiffen enforcement of health and labor standards on nail salons and similar businesses, in the wake of a damaging expose in the *New York Times*.

The year also brought a string of personal and professional challenges. Cuomo's father died at 82, and the governor's girlfriend, Sandra Lee, was diagnosed with breast cancer. Cuomo was on the hot seat after the escape of two murderers from the state prison at Dannemora, with the alleged assistance of prison staff; it was a top-tier national story until one escapee was killed by police and the other was captured. Meanwhile, by summer, Cuomo was mired in a loud feud with de Blasio, with the mayor criticizing the governor for, among other things, his handling of public-housing funds and mayoral control of the city's public schools. "What we've often seen is if someone disagrees with him openly, some kind of revenge or vendetta follows," the mayor told the NY1 network. He made a point of calling reporters into his office to tell them about his strained relationship with Cuomo, which "keeps playing out in ways that I think sometimes are about dealmaking, sometimes about revenge. But it's not about policy. It's not about substance. It's certainly not about the millions of people affected."

In the first half of 2015, a string of polls showed Cuomo's approval ratings falling into the low-to-mid 40s—record lows for his tenure. (Of cold comfort was the fact that de Blasio's ratings were similarly weak.) Other members of the party's liberal wing began to talk up a primary challenge to Cuomo if he were to run for a third term in 2018. One early casualty of the intra-party dissent was Cuomo's 2016 presidential hopes, though these had likely been rendered moot as soon as Hillary Clinton, a fellow New York Democrat, made clear her intention to run.

Senior Senator

Charles Schumer (D)

Elected 1998, term expires Jan. 2017, 3rd term; b. Nov. 23, 1950, Brooklyn; Harvard U., B.A. 1971, J.D. 1974; Jewish; married (Iris Weinshall); 2 children.

Elected Office: NY Assembly, 1975-80; U.S. House, 1981-99.

DC Office: 322 HSOB, 20510, 202-224-6542; Fax: 202-228-3027; Website: schumer.senate.gov.

State Offices: Albany, 518-431-4070; Binghamton, 607-772-6792; Buffalo, 716-846-4111; Melville, 631-753-0978; New York City, 212-486-4430; Peekskill, 914-734-1532; Rochester, 585-263-5866; Syracuse, 315-423-5471.

Committees: *Banking, Housing & Urban Affairs:* Financial Institutions & Consumer Protection; Housing, Transportation & Community Development; Securities, Insurance & Investment. *Finance:* Int'l Trade, Customs & Global Competitiveness; Social Security, Pensions & Family Policy; Taxation & IRS Oversight. *Judiciary:* Crime & Terrorism; Immigration & the Nat'l Interest (RMM); Oversight, Agency Action, Federal Rights & Federal Courts; Privacy, Technology & the Law. *Rules & Administration* (RMM). *Joint Committee on the Library. Joint Committee on Printing.*

Group Ratings

	ADA	ACLU	AFL-CIO	LCV	ITI	COC	HAFA	ACU	CFG	FRC
2014	90%	100%	–	80%	100%	50%	0%	0%	0%	0%
2013	95%	C	100%	100%	C	38%	C	4%	0%	C

National Journal Ratings

	2013 LIB	—	2013 CONS
Economic	93%	—	0%
Social	73%	—	0%
Foreign	71%	—	0%
Composite	90%	—	11%

Key Votes of the 113th Congress

1. Sandy storm spending	Y	5. Student Loan Rates	Y	9. Bipartisan Budget Deal	Y
2. Chuck Hagel Confirmation	Y	6. Employee Non-Discrim'n Act	Y	10. Farm Bill Conference Rept.	Y
3. Gun Background Checks	Y	7. Senate Vote on Judgeships	N	11. Unempl. Comp. Extension	Y
4. Immigration Reform	Y	8. Defense Dept. Spending	Y	12. Keystone Pipeline	N

Election Results

2010 general	Charles Schumer (D)	3,047,111	(66%)	$19,356,984	$117,929
	Jay Townsend (R)	1,479,724	(32%)	$217,593	
2010 primary	Charles Schumer (D)	unopposed			

Prior winning percentages: 2004 (71%), 1998 (55%); House: 1996 (75%), 1994 (73%), 1992 (89%), 1990 (80%), 1988 (78%), 1986 (93%), 1984 (72%), 1982 (79%), 1980 (77%)

When he was just out of law school, Democrat Charles Schumer, New York's senior senator, began immediately running for a seat in the New York Assembly—over the objections of his mother. "Don't run, you'll never win," she is said to have advised her son. Not only did Schumer win; he has not lost an election in the intervening four decades, and is now poised to become the first New Yorker to assume leadership of his party in the Senate since the roles of majority and minority leader were formally created a century ago. When Harry Reid of Nevada, the Senate Democratic leader since 2004, announced his retirement in February 2015, he anointed Schumer over another would-be successor, Democratic Whip Richard Durbin of Illinois—putting an end to a years-long, behind-the-scenes rivalry between Schumer and Durbin. Reid's move quickly prompted Durbin to concede the top job, ensuring Schumer would become at least minority leader in 2017, assuming his all but certain reelection to a fourth term from New York. And if the hard-charging Schumer has his way, he will take over after Senate Democrats have regained the majority they held from 2007-2015, giving him control of the Senate agenda with a new face in the White House.

Schumer, first elected to the Senate in 1998, began his rise in the leadership by helping to engineer that majority as chairman of the Democratic Senatorial Campaign Committee during the 2006 election cycle. He reprised the DSCC role in the 2008 election campaign, then ascending to the No. 3 slot in the leadership (vice chairman of the Democratic Conference) and later assuming responsibility for Senate Democrats' policy and political messaging. If the Schumer-Durbin rivalry was long a subject of speculation among congressional insiders—particularly given that the two were close friends and weekday housemates in a Capitol Hill townhouse for a dozen years—so was the unlikely bond of the New York City-bred, Harvard-educated Schumer with Reid, a one-time amateur boxer who grew up in a small Nevada mining town. If Schumer and Reid share a strategic savvy and an intense drive to succeed, Reid is as uncomfortable in front of the cameras as Schumer is at ease. Throughout his career, Schumer has been widely noted—and sometimes resented—for his ability to attract publicity. Former Senate Majority Leader Bob Dole, a Kansas Republican, once famously wisecracked that the most dangerous place to be in Washington was between Schumer and a television camera.

Schumer isn't the only member of his extended family to draw media attention; his cousin's daughter, Amy Schumer, stars in Comedy Central's *Inside Amy Schumer* and has made a reputation for her raunchy comedy. Charles Schumer grew up in Flatbush, Brooklyn, where his father had a small exterminating business. He graduated first in his class at James Madison High School, also the *alma mater* of Supreme Court Justice Ruth Bader Ginsburg, Sen. Bernie Sanders of Vermont, and former Minnesota Sen. Norm Coleman. He graduated from Harvard College and Harvard Law School, but never practiced law—with his law degree fresh in hand in June 1974, he won an open New York Assembly seat the following November. At 23, he became the state's youngest member of the Assembly since Theodore Roosevelt was elected in the early 1880s.

In 1980, just before turning 30, he was elected to an open Brooklyn seat in Congress. Shortly after his election, Schumer staffers were cautioned by congressional insiders that they had signed on with a political has-been. Due to the 1980 reapportionment, New York stood to lose five House seats—nearly 15 percent of its delegation—and, under the requirements of the Voting Rights Act, the state was under pressure to create a second majority-minority district in Brooklyn. Consequently, the district of the newly arrived Schumer was widely regarded as being on the chopping block. But, exhibiting the prowess that would later help him climb the Senate Democratic leadership ladder, Schumer quickly accumulated a large campaign treasury. It saved him and his district: The neighboring district of a more senior Brooklyn House member, albeit a legislator with a far thinner campaign bankroll, was eliminated instead.

Upon his election, Schumer sought and obtained a seat on the House Banking (now Financial Services) Committee, recognizing its importance to Wall Street, located in lower Manhattan just across the East River from Schumer's home borough. He also served on the Judiciary Committee and chaired the Crime Subcommittee. Schumer sponsored the 1994 crime bill that banned assault weapons and shepherded through the House President Bill Clinton's proposal to add 100,000 police officers across the country. In addition, the legislation created "three strikes" mandatory life terms for repeat violent criminals. Schumer was the House sponsor of the Brady bill, which created waiting periods for handgun purchases and was passed over the strong opposition of the National Rifle Association.

The idea of running for statewide office was never far from his mind. In early 1997, a couple of years after the Democrats had lost their four decade-long hold on the House majority, Schumer considered seeking the governorship. But Republican Gov. George Pataki's strong job approval ratings instead persuaded him to use his $5 million campaign treasury to run against GOP Sen. Alfonse D'Amato. It was by no means obvious that Schumer would win, despite New York's Democratic tilt. D'Amato's initial election in 1980 had been considered something of a fluke, as he benefitted from the coattails of Ronald Reagan's landslide election as president and a three-way split in the Senate candidate field in the general election. But he had won reelection in 1986 and 1992, thanks in part to his assiduous constituent service and his ability to dominate the tabloid wars that are a mainstay of metropolitan New York political campaigns. As chairman of the Banking Committee in the GOP-controlled Senate, he also excelled at raising money.

Schumer started off largely unknown outside his district, and faced serious primary opposition from Geraldine Ferraro, the 1984 vice presidential nominee, and Mark Green, the New York City public advocate and D'Amato's 1986 opponent. By summer, Schumer was leading in polls and was much better financed than his rivals. In September, he won the primary with 51 percent to 26 percent for Ferraro and 19 percent for Green. Schumer immediately launched an attack on D'Amato, saying the incumbent had told "too many lies for too long," which echoed D'Amato's earlier criticisms of his opponents as "too liberal for too long." He also emphasized his support of abortion rights and gun regulation. By mid-October, most polls put the race within the margin of error. Then, in a closed meeting before a Jewish group, D'Amato called Schumer a "putzhead," Yiddish slang for "jerk." When the remark became public, he denied it, before backtracking unconvincingly after his own supporter, former New York City Democratic Mayor Edward Koch, confirmed it. By early November, D'Amato was sagging in the polls. Schumer was the beneficiary of two visits from Clinton and no fewer than four from first lady Hillary Rodham Clinton. Although outspent, Schumer won, 55%-44%.

When Hillary Clinton was elected senator two years later upon the retirement of long-time Democratic Sen. Daniel Patrick Moynihan, speculation centered around how well the ambitious Schumer would take to being to being overshadowed in the media spotlight by a junior colleague regarded as a potential presidential candidate from the time she arrived on Capitol Hill. At times, Schumer did appear irked by the wattage from Clinton's celebrity. But he supported Clinton's bid for the 2008 presidential nomination, and her appointment as secretary of state in the Obama administration made him indisputably New York's lead senator—while underscoring his paramount role in New York politics. When Democratic Gov. David Paterson dithered over appointing a Senate successor to Clinton, Schumer weighed in on behalf of Rep. Kirsten Gillibrand, who received the appointment. Former Tennessee Rep. Harold Ford, Jr., who had moved to New York, mulled making the race. But Schumer helped persuade him not to run. As a result, Gillibrand had only desultory primary opposition and won the 2010 general election easily to fill the balance of Clinton's term. Schumer has since helped Gillibrand blossom into a formidable national political player in her own right.

Conscious of New York's traditional upstate/downstate political divide, Schumer, as a Brooklyn native and resident, vowed when first elected to visit all of the state's 62 counties annually, and constant travel upstate has made him as well-known there as in New York City. In his first re-election, in 2004, his fundraising skills enabled him to raise more than $27 million and win easily, 71%-24%, exceeding the 67%-31% record set by Moynihan in 1988. (Schumer's record was later eclipsed, when Gillibrand received 72 percent when she won a full Senate term in 2012.) With the Senate under Democratic control for only an 18-month period during his first term in the chamber, Schumer reportedly again eyed a run for governor in 2006—when Pataki's retirement left that job open. But the issue was settled when Reid named Schumer as DSCC chairman in 2005, with a seat on the influential Senate Finance Committee as an added enticement to remain on Capitol Hill.

The task facing Schumer in the 2006 election appeared formidable: The lineup of Senate seats up for grabs left Republicans with more target seats than Democrats. But Schumer succeeded in persuading Democratic incumbents from states that President George W. Bush carried in 2004—Jeff Bingaman of New Mexico, Kent Conrad of North Dakota, Ben Nelson of Nebraska, and Bill Nelson of Florida—not to retire. Then he worked on getting strong challengers to Republican incumbents. In Pennsylvania, he aggressively recruited state Treasurer Robert Casey, Jr., son of the late governor known for his strong opposition to abortion rights. The younger Casey, who had set his sights on following his father into the governorship, agreed to run for Senate. Schumer made a pitch over dinner in London to state Auditor Claire McCaskill to compete in Missouri, where she had shown strength in her losing 2004 gubernatorial race. She ran for Senate and won. In Virginia, Schumer backed Jim Webb, a decorated Vietnam veteran who served as Reagan's Navy secretary, over liberal lobbyist Harris Miller, and Webb won a narrow victory in the primary and went on to defeat the heavily favored incumbent, Republican George Allen.

During the campaign, Schumer wrote a book, *Positively American: Winning Back the Middle-Class Majority One Family at a Time*, in which he urged Democrats to offer 50 percent solutions—increase math and reading scores by 50 percent, cut property taxes by 50 percent, and reduce illegal immigration by 50 percent. Schumer's success in helping to win a Democratic majority prompted Reid to ask him to stay on as head of the DSCC in the 2008 election season. As an inducement, Reid created a leadership position for Schumer as vice chairman of the Democratic Conference, although the new post did not come with a staff and a detailed portfolio. Schumer effectively became the confidential adviser to the new majority leader, putting Schumer—himself known for private flashes of temper over the years—in the position of counseling the hot-tempered and difficult Reid.

Schumer again played a key role in producing winning candidates at election time. On top of the six seats gained in 2006, the Democrats had a net gain of eight in 2008, while losing none of their own in either election: A 45-seat minority had become a 59-seat majority in the span of a little over two years. Seldom has one senator made such a difference in the partisan composition of the body. And seldom, if ever, has the No. 3 person in a party's leadership done as much to determine a major party's policy stands and political positioning in the Senate. As Republican Sen. John Cornyn of Texas observed of Schumer—ruefully, but with admiration—"In my opinion, his influence is supreme. He's everywhere."

In the Senate, Schumer has established a solidly liberal voting record; in 2013, it put him in a three-way tie for the most liberal senator, according to *National Journal*'s annual vote rankings. But, in his role as the Senate Democrats' chief strategist, he has evidenced a pragmatism that has won him strong support among the Senate Democrats' moderate wing. In the wake of the Democrats' loss of the Senate majority in November 2014, several moderates—who ended up voting against Reid's reelection as Senate Democratic leader—were reported to have privately urged Schumer to challenge Reid, according to a report in *Politico*. But Schumer, four months before Reid announced his retirement and anointed Schumer as successor, rebuffed the moderates' pleas, citing loyalty. "Reid made me [who I am]," Schumer is reported to have said, underscoring the bond between the two men.

On the Banking Committee, Schumer has been a steadfast ally of a major home state constituency, Wall Street, which has come under sharp attack in recent years from the party's increasingly vocal liberal populist wing. It could complicate Schumer's task as he prepares to assume leadership of Senate Democrats in early 2017; Massachusetts Sen. Elizabeth Warren, the Democrats' most visible and vocal Wall Street critic, was given a post in the Senate Democratic leadership by Reid following the 2014 election. In 1999, Schumer supported the Gramm-Bliley-Leach bill eliminating the barriers between banks and investment banks, a measure that Warren pushed to roll back following her 2012 election.

Schumer has long opposed moves to toughen regulation of the government-sponsored mortgage institutions, Fannie Mae and Freddie Mac, citing the rising rate of homeownership and the possibility of increased interest rates. And he has fought increasing tax rates on so-called carried interest; such a move would fall heavily on the hedge fund operators and private equity firms based in New York's financial district and surrounding areas. Schumer could have asserted his seniority to become the ranking Democrat on the Banking Committee, succeeding retiring Sen. Tim Johnson of South Dakota. But Schumer passed on that post to concentrate on his leadership duties, allowing the less-senior Sherrod Brown of Ohio to assume that position. (Schumer has remained the top Democrat on the Senate Rules and Administration Committee, where, as chairman in January 2013, he played a high-profile role in the arrangements for the second term inauguration of President Barack Obama. He was said to be furious at superstar singer Beyoncé Knowles for lip-synching "The Star-Spangled Banner" without first informing anyone.)

If Schumer has frequently been a key congressional ally for Obama's policy agenda, there have been some highly visible differences with the White House. In the spring of 2015, when Obama sought so-called "fast track" negotiating authority to expedite a 12-nation Asian trade deal, Reid and Schumer opposed the president—who ultimately had to rely heavily on Republicans to pass the measure, while also attracting a handful of Democrats, mostly from export-dependent states. "I don't believe in these agreements anymore," Schumer told the *Wall Street Journal.* "I've changed." Schumer did support a number of major trade agreements in the past, although he voted against the North American Free Trade Agreement as a House member in 1993.

Several months earlier, in the aftermath of the Democrats' drubbing at the polls in 2014, Schumer drew wide attention when he gave a National Press Club speech chastising his party for pushing the Affordable Care Act after getting the $787 billion economic stimulus law through in 2009. "Unfortunately, Democrats blew the opportunity the American people gave them," Schumer said, making clear he still backed Obama's signature legislative achievement. "We took their mandate and put all of our focus on the wrong problem—health care reform." He has been a proponent of focusing Democratic efforts on the middle class; he often says his political reference point is an imaginary Long Island couple convinced that politicians devote too much attention to the very rich and very poor. But a number of Schumer's fellow liberals were incensed at the speech, pointing out the law didn't just help lower-income patients. During the 2009 debate on the health insurance overhaul, Schumer joined other liberals in supporting creation of a government-run insurance option. But, sensing it lacked 60 votes, he worked with Maine Republican moderate Olympia Snowe on a trigger mechanism to create a public option only if private plans did not meet certain criteria. But he dropped those efforts after they failed to win Republican support.

Schumer has fretted on occasion about Obama's readiness to make concessions to the Republicans. But, amid his reputation as a no-holds-barred partisan, aides point to his efforts to find common ground with the Republicans in recent years, most notably on immigration. Schumer has had a longstanding interest in immigration policy reform, going back to his days on the House Judiciary Committee, when he contributed key provisions to immigration laws passed in 1986 and 1990. Although a comprehensive bill was not high on Obama's agenda at the outset of his first term, Schumer worked with Republican Lindsey Graham of South Carolina establishing agreement on concepts for later legislation, including stronger border and workplace enforcement, a guest worker program, and a path to legalization for illegal immigrants in the country.

When immigration moved to the political front burner in 2013, Schumer and Graham were part of a bipartisan, eight-member group—the so-called "Gang of Eight"—that came up with a reworked plan that offered a legalization pathway, a new system for employers in a variety of industries to hire guest workers, and stringent border-security provisions. Schumer sought 70 votes for the measure, and ended up falling just two short: It passed 68-32 in July 2013, with 14 Republicans joining the entire Democratic caucus in backing it. He and other members of the Gang of Eight succeeded in building a coalition of interest groups to support the bill, including the Republican-leaning U.S. Chamber of Commerce. When combined with the backing of agriculture and technology groups, Schumer believed, the Chamber's support would neutralize the furor of far-right conservatives. It was arguably the most noteworthy bipartisan achievement in a Congress that featured few other examples of reaching across the political aisle. But the Republican-controlled House refused to take up the bill or pass anything that would satisfy the Democratic-controlled Senate.

In January 2015, Schumer became co-chairman of a bipartisan working group on tax reform with Ohio Republican Sen. Rob Portman, as talk intensified of the potential for a bipartisan deal that could open the way for the policy goals of both parties: a more business friendly tax code sought by Republicans, and revenue for new domestic infrastructure advocated by Democrats. Schumer's interest in tax reform appeared to be a shift from recent years: When House and Senate negotiators sought a deal on taxes and spending to avoid the so-called "fiscal cliff" in October 2012, Schumer dismissed the idea of a tax code overhaul as "little more than happy talk." Republicans reacted angrily, and an overhaul never made it into the final legislation. At that time, Schumer also reportedly clashed with Finance Committee Chairman Max Baucus, a Montana Democrat, over the potential scope of tax reform.

The Sept. 11, 2001 attacks hit home for Schumer more than for most members of Congress: Growing up in Brooklyn in the 1960s, he watched the World Trade Center towers rise in the distance while under construction. Six weeks before his election to Congress in 1980, he was married in the "Windows on the World" restaurant, which was located on the 107th floor of the north tower. (Schumer's wife, Iris Weinshall, was transportation commissioner from 2002-2007 in the administration of New York City Mayor Michael Bloomberg, and is now chief operating officer of the New York Public Library.) When the hijacked planes struck the World Trade Center on 9/11, the older of his two daughters, Jessica, was attending high school near the twin towers, and it was several hours before Schumer and his wife could determine that she was all right. (Jessica Schumer is now chief of staff and general counsel to the White House Council of Economic Advisers.)

Schumer played a major role in shepherding recovery money through Congress after the Sept. 11 attacks. He immediately requested $20 billion in aid for New York, which Bush readily approved. The Bush administration then turned to Schumer to rally support for its centerpiece anti-domestic terrorism law, the USA Patriot Act. In February 2010, Schumer opposed Obama administration plans to try Khalid Sheikh Mohammed, considered by U.S. intelligence sources to be the mastermind of the Sept. 11 attack, in New York. "My advice to the president is, with a great deal of respect, take New York off your radar screen. Find another location," Schumer declared. The plan to try Mohammed in New York was subsequently scrapped. Schumer also was the lead sponsor of a bill to compensate Sept. 11 responders for health problems they later encountered.

Schumer was up for reelection in 2010, but the outcome was never in doubt. He raised $19 million and overwhelmed Republican Jay Townsend, the owner of a market research firm, 66%-32%. Of greater relevance to his Schumer's political future were the returns in Nevada, where Reid had trailed in the polls for months. The potential for a Reid loss opened the prospect of a Schumer-Durbin battle for the Democrats' top leadership spot. But Reid pulled out a win against a weak opponent, opening the way for another four years of speculation—until Reid announced his retirement and confirmed that Schumer was his choice to succeed him. Two weeks after the 2010 election, Reid assigned Schumer more legislative scheduling and communications duties, giving him the added title of chairman of the Democratic Policy and Communications Center, with the role of sharpening the party's appeal to the middle class.

As he took on more responsibility for the Democrats' messaging following the 2010 election, Schumer taunted Senate Republicans for obstructionism. "Their idea of blocking bills with no fingerprints on them is gone. Everyone sees loud and clear what they're doing," he declared in February 2012. But earlier, during the Bush administration, Schumer led the opposition to judicial nominees whom he and liberal advocacy groups judged to be outside the mainstream. Along with other Democrats, he utilized the filibuster at that time to block the appointment of federal judge nominees who enjoyed majority support, forcing a given nominee to earn 60 votes to be confirmed.

In the late spring of 2015, Schumer—in an interview with the *Washington Post*—signaled that, with the Democrats now back in the minority, the party was not afraid to use obstructionist tactics to exact concessions from the Republican majority—much as Republican Leader Mitch McConnell of Kentucky had utilized such a strategy during the eight years the Republicans were in the minority by keeping his caucus unified on most issues. "There is pretty close to unanimity in our caucus that we are not going to just vote on individual appropriations bills until we have a plan as to how much overall money we're going to spend and where that money is going to be allocated," said Schumer told the newspaper, referring to measures due to come up in the coming months. But it was also seen as a preview of how he might operate as leader if Senate Democrats still find themselves in the minority following the 2016 election.

The above scenario is obviously contingent on Schumer winning another term. Given the results in 2004 and 2010, few expect New York Republicans to be able to mount more than a token challenge—although his new role could make Schumer a more tempting target. In late June 2015, CNBC commentator Lawrence Kudlow, an economist who served in the Reagan administration, was reportedly being wooed by the National Republican Senatorial Committee to take on Schumer. But in a late August radio interview, Kudlow said, "I'm going to run against" Democratic Sen. Richard Blumenthal in 2016 if the Connecticut Senator voted in September for the agreement on Iran's nuclear program. Earlier in August, Schumer voiced opposition to the deal because it eventually would permit Iran to have a nuclear weapon. "After 10 years, if Iran is the same nation as it is today, we will be worse off with this agreement than without it," Schumer said.

Assuming he is either majority or minority leader after the next election, Schumer will be faced with how to deal with the final chapter of his long-running rivalry with Durbin. According to several published accounts, Reid's decision to anoint Schumer as the next leader in late February 2015 was followed by a late-night conversation between Schumer and Durbin on the Senate floor. Durbin is reported to have told his long-time friend that he had earned the leadership mantle, and Schumer, in response, is said to have wept in gratitude. But what was, or wasn't, said next remains unclear. The Durbin camp has contended that, during the conversation, Schumer agreed to support Durbin staying on as whip. But Schumer and his aides have denied that any such deals were made, and Washington Sen. Patty Murray, another member of the Democrats' leadership team, has not ruled out challenging Durbin. The headline of a *Washington Post* story summed up the Democrats' leadership predicament: "Is There a Happy Ending to Chuck Schumer-Dick Durbin Buddy Movie?"

Junior Senator

Kirsten Gillibrand (D)

Appointed Jan. 2009, term expires Jan. 2019, 1st full term; b. Dec. 9, 1966, Albany; Dartmouth Col., B.A. 1988, U.C.L.A., J.D. 1991; Catholic; married (Jonathan); 2 children.

Elected Office: U.S. House, 2007-09.

Professional Career: Practicing atty., 1991-2006; Special counsel, HUD, 2000.

DC Office: 478 RSOB, 20510, 202-224-4451; Fax: 202-228-0282; Website: gillibrand.senate.gov.

State Offices: Albany, 518-431-0120; Buffalo, 716-854-9725; Lowville, 315-376-6118; Mahopac, 845-875-4585; Melville, 631-249-2825; New York City, 212-688-6262; Rochester, 585-263-6250; Syracuse, 315-448-0470.

Committees: *Aging (Special). Agriculture, Nutrition & Forestry:* Commodities, Risk Mgmt., & Trade; Livestock, Marketing & Ag Security (RMM); Nutrition, Specialty Crops, & Ag Research. *Armed Services:* Airland; Emerging Threats & Capabilities; Personnel (RMM). *Environment & Public Works:* Fisheries, Water & Wildlife; Transportation & Infrastructure.

Group Ratings

	ADA	ACLU	AFL-CIO	LCV	ITI	COC	HAFA	ACU	CFG	FRC
2014	80%	100%	–	60%	100%	29%	2%	4%	19%	20%
2013	90%	C	100%	100%	C	38%	C	0%	0%	C

National Journal Ratings

	2013 LIB	—	2013 CONS
Economic	82%	—	8%
Social	73%	—	0%
Foreign	71%	—	0%
Composite	86%	—	14%

Key Votes of the 113th Congress

1. Sandy storm spending	Y	5. Student Loan Rates	N	9. Bipartisan Budget Deal	Y
2. Chuck Hagel Confirmation	Y	6. Employee Non-Discrim'n Act	Y	10. Farm Bill Conference Rept.	N
3. Gun Background Checks	Y	7. Senate Vote on Judgeships	N	11. Unempl. Comp. Extension	Y
4. Immigration Reform	Y	8. Defense Dept. Spending	Y	12. Keystone Pipeline	N

Election Results

2012 general	Kirsten Gillibrand (D)	4,816,880	(72%)	$14,257,872	$18,122	$3,515
	Wendy Long (R)	1,758,089	(26%)	$742,747	$963,484	
2012 primary	Kirsten Gillibrand (D)	unopposed				

Prior winning percentages: 2010 special (63%); House: 2008 (62%), 2006 (53%)

Democrat Kirsten Gillibrand, New York's junior senator, was appointed in 2009 to fill the Senate seat vacated by Hillary Clinton when she was appointed secretary of state—and, in the years since, Gillibrand has been signaling she would eventually like to follow Clinton in pursuit of national office as well. Like most future presidential hopefuls, Gillibrand is coy about such ambitions—saying in 2014 she would consider the White House "someday"—and there are other New Yorkers in line ahead of her, notably Gov. Andrew Cuomo, for whom Gillibrand once worked, as well as Clinton. But Gillibrand has taken many of the steps followed by members of Congress seeking to raise their national profiles, including a memoir and a leadership PAC where the money raised has gone to encourage and aid other women candidates. And she has become an in-demand guest at Washington fundraisers seeking to raise funds for a variety of progressive causes "She's a fresh face in the Senate," one Democratic fundraiser and event planner told *Politico*. "She's young, she's vibrant, she's a mom, she's big on women's issues, she's relatable."

It has been an interesting evolution for an ambitious and aggressive politician who, prior to arriving to Congress, was a private attorney defending Big Tobacco, and who joined the Blue Dog Caucus—a group of conservative Democrats—after first being elected to the House a nearly a decade ago. Gillibrand hails from a politically wired family with bipartisan connections. Her father, Douglas Rutnik, is an attorney and lobbyist who has close ties to a number of leading New York Republicans, including former Sen. Alfonse D'Amato, for whom Gillibrand interned while in college. Her grandmother, Polly Noonan, was a prominent Democratic activist in Albany and longtime companion of Albany Mayor Erastus Corning, who held that office for more than 40 years as part of the political organization run by the legendary Daniel O'Connell. Rutnik also was close to Corning, for whom he was a frequent hunting companion. Gillibrand attended the exclusive all-girls Emma Willard School in Troy, just across the Hudson River from Albany, and graduated from Dartmouth College, where she majored in Asian studies and attained fluency in Mandarin; she was among the first Dartmouth students to visit China after the country was opened to students from the United States.

Gillibrand graduated from law school at the University of California, Los Angeles, and did a United Nations internship in Vienna, Austria. After law school, she clerked for Roger Miner, an Albany-based federal appeals court judge appointed by President Ronald Reagan, but spent most of the 1990s working for Davis, Polk & Wardwell, a major New York City-based law firm. Her clients there included tobacco giant Philip Morris, then the subject of numerous criminal probes and civil lawsuits. Shortly after her Senate appointment in 2009, *The New York Times* reported that her work for Philip Morris included helping to defend the firm against allegations that it lied about the existence of internal research on the health effects of smoking. Gillibrand served toward the end of the Clinton administration as special counsel to Cuomo while he was secretary of the Department of Housing and Urban Development, and then joined another major New York law firm, Boies, Schiller & Flexner, as a partner. Gillibrand raised money for Hillary Clinton's first Senate campaign in 2000, and five years later, launched what seemed to be a quixotic campaign against four-term Rep. John Sweeney in the upstate Albany-Troy region where she had grown up.

In 2005, Sweeney was considered a rising Republican star with a seat on the Appropriations Committee. He had never faced a serious reelection challenge in a district that, for the previous century, had elected Democrats on only the rarest of occasions. But Sweeney developed some vulnerabilities as the campaign got underway: He missed several weeks of votes after he was hospitalized in early 2006 for the treatment of vasculitis, an inflammation of the blood vessels. And he got negative press about a fundraising event in Utah that included a ski vacation and dinner at the home of a pharmaceutical lobbyist. Still, August polls showed Sweeney with a solid lead. However, Gillibrand, aided by a national Democratic wave that enabled the party to regain control of both the House and the Senate, ultimately triumphed in what turned into one of the year's nastier races.

Sweeney called Gillibrand a carpetbagger who lived not in the Hudson Valley-based district but in a Manhattan high-rise, and contrasted his working class background with Gillibrand's prep school pedigree. He also accused her campaign of making anonymous and intimidating phone calls to his wife. In turn, Gillibrand demanded that Sweeney release police reports from two arrests in 1977 and 1978 and from a 2001 automobile accident. Sweeney was buffeted by a couple of unflattering revelations in the closing weeks of the campaign. In October, it was revealed he had traveled to the Northern Mariana Islands with Tony Rudy, an associate of disgraced lobbyist Jack Abramoff, who pleaded guilty to conspiracy charges in a scandal that involved several congressional junkets to the islands. Then, a week before the election, the Albany *Times Union* reported Sweeney's wife had called the police in December 2005 to complain the legislator was "knocking her around." Sweeney's campaign at first insisted the report was "false and concocted by our opposition," but Sweeney eventually conceded that the police had been called to his home. Gillibrand won, 53%-47%.

When she arrived in the House, Gillibrand began posting a "Sunlight Report" of her daily schedule, including meetings with lobbyists; she asserts on her current Web site that she was the first member of Congress to post such information daily. Reflecting her district, her voting record had a conservative tilt. She did vote for a nonbinding resolution calling for withdrawing troops from Iraq, but also supported a bill providing funding for the war without a timetable for troop withdrawal. She won a 100-percent voting score from the National Rifle Association, as Gillibrand said she kept two rifles under her bed, while boasting she "always believed in protecting hunters' rights" as she grew up in a family of hunters. Gillibrand also opposed drivers' licenses for illegal immigrants. Defending the seat in 2008, Gillibrand faced a strong opponent in state Republican Chairman Sandy Treadwell, who spent nearly $6 million of his own money. But she collected $4.6 million, and her moderate-to-conservative stands on issues paid off as she won, 62%-38%.

When Clinton was named President-elect Barack Obama's choice for secretary of state, Gillibrand was hardly the first person to spring to mind as a successor. New York Gov. David Paterson considered appointing Cuomo, then state attorney general, which would have removed Cuomo as a possible primary opponent to Paterson in 2010. (Cuomo later was nominated and elected governor after Paterson opted not to run.) Paterson also gave serious thought to appointing Caroline Kennedy, the daughter of President John F. Kennedy. But after Kennedy performed poorly in an interview with *The New York Times* and during an upstate "listening tour," she withdrew. Two days later, Paterson announced he was appointing Gillibrand, a surprise pick considering that several more senior House members were interested. Arguing in Gillibrand's favor was her moderate politics, as Paterson, a New York City resident elevated to the governorship when Eliot Spitzer resigned amid scandal in 2008, hoped to win upstate support as he considered seeking election in his own right.

On Jan. 23, 2009, Gillibrand, then 42, was announced as Paterson's choice, making her the youngest senator at the time. Things were bumpy for her literally from the start: A picture taken as her appointment was announced showed a beaming D'Amato looking on, irking a number of leading Democrats. While later acknowledging she had invited him to the event as a former senator, Gillibrand insisted to *The New York Times*: "Alfonse D'Amato has never influenced me. I've only had about two conversations with him in my whole life. He's not a personal friend of mine; he's a personal friend of my dad's."

Gillibrand quickly moved to modify some of her positions that were out of step with the party, particularly on gun control and immigration. The day after her appointment, she attended a rally in Harlem, where she won applause by vowing flexibility on gun control. "There're a lot of concerns in many of our city communities about gun violence, about keeping our children safe, and keeping guns out of the hands of criminals," she said later.

Gillibrand subsequently opposed Senate amendments that would have allowed licensed gun owners to carry concealed firearms across state lines and would have repealed the District of Columbia's tough gun laws; in the House, she had supported a bill lifting gun restrictions in the District.

But several Democratic House members—Reps. Steve Israel, Carolyn Maloney, and Carolyn McCarthy—began mulling primary challenges to Gillibrand. The motivations appeared to be a combination of pique at being passed over for the appointment in favor of a colleague with less congressional seniority, as well as concern over Gillibrand's past issue stances. McCarthy was first elected to the House in 1996, three years after her husband was killed and her son seriously wounded when a gunman opened fire in a Long Island commuter train. But the three House members dropped out as potential Senate primary candidates in the ensuing months, with Maloney the last to go—announcing she would not run in August 2009 after twice setting and postponing a date to launch her Senate campaign. At the end of 2009, another possible candidate surfaced: former Tennessee Rep. Harold Ford, who had moved to New York three years earlier to become an adviser to Merrill Lynch after losing a bid for a Senate seat in his home state. But, in March 2010, after a statewide tour, he, too, ruled out running.

Throughout this maneuvering, Gillibrand benefited from the assistance of two powerful patrons: Obama and New York's senior senator, Charles Schumer, a member of the Senate Democratic leadership. The White House, fearing an expensive primary could cost the Democrats a seat in the 2010 general election, mounted a full-court press to clear the field for Gillibrand, with Obama and Schumer personally lobbying would-be challengers to stay out. At the same time, Schumer—who was known for being less than thrilled at having to often share the spotlight with Clinton—seemed to delight in taking his new colleague under his wing. He pressed Senate leaders to give her the committee assignments she desired, put her name next to his on project funding announcements in the state, and introduced her to deep-pocketed Democratic donors. "He does look after me in a lot of ways," Gillibrand told *The New York Times* in May 2009.

With her path seemingly cleared for election to the final two years of Clinton's term, Gillibrand turned her focus to legislating. The reauthorization of the Child Nutrition Act, passed into law in the lame-duck session of 2010, included a number of her proposals, such as banning junk food from schools. She joined with several senators to get a bipartisan bill through committee requiring senators to post online their earmark requests for home-state funding projects. But the issue that initially brought Gillibrand the most attention was her call for repeal of the 17-year-old "don't ask, don't tell" policy barring openly gay military service members. She introduced legislation in July 2009 at a time when interest in the issue was lagging, as it leading champion, Sen. Edward Kennedy of Massachusetts, was dying of cancer. In subsequent months, she lobbied former House colleagues as well as fellow senators, pushed for hearings and set up a website featuring videos of gay and lesbian veterans telling their stories. "If you care about national security, if you care about our military readiness, then you will repeal this corrosive policy," she said in an emotional floor speech shortly before it passed the Senate. It became law soon thereafter, earning her widespread praise from progressive and gay rights groups.

Gillibrand's poll numbers remained lackluster throughout 2009, giving some Republicans hope as the 2010 election approached. But by April 2010, she had amassed a $6 million war chest, and leading potential GOP contenders, such as New York Mayor Rudy Giuliani and former Gov. George Pataki, took a pass. The Republicans ended up nominating former Rep. Joseph DioGuardi. DioGuardi had not held public office since a 1985-1989 stint in the House representing suburban Westchester County, and had been unsuccessful in several subsequent attempts to return to Congress prior to the 2010 contest against Gillibrand. Despite a rough year for the Democrats nationally, Gillibrand had no trouble winning, 63%-35%. In 2012, Gillibrand was up for a full six-year term. Wendy Long, a Manhattan lawyer active in conservative circles, got the Republican nod. Gillibrand spent more than $14 million to her rival's $743,000 and won a commanding 72%-26% victory, a record in a New York Senate race—slightly eclipsing Schumer's 71 percent win two years earlier.

Since winning election in her own right, Gillibrand continued her leftward shift. She was tied in *National Journal*'s rankings for most liberal senator in 2011, and tied for fifth place in 2013. In addition to calling in March 2011 for Obama to begin withdrawing troops from Afghanistan, she introduced a bill to repeal the federal Defense of Marriage Act and appeared in a video backing gay marriage. She pleased good-government advocates in early

2012 when she pushed the Senate version of a bill to require more public disclosure of stock transactions by lawmakers.

While tending to her home base—visiting all of the Empire State's 62 counties—she began burnishing her national image by starting an effort, Off the Sidelines, to mobilize female candidates. It was organized as a leadership PAC, a device that allows members of Congress to raise money to increase their visibility, promote their ideas—and collect political chits. Gillibrand cemented her reputation as a fundraising powerhouse: In 2014, the nonpartisan Center for Responsive Politics reported that Off the Sidelines had outraised all other leadership PACs. "I find her to be very impressive," former Vermont Gov. Howard Dean, who mobilized the Democratic left in the 2004 battle for the presidential nomination, observed of Gillibrand. Dean, quoted by *Politico* in 2013, added, "She often underwhelms people at first sight, [but] when you look under the hood, you find a first-class political mind and someone who has a great deal of skill."

In 2013, combating sexual assault became Gillibrand's major focus. She introduced a bill to remove the military chain of command from handling sexual assault cases. Gillibrand waged a high-profile effort for her proposal, telling Illinois voters during one trip there that they needed to pressure their senator, Democrat Richard Durbin, to sign on as a sponsor. (Durbin was reportedly irked by the move, but eventually did so.) The issue pitted Gillibrand against Missouri Democrat Claire McCaskill. As members of the Armed Services Committee, both aggressively lobbied their colleagues on behalf of rival approaches. Gillibrand's proposal fell five votes short of the 60 needed to overcome a Republican filibuster in March 2014; McCaskill's more incremental alternative, to reform the process for handling sexual assault allegations while keeping them within the military chain of command, passed the Senate unanimously with the support of the Defense Department. Meanwhile, to deal with sexual assaults on college campuses, Gillibrand joined a bipartisan group of senators in introducing a bill in July 2014 to require schools to make public results of anonymous surveys on assaults, while also imposing tough fines on schools failing to comply with the requirements.

In 2014, playing off the name of her leadership PAC, Gillibrand published a memoir: *Off the Sidelines: Raise Your Voice, Change the World,* about her efforts to help get women into politics. The book deviated from the usual tomes on the subject by offering self-help and diet advice, and drew attention when Gillibrand wrote about how some unnamed male colleagues commented about her weight. One expressed concern that she might become "porky," while another assured her that she was attractive even when she was heavier. (Early in her Senate tenure, fitness magazines took note of her 40-pound weight loss.) Gillibrand caused a minor fracas when she called Arlington Virginia a "soulless suburb," irking that community's residents. "Sorry, Arlington, didn't mean to hurt your feelings," she said in a tweet.

FIRST DISTRICT

Lee Zeldin (R)

Elected 2014, 1st term; b. Jan. 30, 1980, East Meadow; State U. of NY Albany, B.A. 2001, Albany Law Schl., J.D. 2003; Jewish; married (Diana); 2 children.

Military Career: U.S. Army, 2003-07 (Iraq); U.S. Army Reserve, 2007-present.

Elected Office: NY Senate, 2011-14.

Professional Career: Practicing atty.

DC Office: 1517 LHOB, 20515, 202-225-3826; Fax: 202-225-3143; Website: zeldin.house.gov.

State Offices: Patchogue, 631-289-1097.

Committees: *Foreign Affairs:* Terrorism, Nonproliferation, & Trade; Middle East & North Africa. *Transportation & Infrastructure:* Aviation; Coast Guard & Maritime Transportation; Railroads, Pipelines, & Hazardous Materials. *Veterans' Affairs:* Disability Assistance & Memorial Affairs; Economic Affairs.

Election Results

2014 general	Lee Zeldin (R)	94,035	(54%)	$1,814,213	$234,953	$4,754,240
	Tim Bishop (D)	78,722	(46%)	$2,988,328	$217,756	$3,505,800
2014 primary	Lee Zeldin (R)	10,283	(61%)			
	George Demos (R)	6,482	(39%)			

Population		Race and Ethnicity		Income	
Total:	722,480	White	77.4%	Median income:	$83,493
Urban:	0.0%	Latino	12.8%		*(24 of 435)*
Suburban:	99.9%	Black	4.4%	Under $50,000	30.2%
Rural:	0.1%	Asian	3.5%	$50,000-$99,999:	28.6%
Land area:	575	Two races	1.5%	$100,000-$199,999:	31.2%
Pop/sq. mi.:	1,255.8	White Ethnic	61.8%	$200,000 or more:	10.1%
Born in state:	77.4%			Poverty Rate	7.0%
		Education			
Age Groups		H.S. grad or less:	38.1%	**Work**	
Under 18:	22.0%	Some college:	27.0%	White collar:	38.8%
18 to 34:	20.4%	College degree, 4 yr.:	18.3%	Blue collar:	41.8%
35 to 64:	41.8%	Post-grad study:	16.6%	Sales and service:	19.4%
Over 64:	15.8%				
		Military		Govt. workers:	20.1%
		Veterans/active duty:	6.5%		

Eastern Long Island

Long Island—"the Island" to most New Yorkers—is the largest and most populous island in the mainland United States. It stretches 118 miles, from the two-century-old Montauk Point lighthouse on a crumbling bluff to Fort Hamilton at the foot of the Verrazano-Narrows Bridge. Rang-

Voter Turnout	
2013 Total Citizen 18+	525,240
2014 House Turnout	172,865
2014 Turnout as % CVAP	32.9%
2012 Turnout as % CVAP	57.4%

ing from 12 to 20 miles wide, Long Island is ringed by gentle hills and cliffs above Long Island Sound and sand-spit beaches that front the Atlantic Ocean. Including the populations of Brooklyn and Queens, some 7.7 million people live on there, more than in all but12 states. Brooklyn, at the island's western end, is urban and thickly settled, while the Hamptons in the east are manicured countryside, preserved as a playground for the New York elite.

More important economically—and politically—are the areas immediately west of the Hamptons: the suburbs created in the post-World War II migration out of the city. Developers looking for cheaper land for aircraft factories, shopping centers, subdivisions and office parks found them first in Nassau County, just east of Queens, and then farther out in Suffolk County. Suffolk attracted young families of Irish and Italian descent looking for more space and less crime. Over the past 30 years, the island's economy soured as defense plants were decimated by the end of the Cold War, and young people fled older suburbs for jobs elsewhere. High taxes and expensive housing remain endemic problems; the median home price in Suffolk County is over $400,000. The Long Island Power Authority has a plan to build wind farms and run underwater cables from Connecticut to bring more energy across Long Island Sound. Solar energy plants are sprouting across the eastern end of the island. More recently the county has been attracting Latinos, who are now 18% of the population (compared to 8% black in Suffolk) and include Salvadorans and Puerto Ricans in lower-income areas. In a sign that some urban problems have accompanied them, Latino advocates in April 2015 filed a class-action suit against Suffolk County contending that they were the victims of police discrimination and harassment.

The 1st Congressional District of New York consists of the eastern end of Long Island and covers eastern Suffolk County. It runs as far west as Smithtown on the North Shore and Patchogue on the South Shore.

2012 Presidential Vote		
Barack Obama (D)	146,708	(50%)
Mitt Romney (R)	145,115	(49%)

2008 Presidential Vote		
Barack Obama (D)	168,771	(51%)
John McCain (R)	156,586	(48%)

Cook Partisan Voting Index: R+2

It includes Shelter Island, located between the north and south forks of Long Island's "fishtail," and Plum Island. The district takes in Brookhaven National Laboratory, a physics research lab. Also in the 1st are the Hamptons and most of Fire Island National Seashore, the only federal wilderness area in New York state and a magnet for gay vacationers for decades. In a transportation innovation, high-speed ferry service for summer weekenders began in May 2015, and connected Port Jefferson with Bridgeport Connecticut in two hours.

Suffolk County was long one of the most conservative parts of New York—Richard Nixon won 70% of the vote here in 1972—but it is not very conservative by today's national standards. Democratic registration has almost drawn even with Republican in recent years. It voted solidly for Democrat Al Gore in 2000 but narrowly for Republican George W. Bush in 2004—a September 11 effect. It narrowly backed Democrat Barack Obama in 2008 and 2012. Like its two adjacent districts, each of which includes parts of Suffolk, this has become a classic swing district under most scenarios.

Lee Zeldin (R)

Republican Lee Zeldin, elected in 2014 against Democratic Rep. Tim Bishop, reversed the outcome of their 2008 matchup when Bishop prevailed in a strong Democratic year. The second time around, Zeldin convinced voters it was time to replace an opponent he called a "backbencher."

Zeldin was raised in Shirley New York, and received his bachelor's degree from the State University at Albany before earning his law degree at Albany Law School. He received an Army commission as a second lieutenant, spent four years on active duty, and deployed to Iraq in 2006 with an infantry battalion of paratroopers from the 82nd Airborne Division; he remains in the Army Reserve, as a major. Zeldin opened a law practice, and in 2010 won election to the state Senate where he became known for his effort to fund a pilot program for soldiers suffering from post-traumatic stress disorder. He also led a bid to scale back a transportation-authority payroll tax and sought to end fees for saltwater fishing.

The national Republican Party sought for years to make inroads in this eastern Long Island swing district. Bishop, who had served since 2003, defeated Zeldin in 2008 by 58%-42%, but the party gap narrowed in subsequent years. President Barack Obama carried the district by only 1,593 votes in 2012. In his second challenge to Bishop, Zeldin said he wouldn't be saddled with the problems that doomed his initial bid—fatigue with George W. Bush's presidency and the Iraq War. In the GOP primary, he defeated perpetual candidate George Demos even though Demos outspent him by more than 3-to-1.

In the general election, a September poll showed Bishop with a 10-point lead. The American Action Network and the National Republican Congressional Committee spent nearly $4 million accusing Bishop of being a corrupt Washington insider, and he aired two separate ads to tell voters he was not under FBI investigation for helping a donor secure a fireworks permit for a bar mitzvah. Bishop struck back by attacking Zeldin for accepting contributions from industries that he said were polluting New York. Democrats and their allies spent $5 million to attack Zeldin as a conservative Albany insider. From their own campaign funds, Bishop outspent Zeldin, $3 million to $1.8 million. But Zeldin scored a key endorsement from *Newsday*, which said that Bishop "does not have a significant voice in Congress" and that "Long Island needs this seat at the Republican table."

Zeldin got 54.4% of the vote and won with surprising ease. He became the House's lone Jewish Republican, a status held by Majority Leader Eric Cantor of Virginia before his primary loss in June 2014 and subsequent resignation. Democrats designated Zeldin as a top target for 2016. One potential red flag for him is that turnout in 2012 was 102,000 votes greater than in 2014, and likely will reach that level in another presidential year.

Preparing for a likely tough reelection, Republican leaders gave Zeldin useful committee assignments: Foreign Affairs, Transportation and Infrastructure, and Veterans Affairs. In February 2015, the House gave voice-vote approval to his amendment to permit states to refuse to comply with Common Core education standards. He became co-chairman of the House Republican Israel Caucus, which has more than 100 members. In April 2015, he said that Obama's conflicts with Israeli Prime Minister Benjamin Netanyahu were an opportunity for House Republicans to increase their Jewish ranks. "President Obama is operating as if he doesn't grasp who truly are America's friends and enemies in that region of the world," he told Bloomberg News. He voiced nostalgia for the leadership of President George W. Bush.

SECOND DISTRICT

Peter King (R)

Elected 1992, 12th term; b. April 5, 1944, New York; St. Francis Col., B.A. 1965, U. of Notre Dame, J.D. 1968; Catholic; married (Rosemary); 2 children.

Military Career: Army Natl. Guard, 1968-73.

Elected Office: Hempstead Town Cncl., 1977-81; Nassau Cnty. comptroller, 1981-92.

Professional Career: Practicing atty., 1968-72, 1978-81; Deputy atty., Nassau Cnty., 1972-74; Exec. asst., Nassau Cnty. exec., 1974-76; Gen. counsel, comptroller, 1977.

DC Office: 339 CHOB, 20515, 202-225-7896; Fax: 202-226-2279; Website: peteking.house.gov.

State Offices: Massapequa Park, 516-541-4225

Committees: *Financial Services:* Capital Markets & Gov't Sponsored Enterprises; Oversight & Investigations; Task Force to Investigate Terrorism Financing. *Homeland Security:* Counterterrorism & Intelligence (Chmn); Cybersecurity, Infrastructure Protection, & Security Technologies; Emergency Preparedness, Response & Communications. *Intelligence (Select)*.

Group Ratings

	ADA	ACLU	AFL-CIO	LCV	ITI	COC	HAFA	ACU	CFG	FRC
2014	0%	0%	–	9%	100%	100%	35%	48%	22%	75%
2013	5%	C	57%	14%	C	85%	C	36%	40%	C

National Journal Ratings

	2013 LIB	—	2013 CONS
Economic	52%	—	47%
Social	52%	—	47%
Foreign	33%	—	67%
Composite	46%	—	54%

Key Votes of the 113th Congress

1. Sandy storm spending	Y	5. Medical Marijuana	N	9. Syrian Rebels Training	Y
2. Violence Against Women Act	Y	6. Farm Bill	Y	10. Keystone pipeline	Y
3. Guantanamo Bay Detainees	N	7. Afghanistan Combat	N	11. Immigration Exec. Action	Y
4. Abortion 20-week ban	Y	8. NSA Phone Data Collection	N	12. Bipartisan budget deal	Y

Election Results

2014 general	Peter King (R) 95,177	(68%)	$811,982	$3,754
	Patricia M. Maher (D)................. 41,814	(30%)	$11,610	(41%)
2014 primary	Peter King (R) ....unopposed			

Prior winning percentages: 2012 (59%), 2010 (72%), 2008 (64%), 2006 (56%), 2004 (63%), 2002 (72%), 2000 (60%), 1998 (64%), 1996 (55%), 1994 (59%), 1992 (50%)

Population		Race and Ethnicity		Income	
Total:	718,587	White	63.5%	Median income:	$85,976
Urban:	27.4%	Latino	22.6%		(21 of 435)
Suburban:	72.6%	Black	9.4%	Under $50,000	27.8%
Rural:	0.0%	Asian	3.1%	$50,000-$99,999:	30.4%
Land area:	208	Two races	1.2%	$100,000-$199,999:	32.7%
Pop/sq. mi.:	3,451.3	White Ethnic	57.9%	$200,000 or more:	9.1%
Born in state:	76.4%			Poverty Rate	6.6%
		Education			
Age Groups		H.S. grad or less:	45.2%	**Work**	
Under 18:	22.1%	Some college:	27.5%	White collar:	32.2%
18 to 34:	21.5%	College degree, 4 yr.:	15.9%	Blue collar:	46.9%
35 to 64:	42.7%	Post-grad study:	11.4%	Sales and service:	21.0%
Over 64:	13.6%				
		Military		Govt. workers:	16.2%
		Veterans/active duty:	6.3%		

South-Central Long Island

At the end of World War II, Suffolk County was largely given over to potato fields. It was also directly in the path of one of the major suburban migrations of our day. On the highways that Robert Moses built to connect his parks to the middle-class parts of New York City came tens of

Voter Turnout	
2013 Total Citizen 18+	496,851
2014 House Turnout	139,330
2014 Turnout as % CVAP	28%
2012 Turnout as % CVAP	55.8%

thousands of young veterans and their families, forsaking the row house neighborhoods where they had grown up for comparatively spacious lots and single-family houses. The first wave of postwar migration moved into Nassau County, starting in 1947, when 300 families moved into 750-square-foot houses that sold for $6,990, with no money down for veterans. The location was Levittown—America's first mass-produced suburb, where delivery trucks dropped off piles of prefabricated materials 60 feet apart, to be picked up by roving teams of specialized workers with power tools. By the time the final house was sold for $9,500 in 1951, Levittown, a former potato field, had become synonymous with instant suburbanization. This wave represented a cross-section of all but the poorest New Yorkers: almost half Catholic, about one-quarter Jewish, and one-quarter Protestant. As Long Island developed its own employment base, the next wave of migration came, this time as far out as Suffolk County. This second wave was more Catholic and less Jewish, more blue-collar (aircraft manufacturers were big Suffolk employers) and less white-collar, more Democratic in ancestral politics.

The 2nd Congressional District of New York takes in Levittown (the median house is now worth $387,000) and Massapequa. These Nassau County areas are generally Republican, but only about one-third of the district's population resides in Nassau. Most of its residents live in more Democratic areas of Suffolk County, where the district stretches from Amityville and Babylon east through Bay Shore and Islip to Sayville and Bayport—one community after another strung out along the Sunrise Highway. Inland, the district takes in Brentwood, which was initially called Modern Times and was an experiment in extreme individualism; all land was private property, including the alleyways. Today, it is majority Hispanic. Two major projects on the Long Island Railroad will increase the frequency of service. For truly rapid rail, advocates hope to build a third track.

2012 Presidential Vote		
Barack Obama (D)	140,817	(52%)
Mitt Romney (R)	128,791	(47%)
2008 Presidential Vote		
Barack Obama (D)	156,145	(51%)
John McCain (R)	145,881	(48%)
Cook Partisan Voting Index: R+1		

The district was hit hard by Superstorm Sandy in late 2012. Fire Island was split in two by the storm surge and has struggled to rebuild. After redistricting changes in 2012, the 2nd moved from marginally Republican to a swing district at the national level.

Peter King (R)

Republican Pete King, first elected in 1992, has grown from a loquacious maverick to a serious counterweight to the Obama administration on domestic security matters. His penchant for quotable quips has made him a constant presence on cable television, and he flirted with a long-shot 2016 presidential bid.

King grew up in Sunnyside, Queens. His parents were Irish immigrants and Democrats, his father a New York City police detective. He went to St. Francis College and law school at the University of Notre Dame, and he clerked one summer at former Republican President Richard Nixon's law firm with a Long Islander named Rudolph Giuliani. After law school, he followed the trek to the suburbs and became part of the Nassau County Republican machine. He worked as a lawyer and staffer in county government. He was elected to the Hempstead town council in 1977, and to county comptroller in 1981. When 22-year Republican Rep. Norman Lent retired in 1992, King ran for the seat and won the GOP primary. In the general election, King ran as a fiscal conservative and abortion rights opponent. He won by just 50%-46% but hasn't had a close reelection.

King's voting record ranks him near the ideological center of the House. He is more conservative on foreign policy than on economic or social issues, but with distinctive interests. He is far to the left of most Republicans on gun control, declaring after the Newtown

Connecticut school massacre that Americans "don't need assault weapons" and renewing his call for background checks for firearm purchases at gun shows. On immigration issues, King is an outspoken conservative. He opposes racial quotas and preferences as well as bilingual education. He supports English-only laws and opposes aid to illegal immigrants. He opposed organized labor in 2009 on its "card-check" bill to facilitate union organizing. He was among the Republicans in 2012 to challenge anti-tax activist Grover Norquist's never-raise-taxes pledge. Norquist angrily accused him of trying to "weasel out" of an agreement; King called Norquist "a lowlife."

King has been an ardent supporter of the Irish Republican Army. He had a role in 1998 peace negotiations, carrying messages between the IRA and the Irish government. His activism on the issue led to an unusually close bipartisan relationship with President Bill Clinton, who helped broker the agreement. But in 2005, after the suspected involvement of Sinn Féin, the IRA's political arm, in a bank robbery and a highly publicized murder, King called for the IRA to disband. He has written three novels about politics and diplomacy in Northern Ireland. In one of them, *Deliver Us From Evil*, a thinly disguised Long Island congressman is the protagonist. "Maybe after I retire from Congress, or get thrown out of Congress, or whatever, I'll be a writer because as I've seen from some newspaper columnists, almost anyone can be a writer," he told the *Long Island Sentinel*.

After the September 11 attacks, in which 160 of his constituents died, King became more of a Republican regular and focused on legislation to prevent a repeat of the attacks. In 2005, GOP leaders tapped King to be chairman of the Homeland Security Committee. The following year, he was the first House Republican to attack the Bush administration's plan to give control of six major U.S. ports to a company in Dubai in the United Arab Emirates, and he subsequently helped to enact tighter controls on port security.

King sharpened his rhetoric on terrorist threats following the election of President Barack Obama. He told *Newsday* in December 2009 that Obama was not tough enough on Muslim extremists: "Part of his liberal DNA is that he does not want to use the word 'terrorism' unless he absolutely has to," he said. He said excessive concerns about discrimination against Muslims had hamstrung authorities in the case of Army Maj. Nidal Malik Hasan, who went on a killing rampage at Fort Hood in Texas. When the Homeland Security Department issued a report in April 2009 about domestic right-wing extremism, King complained that the agency "has never put out a report talking about 'Look out for mosques.'" The Council on American-Islamic Relations called his remarks "bigoted."

After Republicans regained House control in 2010, King pursued hearings on "the radicalization of the American Muslim community and homegrown terrorism." Islamic leaders said they feared a witch hunt, and King acknowledged that his stance carried risks. "It is controversial," he told *The New York Times*. "But to me, it is something that has to be discussed." The hearings opened in March 2011 amid massive publicity and round-the-clock security for King following reports of threats against him. Some Muslim groups accused him of a double standard. King responded, "The fact is, the IRA never attacked the United States. And my loyalty is to the United States."

Under House GOP rules, King was term-limited to chair the committee after 2012. After Boehner denied his request for a waiver, King settled for the chairmanship of Homeland Security's Counterterrorism and Intelligence Subcommittee.

King praised Obama's willingness to kill terrorist leaders with unmanned drone attacks. In 2012, he gave the president credit for preventing another September 11. But in 2014, he blasted Obama for withdrawing troops from Iraq and accused him of helping foster the rise of the Islamic State of Iraq and the Levant (ISIL). He said that the terrorist group was more powerful than al-Qaeda was on September 11 and described the president's handling of that country's situation as "shameful."

Over the years, King has been a provocative and frequent presence on radio and television chat shows. When Republican leaders abruptly pulled from the House floor a $60 billion relief bill for Superstorm Sandy in January 2013, two months after it ravaged the East Coast, King declared on CNN, "There's some dysfunction in the Republican leadership." He suggested on Fox News that New York and New Jersey residents stop donating to his party. Speaker John Boehner eventually pacified King by bringing up two Sandy bills, which passed easily. But King later told *Newsday* that he has felt like a "second-class citizen in the Republican caucus" as it has become more Southern-oriented.

King has picked fights with Texas GOP Sen. Ted Cruz, a leader of the tea party movement. When Cruz attempted to defund the Affordable Care Act, prompting a government shutdown in October 2013, King told MSNBC: "We have to start going after him by name. ... It's really time to speak out against him." After House Majority Leader Eric Cantor unexpectedly lost his primary in 2014, King told the network: We can't allow [Cantor's] defeat last night to allow the Ted Cruzes and the Rand Pauls to take over the party, or their disciples to take over the party. Because this is not conservatism to me." Cruz later told CNN he had never met King, but that too many politicians spent their time attacking each other. That led King to call the senator "ignorant" because he hadn't taken his advice over the years. When Cruz supporters telephoned his office to protest, King accused them of "severe cases of arrested development." In March 2015, he said that Republicans who threatened to shut down the Homeland Security Department to challenge Obama's executive actions on immigration were "delusional."

As one of the few remaining moderate Republicans in Congress, King has occasionally been cited in GOP circles as an example of how the party can make inroads in Democratic territory. Nassau County legislator David Mejias, a Democrat, ran against King in 2006 with an endorsement from the AFL-CIO. In an otherwise dismal year for New York Republicans, King won 56%-44%. National and New York Democrats vowed to challenge him following the 2010 redistricting. But their potential top recruit, Nassau County Prosecutor Kathleen Rice, opted not to run in 2012, and instead was elected in the 4th District two years later. King dispatched weak challengers in 2012 and 2014.

Having declared in September 2013 that he was definitely running for president in 2016, King changed his stance by May 2014 to say he was "certainly looking" at the possibility. "I'm looking at this because I see people like Rand Paul and Ted Cruz, and to me, I don't want the Republican Party going in that direction," he told CNN. But he decided against joining the GOP's huge 2016 presidential field.

THIRD DISTRICT

Steve Israel (D)

Elected 2000, 8th term; b. May 30, 1958, Brooklyn; George Washington U., B.A. 1982; Jewish; separated; 2 children.

Elected Office: Huntington Town Cncl., 1993-2001, maj. ldr., 1997-2001.

Professional Career: Legis. asst., U.S. Rep. Richard Ottinger, 1980-83; Fundraising dir., Touro Law Ctr., 1985-88; Pres., Steve Israel Assoc. Inc., 1992-98; Pres. & CEO, Inst. on Holocaust & Law, 1998-2000.

DC Office: 2457 RHOB, 20515, 202-225-3335; Fax: 202-225-4669; Website: israel.house.gov.

State Offices: Great Neck, 516-505-1448; Melville, 631-777-7391; Queens, 718-875-1675.

Committees: *Appropriations:* Defense; Interior, Environment, & Related Agencies.

Group Ratings

	ADA	ACLU	AFL-CIO	LCV	ITI	COC	HAFA	ACU	CFG	FRC
2014	80%	77%	–	94%	80%	43%	16%	8%	13%	0%
2013	75%	C	95%	93%	C	54%	C	16%	14%	C

National Journal Ratings

	2013 LIB —	2013 CONS
Economic	72% —	28%
Social	79% —	16%
Foreign	69% —	29%
Composite	75% —	26%

Key Votes of the 113th Congress

1. Sandy storm spending	Y	5. Medical Marijuana	Y	9. Syrian Rebels Training	Y
2. Violence Against Women Act	Y	6. Farm Bill	N	10. Keystone pipeline	N
3. Guantanamo Bay Detainees	Y	7. Afghanistan Combat	N	11. Immigration Exec. Action	N
4. Abortion 20-week ban	N	8. NSA Phone Data Collection	N	12. Bipartisan budget deal	Y

Election Results

2014 general	Steve Israel (D)	90,032	(55%)	$3,481,423	$25,447
	Grant Lally (R)	74,269	(45%)	$180,405	
2014 primary	Steve Israel (D)	unopposed			

Prior winning percentages: 2012 (58%), 2010 (56%), 2008 (67%), 2006 (70%), 2004 (67%), 2002 (58%), 2000 (48%)

Population		Race and Ethnicity		Income	
Total:	724,490	White	73.4%	Median income:	$101,695
Urban:	34.5%	Asian	12.9%		*(3 of 435)*
Suburban:	65.5%	Latino	9.2%	Under $50,000	24.9%
Rural:	0.0%	Black	2.9%	$50,000-$99,999:	23.7%
Land area:	224	Two races	1.2%	$100,000-$199,999:	30.4%
Pop/sq. mi.:	3,234.6	White Ethnic	49.9%	$200,000 or more:	20.9%
Born in state:	70.0%			Poverty Rate	5.5%
		Education			
Age Groups		H.S. grad or less:	27.1%	**Work**	
Under 18:	22.6%	Some college:	20.7%	White collar:	50.1%
18 to 34:	17.6%	College degree, 4 yr.:	27.7%	Blue collar:	39.5%
35 to 64:	41.6%	Post-grad study:	24.5%	Sales and service:	10.4%
Over 64:	18.2%				
		Military		Govt. workers:	15.4%
		Veterans/active duty:	5.1%		

Northern Long Island, Eastern Queens

The North Shore of Long Island is "Gatsby country," where peninsulas jutting out into the Sound are covered with vast green lawns leading to the mansions of America's great capitalists. Nineteenth-century millionaires commuted by steam yacht from Manhattan to their estates in what is

Voter Turnout	
2013 Total Citizen 18+	510,769
2014 House Turnout	164,375
2014 Turnout as % CVAP	32.2%
2012 Turnout as % CVAP	60.1%

now Queens or Nassau County. In the early 20th century, the richest people in business and show business spent their leisure time here, playing croquet while their servants unloaded bootleggers' boats at their private docks. Inland, behind the expansive lawns, Long Island was still farm country, with little villages clustered at railroad stations, occasional colonial-era houses, and acres of billboard-strewn wasteland on the highways to New York City. But as the city grew outward, affluent neighborhoods developed in Douglaston on the water, just beyond the middle-class Flushing area of Queens inland, and the Great Neck peninsula became a very affluent, mostly Jewish suburb. Farther out, on Sands Point and Oyster Bay, old estates alternated with more modest homes originally built for servants and newer subdivisions. The Huntington area has had commercial development, and was the site in January 2015 for filming of a comedy, "Sisters," with Tina Fey and Amy Poehler.

The 3rd Congressional District of New York ties together a disparate collection of New York City neighborhoods and suburbs. About one-third of its votes are cast in Suffolk County, where the political leanings are more conservative than elsewhere in the district. A bit more than 10 percent live at the western extreme of the district, in upscale neighborhoods of Queens near the Throgs Neck and Bronx-Whitestone bridges to the Bronx and points north: Douglaston, Bellaire and Beechurst. In May 2015, local residents protested pricey redevelopment at Whitestone Waterpointe. This area is more affluent than other portions of Queens, but is still heavily Democratic. In the middle—politically, as well as geographically—is northern Nassau County. Roughly half of the district's population lives here, many in the posh neighborhoods abutting or near Long Island Sound. This affluence largely continues inland; the median household incomes in places like Jericho and Syosset are close to $140,000 per year. The district as a whole is 2 percentage points less Democratic and has become politically marginal since redistricting in 2012. Barack Obama took the revised district 51%-48% against Mitt Romney.

2012 Presidential Vote		
Barack Obama (D)	155,451	(51%)
Mitt Romney (R)	147,617	(48%)

2008 Presidential Vote		
Barack Obama (D)	182,750	(54%)
John McCain (R)	155,947	(46%)

Cook Partisan Voting Index: EVEN

Steve Israel (D)

Democrat Steve Israel, first elected in 2000, is amiable, ambitious, and an able fundraiser. He won praise from party leaders for his chairmanship of the Democratic Congressional Campaign Committee despite their failure to win a House majority in 2012. They failed to hold off the 2014 GOP onslaught, which left Democrats with 188 House seats, their fewest since 1924. He has continued to work with Democratic Leader Nancy Pelosi on broad political strategy.

Israel grew up in Wantagh, the son of a traveling salesman, and graduated from George Washington University in 1983. While in college, he worked full-time on Capitol Hill, doing constituent work for Rep. Robert Matsui of California, and as a legislative assistant for Rep. Richard Ottinger of New York, both Democrats. After college, Israel returned to Long Island, where he was Suffolk director for the American Jewish Congress, fundraising director for Touro Law School, and assistant for intergovernmental relations to Suffolk County Executive Patrick Halpin. Then he started a public relations and marketing firm and was president of the Institute on the Holocaust and the Law. In 1993, Israel was the only Democrat elected to the Huntington Town Council, where he built a reputation as a bipartisan leader who helped revive the town's finances.

After Rep. Rick Lazio decided to run for the Senate, Israel sought the moderate Republican's seat. He eked out a 45%-41% victory in the Democratic primary. In the general election, he faced Republican Joan Johnson, who had a compelling life story as a 66-year-old African American who grew up under segregation, moved to New York to become a schoolteacher, and later was elected town clerk of Islip. Despite help from Lazio, Johnson was a disappointing candidate and ran an ad, which she was forced to pull, wrongly attacking Israel for voting to raise taxes. Israel won by a surprisingly easy 48%-35%.

Israel believes that national Democrats can learn from the successes of centrist Democrats on Long Island. They have prevailed locally, he said, by taking positions that protected national security, balanced government budgets, and championed civil and human rights. His voting record was moderate in his early years, but he lately has become a reliable Democrat. Israel joined the fiscally conservative Blue Dog Coalition and was one of 28 House Democrats who voted for President George W. Bush's tax cuts in 2001. After irritating Democratic leaders by voting in 2002 for a Republican prescription drug bill, which increased annual Medicaid payments on Long Island, Israel redeemed himself with his party by voting against the GOP's Medicare prescription drug benefit in 2003.

After Democrats lost 63 seats and control of the House in November 2010, Minority Leader Nancy Pelosi picked Israel for the DCCC chairmanship ahead of other rising-star Democrats such as New York's Joe Crowley and Florida's Debbie Wasserman Schultz. The move reflected her confidence in Israel's fundraising skills. Working on four hours of sleep a night, he swiftly erased the DCCC's $20 million debt and began issuing optimistic pronouncements about his party's ability to win the 25 additional seats it needed to reclaim the majority. "We have forced a contrast every step of the way between House Republicans, who are fighting for millionaires, and House Democrats, who are fighting for the middle class," he told *National Journal* in March 2012. The DCCC ended up outraising its Republican counterpart, $184 million to $156 million, although Republicans had the advantage on outside spending.

Democrats netted only eight seats in 2012. But their candidates overall outpolled the Republicans at the ballot box, an admittedly pyrrhic victory and a sign that Republicans had skillfully used post-2010 redistricting to preserve their control of the chamber. "Nationally, House Democrats had a much better night than anyone anticipated. ...We also started to roll back the tea party tide," Israel told the New York political publication *City & State*.

He faced a tougher challenge in 2014: The party controlling the White House during a president's sixth year in office has lost seats in every midterm election but one since 1918. Israel remained upbeat, saying the 2012 results indicated that Republicans faced longer-term structural problems such as an inability to attract Latino voters. He argued that GOP redistricting prowess would have a negative side effect. "Republicans redrew already-safe members into even more Republican districts, driving control of their party more to their base, forcing more primaries, and making it less likely that they can put forward a party agenda that appeals to independents," he wrote to colleagues in a February 2013 memo.

Israel faced some tensions with Congressional Black Caucus Chairman Marcia Fudge of Ohio. She said in June 2014 that the DCCC chairman "doesn't really value ... our caucus." Aides and others traced the friction in part to a 2011 comment of his: "Can we win the House without the CBC? Yes. Do we want to win the House without the CBC? No." Other Black Caucus members, mindful of his support from Pelosi, praised Israel's leadership and pointed to his selection of their colleague Donna Edwards of Maryland to chair the committee's "Red to Blue" program.

Even as political analysts agreed that Democrats' chances of retaking the House were bleak, Israel continued to look on the bright side. In July 2014, he cited to reporters the party's continued strong fundraising, which swelled when House Republicans sued Obama over the Affordable Care Act and grew even more—by $1 million in a single day—with talk about the possible impeachment of the president, much of it stirred up by Democrats themselves, including Israel. He said his party would make regular contrasts between "Republicans who are obsessed with lawsuits and appear to be moving closer to impeachment, and Democrats who are focused on the economy." As it turned out, only two House Republicans lost reelection. In Israel's home state alone, two incumbent Democrats were defeated and the party lost an open seat.

After the historically low outcome, he defended his performance to *The Washington Post*, "We fundamentally made the right decisions, as tough as they were." Israel remained in leadership as the Pelosi-designated head of policy and communications, where he focused on middle-class economic security and opportunity. He voiced continued ambition to move up the leadership ladder.

In 2015, he reclaimed his seat on the Appropriations Committee, where he had taken a leave of absence. On that panel, he has promoted international human rights and sought additional funds for renewable energy. After the December 2012 Newtown Connecticut school massacre, Israel said that he would renew his push to curb the production of plastic gun magazines, which are undetectable by metal detectors. In April 2014, he unveiled a bill aimed at closing what he described as a loophole by adding individuals who commit "violent juvenile acts" to the list of individuals who are excluded from owning a gun.

A student of military history, Israel in 2007 edited the book *Charge! History's Greatest Military Speeches,* and often makes historical comparisons in his speeches. In late 2014 he published a satirical novel with some racy writing, *The Global War on Morris,* about a mild-mannered Long Island pharmaceutical sales rep whom conservatives suspect of raising money for Islamic terrorists. Some unhappy Democrats wondered how the former DCCC chairman found the spare time to work on the book.

Israel has had little trouble winning reelection. After Sen. Hillary Clinton resigned to become secretary of State in 2009, Israel was discussed as a possible successor. But he did not line up as well in polling as others considered by then-Gov. David Paterson, including Rep. Kirsten Gillibrand, who got the appointment. Disappointed, Israel talked openly about challenging Gillibrand in the 2010 Democratic primary for the Senate seat but stayed out after a personal appeal from Obama. When his new district lines became less Democratic, he remained culturally in line with many of the upper-class, substantially Jewish North Shore suburbs where he was on the ballot for the first time. He won reelection in 2012 with 58% of the vote. But the hostile 2014 climate posed more of a challenge. Israel spent $3.5 million, 20 times more than Republican challenger Grant Lally and was held to a 55%-45% win. He took all three counties, but his 63% in Queens was by far his strongest.

FOURTH DISTRICT

Kathleen Rice (D)

Elected 2014, 1st term; b. Feb. 15, 1965, New York; Catholic U. of America, B.A. 1987, Touro Law Cntr., J.D. 1991; Catholic; single.

Elected Office: Nassau Cnty. dist. atty., 2006-15.

Professional Career: Asst. dist. atty., Brooklyn; Asst. U.S. atty., 1999-2005.

DC Office: 1508 LHOB, 20515, 202-225-5516; Fax: 202-225-5758; Website: kathleenrice.house.gov.

State Offices: Garden City, 516-739-3008.

Committees: *Homeland Security:* Emergency Preparedness, Response, & Communications; Transportation Security (RMM). *Veterans' Affairs:* Economic Affairs; Oversight & Investigations.

Election Results

2014 general	Kathleen M. Rice (D) 89,793	(53%)	$3,470,328	$30,218	$45,000
	Bruce Blakeman (R) 80,127	(47%)	$1,658,955	$6,130	
2014 primary	Kathleen M. Rice (D) 7,770	(57%)			
	Kevan Abrahams (D) 5,791	(43%)			

Population		Race and Ethnicity		Income	
Total:	715,109	White	60.5%	Median income:	$89,600
Urban:	90.7%	Latino	17.7%		*(14 of 435)*
Suburban:	9.3%	Black	14.0%	Under $50,000	28.2%
Rural:	0.0%	Asian	5.9%	$50,000-$99,999:	26.4%
Land area:	106	Two races	1.1%	$100,000-$199,999:	31.8%
Pop/sq. mi.:	6,731.6	White Ethnic	45.4%	$200,000 or more:	13.6%
Born in state:	71.2%			Poverty Rate	7.2%
		Education			
Age Groups		H.S. grad or less:	36.0%	**Work**	
Under 18:	22.4%	Some college:	24.5%	White collar:	41.2%
18 to 34:	21.1%	College degree, 4 yr.:	22.1%	Blue collar:	43.8%
35 to 64:	41.0%	Post-grad study:	17.3%	Sales and service:	15.0%
Over 64:	15.6%				
		Military		Govt. workers:	17.0%
		Veterans/active duty:	4.9%		

Long Island: Hempstead

Nassau County has long been on the cutting edge of American suburban life. It is the home of one of the earliest suburbs: Garden City, founded in 1869 with wide avenues and single-family homes. After World War II, it pioneered large-scale suburban development, as freeways replaced

Voter Turnout	
2013 Total Citizen 18+	491,913
2014 House Turnout	170,099
2014 Turnout as % CVAP	34.6%
2012 Turnout as % CVAP	60%

highways, and shopping centers sprang up at intersections. Many of the middle- and upper-income residents continue to depend on the Long Island Railroad to speed them to jobs in New York City. Garden City has maintained high real estate prices and is surrounded by some of Nassau County's key institutions: the county seat of Mineola; Hofstra University in Hempstead, where a new medical school opened in 2011; and Roosevelt Field, where Charles Lindbergh took off for Paris in 1927. The fate of this historic airstrip perhaps typifies the extent of suburbanization in Nassau County: It's now a shopping mall, with a long-standing conflict over the exact spot of Lindbergh's departure, either at an escalator in the Roosevelt Field shopping center or just behind a parking garage near a Best Buy.

The 4th Congressional District of New York comprises Garden City and the towns around it. It is one of six districts in the state that is wholly included within a single county. The 4th takes in several suburbs along the Jericho Turnpike—New Hyde Park, Mineola, Westbury—as well as a large swath of southern Nassau County. This territory includes Hempstead, Uniondale, Rockville Centre and part of ethnically diverse Valley Stream, as well as most of the predominantly Jewish "Five Towns"—the railway suburbs of Lawrence, Inwood (now in the neighboring 5th District), Cedarhurst, Hewlett and Woodmere. In a melancholy shift, the New York

2012 Presidential Vote		
Barack Obama (D) 165,876	(56%)
Mitt Romney (R)................129,049	(43%)
2008 Presidential Vote		
Barack Obama (D) 185,409	(55%)
John McCain (R).................147,208	(44%)
Cook Partisan Voting Index: D+3		

Islanders professional hockey team played its final game at the 43-year-old Nassau Coliseum in April 2015, and planned a reverse migration to the Barclays Center in Brooklyn, which opened in 2012.

Nassau County has traditionally been Republican, and Garden City remains that way. But the county remains on the cutting edge of American suburban life as it becomes more diverse and more Democratic. Hempstead typifies these emerging changes. Once swing territory that served as the political base of Republican Sen. Alfonse D'Amato, today the village is heavily minority-majority; non-Hispanic whites make up just 6.6% of the population. Nearby Roosevelt is only 2% non-Hispanic white. These towns, plus Freeport, combined to give Obama more than 86% of the vote in 2008, almost entirely accounting for his 55% victory in the district. The district includes the old resort areas around Lido Beach and Long Beach and suburban Merrick, Bellmore and Wantagh; these areas are more marginal. The resulting 4th District became about 3 percentage points more Republican after 2012 redistricting, but it still leans Democratic.

Kathleen Rice (D)

Democrat Kathleen Rice, a veteran Nassau County prosecutor who built a reputation for being tough on drunken drivers, was elected in 2014. She replaced retiring nine-term Rep. Carolyn McCarthy, another crime-focused Democrat who was one of the House's most vocal gun-control advocates.

Born in Manhattan and raised in Garden City, Rice was one of 10 children borne by an only-child mother. She graduated from Catholic University in Washington, D.C., and got her law degree from Touro Law Center in Central Islip, Long Island. Rice registered as a Republican in 1984 and did not vote until 2002, *Newsday* reported in 2010. She responded that her lack of voting was a "mistake."

She began her legal career as an assistant district attorney in Kings County under legendary Brooklyn D.A. Charles Hynes, prosecuting burglaries, robberies, and sexual assaults. In 1999, she became an assistant U.S. attorney in Philadelphia, where she handled white-collar crimes, corporate fraud, gun and drug cases, and public corruption. Rice was elected Nassau County's district attorney in 2005, defeating a Republican who had held the job for three decades, and quickly developed a reputation for prosecution of drunken drivers. She worked to pass legislation imposing harsher penalties on drunken drivers who had children in the car or who injured other motorists. She won praise from Mothers Against Drunk Driving and was hailed by New York's *Daily News* as "the nation's toughest prosecutor on DWI offenses." Rice also went after cheating on college admission tests, working to improve test security. She was a co-chair of the Moreland Commission to Investigate Public Corruption during 2013 and 2014, and in 2013 she was named president of the District Attorneys Association of the State of New York.

Rice has increased her political dexterity in recent years. She ran in the five-candidate Democratic primary race for state attorney general in 2010, and trailed eventual winner Eric Schneiderman, 34%-32%, but led the balloting in counties outside of New York City. In Nassau, Rice benefited from strong name recognition. She was the only countywide Democrat to win reelection in 2013.

In her campaign for Congress, Republican nominee Bruce Blakeman ran negative ads against Rice, accusing her of being anti-woman for her workplace policies as district attorney and her refusal to fire a staffer who made sexist and racially offensive comments on Twitter. As a new D.A., Rice told part-timers (many of them women caring for children) that they had to become full-timers or leave the office. She told *Newsday* at the time that the county "deserves victims' advocates that are full time." Rice, however, won the support of numerous women's groups. Blakeman also questioned her role on the Moreland Commission, which was under investigation in a state corruption investigation, though there had been no evidence of wrongdoing by Rice. She won the election relatively narrowly, with 53 of the vote. Her election cemented a Democratic trend in a district that had sent Republicans to the House consistently from 1952 until McCarthy was elected in 1996.

In the House, Rice was assigned to the Veterans' Affairs Committee and the Homeland Security panel, where she became the senior Democrat on the often active Transportation Security Subcommittee. Another freshman from New York, Republican John Katko, chaired that subcommittee. Rice replaced McCarthy, her predecessor, on the House Democrats' gun violence prevention task force, where she emphasized the need to enforce existing laws on gun sales. The first bill she introduced would give preference to companies with high numbers of veterans when awarding Veterans Affairs contracts. The House unanimously passed the bill in May 2015. That month, she was part of a bipartisan House delegation to Israel that met Prime Minister Benjamin Netanyahu, where she endorsed cooperation to enhance the security of both nations.

FIFTH DISTRICT

Gregory Meeks (D)

Elected Feb. 1998, 9th full term; b. Sept. 25, 1953, Harlem; Adelphi U., B.A. 1975, Howard U., J.D. 1978; Methodist; married (Simone-Marie); 3 children.

Elected Office: NY Assembly, 1992-98.

Professional Career: Asst. dist. atty., Queens Cnty., 1978-83; NY St. Commission of Investigations, 1984-85; Judge, NY St. Workers' Compensation Bd., 1985-92.

DC Office: 2234 RHOB, 20515, 202-225-3461; Fax: 202-226-4169; Website: meeks.house.gov.

State Offices: Averne, 347-230-4032; Jamaica, 718-725-6000.

Committees: *Financial Services:* Capital Markets & Gov't Sponsored Enterprises; Financial Institutions & Consumer Credit; Task Force to Investigate Terrorism Financing. *Foreign Affairs:* Europe, Eurasia & Emerging Threats (RMM); Western Hemisphere.

Group Ratings

	ADA	ACLU	AFL-CIO	LCV	ITI	COC	HAFA	ACU	CFG	FRC
2014	80%	72%	–	91%	60%	58%	10%	4%	7%	0%
2013	70%	C	90%	86%	C	46%	C	12%	16%	C

National Journal Ratings

	2013 LIB	—	2013 CONS
Economic	72%	—	28%
Social	73%	—	24%
Foreign	77%	—	23%
Composite	75%	—	26%

Key Votes of the 113th Congress

1. Sandy storm spending	Y	5. Medical Marijuana	Y	9. Syrian Rebels Training	Y
2. Violence Against Women Act	Y	6. Farm Bill	N	10. Keystone pipeline	N
3. Guantanamo Bay Detainees	Y	7. Afghanistan Combat	Y	11. Immigration Exec. Action	NV
4. Abortion 20-week ban	N	8. NSA Phone Data Collection	N	12. Bipartisan budget deal	Y

Election Results

2014 general	Gregory Meeks (D)	75,712	(95%)	$882,334	$18,941
	Allen Steinhardt(I)	3,870	(5%)		
2014 primary	Gregory Meeks (D)	8,119	(80%)		
	Joseph Marthone (D)	2,023	(20%)		

Prior winning percentages: 2012 (90%), 2010 (88%), 2008 (100%), 2006 (100%), 2004 (100%), 2002 (97%), 2000 (100%), 1998 (100%), 1998 special (57%)

Population		Race and Ethnicity		Income	
Total:	768,603	Black	48.5%	Median income:	$58,470
Urban:	99.3%	Latino	20.2%		*(140 of 435)*
Suburban:	0.7%	Asian	12.9%	Under $50,000	43.4%
Rural:	0.0%	White	10.7%	$50,000-$99,999:	31.1%
Land area:	65	Two races	3.1%	$100,000-$199,999:	22.1%
Pop/sq. mi.:	11,861.2	White Ethnic	8.5%	$200,000 or more:	3.4%
Born in state:	49.5%			Poverty Rate	14.6%
		Education			
Age Groups		H.S. grad or less:	48.8%	**Work**	
Under 18:	23.3%	Some college:	27.5%	White collar:	28.0%
18 to 34:	24.7%	College degree, 4 yr.:	15.4%	Blue collar:	51.6%
35 to 64:	39.5%	Post-grad study:	8.3%	Sales and service:	20.4%
Over 64:	12.5%			Govt. workers:	18.5%
		Military			
		Veterans/active duty:	3.0%		

Southeast Queens, Western Nassau

A half-century ago, there was a small black community in southern Queens, near Jamaica Bay. Since then, many African-American families have bought houses and raised their families in neighborhoods that fan east from there. They fought to maintain the relatively spacious streets, relish-

Voter Turnout	
2013 Total Citizen 18+	474,712
2014 House Turnout	79,821
2014 Turnout as % CVAP	16.8%
2012 Turnout as % CVAP	48.3%

ing the plenitude of natural light, safe schools and good neighborhood stores. There is block upon block of low-rise, frame and brick houses, built mostly from the 1920s to the 1950s, in the neighborhoods of Springfield Gardens and Laurelton, St. Albans and Rosedale, Cambria Heights and Queens Village. This part of Queens today is home to New York City's largest concentration of middle-class black homeowners, with a median income higher than white households in Queens. The recession in the housing market hit them disproportionately harder than the rest of New York. In a comeback sign, a developer in March 2014 announced plans for a $225 million residential tower and retail space near the Jamaica rail terminal. Nearby Hollis has played a crucial role in the development of hip-hop music. Producer Russell Simmons hails from there, as do rappers Ja Rule, Young MC and Run-D.M.C.

The 5th Congressional District of New York contains all of these southeast Queens neighborhoods, plus other less affluent sections of southern Queens. It is bounded on the north, more or less, by Jackie Robinson Parkway, and a line running just east of Cross Bay Boulevard to the west. To the east, the Nassau County line has melted away as the unofficial boundary between black and white Long Island. The district now takes in some precincts in southwestern Nassau: Inwood, Valley Stream, Elmont. To the south, it includes Rockaway Peninsula, much of which is occupied by vast swaths of government-financed housing that were planned by Robert Moses in the 1950s and 1960s but never completely rebuilt. The motives weren't always pure; this area was remote from the city in the immediate post-War era and provided what author Lawrence Kaplan referred to as a "dumping ground" for the poor. The peninsula's geography, jutting into the Atlantic Ocean, makes it vulnerable to weather; Hurricanes have hit hard here. Recovery from the Sandy superstorm has remained a work in progress. In May 2015, Queens officials approved zoning changes to expedite recovery. In the middle of all this is John F. Kennedy International Airport, a major hub for air travelers entering the United States. The airport

2012 Presidential Vote		
Barack Obama (D)	200,004	(90%)
Mitt Romney (R)	22,026	(10%)
2008 Presidential Vote		
Barack Obama (D)	206,659	(86%)
John McCain (R)	32,559	(14%)
Cook Partisan Voting Index:	D+35	

has generated 230,000 jobs in the area, and businesses there recently have reported more activity—a hopeful sign for New York's economy. Airlines have invested billions of dollars in modernizing terminals, some of which had sunk to third-world levels.

Richmond Hill and Ozone Park, just northwest of JFK, were previously white ethnic neighborhoods, but now have sizable numbers of Latinos and Asians. South Ozone Park is home to many immigrants from Jamaica, Haiti, the Dominican Republic, and Trinidad and

Tobago. The 5th District is 49% African American, 20% Hispanic, and 13% Asian. A common denominator for these groups is the amount of time that residents spend on the road: The district is among the nation's worst for commuters, at 46.2 minutes of mean travel time to work. Politically, it is in the top 2% of the country's most-Democratic districts. President Barack Obama got 90% of the vote here in 2012.

Gregory Meeks (D)

Democrat Gregory Meeks, first elected in 1998, is a liberal who is more sympathetic to business than are other New York City Democrats—sometimes to the unhappiness of organized labor. In part, that reflects the commercial interests of his international district. Ethics controversies have dogged him in recent years.

Meeks grew up in public housing projects in Harlem. He was inspired by his mother, who went back to school when her four children were older and who encouraged community service volunteerism. Meeks' childhood hero was Supreme Court Justice Thurgood Marshall. After graduating from Adelphi college and Howard University law school, Meeks moved to Far Rockaway. He became an assistant district attorney and a workers' compensation judge. He was elected to the state Assembly in 1992 and became an ally of Democratic Rep. Floyd Flake, a minister whose Allen African Methodist Episcopal Church congregation grew from 1,400 members in 1976 to more than 20,000 members.

When Flake retired, Meeks won a majority of Democratic committee members at a January 1998 endorsement meeting and thus became the party's nominee. Democratic state Sen. Alton Waldon and Assemblywoman Barbara Clark ran as independents. With the support of Flake, Rep. Charles Rangel of New York, and civil rights leaders Al Sharpton and Jesse Jackson, Meeks won with 57% of the vote, to Waldon's 21% and Clark's 13%. Since then, he has had only token opposition.

Meeks has a liberal voting record, but he has been active in the commerce-oriented New Democrat Coalition. He backed the 2005 Central American Free Trade Agreement, along with free trade pacts in 2011 with Colombia, Panama and South Korea. In 2015, he was one of the few outspoken Democratic supporters of President Barack Obama's Trans-Pacific Partnership. These agreements promised new opportunities for JFK airport and its many auxiliary businesses. As a member of the Foreign Affairs Committee, Meeks helped launch a caucus on U.S.-Russia trade and economic relations. In 2015, he became ranking Democrat on the Europe, Eurasia and Emerging Threats Subcommittee.

On local issues, Meeks worked with Republicans in 2012 to enact a bill authorizing construction of natural gas pipelines in the state's portion of the Gateway National Recreation Area. He also sought to help constituents facing foreclosure. "The worst thing that I've seen is families in my office crying because they are about to lose their house," he said at a 2011 town hall meeting. On the Financial Services Committee, he has joined African-American members in seeking to ensure that legislation addresses minorities' issues.

His financial ethics have become fodder for New York's major dailies in recent years. The Federal Election Commission in 2006 reprimanded him for using more than $6,000 in 2004 campaign funds for a personal trainer and other expenses. In 2010, *The New York Times* wrote that despite acknowledging that he has no more than a few thousand dollars in his savings account, he "lives a life worthy of a jet-setter," staying in luxury hotels, driving a taxpayer-leased $1,000-a-month Lexus and buying a $1 million house built by a developer who was a campaign contributor. He told the newspaper that he observed all campaign finance laws, and that "I am not going to raise the money in my district that I need to be a player here in Washington." New York's *Daily News* reported that he described his failure to list $55,000 in personal loans as an "oversight." And *The New York Post* found inconsistencies in his political action committee records, including $325 in monthly rent on a nonexistent Queens office. Meeks blamed the negative attention on conservative groups out to undermine Democrats.

The Post reported in January 2013 that Meeks had ties to several people who were either in jail or under indictment. One friend facing sentencing in a mortgage-fraud scheme, Edul Ahmad, gave Meeks $40,000 in 2007. The congressman said the money was a loan but did not pay it back until after the FBI inquired about it. The House Ethics Committee cleared Meeks of wrongdoing in the matter. A Queens immigration lawyer, Albert Baldeo, who was arrested for campaign finance fraud in a 2010 special-election bid to serve on the city council, told *The Post* he gave Meeks a break on rent for office space in a building he owned because he wanted the congressman to have a presence in his area. House rules prohibit members from receiving below-market rent. Meeks told the newspaper, "My office complied with the law and continues to do so." In February 2015, Baldeo was sentenced to 18 months in prison for witness-tampering. The National Legal and Policy Center, a Washington-based conservative watchdog group that has investigated Meeks, called Baldeo a "Meeks crony."

In May 2015, *The Washington Post* wrote that Meeks was among 10 House members on a bipartisan trip to Azerbaijan, with hundreds of thousands of dollars of expenses and gifts paid by the state-owned oil company. In response to the report that Meeks did not comply with requests by the Office of Congressional Ethics, a Meeks aide said that the House Ethics Committee had told the OCE to "cease its review," and that Meeks was confident that he had complied with the law. In July, the committee dismissed the case.

Meeks has sought party leadership positions, but other New York Democrats have been more successful. His support for the Trans-Pacific trade deal led some national unions and their allies to threaten a primary challenge in 2016.

SIXTH DISTRICT

Grace Meng (D)

Elected 2012, 2nd term; b. Oct. 1, 1975, Queens; U. of MI, B.A. 1997, Yeshiva U., J.D. 2002; Christian; married (Wayne Kye); 2 children.

Elected Office: NY Assembly, 2009-12.

Professional Career: Practicing atty., 2003-2013.

DC Office: 1317 LHOB, 20515, 202-225-2601; Fax: 202-225-1589; Website: meng.house.gov.

State Offices: Forest Hills, Flushing, 718-358-MENG (6364).

Committees: *Foreign Affairs:* Asia & the Pacific; Middle East & North Africa. *Small Business:* Agriculture, Energy & Trade (RMM).

Group Ratings

	ADA	ACLU	AFL-CIO	LCV	ITI	COC	HAFA	ACU	CFG	FRC
2014	75%	77%	–	97%	60%	43%	14%	8%	11%	0%
2013	70%	C	95%	89%	C	46%	C	17%	12%	C

National Journal Ratings

	2013 LIB	—	2013 CONS
Economic	72%	—	28%
Social	77%	—	21%
Foreign	75%	—	25%
Composite	75%	—	25%

Key Votes of the 113th Congress

1. Sandy storm spending	Y	5. Medical Marijuana	Y	9. Syrian Rebels Training	N
2. Violence Against Women Act	Y	6. Farm Bill	N	10. Keystone pipeline	N
3. Guantanamo Bay Detainees	Y	7. Afghanistan Combat	Y	11. Immigration Exec. Action	N
4. Abortion 20-week ban	N	8. NSA Phone Data Collection	N	12. Bipartisan budget deal	Y

Election Results

2014 general	Grace Meng (D) ....unopposed	$518,820
2014 primary	Grace Meng (D) ....unopposed	

Prior winning percentage: 2012 (68%)

Population		Race and Ethnicity		Income	
Total:	721,108	White	39.6%	Median income:	$57,001
Urban:	100.0%	Asian	36.3%		*(151 of 435)*
Suburban:	0.0%	Latino	17.5%	Under $50,000	44.2%
Rural:	0.0%	Black	3.3%	$50,000-$99,999:	30.5%
Land area:	34	Two races	2.4%	$100,000-$199,999:	20.0%
Pop/sq. mi.:	21,344.2	White Ethnic	23.2%	$200,000 or more:	5.2%
Born in state:	43.2%			Poverty Rate	13.5%
		Education			
Age Groups		H.S. grad or less:	41.5%	**Work**	
Under 18:	18.6%	Some college:	21.6%	White collar:	37.8%
18 to 34:	22.4%	College degree, 4 yr.:	22.9%	Blue collar:	45.8%
35 to 64:	43.1%	Post-grad study:	14.1%	Sales and service:	16.4%
Over 64:	15.9%			Govt. workers:	13.1%
		Military			
		Veterans/active duty:	2.5%		

Central Queens: Forest Hills, Flushing

A half-century ago, most of the neighborhoods in New York's outer boroughs were virtually all-white. Most of these areas have filled with descendants of the great mass of immigrants who came from eastern and southern Europe between 1890 and 1924 and from northern Europe earlier—Irish and

Voter Turnout	
2013 Total Citizen 18+	448,526
2014 House Turnout	55,963
2014 Turnout as % CVAP	12.5%
2012 Turnout as % CVAP	42.2%

Italians, Jews and Hungarians, Poles and Czechs and Greeks. This hodgepodge produced many cultural icons of the last half-decade: Paul Simon, the Ramones, Michael Landon, and Donna Karan all trace their roots to Forest Hills. A few parts of Queens were WASPy and high-income. Forest Hills in Queens, with its famous tennis stadium and large Tudor houses, was a notable example.

But the only thing permanent in New York is change. The 1960s saw pitched battles of city politics between John Lindsay, a liberal Manhattan Republican, and his mostly outer-borough opponents. During Lindsay's reign as mayor, middle-class New Yorkers fled the city's high taxes and crime-addled neighborhoods, while Forest Hills was the site of some-times violent protests when Lindsay attempted to place low-income housing projects in the neighborhood. The result was a drop in population; Queens had four congressional districts and large portions of two others at the end of the 1960s, while today it is barely entitled to three. Some of this neighborhood change would have happened anyway. Neighborhoods settled by immigrants in the 1920s were full of old people, and increasing numbers of Afri-can Americans were bound to move out of the old ghettoes. Another constant in New York remains the clashes among various groups, often representing old versus new: In Queens, that has taken on a new feature, as when Mayor Bill DeBlasio in July 2014 moved home-less families—many of them African American—into Elmhurst, sparking protests, chiefly by Chinese Americans.

The 6th Congressional District is based in Queens. It begins near the border of Nas-sau County, at Fresh Meadows, and runs west through Pomonok and the old rail suburbs of Kew Gardens and Forest Hills. It continues west to Rego Park, which has many 1950s high-rise apartments; Middle Village; Glendale; and part of Maspeth. Across Flushing Bay from LaGuardia Airport (which is in the 14th District), it also takes in Flushing, long a modest-income Jewish and white ethnic neighborhood and now with a large Asian neighbor-hood. (Republicans cheered when it elected a Chinese-American Republican to the New York City Council in 2009 but were later disappointed when he switched his party affiliation to Democratic.) West of 138th Street, Queens is dominated by Taiwanese and ethnic Chi-nese from Malaysia, Vietnam, and Thailand; shops have an urban "Chinatown" feel and feature an amazing variety of delicacies. (New York City has three Chinatowns—one each in Manhattan and Brooklyn, with the largest in Queens.) East of 138th Street is predominantly Korean. The district is 36%

2012 Presidential Vote
Barack Obama (D) ....125,495　(68%)
Mitt Romney (R)..................57,455　(31%)

2008 Presidential Vote
Barack Obama (D) ....126,785　(63%)
John McCain (R)..................71,417　(36%)

Cook Partisan Voting Index:　D+13

Asian American, 18% Latino, and only 3% black. While there are pockets of Republican voting, especially around Middle Village and Kew Gardens Hills, it is solidly Democratic.

Grace Meng (D)

The daughter of Taiwanese immigrants, Grace Meng became the first Asian-American woman to represent New York City in Congress when she won election to the House in 2012. *The New York Times* described her as a potential political star. "It's nice to be a woman, and it's nice to be an Asian," she said. "But what's more important is what I can bring back to my district."

Meng was born and raised in Queens. Her parents left Taiwan for the United States in the early 1970s. After debating whether to become a teacher or a lawyer, she chose law, studying history at the University of Michigan and later attending Yeshiva University's Cardozo School of Law. She did pro bono work for Sanctuary for Families, and joined a law firm. She worked as a volunteer on several New York political campaigns, including Hillary Clinton's reelection to the Senate.

Her father, Jimmy Meng, served one term in the state Assembly in 2005 and 2006, and did not seek reelection following reports of legal problems in his 2004 campaign. She sought to take his place, but residency issues forced her out of the race. Two years later, she defeated his successor, Assemblywoman Ellen Young. During her years in Albany, Meng sponsored a measure enacted in 2009 to eliminate the word "Oriental"—a term critics say is outdated and offensive—from state documents referring to people of Asian descent. She also worked to protect senior citizens from higher property taxes.

Meng jumped into the race to succeed retiring 15-term Democratic Rep. Gary Ackerman and won the liberal firebrand's endorsement. Ackerman told The *Times* that her self-effacing style was a factor in his decision. "It's not a matter of being the most flashy or the most self-promoting, but the ability to bring people together," he said. "She's a very likable person, and she's a very quick study. She understands that it's not about her, but the people who sent her there." Significant changes in the district lines were a factor in Ackerman's retirement.

Meng received the backing of the Queens Democratic Party and several Asian-American advocacy groups as well as the powerful New York Hotel and Motel Trades Council. She easily won the Democratic primary in June against three other contenders with 53% of the vote to 25% for runner-up Assemblyman Rory Lancman, who appealed to the district's sizable Jewish constituency. In the small turnout, Meng in effect was elected by the 14,825 votes she received in the primary. She had little trouble in the 2012 general election against Republican Daniel J. Halloran, a member of the New York City Council. The contest became raucous after Halloran accused Meng of running a campaign of "ethnocentrism" based on her roots, referred to her as a "Chinese national" and falsely accused her of having dual citizenship. She won, 68%-31%.

Meng persevered through an embarrassing episode, when her father was arrested in July 2014 and accused of soliciting $80,000 from a friend facing criminal charges, claiming he could bribe prosecutors. After her election, Jimmy Meng pleaded guilty to wire fraud in the bribery case and was sentenced to one month in prison.

In the House, Meng became the only Asian American representing an East Coast district. She was assigned to Foreign Affairs and Small Business, where she became ranking Democrat in 2015 on the Agriculture, Energy and Trade Subcommittee. Even before she took office, she worked on the disaster-relief measure following Superstorm Sandy. She won a provision to permit disaster funds to be used for rebuilding houses of worship damaged or destroyed by the storm. On Foreign Affairs, she filed a bill with Republican Tom Emmer of Minnesota to direct the State Department to speed up visa approvals for international physicians who are slated to work at U.S. hospitals. Following the devastating Nepal earthquake in April 2015, she worked with New York Democratic colleague Joe Crowley to grant protected immigration status on a temporary basis to Nepali nationals residing in the United States so they were not forced to return home to harmful and unsafe conditions. She was a founder and became co-chair of the bipartisan Kids' Safety Caucus.

At home, she has focused on steps to bolster the transportation infrastructure for Queens and to expand tourism in the borough. Meng was reelected without opposition in 2014. She has raised an impressive total of nearly $3 million in her two campaigns.

SEVENTH DISTRICT

Nydia Velázquez (D)

Elected 1992, 12th term; b. March 28, 1953, Yabucoa, PR; U. of PR, B.A. 1974, NY U., M.A. 1976; Catholic; divorced.

Elected Office: NY City Cncl., 1984-86.

Professional Career: Faculty, U. of PR, 1976-81; Adjunct prof., Hunter Col., 1981-83; Special asst., U.S. Rep. Edolphus Towns, 1983; Migration dir., PR Dept. of Labor & Human Resources, 1986-89; Dir., PR Dept. of Community Affairs in the U.S., 1989-92.

DC Office: 2302 RHOB, 20515, 202-225-2361; Fax: 202-226-0327; Website: velazquez.house.gov.

State Offices: Brooklyn, 718-599-3658; New York, 212-619-2606; Southwest Brooklyn, 718-222-5819.

Committees: *Financial Services:* Financial Institutions & Consumer Credit; Housing & Insurance. *Small Business* (RMM).

Group Ratings

	ADA	ACLU	AFL-CIO	LCV	ITI	COC	HAFA	ACU	CFG	FRC
2014	95%	77%	–	91%	40%	42%	16%	8%	13%	0%
2013	95%	C	95%	96%	C	33%	C	16%	20%	C

National Journal Ratings

	2013 LIB	—	2013 CONS
Economic	75%	—	24%
Social	87%	—	7%
Foreign	94%	—	0%
Composite	88%	—	13%

Key Votes of the 113th Congress

1. Sandy storm spending	Y	5. Medical Marijuana	Y	9. Syrian Rebels Training	N
2. Violence Against Women Act	Y	6. Farm Bill	N	10. Keystone pipeline	N
3. Guantanamo Bay Detainees	Y	7. Afghanistan Combat	Y	11. Immigration Exec. Action	N
4. Abortion 20-week ban	N	8. NSA Phone Data Collection	Y	12. Bipartisan budget deal	N

Election Results

2014 general	Nydia Velazquez (D)	56,593	(89%)	$715,659
	Jose Luis Fernandez (R)	5,713	(9%)	$22,205
	Allan Romaguera (C)	1,398	(2%)	
2014 primary	Nydia Velazquez (D)	7,627	(81%)	
	Jeff Kurzon (D)	1,796	(19%)	

Prior winning percentages: 2012 (95%), 2010 (94%), 2008 (90%), 2006 (90%), 2004 (86%), 2002 (96%), 2000 (87%), 1998 (84%), 1996 (85%), 1994 (92%), 1992 (77%)

Population		Race and Ethnicity		Income	
Total:	760,308	Latino	43.8%	Median income:	$48,813
Urban:	100.0%	White	28.0%		*(259 of 435)*
Suburban:	0.0%	Asian	17.6%	Under $50,000	50.6%
Rural:	0.0%	Black	8.3%	$50,000-$99,999:	25.5%
Land area:	23	Two races	1.4%	$100,000-$199,999:	16.7%
Pop/sq. mi.:	32,697.0	White Ethnic	15.2%	$200,000 or more:	7.2%
Born in state:	45.3%			Poverty Rate	26.7%
		Education			
Age Groups		H.S. grad or less:	54.1%	**Work**	
Under 18:	22.9%	Some college:	16.0%	White collar:	36.1%
18 to 34:	29.9%	College degree, 4 yr.:	18.5%	Blue collar:	46.1%
35 to 64:	37.0%	Post-grad study:	11.4%	Sales and service:	17.8%
Over 64:	10.2%			Govt. workers:	8.4%
		Military			
		Veterans/active duty:	1.4%		

Northern Brooklyn, Lower East Side of Manhattan

In 1957, amid a vast wave of Puerto Rican migration to New York, Leonard Bernstein wrote the music for *West Side Story*, which featured Romeo as an Italian American and Juliet as a Manhattan Puerto Rican. Before World War II, there were 60,000 Puerto Ricans in New York City. Three decades later, with

Voter Turnout	
2013 Total Citizen 18+	434,298
2014 House Turnout	63,812
2014 Turnout as % CVAP	14.7%
2012 Turnout as % CVAP	42.5%

cheap airfares and no need to go through passport control, there were 800,000. But as the city's industrial base grew stagnant, the number declined, and young New Yorkers of Puerto Rican descent increasingly returned there or to Florida. By the late 1990s, New York City was experiencing a large influx of Latinos from places not under the U.S. flag. Even though New York still has the largest Puerto Rican population outside of that island, most arriving Hispanics in the city today come from the Dominican Republic, Colombia, Mexico, Panama and Peru.

The 7th Congressional District of New York was designed to stitch together many of these diverse people. Close to three-fourths of the district's population is in Brooklyn, with the remainder split between Queens and Manhattan. In Brooklyn, the district hugs the waterfront and dips inland. But this is New York, so it takes in many other ethnicities as well. Overall, the district is 43% Hispanic and 19% Asian (mostly Chinese). Of the Hispanics, one-third are Puerto Rican. Chinese, predominantly in Brooklyn, were about to overtake Dominicans as the largest foreign-born group in the city, *The New York Times* reported in April 2015.

The district includes the upscale Brooklyn Heights waterfront, with its stunning views of Lower Manhattan, and nearby Carroll Gardens, with young professionals intermingled with Italian immigrants. Further inland is Downtown Brooklyn (originally called *Breuckelen* by the Dutch), which is making progress to attract a critical mass of business and residential development to become a "city that never sleeps" in its own right. To the south is Sunset Park, once the home of Irish, Polish and Norwegian immigrants, and now filled with Chinese, Puerto Ricans, Colombians and Ecuadorans. Tensions between the police and residents of Sunset Park erupted in multiple confrontations in September 2014. The Brooklyn Nets, who moved into the Barclays Center in downtown in 2012, planned to open a basketball practice facility in Sunset Park in the summer of 2015. North of Brooklyn Heights is DUMBO (Down Under the Manhattan Bridge Overpass), with artists in old industrial lofts that have become hot real estate. Just above that is Vinegar Hill.

To the east is the old Brooklyn Navy Yard, which houses a vibrant industrial park with the largest movie and television production complex outside of Hollywood. Williamsburg has many Orthodox Jews and recent Latino arrivals as well as the young and hip. Gentrification has caused housing prices to spike in recent years, and rents for the average studio apartment in DUMBO and Williamsburg have grown higher than the average in Greenwich Village, the Financial District, or the Upper East Side of Manhattan.

Inland, the district takes in Bushwick, a former slum that is now the latest beachhead in Brooklyn's urban renewal and multi-ethnic Cypress Hills. In Manhattan, the 7th District includes parts of the Lower

2012 Presidential Vote
Barack Obama (D) 156,860   (89%)
Mitt Romney (R)...................18,378   (10%)

2008 Presidential Vote
Barack Obama (D) 158,853   (84%)
John McCain (R)...................28,091   (15%)

Cook Partisan Voting Index: D+34

East Side, East Village, Chinatown and Little Italy. The small salient in Queens includes Woodhaven. Politically, the district is in the top 2 percent of the most Democratic districts in the nation, along with two adjacent districts in Queens and Brooklyn (the 5th and 8th.)

Nydia Velázquez (D)

Nydia Velázquez, first elected in 1992, is the ranking Democrat on the Small Business Committee and the first Puerto Rican woman elected to Congress. Her nickname is "*La Luchadora*"—"The Fighter." She also is a senior member of the Financial Services Committee, which oversees companies with many employees who are her constituents.

She grew up in Puerto Rico as one of nine children of sugar-cane field workers. Although her father never finished elementary school, he was a political leader in her hometown of Yabucoa and inspired her to pursue politics as a career. She studied political science at the

University of Puerto Rico and taught there in the 1970s. After graduate school in New York City, she went to work for local Democratic Rep. Edolphus Towns. In 1983, she became the first Hispanic woman elected to the New York City Council.

When her new district was created in 1992, Velázquez was a major contender in the Democratic primary. She had to overcome Rep. Stephen Solarz, who had decided to run in the new district rather than challenge then-Democratic Rep. Charles Schumer. Velázquez was endorsed by Mayor David Dinkins and civil rights leader Jesse Jackson. In a light turnout, she beat Solarz 34%-28%. After the primary, confidential hospital records leaked to a New York City tabloid indicated that Velázquez had attempted suicide in September 1991, was hospitalized and underwent counseling. Evidently, voters had little concern. She won in November with 77% of the vote.

In the House, Velázquez has a solidly liberal voting record, with occasional pro-business votes on economic issues. Velázquez has been a leading voice on issues related to Puerto Rico and the ongoing debate over changing the commonwealth's status. She favors a process that would allow the people of Puerto Rico to determine the status of the island, and has filed legislation authorizing a constitutional convention that would produce a recommendation that would then be subject to a referendum. The results would be submitted to Congress for approval. In the 1990s, Velázquez strongly advocated clemency for several members of the FALN terrorist group who had sought Puerto Rican independence and were imprisoned for 19 years in the deaths of six people. When President Bill Clinton granted clemency in 1999, on condition that they renounce violence, Velázquez said that clemency should be unconditional. The House condemned the clemency move, 311-41.

In 2009, Velázquez became chairwoman of the Hispanic Caucus. Velázquez lauded Obama's choice of a woman with a Puerto Rican background, Sonia Sotomayor, to be the Supreme Court's first Hispanic justice. But she repeatedly has pressed him to move comprehensive immigration reform higher on his agenda. When vehement GOP opposition made clear that such a battle was unwinnable, she worked to separate the DREAM Act, a bill providing a path to legal status for the children of illegal immigrants who attend college or serve in the military. The House approved that bill in late 2010, but Senate supporters could not reach the 60-vote threshold to overcome a filibuster.

Much of her legislative work has focused on the Small Business Committee. During the Bush administration, Velázquez joined with Republicans to reinstate an SBA loan program that had guaranteed lenders a 75% payback if a borrower defaulted on loans of up to $750,000. The White House insisted on abolishing the SBA subsidy and funding the program with higher fees to borrowers and lenders. Velázquez initiated an annual scorecard to show whether the federal government had met its goal of granting 23% of contracts to small businesses.

In 2005, the SBA Office of Advocacy found that the agency had miscoded a significant number of loans to small divisions of large firms and had counted them as small business loans. Velázquez accused the Bush administration of "cooking the books." The following year, she revealed that the government had miscoded $12 billion in contracts and that 22% of contracts went to small businesses. Velázquez charged that the SBA repeatedly fell short of its goal of granting 5% of loans to women. After a government report pointed to chaotic service and a loan approval process that lagged behind demand, she called on SBA Administrator Hector Barreto to resign, and in 2006, he did.

As the panel's chairwoman in 2009, Velazquez praised the Obama administration for requiring the nation's largest banks to report monthly on how much lending they do to small businesses. She criticized an administration proposal to give $30 billion of the Troubled Asset Relief Program to community banks for small business, but without any conditions that the money actually be used for small business loans. "Taking $30 billion and simply handing it to banks—in the hopes that they will make loans—is not sound policy," she said. The administration dropped the idea of using TARP money.

Following the recession, she sought to ensure that small businesses get attention in the recovery. In 2014, she sponsored legislation aimed at helping women-owned small businesses secure federal contracts, and in 2015 she introduced another bill to reopen the Small Business Administration's disaster loan program. In May 2015, *The Washington Post* reported that Velázquez was miffed that the SBA had launched new programs to assist entrepreneurs and had taken the funds from existing programs without informing Congress. "This makes no sense," she said. SBA officials defended their approach as a better way to assist emerging businesses.

A longtime combatant in New York City's political wars, Velázquez has won reelection easily every two years, often without major-party opposition.

EIGHTH DISTRICT

Hakeem Jeffries (D)

Elected 2012, 2nd term; b. Aug. 4, 1970, Brooklyn; Binghamton U., B.A. 1992, Georgetown U., M.P.P. 1994, NY U., J.D. 1997; Baptist; married (Kennisandra); 2 children.

Elected Office: NY Assembly, 2007-2012.

Professional Career: Clerk, Judge Harold Baer, 1997-98; Practicing atty., 1999-2003; Counsel, Viacom, 2004-05; Asst. gen. counsel, CBS Broadcasting, 2006.

DC Office: 1607 LHOB, 20515, 202-225-5936; Website: jeffries.house.gov..

State Offices: Central Brooklyn, 718-237-2211; South Brooklyn, 718-373-0033.

Committees: *Education & the Workforce:* Higher Education & Workforce Training; Health, Employment, Labor & Pensions. *Judiciary:* Courts, Intellectual Property, & the Internet; Regulatory Reform, Commercial & Antitrust Law.

Group Ratings

	ADA	ACLU	AFL-CIO	LCV	ITI	COC	HAFA	ACU	CFG	FRC
2014	90%	77%	–	97%	80%	36%	15%	8%	12%	0%
2013	85%	C	95%	89%	C	46%	C	13%	15%	C

National Journal Ratings

	2013 LIB	—	2013 CONS
Economic	82%	—	17%
Social	85%	—	13%
Foreign	82%	—	17%
Composite	84%	—	16%

Key Votes of the 113th Congress

1. Sandy storm spending	Y	5. Medical Marijuana	Y	9. Syrian Rebels Training	N
2. Violence Against Women Act	Y	6. Farm Bill	N	10. Keystone pipeline	N
3. Guantanamo Bay Detainees	Y	7. Afghanistan Combat	Y	11. Immigration Exec. Action	N
4. Abortion 20-week ban	N	8. NSA Phone Data Collection	Y	12. Bipartisan budget deal	Y

Election Results

2014 general	Hakeem Jeffries (D)................... 77,255	(92%)	$650,169
	Alan Bellone (C)........................... 6,673	(8%)	
2014 primary	Hakeem Jeffries (D).............Unopposed		

Prior winning percentage: 2012 (90%)

Population		Race and Ethnicity		Income	
Total:	737,529	Black	53.4%	Median income:	$45,117
Urban:	100.0%	White	22.1%		*(319 of 435)*
Suburban:	0.0%	Latino	18.1%	Under $50,000	53.5%
Rural:	0.0%	Asian	4.5%	$50,000-$99,999:	26.4%
Land area:	26	Two races	1.2%	$100,000-$199,999:	15.8%
Pop/sq. mi.:	28,260.9	White Ethnic	12.8%	$200,000 or more:	4.2%
Born in state:	53.1%			Poverty Rate	24.7%
		Education			
Age Groups		H.S. grad or less:	47.5%	**Work**	
Under 18:	22.6%	Some college:	23.5%	White collar:	37.5%
18 to 34:	25.7%	College degree, 4 yr.:	18.0%	Blue collar:	48.0%
35 to 64:	38.5%	Post-grad study:	10.9%	Sales and service:	14.4%
Over 64:	13.2%				
		Military		Govt. workers:	17.4%
		Veterans/active duty:	3.3%		

Brooklyn: Bedford-Stuyvesant

African Americans began settling in Brooklyn's Bedford-Stuyvesant neighborhood in the 1930s, with the opening of the subway line that was celebrated in Duke Ellington and Billy

Strayhorn's "Take the 'A' Train." After World War II, the pace accelerated, as crime and crowding in Harlem—as well as a large influx of African Americans from the South—drove black New Yorkers to the aging but solid brownstones of "Bed-Stuy." When job growth slowed, Bed-Stuy faced more

Voter Turnout	
2013 Total Citizen 18+	489,343
2014 House Turnout	83,999
2014 Turnout as % CVAP	17.2%
2012 Turnout as % CVAP	49.3%

than its share of poverty and crime. But after a 1966 visit by New York's two senators, Democrat Robert F. Kennedy and Republican Jacob Javits, Bed-Stuy won a Model Cities designation, which brought federal development funds and the establishment of the Bedford-Stuyvesant Restoration Corporation, the first such community development organization in the United States.

Even as the black community expanded across Brooklyn, Bed-Stuy became almost as powerful a symbol of black New York as Harlem, thanks in part to the films of Spike Lee, a Brooklyn native. His *Do the Right Thing*, shot on Stuyvesant Avenue between Lexington Avenue and Quincy Street, succinctly captured the racial tensions then brewing in the old neighborhood. The neighborhood also gave birth to rappers Jay-Z and Notorious B.I.G., two of the most influential hip hop artists. By the new century, Bed-Stuy was in better shape than many other areas of Brooklyn. The neighborhood's stately, Hopperesque architecture largely avoided the wrecking ball, and community vigilance kept the streets maintained. The revitalized residential area has developed a Caribbean flavor that, combined with modest prices for handsome brownstones and new shops and galleries, has led to a wave of gentrification. The Barclays Center, which opened in 2012 and has gained renown as the downtown home for Brooklyn Nets basketball and New York Islanders hockey, has yielded some cultural impact: Its owners Bruce Ratner and Mikhail Prokhorov announced in May 2015 that they have invested in the large Paramount Theater, a surviving Jazz Age movie house on Flatbush Avenue.

The 8th Congressional District of New York takes the shape of a sideways "U" as it rambles across Brooklyn. It begins in Fort Greene, a rising arts area, and from there runs southeasterly through Clinton Hill, Bed-Stuy and East New York. Less than 10% of the district is in Queens, taking in Lindenwood and Howard Beach, an Italian neighborhood that has remained

2012 Presidential Vote		
Barack Obama (D)	209,422	(89%)
Mitt Romney (R)	23,861	(10%)
2008 Presidential Vote		
Barack Obama (D)	208,317	(86%)
John McCain (R)	32,9901	(14%)
Cook Partisan Voting Index:	D+35	

remarkably unaffected by the demographic shifts elsewhere in the borough. The district runs along the Belt Parkway and the edge of Jamaica Bay through Spring Creek and Canarsie, which have become substantially black neighborhoods mainly due to Caribbean immigrants who prized the backyards and single-family homes.

The 8th also takes in parts of heavily African-American Flatlands and the equally heavily white neighborhoods of Bergen Beach, Marine Park and Mill Basin. It includes the Coney Island peninsula, which was an actual island before the city filled in Coney Island Creek. Today, it is a diverse collection of neighborhoods and home to the famous theme park. Brighton Beach, part of Coney Island, has more Russian Jewish immigrants than any other district in the nation. Superstorm Sandy wreaked havoc here in late 2012, with widespread flooding and power outages. Overall, the district is 57% black and 17% Hispanic. Politically, it is one of the most Democratic districts in the nation.

Hakeem Jeffries (D)

Democrat Hakeem Jeffries, elected in 2012, has brought energy and a spirit of consensus-building to his office. He gained attention in February 2014 when Fox News profiled him as one of the nation's "rising political stars."

Jeffries was born and raised in the Crown Heights neighborhood of Brooklyn and graduated from the State University at Binghamton. He pledged Kappa Alpha Psi, the predominantly African-American fraternity, where he received the nickname "Kool Ha," for his measured speech. "I'd like to think ... I've been able to remain relatively calm, cool, and collected under pressure," Jeffries told *National Journal*. As a senior in college, he solidified his commitment to public service after the not-guilty verdict for two police officers accused in the beating of Los Angeles motorist Rodney King. He went to Georgetown University for a master's degree in public policy and later earned a law degree from New York University. He clerked for a federal judge, and worked for Paul, Weiss, Rifkind, Wharton & Garrison, a law firm known for launching the careers of prominent New York Democrats, such as former Gov. Eliot Spitzer and former Rep. Elizabeth Holtzman.

After two unsuccessful campaigns against an entrenched incumbent in the state Assembly, Jeffries won an open seat in 2006. Within a few years, Jeffries appeared in *City and State* magazine's list of 40 rising political stars under 40. In the legislature, he worked on affordable housing issues and got a bill signed into law forcing the elimination of the New York City Police Department's "stop-and-frisk" database, which contained personal information from each police stop since 2004. He also took on political reforms and introduced legislation to establish an independent congressional redistricting process.

When the House seat opened, Jeffries faced another African-American politician, New York City Councilman Charles Barron, in the Democratic primary. A former Black Panther, Barron had a history of making inflammatory statements against Israel; Jeffries voiced support for Israel and, as a result, benefited from national campaign donations. Even the Democratic Congressional Campaign Committee tapped him as a fundraising "all-star," asking him to help campaign around the country in other important congressional races. Jeffries spent $1.4 million and won the primary race in a rout, defeating Barron 72%-28%. That was tantamount to victory in the heavily Democratic district.

In the House, Jeffries was assigned to the Judiciary, and Education and the Workforce Committees. He focused much of his time on law-enforcement issues. In March 2015, President Barack Obama enacted the Slain Officer Family Support Act, which he introduced with Republican Rep. Peter King of New York. The bill extended the tax deadline for charitable deductions of contributions to the families of two Brooklyn police officers who were killed in Bedford-Stuyvesant in December 2014.

In April 2015, following protests against alleged police excesses in several cities, including Brooklyn, he filed a bill to bar the use of chokeholds, which he called a deprivation of civil rights. "It's not sufficient simply to ban a policy through departmental practice. We've got to elevate it, embed it in law, if we really and truly want to end it," he told CNN. To a group sponsored by Al Sharpton's National Action Network in May 2015, Jeffries criticized New York Mayor Bill de Blasio for the city's continued police enforcement of the "broken windows policing" of minor violations.

Jeffries was reelected in 2014 without major party opposition. He does not discourage suggestions that he has a bright political future that may extend beyond the House.

NINTH DISTRICT

Yvette Clarke (D)

Elected 2006, 5th term; b. Nov. 21, 1964, Brooklyn; Oberlin Col., attended; Christian; single.

Elected Office: NY City Cncl., 2002-07.

Professional Career: Childcare specialist, Erasmus Neighborhood Fed., 1987-89; Legis. aide, Sen. Velmanette Montgomery, 1989-91; Exec. asst., NY Workers' Compensation Bd., 1992-93; Youth program dir., Hosp. League/Local S.E.I.U. 1199 Training & Upgrading Fund, 1993-97; Bus. devel. dir., Bronx Overall Devel. Corp., 1997-2001.

DC Office: 2351 RHOB, 20515, 202-225-6231; Fax: 202-226-0112; Website: clarke.house.gov..

State Offices: Brooklyn, 718-287-1142.

Committees: *Energy & Commerce:* Commerce, Manufacturing, & Trade; Communications & Technology; Oversight & Investigations. *Ethics. Small Business.*

Group Ratings

	ADA	ACLU	AFL-CIO	LCV	ITI	COC	HAFA	ACU	CFG	FRC
2014	95%	77%	–	86%	80%	31%	14%	8%	13%	0%
2013	90%	C	95%	96%	C	38%	C	13%	19%	C

National Journal Ratings

	2013 LIB	—	2013 CONS
Economic	88%	—	12%
Social	68%	—	32%
Foreign	94%	—	0%
Composite	84%	—	16%

Key Votes of the 113th Congress

1. Sandy storm spending	Y	5. Medical Marijuana	Y	9. Syrian Rebels Training	N
2. Violence Against Women Act	Y	6. Farm Bill	N	10. Keystone Pipeline	N
3. Guantanamo Bay Detainees	Y	7. Afghanistan Combat	Y	11. Immigration Exec. Action	N
4. Abortion 20-week ban	N	8. NSA Phone Data Collection	Y	12. Bipartisan Budget Deal	N

Election Results

2014 general   Yvette Clarke (D)........................ 82,659   (89%) $534,976
            Daniel Cavanagh (C) 9,727   (11%)
2014 primary   Yvette Clarke (D).................unopposed

Prior winning percentages: 2012 (87%), 2010 (91%), 2008 (93%), 2006 (90%)

Population		Race and Ethnicity		Income	
Total:	735,408	Black	50.5%	Median income:	$47,355
Urban:	100.0%	White	29.4%		*(276 of 435)*
Suburban:	0.0%	Latino	11.9%	Under $50,000	51.5%
Rural:	0.0%	Asian	6.6%	$50,000-$99,999:	27.0%
Land area:	23	Two races	1.4%	$100,000-$199,999:	16.2%
Pop/sq. mi.:	32,288.3	White Ethnic	15.1%	$200,000 or more:	5.3%
Born in state:	47.9%			Poverty Rate	20.1%
		Education			
Age Groups		H.S. grad or less:	43.0%	**Work**	
Under 18:	22.6%	Some college:	22.0%	White collar:	37.3%
18 to 34:	26.8%	College degree, 4 yr.:	20.3%	Blue collar:	49.6%
35 to 64:	37.9%	Post-grad study:	14.8%	Sales and service:	13.1%
Over 64:	12.6%			Govt. workers:	16.8%
		Military			
		Veterans/active duty:	2.2%		

Brooklyn: Flatbush, Crown Heights

Voter Turnout	
2013 Total Citizen 18+	465,274
2014 House Turnout	92,569
2014 Turnout as % CVAP	19.9%
2012 Turnout as % CVAP	53.2%

Brooklyn. Just saying the word in a comedian's monologue used to elicit laughter. It evoked an accent of twisted English, a raucous, in-your-face style, a sense of humor with an edge, and the chip-on-the-shoulder assertiveness of those sure they will always be in second place. As its name testifies, Brooklyn was a separate community from the 17th century on, and in the 19th century, it was one of the largest cities in the country, with its own celebrities—Henry Ward Beecher, Walt Whitman, John Roebling. By 1898, when the five boroughs were welded into Greater New York, 1 million people lived in Brooklyn. In 1913, a transit agreement was struck to link the city's then-independent lines and triple the track to 619 miles. The agreement helped Brooklyn expand well beyond its established neighborhoods near the Brooklyn Bridge.

Suddenly, Manhattan factory workers no longer had to live in the crowded Lower East Side tenements that social reformer Jacob Riis had exposed in the 1890s. They moved in droves into neighborhoods of three- to five-story apartments and four-family houses. Brooklyn grew from 1.1 million in 1900 to 2.6 million in 1930; in 1900 its population was 63% of Manhattan's, and by 1930, it had well surpassed the island's. The old Brooklynites were mostly Protestant—Dutch, Yankee and German, plus some Catholic Irish. The new Brooklynites were heavily Italian and Jewish, and they populated the sports and entertainment businesses for a long generation, making their hometown nationally famous.

Around the time Jackie Robinson suited up for the Brooklyn Dodgers in 1947 as the first black player in Major League Baseball, Brooklyn was experiencing an influx of African Americans into Brownsville and Crown Heights near Ebbets Field. Just as rapid was the flight of ethnic whites, driven away by "blockbusting," in which unscrupulous real estate brokers stoked white fears, then bought homes cheaply and re-sold them for higher prices. After "Dem Bums" left for Los Angeles in 1958 and Ebbets Field was knocked down and replaced by an apartment complex, Brooklyn's African-American neighborhoods continued to grow.

Brooklyn's growth spurt began tapering off in the 1930s, and its population peaked at 2.7 million in the 1950 census. Today, it has 2.6 million people. Kings County, which is identical to Brooklyn, is New York's largest county, the nation's eighth largest, and its second-most densely populated. Some of its old neighborhoods have been ravaged by crime, but there is also great vitality among upwardly mobile Hispanic, Asian, Caribbean and Russian immigrants, among middle-class blacks, and among new generations of Italians and Jews. A change in zoning laws in 2004 resulted in a burst of new residential and office construction that has reinvigorated Brooklyn's commercial district.

The 9th Congressional District of New York begins southeast of downtown Brooklyn. At the far northwestern tip is the Barclays Center, a large arena that is home to basketball's Brooklyn Nets and, starting in 2015, the New York Islanders hockey franchise that moved from Nassau County. The Center lost to Philadelphia in its bid to host the 2016 Democratic national convention. Deeper into the district are some of Brooklyn's jewels: the Grand Army Plaza, the Parisian-style Eastern Parkway (the world's first six-lane parkway), and Prospect Park, home to the Brooklyn Public Library, the Brooklyn Museum, and the Brooklyn Botanic Garden, with its Japanese landscaping and placid duck ponds.

Park Slope, on Prospect Park's west side, has become increasingly affluent, filling up with young professionals who like the easy commute to Manhattan. On the east side of Prospect Park is Crown Heights, with its mix of modest apartment buildings and nicely restored row houses. Prospect Park South, also adjoining the park, is an affluent neighborhood with yuppies whose stately late Victorian era mansions contrast sharply with the vibrant Caribbean street life just around the corner on Flatbush's Church Avenue. At the southern end of the district are Midwood, Homecrest and Sheepshead Bay, mostly white communities with substantial Jewish populations. Most of these neighborhoods have great diversity. The district's population is 51% black and 11% Hispanic. Politically, the 9th is overwhelmingly Democratic.

2012 Presidential Vote		
Barack Obama (D)	202,361	(85%)
Mitt Romney (R)	33,045	(14%)
2008 Presidential Vote		
Barack Obama (D)	208,746	(84%)
John McCain (R)	38,277	(15%)
Cook Partisan Voting Index:	D+32	

Yvette Clarke (D)

Democrat Yvette Clarke, elected in 2006, is a liberal who concentrates on immigration and other issues important to her diverse constituency. She has become a senior leader of the Congressional Black Caucus.

She was born in the Flatbush section of Brooklyn to immigrant parents from Jamaica. As a young girl, she tagged along to political meetings and events with her mother, Una Clarke, who in 1991 became the first Jamaican elected to the New York City Council. Yvette Clarke attended Oberlin College in Ohio but fell short of graduating by six credit hours. She returned to New York, helped train child care workers, worked as a state legislative aide, and served as business development director for the Bronx Overall Economic Development Corporation. In 2001, when term limits forced her mother off the City Council, Clarke defeated four other candidates to succeed her in the predominately Caribbean area of Flatbush and East Flatbush.

From its creation in 1968 until 2006, the district had been represented by just two people, both Democrats—trailblazer Shirley Chisholm, the first black woman elected to Congress and a 1972 presidential candidate, and Major Owens, who succeeded her in 1982. When Owens announced his retirement, he hoped that his son, Chris, a health industry administrator, would succeed him. But Clarke had her own political family with designs on the seat. Her mother had run unsuccessfully against Owens, an African American, in the 2000 Democratic primary, a bitter contest that exposed divisions between the local Caribbean-American community and the African-American community. Four years later, Yvette Clarke and fellow City Councilwoman Tracy Boyland challenged Owens in the Democratic primary. The incumbent won the low-turnout primary with an unimpressive 45%, to 29% for Clarke and 22% for Boyland.

In the 2006 primary, Clarke had to navigate a competitive primary field. New York City Councilman David Yassky, who is white, jumped in and was called a "colonizer" by Owens for running in a majority-black district that had been created in response to a Voting Rights Act lawsuit. By the end of August, Yassky had raised over $1.3 million, more than the other three candidates combined. Clarke's status as the only woman in the contest and her support among Caribbean Americans were helpful. She stumbled when she was forced to backtrack from her claim that she had graduated from Oberlin. But she picked up the endorsement of the Service Employees International Union's powerful Local 1199, which worked to turn out votes. In the September primary, Clarke defeated Yassky 31%-27%, while Owens got 19%.

In the House, Clarke has had a staunchly liberal voting record and tied for most-liberal member in *National Journal's* 2012 rankings. She was among the Black Caucus members who expressed frustration with what they considered President Barack Obama's lack of focus on helping minorities during his first term. "What we are asking for is that the president use his bully pulpit to look at a more far-reaching, deeper-penetrating jobs initiative. ... The level of unemployment in our communities is unacceptable," she told National Public Radio in March 2010. In December 2014, she was more aggressive than other Black Caucus members in calling for an investigation of reports that House Majority Whip Steve Scalise of Louisiana spoke to a white supremacist group.

One of Clarke's priorities has been immigration, specifically the DREAM Act providing in-state college tuition breaks and other benefits to children of illegal immigrants. In June 2008, the House passed her bill to create an appeals process for individuals alleging denial of rights in homeland security investigations. She traveled to Alabama in November 2011 as part of a Democratic effort to focus attention on the state's aggressive new immigration law, which she blasted as "just a step below apartheid." In February 2015, she was "deeply disappointed" when a federal judge in Texas delayed implementation of the Obama administration plan that would have permitted illegal Caribbean immigrants to apply for work permits.

In 2015, Clarke joined the powerful Energy and Commerce Committee. She worked with other Democrats on legislation to urge the Federal Communications Commission to encourage small businesses to participate in spectrum auctions. In December 2014, she joined members of the Homeland Security Committee in the bipartisan enactment of cybersecurity legislation.

Clarke was also among five House Democrats who were investigated by the House Ethics Committee in 2010 for accepting Caribbean trips from corporations; they were later exonerated. She and the other lawmakers said they were unaware of the corporate funding. Clarke has drawn occasional interest from New York's tabloids. The *Daily News* reported in October 2011 that in the first six months of the year, her office spent the most among New York-area House members—nearly $35,000, compared with her colleague Nydia Velázquez's $2,274—in traveling to and from Washington, D.C. Clarke's office attributed the costs to staffers shuttling back and forth. In May 2015, the *Washington Post* reported that Clarke was among the 10 House members in a bipartisan delegation to Azerbaijan in 2013 that accrued lavish expenses and gifts; they were being investigated by the Ethics Committee, of which she is a member. In July, the committee dismissed the case.

Clarke drew attention in 2012 when she said on Comedy Central's *Colbert Report* that Brooklyn blacks lived in slavery in 1898, more than three decades after emancipation and 71 years after New York State abolished slavery. She also said that the Dutch, who last controlled the city three centuries earlier, were responsible. Her spokeswoman said her boss was just trying to be humorous. It hasn't mattered to voters. In 2014, she was reelected without major-party opposition.

TENTH DISTRICT

Jerrold Nadler (D)

Elected Nov. 1992, 12th full term; b. June 13, 1947, Brooklyn; Columbia U., B.A. 1969, Fordham U., J.D. 1978; Jewish; married (Joyce Miller); 1 child.

Elected Office: NY Assembly, 1977-92.

Professional Career: Legis. asst., NY Assembly, 1972; Law clerk, 1976.

DC Office: 2109 RHOB, 20515, 202-225-5635; Website: nadler.house. gov.

State Offices: Brooklyn, 718-373-3198; Manhattan, 212-367-7350.

Committees: *Judiciary:* Constitution & Civil Justice; Courts, Intellectual Property & the Internet (RMM). *Transportation & Infrastructure:* Highways & Transit; Railroads, Pipelines & Hazardous Materials.

Group Ratings

	ADA	ACLU	AFL-CIO	LCV	ITI	COC	HAFA	ACU	CFG	FRC
2014	100%	94%	–	94%	60%	36%	12%	8%	11%	0%
2013	100%	C	95%	96%	C	31%	C	4%	10%	C

National Journal Ratings

	2013 LIB	—	2013 CONS
Economic	91%	—	0%
Social	73%	—	24%
Foreign	94%	—	0%
Composite	89%	—	11%

Key Votes of the 113th Congress

1. Sandy storm spending	Y	5. Medical Marijuana	Y	9. Syrian Rebels Training	N
2. Violence Against Women Act	Y	6. Farm Bill	N	10. Keystone pipeline	N
3. Guantanamo Bay Detainees	Y	7. Afghanistan Combat	Y	11. Immigration Exec. Action	N
4. Abortion 20-week ban	N	8. NSA Phone Data Collection	Y	12. Bipartisan budget deal	Y

Election Results

2014 general	Jerrold Nadler (D)	89,080	(88%)	$1,276,210
	Ross Brady (C)	12,042	(12%)	
2014 primary	Jerrold Nadler (D)	unopposed		

Prior winning percentages: 2012 (81%), 2010 (76%), 2008 (80%), 2006 (85%), 2004 (81%), 2002 (76%), 2000 (81%), 1998 (86%), 1996 (82%), 1994 (82%), 1992 (81%), 1992 special (100%)

Population		Race and Ethnicity		Income	
Total:	716,682	White	65.7%	Median income:	$81,810
Urban:	100.0%	Asian	16.2%		(27 of 435)
Suburban:	0.0%	Latino	13.0%	Under $50,000	35.5%
Rural:	0.0%	Black	3.1%	$50,000-$99,999:	22.4%
Land area:	16	Two races	1.7%	$100,000-$199,999:	23.9%
Pop/sq. mi.:	45,519.8	White Ethnic	33.3%	$200,000 or more:	18.2%
Born in state:	44.3%			Poverty Rate	17.0%
		Education			
Age Groups		H.S. grad or less:	27.2%	**Work**	
Under 18:	19.6%	Some college:	12.2%	White collar:	60.7%
18 to 34:	30.3%	College degree, 4 yr.:	31.5%	Blue collar:	31.7%
35 to 64:	37.4%	Post-grad study:	29.2%	Sales and service:	7.6%
Over 64:	12.7%				
		Military		Govt. workers:	7.7%
		Veterans/active duty:	2.1%		

Manhattan West Side, Brooklyn Borough Park

Over the course of the 20th century, New York City spread so far beyond its original boundaries in Lower Manhattan that, for a while, it became easy to forget how pivotal the southern end of the island had been in making the city what it is today. That all changed in an instant, on the morning of Sept.

Voter Turnout	
2013 Total Citizen 18+	472,098
2014 House Turnout	101,881
2014 Turnout as % CVAP	21.6%
2012 Turnout as % CVAP	48.7%

11, 2001, when al-Qaida terrorists flew two hijacked jets into the twin towers of the World Trade Center, killing nearly 3,000 people and laying waste to 13 city blocks. The terrorists struck the tallest buildings in the nation's biggest city, toppling a complex whose name embodied American capitalism.

Lower Manhattan has long been home to Wall Street and the Financial District, but over the years, it has represented America's striving spirit in other ways as well. The Brooklyn Bridge, begun in 1869 just a few blocks east of the Twin Towers site and completed in 1883, was half again as long as any bridge then standing and seven times higher than any buildings in the adjoining boroughs. The Holland Tunnel, built in 1927, was the first underwater vehicular tunnel built anywhere in the world. Just offshore are Ellis Island, now split between New York and New Jersey, where members of the great immigration wave first set foot on American soil, and the Statue of Liberty, the symbol of freedom they saw as they sailed in.

The 10th Congressional District of New York includes all of these places. From the Battery, at the southern tip of Manhattan, the 10th runs north up the island's west side, covering the Financial District and many neighborhoods. Battery Park City has attractive, modern apartments and parks, and sophisticated TriBeCa has artists' lofts. Art galleries have thrived in Chelsea, and SoHo has become an international shoppers' paradise. Greenwich Village, home of New York University, has long had a taste for the radical, though some ideas have become mainstream: Led by Jane Jacobs, its successful fight against the proposed Lower Manhattan Expressway popularized historic preservation and urbanism. Clinton is the new, economically diverse incarnation of the old slum known as Hell's Kitchen. The Upper West Side is home to Lincoln Center, while the northern end of the district includes Morningside Heights, site of Columbia University.

The venerable apartment buildings along Central Park West, West End Avenue and Riverside Drive, and the brownstones on the cross streets, house some of the country's most dedicated liberals. These professional people were satirized on *Seinfeld*, the long-running sitcom that resonated far beyond Manhattan. In the 1950s, West Siders took up the reform banner and finally killed off the ailing Tammany Hall Democratic machine. The district includes most of Central Park, which was originally a swampy, rocky slum and whose creation required the displacement of 1,600 poor residents. In 2014, the editors of *Bicycling* magazine ranked the city as the best in the nation for cyclists. In a post-9/11 building spree, the famous Manhattan skyline has gained many new towers, both downtown and in Central Park South.

South from the Battery, the 10th District crosses into Brooklyn and into a very different set of neighborhoods. Borough Park has one of the nation's largest Orthodox Jewish communities, with Yiddish-language ATMs and Russian bathhouses. Jewish New Yorkers have a long history in the city. In the years after World War I, as many as 400,000 Jews a year disembarked at Ellis Island until a 1924 law virtually shut down immigration. Their children moved up faster than those of any new group, despite the widespread prejudice against them in the professions

2012 Presidential Vote		
Barack Obama (D)	173,487	(74%)
Mitt Romney (R)	58,970	(25%)
2008 Presidential Vote		
Barack Obama (D)	196,042	(76%)
John McCain (R)	60,668	(23%)
Cook Partisan Voting Index:	D+23	

and in educational institutions. Today, New York has the largest Jewish population behind Tel Aviv. The political attitudes of Brooklyn's Jews, however, are quite different from those of most American Jews, who are liberal on cultural and economic issues. The Russians, many of whom live close to poverty, are anti-socialist. The Hasidic Jews of Borough Park are conservative and hostile to racial preferences, and they favor tough police treatment of crime. Even with these conservative enclaves, the district remains at the cultural and financial heart of national liberalism and it gave President Barack Obama 76% in 2008 and 74% in 2008.

Jerrold Nadler (D)

Democrat Jerrold Nadler, first elected in 1992, is among the House's most vehement liberals, with a strong civil libertarian bent. He has become increasingly vocal in economic debates and is an outspoken advocate of large public works projects, especially for New York City.

Nadler was born in Brooklyn and moved around with his family as a child. His parents bought a chicken farm in New Jersey, but the business failed, and they moved back to the city. His father ran a gas station on Long Island and owned an auto parts store. Interested in politics from a young age, Nadler campaigned for Democrat Eugene McCarthy for president in 1968 while at Columbia University, where he roomed with Dick Morris, who would later become a top adviser to President Bill Clinton.

After getting his law degree from Fordham University, Nadler ran for the New York Assembly in 1976, at age 29. In the primary, he beat Ruth Messinger, the Democratic nominee for mayor in 1997, by 73 votes. In 1992, he suddenly had the opportunity to run for Congress. Representative Ted Weiss, long an Upper West Side icon, died the day before the September primary, which he won posthumously. The nomination was decided by a convention of almost 1,000 county Democratic committee members. Nadler won 62% of the votes to secure the nomination and thus the election. He has not been seriously challenged since.

In the House, Nadler's leftward leanings are evident in his open fondness for the New Deal. He told a New York audience in October 2012 that President Franklin Roosevelt's economic program "put into practice regulations on corporations and banks to prevent economic catastrophes—regulations that worked until they were dismantled, starting in the 1980s." He said Republicans have been misguided in cutting social programs and in letting large corporations pay little or no taxes. He considers the periodic vote to raise the debt ceiling a form of GOP "blackmail," and in January 2013 advocated a trillion-dollar coin, an idea that had bubbled up from economic blogs. Aides to President Barack Obama shot down the idea. He doesn't confine his criticism to the GOP. After Superstorm Sandy ravaged New York and other states in October 2012, he said the Federal Emergency Management Agency was ill-equipped to handle large urban disasters and that New York City needed higher seawalls and waterproofed electric power facilities.

As a senior Democrat on the Judiciary Committee, Nadler has been a counterweight to lawmakers of both parties seeking expanded police powers to crack down on terrorism. It is not, Nadler insists, because he—as the representative of the Ground Zero site of the September 11 attacks—is unsympathetic to their cause. But he has worked to protect detainees' *habeas corpus* rights. When the House voted in September 2012 to extend a warrantless wiretapping program, he bemoaned how much power it gave to presidents. In 2008, he sponsored a bill requiring the Federal Bureau of Investigation to surmount higher legal hurdles before being allowed to use "national security letters," which are government demands for information not subject to judicial review. A vigorous opponent of the USA Patriot Act, the Bush administration's centerpiece anti-terrorism law, he was a leader of the bipartisan coalition that crossed ideological lines as it downsized the law's scope and renamed it the USA Freedom Act, which the House passed 338-88 in May 2015.

Nadler has little regard for most of the tea party conservatives who support strict interpretations of the Constitution. "You are not supposed to worship your Constitution; you're supposed to govern your government by it," he told *The Washington Post* in January 2011. He led the fight in the House against conservative proposals to ban same-sex marriage and, in early 2013, blasted the National Rifle Association's resistance to gun control legislation. He called the suggestion of putting armed guards in schools "ludicrous and insulting."

In 2014, he became the top Democrat on the Judiciary Subcommittee on Courts, Intellectual Property and the Internet. With Republican Rep. Marsha Blackburn of Tennessee, he filed in May 2015 the "Fair Play, Fair Pay" proposal to require that radio stations pay royalties to the record companies that own copyrights to records that are played over the airwaves.

On foreign policy, Nadler has been a staunch supporter of Israel. He opposed the Iraq war resolution in 2002. Regarding Afghanistan, he said in July 2010: "An intelligent policy is not to try to remake a country that nobody since Genghis Khan has managed to conquer." He was among the Democrats who criticized President Barack Obama in 2011 for intervening militarily in Libya without congressional approval.

Nadler has been supportive of non-military post-September 11 responses. In late 2010, he helped steer into law a long-delayed measure providing more than $4 billion in compensation to first responders suffering health problems—a development he called "without a doubt the proudest moment of my 34-year career in government."

On the Transportation and Infrastructure Committee, Nadler has fought to get more rail competition east of the Hudson and to subsidize Amtrak. His biggest idea has been a rail-freight tunnel under the Hudson. Lack of a rail-freight line means that New York gets only a tiny share of its freight by rail; a new line could mean cheaper freight and therefore lower prices. Nadler also has been a strong proponent of the Obama administration's commitment to high-speed passenger rail, which many Republicans have rejected as a boondoggle. "It simply makes no sense to travel by air between New York and D.C. or Boston, or frankly between any cities within a 500-mile radius," he said. He has been an enthusiastic advocate of major projects in Manhattan, such as the new Second Avenue subway line and construction of the Moynihan rail terminal at Penn Station. Nadler successfully fought developer Donald Trump's attempts to alter the West Side Highway to accommodate his luxury housing project on old rail yards between 59th and 72nd Streets. Trump in turn called Nadler a "hack."

In the long tradition of lawmakers from New York, Nadler has gained the seniority to place him close to the top Democratic slot in each of his committee assignments.

ELEVENTH DISTRICT

Daniel Donovan (R)

Elected May 2015, 1st term; b. Nov. 6, 1956, Staten Island; St. John's U., B.A. 1978, Fordham U., J.D. 1988; Catholic; single; 1 child.

Elected Office: Dist. atty., Richmond Cnty., 2003-15.

Professional Career: Investigator; Youth counselor; Asst. dist. atty., 1989-96; Chief staff, borough pres. Guy Molinari, 1996-2002; Deputy borough pres., Staten Island, 2002-03.

DC Office: 1725 LHOB, 20515, 202-225-3371; Website: donovan. house.gov.

State Offices: Brooklyn, 718-630-5277; Staten Island, 718-351-1062.

Committees: *Foreign Affairs:* Africa, Global Health, Global Human Rights, & Int'l Organizations; Western Hemisphere. *Homeland Security:* Cybersecurity, Infrastructure Protection, & Security Technologies; Emergency Preparedness, Response, & Communications.

Election Results
2015 special	Daniel Donovan (R)	24,797	(58%)	$153,194
	Vincent Gentile (D)	17,049	(40%)	$79,698

Population		Race and Ethnicity		Income	
Total:	728,307	White	62.6%	Median income:	$63,750
Urban:	100.0%	Latino	16.1%		*(86 of 435)*
Suburban:	0.0%	Asian	12.7%	Under $50,000	39.9%
Rural:	0.0%	Black	7.4%	$50,000-$99,999:	29.3%
Land area:	55	Two races	1.0%	$100,000-$199,999:	24.0%
Pop/sq. mi.:	13,192.4	White Ethnic	48.3%	$200,000 or more:	6.8%
Born in state:	64.0%			Poverty Rate	13.7%
		Education			
Age Groups		H.S. grad or less:	43.7%	**Work**	
Under 18:	22.1%	Some college:	23.4%	White collar:	39.8%
18 to 34:	22.7%	College degree, 4 yr.:	19.9%	Blue collar:	43.8%
35 to 64:	40.6%	Post-grad study:	12.9%	Sales and service:	16.5%
Over 64:	14.6%			Govt. workers:	18.7%
		Military			
		Veterans/active duty:	4.2%		

Staten Island, South Brooklyn

Staten Island is part of New York City, yet is a land apart, closer geographically and culturally to New Jersey than to the city's other boroughs. Its inclusion in Greater New York as part of the great 1898 consolidation was something of an afterthought. It was connected to the rest of the city only by

Voter Turnout	
2013 Total Citizen 18+	498,118
2014 House Turnout	107,363
2014 Turnout as % CVAP	21.6%
2012 Turnout as % CVAP	42.7%

ferry or through Bayonne New Jersey, until the Verrazano-Narrows Bridge—one of Robert Moses' last and most impressive infrastructure achievements—opened to traffic in 1964. Hilly Staten Island (or Richmond County) is the state's southernmost county, one-tenth as densely populated as Manhattan. That's after it grew 24% between 1990 and 2013, one of the largest increases in New York state. Its rate of home ownership, 70%, is double that of New York City as a whole.

Ethnically, Staten Island has the highest percentage of residents of Italian ancestry in the nation. The signs on coffee shops read *Caffe* and on delicatessens, *Salumeria*. The Staten Island Ferry docks at St. George, where the Staten Island Yankees, nicknamed the "Baby Bombers," were the first minor league baseball team in New York City. The north and south shores that spread out from there are notable for their pleasant Victorian homes, while the island's west shore is industrial marshland, with plans for the development of a 2,200-acre park—more than twice as large as Central Park—on top of the now-closed Fresh Kills dump. More than 700 acres have reopened as green space, and plans are underway for a solar-energy station. Staten Island's interior consists of scrubland that has rapidly become blocks of suburbia for New Yorkers who like a small-town ambience. In April 2015, a development broke ground in St. George on Empire Outlets, a $350 million mall and entertainment complex. Population growth, plus a shortage of mass transit, has brought significant traffic congestion to the island, which depends on cars more than the other boroughs.

Culturally, Staten Islanders are more conservative than people from the other boroughs, particularly the Manhattanites who live a 20-minute ferry ride away. Not many people here read *The New York Times*; the local paper is the *Staten Island Advance*. Fed up with the city's high income taxes and social programs, Staten Island residents voted in 1993 for secession, but the legislature never acted to carry out their wish. In that same election, Staten Islanders provided the margin of victory for Republican Mayor Rudolph Giuliani. His agenda of cutting crime and welfare rolls soothed the secessionist fervor. The Giuliani years produced an eco-

2012 Presidential Vote
Barack Obama (D) 110,088   (52%)
Mitt Romney (R).................100,811   (47%)

2008 Presidential Vote
John McCain (R).................118,112   (51%)
Barack Obama (D) 112,044   (48%)

Cook Partisan Voting Index: R+2

nomic boom, with a new ferry terminal, additional shops, and hundreds of new houses near cleaned-up beaches. The Wall Street crisis in 2008 reverberated strongly in this land of commuters, heavily dependent on jobs off the island. The median household income on Staten

Island remains higher than the rest of the city, and was less affected by the recession. The island was battered by Superstorm Sandy, which severely damaged or destroyed countless homes here and resulted in 23 deaths, the highest number in any New York borough.

The 11th Congressional District of New York is made up of Staten Island plus Brooklyn neighborhoods with similar demographics. These include heavily Catholic and Italian Bay Ridge, Dyker Heights and part of Bensonhurst, middle-class enclaves with large single-family brownstones that are nowhere near a subway stop and thus impervious to the gentrification spreading across Brooklyn. The entertainment industry has found some memorable characters in these neighborhoods: The Three Stooges (Moe, Curly and Shemp) grew up in Bensonhurst, which also was the home to the fictional Ralph Kramden of *The Honeymooners*. John Travolta danced to fame in the film *Saturday Night Fever* on the streets of Bensonhurst and Bay Ridge.

There are growing numbers of Muslims in Bay Ridge and an influx of newcomers from West Africa, Mexico, South America, Southeast Asia and Russia in white ethnic neighborhoods near St. George. The northern shore of Staten Island has gained African-American population centers on the corners of the island, with a large Hispanic community in between. But Staten Island overall remains New York's whitest borough, with the fewest immigrants. It was only 12% black and 18% Hispanic in 2013. As a whole, the district is 8% black and 16% Hispanic. John McCain carried the district in 2008, the only urban district he carried that year; Barack Obama narrowly won four years later.

Daniel Donovan (R)

Republican Dan Donovan won a special election in May 2015 to take the seat of Republican Michael Grimm, who resigned before taking his oath for a third term after pleading guilty to tax fraud in December 2014. Donovan was elected easily, despite widespread criticism for his decision as Staten Island prosecutor not to bring charges against police officers in the choke-hold death of Eric Garner.

A native of Staten Island, Donovan got a bachelor's degree in criminal justice from St. John's University and a law degree from Fordham University. With his working-class roots, he likes to note that he paid his way through those schools with various jobs. He began his career as a prosecutor with eight years in the office of the Manhattan D.A., where he handled major narcotics cases. He then moved to the political world as chief of staff to Staten Island President (and former Rep.) Guy Molinari. In 2002, he became deputy borough president.

Donovan was elected Richmond County District Attorney in November 2003, becoming the first Republican elected district attorney in New York City in more than 50 years. He was easily re-elected to two additional terms, and became a leader in both state and national associations of district attorneys.

He entered the national spotlight on rocky terms during a national period of controversial deaths of black youths at the hands of the police. Garner, who was notably overweight, had been stopped in July 2014 by police who were suspicious that he was selling cigarettes without a tax. As two officers sought to arrest him, Garner resisted. One of the officers applied a choke-hold for an estimated 15 seconds, a move that was barred by NYPD procedures. Garner gasped, "I can't breathe." As the incident was being filmed by a bystander, Garner fell to the ground where he remained for several minutes until he was taken to a hospital. But he had died prior to arrival. As prosecutor, Donovan investigated the police conduct and made a presentation to a grand jury, but decided not to bring charges.

Grimm, a tough-talking Marine combat veteran and undercover FBI agent, had seemed an ideal Republican for the district. Although an underfunded novice when he challenged first-term Democratic Rep. Michael McMahon in 2010, Grimm was one of the many beneficiaries of the Republican wave that year, and won 51%-48%. He got a seat on the Financial Services Committee and worked energetically on local issues. But he soon became the target of newspaper headlines about possible campaign finance violations. With the Justice Department having opened an investigation, he won reelection in 2012, 52%-47%. Ironically, his opponent, Mark Murphy, was the son of former nine-term Staten Island Democratic Rep. John Murphy, who lost reelection in 1980 after he had been indicted in the FBI's Abscam sting; he later was convicted.

In April 2014, Grimm was indicted on charges that he had lied to federal investigators about having hired undocumented immigrants for his Manhattan health-food restaurant, Healthalicioius. Even though the Republican Party largely abandoned him, he decided to seek reelection. Although he had been widely viewed as an underdog, he won 57%-43% over Democratic challenger Domenic Recchia, a former city councilman from Brooklyn. In December, on the eve of his scheduled trial, Grimm pleaded guilty to a single count of tax fraud. Under pressure from House Speaker John Boehner, Grimm agreed to resign and not take his oath for a third term.

In the special election to replace Grimm, Democrats selected Vincent Gentile, a city council member from Brooklyn who had earlier represented Staten Island in the state senate. The Garner case was rarely mentioned by either candidate or their supporters. Donovan cited grand jury secrecy rules and minimized his role in the case. Gentile faced multiple problems, including scant fundraising, a brief campaign, the unpopularity of Democratic Mayor Bill de Blasio and the predominantly Staten Island electorate; he focused chiefly on economic issues. As the nominee, Gentile largely avoided discussion of the Garner case, apparently because it would not be politically helpful in the special election. Democrats, having failed to recruit their top-flight candidates. threw in the towel on a district that they had held four years earlier. Donovan easily won the contest, 59%-40%. Gentile got 60% of the vote in Brooklyn, but it cast only 22% of the total.

In the House, Donovan joined the Foreign Affairs and Homeland Security committees, and reached out to many of his local Democratic colleagues, though some of them had harshly criticized his handling of the Garner case. He initially took a bipartisan approach, defended the Affordable Care Act, and opposed the Trans-Pacific Partnership plan and accompanying legislation. But the Garner controversy had not disappeared, with the Justice Department having opened an investigation into possible civil rights violations. Further complicating the situation, the Democratic Congressional Campaign Committee made Donovan a leading campaign target for 2016.

TWELFTH DISTRICT

Carolyn Maloney (D)

Elected 1992, 11th term; b. Feb. 19, 1946, Greensboro, NC; Greensboro Col., B.A. 1968; Presbyterian; widowed; 2 children.

Elected Office: NY City Cncl., 1982-92.

Professional Career: Community affairs coord., Bd. of Ed. welfare ed. program, 1972-75; Staff, Bd. of Ed. cntr. for career & occupational ed., 1975-76; Sr. program analyst, NY Assembly committee, 1977-79; Legis. aide, NY Assembly & NY Senate, 1979-82.

DC Office: 2308 RHOB, 20515, 202-225-7944; Fax: 202-225-4709; Website: maloney.house.gov.

State Offices: Astoria, 718-932-1804; Brooklyn, 718-349-5972; New York, 212-860-0606.

Committees: *Financial Services:* Capital Markets & Gov't Sponsored Enterprises (RMM); Financial Institutions & Consumer Credit. *Oversight & Gov't Reform:* Gov't Operations.

Group Ratings

	ADA	ACLU	AFL-CIO	LCV	ITI	COC	HAFA	ACU	CFG	FRC
2014	85%	77%	–	91%	80%	46%	15%	8%	13%	0%
2013	80%	C	95%	96%	C	31%	C	13%	12%	C

National Journal Ratings

	2013 LIB	—	2013 CONS
Economic	78%	—	22%
Social	77%	—	23%
Foreign	90%	—	6%
Composite	82%	—	18%

Key Votes of the 113th Congress

1. Sandy storm spending	Y	5. Medical Marijuana	Y	9. Syrian Rebels Training	N		
2. Violence Against Women Act	Y	6. Farm Bill	N	10. Keystone pipeline	N		
3. Guantanamo Bay Detainees	Y	7. Afghanistan Combat	Y	11. Immigration Exec. Action	N		
4. Abortion 20-week ban	N	8. NSA Phone Data Collection	Y	12. Bipartisan budget deal	Y		

Election Results

2014 general	Carolyn Maloney (D).................90,603	(80%)	$1,457,836	$5,323
	Nick Di Iorio (R).......................22,731	(20%)	$83,762	
2014 primary	Carolyn Maloney (D)............unopposed			

Prior winning percentages: 2012 (81%), 2010 (75%), 2008 (80%), 2006 (84%), 2004 (81%), 2002 (75%), 2000 (74%), 1998 (77%), 1996 (72%), 1994 (64%), 1992 (50%)

Population		Race and Ethnicity		Income	
Total:	720,538	White	67.8%	Median income:	$91,628
Urban:	100.0%	Latino	13.9%		(10 of 435)
Suburban:	0.0%	Asian	11.6%	Under $50,000	30.9%
Rural:	0.0%	Black	4.4%	$50,000-$99,999:	22.1%
Land area:	16	Two races	1.9%	$100,000-$199,999:	25.9%
Pop/sq. mi.:	46,131.4	White Ethnic	36.2%	$200,000 or more:	21.1%
Born in state:	42.9%			Poverty Rate	12.5%
		Education			
Age Groups		H.S. grad or less:	17.8%	**Work**	
Under 18:	11.5%	Some college:	13.0%	White collar:	64.6%
18 to 34:	36.2%	College degree, 4 yr.:	38.7%	Blue collar:	30.6%
35 to 64:	37.8%	Post-grad study:	30.4%	Sales and service:	4.8%
Over 64:	14.5%				
		Military		Govt. workers:	7.4%
		Veterans/active duty:	2.6%		

Manhattan's East Side, Queens Astoria

The Upper East Side of Manhattan is home to people with more accumulated wealth than anywhere else in the world. Its western border was established at Fifth Avenue in 1857, when work began on Central Park (completed in 1873). During the 1880s, the avenues—Fifth, Madison, Park,

Voter Turnout	
2013 Total Citizen 18+	548,398
2014 House Turnout	113,429
2014 Turnout as % CVAP	20.7%
2012 Turnout as % CVAP	50.5%

Lexington, Third, Second, First—were paved, and rich New Yorkers as well as many who had made their money elsewhere, including Pittsburgh steel baron Andrew Carnegie, built mansions on Fifth Avenue. With its elevated train line, Third Avenue was lined with walk-ups for working-class commuters, while the side streets off Fifth Avenue were filled with massive brownstones shielded from the industrial haze along the East River.

The Upper East Side began taking on its present character in 1913, when Grand Central Terminal opened and the New York Central rail line was buried under Park Avenue. What had been a filthy railroad cut became a broad boulevard lined with grand apartment buildings. The federal income tax, passed the same year, had the unintended consequence of encouraging New York's rich to dispense with grand mansions and live, quietly and out of sight, in apartment buildings where doormen protected their privacy. The Upper East Side remains a world apart from ordinary folks. Even during the recession, sales of large, multi-million-dollar apartments in the city swelled in 2009. The neighborhood is overwhelmingly white as well as expensive, with only a 2.7% non-Hispanic black population in 2010.

As the mid-19th century New York diarists Philip Hone and George Templeton Strong noted, on an island as compact as Manhattan, it takes only a generation or so before buildings are torn down and rebuilt. Even today, New York is transformed by gleaming postmodern skyscrapers, although its most enduring landmarks are products of the first half of the 20th century: the Flatiron Building, built in 1902; Grand Central, in 1913; the Chrysler Building, in the 1920s; and the Empire State Building and Rockefeller Center, in the 1930s. The United Nations headquarters, the world's first glass-fronted skyscraper, went up after World War II. In January 2015, the master plan for renovation of UN facilities was virtually completed, with the complex made largely blast-proof. This area was the site of the first public housing project in America: The First Houses were built in lower Manhattan in 1935 during the administration of Mayor Fiorello LaGuardia.

The 12th Congressional District of New York includes the Upper East Side. It begins at East 96th Street, the historic dividing line between Manhattan's wealthiest and poorest neighborhoods, and runs through Murray Hill and Gramercy Park all the way to Houston Street, with a few salients protruding further south. It takes in Alphabet City, with its unique lettered avenue names, almost all of the East Village, with its pricey lofts and busy nightlife, and much of the Lower East Side. Also in the district is a slice of the Bowery, including the former site of the iconic CBGB club, which helped birth New Wave and punk rock. Midtown Manhattan's skyscrapers and the Garment District are also here, along with Times Square and the Theatre District. Roosevelt Island, once dubbed Welfare Island and home to massive hospital and prison complexes, was renamed and transformed in the 1970s into an ethnically diverse residential neighborhood. More than 80% of the district resides in Manhattan.

Across the East River in Queens, the 12th encompasses Long Island City and vibrant, historically Greek Astoria, now with many Asians, Latinos and Arabs. In Brooklyn, the district takes in much of trendy Williamsburg, gritty East Williamsburg, and working-class yet gentrifying Greenpoint. The district's cultural landmarks are among the world's finest: the Museum of Modern Art, the Guggenheim, the Whitney Museum of American Art, and the Frick Collection.

The district historically has been dominated by its affluent and highly educated voters, leaders in securities, publishing, advertising, entertainment, broadcasting

2012 Presidential Vote		
Barack Obama (D)	205,662	(77%)
Mitt Romney (R)	57,489	(22%)
2008 Presidential Vote		
Barack Obama (D)	243,665	(80%)
John McCain (R)	57,332	(19%)
Cook Partisan Voting Index:	D+27	

and communications. Historically, they mistrusted the city's usually Democratic immigrant masses. But as the Republican Party increasingly took on cultural conservatism and its Southern accents, the attitude of the Manhattan elite shifted from its "silk stocking" liberal Republican to leftish Democratic, and the Upper East Side's 10021 zip code was the nation's top zip code for Democratic campaign contributions from 2004 to 2010. (In 2012, it favored former venture capitalist Mitt Romney.) The Upper East Side voted heavily for Democrat Barack Obama twice.

Carolyn Maloney (D)

Democrat Carolyn Maloney, first elected in 1992, is known for her forceful efforts on behalf of women and consumers and has been a prolific legislator on Capitol Hill.

Born and educated in North Carolina, she visited New York at the age of 22, loved it, and "just stayed." She taught adult-education classes in East Harlem and, from 1977 to 1982, was an influential legislative staffer in Albany. She was elected to the New York City Council in 1982. Redistricting in 1992 made the Silk Stocking district more Democratic, and Maloney ran against incumbent Bill Green, an independent Republican who shared Manhattan's cultural liberalism. But he was poorly positioned to appeal to voters in the outer-borough neighborhoods that had been added to the district, who preferred Republicans to be conservative on cultural issues but liberal on economics. Maloney lost the Manhattan part of the district 50%-44% but carried Queens heavily, winning 50%-48% overall.

Maloney has a mostly liberal voting record. She is a senior member of the Financial Services Committee, where she has been a leading voice on banking issues. She had a hand in crafting the Dodd-Frank Wall Street overhaul in 2010, working with Democratic Sen. Richard Durbin of Illinois to achieve a compromise on interchange fees charged on consumers' debit cards. The fees had been an area of contention between merchants worried about their high rates and the financial industry's worries that lower fees would not cover their costs. She also worked to enact her bill to promote more transparent practices by credit card companies and to restrict abusive lending practices. She called the 2009 law "a much-needed correction to a market that is out of balance." Annoyed by Republican efforts to block the confirmation of a Consumer Financial Protection Bureau director, as established in

Dodd-Frank, she unsuccessfully proposed an amendment in July 2011 to have the Treasury secretary assume the CFPB director's duties if a nominee weren't confirmed.

Even though she has many constituents in banking, Maloney had tough rhetoric for bankers who took millions of dollars in bonuses after their firms received federal bailout money in 2008. But she opposed in early 2010 a proposed .25% tax on stock transactions above $100,000. In earlier years, she worked to keep banks from controlling other businesses, sought more oversight of the Federal Reserve, and added privacy provisions to financial modernization bills. She helped to craft reforms tightening rules for foreign investment.

A leader of the Women's Caucus, Maloney drew national attention in February 2012 for walking out of an Oversight and Government Reform Committee hearing on contraception and religious protection after pointing out its all-male witness list. "What I want to know is, where are the women?" she asked. She also blasted GOP efforts to bar funding for Planned Parenthood and prenatal care. When conservatives that year removed expanded protections for lesbians and Native Americans in a reauthorization of the Violence Against Women Act, Maloney called it "as chilling and callous as anything I have seen come before this Congress in modern times." Earlier, she demanded that the Food and Drug Administration permit over-the-counter sales of morning-after birth-control pills, and she opposed separating men and women in basic training in the military. With Republican Rep. Marsha Blackburn of Tennessee, she filed a proposal for a commission to study a national women's museum in Washington; the House approved the bill in May 2014.

In 2007, with Sen. Edward Kennedy of Massachusetts, Maloney initially introduced the Women's Equality Amendment, a latter-day version of the Equal Rights Amendment, which had fallen three states short of constitutional ratification in the 1970s. The House passed her 2008 bill to give eight weeks of paid leave to federal employees for the birth or adoption of a child. Also that year, she published a book called, *Rumors of Our Progress Have Been Greatly Exaggerated: Why Women's Lives Aren't Getting Any Easier—And How We Can Make Real Progress for Ourselves and Our Daughters.*

With part of her district in Lower Manhattan and close to Ground Zero, Maloney was heavily involved in the government response to the September 11 attacks. She was outspoken in urging President George W. Bush to quickly send New York the $20 billion that Congress approved for cleanup and recovery. But her proposal to give a $1,000 tax credit to visitors to the city went nowhere. In 2010, she and several other New York members steered into law a long-delayed measure to compensate September 11 first responders with health problems. "It is so fair, it is so right, it should have passed nine years ago," she said. When gun violence became a prominent topic following the Newtown Connecticut school massacre, she introduced a bipartisan bill to make firearms trafficking a federal crime and to impose stronger penalties for straw purchasers buying guns for convicted felons.

Maloney made a bid for the top Democratic slot on Oversight and Government Reform after Democrats lost the House majority in 2010. The departing chairman, New York's Edolphus Towns, bowed out of the race and threw his support to Maloney, who campaigned vigorously. But she lost to the less senior Elijah Cummings of Maryland on a vote of 33-18 in the Democratic Steering Committee and 119-61 in the Democratic Caucus. Cummings reportedly had the pivotal backing of Minority Leader Nancy Pelosi. In 2015, she was ranking Democrat on the Joint Economic Committee and the Financial Services Subcommittee on Capital Markets and Government Sponsored Enterprises.

Maloney has a firm lock on the district. She was bitterly disappointed when Democratic Gov. David Paterson appointed the less-seasoned Rep. Kirsten Gillibrand to the Senate seat vacated by Hillary Clinton in 2009. Maloney publicly questioned Gillibrand's conservative stance on issues such as gun control and curbing illegal immigration, and she began raising money for a primary challenge in 2010. Gillibrand quickly moved left in the Senate, and in August 2009 Maloney heeded the calls of Obama and senior New York Democrats to give her a clear path to the nomination. Maloney endured a wrenching personal setback the next month, when her husband, Clifton, died on a mountain-climbing expedition in the Himalayas.

As the number-two Democrat on each of her House committees, she is positioned to gain additional influence.

THIRTEENTH DISTRICT

Charles Rangel (D)

Elected 1970, 23rd term; b. June 11, 1930, New York; NY U., B.S. 1957, St. John's U., LL.B. 1960; Catholic; married (Alma); 2 children.

Military Career: U.S. Army, 1948-52 (Korea).

Elected Office: NY Assembly, 1966-70.

Professional Career: Asst. U.S. atty., S. Dist. of NY, 1959-64; Legal counsel, NYC Housing & Redevel. Bd., Neighborhood Conservation Bureau, 1963-68; Gen. counsel, Natl. Advisory Comm. on Selective Svc., 1966

DC Office: 2354 RHOB, 20515, 202-225-4365; Fax: 202-225-0816; Website: rangel.house.gov.

State Offices: New York, 212-663-3900.

Committees: *Ways & Means:* Oversight; Trade (RMM). *Joint Committee on Taxation.*

Group Ratings

	ADA	ACLU	AFL-CIO	LCV	ITI	COC	HAFA	ACU	CFG	FRC
2014	70%	77%	–	63%	40%	38%	14%	11%	18%	0%
2013	85%	C	95%	96%	C	31%	C	13%	11%	C

National Journal Ratings

	2013 LIB	—	2013 CONS
Economic	83%	—	17%
Social	73%	—	24%
Foreign	69%	—	29%
Composite	76%	—	24%

Key Votes of the 113th Congress

1. Sandy storm spending	Y	5. Medical Marijuana	NV	9. Syrian Rebels Training	N
2. Violence Against Women Act	Y	6. Farm Bill	N	10. Keystone pipeline	N
3. Guantanamo Bay Detainees	Y	7. Afghanistan Combat	NV	11. Immigration Exec. Action	N
4. Abortion 20-week ban	N	8. NSA Phone Data Collection	Y	12. Bipartisan budget deal	Y

Election Results

2014 general	Charles Rangel (D) 68,396	(87%)	$1,515,861	$8,777
	Daniel Vila Rivera (G) 9,806	(13%)	$2,302	
2014 primary	Charles Rangel (D) 23,799	(48%)		
	Adriano Espaillat (D) 21,477	(43%)		
	Michael A. Walrond Jr. (D) 3,954	(8%)		

Prior winning percentages: 2012 (91%), 2010 (80%), 2008 (89%), 2006 (94%), 2004 (91%), 2002 (88%), 2000 (92%), 1998 (93%), 1996 (91%), 1994 (97%), 1992 (95%), 1990 (97%), 1988 (97%), 1986 (96%), 1984 (97%), 1982 (97%), 1980 (96%), 1978 (96%), 1976 (97%), 1974 (97%), 1972 (96%), 1970 (87%)

Population		Race and Ethnicity		Income	
Total:	765,391	Latino	52.5%	Median income:	$33,607
Urban:	100.0%	Black	27.1%		*(425 of 435)*
Suburban:	0.0%	White	13.2%	Under $50,000	63.5%
Rural:	0.0%	Asian	4.7%	$50,000-$99,999:	23.4%
Land area:	12	Two races	1.7%	$100,000-$199,999:	10.5%
Pop/sq. mi.:	66,234.8	White Ethnic	8.1%	$200,000 or more:	2.6%
Born in state:	47.2%			Poverty Rate	30.8%
		Education			
Age Groups		H.S. grad or less:	50.5%	**Work**	
Under 18:	21.2%	Some college:	19.8%	White collar:	33.7%
18 to 34:	30.0%	College degree, 4 yr.:	18.2%	Blue collar:	52.3%
35 to 64:	37.4%	Post-grad study:	11.5%	Sales and service:	13.9%
Over 64:	11.4%				
		Military		Govt. workers:	11.8%
		Veterans/active duty:	2.3%		

Upper Manhattan: Harlem, Washington Heights

Harlem, for many years America's most famous black ghetto, is rebounding from decades of grim times. In the late 19th century, Harlem was a commuter neighborhood, first for Germans and then for Jews and Italians. After the turn of the century, real estate speculators began constructing blocks

Voter Turnout	
2013 Total Citizen 18+	473,675
2014 House Turnout	78,353
2014 Turnout as % CVAP	16.5%
2012 Turnout as % CVAP	50.7%

of impressive brownstones, hoping to capitalize on the impending arrival of the subway. But overbuilding led to high vacancy rates, and some landlords agreed to rent to African Americans, as long as they were willing to pay a premium. After generations of being shunted from one neighborhood to the next as the city developed, black residents were willing, and the neighborhood soon turned into the locus of New York City's African-American community. Harlem expanded from its nucleus around Lenox Avenue and 125th Street, while the neighborhood to the east later known as Spanish Harlem grew outward from 116th Street and Pleasant Avenue. Many great black Americans—W. E. B. DuBois, Thurgood Marshall, Ralph Ellison, Joe Louis—lived in Harlem's Sugar Hill.

For a long moment in history, Harlem was a center of writers, professionals and entertainers. The rosters of the Apollo Theater on 125th Street in the 1920s and 1930s were filled with the names of great artists. Then, the *WPA Guide* described Harlem as "the spiritual capital of Black America." But starting with a riot in the summer of 1964, Harlem endured decades of deterioration. Hundreds of brownstones were abandoned or pulled down. As successful black families moved out—to Springfield Gardens in Queens, or Williamsbridge in the Bronx, or to the Westchester or New Jersey suburbs—Harlem's population shifted increasingly toward welfare dependency and criminal gangs, and its population declined by a third between 1970 and 1990.

In the 1990s, Harlem began to recover. The federal government provided $300 million in investment capital, and the huge drop in crime under Republican Mayor Rudolph Giuliani made Harlem real estate valuable again. Brownstones were renovated, vacant city buildings were sold off, neighborhood schools were upgraded, and arts spaces opened. Harlem was made an enterprise zone, with favorable federal and state tax treatment. Younger African Americans began returning, while visitors from overseas, especially Japan and Europe, flocked to the area for historical tours, prompting a boomlet in niche hotels and guest houses. The façade of the Apollo Theater has been restored, a new Harlem pier has been constructed, and supermarkets and chain stores have opened. In 2001, former President Bill Clinton opened his post presidential office at 55 West 125th Street in Harlem.

Politically, Harlem has been heavily Democratic since the 1930s, when black voters switched from the Republican Party of Abraham Lincoln to the Democratic Party of Franklin Roosevelt. Harlem got its own congressional district in 1944 and elected Adam Clayton Powell Jr., minister at the Abyssinian Baptist Church and a brilliant orator. He was chairman of the Education and Labor Committee when it crafted many of the Great Society programs in 1965.

Today, the 13th Congressional District of New York includes not just Harlem but all of Upper Manhattan, south to 100th Street on the west side and 96th Street on the east side. On the west side, the district includes portions of the white, liberal Upper West Side. On the east side, it's Harlem. Spanish Harlem, just to the north, was once Italian (it was Fiorello LaGuardia's political base), later became Puerto Rican, and today is dominated by Mexicans and Dominicans along with some gentrifying whites. The district takes in Washington Heights and

2012 Presidential Vote		
Barack Obama (D)	219,319	(95%)
Mitt Romney (R)	10,558	(5%)
2008 Presidential Vote		
Barack Obama (D)	225,845	(93%)
John McCain (R)	14,850	(6%)
Cook Partisan Voting Index:	D+42	

Inwood, both heavily Latino and the center of Dominican life in New York. Across the Harlem River in the Bronx, the district includes Marble Hill and heavily Hispanic Kingsbridge.

Overall, the district is 27% black and 53% Hispanic, figures that testify to decades of black flight from Harlem and the continuing inflow of immigrants from the Western Hemisphere, and raise questions about the future identity of Harlem and the 13th. This is overwhelmingly Democratic territory. Barack Obama had his second-best showing in the nation in the district in 2012 when he got 95% of the vote. It trailed only the adjacent 15th District in New York.

Charles Rangel (D)

Democrat Charles Rangel, first elected in 1970, once wielded power as the gravel-voiced, highly quotable chairman of the tax-writing Ways and Means Committee. He was forced to step aside in March 2010, and later that year was censured by the House for violations of congressional ethics rules, making Rangel the 23rd House member in history to receive the harshest punishment short of expulsion. As he prepared for his retirement in 2016, he became more active on several issues though he did not regain the top Ways and Means post.

Rangel grew up in Harlem and served in the Army in Korea, where he rescued 40 men from behind the lines in Kunu-ri and was awarded the Bronze Star. He graduated from New York University and St. John's University law school, served as legal counsel in several government agencies, and was elected to the New York Assembly in 1966. He was part of a group of young black politicians—among them Basil Paterson, Carl McCall and Percy Sutton—who for many years dominated Harlem and greatly influenced New York politics. In 1970, Rangel challenged Adam Clayton Powell Jr. in the Democratic primary and narrowly won. Remarkably, these two iconic and often controversial figures will have been the district's only representatives for 72 years. Like most Harlem politicians, Rangel has long argued that government aid and racial preferences are needed to solve Harlem's problems.

In the House, Rangel's fall from grace as chairman of the chamber's most powerful committee was striking given his history as a savvy legislator. When he was on his game, Rangel displayed an effective combination of political shrewdness and personal charm, even allowing for his occasional rhetorical extravagance. When a bipartisan majority voted to end racial preferences in broadcasting in 1995, Rangel lashed out in a letter to Ways and Means Republican Chairman Bill Archer of Texas, saying, "Just like under Hitler, people say they don't mean to blame any particular individuals and groups, but in the U.S. those groups always turn out to be minorities and immigrants." Archer refused to speak to Rangel, then the ranking member of the committee, except in public forums. During the 1990s, Rangel defended President Bill Clinton against impeachment with great vigor, but he did not always get along with Clinton. He resented it when his administration negotiated directly with Republicans, leaving him and other congressional Democrats out of the loop.

Republican Bill Thomas of California succeeded Archer as chairman. With a notoriously acerbic tongue, Thomas made few if any moves toward a legislative partnership with Rangel, and the committee was never able to work in a bipartisan way. Rangel protested when Thomas excluded him from the House-Senate conference committee on the 2003 Medicare prescription-drug bill.

He became Ways and Means chairman in 2007 when Democrats took the House majority for the first time in 12 years. Aside from early successes on trade and increasing the minimum wage, his first two years as chairman were stymied by partisan deadlock as his proposals came under veto threat from President George W. Bush. With Democrat Barack Obama as president in 2009, Rangel moved quickly to enact the long-discussed children's health insurance expansion, and he helped craft $348 billion in tax cuts in the administration's $787 billion economic stimulus bill. He joined other senior House Democrats in extended discussions on health reform. Somewhat less expected was his assertive role on climate change legislation. Environmental legislation traditionally has been under the control of the Energy and Commerce Committee, but Rangel held numerous hearings on a proposed carbon tax, though Ways and Means ultimately deferred on most of the legislative details.

Then, Rangel's influence was diminished by several *New York Times* stories that raised questions about four rent-controlled apartments that Rangel maintained in Harlem and his failure to report rental income from a villa in the Dominican Republic. Perhaps most damaging, *The Times* reported that Maurice Greenberg, one of the biggest shareholders in financially troubled American International Group, in 2007 gave $5 million to a public policy school named for Rangel, and that Rangel in early 2008 backed a provision in a tax bill that saved AIG several million dollars a year. Rangel steadfastly denied wrongdoing; in September 2008, he requested a review by the House Ethics Committee.

While the committee opened an investigation into those allegations, another issue cropped up: corporate-sponsored trips Rangel took to Caribbean islands in 2007 and 2008. The panel eventually concluded that Rangel's staff knew that corporations were helping to finance the trips but failed to reveal that fact when they asked the committee to pre-approve them. Rangel was instructed to reimburse the sponsors for the costs of his travel. Several Democrats were prepared to vote in favor of a Republican resolution seeking to remove Rangel as chairman, but Rangel acted first, saying he wanted to save his fellow Democrats from "having to defend me during their elections" in November. He announced in March 2010 he would take a leave of absence as chairman.

Concluding its nearly two-year investigation, the Ethics Committee in July 2010 announced 13 allegations against Rangel. They included his acceptance of the rent-stabilized apartments from a Manhattan developer, failure to pay taxes on rental income from the Dominican villa, and receipt of contributions for his foundations from companies seeking legislative favors. Rangel acknowledged bookkeeping mistakes and said he failed to properly oversee his finances, but argued that he did nothing to personally benefit or enrich himself. Still, in November, the committee ruled there was sufficient evidence to support the allegations. Rangel indignantly walked out of the proceedings, claiming that he could no longer afford legal representation and that it was unfair to continue. Two days later, the panel voted 9-1 in favor of censure, a form of punishment in which a member is shamed by a public recitation of rules violations on the floor of the House.

With his friends and allies, Rangel lobbied for a milder form of punishment called a reprimand. But the House voted 333-79 for censure. Rangel stood in the well of the House, his hands clasped behind him, while Democratic Speaker Nancy Pelosi read a resolution censuring him for bringing discredit to the House. The last time a censure had occurred was 1983, when Reps. Daniel Crane of Illinois, a Republican, and Democrat Gerry Studds of Massachusetts were censured for carrying on sexual relationships with congressional pages. After his rebuke, Rangel addressed the chamber briefly, saying, "I know in my heart I am not going to be judged by this Congress. I'll be judged by my life in its entirety."

After his censure, Rangel stayed on Ways and Means, and in 2013 took over the ranking member slot on its Trade Subcommittee. But he drew more attention for his frequent jabs at Republicans. He told MSNBC that month that "some of the Southern areas have cultures that we have to overcome" in passing tighter gun restrictions, a statement that angered GOP colleagues from the region.

Rangel has opposed some of the international free trade agreements of recent years but has proven open to compromise on others. He supported the 2011 pacts with Panama and South Korea, but not Colombia, citing its lack of worker protections. In 2000, Rangel worked hard for a bill to cut tariffs on apparel and other imports from sub-Saharan Africa, despite opposition from labor unions, textile interests and fellow members of the Congressional Black Caucus. During 2004, Rangel did not take a position on the Dominican Republic-Central America Free Trade Agreement, though many Democrats opposed the agreement. There are many Dominican and Central American immigrants in New York. After an earthquake devastated an already destitute Haiti in January 2010, Rangel sponsored a trade bill allowing the country to export more apparel to the United States. The bill was signed into law by Obama in May 2010. In 2015, he opposed procedural protections in Congress for the Trans-Pacific Partnership that Obama was preparing to sign, but his role was relatively modest.

One of Rangel's top priorities was a permanent change in the alternative minimum tax to prevent it from ensnaring middle-class taxpayers. After 19 modifications since 1969, the tax was indexed to inflation as part of the New Year's Day 2013 budget compromise aimed at averting the so-called "fiscal cliff." Over the years, he helped write numerous bills to help high-poverty areas like Harlem, including the federal empowerment zone law, the low-income housing tax credit, and increases in the earned income tax credit.

On foreign policy, Rangel has long advocated eliminating sanctions on trade with Cuba. In December 2014, he lauded Obama for his moves to recognize Cuba and encourage additional diplomatic and commercial ties. He favors allowing Haitian and Dominican immigrants into the United States on the same basis as refugees from Cuba. Rangel voted against the Iraq war resolution in 2002 and the following year called for the resignation of Defense

Secretary Donald Rumsfeld. Late in 2002, he advocated a revival of the military draft, contending that "a disproportionate number of the poor and members of minority groups make up the enlisted ranks of the military, while the most privileged Americans are underrepresented or absent." A year later, he filed a bill to require some form of national service, military or civilian, from Americans ages 18 to 26, and found 13 cosponsors. When House Republican leaders brought it to a vote in October 2004, he called it a "political maneuver to kill rumors"—utterly unfounded—"of the president's intention to reinstate the draft after the November election" and voted against it, saying it had had no committee hearings. It was voted down 402-2.

Rangel has remained a major player in New York's city and state politics. In the 2008 presidential contest, Rangel was an early and vocal supporter of home-state Sen. Hillary Clinton in her pitched battle with Obama for the Democratic nomination. Despite pressure from many of his own constituents, he stuck with Clinton until she withdrew from the race.

Until recently, Rangel has been easily reelected every two years. In 1994, he faced primary opposition from the grandson of his predecessor, New York City Councilman Adam Clayton Powell IV. Rangel spent $1.4 million and won 61%-33%. When he was weakened in 2010 by the ethics case, Powell challenged Rangel again in the Democratic primary, along with four other opponents. As a referendum on Rangel's continued fitness for office, the results weren't even close. He won the September primary with 51% of the vote to Powell's 23%.

In 2012, when he ran in a redrawn 13th District with a larger Hispanic population, the primary challenge to Rangel became based more on local demographics than on ethics issues in Washington. His closest competitor was New York State Sen. Adriano Espaillat, who hoped to become the first Dominican-American member of Congress. Espaillat argued that Rangel had overstayed his welcome in Congress, but many of Rangel's surrogates maintained that the incumbent's seniority and experience were valuable to the district. Rangel spent $1.6 million, while former Bill Clinton aide Clyde Williams spent $418,000 and Espaillat spent $328,000. Rangel won by 1,086 votes, 44.5% to 42% for Espaillat and 10% for Williams. As usual, he took his general election in a breeze, with 91% of the vote.

In 2014, Rangel appeared to be in greater jeopardy in his primary rematch after Espaillat had become more familiar to voters and was more competitive financially as he spent $716,000 for the campaign to $1.5 million for Rangel. But the outcome yielded little change in two years. In the four-candidate primary, Rangel won the contest 48%-43%. Espaillat got 51% of the vote in the Bronx, but that borough cast only 14% of the vote.

Even before the 2014 election, Rangel informally said that he was seeking his final term. In early 2015, he offered some praise for Powell, but did not commit to supporting him. He made clear that he would not endorse Espaillat. Also running was influential state Assemblyman Keith Wright, a long-time Rangel protégé.

His departure from the House will mark the end of an era, in many ways. With Rep. John Conyers of Michigan, who was first elected in 1964, Rangel is the only other congressional Democrat who served during the Watergate scandal. The remaining Republican who served at that time is Rep. Don Young of Alaska.

FOURTEENTH DISTRICT

Joseph Crowley (D)

Elected 1998, 9th term; b. March 16, 1962, New York; C.U.N.Y. Queens Col., B.A. 1985; Catholic; married (Kasey); 3 children.

Elected Office: NY Assembly, 1986-98.

DC Office: 1436 LHOB, 20515, 202-225-3965; Fax: 202-225-1909; Website: crowley.house.gov.

State Offices: Bronx, 718-931-1400; Queens, 718-779-1400.

Committees: *Ways & Means:* Human Resources; Oversight.

Group Ratings

	ADA	ACLU	AFL-CIO	LCV	ITI	COC	HAFA	ACU	CFG	FRC
2014	80%	83%	–	91%	60%	54%	10%	4%	7%	0%
2013	95%	C	90%	96%	C	31%	C	4%	12%	C

National Journal Ratings

	2013 LIB	—	2013 CONS
Economic	71%	—	28%
Social	77%	—	21%
Foreign	81%	—	18%
Composite	77%	—	23%

Key Votes of the 113th Congress

1. Sandy storm spending	Y	5. Medical Marijuana	Y
2. Violence Against Women Act	Y	6. Farm Bill	N
3. Guantanamo Bay Detainees	Y	7. Afghanistan Combat	Y
4. Abortion 20-week ban	N	8. NSA Phone Data Collection	Y

9. Syrian Rebels Training	Y
10. Keystone pipeline	N
11. Immigration Exec. Action	N
12. Bipartisan budget deal	Y

Election Results

2014 general	Joseph Crowley (D)	50,352	(88%)	$2,668,960	$3,092
	Elizabeth Perri (C)	6,735	(12%)		
2014 primary	Joseph Crowley (D)	unopposed			

Prior winning percentages: 2012 (83%), 2010 (81%), 2008 (85%), 2006 (84%), 2004 (81%), 2002 (73%), 2000 (72%), 1998 (69%)

Population		Race and Ethnicity		Income	
Total:	727,544	Latino	46.9%	Median income:	$50,804
Urban:	100.0%	White	25.0%		(226 of 435)
Suburban:	0.0%	Asian	16.3%	Under $50,000	49.3%
Rural:	0.0%	Black	10.2%	$50,000-$99,999:	30.5%
Land area:	30	Two races	1.2%	$100,000-$199,999:	16.6%
Pop/sq. mi.:	24,368.0	White Ethnic	14.9%	$200,000 or more:	3.5%
Born in state:	43.3%			Poverty Rate	18.7%
		Education			
Age Groups		H.S. grad or less:	52.9%	**Work**	
Under 18:	20.3%	Some college:	21.8%	White collar:	27.7%
18 to 34:	28.4%	College degree, 4 yr.:	16.3%	Blue collar:	50.9%
35 to 64:	39.0%	Post-grad study:	9.1%	Sales and service:	21.4%
Over 64:	12.3%				
		Military		Govt. workers:	11.5%
		Veterans/active duty:	2.4%		

Eastern Bronx, Northern Queens

Like Brooklyn, the Bronx derives its name from its original European settlements. In this instance, the name comes from the surname of Jonas Bronck, a Swede who emigrated to the New World, started a farm, and once wrote that his new homeland was "a veritable paradise and needs but the industrious

Voter Turnout	
2013 Total Citizen 18+	401,228
2014 House Turnout	57,204
2014 Turnout as % CVAP	14.3%
2012 Turnout as % CVAP	42.1%

hand of man to make it the finest and most beautiful region in the world." His name was given to a nearby river, then to a borough, and eventually to a county. (The Bronx wasn't made a county until 1914.) Even after New York annexed the area that is today the Bronx, the region saw little growth in the late 1800s.

That changed in 1910, when the subways first started connecting these neighborhoods with job sites in Manhattan. The Bronx was rapidly transformed by hundreds of thousands of immigrants flooding to the open spaces northeast of the Harlem River. They established neighborhoods called East Bronx, Morris Park, Schuylerville, and Throgs Neck. Today, these neighborhoods are filling with Latinos, many from Puerto Rico, but many also from the Dominican Republic and other Caribbean and Latin American countries.

Out past Eastchester Bay is City Island, a Cape Cod-like resort area with boat makers and plenty of seafood restaurants that still looks like it did half a century ago. Across the bridges in Queens is College Point, a middle class neighborhood. Further south and west are Jackson Heights, home to Little India and a sizable Latino community; East Elmhurst, where Attorney General Eric Holder grew up; and Woodside, a long-settled enclave with recent arrivals from Central and South America and Asia. Corona was once predominantly Italian and African American (Louis Armstrong, Duke Ellington, and Malcolm X lived here), but today, it is home to many Dominican and Ecuadorian immigrants and also many Asians. Also in northern Queens is Ditmars, increasingly popular with professionals, as well as Steinway, where the plant that makes pianos for North and South American distribution is still located. Prominent locales include the Bronx Zoo and New York Botanical Garden in the Bronx, and LaGuardia Airport and the New York Mets home at Citi Field in Queens.

These Bronx and Queens neighborhoods make up the 14th Congressional District of New York. The district is a polyglot; it is 10% black, 47% Hispanic, and 16% Asian. About 60% of the voters reside in Queens. There was a time, not so long ago, that Republicans were competitive here; George H.W. Bush twice held his Democratic opponent to under 60% of the vote in an earlier iteration of this

2012 Presidential Vote		
Barack Obama (D) 136,783	(81%)
Mitt Romney (R)...................30,978	(18%)
2008 Presidential Vote		
Barack Obama (D) 135,268	(76%)
John McCain (R)...................41,296	(23%)
Cook Partisan Voting Index: D+26		

district. But demographic changes and the swing of Northern white urban voters to the Democrats curtailed GOP expansion, and Barack Obama twice won the district with more than three-fourths of the vote.

Joseph Crowley (D)

Joseph Crowley, an ambitious and garrulous Democrat first elected in 1998, fulfilled a long-held goal to enter his party's leadership ranks in 2012 by becoming Democratic Caucus vice chairman. Once a moderate who chaired the centrist New Democrat Coalition, he has moved leftward in recent years and become an energetic fundraiser. He is a likely contender when the departure of senior Democratic leaders opens positions to a new generation.

Crowley grew up in Woodside, where his family was involved in politics. His uncle, Walter Crowley, was elected to the New York City Council in 1984. When he died in 1985, Joseph Crowley wanted to succeed him, at age 23. But Tom Manton, the boss of the efficient Queens County Democratic Party, chose his chief of staff instead. (Walter's daughter and Joseph Crowley's cousin, Elizabeth, now has a council seat. She lost a congressional bid in the 6th District in 2012.) The following year, Assemblyman Ralph Goldstein from Elmhurst died. Fresh from Queens College, Crowley ran and won, with support from Manton. Crowley was interested in Irish affairs and sponsored the law that requires public school students to be taught about the Irish potato famine. He played guitar and sang tenor with the Budget Blues Boys, a group of assemblymen who performed on cold Albany nights. (He still loves to sing, and once did a version of Bruce Springsteen's "Pink Cadillac" at a USO concert with Springsteen's guitarist, Nils Lofgren.) When political boss Manton decided it was time to transfer his seat in Congress, Crowley cooperated.

In 1998, Manton was the 7th District incumbent. He filed for reelection by the July 16 deadline. Then at 11 a.m. on July 21, he convened a meeting of Queens Democratic committeemen, announced that he was retiring, and got them to vote for Crowley as the Democratic nominee. Manton argued that Crowley, at 36, was in a position to accumulate seniority and power in Washington. Other potential candidates were not notified beforehand and were naturally miffed, but resigned to reality. Crowley said, "What you're hearing is not so much about the process, but sour grapes. What happened here is simply that I was offered an ice cream cone, and I took it." His Republican opponent had no money and no chance. Crowley won in November, 69%-26%.

Once elected, Crowley voted as a centrist Democrat. He was the freshman Democrats' class president that year. Over time, he changed his position from opposing abortion rights to favoring them, a stance in line with the party. Since Republicans reclaimed control of the House, he has become much more of a loyalist. "There needs to be a responsibility from the federal government to help our most vulnerable," he said in May 2012 in criticizing Republican plans to cut the rate of growth for some programs that benefit the poor and elderly.

After the September 11 attacks, Crowley was especially active on homeland security issues. His district lost many firefighters at the collapse of the World Trade Center, including his first cousin, who was a battalion chief. He won passage of an amendment to issue the Public Safety Officers Medal of Valor to the 414 first responders who died that day.

Crowley has worked with Republicans on behalf of business interests to gain approval of bilateral free trade agreements. But he became more of a party regular when he sided with most House Democrats in June 2015 in opposing President Barack Obama's planned Trans-Pacific Partnership. When Republicans called for repeal of the Democrats' 2010 health care overhaul, Crowley organized an effort asking GOP lawmakers who backed repeal to forgo their taxpayer-subsidized health insurance as a matter of principle.

His eventual success in winning a leadership post compensated for two earlier failures. In 2005, he sought the chairmanship of the Democratic Congressional Campaign Committee and highlighted his fundraising connections to Wall Street. But as an ally of Minority Whip Steny Hoyer of Maryland at the time, he was on the wrong side of Minority Leader Nancy Pelosi of California, who was competing with Hoyer to move up the leadership ladder. The DCCC appointment went to Rep. Rahm Emanuel of Illinois, who led Democrats to victory in the 2006 election.

After the 2006 election, Crowley sought to move up to caucus vice chairman. But Pelosi ally John Larson of Connecticut prevailed, 116-87. Crowley did some bridge-building with Pelosi and her allies, serving as chief deputy whip and DCCC vice chairman for finance. When the caucus vice chairmanship opened again after the 2008 election, he expressed interest but deferred when Pelosi backed Rep. Xavier Becerra of California.

For a time, Crowley held sway as head of the New Democrat Coalition, a group of moderate Democrats. Crowley worked chiefly on economic issues and sought closer cooperation with the leadership than did the more confrontational Blue Dog Coalition. He cited his group's success in reshaping elements of the financial regulatory reform bill that passed the House in 2009 and became law a year later. The New Democrats' efforts earned them admiration from the industry's lobbyists—an issue that the investigative reporting organization *ProPublica* highlighted in a lengthy October 2010 article detailing the New Democrats' tight connections with K Street. Crowley found himself fighting allegations that he was the object of a lobbyists' fundraiser right before a vote on the financial bill. The House Ethics Committee ultimately cleared him and two other lawmakers in 2011. The coalition lost about a third of its members in the November 2010 elections, and with Republicans back in control of the House, its influence waned.

In 2012, Crowley finally became caucus vice chairman after his two rivals, Barbara Lee of California and Jared Polis of Colorado, dropped their bids; Crowley was helped by his new-found alliance with Pelosi. Fundraising has been one of Crowley's chief duties. By August 2014, his political action committee had raised nearly $1 million, according to the Center for Responsive Politics. He concentrated his attention on freshmen lawmakers in tough reelection races.

With his seat on the tax-writing Ways and Means Committee, he served as an attack dog against Republican efforts to investigate the Internal Revenue Service for allegedly targeting conservative groups. He stepped outside a May 2013 hearing to tell MSNBC: "Right now, unfortunately, what you are seeing is a breakdown in the process. It's about partisanship once again and trying to somehow link this to the White House." Around the same time, he said that House Oversight and Government Reform Committee Chairman Darrell Issa of California urged the IRS inspector general to tailor a report on the targeting of conservative organizations to Issa's "personal ideology."

Crowley has focused his recent activities on immigration to bolster his standing with Hispanics and Asians. In September 2013, he was one of eight lawmakers arrested at an immigration rally on the National Mall that urged Congress to permit individuals who were illegally in the United States to apply for citizenship. A year later, he joined freshman Democrat Ami Bera of California in urging the International Basketball Federation to end its restrictions against Sikh basketball players who wear turbans as an article of faith. When protestors on social media objected in January 2015 to the appointment of Democratic Rep. Andre Carson of Indiana to the House Select Intelligence Committee, Crowley urged Democrats to support Carson. "We will never be able to grow as a society if we allow this kind of hatred and division to go unchecked," he said.

His local priorities include aid for city hospitals and getting Brazil, Argentina and Chile added to the visa waiver program in the hopes of boosting Queens' tourism; all three countries have sizable populations in the borough. He has worked on a range of foreign policy issues, from extending economic sanctions against Burma's military regime to criminalizing the removal of girls from the United States for genital mutilation, a practice common across Africa and parts of the Middle East and Asia. He co-chairs the House Ad Hoc Committee on Irish Affairs.

He has not faced serious reelection opposition. After Manton died in July 2006, Crowley became Queens Democratic chairman, a job that has enabled him to weigh in on important local political issues. It also has brought him a few headaches. When Democratic Rep. Anthony Weiner resigned in 2011 over texting sexually explicit photos to a woman, Crowley reportedly was the one who chose his potential Democratic successor, Assemblyman David Weprin. But Weprin ran a poor campaign and lost to a Republican, Bob Turner, causing some New York Democrats to blame Crowley.

With Becerra of California term-limited as caucus chairman after the 2016 election, that would be a logical next step for Crowley to move up the leadership ladder—unless a more senior position becomes available.

FIFTEENTH DISTRICT

José Serrano (D)

Elected March 1990, 13th full term; b. Oct. 24, 1943, Mayaguez, PR; C.U.N.Y. Lehman Col., attended; Catholic; divorced; 5 children.

Military Career: U.S. Army Med. Corps, 1964-66.

Elected Office: Dist. 7 Schl. Bd., 1969-74; NY Assembly, 1975-90.

Professional Career: Banker, 1961-69.

DC Office: 2227 RHOB, 20515, 202-225-4361; Fax: 202-225-6001; Website: serrano.house.gov.

State Offices: Bronx, 718-620-0084.

Committees: *Appropriations:* Commerce, Justice, Science & Related Agencies; Financial Services & General Gov't (RMM); State, Foreign Operations & Related Progams.

Group Ratings

	ADA	ACLU	AFL-CIO	LCV	ITI	COC	HAFA	ACU	CFG	FRC
2014	95%	83%	–	94%	60%	38%	12%	8%	11%	0%
2013	100%	C	95%	93%	C	31%	C	12%	12%	C

National Journal Ratings

	2013 LIB	—	2013 CONS
Economic	91%	—	0%
Social	87%	—	7%
Foreign	94%	—	0%
Composite	94%	—	6%

Key Votes of the 113th Congress

1. Sandy storm spending	Y	5. Medical Marijuana	Y	9. Syrian Rebels Training	N
2. Violence Against Women Act	Y	6. Farm Bill	N	10. Keystone pipeline	N
3. Guantanamo Bay Detainees	Y	7. Afghanistan Combat	Y	11. Immigration Exec. Action	N
4. Abortion 20-week ban	N	8. NSA Phone Data Collection	Y	12. Bipartisan budget deal	Y

Election Results

2014 general	José Serrano (D)	54,906	(97%)	$165,919
2014 primary	Jose Serrano (D)	10,346	(91%)	
	Sam Sloan (D)	1,004	(9%)	

Prior winning percentages: 2012 (97%), 2010 (96%), 2008 (97%), 2006 (95%), 2004 (95%), 2002 (92%), 2000 (96%), 1998 (95%), 1996 (96%), 1994 (96%), 1992 (91%), 1990 (93%), 1990 special (92%)

Population		Race and Ethnicity		Income	
Total:	747,271	Latino	66.1%	Median income:	$25,801
Urban:	100.0%	Black	28.1%		*(435 of 435)*
Suburban:	0.0%	White	2.3%	Under $50,000	74.8%
Rural:	0.0%	Asian	1.3%	$50,000-$99,999:	18.9%
Land area:	17	Two races	1.0%	$100,000-$199,999:	5.6%
Pop/sq. mi.:	44,583.9	White Ethnic	2.2%	$200,000 or more:	0.6%
Born in state:	51.1%			Poverty Rate	39.8%
		Education			
Age Groups		H.S. grad or less:	62.9%	**Work**	
Under 18:	28.1%	Some college:	23.9%	White collar:	17.2%
18 to 34:	27.4%	College degree, 4 yr.:	9.4%	Blue collar:	63.0%
35 to 64:	35.7%	Post-grad study:	3.7%	Sales and service:	19.8%
Over 64:	8.7%				
		Military		Govt. workers:	13.2%
		Veterans/active duty:	2.4%		

South Bronx

It may not quite be "the beautiful Bronx," as borough historian Lloyd Ultan calls it, but the Bronx seems to have rebounded from rock bottom. The borough began its modern development in 1906 with the arrival of the first subway, which allowed the children of immigrants to move from grim

Voter Turnout	
2013 Total Citizen 18+	398,765
2014 House Turnout	56,563
2014 Turnout as % CVAP	14.2%
2012 Turnout as % CVAP	47.9%

Lower East Side tenements to spacious walk-up apartments flooded with light. The population grew from 200,000 in 1900 to 1.2 million in 1930. Its population hit nearly 1.5 million in 1950. Four years later, Supreme Court Justice Sonia Sotomayor was born in a South Bronx tenement before her family moved into the nearby Bronxdale Houses public housing project. The years prior to mid-century were the peak days for the Bronx, when Babe Ruth, Lou Gehrig, and Joe DiMaggio knocked home runs out of Yankee Stadium, art deco apartment buildings were built along the Grand Concourse, and shoppers thronged Tremont Avenue stores.

Then, in the mid-1960s, several factors led to the destruction of Bronx neighborhoods. Rent control guaranteed that many owners of low-rent property wouldn't maintain it. Once empty, buildings were torched for the insurance money, sometimes as many as four blocks of buildings a week. At the same time, a decline in low-skill jobs in Manhattan and the Bronx led to a rise in welfare dependency and crime, and empty building shells became the perfect venue for drug dealing. The 13-year, $250 million effort to build the Cross-Bronx Expressway—a brainchild of Robert Moses that crossed 113 streets and avenues, hundreds of utility mains and ten mass-transit lines—only made things worse. A vicious cycle emerged: Crime drove away jobs, which produced more crime. When Tom Wolfe imagined the "wrong turn" that sank a high-flying Wall Street career in *Bonfire of the Vanities*, he set it in the South Bronx.

The borough's eventual saviors were churches and creative community groups that built single-family, pastel bungalows and small-scale apartment projects for the elderly, single-parent families and the homeless. In the 1980s, the South Bronx turned a corner. A building spree created the Bronx's first new wave of housing starts since the 1950s and the first new cluster of private residences since the 1930s. As immigrants from the Dominican Republic, Jamaica, Ecuador and Central America settled in, the population began to rise. After a quarter-century of deterioration, its population grew by almost 11% in the 1990s. Today, around 1.4 million people live in the Bronx, as new immigrants revive neighborhoods that had been given up for dead. Charlotte Street, a former slum, is now Charlotte Gardens, with owner-occupied houses. Businesses—warehouses, distribution centers and small industrial parks—have begun to move back in. The new Yankee Stadium, at $1.5 billion the most expensive baseball stadium ever built, opened in 2009 and focused attention on the area's economic renewal. Still, incomes remain low in the South Bronx, with many people on public assistance, and check-cashing outlets are still easier to find than banks. Unemployment in Bronx County did not fall below double digits until March 2014. In the following year, it dropped to 8.9%.

The 15th Congressional District of New York includes most of the South Bronx. It is bounded by the Harlem River on the west; the East River on the south; the Hutchinson River, Cross Bronx Expressway, and Bronx Park (home of the Bronx Zoo) on the east; and it goes just past Fordham Road on the north. It includes Belmont, the industrial flatlands of Bruckner Boulevard, and Hunts

2012 Presidential Vote		
Barack Obama (D) 171,364	(97%)
Mitt Romney (R).....................5,315	(3%)
2008 Presidential Vote		
Barack Obama (D) 170,490	(95%)
John McCain (R)....................9,375	(5%)
Cook Partisan Voting Index: D+43		

Point, where meat and produce markets supply the city's tony restaurants. It takes in Clason Point and Castle Hill, neighborhoods that inspired the lyrics of pop singer Jennifer Lopez. The district is 28% black, and it has the highest share of Hispanics—66%—of any New York district; it is 2% white. It has long had New York's largest concentration of Puerto Ricans, but about 63% of Hispanics are now from other parts of Latin America. It is also longstanding Democratic territory. The last Republican presidential candidate to carry the Bronx was Calvin Coolidge in 1924. The 15th was the most Democratic district in the nation in 2012, giving Barack Obama almost 97% of the vote.

José Serrano (D)

Democrat José Serrano, who won his seat in a 1990 special election, is known for his jesting about everything from Republicans to his thick mustache. But he gets serious in going against his party when he considers it important for his district—among the country's poorest and most Democratic—or his native Puerto Rico.

Born in Mayagüez, he grew up in the Mill Brook project in Mott Haven. After serving in the Army, he worked at a bank and as a school administrator. Serrano moved up while other Bronx politicians fell by the wayside because of corruption. He was elected to the New York Assembly in 1974 and chaired its Education Committee. In 1985, he ran for Bronx borough president, bucking the Democratic organization, and nearly won. Then in January 1990, Rep. Robert García of the South Bronx was convicted of accepting money from the minority contractor Wedtech. His conviction was later reversed, but his resignation paved the way for Serrano's election to the House.

Serrano once described himself as being "to the left of the left," and he has one of the most liberal voting records in the House. He has long championed legislation to repeal the 22nd Amendment to allow presidents to serve more than two terms in office. As a senior member of the Appropriations Committee, he focuses on bringing as much federal money as he can to his economically struggling district. He chaired its Financial Services Subcommittee when the Democrats controlled Congress and is now its ranking Democrat.

Among Appropriations members he is known as a jokester, always ready to enliven hearings with a quip. At a June 2010 session on the Federal Communications Commission's budget, he said he was doing his part for technology: "This hearing is online live as we speak. And I sent out a Twitter message. I put it on two Facebook pages and an email. So we should get at least 10 people to watch." At a comedy event at the 2012 Democratic National Convention, he joked about keynote speaker Julian Castro and his twin brother Joaquin: "The Florida delegation threatened to walk out when they heard the Castro brothers were speaking at the convention." Serrano told *National Journal* that humor is useful in a highly polarized House. "We take our work seriously, but we shouldn't always take ourselves so seriously," he said.

Serrano was the only House member from New York City who voted in 2008 against the federal bailout for banks and other financial services companies. He said he couldn't justify giving money to the wealthy people he believed created the problem. A big local priority for Serrano has been the environmental restoration of the Bronx River, and he delivered more than $30 million for the effort. (When the river progressed to the point where it could support wildlife, a beaver appeared for the first time in 200 years and was dubbed "José" in honor of Serrano's work.) With Republicans in control of the House, he said he sees one of his chief goals as "trying to avoid as much harm as possible" in spending cuts in the federal budget.

Another of his issues is statehood for Puerto Rico, which he calls an American "colony." A proponent of a long-stalled referendum to determine the island's status, he got a bill through the House in 2010 calling for a two-step process. Unlike fellow Puerto Rican New

York Democrat Nydia Velázquez, he saw great significance in the 2012 vote of islanders in favor of statehood, even though Congress did not authorize the process. "It will demand the attention of Congress, and a definitive answer to the Puerto Rican request for change," he said. He also took credit for working with the late Venezuelan President Hugo Chávez and Citizen Energy Corp. to strike a deal to bring cheaper oil to the South Bronx.

In early 2013, Serrano scoffed at Florida GOP Sen. Marco Rubio's attempts to become a leader on immigration. He told the website *Capital New York* that Rubio, who is of Cuban descent, "has no support in the immigrant or Latino community for his stance on immigration. He's as nasty as the rest of them."

Serrano's attempts to join the Democratic leadership have been stymied. In 1997, Democratic Leader Dick Gephardt passed over him and picked the less-senior Robert Menendez of New Jersey, who was a better fundraiser, to be chief deputy whip. In 1998, Serrano ran for Democratic Caucus vice chairman as "the candidate who refuses to raise money to buy your vote for leadership." He again lost out to Menendez, who went on to become a senator. Serrano was among the New York Democrats who briefly toyed with running against newly appointed Sen. Kirsten Gillibrand in the 2010 primary because of concerns over her centrist voting record. He passed, and Gillibrand moved left once she was in the Senate.

Serrano has become "alienated from the Bronx political establishment," the New York *Observer* reported in February 2015, and Democratic officials reportedly have been seeking another candidate for his seat. But there has been no sign of a recent political challenge to Serrano, or an attempt to show his unpopularity.

SIXTEENTH DISTRICT

Eliot Engel (D)

Elected 1988, 14th term; b. Feb. 18, 1947, Bronx; Hunter-Lehman Col., B.A. 1969, C.U.N.Y. Lehman Col., M.A. 1973, NY Law Schl., J.D. 1987; Jewish; married (Pat); 3 children.

Elected Office: NY Assembly, 1977-88.

Professional Career: Teacher, guidance counselor, NYC public schl., 1969-77; Bronx Democratic dist. ldr., 1974-77.

DC Office: 2464 RHOB, 20515, 202-225-2464; Fax: 202-225-5513; Website: engel.house.gov.

State Offices: Bronx, 718-796-9700; Co-Op City, 718-320-2314; Mt. Vernon, 914-699-4100.

Committees: *Energy & Commerce:* Energy & Power; Health. *Foreign Affairs* (RMM).

Group Ratings

	ADA	ACLU	AFL-CIO	LCV	ITI	COC	HAFA	ACU	CFG	FRC
2014	80%	77%	–	91%	60%	54%	14%	8%	11%	0%
2013	70%	C	95%	93%	C	33%	C	21%	12%	C

National Journal Ratings

	2013 LIB — 2013 CONS		
Economic	85%	—	15%
Social	77%	—	21%
Foreign	71%	—	27%
Composite	78%	—	22%

Key Votes of the 113th Congress

1. Sandy storm spending	Y	5. Medical Marijuana	Y	9. Syrian Rebels Training	Y
2. Violence Against Women Act	Y	6. Farm Bill	N	10. Keystone pipeline	N
3. Guantanamo Bay Detainees	Y	7. Afghanistan Combat	Y	11. Immigration Exec. Action	N
4. Abortion 20-week ban	N	8. NSA Phone Data Collection	N	12. Bipartisan budget deal	Y

Election Results

2014 general Eliot Engel (D) ....unopposed $1,015,032
2014 primary Eliot Engel (D) ....unopposed

Prior winning percentages: 2012 (76%), 2010 (73%), 2008 (80%), 2006 (76%), 2004 (76%), 2002 (63%), 2000 (90%), 1998 (88%), 1996 (85%), 1994 (78%), 1992 (80%), 1990 (61%), 1988 (56%)

Population		Race and Ethnicity		Income	
Total:	730,795	White	39.2%	Median income:	$63,710
Urban:	83.7%	Black	30.4%		*(88 of 435)*
Suburban:	16.3%	Latino	23.4%	Under $50,000	40.3%
Rural:	0.0%	Asian	4.6%	$50,000-$99,999:	28.0%
Land area:	83	Two races	1.7%	$100,000-$199,999:	20.6%
Pop/sq. mi.:	8,783.8	White Ethnic	28.6%	$200,000 or more:	11.1%
Born in state:	57.1%			Poverty Rate	13.0%
		Education			
Age Groups		H.S. grad or less:	37.7%	**Work**	
Under 18:	23.3%	Some college:	23.5%	White collar:	42.9%
18 to 34:	21.6%	College degree, 4 yr.:	19.6%	Blue collar:	44.0%
35 to 64:	39.3%	Post-grad study:	19.2%	Sales and service:	13.2%
Over 64:	15.7%				
		Military		Govt. workers:	16.3%
		Veterans/active duty:	4.1%		

North Bronx, Yonkers, Westchester County

The northeastern Bronx wasn't settled until the early 20th century, when it became a collection of middle-class neighborhoods clustered around subway stops, places where the children of immigrants left behind Manhattan's gloomy tenements and walk-ups and basked in the sunlight, wide avenues, and hilly vistas.

Voter Turnout	
2013 Total Citizen 18+	475,141
2014 House Turnout	100,391
2014 Turnout as % CVAP	21.1%
2012 Turnout as % CVAP	57.2%

Different ethnic groups collected here: Irish in Kingsbridge; well-to-do WASPs and Jews in Riverdale; and middle-class blacks in Williamsbridge. When neighboring areas in the South Bronx began to deteriorate, many residents fled to Westchester County.

The 16th Congressional District of New York includes the bulk of these Bronx neighborhoods, as well as southern Westchester County. It is divided roughly into three parts. South of the Westchester County line and west of the Bronx River Parkway, the district is around 70% white and heavily Democratic. This portion has the century-old Van Cortlandt Park, at 1,146 acres, New York City's fourth-largest park. It also includes leafy Woodlawn, still a magnet for Irish immigrants. The second section of the district starts east of the Bronx River Parkway and extends into Mount Vernon in Westchester. It is overwhelmingly African American. The sprawling Co-op City is here, consisting of 35 buildings that house more than 50,000 residents in 15,000 apartments that were built by a consortium of labor unions in the late 1960s.

The district's third section, in the north, includes Yonkers, which is heavily Hispanic, and population centers stretching from Hastings-on-Hudson on the Hudson River to Mamaroneck on Long Island Sound. The 16th pushes well into Westchester County suburbs, all the way to a short touch of the Connecticut border along the Sound; around 45% of the district is taken from these neighborhoods. It includes a number of affluent suburbs, many within easy reach of Grand Central via the Metro North rail lines—Bronxville, Tuckahoe, Eastchester, New Rochelle, Scarsdale, Larchmont, Mamaroneck and Rye. *Westchester* magazine in 2014 described White Plains, the county seat, as the heart of the county that "combines a suburban environment with urban sophistication for a great living and working experience." About two-thirds of district voters reside in Westchester.

Historically, Westchester was a Republican county, with a successful GOP machine and an electorate of white-collar professionals who naturally preferred the political party that opposed the big city political bosses and labor union leaders. But today, party registration in Westchester is almost

2012 Presidential Vote
Barack Obama (D) 197,364   (74%)
Mitt Romney (R)...................68,373   (26%)

2008 Presidential Vote
Barack Obama (D) 205,767   (73%)
John McCain (R)...................74,524   (26%)

Cook Partisan Voting Index: D+21

majority-Democratic, after an influx of racial and ethnic minorities and of Jews who broke down many barriers to residence after World War II. Countywide, these suburbanites gave Barack Obama 63% of the vote in 2008. Overall, the parts of the richly diverse 16th have had a major transformation. It is 39% non-Hispanic white, 32% African American, and 23% Hispanic—and solidly Democratic.

Eliot Engel (D)

Democrat Eliot Engel, elected in 1988, has remained popular at home by relentlessly staying on top of constituent service and working on issues of interest to his district's foreign-born and low-income residents. In 2013, he became the ranking Democrat on the Foreign Affairs Committee, where he has backed many downtrodden ethnic groups.

Engel is the son of a welder and grew up in the Bronx. As a boy, he was a political junkie who memorized the names of all 100 senators. He graduated from Hunter-Lehman College, got a master's in guidance and counseling from the City University of New York, and then taught and was a guidance counselor in the New York City public schools. After 14 years, he returned to school for a law degree from New York Law School. In 1977, at age 30, he was elected to the New York Assembly in a special election to replace a convicted incumbent. He won election to the House in 1988, replacing Democratic Rep. Mario Biaggi, who also had been convicted of bribery.

Engel's once strongly liberal voting record has become more moderate in recent years, especially on foreign policy. On Foreign Affairs, Engel is limited in what he can accomplish in the minority on the panel, which has a far lower profile than its Senate counterpart. But he has forged a good working relationship with California Republican Ed Royce, the committee's chairman and a fellow staunch supporter of Israel, and they have issued many joint news releases. In April 2014, they won committee support of their bill to require that the Voice of America actively support U.S. policy. But the measure ran into trouble when VOA journalists objected to restraints on their work. They appeared together on CNN in September 2014 to call for greater action against the Islamic State after the group released a video depicting the beheading of an American hostage. Failure to act against ISIS, he warned, would lead to "many more September 11ths."

When a senior Obama administration official was quoted in *The Atlantic* in October 2014 comparing Israeli Prime Minister Benjamin Netanyahu to poultry excrement, Engel issued a statement calling it "counterproductive and unprofessional for administration officials to air their dirty laundry in such a public way." And when Speaker John Boehner enraged some Democrats a few months later by inviting Netanyahu to address a joint session of Congress, Engel said he would attend. Though many Democrats boycotted the speech because they said it was aimed at undermining U.S. negotiations on Iran's nuclear program, Engel cautioned, "the U.S.-Israel relationship is bigger than any of the personalities involved at a given time."

Engel has sought to publicly deflect Republican criticism of the Obama administration. At a January 2013 hearing at which committee members sharply questioned outgoing Secretary of State Hillary Clinton about security flaws that led to the September 2012 attack in Benghazi, Libya, Engel noted that House Republicans had cut diplomatic security funding. On many issues, he worked in a bipartisan fashion with Royce's Foreign Affairs predecessor Ileana Ros-Lehtinen of Florida, including on legislation to rein in Syria's weapons program and promote human rights there. She has called him "a principled man ... an incredible freedom fighter." Engel has written laws relating to Albania and Kosovo, Cyprus and Irish affairs, and was co-author with then-Democratic Sen. Tom Harkin of Iowa of a law that addressed child slave labor in the cocoa fields of Africa.

Engel is not a 1970s-style dove. He supported the Gulf War resolution in 1990, the bombing of Serbia to get a settlement in Bosnia, and the use of force in Iraq in 2002, though he criticized President George W. Bush's handling of that conflict. As chairman of the Western Hemisphere Subcommittee in 2008, he criticized socialist Venezuelan President Hugo Chávez for "provocation" of the United States. He supported continued funding for the war in Afghanistan in 2010 and was one of three lawmakers to participate in a 2011 documentary, *Iranium*, that was intended to sound alarms about Iran's pursuit of nuclear weapons.

On the Energy and Commerce Committee, Engel has worked on a wide range of subjects, from climate change to cell phone theft. He was among a bipartisan group of lawmakers who sponsored a 2009 measure requiring half of all new cars sold in U.S. by 2012 to be flex-fuel vehicles capable of burning any combination of ethanol, methanol, and gasoline. The automobile industry fought the measure, and it was not added to the House-passed energy bill that year. In 2010, he succeeded in enacting a bill that made it illegal to use false caller IDs to trick people into revealing personal information.

Engel has a personal tradition of staking out an aisle seat many hours before the start of the annual State of the Union address so he can shake the president's hand or occasionally give him a hug. In February 2009, CNN anchor Anderson Cooper called Engel "pathetic" for waiting more than 12 hours for President Barack Obama's address to Congress. Engel replied that Cooper was "pathetic" for failing to share his enthusiasm. He later told *The Journal-News* that constituents loved him for it: "It'll be September, October and people will say they saw me on TV."

Engel has had a handful of spirited election opponents. In the 2000 primary, Assemblyman Larry Seabrook attacked Engel for living in suburban Maryland. Engel won 50%-41%. After redistricting made his district more suburban in 2002, Engel had vigorous competition from Rockland County Executive Scott Vanderhoef, a Republican who criticized Engel for voting against tax cuts and defense spending. Engel won 63%-34%. In 2014, he was reelected without major-party opposition in his secure district.

SEVENTEENTH DISTRICT

Nita Lowey (D)

Elected 1988, 14th term; b. July 5, 1937, Bronx; Mt. Holyoke Col., B.S. 1959; Jewish; married (Stephen); 3 children.

Professional Career: Asst. for Econ. Devel. & Neighborhood Preservation, NY secy. of st.; Deputy dir., Div. of Econ. Opportunity, 1975-85; NY asst. secy. of st., 1985-87.

DC Office: 2365 RHOB, 20515, 202-225-6506; Fax: 202-225-0546; Website: lowey.house.gov.

State Offices: New City, 845-639-3485; White Plains, 914-428-1707.

Committees: *Appropriations* (RMM): State, Foreign Operations & Related Programs (RMM).

Group Ratings

	ADA	ACLU	AFL-CIO	LCV	ITI	COC	HAFA	ACU	CFG	FRC
2014	80%	83%	–	94%	60%	50%	12%	4%	7%	0%
2013	75%	C	95%	96%	C	38%	C	4%	15%	C

National Journal Ratings

	2013 LIB	—	2013 CONS
Economic	71%	—	28%
Social	79%	—	16%
Foreign	83%	—	15%
Composite	79%	—	21%

Key Votes of the 113th Congress

1. Sandy storm spending	Y	5. Medical Marijuana	Y	9. Syrian Rebels Training	Y
2. Violence Against Women Act	Y	6. Farm Bill	N	10. Keystone pipeline	N
3. Guantanamo Bay Detainees	Y	7. Afghanistan Combat	N	11. Immigration Exec. Action	N
4. Abortion 20-week ban	N	8. NSA Phone Data Collection	N	12. Bipartisan budget deal	Y

Election Results

2014 general	Nita Lowey (D)	98,150	(56%)	$2,332,093	
	Chris Day (R)	75,781	(44%)	$194,700	$24,978
2014 primary	Nita Lowey (D)	unopposed			

Prior winning percentages: 2012 (64%), 2010 (62%), 2008 (68%), 2006 (71%), 2004 (70%), 2002 (92%), 2000 (67%), 1998 (83%), 1996 (64%), 1994 (57%), 1992 (56%), 1990 (63%), 1988 (50%)

Population		Race and Ethnicity		Income	
Total:	742,344	White	61.9%	Median income:	$87,899
Urban:	23.1%	Latino	20.7%		*(17 of 435)*
Suburban:	76.9%	Black	9.7%	Under $50,000	29.9%
Rural:	0.0%	Asian	6.0%	$50,000-$99,999:	25.1%
Land area:	419	Two races	1.2%	$100,000-$199,999:	30.6%
Pop/sq. mi.:	1,772.7	White Ethnic	43.8%	$200,000 or more:	14.4%
Born in state:	62.6%			Poverty Rate	11.3%
		Education			
Age Groups		H.S. grad or less:	33.4%	**Work**	
Under 18:	25.1%	Some college:	21.7%	White collar:	44.1%
18 to 34:	20.7%	College degree, 4 yr.:	23.3%	Blue collar:	42.9%
35 to 64:	39.7%	Post-grad study:	21.6%	Sales and service:	13.0%
Over 64:	14.4%				
		Military		Govt. workers:	15.2%
		Veterans/active duty:	4.6%		

Northern Westchester, Rockland Counties

Blessed with some of America's loveliest scenery and easily accessible from Manhattan by train, Westchester County has some of America's earliest suburbs, where grand estates were built by millionaires—Jay Gould's Gothic revival Lyndhurst and John D. Rockefeller's spectacular

Voter Turnout	
2013 Total Citizen 18+	473,666
2014 House Turnout	174,062
2014 Turnout as % CVAP	36.7%
2012 Turnout as % CVAP	62.8%

Kykuit. Today, Westchester still looks suburban, but with the patina of age. It has little commuter railroad stations across from faux Tudor drugstores, soda fountains and cobblestone post offices. But it also has shopping malls and plenty of corporate headquarters, from IBM to Pepsi. In recent years, Westchester also has been drawing biotech companies; a former Union Carbide site in Tarrytown—which writer Washington Irving fictionalized into Sleepy Hollow while sending his headless horseman on a chase for schoolmaster Ichabod Crane—has become a bustling hub. Those firms have helped keep unemployment relatively low; the county's jobless rate mostly stayed below 8% during the recession; since mid-2014, the rate has been below 5%. Development slows north of White Plains, where Westchester is crossed by the first of several mountain ridges—the closest the Appalachians come to the ocean. In Ossining, on the Hudson River, looms the famed Sing Sing maximum security prison.

The 17th Congressional District of New York contains northern and western sections of Westchester County: Port Chester, White Plains, Tarrytown, Armonk and Chappaqua, where former President Bill Clinton and presidential candidate Hillary Clinton have a home. Facebook Chairman and CEO Mark Zuckerberg was born in White Plains and grew up in Dobbs Ferry, now the southernmost town in the district on the east bank of the Hudson River. Also here are Yorktown Heights and Peekskill, where George Pataki was mayor before becoming governor. At the Rockefeller State Park Preserve, sheep have been preserved as part of a land study.

Across the Tappan Zee—a stretch in the Hudson River so wide that Henry Hudson believed he had finally discovered the Northwest Passage to the Pacific Ocean upon entering it—the district takes in all of Rockland County, which comprises about 40% of the residents of the 17th. First settled by Dutchmen, Rockland was studded by little towns that grew up as if they were 1,000 miles from Gotham, but which eventually thrived on their proximity to the city once the Palisades Interstate Parkway and Tappan Zee Bridge were built in the 1950s.

Today, Rockland is a triangular stretch of suburbia, wedged between New Jersey, the

2012 Presidential Vote
Barack Obama (D) ....167,884　(57%)
Mitt Romney (R)................123,125　(42%)

2008 Presidential Vote
Barack Obama (D) ....181,757　(58%)
John McCain (R)................129,021　(41%)

Cook Partisan Voting Index: D+5

Hudson River, and the Appalachians. Its demographics have changed; Haverstraw, on the banks of the Hudson, has a large share of Dominicans; Kaser, a village in the inland town of Rampao, has a large community of Romanians. The first span of a new twin-span, eight-lane bridge to replace the deteriorating Tappan Zee was scheduled to open in 2016. The total cost of $3.9 billion is expected to be paid from future toll revenue of the New York Thruway.

Redrawn after the 2010 census, the 17th District is quite different from its predecessor. Its share of non-whites dropped to 37% from 40%, and President Barack Obama's vote share in 2008 dropped 4 percentage points to 58%. Still, this district leans Democratic.

Nita Lowey (D)

Democrat Nita Lowey, first elected in 1988, is a formidable insider among House Democrats. She is a close and persuasive ally of Minority Leader Nancy Pelosi and since 2013 has been the Appropriations Committee's ranking Democrat, the first woman to hold that slot. Her Senate committee counterpart is Barbara Mikulski of Maryland.

Lowey was born in the Bronx. After graduating from Mount Holyoke College with a degree in marketing, she moved to Queens, where she became a homemaker raising three children. She got involved in politics when her neighbor, Mario Cuomo, got Lowey to assist his 1974 campaign for lieutenant governor. He lost that race but was appointed New York secretary of state and hired Lowey as his assistant in 1975. She remained a top official in his administration until she ran for Congress.

In the 1988 Democratic primary for the House seat, Lowey faced Hamilton Fish III, who was politically well connected but, as a former publisher of *The Nation*, was considerably to the left of Lowey. She won 44%-36%. In the general election, two-term Republican Rep. Joseph DioGuardi was dogged by charges of illicit contributions. Lowey won 50%-47%, while spending $657,000 of her own money.

In the House, Lowey's voting record is liberal, although she has been more moderate on foreign policy. She has been a strong advocate of aid to Israel and voted for the 2002 Iraq war resolution. Her ties to Pelosi were evident in 2010 when she defeated Marcy Kaptur of Ohio for the ranking Democratic slot on Appropriations, even though Kaptur had more seniority. As the ranking Democrat on the Appropriations State and Foreign Operations Subcommittee, she has continued to work closely with that panel's chairman, Texas Republican Kay Granger. They have warned the Palestinian Authority that its quest for statehood jeopardized its U.S. funding. Lowey led the opposition in 2011 to a GOP proposal to slash U.S. contributions to international financial organizations. She argued that it would impair companies' access to foreign markets.

On domestic issues, Lowey has been a big supporter of biomedical research and helped increase spending on cancer research at the National Institutes of Health. She has become a vigorous crusader against skin cancer after watching two close friends undergo surgeries and chemotherapy for melanoma, calling for better guidelines on sunscreen. She has worked to combat drunken driving, advocating the increased use of ignition interlock devices to impede repeat offenses. Pursuing her interest in feminist issues, she has backed funds for international family planning, including abortion. She has actively supported the National Endowment for the Arts.

During the early months of the spending debate in 2015, Lowey said that the Republican budget plan provided an insufficient total for government operations and that a new spending agreement would be required with the administration. "Let's get real," she implored the committee in May.

Lowey reportedly played a key behind-the-scenes role in getting the 2010 Dodd-Frank financial industry overhaul law to soften restrictions on derivatives that would have negatively affected New York's banking industry. That law became a controversial part of the 2014 year-end omnibus spending bill when Lowey—working with Mikulski—cut a deal with Republican appropriators to permit an exemption for big banks from derivatives regulation. In exchange, Lowey got an additional $185 million in spending for banking regulators. That agreement raised major objections from Minority Leader Nancy Pelosi and Democratic Sen. Elizabeth Warren of Massachusetts, but the appropriators held firm. Obama went along with the agreement.

Since Lowey first won, the boundaries of her district have been radically altered three times by redistricting but she has been reelected by wide margins. She thought about a Senate bid in 2000, but deferred to first lady Hillary Clinton, and in 2008, she was an enthusiastic supporter of Clinton's presidential campaign. Her party loyalty and avid fundraising led Minority Leader Dick Gephardt to appoint her to chair the Democratic Congressional Campaign Committee for the 2002 election. That year, the GOP's six-seat gain was an acute disappointment to Lowey, who quietly bowed out of the chairmanship. In 2008, she was mentioned as a possible successor in the Senate after Clinton became secretary of State, but the plum fell to Democratic Rep. Kirsten Gillibrand.

Lowey's Republican opponent in 2008 and 2010 was Jim Russell, a Christian conservative. The local GOP in 2010 rescinded its endorsement of Russell after reports that he wrote an anti-integration essay that was posted on former Ku Klux Klan leader David Duke's website. Lowey won 62%-38%. When redistricting gave Lowey a district in 2012 in which just over half of her constituents were new to her, she drew a stronger GOP candidate in Rye Town Supervisor Joe Carvin. But she won an impressive 64% of the vote and further increased her influence in Washington by donating nearly $700,000 to colleagues before the election. In the more Republican-leaning 2014 cycle, Lowey got 56% of the vote against Republican Chris Day, a retired Army captain who served in Iraq and Afghanistan, whom she outspent by more than 10-to-1. Lowey remains entrenched. But she turns 80 in 2017, and her potential retirement could spur a close contest in a state where House Republican candidates recently have become more competitive.

EIGHTEENTH DISTRICT

Sean Patrick Maloney (D)

Elected 2012, 2nd term; b. July 30, 1966, Sherbrooke, QC, Canada; U. of VA, B.A. 1988, J.D. 1992; Catholic; married (Randy Florke); 3 children.

Professional Career: Practicing atty., 1993-97, 2004-06, 2009-present; Staff secy., Pres. Bill Clinton, 1997-2000; Founder & COO, Kiodex, 2000-03; First deputy secy., Gov. Eliot Spitzer, 2007-08.

DC Office: 1529 LHOB, 20515, 202-225-5441; Fax: 202-225-3289; Website: seanmaloney.house.gov.

State Offices: Newburgh, 845-561-1529.

Committees: *Agriculture:* Commodity Exchanges, Energy, & Credit; General Farm Commodities & Risk Mgmt. *Transportation & Infrastructure:* Aviation; Highways & Transit; Water Resources & Environment.

Group Ratings

	ADA	ACLU	AFL-CIO	LCV	ITI	COC	HAFA	ACU	CFG	FRC
2014	55%	50%	–	83%	100%	64%	16%	8%	13%	0%
2013	35%	C	95%	79%	C	69%	C	24%	20%	C

National Journal Ratings

	2013 LIB	—	2013 CONS
Economic	56%	—	44%
Social	59%	—	40%
Foreign	54%	—	45%
Composite	57%	—	43%

Key Votes of the 113th Congress

1. Sandy storm spending	Y	5. Medical Marijuana	Y
2. Violence Against Women Act	Y	6. Farm Bill	N
3. Guantanamo Bay Detainees	N	7. Afghanistan Combat	Y
4. Abortion 20-week ban	N	8. NSA Phone Data Collection	N

9. Syrian Rebels Training	N
10. Keystone pipeline	Y
11. Immigration Exec. Action	N
12. Bipartisan budget deal	Y

Election Results

2014 general	Sean Maloney (D)	88,993	(50%)	$4,161,437	$112,788	$869,462
	Nan Hayworth (R)	85,660	(48%)	$3,386,119	$453,931	$2,183,155
	Scott Smith (I)	4,294	(2%)	$13,985		
2014 primary	Sean Patrick Maloney (D)	unopposed				

Prior winning percentage: 2012 (52%)

Population		Race and Ethnicity		Income	
Total:	718,210	White	70.6%	Median income:	$74,704
Urban:	0.0%	Latino	15.2%		*(45 of 435)*
Suburban:	98.5%	Black	8.5%	Under $50,000	34.0%
Rural:	1.5%	Asian	3.2%	$50,000-$99,999:	29.3%
Land area:	1,441	Two races	2.2%	$100,000-$199,999:	27.6%
Pop/sq. mi.:	498.4	White Ethnic	53.0%	$200,000 or more:	9.1%
Born in state:	70.8%			Poverty Rate	10.5%
		Education			
Age Groups		H.S. grad or less:	36.4%	**Work**	
Under 18:	24.1%	Some college:	29.7%	White collar:	38.3%
18 to 34:	20.9%	College degree, 4 yr.:	19.0%	Blue collar:	44.8%
35 to 64:	41.3%	Post-grad study:	14.8%	Sales and service:	17.0%
Over 64:	13.6%				
		Military		Govt. workers:	18.2%
		Veterans/active duty:	8.0%		

Lower Hudson Valley

The great interior of America can be said to begin where the Hudson River squeezes through a series of Appalachian ridges at the Hudson Highlands. This chokepoint became a barrier to British military power during the Revolutionary War, when American forces put a chain across the river to

Voter Turnout	
2013 Total Citizen 18+	509,256
2014 House Turnout	179,091
2014 Turnout as % CVAP	35.2%
2012 Turnout as % CVAP	57.7%

keep the British from sailing north. Benedict Arnold betrayed his country over control of this part of the Hudson, and the new nation built its Military Academy high on the cliffs at West Point. The Hudson was the impetus for the builders of the Erie Canal and the water-level New York Central Railroad, two great projects that made New York City the port of the American interior.

The 18th Congressional District of New York covers much of the southern Hudson Valley, sprawling across parts of four counties. West of the Hudson, the district takes in all of Orange County, which trails only Rockland as New York's second fastest-growing county, with a 10 percent increase between 2000 and 2013. There, old farming villages like Warwick adjoin mountains, farms and new middle-income subdivisions on the nation's biggest deposit of muck soil outside the Everglades. Orange County, which includes nearly half the population of the district, includes Kiryas Joel, a Hasidic Jewish settlement, many of whose residents moved from Brooklyn to make room for their large families. Three-fifths of its residents live below the poverty line. Its 20,000 residents function almost as a single voting unit, without much regard to partisan affiliation, a fact that has not escaped the notice of the state's top politicians, who regularly court local leaders. Also in Orange, the heirs to railroad baron E.H. Harriman have been battling with the Caesars Entertainment moguls over possible plans to locate a large casino and resort complex next to their parkland.

East of the river, the 18th takes in all of Putnam County and part of Dutchess County, including Poughkeepsie, home of Vassar College, and Wappingers Falls. Poughkeepsie, which has suffered many years of economic hard times, prepared in early 2015 robust economic development plans, including a booming waterfront along the Hudson. Putnam

2012 Presidential Vote		
Barack Obama (D)	149,610	(51%)
Mitt Romney (R)	137,144	(47%)

2008 Presidential Vote		
Barack Obama (D)	162,572	(52%)
John McCain (R)	146,266	(47%)

Cook Partisan Voting Index: EVEN

has become popular with first-time home buyers, who make an 80-minute commute to Grand Central Station. The district also takes in the lightly populated northeastern reaches of Westchester County, around Somers, North Salem and Lewisboro.

The region has proved attractive to middle- and higher-income white-collar workers seeking reasonably priced housing in low-crime areas. *Forbes* magazine in 2012 rated the mid-Hudson Valley one of the best places to raise a family. This has led to robust population growth at a time when many other areas of the state are losing residents. Politically, Putnam County is reliably Republican; the rest of the district is swing territory or leans slightly Democratic, resulting in a district that tends to end up near the national average. President Barack Obama won here with 52% in 2008 and 51% in 2012.

Sean Patrick Maloney (D)

Elected in 2012, freshman Sean Patrick Maloney describes himself as a "Bill Clinton Democrat"—with good reason. He worked as a staffer on both of Clinton's presidential campaigns, and was a top West Wing aide. The former president's brand of centrism and his endorsement helped the 46-year-old lawyer defeat Republican Rep. Nan Hayworth.

Maloney was born in Quebec, Canada, where his father was working in the lumber industry. He grew up in a middle-class section of Hanover New Hampshire, in what he described as a "small Irish-Catholic family" that included five brothers and one sister. In high school, Maloney became interested in 20th century history, especially the civil rights struggle. He attended Georgetown University for two years and then transferred to the University of Virginia, where he studied international relations and stayed on to earn a law degree.

Maloney delayed taking the bar exam to work on Clinton's 1992 campaign as a deputy to Susan Thomases, then the chief scheduler. In 1996, he joined the reelection campaign, this time as director of surrogate travel. When Clinton won a second term, Maloney snagged a job in the administration as the No. 3 official under Chief of Staff John Podesta. Maloney later ascended to the job of staff secretary, responsible for coordinating the flow of information to the president.

When Clinton left office, Maloney took a break from politics and worked as the chief operating officer at Kiodex, a firm that developed risk management tools. After a short stint in legal work, he made his first bid for office in 2006, when he lost badly to Andrew Cuomo in the Democratic primary for New York attorney general. A year later, Maloney became first deputy secretary to Gov. Eliot Spitzer and, later, to David Paterson. Maloney worked to raise revenues by leasing state assets to private companies.

Maloney came under a cloud for possible obstruction of justice following a scheme to release damaging information about then-Senate Majority Leader Joseph Bruno's travel. Although his defenders insisted that Maloney was not involved, his role became an issue in the five-way Democratic primary for the House seat in 2012. *The New York Times* editorial board said that during law-enforcement review of the charges, Maloney "appeared to be most interested in holding back the staff's personal emails from investigators." Still, he won the primary handily against his closest competitor, Cortlandt Town Council Member Richard Becker, 48%-32%.

In the general election, Maloney's challenge to first-term Rep. Hayworth got the attention of the national party, and the Democratic Congressional Campaign Committee and liberal super PACs put money behind his campaign. Maloney and Democrats painted Hayworth as a tea party extremist, citing her votes for Rep. Paul Ryan's budget and for cutting funding for Planned Parenthood. Maloney argued that his moderate politics better suited the district. Hayworth outraised Maloney $3.3 million to $2.2 million and had a comparable edge in Super PAC assistance. But Maloney eked out a win, 52%-48%.

Maloney, who is gay, married in 2014 his longtime partner, Randy Florke, a prominent Realtor and interior designer. After his initial election, the front page of *The Times* featured a photo of Maloney taking his oath of office alongside Florke and their three children. He co-chairs the Congressional LGBT Equality Caucus, and has expressed support for legislation that bars discrimination against people based on their sexual orientation. But Maloney got in trouble for hiring a drone to photograph his wedding. Republicans attacked this activity as a possible violation of Federal Aviation Administration rules, which they contend Maloney should have known as a member of the Transportation and Infrastructure Committee.

In his 2014 year-end report summarizing his work during his first term, Maloney claimed credit for introducing 10 bills that were signed into law. In most of those cases, he appeared to have been a co-sponsor of legislation, which often went through many changes prior to enactment. On a separate official listing of the bills that he introduced in 2013-14, the only one enacted was the naming of a post office in his district.

Maloney won a second term in a rematch with Hayworth. This time, Maloney outspent his opponent, $4.2 million to $3.4 million, and assistance from super PACs gave him another $2 million. He won 49.7%-47.9%, and led in three of the four counties, losing only Putnam. In an unusual move, Republican state Sen. Greg Ball, whose district included much of Putnam

County, crossed party lines to endorse Maloney. Ball, who retired in 2014, said that he had "no stronger ally" on veterans' issues than Maloney. A spokesman for Hayworth said that Ball's action was "revenge" because she "scared him out of running" when Hayworth was elected to the seat in 2010.

NINETEENTH DISTRICT

Chris Gibson (R)

Elected 2010, 3rd term; b. May 13, 1964, Rockville Centre; Siena Col., B.A. 1986, Cornell U., M.P.A. 1995, Ph.D. 1998; Catholic; married (Mary Jo); 3 children. .

Military Career: NY Natl. Guard, 1981-86; U.S. Army, 1986-2010 (Kosovo, Iraq).

Professional Career: Faculty, U.S. Military Academy West Pt.

DC Office: 1708 LHOB, 20515, 202-225-5614; Fax: 202-225-1168; Website: gibson.house.gov.

State Offices: Cooperstown, 607-282-4002; Delhi, 607-746-9537; Ferndale, 845-747-9261; Hyde Park, 845-698-0132; Kinderhook, 518-610-8133; Kingston, 845-514-2322.

Committees: *Agriculture:* Agriculture: Biotechnology, Horticulture, & Research; Conservation & Forestry. *Armed Services:* Readiness; Tactical & Land Air Forces. *Small Business:* Agriculture, Energy & Trade; Contracting & Workforce.

Group Ratings

	ADA	ACLU	AFL-CIO	LCV	ITI	COC	HAFA	ACU	CFG	FRC
2014	30%	38%	–	54%	80%	79%	26%	16%	29%	63%
2013	30%	C	62%	43%	C	77%	C	36%	37%	C

National Journal Ratings

	2013 LIB	—	2013 CONS
Economic	54%	—	45%
Social	54%	—	46%
Foreign	52%	—	47%
Composite	54%	—	46%

Key Votes of the 113th Congress

1. Sandy storm spending	Y	5. Medical Marijuana	N	9. Syrian Rebels Training	N
2. Violence Against Women Act	Y	6. Farm Bill	Y	10. Keystone pipeline	Y
3. Guantanamo Bay Detainees	Y	7. Afghanistan Combat	Y	11. Immigration Exec. Action	Y
4. Abortion 20-week ban	Y	8. NSA Phone Data Collection	Y	12. Bipartisan budget deal	Y

Election Results

2014 general	Chris Gibson (R)	131,594	(64%)	$2,981,041	$865,195	$4,318
	Sean Eldridge (D)	72,470	(36%)	$6,367,880	$1,368,789	
2014 primary	Chris Gibson (R)	unopposed			

Prior winning percentages: 2012 (53%), 2010 (55%)

Population		Race and Ethnicity		Income	
Total:	709,970	White	85.8%	Median income:	$56,757
Urban:	9.1%	Latino	6.7%		(154 of 435)
Suburban:	45.2%	Black	4.0%	Under $50,000	43.8%
Rural:	45.7%	Asian	1.5%	$50,000-$99,999:	32.0%
Land area:	6,903	Two races	1.8%	$100,000-$199,999:	19.8%
Pop/sq. mi.:	102.8	White Ethnic	54.8%	$200,000 or more:	4.4%
Born in state:	76.1%			Poverty Rate	12.5%
		Education			
Age Groups		H.S. grad or less:	42.9%	**Work**	
Under 18:	19.3%	Some college:	30.3%	White collar:	37.6%
18 to 34:	20.8%	College degree, 4 yr.:	14.6%	Blue collar:	41.3%
35 to 64:	42.5%	Post-grad study:	12.2%	Sales and service:	21.1%
Over 64:	17.4%				
		Military		Govt. workers:	19.8%
		Veterans/active duty:	8.3%		

Central Hudson Valley, the Catskills

The Hudson River, an avenue of commerce in colonial days and an inspiration to artists in the early republic, is still one of America's great sights, although it is no longer central to the nation's consciousness and politics. The classic mansions overlooking the river, like Clermont, built by Robert

Voter Turnout	
2013 Total Citizen 18+	557,142
2014 House Turnout	204,173
2014 Turnout as % CVAP	36.6%
2012 Turnout as % CVAP	54.5%

Livingston, who financed the first steamboat, are reminders of the cool serenity of the 18th century mind and the daring nature of its spirit. The Hudson was also a center of American culture during the Romantic era. From Frederick Church's Moorish mansion, Olana, one can see the still-unspoiled river landscape that inspired his art and that of others of the Hudson River School of painters.

The Hudson also gave birth to America's passionate party politics. On a visit to this area in the 1790s, James Madison and Aaron Burr welded the Virginia-New York alliance that changed the course of American political history. Nearby is Kinderhook, the home of Martin Van Buren, the innkeeper's son, who in concert with Andrew Jackson, invented the torchlight parade, the national party convention, and, some argue, the Democratic Party. Later in the 19th century, the Hudson was lined with the palaces of the nation's first great millionaires and the comfortable country homes of New York's gentry. One of the latter, Springwood in Hyde Park, was the birthplace and home of Franklin D. Roosevelt, who, even as president, was most comfortable looking out over his sloping lawn to the river, where he liked to go iceboating in the winter. To the north is the charming town of Rhinebeck, site of the 2010 wedding of Chelsea Clinton and Marc Mezvinsky, the bride the daughter of a former president and two-time presidential candidate, the groom the son of two former members of Congress.

On the other side of the Hudson, the Catskills loom, where Rip Van Winkle was said to have fallen asleep for 20 years after drinking with nine pipe-playing dwarfs. Eventually, the area became part of a great pathway west, along the Erie Lackawanna and Delaware & Hudson railroad lines, with engines steaming over giant viaducts and along narrow river valleys through the mountains. Later in the 19th century, huge kosher hotels were built in Sullivan County in the Catskills, the Jewish resort area popularly known as the Borscht Belt. These thrived when Jews were excluded from other resorts but fell on hard times in the late 20th century. Some survived to cater to Russian-Jewish immigrants and a kosher clientele. Today, there is little passenger train service, and the Catskills are bypassed by major airlines.

The sprawling 19th Congressional District of New York connects these two regions into a single district. It includes seven full counties (Schoharie, Delaware, Sullivan, Ulster, Otsego, Columbia and Greene) and parts of four others (Rensselaer, Dutchess, Montgomery and Broome). It is a collection of small towns and villages, some suburban in nature, and some rural. The largest locale is Kingston (pop. 24,000) and only one other place, Hyde Park, has more than 20,000 residents. It bends around the Albany metropolitan area in the north, taking in a bit of the Mohawk Valley, and the Baseball Hall of Fame in Cooperstown. The district also includes Oneonta, home of the less well-known National Soccer Hall of Fame. Further south, in Ulster County, is Bethel, where the 1969 Woodstock music festival took place. In December 2014, state-imposed restrictions stifled local interests in Schoharie County that saw the potential for hydraulic fracturing of natural-gas deposits.

Ulster, the largest county, is solidly Democratic at the national level, but like most of Upstate New York, Republicans fare better at the local level and even control the county legislature. The district overall was once solidly Republican, part of a tradition that

2012 Presidential Vote		
Barack Obama (D)	157,279	(52%)
Mitt Romney (R)	138,384	(46%)

2008 Presidential Vote		
Barack Obama (D)	175,800	(53%)
John McCain (R)	150,359	(45%)

Cook Partisan Voting Index: D+1

dated to the Civil War (Franklin Roosevelt never carried his home territory except when he ran for the state Senate in 1910). Today, it is swing territory: Barack Obama carried the district twice, with vote totals close to his national averages.

Chris Gibson (R)

Chris Gibson, elected in 2010, has one of the most liberal voting records among House Republicans. After easily winning one of the most expensive races in 2014, he announced in January 2015 he would not seek another term and that he might instead pursue statewide office.

Gibson grew up in Kinderhook, played basketball at Ichabod Crane High School and joined the Army National Guard one day after his 17th birthday. He graduated magna cum laude and got his ROTC commission from Siena College and later earned a Ph.D. in government from Cornell University. Gibson served 24 years in the Army, rose to colonel, was deployed to Kosovo and to Haiti for a humanitarian relief mission, and did four combat tours in Iraq. He taught American politics at the U.S. Military Academy at West Point and was a Hoover National Security Affairs fellow at Stanford University. He wrote a 2008 book, *Securing the State*, about civil-military relations in the Defense Department.

In 2010, Gibson challenged incumbent Democrat Scott Murphy. Murphy had replaced Kirsten Gillibrand, who was appointed to succeed Hillary Clinton in the Senate. He had narrowly won the special election for the seat, 50.2%-49.8%, against Republican state Assembly Leader Jim Tedisco. Gibson focused his campaign on familiar fiscal conservative issues and a tough-on-terrorists national security platform. He slammed Murphy for his votes for Obama's initiatives, while Murphy argued that in the health care deliberations, he had bargained successfully for a reduced tax on medical devices and paper manufacturers, both good for the district.

Murphy tried to distance himself from liberal House Speaker Nancy Pelosi and touted his moderate voting record. He got some attention with an ad depicting Gibson riding an animated cartoon crocodile that eats a middle-class family and asserting that his opponent will "feed on the middle class." Murphy spent $5.3 million to Gibson's $1.7 million. Gibson won handily, 55%-45%.

In the House, Gibson in 2012 was the chamber's most liberal Republican, ahead of 10 Democratic lawmakers, according to *National Journal's* annual rankings. In 2013, the rankings again showed him as the most liberal Republican, outpacing two Democrats.

He and Republican Steven LaTourette of Ohio proposed an unsuccessful amendment in February 2011 aimed at undoing Republican attempts to eliminate several programs. He was one of 16 Republicans in 2012 to back an alternative by Democratic Rep. Jim Cooper of Tennessee, which was based on the bipartisan Simpson-Bowles deficit-reduction commission's recommendations. Gibson joined neighboring Democrat Paul Tonko of New York in sponsoring a bill to improve the tax credit for fuel cell-powered industrial vehicles. He spoke out against New York state's stringent new gun control law in February 2013, calling it a legislative overreach. In the fiscal 2016 defense-policy bill, Gibson cited approval of several of his provisions, including equine therapy for wounded veterans, a report from the Joint Chiefs of Staff on the Global Response Force (which Gibson once commanded), and new systems to counter the impact of improvised explosive devices on the battlefield. A new listing prepared by the Lugar Center, founded by former Republican Sen. Richard Lugar, and a Georgetown University public policy institute ranked Gibson as the most bipartisan member of the House.

In this competitive district, he took his campaigns seriously. 2012, Gibson faced Democratic challenger Julian Schreibman, who, as a CIA lawyer, had successfully prosecuted al-Qaida members for bombing U.S. embassies. Schreibman accused his opponent of favoring an end to Medicare and of being "out of step" with the values of Upstate New York. Gibson responded by emphasizing his work on such important local issues as expanding rural broadband access and eradicating Lyme disease. Gibson enjoyed a significant money advantage. The Democratic tide in New York swung the race closer as Election Day neared, but Gibson pulled out a 53%-47% victory.

Gibson had a far easier time in 2014 with an unusual challenge from Democrat Sean Eldridge, who grew up outside of Toledo Ohio, worked in support of same-sex marriage and had deep pockets from his marriage with *New Republic* owner Chris Hughes. The challenger spent $6.4 million to $3 million for Gibson, and emphasized that the Republican-controlled House had become dysfunctional. Eldridge suffered from repeated campaign gaffes, fueling the impression that he was attempting to buy a congressional seat from his multiple homes elsewhere. The contest generated extensive national media coverage, which was abetted by harsh and sarcastic attacks on Eldridge from the National Republican Congressional Committee. Gibson largely stayed aside as his opponent self-destructed, and won 64%-36%, which seemed a judgment by voters about both candidates. In a withering post-election review, *Vanity Fair* wrote that Eldridge was "not a natural, easygoing campaigner." Eldridge said that he would not run again for elected office, though he voiced continued interest in political activism.

In January 2015, Gibson announced that he would comply with his earlier pledge for term limits. But he remained active politically, with interest in a statewide campaign in 2018—most likely a bid for governor. He criticized Gov. Andrew Cuomo for failing to fulfill his promise to clean up the corruption in Albany. The contest to succeed Gibson in the congressional seat quickly shaped up as competitive.

TWENTIETH DISTRICT

Paul Tonko (D)

Elected 2008, 4th term; b. June 18, 1949, Amsterdam; Clarkson U., B.S. 1981; Catholic; single.

Elected Office: Montgomery Cnty. Bd. of Supervisors, 1976-83, chmn., 1981; NY Assembly, 1983-2007.

Professional Career: NY Dept. of Transportation, 1972-74; NY Dept. of Public Service, 1974-83; Pres. & CEO, NY St. Energy Research & Devel-opment Authority, 2007-08.

DC Office: 2463 RHOB, 20515, 202-225-5076; Fax: 202-225-5077; Website: tonko.house.gov.

State Offices: Albany, 518-465-0700; Amsterdam, 518-843-3400; Schenectady, 518-374-4547.

Committees: *Energy & Commerce:* Energy & Power; Environment & the Economy (RMM); Oversight & Investigations. *Science, Space, & Technology:* Research & Technology.

Group Ratings

	ADA	ACLU	AFL-CIO	LCV	ITI	COC	HAFA	ACU	CFG	FRC
2014	85%	83%	–	97%	80%	36%	14%	4%	6%	0%
2013	95%	C	100%	93%	C	46%	C	12%	13%	C

National Journal Ratings

	2013 LIB	—	2013 CONS
Economic	91%	—	0%
Social	87%	—	7%
Foreign	89%	—	10%
Composite	92%	—	8%

Key Votes of the 113th Congress

1. Sandy storm spending	Y	5. Medical Marijuana	Y	9. Syrian Rebels Training	N
2. Violence Against Women Act	Y	6. Farm Bill	N	10. Keystone pipeline	N
3. Guantanamo Bay Detainees	Y	7. Afghanistan Combat	Y	11. Immigration Exec. Action	N
4. Abortion 20-week ban	N	8. NSA Phone Data Collection	Y	12. Bipartisan budget deal	Y

Election Results

2014 general	Paul Tonko (D)	125,111	(61%)	$871,957
	Jim Fischer (R)	79,104	(39%)	$151,979
2014 primary	Paul Tonko (D)	unopposed		

Prior winning percentages: 2012 (68%), 2010 (59%), 2008 (62%)

Population		Race and Ethnicity		Income	
Total:	724,345	White	79.3%	Median income:	$58,095
Urban:	51.0%	Black	8.2%		*(141 of 435)*
Suburban:	42.3%	Latino	5.5%	Under $50,000	43.0%
Rural:	6.7%	Asian	3.6%	$50,000-$99,999:	31.4%
Land area:	1,742	Two races	2.8%	$100,000-$199,999:	21.0%
Pop/sq. mi.:	415.8	White Ethnic	58.6%	$200,000 or more:	4.6%
Born in state:	76.9%			Poverty Rate	13.6%
		Education			
Age Groups		H.S. grad or less:	34.8%	**Work**	
Under 18:	20.4%	Some college:	29.2%	White collar:	42.3%
18 to 34:	25.3%	College degree, 4 yr.:	20.0%	Blue collar:	42.6%
35 to 64:	39.4%	Post-grad study:	16.0%	Sales and service:	15.1%
Over 64:	14.9%				
		Military		Govt. workers:	21.4%
		Veterans/active duty:	7.4%		

Capital Region: Albany, Schenectady

As readers of novelist laureate William Kennedy know, Albany is an antique city. Its solid row houses recall its 19th-century prosperity. Its once-teeming lumberyards, railroad car shops, restaurants and hotels have the patina of age and the accumulated grime of decades of coal smoke burned during six-

Voter Turnout	
2013 Total Citizen 18+	552,841
2014 House Turnout	204,329
2014 Turnout as % CVAP	37%
2012 Turnout as % CVAP	56.9%

month-long winters. Its history dates to 1609, when Dutch traders from Henry Hudson's ship *Half Moon* set up a fur trading post. Hudson, his son, and seven crew members were set adrift amidst a mutiny in James Bay, Canada, two years later and never seen again, but the trading post endured. The Dutch built Fort Orange on the banks of the Hudson in 1624 so seagoing ships could dock at the edge of the great, gloomy forests near the confluence of the Hudson and the Mohawk. Albany became one of America's biggest lumber towns in addition to serving as New York's state capital.

A few miles upriver, Troy was a steel town rivaling Pittsburgh in the 1840s, greatly advantaged by its proximity to the mouth of the Erie Canal. It is where meat-packer Samuel Wilson supplied beef rations to soldiers during the War of 1812; we know Wilson today as "Uncle Sam." Today, a gentrified Troy is bustling with antique shops. Schenectady, a few miles up the Mohawk, was the site of Charles Steinmetz's fabled General Electric laboratories and long remained a GE town.

In addition to state government, Albany for a while had one of the nation's most famed Democratic political machines, dating to 1921, when Daniel O'Connell, his brothers, and local aristocrat Edwin Corning took control of City Hall; Democrats have lost only a handful of congressional elections here since. The machine was sustained by legions of city and county employees, by a certain creativity when it came to counting votes, and by the raffish atmosphere of the speakeasies during Prohibition. Curiously, the machine made possible the transformation of Albany into the shinier metropolis it is today. Mayor Corning and Republican Gov. Nelson Rockefeller collaborated on a smorgasbord of civic improvement projects: the Empire State Plaza with 11,000 employees in 10 government buildings on 98 acres; the distinctive, ovoid performing arts center known as the Egg; and a renovated Union Station.

The 20th Congressional District of New York includes most of the Albany metropolitan area: all of Albany and Schenectady counties; most of Montgomery County, including Amsterdam; parts of Rensselaer County, including Troy; and much of Saratoga County. The horse-race track at Saratoga Springs, operating since 1863 and reportedly the oldest sports venue in the

2012 Presidential Vote		
Barack Obama (D)	186,460	(59%)
Mitt Romney (R)	122,230	(39%)
2008 Presidential Vote		
Barack Obama (D)	198,650	(58%)
John McCain (R)	135,552	(40%)
Cook Partisan Voting Index:	D+7	

nation, planned in May 2015 a major upgrade in its facility. The presence of state government has kept unemployment in the region lower than other parts of New York, but times were tough here during the recession. State government job cuts haven't helped. The area has been able to rebound through renewable energy jobs and high-tech manufacturing; GE in 2009 opened a plant producing digital X-ray equipment and built another facility to produce advanced batteries. In April 2015, unemployment was at 4.4%. Democratic voters in Albany and Troy outweigh the Republican tilt of the outer counties and make this a comfortably Democratic district. It will vote for the occasional Republican, but Democrats typically get about 60% of the vote.

Paul Tonko (D)

Democrat Paul Tonko, elected in 2008, came to Congress with an extensive background in energy issues and parlayed his expertise into a seat on the powerful Energy and Commerce Committee, where he has dealt with similar issues.

The grandson of Polish immigrants, Tonko was born in the old mill town of Amsterdam New York, where he still lives. He graduated from Clarkson University with a degree in engineering. Attracted from a young age to public service, he built his career in state government, first at the New York Department of Transportation and then as an engineer at the Department of Public Service, the state's utilities regulator. His working-class background gave him an appreciation for the "underdog" that remains the underpinning of his political beliefs.

In 1974, at age 26, he became the youngest person ever elected to the Montgomery County Board of Supervisors. He became board chairman in 1981. Tonko won a seat in the New York Assembly in a 1983 special election and served for nearly a quarter century. He won passage of a law requiring health insurers to cover most mental illnesses and another requiring social workers to report all cases of suspected child abuse to the state. He exercised his greatest influence over state energy policy, serving as chairman of the Assembly's energy committee from 1992 to 2007, when he resigned to head the state's Energy Research and Development Authority.

When the seat opened in 2008, Tonko in the primary faced Phil Steck, an Albany County legislator, and Tracey Brooks, a former staffer for Democratic Sen. Hillary Clinton. Both enjoyed a head start raising money. But most of the local Democratic establishment lined up behind Tonko. He also won important union endorsements, as well as the backing of the state's Working Families Party. With few differences between the candidates on major issues, the local support likely made the difference. Outraised and outspent by both Brooks and Steck, Tonko sailed to victory.

In the general election, Tonko faced Republican Jim Buhrmaster, a Schenectady County legislator who hoped that his appeal to independents would help him overcome the registration advantage for Democrats in the district. But Tonko won with 62% of the vote. Buhrmaster received 35%, and Steck, running as an independent, got 3%.

In the House, Tonko has focused on the issue he knows best, energy policy. Shortly after joining Energy and Commerce in late 2012, he became ranking Democrat on the panel's Environment and the Economy Subcommittee, where he was at the vanguard of defending the Environmental Protection Agency against frequent GOP attacks. He co-chairs the Sustainable Energy and Environment Coalition. In 2011, he sponsored an amendment to a spending bill seeking to protect EPA's authority to regulate carbon emissions. He also sought to undo Republican cutbacks to the Weatherization Assistance Program helping low-income families and the elderly save money by improving their homes' energy efficiency through insulation and by replacing windows and doors. He joined neighboring Republican Rep. Chris Gibson on a bill to simplify the tax credit for fuel cell-powered industrial vehicles. He was among those tied for most-liberal member in 2011, according to *National Journal's* rankings. On the Science, Space and Technology Committee, he battled in 2015 to protect federal research funds that had been directed at upstate New York's manufacturing facilities.

Even as a freshman, while Democrats controlled the House, Tonko was quick to exploit his policy expertise. He got a bill through the House in 2009 creating an $800 million research program in wind energy technologies, which would benefit GE in his district. Another of his bills, which passed the same year, created a research program to improve the efficiency of gas turbines used in power generation systems that convert heat into energy. In 2010, following the BP disaster in the Gulf of Mexico, Tonko got a provision in a House-passed bill to speed up the response to future oil spills.

On other issues, Tonko worked to expand low-income children's access to healthy meals and to improve engineering education in schools. He has sought to promote mental-health parity, as he did in Albany. His efforts to rein in pay for government contractors have won him some attention. In 2012, he and Democratic Rep. Jackie Speier of California called for capping salaries for contracting executives at the rate of the president's annual salary of $400,000, down from a maximum allowable level of $770,000. But Republicans blocked them from offering their amendment to the fiscal 2013 defense bill.

Tonko has had little trouble winning reelection. Albany *Times Union* columnist Marv Cermak described him in 2011 as "a super-duper campaigner who shows up all over the place," and said "If there is a chink in his armor, colleagues and media types agree it's his penchant for long-winded speeches."

TWENTY-FIRST DISTRICT

Elise Stefanik (R)

Elected 2014, 1st term; b. July 2, 1984, Albany; Harvard U., B.A. 2006; Catholic; single.

Professional Career: Staff, Pres. George W. Bush, 2006-09; Staff, V.P. candidate Paul Ryan, 2012; Dir. Communications, Foreign Policy Initiative; Sales, marketing & mgmt operations, Premium Plywood Products.

DC Office: 512 CHOB, 20515, 202-225-4611; Website: stefanik.house .gov.

State Offices: Glen Falls, 518-743-0964; Plattsburgh, 518-561-2324.

Committees: Armed Services: Emerging Threats & Capabilities; Military Personnel; Readiness. *Education & the Workforce:* Workforce Protections; Higher Education & Workforce Training.

Election Results

2014 general	Elise Stefanik (R)	96,226	(55%)	$1,893,160	$848,151	
	Aaron Woolf (D)	59,063	(34%)	$1,993,756	$5,020	$872,569
	Matt Funiciello (Green)	19,238	(11%)	$34,973		
2014 primary	Elise Stefanik (R)	16,489	(61%)			
	Matt Doheny (R)	10,620	(39%)			

Population		Race and Ethnicity		Income	
Total:	716,340	White	91.0%	Median income:	$48,898
Urban:	9.9%	Latino	3.1%		*(257 of 435)*
Suburban:	22.2%	Black	2.8%	Under $50,000	51.0%
Rural:	68.0%	Asian	0.8%	$50,000-$99,999:	30.8%
Land area:	14,858	Two races	1.3%	$100,000-$199,999:	15.9%
Pop/sq. mi.:	48.2	White Ethnic	55.4%	$200,000 or more:	2.3%
Born in state:	77.3%			Poverty Rate	15.1%
		Education			
Age Groups		H.S. grad or less:	48.0%	**Work**	
Under 18:	21.1%	Some college:	31.1%	White collar:	32.1%
18 to 34:	23.1%	College degree, 4 yr.:	11.8%	Blue collar:	45.1%
35 to 64:	40.0%	Post-grad study:	9.1%	Sales and service:	22.8%
Over 64:	15.8%				
		Military		Govt. workers:	21.1%
		Veterans/active duty:	12.4%		

Northern New York: Glens Falls, Watertown

Some early 19th century visionaries believed that the North Country of Upstate New York— a battleground in both the Revolutionary War and the War of 1812—was the land of the future. Financier Gouverneur Morris, French slave trader James LeRay, and Dutch silver speculator David Parish bought up thousands of acres between the Adirondacks and the St. Lawrence River and tried to unload them on farmers unaware of the shortness of the growing season and the unnavigability of the river. These developers left behind grand mansions, but their hopes for huge profits were frustrated when the Erie Canal turned the stream of settlement westward, and Canadians built their new capital of Ottawa far north of the river. But northern New York was not without its business successes: It was in Watertown in 1878 that 26-year-old Frank Woolworth put a sign over a table of odds and ends that read "Any Article 5 Cents," starting America's first retail chain and inventing the concept of discount stores.

Voter Turnout	
2013 Total Citizen 18+	554,187
2014 House Turnout	174,668
2014 Turnout as % CVAP	31.5%
2012 Turnout as % CVAP	47.9%

More recently, the North Country has looked to government for help. The St. Lawrence Seaway proved too small for most oceangoing freighters and remains frozen three months of the year. The locks are slow, and icebreakers would wreck the shoreline. The biggest initiative has been the enlargement of Fort Drum, near Watertown and adjacent to Lake Bonaparte, where despite the Army's preference for warm-weather training sites, a 10,000-person light infantry division, the 10th Mountain Division, has been stationed since 1985. The 10th Mountain performed valiantly in difficult environs in Afghanistan and Iraq. Private developers have built big malls in Watertown and Massena, attracting Canadians, as even New York has lower taxes than Ontario. While the dollar has been cheap, Canadian tourism and shopping here have been strong.

The 21st Congressional District of New York covers most of the North Country, starting at Lake Champlain, running westward along the St. Lawrence Seaway and over the Adirondacks Forest Preserve to Lake Ontario. Lake Placid is here, site of the 1980 Olympic Games and the famous "Miracle on Ice," when a heavily favored Soviet hockey team was upset by an upstart American squad. It stretches to the edges of Saratoga Springs to the southeast, and near Oswego and Syracuse to the southwest. The district has only a few population centers, including Platts-

2012 Presidential Vote
Barack Obama (D) 138,889   (52%)
Mitt Romney (R).................122,471   (46%)

2008 Presidential Vote
Barack Obama (D) 150,232   (52%)
John McCain (R).................135,834   (47%)

Cook Partisan Voting Index: EVEN

burgh on Lake Champlain, Watertown near Lake Ontario, and Gloversville and Glens Falls in the south. Warren County is known as "catheter valley" because of its many medical-device companies that make such products. In 2014, the state of New York reached a tentative land settlement with the St. Regis Mohawk tribe, contingent on agreement by the local counties.

Geographically it is the largest district in New York state and one of the largest in the East. It is ancestrally Republican but more inclined toward moderates than conservatives and increasingly divided in its loyalties to the two major parties. Clinton, Franklin and St. Lawrence counties in the northeast corner along the Vermont border have been solidly Democratic since the early 1990s. The southwestern counties are more heavily Republican. Overall, the district is competitive. Barack Obama twice won the presidential contest with margins approximating his wins nationally.

Elise Stefanik (R)

Republican Elise Stefanik won an open-seat contest in 2014 to take a Democratic-held district. The contest also elevated the politically adept Stefanik—the youngest woman ever elected to Congress—as a rising and prominent Republican star.

Born and raised in Albany, Stefanik grew up among entrepreneurs, with both parents running a wholesale plywood business. She became politically engaged during her college years at Harvard, and upon graduation she landed a job with the Bush administration's Domestic Policy Council. She went on to work in the White House chief of staff's office, and later joined Tim Pawlenty's 2012 presidential campaign as policy director. After Pawlenty withdrew, she worked for Rep. Paul Ryan of Wisconsin when he became the running mate for Mitt Romney, advising him on vice-presidential debate preparation.

After Blue Dog Democratic Rep. Bill Owens announced his retirement, Stefanik unveiled her House bid and secured the backing of the National Republican Congressional Committee's "Young Guns" initiative, which supports new talent. Democrats faced problems in their initial recruiting, and their eventual nominee, Aaron Wolff, was a film-maker who was a resident of Brooklyn. His only claim to the North Country was some land that his family had owned.

With nearly $800,000 in help from Karl Rove's American Crossroads—making a rare intervention in a GOP primary, and mostly through negative ads—Stefanik dispatched Republican Matt Doheny in the June primary, 61%-39%; Doheny, a Wall Street investment banker, had run twice against Owens, and lost each time by 2 percentage points. In the general against Wolff, Stefanik moderated from the customary GOP line on some issues. She signaled willingness to compromise on raising the minimum wage, and proposed expanding Medicare as part of an alternative to the Affordable Care Act. She refused to sign Grover Norquist's anti-tax pledge, arguing that she was beholden to voters, not lobbies.

Still, Stefanik's campaign came under criticism for lacking a district address and for property-tax delinquency in Washington. Woolf stayed competitive on the cash front as each candidate spent about $2 million. Stefanik benefited from nearly $2 million in party-related assistance, far more than Democrats spent for Wolff, who also suffered from an active campaign by Green Party candidate Matt Funicello. With that split between liberal and centrist voters, Stefanik pulled away to a surprisingly comfortable win. She prevailed with a stunning 55% of the vote to 34% for Wolff and 11% for Funicello. Stefanik won 9 of the 12 counties, losing three in the northeast corner of the state.

At age 30, Stefanik drew considerable publicity. CBS News featured her with an online story headlined, "Is Elise Stefanik the future of the GOP?" She told the network: "I think we need to have a tone that reaches out to women, and that's something that I've been very focused on. I also think that we need to do a better job of listening." She recounted that she took the advice of Paul Ryan that "you have one mouth and two ears. Use them in that ratio." Elizabeth Holtzman, a Democrat from Brooklyn who had been the youngest woman elected to the House at age 31 in 1972, gave Stefanik some advice in *Politico*: "Being young gives you a different—and sometimes important—perspective on what is happening. I found I was more open to question the old ways of doing things, and more open to new approaches."

In the House, Stefanik was assigned to the Armed Services and Education and the Workforce committees. Freshman Republicans selected her as their representative on the GOP Policy Committee. She also co-chaired the Congressional STEAM (science, technology, engineering, arts, math and design) Caucus. In May 2015, she introduced her first bill, which would permit local officials to seek a waiver of Environment Protection Agency rules within 90 days for the demolition of a building that is at risk of collapse. The proposal stemmed from a conflict in Malone in her district. She promoted biomass as a potential growth opportunity for the district. Protecting Fort Drum from budget cuts became a priority.

TWENTY-SECOND DISTRICT

Richard Hanna (R)

Elected 2010, 3rd term; b. Jan. 25, 1951, Utica; Reed Col., B.A. 1976; Catholic; married (Kim); 2 children.

Professional Career: Founder & Pres., Hanna Construction; Partner, The Gabriel Group, 1992-2010.

DC Office: 319 CHOB, 20515, 202-225-3665; Fax: 202-225-1891; Website: hanna.house.gov.

State Offices: Binghamton, 607-723-0212; Utica, 315-724-9740.

Committees: *Small Business:* Contracting & Workforce (Chmn); Economic Growth, Tax & Capital Access. *Transportation & Infrastructure:* Aviation; Highways & Transit; Railroads, Pipelines & Hazardous Materials.

Group Ratings

	ADA	ACLU	AFL-CIO	LCV	ITI	COC	HAFA	ACU	CFG	FRC
2014	5%	22%	–	11%	100%	85%	40%	42%	34%	13%
2013	15%	C	42%	11%	C	92%	C	48%	47%	C

National Journal Ratings

	2013 LIB	—	2013 CONS
Economic	50%	—	50%
Social	53%	—	46%
Foreign	52%	—	48%
Composite	52%	—	48%

Key Votes of the 113th Congress

1. Sandy storm spending	Y	5. Medical Marijuana	Y
2. Violence Against Women Act	Y	6. Farm Bill	Y
3. Guantanamo Bay Detainees	N	7. Afghanistan Combat	N
4. Abortion 20-week ban	N	8. NSA Phone Data Collection	N

9. Syrian Rebels Training	Y
10. Keystone pipeline	Y
11. Immigration Exec. Action	Y
12. Bipartisan budget deal	Y

Election Results

2014 general	Richard Hanna (R)................unopposed			$877,661	$85,859	$9,819
2014 primary	Richard Hanna (R).....................16,119	(54%)				
	Claudia Tenney...........................14,000	(46%)				

Prior winning percentages: 2012 (61%), 2010 (53%)

Population		Race and Ethnicity		Income	
Total:	713,145	White	89.0%	Median income:	$46,648
Urban:	29.6%	Latino	3.2%		*(289 of 435)*
Suburban:	41.5%	Black	3.2%	Under $50,000	52.9%
Rural:	28.9%	Asian	2.3%	$50,000-$99,999:	31.1%
Land area:	6,234	Two races	1.8%	$100,000-$199,999:	13.9%
Pop/sq. mi.:	114.4	White Ethnic	47.6%	$200,000 or more:	2.2%
Born in state:	80.7%			Poverty Rate	16.5%
		Education			
Age Groups		H.S. grad or less:	47.1%	**Work**	
Under 18:	20.9%	Some college:	29.6%	White collar:	34.8%
18 to 34:	22.8%	College degree, 4 yr.:	13.4%	Blue collar:	42.2%
35 to 64:	39.6%	Post-grad study:	9.9%	Sales and service:	22.9%
Over 64:	16.7%				
		Military		Govt. workers:	20.1%
		Veterans/active duty:	9.4%		

Central New York: Utica, Binghamton

One of the first American frontiers was the Mohawk River Valley of Upstate New York. But from the establishment of Fort Orange in 1624 in what is now Albany until the Revolutionary War, white settlers did not dare move west along the Mohawk. The British used their Iroquois allies as

Voter Turnout	
2013 Total Citizen 18+	550,244
2014 House Turnout	131,932
2014 Turnout as % CVAP	24%
2012 Turnout as % CVAP	50.7%

a buffer against the French and in turn kept New England Yankees from moving westward. Only after the French were driven from North America in 1759 did the pressures for westward settlement prevail. Once the Revolutionary War started, Iroquois dominion ended. The later digging of the Erie Canal was an engineering feat that hastened the westward push. In 1811, it cost more to ship goods 30 miles inland from New York City than it cost to send them to England. But after eight years of work by 9,000 men, the canal opened in 1825, ahead of schedule and on budget, effectively tying together the nation and guaranteeing the preeminence of New York City in America's economy.

When the New York Central built its water-line rail route, the Mohawk Valley became one of the nation's early industrial centers. The little Oneida County hamlets of Utica and Rome, where the canal builders had to dig through the route's highest ground, became sizable factory towns. Even the utopian Oneida Community, with its believers in plural marriage and communal ownership, operated a stainless steel factory. First settled by New England Yankees, these towns attracted a new wave of immigration from the Atlantic coast in the early 20th century, including many Italian and Polish Americans.

2012 Presidential Vote		
Mitt Romney (R)................136,500	(49%)
Barack Obama (D) 135,172	(49%)

2008 Presidential Vote		
John McCain (R)................148,567	(49%)
Barack Obama (D) 148,418	(49%)

Cook Partisan Voting Index: R+3

The 22nd Congressional District of New York drops from Lake Ontario to the Pennsylvania border in a strip east of Syracuse, as it sprawls through parts of eight counties in central New York, most of them lightly populated. The biggest cities are Utica and Rome in Oneida County and Binghamton in Broome County. This part of Upstate New York has been bypassed by economic growth for decades. Oneida

County's population has dropped 15% since it peaked in the 1970 census, and it continued to lose population from 2000 to 2013. A similar pattern applied in Broome, which has lost about 10% of its population since 1970. In a once economically dynamic area, the largest employer in central New York has become Oneida Nation's Turning Stone Resort Casino, which announced in November 2014 plans for a huge retail outlet and entertainment complex. State government has completed dredging the successor to the Erie Canal in Utica, but barge traffic is not a growth industry.

Politically this part of Upstate New York had been Republican since the party came into existence in the 1850s, and the GOP maintains a registration advantage in every county except for Broome. But the Republican advantage is broad, not deep, and the district as a whole was tightly divided at the presidential level in 2008 and 2012, with President Barack Obama and his GOP opponents getting 49% each time.

Richard Hanna (R)

Republican Richard Hanna is a multimillionaire construction executive who is loyal to his party but does not share the no-compromises militancy of many fellow members of the GOP class of 2010, especially on social issues. "We need to get along," he told the Utica *Observer-Dispatch*. "Compromise is not treason." That approach has ranked him among the most moderate House Republicans.

Hanna is of Lebanese descent; he was born in Utica and graduated from high school in nearby Marcy. When his father died, the 20-year-old Hanna became the main source of income for his mother and four sisters. But he was determined to go to college and earned enough to put himself through Reed College in Oregon. But his money ran out before he could get a master's degree, so he decided to return home and start a business. Since his father had been a carpenter, Hanna started a construction company. For five years, he lived in a barn he built and worked at whatever jobs his fledgling company could pick up. Hanna Construction eventually grew to employ more than 450 people. A licensed pilot, Hanna also volunteered with Angel Flights, a service that provides free transport to the sick and injured in need of long-distance transportation.

In 2008, Hanna ran against freshman Democrat Michael Arcuri, who had taken the seat of veteran Rep. Sherwood Boehlert, a Republican moderate who retired. Hanna did not get much support from national Republicans, but he held Arcuri to a 52%-48% victory, even as Democrat Barack Obama narrowly carried the district. Two years later, Hanna was back for a rematch, running as a fiscal conservative opposed to government bailouts and, like Boehlert, a moderate on cultural issues. He supported abortion rights and civil unions for gay couples, but dubbed the Democrats' health care legislation "ill-conceived."

Arcuri voted for the health care bill in November 2009 but against the final version in March 2010. That cost him the support of the union-controlled Working Families Party, so he created his own Moderate Party to give him a second ballot line. Hanna's business became an issue in the campaign. Arcuri aired an ad questioning Hanna's commitment to restraining government spending, noting his business received $4 million in government contracts. Arcuri also noted that Hanna's firm was cited 12 times for health and safety violations. Hanna responded that he went through proper avenues in obtaining government work, and that any company doing construction work was bound to accrue some violations. Arcuri spent $1.9 million, while Hanna spent $1.3 million, $270,000 of it his own money. Hanna won 53%-47%, carrying eight of 11 counties.

In the House, Hanna has seats on the Transportation and Infrastructure and Small Business committees. A pilot, he urged in May 2015 reauthorization of the Federal Aviation Administration, with an upgrading of aviation programs such as new technologies for unmanned aircraft systems and satellite-based GPS systems. He called for more federal funding for small airports, such as those in Upstate New York. With Democratic Rep. Janice Hahn of California, he filed a bill to re-establish state infrastructure banks to fund local transportation initiatives.

Hanna has had an unpredictable voting record. He opposed moves by conservatives to drastically cut or eliminate programs such as National Public Radio. He strongly favored, however, elimination of the Treasury Department's Home Affordable Modification Program and successfully amended the bill to include details of the mortgage-assistance program's flaws. He collected an "A" rating from the National Rifle Association. After South Carolina

GOP Rep. Jeff Duncan in February 2013 encouraged Remington Arms to relocate its plant from Hanna's district in retaliation for New York's strict new gun laws, Hanna responded that he would work to make sure the plant stayed "right where it began almost 200 years ago."

Hanna has sided with most Democrats on women's rights issues. In 2012, he played a leading role in an effort to revive a reauthorization of the Violence Against Women Act, largely pushed by Democrats. He also was the only GOP House member to appear at a March 2012 rally in support of the Equal Rights Amendment and candidly told the crowd, "Contribute your money to people who speak out on your behalf, because the other side— my side—has a lot of it." In May 2015, Hanna was one of only four Republicans who voted against House passage of the bill to ban abortions in virtually all cases after 20 weeks of pregnancy.

He also has worked across the aisle on gay rights. In April 2015, he was one of three House Republicans who signed a brief to the Supreme Court urging the legalization of same-sex marriage. Earlier, Hanna backed the Court's 2013 ruling that overturned the California initiative that backed same-sex marriage. He has joined the bipartisan "Problem Solvers" coalition led by Democratic Sen. Joe Manchin of West Virginia and former GOP Gov. Jon Huntsman of Utah.

Hanna's reelections have shown strength with moderates, but a strong warning from conservatives. In 2012, he defeated Democrat Dan Lamb, 61%-39%. Two years later, he faced no Democratic opposition. In 2014, he survived a close GOP primary against Assembly-woman Claudia Tenney, who criticized the incumbent's support for gay marriage and his votes to increase the debt ceiling and oppose delay of implementation of the 2010 health care law. She spent only $190,000, of which $119,000 came from loans that she made to her campaign. Tenney had backing from the tea party and conservative talk-show hosts Laura Ingraham and Sean Hannity. Hanna's campaign account spent $862,000 during the cycle, and he had $665,000 support from a Super PAC backed by billionaire investor Paul Singer. Hanna took five of the eight counties and won 53.5%-46.5%.

TWENTY-THIRD DISTRICT

Tom Reed (R)

Elected Nov. 2010, 3rd full term; b. Nov. 18, 1971, Joliet, IL; Alfred U., B.A. 1993, OH Northern U., J.D. 1996; Catholic; married (Jean); 2 children.

Elected Office: Corning mayor, 2008-10.

Professional Career: Clerk, private firm, 1995; Assoc. atty., private firm, 1996-99; Owner, Law Office of Thomas W. Reed II.

DC Office: 2437 RHOB, 20515, 202-225-3161; Fax: 202-226-6599; Website: reed.house.gov.

State Offices: Corning, 607-654-7566; Geneva, 315-759-5229; Ithaca, 607-222-2027; Jamestown, 716-708-6369; Olean, 716-379-8434.

Committees: *Ways & Means:* Select Revenue Measures; Social Security.

Group Ratings

	ADA	ACLU	AFL-CIO	LCV	ITI	COC	HAFA	ACU	CFG	FRC
2014	0%	0%	–	3%	60%	92%	41%	52%	41%	75%
2013	5%	C	30%	4%	C	83%	C	52%	49%	C

National Journal Ratings

	2013 LIB	—	2013 CONS
Economic	49%	—	51%
Social	53%	—	47%
Foreign	24%	—	68%
Composite	43%	—	57%

Key Votes of the 113th Congress

1. Sandy storm spending	Y	5. Medical Marijuana	Y	9. Syrian Rebels Training	Y
2. Violence Against Women Act	NV	6. Farm Bill	Y	10. Keystone pipeline	Y
3. Guantanamo Bay Detainees	N	7. Afghanistan Combat	N	11. Immigration Exec. Action	Y
4. Abortion 20-week ban	Y	8. NSA Phone Data Collection	N	12. Bipartisan budget deal	Y

Election Results

2014 general	Tom Reed (R)	113,130	(62%)	$3,471,224	$698,991	$78,487
	Martha Robertson (D)	70,242	(38%)	$2,300,753	$28,565	
2014 primary	Tom Reed (R)	unopposed				

Prior winning percentages: 2012 (52%), 2010 (57%), 2010 special (57%)

Population		Race and Ethnicity		Income	
Total:	716,427	White	89.4%	Median income:	$44,819
Urban:	14.4%	Latino	3.3%		*(323 of 435)*
Suburban:	20.7%	Black	2.8%	Under $50,000	54.8%
Rural:	64.9%	Asian	2.2%	$50,000-$99,999:	30.1%
Land area:	7,424	Two races	1.5%	$100,000-$199,999:	12.7%
Pop/sq. mi.:	96.5	White Ethnic	39.3%	$200,000 or more:	2.4%
Born in state:	74.8%			Poverty Rate	17.0%
		Education			
Age Groups		H.S. grad or less:	46.1%	**Work**	
Under 18:	20.7%	Some college:	29.6%	White collar:	35.1%
18 to 34:	23.8%	College degree, 4 yr.:	12.2%	Blue collar:	41.5%
35 to 64:	39.1%	Post-grad study:	12.0%	Sales and service:	23.4%
Over 64:	16.4%				
		Military		Govt. workers:	16.0%
		Veterans/active duty:	9.3%		

Southern Tier: Jamestown, Elmira

The Southern Tier of New York is one of the nation's forgotten stretches of territory, yet it has an interesting and distinctive history. Elmira was the hometown of Mark Twain's beloved wife, Olivia, and it is where Twain is buried. On Lake Chautauqua, not far from Lake Erie, a training

Voter Turnout	
2013 Total Citizen 18+	553,927
2014 House Turnout	183,481
2014 Turnout as % CVAP	33.1%
2012 Turnout as % CVAP	50.4%

camp for Methodist Sunday school teachers was founded in 1874. In summers, on wide green lawns and in Victorian-style gazebos, some 25,000 people heard educational talks and inspirational lectures from the likes of William Jennings Bryan. The area has an Indian presence, with small reservations as well as the Seneca-Iroquois National Museum in Salamanca, plus miles and miles of dairy farms. Sheltered by hills, the lands at the edge of Upstate New York's deep lakes constitute the nation's largest grape-growing area outside California and are the headquarters of prime New York wineries.

Corning is the headquarters of Corning Glass Works, a company successful over the years not only in manufacturing but also in its artistic distinction, which is showcased at a well-visited glass museum. Its long-term prospects have improved dramatically, with heavy demand for its fiber optics and other high-tech components. The *Fortune* 500 company also makes key components of the liquid crystal display (LCD) glass used in flat-screen televisions and computers. But the company has been moving jobs overseas, including a controversial decision in 2010 to spend $800 million on a new LCD glass facility in Beijing instead of Corning. The state of New York has tried to improve the region's fortunes, with economic development grants. From December 2009 to December 2014, the unemployment rate in the Southern Tier dropped from 8.6% to

2012 Presidential Vote		
Mitt Romney (R)	137,307	(50%)
Barack Obama (D)	133,940	(48%)
2008 Presidential Vote		
Barack Obama (D)	150,402	(50%)
John McCain (R)	147,906	(49%)
Cook Partisan Voting Index:	R+3	

5.6%, close to the national average. Many local residents criticized as a missed job-creating opportunity the December 2014 decision by state officials with Gov. Andrew Cuomo to ban hydraulic fracturing in this area, which is believed to have large deposits of natural gas.

The 23rd Congressional District of New York is centered on the state's Southern Tier, extending from Chautauqua near the Pennsylvania line almost to Binghamton, more than halfway to the Massachusetts line. To the north, it includes the central Finger Lakes: giant gorges torn into the Earth's crust by expanding glaciers, and then naturally dammed up by the debris deposited when the glaciers retreated. Nearby Seneca Falls was the birthplace of the women's rights movement in 1848, when Boston transplants Elizabeth Cady Stanton and Lucretia Mott produced a Declaration of Sentiments that initiated the push for suffrage. The town is believed to be the inspiration for Bedford Falls in the classic film, *It's a Wonderful Life*. In the small town of Celoron, a statue was constructed to honor Lucille Ball, the hometown native who became a renowned comedian. But in early 2015, many local residents were so frightened by its dramatic features and un-Lucy-like features that they demanded removal of the statue.

The towns here have long had a Democratic tilt, reflecting the Irish and Italian Catholics who settled there, but the countryside was traditionally Protestant and Republican. The addition to the district of the heavily Democratic university town of Ithaca helped turn this into true swing territory at the federal level; Republicans still perform well at most state and local levels. Fun facts: Ithaca is the home of the nation's first electric street lamps, first ice cream sundae and first chicken nuggets—but not all at the same time.

Tom Reed (R)

Republican Tom Reed, who took office in November 2010, is a pragmatic and low-key centrist. He has won the trust of House GOP leaders, who gave him a seat on the Ways and Means Committee. He fell short in his own party leadership bid.

Reed was born in Joliet Illinois, the youngest of 12 children. His father was an Army veteran and Silver Star recipient who fought in World War II and Korea, but he accidentally died of carbon monoxide poisoning while working on his car when Reed was two years old. Reed's surviving family soon moved to Corning New York, where his mother had grown up. She stayed home to take care of the children, relying on her late husband's military death benefits and Social Security checks for financial support. "We struggled but we never went without, so to speak. We were happy," Reed said. As the youngest, Reed grew accustomed to being the last one to get a bath and to sitting on the floor of the family car because there weren't enough seats to go around.

In high school, Reed swam competitively and received offers to compete in college athletics programs. He opted to stay close to home, attending Alfred University in western New York. He majored in political science, and captained the swim team, placing eighth in Division III College National Championships. Reed went to law school at Ohio Northern University College, then worked at a law firm in Rochester. In 1999, he returned to Corning to start his own law firm. He was elected mayor in 2007.

In 2009, Reed challenged freshman Democratic Rep. Eric Massa in the Republican-leaning district. Massa had a reputation as a fierce campaigner, and he seemed to have a good chance to retain his seat. The race turned on its head in March 2010, when Massa abruptly resigned from the House amid allegations from male staff members that he had inappropriately touched them during social events. Democratic Gov. David Paterson scheduled a special election to coincide with the general election in November.

Reed was unchallenged for the Republican nomination. Democrats chose Matthew Zeller, an Afghanistan combat veteran, who argued that he would protect Social Security and create jobs more effectively than would Reed, who focused his message on reducing the deficit and shrinking government. Zeller raised $457,000, compared with Reed's $1 million. Reed had one slip-up in the race. He suggested on Twitter that the district had been shortchanged by the House's failure to vote on the confirmation of Supreme Court Justice Elena Kagan. The Senate votes on judicial confirmations, not the House. By capitalizing on voter angst over excessive spending and on the Republican wave that resulted, Reed won handily, 57%-43%. He served in the final weeks of the lame-duck session.

Despite his centrist tendencies, Reed has mostly stuck with his party on major legislation. He impressed House leaders by getting the support of colleagues for free trade agreements with Colombia, Panama and South Korea. In June 2011, he got a prized seat on Ways and Means, rare for a freshman, and later that year was one of the six GOP members chosen as conferees in payroll tax-cut negotiations. "As you talk to Tom, you realize he is very policy-oriented, that there's a lot of substance there," Ways and Means Chairman Dave Camp of Michigan told *The Buffalo News*. In January 2015, Reed backed a change that Republicans made in House rules to prevent a transfer of funds from the Social Security retirement system as "a short-term Band Aid" to fix the serious financial shortfall in the federal disability program. He also called for simplification of the tax code.

On local issues, Reed added an amendment to the House-passed fiscal 2013 energy and water spending bill to increase money for cleanups at sites such as his district's West

Valley Demonstration Project, a former nuclear fuel reprocessing facility. In Ithaca, the Democratic bastion in the district, Reed may have found an acceptance level, at least on his terms. A small group of protestors in May 2015 interrupted a nearby town hall meeting and serenaded him with their custom-made lyrics about his alleged close ties to the natural gas industry: "Oh Tommy Boy, the pipes we'd be installing. Turn not ye back! An industry implores you." Reed heard them out, thanked them for their commitment to their beliefs and added, "I appreciate that input and obviously we're going to disagree."

In 2012, Reed drew an energetic Democratic challenger in Nate Shinagawa, the 28-year-old vice chairman of the Tompkins County (Ithaca) Legislature. He attacked Reed for his support of hydraulic fracturing for natural gas, contending it would endanger tourism and agriculture in the Finger Lakes region. Reed said he supported an exemption for drilling in the Finger Lakes. He raised more than $2 million to Shinagawa's $829,000 and eked out a win, 52%-48%.

Reed had another competitive campaign in 2014. Martha Robinson, chairwoman of the Tompkins County Legislature, challenged Reed. She advocated liberal views in strong opposition to fossil-fuel production in New York and to changes in the Social Security cost-of-living adjustment. She raised more money than Shinagawa, but was outspent, $3.5 million to $2.3 million. Reed won overwhelmingly, 62%-38%, an indication that he had become entrenched in his seat.

After the 2014 election, Reed ran against two other candidates for chairman of the House Republican Policy Committee, which has been viewed as a stepping-stone to higher leadership positions. He said that he wanted the committee to play a more formal role in working with Republicans on legislation. On the showdown second ballot, Reed lost to Luke Messer of Indiana, 137-90. He remains well-positioned to influence policy at Ways and Means.

TWENTY-FOURTH DISTRICT

John Katko (R)

Elected 2014, 1st term; b. Nov. 9, 1962, Camillus; Niagara U., B.A. 1984, Syracuse U., J.D. 1988; Catholic; married (Robin); 3 children.

Professional Career: Sr. trial atty., U.S. Securities & Exchange Comm., 1991-95; Prosecutor, NY Northern Dist. U.S. atty. office; Asst. U.S. atty., U.S. Justice Dept., 1995-2013.

DC Office: 1123 LHOB, 20515, 202-225-3701; Fax: 202-225-4042; Website: katko.house.gov.

State Offices: Auburn, 315-253-4068; Syracuse, 315-423-5657.

Committees: *Homeland Security:* Counterrorism & Intelligence; Transportation Security (Chmn). *Transportation & Infrastructure:* Highways & Transit; Railroads, Pipelines, & Hazardous Materials; Water Resources & Environment.

Election Results

2014 general	John Katko (R)	118,474	(60%)	$992,698	$1,078,363	$1,863,464
	Dan Maffei (D)	80,304	(40%)	$2,749,173	$386,385	$1,524,289
2014 primary	John Katko (R)	unopposed				

Population		Race and Ethnicity		Income	
Total:	715,192	White	83.2%	Median income:	$51,028
Urban:	31.0%	Black	7.8%		*(221 of 435)*
Suburban:	53.0%	Latino	3.9%	Under $50,000	48.9%
Rural:	15.9%	Asian	2.2%	$50,000-$99,999:	31.3%
Land area:	2,584	Two races	2.2%	$100,000-$199,999:	16.2%
Pop/sq. mi.:	276.8	White Ethnic	54.0%	$200,000 or more:	3.6%
Born in state:	79.6%			Poverty Rate	15.1%
		Education			
Age Groups		H.S. grad or less:	40.1%	**Work**	
Under 18:	21.8%	Some college:	30.9%	White collar:	37.3%
18 to 34:	23.1%	College degree, 4 yr.:	16.3%	Blue collar:	42.5%
35 to 64:	39.8%	Post-grad study:	12.7%	Sales and service:	20.2%
Over 64:	15.2%				
		Military		Govt. workers:	15.9%
		Veterans/active duty:	8.2%		

North-Central New York: Syracuse Metro

Syracuse is a Middle American city in the middle of Upstate New York, halfway between Albany and Buffalo on the Erie Canal and the old New York Central Railroad, which were for years the nation's major east-west transportation routes. Built on a swamp that was a salt spring, Syracuse is the

Voter Turnout	
2013 Total Citizen 18+	542,213
2014 House Turnout	199,222
2014 Turnout as % CVAP	36.7%
2012 Turnout as % CVAP	55.7%

home of many practical-minded inventions—the dental chair, Stickley mission furniture, the drive-in bank teller, and the serrated knife. It is the site of the New York State Fair, which attracts 1 million visitors annually; of Syracuse University, which plays basketball and football inside the Carrier Dome, the largest domed stadium on a college campus; and of the Museum of Automobile History, home to the largest private collection of automobile and automobile-related objects in the world.

Nearby, the agricultural hinterland is rich with specialty crops like wine grapes, and its industrial jobs are mostly high-skill. Still, with the decline in manufacturing, there are 25,000 fewer jobs here than there were in the mid-2000s. Because local housing prices increased only modestly during the real estate boom, the area suffered little from the housing bust. *CNNMoney* named Syracuse the third most affordable housing market in the nation in 2010, with a median home price of $95,000.

The 24th Congressional District of New York includes all of Syracuse and surrounding Onondaga County. West of Syracuse, it includes territory just south of Lake Ontario, including all of Cayuga County, home of abolitionist Harriet Tubman. Near Rochester, in Wayne County, is the village of Palmyra, where Joseph Smith had his vision of the

2012 Presidential Vote		
Barack Obama (D) 171,502	(57%)
Mitt Romney (R)................123,534	(41%)
2008 Presidential Vote		
Barack Obama (D) 181,791	(56%)
John McCain (R)................135,947	(42%)
Cook Partisan Voting Index: D+5		

angel Moroni and saw the golden tablets that led him to found the Mormon Church. To the north, the district takes in part of Oswego County, including the city of Oswego, whose port facilities on Lake Ontario have made it an attractive tourist destination.

Historically, Syracuse was Republican, partly out of antipathy to New York City. In the 1990s, economically ailing Upstate New York trended sharply toward national Democrats even as it voted for Republican Gov. George Pataki. The 24th district today leans Democratic. But like much of Upstate, it has shown competitive tendencies.

John Katko (R)

Republican John Katko, a former federal prosecutor, made a late surge in 2014 and defeated Democratic Rep. Dan Maffei 60% to 40%, a stunning margin in a district that President Barack Obama carried with 57% just two years earlier. Katko leveraged his law-and-order credentials and hammered home the GOP's long-standing characterization of Maffei as a Washington insider. His setback appeared to end Maffei's unusual streak of participating in five consecutive elections with alternating party control of the seat.

Katko grew up in Onondaga County, then attended Niagara University and Syracuse University's law school. He worked for a D.C. law firm before taking a position at the Securities and Exchange Commission. In two decades at the Justice Department, he served as a special assistant U.S. attorney in Virginia's Eastern District and for the narcotics and dangerous drugs section of the criminal division. During that time, he returned home and worked a variety of organize crime and drug enforcement-related prosecutions with the U.S. Attorney's Office for the Northern District of New York in Syracuse. He contends that his successful prosecution of a major gang case led to a significant drop in the violent crime rate in Syracuse.

Katko retired from the Justice Department to challenge Maffei, who was first elected in 2008, lost his seat in the 2010 GOP wave and won it back in 2012—albeit with just 49% of the vote, as President Barack Obama won 57% in the district. Katko won the GOP nomination without opposition.

As with Maffei's previous Republican opponents, Katko tried to depict the congressman as an out-of-touch Beltway insider. He pointed to Maffei's purchase of a $700,000 house in the Washington area. And Katko drew substantial media attention when he noted that Maffei and his wife had their baby in a D.C. hospital, a question that the congressman said was "out of bounds." Katko responded at a debate that Maffei put the name of the hospital in a news release: "You can't have your cake and eat it, too."

As in past campaigns, Maffei emphasized his moderate stripes and nonideological pragmatism. He criticized Obama's handling of the Ebola scare in the United States and voiced unhappiness with the administration's handling of the conflict in Syria.

Maffei and Democrats tried to poke holes in Katko's record as a prosecutor, criticizing him for his handling of a local mayor's sex-offender case as well as for an incident involving a gun that was stolen from Katko in 2000 and used in a robbery that left two people dead. Katko complained that such campaign attacks "destroyed my character." But he overtook his opponent in polls in the race's final week with help from the endorsement of the local digital paper *Syracuse.com*, which said Maffei's performance in office has been "steady but uninspiring. ... It's time to give someone else a chance."

Katko won with surprising ease, 60%-40%, and he took all four counties. Onondaga, which is the largest county, also was the tightest, with 53% for Katko. In January 2015, Maffei told Syracuse.com, "I have no plans to ever be involved as a candidate in electoral politics," though he slightly hedged that he would "never say never."

In the House, Katko was assigned to the Transportation and Infrastructure Committee and the Homeland Security Committee, where he chaired the Transportation Subcommittee. In June 2015, he filed a bill to overhaul the Transportation Security Administration to improve safety at airports. He also took the leadership of a new bipartisan Task Force on Combating Terrorist and Foreign Fighter Travel. In a May 2015 article, he wrote that more resources and a multi-disciplinary approach are needed to confront the Islamic State (ISIS) in the United States. "This is a serious threat to the U.S. homeland that cannot be contained—it must be confronted," he wrote. Katko showed occasional independence from the House GOP position, as when he voted in April 2014 to oppose both the final version of the annual budget plan and a plan to overturn a District of Columbia law that bans workplace discrimination over employees' reproductive decisions but provides no faith-based exemptions.

Katko told his constituents that his chief priorities were at home. When he issued a report on his first 100 days in office, each of his top 10 highlights dealt with Central New York. His number-one priority was the reconstruction of Interstate 81, which needs replacement of its elevated highway in downtown Syracuse, according to many local officials. Given the repeated changes in this seat for the past decade, Katko likely will face a daunting reelection contest in the 2016 presidential cycle. He got good news when Syracuse Democratic Mayor Stephanie Miner in May 2015 decided not to challenge him.

TWENTY-FIFTH DISTRICT

Louise Slaughter (D)

Elected 1986, 15th term; b. Aug. 14, 1929, Harlan Cnty., KY; U. of KY, B.S. 1951, M.S. 1953; Episcopalian; widowed; 3 children.

Elected Office: Monroe Cnty. Legislature, 1976-79; NY Assembly, 1982-86.

Professional Career: Regional coord., NY Dept. of St., 1976-79; Regional coord., Lt. Gov. Mario Cuomo, 1979-82.

DC Office: 2469 RHOB, 20515, 202-225-3615; Fax: 202-225-7822; Website: louise.house.gov.

State Offices: Rochester, 585-232-4850.

Committees: *Rules* (RMM): Rules & Organization of the House.

Group Ratings

	ADA	ACLU	AFL-CIO	LCV	ITI	COC	HAFA	ACU	CFG	FRC
2014	85%	77%	–	94%	40%	36%	12%	12%	11%	0%
2013	95%	C	100%	86%	C	25%	C	10%	11%	C

National Journal Ratings

	2013 LIB	—	2013 CONS
Economic	91%	—	0%
Social	93%	—	0%
Foreign	73%	—	26%
Composite	89%	—	12%

Key Votes of the 113th Congress

1. Sandy storm spending	Y	5. Medical Marijuana	NV	9. Syrian Rebels Training	N
2. Violence Against Women Act	Y	6. Farm Bill	NV	10. Keystone pipeline	N
3. Guantanamo Bay Detainees	Y	7. Afghanistan Combat	Y	11. Immigration Exec. Action	N
4. Abortion 20-week ban	N	8. NSA Phone Data Collection	N	12. Bipartisan budget deal	N

Election Results

2014 general	Louise Slaughter (D)	96,803	(50%)	$796,859
	Mark Assini (R)	95,932	(50%)	$193,193
2014 primary	Louise Slaughter (D)	unopposed		

Prior winning percentages: 2012 (57%), 2010 (65%), 2008 (78%), 2006 (73%), 2004 (73%), 2002 (62%), 2000 (66%), 1998 (65%), 1996 (57%), 1994 (57%), 1992 (55%), 1990 (59%), 1988 (57%), 1986 (51%)

Population		Race and Ethnicity		Income	
Total:	724,587	White	71.5%	Median income:	$51,129
Urban:	71.4%	Black	15.0%		*(219 of 435)*
Suburban:	28.3%	Latino	7.7%	Under $50,000	48.8%
Rural:	0.3%	Asian	3.3%	$50,000-$99,999:	30.6%
Land area:	779	Two races	2.0%	$100,000-$199,999:	16.9%
Pop/sq. mi.:	929.9	White Ethnic	45.3%	$200,000 or more:	3.7%
Born in state:	74.1%			Poverty Rate	16.1%
		Education			
Age Groups		H.S. grad or less:	34.7%	**Work**	
Under 18:	21.6%	Some college:	29.3%	White collar:	42.1%
18 to 34:	24.7%	College degree, 4 yr.:	19.9%	Blue collar:	42.2%
35 to 64:	38.6%	Post-grad study:	16.1%	Sales and service:	15.7%
Over 64:	15.1%				
		Military		Govt. workers:	12.3%
		Veterans/active duty:	6.8%		

Rochester Metro

Rochester, with a metropolitan area of just over 1 million, is a major city of Upstate New York and was one of America's first boomtowns. Here, the Genesee River descends in a 100-foot drop known as High Falls, which powered the city's early industries. Rochester became known as Flour City for

Voter Turnout	
2013 Total Citizen 18+	546,344
2014 House Turnout	192,971
2014 Turnout as % CVAP	35.3%
2012 Turnout as % CVAP	59.1%

the mills that served western New York farmers. Rochester was also the home base of women's suffrage leader Susan B. Anthony and abolitionist Frederick Douglass, and a popular center of 19th century tent revivals.

It became one of the early high-tech cities, after a bank clerk named George Eastman marketed the first still camera and film for Thomas Edison's motion picture camera. Later, Bausch & Lomb developed its lens business in Rochester. The optics and imaging industry continues to be a significant regional employer. The industries it has produced—Bausch & Lomb, Eastman Kodak and Xerox, which started here as Haloid before moving its headquarters to Connecticut in 1969—thrived on technical innovation, precision workmanship, high reliability and customer service. They gave Rochester an affluent and well-educated population as well as fine civic institutions, including the George Eastman House, one of the world's leading repositories of photographic and motion picture history.

In recent decades, Rochester's big employers have fallen on hard times, and young professionals have been leaving the area. Kodak was hard hit by competition from digital cameras, and although it employed 2,300 people in 2013, the workforce was down from 60,000 people in 1981.

2012 Presidential Vote		
Barack Obama (D)	187,753	(59%)
Mitt Romney (R)	125,897	(39%)
2008 Presidential Vote		
Barack Obama (D)	201,019	(59%)
John McCain (R)	136,489	(40%)
Cook Partisan Voting Index: D+7		

In 2012, it filed for bankruptcy and reemerged in September 2013 as what it called "a technology company focused on imaging for business." *The New York Times* reported in March

2015 that of the nearly 200 buildings that had housed Kodak production in Rochester, 80 were destroyed, 59 were sold, and "61 buildings remain, awaiting an uncertain fate."

Xerox maintains a significant presence in the area but employs less than half as many as when its workforce numbered 16,000. The city's population—332,000 in 1950—has dropped in each census since then, to 210,000 in 2013; the overall metropolitan area has grown by less than 10% in the past 40 years.

The 25th Congressional District of New York is a compact district that is entirely within Rochester's Monroe County, which previously had been split among four districts. Heavily Democratic areas in Rochester were combined with more marginal suburbs to create a district that is comfortably but not overwhelmingly Democratic.

Louise Slaughter (D)

Democrat Louise Slaughter, elected in 1986, is the only woman who has chaired the powerful Rules Committee. She has a long history of working on issues important to women and was one of the original authors of the 1994 Violence Against Women Act. In 2014, she barely survived a surprisingly close reelection.

A coal miner's daughter and a descendant of Daniel Boone, she grew up in Kentucky and still speaks with the distinctive phraseology of the mountains. She wound up in New York in the 1950s when she moved there with her husband. Her involvement in community issues led to a career in government. Slaughter became a staffer for Mario Cuomo when he was lieutenant governor in the 1970s, and she won a seat in the Monroe County Legislature in 1976. She was elected to the New York Assembly in 1982.

Four years later, she beat one-term conservative Republican Rep. Fred Eckert, 51%-49%, after charging that he did nothing to free Associated Press reporter Terry Anderson, a Rochester native held hostage in Lebanon for nearly seven years. She carefully tended to local problems and earned the support of area businesses and the local *Democrat and Chronicle* newspaper.

A microbiologist by training, Slaughter opposed proposals to ban human cloning and was an outspoken proponent of federal support for embryonic stem cell research. She introduced a bill in 2009 to limit the non-therapeutic use of pharmaceuticals in livestock. The bill did not move, but hearings on it drew widespread attention. The Food and Drug Administration released guidelines recommending a halt to antibiotics to promote animal growth, a move Slaughter hailed as a step in the right direction.

As a loyal lieutenant of House Speaker Nancy Pelosi, who once called Slaughter "the best politician that I have ever seen," Slaughter helped to bring the first legislation to the House floor for the new Democratic majority in 2007: an overhaul of House rules, largely dictated by Pelosi and her lieutenants. Slaughter hailed the result as "a Congress people can be proud of again." But Republicans quickly cried foul when Democrats next moved to the floor six bills from their campaign agenda, without committee action and with no opportunity for amendments. Her dismissal of procedural objections led to regular flare-ups with ranking Republican David Dreier of California, a partisan master of parliamentary procedure who chaired Rules before and after Slaughter's four-year reign.

Slaughter's ascension as Rules chair capped several years of struggle to move up the Democratic leadership. In 1994, she lost to Barbara Kennelly of Connecticut for vice chair of the Democratic Caucus; in 1996, she was defeated by John Spratt of South Carolina for the ranking Democrat post on the Budget Committee.

During the 2009 health care debate, she was a major advocate of including a government-run insurer to compete with private companies and was sharply critical of the Senate's decision to jettison this so-called public option. When the final compromise reached the House in March 2010, Slaughter wrote a rule for the floor vote that attempted to get around the Senate by deeming the Senate version passed by the House once the House approved a "corrections bill" making changes to the other body's version. Outraged Republicans dubbed the move the "Slaughter Solution," even as Slaughter noted that the GOP occasionally used the strategy in the majority. Her idea eventually was scrapped.

Slaughter has a solidly liberal voting record. She drew widespread attention in April 2011 when she said at a rally that a GOP bill blocking federal financing of abortions had documentation requirements that were "sort of like an old German Nazi movie: 'Show me your papers.'" She is a fiery opponent of international trade agreements that she contends have put Americans out of work. When President Bill Clinton asked her to support the North

American Free Trade Agreement, she responded: "Why are you carrying George Bush's trash?"

She scored an unexpected victory in 2012 when President Barack Obama signed her bill banning insider stock trading by lawmakers, a cause she had championed for years. In 2008, Slaughter capped a years-long campaign by enacting her bill to bar discrimination in employment or health insurance based on the use of genetic information. On local issues, Slaughter has been an outspoken advocate of bringing high-speed rail to her region. She has worked to get USAir to slash the cost of its flights to and from Rochester.

Slaughter has faced occasional challenges at home. In 2002, redistricting placed her in the same district with Democratic Rep. John LaFalce, the party's ranking member on the Banking Committee. Luckily for Slaughter, LaFalce decided to retire. She won 62%-38% against an inexperienced Republican challenger in a solidly Democratic district that stretched to Buffalo. After the 2012 redistricting placed her in a more balanced district, popular Monroe County Executive Maggie Brooks challenged her. Questions arose about whether it was time for the 83-year-old Slaughter to make way for someone younger; the congresswoman had broken her leg in April at an event and earlier had missed numerous votes because of a family matter. Brooks hammered her opponent for being a "Washington insider," but she failed to offer a compelling reason for replacing Slaughter. The incumbent won, 57%-43%.

Slaughter's husband of 57 years, Robert, died in May 2014. No one expected her to be in trouble that fall, but a lackluster local economy and dissatisfaction with Democratic Gov. Andrew Cuomo adversely affected Democrats in her region. In contrast to 2012, when Slaughter outspent Brooks $2.5 million to $1.4 million, the two candidates combined spent slightly less than $1 million in 2014. Slaughter won narrowly with a margin of 871 votes and 50.2% over Gates Town Supervisor Mark Assini, who had previously run unsuccessfully for Congress and wasn't taken seriously by his own party. Assini led in the initial vote count. She told reporters that she had trouble with "messaging," not performance. In January 2015, Assini said that he planned to run again in 2016. In interviews following the election, Slaughter did not commit herself to seeking a 16th term.

TWENTY-SIXTH DISTRICT

Brian Higgins (D)

Elected 2004, 6th term; b. Oct. 6, 1959, Buffalo; S.U.N.Y. Buffalo, B.A. 1984, M.A. 1985, Harvard U., M.P.A. 1996; Catholic; married (Mary Jane); 2 children.

Elected Office: Buffalo City Cncl., 1988-94; NY Assembly, 1999-2004.

Professional Career: Chief of staff, Erie Cnty. Leg., 1994-98; Lecturer, Buffalo St. Col., 2000-03.

DC Office: 2459 RHOB, 20515, 202-225-3306; Fax: 202-226-0347; Website: higgins.house.gov.

State Offices: Buffalo, 716-852-3501; Niagara Falls, 716-282-1274.

Committees: *Foreign Affairs:* Terrorism, Nonproliferation, & Trade; Middle East & North Africa. *Homeland Security:* Border & Maritime Security; Counterterrorism & Intelligence (RMM).

Group Ratings

	ADA	ACLU	AFL-CIO	LCV	ITI	COC	HAFA	ACU	CFG	FRC
2014	90%	77%	-	100%	60%	50%	14%	8%	20%	0%
2013	80%	C	100%	93%	C	54%	C	4%	14%	C

National Journal Ratings

	2013 LIB	—	2013 CONS
Economic	91%	—	0%
Social	87%	—	7%
Foreign	88%	—	12%
Composite	91%	—	9%

Key Votes of the 113th Congress

1. Sandy storm spending	Y	5. Medical Marijuana	Y	9. Syrian Rebels Training	Y
2. Violence Against Women Act	Y	6. Farm Bill	N	10. Keystone pipeline	N
3. Guantanamo Bay Detainees	Y	7. Afghanistan Combat	Y	11. Immigration Exec. Action	N
4. Abortion 20-week ban	N	8. NSA Phone Data Collection	N	12. Bipartisan budget deal	Y

Election Results

2014 general	Brian Higgins (D)	113,210	(68%)	$663,042
	Kathy Weppner (R)	52,909	(32%)	$71,418
2014 primary	Brian Higgins (D)	unopposed		

Prior winning percentages: 2012 (75%), 2010 (61%), 2008 (74%), 2006 (79%), 2004 (51%)

Population		Race and Ethnicity		Income	
Total:	715,554	White	71.5%	Median income:	$44,688
Urban:	81.0%	Black	17.3%		(325 of 435)
Suburban:	19.0%	Latino	5.3%	Under $50,000	54.3%
Rural:	0.0%	Asian	3.0%	$50,000-$99,999:	30.4%
Land area:	281	Two races	2.3%	$100,000-$199,999:	12.9%
Pop/sq. mi.:	2,550.5	White Ethnic	55.4%	$200,000 or more:	2.4%
Born in state:	79.5%			Poverty Rate	19.3%
		Education			
		H.S. grad or less:	39.9%	**Work**	
Age Groups		Some college:	30.6%	White collar:	35.8%
Under 18:	20.7%	College degree, 4 yr.:	16.3%	Blue collar:	47.1%
18 to 34:	25.3%	Post-grad study:	13.2%	Sales and service:	17.1%
35 to 64:	38.2%				
Over 64:	15.8%			Govt. workers:	15.7%
		Military			
		Veterans/active duty:	7.9%		

Buffalo Metro

With its massive 1920s City Hall overlooking the Niagara River and Lake Erie, Buffalo declares itself to be a city of substance. The butt of jokes about the snow from Lake Erie that supposedly keeps it immobilized half the year, Buffalo also can claim credit for building a heavy industrial base in

Voter Turnout	
2013 Total Citizen 18+	544,206
2014 House Turnout	166,124
2014 Turnout as % CVAP	30.5%
2012 Turnout as % CVAP	55.5%

the late 19th and early 20th centuries, as America's No. 1 grain milling center and as a major steel producer. By 1910, it had installed the first electric street light, produced the world's largest office building (Ellicott Square), and erected one of the earliest skyscrapers. It also played a part in producing two presidents: Grover Cleveland was mayor of Buffalo, and Millard Fillmore worked in nearby East Aurora. Today, the area still benefits from cheap hydroelectric power, but the Lackawanna steel mills are shuttered and grain milling waned after the St. Lawrence Seaway opened in the 1950s. Buffalo was eclipsed by the larger Great Lakes industrial cities of Chicago, Detroit and Cleveland.

Buffalo was the nation's 15th-largest city in 1950, when it had a population of 580,000. By 2013, it was 76th-largest, with a population reduced by more than half to about 259,000. The city's unemployment rate hovered around 10% for three years during the recession but dropped to 6.9% in March 2015, with a decreased base of available workers. As a final insult, right across Buffalo's Peace Bridge is the richest part of Canada, the "Golden Horseshoe," from Niagara Falls through Hamilton to Toronto; the NFL's Buffalo Bills franchise has moved some home games to Toronto. Still, Buffalo retains considerable assets: a highskill labor force, inexpensive real estate, including a gentrified and handsome waterfront on a now-cleaner Lake Erie, and some impressive cultural institutions. Niagara Falls and Frank Lloyd Wright properties have helped to make the area a popular tourist destination. In April 2015, thousands of elementary school students refused to take standardized tests: Their parents were unhappy about the lack of feedback and the long-term impact for their kids and schools. Good news, bad news: In 2014, *Forbes* magazine ranked Buffalo as the most affordable place in the nation for

2012 Presidential Vote		
Barack Obama (D)	193,362	(64%)
Mitt Romney (R)	103,743	(34%)

2008 Presidential Vote		
Barack Obama (D)	208,511	(63%)
John McCain (R)	115,092	(35%)

Cook Partisan Voting Index: D+12

home ownership; even though wages are comparatively low, the low prices have helped to make the city a popular destination for recent college graduates, with a 34 percent increase from 2000 to 2012.

The 26th Congressional District of New York includes all of the city of Buffalo and the cities and townships abutting it. The district includes almost two-thirds of Erie County. To the north, it takes in a small slice of Niagara County with Niagara Falls and North Tonawanda. The large number of Eastern European settlers, many of whom hailed from Poland, gave Buffalo a Democratic tilt early on; unlike much of Upstate New York, it began electing Democrats with some regularity in the 1860s, and almost exclusively after the 1930s. Today, the district is solidly Democratic. Barack Obama won here twice with almost two-thirds of the vote. But local Democrats can be quirky: independent presidential candidate Ross Perot won 28 percent of the vote in Buffalo in 1992—his best showing in any urban center.

Brian Higgins (D)

Democrat Brian Higgins, elected in 2004, devotes his energies to reviving the Buffalo area's economy, from seeking money for a new federal courthouse to securing grants to help the local wine industry.

Higgins grew up in Buffalo, the son of a skilled tradesman who was prominent in local politics, serving on the Buffalo City Council and later as commissioner of the New York State Workers Compensation Board. His mother was a schoolteacher. Higgins graduated from Buffalo State College, where he later became an instructor, and got a master's degree in public administration from Harvard. A political junkie, he launched his career in government with staff jobs in the Erie County sheriff's office, the state Assembly, and the county legislature. In 1993, after six years on the Buffalo City Council, he ran for county comptroller and lost. In 1998, he was elected to the Assembly and served three terms. In a district crowded with unionized workers, Higgins often reminded voters that his father and uncle were bricklayers and he stressed his Irish immigrant heritage.

A House seat unexpectedly opened in 2004, when Republican Rep. Jack Quinn retired. Nancy Naples, a former Merrill Lynch executive in Manhattan and a popular local figure with strong name recognition, quickly wrapped up the Republican nomination, while five Democrats battled for their party's nomination. Higgins was the favorite of local and national Democratic leaders, organized labor and *The Buffalo News*, which called him "an unusually productive member of a largely dysfunctional legislative body" in Albany. He won the primary with 44% of the vote.

In the contentious general election, Higgins reminded voters that Naples supported many of President George W. Bush's policies and accused Republicans of shifting the tax burden from the rich to the middle class. He ran on a platform of making health care more widely available. Naples criticized Higgins for supporting tax increases in Albany. Higgins won 51%-49%, about a 3,800-vote victory, in a district that was far more competitive than the current lines.

In the House, Higgins established a centrist voting record with a liberal bent on economic issues. Hoping to kick off a debate about the importance of infrastructure, he introduced a bill in April 2012 calling for $1.25 trillion to be spent over five years to rebuild roads, bridges, railroads, ports and airports. "This isn't a stimulus bill, it's a nation-building bill," he told *The News*. "It's rebuilding this country as we've rebuilt other countries—Iraq and Afghanistan—in recent years." He helped create, and co-chaired, a Revitalizing Older Cities Task Force and has sought tax credits to transform older neighborhoods. In May 2015, he updated his transportation proposal and criticized Congress for its failure to approve long-term action to address the "deplorable status of our infrastructure investment."

After spending his first years with efforts for his district, he was rewarded with a seat on the powerful Ways and Means Committee in 2009. He initially vowed to oppose the December 2010 deal to extend the expiring Bush-era tax cuts because it would not extend the Renewal Communities program, which had brought $150 million in development to the district. But he voted for the deal and said, "The cost of inaction would be far worse for western New York families and seniors." After the Republican takeover of the House in 2011 reduced the number of Democratic seats on Ways and Means, Higgins was forced off the committee. He joined the Homeland Security and Foreign Affairs panels.

In the debate over gun control, Higgins has sided with gun owners, voting in favor of a February 2011 amendment to block federal efforts to demand reports from gun dealers on sales of multiple semi-automatic rifles. But after the Newtown Connecticut elementary school massacre in December 2012, he called for "meaningful reforms" to gun laws.

Since developing skin cancer, Higgins has worked heavily on cancer research, introducing bills to establish a national cancer trust fund and pushing for money for Buffalo's

Roswell Park Cancer Institute. He helped to broker an agreement with the New York Power Authority for local financial aid, including waterfront improvements, in exchange for its long-term right to operate the Niagara Power Project. The issue strained his relationship with Rochester-area Democratic Rep. Louise Slaughter, who disagreed with his strategy.

Higgins has been reelected easily in what has become a safe district. But the declining population of Buffalo could prove perilous during the next redistricting.

TWENTY-SEVENTH DISTRICT

Chris Collins (R)

Elected 2012, 2nd term; b. May 20, 1950, Schenectady; NC St. U., B.S. 1972, U. of AL, Birmingham, M.B.A. 1975; Catholic; married (Mary); 3 children

Elected Office: Erie Cnty. exec., 2007-11.

Professional Career: Westinghouse Electric, 1972-83; Founder & CEO, Nuttall Gear Corp., 1983-97; Entrepreneur, 1998-2007.

DC Office: 1117 LHOB, 20515, 202-225-5265; Fax: 202-225-5910; Website: chriscollins.house.gov.

State Offices: Geneseo, 585-519-4002; Williamsville, 716-634-2324.

Committees: *Energy & Commerce:* Communications & Technology; Health; Oversight & Investigations.

Group Ratings

	ADA	ACLU	AFL-CIO	LCV	ITI	COC	HAFA	ACU	CFG	FRC
2014	0%	0%	–	3%	100%	100%	44%	79%	41%	50%
2013	0%	C	24%	4%	C	85%	C	64%	57%	C

National Journal Ratings

	2013 LIB	—	2013 CONS
Economic	42%	—	57%
Social	34%	—	62%
Foreign	5%	—	86%
Composite	29%	—	71%

Key Votes of the 113th Congress

1. Sandy storm spending	Y	5. Medical Marijuana	Y
2. Violence Against Women Act	Y	6. Farm Bill	Y
3. Guantanamo Bay Detainees	N	7. Afghanistan Combat	N
4. Abortion 20-week ban	Y	8. NSA Phone Data Collection	N

9. Syrian Rebels Training	Y
10. Keystone pipeline	Y
11. Immigration Exec. Action	Y
12. Bipartisan budget deal	Y

Election Results

2014 general	Chris Collins (R)	144,675	(71%)	$366,415	$10,060
	Jim O'Donnell (D)	58,911	(29%)		
2014 primary	Chris Collins (R)	unopposed			

Prior winning percentage: 2012 (51%)

Population		Race and Ethnicity		Income	
Total:	714,863	White	92.1%	Median income:	$57,149
Urban:	12.4%	Latino	2.6%		*(149 of 435)*
Suburban:	65.3%	Black	2.2%	Under $50,000	43.6%
Rural:	22.3%	Asian	1.2%	$50,000-$99,999:	33.0%
Land area:	3,311	Two races	1.3%	$100,000-$199,999:	19.7%
Pop/sq. mi.:	215.9	White Ethnic	54.3%	$200,000 or more:	3.7%
Born in state:	84.8%			Poverty Rate	9.8%
		Education			
Age Groups		H.S. grad or less:	39.9%	**Work**	
Under 18:	20.7%	Some college:	31.3%	White collar:	37.7%
18 to 34:	19.9%	College degree, 4 yr.:	16.3%	Blue collar:	39.8%
35 to 64:	42.6%	Post-grad study:	12.5%	Sales and service:	22.5%
Over 64:	16.8%				
		Military		Govt. workers:	16.0%
		Veterans/active duty:	8.5%		

Northwestern New York: Buffalo and Rochester Suburbs

The destination of the Erie Canal, the great engineering project that made New York the Empire State, is Lake Erie. The final 100 miles of the canal passed through the rolling countryside of western New York when it was scarcely occupied, except by American Indians. Later, the land was settled

Voter Turnout	
2013 Total Citizen 18+	558,207
2014 House Turnout	203,591
2014 Turnout as % CVAP	36.5%
2012 Turnout as % CVAP	58.4%

mostly by New England Yankees, with cultural folkways quite different from those of New York City. By the end of the 19th century, much of the farmland found here had become dominated by heavy industry, especially in Buffalo, where the Yankees were joined by Irish, Italian and Polish immigrants who came to work in the factories. For most of its history, western New York had an economy more prosperous than that of the rest of the country, as is visible in the solid houses and schools, stores and factories built to weather the Upstate winters. But in the past three decades, economic growth has lagged behind the rest of the nation. Many of Buffalo's factories have closed. The slow growth and population decline have frequently spilled over to the suburbs that sprang up around the city in outer Erie County. In some ways, the region has a Midwest flavor, culturally as well as economically. People speak not in the pungent accents of New York City, but in flat Midwestern tones.

The 27th Congressional District of New York covers much of western New York. It extends from the suburbs of Buffalo to suburbs southeast of Rochester. In between are rural areas and small towns, including Attica, scene of a terrible prison uprising in 1970. Prior to the 2012 redistricting, the district was based largely in the Buffalo suburbs and it elected influential national Republicans such as Jack Kemp and Bill Paxon. With population changes, Erie and Niagara counties are now a bare majority, though Erie remains the heart of the district. Politi-

2012 Presidential Vote		
Mitt Romney (R)................180,681	(55%)
Barack Obama (D) 140,136	(43%)
2008 Presidential Vote		
John McCain (R)................186,563	(54%)
Barack Obama (D) 153,875	(45%)
Cook Partisan Voting Index: R+8		

cally, these suburbs are ancestrally Republican country, based on Upstaters' general distrust of New York City. It is the most Republican district in the state by most measures.

Chris Collins (R)

Republican Chris Collins, a self-made multimillionaire, was elected in 2012 by narrowly defeating a first-term Democrat who had won a special election. His promises to bring business sensibilities to Washington proved more effective than the Democrats' attacks on Collins as a cold-hearted tycoon. He seems entrenched in this Republican-leaning district.

As a child, Collins' family moved around the country with his father's job transfers at General Electric. After high school in Hendersonville North Carolina, he earned a bachelor's degree in mechanical engineering from North Carolina State and a master's in business administration from the University of Alabama at Birmingham. He went to work for Westinghouse in Buffalo and planned to spend his career climbing the corporate ladder there, as his father did at GE. When Westinghouse approached Collins about taking over its plant, where he already was the general manager of the industrial gear division, he agreed. He ran the Nuttall Gear Corp., which eventually reverted to private ownership when he sold it.

Former local Rep. Bill Paxon, a House Republican leader in the 1990s, persuaded Collins to get into politics. He challenged veteran Democratic Rep. John LaFalce in 1998, hoping to benefit from dissatisfaction with the local economy, but Collins lost, 57%-41%. He returned to business as an entrepreneur, spending the next 10 years working on almost two dozen financially distressed and bankrupt companies in the Buffalo area.

In 2007, New York Republicans again tapped Collins, this time to run for Erie County executive. "Erie County was effectively bankrupt, and I was now known as a fix-it guy," Collins told *National Journal.* He ran as an independent on a platform of business know-how and won with 64% of the vote. He lost reelection in 2011 in this Democratic county. Collins said his experience at the county level inspired him to head to Washington, where he said he hoped to apply his budget experience. "If there's ever anything that's broken, it is Congress," Collins said. "While I'll be one of 435, I can certainly advocate for the efficiencies I brought into Erie County."

Republicans were eager to unseat Rep. Kathy Hochul, who had won a special election in May 2011. She succeeded GOP Rep. Chris Lee, who abruptly resigned in February after reports that he had responded with a shirtless photo of himself to a personal ad on Craigslist from a woman seeking a "financially and emotionally secure" man. Hochul's 47%-42% victory over Republican Assemblywoman Jane Corwin in the special election benefited from her relentless attacks on GOP Rep. Paul Ryan's proposed federal budget and its controversial changes to Medicare.

In 2012, when redistricting added socially conservative, working-class suburbs to the district, Collins thought he had a chance. Democrats accused Collins of neglecting the county's infrastructure, but he stayed focused on his business background. "Unlike my opponent and President Obama, who think we can tax our way to prosperity, I'm saying we need to grow our way to prosperity, by having a balanced budget and having some certainty for business on the financial side," Collins said. He benefitted from heavy campaign spending from outside GOP groups and beat Hochul, 51%-49%. He was reelected with 71% of the vote against James O'Donnell, who did not report any campaign spending.

In the House, Collins gained a seat on the Energy and Commerce Committee in 2015. He styled himself as a pragmatic problem-solver. In May 2015, when the committee approved its bipartisan 21st Century Cures Act, it included a plan from Collins to simplify the approval of new medical treatments for the market, with adaptive clinical trials that monitor patients. Calling the measure "common sense," he said that his proposal "makes sure these drugs come through the [Food and Drug Administration] process faster." Citing his experience in the biotech industry, he sponsored other measures to the bill to replace what he described as antiquated procedures and encourage medical innovators to get life-saving drugs to patients. Collins promised to use his Energy and Commerce seat to promote hydraulic fracturing for natural gas in New York.

In March 2015, the *Buffalo News* praised Collins as one of 75 House Republicans who supported the plan of Speaker John Boehner to keep open the Homeland Security Department rather than engage in "a suicide charge" against President Barack Obama's proposed immigration regulations. "I didn't come here to lurch from crisis to crisis," Collins said. In June, he joined most House Democrats, and abandoned Obama and most House Republicans, when he voted against a plan to expedite congressional action on the President's proposed Transpacific Partnership trade deal. He objected that the agreement failed to stop overseas currency manipulation. Four other New York Republicans joined him in opposing the proposal.

★ NORTH CAROLINA ★

In early September 2012, North Carolina was at the center of the American political world as the Democratic Party assembled for its quadrennial convention in Charlotte. Politics played a big part in President Barack Obama's choice of the city: North Carolina's electoral votes were determined by the second-smallest percentage margin of any state in 2008 and would be again in 2012. More than at any other time since the Wright Brothers, North Carolina is a national leader. It is the 9th largest state in population, passing Michigan in 2014, and has two of the nation's fastest-growing and most dynamic major metropolitan areas, Charlotte and Raleigh.

North Carolina achieved this status after humble beginnings. In the early republic, when Virginia and South Carolina produced statesmen and spokesmen, and had grand plantation cultures, North Carolina was often called a valley of humility between two mountains of conceit. It joined the Confederacy only after those two neighbors did so. After the Civil War, North Carolina developed its tobacco industry and enticed textile mills south from New England, while its hardwood forests produced raw material for furniture factories. Textile mills were prevalent in the Piedmont region as owners saw in the South an opportunity for cheap land, cheap labor, and state governments eager to foster pro-business, anti-union climates. In the following decades, the industry continued to expand and drastically improved the economy of the South. The mill industry became the main source of industrial paid labor for white southerners, and while it was one of the lowest paying manufacturing industries, the jobs were valued because there were few other employment options other than agricultural or service work. The tobacco-textile-furniture trio enabled North Carolina to grow faster than the national average in the 1920s and 1930s, but the state began to lag in the 1950s. Then, two developments transformed the state. In 1959, Gov. Luther Hodges started Research Triangle Park between Raleigh and Durham. With synergy from accessible universities—Duke, North Carolina, and North Carolina State—the region became one of the leading research centers in the United States. The second development was Charlotte's emergence as the No. 2 city in financial assets, behind only New York, which owes much to state laws allowing statewide branch banking. NationsBank and Wachovia set up headquarters on Tryon Street. NationsBank bought Bank of America and took its name, while during the financial crisis, Wachovia was acquired by Wells Fargo, which kept many of its operations in Charlotte.

These twin developments explain how North Carolina has become one of the fastest-growing and largest states. Its population grew 88% between 1970 and 2010, from 5.1 million to 9.5 million. In the same period, the city of Charlotte grew from 241,000 to 731,000 and Raleigh from 123,000 to 404,000. In 2014, those two cities had populations of 793,000 and 432,000, and are growing more than twice as rapidly as the state. Meanwhile, the old mainstays of North Carolina's economy have faded in importance. The textile industry largely moved offshore, and the federal government's 2004 buyout of tobacco quotas greatly diminished that sector. According to the Bureau of Labor Statistics, from 1992-2012, the textile and apparel industry in North Carolina lost 86.7% of its employees, more than 200,000 jobs. High Point still hosts annual furniture industry shows, but much production has gone elsewhere, including China. North Carolina now ranks highly in biotech employment, and the Triangle—as the Raleigh-Durham area is commonly known—is one of the world's leading biotech, pharmaceutical, medical device, and telecommunications centers. High-tech firms are also sprouting farther west in the Piedmont Triad of Greensboro, Winston-Salem, and High Point, which was prime textile country. And in Charlotte, Bank of America has snapped back after its disastrous purchase of Merrill Lynch. Not surprisingly, the financial crisis hit the state hard. Unemployment peaked at 11.3% in February 2010, and was 5.4% in December 2014. As the state has shifted from old-line manufacturing in textiles and furniture sectors to fast-growing industries, including pharmaceuticals and aerospace, so have its exports. Fitting for a state that was home to the first air flight at Kitty Hawk, the state's top export in 2014 was civilian aircraft engines and parts ($1.2 billion). State officials continue to tout their business-friendly way and *Site Selection* magazine ranked North Carolina the top state in the country in 2014 for landing new plants and industries on a per capita basis. The state has the nation's least-unionized labor force; only 1.9% of North Carolina workers are unionized compared to 11.1% for the nation. It has attracted highly skilled people from

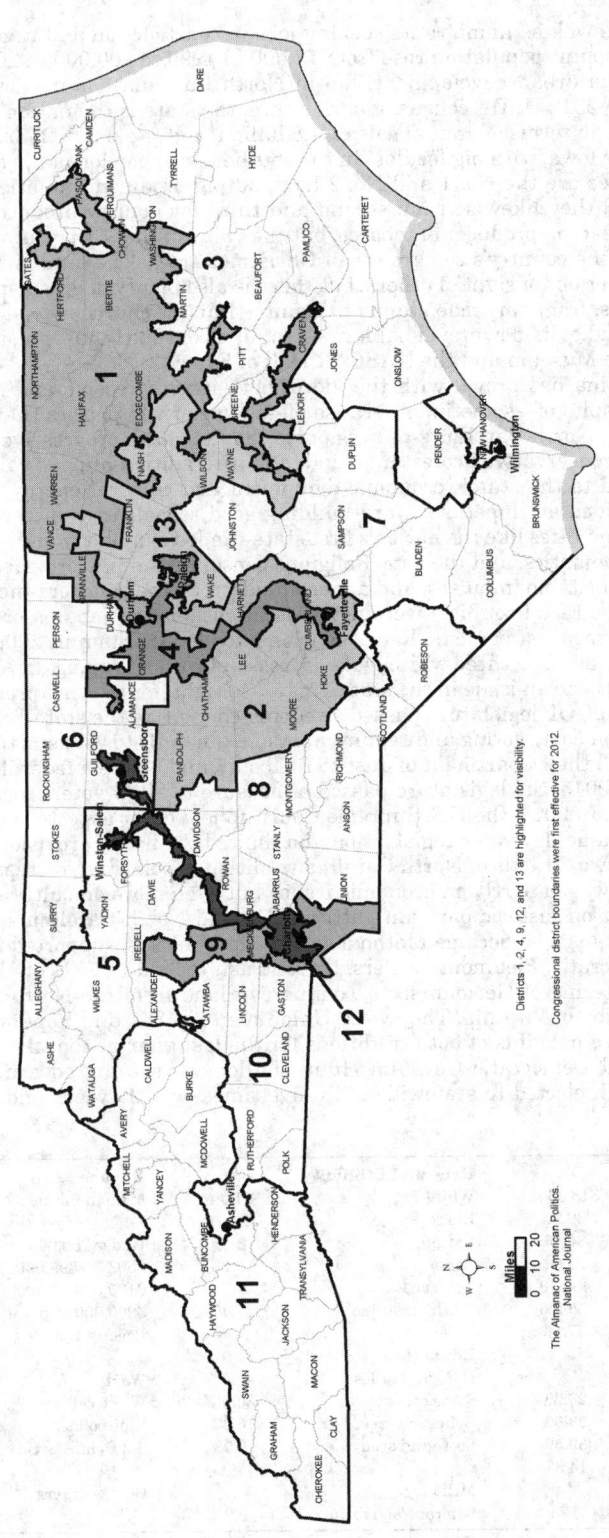

Districts 1, 2, 4, 9, 12, and 13 are highlighted for visibility.

Congressional district boundaries were first effective for 2012.

Miles
0 10 20

The Almanac of American Politics.
National Journal

the Northeast as well as immigrants seeking jobs in construction and in meat and chicken factories. Its Hispanic population rose from 77,000 in 1990 to 800,000 in 2010.

Yet for all its urban development, life in North Carolina has not lost its rural tone. According to the 2012 USDA census of agriculture, the state is the nation's top producer of poultry and eggs in terms of annual sales, $4.8 billion, and ranks No. 2 ($2.9 billion) for hog production, after Iowa, with big feedlots in the southeastern portion of the state. Duplin and Sampson counties are the No. 1 and No. 2 hog and pig producing counties in the country, respectively, and they likewise rank second and third for poultry production. The state is still the fourth leading producer of tobacco, but the value of that crop was only $700 million. Ashe County is the country's top grower of Christmas trees. The land is so thickly settled that you are never out of sight of others, but there is also plenty of green space and reminders of rural roots, from barbecue stands to country Baptist churches to stock car tracks. If Charlotte is proud of its downtown bank towers and modern art museum, it is also proud of its Billy Graham Museum and the NASCAR Hall of Fame.

North Carolina has grown with the aid of both its progressive and tradition-minded citizens, and in spite of—sometimes because of—the polarized politics that have developed between the two. North Carolina's professionals tend to share progressive values; its business people and conservative Protestants tend to share tradition-minded values. Both groups have contributed to the state's economic dynamism and cultural energy. Liberal progressivism has provided an impetus toward building good schools and universities, as well as highways and amenities like the nation's first state-funded symphony and state high schools for science, mathematics, and the arts. Religious conservatism has provided a communitarian spirit and charitable impulses, and a moral undertone that anchors those who might go astray. The state's racial conflicts were never as intense as in Alabama or Mississippi, but the legacy of segregation persists. Racial tensions divided Durham in 2006, when its prosecutor baselessly accused three white Duke lacrosse players of raping an African-American dancer. Race has been an issue in the state's moves to tighten its voting procedures. In 2013, the newly minted GOP legislature passed sweeping changes to the state's election laws that included a curb on early voting and requirement of a photo ID to vote starting in 2016. Civil rights groups and the Department of Justice filed suit, and before a federal trial was scheduled to begin in 2015, the legislature passed a measure to allow voters to sign affidavits in lieu of photo IDs. In 2014, the U.S. Supreme Court upheld other aspects of the controversial law that ended same-day voter registration and limited the use of provisional ballots.

From these two strands of North Carolina tradition, a polarized, increasingly party-line politics evolved, waged partly on economic issues but even more on cultural attitudes. This politics was built on historic partisan patterns. Coastal North Carolina settlers tended to be British Anglicans who became Methodists and slaveholders, supported the Confederacy, and voted Democratic. Piedmont settlers, by contrast, tended to be Scots-Irish Presbyterians, with a scattering of German sects, coming overland from the Northeast through the Shenandoah Valley of Virginia. They were Union men in 1861 and Republicans ever after. The most-effective paladins of both traditions for the last quarter-century, Republican Sen. Jesse Helms and Democratic Gov. Jim Hunt, the longest serving governor in the state's history, were each elected to statewide office five times over 25 years and, in 1984, waged

Population		Race and Ethnicity		Income	
Total:	9,848,060	White	64.9%	Median income:	$41,208
Urban:	39.9%	Black	21.4%		*(46 of 50)*
Suburban:	34.1%	Latino	8.6%	Under $50,000	53.7%
Rural:	26.0%	Asian	2.2%	$50,000-$99,999:	29.1%
Land area:	48,618	Two races	1.7%	$100,000-$199,999:	13.6%
Pop/sq. mi.:	202.6	White Ethnic	17.4%	$200,000 or more:	3.6%
Born in state:	57.4%			Poverty Rate	13.1%
		Education			
Age Groups		H.S. grad or less:	40.8%	**Work**	
Under 18:	23.2%	Some college:	30.8%	White collar:	35.9%
18 to 34:	23.0%	College degree, 4 yr.:	18.4%	Blue collar:	41.8%
35 to 64:	39.5%	Post-grad study:	9.9%	Sales and service:	22.3%
Over 64:	14.3%				
		Military		Govt. workers:	14.8%
		Veterans/active duty:	9.9%		

what was then the most expensive Senate race in U.S. history. Once bitter rivals, they later reconciled. Helms did not seek reelection in 2002 and died in 2008. Hunt left office in 2001 but remained a driving force among state Democrats, delivering a speech celebrating North Carolina's accomplishments at the national convention in 2012.

Voter Turnout			
2013 Total Citizen 18+			7,101,056
2014 Highest Statewide Turnout			2,915,281
2014 Turnout as % CVAP			41.1%
2012 Turnout as % CVAP			64.3%
Legislature			
Senate:	34R	16D	
House:	74R	45D	1V

Over the past four decades, Republicans tended to win federal elections in North Carolina, and Democrats tended to do well in state elections. In five elections, Helms never got more than 55% of the vote, but Republicans carried the state for president in every election from 1968 to 2004, except 1976. George W. Bush won 56%-43% in 2000 and, despite the presence of North Carolinian John Edwards on the Democratic ticket, he won 56%-44% in 2004. In 2008, federal and state voting started to converge with very narrow divisions between the parties. Obama's organization spotted North Carolina's potential early, and after beating Hillary Clinton 56%-42% in the primary with big margins among blacks and upscale professionals, he made North Carolina a target state in the general election. Increased voter turnout was one result: Presidential year turnout in North Carolina increased 55% from 2000 to 2012, more than any other state except much faster-growing Nevada. Blacks who had not previously voted, Hispanics who had recently become citizens, and upscale professionals who had recently moved from elsewhere flocked to the polls, and Obama narrowly won North Carolina's 15 electoral votes, 49.7%-49.4%. Also that year, Democrats elected Bev Perdue governor and Kay Hagan senator against Republican incumbent Elizabeth Dole. Democrats held the governorship for 28 of the 42 years from 1971 to 2012, with Hunt elected four times, Michael Easley twice, and Perdue once. After Democrats raised the sales and income taxes in 2009, voters in 2010 replaced big Democratic margins in the legislature with big Republican margins, giving the GOP control for the first time since Reconstruction. Republican Pat McCrory took over the statehouse after he was elected in 2012, when Obama failed to carry the state in his reelection bid. Although Republicans hold the executive mansion, control both chambers of the General Assembly, hold the state's two Senate seats and 10 of its 13 congressional districts, Democrats still outnumber Republicans in party registration 2.6 million to 1.9 million. Below the governor, Democrats maintained the offices of attorney general (Republicans didn't even field a candidate in 2012), secretary of state, and treasurer. Both parties in the state, it seems, have reasons to remain a bit humble.

Presidential Politics After 1980, North Carolina was not a competitive state in presidential elections. Democrats hoped to change that in 2004 when John Kerry named Sen. John Edwards of North Carolina as his running mate. But Edwards had won just one election in the state, with 51% of the vote in 1998, and his appeal proved limited. The Kerry-Edwards campaign took its ads off the air in North Carolina in August, and Edwards himself returned to the state only to vote early, in October.

2012 Presidential Vote		
Mitt Romney (R)..............2,270,395		(50%)
Barack Obama (D) 2,178,391		(48%)
2012 Presidential Primary		
Mitt Romney (R)................638,601		(66%)
Ron Paul (R) 108,217		(11%)
Rick Santorum (R) 101,093		(10%)
Newt Gingrich (R)...............74,367		(8%)
2008 Presidential Vote		
Barack Obama (D) 2,142,651		(50%)
John McCain (R)..............2,128,474		(49%)

The 2008 campaign was quite another matter. North Carolina's presidential primary, held on the same day in May as its state primary, had played a serious role in presidential politics only once before. In 1976, after five straight losses, Ronald Reagan won his first major victory over Gerald Ford in the Republican primary, reenergizing his campaign that went all the way to the convention in Kansas City. Then in 2008, Barack Obama's campaign, quick to spot opportunities, staked out North Carolina as a target, first in the primary and then in the general election. The state had a large African-American population (22%), much of which had never been politically organized. Its universities and its 2007 state law authorizing same-day registration and early voting meant that a large student vote could be mobilized. The recent arrivals of many Hispanics—8% of the population in 2010—and affluent professionals provided other opportunities. The results justified Obama's calculations. New registrations in the first three months of 2008 were nearly triple the number in the same months of 2004.

Hillary Clinton, fresh from March and April victories in Ohio, Texas, and Pennsylvania, was still in the race and was endorsed by Gov. Mike Easley. But on May 6, Obama won by a solid 56%-42%, carrying not only the five congressional districts with high black percentages but also two others with affluent white populations in the Research Triangle and Charlotte areas. Clinton carried rural whites in the east and west of the state. His big margin in North Carolina, and Clinton's small margin of victory the same day in Indiana, prompted Tim Russert of NBC News to declare that the nomination race was decided for Obama.

In the fall, John McCain's campaign was reluctant to spend resources in North Carolina, given its past voting behavior, and Democrats made good use of their early lead in organizing. Early voting was heavy; accounting for 57% of votes cast, and turnout was up 23% from 2004, the largest percentage gain in any state. McCain got 9% more votes than George W. Bush had four years before. But Obama got 40% more votes than the Kerry-Edwards ticket, with especially large increases in heavily black eastern counties, the Research Triangle, and metro Charlotte. Obama carried the state 49.7%-49.4%. Black voters went 95%-5% for Obama, while whites voted 64%-35% for McCain. Obama carried 56% of those with graduate degrees, 44% of those with incomes over $100,000, and 74% of those under 30, while white evangelical Protestants voted 74% for McCain.

In 2012, North Carolina's May primary was too late to have much impact. Mitt Romney won with 66% of the vote. Despite Republican claims that the Obama campaign was abandoning the state, North Carolina was still a target for Obama organizational efforts even if it got little in the way of candidate appearances after the Charlotte convention. Turnout was up again, but by only 5% from 2008, and Obama's percentage declined, but by only 1.3%. But that was enough to give Romney a 50%-48% victory. Obama won 96% of blacks, but his percentages declined among those with graduate degrees and the young. His campaign increased turnout and Democratic percentages in rural counties in eastern North Carolina with large black percentages, but Obama lost ground in the big metro areas and small-town western North Carolina. The new North Carolina is likely to be a battleground in the next competitive presidential race.

Congressional Districts North Carolina won a 12th House seat in the 1990 census and a 13th seat in 2000, when it beat out Utah for the last seat in the House by just 856 people. In the 2010 census, the state almost gained a 14th seat, but its population came in about 16,000 short of what it needed to take

114th Congress Lineup	
10 R	3 D
113th Congress Lineup	
9 R	4 D

the nation's 435th seat from Minnesota. In the 1990s, North Carolina was the epicenter of race-based redistricting litigation, home to a legal controversy over a long, skinny new black-majority 12th District that went to the U.S. Supreme Court four times. In 2002, Democrats created an ugly new 13th District in the northern Piedmont, which ended up electing Democrat Brad Miller, not coincidentally the chair of the Senate redistricting committee. Even after the Republican surge in 2010, Democrats enjoyed a 7-6 seat advantage—including four relatively centrist Democrats.

But in 2011, North Carolina was the site of Democrats' worst redistricting devastation, the seeds of which were sown 15 years prior. In 1996, Democrats in charge of the General Assembly exempted redistricting matters from new gubernatorial veto powers, reasoning they would always hold the legislature but voters might occasionally elect a Republican governor. In the ultimate tale of unintended consequences, Republicans shocked even themselves by taking over the legislature by large margins in 2010 (31-19 in the Senate, 67-52-1 in the House), rendering Democratic Gov. Bev Perdue helpless to foil their map makeover. With an Obama-appointed Justice Department the only obstacle potentially standing in their way, Republicans went to work.

In July 2011, Republicans quickly released and passed a new plan that cleverly unraveled and reversed the Democrats' 2002 map, and then some. They packed Democratic voters into just three of the state's 13 seats: an African-American majority 1st District covering parts of rural northeastern counties and heavily black neighborhoods in Durham, an almost comically gerrymandered and liberal 4th District connecting via tentacles the academic haven of Chapel Hill, black neighborhoods in Raleigh and faraway Fayetteville, and an even more tightly packed African-American majority 12th District knifing along the I-85 corridor in a strip from Charlotte to Winston-Salem and Greensboro. Republicans drew the other 10 seats at least 10 percentage points more Republican than the national average. They were all comfortably Republican, but balanced enough in sharing GOP voters that none of them were in the top 20% of the nation's most Republican districts.

Their handiwork eviscerated four of the state's seven Democrats. The map double-bunked Chapel Hill Democrat David Price and Raleigh Democrat Miller in the 4th District. It carved the burgeoning progressive mountain mecca of Asheville out of Democrat Heath Shuler's western 11th District, and black neighborhoods in Charlotte and Fayetteville out of Democrat Larry Kissell's southern tier 8th District. Republicans even purged Democrat Mike McIntyre's Robeson County home base, as well as black neighborhoods in Wilmington, from his southeastern 7th District. Republican freshman Renee Ellmers, who had defeated Democrat Bob Etheridge in the suburban Raleigh 2nd District in 2010, received a much safer seat.

A furious state Democratic Party and the NAACP sued in state court to block the map. But the Justice Department's preclearance of the lines undercut the groups' claims of racial gerrymandering, and a state panel ruled the map could proceed. Miller and Shuler opted to retire, while Kissell lost 53%-45% in the 8th District. Impressively, McIntyre beat the odds in a radically redrawn 7th District, winning by just 654 votes while Obama lost the district 59%-40%, the Democrats' only silver lining. Astonishingly, Democrats won a majority of the state's votes in House races, but just four of 13 seats. In the 2014 cycle, McIntyre bowed to the inevitable and retired, and a Republican won in a rout. The only remaining Carolina blue were the two African-American districts and Price's liberal bastion. The state likely will get its 14th district after the 2020 Census. Unless the courts intervene, as some Democrats hope, that may be their next opportunity to gain a seat.

Governor

Pat McCrory (R)

Elected 2012, term expires 2017; b. Oct. 17, 1956, Columbus, OH; Catawba Col., B.A. 1978; Christian; married (Ann).

Elected Office: Charlotte City Cncl., 1989-95; Charlotte mayor, 1995-2009.

Professional Career: Sr. econ. development consultant, Duke Energy, 1978-2008; Partner, McCrory & Co., 2007-present; Sr. dir. of strategic initiatives, Moore & Van Allen, 2010-12.

Office: 20301 Mail Service Center Raleigh, 27699-0301, 919-814-2000; Fax: 919-733-2120; Website: governor.nc.gov.

Election Results

2012 general	Pat McCrory (R)	2,440,707	(55%)
	Walter Dalton (D)	1,931,580	(43%)
	Barbara Howe (Lib)	94,652	(2%)
2012 primary	Pat McCrory (R)	748,180	(83%)
	Paul Wright (R)	47,403	(5%)

Pat McCrory is a rare GOP politician who readily describes himself as an "Eisenhower Republican." As the seven-term mayor of Charlotte, McCrory had to adopt the "middle way" philosophy of the 34th president to move his agenda through a Democratic city council, but that approach has not worked as well for Gov. McCrory in dealing with an assertive and conservative Republican-controlled state legislature.

McCrory was born in Columbus Ohio. His father was an engineer and entrepreneur who once served on the city council in nearby Worthington. When he was nine years old, McCrory's family moved to Jamestown North Carolina, where he later became his high school's student body president. He attended Catawba College and initially planned to become a teacher, but instead decided to work for Duke Energy, a power company where he'd had summer jobs. He rose through a variety of recruiting and training jobs to become a senior adviser with the company's business and economic development group. His political career began in 1989, when he was elected to an at-large seat on the Charlotte City Council. After six years, McCrory ran for mayor and won, becoming at 39 the city's youngest-ever chief executive. He presided over an economic development boom in the city that helped fuel his popularity and helped produce its 25-year land use plan, as well as the LYNX light rail system, which shuttled delegates to the 2012 Democratic National Convention held in the Time Warner Cable Arena in the shadow of the city's gleaming "Uptown" skyscrapers. He also successfully worked in 2006 to bring NASCAR's new hall of fame to Charlotte, beating out several competing suitors.

In his first run for governor in 2008, McCrory called for a 50-year transportation plan for the state. He attacked Bev Perdue, then lieutenant governor, for her opposition to offshore oil drilling, which many North Carolina voters supported. She backed off and said she would appoint a panel to study the issue. Perdue supported increasing the number of college scholarships for North Carolina students, while McCrory emphasized vocational training, saying that four-year college programs did not interest all high school graduates. Endorsed by teachers' unions grateful for her efforts in the legislature, Perdue criticized McCrory's support for government vouchers for private school tuition. It was a hard-fought election, with Perdue winning 50%-47%. She clearly benefited from the voter registration and turnout efforts of Democrat Barack Obama's presidential campaign, which targeted North Carolina. McCrory carried the Charlotte area, while Perdue solidly carried the Triangle and Triad areas and ran far ahead on her home turf in eastern North Carolina. She won Wake County, the top vote producer in the state and home to the state capital, but also a burgeoning number of suburban communities that are emblematic of North Carolina's transition to a more metropolitan state.

Perdue faced serious fiscal problems when she took office in 2009. With the state's unemployment rate above 11% and facing a record $4.7 billion budget shortfall, Perdue called for tax increases to avoid deep cuts to public schools. She invoked former Gov. Terry Sanford, a revered figure among the state's liberals, who had taken a similar step. But her approval rating fell by half—from 60% to 30%—in less than six months. Republicans gained control of both chambers of the legislature in the November 2010 elections, marking the first time since 1870 that the GOP had the majority in both houses. As Perdue prepared for reelection in 2012, she was in difficult shape. Despite avoiding the ethics problems of her predecessor, Michael Easley, her administration was the subject of state and federal investigations into whether she properly reported campaign flights. She announced in January 2012 that she would not seek a second term.

McCrory had prepared for a rematch with Perdue, criticizing her March 2011 veto of a Republican-passed bill to challenge the federal health care law. He courted conservative activists who were skeptical of his support for a sales tax hike to help finance LYNX. He easily beat five other candidates in the May 2012 Republican primary with 83% of the vote. With Perdue out of the picture, North Carolina Democrats nominated Lt. Gov. Walter Dalton, who had to overcome the baggage of being Perdue's second-in-command. McCrory played up his connections to the business community in bringing jobs to the state while keeping a low profile on hot-button social issues such as same-sex marriage. He also called for more offshore energy drilling and supported a controversial natural gas extraction method known as hydraulic fracturing or "fracking," which Dalton questioned. Throughout the race, McCrory maintained a commanding lead in fundraising and was ahead in polls. He won, 55%-43%, finishing well ahead of Republican presidential candidate Mitt Romney's 50% showing in the state. This time around, McCrory carried Wake County, even though Obama had bested Romney there. He narrowly won Charlotte's Mecklenburg County and racked up huge margins in the adjacent suburban and exurban Carrabus, Gaston and Union counties.

In his inaugural address, McCrory said, "Government should not be a barricade or an obstacle to progress," and vowed to create a friendly climate for business. He set off a tempest when he said in a radio interview that he was drafting legislation to shift higher education funding toward career-oriented fields and away from academic pursuits "that have no chance of getting people jobs." One of the first pieces of legislation McCrory signed in February 2013 was a measure cutting unemployment benefits by about one-third and reducing the eligibility time for receiving benefits. With McCrory's support, the legislature in 2013 also passed the state's largest tax reform package in more than a generation, changing a progressive income tax code with three tiers to a single, lower flat rate. At the time, the state had the highest personal tax rate in the Southeast. The measure also raised the standard deduction, but eliminated dozens of deductions and credits including the earned income tax credit for the working poor and deductions for medical expenses, retirement income, child-care expenses and college 529 plans. It also slashed the state corporate tax. McCrory signed the controversial Voter Information Verification Act in 2013, which cut early voting days, ended same-day voter registration, limited the use of provisional ballots and required government-issued photo IDs to vote. In 2014, McCrory and the legislature approved a plan that raised teachers' salaries by an average of seven percent, but was more generous to some early career teachers to boost recruitment and retention.

By 2015, relations between McCrory and the legislature had become severely strained. McCrory won a lawsuit he brought against the legislature over the governor's appointment powers and the General Assembly's ability to create independent commissions and select their membership. Republican leaders decried the decision. They backed a plan to drop the state's corporate tax even further to boost job growth. McCrory said the proposal would "divide" the state and "break the bank." The governor proposed an infrastructure plan financed by nearly $3 billion in bonds to stimulate growth that received a cool reception from GOP lawmakers. McCrory also got into a veto war over social issues. He vetoed a bill that he said would impede undercover investigations and could curb whistleblowers, siding with animal rights groups and the AARP. They said the measure would deter employees from reporting violations in workplace standards at factory farms and nursing homes. The legislature overrode his veto. The governor agreed to a bill increasing the waiting period for abortion to 72 hours from 24 hours. In his 2012 campaign, McCrory had said he wouldn't restrict abortions but later argued the longer waiting period didn't constitute a restriction. Early in 2015, Republican legislative leaders pulled back from a Religious Freedom Restoration Act after major corporations in the state voiced concerns. Among others, technology leader IBM, which has thousands of employees at the company's Research Triangle campus and elsewhere in the state, came out against the legislation saying that it would allow discrimination against gays and lesbians. McCrory had also questioned the need for such legislation. But the legislature came back later and passed a bill allowing local magistrates to opt out of performing same-sex marriages. Although he reiterated his personal opposition to gay marriage, McCrory vetoed the GOP lawmakers' bill saying that state officials were required to obey a federal court decision legalizing same-sex unions in the state. The conservative North Carolina Values Coalition called McCrory's veto "outrageous" and the state legislature overrode him again.

McCrory's differences with the GOP legislature were not just driven by philosophy, but also by an urban-rural friction. Many of the Republican lawmakers and their leaders were from rural districts, while McCrory cut his political teeth in the state's biggest city. When McCrory and his allies sought an infusion of funds for the state's incentive programs to attract new businesses, Republican lawmakers countered with less money. "The governor needs to accept responsibility for rapidly draining his jobs incentive fund and directing close to 90 percent of the state's incentive money to its richest three counties, including his own," said GOP Senate Majority Leader Harry Brown in a statement. "These counties already receive a disproportionate share of sales tax and transportation funds, and it's time for the 97 other counties in this state to be treated with respect." Republican lawmakers also backed plans to shift sales tax revenues from major urban centers like Charlotte to rural counties. Sen. Brown, an author of one of the GOP proposals, said there are "two North Carolinas, one that is booming and one that is busting." McCrory called proposals to redistribute sales tax revenues to rural areas "class warfare," and told a Charlotte radio talk show, "It's almost John Edwards-type language being used by my own party." When North Carolina Democratic Sen. Edwards sought the 2004 Democratic presidential nomination he often spoke in populist language about "two Americas." With an eye towards running for reelection in 2016, when he is likely to face the popular four-term Democratic Attorney General Ray Cooper, McCrory understood he must do well among the state's metropolitan and suburban voters to win a second term. And McCrory sounded like he wants another four years. In a 2015 interview with the NBC television affiliate in Charlotte, McCrory said, "I love the job. I love the honor and privilege, and I think we're doing a good job. And I don't want to stop that now."

Senior Senator

Richard Burr (R)

Elected 2004, term expires Jan. 2017, 2nd term; b. Nov. 30, 1955, Charlottesville, VA; Wake Forest U., B.A. 1978; Methodist; married (Brooke); 2 children.

Elected Office: U.S. House, 1995-2005.

Professional Career: Natl. sales mgr., Carswell Distributing, 1978-94.

DC Office: 217 RSOB, 20510, 202-224-3154; Fax: 202-228-2981; Website: burr.senate.gov.

State Offices: Asheville, 828-350-2437; Gastonia, 704-833-0854; Rocky Mount, 252-977-9522; Wilmington, 910-251-1058; Winston-Salem, 336-631-5125.

Committees: *Finance:* Energy, Natural Resources & Infrastructure; Fiscal Responsibility & Economic Growth; Health Care. *Health, Education, Labor & Pensions:* Children & Families; Primary Health & Retirement Security. *Intelligence (Select)* (Chmn).

Group Ratings

	ADA	ACLU	AFL-CIO	LCV	ITI	COC	HAFA	ACU	CFG	FRC
2014	10%	0%	–	0%	33%	100%	57%	88%	74%	100%
2013	10%	C	22%	15%	C	63%	C	84%	67%	C

National Journal Ratings

	2013 LIB	—	2013 CONS
Economic	24%	—	74%
Social	19%	—	79%
Foreign	37%	—	62%
Composite	28%	—	73%

Key Votes of the 113th Congress

1. Sandy storm spending	N	5. Student Loan Rates	Y	9. Bipartisan Budget Deal	N
2. Chuck Hagel Confirmation	N	6. Employee Non-Discrim'n Act	N	10. Farm Bill Conference Rept.	N
3. Gun Background Checks	N	7. Senate Vote on Judgeships	Y	11. Unempl. Comp. Extension	N
4. Immigration Reform	N	8. Defense Dept. Spending	N	12. Keystone Pipeline	Y

Election Results

2010 general	Richard Burr (R)	1,458,046	(55%)	$6,274,147	$1,041,248	$3,606
	Elaine Marshall (D)	1,145,074	(43%)	$2,845,246	$50,413	
	Michael Beitler (Lib)	55,687	(2%)	$16,815		
2010 primary	Richard Burr (R)	297,993	(80%)			
	Brad Jones (R)	37,616	(10%)			
	Eddie Burks (R)	22,111	(6%)			

Prior winning percentages: 2004 (52%); House: 2002 (70%), 2000 (93%), 1998 (68%), 1996 (62%), 1994 (57%)

Republican Richard Burr, North Carolina's senior senator, was first elected to the Senate in 2004 after serving 10 years in the House. A hard-working and conscientious conservative, Burr has not built the national profile of other senators and has been stymied in his attempts to enter the Senate GOP leadership ranks. But his ascension to the chairmanship of the Senate Intelligence Committee in 2015 offered him a chance to prominently shape debates over surveillance and terrorism. He faces reelection in 2016, and while North Carolina has been trending more liberal in recent years, Democrats have a short bench in the state. Former Sen. Kay Hagan's decision not to run against him left them with no obvious frontrunner.

A distant relative of Vice President Aaron Burr, Richard Burr grew up a minister's son in Winston-Salem, was a star football player at Reynolds High School and Wake Forest University, and then worked in sales for national wholesaler Carswell Distributing. In 1992, Burr ran against Rep. Steve Neal, a Democrat first elected in 1974. Although outspent 3-to-1, he lost by a relatively narrow 53%-46%. Neal retired in 1994 and Burr ran again, this time winning a solid 57 percent of the vote. He did not have a serious challenger in the next four House elections.

In the House, Burr had a mostly conservative voting record. On the Energy and Commerce Committee, his early cause was streamlining the Food and Drug Administration's drug and medical device approval process, which he argued would speed lifesaving products to the market. For over two years, he worked with the agency, doctors, patients, consumer groups, and the pharmaceutical industry to come up with a consensus. With broad bipartisan support, his FDA Modernization Act became law in 1997. He also helped to set up the National Institute for Biomedical Imaging and Bioengineering at the National Institutes of Health. After the September 11 attacks, he sponsored laws to improve defenses against bioterrorism. He sought a crackdown on illegal textile imports but backed President George W. Bush's call for trade promotion authority after securing promises that the local textile industry would have a seat at the table. He called it a difficult vote but said it could help make U.S. textiles more competitive internationally. The North Carolina textile industry has since seen a steep decline. A decade later, with the other party in the White House, Burr was more skeptical of expanding trade. He voted against giving President Obama fast-track authority for the Trans-Pacific Partnership, the only Republican on the Senate Finance Committee to do so.

In 2004, a major issue for Burr was a plan to end the tobacco quota system in place since 1938 with a government buyout of quota holders. The entire North Carolina delegation favored it; tobacco quotas had been cut back in recent years and seemed likely to be again. At issue was whether the buyout should be coupled with FDA regulation of tobacco. The Senate passed a corporate tax bill with both the buyout and FDA regulation. In the House, Burr favored the buyout without FDA regulation, arguing that the toxicity of cigarettes should be regulated by the Centers for Disease Control and Prevention and that package labeling should fall under the Federal Trade Commission. Burr was appointed to the conference committee, where he held out for the buyout without FDA regulation; the Senate yielded, and the bill was enacted to reflect his preferences.

Burr had promised to serve only five terms in the House and by the early 2000s, he wanted to run for the Senate. In 2002, when GOP Sen. Jesse Helms retired, he deferred to fellow Republican Elizabeth Dole, who had the backing of the Bush White House. Two years later, Democratic Sen. John Edwards was running for president, and Burr had the shot he was waiting for. He had $2 million in his campaign treasury and, this time, had the support of White House political strategist Karl Rove.

He had serious opposition from Erskine Bowles, the White House chief of staff under President Bill Clinton who had lost the 2002 Senate race 54%-45% to Dole. Bowles had deep roots in North Carolina. His father Hargrove "Skipper" Bowles was the Democratic nominee for governor in 1972, and his wife, Crandall Close, headed Springs Industries, a large textile firm started by her family. As Clinton's top aide, Bowles negotiated the 1997 legislation that helped produce a balanced federal budget for the first time in years. And he had earned the respect of Republican leaders even as they seethed with mistrust of Clinton.

Bowles started running ads in May and led in polls until September. Both candidates spent about $13 million. Burr held back on ads until then and, having conserved resources, had a money advantage in the last two months. Bowles ran on a 10-point economic program and touted his ability to work with both parties while depicting Burr as the king of the special interests, especially the pharmaceutical and tobacco companies. Republicans made much of Burr's role in blocking FDA regulation of tobacco. For his part, Burr linked Bowles to Clinton's policies on tax increases, welfare for immigrants, and trade with China.

On Election Day, Bush carried North Carolina 56%-44% in his reelection bid, and Burr beat Bowles 52%-47%. Bowles won big majorities in rural black-majority counties and in the counties with Durham and Chapel Hill. Burr carried almost every rural county in the Piedmont and the mountains. Later, when he co-chaired President Barack Obama's fiscal commission, Bowles said of Burr: "I think by the grace of God we both ended up in the exact right jobs for North Carolina. ... I can tell you from firsthand experience nobody works harder or is smarter than this guy in Washington."

In the Senate, Burr has shown little interest in self-promotion. He told *The Charlotte Observer* in 2009: "I tend to be more of a policy guy than I am a guy who shows up on the 24-hour talk shows or a guy who goes to the floor and speaks." He has leaned conservative on cultural issues and initially toward the center on foreign policy, although he has moved further to the right in that area since Democrat Barack Obama became president.

In taking the Intelligence chairmanship, Burr was expected to maintain better relations with the Obama administration's spy agency chiefs than the previous Democratic chairman, California's Dianne Feinstein. In contrast to Feinstein and other Democrats, who said they didn't know about the CIA's abuse of terrorist detainees, he told *McClatchy* Newspapers: "We're going to focus on real-time oversight, so nobody can ever say again that they forgot or they weren't briefed or they didn't know," Burr said.

In late 2014 Burr lambasted the conclusions of a committee report that the CIA's torture program had proven ineffective, calling it "fiction" and arguing in a letter with his GOP committee colleagues that the program "was an effective means of gathering significant intelligence information and cooperation from a majority of these CIA detainees." He had fought the report's declassification.

Burr resisted reining in those agencies' power in the face of domestic snooping revelations, and fought hard to turn back attempts at greater openness when sections of the USA Patriot Act came up for reauthorization. "I personally don't believe that anything that goes on in the Intelligence Committee should ever be discussed publicly," he told reporters in March 2014. "If I had my way, with the exception of nominees, there would never be a public intelligence hearing."

In 2015, Burr helped lead the charge to reauthorize the full Patriot Act, fighting against bipartisan efforts to curtail the program's bulk collection of Americans' phone records. He and Senate Majority Leader Mitch McConnell did all they could to renew the act without making changes, even after the House passed a bill with reforms by overwhelming bipartisan margins. After trying to force a short-term extension to the bill failed and the Patriot Act expired on June 1, McConnell relented and allowed a vote. Burr was one of just 32 senators to vote against the reforms. "I am disappointed in the final bill and, quite frankly, am very concerned about the new system's ability to keep up with the threats we face," he said.

Burr occasionally has shown a willingness to take on far-right colleagues; he said in July 2013 that talk of shutting down the federal government over the Affordable Care Act was "the dumbest idea I've ever heard." A year later, he worked with Republicans Orrin Hatch of Utah and Tom Coburn of Oklahoma on a comprehensive alternative to the law. It retained many of the law's most popular elements but guaranteed coverage to people with pre-existing medical conditions only if they maintained "continuous coverage." The measure drew widespread media attention but failed to gain any political traction.

In 2005, Burr won enactment of a bill to create the Biomedical Advanced Research and Development Authority to develop vaccines and other countermeasures to biological terrorism or a pandemic, and he cosponsored reauthorization of the bill in 2009 with the late Democratic Sen. Edward Kennedy of Massachusetts. He was an original cosponsor of the food safety bill that passed in 2010. More recently, Burr was part of a bipartisan group of senators that struck a deal in 2013 to keep down student loan interest rates by tying those rates to the government's cost of borrowing. It passed the Senate on an 81-18 vote and was signed into law.

Burr also seems to have a soft spot for animals. He sponsored a bill to bar the National Institutes of Health from recalling chimpanzees from their haven in Keithville Louisiana, for medical research. And in 2010, he cosponsored successful legislation that criminalized so-called animal crush videos, which depict small animals being tortured to death. He also has worked on ways to manage the wild horse population around the Outer Banks.

As the ranking minority member on the Veterans' Affairs Committee, Burr in 2012 cosponsored a bipartisan bill that became law aimed at ensuring veterans receive dignified burials. He and other lawmakers introduced the bill after a World War II veteran was found buried in a cardboard box in Florida. Burr also cosponsored with Republican Sens. Lindsey Graham of South Carolina and John McCain of Arizona a revision of the GI Bill of Rights that would allow veterans to transfer half their benefits to spouses or children after six years and all of them after 12 years. The Senate ultimately passed a bill that went even further, allowing veterans with three years of service to get tuition at the most expensive of their state's public colleges. In December 2010, Burr surprised his conservative supporters when he voted to end the "don't ask, don't tell" ban on openly gay service personnel. In 2014 he said the judge who'd struck down his state's gay marriage ban was "most qualified;" the next year he voted to give legally married same-sex spouses Social Security and veterans benefits they have earned.

After a scandal erupted at the Veterans' Affairs Department in 2014 over mismanagement and overly long wait times for treating patients, Burr found himself at the center of an acrimonious spat. He wrote an open letter that the staff at various veterans groups "has ignored the constant VA problems expressed by their members and is more interested in their own livelihoods and Washington connections than they are to the needs of their own members." His comments outraged those groups; an official at Disabled American Veterans said the senator "shows no interest in pursuing serious policy solutions, preferring instead to launch cheap political attacks on the integrity of leaders of veterans organizations that do not agree with him."

One area where Burr takes a strong conservative line is immigration. In 2006, he voted against the Senate immigration overhaul bill because he said it would lead to "blanket amnesty" for illegal immigrants. During negotiations on the compromise bill the following year, Burr supported the "touchback" amendment that would have forced illegal immigrants to return to their home countries before applying for visas. When the amendment was voted down, he voted against allowing the compromise bill to advance. Unlike some conservatives, however, he said in January 2013 that he would keep an open mind about a comprehensive immigration reform proposal drafted by a bipartisan group of senators. But he ultimately voted against the Senate-passed measure, saying it didn't do enough to secure the border.

During the financial crisis in 2008, Burr voted with many Democrats for the $700 billion government rescue of the financial industry, but he later had reservations and opposed release of the second half of the money from the Troubled Asset Relief Program. He also attracted some unfavorable attention during the crisis when he said he had advised his wife to withdraw as much cash as possible out of ATMs.

Burr cast a controversial vote in early 2012. When a bill aimed at banning insider trading by members of Congress was brought up on the Senate floor, there was little doubt it would pass. The legislation gained momentum after Congress was shamed into acting after a *60 Minutes* exposé on the practice. On a 96-3 vote, Burr was one of the three dissenters and received widespread criticism. The left-leaning blog *Huffington Post* reported that Burr stood to gain from his natural gas tax-credit bill because he had personal investments in the natural gas industry. Burr denied any attempt to profit from past legislation. Defending his actions on a local radio show, Burr said that insider trading bans were already on the books.

Burr has had an interest in moving up in the Senate leadership. In 2007, he lost a bid for Republican Conference chairman to Lamar Alexander of Tennessee on a 31-16 vote. But in January 2009, he was named chief deputy whip. In October 2011, Burr said he intended to run for Senate Republican whip, the No. 2 slot in the GOP leadership chain. However, in March 2012, Burr changed his mind and said he'd rather focus on legislation, clearing the way for Texas' John Cornyn to take the job.

When he came up for reelection in 2010, there was some speculation that Burr would encounter serious opposition, considering Obama's victory in North Carolina in 2008 and Dole's defeat for reelection to the Senate. Moreover, polls showed Burr had a low profile in the state. But the strongest possible Democratic challenger, state Attorney General Roy Cooper, widely respected for his work in the case of three Duke University lacrosse players falsely accused of rape, declined to run. Burr's opponent became Secretary of State Elaine Marshall.

Marshall emerged from the primary contest with little money and spent $2.8 million altogether. Burr raised $11 million. Marshall hit him for supporting the Wall Street bailout and dubbed him "Bank Run" Burr for his ATM advice to his wife. None of this got much traction. Marshall also got no help from the Democratic Senatorial Campaign Committee, which was busy defending a dozen Democratic-held seats that year. Burr won 55%-43%, losing in Charlotte, Fayetteville, and all the black-majority counties, but carrying virtually everything else. A prolific fundraiser, Burr in 2012 was named in *Washingtonian* magazine's anonymous survey of congressional staffers as one of the Senate's biggest "party animals," in recognition of his frequent money-raising events.

Rumors abounded in North Carolina in 2014 that Burr might retire in 2016 rather than face a challenge from a top-tier Democratic recruit such as Anthony Foxx, a former Charlotte mayor who became Secretary of Transportation, or former Sen. Kay Hagan. But Burr said the rumors weren't true, and that Foxx had assured him he wouldn't run. While he started his reelection cycle with little campaign cash, Burr kicked his fundraising into high gear as soon as the calendar turned to 2015, raising $1 million at a single fundraiser. Even though Hagan announced that she wouldn't run and the Democratic bench is relatively weak, Burr was not entirely out of the woods. North Carolina will be a swing state in the presidential contest, meaning that Democrats will spend heavily and will work to ensure that their down ballot slate of candidates is competitive.

Junior Senator

Thom Tillis (R)

Elected 2014, term expires Jan. 2021, 1st term; b. Aug. 30, 1960, Jacksonville, FL; U. of MD, B.A. 1997; Catholic; married (Susan); 2 children.

Elected Office: Board of Commissioners, Cornelius, NC, 2003-05; NC House, 2007-14.

Professional Career: Life insurance company consultant, 1981-82; Executive and mgr., PricewaterhouseCoopers, IBM, 1983-2009.

DC Office: 185 DSOB, 20510, 202-224-6342; Fax: 202-228-2563; Website: tillis.senate.gov.

State Offices: Charlotte, 704-334-2448; Greenville, 252-329-0371; Raleigh, 919-856-4630.

Committees: *Aging (Special). Agriculture, Nutrition & Forestry:* Livestock, Marketing & Agriculture Security; Nutrition, Specialty Crops & Agricultural Research; Rural Development & Energy. *Armed Services:* Emerging Threats & Capabilities; Personnel; Seapower. *Judicary:* Antitrust, Competition Policy & Consumer Rights; the Constitution; Immigration & the National Interest; Privacy, Technology & the Law. *Veterans' Affairs.*

Election Results

2014 general	Thom Tillis (R)	1,423,259	(49%)	$10,513,963	$13,033,391	$37,000,532
	Kay Hagan (D)	1,377,651	(47%)	$24,851,013	$7,789,136	$20,462,687
	Sean Haugh (Lib)	109,100	(4%)			
2014 primary	Thom Tillis (R)	223,174	(46%)			
	Greg Brannon (R)	132,630	(27%)			
	Mark Harris (R)	85,727	(18%)			

Republican Thom Tillis, North Carolina's junior senator, benefited from Republicans' 2014 wave election and heavy support from outside groups to pull off a narrow win over Democratic Sen. Kay Hagan.

Tillis was born in Jacksonville Florida, but by the time he was 17 had moved with his family 20 times as his father took new jobs, at one point living in a trailer park. He became interested in technology and, after earning a degree at the University of Maryland-Baltimore College, worked for the now-defunct Wang Laboratories before joining the international accounting and consulting firm PriceWaterhouseCoopers. He remained there when IBM took it over, advising banks and other corporations.

Tillis moved to Cornelius, a Charlotte suburb, in 1998 and served as a town commissioner. He was elected to the state House in 2006 and rose quickly through the ranks. In 2011, colleagues elected him the fifth Republican speaker in state history. He brought what he called a business leader's sensibility to the job: "A democratic institution is by definition not a business. But there is the business of running the Legislature, which I think we're doing pretty well," he told *North Carolina Business* in 2012.

He helped enact laws that included a restructuring of North Carolina's tax code that entailed reductions in personal and business income taxes, elimination of the estate tax, and a cap on the gasoline tax. Democrats attacked him for those moves and for cutting funds from the University of North Carolina system, as well as dragging his feet on public school-teacher pay increases—charges that became a prominent feature in Hagan's subsequent ads. But Tillis couldn't please everyone, as some on the right griped that he wasn't going far enough in pushing through changes in the state.

Republicans were eager to defeat Hagan, who had ousted Republican Sen. Elizabeth Dole in the strong Democratic year of 2008 and who, despite a reputation as a cautious centrist, was willing to back President Obama on his chief legislative priorities. Tillis, a programmatic social and fiscal conservative but not a fire-breather, had no trouble picking up the support of the state's GOP establishment. With their help he prevailed in an eight-way primary with 46 percent of the vote, getting past the 40 percent threshold necessary to avoid a runoff against an Evangelical preacher who'd led the state's referendum against gay marriage and a Tea Party candidate and acolyte of former Rep. Ron Paul of Texas.

But while Tillis won the primary comfortably, pressure from conservatives in the statehouse kept him more focused on his day job than was helpful for a candidate in a nationally targeted race. After months of debate over state budget proposals where he repeatedly fought with the more hardline conservatives running the state senate, he finally wrapped up a special legislative session in Raleigh in July and was able to turn his full attention to Hagan.

He had help from outside right-leaning groups like American Crossroads, Americans for Prosperity, and the U.S. Chamber of Commerce that spent months and multiple millions of dollars attacking Hagan in television ads and boosting Tillis. The contest stands as the most expensive Senate race in history despite Tillis's comparatively modest fundraising—$111 million spent in total, according to a Brookings Institution study. Hagan outspent Tillis by $25 million to $11 million, and without the outside groups' heavy support, it's unlikely Tillis would have been able to stay competitive throughout the race.

Tillis's main campaign objective was to tie Hagan to Obama, highlighting her support for the Affordable Care Act. He accused his rival of skipping an Armed Services Committee hearing on the threat of ISIS to raise money, a particularly potent attack in a state with a large military population and 800,000 veterans statewide. Hagan responded by emphasizing her opposition to a statewide ban on same-sex marriage, which Tillis said he would continue to defend.

Democrats had the edge in the race in public and private polling for much of the year, as Hagan and her allies relentlessly attacked Tillis on education and his opposition to increasing minimum wage in TV ads. But the last few weeks of the 2014 election featured a notable shift to Republicans nationwide. And as Hagan turned her attention toward base turnout, focusing on minimum wage increases, equal pay legislation for women, and Republicans' push to constrain ballot access in the state, Tillis tightened up his message and drilled Hagan on national security issues like ISIS and Ebola as well as problems at the Veterans' Administration.

Tillis ended up edging Hagan by 48.8%-47.2%, Republicans' closest win of the election cycle. Polls showed neither candidate was well-liked by election day—but President Obama's low popularity in the state likely was the crucial blow for Hagan.

Since winning his Senate seat Tillis has mostly kept a low profile, though his first big headline proved embarrassing. The new senator became a late-night comedy punch line in February 2015 for arguing the government should not require food workers to wash their hands after using the bathroom, saying "the market will take care of that" by causing businesses that didn't to fold. The Daily Show's Jon Stewart jumped on the comments, calling him "Sen. Dunghands Von Fecalfingers."

Tillis has remained a steadfast conservative since his election. He used his first Senate speech to call for offshore oil drilling, voted against Attorney General Loretta Lynch's confirmation, backed a state push to add anti-abortion "choose life" license plates, cosponsored a bill barring anyone with gang ties from receiving immigration benefits, and called the Department of Justice's investigation into the constricting voting laws and gerrymandered congressional map he'd helped pass in the statehouse a "waste of resources." He's also tended to parochial North Carolina issues, pushing for federal funding to expand and improve North Carolina's highway system, and fighting the military's plans to shutter programs and bases in North Carolina. Despite his opposition to same-sex marriage he voted for a bill to give legally married same-sex spouses Social Security and veterans benefits they have earned.

FIRST DISTRICT

G.K. Butterfield (D)

Elected July 2004, 6th full term; b. April 27, 1947, Wilson; NC Central U., B.A. 1971, J.D. 1974; Baptist; divorced; 3 children.

Military Career: Army, 1968-70.

Elected Office: NC Superior Court, 1988-2001, 2002-04; NC Supreme Court, 2001-02.

Professional Career: Practicing atty., 1974-88.

DC Office: 2305 RHOB, 20515, 202-225-3101; Fax: 202-225-3354; Website: butterfield.house.gov.

State Offices: Durham, 919-908-0164; Wilson, 252-237-9816.

Committees: *Energy & Commerce:* Commerce, Manufacturing & Trade; Communications & Technology; Health.

Group Ratings

	ADA	ACLU	AFL-CIO	LCV	ITI	COC	HAFA	ACU	CFG	FRC
2014	75%	77%	–	91%	80%	43%	9%	4%	4%	0%
2013	75%	C	95%	86%	C	42%	C	16%	10%	C

National Journal Ratings

	2013 LIB	—	2013 CONS
Economic	72%	—	28%
Social	73%	—	24%
Foreign	66%	—	32%
Composite	71%	—	29%

Key Votes of the 113th Congress

1. Sandy storm spending	Y	5. Medical Marijuana	Y	9. Syrian Rebels Training	Y
2. Violence Against Women Act	Y	6. Farm Bill	N	10. Keystone pipeline	N
3. Guantanamo Bay Detainees	Y	7. Afghanistan Combat	N	11. Immigration Exec. Action	N
4. Abortion 20-week ban	N	8. NSA Phone Data Collection	N	12. Bipartisan budget deal	Y

Election Results

2014 general	G.K. Butterfield (D)	154,333	(73%)	$703,902
	Arthur Rich (R)	55,990	(27%)	$17,822
2014 primary	G.K. Butterfield (D)	60,847	(81%)	
	Dan Whittacre	14,147	(19%)	

Prior winning percentages: 2012 (75%), 2010 (59%), 2008 (70%), 2006 (100%), 2004 (64%), 2004 special (71%)

Population		Race and Ethnicity		Income	
Total:	724,668	Black	51.9%	Median income:	$32,916
Urban:	40.8%	White	35.7%		(428 of 435)
Suburban:	10.5%	Latino	8.4%	Under $50,000	66.6%
Rural:	48.6%	Asian	1.3%	$50,000-$99,999:	24.2%
Land area:	5,337	Two races	1.8%	$100,000-$199,999:	7.9%
Pop/sq. mi.:	135.8	White Ethnic	8.6%	$200,000 or more:	1.3%
Born in state:	69.4%			Poverty Rate	26.9%
		Education			
Age Groups		H.S. grad or less:	50.4%	**Work**	
Under 18:	23.1%	Some college:	29.7%	White collar:	30.5%
18 to 34:	25.3%	College degree, 4 yr.:	12.3%	Blue collar:	44.7%
35 to 64:	36.8%	Post-grad study:	7.7%	Sales and service:	24.8%
Over 64:	14.8%			Govt. workers:	18.5%
		Military			
		Veterans/active duty:	8.9%		

Northeastern North Carolina: Durham, Greenville

In colonial days, the eastern portion of North Carolina was a smaller version of the Chesapeake Bay colonies of Virginia and Maryland. A fertile land laced by rivers and inlets, it had tobacco plantations and farms with docks on waterways accessible to the ocean and so to London.

Voter Turnout	
2013 Total Citizen 18+	525,160
2014 House Turnout	210,323
2014 Turnout as % CVAP	40%
2012 Turnout as % CVAP	65%

Vestiges of its 18th-century past can still be seen in New Bern with its reconstructed Tryon Palace, the governor's house when this was the capital, and in the tiny, well-preserved town of Edenton on Albemarle Sound, where 51 women in 1774 protested the taxing of tea and cloth. It is considered the first women's political protest on American shores. In 1890, James B. Duke founded the American Tobacco Co. in Durham, and began mass production of cigarettes.

Today, East Carolina survives with remnants of Tobacco Road and is still largely inhabited by the descendants of the original white settlers and black slaves of 250 years ago. They live in small towns and cities. Tobacco was a labor-intensive crop that for many years produced yields of $4,000 an acre; a family lucky enough to have a tobacco quota could make a living off 40 acres. In 2004, Congress enacted a $10 billion buyout of quota holders. Although North Carolina still produces nearly three-fourths of the nation's crop, tobacco's production and political influence have diminished. Hog farming in this area makes North Carolina the second-largest producer behind Iowa. Food-processing plants are replacing textile mills. Reser's Fine Foods began operations locally in 1950 with a potato-salad recipe, and now has nearly 5,000 employees who produce deli foods and salads at 16 facilities in the United States and Mexico, including tortillas at its home base in Halifax. The recession lingered in this region; Rocky Mount's unemployment rate remained in double digits in mid-2014, before dropping to 8.3 percent in February 2015.

The 1st Congressional District of North Carolina covers much of the old tobacco country of East Carolina. Its odd shape resembles a misshapen ostrich in the process of placing its head in the sand, and has been ranked among the most gerrymandered districts in the nation. The head of the bird is in Durham, where the district takes in Duke University. Duke provides an anchor for the Research Triangle area, whose facilities attract scientists from across the globe in a wide variety of studies and were ranked fourth in the nation in 2015 for tech jobs. The district includes most of the heavily African-American precincts on the eastern side of Durham County, which is the only urban area in the district and includes about one-fourth of its residents. The white and black portions of Durham are both overwhelmingly Democratic.

The neck of the bird runs up Interstate 85, into the body of the district: a swath of mostly rural, heavily African-American counties in the northeastern portion of the state. The remnants of Soul City, civil rights leader Floyd McKissick's planned 5,000-resident majority-black community from the 1970s, are in Warren County. It never really took off; today a few hundred residents occupy the houses there, while its only industrial building was annexed by the Warren County Correctional Institution. The district's various "limbs" and "feathers" take in heavily Democratic precincts in a variety of small towns and cities along North Carolina's coastal plain: Elizabeth City, Greenville, Washington, Wilson, Rocky Mount and Goldsboro, including Seymour Johnson Air Force Base.

2012 Presidential Vote

Barack Obama (D)	251,853	(73%)
Mitt Romney (R)	90,551	(26%)

2008 Presidential Vote

Barack Obama (D)	235,289	(71%)
John McCain (R)	96,353	(29%)

Cook Partisan Voting Index: D+19

New Bern birthed Pepsi-Cola, and Mount Olive makes famous pickles. The district is 54% African-American overall, and one of three solidly Democratic North Carolina districts where President Barack Obama twice got more than 70% of the vote.

G.K. Butterfield (D)

Democrat G.K. (George Kenneth) Butterfield, who won a special election in July 2004, rarely makes headlines but has been a key behind-the-scenes strategist for Democratic leaders and the Congressional Black Caucus. He took over in 2015 as Black Caucus chairman with a pledge to maintain its role as "conscience of the Congress."

Butterfield grew up in Wilson County, where his father was a dentist and the first black elected official in Wilson in the 20th century; he lost his seat when the white majority switched voting procedures to at-large elections. His mother was a schoolteacher for 48 years. In 1963, young Butterfield joined his father in Washington when Martin Luther King Jr., delivered his "I have a dream" speech. He got his bachelor's and law degrees from North Carolina Central University and participated in many registration drives after enactment of the Voting Rights Act. As a civil rights lawyer, Butterfield took on voting rights cases. He joined hospital employees at Duke University in their drive to organize a union. As a Superior Court judge for 12 years, he handled thousands of civil and criminal cases in 46 counties until February 2001, when Democratic Gov. Michael Easley appointed him to the state Supreme Court. After Butterfield lost election in 2002 to a full term, Easley appointed him as a special Superior Court judge.

In the July 2004 special election, party caucuses selected the nominees, and the six-week contest in the safe Democratic district received little local or national attention. Butterfield said that his priorities would be strengthening the rural economy and halting U.S. job losses. He won 71%-27% and has not been seriously challenged since.

In the House, Butterfield has a liberal voting record, particularly on economic matters. He has focused on an array of racial-discrimination issues. He helped to settle claims of up to 74,000 African-American farmers who were discriminated against when applying for Agriculture Department loans and programs between 1983 and 2010. He lobbied to include an exhibit in the Capitol Visitor Center on the slave labor that was employed in building the Capitol and on the careers of the 22 African Americans who served in Congress during and after Reconstruction. He pushed for the 2006 renewal of the Voting Rights Act, noting that his father lost his seat on the local city council in 1957 because of a discriminatory voting law change. He pressed Obama administration officials in early 2013 for the appointment of an African-American federal judge for North Carolina's Eastern District.

A longtime friend of Democratic Rep. James Clyburn of South Carolina, Butterfield managed his successful campaign for majority whip in 2006. Butterfield became a chief deputy whip under Clyburn and has retained the position with Democrats in the House minority. A long-time leader of the Black Caucus, he has been less confrontational toward President Barack Obama than other CBC members. Along with Clyburn, he was one of six who supported the 2010 funding of the wars in Iraq and Afghanistan.

As caucus chairman, Butterfield led a delegation to Ferguson Missouri to celebrate Martin Luther King's birthday in January 2015 and to call for "transformative changes" nationwide in police practices. He urged "coordination and respect" within the community. During a February 2015 meeting of CBC members with Obama, he told the president that "black America continues to be in a state of emergency." Separately, Obama pressed hard on Butterfield to support his Trans-Pacific Partnership trade initiative.

With his connections to Democratic leaders, Butterfield has a seat on the influential Energy and Commerce Committee, where he has worked to prohibit states from passing on their Medicaid costs to counties. In his district, many counties spend more of their property-tax revenues on Medicaid than on public schools. When the House passed in 2009 the Democrats' proposed cap-and-trade system of carbon emissions swapping, he got assurance that more of the revenue would be used to help low-income areas. However, the bill stalled in the Senate. He worked with Republican Rep. Michael McCaul of Texas to enact in 2012 a bill allowing pharmaceutical companies to receive faster Food and Drug Administration reviews of profitable drugs in return for developing treatments for rare pediatric diseases.

The independent Office of Congressional Ethics investigated Butterfield and five other House members after *The Wall Street Journal* reported in 2010 that the members did not return unused portions of their travel allowances. But the House Ethics Committee in January 2011 declined to take action against the members.

SECOND DISTRICT

Renee Ellmers (R)

Elected 2010, 3rd term; b. Feb. 9, 1964, Ironwood, MI; Oakland U., B.S. 1990; Catholic; married (Brent); 1 child.

Professional Career: Surgical intensive care nurse, Beaumont Hosp.; Clinical dir., Trinity Wound Care Ctr., 2007-10.

DC Office: 1210 LHOB, 20515, 202-225-4531; Fax: 202-225-5662; Website: ellmers.house.gov.

State Offices: Asheboro, 336-626-3060; Dunn, 910-230-19100.

Committees: *Energy & Commerce:* Communications & Technology; Energy & Power; Health.

Group Ratings

	ADA	ACLU	AFL-CIO	LCV	ITI	COC	HAFA	ACU	CFG	FRC
2014	0%	0%	–	3%	100%	86%	51%	72%	51%	75%
2013	0%	C	14%	0%	C	77%	C	76%	62%	C

National Journal Ratings

	2013 LIB	—	2013 CONS
Economic	29%	—	70%
Social	16%	—	74%
Foreign	15%	—	77%
Composite	23%	—	77%

Key Votes of the 113th Congress

1. Sandy storm spending	N	5. Medical Marijuana	Y	9. Syrian Rebels Training	Y
2. Violence Against Women Act	N	6. Farm Bill	Y	10. Keystone pipeline	Y
3. Guantanamo Bay Detainees	N	7. Afghanistan Combat	N	11. Immigration Exec. Action	Y
4. Abortion 20-week ban	Y	8. NSA Phone Data Collection	N	12. Bipartisan budget deal	Y

Election Results

2014 general	Renee Ellmers (R)	122,128	(59%)	$1,820,394	$204,211
	Clay Aiken (D)	85,479	(41%)	$1,178,594	
2014 primary	Renee Ellmers (R)	21,412	(59%)		
	Frank Roche	15,045	(41%)		

Prior winning percentages: 2012 (56%), 2010 (50%)

Population		Race and Ethnicity		Income	
Total:	777,683	White	66.8%	Median income:	$50,713
Urban:	26.8%	Black	15.8%		(230 of 435)
Suburban:	42.2%	Latino	10.7%	Under $50,000	49.3%
Rural:	31.0%	Asian	3.6%	$50,000-$99,999:	30.1%
Land area:	2,743	Two races	2.0%	$100,000-$199,999:	16.7%
Pop/sq. mi.:	283.6	White Ethnic	19.0%	$200,000 or more:	3.9%
Born in state:	52.2%			Poverty Rate	16.2%
Age Groups		**Education**			
		H.S. grad or less:	38.6%	**Work**	
Under 18:	26.0%	Some college:	32.2%	White collar:	38.7%
18 to 34:	22.2%	College degree, 4 yr.:	18.6%	Blue collar:	40.4%
35 to 64:	38.7%	Post-grad study:	10.6%	Sales and service:	20.9%
Over 64:	13.1%				
		Military		Govt. workers:	18.0%
		Veterans/active duty:	16.3%		

Central North Carolina: Fayetteville area

Most Easterners have heard of the Fall Line, but few appreciate what it is: a low, 900-mile long escarpment, running roughly along U.S. Route 1. The major rivers that cross the drop-off form a series of waterfalls from Paterson New Jersey through Columbus Georgia. These rapids and falls birthed many of today's major Southern cities, first as the final stopping point for oceangoing vessels supplying goods to the frontier, then as manufacturing centers in the days when falls powered early industries. Richmond, Fayetteville, Columbia and Augusta are among the cities in the South that owe their existence to these cataracts, to varying degrees. There are more falls along these rivers to the west, as the landscape transforms from the broad, flat coastal plain to the rolling hills of the Piedmont, which are really the foothills of the long ridges of the Appalachian Mountains.

Voter Turnout	
2013 Total Citizen 18+	536,045
2014 House Turnout	207,607
2014 Turnout as % CVAP	38.7%
2012 Turnout as % CVAP	61.2%

The Piedmont is a geographic feature that helped define North Carolina politically. It was settled not by the aristocratic planters who typified the Southern lowlands, but by the more hardscrabble Scots-Irish who colonized the Piedmont and Appalachian regions. These settlers clustered in small towns, usually around a mill or a factory. Even today, there isn't a large population center between High Point and the Sandhills region toward Fayetteville. Instead, the landscape is a collection of small towns, places like Asheboro and Siler City, burial place of Francis Bavier, best known as Aunt Bee on *The Andy Griffith Show*. Wyeth Vaccines is the largest employer in Sanford, while medical device manufacturer Teleflex has a sizable presence in Asheboro. In Moore County, ancient sand dunes begin the Sandhills, formed when the edge of today's Piedmont was North Carolina's coastline. Today, it hosts several world-famous golf resorts near Pinehurst.

The 2nd Congressional District of North Carolina takes in these Piedmont towns. This was once a swing area of the state, but now the Piedmont, where about half the district's population lives, is solidly Republican, especially Randolph County. Another quarter of the population lives at the southern end of the district, in and around Fort Bragg and the military-focused Fayetteville. This territory has split nearly evenly between recent presidential candidates. The final quarter lives in the suburbs and exurbs of Raleigh, in Wake and Harnett counties. Wake has the most pronounced Democratic base in the 2nd, and is the largest county. In 2014, RealtyTrac rated Cary as the "nicest" housing market in the nation. MetLife opened a 40-acre campus there in February 2015, and global high-tech companies have been moving into the city. Overall, the district's voters lean solidly Republican, as is the case with each of the state's 10 GOP-held districts.

2012 Presidential Vote		
Mitt Romney (R)	184,507	(58%)
Barack Obama (D)	132,381	(41%)

2008 Presidential Vote		
John McCain (R)	169,518	(56%)
Barack Obama (D)	131,886	(43%)

Cook Partisan Voting Index: R+10

Renee Ellmers (R)

The representative from the 2nd District is Republican Renee Ellmers, who has been among the most hostile anti-Obama conservatives elected in 2010 but has had a more amiable relationship with her party leaders than others in her class.

Ellmers grew up in the blue-collar Detroit suburb of Madison Heights, where her father worked in the auto industry. To pay her way through college, she trained as a medical assistant and worked full- and part-time jobs while taking classes. In 1990, she graduated from Oakland University in Rochester Michigan, with a bachelor's degree in nursing. She worked as a nurse in the surgical intensive care unit at Beaumont Hospital, where she met her husband, surgeon Brent Ellmers. Shortly after the birth of their son, Ben, they visited family members in Cary, the fast-growing suburb just west of Raleigh, and decided to move to the state. They settled in Dunn, in Harnett County, where Ellmers worked as a nurse in her husband's practice at the Trinity Wound Care Center. She got involved in the Dunn Chamber of Commerce, and was chairwoman-elect when she ran for Congress.

As the 2010 election approached, state and national Republicans had not mounted a challenge to Rep. Bob Etheridge, a veteran Democrat with a somewhat moderate record in a district that had voted for Barack Obama in 2008. Meanwhile, Ellmers was appalled that her congressman had supported the Democrats' health care legislation then wending its way to passage. "So rather than sit at home yelling at the TV set, which I did, I decided I needed to get involved," she told *The Sanford Herald*. A political novice, Ellmers started going to county GOP meetings and joined a bus tour organized by Americans for Prosperity as it protested the legislation. Though unnoticed by national Republican strategists, she built enough of an organization to win the May GOP primary with 55% of the vote against two businessmen who got 26% and 19%.

Ellmers cast the general election as a stark choice between the Obama agenda and a different direction for the country. "I'm a mother, wife, and nurse, and I never dreamed I'd be running for Congress, but it's time to put a stop to the Obama rubber stamp in Congress and Washington politics as usual," she said, noting that Etheridge had voted with his party more than 95% of the time. In June, she got a big break from Etheridge. When two young Republican operatives approached him outside the House office buildings and asked whether he supported "the Obama agenda," Etheridge asked them repeatedly, in angry tones, who they were, and grabbed one by the wrist and the other, briefly, by the neck. The operatives captured the encounter on videotape and posted it on *YouTube*. Etheridge quickly apologized, but after the video got 3 million hits, contributions poured into Ellmers' campaign.

Republican groups followed up with $360,000 worth of attack ads highlighting the incident. Ellmers was endorsed by former Alaska Gov. Sarah Palin, popular with the emerging tea party. National Republicans remained skeptical whether she was ready for prime time. Etheridge had a big money advantage, spending $1.9 million to Ellmers' $890,000, but Ellmers won, 49.5%-48.7%. A recount showed no significant change, and Etheridge conceded.

In the House, Ellmers has taken an interest in small business and health care issues that had been at the center of her career. After the Democratic Congressional Campaign Committee targeted Ellmers for her vote for a budget plan that included an overhaul of Medicare, she defended her position in town hall meetings. Ellmers insisted that overturning the 2010 health care law would help revive the economy. She charged that the 15-member Independent Payment Advisory Board, established under the health care law, would have the ability to deny surgery to a patient, a charge that the *News & Observer* newspaper declared to be false.

Ellmers called for a congressional inquiry into federal funding for Planned Parenthood. But her views on social issues moderated. Although she had opposed same-sex marriage, she spoke out against a 2012 North Carolina ballot measure to ban gay marriage in the state constitution; she said the initiative was too broadly written and should not include civil unions. She has chaired the Republican Women's Policy Committee, and has sought to unify the views of GOP women in the House. They worked to find common ground among Republicans on the bill to restrict abortions after 20 weeks, which the House passed in May 2015 after resolving earlier objections from Ellmers and her group. "We have to be compassionate to women when they're in a crisis situation," she told Bloomberg News. Despite her insistence that she remained pro-life on abortion, her efforts generated strong pushback from conservative activists, who threatened a GOP primary challenge.

She has been an ally of House Speaker John Boehner, and has frequently joined GOP leadership press conferences. She supported the leaders' sweeping "cut, cap, and balance" package that included a constitutional amendment mandating a balanced budget. Unlike some conservative deficit hawks, Ellmers backed the Boehner-Obama budget compromise that raised the debt limit. In August 2011, *The New York Times* described Ellmers: "Her loyalty, relentless cheer, and folksy locution ... have combined to make her one of the Republican leadership's greatest freshman allies, and a rising star in the conference."

In 2013, Ellmers was rewarded with a seat on the Energy and Commerce Committee. Continuing her work on health care issues, she sought bipartisan opportunities. With Democratic Rep. G.K. Butterfield from her home state, she filed a bill to expedite the ability of Medicare beneficiaries to use more advanced medical devices. She and Democratic Rep. Jerry McNerney of California sponsored a proposal to enhance the reliability of the nation's energy grid, which became part of the committee's package to boost energy independence. On a local issue, she strongly opposed the plan by the Air Force to inactivate the C-130 transports based at Fort Bragg, and won House passage in May 2015 of her amendment to the defense-spending bill requiring review by the Defense secretary.

Ellmers has twice won reelection comfortably, although she has not cracked the 60 percent ceiling in her vote. Her 2014 campaign received considerable attention because her opponent was well-known pop singer Clay Aiken, who got his start on the "American Idol" television series. Aiken, who ran a spirited campaign and promised bipartisanship, spent $1.2 million to $1.8 million for Ellmers. The incumbent was never at serious risk of losing her seat. Ellmers won 59%-41% and took seven of the nine counties, some by a margin of more than three-to-one. Aiken narrowly led in Wake and Hoke counties. Earlier in 2014, she defeated 59%-41% a primary challenge from economic commentator Frank Roche, who criticized her support for immigration reform. In April 2015, Jim Duncan, a retired high-tech executive and past chairman of the Chatham County Republican Party, said he would challenge Ellmers in the 2016 primary.

THIRD DISTRICT

Walter Jones (R)

Elected 1994, 11th term; b. Feb. 10, 1943, Farmville; NC St. U., 1962-65, Atlantic Christian Col., B.A. 1966; Catholic; married (Joe Anne); 1 child.

Military Career: NC Natl. Guard, 1967-71.

Elected Office: NC House, 1982-92.

Professional Career: Mgr., Walter B. Jones Office Supply Co., 1967-73; Salesman, Dunn Assoc., 1973-82; Pres., Benefit Reserves Inc., 1989-94; Pres., Judson Co., 1990-94.

DC Office: 2333 RHOB, 20515, 202-225-3415; Fax: 202-225-3286; Website: jones.house.gov.

State Offices: Greenville, 252-931-1003.

Committees: *Armed Services:* Military Personnel; Tactical Air & Land Forces.

Group Ratings

	ADA	ACLU	AFL-CIO	LCV	ITI	COC	HAFA	ACU	CFG	FRC
2014	40%	44%	–	17%	40%	25%	71%	76%	88%	57%
2013	30%	C	38%	18%	C	33%	C	84%	78%	C

National Journal Ratings

	2013 LIB	—	2013 CONS
Economic	51%	—	49%
Social	47%	—	52%
Foreign	56%	—	44%
Composite	52%	—	49%

Key Votes of the 113th Congress

1. Sandy storm spending	N	5. Medical Marijuana	Y
2. Violence Against Women Act	N	6. Farm Bill	N
3. Guantanamo Bay Detainees	N	7. Afghanistan Combat	Y
4. Abortion 20-week ban	Y	8. NSA Phone Data Collection	Y

9. Syrian Rebels Training	N
10. Keystone pipeline	NV
11. Immigration Exec. Action	Y
12. Bipartisan budget deal	N

Election Results

2014 general	Walter Jones (R)	139,415	(68%)	$677,381	$99,999	$532,422
	Marshall Adame (D)	66,182	(32%)	$23,909		
2014 primary	Walter Jones (R)	22,616	(51%)			
	Taylor Griffin (R)	20,024	(45%)			

Prior winning percentages: 2012 (63%), 2010 (72%), 2008 (66%), 2006 (69%), 2004 (71%), 2002 (91%), 2000 (61%), 1998 (62%), 1996 (63%), 1994 (53%)

Population		Race and Ethnicity		Income	
Total:	749,521	White	70.5%	Median income:	$44,147
Urban:	35.9%	Black	20.3%		*(332 of 435)*
Suburban:	21.6%	Latino	5.8%	Under $50,000	55.4%
Rural:	42.5%	Asian	1.2%	$50,000-$99,999:	30.3%
Land area:	6,556	Two races	1.6%	$100,000-$199,999:	12.2%
Pop/sq. mi.:	114.3	White Ethnic	22.5%	$200,000 or more:	2.1%
Born in state:	52.5%			Poverty Rate	17.3%
		Education			
Age Groups		H.S. grad or less:	40.9%	**Work**	
Under 18:	21.1%	Some college:	37.8%	White collar:	31.3%
18 to 34:	29.1%	College degree, 4 yr.:	13.8%	Blue collar:	45.5%
35 to 64:	35.4%	Post-grad study:	7.5%	Sales and service:	23.2%
Over 64:	14.3%				
		Military		Govt. workers:	20.3%
		Veterans/active duty:	19.6%		

Coastal North Carolina: Jacksonville, Wilmington

Nearly 500 years ago, Giovanni da Verrazzano, a Florentine explorer under the flag of France, sailed past the Gulf Stream and landed on a sand-spit island he thought was the outer edge of China. It was the Outer Banks of North Carolina. These are probably America's most unstable barrier islands,

Voter Turnout	
2013 Total Citizen 18+	571,676
2014 House Turnout	205,597
2014 Turnout as % CVAP	36%
2012 Turnout as % CVAP	56%

constantly changing shape and cut by new inlets as they are battered by ocean currents and storm winds. The islands were settled early by Europeans. Sir Walter Raleigh's Roanoke colony was founded here in 1587, near present-day Manteo, then vanished shortly thereafter when supply ships diverted themselves to loot Spanish galleons rather than deliver their badly needed cargo. Edward Teach, better known as Blackbeard, and other pirates lurked in Pamlico and Albemarle sounds behind the islets.

History is very much alive on the Outer Banks. An antique form of English is spoken by some on Ocracoke Island, reachable only by ferry and largely insulated from the commercialization of the upper islands. A pack of feral horses—believed to be the last remaining descendants of late-16th century Spanish mustangs—roams free in a 12,000-acre sanctuary in Corolla. The 208-foot lighthouse on Cape Hatteras, America's tallest, looks out on some of the most treacherous currents in the Atlantic. The sands along Kitty Hawk, with their winds, brought the Wright brothers to the Outer Banks to undertake mankind's first heavier-than-air flight in December 1903. The Outer Banks are prime vacation and retirement country, with affluent beachfront communities on both the coastal and sound side. Kill Devil Hills has the most millionaires per capita in the state. In 2015, CNN rated the Ocracoke campground at Cape Hatteras among the prettiest beaches in the nation. There are plans for wind farms off-shore. Rising sea levels on the Outer Banks have raised concerns by residents and activists worried about climate change.

Further south, amid swamps, is the Marine Corps' Camp Lejeune, home base for one-fifth of the roughly 200,000 Marines and the Corps' largest base. On the other side of the Croatan National Forest is Cherry Point, the world's largest Marine Corps air station. The flatlands of East Carolina have long been tobacco- and peanut-growing country and also have become hog-raising land. This is also the only part of the world where Venus flytrap plants grow wild.

The 3rd Congressional District of North Carolina covers the Outer Banks and the coastal plain of North Carolina from the Virginia border nearly to South Carolina. Most of the district is solidly Republican. Although the district is hostile to national Democrats, Gov. Michael Easley in 2004 and Gov. Bev

2012 Presidential Vote		
Mitt Romney (R)	187,555	(59%)
Barack Obama (D)	126,503	(40%)

2008 Presidential Vote		
John McCain (R)	174,150	(56%)
Barack Obama (D)	133,260	(43%)

Cook Partisan Voting Index: R+11

Perdue in 2008, among other Democrats, have carried it. Minority communities of Wilmington in New Hanover County are a Democratic bastion. Barack Obama got 43% of the vote in 2008 and 40% in 2012.

Walter Jones (R)

Republican Walter Jones, first elected in 1994, is one of his party's leading iconoclasts. An evangelical Christian and devout social conservative, he has been the GOP's most fervently antiwar House member and happens to represent many military members and retirees. Party leaders often treat him as an outcast.

Jones grew up in eastern North Carolina, attended North Carolina State and Atlantic Christian College, and served in the National Guard. His father, Walter Jones Sr., was a Democratic representative with a similar district. The senior Jones served for a quarter-century and chaired the Merchant Marine and Fisheries Committee. The younger Jones, then a Democrat, was elected in 1982 to the state House, where he often broke with party leaders.

In 1992, he ran in the new black-majority 1st District after his father retired. He led the primary with 38% but lost the runoff to Democrat Eva Clayton, an African-American woman who got 55% to Jones' 45%. In April 1993, Jones switched to the Republican Party and announced he was running in the 3rd District. This pitted him against four-term Rep. Martin Lancaster, a Democrat who had worked earnestly on local projects. But Lancaster voted for President Bill Clinton's budget and tax bills and his crime legislation, while failing to persuade Clinton to drop the cigarette tax from health care legislation. Jones ran an ad showing Lancaster jogging with Clinton, with the voiceover message: "How'd Martin Lancaster get so out of touch? Well, look who he's running around with in Washington." Jones won 53%-47%.

In the House, Jones' voting record began consistently conservative and hawkish, but over the years has moderated. He had a remarkable conversion on the issue of the war in Iraq. Jones voted in 2002 to authorize the use of force in Iraq, as did all but six House Republicans. He even led the 2003 effort, widely spoofed by late-night comics, to rename the House cafeteria's French fries as "freedom fries" after France declined to support the invasion. Not long afterward, he was profoundly affected by a local Marine's funeral, setting the stage for an unlikely conversion to passionate war critic.

As the war dragged on, Jones supported Democratic proposals for a timetable to withdraw troops from Iraq, and he opposed President George W. Bush's troop surge. But he drew the line at a Democratic plan to attach conditions to future war funding, saying that attempts to "starve" the war to bring it to a close were wrong. Jones also began writing letters to the families of every soldier killed in Iraq and Afghanistan. By February 2013, he had sent more than 10,800 letters, calling them his "mea culpa to my Lord" for voting for the war. He also began work on a book, *My Daddy's Not Dead Yet*, whose title came from a little boy who feared his Marine father would be killed in Iraq.

His independence from his party has cost him top Republican posts on the Armed Services Committee. After punishment by GOP leaders, Democrats approached Jones about switching parties, but he declined, saying his opposition to abortion rights would make him ill at ease in the party. "I'm a Pat Buchanan American," he said in 2009. "I want to stop trying to take care of the world and fix this country." House Republican leaders, again exasperated with Jones in late 2012, kicked him off the Financial Services Committee as they organized for the new Congress; GOP leadership aides said it wasn't because of ideology but because he had not raised enough campaign money for the party. Jones retained his seat on Armed Services, but without a subcommittee chairmanship.

When his party assumed the House majority in 2011, Jones was the chamber's most liberal Republican that year, according to *National Journal's* rankings. He has twice refused to support John Boehner for House speaker, casting his vote in 2013 for former Comptroller General David Walker, a deficit hawk, and in 2015 for Republican Rep. Dan Webster of Florida. In December 2010, he was one of just three Republicans to support a Democratic bill extending the Bush-era tax cuts for low- and middle-income Americans but not for the highest-earners. After the Supreme Court's *Citizens United* decision on campaign finance, Jones co-sponsored a bill backed by President Barack Obama aimed at restricting corporate spending on campaign ads.

In 2011, Jones was part of a bipartisan and bicameral group to call for nearly $1 trillion in defense savings over 10 years to reduce the deficit. He got the Pentagon to investigate substandard mental health treatment for soldiers returning from Iraq and Afghanistan to Camp Lejeune. He drew headlines in March 2012 when, at an Armed Services hearing, he used an ethnic stereotype in questioning the need to borrow from China to finance the war: "The Chinese—Uncle Chang—is lending us the money to pay what we are spending in Afghanistan," he said. In December 2014, he lamented that House Republicans were not pursuing the possible impeachment of Obama for his executive actions on immigration. With Democratic Rep. Jim McGovern of Massachusetts, Jones organized a constitutional war study group to promote discussion of congressional powers. In May 2015, they urged Boehner to schedule House action on Obama's request for an authorization of military force against the Islamic State.

At home, Jones occasionally has joined battles on local cultural matters. He called for the state school superintendent to remove from an elementary school a book about two gay princes who get married, and he complained in January 2013 about a federal grant to Craven Community College to acquire 25 books and a DVD series educating Americans about Muslim culture.

His outspoken criticism of the Iraq war brought Jones a serious primary challenge in 2008 from Onslow County Commissioner Joe McLaughlin, a former Army Ranger. McLaughlin called Jones "a poster boy for the Left." Jones seemed to benefit from Iraq fatigue among voters, even among military families. McLaughlin was significantly outspent, and Jones won 59%-41%. His next competitive contest came in the 2014 primary against Republican Taylor Griffin, a native of eastern North Carolina who worked more than a decade in Washington, both in government and as a lobbyist. He returned home to challenge Jones as too close to Obama in his views. The margin narrowed to 51%-45%. Those recent contests and the continued independence of Jones suggest continued vulnerability in a GOP primary. For 2016, he got an early challenge from Phil Law, a supervisor for Hewlett-Packard who earlier served four years in the Marines. Griffin was also preparing another campaign.

FOURTH DISTRICT

David Price (D)

Elected 1996, 14th term; b. Aug. 17, 1940, Erwin, TN; U. of NC, B.A. 1961, Yale U., B.D. 1964, Ph.D. 1969; Baptist; married (Lisa); 2 children.

Elected Office: U.S. House, 1986-94.

Professional Career: Legis. aide, U.S. Sen. Bartlett, 1963-67; Prof., Yale U., 1969-73, Duke U., 1973-86, 1995-96; Exec. dir., NC Dem. Party, 1979-80, chmn., 1983-84; Staff dir., DNC Comm. on Pres. Nominations, 1981-82.

DC Office: 2162 RHOB, 20515, 202-225-1784; Fax: 202-225-2014; Website: price.house.gov.

State Offices: Chapel Hill, 919-967-7924; Fayetteville, 910-323-0260; Raleigh, 919-859-5999.

Committees: *Appropriations:* Homeland Security; Military Construction, Veterans Affairs & Related Agencies; Transportation, HUD & Related Agencies (RMM).

Group Ratings

	ADA	ACLU	AFL-CIO	LCV	ITI	COC	HAFA	ACU	CFG	FRC
2014	90%	83%	–	97%	60%	50%	6%	0%	2%	0%
2013	80%	C	90%	93%	C	31%	C	8%	10%	C

National Journal Ratings

	2013 LIB	—	2013 CONS
Economic	90%	—	9%
Social	79%	—	16%
Foreign	83%	—	15%
Composite	85%	—	15%

Key Votes of the 113th Congress

1. Sandy storm spending	Y	5. Medical Marijuana	Y	9. Syrian Rebels Training	Y
2. Violence Against Women Act	Y	6. Farm Bill	N	10. Keystone pipeline	N
3. Guantanamo Bay Detainees	Y	7. Afghanistan Combat	N	11. Immigration Exec. Action	N
4. Abortion 20-week ban	N	8. NSA Phone Data Collection	N	12. Bipartisan budget deal	Y

Election Results

2014 general   David Price (D) 169,946   (75%) $688,801
             Paul Wright (R) 57,416   (25%)
2014 primary   David Price (D) .... unopposed

Prior winning percentages: 2012 (74%), 2010 (57%), 2008 (63%), 2006 (65%), 2004 (64%), 2002 (61%), 2000 (62%), 1998 (57%), 1996 (54%), 1992 (65%), 1990 (58%), 1988 (58%), 1986 (56%)

Population		Race and Ethnicity		Income	
Total:	769,734	White	47.4%	Median income:	$49,637
Urban:	67.6%	Black	32.6%		*(246 of 435)*
Suburban:	24.7%	Latino	11.9%	Under $50,000	50.3%
Rural:	7.7%	Asian	5.2%	$50,000-$99,999:	30.1%
Land area:	1,256	Two races	2.0%	$100,000-$199,999:	14.6%
Pop/sq. mi.:	612.9	White Ethnic	17.0%	$200,000 or more:	5.1%
Born in state:	46.6%			Poverty Rate	18.2%
		Education			
Age Groups		H.S. grad or less:	30.7%	**Work**	
Under 18:	22.6%	Some college:	27.0%	White collar:	44.8%
18 to 34:	31.3%	College degree, 4 yr.:	25.2%	Blue collar:	39.5%
35 to 64:	35.9%	Post-grad study:	17.1%	Sales and service:	15.7%
Over 64:	10.2%			Govt. workers:	18.9%
		Military			
		Veterans/active duty:	10.8%		

Central North Carolina: Raleigh, Chapel Hill

Back in the 1950s, few people would have predicted that the countryside around Raleigh and Durham would become one of America's high-tech boom areas. But Democratic Gov. Luther Hodges did, and he started the 6,900-acre Research Triangle Park as a research and development industrial park

Voter Turnout	
2013 Total Citizen 18+	537,332
2014 House Turnout	227,362
2014 Turnout as % CVAP	42.3%
2012 Turnout as % CVAP	68.6%

between the musty state capital of Raleigh and the Lucky Strike-manufacturing city of Durham. With the drawing power of three universities—North Carolina State in Raleigh, Duke in Durham, and the University of North Carolina in Chapel Hill—Research Triangle Park slowly began attracting top R&D organizations, which in turn spawned a dynamic entrepreneurial sector. Today, this is among the top high-tech centers in the nation, with big-name employers that include IBM, Credit Suisse, Merck & Co., Verizon, GlaxoSmithKline, Cisco Systems, Nortel, and RTI International. A sleepy metro area that once trailed the nation in income is now a vibrant, affluent metropolis and the prime engine of North Carolina's growth. The Raleigh-Durham airport, which had four gates in the 1970s, opened a new terminal in 2011. Local planners are working on a light-rail system for the area. In 2011, voters in Durham approved a half-cent sales tax to help pay for it. But officials in Wake County rejected a referendum in 2012 to vote on a similar tax.

Still, the region prides itself on its homier touches. Barbecue is a serious business here. The state is split between proponents of Eastern Carolina barbecue (vinegar-based) and Lexington style (vinegar-plus-tomato), and controversy engulfed the statehouse when bills were introduced to declare the Lexington Barbecue Festival the state's official festival. The all-you-can-eat buffet at Bullock's in Durham is a regular stop for celebrities and politicians. College basketball is the other major preoccupation here, and UNC, N.C. State, and Duke (in the neighboring 1st District) have fielded more March Madness contenders than any similarly sized area.

The combination of upscale and down-home has proved to be a popular draw. From 1990 to 2014, the Raleigh-Durham-Cary metro area more than doubled in population, from 855,000 to 2.1 million. Many of the new arrivals are from the North; locals joke that the fast-growing town of Cary is an acronym for "Containment Area for Retired Yankees." The new arrivals are changing the politics of the region as well. Just as Northern immigrants helped bring Republicanism to the South in the 1950s and 1960s, today they have made this the most heavily Democratic region in the state.

The 4th Congressional District of North Carolina is anchored by the Research Triangle, and about 30% of the residents are located in southwest Durham County, southern Orange County, or in the arms that jut off into the old textile cities of Hillsborough and Burlington (the "Hosiery Center of the South"). This part of the Triangle has one of the highest concentrations of Ph.D.s in the nation, many earning livelihoods in academia, the sciences, and social services. About 40% of the district's residents are in Democratic precincts in Raleigh-based Wake County. The final share lives in a tendril that snakes through central North Carolina—at one point it narrows to a mere point on the Cape Fear River—on a journey to the Democratic portions of Fayetteville. The 4th is by far the most heavily Democratic district with a non-Hispanic white majority population in the South, and it elects the only white House Democrat in a coastal state between northern Virginia and Tallahassee. Like the minority-majority 1st and 12th districts, Republicans creatively gerrymandered this district to maximize its Democratic vote.

2012 Presidential Vote		
Barack Obama (D)	263,003	(72%)
Mitt Romney (R)	96,300	(27%)
2008 Presidential Vote		
Barack Obama (D)	246,527	(72%)
John McCain (R)	92,456	(27%)
Cook Partisan Voting Index:	D+20	

David Price (D)

Democrat David Price was first elected in 1986, lost the seat in 1994, and regained it in 1996. Since his return, he has distinguished himself as an influential spender and a thoughtful voice on anti-terrorism and border security in addition to education and science issues.

Price grew up in East Tennessee, the son of a school principal and an English teacher. He is an interesting blend of political scientist, practical politician and lay Baptist preacher. He attended the University of North Carolina at Chapel Hill, worked as a young aide on Capitol Hill, earned a degree in divinity and a doctorate in political science at Yale University, and taught there for four years. In 1973, he became a political science professor at Duke. He was executive director of the North Carolina Democratic Party in the 1980 election season and chairman in 1983-84. With Democratic Gov. Jim Hunt, Price helped develop North Carolina's robust straight-ticket politics.

In 1986, he ran for the House and beat Republican freshman Rep. Bill Cobey. In 1994, Price lost the seat, 50.4%-49.6%, to Fred Heineman, a former New York City police officer and Raleigh police chief in the 1970s. Two years later, Price outspent Heineman in a rematch, winning 54%-44%.

Price has written four books about Congress, including *The Congressional Experience,* which focuses on his life as a lawmaker. The polarization of the two chambers has made him pessimistic about finding agreement to solve the nation's fiscal problems. "Our capacity to take them on in the bipartisan fashion that history teaches us is almost always necessary is far weaker" than it was in the 1990s, he said in 2010.

His Education Affordability Act, which he considers his proudest achievement, was folded into the 1997 Balanced Budget Act. It made interest on student loans tax-deductible and allowed penalty-free withdrawals from individual retirement accounts for education expenses.

From 2007 through 2010, Price chaired the Homeland Security Appropriations Subcommittee. He consistently sought higher levels of spending for homeland security measures, like support for first responders, than were requested by the Bush administration. In 2007, the House passed Price's bill establishing a code of conduct for private security contractors in Iraq and Afghanistan. A target of the bill was North Carolina-based Blackwater, whose controversial activities in Iraq included the shooting of 17 people in a Baghdad square. After President Barack Obama took office, Price crafted bills that rejected the administration's proposal to hold criminal trials for terror suspects in New York City and restored budget cuts that the administration had made to the Coast Guard. In 2010, he called increased drug trafficking and violence on the U.S. border "an emergency" that merited as much attention as the wars in Afghanistan and Iraq.

As the subcommittee's ranking member with Democrats in the minority, Price worked in 2012 to pass a bipartisan spending bill for homeland security. But when it came to the House floor, he sharply criticized two amendments that were added by Republican Rep. Steve King of Iowa. One of them barred the use of federal money to provide translation services to people who cannot speak English well, a move that Price said "breaks faith with all immigrant constituencies." The bill subsequently passed on a largely party-line vote. In opposing a three-month extension of the federal debt limit in January 2013, he said it "is not an end to government by crisis—it is a continuation of it."

Price has been active on campaign finance law. He sponsored the "stand by your ad" requirement for candidates to appear in the full frame of television ads reading their disclaimers on the air, so they would more likely be held responsible for negative ads. His proposal became part of the campaign reform law in 2002. He wants a similar requirement for Internet ads and said the Supreme Court's March 2010 *Citizens United* decision allowing unlimited spending by corporations contributed to the flow of misleading ads. "The least we can do is inform viewers who has bought the ads they are seeing," he said. The same year, he sponsored a bill to make small political donors more important by matching contributions under $200 to presidential campaigns on a 4-to-1 basis.

In a January 2015 column co-authored by Democratic Rep. Chris van Hollen of Maryland, Price promoted their bill to clarify and strengthen the ban on candidate coordination with outside spending groups. "The unchecked and rapid rise of new organizations solely designed to circumvent campaign finance law should be a call to action for Congress," they wrote in *The Hill*.

In the appropriations process, Price has nurtured local projects, including $272 million for a new Environmental Protection Agency complex in Research Triangle Park as well as a variety of defense- and technology-related programs for colleges in his district. But he voiced regret that such funding has become more difficult to secure. Speaking to UNC researchers in October 2014, he said, "I've never seen things so locked up in terms of some people just having the ideology that will not let them bend. That's pretty unusual in American politics," the *Daily Tarheel* reported.

Since his return to the House in 1996, Price has been reelected by wide margins. After Democratic Rep. Brad Miller decided to retire rather than face Price in a primary following the 2012 redistricting, he won with 74 percent of the vote, his highest ever. In 2014, he raised his showing to 75 percent.

FIFTH DISTRICT

Virginia Foxx (R)

Elected 2004, 6th term; b. June 29, 1943, Bronx, NY; U. of NC, A.B. 1968, M.A.C.T. 1972, U. of NC, Greensboro, Ed.D. 1985; Catholic; married (Thomas); 1 child.

Elected Office: Watauga Bd. of Ed., 1976-88; NC Senate, 1994-2004.

Professional Career: Owner, Grandfather Mountain Nursery, 1976-2004; Prof., Asst. Dean of Gen. Col., Appalachian St. U., 1976-85; Pres., May-land CC, 1987-94.

DC Office: 2350 RHOB, 20515, 202-225-2071; Fax: 202-225-2995; Website: foxx.house.gov.

State Offices: Boone , 828-265-0240; Clemmons, 336-778-0211.

Committees: *Education & the Workforce:* Health, Employment, Labor & Pensions; Higher Education & Workforce Training (Chmn). *Rules* (VChmn): Legislative and Budget Process.

Group Ratings

	ADA	ACLU	AFL-CIO	LCV	ITI	COC	HAFA	ACU	CFG	FRC
2014	5%	0%	–	3%	100%	71%	73%	88%	90%	100%
2013	0%	C	10%	4%	C	85%	C	92%	84%	C

National Journal Ratings

	2013 LIB	—	2013 CONS
Economic	10%	—	88%
Social	16%	—	74%
Foreign	15%	—	77%
Composite	17%	—	83%

Key Votes of the 113th Congress

1. Sandy storm spending	N	5. Medical Marijuana	N	9. Syrian Rebels Training	Y
2. Violence Against Women Act	N	6. Farm Bill	Y	10. Keystone pipeline	Y
3. Guantanamo Bay Detainees	N	7. Afghanistan Combat	N	11. Immigration Exec. Action	Y
4. Abortion 20-week ban	Y	8. NSA Phone Data Collection	N	12. Bipartisan budget deal	Y

Election Results

2014 general	Virginia Foxx (R)....................... 139,279	(61%)	$693,139
	Josh Brannon (D)........................ 88,973	(39%)	$9,946
2014 primary	Virginia Foxx (R)........................ 49,572	(75%)	
	Philip Doyle (R)........................... 16,175	(25%)	

Prior winning percentages: 2012 (58%), 2010 (66%), 2008 (58%), 2006 (57%), 2004 (59%)

Population		Race and Ethnicity		Income	
Total:	745,928	White	75.3%	Median income:	$42,904
Urban:	31.7%	Black	12.5%		*(346 of 435)*
Suburban:	42.1%	Latino	9.1%	Under $50,000	56.0%
Rural:	26.1%	Asian	1.4%	$50,000-$99,999:	28.2%
Land area:	3,093	Two races	1.4%	$100,000-$199,999:	12.6%
Pop/sq. mi.:	241.1	White Ethnic	16.1%	$200,000 or more:	3.2%
Born in state:	63.7%			Poverty Rate	19.0%
Age Groups		**Education**		**Work**	
Under 18:	21.4%	H.S. grad or less:	44.0%	White collar:	35.6%
18 to 34:	22.1%	Some college:	29.1%	Blue collar:	40.4%
35 to 64:	40.2%	College degree, 4 yr.:	17.3%	Sales and service:	24.0%
Over 64:	16.3%	Post-grad study:	9.5%		
				Govt. workers:	12.8%
		Military			
		Veterans/active duty:	8.2%		

Northwest North Carolina: Winston-Salem

From the Atlantic Ocean, the terrain of North Carolina rises slowly through the Piedmont, a transitional land of modest hills that lies between the coastal plain and the Blue Ridge Mountains. The Blue Ridge, named for the mysterious blue haze that blankets it, provides the headwaters of the

Voter Turnout	
2013 Total Citizen 18+	558,167
2014 House Turnout	228,252
2014 Turnout as % CVAP	40.9%
2012 Turnout as % CVAP	64.5%

New River—somewhat ironically named given that it is the oldest river in North America—which cuts majestic crevasses as it flows north to West Virginia. The lower Piedmont lands of North Carolina were first settled by independent-minded Scots-Irish farmers and by followers of British and German sects like the Moravians. This was hardscrabble farm country before the Civil War, with few slaves. By the late-19th century, it was becoming industrialized, with textile mills alongside streams, furniture factories not far from hardwood forests, and R.J. Reynolds' cigarette factories in the growing city of Winston-Salem.

Today, the Winston-Salem area's pharmaceutical companies, banking institutions and high-skill Piedmont factories have emerged from the recession. The unemployment rate in March 2015 was 5.1 percent, half of what it was four years earlier. At a former R.J. Reynolds Tobacco plant, the Wake Forest Innovation Quarter focuses on medical education and biotech research; it is a $517 million partnership among the city, state, university and the private developer, with about 3,000 workers. "The idea was to build a place with a lot of intellectual energy and make it possible for people to work here and live a few blocks away," the head of the medical center told *The New York Times*. Krispy Kreme Doughnuts and the Hanes Corp. are headquartered in Winston-Salem. In 2014, Caterpillar continued to expand its work force at its massive mining-truck axle plant.

Large swaths of the region remain rural, from chicken-raising Wilkes County to Appalachian State University in Boone (named for Daniel), a center for resurgent pride in the culture of Appalachia, a region often the target of either pity or condescension.

All of these places are within the boundaries of the 5th Congressional District. The 5th begins in the heart of the Piedmont: the

2012 Presidential Vote		
Mitt Romney (R)................208,867	(59%)
Barack Obama (D) 140,660	(40%)

2008 Presidential Vote		
John McCain (R)................197,556	(57%)
Barack Obama (D) 146,200	(42%)

Cook Partisan Voting Index: R+11

suburbs of Forsyth County, although Winston-Salem splits its minority population with the Democratic 12th District. A little less than half of the district's residents live here. To the west, it takes in small cities and towns in the heavily Republican Piedmont and mountain areas. Salients jut out to take in the Democratic precincts of Statesville and Hickory. The only other area of Democratic strength is in Watauga County, with the university. Otherwise, it is a solidly Republican district.

Virginia Foxx (R)

Republican Virginia Foxx, first elected in 2004, is one of Congress' most vocal conservatives and earned a leadership position in 2012 as House Republican Conference secretary. Her GOP admirers call her a passionate voice of reason, while her liberal critics dismiss her as a loose cannon. She is influential on higher-education policy.

Foxx grew up in the hardscrabble hollows of Western North Carolina; she lived in a home that didn't have running water or electricity until she was 14. She got her bachelor's in English from the University of North Carolina in Chapel Hill and her doctorate in education from UNC-Greensboro, and had a diverse background before she was elected to Congress. She owned a nursery and landscape company, and she taught sociology and was assistant dean of the General College at Appalachian State University. Later, she was president of Mayland Community College. She served 12 years on the Board of Education of Watauga County. In 1994, Foxx was elected to the state Senate, where she served 10 years and sponsored a constitutional amendment to ban same-sex marriage and a bill to deny Social Security benefits to undocumented aliens. She actively supported gun rights and home schooling, and she opposed abortion rights.

In 2004, Foxx was one of five candidates in a hotly contested Republican primary for an open seat. Winston-Salem Councilman Vernon Robinson, a retired Air Force officer who campaigned as "the black Jesse Helms," finished first with 24% of the vote. Foxx was second, with 22%, just 511 votes ahead of Ed Broyhill, the son of former Republican Sen. James Broyhill.

In a hard-fought, four-week runoff campaign, Robinson aired several controversial ads highlighting his tough position on illegal immigrants. Foxx warned voters that Robinson's aggressive style would make him a weak general election candidate who would lose the district for the GOP. She won 55%-45%. In the general election, Foxx won relatively easily, 59%-41%.

In the House, Foxx has a solidly conservative voting record and is close to GOP leaders. She joined their team when she defeated Jeff Denham of California to become one of three women to take leadership roles when the party was smarting from its losses on the gender gap in the 2012 elections.

Foxx has not been afraid to speak her mind in her home-spun style. During the health care debate in 2009, she remarked that the public had more to fear from the legislation than from terrorists. In 2011, she attached an amendment to a House-passed health bill forbidding medical schools from teaching doctors how to perform abortions as a condition of the schools receiving federal grant money. During debate on a hate crimes bill named for Matthew Shepard, a Wyoming man tortured and murdered allegedly because of his sexual orientation, she said naming the bill for Shepard was "a hoax" because, she argued, he wasn't gay. She later apologized.

When Democrats proposed legislation putting limits on executive bonuses at companies receiving government bailout money, she said: "The Democrats have a tar baby on their hands, and they simply can't get away from it." Democrats called the use of "tar baby" racially loaded and objectionable. Republican leaders saw her as a useful attack dog and put her on the Rules Committee.

On the Education and the Workforce Committee, Foxx chairs the Higher Education Sub-committee. She has said the Education Department imposes burdensome regulations on colleges. Foxx is an advocate of for-profit colleges and community colleges. In early 2015, she disagreed with the administration's plan to tighten standards on grants and loans to students at for-profit colleges. Appearing on G. Gordon Liddy's radio show in 2012, she expressed her disdain for people taking out student loans. "I have very little tolerance for people who tell me that they graduate with $200,000 of debt or even $80,000 of debt, because there's no reason for that." President Barack Obama later repeated her remarks at a campaign stop at the University of North Carolina. "Can you imagine saying something like that?" he asked. Despite the rhetoric from both sides, Foxx found common ground with Obama in 2013 during renewal of the student-loan program. They tied the rate to the 10-year Treasury bond in what Foxx termed a "market-based approach."

Foxx was one of only 11 House members who voted against a $52 billion relief bill following Hurricane Katrina in 2005 because, she said, there was too little accountability in how the money would be spent. She has been more generous with local projects, taking credit for $500,000 for a teapot museum in Sparta, which President George W. Bush later criticized as wasteful spending. Foxx said in 2007 that she would no longer seek earmarks.

In her safely Republican district, Foxx has been reelected by modest margins against low-profile opponents. In most cases, her victory margin has been close to the 59 percent of the vote that Mitt Romney received in her district in 2012. *The Winston-Salem Journal*, the largest paper in her district, endorsed her Democratic challenger, Elisabeth Motsinger, in 2012. The newspaper said Foxx "has accomplished little" for the district and "represents the calcification of the political process and is therefore an impediment to reasoned political compromise." Regardless, she remained popular with her political base.

SIXTH DISTRICT

Mark Walker (R)

Elected 2014, 1st term; b. May 20, 1969, Dothan, AL; Trinity Baptist Col., attended 1987-88, Piedmont Internat'l. U., B.A. 1999; Baptist; married (Kelly); 3 children.

Professional Career: Sales & business mgr., automotive company, 1991-96; Church minister & official, 1998-2014.

DC Office: 312 CHOB, 20515, 202-225-3065; Fax: 202-225-8611; Website: walker.house.gov.

State Offices: Graham, 336-229-0159; Greensboro, 336-333-5005.

Committees: *Homeland Security:* Emergency Preparedness, Response & Communications; Transportation Security. *House Administration. Oversight & Government Reform:* Health Care, Benefits & Administrative Rules; Information Technology.

Election Results

2014 general	Mark Walker (R)	147,312	(59%)	$824,586	$18,476	$107,845
	Laura Fjeld (D)	103,758	(41%)	$893,425	$2,805	
2014 runoff	Mark Walker (R)	18,849	(60%)			
	Phil Berger, Jr.	12,527	(40%)			
2014 primary	Phil Berger, Jr. (R)	15,127	(34%)			
	Mark Walker (R)	11,123	(25%)			
	Bruce VonCannon (R)	5,055	(12%)			
	Zack Matheny (R)	5,043	(11%)			
	Jeff Phillips (R)	3,494	(8%)			

Population		Race and Ethnicity		Income	
Total:	760,762	White	74.3%	Median income:	$49,980
Urban:	39.9%	Black	15.7%		*(242 of 435)*
Suburban:	38.9%	Latino	5.9%	Under $50,000	50.0%
Rural:	21.2%	Asian	1.6%	$50,000-$99,999:	31.6%
Land area:	2,896	Two races	1.9%	$100,000-$199,999:	14.6%
Pop/sq. mi.:	262.7	White Ethnic	15.0%	$200,000 or more:	3.8%
Born in state:	63.7%			Poverty Rate	15.1%
		Education			
Age Groups		H.S. grad or less:	40.9%	Work	
Under 18:	21.8%	Some college:	29.2%	White collar:	37.2%
18 to 34:	20.0%	College degree, 4 yr.:	19.1%	Blue collar:	40.6%
35 to 64:	42.0%	Post-grad study:	10.7%	Sales and service:	22.1%
Over 64:	16.1%				
		Military		Govt. workers:	12.3%
		Veterans/active duty:	8.5%		

North-Central North Carolina: Greensboro

For more than half a century, furniture store managers and owners from all over the country twice a year have converged on the huge Furniture Mart in High Point, the center of the U.S. furniture business. The giant trade show put on by manufacturers now attracts about 75,000 visitors and 2,000

Voter Turnout	
2013 Total Citizen 18+	567,125
2014 House Turnout	251,070
2014 Turnout as % CVAP	44.3%
2012 Turnout as % CVAP	67.4%

exhibitors. The furniture business grew here early in the 20th century because of the hardwoods in the mountains not far to the west and the abundance of low-wage labor in the flatlands not far to the east. For many years, the furniture business has proven more resilient than textiles and tobacco, but lately it has faced serious competition from China. According to projections from the North Carolina Commission on Workforce Development, it stands to lose more than 3,000 jobs between 2012 and 2016.

The Triad area—Greensboro, High Point, and Winston-Salem—has scrambled for new sources of economic growth to keep pace with booming Raleigh-Durham and Charlotte. In 2009, FedEx opened a hub at Piedmont Triad International Airport, between Winston-Salem and Greensboro, which was followed in 2011 by a new "super hub" ground sorting facility that can handle 24,000 packages per hour. That has led other firms to plan distribution centers to utilize the "aerotropolis."

The 6th Congressional District of North Carolina is centered on greater Greensboro and High Point, which collectively contain about two-fifths of its residents. The Furniture Mart itself is physically located within the 12th district, but the 6th takes in other parts of High Point. It also includes much of downtown Greensboro, including the site of the Woolworth's where, on Feb. 1, 1960, four young black men sat down at a segregated lunch counter and asked for coffee. They were refused service, and the ensuing sit-ins helped desegregate the department store's eateries that year.

Another fifth of the population lives in Alamance, Orange and Durham counties, and the district's remaining residents are in the tier of counties stretching along the Virginia border from Granville in the east to Surry in the west. The counties are largely rural, with a smattering of small towns and cities like Mount Airy, the model for Mayberry in *The Andy Griffith Show*. In an unusual move for the locally declining textile industry, Hanes-Brands announced in December 2014 the hiring of 75 additional workers at its factory that manufactures socks in Mount Airy. The district is solidly Republican. Democrats have a 6-point registration advantage, but Republicans routinely carry the district in statewide races, usually by more than their overall margin.

2012 Presidential Vote
Mitt Romney (R)................216,610   (58%)
Barack Obama (D) 152,720   (41%)

2008 Presidential Vote
John McCain (R)................201,509   (56%)
Barack Obama (D) 156,585   (43%)

Cook Partisan Voting Index: R+10

Mark Walker (R)

Republican Mark Walker, an ordained minister running as a Washington outsider, was elected in 2014 to succeed 30-year veteran GOP Rep. Howard Coble, who retired. Walker cited President Ronald Reagan as a chief inspiration, especially on foreign policy, and framed his campaign in religious terms. "Our nation seems to have forgotten that our freedom isn't a derivative of the federal government, but rather it comes from our Creator, God Almighty," he said on his campaign website.

Walker was born in Dothan Alabama, and grew up in Pensacola Florida, where his father was a minister. He got his bachelor's degree in religious studies at Piedmont Baptist College. Most of his professional career was spent serving churches in the Greensboro region, most recently at Lawndale Baptist Church. He also devoted time to helping local and state Republicans in campaigns, and engaging in civic affairs.

When Coble announced his retirement in 2013, the GOP-leaning open seat attracted a scrum of nine Republican candidates. The initial front-runner was Phil Berger Jr., the district attorney for Rockingham County and son of a state senator. Boosted by name recognition and endorsements from the GOP establishment, including Coble, Berger topped the primary field in May at 34% of the vote, with Walker at 25%.

In the July runoff, Walker built up his campaign base in Guilford County while underscoring his outsider credentials. He rejected signing on to activist Grover Norquist's anti-tax pledge because he said he did not want to be beholden to "a guy in Washington." The race was unusual in that Walker aimed to get the edge on the ground with door-to-door contacts rather than to seek support of national tea party groups, and he openly pledged to decline money from political action committees. Berger took a more negative approach with his ads, which may have cost him support. With turnout low and much of the vote from other candidates in May turning toward the insurgent, Walker won 60%-40%. He took 65% of the vote in Guilford County, which cast 55% of the total vote in the runoff.

The general election was a breeze for Walker in this Republican stronghold. Democratic challenger Laura Fjeld took three counties at the eastern end of the district, but Walker won 59%-41%. Surprisingly, Fjeld spent nearly $900,000, which was slightly more than the total that Walker spent in his three contests. But her money appeared to do little more than attract the Democratic base vote.

He initially got seats on the Homeland Security, and Oversight and Government Reform Committees. In April, he got an assignment to the House Administration Committee, where party leaders typically make sure that they can rely on its members to perform housekeeping tasks. During Walker's first month in office, the House passed his Human Traffic Detection Act, which was designed to improve the training of workers at the Homeland Security Department to intercept human traffickers and their victims. "We must act to end this unconscionable industry," said Walker, who added that North Carolina was a leading state for the illicit trade. The bill passed by voice vote, and he noted the assistance of second-term Rep. Mark Meadows of North Carolina. Walker was the first freshman Republican to pass a bill in 2015.

SEVENTH DISTRICT

David Rouzer (R)

Elected 2014, 1st term; b. Feb. 16, 1972, Landstuhl, Germany; NC State U., B.S. 1994; Baptist; single.

Elected Office: NC Senate 2009-12.

Professional Career: PAC coordinator, 1996; Congressional aide, 1996-2000, 2001-05; University official, 2000-01; Administrator, U.S. Dept. of Agriculture, 2005-06; Owner, consulting company, 2006-present; Owner, cleaning products business, 2009-present.

DC Office: 424 CHOB, 20515, 202-225-2731; Fax: 202-225-5773; Website: rouzer.house.gov.

State Offices: Bolivia, 910-253-6111; Smithfield, 919-938-3040; Wilmington, 910-395-0202.

Committees: *Agriculture:* Livestock & Foreign Agriculture (Chmn); Nutrition. *Transportation & Infrastructure:* Coast Guard & Maritime Transpor-tation; Economic Development, Public Buildings & Emergency Management; Water Resources & Environment.

Election Results

2014 general	David Rouzer (R) 134,431	(59%)	$1,452,826	$30,272	$7,122
	Jonathan Barfield, Jr. (D)........... 84,054	(37%)	$60,461		
	Wesley Casteen (Lib)................... 7,850	(4%)	$29,125		
2014 primary	David Rouzer (R) 23,010	(53%)			
	Woody White (R) 17,389	(40%)			
	Chris Andrade (R)........................ 3,000	(7%)			

Population		Race and Ethnicity		Income	
Total:	762,540	White	69.2%	Median income:	$45,545
Urban:	22.2%	Black	17.5%		(309 of 435)
Suburban:	42.0%	Latino	9.7%	Under $50,000	54.7%
Rural:	35.9%	Amer. Indian	1.6%	$50,000-$99,999:	30.1%
Land area:	5,019	Two races	1.5%	$100,000-$199,999:	12.7%
Pop/sq. mi.:	151.9	White Ethnic	18.5%	$200,000 or more:	2.5%
Born in state:	60.9%			Poverty Rate	19.3%
		Education			
Age Groups		H.S. grad or less:	43.9%	**Work**	
Under 18:	23.3%	Some college:	32.5%	White collar:	32.5%
18 to 34:	19.7%	College degree, 4 yr.:	16.0%	Blue collar:	40.4%
35 to 64:	40.6%	Post-grad study:	7.6%	Sales and service:	27.0%
Over 64:	16.4%			Govt. workers:	15.8%
		Military			
		Veterans/active duty:	10.5%		

Southeast North Carolina: Wilmington

At the end of the 19th century, North Carolina's lengthy attachment to the Democratic Party and white supremacy seemed to be weakening. A fusion ticket of Populists and Republicans had taken over the state legislature in 1894, and the state elected a rotund, racially egalitarian Republican named Daniel Russell as governor two years later. At the epicenter of this not-so-quiet revolution was Wilmington, which Russell had represented in Congress as a member of the Greenback Party in the 1870s. Wilmington was a bustling majority-black city then, the largest and fastest-growing city in the state, and a seem-

Voter Turnout	
2013 Total Citizen 18+	547,737
2014 House Turnout	226,504
2014 Turnout as % CVAP	41.4%
2012 Turnout as % CVAP	62.7%

ing model for the "New South" that many were talking about. Blacks often served on juries and ate in restaurants alongside whites; the business community produced a thriving black middle class.

It was truly revolutionary, but the changes fell short. The run-up to the 1898 elections was marked by increasing violence and assertion of racial supremacy by many whites. Republican Sen. Jeter Pritchard asked President William McKinley to send in federal troops to protect the integrity of the elections. But it was determined that such a request had to come from the governor, who declined. In the ensuing election, Democrats recaptured the statehouse, though a biracial governing coalition was elected in Wilmington. But this, too, was short-lived. A white mob instigated a violent protest, and hundreds of African Americans fled to the nearby woods and swamps. The biracial government was forced to resign at gunpoint in the only violent *coup d'état* in American history. As many as 2,000 more blacks fled the city shortly thereafter, making Wilmington a majority-white city, which it remains to this day. The episode marked the beginning of Wilmington's decline; its population didn't recover until 1920.

The coastal counties of southern North Carolina grew smartly in the 2000s, but that growth tapered off during the recession. In the six months starting with October 2014, the unemployment rate was below 5 percent. The military keeps things afloat. South of Wilmington, the Army runs the 16,000-acre Military Ocean Terminal at Sunny Point, the Army's main deep-water port on the East Coast. It is the largest military ammunition port in the world, and often is referred to as "the FedEx of the sea" because it is almost always open. Tourism is thriving, thanks to the beaches north and south of Wilmington, and the region has some of the busiest American movie- and television-production facilities outside Los Angeles. The popular teenage TV drama series *One Tree Hill* and *Dawson's Creek* were among the projects shot there.

The 7th Congressional District of North Carolina covers much of this territory. It is ancestrally Democratic, and it was the final white-majority district in the state that hadn't elected a Republican since Reconstruction. Redistricting in 2012 made the 7th the second-most Republican district in the state, and that anomaly was resolved in 2014.

2012 Presidential Vote		
Mitt Romney (R)..................202,163	(59%)
Barack Obama (D) 136,240	(40%)

2008 Presidential Vote		
John McCain (R)..................187,709	(58%)
Barack Obama (D) 135,480	(42%)

Cook Partisan Voting Index: R+12

David Rouzer (R)

With his election to an open seat in 2014, Republican David Rouzer became the first Republican to represent southeastern North Carolina since the late 19th century. He came close to defeating the 7th District Democratic incumbent in 2012, losing by fewer than 700 votes. He styles himself as an expert in public relations and legislative strategy.

Rouzer was born in Landstuhl, Germany, and raised in Durham. He attended North Carolina State University's College of Agriculture, where he received his bachelor's degree in three majors: agricultural business management, agricultural economics and chemistry. He spent much of his career in Washington as an aide to two home-state Republican senators, Jesse Helms and Elizabeth Dole; as a Bush administration appointee in the Agriculture Department; and as a lobbyist for tobacco companies.

During four years in the state Senate, Rouzer co-chaired the Agriculture and Environment Committee. He became known for his vocal support of a North Carolina law banning the state's use of scientific predictions of how much sea level will rise in developing coastal policy. The law, passed in 2012, drew criticism from environmental groups, which said it amounted to denial of scientific evidence of climate change.

Centrist Democratic Rep. Mike McIntyre had been targeted by the GOP for 2014. The independent and once-untouchable incumbent barely survived the 2012 challenge from Rouzer, who had more than $4 million in support from party groups; McIntyre had $1.9 million in party assistance, and spent $2.3 million of his campaign funds. When he announced his retirement after nine terms, the seat became a relatively easy pickup for Republicans, despite a Democratic voter-registration advantage. Rouzer's chief opponent in the primary was attorney Woody White. The two men agreed on many issues, including repeal of the 2010 health care law. Not surprisingly given the stakes, the campaign got nasty: White accused Rouzer of being a Beltway lobbyist, and Rouzer derided White's work as a trial lawyer. With more money, more establishment support and more name recognition, Rouzer defeated White 53%-40%.

In the general election, Rouzer campaigned as an unabashed conservative. As in his 2012 run, Rouzer argued for a strong military, less regulation and a simplified tax code, preferably a flat tax. Both Rouzer and Democratic nominee Jonathan Barfield said they supported air strikes on Syria. But Barfield, a commissioner in New Hanover County and a local real estate agent, said he did not want to see U.S. boots on the ground. Rouzer spent nearly $1.5 million for the entire campaign, compared with $60,000 for Barfield, and won 59%-37%.

In the House, Rouzer got a rare chairmanship for a freshman at the Agriculture Subcommittee on Livestock and Foreign Agriculture. With no major farm legislation expected for a few years, that panel may focus chiefly on oversight and planning. He talked up two familiar proposals from the conservative arsenal: shutting down the Education Department and requiring drug tests for welfare recipients. With seven North Carolina Republicans newly elected since 2012, he may spend time deciding what kind of niche he hopes to fill in the House.

EIGHTH DISTRICT

Richard Hudson (R)

Elected 2012, 2nd term; b. Nov. 4, 1971, Franklin, VA; U. of NC, Charlotte, B.A. 1996; Protesant; married (Renee).

Professional Career: Deputy chief of staff, Rep. Robin Hayes, 2000-05; Chief of staff, Rep. Virginia Foxx, 2005-06; Chief of staff, Rep. John Carter, 2006-08; Chief of staff, Rep. Mike Conaway, 2008-11; Pres., Cabarrus Marketing Group, 2011-present

DC Office: 429 CHOB, 20515, 202-225-3715; Website: hudson.house.gov.

State Offices: Concord, 704-786-1612; Rockingham, 910-997-2070.

Committees: *Energy & Commerce:* Energy & Power; Environment & the Economy; Oversight & Investigations.

Group Ratings

	ADA	ACLU	AFL-CIO	LCV	ITI	COC	HAFA	ACU	CFG	FRC
2014	0%	0%	–	3%	100%	86%	72%	88%	78%	100%
2013	0%	C	14%	4%	C	69%	C	88%	78%	C

National Journal Ratings

	2013 LIB	—	2013 CONS
Economic	8%	—	91%
Social	0%	—	87%
Foreign	5%	—	86%
Composite	8%	—	92%

Key Votes of the 113th Congress

1. Sandy storm spending	N	5. Medical Marijuana	N	9. Syrian Rebels Training	Y
2. Violence Against Women Act	N	6. Farm Bill	Y	10. Keystone pipeline	Y
3. Guantanamo Bay Detainees	N	7. Afghanistan Combat	N	11. Immigration Exec. Action	Y
4. Abortion 20-week ban	Y	8. NSA Phone Data Collection	N	12. Bipartisan budget deal	Y

Election Results

2014 general	Richard Hudson (R)	121,568	(65%)	$1,143,349
	Antonio Blue (D)	65,854	(35%)	$6,278
2014 primary	Richard Hudson (R)	unopposed		

Prior winning percentage: 2012 (53%)

Population		Race and Ethnicity		Income	
Total:	744,074	White	63.0%	Median income:	$40,669
Urban:	21.8%	Black	18.8%		*(382 of 435)*
Suburban:	36.5%	Latino	8.7%	Under $50,000	59.4%
Rural:	41.6%	Amer. Indian	7.0%	$50,000-$99,999:	29.0%
Land area:	3,570	Two races	1.7%	$100,000-$199,999:	10.1%
Pop/sq. mi.:	208.4	White Ethnic	12.0%	$200,000 or more:	1.5%
Born in state:	68.0%			Poverty Rate	20.5%
		Education			
Age Groups		H.S. grad or less:	50.7%	**Work**	
Under 18:	24.5%	Some college:	31.5%	White collar:	28.0%
18 to 34:	21.1%	College degree, 4 yr.:	12.5%	Blue collar:	42.7%
35 to 64:	40.3%	Post-grad study:	5.3%	Sales and service:	29.3%
Over 64:	14.0%				
		Military		Govt. workers:	14.4%
		Veterans/active duty:	8.6%		

South-Central North Carolina: Eastern Charlotte Suburbs

In the Carolina Piedmont, from Atlanta to Durham along Interstate 85, lie the remnants of America's once-mighty textile industry. These sites included Concord and Kannapolis, the latter named for its founding company, Cannon Mills.

Voter Turnout	
2013 Total Citizen 18+	533,507
2014 House Turnout	187,422
2014 Turnout as % CVAP	35.1%
2012 Turnout as % CVAP	58.6%

While eastern Carolina was settled by Englishmen, the Piedmont was settled mainly by Scots and diverse groups like Quakers and Moravian sects, coming down the Blue Ridge from Pennsylvania through Virginia. These migratory patterns were reflected in Civil War divisions and continue to some degree in current voting habits. The textile mill towns along the interstate were anti-secession and are now Republican. The coastal counties through the Sandhills to the outskirts of Charlotte were heavily Confederate and still have Democratic tendencies at the local and state levels, although those traditional allegiances have lessened.

Parts of both of these areas are in the 8th Congressional District, but they recently have moved in very different directions. The most populous area in the district is Cabarrus County, which includes the southern end of the textile corridor around Kannapolis and Concord. In recent years, Cabarrus, fed by migration from Charlotte, has moved beyond its small-town roots and become a booming exurban county, growing by 40% from 2000 to 2013. Concord, with an influx of high-tech jobs, has been the seventh-fastest growing city in the nation since 2008. A former Philip Morris cigarette factory in Concord was taken over by Alevo, a Swiss manufacturer of cutting-edge battery technology, and reopened in October 2014 with promises of 2,500 jobs in three years. In March 2015, city leaders in Kannapolis purchased 49 acres in downtown and planned a massive economic revitalization. Cabarrus casts one-fifth of the district's votes and is heavily Republican.

The southeastern portion of the district remains more rural and includes Democratic-leaning Robeson County. Rural Scotland County had the lowest household income in the state. Redistricters in 2011 removed Democratic precincts around Fayetteville and in Hoke County.

2012 Presidential Vote		
Mitt Romney (R)	178,977	(58%)
Barack Obama (D)	126,065	(41%)
2008 Presidential Vote		
John McCain (R)	170,657	(57%)
Barack Obama (D)	123,885	(42%)
Cook Partisan Voting Index:	R+11	

What had been a political swing area has become a much more Republican district. In a testament to the power of redistricting, the district under its old lines gave 47% of the vote to John McCain in 2008. In the new GOP-drawn 8th district, he would have received 57%.

Richard Hudson (R)

Republican Richard Hudson, a former senior congressional staffer, defeated a Democratic incumbent in 2012, with a boost from redistricting. Democratic Rep. Larry Kissell had a relatively conservative voting record and had weathered the 2010 Republican wave. But the GOP-led redrawing of district lines plus demographic changes gave Kissell an all but unwinnable predicament.

Hudson grew up in the Charlotte area, and has a good political blood line. He helped his grandfather run for the Roanoke Rapids City Council, where he served for 30 years. Hudson became student-body president at the University of North Carolina at Charlotte, where he got a bachelor's degree. He volunteered putting up yard signs for another role model, conservative Republican Sen. Jesse Helms.

After college, Hudson continued to work behind-the-scenes in politics. In Washington, he served as chief of staff to GOP Reps. Mike Conaway and John Carter of Texas and Virginia Foxx of North Carolina. He was deputy chief of staff for local Rep. Robin Hayes, who lost to Kissell in 2008. In November 2011, two months after moving back to the district, he said he had a sense that God had a higher purpose for his life and was calling him to run for Congress.

Republicans made Kissell's seat a top 2012 takeover target after the favorable work of GOP mapmakers. Although Hayes passed on a bid, the race drew five Republican candidates, including Hudson. He led the first round in the primary with 32%, setting up a runoff with former Iredell County Commissioner Scott Keadle. When Keadle tried to portray Hudson as a Washington insider out of touch with the needs of the district, Hudson maintained that his experience on Capitol Hill created connections that would allow him to be more effective than most freshmen. He also got endorsements from former Arkansas Gov. Mike Huckabee and former Pennsylvania Sen. Rick Santorum. Hudson cruised to a runoff win, 64%-36%.

In the general election, Hudson turned the tables by painting Kissell as the Beltway insider. He blamed the incumbent for moving the country toward "skyrocketing debt" and for "out-of-control spending." To find work for the district's many laid-off textile workers, he promised to work for full funding of job retraining programs. He accused his rival of flip-flopping to try to save his seat. "I don't know where my opponent stands on many issues, it depends which day of the week it is," he told *The Fayetteville Observer*.

Kissell stressed his vote as one of 39 Democrats who opposed President Barack Obama's health care initiative and touted a provision he inserted into the economic stimulus bill requiring the Transportation Security Administration to buy U.S.-made uniforms. He boasted of getting the National Rifle Association's endorsement. But his efforts to run as a conservative Blue Dog and to distance himself from Obama alienated black voters. Hudson captured the seat, 53%-45%.

In his first term, Hudson claimed credit for enacting two bills in 2014 from the Homeland Security Committee, on which he served. One was designed to promote greater transparency and accountability at the TSA. The other limited to $11.20 per round-trip the passenger security fee on airline flights. In January 2015, he joined the influential Energy and Commerce Committee, where he pledged to unleash the energy resources of North Carolina and to replace the Affordable Care Act with "a health care system that puts patients first." He helped to form the Atlantic Offshore Energy Caucus, which was designed to promote policies that explore and expand energy production on the Outer Continental Shelf. He stayed active on the partisan front as chairman of the agriculture policy group of the House Republican Policy Committee.

He breezed to reelection in 2014 with 65% of the vote against Democratic challenger Antonio Blue, the mayor of Dobbins Height, a tiny town (pop. 855) in Richmond County. Blue said he campaigned actively, but he spent barely $6,000, compared with $1.1 million by Hudson.

NINTH DISTRICT

Robert Pittenger (R)

Elected 2012, 2nd term; b. Aug. 15, 1948, Dallas, TX; U. of TX, B.A. 1970; Christian; married (Suzanne Bahakel Pittenger); 4 children.

Elected Office: NC Senate, 2003-08.

Professional Career: Asst. to the pres., Campus Crusade for Christ, 1970-85; Owner, Robert Pittenger Co., 1989-present.

DC Office: 224 CHOB, 20515, 202-225-1976; Fax: 202-225-3389; Website: pittenger.house.gov.

State Offices: Charlotte, 704-362-1060; Mooresville, 704-696-8188.

Committees: *Financial Services:* Financial Institutions & Consumer Credit; Monetary Policy & Trade.

Group Ratings

	ADA	ACLU	AFL-CIO	LCV	ITI	COC	HAFA	ACU	CFG	FRC
2014	5%	0%	–	3%	100%	86%	78%	92%	85%	100%
2013	0%	C	15%	4%	C	92%	C	92%	80%	C

National Journal Ratings

	2013 LIB	—	2013 CONS
Economic	13%	—	85%
Social	0%	—	87%
Foreign	33%	—	67%
Composite	18%	—	82%

Key Votes of the 113th Congress

1. Sandy storm spending	N	5. Medical Marijuana	N
2. Violence Against Women Act	N	6. Farm Bill	N
3. Guantanamo Bay Detainees	N	7. Afghanistan Combat	N
4. Abortion 20-week ban	Y	8. NSA Phone Data Collection	N

9. Syrian Rebels Training	Y
10. Keystone pipeline	Y
11. Immigration Exec. Action	Y
12. Bipartisan budget deal	Y

Election Results

2014 general	Robert Pittenger (R)..............unopposed	$952,895
2014 primary	Robert Pittenger (R)....................29,505	(68%)
	Mike Steinberg (R).......................14,146	(32%)

Prior winning percentage: 2012 (52%)

Population		Race and Ethnicity		Income	
Total:	780,211	White	73.8%	Median income:	$69,972
Urban:	58.8%	Black	13.4%		*(63 of 435)*
Suburban:	40.2%	Latino	6.8%	Under $50,000	35.4%
Rural:	1.0%	Asian	4.0%	$50,000-$99,999:	30.2%
Land area:	979	Two races	1.7%	$100,000-$199,999:	24.4%
Pop/sq. mi.:	797.2	White Ethnic	26.6%	$200,000 or more:	9.9%
Born in state:	40.2%			Poverty Rate	7.9%
		Education			
Age Groups		H.S. grad or less:	24.3%	**Work**	
Under 18:	25.2%	Some college:	27.4%	White collar:	47.2%
18 to 34:	20.3%	College degree, 4 yr.:	32.3%	Blue collar:	39.5%
35 to 64:	42.9%	Post-grad study:	16.1%	Sales and service:	13.4%
Over 64:	11.5%				
		Military		Govt. workers:	8.2%
		Veterans/active duty:	7.2%		

Charlotte Metro

"An agreeable village but in a damn rebellious country," recorded British Revolutionary War Gen. Charles Cornwallis when, before the unpleasantness at Yorktown, he visited Charlotte. Settled by Scots-Irish and German colonists who came down from Pennsylvania along the Blue Ridge Moun-

Voter Turnout	
2013 Total Citizen 18+	542,784
2014 House Turnout	173,668
2014 Turnout as % CVAP	32.0%
2012 Turnout as % CVAP	73.4%

tains, Charlotte is a rapidly growing metropolitan area with nearly 1.8 million people in 2014, a 33 percent increase since 2000. It hosted the 2012 Democratic National Convention, having been chosen to illustrate President Barack Obama's eagerness to reclaim the South for his party. (Obama didn't hold on to North Carolina, but he did carry both Virginia and Florida a second time.) Before the California gold rush, Charlotte was the gold-mining capital of the country; in 1837, the U.S. Mint established a branch here. And the city continues its preoccupation with the financial sector today. It is headquarters to one of the nation's biggest banks, Bank of America. But it was not immune to the tumult in the financial markets. Charlotte-based Wachovia, which was the area's second-largest employer, was taken over in early 2009 by San Francisco-based Wells Fargo, a move that likely saved Wachovia from failure.

There have been signs of recovery. *The Charlotte Observer* reported that more than 20 financial firms had opened, launched satellite offices, or expanded in the city in a two-year span. And for a city its size, Charlotte has a respectable share of *Fortune* 500 companies. Nine are headquartered in the Charlotte area, including Bank of America, Lowe's, Family Dollar Stores, Duke Energy, and Sonic Automotive. Duke Energy in 2012 completed its merger with Raleigh-based Progress Energy, creating the nation's biggest electric utility. The city remains the center of the nation's biggest textile manufacturing region. The downside of this rapid growth is that the city has had the worst sprawl of 15 fast-growing metro areas. In May 2015, the state transportation department reached agreement with a private contractor to add two toll lanes in each direction for 26 miles on Interstate 77, with scheduled completion in late 2018. Some local residents objected to the tolls. High-end homes have sold rapidly in Davidson, a few miles up the interstate.

Charlotte has promoted cultural development and entertainment worthy of its growing business stature. It boasts a $50 million performing arts center across from the 60-story Bank of America tower. It is home to the Carolina Panthers professional football team and the Charlotte Bobcats basketball franchise, owned by the legendary Michael Jordan, who played his college basketball at the University of North Carolina in Chapel Hill. In 2010, the NASCAR Hall of Fame opened in Charlotte. The city has a boosterish pride in its capacity for accommodation. It is proud that it responded amicably to a busing order approved in a landmark Supreme Court case in 1971, and that it twice elected an African-American Democrat as mayor, Harvey Gantt. The city continues to diversify, with a rapidly increasing 13 percent Hispanic population. In 2013, Mecklenburg County exceeded one million residents and became majority-minority population.

The 9th Congressional District is a microcosm of the changes that have taken place in the South in the past century. In 1928, it elected Republican Charles A. Jonas to Congress. It was considered a fluke—he lost two years later—but in truth it was a precursor of trends in urban areas across the region in another 20 years. In 1952, the congressman's son, Charles R. Jonas, won the Charlotte district again, and this time held it for another nine elections; Republicans haven't given it up since. As Charlotte and other urban areas moved toward Republicans—the rural areas didn't start to become reliably Republican for another 40 years—the party became competitive across the South.

Today, the urban core of Mecklenburg County leans Democratic; Barack Obama won 61 percent of the vote here in 2012. GOP strength in the 9th comes from exurban and rural areas in Union County to the south and Iredell County to the north. They combined to give John McCain about two-thirds of the vote in 2008. Overall, the Republican Party enjoys an 8 percentage point registration advantage here.

2012 Presidential Vote		
Mitt Romney (R)................215,861	(56%)
Barack Obama (D) 163,883	(43%)

2008 Presidential Vote		
John McCain (R)................190,650	(54%)
Barack Obama (D) 160,219	(45%)

Cook Partisan Voting Index: R+8

Robert Pittenger (R)

Republican Robert Pittenger, first elected in 2012, was a real estate entrepreneur who defeated 10 other candidates in the GOP primary that year. He is a member of the Financial Services Committee, talks about bipartisanship, and has fit comfortably in the GOP establishment.

A Texas native, Pittenger's father was a lawyer and real estate agent. While attending the University of Texas in Austin, Pittenger held three jobs before graduating with degrees in psychology and political science. After graduation in 1970, he worked for Campus Crusade for Christ, an evangelical Christian organization, where he served 10 years as assistant to the president. In 1972, as a public relations officer for the group, he helped to organize Explo, a weeklong conference that attracted nearly 100,000 high school and college students and became known as the "Christian Woodstock." Pittenger trekked to Africa, Asia and South America to promote Campus Crusade's work.

In 1985, Pittenger and his wife moved to Charlotte, Suzanne's hometown, to raise their family. He started a real estate business and invested in undeveloped regions in the country that were prone to growth. Within 23 years, he grew the business to acquire holdings in Austin, San Antonio, Nashville, Raleigh and Charleston South Carolina.

Pittenger ran for the state Senate in 2002 and won. He was a strong conservative advocate on economic and social issues. On his first day, he introduced legislation to reform medical liability laws, and 3,000 doctors from across the state rallied in support. However, the Democratic-controlled Senate proved challenging for the Republican, and the nonpartisan North Carolina Center for Public Policy ranked his effectiveness as 49th out of 50 in 2007. In 2008, Pittenger left the Senate and ran unsuccessfully for lieutenant governor.

When the House seat opened in 2012, Pittenger decided to run. He partially financed his campaign with $2.3 million from his personal fortune. In the Republican primary, Pittenger poured $324,000 into radio and television ads on a single day in April, nearly equaling the amount that his chief opponent, former Mecklenburg County Sheriff Jim Pendergraph, spent on his entire campaign. Their bruising primary runoff was chiefly characterized by mudslinging. Pittenger accused Pendergraph of being a Democrat and Pendergraph supporters accused Pittenger of buying the election. They highlighted Pittenger's 2003 vote in the state legislature on a land annexation that benefited his real estate company. The issue was brought before an independent ethics committee in the Senate, but no charges resulted. Pittenger won the runoff 53%-47%. In the general election, Pittenger defeated Democrat Jennifer Roberts, a Mecklenburg County commissioner, 52%-46%. His vote share was four points less than GOP presidential nominee Mitt Romney received in the district that day. Roberts led 50%-47% in Mecklenburg, which cast 72% of the vote, but Pittenger won Union and Iredell by 2-to-1 margins.

Pittenger has pursued an array of issues in the House. On the Financial Services Committee, he was named vice chairman in March 2015 of its Task Force to Investigate Terrorism Financing. The next month, the House approved his bipartisan bill to strengthen the voice of the small business community in the actions of federal banking regulators. Following up on his interest in religious issues, he has served on the Congressional-Executive Commission on China, which monitors human rights and the rule of law in China. He co-chairs the Congressional Task Force on Terrorism and Unconventional Warfare, which has met with international security experts to advocate increased global cooperation on security and intelligence. In February 2015, he visited Israeli Prime Minister Benjamin Netanyahu and defended him against protests about his planned speech to Congress the next month. "He is the Winston Churchill of the day, warning the world about Iran," Pittenger said. He also co-chairs the bipartisan United Solutions caucus, whose mostly junior members have sought to move forward on fiscal issues, including entitlement spending and tax reform.

In the Republican primary in 2014, Pittenger faced tea party challenger Michael Steinberg and won with 68% of the vote. Pittenger had stirred tea party protests when he responded negatively to a question at a town hall meeting in August 2013 on whether he would support a government shutdown to "defund Obamacare." He was reelected without Democratic opposition in 2014.

TENTH DISTRICT

Patrick McHenry (R)

Elected 2004, 6th term; b. Oct. 22, 1975, Charlotte; NC St. U., attended, Belmont Abbey Col., B.A. 1999; Catholic; married (Giulia McHenry).

Elected Office: NC House, 2002-04.

Professional Career: Real estate broker, 2000-02; Special asst. to the U.S. Secy. of Labor, 2001.

DC Office: 2334 RHOB, 20515, 202-225-2576; Fax: 202-225-0316; Website: mchenry.house.gov.

State Offices: Black Mountain, 828-669-0600; Gastonia, 704-833-0096; Hickory, 828-327-6100.

Committees: *Financial Services* (VChmn): Capital Markets & Government Sponsored Enterprises; Oversight & Investigations.

Group Ratings

	ADA	ACLU	AFL-CIO	LCV	ITI	COC	HAFA	ACU	CFG	FRC
2014	0%	5%	–	3%	100%	85%	65%	88%	78%	88%
2013	5%	C	16%	0%	C	92%	C	80%	73%	C

National Journal Ratings

	2013 LIB	—	2013 CONS
Economic	17%	—	82%
Social	27%	—	71%
Foreign	14%	—	86%
Composite	20%	—	80%

Key Votes of the 113th Congress

1. Sandy storm spending	N	5. Medical Marijuana	N	9. Syrian Rebels Training	Y
2. Violence Against Women Act	Y	6. Farm Bill	Y	10. Keystone pipeline	Y
3. Guantanamo Bay Detainees	N	7. Afghanistan Combat	N	11. Immigration Exec. Action	Y
4. Abortion 20-week ban	Y	8. NSA Phone Data Collection	Y	12. Bipartisan budget deal	Y

Election Results

2014 general	Patrick T. McHenry (R)	133,504	(61%)	$1,021,565
	Tate MacQueen, IV (D)	85,292	(39%)	$82,886
2014 primary	Patrick T. McHenry (R)	29,400	(78%)	
	Richard Lynch (R)	8,273	(22%)	

Prior winning percentages: 2012 (57%), 2010 (71%), 2008 (58%), 2006 (62%), 2004 (64%)

Population		Race and Ethnicity		Income	
Total:	739,282	White	79.2%	Median income:	$42,148
Urban:	29.5%	Black	11.7%		*(355 of 435)*
Suburban:	46.1%	Latino	5.5%	Under $50,000	57.8%
Rural:	24.5%	Asian	1.5%	$50,000-$99,999:	27.8%
Land area:	2,528	Two races	1.6%	$100,000-$199,999:	11.9%
Pop/sq. mi.:	292.4	White Ethnic	18.3%	$200,000 or more:	2.4%
Born in state:	63.7%			Poverty Rate	17.7%
		Education			
Age Groups		H.S. grad or less:	44.6%	**Work**	
Under 18:	21.8%	Some college:	31.1%	White collar:	32.3%
18 to 34:	20.5%	College degree, 4 yr.:	16.5%	Blue collar:	41.9%
35 to 64:	41.3%	Post-grad study:	7.7%	Sales and service:	25.8%
Over 64:	16.3%			Govt. workers:	12.7%
		Military			
		Veterans/active duty:	8.9%		

West-Central North Carolina: Gastonia, Asheville

In 1790, one of the most important decisions in North Carolina's history was made—in Pennsylvania. That was when 19-year-old Michael Schenck decided to leave his family farm in Lancaster, Pa., and settle in Western North Carolina. In 1813, on a small creek west of Lincolnton, Schenck built the

Voter Turnout	
2013 Total Citizen 18+	555,745
2014 House Turnout	218,796
2014 Turnout as % CVAP	39.4%
2012 Turnout as % CVAP	61.1%

first cotton mill south of the Potomac River. In 1816, he brought in investors and erected the Lincoln Cotton Mills on the South Fork of the Catawba River, which operated until the Civil War. The North Carolina textile industry was born and soon dominated in an area that had specialized in corn, cotton and whiskey production. After the Civil War, the surfeit of cheap labor and fast-flowing streams on the Piedmont made it a perfect locus for manufacturing. By the end of the 19th century, North Carolina had more textile plants than Connecticut, Maine or Vermont. These companies relied on the "Rhode Island model" of development, where towns were put up around the mills and whole families were placed in small, company-owned homes. These towns spread all across the Piedmont; some grew into substantial cities, while others remained hamlets.

Ground zero for the industry was Gaston County and nearby towns. By the 1930s, there were 570 mills within a 100-mile radius of Gastonia. The relationship between workers and management was often uneasy. Gastonia was the site of a massive strike at Loray Mills in the late 1920s, led by the communist-dominated United Textile Workers, which erupted in violence and resulted in the deaths of the local police chief and Ella May Wiggins, the unofficial balladeer of the union who penned tunes such as "A Mill Mother's Song" and "The Big Fat Boss and the Workers."

Today, the textile industry is in decline, but the western Piedmont continues to excel in making things. The Wuxi Taiji Paper Industry Co., which makes spiral-wound cardboard tubes, recently put a plant in Conover. Tenowo completed a $7.2 million expansion of its nonwoven textile production at the Lincoln County plant. The unemployment rate here had been 13.3 percent in January 2010. But it dropped to 5.8 percent in April 2015 with a boost from new manufacturing facilities, including a plant by Owens Corning. Developers have found new uses for abandoned mills.

The 10th Congressional District of North Carolina is centered on Gastonia, where a little more than a quarter of the district's votes are cast. To the north, it takes in Lincoln County and most of Hickory's Catawba County, although not the heavily Democratic precincts in downtown Hickory. To the west are heavily Republican Cleveland and Rutherford counties. In the 2011 redistricting, the 10th gained most of heavily Democratic Asheville, a popular retirement mecca with its well-preserved historic structures in styles ranging from Gothic Revival to Art Deco. Before the new lines were drawn in the 2010 reapportionment, Republicans had a seven percent registration advantage in the 10th, but

2012 Presidential Vote		
Mitt Romney (R)	197,818	(58%)
Barack Obama (D)	139,165	(41%)
2008 Presidential Vote		
John McCain (R)	190,495	(57%)
Barack Obama (D)	140,427	(42%)
Cook Partisan Voting Index:	R+11	

now Democrats enjoy a four percent edge. To be sure, this includes a sizable number of Democrats who routinely vote Republican, and the district retains a strong GOP tilt. Other than Asheville-based Buncombe, the other six counties remain solidly Republican. Mitt Romney took 58 percent of the vote here in 2012.

Patrick McHenry (R)

Patrick McHenry, a Republican first elected in 2004, has evolved from a highly partisan GOP guerilla fighter in his early years in the House into a leadership insider seeking to move the party's agenda. That evolution was confirmed in June 2014, when new Majority Whip Steve Scalise tapped McHenry to be his chief deputy whip.

McHenry grew up in Cherryville as the youngest of five children and graduated from Belmont Abbey College, where he was president of the state College Republicans. After school he worked as a real estate broker. As a young conservative, he cut his political teeth on his strenuous opposition to the Clintons. He once dressed up in an Abraham Lincoln costume at a North Carolina appearance by Bill Clinton after Clinton was accused by Republicans of rewarding big contributors with overnight stays in the Lincoln Bedroom in the White House. In 2000, he ran a website, *notHillary.com*, opposing Hillary Clinton's Senate candidacy in New York. McHenry worked on several Republican campaigns in North Carolina. In 2001, he was appointed to a job in the Labor Department, and in 2002, he was elected to the state House.

McHenry ran for Congress after Republican Rep. Cass Ballenger announced his retirement, leaving an open seat for the first time in 18 years. In the Republican primary, his chief competition was Catawba County Sheriff David Huffman, and both made conservative Christian values their main issue. Huffman finished first with 35% and McHenry second with 26%. North Carolina holds runoffs when no candidate gets 40% in the primary, and the four-week campaign took a negative turn.

Huffman questioned McHenry for hosting noisy late-night parties at his house, which also served as a residence for his campaign staff, a claim rebutted by McHenry's neighbors. McHenry accused Huffman of campaign finance irregularities. He ran an energetic, door-to-door grassroots campaign, billing himself as a "pro-life, pro-gun, anti-gay-marriage" Christian conservative. He won the runoff by just 85 votes after a recount. Huffman carried Catawba County 59%-41%. But McHenry rolled up huge majorities in the counties south of Interstate 40 and close to his Gaston County home. He then easily won the general election.

At age 29, McHenry was the youngest member of the House when he arrived. Instead of keeping a low profile and doing constituent work to sew up his seat, as freshmen usually do, he made repeat appearances on talk shows to serve up red meat and sound bites. On the House floor, he took on Democrats no matter how powerful or senior. In 2007, he accused Speaker Nancy Pelosi of California of abusing her office by using military jets to fly home to San Francisco during congressional recesses, although former Republican Speaker Dennis Hastert had also used military planes for his Illinois commute. (Current Speaker John Boehner of Ohio takes commercial flights.) And in 2009, he sidled up to the "birther" movement by saying at a town hall forum that "I haven't seen evidence one way or the other" of President Barack Obama's U.S. citizenship. He backed away from the comment the next day.

His House colleagues sometimes grew weary of McHenry's hijinks. After he repeatedly took to the floor to criticize other lawmakers' earmarks in spending bills, the House in 2007 voted down, 249-174, one of McHenry's earmarks—$129,000 to expand a Christmas crafts store in Mitchell County.

His political style has since softened, thanks in part to his securing of a subcommittee gavel. When Republicans took control of the House in January 2011, McHenry became chairman of a new subcommittee specializing in government bailouts, such as the Troubled Asset Relief Program for the financial industry. He told *The Charlotte Observer* that TARP was "a very uneven response from the federal government," with some banks bailed out and others, notably Charlotte-based Wachovia, forced to merge. He got into a hostile exchange at a May 2011 hearing with Elizabeth Warren, then a Harvard professor who helped create the Consumer Financial Protection Bureau as part of the Dodd-Frank financial services overhaul. The two squabbled over the amount of time she was supposed to testify, with McHenry snapping at one point, "You're making this up, Ms. Warren." Supporters of Warren, a liberal Democrat who was later elected to the Senate from Massachusetts, posted thousands of angry comments on McHenry's Facebook page.

On the Financial Services Committee, he won enactment of his bill allowing financial institutions involved in multiple transactions to combine them into one contract, something helpful to the banking industry in Charlotte. The House also passed his measure in 2011 to terminate the Home Assistance Mortgage Program, which assists eligible homeowners with mortgage loan modifications. The bill drew a veto threat from the White House, and the Senate never took it up. The following year, McHenry was successful in passing a provision in the 2012 jobs bill that allowed companies to more easily raise equity through social media and online platforms. The bill was signed into law by Obama.

As he has become more effective as a legislator, others have taken notice. McHenry in 2012 was named one of *Time* magazine's "40 Under 40" civic leaders who is "at work trying to fix a broken system" and restore public faith in government. He was influential behind the scenes, helping his Louisiana friend Scalise get elected in 2012 as chairman of the Republican Study Committee, the caucus of the House's most conservative members.

When Scalise became majority whip in the fallout from Eric Cantor's surprise primary defeat in June 2014, he repaid the favor. He replaced Illinois' Peter Roskam—who had unsuccessfully challenged Scalise for the whip's job—with McHenry. In the whip race, Scalise had made an issue of putting more red-state lawmakers in key posts. Like Scalise, McHenry subsequently spent much of his time courting his long-time conservative allies, not always successfully. The North Carolina delegation has included troublemakers for the GOP leadership, including Rep. Mark Meadows, who represents the district adjacent to McHenry's and was temporarily stripped of a subcommittee chairmanship in June 2015. For his new job, McHenry abandoned his earlier presence on the media circuit and went underground, *The Wall Street Journal* reported. "Some [lawmakers] know on day one how to be effective in this institution; others, it takes time—and I was in that camp," McHenry told the *Journal* in May 2015.

McHenry's lifetime rating from the American Conservative Union through 2012 was 98%, the highest of any North Carolinian. Given the economic plight of the textile industry, McHenry had often voted against free trade deals, as he did in 2005 on a pact proposed with Central America and in 2010 on a Haiti trade relief bill. But his leadership post created a new twist in early 2015 as he engaged in countless discussions to rally support by GOP members for the trade promotion authority request from Obama. His growing experience at the leadership table highlighted a comment about his new job that he made in an earlier interview with the *Raleigh News-Observer*: "It's the opportunity to shape outcomes is what is meaningful." In early 2015, he became a prominent supporter of Jeb Bush's presidential campaign.

McHenry has had little trouble at election time. He had two GOP primary challengers in 2010 and 2012 but won both contests easily. In the 2012 general election, he beat Democrat Patsy Keever with 57% of the vote. The redistricting changes that added Asheville to his district resulted in his closest victory in five campaigns, but he seemed secure. In 2014, he took 61% against a weakly-financed challenger.

ELEVENTH DISTRICT

Mark Meadows (R)

Elected 2012, 2nd term; b. July 28, 1959, Verdun, France; FL St. U., attended, U. of South FL, B.S. 1983; Christian; married (Debbie); 2 children.

Professional Career: Dir., customer relations & public safety, Tampa Electric, 1983-86; Owner, sandwich shop, 1986-90; Real-estate developer, 1990-12.

DC Office: 1024 LHOB, 20515, 202-225-6401; Fax: 202-226-6422; Website: meadows.house.gov.

State Offices: Lenoir, 828-426-8701; Hendersonville, 828-693-5660; Spruce Pine, 828-765-0573; Waynesville, 828-452-6022.

Committees: *Foreign Affairs:* Africa, Global Health, Global Human Rights & International Organizations; Middle East & North Africa. *Oversight & Government Reform:* Government Operations (Chmn); Health Care, Benefits & Administrative Rules. *Transportation & Infrastructure:* Aviation; Economic Development, Public Buildings & Emergency Management; Highways & Transit.

Group Ratings

	ADA	ACLU	AFL-CIO	LCV	ITI	COC	HAFA	ACU	CFG	FRC
2014	0%	11%	–	3%	80%	54%	85%	96%	88%	100%
2013	5%	C	10%	4%	C	77%	C	88%	85%	C

National Journal Ratings

	2013 LIB	—	2013 CONS
Economic	15%	—	84%
Social	13%	—	84%
Foreign	15%	—	77%
Composite	16%	—	84%

Key Votes of the 113th Congress

1. Sandy storm spending	N	5. Medical Marijuana	N	9. Syrian Rebels Training	N
2. Violence Against Women Act	N	6. Farm Bill	Y	10. Keystone pipeline	Y
3. Guantanamo Bay Detainees	N	7. Afghanistan Combat	N	11. Immigration Exec. Action	Y
4. Abortion 20-week ban	Y	8. NSA Phone Data Collection	Y	12. Bipartisan budget deal	N

Election Results

2014 general	Mark Meadows (R)	144,682	(63%)	$332,786	$31,181
	Tom Hill (D)	85,342	(37%)	$14,966	
2014 primary	Mark Meadows (R)	unopposed			

Prior winning percentage: 2012 (57%)

Population		Race and Ethnicity		Income	
Total:	737,318	White	87.5%	Median income:	$39,355
Urban:	21.9%	Latino	5.8%		*(396 of 435)*
Suburban:	33.2%	Black	2.8%	Under $50,000	60.5%
Rural:	44.9%	Amer. Indian	1.4%	$50,000-$99,999:	28.5%
Land area:	5,960	Two races	1.4%	$100,000-$199,999:	9.1%
Pop/sq. mi.:	123.7	White Ethnic	16.9%	$200,000 or more:	1.9%
Born in state:	61.1%			Poverty Rate	19.0%
		Education			
Age Groups		H.S. grad or less:	45.8%	**Work**	
Under 18:	19.9%	Some college:	31.7%	White collar:	30.5%
18 to 34:	19.1%	College degree, 4 yr.:	14.0%	Blue collar:	44.2%
35 to 64:	40.4%	Post-grad study:	8.4%	Sales and service:	25.3%
Over 64:	20.6%			Govt. workers:	15.3%
		Military			
		Veterans/active duty:	10.1%		

Western North Carolina: Asheville

Steeped in the hues that gave them the name Blue Ridge, the heavily wooded mountains of North Carolina seem placid and ancient. Geologically, they are some of the oldest ranges in the world; they began forming 400 million years ago, when plant life was just beginning to spread across the con-

Voter Turnout	
2013 Total Citizen 18+	571,960
2014 House Turnout	230,024
2014 Turnout as % CVAP	40.2%
2012 Turnout as % CVAP	59.8%

tinents. Along with the Great Smoky Mountains, which cross into Tennessee, they have become popular tourist destinations. In the early 20th century, this hardscrabble country, around the county seats of Lenoir and Morganton, became a manufacturing area. Textile mill owners moved their operations from New England to Western North Carolina for its low-wage workforce. After the collapse of the residential furniture industry in Grand Rapids Michigan, during the Depression, furniture manufacturing took hold in the region because of the abundance of hardwood forests.

But textiles are a low-wage industry that typically represents the first stage in industrial development, migrating to cheaper venues when wages rise. And furniture has faced competition from Asia. So the region has increasingly turned to technology. In the 1990s, the boom industry in the Catawba Valley was fiber optics, with new factories that helped reduce unemployment. Google built a $600 million data center in Lenoir. Apple and Facebook soon followed with similar facilities in Maiden and Forest City, which are nearby in the 10th District. The proximity of Charlotte's airport, about an hour away on freeways, has helped. The recent influx of newcomers, including many Hispanics and Laotians, prompted some anti-immigrant backlash in this previously insular region, including the occasional rejection of school bond proposals that would disproportionately help immigrants. The unemployment rate in both Buncombe and Henderson counties fell below 5% in mid-2014.

The 11th District of North Carolina includes the Catawba Valley and consists of small, mountainous counties in far western North Carolina. The local politics had been volatile. From 1978 through 2012, the western North Carolina district switched between the parties seven times and threw out six incumbents. Republicans redistricters after the 2010 census worked hard to make sure that it wouldn't switch hands anytime soon. About a third of the district's residents live in the stretch of counties along the Tennessee border. These include some of the most reliably Republican locales in the nation: Avery County has never voted for a Democratic presidential candidate since it was created in 1912. Another third of the district comes from the Asheville and Hendersonville areas, but

2012 Presidential Vote		
Mitt Romney (R)................205,502	(61%)
Barack Obama (D) 127,852	(38%)
2008 Presidential Vote		
John McCain (R)................197,003	(58%)
Barack Obama (D) 137,010	(40%)
Cook Partisan Voting Index: R+13		

redistricters removed Democratic precincts in Asheville and kept Republican areas of Buncombe County. Retiree-friendly Henderson County, which grew by 22% from 2000 to 2013, is heavily Republican. The district is the most Republican in the state. John McCain got 58% of the vote in 2008, and Mitt Romney won 61% in 2012.

Mark Meadows (R)

Businessman and longtime Republican activist Mark Meadows, elected in 2012, was one of three North Carolina Republicans who took Democratic-held seats that year with a significant boost from the redistricting plan drawn by the GOP-controlled Legislature. He voted against John Boehner for speaker in January 2015 and made other maverick moves that alienated party leaders. He was stripped of his subcommittee chairmanship the following June, but an angry rank-and-file reaction restored his post a few days later.

Meadows was born in the 42nd Army Field Hospital in Verdun, France, while his father was stationed abroad. His father was a draftsman; his mother, a surgical nurse. He attended high school in the Tampa area, where he met his wife, Debbie, and went on to get a degree in business management from the University of South Florida. After college, he worked for

Tampa Electric, but he and his wife dreamed of living in North Carolina. They said to each other, "Wouldn't it be great to retire to the mountains one day?" Instead of retiring, they just moved there in 1986. He and Debbie started a small sandwich shop in the resort town of Highlands, and ran it for a few years before they sold it and turned to real estate investments.

A self-described history buff, Meadows says that his observations of history and experiences as a businessman drew him to conservative politics. He was the only person who showed up for a precinct meeting of his local Republican Party in rural North Carolina, thus becoming precinct chairman and eventually county chairman. He worked on behalf of GOP candidates for 25 years and was a delegate to party conventions.

In 2010, Republicans captured control of North Carolina's General Assembly for the first time since Reconstruction. With decennial redistricting, they aimed at reversing the Democrats' 7-6 majority in the state's House delegation. Rep. Heath Shuler's 11th District was one of four targeted, and it was revamped to become significantly more conservative. Shuler, who had challenged Nancy Pelosi for minority leader following the 2010 elections, decided to retire.

Meadows faced six Republicans in the May primary. He led with 38% of the vote. In the runoff campaign, Meadows faced tea party activist Vance Patterson. Both men stressed their opposition to increases in federal spending and regulation. In a turnout of 23,000 voters, Meadows trounced Patterson 76%-24%, and essentially won the seat.

In November, Meadows faced Shuler's former chief of staff, Hayden Rogers, who easily won his primary and received significant financial backing from local business and labor interests. A moderate western North Carolina native, he was regarded as the Democrats' best chance to retain the seat. Rogers ran ads espousing his "mountain values" and sought to depict his opponent as wealthy and out of touch. He spent $726,000, but received little national-party assistance. Meadows played up his business background; his ads, which focused heavily on opposition to President Barack Obama, struck a chord with district voters. He took 12 of the 17 counties and won, 57%-43%.

In the House, Meadows joined other conservative activists. In January 2015, he was one of nine founding members of the Freedom Caucus, which pressed House Republicans to pursue a more conservative agenda. Also that month, he was one of 25 Republicans who did not vote for John Boehner for speaker; he explained that he was reflecting the widespread view of his constituents that they wanted a new direction. Meadows took an interest in investigative work, and he became chairman in 2015 of the Oversight and Government Reform Subcommittee on Government Operations, whose jurisdiction includes federal employees. He created a "tip line" for them to report problems. In March 2015, the committee approved his bill to prohibit government workers from using their computers to surf pornographic websites. He threatened prosecution of District of Columbia officials if they implemented a voter referendum to legalize marijuana.

Meadows seemed to have grown more aware of the benefits of being a team player. When a reporter for *The Hill* asked his view of Boehner after getting the chairmanship, Meadows responded, "He is a man of integrity." In August 2013, Meadows initiated a letter from dozens of House Republican to party leaders urging that they use a deadline for renewal of federal spending as leverage to shut down the new health reform law. After many local businesses complained to him about the adverse financial impact of the October 2013 government shutdown, including national parks, Meadows later conceded that "history shows us that the answer" is that he and other proponents had a flawed strategy. But his June vote against a rule on trade legislation supported by the leadership—on top of his vote against Boehner plus his failure to pay dues to the National Republican Congressional Committee—led Oversight and Government Reform Chairman Jason Chaffetz of Utah to take away his subcommittee chairmanship. After angry conservatives threatened retaliatory moves to weaken his control of the committee, Chaffetz quickly reversed himself and Meadows regained his gavel. On the eve of the August recess, he stirred the pot again with a resolution to oust Boehner as speaker. Meadows had one co-sponsor and said that he hoped for a "family discussion."

Despite his occasionally shaky start, Meadows won 63%-37% against token reelection opposition from Tom Hill, a retired aerospace engineer who spent $15,000 on his campaign. For now, Democrats appear to have thrown in the towel on this district.

TWELFTH DISTRICT

Alma Adams (D)

Elected 2014, 1st full term; b. May 27, 1946, High Point; NC A&T U., B.S. 1968, M.S. 1972, Ohio St. U., Ph.D. 1981; Baptist; divorced; 2 children.

Elected Office: Guilford Cty., Schl. Bd., 1984-86; Greensboro City Cncl., 1987-94; NC House, 1994-2014.

Professional Career: Professor, Bennett Col., 1972-2012.

DC Office: 222 CHOB, 20515, 202-225-1510; Fax: 202-225-1512; Website: adams.house.gov.

State Offices: Charlotte, 704-344-9950; Greensboro, 336-275-9950.

Committees: *Agriculture:* Nutrition. *Education & the Workforce:* Higher Education & Workforce Training; Workforce Protections. *Small Business:* Investigations, Oversight & Regulations (RMM). *Joint Economic Committee.*

Election Results

2014 general	Alma Adams (D)	130,096	(75%)	$743,807	$172,827
	Vince Coakley (R)	42,568	(25%)	$366,909	
2014 primary	Alma Adams (D)	15,235	(44%)		
	Malcolm Graham (D)	8,180	(24%)		
	George Battle (D)	4,342	(13%)		
	Marcus Brandon (D)	2,856	(8%)		
	James "Smuggie" Mitchell (D)	1,775	(5%)		
	Curtis Osborne (D)	1,733	(5%)		

Prior winning percentage: 2014 special (75%)

Population		Race and Ethnicity		Income	
Total:	773,617	Black	48.3%	Median income:	$35,679
Urban:	75.9%	White	29.9%		*(418 of 435)*
Suburban:	24.0%	Latino	15.2%	Under $50,000	65.6%
Rural:	0.1%	Asian	4.4%	$50,000-$99,999:	24.4%
Land area:	804	Two races	1.6%	$100,000-$199,999:	8.2%
Pop/sq. mi.:	962.7	White Ethnic	8.4%	$200,000 or more:	1.7%
Born in state:	53.8%			Poverty Rate	27.3%
		Education			
Age Groups		H.S. grad or less:	45.8%	**Work**	
Under 18:	25.5%	Some college:	30.8%	White collar:	27.5%
18 to 34:	29.2%	College degree, 4 yr.:	16.3%	Blue collar:	47.8%
35 to 64:	35.7%	Post-grad study:	7.0%	Sales and service:	24.7%
Over 64:	9.6%			Govt. workers:	10.9%
		Military			
		Veterans/active duty:	6.6%		

Charlotte—Greensboro—Winston-Salem Corridor

"This is perhaps the Negro's temporary farewell to Congress," began the peroration of the last speech given by George White, an African-American lawyer from Tarboro, N.C., and a Republican, in his last days in the House in 1901. Segregation was being imposed by law, and blacks were informally but

Voter Turnout	
2013 Total Citizen 18+	501,654
2014 House Turnout	172,664
2014 Turnout as % CVAP	34.4%
2012 Turnout as % CVAP	63.5%

effectively driven from the voting rolls in the rural South. White had opted not to run for reelection because he believed that Democrats would not validate his win even if he received the most votes. The conclusion of White's speech proved prophetic: "Phoenix-like he will rise up some day and come again. These parting words are in behalf of an outraged, heart-broken, bruised, and bleeding, but God-fearing people, faithful, industrious, loyal people—rising people, full of potential force."

It took 28 years, but eventually another black candidate was elected to Congress (from Chicago), and another 44 years before an African American won in the South (in Atlanta). When White said his farewell, most North Carolina blacks lived on farms or in tiny towns. Through the 20th century, few moved to the textile towns, where most mills hired only whites, but some moved to its larger cities. In the years after the Voting Rights Act of 1965, their "potential force" began to be felt as they elected members to the state legislature. Some black candidates were successful with white-majority constituencies, notably Charlotte Mayor Harvey Gantt. But no African American from North Carolina succeeded White in Congress until the Democratic legislature after the 1990 census drew two irregularly shaped black-majority districts. The 1982 amendments to the Voting Rights Act had taken effect, which effectively forced Southern states to draw more majority-minority districts. That resulted in the election in 1992 of Eva Clayton in the mostly rural and small-town 1st District and of Melvin Watt in the 12th District.

This 12th Congressional District of North Carolina was the most litigated district in the country during the 1990s and was the focus of no fewer than four cases that went to the Supreme Court. It originally comprised a series of scattered black precincts connected in some places by nothing wider than the lanes of Interstate 85, and it stretched 160 miles from Gastonia all the way to Durham. In the current Republican-drawn version, the 12th is a bit shorter but remains a snake-like agglomeration that roughly parallels I-85 and includes parts of Charlotte, Greensboro, Winston-Salem, Salisbury, Lexington and High Point. The district, which continues to be listed among the most gerrymandered in the nation, concentrates Democratic strength of any color, helping to make nearby districts more Republican.

The Charlotte-area precincts, including the major banking center in downtown, account for almost half of the district's population and are 50% black. Another third of the district's population is in the Greensboro and Winston-Salem areas, while the balance resides in the sparsely populated (and Republican-leaning) small towns and cities connecting these urban areas. Overall, 54% of the district's population is black, and 15% is Hispanic. Politically, it is among the most Democratic districts in the nation.

2012 Presidential Vote		
Barack Obama (D)	250,719	(79%)
Mitt Romney (R)	66,291	(21%)
2008 Presidential Vote		
Barack Obama (D)	231,627	(78%)
John McCain (R)	62,885	(21%)
Cook Partisan Voting Index: D+26		

Alma Adams (D)

Democrat Alma Adams was elected in 2014 to take the seat vacated by Rep. Melvin Watt, whom President Barack Obama nominated to head the Federal Housing Finance Agency. Because of Watt's early departure, Adams also won a special election and served the final few weeks of Watt's term. She became the 100th woman—a record number—to serve in the 113th Congress.

Adams arrived in Washington as a rarity: a lawmaker with a fine-arts background. She grew up in New Jersey, with her single mother who did domestic work. She got her bachelor's degree from North Carolina A&T State University, a master's and her doctorate in art education and multicultural education from Ohio State University. Until 2012, she taught art history at Bennett College, a historically black women's college. She got her first taste of politics in the 1980s, with election to the Guilford County School Board and the Greensboro City Council. A single mother from a working-class African-American community, she focused on educational and housing disparities in the state. She helped to organize Greensboro for the 1988 presidential campaign of Jesse Jackson. In 1994, she was appointed to fill a seat in the state Assembly, where she served 10 terms, chaired the North Carolina Legislative Black Caucus and became known as "the minimum-wage lady" because of her advocacy.

The departure of Watt, who had held the seat since 1993, set off a scramble. Seven Democrats jumped into the race. Adams was in a strong position for contributions, endorsements and name recognition. She was backed by progressive and abortion-rights organizations that funneled at least $186,000 to super PACs that took aim at her top Democratic rival, Malcolm Graham. Organized labor was another major ally.

In a heavily Democratic district, the candidates' messaging skewed left, and they largely agreed on the core issues: supporting the Affordable Care Act, opposing the decision of GOP Gov. Pat McCrory to block Medicaid expansion, and taking aim at Republican efforts to curtail early voting. Adams emphasized her role as a legislator in the Democratic pushback against the GOP majority in a state where partisan politics have become fractious.

Adams' tactics paid off. She easily topped the field in the May primary with 44% to 24% for Graham. Her victory in the general election was a foregone conclusion; she got 75% against Republican Vince Coakley. Citing the cost, McCrory had declined to call a special election before the general, a move that Democrats condemned.

Like Florida Democratic Rep. Frederica Wilson, Adams is known for her hats; she said that she has 903 of them, as of February 2015. "It's a part of my wardrobe," she told National Public Radio. "I started wearing hats because I was sick a lot. And I remember my grandmother telling me, 'Cover your noggin; you'll stay healthy.'"

In the House, she was assigned to the Education and the Workforce and Agriculture committees. On Small Business, she was the ranking Democrat on the Oversight Subcommittee. She quickly displayed her activism on numerous issues. With Republican Rep. Bradley Byrne of Alabama, she founded the Historically Black Colleges and Universities Caucus. She introduced in March 2015 with Democratic Rep. Rosa DeLauro the Paycheck Fairness Act for gender equality on wages, and she filed in May a bill to raise the federal minimum wage to $12 hourly by 2020. She said that voting must be made easier for all Americans, and claimed that mandatory voter ID laws did the opposite. In May 2015, the House approved her amendment to the defense spending bill calling on the Pentagon to assure that service members have the resources and treatment for post-traumatic stress disorder.

THIRTEENTH DISTRICT

George Holding (R)

Elected 2012, 2nd term; b. April 17, 1968, Raleigh; Wake Forest U., B.A. 1990, J.D. 1996; Baptist; married (Lucy Herriott); 4 children.

Professional Career: Practicing lawyer, 1996-99; Legis. aide, Sen. Jesse Helms, 1999-2001; Practicing lawyer, 2001-02; Asst. U.S. atty., E. Dist. of NC, 2002-06; U.S. atty., E. Dist. of NC, 2006-11.

DC Office: 507 CHOB, 20515, 202-225-3032; Website: holding.house. gov.

State Offices: Fremont, 919-440-5247; Raleigh, 919-782-4400.

Committees: *Ways & Means:* Human Resources; Oversight.

Group Ratings

	ADA	ACLU	AFL-CIO	LCV	ITI	COC	HAFA	ACU	CFG	FRC
2014	5%	0%	–	3%	80%	86%	79%	96%	86%	100%
2013	0%	C	10%	4%	C	83%	C	92%	86%	C

National Journal Ratings

	2013 LIB	—	2013 CONS
Economic	2%	—	97%
Social	0%	—	87%
Foreign	0%	—	95%
Composite	4%	—	96%

Key Votes of the 113th Congress

1. Sandy storm spending	N	5. Medical Marijuana	N	9. Syrian Rebels Training	Y
2. Violence Against Women Act	N	6. Farm Bill	Y	10. Keystone pipeline	Y
3. Guantanamo Bay Detainees	N	7. Afghanistan Combat	N	11. Immigration Exec. Action	Y
4. Abortion 20-week ban	Y	8. NSA Phone Data Collection	N	12. Bipartisan budget deal	N

Election Results

2014 general	George Holding (R)..................153,991	(57%)	$1,415,887
	Brenda Cleary (D)..................114,718	(43%)	$73,203
2014 primary	George Holding (R)...............unopposed		

Prior winning percentage: 2012 (57%)

Population		Race and Ethnicity		Income	
Total:	782,722	White	71.6%	Median income:	$63,686
Urban:	43.5%	Black	16.4%		*(89 of 435)*
Suburban:	39.9%	Latino	8.0%	Under $50,000	38.5%
Rural:	16.6%	Asian	1.8%	$50,000-$99,999:	33.8%
Land area:	2,249	Two races	1.8%	$100,000-$199,999:	21.3%
Pop/sq. mi.:	348.0	White Ethnic	21.9%	$200,000 or more:	6.4%
Born in state:	52.7%			Poverty Rate	9.7%
		Education			
Age Groups		H.S. grad or less:	31.7%	**Work**	
Under 18:	24.8%	Some college:	30.3%	White collar:	44.7%
18 to 34:	19.1%	College degree, 4 yr.:	24.5%	Blue collar:	38.1%
35 to 64:	43.5%	Post-grad study:	13.4%	Sales and service:	17.2%
Over 64:	12.7%			Govt. workers:	15.8%
		Military			
		Veterans/active duty:	9.5%		

East-Central North Carolina: Raleigh Metro, Rocky Mount

A generation ago, Raleigh was a sleepy state capital, moderately prosperous but not very big or showy, while the small cities to the east—Rocky Mount, Wilson, and Goldsboro—had economies built around tobacco and textile factories and the railroad. Just a few miles from the center of town,

Voter Turnout	
2013 Total Citizen 18+	552,164
2014 House Turnout	268,709
2014 Turnout as % CVAP	48.7%
2012 Turnout as % CVAP	72.8%

farm fields started, dotted by country towns with barbecue restaurants and churches. Today, the booming metropolitan areas of North Carolina have spread far beyond the old city and county lines into the adjacent counties. Wake County, which includes Raleigh, grew 51% between 2000 and 2013, reaching a population of close to 1,000,000; Raleigh is about 45% of the total and also is fast-growing. Rural roads are clogged in the morning with commuters headed for jobs in new office parks, and income levels have risen far above what they once were.

Much of this territory makes up the 13th Congressional District of North Carolina. Almost two-thirds of its residents live in Wake County. Republican redistricters in 2011 significantly revised its lines to remove downtown Raleigh and add Republican areas outside Wake County. Raleigh neighborhoods include the Hayes Barton Historic District—a post-World War I suburb now on the National Register of Historic Places—and Anderson Heights, another upscale subdivision near the Carolina Country Club. Roseville is a fast-growing boom town in northern Wake County, where farmlands have been converted in a few years into subdivisions and commercial development. Raleigh has long had an active Lebanese community, now with about 16,000 residents, which celebrates an annual cultural festival. Zebulon is a growing business area, including a new plant where the pharmaceutical firm GlaxoSmithKline employs nearly 1,000 and is producing respiratory drugs and inhalers.

2012 Presidential Vote		
Mitt Romney (R)..................219,397	(56%)
Barack Obama (D).............167,355	(43%)

2008 Presidential Vote		
John McCain (R)..................197,407	(54%)
Barack Obama (D).............164,075	(45%)

Cook Partisan Voting Index: R+8

The district draws in the affluent Republican suburbs and exurbs that surround Raleigh. It includes a collection of crossroads towns and GOP-leaning portions of Rocky Mount, Wilson and Goldsboro. This has become a reliably Republican district.

George Holding (R)

Former federal prosecutor George Holding was elected in 2012 after winning a competitive Republican primary. He has not faced a significant Democratic challenge. The change in the district lines all but guaranteed GOP success and led five-term Democratic Rep. Brad Miller to retire.

Holding grew up in Raleigh in a wealthy family. He gave his first public speech at age 11 to dedicate a statue of his recently deceased father, a prominent banker. He entered Massachusetts' prestigious Groton School and he graduated from Wake Forest University. During those years, Holding developed an interest in conservative ideas and worked as a summer intern for his state's conservative Republican Sen. Jesse Helms. Holding remembers Helms as someone who stuck to his core principles and yet took the time to learn about an issue before casting his vote. Holding graduated from Wake Forest law school, where he met his British wife, Lucy Herriott. After clerking for a federal judge and working at a law firm, he re-joined Helms as a legislative counsel, concentrating on business, tax and tobacco issues.

In 2006, President George W. Bush nominated Holding as U.S. attorney for eastern North Carolina. His territory included Raleigh, which led to prosecution of numerous politicians, including former Gov. Mike Easley for campaign finance irregularities, and former state House Speaker Jim Black for accepting illegal funds. His most prominent case was that of former Democratic Sen. John Edwards, and the nearly $1 million that his supporters paid to Edwards's mistress, Rielle Hunter, during his 2008 presidential campaign. Holding initiated the prosecution against Edwards but resigned to run for Congress before the case was argued in court. In June 2012, a jury deadlocked on five of the six felony counts, prompting the Justice Department to drop the charges. Holding, defending the prosecution, said that Edwards' conduct called out for action.

His campaign for the House seat featured feel-good ads, including one about a World War II-era nurse who tended to soldiers despite shrapnel tearing through a tent, and another praising Thomas Edison's entrepreneurial spirit that led to the invention of the light bulb. But the primary turned acrimonious. Holding's main opponent was Wake County Commission Chairman Paul Coble, a nephew of Helms. Coble accused Holding of politicizing Edwards' indictment and set up a website accusing Holding of taking "dirty money" from trial lawyers who supported President Barack Obama's health care legislation. Holding's massive financial advantage helped him notch a victory, 44%-34%.

In the general election, Democrat Charles Malone accused Holding of being "surrounded by wealth" and therefore out of touch. But Malone spent only $18,000, about 1% of what Holding spent, and his message had little resonance. Holding won, 57%-43%.

Holding fit comfortably in the Republican establishment in the House, though he had the second-most conservative voting record in *National Journal's* 2013 rankings. He took an interest in India, meeting there with President Narendra Modi, and became co-chairman of the India Caucus in 2015. In a significant career move, he won a seat on the House Ways and Means Committee and listed tax reform as a top priority, "including closing loopholes and stopping fraud." In April 2015, the House approved by voice vote his IRS Bureaucracy Reduction and Judicial Review Act, which he said would streamline Internal Revenue Service reviews by "allowing groups to declare their tax-exempt status rather than wait for endless amounts of time to gain approval." He called the IRS "an agency in turmoil." In October 2013, C-SPAN's camera captured Holding while he appeared to be dozing as he presided over the House during late-afternoon speeches, certainly not the first lawmaker to catch a few winks on the House floor.

Holding was reelected in 2014 with another 57%-43% win over another under-funded Democratic opponent, health care consultant Brenda Cleary. In 2015, he helped to lead the "Project Listen" Initiative of the state Republican party, which focused on "issue research" and "brand assessment" in preparation for the 2016 election.

★ NORTH DAKOTA ★

In late 1804, members of the Lewis and Clark Expedition paddled up the Missouri River and reached what is now North Dakota. The explorers bivouacked for the winter across the river from what is now the state capital of Bismarck and spent 146 nights in North Dakota. On the Lewis and Clark Trail, you can still see traces of the pristine landscape that met the expedition—a vast unfenced land where the Indians built a civilization based on the buffalo and the horse, a Spanish import. Just a hundred years later, railroads were constructed across the prairie, and the Sioux were herded onto reservations; it was from Fort Abraham Lincoln, built on the site of an old Mandan Indian village in central North Dakota, that the post's commander, George A. Custer, rode out to his routing and death at Little Bighorn. By the time President Theodore Roosevelt visited the state, he needed perseverance to find a buffalo to shoot. North Dakota is relentlessly flat, its lush, green farmland pockmarked in places by placid blue "prairie pothole" lakes carved by glaciers; its flatness encourages flooding, as in the massive Grand Forks flood in April 1997 as well as the creeping expansion of Devils Lake, which for a while in the 1990s threatened to overwhelm the eponymous city.

North Dakota was admitted to the Union in 1889, on the same day as South Dakota (no one knows which is the 39th state and which is the 40th), and settlers poured in. Its rolling prairies turned out to be some of the best wheat-growing acreage in the world, and while wheat—mostly spring wheat but also durum (used in pasta)—remains the biggest crop, it is not the only one. North Dakota ranks first in production of dry edible beans, oats, and dry peas; it ranks high in the production of sunflowers, barley, sugar beets, and rye. There is also plenty of cattle ranching on the arid plains in the western half of the state. While North Dakota's cold climate discouraged many Americans from settling this far north, it was no deterrent to emigrants from Germany, Norway, Bohemia (now the Czech Republic), Iceland, and Russia. North Dakota's population shot up from 191,000 in 1890 to 319,000 in 1900 and to 647,000 in 1920. For the next nine decades, its population oscillated in the 600,000s, peaking at 680,000, dropping to 618,000 in 1970, and then wobbling along until it started to rise dramatically after 2007, reaching 739,482 in the Census estimate for 2014—about a century after it reached the 600,000 mark. Just a decade after escalating worries about an emptying-out of the northern plains, North Dakota saw the fastest-growing population of any state, rising by 7.6% between 2010 and 2013.

Behind those numbers are two stories. The contraction owed to the state's dependence on an agriculture sector growing ever more productive and efficient, and thus requiring less labor. The subsequent rise came from a new economic engine: oil and natural gas from the Bakken shale formation in the western part of the state. North Dakota had seen other energy booms before. In the 1970s, it developed lignite coal just west of Bismarck, which bequeathed six electric power plants and a coal gasification facility. The state also has six ethanol and three biodiesel plants, and wind energy supplies 12% of North Dakota's electricity. But all this pales compared to Bakken. It was discovered in 1951 and named after a Williston-area farmer, but it remained untapped for many years. Then, in 2006, oil producers began using extended-reach horizontal drilling to reach more deposits along with hydraulic fracturing to break up the shale in which the oil is embedded. "Satellite photos of western North Dakota at night, aglitter like a metropolis with lighted rigs and burning flares, crystallized its rapid transformation from tight-knit agricultural society to semi-industrialized oil powerhouse," the *New York Times* wrote. After a twenty-fold increase in six years, North Dakota surged to No. 2 in the nation in petroleum production; natural gas production rose as well. At its peak in 2014, oil production contributed $50 million a day to North Dakota's economy, with more than $11 million daily in oil and gas taxes for the state, according to the North Dakota Petroleum Council. Unemployment stood at a national low of 3.1 percent in March 2015, up slightly from a year earlier.

Fueling this boom has been a surge of men (and many fewer women) to western North Dakota, lured by annual earnings of $100,000; many live in RVs or modular living pods lined up on farm fields, because Williston, improbably, has the nation's highest average rent for an entry-level apartment. Trucks carrying water in for fracking and oil out for refining jam the two-lane roads and buckle the pavement; there are long lines at stores and fast-food takeout lanes, and schools are strained. In Williston, "the first thing you see leaving the Amtrak

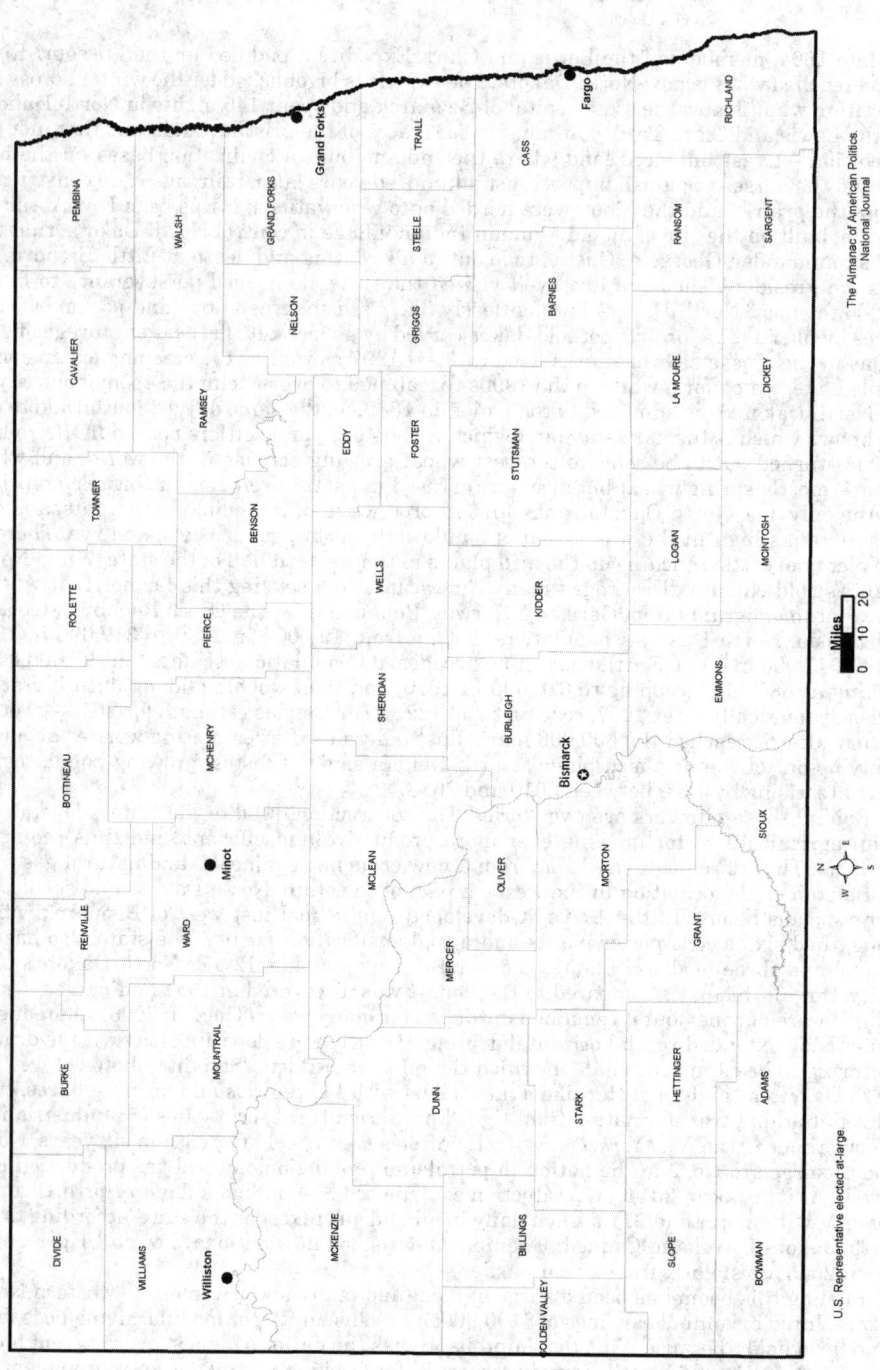

U.S. Representative elected at-large.

station is two strip clubs that cater to the wave of men coming into town from the oil fields, their pockets stuffed with cash," NPR reported. This milieu has spawned human and drug trafficking, organized crime and homicides—a situation worrisome enough that the FBI opened a permanent office there.

Voter Turnout	
2013 Total Citizen 18+	549,624
2014 Highest Statewide Turnout	248,670
2014 Turnout as % CVAP	45.2%
2012 Turnout as % CVAP	60.2%
Legislature		
Senate:	32R	15D
House:	71R	23D

Other factors have tempered enthusiasm about the oil patch, at least somewhat. One is the volatility of the energy markets. In 2015, amid persistently low petroleum prices, the number of drilling rigs in North Dakota dropped below 100 for the first time in five years, a sign of decreased confidence within the industry about the prospects for strong economic returns. The second is the environmental impact. In 2013, a pipeline spilled more than 20,000 barrels of crude into a wheat field; later that year, a mile-long train carrying crude exploded into a giant fireball after colliding and derailing. In 2014, 1 million gallons of saltwater produced by oil extraction leaked from a pipeline and headed toward a Native American reservation. Worker deaths have spiked, and the lack of government regulation has been questioned. The *New York Times* calculated that North Dakota regulators have collected just one-thirtieth the fines on industry that Texas collected over the same period.

Until recently, dependence on agriculture, not oil, shaped North Dakota's politics. Farmers, as much as they like to extol their way of life, are seldom content with the workings of the market. When prices are high, it is often because of low production; when they are low, farmers seek protection. The boosterish optimism of the first settlers was soon followed by cries, reverberating with varying intensity, for government protection against market forces. Since commodity prices tend to fall during periods of economic growth, there was often a countercyclical force at work in North Dakota politics—a tendency to vote against the national trends and a radical strain going back to the 1910s. That strain also owes much to the Scandinavian and German origins of many of the state's early settlers, who produced orderly small towns and grain cooperatives and supported the Nonpartisan League, which operated as an independent force from its founding in 1915 to its alliance with the Democratic Party in 1956.

The NPL appealed to marginal farmers, cut off in many cases from the wider American culture by language barriers and seemingly at the mercy of the grain millers in Minneapolis, the railroads in St. Paul, the banks in New York City, and the commodity traders in Chicago. The NPL's program was socialist—government ownership of railroads and grain elevators— and its members, like most North Dakota ethnics, opposed going to war with Germany in 1917 and in 1940-41. The NPL often determined the outcome of the usually decisive Republican primary, but sometimes swung its support to the otherwise heavily outnumbered Democrats, instituting reforms and creating the state-owned Bank of North Dakota and a state grain elevator. The merger of the NPL into the Democratic Party was symbolized by the election in 1960 of Democratic Sen. Quentin Burdick, whose father Usher Burdick had served 20 years in the House as an NPL-endorsed Republican. North Dakota's leading Democrats of recent decades, Sens. Kent Conrad and Byron Dorgan and Rep. Earl Pomeroy, championed a politics of NPL lineage: boosterish of government farm programs, wary of if not hostile to American military involvement abroad, and a cheerful championing of the little guy from North Dakota against out-of-state corporations.

One reason Democrats thrived for years while the state steadily voted Republican for president is that politics is personal in a place where most everyone knows everyone else. For years voter registration has been automatic because people spotted anyone who was not eligible. People live longer here too. The 2010 census reported that North Dakota tied for the highest proportion of residents ages 85 and older, and tiny McIntosh County had the second highest proportion of any county, due in part to years of out-migration. Communal closeness has produced an innate cultural conservatism in North Dakota, with divorce rates well below the national average. North Dakota's odd combination of light taxation and regulation on the one hand and the state-owned Bank of North Dakota on the other has encouraged business start-ups. But if state government has applied a light touch on industry, it has exerted a stricter influence on social matters: Republican Gov. Jack Dalrymple signed what was widely regarded as the nation's strictest anti-abortion law, including one provision that could curb abortions as early as six weeks into a pregnancy. (North Dakota voters, however,

Population		Race and Ethnicity		Income	
Total:	723,393	White	88.5%	Median income:	$52,888
Urban:	40.6%	Amer. Indian	5.6%		(26 of 50)
Suburban:	5.2%	Latino	2.2%	Under $50,000	45.1%
Rural:	54.2%	Asian	1.0%	$50,000-$99,999:	32.7%
Land area:	69,001	Two races	1.7%	$100,000-$199,999:	17.9%
Pop/sq. mi.:	10.5	White Ethnic	23.0%	$200,000 or more:	4.2%
Born in state:	65.1%			Poverty Rate	11.8%
		Education			
Age Groups		H.S. grad or less:	36.0%	**Work**	
Under 18:	22.2%	Some college:	36.9%	White collar:	34.3%
18 to 34:	27.2%	College degree, 4 yr.:	20.0%	Blue collar:	39.6%
35 to 64:	36.4%	Post-grad study:	7.2%	Sales and service:	26.1%
Over 64:	14.2%				
		Military		Govt. workers:	16.1%
		Veterans/active duty:	9.4%		

rejected a ballot measure in November 2014 that would have defined life as beginning at conception.)

Exit polls in 2004 showed George W. Bush running stronger among young voters than with the elderly in North Dakota, the opposite of the pattern in most states. This may reflect that older voters have fond memories of NPL and support a strong government hand in agriculture, while younger North Dakotans are more trusting of the marketplace. Barack Obama cut into the young vote here in 2008, but the state followed the strong Republican trend of 2010. That year, populist Democratic Sen. Byron Dorgan retired after 41 years in statewide office and was succeeded by Republican Gov. John Hoeven, who won an impressive 76%-22% victory. Meanwhile, Democrat Pomeroy was defeated 55%-45% after spending 18 years in the House and eight years before that as tax commissioner.

In the 2012 presidential contest, Mitt Romney carried the state 58%-39%, and Dalrymple was reelected, 63%-34%. Republican Kevin Cramer won the state's one House seat, 55%-42%. But in the race for the Senate seat vacated by Democrat Kent Conrad, Democrat Heidi Heitkamp edged Republican Rep. Rick Berg 50%-49%. Heitkamp, a former attorney general who lost to Hoeven in 2000, campaigned personally all over the state and promised to oppose Obama on gun control and the Keystone XL pipeline, which would cut across North Dakota. Her victory was evidence that even in the new North Dakota, the personal touch can be decisive in a small state. One other result shows that North Dakota in the Bakken age has not forgotten farming: By 67%-33%, voters approved a "right to farm" constitutional amendment that banned any law limiting farmers' right "to employ agricultural technology, modern livestock production, and ranching practices."

Presidential Politics For the first time since 1964, North Dakota was viewed as a competitive state in the presidential election in 2008. It had given George W. Bush more than 60% of its votes in 2000 and 2004, but by 2008 this historically dovish state was plainly unhappy with the incumbent. Although only 1% of its residents are African-American (most live on military bases; the biggest minority is American Indians, at 6%), North Dakota was plainly intrigued by Barack Obama. With the state scheduled to hold caucuses on Super Tuesday, February 5,

2012 Presidential Vote

Mitt Romney (R)	188,163	(58%)
Barack Obama (D)	124,827	(39%)

2012 Presidential Caucus

Rick Santorum (R)	4,510	(40%)
Ron Paul (R)	3,186	(28%)
Mitt Romney (R)	2,691	(24%)
Newt Gingrich (R)	962	(8%)

2008 Presidential Vote

John McCain (R)	168,601	(53%)
Barack Obama (D)	141,278	(45%)

the Obama campaign moved in early, bought television time, and set up offices with paid staff and volunteers in Fargo, Grand Forks, Bismarck, and Minot. The effort paid off on Caucus Day. Altogether, 19,012 North Dakotans participated in the Democratic caucuses and only 9,566 in the Republican caucuses.

Obama outpolled Hillary Clinton 61%-37%. On the Republican side, Mitt Romney's 36% of the vote put him ahead of John McCain's 23%, Ron Paul's 21%, and Mike Huckabee's 20%. In the general election, McCain prevailed 53%-45%, far below Bush's percentages. Obama carried Cass (Fargo) and Grand Forks (home to the University of North Dakota) counties and thus was able to carry the eastern Red River basin portion of the state, which has North Dakota's most prosperous farmland. He also won three counties with heavy American Indian populations and reservations, Benson, Rolette and Sioux. McCain carried Burleigh (Bismarck) and Ward (Minot) counties, the western part of the state where oil and natural gas production from the Bakken shale formation is transforming the state, and most of North Dakota's other rural counties.

In 2012 the picture was different. North Dakota Republicans caucused on March 6, and 11,349 people participated. Rick Santorum led with 40% to 28% for Paul and 24% for Romney. In the general election, Obama had far less appeal than he had had four years before. North Dakotans disliked his energy policies and feared that in a second term his regulators might inhibit or ban hydraulic fracturing, and Romney carried the state 58%-39%. Obama carried only six counties, the three with major Indian reservations and three small rural ones in the Red River Basin.

Governor

Jack Dalrymple (R)

Assumed office Dec. 2010, term expires Jan. 2017, 1st full term; b. Oct. 16, 1948, Minneapolis, MN; Yale U., B.A. 1970; married (Betsy); 4 children.

Elected Office: ND House, 1985-2000; ND lt. gov., 2000-10.

Professional Career: Chmn., ND Trade Office; Chmn., Gov. Commission on Ed. Improvement.

Office: 600 E. Boulevard Ave., Bismarck, 58505-0001, 701-328-2200; Fax: 701-328-2205; Website: governor.nd.gov.

Election Results

2012 general	Jack Dalrymple (R)	200,525	(63%)
	Ryan Taylor (D)	109,048	(34%)
2012 primary	Jack Dalrymple (R)	unopposed	

North Dakota's Republican governor is Jack Dalrymple, who moved up from lieutenant governor in December 2010 to succeed John Hoeven after Hoeven was elected to the Senate. Dalrymple has presided over a huge, oil-driven economic boom—*The New York Times Magazine* dubbed the state "the luckiest place on earth"—and in 2012 he was elected to a full four-year term in his own right.

Dalrymple grew up in Casselton, a farming town of about 2,000 people west of Fargo that has the unique status of producing four of the state's other governors: Andrew Burke (1891-92), William Langer (1933-34, 1937-39), William Guy (1961-73), and George Sinner (1985-92). Dalrymple's family farm was established in 1875 as the state's first large-scale wheat farm. After leaving to get a bachelor's degree from Yale University, he returned to manage its operations. He eventually worked with other farmers to found the Dakota Growers Pasta Co., a mill and processing plant, serving as its initial board chairman. The company was sold in 2010 to a Canadian grain and food processing company. Also during that time period, he helped establish ShareHouse Inc., a Fargo residential treatment program for alcohol and drug addiction.

Dalrymple entered politics in 1984, when he ran successfully for a state House seat. He served eight terms and spent six years chairing the House Appropriations Committee. Dalrymple made two stabs at higher office: In 1988, he ran for the U.S. Senate seat held by Democrat Quentin Burdick, but he lost in the GOP primary to state House Republican Leader Earl Strinden. Four years later, after Burdick's death, he ran against Democrat Kent Conrad in a December special election to fill the remaining two years of Burdick's term. (At the time, Conrad, elected to the Senate in 1986, was an incumbent who had announced he would not seek reelection in 1992. Democrat Byron Dorgan went on to win the seat that year.

But after Burdick died, Conrad had a change of heart about retiring and ran in the special election for Burdick's seat.) Dalrymple attacked Conrad for broken promises, but the senator was more of a known quantity with far more money than Dalrymple. Conrad won, 63%-34%.

When Hoeven ran for governor in 2000 to replace retiring Republican Gov. Ed Schafer, he came under pressure to choose a woman as his running mate. But Hoeven told the *Grand Forks Herald* that none of the women he approached believed they could balance the task of lieutenant governor with their personal lives, so he turned to Dalrymple. Hoeven said that having a running mate from the state's more populous eastern region helped balance the ticket because he was from the western part. Hoeven defeated Democrat Heidi Heitkamp, the state's attorney general, 55%-45%.

As lieutenant governor, Dalrymple was given the task of courting international business for the state, helping in 2009 to arrange a $5 million contract with South Korea for 275,000 bushels of U.S. soybeans. He also worked closely with his former colleagues in the legislature on budget issues, winning praise for his understanding of negotiating successful deals.

As North Dakota's economy thrived, Hoeven became extremely popular, easily winning reelection in 2004 and 2008 and running up record approval ratings. He was considered the logical choice among Republicans to run for the Senate after Dorgan announced he would retire in 2010. Hoeven resigned as governor shortly after winning the election, leaving Dalrymple, the state's longest-serving lieutenant governor, as his successor.

The new governor announced that his focus would be on energy and infrastructure, saying he wanted to create one central division of state government to concentrate on developing all of North Dakota's energy sectors. He also signed into law in March 2011 a bill making the University of North Dakota's sports team name, Fighting Sioux, a matter of state law. The measure came in defiance of the National Collegiate Athletic Association, which opposes the use of Indian names and symbols. Eight months later, however, Dalrymple asked lawmakers to reverse the decision after it had jeopardized the university's plans to join the Big Sky athletic conference.

Heavy flooding on the Missouri River in the summer 2011 led Dalrymple to propose a $569 million plan to provide disaster aid to flood-stricken areas while helping western North Dakota towns struggling to cope with the oil boom. It established a loan program for flood victims and provided funding for city and county infrastructure improvements. It also set aside $1 million for a potential lawsuit against the Environmental Protection Agency over the possible regulation of hydraulic fracturing, the drilling technique widely used in North Dakota's oil fields. It swiftly became law. In July 2012, Dalrymple proposed an even larger $2.5 billion road and infrastructure plan that included more than $1 billion for new highways. The governor also supported the legislature's decision to reject a state-run health insurance exchange established by the new federal health care overhaul law.

With North Dakota leaning so heavily Republican, Dalrymple was considered a strong favorite for election to the post in 2012. His Democratic opponent was Ryan Taylor, the state Senate minority leader. He accused Dalrymple of putting away too much money in rainy day funds that he said would be better spent on education. Dalrymple campaigned on his emphasis on infrastructure to cope with the expected population growth while keeping taxes low. He won easily, with 63% of the vote.

In his January 2013 State of the State address, Dalrymple touted the "incredible moment in our state's history," when it enjoyed a record-level budget surplus and the nation's lowest unemployment rate. He drew national attention two months later when he signed the nation's toughest anti-abortion legislation into law. It bars abortion as soon as a fetal heartbeat is "detectable," which can be as early as six weeks into a pregnancy—a much shorter time period than the roughly 24-week time frame established in the Supreme Court's *Roe v. Wade* decision legalizing abortion. "Although the likelihood of this measure surviving a court challenge remains in question, this bill is nevertheless a legitimate attempt by a state legislature to discover the boundaries of *Roe v. Wade*," Dalrymple said in a statement.

In 2015, as other Republican-led states were facing a backlash against laws they'd passed that might allow businesses to discriminate against gay customers, Dalrymple took the legislature to task for failing to act on a different but related issue—a measure that would have barred discrimination based on sexual orientation in housing, government, public services and the workplace. For the third time in six years, lawmakers rejected such a bill in 2015; after it failed, Dalrymple said that "discrimination based on an individual's sexual orientation is not acceptable" and issued a "reminder" memo that his administration's policy is not to discriminate based on sexual orientation in the state's 17 cabinet agencies.

Dalrymple expressed confidence in the face of an increasingly uncertain future for the state's oil and gas industry. Despite plunging prices, Dalrymple said, his agenda of tax relief and infrastructure spending would be undeterred. "In the end, our growth may be slowed, but it will not stop," he said. In August 2015, Dalrymple announced that he would not seek reelection in 2016. Voters faced an open-seat contest for the first time since 2000.

Senior Senator

John Hoeven (R)

Elected 2010, term expires Jan. 2017, 1st term; b. March 13, 1957, Bismarck; Dartmouth, B.A. 1979, Northwestern U. Kellogg Grad. Schl., M.B.A. 1981; Catholic; married (Mikey); 2 children.

Elected Office: ND gov., 2000-10.

Professional Career: Exec. V.P., First Western Bank, 1986-93; Pres. & CEO, Bank of ND, 1993-2000.

DC Office: 338 RSOB, 20510, 202-224-2551; Fax: 202-224-7999; Website: hoeven.senate.gov.

State Offices: Bismarck, 701-250-4618; Fargo, 701-239-5389; Grand Forks, 701-746-8972; Minot, 701-838-1361; Williston, 701-580-4535.

Committees: *Agriculture, Nutrition & Forestry:* Commodities, Risk Management & Trade; Rural Development & Energy; Nutrition, Specialty Crops, Food & Ag Research (Chmn). *Appropriations:* Homeland Security (Chmn); Agriculture, Rural Development, Food and Drug Administration & Related Agencies; Energy & Water Development; Interior, Environment & Related Agencies; Military Construction, Veterans Affairs & Related Agencies. *Energy & Natural Resources:* Energy; National Parks; Public Lands, Forests, and Mining. *Indian Affairs.*

Group Ratings

	ADA	ACLU	AFL-CIO	LCV	ITI	COC	HAFA	ACU	CFG	FRC
2014	10%	6%	–	0%	66%	100%	41%	68%	47%	86%
2013	10%	C	33%	23%	C	88%	C	60%	58%	C

National Journal Ratings

	2013 LIB	—	2013 CONS
Economic	40%	—	58%
Social	21%	—	77%
Foreign	28%	—	70%
Composite	31%	—	69%

Key Votes of the 113th Congress

1. Sandy storm spending	Y	5. Student Loan Rates		9. Bipartisan Budget Deal	Y
2. Chuck Hagel Confirmation	N	6. Employee Non-Discrim'n Act	N	10. Farm Bill Conference Rept.	Y
3. Gun Background Checks	N	7. Senate Vote on Judgeships	Y	11. Unempl. Comp. Extension	N
4. Immigration Reform	Y	8. Defense Dept. Spending	N	12. Keystone Pipeline	Y

Election Results

2010 general	John Hoeven (R)	181,689	(76%)	$2,909,158	$25,107
	Tracy Potter (D)	52,955	(22%)	$28,279	$67,564
2010 primary	John Hoeven (R)	unopposed			

Prior winning percentages: Governor: 2008 (74%), 2004 (71%), 2000 (55%)

North Dakota's senior senator, John Hoeven, in 2010, became the first Republican elected to the Senate from that state in 30 years. His election heralded the political evolution of a jurisdiction in which a majority of voters, while not supporting a Democratic presidential candidate since Lyndon Johnson in 1964, nonetheless had consistently sent Democrats to Capitol Hill to represent them in the intervening years. But in 2010, amid an oil and gas boom that transformed North Dakota into one of the nation's most economically flourishing states, the Republican tilt at the top of the ticket spread to the congressional delegation: Hoeven, who had presided over the state's new prosperity during a decade as governor, was overwhelmingly elected to the Senate, and voters also chose a Republican to fill the state's at-large House seat for the first time since 1978.

Ironically, the man credited with helping to put North Dakota firmly in the red state column publicly declared himself a Democrat as recently as four years before his 2000 election as governor. In a 1996 letter to a local newspaper, Hoeven, then president of the Bank of North Dakota—the only state-run bank in the country—declared, "I have always been moderate in my political views, but now that I am considering elective office, I realize I must join a political party and stick to it." He continued, "I have decided to join the Democratic-NPL Party because I believe that is the best fit for my views." The bank that Hoeven was running at the time had been created in 1919 at the initiative of the Nonpartisan League, a coalition of reformers and radicals that was a major force in North Dakota for the first half of the 20th century (and which merged with state Democrats in 1960 to create what is now known as the Democratic-NPL Party).

When the letter surfaced during Hoeven's 2010 Senate bid, his campaign manager, Don Larson, told *Talking Points Memo* that, shortly after writing the letter, Hoeven "realized his views were more in line with the Republicans than the Democrats. So he got involved with the Republican Party, became a Republican district chairman, helped Republican candidates around North Dakota, and then ran for and won the governorship. Before that, he had not been involved in politics at all, either as a Republican or a Democrat." Throughout his tenure as governor and senator, Hoeven has been in the conservative Republican mainstream on most social issues, ranging from abortion to gun control. But, unlike his colleagues in the Senate Republicans' tea party wing, Hoeven has been open to committing increased funds for education and infrastructure; while he was governor, the state budget increased dramatically, with much of the added spending directed toward those categories.

Hoeven was born in Bismarck and grew up in Minot. His father was a banker who in 1969 took over the First Western Bank & Trust of Minot, which became a family business. John Hoeven started working there as a bookkeeper at age 15. He graduated from Dartmouth College and went on to earn an M.B.A. from Northwestern University. In 1981, he returned home to become First Western Bank's executive vice president. In 1993, he was chosen to head the state-owned Bank of North Dakota by a board that included his predecessor as governor, Republican Ed Schafer, and also Attorney General Heidi Heitkamp, a Democrat who is now the state's junior senator. Under Hoeven's stewardship, the bank's worth rose from $990 million to $1.6 billion, and its loan portfolio increased from $200 million to $1 billion.

In 2000, after Schafer retired as governor, Hoeven ran for the post against Heitkamp. He cited his work attracting and retaining local jobs and organizing the effort to keep Minot Air Force Base off the government's base closure list. He called for economic development in the state with an emphasis on the technology industry and on improving education, and he pledged more money for teacher training and salaries. He won 55%-45%, as Heitkamp was compelled to all but forfeit the campaign after she was diagnosed with breast cancer.

As governor, Hoeven used North Dakota's burgeoning state revenues to fund programs to stimulate economic development. In his first years, he combined several state agencies into a Commerce Department. In 2002, he announced an ambitious research and development program, borrowing $50 million for university projects to help commercialize new technology. From 2005 to 2007, more than $40 million in state funds and double that amount in private funds were invested in the Center of Excellence in Life Sciences and Advanced Technologies and other research centers. Much of this was aimed at exploiting North Dakota's considerable energy resources, including oil, coal, ethanol, wind, and hydrogen. In 2002, Hoeven announced his EmPower North Dakota energy plan, aiming to build three new biodiesel plants by 2015 and to have wind supply 10 percent of the state's electricity by 2015 (up from 5 percent).

During his second term, Hoeven submitted budgets with reductions in local property taxes that also provided for big increases in education spending, with the latter targeted at raising teachers' salaries. He had no trouble winning a second term in 2004 over former state Sen. Joseph Satrom, 71%-27%, and national Republicans were hoping that he would take on one of the state's two Democratic senators. But he opted not to challenge Sen. Kent Conrad in 2006 and, in November 2008, won reelection to a third term by easily defeating state Sen. Tim Mathern, capturing nearly 75 percent of the vote. Before the 2008 election, Hoeven brushed aside speculation that he would run against the state's other senator, Democrat Byron Dorgan or at-large Democratic Rep. Earl Pomeroy in 2010, but did not pledge to serve out his third term.

One poll, at the end of 2009, showed Hoeven with a stratospheric 87-percent approval rating, with the same poll showing him leading Dorgan by a 58%-36% margin in a hypothetical matchup. By all indications, Dorgan was planning to run for a fourth term—he had been raising money for the campaign—until he stunned Senate colleagues in January 2010 by saying he had decided to retire after reflecting over the Christmas holidays. Shortly thereafter, Hoeven announced he was running for the newly open Senate seat, criticizing President Barack Obama's economic agenda and what he called an overly bureaucratic health care overhaul. "Washington's approach is to put a 2,000-page bill between you and your doctor," he said. He didn't have to campaign very hard. Both Pomeroy and Heitkamp declined to run for the Senate seat, leaving the Democrats without a top-tier candidate. The eventual Democratic nominee, Tracy Potter, a state senator from Bismarck, struggled to raise money and achieve any momentum. Hoeven spent $4 million to just $28,000 for Potter, and won by a better than 3-1 margin, 76%-22%.

As a freshman senator, Hoeven has continued his focus on energy issues, advocating efforts to develop a national energy plan similar to his home state's EmPower North Dakota, an approach that encompasses renewable as well as traditional energy resources. With regard to the latter, Hoeven has been an outspoken critic of Obama's decision to block construction of the Keystone XL oil pipeline designed to run from Canada to the Gulf Coast—while also carrying a projected 100,000 barrels a day produced in the oilfields of western North Dakota and neighboring Montana. In March 2012, Hoeven offered a bill to reinstate the project, and, while 11 Democrats crossed over to support the bill, it still failed to reach the 60-vote threshold needed to end a threatened filibuster. With the Senate in Republican control following the 2014 election, Hoeven sponsored the bill and led the effort to allow the pipeline to move ahead—which, this time around, cleared both the House and Senate. Pipeline advocates fell five votes short in March 2015 of the two-thirds majority needed to override Obama's veto.

Upon his arrival on Capitol Hill, Hoeven was immediately given a prized slot on the Senate Appropriations Committee, and also was named to the Agriculture Committee, where he was a conferee on the 2014 farm bill that renewed federal agriculture and nutrition programs for five years. Hoeven supported an earlier version of the bill that cleared the Senate in June 2012, which ended direct payments to farmers but included a new form of crop insurance favored by farm state senators outside the South. Both of these features were included in the final farm bill that was approved in 2014. Hoeven also worked to ensure that the legislation contained an extension of the sugar program contained in past farm bills—important to North Dakota, one of the nation's leading producers of sugar beets, but controversial among critics who complain it has made sugar significantly more expensive for U.S. consumers.

In early 2015, as the Agriculture Committee was preparing to reauthorize the 2010 Healthy Hunger-Free Kids Act, Hoeven found himself on a potential collision course with first lady Michelle Obama and her campaign to reduce childhood obesity. Hoeven introduced a measure that would relax Agriculture Department rules for schools with regards to serving whole grain products and reducing sodium levels. "We all want to work with the spirit of the Healthy Hunger-Free Kids Act," Hoeven told a gathering of the School Nutrition Association. "But we've got to have the flexibility to do it right."

While he has targeted federal regulations he feels have stifled innovation and are onerous for state and local governments, Hoeven is no conservative absolutist. After Hurricane Irene hit the East Coast in the summer of 2011, he was one of 10 Republicans to support a $6.9 billion increase in Federal Emergency Management Agency funding. He showed a willingness to cross party lines when he joined 14 other Republicans to vote for a reauthorization of the Violence Against Women Act in April 2012. In the early months of 2013, Hoeven expressed support for the idea of bipartisan immigration reform being pushed by Republican Sens. Marco Rubio of Florida and John McCain of Arizona, and, during the same period, was one of just 12 Republicans to vote for a successful measure to raise the limit on how much debt the government can acquire. At the end of 2013, he was one of only nine Senate Republicans to back a budget deal crafted by the chairmen of the Senate and House Budget committees—Washington Democrat Patty Murray and Wisconsin Republican Paul Ryan, respectively—that was criticized by conservative groups as permitting too much spending.

Hoeven turned 58 in 2015, and aides put out the word in June that he would seek reelection when his current term is up in 2016. He is considered an overwhelming favorite to win another term, and there are no obvious, let alone high-profile challengers, in sight. One name that has been floated is state Sen. George Sinner, who lost a contest to the state's at-large House member, Kevin Cramer, in 2014. Sinner has the advantage of name recognition over other potential Democratic challengers as the son and namesake of a former Democratic governor who served from 1984 to 1992. The more likely scenario is that Hoeven has an easy road to a second term.

Junior Senator

Heidi Heitkamp (D)

Elected 2012, term expires Jan. 2019, 1st term; b. Oct. 30, 1955, Mantador; U. of ND, B.A. 1977, Lewis & Clark Law Schl., J.D. 1980; Catholic; married (Darwin Lange); 2 children.

Elected Office: ND atty. gen., 1992-2000; tax commissioner, 1986-92.

Professional Career: Dir., Dakota Gasification, 2001-12; Atty., ND Tax Commissioner Office, 1981-86; Atty., U.S. Environmental Protection Agency, 1980-81.

DC Office: SH-110 HSOB, 20510, 202-224-2043; Fax: 202-224-7776; Website: heitkamp.senate.gov.

State Offices: Bismarck, 701-258-4648; Dickinson, 701-225-0974; Fargo, 701-232-8030; Grand Forks, 701-775-9601; Minot, 701-852-0703.

Committees: *Agriculture, Nutrition & Forestry:* Commodities, Risk Management & Trade; Rural Development & Energy (RMM); Conservation, Forestry & Natural Resources. *Banking, Housing & Urban Affairs:* Economic Policy; Housing, Transportation & Community Development; National Security & International Trade & Finance (RMM). *Homeland Security & Governmental Affairs:* Permanent Subcommittee on Investigations; Regulatory Affairs & Federal Management (RMM). *Indian Affairs. Small Business & Entrepreneurship.*

Group Ratings

	ADA	ACLU	AFL-CIO	LCV	ITI	COC	HAFA	ACU	CFG	FRC
2014	75%	100%	–	40%	100%	50%	5%	16%	11%	0%
2013	70%	C	100%	69%	C	38%	C	12%	2%	C

National Journal Ratings

	2013 LIB	—	2013 CONS
Economic	52%	—	47%
Social	48%	—	51%
Foreign	56%	—	42%
Composite	53%	—	47%

Key Votes of the 113th Congress

1. Sandy storm spending	5. Student Loan Rates	9. Bipartisan Budget Deal Y
2. Chuck Hagel Confirmation Y	6. Employee Non-Discrim'n Act Y	10. Farm Bill Conference Rept. Y
3. Gun Background Checks N	7. Senate Vote on Judgeships N	11. Unempl. Comp. Extension Y
4. Immigration Reform Y	8. Defense Dept. Spending Y	12. Keystone Pipeline Y

Election Results

2012 general	Heidi Heitkamp (D)	161,163	(50%)	$5,493,544	$1,175,717	$6,236,825
	Rick Berg (R)	158,282	(50%)	$6,344,251	$1,896,755	$7,730,094
2012 primary	Heidi Heitkamp (D)	unopposed				

Democrat Heidi Heitkamp, North Dakota's junior senator, was one of the more surprising success stories of the 2012 election: Her victory enabled the Democrats to hang onto a seat that, at the beginning of the cycle, was widely regarded as a prime Republican pickup opportunity due to the retirement of long-serving Sen. Kent Conrad. In narrowly winning in a red state, Heitkamp kept her distance from President Barack Obama—and ran 11 points ahead of him on Election Day—while vowing to place pragmatic legislating above politics in a Congress beset by partisanship and legislative gridlock. Heitkamp arrived on Capitol Hill in early 2013 to join a group of nearly a dozen Democratic senators with centrist leanings representing traditionally Republican states. But a combination of retirements and defeats in 2014 cut this number in half, reducing the Democrats to a Senate minority—and prompting Heitkamp to eye a run for governor, a job she had sought more than a decade earlier.

Born in Breckenridge Minnesota, Heitkamp (her formal given name is Mary Kathryn) grew up just over the Minnesota state line in Mantador North Dakota. (population 64 in 2010). Her mother was the school cook and custodian, and her father held a series of jobs ranging from truck driver to construction worker. Heitkamp was the fourth of seven children. "Being right in the middle of seven bossy people—does that prepare me for being bipartisan, collaborative, and a compromiser?" she asked rhetorically in a 2014 interview with the *Daily Beast.* "I've been compromising and collaborating all my life."

Heitkamp studied political science at the University of North Dakota and then earned a degree from the Lewis & Clark College Law School in Portland Oregon. She briefly worked for the Environmental Protection Agency as an attorney before moving to the North Dakota State Tax Commissioner's Office. It was there that she met Conrad, then tax commissioner. He became her political mentor, and, when he left to successfully run for Senate in 1986, she subsequently ran for tax commissioner in 1988 "with a push" from him. (She had previously waged an unsuccessful bid for state auditor.) She won the tax commissioner's post with 66 percent of the vote and served until 1992, when she ran for attorney general when that office opened. She captured 62 percent, and was easily reelected four years later. As attorney general, Heitkamp was best known for leading the state's legal efforts against tobacco companies that ultimately led to a national settlement in 1998. She also has cited efforts to revamp the state's juvenile justice system and to improve the anti-domestic violence system as highlights of her tenure.

Heitkamp hoped to parlay those accomplishments into becoming governor in 2000, but lost to Republican John Hoeven—now her senior colleague in the state's Senate delegation—by 55%-45%. Her ability to compete was hindered by a diagnosis of breast cancer in August of the election year. She took a month off the campaign trail to undergo treatment and has been in remission since, but that time away eroded whatever advantage she had in the contest. After that disappointing race, Heitkamp took a job as a director for Dakota Gasification, a company that operates a synthetic fuels plant, and sometimes filled in for her brother, Joel, a former state senator, as host of a radio talk show. When long-time Democratic Sen. Byron Dorgan retired in 2010, opening the seat ultimately won by Hoeven, Heitkamp was urged to run, but declined. "My life, my family and my friends are here in North Dakota. In the final analysis, I simply could not compete for a job that would require me to spend so much time in Washington, away from my family and the people and the place that I love," Heitkamp said in March 2010. Many in the state's political establishment took it as an indication that Heitkamp was eyeing a run for governor in 2012. But she was reportedly urged by Conrad to change her mind and run to succeed him instead, prompting her to announce for Senate in November 2011.

Prior to her announcement, other potential Democratic Senate candidates included former Rep. Earl Pomeroy, who had lost his at-large House seat in 2010 after almost two decades in Congress. Pomeroy had been ousted by Republican Rick Berg, a former majority leader of the North Dakota House. In the view of many observers, Berg's upset of Pomeroy—coupled with Hoeven's election to an open Senate seat the same year—cemented North Dakota's status as a red state. Just months after being sworn in as a freshman member of the House, Berg announced in May 2011 that he would run for Senate.

Given the evolving politics of a state undergoing an oil and gas boom, Berg initially was seen as a strong favorite. But he was hurt by what was viewed by political insiders as a poorly run campaign—and, just as he worked to tie Heitkamp to Obama, she in turn sought to link him to a Congress whose approval ratings were even lower than the president's. Meanwhile, Heitkamp stressed her independence from her party on issues such as energy, including her support for the controversial Keystone XL pipeline, and spending, where she backed a constitutional balanced budget amendment with an exemption for wartime spending, Social Security, and Medicare. Heitkamp walked a fine line on Obama's health care legislation, which was unpopular in the state. In a widely noticed TV ad, she said the law contained "good and bad" and "needs to be fixed," but rebuked her opponent for voting to repeal it. "Rick Berg voted to go back to letting insurance companies deny coverage to kids, or for preexisting conditions," she said. "... I don't ever want to go back to those days." The ad contained a pointed reference to her own health struggles: "I'm Heidi Heitkamp, and 12 years ago I beat breast cancer. When you live through that, political attack ads seem silly."

If Heitkamp, during her years in public office, had developed a reputation for what is known in the state as "North Dakota nice," she did not hesitate to take off the gloves in what became one of the nastiest political contests in state history. Berg was among the wealthiest members of Congress thanks to his real estate holdings, and Heitkamp called attention to his ties to a company that owns and manages rental housing—and which had drawn numerous tenant complaints and been cited for fire safety violations. When Berg contended he had "absolutely no involvement" with the management of the company, her campaign released an ad listing documents it said tied him to the firm, and asking whether he could be trusted on other issues. "Maybe it shouldn't be a surprise that Rick Berg would use his business experience to privatize Social Security," Heitkamp asserted in the ad. "He's voted time and again to risk Social Security funds in the stock market. Rick Berg, treating seniors the same way he treats his tenants." Privately, even some Democratic consultants considered the ad to be something of a stretch, *Politico* reported.

Heitkamp held a lead in the polls during the summer of 2012, and although the race tightened as Election Day approached, she held on to win the closest Senate race in the country that year, 50.23% to 49.33%, or just under 3,000 votes out of nearly 321,000 cast. Berg carried most of the state's central and western counties, including the area around Bismarck, but Heitkamp won the county that includes Fargo along the border with Minnesota, and dominated the eastern side of the state. Heitkamp became the first woman ever elected to the Senate from North Dakota (the widow of long-time Democratic Sen. Quentin Burdick had filled the seat by appointment for three months following his death in 1992).

Once sworn in, Heitkamp continued to distance herself from Obama, telling ABC News in January 2013 that she was concerned that the president was taking his focus off the economy to address issues such as climate change and gun control. "The one thing that has gotten lost by everyone is, one of the best ways that we can perform here is by getting people back to work, making sure that this economic recovery, slow as it is, gets amped up and moves forward," she declared. She joined a bipartisan group of senators seeking quick action on the Keystone pipeline; ultimately, she joined seven other Democrats and all Republicans in an unsuccessful effort in early 2015 to override Obama's veto of a bill allowing the pipeline to go forward. And she won praise early on for her self-deprecating remarks at a Washington dinner sponsored by the media. "You're asking yourself, 'How did this middle-aged, red-headed Democrat win a United States Senate seat in a red state that the president lost by 21 points?'" she said. "To you, I'm like a unicorn …You just wanted to tell your family that you saw me in person, and I am the last of my species."

But not many Democrats were laughing when Heitkamp, after three months on Capitol Hill, joined three other red state Democratic senators in voting to block compromise legislation that would have expanded background checks for gun owners. The measure was brought up in the wake of the December 2012 Newtown Connecticut school shooting in which two dozen were killed by a deranged gunman. Largely due to the Democratic defections, it fell five votes short of the needed 60-vote supermajority to proceed. Writing in *The Washington Post* two days later, an outraged William Daley, Obama's former White House chief of staff, accused Heitkamp of buckling to the gun lobby and said he wanted his $2,500 donation to her campaign returned. "I have had a long career in government and politics, but I don't donate heavily to political campaigns. When I contribute, it's because I know the candidate well or am really impressed with the person. Heidi Heitkamp was one of the latter: She struck me as strong-willed, principled and an independent thinker. But this week, Heitkamp betrayed those hopes," declared Daley, son and brother of former mayors of Chicago—a city wracked by gun violence in recent years.

Heitkamp voted against the measure even though it had been crafted by West Virginia Sen. Joe Manchin, a fellow Democratic moderate from a red state. "I think Joe's worked very hard to forge a compromise, but in the end it's not what any other senator believes. It's about what the people of North Dakota believe," she told *The New York Times*. The bottom line, she added, is that "I'm going to represent my state." She later told *The Daily Beast*, "I made a judgment call that [the proposed law's] main purpose was to put more restrictions on law-abiding gun owners as opposed to really capturing criminals."

On a less controversial issue of importance to her home state constituency, Heitkamp pushed for measures to assist Native Americans; nearly 6.5 percent of the North Dakota population consists of American Indians, according to the 2010 census. She introduced a bill when Congress convened in January 2015—to create a commission on Native American children and explore solutions to the challenges they face. She also teamed with Kansas Republican Jerry Moran to bar the IRS from taxing tribal programs aimed at increasing the health and safety of Native American families. Nationally, as a partisan budget stalemate led to a 16-day government shutdown toward the end of her first year in the Senate, Heitkamp was part of a 14-member bipartisan group of senators organized by Maine moderate Republican Susan Collins; the group's efforts were credited with helping to bring an end to the standoff. Her voting record for 2013 put her squarely in the middle of the Senate: She was tied with another red state centrist, Missouri Democrat Claire McCaskill, as the 49th most liberal senator, according to *National Journal* vote rankings.

Four of Heitkamp's red state Democratic colleagues were defeated for reelection in 2014, prompting a number of the remaining band of moderates—including Heitkamp—to vote against Nevada Sen. Harry Reid continuing as Senate Democratic leader. "The clearest message from the recent election is that Congress needs to change and get to work. We need to show the American people that we hear them by implementing real, tangible changes to help restore trust," Heitkamp said in a statement afterward. A couple of the other moderates who voted against Reid, Manchin and McCaskill, contemplated runs for governor in 2016 but ultimately opted to remain in Washington—much to the relief of Democratic strategists fearful that such departures would complicate Democratic efforts to regain the Senate majority lost in 2014. But Heitkamp again looked toward Bismarck, and her gaze seemed to remain fixed on the governorship through much of 2015, even as she remained publicly mum as to her intentions.

"What I'm doing right now is trying to figure out how I can get things done for North Dakota in the United States Senate," she said during a meeting with the editorial board of the *Fargo Forum* early in 2015. "I am very interested in seeing how this new Congress can and cannot work, and so I am really focused." But Heitkamp did say "the proof is in the past" regarding her desire to be governor, a reference to her failed bid in 2000. She also called the governor's post "the greatest honor that you can have from the people of North Dakota," and noted it was not unusual to move from senator to governor in recent years. In part, Heitkamp's decision appeared to hinge on whether Republican Jack Dalrymple, elevated from lieutenant governor to governor upon Hoeven's election to the Senate, ran for a second full term. In late August, Dalrymple announced that he would not seek reelection. Even before that, North Dakota Republicans were taking no chances: A bill passed by the legislature and signed by Dalrymple changed state law, effective August 2015, so that future Senate vacancies would be filled by special election rather than gubernatorial appointment. It would bar Heitkamp from appointing her successor if she were elected governor, while giving the Republicans a good shot at grabbing her Senate seat.

Regardless, Heitkamp's office announced in July 2015 that the senator would have hip replacement surgery in August, a procedure that would complicate her run for governor. She continued to keep the door open to running in 2016.

REPRESENTATIVE-AT-LARGE

Kevin Cramer (R)

Elected 2012, 2nd term; b. Jan. 21, 1961, Rolette; Concordia Col. (MN), B.A. 1983, U. of Mary, M.S. 2003; Evangelical Christian; married (Kris); 5 children.

Elected Office: ND Public Service Commission, 2003-12.

Professional Career: Dir., Harold Schafer Leadership Foundation, 2001-03; Dir., ND tourism, 1993-97; Chmn., ND Republican Party, 1991-93.

DC Office: 1032 LHOB, 20515, 202-225-2611; Fax: 202-226-0893; Website: cramer.house.gov.

State Offices: Bismark, 701-224-0355; Fargo, 701-356-2216; Grand Forks, 701-738-4880; Minot, 701-839-0255.

Committees: *Energy & Commerce:* Communications & Technology; Environment & the Economy; Oversight & Investigations.

Group Ratings

	ADA	ACLU	AFL-CIO	LCV	ITI	COC	HAFA	ACU	CFG	FRC
2014	0%	0%	–	0%	80%	93%	38%	68%	48%	86%
2013	5%	C	29%	4%	C	77%	C	64%	45%	C

National Journal Ratings

	2013 LIB	—	2013 CONS
Economic	44%	—	55%
Social	34%	—	62%
Foreign	43%	—	57%
Composite	41%	—	59%

Key Votes of the 113th Congress

1. Sandy storm spending	Y	5. Medical Marijuana	NV	9. Syrian Rebels Training	Y
2. Violence Against Women Act	Y	6. Farm Bill	Y	10. Keystone pipeline	Y
3. Guantanamo Bay Detainees	N	7. Afghanistan Combat	N	11. Immigration Exec. Action	Y
4. Abortion 20-week ban	Y	8. NSA Phone Data Collection	Y	12. Bipartisan budget deal	Y

Election Results

2014 general	Kevin Cramer (R)	138,100	(56%)	$1,505,728	$17,215	$100,611
	George B. Sinner (D)	95,678	(39%)	$929,147	$15,285	$39,780
	Jack Seaman (Lib)	14,531	(6%)	$10,845		
2014 primary	Kevin Cramer (R)	unopposed				

Prior winning percentage: 2012 (55%)

Republican Kevin Cramer was elected to the House in 2012 in his fourth attempt to win North Dakota's at-large seat. A former state GOP chairman and a strong conservative, he succeeded Rick Berg, who was narrowly defeated that year when he ran for the Senate. Cramer serves on the Energy and Commerce Committee, where he tends to his home-state's oil and gas interests.

Voter Turnout	
2013 Total Citizen 18+	549,624
2014 House Turnout	248,670
2014 Turnout as % CVAP	45.2%
2012 Turnout as % CVAP	60.2%

Cramer grew up in Kindred, southwest of Fargo. His father, a "fix-it guy" who didn't graduate from high school, was an electricity lineman, and his mother worked multiple jobs, from caring for seniors to pumping gas. Throughout high school, Cramer worked for the same electric cooperative as his father. He attended the Lutheran Church-owned Concordia College in Minnesota, where he became a pre-seminary student majoring in social work. But he soon found another calling. His time there coincided with Ronald Reagan's presidency, and Cramer said he was inspired to get involved in politics by Reagan, whom he described as a "joyful conservative."

After working for an unsuccessful Republican tax commissioner candidate in North Dakota, Cramer was a campaign aide to Sen. Mark Andrews in his failed 1986 reelection bid. He took a job with the state Republican Party, and rose to executive director in 1990. A year later, at age 30, he was the youngest-ever state party chairman. As a self-professed leader of a GOP "youth movement," he was courted by national party bigwigs, including Vice President Dan Quayle. Looking back, Cramer said, he was "naïve enough" to be "quite bold—you might say reckless, even."

Cramer became state tourism director in 1993. From that perch, he first ran for the House seat in 1996, with persuasion from then-House Majority Leader Dick Armey of Texas, a North Dakota native. Cramer lost to Democratic Rep. Earl Pomeroy, 55%-43%. After the loss, Cramer became the state's economic development director. He ran for the House seat a second time in 1998, but again lost to Pomeroy, with 41% of the vote. He now calls that run a political mistake that eventually cost him the state party's endorsement when he ran for the seat again in 2010. That year, in his third try, he dropped out before the GOP primary. From 2003 to 2012, he served on North Dakota's public service commission, helping to oversee an energy-driven boom in the state economy. He also worked for a foundation offering faith-based training for students at the University of Mary, where he received a master's in management.

When Berg vacated the House seat to run for the Senate, Cramer decided to try again, spurning the state party's endorsement in favor of taking his campaign directly to the primary. He edged out party-backed candidate Brian Kalk, a fellow public service commissioner, 55%-45%. That set him up to run against Democrat Pam Gulleson, a former state House member, in the general election. Cramer ran as a strong social conservative, saying on his campaign website, "I hope you know that my public service is an extension of my service to Christ." He calls himself "a strong advocate for the free market system."

Earlier in the year, the Sierra Club and the Dakota Resource Council filed a lawsuit alleging that Cramer and Kalk should be disqualified from regulating coal since both had taken campaign donations from the industry in their House races. Gulleson sought to make an issue of the lawsuit. She was competitive financially, but the state's growing Republican tilt gave the win to Cramer, 55% to 42%.

In the House, Cramer advocated for a host of North Dakota interests. He often said "you're welcome" to President Barack Obama for the huge economic boost from oil and gas drilling in North Dakota, most of which is on private or state land. He urged Obama to open more federal lands to production for additional economic and energy security. He was one of the few congressional Republicans to support Obama on normalizing relations with Cuba. In addition to the opportunity for farm sales, he said that the move was "an opportunity to influence an oppressed country." In April 2015, he joined 70 other House members in a letter to the Obama Administration assuring that lean red beef is classified as part of a healthy diet.

In 2015, Cramer took a seat on Energy and Commerce, which he called a "heavy lift" and "awesome privilege." Historically, the panel often has been friendly with energy interests. Of legislation approved by the committee, he particularly noted proposals designed to protect electricity consumers from higher costs imposed by Environmental Protection Agency regulation of power plants.

Democrats nominated state Sen. George Sinner, the son of former governor George Sinner, to challenge the incumbent in 2014. The challenger complained that Cramer's campaign ads were filled with lies and he proposed "truth in politics" legislation in which the Federal Election Commission would regulate the truthfulness of those ads. Cramer responded that the proposal would violate the free-speech guarantee of the First Amendment. Cramer outspent Sinner $1.5 million to $929,000, and won 56%-39%. He ran well across the state and won all of the urban centers. Sinner took eight rural counties. Cramer may be well-positioned to run for the Senate when opportunity knocks.

★ OHIO ★

Ohio was the first entirely American state. The original 13 started as British colonies, and the next three—Vermont, Kentucky, and Tennessee—were spun off from them. But Ohio sprang Athena-like from the head of Congress, as the first state formed from the Northwest Territory. The Northwest Ordinance of 1787 established 6-mile-square townships, which imposed geometric order on diverse new American landscapes to the west. It set aside one square mile per township for public schools, and the land was soon peppered with schoolhouses and small colleges, the foundation stones of a literate republic. The ordinance prohibited slavery at a time when most northern states still had it, opening the way for free labor to clear fields, raise crops, and build mills and factories. In less than half a century, the former wilderness wrested from Indian and British control only in 1796 was one of the most productive parts of the young republic. In the years after the Civil War, Ohio became one of the great industrial states, the original headquarters of John D. Rockefeller's Standard Oil, the site of major steel mills along the narrow Cuyahoga and Mahoning rivers, and the location of the biggest soap companies, machine tool makers, and tire manufacturers. Dayton was the home of the Wright brothers, who developed the airplane; Akron was the home of Harvey Firestone, B. F. Goodrich and F. A. Seiberling—the great tire manufacturers. Cincinnati was and is the headquarters of Procter & Gamble.

Ohio was settled by New Englanders in the northeast (in the Western Reserve) and by Virginians in the south, creating a split between the Southern-accented counties south of the National Road and U.S. 40 and the Yankee-accented cities and towns to the north. In the middle were the Amish, who moved west from Pennsylvania, and in 2013, Ohio was home to more than 65,000 Amish in 485 congregations, the most in the country. They form a near majority in Holmes County, where their horse-drawn buggies are a common sight. The state was also similarly split between Butternut and Copperhead territory that didn't want to fight the Civil War and Yankee territory that fiercely prosecuted the war. This split heritage made Ohio politically a closely divided state—and a nationally pivotal one. Ohio produced the winning candidate for president in 1896 and 1900, William McKinley, who inaugurated a 34-year period of mostly Republican national majorities. McKinley's Republicans were for high tariffs and hard money and had a friendly regard for workers and even some unions, but they had no patience with large unions. They preached a nationalist Americanism tempered by wariness about making major commitments abroad. Republicans were the majority in this increasingly industrial Ohio, losing rural Butternut counties but carrying the big industrial cities of the north.

Then came the Depression of the 1930s, and Ohio became the scene of class warfare, with sit-down strikes and victories for the CIO industrial unions in autos, steel, and tires. CIO cities—Cleveland, Akron, Youngstown, and Toledo—moved sharply toward the Democrats, while places with fewer union members, such as Cincinnati and Columbus, stayed Republican. The political fighting was fierce, and the stakes were high. CIO leaders hoped to organize the entire workforce, but Republican leaders like Ohio's Sen. Robert Taft feared union control of business would imperil freedoms and throttle the economy. In the 1930s and 1940s, the unions made great gains, but Taft held them off, reducing union power with the Taft-Hartley Act of 1947 and his own reelection after hotly contested campaigns in 1944 and 1950. Ohio thrived in the industrial economy after World War II, with new auto and auto-parts plants going up and its population rising. In those years it was often said that Ohio was a great test market, close to the national average in income levels, urban-rural balance, and ethnic mix, as well as partisan proclivities. The typical American voter, wrote Richard Scammon and Ben Wattenberg in 1970, was a Dayton housewife whose brother-in-law was a machinist and who was hoping one of her children might go to college. But Ohio is not so typical today. It remains industrial in an increasingly post-industrial country. The number of manufacturing jobs plummeted in the last two decades. Between 1970 and 2010, Ohio's population grew by only 8%, a lower rate than any other state except New York, West Virginia, Pennsylvania, and Iowa. The state's demographics are increasingly atypical. Blacks make up 12% of the population, a reflection of the great northward migration of 1940-65, but Hispanics make up only 3%, as Ohio largely missed out on the Hispanic wave of 1982-2007. Cultural liberalism has a far smaller constituency in Ohio than it does on either coast or even in nearby Illinois and Michigan; except around Columbus, affluent suburbanites

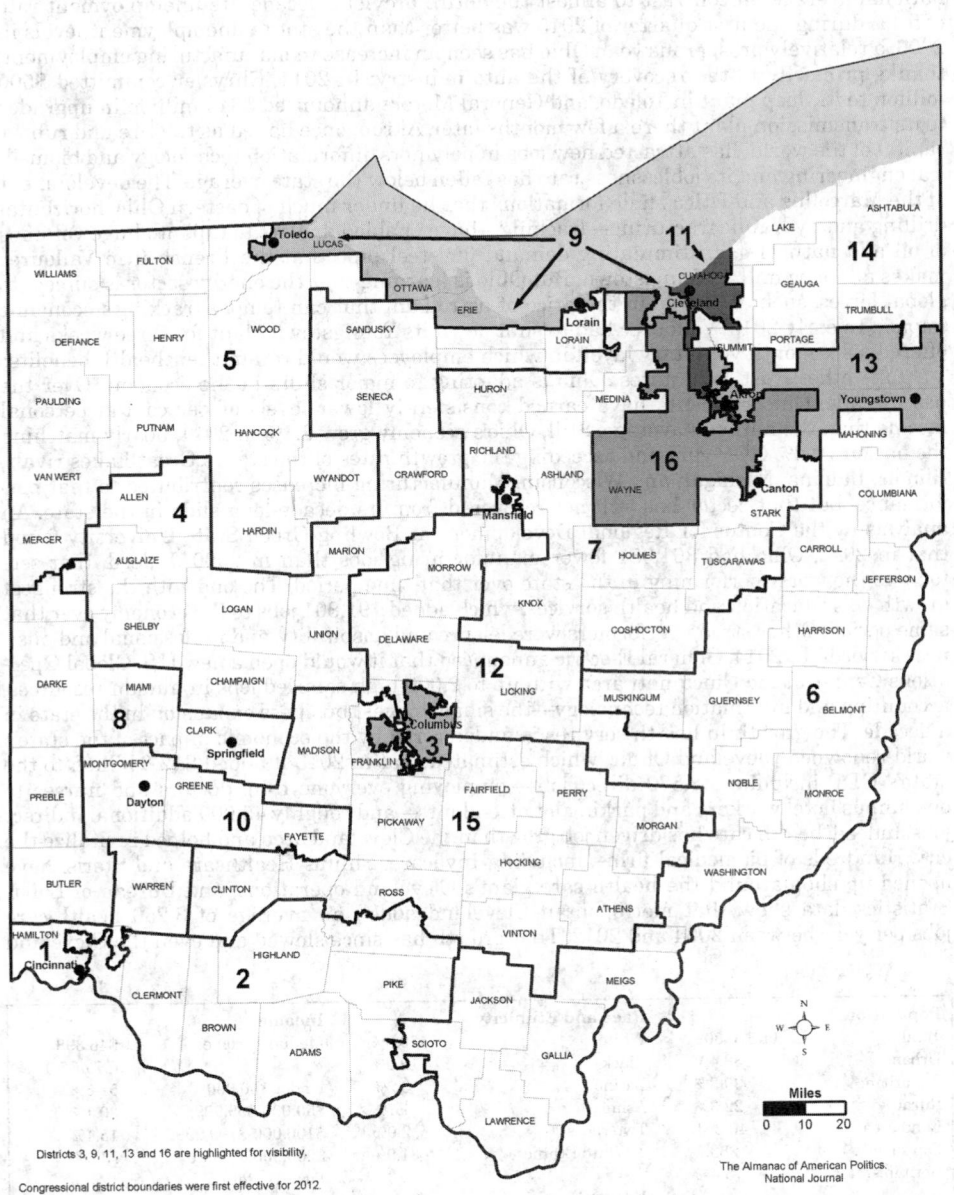

Districts 3, 9, 11, 13 and 16 are highlighted for visibility.

Congressional district boundaries were first effective for 2012.

haven't been trending Democratic in large numbers. At the same time, Ohio's white blue-collar workers have remained more Democratic than in most other states, except for those in rural counties along the Ohio River facing West Virginia and Kentucky.

Change has come to Ohio again. The state's unemployment peaked at 11% at the start of 2010, but that rate has since steadily fallen and in 2014, its overall level was below the national average, in contrast to almost the entire previous decade. Its unemployment rate of 5.1% during the first quarter of 2015 was better than the state's unemployment levels in 2006, a relatively prosperous year. Ohio has seen an increase in manufacturing employment, thanks primarily to the recovery of the auto industry: In 2011, Chrysler committed $500 million to its Jeep plant in Toledo, and General Motors announced $343 million in upgrades to its transmission plant there a few months later. Akron, once hailed as the tire and rubber capital of the world, has attracted new jobs in polymers, information technology and biomedical engineering and its joblessness rate has fallen below the state average. The development of the Marcellus and Utica shale formations that lie under much of eastern Ohio, horizontal drilling and hydraulic fracturing—fracking—have enabled drillers to tap into huge volumes of oil and natural gas, stimulating demand for steel pipe that the French firm Vallourec makes at a new mill in Youngstown. But Ohio is learning that the energy sector is subject to global forces, such as a drop in the price of petroleum that can temper fracking's economic impact. In early 2015, Vallourec had to shut down its Youngstown plant for three weeks and offered a six-month voluntary layoff in which employees would retain their health benefits.

Like other Rust Belt states, Ohio is adapting to major shifts in the economy. Over the past decade, Ohio residents have earned consistently lower levels of per capital personal income than the national average. Still, Ohio's economy grew 2.1% in 2014, nearly matching the nation's 2.2% GDP gain and exceeding the growth rates of the state's Great Lakes rivals, Illinois, Indiana, Michigan and Wisconsin. Manufacturing increases contributed to that performance, but that sector has still not recovered from its decade-long slide in the state. An analysis by the Center for Regional Development at Bowling Green State University found that in 2013, Ohio had 361,081 fewer manufacturing jobs than in 2000. Indeed, that sector was the worst performing in the state over that time period. The one with the strongest growth was education and health services, which added 191,801 jobs to the economy over that same period. Other strong performers were leisure and hospitality, and professional and business services. In 2014, General Electric announced that it would open a new U.S. Global Operations Center in the Cincinnati area with up to 2,000 high salaried jobs in human resources, accounting and information technology—the single biggest business expansion in the state in a decade. The growth in health services is underscored by the economic impact of the state's world-renowned Cleveland Clinic, which estimated that in 2013 it added $12.6 billion to the state's GDP including 48,570 direct jobs—employing everyone from doctors and nurses to on-campus hotel workers and parking lot attendants—and roughly 45,000 additional indirect jobs. Indeed, health care has driven job growth in the Cleveland area and helped revitalize the city. Hundreds of biomedical firms, including Invacare, Philips Healthcare and Steris, have opened up shop around the health care giant's Cleveland operations, and Bureau of Labor Statistics data show that metropolitan Cleveland added an average of 3,250 health-care jobs per year between 2004 and 2012. That growth has since slowed and even the Cleveland

Population		Race and Ethnicity		Income	
Total:	11,570,808	White	80.9%	Median income:	$46,398
Urban:	38.4%	Black	12.0%		(37 of 50)
Suburban:	39.3%	Latino	3.2%	Under $50,000	51.6%
Rural:	22.3%	Asian	1.7%	$50,000-$99,999:	30.1%
Land area:	40,861	Two races	2.0%	$100,000-$199,999:	15.1%
Pop/sq. mi.:	283.2	White Ethnic	31.9%	$200,000 or more:	3.3%
Born in state:	75.4%			Poverty Rate	12.3%
		Education			
Age Groups		H.S. grad or less:	45.2%	**Work**	
Under 18:	22.9%	Some college:	28.7%	White collar:	34.9%
18 to 34:	22.2%	College degree, 4 yr.:	16.4%	Blue collar:	41.6%
35 to 64:	39.8%	Post-grad study:	9.7%	Sales and service:	23.5%
Over 64:	15.1%				
		Military		Govt. workers:	12.4%
		Veterans/active duty:	8.7%		

Clinic was not immune to the transitions in health care, undergoing budget cuts and offering employee buyouts in 2014, as it adapted to changes brought on at least in part by the Affordable Care Act.

Voter Turnout	
2013 Total Citizen 18+	8,705,986
2014 Highest Statewide Turnout	3,055,913
2014 Turnout as % CVAP	35.1%
2012 Turnout as % CVAP	64.2%
Legislature	
Senate:	23R 10D
House:	65R 34D

Cleveland still has its challenges. In 2015, it signed a consent decree with the Department of Justice to impose new standards and monitoring on the use of force by the city's police department. This followed two separate incidents in which officers gunned down an unarmed couple in a car chase and a child at a park. But the city once dubbed the "mistake by the lake" as a symbol of 1960's and '70's urban decline is turning things around. In 2013, after some delay, Cleveland opened its renovated downtown convention center and adjacent Global Center for Health Innovation, designed to attract health-related trade shows, meetings and conferences. In 2014, about one-third of the convention events were health related and the next-door office complex, known as the "Globe," has occupants like the Cleveland Clinic, GE Healthcare, Hyland Software, Johnson Controls and the Healthcare Information and Management Systems Society. That year Cleveland also saw the return of prodigal son and professional basketball superstar LeBron James, which not only helped boost the spirits of many of the city's long-suffering sports fans, it also may have given a shot to the downtown economy. As the website *Quartz* noted, the return of "King James" (whose hometown is Akron) to play for the Cleveland Cavaliers was not transformative, but it probably provided some stimulus. Nearby bars and restaurants saw their receipts rise as much as 200 percent on game nights. From April 2014 to April 2015, employment in Cleveland's leisure and hospitality sector jumped nearly 10 percent. That's not all due to James, but the job growth in that sector was four times what it was in Columbus and Cincinnati during that same period. And while Cuyahoga County continued to lose population in the latest decade—down an estimated 20,294 residents from 2010 to 2014, second nationally only to Wayne County (Detroit), where the population plunged by 55,780—downtown Cleveland is literally blossoming. In 2014, residential occupancy rates downtown exceeded 98 percent, and many of the people who were moving into those apartments and condos were college-educated millennials, the lifeblood of urban revival. A study by Cleveland State University researchers found that from 2006 to 2013, the number of college-educated city residents between the age of 25 and 34 had doubled compared to just a 30% increase for the Cuyahoga County suburbs. During that time, the percentage of young adults with a bachelor's degree or higher in Cleveland jumped from 15% to 26%. And landscape architect James Corner, who designed Manhattan's celebrated High Line, has been commissioned to turn Cleveland's asphalt and traffic-snarled Public Square into a lush urban park scheduled to open in the summer of 2016, when Cleveland will host the Republican National Convention, the first major party gathering in the city since the GOP nominated Alf Landon there in 1936.

Post New Deal, there have been two politically distinct parts of Ohio. Northeast Ohio—centered on Cleveland and extending west to Toledo and south and east to the factory towns of Akron and Canton, Youngstown, and Warren—has been the state's Democratic heartland, with the highest percentages of union members and African-Americans. The other part of Ohio—south and west of the industrial belt and including Columbus, Cincinnati, and Dayton—was never as heavily unionized and in national elections has tended to vote Republican, much like most of Indiana, although not always by wide margins. There have been some changes in these patterns in recent years. Metro Columbus has trended Democratic and provided key votes for Barack Obama in 2008 and 2012. At the same time, the hill country along the Ohio River—coal country and now shale oil country—has trended Republican, while northwest Ohio, with its auto and auto-parts plants, swung marginally toward Obama in both elections. The result is a state that has not voted for a presidential loser since 1960, and is likely to remain a major battleground for the two parties for some time.

Presidential Politics Almost from its beginnings, Ohio has been crucial in presidential politics. That's one reason so many natives of this large and politically competitive state found their way onto national tickets between the Civil War and World War II, and why presidential candidates in recent times have found their way so many times to Ohio. It has almost always been more Republican, but usually just slightly more Republican, than the nation as a whole. No Republican has ever been elected president without carrying Ohio. No Democrat, given recent electoral vote arithmetic, can be sure of winning without it.

In 2004, both George W. Bush and John Kerry recognized Ohio's importance. The Kerry campaign ran a spectacularly successful registration and turnout drive aimed at black neighborhoods in central cities and at university communities. The Democratic popular vote margin increased by 60,000 votes in Cleveland's Cuyahoga County, and was up in the counties containing Columbus,

2012 Presidential Vote		
Barack Obama (D) 2,827,710		(51%)
Mitt Romney (R)..............2,661,433		(48%)
2012 Presidential Primary		
Mitt Romney (R).................460,831		(38%)
Rick Santorum (R) 448,580		(37%)
Newt Gingrich (R).............177,183		(15%)
Ron Paul (R) 113,256		(9%)
2008 Presidential Vote		
Barack Obama (D) 2,940,044		(52%)
John McCain (R)..............2,677,820		(47%)

Cincinnati, Akron, Toledo, Lorain, Youngstown, and Warren. But the Bush campaign ran a registration and turnout organization in all 88 counties, which produced a margin of 119,000 votes (51%-49%) over Kerry. Turnout in the state's rural areas was strong, helped along by a ballot initiative to prohibit gay marriage in the state.

In 2008, Republicans hoped that Barack Obama would be a weak candidate in a state where he had lost the Democratic primary to Hillary Clinton. John McCain introduced Sarah Palin as his vice presidential nominee in Dayton, and there were intensive organizational efforts by both campaigns. Turnout, up 20% in 2004 despite low population growth, rose only 4% more in 2008. Obama carried the state 52%-47%, a slightly larger margin than either of Bush's. Young voters went 61% for Obama, providing about two-thirds of his popular vote margin.

By 2012, turnout fell 2% compared to 2008 and 1% fewer Ohioans voted in 2012 than in 2004. The Obama campaign emphasized his support for the Chrysler and General Motors bailouts and hit Mitt Romney for his *New York Times* opinion article headlined, "Let Detroit go bankrupt," in which Romney proposed a managed bankruptcy that included some steps that the Obama administration ultimately took. The evidence from the election results and exit polls is mixed. Obama's statewide margins hardly varied—51%-47% in 2008, 51%-48% in 2012. Romney received 16,000 fewer votes than John McCain had, but Obama received 112,000 fewer votes than in 2008. The 2008 and 2012 exit polls showed Obama losing ground primarily among men age 45 to 64, college graduates, and people earning $50,000 to $100,000. In heavily auto-dependent northwest Ohio, Obama lost ground from 2008, but ran well ahead of Kerry's showing in 2004. But Obama lost much ground in the coal and shale-oil counties of southeastern Ohio compared to both elections. Numerically both shifts seem small next to Obama's gains in the Columbus media market. Columbus, with its post-industrial economy, has been growing much more than the rest of Ohio, and affluent voters there seem to have been attracted to Obama. Metro Columbus voted 52%-48% for Bush in 2004 and 53%-45% for Obama in 2012.

In 1996, Ohio switched its presidential primary from May to March and voted on the same day as Illinois, Michigan, and Wisconsin. But even then, just four weeks after New Hampshire, the race was already over. For the 2000 election, the state legislature moved the date to March 7, and Ohio was seriously contested. Bush and Gore won overwhelming victories as they clinched their parties' nominations. In 2004, Ohio held its primary on March 2, with seven other states; Kerry won easily here and elsewhere, and clinched the Democratic nomination nine months before the general election.

In 2008, the Republican contest was effectively over when Ohio voted on March 4. Mike Huckabee remained an active candidate, but McCain beat him 60%-31%, carrying all 88 counties. There was a spirited contest on the Democratic side. Fresh from a series of stunning victories in February, Obama hoped to end Clinton's candidacy by beating her in Ohio and Texas. But, casting herself as a fighter for working families, Clinton rallied and won an impressive 53%-45% victory in Ohio, which, with a narrower win in Texas, kept her in the race for three more months. Obama carried only five counties, including the cities of Cleveland, Columbus, Cincinnati, and Dayton, and he won only five of 18 congressional districts. He was particularly weak in white working-class areas—the west side of Cleveland and its close-in suburbs, the Mahoning Valley steel country around Youngstown and Warren, and the Democratic-leaning small industrial counties along the Ohio River. Clinton got as much as 80% of the vote in some counties, evidence of Obama's weakness in Appalachia.

In 2012, the March 7 GOP primary was a pivotal contest between Romney and Rick Santorum. Although 10 states held a contest on that Super Tuesday, after narrowly defeating

Santorum in the Michigan primary a week earlier, Ohio was an opportunity for Romney to demonstrate his appeal in larger states that would be crucial to carry in the general election. For Santorum, it was a chance to prove that outside of Romney's native Michigan, he had the ability to appeal to blue-collar workers that could play a critical role in the fall. Romney won narrowly, 38%-37%; Newt Gingrich finished third with 15% and Rand Paul took 9%. Romney carried Cleveland and the rest of northeast Ohio, Franklin (Columbus) and Delaware (suburban-exurban Columbus) counties, and the southwest corner of the state (Cincinnati-Dayton). Santorum carried the rest of the state, but without a major metro, fell short. The victory set Romney on an uninterrupted path to the GOP nomination.

Congressional Districts Ohio lost one House seat in the reapportionment following the 2000 census and two seats after the 2010 census, reducing the delegation to 16 members, the fewest since Ohio was frontier country in the 1820s. In 2001, Republicans kept most of the districts relatively intact. Over

114th Congress Lineup	
12 R	4 D
113th Congress Lineup	
12 R	4 D

the next 10 years, the map remained somewhat competitive: Democrats won a 10-8 majority in 2008 and Republicans a 13-5 majority in 2010.

In 2011, Republicans became victims of their own 2010 success. Faced with the loss of two seats overall, they had only conventional Democrats left to target in their seemingly secure bases: Marcy Kaptur in Toledo, Dennis Kucinich and Marcia Fudge in Cleveland, Betty Sutton near Akron, and Tim Ryan near Youngstown. All five seats were badly underpopulated, but Fudge's black-majority district was sacrosanct. Eliminating any two others meant displacing thousands of Democratic voters in the northeast. Furthermore, for decades, Republicans had cracked Columbus into multiple districts to shortchange Democrats. But the state capital was growing and attracting progressive-minded voters at such a rate that neither the Republican-held 12th nor 15th might hold until 2020.

So for three months, Republican legislative aides bunkered in a clandestine Columbus hotel room. Under the watchful guidance of House Speaker John Boehner of Ohio, they hatched an innovative scheme. Republicans would pack Democrats into a new Columbus 3rd District, merge Kaptur and Kucinich in a skinny 9th District stretching 100 miles along Lake Erie, and throw Sutton into a nearby 16th District favoring freshman Republican Jim Renacci. They would also sacrifice by merging two of their own, Dayton area Republicans Mike Turner and Steve Austria. But the creation of a Columbus Democratic vote sink would produce a beneficial ripple effect, allowing Republicans to shore up their freshmen and keep a 12-4 advantage.

The legislature and Gov. John Kasich easily approved the plan. But in Ohio, all non-spending bills that pass with less than two-thirds support are subject to a veto referendum in the next election if opponents collect sufficient signatures on petitions. Under siege, Republicans plotted minor changes designed to appease enough Democrats to attain two-thirds in the state House. As Democrats realized that collecting the 230,000 required signatures didn't arouse their base like collective bargaining had, a few became more inclined to deal. On the revised map, 21 Democrats caved and voted with Republicans.

The second draft catered to urban legislators by uniting more of Toledo and Dayton—changes that benefited Kaptur and Turner in their pairings with neighboring incumbents. Kucinich appealed to his left-leaning national fundraising network, but was steamrolled by Kaptur's loyal Toledo base. Austria, a low-key sophomore, retired. Boehner was on a roll at home. Republicans got the 12-4 delegation they envisioned in a state that Barack Obama twice won. In addition, voters defeated by 63%-37% a seemingly benign ballot initiative to transfer future redistricting authority to an independent citizens' commission.

Proposed reforms of Ohio's redistricting procedures took on new life after the 2014 election. Spurred by Republican Secretary of State Jon Husted, who had earlier served as the state's Speaker of the House, a bipartisan coalition voted for a compromise plan that transferred redistricting authority from a handful of statewide elected officials to a broader group that would require support from both parties. But the plan, which was subject to voter approval in a November 2015 statewide referendum, has limitations. If a plan did not receive minority-party support, it would still take effect—but for only four years, instead of 10. At Boehner's urging, the new procedures would not apply to the state's congressional map, at least initially. In short, the revisions had become a work in progress. Whatever the procedures, House Republicans appear to have maxed out. They likely will pay the price after the 2020 census, when the state is expected to lose another seat.

Governor

John Kasich (R)

Elected 2010, term expires Jan. 2019, 2nd term; b. May 13, 1952, McKees Rocks, PA; OH St. U., B.A. 1974; Christian; married (Karen Waldbillig Kasich); 2 children.

Elected Office: OH Senate, 1978-82; U.S. House, 1983-2001.

Professional Career: Admin. asst., OH Sen. Donald Lukens, 1975-77; Managing dir., investment banking div. of Lehman Brothers/Barclays Capital, 2001-08; Commentator, FOX News/Heartland with John Kasich, 2001-09; Presidential fellow, OH St. U. 2002-09.

Office: Riffe Center, 30th Fl., 77 S. High St., Columbus, 43215-6117, 614-466-3555; Website: governor.ohio.gov.

Election Results

2014 general	John Kasich (R)	1,944,848	(64%)
	Ed FitzGerald (D)	1,009,359	(33%)
	Anita Rios (G)	101,706	(3%)
2014 primary	John Kasich (R)	unopposed	

Prior winning percentages: 2010 (49%); House: 1998 (67%), 1996 (64%), 1994 (66%), 1992 (72%), 1990 (72%), 1988 (80%), 1986 (73%), 1984 (70%), 1982 (50%)

"I'm a normal guy that has a big job," says Republican Gov. John Kasich, who was first elected as Ohio's chief executive in 2010. It's a line that Kasich often uses, displaying a sense of self-awareness unusual for politicians. But it's a trait that has served him well, helping him win nine terms in the House of Representatives where he rose to become chairman of the Budget Committee, a position that put him at the center of his party's budget-balancing confrontations with President Bill Clinton in the 1990s. He was back in the thick of controversy on fiscal matters when, as governor, he called for drastic reductions in the size and cost of state government, but demonstrated sharp political skills that got him reelected in 2014.

Kasich has spent much of his adult life in politics. He grew up the son of a mail carrier in working-class McKees Rocks Pennsylvania and is of Hungarian, Czech, and Croatian ancestry. After graduating from Ohio State University with a bachelor's in political science, he worked for a state legislator. In 1978, at age 26, Kasich ran a strenuous door-to-door campaign and beat a Democratic state senator, becoming the youngest person ever elected to that chamber. He ran for the House four years later and, with the help of a favorable redistricting plan, ousted Democrat Bob Shamansky. As a brash new member of Congress, Kasich caused his first commotion on the Armed Services Committee, where he was the leading Republican opponent of the B-2 bomber and teamed with California Democrat Ron Dellums in drastically reducing its production. Although he was raised a Catholic, after a drunk driver killed his parents in 1987, he turned to evangelical Christianity.

Kasich got a seat on the Budget Committee in 1989 and won the ranking Republican spot four years later with the help of Rep. Newt Gingrich of Georgia, then an ascendant figure in the GOP. In that Democratic Congress, Kasich led the Republicans' charge to "cut spending first," which laid the groundwork for the defeat of Clinton's 1993 economic stimulus legislation. He advanced a budget alternative with no tax increases or Social Security cuts, but it did contain means-testing and serious cuts in discretionary spending. In 1994, he and Democrat Tim Penny of Minnesota put together spending cut bills that the House narrowly defeated. He offended some conservatives by supporting Clinton's assault weapons ban and the 1994 crime bill. The serious and detailed work Kasich did on the budget was an indispensable ingredient in his successes in 1995 and 1996 after Republicans regained control of Congress. Kasich and House Republicans pushed to curb discretionary spending, and their persistence helped lead to the Balanced Budget Act of 1997, a sweeping deal that combined tax cuts with reductions in Medicare and Medicaid payments to health care providers and added money for higher education assistance and the creation of the State Children's Health Insurance Program for kids living in poverty. Kasich remained popular in his Columbus-area district, winning reelection eight times.

He turned down chances to run for statewide office, but in 1999, after writing a book, *Courage Is Contagious,* profiling Americans who have sought to improve their communities, Kasich formed a presidential exploratory committee. "A mailman's kid can change the world," he said ebulliently as he issued an anti-establishment call to return power to the people. But he faced huge obstacles, including fundraising and his often-undisciplined personality. He abandoned his bid by July of that year. In addition to working at financial giant Lehman Brothers he dabbled in television, hosting a Fox News talk show, *From the Heartland with John Kasich,* until 2007.

After leaving the House in 2001, Ohio's dire economic situation during the Great Recession helped lure Kasich back into politics. In June 2009, he announced his challenge to Democratic Gov. Ted Strickland, who just a year earlier had been popular enough to be considered as a potential running mate for Barack Obama. "We have to face facts. We've drifted in Ohio, and it just hasn't been one political party," Kasich said. He cited the need to balance the state budget as well as cut bureaucracy that he said was hampering business growth, and he jumped to an early lead in the polls. Strickland fought back vigorously. With the help of Bill Clinton, during the spring of 2010 he out-raised not only Kasich, but also every other Democratic governor facing reelection. The governor and his allies attacked Kasich's congressional voting record; especially his support of free trade agreements that they said had cost the state jobs. They also highlighted his tenure as a managing director at Lehman Brothers, which had gone bankrupt. News articles described a wealthy lifestyle at odds with Kasich's regular-guy portrayal of himself—his 4,400-square-foot home in suburban Columbus and 2008 tax returns showing an income of $1.4 million, including almost $600,000 from Lehman. Kasich rebutted such arguments by saying they were evidence of his "hard work." But his lead in the polls shrank by October. In the end, though, he was able to pull out a 49%-47% victory. Strickland took Cuyahoga County, which includes Cleveland, 61%-36%, and Franklin County, which includes Columbus, 53%-44%, along with most of the blue-collar counties in southeastern Ohio that he had earlier represented as a House member. But Kasich prevailed in Hamilton County, which includes Cincinnati, 50%-47%, and dominated the rest of the state.

As governor, Kasich immediately made clear his willingness to break with the previous administration. He rejected a passenger rail line through the state that Strickland had pushed, calling it a waste of taxpayer money. He joined other new GOP governors in seeking to curtail the influence of public employee unions, calling for a ban on strikes by teachers and embracing a limit on collective bargaining. And he drew opposition to his proposed $55.5 billion budget, which called for sharing services among agencies, pooling health care costs, and reducing prevailing-wage requirements on public construction contracts. It also called for a 25% reduction in local government funding. Rather than go on the defensive, an upbeat Kasich sought to sell his approach to closing an $8 billion budget gap as being done "with no smoke and mirrors" and promoting growth over the long term. He got his budget passed in June with few major changes, and the national media began recognizing him as a successful example of the new crop of young GOP state chief executives. But at home his job approval rating sank. Polls also showed strong public opposition to his move to limit collective bargaining with public-sector unions, including police and firefighters, as a way to cut costs, a controversial idea popular with other GOP governors. Kasich and fellow Republicans offered to meet with unions to discuss a compromise to avoid putting the issue on the ballot as a referendum that November, but the unions rebuffed him, firmly opposed to the concept. Voters subsequently didn't just vote down Kasich's collective-bargaining law; they rejected it overwhelmingly, 62% to 38%. Kasich seized the moment and with a touch of humility he didn't often display, told reporters after the defeat, "I respect what the people have to say in an effort like this. And as a result of that, it requires me to take a deep breath and to spend some time to reflect on what happened here."

Kasich tried a new budgetary tack in 2012, calling for a higher tax on oil and gas companies that extract from wells using the controversial method of hydraulic fracturing. Most of the tax revenue would fund an across-the-board income tax reduction. State GOP lawmakers, however, balked at the idea. Kasich departed from his fiscally conservative ways in 2013 by embracing Medicaid expansion over the opposition of the Republican legislature. The state's improving economy corresponded with a rise in his job approval rating, but surveys also indicated that a successful reelection bid was far from assured. Kasich responded by taking some popular steps. He created JobsOhio, a private non-profit economic development entity to be funded with state liquor proceeds, and he signed a bipartisan law that reformed criminal sentencing laws to ease prison overcrowding. In 2014, he helped craft a compromise on state mandates on utility companies that froze, rather than eliminated, the requirements that they use renewable sources to generate a portion of their energy.

Democrats were initially hopeful for their nominee, Cuyahoga County Executive Ed FitzGerald, a former FBI agent. But FitzGerald stumbled through a series of embarrassing disclosures, including that he had not had a valid license in a decade and a police report from 2012 that said he had been in a car at 4:30 a.m. with a woman who was not his wife. Several senior staffers left his campaign and he struggled raising funds. Kasich ignored his Democratic opponent, didn't debate him—the first time since 1978 there wasn't at least one gubernatorial debate in Ohio—and was able to campaign as a recovery Republican who had guided his state's economic turnaround. He won a sweeping reelection victory with 64% of the vote, capturing majorities in normally Democratic Cuyahoga and Franklin counties. He lost only two of the state's 88 counties, both rural ones along the Ohio River. Kasich won among men, women, every age cohort, high school graduates and post-graduate degree holders, and captured two-thirds of self-described independents and one-quarter of the black vote. He even won a majority of union household members who had so fiercely fought his labor reform initiative just two years earlier.

In 2015, Kasich signed a budget bill that continued his Medicaid expansion, cut the state's top personal income tax rate to just below 5 percent, provided tax relief to small businesses, raised cigarette taxes 35 cents a pack and boosted state aid to K-12 education by $955 million over two years. He failed to win approval for his proposed tax increase on oil-and-gas drillers and he had initially sought a $1-a-pack hike in cigarette taxes along with a broader reduction in income taxes. He made good use of his line-item veto, cutting more than 40 provisions in the budget, including several specific benefits lawmakers had sought for business and industry, including power plants, big box retailers and nursing homes. The bill also included new restrictions on abortion clinics. Also tucked into the spending measure was a provision allowing many Cleveland bars to remain open until 4 a.m. when the city hosts the 2016 Republican National Convention. At a signing ceremony, Kasich said the budget delivers more money to people in need without endangering Ohio's finances. "Here in this state, we're minding the store," Kasich said. "We've got our eyes firmly fixed on the horizon. We know that we can be better and stronger."

Kasich's own horizon extends to Washington and the White House, but his quest for the 2016 GOP presidential nomination seemed likely to be an uphill battle. Four-plus years in Columbus have helped shape him into a more disciplined politician. But he remains a font of ideas, and interviewing Kasich can sometimes feel like taking a drink from a fire hose. His sincere and sunny demeanor is appealing, especially for Republicans who believe that their party needs to soften its image and display more tolerance. Prevailing in a crowded and talented field of GOP candidates, would show that "a mailman's kid can change the world," or at least the political world.

Senior Senator

Sherrod Brown (D)

Elected 2006, term expires Jan. 2019, 2nd term; b. Nov. 9, 1952, Mansfield; Yale U., B.A. 1974, OH St. U., M.A. 1979, M.A. 1981; Lutheran; married (Connie Schultz); 4 children.

Elected Office: OH House, 1974-82; OH secy. of st., 1982-90; U.S. House, 1993-2007.

Professional Career: Prof., OH St. U. Mansfield, 1979, 1981, 1991.

DC Office: 713 HSOB, 20510, 202-224-2315; Fax: 202-228-6321; Website: brown.senate.gov.

State Offices: Cincinnati, 513-684-1021; Cleveland, 216-522-7272; Columbus, 614-469-2083; Lorain, 440-242-4100.

Committees: *Agriculture, Nutrition & Forestry:* Commodities, Risk Markets, & Trade; Rural Development & Energy; Nutrition, Specialty Crops & Agricultural Research. *Banking, Housing & Urban Affairs* (RMM). *Finance:* Health Care; Social Security, Pensions & Family Policy (RMM). *Veterans' Affairs.*

Group Ratings

	ADA	ACLU	AFL-CIO	LCV	ITI	COC	HAFA	ACU	CFG	FRC
2014	95%	100%	–	80%	100%	13%	5%	4%	9%	0%
2013	95%	C	100%	100%	C	50%	C	4%	2%	C%

National Journal Ratings

	2013 LIB	—	2013 CONS
Economic	75%	—	19%
Social	73%	—	0%
Foreign	71%	—	0%
Composite	83%	—	17%

Key Votes of the 113th Congress

1. Sandy storm spending	Y	5. Student Loan Rates	N	9. Bipartisan Budget Deal	Y
2. Chuck Hagel Confirmation	Y	6. Employee Non-Discrim'n Act	Y	10. Farm Bill Conference Rept.	Y
3. Gun Background Checks	Y	7. Senate Vote on Judgeships	N	11. Unempl. Comp. Extension	Y
4. Immigration Reform	Y	8. Defense Dept. Spending	Y	12. Keystone Pipeline	N

Election Results

2012 general	Sherrod Brown (D)	2,762,690	(51%)	$24,576,288	$3,447,764	$16,227,889
	Josh Mandel (R)	2,534,712	(45%)	$18,868,809	$7,226,232	$11,782,303
	Scott Rupert (I)	250,616	(5%)	$6,337)		
2012 primary	Sherrod Brown (D)	unopposed				

Prior winning percentages: 2006 (56%); House: 2004 (67%), 2002 (69%), 2000 (65%), 1998 (62%), 1996 (60%), 1994 (49%), 1992 (53%)

He may lack the national profile of such like-minded colleagues as Massachusetts' Elizabeth Warren and Vermont's Bernie Sanders, but Sherrod Brown—Ohio's senior senator—has emerged as an outspoken and influential member of the Democrats' liberal populist wing. At the beginning of 2015, Brown became the ranking Democrat on the Banking Committee, where he has fought to limit the size of the nation's largest banks. If his party regains the Senate majority in the 2016 election, Brown would be in line to chair the panel, a prospect that unnerves officials of major financial institutions. Meanwhile, amid the protracted and ultimately unsuccessful effort by progressive groups to draft Warren to run for president in 2016, questions were asked about why these same groups had not urged Brown to do so. "If Ohio's senior senator were named Sharon Brown instead of Sherrod Brown, progressives would have a plausible political pin-up and a serious alternative to the tawdry boredom of Hillary Clinton's joyless plod toward her party's presidential nomination," columnist George Will opined in August 2014, suggesting the Democrats' determination to nominate a woman for president was a major impediment to a draft-Brown effort.

For his part, Brown, who has spent all but a couple of the last 40 years in elective office, insists he has "zero interest" in trying to move up further. "I don't think you can do your job well in the Senate if you're looking over your shoulder wanting to be president," he told *The Washington Post* in early 2015. The Senate seat he has occupied since his 2006 election was held from the mid-1970s through the mid-1990s by the late Howard Metzenbaum, to whom Brown is sometimes compared. Metzenbaum, a self-made multimillionaire, was nonetheless a populist who fought conservatives and big business, and was dubbed "the last angry liberal." Like his predecessor, Brown can be rhetorically combative; in a March 2011 floor speech, he likened the GOP's push in some states to restrict collective-bargaining rights to the anti-union efforts of Adolf Hitler and Joseph Stalin, a remark for which he later apologized. More recently, in May 2015, Brown suggested President Barack Obama was guilty of sexism because he had referred to Warren by her first name during the heated debate over granting Obama so-called "fast track" trade negotiating authority. The White House figuratively rolled its eyes, noting the president also refers to male senators with whom he has a personal relationship by their first names.

Behind such rhetoric is a personal style that is often cheerful and informal. Brown loves to chat about baseball; he has a personal email address that begins with "DamnYankees", and he took his wife to Chicago's Wrigley Field on their honeymoon. In addition to his fondness for wearing sneakers (American-made) with his suits, he is known for a voice that sounds perpetually hoarse and a mop of tousled hair that frequently appears in need of a comb. Brown is so often described as "rumpled" that it sometimes appears to be part of his given name. He also is known as an energetic cheerleader for his state, dropping the names of Ohio localities in his floor speeches, while amassing a solid constituent-service record.

Brown grew up in Mansfield in north central Ohio, halfway between Cleveland and Columbus. The son of a physician, he graduated from Yale in 1974, and went directly to the campaign trail, winning a seat in the Ohio House in November as he was turning 22. He earned master's degrees in education and public administration from Ohio State University while serving in the legislature. In 1982, he was elected Ohio secretary of state and worked to increase voter registration and turnout. After serving two terms, he lost that office in 1990 to Republican Bob Taft, a scion of Ohio's most famous political family and later the state's governor. It didn't take long for Brown to make a political comeback, winning the open 13th District House seat in 1992. The district stretched from the western suburbs of Cleveland south to Akron; with solid labor support, Brown campaigned hard against the North American Free Trade Agreement, which would come before Congress in 1993, while championing universal health care. He won 53%-35%. He had a close call in the Republican wave year of 1994, winning by only 49%-46%, but, after that, was regularly reelected with more than 60 percent of the vote.

For many years, Brown wore a self-designed lapel pin of a canary in a cage, to commemorate underground miners who were at risk back in the days before labor unions and government safety inspections. He had a consistently liberal voting record in the House. On trade, he was one of the most voluble pro-labor and "fair trade" members from the Great Lakes area, attacking the string of trade agreements and free trade policies that followed NAFTA. In 2005, he helped to lead the effort to defeat the Central American Free Trade Agreement, which cleared the House by just two votes. One of two books he published during his House years was entitled *Myths of Free Trade: Why American Trade Policy Has Failed.* (The other was *Congress on the Inside: Observations from the Majority and the Minority,* reflecting his experiences before and after the House switch to Republican control in 1994.) During a period of widespread calls to allow import of Canadian pharmaceuticals to drive down prices in the United States, Brown also sponsored bus trips to Canada for consumers to buy prescription drugs.

Brown had had his eye on a return to statewide office, but, in 2005, he initially said he would not challenge two-term Republican Sen. Mike DeWine, who had won the seat in 1994 when Metzenbaum retired. That left Iraq War veteran Paul Hackett as the Democratic frontrunner. Hackett was an attractive candidate, but there were questions about whether he could raise enough money, and his shoot-from-the-hip style aroused concerns about how he would play statewide. Brown reconsidered and entered the race in October 2005. Although incensed, Hackett withdrew from the race, and Brown breezed to the Democratic nomination.

DeWine, meanwhile, won a lackluster 72 percent in the GOP primary against two little-known opponents, a reflection of conservative dissatisfaction with him on issues such as gun control. He also was seeking reelection in a hostile political environment: There was an undertow from various scandals associated with the Republican-controlled state government, plus the drag from the unpopular Bush administration. Brown charged that DeWine was a "rubber stamp" for President George W. Bush and tied him to Bush's Iraq policy. DeWine focused on his accomplishments and his ability to work across party lines, hoping to heighten the contrast between himself and the more sharply partisan Brown, whose legislative effectiveness had been limited under Republican House rule. Brown won 56%-44%, dominating nearly all of Ohio's population centers. He also carried everything east of Interstate 77, where his high-profile opposition to free trade resonated in the coal and steel counties.

In the Senate, Brown's voting record has been as unfailingly liberal as it was in the House, even though he now represents a state that, as a whole, has long been politically marginal. In 2013, *National Journal*'s annual vote rankings put Brown among the 15 most liberal senators. Of that group, 12 came from solidly blue states, leaving Brown as one of just three representing a battleground jurisdiction. As in the House, his focus has been on trade issues. "In a place like Mansfield, Ohio, where I grew up, which used to have six or eight major manufacturers and five dozen small manufacturers, most of them are gone. The rest of them, by and large, will be gone, if we don't take care of worker enforcement on trade law and if we don't help those workers that lose their jobs," he told the *Huffington Post* in a May 2015 interview. When he sought reelection in 2012, a sign posted outside his Columbus campaign headquarters was less nuanced: "Only vehicles assembled by union workers in North America are welcome in this parking lot."

Early in 2009, as Congress passed a $787 billion measure—which Brown felt should be even larger—he fought to include requirements that the money be used on American-made goods. The provision was included in the versions of the bill that passed the House and Senate, but the final legislation allowed goods to be purchased from some of America's largest trading partners. Also in 2009, Brown called on Obama to take a tougher stance with China on trade, saying the White House should prod the Chinese government to allow its currency to float rather than keep it pegged to the dollar, a change that would have the effect of raising prices for Chinese goods. He led a subsequent effort in 2012 to persuade Obama to file a series of trade cases against China regarding the auto industry, accusing Beijing of unfairly subsidizing Chinese auto parts makers.

In 2013, Brown won a prized seat on the Finance Committee, enabling him to have an even bigger say on trade matters. When the fight was joined in the spring of 2015 over granting Obama fast track negotiating authority to pursue a 12-nation Asian trade deal, Brown showed up at the Finance Committee with no less than 88 amendments in an effort to both modify the measure and slow down its progress. The fast track measure ultimately cleared the Senate, but Brown could claim a small victory when his "Level the Playing Field Act" made it into both the House and Senate bills to reauthorize the U.S. Customs Service and Border Patrol. The measure was intended to strengthen the hand of the Commerce Department and International Trade Commission against foreign producers selling in the United States below market price or receiving subsidies from their home nations; Brown complained enforcement of antidumping and countervailing duty statutes had been weakened through court challenges by foreign producers.

At the outset of 2015, when New York's Charles Schumer passed on becoming the top Democrat on the Banking Committee to concentrate on his duties in the Senate leadership, the slot went to Brown. While Brown and Schumer share a voting record that puts them on the left end of the Senate spectrum, Schumer—reflecting the presence of Wall Street in his home city—has been supportive of the nation's financial industry. Brown, on the other hand, has sided with Warren in favor of reinstituting some of the barriers between banks and other financial institutions dropped in 1999 when the Depression-era Glass-Steagall Act was repealed. Brown worked on the Dodd-Frank financial industry regulation bill in 2010, and unsuccessfully pushed a proposal to limit the size of banks deemed "too big to fail" in the wake of the government bailout of financial firms during the 2008 crash. He called for capping banks at holdings of no more than 2 percent of the gross domestic product or 10 percent of insured bank deposits nationally. The cap would have affected three large banks: Bank of America, Wells Fargo, and JP Morgan Chase.

Prior to the 2014 election, with control of the Senate in the balance, one bank executive anonymously told *The Washington Post* that the prospect of Brown becoming committee chairman was "frightening," complaining the senator had showed no interest in finding common ground with large banks. Brown's attitude toward such institutions guided his actions on a couple of Obama's major appointments. In 2013, Brown got 20 fellow Democrats to sign a letter supporting Janet Yellen as the next chair of the Federal Reserve; she was later appointed by Obama. Obama's preferred choice, former Treasury Secretary Larry Summers, was seen by Brown and a number of other Democrats as overly close to Wall Street. Similar objections prompted Brown to oppose confirmation of Mary Jo White as chair of the Securities and Exchange Commission earlier that year.

Brown did vote for Obama's signature legislative achievement, the Affordable Care Act when it cleared Congress in 2010, even though he had earlier joined other liberals in pushing for inclusion of a government-run insurance option. When the public insurance option was dropped as politically endangering passage of the measure, Brown said that at least the final version contained "good insurance reform." Later that year, Brown opposed Obama's deal to allow the Bush-era tax cuts to continue even for the top income-earners, but wound up voting for final passage of that legislation because it also contained extended unemployment benefits for 13 months. "My principle of not wanting tax cuts for the rich doesn't help an unemployed worker," he told *Politico*.

Brown says one of his proudest achievements in the Senate was a bill passed with the help of the late Massachusetts Sen. Edward Kennedy. During reauthorization of the Food and Drug Administration in 2009, Brown won passage of an amendment creating incentives for pharmaceutical companies to produce drugs for diseases common in the developing world. Within weeks of it going into effect, an international aid group reported a flood of new TB drugs on the market.

Closer to home, Brown, as a liberal from a coal-producing state, has tread carefully on environmental issues, while again seeking to protect U.S. interests in the international marketplace. In early 2011, when Obama announced the Environmental Protection Agency would issue new regulations for carbon emissions, Brown said he would insist on protections for U.S. manufacturers. A year earlier, as a negotiator on a climate change bill that the Senate worked on but failed to pass, he was point man for a bloc of Democrats who dubbed themselves the "Brown Dogs"—and likewise refused to support the bill without protections for U.S. firms. Brown surprised environmental groups in 2007 when he said nuclear power is safe and should be an option; more recently, he has worked to make Ohio a leader in wind energy production.

In the 2012 election, Brown was the target of one of the most expensive outside efforts ever to defeat a member of Congress, as conservative groups poured $40 million into attacking him; GOP strategist Karl Rove's Crossroads GPS was responsible for $12 million of that. His Republican opponent was 35-year-old Josh Mandel, who broke a pledge to serve a full term as state treasurer by challenging Brown less than two years into his tenure. Mandel raised $19 million on his own and served up plenty of stinging rhetoric, calling Brown's support for the auto industry bailout "un-American" and labeling the senator "a liar" during a debate.

Brown and his allies accused Mandel of not being ready for the Senate, pointing to Mandel statements that fact-checking watchdogs had labeled as false. The senator called his rival "the king" of "Pants on Fire," a reference to the website *PolitiFact's* lowest rating for truthfulness. (Brown later had his own problems on this front, thanks to *The Washington Post's* counterpart to *PolitiFact.* During the 2015 trade debate, the *Post* awarded Brown "four Pinocchios" for repeatedly attributing a quote to former President George H.W. Bush that Bush had never made.) Brown's campaign and outside liberal groups came up with $35 million, and, boosted by Obama's substantial political investment in Ohio, turned what was a neck-and-neck race in August into a 51%-45% win. Mandel won most counties, but Brown dominated the major population centers, winning 69 percent in Cleveland's Cuyahoga County and 61 percent in Columbus' Franklin County.

The campaign caused professional complications for Brown's wife, Pulitzer Prize-winning columnist Connie Schultz, whom he had married in 2004 (his second marriage). In 2011, Schultz resigned after 18 years with the *Cleveland Plain Dealer,* telling colleagues that "in recent weeks, it has become painfully clear that my independence, professionally and personally, is possible only if I'm no longer writing for the newspaper that covers my husband's Senate race on a daily basis." She remains a nationally syndicated columnist. Schultz apologized for failing to mention earlier that, during a tea party event at which she was present, Mandel had attended and she had videotaped him. Schultz had taken a leave of absence from the paper during Brown's first Senate campaign in 2006. Her experiences provided material for a book, published in 2007, entitled *...And His Lovely Wife: A Memoir From the Woman Beside the Man.*

Junior Senator

Rob Portman (R)

Elected 2010, term expires Jan. 2017, 1st term; b. Dec. 19, 1955, Cincinnati; Dartmouth Col., B.A. 1979, U. of MI, J.D. 1984; Methodist; married (Jane); 3 children.

Elected Office: U.S. House, 1993-2005.

Professional Career: White House Legis. Affairs Dir., 1989-91; U.S. trade rep., 2005-06; Dir., Office of Mgmt. & Budget, 2006-07; Practicing atty., 1984-88, 2007-10.

DC Office: 448 RSOB, 20510, 202-224-3353; Fax: 202-224-9075; Website: portman.senate.gov.

State Offices: Cincinnati, 513-684-3265; Cleveland, 216-522-7095; Columbus, 614-469-6774, Toledo, 419-259-3895.

Committees: *Budget. Energy & Natural Resources:* Energy; National Parks; Water & Power. *Finance:* Taxation & IRS Oversight; International Trade, Customs, & Global Competitiveness; Fiscal Responsibility & Economic Growth (Chmn). *Homeland Security & Governmental Affairs:* Investigations (Permanent), (Chmn); Regulatory Affairs & Federal Management.

Group Ratings

	ADA	ACLU	AFL-CIO	LCV	ITI	COC	HAFA	ACU	CFG	FRC
2014	25%	6%	–	0%	33%	75%	55%	68%	77%	79%
2013	15%	C	39%	8%	C	75%	C	64%	71%	C

National Journal Ratings

	2013 LIB	—	2013 CONS
Economic	29%	—	69%
Social	32%	—	67%
Foreign	24%	—	73%
Composite	29%	—	71%

Key Votes of the 113th Congress

1. Sandy storm spending — N
2. Chuck Hagel Confirmation — N
3. Gun Background Checks — N
4. Immigration Reform — N
5. Student Loan Rates — Y
6. Employee Non-Discrim'n Act — Y
7. Senate Vote on Judgeships — Y
8. Defense Dept. Spending — N
9. Bipartisan Budget Deal — Y
10. Farm Bill Conference Rept. — Y
11. Unempl. Comp. Extension — Y
12. Keystone Pipeline — Y

Election Results

2010 general	Rob Portman (R)	2,168,742	(57%)	$5,257,618	$2,130,768	$130,822
	Lee Fisher (D)	1,503,297	(39%)	$6,356,737	$301,371	$787,794
2010 primary	Rob Portman (R)	unopposed				

Prior winning percentages: House: 2004 (72%), 2002 (74%), 2000 (74%), 1998 (76%), 1996 (72%), 1994 (77%), 1993 special (70%)

For Republican Rob Portman, Ohio's junior senator, election to the Senate in 2010 was the latest stop for a consummate insider whose career has alternated between the two ends of Pennsylvania Avenue in official Washington: Capitol Hill and the White House. After service in the administration of President George H.W. Bush—to whom Portman occasionally has been compared, in terms of both his center-right views and even-keeled modesty—Portman won a Cincinnati-based House seat in a 1993 special election, only to head back down Pennsylvania Avenue a dozen years later when he was appointed U.S. Trade Representative and later director of the Office of Management and Budget by President George W. Bush. For a time following his arrival in the Senate, it appeared that another White House stint might be in Portman's future: He was on a short list of possible running mates to Republican presidential nominee Mitt Romney in 2012, and, early in the 2016 election cycle, Portman made the requisite visits to Iowa and New Hampshire, where the earliest contests for national convention delegates take place, as he mulled a presidential bid himself.

But in December 2014, Portman cited the newly acquired GOP majority in the Senate as a key factor in announcing his decision not to seek the presidency. "It's just not possible to be involved with policy issues" and simultaneously gear up for a national campaign, he told reporters. While some questioned how saleable Portman might have been in a GOP presidential nominating contest given some of his more moderate views, his decision was good news for Republicans looking to hang onto a Senate seat in the battleground state of Ohio in 2016. However, notwithstanding Portman's considerable legislative and political skills, his seat remains high up on Democratic lists as a takeover target. Meanwhile, as trade moved to the front of the congressional agenda in 2015, Portman found himself having to navigate between his high-profile past as a negotiator of trade agreements and the widespread skepticism toward such deals in a state where "free trade" is widely blamed for reduced employment and a shrinking manufacturing base.

Portman grew up in Cincinnati, where his father in 1960 started a forklift distribution company employing five people. The privately held Portman Equipment Co. eventually grew into a 350-person operation with annual revenues of $65 million before being sold to a Dutch conglomerate in 2004. In his youth, Portman worked summers at the company, sweeping floors and grinding old paint off trucks. While at Dartmouth College, he hung out with a crowd nicknamed the "Granola Gang" known for its love of the outdoors; many of its members later volunteered for the Peace Corps or went to work in the field of renewable energy. He took a semester off to work for Cincinnati area Rep. Willis Gradison, a member of the House Ways and Means Committee whom Portman would later succeed. After graduating from Dartmouth, Portman worked for George H.W. Bush's 1980 campaign for the Republican presidential nomination, as part of the advance team setting up events. It was the beginning of a long association with the Bush family.

Portman earned a law degree at the University of Michigan in 1984, and was quickly hired by a leading Washington lawyer/lobbying firm, Patton, Boggs and Blow, as a trade attorney. He returned to Cincinnati in 1987 to practice law before coming back to Washington in 1989 as an associate White House counsel and then head of the Office of Legislative Affairs under George H.W. Bush. Portman was back practicing law in Cincinnati when, in January 1993, Gradison resigned his 2nd District House seat to become head of a Washington-based trade association. Portman ran to fill the vacancy, and had help from former first lady Barbara Bush, who made a radio ad for him. He won a seven-candidate primary with 36 percent to 30 percent for the second place-finisher: former Rep. Bob McEwen, who had been ousted in a neighboring district in 1992. The special election in the predominantly Republican district was anticlimactic; Portman won with 70 percent and was easily reelected six times from 1994 through 2004.

In the House, Portman got on the Ways and Means and Budget committees and became known for his fiscal conservatism and his ability to work across the aisle. He co-chaired the National Commission on Restructuring the Internal Revenue Service and won broad support for repeal of the 3 percent excise tax on telephone service. He worked with Democrats, notably his current Senate colleague, Ben Cardin of Maryland (then a House member also serving on the Ways and Means panel), on issues ranging from land conservation to welfare reform to pensions. He helped revise 401(k) rules to make it easier for small businesses to offer pension plans, but he got nowhere with a 2002 attempt to repeal the alternative minimum tax. He also sponsored the bill to create a National Underground Railroad Museum in Cincinnati; Portman's ancestors include Quaker abolitionists who were active in Underground Railroad.

In 2005, President George W. Bush appointed Portman as the U.S. trade representative, in charge of negotiating free trade agreements and representing U.S. interests in global talks on reducing trade barriers. A year later, Bush appointed him director of the Office of Management and Budget, a position that requires immersion in the arcana of federal spending. Bush nicknamed him "The Mule," in tribute to his persistence. Portman succeeded in pushing the budget more toward balance, although he later told *The Hill* newspaper that he was frustrated he couldn't do more. "I wanted to offer a balanced budget over five years, and a lot of people didn't," he said. He left the agency in 2007 and returned to the Cincinnati area, where he joined a law firm, taught a class at Ohio State University's John Glenn School of Public Affairs, and coached his daughter's soccer team.

Just after Republican Sen. George Voinovich announced in January 2009 that he would not run for a third term, Portman entered the contest, saying his focus would be on job creation. The timing of his candidacy did not seem propitious. Despite his stint in Cabinet-level positions during the George W. Bush administration, he had virtually no name recognition beyond the Cincinnati media market. And President Barack Obama had just come to office, while moving Ohio into the Democratic column in 2008. Soon, two Democratic officials who had run statewide joined the race: Lt. Gov. Lee Fisher and Secretary of State Jennifer Brunner. Polls showed Portman trailing both. Unfazed, he campaigned around the state in blue jeans and a windbreaker, putting out a six-point jobs program and opposing the Democrats' $787 billion stimulus bill and their health care overhaul—albeit doing so affably. Portman raised serious money, $16.5 million, and he also benefited from a fractious Democratic primary in May 2010, which Fisher won, 56%-44%.

In the fall campaign, Fisher derided Portman's long friendship with the Bush family, telling *The Columbus Dispatch*, "Rob Portman had his hands on the steering wheel as George W. Bush drove us off the cliff and into the deepest economic ditch in most of our lives." But Fisher had little money—much of the $6.4 million he raised was spent on the primary—and his position as Gov. Ted Strickland's "jobs czar" in 2007 and 2008 proved a liability rather than an asset. Portman asserted that Ohio lost 400,000 jobs while Fisher held the post. Portman fended off criticism of his work as trade representative by saying he would make enforcement of trade laws a high priority. He was not a particular favorite of tea party activists, but they didn't campaign against him. By October, the race was off everyone's list of competitive contests. Far behind in the polls and out of money, Fisher lost to Portman, 57%-39%. Portman carried 82 of the state's 88 counties, and ran even in usually Democratic northeast Ohio.

In the Senate, Portman's government experience and personable demeanor quickly earned him respect as well as affection from members of both parties. In an institution where some adults have a reputation for exhibiting juvenile behavior, Portman is regularly described as a "grownup." It's a description he self-deprecatingly waves off, quipping, "When your hair starts to turn more gray, as mine as has been, people are going to call you a grownup." His voting record has been conservative, but not extremely so. He attracted widespread attention in March 2013 when he reversed his opposition to same-sex marriage after he disclosed that his 21-year-old son, Will, had come out as gay. It made Portman the first Republican senator to support same-sex marriage. Some conservatives vowed to oppose him for renomination in 2016, but a serious primary challenger is not likely to emerge.

"Every week, sometimes every day, somebody will talk to me about it," Portman said of the gay marriage issue in a 2014 interview with the *Associated Press*. He added, "I feel very comfortable in taking a position of respecting people for who they are, which is what I think ultimately same-sex marriage is about." (Also present for that interview was his wife, Jane, whom he married in 1986. Jane Portman grew up in a Democratic family in North Carolina and has a resume that includes an internship in Jimmy Carter's White House and a stint as a staffer to South Dakota Democratic Sen. Tom Daschle in the mid-1980s. She has laughingly referred to the "consolidation agreement" when she and Rob Portman married: She agreed to become a Republican and he agreed to become a Methodist.)

Just months after Portman was sworn into the Senate, a standoff between the Obama White House and Republican leaders on Capitol Hill over raising the federal debt limit resulted in a deal that created the Joint Committee on Deficit Reduction—the so-called "Supercommittee"—consisting of 12 members of the House and Senate, evenly divided between the two parties. Portman was one of three Senate Republicans appointed to the panel, which was charged with finding an additional $1.5 trillion in budget savings over a 10-year period. As the late November 2011 deadline for the committee to act approached, efforts to come up with an agreement faltered. Portman and Massachusetts Sen. John Kerry—a Democratic member of the panel who later was named Secretary of State—are devoted cyclists, and took numerous bike rides together as they informally discussed ways to move forward. But the deadline passed with the panel in a partisan deadlock, ultimately triggering $1.2 billion in across-the-board, automatic budget cuts that kicked in during the early part of 2013.

In the wake of that experience, Portman teamed with Montana's Jon Tester on a 2012 bill to end the practice of government shutdowns, and found ways to work with other Democrats as well. He closely cooperated with Missouri's Claire McCaskill on a Homeland Security and Governmental Affairs Committee inquiry into the Obama administration's public relations spending. Portman and McCaskill also worked on legislation aimed at streamlining the process for federal permits. And he partnered with Arkansas Democrat Mark Pryor, who later lost his bid for reelection in 2014, on a bill to reform the federal regulatory process that drew support from Republicans as well as some conservative Democrats. A four-year legislative effort, in tandem with New Hampshire Democratic Sen. Jeanne Shaheen, to pass legislation to encourage more energy efficient buildings finally met with success in early 2015, when Obama signed a scaled-down version of the legislation. The bill was initially brought to the floor in September 2013, but become entangled in debates over two perennial flashpoints: the Affordable Care Act and Keystone XL pipeline. It failed again in May 2014 after Republicans insisted on being able to offer controversial amendments to block environmental regulations.

On the political front, Portman again demonstrated his fundraising prowess, raising more money for the National Republican Senatorial Committee than any other freshman. He was urged to seek the chairmanship of the NRSC for the 2013-2014 cycle, but declined. He did agree to serve as one of two vice chairs of the committee, and played an active role in the successful effort to gain a Republican Senate majority. In 2012, Portman had thrown his Ohio organization behind Romney before the state's crucial March 6 Republican primary, which the former Massachusetts governor won by just over 10,000 votes. He and Romney got along well, and Portman later took on the role of Obama in Romney's debate preparation sessions, having earlier portrayed other Democrats in similar mock debates. But Portman's close association with the unpopular George W. Bush was probably a mark against him in the vice presidential sweepstakes, along with the perception that his personality is—well, bland. Those who know him say such characterizations are off the mark; in fact, he has a reputation as a prankster, and his outdoors exploits include smuggling a kayak into China in the 1980s to paddle the Yangtze River.

In the spring of 2015, Portman found himself at odds with members of his own party as he pushed an amendment to Obama's request for so-called "fast track" negotiating authority to expedite a 12-nation Asian trade agreement. Teaming with a fellow Finance Committee member, Michigan Democrat Debbie Stabenow, Portman sought an amendment to require the White House to establish "enforceable rules" to combat currency manipulation. "We need a more level playing field," Portman told the *Cincinnati Enquirer*, contending his currency provision would help ensure that "other countries aren't cheating." His amendment was backed by the nation's domestic automakers, who have charged in recent years that they are being undercut by Japan's undervaluing of the yen. But Portman's currency amendment was strongly opposed by the committee chairman, Utah Republican Orrin Hatch, as well as another committee member, Senate Majority Whip John Cornyn of Texas, who clashed with Portman over it during a committee session. The *Wall Street Journal*'s conservative editorial page called the proposal a "killer amendment"—a charge strongly disputed by Portman—while suggesting the senator was "abandoning his policy chops in favor of re-election politics."

With lobbying from the White House, which teamed with congressional Republican leaders to pass the fast track proposal over the objection of many leading congressional Democrats, the Finance Committee rejected Portman's currency amendment by 15-11. It later was proposed on the Senate floor, and was defeated 51-48, with Portman and only 11 other Republicans joining a majority of Democrats in supporting it. If Portman took heat from fellow Republicans for pushing the currency proposal, he was criticized by Democrats for supporting the final passage of the measure to give the president fast-track negotiating authority. Among the critics: his two potential Democratic opponents in 2016, Strickland and Cincinnati Councilman P.G. Sittenfeld, both of whom said they would have voted against giving the president such authority.

Strickland is the favorite to win the Democratic Senate nomination. After serving six terms in the House, he was elected governor in 2006, but was ousted in the 2010 by current Republican Gov. John Kasich. While seen as a formidable challenger to Portman, Strickland, if elected, would be 75 when sworn into office in January 2017—which would appear to make him the oldest popularly elected freshman senator in history. Strickland is also coming off a stint as an official of the Center for American Progress, a Washington think tank, and has taken heat back home for several statements he made while there—including defending Obama's policy on coal.

If Portman's day job doesn't work out in the long term, he could fall back on being an innkeeper and restaurateur: He is part owner of the Golden Lamb Inn in Lebanon, located just outside Cincinnati and which is Ohio's oldest continuously operated business. Opened in 1803, it was purchased in 1926 by Portman's maternal grandfather and is now owned by Portman and his siblings; Portman's share of it is valued between $1 million and $5 million, according to Senate financial disclosure reports. A dozen presidents have stayed at the hotel—Romney visited three weeks before the 2012 election—and many other national and statewide candidates have held rallies there, seeking support in the bellwether precincts of southwestern Ohio.

FIRST DISTRICT

Steve Chabot (R)

Elected 2010, 10th term; b. Jan. 22, 1953, Cincinnati; Col. of William & Mary, B.A. 1975, Northern KY U., J.D. 1978; Catholic; married (Donna); 2 children.

Elected Office: Cincinnati City Cncl., 1985-90; Hamilton Cnty. Commission, 1990-94; U.S. House, 1995-2009.

Professional Career: Teacher, St. Joseph Schl., 1975-76; Practicing atty., 1978-94.

DC Office: 2371 RHOB, 20515, 202-225-2216; Fax: 202-225-3012; Website: chabot.house.gov.

State Offices: Cincinnati, 513-684-2723; Warren County, 513-421-8704.

Committees: *Foreign Affairs:* Asia & the Pacific; Middle East & North Africa. *Judiciary:* Courts, Intellectual Property & the Internet; Crime, Terrorism, Homeland Security, & Investigations. *Small Business* (Chmn).

Group Ratings

	ADA	ACLU	AFL-CIO	LCV	ITI	COC	HAFA	ACU	CFG	FRC
2014	5%	0%	–	3%	100%	71%	84%	92%	93%	100%
2013	5%	C	10%	7%	C	85%	C	96%	96%	C

National Journal Ratings

	2013 LIB	—	2013 CONS
Economic	0%	—	98%
Social	0%	—	87%
Foreign	0%	—	95%
Composite	3%	—	97%

Key Votes of the 113th Congress

1. Sandy storm spending	N	5. Medical Marijuana	N	9. Syrian Rebels Training	Y
2. Violence Against Women Act	N	6. Farm Bill	N	10. Keystone pipeline	Y
3. Guantanamo Bay Detainees	N	7. Afghanistan Combat	N	11. Immigration Exec. Action	Y
4. Abortion 20-week ban	Y	8. NSA Phone Data Collection	Y	12. Bipartisan budget deal	N

Election Results

2014 general	Steve Chabot (R)	124,779	(63%)	$636,369
	Fred Kundrata (D)	72,604	(37%)	$309,874
2014 primary	Steve Chabot (R)	unopposed		

Prior winning percentages: 2012 (58%), 2010 (51%), 2006 (52%), 2004 (60%), 2002 (65%), 2000 (53%), 1998 (53%), 1996 (54%), 1994 (56%)

Population		Race and Ethnicity		Income	
Total:	724,914	White	70.7%	Median income:	$50,461
Urban:	56.9%	Black	22.0%		(234 of 435)
Suburban:	42.2%	Latino	2.9%	Under $50,000	49.5%
Rural:	0.9%	Asian	2.4%	$50,000-$99,999:	27.6%
Land area:	732	Two races	1.9%	$100,000-$199,999:	17.1%
Pop/sq. mi.:	989.8	White Ethnic	22.8%	$200,000 or more:	5.7%
Born in state:	72.1%			Poverty Rate	17.9%
		Education			
		H.S. grad or less:	40.9%	**Work**	
Age Groups		Some college:	27.4%	White collar:	38.8%
Under 18:	24.8%	College degree, 4 yr.:	19.2%	Blue collar:	43.0%
18 to 34:	22.8%	Post-grad study:	12.6%	Sales and service:	18.2%
35 to 64:	39.0%				
Over 64:	13.3%			Govt. workers:	10.0%
		Military			
		Veterans/active duty:	7.9%		

Western/Northern Cincinnati Metro

Cincinnati, with its long-settled good looks, was Ohio's first major metropolis, a heavily German beehive of riverboats and sausage factories, nicknamed in the 1850s "Porkopolis." In the 19th century, it was the nation's fourth-largest city, and at

Voter Turnout	
2013 Total Citizen 18+	525,990
2014 House Turnout	197,383
2014 Turnout as % CVAP	37.5%
2012 Turnout as % CVAP	68.5%

the outbreak of the Civil War, it was a chief destination for slaves on the Underground Railroad. The National Underground Railroad Freedom Center is now located downtown. In the middle of the city is Mill Creek, lined with factories and so badly polluted that it is unfit for people to swim in or fish to live in. The advocacy group American Rivers named it the most endangered urban river in North America in 1997, and little has changed since then. On the hills to the west, above the restored Union Terminal housing several museums, are the modest streetcar suburbs of the 19th century and the early years of the 20th.

The Cincinnati area was the site of great innovations: the first professional baseball team, the Red Stockings, who began playing in 1869; and the nation's first concrete skyscraper, the 15-story Ingalls building built in 1902. Not all of these innovations have been salutary; the first train robbery in America occurred in North Bend, just to the west. Cincinnati spawned not flashy but solid industries, including America's biggest concentration of machine tool makers, an industry that's now a fraction of its once-robust size, and the Procter & Gamble soap business, with its twin-towered headquarters at the edge of downtown.

Today, downtown Cincinnati's spruced-up Fountain Square shows off well-maintained skyscrapers plus a revival of museums, arts institutions, and retail shops. Its first-class restaurants still attract a dressy clientele. Old ethnic neighborhoods on the west side, crowded with brick row houses on steep hills, maintain their thick local accents and special foods, from German sauerbraten to Cincin-

2012 Presidential Vote		
Mitt Romney (R)..................190,501	(52%)
Barack Obama (D) 168,195	(46%)
2008 Presidential Vote		
John McCain (R)..................188,145	(52%)
Barack Obama (D) 171,639	(47%)
Cook Partisan Voting Index: R+6		

nati chili. (Go for the 5-way at Skyline!) Yet crime is a problem, and there has been ongoing flight to the suburbs. With fewer recent immigrants than comparable Northern cities, Cincinnati's population has declined in every decade since the 1940s, falling 10 percent to 298,000, from 2000 to 2013. In May 2015, a local officer of the Federal Reserve Bank gave an optimistic forecast of the local economy, including increased capital spending, two hospital expansions and the opening of General Electric's Global Operations Center.

The 1st Congressional District of Ohio includes almost all of Cincinnati, except for parts of its affluent eastern side. It contains most of Cincinnati's distinctive neighborhoods, like Over-the-Rhine, named for its heavily German-American early population and its proximity across the Miami and Erie Canal from downtown. This was a premier entertainment district until the late 1910s, when Prohibition shut down the breweries, and it later drew African Americans displaced from their neighborhoods by the construction of Interstate 71. It was the epicenter of race riots in 2001, but is now gentrifying. The district takes in Avondale, once the center of Cincinnati's Jewish population, but now more than 90% are African American and more than 40% live in poverty; Hebrew Union College, the oldest extant Jewish seminary in the Americas, is just to the west of the neighborhood. In December 2014, *The Cincinnati Enquirer* enthusiastically reported a "development revival" in Avondale.

Historically, Cincinnati was a pro-Union island of Republicanism in a sea of Democratic sentiment. Today, the reverse is true. It has an overwhelmingly Democratic urban core, but beyond that, the rest of the district is mostly Republican. The 1st includes most of the heavily Republican middle-class suburbs and exurbs to the west of the city and some Democratic-leaning inner suburbs to the north. The other large piece is overwhelmingly Republican Warren County, suburban territory that is prospering and has the second-highest median household income in the state. City-dwellers now comprise about one-third of the district, Warren County is a bit less than one-third and the Hamilton suburbs are the remainder. The overall effect has made this a leans-Republican district; John McCain and Mitt Romney each got 52 percent of the district vote, while each narrowly lost the state overall.

Steve Chabot (R)

Republican Steve Chabot first came to the House as part of the historic GOP Class of 1994. After losing reelection in 2008, he returned two years later as the most senior member of another huge freshman class. He reclaimed his status as one of the chamber's most conservative members, and now serves as Small Business Committee chairman.

Chabot grew up in the Cincinnati area and graduated from La Salle High School, where he says he "got the bug" for politics after serving on the student council. Then came the Watergate scandal. "A lot of people my age got turned off from politics because of all that," Chabot told *National Journal*. "I wasn't that way. I thought we needed honest people in government." He earned a degree in history and physical education from the College of William & Mary. He then took night classes at Northern Kentucky University to get his law degree while teaching at an elementary school during the day. Chabot won a seat on the Cincinnati City Council, where he served for four years. He followed that with a four-year stint on the Hamilton County Commission. During that time, Chabot tried to find innovative ways to reduce the cost of government, such as using jail inmates for some public services.

In 1994, he was among the successful conservative Republicans who ended 40 years of Democratic control of the House. In his 14 years on Capitol Hill, Chabot took principled and politically risky stands opposing federal spending on projects in his district and was a leader on social issues, particularly opposition to abortion rights. In 2003, he helped enact a ban on "partial-birth" abortions, and he also pushed a bill to prevent minors from crossing state lines to get abortions. Chabot was a House manager during the 1998 impeachment of President Bill Clinton. In retrospect, Chabot said, he is most proud of his work in fighting wasteful spending.

Chabot lost his seat in 2008, when Democrat Steve Driehaus defeated him by 5 percentage points. Spoiling for a rematch, Chabot in 2010 criticized the incumbent for voting with the Democratic majority on President Barack Obama's health care initiative and the $787 billion economic-stimulus package. For his part, Driehaus defended the actions of the Democrats, including the health care overhaul, which he called "the right thing" to do. On the stump, he asked voters to give Obama and the Democrats more time to implement change. But Driehaus had trouble generating much voter excitement for his reelection, and in October, the Democratic Congressional Campaign Committee pulled the plug on further spending on television ads for him. Each candidate raised about $2 million. Chabot won, 52%-46%.

When he returned to the House, Chabot used his seniority to claim the chairmanship of the Foreign Affairs Subcommittee on the Middle East and South Asia. He criticized the Obama administration's policies in the region and called its explanation of events before and after the deadly September 2012 attack at the U.S. consulate in Benghazi, Libya, "hamhanded at best and a cover-up at worst." In 2013, he became chairman of the Asia and the Pacific Subcommittee. With Democratic Rep. Joe Crowley, he filed in January 2014 the Burma Human Rights and Democracy Act, which restricted military aid to that country and signaled the Obama administration to move more cautiously to normalize relations.

On domestic issues, he introduced a bill in 2012 to revamp the Section 8 housing initiative for low-income residents, calling it "a broken program that rewards dependency on government with our tax dollars." He also crusaded against federal funding of Cincinnati's streetcar project on economic grounds. In 2014, Chabot enacted a bipartisan bill to strengthen the law school clinic certification program of the Patent and Trademark Office, which he said would encourage entrepreneurial innovation.

He drew attention in August 2011, when his staff ordered police to seize the cameras of two Democratic activists who were videotaping one of Chabot's town hall meetings. After an outpouring of criticism from across the political spectrum—tea party leader Judson Phillips called Chabot a "moron"—he allowed taping of subsequent events.

With Republican Sam Graves of Missouri term-limited as Small Business chairman after 2014, Chabot played up his conservative bona fides to take over the gavel. "If there's one thing government can do for small business, it's to get the heck off their backs," Chabot told the Associated Press. In addition to scrutinizing the Internal Revenue Service and Environmental Protection Agency, he said that he would try to streamline the Small Business Administration's lending process. "It's cumbersome, it takes too long, there's far too much paperwork. It just intimidates a lot of people," he said. Chabot has benefited in the House from having Speaker John Boehner as his colleague in the adjacent 8th District, even though they don't always agree on issues.

Since redistricting has made the 1st District substantially more Republican by adding solidly GOP Warren County, Chabot has won reelection easily. "Unless Steve Chabot commits a felony, he will be there for as long as he wants to be," Hamilton County Democratic Party Chairman Tim Burke lamented to *The Cincinnati Enquirer.*

SECOND DISTRICT

Brad Wenstrup (R)

Elected 2012, 2nd term; b. June 17, 1958, Cincinnati; U. of Cincinnati, B.A. 1980, William M. Scholl Col. of Podiatric Medicine, B.S. D.P.M. 1985; Catholic; married (Monica Klein Wenstrup) 1 child.

Military Career: Army Reserves, 1998-2011 (combat surgeon, Iraq, 2005-06).

Professional Career: Physician, Wellington Orthopaedic & Sports Medicine, 1999-2013; Private practice, 1986-99.

DC Office: 1318 LHOB, 20515, 202-225-3164; Website: wenstrup. house.gov.

State Offices: Cincinnati, 513-474-7777; Peebles, 513-605-1380.

Committees: *Armed Services:* Readiness. *Veterans' Affairs:* Economic Opportunity (Chmn); Health. *Intelligence (Permanent):* Dept. of Defense Intelligence & Overhead Architecture; Emerging Threats.

Group Ratings

	ADA	ACLU	AFL-CIO	LCV	ITI	COC	HAFA	ACU	CFG	FRC
2014	5%	0%	–	3%	100%	79%	74%	88%	69%	100%
2013	0%	C	10%	7%	C	85%	C	96%	90%	C

National Journal Ratings

	2013 LIB	—	2013 CONS
Economic	16%	—	84%
Social	16%	—	74%
Foreign	15%	—	77%
Composite	19%	—	81%

Key Votes of the 113th Congress

1. Sandy storm spending	N	5. Medical Marijuana	N	9. Syrian Rebels Training	Y
2. Violence Against Women Act	N	6. Farm Bill	N	10. Keystone pipeline	Y
3. Guantanamo Bay Detainees	N	7. Afghanistan Combat	N	11. Immigration Exec. Action	Y
4. Abortion 20-week ban	Y	8. NSA Phone Data Collection	N	12. Bipartisan budget deal	N

Election Results

2014 general	Brad Wenstrup (R)	132,658	(66%)	$865,102	
	Marek Tyszkiewicz (D)	68,453	(34%)	$169,159	$20,934
2014 primary	Brad Wenstrup (R)	unopposed			

Prior winning percentage: 2012 (59%)

Population		Race and Ethnicity		Income	
Total:	727,391	White	86.8%	Median income:	$50,802
Urban:	50.9%	Black	8.1%		(227 of 435)
Suburban:	22.5%	Latino	1.5%	Under $50,000	49.1%
Rural:	26.7%	Asian	1.3%	$50,000-$99,999:	29.9%
Land area:	2,889	Two races	2.1%	$100,000-$199,999:	16.3%
Pop/sq. mi.:	251.8	White Ethnic	22.4%	$200,000 or more:	4.6%
Born in state:	75.1%			Poverty Rate	15.5%
		Education			
Age Groups		H.S. grad or less:	43.5%	**Work**	
Under 18:	23.1%	Some college:	26.4%	White collar:	38.7%
18 to 34:	21.2%	College degree, 4 yr.:	19.0%	Blue collar:	40.1%
35 to 64:	40.9%	Post-grad study:	11.1%	Sales and service:	21.2%
Over 64:	14.7%				
		Military		Govt. workers:	11.9%
		Veterans/active duty:	8.5%		

Eastern Cincinnati Metro, Southern Ohio

Back in the 1850s, Cincinnati, with its large German population, was heavily Republican and anti-slavery. The city's ethnic character and political preference, like its physical appearance, remained pretty well fixed from that time until fairly recently.

Voter Turnout	
2013 Total Citizen 18+	550,185
2014 House Turnout	201,111
2014 Turnout as % CVAP	36.6%
2012 Turnout as % CVAP	65.7%

Cincinnati attracted fewer southern and eastern European immigrants than did Great Lakes industrial cities like Cleveland, Detroit and Chicago, so the New Deal failed to alter the political dynamic here as much as it did in those cities. The Appalachians who settled here in the 1940s to work in the factories were typically Republicans. Economically, it was never a strong union town, and culturally it is conservative. It is the only 1 million-plus metro area in the nation that has voted at least 50% Republican in every presidential election since 1992.

Ohio's 2nd Congressional District includes the eastern edge of Cincinnati, taking in Hyde Park Square, with its farmer's market and many shops and boutiques; most of the largely affluent suburbs of eastern Hamilton County; and the fast-growing suburbs of Clermont County. In once-rural Clermont, Miami Township has become a bedroom community and a center of commercial development along the Interstate 275 loop.

The district ranges farther east on the Ohio River, all the way to the old industrial city of Portsmouth. These are distinctly different places—"the richest to the poorest, and everything in between," as one area mayor put it. Chillicothe, on the Scioto River, was the first capital of Ohio. Hillsboro briefly made headlines in 1954 when Philip Partridge, a white city engineer, decided that desegregation in the wake of the recent *Brown v. Board of Education* decision by the Supreme Court was not proceeding quickly enough, and forced the city's hand by burning down the school for African-American children. Partridge went to prison for arson, but the

2012 Presidential Vote		
Mitt Romney (R)................194,385	(55%)
Barack Obama (D) 155,036	(44%)
2008 Presidential Vote		
John McCain (R).................195,959	(54%)
Barack Obama (D) 160,158	(44%)
Cook Partisan Voting Index: R+8		

schools were integrated two years later, and his family later received a citation from the National Underground Railroad Freedom Center. The city of Ripley was a hub for the Underground Railroad, a natural point of egress from the South since the Ohio River narrows near the city. In 1838, escaped slave Eliza Harris leapt from one ice floe to the next, while carrying her 2-year-old son, to cross the river and make it to the city; a young abolitionist and Underground Railroad participant named Harriet Beecher Stowe lived in Cincinnati at the time and likely borrowed from Harris' experiences to create one of the most riveting scenes in *Uncle Tom's Cabin*.

The metropolitan parts of the district, with more than 70% of the people, are mostly affluent and Republican. The counties farther east are less well off, with most of the old factories gone and with pockets of high unemployment and poverty. In April 2015, the unemployment rate was 4.1% in Clermont County, compared with 7.1% in Portsmouth-based Scioto, the third-highest in the state. Pike County has a lengthy Democratic tradition. The district still leans substantially Republican, and Democrats have rarely competed here.

Brad Wenstrup (R)

A foot surgeon and Iraq War veteran, Republican Brad Wenstrup exploited the anti-incumbent sentiment to upset often controversial Rep. Jean Schmidt in the 2012 primary in the heavily Republican district. He has served more quietly than his predecessor and has shown influence on national security issues.

Wenstrup was born and raised in Cincinnati. His father is an optician, and his mother worked at a Stein Mart department store. As early as second grade, Wenstrup thought about a career in medicine as well as serving in the military. "There were two shows I would watch with my dad. One was *Combat!*, and the other was called *Medical Center*. And I knew at an early age I wanted to be a doctor, but the idea of serving never really left my mind," Wenstrup recalled. He got his bachelor's degree from the University of Cincinnati and a medical degree from the Scholl College of Podiatric Medicine in Chicago.

Wenstrup opened his practice in 1986, and it was incorporated into Wellington Orthopaedic & Sports Medicine in 1999. He joined the Army Reserve in 1998 and became a combat surgeon in Iraq in 2005 and 2006. "I tell people, it's the worst thing I ever had to do, but the best thing I ever got to do," he said. Not long after the prisoner-abuse scandal at the Abu Ghraib prison erupted, he was stationed at a combat support hospital within the prison walls. He treated U.S. troops, civilians and some enemy combatants.

Politics grew more intriguing to Wenstrup when he returned from Iraq. "I started to see people in Washington making military decisions that have never served, making health care plans that have never seen a patient or dealt with insurance companies or Medicaid and Medicare," he said. He ran for mayor of Cincinnati in 2009 against incumbent Democrat Mark Mallory. Though Wenstrup lost, he took a respectable 46% of the vote in the Democratic-leaning city. The strong showing raised his profile and opportunities.

In 2011, he launched a primary challenge to Schmidt, who had experienced electoral troubles. In 2006, she faced a tough primary challenge and won with just 48% of the vote. In the 2006 and 2008 general elections, she got just 50% and 45%, respectively. She had sometimes offended colleagues in Washington and Ohio and was dubbed "Mean Jean" in the blogosphere.

In February 2012, Wenstrup got a key endorsement from the Ohio Liberty Council, a coalition of tea party groups. The anti-incumbent super PAC, Campaign for Primary Accountability, spent money against Schmidt. Wenstrup criticized her for owing money to lawyers at the Turkish Coalition of America while she sat on the House Foreign Affairs Committee. The Schmidt campaign said the money was donated before she served on the committee and that Schmidt had reimbursed some of the attorneys' fees. Wenstrup ran an ad attacking her votes to raise the debt limit and to support the Wall Street bailout, while mentioning that Schmidt planted a kiss on President Barack Obama at the State of the Union address. He won the nomination, 49%-43%. In November, he faced token opposition in Democrat William Smith, a former postal worker who spent no campaign money, and won, 59%-41%. He was reelected with 66% of the vote in 2014.

In the House, with help from Speaker John Boehner, who serves a nearby district, Wenstrup got seats on the Armed Services and Veterans' Affairs committees, and chairs the VA Subcommittee on Economic Opportunity, and he joined the Intelligence panel in 2015. When Congress completed action on the defense spending bill in December 2014, he cited the additional funding for Reserve and National Guard equipment, new funds to combat suicide within the ranks, and the continued prohibition on transfer of any detainees from the Guantanamo prison facility to the United States. In February 2015, Wenstrup said that Congress had "a constitutional responsibility" to debate President Barack Obama's request to authorize the use of military force against the Islamic State. In May, he praised the Veterans Affairs Department for integrating its record-keeping with Ohio's automatic prescription reporting system, and he highlighted his discussions of the problem with VA officials during the previous two years.

As a doctor, Wenstrup has advocated replacing the 2010 health care law with market-based solutions that protect the doctor-patient relationship. He opposed regulations on coal that would force businesses to pay higher energy prices. With Sen. Rob Portman and Rep. Bill Johnson, he demanded in May 2015 that the Energy Department provide more details of its plan to decontaminate and decommission the Portsmouth Gaseous Diffusion Plant; the uranium clean-up project employed nearly 2,000 workers.

THIRD DISTRICT

Joyce Beatty (D)

Elected 2012, 2nd term; b. March 12, 1950, Dayton; Central S. U., B.A. 1972, Wright St. U., M.S. 1975; Baptist; married (Otto Jr.); 2 children.

Elected Office: OH House, 1999-2008.

Professional Career: Sr.V.P., OH St. U., 2008-2013; Pres., Joyce Beatty & Assocs., 1992-2013; Dir., Montgomery Cnty. Dept. of Comm. Human Services, 1983-92; Dir., adult & elderly services, Montgomery Cnty. Mental Health Bd., 1983; Prof., Capital U., 1979-92; Prof., Sinclair Comm. Col., 1975-83; Caseworker, City of Dayton, 1971-75.

DC Office: 133 CHOB, 20515, 202-225-4324; Fax: 202-225-1984; Website: beatty.house.gov.

State Offices: Columbus, 614-220-0003.

Committees: *Financial Services:* Housing & Insurance; Oversight & Investigations.

Group Ratings

	ADA	ACLU	AFL-CIO	LCV	ITI	COC	HAFA	ACU	CFG	FRC
2014	85%	77%	–	97%	40%	43%	12%	4%	6%	0%
2013	80%	C	100%	93%	C	38%	C	12%	14%	C

National Journal Ratings

	2013 LIB	—	2013 CONS
Economic	75%	—	25%
Social	73%	—	24%
Foreign	86%	—	13%
Composite	79%	—	21%

Key Votes of the 113th Congress

1. Sandy storm spending	Y	5. Medical Marijuana	Y	9. Syrian Rebels Training	Y
2. Violence Against Women Act	Y	6. Farm Bill	N	10. Keystone pipeline	N
3. Guantanamo Bay Detainees	Y	7. Afghanistan Combat	Y	11. Immigration Exec. Action	N
4. Abortion 20-week ban	N	8. NSA Phone Data Collection	NV	12. Bipartisan budget deal	Y

Election Results

2014 general	Joyce Beatty ....(D)	91,769	(64%)	$612,031	$2,816
	John Adams.......................................(R)	51,475	(36%)	$3,059	
2014 primary	Joyce Beatty (D)....................unopposed				

Prior winning percentage: 2012 (68%)

Population		Race and Ethnicity		Income	
Total:	739,980	White	55.4%	Median income:	$41,020
Urban:	72.2%	Black	31.8%		*(376 of 435)*
Suburban:	27.6%	Latino	6.1%	Under $50,000	58.0%
Rural:	0.2%	Asian	2.7%	$50,000-$99,999:	29.1%
Land area:	408	Two races	3.3%	$100,000-$199,999:	10.8%
Pop/sq. mi.:	1,814.0	White Ethnic	21.4%	$200,000 or more:	2.1%
Born in state:	68.4%			Poverty Rate	23.3%
		Education			
Age Groups		H.S. grad or less:	44.3%	**Work**	
Under 18:	24.7%	Some college:	29.1%	White collar:	33.3%
18 to 34:	29.3%	College degree, 4 yr.:	17.5%	Blue collar:	45.7%
35 to 64:	36.1%	Post-grad study:	9.1%	Sales and service:	21.0%
Over 64:	9.9%				
		Military		Govt. workers:	14.2%
		Veterans/active duty:	7.6%		

Columbus Metro

In 1972, the first *Almanac of American Politics* noted that Columbus had just surpassed Cincinnati to become Ohio's second-largest city. Today, Columbus is by far the largest city in the state. Franklin County grew by a brisk 9% during the 2000s and another 4% in the three subsequent years, while

Voter Turnout	
2013 Total Citizen 18+	514,384
2014 House Turnout	143,261
2014 Turnout as % CVAP	27.9%
2012 Turnout as % CVAP	61%

four of the seven counties abutting it enjoyed double-digit growth rates. The reasons are simple: location, location, location...and government. Not only the geographical center of Ohio, the city lies just a one-day truck drive from more than half of the nation's population, making it the perfect location for a Midwestern hub. It is also the capital of the nation's seventh-most-populous state and home to the state university system's flagship campus: The Ohio State University (fans of college sports know that "The" is not to be dropped from the school's name).

In a region known for its blue-collar accents, Columbus has retained a distinctly white-collar flavor and attracted the type of upscale, enterprising people who have produced much of America's growth in recent years. It is home to five Fortune 500 companies: Nationwide Insurance, American Electric Power, Limited Brands (parent company to Victoria's Secret and Bath & Body Works), Momentive Specialty Chemicals and the big-box chain Big Lots. The area is the home of the Battelle Memorial Institute, the think tank that helped invent photocopying, compact discs and the Universal Product Code. Columbus has been rated as one of the best cities for a start-up business.

The city's rapidly growing foreign-born population—Latinos, Koreans, Ethiopians, Chins, Russian Jews and Somalis—exceeds that of Cleveland or Detroit. It isn't just ethnic diversity: Columbus sits just 90 miles north of the Mason-Dixon Line, and one is as likely to hear an Appalachian twang as a Great Lakes accent. The city's diverse climate—hot in the summer, cold in the winter—has driven innovation as well: The capitol building was one of the first in the country to include forced-air heating, while the former Lazarus department store was the first to enjoy air-conditioning. This population growth brought political change. Columbus had been Democratic during the Civil War years—making it all the more surprising that it contained a critical stop on the Underground Railroad—but became reliably Republican in

2012 Presidential Vote		
Barack Obama (D) 217,969	(70%)
Mitt Romney (R)..................90,434	(29%)

2008 Presidential Vote		
Barack Obama (D) 209,273	(67%)
John McCain (R)..................97,286	(31%)

Cook Partisan Voting Index: D+17

the late 1800s. As the metropolitan area grew, more people headed for the suburbs, and one of the largest Republican cities in the country slowly became Democratic again. It competed actively to host the 2016 Democratic convention, but the nod went to Philadelphia.

The 3rd Congressional District represents a bow by Republicans to these new political and demographic realities. Columbus had traditionally been split between the 12th and 15th districts, enabling suburban areas to trump Democratic-leaning portions of the city even in landslide Democratic years. By 2010, the city had become so solidly Democratic that the suburbs no longer outweighed it, and the region's rapid growth meant that either another district had to be extended into the area or a new one had to be created.

Republicans chose to protect the 12th and 15th, and create a Democratic "vote sink" in Franklin County, the only district in the state entirely contained in a single county. The 3rd takes in the skyscrapers of downtown Columbus; heavily Jewish Bexley, the site of the governor's mansion; the capitol, with the statue of President William McKinley out front; the university neighborhoods; city slums; and the Democratic portions of upscale New Albany and Westerville. The district includes working-class, mixed-race communities to the west of the city, like Greater Hilltop and Franklinton. These sometimes disparate areas have Democratic voting patterns in common. It is the second-most Democratic district in Ohio. Barack Obama won over two-thirds of the vote here in 2008 and improved on that showing four years later.

Joyce Beatty (D)

Democrat Joyce Beatty's election to the House in 2012 gave Ohio its first two African-American members of Congress serving together. The other is Cleveland Democrat Marcia Fudge. Among the differences between them is that Beatty represents a growing constituency.

Beatty is the daughter of a brick mason and stay-at-home mom. Her parents moved from the inner city to a predominately white neighborhood with better schools when Beatty was young, and she and her family were the only blacks on their street in Dayton. Her high school became integrated in her freshman year. Beatty's parents constantly stressed the importance of civil rights for women and African Americans, and her interest in politics was fueled by hearing Jesse Jackson speak at the 1984 Democratic National Convention.

She did her undergraduate work in speech and psychology at Central State University and later earned a master's degree in counseling from Wright State University, both in Ohio. She had several jobs in local and county government and academia, eventually becoming senior vice president for engagement and outreach at Ohio State University. She also owned a management consulting business and a clothing store in downtown Dayton. Beatty served in the Ohio House for nearly a decade, including a stint as minority leader from 2006 to 2008. She was instrumental in passing legislation that helped women without health insurance get cancer screenings, that reined in home foreclosures, and that encouraged financial literacy education. Her husband, Otto Beatty Jr., is an attorney and was a member of the state House for nearly two decades until he resigned and was succeeded by his wife; their two sons are both attorneys.

When she entered the race in the new Columbus-based district, Beatty cited her knowledge of how to "make a payroll" and her ability to work with businesses and labor unions to bring jobs to central Ohio. She made education a central focus of her campaign, drawing on her background to call for making college more affordable and bringing public-private partnerships to the area to work on job training initiatives with community colleges and training centers. Instead of traditional town hall-style meetings, Beatty held what she called "listening tours," bringing in "everyday folks," such as small business owners and educators, to speak to voters.

With the endorsement of Columbus Mayor Michael Coleman and strong financial support from labor unions, Beatty in March defeated three other candidates in the Democratic primary. Her toughest opponent was former Rep. Mary Jo Kilroy, who had served in the 15th District for one term until her defeat in 2010. Beatty won the primary 38%-35%. In the general election, she had no trouble with Republican Chris Long, a Reynoldsburg City Council member. Beatty won, 68%-26%.

Well before the election, Beatty had drawn the attention of national Democrats. House Minority Leader Nancy Pelosi traveled to her district to join her at a forum on health care policy, and Beatty spoke at the Democratic convention in Charlotte on the role of women in the economy.

In the House, Beatty joined the Financial Services Committee, which is a useful connection to the robust financial sector in Columbus. She focused on home mortgage financial literacy, financial oversight, affordable housing and consumer access to credit. She has been a leading advocate for placing a woman on the $20 bill, and praised Treasury Secretary Jacob Lew for a step toward "gender equality" when he announced in June 2015 that a woman would be placed on the $10 bill. She urged reauthorization of the Export-Import Bank, and said that it supported $67 million in exports by 13 businesses in her district.

During her first term, Beatty secured nearly $4 million to address Columbus's infant mortality rate, which is one of the highest in the country. She praised the Big Ten universities when they adopted a plan similar to what she had advocated to guarantee that students who receive athletic scholarships may keep the award until they graduate. She cosponsored bipartisan legislation to combat sex trafficking, which passed the House in 2014 and 2015. Beatty faced a nominal reelection challenge in her safe district.

FOURTH DISTRICT

Jim Jordan (R)

Elected 2006, 5th term; b. Feb. 17, 1964, Troy; U. of WI, B.A. 1986, OH St. U., M.Ed. 1991, Capital U., J.D. 2002; Christian; married (Polly); 4 children.

Elected Office: OH House, 1994-2000; OH Senate, 2000-06.

Professional Career: Asst. wrestling coach, OH St. U., 1987-95; Wrestling camp coach, clinician, 1987-2006.

DC Office: 1524 LHOB, 20515, 202-225-2676; Fax: 202-226-0577; Website: jordan.house.gov.

State Offices: Lima, 419-999-6455; Norwalk, 419-663-1426.

Committees: *Judiciary:* Constitution & Civil Justice; Intellectual Property, & the Internet. *Oversight & Government Reform:* Health Care Benefits, & Administrative Rules (Chmn); Government Operations. *Select Benghazi Committee.*

Group Ratings

	ADA	ACLU	AFL-CIO	LCV	ITI	COC	HAFA	ACU	CFG	FRC
2014	5%	0%	–	3%	80%	43%	90%	100%	100%	100%
2013	5%	C	10%	7%	C	85%	C	100%	97%	C

National Journal Ratings

	2013 LIB	—	2013 CONS
Economic	0%	—	98%
Social	13%	—	84%
Foreign	34%	—	60%
Composite	18%	—	83%

Key Votes of the 113th Congress

1. Sandy storm spending	N	5. Medical Marijuana	N	9. Syrian Rebels Training	N
2. Violence Against Women Act	N	6. Farm Bill	N	10. Keystone pipeline	Y
3. Guantanamo Bay Detainees	N	7. Afghanistan Combat	N	11. Immigration Exec. Action	Y
4. Abortion 20-week ban	Y	8. NSA Phone Data Collection	Y	12. Bipartisan budget deal	N

Election Results

2014 general	Jim Jordan (R)	125,907	(68%)	$1,016,223	
	Janet Garrett (D)	60,165	(32%)	$44,108	$22,552
2014 primary	Jim Jordan (R)	unopposed			

Prior winning percentages: 2012 (58%), 2010 (71%), 2008 (65%), 2006 (60%)

Population		Race and Ethnicity		Income	
Total:	709,122	White	88.3%	Median income:	$47,605
Urban:	17.3%	Black	5.4%		*(272 of 435)*
Suburban:	24.5%	Latino	3.3%	Under $50,000	52.3%
Rural:	58.2%	Asian	0.7%	$50,000-$99,999:	32.4%
Land area:	4,116	Two races	2.0%	$100,000-$199,999:	13.0%
Pop/sq. mi.:	172.3	White Ethnic	27.2%	$200,000 or more:	2.3%
Born in state:	82.3%			Poverty Rate	13.4%
		Education			
Age Groups		H.S. grad or less:	52.3%	**Work**	
Under 18:	22.9%	Some college:	30.5%	White collar:	28.5%
18 to 34:	20.5%	College degree, 4 yr.:	10.7%	Blue collar:	38.6%
35 to 64:	40.9%	Post-grad study:	6.5%	Sales and service:	32.8%
Over 64:	15.8%				
		Military		Govt. workers:	11.7%
		Veterans/active duty:	10.0%		

Central Ohio: Lima, Sandusky

Central and western Ohio look mostly like farmland to the traveler. Yet this is manufacturing country, indeed one of America's premier manufacturing areas, where the economy is based on factories in small towns and on rural highways. These places seem far from anywhere important, yet the

Voter Turnout	
2013 Total Citizen 18+	542,474
2014 House Turnout	186,072
2014 Turnout as % CVAP	34.3%
2012 Turnout as % CVAP	60.7%

region has been quietly prosperous most of the years since World War II. While there have been some manufacturing job losses, most of this area emerged from the recession in better shape than other parts of the state. Each population center has its own "pet" industry: In Lima, the Joint Systems Manufacturing Center has been building versions of the Abrams tank for 30 years, and Ford spent $500 million to develop "EcoBoost" technology for its F-150 pick-up truck at a plant there. Dannon yogurt operates a food-processing facility in Minster. In Jackson Center, Airstream expanded its iconic trailers in 2014. Honda has invested more than $6 billion in Marysville and East Liberty since it opened its first plant in Union County, for motorcycles, in 1979. Today, it employs 13,700 Ohioans and is the largest automobile employer in the state. In April 2015, Honda announced a local workforce training initiative. Ethanol production is a growth industry in the area, and a small but growing Hispanic population is limiting the effects of native outmigration. Still, not all is well. Monthly production of the Abrams tank was scheduled to drop in 2015 from double digits to no more than three and significant job cutbacks were expected at the unique JSMC, which was preparing for a new generation of tanks.

These small towns have historical significance. Marion is the home of President Warren G. Harding and socialist Norman Thomas; the latter, as a young boy, delivered the newspaper edited by the former. Fremont, settled by abstemious Yankees, was the home of President Rutherford B. Hayes, whose wife, Lucy, served only lemonade in the White House. Today it is home to an aromatic Heinz ketchup plant. Tiny Milan is the birthplace of the great inventor and capitalist Thomas Edison, while Tiffin still has St. Paul's United Methodist Church, the first public building in the United States to be wired for electricity.

This terrain in central Ohio makes up the 4th Congressional District. The district has been extended north and east into Seneca, Sandusky, Erie and Lorain counties, and

2012 Presidential Vote		
Mitt Romney (R)	185,521	(56%)
Barack Obama (D)	139,189	(42%)
2008 Presidential Vote		
John McCain (R)	187,326	(54%)
Barack Obama (D)	150,274	(44%)
Cook Partisan Voting Index: R+9		

the outer Cleveland suburbs. But it has been carefully wedged into the countryside to avoid metro areas, including Dayton and Toledo. The GOP lean of the small towns mitigate the impact of places like Oberlin College, one of the most liberal colleges in the country and the first to admit women and African Americans. Overall, the 4th is the second strongest Republican district in Ohio, behind the adjacent 8th District of Speaker John Boehner.

Jim Jordan (R)

Republican Jim Jordan, first elected in 2006, has endeared himself to conservatives while annoying his party's leaders as the confrontational chairman of the Republican Study Committee, and later with more informal groups. He has been a leader of the House Freedom Caucus, which was organized in 2015 as a forum for the most conservative members on economic and social policy and in their hostility to President Barack Obama.

Jordan grew up in Champaign County and graduated from Graham High School, where he was a championship wrestler. At the University of Wisconsin, Jordan won two NCAA wrestling championships in the 134-pound weight class and was inducted into the Badger Hall of Fame. After graduating with an economics degree, Jordan worked as an assistant wrestling coach at Ohio State University, where he earned a master's degree in education before completing a law degree at Capital University. Within a few years, he began thinking about elected office. "You get married and have kids, and you get sick of having the government take your money and tell you what to do," he told columnist George Will in 2011. He won a state House seat in 1994, and served there six years before he won a tough primary in 2000 for the state Senate. In the Legislature, his solidly conservative record included legislation creating Ohio's "Choose Life" license plates, a ban on same-sex marriage, and government vouchers for private-school tuition.

Jordan ran for House when Republican Rep. Michael Oxley retired as chairman of the Financial Services Committee. In the six-way Republican primary, he had the most name recognition plus support from Ohio Right to Life, the National Rifle Association, and the national anti-tax group Club for Growth. Findlay real estate developer Frank Guglielmi spent $1.6 million of his own money and saturated the television airwaves with ads, far more than the rest of the field. While money mattered, so did geography and connections. Jordan won with 51%, carrying eight of 11 counties. Guglielmi carried only his home county and one other to finish second with 30%. Despite the tough political environment for Republicans in 2006, Democrats barely mounted a competitive campaign. Jordan beat Lima attorney and Vietnam veteran Rick Siferd 60%-40%.

In the House, Jordan established an unfailingly conservative voting record, with eight perfect scores and a 100% lifetime rating from the American Conservative Union through 2014. "With the exception of the military, the federal government doesn't do anything very well," he told the *Mansfield News Journal*. He said he weighs all issues based on whether they benefit families; he is a father of four whose desk calendar is crowded with his children's athletic schedules.

With his right-wing bona fides well established, Jordan succeeded Georgia's Tom Price as head of the 170-member Republican Study Committee in 2011 when the GOP reclaimed control of the House. "He approaches the world of politics like a wrestling match, with the same kind of intensity, preparation, training, and focus," Price told *The Plain Dealer* of Cleveland. Jordan had been chairman of the group's budget task force. He beat back a challenge from Texan Louie Gohmert, who accused him of being a "wing man" for John Boehner, the GOP leader from a neighboring Ohio district. Boehner, in fact, made a campaign appearance for him in Lima the final weekend of the 2010 campaign. But Jordan vowed to be independent of the leadership, saying his group would lobby lawmakers just as vigorously as did the Republicans' formal whip team.

Under Jordan's guidance, the RSC in 2011 unveiled a congressional budget plan that called for spending cuts of $2.5 trillion over 10 years. It would have held non-security discretionary spending to fiscal 2008 levels in the first year and at 2006 levels in subsequent years. When the House approved a measure in March to keep the government running temporarily as Boehner and Obama tried to hammer out an agreement on spending cuts, Jordan was openly scornful. "We must do more than cut spending in bite-sized pieces," he said.

He denied speculation that he and allies were eager to shut down the government, a move that had disastrous political consequences for Republicans in 1995, and he said he was not out to undercut Boehner. But anonymous Republicans and lobbyists told *The Columbus Dispatch* that they were worried about the growing divide between Jordan and Boehner. GOP Rep. Steven LaTourette, a Boehner ally, referred to the RSC in an Associated Press interview: "My experience with things that don't bend is that they break." When Republicans and Obama once again failed to reach a budget deal in early 2013, and triggered across-the-board spending cuts under the sequester, Jordan shrugged that it "won't be the end of the world" and marked an important step toward savings.

Jordan dug in his heels a few months later during the showdown over whether to raise the federal debt limit. But he apologized to Republicans at a closed-door meeting after one of his staffers sent an email to conservative groups identifying which lawmakers were undecided about voting for the increase. *The Dispatch* reported that Boehner's allies in Ohio were considering retaliation through a redistricting plan that would make Jordan's seat substantially more competitive. Boehner denied any such effort, and his new district was securely Republican, though it moved well beyond Jordan's base in western Ohio. Despite his stature among the rebels and his continued poor-mouthing of GOP leaders, Jordan pointedly was not among the conservatives who voted for alternatives when Boehner was reelected as House speaker in 2013 and 2015.

Jordan has focused his legislative work on the Oversight and Government Reform Committee, where he became chairman in 2015 of the Health Care, Benefits and Administrative Rules Subcommittee. "Uncovering and investigating government abuse has been my passion in Congress," Jordan said when he took the position.

As the founding chairman in January 2015 of the House Freedom Caucus, whose chief purpose was to move the Republican agenda to the right, he created another base for friction with Boehner. Those divisions were apparent on several issues in the next few months, notably opposition by Jordan and many in the Freedom Caucus to giving trade promotion authority to Obama, and their demand that new limits on national security data collection go even further. Unlike some of his more junior and outspoken colleagues, though, he was less interested in casting the conflict in personal terms. He typically defers to other conservatives who are more eager to pinpoint Boehner as the problem.

The new boundaries of his 4th District have been little problem to Jordan. He was reelected in 2014 with 68 percent of the vote against weak opposition.

FIFTH DISTRICT

Bob Latta (R)

Elected Dec. 2007, 4th full term; b. April 18, 1956, Bluffton; Bowling Green St. U., B.A. 1978, U. of Toledo Col. of Law, J.D. 1981; Catholic; married (Marcia); 2 children.

Elected Office: Wood Cnty. commissioner, 1991-96; OH Senate, 1997-2001; OH Gen. Assembly, 2001-07.

Professional Career: Atty., 1981-91.

DC Office: 2448 RHOB, 20515, 202-225-6405; Fax: 202-225-1985; Website: latta.house.gov.

State Offices: Bowling Green, 419-354-8700; Defiance, 419-782-1996; Findlay, 419-422-7791.

Committees: *Energy & Commerce:* Communications & Technology (VChmn); Energy & Power; Environment & the Economy.

Group Ratings

	ADA	ACLU	AFL-CIO	LCV	ITI	COC	HAFA	ACU	CFG	FRC
2014	0%	0%	–	3%	100%	86%	64%	84%	69%	100%
2013	0%	C	14%	0%	C	85%	C	76%	76%	C

National Journal Ratings

	2013 LIB	—	2013 CONS
Economic	6%	—	94%
Social	0%	—	87%
Foreign	5%	—	86%
Composite	7%	—	93%

Key Votes of the 113th Congress

1. Sandy storm spending	N	5. Medical Marijuana	N
2. Violence Against Women Act	N	6. Farm Bill	Y
3. Guantanamo Bay Detainees	N	7. Afghanistan Combat	N
4. Abortion 20-week ban	Y	8. NSA Phone Data Collection	N

9. Syrian Rebels Training	Y
10. Keystone pipeline	Y
11. Immigration Exec. Action	Y
12. Bipartisan budget deal	Y

Election Results

2014 general	Bob Latta (R)............................. 134,449	(67%)	$777,771	$1,894
	Robert Fry (D)............................ 58,507	(29%)	$59,444	
	Eric Eberly (Lib)........................... 9,344	(5%)		
2014 primary	Bob Latta (R)........................unopposed			

Prior winning percentages: 2012 (57%), 2010 (68%), 2008 (64%), 2007 special (57%)

Population		Race and Ethnicity		Income	
Total:	730,642	White	90.4%	Median income:	$50,823
Urban:	15.0%	Latino	4.3%		*(225 of 435)*
Suburban:	35.3%	Black	2.7%	Under $50,000	49.1%
Rural:	49.7%	Asian	0.9%	$50,000-$99,999:	32.8%
Land area:	5,456	Two races	1.5%	$100,000-$199,999:	15.4%
Pop/sq. mi.:	133.9	White Ethnic	29.3%	$200,000 or more:	2.7%
Born in state:	79.8%			Poverty Rate	12.6%
		Education			
Age Groups		H.S. grad or less:	44.2%	**Work**	
Under 18:	23.5%	Some college:	31.2%	White collar:	31.8%
18 to 34:	22.3%	College degree, 4 yr.:	14.8%	Blue collar:	38.9%
35 to 64:	39.0%	Post-grad study:	9.9%	Sales and service:	29.3%
Over 64:	15.2%				
		Military		Govt. workers:	12.6%
		Veterans/active duty:	8.5%		

Northwest Ohio: Toledo Area, Bowling Green

Undergirded by limestone, as flat and fertile as any place in America, northwest Ohio was economically productive from the time it was settled. But that settlement came relatively late. A series of conflicts with Native Americans played a large role in the delay. In 1791, near Fort Recovery in Mercer

Voter Turnout	
2013 Total Citizen 18+	550,778
2014 House Turnout	202,300
2014 Turnout as % CVAP	36.7%
2012 Turnout as % CVAP	65.7%

County, the United States Army was routed by a confederation of Indian tribes: Only 48 of the 1,000 soldiers led into battle escaped unharmed, and a full quarter of them died. Three years later, the Battle of Fallen Timbers near present-day Maumee put a temporary end to outright conflict between Indians and Americans, and the ensuing Treaty of Greenville set aside northwestern Ohio for Native American use; the area wasn't made formally available for white settlement until the end of Tecumseh's War some 20 years later. But the area was still inhospitable for pioneers. What we know today as fecund farmland was actually part of a giant swamp in the early 1800s. The Great Black Swamp, left behind by a retreating glacier thousands of years earlier, ran from present-day Sandusky southwest to Findlay and west to the outskirts of Fort Wayne Indiana. It wasn't drained until the mid-1800s, and very few of the towns here were founded before 1840.

Today, this is prime industrial country. Its limestone, rail connections, and location near the Great Lakes have spurred the growth of a factory economy that financially is far more important than agriculture. After the first settlements took hold, northwest Ohio grew steadily for many decades, with Germany supplying many of the immigrants. In the 1950s and 1960s, its small factories supplied the big auto plants in Detroit and Ohio. Growth lagged noticeably in the 1980s, when the domestic industry collapsed, but rebounded somewhat as small firms sold not only to the Big Three but to foreign customers. Honda has dozens of suppliers in the area, although many parts companies have continued to cut back with the continuing troubles in the domestic auto industry.

The 5th Congressional District of Ohio sweeps across northwest Ohio, from northern Fulton County, past the university town of Bowling Green and the Toledo suburb of Perrysburg, to the towns of Defiance and Napoleon and to Ohio's border with Michigan and Indiana. It takes in Findlay, home of Marathon Petroleum, as well as several lightly populated counties in the northwest. Its factories are numerous and widespread: Bowling Green is the site of the state's first wind turbines, and locals now call it "Blowing Green." Celina Aluminum Precision Technology is a Honda supplier, and Napoleon is home to Isofoton North America, which supplies solar energy products. Napoleon has the world's largest Campbell soup plant, which in 2014 was named the most environmentally sustainable plant in Ohio. Upper Sandusky (which is more than 60 miles inland from Sandusky on Lake Erie) is home to over 40 industrial firms. Residents in parts of Lucas County, and nearby Fulton and Henry counties, have objected to a proposed gas transmission pipeline. In May 2015, a report from Bowling Green University warned that, with robotics and other enhanced productivity, manufacturing could not be relied on to create as many middle-class jobs in the future.

2012 Presidential Vote		
Mitt Romney (R)................195,060	(54%)
Barack Obama (D) 159,659	(44%)
2008 Presidential Vote		
John McCain (R)................194,787	(52%)
Barack Obama (D) 171,859	(46%)
Cook Partisan Voting Index: R+7		

This had been a solidly Republican district, though it now includes parts of Lucas County that lean Democratic. It remains comfortably Republican—like each of the 12 GOP-held districts in Ohio.

Bob Latta (R)

Republican Bob Latta, who won a special election for his seat in 2007, is the son of Delbert Latta, who held the seat for 30 years. The younger Latta is conservative like his father and meshes well with the younger, like-minded Republicans who arrived in subsequent House elections. He has sought to address environmental concerns of Lake Erie.

Bob Latta was born in Ohio but split his early years between his native Bluffton and Washington D.C. Helping his father's campaigns, Latta says he learned the business of catering to constituents. Young Latta was frequently interrupted during his homework to answer their phone calls and remembers his father following up with federal agencies to try to get results from the vast government bureaucracy. Latta also spent time driving around the district with his dad, going to meetings and events. During college at Bowling Green State University, he volunteered in his father's office, where he met his wife, Marcia, who worked for his father. When he graduated from law school at the University of Toledo, his father had one bit of career advice for him: Don't get into politics.

He did his best to follow that guidance and practiced law for several years. But when his father retired in 1988, the 31-year-old couldn't pass on the opportunity to try to follow in his footsteps. First, he had to get by Paul Gillmor, a Republican state senator who had been waiting for a congressional seat to open up during Del Latta's long tenure. In the primary contest with Gillmor, Bob Latta argued that, like his father, he would start out young and eventually gain enough seniority to preside over powerful committees. After a spirited race, Gillmor beat Latta by just 27 votes out of 57,361 cast.

Latta retreated to local politics, first getting elected to the Wood County Commission and then to the Ohio Legislature, where he served in both the Senate and then the Assembly—an unusual sequence. One of his major efforts was to repeal the estate tax, which he succeeded in doing for 78 percent of Ohioans. An avid hunter, Latta championed conservation issues, including longer hunting seasons and expanded wildlife reserves.

In September 2007, Gillmor died at his Washington home, apparently from a fall down stairs. Latta entered the contest for the open seat, but had to win two hard-fought contests. His major primary opponent was state Sen. Steve Buehrer, who was backed by the national anti-tax group Club for Growth, which ran several ads attacking Latta as an advocate of higher taxes. Latta attacked Buehrer for accepting donations from a former fundraiser for President George W. Bush in Ohio, Tom Noe, a convicted money launderer. But it came to light that Latta had also taken money from Noe. In the end, Latta defeated Buehrer by only 2,542 votes out of 74,191 cast.

Latta's Democratic opponent, Robin Weirauch, a former public administrator who had twice run against Gillmor, had backing from national labor unions and the fundraising group EMILY's list. She attacked Latta on economic issues and on his support for the Iraq war. Despite Weirauch's best efforts to capitalize on the anti-Washington sentiment that year, she fell short in the solidly Republican district. Latta won 57%-43%.

In the House, Latta has been solidly conservative, often dismissing Democratic proposals as "socialist." He introduced bills to eliminate automatic pay raises for lawmakers, to permanently repeal the estate tax, and to issue a Ronald Reagan commemorative coin. He took a prized seat on the Energy and Commerce Committee in 2010, having earlier made energy independence his central issue. He successfully amended a House-passed air-quality bill in September 2011 to require the Environmental Protection Agency to take industry costs into account in setting standards under the Clean Air Act. The proposal never moved in the Senate, and in December it landed Latta on the *Los Angeles Times* editorial board's list of the "10 biggest enemies of the Earth."

Latta has taken an increasing interest in technology. He was the first House member to release an iPhone app in 2010 and became vice chairman of Energy and Commerce's Communications and Technology Subcommittee in 2013. He tried unsuccessfully in February 2011 to amend a spending bill to cut the National Institute of Standards and Technology's budget by $10 million and introduced a resolution the following month declaring that to continue aggressive growth in the telecommunications and technology industries, the federal government "should get out of the way and stay out of the way." He co-chairs the Republican New Media Caucus.

As vice chairman of the Congressional Sportsmen's Caucus, Latta drew headlines in 2009 for castigating an Obama administration proposal to reclassify pocketknives that can be sprung open with one hand as switchblades. Both chambers passed bills overturning the rule, and it was signed into law. In May 2015, he reintroduced his Protect Our Great Lakes Act, which is designed to reduce algal blooms by prohibiting the discharge of dredged material into the lakes. The House passed in February his related Drinking Water Protection Act, which requires the Environmental Protection Agency to submit a plan to Congress that assesses and manages risks of algal toxins in drinking water.

Latta has won reelection by wide margins. His father was known for his constituent-service work, and his son has sought to replicate that by personally reading and signing each piece of outgoing mail from his office. His closest race was in 2012. The Toledo *Blade* endorsed his Democratic opponent, Angela Zimmann, a college professor, and said Latta "has not been pragmatic or constructive." Latta outspent her nearly 3-to-1 and won convincingly, 57%-39%.

SIXTH DISTRICT

Bill Johnson (R)

Elected 2010, 3rd term; b. Nov. 10, 1954, Roseboro, NC; Troy U., B.S. 1979, GA Inst. of Tech., M.S. 1984, U.S. Air Force Squadron Officers Col., U.S. Air Force Air Command & Staff Col.; Protestant; married (LeeAnn); 4 children.

Military Career: Air Force, 1973-99.

Professional Career: Pres., Johnson-Schley Mgmt. Group, 1999-2003; Owner, J2 Business Solutions, 2003-06; Dir., Lockheed Martin, 2005; CIO, Stoneridge Inc., 2006-10.

DC Office: 1710 LHOB, 20515, 202-225-5705; Fax: 202-225-5907; Website: billjohnson.house.gov.

State Offices: Cambridge, 740-432-2366; Ironton, 740-534-9431; Marietta, 740-376-0868; Salem, 330-337-6951.

Committees: *Energy & Commerce:* Environment & the Economy; Energy & Power; Communications & Technology. *Science, Space, & Technology:* Research & Technology; Space.

Group Ratings

	ADA	ACLU	AFL-CIO	LCV	ITI	COC	HAFA	ACU	CFG	FRC
2014	0%	0%	–	6%	100%	86%	53%	72%	51%	100%
2013	5%	C	14%	0%	C	85%	C	76%	68%	C

National Journal Ratings

	2013 LIB	—	2013 CONS
Economic	26%	—	73%
Social	0%	—	87%
Foreign	15%	—	77%
Composite	17%	—	83%

Key Votes of the 113th Congress

1. Sandy storm spending	N	5. Medical Marijuana		N	9. Syrian Rebels Training	Y
2. Violence Against Women Act	N	6. Farm Bill		Y	10. Keystone pipeline	Y
3. Guantanamo Bay Detainees	N	7. Afghanistan Combat		N	11. Immigration Exec. Action	Y
4. Abortion 20-week ban	Y	8. NSA Phone Data Collection		Y	12. Bipartisan budget deal	Y

Election Results

2014 general	Bill Johnson (R)	111,026	(58%)	$1,920,522	$46,939	$39,310
	Jennifer Garrison (D)	73,561	(39%)	$902,867		
	Dennis Lambert (Green)	6,065	(3%)			
2014 primary	Bill Johnson (R)	unopposed				

Prior winning percentages: 2012 (53%), 2010 (50%)

Population		Race and Ethnicity		Income	
Total:	713,464	White	94.9%	Median income:	$41,719
Urban:	5.4%	Black	2.4%		(363 of 435)
Suburban:	22.8%	Latino	0.8%	Under $50,000	57.5%
Rural:	71.8%	Asian	0.3%	$50,000-$99,999:	29.9%
Land area:	6,506	Two races	1.4%	$100,000-$199,999:	11.0%
Pop/sq. mi.:	109.7	White Ethnic	30.7%	$200,000 or more:	1.6%
Born in state:	69.7%			Poverty Rate	17.9%
		Education			
Age Groups		H.S. grad or less:	56.5%	**Work**	
Under 18:	21.6%	Some college:	28.3%	White collar:	27.6%
18 to 34:	19.3%	College degree, 4 yr.:	9.5%	Blue collar:	42.3%
35 to 64:	41.4%	Post-grad study:	5.6%	Sales and service:	30.1%
Over 64:	17.7%			Govt. workers:	12.8%
		Military			
		Veterans/active duty:	10.7%		

Ohio River Valley: Steubenville

In the years after the American Revolution, shipping goods downriver by raft was cheaper than sending them over the Appalachian Mountains, and so the Ohio River became a great highway of commerce. From Pittsburgh, where the Allegheny and Monongahela Rivers meet to form the Ohio, the

Voter Turnout	
2013 Total Citizen 18+	556,323
2014 House Turnout	190,652
2014 Turnout as % CVAP	34.3%
2012 Turnout as % CVAP	57.0%

river led south and west toward the Mississippi and the great port of New Orleans. For hundreds of miles, it twisted this way and that through mountains and rolling hills, land that marked the boundary between post-Revolutionary Virginia and the Northwest Territory, between slaveholding territory and free soil as determined by the Confederation Congress of 1787. Across this boundary, settlers made their way in those years to Ohio—Yankees and, in larger numbers, Virginians.

By the late 19th century, the Ohio was an industrial river. Coal was nearby, barge transportation was available, and railroads were built in the narrow valleys between the hills. Steel mills went up on the riverfront. This produced prosperity for a while, but it also produced pollution—Steubenville on the Ohio River once had the nation's dirtiest air—and after the old-line steel industry fell on hard times, the Ohio River was lined with some of the most impoverished parts of America. Even with mandates from the Clean Air Act, the pollution in much of the area from coal-fired power plants remains. But the positive news is that many local landowners have recently reaped a windfall after rising prices made feasible the extraction of oil and natural gas from the Marcellus and Utica shale beds miles under their land; the ranks of these "shale-ionaires" are expected to grow. Economists advised local communities to use this shot of prosperity to make long-term plans for the area. Southeast Ohio suffers from poor highways, and poor air quality in some parts.

The 6th Congressional District of Ohio is made up of a string of counties running 325 miles along the Ohio River, plus part of the Mahoning Valley. It includes Canfield and a few small suburbs of Youngstown in Mahoning County, and it takes in East Liverpool, where bank robber and Public Enemy No. 1 Charles Arthur "Pretty Boy" Floyd was shot by FBI agents in a cornfield. Nearby is

2012 Presidential Vote		
Mitt Romney (R)	176,602	(55%)
Barack Obama (D)	136,518	(43%)

2008 Presidential Vote		
John McCain (R)	177,072	(53%)
Barack Obama (D)	149,039	(45%)

Cook Partisan Voting Index: R+8

Steubenville, once known as "Sin City" and home to Rat Pack crooner Dean Martin. The district curves along the lightly populated stretch of the river south from Marietta, past the old industrial town of Ironton, and extends to Wheelersburg, which is near Portsmouth and not quite in the Cincinnati metropolitan area.

This mix of communities has made a Republican district with a cultural conservatism much like that of West Virginia and eastern Kentucky across the river. The population is 95 percent white, the third highest in the nation.

Bill Johnson (R)

Republican Bill Johnson defeated two-term Democratic Rep. Charlie Wilson in 2010 and then beat him in a rematch two years later to dispel Democratic accusations that he was a fluke. Wilson died at age 70 in 2013, highlighting the Democrats' need for younger faces. Prior to Congress, Johnson was a career officer in the Air Force, then became a business consultant and founded an anti-tax group.

Johnson was born in Roseboro, North Carolina, and raised on his family's cotton and tobacco farm. He joined the Air Force when he was just 17. While serving, he graduated with a degree in computer science from Alabama's Troy University. In the military, he was stationed at many bases; as a director at U.S. Special Operations Command, he briefed congressional and intelligence officials. He retired from the military in 1999 as a lieutenant colonel, dealing with communications and computer systems.

Johnson earned his master's degree in computer science from Georgia Tech. After leaving the Air Force, he worked for a number of high-technology companies. He became an information-technology consultant, especially for the military. He moved to Ohio in 2006, when he began working for Stoneridge, which makes electronic components for automobiles. Upset that shoppers were pouring across the border into Pennsylvania to buy certain goods free of sales taxes, Johnson in 2009 founded an organization called the Ohio Sales Tax Reform Incentive with the goal of creating tax holidays for shoppers.

Initially, Johnson considered running against Democratic Rep. Tim Ryan in the adjacent district. But in challenging Wilson, he picked a much less Democratic district. In the GOP primary, he defeated Donald Allen, a veterinarian, 43%-37%; former Belmont County Sheriff Richard Stobbs got 20%.

Johnson tried to characterize Wilson as a puppet of liberal House Speaker Nancy Pelosi and out of touch with his constituents. In their only debate, Wilson accused Johnson's company of exporting jobs overseas, while Johnson replied that the company created jobs in Ohio. The Republican called Wilson's attacks "the desperate act of a career politician who cannot defend his record for his tax-and-spend policies." Wilson had a large fundraising advantage, but the race tightened in the final weeks.

In mid-October, the Democratic Congressional Campaign Committee stepped in to buy advertising for Wilson. Meanwhile, Johnson benefited from ads by the U.S. Chamber of Commerce that attacked Wilson as "Party-Line Charlie." Wilson cast fiscally conservative votes and backed gun rights, but he also voted for President Barack Obama's overhaul of health care policy and the Democrats' $787 billion economic stimulus bill. Johnson won, 50%-45%. Wilson outspent Johnson almost 2-to-1, but each of them benefited from national party spending.

In the House, Johnson's voting record moved closer to the center, as he adopted more Democratic positions on foreign policy. But he remained an adamant Obama administration critic. He won House passage in September 2012 of his "Stop the War on Coal Act," which barred the Environmental Protection Agency from restricting greenhouse gas emissions, quashed stricter fuel efficiency standards for cars, and gave states control over disposal of coal byproducts. The vote coincided with GOP presidential candidate Mitt Romney's attacks on Obama over coal. Johnson also introduced a bill to prevent the rewriting of a Bush administration regulation that allows mining companies to dump debris in stream beds that fill up in rainy seasons but go dry at other times.

In 2013, Johnson got a seat on the Energy and Commerce Committee, where he was in a better position to act on coal and promote energy independence. In January 2015, the House passed his bill to expedite exports of liquefied natural gas by setting a deadline for federal approval. After a trip to four European nations in May, he said that they are "begging" for U.S. energy exports so that they can reduce their dependence on Russia.

Wilson sought a comeback in 2012, and loaned his campaign more than $400,000 to try to keep pace with Johnson, who tried to preserve his outsider status by running ads referring to his rival as "Congressman Charlie Wilson." Wilson got about $2 million in help from the DCCC in the race's closing weeks, but the anti-tax lobbying group Americans for Tax Reform spent more than $3 million on Johnson's behalf. Johnson won again, 53%-47%. In 2014, Johnson faced Democrat Jennifer Garrison, a lawyer who served six years in the state Assembly and described herself as "pro-life, pro-gun and pro-coal." She called Johnson "the face of Washington dysfunction." Johnson outspent her $1.9 million to $900,000. He won 58%-39% and took 17 of the 18 counties. Democrats may decide to send their campaign money elsewhere.

SEVENTH DISTRICT

Bob Gibbs (R)

Elected 2010, 3rd term; b. June 14, 1954, Peru, IN; OH St. U. Ag. Tech. Inst., A.S. 1974; Methodist; married (Jody Cox); 3 children.

Elected Office: OH House, 2003-08; OH Senate, 2008-10.

Professional Career: Technician, OH Ag. Research & Devel. Ctr., 1974-78; Owner, Hidden Hollow Farms, 1978-2004; Owner, Gibbs Enterprises.

DC Office: 329 CHOB, 20515, 202-225-6265; Fax: 202-225-3394; Website: gibbs.house.gov.

State Offices: Ashland, 419-207-0650; Canton, 330-737-1631.

Committees: *Agriculture:* Nutrition; General Farm Commodities & Risk Management. *Transportation & Infrastructure:* Highways & Transit; Coast Guard & Maritime Transportation; Water Resources & Environment (Chmn).

Group Ratings

	ADA	ACLU	AFL-CIO	LCV	ITI	COC	HAFA	ACU	CFG	FRC
2014	0%	0%	–	3%	80%	86%	54%	71%	58%	88%
2013	0%	C	14%	4%	C	77%	C	76%	69%	C

National Journal Ratings

	2013 LIB	—	2013 CONS
Economic	34%	—	65%
Social	16%	—	74%
Foreign	5%	—	86%
Composite	22%	—	78%

Key Votes of the 113th Congress

1. Sandy storm spending	N	5. Medical Marijuana	N	9. Syrian Rebels Training	Y
2. Violence Against Women Act	Y	6. Farm Bill	Y	10. Keystone pipeline	Y
3. Guantanamo Bay Detainees	N	7. Afghanistan Combat	N	11. Immigration Exec. Action	Y
4. Abortion 20-week ban	Y	8. NSA Phone Data Collection	N	12. Bipartisan budget deal	Y

Election Results

2014 general	Bob Gibbs (R)	...........................unopposed	$499,405
2014 primary	Bob Gibbs (R)	...........................unopposed	

Prior winning percentages: 2012 (56%), 2010 (54%)

Population		Race and Ethnicity		Income	
Total:	719,276	White	92.1%	Median income:	$48,382
Urban:	25.5%	Black	3.5%		*(264 of 435)*
Suburban:	34.6%	Latino	1.7%	Under $50,000	51.3%
Rural:	39.9%	Asian	0.5%	$50,000-$99,999:	32.5%
Land area:	3,250	Two races	1.9%	$100,000-$199,999:	14.2%
Pop/sq. mi.:	221.3	White Ethnic	33.0%	$200,000 or more:	2.0%
Born in state:	82.6%			Poverty Rate	13.0%
		Education			
Age Groups		H.S. grad or less:	52.8%	**Work**	
Under 18:	23.6%	Some college:	27.2%	White collar:	28.8%
18 to 34:	19.8%	College degree, 4 yr.:	13.0%	Blue collar:	41.0%
35 to 64:	40.1%	Post-grad study:	7.0%	Sales and service:	30.2%
Over 64:	16.4%				
		Military		Govt. workers:	10.6%
		Veterans/active duty:	9.2%		

North-Central Ohio: Canton, Cleveland Suburbs

A little more than a century ago, Canton was at the center of American politics. It was already an industrial city, but without the huge steel mills of Youngstown or Cleveland. Its high-skill workers were fashioning new kinds of plows and reapers, making watches, and, beginning in 1899, roller

Voter Turnout	
2013 Total Citizen 18+	544,437
2014 House Turnout	143,959
2014 Turnout as % CVAP	26.4%
2012 Turnout as % CVAP	60.2%

bearings. It did not attract masses of immigrants, its factories did not run on harsh stop-watch discipline, and the class-warfare politics of other northern Ohio industrial cities did not take root here. Canton's most famous citizen was Republican President William McKinley, who rose to the rank of major at age 22 in the Civil War, and was later elected to Congress. As the Republican nominee for president in 1896, McKinley campaigned from his front porch in Canton, meeting with delegations brought in by train from around the country. This spectacle, displaying both technological virtuosity and personal modesty, sounded a reverberating note in American politics, as did the McKinley platform—the "full dinner pail," the gold standard, and the enforcement of law and order in labor relations—a platform that mostly severed the Democrats' ties to northern blue-collar whites until the 1930s.

Today, Canton remains based in manufacturing, but has been troubled by job losses, including those stemming from the crash of the domestic auto industry in 2009. It has become best known as the home of the Professional Football Hall of Fame, with a roof shaped like a football. The Canton Bulldogs were one of the first teams in the Ohio League, the predecessor to the modern NFL. In May 2015, the NFL unveiled ambitious plans for a Hall of Fame village in Canton.

The 7th Congressional District of Ohio is a hodgepodge of counties forming a crescent across northeastern Ohio and avoiding Democratic areas of Cleveland, Akron and Lorain. It includes all of Canton, the old Ohio and Erie Canal town of Massillon, and most of Stark County, which has about a third of the district's population. The rest is in the lightly populated swath of counties arching around almost to Lake Erie. Much of the area west and southwest of Canton is a part of the Appalachian Plateau. Holmes County, whose more than 30,000 Amish residents are the largest such community in the world, is on its way to becoming the first Amish-majority county in the nation. Ashland is a smaller rural county, where Johnny Appleseed once lived on what is now

2012 Presidential Vote
Mitt Romney (R)..............179,375 (54%)
Barack Obama (D) 147,567 (44%)

2008 Presidential Vote
John McCain (R)...............173,095 (51%)
Barack Obama (D) 159,263 (47%)

Cook Partisan Voting Index: R+6

the campus of Ashland University. The district extends through Medina County in the outer reaches of the Cleveland metropolitan area, up to North Ridgeville and Avon near Lake Erie. The Stark County portions of the district are Democratic, but the rest of it is mostly Republican, and the net result is that the 7th District leans Republican.

Bob Gibbs (R)

Republican Bob Gibbs, elected in 2010, is a hog farmer and ex-state farm bureau president who takes agriculture seriously. The elimination of government regulations is his other main interest. He chairs the Transportation and Infrastructure Water Resources and Environment Subcommittee, which remains a prime source of congressional pork—or, as his website describes his domain, "cost effective water infrastructure improvements that provide jobs."

Gibbs grew up on the west side of Cleveland, "as far away from agriculture as you can get," he says. But he was drawn to farming at a young age. After working in the garden center of his high school, he enrolled in Ohio State University's Agricultural Institute, becoming part of its first graduating class in 1974. After college, Gibbs founded Hidden Hollow Farms and later served as president of the Ohio Farm Bureau Federation for two terms. On his Holmes County property, he mostly produces market hogs. "In agriculture, you have a lot of challenges," Gibbs said. "Every day on the farm, you have chores you have to do. I taught myself how to weld, do electrical work, accounting. There's so much you can do. It's not just the same thing every day." His time with the Farm Bureau sparked his interest in politics.

In 2002, Gibbs won a seat in the Ohio House, and he was elected in 2008 to the Senate, where he chaired the Ways and Means Committee. He focused on agriculture, small business, and private property issues. In 2005, he introduced a bill barring the use of eminent domain takings for private entities, which allows the transfer of land from one private owner to another to further economic development. He co-authored a 21 percent cut in Ohio's personal income tax rates.

In 2010, Gibbs challenged two-term Democratic Rep. Zack Space, a moderate and a prolific fundraiser. He and Space attacked each other on climate change, health care reform, and the "don't ask, don't tell" policy prohibiting gay men and women from serving openly in the military. Republicans blasted Space for his vote for the 2009 House-passed bill to create a cap-and-trade system to reduce greenhouse-gas emissions blamed for global warming. Gibbs said he doesn't believe human activity causes climate change. Space ran ads with footage of Gibbs telling an audience, "I'm a free-trader," and tying him to trade deals that Space said have sent Ohio jobs overseas. Space outspent Gibbs, $2.9 million to $1.1 million; each had more than $1 million in help from his national party. Gibbs won easily, 54%-40%.

In the House, Gibbs was among the Class of 2010 members most likely to vote with Ohioan John Boehner and the House leadership. One notable exception was the budget and tax compromise to avert the so-called fiscal cliff in January 2013. "It stifles our already fragile economy, keeping the private sector from prospering. ... [It] is absolutely not the answer to our economic crisis," he said. He also broke from the leadership that year to oppose the farm bill, which he said unfairly benefited farmers in the South at the expense of those in the Midwest.

On the Transportation and Infrastructure Committee, new congressional restrictions on spending "earmarks" have reduced the opportunities to mandate new water projects. With a final House vote of 412-4, he enacted in 2014 the Water Resources Reform and Development Act, the first such reauthorization since 2007. The law reformed the review process of the Army Corps of Engineers for the nation's ports and flood control projects, "deauthorized" $18 billion in inactive projects and included no specific earmarks. But it gave clear guidance to the Army Corps for new projects. "Typically, it would take 10 to 15 years to complete the studies necessary prior to beginning construction. WRRDA will reduce that time to three years so that projects are able to begin as they are needed and create jobs," Gibbs summarized. He noted, in particular, the importance of the health of Great Lakes ports. A year later, Gibbs said that he was "disappointed at the pace and the prioritization" with which the Army Corps was implementing the new law.

His work on water resources has given him a prominent perch to blast the Environmental Protection Agency. The House in 2011 passed his "Reducing Regulatory Burdens Act," which prevented the implementation of a court order requiring pesticide applications in and around U.S. waters to be covered by Clean Water Act permits. Gibbs said the requirement was unnecessary and redundant. The Sierra Club called his measure "damaging and dangerous," and it never moved in the Senate. In a May 2013 report to constituents headlined "Washington Doesn't Like Me Very Much," Gibbs wrote of the Obama administration, including its excessive regulations, "There is absolutely no excuse for the kind of corruption coming out of this White House." In May 2015, the House passed, 261-155, his bill to nullify the EPA's proposed "Waters of the United States" rules, which Gibbs described as "a vast expansion of federal jurisdiction." The Senate was considering a companion bill. Interest groups engaged actively on both sides of the issue.

The radically reshaped district following redistricting, in which six of the 10 counties were completely new to Gibbs, prompted Space to consider a rematch in 2012. But the Democrat didn't want to risk a second loss in his political career, according to *The Cook Political Report*. Instead, Democrats nominated Joyce Healy-Abrams, who ran a corporate record-keeping business and whose brother, William Healy, was mayor of Canton. She spent $905,000, to $1.3 million for Gibbs. Healy-Abrams won 55% of the vote in Stark, but Gibbs rolled up big majorities in the other counties, and won 56%-44%. In a sign that he had settled into his revamped district, Gibbs was re-elected without opposition in 2014 and built up his campaign fund to nearly $1 million.

EIGHTH DISTRICT

John Boehner (R)

Elected 1990, 13th term; b. Nov. 17, 1949, Cincinnati; Xavier U., B.S. 1977; Catholic; married (Debbie); 2 children.

Military Career: Navy, 1969.

Elected Office: Union Township Bd. of Trustees, 1981-85, pres., 1984; OH House, 1984-90.

Professional Career: Pres., Nucite Sales Inc., 1976-90.

DC Office: 1011 LHOB, 20515, 202-225-6205; Fax: 202-225-0704; Website: johnboehner.house.gov.

State Offices: Butler County, 513-779-5400; Miami County, 937-339-1524; Clark County, 937-322-1120.

Vote Ratings and Key Votes: As Speaker, Boehner rarely votes in the House.

Key Votes of the 113th Congress
1. Farm Bill   Y   3. Syrian Rebels Training   Y

2. NSA Phone Data Collection   N   4. Bipartisan Budget deal   Y

Election Results
2014 general	John Boehner (R)	126,539	(67%)	$17,106,254	$267,825	$327,484
	Tom Poetter (D)	51,534	(27%)	$192,079	$35,771	
	Jim Condit Jr. (CNP)	10,257	(5%)			
2014 primary	John Boehner (R)	47,261	(72%)			
	J.D. Winteregg (R)	15,030	(23%)			
	Eric Gurr (R)	3,812	(6%)			

Prior winning percentages: 2012 (84%), 2010 (66%), 2008 (68%), 2006 (64%), 2004 (69%), 2002 (71%), 2000 (71%), 1998 (71%), 1996 (70%), 1994 (100%), 1992 (74%), 1990 (61%)

Population		Race and Ethnicity		Income	
Total:	721,486	White	87.4%	Median income:	$50,750
Urban:	19.2%	Black	5.8%		*(229 of 435)*
Suburban:	60.4%	Latino	3.1%	Under $50,000	49.2%
Rural:	20.4%	Asian	1.7%	$50,000-$99,999:	31.6%
Land area:	2,591	Two races	1.6%	$100,000-$199,999:	16.3%
Pop/sq. mi.:	278.5	White Ethnic	22.2%	$200,000 or more:	2.9%
Born in state:	74.5%			Poverty Rate	13.8%
		Education			
Age Groups		H.S. grad or less:	48.3%	**Work**	
Under 18:	23.9%	Some college:	28.8%	White collar:	32.7%
18 to 34:	21.7%	College degree, 4 yr.:	14.9%	Blue collar:	41.5%
35 to 64:	39.3%	Post-grad study:	7.9%	Sales and service:	25.8%
Over 64:	15.0%			Govt. workers:	11.5%
		Military			
		Veterans/active duty:	8.9%		

West-Central Ohio: Cincinnati and Dayton Suburbs, Springfield

Since the early 20th century, the far west edge of Ohio—where U.S. 40, the old National Road, heads straight as an arrow in its last miles across Ohio and into Indiana—was some of the nation's prime industrial country. The Great and Little Miami rivers drain south into the Ohio, the Miami and Erie

Voter Turnout	
2013 Total Citizen 18+	536,758
2014 House Turnout	188,330
2014 Turnout as % CVAP	35.1%
2012 Turnout as % CVAP	63.5%

Canal system continues its northward march to Toledo, and U.S. 40 jogs southward twice to go over the Miami and Stillwater river dams (built after a flood in 1913 that killed 367 people and 1,420 horses in Dayton). The small cities and towns around and between Dayton and Cincinnati were rising industrial country a century ago, and in the years since, they have weathered depression and recession and sought to adapt to changing markets and circumstances. Butler County, in between the two cities, was dominated by the large factory towns of Hamilton and Middletown.

In recent years, major employers, including International Paper, have shut down operations, but other, smaller businesses have started up, and the county's population has grown with the outflow of people from Cincinnati and Dayton. The center of growth has been West Chester Township, situated on Interstate 75 south of Wright-Patterson Air Force Base. It has attracted a new GE Aviation facility, and an Amylin Pharmaceuticals facility, which produces diabetes medication; the ownership of Amylin switched in 2013 from Bristol-Myers to AstraZeneca. Butler County was largely settled by people from south of the Ohio River, who carried Democratic voting habits with them. Since then, it has followed most of the new South and become reliably Republican. The county has had an economic boon, with retail vendor licenses increasing from 359 in 2013 to 634 in 2014.

The 8th Congressional District of Ohio includes all of Butler County. It extends north along the Indiana border to take in Preble and Darke County, the birthplace of Phoebe Ann Moses, later known as sharpshooter Annie Oakley. The district includes some townships in southern Mercer County, near Fort Recovery. The district now includes Clark County, including economically depressed Springfield, where manufacturing has collapsed and the remaining residents are disproportionately aging. Its declining population is at a 90-year low, and it was rated by Gallup in 2011 as the unhappiest city in the United States. Still, a small uptick in new businesses in 2014 led some locals to ask, "Why

2012 Presidential Vote		
Mitt Romney (R)	211,446	(62%)
Barack Obama (D)	124,407	(36%)
2008 Presidential Vote		
John McCain (R)	210,503	(60%)
Barack Obama (D)	133,188	(38%)
Cook Partisan Voting Index: R+15		

not Springfield?" That city votes Democratic, but its presence does not alter the partisan balance of the district, which remains the most Republican in Ohio. Mitt Romney got 62% of the vote here in 2012; his next best showing was 56% in the adjacent 4th.

John Boehner (R)

John Boehner, a Republican first elected in 1990, has been the speaker of the House since January 2011. He is sometimes compared to Don Draper, hero of the acclaimed TV series *Mad Men*: Both are no-nonsense, cigarette-puffing leaders who adapt to changing circumstances—in Boehner's case, by consolidating the largest GOP majority since 1928, shaping his chamber's rightward shift and surviving occasional challenges by maverick conservatives. It's not always pretty, but he usually gets the job done.

Boehner grew up in Reading, just north of Cincinnati, the second-oldest of 12 children in a home with two bedrooms. His father ran Andy's Café, a neighborhood restaurant and bar. Playing at a much heavier weight than he is now, he was a linebacker for Cincinnati's Archbishop Moeller High School on a team coached by Gerry Faust, before Faust went on to coach at Notre Dame. Boehner worked at various jobs after high school and enlisted in the Navy, from which he was discharged because of a back injury. He spent six years working his way through Xavier University as a janitor, and was the first college graduate in his family. He moved to Butler County, where he worked for the Merrell Dow pharmaceutical firm and met Dave Kessler, owner of Nucite, a small plastic packaging company. Kessler hired Boehner as a salesman and within a year after graduation, he was making $74,000—and complaining about high taxes and government paperwork. Kessler's children were uninterested in the business and he sold it to Boehner, who was also developing an interest in politics. He served on the Union Township Board of Trustees and in 1984, at age 34, was elected to the Ohio House.

In 1990, he ran against Republican Rep. Donald (Buz) Lukens, who inexplicably sought reelection after he was convicted of having sex with a 16-year-old girl. Also running was former Rep. Tom Kindness, who had run unsuccessfully for the Senate in 1986 and was a lobbyist in Washington. Boehner won the primary with 49%, to 32% for Kindness and 17% for Lukens. The win was tantamount to victory in the heavily Republican district, and Boehner has since been reelected without difficulty.

In the House, Boehner is known for his perpetual tan (President Barack Obama jokingly described him as a fellow "person of color"), and an emotional side that leads him to get teary-eyed on occasion. He has a consistently conservative voting record, though his record as a committee chairman showed that he can be pragmatic and apt to look for compromise, including across the aisle. That has been a reason why younger conservative Republicans have twice made hastily organized efforts to oppose his reelection as Speaker and discussed plans to topple him in a coup. Sometimes, he has found his options limited as the House has become increasingly populated with take-no-prisoners conservatives who have not shared his interest or skill in consensus-building.

The irony of Boehner's struggles with his unruly and uncompromising GOP caucus is he had been a young rebel himself. In 1991, he joined the Gang of Seven, freshmen Republicans who insisted on naming all 355 members who had overdrafts at the House bank, a scandal that revealed that members had routinely abused their tax-subsidized banking privileges. He assailed members of both parties who supported a congressional pay raise. Boehner's rabble-rousing Gang of Seven infuriated House veterans but struck a chord with the public; the junior lawmakers earned recognition beyond their years of service. In the process, Boehner became an ally of Minority Whip Newt Gingrich, who was pursuing his goal of ousting the entrenched Democratic majority that seemed at little risk.

Boehner worked with Gingrich in putting together the 10-point Contract with America, unveiled in late September 1994 while most political insiders still doubted that Republicans could break the Democrats' 40-year lock on the House majority. But Gingrich took advantage of young, outlying Republican talent around the country and gave them positive themes and plenty of money to run on. When Republicans defied expectations and won the majority, Boehner ran for chairman of the Republican Conference, and with Gingrich's backing, he beat California Rep. Duncan Hunter 122-102. That made Boehner the No. 4 person in the party leadership with the responsibility of preparing the party's message and coordinating with GOP-allied outside groups.

The Gingrich years were a turbulent time for Boehner. An ethics investigation of Gingrich instigated by the Democrats placed Boehner in the middle of a legal altercation after a Florida couple taped one of his cell phone conversations with Republican leaders while he was driving through the state. The tape eventually reached Rep. Jim McDermott of Washington, the senior Democrat on the Ethics Committee, who made the contents available to *The New York Times*. In 1998, Boehner sued McDermott in federal court for invasion of privacy. The two could not agree on a settlement, and the case wound its way through the courts for several years; the Supreme Court denied final review in 2008 and a federal judge ordered McDermott to pay Boehner more than $1 million in legal fees.

By 1997, many rank-and-file House Republicans had lost confidence in the leadership team, especially the brilliant but erratic Gingrich. Boehner and other leaders secretly discussed whether to try to force out Gingrich as speaker. When their plotting became public, the plan dissolved, and the plotters took the heat for appearing to be disloyal and self-serving. Boehner suffered a major setback. After the 1998 elections, Gingrich lost power and Boehner lost the conference chairmanship to J.C. Watts, an African American from Oklahoma who argued that Republicans needed more diverse leadership.

Boehner later told *The New Yorker* that he immediately began to plan his comeback. "I just walked out of the room, I looked at [longtime aide] Barry [Jackson] and I said, 'We're just gonna put our heads down, and we're gonna work our way back.' And we did." He plunged into his role as a subcommittee chairman on the Education and the Workforce Committee. In six months, the subcommittee passed eight bills restructuring employer-run health insurance plans. Pleased by Boehner's initiative and dismayed that other committees had not been as effective, Speaker Dennis Hastert of Illinois adopted many of the subcommittee's bills as part of the Republican health care agenda. After the 2000 election, Boehner became chairman of the full committee.

When George W. Bush became President in 2001, he made an overhaul of education policy a top priority, putting Boehner in the driver's seat of the new administration's chief domestic initiative. The new chairman established a working relationship with the senior Democrat on the panel, George Miller of California. Miller believed that current programs weren't helping disadvantaged children keep up with their peers, and Boehner shared his concern. While other committees dissolved into partisan stalemate, Boehner and Miller worked together on the House version of Bush's No Child Left Behind Act, which included the president's mandates for annual testing and increased accountability. It passed the committee and was approved by the House, 384-45. Boehner and Miller then worked with their Senate counterparts, led by Ted Kennedy, on a final compromise that won overwhelming support. A few months after the September 11 attacks, Bush's bill-signing with Boehner and the Democrats was a feel-good moment.

In January 2005, as bankrupt airlines began ceding their pension obligations to the federal Pension Benefit Guaranty Corporation, Boehner - once again with bipartisan support— pushed for a comprehensive solution to pension problems around the country and then played a leading role in months of painstaking House-Senate negotiations. The legislation, passed in summer 2006, represented a major change in pension law, closing loopholes that had permitted many companies to underfund their plans. It set deadlines for them to make payments, and created automatic enrollment in 401(k) plans for many workers.

In the fall of 2005, the House Republican leadership again was mired in turmoil. Majority Leader Tom DeLay was forced to step down after being indicted in Texas for alleged campaign fundraising violations. Hastert named Majority Whip Roy Blunt of Missouri to serve as acting leader. Boehner had been quietly planning for a return to the leadership and privately voiced doubts that Republicans could retain their House majority. In January 2006, he announced he would run against Blunt for majority leader and offered a 37-page campaign manifesto that called for "one big, bold goal" each year and more reliance on committees to generate legislation. Blunt led with 110 votes to 79 for Boehner and 40 for Rep. John Shadegg of Arizona on the first ballot. On the second ballot, Boehner picked up most of Shadegg's votes and beat Blunt 122-109. Boehner was back, now as the No. 2 leader in the House. Within a year, Republicans had lost control of the House and Boehner took over as party leader.

In contrast to the reserved Hastert, Boehner was sociable and adept at the glad-handing side of politics. He regularly held court just off the House floor with reporters and fellow members, puffing on the ever-present cigarette. As majority leader, he focused on lobbying reform and a crackdown on spending earmarks, which had exploded under Republican rule and damaged the party's credibility for fiscal restraint. In the 2006 election, he campaigned around the country, but Republicans lost 31 seats and their House majority to the Democrats.

In the wake of that dismal defeat, Hastert announced that he would resign. Boehner ran for minority leader and defeated Mike Pence of Indiana, 168-27. In January 2007, Boehner gracefully handed over the gavel to Nancy Pelosi, the new Democratic speaker. As minority leader, he occasionally cooperated with Democratic leaders, notably on the 2008 economic stimulus bill and Iraq War funding. But under Pelosi (as under Hastert), the minority party played little role in shaping legislation. He led the charge to oust Ways and Means Committee Chairman Charles Rangel of New York after questions were raised about Rangel's ethics and financial dealings. On immigration reform, he dropped his earlier advocacy of a middle ground and joined Republican hard-liners who emphasized border security and opposed a path to citizenship for illegal immigrants.

A low moment for Boehner came in the spring of 2008 with the loss of three longtime Republican-held seats in special elections. Boehner tried to buck up his party with assurances that the upcoming November elections were "not going to be as bad as people think." He turned the focus to the soaring price of oil to spotlight policy differences between the two parties. But in the general election that November, Republicans lost 21 more House seats— including three in Ohio, an abysmal showing and a setback for Boehner, whose only words of encouragement were that it could have been worse, given the party's low public approval and Bush's unpopularity.

His early dealings with Obama did not bode well for bipartisanship. After a meeting at the White House in January 2009, Obama rejected an alternative economic stimulus plan by Boehner and other GOP leaders, saying, "elections have consequences," and "I won." Boehner rallied Republicans to oppose the Democrats' $787 billion stimulus bill and all 177 voted against it. With the GOP lacking any real power, Boehner characterized House Republicans as an "entrepreneurial insurgency" that would oppose Democratic policies through all means at their disposal. He assembled solid blocs of opposition to the Democrats' cap-and-trade bill to curb carbon emissions (only eight Republicans voted for it) and their overhaul of health care policy (one Republican voted yes) in 2009, although he was unable to attract enough moderate Democrats to stop the bills from passing. Many of those Democrats, and their party, would soon pay a price.

Planning for the 2010 elections began early. In February 2009, Boehner backed the idea of National Republican Congressional Committee Chairman Pete Sessions to put 80 Democratic seats in play. While visiting GOP Rep. Kevin McCarthy's district in Bakersfield, California, Boehner was struck by the enthusiasm of tea party activists at a rally on tax day in April 2009 and he embraced their role in the party. In November 2010, Republicans gained a stunning 63 House seats, a bigger switch than Gingrich commanded in 1994 and more than either party had gained since 1948. Boehner called the election a repudiation of Obama's policies of 2009 and 2010. Even before his formal takeover as the leader of the new House majority, Boehner negotiated with Obama and the Senate a December 2010 agreement to continue the 2001 and 2003 Bush-era tax cuts for all taxpayers, including the high-income earners whom Obama had wanted to exclude.

In the early days of his reign as speaker, Boehner led the House in a vote to repeal Obama's health care legislation, which was largely symbolic considering Democrats still controlled the Senate and the White House. He let the GOP freshmen kill a multibillion-dollar defense project important to his district in the name of cutting government spending. His next task was much harder: negotiating a budget deal with the Democrats that would avert a government shutdown, but also mollifying the 87 Republican freshmen, many of whom were unfamiliar with, or disinclined toward, the process of cross-party compromise. Many of them wanted the full $100 billion in spending cuts that they had campaigned on, while Obama and the Democrats pushed for far less. Ultimately, Boehner reached a deal with Obama for $38 billion in spending cuts.

The road ahead only became more difficult. In the spring of 2011, Boehner began discussing a "grand bargain" on taxes and spending with Obama without telling others in the GOP leadership. When he informed Majority Leader Eric Cantor, the Virginian argued fiercely against any deal, saying the matter should be left to voters in 2012; rank-and-file Republicans spoiled for a confrontation. That led to several months of stalemate over raising the federal debt limit, including conflicts with Cantor. The bipartisan deal in August 2011 included spending cuts, but left the issue of long-term fiscal matters in the hands of a bipartisan "super committee" of House and Senate members. That panel deadlocked, postponing the issue until after the 2012 elections.

In the ensuing lame-duck session, Boehner and Cantor sought to negotiate a tax and spending compromise directly with the White House to avoid a so-called "fiscal cliff" of automatic deep cuts and big tax hikes. Unable to do so, they proposed a "Plan B" designed to limit looming tax hikes to people with annual incomes over $1 million. It was pulled for lack of support, mostly among conservatives who said the proposed spending cuts didn't go far enough. Senate Minority Leader Mitch McConnell ended up taking the reins on cutting a similar deal with Vice President Joe Biden. In a subsequent interview with *The Wall Street Journal*, Boehner blamed the president. "He's so ideological himself, and he's unwilling to take on the left wing of his own party," he said. That, the speaker added, explained why Obama originally agreed with Boehner's proposal to raise the retirement age for Medicare, and then reversed himself. "He admitted in meetings that he couldn't sell things to his own members," Boehner said.

In early 2013, he refused to talk with Obama about a way to avoid steep automatic spending cuts from kicking in across all federal agencies. The dispute, he told reporters, amounted to a difference over "how much more money do we want to steal from the American people to fund more government. I'm for no more." Such tough talk endeared him to many of his party's right wing. "He's doing exactly what he said he was going to do, and I think it's working to our favor and to his," South Carolina Republican Rep. Mick Mulvaney, a frequent Boehner critic, told *The New York Times*.

Other Republicans laud Boehner for being consistent in his conservatism and for being in front of issues that later became GOP doctrine, such as banning earmarks on spending bills and pressing for broader cuts in spending and the federal deficit. "He was tea party before there was a tea party," fellow Ohio GOP Rep. Pat Tiberi, one of his closest allies, told *The Cincinnati Enquirer*. They also appreciate his candor; he famously referred to the $700 billion Wall Street rescue bill in 2008—which he reluctantly supported—as a "crap sandwich." And they admire his impressive fundraising ability: He took in nearly $13 million in the 2010 election season, almost twice that amount in 2012, and another $21.1 million in 2014. After House Republicans kept their majority but lost seats in the November 2012 elections, lobbyist and former GOP leadership aide John Feehery told the Associated Press, "No one else can right now do the job of bringing everyone together" within the party.

Since taking command of House Republicans, Boehner has had conflicts with detractors across the political spectrum. But those tiffs have not prevented him from finding common ground. He had a frosty relationship with Senate Democratic Leader Harry Reid of Nevada, whose description of Boehner as a "dictator" in December 2012 led the speaker to later snap undiplomatically at Reid, "Go f--- yourself." With Pelosi, they often communicated by memo or through the news media. But he also has found opportunities to work with each of them, such as an unexpected bipartisan, bicameral deal in April 2015 to resolve a Medicare spending problem that had festered for more than a decade, including when Reid and Pelosi were in charge of Congress.

Others have taken their shots at Boehner. New Jersey Republican Gov. Chris Christie tore into him for postponing a January 2013 vote on Hurricane Sandy relief funding; the speaker promptly passed two bills, to the dismay of many conservatives. Former Ohio GOP Rep. Bob Ney, who went to prison for ethics violations, accused Boehner in a 2013 memoir of being far more interested in playing golf than passing legislation. The speaker called the charges "baseless and false." Obama, for his part, has professed to like Boehner personally, though the president rarely indulged in social niceties, including their mutual fondness for golf.

Even his limited dealings with Obama enraged and emboldened a cadre of conservatives. Though 12 Republicans voted against giving him a second term as speaker, making for a few tense minutes on the opening day in January 2013, he won with six votes to spare. The situation repeated itself two years later to an even greater extent. That vote came a few weeks after Boehner worked with Obama for the bipartisan enactment of a massive spending bill. Sarah Palin told the right-wing Breitbart website that he and other GOP leaders "just flipped American voters the bird by sidelining the new Congress we just elected." Twenty-five Republicans voted for someone other than Boehner, with 12 of the votes going to Rep. Daniel Webster of Florida. It was four votes short of the 29 needed to send the vote to a second count, and the largest number of members who had voted against a major-party's speaker nominee since 1860. A number of the dissenters informed Boehner ahead of time, saying they were under heavy pressure from angry constituents. Boehner responded by removing Webster and a handful of fellow perpetrators from committee and party assignments.

At home, Boehner faced two tea party challengers in May 2014; J.D. Winteregg raised more than $300,000 for his effort. Unlike Cantor, who paid the price for being oblivious to his tea party challenger in Virginia a few weeks later, Boehner kept in contact at home and aired television ads; he defeated Winteregg 71%-23%.

Boehner has not been afraid to take hardline positions. Not long after the 2015 speaker's vote, he said he was willing to let a funding bill for the Homeland Security Department lapse because the House version blocked funds from enforcing an Obama executive order on immigration—and Senate Democrats, now in the minority, refused to permit debate on that version in their chamber. "The House has acted. We've done our job," Boehner said. "Senate Democrats are the ones putting us in this precarious position. It's up to Senate Democrats to get their act together." Intent on avoiding another government shutdown, Boehner eventually threw in the towel, to the relief of many Republicans. Meanwhile, he invited Israeli Prime Minister Benjamin Netanyahu to address a joint session of Congress without informing the White House. Many Democrats viewed the move as an attempt to torpedo negotiations with Iran over curbing its nuclear aspirations and they boycotted the speech. Netanyahu, who was weeks away from his own reelection vote, ardently opposed those talks. Boehner, who made little secret of his reservations, told Fox News that Obama "doesn't quite understand that we're trying to strengthen his hand."

His collaboration with McConnell on a set of legislative victories in the first half of 2015 broke the logjam with Obama and relieved some of the internal tensions. He negotiated for days with Pelosi in June 2015 on Obama's request for trade promotion authority, only for Pelosi to succumb to internal Democratic pressure to oppose her own deal; in that case, Boehner emerged triumphant in passing the bill to prepare for Obama's prospective Trans Pacific Partnership agreement, which many businesses viewed as vital. In a mid-year review of accomplishments, Boehner also cited Medicare reform, the end of bulk collection of phone records for national security purposes, safeguards against cyber attacks, and penalties for human trafficking. "We're going to stay focused, keep doing our jobs and continue making progress on behalf of the American people," he wrote.

Boehner clearly was eager for the election of a Republican president in 2016 so that he could exercise his legislative skills on behalf of a shared agenda of broader issues, including tax reform, budget discipline and military strength.

Other observers of Congress agreed that Boehner has done the best he can in difficult circumstances. "I am of the view—intensely unpopular among many conservatives—that John Boehner has been a pretty good speaker, that his is a nearly impossible job, and that 99 percent of those who castigate him as a weakling and a sellout—officeholders and free-range critics alike—could not hope to perform half as well as he has," Kevin D. Williamson wrote for the conservative *National Review* in January 2015.

NINTH DISTRICT

Marcy Kaptur (D)

Elected 1982, 17th term; b. June 17, 1946, Toledo; U. of WI, B.A. 1968, U. of MI, M.A. 1974, MA Inst. Tech., 1981-82; Catholic; single.

Professional Career: Urban planner, Lucas Cnty. Planning Comm., 1969-75; Urban planning consultant, 1975-77; White House Asst. Dir. for Urban Affairs, 1977-80; Deputy secy., Natl. Consumer Coop. Bank, 1980-81.

DC Office: 2186 RHOB, 20515, 202-225-4146; Fax: 202-225-7711; Website: kaptur.house.gov.

State Offices: Toledo, 419-259-7500; Lorain, 440-288-1500; Lakewood, 216-767-5933.

Committees: *Appropriations:* Defense; Energy & Water Development (RMM); Homeland Security.

Group Ratings

	ADA	ACLU	AFL-CIO	LCV	ITI	COC	HAFA	ACU	CFG	FRC
2014	80%	77%	–	91%	60%	50%	6%	0%	2%	0%
2013	75%	C	100%	82%	C	33%	C	8%	10%	C

National Journal Ratings

	2013 LIB	—	2013 CONS
Economic	75%	—	25%
Social	65%	—	35%
Foreign	71%	—	29%
Composite	70%	—	30%

Key Votes of the 113th Congress

1. Sandy storm spending	Y	5. Medical Marijuana	Y	9. Syrian Rebels Training	Y
2. Violence Against Women Act	Y	6. Farm Bill	N	10. Keystone pipeline	N
3. Guantanamo Bay Detainees	Y	7. Afghanistan Combat	Y	11. Immigration Exec. Action	N
4. Abortion 20-week ban	N	8. NSA Phone Data Collection	N	12. Bipartisan budget deal	Y

Election Results

2014 general	Marcy Kaptur (D)	108,870	(68%)	$652,304	$13,783
	Richard May (R)	51,704	(32%)		
2014 primary	Marcy Kaptur (D)	unopposed			

Prior winning percentages: 2012 (73%), 2010 (59%), 2008 (74%), 2006 (74%), 2004 (68%), 2002 (74%), 2000 (75%), 1998 (81%), 1996 (77%), 1994 (75%), 1992 (74%), 1990 (78%), 1988 (81%), 1986 (78%), 1984 (55%), 1982 (58%)

Population		Race and Ethnicity		Income	
Total:	715,447	White	70.5%	Median income:	$40,150
Urban:	66.0%	Black	14.9%		*(389 of 435)*
Suburban:	23.5%	Latino	9.8%	Under $50,000	60.3%
Rural:	10.5%	Asian	1.5%	$50,000-$99,999:	27.6%
Land area:	506	Two races	3.1%	$100,000-$199,999:	10.5%
Pop/sq. mi.:	1,413.7	White Ethnic	42.7%	$200,000 or more:	1.6%
Born in state:	76.3%			Poverty Rate	22.3%
		Education			
Age Groups		H.S. grad or less:	47.2%	**Work**	
Under 18:	22.3%	Some college:	31.4%	White collar:	29.9%
18 to 34:	23.6%	College degree, 4 yr.:	14.2%	Blue collar:	46.1%
35 to 64:	39.6%	Post-grad study:	7.2%	Sales and service:	24.0%
Over 64:	14.5%				
		Military		Govt. workers:	11.5%
		Veterans/active duty:	8.7%		

Lakefront: Toledo, Cleveland Suburbs

Lake Erie, the southernmost and shallowest of the Great Lakes, played a critical role in the history of America's interior. It was discovered late by Europeans: When explorer Louis Joliet first set eyes on it in 1669, it was the last Great Lake to be discovered.

Voter Turnout	
2013 Total Citizen 18+	543,108
2014 House Turnout	160,715
2014 Turnout as % CVAP	29.6%
2012 Turnout as % CVAP	59.4%

For decades, its shoreline was the locus of a four-way battle among French, Indian, British and American claimants. Additional conflicts over various claims to the area made by the various American colonies bubbled underneath. Once the federal government finally assumed full control of the Lake Erie shoreline in 1800, development proceeded quickly.

Cleveland, at the mouth of the Cuyahoga River, had a population of 1,000 in 1830. Hamlets sprang up on the shoreline, usually at the mouths of rivers: Huron, at the mouth of the Huron River, in 1804; Lorain, at the mouth of the Black River, in 1807; Sandusky, at the mouth of the Sandusky River, in 1818; and Toledo, at the mouth of the Maumee River, in 1833. Toledo and Cleveland became the biggest cities here once the Ohio & Erie and Miami & Erie canals were completed. But all of the towns benefited from the trade that flowed from the Atlantic seaboard, up the Erie Canal to Buffalo, across the lake, and down through the canals into the burgeoning American interior.

The canal traffic declined in the late-1800s, but Lake Erie retained an important role in the U.S. economy. Erie contains only 2% of the water of the Great Lakes, but 50% of its fish. It houses one of the largest commercial freshwater fisheries in the world; a sizable yellow perch commercial yield is hauled in annually. Port Clinton, on Lake Erie, bills itself as the "Walleye Capital of the World" and drops a plastic walleye in place of a glittering ball on New Year's Eve. Gritty Lorain has managed to survive as a steel town; U.S. Steel Corp. in 2011 announced a huge expansion of its plant that makes pipes for natural gas companies. Lorain and neighboring Sheffield have a growing Hispanic population, and Lorain is more than 15% Puerto Rican. Chrysler has manufactured all of its highly profitable Jeep Wranglers in Toledo for several decades, and recently has employed about 6,000. In May 2015, company officials confirmed that manufacturing of the next generation of the vehicle will remain in Toledo. The region's manufacturing base is slowly giving way to the high-tech economy, which in turn helps to produce innovative ways to clean up the environmental degradation left behind by earlier industries: The canals brought in invasive species—most recently Asian carp—while runoff from farms still promotes algae blooms. Pollution poses a continued threat to the native fisheries.

The 9th Congressional District of Ohio sprawls across the Lake Erie shoreline, rarely venturing more than 10 miles inland and sometimes less than a mile or two. It begins in Toledo, and goes east through Port

2012 Presidential Vote		
Barack Obama (D)	217,169	(68%)
Mitt Romney (R)	99,213	(31%)

2008 Presidential Vote		
Barack Obama (D)	227,406	(67%)
John McCain (R)	107,499	(32%)

Cook Partisan Voting Index: D+15

Clinton and Sandusky, home to the giant Cedar Point amusement park, with some of the country's fastest roller coasters. A plurality of its residents are in Cuyahoga County, where the district takes in western Cleveland, including Hopkins International Airport. This portion includes some inner suburbs, such as Lakewood, with its large collection of Victorian-era houses; and Brooklyn, home to the first seatbelt law in the country in 1966. The two ends of the district are geographically distant, but they share two things: generally blue-collar economies and Democratic voting patterns. Barack Obama got more than two-thirds of the vote here in both 2008 and 2012.

Marcy Kaptur (D)

Democrat Marcy Kaptur, first elected in 1982, is now the most senior Democratic woman in the House—a distinction not lost on her in her occasional clashes with Minority Leader Nancy Pelosi. Kaptur is a plainspoken Democrat and a dedicated opponent of free trade who does not always toe the party line, but whose old-fashioned ways have proven popular at home.

Kaptur grew up in a blue-collar neighborhood in Toledo, the daughter of Polish-American parents who worked at local auto plants. The family also operated a small grocery store, but her father sold it to get a job with health benefits. "It broke his heart," she said. She has spent almost her entire career in public service. She and her brother, Steve, live in the house where they grew up. She graduated from the University of Wisconsin, the first in her family to attend college, got a master's degree from the University of Michigan, then spent eight years as an urban planner in Toledo. She worked on urban revitalization in the Jimmy Carter White House, returning home in 1980 with thoughts of running for elected office. In 1982, she challenged first-term Republican Rep. Ed Weber for the House seat and won 58%-39%, despite being outspent 3-to-1.

Kaptur has long been convinced that Toledo and places like it have lost jobs and industry because of unfair trade practices and low-wage competition from countries like Mexico and China. She was featured prominently in controversial liberal filmmaker Michael Moore's 2009 movie *Capitalism: A Love Story*. "I have always said there's a great injustice being done here, because the power rests with a handful of megabanks and millions of Americans are being affected," she told the Toledo *Blade* when the film opened.

Kaptur was a dedicated opponent of the 1993 North American Free Trade Agreement in Congress. She criticized Democratic President Bill Clinton for ignoring Democrats opposed to NAFTA. She became a national figure in 1995 when she appeared before Texas businessman Ross Perot's United We Stand Party and made a rousing speech on trade that had delegates cheering. Perot, running as a third-party candidate for president in 1996, offered her the vice presidential nomination a year later, but she turned it down. She was a vocal opponent of normal trade relations with China and the 2005 Central American Free Trade Agreement.

Reflecting on those early trade wars years later, Kaptur criticized Pelosi's support of NAFTA. "That's where the real knife was put in the flesh," she said. When Pelosi announced in May 2007 an agreement with Treasury Secretary Hank Paulson on principles for international trade policy, an uninvited Kaptur glared from the back of the room. In 2002, she ran a quixotic, one-day campaign for minority leader against Pelosi but, predictably, got nowhere against the powerful California Democrat. In 2008, Kaptur challenged Pelosi ally Xavier Becerra of California for the leadership post of Democratic Caucus vice chairman and lost badly, 175-67. But Kaptur backed her for minority leader in 2011 when her hold on power within the caucus was at its most tenuous. One of the dissenting Democrats, Daniel Lipinski of Illinois, cast his vote for Kaptur in a symbolic tribute to her as a "strong voice for American workers."

Kaptur strongly opposed trade agreements with Colombia, Panama and South Korea that passed the House in 2011. Kaptur took to the House floor during the debate to point out that the number of cars that the U.S. imported from South Korea dwarfed the number of American cars bought by people in the Northeast Asian nation. "These unfair, unbalanced agreements will not have a demonstrable, positive impact on job creation. We have lost six million manufacturing jobs in the past decade. Enough is enough," she said. When the House narrowly voted in June 2015 to give trade promotion authority to President Barack Obama, she slammed proponents who she said sold out "working families and American industries that have been the backbone of the U.S. economy for decades."

When Washington Rep. Norm Dicks retired in 2012, Kaptur hoped to succeed him as the ranking Democrat on Appropriations. But the post instead went to Nita Lowey of New York, a more predictable liberal and a favorite of Pelosi's. Although the minority leader officially remained neutral, Lowey was widely perceived to have her friend's backing. Kaptur became ranking Democrat on the Energy and Water Development Subcommittee. She is a strong advocate of alternative energy sources such as ethanol and biofuels for Ohio. She made Democrats work for her vote on energy and climate change legislation in 2009. Sponsors of the bill agreed to her demand to establish a new federal power authority with up to $3.5 billion to lend to alternative energy projects in Ohio and other Midwestern states. Kaptur has promoted solar energy, a growing industry in Toledo. In May 2015, she criticized Ohio Gov. John Kasich for freezing an intended increase in the state's renewable energy mandate. He "shouldn't lead us backwards," she said.

Kaptur departs from party orthodoxy on abortion. She opposes federal funding for the procedure, though she has also voted against proposals to deny federal money to Planned Parenthood. She contended that federal funds were not being used for abortions, and that Planned Parenthood has provided valuable medical care for women.

Kaptur keeps close tabs on her district. A constituent gave her the idea to sponsor the legislation that created the World War II Memorial on the National Mall. On Appropriations, she has focused on improvements to bridges, roads, and rail and port facilities in her district. In 2010 she ranked 24th among the top earmark recipients in the House, according to the group Taxpayers for Common Sense. She once challenged Republicans on the committee to limit farm payments, but when they threatened her favorite spending projects, she backed off. "I may be blockheaded sometimes, but I'm not stupid," Kaptur said.

Kaptur, who wrote a book on women in Congress, is exceedingly popular in the Toledo area and rarely has faced a credible challenge. In 2012, Ohio lost two congressional seats, and state Republicans drawing the new map put her in a district with Cleveland-based Democratic Rep. Dennis Kucinich. Though the ultraliberal Kucinich's bids for president had made him a national hero to hard-core progressives, he had a reputation at home for being more interested in hobnobbing with celebrities than accomplishing much for the district. He didn't help himself by briefly toying with the idea of running in Washington state.

Kaptur defeated Kucinich in the Democratic primary, 56%-40%, putting an end to his 16-year House career. (In Toledo's Lucas County, she took 94% to his 4%.) She had an even easier time in the general election against Republican Samuel Wurzelbacher, better known as "Joe the Plumber" for his role in a 2008 presidential debate. *The Cook Political Report* called his candidacy "one of the biggest pipe dreams of the year," and Kaptur trounced him, 73%-23%. In 2014, she had no primary opposition and breezed to reelection with 68% of the vote. She appears secure, at least until the next redistricting.

TENTH DISTRICT

Mike Turner (R)

Elected 2002, 7th term; b. Jan. 11, 1960, Dayton; OH N. U., B.A. 1982, Case Western Reserve U., J.D. 1985, U. of Dayton, M.B.A. 1992; Protestant; separated; 2 children.

Elected Office: Dayton mayor, 1993-2001.

Professional Career: Practicing atty.

DC Office: 2239 RHOB, 20515, 202-225-6465; Fax: 202-225-6754; Website: turner.house.gov.

State Offices: Dayton, 937-225-2843.

Committees: *Armed Services:* Tactical Air & Land Forces (Chmn); Strategic Forces. *Oversight & Government Reform:* Transportation & Public Assets. *Intelligence (Permanent):* Department of Defense Intelligence & Overheard Architecture; Emerging Threats.

Group Ratings

	ADA	ACLU	AFL-CIO	LCV	ITI	COC	HAFA	ACU	CFG	FRC
2014	0%	0%	–	3%	80%	86%	44%	48%	44%	88%
2013	0%	C	38%	7%	C	77%	C	48%	50%	C

National Journal Ratings

	2013 LIB	—	2013 CONS
Economic	51%	—	49%
Social	48%	—	50%
Foreign	34%	—	60%
Composite	46%	—	54%

Key Votes of the 113th Congress

1. Sandy storm spending	Y	5. Medical Marijuana	N	9. Syrian Rebels Training	Y
2. Violence Against Women Act	Y	6. Farm Bill	Y	10. Keystone pipeline	Y
3. Guantanamo Bay Detainees	N	7. Afghanistan Combat	N	11. Immigration Exec. Action	Y
4. Abortion 20-week ban	Y	8. NSA Phone Data Collection	N	12. Bipartisan budget deal	Y

Election Results

2014 general	Mike Turner (R)	130,752	(65%)	$931,476
	Robert Klepinger (D)	63,249	(32%)	
	David Harlow (Lib)	6,605	(3%)	
2014 primary	Mike Turner (R)	32,550	(80%)	
	John Anderson (R)	8,214	(20%)	

Prior winning percentages: 2012 (60%), 2010 (68%), 2008 (63%), 2006 (59%), 2004 (62%), 2002 (59%)

Population		Race and Ethnicity		Income	
Total:	723,987	White	76.0%	Median income:	$45,903
Urban:	66.8%	Black	17.0%		*(302 of 435)*
Suburban:	28.3%	Latino	2.3%	Under $50,000	53.5%
Rural:	4.9%	Asian	2.1%	$50,000-$99,999:	28.5%
Land area:	1,594	Two races	2.3%	$100,000-$199,999:	15.0%
Pop/sq. mi.:	454.1	White Ethnic	24.1%	$200,000 or more:	3.0%
Born in state:	69.9%			Poverty Rate	17.6%
		Education			
		H.S. grad or less:	39.1%	**Work**	
Age Groups		Some college:	33.5%	White collar:	38.6%
Under 18:	22.1%	College degree, 4 yr.:	15.8%	Blue collar:	41.7%
18 to 34:	23.4%	Post-grad study:	11.6%	Sales and service:	19.7%
35 to 64:	38.4%				
Over 64:	16.0%	**Military**		Govt. workers:	15.0%
		Veterans/active duty:	11.2%		

Dayton Area

The underestimated Dayton can hold its own against bigger cities for fostering creative American genius in commerce. It has strong traditions of tinkering and innovation, practical organization and mechanical dreaming, as well as small-town neighborliness.

Voter Turnout	
2013 Total Citizen 18+	550,930
2014 House Turnout	200,606
2014 Turnout as % CVAP	36.4%
2012 Turnout as % CVAP	65.4%

Just south of the old National Road that spans the Midwest was the home of James Ritty, who in 1879 invented the cash register, that indispensable instrument of retail trade that led to the establishment in 1884 of the National Cash Register Co. Tom Watson Sr., an employee of NCR, feuded with owner John Henry Patterson and went off in a huff to found IBM. In 1887, George Huffman moved the Davis Sewing Machine Co. to Dayton, and in 1892 began producing Huffy bicycles. Around the same time, Wilbur and Orville Wright experimented with kites and gliders and constructed the first wind tunnel in the world and the first heavier-than-air flying machine, which they took to windy Kitty Hawk, North Carolina, for a test flight in 1903. A few years later, Dayton's Charles Kettering invented the automatic starter for cars and became one of the leaders of the budding automobile industry. Not long ago, Montgomery County was home to the most patents per capita of any county in the United States. Boston now has that title.

In the past few decades Dayton's economy sputtered, but it revived starting in 2010. General Motors, the area's largest employer, suffered cutbacks in the 1970s and other manufacturing jobs were dwindling. During the most recent recession, DHL closed an air cargo hub at the Wilmington Air Park in Clinton County, costing the region 10,000 jobs. Then, in a major psychological and economic blow for the city, NCR announced in 2009 that it was leaving after 125 years, taking away Dayton's last *Fortune 500* company and the 1,300 jobs it provided. The economic picture has brightened in the past few years. *Forbes* named Dayton the most affordable city in the country in 2012. General Electric has a new center to develop advanced electric power systems for aircraft, ships, and hybrid auto-mobiles, including a partnership with Boe-

2012 Presidential Vote		
Mitt Romney (R)..............179,772	(50%)
Barack Obama (D) 172,981	(48%)
2008 Presidential Vote		
Barack Obama (D) 183,272	(49%)
John McCain (R)................183,268	(49%)
Cook Partisan Voting Index: R+3		

ing. Dayton-area universities and Wright-Patterson Air Force Base increasingly make the area a magnet for high-tech companies. In 2011, the Dayton area had the third-highest increase in high-tech jobs in the country. For 2014, *Site Selection* magazine ranked Dayton as number-two, behind Greensboro, North Carolina, for business expansion projects in cities with a population of less than 1 million. In May 2015, its unemployment rate of 4.9 percent was below the national average.

The 10th Congressional District of Ohio includes all of Dayton and surrounding Mont-gomery County. To the east, it includes Greene County, including upscale Beaver Creek and middle-class Fairborn. It also takes in the city of Washington Court House, a town whose street grid is arrayed in a northwesterly-southeasterly direction (rather than the classic north/east orientation) so that each face of its centrally located courthouse gets some sun-shine during the day. Overall, this is a Republican-leaning district, although not overwhelm-ingly so. John McCain won the district with 49% in 2008 and Mitt Romney squeezed by with 50% in 2012.

Mike Turner (R)

Mike Turner, a Republican first elected in 2002, is a former Dayton mayor who has shown a stronger interest in urban issues than most House Republicans. He has been an active member of the Republican majority on national security issues, an area in which his influ-ence has steadily increased.

Turner grew up in Dayton, where his father worked for 42 years for General Motors. He graduated from Ohio Northern University, Case Western law school, and the University of Dayton business school and became a corporate lawyer. In 1993, at age 33, he narrowly defeated a scandal-tainted Democratic incumbent to win the first of two terms as Dayton mayor. He created Rehabarama, an acclaimed private-public partnership to rehabilitate neglected housing in Dayton's historic neighborhoods. He narrowly lost a bid for reelection in 2001.

Ohio and national Republican leaders recruited him to challenge Democratic Rep. Tony Hall, who had served 12 terms but was vulnerable after post-2000 census redistricting made his turf considerably more Republican. In early 2002, Turner announced he was running for Congress. A week later, President George W. Bush nominated Hall as ambassador to the United Nations' Food and Agriculture Organization in Rome.

In the Republican primary, Turner had fierce opposition from newspaper publisher Roy Brown, grandson and son of former Reps. Clarence Brown and Clarence Brown Jr., who had represented a neighboring district from 1938 to 1982. Brown spent $1.3 million of his own money, largely on ads attacking Turner's record on taxes and lambasting him for being insufficiently conservative. Brown owned 10 local newspapers, and Turner contended that Brown's campaign guided his newspapers' coverage of the race. A few days before the primary, the Ohio Election Commission ruled that Brown violated state law with false statements in a televised ad. Voters evidently shared that view. Turner defeated Brown 80%-14%.

The general election was comparatively sedate. The Democratic nominee was Rick Carne, Hall's chief of staff. With little support from his national party, he raised nearly $600,000, including a local appearance by Dayton native Martin Sheen, who played Presi-dent Josiah Bartlet on the popular *West Wing* television series. Turner won 59%-41%.

In the House, Turner has supported his party on most major issues but he is among the more moderate House Republicans. He has voted against conservative efforts to sharply cut science funding and to eliminate such agencies as the Legal Services Corporation and the National Endowment for the Arts. He has helped to save the Community Development Block Grant program.

In 2013, he became chairman of the Armed Services Committee's Tactical Air and Land Forces Subcommittee. That has enabled him to offer protection against Defense Department cuts for Wright-Patterson Air Force Base, which is the largest single-site employer in Ohio, and for the Lima Army Tank Plant. He has worked to make Dayton into a center for unmanned aerial vehicle research and testing, and he has been strongly critical of the Obama administration's funding cuts for missile defense. He has accused the administration of being in a "dream-like trance" in ignoring the threat from North Korea. In December 2014, he became president of the inter-parliamentary organization of legislators from the countries of the North Atlantic Alliance. He became a member of the House Intelligence Committee in 2015, where he worked to continue the National Air and Space Intelligence Center headquartered at Wright-Patt. On the 2015 defense spending bill, he was a leader of the strategy to ignore earlier requirements to "sequester" spending until the deficit was reduced. The veto threat from President Barack Obama, he said, "ignores the real security risks facing our nation."

Turner and Democratic Rep. Niki Tsongas of Massachusetts created the bipartisan Military Sexual Assault Prevention Caucus. Turner earlier collaborated with then-Democratic Rep. Jane Harman of California to review the military's handling of sexual assault charges. He has tried for years to get Congress to pass a law aimed at protecting service members from losing custody of their children because of military deployments; the measure passed the House and stalled in the Senate. In 2014, Turner considered a bid to fill the opening as chairman of the Armed Services Committee. He deferred, but made clear his interest in the next such vacancy.

Turner has remained focused on urban issues and formed a caucus of former mayors serving in Congress. He has worked on House-passed legislation to accelerate the cleanup of polluted brownfields by making it easier for communities to apply for federal grants. He has promoted the kind of public-private partnerships that he used for economic development in Dayton. In 2009, Turner was one of seven House Republicans to support a bill that would give bankruptcy judges the power to restructure the terms of home mortgages. Then-Minority Leader John Boehner, who serves in an adjacent district, called the bill "just the worst idea in the world."

In 2008, Ohio Democrats made an issue of the fact that Turner had not disclosed a five-year business relationship between his wife, Lori Turner, and home builder Tom Peebles, who had contributed to Turner's campaign. Turner asked for a ruling from the House Ethics Committee, which concluded he did not have to disclose the relationship. Turner was reelected that year 63%-37%. He has not been seriously challenged since, and spent much of his time in 2012 as an aggressive surrogate for GOP presidential nominee Mitt Romney.

ELEVENTH DISTRICT

Marcia Fudge (D)

Elected Nov. 2008, 5th term; b. Oct. 29, 1952, Cleveland; OH St. U., B.S. 1975, Cleveland St. U., J.D. 1983; Christian; single.

Elected Office: Warrensville Heights mayor, 2000-08.

Professional Career: Practicing atty.; Aide, U.S. Rep. Stephanie Tubbs Jones, 1991-2000.

DC Office: 2344 RHOB, 20515, 202-225-7032; Fax: 202-225-1339; Website: fudge.house.gov.

State Offices: Warrensville Heights, 216-522-4900; Akron, 330-835-4758.

Committees: *Agriculture:* Biotechnology, Horticulture & Research; Nutrition. *Education & the Workforce:* Early Childhood, Elementary & Secondary Education (RMM); Workforce Protections.

Group Ratings

	ADA	ACLU	AFL-CIO	LCV	ITI	COC	HAFA	ACU	CFG	FRC
2014	85%	66%	–	89%	60%	43%	16%	4%	6%	0%
2013	85%	C	100%	89%	C	38%	C	17%	20%	C

National Journal Ratings

	2013 LIB	—	2013 CONS
Economic	75%	—	25%
Social	65%	—	35%
Foreign	77%	—	23%
Composite	72%	—	28%

Key Votes of the 113th Congress

1. Sandy storm spending	Y	5. Medical Marijuana	Y	9. Syrian Rebels Training	N
2. Violence Against Women Act	Y	6. Farm Bill	N	10. Keystone pipeline	N
3. Guantanamo Bay Detainees	Y	7. Afghanistan Combat	NV	11. Immigration Exec. Action	N
4. Abortion 20-week ban	N	8. NSA Phone Data Collection	Y	12. Bipartisan budget deal	N

Election Results

2014 general	Marcia Fudge (D)..................... 137,105	(80%)	$497,385
	Mark Zetzer (R) 35,461	(21%)	
2014 primary	Marcia Fuge (D)....................unopposed		

Prior winning percentages: 2012 (89%), 2010 (83%), 2008 (85%), 2008 special (unopposed)

Population		Race and Ethnicity		Income	
Total:	692,794	Black	53.9%	Median income:	$33,935
Urban:	78.4%	White	37.9%		(424 of 435)
Suburban:	21.6%	Latino	3.6%	Under $50,000	64.1%
Rural:	0.0%	Asian	2.2%	$50,000-$99,999:	22.1%
Land area:	356	Two races	2.0%	$100,000-$199,999:	10.2%
Pop/sq. mi.:	1,945.8	White Ethnic	24.2%	$200,000 or more:	3.6%
Born in state:	73.2%			Poverty Rate	27.6%
		Education			
Age Groups		H.S. grad or less:	43.7%	**Work**	
Under 18:	22.3%	Some college:	28.9%	White collar:	36.9%
18 to 34:	24.4%	College degree, 4 yr.:	15.1%	Blue collar:	44.9%
35 to 64:	38.1%	Post-grad study:	12.2%	Sales and service:	18.2%
Over 64:	15.2%				
		Military		Govt. workers:	12.8%
		Veterans/active duty:	7.2%		

Cleveland, Akron

Like most great American cities, Cleveland grew in great bursts of migration, during periods when the economy expanded and attracted low-wage workers from around the country and the world. After the Ohio and Erie Canal connected Lake Erie with the Ohio River in the 1830s, Cleveland became a criti-

Voter Turnout	
2013 Total Citizen 18+	523,760
2014 House Turnout	172,566
2014 Turnout as % CVAP	32.9%
2012 Turnout as % CVAP	68.5%

cal destination for goods traveling from the north to the interior and vice versa. Its greatest surge of growth started in the 1890s and lasted through the 1920s, when the city was transformed from a bustling city of 250,000 to a burgeoning metropolis of over 900,000. Tens of thousands of immigrants from central and southern Europe arrived, looking for jobs in the steel and automobile factories. Bohemians came to the tightly packed neighborhoods along Broadway, Hungarians settled in the northeast, Jews lived north of University Circle along East 105th Street, and Italians ran produce markets along Mayfield Road. As heavy industries geared up for World War II and enjoyed years of prosperous growth afterward, another surge of immigrants came, this time from the South. African Americans settled in on the east side and grew from just 2% of Cleveland's population in 1910 to 38% by 1970.

These bursts of migration led to political changes. A string of ethnic mayors— Frank Lausche, Anthony Celebrezze, Ralph Locher—was followed by the election in 1967 of Carl Stokes, the nation's first black big-city mayor. Cleveland had racially polarized politics for much of the 1970s. Even so, the west

2012 Presidential Vote		
Barack Obama (D) 299,107	(83%)	
Mitt Romney (R)..................57,787	(16%)	
2008 Presidential Vote		
Barack Obama (D) 303,512	(82%)	
John McCain (R)..................63,649	(17%)	
Cook Partisan Voting Index: D+30		

side stayed mostly white, and Cleveland did not have a black majority until the 2000 census, when its declining population was 51% black; its 2013 population declined to 390,000 and was only 43% of what it was in 1930. In 2010, the Census Bureau reported that Cleveland was second to Detroit as the poorest of the nation's big cities, with more than half of children living in poverty. Despite steady increases in international migration, the population loss in Cuyahoga County since 2010 has been second in the nation, trailing only Wayne County (Detroit).

The 11th Congressional District of Ohio includes most of the east side of Cleveland, plus the suburbs just to the east. Some of these areas—East Cleveland, Warrensville Heights—are mostly black. Others, like Shaker Heights, are mostly white. Still others, like the old Slavic enclave of Garfield Heights, are mostly populated by the heirs of the ethnic whites who settled Cleveland in the early 20th century. The district includes exurbs of Cleveland, plus heavily minority and Democratic segments of Akron and a few of its suburbs. Akron, too, has benefited from immigration, with many refugees from Myanmar and Bhutan who have moved into the North Hill neighborhood. Summit County is less than 20% of the district population. The 11th exists for two reasons: To provide a minority-majority district in compliance with the Voting Rights Act, and to satisfy the desire of Republicans in control of redistricting to place as many Democrats as possible in a single district and protect Republicans in nearby districts. The 11th is 54% black, and among the five percent most heavily Democratic districts in the nation.

Marcia Fudge (D)

Democrat Marcia Fudge in 2008 succeeded her former mentor and friend, Rep. Stephanie Tubbs Jones, who died from a cerebral aneurysm. Fudge parlayed her organizational and networking skills into an active leadership of the Congressional Black Caucus in 2013-14. Her legislative focus has been on education.

Fudge, like many African Americans of her generation, was greatly influenced by the civil rights movement and got active politically when she was young. She grew up in Cleveland, but her family moved to the suburb of Shaker Heights when she was 12. During high school, Fudge volunteered with "Young Folks for Stokes," a coalition of young people helping to elect Carl Stokes mayor of Cleveland. She helped with get-out-the-vote efforts and distributing campaign literature. After graduating from Ohio State University with a degree in business administration, she received her law degree from Cleveland State University. She practiced mainly criminal defense law in the Cleveland area, along with some probate and corporate work, until she went to work for Tubbs Jones.

Fudge and Tubbs Jones first met as members of the national Delta Sigma Theta Sorority alumnae association. Fudge later served as national president of the group of predominately African-American women. When Tubbs Jones became the Cuyahoga County prosecutor in 1991, Fudge became her administrative assistant. When her boss was elected to Congress in 1998, Fudge joined her in Washington as chief of staff.

After a few years, Fudge felt the pull of elected office. When the Warrensville Heights mayor resigned, she won and became the first African-American woman to be elected mayor of the city. Fudge focused on economic development and claimed credit for creating 3,000 jobs and bringing in $500 million for development and infrastructure.

Tubbs Jones died unexpectedly just a few days before the Democratic National Convention, after winning the 2008 Democratic primary for reelection. Fudge called each member of the district's Democratic Executive Committee, which was in charge of selecting a replacement on the ballot. She explained why she would be the best choice to carry on Tubbs Jones' legacy, and the strategy paid off. There were four candidates, and the committee nominated Fudge with 175 votes. Former state Sen. C.J. Prentiss was a distant second, with 64 votes. She won the general election with 85% of the vote. She had no Republican challenger for the special election, allowing her to be sworn in before other freshmen that year.

In the House, Fudge has been a staunch and passionate liberal. In urging an extension of unemployment benefits in July 2010, she said on the House floor, "I hope you can't sleep until you understand that our former coworkers, our neighbors, our friends, our family are hurting." Representing an urban area, she has been outspoken on the Agriculture Committee in defending food stamps. When committee Republicans called for cutting the program by $16.5 billion over 10 years, she said at a panel discussion in January 2013 that the lawmakers "literally do not believe there is poverty in this country." In 2015, she became ranking Democrat on the Education and the Workforce Subcommittee on Early Childhood, Elementary and Secondary Education, where her objective was to provide resources and opportunity for all students regardless of income. She said that it was vital for Congress to listen to educators before it made changes in the No Child Left Behind Act. With Republican Rep. Chris Gibson of New York, she filed a bill in April 2015 to permit eligible students to use Pell Grants to pay for college credits while they are still in high school.

During her two years as chair of the CBC, she continued her advocacy on behalf of low-income African Americans in assailing the budget sequester that imposed automatic across-the-board spending cuts after the two parties failed to reach a budget agreement. "If we allow this sequester to happen, we're saying that our political agendas are more important than the ability to take care of our families," she said. When lawmakers unveiled a statue of civil rights icon Rosa Parks at the Capitol, she noted the irony of the event occurring on the same day that several conservative Supreme Court justices raised sharp questions about the Voting Rights Act.

Fudge earlier drew attention for her proposal to rein in the powers of the independent Office of Congressional Ethics. The OCE found in 2009 that Fudge's chief of staff "improperly influenced" information that a group called Carib News Foundation gave the House Ethics Committee about an annual Caribbean trip that the group had sponsored for Black Caucus members. Fudge introduced a bill seeking to place limits on the OCE's jurisdiction and to bar "premature publication" of its findings.

At home, Fudge focused on the continuing urban decay and tensions in Cleveland. In May 2015, she embraced as "a turning point" for police-community relations the consent decree between the city and the Justice Department that promised systemic changes. In her overwhelmingly Democratic district, Fudge has faced token opposition in primary and general elections.

TWELFTH DISTRICT

Pat Tiberi (R)

Elected 2000, 8th term; b. Oct. 21, 1962, Columbus; OH St. U., B.A. 1985; Catholic; married (Denice); 4 children.

Elected Office: OH House, 1992-2000, maj. ldr., 1999-2000.

Professional Career: Staff asst., U.S. Rep. John Kasich, 1984-92; Realtor, ReMax Achievers, 1995-2000.

DC Office: 1203 LHOB, 20515, 202-225-5355; Fax: 202-226-4523; Website: tiberi.house.gov.

State Offices: Worthington, 614-523-2555.

Committees: *Ways & Means:* Select Revenue Measures; Trade (Chmn).

Group Ratings

	ADA	ACLU	AFL-CIO	LCV	ITI	COC	HAFA	ACU	CFG	FRC
2014	5%	0%	–	6%	60%	93%	53%	64%	59%	88%
2013	0%	C	29%	4%	C	92%	C	56%	59%	C

National Journal Ratings

	2013 LIB	—	2013 CONS
Economic	28%	—	72%
Social	38%	—	59%
Foreign	5%	—	86%
Composite	26%	—	74%

Key Votes of the 113th Congress

1. Sandy storm spending	N	5. Medical Marijuana	N	9. Syrian Rebels Training	Y
2. Violence Against Women Act	Y	6. Farm Bill	Y	10. Keystone pipeline	Y
3. Guantanamo Bay Detainees	N	7. Afghanistan Combat	N	11. Immigration Exec. Action	Y
4. Abortion 20-week ban	Y	8. NSA Phone Data Collection	N	12. Bipartisan budget deal	Y

Election Results

2014 general	Patrick Tiberi (R)	150,573	(68%)	$2,358,505	$4,631
	David Tibbs (D)	61,360	(28%)		
	Bob Hart (Green)	9,148	(4%)	$4,741	
2014 primary	Patrick Tiberi (R)	unopposed			

Prior winning percentages: 2012 (63%), 2010 (56%), 2008 (55%), 2006 (57%), 2004 (62%), 2002 (64%), 2000 (53%)

Population		Race and Ethnicity		Income	
Total:	744,647	White	87.8%	Median income:	$61,180
Urban:	25.4%	Black	4.5%		*(112 of 435)*
Suburban:	56.9%	Asian	3.0%	Under $50,000	40.7%
Rural:	17.8%	Latino	2.0%	$50,000-$99,999:	30.5%
Land area:	2,156	Two races	2.4%	$100,000-$199,999:	23.1%
Pop/sq. mi.:	345.4	White Ethnic	29.2%	$200,000 or more:	5.7%
Born in state:	73.3%			Poverty Rate	11.1%
		Education			
Age Groups		H.S. grad or less:	36.0%	**Work**	
Under 18:	24.5%	Some college:	25.6%	White collar:	44.8%
18 to 34:	21.5%	College degree, 4 yr.:	24.2%	Blue collar:	38.7%
35 to 64:	41.1%	Post-grad study:	14.2%	Sales and service:	16.6%
Over 64:	12.9%				
		Military		Govt. workers:	13.4%
		Veterans/active duty:	8.0%		

Central Ohio: Northern Columbus Metro

Columbus was long the forgotten city in Ohio. Overshadowed by its much larger cousins for most of its existence—Cincinnati to the south and Cleveland to the north—it was best-known to most Americans as the subject of James Thurber's biting satire, *My Life and Hard Times*. It remained a surprisingly

Voter Turnout	
2013 Total Citizen 18+	543,850
2014 House Turnout	221,081
2014 Turnout as % CVAP	40.7%
2012 Turnout as % CVAP	69.4%

small town for the capital of such an important state; its population in 1920 was roughly the same as Akron's. Today, Columbus is a major metropolis and, with 823,000 people in 2013, has breezed past the total of Cleveland and Cincinnati (though those two cities still have more populous metropolitan areas). Columbus' Franklin County passed the 1 million mark in the 1990s and has grown to 1.2 million.

With this explosive growth has come sprawl in all directions. Most American cities grew up around a coastline or river, which tended to direct its growth (think of Miami's unusual shape). But Columbus, with its location near the geographic center of the state, was selected as the state capital in 1812 mainly as a way of placating various other aspirants for the designation. The plains to the north and west do little to inhibit growth, while the rolling hills that mark the end of the Appalachian Plateau to the south and east were worn down by glaciers in the last ice age and provide no meaningful barrier to expansion.

The 12th Congressional District contains a slice of the city that takes in the northern portions of the University District—bordering the football stadium of Ohio State University—filled with pre-World War II Craftsman-style bungalows, as well as the more spacious homes of Clintonville, one of the original "streetcar" communities. It takes in suburbs to the north and east: Worthington, increasingly indistinguishable from the encroaching city; newly fashionable Dublin; Gahanna; and upscale New Albany. This portion of the district, contained in Franklin County, casts about a third of its votes. To the north is fast-growing Delaware County, home to the highly-rated Columbus Zoo and heavily Republican. It last voted for a Democratic presidential candidate in 1916. Westerville, Powell, Lewis Center and Galena are all upscale suburbs that help give Delaware the highest median income of any county in Ohio.

2012 Presidential Vote		
Mitt Romney (R)	207,339	(54%)
Barack Obama (D)	167,507	(44%)

2008 Presidential Vote		
John McCain (R)	201,582	(54%)
Barack Obama (D)	167,884	(45%)

Cook Partisan Voting Index: R+8

The rest of the district is outside Columbus' orbit. Licking County is home to picturesque Granville and Denison, its small liberal arts college. Industrial parks across the country have been the magnet to attract new manufacturing companies, with programs to encourage high school students about the benefits of a career in skilled trades. With its customary secrecy, Amazon has built three huge data centers in the Columbus area, creating an expectation that a larger computing center may follow. Newark is an old manufacturing town in decay, but some industries hold on. Mansfield, where the microwave oven was invented in 1955, has an old reformatory with imposing gothic architecture that was made famous as Shawshank Prison in the 1994 film. Zanesville, with its famous "Y"-shaped bridge, provides the only real center of Democratic voting strength outside of Franklin County. Franklin is the largest population center in the district, but Delaware and Licking are not far behind.

Republicans in charge of redistricting in 2011 painstakingly redrew Franklin County to include the new 3rd district filled with Democratic precincts and reinforced neighboring districts with Republican-leaning rural areas. That produced a significant shift in the 12th. A district that Barack Obama won in 2008 with 54% was transformed into one that John McCain would have won with 54%; Mitt Romney replicated that number in 2012.

Pat Tiberi (R)

Republican Pat Tiberi, elected in 2000, is one of Speaker John Boehner's closest allies. He has reaped the benefits by swiftly gaining influence on the powerful Ways and Means Committee, and has returned the favor by increasingly challenging Boehner's critics in the Republican Conference.

The son of Italian immigrants, Tiberi grew up in Columbus and graduated from Ohio State University. He worked as a real estate agent and then as an aide to Republican Rep. John Kasich (now governor) for eight years. He recalled to *The Columbus Dispatch* that Kasich won him over by blasting AC/DC's hard rock on the car radio. "I thought, 'Man, this guy listens to the same music, and he's a Republican congressman,'" Tiberi said. "It broke my entire image of what a Republican congressman is."

Kasich helped Tiberi win a seat in the state House, where he became majority leader and supported business-friendly legislation and tort law changes. In 1999, Kasich, then chairman of the Budget Committee, announced his retirement from the House. Tiberi won support to replace his mentor from most of the Republican establishment and the U.S. Chamber of Commerce. He faced a noisy but ineffective primary challenge from state Sen. Gene Watts, who sought to rally conservatives. Tiberi won 73%-21%.

The resounding victory gave him a big boost heading into the general election against Maryellen O'Shaughnessy, a Democratic Columbus City Council member. She had a compelling personal story as the single mother of a 10-year-old son. Tiberi played up his Columbus roots and his membership in the Ohio State marching band and held O'Shaughnessy responsible for negative Democratic Party ads that labeled him a defender of insurance companies on the issue of affordable prescription drugs. This was one of the most-watched House races in the nation during that politically tight year. With more campaign help from Kasich, Tiberi won 53%-44%.

In the House, Tiberi's voting record has been faithfully Republican but has grown slightly less conservative since his party and his friend Boehner regained control of the House. He was one of only seven Republicans to vote against denying funding for National Public Radio in 2011; in 2012, he refused to go along with House-passed amendments to bar federal funding for political science research and to reduce money for renewable energy projects. Earlier, he supported expansion of the Children's Health Insurance Program, and a Democratic overhaul of food safety laws in 2009. At Boehner's urging, he backed the final version of the Troubled Asset Relief Program in 2008 after initially opposing it.

In the majority, Tiberi became chairman of the Select Revenue Subcommittee at Ways and Means, and pledged to scrap the income tax code and replace it with a simpler version. He blamed the disinterest of the Obama administration for the lack of progress. In January 2015, he switched to chairman of the Trade Subcommittee. He spent the next six months in arduous negotiations to gain House support for trade promotion authority for President Barack Obama and eventually to count the votes until he, Ways and Means Chairman Paul Ryan of Wisconsin and GOP leaders were confident they had secured a majority. He also tried to rally public support. "The pie's going to get smaller because the world is a smaller place. Either we engage and move ahead, or we fall behind," he told business officials in New Albany.

As Republicans sought ways to reduce gun violence in schools after the December 2012 elementary school massacre in Newtown Connecticut, Tiberi came up with a novel proposal: He introduced a bill to encourage off-duty police officers to serve as substitute teachers by giving them a break on their income taxes.

Befitting his background as a former congressional aide, Tiberi has a reputation as an effective behind-the-scenes operator. He was campaign manager for Boehner's successful bid for majority leader in early 2006, and he later helped Boehner fix organizational problems at the National Republican Congressional Committee. He and Oklahoma Republican Tom Cole served as vote-counters for Cathy McMorris Rodgers of Washington, another favorite of Boehner, in her successful November 2012 bid to chair the Republican Conference. When more than two dozen House Republicans voted for someone other than Boehner in the January 2015 selection of the speaker, Tiberi was reported to be among Boehner's close allies urging penalties for the rebels and making the case that the speaker had broad party support. In the following weeks and months, Tiberi's fingerprints were evident in disciplinary actions against lawmakers who abandoned the GOP on what were viewed as routine parliamentary votes.

Tiberi had easily won reelection with his district's earlier narrow partisan balance. But he welcomes the new district lines that became "the most dramatic partisan makeover in the state," according to *The Cook Political Report,* with the Democratic portions around Columbus shifted elsewhere. In the redrawn 12th, he has not faced significant opposition. In July 2015, he stepped forward as the chair of the steering committee for Kasich's presidential campaign.

THIRTEENTH DISTRICT

Tim Ryan (D)

Elected 2002, 7th term; b. July 16, 1973, Niles; Bowling Green St. U., B.A. 1995, Franklin Pierce Law Ctr., J.D. 2000; Catholic; married (Andrea), 3 children.

Elected Office: OH Senate, 2000-02.

Professional Career: Aide, U.S. Rep. Jim Traficant, 1995-97.

DC Office: 1421 LHOB, 20515, 202-225-5261; Fax: 202-225-3719; Website: timryan.house.gov.

State Offices: Akron, 330-630-7311; Warren, 800-856-4152; Youngstown, 330-740-0193.

Committees: *Appropriations:* Defense; Transportation, HUD & Related Agencies. *Budget.*

Group Ratings

	ADA	ACLU	AFL-CIO	LCV	ITI	COC	HAFA	ACU	CFG	FRC
2014	80%	88%	–	86%	80%	43%	15%	13%	13%	0%
2013	80%	C	95%	93%	C	31%	C	20%	12%	C

National Journal Ratings

	2013 LIB	—	2013 CONS
Economic	71%	—	29%
Social	69%	—	28%
Foreign	58%	—	42%
Composite	67%	—	34%

Key Votes of the 113th Congress

1. Sandy storm spending	Y	5. Medical Marijuana	Y	9. Syrian Rebels Training	Y
2. Violence Against Women Act	Y	6. Farm Bill	N	10. Keystone pipeline	N
3. Guantanamo Bay Detainees	Y	7. Afghanistan Combat	NV	11. Immigration Exec. Action	N
4. Abortion 20-week ban	N	8. NSA Phone Data Collection	N	12. Bipartisan budget deal	Y

Election Results

2014 general	Tim Ryan (D)	120,230	(69%)	$787,870
	Thomas Pekarek (R)	55,233	(32%)	
2014 primary	Tim Ryan (D)	45,585	(85%)	
	John Luchansky (D)	8,016	(15%)	

Prior winning percentages: 2012 (73%), 2010 (54%), 2008 (78%), 2006 (80%), 2004 (77%), 2002 (51%)

Population		Race and Ethnicity		Income	
Total:	719,201	White	82.0%	Median income:	$40,835
Urban:	50.8%	Black	11.5%		*(379 of 435)*
Suburban:	48.3%	Latino	2.7%	Under $50,000	59.0%
Rural:	0.9%	Asian	1.3%	$50,000-$99,999:	29.4%
Land area:	1,064	Two races	2.1%	$100,000-$199,999:	9.8%
Pop/sq. mi.:	675.8	White Ethnic	43.3%	$200,000 or more:	1.8%
Born in state:	77.4%			Poverty Rate	19.8%
		Education			
Age Groups		H.S. grad or less:	50.9%	**Work**	
Under 18:	19.7%	Some college:	27.5%	White collar:	29.0%
18 to 34:	23.8%	College degree, 4 yr.:	14.7%	Blue collar:	45.5%
35 to 64:	39.9%	Post-grad study:	7.0%	Sales and service:	25.4%
Over 64:	16.7%				
		Military		Govt. workers:	11.9%
		Veterans/active duty:	9.1%		

Northeast Ohio: Youngstown, Akron Area

For nearly a century, the Mahoning Valley—between the Lake Erie docks that unload iron ore from Great Lakes freighters and the coalfields of western Pennsylvania and West Virginia—was a steel capital of the United States. The first blast furnace opened in 1803, and the first coal mine

Voter Turnout	
2013 Total Citizen 18+	561,807
2014 House Turnout	175,463
2014 Turnout as % CVAP	31.2%
2012 Turnout as % CVAP	60.5%

opened in 1826. Canals followed, and in 1892 the first steel mill was built. The valley soon filled up with mills, converters and furnaces. But big-steel management and unions allowed foreign producers to gain a technological edge in the 1950s and 1960s, and worldwide overcapacity in steel grew as almost every developing country decided it needed its own steel mills. After a 119-day strike in 1959, an agreement between the United Steelworkers and management boosted wages and fringe benefits to levels that helped price domestic steel out of the market. Import restrictions kept the furnaces hot for a while, but the oil shock of the 1970s produced sharply higher energy prices and a collapse in the U.S. auto and steel markets. Every plant in the Mahoning Valley closed, with a loss of 40,000 jobs; the public schools were closed for a few months because city revenues fell so precipitously. In the early 1980s, Youngstown had one of the nation's highest unemployment rates.

Steel has since revived, although not at its previous peak and not in Youngstown. The high-wage living standard vanished. Organized crime infiltrated local government, and a federal investigation in the late 1990s led to more than 70 convictions; among those sentenced were a prosecutor, a sheriff and a congressman. In 2010, Youngstown's population was 67,000, only a little more than a third its size in the 1950s. The city is struggling to rebound, though it has managed to attract a few high-tech firms, including the fast-growing Turning Technologies software company, whose goal is to make technology more affordable and user-friendly. It has become a locus for shale drilling, but young people looking for opportunities continue to leave. Still, there is some benefit to the weak economy. In the first quarter of 2015, according to the National Association of Realtors, the Youngstown-Warren area had the lowest home prices in the nation. The median price for single-family home sales was $64,300.

The 13th Congressional District of Ohio encompasses most of the Mahoning Valley industrial area: Youngstown (though not its southern Mahoning County suburbs), Warren, and most of Trumbull County. It includes nearly all of Portage County and the less-minority parts of Summit County and Akron. Mahoning, Trumbull and Summit have similar shares of the population. It contains two loci of 1970s protest—Kent State University, where four war-protesting students were killed by National Guardsmen, and Lordstown, site of the General Motors plant where workers purposely built shoddy cars to protest the tedium of the assembly line.

2012 Presidential Vote		
Barack Obama (D)	212,082	(63%)
Mitt Romney (R)	120,913	(36%)

2008 Presidential Vote		
Barack Obama (D)	221,979	(62%)
John McCain (R)	127,497	(36%)

Cook Partisan Voting Index: D+11

This Rustbelt patchwork is the least Democratic and least urban of the four Democratic districts in Ohio. Barack Obama twice won a bit more than 60 percent of the vote.

Tim Ryan (D)

Tim Ryan, a Democrat elected in 2002 at age 29, has been a pro-union, anti-abortion centrist who is usually a party regular. That combination has propelled other Ohioans to higher office, but Ryan so far has rejected opportunities to go that route.

Ryan grew up in Niles, was a star quarterback before a knee injury ended his career, and graduated from Bowling Green State University. His first job was with Rep. James Traficant, a blue-collar and often maverick Democrat. In 2000, after graduating from Franklin Pierce Law Center, Ryan was elected to the state Senate. His opening to run for Congress came when the increasingly flaky Traficant was forced to resign in disgrace after his conviction in 2002 for racketeering and bribery. For years, Traficant had been a colorful if coarse figure in the House, whose ranting orations ("Beam me up, Scotty" was his expression of incredulity at hearing an opposing viewpoint) were a regular source of fascination for C-SPAN viewers.

Akron-based Rep. Tom Sawyer, a Democrat who had been thrown into the district by redistricting, seemed to have the inside track to succeed Traficant. By standard measures, Sawyer should have easily won the primary: He outspent Ryan nearly 6-to-1 and he had the perks of incumbency. But his record gave Ryan an opening. Sawyer had voted for the 1993 North American Free Trade Agreement, and he was one of the few Rust Belt Democrats to vote for normalizing trade relations with China. Ryan hammered on these votes in the Mahoning Valley, where it is gospel that free trade drove the region's high-paying jobs abroad. Ryan also got the endorsement of the National Rifle Association in a district with many hunters. In a district with greater intensity in Youngstown than in its slice of Akron, Ryan defeated Sawyer 41%-27%.

The Republican nominee was state Rep. Ann Womer Benjamin. Ryan slammed her and the Republican Legislature for votes that had led to higher tuition at state universities. Republicans fired back with ads highlighting several disorderly conduct charges lodged against Ryan while he was in college. The district's Democratic leanings and Ryan's labor support proved decisive. He won 51% of the vote to 34% for Womer Benjamin and 15% for Traficant, who ran as an independent even though he'd been carted off to jail.

Ryan has leaned to the left on economic and foreign policy. His splits with Democrats on abortion rights and gun control have placed him closer to the center on social issues, and he has worked with others to seek common ground. After the deadly school massacre in Newtown Connecticut, he held meetings with gun enthusiasts and law enforcement officials to try to "thread the needle" on a solution to gun violence. With Democratic abortion-rights advocate Rosa DeLauro of Connecticut, he sponsored the "Reducing the Need for Abortion and Supporting Parents Act," with federal dollars to fight teen pregnancy and increased aid for women who become pregnant; Democratic activists depicted this as a move toward party consensus on a difficult issue. He refused to join most Republicans in 2011 in voting to defund Planned Parenthood. In January 2015, he said that his position "evolved" further. "I have come to believe that we must trust women and families—not politicians—to make the best decisions for their lives," he wrote in the *Akron Beacon-Journal*.

In 2006, Ryan endeared himself to rising House Speaker Nancy Pelosi when he was a vocal backer of powerful Pennsylvania Democrat John Murtha in his unsuccessful bid for majority leader against Steny Hoyer of Maryland. That earned Ryan a coveted seat on the House Appropriations Committee. He immediately went to work securing earmarked projects for his hard-pressed district. Those practices ended when John Boehner from politically distinct southwest Ohio ended earmarks after Republicans regained control in 2011. Reflecting his district, Ryan has remained a harsh critic of international trade deals. For several years, he sponsored the Chinese Currency Act, a proposal to counter China's alleged manipulation and undervaluation of its currency. He co-chairs the Congressional Manufacturing Caucus, which seeks to revive the nation's industrial base and to revise its trade policy.

Ryan has drawn attention not from legislation, but from meditation. He attended a five-day retreat after the 2008 election, turning off his two BlackBerrys and gradually reducing how often he talked until he maintained a 36-hour period of silence. "My mind and body were in the same place at the same time, synchronized in a way I had rarely experienced," he told the *Beacon Journal*. He wrote a book in 2012, *A Mindful Nation: How a Simple Practice Can Help Us Reduce Stress, Improve Performance, and Recapture the American Spirit*, and he now spends 45 minutes a day practicing "mindfulness"—something he says stressed-out Washingtonians and corporate executives should try. He expanded his spiritual revival to include healthier eating, with a book scheduled for release later in 2015, *The Real Food Revolution: Healthy Eating, Green Groceries, and the Return of the American Family Farm*. In a *New York* magazine profile in January 2015, Marin Cogan profiled Ryan's new focus: "He's introduced bills to add holistic and alternative-medicine programs for the treatment of veterans, to teach schoolchildren social and emotional skills through better self-awareness, to fund 'integrated nutrition curricula' in medical schools—and that's just in the last Congress." But not everything he puts in his body has been good for him. Ryan drew unwanted attention in 2012 when he was arrested in August for public intoxication in Virginia. The charges were later dismissed.

Ryan has not faced serious reelection problems. His political problem has been a repeated refusal to step up the political ladder. He considered a run for the Senate in 2006 but decided against challenging the more senior Democrat Sherrod Brown. Democratic Gov. Ted Strickland discussed a shared ticket with Ryan in 2010, but Ryan decided to remain in the House, largely because of his new assignment on Appropriations. He again took a serious look at running for governor in 2014 after Strickland said that he wouldn't run, but announced in March 2013 that the risk still wasn't worth giving up his Appropriations seat. In February 2015, he turned down the opportunity to run for the Senate the next year, with the explanation, "With my new and growing family, I feel now is the time to be close to home." In his early 40s and with a thin bench of Ohio Democrats, he likely will have other opportunities.

FOURTEENTH DISTRICT

David Joyce (R)

Elected 2012, 2nd term; b. March 17, 1957, Cleveland; U. of Dayton, B.S. 1979, J.D. 1982; Catholic; married (Kelly); 3 children.

Elected Office: Prosecutor, Geauga Cnty., 1988-2013.

Professional Career: Public defender, Geauga Cnty., 1985-88; Public defender, Cuyahoga Cnty., 1983-84.

DC Office: 1124 LHOB, 20515, 202-225-5731; Fax: 202-225-3307; Website: joyce.house.gov.

State Offices: Painesville, 440-352-3939; Twinsburg, 330-425-9291.

Committees: *Appropriations:* Interior; Military Construction & Veterans Affairs; Transportation, HUD & Related Agencies.

Group Ratings

	ADA	ACLU	AFL-CIO	LCV	ITI	COC	HAFA	ACU	CFG	FRC
2014	0%	0%	–	6%	80%	93%	44%	56%	46%	63%
2013	15%	C	45%	7%	C	92%	C	40%	47%	C

National Journal Ratings

	2013 LIB	—	2013 CONS
Economic	49%	—	50%
Social	51%	—	48%
Foreign	34%	—	60%
Composite	46%	—	54%

Key Votes of the 113th Congress

1. Sandy storm spending	N	5. Medical Marijuana	Y	9. Syrian Rebels Training	Y
2. Violence Against Women Act	Y	6. Farm Bill	Y	10. Keystone pipeline	Y
3. Guantanamo Bay Detainees	N	7. Afghanistan Combat	N	11. Immigration Exec. Action	Y
4. Abortion 20-week ban	Y	8. NSA Phone Data Collection	N	12. Bipartisan budget deal	Y

Election Results

2014 general	David Joyce (R)	 135,736	(63%)	$2,623,918	$308,462	$31,705
	Michael Wager (D)	 70,856	(33%)	$1,042,191		$82,081
	David Macko (Lib)	 7,988	(4%)			
2014 primary	David Joyce (R)	 27,547	(55%)			
	Matt Lynch (R)	 22,546	(45%)			

Prior winning percentage: 2012 (54%)

Population		Race and Ethnicity		Income	
Total:	725,681	White	90.8%	Median income:	$59,111
Urban:	8.0%	Black	3.6%		*(136 of 435)*
Suburban:	77.3%	Latino	2.5%	Under $50,000	42.4%
Rural:	14.7%	Asian	1.7%	$50,000-$99,999:	32.4%
Land area:	1,595	Two races	1.3%	$100,000-$199,999:	19.8%
Pop/sq. mi.:	454.9	White Ethnic	51.5%	$200,000 or more:	5.4%
Born in state:	76.3%			Poverty Rate	9.0%
		Education			
Age Groups		H.S. grad or less:	39.4%	**Work**	
Under 18:	22.5%	Some college:	27.2%	White collar:	39.3%
18 to 34:	18.2%	College degree, 4 yr.:	20.9%	Blue collar:	40.1%
35 to 64:	41.9%	Post-grad study:	12.5%	Sales and service:	20.6%
Over 64:	17.4%				
		Military		Govt. workers:	9.6%
		Veterans/active duty:	9.1%		

Northeast Ohio: Cleveland Akron Suburbs, Ashtabula

The imprint of the westward track of New England Yankee migration is still apparent today on the shores of Lake Erie in northern Ohio. The British crown had granted the Colony of Connecticut all of the land due west of its borders in 1662. Connecticut ceded most of this land in 1786 in exchange

Voter Turnout	
2013 Total Citizen 18+	550,063
2014 House Turnout	214,580
2014 Turnout as % CVAP	39.0%
2012 Turnout as % CVAP	69.7%

for the newly created federal government taking over its Revolutionary War debts, but it retained a 3 million-acre claim in Ohio for its excess population, which became known as the Western Reserve. As European claims to North America subsided and Native Americans were placed on reservations or relocated, these Yankees, cooped up in New England for 200 years, moved west, through Upstate New York, across Ohio and Michigan to Chicago, and on to Kansas and California.

During the Civil War, the Western Reserve, ceded by Connecticut to the federal government in 1800, produced some of the nation's strongest opposition to slavery and hardiest support of the Union armies and the Republican Party; Lake Erie ports were prime transit points for the Underground Railroad to Can-

ada. Its thrifty, hardworking, well-educated citizens built communities with fine schools and, with their accumulated savings, invested in what became some of the nation's leading industries. Now, like Connecticut and Massachusetts, northeastern Ohio is moving toward a post-industrial economy. Factory employment has dropped. Small, adaptive business units with highly skilled

2012 Presidential Vote		
Mitt Romney (R)	192,895	(51%)
Barack Obama (D)	180,026	(48%)
2008 Presidential Vote		
John McCain (R)	190,154	(50%)
Barack Obama (D)	188,635	(49%)
Cook Partisan Voting Index:	R+4	

workers are the growth sectors. In May 2015, a private economic development report found that northeast Ohio will need to find 49,000 manufacturing workers to meet the expected demand in the next decade.

The 14th Congressional District of Ohio takes in parts or all of seven counties of northeast Ohio and the old Western Reserve. It includes the affluent suburbs of eastern and southern Cleveland-based Cuyahoga County; the comfortable suburbs in northern Summit County; some of Portage County to the east; and prosperous suburbs in Geauga County. Lake County, northeast of Cleveland, is the most populous. Ashtabula, home to 18 covered bridges and several wineries, is in the district, as is the northern part of Trumbull County, which is industrial. Historically, the area was Republican, but it has been politically competitive since the 1930s, as Cleveland and the industrial centers on Lake Erie became more Democratic. The current 14th District has enough Republican territory to give a GOP lean. Along with the Dayton-based 10th, it is the most competitive district in Ohio.

David Joyce (R)

Former prosecutor Dave Joyce was elected in 2012 against a weak opponent after nine-term GOP Rep. Steven LaTourette unexpectedly retired following the primary. Joyce quickly showed his legislative skills when he got a seat on the Appropriations Committee and became, like his predecessor, an ally of Speaker John Boehner.

Joyce, born in Cleveland as the third of four children in a deeply religious Irish-Catholic family, is the son of a coal salesman. At high school in Geauga County, he ran track and played defensive tackle and fullback on the football team. At one point in his youth he considered the priesthood, but he instead studied accounting at the University of Dayton. He also earned a law degree at Dayton, expecting to get a job at one of the big national accounting firms. During interviews with potential employers, he was told he would have little opportunity for trial work. So he took a job as a public defender in Cuyahoga County, eventually moving to nearby Geauga County.

Joyce rose through the ranks quickly and, at age 30, he was elected as the youngest prosecutor in the county's history. Joyce collaborated with LaTourette, who was then the prosecutor in neighboring Lake County, on a locally famous murder case involving a cult leader, as well as on a failed effort in 1990 to ban from record stores an album by the hip-hop group 2 Live Crew. Joyce got involved in politics by working on phone banks for then-Cleveland Mayor George Voinovich's reelection bid in 1983 and worked his way up the local Republican organization. In 1999, he organized "Prosecutors for Bush," in support of George W. Bush's presidential campaign.

On July 30, 2012, the 58-year-old LaTourette made a stunning announcement that he would not seek reelection in November, despite having won the GOP primary. Without giving specifics, he said that the political climate "has increased the toll that it takes on a person." Some Capitol Hill insiders speculated that LaTourette was miffed because he was unlikely to be tapped to fill the opening as chairman of the Transportation and Infrastructure Committee, where he had been a long-time member; instead, Bill Shuster of Pennsylvania got that post in January 2013. Another suggested explanation was that LaTourette had felt increasingly isolated as a moderate Republican who was friendly with organized labor. LaTourette offered little insight on his decision.

Republicans faced the immediate challenge of qualifying a new candidate for the ballot for the 14th District. A group of 14 Republican leaders selected Joyce, a friend of LaTourette who had a credible background and no political record to attack. Democrats offered immeasurable assistance by nominating Dale Blanchard, an obscure accountant and a 10-time candidate for Congress, who continued to run despite pressure to step aside for a stronger challenger. Blanchard failed to report any money raised during the campaign. Joyce spent $672,000, despite not entering the race until mid-August. He ran a mostly positive campaign and generally did not engage Blanchard. He won, 54%-39%.

Joyce has had a more conservative record than his predecessor. With a boost from Boehner, he got a seat on the Appropriations Committee, where he said that his priority is to reduce the size and scope of government. Befitting his district, he hasn't taken the hard line of many GOP newcomers, acknowledging the important role of infrastructure for example. Joyce filed a bill that he said would cut $200 billion in government waste and duplicative programs. But he also has cited his bipartisan efforts to restore the Great Lakes with $300 million in both 2013 and 2014, and his attempts to secure the same amount for 2015. With Democratic Rep. Dan Lipinski of Illinois, he cosponsored a bill to strengthen Buy America rules on the purchase of transportation infrastructure.

After handing Joyce his seat on a silver platter in 2012, Democrats promised a more serious effort in 2014. They failed again, for reasons that went far beyond the usual excuse of redistricting by Ohio Democrats. In the Republican primary, Joyce won 55%-45% over pro-life state Rep. Matt Lynch, who criticized GOP congressional leaders for "falling apart" in budget negotiations and was helped by tea party groups. Joyce had more than $600,000 in help from the U.S. Chamber of Commerce, American Hospital Association and a Super PAC run by LaTourette. Michael Wager won the Democratic nomination without opposition. He had the credentials of an attorney, active Democratic fund-raiser, and former chairman of the

Cleveland-Cuyahoga County Port Authority. Joyce spent $2.6 million compared with $1 million for Wager, who ran ads that called his opponent "greedy" and criticized him for flying first-class. Despite the early party hype, including his plan to raise at least $2 million, Wager was a weak challenger in what became a poor year for Democrats in Ohio. Joyce won, 63%-33%.

FIFTEENTH DISTRICT

Steve Stivers (R)

Elected 2010, 3rd term; b. March 24, 1965, Ripley; OH St. U., B.A. 1989, M.B.A. 1996; United Methodist; married (Karen); 2 children.

Military Career: OH Army Natl. Guard, 1988-2008.

Elected Office: OH Senate, 2003-08.

Professional Career: Legis. aide; Lobbyist.

DC Office: 1022 LHOB, 20515, 202-225-2015; Fax: 202-225-3529; Website: stivers.house.gov.

State Offices: Hilliard, 614-771-4968; Lancaster, 740-654-2654; Wilmington, 937-283-7049.

Committees: *Financial Services:* Capital Markets and Government Sponsored Enterprises; Housing & Insurance. *Rules:* Rules and Organization of the House (Chmn).

Group Ratings

	ADA	ACLU	AFL-CIO	LCV	ITI	COC	HAFA	ACU	CFG	FRC
2014	0%	0%	–	6%	80%	86%	51%	63%	54%	75%
2013	0%	C	24%	4%	C	92%	C	56%	56%	C

National Journal Ratings

	2013 LIB	—	2013 CONS
Economic	44%	—	55%
Social	47%	—	52%
Foreign	34%	—	60%
Composite	43%	—	57%

Key Votes of the 113th Congress

1. Sandy storm spending	N	5. Medical Marijuana	N	9. Syrian Rebels Training	Y
2. Violence Against Women Act	Y	6. Farm Bill	Y	10. Keystone pipeline	Y
3. Guantanamo Bay Detainees	N	7. Afghanistan Combat	N	11. Immigration Exec. Action	Y
4. Abortion 20-week ban	Y	8. NSA Phone Data Collection	N	12. Bipartisan budget deal	Y

Election Results

2014 general	Steve Stivers (R) 128,496	(66%)	$2,020,213	$11,148
	Richard Scott Wharton (D).......... 66,125	(34%)	$127,340	$4,051
2014 primary	Steve Stivers (R) 36,569	(90%)		
	Charles Chope (R)......................... 3,999	(10%)		

Prior winning percentages: 2012 (62%), 2010 (54%)

Population		Race and Ethnicity		Income	
Total:	742,133	White	90.4%	Median income:	$53,720
Urban:	25.6%	Black	3.1%		*(179 of 435)*
Suburban:	46.4%	Asian	2.4%	Under $50,000	46.3%
Rural:	28.0%	Latino	1.8%	$50,000-$99,999:	31.8%
Land area:	3,666	Two races	2.1%	$100,000-$199,999:	18.6%
Pop/sq. mi.:	202.4	White Ethnic	27.9%	$200,000 or more:	3.3%
Born in state:	77.6%			Poverty Rate	13.5%
		Education			
Age Groups		H.S. grad or less:	43.7%	**Work**	
Under 18:	22.1%	Some college:	27.4%	White collar:	38.3%
18 to 34:	24.3%	College degree, 4 yr.:	18.3%	Blue collar:	40.2%
35 to 64:	39.9%	Post-grad study:	10.6%	Sales and service:	21.6%
Over 64:	13.7%				
		Military		Govt. workers:	16.9%
		Veterans/active duty:	8.7%		

Central Ohio: Southern Columbus Metro, Athens

John Kennedy, campaigning for president in Columbus in 1960, was met by large, raucous crowds. He later quipped that Columbus was the city where he received the loudest cheers and the fewest votes. Indeed, Kennedy's 19-point loss in Franklin County was his worst showing in a major urban county in

Voter Turnout	
2013 Total Citizen 18+	563,728
2014 House Turnout	194,621
2014 Turnout as % CVAP	34.5%
2012 Turnout as % CVAP	63.7%

Ohio, affirmation of Franklin's deep Republican roots. Back then, it usually voted Democratic only during a Democratic landslide, as in 1936 and 1964. Columbus had attracted few of the Eastern European immigrants and labor unions that made Cleveland and northeastern Ohio so Democratic after the 1930s. But where JFK and others failed, later Democrats succeeded: Franklin County voted for Bill Clinton and then narrowly for Al Gore in 2000. It gave Barack Obama 60% of the vote in 2008 and 61% in 2012.

These shifts in the past two decades changed the composition of the 15th Congressional District of Ohio, which went from heavily Republican to Democratic-leaning. After the 2010 census, state Republicans in control of redistricting responded by making radical changes. Only about 39% of the old 15th was preserved: half of the Short North neighborhood just north of downtown, an up-and-coming neighborhood with a large gay population and many of the city's fashionable new clubs and restaurants; the old money suburb of Upper Arlington; and the up-and-coming suburbs of Hilliard and Grove City.

2012 Presidential Vote		
Mitt Romney (R)	180,487	(52%)
Barack Obama (D)	161,187	(46%)
2008 Presidential Vote		
John McCain (R)	183,131	(52%)
Barack Obama (D)	161,569	(46%)
Cook Partisan Voting Index:	R+6	

Almost 60% of the district's residents live outside of Columbus and its suburbs, in a vast swath of mostly Republican counties stretching from the exurbs of Cincinnati nearly to West Virginia—disparate areas stitched together to help prevent a non-Columbus Republican politician from amassing a powerbase in a primary election. It includes Athens County, the only Democratic county in the bunch and home of Ohio University, the oldest college west of the Appalachians, but also the poorest county in the state. The district now has a distinct Republican lean.

Steve Stivers (R)

Republican Steve Stivers, elected in 2010, is a pro-abortion rights centrist who has become an up-and-comer in the GOP. In January 2015, *The Columbus Dispatch* praised him for "the strong leadership skills of a congenial representative who has a clear vision of what's best for the nation and the ability to say 'no' without making enemies."

Stivers grew up in the Cincinnati suburbs, moved to Columbus to attend Ohio State University, and never left, except for deployments with the Ohio Army National Guard. For most of his career, he was associated with the Ohio Legislature. He was a staffer in the state Senate, and in 1995 began working as a lobbyist for BankOne, which was based in Columbus (and later absorbed into Bank of America). He was appointed by the Senate in 2003 to fill the seat of a retiring state senator. Soon afterward, he served tours in Kuwait and Iraq, for which he received a Bronze Star. He remains a colonel in the Ohio Army National Guard. In the 2006 election, he ran his campaign from Iraq and won. Stivers was vice chairman of the Finance Committee, supporting state budgets that cut property taxes and froze tuition at state universities.

When Republican Rep. Deborah Pryce retired in 2008, Democrats nominated Franklin County Commissioner Mary Jo Kilroy, who lost to Pryce by 1,055 votes two years earlier. Minority Leader John Boehner urged Stivers to run. After initially declining amid speculation that he wanted to be Ohio Senate president, he entered the contest.

He campaigned as a moderate, with a blend of support for abortion rights and fiscal discipline plus his military experience. He supported a two-year federal budget process similar to Ohio's and line-item veto power for the president. Kilroy emphasized her background as a former Columbus school board president and slammed Stivers for his stint as a bank lobbyist. Stivers portrayed Kilroy as "way outside the mainstream," too liberal for the district, and a captive of big labor. In a strongly Democratic year, Kilroy won by a narrower than expected 46%-45%.

In her one term, Kilroy was a faithful supporter of the majority Democrats' programs, including the economic stimulus bill, the cap-and-trade bill to reduce carbon emissions, and the health care overhaul. Stivers, who continued to run for the seat in anticipation of a 2010 rematch, called the health law's mandate to buy insurance "very dangerous" and said the legislation would be a heavy burden on small business. Kilroy portrayed him as a flip-flopper, arguing that he had supported an individual mandate and a carbon emissions bill in the past. She charged that he had supported a national sales tax to replace the income tax, and she again ran ads attacking him as a lobbyist.

Kilroy-Stivers redux turned out to be a great disappointment for national Democrats. They raised roughly $2.7 million each, but the Democratic Congressional Campaign Committee abandoned the race in October as unwinnable. Stivers prevailed 54%-41%.

In the House, Stivers established himself as a Boehner loyalist and "the type of sensible moderate that most Ohioans want to see," *The Dispatch* said in endorsing him for reelection. He joined the centrist Main Street Partnership as well as the conservative Republican Study Committee. He opposed conservatives' attempts to abolish or slash funding for the National Endowment for the Arts and the Legal Services Corporation, and to enforce the Davis-Bacon Act's prevailing union wage requirements. On the Financial Services Committee, Stivers has worked with other Republicans in attempts to limit the Dodd-Frank banking overhaul law. In his attempt to boost the housing market, the House in April 2015 passed his bipartisan Capital Access for Small Community Financial Institutions bill. He also has pressed his proposal to permit credit unions to apply for membership with the Federal Home Loan Banks. In 2015, he also got an assignment to the House Rules Committee, the "arm of the leadership," where Stivers can be eyes and ears for Boehner.

Stivers has become deeply involved in party activities, initially working with Rep. Steve Scalise on recruiting GOP candidates for the National Republican Congressional Committee; in 2013, he became the NRCC's vice chair for finance. When Scalise was selected as GOP Whip in 2014, Stivers became one of his top deputies. At Boehner's behest, Stivers served on a party task force on cybersecurity and worked with other allies of the speaker to find ways to boost infrastructure spending. After Stivers introduced a bill to use projected revenue from offshore drilling leases to back the sale of government bonds for highways, Boehner embraced that approach.

With his Republican-leaning district, Stivers no longer has to worry about close campaigns. At the end of 2014, his campaign fund had a balance of nearly $1 million, allowing Stivers to spread his wings more broadly.

SIXTEENTH DISTRICT

Jim Renacci (R)

Elected 2010, 3rd term; b. Dec. 3, 1958, Monongahela, PA; Indiana U. of PA, B.A. 1980; Catholic; married (Tina); 3 children.

Elected Office: Wadsworth City Cncl., 1999-2003; City of Wadsworth mayor, 2004-08.

Professional Career: CEO, LTC Mgmt. Services, 1985-2003; CEO, LTC Companies Group, 2003-10.

DC Office: 328 CHOB, 20515, 202-225-3876; Fax: 202-225-3059; Website: renacci.house.gov.

State Offices: Wadsworth, 330-334-0040; Parma, 440-882-6779.

Committees: *Ways & Means:* Select Revenue Measures; Social Security.

Group Ratings

	ADA	ACLU	AFL-CIO	LCV	ITI	COC	HAFA	ACU	CFG	FRC
2014	0%	0%	–	3%	100%	93%	55%	64%	42%	88%
2013	0%	C	14%	4%	C	85%	C	72%	69%	C

National Journal Ratings

	2013 LIB	—	2013 CONS
Economic	38%	—	61%
Social	34%	—	62%
Foreign	5%	—	86%
Composite	28%	—	72%

Key Votes of the 113th Congress

1. Sandy storm spending	N	5. Medical Marijuana	N	9. Syrian Rebels Training	Y
2. Violence Against Women Act	Y	6. Farm Bill	Y	10. Keystone pipeline	Y
3. Guantanamo Bay Detainees	N	7. Afghanistan Combat	N	11. Immigration Exec. Action	Y
4. Abortion 20-week ban	Y	8. NSA Phone Data Collection	N	12. Bipartisan budget deal	Y

Election Results

2014 general	Jim Renacci (R)	132,176	(64%)	$1,444,488	$3,087	$25,508
	Pete Crossland (D)	75,199	(36%)	$35,026	$23,513	
2014 primary	Jim Renacci (R)	unopposed				

Prior winning percentages: 2012 (52%), (2010 (52%)

Population		Race and Ethnicity		Income	
Total:	720,643	White	92.7%	Median income:	$60,353
Urban:	32.4%	Latino	2.0%		(126 of 435)
Suburban:	54.7%	Asian	2.0%	Under $50,000	41.0%
Rural:	12.9%	Black	1.6%	$50,000-$99,999:	33.8%
Land area:	1,075	Two races	1.6%	$100,000-$199,999:	20.6%
Pop/sq. mi.:	670.5	White Ethnic	47.4%	$200,000 or more:	4.6%
Born in state:	78.5%			Poverty Rate	8.2%
Age Groups		**Education**			
Under 18:	22.5%	H.S. grad or less:	40.0%	**Work**	
18 to 34:	18.1%	Some college:	29.0%	White collar:	39.1%
35 to 64:	41.3%	College degree, 4 yr.:	20.1%	Blue collar:	39.2%
Over 64:	18.1%	Post-grad study:	10.9%	Sales and service:	21.7%
		Military		Govt. workers:	11.4%
		Veterans/active duty:	9.7%		

Northern Ohio: Cleveland/Akron/Canton Suburbs

The rapidly growing Cleveland of the early-1900s—it went from 93,000 residents in 1870 to over 900,000 in 1930—was crammed into a compact area. The eclectic mix of newcomers that populated the city sorted itself into Cleveland's so-called "cosmo wards:" Italians in Big Italy to the south-

Voter Turnout	
2013 Total Citizen 18+	547,411
2014 House Turnout	207,375
2014 Turnout as % CVAP	37.9%
2012 Turnout as % CVAP	67.9%

east of Public Square; Croats, Serbs and Slovenians in the St. Clair area on the northeast side of town; Irish in Whiskey Island to the west of downtown; Russians, Germans, Poles and Slovaks in the Ohio City and Tremont areas near present-day Newburgh Heights; and Czechs and Poles in Praha and Slavic Village to the north of present-day Garfield Heights. The cosmo wards began to empty out in the 1950s as the original immigrants died off and their children fled to the suburbs. Today, Cleveland's population is in decline. Only 14 percent of the population of Greater Cleveland now lives in the city itself, the lowest share since before the Civil War.

The now-graying great-grandchildren of those immigrants live in places like those found in the 16th Congressional District of Ohio, a political creation whose precincts are bound more by Republican voting habits than by any coherent geographic locale. About 40 percent of the district's votes are cast in Cuyahoga County and Cleveland's western outer suburbs: comfortable places

2012 Presidential Vote

Mitt Romney (R)	199,697	(54%)
Barack Obama (D)	169,106	(45%)

2008 Presidential Vote

John McCain (R)	196,843	(51%)
Barack Obama (D)	181,055	(47%)

Cook Partisan Voting Index: R+6

like Westlake, a stone's throw from Lake Erie, plus Strongsville and North Royalton, where median incomes exceed the national average. Many residents here tend to be descended from the Hungarians and Bohemians who settled southwest of Public Square, near present-day Brooklyn.

The district also takes in exurban Medina County, Portage and Stark (but not including Canton) counties, and Wayne County, home to the College of Wooster and the headquarters of Smuckers. Nerdwallet.com ranked Wooster the sixth best small city in the nation. The local Rubbermaid distribution center, which closed in 2013, was taken over in May 2015 by Akron-based GOJO Industries, the inventor of Purell hand sanitizer. The southern part of Wayne County is Amish country, where people drive horse-drawn tractors, eschew automobiles and electricity (except from their own generators), and quit school after the eighth grade. Tourism has been a growth industry in the Amish region, with a profusion of restaurants, bed-and-breakfasts, and gift shops. The 16th leans Republican just enough to avoid serious Democratic challenges.

Jim Renacci (R)

Republican Jim Renacci, first elected in 2010 against a Democratic incumbent, is a committed conservative but he works with Democrats more than many of his Class of 2010 GOP colleagues. He survived a 2012 contest against Democratic Rep. Betty Sutton after their districts were combined in redistricting. Life has become easier for him with a relatively safe district and a seat on the tax-writing Ways and Means Committee.

Renacci grew up in a working-class family outside Pittsburgh. His mother was a nurse, and his father was a railroad worker who lost his job when Renacci was eight years old. "Very early on, I understood the meaning of balancing a family budget," he said. Renacci graduated from Indiana University of Pennsylvania, the first in his family to finish college, and became very entrepreneurial. According to his congressional website, Renacci during his 30-year business career "owned and operated over 60 entities, created more than 1,500 jobs and employed over 3,000 people."

As a certified public accountant, he worked for an accounting firm in Pittsburgh with nursing home clients. In 1984, he moved to Wadsworth, Ohio, and started a chain of nursing homes. He sold the chain and formed a company specializing in financial consulting for troubled businesses. Along the way, he accumulated a diverse portfolio of investments, including a share in the Columbus Destroyers, an Arena League football team, a concert promotion firm, and several Harley-Davidson dealerships. He also spent five years as a volunteer firefighter in Wadsworth. He was elected to the Wadsworth Council in 1999 and served as mayor from 2004 to 2008.

As the 2010 election approached, Renacci decided to challenge Democrat John Boccieri, who was elected two years earlier after longtime Republican Rep. Ralph Regula retired. Boccieri had served in the Ohio Legislature, was a former professional baseball player, and an Air Force reservist who served in Iraq and Afghanistan. He had a respectable victory of 55%-45% in 2008. On the surface, he did not seem an easy target for Renacci.

But Boccieri had voted for President Barack Obama's $787 billion economic stimulus bill and for the Democrats' cap-and-trade bill to curb carbon emissions. He initially opposed the health care overhaul bill when it passed the House in November 2009, but voted for the final version in 2010. With help from national Republicans, Renacci campaigned on a theme that Obama administration policies were killing job creation. Democrats referred to Renacci as the "millionaire CEO," who made his fortune off the government and taxpayers. They criticized him for a dispute over taxes in 2000 with Ohio authorities in which Renacci accepted a settlement requiring him to pay $1.3 million. Renacci spent $2.4 million on his campaign, but Boccieri remained competitive with $2.1 million. The outcome wasn't close. Renacci won 52%-41%, carrying every county in the district.

In the House, Renacci has been firmly conservative on economic issues, but has moved toward the middle on social and foreign policy issues. On the Financial Services Committee, he became friends with Democrat John Carney of Delaware. The two formed a bipartisan breakfast club that grew to 14 members and developed several bills aimed at job creation. "We need to be able to work together," Renacci told *The New York Times*. He later teamed up with another Financial Services member, Minnesota's Keith Ellison—one of the chamber's most liberal Democrats—on a bill allowing utility and telecommunications companies to report their customers' on-time payments to credit-reporting agencies. In May 2015, he coauthored a column for CNN with Democratic Rep. Earl Blumenauer of Oregon on the "looming transportation funding crisis" in which they called for "a long-term, sustainable solution to give the American people the infrastructure they deserve and the jobs the economy needs." But he opposed the New Year's Day 2013 compromise on taxes and spending aimed at avoiding the so-called "fiscal cliff," saying that it "spends too much, taxes too much, and cuts far too little."

In the 2011 redistricting that eliminated two House seats in Ohio, the Republican-held Legislature merged Renacci and Sutton into a single district west of Cleveland that dropped south toward the center of the state. They made sure that the fight would play out more on the turf of Renacci than Sutton. Sutton could have run in the 13th District against fellow Democratic Rep. Tim Ryan but opted to take on Renacci. That earned her the appreciation of the Democratic Congressional Campaign Committee. Renacci outspent Sutton, $3.3 million to $2.6 million. Outside groups poured in more than $10 million, which was split about evenly between the two parties. The new district's GOP lean proved too much for Sutton, and Renacci won 52%-48%.

Having defeated Democratic incumbents in consecutive elections, Renacci in 2013 gained a prized seat on Ways and Means. Unlike most of the committee Republicans, he was willing to discuss the need for higher taxes, including a possible hike in the gasoline tax to pay for highway and bridge construction and repair. "It's easy to sit here in Washington and do nothing. I'd rather be somebody who is going to get something accomplished," he told CNN in May 2015. He also has called for unspecified reforms in Social Security and Medicare to protect the retirement systems.

In 2014, he outspent his Democratic opponent, former state Rep. Pete Crossland, by a 40-to-1 margin and won 64% of the vote.

★ OKLAHOMA ★

Oklahoma, the subject of the classic Broadway musical, is one of the newest states, the 46th to be admitted to the Union, in 1907. Its Capitol, located atop a large oil field, opened in 1917, though the dome was not finally finished until 2002. As that chronology suggests, Oklahoma's history has been a story of sudden stops and starts. It was settled in a rush, first by the Five Civilized Tribes—Chickasaw, Choctaw, Creek, Cherokee, and Seminole—driven west by Andrew Jackson's troops on the Trail of Tears in the 1830s. Then came white settlers. One morning in April 1889, in the great land rush memorialized by novelist Edna Ferber and Hollywood movies, thousands of homesteaders drove their wagons across the territorial line at the sound of a gunshot, the most adventurous or unscrupulous of them literally jumping the gun—the Sooners. In 1905, a convention of the Civilized Nations sought to have eastern Oklahoma admitted as a separate state of Sequoyah. The federal government turned a deaf ear and ended the tribal government, parceled out reservation land to tribe members, and combined the Indian and Oklahoma Territories as a single state.

The Rodgers and Hammerstein musical was set in a mythical Oklahoma on the brink of statehood in 1906. Soon thereafter, the territory rapidly filled up with farmers, rising from 1.5 million people in 1907 to 2.4 million in 1930. Oil helped. The first well was drilled here in 1897, and by 1920 Tulsa was an oil boom town complete with art deco skyscrapers. Then in the 1930s came a decade of bust—and dust—as soil loosened by erosion was whipped into giant swirling clouds: the Dust Bowl. "People sat in Oklahoma City, with the sky invisible for three days in a row, holding dust masks over their faces and wet towels to protect their mouths at night, while the farms blew by," wrote author John Gunther. Okies headed in droves west on U.S. 66 to greener California, and Oklahoma's population steadily declined, falling to 2.2 million in 1950. It did not reach its 1930 level again until 1970.

Then came another oil boom. As the oil shocks of 1973 and 1979 sent prices up, Oklahoma's population rose from 2.5 million in 1970 to 3 million in 1980. The collapse of oil prices in the 1980s produced another bust. Oklahoma's rig count went from 882 in 1982 to 232 in 1983. The 1990 census reported just 3.1 million Oklahomans. In the 1990s, Oklahoma began building a more diversified economy, with high-tech employers as well as oil and gas firms. Population rose 10% in the 1990s and 9% from 2000 to 2010, to 3.75 million. High oil prices made it worthwhile to squeeze more from marginal wells and horizontal drilling allowed more production with the same number of rigs. Oklahoma has been a leader in hydraulic fracturing—so-called "fracking"—and horizontal drilling to extract natural gas embedded in shale rock. It's now the fourth-ranking state in natural gas production, and the state's rig count remained stable in 2014 even as the numbers dropped elsewhere. Chesapeake Energy, Devon Energy, SandRidge Energy, and Continental Resources, all headquartered in Oklahoma City, increased natural gas production sharply. But their extraction has also apparently increased earthquakes—585 tremors above 3.0 in 2014, up from an average of 1.5 a year prior to the mid-2000s. The state government now acknowledges the connection: The Oklahoma Geological Survey calls a link between drilling and earthquakes "very likely," and the state has launched an interactive website that overlays earthquake sites with the locations of drilling-related wells. "Oklahoma state agencies already are taking action to address this issue and protect homeowners," Republican Gov. Mary Fallin said. But she also joined Texas in signing legislation to prevent Oklahoma cities and counties from banning fracking on their own.

The influx of energy revenue has juiced the state's capital. The area around its stockyards, the nation's largest, has become a tourist attraction, and civic leaders have channeled the North Canadian River (and renamed it the Oklahoma) to create North America's premier rowing center, even if the arid landscape does not match verdant Henley-on-Thames. Even as Oklahoma harnesses its fossil-fuel legacy, it has also been one of the leading states in developing wind power, nearly reaching its 2015 goal in 2012 of having 15% of electricity produced by renewable energy sources. Utilities offer customers electricity produced from wind, although at slightly higher-than-ordinary rates.

Another natural Oklahoma resource—extreme weather—has had a more destructive effect. Between 1890 and 2013, metropolitan Oklahoma City saw at least 156 tornadoes— about one each year, including the 2013 EF5 that killed 24 in and around Moore Oklahoma. Despite its oil riches, the state has its share of problems. Oklahoma has the third-highest

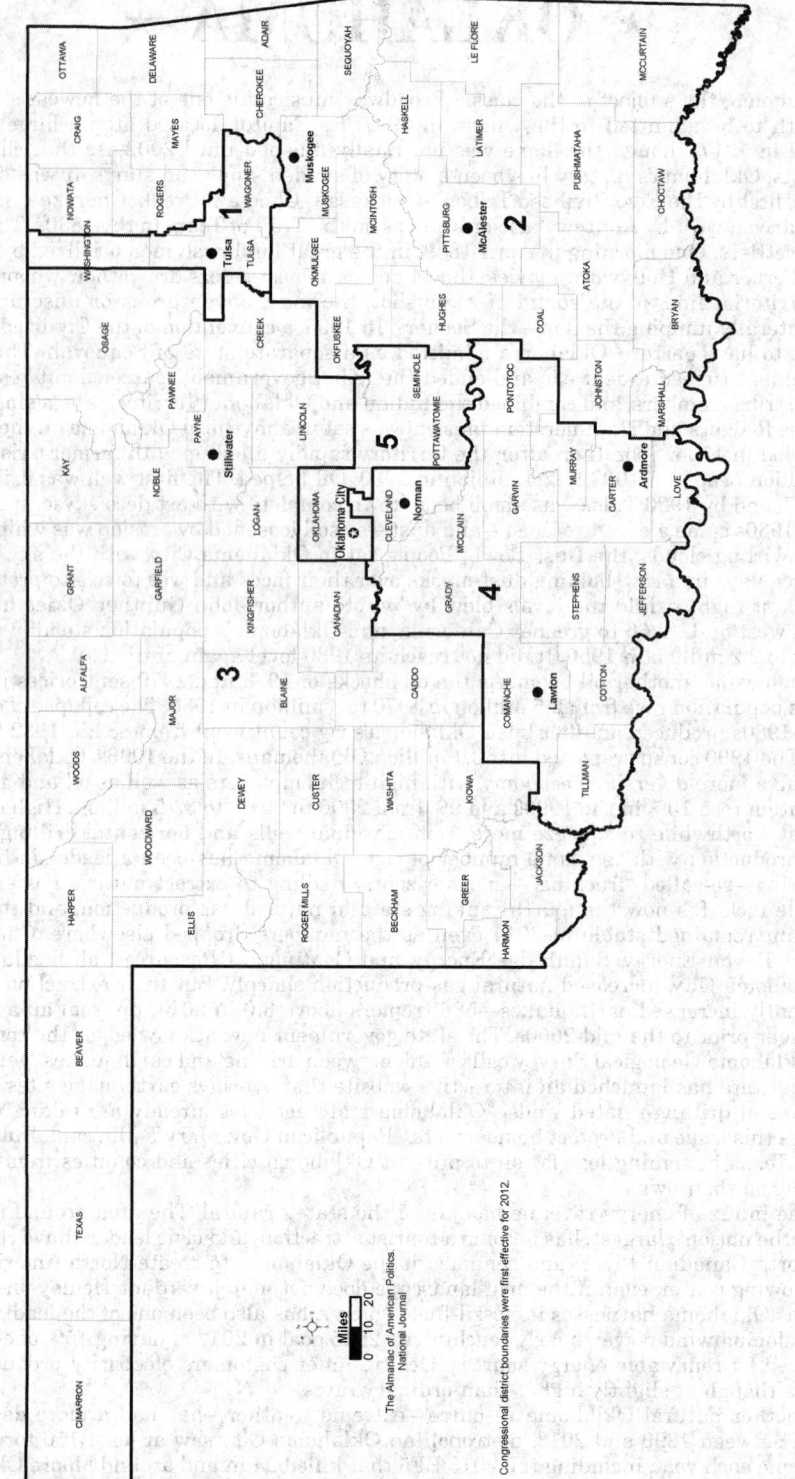

Miles
0 10 20

percentage of divorced residents in the nation, and its health system was ranked 49th in the nation by the Commonwealth Fund. Oklahoma has above-average rates of teenage pregnancy and crime, and a low rate of college graduates. Two studies found that Oklahoma police killed people in 2015 more often than those in any other state, a pattern crystallized that year by the high-profile case of Tulsa reserve deputy Robert Bates, a 73-year-old insurance executive who mistakenly shot an unarmed black man when he meant to use his service taser. On the other hand, unemployment in the state has been mild—peaking at 7.1% and sinking below 4.0 by early 2015—due in part to a more stable housing market, oil and gas resources and some good years for agriculture, conditions that Oklahoma shares with many of its Great Plains neighbors. The state got a psychic boost in 2012 when the Oklahoma City Thunder—the first major league pro sports team based in the state—reached the NBA Finals.

Amid all this change, Oklahoma's Indian identity has persisted. With only one small reservation, Oklahomans of Indian ancestry—9% of the population—have made their way forward in the larger society but still cherish their heritage. There has been much intermarriage over the years, and many Oklahomans—and not a few of its politicians—proudly claim Indian blood. (Such murky ancestral ties would eventually cause problems for Massachusetts Sen. Elizabeth Warren, an Oklahoma native whose claims of Native American family history came under scrutiny.) There is an ongoing struggle to keep the Cherokee, Choctaw, Chickasaw, and Seminole languages from dying out—you can see street signs in the Cherokee alphabet in Tahlequah, the Cherokees' historical capital. In the 2010 census, 9% of Oklahomans reported being of Native ancestry, the third highest of any state. Indians are most numerous in the eastern part of the state. Hispanics, who account for 10% of the state's population, are concentrated in the two big cities and in meatpacking counties in the west. Just 8% identified as black, and most live in Oklahoma City and Tulsa. The latter was the site of the Tulsa race riot of 1921, "a firestorm of hatred and violence that is perhaps unequaled in the peacetime history of the United States," as historian John Hope Franklin called it. The largely forgotten event destroyed nearly 40 square blocks of African-American homes and businesses and likely killed between 75 and 100 people. More than seven decades later, on April 19, 1995, the state's other major city, Oklahoma City, was the site of mass carnage when a truck bomb blew apart the Alfred P. Murrah Federal Building, killing 168.

Historically, Oklahoma was a Democratic state, with big Democratic margins in eastern counties and in Little Dixie in the southeast. But northwestern Oklahoma, settled by Kansans, has always been Republican, and starting in the 1950s, Tulsa and Oklahoma City leaned Republican too. Today, only vestiges of its Democratic heritage remain. There were still more registered Democrats than Republicans until 2014, and Oklahoma elected a popular Democratic governor, Brad Henry, in 2002 and 2006. From the 1960s through the 2000s, Oklahoma politics was a struggle between Oklahoma City and Tulsa Republicans and rural Democrats. Then, in the last decade, parts of the state outside the metro regions, like Texas outside its big metro areas, have moved away from their Democratic heritage and become, in the last two presidential and U.S. Senate races, more Republican than the two big metro areas.

Population		Race and Ethnicity		Income	
Total:	3,850,568	White	68.2%	Median income:	$43,777
Urban:	32.8%	Latino	9.2%		(40 of 50)
Suburban:	24.0%	Black	7.2%	Under $50,000	53.8%
Rural:	43.3%	Amer. Indian	6.6%	$50,000-$99,999:	30.0%
Land area:	68,595	Two races	7.0%	$100,000-$199,999:	13.3%
Pop/sq. mi.:	56.1	White Ethnic	17.8%	$200,000 or more:	2.9%
Born in state:	61.1%			Poverty Rate	15.6%
		Education			
Age Groups		H.S. grad or less:	45.6%	**Work**	
Under 18:	24.6%	Some college:	30.6%	White collar:	32.5%
18 to 34:	23.9%	College degree, 4 yr.:	16.1%	Blue collar:	42.4%
35 to 64:	37.3%	Post-grad study:	7.7%	Sales and service:	25.1%
Over 64:	14.2%				
		Military		Govt. workers:	16.8%
		Veterans/active duty:	9.9%		

This evolution has made Oklahoma one of America's most Republican states. It has not voted Democratic for president since 1964. Since 1966, it has elected only one Democratic senator, David Boren. It elected all-Republican House delegations in 1996 and 1998 and since 2012 after Boren's son, Dan Boren, retired from the House at age 39. In 2008, Oklahoma voted 66% for John

Voter Turnout	
2013 Total Citizen 18+	2,775,109
2014 Highest Statewide Turnout	824,831
2014 Turnout as % CVAP	29.7%
2012 Turnout as % CVAP	48.6%

Legislature			
Senate:	40R	8D	
House:	71R	28D	2V

McCain, his highest percentage in any state, and in 2012, it voted 67% for Mitt Romney. Both Republican nominees carried all 77 counties with at least 58% of the vote. Democrats long controlled the state legislature, but they lost their majority in the state House in 2004 and in the state Senate in 2008, and Republicans currently have more than 2- 1 majorities. In 2010, more than 70% of voters approved a state constitutional amendment to prevent courts from considering sharia law in judicial decisions, despite little evidence that any were doing so. Gov. Fallin and Sens. Jim Inhofe and James Lankford, all Republicans, won their most recent elections with 56%, 68%, and 68%, respectively.

Presidential Politics Since the FDR era, Oklahoma has voted only twice for a Democratic presidential candidate: Harry Truman in 1948 and Lyndon Johnson in 1964. While Tulsa and Oklahoma City have long been Republican strongholds, starting in 2004 the counties outside the two big metro areas have been voting more Republican than the state average in presidential elections. The last Democratic nominee to carry a county in Oklahoma was Al Gore in 2000 (he won nine). In the next three elections, Republican nominees won 66% or 67% of the vote and carried all 77 counties. In the 1990s the state was more competitive. In 1992, George H. W. Bush beat out Bill Clinton 43%-34%, but Clinton actually captured a majority of counties, 41. Most of those counties were in

2012 Presidential Vote		
Mitt Romney (R)	891,325	(67%)
Barack Obama (D)	443,547	(33%)

2012 Presidential Primary		
Barack Obama (D)	64,389	(57%)
Randall Terry (D)	20,312	(18%)
Jim Rogers (D)	15,546	(14%)
Darcy Richardson (D)	7,201	(6%)

2012 Presidential Primary		
Rick Santorum (R)	96,849	(34%)
Mitt Romney (R)	80,356	(28%)
Newt Gingrich (R)	78,730	(27%)
Ron Paul (R)	27,596	(10%)

2008 Presidential Vote		
John McCain (R)	960,165	(66%)
Barack Obama (D)	502,496	(34%)

the region's old Indian Territory, where in-migration from Texas, Arkansas and especially Mississippi brought with it Democratic traditions and the region became known as "Little Dixie."

For 2004, the legislature scheduled the primary for February, a week after New Hampshire. Democrats John Edwards and Wesley Clark, both desperate for a win after John Kerry's triumphs in Iowa and New Hampshire, targeted Oklahoma. Clark won here—his first and only electoral victory—but with just 29.9% to 29.5% for Edwards and 27% for Kerry. Kerry carried the counties including Oklahoma City, Tulsa, and Norman (home of the University of Oklahoma) and not much else. Clark, a retired four-star general, got big pluralities in the counties around Fort Sill and Altus Air Force Base and not much else. Edwards carried most suburban and rural counties, but generally not by big pluralities.

In 2008, Oklahoma was joined by many other states in voting on Super Tuesday on Feb. 5 and did not attract much attention. In the Democratic primary, Hillary Clinton was the early favorite and beat Barack Obama 55%-31%. Edwards got 10% although he had already dropped out of the race. Obama carried Oklahoma County (Oklahoma City), and Clinton carried the other 76 counties, with very big margins in eastern Oklahoma counties near her longtime home in Arkansas. Edwards finished second in three rural counties. Turnout was 417,000, a record, significantly higher than 2004, when almost 300,000 ballots were cast.

The Republican race was much closer. Fresh off victories in New Hampshire and Florida, John McCain won with 37% to 33% for Mike Huckabee and 25% for Mitt Romney. Huckabee carried the eastern portion of the state, with a high of 59% in Adair County, on the border of his home state of Arkansas. McCain ran strongest in the western part of the state, with his best showing, 50%, in rural Ellis County. Turnout was 335,000, a record and 27% above the previous high in 1996. Republican turnout was down to 286,000 in 2012, when the primary was held on March 6. Rick Santorum beat Romney 34%-28%, running narrowly ahead in the two primary metro areas and leading by a bit more in the rest of the state. Romney won only two counties: Oklahoma (Oklahoma City) and Payne. Newt Gingrich finished a close third, only 1,600 votes behind Romney.

Congressional Districts Oklahoma redistricting following the 2010 census was a breeze compared to the previous cycle, when enough Democrats remained to stake their claim to House seats. Republicans controlled the process for the first time, and they had little incentive to rock the boat. Democrat Dan Boren, whose family name is revered in state politics, was the sole Democrat in the delegation, but he voted with Republicans more often than any other Democrat in the House.

114th Congress Lineup	
5 R	0 D
113th Congress Lineup	
5 R	0 D

All five incumbents, including Boren, agreed to minimal changes in their districts, and legislators passed them with a yawn. Then, Boren surprised observers and made the GOP job even easier by announcing his retirement at age 37, from what had long been known as the Little Dixie district—a Democratic stronghold in the southeast. Fiercely conservative Republican Markwayne Mullin easily picked up the seat the following November. It may be many years before another Democrat is elected from anywhere in Oklahoma.

Governor

Mary Fallin (R)

Elected 2010, term expires Jan. 2019, 2nd term; b. Dec. 9, 1954, Warrensburg, MO; OK Baptist U., attended, OK St. U., B.S. 1977, U. of Central OK, attended; Christian; married (Wade Christensen); 6 children.

Elected Office: OK House, 1990-94; OK lt. gov., 1994-2006; U.S. House, 2007-11.

Professional Career: OK Dept. of Tourism & Rec.; OK Securities Comm.; OK Office of Personnel Mgmt., 1977-82; Hotel mkting. & mgmt., 1983-90.

Office: OK State Capitol, 2300 N. Lincoln Blvd., Rm. 212, Oklahoma City, 73105, 405-521-2342; Fax: 405-521-3353; Website: ok.gov/governor.

Election Results

2014 general	Mary Fallin (R)	460,298	(56%)
	Joe Dorman (D)	338,239	(41%)
	Kimberly Willis (I)	17,169	(2%)
2014 primary	Mary Fallin (R)	200,035	(76%)
	Chad Moody (R)	40,839	(15%)
	Dax Ewbank (R)	24,020	(9%)

Prior winning percentages: 2010 (60%); House: 2008 (66%), 2006 (60%)

Oklahoma's governor is Mary Fallin, a Republican elected in 2010 as the state's first female chief executive and easily reelected in 2014. A former lieutenant governor and House member, she has delighted conservatives in her deep-red state with an emphasis on trimming government, curbing abortion rights, and relaxing handgun restrictions. She also gained a national profile as chair of the National Governors Association in 2013 and 2014.

Fallin was born in Missouri but raised in Tecumseh. Her mother and father were Democrats and each served as mayor of the town. After graduating from Oklahoma State University, Fallin managed hotel properties and was a commercial real estate broker. In 1990, she was elected to the state House, where she championed victims' rights and health care reform.

She became lieutenant governor four years later, making her the first Republican and the first woman to hold the office in Oklahoma. During her three terms, she expanded her reach well beyond the office's traditional ribbon-cutting responsibilities. With a focus on economic development, she compiled a pro-business record and played a key role in bringing the right-to-work issue to a successful statewide vote. In 1998, her star dimmed a bit when, in the course of a bitter divorce, she was accused of having a sexual relationship with a state trooper assigned to her security detail; both of them denied the charge.

Fallin decided to run for the seat of GOP Rep. Ernest Istook, who was making a bid for governor in 2006. She joined a wide-open, six-way primary that included state Corporation Commissioner Denise Bode and Oklahoma City Mayor Mick Cornett. In the initial July balloting, Fallin led with 35% to Cornett's 24% and Bode's 19%. In the subsequent runoff, Fallin, with a big fundraising advantage, defeated Cornett, 63%-37%, even though Oklahoma County cast 93% of the vote. Fallin easily won the general, 60%-37%, and became the first woman sent to Washington by Oklahoma since 1922.

In June 2007, she saw her first bill pass in the House, a revamping of federal grants for women's business centers. She joined a group of 38 Republicans who staked out negotiating positions in opposition to the Democrats' proposal to expand the State Children's Health Insurance Program. In 2008, she was part of a House Republican delegation that traveled to Alaska to try to bolster the case for oil drilling in the Arctic National Wildlife Refuge. Fallin became politically active on the executive committee of the National Republican Congressional Committee, which was chaired by fellow Oklahoman Tom Cole. In the 2008 presidential contest, she was an enthusiastic backer of Alaska Gov. Sarah Palin as the GOP vice presidential nominee, calling her "an excellent model for other women."

With two-term Democratic Gov. Brad Henry ineligible to seek a third term, Fallin announced her candidacy for governor in February 2009. She raised an impressive $2.4 million before the July 2010 primary. Her main opponent was state Sen. Randy Brogdon of Owasso, who sought to generate tea party support by making an issue of her 2008 vote for the bailout of the financial industry. Fallin, however, capitalized on her friendship with Palin and several other big-name Republicans, including then-Govs. Tim Pawlenty of Minnesota and Jan Brewer of Arizona. She drew 55% in the primary, easily avoiding a runoff.

The general election was a two-woman race—Fallin against Democratic Lt. Gov. Jari Askins. To stay competitive in fundraising, Fallin loaned her campaign $1.1 million and emphasized job creation through lower taxes as well as reducing excessive workers' compensation and legal fees. She also suggested cutting the number of state agencies from more than 500 to levels similar to those in Oregon and Kansas, which each had around 130. In October, Fallin suggested she was more qualified than Askins as a result of her experience "being a mother, having children, raising a family." Askins was single and had no children, but Fallin said she didn't intend her remarks as an attack. The controversy didn't end up hurting her; Fallin won handily, 60%-40%, capturing every county except Askins' home of Stephens County and three nearby south-central Oklahoma counties.

Fallin's first budget had a 3% reduction for core state agencies, such as public safety and education, and a steeper 5% cut for others. Despite her opposition to President Barack Obama's health care overhaul while in the House, she supported a state bill to set up a framework for the insurance exchanges called for in the federal legislation. At the emphatic urging of the legislature's Republican leaders, though, she eventually rejected setting up an exchange. She also joined numerous other Republican governors in rejecting an expansion of Medicaid. Fallin hit turbulence in February 2013, when she pushed a bill that would have allowed cities and towns to enact stricter smoking bans than exist in state law, which is permitted in many states. She said that smoking was "a personal issue for me," having lost both of her parents in smoking-related deaths, but a Senate committee rejected the measure.

For the most part, though, Fallin got what she wanted. The number of state employees dropped more than 3% in 2011, and she oversaw the consolidation of five state agencies into a single Office of Management and Enterprise Services. Among her other stated goals she met in 2012 were opening new mental health centers; increasing the number of college graduates; requiring state agencies to reduce energy consumption; and launching a plan to fix structurally deficient state highway bridges. She also got an additional $1 million to reduce infant mortality rates. On social issues, Fallin in 2012 signed a bill making Oklahoma the 25th state to adopt an open-carry firearms law. Earlier, she signed legislation to make it a felony for doctors to perform abortions after a woman reaches 20 weeks of pregnancy and to bar Oklahoma health insurance plans from offering coverage for elective abortions under the federal health care law.

In May of 2013, Fallin found herself in the national spotlight after a deadly tornado struck the Oklahoma City suburbs, killing 24 people. Fallin toured toppled school buildings, consoled victims, and quickly became the face of the state's collective determination to rebuild on television news shows. Her response to the crisis prompted *The Daily Beast* to remark, "Gov. Mary Fallin looks like the star Sarah Palin was supposed to be." But Fallin also drew some scrutiny for her out-of-state travel. *The Oklahoman* newspaper reported in 2012 that her office had spent more than $273,000 on trips, including visits to Arizona for college football bowl games and to Ireland for her daughter's wedding. (She paid her own expenses to Ireland, but her security detail cost taxpayers more than $13,000.)

Nevertheless, her efforts proved popular among Oklahomans, which made her reelection bid against Democratic state Rep. Joe Dorman a breeze. Dorman complained that the state didn't fund schools adequately and attacked Fallin for initially supporting the Common Core academic standards for math and English only to oppose them when they became a national target of conservatives' wrath. But she won easily, 56%-41%, carrying 71 of the state's 77 counties in the lowest-turnout gubernatorial election in the state since 1978. Not a single Democrat won a statewide or congressional office, and the legislature remained overwhelmingly Republican.

Budget woes dominated the start of her second term in 2015, with a budget gap fed by a decline in oil and gas tax revenues and a scheduled income tax decrease. By the time Fallin and lawmakers reached a deal, the shortfall had ballooned to more than $600 million, which they agreed to close through cuts to agencies of 5% to 7% and by drawing from the state's rainy day fund. One of the rare increases in the budget was for corrections, which got an additional $14 million to ease overcrowding. Heavy rains and flooding in May 2015 caused more budgetary worries.

Fallin pleased conservatives when she signed a bill to outlaw an abortion method that critics call "dismemberment," as well as an extension to the mandatory waiting period for an abortion from 24 hours to 72. She also signed a law establishing a backup method of execution—nitrogen gas—amid the state's increasing difficulty in acquiring lethal-injection drugs. A controversial lethal injection in the state in 2014—when it took 43 minutes to execute a writhing convicted murderer, Clayton Lockett—made the issue particularly urgent. Fallin ordered an investigation of the Lockett case that found problems with the execution process.

In tune with her state's energy industry, Fallin issued an executive order opposing proposed federal regulations on carbon emissions from power plants. She also signed a bill to sunset a property-tax exemption for new wind-energy development, saving an estimated $500 million in foregone revenues over 10 years. But she irritated gun-rights supporters by vetoing a bill that would have prevented private businesses from banning the otherwise legal carrying of guns in public places. Critics said the bill could have made it hard for the state to attract major sporting and entertainment events. Meanwhile, Fallin signed a law mandating that school districts develop programs to prevent sexual assault.

Senior Senator

James Inhofe (R)

Elected Nov. 1994, term expires Jan. 2021, 4th full term; b. Nov. 17, 1934, Des Moines, IA; U. of Tulsa, B.A. 1973; Presbyterian; married (Kay); 4 children (1 deceased).

Military Career: Army, 1957-58.

Elected Office: OK House, 1967-69; OK Senate, 1969-77, Repub. ldr., 1975-77; Tulsa mayor, 1978-84; U.S. House, 1987-95.

Professional Career: Businessman, land developer, 1962-86.

DC Office: 205 RSOB, 20510, 202-224-4721; Fax: 202-228-0380; Website: inhofe.senate.gov.

State Offices: Enid, 580-234-5105; McAlester, 918-426-0933; Oklahoma City, 405-608-4381; Tulsa, 918-748-5111.

Committees: *Armed Services*: Airland; Readiness & Management Support; Strategic Forces. *Environment & Public Works* (Chmn: ex officio member of each subcommittee).

Group Ratings

	ADA	ACLU	AFL-CIO	LCV	ITI	COC	HAFA	ACU	CFG	FRC
2014	5%	0%	–	3%	33%	100%	79%	92%	92%	100%
2013	0%	C	6%	8%	C	86%	C	72%	94%	C

National Journal Ratings

	2013 LIB	—	2013 CONS
Economic	0%	—	95%
Social	0%	—	92%
Foreign	13%	—	86%
Composite	7%	—	93%

Key Votes of the 113th Congress

1. Sandy storm spending	N	5. Student Loan Rates	Y	9. Bipartisan Budget Deal	N	
2. Chuck Hagel Confirmation	N	6. Employee Non-Discrim'n Act	N	10. Farm Bill Conference Rept.	N	
3. Gun Background Checks	N	7. Senate Vote on Judgeships	Y	11. Unempl. Comp. Extension	N	
4. Immigration Reform	N	8. Defense Dept. Spending	N	12. Keystone Pipeline	Y	

Election Results

2014 general	Jim Inhofe (R)	558,166	(68%)	$5,152,276	$7,250
	Matt Silverstein (D)	234,307	(29%)	$471,194	
2014 primary	Jim Inhofe (R)	231,131	(88%)		

Prior winning percentages: 2008 (57%), 2002 (57%), 1996 (57%), 1994 special (55%); House: 1992 (53%), 1990 (56%), 1988 (53%), 1986 (55%)

Republican James Inhofe, Oklahoma's senior senator and one of the most experienced Republicans in Congress, was elected to the House in 1986 and to the Senate in 1994. He vehemently rejects the science of climate change and his military views are hawkish. He returned to the chairmanship of the Environment and Public Works Committee in 2015.

Inhofe grew up in Tulsa, served in the Army, and worked in real estate and insurance. He was elected to the state House in 1966, and to the Senate in 1969. As a state legislator, he promoted the balanced budget constitutional amendment. He ran for governor in 1974 and lost to David Boren, 64%-36%. In 1976, he ran for the House against Democratic Rep. Jim Jones and lost. From 1979 to 1984, he was mayor of Tulsa. When Jones ran unsuccessfully for the Senate in 1986, Inhofe was elected to his House seat. He was re-elected three times, but with uninspiring margins. Negative publicity from a family business lawsuit and charges of campaign finance irregularities impaired his support in what was even then a strongly Republican district.

Inhofe's greatest achievement in the House was reforming the arcane discharge petition rule. For years, House rules kept secret the names of signers of petitions to force bills stuck in committees to the floor for action; anonymity allowed lawmakers to claim they had worked to bring legislation to the floor when they in fact had done the opposite. That was changed in 1993, and one of the first bills to benefit from the new rules was an aviation liability reform bill, co-sponsored by flying buff Inhofe, that limited the liability of small airplane manufacturers in lawsuits resulting from crashes.

In 1994, Inhofe jumped into the special election that was held when conservative Democrat Boren resigned to become president of the University of Oklahoma. Rep. Dave McCurdy, a moderate Democrat, was the initial frontrunner. But President Bill Clinton's unpopularity among conservatives was too much for McCurdy, who had voted for 1993 budget increases and tax hikes, and for the 1994 crime bill with its ban on assault weapons. Inhofe won by a solid 55%-40%. In the Senate, Inhofe was president of the GOP freshman class of 11 senators. In 1996, he won a six-year term over James Boren, David Boren's cousin, 57%-40%.

Inhofe has a solidly conservative voting record and is blunt, even acerbic, at times. "I'm not afraid of controversy. I'm not afraid to say what's on my mind and what's on a lot of people's minds," he says. He speaks his mind in pungent terms, with his barbs often targeted at his opponents in the green movement. He once accused Clinton Environmental Protection Agency chief Carol Browner of "Gestapo tactics." Environmentalists often hit back; activist Robert F. Kennedy Jr. in 2012 called Inhofe "big oil's top call girl."

Inhofe has been a leader of the GOP faction that disputes the scientific evidence that carbon dioxide emissions cause catastrophic climate change. In 2003, Inhofe said that the idea that man-made emissions have caused global warming was "the greatest hoax ever perpetrated on the American people." After emails in 2009 revealed attempts by some scientists to bolster the case for global warming, he said in March 2010 that "the world's first climate billionaire is running for cover. Yes, I'm talking about Al Gore. He's under siege these days." Inhofe published a book in 2012, *The Greatest Hoax: How the Global Warming Conspiracy Threatens Your Future.*

Inhofe chaired the Environment committee from 2003 to 2007, when Republicans last controlled the Senate. He devoted much of his attention to reauthorization of the highway bill, which is a prime responsibility of the panel. By early 2004, Inhofe had hammered out an agreement in the Senate for a six-year, $318 billion transportation bill. House Transportation Chairman Don Young was seeking a $375 billion bill, while the Bush administration wanted to cap spending at $256 billion. Inhofe argued that money was needed to maintain the highway system and would be funded entirely by user fees, primarily the gas tax. The House-passed bill was $275 billion. The two versions had significant political differences. Inhofe's goal was to guarantee that every state got 95 percent of its gas tax money back; if total spending was decreased, other states would lose projects. With the conflict deadlocked, the issue was deferred to 2005. By that time, GOP leaders were eager to cut a final deal with Bush, and Inhofe agreed to a scaled-down bill of $286 billion.

Representing a major petroleum-producing state, Inhofe has been an avid proponent of oil drilling in the Arctic National Wildlife Refuge, plus more oil and gas exploration throughout the nation. He has low regard for the Endangered Species Act. "America has adopted an attitude that places more value on the life of a critter than on a human being," he once said.

After Democrats won control of the Senate, Inhofe in January 2007 withstood a backroom challenge from Virginia Republican John Warner to become the ranking minority member on the committee. Prospects for his cooperation with incoming Democratic Chairman Barbara Boxer, a liberal from California, initially seemed to be nil. He spoke out strongly against her bill to impose a mandatory cap on carbon dioxide emissions. When that proposal died in the Senate in 2008, he said that it showed "momentum is going our way." But he insisted that his working relations were good. Indeed, after they worked together in 2012 to pass a two-year highway and surface transportation bill, Boxer told reporters that Inhofe "has been just the best partner for me as chairman...in the best traditions of how the highway bill has been done until now."

Inhofe co-sponsored a bill to stop the EPA from regulating carbon dioxide emissions and limiting states' authority to do so. The Senate rejected it, 47-52, in March 2013. After the April 2010 BP oil spill in the Gulf of Mexico, he opposed a Democratic initiative to remove the $75 million cap on damages for offshore drilling accidents.

Inhofe took the top GOP post on Armed Services in 2013 after Arizona's John McCain stepped aside because of party-imposed term limits. Inhofe began by crusading against his former Senate colleague, Nebraska Republican Chuck Hagel, to become secretary of Defense after having earlier praised Hagel. While other senators questioned Hagel's support for Israel as a cause for concern, Inhofe went even further: He suggested that Hagel was "cozy" with countries promoting terrorism because Iran had expressed support for his nomination. That led Missouri Democrat Claire McCaskill to respond, "Senator Inhofe, be careful. What if some horrible organization said tomorrow that you were the best guy that they knew?"

Inhofe regularly blasted Obama on national security matters. He accused Obama in February 2014 of telling an "outrageous lie" during an interview about the 2012 attack on a consulate in Benghazi, Libya, and alleged the administration was mounting a Watergate-style cover-up about the incident. He implored his colleagues later that year to give the president formal authority to take military action in Syria. As he told MSNBC: "Let's give him that authority so, at the last minute, he can't say, 'Well, I'm not sure I have that authority.' He's inclined to do that."

On another military issue, Inhofe added a provision to the fiscal 2011 defense authorization law barring commanders from collecting information about weapons privately owned by troops. The measure led a group of senior retired generals and admirals in 2012 to ask that the law be changed because it interfered with efforts to prevent military suicides. Inhofe said he disagreed with that view, but he did not block efforts to modify it.

Inhofe has been a leader in the movement to make English the country's official language. During the 2006 debate on overhauling immigration policy, he got the Senate to pass his amendment. "This is not just about preserving our culture and heritage, but also about bettering the odds for our nation's newest potential citizens," he said. His contrarian streak has not slackened in the least. In June 2009, he refused to meet with Supreme Court nominee Sonia Sotomayor on the grounds that he had decided to oppose her.

In January 2015, McCain reclaimed the top Republican position at Armed Services and Inhofe returned as Environment Committee chairman. His agenda as the Environment Committee chairman included attacks on the EPAs "job-killing regulations" through tough oversight hearings, along with an update of the Toxic Substances Control Act. He urged EPA to withdraw proposed regulations on pollution discharges into federally protected waterways. On climate change, he added some apparent nuances. "Climate is changing, and climate has always changed. There's archeological evidence of that. There's biblical evidence of that.

There's historic evidence of that," he told the Senate. But his basic skepticism remained. In February, he tossed a snowball on the Senate floor during a speech on climate change. Citing recent records of unseasonably warm weather, he said, "Now, the script has flipped." He expressed his desire for "a long term transportation bill—a sizeable and robust one," a goal that he continued to share with Sen. Boxer, now the committee's ranking Democrat.

At home, Inhofe was twice reelected by almost identical margins, both somewhat smaller than Republican presidential margins in Oklahoma. In 2002, he beat former Gov. David Walters, who had years earlier pleaded guilty to a misdemeanor count of violating campaign finance laws, 57%-36%. In 2008, he beat state Sen. Andrew Rice, 57%-39%, carrying all but four counties in the Muskogee area. In 2014, he was reelected with a more convincing 68% of the vote against little-known Democratic challenger Matt Silverstein. Inhofe's share of the vote that day was 0.1 percent larger than that of newly elected Sen. James Lankford, who got 67.9 percent to fill the remaining two years of the term of Sen. Tom Coburn, who resigned for health reasons.

Inhofe has for years regularly flown airplanes and is one of the few certified commercial pilots in Congress. He flew around the world following the historic route of Wiley Post, the first pilot to fly solo around the globe. But he encountered problems in October 2006 when the small plane he was flying spun out of control and suffered significant damage on landing in Tulsa, though he and an aide escaped injury. His penchant for daredevil stunts in the air is well-known around the Capitol, and few of his aides will take him up on his offers of airplane rides. In October 2010, his flouting of air safety rules became a serious issue. Inhofe set his six-seat Cessna down on a runway clearly marked closed at a South Texas airport, and just narrowly missed hitting a group of construction workers during an aborted landing attempt. The Federal Aviation Administration ordered him to take remedial flying lessons, but did not take away his pilot's license. Inhofe was a chief backer of a bill signed into law by Bush in 2007 that raised the mandatory retirement age for airline pilots from 60 to 65.

In November 2013, Inhofe's son Perry died when the small, single-engine plane he was flying crashed in Oklahoma. Discussing how the loss affected him, he told NBC News: "You don't change in terms of your positions, in terms of what you believe in, but you change in terms of your understanding of individuals." The previous month, Sen. Inhofe had quadruple bypass surgery to repair extreme blockages in his arteries. As of November 2014, he became one of five Senators at least 80 years old.

Junior Senator

James Lankford (R)

Elected 2014, term expires Jan. 2017, 1st term; b. March 4, 1968, Dallas, TX; U. of TX, B.S. 1990, Southwestern Theological Baptist Seminary, M.Div. 1994; Baptist; married (Cindy); 2 children.

Professional Career: Youth camp dir., Baptist Gen. Convention of OK, 1995-2009.

DC Office: 316 HSOB, 20510, 202-224-5754; Website: lankford.senate.gov.

State Offices: Oklahoma City, 405-231-4941; Tulsa, 918-581-7651.

Committees: *Appropriations:* Commerce, Justice, Science & Related Agencies; Energy & Water Development; Financial Services & General Government; Labor, Health & Human Services, Education & Related Agencies; State, Foreign Operations & Related Programs. *Homeland Security & Governmental Affairs:* Investigations; Federal Spending Oversight & Emergency Management; Regulatory Affairs & Federal Management (Chmn). *Indian Affairs. Intelligence.*

Group Ratings (House)

	ADA	ACLU	AFL-CIO	LCV	ITI	COC	HAFA	ACU	CFG	FRC
2014	5%	0%	–	0%	100%	54%	80%	94%	100%	100%
2013	0%	C	19%	4%	C	85%	C	80%	70%	C

National Journal Ratings (House)

	2013 LIB	—	2013 CONS
Economic	34%	—	65%
Social	0%	—	87%
Foreign	15%	—	77%
Composite	20%	—	80%

Key Votes of the 113th Congress (House)

1. Sandy storm spending	N	5. Medical Marijuana	NV 9. Syrian Rebels Training Y
2. Violence Against Women Act	N	6. Farm Bill	Y 10. Keystone pipeline Y
3. Guantanamo Bay Detainees	N	7. Afghanistan Combat	NV 11. Immigration Exec. Action Y
4. Abortion 20-week ban	Y	8. NSA Phone Data Collection	N 12. Bipartisan budget deal Y

Election Results

2014 special	James Lankford (R)	557,002	(68%)	$4,384,320	$115,524	$420,310
general	Constance Johnson (D)	237,923	(29%)	$148,658		
	Mark Beard (I)	25,965	(3%)			
2014 special	James Lankford (R)	152,658	(57%)			
primary	T.W. Shannon (R)	91,772	(34%)			

Prior winning percentages: House: 2012 (59%), 2010 (63%)

Just a few years ago, Republican James Lankford was a little-known church youth camp director without any political experience. Since then, he has won a seat in the House, a leadership position in his party, and—in 2014—the Senate seat held by Republican Tom Coburn, who resigned because of health concerns.

Lankford grew up impoverished in Dallas. His parents divorced when he was 4 years old. With his mother and older brother, he moved into the garage behind his grandparents' house. Lankford says that he became a follower of Christ when he was 8 and that his religion has helped him endure tough times. He graduated from the University of Texas with a degree in secondary education, then attended the Southwestern Baptist Theological Seminary and earned a master's degree in divinity.

In 1995, Lankford began working for the Baptist General Convention of Oklahoma. A year later, he was made director of the Falls Creek Christian youth summer camp that touts itself as the largest summer camp in the country. He was in charge of organizing activities for more than 50,000 campers each summer. He served there until 2009, when he resigned to run for the seat of GOP Rep. Mary Fallin after she decided to run for governor. With grassroots support largely among Christians, Lankford led the initial voting, then won a stunning 65 percent in the primary runoff against state Rep. Kevin Calvey, who had the backing of national Republicans. He easily defeated Democratic lawyer Billy Coyle with 63 percent of the vote in the general election in his comfortably Republican district, even though it is the least conservative of Oklahoma's five districts.

In the House, Lankford was given a seat on the Oversight and Government Reform panel and won committee passage of several bills, including a measure setting new standards to promote transparency in the awarding of federal grants. On the Budget Committee, he became a firm supporter of Republican Chairman Paul Ryan's push to cut spending. *Politico* named him, along with California Democrat Karen Bass, as the freshman "most likely to succeed." When Georgia's Tom Price decided to run for GOP Conference chairman after the 2012 election, Lankford quietly lined up support from colleagues to succeed Price as chairman of the Republican Policy Committee. Making the case that he provided fresh blood from the big Class of 2010, he was elected without opposition to the party's fifth-ranking post, a sign of respect from relentlessly ambitious colleagues. In his leadership post, he tried to define agenda items beyond the typical week-ahead congressional perspective, and he said that he served as "eyes and ears" for Speaker John Boehner in the Republican Conference. But he had little time to make an impact.

When Coburn, a medical doctor who had been battling prostate cancer, announced in January 2014 that he would resign at the end of that year rather than serve the final two years of his term, Lankford jumped into the race. Despite his earlier backing from tea-party interests, he rankled some in the movement for joining the GOP leadership and for voting in favor of raising the federal debt ceiling. Several of the tea party's most visible figures coalesced around Republican T.W. Shannon, the former speaker of the Oklahoma House. An African-American who also is a member of the Chickasaw tribe, Shannon drew support from some national conservative groups, and leading figures such as former vice presidential nominee Sarah Palin and Senators Ted Cruz of Texas and Mike Lee of Utah.

Coburn called Lankford "a man of absolute integrity," though he did not formally endorse him. Lankford drew on his long-standing support from the Southern Baptist community, including former Arkansas Governor Mike Huckabee, and defeated Shannon by an unexpectedly strong 57%-34%. The outcome was a surprise, in particular, for conservative groups that were planning a big push for Shannon in an August runoff, which would have resulted if no candidate got more than 50 percent of the vote. In solidly conservative Oklahoma, the GOP nomination assured Lankford's election in November, when he got 67.9% of the vote against Democratic state Rep. Connie Johnson, who was the first woman and the first African-American nominee to the Senate from Oklahoma.

In the Senate, Lankford got seats on the Appropriations, Homeland Security and Governmental Affairs, Intelligence and Indian Affairs committees. He took a particular interest in defending freedom of religion. When the Senate in May 2015 approved trade promotion authority for President Barack Obama, Lankford won inclusion of his amendment that U.S. trading partners should encourage religious freedom. He noted that a panel recently had urged the State Department to designate Vietnam as a country of particular concern because it had violated religious freedom. In March, he introduced resolutions of disapproval that were designed to reject two measures from the District of Columbia city council that were designed to protect the right to an abortion and the rights of gay student groups. Lankford voiced concern that those policies could restrict the rights of others, including religious groups.

On the Homeland Security Subcommittee on Regulatory Affairs and Federal Management, which he chairs, Lankford worked with Democratic Sen. Heidi Heitkamp of North Dakota, the panel's ranking minority member, on a proposal to make it easier for citizens to register their concerns to federal agencies about proposed regulations. He worked with other libertarian-minded Republicans to reduce mandatory questionnaires from the Census Bureau that they viewed as too intrusive into personal freedom.

Lankford's victory in 2014 earned him the right to serve the remaining two years of Coburn's term. He must run in 2016 for a full six-year term, a race in which he is heavily favored.

FIRST DISTRICT

Jim Bridenstine (R)

Elected 2012, 2nd term; b. June 15, 1975, Ann Arbor, MI; Rice U., B.A. 1998, Cornell U., M.B.A. 2009; Baptist; married (Michelle Ivory Bridenstine); 3 children.

Military Career: Navy, 1998-2007; Navy Reserve, 2010-present.

Professional Career: Defense consultant, Wyle Labs., 2007-08; Dir., Tulsa Air & Space Museum, 2008-10.

DC Office: 216 CHOB, 20515, 202-225-2211; Website: bridenstine.house.gov.

State Offices: Tulsa, 918-935-3222.

Committees: *Armed Services:* Seapower & Projection Forces; Strategic Forces. *Science, Space, & Technology:* Environment (Chmn); Oversight.

Group Ratings

	ADA	ACLU	AFL-CIO	LCV	ITI	COC	HAFA	ACU	CFG	FRC
2014	5%	11%	–	3%	60%	57%	91%	96%	98%	100%
2013	15%	C	19%	7%	C	62%	C	88%	97%	C

National Journal Ratings

	2013 LIB	—	2013 CONS
Economic	26%	—	73%
Social	31%	—	67%
Foreign	15%	—	77%
Composite	26%	—	74%

Key Votes of the 113th Congress

1. Sandy storm spending	N	5. Medical Marijuana	N	9. Syrian Rebels Training	N
2. Violence Against Women Act	N	6. Farm Bill	N	10. Keystone pipeline	Y
3. Guantanamo Bay Detainees	N	7. Afghanistan Combat	N	11. Immigration Exec. Action	Y
4. Abortion 20-week ban	Y	8. NSA Phone Data Collection	Y	12. Bipartisan budget deal	N

Election Results

2014 general   Jim Bridenstine (R) ....unopposed $365,520 $4,693
2014 primary Jim Bridenstine (R) ....unopposed

Prior winning percentage: 2012 (63%)

Population		Race and Ethnicity		Income	
Total:	773,208	White	66.7%	Median income:	$48,746
Urban:	53.1%	Latino	10.1%		*(260 of 435)*
Suburban:	33.8%	Black	9.0%	Under $50,000	51.0%
Rural:	13.1%	Amer. Indian	5.7%	$50,000-$99,999:	30.5%
Land area:	2,557	Two races	6.2%	$100,000-$199,999:	15.1%
Pop/sq. mi.:	302.4	White Ethnic	19.6%	$200,000 or more:	3.5%
Born in state:	58.4%			Poverty Rate	15.3%
		Education			
Age Groups		H.S. grad or less:	38.9%	**Work**	
Under 18:	25.3%	Some college:	32.4%	White collar:	34.8%
18 to 34:	23.4%	College degree, 4 yr.:	19.7%	Blue collar:	43.4%
35 to 64:	38.1%	Post-grad study:	8.9%	Sales and service:	21.9%
Over 64:	13.2%				
		Military		Govt. workers:	10.1%
		Veterans/active duty:	8.8%		

Tulsa Area

The gushers of the 1905 Glenn Pool discovery made Tulsa one of America's oil boomtowns, settled not just by people from the immediate hinterland but also by Midwesterners and New Englanders of Yankee stock. In the 1920s, as its art deco skyscrapers rose on the heights above the Arkansas River, it

Voter Turnout	
2013 Total Citizen 18+	545,052
2014 House Turnout	0
2014 Turnout as % CVAP	0.0%
2012 Turnout as % CVAP	53.5%

was still a raw town, but one bent on becoming more cultured. It was optimistic and ready to seek economic change, yet culturally and politically conservative, with a Yankee elite and an American Indian heritage recalled today in one of the nation's best collections of Western art at the Gilcrease Museum—left by oil millionaire Thomas Gilcrease, who was one-eighth Creek Indian.

In recent decades, Tulsa has boomed and occasionally busted. In 2003, voters approved a $900 million initiative funded by a one-cent sales tax increase, as part of Tulsa's efforts to diversify. That has become the "Vision 2025" tax of six-tenths of a cent. The tax has helped pay for everything from Arkansas River protection work to new university buildings to upgrades at city parks and golf courses. In 1992, American Airlines completed a $480 million expansion and renovation of its maintenance center a few miles away from the city, with an increase from 11 to 20 hangar bays. That move spurred other aerospace-related development in Tulsa, which has become the base of the Oklahoma Aerospace Alliance. More than 300 aerospace firms in the state have an annual output of about $13 billion, including more than 20,000 workers in Tulsa. The American hub employs 5,700 people at the primary maintenance base for the world's largest airline. The next two largest companies are NORDAM, which makes aerospace components, and Spirit AeroSystems, a Boeing supplier.

Tulsa, also the home of Oral Roberts University, has remained cosmopolitan but conservative. A travel writer for *The Washington Post* once termed Tulsa "a fine replica of European grandeur." People here do not resent the oil companies or the new rich; they identify with them. In 2015, WalletHub ranked Tulsa as the second-best city to start a business, trailing only Shreveport Louisiana.

The 1st Congressional District of Oklahoma includes Tulsa, Wagoner and Washington counties, and small slices of Rogers and

2012 Presidential Vote		
Mitt Romney (R)................188,961	(66%)
Barack Obama (D) 98,321	(34%)

2008 Presidential Vote		
John McCain (R)................204,009	(64%)
Barack Obama (D) 113,909	(36%)

Cook Partisan Voting Index: R+18

Creek counties—just about all of the Tulsa metropolitan area. The political tradition here is heavily Republican, strengthened in recent decades by opposition to national Democrats' cultural liberalism. Mitt Romney got 66 percent of the vote here in 2012, but the 1st ranked only fourth among the five Oklahoma districts in its vote for Romney, as well as for John McCain in 2012.

Jim Bridenstine (R)

Tea party-backed Jim Bridenstine, first elected in 2012 when he upset a five-term incumbent in the Republican primary, has become a leader of House GOP rebels. In his conservative district, Bridenstine's hard-nosed tactics have played well.

The son of an accountant and a schoolteacher, Bridenstine was born in Ann Arbor, Michigan. His family moved to Arlington, Texas, and then to Jenks, a suburb of Tulsa, when he was in high school. He attended Rice University in Houston on a partial swimming scholarship. But a shoulder injury forced him to leave the sport after his sophomore year, and he focused on his triple-major in business administration, economics and psychology.

After graduating from Rice, he joined the Navy and became a pilot of the E-2 Hawkeye, an airborne command and control plane. As a naval officer, he served tours of duty in Iraq and Afghanistan, flying combat missions and logging more than 1,900 flight hours. He transitioned to flying the F-18 Hornet with the Naval Strike and Air Warfare Center in Nevada. During that time, he bought a small ranch in Nevada and began to raise alpacas, a small South American mammal that produces fur used for knitted and woven items. After leaving active duty, Bridenstine and his wife, Michelle, worked in Orlando Florida at defense consulting firm Wyle Laboratories. Simultaneously, he earned his M.B.A. from Cornell University, flying to New York every other weekend for classes. In 2008, they returned to Tulsa, where he became director of the city's Air and Space Museum.

In September 2011, Bridenstine launched a long-shot primary campaign against veteran Rep. John Sullivan. The incumbent had a very conservative voting record and had won at least 60% of the vote in his prior three reelection campaigns. Bridenstine painted Sullivan as an out-of-touch career politician with a proclivity for missing votes. Sullivan had been admitted to a rehabilitation center to be treated for alcoholism after the death of his daughter, which he said explained his missed votes.

Sullivan accused Bridenstine of operating the Air and Space Museum at a loss and putting it in financial jeopardy, a charge Bridenstine disputed, responding that his project to bring a space shuttle to the museum was a secure venture that raised the museum's visibility. Sullivan outspent Bridenstine $990,000 to $244,000. But Bridenstine won, 54%-46%. "So many things came together in a perfect storm," he told *National Journal.* "I think the electorate was looking for viable candidates who would oppose incumbents." In the general election, Bridenstine easily dispatched Democratic businessman John Olson, with 63% of the vote. A strong believer in term limits, he vowed to serve no more than three terms in the House.

He got off to an early start as a House rebel, casting his first vote in January 2013 for Majority Leader Eric Cantor of Virginia for speaker rather than for returning John Boehner. His office issued a statement that his vote "should not have been a surprise to anyone who followed his campaign."

He focused his legislative attention on the Armed Services Committee, plus Science, Space and Technology, where he became chairman of the Environment Subcommittee in 2015. On the annual defense spending bill that the House passed in May 2015, Bridenstine worked on military-space provisions, including funding of the Air Force's Satellite Communications Pathfinder program. Also that month, the House passed his Weather Research and Forecasting Innovation Act, which he co-authored with fellow Oklahoma Republican Frank Lucas. The measure was designed to provide additional warnings to states such as Oklahoma that have suffered devastating effects of severe weather, such as tornadoes and hurricanes. In 2013, he filed a bill to repeal the 16th Amendment to the Constitution, which permitted the federal income tax; he called the tax code unfair and too complicated. He took his often controversial remarks to the House floor, as with a June 2013 speech in which he called President Barack Obama "not fit to lead," in part because of his "lies" about the Internal Revenue Service and the attack on the American consulate in Benghazi, Libya.

Bridenstine was reelected without opposition in 2014. In January 2015, he again voted against Boehner for speaker, criticizing him for having "relinquished the power of the purse" to Obama in the bipartisan spending deal during the 2014 lame-duck session. He was among several conservative House Republicans who became targets of radio advertisements in March 2015 by the Boehner-affiliated American Action Network urging their vote for the spending bill for the Homeland Security Department.

According to a May 2015 report in *The Washington Post*, Bridenstine was part of a bipartisan delegation to Azerbaijan that the House Ethics Committee was investigating for excessive gifts and possible non-compliance with House rules. He reportedly was the only one in the group who disclosed the gift in his financial disclosure report. He told the *Post* that he had offered to pay for the cost of two rugs, but ultimately returned them to Azerbaijan officials. He said that he joined the trip because the Oklahoma National Guard has joint activities with Azerbaijan's armed forces. The Ethics Committee included Bridenstine when it announced in June that it was investigating those nine members.

SECOND DISTRICT

Markwayne Mullin (R)

Elected 2012, 2nd term; b. July 26, 1977, Tulsa; MO Valley Col., attended 1996, OK St. U. Inst. of Tech., A.D. 2010; Pentecostal; married (Christie); 5 children.

Professional Career: Owner, Mullin Plumbing, 1996-present.

DC Office: 1103 LHOB, 20515, 202-225-2701; Fax: 202-225-3038; Website: mullin.house.gov.

State Offices: McAlester, 918-423-5951; Muskogee, 918-687-2533.

Committees: *Energy & Commerce:* Commerce, Manufacturing & Trade; Energy & Power; Oversight & Investigations.

Group Ratings

	ADA	ACLU	AFL-CIO	LCV	ITI	COC	HAFA	ACU	CFG	FRC
2014	0%	5%	–	0%	100%	85%	59%	84%	66%	100%
2013	5%	C	19%	0%	C	69%	C	80%	75%	C

National Journal Ratings

	2013 LIB	—	2013 CONS
Economic	24%	—	75%
Social	0%	—	87%
Foreign	5%	—	86%
Composite	14%	—	87%

Key Votes of the 113th Congress

1. Sandy storm spending	N	5. Medical Marijuana	N	9. Syrian Rebels Training	Y
2. Violence Against Women Act	N	6. Farm Bill	Y	10. Keystone pipeline	Y
3. Guantanamo Bay Detainees	N	7. Afghanistan Combat	N	11. Immigration Exec. Action	Y
4. Abortion 20-week ban	Y	8. NSA Phone Data Collection	Y	12. Bipartisan budget deal	N

Election Results

2014 general	Markwayne Mullin (R)	110,925	(70%)	$955,584
	Earl Everett (D)	38,964	(25%)	
	Jon Douthitt (I)	8,518	(5%)	
2014 primary	Markwayne Mullin (R)	26,224	(80%)	
	Darrel Robertson (R)	6,667	(20%)	

Prior winning percentage: 2012 (57%)

Population		Race and Ethnicity		Income	
Total:	747,973	White	65.8%	Median income:	$37,949
Urban:	0.0%	Amer. Indian	13.0%		*(404 of 435)*
Suburban:	13.8%	Latino	4.6%	Under $50,000	61.7%
Rural:	86.2%	Black	3.4%	$50,000-$99,999:	27.3%
Land area:	20,439	Two races	12.8%	$100,000-$199,999:	9.5%
Pop/sq. mi.:	36.6	White Ethnic	15.3%	$200,000 or more:	1.5%
Born in state:	62.1%			Poverty Rate	20.6%
		Education			
Age Groups		H.S. grad or less:	54.6%	**Work**	
Under 18:	23.9%	Some college:	29.2%	White collar:	27.6%
18 to 34:	20.9%	College degree, 4 yr.:	11.0%	Blue collar:	42.4%
35 to 64:	37.8%	Post-grad study:	5.1%	Sales and service:	30.0%
Over 64:	17.5%				
		Military		Govt. workers:	20.4%
		Veterans/active duty:	9.7%		

East Oklahoma: Tulsa Suburbs, Muskogee

The land that is now northeast Oklahoma used to be Indian territory, the place where in the 1830s the Five Civilized Tribes were driven from Georgia and Alabama over the Trail of Tears. A sizable minority here report their race as American Indian. The Native American identity is highest in

Voter Turnout	
2013 Total Citizen 18+	560,277
2014 House Turnout	158,407
2014 Turnout as % CVAP	28.3%
2012 Turnout as % CVAP	45%

the hilly counties west of the Ozarks of Arkansas, where county names—Cherokee, Osage, Sequoyah—recall the Civilized Tribes. The street signs in scenic Tahlequah, the Cherokee capital since 1839, are written in both English and Cherokee. The Creek Nation chose its tribal site in Okmulgee in the belief that tornadoes would not strike the area; history has proven the choice correct so far—tornadoes have done minimal damage here. South of Indian country is Oklahoma's Little Dixie, settled between 1889 and 1907 by white Southerners, most of them poor. Some of the county names—such as Le Flore—are borrowed straight from Mississippi.

This pleasant land of gentle hills and man-made lakes recently has grown at a healthy pace with population spread from Tulsa. Interstate highways and turnpikes connect people to jobs in more-vibrant metropolitan areas, while dam-made lakes have spurred resort and retirement communities. Still, traditional cultural attitudes and folkways remain strong. When Oklahoma voted in 2002 to outlaw cockfighting, voters in many Little Dixie towns turned out in large numbers to oppose the ban. The most populated city here is Muskogee, an old railroad community with a manufacturing economy that has slowed in recent years, though recent increases in sales tax receipts have shown local revival. In 2014, Pryor received the Most Innovative City Award from the National League of Cities for its health and fitness programs. Bicyclists from the Cherokee Nation have an annual three-week bicycle trip for 950 miles across seven states to retrace the Trail of Tears.

2012 Presidential Vote		
Mitt Romney (R)	170,983	(68%)
Barack Obama (D)	81,179	(32%)
2008 Presidential Vote		
John McCain (R)	179,566	(66%)
Barack Obama (D)	93,712	(34%)
Cook Partisan Voting Index:	R+20	

The 2nd Congressional District includes eastern Oklahoma. It takes in Muskogee; Claremore, Will Rogers' hometown; and McAlester, former House Speaker Carl Albert's hometown. McAlester is the site of a massive Army ammunition plant that manufactures non-nuclear bombs and is the largest local employer. Tiny Spavinaw in the northeast corner was the birthplace of baseball legend Mickey Mantle. The area was ancestrally Democratic, but in the 1980s, it trended Republican and has remained that way; today it is as solidly Republican as most of Oklahoma.

Markwayne Mullin (R)

Republican plumber Markwayne Mullin, elected in 2012, took the seat of one of the House's few remaining conservative Southern Democrats. He has been an outspoken conservative, but usually a reliable vote for the GOP leadership.

Mullin was born in Tulsa and grew up in Westville, a small town on the Arkansas line, as the youngest of seven children. His father ran a small plumbing business, which Mullin took over at age 19 after briefly attending Missouri Valley College. He expanded the company from six employees to more than 100. He also hosted a local talk show advising callers on home repair. Mullin, a Cherokee, operates the Oklahoma Fight Club in Broken Arrow, a training center for jujitsu and mixed martial arts. He earned an associate's degree in business in 2010 from the Oklahoma State University Institute of Technology in Okmulgee.

Mullin was one of six candidates for the Republican nomination for the open seat of retiring Democratic Rep. Dan Boren. Arguing against excessive regulation and saying it was "time to fire Barack Obama," he was the first to jump into the race and became the front-runner. His fundraising outpaced that of his GOP rivals, although a good portion of his war chest was self-financed. In the June primary, he coasted to a first-place finish with 42% of the vote and then faced George Faught, a Republican state House member who earned 23%, in a runoff. Faught accused Mullin of carpet-bagging when property records showed that he had claimed homestead tax exemptions in Wagoner County, outside the district. Mullin labeled Faught a career politician and won the runoff handily, 57%-43%.

Democrats nominated Rob Wallace, a former assistant U.S. attorney. In September, news broke that Mullin Plumbing had received about $370,000 in federal economic stimulus money for housing projects with the Cherokee and Muscogee nations. Mullin had campaigned heavily against President Barack Obama's stimulus program, and Wallace accused him of acting like an "out-of-touch, typical Washington politician." Mullin claimed not to know that the projects got stimulus money, but documents from the Cherokee Nation obtained by the *Tulsa World* contradicted that assertion.

Some of Mullin's business practices came under fire. Based on a tip from an employee, federal agents raided Mullin Plumbing and discovered a stocked gun safe belonging to another employee, who was a convicted felon and ultimately pleaded guilty to possession of a firearm. Mullin admitted he had not performed a background check, and that he had shot guns with the employee. Wallace also hit Mullin on illegal immigration, picking up on his statement that he "did not use E-Verify," and raising the possibility that Mullin employed illegal immigrants. Those attacks mostly fell flat. Mullin outspent Wallace, $1.7 million to $1.2 million, and won, 57%-38%.

In the House, Mullin increased his legislative activity when he was assigned to the Energy and Commerce Committee in January 2015. He said he would provide an "Oklahoma business owner perspective" as the committee handles its broad agenda of regulatory and health-care issues. He later cited his work on committee legislation to limit the Obama administration's proposed "Clean Power Plan" that would impose big increases in electricity rates. In December 2014, he introduced his Fines in Need of Extensive Reform (FINER) Act to require more transparency by federal regulators and change how their fines are handled.

Mullin has taken a personal approach to his work. He used his physical fitness expertise to bond with members from both parties, including early morning interval training exercises at the House gym and the formation with Democratic Rep. Donald Payne of New Jersey of the Men's Health Caucus. He posts a "Mullin' It Over Column" on his office website most weeks, with informal and home-spun views on his life in Washington and at home.

THIRD DISTRICT

Frank Lucas (R)

Elected May 1994, 11th full term; b. Jan. 6, 1960, Cheyenne; OK St. U., B.S. 1982; Baptist; married (Lynda); 3 children.

Elected Office: OK House, 1988-94.

Professional Career: Farmer & rancher.

DC Office: 2405 RHOB, 20515, 202-225-5565; Fax: 202-225-8698; Website: lucas.house.gov.

State Offices: Yukon, 405-373-1958.

Committees: *Agriculture:* Commodity Exchanges, Energy & Credit; Conservation & Forestry; General Farm Commodities & Risk Management. *Financial Services:* Financial Institutions & Consumer Credit; Monetary Policy & Trade. *Science, Space, & Technology* (VChmn): Research & Technology; Space.

Group Ratings

	ADA	ACLU	AFL-CIO	LCV	ITI	COC	HAFA	ACU	CFG	FRC
2014	0%	0%	–	6%	100%	93%	49%	68%	64%	100%
2013	0%	C	24%	11%	C	77%	C	64%	53%	C

National Journal Ratings

	2013 LIB	—	2013 CONS
Economic	50%	—	50%
Social	16%	—	74%
Foreign	32%	—	67%
Composite	35%	—	66%

Key Votes of the 113th Congress

1. Sandy storm spending	Y	5. Medical Marijuana	N	9. Syrian Rebels Training	Y
2. Violence Against Women Act	N	6. Farm Bill	Y	10. Keystone pipeline	Y
3. Guantanamo Bay Detainees	N	7. Afghanistan Combat	N	11. Immigration Exec. Action	Y
4. Abortion 20-week ban	Y	8. NSA Phone Data Collection	N	12. Bipartisan budget deal	Y

Election Results

2014 general	Frank Lucas (R)	201,744	(75%)	$1,253,709	$2,151
	Timothy Ray Murray (D)	53,472	(20%)		
	William Sanders (I)	12,787	(5%)		
2014 primary	Frank Lucas (R)	54,816	(83%)		
	Robert Hubbard (R)	7,917	(12%)		
	Timothy Murray (R)	3,442	(5%)		

Prior winning percentages: 2012 (75%), 2010 (78%), 2008 (70%), 2006 (67%), 2004 (82%), 2002 (76%), 2000 (59%), 1998 (65%), 1996 (64%), 1994 (70%), 1994 special (54%)

Population		Race and Ethnicity		Income	
Total:	767,552	White	76.0%	Median income:	$47,563
Urban:	6.5%	Latino	8.4%		*(273 of 435)*
Suburban:	20.0%	Amer. Indian	5.0%	Under $50,000	51.8%
Rural:	73.6%	Black	3.8%	$50,000-$99,999:	31.5%
Land area:	30,294	Two races	5.5%	$100,000-$199,999:	13.8%
Pop/sq. mi.:	25.3	White Ethnic	18.0%	$200,000 or more:	2.8%
Born in state:	64.2%			Poverty Rate	14.3%
		Education			
Age Groups		H.S. grad or less:	48.2%	**Work**	
Under 18:	24.5%	Some college:	29.7%	White collar:	31.0%
18 to 34:	23.9%	College degree, 4 yr.:	15.2%	Blue collar:	39.5%
35 to 64:	36.9%	Post-grad study:	6.9%	Sales and service:	29.5%
Over 64:	14.7%				
		Military		Govt. workers:	18.4%
		Veterans/active duty:	10.0%		

Western and Central Oklahoma: Suburbs of Oklahoma City and Tulsa

Settled at the turn of the 20th century, western Oklahoma is a fertile land forever at the mercy of the elements. The western plains are scorching hot under the summer sun and blown frozen by bitter winter winds. Visitors to the Tallgrass Prairie Preserve, maintained by the Nature Conservancy near

Voter Turnout	
2013 Total Citizen 18+	558,744
2014 House Turnout	169,605
2014 Turnout as % CVAP	30.4%
2012 Turnout as % CVAP	48.7%

Pawhuska, can experience what settlers found when they arrived here: a swaying ocean of 10-foot-high grasses filled with insects emitting a dull, incessant roar. Many rural counties here are not much more populated than they were 100 years ago. Today, local entrepreneurs see the possibility of economic revival in another abundant natural resource: the wind. Kansas company TradeWind has purchased multiple wind farm properties in western Oklahoma. The region is home to the world's largest plot of switchgrass, and there are hopes that it too can become a profitable source of alternative energy. Solar power also has started up in the Panhandle. In June 2015, a subsidiary of Arkansas Electric Cooperatives brought a 1-megawatt solar project to its headquarters in Hooker. In 2010, the state government set a goal of making Oklahoma 15% dependent on renewable energy by 2015. Early signs were that the state was ahead of schedule, the *Daily Oklahoman* reported.

The 3rd Congressional District includes Oklahoma's western plains and roughly half of the state's land. It includes the university town of Stillwater, and Osage County, site of the state's lone Indian reservation. A few of the southern counties, settled by farmers crossing the Red River from Texas, are ancestrally Democratic. But farmers coming south from Kansas settled most of these plains, and they were heavily Republican. Farther west in the Panhandle is Beaver County, which claims to be the cow-chip-throwing capital of the world. An increasing number of Hispanics are moving here to work on hog farms and in meatpacking plants. One of the largest oper-

2012 Presidential Vote		
Mitt Romney (R)	199,390	(74%)
Barack Obama (D)	70,346	(26%)
2008 Presidential Vote		
John McCain (R)	215,128	(73%)
Barack Obama (D)	79,941	(27%)
Cook Partisan Voting Index:	R+26	

ations is Seaboard Corp.'s plant in Guymon, which has more than 3,000 employees. Texas County, a wheat-growing area in the Panhandle, is almost 46% Hispanic, by far the highest percentage in the state. This is the most Republican district in the state, and among the top 10 for the GOP nationwide.

Frank Lucas (R)

Republican Frank Lucas, who won a 1994 special election, is a soft-spoken, unflashy farmer and rancher. As chairman of the Agriculture Committee until 2015, he sought to bridge deal-oriented lawmakers from farm states and budget-conscious conservatives. He has moved to create new niches at the Financial Services and Science committees.

Lucas' family roots in western Oklahoma extend more than 100 years; he owns a 480-acre farm and cattle ranch in Roger Mills County. He studied agricultural economics at Oklahoma State University, where he was active in the College Republicans and student government. He was elected to the Oklahoma House in 1988 at age 28 after losing two races. He shared an office there with Jim Reese, who became the state's secretary and commissioner of agriculture. "He's not a showboat," Reese told *The New York Times* in 2012. "He just goes about doing his work and tries to work with everybody and is not about getting credit for himself."

He ran for Congress when veteran conservative Democrat Glenn English resigned to head the National Rural Electric Cooperative Association. Lucas faced two rounds of serious competition. In the primary, he trailed state Sen. Brooks Douglass, who campaigned from his Oklahoma City base, 36%-34%. In the runoff, Lucas ridiculed "some Johnny-come-lately dressed up like a drugstore cowboy" and carried the rural areas to win 56%-44%. In the general, he faced Dan Webber, the 27-year-old press secretary to Democratic Sen. David Boren. Lucas ran an ad depicting the Capitol and saying, "This is where Dan Webber has worked his entire adult life." The ad displayed a picture of Oklahoma farmland and said, "This is where Frank Lucas has worked his entire adult life." Lucas won 54%-46%. Since then, he has been reelected by wide margins.

Lucas' voting record is mostly conservative. He has broken from conservative orthodoxy on economic matters. In 2011, he voted against GOP amendments to abolish or cut funding for federal programs such as rural airport subsidies and the Economic Development Administration. The Club for Growth threatened to recruit a primary opponent in 2014 after he scored in the bottom third among Republicans in the anti-tax group's legislative ratings in 2011 and 2012. He said that the criticism didn't bother him. "Any time I have to choose between the influences of D.C. political groups and my fellow Oklahomans, I will always side with my fellow Oklahomans," he told the *Tulsa World*.

His main focus has been the Agriculture Committee. During drafting of the 2002 farm bill, Lucas helped to unravel the 1996 Freedom to Farm Act and its rollback of government subsidies, although he had once embraced the law and its conservative philosophical underpinnings. Lucas helped write provisions to control erosion, aid farmers hit by drought, and protect air and water quality. He successfully fought a plan to reduce the number of Farm Service Agency field offices. In the minority during work on the 2008 farm bill, Lucas strongly opposed an overhaul of farm programs as "a threat to the nutrition of the whole, entire world," and he mostly succeeded in preserving subsidies for his district, which ranked 14th in subsidies between 1995 and 2009. With an eye on his district, Lucas helped to write the final provisions in the 2005 energy bill governing rural grants and biodiesel tax credits. He has been a proponent of government support for alternative fuels, particularly switchgrass.

He became ranking Republican on the committee in 2009 and rose to chairman in 2011. He found himself leading a committee full of freshmen and new members who did not share his bipartisan leanings. "Not everyone on the committee understands the history of farm bills, which have never been partisan by nature," he told *National Journal*. "Getting them to understand the culture is a process." He worked closely with Agriculture's ranking Democrat Collin Peterson of Minnesota to report a five-year farm bill from the committee in July 2012. Their plan called for reducing spending on agriculture programs by $35 billion over 10 years.

But the measure never came to a vote that year in the full House. Some conservatives wanted deeper cuts to the food stamp program, which Democrats fiercely resisted. In a closed-door GOP meeting, House Speaker John Boehner reportedly criticized the committee bill's dairy provisions—which contained a new market stabilization plan that major milk processors strongly opposed—as "communism." The delays frustrated Lucas, who labored for months to strike a deal acceptable to House GOP leaders, whom he referred to as "the management." After failing to reach a compromise in the 2012 lame-duck session, Lucas took another crack at trying to work out a deal in 2013.

By that summer, Lucas again thought he had found a political recipe to pass a bill. The legislation he managed to get to the floor looked to be a conservatives' dream: It cut spending $40 billion over 10 years, including $20 billion from the food stamp program, and it had bipartisan support from Peterson and many other farm-state Democrats. Discontented conservatives passed an amendment to give states the option of imposing work requirements on food stamp recipients, a move that shattered the delicate political coalition behind the bill. Lucas made a desperate last-minute plea on the House floor, but the farm bill failed on final passage, 195-234. Sixty-two Republicans voted against it while only 24 Democrats voted for it.

Back in his district in June 2013, the *Tulsa World* reported, conservative activists showed up at a Lucas town-hall meeting in Skiatook to protest his bill. He was the target of radio ads from Washington-based Heritage Action threatening to recruit a "real conservative" to run against him in 2014. "I'm under attack by those people," Lucas said. "They're coming after me. They are all special interest groups that exist to sell subscriptions, to collect seminar fees, and to perpetuate their goals." At one point, he lamented, "it shouldn't be this hard to pass a farm bill."

When he finally passed the bill in 2014, which Lucas called his "single biggest accomplishment" as chairman, he said that its "fundamental guise" was that it became an insurance measure in place of the direct payment program for farm commodities. "When things are beyond our control, or has been the case occasionally in my lifetime, have been manipulated by outside forces, outside governments or even sometimes government actions here at home—then these safety nets are necessary," as he explained the bill. The House passed the bill, 251-166, with bipartisan support in January 2014.

On the Financial Services Committee, Lucas has been a reliable supporter of the banking and insurance industries. The liberal Center for American Progress complained in

December 2010 when Lucas hired a former U.S. Chamber of Commerce lobbyist as the senior staffer to oversee the Commodity Futures Trading Commission, which was charged with implementing the new law cracking down on the financial industry, including provisions on over-the-counter derivatives.

As he prepared his term-limited exit from the Agriculture Committee helm, Lucas found himself, like other term-limited House GOP chairmen, looking for opportunities to remain relevant. Some members urged him to challenge Jeb Hensarling of Texas, the hard-edged chairman at Financial Services. But it's difficult to knock out a sitting chairman, especially one who has the support of the huge Texas delegation and where party leaders had no obvious reason to make a change.

When Hensarling refused to give him a subcommittee chairmanship, Lucas pursued another Texas chairman—Lamar Smith at Science, Space and Technology—and became vice chairman of that committee, though neither explained publicly what the job entailed. In early 2015, Lucas worked to build bridges on the panel to pass legislation. With fellow Oklahoma Republican Jim Bridenstine, Lucas shaped a bipartisan bill to improve weather forecasting. Lucas worked again with his Democratic ally Peterson on a bill to create a science advisory board to promote fairness and independence at the Environmental Protection Agency.

Back home, the real trouble for the easygoing Lucas seems to be on his ranch. He broke his nose years ago when a cow slammed a gate on him, and he lost a tooth while trying to attach an identification tag to a 250-pound heifer. When drought hit Oklahoma hard in 2011, he found himself forced to sell off some of his herd. "Watching my wife agonize over her mama cows, that's never any fun," he told the *Times*.

FOURTH DISTRICT

Tom Cole (R)

Elected 2002, 7th term; b. April 28, 1949, Shreveport, LA; Grinnell Col., B.A. 1971, Yale U., M.A. 1974, U. of OK, Ph.D. 1984; Methodist; married (Ellen); 1 child.

Elected Office: OK Senate, 1988-91.

Professional Career: Staff, U.S. Rep. Mickey Edwards, 1982-84; OK GOP chmn., 1985-89; Exec. dir., NRCC, 1991-95; OK secy. of st., 1995-99; Chief of staff, RNC, 1999-2000; Pol. consultant, 2000-02.

DC Office: 2467 RHOB, 20515, 202-225-6165; Fax: 202-225-3512; Website: cole.house.gov.

State Offices: Ada, 580-436-5375; Lawton, 580-357-2131; Norman, 405-329-6500.

Committees: *Appropriations:* Defense; Interior, Environment & Related Agencies; Labor, Health & Human Services, Education & Related Agencies (Chmn). *Budget. Rules.*

Group Ratings

	ADA	ACLU	AFL-CIO	LCV	ITI	COC	HAFA	ACU	CFG	FRC
2014	0%	5%	–	6%	100%	93%	45%	64%	53%	88%
2013	0%	C	33%	11%	C	83%	C	56%	49%	C

National Journal Ratings

	2013 LIB		2013 CONS
Economic	50%	—	49%
Social	43%	—	54%
Foreign	40%	—	59%
Composite	45%	—	55%

Key Votes of the 113th Congress

1. Sandy storm spending	Y	5. Medical Marijuana	N	9. Syrian Rebels Training	Y
2. Violence Against Women Act	Y	6. Farm Bill	Y	10. Keystone pipeline	Y
3. Guantanamo Bay Detainees	N	7. Afghanistan Combat	N	11. Immigration Exec. Action	Y
4. Abortion 20-week ban	Y	8. NSA Phone Data Collection	N	12. Bipartisan budget deal	Y

Election Results

2014 general	Tom Cole (R)	117,721	(71%)	$1,147,517
	Bert Smith (D)	40,998	(25%)	
	Dennis B. Johnson (I)	7,549	(5%)	
2014 primary	Tom Cole (R)	40,762	(84%)	
	Anna Flatt (R)	7,510	(16%)	

Prior winning percentages: 2012 (68%), 2010 (unopposed), 2008 (66%), 2006 (65%), 2004 (78%), 2002 (54%)

Population		Race and Ethnicity		Income	
Total:	776,394	White	72.9%	Median income:	$49,738
Urban:	39.4%	Latino	7.8%		*(245 of 435)*
Suburban:	28.1%	Black	6.1%	Under $50,000	50.3%
Rural:	32.5%	Amer. Indian	5.1%	$50,000-$99,999:	33.0%
Land area:	10,254	Two races	5.9%	$100,000-$199,999:	14.2%
Pop/sq. mi.:	75.7	White Ethnic	18.3%	$200,000 or more:	2.6%
Born in state:	60.7%			Poverty Rate	15.1%
		Education			
Age Groups		H.S. grad or less:	44.9%	**Work**	
Under 18:	23.9%	Some college:	31.7%	White collar:	34.1%
18 to 34:	25.6%	College degree, 4 yr.:	15.4%	Blue collar:	43.0%
35 to 64:	37.2%	Post-grad study:	8.0%	Sales and service:	23.0%
Over 64:	13.3%				
		Military		Govt. workers:	21.1%
		Veterans/active duty:	13.9%		

South-Central Oklahoma: Parts of Oklahoma City, Norman

In the years after 1900, the brown hills west of Oklahoma City and north of the Red River suddenly filled up with farmers riding north from Texas, past the quenched green lands of the east toward the bare pasturelands of the west. The first settlers here arrived just as the buffalo were dying out,

Voter Turnout	
2013 Total Citizen 18+	574,175
2014 House Turnout	166,268
2014 Turnout as % CVAP	29%
2012 Turnout as % CVAP	46.1%

down from an estimated 60 million animals to no more than 1,000. So in 1901, Republican President William McKinley established the nation's first wildlife preserve in the Wichita Mountains, 25 miles northwest of Lawton. Fifteen bison were donated by the New York Zoological Society and arrived at the preserve via rail in 1907—a major factor in the survival of the species. Today, this habitat supports grazing for Rocky Mountain elk, white-tailed deer and Texas longhorn cattle.

Government has played a role in the survival of the people, too. Population in southwest Oklahoma clusters around major government institutions: the University of Oklahoma in Norman, which was the world's first school of petroleum geology and is now home to the National Weather Center; Tinker Air Force Base in southern Oklahoma City; and the Army Field Artillery School at Fort Sill in Lawton. Fort Sill is the home of the Army Air Defense Artillery School, which was relocated from Fort Bliss, Texas, in 2009. With 118,000 people, Norman is the third-largest city in Oklahoma. Commercial development has been underway at University North Park, a site for six new office buildings on 60 acres that the univer-

sity sold to private interests. In March 2015, the city considered a $143 million package of capital improvements for the community, as proposed by Norman Forward. The area to the south of Norman is rural. The tiny community of Elmore City, with its prohibition of dancing, became the inspiration for the 1984 movie *Footloose* (dancing was legalized in the town in 1980).

2012 Presidential Vote		
Mitt Romney (R)	175,956	(67%)
Barack Obama (D)	86,357	(33%)

2008 Presidential Vote		
John McCain (R)	191,402	(66%)
Barack Obama (D)	97,901	(34%)

Cook Partisan Voting Index: R+19

The 4th Congressional District of Oklahoma begins smack dab in the middle of the state not far from the capitol in Oklahoma City, and spreads south and west to cover half of Oklahoma's Red River Valley. Demographically, this district is becoming more suburban, but the cultural tone remains countrified. The area is at the heart of Tornado Alley. Moore, outside Oklahoma City, has been the site of several deadly strikes, including one in 1999 that remains the strongest ever recorded. In May 2013, an EF-5 tornado struck Moore, killing 24 people, damaging at least 12,000 buildings, and leveling entire neighborhoods, including two elementary schools; its estimated $2 billion in damage placed it among the most costly tornados in the nation's history. Ancestrally, this is Democratic country. But Norman, Lawton and the Oklahoma City fringe have voted solidly Republican since the 1990s. This remains a strongly Republican district.

Tom Cole (R)

Tom Cole, first elected in 2002, is a politically savvy Republican who is a frequent source for reporters seeking to understand the GOP's inner workings. After a falling-out with then-Minority Leader John Boehner over Cole's rocky stewardship of the National Republican Congressional Committee, he has become a key Boehner ally and an increasingly active policy leader for the GOP. Cole was rated the "wisest" House Republican by *Washingtonian* magazine in 2014.

Cole grew up in Moore, south of Oklahoma City. He is a fifth-generation Oklahoman, and his mother was a state representative and senator. He is a member of the Chickasaw Nation tribe; more than half of the nation's Chickasaw Indians live in his district. Oklahoma GOP colleague Markwayne Mullin and Cole are the only American Indians in Congress. Cole's father served in the Air Force and later worked at Tinker Air Force Base. Cole graduated from Grinnell College, got a master's degree at Yale University, and a Ph.D. in British history at the University of Oklahoma, studying for a year at the University of London. From 1985 to 1989, he was the Oklahoma Republican Party chairman. In 1988, he was elected to the state Senate.

He moved to Washington in 1991 to become executive director of the NRCC, and over the next few years held jobs as chief of staff for the Republican National Committee in the 2000 election, the appointed Oklahoma secretary of state, and the president of a polling and political consulting firm in Oklahoma City. In 2002, when Republican Rep. J.C. Watts announced that he would not seek reelection, Cole was the early frontrunner. Despite his party connections and an endorsement from Watts, he faced formidable opposition from attorney Marc Nuttle. The two shared positions on most issues and extensive party connections. Nuttle had been Cole's predecessor at the NRCC and worked on Pat Robertson's 1988 presidential campaign. Nuttle and Cole also had worked together to pass an Oklahoma right-to-work law in a 2001 referendum. In the showdown between the strategists, Cole won 60%-33%.

In the general election, he had tough competition from former state Senate Majority Leader Darryl Roberts, who appealed to the "yellow dog" Democratic tradition that had remained strong in the Red River counties. Cole countered by linking Roberts to past Democratic presidential nominees he had supported, and described him as "pro-tax, pro-abortion, and pro-lawsuit." Cole won 54%-46%, and has been reelected with ease.

In the House, Cole has a mostly conservative voting record, though he occasionally has been ranked the least-conservative Republican in the Oklahoma delegation. He is a member of the GOP whip team. In a sign of his increasing value to Boehner, he returned in 2013 to the leadership-driven Rules Committee. "He doesn't play coy and he has good relationships on both sides of the aisle," University of Oklahoma political science professor Keith Gaddie told Oklahoma City's *Journal Record Legislative Report*. Colleagues value his understanding of politics. "He's an excellent political mechanic—one of the best," Oklahoma Sen. Jim Inhofe told *The Oklahoman*. "I never question his wisdom when he says something out of the norm."

Cole began his House career on the Armed Services Committee, a seat of obvious importance to the district. He has been actively involved in issues related to American Indians. The House in 2012 took up his bill to help foreign businesses invest in tribal enterprises, but it did not achieve the two-thirds majority required to get on a fast-track for passage. In the wake of an influence-peddling scandal involving Republican lobbyist Jack Abramoff, who represented several tribes, Cole strongly opposed the proposed limits on the right of tribes to contribute to political campaigns.

Cole differs from his younger conservative colleagues in his willingness to defend some government spending. From his plum seat on the Appropriations Committee, he tends to the needs of his district's military installations and supports federal programs that help his constituents. During the late 2012 negotiations over tax and spending to avoid the so-called "fiscal cliff," he urged his party to accept a tax-cut extension for all but the highest-earning Americans, a position that many Republicans subsequently adopted, leading to the bill's enactment. On the other hand, he led the fight that succeeded in 2014 to end taxpayer subsidies of political conventions. The appropriator has warned about the need to control entitlement spending. In a bill filed with Democratic Rep. John Delaney of Maryland, he has called for a bipartisan commission to recommend steps to guarantee the solvency of Social Security for decades to come. "Without immediate changes that modernize the current system, Social Security will not be able to pay the benefits that American workers have earned and have come to rely upon," Cole warned in March 2015.

In late 2013, Cole took an expanded role in critical budget talks with Senate Democrats, as one of four House Republicans appointed by Boehner to a conference committee seeking to end the partisan brinkmanship that had led to a 16-day government shutdown in October, which the public largely blamed on the House GOP. Earlier battles over taxes and spending had resulted in automatic, across-the-board cuts and threatened the nation's credit rating— all of which helped to produce historic lows in public confidence in the federal government. Working with Budget Committee Chairman Paul Ryan of Wisconsin, Cole was a skillful conciliator trusted by mainstream Republicans and conservative enough to maintain credibility with the restive tea party faction. A profile on the *Politico* website in October 2013 likened him to "the friendly uncle sent out to smoke a cigar and explain to the neighbors what all the noise is about in the basement," and called him "an important arbiter in upcoming budget talks."

In 2015, Cole became an Appropriations "cardinal" as chairman of the Subcommittee on Labor, Health and Human Services, Education and Related Agencies. In recent years, this spending bill typically made little progress toward agreement with Senate Democrats and instead became part of a status quo "continuing resolution" in the new fiscal year. With Republican Sen. Roy Blunt of Missouri, a Cole ally when he served in the House, taking over as chairman of the counterpart Senate panel, the door was opened to possible House-Senate consensus.

Campaign politics have been part of Cole's portfolio in the House. Following the dismal 2006 election for Republicans, he was elected chairman of the NRCC, in which he led GOP efforts to regain the House majority in 2008. Cole defeated Texan Pete Sessions, 102-81, to take over the committee, where he had cut his teeth as a political strategist years earlier. He expanded the playing field of competitive seats, but his chairmanship was a dismal time for the GOP. The party suffered a rough transition to the minority with many retirements, and the committee was $19 million in debt. Cole and the Republicans raised $116 million that cycle, compared with $171 million for the Democrats. Making matters worse, the committee discovered that its longtime treasurer had embezzled hundreds of thousands of dollars. The biggest obstacle was largely out of Cole's control: President George W. Bush's low public approval ratings, which made reelection an uphill climb for Republicans in competitive seats. The party lost 24 seats during the cycle.

In that period, the relationship between Cole and Boehner was marked by public sniping over who was to blame for the party's electoral failure. Boehner believed that Cole's top staffers at the NRCC were not sufficiently aggressive at fundraising and candidate recruitment, and created an advisory group to look over his shoulder. When Cole sought another two years as chairman, Sessions had the active support of Boehner. Sensing that he could lose a showdown of House Republicans, Cole withdrew. In a spirit of conciliation, Boehner gave Cole the seat on Appropriations. Cole found his way back into Boehner's good graces through aggressive fundraising, plus his savvy combination of legislative skills and political instincts. He called Republicans who voted against Boehner for speaker in January 2015 "pretty unprofessional and very disappointing." Some Republicans speculate that Cole could be part of a future leadership team.

FIFTH DISTRICT

Steve Russell (R)

Elected 2014, 1st term; b. May 25, 1963, Oklahoma City; Ouachita Baptist U., B.A. 1985, Command & General Staff Col., M.A. 1998; Baptist; married (Cindy); 5 children.

Military Career: Army, 1985-2006. (Kosovo, Kuwait, Afghanistan and Iran).

Elected Office: OK Senate, 2008-12.

Professional Career: Motivational speaker & author, 2007-14; Founder/owner, Two River Arms gun company, 2010-14.

DC Office: 128 CHOB, 20515, 202-225-2132; Fax: 202-226-1463; Website: russell.house.gov.

State Offices: Del City, 405-602-3074.

Committees: *Armed Services:* Readiness; Seapower & Projection Forces. *Education & the Workforce:* Early Childhood, Elementary & Secondary Education; Workforce Protections. *Oversight & Government* Reform: Interior; National Security (VChmn).

Election Results

2014 general	Steve Russell (R)	95,632	(60%)	$845,411	$153,301
	Al McAffrey (D)	57,790	(36%)	$176,110	
2014 primary runoff	Steve Russell (R)	19,371	(59%)		
	Patrice Douglas (R)	13,315	(41%)		
2014 primary	Steve Russell (R)	14,597	(27%)		
	Patrice Douglas (R)	13,440	(25%)		
	Clark Jolley (R)	9,226	(17%)		
	Mike Turner (R)	7,757	(14%)		
	Shane Jett (R)	7,019	(13%)		
	Harvey Sparks (R)	2,895	(5%)		

Prior winning percentages: 2012 (59%), 2010 (63%)

Population		Race and Ethnicity		Income	
Total:	785,441	White	59.6%	Median income:	$44,597
Urban:	63.2%	Latino	14.9%		*(326 of 435)*
Suburban:	23.8%	Black	13.5%	Under $50,000	54.6%
Rural:	13.1%	Amer. Indian	4.2%	$50,000-$99,999:	27.7%
Land area:	2,614	Two races	5.0%	$100,000-$199,999:	13.9%
Pop/sq. mi.:	300.5	White Ethnic	15.9%	$200,000 or more:	3.8%
Born in state:	59.9%			Poverty Rate	18.7%
		Education			
Age Groups:		H.S. grad or less:	41.4%	**Work**	
Under 18:	25.4%	Some college:	29.9%	White collar:	34.1%
18 to 34:	25.4%	College degree, 4 yr.:	19.0%	Blue collar:	43.5%
35 to 64:	36.6%	Post-grad study:	9.6%	Sales and service:	22.4%
Over 64:	12.6%			Govt. workers:	15.2%
		Military			
		Veterans/active duty:	9.2%		

Oklahoma City Area

Oklahoma City, like many state capitals, was not the spontaneous creation of commerce but the deliberate creation of government, sited in the geographic center of the state on what turned out to be oil land. Rigs were pumping crude on the grounds of the Capitol until 1989. The land here is browner

Voter Turnout	
2013 Total Citizen 18+	536,861
2014 House Turnout	159,133
2014 Turnout as % CVAP	29.6%
2012 Turnout as % CVAP	50%

and more eroded by creeks than the rolling Oklahoma farmland to the east. Oklahoma City's population grew briskly from 506,000 in 2000 to 611,000 in 2013, a 21% increase, and the city now extends into four counties. Soaring farm commodities prices helped to keep the economy strong while much of the nation was mired in recession. Oklahoma City's unemployment rate has been among the lowest in the nation: 3.2% in April 2015. The commercial real estate market is growing, with a number of high-end stores setting up shop. The increase in sales tax revenue had dropped to 4% in early 2015.

2012 Presidential Vote		
Mitt Romney (R)	156,035	(59%)
Barack Obama (D)	107,344	(41%)
2008 Presidential Vote		
John McCain (R)	170,003	(59%)
Barack Obama (D)	116,877	(41%)
Cook Partisan Voting Index:	R+12	

Oklahoma City is best known nationally for a profound tragedy: the day in April 1995 when a bomb destroyed the Alfred P. Murrah Federal Building, killing 168 people and injuring more than 680. Five years later, the Oklahoma City National Memorial opened on the site of the blast. Domestic terrorist Timothy McVeigh, a militia movement sympathizer, was put to death in 2001 for his crime. Local pride spiked in 2008 when the Seattle SuperSonics of the National Basketball Association relocated to the city and became the Oklahoma City Thunder, the state's first major sports franchise. The team's successful run to the NBA finals in 2012 energized and expanded the city's fan base. Oklahoma City Mayor Mick Cornett told *GQ* that the team helped to promote the city: "Nobody in Paris is waking up thinking about Oklahoma City. But they *might* be watching an international game and see us playing the Lakers." In June 2015, a new owner made plans to redevelop the historic First National Center in downtown.

The 5th Congressional District is centered in Oklahoma City and includes most of Oklahoma County. It also takes in Pottawatomie and Seminole counties to the east. Oklahoma County, which is the bluest in the state, casts more than 90% of the vote. The district overall is solidly Republican.

Steve Russell (R)

Republican Steve Russell, elected in 2014, is accustomed to a fight. He survived several life-threatening events as a child, was part of the military unit that captured Saddam Hussein in Iraq, and won the nomination for the House in a runoff after a combative primary. He succeeded James Lankford, who was elected to the Senate.

Russell nearly died soon after birth because his blood type differed from that of his mother. At age seven, he almost perished again, in a deadly tornado, while he was visiting his grandparents. Later that year, Russell suffered a ruptured appendix and underwent two surgeries, spending weeks in intensive care. After graduating high school (where he was voted most likely to succeed), Russell graduated from Ouachita Baptist University on an ROTC scholarship. He was commissioned as a second lieutenant in the Army Infantry and ultimately reached the rank of lieutenant colonel.

In the military, Russell served in Kosovo, Kuwait, Afghanistan and Iraq, where his unit was part of the effort to find Saddam. Decorated several times for his service, he retired from the military in 2006 and returned to Oklahoma, where he wrote a book, *We Got Him! A Memoir of the Hunt and Capture of Saddam Hussein.*

In 2008, Russell won a seat in the Oklahoma state Senate, winning a runoff after a highly contested four-way primary. In the legislature, Russell focused on two issues important to him—veterans and abortion—and authored a law that made Oklahoma-serving military members exempt from taxes. He declined to run for reelection in 2012 so he could promote his book and start a small rifle-manufacturing business, Two River Arms.

In 2014, Russell led the six-way Republican primary with 27% of the vote, and faced a runoff with runner-up, Patrice Douglas, commissioner of the Oklahoma Corporation Commission. Douglas was the initial frontrunner, as she was better-funded and had more establishment Republican connections. Russell benefited from tea party backing. Both the Russell and Douglas campaigns claimed to have Lankford's support, though Lankford said he hadn't endorsed either of them. Douglas spent $1 million, compared to about $400,000 that Russell spent for the nomination. Russell won the runoff easily, with 59% of the vote. The outcome in November against Democrat Al McAffrey, the first openly gay legislator in Oklahoma, was a foregone conclusion. Russell won 60%-36%.

In the House, Russell was assigned to the Education and the Workforce and Oversight and Government Reform committees, and he was selected to fill a vacancy on Armed Services in March. He was the freshman representative on the GOP Steering Committee that made House committee assignments, and supported John Boehner for speaker based, he said, on the need for "continuity of leadership." Russell continued the practice of retired GOP Sen. Tom Coburn of Oklahoma to issue regular "Waste Watch" reports on government spending. He voted with House Republicans on most major issues, except for his opposition to trade promotion authority for President Barack Obama, who he said had "exhibited poor leadership in foreign affairs."

In an interview with *The New York Times* in March 2015, Russell said that a difficult part of serving in Congress is the role of outside groups that profit from conflict. "There's people enriching themselves, making millions in this town off fomenting division and conflict. And I think that's shameful," he said.

★ OREGON ★

Oregon is an experimental commonwealth, a laboratory of reform, a maker of national trends—with varying results. Bike trails now exist throughout the country; bike boulevards are catching on, but not as prevalent, yet. You can find light-rail trams in many central cities, but not so many solar energy-powered, plug-in stations for electric cars. Oregon produces (or has manufactured in China) Nike sneakers and Pendleton shirts, but its handcrafted ales don't travel far from the Oregon Brewers Festival. For all its modern advances, however, you can still see much of the same Oregon that Lewis and Clark saw in 1805, when they came down the Columbia River gorge, past the Willamette River to the Pacific Ocean. A few years later, in 1811, John Jacob Astor set up his fur trading post at Astoria. But few Americans came overland until the 1840s, when New England Yankees drove wagons along the Oregon Trail and floated down the Columbia to the well-watered Willamette Valley.

In this remote spot, nearly 2,000 miles from the Mississippi River frontier and 700 miles from the small Mexican settlements in California, they built an orderly, productive society—a kind of western New England. It grew steadily, with a few booms—in the early 1900s as timber harvesting surged, during World War II, when Kaiser shipyards in Portland and Vancouver churned out "Liberty" and "Victory" ships, and then again in the 1970s, when homebuilding skyrocketed and Oregon's natural environment began to be widely appreciated. The settlers brought New England town-meeting attitudes to Oregon. This was the second state to give people direct decision-making via the initiative and referendum; South Dakota did it first, but Oregon's measure was widely copied, and it has used the procedure more than any other state. It pioneered the election of U.S. senators by popular vote and, with Michigan in 1908, the recall of elected officials. It was the first state to institute Labor Day. In recent decades, it was first to sanction assisted suicide and to adopt mail-in ballot elections.

Oregon grew much faster than the national average in the 1940s, when war industries brought thousands of people to the West Coast, and again in the 1970s, when the pleasant environment attracted so many young people the state's population shot up 26%. Containing growth became the hot local issue. "Come and visit us again and again," Republican Gov. Tom McCall told outsiders. "But for heaven's sake don't come here to live." At McCall's prodding, the legislature in 1973 passed a law that in many ways limited development, and in the 1990s, the Portland metropolitan area sharply restricted growth and sprawl. These measures were popular in Portland and the university towns of Eugene and Corvallis and to a lesser extent in the suburbs. The lumber industry, which for decades accounted for most of Oregon's exports, was already sliding when it took another major blow in the 1990s from federal land-use restrictions imposed to protect the threatened spotted owl. Productivity gains from technology advances and greater automation also contributed to slack employment in the timber sector. But Oregon has remained a leader in producing Christmas trees, mainly in the counties around Salem and mostly for sale in arid California.

Such policies, even as they devastated the economies of some rural areas, attracted environment-minded migrants to Portland and the university towns. And some of those newcomers helped build the state's new economy. Oregon struggled in the 1980s as it began the transition from a resource-based economy centered on timber, fishing and agriculture, to one that placed more emphasis on manufacturing and high-technology. Indeed, the growth of high-tech companies around Portland was such that the area became known as Silicon Forest, where Intel, the largest tech employer in the state, shares the stage with homegrown firms like Mentor Graphics, FEI Co. and Rentrack Corp. Unemployment spiked during the 2007-09 recession to a peak of 11.6% in May 2009. The tech industry accounted for a disproportionate amount of the state's jobs gains in the most recent economic rebound. And those jobs were high paying: The Oregon Office of Economic Analysis reported in 2013 that the average high tech salary in the state was roughly $94,000, while the state's overall average wage was just over $44,000. That year, tech workers accounted for 12 percent of the state's entire payroll, an amount equal to the share of Oregon wages that employees in wood products businesses earned in the 1970s, during the peak of the timber industry. Oregon is also a top exporter, roughly $21 billion worth in 2014. Three of the state's top four export products were in high-tech fields: processors and controllers for electronic integrated circuits (first), machines for manufacturing semiconductors (third) and digital processing units (fourth).

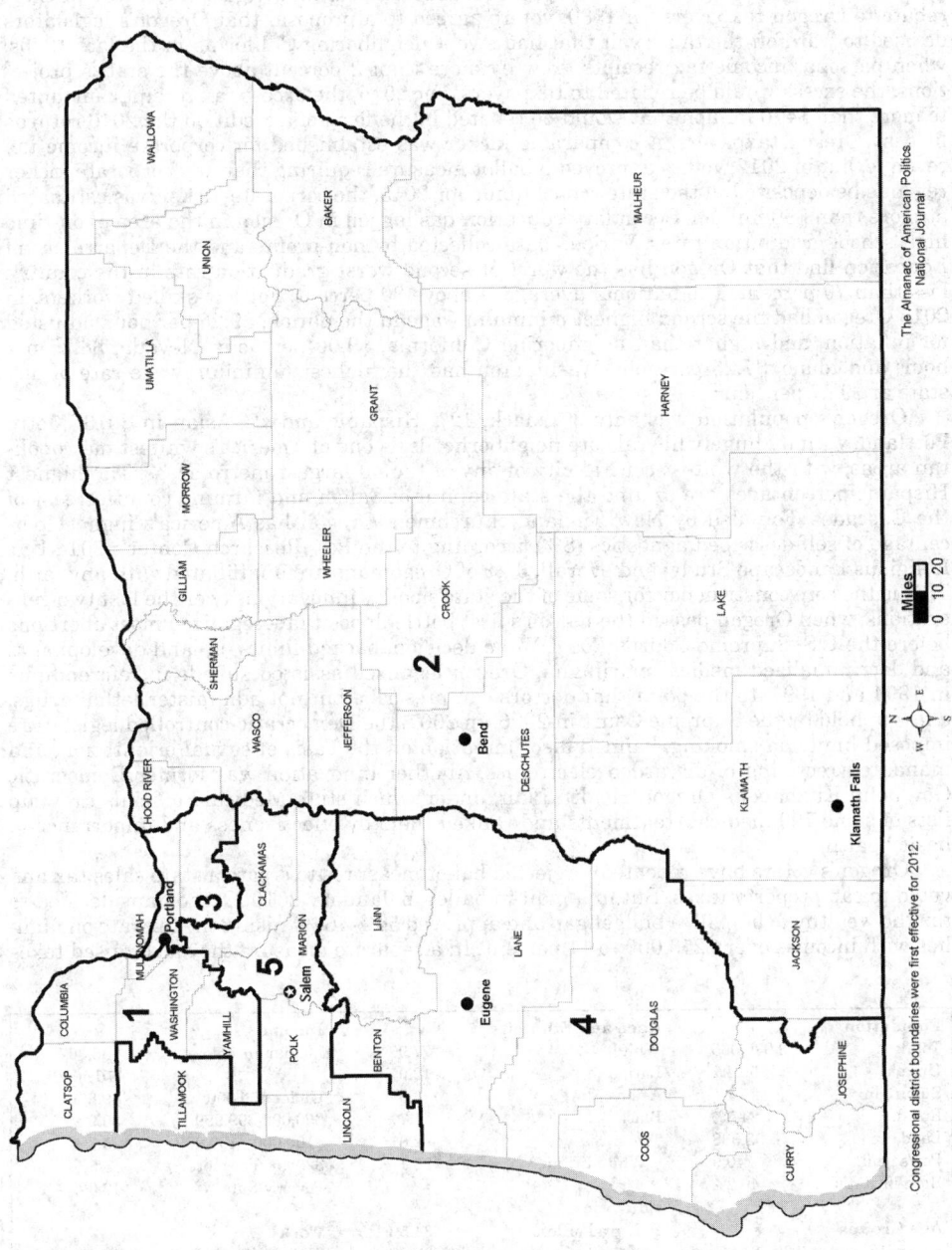

Congressional district boundaries were first effective for 2012.

The Almanac of American Politics.
National Journal

The state's second biggest export was wheat. The state's largest trading partners are China, Canada, Malaysia, Japan and South Korea.

In 2014, Oregon's GDP grew by 3.6%, the sixth best performance in the country, and by April 2015 its unemployment rate fell to 5.2%, a mark comparable to pre-recession levels in the state. That kind of growth caused state revenues to soar and trigger the state's "kicker" rebate to Oregon taxpayers. In 1980, voters agreed to a proposal that Oregon's legislators devised to ward off the tax revolt that had swept neighboring California in the late 1970s: when personal income tax receipts grew by more than 2 percent above the state's projections, the excess would be rebated to taxpayers. For 2015, the excess tax receipts amounted to more than $470 million that would be rebated in the form of a credit on the 2016 returns filed by Oregon taxpayers. A comparable kicker was established for corporate income tax revenue, but in 2012, voters approved a ballot measure requiring that any corporate kicker revenue be deposited in the state school fund. For 2015, the corporate kicker was estimated at more than $90 million. Secondary education has lagged in Oregon in the area of on-time high school graduation rates. Various data collected by non-profits and the Department of Education find that Oregon has the worst or second-worst graduation rate in the country, less than 70 percent. The national average is above 80 percent. For low-skilled workers, in 2015 Oregon had the second highest minimum wage in the nation, $9.25 per hour, adjusted for inflation, and higher than neighboring California, $9.00 per hour; Nevada, $8.25 per hour; and Idaho, $7.25 per hour. Washington had the highest minimum wage rate of any state at $9.47 per hour.

Oregon's population was only 2% black, 12% Hispanic and 4% Asian in 2013. Metro Portland, with its hugely liberal core neighborhoods, is one of America's whitest metropolitan areas, with the whitest central city of any of the 40 largest metro areas. The highest Hispanic percentages are around the state capital of Salem and farming counties east of the Cascades. Founded by New England churchmen, Oregon has America's highest percentage of self-described agnostics (8%) according to the Pew Research Center's 2014 U.S. Religious Landscape Study; and overall, 31% of Oregonians are unaffiliated with any faith. This is the core constituency for some of the state's policy innovations over the last two generations, when Oregon passed the nation's first bottle-deposit law, legalized most abortions before the U.S. Supreme Court's *Roe v. Wade* decision, backed limits on land development, and decriminalized medical marijuana. Oregon legalized assisted suicide in referendums in 1994 and 1997, to the point that doctors can prescribe but not administer lethal drugs, a law upheld by the Supreme Court in 2006. In 2007, the Democratic-controlled legislature imposed limits on smoking, banned discrimination on the basis of sexual orientation, and mandated recycling of discarded electronics. Another innovation was former Democratic Gov. John Kitzhaber's Oregon Health Plan, under which state Medicaid officials drew up lists of some 700 medical treatments and ranked them by effectiveness and importance to basic health.

Oregon's voters have repeatedly rejected ballot measures to create a state sales tax and voted to cap property taxes. But in a mail-in ballot in January 2010, Oregonians decided to tax the wealthy to help fill a budget gap and approved 54%-46%, raising the tax rate on families with incomes over $250,000 to 11 percent. In a separate measure they also raised taxes

Population		Race and Ethnicity		Income	
Total:	3,930,065	White	77.9%	Median income:	$56,307
Urban:	50.4%	Latino	12.0%		(16 of 50)
Suburban:	25.1%	Asian	3.9%	Under $50,000	49.8%
Rural:	24.5%	Black	1.7%	$50,000-$99,999:	30.9%
Land area:	95,988	Two races	2.8%	$100,000-$199,999:	15.8%
Pop/sq. mi.:	40.9	White Ethnic	26.1%	$200,000 or more:	3.5%
Born in state:	46.2%			Poverty Rate	12.0%
		Education			
Age Groups		H.S. grad or less:	34.5%	**Work**	
Under 18:	21.9%	Some college:	34.8%	White collar:	36.7%
18 to 34:	22.9%	College degree, 4 yr.:	19.3%	Blue collar:	42.3%
35 to 64:	39.8%	Post-grad study:	11.5%	Sales and service:	20.9%
Over 64:	15.4%				
		Military		Govt. workers:	13.7%
		Veterans/active duty:	9.3%		

on corporations. Nike founder and Chairman Phil Knight campaigned against the hikes, calling them "Oregon's Assisted Suicide Law II." By 2012, 55,000 Oregonians had a medical marijuana card; penalties for possession of up to one ounce of the substance are the equivalent of a traffic ticket. In 2014, Oregon's voters handily approved a measure legalizing recreational marijuana use among adults 21 years

Voter Turnout	
2013 Total Citizen 18+	2,854,921
2014 Highest Statewide Turnout	1,469,717
2014 Turnout as % CVAP	51.5%
2012 Turnout as % CVAP	63%

Legislature		
Senate:	18D	12R
House:	35D	25R

old and older. That same year, Oregonians barely rejected a ballot measure requiring labels on genetically engineered foods by 837 votes out of more than 1.5 million cast. Not only was it one of the closest elections in the state's history, it was also Oregon's most well-funded ballot proposition fight: opponents raised almost $21 million, including some $6 million from Monsanto. Proponents raised about $8.2 million. Sometimes Oregon's liberals have moved faster than the state's voters. In 2004, Portland's Multnomah County Commission chairman ordered clerks to issue marriage licenses to same-sex couples. Opponents gathered signatures and voters approved an amendment to the state constitution banning same-sex marriage by a 57%-43% margin. The legislature did endorse domestic partnerships in 2007, and in 2014 a federal District Court judge struck down the constitutional amendment and legalized same-sex marriage in the state.

The voting in these elections and on many ballot propositions has followed a similar pattern. Huge margins for liberal candidates and positions in Portland and the university towns of Eugene and Corvallis contrast with huge conservative margins in counties east of the Cascades and in much of southwestern Oregon, where discontent over the policies that decimated the logging industry has lingered. In the last three presidential elections, Democrats won 72%, 77%, and 75% in Multnomah County, while Republicans carried the counties east of the Cascades with 63%, 56%, and 60%. The 2010 election produced a 30-30 tie in the state House, which led to the election of Democratic and Republican co-speakers. Voting in all the state's elections is by mail, which voters authorized in a 1998 referendum. Since then, Democrats have regained control. There are no polls open on Election Day and voters have until the night of the election to get their ballots to an election clerk. Proponents of mail-in ballots argue that they increase the percentage of people who vote, which has always been high in Oregon anyway, and that they give voters time to read over and think about ballot initiatives. Opponents say that mail-in voting increases the possibility of fraud. Gradually, other states have followed Oregon's lead: Washington state approved mail-in-only voting in 2011 and Colorado adopted the system for the 2014 elections.

Presidential Politics Oregon was once the most Republican state in the West, the only one voting for Thomas Dewey over Harry Truman in 1948 and voting for other losing Republican nominees in 1960 and 1976. By the late 1980s, it had become one of the most Democratic states, voting for Democrats who lost the race for president in 1988, 2000, and 2004. For a time, the unpopularity of Clinton administration logging policies in much of Oregon threatened to make the state competitive, and Al Gore carried it by only 47.0%-46.5% in 2000, with 5% for Green Party candidate Ralph Nader. Nader was not on the ballot in 2004, and John Kerry won here 51%-47%. During most of the 2008 and 2012 election cycles, Oregon seemed solidly Democratic, though a few polls suggested it might be competitive.

But it wasn't, and Barack Obama carried the state by 57%-40% in 2008 and by a reduced 55%-42% in 2012.

Oregon once had an important presidential primary held in late May. In 1948, Oregon ended Republican Harold Stassen's presidential prospects, when he lost 52%-48% to Dewey. In 1968, Oregon gave Democrat Robert Kennedy the only defeat in his electoral career when it voted 44%-38% for Eugene McCarthy. Oregon in those days was part of any West Coast campaign swing, just before the California primary, at a time when candidates were not used to routinely

2012 Presidential Vote
Barack Obama (D) 970,488 (55%)
Mitt Romney (R)................754,175 (42%)

2012 Presidential Primary
Mitt Romney (R)................204,176 (72%)
Ron Paul (R) 36,810 (13%)
Rick Santorum (R) 27,042 (10%)
Newt Gingrich (R)................15,451 (5%)

2008 Presidential Vote
Barack Obama (D) 1,037,291 (57%)
John McCain (R)................738,475 (40%)

crisscrossing the country and, like NFL teams in the 1950s, scheduled West Coast contests together to minimize travel time.

For 1996, Oregon scheduled its primary for Super Tuesday in March, but it was overshadowed by bigger contests in the South. In 2000 and 2004, the primary was held again in May, well after the parties' nominees were determined. But in 2004, Ohio Democrat Dennis Kucinich spent four weeks campaigning in Oregon, hoping to rally a constituency with his New Age ideas, which included a proposed U.S. Department of Peace. He nonetheless lost to Kerry 79%-16%. In 2008, the primary was again held in May, when the race between Obama and Hillary Clinton was still raging. Obama carried Oregon 59%-41%, with especially large margins in Multnomah County and the university towns. John McCain, already the GOP's de facto nominee by the time of the primary, defeated Ron Paul, 85%-15%. The May 2012 primary again came after the Republican race was decided, and Mitt Romney defeated Ron Paul, 71%-13%, out of 287,955 ballots cast.

Congressional Districts Oregon narrowly missed gaining a sixth seat in the 2010 census, but in 2011, its legislature accomplished something it hadn't been able to do in over 100 years: It passed its own congressional redistricting plan. The odds were that the remap would go to court, since Democrats controlled the governorship and the state Senate, and the parties were tied at 30 seats apiece in the state House.

Republicans pushed for the 1st District, which needed to shed about 36,000 residents, to cede heavily Democratic Portland west of the Willamette River to the Democratic 3rd District. But suburban migration had given Democrats a comfortable cushion in the 1st anyway, and there was a compromise to be had: Democrats wanted to shift Corvallis, home of Oregon State University, to the Eugene-based 4th District in case Democrat Peter DeFazio retired. In the deal, Democrats

114th Congress Lineup	
1 R	4 D
113th Congress Lineup	
1 R	4 D

let the Portland-based 3rd pick up some of Democrat Kurt Schrader's already tiny share of Portland, keeping his 5th District competitive. Legislators barely touched the huge and politically secure eastern Oregon 2nd District of Republican Greg Walden. Traditionally progressive Oregon is now the last West Coast state without an independent redistricting commission of some kind.

Governor

Kate Brown (D)

Assumed office Feb. 2015, term expires Jan. 2017; b. June 21, 1960, Torrejón de Ardoz, Spain; U. of CO Boulder, B.A. 1981, Northwestern Schl. of Law, J.D. 1985; married (Dan); 2 children.

Elected Office: OR House, 1991-96; OR Senate, 1997-2008, maj. ldr., 2004; OR Secy. of St., 2008-15.

Professional Career: Practicing atty.; Instructor, Portland St. U.

Office: 160 State Capitol, 900 Court St., Salem, 97301-4047, 503-378-4582; Website: oregon.gov/gov.

Democrat Kate Brown was sworn in as Oregon governor in February 2015 following the resignation of John Kitzhaber, who had just been reelected in November to a fourth term. Kitzhaber, a Democrat, became enmeshed in a scandal over the awarding of state consulting work to his fiancée that prompted multiple investigations. Because Oregon has no lieutenant governor, Brown was next in line as secretary of state, a job she had held since 2009. Brown's ascension to the job drew considerable national attention not just because of the circumstances that led to Kitzhaber's departure, but because she is the nation's first openly bisexual governor.

She was born in Spain, where her father served in the Air Force, but raised in Minnesota. She received a bachelor's degree in environmental conservation, with a certificate in women's studies, from the University of Colorado at Boulder, then obtained her law degree from Lewis & Clark College. She practiced family law in Portland and worked for a non-profit legal services group. Brown got her start in politics in 1991, when, while working as an advocate for the Women's Rights Coalition, she was appointed by the Multnomah County Board of Commissioners to fill a vacancy in the Oregon House. A year later, the state representative that Brown replaced, Judy Bauman, wanted her seat back and challenged Brown in the Democratic primary. Bauman was more politically connected, but Brown went door-to-door and waged a vigorous grassroots campaign and won the primary by seven votes. In 1996, Brown won a seat in the Oregon Senate and quickly was named its Democratic caucus leader. Brown married in 1997, and publicly acknowledged her bisexuality after the *Oregonian* reported on it when she was a state lawmaker. "Some days I feel like I have a foot in both worlds, yet never really belonging to either," she wrote in an essay for a website tracking gay and lesbian elected officials. She rose to majority leader in 2004, becoming the first woman to occupy that post. In that position, Brown championed government transparency and helped create the state's new online database for campaign transactions, which replaced the state's outdated public campaign finance reporting system. In 2007, she pushed an ethics law limiting the value of lobbyist gifts to lawmakers to $50. She announced her candidacy for secretary of state in 2007 and won election a year later in a 51%-46% victory over Republican Rick Dancer, a former TV journalist.

During her time in office, she drew attention for helping Oregon implement an online voter-registration system—it was the fourth state to do so in 2010—and for using iPad technology to make voting more accessible to people with disabilities. But in 2012, she came under fire when her office notified two candidates for labor commissioner that their elections would be held in November instead of the following May, a move that critics said appeared to be aimed at helping the Democratic candidate. *The Oregonian* endorsed Republican Knute Buehler for the job. The election switch "isn't, by itself, justification to turn Brown out of office," it said. "But it has eroded public confidence in Brown, if not the office itself, and it's one reason for voters to give serious consideration to Buehler, who is anything but rigidly partisan." Brown won reelection anyway.

Kitzhaber was a prominent figure in Oregon politics: He was elected to a second stint as governor in 2010, having served from 1995 to 2003. In recent years, he drew attention by working out a unique deal with the Obama administration that called for the federal government to help the state patch a $2 billion hole in its Medicaid budget in return for keeping the program's growth rate at 2% slower than the rest of the nation. But he ran into trouble when Oregon's health-care exchange system proved to be a disaster, and won reelection in 2014 with just under 50% of the vote. The summer before his reelection, Kitzhaber became engaged to Cylvia Hayes, who ran an environmental consulting business. Hayes made headlines shortly thereafter when *Willamette Week* reported that in 1997, while she was a college student, she accepted $5,000 to marry an Ethiopian immigrant so he could retain U.S. residency and pursue a college education. But her involvement with the governor became a serious problem for him in early 2015, when authorities began looking into whether she had benefited financially from her relationship with him and whether she had properly disclosed the consulting fees she had been paid. "We knew there was a gray area, and we took intentional steps to try to clearly separate her volunteer activities as first lady from her paid professional work," Kitzhaber said at a January news conference at which he vowed not to resign. As Kitzhaber's political troubles mounted he became beleaguered: He twice made plans to resign, only to then change his mind. Even when he announced his final decision, he sent a mixed message. While he acknowledged he had "become a liability to the very institutions and policies to which I have dedicated my career," he said he was confident he had not been "dishonest or dishonorable."

In taking over for Kitzhaber, Brown stressed the need to restore trust in government. She called on lawmakers to strengthen the Oregon Government Ethics Commission and said neither she nor any members of her household and staff would accept any outside business. She won approval for a new law that automatically registers voters when they obtain or renew their drivers' licenses or any other state identification card, the nation's first state law to make voter registration automatic. The enactment of the new voting law is a culmination of Brown's reform efforts—she initially crafted and pushed the measure in 2013 when she was secretary of state. New registrants will be notified they've been added to the voting rolls and given 21 days to opt out of registering. The legislature also set up a campaign finance task force after it sidelined campaign spending limits the governor had personally lobbied lawmakers to approve. Brown also won approval for her proposals to strengthen the state's Ethics Commission, limiting the governor's appointments to the commission as well as the amount of time it could take to conduct investigations. At the same time, the reforms would require greater disclosure for the commission's investigative work. Brown signed a number of progressive measures approved by the state legislature including: mandatory paid sick leave for most Oregon workers; a bill making it illegal for employers to ask about applicants' criminal background on job applications; a new system for collecting data about racial profiling by law enforcement officers; an employee-funded workplace-based retirement savings program, and a gun control measure that requires a background check for most private sales.

Brown had some difficulty leading a squabbling state Senate and House of Representatives, both controlled by Democrats, on some issues. Efforts to raise the minimum wage fell victim to differences between the two chambers. Brown's biggest disappointment probably was the failure of the legislature to adopt a major transportation bill. Early in her tenure, Brown signed a contentious bill extending Oregon's clean fuels program, which infuriated Republican lawmakers. But in order to gain a transportation-funding bill, she agreed to trade away the clean fuels standards extension she had signed for an increase in the gas tax to pay for roadway construction and repair. That idea angered environmentalists. She tried to work with Senate leaders to craft a compromise, but when House Democrats balked at any bargain, Brown had to concede defeat. Notwithstanding that setback, legislators welcomed Brown's more collegial approach towards governing compared to her predecessor, Kitzhaber, who was seen as aloof and arrogant in his dealings with lawmakers in Salem. Republican state Sen. Jeff Kruse told the *Oregonian*, "We traded up; John was King John. He did not play well in the sandbox with others." With the generally favorable reviews she's won, Brown appears likely to run in the 2016 special election for the remainder of Kitzhaber's term. Her potential GOP challengers could include former state Rep. Dennis Richardson, the Republican who lost to Kitzhaber in the 2014 election, and Allen Alley who lost the 2010 GOP gubernatorial primary to Chris Dudley. Whoever the opponent is, Brown will be favored to win in 2016: Republicans haven't won an Oregon governor's race since 1986.

Senior Senator

Ron Wyden (D)

Elected Jan. 1996, term expires Jan. 2017, 3rd full term; b. May 3, 1949, Wichita, KS; Stanford U., B.A. 1971, U. of OR, J.D. 1974; Jewish; married (Nancy Bass-Wyden); 5 children.

Elected Office: U.S. House, 1981-96.

Professional Career: Co-dir. & co-founder, OR Gray Panthers, 1974-80; Dir., OR Legal Svcs. for the Elderly, 1977-79; Instructor, U. of OR, 1976, Portland St. U., 1979, U. of Portland, 1980.

DC Office: 221 DSOB, 20510, 202-224-5244; Fax: 202-228-2717; Website: wyden.senate.gov.

State Offices: Bend, 541-330-9142; Eugene, 541-431-0229; La Grande, 541-962-7691; Medford, 541-858-5122; Portland, 503-326-7525; Salem, 503-589-4555.

Committees: *Budget. Energy & Natural Resources:* Nat'l Parks; Public Lands, Forests, & Mining (RMM); Water & Power. *Finance* (RMM): Int'l Trade, Customs & Global Competitiveness (RMM); Taxation & IRS Oversight; ex officio member on all remaining subcommittees. *Intelligence (Select). Joint Committee on Taxation.*

Group Ratings

	ADA	ACLU	AFL-CIO	LCV	ITI	COC	HAFA	ACU	CFG	FRC
2014	95%	100%	–	80%	100%	25%	3%	4%	15%	0%
2013	90%	C	94%	100%	C	38%	C	4%	0%	C

National Journal Ratings

	2013 LIB	—	2013 CONS
Economic	82%	—	8%
Social	71%	—	27%
Foreign	49%	—	49%
Composite	70%	—	30%

Key Votes of the 113th Congress

1. Sandy storm spending	Y	5. Student Loan Rates	Y	9. Bipartisan Budget Deal	Y
2. Chuck Hagel Confirmation	Y	6. Employee Non-Discrim'n Act	Y	10. Farm Bill Conference Rept.	Y
3. Gun Background Checks	Y	7. Senate Vote on Judgeships	N	11. Unempl. Comp. Extension	Y
4. Immigration Reform	Y	8. Defense Dept. Spending	N	12. Keystone Pipeline	N

Election Results

2010 general	Ron Wyden (D)	825,507	(57%)	$8,520,594	$46,609
	Jim Huffman (R)	566,199	(39%)	$2,204,734	$15,534
2010 primary	Ron Wyden (D)	333,652	(90%)		
	Loren Hooker (D)	25,152	(7%)		

Prior winning percentages: 2004 (63%), 1998 (61%), 1996 special (48%); House: 1994 (73%), 1992 (77%), 1990 (81%), 1988 (99%), 1986 (86%), 1984 (72%), 1982 (78%), 1980 (72%)

Ron Wyden, Oregon's senior senator, was elected to the Senate in January 1996 after serving in the House. In 2013, he became chairman of the Senate Energy and Natural Resources Committee; just over a year later, he took the gavel at the even higher-profile Finance Committee, bringing along his reputation for trying to craft bipartisan deals on highly polarizing issues. He continued in 2015 as the panel's ranking Democrat.

Both of Wyden's parents were Jewish and fled Nazi Germany. He grew up in California, graduated from Stanford University, and moved to Oregon to attend the University of Oregon law school. After graduating in 1974, he founded the Oregon chapter of the Gray Panthers, an advocacy group for the elderly. His first foray into electoral politics was sponsoring a successful referendum reducing the price of dentures. In 1980, at age 31, he boldly launched a primary challenge to Robert Duncan in the 3rd Congressional District, which covered most of Portland, and won 60%-40%. He went on to easily capture the seat in the heavily Democratic district.

Wyden's path to the Senate was opened by the Senate Ethics Committee's decision in September 1995 to expel Republican Sen. Bob Packwood for sexual harassment of former aides and lobbyists. Wyden, who had long been eyeing the seat, decided to run in the special election to replace Packwood. With his home base in Portland, where the local television broadcasts reach most of the state, Wyden had greater name identification than his rivals. But he had spirited opposition in the Democratic primary from Eugene-based Rep. Peter DeFazio, who carried his own district overwhelmingly, holding Wyden to a 50%-44% win. The Republican nomination went to state Senate President Gordon Smith, a frozen-vegetable tycoon from eastern Oregon who spent $2 million of his own money. Most polls suggested a dead heat, and negative ads flooded the airwaves. Wyden picked up strength the week before the Jan. 30 mail-in deadline and won, 48%-47%.

Ten months later, Smith won the state's other Senate seat, marking the first time two senators were elected who had run against each other in the same year. With the departure of Packwood and Republican Mark Hatfield, Oregon lost 56 years of Senate seniority in short order and gained two senators who everyone expected would be bitter enemies. Instead they became friends and collaborators, holding dozens of joint town meetings across Oregon and having lunch every Thursday with their chiefs of staff. The bipartisan working alliance between the two ended in 2008, when Smith lost his reelection bid to Democrat Jeff Merkley.

Wyden has displayed a genius for coming up with sensible-sounding ideas no one else had thought of and for making the counterintuitive political alliances that prove helpful in passing bills. For instance, in early 2009, Wyden and Maine Republican Sen. Olympia Snowe astutely predicted that high-dollar bonuses and "golden parachutes" for executives of financial companies being bailed out by American taxpayers would be unpopular with the public, and they won passage of a provision in that year's economic stimulus bill to prevent such payments. But the stipulation was left out of the final bill at the insistence of the Obama administration, which said employees might sue to keep their bonuses. Sure enough, in

March 2009 came an outpouring of public anger over bonuses paid to employees of troubled insurance giant AIG, which would have been prevented by their provision. He later became one of 13 Democrats who joined Republicans in trying to end the Troubled Asset Relief Program in January 2010.

In 1997, he and Iowa Republican Charles Grassley called for disclosure of the names of senators who place holds on legislation, to block them from consideration. It took years, but finally, in January 2011, the Senate voted 92-4 to require public disclosure of holds after two days, ending the ability of a single senator to secretly stop legislation from advancing. Wyden voted against the Iraq war resolution in 2002 and opposed Obama's plan to add troops in Afghanistan in 2009. He also voted against the $700 billion bailout of the financial industry in 2008.

Another Wyden cause has been the Internet. He and former California Republican Rep. Christopher Cox sponsored the three-year ban on Internet taxation that passed in 1998. In 2001, they sought to extend the ban permanently but also set up a procedure to allow states to tax Internet sales if they adopted uniform sales tax rules and provided a means to remit sales taxes electronically. In 2004, the Senate passed a four-year extension that grandfathered in pre-1998 taxes and permitted states to apply telephone taxes to voice-over-Internet protocol (VOIP) services. Wyden has also worked on Internet privacy issues and on anti-spam legislation, which passed in 2003. In 2010, he worked to block action on a bill that would allow the government to bar credit card companies and ad networks from dealing with websites that engage in copyright infringement. Wyden told *Wired* that the approach was "like using a bunker-busting cluster bomb when what you really need is a precision-guided missile. The collateral damage of this statute could be American innovation, American jobs, and a secure Internet."

Health care has long captured Wyden's interest. He was one of 11 Senate Democrats to vote for the Republican-authored Medicare prescription drug law in 2003 in the face of criticism from fellow Democrats. "It wasn't a bill I would have written. But I thought it was the right thing to do to get started," he said. He won amendments creating a national commission on health care and extending a managed care option for rural Oregon. Later, with Snowe, he sponsored a bill to allow the federal government to negotiate drug prices with pharmaceutical companies. As Obama's health care law was being debated, Wyden joined Republican Robert Bennett of Utah on a bill to replace the tax exclusion for employer-provided health insurance with a tax deduction for individuals to buy insurance from private insurers. They lined up six Democratic and four Republican co-sponsors and argued in 2009 that their approach would produce a bipartisan health care bill that included universal coverage. Wyden presciently predicted that the more government-heavy approach Obama favored would be a hard sell. But the Obama administration and key Senate committee chairmen disagreed that changes in tax incentives alone would achieve the goal of insuring millions of Americans without health insurance.

Wyden surprised much of Washington in December 2011 when he joined forces with Rep. Paul Ryan of Wisconsin to offer a plan to partially privatize and radically transform Medicare. The Democratic Party had already campaigned against—and strongly condemned—Ryan's budget blueprint to change Medicare, and Wyden's move undermined the party's message. The Obama White House said the plan would "end Medicare as we know it." Wyden and Ryan's plan would have allowed insurers to compete with traditional Medicare and give patients subsidies that they could use for either fee-for-service Medicare or private insurance. Ryan was later chosen as Republican Mitt Romney's running mate in the 2012 presidential race. In arguing that the Ryan Medicare plan had bipartisan support, the Romney campaign frequently cited Wyden. But by then, Wyden had mostly disavowed his previous support, and later voted against the Ryan budget in the Senate.

For some years, Wyden has promoted a restructuring of the tax code akin to the reform bill of 1986, including reductions in tax rates and an expansion of the tax base by eliminating tax preferences and deductions. In 2010, he and Republican Judd Gregg of New Hampshire sponsored a measure with three income tax brackets (15%, 25%, 35%), a lower corporate tax rate, and immediate expensing of inventory and equipment for businesses with receipts under $1 million. Wyden reintroduced the bill in 2011, undaunted by the conventional wisdom that Congress is too politically polarized to accomplish major tax reform. (So far, though, that conventional wisdom has proven correct.)

Wyden, an Intelligence Committee member, has been a major player in the emerging area of national-security surveillance. In 2011, Wyden joined Democratic Sen. Mark Udall of

Colorado in introducing an amendment to force the Justice Department's inspector general to estimate how many Americans were having email and phone calls monitored as part of anti-terrorism efforts, but the Senate Intelligence Committee shot down the proposal. In early August 2011, Wyden placed a temporary hold on the intelligence authorization bill over lack of transparency about surveillance. In March 2013, he was the only Democrat to stand on the floor with Republican Sen. Rand Paul of Kentucky while Paul filibustered John Brennan's CIA director nomination, a protest of the Obama White House's use of controversial drone strikes. Wyden did vote to confirm Brennan, but he called on the administration to produce more documents about its drone policy. At a March 2014 hearing, Wyden blasted intelligence officials for what he called a "pattern of deception" and for creating a "culture of misinformation." Wyden has also joined Paul to seek declassification of 28 pages of the 9/11 commission report, so far unsuccessfully. But Wyden celebrated a significant win in 2015 with passage of the USA Freedom Act, which reined in the government's ability to collect phone data.

Wyden's ascension to the chairmanship of Finance became possible when Montana's Max Baucus was named U.S. ambassador to China in early 2014 and their ambitious colleague, New York's Chuck Schumer, decided not to challenge Wyden (cannily: In 2015, with the looming retirement of Democratic leader Harry Reid of Nevada, Schumer became the heir apparent for party leader.) Wyden signaled that he would run the committee with a lighter touch than the sometimes irascible Baucus, including letting subcommittee chairs know that they would have more freedom to hold their own hearings. He worked with Utah's Orrin Hatch, the panel's ranking Republican, on a proposal to rescue the Highway Trust Fund in part by instituting a series of measures aimed at achieving better compliance with existing tax laws, a move that drew criticism from House Ways and Means Committee Chairman Dave Camp of Michigan.

During his short-lived chairmanship of Finance—before transitioning to ranking member once the Democrats lost the Senate—Wyden didn't get much of what he wanted, with the *Washington Post* writing that he was "shoved aside by his majority leader, snubbed by his House counterpart and handcuffed by his president." The newspaper even quoted a former aide to Reid, Jim Manley, being dismissive of Wyden's leadership style: "He's prone to quixotic causes and never really got into the nitty-gritty of the legislative process," Manley said.

But with the Trans-Pacific Partnership trade deal with Asian nations heading to completion in 2015, Wyden has been in the spotlight. Representing a state that's unusually strong in exports, from agriculture to manufacturing to high-tech products, Wyden had already been one of his party's most notable free-trade voices, and that role was only heightened during the TPP debate. Oregon is "the face of the opportunity to grow more good-paying jobs" from trade, Wyden told the *Post*. Those to his left expressed their dismay, from activists back home chasing him with a blimp and an RV to AFL-CIO president Richard Trumka, who made a special visit to Portland to scold Wyden and other free-trade backers in the delegation. "People like Ron Wyden will get a chance to stand with Corporate America or with working Oregonians," Trumka said.

As if this portfolio of major issues weren't enough, Wyden has taken up a varied array of other topics. He has asked the U.S. International Trade Commission to track the importation of e-cigarettes, proposed ending the federal ban on hemp production, advocated reforming the federal excise tax on craft beer, introduced legislation to require the Pentagon to pay for military dogs to return to the United States after completing their service, and proposed, with Merkley, a bill to slap a fee on outdated rail cars used to transport petroleum. Wyden has been a staunch defender of Oregon's landmark assisted-suicide law, fighting various attempts to nullify the law over the years. In a hotly contested issue back home, Wyden irritated his allies in the environmental movement by backing a proposed liquefied natural gas terminal at the Port of Coos bay; he touted its potential for jobs, but opponents said it would encourage significant greenhouse-gas emissions.

Wyden's attention to state issues, and to keeping up his visibility at home—he holds open forums in all 36 counties every year, even in heavily Republican eastern Oregon—has paid off at election time. He won a full term in November 1998 by 61%-34%. In 2004, he won reelection easily against a little known candidate 63%-32%. In 2010, he was opposed by Lewis and Clark law professor James Huffman. After the May primary, Wyden had $3.7 million and Huffman $224,000. In a heavily Republican year, Wyden won by the reduced margin of 57%-39%. His hard work in eastern Oregon paid off as he lost there by only 51%-46%.

Wyden underwent prostate surgery in December 2010 and made a quick recovery, voting on the Senate floor two days later. At age 63, Wyden had his fifth child—and his third with his current wife—in December 2012. His wife, Nancy Bass Wyden, co-owns New York City's venerated Strand Bookstore. Her holdings have enabled the couple to rank 22nd on the annual Roll Call list of richest lawmakers.

Junior Senator

Jeff Merkley (D)

Elected 2008, term expires Jan. 2021, 2nd term; b. Oct. 24, 1956, Myrtle Creek; Stanford U., B.A. 1979, Princeton U., M.P.A. 1982; Lutheran; married (Mary Sorteberg); 2 children.

Elected Office: OR House, 1999-2008, speaker, 2007-08.

Professional Career: Pres. fellow, Office of the Secy. of Defense, 1982-85; Natl. security analyst, CBO, 1985-89; Exec. dir., Portland Habitat for Humanity, 1991-94; Dir. of housing development, Human Solutions, 1995-96; Pres., World Affairs Cncl. of OR, 1996-2003.

DC Office: 313 HSOB, 20510, 202-224-3753; Fax: 202-228-3997; Website: merkley.senate.gov.

State Offices: Bend, 541-318-1298; Eugene, 541-465-6750; Medford, 541-608-9102; Pendleton, 541-278-1129; Portland, 503-326-3386; Salem, 503-362-8102.

Committees: *Appropriations:* Agriculture, Rural Development, FDA & Related Agencies (RMM); Energy & Water Development; Interior, Environment & Related Agencies; Labor, HHS, Education & Related Agencies; State, Foreign Operations & Related Programs. *Banking, Housing & Urban Affairs:* Economic Policy; Financial Institutions & Consumer Protection (RMM); Housing, Transportation & Community Development. *Budget. Environment & Public Works:* Clean Air & Nuclear Safety; Superfund, Waste Mgmt. & Regulatory Oversight; Transportation & Infrastructure.

Group Ratings

	ADA	ACLU	AFL-CIO	LCV	ITI	COC	HAFA	ACU	CFG	FRC
2014	95%	100%	–	80%	100%	25%	3%	8%	9%	0%
2013	90%	C	94%	100%	C	38%	C	4%	1%	C

National Journal Ratings

	2013 LIB	—	2013 CONS
Economic	75%	—	19%
Social	64%	—	34%
Foreign	58%	—	36%
Composite	68%	—	32%

Key Votes of the 113th Congress

1. Sandy storm spending	Y	5. Student Loan Rates	Y	9. Bipartisan Budget Deal	Y
2. Chuck Hagel Confirmation	Y	6. Employee Non-Discrim'n Act	Y	10. Farm Bill Conference Rept.	Y
3. Gun Background Checks	Y	7. Senate Vote on Judgeships	N	11. Unempl. Comp. Extension	Y
4. Immigration Reform	Y	8. Defense Dept. Spending	Y	12. Keystone Pipeline	N

Election Results

2014 general	Jeff Merkley (D)	814,537	(56%)	$11,147,553	$198,099	$1,320,547
	Monica Wehby (R)	538,847	(37%)	$3,896,848	$747,941	$322,424
	Mike Montchalin (Lib)	44,916	(3%)			
	Christina Jean Lugo (Green)	32,434	(2%)			
2014 primary	Jeff Merkley (D)	256,365	(93%)			

Prior winning percentage: 2008 (49%)

Democrat Jeff Merkley, Oregon's junior senator, was elected in 2008 and reelected six years later. Merkley shares with President Barack Obama a background as a community activist and advocate for affordable housing—but politically, he is to the left of Obama and a good many of his Senate colleagues.

Merkley was born in Myrtle Creek to parents who worked at a local sawmill. The sawmill closed when he was 2 years old, and his father went to work as a logger and a homebuilder in the neighboring town of Roseburg. When those jobs disappeared, the family moved to Portland, where his father took a job as a mechanic. "My parents lived with an ethic of making sure they saved and spent very little money on frills," he says. In high school, Merkley spent a summer in Ghana as part of the American Field Service Exchange Program. The first in his family to attend college, he pursued international affairs as an undergraduate at Stanford University. He spent a trimester in Florence, Italy, and a summer hitchhiking around Israel. After graduation, he took an internship with the Carnegie Endowment for International Peace. In the summer of 1980, Merkley and a fellow intern traveled through war-torn Central America by bus. He earned a master's degree in public policy from Princeton University, landed a presidential fellowship at the Pentagon in 1982, and then worked as an analyst in the Congressional Budget Office.

Merkley moved back to Portland in the early 1990s and took a job as director of the city's Habitat for Humanity chapter, where he concentrated on affordable housing and skills training for at-risk youth and low-income families. In 1998, he was elected to the state House, campaigning on his desire to improve Oregon's school system. In 2003, he was chosen by his peers as the Democratic House minority leader, and fellow House members cited his consensus-building ability. But the state House was plagued by bitter partisanship between the two parties, making it difficult to get anything done. Merkley demonstrated a competitive edge by aggressively campaigning on behalf of Democratic House candidates in 2006, including a controversial television ad that accused Republican House Speaker Karen Minnis of covering up suspected sexual misconduct by her brother-in-law. State Republicans condemned the ad as too personal. Yet Democrats won control of the Oregon House for the first time in 16 years, and Merkley was unanimously elected speaker.

During his tenure as speaker, the legislature passed several reforms, including an expanded indoor smoking ban and greater rights for same-sex couples. He also pushed through an ethics bill aimed at curbing gifts and other perks from lobbyists to lawmakers. In 2007, Merkley fought Oregon's payday loan industry with a bill that imposed an interest rate cap of 36 percent annually on consumer loans of less than $50,000. He also negotiated the establishment of a state rainy-day fund to protect schools and other state services from recessions; an increase in the state's corporate minimum tax paid for the fund. *The Oregonian* called the session "one of the most successful legislative sessions of recent years."

Merkley got the attention of Democratic Senatorial Campaign Committee Chairman Charles Schumer of New York, who recruited him to challenge incumbent GOP Sen. Gordon Smith in the 2008 election. National Democrats thought Merkley would appeal to the same voters who had elected the moderate and pragmatic Smith to two Senate terms. Despite the endorsements and financial backing of his national party, Merkley faced stiff primary competition from liberal activist and political consultant Steve Novick, who had opposed Merkley's elevation to House minority leader in 2003. Merkley initially ignored Novick and focused his campaign on Smith. But Novick labeled Merkley as pro-war for a vote he cast in favor of a 2003 resolution that praised both President George W. Bush and American troops for courage in the war against Iraq. Merkley narrowly defeated Novick, 45%-42%. Novick won liberal Multnomah County around Portland by 12 percentage points, but Merkley's large victories in rural areas gave him the nomination.

The general election was one of the most expensive and closely watched contests of 2008. Smith had broken with his party by voting for higher automobile mileage standards and against oil drilling in the Arctic National Wildlife Refuge. To combat Smith's centrist appeal, Merkley allied himself with Obama and his presidential campaign theme of change. The message resonated in a state where Bush's approval ratings were particularly weak. In late October, Merkley aired a television ad that featured Obama urging voters to bring about "real change" by casting their ballots for Merkley. Smith touted his reputation for bipartisanship, particularly his good relationship with fellow Oregon Sen. Ron Wyden, a Democrat. He attempted to distance himself from Bush, running ads that featured Wyden, Democratic icon Sen. Edward Kennedy of Massachusetts, and even Obama. In one of the campaign season's oddest attack ads, the National Republican Senatorial Committee aired an unflattering clip of Merkley gobbling a hot dog and fielding questions about Russia's invasion of Georgia with his mouth full. In addition to capturing an inelegant moment for Merkley, the ad also caught him uninformed on the issue. Smith later condemned the ad. Ultimately, Merkley defeated Smith, 49%-46%, with Constitution Party candidate Dave

Brownlow, a libertarian with almost no campaign budget, getting 5 percent. Smith out-raised Merkley $13 million to $7 million, but the DSCC and other outside groups poured $11 million into the race. The election gave Oregon two Democrats in the Senate for the first time in 40 years.

Merkley was the most liberal senator in 2011 in *National Journal's* annual rankings; he dropped to 34th in 2012, just ahead of Wyden, after taking centrist stands on foreign policy. He won a coveted seat on the Appropriations Committee in 2013, making him the only Oregonian in the House or Senate to serve on a spending panel. During the 2010 debate on the health care overhaul, Merkley was among a group of Democrats who unsuccessfully pushed for a Senate vote on a government-run "public option" to compete with private insur-ers. He opposed the subsequent year's deal to raise the federal debt ceiling, arguing that it cut spending by too much. He successfully amended the Senate-passed 2012 farm bill to make it easier for organic farmers to obtain federal crop insurance.

In early 2013, Merkley took over as chairman of the Economic Policy Subcommittee on Banking, Housing, and Urban Affairs. He said he planned to focus on "crowd-funding," which enables small businesses to use the Internet to gather investments without being subject to stringent Securities and Exchange Commission funding rules. Earlier, Merkley was one of just 11 Democrats to oppose Ben Bernanke's confirmation as Federal Reserve chairman in January 2010, contending Bernanke was partly at fault for the recession and was the wrong person to trust with an economic recovery. During the debate on the Dodd-Frank financial industry overhaul, he joined forces with Democrat Carl Levin of Michigan to craft a tough version of the "Volcker Rule" banning banks from engaging in risky investment practices that may have contributed to the crisis. Their provision remained in the final bill, though in watered-down form to attract Republican support. He currently serves as ranking member of the Subcommittee on Financial Institutions and Consumer Protection and as a member of the Budget Committee.

Also in 2013, Merkley secured the chairmanship of the new Environment and Public Works Subcommittee on Green Jobs and the New Economy. He planned to try to duplicate some of Oregon's moves to increase renewable energy development and create jobs. He sup-ported a permanent ban on offshore drilling on the West Coast and unveiled an energy plan in 2010 that relied on electric cars and increased mass transit to make the United States independent of foreign oil in two decades. He also joined Maine Republican Olympia Snowe on a bill in 2011 to give the president additional emergency authority to reduce gasoline prices, and he worked with Wyden on a measure to extend federal payments to timber-dependent counties.

Merkley made some of his biggest impact with his sponsorship of the Employment Non-Discrimination Act, introduced in April 2013 to protect members of the LGBT community from job discrimination. Equivalent legislation went nowhere in the Republican-controlled House, but the measure notched an impressive victory in the Senate, passing in November 2013 with bipartisan backing, 64-32. He is expected to continue to play a key role in the future in the wake of the Supreme Court ruling legalizing same-sex marriage; discrimina-tion in employment and public accommodations is poised to become the new battleground over LGBT rights.

Like other members of his Democratic freshman class, Merkley chafed at the Senate's procedures. He told *The New Yorker* in 2010 that he winces when he hears the chamber described as the world's greatest deliberative body, "because the amount of real deliberation, in terms of exchange of ideas, is so limited." He joined Democrats Tom Udall of New Mexico and Amy Klobuchar of Minnesota on a proposal to ban filibustering of motions to proceed to legislation. Their measure also required senators opposing a bill to stay on the Senate floor, as well as limiting debate on nominations to two hours and targeting "secret holds" that permit senators to anonymously block legislation. When Senate leaders announced a bipartisan agreement in January 2011 that retained the filibuster, he expressed skepticism that the deal would lead to significant change. His proposal to make senators come to the floor to carry out filibusters fell 18 votes short of the number needed for passage. He and Udall tried again in 2013. Initially, Senate leaders resisted their efforts, until later that year Senate Majority Leader Harry Reid of Nevada pushed through a no-filibuster rule for most judicial and executive-branch appointments.

Republicans had hopes of unseating Merkley in 2014, nominating as his opponent Monica Wehby, a pediatric neurosurgeon with moderate positions. But media reports alleged that Wehby had "stalked" her ex-husband and a former boyfriend. No charges were ever filed, and Wehby blamed Democrats for trying to "shred" her family. But she never recovered from those allegations. Freedom Partners, a group aligned with billionaire libertarians Charles and David Koch, poured money into the race, but it proved to be a double-edged sword, as it gave Merkley an angle of attack—that Wehby was beholden to the controversial industrialists. Merkley campaigned hard, visiting as many as eight cities in a single day of campaigning, and Freedom Partners pulled out more than a month away from the election. Merkley won easily with 56 percent.

Merkley broke with most of the Oregon congressional delegation—and his own president—in opposing the Trans-Pacific Partnership trade deal. While trade receives notable support in export-friendly Oregon, even from Democrats, and while Obama pledged that the deal would be more pro-worker and pro-environment than past agreements, Merkley didn't buy that argument. "Here we are repeating the same basic structure of the other agreements with no changes for America and therefore no improvement for the workers," he said in a floor speech.

Meanwhile, Merkley has taken a leading role on two veterans' issues. Joining with Republican Sen. Steve Daines of Montana, Merkley sponsored a bill to ease medicinal cannabis access for veterans, and in May 2015 it passed the full Appropriations Committee. And with his fellow Oregon Democrat Wyden, he sought to block David Shulkin, Obama's nominee for undersecretary for health at the VA, as leverage to expand coverage to National Guard members for health problems related to the Vietnam-era herbicide Agent Orange while serving stateside.

FIRST DISTRICT

Suzanne Bonamici (D)

Elected Jan. 2012, 2nd full term; b. Oct. 14, 1954, Detroit, MI; Lane Comm. Col., A.A. 1978, U. of OR, B.A. 1980, J.D. 1983; no religious affiliation; married (Michael Simon); 2 children.

Elected Office: OR House, 2007-08; OR Senate, 2008-11.

Professional Career: Atty., Federal Trade Commission, 1983-86; Practicing atty., 1986-89; Legis. aide, 2001-06.

DC Office: 439 CHOB, 20515, 202-225-0855; Website: bonamici. house.gov.

State Offices: Beaverton, 503-469-6010.

Committees: *Education & the Workforce:* Early Childhood, Elementary, & Secondary Education; Health, Employment, Labor & Pensions. *Science, Space, & Technology:* Environment (RMM); Research & Technology.

Group Ratings

	ADA	ACLU	AFL-CIO	LCV	ITI	COC	HAFA	ACU	CFG	FRC
2014	85%	94%	–	97%	60%	43%	8%	4%	6%	0%
2013	90%	C	95%	96%	C	31%	C	12%	10%	C

National Journal Ratings

	2013 LIB	—	2013 CONS
Economic	80%	—	19%
Social	93%	—	0%
Foreign	90%	—	6%
Composite	90%	—	10%

Key Votes of the 113th Congress

1. Sandy storm spending	Y	5. Medical Marijuana	Y
2. Violence Against Women Act	Y	6. Farm Bill	N
3. Guantanamo Bay Detainees	Y	7. Afghanistan Combat	Y
4. Abortion 20-week ban	N	8. NSA Phone Data Collection	Y

9. Syrian Rebels Training	Y
10. Keystone pipeline	N
11. Immigration Exec. Action	N
12. Bipartisan budget deal	Y

Election Results

2014 general	Suzanne Bonamici (D)	160,038	(57%)	$897,513	$4,948
	Jason Yates (R)	96,245	(35%)	$22,238	
	James Foster (Lib)	11,213	(4%)		
	Steven Cody Reynolds (Green)	11,163	(4%)		
2014 primary	Suzanne Bonamici (D)	unopposed			

Prior winning percentage: 2012 special (54%)

Population		Race and Ethnicity		Income	
Total:	796,901	White	73.6%	Median income:	$61,908
Urban:	54.9%	Latino	14.0%		*(99 of 435)*
Suburban:	34.4%	Asian	6.8%	Under $50,000	40.8%
Rural:	10.7%	Black	1.5%	$50,000-$99,999:	31.7%
Land area:	2,101	Two races	2.8%	$100,000-$199,999:	22.0%
Pop/sq. mi.:	379.3	White Ethnic	24.4%	$200,000 or more:	5.5%
Born in state:	45.3%			Poverty Rate	11.3%
		Education			
Age Groups		H.S. grad or less:	30.5%	**Work**	
Under 18:	23.6%	Some college:	32.8%	White collar:	42.7%
18 to 34:	22.8%	College degree, 4 yr.:	23.1%	Blue collar:	38.9%
35 to 64:	40.8%	Post-grad study:	13.5%	Sales and service:	18.4%
Over 64:	12.7%				
		Military		Govt. workers:	10.0%
		Veterans/active duty:	7.9%		

Northwest Oregon: Western Portland Area

Just over the hills from downtown Portland are the valleys and interstices between green mountains of suburban Washington County. This was once farm country, with 39,000 people in 1940; now it has almost 555,000 and is an integral part of metro Portland. Its population zoomed up 70% between

Voter Turnout	
2013 Total Citizen 18+	551,190
2014 House Turnout	279,253
2014 Turnout as % CVAP	50.7%
2012 Turnout as % CVAP	65.1%

1990 and 2010, and it enjoys a high-tech, healthy-lifestyle affluence. Its towns are cushioned by protected forests and anchored by major employers that include Tektronix, Intel, IBM and Columbia Sportswear. Near Beaverton is the world headquarters of Nike, housed in 22 buildings spread over 200 acres. Like Silicon Valley, the Silicon Forest has an environment that appeals to a highly skilled workforce. Nestled at the foot of mountains, it is woodsy and even rustic, but is outfitted with all the comforts of modern life. The Asian population of the county is 7%, with 12.5% in Beaverton.

The companies went through a rough patch in the 2007-09 recession, cutting jobs and sending unemployment in the Portland area well above 10% though 2010. Tektronix, the testing and measurement technology company, had five rounds of layoff from 2008 to 2012, cutting its Oregon workforce in half to 1,000, according to *The Oregonian* newspaper. But the Portland area has since been on the rebound, and unemployment dropped to 4.4% in April 2015. Nike continues to expand, and employs about 8,000 people in Oregon. Intel, which employs 18,600 in the state, opened a new office building in October 2014 at its 530-acre campus in Hillsboro. Biotech firm Genentech also has a presence in Hillsboro.

The 1st Congressional District of Oregon includes part of Portland and all of suburban Washington County. It extends nearly 100 miles northwest from Portland along the Columbia River to the rain-swept port of Astoria on the Pacific Coast, where Lewis and -Clark spent the winter of 1805-06. (The event is memorialized in the Lewis and Clark National Historical Park.) Yamhill County and Beaverton are known for wineries. In June 2015, Astoria was invaded by several hundred sea lions. Its initial response of a fake motorized whale proved unsuccessful. Astoria, which retains many century-old buildings, has been a popular site to shoot movies, including *Goonies*, a 1980s small-town cult classic.

2012 Presidential Vote

Barack Obama (D)	200,993	(57%)
Mitt Romney (R)	140,462	(40%)

2008 Presidential Vote

Barack Obama (D)	211,153	(60%)
John McCain (R)	133,544	(38%)

Cook Partisan Voting Index: D+7

Like Oregon overall, the 1st District was historically New England Republican, electing only Republicans to Congress from 1892 to 1972. But like New England, it trended left on cultural issues, and since 1974 it has elected only Democrats. The redistricting plan made the 1st District a bit less Democratic than before, but the GOP remains the underdog.

Suzanne Bonamici (D)

The congresswoman from the 1st District is Suzanne Bonamici, a Democrat who won a special election in January 2012. She has had a mostly liberal record, but has been responsive to the needs of local businesses.

Bonamici was born in Detroit and grew up in the small town of Northville, Michigan. Her father worked at a local bank, and her mother was a piano teacher. After high school, Bonamici traveled with friends in a van to Oregon, fell in love with the state, and moved to Eugene. "It was a very '70s thing to do," Bonamici told *The Oregonian*. She began attending Lane Community College and worked at a legal-aid center in Eugene. Bonamici earned both her bachelor's and law degrees from the University of Oregon. She moved to Washington, D.C., to take a job as a consumer protection lawyer at the Federal Trade Commission. During that time, Bonamici met her husband, Michael Simon, and the two relocated to Oregon in 1986. Bonamici worked as a lawyer in private practice. In 2001, Bonamici took a job as a legislative assistant in the Oregon House of Representatives. Five years later, she won her own state House seat and focused on consumer protection. In 2008, she was elected to the state Senate.

When a special election was called following the resignation of Democrat David Wu, who stepped down amid charges of improper sexual advances, Bonamici jumped into the Democratic primary. She faced off against state Labor Commissioner Brad Avakian and state Rep. Brad Witt, both of whom said they would oppose U.S. trade pacts with Colombia, Panama and South Korea that were being debated in Congress. Bonamici initially declined to take a position and drew criticism for indecisiveness. She then came out in favor of the South Korea pact. She raised the most money of the three candidates and won with 66% of the vote.

In the general election, Bonamici faced Rob Cornilles, a sports business consultant who lost 55%-42% to Wu in 2010. Cornilles played up his business experience and kept his distance from the national GOP. He praised the Democrats in the Oregon delegation, touted his endorsements from Democratic mayors, and refused to take the customary no-new-taxes pledge made by most Republicans in Congress. Bonamici ran an ad attacking Cornilles for an old federal tax lien against his business over failure to pay payroll taxes. She emphasized the need to tax the highest-earning Americans and to end corporate tax breaks in order to fund education and infrastructure projects.

Bonamici had the advantage in a Democratic-leaning district. But the Democratic Congressional Campaign Committee moved aggressively early on, sinking $1 million into the contest and painting Cornilles as a tea party extremist. The DCCC, EMILY's List, and other liberal interest groups poured millions into the race, while national Republican groups spent little and mostly stayed away. Bonamici won, 54%-40%.

In the House, Bonamici has mostly been a reliable Democratic vote. As a member of the Education and the Workforce Committee, she has focused on making college more affordable and reforming the No Child Left Behind Act. On the renewal of student-loan legislation in 2014, she worked with others to add increased financial counseling for recipients. She was a founder of the bipartisan Congressional STEAM Caucus, which encourages innovation in science, technology, engineering, art and design and math education. As the ranking Democrat on the Science, Space and Technology Subcommittee on Environment, she has focused on global climate change. With an eye toward Nike—the apparel and shoemaker's headquarters is in her district—she offered a bill to suspend a duty on leathered footwear. She pushed a bill to crack down on online payday loans, arguing that predatory lending practices are driving up consumer debt.

In June 2015, Bonamici was one of 28 House Democrats who voted to give trade promotion authority to President Barack Obama, whose prospective Trans-Pacific Partnership could be an economic boon for West Coast companies and ports. "Our economy is increasingly global, and trade done right creates jobs, helps businesses grow and puts our country on stronger economic footing," she said. She cited the benefits for local farmers, including wheat and potato growers. Bonamici accompanied Obama a month earlier on a visit to Nike headquarters, where he said that the deal would benefit Oregon companies and "help level the playing field." In an appearance in Portland a few days later, AFL-CIO President Richard Trumka warned that he was "blowing the whistle, quite frankly" on Bonamici and other Portland-area Democrats in Congress for being on "the wrong side" of TPA, which he said most Oregonians opposed.

Bonamici has twice been reelected easily. Following her votes on international trade in 2015, she faced the risk of a primary challenge from a candidate backed by organized labor or a loss of enthusiasm among her local base. She can expect continued support from the local business community.

SECOND DISTRICT

Greg Walden (R)

Elected 1998, 9th term; b. Jan. 10, 1957, The Dalles; U. of OR, B.S. 1981; Episcopalian; married (Mylene); 2 children (1 deceased).

Elected Office: OR House, 1989-95, maj. ldr., 1991-93; OR Senate, 1995-97.

Professional Career: Press secy., U.S. Rep. Denny Smith, 1981-84, chief of staff, 1984-86; Owner, Columbia Gorge Broadcasters Inc., 1986-2008.

DC Office: 2185 RHOB, 20515, 202-225-6730; Fax: 202-225-5774; Website: walden.house.gov.

State Offices: Bend, 541-389-4408; La Grande, 541-624-2400; Medford, 541-776-4646.

Committees: *Energy & Commerce:* Communications & Technology (Chmn).

Group Ratings

	ADA	ACLU	AFL-CIO	LCV	ITI	COC	HAFA	ACU	CFG	FRC
2014	0%	0%	–	3%	100%	93%	48%	56%	39%	75%
2013	0%	C	14%	0%	C	77%	C	64%	55%	C

National Journal Ratings

	2013 LIB	—	2013 CONS
Economic	29%	—	70%
Social	47%	—	52%
Foreign	24%	—	68%
Composite	35%	—	65%

Key Votes of the 113th Congress

1. Sandy storm spending	N	5. Medical Marijuana	Y	9. Syrian Rebels Training	Y
2. Violence Against Women Act	Y	6. Farm Bill	Y	10. Keystone pipeline	Y
3. Guantanamo Bay Detainees	N	7. Afghanistan Combat	N	11. Immigration Exec. Action	Y
4. Abortion 20-week ban	Y	8. NSA Phone Data Collection	N	12. Bipartisan budget deal	Y

Election Results

2014 general	Greg Walden (R)	202,374	(70%)	$3,463,666	$47,641	$503
	Aelea Christofferson (D)	73,785	(26%)	$134,512		
	Sharon Durbin (Lib)	10,491	(4%)			
2014 primary	Greg Walden (R)	62,957	(76%)			
	Dennis Linthicum (R)	19,936	(24%)			

Prior winning percentages: 2012 (69%), 2010 (74%), 2008 (70%), 2006 (67%), 2004 (72%), 2002 (72%), 2000 (74%), 1998 (61%)

Population		Race and Ethnicity		Income	
Total:	778,062	White	81.2%	Median income:	$42,583
Urban:	29.4%	Latino	12.8%		*(350 of 435)*
Suburban:	7.3%	Amer. Indian	1.6%	Under $50,000	57.0%
Rural:	63.3%	Asian	1.1%	$50,000-$99,999:	29.3%
Land area:	50,794	Two races	2.4%	$100,000-$199,999:	11.6%
Pop/sq. mi.:	15.3	White Ethnic	24.9%	$200,000 or more:	2.0%
Born in state:	44.5%			Poverty Rate	18.0%
		Education			
Age Groups		H.S. grad or less:	40.2%	**Work**	
Under 18:	22.2%	Some college:	35.6%	White collar:	31.0%
18 to 34:	20.1%	College degree, 4 yr.:	15.5%	Blue collar:	45.8%
35 to 64:	39.2%	Post-grad study:	8.7%	Sales and service:	23.2%
Over 64:	18.6%				
		Military		Govt. workers:	15.2%
		Veterans/active duty:	11.9%		

Eastern Oregon: Medford, Bend

The Cascade Mountains that wall off eastern Oregon from the rest of the state are a magnificent chain of once active volcanic mountains that drain almost every drop of moisture out of the air blowing in from the Pacific Ocean. They separate green, wet, western Oregon from brown, parched

Voter Turnout	
2013 Total Citizen 18+	575,266
2014 House Turnout	287,425
2014 Turnout as % CVAP	50%
2012 Turnout as % CVAP	60.9%

eastern Oregon. The eastern part has 70% of the state's land, but only around half a million of its 4 million people, many of whom still make their living off the land: beef and dairy cattle, timber and lumber, fish from the Columbia River, and wheat and sugar beets from the irrigated plains. The effect of the Cascades can be felt in the one place they are breached—at the Columbia River Gorge. Here, funneled winds pound in steadily from the west, making the confluence of the Columbia and Hood rivers the best windsurfing site in the United States. One of the world's largest wind farms, Shepherds Flat, became operational here in 2012.

The 2nd Congressional District of Oregon covers nearly three-fourths of the state: everything east of the Cascades and the southernmost valley between the Cascades and the Coast Range. Much of this land is forested and unpopulated. Harney County, with a land area larger than that of nine states, had just 7,422 residents in 2010. In the town of The Dalles, housing prices spiked after Internet giant Google purchased 30 acres of riverfront land for a $600 million, 100-employee data center in 2005. Facebook four years later picked Prineville, to the south, for its own data center. After getting a property tax exemption from Gov. Kate Brown, Apple launched in April 2015 a major expansion of a data center in Prineville that it had built in 2012. In the town of Bend, sawmills have closed, but the wilderness and high desert plateau have attracted software developers, outdoor activity, upscale tourists and telecommuters.

The 2nd District is heavily Republican. This is part of the leave-us-alone Rocky Mountain Basin, not the hipster West Coast. Court decisions protecting the spotted owl hurt the logging industry here. International competition has hurt the timber industry, with Oregon lawmakers blaming Chinese manufacturers for setting artificially low prices for timber-related products. In 2009, rural Jackson County saw its last remaining large sawmill dismantled; it had 91 in its heyday. An unusual coalition of timber industry leaders, environmentalists and government officials joined forces to save the last remaining lumber mill in Grant County in 2012. There

2012 Presidential Vote		
Mitt Romney (R)	196,568	(56%)
Barack Obama (D)	139,940	(40%)
2008 Presidential Vote		
John McCain (R)	191,689	(54%)
Barack Obama (D)	154,051	(43%)
Cook Partisan Voting Index:	R+10	

is a "growing sense that healing eastern Oregon's overgrown forests can't be done without sawmills, loggers and truck drivers to cut, remove and process logs," *The Oregonian* wrote in 2012.

Greg Walden (R)

Greg Walden, elected in 1998, has emerged as one of the Republican Party's most highly regarded inside strategists and a trusted ally of House Speaker John Boehner. As chairman of the National Republican Congressional Committee, he led the successful GOP effort to expand its majority in 2014, and signed up for another term in the far more challenging election environment expected in 2016.

Walden grew up on an 80-acre cherry orchard near The Dalles in the Columbia Gorge. His father ran radio stations that had been in the family since the 1930s and also served in the state House. Walden followed both pursuits. As a young man, he was a disc jockey and talk show host. Then, he got involved in politics as the press secretary and chief of staff for local Republican Rep. Denny Smith from 1981 to 1987. Walden returned to Hood River to run the family's five-station broadcast business, Columbia Gorge Broadcasters. In 1988, he was elected to the state House, eventually becoming majority leader.

When the 2nd District seat opened in 1998, Walden ran and faced substantial primary opposition from Perry Atkinson, a Christian broadcaster who was backed financially by Gary Bauer's Campaign for Working Americans. Walden stayed competitive by raising $500,000 and prevailed over Atkinson with 55% of the vote. In the anticlimactic general election against a conservative Democrat, Walden won 61%-35%. He has not faced a serious reelection challenge in his comfortably Republican district.

In the House, he is a conservative on fiscal issues but more of a moderate on cultural issues. Walden caught the eye of Republican leaders with his political knowledge, knack for forming friendships and devotion to the party agenda. In 2011, *The Oregonian* newspaper wrote that Walden is known for being "reliable, self-deprecating, and largely without ego." He is close to Republican Pete Sessions of Texas, and when Sessions took over as NRCC chairman, he made Walden his deputy. In early 2010, still in the minority, Boehner picked Walden to be chairman of the Republican leadership, a post that had been vacant since Ohio's Rob Portman left the House five years earlier. When Republicans reclaimed the majority that fall, Walden helped steer the GOP's transition to power, handling issues ranging from rules changes governing debate to steps to economize on House operations.

After the 2012 election, Boehner tapped Sessions as Rules Committee chairman and Walden was unanimously elected chairman of the NRCC. His term hit some bumps: The NRCC came under criticism for what members of both parties said was an unseemly May 2014 fundraising email about the select committee investigating the deadly 2012 terrorist attacks at U.S. facilities in Benghazi Libya. "There are times when I'm taken aback because that's not the person I knew growing up and I don't think they are always things he believes," Democratic Oregon Rep. Earl Blumenauer, who served with Walden's father in the state Legislature, told *The Oregonian*.

Although the midterm environment was considered highly favorable for his party, Walden's confidence in a wave election startled even fellow Republicans. Walden touted a "Drive for 245," which would require a double-digit increase in Republican seats. Some Republicans dismissed it as an unrealistic fundraising ploy, and lamented the Democrats' ability to out-raise them even as they acknowledged lacking a figure who brought in funds as proficiently as President Barack Obama. Two junior Republicans floated the idea of challenging Walden for another term. Some anonymous Republicans wondered in print whether he was too nice.

All of that talk disappeared after Republicans exceeded Walden's goals to reap its largest House majority since the Truman administration. Their 247 seats were the most for the party since 1928. Walden was unopposed for another term as NRCC chairman. His eyes may be on a bigger prize: With Fred Upton of Michigan term-limited as Energy and Commerce Committee Chairman after 2016, Walden is among those interested in succeeding him, though he might need to leap-frog three senior committee Republicans.

Walden has kept busy on the policy side. In January 2011, he took over as chairman of the Energy and Commerce Telecommunications Subcommittee, a prime niche for an ex-broadcaster. As a critic of Federal Communications Commission and its two chairmen since then, his appointment signaled to the Obama administration that Republicans would wage a fierce battle against the regulators. Later that year, Walden introduced legislation that would require the FCC to justify any rule change by identifying market implications or potential harm to consumers. He would require the FCC to disclose the text of its proposals before a vote. Walden's bill passed the House in March 2012, but the Democratic-controlled

Senate did not take it up. Walden authored a bill to provide more spectrum for wireless broadband. As part of payroll-tax negotiations in February 2012, he helped broker a deal to raise $15 billion from spectrum auctions.

Walden vowed to upend the FCC's proposed Internet rules, known as "network neutrality," which prohibit tiered pricing by phone and cable companies that many Republicans regard as excessive interference in the market. The bill passed the House in 2011 but died in the Senate. Walden then co-authored a letter to Obama asking him to halt net neutrality rules expected to take effect. The administration ignored his letter. In February 2015, the FCC under Chairman Tom Wheeler finally issued its net neutrality rules. Republicans strongly objected. The FCC's actions did not end the debate, Walden said. "Resorting to Great Depression-era rules will trigger a stampede to the courts, unleashing years of lawsuits and uncertainty at a time when U.S. leadership and the Internet economy are more important than ever." He pursued his own legislative alternative. But the Obama administration's embrace of Wheeler left his critics with few options.

In 2007, Walden was a leader of a coalition to stifle efforts to restore the Fairness Doctrine in broadcasting, which required broadcasters to offer multiple viewpoints on controversial issues of the day. The rule was abandoned in 1987, and liberals have pushed to revive it to counter the influence of popular conservative talk show hosts like Rush Limbaugh. Recalling his own days in broadcasting, Walden told *The Oregonian* that it was difficult to figure out who qualified to offer opposing viewpoints when his father read editorials on the air, so the family stopped airing editorials altogether. Political chatter over the broadcast network tends to be conservative, he said, but that should not matter. "Is it more conservative than liberal? Yeah," Walden told the newspaper. "Are there a lot more country-western stations than polka stations? Yeah. Listeners make these determinations. The marketplace decides." Walden won this battle, as the FCC removed the Fairness Doctrine from the agency's rules.

Walden has had a hand in national issues with strong implications in his rural district. He played a central role in 2003 in assembling bipartisan support for the Healthy Forests Restoration Act, which was a legislative response to wildfires raging across the West worsened by unlogged dry timber. He also successfully reopened the flow of water to farmers in the Klamath Basin. The House passed his bill to expand the Mount Hood wilderness area, which became part of a 2009 omnibus public-lands law. Walden has worked to curb regulations under the Endangered Species Act by encouraging a greater role for outside scientists to review government proposals. In recent years, he has tried to restore timber payments to rural counties, joining forces with home-state Democratic Sen. Ron Wyden. Walden found an unexpected vehicle for action in March 2015, when he successfully added to a widely supported and time-urgent Medicare bill his plan, cosponsored by Oregon Democratic Rep. Peter DeFazio, to provide hundreds of millions of dollars of aid to rural counties that have suffered from reduced timber sales.

Managing his full platter of policy and political priorities has been a tough juggling act for Walden, who has managed to keep all the balls in the air. But as he rises further up the ladder of influence, the risks and the rewards grow larger.

THIRD DISTRICT

Earl Blumenauer (D)

Elected May 1996, 10th full term; b. Aug. 16, 1948, Portland; Lewis & Clark Col., B.A. 1970, J.D. 1976; no religious affiliation; married (Margaret); 4 children..

Elected Office: OR House, 1973-78; Multnomah Cnty. Comm., 1978-86; Portland City Cncl., 1986-96.

Professional Career: Asst. to pres., Portland St. U., 1970-77; Portland Community Col. Bd. of Dir., 1975-81.

DC Office: 1111 LHOB, 20515, 202-225-4811; Fax: 202-225-8941; Website: blumenauer.house.gov.

State Offices: Portland, 503-231-2300.

Committees: *Ways & Means:* Health; Social Security; Trade.

Group Ratings

	ADA	ACLU	AFL-CIO	LCV	ITI	COC	HAFA	ACU	CFG	FRC
2014	80%	61%	–	94%	80%	31%	20%	8%	26%	0%
2013	90%	C	95%	96%	C	38%	C	12%	19%	C

National Journal Ratings

	2013 LIB	—	2013 CONS
Economic	86%	—	13%
Social	87%	—	7%
Foreign	94%	—	0%
Composite	91%	—	9%

Key Votes of the 113th Congress

1. Sandy storm spending	Y	5. Medical Marijuana	Y
2. Violence Against Women Act	Y	6. Farm Bill	N
3. Guantanamo Bay Detainees	Y	7. Afghanistan Combat	Y
4. Abortion 20-week ban	N	8. NSA Phone Data Collection	Y

9. Syrian Rebels Training	Y
10. Keystone pipeline	NV
11. Immigration Exec. Action	N
12. Bipartisan budget deal	Y

Election Results

2014 general	Earl Blumenauer (D)................	211,748	(72%)	$1,177,555	
	James Buchal (R)........................	57,424	(20%)	$8,378	$298
	Michael Meo (Green)...................	12,106	(4%)		
	Jeffrey Langan (Lib).....................	6,381	(2%)		
2014 primary	Earl Blumenauer (D)............unopposed				

Prior winning percentages: 2012 (75%), 2010 (70%), 2008 (75%), 2006 (73%), 2004 (71%), 2002 (67%), 2000 (67%), 1998 (84%), 1996 (67%), 1996 special (68%)

Population		Race and Ethnicity		Income	
Total:	797,199	White	73.0%	Median income:	$54,300
Urban:	73.1%	Latino	10.9%		(176 of 435)
Suburban:	25.0%	Asian	6.4%	Under $50,000	46.9%
Rural:	1.9%	Black	5.2%	$50,000-$99,999:	30.9%
Land area:	953	Two races	2.9%	$100,000-$199,999:	17.5%
Pop/sq. mi.:	836.3	White Ethnic	28.6%	$200,000 or more:	4.7%
Born in state:	44.6%			Poverty Rate	18.0%
		Education			
Age Groups		H.S. grad or less:	30.3%	Work	
Under 18:	20.6%	Some college:	31.9%	White collar:	41.0%
18 to 34:	26.4%	College degree, 4 yr.:	23.3%	Blue collar:	40.9%
35 to 64:	41.2%	Post-grad study:	14.4%	Sales and service:	18.1%
Over 64:	11.8%				
		Military		Govt. workers:	12.2%
		Veterans/active duty:	7.1%		

Greater Portland

Postmodern skyscrapers rising above the riverfront and below a range of hills: This is downtown Portland. The city—which would have been named Boston if a coin toss had gone the other way—started here, along the Willamette River just before it flows into the Columbia. Downtown Portland was once a

Voter Turnout	
2013 Total Citizen 18+	575,676
2014 House Turnout	292,757
2014 Turnout as % CVAP	50.9%
2012 Turnout as % CVAP	64.9%

dowdy place, proper in a New England kind of way, with a few formal buildings above the warehouses and factories. But in the last 30 years, there has been an explosion of affluence and creativity here, symbolized by handsome high-rises—the pyramid-crested brick KOIN Tower, the wedge-shaped Justice Center—restored Victorian storefronts, a downtown transit trolley, and a light-rail line known as MAX (for Metropolitan Area Express).

Out on the Pacific Rim, Portland increasingly makes its living on foreign trade with Asia. It has become a home to high-tech industries, particularly in the Silicon Forest suburbs. Local government also has produced change. Metro, the regional agency established in 1979 just as growth was accelerating, is a counterweight against the endless population spread outward. The city encouraged development of high-density commercial space and housing around transit stops, and bicycle paths wind throughout the metropolitan area.

In a May 2015 Bike Score ranking, Portland was third as the nation's most bicycle-friendly large city, behind Minneapolis and San Francisco, though it remained first in the share of commuters who bicycle to work. Local leaders have sought to make Portland the nation's leader for biodiesel and other renewable fuels. In 2012, Beaver Biodiesel and Whole Energy Fuels Corp. set up shop in Portland for integrated biodiesel produc-

2012 Presidential Vote		
Barack Obama (D) 268,004	(72%)
Mitt Romney (R)...................91,733	(25%)
2008 Presidential Vote		
Barack Obama (D) 274,294	(73%)
John McCain (R)...................91,217	(24%)
Cook Partisan Voting Index: D+22		

tion. In becoming a city focused on renewable energy, Portland has attracted political and cultural liberals. In 2015, Portland ranked third in the nation in the Clean Tech Leadership Index. The city's hipster sensibility has been satirized on AMC's television show *Portlandia*, which features Carrie Brownstein and Fred Armisen, who called the show "an exaggerated, dreamy version" of the city. In March 2015, a Gallup survey ranked the Portland metro area second behind San Francisco in the share of its population that is gay, lesbian, bisexual or transgender.

The 3rd Congressional District of Oregon includes most of Portland, including downtown. It also takes in Multnomah County east of the city and some of suburban Clackamas County to the south, which includes a bit more than 10% of its voters. Politically, the 3rd remains dominated by liberals. In 2012, President Barack Obama got 75% of the vote in Multnomah County and 72% in the district.

Earl Blumenauer (D)

Democrat Earl Blumenauer, who won a special election in 1996, is best known for his role as Congress' point person on "smart growth" planning strategies that combat urban sprawl and promote alternatives to driving. On the Ways and Means Committee, he has become a leader in promoting international trade. He is known for his distinctive bow ties.

Blumenauer grew up in Portland and graduated from Lewis and Clark College and its Northwestern Law School. In his teens, he was inspired by the civil rights and anti-war movements of the 1960s. In college, he headed a statewide campaign to lower Oregon's voting age. He has held public office almost all of his adult life. In 1972, at age 23, he was elected to the Oregon House. He was elected as a Multnomah County commissioner in 1978 and as a Portland city councilor in 1986; during the latter period, he also served as commissioner of public works.

He championed many of the policies that have made Portland distinctive—regional light-rail transit, curbside recycling, and aggressive land-use planning. He encouraged bicycle riding and "regional rail summits," which bring neighborhood residents into the planning for higher densities at transit nodes. Blumenauer has had some setbacks, notably when he lost the 1992 mayoral race. But he was the obvious successor when Ron Wyden was elected to the Senate, and he won the special election 68%-25%. His campaign slogan was "Vote Earl, Vote Often." In his Democratic bastion, he has never drawn less than 67% of the vote since and has not faced a serious primary challenge.

In the House, Blumenauer has had a consistently liberal voting record. He and Colorado's Jared Polis were lead sponsors of the 2013 bill allowing states to legalize medical marijuana and to regulate it in a manner similar to alcohol. "We're still arresting two-thirds of a million people for use of a substance that a majority feel should be legal," Blumenauer told The Associated Press. In June 2015, the House narrowly defeated a proposal that he co-sponsored to give states the authority to legalize marijuana. He urged the attorney general to reclassify marijuana as a drug to give researchers more opportunities for research.

Blumenauer rides his bicycle everywhere he travels around Washington from his Capitol Hill apartment. He formed a Congressional Bike Caucus and fought for showers for bike commuters at the Capitol. Blumenauer was astonished to find that the House subsidized parking for employees, but not mass transit; now, employees can get subsidized transit fares. He is interested in what seem like quixotic projects now but may seem less so in time: an interstate highway system for bicycle paths and less dependence on driving as a tool to improve public health. "The rise of bicycles is a metaphor for change in this country," Blumenauer says. He has been active in promoting healthier school lunches. To rescue the depleted highway trust fund, he has called for a 15-cent hike per gallon in the gas tax over a three-year period, plus eventual movement toward a mileage-based tax. "There is a looming transportation funding crisis before us," he wrote with Republican Rep. Jim Renacci of Ohio in a May 2015 opinion column for CNN.

The sometimes nerdy policy wonk has developed an audience for his gospel of livability and civic values, including the Obama administration, which has embraced some of his concepts. With his seat on the tax-writing Ways and Means Committee, he has given the panel a new focus on the environment and urban planning. His call for tax subsidies for bicycle commuting was included in the Troubled Asset Relief Program law of 2008. Committee Chairman Paul Ryan of Wisconsin has dismissed his ideas as "central planning."

On economic issues, he has actively promoted trade across the Pacific, a key element of Portland's economy. He was an outspoken supporter of approving Trade Promotion Authority for President Barack Obama, noting in June 2015 that "Oregon will not only be able to export more of its products, but also its values," including human rights, worker rights and environmental protections. He was caustic in criticizing other House Democrats, including party leaders, for their initial votes against extending trade adjustment assistance for workers adversely affected by overseas trade deals. "Political gamesmanship within our party won out over substance," he said. He complained to the Obama administration that tariffs imposed on U.S.-designed footwear imported from Asia discriminate against companies like Oregon's Nike.

Blumenauer chairs the Congressional Public Broadcasting Caucus and has been an outspoken critic of Republican proposals to strike funding for National Public Radio, citing polls showing strong public support for the operation. During the earlier health care debate, he promoted legislation to allow doctors to charge Medicare for end-of-life consultations, a proposal that former Alaska Gov. Sarah Palin famously charged would lead to "death panels." He staged a retaliation of sorts in 2011, when he questioned the Park Service about whether Palin received preferential treatment during her widely publicized bus tour of national historic sites. The Internet-savvy Blumenauer sets his BlackBerry to notify him when he is mentioned in a blog posting, and he responds on a regular basis.

He seriously considered running for mayor of Portland in 2004 but decided against it and has deferred on statewide opportunities.

FOURTH DISTRICT

Peter DeFazio (D)

Elected 1986, 15th term; b. May 27, 1947, Needham, MA; Tufts U., B.A. 1969, U. of OR, M.A. 1977; Catholic; married (Myrnie Daut)..

Military Career: U.S. Air Force Reserve, 1967-71.

Elected Office: Lane Cnty. Bd. of Commissioners, 1983-86, chmn, 1985-86.

Professional Career: Dist. dir., U.S. Rep. James Weaver, 1977-82.

DC Office: 2134 RHOB, 20515, 202-225-6416; Fax: 202-226-3493; Website: defazio.house.gov.

State Offices: Coos Bay, 541-269-2609; Eugene, 541-465-6732; Roseburg, 541-440-3523.

Committees: *Transportation & Infrastructure:* (RMM: ex officio member of each subcommittee).

Group Ratings

	ADA	ACLU	AFL-CIO	LCV	ITI	COC	HAFA	ACU	CFG	FRC
2014	90%	83%	–	100%	60%	36%	17%	12%	22%	0%
2013	95%	C	90%	93%	C	38%	C	12%	16%	C

National Journal Ratings

	2013 LIB	—	2013 CONS
Economic	66%	—	33%
Social	69%	—	28%
Foreign	90%	—	6%
Composite	76%	—	24%

Key Votes of the 113th Congress

1. Sandy storm spending	Y	5. Medical Marijuana	Y	9. Syrian Rebels Training	N
2. Violence Against Women Act	Y	6. Farm Bill	N	10. Keystone pipeline	N
3. Guantanamo Bay Detainees	Y	7. Afghanistan Combat	Y	11. Immigration Exec. Action	N
4. Abortion 20-week ban	N	8. NSA Phone Data Collection	Y	12. Bipartisan budget deal	N

Election Results

2014 general	Peter DeFazio (D)..................... 181,624	(59%)	$1,277,585	$1,481	$336,355
	Art Robinson (R)....................... 116,534	(38%)	$611,659	$418,031	
	David Chester (Lib)...................... 4,676	(2%)			
	Michael Beilstein (Green) 6,863	(2%)			
2014 primary	Peter DeFazio (D)..................unopposed				

Prior winning percentages: 2012 (59%), 2010 (54%), 2008 (82%), 2006 (62%), 2004 (61%), 2002 (64%), 2000 (68%), 1998 (70%), 1996 (66%), 1994 (67%), 1992 (71%), 1990 (86%), 1988 (72%), 1986 (54%)

Population		Race and Ethnicity		Income	
Total:	772,196	White	85.5%	Median income:	$42,103
Urban:	43.6%	Latino	6.8%		*(356 of 435)*
Suburban:	19.6%	Asian	2.2%	Under $50,000	57.1%
Rural:	36.8%	Amer. Indian	1.4%	$50,000-$99,999:	29.5%
Land area:	10,663	Two races	3.2%	$100,000-$199,999:	11.2%
Pop/sq. mi.:	72.4	White Ethnic	25.9%	$200,000 or more:	2.2%
Born in state:	46.5%			Poverty Rate	20.9%
		Education			
Age Groups		H.S. grad or less:	35.9%	**Work**	
Under 18:	19.5%	Some college:	38.0%	White collar:	34.3%
18 to 34:	23.6%	College degree, 4 yr.:	15.8%	Blue collar:	42.9%
35 to 64:	38.6%	Post-grad study:	10.4%	Sales and service:	22.8%
Over 64:	18.2%			Govt. workers:	17.3%
		Military			
		Veterans/active duty:	11.2%		

Southwest Oregon: Eugene, Albany

Eugene is nestled in the southernmost bit of lowland in Oregon's Willamette Valley, and is surrounded by mountains on three sides. It is a farming center, a lumber provider, and most notably, a university town. In 1876, the University of Oregon was established, a symbol of the state's strong Yankee cultural ethic. Eugene and next-door Springfield, which has become a center for the manufacture of computer chips, have grown into comfortable midsized towns. Eugene has bicycle paths along the riverbanks and its main streets. It likes to bill itself as the "Running Capital of the Universe"—Phil Knight and his former University of Oregon track coach, Bill Bowerman, started Nike here, the first soles formed on a waffle iron. Now the third-largest city in Oregon, Eugene has small-town ambience and urban sensibilities, and its liberal voters have been vital to Democrats statewide. The 1978 comedy *National Lampoon's Animal House* was filmed at the University of Oregon after many universities declined to provide a location for the movie over its raunchy content. Knight has poured millions of dollars into University of Oregon facilities. The student online news site *Daily Emerald* in 2012 put the donation number at a whopping $300 million. In June 2015, downtown Eugene had high-speed fiber optic Internet technology, even before such service was available in downtown Portland.

Beyond Eugene and Springfield are southwest Oregon's green-clad mountains, and for years, the region cut more timber than anywhere else in the country. But Timber Country, including forest-product businesses,

Voter Turnout	
2013 Total Citizen 18+	597,613
2014 House Turnout	310,179
2014 Turnout as % CVAP	51.9%
2012 Turnout as % CVAP	61.1%

2012 Presidential Vote

Barack Obama (D) 188,563	(51%)
Mitt Romney (R)................163,931	(45%)

2008 Presidential Vote

Barack Obama (D) 210,108	(54%)
John McCain (R)................165,368	(43%)

Cook Partisan Voting Index: D+2

has struggled. Recent economic development has been diverse, with gains in health care, tourism and retiree migration from California. Springfield is the putative home of the popular television show "The Simpsons," according to its creator, Oregon native Matt Groening. The largest employer in the real Springfield is Peace Health, a Catholic health care and hospital system. Renewable energy company Ocean Power Technologies is working on a project to generate electricity for 1,000 homes through ocean wave motion. Plans for a liquefied natural gas terminal in Coos Bay drew protests in early 2015. Protests for years have stalled plans for a near-by natural-gas pipeline.

The 4th Congressional District of Oregon includes Eugene, Springfield and surrounding Lane County. It also includes Oregon's other main college town, Corvallis, home to Oregon State University. South along Interstate 5 it takes in Roseburg in Douglas County. Also in the 4th is the southern half of Oregon's stunning Pacific coastline, to the California border. Eugene is heavily Democratic, while Douglas County and Roseburg vote Republican; the travails of the logging industry hurt the Democrats here. The 4th is Democratic-leaning, but far more blue-collar and less liberal than the Portland area's districts.

Peter DeFazio (D)

Peter DeFazio, a Democrat first elected in 1986, is a persistent—and sometimes outspoken—populist who doesn't mind showing his independence from his party or loudly criticizing the conservative ideas he disdains. Oregon's longest-serving House member, he has shown legislative skills as the top Democrat on the Natural Resources Committee and, since January 2015, on the Transportation and Infrastructure Committee.

DeFazio grew up in Massachusetts, moved to Oregon for graduate school, was a bike mechanic, and went to work for Democratic Rep. Jim Weaver. In 1982, DeFazio moved to Springfield and won a seat on the county commission. When Weaver retired in 1986, DeFazio won his House seat in close contests. He beat Bill Bradbury 34%-33% in the primary and took the general election 54%-46%.

DeFazio has compiled a record that seems to satisfy both Eugene and the rest of the district: He's liberal on most issues, yet moderate on social issues. An original founder of the loose-knit Progressive Caucus, he has not been shy to express his anger that millions of working Americans suffered during the boom years before the economic collapse in 2008 and the recession. DeFazio is known for sarcasm and his tendency to yell during debates. He dismissively referred to Treasury Secretary Timothy Geithner, whom he considered overly protective of Wall Street, as "Timmy." Referring to the GOP's fiscal policy, he told MSNBC in 2009: "Tax cuts solve all problems. I mean, we are pretty soon going to fill potholes with tax cuts." But in an acknowledgment of the need to keep himself in check, he told *The Oregonian* in 2013 that he keeps a blood-pressure cuff attached to his iPad.

DeFazio often takes idiosyncratic or maverick views. With Democratic Rep. Louise Slaughter of New York, he has long sought to remove the antitrust exemption from the health insurance industry. He introduced a bill in 2011 allowing people to opt out of the health care law's individual mandate reviled by Republicans—but only if they waived the right to any government-backed medical help for at least three years. He has called for abolishing the Selective Service System, the independent federal agency that manages draft registration. DeFazio blames his failures on his colleagues' desire not to appear weak on defense. He voted against climate legislation in 2009 putting caps on carbon emissions because he said there were better ways to reduce greenhouse gas emissions, such as a carbon tax. And he introduced a bill calling for a tax on large stock and derivative transactions that drew predictable enmity from Wall Street and business-minded Democrats. Sometimes, his views are enacted: He took the lead in 2007 in the House effort to permit airline pilots to carry guns in the cockpit, and although the Bush administration initially opposed it, DeFazio won by an astonishing 250-175. The Senate later followed suit.

When Democrats won control of the House in 2006, DeFazio became chairman of Transportation and Infrastructure's Highways and Transit Subcommittee. He was the only member of Congress to oppose the final 2009 economic stimulus bill after backing the original House version, saying it did not sufficiently boost transportation spending. He worked to get $1.1 billion authorized for Oregon projects in the 2012 two-year surface transportation bill. He also made sure the measure contained a temporary extension of federal payments for Oregon counties. DeFazio has called for replacing the federal gasoline tax with a per-barrel tax on oil companies. "What if we got rid of the tax that people don't like and move it upstream to something that most people don't like—the oil industry?" he asked *The Oregonian*.

In July 2013, after Rep. Edward Markey of Massachusetts was elected to the Senate, DeFazio took over as ranking Democrat on the Natural Resources Committee. He promised to "push for a 21st century energy policy that promotes conservation and the development of renewable resources on federal lands and waters," but the next 18 months turned out to be an unusually quiet legislative period. In May 2014, the committee passed his bipartisan bill to save West Coast fishermen millions of dollars by refinancing high-interest federal loans for fishing vessels in a program that had been created in 2003 to address over-capacity; the House failed to act. DeFazio strongly objected to Republican efforts to revise the Endangered Species Act.

The top Democratic post on Transportation and Infrastructure opened after the 2014 election when West Virginia Rep. Nick Rahall lost reelection. DeFazio initially faced a challenge from northern California's John Garamendi, who was very junior in seniority but argued that he could work more successfully with Republicans. Garamendi failed to generate support and dropped his bid. When he took over, DeFazio urged Congress to get serious about fixing the nation's decaying transportation facilities and stop "relying on short-term patches for long-standing problems." He called for financing the highway trust fund with a one-time 14% transition tax on foreign earnings by U.S. companies, followed by a 19% minimum tax on their global profits. He pledged bipartisan cooperation and said that his goals were "job creation, increased efficiency and strategic growth."

Long before it became the consensus position for congressional Democrats, he had been a vocal foe of international trade deals. He opposed the Clinton-era North American Free Trade Agreement and later was a leader in the fight against normal trade relations with China. In June 2015, he was an outspoken foe of granting Trade Promotion Authority to President Barack Obama to expedite his prospective Trans-Pacific Partnership. The agreement, he said, would have "relegated Congress to be used as a doormat... [for an agreement that] has been negotiated in secret and will export jobs, drive down U.S. wages, and undermine U.S. sovereignty." When Obama made a last-ditch plea to House Democrats at the Capitol prior to the initial failed vote on the plan, DeFazio told reporters, "The president tried to both guilt people and impugn their integrity. I was insulted." But the House reversed itself the following week, with support from the other three House Democrats from Oregon.

Until 2010, DeFazio routinely won reelection by more than 60% in his marginal district. That year, Republican Art Robinson held him to 54% of the vote after getting a boost from outside interest groups' ads tying DeFazio to liberal House Speaker Nancy Pelosi. He beat Robinson again with 59% in 2012 after first crushing Robinson's son, Matthew, 90%-10%, in the Democratic primary. And in Republican-friendly 2014, he beat Robinson once more with 59%.

After GOP Sen. Bob Packwood resigned in 1995, DeFazio ran in the special election. His opposition to gun control and NAFTA provided clear contrasts to Portland liberal Democratic Rep. Ron Wyden. The better-funded Wyden won the primary 50%-44% and prevailed in the general. DeFazio seems comfortable in serving as the occasional lone wolf in the Oregon delegation, even as he has gained more influence in his committee work.

FIFTH DISTRICT

Kurt Schrader (D)

Elected 2008, 4th term; b. Oct. 19, 1951, Bridgeport, CT; Cornell U., B.A. 1973, U. of IL Urbana-Champaign, B.S. 1975, D.V.M. 1977; Episcopalian; divorced; 5 children.

Elected Office: OR House, 1997-2003; OR Senate, 2003-08.

Professional Career: Former aide, AK gov.; Veterinarian, 1978-2008.

DC Office: 2431 RHOB, 20515, 202-225-5711; Fax: 202-225-5699; Website: schrader.house.gov.

State Offices: Oregon City, 503-557-1324; Salem, 503-588-9100.

Committees: *Energy & Commerce:* Environment & the Economy; Health.

Group Ratings

	ADA	ACLU	AFL-CIO	LCV	ITI	COC	HAFA	ACU	CFG	FRC
2014	55%	72%	–	60%	80%	71%	12%	12%	6%	0%
2013	70%	C	86%	71%	C	69%	C	21%	9%	C

National Journal Ratings

	2013 LIB	—	2013 CONS
Economic	57%	—	43%
Social	60%	—	39%
Foreign	74%	—	26%
Composite	64%	—	36%

Key Votes of the 113th Congress

1. Sandy storm spending	Y	5. Medical Marijuana	Y	9. Syrian Rebels Training	Y
2. Violence Against Women Act	Y	6. Farm Bill	Y	10. Keystone pipeline	N
3. Guantanamo Bay Detainees	Y	7. Afghanistan Combat	Y	11. Immigration Exec. Action	N
4. Abortion 20-week ban	N	8. NSA Phone Data Collection	Y	12. Bipartisan budget deal	N

Election Results

2014 general	Kurt Schrader (D)	150,944	(54%)	$1,325,699	$3,810
	Tootie Smith (R)	110,332	(39%)	$61,232	$1,110
	Marvin Sannes (I)	7,674	(3%)		
	Raymond Baldwin (CNP)	6,208	(2%)		
2014 primary	Kurt Schrader (D)	41,078	(84%)		
	Anita Brown (D)	7,913	(16%)		

Prior winning percentages: 2012 (54%), 2010 (51%), 2008 (54%)

Population		Race and Ethnicity		Income	
Total:	785,707	White	76.3%	Median income:	$53,431
Urban:	50.3%	Latino	15.6%		(181 of 435)
Suburban:	38.5%	Asian	2.7%	Under $50,000	46.7%
Rural:	11.2%	Amer. Indian	0.9%	$50,000-$99,999:	33.1%
Land area:	3,217	Two races	2.7%	$100,000-$199,999:	17.0%
Pop/sq. mi.:	244.3	White Ethnic	24.3%	$200,000 or more:	3.2%
Born in state:	50.2%			Poverty Rate	15.3%
		Education			
Age Groups		H.S. grad or less:	35.9%	**Work**	
Under 18:	23.4%	Some college:	35.6%	White collar:	32.8%
18 to 34:	21.6%	College degree, 4 yr.:	18.3%	Blue collar:	43.9%
35 to 64:	39.2%	Post-grad study:	10.2%	Sales and service:	23.2%
Over 64:	15.8%			Govt. workers:	14.6%
		Military			
		Veterans/active duty:	10.1%		

West-Central Oregon: Salem, Clackamas County

The Willamette Valley was the great Promised Land at the end of the Oregon Trail, shielded from the cold storms of the Pacific by mountains but squeezing most of the moisture out of the clouds in the form of rain, fog and persistent mist. New England Yankees planted small towns they called Salem

Voter Turnout	
2013 Total Citizen 18+	555,176
2014 House Turnout	281,088
2014 Turnout as % CVAP	50.6%
2012 Turnout as % CVAP	63.3%

and Oregon City, founded schools and colleges, built tall-spired churches and eventually Salem's distinctive Art Deco state capitol. This was one of the few valleys in the West that settlers found readily suitable for agriculture. The Willamette Valley's soil is fertile, and the plain created by the waters of the Willamette sweeping down from the mountains is broad, although industrial runoff has made the river among the most polluted in the nation. The Willamette Valley is home to a burgeoning wine industry, known especially for its pinot noir.

Salem and Eugene are battling for the distinction of Oregon's second-largest city, after Portland. Salem, the state capital, has pulled slightly ahead; its 20% Hispanic population is more than twice the share in Eugene. Like the rest of the state, Salem was slow to rebound from the recession; in April 2015, its 5.5% jobless rate was near the national average. In

June 2015, Microsoft announced that it will build in Wilsonville its giant new touch screen—in separate 55-inch and 84-inch versions. The company gained a local presence in 2012 when it purchased a Pixel facility. Also based in growing Wilsonville is Mentor Graphics, whose 1,000 employees make software to produce computer chips.

The 5th Congressional District of Oregon includes much of the northern Willamette Valley. The district spreads south to Salem, also home of Willamette University, the oldest university in the West, and crosses the Coast Range to take in Lincoln and Tillamook counties, which are fishing, logging, and cheese-making communities. In the thinly populated coastal areas, Newport is a busy port, where the Coast Guard announced in 2014 that it was closing its aviation facility because of budget pressures. Historically, the valley was Republican, but it has been trending Democratic. Overall, the 5th is a competitive district. President Barack Obama was held to a 50%-47% win in 2012.

2012 Presidential Vote		
Barack Obama (D) 172,986	(50%)
Mitt Romney (R)................161,482	(47%)
2008 Presidential Vote		
Barack Obama (D) 187,682	(53%)
John McCain (R).................156,657	(44%)
Cook Partisan Voting Index: EVEN		

Kurt Schrader (D)

Kurt Schrader, a Democrat elected in 2008, juggles priorities in a district that is divided between urban and rural. A veterinarian and organic farmer, he joined the Energy and Commerce Committee in 2015 to deal more broadly with health-care and energy issues.

Schrader was born in Bridgeport, Connecticut, where his father was a chemical engineer. He studied government at Cornell University, where he met his wife, Martha, also a student. Schrader pursued his passion for veterinary medicine at the University of Illinois. After college, the couple settled in Oregon. Schrader ran two veterinary clinics in Canby. From his farm, he sold organic fruits and vegetables. Schrader entered politics as a member of the Canby planning commission for 15 years, assisting in development of the city's land use plan. In 1997, he won a seat in the state House, and six years later was elected to the state Senate. There, he was co-chairman of the Joint Ways and Means Committee, with jurisdiction over taxation. His major focus was improving public education, and he pushed legislation to tax new construction to pay for schools. He developed a reputation as a conservative Democrat and opposed his party on increasing the minimum wage. His wife was his chief of staff in his early years in the Legislature, and later served on the Clackamas County Commission. They divorced in 2011.

When Democratic Rep. Darlene Hooley announced her retirement in 2008, Schrader lent his campaign $130,000 during the primary and won over 50% of the vote against three opponents. In the general election, he faced Republican shipping entrepreneur Mike Erickson, who had challenged Hooley two years earlier. Erickson lent his campaign $1.6 million and managed to win the Republican primary, in spite of his opponent publicizing allegations that Erickson had impregnated a woman in 2000 and then paid for an abortion. Erickson admitted to the relationship but denied paying for an abortion. The general election was initially considered wide open. This was George W. Bush territory in 2000 and 2004, but a surge in new Democratic voters gave Democrats their first voter-registration advantage in 12 years.

Erickson was unable to shake the allegations about his earlier relationship, and he limited his public appearances during the campaign. Schrader received endorsements from the Oregon Farm Bureau and several newspapers, and got financial help from the Democratic Congressional Campaign Committee. Erickson outspent Schrader by more than $1 million, but Schrader prevailed 54%-38%.

In the House, Schrader has been willing to go his own way from his party. In 2013, he became the fiscally conservative Blue Dog Coalition's co-chair for communications and outreach. Two years later, he became co-chair for administration. He was one of 22 House Democrats in 2012 to support fellow Blue Dog Jim Cooper's unsuccessful budget proposal based on the bipartisan Simpson-Bowles commission's recommendations. He has voted for Republican alternatives to weaken the 2010 health care law by allowing consumers to purchase insurance plans that don't meet the terms of that law. He originally cosponsored the DREAM Act for children of illegal immigrants but later voted against it, saying he wanted a more comprehensive immigration-reform solution. In January 2015, he voted for the first time for the Keystone XL pipeline from Canada, the only Democrat from Oregon to support the project. In June 2015, he was among only 28 House Democrats voting for trade promotion authority, though three of them were from Oregon.

Schrader has been an outspoken critic of the Supreme Court's *Citizens United* decision in 2010 that eased campaign finance restrictions, and has proposed a constitutional amendment to allow congressional regulation of campaign contributions and spending. He joined the non-partisan No Labels group, which has urged a bipartisan congressional agenda. He attracted local support by joining a bipartisan plan to place 1.6 million acres of federal lands in Western Oregon into a state trust focused on timber production.

With his new seat on the influential Energy and Commerce Committee in January 2015, Schrader promised more spending on renewable energy and access to quality health coverage without increased government regulations. He praised the panel's bipartisan handling of several bills in the next few months, and seemed to take some credit.

National Republicans went after Schrader's seat in 2010 and recruited state Rep. Scott Bruun, who accused Schrader of not being the fiscal hawk he portrayed himself as and going "on a world-class spending spree with your money." Schrader parried that Bruun wanted to privatize Social Security, and he out-raised Bruun, $1.9 million to $1.2 million. Schrader won 51%-46%, benefiting from the huge Democratic vote in Multnomah while carrying Benton and Clackamas counties and staying even in Marion County.

The 2012 redistricting made Schrader's district slightly more favorable to Republicans by leaving only a sliver of Multnomah and adding more of Clackamas. The GOP, however, didn't help Republican Fred Thompson, allowing Schrader to win 54%-43%. In 2013, Schrader's home-state colleague Greg Walden took over as chairman of the National Republican Congressional Committee, with plans to take more seriously winning back the seat in 2014. Republicans nominated Clackamas Commissioner Tootie Smith, a conservative who once raffled off a Glock pistol to raise campaign funds. But she spent only $61,000 while Schrader spent $1.3 million. He won 54%-39% and led in all seven counties, his most impressive win yet.

★ PENNSYLVANIA ★

The state where the Founders declared their independence and wrote the Constitution started out as a Quaker haven, founded in 1682 by the pacifist William Penn, son of an admiral to whom King Charles II owed political debts. Pennsylvania's policy of tolerance attracted Englishmen of many religious sects and thousands of pietist Germans—ancestors of the Pennsylvania Dutch. Soon, Pennsylvania became the major settlement in the Middle Colonies and Philadelphia the largest colonial port. In the 18th century, bordermen from Scotland, the north of England, and Northern Ireland landed in Philadelphia and crossed the corduroy ridges of the Appalachians and settled the mountainous interior. The geometric lines William Penn had obtained from the king included two major river systems—the wide Delaware estuary with its thriving commerce and rich hinterland, and the golden triangle where the Allegheny and Monongahela Rivers joined to form the Ohio, still today important geographical features defining the eastern and western parts of the state. Philadelphia was the natural host for the Continental Congresses that began meeting in 1774 and in the early republic it seemed destined to become the London of America, the metropolis of government and commerce and culture. Pittsburgh, founded in 1758, was the young republic's key frontier metropolis, the fulcrum point of American expansion.

But Philadelphia—and Pennsylvania—failed to maintain the central position the Founders expected. As part of a political deal, the young republic's capital was located on a site along the Potomac River. And the Erie Canal from the Hudson to Lake Erie, completed in 1825, channeled trade away from Philadelphia to New York. Philadelphia's Quaker tradition, tolerant of diversity, was overshadowed in intellectual life by New England's Puritan tradition, morally stern, angrily intolerant, ready to use the state to impose cultural values from abolition to prohibition. So Pennsylvania evolved into America's early capital of energy and heavy industry. Northeast Pennsylvania was the nation's primary source of anthracite, the hard coal used for home heating, and western Pennsylvania was laced with bituminous coal, the soft coal used in steel production. Connected with Philadelphia by the Pennsylvania Railroad, Pittsburgh was the center of the nation's steel industry by 1890; it became synonymous with industrial prosperity and, led by its adopted son, steel mogul Andrew Carnegie, for philanthropy as well. Immigrants poured in from Europe and from the surrounding hills to work in western Pennsylvania's mines and factories, a hardscrabble environment that would produce a disproportionate share of football stars, from Johnny Unitas to Joe Namath to Dan Marino, Jim Kelly, and Joe Montana.

Pennsylvania was the nation's second-largest state from the first census in 1790 up through 1940, but it stopped growing rapidly during the Depression and in some parts of the state, growth has never returned. After World War II, both home heating and industry shifted away from coal. Only the embers remain, or, the fires: The Red Ash colliery fire, ignited in 1915, burns on beneath the hills above Wilkes-Barre, as do a few dozen other fires in abandoned coal mines. Similarly, Pennsylvania steel began a sharp decline in the 1960s. Big steel got import quotas as long ago as 1969—Pennsylvania has been a protectionist state since the first Bessemer converter furnaces were lit—but they didn't create jobs. By the time quotas lapsed in the 1990s, the industry had modernized, but mostly in huge new Indiana mills and in small mini-mills scattered far from the factories that once lined the Monongahela.

The result has been the slowest population growth of any major state: There were 9.6 million Pennsylvanians in 1930 and 12.7 million in 2010. Pennsylvania cast 36 electoral votes for Franklin Roosevelt in 1940 and cast only 20 for Barack Obama in 2012. In 1960, it had 30 House members, as many as California and more than Texas. Now it has 18 to California's 53 and Texas' 36. For the most part, people growing up here have been as likely to leave as to stay, and few outsiders moved in (Pennsylvania has fewer Hispanics than most of its neighbors, at just 6%). Meanwhile, the state has grown increasingly old; only three others (Florida, West Virginia and Maine) have a higher percentage of residents age 65 and over. Old, too, is some of the state's infrastructure—half of all housing units in the state were built before 1960, and Pennsylvania ranks first in the nation in the percentage of bridges that are rated deficient.

In the last two decades, Pennsylvania has begun to perk up. Big hospitals have replaced big steel mills as employers in metro Pittsburgh and metro Philadelphia, and the surrounding

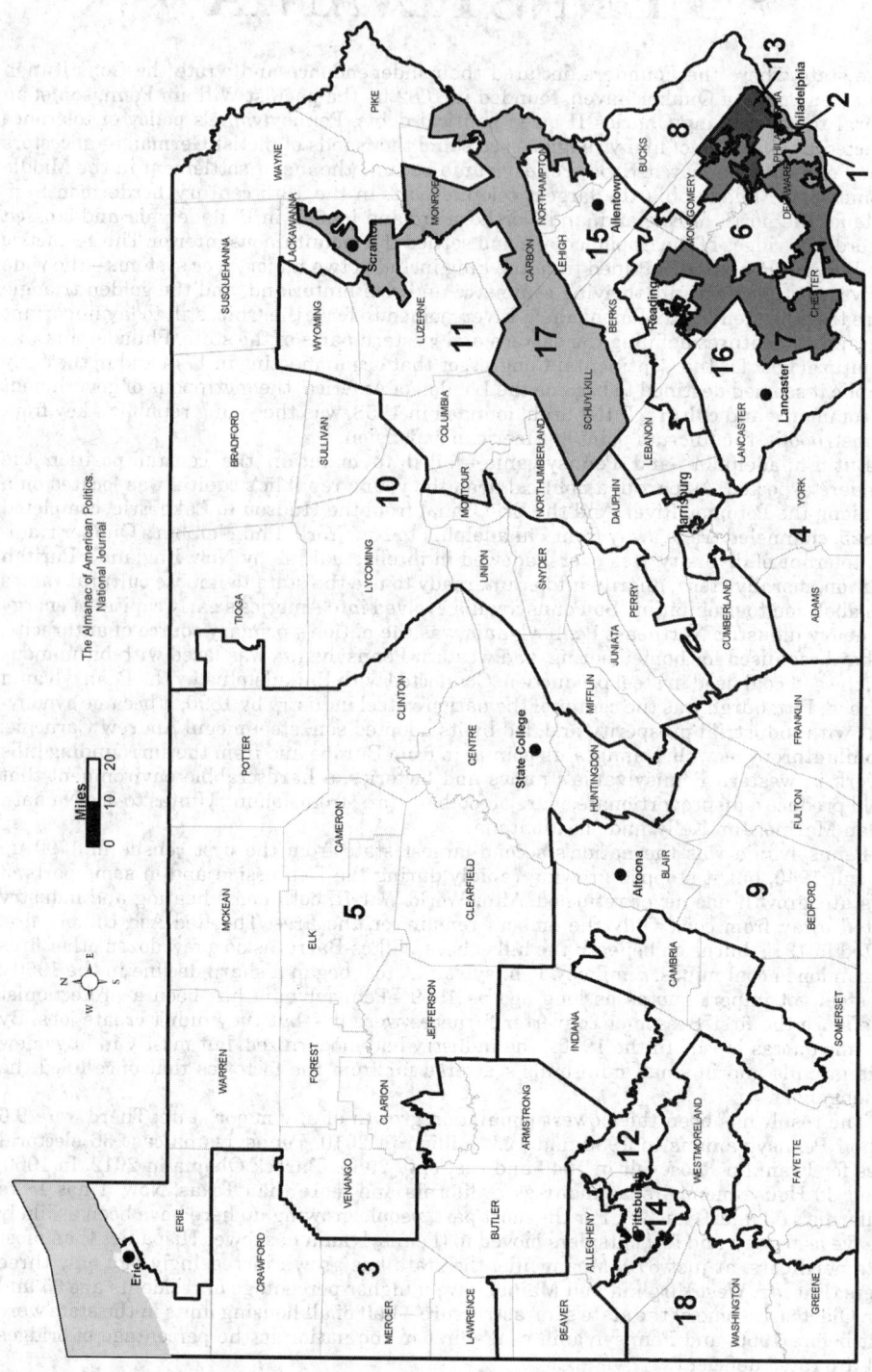

The Almanac of American Politics.
National Journal

Congressional district boundaries were first effective for 2012.

Districts 1, 2, 7, 13 and 17 are highlighted for visibility.

SEE INSET for Greater Philadelphia.

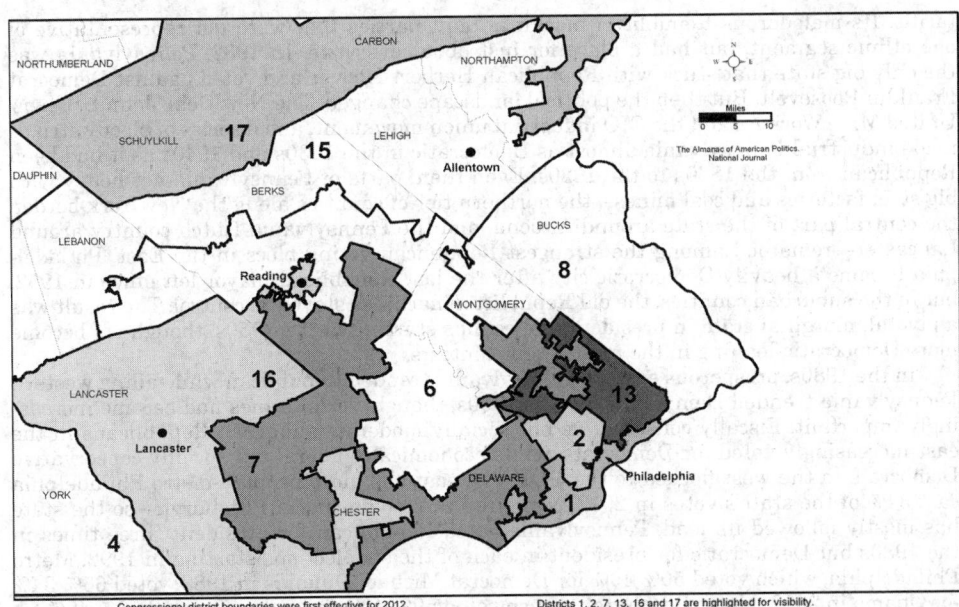

Congressional district boundaries were first effective for 2012. Districts 1, 2, 7, 13, 16 and 17 are highlighted for visibility.

countryside has experienced diversified economic growth. Some municipalities have become insolvent because of unwise investment in unprofitable facilities—an incinerator in Harrisburg, parking structures in Scranton. Pennsylvania has held taxes down more than many of its Northeastern neighbors, and there has been significant growth in the counties along its eastern border and in York County north of Baltimore. New Yorkers are moving a couple of miles farther out on Interstate 80 to retire near the Delaware Water Gap and the Poconos, and Hispanics from New York and North Jersey are moving out Interstate 78 to work in Reading, Allentown and Bethlehem, where a big Sands casino opened in 2009 on what was once Bethlehem Steel property. Metro Philly, and even the central city of Philadelphia, grew in population from 2000 to 2014. "While its public school system remains a mess, its crime rate elastic and its poverty rate high, Philadelphia has been revitalized over the last decade and a half, with celebrity chefs, a vibrant technology sector and thriving art scene, all boxes to check for cities on the move these days," the *New York Times* wrote upon the city's selection as the site of the 2016 Democratic convention.

James Carville once famously described the state as Pittsburgh and Philadelphia with Alabama in between. But today, rural Pennsylvania, once the site of the world's first oil well and first commercial nuclear power plant, is once again becoming a major economic engine. The Marcellus Shale beneath 60% of Pennsylvania and much of upstate New York contains the nation's largest reserves of natural gas embedded in hard rock. It can be brought to the surface by hydraulic fracturing—better known as "fracking"—in which water under high pressure is injected into the shale, fracturing it and releasing gas previously locked inside. With the development of horizontal drilling, fracking became commercially feasible in 2004, and there are now wells through much of the western and northern parts of the state. Environmental groups have charged that fracking can pollute drinking water sources, but development is still going forward. Pennsylvania imported 75% of its natural gas in 2007, but was exporting it by 2012, and a new fee generated $200 million in state revenue. While New York state, heeding Manhattan environmentalists, bans fracking, in Pennsylvania it is generating jobs—234,000 jobs according to the Marcellus Shale Coalition—and the state recently installed its first of a planned 17 compressed natural gas stations on the Pennsylvania Turnpike. Many counties in western Pennsylvania that had been languishing for years are suddenly crackling with activity, although some studies suggest a growing risk not just of environmental contamination but also higher crime, traffic casualties and other social ills.

For generations after the Civil War—whose turning point is often pegged to quiet Gettysburg—Pennsylvania was the most Republican of the large states, due in part to the legacy of Abraham Lincoln and the Union, and due in part to the steel industry and high tariffs. Its malodorous Republican machines built parties that were not representative of one ethnic segment, but had a place for just about everyone. In 1932, Pennsylvania was the only big state that stuck with Republican Herbert Hoover and voted against Democrat Franklin Roosevelt. But then the political landscape changed. The New Deal, John L. Lewis' United Mine Workers and the CIO industrial union movement, and a series of bloody strikes made industrial Pennsylvania almost as Democratic in the 1930s and 1940s as it had been Republican from the 1860s to the 1920s. Even then, parts of Pennsylvania not heavy with big steel factories and coal mines—the northern tier of counties along the New York border, the central part of the state around Altoona, and the Pennsylvania Dutch country around Lancaster—remained among the strongest Republican voting blocs in the East. Philadelphia became a heavily Democratic city after the last Republican mayor left office in 1952, but in the suburban counties, the old Republican machines stayed in control. The result was a pivotal, marginal state in presidential elections starting in the 1950s, though it's become more Democratic-leaning in the most recent contests.

In the 1980s, prosperous eastern Pennsylvania trended Republican while ailing western Pennsylvania trended Democratic. By the 1990s, though, social issues had become increasingly important. Fiscally conservative but socially moderate suburban Republicans in the east increasingly voted for Democrats, while economically liberal but socially conservative Democrats in the west flocked to the GOP. The east has more people—metro Philadelphia cast 34% of the state's votes in 2012, compared to 20% for metro Pittsburgh—so the state has mostly followed its lead. Pennsylvania voted Republican for president three times in the 1980s but Democratic for president in each of the six elections starting in 1992. Metro Philadelphia, which voted 50%-49% for Democrat Michael Dukakis in 1988, voted 65%-34% for Obama in 2012. Metro Pittsburgh, which voted 59%-40% for Dukakis, voted 50%-49% for Mitt Romney in 2012.

For the better part of four decades, Pennsylvania had two Republican senators, except when Democrat Harris Wofford won a 1991 special election following the death of Republican John Heinz that presaged the presidential victory of Bill Clinton a year later. Wofford lost in the Republican wave of 1994, and for a dozen years, Pennsylvania had two Republicans, though very different ones—moderate Arlen Specter and conservative Rick Santorum. In 2006, Santorum lost 59%-41% to Democrat Bob Casey Jr., and in April 2009, Specter switched parties to become a Democrat rather than face Rep. Pat Toomey in the GOP primary. In 2010, Specter lost the Democratic primary to Rep. Joe Sestak, who went on to lose the general election, 51%-49%, to Toomey. With Casey's reelection in 2012, Pennsylvania remains a split-party Senate delegation. Its House contingent, by contrast, leans 13-5 Republican, thanks to effective GOP line-drawing after the 2010 Census.

As for the governorship, 2014 saw the end of one of the nation's most striking and durable political patterns. Starting shortly after World War II, Pennsylvania voters chose to rotate the governorship between the two parties like clockwork every eight years—a pattern that began even before the state allowed two-term governorships. In 1986, Pennsylvanians elected Democrat Bob Casey, who, like his son the future senator, was a strong opponent of abortion rights. In 1994, they elected pro-abortion rights Republican Tom Ridge.

Population		Race and Ethnicity		Income	
Total:	12,773,801	White	79.1%	Median income:	$53,952
Urban:	37.3%	Black	10.4%		(22 of 50)
Suburban:	47.7%	Latino	5.9%	Under $50,000	47.8%
Rural:	14.9%	Asian	2.8%	$50,000-$99,999:	30.6%
Land area:	44,743	Two races	1.5%	$100,000-$199,999:	17.1%
Pop/sq. mi.:	285.5	White Ethnic	44.2%	$200,000 or more:	4.4%
Born in state:	73.5%			Poverty Rate	11.2%
		Education			
Age Groups		H.S. grad or less:	47.2%	Work	
Under 18:	21.3%	Some college:	24.1%	White collar:	36.5%
18 to 34:	22.3%	College degree, 4 yr.:	17.5%	Blue collar:	42.0%
35 to 64:	40.1%	Post-grad study:	11.2%	Sales and service:	21.6%
Over 64:	16.4%			Govt. workers:	10.7%
		Military			
		Veterans/active duty:	8.2%		

In 2002, they elected Democrat Ed Rendell, the ebullient former mayor of Philadelphia who had issued bonds to finance sports stadiums, museum wings, hospital additions, and factory expansions. In 2010, they elected Republican Tom Corbett, then attorney general. But Corbett struggled, including having to face questions about his handling of the Penn State child sexual-abuse scandal when he was attorney general. This gave Democrat Tom Wolf an opening to oust him in 2014. Despite the heavy Republican tide nationally—and despite Republicans all but completing a down-ballot sweep of western Pennsylvania—Wolf won, 55%-45%.

Voter Turnout			
2013 Total Citizen 18+			9,710,994
2014 Highest Statewide Turnout			3,495,866
2014 Turnout as % CVAP			36%
2012 Turnout as % CVAP			59.4%
Legislature			
Senate:		30R	19D	1V
House:		118R	80D	5V

Presidential Politics Pennsylvania has been seriously contested in just about every presidential election since 1976; only once in that time, in 2008, has any candidate received more than 52% of its votes or won by a double-digit percentage margin. George H. W. Bush carried the state 51%-48% in 1988 and his son lost it by an identical margin in 2004. The difference in those two contests vividly illustrates the political shifts in the state. In 1988, Democratic nominee Michael Dukakis won 15 of the state's 67 counties, most of those in the western region

2012 Presidential Vote		
Barack Obama (D) 2,990,274		(52%)
Mitt Romney (R)..............2,680,434		(47%)
2012 Presidential Primary		
Mitt Romney (R).................468,374		(58%)
Rick Santorum (D) 149,056		(18%)
Ron Paul (D) 106,148		(13%)
Newt Gingrich (D)...............84,537		(10%)
2008 Presidential Vote		
Barack Obama (D) 3,276,363		(54%)
John McCain (R)..............2,655,885		(44%)

of the state where white working class and union voters who worked in the steel mills around Pittsburgh remained true to their Democratic roots. Dukakis also won Philadelphia by a comfortable 2-1 margin, but he failed to carry any of the suburban counties that ring the city. In 2004, John Kerry won 13 counties, including Philadelphia, but he also carried three of the four large counties that surround the city, including the affluent "Main Line" suburbs in Bucks and Montgomery along with the more blue-collar Delaware. Kerry also did well in the industrial Lehigh Valley. Like Dukakis, Kerry won Lackawanna, home to Scranton, a former mining city. But Kerry also won counties like Northampton and Monroe that were beginning to become long-distance exurbs for the New York City metropolitan area. At the same time, Democratic allegiances in Western Pennsylvania were fraying as the national party adopted a distinctly liberal posture on social issues, and Kerry won only five counties in that region compared to 12 that went for Dukakis. By the 2008 general election, the only counties that Barack Obama carried on the state's western frontier were Allegheny, where Pittsburgh was transforming itself from a steel town to a technology center, and the Democratic bastion of Erie.

Obama lost the April 2008 Democratic primary to Hillary Clinton, and his comment in a closed fundraiser about people in small towns who were "bitter" about their economic straits and who "cling to guns or religion" seemed likely to hurt him in the small towns and coal and steel country outside metro Philadelphia in the general election. But the strong Democratic trend in the Philadelphia suburbs helped Obama to a 54%-44% victory. He ran worse than Kerry had in metro Pittsburgh four years earlier, but he swept metro Philadelphia 66%-33% and improved on Kerry's showing in the fast-growing counties in the Lehigh Valley. The old anthracite area around Scranton, where Vice President Joe Biden was born, delivered handsome majorities to the Obama-Biden ticket, as did Jewish and Latino voters—even though he had lost them in the primary. White Catholics voted 54% for McCain and white Protestants 61% for him, but African-Americans voted 95% for Obama, and voters registering no religion—11% of the total—voted 84% for Obama. Those with incomes over $200,000, a group heavily concentrated in the Philadelphia suburbs, voted 58% for Obama.

In 2012, Obama still carried the state 52%-47%, close to his national average, but Mitt Romney carried metro Pittsburgh 50%-49%, the first GOP nominee to do since Richard Nixon in 1972. But Obama won metro Philadelphia 65%-34%and limited Romney's margin in the rest of the state to 55%-44%. Romney won 56% of white Catholics and 64% of white Protestants, but blacks voted 93% for Obama and he carried those with no religion—now 12% of voters—with 74%. Exit polls indicate that Obama increased his percentage among voters with incomes under $50,000 but lost ground with those with incomes over $200,000, who voted 55% for Romney.

Pennsylvania's presidential primary was a battleground in 2008. By April, Obama had a narrow lead in delegates, but Clinton had won in Ohio and Pennsylvania looked, demographically and politically, a lot like the Buckeye State. Videotapes of divisive, black-versus-white speeches by Obama's longtime pastor, the Rev. Jeremiah Wright (who grew up in Philadelphia), were played over and over on cable television, and Obama responded in a widely hailed speech on race relations in Philadelphia. Moreover, it was plain from earlier results in Ohio, Virginia, Tennessee, and Georgia that he was particularly weak in Jacksonian America, in the Appalachian chain that stretches from Alabama and Georgia in the south to southwestern Pennsylvania. Obama did have the support of Democratic Sen. Bob Casey, a moderate, giving him hope of carrying Casey's Scranton base. But Clinton had the support of Gov. Ed Rendell, who had strong appeal in metro Philadelphia, especially in the suburban counties that Obama targeted.

Some 2.3 million registered Democrats voted, with more than 130,000 voters switching their party registration to do so—far above the 1.3 million to 1.5 million turnouts in Democratic primaries from 1972 to 1992, and triple the 700,000-odd turnouts in 2000 and 2004, when Pennsylvania voted after the contest was long over. Clinton won a convincing 55%-45% victory. As in earlier contests in other states, she ran strongest among older and downscale voters, and she won among Jewish and Latino voters. Obama carried only seven counties—Philadelphia, Delaware, and Dauphin, with large black populations; Chester and Lancaster, relatively affluent areas; and Centre and Union, dominated by Penn State and Bucknell universities. The Republican primary was an afterthought, and John McCain won 73% of the roughly 800,000 votes cast.

In 2012, Romney's victories over Rick Santorum in Michigan, Ohio, Illinois, and Wisconsin gave him a wide lead in the delegate count. Santorum said he looked forward to fighting it out in his native Pennsylvania, but early polling was discouraging, and two weeks before Pennsylvania voted, Santorum announced he was suspending his campaign. He still won 18% of the vote, but Romney won 58% and carried all 67 counties.

Congressional Districts Pennsylvania lost two seats following the 2000 census and another after 2010. At 18 seats, the Keystone State now has half the House members it had at its peak in 1930. Republicans held the governorship and legislative majorities in both 2001 and 2011, and were in firm control of redistricting. But in 2001, under heavy pressure from White House strategist Karl Rove, they overreached. Republicans could have eliminated two of the Democrats' 10 seats and called it a day; instead they attempted to claim 13 of 19 seats by pairing three sets of Democratic incumbents, drawing Democrat Tim Holden into Republican George Gekas' seat, and creating two new Republican seats in the Pittsburgh and Philadelphia suburbs. But in 2002, Holden upset the septuagenarian Gekas, who proved politically rusty. Then, four years later, Democrats defeated four Republican incumbents in a strong Democratic year, proving Republicans had spread themselves too thin; two GOP incumbents who lost that year were damaged by scandals. In 2008, Democrats defeated a fifth Republican, Phil English, in the Erie area. Still, Republicans showed the utility of that old map in 2010, when they picked up five seats and turned Democrats' 12-7 edge upside-down.

114th Congress Lineup	
13 R	5 D
113th Congress Lineup	
13 R	5 D

By 2011, Republicans had learned their lesson. Needing to cut a seat while protecting 12 of their own, including five in districts Obama had carried in 2008, Republicans set about to axe only one Democrat. By process of elimination, the choice was easy. Merging any two of the three Philadelphia Democrats would have displaced too many Democratic voters into suburban Republican seats. Democrat Mike Doyle's Pittsburgh seat was too Democratic to break apart. Holden, in the Harrisburg area, had already proven he could run ahead of party lines in 2002 and no neighboring Republican wanted to face him. That left junior Democrats Jason Altmire in the 4th District and Mark Critz in the 12th District, who could easily be merged in the slow-growing, Republican-trending counties north and east of Pittsburgh.

After months of closed-door negotiations among finicky incumbents, Republicans unveiled their proposal and GOP Gov. Tom Corbett signed it less than 10 days later. The plan ruthlessly sewed the state, particular the Philadelphia suburbs, into a crazy quilt. Montgomery County, about the population of one district, was split five ways to boost the suburban Republican trio of Jim Gerlach, Mike Fitzpatrick and Pat Meehan, who were happy to feed their trickiest inner suburbs to Philadelphia's Democrats. In the northeast, Republicans stuffed Blue Dog Holden's 17th District with the liberal labor bastions of Scranton, Wilkes-Barre and Easton to relieve pressure on freshman Republican Lou Barletta in the 11th District and Charlie Dent in the Lehigh Valley's 15th.

In the west, Republicans split Erie to shore up freshman Mike Kelly and carefully merged Altmire and Critz in such a way that neither Democrat could plausibly run elsewhere but either would still be vulnerable in a general election. Sure enough, Critz defeated Altmire in a bitter primary and Republican Keith Rothfus defeated Critz in November. Back east, Holden lost his primary to a more liberal Democrat, and in November, Republicans held onto their other 12 seats without much of a fight.

Pennsylvania is House Democrats' redistricting dilemma in a nutshell. Statewide, Democrats in 2012 won about 83,000 more votes in House races than Republicans, but Republicans won 13 of 18 districts and look more secure in their seats than they did at the outset of the last decade. Retirements may be their biggest threat. Most of the GOP-held seats have enough advantage for incumbents to survive if they do their work, but open seats pose greater jeopardy. They easily survived when Gerlach called it quits in 2014 in the Chester County-based 6th District. Fitzpatrick's planned departure in 2016 from the "swing" Bucks County 8th District might be a more serious GOP problem. The state's projected loss of a seat in the next reapportionment likely would pose more challenges for Republicans. The five Democratic-held seats are secure in a general election, but some of the incumbents could be at risk in a primary under certain circumstances.

Governor

Tom Wolf (D)

Elected 2014, term expires Jan. 2019, 1st term; b. Nov. 17, 1948, York; Dartmouth Col., B.A. 1972, U. of London, M.A. 1978, MA Inst. of Technology, PhD 1981; Episcopalian; married (Frances); 2 children.

Professional Career: Peace Corps, India; CEO & pres., Wolf Organization, 1986-2006, Chmn. & CEO, 2009-present; Secy. of revenue, Gov. Ed Rendell cabinet, 2007-2009.

Office: Governor's Office, 508 Main Capitol Building, Harrisburg, 17120, 717-787-2500; Fax: 717-772-8284; Website: governor.pa.gov.

Election Results

2014 general	Tom Wolf (D)	1,920,355	(55%)
	Tom Corbett (R)	1,575,511	(45%)
2014 primary	Tom Wolf (D)	488,917	(58%)
	Allyson Schwartz (D)	149,027	(18%)
	Rob McCord (D)	142,311	(17%)
	Kate McGinty (D)	64,754	(8%)

Pennsylvanians elected Democrat Tom Wolf as their governor in 2014. Wolf, a wealthy latecomer to politics, capitalized on the unpopularity of GOP Gov. Tom Corbett just four years after Corbett had won the job with 55% of the vote. By winning, Wolf shattered Pennsylvania's rigid, post-World War II pattern of the two parties trading off the governorship every eight years.

Born in York and raised in Mount Wolf—named for his great-great-grandfather—Wolf acquired degrees from Dartmouth College, the University of London, and the Massachusetts Institute of Technology. During that time, he interrupted his studies to join the Peace Corps, serving two years in a village in India. After graduation, Wolf went to work for the family business, initially employed as a forklift operator at the Wolf Organization, a cabinet and building-materials company. In 1985, Wolf and two cousins bought the company and more than doubled its size. After selling the company to a private-equity firm in 2006, Wolf was tapped by Democratic Gov. Ed Rendell to be state revenue secretary in 2007 and 2008. Wolf intended to mount a campaign for governor to succeed Rendell, who was term-limited, but when the family business was on the brink of bankruptcy and collapse, Wolf abandoned the campaign and repurchased the company, refocusing its business model and restoring it to financial solvency. He stepped down as CEO in 2013 to focus on his 2014 bid for governor.

Democratic Rep. Allyson Schwartz was anointed the early front-runner in the primary, and state Treasurer Rob McCord and former state Environmental Protection Secretary Kathleen McGinty also ran. But Wolf poured $10 million of his own money into the race, allowing him to blanket the airwaves from January 2014 until the May primary, which Wolf won easily with 58 percent of the vote. (Wolf later tapped McGinty as his chief of staff. In August 2015, she launched her campaign for the seat of Republican Sen. Pat Toomey.)

In the general, Wolf had the air and campaign strategy of an incumbent, bolstered by double-digit leads in the polls. Corbett touted his tax cuts and his efforts to reduce the size of government, rein in spending, and bring businesses back to Pennsylvania. But Wolf hammered away at weak job growth under Corbett and accused him of slashing school funding. Wolf said that unlike Corbett, he would tax the fast-growing natural gas industry. Scrutiny of Corbett's role as attorney general in the investigation of former Penn State assistant football coach Jerry Sandusky on accusations of child molestation became another albatross for Corbett. Ultimately, Wolf won the high-spending race with 55%. Typical of the electoral turnabout was Allegheny County, Corbett's home turf, which he won narrowly in 2010 but lost by 60,000 votes in 2014.

Symbolically, Wolf came into office stressing transparency; he introduced a website to track expenses by cabinet secretaries and signed a gift ban, and he refused the gubernatorial salary and residence and paid out of pocket for office space for the state police officers assigned to protect him. But the tougher issues for the state were flat revenues and rising costs for Medicaid and pensions, which had led credit-rating agencies to lower the state's ratings. Wolf came into office facing a $2 billion budget gap. He proposed raising the personal income tax from 3.07% to 3.7% and the basic sales tax from 6% to 6.6% while also eliminating some sales-tax exemptions; these increases would be at least partially offset by reductions in school property taxes. Wolf proposed cutting the corporate net income tax in half over three years, while instituting a 5% severance tax for drilling and an increase in cigarette taxes. He pledged to increase spending on both higher education and K-12 schools. A Franklin & Marshall poll in March showed 59% of those surveyed supported Wolf's general approach, but to make it a reality, the governor needed to get it through two Republican-controlled and increasingly conservative legislative chambers.

Senior Senator

Robert Casey Jr. (D)

Elected 2006, term expires Jan. 2019, 2nd term; b. April 13, 1960, Scranton; Col. of the Holy Cross, B.A. 1982, Catholic U., J.D. 1988; Catholic; married (Terese); 4 children.

Elected Office: PA auditor gen., 1997-2005; PA st. treas., 2005-07.

Professional Career: Practicing atty., 1988-96.

DC Office: 393 RSOB, 20510, 202-224-6324; Fax: 202-228-0604; Website: casey.senate.gov.

State Offices: Bellefonte, 814-357-0314; Erie, 814-874-5080; Harrisburg, 717-231-7540; Lehigh Valley, 610-782-9470; Philadelphia, 215-405-9660; Pittsburgh, 412-803-7370; Scranton, 570-941-0930.

Committees: *Aging (Special). Agriculture, Nutrition, & Forestry:* Conservation, Forestry & Natural Resources; Livestock, Marketing & Ag Security; Nutrition, Specialty Crops, & Ag Research (RMM). *Finance:* Energy, Natural Resources & Infrastructure; Taxation & IRS Oversight (RMM). *Health, Education, Labor & Pensions:* Children & Families (RMM); Employment & Workplace Safety. *Joint Economic Committee.*

Group Ratings

	ADA	ACLU	AFL-CIO	LCV	ITI	COC	HAFA	ACU	CFG	FRC
2014	85%	86%	–	60%	100%	50%	3%	8%	20%	14%
2013	70%	C	100%	85%	C	50%	C	8%	5%	C

National Journal Ratings

	2013 LIB	—	2013 CONS
Economic	59%	—	39%
Social	62%	—	37%
Foreign	58%	—	36%
Composite	61%	—	39%

Key Votes of the 113th Congress

1. Sandy storm spending	Y	5. Student Loan Rates	Y	9. Bipartisan Budget Deal	Y
2. Chuck Hagel Confirmation	Y	6. Employee Non-Discrim'n Act	NV	10. Farm Bill Conference Rept.	N
3. Gun Background Checks	Y	7. Senate Vote on Judgeships	N	11. Unempl. Comp. Extension	Y
4. Immigration Reform	Y	8. Defense Dept. Spending	Y	12. Keystone Pipeline	Y

Election Results

2012 general	Robert Casey (D)	3,021,364	(54%)	$14,342,086	$1,214,669	$1,832,382
	Tom Smith (R)	2,509,132	(45%)	$21,206,326	$1,756,341	$803,659
2012 primary	Robert Casey (D)	565,488	(81%)			
	Joseph Vodvarka (D)	133,683	(19%)			

Prior winning percentage: 2006 (59%)

Robert Casey Jr., Pennsylvania's senior senator, is the son and namesake of a former governor of the Keystone State, and, in 2002, sought unsuccessfully to follow his late father's footsteps into the governor's mansion. He appeared to be waiting to make another run at that job when, in 2005, New York Sen. Charles Schumer—then head of the Democratic Senatorial Campaign Committee—convinced him instead to take a run at ousting two-term Republican Sen. Rick Santorum. The elder Casey, who served in the statehouse from 1986-1994, was an anti-abortion Democrat who clashed with national party leaders over that issue, and, in turn, Schumer's push to recruit the younger Casey rankled a number of the state's socially liberal Democratic activists. In his voting record since assuming the Senate seat, Casey has made moves to assuage the latter group—softening his anti-abortion stance somewhat around the edges, even as he told the Philadelphia-based *Inquirer* in 2014, "I'm a pro-life Democrat, always have been, always will be."

Casey won a second Senate term in 2012, but faced a tougher than expected challenge from a largely unknown—but personally wealthy—Republican after the GOP failed to recruit a better-known candidate. It's likely to put him higher in the sights of national Republican strategists when he next faces the voters in 2018. Born in the former coal town of Scranton in northeast Pennsylvania, the oldest son in a large Irish-Catholic family, Casey grew up in the Green Ridge neighborhood—also the boyhood home of Vice President Joe Biden. (Biden moved away two years before Casey's birth.) Robert Casey Sr. served as a state senator and Pennsylvania's auditor general, while losing three Democratic primaries for governor before finally winning that office. He was a feisty, tradition-minded practitioner of New Deal-style politics, but was best known nationally for his steadfast opposition to abortion rights. In 1992, he was prevented from speaking at the Democratic National Convention, a decision related to his abortion stance but also brought on by his skepticism about Bill Clinton as the right candidate. (The younger Casey, after backing Barack Obama over Hillary Clinton in the Pennsylvania Democratic primary in 2008, is firmly in the Clinton camp for 2016.)

Like his father, Casey Jr. graduated from the College of the Holy Cross in Massachusetts. He taught in an inner-city Philadelphia school for the Jesuit Volunteer Corps and got his law degree from Catholic University in Washington, D.C. He practiced law in Scranton, and then began his political career by winning election in 1996 as state auditor general, the same post his father had held a couple of decades earlier. He was reelected in 2000, and, two years later, running as a cultural conservative with strong labor support, he lost a bitter and expensive primary for governor to former Philadelphia Mayor Ed Rendell. Casey's tightly scripted campaign and negative ads tarnished his image, but he showed resilience by returning in 2004 to win the state treasurer's office after his second term as auditor general had come to a close.

A year later, national Democrats were looking for a strong challenger to Santorum, a high-profile social conservative with a red-state following and a blue-state constituency. First in the House and then in the Senate, Santorum showed a knack for winning elections against tough odds—but the state's political landscape had shifted considerably since his first election to the Senate in 1994. Schumer wanted Casey to run and quickly cleared the field to avoid a cash-draining primary. While Casey's opposition to abortion rights made him anathema to many cultural liberals in the Philadelphia area, Schumer believed Casey could make inroads into Santorum's culturally conservative and "pro-life" base—particularly in the western part of the state, where Santorum resided. Meanwhile, as the Democratic alternative to Santorum, Casey would be acceptable to "pro-choice" voters in suburban Philadelphia, Schumer reasoned. The national party's heavy-handed involvement in recruiting Casey rankled many Democrats in the state. But resistance to Casey's candidacy faded in the run-up to the election, as he maintained a steady and sizable lead over Santorum in the polls.

Though Santorum was being mentioned as a potential presidential candidate, his standing at home was tenuous. As early as April 2005, he trailed Casey by double digits in the polls. That summer, he released a book titled, *It Takes a Family: Conservatism and the Common Good*. Coming a year before he stood for reelection, it was perhaps not the best timing for a frank discourse on some of the most divisive cultural issues of the day. And Santorum's support of the unpopular Bush administration was not politically helpful to him in 2006, as Casey hammered him for voting "98 percent of the time" with President George W. Bush. He also characterized Santorum as having close ties to the oil, pharmaceutical, and insurance industries. In addition, Democrats sought mileage from the issue of Santorum's residence—an issue Santorum had used against his opponent in his first House campaign in 1990—and questioned whether his Virginia home disqualified him from casting a vote in Penn Hills, the Pittsburgh suburb where Santorum owned a home and was registered to vote. They also criticized Santorum for using Penn Hills school district taxpayer dollars to educate his children in a Pennsylvania-based online charter school, even though they spent much of their time in Virginia.

As Casey and Santorum clashed on issues ranging from the war in Iraq to immigration to Social Security, Casey's socially conservative positions—at the time, he opposed gun control and same-sex marriage—helped cut into Santorum's advantage outside the state's metropolitan areas. Together the two candidates raised $43 million. Santorum outspent Casey by more than $8 million, but it wasn't enough. Casey won 59%-41%, to become the first Pennsylvania Democrat elected to a full Senate term since 1962. He won by huge margins in Pittsburgh's Allegheny County and in Philadelphia, while holding his own in the Republican "T" that stretches from Pennsylvania Dutch country around Lancaster to the northern tier of sparsely populated counties along the New York border. Schumer's earlier political calculations proved to be correct, as Casey also swept the populous Philadelphia suburbs, winning 62 percent in Delaware and Montgomery counties, 59 percent in Bucks County, and 55 percent in Chester County.

In the Senate, Casey has been a reliable supporter of his party's agenda, while moving leftward on several hot-button issues since his first election. He angered some anti-abortion groups in April 2011 when he voted against denying federal funds to Planned Parenthood, saying the group provides many family planning services beyond abortion. He used a similar line of argument in July 2014 when he supported a bill to overturn the Supreme Court's so-called "Hobby Lobby" decision, a move that also irked some abortion foes. The legislation was an effort to put congressional Democrats on record in favor of forcing most businesses to offer employees a full range of contraceptive coverage, even if the businesses' owners raised religious objections. "The health-care service that's at issue here is contraception, which means prior to conception," Casey told the *Inquirer*. One political scientist viewed it as part of Casey's continuing effort to find a balance between his party's pro-abortion rights orthodoxy and his anti-abortion stance. "He has remained a pro-life Democrat, but one who has stretched the bounds of that definition," Christopher Borick of Muhlenberg College told the newspaper.

Casey did hold to his traditional anti-abortion stand in the spring of 2015, as he joined just three other Democrats in voting with most Republicans to advance a bill relating to human trafficking. Most Democrats were supporting a filibuster of the measure over a provision they believed would expand the scope of the so-called Hyde amendment, which bars federal dollars from being spent on abortions. But, two years earlier, Casey had reversed himself on two other social issues of perennial controversy: gun control and same-sex marriage. In April 2013, he supported a measure—co-authored by his Pennsylvania Republican colleague, Pat Toomey—to expand background checks for gun owners. The bill, proposed following the December 2012 school shooting in Newtown Connecticut in which more than two dozen were killed, failed to overcome a filibuster. The same month, Casey dropped his opposition to same-sex marriage. While he was among the last group of Senate Democrats to do so, his statement came more than two years before the 2015 Supreme Court ruling legalizing same-sex marriage across the country.

Casey, who acquired a sought-after seat on the Senate Finance Committee shortly after his 2012 reelection, has shared the skepticism of other Democrats from Rust Belt states toward international trade deals. "Our workers are losing over and over again when you have these trade agreements," Casey told the Allentown-based *Morning Call*. He voted against South Korea, Panama, and Colombia trade agreements that became law in October 2011, and, in the spring of 2015, was among the large majority of Democrats to oppose giving Obama "fast track" negotiating authority to expedite a 12-nation Asian trade agreement. Casey did push successfully in 2011 for an extension of trade adjustment assistance, designed to assist workers whose jobs have been lost due to foreign trade. In 2012, he offered a bill to withhold federal funds to call centers that shift jobs overseas.

In May 2012, Casey and Schumer combined on legislation aimed at preventing U.S. business executives from giving up their citizenship to evade taxes. The legislation stirred controversy, as the bill's sponsors singled out Facebook co-founder Eduardo Saverin, who had renounced his citizenship before the social networking company went public and new taxes kicked in. The conservative editorial page of *The Wall Street Journal* condemned it, and anti-tax activist Grover Norquist declared that similar legislation "existed in Germany in the 1930s." Saverin, who moved to Singapore, claimed he still paid hundreds of millions in U.S. taxes.

As part of his move to the Finance Committee, Casey gave up his slot on the Foreign Relations Committee. While on that panel, he visited Pakistan in August 2011 and urged government officials to limit exports of chemicals used to make improvised explosive devices, which have been responsible for the deaths of numerous U.S. soldiers in Afghanistan. A year earlier, he pushed Pakistani President Asif Ali Zardari to improve customs enforcement at border crossings, in the wake of news reports that caravans of Pakistani trucks carrying bomb-making materials were crossing into Afghanistan through the Khyber Pass. Another cause during his time on the Foreign Relations panel was the plight of Afghan women. In 2014, the "Scranton Restaurant" opened in western Afghanistan's Herat Province as the country's first female-only restaurant, with assistance from two famous Scranton natives, Casey and Biden, and donations from dozens of Scranton residents.

Closer to home, Casey, who also serves on the Health, Education, Labor and Pensions Committee, has consistently promoted legislation to award grants to states that provide high-quality, full-day pre-kindergarten programs. He reintroduced the legislation in 2015 after earlier proposing it in 2007 and 2013, while complaining Congress has ignored the business community's support for investment in early childhood education. "It's been terribly frustrating," he told the Easton *Express-Times*. He also has sought an expansion of the federal child care tax credit, saying the current credit—which begins to phase out after the first $15,000 in income—does not do enough to benefit middle-class families. And he has been an avid booster of funding for the State Children's Health Insurance Program, similar to a program his father instituted in Pennsylvania in 1992.

Like other coal-state senators, Casey has had his differences with the Obama administration on environment and energy policy. Responding in late 2014 to the administration's proposed climate change rules, Casey, emphasizing his commitment to environmental protection, said that a plan by the Environmental Protection Agency was necessary; Obama has sought to deal with climate change via EPA regulation in the absence of congressional action. But, in a 22-page letter to EPA officials, Casey asked for revisions in the plan, saying it set the carbon emissions target for Pennsylvania too high. "Our Commonwealth powers the electricity needs of states across the mid-Atlantic. We should be treated sensibly and fairly," he wrote. In early 2015, he also was one of only eight Democrats to support an unsuccessful effort to override Obama's veto of the Keystone XL pipeline, a project opposed by environmentalists. However, in 2011, Casey sponsored a bill to authorize the federal government to regulate the controversial natural gas drilling technique known as hydraulic fracturing or "fracking," which environmentalists blame for contaminating groundwater in Pennsylvania and elsewhere.

Republicans hoped to unseat Casey in 2012, but they had a hard time recruiting a top-tier candidate to take on the well-funded incumbent. None of their four primary candidates had significant name recognition. Businessman Steve Welch received the support of

Republican Gov. Tom Corbett, but lost the primary to former coal company executive Tom Smith—who spent almost $5 million of his own money and won the nomination with almost 40 percent of the vote. At the outset, Smith was given little chance to beat Casey. But, as a precaution, Casey kept his distance from Obama, whose popularity in the state had waned; in late November 2011, he failed to attend a speech Obama gave in Scranton. Casey's office said the senator had to be in Washington for floor votes.

A June 2012 Quinnipiac poll showed Casey with a comfortable lead of almost 20 points. Smith went on the attack, calling Casey "Senator Zero" and claiming he had accomplished little in the Senate. Casey's supporters worried he was underestimating Smith. "They've run a non-campaign up until now," Rendell told the Scranton *Times-Tribune* just weeks before the general election. Around that time, Smith personally invested another $10 million into his campaign, flooding the airwaves with attack ads. Despite his tea party support, Smith characterized himself as a former "union coal miner with big dreams," and in the campaign's only debate, he portrayed Casey as tight with the Obama administration. Casey sought to demonstrate his independence by highlighting his opposition to the Obama-sponsored trade deals. Still, an October Quinnipiac poll found Casey's lead had narrowed to just 3 points. Casey won endorsements from most of the state's major newspapers, including the conserva- tive *Pittsburgh Tribune-Review.* Smith outspent him, $21 million to $14 million, but Casey hung on to win, 54%-45%. He ran only slightly ahead of Obama, who garnered 52 percent in winning the state.

While Casey has endorsed Hillary Clinton in 2016, he also appears to have developed a bipartisan friendship with a leading Republican presidential contender, Florida Sen. Marco Rubio. In early 2015, Casey and Rubio co-authored legislation to boost computer science education in schools, and they previously sponsored a bill to help veterans own small businesses. In 2013, they co-authored an op-ed piece in *Politico*, seeking support for legislation they had sponsored to boost political and military opposition to the Assad regime in Syria.

Junior Senator

Pat Toomey (R)

Elected 2010, term expires Jan. 2017, 1st term; b. Nov. 17, 1961, Provi- dence, RI; Harvard U., B.A. 1984; Catholic; married (Kris); 3 children.

Elected Office: Allentown Gov't Study Comm., 1994-96; U.S. House, 1999-2005.

Professional Career: Investment banker, Chemical Bank, 1984-86; Investment banker, Morgan Grenfell, 1986-90; Financial consultant, Springfield Ltd., 1990-91; Restaurateur, 1990-2001; Pres., Club for Growth, 2005-09.

DC Office: 248 RSOB, 20510, 202-224-4254; Fax: 202-228-0284; Web- site: toomey.senate.gov.

State Offices: Allentown, 610-434-1444; Erie, 814-453-3010; Harrisburg, 717-782-3951; Johnstown, 814-266-5970; Pittsburgh, 412-803-3501; Scranton, 570-941-3540; Philadelphia, 215-241-1090.

Committees: *Banking, Housing & Urban Affairs:* Economic Policy; Financial Institutions & Consumer Protection (Chmn); Securities, Insurance & Investment. *Budget. Finance:* Health Care (Chmn); Social Security, Pensions & Family Policy; Taxation & IRS Oversight.

Group Ratings

	ADA	ACLU	AFL-CIO	LCV	ITI	COC	HAFA	ACU	CFG	FRC
2014	15%	6%	–	0%	33%	88%	67%	88%	86%	79%
2013	5%	C	11%	8%	C	75%	C	80%	93%	C

National Journal Ratings

	2013 LIB	—	2013 CONS
Economic	10%	—	87%
Social	30%	—	68%
Foreign	18%	—	80%
Composite	21%	—	80%

Key Votes of the 113th Congress

1. Sandy storm spending	N	5. Student Loan Rates	Y	9. Bipartisan Budget Deal	N
2. Chuck Hagel Confirmation	N	6. Employee Non-Discrim'n Act	Y	10. Farm Bill Conference Rept.	N
3. Gun Background Checks	Y	7. Senate Vote on Judgeships	Y	11. Unempl. Comp. Extension	N
4. Immigration Reform	N	8. Defense Dept. Spending	N	12. Keystone Pipeline	Y

Election Results

2010 general	Pat Toomey (R)	2,028,945	(51%)	$16,958,449	$3,581,634	$10,677,656
	Joe Sestak (D)	1,948,716	(49%)	$13,441,119	$2,128,034	$12,505,385
2010 primary	Pat Toomey (R)	668,409	(81%)			
	Peg Luksik (R)	151,802	(19%)			

Prior winning percentages: House: 2002 (57%), 2000 (53%), 1998 (55%)

Before he narrowly won election in 2010 as Pennsylvania's junior senator, Republican Pat Toomey spent several years as the president of the Club for Growth, a national organization that spends generously to support conservative candidates who share its views. It has frequently backed candidates opposed by the local party establishment in Republican primary contests, sometimes taking on incumbent Republicans in the process. As head of the group, Toomey's view was that the GOP was courting political disaster because it had abandoned conservative principles. During his first term in the Senate, Toomey has remained steadfast in his devotion to the Club for Growth's core principles of lower taxes and less spending. But, facing a 2016 reelection battle in a state that has become reliably blue in presidential elections, Toomey has moved perceptibly to the center on some social issues. Perhaps the most noteworthy example came in 2013, when Toomey—a gun rights supporter with an "A" rating from the National Rifle Association—broke with his party to sponsor expanded background checks for gun owners.

Toomey is one of just four Republican senators from the 13 states in the New England and Mid-Atlantic regions, and the political complexion of the vast majority of those states—blue or purple—has placed Toomey near the top of national Democrats' lists of takeover prospects as the party seeks to regain the Senate majority in 2016. Toomey is a New Englander by birth: He grew up in Providence Rhode Island, the third of six children of a union worker and a part-time church secretary. He graduated from Harvard University, about 40 miles up the road from where he grew up, thanks to scholarship money and earnings from part-time jobs. After college, he worked in investment banking—founding a successful international financial services consulting firm in 1990 and amassing considerable wealth. After six years on Wall Street, Toomey moved to Allentown, where he joined his brothers to start Rookies Restaurant and Sports Bar, which grew into a chain with outlets across the state. In 1994, he was elected to the Allentown Government Study Commission, where he pushed to lower taxes and to require a supermajority vote by the city council to raise taxes.

In 1998, Toomey ran for the seat of retiring Democratic Rep. Paul McHale. One of six candidates in the Republican primary, he advocated individual Social Security investment accounts, a flat tax to replace the current income tax system, and term limits for members of Congress; he promised to serve only six years. He won the close primary with 27 percent, just ahead of the 1996 nominee, Bob Kilbanks, with 25 percent, and state Sen. Joseph Uliana, with 23 percent. In the general election, he bested the Democratic nominee, state Sen. Roy Afflerbach, 55%-45%. He was reelected 53%-47% in 2000 and 57%-43% in 2002 in a district that had voted Democratic for president since 1992.

As a member of the House, Toomey focused primarily on economic issues, pushing to limit spending and to force Congress to set aside money for debt reduction. Toomey kept his term limit pledge in 2004 and instead ran for the Senate seat held by then-Republican Arlen Specter. Specter was supported by President George W. Bush as well as his conservative Pennsylvania colleague, Sen. Rick Santorum. Specter raised far more money than Toomey while spotlighting the projects he had obtained for the state over his 24 years in the Senate. Toomey criticized Specter's voting record as too liberal and emphasized the latter's support from trial lawyers. The result was exceedingly close. Specter won 51%-49%, 17,000 votes out of over 1 million cast. Specter carried metro Philadelphia, his home, with 57 percent, but Toomey carried metro Pittsburgh with 58 percent.

In 2005, Toomey signed on as the head of the Club for Growth, a post he held until 2009, and which enabled him to make contacts around the country with conservative activists and major fundraisers. He defended the Club's strategy in 2008 after Oklahoma Rep. Tom Cole, then chair of the National Republican Congressional Committee, excoriated the Club for Growth's involvement in a contentious Ohio congressional primary. "The problem I have with the Club is I think they're stupid," Cole told *The New York Times.* "They spend more money beating Republicans than Democrats." In a *Wall Street Journal* op-ed piece entitled "In Defense of RINO Hunting," - an acronym for Republican In Name Only—Toomey shot back: "Republicans would be better off, the argument goes, if the Club PAC spent its money targeting Democrats instead of liberal Republicans. This is the argument of politicians who care more about maintaining power than using that power to implement conservative policies."

Toomey decided to challenge Specter again in the 2010 election after the incumbent cast one of three Republican votes for the Democrats' $787 billion economic stimulus bill in 2009. But in April 2009, Specter announced he was switching parties to become a Democrat, saying he did not want to put his service at the mercy of Republican primary voters. (Specter had started his political career as a Democrat, switching to the GOP in the mid-1960s when he ran for Philadelphia district attorney.) Unfortunately for Specter, his path to the Democratic nomination was not clear, despite his backing from party heavyweights. Two-term Democratic Rep. Joe Sestak, a retired Navy admiral, subsequently entered the race, despite pressure from the Obama White House and the Senate Democratic leadership to clear the field for Specter. Sestak won the primary, 54%-46%, carrying all but three counties: Philadelphia and those containing Harrisburg and Scranton (Sestak's refusal to yield to the wishes of Democratic leaders left intraparty scars that affected the run-up to the 2016 contest, in which Sestak was seeking a rematch against Toomey.)

Toomey had no problem winning the Republican primary, capturing 81 percent. The general election presented a clear contrast on issues: Sestak had voted not only for the stimulus bill, but for the Democrats' health care overhaul and their cap-and-trade bill to limit carbon emission. Toomey called for extending the Bush-era tax cuts for everyone, including the wealthiest bracket, and for lower corporate and capital gains tax rates. He spent $17 million, while Sestak spent $12 million, much of it in the primary. In a year in which Republicans rode a political wave to take control of the House and make significant gains in the Senate, Toomey beat Sestak, 51%-49%, while Republican Tom Corbett was elected governor. Toomey lost metro Philadelphia, 62%-38%, but carried metro Pittsburgh, 53%-47%, and the rest of the state, 59%-41%.

In the Senate, Toomey has shown a preference for policy over sound bites, and perhaps as a result, is not a frequent figure on cable television. Notwithstanding his Club for Growth background, he has won praise for articulating conservative ideals in a manner that has not offended those who may disagree. Toomey replaced South Carolina's Jim DeMint in 2012 as chairman of the Republican Steering Committee, the caucus of the Senate's conservatives, when DeMint resigned from the Senate to become president of the conservative Heritage Foundation. Toomey reached out to centrists, such as Maine's Susan Collins, who had stopped coming to the group's weekly luncheons after DeMint's uncompromising views rubbed them the wrong way. Keeping up an effort he had begun in the House, Toomey joined with a Democratic centrist, Missouri Sen. Claire McCaskill, in a letter urging colleagues to abandon so-called earmarks in appropriations bills to fund pet projects. He later introduced legislation making an earmark ban permanent; it did not pass, but a combination of opposition to earmarks from the White House and House Republican leaders has placed a *de facto* ban on the practice.

Toomey showed few signs of retreating from his hardline conservatism on economic matters, while floating a couple of far-reaching plans to reduce the deficit that gained him attention. During the first year of his term, a standoff developed between President Barack Obama and Republican congressional leaders over raising the federal debt ceiling. Toomey disputed warnings from the Treasury Department and business leaders that a failure to raise the debt ceiling risked a financial default; he argued the United States could prioritize its payments in the event of a debt ceiling breach to avoid a true default. Toomey voted against the bill that ended the crisis by raising the federal debt ceiling. He was, however, one of three Republican senators appointed to the Joint Committee on Deficit Reduction—the so-called "Supercommittee"—that was created by the legislation raising the debt limit. The committee, evenly divided between Democrats and Republicans and House and Senate, was charged with coming up with at least $1.2 trillion in budget savings over a 10-year period.

The committee's efforts ended in partisan stalemate prior to a November deadline set by the legislation. Toomey, with the support of several other Republicans, floated a proposal to raise $400 billion in revenue—the majority of it coming from a reduction in tax breaks—coupled with $800 million in spending cuts. But the Democrats reportedly rejected Toomey's plan because it did not phase out the Bush era tax cuts for the wealthiest Americans, which budget analysts said would cost $800 billion over the next decade. Earlier, as a member of the Senate Budget Committee, Toomey offered an alternative to a controversial deficit reduction plan by House Budget Chairman Paul Ryan that would have transformed Medicare into a voucher-like system. Toomey's proposal aimed to balance the budget in nine years with defense cuts already proposed by then-Defense Secretary Robert Gates, along with an overhaul of Medicaid into a block grant program. His plan did not touch two popular entitlement programs, Medicare and Social Security. Still, the plan went down to defeat in May 2011 by a vote of 55-42, with no Democratic support.

In 2013, Toomey won a coveted seat on the Finance Committee. At the same time, he supported the January 2013 compromise on taxes and spending to avoid the so-called "fiscal cliff." But he blunted criticism from conservatives who didn't like the deal by declaring that Republicans needed to be ready to shut down the government in future debates over raising the deficit. "We absolutely have to have this fight over the debt limit," he said. In October of that year, Toomey was one of just 18 senators to vote against the spending deal to end a 16-day federal government shutdown, saying he opposed the new borrowing it allowed.

It is on social issues that Toomey's first-term record often has been unpredictable. He surprised some of his supporters in late 2010 by *favoring* repeal of the ban on openly gay service personnel in the military. "My highest priority is to have the policy that best enables our armed services to do their job," he told the Allentown *Morning Call*. Toomey did reiterate shortly before the Supreme Court's 2015 ruling on same-sex marriage that he believes marriage should be between a man and a woman. But he has voted during his first term to extend domestic violence protections to gay, lesbian and transgender victims; ban workplace discrimination against gay employees, and require that groups receiving federal money to aid homeless youth are not discriminating based on sexual orientation.

But it was Toomey's teaming with West Virginia Democrat Joe Manchin on a compromise on gun control in April 2013 that rippled across Capitol Hill. Their proposal called for expanding background checks to gun shows and online sales while maintaining record-keeping provisions that law enforcement officials said were essential in tracking criminal gun use. Toomey said that, while the volatile issue was "not something I sought," he considered it important to take action. It followed the December 2012 school shooting in Newtown Connecticut, in which a deranged gunman killed 26, most of them children. The Manchin-Toomey proposal fell five votes short of the 60-vote supermajority needed to overcome a filibuster, as only three other Republicans joined Toomey in supporting the measure, which was strongly opposed by the NRA. Two years later, at an event where he was honored by the families of the Newtown victims, Toomey said that, despite the fallout from his conservative base, he would "do it again in a heartbeat," according to *The Washington Post*. Speaking shortly after the shootings at a Charleston South Carolina church in which nine were killed, Toomey said he regretted his bill hadn't passed and "that it took me so long before I raised my voice on this very important issue."

National Democratic leaders spent much of the first part of 2015 seeking an alternative candidate to Sestak to take on Toomey. Not only is there lingering anger that Sestak ignored their 2010 admonitions not to take on Specter; Sestak is seen as a maverick who, on several occasions, has lent support to candidates opposing his former House colleagues. "He does his own thing," Rep. Robert Brady, who also chairs the Philadelphia Democratic Committee, told *Politico*. "There's not a lot of love there." After months of trying, the Democrats had little success recruiting another candidate. Members of the Senate Democratic leadership reportedly urged Josh Shapiro, a well-regarded county commissioner in Philadelphia's Main Line suburbs, to run. But Shapiro declined in the late spring of 2015. Allentown Mayor Ed Pawlowski announced his Senate candidacy in April, only to suspend it in July after FBI agents searched City Hall and questioned officials in connections with a grand jury investigation, according to the Allentown *Morning Call*. In August, Katie McGinty entered the contest with hopes to rally the support of feminists, organized labor and her environmental base as a former top aide to Vice President Al Gore. But Republicans pointed out that she ran a distant fourth in the 2014 primary for governor.

Amid this maneuvering, there were Democrats who argued that Sestak, given his military background and narrow loss to Toomey in a year not kind to Democrats, would be a formidable challenger in November, notwithstanding his scratchy relations with the Democratic establishment. Former Gov. Ed Rendell, among those who have acknowledged reservations about Sestak, told the Philadelphia *Inquirer* that Toomey "should be a stronger candidate in '16 than he was in '10—except one problem: Hillary Clinton." It was a reference not only to the prospect of Clinton at the top of the ticket in Pennsylvania, but also the fact that the state has not voted Republican in a presidential election since 1988. Toomey continues to believe in term limits, and has said that, if reelected in 2016, it would likely be his last term—even though he would be a relative youngster of 61 in 2022.

FIRST DISTRICT

Robert Brady (D)

Elected May 1998, 9th full term; b. April 7, 1945, Philadelphia; St. Thomas More H.S.; Catholic; married (Debra); 2 children.

Elected Office: 34th Ward Dem. exec.cmte. mbr., 1967-present, ward ldr., 1980.

Professional Career: Carpenter; Sgt-at-arms, Philadelphia city cncl., 1975-83; Philadelphia deputy mayor for labor, 1984-87; Chmn., Philadelphia Dem. Party, 1986-present; Legis. rep., Metro. Regional Cncl. of Carpenters & Joiners, 1987-98; Lecturer, U. of PA, 1997-present.

DC Office: 102 CHOB, 20515, 202-225-4731; Fax: 202-225-0088; Website: brady.house.gov.

State Offices: Chester, 610-874-7094; Philadelphia S. Broad St., 215-389-4627, Memphis St., 215-426-4616, E. Clearfield St., 267-519-2252.

Committees: *Armed Services:* Military Personnel. *House Administration* (RMM). *Joint Committee on the Library.*

Group Ratings

	ADA	ACLU	AFL-CIO	LCV	ITI	COC	HAFA	ACU	CFG	FRC
2014	90%	83%	–	94%	60%	57%	13%	4%	9%	0%
2013	90%	C	100%	89%	C	46%	C	16%	14%	C

National Journal Ratings

	2013 LIB	—	2013 CONS
Economic	75%	—	24%
Social	87%	—	7%
Foreign	79%	—	20%
Composite	82%	—	18%

Key Votes of the 113th Congress

1. Sandy storm spending	Y	5. Medical Marijuana	Y	9. Syrian Rebels Training	Y
2. Violence Against Women Act	Y	6. Farm Bill	N	10. Keystone pipeline	Y
3. Guantanamo Bay Detainees	Y	7. Afghanistan Combat	Y	11. Immigration Exec. Action	N
4. Abortion 20-week ban	N	8. NSA Phone Data Collection	Y	12. Bipartisan budget deal	Y

Election Results

2014 general	Robert Brady (D)	131,248	(83%)	$750,831	$43,827
	Megan Rath (R)	27,193	(17%)	$42,005	
2014 primary	Robert Brady (D)	unopposed			

Prior winning percentages: 2012 (85%), 2010 (unopposed), 2008 (91%), 2006 (100%), 2004 (86%), 2002 (86%), 2000 (88%), 1998 (81%), 1998 special (74%)

Population:		Race and Ethnicity:		Income:	
Total:	725,059	White	42.2%	Median income:	$40,731
Urban:	90.1%	Black	32.8%		*(380 of 435)*
Suburban:	9.9%	Latino	15.9%	Under $50,000	58.8%
Rural:	0.0%	Asian	6.8%	$50,000-$99,999:	27.0%
Land area:	93	Two races	2.0%	$100,000-$199,999:	11.5%
Pop/sq. mi.:	7,826.4	White Ethnic	31.5%	$200,000 or more:	2.6%
Born in state:	65.8%			Poverty Rate	25.4%
		Education			
Age Groups		H.S. grad or less:	52.5%	**Work**	
Under 18:	24.1%	Some college:	21.7%	White collar:	35.8%
18 to 34:	29.2%	College degree, 4 yr.:	16.0%	Blue collar:	47.1%
35 to 64:	35.7%	Post-grad study:	9.8%	Sales and service:	17.1%
Over 64:	11.1%				
		Military		Govt. workers:	11.3%
		Veterans/active duty:	5.3%		

Parts of Philadelphia and Delaware County

Everywhere in Center City Philadelphia, American history is close at hand. Independence Hall is where Americans in the 1780s drew up the Constitution, and not far away are the restored townhouses of Society Hill. In 2003, the National Constitution Center opened on Independence Mall. Nearby sits

Voter Turnout	
2013 Total Citizen 18+	502,437
2014 House Turnout	158,441
2014 Turnout as % CVAP	31.5%
2012 Turnout as % CVAP	59.6%

the Liberty Bell and its signature crack. City founder William Penn was a Quaker, a member of one of the 17th century sects that prized reason, and he imposed order on his new environment: no cow-path street patterns here, but a grid of numbered and named streets. Penn's "City of Brotherly Love" grew to be a commercial and industrial metropolis that spread out over the countryside until it was the young nation's largest city.

For all its historical grandeur, Philadelphia seldom has had a city government to be proud of. The city lurched toward bankruptcy under Democratic Mayor Wilson Goode. In 1991, Democrat Ed Rendell was elected mayor, and did well enough to be elected governor in 2002. Unfortunately, Rendell's push for reform stalled in the mid-1990s. Philadelphia has an inordinately expensive government. Its employees' retirement fund was only 47 percent funded in January 2015, and there were more retirees and beneficiaries than employees who were making contributions. It has had crime-ravaged neighborhoods, with homicides topping 330 in 2012, a four-year high. But the murders dropped 25 percent the next year. There are signs of renewal. Center City remains attractive to young professionals—a growing number with families—and population in that area increased 26 percent from 1990 to 2010. A $575 million gallery project is underway as part of an expected $1.5 billion in development between City Hall and Independence Mall by 2017.

The 1st Congressional District of Pennsylvania contains parts of Center City and eastern sections of Philadelphia along the Delaware River. Much of 18th century Philadelphia is here: Independence Hall; the U.S. Mint; and historic Christ Church, where George Washington and Benjamin Franklin worshiped. It also takes in Chinatown, Society Hill, the Northern Liberties village, Penn's Landing and Old City, with its flourishing night life. The 1st includes once heavily Italian South Philadelphia. Nearby the district takes in the city's stadium and arena complex, as well as Pat's and Geno's, well-established haunts for late-night cheesesteaks. Along the Delaware River into Delaware County, it covers

2012 Presidential Vote
Barack Obama (D) 244,505   (82%)
Mitt Romney (R)...................50,211   (17%)

2008 Presidential Vote
Barack Obama (D) 244,543   (78%)
John McCain (R)...................67,747   (22%)

Cook Partisan Voting Index: D+28

impoverished Chester, where the school system went bankrupt in 2012. A new school superintendent improved academic performance and reduced crime. But the system remained deep in debt.

To keep the neighboring 2nd District an African-American majority, redistricting decreased the black population of the 1st to 36 percent. But this is still a majority-minority and strongly Democratic district.

Robert Brady (D)

Democrat Robert Brady, elected in 1998, is the personification of Philadelphia's old-fashioned urban politics, and is one of the few remaining white ethnic party bosses in big-city America. He worked behind the scenes to help his city land the 2016 Democratic National Convention.

Brady grew up in Overbrook Park in West Philadelphia, with an Italian mother and an Irish father who was a policeman. After high school, he went to work as a carpenter, quickly rose through the ranks of the carpenters' union, and remains a dues-paying member. He entered politics at age 22, when the local ward leader wouldn't replace a burned-out streetlight. Brady was elected to the 34th Ward Democratic Executive Committee, and in 1980 he was elected ward leader. In 1986, he became chairman of the Philadelphia Democratic Party.

He depicts himself as a roll-up-your-sleeves guy who represents working-class voters, and says he's proud to be the boss of what he calls the nation's largest big-city machine—or, as he calls it, an "organization." Brady is known for making "arrangements" with others— "they're always arrangements, never deals," he insists. "Governors come and go, mayors come and go, but he's the party chair," Ed Rendell, a former Philly mayor and Pennsylvania governor, told *Politico.*

In 1997, Brady ran for an open seat. The district's ward leaders determined the nomination for the special election. Not surprisingly, they favored Brady. With the endorsement of many black leaders and a strong Election Day organization, he won the special election with 74 percent of the vote. The same year he married his wife, Deb, a former Eagles cheerleader who later took a position on the city's housing authority board.

After his election to the House, Brady's focus remained back home. "Ninety-five percent of my day is not Congress," he once said. In 2009, he helped settle a transit strike that plagued the city's traffic for a week; a year later, he worked to end a 28-day walkout by staffers at Temple University Hospital. His ties to City Hall and to local unions gave him credibility with both sides. Brady has worked to resolve local intra-party conflicts. After he helped rescue Philadelphia's annual bike race in January 2013, *Philadelphia Daily News* columnist Stu Bykofsky wrote: "If anyone in Philadelphia is Mr. Democrat, it is Big Bob. ... He's been called a fixer, but I think of him as a peacemaker, a problem-solver, a blue-collar realist with iron pants."

Brady has a liberal voting record and keeps a low profile in Washington. On most days that the House is in session, he commutes from home. For "the most powerful man in Philadelphia," *Philadelphia* magazine once wrote, "Washington gas-bagging is not his thing." His initiatives reflect his local orientation. He boasts of once refusing to take a phone call from President Bill Clinton because he was busy dealing with a woman asking if he could send someone to fix her toilet. He says he decided that he was in favor of abortion rights after asking his mother. His loyalty to unions led him to buck environmentalists and most Democrats to vote for drilling in the Arctic National Wildlife Refuge.

In 2007, House Speaker Nancy Pelosi may have found the perfect job for him. Brady became chairman of the House Administration Committee, the so-called "Mayor of Capitol Hill" who oversees operations of the House and doles out favors such as choice office space. He helped get a bill through the House in 2009 to honor African Americans who had been slave laborers during the original construction of the Capitol building. After the fatal crash just north of the Philly train station in May 2015, an angry Brady criticized Amtrak for failing to have a safety system in place. He pays less attention to his assignment with the Armed Services Committee, though the decision of California Rep. Loretta Sanchez to run for the Senate will leave Brady as the panel's second-ranking Democrat.

In 2013, he began making calls to other leading local Democrats about hosting the 2016 convention. In February 2015, the Democratic National Committee picked the City of Brotherly Love over New York and Columbus, Ohio. "Did Bob Brady raise a lot of money? No, I raised the most money," Rendell added. "Did he do any work to put the bid together? No. But without Bob Brady bringing us all together and saying, 'Come on guys, let's roll,' we never would have been here."

Brady ran for Philadelphia mayor in 2007. He joined the field late and had significant opposition in the primary, including from three veteran local black officials who had operated largely outside Brady's organization. Brady's platform was standard fare, including a call for more open government, safer streets, improved schools, and lower taxes. Democratic ward leaders endorsed him in overwhelming numbers but with varying enthusiasm. And his campaign ran into an unusual stumbling block: a lawsuit seeking to remove Brady from the ballot because he did not include his union pension on a candidate disclosure form. Brady revealed in court that his pension benefits were accruing as though he was working a full work week, a curiosity given the fact that he was serving in Congress. He paid nearly $20,000 in fines for violating the city's campaign finance laws. And he finished a distant third in the primary, with 15 percent of the vote.

In Philadelphia's Byzantine politics, Brady's weak performance—he even lost his home ward in Overbrook—raised questions about his political vulnerability. There was talk of a 2008 primary challenge to his House seat from an African-American candidate, but it never materialized. He was unopposed in 2010 after his would-be GOP challenger, tea party activist Pia Varma, was removed from the ballot for insufficient valid signatures on her nominating petitions. She accused Republicans of colluding with Brady to keep her off the ballot, a charge the city GOP chairman denied. Brady took 85% of the vote in 2012 against Republican John Featherman, who released a campaign video featuring a nude actress purporting to tell "the naked truth" about Brady. Two years later, he won with 83% over Republican Megan Rath.

SECOND DISTRICT

Chaka Fattah (D)

Elected 1994, 11th term; b. Nov. 21, 1956, Philadelphia; U. of PA, B.A. 1977, M.A. 1986; Baptist; married (Renee Chenault-Fattah); 4 children.

Elected Office: PA House, 1983-88; PA Senate, 1989-94.

Professional Career: Asst. dir., House of Umoja, 1977-79; City of Philadelphia, special asst. to dir. of housing & comm. dev., 1980, special asst. to managing dir., 1981.

DC Office: 2301 RHOB, 20515, 202-225-4001; Fax: 202-225-5392; Website: fattah.house.gov.

State Offices: Philadelphia, 215-871-4455.

Committees: *Appropriations:* Commerce, Justice, Science & Related Agencies; Financial Services; Labor, HHS, Education & Related Agencies.

Group Ratings

	ADA	ACLU	AFL-CIO	LCV	ITI	COC	HAFA	ACU	CFG	FRC
2014	90%	61%	–	86%	60%	57%	11%	4%	9%	0%
2013	90%	C	95%	89%	C	38%	C	8%	18%	C

National Journal Ratings

	2013 LIB	—	2013 CONS
Economic	91%	—	0%
Social	87%	—	7%
Foreign	85%	—	14%
Composite	90%	—	10%

Key Votes of the 113th Congress

1. Sandy storm spending	Y	5. Medical Marijuana	Y	9. Syrian Rebels Training	Y
2. Violence Against Women Act	Y	6. Farm Bill	N	10. Keystone pipeline	N
3. Guantanamo Bay Detainees	Y	7. Afghanistan Combat	Y	11. Immigration Exec. Action	N
4. Abortion 20-week ban	N	8. NSA Phone Data Collection	Y	12. Bipartisan budget deal	Y

Election Results

2014 general	Chaka Fattah (D)	181,141	(88%)	$524,914
	Armond James (R)	25,397	(12%)	$12,536
2014 primary	Chaka Fattah (D)	unopposed		

Prior winning percentages: 2012 (89%), 2010 (89%), 2008 (89%), 2006 (89%), 2004 (88%), 2002 (88%), 2000 (98%), 1998 (87%), 1996 (88%), 1994 (86%)

Population		Race and Ethnicity		Income	
Total:	712,372	Black	58.1%	Median income:	$34,928
Urban:	92.4%	White	29.4%		*(421 of 435)*
Suburban:	7.6%	Latino	5.5%	Under $50,000	62.7%
Rural:	0.0%	Asian	4.5%	$50,000-$99,999:	21.1%
Land area:	77	Two races	1.6%	$100,000-$199,999:	11.0%
Pop/sq. mi.:	9,306.5	White Ethnic	17.7%	$200,000 or more:	5.1%
Born in state:	67.2%			Poverty Rate	27.5%
		Education			
Age Groups		H.S. grad or less:	45.6%	Work	
Under 18:	20.1%	Some college:	21.9%	White collar:	43.5%
18 to 34:	31.3%	College degree, 4 yr.:	16.4%	Blue collar:	43.8%
35 to 64:	35.3%	Post-grad study:	16.2%	Sales and service:	12.7%
Over 64:	13.3%				
		Military		Govt. workers:	12.5%
		Veterans/active duty:	5.4%		

North and West Philadelphia

Looking out over the Schuylkill River north of Center City Philadelphia, you can still see the landscape painted 100 years ago by Philadelphia artist Thomas Eakins: the tightly packed but formidable rowhouses, the old fieldstone houses of Germantown, and the boat houses below the small

Voter Turnout	
2013 Total Citizen 18+	540,076
2014 House Turnout	206,538
2014 Turnout as % CVAP	38.2%
2012 Turnout as % CVAP	69.2%

Greek temples of the Water Works. Here are some of Philadelphia's long-established black neighborhoods: West Philadelphia, across the Schuylkill on either side of Market Street; and North Philadelphia, on either side of Broad Street. Pennsylvania was the first state to abolish slavery, thanks to William Penn and his Quaker legacy, and Philadelphia has been home to a large African-American community since before the Civil War. That heritage is reflected in places like the John Coltrane House, a national historic landmark in celebration of the jazz innovator's early years here.

Northwest Philadelphia includes distinguished old neighborhoods such as Chestnut Hill, with its cobblestone streets and classic architecture. East Falls was the childhood home of Grace Kelly, who grew up to be a Hollywood starlet and princess of Monaco. Kelly Drive, which runs along the Schuylkill River, was named after Grace's brother, former City Councilman John Kelly Jr. Some neighborhoods here continue to suffer from poverty and blight. But in recent years, city officials have made a concerted effort to bring young, affluent people back to the city. Philadelphia grew by 8,500 people from 2000 to 2010, and has gained another 24,000 since then. In April 2015, local officials said Center City ranked second only to midtown Manhattan for the number of residents living in the heart of a city.

The 2nd Congressional District of Pennsylvania takes in the African-American neighborhoods in North and West Philadelphia. It extends east to City Hall, an ornate building where a statue of city founder William Penn stands 37 feet high, and includes well-heeled Rittenhouse Square, the Philadelphia Zoo (America's first), the University of Pennsylvania, and Drexel University. It also includes most of lush Fairmount Park, the largest landscaped urban park in the world, which climaxes at the Philadelphia Museum of Art, where a *Rocky*-like run up the steps has become *de rigueur* for tourists. The 2nd, which is 58% black but only 6% Hispanic, also covers wealthier suburbs on the Main

2012 Presidential Vote		
Barack Obama (D) 338,343		(90%)
Mitt Romney (R)...................33,530		(9%)
2008 Presidential Vote		
Barack Obama (D) 347,883		(91%)
John McCain (R)...................33,395		(9%)
Cook Partisan Voting Index: D+38		

Line, including Ardmore and Bala Cynwyd. These Montgomery County voters are about 12% of the district. This is among the five most Democratic districts in the nation, with a 90% vote for Barack Obama in 2012.

Chaka Fattah (D)

Chaka Fattah, a Democrat first elected in 1994, has a more nationally oriented focus than Rep. Robert Brady, the city's other congressman. Fattah works on housing, education, and other urban-centric issues while persistently championing a bill that would abolish the income tax and replace it with a levy on all financial transactions. On July 29, 2015, he was indicted by a federal grand jury in Philadelphia for bribery, bank fraud, filing false statements and other offenses related to the financing of his 2007 campaign for mayor. He immediately stepped aside as the ranking Democrat of an Appropriations subcommittee. Since prior to his indictment, Fattah's wife, Renee Chenault-Fattah, has been on leave from her job as a local television news anchor in Philadelphia.

Fattah was born Arthur Davenport, one of six children of a poor single mother in Philadelphia. She changed his name after she married community activist David Fattah; his first name was taken from a Zulu warrior. His parents were politically active, producing a magazine for African Americans and opening their home as a neighborhood gathering spot for teens at risk of joining street gangs. Fattah dropped out of high school, but later got an equivalent diploma and went on to earn a master's degree in government administration at the University of Pennsylvania. At age 25, he was elected to the Pennsylvania General Assembly, at the time its youngest member ever. Six years later, he was elected to the state Senate.

In 1991, Democratic Rep. William Gray, the powerful House majority whip, resigned to become head of the United Negro College Fund. In the special election to succeed him, local Democratic ward leaders nominated Councilman Lucien Blackwell, a former longshoreman and labor union stalwart. Fattah ran under the Consumer Party label while state Welfare Secretary John White ran as an independent. Blackwell won with 39% to 28% for Fattah and 27% for White.

In 1994, Fattah ran again, this time taking on the Democratic establishment in the primary. Blackwell relied mostly on ward politicians. Fattah was endorsed by the Black Clergy of Philadelphia and Vicinity. This time Fattah won, 58%-42%.

The Philadelphia Inquirer has called the liberal Fattah "a policy wonk with savvy." He occasionally shows his independence from his party; he was one of just 22 Democrats to support a failed 2011 amendment to implement a budget based on the recommendations of the bipartisan Simpson-Bowles deficit reduction commission. He has focused on increasing education spending for low-income students.

His "Debt Free America Act" would eliminate the federal tax code and replace all individual and corporate taxes with a system that would tax all financial transactions, an idea that generated some interest among Republicans. But most Democrats are leery of anything that looks like a consumption tax, and his bill has not moved beyond the talking stage. It did, however, spawn an Internet rumor in 2010 that the Obama administration was behind it as part of a plot to take money from Social Security recipients. To end the periodic wrangling over raising the federal debt limit, he filed a bill in 2013 giving the administration the power to raise the limit without having to go through Congress.

Fattah has used his post on the Appropriations Committee to secure money to curb witness intimidation in Philadelphia, to combat the use of unsafe blood supplies that transmit HIV/AIDS in Africa, and to increase the number of minorities working on defense programs. He started an initiative in 2012 to have federal agencies cooperatively examine the future of neuroscience research. He sought to become Appropriations' top Democrat in 2010, but lost a 26-18 vote of the leadership-run Democratic Steering Committee to Norm Dicks of Washington, who had more seniority. Fattah settled for the ranking Democratic post on the subcommittee funding the Commerce and Justice departments and science programs. He has been a strong advocate of medical research, especially for neuroscience and research of the brain. In July 2014, the House passed Fattah's bill to name the 30th Street Station in honor of his predecessor Gray, who died a year earlier.

Fattah lost a campaign for Philadelphia mayor in 2007. The move prompted grumbling among local Democrats planning to run for mayor that he was giving up his clout as an appropriator, and even some threats that Fattah would face a primary challenge for his House seat. Also in the crowded mayoral primary was Brady, of the neighboring 1st District, former City Councilman Michael Nutter, and wealthy businessman Thomas Knox. Fattah began the race as the front-runner, but his campaign struggled to raise money and drew criticism over his refusal to release his income tax returns. Nutter was the eventual winner with 37% of the vote. Fattah finished fourth with 15%.

Fattah's son, Chaka "Chip" Fattah Jr., was indicted in August 2014 as part of an alleged scheme to defraud banks and the Internal Revenue Service of several hundred thousand dollars. According to the charges, he had launched a consulting firm, Dreamchasers, with the hope of gaining school-district contracts for at-risk students.

But that was only one early sign of Rep. Fattah's troubles. Later that month, longtime aide Gregory Naylor pleaded guilty to a scheme to obtain an illegal loan for a 2007 mayoral campaign and pay it back with federal grant money. In November 2014, Thomas Lindenfeld, another former aide, pleaded guilty to corruption charges in Philadelphia. Federal prosecutors didn't identify the candidate involved, but Philadelphia media outlets speculated that it was Fattah, and news stories began to report on possible successors if the issue drove him from Congress. Fattah declined to discuss the issue, telling a local radio station: "The one thing is, I'm not a lawyer, I'm not going to engage in it. I'm not going to respond to an allegation that hasn't been made."

After additional months of investigation, Fattah was indicted on the eve of the August 2015 recess for what prosecutors described as an extensive effort to conceal improper financing of his campaign for mayor, including an illegal loan, plus misuse of federal and charitable funds. Fattah denied any wrong doing and said that he will not resign his seat. But he could face his first serious Democratic primary since he was first elected.

THIRD DISTRICT

Mike Kelly (R)

Elected 2010, 3rd term; b. May 10, 1948, Pittsburgh; U. of Notre Dame, B.A. 1970; Catholic; married (Victoria); 4 children.

Elected Office: Butler City Cncl., 2006-09.

Professional Career: Butler Area Schl. Bd., 1992-96; Owner, mgr., Kelly Chevrolet-Cadillac Inc.

DC Office: 1519 LHOB, 20515, 202-225-5406; Fax: 202-225-3103; Website: kelly.house.gov.

State Offices: Butler, 724-282-2557; Erie, 814-454-8190; Kittanning, 724-282-2557; Meadville, 814-454-8190; Sharon, 724-342-7170.

Committees: *Ways & Means:* Oversight; Select Revenue Measures; Social Security.

Group Ratings

	ADA	ACLU	AFL-CIO	LCV	ITI	COC	HAFA	ACU	CFG	FRC
2014	0%	0%	–	3%	100%	93%	50%	64%	49%	100%
2013	0%	C	19%	4%	C	92%	C	64%	58%	C

National Journal Ratings

	2013 LIB	—	2013 CONS
Economic	40%	—	59%
Social	16%	—	74%
Foreign	15%	—	77%
Composite	27%	—	73%

Key Votes of the 113th Congress

1. Sandy storm spending	N	5. Medical Marijuana	N
2. Violence Against Women Act	N	6. Farm Bill	Y
3. Guantanamo Bay Detainees	N	7. Afghanistan Combat	N
4. Abortion 20-week ban	Y	8. NSA Phone Data Collection	N

9. Syrian Rebels Training	Y
10. Keystone Pipeline	Y
11. Immigration Exec. Action	Y
12. Bipartisan Budget Deal	Y

Election Results

2014 general	Mike Kelly (R)............................113,859	(61%)	$1,468,975	$11,633
	Dan LaVallee (D) 73,931	(39%)	$407,605	
2014 primary	Mike Kelly (R).......................unopposed			

Prior winning percentages: 2012 (55%), 2010 (56%)

Population		Race and Ethnicity		Income	
Total:	703,010	White	91.2%	Median income:	$46,627
Urban:	19.5%	Black	4.4%		*(290 of 435)*
Suburban:	48.3%	Latino	2.1%	Under $50,000	53.0%
Rural:	32.2%	Asian	0.8%	$50,000-$99,999:	30.3%
Land area:	4,072	Two races	1.3%	$100,000-$199,999:	13.9%
Pop/sq. mi.:	172.6	White Ethnic	46.1%	$200,000 or more:	2.7%
Born in state:	82.4%			Poverty Rate	14.3%
		Education			
Age Groups		H.S. grad or less:	51.8%	**Work**	
Under 18:	20.8%	Some college:	24.0%	White collar:	32.3%
18 to 34:	20.8%	College degree, 4 yr.:	15.6%	Blue collar:	42.5%
35 to 64:	41.0%	Post-grad study:	8.5%	Sales and service:	25.2%
Over 64:	17.4%				
		Military		Govt. workers:	10.4%
		Veterans/active duty:	10.0%		

Northwest Pennsylvania: Erie, Pittsburgh Exurbs

The best natural harbor on Lake Erie is in Erie, Pennsylvania, protected by the Presque Isle ("almost an island") peninsula—a cowlick-shaped, seven-mile-long sand spit blanketed by mature forest, with a lighthouse dating to 1872. Erie is in Pennsylvania's far northwest corner, only about 100

Voter Turnout	
2013 Total Citizen 18+	550,851
2014 House Turnout	187,790
2014 Turnout as % CVAP	34.1%
2012 Turnout as % CVAP	56.3%

miles from Cleveland. There are farmlands here, and even some woods, but the land between the Great Lakes and the basin of the Ohio River has been prime heavy industry territory for more than a century. The jeep, which Gen. George Marshall called America's greatest contribution to World War II, was invented in Butler County. In the 1990s, under Republican Gov. Tom Ridge, who grew up in Erie, the state invested $100 million in the city's waterfront to develop a cruise ship terminal, hotel and convention center, a ballpark for the double-A Erie SeaWolves baseball team, and a renovated Warner Theatre. The effort spruced up a dying downtown, but it didn't buffer Erie from a subsequent economic downturn, during which International Paper, American Meter, Gunite/EMI and American Sterilizer laid off

employees and closed plants. General Electric Transportation, one of the area's largest employers, also had major cutbacks. Nor did that extensive development have a discernible effect on population, which has had a steady 8% percent decline from 1990 to its 2013 total of 100,671. The jobless rate for the Erie area has dropped by half since 2010, reaching 5.5% in May 2015.

2012 Presidential Vote		
Mitt Romney (R)	171,114	(56%)
Barack Obama (D)	132,486	(43%)
2008 Presidential Vote		
John McCain (R)	168,940	(52%)
Barack Obama (D)	149,804	(46%)
Cook Partisan Voting Index:	R+8	

The 3rd Congressional District of Pennsylvania occupies the northwest corner of the state. It takes in part of Erie and surrounding Erie County, and covers Meadville, where the company Talon invented the zipper, and Grove City and Grove City College, a Christian liberal arts school. It includes New Castle and the old glass industry borough, Ford City. The district dips south to politically conservative Butler and Armstrong counties, which include the northern exurbs of Pittsburgh. Butler and Erie counties are the population centers.

Redistricting changes in 2011 were designed to give a modest boost to Republicans, and they did. Mitt Romney won the 3rd with 56% of the vote in 2012.

Mike Kelly (R)

Republican Mike Kelly, who won his seat in 2010, is an ex-college football player who has been known for his fiery pep talks to colleagues behind closed doors. But he is mostly loyal to his party and to House Speaker John Boehner of Ohio.

Kelly was born in Pittsburgh and his family moved to Butler four years later, where his father started a small automobile business, working seven days a week. "He took the cars off the trains himself, and he serviced them himself. And he built a business, based around a strong work ethic, which was similar to his parents. It's pretty much the story of western Pennsylvania," Kelly said. In high school, Kelly was an all-state football player and was recruited to play for the University of Notre Dame. But he tore a knee during his freshman year and dislocated it again in his sophomore season, ending his football career. "It was over very quickly," he recalled. After college, he worked in the family business, Kelly Chevrolet-Cadillac, as a salesman, eventually becoming general manager. He bought the dealership from his father, and expanded it to include Hyundai and Kia autos. In 2005, Kelly was elected to the Butler City Council.

As the 2010 midterm election approached, Kelly decided to take on Rep. Kathy Dahlkemper, a Democrat who in 2008 had narrowly knocked off seven-term GOP Rep. Phil English, 51%-49%. Dahlkemper opposed abortion rights, but she took heat from conservatives for voting for the Democrats' health care reform law, which many anti-abortion activists believed opened the door to taxpayer-funded abortions. Dahlkemper also voted for President Barack Obama's $787 billion economic stimulus bill.

In the May primary, Kelly's toughest opponent proved to be Paul Huber, former chief executive of Seco/Warwick, a maker of industrial furnaces. Kelly ran an ad accusing Huber of outsourcing jobs. Huber asserted that he never outsourced jobs while running his company. Kelly eked out a victory by 954 votes out of 54,000 cast.

In the general election, Dahlkemper outspent Kelly by about 3-to-2. He stressed his football background, which was an asset in the football mecca of western Pennsylvania. He promised to cut government spending and curtail interference with small business. Dahlkemper ran an ad playing on populist themes, calling Kelly a multimillionaire who has "millions invested in Wall Street and big gas-and-oil companies." Kelly was more determined to serve in Congress after the 2008 restructuring of the auto industry resulted in government meddling in his family-owned business. With the strong Republican wave at his back, Kelly won 56%-44%.

In the House, Kelly has been conservative on foreign policy and more centrist on economic matters. With his strong pro-business bent, he voted against a 2012 amendment to eliminate the Economic Development Administration. Republicans laud his passion. During the 2011 fight over raising the debt limit, he gave what Rep. Peter King of New York called a well-delivered "Knute Rockne-type speech" to rally conservatives. "Mike Kelly's the one that steps up to the microphone and says, 'Hey, we're all in this together. ... Nobody in this room is going to get everything they want. Let's go do this,'" Republican Rep. Austin Scott of Georgia told the *Pittsburgh Tribune-Review*. Kelly complained to *The Washington Post* in September 2012 about what he called the media's favorable coverage of President Barack Obama, saying that the president "has gotten more free passes than a 12-year-old boy at a fair." He got national attention in December 2014 when he delivered the Republican weekly address and offered Obama a lump of coal for Christmas to bolster the nation's economic revival.

Kelly won a seat on the tax-writing Ways and Means Committee in 2013. The panel approved in March 2015 his bill to remove protections for Internal Revenue Service employees who improperly review or reveal taxpayer information. In June, the committee approved his bill to improve the transparency of Medicare Advantage programs for the individuals who have enrolled. Kelly has been a vocal advocate of expanded international trade, which he said is a boost for workers and assures that the nation "is leading, shaping, and dominating the global economy." In 2015, he co-founded the bipartisan Retirement Security Caucus to encourage more savings.

At home, Kelly has restored the Republican proclivity of his district. He won reelection with 55% and 61% of the vote against active Democratic challengers.

FOURTH DISTRICT

Scott Perry (R)

Elected 2012, 2nd term; b. May 27, 1962, San Diego, CA; PA St. U., B.S. 1991, U.S. Army War Col., M.S.P. 2012; Christian; married (Christy); 2 children.

Military Career: PA Army Natl. Guard, 1980-present.

Elected Office: PA House, 2007-12.

Professional Career: Dock worker, Dauphin Distribution, 1981-82; Ins. sales agent, 1984-85; Co-owner, Hydrotech Mechanical Services, 1993-present.

DC Office: 1207 LHOB, 20515, 202-225-5836; Website: perry.house.gov.

State Offices: Gettysburg, 717-338-1919; Wormleysburg, 717-635-9504; York, 717-600-1919.

Committees: *Foreign Affairs:* Asia & the Pacific; Terrorism, Nonproliferation & Trade. *Homeland Security:* Cybersecurity, Infrastructure Protection & Security Technologies; Oversight & Mgmt. Efficiency (Chmn). *Transportation & Infrastructure:* Economic Development, Public Buildings & Emergency Management; Highways & Transit; Railroads, Pipelines & Hazardous Materials.

Group Ratings

	ADA	ACLU	AFL-CIO	LCV	ITI	COC	HAFA	ACU	CFG	FRC
2014	10%	0%	–	3%	100%	71%	78%	96%	78%	88%
2013	5%	C	10%	7%	C	85%	C	92%	90%	C

National Journal Ratings

	2013 LIB	—	2013 CONS
Economic	2%	—	97%
Social	0%	—	87%
Foreign	5%	—	86%
Composite	6%	—	94%

Key Votes of the 113th Congress

1. Sandy storm spending	N	5. Medical Marijuana	Y	9. Syrian Rebels Training	N
2. Violence Against Women Act	N	6. Farm Bill	N	10. Keystone pipeline	Y
3. Guantanamo Bay Detainees	N	7. Afghanistan Combat	N	11. Immigration Exec. Action	Y
4. Abortion 20-week ban	Y	8. NSA Phone Data Collection	Y	12. Bipartisan budget deal	Y

Election Results

2014 general	Scott Perry (R) 147,090	(75%)	$460,840
	Linda Deliah Thompson (D)........ 50,250	(25%)	$8,787
2014 primary	Scott Perry (R) ....unopposed		

Prior winning percentage: 2012 (60%)

Population		Race and Ethnicity		Income	
Total:	710,120	White	82.5%	Median income:	$56,287
Urban:	46.5%	Black	7.3%		*(156 of 435)*
Suburban:	51.5%	Latino	6.1%	Under $50,000	44.0%
Rural:	2.0%	Asian	1.9%	$50,000-$99,999:	34.1%
Land area:	1,533	Two races	1.9%	$100,000-$199,999:	18.4%
Pop/sq. mi.:	463.3	White Ethnic	27.8%	$200,000 or more:	3.5%
Born in state:	65.8%			Poverty Rate	11.0%
		Education			
Age Groups		H.S. grad or less:	50.1%	**Work**	
Under 18:	22.1%	Some college:	25.4%	White collar:	33.5%
18 to 34:	20.4%	College degree, 4 yr.:	15.6%	Blue collar:	41.2%
35 to 64:	41.8%	Post-grad study:	9.0%	Sales and service:	25.3%
Over 64:	15.7%				
		Military		Govt. workers:	12.4%
		Veterans/active duty:	9.5%		

South-Central Pennsylvania: York, Harrisburg

The Mason-Dixon Line, the historic boundary between Maryland and Pennsylvania, runs
through pleasant rolling farmlands, west of the
Susquehanna River, and through the Appalachian
Mountains. The area was home to the westernmost
capital of the United States during the Revolution-

Voter Turnout	
2013 Total Citizen 18+	538,368
2014 House Turnout	197,340
2014 Turnout as % CVAP	36.7%
2012 Turnout as % CVAP	58%

ary War: the city of York, where the Continental Congress passed the Articles of Confederation and received word from Benjamin Franklin in Paris that the French would help the
colonies with money and ships. Nearly a century later, Robert E. Lee's Confederate troops
crossed over this invisible line and were repelled at the Battle of Gettysburg in July 1863.
Not much today suggests that these hills were either a frontier or the object of bloody struggle. This is where former President Dwight Eisenhower, of Pennsylvania Dutch stock, chose
to quietly spend his retirement years. The Pennsylvania Gaming Control Board in 2011
rejected a proposal to build a casino within a half-mile of Gettysburg National Military
Park. Civil War experts such as documentary filmmaker Ken Burns and historian James
McPherson opposed the plan.

Today, York is the site of a large Harley-Davidson manufacturing plant, though it has
become more machine-operated and its payroll downsized from 2,000 workers in 2009 to
1,200 in early 2013. Hanover, in York County, is a snack headquarters, home to Snyder's
of Hanover and potato chip giant Utz. The city has a growing Hispanic population, many
of whom work the abundant orchards near Gettysburg. Harrisburg, the capital of Pennsylvania, features a string of mansions-turned-lobbying headquarters lining the banks of the
Susquehanna and boasts Pennsylvania's marvelously restored Capitol building. Despite the
presence of state government, its economy is weaker than nearby cities and the city has run
up heavy debts. Harrisburg filed for bankruptcy in October 2011 but it was rejected by the
state. In August 2012, its $1.5 billion debt was the largest per capita in the nation. In June
2014, the state enacted a bill to assist cities to restructure their finances with additional
taxing powers. But Harrisburg retained much of its debt, and had no apparent repayment
terms. Early in 2015, York faced problems
in the financing of its school system. In May
2015, the York-Harrisburg area was the fifth-
cheapest housing market in the nation, with
a median home sales price of $151,000.

2012 Presidential Vote		
Mitt Romney (R)	177,707	(57%)
Barack Obama (D)	129,243	(42%)
2008 Presidential Vote		
John McCain (R)	173,044	(54%)
Barack Obama (D)	145,023	(45%)
Cook Partisan Voting Index:	R+9	

The 4th Congressional District is in the
south-central part of the state and includes
all of Adams and York counties and portions of Cumberland and Dauphin counties.
It takes in a small slice of downtown Har-
risburg along the Susquehanna. That section of Harrisburg is Democratic, but it does not
jeopardize the traditionally Republican makeup of the district.

Scott Perry (R)

Republican Scott Perry won the 4th District House seat in 2012 after easily prevailing in a
crowded primary in which he started as an underdog. Considerably more conservative than
his predecessor, he ran on an agenda of a leaner federal government, gun rights and traditional marriage, and emphasized his lengthy military career.

Perry was born in San Diego but moved at age 7 to central Pennsylvania, where he
lived in a home without electricity or plumbing; he took baths in a steel tub on the front
porch. He grew up in what he described to *National Journal* as a "little dysfunctional and
a little disjointed family." Perry was the child of a single mother and has met his biological
father just once. The family fell on hard times when both his mother, a flight attendant, and
stepfather, a pilot, lost their airline jobs. After graduating from high school, Perry worked
as an auto mechanic before enlisting in the Pennsylvania Army National Guard, where
he remains active. After being commissioned as a second lieutenant in the field artillery,
he transferred to Army aviation. He flew numerous aircraft and became an instructor pilot.

He distinguished himself as a helicopter pilot and rose to the rank of colonel. While serving as state representative, he served for a year in Iraq in 2009, flying 44 missions. He has commanded the Fort Indiantown Gap National Training Site. In October 2014, the state Senate confirmed him as a brigadier general.

As a young man, Perry held a series of jobs, including as a dockhand, an insurance sales agent, and a designer and drafter at an engineering firm. He graduated with a bachelor's in business administration from Penn State University, where a political science course sparked his interest in politics. He and a partner founded Hydrotech Mechanical Services and built it into a contracting firm specializing in meter calibration and line work for municipalities. The venture hit a snag in 2002 when the Pennsylvania attorney general's office accused Perry of falsifying reports to the state Environmental Protection Department. Instead of fighting the charge, Perry entered the state's Accelerated Rehabilitative Disposition Program, a pretrial avenue similar to probation, available to first-time offenders. The matter ended with a $5,000 fine and his record being expunged. Perry maintains his innocence on the charge, asserting that an overzealous "bureaucrat" was the culprit.

His legal ordeal inspired Perry to get more involved in politics. As a past president of the Pennsylvania Young Republicans and a member of a local board dealing with planning and water issues, he was elected to the state House in 2006. There, Perry expanded the law allowing residents to use deadly force in self-defense, which requires that an assailant display a weapon. He bucked Republican Gov. Tom Corbett by proposing legislation that would have declined federal money to fund insurance exchanges under the 2010 health care law.

When he ran for the House, Perry's past legal troubles became an issue in the seven-person Republican primary field but they never got traction. He garnered endorsements from Corbett and GOP Sen. Pat Toomey. Retiring Rep. Todd Platts offered kind words about him in a mailer to voters, but not an endorsement. He also benefited from his military background. Perry was outspent 2-to-1, but won 54% of the primary vote, far ahead of York County Commissioner Christopher Reilly, the runner-up with 19%. In November, he had no trouble in this heavily Republican district, defeating Democrat Harry Perkinson, an engineer who had little national party support, 60%-34%.

In the House, Perry serves on three committees: Foreign Affairs, Homeland Security, and Transportation and Infrastructure. He is a co-founder of the post-9/11 veterans' caucus. In 2014, when the Iraqi military lost control of major parts of their country, he voiced bitterness as he recalled his own service. "Right now I wonder what that was all about. What was the point of all of that?" In February 2015, he criticized President Barack Obama's "lack of leadership" in dealing with terror threats overseas and worried publicly about the potential threat to the homeland from domestic jihadists. But he backed away from an earlier charge that Obama was "working collaboratively with what I would say is the enemy of freedom."

In May 2015, after touring a hydropower equipment manufacturing facility in his district, he voiced strong support for expanding that resource at home. In June 2015, he joined the minority of House Republicans who voted against trade promotion authority; he said the proposal failed to provide sufficient accountability and transparency in trade negotiations. He has filed legislation to legalize a marijuana-based oil that has been shown to reduce seizures in children with debilitating epilepsy.

At home, Perry faced Harrisburg Democratic Mayor Linda Thompson in the 2014 election. She campaigned against the "dysfunction" in Congress, but raised less than $9,000 and was not well known outside of her home base. Perry won 75%-25%, though Thompson got 58% of the small vote in Dauphin County.

FIFTH DISTRICT

GlennThompson (R)

Elected 2008, 4th term; b. July 27, 1959, Bellefonte; PA St. U., B.S. 1981, Temple U., M.Ed. 1988; Protestant; married (Penny Ammerman-Thompson); 3 children.

Elected Office: Bald Eagle Area Schl Bd., 1990-95.

Professional Career: Therapist, Williamsport Hosp., 1982-95; Adjunct faculty, Cambria Cnty. Comm. Col., 1997-99; Mgr., Susquehanna Health Rehabilitation Services, 1995-2008; Centre Cnty. GOP chmn., 2002-08; Firefighter & EMT.

DC Office: 124 CHOB, 20515, 202-225-5121; Fax: 202-225-5796; Website: thompson.house.gov.

State Offices: Bellefonte, 814-353-0215; Titusville, 814-827-3985.

Committees: *Agriculture:* Biotechnology, Horticulture, & Research; Conservation & Forestry (Chmn); Nutrition. *Education & the Workforce:* Early Childhood, Elementary & Secondary Education; Workforce Protections. *Natural Resources:* Energy & Mineral Resources; Federal Lands.

Group Ratings

	ADA	ACLU	AFL-CIO	LCV	ITI	COC	HAFA	ACU	CFG	FRC
2014	0%	0%	–	3%	100%	93%	43%	48%	46%	88%
2013	5%	C	24%	4%	C	92%	C	56%	52%	C

National Journal Ratings

	2013 LIB	—	2013 CONS
Economic	41%	—	58%
Social	34%	—	62%
Foreign	15%	—	77%
Composite	32%	—	68%

Key Votes of the 113th Congress

1. Sandy storm spending	N	5. Medical Marijuana	N	9. Syrian Rebels Training	Y
2. Violence Against Women Act	Y	6. Farm Bill	Y	10. Keystone pipeline	Y
3. Guantanamo Bay Detainees	N	7. Afghanistan Combat	N	11. Immigration Exec. Action	Y
4. Abortion 20-week ban	Y	8. NSA Phone Data Collection	Y	12. Bipartisan budget deal	Y

Election Results

2014 general	Glenn Thompson (R).................. 115,018	(64%)	$1,098,206
	Kerith Strano Taylor (D)............. 65,839	(36%)	$159,848
2014 primary	Glenn Thompson (R).............unopposed		

Prior winning percentages: 2012 (63%), 2010 (68%), 2008 (57%)

Population		Race and Ethnicity		Income	
Total:	701,630	White	93.1%	Median income:	$45,001
Urban:	19.0%	Black	2.2%		*(320 of 435)*
Suburban:	13.1%	Asian	1.7%	Under $50,000	54.9%
Rural:	67.9%	Latino	1.7%	$50,000-$99,999:	31.2%
Land area:	11,265	Two races	1.0%	$100,000-$199,999:	11.9%
Pop/sq. mi.:	62.3	White Ethnic	37.8%	$200,000 or more:	2.0%
Born in state:	80.4%			Poverty Rate	16.4%
		Education			
Age Groups		H.S. grad or less:	55.1%	**Work**	
Under 18:	19.2%	Some college:	22.6%	White collar:	31.5%
18 to 34:	25.2%	College degree, 4 yr.:	13.7%	Blue collar:	40.8%
35 to 64:	38.6%	Post-grad study:	8.6%	Sales and service:	27.7%
Over 64:	17.0%				
		Military		Govt. workers:	13.1%
		Veterans/active duty:	9.7%		

North-Central Pennsylvania: State College, Erie Suburbs

North central Pennsylvania, isolated from the rest of the country by mountains and off the main east-west rail and highway lines until the 1970s, is one of those empty spaces that make even the North-eastern states seem lightly populated compared to the densely packed terrain of Western Europe or

Voter Turnout	
2013 Total Citizen 18+	557,199
2014 House Turnout	180,857
2014 Turnout as % CVAP	32.5%
2012 Turnout as % CVAP	52.1%

East Asia. This is a prime area for hunting, fishing and snowmobiling. There are wide-open spaces like the Allegheny National Forest, which sprawls across four counties and is a popular recreational area. Neatly preserved Ridgway holds the largest chainsaw carving event in the world.

The recent downturn in manufacturing hit the area hard, but the production of natural gas deep underground in the Marcellus Shale formation has generated considerable optimism locally. The company PVR Partners completed construction in 2012 of a natural gas trunk line for Marcellus Shale producers. Even with the worldwide decline in oil and gas prices, production in the Marcellus Shale increased by more than 50 percent in 2013 and PVR reported 101 new well connections. In Erie County, the General Electric Transportation plant had employed 5,500 people. In 2012, GE Transportation announced it was moving its executive headquarters to Chicago, though Erie remained headquarters for the company's locomotive business and a key manufacturing and engineering site. In April 2013, the company announced 950 layoffs at the local facility. Punxsutawney in Jefferson County is home of the legendary groundhog Phil, who predicts the arrival of spring every February 2 by looking for his shadow on Gobbler's Knob. The 1993 movie *Groundhog Day* sparked a tourism boomlet in the small town, even though the movie was filmed in Woodstock Illinois.

The economy of Centre County in the Nittany Valley has been more resilient thanks to Pennsylvania State University. Penn State's cutting-edge facilities have spawned a high-skills job market. The university was long known for its powerful football teams coached by Joe Paterno. Scandal rocked the university in 2011 when former defensive coordinator Jerry Sandusky was charged with 40 counts of child molestation and related crimes. The athletic director was charged with perjury and failure to report what he knew about Sandusky's behavior. Criminal charges also were brought against the university president. Once an iconic figure in these parts, Paterno was fired for "failure of leadership" and failing to do more to stop Sandusky; he died just two and a half months later. Sandusky was sentenced to up to 60 years in prison, and the National Collegiate Athletic Association imposed stiff sanctions on Penn State football. In January 2015, the university reached a settlement with the NCAA in which the sanctions were rescinded and a new "integrity agreement" took effect. The criminal charges against the former university officials had not yet gone to trial. Even during the sanctions, football Saturdays remained a local religion with a huge economic impact in Happy Valley.

2012 Presidential Vote		
Mitt Romney (R)	165,469	(57%)
Barack Obama (D)	120,026	(41%)

2008 Presidential Vote		
John McCain (R)	160,364	(52%)
Barack Obama (D)	146,574	(47%)

Cook Partisan Voting Index: R+8

The 5th Congressional District of Pennsylvania is rural and sprawling. At its opposite ends, Erie and Centre counties are the most populous and the least Republican. The district remains secure for the GOP.

Glenn Thompson (R)

Republican Glenn Thompson, who won the seat in 2008, is an amiable centrist and the only Pennsylvanian to serve on the House Agriculture Committee. He tries to protect farmers, as well as energy interests, from what he sees as excessive regulation.

A lifelong resident of Centre County, Thompson was born in Bellefonte, Pennsylvania. Staying close to home for college, he attended nearby Penn State. After graduating, he launched his career in health care at Williamsport Hospital, which later became part of the community health network Susquehanna Health, where he worked as a rehabilitation services manager. He also worked as a licensed nursing home administrator. As his congressional website states about his career, "GT has touched the lives of thousands of individuals facing life altering conditions. As a result, he ... has become a strong advocate for increased access, affordability, quality of care, and patient choice." Thompson served as a member of the board of the Bald Eagle Area School District from 1990 to 1996. He ran twice for state representative, both times unsuccessfully, but was elected to three terms as chairman of the Centre County Republican Party.

When the House seat opened, Thompson jumped into the nine-candidate primary. His hopes at first appeared dim against the robust spending by rivals. Businessmen Matt Shaner and Derek Walker financed their own campaigns, and took to the airwaves to reach voters across the expansive district. Thompson instead hit the pavement, crisscrossing the district in a low-key campaign that emphasized his Republican positions and focused on rural issues. He opposed tolls on Interstate 80 and called for expanding rural Medicare initiatives. He spoke of the Iraq war in personal terms; his son, Logan, was injured by a landmine in late 2007 while serving there.

Two developments late in the campaign helped Thompson to break out of the pack. Less than two weeks before the primary, retiring GOP Rep. John Peterson threw his support behind Thompson as the candidate who would follow in his footsteps and who best understood rural issues. The following week, the Clearfield County district attorney filed charges against Walker for allegedly breaking into his ex-girlfriend's apartment. Thompson eked out a small victory. Vastly outspent, he won 19% of the vote to beat Walker by 835 votes.

The general election was a breeze by comparison. Thompson's opponent, Clearfield County Commissioner Mark McCracken, raised only $94,000 and received little help from national or state Democrats. Thompson won 57%-41%. He has had little trouble winning reelection.

In the House, Thompson sticks with his party on major votes but has shown some independence. He dissed tea party advocates by voting to raise the federal debt limit in 2011, to preserve rural air subsidies in 2012, and to support the tax and spending legislation that averted the so-called "fiscal cliff" in 2013. He called the latter "not perfect, but a pretty good deal." In December 2014, he successfully included in the year-end spending bill $155 million for the Essential Air Service program, which promotes rural airports and is opposed by many conservatives.

Rural causes have been a priority for Thompson. On the Agriculture panel, he has chaired the Subcommittee on Conservation and Forestry. He worked to strengthen voluntary conservation programs as part of the farm bill that was enacted in 2014. With many dairy farmers in his district, he filed a bill in May 2015 with Democratic Rep. Joe Courtney of Connecticut to reaffirm the requirement that milk is offered with each school meal.

Thompson also has a seat on the Natural Resources Committee, and has pushed for more natural gas drilling in the Marcellus Shale formation. He dismissed concerns of environmentalists that the gas-drilling technique called hydraulic fracturing is contaminating groundwater. He was highly critical of the Environmental Protection Agency's efforts to protect the Chesapeake Bay from agricultural-related pollution, accusing the EPA of a "quixotic quest to impose unreasonable regulatory mandates." In an October 2012 op-ed column, he wrote that the recent closing of numerous coal facilities in his district was a "real-world impact of EPA's regulatory onslaught." In March 2015, he attacked EPA for its proposed Waters of the U.S. rules, which he said would have severe implications for farmers.

Thompson retains his interest in education issues as a member of the Education and the Workforce Committee. He has co-chaired both the Career and Technical Education Caucus and the Natural Gas Caucus. In 2015, he took on some security and trade issues as co-chair of the German-American Caucus.

SIXTH DISTRICT

Ryan Costello (R)

Elected 2014, 1st term; b. Sept. 7, 1976, Phoenixville; Ursinus Col., B.A. 1999, Villanova U., LL.B. 2002; Presbyterian; married (Christine); 1 child.

Elected Office: E. Vincent Township Bd. of Supervisors, 2002-07; Chester Cnty. recorder of deeds, 2008-11; Chester Cnty. Bd. of Comm., 2011-13.

Professional Career: Practicing atty., 1980-2002.

DC Office: 427 CHOB, 20515, 202-225-4315; Website: costello.house.gov.

State Offices: West Chester, 610-696-2982; Wyomissing, 610-376-7630.

Committees: *Transportation & Infrastructure:* Aviation; Economic Development, Public Buildings & Emergency Mgmt; Highways & Transit. *Veterans' Affairs:* Disability Assistance & Memorial Affairs; Economic Opportunity.

Election Results

2014 general	Ryan Costello (R)	119,643	(56%)	$1,674,283	$899,168	
	Manan Trivedi (D)	92,901	(44%)	$943,661	$17,163	$77,967
2014 primary	Ryan Costello	unopposed				

Population		Race and Ethnicity		Income	
Total:	721,522	White	85.2%	Median income:	$73,826
Urban:	20.1%	Latino	4.7%		*(49 of 435)*
Suburban:	79.4%	Asian	4.2%	Under $50,000	33.7%
Rural:	0.6%	Black	4.1%	$50,000-$99,999:	30.5%
Land area:	1,073	Two races	1.7%	$100,000-$199,999:	26.3%
Pop/sq. mi.:	672.1	White Ethnic	50.2%	$200,000 or more:	9.4%
Born in state:	72.0%			Poverty Rate	7.8%
		Education			
Age Groups		H.S. grad or less:	36.0%	**Work**	
Under 18:	23.3%	Some college:	21.7%	White collar:	44.4%
18 to 34:	20.3%	College degree, 4 yr.:	25.5%	Blue collar:	39.1%
35 to 64:	41.0%	Post-grad study:	16.7%	Sales and service:	16.4%
Over 64:	15.4%			Govt. workers:	8.7%
		Military			
		Veterans/active duty:	7.6%		

Southeast Pennsylvania: Philadelphia Exurbs, Reading Area

The gentle hills of southeastern Pennsylvania, settled in the 18th century by Quaker townsmen, Welsh farmers, German peasants and members of pietistic sects who became known as the Pennsylvania Dutch, were America's first polyglot interior. Before and after independence, a diverse lot

Voter Turnout	
2013 Total Citizen 18+	534,446
2014 House Turnout	212,544
2014 Turnout as % CVAP	39.8%
2012 Turnout as % CVAP	64.7%

looking for tolerance in the area above Philadelphia and the Delaware River found a land that yielded riches, first in crops, then in ironworking. In Revolutionary times, the area was countryside, a long day's ride from the markets and docks of Philadelphia. Then, rail lines were built from Philadelphia: The Main Line of the Pennsylvania Railroad headed west to industrial Pittsburgh and the Midwest, and the Reading Railroad headed northwest through Berks County and the anthracite coalfields beyond. Factories were built in some of the towns, and many farms continued to thrive, but by the late 19th century, some of the land had become commuter territory. The area along the Main Line was affluent suburbia for the masses, or a large part of them.

Much of this area has a kinship with Philadelphia, but it also offers idyllic, rustic living. Country music pop star Taylor Swift grew up on a Christmas tree farm in the region. Chester is the wealthiest county in the state, and its $86,000 median household income was among the highest in the nation. Its robust 3.3% jobless rate in April 2015 was among the lowest in Pennsylvania. At 4.4% in the same period, Berks County had an impressive turnaround from the recession when its unemployment rates were among the highest in the state.

2012 Presidential Vote		
Mitt Romney (R)................174,415	(51%)
Barack Obama (D) 166,030	(48%)
2008 Presidential Vote		
Barack Obama (D) 187,056	(53%)
John McCain (R)................161,943	(46%)
Cook Partisan Voting Index: R+2		

The 6th Congressional District of Pennsylvania is an oddly shaped configuration that includes parts of the countryside in Chester County and the northwest corner of Montgomery County. It stretches through the middle of Berks County, but does not include the city of Reading. And it includes part of heavily Republican Lebanon County. Berwyn, Devon, Malvern, and Paoli, sometimes referred to as the Upper Main Line, are all in the district. The new 6th takes in fast-growing Phoenixville and the commercial hub of West Chester. Chester is the population center, with nearly half of the population, followed by Berks and Montgomery. The district had been the site of some of the closest House races in recent years, but the 2012 shifts made the 6th about five points more Republican. Like the other four artfully drawn Republican-held seats in the suburbs and exurbs of Philadelphia, redistricting changes left the district GOP-friendly but competitive under the right circumstances.

Ryan Costello (R)

Ryan Costello sealed the suburban Philadelphia battleground for Republicans in 2014 by keeping GOP control of the 6th District, which has become less friendly to Democrats. The self-styled moderate won a comfortable 56 percent of the vote against Manan Trivedi, a physician who served with the Marines in the Iraq War and was a campaign adviser for President Barack Obama.

Costello, the son of two public-school teachers, grew up in Chester County. He got his bachelor's from Ursinus College and his law degree from Villanova. He served on the East Vincent Township Board of Supervisors, where he was elected chairman, and then as recorder of deeds in Chester. He later was elected to Chester's Board of Commissioners, the three-member governing body of the county, and was chosen internally as chairman. Costello touted a record of balancing budgets of more than $500 million, cutting spending, and improving the county's 911 emergency call system. After six-term GOP Rep. Jim Gerlach retired, Costello ran unopposed for the GOP nomination.

Democrats, who had eagerly eyed the seat, placed Trivedi (who had lost to Gerlach in 2010 and 2012) on its "Red to Blue" program in hopes of a pickup. But they faced several obstacles, including that redistricting had made the district more conservative. Costello benefited from about $1 million in combined outside spending by the National Association of Realtors, the National Rifle Association and the U.S. Chamber of Commerce. Trivedi, by contrast, had little spending by groups on the left. He questioned Costello's ethics, accusing him of steering a lucrative health care contract for the county to the company of a campaign donor; the Costello camp denied the charge.

Costello cast Trivedi as a creature of Washington and its liberal Democrats. He issued a tongue-in-cheek bet to Trivedi over a Washington-Philadelphia football game, suggesting Trivedi's home team was in the nation's capital. A National Republican Congressional Committee ad linked Trivedi to House Minority Leader Nancy Pelosi, saying he shared her support of "Obamacare on steroids." Costello's victory was evenly split: 55% each in Chester and Montgomery, 57% in Berks, and 69% in smaller Lebanon.

With assignments to the Transportation and Infrastructure and Veterans' Affairs committees, Costello placed a high priority on oversight of the VA. He followed up on continuing problems at the Philadelphia regional office and worked with Veteran' Affairs Committee Chairman Jeff Miller of Florida on legislation to authorize the VA secretary to fire any agency employee for bad performance or misconduct. In March, Costello cited his work on the bipartisan passage of the Passenger Rail Reform and Investment Act, which would upgrade three rail stations in southeast Pennsylvania. He opposed proposed cuts to Amtrak. In January, he broke with most House Republicans by voting against the plan to deport the grown children of illegal immigrants who had lost protected status. He said that he hoped to support immigration reform measures.

The Democratic Congressional Campaign Committee placed Costello on its "one-term wonders" list of 15 GOP freshmen whom it planned to target in the 2016 campaign.

SEVENTH DISTRICT

Pat Meehan (R)

Elected 2010, 3rd term; b. Oct. 20, 1955, Cheltenham; Bowdoin Col., B.A. 1978, Temple U., J.D. 1986; Catholic; married (Carolyn); 3 children.

Elected Office: Delaware Cnty. dist. atty., 1996-2001.

Professional Career: Practicing atty., 1986-91, 2008-10; Counsel, Sen. Arlen Specter, 1991-94; Campaign aide, Sen. Rick Santorum, 1994; U.S. atty., 2001-08.

DC Office: 434 CHOB, 20515, 202-225-2011; Fax: 202-226-0280; Website: meehan.house.gov.

State Offices: Springfield, 610-690-7323.

Committees: *Ethics. Ways & Means:* Human Resources; Oversight.

Group Ratings

	ADA	ACLU	AFL-CIO	LCV	ITI	COC	HAFA	ACU	CFG	FRC
2014	0%	5%	–	6%	100%	100%	39%	48%	31%	88%
2013	10%	C	48%	7%	C	92%	C	40%	51%	C

National Journal Ratings

	2013 LIB	—	2013 CONS
Economic	49%	—	51%
Social	53%	—	46%
Foreign	15%	—	77%
Composite	41%	—	60%

Key Votes of the 113th Congress

1. Sandy storm spending	Y	5. Medical Marijuana	N	9. Syrian Rebels Training	Y
2. Violence Against Women Act	Y	6. Farm Bill	N	10. Keystone pipeline	Y
3. Guantanamo Bay Detainees	N	7. Afghanistan Combat	N	11. Immigration Exec. Action	Y
4. Abortion 20-week ban	Y	8. NSA Phone Data Collection	N	12. Bipartisan budget deal	Y

Election Results

2014 general	Patrick Meehan (R).................. 145,869	(62%)	$1,332,058	$20,492
	Mary Ellen Balchunis (D) 89,256	(38%)	$94,266	
2014 primary	Pat Meehan (R)......................unopposed			

Prior winning percentages: 2012 (59%), 2010 (55%)

Population		Race and Ethnicity		Income	
Total:	722,495	White	85.9%	Median income:	$81,186
Urban:	26.7%	Black	5.5%		(28 of 435)
Suburban:	73.3%	Asian	3.9%	Under $50,000	30.1%
Rural:	0.0%	Latino	3.2%	$50,000-$99,999:	29.6%
Land area:	732	Two races	1.3%	$100,000-$199,999:	28.5%
Pop/sq. mi.:	987.1	White Ethnic	59.0%	$200,000 or more:	11.8%
Born in state:	74.4%			Poverty Rate	5.6%
		Education			
Age Groups		H.S. grad or less:	36.4%	**Work**	
Under 18:	22.6%	Some college:	23.0%	White collar:	46.3%
18 to 34:	20.0%	College degree, 4 yr.:	23.5%	Blue collar:	37.7%
35 to 64:	41.3%	Post-grad study:	17.1%	Sales and service:	16.0%
Over 64:	16.2%				
		Military		Govt. workers:	7.9%
		Veterans/active duty:	7.0%		

Southern and Western Philadelphia Suburbs: Delaware County

A century ago, Delaware County, southwest of Philadelphia, was already filling up, with industrial towns strung out along the rail lines paralleling the Delaware River and residential suburbs along the inland commuter rail lines. Politics in Delaware County in those days was run by a

Voter Turnout	
2013 Total Citizen 18+	540,354
2014 House Turnout	235,125
2014 Turnout as % CVAP	43.5%
2012 Turnout as % CVAP	67.8%

Republican machine headed by state Sen. John McClure. Such was his power that, in 1960, presidential candidate Richard Nixon stopped by the ailing McClure's home to pay homage. McClure exercised his influence through the War Board, a 15-member panel that decided on all nominations for public office. The board technically went out of business in 1975, but one of its products, Tom Judge, remained county Republican chairman till 2010.

In recent decades, the area has undergone significant demographic and political change: Blacks have moved out of Philadelphia into adjacent Delaware County suburbs in large numbers, and cultural liberalism has led many affluent suburbs to vote Democratic. In the 1988 presidential race, Delaware County voted 60%-39% for Republican George H.W. Bush, but in 2012, it voted by the identical margin for Democrat Barack Obama. A driving economic force here is Boeing's plant in Ridley Park, with 6,200 employees, where the V-22 Osprey is assembled. In 2013, Boeing won a $4 billion contract from the Army to produce as many as 38 additional Chinook helicopters, which have been built since the early 1960s.

Along with many upscale residents, suburban Philly includes blue-collar, white ethnics with roots in the city. These cultural remnants of the city extended outward—the cheesesteak restaurant Tony Luke's has a branch in the Springfield Mall. Much of the 2012 film *Silver Linings Playbook* was set and filmed here, and the movie depicts an off-kilter Italian-American family obsessed with Philadelphia Eagles football. The area is also filled with colonial history. The Brandywine Battlefield was where George Washington and Gen. Henry Knox unsuccessfully tried to prevent British forces from taking Philadelphia during the Revolutionary War. Valley Forge is where Washington and his men spent the terrible winter and spring of 1777-78. The I-495 bridge over the Christina River closed for emergency repairs during the summer of 2014 and caused major inconvenience during two months of repairs southbound and nearly three months northbound.

The 7th Congressional District of Pennsylvania covers most of Delaware County, which is a bit more than half of the population of the district, though the black neighborhoods remain mostly in the 1st District. It takes in parts of Chester County, such as the refined farm country of Chadds Ford, home to generations of Wyeth artists. The district also includes parts of Berks and Montgomery counties. The new, unconventional shape of the 7th made it one of the most highlighted gerrymanders in the nation in post-2010 census redistricting. *The Patriot-News* of Harrisburg called it "some sort of amorphous modern art drawing." *The Washington Post* described it as "Goofy Kicking Donald Duck." The *Philadelphia Daily News* complained that it was "a new poster child for why we must find a better way to do redistricting." Republicans in charge of redistricting stretched it much farther west to include parts of conservative Lancaster County. And they placed Demo-

2012 Presidential Vote
Mitt Romney (R)................183,343   (50%)
Barack Obama (D) 176,658   (49%)

2008 Presidential Vote
Barack Obama (D) 194,026   (53%)
John McCain (R)................171,283   (46%)

Cook Partisan Voting Index: R+2

cratic Swarthmore in the Philadelphia-based 1st District. Despite modest changes in the GOP's favor, the district remained marginal territory. Mitt Romney took the 2012 presidential vote, 50%-49%.

Pat Meehan (R)

Pat Meehan, elected in 2010, is a moderate Republican in the mold of the late Sen. Arlen Specter, his former boss. He has displayed influence in his work on House committees and emphasized his approach as a pragmatic problem-solver.

Meehan grew up in Cheltenham Township, in Montgomery County. His father was a construction worker, his mother a secretary. Meehan began saving for college when he was 13, working as a caddy at a golf course. He helped pay his tuition at Bowdoin College in

Maine by working at a rubber factory, where he shoveled rubber pellets into an incinerator. He played hockey in college and for two years worked as a referee in the National Hockey League, a job that he says was good training for politics. He learned to stand behind controversial calls, to be fair in the public spotlight, and to know when to break up a fight and when to let the players slug it out, Meehan said. Standing up to angry hockey players also made going to law school seem less intimidating for him.

Meehan graduated from Temple University law school, then went to work at the large law firm founded by Philadelphia Mayor Richardson Dilworth (1956-62). He left the firm to become counsel to Specter, long before the cantankerous senator switched parties to become a Democrat. In 1994, Meehan was the campaign manager for Republican Rick Santorum when he defeated Democratic Sen. Harris Wofford.

With his solid Republican credentials, Meehan was elected district attorney in Delaware County in 1995. That job gave him substantial publicity for the successful prosecution of millionaire John DuPont in the murder of Olympic wrestler Dave Schultz. He also created a special victims unit that allowed domestic violence cases to be prosecuted without victims having to testify in open court. In 2001, on Specter's recommendation, Meehan was appointed U.S. attorney for the Philadelphia office. He won corruption convictions against several high-profile local politicians, Republicans as well as Democrats, some resulting from wiretaps in the office of Philadelphia Mayor John Street, who was not charged with any crime.

When Democratic Rep. Joe Sestak challenged Specter for his Senate seat in 2010, Meehan ran for Sestak's House seat. Although the district was trending Democratic, Meehan had an edge as a familiar prosecutor with moderate positions on cultural issues. With his Philadelphia-area contacts, he raised $3 million, almost twice that raised by his Democratic opponent, Bryan Lentz, an Iraq war veteran and two-term state representative from Swarthmore. Both national parties spent lavishly on the contest.

The candidates differed on economic issues, with Meehan favoring extension of the 2001 and 2003 tax cuts for all taxpayers, and Lentz saying he would carve out an exception for high-income earners. Meehan was endorsed by the union that represented workers at Boeing's Ridley Park plant. Meehan criticized Lentz for casting ghost votes—having someone else vote for him—in Harrisburg. Lentz's campaign manager vehemently denied it, but then backtracked when Meehan produced testimony from a witness in the spectator's gallery at the state Capitol. Meehan charged that Democratic volunteers placed a third-party conservative on the general election ballot to try to draw votes from him. Meehan won 55%-44%, carrying all three counties that were then in the district.

In the House, Meehan quickly became a leadership ally. But he showed plenty of independence, especially on legal issues. He was one of 17 Republicans to oppose a House-passed amendment in 2012 barring the use of federal funds to defend legal challenges to a provision of the health care law. On the Homeland Security Committee, he chaired the panel on cybersecurity, a timely topic. He won House passage in 2012 of his bill to set guidelines for the Homeland Security Department's sharing of information with state and local law enforcement about threats involving chemical, biological and nuclear weapons. The House also passed his bill to boost penalties for people trafficking in counterfeit drugs. In December 2014, he worked with a broad bipartisan group of lawmakers to enact a legislative package to modernize and strengthen the nation's cybersecurity defense. Noting that the cyber capabilities of both state and non-state adversaries of the United States were costing billions of dollars, he described the new law as "a major achievement to improve our nation's cybersecurity defenses, improve coordination between government and private sector and protect the personal data of millions of American consumers." Meehan worked on a local bill to deepen the Delaware River to increase ship traffic. On a lighter note, he participated in the annual congressional hockey game between lawmakers and lobbyists.

In January 2015, Meehan got a coveted seat on the Ways and Means Committee. In March, he won committee approval of his bill to assure that organizations denied tax-exempt status had the right to file an administrative appeal. In April, he was among the first Republicans to support the campaign to place a woman on the nation's currency and break what Meehan called the "green ceiling." He organized activities to repeal the controversial medical devices tax in the health care overhaul. He also got a seat on the Ethics Committee, which is not a place to make friends in the House but is a useful slot for a former prosecutor.

After redistricting, his Democratic opponent in 2012, Radnor Township Democratic Chair George Badey, tried to highlight Meehan's conservative votes, such as his support of

House Budget Committee Chairman Paul Ryan's budget. But Meehan was endorsed by the Philadelphia building and construction trades council, an influential union that opposed him in 2010, and he coasted to a 59%-41% victory. In 2014, he was reelected with 62% against Mary Ellen Balchunis, a political science professor at LaSalle University.

EIGHTH DISTRICT

Mike Fitzpatrick (R)

Elected 2010, 4th term; b. June 28, 1963, Philadelphia; St. Thomas U., B.A. 1985, Dickinson Schl. of Law, J.D. 1988; Catholic; married (Kathy); 6 children.

Elected Office: Bucks Cnty. Commission, 1994-2004; U.S. House, 2005-07.

Professional Career: Practicing atty., 2007-10.

DC Office: 2400 RHOB, 20515, 202-225-4276; Fax: 202-225-9511; Website: fitzpatrick.house.gov.

State Offices: Langhorne, 215-579-8102.

Committees: *Financial Services:* Financial Institutions & Consumer Credit; Oversight & Investigations (VChmn); Task Force to Investigate Terrorism Financing (Chmn).

Group Ratings

	ADA	ACLU	AFL-CIO	LCV	ITI	COC	HAFA	ACU	CFG	FRC
2014	10%	5%	–	29%	100%	92%	33%	40%	29%	88%
2013	10%	C	43%	25%	C	92%	C	36%	42%	C

National Journal Ratings

	2013 LIB	—	2013 CONS
Economic	53%	—	47%
Social	51%	—	48%
Foreign	50%	—	50%
Composite	52%	—	49%

Key Votes of the 113th Congress

1. Sandy storm spending	Y	5. Medical Marijuana	N	9. Syrian Rebels Training	Y
2. Violence Against Women Act	Y	6. Farm Bill	Y	10. Keystone pipeline	Y
3. Guantanamo Bay Detainees	N	7. Afghanistan Combat	N	11. Immigration Exec. Action	Y
4. Abortion 20-week ban	Y	8. NSA Phone Data Collection	Y	12. Bipartisan budget deal	Y

Election Results

2014 general	Michael G. Fitzpatrick (R).........	137,731	(62%)	$2,089,893	$631,626	$1,059
	Kevin Strouse (D)	84,767	(38%)	$1,346,514	$2,413	
2014 primary	Mike Fitzpatrick (R) ....unopposed					

Prior winning percentages: 2012 (57%), 2010 (54%), 2004 (55%)

Population		Race and Ethnicity		Income	
Total:	708,333	White	86.7%	Median income:	$73,522
Urban:	0.0%	Latino	4.3%		(51 of 435)
Suburban:	100.0%	Asian	4.0%	Under $50,000	33.5%
Rural:	0.0%	Black	3.6%	$50,000-$99,999:	31.2%
Land area:	699	Two races	1.3%	$100,000-$199,999:	26.6%
Pop/sq. mi.:	1,013.4	White Ethnic	56.7%	$200,000 or more:	8.7%
Born in state:	69.1%			Poverty Rate	6.1%
		Education			
Age Groups		H.S. grad or less:	37.8%	**Work**	
Under 18:	21.8%	Some college:	25.1%	White collar:	41.2%
18 to 34:	18.8%	College degree, 4 yr.:	22.6%	Blue collar:	40.4%
35 to 64:	43.4%	Post-grad study:	14.5%	Sales and service:	18.4%
Over 64:	16.1%				
		Military		Govt. workers:	8.8%
		Veterans/active duty:	7.4%		

Northern Philadelphia Suburbs: Bucks County

Bucks County was one of Pennsylvania founding father William Penn's three original settlements and the launching point for George Washington's crossing of the frigid Delaware River to surprise English and Hessian forces on Christmas Day 1776. But it has had a split personality from the

Voter Turnout	
2013 Total Citizen 18+	532,932
2014 House Turnout	222,498
2014 Turnout as % CVAP	41.7%
2012 Turnout as % CVAP	67.8%

start. Upper Bucks County was at once a bucolic paradise of rolling hills and creeks and, after Penn's secretary, James Logan, built the Durham Furnace iron works in 1727, it became one of the nation's major industrial sites. In the 1920s, Bucks County's well-settled farmland, old fieldstone houses and covered bridges captured the imagination of writers and artists, attracting the New York theatrical crowd—Oscar Hammerstein, Moss Hart, Dorothy Parker and S. J. Perelman. Doylestown, the county seat of Bucks, has beautiful old homes and several impressive museums. New Hope remains a popular weekend spot, with its hip boutiques and restaurants.

After World War II, its location between Philadelphia and Trenton, New Jersey, brought industrial Lower Bucks County to the forefront. The ocean-navigable Delaware River and several rail lines resulted in huge new developments: U.S. Steel's Fairless Works, one of the few big postwar steel plants, and the Levitt organization's second Levittown in what had been a swamp between U.S. 13 and U.S. 1. The steel mill closed in 1991 and a wind turbine plant on part of the site was the venue for a visit from President Barack Obama in April 2011. The county has a growing biotechnology sector; Discovery Laboratories is based in Warrington.

Historically, Bucks County was heavily Republican, but it has become marginal. Development in Bucks came after the New Deal, unlike other suburban Philadelphia counties where most blue-collar immigration occurred decades earlier. Lower Bucks around Fairless Works and Levittown, with its tightly packed homes filled with blue-collar workers, became Democratic. Upper Bucks, faster-growing and attracting trendy New Yorkers, has increasingly favored Democratic policies such as green space programs to keep developers away.

The 8th Congressional District of Pennsylvania includes all of Bucks County. Its small part of northern Montgomery County is slightly more than 10 percent of the district.

2012 Presidential Vote		
Mitt Romney (R)	178,195	(49%)
Barack Obama (D)	177,940	(49%)
2008 Presidential Vote		
Barack Obama (D)	198,668	(53%)
John McCain (R)	170,830	(46%)
Cook Partisan Voting Index: R+1		

Bucks has a notably small minority population and the third-highest income of any county in the state. Compared with surrounding districts, the Bucks County-based 8th is relatively compact. The district has hosted some of the most hotly contested House races in the country, and it remains competitive.

Mike Fitzpatrick (R)

Republican Mike Fitzpatrick was first elected in 2004, defeated in 2006, and elected again in 2010. Despite an occasional flirtation with tea party-inspired partisan rhetoric, his voting record is solidly in line with Pennsylvania's other GOP moderates. A term-limits supporter, he unexpectedly announced at the end of a 2014 campaign debate that he would not run again after having served eight years. "There are many in Bucks County who want to serve and they should have the opportunity to do that," he said.

Fitzpatrick grew up in Bucks County's Levittown, one of seven children. An Eagle Scout, he graduated from St. Thomas University in Miami and got his law degree at Penn State. From 1994 to 2004, he served on the Bucks County Commission, where he worked on land preservation and had a reputation for supporting environmental causes. Rep. Jim Greenwood, a moderate Republican, announced after the primary in 2004 that he had accepted an offer to head the Biotechnology Industry Organization. Local GOP leaders chose Fitzpatrick to replace him. He won the general election 55%-43%.

In his first bid for reelection in 2006, Fitzpatrick was challenged by Democrat Patrick Murphy, an Army lawyer and Iraq war veteran who was the son of a Philadelphia policeman. Murphy favored an end to the war at a time when anti-war sentiments were running high.

Fitzpatrick tried to distance himself from the Bush administration's policies in Iraq. When Fitzpatrick ran an ad questioning Murphy's claim that he had worked as a Justice Department prosecutor, Murphy declared at a forum, "Mike, you are a liar and a coward." Murphy won 50.3%-49.7%, with a vote margin of 1,518 votes out of almost 250,000 votes cast.

Fitzpatrick returned to private law practice. He was later diagnosed with colon cancer; after treatment, doctors gave him a clean bill of health in 2010. That year was shaping up to be a favorable political climate for Republicans, and Fitzpatrick decided to try to get the seat back. He defeated three opponents in the primary with 77% of the vote. In the general election, Fitzpatrick emphasized not the environmental issues he had in the past, but his opposition to the Obama administration. "Cash for clunkers, Obamacare, stimulus—no jobs. We've wasted a lot of money in the last few years," he told *The New York Times*.

Like many Democrats in 2010, Murphy would have allowed the Bush-era tax cuts to expire for high-income earners while extending them for other taxpayers. Murphy attacked Fitzpatrick for "Fitzflops"—formerly cosponsoring and now opposing a bill making it easier to organize workplaces by eliminating the secret ballot in union elections, and earlier bragging about being one of the House's most liberal Republicans but now campaigning as a tea partier. Murphy was appealing to many Democratic insiders who hoped that he might someday run statewide. He had raised his profile in the House as the leader of the effort to repeal the ban on openly gay service personnel in the military. Murphy spent $4.3 million, more than twice the $2 million Fitzpatrick spent. But Fitzpatrick won by a decisive 54%-46%.

Back in the House, Fitzpatrick was the Pennsylvania delegation's most liberal Republican in 2011 and 2012, according to *National Journal's* vote ratings. Showing his unpredictability, he sponsored a successful bill requiring schools and libraries to restrict minors' access to social networking sites and chat rooms. He opposed a House-passed bill that replaced automatic spending cuts with targeted reductions aimed at decreasing eligibility for food stamps and eliminating programs created in the 2010 health care law. The House passed his bill in 2012 to overturn President Barack Obama's executive order giving an across-the-board pay hike to members of Congress and some federal workers. He also enacted a measure to extend death benefits to the families of emergency service workers for non-profit organizations.

Fitzpatrick took on a wide-ranging assignment in 2015 as chairman of a bipartisan task force of the Financial Services Committee to investigate terrorist financing. The immediate focus was an effort, including possible legislation, to stop financing from reaching terrorist groups such as the Islamic State. His focus was "terrorist financing, evaluating the security of the U.S. banking system and asking the tough questions as to whether or not we are doing enough," Fitzpatrick told philly.com in March 2015. He said that his investigation was spurred by a six-day trip that he took to the Mideast the previous October during which he spoke with experts in the region.

At home, his Democratic opponent in 2012 was attorney Kathy Boockvar. The National Republican Congressional Committee landed in hot water by seeking to link Boockvar to the controversial movement to free convicted cop-killer Mumia Abu-Jamal. Her husband had once done legal work for a witness who recanted her testimony in the case. That led former Democratic Gov. Ed Rendell, still a popular figure in the area, to condemn Fitzpatrick. But the incumbent outspent Boockvar by nearly 2-to-1 and won, 57%-43%.

In 2014, Democrats recruited and talked up Kevin Strouse, a former Army Ranger who served in Afghanistan and Iraq and later worked at the Central Intelligence Agency. He discussed the need for innovation, education and worker training to succeed in the global economy. One downside for Strouse: His roots were in Delaware County, which is on the other side of the Philadelphia suburbs. Fitzpatrick got a boost from more than $500,000 in spending by gun-control groups, including the Super PACs of former Democratic Rep. Gabby Giffords and independent ex-New York City mayor Michael Bloomberg. He didn't need the help. Fitzpatrick won his House swan-song, 62%-38%.

Once Fitzpatrick affirmed his retirement plans for 2016, candidates and potential candidates began expressing their interest in what was expected to be an expensive and hard-fought campaign to replace him.

NINTH DISTRICT

Bill Shuster (R)

Elected May 2001, 7th full term; b. Jan. 10, 1961, McKeesport; Dickinson Col., B.A. 1983, American U., M.B.A. 1987; Lutheran; divorced; 2 children.

Professional Career: Mgr., Goodyear Tire & Rubber Co., 1983-87; Dist. mgr., Bandag Inc., 1987-90; Owner & gen. mgr., Shuster Chrysler, 1990-2001.

DC Office: 2268 RHOB, 20515, 202-225-2431; Fax: 202-225-2486; Website: shuster.house.gov.

State Offices: Chambersburg, 717-264-8308; Hollidaysburg, 814-696-6318; Indiana, 724-463-0516.

Committees: *Armed Services:* Emerging Threats & Capabilities. *Transportation & Infrastructure* (Chmn: ex officio member of each subcommittee).

Group Ratings

	ADA	ACLU	AFL-CIO	LCV	ITI	COC	HAFA	ACU	CFG	FRC
2014	0%	0%	–	6%	80%	79%	60%	57%	61%	86%
2013	0%	C	29%	11%	C	92%	C	64%	75%	C

National Journal Ratings

	2013 LIB	—	2013 CONS
Economic	34%	—	66%
Social	38%	—	59%
Foreign	5%	—	86%
Composite	28%	—	72%

Key Votes of the 113th Congress

1. Sandy storm spending	N	5. Medical Marijuana		9. Syrian Rebels Training	NV

1. Sandy storm spending   N
2. Violence Against Women Act   Y
3. Guantanamo Bay Detainees   N
4. Abortion 20-week ban   Y

5. Medical Marijuana   NV
6. Farm Bill   N
7. Afghanistan Combat   N
8. NSA Phone Data Collection   N

9. Syrian Rebels Training   Y
10. Keystone pipeline   Y
11. Immigration Exec. Action   Y
12. Bipartisan budget deal   Y

Election Results

2014 general	Bill Shuster (R)	110,094	(64%)	$3,924,437	$54,462	$10,000
	Alanna Hartzok (D)	63,223	(37%)	$22,255		
2014 primary	Bill Shuster (R)	24,106	(53%)			
	Art Halvorson (R)	15,761	(35%)			
	Travis Schooley (R)	5,802	(13%)			

Prior winning percentages: 2012 (62%), 2010 (73%), 2008 (64%), 2006 (60%), 2004 (69%), 2002 (71%), 2001 special (52%)

Population		Race and Ethnicity		Income	
Total:	701,622	White	93.3%	Median income:	$45,942
Urban:	23.0%	Black	3.0%		(301 of 435)
Suburban:	37.8%	Latino	1.8%	Under $50,000	54.0%
Rural:	39.2%	Asian	0.6%	$50,000-$99,999:	32.0%
Land area:	6,424	Two races	1.2%	$100,000-$199,999:	12.2%
Pop/sq. mi.:	109.2	White Ethnic	39.6%	$200,000 or more:	1.7%
Born in state:	80.7%			Poverty Rate	15.6%
		Education			
Age Groups		H.S. grad or less:	59.7%	**Work**	
Under 18:	20.7%	Some college:	22.9%	White collar:	28.8%
18 to 34:	20.6%	College degree, 4 yr.:	11.4%	Blue collar:	42.5%
35 to 64:	40.4%	Post-grad study:	5.9%	Sales and service:	28.7%
Over 64:	18.3%			Govt. workers:	12.7%
		Military			
		Veterans/active duty:	10.4%		

South-Central Pennsylvania: Pittsburgh Exurbs, Altoona

The old towns of south central Pennsylvania look much as they did a century ago: farmhouses and red barns set amidst rolling hills in the shadow of mountain ridges, seemingly isolated from the pulsing rhythms of modern America. During the 18th century, the Appalachian Mountains provided

Voter Turnout	
2013 Total Citizen 18+	551,831
2014 House Turnout	173,317
2014 Turnout as % CVAP	31.4%
2012 Turnout as % CVAP	50.6%

Quaker Pennsylvania with a rampart against Indian attacks, and allowed the commonwealth to become the richest and most populous of the colonies. But the mountains also became a barrier to commerce for later pioneers, and it took the aggressive capitalists who built the Pennsylvania Railroad to get trains over the ridges. Though Pennsylvania's rail links remained important, a war-bound nation in 1940 opened the road of the future here: the Pennsylvania Turnpike, the first highway in America that was able to move vehicles dependably at high speeds over long distances.

The region made history again much later, although without the happy ending: On Sept. 11, 2001, United Airlines Flight 93 crashed into an empty former coalfield near Shanksville in Somerset County, killing all 40 passengers and crew on board. To Americans, the crash site became a symbol of both sadness and pride at the passengers' effort to wrest back control of the plane and possibly thwart a greater disaster, initiated by the now-famous cry of "Let's roll!" The National Park Service opened a memorial to Flight 93 for the 10th anniversary of the attacks.

The 9th Congressional District takes in a wide swath of south and central Pennsylvania, including six full counties and parts of six others. Most of the 9th is not coal country and was thus spared the boom-bust cycles of northeastern Pennsylvania. But this is still a slow-growth, low-income area today. Blair County includes the city of Altoona, which continues to wither, from 82,000 people in 1930 to 45,800 in 2013. In January 2015, the Louisiana-based Albemarle Corp. announced plans to sell its chemical plant outside of the city; it abandoned its 2013 plan for a $30-million expansion. The largest and fastest-growing full county in the district is Franklin, where several international manufacturers have built local plants; its population jumped 17 percent from 2000 to 2013. In December 2014, the *Pittsburgh Post-Gazette* reported that Pennsylvania Turnpike managers were reviewing options to build new tunnels to replace two existing 6,070-foot tunnels through the mountains in Somerset County. The original tunnels, opened in the late 1930s and in 1965, were described as deteriorating and lacking adequate capacity.

Politically, this part of Pennsylvania has been solidly Republican since 1860, and has not come close to electing a Democrat to Congress for decades. Republicans in charge of 2011 redistricting allowed the 9th to lose some GOP voters to shore up nearby districts. But this is still the strongest GOP district in the state. Mitt Romney took 63 percent of the vote in 2012.

2012 Presidential Vote		
Mitt Romney (R)	176,451	(63%)
Barack Obama (D)	100,765	(36%)

2008 Presidential Vote		
John McCain (R)	170,578	(58%)
Barack Obama (D)	120,644	(41%)

Cook Partisan Voting Index: R+14

Bill Shuster (R)

Republican Bill Shuster won a May 2001 special election to succeed his father, Bud Shuster, the powerful chairman of the Transportation and Infrastructure Committee in the 1990s. With the support of GOP leaders, the younger Shuster took over as head of the panel in 2013 after becoming an important figure on transportation issues in his own right.

Bill Shuster grew up in the Pittsburgh area, where his father started a successful business. After getting a bachelor's degree from Dickinson College and a master's in business administration from American University, he took over the family's car dealership, Shuster Chrysler in East Freedom, near Altoona. He sold the business in 2002.

Bud Shuster resigned from the House in January 2001, unhappy that Republican leaders refused him an exemption from term limits on committee chairmen. The contest for the House seat was decided for all practical purposes at a district-wide Republican convention. Facing nine other contenders, Bill Shuster, with back-room help from his father, ran an insider campaign that took advantage of his father's name and years of service. Despite local grumbling about a Shuster dynasty, opponents failed to coalesce behind a candidate. Shuster won 69 of the 133 votes, two more than the required majority.

National Democrats ignored the race in the heavily Republican district. But Democratic nominee H. Scott Conklin campaigned vigorously as an opponent of abortion rights and gun control. Shuster won by a closer than expected 52%-44%. National Republicans attributed the narrow margin to residual intra-party ill will over Shuster's nomination.

In the House, Shuster has a solidly conservative voting record, though his predilection toward grabbing federal funding for his area has led him to oppose conservatives' amendments to cancel or cut federal programs. In 2011, he took the gavel of the Railroads, Pipelines, and Hazardous Materials Subcommittee. He favored high-speed rail, but only in the busy Northeast corridor, and said that it should be privatized—an idea many Democrats consider unworkable. He also takes a dim view of funding bike and pedestrian projects that many urban Democrats champion as essential. "When you start getting into the inner city, the federal government has less of a role to play," he said at a January 2012 transportation conference. He sponsored a measure that became law that year cracking down on unauthorized intercity bus operators, a priority of authorized bus companies and their unions. He added an amendment to an aviation bill in March 2011 requiring the Federal Aviation Administration to give more weight to economic factors before adopting safety rules. Safety groups sharply criticized the proposal, but it narrowly passed.

His loyalty to the House GOP agenda earned Shuster a spot on its whip team and Republican leaders occasionally have called on him for behind-the-scenes assistance. Shuster occasionally reaches across the aisle, joining with Vermont Democrat Peter Welch in 2011 in an effort to impose limits on credit card swipe fees.

In his father's tradition, Shuster has been an avid practitioner of earmarked spending for his district, a practice that in recent years has been attacked by budget conservatives as wasteful. But he reluctantly went along when then-Minority Leader John Boehner led the House Republicans' push to ban the practice. Democrats lampooned Shuster in March 2009 for taking credit for $9 million sent to his district from President Barack Obama's economic stimulus bill, even though he had voted against the legislation. He was less amenable to funding for Berkeley, California. He tried unsuccessfully to cut $2 million for the city from an appropriations bill in 2008 after the city told Marine recruiters they were unwelcome to set up shop there; Shuster called Berkeley "ground zero for radicals and leftist zealots."

Taking the helm of Transportation and Infrastructure in 2013, he vowed to cut through the polarization that marked the tenure of the previous chairman, Florida's John Mica. Shuster told the *Pittsburgh Tribune-Review* that he would even consider abandoning the Republican no-new-taxes pledge to fund transportation projects. Though he initially said he was open to a vehicle-miles-traveled fee, he abandoned that idea in late 2014 along with an increase in the federal gasoline tax, citing public and political opposition, not least among House Republicans.

Shuster has been more approachable and pragmatic than his father, who ran the committee with an iron fist. "He's a lot more personable than his father," Roger Beckner, a former chairman of the Franklin County Republican Party, told *The Washington Post* in 2014. Part of that is by necessity: Unlike his father, he can no longer use earmarks on transportation authorization bills to help smooth deal-making. He also has an altered budget environment in which to work, partly due to a slowing in the growth of revenues from the gasoline tax. Former Democratic Rep. Jim Oberstar of Minnesota, who chaired the panel from 2007 to 2011 and died in May 2014, told *The Morning Call* of Allentown that Shuster "has all the right instincts, all the right views of the policy direction. ... But his ability to move on his instincts and judgments will be entirely limited by the House Republican leadership."

During his first two years as chairman, Shuster failed to get a multi-year transportation reauthorization bill through the House. Lawmakers in July 2014 passed a version that extended only through May 2015. Conservative groups opposed it for using what they called "budget gimmicks," and even supporters said it was little more than a Band-Aid. But Shuster hit it off with Obama's Transportation secretary, Anthony Foxx, raising hopes that they could get a longer-term bill into law before the start of the 2016 presidential campaign. The two even held a joint "Twitter Town Hall" discussion in February 2015 to try to drum up support. "The timing is right for me and Secretary Foxx," Shuster said. Amid a continuing deadlock and less money than Shuster wants to spend, Congress agreed in May 2015 to a two-month extension of the highway programs. In July, the House passed another extension until Dec. 18.

Shuster had better success in enacting a bipartisan $12.3 billion water projects bill in 2014. In rolling out that measure a year earlier, he again took to social media, posting a slickly produced video on YouTube in which he explained how the measure would create jobs. In a nod to the GOP's fiscally oriented conservatives, the bill called for deauthorizing money that had been inactive for years but remained on the books.

At home, Shuster had an unusually strong primary challenge in 2004 from Michael DelGrosso, a management consultant whose family owns a Blair County tomato sauce company. He said that the district needed a new economic approach. DelGrosso carried Blair County and three nearby counties in the northern part of the district, but Shuster ran strongly elsewhere and squeezed by with a 51%-49% win. Shuster drew another aggressive primary challenge in 2014 from Art Halvorson, a retired Coast Guard official with tea party ties. He attacked the congressman as a loyal lieutenant of Speaker John Boehner and said the district needed to be represented by someone not named Shuster for a change. Shuster spent more than $700,000 on TV ads and took 11 of the 12 counties as he won the primary, 53%-35%.

In April 2015, Shuster faced a potentially damaging news story when *Politico* reported that he was dating an influential lobbyist who works for Airlines for America, a large trade association with extensive interest in legislation before his committee. In a statement, Shuster acknowledged that he had a private and personal relationship with the lobbyist, Shelley Rubino, but that she "doesn't lobby my office, including myself and my staff." Shuster was divorced in 2014.

TENTH DISTRICT

Tom Marino (R)

Elected 2010, 3rd term; b. Aug. 15, 1952, Williamsport; Lycoming Col., B.A. 1985, Dickinson Schl. of Law, J.D. 1988; Catholic; married (Edie); 2 children.

Elected Office: Lycoming Cnty. dist. atty., 1992-2002.

Professional Career: U.S. atty., 2002-07; Practicing atty., 2007-10.

DC Office: 410 CHOB, 20515, 202-225-3731; Fax: 202-225-9594; Website: marino.house.gov.

State Offices: Hamlin, 570-689-6024; Selinsgrove, 570-374-9469; Williamsport, 570-322-3961.

Committees: *Foreign Affairs:* Asia & the Pacific; Europe, Eurasia & Emerging Threats. *Homeland Security:* Cybersecurity, Infrastructure Protection, & Security Technologies; Emergency Preparedness, Response & Communications. *Judiciary:* Courts, Intellectual Property & the Internet; Regulatory Reform, Commercial & Antitrust Law (Chmn).

Group Ratings

	ADA	ACLU	AFL-CIO	LCV	ITI	COC	HAFA	ACU	CFG	FRC
2014	0%	5%	–	3%	100%	93%	51%	64%	46%	100%
2013	0%	C	24%	7%	C	85%	C	60%	63%	C

National Journal Ratings

	2013 LIB	—	2013 CONS
Economic	43%	—	57%
Social	38%	—	59%
Foreign	15%	—	77%
Composite	34%	—	66%

Key Votes of the 113th Congress

1. Sandy storm spending	Y	5. Medical Marijuana	N	9. Syrian Rebels Training	Y
2. Violence Against Women Act	N	6. Farm Bill	Y	10. Keystone pipeline	Y
3. Guantanamo Bay Detainees	N	7. Afghanistan Combat	Y	11. Immigration Exec. Action	Y
4. Abortion 20-week ban	Y	8. NSA Phone Data Collection	N	12. Bipartisan budget deal	Y

Election Results

2014 general	Tom Marino (R)	112,851	(63%)	$952,468	$2,922
	Scott Brion (D)	44,737	(25%)	$191,354	
	Nick Troiano (I)	22,734	(13%)	$165,290	
2014 primary	Tom Marino (R)	unopposed			

Prior winning percentages: 2012 (66%), 2010 (55%)

Population		Race and Ethnicity		Income	
Total:	707,291	White	91.1%	Median income:	$50,007
Urban:	14.2%	Latino	3.6%		*(241 of 435)*
Suburban:	24.1%	Black	3.1%	Under $50,000	50.0%
Rural:	61.7%	Asian	0.7%	$50,000-$99,999:	33.8%
Land area:	7,849	Two races	1.3%	$100,000-$199,999:	13.8%
Pop/sq. mi.:	90.1	White Ethnic	39.7%	$200,000 or more:	2.5%
Born in state:	69.5%			Poverty Rate	11.6%
		Education			
Age Groups		H.S. grad or less:	54.6%	**Work**	
Under 18:	20.7%	Some college:	25.0%	White collar:	29.9%
18 to 34:	20.3%	College degree, 4 yr.:	12.6%	Blue collar:	41.4%
35 to 64:	40.8%	Post-grad study:	7.7%	Sales and service:	28.7%
Over 64:	18.2%				
		Military		Govt. workers:	11.6%
		Veterans/active duty:	10.4%		

Northeast Pennsylvania

The northeast corner of Pennsylvania is a land of crevassed valleys and rugged mountains, criss-crossed by giant viaducts built for the railroads linking the East Coast with the Great Lakes and the mines that produced the region's anthracite

Voter Turnout	
2013 Total Citizen 18+	551,460
2014 House Turnout	180,322
2014 Turnout as % CVAP	32.7%
2012 Turnout as % CVAP	51.2%

coal. Except for a row of anthracite coal cities from Scranton to Wilkes-Barre, this part of Pennsylvania still has a throwback look to it. The region has numerous long-established small towns, with solidly built courthouses and banks and elderly citizens. It's a part of the Northeast that seems worlds away from the region's huge central cities and growing suburbs. Notable towns include Williamsport, home of the Little League World Series, and Lewisburg, home of Bucknell University. Only at the eastern edge has there been significant growth. Pike County on the Delaware River was the state's second-fastest growing county from 2000 to 2010, increasing in population by 24 percent, with many of its new residents fleeing high taxes in New Jersey and New York. In Pike, Milford is the home of Gifford Pinchot, who served two terms as governor and became a founder of the conservation movement and the first chief of the Forest Service under President Theodore Roosevelt. The Pocono Mountains are a destination for weekend skiers and, for a few days each November, for bear hunters. Seeking to revive tourism, business leaders in the Poconos in 2015 styled the area as the nation's indoor water-park capital.

The 10th Congressional District of Pennsylvania includes the less-populated areas of northeast Pennsylvania. (Democratic-leaning Scranton in the neighboring 17th District is surrounded by the 10th.) The area's most consequential member of Congress was probably David Wilmot, a founding member of the Republican Party who in the 1840s introduced the Wilmot Proviso barring slavery from the New Mexico and California territories acquired in the Mexican War, raising the issue that led proximately to the Civil War. Most people in this part of Pennsylvania have

2012 Presidential Vote		
Mitt Romney (R)	170,273	(60%)
Barack Obama (D)	109,011	(39%)
2008 Presidential Vote		
John McCain (R)	169,585	(57%)
Barack Obama (D)	126,919	(42%)
Cook Partisan Voting Index:	R+12	

been Republicans ever since. It dips deep into central Pennsylvania west of Harrisburg in the conservative rural counties of Juniata and Mifflin. Williamsport-based Lycoming County is the population center. Overall, this is the second-most Republican district in the state.

Tom Marino (R)

Republican Tom Marino, who defeated a Democratic incumbent in 2010, is a former prosecutor who cultivates an image at home as an aggressive guardian of taxpayer interests. "There are few as tough as Tom Marino," a 2012 campaign ad boasted. In Washington, he has kept a low profile as he dealt chiefly with law enforcement and regulatory issues and largely avoided intra-mural scuffles.

Marino was born and raised in Williamsport. His father was a janitor and a firefighter, and his mother was a homemaker. After high school, Marino held jobs in manufacturing and managed a bakery for several years before enrolling at Williamsport Area Community College at age 30 and then graduating from Lycoming College. He earned a law degree at Penn State University. In 1992 he was elected district attorney for Lycoming County. After holding that post for a decade, he was appointed as the U.S. attorney for Pennsylvania's Middle District, which includes Scranton and Harrisburg.

As a federal prosecutor, he was involved in a case that became an issue in his 2010 campaign. Marino had served as a reference for Louis DeNaples on an application for a gambling license for the Mount Airy Casino Resort while his office was investigating DeNaples on another matter. After Marino resigned as U.S. attorney in 2007, he became an in-house counsel for DeNaples on some of his non-casino businesses. When his role in the application surfaced during the campaign, Marino said that he had received authorization from the Justice Department. When the Associated Press challenged him, Marino responded that he never asked for permission but that his role at the time was understood to be above-board and ethical as long as he didn't use his job title in the reference. Two-term Democratic Rep. Chris Carney raised questions about Marino's character and trustworthiness in what became a bitterly negative campaign. Two factors bolstered Marino: Carney's support for the 2010 health care overhaul was unpopular in this conservative stronghold, and $1.7 million in late spending on behalf of Marino by national Republican and business groups had an impact in in the low-cost advertising market. In a big Republican year, Marino won, 55%-45%.

In the House, Marino has been generally conservative, although he voted against like-minded Republicans on their efforts to cancel some federal programs, including subsidies to rural airports. He has pushed successfully every two years for House action on his *Responsibly and Professionally Invigorating Development* (Rapid) Act, which requires federal agencies to act promptly on proposals for infrastructure or energy construction.

In 2015, Marino became chairman of the Judiciary Subcommittee on Regulatory Reform, Commercial and Antitrust Law. He called for actions to reduce the adverse economic impact of federal regulations. In June, as the committee was considering reforms in the criminal justice system, he hosted Judiciary Chairman Bob Goodlatte of Virginia on a tour of the federal penitentiary at Lewisburg. Marino filed a constitutional amendment to limit lawmakers to 12 years in the House and 12 years in the Senate. With Democratic Rep. Scott Peters of California, he called for changes in House rules to require that any House bill may be considered after 60 days. With 5,884 House bills having been introduced in 2013-14, that could force House members to spend much more time at the Capitol.

In 2012, Marino rolled to a 66%-34% win over Democrat Phil Scollo, an insurance consultant who got off to a late start. In 2014, 25-year-old independent Nick Troiano focused on the need for bipartisan action to fix the federal deficit. But his 13% of the vote appeared to come chiefly from Democratic businessman Scott Brion, who lost to Marino, 63%-25%.

The heated claims from the 2010 campaign continued to simmer. Carney told *The Daily Item* of Sunbury in March 2013, "the problem is, he has no one in the 10th District to challenge him. So he gets away with just saying things." Marino shot back, "If Chris Carney would have listened to the people he represented instead of Obama and [Minority Leader Nancy] Pelosi, maybe his political prospects would be brighter today." Following the 2014 election, Marino said that the allegations that had been raised against him by Carney and later by Scollo were "lies," adding that "there was nothing unethical or illegal" and his actions had not been under investigation.

ELEVENTH DISTRICT

Lou Barletta (R)

Elected 2010, 3rd term; b. Jan. 28, 1956, Hazleton; Bloomsburg U., attended; Catholic; married (Mary Grace); 4 children.

Elected Office: Hazleton City Cncl., 1998-2000; Hazleton mayor, 2000-10.

Professional Career: Co-owner, Interstate Road Marketing, 1984-2000.

DC Office: 115 CHOB, 20515, 202-225-6511; Fax: 202-226-6250; Website: barletta.house.gov.

State Offices: Carlisle, 717-249-0190; Harrisburg, 717-525-7002; Hazleton, 570-751-0050; Sunbury, 570-988-7801.

Committees: *Education & the Workforce:* Health, Employment, Labor & Pensions; Higher Education & Workforce Training. *Homeland Security:* Border & Maritime Security; Counterterrorism, Infrastructure Protection, & Security Technologies. *Transportation & Infrastructure:* Economic Development, Public Buildings & Emergency Mgmt. (Chmn); Highways & Transit; Railroads, Pipelines & Hazardous Materials.

Group Ratings

	ADA	ACLU	AFL-CIO	LCV	ITI	COC	HAFA	ACU	CFG	FRC
2014	0%	0%	–	3%	100%	92%	40%	52%	39%	88%
2013	0%	C	38%	4%	C	92%	C	52%	51%	C

National Journal Ratings

	2013 LIB	—	2013 CONS
Economic	47%	—	53%
Social	43%	—	54%
Foreign	24%	—	76%
Composite	39%	—	62%

Key Votes of the 113th Congress

1. Sandy storm spending	Y	5. Medical Marijuana	N	9. Syrian Rebels Training	Y
2. Violence Against Women Act	Y	6. Farm Bill	Y	10. Keystone pipeline	NV
3. Guantanamo Bay Detainees	N	7. Afghanistan Combat	N	11. Immigration Exec. Action	Y
4. Abortion 20-week ban	Y	8. NSA Phone Data Collection	NV	12. Bipartisan budget deal	Y

Election Results

2014 general	Lou Barletta (R)	122,464	(66%)	$1,101,031
	Andy Ostrowski (D)	62,228	(34%)	
2014 primary	Lou Barletta (R)	unopposed		

Prior winning percentages: 2012 (59%), 2010 (55%)

Population		Race and Ethnicity		Income	
Total:	705,647	White	87.2%	Median income:	$51,135
Urban:	31.9%	Latino	4.7%		*(218 of 435)*
Suburban:	44.6%	Black	4.7%	Under $50,000	48.8%
Rural:	23.6%	Asian	1.4%	$50,000-$99,999:	32.9%
Land area:	3,300	Two races	1.5%	$100,000-$199,999:	15.1%
Pop/sq. mi.:	213.9	White Ethnic	46.1%	$200,000 or more:	3.2%
Born in state:	77.5%			Poverty Rate	12.9%
		Education			
Age Groups		H.S. grad or less:	51.1%	**Work**	
Under 18:	20.4%	Some college:	25.7%	White collar:	32.6%
18 to 34:	21.9%	College degree, 4 yr.:	14.5%	Blue collar:	43.1%
35 to 64:	40.2%	Post-grad study:	8.7%	Sales and service:	24.2%
Over 64:	17.6%				
		Military		Govt. workers:	14.5%
		Veterans/active duty:	10.3%		

North-Central Pennsylvania: Harrisburg Area, Wilkes-Barre Suburbs

The small town of Carlisle has a unique history as one of the unsung stories of rural Pennsylvania. In 1912, the most dominant college football team in the nation belonged to the Carlisle Indian Industrial School. The team of Native Americans starred Olympian Jim Thorpe and was coached by

Voter Turnout	
2013 Total Citizen 18+	547,269
2014 House Turnout	184,692
2014 Turnout as % CVAP	33.7%
2012 Turnout as % CVAP	53.3%

Glenn Scobey "Pop" Warner. "They didn't just change football. They changed prevailing ideas about Indians," wrote author Sally Jenkins in her book, *The Real All Americans*. The epic 1912 game between the Carlisle Indians and the U.S. Military Academy at West Point—which featured Dwight Eisenhower at linebacker—became an extension of fighting between white expansionists and Native Americans. This time, the Carlisle underdogs won, 27-6.

The 11th Congressional District of Pennsylvania stretches from Wyoming County in the northeast to Cumberland County in the south, taking in Carlisle, some of Harrisburg's suburbs, and a slice of the capital city. Today, Carlisle is home to Dickinson College and the U.S. Army War College. Luzerne is the largest county, but the district skirts Wilkes-Barre. Also in the district is Hazleton, a small city that

has gained national notoriety for its crackdowns on illegal immigrants, which have been repeatedly contested in the courts and not implemented. Hazleton also is the site for much of the nation's supply of anthracite coal. Another hot issue in the region is whether natural gas extraction in the underground Marcellus Shale formation will irrevocably contaminate the Susquehanna River.

2012 Presidential Vote		
Mitt Romney (R)	157,842	(54%)
Barack Obama (D)	130,429	(45%)
2008 Presidential Vote		
John McCain (R)	158,939	(52%)
Barack Obama (D)	144,964	(47%)
Cook Partisan Voting Index:	R+6	

The 11th had leaned Democratic for decades. But the Republican redistricting in 2011 removed Scranton and other Democratic urban centers. The district now has a distinct Republican lean.

Lou Barletta (R)

Republican Lou Barletta won in his third challenge to 13-term Democrat Paul Kanjorski. Although he has been a vociferous critic of illegal immigration, he has worked on bipartisan measures on other issues and much of his overall voting record has been centrist.

Barletta hails from Hazleton, where he was mayor for a decade. As a youth, he worked with his parents and three brothers in his family's businesses: A. Barletta and Sons Road Construction and Barletta Heating Oil. He attended Bloomsburg University, but he left early to follow a dream of becoming a professional baseball player. After an unsuccessful tryout with the Cincinnati Reds—"I couldn't hit a curve ball," he told *The Patriot-News* of Harrisburg—he returned to Hazleton, where he opened a pavement-marking business.

In 1998, Barletta was elected to the Hazleton City Council, and two years later became mayor. He inherited a budget shortfall and helped return the city to financial health. In 2006, Barletta made national news when he signed a law allowing the city to deny business permits to employers who hired illegal immigrants and to fine landlords who rented to them. The following year, a federal District Court judge struck down the law, and it has been regularly contested in the courts.

Barletta first challenged Kanjorski in 2002. He lost, but he maintained ties to national Republicans. In 2004, President George W. Bush appointed him to the United Nations Advisory Committee on Local Authorities. Two years later, the Republican National Committee tapped Barletta to work on outreach to Catholics. He lost to Kanjorski again in 2008 but narrowed the outcome to 52%-48%.

In 2010, he campaigned with ads that characterized Kanjorski as a "couch potato" and asserted, "Paul Kanjorski has just been around too long." The Kanjorski campaign appealed to the district's many senior citizens with ads accusing Barletta of supporting the privatization of Social Security, even though he opposed private Social Security accounts. Kanjorski's ads warned, "The Barletta campaign sends an offensive message to the thousands of area seniors: Get out of the way because your time may have passed." Kanjorski outspent

Barletta, $2.1 million to $1.3 million. Both national parties and their allies spent heavily on the contest. The Republican tide of 2010 gave Barletta enough lift to win, 55%-45%.

In the House, Barletta has been a moderate who backs his party on big votes, like most of the Pennsylvania Republicans. On immigration, however, he has taken a hard line. When others in the GOP saw the 2012 presidential election results as a sign that they needed to reach out to Latino voters, Barletta was having none of it. After a bipartisan Senate group came out in February 2013 with a comprehensive immigration reform proposal, he scoffed that it was "amnesty that America can't afford." He told *The Morning Call* of Allentown that courting Hispanics is a waste of time for his party. "The Republican Party is not going to compete over who can give more social programs out," he said. "They will become Democrats because of the social programs they'll depend on."

Barletta was equally dismissive of Democratic gun control efforts following the Newtown, Connecticut, elementary school massacre in 2012. "Would banning spoons stop obesity?" he asked on ABC News' *This Week*. He and neighboring Pennsylvania Republican Tom Marino irked local activists in 2011 when they banned non-journalists from taping their town hall meetings. In September 2012, the House passed his bill to lower interest rates on disaster loans issued by the Small Business Administration.

On the Transportation and Infrastructure Committee, Barletta chairs the Economic Development Subcommittee, which oversees all federal buildings and the Federal Emergency Management Agency. Based on the experience of his district with hurricanes and other natural disasters, he has sought steps to improve disaster relief. In March 2015, he introduced with the committee's bipartisan leaders a bill to assess and modernize FEMA operations. In May, he filed another bipartisan committee bill to reform management of federal office space, which he said would save billions of dollars annually. In June 2015, he voted to give President Barack Obama trade promotion authority to expedite international trade deals, but only after Barletta said that he won provisions to protect Americans from foreign guest workers and prevent illegal dumping of cheaper foreign products, including steel.

The Cook Political Report called Barletta "the biggest winner in Pennsylvania's redistricting" after state Republicans jettisoned Democratic precincts and stretched the 11th District to the conservative Harrisburg suburbs. Since then, he has won with 59% and 66% against lightly funded opponents.

TWELFTH DISTRICT

Keith Rothfus (R)

Elected 2012, 2nd term; b. April 25, 1962, Endicott, NY; S.U.N.Y. Buffalo, B.S. 1984, U. of Notre Dame, J.D. 1990; Catholic; married (Elsie); 6 children.

Professional Career: Systems programmer, IBM, 1985-88; Practicing atty., 1991-2010; Assoc. dean, Regent U. Schl. of Law, 1993-97; Bush administration faith-based initiatives official, 2004-07; Staff, U.S. Dept. of Homeland Security, 2006-07.

DC Office: 1205 LHOB, 20515, 202-225-2065; Website: rothfus.house. gov.

State Offices: Beaver, 724-359-1626; Johnstown, 814-619-3659; Pittsburgh, 412-837-1361.

Committees: *Financial Services:* Financial Institutions & Consumer Credit; Housing & Insurance; Task Force to Investigate Terrorism Financing.

Group Ratings

	ADA	ACLU	AFL-CIO	LCV	ITI	COC	HAFA	ACU	CFG	FRC
2014	5%	0%	–	3%	80%	71%	66%	76%	67%	100%
2013	5%	C	14%	7%	C	77%	C	80%	82%	C

National Journal Ratings

	2013 LIB	—	2013 CONS
Economic	24%	—	75%
Social	0%	—	87%
Foreign	5%	—	86%
Composite	14%	—	87%

Key Votes of the 113th Congress

1. Sandy storm spending	N	5. Medical Marijuana	N	9. Syrian Rebels Training	N
2. Violence Against Women Act	N	6. Farm Bill	N	10. Keystone pipeline	Y
3. Guantanamo Bay Detainees	N	7. Afghanistan Combat	N	11. Immigration Exec. Action	Y
4. Abortion 20-week ban	Y	8. NSA Phone Data Collection	Y	12. Bipartisan budget deal	Y

Election Results

2014 general	Keith Rothfus (R)...................... 127,993	(59%)	$1,807,454	$160,206
	Erin McClelland (D) 87,928	(41%)	$376,715	$8,840
2014 primary	Keith Rothfus (R).................unopposed			

Prior winning percentage: 2012 (52%)

Population		Race and Ethnicity		Income	
Total:	703,938	White	93.1%	Median income:	$54,765
Urban:	29.2%	Black	3.1%		*(168 of 435)*
Suburban:	58.0%	Asian	1.3%	Under $50,000	45.8%
Rural:	12.8%	Latino	1.0%	$50,000-$99,999:	31.5%
Land area:	2,145	Two races	1.2%	$100,000-$199,999:	18.8%
Pop/sq. mi.:	328.1	White Ethnic	57.2%	$200,000 or more:	4.0%
Born in state:	83.4%			Poverty Rate	9.6%
		Education:			
Age Groups:		H.S. grad or less:	43.0%	**Work:**	
Under 18:	20.4%	Some college:	25.2%	White collar:	39.0%
18 to 34:	18.4%	College degree, 4 yr.:	19.5%	Blue collar:	40.7%
35 to 64:	41.8%	Post-grad study:	12.3%	Sales and service:	20.3%
Over 64:	19.3%				
		Military:		Govt. workers:	9.5%
		Veterans/active duty:	9.8%		

Northern Pittsburgh Suburbs, Johnstown Area

The mountains and valleys within a 100-mile radius of Pittsburgh comprise one of America's most beautiful—and economically troubled—regions. This has been tough, hard-working country ever since Scots-Irish farmers settled here in the 1790s. Their first big product was whiskey—this was the site of

Voter Turnout	
2013 Total Citizen 18+	552,979
2014 House Turnout	215,921
2014 Turnout as % CVAP	39.0%
2012 Turnout as % CVAP	63.0%

the Whiskey Rebellion of 1794—but historically the most important product was bituminous coal. Discovered in the 19th century, it was the basic energy source for the production of iron and steel. Johnstown was once known as the "Cradle of the American Steel Industry," but it has been on a long downhill slide since the 1979 oil shock. Its population fell from 67,000 in 1920 to about 20,000 in 2013, a decline similar to that of many communities in the region. Johnstown is ranked as the poorest city in Pennsylvania.

Johnstown was the site of the flood of May 1889, when water from the ruptured South Fork Dam cascaded down steep valley walls, gaining speed during an 18-mile trip, and poured into the little industrial city with a force equal to Niagara Falls. "Everyone heard shouting and screaming, the ear-splitting crash of buildings going down, glass shattering, and the sides of houses ripping apart," historian David McCullough wrote of the flood that killed more than 2,200 people in a disaster that lasted just 10 minutes. In May 2015, an area capital campaign announced plans to improve the flood museum. Even after the death in 2010 of its long-time Democratic Rep. John Murtha, Johnstown continued to receive a disproportionate share of

Defense Department contracts. With government aid, companies in the area have developed improved batteries and energy storage.

Southwestern Pennsylvania is also football country: Joe Namath is a grandchild of a Hungarian immigrant steelworker from Beaver Falls, and Hall of Fame quarterbacks Joe Montana and Dan Marino also hail from the region.

2012 Presidential Vote		
Mitt Romney (R).................200,093	(58%)
Barack Obama (D) 141,753	(41%)

2008 Presidential Vote		
John McCain (R).................194,401	(54%)
Barack Obama (D) 161,068	(45%)

Cook Partisan Voting Index: R+9

The 12th Congressional District stretches from the Ohio border to the Pennsylvania heartland. It covers the shrinking rust belt cities of Aliquippa and Beaver Falls, more upscale northern Pittsburgh suburbs in Allegheny County, Johnstown in Cambria County, and part of nearby Somerset County. With the shifting political climate in the area, the district clearly favors the GOP.

Keith Rothfus (R)

Republican Keith Rothfus won the seat in 2012, succeeding two House Democrats who had represented local districts before redistricting revamped the area surrounding Pittsburgh and forced them to run in a district where many voters were new to them. The fiscally conservative Rothfus brought a new style less focused on aid from Washington.

Rothfus grew up in Endicott New York, near Binghamton and the Pennsylvania border, and was a teen-age acolyte of Republican presidential candidate Ronald Reagan in 1980. "When Ronald Reagan started talking about empowering people in the private sector, keeping tax rates low, it made a lot of sense to me," he told *National Journal*. "He brought peace through strength. He respected traditional values."

Rothfus got a bachelor's degree in information systems from Buffalo State College, part of the State University of New York. He worked for IBM for three years, then got a law degree from Notre Dame. He began his law career as a litigator in Pittsburgh and became an associate dean at the Regent University School of Law. He later negotiated commercial contracts and established a private practice in Pittsburgh. He became increasingly involved in politics, working on faith-based initiatives at the Homeland Security Department in the George W. Bush administration.

Although he was long interested in public policy, Rothfus said he never thought he would run for office. That changed in 2009, when he looked for six months for a candidate to support in his congressional district before putting his own name forward. Passage in Congress of the $787 billion economic stimulus in 2009—and the debt it added—heightened his interest. The challenge was daunting: Not only did Rothfus run in a district that leaned Democratic, but he was an underdog in the Republican primary against former U.S. Attorney Mary Beth Buchanan. With tea party support, Rothfus pulled an upset in the 2010 primary. Then, he nearly won a shocker on Election Day, falling to the well-funded Democratic Rep. Jason Altmire 51%-49%.

That close contest encouraged him to run again in 2012. This time, he faced Rep. Mark Critz, a long-time staffer to former Defense Appropriations Subcommittee Chairman John Murtha and heir to his seat when Murtha died in 2010. In the 2012 Democratic primary, Critz defeated Altmire 51%-49%, by rolling up huge leads in Cambria and Somerset even though Altmire won the Pittsburgh-area counties. In the newly drawn 12th District, made considerably more favorable to the GOP after redistricting, Critz stressed his support for gun owners' rights and opposition to abortion rights, and he sought to tie Rothfus to House Budget Committee Chairman Paul Ryan's plans to overhaul Medicare. Rothfus linked Critz to President Barack Obama and listed as his top priorities the "Three Rs:" repealing "Obamacare," reforming tax and spending policies, and rolling back regulation. He called for transforming southwest Pennsylvania into an energy capital. With his strength in Allegheny and Westmoreland counties that overcame Critz's big leads in the eastern part of the district, Rothfus won 52%-48%.

In the House, Rothfus centered his work at the Financial Services Committee. He said that he wanted to be a conciliator and deal-maker at a time of polarization in Congress. "I have a reputation in my professional work, negotiating contracts, where I've gone into deals where other people haven't closed the deal, and I've been able to get it done," he said. "We need to work with people of goodwill in both parties and start to tackle problems we have." In March 2015, Rothfus filed proposals to permit mutual banks and savings associations to engage in a broader range of financial services, which would require changes in the 2010 Dodd-Frank law. The National Association of Manufacturing praised his support for manufacturing and innovation. In April 2015, he joined the Financial Services task force that was investigating terrorism financing.

At home, Rothfus protested the Defense Department's decision in 2014 to transfer to the Army control of Apache helicopters at the National Guard complex in Johnstown and in three other states. He breezed to reelection in 2014 with 59 percent of the vote against Democratic health care expert Erin McClelland, despite the support she received from party and union spending.

THIRTEENTH DISTRICT

Brendan Boyle (D)

Elected 2014, 1st term; b. Feb. 6, 1977, Philadelphia; U. of Notre Dame, B.A. 1999, Harvard U., M.P.P. 2005; Catholic; married (Jennifer); 1 child.

Elected Office: PA House, 2009-14.

Professional Career: Radio broadcaster; Mgmt. consultant; Adjunct prof., Drexel U.

DC Office: 118 CHOB, 20515, 202-225-6111; Fax: 202-226-0611; Website: boyle.house.gov.

State Offices: Glenside, 215-517-6572; Norristown, 484-681-2563; Northeast Philadelphia, 215-335-3355; Philadelphia, 267-335-5643.

Committees: *Foreign Affairs:* Middle East & North Africa. *Oversight & Gov't Reform:* Health Care, Benefits & Administrative Rules; Transportation & Public Assets.

Election Results

2014 general	Brendan Boyle (D)	123,601	(67%)	$926,281	$381,494	$52,545
	Dee Adcock (R)	60,549	(33%)			
2014 primary	Brendan Boyle (D)	24,524	(41%)			
	Marjorie Margolies (D)	16,528	(27%)			
	Valerie Arkoosh (D)	10,066	(17%)			
	Daylin Leach (D)	9,313	(15%)			

Population		Race and Ethnicity		Income	
Total:	710,615	White	61.3%	Median income:	$54,355
Urban:	63.3%	Black	17.4%		*(175 of 435)*
Suburban:	36.7%	Latino	10.7%	Under $50,000	46.1%
Rural:	0.0%	Asian	8.3%	$50,000-$99,999:	28.7%
Land area:	188	Two races	2.1%	$100,000-$199,999:	20.3%
Pop/sq. mi.:	3,789.9	White Ethnic	45.9%	$200,000 or more:	4.9%
Born in state:	68.8%			Poverty Rate	13.6%
		Education			
Age Groups		H.S. grad or less:	43.8%	**Work**	
Under 18:	22.6%	Some college:	24.1%	White collar:	37.9%
18 to 34:	22.5%	College degree, 4 yr.:	19.5%	Blue collar:	44.9%
35 to 64:	39.6%	Post-grad study:	12.6%	Sales and service:	17.3%
Over 64:	15.3%				
		Military		Govt. workers:	11.3%
		Veterans/active duty:	6.9%		

Montgomery County, Northeast Philadelphia

Montgomery County is the proximate hinterland of Philadelphia: rolling hills cut on one side by the Schuylkill River and at intervals by the Pennsylvania and Reading Railroad lines radiating outward from Center City. Older suburbs, both rich and modest, grew up around rail stations, with

Voter Turnout	
2013 Total Citizen 18+	499,299
2014 House Turnout	184,150
2014 Turnout as % CVAP	36.9%
2012 Turnout as % CVAP	63.6%

comfortable houses within walking distance for commuters. Farther out are 18th and 19th century villages, once surrounded by farm fields, now encroached by subdivisions where people depend on cars, not rail lines, to get to work. Montgomery County is the second most affluent county, behind Chester, in the state. It is the state's third most populous county, behind Philadelphia and Allegheny. Its unemployment rate was 3.7 percent in April 2015—a bit lower than neighboring Bucks and Delaware counties.

Nearby, Northeast Philadelphia is quite a different place. This is relatively new urban territory, with more than half its houses built after 1950. Many of Philadelphia's Hispanics live in the industrial river wards along the Delaware River, but other wards of Northeast Philadelphia remained mostly white and blue-collar. Some industries have settled here, such as Teva Pharmaceuticals USA, which is the largest generic drug manufacturer in the world.

The 13th Congressional District of Pennsylvania includes southeastern and central Montgomery County and parts of Northeast Philadelphia. About 60 percent of the voters are in Montgomery. It extends north in two arms, one to Norristown and King of Prussia and the other to Lansdale. Expansion of the mall at King of Prussia will make it the nation's second-largest in 2016, behind only the Mall of America in Minnesota. It includes the old communities of Elkins Park and Glenside. Israeli Prime Minister Benjamin Netanyahu attended high school and was active on the debate team in Cheltenham, which has had a large concentration of Jews. ABC aired a comedy series, "The Goldbergs," which was based in the small borough of Jenkintown. In Horsham, the closing of the Willow Grove Naval Air Station has resulted in plans for a large housing development following an environmental clean-up of the area. Northern parts of the county have been parceled out to the 6th, 7th and 8th Districts.

Historically, Montgomery was Republican, with a style of politics set for years by Ivy League-educated Republican men. But in the 1990s, the county swung toward the Democrats in national politics, with abortion rights and other cultural issues usually trumping economic concerns. A feisty Republican organization in Northeast Philadelphia has won some elections and shown facility in making deals to get its share of patronage. The 13th is one of five solidly Democratic districts in Pennsylvania. President Barack Obama won 66 percent of its vote in 2012.

2012 Presidential Vote		
Barack Obama (D)	210,902	(66%)
Mitt Romney (R)	105,024	(33%)
2008 Presidential Vote		
Barack Obama (D)	217,033	(65%)
John McCain (R)	115,479	(34%)
Cook Partisan Voting Index:	D+13	

Brendan Boyle (D)

Democrat Brendan Boyle in 2014 took an unconventional route to victory in the 13th District by sweeping the north Philadelphia wards while his higher-spending rivals in the Democratic primary focused on upscale Montgomery County. He had no trouble with Republican Carson Dee Adcock, who was backed by health care groups, to replace Democratic Rep. Allyson Schwartz.

Boyle became one of the youngest members of Congress at age 37 and looked even younger. Raised by working-class parents in northeast Philadelphia, he was the first in his family to go to college. After his bachelor's in government at Notre Dame, he got a master's degree in public policy at Harvard's John F. Kennedy School of Government. In 2008, he was elected to the state House. His brother, Kevin, was elected two years later, making them the first pair of siblings to serve together in the state House. He owned a swimming pool equipment distribution company.

When Schwartz ran unsuccessfully in the Democratic primary for governor, Boyle was one of four Democrats seeking to replace her. They included former Rep. Marjorie Margolies, who is Chelsea Clinton's mother-in-law. The resulting primary battle cost more than $5 million, one of the most expensive in the nation, with Bill Clinton offering fundraising help for Margolies. Boyle was financially outgunned by the three other Democratic contenders, especially Valerie Arkoosh, a well-funded doctor. Each spent at least $1.5 million in the primary, while Boyle spent only $900,000 for his entire campaign.

But he succeeded with old-school populism, plus a crucial endorsement by Rep. Robert Brady, the boss of the Philadelphia Democratic organization. Boyle hit the pavement and held 225 voter events that played up his grass-roots candidacy, noting that his father was a public-transit maintenance worker and his mother a school crossing guard. He got a boost from union support, with a labor-backed PAC spending $350,000 on Boyle's behalf. In a campaign ad, he noted that his three Montgomery County opponents were millionaires.

His rivals targeted his legislative record on women's health, namely his support for a bill that called for the renovation of health centers but reportedly led to the closing of several abortion clinics. NARAL, a leading abortion-rights group, accused him of "tap dancing around votes he took that would throw roadblocks in front of women seeking reproductive health care." Boyle's route to victory went decidedly through Philadelphia County, where he got 70% of the vote, with Brady's help. He called himself "a Northeast guy." By contrast, Boyle finished a distant fourth with only 16% in Montgomery, which cast 54% of the primary vote. But that was enough to give him the victory with 41%, to 27% for runner-up Margolies, whose Clinton ties were not enough to overcome a disorganized campaign.

In the general election, Adcock spent $500,000 and a group of anesthesiologists spent another $300,000 on her behalf. But the contest was never in doubt. Boyle won 67%-33%, and won 75% of the vote in Philadelphia. The chief reelection risk that he faces is the prospect of liberal groups uniting around a Montgomery County Democrat in the primary.

In the House, he won assignments to the Foreign Affairs and Oversight and Government Reform committees. He joined a delegation to Dubai for a briefing on the Islamic State and the situation in the Persian Gulf. At the St. Patrick's Day reception at the White House in March, President Barack Obama gave a shout-out to Boyle, plus his brother and father. He told the immigrant story of their father, who was born in Donegal.

FOURTEENTH DISTRICT

Mike Doyle (D)

Elected 1994, 11th term; b. Aug. 5, 1953, Pittsburgh; PA St. U., B.S. 1975; Catholic; married (Susan); 4 children.

Elected Office: Swissvale Borough Cncl., 1977-81.

Professional Career: Ins. agent, 1975-77; Exec. dir., Turtle Creek Valley Citizens Union, 1977-79; Chief of staff, PA Sen. Frank Pecora, 1979-94; Co-founder/owner, Eastgate Ins. Agency, 1983-present.

DC Office: 239 CHOB, 20515, 202-225-2135; Fax: 202-225-3084; Website: doyle.house.gov.

State Offices: Coraopolis, 412-264-3460; McKeesport, 412-664-4049; Penn Hills, 412-241-6055; Pittsburgh, 412-390-1499.

Committees: *Energy & Commerce:* Communications & Technology; Energy & Power; Environment & the Economy.

Group Ratings

	ADA	ACLU	AFL-CIO	LCV	ITI	COC	HAFA	ACU	CFG	FRC
2014	90%	77%	–	89%	40%	50%	11%	9%	7%	0%
2013	95%	C	100%	82%	C	25%	C	13%	12%	C

National Journal Ratings

	2013 LIB	—	2013 CONS
Economic	81%	—	18%
Social	87%	—	7%
Foreign	79%	—	20%
Composite	84%	—	16%

Key Votes of the 113th Congress

1. Sandy storm spending	Y	5. Medical Marijuana	Y	9. Syrian Rebels Training	N
2. Violence Against Women Act	Y	6. Farm Bill	N	10. Keystone pipeline	Y
3. Guantanamo Bay Detainees	Y	7. Afghanistan Combat	Y	11. Immigration Exec. Action	NV
4. Abortion 20-week ban	N	8. NSA Phone Data Collection	Y	12. Bipartisan budget deal	Y

Election Results

2014 general	Mike F. Doyle (D)	...................unopposed	$861,701
2014 primary	Mike F. Doyle (D)	 56,796	(84%)
	Janis Brooks	 10,744	(16%)

Prior winning percentages: 2012 (77%), 2010 (69%), 2008 (91%), 2006 (90%), 2004 (100%), 2002 (100%), 2000 (69%), 1998 (68%), 1996 (56%), 1994 (55%)

Population		Race and Ethnicity		Income	
Total:	704,276	White	70.7%	Median income:	$41,213
Urban:	62.2%	Black	21.5%		*(373 of 435)*
Suburban:	37.8%	Asian	2.8%	Under $50,000	58.0%
Rural:	0.0%	Latino	2.1%	$50,000-$99,999:	28.0%
Land area:	373	Two races	2.5%	$100,000-$199,999:	11.4%
Pop/sq. mi.:	1,889.5	White Ethnic	51.2%	$200,000 or more:	2.5%
Born in state:	78.4%			Poverty Rate	19.2%
		Education			
Age Groups		H.S. grad or less:	41.0%	Work	
Under 18:	17.3%	Some college:	26.9%	White collar:	38.9%
18 to 34:	28.5%	College degree, 4 yr.:	18.7%	Blue collar:	46.4%
35 to 64:	37.7%	Post-grad study:	13.4%	Sales and service:	14.6%
Over 64:	16.5%				
		Military		Govt. workers:	9.4%
		Veterans/active duty:	8.8%		

Pittsburgh Metro

The Golden Triangle is the inevitable focus of Pittsburgh, the tip of land where the Allegheny and Monongahela rivers come together to form the Ohio. It has been a strategic site for more than 200 years. During the French and Indian War, British Gen.

Voter Turnout	
2013 Total Citizen 18+	562,251
2014 House Turnout	148,351
2014 Turnout as % CVAP	26.4%
2012 Turnout as % CVAP	59.7%

Edward Braddock's army was heading to Fort Duquesne, with George Washington helping lead the way, when it was ambushed and famously defeated in 1754. A few years later, the first American city west of the Appalachian chain was carved out of the wilderness and named after the English statesman William Pitt. Pittsburgh did nicely when railroads became ascendant, since rail lines tend to run along the riverside.

Then Andrew Carnegie, a Scottish immigrant, foresaw that steel would replace iron for railroad bridges. He built a steel factory in Pittsburgh, one blessed with ready deposits of coal and access to iron ore from the Great Lakes. Carnegie built his capacity to the point that when he sold out in 1901, the resulting U.S. Steel Corp. held a near-monopoly. But as the steel industry and other blue-collar industries contracted over the years, so did Pittsburgh. In 1940, it was the nation's 10th largest city, with 672,000 people. In 2014, it was the 62nd largest, with 305,000 people. But the population loss has been easing, with an increase in young people. Local universities and hospitals now have far more workers than downsized U.S. Steel. Economic diversity helped Pittsburgh survive the recession better than other Rust Belt cities. The University of Pittsburgh Medical Center is the largest employer in the region, with the UPMC acronym on the old U.S. Steel skyscraper. In March 2015, local icon H.J. Heinz purchased Chicago-based Kraft Foods, with plans to retain their separate headquarters.

The city has a rich cultural heritage. Pop artist Andy Warhol grew up in Pittsburgh and the Warhol Museum is located in the downtown area. The predominantly black Hill District inspired playwright August Wilson's chronicles, and along the Monongahela River is the town of Clairton, where *The Deer Hunter* was filmed.

2012 Presidential Vote
Barack Obama (D) 230,768   (68%)
Mitt Romney (R).................103,964   (31%)

2008 Presidential Vote
Barack Obama (D) 243,829   (67%)
John McCain (R).................116,437   (32%)

Cook Partisan Voting Index: D+15

The 14th Congressional District of Pennsylvania includes Pittsburgh and the mostly working class suburbs to the east, south and west. All of it is in Allegheny County, except for 2 percent who live in the northwest corner of Westmoreland. It is heavily Democratic, with the two adjacent districts having become more Republican.

Mike Doyle (D)

Mike Doyle, an ardently pro-labor Democrat first elected in 1994, has become a senior member of the Energy and Commerce Committee and the most liberal member of Pennsylvania's House delegation, especially on economic issues.

Of Irish and Italian descent, Doyle grew up in the Monongahela Valley town of Swissvale and worked in steel mills during summers off from Penn State. He became an insurance agent and was elected to the Swissvale Borough Council at age 24. In 1978, he became chief of staff to state Sen. Frank Pecora, a Republican. In 1994, Doyle, who followed his boss in switching to the Democratic Party, ran for the House seat vacated by Republican Rep. Rick Santorum, who was elected to the Senate. With endorsements from labor unions and community leaders, he won the seven-candidate primary. In November, he faced John McCarty, an aide to the late Republican Sen. John Heinz. McCarty was pro-abortion rights and Doyle opposed abortion rights. Doyle also campaigned for sweeping health care changes. In a Republican year, he won 55%-45%.

In the House, Doyle initially had a mixed voting record, often on the right on cultural issues and on the left on economics. During the four years when his party controlled the House and emphasized economics, he became much more of a progressive populist. As a pro-life Catholic, he helped broker the deal on abortion during the final days of the 2010 health care debate that brought on board other anti-abortion members of his party. When Republicans regained control, he complained that GOP budgets would "eviscerate" social services.

Doyle rarely has sought attention or caused much of a ruckus. One notable exception was the 2011 debate over raising the federal debt limit, when in a private meeting he reportedly compared Republicans' negotiating tactics to those of terrorists. Conservative bloggers and commentators heaped criticism on him, and he said, "I wasn't out to defame anybody."

On Energy and Commerce, his focus has been on high-tech initiatives, including increased availability of broadband services in underserved areas. He has been a leading advocate of the "Do Not Call" restrictions on telephone marketers, and enacted a bill to make the national list permanent. Doyle has worked to reduce foreign imports, and he pushed a bill to create a national historic site at the former U.S. Steel facilities along the Monongahela River. Doyle founded and co-chairs of the House Distributed Generation Caucus, which promotes decentralized power generation technology that is fuel efficient and environmentally friendly. He also co-chairs the Robotics Caucus.

During the 2009 debate over cap-and-trade legislation, which would have capped carbon emissions while allowing companies to trade emissions credits, he vigorously advocated the interests of steel and other job-creating Rust Belt industries, even as he worked out a compromise with environmentalists. The House-passed bill died in the Senate, largely because of opposition from Rust Belt Democrats. When Republicans in 2011 voted to slash the Environmental Protection Agency's power to regulate emissions, Doyle accused the GOP of "scaring American people" into wrongly believing that failure to curb EPA's authority would cause gas prices to rise. During debate over the Keystone XL pipeline, he unsuccessfully offered an amendment that would have required at least three-quarters of the iron and steel in the pipeline to be made in North America.

Before the practice was banned, Doyle was an avid earmarker of spending projects for his district. One of his favorite beneficiaries was the Doyle Center for Manufacturing Technology in South Oakland, which was started in 2003 by a $1.5 million federal grant he helped secure. He also is active on funding autism research and cracking down on illegal dog-breeding "puppy mills." His colleagues appreciate his managing the Democrats' team in the annual congressional charity baseball game.

In January 2015, Doyle was named to the Democrats' Policy and Communications Committee, which was formed to develop a united and more effective caucus message. He has been politically untouchable at home, though the downsides for his party are that he has become the only House Democrat from southwest Pennsylvania and that his district is surrounded by two Republican-held districts. When he was elected in 1994, he was one of five Democrats (with no Republicans) from roughly the same region. That shift helps to illustrate why they are in the minority.

FIFTEENTH DISTRICT

Charlie Dent (R)

Elected 2004, 6th term; b. May 24, 1960, Allentown; PA St. U., B.A. 1982, Lehigh U., M.P.A. 1993; Presbyterian; married (Pamela); 3 children.

Elected Office: PA House, 1991-99; PA Senate, 1999-2005.

Professional Career: Development officer, Lehigh U., 1986-90.

DC Office: 2211 RHOB, 20515, 202-225-6411; Fax: 202-226-0778; Website: dent.house.gov.

State Offices: Allentown, 610-770-3490; Annville, 717-867-1026; Hamburg, 610-562-4281; Hershey, 717-533-3959.

Committees: *Appropriations:* Labor, HHS, Education & Related Agencies; Military Construction, Veteran Affairs & Related Agencies (Chmn); State, Foreign Operations & Related Programs (VChmn). *Ethics* (Chmn).

Group Ratings

	ADA	ACLU	AFL-CIO	LCV	ITI	COC	HAFA	ACU	CFG	FRC
2014	0%	11%	–	3%	100%	100%	36%	54%	37%	75%
2013	5%	C	24%	4%	C	92%	C	56%	43%	C

National Journal Ratings

	2013 LIB	—	2013 CONS
Economic	51%	—	49%
Social	43%	—	54%
Foreign	15%	—	77%
Composite	38%	—	62%

Key Votes of the 113th Congress

1. Sandy storm spending	Y	5. Medical Marijuana	N	9. Syrian Rebels Training	N
2. Violence Against Women Act	Y	6. Farm Bill	Y	10. Keystone pipeline	Y
3. Guantanamo Bay Detainees	N	7. Afghanistan Combat	N	11. Immigration Exec. Action	Y
4. Abortion 20-week ban	N	8. NSA Phone Data Collection	N	12. Bipartisan budget deal	Y

Election Results

2014 general   Charlie Dent (R) ....unopposed $1,059,973 $52,493
2014 primary   Charlie Dent (R) ....unopposed

Prior winning percentages: 2012 (57%), 2010 (54%), 2008 (59%), 2006 (54%), 2004 (59%)

Population		Race and Ethnicity		Income	
Total:	713,008	White	79.1%	Median income:	$57,598
Urban:	41.4%	Latino	13.2%		*(144 of 435)*
Suburban:	55.5%	Black	3.2%	Under $50,000	43.1%
Rural:	3.1%	Asian	2.4%	$50,000-$99,999:	34.1%
Land area:	1,290	Two races	1.9%	$100,000-$199,999:	18.6%
Pop/sq. mi.:	552.8	White Ethnic	35.8%	$200,000 or more:	4.2%
Born in state:	67.9%			Poverty Rate	12.1%
		Education			
Age Groups		H.S. grad or less:	47.6%	**Work**	
Under 18:	20.9%	Some college:	24.5%	White collar:	35.7%
18 to 34:	21.9%	College degree, 4 yr.:	16.8%	Blue collar:	41.2%
35 to 64:	40.7%	Post-grad study:	11.0%	Sales and service:	23.1%
Over 64:	16.5%				
		Military		Govt. workers:	9.8%
		Veterans/active duty:	8.1%		

East-Central Pennsylvania: Allentown

Billy Joel's song "Allentown" was a source of both controversy and praise upon its release in 1982. Its grim picture of closed factories, joblessness and human despair resonated with some area residents, while others found the song derisive and inaccurate. Joel was actually singing about the neighboring town of Bethlehem and the struggles of Bethlehem Steel, which was dissolved in 2003. Fences were mended when a petition drive helped bring Joel to play a concert at Lehigh University's Stabler Arena in 1982, and the mayor of Allentown gave him a key to the city. The empathy Joel showed towards the region's economic plight has generated mostly pleasant memories.

Voter Turnout	
2013 Total Citizen 18+	543,744
2014 House Turnout	128,285
2014 Turnout as % CVAP	23.6%
2012 Turnout as % CVAP	58.3%

Today's Lehigh Valley has a much more diverse economy, with a mix of regional health care networks, telephone call centers for insurance companies and banks, and long-surviving industries, including the energy company PPL. The valley's population increased almost 12% from 2000 to 2010. Commuters seeking to avoid big-city housing costs are connected by Interstate 78 to New York City and by the Northeast Extension to Philadelphia. The region has a cluster of colleges—Lehigh, Muhlenberg, and Moravian—and a strong newspaper in *The Morning Call* of Allentown. It has Dorney Park, one of the nation's oldest amusement parks. But recovery from the recent recession has been slow. A 2013 joint report by two Lehigh Valley community groups found that the area was shedding manufacturing jobs, and that even the health care sector was struggling. The unemployment rate of 7.2% in April 2015 was down from 13% three years earlier, but still ranked among the highest in the state. The 2014 opening of a new $200 million hockey arena was described as "the biggest happening in 30 years in Allentown." In 2015, waterfront development along the Lehigh River was underway.

The 15th Congressional District includes most of the Lehigh Valley, covering Allentown and Bethlehem. The two eastern counties include about 70% of the population. The district extends west almost to Harrisburg and takes in parts of Berks, Lebanon and Dauphin counties. It includes Hershey, the town erected by chocolate magnate Milton S. Hershey as a planned, utopian village for his factory workers and their families. The surrounding area is fed by a steady flow of tourists to the Hersheypark amusement site. In 2012, the chocolate maker announced a $300 million expansion of its West Hershey plant. With automation and increased efficiency, which will permit production of 70 million Kisses each day, the changes were expected to cut about 500 jobs from the payroll. The city of Middletown in the district has leafy, gridded streets and handsome homes that give no hint that it is the location of the Three Mile Island nuclear

2012 Presidential Vote		
Mitt Romney (R) 156,165	(51%)
Barack Obama (D) 147,240	(48%)
2008 Presidential Vote		
Barack Obama (D) 165,928	(52%)
John McCain (R)................148,581	(47%)
Cook Partisan Voting Index: R+2		

plant, which in 1979 was the site of the worst nuclear accident in U.S. history. The 15th District leans Republican. Like other GOP-held districts in the Philadelphia area, it can be competitive.

Charlie Dent (R)

Charlie Dent, elected in 2004, is prominent in the dwindling ranks of moderate House Republicans. He is admired by more conservative colleagues for his survival skills. He has gained clout as a new subcommittee chairman on the Appropriations Committee, and respect for his willingness to serve as chairman of the House Ethics Committee.

Dent grew up in Allentown, graduated from Penn State and got a graduate degree in public administration at Lehigh University, where he later worked as a development officer. In 1990, he was elected to the state House and in 1998 to the state Senate. When Republican Rep. Pat Toomey decided to run against Sen. Arlen Specter in the 2004 Republican primary, Dent was the front-runner to succeed him.

Dent's lifelong residence in the Lehigh Valley was a sharp contrast to the background of the Democratic nominee, businessman Joe Driscoll. Driscoll grew up in Massachusetts, where he went sailing with the Kennedys and made enough money to spend $2 million on his campaign. He lived for years in posh Lower Merion in Montgomery County, just outside Philadelphia. Dent framed the campaign as a contest between a native son and a carpetbagging outsider who thought of the Lehigh Valley as "a speed bump on his way to Congress." Driscoll sought to deflect the residency issue with aggressive criticism of the Bush administration, asserting that a vote for Dent was an endorsement of President George W. Bush's policies. Dent's moderate record, which included support for abortion rights, made it difficult to tie him to Bush, and he insisted that he would be an independent voice in Washington. Dent won 59%-39%.

In the House, Dent has one of the least conservative voting records among Republicans. He has been a co-chairman of the Tuesday Group, a caucus of moderates in a GOP Conference dominated by conservatives. (He prefers the term "center-right" to "moderate.") In the early years of President Barack Obama, he broke from the majority of Republicans to vote for expanding the Children's Health Insurance Program, allowing the Food and Drug Administration to regulate tobacco and overhauling food safety laws.

Dent has stuck with the GOP on most broad-based economic issues, even refusing Obama's personal entreaties to support the economic stimulus bill in 2009. Republican leaders have come to regard him as a useful swing vote. He was among the 85 Republicans who joined with 172 Democrats on New Year's Day 2013 to pass the compromise bill on spending and taxes to avert the so-called fiscal cliff, and he was among the 49 Republicans who joined with 192 Democrats to pass a relief bill for states hit by Hurricane Sandy. After the House passed a reauthorization of the Violence Against Women Act in February 2013, he told *The New York Times,* "At a time like this, we have to show we can get something done." He and Rep. Peter King of New York were the only Republicans who voted for a Democratic proposal that would have avoided the October 2013 government shutdown. "When you're in this business of governing, sometimes you must step up and govern," he told the *Times* that month.

In 2011, Dent got a seat on the influential Appropriations Committee. That post was in part a reward for his willingness to serve on the Ethics Committee, regarded by most lawmakers as an unpalatable chore. In 2015, he became an Appropriations "cardinal" in charge of the bill funding Military Construction and Veterans' Affairs, which is the third largest of the 12 spending bills. During his first year as chairman, he won House approval of the annual spending bill on April 30. Dent summarized the following features: enhanced transparency and accountability at the Department of Veterans Affairs through further oversight, increased funding for the inspector general's independent audits and investigations, modernization of the VA's electronic health records with restrictions on its funding until progress has been shown on the system's functionality, and rejection of additional spending for VA hospital construction pending review of the new hospital in Colorado, which resulted in a $930 million cost overrun.

Also in 2015, Boehner moved him up to chairman of the Ethics Committee. "Charlie Dent is the epitome of what an Ethics Committee chairman should be: he is thoughtful and well-respected on both sides of the aisle for his integrity and good judgment," Boehner said.

Dent continued to emphasize his independence on hot-button social issues. In May 2014, he reversed his earlier opposition to same-sex marriage. "Life is too short to have the force of government stand in the way of two adults whose pursuit of happiness includes marriage," he said. He has worked with a bipartisan group that has sought to update the Voting Rights Act after the Supreme Court overturned a key section on enforcement. In May 2015, he was one of four House Republicans who voted against the bill prohibiting most abortions after 20 weeks.

In 2010, Dent faced his toughest reelection opponent in Bethlehem Mayor John Callahan. The race was a statistical dead heat in polls a month before the election, and former President Bill Clinton and Vice President Joe Biden both made campaign stops for Callahan. But Dent was able to paint Callahan as fiscally irresponsible while portraying himself as a restraint on government spending. Dent pulled off a surprisingly easy 54%-39% victory. In 2012, he reaped the benefits of a redrawn district stretching along Interstate 78 to the deeply Republican outskirts of Harrisburg and Lebanon. Lehigh County Democratic Chair Rick Daugherty raised virtually nothing, and Dent won 57%-43%. In 2014, he ran unopposed, the first time that he exceeded 59% of the vote.

SIXTEENTH DISTRICT

Joe Pitts (R)

Elected 1996, 10th term; b. Oct. 10, 1939, Lexington, KY; Asbury Col., B.A. 1961, West Chester U., M.Ed. 1972; Protestant; married (Virginia); 3 children.

Military Career: U.S. Air Force, 1963-69 (Vietnam).

Elected Office: PA House, 1973-97.

Professional Career: H.S. teacher, 1961-63, 1969-72; Owner, Landscape & Nursery Co., 1974-90.

DC Office: 420 CHOB, 20515, 202-225-2411; Fax: 202-225-2013; Website: pitts.house.gov.

State Offices: Lancaster, 717-393-0667; Reading, 610-374-3637; Unionville, 610-444-4581.

Committees: *Energy & Commerce:* Energy & Power; Environment & the Economy; Health (Chmn).

Group Ratings

	ADA	ACLU	AFL-CIO	LCV	ITI	COC	HAFA	ACU	CFG	FRC
2014	5%	0%	–	6%	100%	86%	67%	88%	82%	100%
2013	0%	C	10%	4%	C	85%	C	92%	79%	C

National Journal Ratings

	2013 LIB —	2013 CONS
Economic	8% —	92%
Social	0% —	87%
Foreign	5% —	86%
Composite	8% —	92%

Key Votes of the 113th Congress

1. Sandy storm spending	N	5. Medical Marijuana	N	9. Syrian Rebels Training	N
2. Violence Against Women Act	N	6. Farm Bill	N	10. Keystone pipeline	Y
3. Guantanamo Bay Detainees	N	7. Afghanistan Combat	N	11. Immigration Exec. Action	Y
4. Abortion 20-week ban	Y	8. NSA Phone Data Collection	N	12. Bipartisan budget deal	Y

Election Results

2014 general	Joe Pitts (R)	101,722	(58%)	$1,314,732	$1,265	$6,118
	Tom Houghton (D)	74,513	(42%)	$152,537		
2014 primary	Joe Pitts (R)	unopposed				

Prior winning percentages: 2012 (58%), 2010 (65%), 2008 (56%), 2006 (57%), 2004 (64%), 2002 (88%), 2000 (67%), 1998 (71%), 1996 (59%)

Population		Race and Ethnicity		Income	
Total:	712,447	White	74.3%	Median income:	$54,033
Urban:	39.5%	Latino	16.8%		*(178 of 435)*
Suburban:	60.3%	Black	5.4%	Under $50,000	46.2%
Rural:	0.2%	Asian	1.6%	$50,000-$99,999:	33.5%
Land area:	1,138	Two races	1.6%	$100,000-$199,999:	16.9%
Pop/sq. mi.:	626.0	White Ethnic	25.8%	$200,000 or more:	3.4%
Born in state:	69.8%			Poverty Rate	14.5%
		Education			
Age Groups		H.S. grad or less:	53.3%	**Work**	
Under 18:	24.9%	Some college:	20.8%	White collar:	32.5%
18 to 34:	22.0%	College degree, 4 yr.:	17.0%	Blue collar:	40.2%
35 to 64:	38.3%	Post-grad study:	9.0%	Sales and service:	27.4%
Over 64:	14.8%			Govt. workers:	8.7%
		Military			
		Veterans/active duty:	8.0%		

South-Central Pennsylvania: Lancaster, Reading

The Pennsylvania Dutch Country, settled by Germans in the 18th century when it was Pennsylvania's frontier, remains a distinctive part of America. These Germans were Amish and Mennonite, pietistic sects seeking religious liberty and determined to farm rich lands in the same intensive way they had in Germany. Today, many of their descendants—the Eisenhower family is the most famous example—have blended into mainstream America. But in the Dutch area around Lancaster, many "Plain People" still live in the old way, though today they

Voter Turnout	
2013 Total Citizen 18+	509,073
2014 House Turnout	176,235
2014 Turnout as % CVAP	34.6%
2012 Turnout as % CVAP	58.3%

are still willing to use some modern devices, such as battery-powered electricity. Tourists can still see families of Plain People clad in black, clattering over the back roads in horse-drawn carriages, with scrupulously tended farms set amid rolling hills and barns decorated with hex signs.

Beneath the surface, Amish communities are facing the strains of modernity and economic dislocation. In October 2006, five Amish girls were killed and five others seriously wounded by a gunman at their one-room schoolhouse in Nickel Mines. Remarkably, more than 30 Amish people—including parents of several victims—attended the burial of the shooter in an act of forgiveness. With the rich soil, fruits and vegetables are a pillar of the local economy. And with an easy drive from Philadelphia, Baltimore and Washington, the area is home to many outlet malls; that seems fitting, given that the first Woolworth's store opened in Lancaster in 1879. Pennsylvania Dutch Country draws more than 8 million tourists annually. In early 2015, the jobless rate in both Chester and Lancaster counties had fallen below 4%.

The 16th Congressional District of Pennsylvania includes most of Lancaster County, parts of southwestern Chester County, and a small slice of urban Reading in Berks County. An old industrial town that inspired John Updike's *Rabbit* novels and ranked recently among the poorest cities in the nation, Reading is now 58% Hispanic. Lancaster County remains solidly Republican, is the second-fastest growing county in the state and includes nearly 75% of the population in the 16th District, which continues to lean Republican. (Amish rarely vote, but their

2012 Presidential Vote		
Mitt Romney (R)	153,452	(52%)
Barack Obama (D)	135,469	(46%)
2008 Presidential Vote		
Barack Obama (D)	151,172	(50%)
John McCain (R)	148,895	(49%)
Cook Partisan Voting Index:	R+4	

social views seem consistent with the overall local attitudes.) Like the other Republican-held districts in southeast Pennsylvania, the 16th was carefully drawn to share the heavily Republican precincts among those five districts.

Joe Pitts (R)

Joe Pitts, a Republican elected in 1996, is the dean of the Pennsylvania GOP delegation and one of its most rock-solid conservatives. He has a prominent platform for his free-market, anti-abortion views as chairman of the Energy and Commerce Health Subcommittee.

Pitts was born in Kentucky and spent time in the Philippines with his parents, where they served as religious missionaries. His father had been an Army chaplain in the South Pacific during World War II. He joined the Air Force after college and served three tours of duty, flying 116 B-52 combat missions in Vietnam. He returned home to become a math and science teacher in Malvern in Chester County, and later owned a landscape nursery. In 1972, at age 33, he was elected to the Pennsylvania General Assembly. In 1989, he became chairman of the Appropriations Committee, and oversaw the restoration of the Pennsylvania Capitol. Pitts and his daughter have exhibited their artwork at local galleries.

When Republican Rep. Bob Walker, a key ally of Newt Gingrich and a conservative reformer of that era in the House, retired after serving 20 years, Pitts ran for the seat. In the primary, he styled himself as a "true conservative," speaking out in favor of home schooling and against gambling. He raised the most money and won with 45% of the vote against four other candidates. In November, he easily defeated newspaper publisher James Blaine, a descendant of James G. Blaine, the GOP presidential nominee in 1884.

In the House, Pitts has often been the Pennsylvania House delegation's most conservative member, according to *National Journal*'s annual rankings. He helped to organize and has chaired the conservatives' values action team. He has been especially vocal in his opposition to the health care overhaul of 2010. After taking the helm of Energy and Commerce's Health Subcommittee, he quickly moved a series of bills through the House in 2011 aimed at dismantling the law by repealing mandatory funding for state-based insurance exchanges and school-based health center construction. None of the measures passed the Democratic controlled Senate. House GOP leaders' intense interest in health care has limited his authority. When his party rolled out its alternative to the health care law in 2012, Pitts made clear that it came straight from the leadership, saying that some decisions were "above my pay grade."

When Democrats earlier passed the law, he was among the anti-abortion lawmakers who pushed unsuccessfully for a ban on federal funding for insurers that cover abortions. After Republicans took control, the House passed his bill to bar funding for health plans that provide abortion services, a measure that provoked strong condemnation from liberals. He also has been a chief proponent of legislation to ban human cloning. In 2015, he helped Energy and Commerce to prepare the bipartisan 21st Century Cures initiative to speed new cures and treatments to patients.

Pitts has been active on overseas issues. With his appreciation for both human rights and national defense, Pitts founded two diverse groups: the Religious Prisoners Congressional Task Force to plead for human rights around the world, and the Electronic Warfare Working Group, to encourage more congressional support for military technology. In 2008, he urged a boycott of the Olympics in Beijing until China improved its human rights record. After the 2012 presidential election, he rebuked losing Republican nominee Mitt Romney for not hitting President Barack Obama harder on foreign policy. Pitts has worked across the ideological spectrum in support of a negotiated settlement for the people of Tibet.

On domestic policy, his frequent sponsorship of legislation aimed at curtailing gay rights led the liberal Center for American Progress to call him a "close runner-up" on its list of Congress' most anti-gay members in 2012. He has been a champion of nuclear power, and he has filed legislation to reduce the time required for federal approval of new reactors.

Pitts originally promised not to serve more than five terms, but later changed his mind. In 2006, he had a tough reelection against former corporate executive Lois Herr, who ran on an anti-Iraq war platform. But Pitts won 57%-40%. He faced Herr in a rematch in 2010, and this time focused on Pitts' legislative record, contending that he had passed just three of his bills in 15 years. Pitts waved off the criticism, and won 65%-35%. After redistricting shifted liberal suburbanites into his district, his winning percentage dipped to 55% in 2012. Against Democratic former state Rep. Thomas Houghton in 2014, he got 58% of the vote. With Pitts among the 18 oldest members of the House, the contest for his successor could be competitive when the seat becomes open.

SEVENTEENTH DISTRICT

Matt Cartwright (D)

Elected 2012, 2nd term; b. May 1, 1961, Erie; Hamilton Col., B.A. 1983, U. of PA, J.D. 1986; Catholic; married (Marion Munley); 2 children.

Professional Career: Practicing atty., Munley, Munley & Cartwright, 1986-2012.

DC Office: 1419 LHOB, 20515, 202-225-5546; Website: cartwright. house.gov.

State Offices: Easton, 484-546-0776; Pottsville, 570-624-0140; Scranton, 570-341-1050; Wilkes-Barre, 570-371-0317.

Committees: *Natural Resources:* Energy & Mineral Resources; Federal Lands. *Oversight & Gov't Reform:* Health Care, Benefits & Administrative Rules (RMM); Interior.

Group Ratings

	ADA	ACLU	AFL-CIO	LCV	ITI	COC	HAFA	ACU	CFG	FRC
2014	95%	83%	–	97%	40%	43%	14%	8%	11%	0%
2013	85%	C	95%	96%	C	31%	C	12%	13%	C

National Journal Ratings

	2013 LIB	—	2013 CONS
Economic	91%	—	0%
Social	85%	—	13%
Foreign	71%	—	27%
Composite	85%	—	16%

Key Votes of the 113th Congress

1. Sandy storm spending	Y	5. Medical Marijuana	Y	9. Syrian Rebels Training	Y
2. Violence Against Women Act	Y	6. Farm Bill	N	10. Keystone pipeline	N
3. Guantanamo Bay Detainees	Y	7. Afghanistan Combat	N	11. Immigration Exec. Action	N
4. Abortion 20-week ban	N	8. NSA Phone Data Collection	Y	12. Bipartisan budget deal	Y

Election Results

2014 general	Matt Cartwright (D).................93,680	(57%)	$878,616	$2,717
	David Moylan (R)........................71,371	(43%)	$93,600	
2014 primary	Matt Cartwright (D).............unopposed			

Prior winning percentage: 2012 (60%)

Population		Race and Ethnicity		Income	
Total:	699,632	White	83.8%	Median income:	$45,896
Urban:	33.2%	Latino	7.6%		*(303 of 435)*
Suburban:	48.6%	Black	5.3%	Under $50,000	53.2%
Rural:	18.2%	Asian	1.7%	$50,000-$99,999:	29.6%
Land area:	1,807	Two races	1.3%	$100,000-$199,999:	14.7%
Pop/sq. mi.:	387.2	White Ethnic	59.5%	$200,000 or more:	2.5%
Born in state:	69.0%			Poverty Rate	14.7%
		Education			
Age Groups		H.S. grad or less:	52.5%	**Work**	
Under 18:	20.9%	Some college:	26.8%	White collar:	29.2%
18 to 34:	20.6%	College degree, 4 yr.:	13.5%	Blue collar:	45.3%
35 to 64:	41.0%	Post-grad study:	7.2%	Sales and service:	25.5%
Over 64:	17.4%				
		Military		Govt. workers:	13.0%
		Veterans/active duty:	9.0%		

North-Central Pennsylvania: Scranton/Wilkes-Barre, Allentown

"Coal is the theme song of this city in the hills," the *WPA Guide* said of Scranton in 1940, but even as those words were written, the anthracite kingdom around Scranton and Wilkes-Barre was crumbling. In the 19th century, anthracite had become America's main home heating fuel, and the valley

Voter Turnout	
2013 Total Citizen 18+	538,343
2014 House Turnout	165,051
2014 Turnout as % CVAP	30.7%
2012 Turnout as % CVAP	51.7%

along the East Branch of the Susquehanna River was the No. 1 source of anthracite. Thousands of immigrants flocked to the valley, settling in a chain of little cities north and south of Wilkes-Barre and Scranton. They took jobs with long hours, modest pay, poor working conditions and high death rates—facts of life that made the violently pro-union Molly Maguires popular here and that spawned periodic clashes between workers and the Pinkerton security forces hired by the industrial moguls. Author John O'Hara grew up in Pottsville and wrote about tough-talking miners in the 1930s and 1940s.

While the supply of coal was endless, demand proved fleeting. Anthracite production peaked in 1917, with long strikes in 1922 and 1925 quickening the conversion to oil and gas. Demand for anthracite began to fall in the 1920s and plummeted in the 1940s. The counties containing Wilkes-Barre and Scranton, Luzerne and Lackawanna, had 755,000 people in 1930 and 534,000 in 2013. Scranton was known from 2005 until 2013 as the location of the fictitious Dunder Mifflin Paper Company on *The Office*, the hit NBC comedy series. It is the birthplace of Vice President Joe Biden, and Hillary Clinton's paternal grandparents were natives. Pottsville is the home of Yuengling lager (known locally as "Vitamin Y").

Scranton's $16 million budget shortfall in 2012 threatened to push the city into bankruptcy. The city owed more than $2 million to its health insurer, Blue Cross of Northeastern Pennsylvania. Nearly out of cash, the mayor hatched a plan in July to pay all municipal workers, including himself, a federal minimum wage of $7.25 an hour for two weeks. The city of Cheyenne Wyoming ran an ad in *The Times-Tribune* local newspaper inviting underpaid Scranton police officers to apply for openings on the Cheyenne police force. Scranton officials kept the city afloat by issuing $26 million in bonds and getting financial aid from the state. In January 2015, the city tripled to $3 a week its local services tax for all workers in the city. The police and firefighter pension funds were near insolvency. In May 2015, state Auditor

General Edward DePasquale warned that Scranton would go bankrupt in two years if its pension debt is not addressed.

The 17th Congressional District takes in the Democratic strongholds Scranton and Wilkes-Barre, drops south to Easton and Bethlehem in Northampton, then shifts west to Pottsville and Republican-leaning Schuylkill County. It also covers parts of marginal Carbon County and Democratic-leaning Monroe County. In Easton, old industrial buildings have become a magnet for artists seeking inexpensive loft and warehouse space. The district was carefully drawn by Republican redistricters to include Democratic bastions and protect nearby GOP districts.

2012 Presidential Vote		
Barack Obama (D) 156,015	(55%)
Mitt Romney (R)................121,867	(43%)

2008 Presidential Vote		
Barack Obama (D) 174,418	(57%)
John McCain (R)................128,540	(42%)

Cook Partisan Voting Index: D+4

Matt Cartwright (D)

Scranton lawyer and political newcomer Matt Cartwright was elected in 2012 after he toppled 10-term Rep. Tim Holden in the 2012 Democratic primary by running to the left in a redrawn district that contained extensive new territory for the incumbent.

Cartwright was born in Erie. His mother earned a law degree but didn't practice law. His father served in the Army during World War II, and his wartime experience with radar technology led to a job with General Electric. His father's GE work eventually led the family to relocate to Toronto. "I was the token Yankee. And they tried to teach me to play cricket, of all things. But I rebelled and I organized a softball league," he told *National Journal.* Cartwright earned his bachelor's degree from Hamilton College in 1983. During his undergraduate years, he studied at the London School of Economics and Political Science, where he met his future wife, Marion Munley.

He earned his law degree from the University of Pennsylvania. "I wanted to make something of myself, and I knew I was lousy at math," he said of his decision to pursue law. Cartwright practiced law in Philadelphia for several years while his wife worked as a judicial clerk. The couple later moved to Scranton to join the law firm of his father-in-law, Robert Munley. Cartwright represented consumers tangling with large corporations on a variety of civil claims. He served on the board of governors of the American Association for Justice, a trial lawyers' group.

In 2012, Cartwright decided to take on Holden. During Republican-orchestrated redistricting in 2011, Holden's hometown areas of St. Clair and Pottsville were joined with unfamiliar territory in Scranton. Although Holden had represented part of Harrisburg, the capital city was jettisoned from the new district. Cartwright's campaign estimated that 86% of the district's likely Democratic voters were new to Holden. "I had always thought about running for high political office, and I was kind of waiting for the stars to line up," Cartwright said. "And, you know, they don't hold the door open for you. You kind of have to muscle your way in."

By March, Cartwright had raised around $600,000, much of it from fellow trial lawyers. He got help from the anti-incumbent super PAC Campaign for Primary Accountability. Cartwright ran as a progressive, pushing for environmental protections and criticizing corporate tax breaks. The two candidates also differed on health care. Cartwright supported the 2010 overhaul; Holden had voted against it while serving a more conservative district.

Holden ran a hard-hitting ad insinuating that Cartwright's law firm contributed money to jailed Luzerne County Judge Michael Toole in exchange for a favorable verdict in a malpractice case. *The Citizens' Voice* newspaper of Wilkes-Barre pointed out that the political contribution was four years before the malpractice verdict and six years before Toole pleaded guilty to corruption charges.

The new Democratic district was better suited to Cartwright's liberal views than Holden's centrism. He won the primary, 57%-43%. Scranton native and Vice President Joe Biden called to offer his congratulations. Cartwright won Lackawanna and Luzerne with more than 70% of the vote in each county. Holden took 85% in his home base of Schuylkill, but it wasn't enough. In the general election, Cartwright faced Scranton Tea Party founder Laureen Cummings. In Democratic territory, Cartwright had a distinct advantage and won easily, 60%-40%.

With Rep. Joaquin Castro of Texas, Cartwright was elected one of two presidents of the Democratic freshman class. He was assigned to the Natural Resources Committee, and the Oversight and Government reform panel, where he is the ranking Democrat on the Healthcare, Benefits, and Administrative Rules Subcommittee. During his first two years, he took credit for having developed and introduced 60-plus bills, more than any other House Democrat. True to his campaign promise, he mostly voted the party line. In May 2015, he joined Democratic Rep. Rick Nolan of Minnesota on his proposed constitutional amendment to reverse the Supreme Court's ruling in the *Citizens United* case that overturned restrictions of federal campaign financing.

Cartwright was reelected against Republican David Moylan, the Schuylkill County coroner. Even though Cartwright out-spent the challenger nearly 10-to-1, his 57% of the vote was smaller than during his first election.

EIGHTEENTH DISTRICT

Tim Murphy (R)

Elected 2002, 7th term; b. Sept. 11, 1952, Cleveland, OH; Wheeling Jesuit U., B.S. 1974, Cleveland St. U., M.S. 1976, U. of Pittsburgh, Ph.D. 1979; Catholic; married (Nan Missig); 1 child.

Military Career: U.S. Navy Reserve Medical Service Corps, 2009-present.

Elected Office: PA Senate, 1997-2003.

Professional Career: Practicing psychologist, 1976-2002.

DC Office: 2332 RHOB, 20515, 202-225-2301; Fax: 202-225-1844; Website: murphy.house.gov.

State Offices: Greensburg, 724-850-7312; Pittsburgh, 412-344-5583.

Committees: *Energy & Commerce:* Environment & the Economy; Health; Oversight & Investigations (Chmn).

Group Ratings

	ADA	ACLU	AFL-CIO	LCV	ITI	COC	HAFA	ACU	CFG	FRC
2014	0%	0%	–	6%	100%	85%	50%	56%	47%	100%
2013	0%	C	29%	0%	C	92%	C	68%	48%	C

National Journal Ratings

	2013 LIB	—	2013 CONS
Economic	34%	—	66%
Social	38%	—	59%
Foreign	5%	—	86%
Composite	28%	—	72%

Key Votes of the 113th Congress

1. Sandy storm spending	N	5. Medical Marijuana	N	9. Syrian Rebels Training	Y
2. Violence Against Women Act	N	6. Farm Bill	Y	10. Keystone pipeline	Y
3. Guantanamo Bay Detainees	N	7. Afghanistan Combat	N	11. Immigration Exec. Action	Y
4. Abortion 20-week ban	Y	8. NSA Phone Data Collection	N	12. Bipartisan budget deal	Y

Election Results

2014 general	Tim Murphy (R)	unopposed	$1,156,372
2014 primary	Tim Murphy (R)	unopposed	

Prior winning percentages: 2012 (64%), 2010 (67%), 2008 (64%), 2006 (58%), 2004 (63%), 2002 (60%)

Population		Race and Ethnicity		Income	
Total:	710,784	White	93.3%	Median income:	$59,277
Urban:	18.6%	Black	2.3%		(132 of 435)
Suburban:	72.1%	Asian	1.6%	Under $50,000	41.6%
Rural:	9.3%	Latino	1.4%	$50,000-$99,999:	32.6%
Land area:	1,898	Two races	1.1%	$100,000-$199,999:	20.5%
Pop/sq. mi.:	374.4	White Ethnic	61.1%	$200,000 or more:	5.3%
Born in state:	81.1%			Poverty Rate	9.1%
		Education			
Age Groups		H.S. grad or less:	40.0%	**Work**	
Under 18:	19.8%	Some college:	25.3%	White collar:	40.1%
18 to 34:	18.5%	College degree, 4 yr.:	21.6%	Blue collar:	38.8%
35 to 64:	42.9%	Post-grad study:	13.1%	Sales and service:	21.0%
Over 64:	18.8%				
		Military		Govt. workers:	9.3%
		Veterans/active duty:	9.3%		

Southwestern Pittsburgh Suburbs

Pittsburgh was built on the unlikeliest terrain of any major U.S. city. Just about the only level places in the city or its suburbs are the bottomlands along the rivers. Everything else is built on hills that approach the magnitude of mountains. Only a pro-pitious location, where the Allegheny and Monon-

Voter Turnout	
2013 Total Citizen 18+	558,082
2014 House Turnout	166,076
2014 Turnout as % CVAP	29.8%
2012 Turnout as % CVAP	62.6%

gahela rivers join to form the Ohio, and the confluence of economically valuable natural resources—coal from the mountains and iron ore from the Great Lakes—can explain why a large metropolitan area sprang up there. The cities and towns of greater Pittsburgh are separated from each other not just by miles but by altitude. So, the region's high-income sub-urbs and its gritty factory towns are not concentrated in one quarter, but are scattered all around. This is long-settled country, with many more old towns than sparkling new suburbs.

Unlike the economically diverse Pittsburgh-based Allegheny County, Washington and Westmoreland counties here are more depen-dent on manufacturing and more susceptible to industry-wide cuts.

The 18th Congressional District of Penn-sylvania covers the southern part of the Pittsburgh metropolitan area. It includes substantial portions of southern Allegheny

2012 Presidential Vote		
Mitt Romney (R)................201,320	(58%)
Barack Obama (D) 142,394	(41%)

2008 Presidential Vote
John McCain (R).................196,869 (55%)
Barack Obama (D) 156,794 (44%)

Cook Partisan Voting Index: R+10

and Westmoreland counties, which are the population centers, plus smaller and more rural Washington and Greene counties in the southwest corner of the state along the West Vir-ginia border. Westmoreland votes most heavily Republican of the four counties. The district gained GOP voters in the 2011 redistricting, and leans strongly Republican.

Tim Murphy (R)

Republican Tim Murphy, elected in 2002, has used his background as a psychologist and his seat on the Energy and Commerce Committee to play a role in debates over health care. He is a fairly reliable Republican, but occasionally shows independence and draws just enough backing from labor unions to avoid serious Democratic challenges.

Murphy grew up in Cleveland in a family of 11 children. He took up the guitar as a teenager, and was accomplished enough to play in bands that opened for folk legend John Hartford and banjo master Earl Scruggs. He graduated from Wheeling Jesuit University, got a Ph.D. from the University of Pittsburgh and became a child psychologist. He worked in several Pittsburgh-area hospitals and was an adjunct faculty member in public health and pediatrics at the University of Pittsburgh. He became well-known locally as "Dr. Tim," offering advice in television appearances and on radio talk shows. He co-authored the book, *The Angry Child: Regaining Control When Your Child is Out of Control.* After his election to

Congress, he co-authored another book (which was not about Congress) titled, *Overcoming Passive-Aggression.*

In 1996, Murphy was elected to the state Senate, where he sponsored a Patients' Bill of Rights and increased funding for medical research. Running for the House in a vacant district after redistricting, he presented himself as an experienced and accomplished legislator who opposed abortion rights and supported gun ownership. With extensive support from state and national Republicans, he ran unopposed in the Republican primary. In the general election, he outspent Democratic nominee Jack Machek, a school district administrator, by nearly 8-to-1. Murphy won 60%-40%, an impressive showing in an open seat race in an area that had mostly sent Democrats to Congress.

In the House, Murphy is an active legislator but he has kept a fairly low profile. "He's measured. He doesn't provoke controversy," Franklin & Marshall University politics professor G. Terry Madonna told the *Pittsburgh Post-Gazette.* In 2007 and 2009, he backed the Democrats' plan to expand the Children's Health Insurance Program, and he has supported several priorities of labor unions, including a bill to make unionizing easier by eliminating the secret ballot in worksite elections. But he reversed his position and mollified business groups on that issue in 2012, prompting the conservative *Pittsburgh Tribune-Review*'s editorial page—which frequently jabs at him—to call him "a weasel." He took enough conservative fiscal positions on other issues that year to lift his rating on the Club for Growth's legislative scorecard to 68%; his lifetime rating from the anti-tax group had been just 50%.

With a seat on Energy and Commerce, where he has chaired the Oversight and Investigations Subcommittee since 2013, Murphy has focused on programs for military veterans with mental illness and on improving security for their medical records. After the Newtown, Connecticut, elementary school massacre in December 2012 focused attention on mental illness and violence, his oversight panel conducted a thorough overview of federal programs to determine what role mental illness plays in outbreaks of violence. In December 2013, he introduced what he called his landmark mental health reform legislation, the Helping Families in Mental Health Crisis Act. In recent years, he worked with Texas Democrat Gene Green to win House passage of a bill to address the shortage of doctors in underserved communities. Murphy co-chairs the Mental Health Caucus and is a founding member of the GOP Doctors Caucus. He serves in the Navy Reserve Medical Service Corps at Walter Reed National Military Medical Center, where he treats service members with traumatic brain injury.

On energy issues, Murphy pressed a bipartisan effort in 2011 to convince Interior Secretary Ken Salazar not to impose regulatory burdens on companies using hydraulic fracturing, better known as "fracking," to extract natural gas. Environmentalists claim the technique is responsible for groundwater contamination. Murphy later announced his interest in promoting small "modular" nuclear reactors that could power individual neighborhoods. He also formed a bipartisan energy working group that created a plan to free the United States from dependence on foreign oil. The proposal would expedite exploration of oil and gas resources, and invest new revenues from leasing and royalties into rebuilding roads, bridges, locks and dams.

On other issues, he has advocated on behalf of domestic manufacturers who have sought relief from years of underpriced Chinese imports. He sponsored with Ohio Democratic Rep. Tim Ryan a House-passed bill to permit the Commerce Department to impose countervailing duties on imported goods from countries found to have undervalued their currency. But he voted with most Republicans in June 2015 to give trade promotion authority to President Barack Obama. He has sought to keep open his district's 911th Airlift Wing in Moon Township, which employs about 300 civilians and more than 1,300 Air Force reservists and which the Pentagon threatened to shut down in 2012.

Murphy has not been seriously challenged for reelection. In 2012, he drew a GOP primary opponent—Evan Feinberg, a 28-year-old tea party favorite who brandished endorsements from his former bosses, Kentucky Sen. Rand Paul and Oklahoma Sen. Tom Coburn. Feinberg failed to gain much traction, and Murphy won 63%-37%. He then coasted in November with 64% over underfunded Democrat Larry Maggi. In 2014, Murphy was reelected without opposition.

★ RHODE ISLAND ★

Rhode Island has endured a slow economic recovery and continuing scandals in high office. But with the election of the state's first female governor, there are hopes that it will be able to set a new course. "Little Rhody," the nation's smallest state in size, has always had its quirks. The official state appetizer is "Rhode Island style" calamari, fried squid tossed with hot peppers. Indeed, Rhode Island fishing fleets haul in about half the squid caught on the East Coast, making it one of the state's most important commercial fisheries along with lobster harvesting. Rhode Island has often been set apart, with a turbulent history, from its very beginning. It was founded by Roger Williams as a refuge for religious dissenters, "the sewer of New England," as the orthodox Puritan Cotton Mather put it. It has been a successful trading community since the late 17th century and a leader in manufacturing since Samuel Slater replicated from memory an English water-powered cotton textile mill in Pawtucket in 1791.

Rhode Island profited from slavery (two-thirds of America's slaves arrived from Africa on ships owned by Rhode Islanders) and war (the state boomed during the Civil War), and it carried its tradition of tolerating just about anything into its politics. Rhode Island refused to pay its share for the Revolutionary War and declined to send delegates to the 1787 Constitutional Convention. It delayed joining the union until the other 12 states had, prompting George Washington to say, "Rhode Island still perseveres in that impolitic, unjust—and one might add without much impropriety—scandalous conduct, which seems to have marked all her public counsels of late."

In the 1930s, Rhode Island had something resembling a political revolution. Thousands of immigrants from Ireland, Italy, Portugal, and French Canada came to the state to work in textile mills, and this colony founded by dissident Protestants became the most heavily Catholic state in the nation. Yankee Republicans tried to appeal to Catholics by running French Canadians for office. But national events—Catholic Democrat Al Smith's presidential candidacy in 1928 and Franklin Roosevelt's New Deal—moved the Catholics toward the Democrats. Then came the revolution. Although they had won only 20 of the 42 state Senate seats, the Democrats under Gov. Theodore Green refused to seat two Republicans in 1935. With the lieutenant governor's tiebreaker, they voted Democrats into the seats and proceeded in 14 minutes to declare the state Supreme Court vacant, to abolish state boards that controlled Democratic cities, to increase the power of the governor, and to reorganize state government to purge Republicans. This ended the political control of Rhode Island's "Five Families"—the Browns, Metcalfs, Goddards, Lippitts, and Chafees—who owned or ran many of the textile mills, the Rhode Island Hospital Trust (long the largest bank), the *Providence Journal-Bulletin*, Brown University, the Rhode Island School of Design, and the state Republican Party. Democrats have won most elections ever since, with the lion's share of votes from Rhode Island's Catholic faithful.

From 1940 to 1980, Democrats won every election for House seats. The state's Democratic percentages in presidential elections from 1968 to 2012 were rivaled only by those of Massachusetts. But this is tempered by what political analyst Nate Silver calls elasticity: Rhode Island has the largest percentage of voters willing in the right circumstances to vote for the other party. This was evident as long ago as 1964, when Rhode Islanders voted 81% for Lyndon Johnson and 61% for incumbent Republican Gov. John Chafee, who later was elected to the Senate four times. And starting in 1992, Republicans Lincoln Almond and Donald Carcieri were elected governor twice each, and in 2010, Lincoln Chaffee, John Chafee's son, was elected as an independent. It wasn't until 2014 that Democrats returned to the governor's chair when Gina Raimondo, the first female governor of Rhode Island, was elected. Rhode Island today has a diverse ethnic and racial mix. In 2013, it was 5% African-American, 12% Hispanic, and 4% Asian. Some 20% describe their ancestry as Irish, 19% as Italian, 17% as French or French Canadian, 13% as English, and 10% as Portuguese (mainly from the Azores). A study by the Pew Research Center found that 42% are Catholic, the highest percentage of any state in the country. And most people in that category identify as Democrats. Democrats currently hold all of the state's four seats in Congress. Sens. Jack Reed, first elected in 1996, and Sheldon Whitehouse, elected in 2006, seem well-positioned to hold on as long as their Democratic predecessors John Pastore and Claiborne Pell (24 and 36 years, respectively).

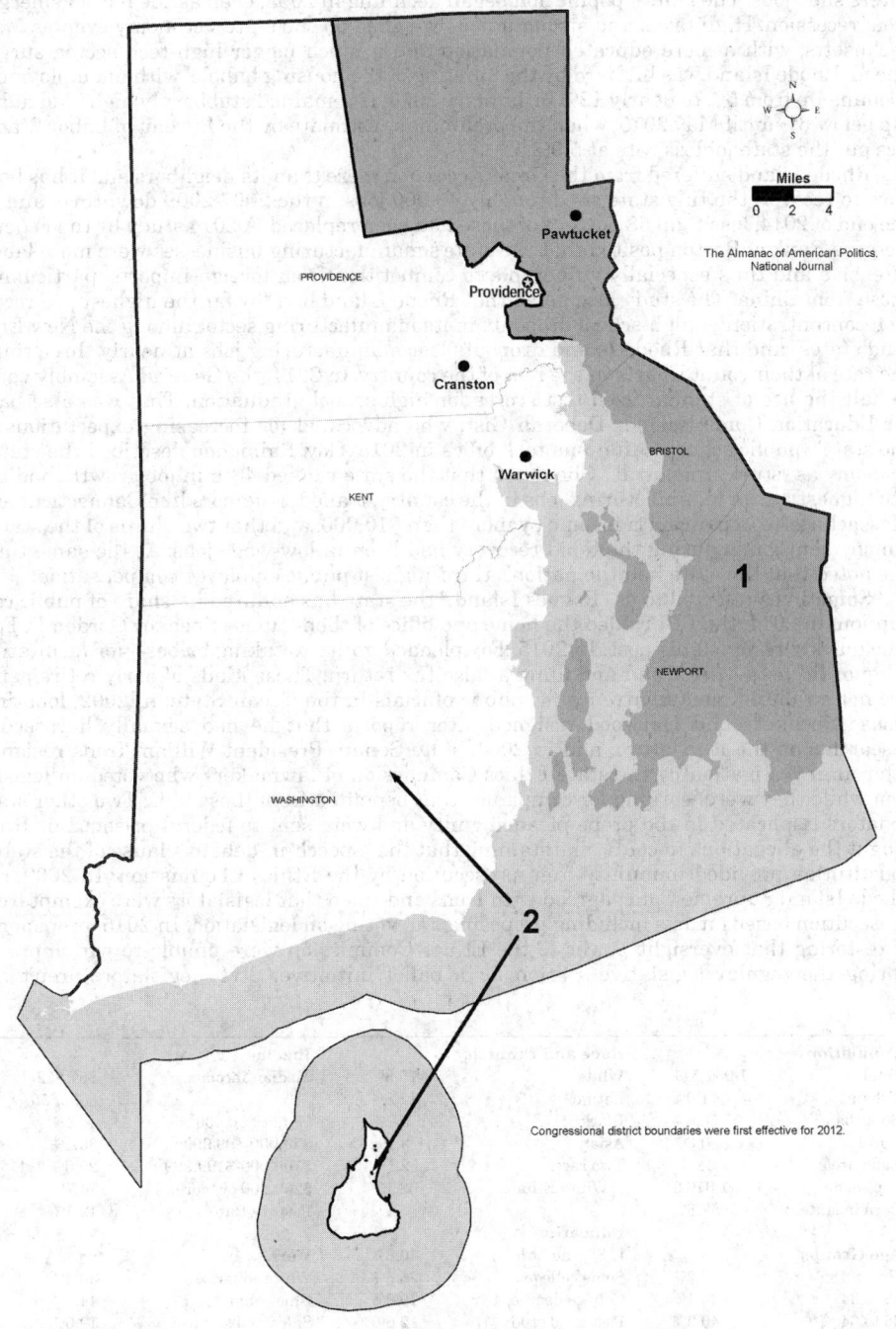

The Almanac of American Politics.
National Journal

Congressional district boundaries were first effective for 2012.

Rhode Island has gone through a long and often painful economic transformation, from blue collar to white collar, from textiles toward high tech. In the early 1990s, it suffered job losses when the naval air base at Quonset Point and the state's costume jewelry manufacturers shed jobs. The state's population began declining in 2003, even as the nation emerged from recession. High taxes and strong unions weighed on the state's economy even as Massachusetts, with a more educated population and a much bigger high-tech sector, surged ahead. Rhode Island was hit hard by the bursting of the housing bubble, with unemployment zooming up from 5% to nearly 12% in January 2010. It remained stubbornly high, and didn't dip below 6% until May 2015, when the preliminary estimate by the Bureau of Labor Statistics put the state jobless rate at 5.9%.

Rhode Island suffered from the Great Recession more than its neighbors and it has been slow to recover: the tiny state shed roughly 40,000 jobs in the 2007-2009 downturn, and by the end of 2014, less than 58 percent of those had been replaced. A 2014 study by the Federal Reserve Bank of Boston posited that the state's manufacturing businesses were more labor-intensive and thus especially vulnerable to competition from foreign imports, particularly those from China. The study also noted that Rhode Island had "by far the highest pre-recession concentration of high-school dropouts in its manufacturing sector among the New England states" and that Rhode Island dropouts lost manufacturing jobs at nearly three times the rate of their counterparts in the rest of the country. In 2014, the General Assembly voted to halt the use of standardized test scores for high school graduation. That was a setback for Education Commissioner Deborah Gist, who advocated for increasing expectations in the state's public schools. After she took office in 2015, Gov. Raimondo described the state's economy as "stuck in neutral." She noted that the state ranked 48th in job growth, had the 4th highest loss of manufacturing jobs in the country, trailed neighbors like Connecticut and Massachusetts in per capita income by more than $10,000, and that two-thirds of the state's employment gains during the tepid recovery had been in low-wage jobs. At the same time, she noted that the state had the nation's third-highest public employee compensation.

Sometimes referred to as "Rogues Island," the state has endured its share of public corruption. In 2014, the FBI raided the home and office of then- House Speaker Gordon D. Fox, who quickly resigned his post. In 2015, Fox pleaded guilty to taking bribes—for facilitating a liquor license—wire fraud and filing a false tax return. These kinds of early retirements are not an uncommon occurrence for public officials in the Ocean State: in 2002, longtime House Speaker John Harwood resigned after reports that he had sexually harassed a researcher in the legislature; and in 2004, state Senate President William Irons resigned after an investigation by the state Ethics Commission of lawmakers who voted on legislation while they were working for companies that benefited from those bills. Two other state senators implicated in the probe pleaded guilty and were sent to federal prison. But Irons fought the allegations in court, maintaining that the "speech-in-debate" clause of the state's constitution provided immunity from prosecution by the Ethics Commission. In 2009, the Rhode Island Supreme Court agreed with Irons and ruled that legislators were exempt from prosecution based on acts including proposing and voting on legislation. In 2015, proponents of restoring that oversight power to the Ethics Commission were unable to win approval during the regular legislative session for a ballot initiative. State legislators aren't the

Population		Race and Ethnicity		Income	
Total:	1,051,511	White	75.8%	Median income:	$57,812
Urban:	41.0%	Latino	12.8%		(13 of 50)
Suburban:	58.4%	Black	5.2%	Under $50,000	45.1%
Rural:	0.6%	Asian	3.1%	$50,000-$99,999:	30.2%
Land area:	1,034	Two races	2.1%	$100,000-$199,999:	20.0%
Pop/sq. mi.:	1,016.9	White Ethnic	68.1%	$200,000 or more:	4.7%
Born in state:	57.8%			Poverty Rate	12.1%
		Education			
Age Groups		H.S. grad or less:	40.8%	**Work**	
Under 18:	20.2%	Some college:	26.8%	White collar:	36.8%
18 to 34:	24.1%	College degree, 4 yr.:	19.8%	Blue collar:	44.2%
35 to 64:	40.2%	Post-grad study:	12.6%	Sales and service:	19.0%
Over 64:	15.5%			Govt. workers:	12.1%
		Military			
		Veterans/active duty:	7.7%		

only ones who have run afoul of the law in Rhode Island. Former Gov. Edward DiPrete served time after pleading guilty to bribery and extortion charges in 1998; and two chief justices of the state Supreme Court, Joseph Bevilacqua and Thomas Fay, resigned while they were under investigation in 1986 and 1992, respectively. The lore of Election Day vote buying in Rhode Island is so rich that a

Voter Turnout			
2013 Total Citizen 18+			777,825
2014 Highest Statewide Turnout			324,055
2014 Turnout as % CVAP			41.7%
2012 Turnout as % CVAP			57.9%
Legislature			
Senate:	32D	5R	1V
House:	63D	11R	I1

Democratic controlled legislature with the support of African-American members passed a law in 2011 requiring that residents show a photo ID to vote. (States in the South that have adopted that election law change have had to face the scrutiny of the Department of Justice.) Some analysts suspect the law was partially motivated by a desire to dampen the turnout of newly arrived and growing numbers of Hispanic voters. Those without a photo ID can still cast a provisional ballot.

And then there's the colorful former mayor of Providence, now a popular radio talk show host, Buddy Cianci, who jokes about the five years he spent in a "federally funded gated community." In 1984, Cianci resigned as mayor and was convicted of assaulting with a fire log a man whom he accused of having an affair with his wife. Cianci was reelected mayor in 1990, then resigned again and was convicted on federal racketeering charges in 2002. In 2014, the former Democrat attempted a second political comeback, but lost his bid as an independent to return to power in Providence—his first defeat in seven runs for mayor—to Jorge Elorza, a former Housing Court judge. A teacher's union lobbyist in Rhode Island told Boston Public Radio that the state's residents can take a perverse pride in their reputation for political chicanery: "I like the idea of being able to tell my colleagues across the country, 'Yeah, that's right, we're from Rhode Island, get used to it.'" Many in the state may do so, but not enough in Providence to bring back Buddy.

Presidential Politics Rhode Island is one of the most Democratic states in presidential elections. It voted 61%-32% for Al Gore in 2000—his best state in the country—but gave John Kerry from neighboring Massachusetts a somewhat smaller margin of 59%-39% in 2004. The state voted 63%-35% for Barack Obama in both 2008 and 2012, his best margins after the District of Columbia, Obama's native Hawaii, Vermont, and New York. Rhode Island's Catholics are heavily Democratic and more likely to favor abortion rights, so like many other Catholic Democrats nationwide, they vote with their party rather than with their bishop.

2012 Presidential Vote		
Barack Obama (D)	279,677	(63%)
Mitt Romney (R)	157,204	(35%)
2012 Presidential Primary		
Mitt Romney (R)	9,178	(63%)
Ron Paul (R)	3,473	(24%)
Newt Gingrich (R)	880	(6%)
Rick Santorum (R)	825	(6%)
2008 Presidential Vote		
Barack Obama (D)	296,571	(63%)
John McCain (R)	165,391	(35%)

For years, Rhode Island held a presidential primary on the same day as Massachusetts. In 2008, the state voted on March 4, the same day as Vermont, Ohio, and Texas. At that point, the Republican contest was effectively decided, although Mike Huckabee remained in the race and lost to John McCain by a predictably large 64%-21%. On the Democratic side, Obama and Hillary Clinton were locked in a tight contest and Rhode Island was a battleground like every other state. The economic divide seemed fairly apparent in the results. As in Massachusetts, Obama carried upscale towns and city neighborhoods, while Clinton ran well in blue-collar areas that had not shared in recent prosperity. She won the state 58%-40% and, with her narrower victories in Ohio and Texas, could claim to have won the majority of the March 4 primaries. That outcome kept her in the race for three more months.

In 2012, Rhode Island held its Republican primary on April 24, after Rick Santorum had left the race, and Mitt Romney won 63% of the votes; 24% voted for Ron Paul. Turnout was miniscule—14,564 in a state of more than 1 million people.

Congressional Districts Rhode Island held onto its two districts in the 2010 census, though not by much, and now houses the least populous districts in the country. Redistricting hasn't been much of a problem since the state lost its third seat in 1932: Providence

is split and both districts are overwhelmingly Democratic—
though a Republican occasionally has been elected. In 2011, the
legislature approved a new 18-member Special Commission on
Reapportionment, an advisory panel comprising eight legislators and six citizens appointed by the majority leaders (Democrats), and four legislators appointed by the minority.

114th Congress Lineup	
0 R	2 D
113th Congress Lineup	
0 R	2 D

The commission needed to shift only about 7,000 residents from the 1st District to the
2nd, and could have easily done so by tweaking a few lines in Providence. But freshman
Democrat David Cicilline was polling abysmally in the 1st. His ally, state House Speaker
Gordon Fox, prevailed on the commission to draft a map shifting three northern towns Cicilline had lost in 2010—Smithfield, North Smithfield, and Burrillville—into Langevin's 2nd
District in exchange for more of liberal Providence, moving nearly 100,000 residents. Langevin, though popular, would have none of it. The commission proposed exchanging only
Burrillville for a smaller share of Providence, giving Cicilline only an extra percentage point
of insurance. The legislature and governor approved. Since then, Cicilline and Langevin
have won easily. The state already is preparing for a political nightmare when the 2020 census likely will strip its second House seat, and the two Democrats—or their successors—will
be forced to run against each other, unless one steps aside.

Governor

Gina Raimondo (D)

Elected 2014, term expires Jan. 2019, 1st term; b. May 17, 1971, Smithfield; Harvard U., B.A. 1993, Rhodes Scholar, Oxford U., PhD, Yale Law
Schl., J.D. 1998; Catholic; married (Andy Moffitt); 2 children..

Elected Office: RI treasurer, 2010-14.

Professional Career: Clerk, Judge Kimba Wood; Founder & sr. v.p.,
Village Ventures; Co-founder, Point Judith Capital.

Office: Office of the Governor, 82 Smith St., 02903, 401-222-2080; Fax:
401-222-8096; Website: governor.state.ri.us.

Election Results

2014 general	Gina Raimondo (D)	131,899	(41%)
	Allan Fung (R)	117,428	(36%)
	Robert Healey (Mod.)	69,278	(21%)
2014 primary	Gina Raimondo (D)	53,990	(42%)
	Angel Taveras (D)	37,326	(29%)
	Clay Pell (D)	34,515	(27%)

Democrat Gina Raimondo—a Harvard graduate, Rhodes scholar, lawyer and venture
capitalist—was elected Rhode Island's first female governor in 2014. Petite in stature, less
than 5-foot-3, she has managed to bring big changes to a state where politics can be a rough-
and-tumble sport. Raimondo was prepared for that too, having played rugby in college.

Raimondo's personal history reads like the script for a made-in-Rhode Island public
service ad. Her grandfather arrived from Italy at age 14, learning English by studying at
the Providence Public Library. Her father is a World War II Navy veteran from a family of
butchers and used the GI Bill to become the first in his family to attend college. She grew
up in a tight-knit family in Smithfield and graduated with honors from Harvard, where she
was named top economics student in her class; received a doctorate from Oxford University
on a Rhodes scholarship; and earned her law degree from Yale Law School. She clerked for a
federal judge and then entered the venture-capital business.

Raimondo was elected Rhode Island treasurer in 2010 and set about fixing the state's
public-employee pension system. Central Falls filed for bankruptcy in 2011 under the weight
of underfunded pensions—its retiree health benefit liability was five times the city's annual
revenues. In 1991, Providence Mayor Buddy Cianci handed out 6% annual increases in pension benefits to hundreds of that city's employees that began to cut into its finances 20 years
later. Raimondo warned that Rhode Island had the largest unfunded pension debt per capita

of any state: it was spending 10 cents of every dollar in tax revenue on the pensions of 21,000 public employees and that amount of money for retirees was due to double in less than five years. In 2011, Raimondo crafted a pension law that froze automatic cost-of-living increases and raised retirement ages, angering public employee unions. Additional reform legislation that forced some state workers and teachers to move a portion of their retirement savings into 401(k)-style accounts was passed with bipartisan support and signed into law in 2012.

At first, it appeared the Democratic primary race for governor was headed toward a battle between Raimondo, running as a fiscal reformer, and Providence Mayor Angel Taveras, running as a progressive who would win support from labor unions. But when former U.S. Education Department official Clay Pell, grandson of the late Sen. Claiborne Pell and scion of one of Rhode Island's most prominent families, got into the race, union support was divided, with firefighters, police, supermarket clerks, and city employees backing Taveras, and the teachers union—unhappy with Taveras's support of charter schools—siding with Pell. Raimondo benefited from the split and won the primary with 42 percent of the vote.

Raimondo sought to mend fences with organized labor in the general election and she stumped to raise the state minimum wage to $10.10 an hour. She was helped by the fact that her Republican opponent, Cranston Mayor Allan Fung, had come out against raising the minimum wage and in favor of "right-to-work" legislation that would ban union shops from requiring workers to pay union dues. In a state where more than one-in-seven workers carry a union card, the highest rate in New England, that idea was a non-starter with many voters. Each candidate claimed to be the better protector of the middle class. Fung pledged to cut taxes and spending. Raimondo called it "wrong-headed economic theory." She ended up winning 41%-36%. Perennial candidate Robert J. Healey Jr., won 21%, surprising local analysts. Some attributed Healey's relative success to the name recognition he's earned from his many campaigns; he first ran for governor in 1986 and has run for several other offices since. In 2010 he captured 39% of the vote running for lieutenant governor on a platform to abolish the office if elected.

Rhode Island has one of strongest state legislatures in the country and the powers of its chief executive are circumscribed by the state constitution. The governor has limited authority when it comes to state appointments, which must be approved the state Senate, and lacks a line-item veto that 44 other governors enjoy. The budget process is also set up in a way that empowers the legislature to make additions and cuts. The governor can only sign or veto the entire final budget. And a veto usually prompts the General Assembly to override, which only requires the votes of three-fifths of those present. Raimondo got off to an inauspicious start in her early days in office when she criticized the Assembly's budget process at a Washington, D.C. conference, saying, "For too long, what's happened in Rhode island—and it may happen in other statehouses—is the governor proposes a budget and then the General Assembly takes the budget and—often in the dark of night, in a quiet room—the lobbyists and the General Assembly get together and they hack it up every which way and out pops a budget." That brought a rebuke from House Speaker Nicholas Mattielo, who told the *Providence Journal* that he was "disappointed the governor provided an inaccurate depiction of the budget process to her Washington audience." Within days, Raimondo called Mattielo to apologize and then went to his state House office to smooth things over.

After that flap, Raimondo quietly worked with lawmakers on the budget she proposed. It emerged largely intact, winning unanimous approval in the House from 63 Democrats, 11 Republicans and one independent. The Senate approved the budget by a vote of 35-3, with only a handful of Republicans dissenting. The budget created new economic development programs Raimondo proposed to promote job growth, exempted most Social Security benefits from state taxes, removed the sales taxes on energy for businesses, cut Medicaid spending, increased funding for K-12 education, raised the tax on cigarettes by 25 cents to $3.75 a pack, lowered the state's corporate minimum tax and established a state infrastructure bank. Mattielo, a Democrat, praised the budget and said it gave "a clear shot in the arm to business." The other major accomplishment of the General Assembly that Rhode Island businesses did not like was raising the state minimum wage to $9.60 an hour, although that was 50 cents less than what Raimondo had proposed in her campaign.

The budget also authorized the state to settle the lawsuit brought by unions challenging its pension reforms. Earlier, the state and the unions had averted a trial and agreed to soften the public pension reforms by modifying retirement ages, increasing defined benefits for longtime public employees and permitting more chances for inflation adjustments. While Raimondo said the state "had a very strong case," the settlement allowed her to remove the uncertainty hanging over the state pension structural reforms, which she maintained remained intact after the settlement. As Raimondo told *New York Times* columnist Frank Bruni shortly before taking office, "My own rhetoric is not so 'us versus them.' I don't like fighting."

Senior Senator

Jack Reed (D)

Elected 1996, term expires Jan. 2021, 4th term; b. Nov. 12, 1949, Providence; U.S. Military Acad. West Point, B.S. 1971, Harvard U., M.P.P. 1973, J.D. 1982; Catholic; married (Julia); 1 child.

Military Career: U.S. Army, 1967-79; U.S. Army Reserve, 1979-91..

Elected Office: RI Senate, 1985-91; U.S. House, 1991-97.

Professional Career: Assoc. prof., U.S. Military Acad. at West Point, 1977-79; Practicing atty., Southerland, Asbill & Brennan, Edwards & Angell, 1982-90.

DC Office: 728 HSOB, 20510, 202-224-4642; Fax: 202-224-4680; Website: reed.senate.gov.

State Offices: Cranston, 401-943-3100; Providence, 401-528-5200.

Committees: *Appropriations:* Commerce, Justice, Science & Related Agencies; Defense; Interior, Environment & Related Agencies; Labor, HHS, Education & Related Agencies; Military Construction, Veterans Affairs & Related Agencies; Transportation, HUD & Related Agencies (RMM). *Armed Services* (RMM: ex officio member of each subcommittee). *Banking, Housing & Urban Affairs:* Financial Institutions & Consumer Protection; Housing, Transportation & Community Development; Securities, Insurance & Investment. *Intelligence (Select):* ex officio.

Group Ratings

	ADA	ACLU	AFL-CIO	LCV	ITI	COC	HAFA	ACU	CFG	FRC
2014	90%	93%	–	80%	100%	38%	2%	4%	17%	0%
2013	100%	C	100%	92%	C	50%	C	4%	9%	C

National Journal Ratings

	2013 LIB	—	2013 CONS
Economic	75%	—	19%
Social	73%	—	0%
Foreign	71%	—	0%
Composite	83%	—	17%

Key Votes of the 113th Congress

1. Sandy storm spending	Y	5. Student Loan Rates	N	9. Bipartisan Budget Deal	Y
2. Chuck Hagel Confirmation	Y	6. Employee Non-Discrim'n Act	Y	10. Farm Bill Conference Rept.	N
3. Gun Background Checks	Y	7. Senate Vote on Judgeships	N	11. Unempl. Comp. Extension	Y
4. Immigration Reform	Y	8. Defense Dept. Spending	Y	12. Keystone Pipeline	N

Election Results

2014 general	Jack Reed (D)	223,675	(71%)	$4,649,761	$5,576	$4,115
	Mark Zaccaria (R)	92,684	(29%)	$54,031		
2014 primary	Jack Reed (D)	unopposed				

Prior winning percentages: 2008 (73%), 2002 (78%), 1996 (63%); House: 1994 (68%), 1992 (71%), 1990 (59%)

Since first elected in 1996, Democrat Jack Reed, Rhode Island's senior senator, has been one of the chamber's lowest-profile members—but also has been numbered among its most respected policy wonks, making his influence felt on banking issues as well as national security matters. Reed is a graduate of the United States Military Academy, and, as such, is among the few senators of his generation with military experience. Perennially mentioned as a candidate for defense secretary during the administration of President Barack Obama, Reed waved off the overtures—in the apparent hope of one day chairing the Senate Armed Services Committee. He became the Armed Services panel's top Democrat in 2015 upon the retirement of Michigan's Carl Levin, putting Reed in line to chair the committee if and when the Democrats regain the Senate majority they lost in 2014.

Rhode Island has had a tendency over the past century to send scions of the state's blue-blooded families to the Senate; Theodore Green, Reed's predecessor once removed, traced his ancestry to the colonists who arrived with Roger Williams, Rhode Island's founder, in 1636. Reed is an exception to this political pattern: He grew up in working-class Cranston, immediately west of Providence, as the second of three children of a school custodian and a housewife. Disappointed that she never got to go to college, Mary Reed prepared her children for success in school. She insisted on music and art classes for Jack beginning at age 5. But her son was fascinated by history and World War II as a child, eventually deciding he wanted to attend the U.S. Military Academy in West Point New York. At LaSalle Academy, a Catholic prep school in Providence, he played football, although he was small for the sport (he today stands at 5 feet, 7 inches.) He also ran track, while also working for the school newspaper and winning election to the student council.

After graduating from West Point, in 1971, Reed served in the 82nd Airborne Division as a paratrooper, and also received a master's degree from Harvard's Kennedy School of Government while in the Army. After eight years of active duty (he spent an additional 12 years in the Army Reserve, retiring with the rank of major), Reed enrolled in Harvard Law School. Throughout his life, he has maintained connections to West Point, teaching there briefly in the late 1970s, serving on the academy's governing board, and choosing its chapel as the site of his wedding in April 2005.

Following graduation from law school, Reed was an associate at a Washington, D.C. law firm before returning to Rhode Island in 1983 to work for Providence-based Edwards & Angell, then one of the state's oldest and most prominent law firms. A year later, at 35, Reed won public office for the first time, beating an incumbent in the primary for the state Senate, where he served six years. During his tenure, Reed headed a commission that investigated a corruption scandal involving the Rhode Island Housing and Mortgage Finance Corporation, a state agency created to make affordable loans to low-income Rhode Islanders. When Republican Claudine Schneider gave up her House seat in 1990 to run against Sen. Claiborne Pell, Reed made a run for Congress. He captured 49 percent of the vote in a four-way field. Former Rep. Edward Beard, a colorful figure who had served three terms in the House prior to being ousted by Schneider in 1980, ran a distant second with 27 percent. In the general election, Reed won the district, covering the western section of the state, by 59%-41%. He was reelected twice by margins exceeding 2-1.

In 1995, when Pell announced his retirement after six terms, Reed ran to succeed him. Reed had no serious competition for the Democratic nomination and faced state Treasurer Nancy Mayer in the general election. National Republicans spent nearly $1 million on ads attacking Reed as a liberal for opposing bills requiring welfare recipients to work and for supporting labor unions—not especially harmful charges in largely liberal, heavily unionized Rhode Island. Reed spent $2.7 million to Mayer's $773,000. His biography was his message: Reed launched his campaign in a public school conference room named for his late father, he stressed his bootstraps rise from a working-class background, and he called for education spending to help others achieve the same success. He won 63%-35%. He has not had serious competition in three reelection bids since, winning a fourth term in November 2014 with 71 percent of the vote.

Reed has served on the Armed Services Committee since January 1999, two years after his initial election to the Senate. When he was given a sought-after seat on the Appropriations Committee in 2007, he received a waiver from the Democratic leadership to remain on the Armed Services panel. His influence and clout on defense issues is such that former Defense Secretary Robert Gates said Reed was instrumental in persuading him to stay on the job in the early years of the Obama administration. "In terms of reaching out to me, and whether I would stay on, Obama couldn't have picked a person I was more willing to listen to or respected more than Jack," Gates told *Rhode Island Monthly* in November 2012. In fact, Gates said he had proposed Reed to Obama as a candidate for defense secretary. But the president "shook his head—he clearly has the highest respect for Jack—and he said, 'I can't lose him in the Senate,'" Gates recalled.

Obama's sentiments at the time were likely driven as much by concerns over the partisan makeup of the Senate as by respect for Reed. At the end of 2008, the governorship of Rhode Island was in GOP control: If the governor had appointed a Republican to replace Reed, it could have upset the new administration's aim to have a 60-vote, filibuster-proof Democratic Senate majority in place. Rhode Island law has since been changed to provide for a special election in the case of a Senate vacancy, but Reed—on at least two occasions in recent years—has reportedly rejected opportunities to become defense secretary. The most recent occurred just after the 2014 election, when Defense Secretary Chuck Hagel was eased out. A Reed spokesman told the *Providence Journal* at that time that Reed "has made it very clear that he does not wish to be considered for secretary of defense or any other Cabinet position. He just asked the people of Rhode Island to hire him for another six-year term and plans to honor that commitment."

Six years earlier, Reed was briefly regarded as a possible vice presidential choice: When Obama was a Democratic presidential candidate, Reed accompanied him on a 2008 trip to Iraq and Afghanistan, and Obama later considered him as a potential running mate until Reed ruled himself out. (Reed's working-class upbringing as well as his military service and expertise were seen as his upsides as a candidate for national office. Among the downsides: His low-key rhetorical style hardly fit the attack-dog role that vice presidential candidates often must play.) During Obama's first year, as the new president was mulling strategy in Afghanistan, Reed expressed doubts about sending more troops and said the burden of proof was on commanders to justify a troop increase. Reed has traveled to Iraq and Afghanistan frequently, often straying from the safe zones—thanks to his military background and his close relationships with many military commanders. "I talk to people in the field, diplomats and soldiers," he told *National Journal* in 2010. "I go recognizing, frankly, everyone has an institutional agenda. I try to approach all these things with a questioning mind." He made his 14th visit to Afghanistan in January 2013, and expressed confidence in the ability to withdraw a significant number of troops there by 2014.

During the administration of President George W. Bush, Reed in October 2002 opposed the Iraq war resolution; he argued that Defense Secretary Donald Rumsfeld grossly under-estimated the strength of anti-American insurgents in Iraq and failed to send in adequate troops and equipment. In 2005, after a trip to Iraq, he said: "I think my criticism has been accurate, certainly in the operations in this region, in that we didn't organize ourselves for the appropriate occupation and stabilization" following the overthrow of Iraqi leader Saddam Hussein. Reed was at the forefront of Democratic efforts in 2006 to convince Bush to redeploy the forces in Iraq. With Levin, he sponsored a bill calling for a "phased redeployment" in six months, with no deadline for complete withdrawal and with some U.S. forces remaining to train Iraqi security forces. The Levin-Reed amendment lost 60-39. After Bush's successful troop surge in 2007, Reed continued to push for alternatives that would leave only a residual force in Iraq. But most Republicans were opposed, and Reed failed to gain the 60 votes required to force a final vote.

Reed has long backed efforts to permanently increase the size of the Army. In 2004, he and Hagel, then a Nebraska Republican senator, called for an increase of 30,000 troops, and the Senate agreed to 20,000. In 2006, Reed worked with the Republican leadership to add $3.7 billion for more soldiers and Marines, and he sponsored an amendment to add $10 billion to replace damaged or destroyed equipment. While, in 2012, Reed did defend Obama's plans to shrink the size of the Army and Marines, he has more recently expressed concern about the impact on the armed forces of the 2011 Budget Control Act—passed to end a standoff between Obama and Republican congressional leaders over raising the federal debt ceiling. The 2011 BCA created automatic spending cuts—so-called sequestration—while putting both defense and domestic spending limits in place.

In a joint letter in early 2015, Reed and Arizona Republican John McCain, the chairman of the Armed Services Committee, told leaders of the Senate Budget Committee that those limits "which require nearly $1 trillion of defense spending cuts over 10 years... have become a national security crisis of the first order." Reed and McCain acknowledged some legislators "insist that our nation cannot afford to spend more on defense at this time," but added: "[All] four of the military service chiefs testified that American lives are being put at risk by the caps on defense spending mandated in the [Budget Control Act]. At a time when real worldwide threats are growing, we are compounding those dangers with a national security crisis of our own making."

On most issues, Reed has had a solidly liberal voting record. In February 2009, a *National Journal* examination of roll call votes dating to the 1980s found him to be the most liberal senator, slightly ahead of Barbara Boxer of California and Edward Kennedy of Massachusetts. Since then, he has remained among the 20 most-liberal senators. He has supported extensions of unemployment benefits and work-share programs, like those in Rhode Island, in which employers reduce the hours of full-time employees to avoid layoffs during financial hard times. He also has been instrumental in efforts to extend low interest rates for college student loans.

Sometimes overlooked in Reed's high-profile status as a defense expert is his grounding in financial issues. The retirement of South Dakota's Tim Johnson at the end of 2014 made Reed the longest-serving Democrat on the Senate Banking Committee, but he opted instead to become the ranking Democrat on the Armed Services panel. In his Banking Committee portfolio, he played a key role in the crafting of the Dodd-Frank financial regulation law in 2010. When discussion of that legislation began, Reed already had drafted a bill to regulate the derivatives markets. The Banking Committee chairman, Connecticut Democrat Christopher Dodd, asked Reed to work with New Hampshire Republican Judd Gregg on the derivatives issue. According to *Act of Congress,* a book by *Washington Post* editor Robert Kaiser on the making of the Dodd-Frank financial regulatory law, Reed spent months working with Gregg to craft a regulatory framework in the complex area of derivatives—financial contracts based on the value of other assets, from interest rates to corn and soybeans. "Reed was an atypical senator," Kaiser wrote. "A small, compact man with a formidable intellect, he did mountains of homework. He mastered complicated issues."

Two years earlier, as his home state was buffeted by the Great Recession—Rhode Island had one of the highest unemployment rates in the nation, and was among the top 10 states in terms of subprime mortgage foreclosures—Reed played a quiet, but major role in securing an agreement on a foreclosure rescue bill. Reed, accompanied by Dodd, met with Alabama Sen. Richard Shelby, the Banking Committee's top Republican, to broker the final terms of the 2008 foreclosure rescue plan. It widened access to federally insured mortgages without tapping taxpayer money—a condition on which Shelby insisted—while, at the same time, allowing Reed to include an affordable housing fund that he had been seeking since his reelection to a second term in 2002. Noting that Reed had finally found the right political opportunity to turn the latter proposal into reality, a fellow Banking Committee member, New York Democrat Charles Schumer, told *The New York Times,* "Once again, Jack does it in his quiet, steadfast way, and it is extremely effective."

In 2005, Reed, whom friends long joked was married to his work, married for the first time in his mid-50s. His wife, Julia Hart, was working in the Senate's Interparliamentary Services Office when she and Reed met in 2002—on a congressional delegation trip to Afghanistan. The couple has a daughter who turned eight in 2015. Reed holds a Senate seat in which the previous occupants have enjoyed long tenures. Green served 24 years and retired at the age of 93; Pell served for 36, retiring at 77. Based on those precedents—and Rhode Island's blue voting patterns—Reed, beginning his fourth term, could remain a quiet force in the Senate for years to come.

Junior Senator

Sheldon Whitehouse (D)

Elected 2006, term expires Jan. 2019, 2nd term; b. Oct. 20, 1955, New York, NY; Yale U., B.A. 1978, U. of VA, J.D. 1982; Episcopalian; married (Sandra); 2 children.

Elected Office: RI atty. gen., 1999-2003.

Professional Career: RI special asst. atty. gen., 1984-90; Legal counsel, Gov. Bruce Sundlun, 1991; Policy dir., Gov. Bruce Sundlun, 1992; Dir., RI Dept. of Business Regulation, 1992-94; U.S. atty. for RI, 1994-98; Practicing atty., 2003-06.

DC Office: 530 HSOB, 20510, 202-224-2921; Fax: 202-228-6362; Website: whitehouse.senate.gov.

State Offices: Providence, 401-453-5294.

Committees: *Aging (Special). Budget. Environment & Public Works:* Clean Air & Nuclear Safety; Fisheries, Water & Wildlife (RMM); Transportation & Infrastructure. *Health, Education, Labor & Pensions:* Employment & Workplace Safety; Primary Health & Retirement Security. *Judiciary:* Crime & Terrorism (RMM); Oversight, Agency Action, Federal Rights & Federal Courts; Privacy, Technology & the Law; the Constitution.

Group Ratings

	ADA	ACLU	AFL-CIO	LCV	ITI	COC	HAFA	ACU	CFG	FRC
2014	95%	93%	–	80%	100%	25%	2%	4%	19%	0%
2013	100%	C	100%	92%	C	50%	C	4%	9%	C

National Journal Ratings

	2013 LIB	—	2013 CONS
Economic	74%	—	25%
Social	73%	—	0%
Foreign	71%	—	0%
Composite	82%	—	18%

Key Votes of the 113th Congress

1. Sandy storm spending	Y	5. Student Loan Rates	N	9. Bipartisan Budget Deal	Y
2. Chuck Hagel Confirmation	Y	6. Employee Non-Discrim'n Act	Y	10. Farm Bill Conference Rept.	N
3. Gun Background Checks	Y	7. Senate Vote on Judgeships	N	11. Unempl. Comp. Extension	Y
4. Immigration Reform	Y	8. Defense Dept. Spending	Y	12. Keystone Pipeline	N

Election Results

2012 general	Sheldon Whitehouse (D)	271,034	(65%)	$4,933,336	$4,103	$183,165
	B. Barrett Hinckley (R)	146,222	(35%)	$1,667,195	$9,084	
2012 primary	Sheldon Whitehouse (D)	unopposed				

In May 2015, Democrat Sheldon Whitehouse, Rhode Island's junior senator, delivered the 100th in a series of weekly Senate floor speeches on the dangers he believes are posed by climate change—a green poster with a satellite photo of Earth and the slogan "Time To Wake Up" perched on an easel behind him. The ritual served to underscore that Whitehouse, since first being elected in 2006 from one of the country's bluest states, has emerged as one of the Senate's most vocal liberals—particularly on climate change, but also on other hot-button topics ranging from gun control to campaign finance reform to income equality.

Whitehouse is only the latest in a series of outspoken congressional liberals in recent decades to come from a background of wealth and privilege. He is a descendant of Charles Crocker, one of California's "Big Four" men who built the Central Pacific Railroad; the latter connected with the Union Pacific line at Promontory Summit, Utah, in 1869 to form the nation's first transcontinental railroad. Whitehouse's grandfather was a diplomat, and so was his father, Charles Whitehouse, a World War II Marine Corps pilot who was U.S. ambassador to Laos and Thailand in the 1970s. Sheldon Whitehouse was born in New York City and spent his formative years overseas, including in Cambodia, South Africa, the Philippines, and Guinea; as a teenager, he taught English to Vietnamese children in Saigon. He graduated from St. Paul's preparatory school, Yale University, and the University of Virginia Law School.

After clerking for an appeals court judge, Whitehouse moved to Rhode Island in 1984 to take a job as an assistant state attorney general. He was appointed a top staffer to newly elected Democratic Gov. Bruce Sundlun in 1991, and subsequently served two years as the head of the state's department of business regulation under Sundlun. In 1994, on the recommendation of Democratic Sen. Claiborne Pell, a family friend, Whitehouse was appointed U.S. attorney for Rhode Island. Whitehouse launched an undercover investigation that resulted in the conviction of Providence Mayor Buddy Cianci on corruption charges. He also focused on environmental cleanup, leading an investigation that resulted in the largest fine in state history for an oil spill in Narragansett Bay.

In 1998, Whitehouse ran for state attorney general. In the three-way Democratic primary, his opponents portrayed him as an inexperienced, fox-hunting patrician trying to buy his way into public office. But Whitehouse was better known in the state than his two opponents, and he got the nomination, capturing about half of the total vote. In the general election, the Republican nominee, state Treasurer Nancy Mayer forced Whitehouse to concede he had tried drugs as a student, and questioned whether he was tough enough for the job. Whitehouse later told *The Providence Journal:* "The book on me was, 'Smart kid, works hard, but, you know, has no common touch, can't relate to people, will be a disaster.' In fact, I got advice from some political types to run sort of a Rose Garden strategy. You know, 'Don't go out, don't let people see you, 'cause if they see you, they're not going to like you. Just mail your resume around, you know, and spend a lot of money on television.'" But the tide began to turn after Mayer ran highly negative ads on the drug issue that backfired in the absence of evidence that the incident was more than a short chapter from Whitehouse's distant past. He overwhelmingly won the election, 67%-33%.

By 2002, Whitehouse was viewed as a strong contender for governor. He ran but lost the Democratic primary by 926 votes to former state Sen. Myrth York, who outspent Whitehouse by 2-1. York, who had been the Democratic gubernatorial nominee in 1994 and 1998, went on to lose for a third time in November against Republican Donald Carcieri. The Democratic primary battle clearly left scars: When Whitehouse challenged Republican incumbent Lincoln Chafee in 2006, York broke with her party and endorsed Chafee.

Whitehouse had considered running for the Senate in 1999, when four-term incumbent John Chafee announced he would not seek a fifth term. But then, Chafee—who had been a roommate of Whitehouse's father while they were undergraduates at Yale—died in November 1999. Republican Gov. Lincoln Almond appointed the senator's son, Lincoln Chafee, then mayor of Warwick, to fill the vacancy, and Chafee the following year was elected to a full term. In the Senate, Chafee sided with Democrats often enough that there was frequent speculation that he would switch parties. (He would later run successfully for governor as an independent, before becoming a Democrat and announcing a longshot bid for the 2016 presidential nomination.) In 2006, Chafee—still a Republican—was opposed in the primary by Cranston Mayor Steve Laffey, a conservative and a sharp-elbowed campaigner backed by a national anti-tax group, the Club for Growth. Though Chafee won the September primary, 54%-46%, he had little cash left after that fight.

After deciding to take on Lincoln Chafee in 2006, Whitehouse had a relatively easy time in the Democratic primary. The general election pitted two candidates of fairly similar views who shared an upper-crust background: Chafee was an offshoot of one of Rhode Island's most prominent families, whose members had held high office in the state going back to the 1870s. In 2006, there was little daylight between Chafee and Whitehouse on the issues—both backed federal funding of embryonic stem cell research, abortion rights, and gun control. So Whitehouse campaigned against the then-unpopular Bush administration, running ads with the tagline, "Finally, a Whitehouse in Washington you can trust." Whitehouse won, 54%-46%. He overwhelmingly won Providence and the fading industrial cities—Central Falls, Pawtucket, and Woonsocket—in the northeastern section of the state. Chafee won in Warwick, where he had been mayor, while also carrying a couple of major jurisdictions in the less populated western section of the state. The two candidates ran close to each other in the towns that line the east side of Narragansett Bay.

Whitehouse was one of eight new Democratic senators whose election gave the party a majority in the Senate. He quickly gained recognition as a fierce critic of the Bush administration in President George W. Bush's final two years in office. As a former U.S. attorney himself, Whitehouse blasted Attorney General Alberto Gonzalez for firing U.S. attorneys for what Democrats alleged were political motivations. After Gonzalez resigned, Whitehouse opposed the nomination of Michael Mukasey as attorney general for refusing to say whether water boarding was an illegal tactic against terrorism detainees.

With President Barack Obama in office, Whitehouse became a stalwart administration defender. His voting record put him on the Senate's liberal end: *National Journal* vote rankings for both 2012 and 2013 rated him among the Senate's top 20 most liberal members. In 2011, he gave the keynote speech at the Netroots Nation conference of liberal bloggers, and successfully worked to lure the following year's conference to Providence. During the first year of the Obama administration, he supported the $787 billion economic stimulus bill, and even said he would like to see a second stimulus bill focused entirely on the nation's infrastructure. Later, Whitehouse loudly clamored for a Senate vote on the administration's so-called "Buffett Rule" imposing higher taxes on the wealthiest Americans. Republicans blocked it from clearing the necessary 60-vote hurdle in April 2012.

Whitehouse's tendency toward hyperbole has occasionally sparked controversy. He irked conservatives when he said on the Senate floor that opposition to Obama's health care reform measure was driven in part by "right-wing militias and Aryan support groups." Later, in October 2012, he charged that House Budget Committee Chairman Paul Ryan's budget blueprint "gets rid of Medicare in 10 years and turns it into a voucher program," which the fact-checking site *PolitiFact* rated as false.

PolitiFact has been kinder to his regular floor speeches on climate change, rating as "mostly true" claims he has made on issues ranging from rising sea levels to warmer oceans to eroding coastlines. "We're not a very big state, so we don't have a lot of land to give away to the sea," Whitehouse told the *Associated Press*, noting that Rhode Island finds itself "on the receiving end" of the climate change problem because it doesn't have coal mines or oil drilling. He began to give his weekly speeches on climate change in January 2013, accusing Congress of "sleepwalking through history." At the end of 2014, he claimed he had never had to give the same speech twice because of the breadth of the topic. Whitehouse credits his wife, a marine scientist, with helping him to recognize the importance of oceans in everyone's lives. In the process, he has become perhaps Congress' most persistent voice on the hazards of climate change. "I consider myself vocal [on climate change], but nobody is more vocal than Sheldon Whitehouse," said Connecticut Sen. Richard Blumenthal, a fellow Democratic liberal. "He's in a league of his own."

In 2013, Whitehouse and now-retired California Democratic Rep. Henry Waxman, long a key congressional player on environmental issues, formed a climate change task force. He is also pushing for creation of a National Endowment for the Oceans, Coasts and Great Lakes, pointing to the example of the late Rhode Island Sen. Claiborne Pell—a Democrat who was largely responsible for creation of the National Endowment for the Arts and the National Endowment for the Humanities. Whitehouse's passion on this topic is such that he suggested, in a May 2015 op-ed piece in *The Washington Post,* that the fossil fuel industry's efforts to discredit climate science may constitute deliberate deception similar to what the tobacco industry perpetrated in previous decades. In 2006, a federal judge found the tobacco industry guilty of fraud in a civil lawsuit brought under the Racketeer Influenced and Corrupt Organizations Act (RICO), and Whitehouse contended fossil fuel companies may be a ripe target for a civil lawsuit under RICO as well.

But some of Whitehouse's proposals, such as imposing a carbon fee on industries that emit carbon pollution, would face steep political hurdles even in a Democratic-controlled Congress, and he has pursued some more conciliatory approaches to advance his cause. In 2014, Whitehouse formed an alliance with West Virginia Sen. Joe Manchin, a centrist Democrat from a major coal-producing state. Manchin visited Rhode Island to see the effect of climate change firsthand and Whitehouse toured coal and energy resources in West Virginia. They made plans to work together on legislation to invest in technology for cleaner fossil fuel energy. Whitehouse has shown an ability to reach across the aisle on other issues. When cyber security legislation became hung up in partisan battles in 2012, Whitehouse worked with conservative Arizona GOP Sen. Jon Kyl to hammer out a compromise, which Senate Majority Leader Harry Reid then refused to advance. As head of the Senate Judiciary Subcommittee on Crime and Terrorism in 2014, Whitehouse also worked with the subcommittee's ranking member, South Carolina Republican Lindsey Graham, on cybersecurity legislation.

Much of Whitehouse's energy, however, has been devoted to keeping the flame alive on a host of liberal causes unlikely to be enacted into law anytime soon. He has become the ideological heir to former Wisconsin Democratic Sen. Russ Feingold, who lost a bid for reelection in 2010, in seeking to control the influence of money in elections. He has taken on gun rights advocates: When the National Rifle Association's Wayne LaPierre asserted at a January 2013 committee hearing that only 62 firearm purchases denied by the federal instant-check system had been referred for prosecution, Whitehouse shot back that the actual number was 11,700 in 2012, or "a lot more than 62."

Conservative groups have pushed back on occasion. In June 2014, a tea party group filed a complaint with the Senate Ethics Committee, accusing Whitehouse of breaking ethics rules by pressuring the Obama administration to target conservative groups, according to *The Hill.* The Tea Party Patriots pointed to an April 2013 hearing at which it charged Whitehouse had "publicly berated" the Internal Revenue Service and Justice Department for not prosecuting conservative groups, classified under tax law as social welfare organizations, for engaging in electioneering activity. The complaint was filed about a year after controversy broke out over the IRS targeting tea party groups for audits. Whitehouse defended his actions as proper, with a spokesman saying the senator "noticed that certain legal declarations appear to have violated [federal statutes] making false statements a crime ... Bringing those potential crimes to the attention of the relevant federal authorities is perfectly appropriate for a senator, indeed any citizen who thinks they may be witness to a crime."

Whitehouse entered the 2012 campaign season as a clear favorite in heavily Democratic Rhode Island. His Republican opponent was software executive Barry Hinckley, who campaigned as a moderate on social issues despite calling for the repeal of the health care reform law and supporting offshore oil drilling. But he faced an uphill battle, and Whitehouse won 65%-35%. When Attorney General Eric Holder announced his resignation in the fall of 2014, Whitehouse's name surfaced briefly as a possible candidate to replace him. Whitehouse quickly disavowed interest, saying in a statement to *Politico,* "It would be a great honor to be considered for attorney general of the United States, but my heart's desire is representing Rhode Island in the Senate, and I have no interest in other positions."

FIRST DISTRICT

David Cicilline (D)

Elected 2010, 3rd term; b. July 15, 1961, Providence; Brown U., B.A. 1983, Georgetown U., J.D. 1986; Jewish; single.

Elected Office: RI House, 1995-2003; Providence mayor, 2003-11.

Professional Career: Public defender, 1986-87; Practicing atty; Faculty, Roger Williams Law Schl.

DC Office: 2244 RHOB, 20515, 202-225-4911; Fax: 202-225-3290; Website: cicilline.house.gov.

State Offices: Pawtucket, 401-729-5600.

Committees: *Foreign Affairs:* Africa, Global Health, Global Human Rights & Int'l Organizations; Middle East & North Africa. *Judiciary:* Courts, Intellectual Property, & the Internet; Regulatory Reform, Commercial & Antitrust Law.

Group Ratings

	ADA	ACLU	AFL-CIO	LCV	ITI	COC	HAFA	ACU	CFG	FRC
2014	95%	88%	–	94%	40%	38%	18%	8%	11%	0%
2013	90%	C	95%	96%	C	38%	C	16%	19%	C

National Journal Ratings

	2013 LIB	—	2013 CONS
Economic	88%	—	12%
Social	93%	—	0%
Foreign	79%	—	20%
Composite	88%	—	12%

Key Votes of the 113th Congress

1. Sandy storm spending	Y	5. Medical Marijuana	Y	9. Syrian Rebels Training	N
2. Violence Against Women Act	Y	6. Farm Bill	N	10. Keystone pipeline	N
3. Guantanamo Bay Detainee	Y	7. Afghanistan Combat	Y	11. Immigration Exec. Action	N
4. Abortion 20-week ban	N	8. NSA Phone Data Collection	Y	12. Bipartisan budget deal	N

Election Results

2014 general	David Cicilline (D)	87,060	(60%)	$1,212,281
	Cormick Lynch (R)	58,877	(40%)	$12,853
2014 primary	David Cicilline (D)	33,350	(62%)	
	Matt Fecteau (D)	20,460	(38%)	

Prior winning percentages: 2012 (53%), 2010 (51%)

Population		Race and Ethnicity		Income	
Total:	528,341	White	71.7%	Median income:	$50,796
Urban:	47.2%	Latino	14.7%		(228 of 435)
Suburban:	52.8%	Black	6.4%	Under $50,000	49.2%
Rural:	0.0%	Asian	3.7%	$50,000-$99,999:	29.4%
Land area:	274	Two races	2.4%	$100,000-$199,999:	16.8%
Pop/sq. mi.:	1,927.5	White Ethnic	64.1%	$200,000 or more:	4.7%
Born in state:	51.4%			Poverty Rate	16.5%
		Education			
Age Groups		H.S. grad or less:	43.1%	**Work**	
Under 18:	20.1%	Some college:	25.5%	White collar:	36.0%
18 to 34:	25.1%	College degree, 4 yr.:	18.7%	Blue collar:	44.2%
35 to 64:	39.1%	Post-grad study:	12.8%	Sales and service:	19.9%
Over 64:	15.7%				
		Military		Govt. workers:	10.5%
		Veterans/active duty:	7.8%		

Eastern Rhode Island: Parts of Providence, Newport

The 1st Congressional District is the eastern half of Rhode Island, divided from the state's other congressional district by a boundary line that cuts through the state capital of Providence and extends about 40 miles from Woonsocket along the Massachusetts border to Newport and Little Compton

Voter Turnout	
2013 Total Citizen 18+	380,716
2014 House Turnout	146,353
2014 Turnout as % CVAP	38.4%
2012 Turnout as % CVAP	56.3%

along the Atlantic Ocean. The district takes in much of Providence, including the elite East Side and College Hill around Brown University. In recent years, the once down-on-its-luck city has been revived, with a more accessible waterfront, active night life, and restoration of neighborhoods around the state capitol. The district captures all of next-door Pawtucket, whose Slater Mill is known as the birthplace of the American Industrial Revolution. Hasbro, the nation's second-largest toy company, has partnered with Hollywood to produce blockbuster films like *Transformers* and *Battleship* based on its products.

The onetime textile mill towns of the Blackstone Valley, Woonsocket and Central Falls are in the 1st, along with high-income Barrington and Bristol along the eastern coast of Narragansett Bay. To the south, on the ocean, is the old city of Newport, with its restored 18th-century houses and summer "cottages" that are more like mansions. Newport has been home to the America's Cup races and has hosted a popular jazz festival every summer since 1954, with productions occasionally elsewhere. It is also the site of the oldest synagogue in North America, where George Washington once told a congregation that the United States gives "to bigotry no sanction, to persecution no assistance."

Budget woes hit hard in Rhode Island's towns and cities. Central Falls declared bankruptcy in August 2011, becoming the second city in the nation to exhaust its pension fund; it significantly cut benefits for retirees under court direction. In 2012, Providence, on the brink of bankruptcy, averted fiscal disaster by cutting back pensions and education spending, and raising property taxes. Ethnically, the 1st District is the more

2012 Presidential Vote		
Barack Obama (D)	141,306	(66%)
Mitt Romney (R)	68,723	(32%)
2008 Presidential Vote		
Barack Obama (D)	149,420	(68%)
John McCain (R)	71,436	(32%)
Cook Partisan Voting Index:	D+15	

French-Canadian and the less Italian of Rhode Island's two congressional districts. Politically, it is the more strongly Democratic district, though each should be secure.

David Cicilline (D)

Democrat David Cicilline was elected in 2010 to fill the seat of retiring Democratic Rep. Patrick Kennedy. The former mayor of Providence, Cicilline's popularity plummeted with news of his messy stewardship of the city's finances, but he recovered in time to win reelection at home and establish a socially liberal niche as a gay lawmaker.

Cicilline was born in Providence, the middle of five children. His parents eloped when his mother was 16 and his father 17. His mother is Jewish and his father Catholic, and Cicilline grew up celebrating the traditions of both religions. He now identifies as Jewish. His father was a criminal-defense attorney. Cicilline was interested in politics from a young age. When he was 10, he wrote letters to his elected representatives when he had something on his mind, and at 14 he had his parents drop him off at city council meetings so he could participate in the public comment period.

Cicilline attended Brown University, where he majored in political science and founded, along with classmate John F. Kennedy Jr., a chapter of the College Democrats. He was active in student government and worked two jobs waiting tables. Cicilline came out as gay in college and says he was fortunate to have a supportive family. After getting a law degree from Georgetown University, he worked in Washington as a public defender for juveniles. In addition to defending the youths in court, Cicilline sometimes enrolled them in school, substance-abuse treatment and other support services.

He returned to Rhode Island to campaign for the state Senate. He lost that bid but ran for the state House two years later and won. In the legislature, he supported a variety of liberal policies. He pushed to raise the legal age to buy a gun from 13 to 18, introduced a bill creating a needle exchange program for drug users, and fought attempts to restrict abortion rights.

In 2002, Cicilline was elected to the first of two terms as mayor of Providence, becoming the first openly gay mayor of a state capital city. He campaigned as a reformer, promising to clean up the city after the two-decade reign of Buddy Cianci, who was convicted of corruption. In office, Cicilline sought to end cronyism in the police department and expanded after-school programs. As the city's revenue shriveled in the recession, he laid off nearly 500 city employees and raised property taxes. Cicilline also served as president of the National Conference of Democratic Mayors.

When Kennedy decided not to seek reelection, Cicilline ran for the seat. He won the primary with 37% of the vote against three opponents. In the general election, Cicilline campaigned as a pragmatist focused on creating jobs. Republican state Rep. John Loughlin focused on the state's poor economy and said that he would balance the federal budget. Cicilline spent $2 million compared to $800,000 for Loughlin, and won 51%-45%. The unexpectedly close outcome in a heavily Democratic district highlighted Republican strength in 2010 and some residual problems for Cicilline.

In 2011, Cicilline became the fourth openly gay member of Congress. He established a solidly liberal voting record but also co-founded the Common Ground Caucus, a bipartisan group of House members that meet regularly to foster greater cooperation. He spoke out forcefully against proposed GOP budget cuts to programs for low-income citizens, and he tried without success to amend spending bills to take money from Afghanistan reconstruction and apply it to deficit reduction.

Cicilline spent his first term under a cloud. *The Providence Journal* reported in early 2011 that the city had a $180 million deficit for the next two fiscal years and that its reserve fund was almost depleted. A nonpartisan bond rating agency, Fitch Ratings, downgraded the city's rating and criticized Cicilline's administration for "imprudent budgeting decisions." Cicilline said he was forced to use reserve money to prevent sharp cuts to city programs. A Brown University poll showed his approval at an unhealthy 17 percent, and he went on an apology tour to acknowledge he should have been more forthcoming about Providence's fiscal problems.

Cicilline serves on the Foreign Affairs and Judiciary committees. He has made immigration reform a priority. The current system is broken, he told a January 2014 rally at a South Providence church. "It hurts families. It hurts our communities and it undermines opportunities for economic growth. And we need to fix it now."

His liberal agenda likely has no prospects in a Republican-controlled Congress, but it gives Democrats and progressives talking points in the political debate. In June 2015, following the shooting deaths of nine people in a Charleston South Carolina church, he filed legislation to prohibit gun purchases by children, people with a criminal record and those with a mental illness. "While I understand that some in Congress would prefer not to have this debate right now, it is critical that we find the political will to finally address these urgent concerns," Cicilline said. The same month, he filed a bill for automatic voter registration in the 50 states, which shifts the burden for registering from the individual to the state. The proposal gives citizens a 21-day period to opt out of registration.

In 2012, he turned back a Democratic challenge from businessman Anthony Gemma, who was the runner-up in the 2010 primary. Gemma accused Cicilline of voter fraud. The incumbent called the allegation "absolutely absurd" and won 62%-38%. His general election rival was Republican Brendan Doherty, a former state police superintendent. Cicilline outspent Doherty, $2.4 million to $1.5 million, and each received generous party support. Cicilline sought to link Doherty to GOP presidential nominee Mitt Romney, which resonated in the Democratic-dominated district. He again won modestly, 53%-41%, while President Barack Obama took the district with 66% of the vote. He improved his performance in 2014 with a 60% win over Republican Cormick Lynch, an Iraq war veteran who was outspent 100-to-1.

SECOND DISTRICT

Jim Langevin (D)

Elected 2000, 8th term; b. April 22, 1964, Providence; RI Col., B.A. 1990, Harvard U., M.P.A. 1994; Catholic; single.

Elected Office: RI House, 1989-95; RI secy. of st., 1995-2001.

DC Office: 109 CHOB, 20515, 202-225-2735; Fax: 202-225-5976; Website: langevin.house.gov.

State Offices: Warwick, 401-732-9400.

Committees: *Armed Services:* Emerging Threats & Capabilities (RMM); Seapower & Projection Forces. *Homeland Security:* Cybersecurity, Infrastructure Protection & Security Technologies.

Group Ratings

	ADA	ACLU	AFL-CIO	LCV	ITI	COC	HAFA	ACU	CFG	FRC
2014	80%	77%	–	94%	80%	43%	14%	8%	13%	0%
2013	75%	C	95%	86%	C	46%	C	13%	13%	C

National Journal Ratings

	2013 LIB	—	2013 CONS
Economic	89%	—	10%
Social	87%	—	7%
Foreign	65%	—	35%
Composite	82%	—	19%

Key Votes of the 113th Congress

1. Sandy storm spending	Y	5. Medical Marijuana	Y	9. Syrian Rebels Training	Y
2. Violence Against Women Act	Y	6. Farm Bill	N	10. Keystone pipeline	N
3. Guantanamo Bay Detainee	Y	7. Afghanistan Combat	N	11. Immigration Exec. Action	N
4. Abortion 20-week ban	N	8. NSA Phone Data Collection	N	12. Bipartisan budget deal	Y

Election Results

2014 general	James R. Langevin (D)	105,716	(62%)	$811,117
	Rhue Reis (R)	63,844	(38%)	$13,548
2014 primary	James R. Langevin (D)	unopposed		

Prior winning percentages: 2012 (56%), 2010 (60%), 2008 (70%), 2006 (73%), 2004 (75%), 2002 (76%), 2000 (62%)

Population		Race and Ethnicity		Income	
Total:	523,170	White	80.0%	Median income:	$61,822
Urban:	34.7%	Latino	11.0%		*(101 of 435)*
Suburban:	64.1%	Black	3.9%	Under $50,000	40.9%
Rural:	1.1%	Asian	2.6%	$50,000-$99,999:	31.0%
Land area:	655	Two races	1.8%	$100,000-$199,999:	23.2%
Pop/sq. mi.:	799.2	White Ethnic	71.9%	$200,000 or more:	4.8%
Born in state:	64.2%			Poverty Rate	12.1%
		Education			
Age Groups		H.S. grad or less:	38.4%	**Work**	
Under 18:	20.3%	Some college:	28.3%	White collar:	37.7%
18 to 34:	23.1%	College degree, 4 yr.:	20.9%	Blue collar:	44.2%
35 to 64:	41.2%	Post-grad study:	12.4%	Sales and service:	18.1%
Over 64:	15.3%				
		Military		Govt. workers:	13.7%
		Veterans/active duty:	8.2%		

Western Rhode Island: Parts of Providence, Warwick, Cranston

The 2nd Congressional District is the western half of Rhode Island. Most of its population is concentrated in towns like working-class Cranston and more upscale Warwick, which, despite their British names, are inhabited mostly by people with Irish, Italian, French and Portuguese surnames. Cranston

Voter Turnout	
2013 Total Citizen 18+	397,109
2014 House Turnout	169,904
2014 Turnout as % CVAP	42.8%
2012 Turnout as % CVAP	59.4%

is reportedly the inspiration for FOX's long-running animated comedy *Family Guy*, set in the fictitious town of Quahog. The 2nd includes the fastest-growing part of the state, South County, which is not an official place but the common name for Rhode Island south of East Greenwich. This area takes in the affluent suburbs and beachfront communities along Narragansett Bay, the Kingston home of the University of Rhode Island, and the area around Westerly, where many residents work at the General Dynamics Electric Boat shipyards in Groton, Connecticut. Electric Boat also employs about 3,300 people several miles up the coast in Quonset, Rhode Island. That includes about 450 slots that were created in 2014 for work on new Virginia-class attack submarines, which were scheduled for two-a-year production for the next five years. The April 2015 unemployment rate of 4.9% in the state's second-largest city, Warwick, was considerably lower than the statewide rate of 6.1% at that time.

Another important segment of the economy is sailing and tourism. In addition to Rhode Island's rolling farmland (although there is not that much acreage), the district includes the communities along the bay and the ocean, where many people still make their living building boats and catching fish. After years of discussion, regulatory hurdles and opposition from local residents, construc-

2012 Presidential Vote		
Barack Obama (D)	138,371	(60%)
Mitt Romney (R)	88,481	(38%)
2008 Presidential Vote		
Barack Obama (D)	147,123	(60%)
John McCain (R)	93,951	(39%)
Cook Partisan Voting Index:	D+8	

tion began in April 2015 on the nation's first off-shore wind farm near Block Island, a project that the state hoped would position it as a leader in renewable energy. The five-turbine, 30-megawatt facility would use a submarine cable to connect to the mainland. Developers planned to follow up with a second larger and less costly farm.

This remains a comfortably Democratic district, which President Barack Obama won with 60% in 2012.

Jim Langevin (D)

Democrat Jim Langevin, elected in 2000, is the first quadriplegic to serve in Congress and he has worked on behalf of others with similar physical challenges. He has been an active and respected participant on cybersecurity and other national security issues as a member of the Armed Services and other national security committees.

Langevin grew up in Warwick and as a boy hoped to become an FBI agent. But in 1980, at age 16, when he was a police cadet in the Boy Scout Explorer program, he was shot by a police officer when a gun accidentally discharged. The bullet went through his upper back and throat and damaged the upper part of his spinal column, making him a quadriplegic. After the accident, Langevin received $2.2 million in a settlement with the city of Warwick. Although he disliked the attention it brought him, he says he became determined to do something meaningful with his life. He worked as an intern in the state House and for Democratic Sen. Claiborne Pell. In 1988, while a student at Rhode Island College, he was elected to the state House of Representatives, where he styled himself a reformer. After finishing his undergraduate degree, he got a master's degree in public administration from the John F. Kennedy School of Government at Harvard. In 1994, Langevin was elected Rhode Island's secretary of state.

When Democratic Rep. Bob Weygand ran for the Senate in 2000, Langevin ran for his House seat. In a four-way Democratic primary, Langevin's most strenuous opposition came from Kate Coyne-McCoy, executive director of the Rhode Island Association of Social Workers, who made an issue of Langevin's opposition to abortion rights. Although Langevin had support from many Democratic leaders and some unions, and won the party's endorsement at the April convention, Coyne-McCoy waged an aggressive campaign financed by unions, health care workers and EMILY's List.

Langevin called her positions "unrealistic and extreme." Coyne-McCoy said, "There's no such thing as being too liberal." He favored less stringent forms of gun control and said, "No one has to tell me how dangerous weapons can be." He spoke often about the accident that paralyzed him. "Certainly, being disabled is part of who I am, but it doesn't define me," he said. Langevin won the primary. In the general election, he was opposed by Rodney Driver, nominee of the Conscience for Congress Party and a retired mathematics professor who spent $300,000 of his retirement savings on his campaign. Langevin won easily, 62%-21%.

The House chamber in the Capitol was made wheelchair-accessible for Langevin, with two of the fixed seats in the front removed to give him space to maneuver and to talk to colleagues. At his urging, then-Democratic Speaker Nancy Pelosi agreed to more far-reaching structural changes in 2009 to make all parts of the chamber, including the speaker's rostrum, accessible. In July 2010, on the 20th anniversary of the Americans with Disabilities Act, Langevin became the first person in a wheelchair to preside over the House. When an audit in 2012 revealed that sidewalks around the House offices were far out of ADA compliance, he pledged to address the issue.

Langevin, a member of Democratic Rep. Steny Hoyer's senior whip team, has been liberal on economic issues and more centrist on cultural and foreign policy issues, an apt reflection of his district's ethnic communities. In 2005, he was one of only three House Democrats from New England to join conservatives in the controversial case of Terri Schiavo, a severely brain-damaged Florida woman at the center of a court battle over removing her life-sustaining feeding tube. But he returned to the liberal fold on embryonic stem cell research, which was opposed by anti-abortion groups. Langevin, who took the view that the research might alleviate suffering from certain diseases and injuries, drew heat from the Roman Catholic bishop of Providence for his position.

Langevin has sponsored several gun control bills, including increased inspections of firearms dealers' sales records and stiffened penalties for dealers who have been untruthful. He has called universal health care coverage his top priority. In 2006, Langevin won passage of a bipartisan bill that established a respite program for caregivers of individuals with special needs. He was a staunch supporter of the Democrats' health care initiative in 2009 and 2010, which sought to cover millions of uninsured households.

On the Armed Services Committee, where he chaired the Subcommittee on Strategic Forces, Langevin sponsored a measure in 2010 allowing the Pentagon to convert jobs held by private contractors to full-time civilian positions. He led efforts to boost spending for missile defense systems above the level requested by the Obama administration. He worked successfully in 2012 with Connecticut independent Sen. Joe Lieberman to thwart the administration's proposed cut in production of Virginia-class submarines in Connecticut and Rhode Island. He has been the ranking Democrat on the Emerging Threats and Capabilities Subcommittee.

Langevin has been the chief House sponsor of a bill to establish cybersecurity offices in the White House and Homeland Security Department and give the president emergency powers to act during a cybersecurity crisis. The House passed the bill in 2010, but it died in the Senate. He later sought to amend the fiscal 2012 defense authorization bill for the new office, but he failed on a largely party-line vote. After being term-limited on the House Intelligence Committee, he returned in 2015 to the Homeland Security Committee where he is dealing with some similar issues. In June 2015, he called for the resignation of Katherine Archuleta, director of the Office of Personnel Management, after she failed to take responsibility or suggest steps to respond to the massive cyberattack on OPM records for millions of federal employees. Her failure to create a risk-based cyber strategy was "simply unacceptable," Langevin said.

In January 2015, he was listed among 35 non-freshmen members of the House who have never had their own bill enacted. His aides and sympathetic observers noted that Langevin has contributed to numerous bills that have had multiple authors. Also, he has served only four years in the majority in a chamber where minority-party members find it more difficult to claim sponsorship of enacted bills.

State and national Democrats urged Langevin to challenge Republican Sen. Lincoln Chafee in 2006, but abortion rights groups objected to his candidacy. Democrat Sheldon Whitehouse challenged Chafee and won. Langevin has not faced serious reelection challenges.

★ SOUTH CAROLINA ★

History is inescapable anywhere, but especially so in the South—as Americans were reminded once again in 2015, when South Carolina vaulted into the headlines for something very current, and also very old. A gunman with a history of white supremacist beliefs entered a historic African-American church in Charleston, sat down for Bible study, and then systematically gunned down nine black worshippers—including the pastor, state Sen. Clementa Pinckney. Amid the mourning, an old debate about an old subject—race and Confederate heritage—reemerged. Critics said the state should finally do what it had previously balked at doing—remove the Confederate battle flag from the state capitol grounds in Columbia, where it had flown, in one way or another, since the heat of the civil-rights conflict in 1962. Republican Gov. Nikki Haley, who prior to the killings had shown little interest in following her predecessors' (failed) efforts to pull down the flag, offered her support for removal, and the tide began to turn. The Legislature gave its approval, and on July 10, 2015, the flag was lowered from the statehouse grounds for good.

This was only the latest chapter of South Carolina's history of tragedy and tumult. The state's early influence was the slave-majority, sugar-producing island of Barbados, which produced its original settlers; until 1855, South Carolina was the only southern colony or state with a black majority. Carolina plantation owners were tolerant of some groups, opening their colony to French Huguenots and Sephardic Jews, but they were also slave masters of giant plantations that produced rice and indigo. Indeed, the predecessor of the very same church where the 2015 shootings occurred was the epicenter of the 1822 slave rebellion led by Denmark Vesey, which was ended with the execution of Vesey and numerous lieutenants, as well as the destruction of the church. (Before his death, Pinckney had been active in erecting a memorial to Vesey.) The Lowcountry planters maintained control of the legislature, and therefore the state's two U.S. Senate seats and presidential electors, up through 1860. In that year and the next, South Carolina did more than any other state to precipitate the Civil War. Angry Charlestonians forced the Democratic National Convention to adjourn without selecting a nominee; separate Northern and Southern conventions were then held in other cities. In December, after the election of Abraham Lincoln, the South Carolina legislature voted to secede from the Union and was soon followed by other states. And in April 1861, a cannon on the Battery in Charleston fired on Union troops at Fort Sumter, and so the war came.

Defeat in the Civil War transformed South Carolina. The state's slaves, 57% of the population in 1860, were freed. One of the wealthiest states became one of the poorest. Some 30% of military-age white males were killed. Reconstruction briefly gave black Republicans political control, but the backlash was fierce once federal troops left: strict racial segregation and voting restrictions, like the poll tax, which kept most South Carolinians disenfranchised. As late as 1944, in a state of 2 million people, only 103,000 voted for president, with 88% of them voting Democratic. The Lowcountry languished in poverty, with malnutrition on coastal islands. The one silver lining was architectural—the old mansions of Charleston were not replaced by commercial buildings, and instead were saved by the nation's first local historic preservation movement (and rebuilt after Hurricane Hugo in 1989). Mostly white Upstate South Carolina took the economic and political lead, led by a growing textile industry and politicians like Pitchfork Ben Tillman (governor 1890-94, senator 1895-1918) and his close friend's son, Strom Thurmond (governor 1947-51, senator 1954-2003).

In the last few decades, this once underdeveloped state has taken steps forward. In the 1950s, South Carolina repealed its poll tax, and turnout surged as South Carolina became competitive in the presidential elections of 1952 and 1960. Clemson University was peaceably desegregated during the governorship of Democrat Ernest Hollings (1959-63). Most South Carolina whites opposed integration, but unlike in Alabama and Mississippi the effort was not punctuated by violence. The Civil Rights Act of 1964 and the Voting Rights Act of 1965 ended legal segregation of public accommodations and workplaces and brought blacks into the electorate. Democratic (and later Republican) Sen. Thurmond, who staged a record-setting filibuster of the 1957 Civil Rights Act, started appointing black staffers and a black federal judge in the late 1960s and early 1970s. By 2010, the state elected Haley, a daughter of immigrants from India, and then Tim Scott, an African-American, to the House and later to the Senate, respectively; in this strongly conservative state, their conservative views were

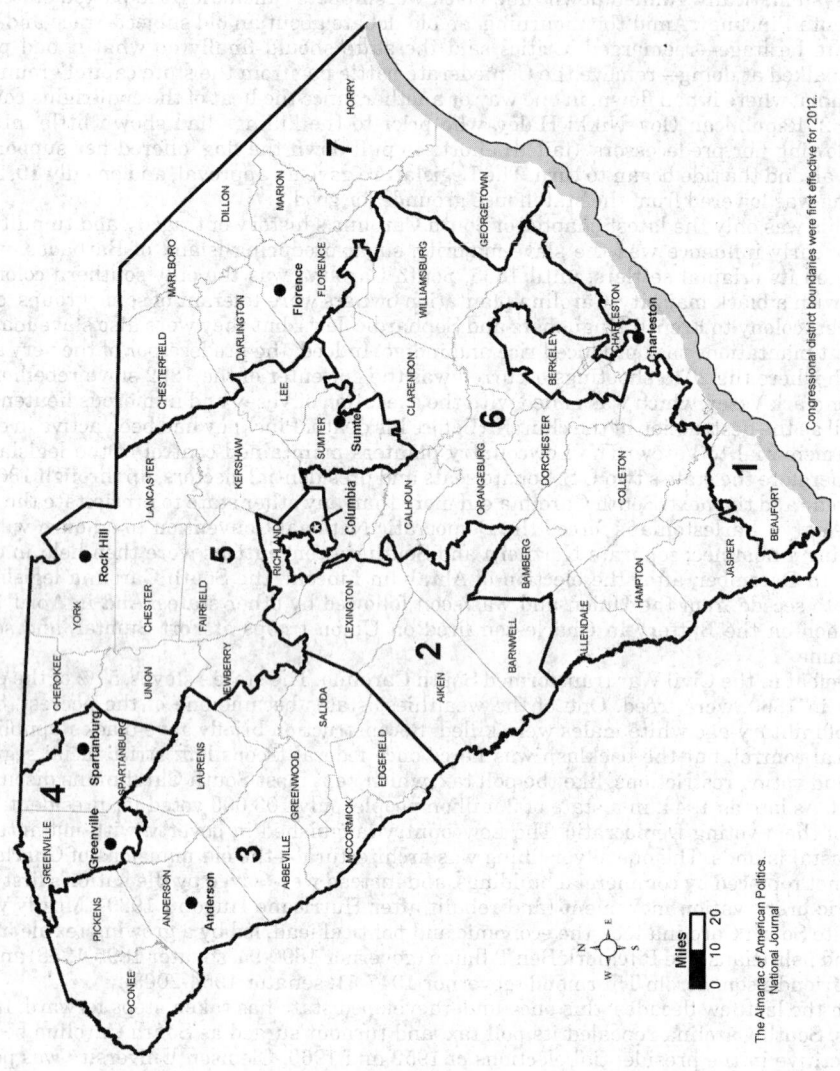

Congressional district boundaries were first effective for 2012.

The Almanac of American Politics.
National Journal

all that mattered. But by 2015, there was only one female state senator in South Carolina, and at the time of the church shooting, South Carolina was one of only five states without a law against hate crimes.

In many ways, the biggest change has been economic. Forty years ago, much of South Carolina's economy depended on military bases and big textile mills in the Interstate 85 corridor around Greenville and Spartanburg. Then South Carolina became the most aggressive state in the South in seeking new industry. It advertised its business climate, with one of the nation's lowest rates of unionization and taxation and a willingness to splurge on tax incentives. Crucially, Hollings as governor spearheaded the creation of the state's technical colleges, which today educate and train more than 250,000 people a year. Michelin opened the first of several South Carolina plants in 1975, and the first BMW vehicles rolled off the Spartanburg assembly line in 1992. As recently as May 2015, Volvo chose a South Carolina site 30 miles northwest of Charleston as the location of its first North American assembly plant, lured by business-friendly laws and $200 million in incentives. Smaller companies built factories throughout much of the Upstate and middle of the state. Navy bases were the mainstay of Charleston's economy in the 1970s, but the bases were closed in the early 1990s. Charleston has not only survived but thrived, thanks in large part to the creative energy of longtime Mayor Joseph P. Riley Jr., first elected in 1975 and reelected to a 10th term in 2011. With a keen aesthetic eye, he has made the city's historic center a magnet for tourists, and he has helped Charleston to become a major port, which is especially important to Michelin and BMW. Meanwhile, shuttered military bases became a center of aircraft production, first with Vought Aircraft and Alenia Aeronautica, and then when Boeing in 2009 chose North Charleston to build a 3,800-worker plant to assemble its 787 Dreamliner.

Such industrial expansion has improved South Carolina's fundamentals, but only to a certain degree. Per capita personal income ranked 48th in the nation in 2014, or 20 percent below the national average. The poverty rate was 17.2 percent, compared to 14.8 nationally. South Carolina ranked in the top one-fifth of states for uninsured residents, and its percentage of residents with a college degree trailed the national average. Unemployment hit a peak of 11.7 percent in the Great Recession and fell only to 6.8 percent by May 2015, more than a percentage point above the national average.

That said, South Carolina's changing economic base has transformed the state from an inward-looking state to a more outward-looking one. Through the 1960s, few people except military personnel moved in. That has changed as the economy has grown. Most of the newcomers are white, largely with conservative attitudes—the state has the sixth largest percentage of "very religious" residents, according to Gallup—but with less attachment to the state's ancient traditions. In 2010, South Carolina's population was 28% black, far below the near-majority of the 1940s, and 5% Hispanic and 1% Asian. The fastest growth in recent years has been in the coastal resort areas around Hilton Head and Myrtle Beach and in suburban counties outside Charleston and Charlotte North Carolina. These booming areas bring in millions of tourists every year, along with thousands of new residents, many of them affluent retirees eager to spend days with pleasant weather on the golf course.

Population		Race and Ethnicity		Income	
Total:	4,774,839	White	63.9%	Median income:	$43,749
Urban:	33.8%	Black	27.7%		*(41 of 50)*
Suburban:	42.9%	Latino	5.2%	Under $50,000	55.2%
Rural:	23.3%	Asian	1.3%	$50,000-$99,999:	29.0%
Land area:	30,061	Two races	1.5%	$100,000-$199,999:	13.3%
Pop/sq. mi.:	158.8	White Ethnic	18.0%	$200,000 or more:	2.6%
Born in state:	57.8%			Poverty Rate	15.0%
		Education			
Age Groups		H.S. grad or less:	43.7%	**Work**	
Under 18:	22.6%	Some college:	30.2%	White collar:	32.8%
18 to 34:	23.1%	College degree, 4 yr.:	16.6%	Blue collar:	43.7%
35 to 64:	39.1%	Post-grad study:	9.5%	Sales and service:	23.4%
Over 64:	15.2%			Govt. workers:	16.1%
		Military			
		Veterans/active duty:	10.3%		

Economically and culturally, South Carolina has been part of the booming South Atlantic region, filling up with new retirement condominiums, time shares, factories, office buildings, and giant shopping centers.

This demographic change has moved South Carolina politically toward the Republicans. South Carolina voted for Republicans Barry Goldwater in 1964 and Richard Nixon in 1968; it has only once voted for a Democrat since—son of the South Jimmy Carter in 1976. With some bare-knuckled help from wunderkind strategist Lee Atwater, former Gov. Carroll Campbell built a Republican Party capable of electing statewide officials and legislative majorities. In 1988, Campbell and Atwater, who was by then George H.W. Bush's campaign manager, set up the early Republican presidential primary on the Saturday before Super Tuesday, which enabled Bush to clinch the nomination that year. It did the same for Bob Dole in 1996, for George W. Bush in 2000, and for John McCain in 2008. But in 2012, South Carolina Republicans' choice of Newt Gingrich was replicated only in Gingrich's former home state of Georgia.

South Carolina's Democrats were once competitive. Sen. Hollings served 38 years, 36 of them as a junior senator—a record. And Rep. Jim Clyburn of the black-majority 6th District is the third-ranking member of the House Democratic leadership. But politics still cleaves the electorate along racial lines, and the hard math of the population figures—with whites an easy majority—makes it difficult for Democrats to win statewide in South Carolina any more. In November 2012, according to a Reuters/Ipsos survey, South Carolina whites voted 78% for Mitt Romney and blacks voted 99% for Barack Obama.

Voter Turnout	
2013 Total Citizen 18+	3,566,286
2014 Highest Statewide Turnout	1,246,301
2014 Turnout as % CVAP	34.9%
2012 Turnout as % CVAP	55.9%

Legislature			
Senate:	28R	17D	1V
House:	77R	46D	1V

Presidential Politics In presidential elections, South Carolina has been reliably Republican for a long time. It was the only Deep South state to vote for Richard Nixon over George Wallace in 1968. Since then, it has voted Democratic only once, for Jimmy Carter in 1976.

The primaries are not so predictable. South Carolina was decisive in determining the Republican nomination from 1988 to 2008. And with an early spot on the calendar, it also played a major role in the 2008 Democratic race. In 1987, Republican operative Lee Atwater craftily scheduled the Republican primary for the Saturday before Super Tuesday, a collection of mostly Southern primaries that many Democrats hoped would move their party toward choosing a moderate Southerner. Instead, South Carolina moved Republicans toward choosing a moderate Southern Republican, George H.W. Bush of Texas, who won a 49%-21%-19% victory here over Bob Dole and Pat Robertson, a foretaste of the Southern sweep that clinched Bush's nomination four days later. In 1992, Bush beat Pat Buchanan 67%-26%, squashing Buchanan's claims to Southern support. Four years later, Dole, after his disappointing showings elsewhere, won an impressive 45%-29% victory over Buchanan. And in 2000, former governors Carroll Campbell and David Beasley supported George W. Bush, as he beat John McCain 53%-42%. In 2004, Democrats held a primary on Feb. 3, a week after the New Hampshire primary. Native son John Edwards won 45% of the vote, more than John Kerry's 30%, but not the landslide he wanted.

The state's two political parties—not the state government—conduct presidential primaries in South Carolina, and they can choose to hold them on different days. In 2008, South Carolina Republicans responded by moving their primary to January 19 to protect the state's first-in-the-South status. On the other side, the Democratic National Committee chose South Carolina as the only state other than New Hampshire to hold a pre-February 5 primary, and South Carolina Democrats picked Jan. 26. Candidates started coming into the state early. The state's two senators split, with Lindsey Graham once again backing McCain strongly, and Jim DeMint endorsing Mitt Romney. On the Democratic side, the most

2012 Presidential Vote		
Mitt Romney (R)	1,071,645	(55%)
Barack Obama (D)	865,941	(44%)

2012 Presidential Primary		
Newt Gingrich (R)	244,065	(40%)
Mitt Romney (R)	168,123	(28%)
Rick Santorum (R)	102,475	(17%)
Ron Paul (R)	78,360	(13%)

2008 Presidential Vote		
John McCain (R)	1,034,896	(54%)
Barack Obama (D)	862,449	(45%)

coveted endorsement was that of Rep. James Clyburn, then the House majority whip and an African-American who could be a force in a primary whose electorate was likely to be about 50% black. Candidates and surrogates thronged to his 16th annual fish fry in Columbia in April, where the crowd consumed 1,200 pounds of whiting. Clyburn frustrated all sides by not endorsing before the Democratic primary.

Initially, Romney spent large sums and made frequent trips to the state, but he later focused on the Nevada caucuses that were held the same day. Mike Huckabee, fresh from his victory in the Iowa caucuses, looked forward to competing in another state with a large evangelical Protestant population and hoped to expand his appeal beyond that base. Fred Thompson decided to stake his campaign on South Carolina. McCain focused on the Low Country on the Atlantic Coast, while Huckabee and Thompson focused on the Up Country and Piedmont regions and rural areas. South Carolina proved to be a pivotal point in the campaign. Romney finished fourth, with 15% of the vote. Thompson, for all his folksiness, failed to break Huckabee's connection with religious conservatives and finished third with 16%. After the results were in, he quietly left the race. At the top of the ballot, McCain finished ahead of Huckabee by only 33%-30%. Huckabee got 43% from evangelical Protestants and carried the Up Country and Piedmont. McCain carried the Low Country, including the Charleston metro area. He also won the Columbia media market. McCain's victory established him as the front-runner for the nomination and gave him momentum that he carried into the Florida primary 10 days later, where he narrowly defeated Romney.

The Democrats had a three-candidate contest in South Carolina. Edwards, who was born there, visited the state most frequently and assured voters he understood their plight. Barack Obama also visited and hoped that African-American voters would support him. Hillary Clinton did not concede black votes and particularly targeted black women. This was the first contest with significant numbers of African-American voters, and observers watched the polls closely. At the outset, the state's black voters seemed split about evenly between Obama and Clinton. But Obama's victory in the Iowa caucuses convinced many skeptical blacks that whites would vote for him and he would have a serious chance to win. By early January, Obama appeared to be sweeping African-American voters. Former President Bill Clinton, campaigning for his wife, was desperate to turn things around and remarked that Obama's claim to have strongly opposed the Iraq war was "a fairy tale," a remark that some perceived as applying more generally to the Obama campaign. It stirred days of controversy.

Turnout in the Democratic primary on Jan. 26 was 532,000 voters, 19% more than in the Republican contest. Obama won a crushing victory with 55% of the vote, winning 78% among blacks and a not- inconsiderable 24% among whites. Obama carried all but two counties at opposite ends of the state. Clinton was second, with 26% of the vote. She won about 36% among whites and 19% among blacks, and she carried only Horry County (the Grand Strand) with its retirement communities and relatively small black population. Edwards was a poor third, with only 18%, carrying his boyhood home of Oconee County and nothing else. His third-place finish in the one primary state that he'd won four years earlier ended his campaign. Years later in his memoir, Clyburn, who had voted for Obama, wrote that he received a 2 a.m. phone call the day after the primary from the ex-president blaming him for his wife's defeat and vowing, "If you bastards want a fight, you damn well will get one." Not long after that phone call, Clinton downplayed Obama's big win, noting that civil rights leader Jesse Jackson carried South Carolina in his two unsuccessful bids for the Democratic nomination in 1984 and 1988, a remark that seemed racially disparaging to many Democrats.

The 2012 Republican primary was held on Jan. 21, 10 days after New Hampshire. Chastened by his showing four years earlier, Romney only sporadically visited, but stepped up his efforts after being declared the winner in Iowa and New Hampshire. Rick Perry and Newt Gingrich saw South Carolina as a must-win state for their campaigns, particularly after their weak finishes in Iowa and New Hampshire. Rick Santorum, after what was reported as his near-win in Iowa, hoped that his cultural conservatism would help him in South Carolina. Endorsements mattered less this time than debates. Romney led in some pre-primary polls, but the hot candidate turned out to be Gingrich. In the South Carolina debates, he turned his fire not so much on Romney as on the news media and liberal elites. This struck a chord with the state's Republicans, and Perry dropped out of the race and endorsed Gingrich. Romney didn't help himself in the debates by repeatedly dodging questions about whether or when he would release his tax returns. Turnout was 604,000, a South Carolina record, and Gingrich won 40% to 28% for Romney, 17% for Santorum, and 13% for Ron Paul. Gingrich carried all of the counties but three; Romney carried Charleston, Richland (Columbia), and Beaufort (Hilton Head) counties, with their relatively affluent Republican electorates.

Few national political reporters return to South Carolina after the primaries. While North Carolina was seriously contested in both 2008 and 2012, South Carolina was not. Spontaneous enthusiasm for Obama produced high black turnout, but about three-quarters of whites voted for McCain and Romney, who carried the state by near-identical margins of 54%-45% and 55%-44%, respectively.

Congressional Districts South Carolina gained a seventh House seat in the reapportionment of 2010, making the largest delegation since the 1910 census. Republicans held the governorship and solid majorities in both houses of the legislature. They also held five of six House seats after shoring up their incumbents

114th Congress Lineup	
6 R	1 D
113th Congress Lineup	
6 R	1 D

while adding a sixth Republican seat. So in June 2011, the state House passed a proposal adding a new 7th District in the Pee Dee region anchored by Myrtle Beach and surrounding Horry County, a rapidly growing Republican bastion.

But something unexpected happened on the road to full passage. The state Senate, including ambitious Republicans from the Lowcountry region, surprised the House with its own scheme, placing the new 7th District in the Charleston suburbs and Beaufort to the south. The map's plotters had brought on board several Democrats who believed the Senate version would give them a better shot in the 7th District, and they passed it 22-20. The impasse created by Republicans' infighting threatened to send the entire matter to federal court, where it was possible judges would insist on creating a second black majority seat in addition to Democrat Jim Clyburn's 6th District. After all, African-Americans were 28% of the state's population in 2010.

Republicans in the two chambers reached a compromise, greased by support from Upstate legislators, to place the 7th District in the Pee Dee, which would have the most blacks of any district in the state other than Clyburn's. The Charleston-based 1st District would pick up Beaufort, and 2nd District Republican Joe Wilson, who had taken only 53 percent in 2010, would shed some African-American counties to Clyburn. Gov. Nikki Haley signed the map, and the Obama Justice Department tersely granted preclearance. A group of six Democratic voters sued to block the map on the grounds it failed to create a new African-American seat, but a three-judge panel upheld the map in March 2012, and the Supreme Court affirmed the ruling in October. Even though it is the least partisan of the six Republican districts, Tom Rice has easily held the new 7th District for the GOP.

Governor

Nikki Haley (R)

Elected 2010, term expires Jan. 2019, 2nd term; b. Jan. 20, 1972, Bamberg; Clemson U., B.S. 1994; Methodist; married (Michael); 2 children.

Elected Office: SC House, 2004-10.

Professional Career: Accounting supervisor, FCR Inc., Charlotte, NC, 1994-96; Chief financial officer, Exotica Intl., Lexington, SC, 1996-2004.

Office: 1205 Pendleton St., Columbia, 29201, 803-734-2100; Fax: 803-734-5167; Website: governor.sc.gov.

Election Results

2014 general	Nikki Haley (R)	696,645	(56%)
	Vincent Sheheen (D)	516,166	(41%)
2014 primary	Nikki Haley (R)	unopposed	

Prior winning percentage: 2010 (51%)

South Carolina's governor is Nikki Haley, a conservative, Indian-American Republican elected in 2010. As the first woman and first racial minority to become the deeply conservative state's chief executive, she is at the forefront of the national Republican Party's efforts to tout an image of inclusiveness. Despite a lackluster first term, she won reelection in 2014 by a wider margin, then took a leading role in removing the Confederate battle flag from the state capitol complex, which brought her renewed national attention.

Haley was born Nimrata Nikki Randhawa to Sikh parents who had emigrated from India to Bamberg South Carolina. Her father was a biology professor, while her mother started a gift shop in town. Her upbringing in the small, blue-collar community south of Columbia was at times difficult. Although male Sikhs normally do not cut their hair, her brothers had theirs trimmed after they were viciously taunted at school. When she was 5 years old, she and her older sister entered a beauty pageant in which one white winner and one black winner had historically been crowned; the judges disqualified the girls because they were considered to be neither. Haley worked at her mother's shop and took over the bookkeeping there at age 13, going on to get an accounting degree at Clemson University, where she met her husband, Michael Haley. She said she subsequently converted to Christianity, though later news reports noted that they were wed in two ceremonies, one Sikh and one Methodist. She worked for a waste management and recycling company before returning to her mother's business, which had branched out into clothing and jewelry.

In 2004, Haley decided to challenge Republican state Rep. Larry Koon, who had been in office since 1975. She was the target of slurs but brushed them off, saying she wouldn't let them distract her. Haley ran as a dedicated fiscal conservative who was strongly opposed to raising taxes; she managed to hold Koon to less than 50% of the vote, forcing a runoff. She won that matchup with 55% to become the first Indian-American Republican state legislator in the United States. She easily won reelection in 2006 and 2008.

She developed a reputation as a staunch fiscal conservative and became a loyal ally of Republican Gov. Mark Sanford. She was named majority whip in 2006; she also chaired a subcommittee of the powerful Labor, Commerce, and Industry Committee. She sought to lead the full committee in 2009 but angered her party's leaders by seeking to push regulations on the state's payday lending industry and by openly criticizing the House's reluctance to cast recorded votes. She was reassigned to another committee, a move she characterized as punishment.

Haley in May 2009 announced her intention to succeed Sanford, running as an outsider and reformer. "I know what good government can look like," she said. "I'm running for governor so the people of the state will know what it feels like." She said she drew inspiration from Louisiana Gov. Bobby Jindal, who is also Indian-American, and she remained a protégé of Sanford's. The next month, though, Sanford became a political embarrassment when he disappeared from work for several days and then admitted to an affair with a woman living in Argentina. (His staff's initial explanation that he had been "hiking the Appalachian Trail" subsequently entered the lexicon as a euphemism for adultery.)

After that, Haley sought to distance herself from Sanford, taking his photographs down from her campaign website. But she endured other challenges in what would become one of the country's ugliest primary battles. She faced three other prominent Republican candidates: Attorney General Henry McMaster, Lt. Gov. André Bauer, and Rep. Gresham Barrett. No one, however, was able to emerge as a front-runner, and Barrett began running an ad calling himself "a Christian family man who won't embarrass us," while Haley was accused of de-emphasizing her upbringing as a Sikh.

In the final weeks of the campaign, a Republican blogger and former Sanford aide claimed he had had "inappropriate sexual contact" with Haley. She denied the charge, and the blogger produced no proof. Several days later, a Republican lobbyist who worked for Bauer said he also had had a sexual encounter with Haley, who again denied the allegations. "This is South Carolina politics at its worst," her spokesman said. Bauer came under suspicion for having started the rumors, a charge he strongly denied. But Haley, appearing to get the benefit of the doubt from voters, started climbing in the polls. She also collected the endorsement of former Alaska Gov. Sarah Palin, as well support from Jenny Sanford, who had won widespread admiration among South Carolinians for her graceful conduct during her husband's scandal.

A few days before the primary, the race made negative headlines for another reason. GOP state Sen. Jake Knotts said on a radio show, "We already got one raghead in the White House. We don't need another in the governor's mansion." Knotts apologized, and primary voters were wholly unmoved by the display of bigotry. Haley won with 49% of the vote, to 22% for Barrett, 17% for McMaster, and 12% for Bauer.

Haley had little time to savor her triumph, which, under normal circumstances, would have sealed her general election victory in the overwhelmingly Republican state. Reports surfaced that she had been late in paying income taxes and that her family's clothing business had been hit with liens for failing to pay taxes. Then, *The State* reported that the foundation arm of a medical center—an entity she had backed in its fight to open a heart surgery center—had created a fundraising job for her paying more than $100,000 a year. Her Democratic opponent, lawyer and state Sen. Vincent Sheheen, accused her of hypocrisy. She denied any wrongdoing and attacked him for voting to regulate payday lenders while being part of a law firm that made money from suing them.

With help from tea party activists, she beat Sheheen 51%-47%, losing populous Charleston County and Richland County—home of state capital Columbia—but dominating the northwestern counties around Greenville, Spartanburg, and Anderson as well as the affluent coastal areas in the northeast. Potential Republican presidential candidates wooed her for support, and she agreed to appear at a rally with Minnesota GOP Rep. Michele Bachmann, the tea party's unofficial doyenne in the House.

Haley's former colleagues welcomed her—a sharp contrast to Sanford, who often clashed with the legislature. Lawmakers passed a measure that she signed into law cutting the state's Medicaid spending by 3% in response to a health services' budget deficit of $225 million. In the House, though, lawmakers turned back most of her recommendations. Meanwhile, Haley's personnel moves drew considerable controversy. *The State* reported in March that almost half the 59 people she had appointed to state boards and commissions had donated to her campaign. And, drawing national publicity, she yanked philanthropist Darla Moore from the University of South Carolina Board of Trustees and replaced her with one of her campaign donors, even though Moore had given more than $70 million to the school. The governor said that Moore hadn't shown enough interest in the job.

Haley's popularity surged outside of South Carolina. She was featured in *Vogue* and *Marie Claire*, and she penned an autobiography. She endorsed Mitt Romney in the hotly contested South Carolina Republican presidential primary. Though Romney lost the race by double digits to former House Speaker Newt Gingrich, she acted as a surrogate for him as he locked up the nomination. She was later given a speaking slot at the party's national convention, her youth and diverse background making her an attractive figure for Republicans nationally. She has expressed a fondness for singer Joan Jett, telling *Marie Claire* that the 1980s rocker opened doors for women.

Things were not as rosy at home. Haley was criticized for taking a $158,000 state-funded trip to Europe and the Paris Air Show. In 2011, an old issue surfaced when former state economic adviser John Rainey filed a lawsuit claiming that Haley broke ethics laws by working as a lobbyist for her employers while serving in the state House. Haley said the allegations were false, calling Rainey a "racist, sexist bigot." In July 2012, the legislature's House Ethics Committee cleared her of wrongdoing. Haley faced additional scrutiny when *the Post and Courier* reported that she tried to direct the state health planning committee to forego participating in a health exchange as required under the new federal health care law. Reports surfaced that her office deleted some emails regarding the matter. Members of the state health committee denied any undue influence from the governor, and Haley implemented a new administration policy to save all internal emails.

In 2012, Haley battled with the legislature over the budget. Haley exercised her veto on 81 budget funds, but only 34 of the vetoes were sustained. She took substantial heat for vetoing money for rape crisis centers, a decision that was overridden. The legislature also voted to override her veto that cut arts funding. She told local reporters that she still saved the state money. "Did I get all that I wanted? ... No, but did I get to see them take a lot of that pork and irresponsible spending out of the budget? Yes." Haley also drew national attention for signing a tough, new voter ID law. In December 2011, the Obama Justice Department rejected the law, claiming it would hinder minority voting rights. She called the decision "outrageous" and "clearly political." A three-judge U.S. District Court panel ruled that the law could not take effect until 2013, because there was too little time to put it into effect before the 2012 elections.

In January 2013, she named Rep. Tim Scott to succeed retiring GOP Sen. Jim DeMint, making Scott the Senate's first black Republican in more than three decades. The decision proved popular, to Haley's benefit. But Sheheen returned for a rematch, and his close showing in 2010 suggested that he might have an opening. He highlighted what he called Haley's mismanagement of a data breach in 2012 at the state Department of Revenue that affected 6.4 million taxpayers, as well as the handling of child abuse and neglect cases. He also criticized Haley for not paying enough attention to shoring up the state's infrastructure. Haley touted her accomplishments on economic development, including the creation of more than 56,000 new jobs during her tenure and a 13-year low for the state's unemployment rate. When Sheheen said in an event in Florence that his party would escort Haley out the door—he mangled the word so that some thought he said "whore"—Republicans made hay of it, but the comment mattered little in the end. On a staunchly Republican election day in a strongly conservative state, Haley was able to improve her showing by five percentage points, defeating Sheheen, 56%-41%.

In June 2015, after a gunman with a history of white-supremacist writings was arrested for killing nine worshippers at a historic African-American church in Charleston, South Carolina was thrust uncomfortably into the national spotlight. Amid the grief, attention turned to the question of why the Confederate battle flag continued to fly from a memorial near the state capitol. Past efforts to remove the flag from the capitol grounds, including a boycott of the state, had always come to naught, and seeking the flag's removal had come to be seen as politically toxic; before the shooting, Haley had shown no interest in seeking removal of the flag. But after the slaughter, the mood changed. The turning point came when Haley, in a speech praised for its forcefulness and eloquence, called for the Legislature to pass a law to get rid of the flag from the capitol grounds. "For those who wish to respect the flag on private property, no one will stand in your way," she said. "But the statehouse is different. The events this past week call on us to look at this in a different way. ... We are not going to allow this symbol to divide us any longer. ... The fact that it causes so [much] pain is enough to move it from the capitol grounds. It is, after all, a capitol that belongs to all of us." Haley's call won plaudits from across the ideological spectrum. "True political bravery would have been calling for the flag to be removed during her 2010 or 2014 campaigns, which she pointedly did not do," wrote *Washington Post* political reporter Chris Cillizza. "But politics is not always about being first. Oftentimes it's simply about not being last or, at least, not being perceived as late. By that measure, Haley succeeded." After emotional debate, state lawmakers voted to follow her lead, and on July 10, 2015, the flag was lowered and the pole removed from the site.

Senior Senator

Lindsey Graham (R)

Elected 2002, term expires Jan. 2021, 3rd term; b. July 9, 1955, Central; U. of SC, B.A. 1977, J.D. 1981; Baptist; single.

Military Career: Air Force, 1982-88; SC Air Natl. Guard, 1989-94 (Operation Desert Storm); Air Force Reserve, 1995-present.

Elected Office: SC House, 1992-94; U.S. House, 1995-2003.

Professional Career: U.S. Air Forces Europe Circuit Trial Counsel, 1984-88; Asst. Oconee Cnty. atty., 1988-92; Practicing atty., 1988-94; Judge advocate, McEntire Air Natl. Guard Base, 1989-94; Central, SC, city atty., 1990-94.

DC Office: 290 RSOB, 20510, 202-224-5972; Fax: 202-224-3808; Website: lgraham.senate.gov.

State Offices: Columbia, 803-933-0112; Florence, 843-669-1505; Greenville, 864-250-1417; Mt. Pleasant, 843-849-3887; Pendleton, 864-646-4090; Rock Hill, 803-366-2828.

Committees: *Appropriations:* Commerce, Justice, Science & Related Agencies; Defense; Energy & Water Development, Homeland Security; Labor, Health & Human Services, Education & Related Agencies; State, Foreign Operations & Related Programs (Chmn). *Armed Services:* Emerging Threats & Capabilities; Personnel (Chmn); Strategic Forces. *Budget. Judiciary:* Constitution; Crime & Terrorism (Chmn); Oversight, Agency Action, Federal Rights & Federal Courts; Privacy, Technology & the Law.

Group Ratings

	ADA	ACLU	AFL-CIO	LCV	ITI	COC	HAFA	ACU	CFG	FRC
2014	10%	40%	–	0%	66%	100%	47%	74%	58%	93%
2013	20%	C	33%	31%	C	63%	C	68%	65%	C

National Journal Ratings

	2013 LIB	—	2013 CONS
Economic	28%	—	71%
Social	39%	—	60%
Foreign	38%	—	61%
Composite	36%	—	65%

Key Votes of the 113th Congress

1. Sandy storm spending	N	5. Student Loan Rates	Y	9. Bipartisan Budget Deal	N
2. Chuck Hagel Confirmation	N	6. Employee Non-Discrim'n Act	N	10. Farm Bill Conference Rept.	Y
3. Gun Background Checks	N	7. Senate Vote on Judgeships	Y	11. Unempl. Comp. Extension	N
4. Immigration Reform	Y	8. Defense Dept. Spending	N	12. Keystone Pipeline	Y

Election Results

2014 general	Lindsey Graham (R)	672,941	(55%)	$11,464,087	$597,771	$7,725
	Brad Hutto (D)	456,726	(38%)	$522,454		
	Thomas Ravenel (I)	47,588	(4%)			
	Victor Kocher (Lib)	33,839	(3%)	$12,931		
2014 primary	Lindsey Graham (R)	178,093	(56%)			
	Lee Bright (R)	48,704	(15%)			
	Richard Cash(R)	26,246	(8%)			
	Det Bowers (R)	23,071	(7%)			
	Nancy Mace (R)	19,560	(6%)			
	Bill Connor (R)	16,847	(5%)			

Prior winning percentages: 2008 (58%), 2002 (54%); House: 2000 (68%), 1998 (100%), 1996 (60%), 1994 (60%)

Republican Lindsey Graham, South Carolina's senior senator, was elected to the House in 1994 and to the Senate in 2002. He and his close friend, Arizona Republican John McCain, are the Senate's two high-profile defense hawks; on domestic issues, Graham sometimes confounds conservatives by collaborating with Democrats, but he also can be a lacerating critic of the other party. Graham announced his bid for the White House in June 2015, with McCain quickly endorsing him.

Graham grew up in Pickens County, where his parents owned a tavern in the textile mill town of Central. Both his parents died young, while Graham was still attending the University of South Carolina, and he became his younger sister's legal guardian so that she could receive his military benefits. He was the first in his family to graduate from college, and then received a law degree from the University of South Carolina. He was an Air Force prosecutor who worked on assignments overseas, including one case that led to major changes in the service's drug testing program for soldiers. In 1988, he returned home and practiced law in Seneca. In 1992, he was elected to the state House. Graham was called up to active duty and served stateside during the Gulf War. He joined the Air Force Reserve in 1995 where he served as a senior instructor in the Air Force's JAG school and also as a reserve judge on the Air Force Court of Criminal Appeals. He was awarded the Bronze Star in 2014 for meritorious service for his role as a senior legal adviser to the Air Force during combat operations in Afghanistan. Graham retired from the reserves in June 2015 just as he was launching his presidential campaign.

In 1994, with the retirement of 20-year Democratic Rep. Butler Derrick, Graham ran for the House. Both parties had contested primaries, and Graham won the Republican primary with 52 percent of the vote. In the general election, he faced state Sen. Jim Bryan. Graham called for term limits, supported more defense spending, and opposed gays in the military. His attitude toward the Clinton administration and the Democratic leadership was unequivocal. He said, "I'm one less vote for an agenda that makes you want to throw up." Graham won 60%-40%, a smashing victory in a district represented only by Democrats since Reconstruction.

In the House, Graham had a solidly conservative voting record but did not always support the Republican leadership. In the summer of 1997, he was among a small group of junior House members who plotted with some senior lawmakers to try to oust Speaker Newt Gingrich, who by then had lost the confidence of his Republican troops. The attempt failed. In a Republican Conference meeting, when Majority Leader Dick Armey of Texas, one of the plotters, asserted that no member of the leadership was involved, Graham challenged that assertion as false.

As a member of the House Judiciary Committee, Graham played a major role in the 1998 impeachment of President Bill Clinton. In the Senate trial, Graham's folksy manner and clear description of Clinton's offenses—"Where I come from, a man who calls someone up at 2:30 in the morning is up to no good"—made him one of the most effective GOP impeachment managers. In 2000, Graham was one of McCain's staunchest supporters in his first bid for the presidency.

In 2002, Graham ran for the Senate seat of Republican Sen. Strom Thurmond, who was in his 90s and did not seek a ninth term. There had not been an open South Carolina Senate seat since 1941. In this now heavily Republican state, Graham had no opposition in the Republican primary. His work on impeachment and in the McCain campaign made him well-known and popular statewide, and he had the endorsements of three former governors and Thurmond. Democrats portrayed him as lacking in substance and recruited Alex Sanders, president of the College of Charleston who in 1985 was appointed to the state Court of Appeals.

Sanders was a gifted raconteur, charming and well-connected around the state. He was a solid fundraiser as well, eventually raising $4.2 million, below Graham's $6.2 million, but a considerable achievement for a candidate consistently behind in the polls. Sanders supported the Bush tax cuts and military action in Iraq, but he opposed the death penalty, on religious grounds, as well as a constitutional amendment to allow criminalization of flag burning. Graham hammered him on the death penalty and the flag amendment but most of all tried to label him as a liberal, saying Sanders would advance the agenda of Sens. Hillary Clinton of New York and Edward Kennedy of Massachusetts. Graham won 54%-44% and took the place of a senator first elected in the year before he was born. Graham and Clinton have long had a love-hate relationship - she's cited him as one of the Republicans she worked best with while in the Senate and called him after the Charleston murders, but he's been a vocal critic of her tenure as secretary of State.

Graham has long combined a foreign policy hawkishness with sometimes surprising breaks with his party on domestic issues. Graham was the only Judiciary Committee Republican to support President Barack Obama's choice of Sonia Sotomayor for the Supreme Court in 2009, saying the president deserved the prerogative to nominate a qualified person of his choice even if the GOP disagreed with her ideology. He took the same position a year later when Obama nominated Solicitor General Elena Kagan for the court. In addition to praising her intellect, he said, "She's funny, and that goes a long way in my book." After the Supreme Court legalized gay marriage nationwide he said the party should accept the ruling and drop language calling for a constitutional amendment barring gay marriage nationwide from its platform.

In February 2009, Graham said he supported a limited nationalization of some banks and Obama's proposal to "stress-test" banks. "I'm not going to be the Herbert Hoover of 2009, saying 'Just let the free market work it out,'" he told the *Charlotte Observer*. And he incensed tea party activists by declaring to *The New York Times* in 2010 that the movement would "die out" because it "can never come up with a coherent vision for governing the country." When Kentucky GOP Sen. Rand Paul staged a 13-hour talking filibuster in March 2013 in partial protest of the administration's use of unmanned drones to kill U.S. citizens, Graham dismissed Paul's concerns to the Associated Press as "paranoia between libertarians and the hard left that is unjustified."

Graham shored up his standing among conservatives by turning aggressively confrontational on several high-profile issues, many of them involving national security. He and McCain led a successful push to derail U.N. Ambassador Susan Rice's chances to become secretary of State after they sharply questioned her role in responding to the deadly September 2012 terrorist consulate attack in Benghazi Libya. Graham told Fox News that outgoing Secretary of State Hillary Clinton "got away with murder" for not foreseeing the threat in Benghazi. The two senators also were at the forefront of opposing the nomination of their former colleague, Republican Chuck Hagel of Nebraska, to become secretary of Defense because of what they considered his insufficient support for Israel and hawkishness on Iran, although Hagel eventually was confirmed.

After Obama's decision in June 2014 to swap imprisoned Army Sgt. Bowe Bergdahl for five Taliban leaders held captive at Guantanamo Bay, Graham said the president could be impeached if he agreed to any such exchanges in the future. And he warned that same month that the "seeds of 9/11 are being planted all over Iraq and Syria" in calling for a more aggressive U.S. response in both nations.

Graham's sharp turn to the right extended to fiscal and social policy. During the 2012 showdown over spending and taxes, he faulted Obama for not "manning up" and told Fox News his party needed to take a tough approach on the next vote to raise the federal debt limit. "We're not going to let Obama borrow any more money, or any American Congress borrow any more money, until we fix this country from becoming Greece," he said. Meanwhile, Graham took a hard line against new gun control measures including a ban on assault weapons, instead introducing a bill to strengthen mental health provisions in gun background checks. Graham stuck by his view that tighter gun control wasn't necessary in the wake of the murders of nine African-American churchgoers by a white man in Charleston in June 2015, though he suggested he supported more enforcement of background check laws already on the books. Breaking with some other Republican candidates he said there's "no doubt" the murders were racially motivated, but demurred when asked if he thought the Confederate Flag should be removed from official use in the state, calling it "part of who we are." He backed South Carolina Gov. Nikki Haley when she called for the removal of the Confederate flag from statehouse grounds after the Charleston murders.

Graham has continued to work in a bipartisan fashion on immigration, an issue with which he has long grappled. In 2006 and 2007, Graham supported the McCain-Kennedy and Kennedy-Kyl immigration bills, positions that got him in considerable trouble with conservatives who opposed giving illegal immigrants a process to achieve citizenship. Radio talk show host Rush Limbaugh belittled him as "Lindsey Grahamnesty," and the Greenville County Republican Party voted to censure him. Graham's public comments suggesting that immigration bill opponents were "bigots" did not help his cause.

Undeterred, Graham joined a group of senators, four Democrats and four Republicans, that hammered out a plan in early 2013 to tighten border security, visa tracking, and workplace verification in exchange for providing a path toward citizenship for the country's estimated 11 million undocumented workers. "I am confident, very confident, that if I help solve this problem in a way that we won't have 20 million illegal immigrants 20 years from now, not only will I get reelected, I can look back and say I was involved in something that was important," he told McClatchy Newspapers. The bill passed by a wide margin in the Senate but House GOP leaders refused to take it up in the face of withering criticism from conservative talk radio.

Graham earlier had worked with Democratic Sen. Charles Schumer of New York on immigration, coming up with a plan to toughen border security and require biometric Social Security cards to ensure illegal immigrants could not get jobs. But Graham later joined conservatives in calling for an end to birthright citizenship, a position that incensed his usual immigration allies. "He has either taken leave of his senses or of his principles," former Bush speechwriter Michael Gerson wrote in *The Washington Post*. Graham joined Republicans in opposing the DREAM Act giving the children of illegal immigrants a potential path to citizenship in December 2010.

Graham also supports action to combat climate change, though he's been less active on the issue in recent years. He had worked with Massachusetts Democratic Sen. John Kerry and Connecticut independent Sen. Joe Lieberman on a method of pricing carbon that would be an alternative to the House's 2009 bill creating a cap-and-trade system for companies emitting the greenhouse gases. But Graham angrily pulled out of those discussions in April 2010 when Majority Leader Harry Reid planned to bring an immigration bill to the Senate floor before taking up the energy and climate change measure. After he launched his presidential candidacy in 2015 he told CNN that "Climate change is real" and promised "If I'm president of the United States, we're going to address climate change, CO2 emissions in a business-friendly way."

Since his arrival in the Senate, Graham has been interested in solutions to the Social Security solvency issue. In 2003, he unveiled his own plan: personal retirement accounts, with higher taxes for workers who do not choose them. The proposal was sharply criticized by some conservatives, but Graham persisted. He participated in private meetings with both Democratic and Republican senators, and he insisted that raising the payroll tax limit was necessary if a plan was to get Democratic support. He later recruited two freshman senators who were tea party favorites, Paul and Mike Lee of Utah, to work with him on Social Security.

Comparing his political style to McCain's, Graham told *The New York Times:* "I've never been a Luke Skywalker; I'm a much more calculating guy than that. I understand that you just don't charge into these things based on some moral belief that you're right and the other guy's wrong." Without much of a threat to his own reelection bid, Graham in 2008 traveled the country with McCain, the Republican presidential nominee. McCain, Graham, and Lieberman formed a bipartisan triumvirate on the campaign trail, dubbed the "Three Amigos." Graham's support was helpful to McCain in the pivotal January 2008 South Carolina primary, in which McCain redeemed his 2000 loss by winning with 33 percent of the vote. "There's nobody I trust more than Lindsey Graham," McCain told the Myrtle Beach *Sun News*. Graham was said to be the member of McCain's inner circle who was the most enthusiastic about him tapping Lieberman as his running mate, according to the 2010 book about the campaign, *Game Change*. But McCain settled on Alaska Gov. Sarah Palin after Graham began privately floating the idea of Lieberman with social conservatives, enraging Limbaugh and others when word leaked out.

Graham's departures from party orthodoxy fueled talk of a primary challenger in 2014, and D.C.-based groups like the Club for Growth had him high on their target list. But Graham worked assiduously behind the scenes to befriend or scare off serious potential challengers, and managed to ward off any big-name opponents.

Graham avoided the fate of other GOP colleagues sweating out tea-party challenges by running a flawless campaign. He raised more than $12 million and put together an impressive on-the-ground operation featuring more than 5,000 precinct captains and six field offices around South Carolina. He kept his most prominent potential opponents out of the race - he helped Rep. Mick Mulvaney land a seat on the House Financial Services Committee, for instance. "When the members of the congressional delegation needed something for their district, their first call was to Lindsey Graham and it was to his cell phone. Lindsey Graham has been accessible to that federal delegation from day one," said former South Carolina Republican Party Chairman Katon Dawson, who ran a super PAC backing Graham.

On the campaign trail, Graham didn't try to deny that Washington had grown dysfunctional—but portrayed himself as one of those brave enough to seek a solution. "I'm trying to tell the tea party, I understand your frustration, but being frustrated is not enough," he told *The Atlantic*. He also emphasized the areas where he agreed with the conservative base, introducing a bill banning abortions after 20 weeks of pregnancy in the Senate and trumpeting his battles with the Obama Administration on national security, ripping the President on his handling of Benghazi, Russia, Syria, Iraq and Israel. Graham drew six minor challengers, and walked away from the June primary with 56 percent. From there, he had little trouble in the general election.

Even before he won another term, Graham mused about dipping his toe in a bid for the White House. "If I get through my general election, if nobody steps up in the presidential mix, if nobody's out there talking—me and McCain have been talking—I may just jump in to get to make these arguments" about a hawkish foreign policy, he told *The Weekly Standard*.

Many remained doubtful he'd run, but Graham proved his skeptics wrong when he launched his campaign in June 2015 at a rally in his hometown. The senator promised a heavy focus on national security. "I want to be president to protect our nation that we all love so much from all threats foreign and domestic," he said in his announcement speech. Graham began the campaign as a long-shot candidate, and faced questions about his bachelorhood—which he didn't put to rest when he declared he'd have a "rotating first lady" if he won.

Junior Senator

Tim Scott (R)

Appointed Jan. 2013, 1st term; b. Sept. 19, 1965, North Charleston; Presbyterian Col., attended, Charleston Southern U., B.S. 1988; Christian; single.

Elected Office: Charleston Cnty. Cncl., 1995-2008, chmn., 2007-08; SC House, 2009-10; U.S. House, 2011-13.

Professional Career: Partner, real estate firm; Owner, Tim Scott Allstate.

DC Office: 520 HSOB, 20510, 202-224-6121; Fax: 202-228-5143; Website: scott.senate.gov.

State Offices: Columbia, 803-771-6112; Greenville, 864-233-5366; North Charleston, 843-727-4525.

Committees: *Aging (Special). Banking, Housing & Urban Affairs:* Housing, Transportation & Community Development (Chmn); Financial Institutions & Consumer Protection; Securities, Insurance & Investment. *Finance:* Health Care; Social Security, Pensions & Family Policy; Taxation & IRS Oversight. *Health, Education, Labor & Pensions:* Employment & Workplace Safety; Primary Health & Retirement Security. *Small Business & Entrepreneurship.*

Group Ratings

	ADA	ACLU	AFL-CIO	LCV	ITI	COC	HAFA	ACU	CFG	FRC
2014	10%	0%	–	0%	33%	75%	86%	96%	90%	100%
2013	0%	C	0%	0%	C	75%	C	96%	94%	C

National Journal Ratings

	2013 LIB	—	2013 CONS
Economic	5%	—	93%
Social	0%	—	92%
Foreign	2%	—	96%
Composite	4%	—	96%

Key Votes of the 113th Congress

1. Sandy storm spending	N	5. Student Loan Rates	Y	9. Bipartisan Budget Deal	N
2. Chuck Hagel Confirmation	N	6. Employee Non-Discrim'n Act	N	10. Farm Bill Conference Rept.	N
3. Gun Background Checks	N	7. Senate Vote on Judgeships	Y	11. Unempl. Comp. Extension	N
4. Immigration Reform	N	8. Defense Dept. Spending	N	12. Keystone Pipeline	Y

Election Results

2014 general	Tim Scott (R)	757,215	(61%)	$4,384,151 $36,410
	Joyce Dickerson (D)	459,583	(37%)	$74,517
2014 primary	Tim Scott (R)	275,018	(90%)	
	Randall Young (R)	30,646	(10%)	

Prior winning percentages: House: 2012 (62%), 2010 (65%)

Republican Tim Scott was named South Carolina's junior senator in January 2013 after GOP Sen. Jim DeMint unexpectedly resigned to head the conservative Heritage Foundation think tank. He was elected with ease in 2014 to serve the remaining two years of DeMint's term, becoming the first black GOP lawmaker to be elected statewide in the South since Reconstruction and the Senate's first black Republican since 1979. He previously served one term in the House.

Scott and his siblings were raised by a single mother who worked 16-hour days as a nurse's assistant. Scott got his first job at age 13. He was on the verge of flunking out of high school when he met the man who he says changed his life—John Moniz, the owner of the fast-food Chick-fil-A restaurant next to the movie theater where Scott worked and where he would regularly buy french fries, the only food he could afford. Moniz, who considered himself a born-again Christian, became a father figure for Scott, teaching him the value of personal discipline and hard work. In a speech at the 2012 Republican National Convention, Scott said Moniz taught him that "having a job is a good thing, but creating jobs was even better." Scott finished high school and went on to earn a partial football scholarship to Presbyterian College. He eventually transferred to Charleston Southern University, where he earned a bachelor's degree in political science.

Scott ran an insurance company and owned part of a real estate agency. His first elected office was a seat on the Charleston County Council in 1995. Just after his election, he received a handwritten note of congratulations from Republican Sen. Strom Thurmond of South Carolina, who had run for president on a pro-segregation platform in 1948. Thurmond's past didn't stop Scott from accepting the job as statewide co-chairman of Thurmond's final senatorial campaign in 1996. Asked how an African-American could help Thurmond, Scott told *The New York Times*, "The Strom Thurmond I knew had nothing to do with that" and noted that Thurmond's views on race had evolved. Scott also said that Thurmond taught him the value of constituent service.

In 2010, Scott ran for the 1st District House seat that became vacant with GOP Rep. Henry Brown's retirement. In the GOP primary, he faced opposition from candidates with better name recognition, including Carroll Campbell III, son of former South Carolina Gov. Carroll Campbell, Jr.; and Paul Thurmond, the former senator's son. But Scott got help from national Republican organizations. He came in first in the primary, and Thurmond took second, but neither got the necessary 50 percent to avoid a runoff. There were few policy differences between the two, although Thurmond did not share Scott's willingness to abide by term limits and to swear off earmarked spending. Scott claimed that in his 15 years in elected office, he never voted for a tax increase. His conservative credentials won him praise from prominent Republicans such as former Alaska Gov. Sarah Palin and former House Speaker Newt Gingrich of Georgia. In the runoff election, Scott defeated Thurmond, 68% to 32%. In the general election, he easily beat Democrat Ben Frasier, a retired federal worker, 65% to 29%. His race appeared to be a non-issue for the district's voters, about 70 percent of whom were white. He was reelected easily in 2012 with 62 percent.

As a House member, Scott's voting record was only marginally less conservative than the rest of South Carolina's deeply conservative delegation. He was not as outspoken as the delegation's other members or as Florida Republican Rep. Allen West, the chamber's other black Republican during his first term. But he did join conservatives in refusing to support a 2011 bill to raise the federal debt limit, a 2012 tax and spending compromise to avert a so-called "fiscal cliff," and several leadership-backed spending bills to keep the government running. Republican leaders professed not to mind; they realized his obvious value to their party and heaped praise on him. "He is leadership personified. He has a lot of magnetism and a lot of charisma," Majority Leader Eric Cantor of Virginia told *National Journal*. Scott served as a deputy whip and a freshman-class liaison to the leadership, and he was given a seat on the influential Rules Committee.

After some Tea Party candidates DeMint backed choked away winnable Senate races in 2012 and contributed to Republicans' failure to win Senate control, he announced in December that he would leave to join Heritage rather than finish his second term.

Speculation about who South Carolina GOP Gov. Nikki Haley would appoint revolved around Scott, especially in light of the party's dismal electoral showing among African-American voters. Less than two weeks after DeMint's announcement, Haley, who is Indian-American, chose Scott over four other finalists, a decision she said was based on his devotion to the state and his ability to advocate for it. "It is very important to me, as a minority female, that Congressman Scott earned this seat," she said. His selection proved extremely popular with Republicans.

Scott joined Republicans in cosponsoring a balanced-budget amendment to the Constitution, saying that President Barack Obama "is committed to spending money we don't have, our children don't have, and our grandchildren don't have." But he largely eschewed fierce rhetoric. "It's really hard to offend someone into changing their minds," he told The *Washington Post* in May 2014.

Scott mostly shunned the spotlight, turning down a number of opportunities to raise his national profile, and didn't seek to highlight his race. He concentrated his time on getting to know the state, holding numerous local town halls and doing things like volunteering incognito at a local Goodwill store to talk to local constituents about their problems without tipping them off that he was a politician. The lack of a serious primary or general election challenge in 2014 helped him fly under the national radar—he won his first statewide election with 61 percent of the vote.

But when major race-related events shook South Carolina in 2015, Scott embraced his unique position. After a white policeman killed Walter Scott [no relation], an unarmed black man in Scott's hometown of North Charleston in April 2015, the senator was one of the first to call for legislation for body cameras for policemen and introduced a bill in Congress to provide millions for local police departments to acquire them. Similar legislation became law in South Carolina in early June. And weeks later when nine African-American churchgoers were murdered by a white supremacist in Charleston, Scott joined Gov. Haley and other South Carolina leaders to back a move to remove the Confederate flag from statehouse grounds. His emotional speech on the Senate floor generated widespread coverage, as he choked up when repeating comments from a relative of a victim that "this evil attack would lead to reconciliation, restoration, and unity in the nation."

He joined with New Jersey Democratic Sen. Cory Booker, the Senate's only other African American, to introduce a bill for tax credits for businesses to create more apprenticeship programs. The idea received bipartisan praise—Hillary Clinton held an event in his hometown to talk up the idea in a June 2015 campaign stop. He's been part of a bipartisan working group focused on criminal justice and sentencing reform. He also has been a loud advocate for school choice, a more partisan issue. Scott believes it can help improve education for poor and minority children. "There is a trend that can be broken at its foundation if we focus first on education and second on work skills," he said on ABC's "This Week" in mid-2015.

His critics point out that he has received "F" ratings from the NAACP on its annual scorecards, supports voter ID laws many civil rights groups view as discriminatory against minorities, and refused to endorse a congressional fix to the Voting Rights Act after the Supreme Court struck down a key enforcement provision of the law.

As the 2016 presidential race started to heat up, polls showed Scott to be South Carolina's most popular politician—both statewide and among Republicans. As in 2012, he decided to hold a series of town halls with the presidential prospects, this time partnering with Rep. Trey Gowdy. Many candidates jumped at the chance to appear alongside the potential king-makers. Unlike in 2012, Scott didn't rule out endorsing a candidate.

Scott will also be on the ballot in 2016 as he must run for a full six-year term. He is unlikely to face serious competition.

FIRST DISTRICT

Mark Sanford (R)

Elected May 2013, 4th full term; b. May 28, 1960, Ft. Lauderdale, FL; Furman U., B.A. 1983; U. of VA, M.B.A. 1988; Episcopalian; divorced; 4 children.

Military Career: Air Force Reserves, 2002-11

Elected Office: U.S. House, 1995-2001; SC gov., 2003-11.

Professional Career: Real estate investor, 1988-1992; Owner, Norton & Sanford real estate investment firm, 1992-2002; Commentator, FOX News, 2011-13; real estate investor, 2011-13.

DC Office: 2201 RHOB, 20515, 202-225-3176; Website: sanford.house.gov.

State Offices: Beaufort, 843-521-2530; Mount Pleasant, 843-352-7572.

Committees: *Budget. Transportation & Infrastructure:* Aviation; Coast Guard & Maritime Transportation; Water Resources & Environment.

Group Ratings

	ADA	ACLU	AFL-CIO	LCV	ITI	COC	HAFA	ACU	CFG	FRC
2014	20%	27%	–	9%	100%	50%	78%	88%	82%	63%
2013	10%	C	9%	8%	C	78%	C	100%	95%	C

National Journal Ratings

	2013 LIB	—	2013 CONS
Economic	26%	—	74%
Social	52%	—	48%
Foreign	53%	—	46%
Composite	44%	—	56%

Key Votes of the 113th Congress

1. Guantanamo Bay Detainees	Y	5. Afghanistan Combat Y	9. Immigration Exec. Action Y
2. Abortion 20-week ban	Y	6. NSA Phone Data Collection Y	10. Bipartisan budget deal N
3. Medical Marijuana	Y	7. Syrian Rebels Training N	
4. Farm Bill	N	8. Keystone pipeline Y	

Election Results

2014 general   Mark Sanford (R)..................... 119,392   (93%) $1,317,225 $130,231 $957,238
2014 primary Mark Sanford (R)..................unopposed

Prior winning percentages: 2013 special (54%), Governor: 2006 (55%), 2002 (53%); House: 1998 (91%), 1996 (96%), 1994 (66%)

Population		Race and Ethnicity		Income	
Total:	715,200	White	70.5%	Median income:	$59,318
Urban:	48.9%	Black	18.4%		*(131 of 435)*
Suburban:	46.1%	Latino	6.9%	Under $50,000	42.7%
Rural:	5.0%	Asian	1.7%	$50,000-$99,999:	32.3%
Land area:	2,374	Two races	1.9%	$100,000-$199,999:	20.0%
Pop/sq. mi.:	301.3	White Ethnic	25.8%	$200,000 or more:	5.1%
Born in state:	42.9%			Poverty Rate	13.3%
		Education			
Age Groups		H.S. grad or less:	29.5%	**Work**	
Under 18:	22.0%	Some college:	32.1%	White collar:	38.6%
18 to 34:	24.0%	College degree, 4 yr.:	23.8%	Blue collar:	44.1%
35 to 64:	38.5%	Post-grad study:	14.6%	Sales and service:	17.3%
Over 64:	15.5%				
		Military		Govt. workers:	17.6%
		Veterans/active duty:	14.1%		

Lowcountry: Charleston, Hilton Head

Looking out across the harbor to Fort Sumter are the glorious mansions of the Battery, gazing on the same view that the hot-blooded young swells of Charleston did in April 1861, when they fired the shots that began the Civil War. Today, there are few more beautiful urban scenes in America than the

Voter Turnout	
2013 Total Citizen 18+	534,093
2014 House Turnout	127,815
2014 Turnout as % CVAP	23.9%
2012 Turnout as % CVAP	57.2%

pastel "single houses" of Charleston, built flush with the sidewalk, turning their shoulders to the streets, with open piazzas inside their iron gateways facing south to catch the breeze. Founded in 1670, Charleston was blessed with one of the finest harbors on the Atlantic, at the point where, Charlestonians like to say, the Ashley and Cooper rivers meet to form the Atlantic Ocean. It was one of the South's two leading cities during the Civil War. Cargoes of rice, indigo, cotton, and slaves crossed its docks, enriching the white planters and merchants who dominated the state's economic and political life. After the war, Charleston became an economic backwater, enabling the old buildings to survive. The loving restorations of recent years have made the center city look better than ever and have attracted a considerable tourist trade.

Charleston's old society—descended from planters from Barbados, French Huguenots, Sephardic Jews, and the second sons of English gentry—was once a leading force in American political life. The hotheads in the gallery disrupted the 1860 Democratic National Convention here so boisterously that it adjourned and reconvened in Baltimore, while Southern Democrats split off and nominated their own candidate, enabling Abraham Lincoln to win with 38 percent of the popular vote. The history of black South Carolinians, memorialized in George Gershwin's *Porgy and Bess*, is noteworthy, but the tale of slavery, once hidden under a blanket of politeness, is only now emerging. Many, though not all, plantations near Charleston are adding programs on the history of slavery to tours once dominated by romantic tales of the old South. The decision by Gov. Nikki Haley to remove the Confederate flag from the state capital following the June 2015 shootings at a black church in downtown Charleston seemed likely to accelerate that local rethinking.

The 1st Congressional District of South Carolina stretches along the coast from Charleston down to Hilton Head. It includes the coastal parts of Beaufort County taking in the old county seat of Beaufort and the carefully manicured developments of Hilton Head Island, plus parts of burgeoning inland suburbs in Berkeley and Dorchester counties. It includes the heavily white Battery and the area west of the Ashley River, but not the heavily African-American areas to the north in downtown Charleston. About 40% of the population is in Charleston, another 40% in the inland counties, and 20% in Beaufort. The district takes in the Marine Corps' Parris Island training base and air station, which is the base for five squadrons of the F-35 Joint Strike Fighter. This part of the district distinctively blends old and new. Beaufort's old mansions and evocative Spanish moss provided the backdrop for novelist Pat Conroy, while the posh condominium developments and golfing resorts around Hilton Head help drive up Beaufort County's population, which doubled between 1990 and 2013. On nearby St. Helena Island, slave owners escaping the heat and the mosquitoes

ran largely absentee operations, thus allowing Gullah culture—a fusion of English and
African elements—to thrive.

This is comfortable Republican country,
but the conservatism of the Lowcountry—
the term for South Carolina's coastal counties, including Charleston—is more economic
and less cultural than the conservatism of
the Upstate region. Many voters here favor
environmental restrictions and efforts to
curb sprawl.

2012 Presidential Vote		
Mitt Romney (R)................174,391	(58%)
Barack Obama (D) 119,833	(40%)

2008 Presidential Vote		
John McCain (R).................156,560	(56%)
Barack Obama (D) 119,461	(43%)

Cook Partisan Voting Index: R+11

Mark Sanford (R)

Republican Mark Sanford won a May 2013 special election to represent the 1st District,
completing an extraordinary political comeback. A disgraced former governor whose personal life became a national punch line, Sanford recaptured his old House seat in hopes of
rebuilding his earlier persona as one of the GOP's most stringent fiscal conservatives. His
re-entry to Congress was notably tame.

Sanford grew up in Fort Lauderdale, Florida, the son of a heart surgeon. The family
spent summers and vacations on a 3,000-acre farm in Beaufort County, once known as Coo-
saw Plantation, and moved there permanently when Mark was 18. He graduated from Furman University and the University of Virginia business school. He worked in real estate
investment in New York and later started his own firm in Charleston.

When the seat was open in 1994, Sanford, with no political experience, ran for the House.
He campaigned as an outsider and pledged to serve only three terms, to take no political
action committee money, to vote for no tax increases, and to refuse any salary increase until
the federal budget was balanced. He won a primary runoff 52%-48% and then easily prevailed in the general election with 66% of the vote. In the House, Sanford became a voice for
reduced federal spending, and he declined to seek pork barrel projects for his district.

After honoring his term-limit pledge, Sanford in 2002 launched a campaign for governor. He beat two better-known Republicans in the primary, then faced Democratic Gov. Jim
Hodges, who played up his modest background and called Sanford a wealthy Charleston
plantation owner from South Florida. One of his ads attacked Sanford for having voted
"against programs for disabled kids." But then it was revealed that Hodges had transferred
$300,000 from a fund for emotionally disturbed children to the operating account for the
governor's office. Campaigning in khakis and a plaid shirt, Sanford promised to end politics
as usual and won 53%-47%.

As governor, Sanford had an extremely strained relationship with the Republican-controlled
legislature. In 2004, he issued 106 budget vetoes to cut spending and the House overrode 105 of
them. He angered legislators by sneaking two piglets into the State House—which he dubbed
"Pork" and "Barrel"—to symbolize the legislature's wasteful spending; the pigs defecated on the
carpet. But the public loved the stunt. *Time* magazine in 2005 named Sanford one of the three
worst governors in the nation, listing as evidence Standard & Poor's decision to lower South
Carolina's bond rating. Sanford dismissed the story as an attack by a liberal magazine.

Seeking a second term in 2006, Sanford easily won the GOP primary and faced Democratic challenger Tommy Moore, a state senator and veteran legislative dealmaker who
emphasized his ability to bring people together. Sanford framed the race as a choice between
his outsider's approach and the state's business-as-usual political culture. He raised more
than $8 million, compared with Moore's $3 million, and won 55%-45%.

Sanford's tightfisted budgeting, popular with some national conservatives, stirred talk
of a possible place for him on the Republican national ticket in 2008. During a July 2008
interview on CNN, host Wolf Blitzer asked Sanford to specify distinctions between Republican presidential candidate John McCain and President George W. Bush on the economy.
Sanford drew a blank for several seconds, before citing the North American Free Trade
Agreement. Blitzer pointed out Bush and McCain agreed on free trade. The clip of Sanford's
flub replayed for days, probably sinking Sanford's chances of joining the ticket. His political
future soon worsened.

In June 2009, reports surfaced that Sanford had not been at work for several days.
As legislators wondered where he was, Sanford's spokesman reported that the governor
was in the mountains hiking the Appalachian Trail. But a reporter for *The State*, acting on

a tip, staked out Atlanta's Hartsfield-Jackson airport and confronted Sanford, who admitted that he had not been hiking. Back in Columbia that afternoon, Sanford said in a rambling, unscripted news conference that he had been carrying on an extramarital affair with a woman from Argentina. He made clear he intended to remain as governor, although he resigned as chairman of the Republican Governors Association.

A few days later, Sanford gave an interview to the Associated Press in which the married governor and father of four called his mistress, Maria Belen Chapur, his "soul mate." More than half of the Republicans in the state Senate called for Sanford's resignation. Several members of the state's congressional delegation either publicly or privately urged him to step down. But he refused and finished out his term. The phrase "hiking the Appalachian Trail" entered the vernacular as slang for infidelity, and Sanford seemed to be washed up in politics. He took the well-traveled road of failed political conservatives to a commentator's job at FOX News, and he became engaged to Chapur.

When GOP Rep. Tim Scott was appointed to fill a vacancy in the Senate, Sanford decided to run for his House seat. Despite his obvious negatives, Sanford had reason to be optimistic: A Democrat had not represented the district since the early 1970s, and Republican Mitt Romney won 58 percent of the vote in the 2012 presidential election.

Sanford had plenty of competition in the primary. But he led the 15 GOP candidates in the first round of voting and took the runoff from Curtis Bostic, a former Charleston County Council member, 57%-43%. That set up a contest with Democratic businesswoman Elizabeth Colbert Busch, the sister of political satirist Stephen Colbert. Her brother's fame lent her considerable name recognition, and she stressed her moderate credentials. Sanford, meanwhile, could not escape his scandal. Revelations that his ex-wife, Jenny Sanford, had accused him of trespassing at her home prompted the National Republican Congressional Committee to withdraw its support of Sanford. He claimed he had just dropped by the house while his ex-wife was away to keep his son company during the Super Bowl.

Still, Colbert Busch would have had to run a perfect race to win, and she didn't. The political novice failed to connect with voters, her campaign themes seemed uninspired, and she made relatively few public appearances compared to the ubiquitous and people-friendly Sanford. He won 54%-45% and said of his unlikely comeback victory, "I am an imperfect man saved by God's grace."

Back in Congress, Sanford learned that many subcommittee chairmen were reluctant to have him on their panels, fearing he could cause an unwanted distraction. House Speaker John Boehner helped smooth things over. Sanford now serves on the Budget Committee and the Transportation and Infrastructure panel. He avoided wading into splashy sound-bite fights and dutifully attended hearings; his perseverance was rewarded in June 2014 when the House passed his bill to end the Transportation Security Agency's practice of paying higher wages to workers for skills they don't use at their jobs.

Sanford remained a strong fiscal conservative but ranked toward the middle on social and foreign-policy issues. He broke from the GOP in June 2013 on a Democratic measure that would have blocked the TSA's "behavior-detection program," which some minorities say amounts to ethnic profiling. He also was one of just 10 Republicans to oppose a Homeland Security funding bill that tightened restrictions on illegal immigrants. "I've always thought that Mark may be more of a libertarian than a Republican," Richard Quinn, a South Carolina GOP consultant, told McClatchy News Service.

Sanford's political life regained some normalcy. In 2014, he was reelected without major-party opposition. In June 2015, he issued a statement supporting the decision by Gov. Nikki Haley to remove the Confederate flag from the State House grounds. He quoted a biblical passage: "All things are lawful, but all are not profitable ... but all do not edify." Also that month, he showed his libertarian instincts when he cosponsored with Democratic Barbara Lee of California an amendment to eliminate proposed travel restrictions to Cuba. The amendment was defeated, 176-247, on a mostly party-line vote.

But Sanford's personal life continued to draw headlines. In September 2014, he announced in a rambling 2,346-word post on Facebook that he and Chapur were breaking up. He said the "agony of divorce" and a custody fight with his ex-wife had proven too much of a strain. "No relationship can stand forever this tension of being forced to pick between the one you love and your own son or daughter, and for this reason Belén and I have decided to call off the engagement," he wrote. The publicity startled Chapur, who later said that she had asked that he not make public the details of their split. But that didn't end the saga. In June 2015, *The Washington Post* reported that the couple attended a private reception at the Library of Congress and introduced themselves to other guests.

SECOND DISTRICT

Joe Wilson (R)

Elected Dec. 2001, 7th full term; b. July 31, 1947, Charleston; Washington & Lee U., B.A. 1969, U. of SC, J.D. 1972; Presbyterian; married (Roxanne); 4 children.

Military Career: Army Reserve, 1972-75; SC Natl. Guard, 1975-2003.

Elected Office: SC Senate, 1985-2001.

Professional Career: Practicing atty., 1972-2001.

DC Office: 2229 RHOB, 20515, 202-225-2452; Fax: 202-225-2455; Website: joewilson.house.gov.

State Offices: Aiken, 803-642-6416; West Columbia, 803-939-0041.

Committees: *Armed Services:* Emerging Threats & Capabilities (Chmn); Tactical Air & Land Forces. *Education & the Workforce:* Health, Employment, Labor & Pensions. *Foreign Affairs:* Middle East & North Africa; Terrorism, Nonproliferation & Trade.

Group Ratings

	ADA	ACLU	AFL-CIO	LCV	ITI	COC	HAFA	ACU	CFG	FRC
2014	0%	0%	–	3%	100%	93%	70%	88%	69%	100%
2013	5%	C	10%	4%	C	85%	C	88%	78%	C

National Journal Ratings

	2013 LIB	—	2013 CONS
Economic	10%	—	88%
Social	16%	—	74%
Foreign	15%	—	77%
Composite	17%	—	83%

Key Votes of the 113th Congress

1. Sandy storm spending	N	5. Medical Marijuana	N	9. Syrian Rebels Training	Y
2. Violence Against Women Act	N	6. Farm Bill	Y	10. Keystone pipeline	Y
3. Guantanamo Bay Detainees	N	7. Afghanistan Combat	N	11. Immigration Exec. Action	Y
4. Abortion 20-week ban	Y	8. NSA Phone Data Collection	Y	12. Bipartisan budget deal	Y

Election Results

2014 general	Joe Wilson (R)	121,649	(62%)	$964,754
	Phil Black (D)	68,719	(35%)	
	Harold Geddings III (I)	4,158	(2%)	
2014 primary	Joe Wilson (R)	43,528	(82%)	
	Eddie McCain (R)	9,818	(18%)	

Prior winning percentages: 2012 (82%), 2010 (53%), 2008 (54%), 2006 (63%), 2004 (65%), 2002 (84%), 2001 special (73%)

Population		Race and Ethnicity		Income	
Total:	671,907	White	67.0%	Median income:	$51,984
Urban:	23.9%	Black	24.8%		*(209 of 435)*
Suburban:	61.4%	Latino	5.0%	Under $50,000	47.9%
Rural:	14.7%	Asian	1.7%	$50,000-$99,999:	32.0%
Land area:	3,354	Two races	1.2%	$100,000-$199,999:	16.9%
Pop/sq. mi.:	200.3	White Ethnic	17.0%	$200,000 or more:	3.1%
Born in state:	52.7%			Poverty Rate	13.6%
		Education			
Age Groups		H.S. grad or less:	37.8%	**Work**	
Under 18:	23.1%	Some college:	29.9%	White collar:	37.3%
18 to 34:	22.9%	College degree, 4 yr.:	20.3%	Blue collar:	42.1%
35 to 64:	40.1%	Post-grad study:	12.0%	Sales and service:	20.6%
Over 64:	13.9%			Govt. workers:	18.9%
		Military			
		Veterans/active duty:	12.6%		

West-Central South Carolina: Parts of Columbia Metro, Aiken

In 1786, soon after the Revolutionary War, the South Carolina Legislature decided to move the state capital away from the Charleston aristocracy and into the interior, away from a city named after a king to a new city named after a discoverer of America. So began Columbia. The State House was

Voter Turnout	
2013 Total Citizen 18+	501,861
2014 House Turnout	194,808
2014 Turnout as % CVAP	38.8%
2012 Turnout as % CVAP	55.6%

built on high ground above the Congaree River in a town of one-and-a-half story houses with first-floor porticos, dormers and raised brick basements—"Columbia cottages." In 1865, Gen. William Tecumseh Sherman's army burned almost everything here but the State House—something remembered by a local Presbyterian minister's eight-year-old son, whose name was Thomas Woodrow Wilson. Columbia recovered but grew slowly, with the state government, the state university, the Army's Fort Jackson, and local insurance companies providing steady employment.

Columbia's politics were personified by Jimmy Byrnes, the Democrat who was first elected to Congress in 1910 and returned from top posts in President Franklin D. Roosevelt's Washington to serve as governor. Byrnes adamantly opposed the *Brown v. Board of Education* decision in 1954. Since then, upwardly mobile white South Carolinians, transplanted from underdeveloped rural areas to comfortable two-car-garage subdivisions, have turned Republican, first in national elections and then at the state and local levels. Metro Columbia is competitive: Richland County, which was 47% African-American in 2013, votes Democratic, but across the river, Lexington County, the home of South Carolina Gov. Nikki Haley, is heavily Republican.

The 2nd Congressional District of South Carolina includes parts of metro Columbia, excluding black neighborhoods in central and north Columbia that are in the black-majority 6th District. It contains the city's affluent white neighborhoods and the spread-out towns and countryside beyond. It includes all of Lexington and Aiken counties. Aiken, with its horsey trappings for polo and steeplechase, has long attracted affluent transplants. The district takes in Barnwell County and the Savannah River Site, which from 1954 to 1991 was one of the nation's nuclear weapons manufacturing complexes. Since then, it has been undergoing a multi-billion-dollar cleanup, an important economic driver regionally. Employment at Savannah River dropped to 11,000 people in 2012.

2012 Presidential Vote		
Mitt Romney (R)	171,829	(62%)
Barack Obama (D)	101,354	(37%)
2008 Presidential Vote		
John McCain (R)	172,967	(62%)
Barack Obama (D)	101,229	(37%)
Cook Partisan Voting Index: R+16		

The 2011 redistricting increased the Republican presidential vote in 2008 from 54% to 62% for this district, while the white population grew from 62% to 70%.

Joe Wilson (R)

Republican Joe Wilson, who won his seat in a December 2001 special election, has a reputation as a hard-working fiscal and defense hawk. But mostly he is known as the lawmaker who breached congressional decorum in a spectacular way in 2009 by shouting, "You lie!" during President Barack Obama's health care address to a joint meeting of Congress.

Wilson grew up in Charleston and graduated from Washington & Lee University and the University of South Carolina law school. He got his Republican stripes as an aide to Rep. Floyd Spence and then for Sen. Strom Thurmond. Wilson was deputy general counsel at the Energy Department during the Reagan administration. He practiced law in West Columbia for 25 years while working on several political campaigns. In 1984, he was elected to the state Senate, where he chaired the Transportation Committee. Throughout this period, he served 31 years as a staff judge advocate in the South Carolina Army National Guard. All four of Wilson's sons have been Eagle Scouts and served in the military, two of them in Iraq. His son, Alan, was reelected state attorney general in 2014.

In 2001, when Spence died after more than 30 years in the House, Wilson became the front-runner to replace his longtime friend and mentor. In his campaign, he pledged to continue Spence's focus on defense. He won the Republican primary with 76% of the vote and defeated his Democratic opponent easily, 73%-25%.

With a seat on the Armed Services Committee, he has concentrated on military issues. In 2011, he became chairman of the Military Personnel Subcommittee. In the fiscal 2013 defense authorization bill, he succeeded in keeping alive some of the Air Force's Global Hawk unmanned surveillance planes after the Pentagon had sought to retire them. At a January 2013 hearing, Wilson rebuked outgoing Secretary of State Hillary Clinton for not going on Sunday talk shows to discuss the terrorist attack in Benghazi, Libya, saying one of her priorities should have been "telling correct information" to the public.

Wilson criticized Obama for "holding our military hostage" with the across-the-board defense cut "sequester" that took effect that year after the president and Congress failed to reach a comprehensive spending deal. Wilson has advocated a closer military relationship with India, and he traveled frequently to Iraq and Afghanistan to review those conflicts when U.S. forces were engaged. In 2015, he took over as chairman of the Emerging Threats and Capabilities Subcommittee at Armed Services.

Wilson was unknown outside of his district, and barely known in Washington, before his outburst during Obama's September 2009 speech in the Capitol. As Obama was answering what he called critics' "bogus claims" of his health care legislation, Wilson called out, "You lie!" His behavior provoked stinging criticism on editorial pages and talk shows around the country. He apologized to Obama in a phone call but rebuffed Democratic demands for a more public apology from the well of the House. His South Carolina colleague, then-Democratic Majority Whip James Clyburn, alleged there was a taint of racism in Wilson's reaction, noting that no other president in memory had been the target of a similar breach in protocol during a joint session. Democrats pushed for a floor vote to sanction Wilson, and the House passed a "resolution of disapproval" on a mostly party-line vote.

Wilson took some heat at home in 2010 after he refused to sign a letter requesting an appropriations earmark for a $400,000 study of dredging in the Port of Charleston, a project aimed at making the port capable of accommodating larger ships that will cross the enlarged Panama Canal. The letter was submitted to the Appropriations committees from the South Carolina congressional delegation, but Wilson and then-Sen. Jim DeMint declined to sign because they objected to earmarking. When the study was refused, civic and business leaders who saw the project as vital to the state's future economic growth were enraged. The Obama administration decided to pursue the study the following year, and Wilson praised the move.

On other issues with strong local interest, Wilson typically has joined most other South Carolina Republicans in opposing trade promotion authority for presidents. In 2011, he refused to support a trade deal with South Korea, which competes against his state's textile industry. Ironically, despite their antipathy for Obama, Wilson and three other House Republicans from South Carolina voted in June 2015 to give him trade promotion authority for the prospective Trans-Pacific Partnership. In March 2010, Wilson criticized the Obama administration's decision to withhold funding for the Yucca Mountain nuclear waste depository in Nevada, saying that the Savannah River Site would be stuck indefinitely holding 7,200 containers of spent nuclear waste. His legislation to reverse the decision failed to advance.

On the Education and the Workforce Committee, Wilson in 2003 won House passage of a bill to expand college loan forgiveness for math, science, and special education teachers who work in impoverished areas. He also worked with Democrats to make permanent the child adoption tax credit. But he failed to get the top Republican slot on the committee when it came open in 2009. Although he had more seniority, he lost out to John Kline of Minnesota.

Over the years, Wilson has been reelected by wide margins. His district includes some of the strongest tea party bastions in the state. In the 2014 primary, he got 82 percent of the vote against Eddie McCain, who ran as a Libertarian when Wilson won the 2001 special election. Wilson's willingness to counsel South Carolina's four Republicans elected in 2010 led them to dub him "the Scoutmaster."

THIRD DISTRICT

Jeff Duncan (R)

Elected 2010, 3rd term; b. Jan. 7, 1966, Greenville; Clemson U., B.A. 1988; Southern Baptist; married (Melody); 3 children.

Elected Office: SC House, 2002-10.

Professional Career: Asst. V.P., M.S. Bailey & Son, 1989-93; Asst. V.P., Palmetto Bank, 1993-95; Pres., J. Duncan & Assocs., 1995-2010.

DC Office: 106 CHOB, 20515, 202-225-5301; Fax: 202-225-3216; Website: jeffduncan.house.gov.

State Offices: Anderson, 864-224-7401; Laurens, 864-681-1028.

Committees: *Foreign Affairs:* Asia & the Pacific; Western Hemisphere (Chmn). *Homeland Security:* Border & Maritime Security; Oversight & Management Efficiency. *Natural Resources:* Energy & Mineral Resources (VChmn); Water, Power & Oceans.

Group Ratings

	ADA	ACLU	AFL-CIO	LCV	ITI	COC	HAFA	ACU	CFG	FRC
2014	10%	16%	–	3%	60%	43%	92%	100%	100%	88%
2013	5%	C	10%	7%	C	69%	C	100%	97%	C

National Journal Ratings

	2013 LIB	—	2013 CONS
Economic	5%	—	94%
Social	16%	—	74%
Foreign	0%	—	95%
Composite	10%	—	90%

Key Votes of the 113th Congress

1. Sandy storm spending	N	5. Medical Marijuana	Y	9. Syrian Rebels Training	N
2. Violence Against Women Act	N	6. Farm Bill	N	10. Keystone pipeline	Y
3. Guantanamo Bay Detainees	N	7. Afghanistan Combat	N	11. Immigration Exec. Action	Y
4. Abortion 20-week ban	Y	8. NSA Phone Data Collection	Y	12. Bipartisan budget deal	N

Election Results

2014 general	Jeff Duncan (R)	116,741	(71%)	$582,705
	Barbara Jo Mullis (D)	47,181	(29%)	$19,574
2014 primary	Jeff Duncan (R)	unopposed		

Prior winning percentages: 2012 (67%), 2010 (62%)

Population		Race and Ethnicity		Income	
Total:	663,437	White	75.1%	Median income:	$40,365
Urban:	18.2%	Black	17.6%		*(386 of 435)*
Suburban:	41.1%	Latino	4.0%	Under $50,000	59.0%
Rural:	40.7%	Asian	0.7%	$50,000-$99,999:	28.1%
Land area:	4,812	Two races	2.2%	$100,000-$199,999:	11.4%
Pop/sq. mi.:	137.9	White Ethnic	18.7%	$200,000 or more:	1.5%
Born in state:	67.4%			Poverty Rate	19.2%
		Education			
Age Groups		H.S. grad or less:	49.3%	**Work**	
Under 18:	21.6%	Some college:	30.5%	White collar:	29.5%
18 to 34:	22.3%	College degree, 4 yr.:	12.8%	Blue collar:	40.8%
35 to 64:	39.3%	Post-grad study:	7.4%	Sales and service:	29.7%
Over 64:	16.8%			Govt. workers:	15.6%
		Military			
		Veterans/active duty:	9.0%		

Northwestern South Carolina: Anderson, Greenwood Suburbs

The Upstate in South Carolina was many days' travel by wagon from the Lowcountry plantations along the coast. It was first settled by Scots-Irish farmers, including the family of future Vice President John C. Calhoun, around the time of the Revolutionary War. The pioneers wanted to make big

Voter Turnout	
2013 Total Citizen 18+	505,014
2014 House Turnout	164,009
2014 Turnout as % CVAP	32.5%
2012 Turnout as % CVAP	52.5%

plantations of these forests, but the land was too hilly for the labor-intensive rice crops grown in the Lowcountry and sometimes too cold for cotton. So relatively few slaves were brought here, and the land became mostly small farms. Today, the racial and cultural tone of the Upstate shows traces of these roots. Clemson University was founded here by Calhoun's son-in-law and is one of the state's two land-grant institutions. (South Carolina State, a historically black university, is the other, located in Orangeburg.) This is a mostly white part of the South, with a hell-of-a-fella tone to daily life and a tradition-minded slice of Middle America.

Yet it is not untouched by change. The textile factories and mills have been shutting down, and a way of life in many of these rural areas has vanished with them. During the recession, Greenwood County suffered the largest increase in the poverty rate for any county in the nation, and its median household income dropped 28% during the same period. On the positive side, high-tech manufacturers like BMW, Michelin and GE have expanded, with growth throughout the Upstate. Interstate 85—once the Main Street of America's textile belt—travels through a booming corridor that runs from Raleigh-Durham to Atlanta, including the northwest corner of South Carolina.

The 3rd Congressional District of South Carolina follows the Georgia border from Augusta through the tree-harvesting country around McCormick County to mountains along the North Carolina border. The southern part of the 3rd has a few heavily African-American areas, like Edgefield County, where the late Sen. Strom Thurmond first won public office in the 1930s. (The former segregationist served until he was 100 years old, retiring in 2002 as the oldest member of Congress.) Edgefield has grown as part of the metropolitan area around Aiken and Augusta, Georgia.

This part of South Carolina, ancestrally Democratic, began trending Republican in the 1950s as cultural issues became more important in this fervently religious region;

2012 Presidential Vote		
Mitt Romney (R).................170,084		(65%)
Barack Obama (D)...............89,439		(34%)
2008 Presidential Vote		
John McCain (R).................169,177		(64%)
Barack Obama (D)...............93,523		(35%)
Cook Partisan Voting Index: R+18		

Thurmond switched to the GOP in 1964. Newt Gingrich swept the district's counties in the 2012 Republican presidential primary over Mitt Romney. Still, Romney won 65% of the vote against President Barack Obama, his best showing in a South Carolina district.

Jeff Duncan (R)

Republican Jeff Duncan was elected in 2010 to an open seat. His deeply-held conservative beliefs can prompt fierce rhetoric, which angers Democrats but plays well among his like-minded colleagues and at home.

Duncan was born in Greenville. His family moved frequently, mostly in the Carolinas, as they followed his father's job as a textile industry manager tasked with turning around underperforming plants. He got his bachelor's at Clemson University, where he played wide receiver on the football team, majored in political science and interned one summer for local legend Sen. Strom Thurmond, which Duncan called a "tremendous experience." After college, he worked as a community banker and then for a real estate auction company, which inspired him to start his own real-estate marketing firm that specialized in auctions.

In the South Carolina House for eight years, he worked on updating the funding formula for education and on lowering taxes. In 2007, he sponsored a bill allowing gun owners with concealed-carry permits to bring guns onto school campuses, arguing that if students had been armed at Virginia Tech that year, they could have returned fire on the deranged student who killed 33 people. The bill died on the House floor. In 2009, Duncan sponsored a bill creating an alternative state budget that did not use federal stimulus money, as a way of protesting President Barack Obama's $787 billion measure. Then-Gov. Mark Sanford recognized him as a "Taxpayer's Hero."

Duncan entered a six-candidate GOP field for the House seat in 2010. He was endorsed by the anti-tax group Club for Growth, built a 2-to-1 fundraising advantage and prevailed in a runoff with 51% of the vote against businessman Richard Cash. In the general election, he faced token Democratic opposition from Air Force veteran Jane Dyer, a FedEx pilot, who had little chance in the solidly Republican district. He won, 62%-36%, then widened his vote to 67% and 71% in his reelections.

Duncan believes in the "Jeffersonian principles of limited governments, free markets, and individual liberties" and thinks that the federal government has gone beyond its constitutional authority, he told *National Journal*. He would shift some of its powers to the states. "If the government would get out of the way, business would come back," he said. He has faithfully followed that approach in Congress. In 2011, he became the first member of Congress to receive a perfect score from the conservative activist group Heritage Action. In 2012, he enacted a bill that called for a strategy to address the Iranian threat in the Western Hemisphere. He became chairman of the Foreign Affairs Subcommittee on the Western Hemisphere in 2015.

Duncan has drawn attention for some of his outspoken comments. At a Foreign Affairs Committee hearing in January 2013 on the terrorist attack in Benghazi Libya, he rebuked outgoing Secretary of State Hillary Clinton for "gross negligence" in allowing the consulate there to "become a death trap." He tweeted in 2012 that 83% of doctors considered leaving the profession because of Obama's health care law, which became widely circulated in the blogosphere. The fact-checking site *PolitiFact* found it was based on a survey that did not specifically mention the law and labeled it "false."

A member of the Tea Party Caucus, Duncan has been part of the cadre of conservatives who have voted against GOP leadership priorities, including the debt limit increase in August 2011 and the bill to reopen the government after the shutdown later that year. In January 2015, he was the only South Carolina Republican who voted against giving John Boehner another term as speaker. "I believe a new speaker of the House would send the signal to the American people that we're hearing their concerns while also letting the president know that Congress is committed to upholding the rule of law," he said in a statement a few hours before the vote. He suffered no immediate payback for his vote.

Duncan reportedly is interested in running for governor in 2018.

FOURTH DISTRICT

Trey Gowdy (R)

Elected 2010, 3rd term; b. Aug. 22, 1964, Greenville; Baylor U., B.A. 1986, U. of SC, J.D. 1989; Baptist; married (Terri Dillard Gowdy); 2 children.

Elected Office: Solicitor, SC 7th Circuit, 2001-10.

Professional Career: Prosecutor, U.S. Atty. Office SC, 1994-2000.

DC Office: 1404 LHOB, 20515, 202-225-6030; Fax: 202-226-1177; Website: gowdy.house.gov.

State Offices: Greenville, 864-241-0175; Spartanburg, 864-583-3264.

Committees: *Ethics. Judiciary:* Crime, Terrorism, Homeland Security & Investigations; Immigration & Border Security (Chmn). *Oversight & Government Reform:* Government Operations; Health Care, Benefits & Administrative Rules. *Select Benghazi Committee* (Chmn).

Group Ratings

	ADA	ACLU	AFL-CIO	LCV	ITI	COC	HAFA	ACU	CFG	FRC
2014	5%	0%	–	3%	80%	50%	87%	92%	95%	100%
2013	5%	C	10%	7%	C	85%	C	100%	97%	C

National Journal Ratings

	2013 LIB	—	2013 CONS
Economic	0%	—	98%
Social	31%	—	67%
Foreign	0%	—	95%
Composite	12%	—	88%

Key Votes of the 113th Congress

1. Sandy storm spending	N	5. Medical Marijuana	N	9. Syrian Rebels Training	N
2. Violence Against Women Act	N	6. Farm Bill	N	10. Keystone pipeline	Y
3. Guantanamo Bay Detainees	N	7. Afghanistan Combat	N	11. Immigration Exec. Action	Y
4. Abortion 20-week ban	Y	8. NSA Phone Data Collection	Y	12. Bipartisan budget deal	N

Election Results

2014 general	Trey Gowdy (R)	126,452	(85%)	$588,778
	Curtis McLaughlin (Lib)	21,969	(15%)	
2014 primary	Trey Gowdy (R)	unopposed		

Prior winning percentages: 2012 (65%), 2010 (63%)

Population		Race and Ethnicity		Income	
Total:	690,796	White	69.4%	Median income:	$46,532
Urban:	47.1%	Black	19.3%		(293 of 435)
Suburban:	51.5%	Latino	7.4%	Under $50,000	52.9%
Rural:	1.4%	Asian	2.2%	$50,000-$99,999:	29.3%
Land area:	1,445	Two races	1.5%	$100,000-$199,999:	14.8%
Pop/sq. mi.:	478.2	White Ethnic	19.4%	$200,000 or more:	3.0%
Born in state:	56.2%			Poverty Rate	17.5%
		Education			
Age Groups		H.S. grad or less:	40.5%	**Work**	
Under 18:	23.9%	Some college:	29.6%	White collar:	35.0%
18 to 34:	22.8%	College degree, 4 yr.:	19.2%	Blue collar:	41.9%
35 to 64:	39.2%	Post-grad study:	10.7%	Sales and service:	23.1%
Over 64:	14.1%			Govt. workers:	11.3%
		Military			
		Veterans/active duty:	8.4%		

Greenville/Spartanburg Area

Voter Turnout	
2013 Total Citizen 18+	495,832
2014 House Turnout	149,049
2014 Turnout as % CVAP	30.1%
2012 Turnout as % CVAP	56.6%

A century ago, Northern investors seeking sites for textile mills looked at the Upstate of South Carolina and found what was described then as "mild climate, abundant water power, proximity to the cotton fields, and plenty of native labor already accustomed to a low standard of living." As mills fled New England, textile factories settled along the Southern Railway and Seaboard Coast Line tracks between Charlotte and Atlanta, especially in the Piedmont of South Carolina. The textile country might look bucolic, but Greenville, Spartanburg and the dozens of mill towns thick in the surrounding countryside became as industrial as Lancashire or the Ruhr. In the days before child labor laws, factory work sometimes began at age 6, condemning workers to a life of illiteracy. Escapes to a brighter future, such as the brilliant but brief baseball career of West Greenville's "Shoeless" Joe Jackson, were rare.

Today, this same stretch of land along Interstate 85, which parallels the Southern Railway, remains one of the largest textile-producing areas in the United States, even though most mills have shut down and those remaining are unlikely to survive. From 1973 to 2011, increasing imports and the productivity gains from technological changes reduced the state's textile and apparel jobs by 185,213—a more than 89% percent drop, according to the Heritage Foundation think tank (although Heritage also found that total South Carolina employment grew by 187% in that period). Many of those textile jobs went to China, and more recently to Vietnam.

Many former textile workers have taken jobs with the new companies discovering the region's virtues. Financial sweeteners, tax incentives, the absence of unions, and solid infrastructure—airports, interstate highways, and the busy Port of Charleston—attracted an enormous BMW plant in Spartanburg. In March 2014, the company announced an expansion that will increase production capacity in 2016 to 450,000 vehicles, its biggest plant worldwide. The payroll at the plant is expected to reach close to 9,000 people. Michelin is also headquartered here. Greenville's revitalized downtown boasts fancy hotels and restaurants, many featuring Korean, Thai and Vietnamese cuisine—each catering to the new corporate manager class.

The 4th Congressional District of South Carolina includes most of Greenville and Spartanburg counties, with more than 60 percent living in Greenville. Along with Anderson (not in the district), Greenville and Spartanburg comprise the largest population area in South Carolina, with more than 1 million residents. Greenville County is the most populous county in the state. Culturally, the 4th ranges from conservative to very conservative, with strong influence from Greenville's many evangelical and fundamentalist churches. Bob Jones University is here as well; it has dropped its longtime ban on interracial dating, but students are still prohibited from smoking, drinking, dancing, and wearing jeans or shorts to class. Here, the real political divide is between religious and economic conservatives. But large new subdivisions have sprouted between Greenville and Spartanburg, and newcomers have brought religious diversity. Greenville has growing numbers not only of Catholics and Jews, but also of Muslims, Buddhists, Hindus, Baha'is, and even has a gay-oriented church. Hispanics have grown to 9 percent of Greenville County's population, one of the largest countywide totals in the state. Still, the 4th is heavily Republican, like most of Upstate.

2012 Presidential Vote		
Mitt Romney (R)	170,623	(62%)
Barack Obama (D)	99,359	(36%)
2008 Presidential Vote		
John McCain (R)	164,141	(61%)
Barack Obama (D)	102,157	(38%)
Cook Partisan Voting Index:	R+15	

Trey Gowdy (R)

Republican Trey Gowdy, elected in 2010, likes to call himself "a prosecutor, not a politician." He has doggedly pressed investigations of the Obama administration, but he has a politician's gregarious personality. Speaker John Boehner named him to head a select committee investigating the Obama administration's handling of the 2012 terrorist attacks in Benghazi, Libya, an issue that has been a *cause celebre* for conservatives. He also has been on the front-lines of the GOP's handling of immigration issues.

Gowdy grew up in Spartanburg. His father grew up poor but put himself through medical school and became a pediatrician. The family was well-off financially, but young Trey was encouraged to get jobs mowing lawns and bagging groceries. His academic performance in his younger years was "extraordinarily average," Gowdy told *National Journal*. As a teenager, he was inspired by Ronald Reagan's 1980 campaign for president and by a stint as a Senate page, sponsored by home-state Sen. Strom Thurmond. Gowdy graduated from Baylor and earned a law degree from the University of South Carolina.

In 1994, Gowdy became a prosecutor for the U.S. Attorney's Office in Greenville, where he worked on cases ranging from drug trafficking to murder. In 2000, he was elected as county solicitor and was reelected twice. In that role, he sought the death penalty in seven cases and won them all. Much of the job was managerial, but Gowdy says he tried about half of the cases that came through his office himself, with a focus on violence against women and drunken driving. Gowdy, who named his dogs Judge, Jury, and Bailiff, says that being a prosecutor was "the best job I will ever have in my life."

He challenged six-term GOP Rep. Bob Inglis in the 2010 Republican primary after the incumbent had tacked to the left on several issues. Gowdy portrayed his opponent as a Washington insider whose positions were out of step with the district's conservative voters. He criticized Inglis for earmarking funds in appropriations bills, for his opposition to President George W. Bush's 2007 troop surge in Iraq, and for his stand against oil exploration in Alaska's Arctic National Wildlife Refuge. Gowdy declared that he was running against the "sins of Congress," rather than an individual.

Gowdy led the initial five-candidate balloting, and soundly defeated Inglis in a runoff, 71%-29%. The outcome was a concrete early sign that the restless mood of voters in 2010 would spell trouble for incumbents that year, chiefly Democrats. In November, Gowdy breezed past Democrat Paul Corden, a retired businessman and Vietnam veteran, 63%-29%. He has been reelected with comparable margins.

In the House, Gowdy has been a committed conservative. He has a firm belief in "a limited government that inspires trust and demands accountability." He usually is willing to offer opinions to reporters and to lavishly compliment his colleagues, and he despairs of the lack of civility in Congress. "We, Republicans and Democrats, are as kind and polite to each other as you could possibly be," he told a local audience in 2012. "That changes the moment the cameras come on." As chairman of the Oversight and Government Reform Committee's panel on the District of Columbia, he surprised city officials by not taking as heavy-handed an approach to monitoring the city as some GOP predecessors.

At the same time, Gowdy has been as ferocious as any of his Class of 2010 colleagues in taking on the Obama administration. He called for Attorney General Eric Holder to resign or be impeached for his failure to rein in the "Operation Fast and Furious" gun-tracking program. He dismissed as "mind-numbingly stupid" the assertion by Minority Leader Nancy Pelosi that the House panel's investigation of the program was linked to voter suppression. At a 2011 hearing on Nuclear Regulatory Commission Chairman Gregory Jaczko's alleged mistreatment of colleagues, he upbraided Jaczko: "When you have four eyewitnesses that testify to someone under oath, you know what they call a defendant after that? An inmate."

In 2013, Gowdy won a plum assignment as chairman of the Judiciary Committee panel on immigration. He told *GreenvilleOnline.com* that he wanted to develop an immigration reform bill that reflects "the humanity that I think defines us as a people and the respect for the rule of law that defines us as a republic." But even though the Senate passed a bipartisan bill in 2013, House Republicans could not agree among themselves about what should be included in the measure, and the effort eventually fell apart.

Gowdy was one of the most outspoken critics of the 2010 health care overhaul, blasting the president for falsely claiming that people would be able to keep their insurance under the law. "The president already has a Nobel Prize for peace; I think he's shooting for one in fiction," he told Fox News in November 2013. He later sponsored a bill that would authorize Congress to sue the president for failing to "faithfully execute" federal laws, including those with which the chief executive disagrees. It passed the House on a largely party-line vote in March 2014 but died in the Democratic-controlled Senate. "To me, it's not a political issue," Gowdy said. "Do you think the chief executive should have to actually enforce the law? I would think every member of the House and Senate would support that." In June 2015, he supported trade promotion authority for President Barack Obama, arguing that it would benefit his trade-dependent home state.

But it was the Benghazi investigation that thrust Gowdy into the spotlight. After the Oversight and Government Reform Committee spent months pursuing allegations that the administration bungled the response to the attack and lied to Congress about it, House GOP leaders created a select committee headed by Gowdy. "Trey Gowdy is as dogged, focused, and serious-minded as they come," House Speaker John Boehner said in announcing the decision. Gowdy later cautioned Republicans against seeking to raise money off "the backs of four murdered Americans," but the issue proved too enticing to party officials seeking to galvanize the base. After House Democrats initially denounced the select committee as a partisan stunt, they agreed to participate, and the panel convened closed-door hearings in summer 2014.

In 2015, the Benghazi panel became riven by partisan strife. The House Intelligence Committee released a bipartisan report that concluded there was no wrongdoing by Obama administration officials. The panel's ranking Democrat, Elijah Cummings of Maryland, accused Gowdy of holding secret meetings with witnesses and then withholding or downplaying information from those interviews that undermined the GOP's investigation. Cummings and other Democrats objected to Gowdy's plan to subpoena 22 witnesses without a debate or vote. Gowdy responded that he had tried to work out a deal with Democrats over subpoenas, only to be rebuffed.

As the months passed, the investigation seemed to focus increasingly on presidential candidate Hillary Clinton, the former secretary of State. Gowdy and his GOP colleagues relentlessly pursued Clinton's involvement with Benghazi wherever it led, including the emails that she had sent while in office via a private server, her decision to wipe her computer clean of those files, the emails that were retained by confidants, and the broader circumstances that left Ambassador to Libya Christopher Stevens and three other officials murdered. In his fact-gathering, Gowdy appeared to be preparing details and conclusions that might have an impact on the 2016 presidential campaign. In June 2015, Cummings accused Gowdy of using the investigation as a "fundraising tool."

Gowdy was approached about potentially challenging South Carolina Republican Sen. Lindsey Graham in a 2014 primary, but demurred. He told conservative talk radio host

Laura Ingraham, "I do not want to stay in Washington. I am where I want to be right now, which is South Carolina, dreading driving to the airport [to fly to D.C.] tomorrow." Graham returned the favor in February 2015 by saying that if he were president, he would nominate Gowdy to serve on the Supreme Court. For now, Gowdy's future seems wide open.

FIFTH DISTRICT

Mick Mulvaney (R)

Elected 2010, 3rd term; b. July 21, 1967, Alexandria, VA; Georgetown U., B.S. 1989, U. of NC, Chapel Hill, J.D. 1992; Catholic; married (Pamela); 3 children.

Elected Office: SC House, 2007-09; SC Senate, 2009-11.

Professional Career: Practicing atty., 1993-2000; Real estate firm owner, 2000-10.

DC Office: 2419 RHOB, 20515, 202-225-5501; Fax: 202-225-0464; Website: mulvaney.house.gov.

State Offices: Gaffney, 864-206-6004; Rock Hill, 803-327-1114; Sumter, 803-774-0186.

Committees: *Financial Services:* Financial Institutions & Consumer Credit; Monetary Policy & Trade (VChmn); Oversight & Investigations. *Oversight & Government Reform:* Government Operations; Health Care, Benefits & Administrative Rules (VChmn).

Group Ratings

	ADA	ACLU	AFL-CIO	LCV	ITI	COC	HAFA	ACU	CFG	FRC
2014	10%	0%	–	3%	80%	57%	86%	95%	95%	63%
2013	5%	C	10%	7%	C	85%	C	100%	97%	C

National Journal Ratings

	2013 LIB	—	2013 CONS
Economic	0%	—	98%
Social	31%	—	67%
Foreign	50%	—	49%
Composite	28%	—	72%

Key Votes of the 113th Congress

1. Sandy storm spending	N	5. Medical Marijuana	Y	9. Syrian Rebels Training	N
2. Violence Against Women Act	N	6. Farm Bill	N	10. Keystone pipeline	Y
3. Guantanamo Bay Detainees	N	7. Afghanistan Combat	NV	11. Immigration Exec. Action	Y
4. Abortion 20-week ban	Y	8. NSA Phone Data Collection	Y	12. Bipartisan budget deal	N

Election Results

2014 general	Mick Mulvaney (R)	103,078	(61%)	$1,136,134
	Tom Adams (D)	66,802	(39%)	$47,455
2014 primary	Mick Mulvaney (R)	unopposed		

Prior winning percentages: 2012 (56%), 2010 (55%)

Population		Race and Ethnicity		Income	
Total:	678,788	White	65.6%	Median income:	$42,920
Urban:	11.1%	Black	27.8%		*(345 of 435)*
Suburban:	61.5%	Latino	4.1%	Under $50,000	56.3%
Rural:	27.5%	Asian	1.1%	$50,000-$99,999:	27.9%
Land area:	5,089	Two races	1.0%	$100,000-$199,999:	13.8%
Pop/sq. mi.:	133.4	White Ethnic	15.5%	$200,000 or more:	2.0%
Born in state:	58.9%			Poverty Rate	17.5%
		Education			
Age Groups		H.S. grad or less:	48.7%	**Work**	
Under 18:	23.8%	Some college:	29.2%	White collar:	32.1%
18 to 34:	21.0%	College degree, 4 yr.:	14.3%	Blue collar:	41.2%
35 to 64:	40.4%	Post-grad study:	7.8%	Sales and service:	26.7%
Over 64:	14.8%			Govt. workers:	15.9%
		Military			
		Veterans/active duty:	10.8%		

North-Central South Carolina: Charlotte Suburbs, Sumter County

Some of the fiercest battles of the Revolutionary War were fought in South Carolina's Upstate, on hilly lands just being settled by Scots-Irish farmers moving up from the Lowcountry or down the Virginia Piedmont valley. This was a country of violent passions and unclear lines. Carolinians

Voter Turnout	
2013 Total Citizen 18+	504,872
2014 House Turnout	175,145
2014 Turnout as % CVAP	34.7%
2012 Turnout as % CVAP	57.6%

argued for years over which side of the North and South Carolina boundary Andrew Jackson was born on in 1767. Ever since, the fighting spirit and Calvinist faith of Upstate Carolinians have not wavered. This "Olde English District" remains intensely religious and pro-military, but it is no longer impoverished. For many years, the dominant industry here was textiles, traditionally the first factory enterprise of industrializing countries, with low pay and poor working conditions. But since the 1980s, the number of textile jobs has declined markedly while more sophisticated manufacturing has boomed. Smaller towns suffered massive unemployment in the 2007-09 recession—over 20% in some small counties—but there has been rapid growth south of Charlotte in York and Lancaster counties. Located 30 miles from downtown Charlotte and with an average home price of about $139,000 in 2015, Rock Hill has become an attractive destination for city workers looking for affordable housing.

Just to the west in Cherokee County, Gaffney is the heart of South Carolina peach country. It is home to the famed Peachoid, a four-story water tower tank off Interstate 85 that is shaped like a peach. (South Carolina has shipped more peaches than neighboring Georgia since the 1950s, despite the latter's Peach State nickname.) In the Netflix drama *House of Cards*, the fictional majority whip played by Kevin Spacey represents this district and, in one episode, hurries home to handle the crisis of a constituent dying in a highway crash after getting distracted by the erotic-looking sculpture.

The 5th Congressional District consists of all or part of 11 counties, mostly in the Upstate and some in the Midlands. Over half the population is in Lancaster and York counties and in Cherokee County, along I-85 and in the Charlotte exurbs. Politically, this homeland of Andrew Jackson is ancestrally Democratic but has become increasingly Republican. Much of the population growth in York and Lancaster comes from Charlotte suburban commuters with no ancestral ties here but with strong conservative views. In the outskirts of Columbia, the rural counties of Fairfield and Lee are majority-black, and

2012 Presidential Vote		
Mitt Romney (R)...............158,537	(55%)
Barack Obama (D) 124,561	(43%)
2008 Presidential Vote		
John McCain (R)................151,486	(55%)
Barack Obama (D) 120,018	(44%)
Cook Partisan Voting Index: R+9		

Sumter is 48% black. The district is 26% black. Overall, this has been a Republican district in presidential elections, although it voted only 55% for Mitt Romney in 2012.

Mick Mulvaney (R)

Republican Mick Mulvaney was elected in 2010 by toppling 28-year Democratic incumbent John Spratt, the chairman of the House Budget Committee. He has been a frequent critic of his party's leaders, though less outspoken than other classmates in demanding their removal. He sought to chair the influential Republican Study Committee in 2015, but lost to a more establishment candidate.

Mulvaney grew up in Charlotte, North Carolina, where his father left teaching to run a homebuilding business. His views were also shaped by listening to his grandparents' stories about economic hardships during the Great Depression and by his first political hero, Ronald Reagan. At age 13, he stuffed envelopes and was inspired by Reagan's 1980 campaign for president. "I remember seeing Reagan on TV and being able to understand what he was talking about," said Mulvaney. He got his bachelor's degree from Georgetown's School of Foreign Service, where he took a course from former Secretary of State Madeleine Albright and was voted student body president.

After getting his law degree from the University of North Carolina, he practiced at a large firm in Charlotte and then opened his own practice. Mulvaney sold the firm in 2000 to join his father's homebuilding business. He dabbled in politics, working in George W. Bush's first presidential campaign. In 2002, Mulvaney settled with his family across the state line in Lancaster County.

In 2006, he won a seat in the South Carolina House. Two years later, he was elected to the state Senate. He was one of 10 senators who supported Republican Gov. Mark Sanford's decision to reject federal economic stimulus money, and he usually supported Sanford's budget-cutting over the policies of GOP legislative leaders. In November 2009, he attended a town hall meeting where Spratt was jeered and booed when he explained his vote for the Democrats' health care bill. "I decided to run while sitting at the back of that meeting," Mulvaney told the Associated Press.

Serving as chairman of the Budget Committee did not help Spratt at home in the first two years of Barack Obama's presidency, as his district became a hotbed of dissent from the administration's agenda. On the stump, Spratt told voters, "It makes sense to reelect a seasoned old-timer like myself, who has been around the track a few times and knows how to get things done in Washington." Mulvaney slammed Spratt for his support of the Democrats' health care overhaul, the $787 billion economic stimulus bill, and cap-and-trade legislation limiting carbon emissions. He insisted that he liked and respected Spratt, but said, "Times have changed, and I think it's time for us to change congressmen." He spent $1.5 million to $2.5 million for Spratt. Outside spending by groups allied with Republicans narrowed the gap. Mulvaney won by a solid 55%-45%. In the area closest to Charlotte—York, Lancaster and Cherokee counties—he won 63% of the vote, a stunning outcome against a veteran incumbent. He has been reelected easily against under-funded challengers.

In the House, Mulvaney occasionally moved toward the center on social and foreign policy matters, but he has been a devout conservative on fiscal matters. In his first term, he often bucked his party leadership in the name of fiscal discipline and voted against several spending bills backed by House Speaker John Boehner. "My no votes are not motivated by a desire to poke my leadership in the eye," he told *National Journal*. "There's a certain value to a small group of people representing true north on the compass." Mulvaney was an author of the "cut, cap, and balance" proposal that Republican deficit hawks and tea partiers supported during the debate over raising the debt limit. The plan—which passed the House only to be tabled in the Senate—included a spending cap and a balanced budget amendment to the Constitution. He has parted ways with many conservatives in his attempts to restrain defense spending, despite his state's historic ties to the military. In 2013, the House adopted his amendment to cut the Pentagon's budget by $3.5 billion on a 215-206 vote.

Mulvaney was highly critical of Boehner's unsuccessful "Plan B" maneuver on taxes and spending to avert a so-called "fiscal cliff" before a bipartisan deal with the White House was struck in January 2013. Mulvaney called the final compromise "a formula for economic collapse." When it came time a few days later to reelect Boehner as speaker, he declined to cast a vote as a "silent protest." Subsequent news reports named him as one of the leaders of a failed plot to oust Boehner as speaker, although he later contended that he and Boehner patched up their differences. Mulvaney was given a seat on the Financial Services Committee, giving the Charlotte area's banks another strong ally. That move came with the help of South Carolina Sen. Lindsey Graham, who hoped (correctly, it turned out) that it would discourage Mulvaney from mounting a 2014 primary challenge. On the eve of the October 2013 government shutdown, he said that Republicans were too eager to use gimmicks rather than to take hard votes to reduce spending.

In late 2014, Mulvaney sought the chairmanship of the RSC, the in-house group of the chamber's most conservative members that expanded to include more than two-thirds of the Republican Conference. After Maryland GOP Rep. Andy Harris dropped out of the race following the death of his wife, Mulvaney appeared to be the frontrunner against three other colleagues. But he faced questions over whether he could unify the group's defense hawks and anti-interventionist libertarians. "I'm trying to find a way to bridge those two groups because they are both very real groups in the RSC," he said. Some RSC members expressed unease about his endorsement of a pathway to legal status for immigrants living in the country illegally. "The concern I have about Mulvaney is he seems to be forward-leaning on amnesty, and I don't think that's an RSC value," said Rep. John Fleming of Louisiana.

Ultimately, the expanded ranks of the RSC made the vote a referendum on the House GOP leadership. With the ideological splits among conservatives, Mulvaney found himself on the wrong side. RSC members chose Bill Flores of Texas, a less confrontational or publicity-seeking member and a selection that was welcomed by Boehner and his allies.

Perhaps soured by that experience, Mulvaney voted for Boehner as speaker in January 2015. In a statement, he cited lessons from the earlier failed effort to unseat Boehner. "First, I learned two years ago that people lie about how they are going to vote. And you cannot go into this kind of fight with people you do not trust," he wrote in a statement. He dismissed the 2015 vote as "an effort driven as much by talk radio as by a thoughtful and principled effort to make a change. It was poorly considered and poorly executed, and I learned first-hand that is no way to fight a battle."

His independence from both the RSC and the hard-core Boehner critics left Mulvaney positioned to build new coalitions for his conservative views on banking and fiscal issues. In 2015, he became a leader of the opposition to renewal of the Export-Import Bank, which set Mulvaney at odds with other Republican South Carolinians worried about the impact for home-state industries such as Boeing.

SIXTH DISTRICT

James Clyburn (D)

Elected 1992, 12th term; b. July 21, 1940, Sumter; SC St. U., B.A. 1962; African Methodist Episcopal; married (Emily); 3 children.

Professional Career: Teacher, 1962-66; Dir., Charleston Neighborhood Youth Corps, 1966-68; Exec. dir., SC Comm. for Farm Workers, 1968-71; Asst., Gov. West, 1971-74; SC Human Affairs Comm., 1974-92.

DC Office: 242 CHOB, 20515, 202-225-3315; Fax: 202-225-2313; Website: clyburn.house.gov.

State Offices: Columbia, 803-799-1100; Kingstree, 843-355-1211; Santee, 803-854-4700.

Group Ratings

	ADA	ACLU	AFL-CIO	LCV	ITI	COC	HAFA	ACU	CFG	FRC
2014	75%	77%	–	91%	80%	64%	6%	0%	2%	0%
2013	80%	C	100%	79%	C	45%	C	13%	15%	C

National Journal Ratings

	2013 LIB	—	2013 CONS
Economic	70%	—	29%
Social	73%	—	24%
Foreign	62%	—	38%
Composite	69%	—	31%

Key Votes of the 113th Congress

1. Sandy storm spending	Y	5. Medical Marijuana	Y	9. Syrian Rebels Training	Y
2. Violence Against Women Act	Y	6. Farm Bill	N	10. Keystone pipeline	Y
3. Guantanamo Bay Detainees	Y	7. Afghanistan Combat	Y	11. Immigration Exec. Action	N
4. Abortion 20-week ban	N	8. NSA Phone Data Collection	Y	12. Bipartisan budget deal	Y

Election Results

2014 general	James Clyburn (D)	125,747	(73%)	$2,184,698	$9,392
	Anthony Culler (R)	44,311	(26%)		
2014 primary	James Clyburn (D)	37,184	(86%)		
	Karen Smith (D)	6,086	(14%)		

Prior winning percentages: 2012 (94%), 2010 (63%), 2008 (67%), 2006 (64%), 2004 (67%), 2002 (67%), 2000 (72%), 1998 (73%), 1996 (69%), 1994 (64%), 1992 (65%)

Population		Race and Ethnicity		Income	
Total:	678,025	Black	56.5%	Median income:	$33,001
Urban:	38.8%	White	36.4%		*(427 of 435)*
Suburban:	22.5%	Latino	4.7%	Under $50,000	67.6%
Rural:	38.7%	Asian	0.9%	$50,000-$99,999:	24.5%
Land area:	5,444	Two races	1.0%	$100,000-$199,999:	6.7%
Pop/sq. mi.:	124.5	White Ethnic	8.6%	$200,000 or more:	1.2%
Born in state:	69.5%			Poverty Rate	27.3%
		Education			
Age Groups		H.S. grad or less:	52.0%	**Work**	
Under 18:	22.4%	Some college:	30.0%	White collar:	27.5%
18 to 34:	28.1%	College degree, 4 yr.:	11.4%	Blue collar:	46.3%
35 to 64:	36.1%	Post-grad study:	6.6%	Sales and service:	26.2%
Over 64:	13.5%				
		Military		Govt. workers:	19.2%
		Veterans/active duty:	10.1%		

Central South Carolina: Parts of Charleston and Columbia

South Carolina's coastal lowlands and islands are laced with sluggish rivers and swamps. Its early settlers, planters from Barbados, brought thousands of slaves from Africa, and Colonial South Carolina quickly became one of the richest parts of North America, with dazzling Georgian archi-

Voter Turnout	
2013 Total Citizen 18+	511,179
2014 House Turnout	173,432
2014 Turnout as % CVAP	33.9%
2012 Turnout as % CVAP	56.5%

tecture in Charleston and classic plantation gardens. The planters built great irrigation systems and grew rice, cotton and the dye-plant indigo, all heavily in demand in Britain and elsewhere. All this wealth, of course, was built on the slave labor of countless African Americans. In colonial times, a majority of South Carolinians were slaves, as were a majority of lowlands residents. South Carolina's black heritage has left a lasting imprint on American culture. Gullah, a mixture of English, French and African dialects, is still spoken on the Sea Islands, and Gullah customs survive—oyster roasts and sweet potato feasts at Christmas, handmade dolls and sweetgrass baskets. The poverty that was the almost universal lot of lowland blacks after the Civil War has eased only in the last generation, as development came to the coast and cultural isolation dissipated. But many African Americans decided not to wait for progress. They long ago abandoned South Carolina for opportunities in the North.

The 6th Congressional District of South Carolina, created in 1992 as a black-majority district, takes in the black central city neighborhoods of Charleston, North Charleston, and Columbia, but leaves out their affluent white areas, both urban and suburban, which are in the adjacent 1st and 2nd Districts. Columbia-based Richland has about 30% of the population; Charleston and Orangeburg are close to 15% each. The 6th includes most of Orangeburg County, home of the historically black South Carolina State University. Orangeburg was the scene of a massacre in February 1968, when three black students were killed and 27 were wounded by police while protesting a segregated bowling alley.

At the Emanuel African Methodist Episcopal Church in downtown Charleston on June 17, 2015, a 21-year-old white gunman opened fire on a Bible study group and killed nine people before he escaped and was captured a few hours later driving in North Carolina. The victims included the church pastor, Clementa Pinckney, who also was a state senator. The church was one of the oldest and most respected black churches in the South. "Emanuel A.M.E. Church is the rock upon which the A.M.E. Church throughout the South is built," local Rep. James Clyburn said at a prayer vigil the next day. Dylan Roof, who was charged with the nine murders, had earlier produced amateur videos that featured white-supremacist objects and themes.

Eulogizing Pinckney at a funeral service in the church, President Barack Obama delivered a stirring speech that addressed the age-old local themes of inequality, violence and the impact of racial bias. "For too long, we've been blind to the way past injustices continue to shape the present," Obama said. "Perhaps we see that now. Perhaps this tragedy causes us to ask some tough questions about how we can permit so many of our children to languish in poverty, or attend dilapidated schools, or grow up without prospects for a job or for a career."

In Orangeburg, the Dubai-based Economic Zones World announced plans in 2007 to build a 1,300-acre industrial and warehouse facility that was expected to generate 8,000 jobs during the next decade. When company leaders met local officials in February 2015 to discuss the status of the project, little progress had been made other than plans for a new interchange from Interstate

2012 Presidential Vote		
Barack Obama (D) 206,857	(73%)
Mitt Romney (R)...................73,588	(26%)
2008 Presidential Vote		
Barack Obama (D) 202,724	(72%)
John McCain (R)...................74,764	(27%)
Cook Partisan Voting Index: D+21		

95. In North Charleston, Boeing unveiled in 2012 its first 787 Dreamliner made in a new assembly and delivery plant. The facility was the source of controversy after the National Labor Relations Board complained that moving the assembly outside Washington state was designed to circumvent tighter labor laws. Gov. Nikki Haley railed against the ruling, as did Republican presidential candidates.

Republicans packed the 6th District with African-American Democrats, ensuring that six of the state's seven congressional seats would solidly favor Republicans. The black population increased under the new lines from 54% to 57%, with the district borders shifting southward to the Georgia-South Carolina border. Obama got 73% of the vote in 2012.

James Clyburn (D)

James Clyburn, a Democrat elected in 1992, is the highest ranking African American in Congress and the dean of his state's otherwise all-Republican delegation. He is the assistant minority leader, the third-ranking position in the House Democratic leadership—a job created for him after his party lost its House majority in 2011.

Clyburn grew up in Sumter, the son of a minister, and was educated at a private, all-black boarding school. As a young man, he joined the Student Nonviolent Coordinating Committee, which took its cues from the Rev. Martin Luther King Jr.'s Southern Christian Leadership Conference. In 1960, he was one of seven people who organized the state's first sit-ins, at a five-and-dime store in the Orangeburg town square. He met his wife while in jail for three days. Clyburn worked as a teacher, as an employment counselor, and in government antipoverty programs. In 1970, he ran for the South Carolina House and lost narrowly. Democratic Gov. John West appointed Clyburn as state Human Affairs commissioner, and he served 18 years, under two Democratic and two Republican governors. He ran twice for secretary of state, in 1978 and 1986, losing narrowly.

Then, the new black-majority 6th District was created. Clyburn ran for the seat and in the Democratic primary won 56% of the vote against four African-American opponents, all with serious claims to the nomination. Clyburn was better known, ran first or second in every part of the district, and piled up 88% of the vote in his home county of Sumter. Clyburn became the first African American to represent South Carolina in Congress since George Washington Murray (a distant relative of his) left in 1897. He has not faced serious opposition for reelection.

In the House, Clyburn established a moderate-to-liberal voting record and, in his early years, focused on local priorities. He also joined the moderate New Democrat Coalition at its inception in 1997, the only African-American House member to do so. Like other South Carolina lawmakers, he is a proponent of expanding the use of nuclear power, which provides more than half of the state's electricity. On the Appropriations Committee from 1998 to 2006, Clyburn focused on securing federal funds to develop the Interstate 95 corridor, which passes through rural counties in the district that historically were dependent on tobacco and cotton. The House twice passed his bill to create a Gullah/Geechee Cultural Heritage Corridor from northern Florida to North Carolina.

As chairman of the Congressional Black Caucus in 1999, he urged the Democratic National Committee to become more responsive to African Americans. After the 2002 election, he ran for vice chairman of the Democratic Caucus, arguing that the leadership needed to better reflect the party's diversity. He prevailed with 95 votes to 56 for New York Rep. Gregory Meeks and 53 for California Rep. Zoe Lofgren. In 2006, he was elected Democratic Caucus chairman, the No. 4 position in the party leadership, and later that year, after Democrats won control of the House, he was chosen majority whip, the No. 3 post. Then-Rep. Rahm Emanuel of Illinois also wanted to be whip but had less seniority than Clyburn, and he backed down at the urging of House Speaker Nancy Pelosi, who favored Clyburn. Emanuel took Clyburn's spot as Democratic Caucus chairman in recognition of his success in the 2006 election, when he chaired the Democratic Congressional Campaign Committee.

Clyburn sought enhanced influence for his whip organization in crafting policy, a way of getting more points of view from across party factions into the process of drafting major legislation. In 2007, he held a series of "listening sessions" with Democrats to explore options for an immigration bill. He led the Hurricane Katrina Task Force, which met regularly with local officials to coordinate the House's response to the devastation caused by Hurricane Katrina in 2005. "I truly believe that if the demographics of the affected areas had been different, the response of the federal government would have been different," he said in a 2007 speech in Baton Rouge. Clyburn also finessed a solution to a longstanding complaint by the CBC that they were prevented from advancing in the Democratic caucus because they couldn't pay their "dues" by raising large amounts of political donations in their disproportionately low-income districts. Clyburn convinced Pelosi to adopt a modified system that rewarded Democrats for non-financial contributions, such as making appearances for candidates and doing press interviews.

As the most prominent black politician in the state, Clyburn has been a player in South Carolina's often pivotal Democratic presidential primary. In 2004, after his first choice candidate, Rep. Dick Gephardt of Missouri, withdrew after the Iowa caucuses, Clyburn endorsed front-runner John Kerry rather than South Carolina native John Edwards. Although he did not take sides in the 2008 primary, he clashed with Hillary Clinton when she seemed to suggest that President Lyndon Johnson, in signing the Civil Rights Act of 1964, had a more important role than King and other key civil rights figures at the time. He later wrote in his 2014 memoir *Blessed Experiences: Genuinely Southern, Proudly Black* that an angry Bill Clinton called to blame him for his wife's defeat in the primary.

As the leader of an older generation of civil rights leaders, he was initially skeptical that Barack Obama could win the nomination. When Obama clinched it in June 2008, Clyburn told a radio interviewer that he went home to watch it alone on television "because what I was feeling was indescribable, and I was afraid that I would not be able to control my emotions."

After the election, Clyburn got into a conflict with Republican Gov. Mark Sanford, who said that he would not use all of the money available to South Carolina from the economic stimulus bill enacted in February 2009. Clyburn called the action a "slap in the face" to the predominately black constituents who would benefit. He also wrote a clause into the $787 billion stimulus bill that enabled state legislatures to bypass governors who rejected the money. Clyburn took on another South Carolina conservative, House colleague Joe Wilson, after Wilson infamously called out "You lie!" during Obama's health care address to Congress in 2009. Clyburn pressed a resolution formally reproaching Wilson for a breach of House rules, which passed on a largely party-line vote.

When Democrats lost the House majority in 2010, they no longer controlled the speakership and so lost one spot in their leadership lineup. Pelosi became leader, the top job in the minority. But a battle shaped up for the No. 2 position of minority whip between Clyburn and former Majority Leader Steny Hoyer of Maryland. Both had a legitimate claim: Clyburn had already been doing the whip's job for four years in the majority, and for his part, Hoyer had a right to remain in the No. 2 role, as he had in the majority. An intense, behind-the-scenes rivalry unfolded, with each camp touting his greater level of support in the caucus. To avoid a divisive outcome, Pelosi created the new job of assistant leader and made it the No. 3 post in the minority hierarchy. Clyburn was named assistant leader, and Hoyer became minority whip.

Clyburn's new job wasn't well-defined, but he used it to become one of his party's main messengers. After the Newtown, Connecticut, elementary school massacre, he compared the push for gun control to the civil rights movement. When Obama's health care law was a hot topic on the 2012 campaign trail, he told a gathering of South Carolina Democrats, "Do not be afraid to use the term 'Obamacare.' You should be proud of Obamacare." He spoke out forcefully against state voter-identification laws that he and other critics said disenfranchised minority voters. But he wasn't always on the same page as other Democrats; an Obama campaign spokeswoman disavowed his May 2012 remark that Republican Mitt Romney's private equity firm Bain Capital was guilty of "raping" other companies.

When Republicans regained House control in 2011, Clyburn went to bat for low-income minorities. At a meeting in June 2011, according to Robert Draper's book *Do Not Ask What*

Good We Do, he listened to Majority Leader Eric Cantor of Virginia propose turning food stamps into a block grant program and allowing states to do what they wanted with the money. "If you knew the history of my state, you wouldn't be in favor of that," Clyburn reportedly responded. Cantor never mentioned the idea again, although Budget Committee Chairman Paul Ryan resurrected it as part of his 2012 budget proposal.

Black Caucus members in February 2013 suggested Clyburn as a potential replacement for Rep. Ray LaHood as secretary of Transportation, but his spokesman shot down the idea. Several months later, he joined other Black Caucus members in blasting a Supreme Court decision that struck down a key portion of the 1965 Voting Rights Act. "Even before I came to Congress, there has been a drift away from the Voting Rights Act," he said. "And I think it is just the Supreme Court using an excuse to do what they didn't have good excuse to do before."

For months before Republicans added to their majority in the November 2014 midterm elections, Clyburn repeatedly predicted that the GOP would find "some reason" to impeach Obama. "These Republicans have decided that this president must have an asterisk by his name when he leaves office, irrespective of whether or not he gets convicted," he told MSNBC. Republican leaders repeatedly rejected such assertions. But most of his attention came from publishing *Blessed Experiences*. He told *The Post & Courier* of Charleston that writing the book made him realize he was "much more faith-based than I thought I was. ... I just found out those teachings in that parsonage [during childhood] shaped me more than I ever thought, and I don't know if I would have come to grips with that if I had not written this book."

SEVENTH DISTRICT

Tom Rice (R)

Elected 2012, 2nd term; b. Aug. 4, 1957, Charleston; U. of SC, B.A. 1975, M.A. 1979, J.D. 1982; Episcopalian; married (Wrenzie); 3 children.

Elected Office: Horry Cnty. Cncl., 2010-12.

Professional Career: Staff accountant, Deloitte Haskins & Sells, 1982-84; Practicing lawyer, 1984-present.

DC Office: 223 CHOB, 20515, 202-225-9895; Fax: 202-225-9690; Website: rice.house.gov.

State Offices: Florence, 843-679-9781; Myrtle Beach, 843-445-6459.

Committees: *Budget. Small Business:* Investigations, Oversight & Regulations; Economic Growth, Tax and Capital Access (Chmn); Health & Technology. *Transportation & Infrastructure:* Highways & Transit; Railroads, Pipelines & Hazardous Materials; Water Resources & Environment.

Group Ratings

	ADA	ACLU	AFL-CIO	LCV	ITI	COC	HAFA	ACU	CFG	FRC
2014	0%	0%	–	0%	100%	79%	67%	88%	75%	75%
2013	5%	C	14%	0%	C	85%	C	80%	76%	C

National Journal Ratings

	2013 LIB — 2013 CONS		
Economic	15%	—	85%
Social	16%	—	74%
Foreign	0%	—	95%
Composite	13%	—	87%

Key Votes of the 113th Congress

1. Sandy storm spending	N	5. Medical Marijuana	Y	9. Syrian Rebels Training	Y
2. Violence Against Women Act	N	6. Farm Bill	Y	10. Keystone pipeline	Y
3. Guantanamo Bay Detainees	N	7. Afghanistan Combat	N	11. Immigration Exec. Action	Y
4. Abortion 20-week ban	Y	8. NSA Phone Data Collection	Y	12. Bipartisan budget deal	Y

Election Results

2014 general	Tom Rice (R)............................ 102,833	(60%)	$830,874
	Gloria Bromell Tinubu (D) 68,576	(40%)	$229,052 $200
2014 primary	Tom Rice (R).........................unopposed		

Prior winning percentage: 2012 (56%)

Population		Race and Ethnicity		Income	
Total:	676,686	White	63.4%	Median income:	$38,707
Urban:	47.0%	Black	29.6%		*(401 of 435)*
Suburban:	16.2%	Latino	3.9%	Under $50,000	61.1%
Rural:	36.8%	Asian	1.0%	$50,000-$99,999:	28.4%
Land area:	5,540	Two races	1.6%	$100,000-$199,999:	8.5%
Pop/sq. mi.:	122.1	White Ethnic	18.6%	$200,000 or more:	2.1%
Born in state:	57.8%			Poverty Rate	22.3%
		Education			
Age Groups		H.S. grad or less:	49.8%	**Work**	
Under 18:	21.4%	Some college:	29.8%	White collar:	27.3%
18 to 34:	20.8%	College degree, 4 yr.:	13.4%	Blue collar:	50.3%
35 to 64:	40.1%	Post-grad study:	7.0%	Sales and service:	22.4%
Over 64:	17.8%				
		Military		Govt. workers:	14.5%
		Veterans/active duty:	9.7%		

Pee Dee/Waccamaw Region: Myrtle Beach, Florence, Georgetown

The Pee Dee region of South Carolina, named for the river that lazily winds its way through the northern lowlands of the Palmetto State (and originally the Pee Dee Indian tribe), is a diverse swath of tobacco and soybean farms, textile mills, and ocean beaches. It was here that Gen. Francis

Voter Turnout	
2013 Total Citizen 18+	513,435
2014 House Turnout	171,524
2014 Turnout as % CVAP	33.4%
2012 Turnout as % CVAP	55.1%

Marion pioneered guerilla warfare techniques against British soldiers during the American Revolutionary War. Marion's penchant for conducting lightning fast raids on larger British forces and then vanishing into the swamps earned him the name "Swamp Fox." Marion later became an inspiration for Benjamin Martin, the hero of the Mel Gibson movie *The Patriot*. The Confederate Navy made use of the river's long navigable stretches by placing the Mars Bluff Naval Yard on its banks, nearly 100 miles inland.

The 7th Congressional District, which is the state's newest district, takes in almost the entire Pee Dee region. Brisk population growth in Myrtle Beach meant that a district likely would need to be anchored in the area. State Republicans in control of redistricting in 2011 were happy to create the district that is solidly Republican. Democrats and African-American legislators hoped that the Obama administration would invoke the Voting Rights Act to force the state to draw an additional minority-majority district, but the administration ultimately concluded that the state was not required to do so.

The 7th District consists of two distinct areas of roughly equal population. The inland counties remain reminiscent of the Old South. Crossroads communities and farms dot the landscape, and on Labor Day weekend the Bojangles' Southern 500 fills the air around Darlington with the roars of stock car engines. Florence, historically the hub of the Pee Dee, is the only city in this portion of the district with a population in excess of 30,000. Unlike the rest of the area, Florence has experienced real economic development over the past decade. QVC home shopping network has a distribution center there.

The second half of the district is coastal. A century ago, this was largely uninhabited forestland, and Myrtle Beach wasn't incorporated until 1938. Today, the two coastal counties of the Pee Dee—Horry and Georgetown—are home to the 60-mile Grand Strand, comprising miles of beachfront and golf courses and drawing 15 million vacationers annually. The two counties' combined vote is half of the total for the district. From 2000 to 2013, Horry grew 47% to 294,000 people. The coastal areas of the district are overwhelmingly

Republican. The inland portions of Florence and Darlington are more competitive. Rural Marion and Marlboro counties are majority-black, and they vote Democratic. The district is 29% black, the largest in the state other than the black-majority 6th District. With shifts of black communities from the 5th District, this could have been more of a minority-influence district, but a black-majority district likely would have required creative mapmaking. Overall, the 7th is Republican, but not overwhelmingly so. Mitt Romney won 55% of the vote here in 2012.

2012 Presidential Vote

Mitt Romney (R)	152,577	(55%)
Barack Obama (D)	124,601	(45%)

2008 Presidential Vote

John McCain (R)	145,646	(54%)
Barack Obama (D)	123,077	(45%)

Cook Partisan Voting Index: R+7

Tom Rice (R)

Republican Tom Rice won South Carolina's newest district in 2012 with a focus on his business background and conservative politics in the growing region. He also secured a key endorsement from GOP Gov. Nikki Haley. Compared to the often raucous members of the state's congressional delegation, Rice has been more low-profile and studious.

Growing up amid the sand dunes of Myrtle Beach, Rice spent every day playing on the beach. His mother was a schoolteacher; his father, a repairman, died when he was young. Rice worked every summer after he turned 12, busing tables at the local tourist restaurants. At the University of South Carolina, he volunteered with Big Brothers Big Sisters. He stayed at the university to earn his master's in accounting and a law degree, returning home every summer to work at the beach.

Rice moved to Charlotte, North Carolina, to work for the accounting giant Deloitte. After gaining experience on larger cases, he returned home to practice tax law and eventually open his own practice. Rice served on the board of the Myrtle Beach Haven homeless shelter and, during his 10-year term as president, helped it build an expanded facility.

He ran successfully for Horry County Council chairman in 2010. In that role, he focused on rebuilding the Myrtle Beach Regional Economic Development Corporation and bringing jobs to the county. He brought a similar focus to Congress. "This country is in a critical state," Rice said. "We have to change, or we will bankrupt ourselves." To compete internationally, he argues, the government must create a more business-friendly climate by slashing regulations.

In 2012, Rice entered the crowded GOP primary field and came in second to former Lt. Gov. André Bauer. His opponent, the conservative favorite, had come under attack for comparing public school children who receive free lunches to stray animals who should not be fed. Bauer raised almost double the amount of campaign cash as Rice and labeled him a "moderate" in a wave of attack ads. But in the runoff, Rice crushed Bauer, 56%-44%, thanks in part to a powerful endorsement from the popular Haley.

In the general election, Rice faced ex-Georgia state Rep. Gloria Bromell Tinubu, who had been the underdog in the Democratic primary running on a platform of union advocacy. A South Carolina native and former economics professor at the mostly African-American Spelman College in Atlanta, she had served in the Georgia state House. Rice ran on the issues of job creation, increased military spending, protection of gun owners' rights, and simplification of immigration laws. He got support from the state tea party and National Right to Life Committee. He campaigned with House Speaker John Boehner and home-state GOP Sen. Lindsey Graham. Rice outspent Bromell Tinubu a bit more than 2-to-1 and won 56%-44%, the same outcome as in the primary. His entire margin of victory came from his base in Horry County, where he led 65%-35%. In the rest of the district, he trailed slightly.

Rice was active on the Transportation and Infrastructure Committee, where he was outspoken in his calls for raising the gasoline tax by as much as 13 cents per gallon to pay for improvements to highways and bridges. "Infrastructure is the foundation of which competitiveness is based," he said. In a vital caveat, he said that the increase should be offset by cuts in income taxes. He also serves on the Budget Committee and on Small Business, where he chairs the Economic Growth, Tax and Capital Access Subcommittee. He disagreed with neighboring GOP Rep. Mick Mulvaney, who sought to shut down the Export-Import Bank. "In a perfect world, I wish it wasn't there. And I wish that banks would step up to fill the void. But the problem is it's not a perfect world," Rice said.

In a 2014 rematch for reelection, Bromell Tinubu spent only $229,000, which was one-third her total in 2012. This time, Rice won 60 percent of the vote.

★ SOUTH DAKOTA ★

South Dakota is renowned for its natural beauty: you can see bison, bighorn sheep and elk at Custer State Park, ranked by Austin Adventures as one of the 10 best places for wildlife viewing in the world. But today the state is also prominent in the financial realm, and names like Citibank, Wells Fargo and Capital One are easily spotted on office buildings in Sioux Falls.

Lewis and Clark encountered herds of buffalo as they paddled up the Missouri River in the fall of 1804 through land where the Oglala Sioux became masters of the horses the Spaniards had imported to North America 350 years earlier. Fort Pierre was established as a fur-trading post in 1817 and Congress established the Dakota Territory in 1861, but few white men settled here until the 1880s. The Sioux remained dominant and their warrior chief Sitting Bull, now buried on a bluff above the Missouri River, destroyed Gen. George Armstrong Custer and his 7th Cavalry troops at Little Big Horn in 1876. Fourteen years later, many of the remaining Oglala Sioux Indians in South Dakota were massacred at Wounded Knee. After half a century of disease and a decade of defeat fighting the westward advance of white settlement, the Sioux were a traumatized people and in many ways, still are.

Indians are 8% of South Dakota's population; most live on reservations with proud traditions but terrible poverty. Isolated from the mainstream economic marketplace, they are beset by high rates of alcoholism and suicide. The life expectancy among the Lakota and Oglala Sioux on the Rosebud and Pine Ridge Indian reservations is 47 years for the average male, compared to almost 79 years nationwide, and lower than life expectancy rates in sub-Sahara Africa. Unemployment rates on reservations have regularly exceeded 80 percent. Incremental progress in infant mortality and preserving Sioux culture has been made over the years, and in 2007 the state added to school curricula units on the language and culture of the Lakota and other Indians. The Lakota of the frontier days were immortalized in the acclaimed 1990 film "Dances With Wolves," which won seven Academy Awards, including one for best picture, and stared Kevin Costner. The movie featured extensive Lakota dialogue and much of it was filmed in South Dakota.

Once the Sioux were forced to surrender their territory, white settlement of South Dakota came fast. After gold was first discovered in the Black Hills in 1874, the mountains swarmed with settlers. Deadwood became a city of 20,000 where Calamity Jane ruled the saloons and Wild Bill Hickok was shot in the back while holding two pair—aces and eights. Because barbed wire could not fence in the buffalo, ranchers massacred them so thoroughly that when Teddy Roosevelt visited the Dakota Territory in 1884, he had a hard time finding one to shoot. It was not long before the railroad came through and then permanent settlers, many of them German and Scandinavian immigrants recruited by the railroads. They built sod houses, broke the land, and set down roots, a story told by Jon Lauck in *Prairie Republic: The Political Culture of Dakota Territory 1879-1889*.

There were 98,000 South Dakotans in 1880; 401,000 in 1900; and 636,000 in 1920—at which point settlement pretty much stopped. Farmers settled the eastern third of the state, sectioned off Midwestern-style into 640-acre square miles. But moving westward, before a traveler reaches the Missouri River in the middle of the state, green turns to brown, cultivation grows sparse, and then just stops. The West River plains are open grazing land, scarcely touched by the white men who were so eager to establish dominion over them a century ago. The land is punctuated, not by roads meeting every mile at precise angles, but by buttes, gullies, and grasslands sweeping to the horizon with no sign of human habitation except the occasional missile silo that once pointed toward the Soviet Union.

South Dakota's political patterns were fairly well set by the early 1900s. Its early settlers were mostly Midwesterners who brought their Republicanism with them, of New England Yankee and German stock primarily, and also some Norwegians. Voters here never had much use for the Non-Partisan League, which caught on in North Dakota, and there was never anything here comparable to the Farmer-Labor Party of Minnesota. But the nature of the farm economy—its dependence on the great railroads and milling companies and on the vagaries of international markets—meant that South Dakota was subject to periodic farm revolts. It voted for populists and William Jennings Bryan in the 1890s, but then switched to Republicans. In the summer of 1927, when the sculpting of Mount Rushmore began, it welcomed President Calvin Coolidge when he vacationed in Custer State Park, where he

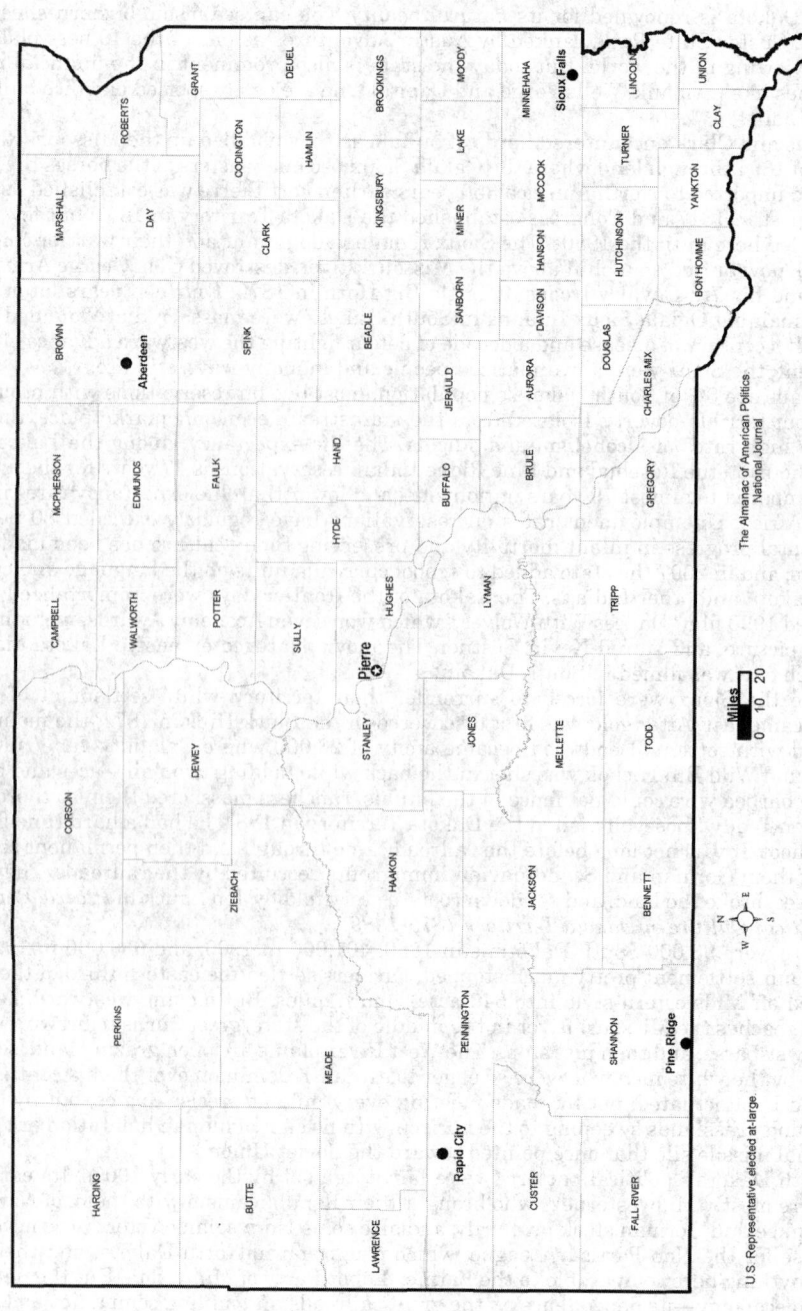

The Almanac of American Politics
National Journal

Miles
0　10　20

U.S. Representative elected at-large

announced he would not seek another term in 1928. South Dakota briefly supported the early New Deal and it revolted against the Eisenhower administration in the late 1950s by electing to Congress a young Dakota Wesleyan University professor named George McGovern. South Dakota shared the isolationist impulse of much of the Great Plains. McGovern's opposition to the Vietnam War in the late 1960s was not a liability here. For a moment in the mid-1970s, Democrats seemed on the verge of becoming the majority party.

Then South Dakota moved sharply to the Republicans, beginning with the administration of Gov. Bill Janklow, elected in 1978 and 1982 and then again in 1994 and 1998. In 1979, Sioux Falls banker Thomas Reardon suggested that the state get rid of its usury law limiting interest rates; inflation was driving market rates over most states' usury limits and choking off credit to consumers. Janklow and the legislature repealed the usury laws and in 1981 passed laws enticing Citibank to move its credit-card operations to Sioux Falls, where it could charge market interest rates—all in a state with no corporate or personal income taxes, and a community with a literate, low-wage work force. The Citibank operation has grown from 500 employees to 2,900, rivaling the meatpacker John Morrell, with 3,400 employees as a main source of jobs in a growing Sioux Falls metropolitan area whose population is almost 250,000. It didn't take long for Wells Fargo, Capital One, and other financial institutions to move their credit-card operations to the Sioux Falls metro. MetaBank, one of the leading issuers of gift cards and pre-paid paid credit cards, made its base in Sioux Falls in 2004. Now more than 16,000 people in the metropolitan area work in financial services.

A secondary industry that has popped up in Sioux Falls is mail-order pharmaceuticals. Cigna Home Delivery Pharmacy and MedVantx have set up operations there to take advantage of the logistics network that was built to enable credit-card companies to deliver replacement cards quickly and securely to their customers. Companies that promise prompt delivery of prescriptions to patients can use the same timely distribution system. The arrival of Citibank, and the other banks that followed, gave Sioux Falls and South Dakota something else besides employment opportunities; it enabled residents of an aging agricultural state to gain exposure to and experience in the 21st Century economy of finance. Such good fortune does not come to many rural communities that often struggle to just hang on and maintain their population. As Amy Sullivan cogently observed in *National Journal's Next Economy*: "Without Citibank, a local college graduate who wanted to work in high-level banking would probably end up moving to Chicago or New York City to gain the necessary training. Instead, Sioux Falls has an entire managerial class that trained locally—and stayed local." The Federal Deposit Insurance Corp. reported that in the first quarter of 2015, 73 financial institutions in South Dakota held almost $3 trillion in bank assets, more than any other state.

All this has given South Dakota prosperity and a mixed economy. It ranks high in credit ratings, low in foreclosures, and high in repaying college loans. Its residents and those in North Dakota spend less time commuting to work than Americans elsewhere. Its wage levels have risen to the point that per capita personal income in 2014 was $46,345, which ranked 21st in the nation, and was higher than the overall U.S. per capita personal income of $46,129. The decline in commodity prices for crops like corn and soybeans—the state's two largest accounting for $4.7 billion in production value in 2014—has been a drag on

Population		Race and Ethnicity		Income	
Total:	844,877	White	84.6%	Median income:	$54,453
Urban:	37.1%	Amer. Indian	8.4%		*(21 of 50)*
Suburban:	5.1%	Latino	2.8%	Under $50,000	51.0%
Rural:	57.8%	Black	1.2%	$50,000-$99,999:	32.8%
Land area:	75,811	Two races	2.2%	$100,000-$199,999:	12.6%
Pop/sq. mi.:	11.1	White Ethnic	19.9%	$200,000 or more:	3.7%
Born in state:	64.3%			Poverty Rate	14.2%
		Education			
Age Groups		H.S. grad or less:	39.8%	**Work**	
Under 18:	24.7%	Some college:	33.7%	White collar:	33.6%
18 to 34:	23.2%	College degree, 4 yr.:	18.9%	Blue collar:	43.0%
35 to 64:	37.4%	Post-grad study:	7.6%	Sales and service:	23.4%
Over 64:	14.7%				
		Military		Govt. workers:	15.5%
		Veterans/active duty:	9.9%		

the state's economy recently. In 2014, South Dakota's farm income decreased almost 21% compared to 2013, which was the primary cause of the tepid growth rate in total personal income in 2014. South Dakota nonfarm income grew 3.9%, slightly less than the national average growth rate of 4.1% in 2014. The state was not much affected by the recession. Unemployment rose to only 5.3%

Voter Turnout	
2013 Total Citizen 18+	623,276
2014 Highest Statewide Turnout	279,412
2014 Turnout as % CVAP	44.8%
2012 Turnout as % CVAP	58.9%

Legislature		
Senate:	27R	8D
House:	58R	12D

for four months in 2009 and was 3.8% in June 2015 and 3.2% in the Sioux Falls metropolitan area. Out-of-state firms have been setting up operations in South Dakota—Minnesota's Eagle Creek Software Services opened a technology center in Vermillion in 2014 with plans for an eventual 1,000 jobs; Bel Brands, a French company, built a 170,000- square-foot cheese processing plant in Brookings that opened in 2014; Minneapolis-based Twin Cities Fan, the largest maker of industrial fans in North America, undertook a major expansion in Brookings in 2013 and it has another facility in Aberdeen. Attractions such as Mount Rushmore and Custer State Park in the Black Hills helped boost tourism, which Gov. Dennis Daugaard said accounted for one out of every 11 jobs in the state in 2013. One challenge facing South Dakota's economy has been the lack of skilled workers: State government paid for training for welders and machinists and hired headhunting firms to find skilled workers from out of state. South Dakota's population rose 8% from 2000 to 2010, the highest rate in the Midwest, and another 4.8% between 2010 and 2014.

Overall, the greatest growth has been in and around Sioux Falls, and South Dakota can no longer be thought of as just a farm state. It is coming to resemble the Rocky Mountain States, with most people concentrated around a few prosperous and growing cities and towns, while vast acreage remains vacant, punctuated by infrequent farm and ranch houses. Sioux Falls' Minnehaha County and Lincoln County just to the south—the latter grew 15% from 2010 to 2014, more than three times the statewide growth rate—had 27% of the state's population in 2014. Five other counties containing the metro areas of Aberdeen, Brookings, Rapid City and Watertown contained another 28%. When Barack Obama traveled to the Lake Area Technical Institute in Watertown in May 2015 to deliver a commencement address, it made South Dakota the 50th state that he visited as president.

There was a much bigger event in the state's life earlier that year when a federal judge delivered a potentially landmark ruling in favor of Native American family rights. The decision came about as a result of a class action lawsuit that the American Civil Liberties Union brought in 2013 on behalf of two tribes and Native American parents in Pennington County. The suit charged that hundreds of children had been removed from their homes by state officials and placed into foster care after child custody hearings that at times lasted only a minute and where parents were not adequately advised of their rights. And in those custody hearings, the state prevailed a remarkable 100 percent of the time. U.S. District Court Chief Judge Jeffrey Viken ruled in 2015 that officials at the South Dakota Department of Social Services and other state agencies "failed to protect Indian parents' fundamental rights" when they removed their children after cursory hearings and placed them mostly in white foster care homes. The Indian Child Welfare Act of 1978 requires that state officials should place Indian children with their relatives or tribes if they are removed from their parents' custody. But a 2011 investigation by National Public Radio found that in South Dakota nearly 700 Native American children a year were routinely placed in nonnative homes, even when native homes and relatives were available. Advocates for Native American rights expect that Judge Viken's ruling will influence the way courts nationwide treat similar cases.

Politically, South Dakota has been mostly Republican. The last time it elected a Democratic governor was 1974. In the Democratic primary that year, Lt. Gov. William Dougherty unsuccessfully challenged incumbent Richard Kneip, who had backed efforts to reinstate the income tax in South Dakota. The proposal won approval in the state House of Representatives, but when the state Senate deadlocked on the measure, Dougherty cast the deciding vote against it. Dougherty was no conservative and his vote on the income tax probably had to do with his ambitions for higher office. While he lost the primary to Kneip, he made his mark in state politics in other ways: he directed Robert F. Kennedy's upset victory in the 1968 South Dakota Democratic presidential primary and accomplished the same feat for his brother Teddy in 1980.

In this small state people expect to meet and chat with their elected officials repeatedly, and personal campaigning has enabled Democrats to be competitive in congressional elections. Back in 1978, the 29-year-old Tom Daschle's personal campaigning enabled him to beat Congressional Medal of Honor recipient Leo Thorsness by exactly 139 votes in a House race. That led to Daschle's election to the Senate in 1986 and his elevation to Senate Democratic leader in 1995. Only the burden of having to defend his steadfast opposition to then-popular George W. Bush and the assiduous personal campaigning of John Thune ended his electoral career in 2004 by a grand total of 4,508 votes. South Dakota's other Senate seat was held by Democrat Tim Johnson, elected in 1996 by 8,579 votes over Republican Larry Pressler. Helped by a major turnout drive on the Pine Ridge Indian Reservation, Johnson was reelected in 2002 over Thune by just 524 votes. Thune's gracious handling of his 2002 defeat helped him come back and defeat Daschle two years later. Briefly, from June 2004 to January 2005, South Dakota had an all-Democratic congressional delegation—with Daschle and Johnson in the Senate and Stephanie Herseth Sandlin in the House—for only the second time in its history. Johnson suffered a disabling brain hemorrhage in December 2006 and his determined recovery generated wide sympathy; he was reelected 62%-38% in 2008 but announced in 2013 he would not seek reelection and was replaced by former GOP Gov. Mike Rounds in 2014.

Presidential Politics South Dakota has voted Democratic for president just four times since statehood—in 1896, 1932, 1936, and 1964. But it was fairly close in five of the seven elections between 1972, when South Dakota's George McGovern was the Democratic nominee, and 1996, when Democrat Bill Clinton came within 3% of winning. In 2000, Al Gore's environmental policies were unpopular here and Republican George W. Bush carried the state, 60%-38%. In 2004, Bush once again carried the state, also 60%-38%, winning every county except those with Indian reservations and the University of South Dakota. In 2008, with no contest generating the interest that the Tom Daschle-John Thune Senate matchup had four years earlier, turnout was down 2%, contrary to the national trend. Republican John McCain carried the state by just 53%-45%. Barack Obama won the Indian reservations, several counties in the northeast and southeast, and he won Sioux Falls' Minnehaha County by 587 votes out of 80,000 cast. In 2012, South Dakota gave Republican Mitt Romney a 58%-40% victory over Obama, and Romney carried Minnehaha County 53%-45%.

2012 Presidential Vote		
Mitt Romney (R)	210,610	(58%)
Barack Obama (D)	145,039	(40%)
2012 Presidential Primary		
Mitt Romney (R)	33,872	(66%)
Ron Paul (R)	6,657	(13%)
Rick Santorum (R)	5,844	(11%)
2008 Presidential Vote		
John McCain (R)	203,054	(53%)
Barack Obama (D)	170,924	(45%)

In 1988, South Dakota switched its presidential primary from the traditional June date to February, just one week after New Hampshire's primary. It proved to be a boost for Great Plains candidates who did not fare well elsewhere: Republican Bob Dole in 1988 and 1996, Democrat Dick Gephardt in 1988, and Democrats Bob Kerrey and Tom Harkin in 1992. But in 1996, it attracted few candidates, and the South Dakota Legislature decided to save $400,000 in election costs by reverting to a June primary.

As it turned out, there was a robust race for the 2008 Democratic nomination up through June 3, when South Dakota and Montana voted. Obama had long since won the endorsements of leading South Dakota Democrats—Sen. Tim Johnson, Daschle, and McGovern. Rep. Stephanie Herseth Sandlin switched to Obama after her initial preference, John Edwards, dropped out. Obama campaigned only briefly in South Dakota, while Hillary Clinton, Bill Clinton, and daughter Chelsea Clinton crisscrossed the state in the two weeks before the primary. It paid off. Clinton won 55%-45%. She ran especially strong in the eastern counties and lost on the Indian reservations. It was her only victory north of the 42nd parallel and west of Indiana and Michigan, and it raised the question of whether she might have won the nomination if more states in the region had held primaries rather than the caucuses in which the better-organized Obama campaign prevailed. Too late to matter in the GOP contests in 2008 and 2012, McCain and Romney swept the state winning, 70% and 66%, respectively. Ron Paul finished second both times.

Governor

Dennis Daugaard (R)

Elected 2010, term expires Jan. 2019, 2nd term; b. June 11, 1953, Garretson; U. of SD, B.S. 1975, Northwestern U., J.D. 1978; Lutheran; married (Linda); 3 children.

Elected Office: SD Senate, 1996-2002; SD lt. gov., 2002-10.

Professional Career: Business devel. & V.P., U.S. Bank, Sioux Falls, 1981-90; Devel. dir., Children's Home Foundation, 1990-2002; Exec. dir., Children's Home Society, 2002-09.

Office: 500 E. Capitol Ave., Pierre, 57501, 605-773-3212; Website: sd.gov/governor.

Election Results

2014 general	Dennis Daugaard (R)	195,477	(71%)
	Susan Wismer (D)	70,549	(25%)
	Mike Myers (I)	11,377	(4%)
2014 primary	Dennis Daugaard (R)	60,017	(81%)
	Lora Hubbel (R)	14,196	(19%)

Prior winning percentage: 2010 (62%)

First elected in 2010, Dennis Daugaard is a conservative Republican who has been a leader in criminal justice reform and approved an increase in the state gasoline tax. He's also garnered national attention for approving legislation allowing teachers to carry guns and enacting tough restrictions on abortion.

Daugaard grew up on his family's dairy farm near Garretson in eastern South Dakota. His grandparents, who emigrated from Denmark, started the farm in 1911. Both of his parents were born deaf, so he principally communicated with them through sign language. He graduated from the University of South Dakota in 1975, and earned his law degree from Northwestern University in 1978. He spent a year at a small law firm in Chicago, and then left the firm to concentrate on real estate and settlement negotiations. He returned to South Dakota in 1981, marrying his high school girlfriend, Linda, and working as a trust officer at U.S. Bank in Sioux Falls for nine years. In 1990, he became director of development at the Children's Home Foundation, the fundraising arm of the Children's Home Society providing help to victims of abuse and neglect. He became the society's executive director in 2002.

Daugaard made his initial bid for public office in 1996, when he won a seat in the state Senate. He was reelected easily in 1998 and 2000. He focused on issues affecting people with disabilities and children, sponsoring an unsuccessful bill in 1999 that would have charged youths under 21 if they were caught driving with any amount of alcohol in their blood. In 2002, Mike Rounds, a former state Senate president, asked him to join his gubernatorial ticket as lieutenant governor. They won with 57% of the vote and were reelected in 2006 with 62%. As lieutenant governor, Daugaard chaired the Worker's Compensation Advisory Board and a task force on health care, and also served on a commission to revise the state constitution.

Daugaard was widely seen as the front-runner to replace the term-limited Rounds. But a February 2010 poll showed he had less than 50% support and that one-third of voters remained unsure what they thought of him. He sought to boost his image by vowing not to raise taxes except to cope with the aftermath of a flood or other emergencies. He also called for increasing the value of the state's economic development fund providing low-interest loans to start-up companies expanding or relocating to the state, while also continuing to expand wind, ethanol, and other alternative energy sources. At the same time, he pushed for a strong increase in science and math education for students. He easily won the June GOP primary with just over 50% of the vote, having far outspent four opponents. His general election opponent was Scott Heidepriem, the state Senate's minority leader. Heidepriem campaigned as an independent Democrat skilled at building consensus, and in recognition of the uphill challenge facing his party, chose a Republican businessman as his running mate. He tried to tie Daugaard to Rounds' policies, which he asserted had led to a ballooning in government's size and cost. He also accused Rounds' administration of not doing enough to promote ethanol production and wind energy. He was able to remain competitive on fundraising, but was unable to overcome the state's Republican bent, and Daugaard won in a landslide, 62%-38%.

With a more hands-on management style than Rounds, Daugaard focused on fiscal matters during his early months in office, proposing a budget that would cut about 10% of almost every aspect of state government. His proposal went deeper than one Rounds had proposed in December that relied on reserve money to limit cuts to 5% for such programs as elementary education and Medicaid. Daugaard rejected that approach. "Using reserves sounds good, but it's just kicking the can down the road," said the governor. Lawmakers heeded his concerns and passed a budget in March making cuts of 10% or more. Daugaard also vetoed a bill limiting the co-payments that insurance companies charge for visits to chiropractors, but the legislature overrode the veto.

The issue that brought Daugaard national attention was a bill he signed into law in March 2011 instituting the nation's longest waiting period at the time—three days—for women seeking an abortion after meeting with a doctor. The measure also required women to visit an anti-abortion counseling center. Abortion rights groups called the law unconstitutional and vowed to challenge it in court. But an undaunted Daugaard signed another bill two years later that said weekends and holidays did not count as part of the three-day waiting period. That meant that a woman theoretically could wait as long as six days if seeking abortion services before a three-day weekend. Another bill that the governor signed in the wake of the December 2012 Newtown Connecticut elementary school massacre also brought him significant publicity. The measure, which had the backing of the National Rifle Association, made South Dakota the first state to authorize school employees to carry guns on the job. The law left it up to individual school districts to arm teachers; Daugaard said he didn't think many would choose that option, but wanted to make it available to them.

Daugaard declined in September 2012 to set up an insurance exchange as part of the federal health care law and said the state would not join in the law's expansion of Medicaid. When South Dakota's economy picked up and the state ended with a $50 million surplus in 2012, he defended his steep budget cuts telling the *Argus Leader*, "One can't budget in hindsight." Daugaard applied his tight-fisted philosophy to the South Dakota corrections system, and determined that the state was facing a budget crunch because it was going to have to increase prison capacity if it kept incarcerating felons at its current rate. He won bi-partisan approval from the state legislature in 2013 for the Public Safety Improvement Act to reduce the growth of the state's prison population primarily by not locking up offenders with minor drug-possession charges. The measure also redirected budget funds to programs to reduce recidivism.

Campaigning for a second term in 2014, Daugaard ran on his budget-balancing ways and his bipartisan public-safety reforms. He also touted his success in attracting businesses to the state. He faced Democratic state Rep. Susan Wismer, the first woman to win a major party's nomination for South Dakota governor. She criticized Daugaard for refusing to support Medicaid expansion to provide health care for tens of thousands of uninsured South Dakotans and attacked budget cuts as excessive and harmful to K-12 education. But she was unable to put Daugaard on the defensive and struggled to build support for her candidacy beyond her northeastern South Dakota base. Voters gave Daugaard a historic victory. He beat Wismer 70%-25%, and that 45-point spread was the largest margin of victory in any South Dakota governor's race. At the same time Daugaard was winning a landslide, 55% of voters approved a ballot initiative increasing the state minimum wage to $8.50 an hour, which he had opposed.

At the start of his second term, the politician who vowed in his 2010 campaign not to raise taxes in his first term except to deal with an emergency signed a six-cent increase in the gasoline tax to 28 cents a gallon to fund road and bridge repairs. Daugaard had favored a larger increase spread over several years, but when Republican lawmakers in the GOP-controlled state legislature balked, he agreed to a compromise. The measure also increased the state's motor vehicle excise tax from 3% to 4% percent, boosted license plate fees by 20% and raised the state speed limit from 75 to 80 mph. Following up on his efforts to reduce the state's prison population, Daugaard also enacted juvenile justice reform in early 2015. That measure was expected to cut the number of those in state juvenile facilities in half by 2020, by diverting more youth without a criminal record from the juvenile system and expanding access to community-based substance-abuse programs. Daugaard kept to his conservative moorings in approving a modest budget with a slim 2 percent increase in funding for education and signing a bill authorizing a lower minimum wage, $7.50 an hour, for youth under 18.

Senior Senator

John Thune (R)

Elected 2004, term expires Jan. 2017, 2nd term; b. Jan. 7, 1961, Pierre; Biola U., B.A. 1983, U. of SD, M.B.A. 1984; Protestant; married (Kimberley); 2 children.

Elected Office: U.S. House, 1997-2003.

Professional Career: Legis. asst., U.S. Sen. James Abdnor, 1985-86; Special asst., U.S. Small Business Admin., 1987-89; Exec. dir., SD Republican Party, 1989-91; SD railroad dir., 1991-93; Exec. dir., SD Municipal League 1993-96.

DC Office: 511 DSOB, 20510, 202-224-2321; Fax: 202-228-5429; Website: thune.senate.gov.

State Offices: Aberdeen, 605-225-8823; Rapid City, 605-348-7551; Sioux Falls, 605-334-9596.

Committees: *Agriculture, Nutrition & Forestry:* Commodities, Risk Mgmt. & Trade; Livestock, Marketing & Ag Security; Rural Development & Energy. *Commerce, Science & Transportation* (Chmn: ex officio member of each subcommittee). *Finance:* Energy, Natural Resources & Infrastructure; Int'l Trade, Customs & Global Competitiveness; Taxation & IRS Oversight.

Group Ratings

	ADA	ACLU	AFL-CIO	LCV	ITI	COC	HAFA	ACU	CFG	FRC
2014	10%	0%	–	20%	33%	100%	61%	84%	59%	93%
2013	5%	C	22%	8%	C	75%	C	88%	80%	C

National Journal Ratings

	2013 LIB	—	2013 CONS
Economic	24%	—	74%
Social	14%	—	84%
Foreign	12%	—	87%
Composite	18%	—	83%

Key Votes of the 113th Congress

1. Sandy storm spending N	5. Student Loan Rates Y	9. Bipartisan Budget Deal N
2. Chuck Hagel Confirmation N	6. Employee Non-Discrim'n Act N	10. Farm Bill Conference Rept. Y
3. Gun Background Checks N	7. Senate Vote on Judgeships Y	11. Unempl. Comp. Extension N
4. Immigration Reform N	8. Defense Dept. Spending N	12. Keystone Pipeline Y

Election Results

2010 general	John Thune (R) .... unopposed	$5,382,436	$2,444	
2010 primary	John Thune (R) .... unopposed			

Prior winning percentages: 2004 (51%); House: 2000 (73%), 1998 (75%), 1996 (58%)

He first came to national notice in 2004, when he ousted the Senate Democratic leader, Tom Daschle. Since then, Republican John Thune, now South Dakota's senior senator, has ascended to the No. 3 spot in his party's Senate leadership, while becoming the subject of perennial speculation for a spot on the GOP national ticket. His good looks, conservative beliefs and ease in conveying the party's message fueled speculation about him as a possible vice-presidential running mate in 2008 and 2012, although his status as a resident of a dependably Republican, sparsely populated state likely worked against him. At one point, he seriously eyed the top spot on the ticket and said, shortly after winning reelection to a second Senate term, that he was "taking a look" at seeking the party's 2012 presidential nomination. But, just three months later, in February 2011, Thune issued a statement saying he would not run for president.

If outside the Beltway political factors—his limited political base, as well as the difficulty of competing with the fundraising network of frontrunner Mitt Romney—may have played a role in keeping Thune out of the 2012 presidential race, Capitol Hill considerations appear to have influenced Thune's decision to stay out of the 2016 presidential contest. With the Republicans back in control of the Senate majority for the first time since the first two years following Thune's initial election, he was elevated in 2015 to the chairmanship of the Commerce, Science and Transportation Committee. It is a role that gives Thune jurisdiction over a wide variety of key issues, ranging from telecommunications to insurance to product safety, in addition to highways and railroads. "I am not actively pursuing [the presidency] at the moment; I've got my work cut out for me in the Senate," Thune told *The Hill* in December 2014. "I think being in the majority, and if all things work out here, the committee chairmanship, is going to keep me extremely busy." Since South Dakota law forbids him from running simultaneously for his Senate seat and the White House, a presidential run in 2016—a year in which he is up for reelection—would force him to surrender his newly acquired clout.

Thune grew up in Murdo, on the dusty plains west of the Missouri River, a small town with a cluster of restaurants and motels at the interchange of Interstate 94 and U.S. 83. His father, the son of a Norwegian immigrant and a Navy veteran of World War II, was a teacher and the family was Democratic. Thune graduated from Biola University in La Mirada, Calif., and then earned an M.B.A. from the University of South Dakota. The genesis of Thune's political career dates back to when, as a high school freshman, he was spotted at a grocery store checkout counter by Republican Rep. Jim Abdnor, who recalled the young man had missed only one of six free throws in his high school basketball game the previous night. They kept in touch, and years later, when Abdnor was in the Senate (Abdnor won the seat in 1980 by ousting onetime Democratic presidential nominee George McGovern), he hired Thune on his Washington staff. Thune joined Abdnor's staff in 1985, a year after finishing business school, and worked there until Abdnor lost a bid for reelection to Democrat Tom Daschle in 1986. Thune then spent a couple of years working for the Small Business Administration.

Thune returned to South Dakota in 1989 and became executive director of the state Republican Party. In 1991, he was appointed state railroad director by Gov. George Mickelson and in 1993 he became director of the South Dakota Municipal League, which represents incorporated municipalities around the state. In 1996, at the age of 35, Thune entered a race for the state's at large House seat, which was open due to Democratic Rep. Tim Johnson's decision to run for Senate. The favorite in the Republican primary was Lt. Gov. Carole Hillard. But Thune attracted the support of religious conservatives and won the primary 59%-41%. In the general election, he faced Democrat Rick Weiland, a former state director for Daschle. Thune opposed all tax increases and promised to serve only three terms. He won 58%-37%. In the House, Thune was chosen as freshman class representative to the Republican leadership. He was reelected, 75%-25%, in 1998, the largest percentage margin ever for a statewide candidate in South Dakota. He did almost as well—73 percent— winning a third term in 2000.

As he bumped up against his self-imposed three-term limit in the House, Thune considered running for the open governor's seat in 2002, and was seen as a heavy favorite to win. But, at a White House dinner in April 2001, President George W. Bush urged Thune instead to challenge Johnson, who had won in 1996 by ousting Republican Sen. Larry Pressler. Daschle, who had become Senate Democratic leader in 1995, had vowed to do everything he could to protect Johnson, and got him a seat on the influential Appropriations Committee. Thune decided to challenge Johnson in 2002, clearing the way for Republican Mike Rounds—now Thune's junior colleague in the state's Senate delegation—to make a successful bid for governor. In taking on Johnson, Thune argued South Dakota would be better off with a bipartisan Senate delegation. Johnson countered that he and Daschle made a uniquely powerful team, and emphasized votes he had cast for Bush administration policies in a state that had not voted for a Democratic presidential nominee since 1964. Johnson and Thune spent about $6 million each, a record amount for South Dakota, and the national parties and independent groups spent much more.

The election was the closest Senate race in the nation that year. During most of Election Night and into the morning, Thune led. Then the last two precincts came in, from Shannon County, which includes most of the Pine Ridge Indian Reservation. It voted for Johnson by a better than 9-1 margin, putting him over the top by a margin of 524 votes—in percentage terms, 50.1%-49.9%. Many Republicans urged Thune to contest the election results, but he declined, and went to work as a lobbyist and consultant in Washington. He was encouraged by Republican leaders and family members to run in 2004 against Daschle, who had beaten lightly funded opponents in 1992 and 1998. Daschle had been majority leader for 18 months in which his party controlled the Senate in 2001-2002, and he remained pivotal as minority leader the next two years, when Republicans controlled the Senate by just 51-49. In South Dakota, Thune's favorable ratings remained high after his narrow 2002 defeat; early GOP polls showed him running slightly ahead of Daschle, and it was clear Thune would enjoy the full support of the Bush White House. Bush, who had carried South Dakota 60%-38%

in 2000, was at the top of the ballot that year. In January 2004, Thune announced he would take on Daschle.

Thune sought to portray Daschle as the chief obstructionist to the Bush agenda in the Senate. To underscore the Republicans' determination to oust the incumbent, Majority Leader Bill Frist of Tennessee traveled to South Dakota to stump for Thune, breaking with Senate tradition of party leaders refraining from campaigning against each other. Daschle ran ads in the summer of 2003, arguing that a freshman senator could not hope to match his influence in Washington, and emphasizing the federal largesse he had brought to South Dakota. He also cited his support of some Bush initiatives. But Daschle was hobbled politically by the same balancing act as several other Democratic congressional leaders before and since—serving as a spokesman for national Democratic policies without putting off voters in a Republican-leaning or battleground state. "Sen. Daschle at the time was using his leadership position in a way that was contrary to where a majority of South Dakotans were," Thune observed during a CSPAN interview nearly a decade after that campaign. "Eventually, that caught up with him."

During the 2004 contest, Thune portrayed Daschle as a political insider who lived in a $2 million house in Washington and had lost touch with the folks back home. The state Republican Party sent a mailer attacking the work of Daschle's wife, an aviation industry lobbyist. It was the most expensive congressional election of the year, as both national parties and numerous third-party interest groups poured millions of dollars into South Dakota. By the end, they had spent $35 million. The closely fought race brought a huge turnout, up 23 percent from 2000. Thune won 51%-49%, the first defeat for a Senate party leader since Democrat Ernest McFarland of Arizona lost to Republican Barry Goldwater in 1952. The popular vote margin was 4,508—small, but more than eight times the margin by which Thune had lost to Johnson two years earlier. The contours of the vote were similar to 2002, although Thune increased his share of the vote significantly in the Pine Ridge and Rosebud Indian reservations—where his decision not to challenge the election outcome two years earlier may have earned him goodwill.

Nationally, Thune was celebrated by Republicans as a giant-killer. He became a talk show favorite, a fundraising star, and a celebrity among Republican freshmen—and quickly rose in the ranks. Named chief deputy whip at the end of 2006, he served as vice-chairman of the Senate Republican Conference before moving up to Republican Policy Committee chairman in June 2009, following the resignation of scandal-plagued John Ensign of Nevada. In early 2012, Thune became chairman of the Republican Conference after Tennessee Sen. Lamar Alexander chose to relinquish that post. It makes Thune the third-ranking member of the Senate Republican leadership, behind Majority Leader Mitch McConnell of Kentucky and Majority Whip John Cornyn of Texas.

In the Senate, Thune has established a mostly conservative voting record, especially on cultural issues. In July 2009, he tried to amend the annual defense authorization bill with a provision allowing holders of concealed weapons permits in one state to carry their weapons to other states with similar laws. It received 58 votes, but not the 60 needed to stop a filibuster and pass. His lifetime rating from the American Conservative Union through 2013 was just under 87 percent, 2.5 percentage points higher than Ohio's Rob Portman, another Republican senator perennially mentioned as a possibility for president or vice president. Like Portman, Thune is credited with projecting a positive political demeanor. "He is conservative, but his message usually is not bombastic, and he doesn't say things that scare off moderates and independents," the largest newspaper in Thune's home state, the Sioux Falls-based *Argus Leader*, observed in January 2013.

Taking over as Commerce Committee chairman in 2015, Thune was expected to place a significant amount of his focus on railroads, which had been a specialty of his lobbying days. He has said he is especially concerned about the intersection of rail freight with agriculture. "In all my years of working on rail matters, I've never seen [agricultural] producers more concerned than they are now regarding the restricted capability to move grain to the marketplace," he said at a September 2014 hearing on rail congestion. Meanwhile, he sought a middle ground on raising the federal gasoline tax, as he faced the task of resolving a partisan stalemate that has blocked passage for several years of a long-term surface transportation reauthorization. "I don't favor increasing any tax, but I think we have to look at all options," Thune told Fox News, as he and other Republicans pushed the idea of finding cuts elsewhere to offset the need for increased revenue to deal with the nation's aging infrastructure.

As chairman, Thune was quickly confronted by another subject within the committee's broad jurisdiction—so-called network neutrality, the concept that all Internet content should be treated equally. At a hearing in March 2015, he blasted the 3-2 decision by the Federal Communications Commission—with the three Democrats appointed by President Barack Obama voting in the affirmative—to classify Internet providers as public utilities, as telephone companies now are. Thune accused the three Democrats of opting for the "most radical, polarizing and partisan path possible," while telling them, "Instead of working with me and my colleagues in the House and Senate on a bipartisan basis to find a consensus, the three of you chose an option that I believe will only increase political, regulatory, and legal uncertainty, which will ultimately hurt average Internet users." Thune has authored a bill to give Congress authority to create rules for an open Internet while limiting FCC authority, but has acknowledged the legislation is not likely to go far without Democratic support. Earlier, in an effort to head off the FCC's move, he outlined 11 principles for network neutrality legislation, including barring Internet service providers from selectively slowing down traffic or creating special "fast lanes" for sites that pay more.

Besides chairing the Commerce panel, Thune holds one of the most sought-after assignments in the Senate: a slot on the Finance Committee. Most recently, he has intensified a push for legislation he has sponsored to repeal the estate tax. In an op-ed published in the *Rapid City Journal*, in early 2015, Thune blasted the tax as a "nightmare" that "violates the basic premise of the American dream," while declaring: "The federal government shouldn't force grieving families to pay a tax on their loved one's life savings, built from income that has already been taxed by Uncle Sam. Death shouldn't be a taxable event." However, the Annenberg Public Policy Center's *FactCheck.org* found that Thune's op-ed "grossly inflated an out-of-date statistic about the percentage of businesses forced to liquidate because of the tax." *FactCheck.org* contended that only a "tiny fraction" of farms in South Dakota and nationwide were liable for the tax in 2013. On fiscal matters, Thune has supported proposals for a biennial budget and a presidential line-item veto. And while he has supported many earmarks for projects in his state over the years, he voted in 2010 in favor a two-year moratorium on earmarks.

As a member of the Agriculture Committee, Thune helped author a section of the 2008 farm bill establishing a permanent disaster program to provide financial aid to farmers whose crops are harmed by natural disasters. It provided payments to farmers through 2011; Thune pushed successfully for these provisions to be reauthorized in the 2014 farm bill, and made retroactive to 2012 to cover losses from that year's drought in the Upper Midwest. On an energy initiative helpful to his state, Thune in July 2009 won passage of an amendment to the defense bill requiring the Air Force to obtain half of its domestic jet fuel from synthetic blends produced in the United States. And on a transportation issue of key importance to South Dakota, Thune has split with fellow conservatives who have sought to kill the Essential Air Service program, which ensures small airports continue to get commercial flights.

One of Thune's first legislative efforts after arriving in the Senate was intensely local. In May 2005, Ellsworth Air Force Base near Rapid City, with nearly 4,000 local jobs and half of the nation's B-1 bombers, was placed on the base closing list, despite Thune's campaign promise that a Republican senator with good relations with the Bush administration could protect Ellsworth. With his South Dakota Democratic colleagues—Johnson and Democratic Rep. Stephanie Herseth Sandlin—Thune made the case to save the base to the base closing commission, the Pentagon, and White House officials. They generated a crowd of more than 10,000 and a pep-rally atmosphere at a commission hearing in Rapid City, and the base survived.

After close Senate races in 2002 and 2004, Thune prepared early for his 2010 reelection campaign, visiting the state often and raising $6 million by February 2010. Leading South Dakota Democrats took a pass on the contest, and the party did not field a candidate. Thune became only the third Republican senator to run unopposed since direct election of senators began in 1913. He may not have much more opposition in seeking a third term in 2016. Herseth Sandlin, who lost her House seat in the 2010 election but remains popular in the state, and former U.S. Attorney Brendan Johnson—Tim Johnson's son—are the leading names mentioned as Democratic challengers. But both took a pass in 2014 when Tim Johnson retired, and Brendan Johnson ruled himself out for 2016 against Thune. "It's certainly something that I would consider in the future," Johnson told *Roll Call*. "But it's not anything that I have any sort of plan or interest in doing at the moment." By mid-2015, Thune had amassed a campaign war chest of over $10 million; an extraordinary amount by South Dakota standards and probably enough to keep away credible opposition.

Thune is young by the standards of the Senate—he will turn 55 in January 2016—and he could be an influential presence on Capitol Hill for years to come. But he acknowledged in an interview with *Politico* in early 2015 that his opportunity to pursue the presidency may have closed. "That might have been the window. You never know," Thune said of his decision not to run in 2012. "Timing's everything."

Junior Senator

Mike Rounds (R)

Elected 2014, term expires Jan. 2021, 1st term; b. Oct. 24, 1954, Huron; SD St. U., B.S. 1977; Catholic; married (Jean); 4 children.

Elected Office: SD Senate, 1991-2000, maj. ldr., 1995-2000; SD governor, 2003-10.

Professional Career: Insurance & real estate exec.

DC Office: 502 HSOB, 20510, 202-224-5842 or 844-975-5268 (toll free); Fax: 202-224-7482; Website: rounds.senate.gov.

State Offices: Aberdeen, 605-225-0366; Pierre, 605-224-1450; Rapid City, 605-343-5035; Sioux Falls, 605-336-0486.

Committees: *Armed Services:* Airland; Readiness & Mgmt. Support; SeaPower. *Banking, Housing & Urban Affairs:* Economic Policy; Financial Institutions & Consumer Protection; Housing, Transportation & Community Development. *Environment & Public Works:* Fisheries, Water & Wildlife; Superfund, Waste Mgmt. & Regulatory Oversight (Chmn). *Veterans' Affairs.*

Election Results

2014 general	Mike Rounds (R)	140,741	(50%)	$5,176,534	$990,789	$1,631,470
	Rick Weiland (D)	82,456	(30%)	$2,314,172	$1,317,788	$838,501
	Larry Pressler (I)	47,741	(17%)	$647,409		$738,649
	Gordon Howie (I)	8,474	(3%)	$63,762	$148,298	
2014 primary	Mike Rounds (R)	41,372	(56%)			
	Stace Nelson (R)	13,591	(18%)			
	Larry Rhoden (R)	13,178	(18%)			
	Annette Bosworth (R)	4,283	(6%)			

Republican Mike Rounds, South Dakota's junior senator, is a former two-term governor who in 2014 was initially expected to walk away with the seat that Democratic Sen. Tim Johnson was vacating after three terms. Rounds did end up winning comfortably, but only after a contest that for a time became one of the most unpredictable races of the election cycle. His swearing-in gave South Dakota—a state that has voted reliably Republican in presidential races, but which has had a history of sending Democrats to the Senate and the House—its first all-GOP congressional delegation in more than a half century.

Rounds, named for an uncle who was killed in World War II, was born in Huron, but has lived in Pierre, the state capital, since he was 3. The eldest of 11 siblings, Rounds earned a degree in political science from South Dakota State University. In 1990, he was elected to the South Dakota Senate, rising to become majority leader during his last six years in that body, which he left in 2000 due to term limits. In 2002, he ran for governor, and won the Republican gubernatorial primary in one of the biggest political upsets in state history. Rounds faced former Lt. Gov. Steve Kirby and state Attorney General Mark Barnett, who waged a highly negative campaign against each other. Barnett criticized Kirby for investing $1 million in a Massachusetts firm, Collagenesis, which had been accused of charging a large amount of money for skin it obtained as donations from tissue banks at a time when there was a shortage of skin for grafts for burn victims. But Barnett's attack ads against Kirby were so negative that they backfired, benefiting Rounds—who won with 44 percent, to 30 percent for Barnett and 26 percent for Kirby. That fall, Rounds won the general election over Democrat Jim Abbott, who had been president of the University of South Dakota, capturing 57 percent of the vote.

As governor, Rounds enjoyed high approval ratings, but they slumped in the spring of 2006 after he signed a controversial law banning all abortions except those necessary to save the mother's life. The law was challenged in court and never took effect, and Rounds' approval ratings recovered. The statute—criticized because it did not include exceptions for rape, incest, or the health of the mother—was repealed by voters in a state referendum, 55%-45%, on the same day that Rounds won his second term by garnering 62 percent of the vote. Barred from seeking a third consecutive term in 2010, Rounds was urged by some Republicans to challenge Johnson in 2008, but declined to do so. Johnson suffered a cerebral hemorrhage at the end of 2006 that required brain surgery, but had recovered and said he would seek a third term. At the end of 2010, Rounds returned to the insurance and real estate firm, Fischer Rounds & Associates, where he was a partner—and where he had put his ownership interest in a blind trust after being elected governor.

As it became clear that Johnson would not seek reelection in 2014, Rounds made plans to run. The Democrats hoped that former three-term Rep. Stephanie Herseth Sandlin would run, but she declined. Although she had been defeated for reelection in the Republican wave year of 2010, she was the offshoot of a prominent South Dakota political family, and remained popular in the state. U.S. Attorney Brendan Johnson, son of the retiring senator, also declined to run—at which point, national Democrats all but threw in the towel on keeping the seat out of Republican hands. Rick Weiland, a former congressional aide and a two-time unsuccessful candidate for the state's at-large House seat, became the Democratic nominee. Rounds won a five-way Republican primary with 56 percent, with state Senate Majority Whip Larry Rhoden running a distant second with 18 percent. In July, one poll showed Rounds leading in the general election by a 2-1 margin.

But Weiland began hammering Rounds on his handling, while governor, of the so-called EB-5 program—which allows foreigners to obtain U.S. green cards by investing $500,000 in U.S. business projects that create jobs. The highest profile EB-5 project in the state was a beef processing plant, Northern Beef Packers that received almost $100 million from EB-5 funding, but nonetheless went bankrupt in 2013, a year after it opened. The problem for Rounds was that, a month before left office as governor, his economic development secretary, Richard Benda, had signed a contract with a private firm, SDRC, to take over the state's EB-5 program. Benda subsequently went to work for that firm. It was later revealed that Benda planned to go to work for SDRC—but didn't disclose his plans—while signing contracts on behalf of the state that benefitted that firm. A complex scandal erupted when Benda committed suicide in 2013 after the South Dakota attorney general, in a draft indictment, accused Benda of diverting a $550,000 state grant for his own enrichment.

Rounds began to drop in the polls in the wake of voter anger over the EB-5 scandal, as he ultimately acknowledged he had been aware of Benda's conflict of interest in the final days of his gubernatorial term. Some Republicans fretted Rounds was not doing enough to defend himself, as Rounds also got into a public dispute with national GOP strategists over whether to run negative ads in the state—a move that Rounds opposed, largely because he had never used them in his past races. Public polling revealed another problem; an independent candidate—former Republican Sen. Larry Pressler—was beginning to show some strength and was making the race a three-way contest. Pressler had held the seat for 18 years until losing it to Johnson in 1996. A Rhodes Scholar and Vietnam War veteran who was regarded as something of an oddball by colleagues during his years on Capitol Hill, had moved back to South Dakota after living in Washington for a decade and a half. He ran as a maverick committed to reforming the way things are done in Washington.

With Pressler not saying with which party he would caucus if he won, the Democratic Senatorial Campaign Committee began running ads attacking Rounds—prompting Weiland to charge the DSCC was seeking to undercut him and boost Pressler. Meanwhile, Rounds went along with national GOP strategists and began running ads contrasting his views on the Affordable Care Act and the Keystone XL pipeline with those of Pressler and Weiland. Rounds began pulling away in the polls, and, on Election Day, won comfortably, taking 50 percent to 30 percent for Weiland and 17 percent for Pressler.

Rounds arrived in Washington having campaigned on a solidly conservative pro-gun rights, anti-abortion and anti-same sex marriage platform; he advocated repeal of the Affordable Care Act and suggested during the campaign that the Department of Education should be abolished. He was the one former governor elected to the Senate in 2014, bringing the total of ex-governors in that chamber to 10. Rounds struck a bipartisan tone as he was named a co-chair of the Former Governors Caucus, along with Democrat Jeanne Shaheen of New Hampshire and independent Angus King of Maine, early in 2015.

"Former governors are accustomed to making decisions and working across party lines to get things done," he said in a statement. "Our shared background helps us find common ground without checking our credentials at the door." Earlier, in an appearance on NBC's "Meet the Press" shortly after his election, he said other former governors in the Senate had warned him that he should be prepared to be frustrated. "They've said time and again, 'Look, you've got to get in and you've got to go to work on it because you've been measured on results already'. Washington has not been," he said. Referring to Capitol Hill, he added: "There's no time frame there. There's nobody there that seems to understand that the people outside of Washington expect results."

REPRESENTATIVE-AT-LARGE

Kristi Noem (R)

Elected 2010, 3rd term; b. Nov. 30, 1971, Watertown; SD St. U., B.A. 2011; Evangelical Christian; married (Bryon); 3 children.

Elected Office: SD House, 2007-11.

Professional Career: Farmer, rancher.

DC Office: 2422 RHOB, 20515, 202-225-2801; Fax: 202-225-5823; Website: noem.house.gov.

State Offices: Aberdeen, 605-262-2862; Rapid City, 605-791-4673; Sioux Falls, 605-275-2868; Watertown, 605-878-2868.

Committees: *Ways & Means:* Human Resources; Oversight.

Group Ratings

	ADA	ACLU	AFL-CIO	LCV	ITI	COC	HAFA	ACU	CFG	FRC
2014	0%	5%	–	3%	100%	86%	51%	75%	58%	100%
2013	0%	C	14%	4%	C	77%	C	64%	57%	C

National Journal Ratings

	2013 LIB	—	2013 CONS
Economic	40%	—	60%
Social	13%	—	84%
Foreign	24%	—	68%
Composite	28%	—	73%

Key Votes of the 113th Congress

1. Sandy storm spending	N	5. Medical Marijuana	N	9. Syrian Rebels Training	Y
2. Violence Against Women Act	N	6. Farm Bill	Y	10. Keystone pipeline	Y
3. Guantanamo Bay Detainees	N	7. Afghanistan Combat	NV	11. Immigration Exec. Action	Y
4. Abortion 20-week ban	Y	8. NSA Phone Data Collection	N	12. Bipartisan budget deal	Y

Election Results

2014 general	Kristi Noem (R)	183,834	(67%)	$1,684,069	$2,911
	Corinna Robinson (D)	92,485	(33%)	$167,102	
2014 primary	Kristi Noem (R)	unopposed			

Prior winning percentages: 2012 (57%), 2010 (48%)

Population		Race and Ethnicity		Income	
Total:	844,877	White	84.6%	Median income:	$54,453
Urban:	37.1%	Amer. Indian	8.4%		*(255 of 435)*
Suburban:	5.1%	Latino	2.8%	Under $50,000	51.0%
Rural:	57.8%	Black	1.2%	$50,000-$99,999:	32.8%
Land area:	75,811	Two races	2.2%	$100,000-$199,999:	12.6%
Pop/sq. mi.:	11.1	White Ethnic	19.9%	$200,000 or more:	3.7%
Born in state:	64.3%			Poverty Rate	14.2%
		Education			
Age Groups		H.S. grad or less:	39.8%	**Work**	
Under 18:	24.7%	Some college:	33.7%	White collar:	33.6%
18 to 34:	23.2%	College degree, 4 yr.:	18.9%	Blue collar:	43.0%
35 to 64:	37.4%	Post-grad study:	7.6%	Sales and service:	23.4%
Over 64:	14.7%				
		Military		Govt. workers:	15.5%
		Veterans/active duty:	10.2%		

Republican Kristi Noem, first elected in 2010 by eking out a win over Democratic Rep. Stephanie Herseth Sandlin, is a conservative and telegenic outdoorswoman. Her frontier touches have evoked comparisons to former Alaska Gov. Sarah Palin. But she has been more of a team player and serious student of policy, especially its rural impact.

Voter Turnout	
2013 Total Citizen 18+	623,276
2014 House Turnout	276,319
2014 Turnout as % CVAP	44.3%
2012 Turnout as % CVAP	58.9%

Noem was born in Hamlin County, South Dakota. She attended college but returned home to help run the family farm after her father died in a fall into a grain bin while trying to unclog a feeder line, an accident that she discussed in her first campaign ad. An avid hunter of elk, pheasant and other game, Noem owned a hunting lodge and worked a variety of jobs, including a stint as a restaurant manager. When she was elected to Congress, the 38-year-old Noem raised Angus cattle and quarter horses on a ranch she shared with her husband, Bryon.

After developing an interest in conservative causes, including unhappiness with the estate tax bill that her family received after her father died, Noem ran for the South Dakota House and narrowly won in 2006. She became a forceful figure in the legislature, earning her GOP colleagues' respect when she questioned a Democratic state senator's sponsorship of a bill to expand casino-style gambling in the state while the senator's law firm was representing an American Indian tribe. She became assistant majority leader.

Noem decided to challenge Herseth Sandlin in February 2010 after becoming disenchanted with rising federal spending and the ballooning debt. In the GOP primary, two-term Secretary of State Chris Nelson had more name recognition and experience, and state Rep. Blake Curd raised more money. But Noem, who emphasized that she didn't plan to make politics a career, struck a chord with voters. One of them told *The Washington Post*, "She's the mama grizzly that we hope for." She talked more about South Dakota issues than national matters. Noem won the June primary with 42%, to Nelson's 35% and Curd's 23%.

After her victory, Noem began collecting substantial campaign contributions from out-of-state Republican interests, enabling her to out-raise Herseth Sandlin early in the campaign. She drew campaign help from operatives associated with popular Republican Sen. John Thune. Outside conservative groups poured about $2 million into the race, more than three times what Herseth Sandlin collected from outside liberal groups. Noem sought to tie her opponent to House Speaker Nancy Pelosi and promised to cut spending and help small businesses create jobs.

Herseth Sandlin, a leader of the Blue Dog Coalition of fiscally conservative House Democrats, touted her credentials as a moderate who opposed Pelosi on several high-profile measures, including the health care overhaul. She played down her party affiliation, leaving it out of her campaign literature entirely. The incumbent received help from the state's Democratic Party, which sought to make an issue of Noem's 20 speeding tickets and other traffic violations over two decades; she also received six notices for failing to appear in court. She responded to the criticism by saying that she is not proud of her driving record and is working to be a better example to young drivers. Her driving seemed to matter little to voters: Noem won 48%-46%.

In Washington, Noem was named one of two freshman class representatives to the GOP leadership. She joined fellow GOP freshman Stephen Fincher of Tennessee in 2011 in opposing the Environmental Protection Agency's proposal to regulate dust as part of air quality standards, arguing it would hurt farmers and ranchers. She joined her party in backing a budget that eliminated an Agriculture Department flood control program, but later requested federal disaster aid to cope with South Dakota's spring flooding—a move that led state Democrats to accuse her of hypocrisy. She worked on other issues of local interest, including a measure to transfer ownership of nine cemeteries in the Black Hills from the federal government to the communities that have managed them. It passed the House in 2012 but the Senate didn't act on the bill.

Noem became a favorite with activists on the right, drawing a cheer at the Conservative Political Action Conference in February 2011 when she declared, "A lot of us freshmen don't have a whole lot of knowledge, necessarily, about the way that Washington, D.C., is operated. And, frankly, we don't really care." Though she voted mostly in accordance with the Republican leadership's wishes, she made sure to distance herself from them at times. At a December 2012 town hall meeting, she told voters that she understood their anger toward House Speaker John Boehner for striking a deal with the Obama White House on taxes and spending to avoid a so-called "fiscal cliff." She said, "What bothers me is that we don't get out there and tell the American people that the House has already passed these bills that extended all the tax rates."

But Noem kept open bridges to GOP leaders. She was appointed to the House-Senate conference committee that hammered out the final terms of the farm bill enacted in February 2014. Responding to the millions of dollars in livestock costs that resulted from an early blizzard in October 2013, she won approval of a livestock disaster program that was retroactive. Noem also authored a provision that gave the Farm Service additional tools to fight the pine beetle, which had caused considerable damage in the Black Hills. In 2015, she scored a coup by gaining a seat on the Ways and Means Committee. She said that the "abysmal" customer service by the Internal Revenue Service was "inexcusable."

As a co-chair of the Congressional Caucus on Women's Issues, she has worked on a bipartisan basis on policies that affect low-income children. "There's so many times I've been in on a discussion on a bill or policy where if the women weren't in the room, it wouldn't have been an adequate solution; it wouldn't have been something that worked for our country," she told the Christian Broadcasting Network.

After Herseth Sandlin declined a rematch in 2012, Noem was challenged by Democrat Matt Varilek, a former aide to Democratic Sen. Tim Johnson. Varilek impressed local observers by raising close to $1 million and hitting Noem on missing Agriculture Committee hearings. Still, Noem raised $2.8 million and won by a comfortable 57%-43%. In 2014, challenger Corinna Robinson raised only $167,000 and Noem breezed to a third term with 67% of the vote.

Noem gave serious thought to running for the Senate in 2014, even after former Republican Gov. Mike Rounds said that he was seeking the seat of retiring Sen. Johnson. With Thune's ambition and Noem's youth, it's a reasonable bet that she eventually will make a Senate bid. Meanwhile, she likely will remain a Democratic target. Noem knows how to balance a busy schedule. While serving in the Legislature and in the House and raising three children on the ranch, she completed her undergraduate course work at South Dakota State University. She got her bachelor's degree in December 2011.

★ TENNESSEE ★

Tennessee has had a fighting temperament since the days before the Revolutionary War, when the first settlers crossed the Appalachian ridges and headed for the rolling country in the watersheds of the Cumberland and Tennessee rivers. Tennessee became a state in 1796, and its first congressman was a 29-year-old lawyer who was the son of Scots-Irish immigrants named Andrew Jackson. Jackson, who killed two men in duels, was a general who led Tennessee volunteers—it's still called the Volunteer State—to battle against the Creek Indians at Horseshoe Bend in 1814 and against the British at New Orleans in 1815. He was the first president from an interior state, elected in 1828 and 1832, and founder of the Democratic Party, now the oldest political party in the world. Jackson was a strong advocate of the Union, but Tennessee eventually decided to join the Confederacy. But this is a state with a certain civility: Both Confederate and Union generals paid respectful calls on the widow of President James K. Polk, who stayed carefully neutral, in her Nashville mansion.

Tennessee also was a cultural battleground for much of the 20th century. On one side were the Fugitives, writers like John Crowe Ransom and Allen Tate, who contributed to "I'll Take My Stand," a manifesto calling for retaining the South's rural economy and heritage. The state is also known for the momentous 1925 Scopes Trial, after high school biology teacher John T. Scopes in Dayton defied a state ban on teaching evolution in public schools. The legal confrontation in the Rhea County Courthouse garnered huge media attention and became known as "The Trial of Century," featuring William Jennings Bryan for the prosecution and renowned Chicago attorney Clarence Darrow, a member of the American Civil Liberties Union, for the defense. Bryan won the trial and died of apoplexy five days later. But Darrow is said to have won the argument by effectively presenting before a national audience the case for evolution in the debate over creationism, one that continues to inspire passions and lawsuits in local school districts today. In 1960, John Lewis, a student at Fisk University organized sit-in protests at segregated lunch counters at Kress, Woolworth and McClellan stores in Nashville. The protests sparked confrontations, arrests and ultimately a bombing that destroyed the home of the defense attorney for the protestors. That prompted Nashville Mayor Ben West to make a public appeal calling for an end to discrimination in the city. Within a few weeks, stores began to integrate their lunch counters and Nashville later became the first major city in the South to desegregate public facilities. The Nashville sit-in campaign became a template for student-run civil rights efforts throughout the South that Lewis, who eventually became a Georgia congressman, would heroically lead. Against this backdrop were business leaders and politicians who made Tennessee the fastest-growing state of the interior South. The state gave birth to the first supermarket (Piggly Wiggly), Holiday Inn, and Moon Pies, and is the home of FedEx. Both of these major influences remain strong in this elongated state, despite the long distance between its two ends: Johnson City in East Tennessee is closer to Dover, Delaware, than it is to Memphis, and Memphis is closer to Dallas, Texas, than to Johnson City.

Music is another strong Tennessee tradition. East Tennessee is one of the original homes of bluegrass music and mountain fiddling. Gospel music has long been centered in Nashville, which is also home to the Southern Baptist Convention and a center for religious publishing. The Gideon's International, HarperCollins Christian Publishing and Lifeway Christian Resources, which also operates more than 180 Christian bookstores in dozens of states, all have their headquarters here. Justifiably, Nashville is known as the "buckle in the Bible Belt." Country music got its commercial start in Nashville, with broadcasts of the Grand Ole Opry from Ryman Auditorium in 1925, and it remains the capital of country music today. The Mississippi lowlands around Memphis, which is economically and culturally the metropolis of the Mississippi Delta, gave birth to the blues in the years from 1890 to 1920, and the blues were in turn the inspiration for the jazz musicians of Beale Street in the 1920s and for Elvis Presley's rock 'n' roll in the 1950s and 1960s. Presley's Graceland mansion is now one of the nation's major tourist destinations, and the state tourism bureau celebrated when Tennessee drew more than 100 million visitors for the first time in 2014.

While Tennessee's economy trailed the nation's through much of the 20th century, its open climate for entrepreneurism enabled it to grow mightily in the 1980s and 1990s. The absence of strong unions and of bitter racial discord—notwithstanding the assassination of

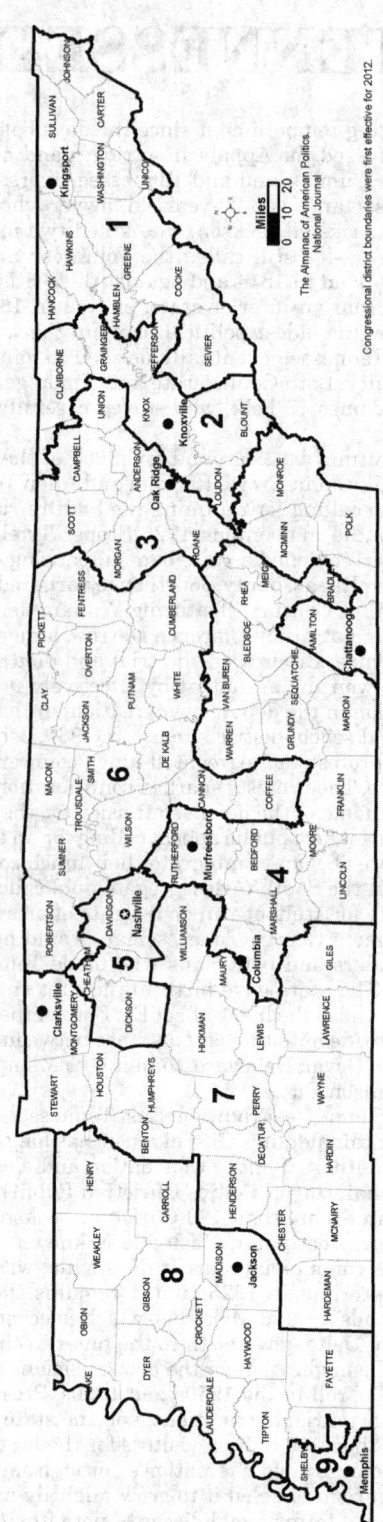

The Almanac of American Politics.
National Journal

Congressional district boundaries were first effective for 2012.

Martin Luther King in Memphis in 1968, Tennessee mostly avoided the violent battles of the 1950s and 1960s civil rights struggles—and the presence of skilled labor made Tennessee attractive. Republican Gov. Lamar Alexander (now a senator) was a deft salesman in his efforts to bring foreign auto plants to Middle Tennessee and in 1983, Nissan opened a plant in Smyrna, south of Nashville. It has since built another and relocated its U.S. headquarters to Tennessee. Volkswagen built a $1 billion "green" plant for its Passat in Chattanooga. Auto employment in Tennessee peaked in December 2006, but after the 2007-09 recession, the state's recovery lagged. In 2014, the Chattanooga Volkswagen workers narrowly rejected a United Auto Workers campaign to unionize the plant, an effort that gained national attention and opposition from Republicans and conservative groups. Tennessee Sen. Bob Corker said he'd been "assured" that the German automaker would expand its manufacturing operations in Chattanooga rather than Mexico if workers voted no, even though Volkswagen maintained the vote would not affect its decision. After the UAW's defeat, Volkswagen announced that it would invest $600 million to increase auto production in Chattanooga, which could create as many as 2,000 new jobs.

Tennessee's economy gained about 51,000 jobs in 2014, and the state unemployment rate dropped from 8.2% in 2013 to 6.9% in 2014. But those numbers were still above the national average. The Center for Business and Economic Research at the University of Tennessee projected that the state would continue to see employment gains in 2015 and 2016, but that growth in professional and business services and the leisure and hospitality sector would outpace gains in manufacturing. Despite the employment gains, the state had not fully recovered from the Great Recession: Inflation-adjusted incomes for most workers were still lagging and labor force participation is about 3 percentage points lower than it had been 10 years ago. The UT researchers reported that, "The post-recession period (2009- 2013) can better be described as a continuation of ongoing structural change rather than recovery." Manufacturing has gone from being the second largest employment sector in the state to the fourth. In the long-term, the state faces challenges to compete in the global economy and resume its earlier growth rates because its workforce is neither highly skilled nor particularly healthy. In 2013, the portion of Tennesseans with at least a high school diploma was 85.6%, almost matching the national average of 86.6%. But the share of Tennesseans with at least a bachelor's degree was only 24.8%, compared to 29.6% nationally. And according to the 2014 edition of *America's Health Rankings*, Tennessee was 45th among all states in overall health status. That poor showing was attributed to high rates of obesity, diabetes and smoking.

According to the Center for Business and Economic Research, the economic readjustment in the state is increasing income disparities between low-wage and high-wage workers. Its research found that inflation-adjusted incomes in the low-paying business and industrial sectors that employ large numbers of Tennesseans have been falling in recent years, while inflation-adjusted incomes in high-paying jobs that employ relatively few people have been rising. And jobs near median pay scales in construction and manufacturing are declining. Those low-wage workers must also deal with a state tax code that a 2015 Federal Reserve Board study found was the most regressive in the country. The Fed study claimed that while Tennessee has some of the lowest overall tax rates in the country, its heavy reliance upon the sales tax to supply the state with more than half its annual revenue means that a disproportionate share of the taxes paid comes from low- and middle-income taxpayers. Tennessee is one of seven states that do not have a payroll or state income tax. The Fed study said that low-income people often pay 10% or more of their income in sales and property taxes (often paid through rent), while wealthy Tennesseans may pay as little as 2-3% of their income in state taxes, because much of what they earn income from is not taxed. And unlike most states that exempt food and clothing from sales taxes, Tennessee does not. But the state's voters are overwhelmingly opposed to establishing any tax on payroll or income even it could reduce the overall tax burden for many low- and middle-income households. In 2014, Tennesseans voted by almost a 2-1 margin to ratify an amendment to the state constitution banning the adoption of any state or local personal income or payroll tax.

Tennessee has long been a political battleground. Jackson's Democrats had staunch opposition from the Whigs, many of them former Jackson allies, and for more than a century, its political divisions were rooted in Civil War loyalties. Tennessee had two referenda on secession, rejecting it 55%-45% in February 1861, but embracing it 69%-31% in June after the attack on Fort Sumter. Most East Tennessee counties voted heavily for the Union both times and have remained heavily Republican ever since; the 2nd Congressional District has never elected a Democratic congressman in all the years since. Pro-secession counties in Middle and West Tennessee long voted heavily Democratic, some even for liberal presidential candidates like George McGovern and Michael Dukakis. Within the limits of these enduring party loyalties, political entrepreneurs have set the tone for the state. From the 1920s to 1948,

Voter Turnout		
2013 Total Citizen 18+		4,831,581
2014 Highest Statewide Turnout		1,374,065
2014 Turnout as % CVAP		28.4%
2012 Turnout as % CVAP		51.2%
Legislature		
Senate:	28R	5D
House:	72R	26D 1V

Memphis political boss Ed Crump used his total control of Democratic primary votes there to elect governors and senators. (Crump, unlike other Southern Democrats, allowed blacks to vote; they voted his way.)

The Tennessee Valley Authority and the cheap electric power it generated provided an institutional base for reform-minded liberal Democrats Estes Kefauver and Albert Gore Sr., who beat incumbents in primaries when they were elected to the Senate in 1948 and 1952, respectively. They were soon national figures, with reliable enough backing from Tennessee's yellow-dog Democratic majority to vote for civil rights bills and to refuse to sign the segregationist Southern Manifesto. Kefauver died in 1963, and Gore was defeated in 1970, but he lived to see his son twice elected vice president before his death in 1998.

In the last half-century, the balance has shifted toward the Republicans. Democrats' cultural liberalism strained the ancestral loyalties of rural voters in West and Middle Tennessee, and the surging growth in the ring of counties around Nashville in the last two decades created a new voting bloc that is conservative on both economic and cultural issues. Over the past dozen years, Tennessee experienced the sort of voter backlash the rest of the country witnessed in 2010. In 1994, Democratic Gov. McWherter created TennCare, an extension of Medicaid, which accelerated spending far beyond projections in the next several years. Republican Gov. Don Sundquist succeeded McWherter in 1994 and was popular until he tried to pass a state income tax in his second term. When the Democratic legislature seemed on the verge of approving the tax in 2001, protesters stormed the Capitol. In 2002, Sundquist was turned out of office, losing to Democrat Phil Bredesen, a former mayor of Nashville and a health care entrepreneur, who Sundquist had defeated eight years earlier. Bredesen quashed all talk of an income tax, but two years later, as George W. Bush was handily carrying the state in the presidential election, for the first time since Reconstruction, Tennessee voters elected a Republican majority in the state Senate. Republicans won a 50-to-49 majority in the state House of Representatives in 2008, the first time since Reconstruction, but they were thwarted from taking control in 2009, when a renegade GOP lawmaker won election as speaker with the support of all 49 Democratic legislators. In 2010, Republicans regained their majority. In the 2012 election, with President Barack Obama at the top of the Democratic ticket, Republicans won supermajorities in the state Senate and House.

In the space of a decade, Democrats went from controlling all three branches of state government to being barely relevant in the capital. They've suffered landslide defeats in the last two governor's races. State Supreme Court Justices, who must face judicial retention elections, have the unique responsibility of appointing the state's attorney general. In 2014

Population		Race and Ethnicity		Income	
Total:	6,495,978	White	75.3%	Median income:	$42,499
Urban:	41.1%	Black	16.6%		(42 of 50)
Suburban:	29.4%	Latino	4.6%	Under $50,000	55.0%
Rural:	29.5%	Asian	1.4%	$50,000-$99,999:	29.2%
Land area:	41,235	Two races	1.7%	$100,000-$199,999:	12.7%
Pop/sq. mi.:	157.5	White Ethnic	17.3%	$200,000 or more:	3.1%
Born in state:	61.1%			Poverty Rate	15.0%
		Education			
Age Groups		H.S. grad or less:	47.3%	**Work**	
Under 18:	23.0%	Some college:	27.9%	White collar:	33.7%
18 to 34:	22.7%	College degree, 4 yr.:	15.6%	Blue collar:	42.1%
35 to 64:	39.7%	Post-grad study:	9.2%	Sales and service:	24.2%
Over 64:	14.6%				
		Military		Govt. workers:	14.2%
		Veterans/active duty:	9.3%		

they named GOP Gov. Bill Haslam's legal counsel, Herbert Slatery, rejecting Democratic Attorney General Bob Cooper's request for a second eight-year term. It was the first time since Reconstruction that a Republican had held that legal post. With little influence by the governor over legislation in the Capitol, Republican lawmakers have few restraints on pushing conservative positions that at times frustrate even Haslam. White Democratic males from rural areas once held sway over state politics, but that turf is now dominated by Republicans, and Democrats have become largely an urban party, as in other Southern states. Democrats hold the mayor's office in the state's largest cities, including Memphis, Nashville, Chattanooga and Knoxville. With rural areas safely in Republican hands, Democrats will need to breach the GOP bastions in the state's metropolitan suburbs and exurbs. That will take a battle of Jacksonian proportions.

Presidential Politics Most of Tennessee is part of the Jacksonian belt of America running along the Appalachians, territory that seemed immune to Barack Obama's appeal in 2008. In the general election, Obama carried Memphis' Shelby County, which is about half African-American, and Nashville's Davidson County, but he won only four of the state's other 93 counties, each of them a declining-population rural area where Democratic loyalties go back to the Civil War. Republican John McCain won the state 57%-42%, carrying white voters 63%-

2012 Presidential Vote		
Mitt Romney (R)..............1,462,330		(59%)
Barack Obama (D) 960,709		(39%)
2012 Presidential Primary		
Rick Santorum (R) 205,809		(37%)
Mitt Romney (R).................155,630		(28%)
Newt Gingrich (R)..............132,889		(24%)
Ron Paul (R) 50,156		(9%)
2008 Presidential Vote		
John McCain (R)..............1,479,178		(57%)
Barack Obama (D) 1,087,437		(42%)

34% and white evangelical Protestants (52% of the electorate) 75%-22%. It was one of four states where McCain got a higher percentage of the vote than George W. Bush had four years earlier. In 2012, Mitt Romney improved on McCain's showing, carrying the state 59%-39%. It was one of only two states (the other is Arkansas) with rising Republican percentages in five consecutive presidential elections. Obama carried Shelby and Davidson counties again, plus just two small rural counties.

For 2008, Tennessee set its primary on Super Tuesday, February 5. But it did not see much campaigning. Hillary Clinton was well ahead in polls and won a solid 54%-40% victory. Turnout was a record high, 625,000, and 29% of voters were African-American. Obama carried Shelby and Davidson counties, plus Hamilton (Chattanooga), Williamson (Nashville suburbs), and four small rural counties. Clinton carried the rest, getting as much as 86% in yellow-dog Democratic Grundy County. Obama carried the Memphis- and Nashville-based 5th and 9th congressional districts by 64%-34%; Clinton carried the other seven congressional districts 61%-32%, a margin comparable to those in similar districts she won in Kentucky, West Virginia, and southwest Virginia.

On the Republican side, everyone assumed that Fred Thompson, who announced his candidacy in September 2007, would carry his home state. But he dropped out of the race after his weak showing in South Carolina, and the remaining candidates put Tennessee on their schedules. Mike Huckabee carried most of rural Tennessee and Shelby County and won with 34% of the vote. McCain carried Knoxville and its suburbs and got his highest percentage in the county that includes Fort Campbell, for a total of 32%. Romney carried most of metro Nashville and got 24%. In 2012, Tennessee voted on March 6, the same day as Georgia. Rick Santorum won with 37%, well ahead of Romney's 28% and Newt Gingrich's 24%.

Congressional Districts Republicans swept the governorship and both houses of the legislature in 2010, earning unbridled authority to reverse the jig-sawed map Democrats had drawn in 2002. Back then, legislators lopped off heavily Republican Williamson County outside Nashville from Democrat Bart

114th Congress Lineup	
7 R	2 D
113th Congress Lineup	
7 R	2 D

Gordon's 6th District, kept parts of Memphis in Democrat John Tanner's 8th District, and added six ancestrally Democratic counties to the rural 4th District to help Democrat Lincoln Davis win an open seat. The fragile arrangement produced a 5-4 Democratic edge for eight years. But Tennessee's cultural shift away from Democrats rendered the map a ticking time bomb even before the next redistricting. In 2010, Republicans defeated Davis and picked up Gordon and Tanner's open seats with double-digit wins to romp to 7-2 control of the delegation.

In early 2011, there was chatter that Republicans would seek even more revenge by splitting Nashville Democrat Jim Cooper's 5th District four ways. But Republicans determined the move too risky and, in January 2012, passed a map strengthening Cooper and straightening most district lines across the state. They also helped a few of their own: The heavily Republican Memphis suburbs, an occasional primary nuisance to Nashville-based 7th District Republican Marsha Blackburn, were transferred to the 8th District to shore up freshman Stephen Fincher. Southeast of Nashville, Rutherford County was cut out of Republican Diane Black's 6th District to remove an old primary foe. Democrats comfortably control the Memphis-based 9th plus the 5th. For now, the seven GOP-held seats seem secure at least until the redistricting in 2022.

Governor

Bill Haslam (R)

Elected 2010, term expires Jan. 2019, 2nd term; b. Aug. 23, 1958, Knoxville; Emory U., B.A. 1980; Presbyterian; married (Crissy); 3 children.

Elected Office: Knoxville mayor, 2003-11.

Professional Career: Mgr., dir., & pres., Pilot Corp., 1980-2003; Pres. of e-strategies, consultant, Saks Inc., 1999-2001.

Office: State Capital, 1st Floor, 600 Charlotte Ave., Nashville, 37243, 615-741-2001; Website: tn.gov/governor.

Election Results

2014 general	Bill Haslam (R)	951,796	(70%)
	Charles V. "Charlie" Brown (D)	309,237	(23%)
	John Jay Hooker (I)	30,579	(2%)
	Shaun Crowell (Const.)	26,580	(2%)
2014 primary	Bill Haslam (R)	570,997	(88%)
	Mark "Coonrippy" Brown (R)	44,165	(7%)

Prior winning percentage: 2010 (65%)

As mayor of Knoxville and then governor of Tennessee, Republican Bill Haslam has won plaudits for his practical, hands-on approach to governing and his low-key personal manner. But that hasn't won over enough conservative members of his own party in the GOP-controlled state legislature to gain approval for some of his key policy initiatives.

Haslam is a product of Knoxville's most influential and powerful family. His father, James, made a fortune by building a single gas station into a chain of Pilot stations, which expanded into an empire of more than 650 travel centers and truck stops in 43 states and Canada. Pilot Flying J was the country's seventh largest private company in 2014 with some 21,000 employees and sales of more than $38 billion, according to *Forbes* magazine. *Forbes* estimated that Gov. Haslam, who has a 15% stake in the family business, had a net worth of $1.8 billion in 2015, making him the richest public official in the United States. The family has financed numerous projects around the state, many of them at the University of Tennessee. Republican Sen. Lamar Alexander once served on the company's board, and GOP Sen. Bob Corker was a college roommate of James Haslam III, Bill's older brother, who in 2012 became owner of the Cleveland Browns football team. In 2014, the company paid $92 million to avoid criminal prosecution and settle a federal investigation into allegations that it schemed to defraud customers of rebates.

Bill Haslam was a teenager attending the prestigious Webb School in Knoxville when his mother suddenly died at the age of 42. Her death prompted Haslam to examine his faith more deeply and he became active in Young Life, a Christian outreach ministry for high school students. Haslam went to Emory University, where he met his wife, Crissy Garrett, a

Memphis native, whose father trained with famed heart surgeon Michael DeBakey. Before graduating in 1980 with a history degree, Haslam thought he might teach high school history for a couple of years and then go to seminary. But one day when he was jogging with his father he asked about a possible role in the family business. His father encouraged the idea. Haslam worked in different aspects of the company and became its president in 1995, but he was always unsure about making his entire career at Pilot and in 1999 he became the chief executive officer of Saks Direct, the online retail arm of Saks Fifth Avenue. In 2001, Haslam left that post and became a consultant for Saks. According to a lengthy profile of the Haslam family in the *Knoxville News Sentinel*, Haslam was taking a break in Florida in 2001, when he happened to go on a bike ride with Corker, a longtime family friend and the newly elected mayor of Chattanooga, who was also on vacation. During the bike ride, Corker described the impact a mayor can have, which piqued Haslam's interest. Haslam floated the idea of running for mayor of Knoxville to a group of friends he regularly meets with from Cedar Springs Presbyterian Church. The feedback he got was more encouraging than he anticipated and he decided to run in 2003.

His Democratic opponent, Madeline Rogero, a nonprofit executive and former Knox County commissioner, depicted him as an inexperienced elitist. He won by 2,000 votes out of nearly 30,000 cast, even though he raised nearly four times as much money as his opponent. He responded to criticism by promising to involve the community in decision-making and to run an open government. He reached out to Rogero and her supporters and embraced some of the issues she championed, such as environmental sustainability. He brought together interested groups to work out a plan for South Knoxville's waterfront and to end homelessness, and he brought the city's finances under control, getting property taxes to the lowest levels in 50 years. He even hired Rogero to serve as the city's director of community development. He gained a reputation as a moderate with a hands-off management style and was reelected in 2007 with 87% of the vote.

Haslam was one of several prominent Republicans interested in succeeding term-limited Democrat Phil Bredesen as governor in 2010, but all waited to see whether former Senate Majority Leader Bill Frist would run. When Frist opted out in January 2009, Haslam announced his bid. He was part of a Republican field that eventually included Chattanooga-area Rep. Zach Wamp and Lt. Gov. Ron Ramsey, both of whom ran to Haslam's right. The Haslam family's company became a frequent punching bag. In April 2009, state Attorney General Bob Cooper announced that Pilot was among 16 companies and individuals that settled claims of gasoline price gouging, prompting criticism from Democrats. "When you have that many employees, there are bound to be occasional issues," Haslam responded. Wamp in particular went after Haslam, accusing him of a breach of ethics by mixing personal money with city funds to develop a movie theater. Haslam responded he was a buyer of last resort and that city legal and ethics officials agreed that the arrangement posed no conflict of interest.

Neither Wamp nor Ramsey could match Haslam's financial advantages. He spent over $9 million, more than Wamp and Ramsey combined, and maintained a double-digit lead in polls while collecting endorsements from the state's largest newspapers, which praised his pragmatism. He easily won the August primary with 47% of the vote, to 29% for Wamp, and 22% for Ramsey. Wamp, who had developed a reputation for occasional displays of temper while in the House, chafed at the result. "The best candidate doesn't always win," he fumed on primary night.

Haslam was widely regarded as the favorite in the general election over Democrat Mike McWherter, a businessman and the son of former Gov. Ned Ray McWherter. The Democrat portrayed himself as a fresh-faced political outsider. Haslam outlined a platform that called for issuing annual report cards on progress in five key areas: jobs and economic development, education and workforce development, fiscal strength, health, and public safety. McWherter criticized Haslam's plan as short on specifics on spending cuts, and he picked up where the primary candidates had left off in attacking Pilot, charging that the company was linked to a German firm that had done business in Iran and Libya. Haslam's campaign dismissed the charge as "desperate." Haslam again had the financial advantage, outspending McWherter by 6-to-1. He won a lopsided 65%-33%, the largest margin of victory for an open-seat race in Tennessee since the 1970s. He lost only the counties containing Memphis and Nashville and three rural counties out of the state's 95.

Haslam came into office determined to replicate the inclusive style he used as mayor. Unlike other Republican governors who demonized teachers' unions, he met with teachers over lunch around the state to seek their input. He promised to fully fund elementary education programs but asked state departments to provide cuts of up to 3%. At the same time, however, he showed his affinity with conservatives by proposing new restrictions to the state's consumer protection law, including a ban on class-action lawsuits. He also sought to develop a broad-based illegal immigration bill that would include enhanced powers for law enforcement modeled after the state of Arizona's controversial law, though he subsequently did little to make the issue a priority. His budget, which cut $1 billion in spending, passed with overwhelming support. His administration worked out a deal in October with online retailer Amazon to add $350 million in new distribution locations in the state, with the potential to create 3,500 jobs, in exchange for tax breaks.

With Tennessee's economic climate improving, Haslam in 2012 called for relatively small but politically popular reductions in both the state sales tax on food and the state inheritance tax. He also called for more spending in other areas, including cash grants to businesses to expand or locate in the state and a 2.5% pay hike for state employees. After saying he would "probably" sign a controversial bill to protect teachings of "weaknesses" in evolution and other scientific theories, he let it become law without his signature. But he disappointed social conservatives by using his first veto on a measure that would have allowed campus organizations at Vanderbilt University to discriminate on the basis of race, gender, sexual orientation, and religion. Religious groups argued that they should be able to require members and leaders to adhere to their beliefs. He also angered conservatives by retaining Democratic as well as gay employees and hiring a Muslim woman as a state economic development official. He brushed aside the criticism, telling the *Knoxville News Sentinel*: "In the end I think it is about, how do we get the very best people to work for the state of Tennessee."

To the delight of Republicans in the legislature, in December 2012 Haslam decided against creating a state-based health insurance exchange as part of President Barack Obama's new health care law. He also announced plans to push a limited school voucher program, though he pulled the plug after Senate Republicans sought a more expansive bill. While Haslam maintains that his ties with Republican leaders in the legislature are solid, his relationship with at least some of the GOP lawmakers aligned with the tea party have been strained. Rep. Rick Womick called Haslam "a traitor to the party" over his past efforts to defeat a few of his legislative opponents in party primaries. Republican Senate Speaker Ron Ramsey and some conservative GOP supporters, including Americans for Prosperity, an advocacy group funded by billionaires Charles G. and David H. Koch, sought to oust three state Supreme Court justices who had to face judicial retention elections in August 2014. The justices, critics argued, bore responsibility for appointing Democrat Bob Cooper to be Tennessee attorney general, who in turn did not join other state attorneys general in a lawsuit challenging the Affordable Care Act. Haslam refused to aid Ramsey's effort, which was ultimately unsuccessful and all three justices won their elections. Haslam's own reelection bid in 2014 was a breeze. His opponent, Oakdale retiree Charlie Brown, won the Democratic primary by more than 35,000 votes, defeating Sullivan County Mayor John McKamey and two other candidates. A political unknown, Brown, 72, didn't mount much of a campaign, which at times seemed to consist primarily of a Facebook page. He drew press attention when he said he'd like to strap Haslam into the electric chair and "give him about half the jolt." Haslam campaigned touting a successful first term and defeated Brown 70%-23% in a low-turnout election. After his victory, Haslam was elected chairman of the Republican Governors Association to oversee the group's efforts in gubernatorial contests in Kentucky, Louisiana and Mississippi in 2015.

Searching for a way to extend health coverage without backing Medicaid expansion, Haslam crafted Insure Tennessee, a proposal that would set up two programs for those with incomes up to 138% of the poverty rate: One, vouchers for people whose employers offer insurance that they cannot afford; and two, savings accounts that people could tap to pay health costs after making prudent choices, like not relying on emergency room care. Haslam called a special session of the legislature in early 2015 to consider his proposal, but when it met in February a state Senate committee rejected the measure and the effort died. After the defeat, Senate Speaker Ramsey—who also holds the post of lieutenant governor—cited the lack of written guarantees from the Obama administration that the state would not face added costs in extending coverage. "Tennessee has always been a well-run, fiscally-responsible state," said Ramsey. "We could not in good conscience put our stamp of approval on a mere verbal agreement with the Obama administration." The Tennessee chapter of Americans for Prosperity mobilized 200 activists to lobby lawmakers to reject the plan. Haslam told reporters that he and his staff had worked tirelessly to win approval for his proposal and that "It was a little embarrassing to do all that and come away with nothing."

During the regular session of the legislature, Haslam won approval for his budget that included $166 million in incentives for Volkswagen to expand its Chattanooga plant, but another Senate committee overwhelmingly rejected a resolution that would have enabled him to implement his version of Medicaid expansion. Haslam had urged Republican lawmakers to move past the national politics of Medicaid, but they remained steadfastly opposed. Critics voiced concerns that Haslam's plan would drain state revenues. Democratic lawmakers urged Haslam to call another special session to push through his proposal, but the pragmatic governor demurred. He said he and his supporters first needed to show that they had changed some minds of the proposal's skeptics before making another run at extending health coverage to the state's working poor. The governor said he would "pull some people together over the summer [of 2015]" to discuss options for moving forward.

Haslam acquiesced to conservative social measures that the GOP supermajorities in the state legislature sent to his desk in 2015. He signed a bill requiring a 48-hour waiting period before an abortion could be performed, and he signed another bill requiring medical facilities or physician's offices to be licensed as ambulatory surgical treatment centers if they perform more than 50 abortions in a year. Those measures came after voters in 2014 endorsed an amendment to the state constitution giving state lawmakers more power to regulate abortions. Under pressure from the legislature, Haslam also signed a measure preventing local governments from barring people with handgun-carry permits from bringing weapons to playgrounds, parks and sports fields. As mayor of Knoxville, Haslam had backed a ban on guns in city parks, but he faced the prospects that if he vetoed the bill Republican lawmakers would override him. Dubbed "Mr. Nice Guy" for his genial manner, an editorial in the *Chattanooga Times Free Press* said Haslam needed to get "some steel-toed boots" to "kick the not-so-nice guys out of the way."

Senior Senator

Lamar Alexander (R)

Elected 2002, term expires Jan., 2021, 3rd term; b. July 3, 1940, Maryville; Vanderbilt U., B.A. 1962, N.Y.U., J.D. 1965; Presbyterian; married (Honey); 4 children.

Elected Office: TN gov., 1979-87.

Professional Career: Pres., U. of TN, 1988-91; U.S. Edu. Sect., 1991-93; Co-dir., Empower America, 1994-95; Prof., Harvard U. JFK Schl. of Govt., 2001-02.

DC Office: 455 DSOB, 20510, 202-224-4944; Fax: 202-228-3398; Website: alexander.senate.gov.

State Offices: Chattanooga, 423-752-5337; Jackson, 731-664-0289; Knoxville, 865-545-4253; Memphis, 901-544-4224; Nashville, 615-736-5129; Tri-Cities, 423-325-6240.

Committees: *Appropriations:* Energy & Water Development (Chmn); Interior, Environment & Related Agencies; Labor, Health & Human Services, Education & Related Agencies; Transportation, HUD & Related Agencies. *Energy & Natural Resources:* Energy; National Parks. *Health, Education, Labor & Pensions* (Chmn): Children & Families; Employment & Workplace Safety; Primary Aging & Health. *Rules & Administration.*

Group Ratings

	ADA	ACLU	AFL-CIO	LCV	ITI	COC	HAFA	ACU	CFG	FRC
2014	5%	6%	–	20%	66%	100%	46%	76%	68%	79%
2013	5%	C	39%	31%	C	100%	C	60%	67%	C

National Journal Ratings

	2013 LIB	—	2013 CONS
Economic	39%	—	60%
Social	36%	—	63%
Foreign	30%	—	69%
Composite	36%	—	65%

Key Votes of the 113th Congress

1. Sandy storm spending	Y 5. Student Loan Rates	Y 9. Bipartisan Budget Deal N
2. Chuck Hagel Confirmation	N 6. Employee Non-Discrim'n Act	N 10. Farm Bill Conference Rept. Y
3. Gun Background Checks	N 7. Senate Vote on Judgeships	Y 11. Unempl. Comp. Extension N
4. Immigration Reform	Y 8. Defense Dept. Spending	N 12. Keystone Pipeline Y

Election Results

2014 general	Lamar Alexander (R)	849,629	(62%)	$9,378,379	$973,069	$294,406
	Gordon Ball (D)	437,251	(32%)	$971,372		
	Joe Wilmoth (CNP)	36,063	(3%)			
2014 primary	Lamar Alexander (R)	330,088	(50%)			
	Joe Carr (R)	269,169	(41%)			
	George Flinn (R)	34,207	(5%)			

Prior winning percentages: 2008 (65%), 2002 (54%); Governor: 1978 (56%), 1982 (60%)

Lamar Alexander, a former governor of Tennessee, Education secretary, and Republican presidential aspirant, was elected to the Senate in 2002. His biography isn't all that sets him apart: He holds the unusual distinction of attaining a high-ranking Senate GOP leadership post only to later resign from it, because he said the job interfered with his attempts at bipartisanship. In 2015, he took over the chairmanship of the Health, Education, Labor and Pensions (HELP) Committee.

Alexander grew up Maryville, in East Tennessee between Knoxville and the Smoky Mountains, the son of a principal and a teacher. He started piano lessons at age 4 and still plays. He went to Vanderbilt University, where in the early 1960s he wrote editorials for the school newspaper urging integration. He went on to get a law degree from New York University and then clerked for Judge John Minor Wisdom of the 5th U.S. Circuit Court of Appeals. In 1966, he wrote to Republican Howard Baker, volunteering to work in Baker's Senate campaign against Democrat Frank Clement. Instead, Baker gave him a job on his Washington staff. In 1969, on Baker's recommendation, Alexander got a job working for President Richard Nixon's congressional liaison, Bryce Harlow. On a trip back to Tennessee in 1970, he met Memphis dentist Winfield Dunn, who was running for governor, and Alexander agreed to manage his campaign. Dunn became the first Republican elected governor in 50 years.

Back then, Tennessee governors were limited to one four-year term, and Alexander decided that next time, he would be the candidate. So in 1974, at age 34, he ran for governor. He ran a conventional campaign and in that Watergate year, he lost to Democratic Rep. Ray Blanton, 55%-44%. He ran again in 1978—by then, Tennessee had changed its law to allow two consecutive terms—and undertook a more colorful campaign strategy. Wearing a red plaid shirt that would become his signature, Alexander walked 1,000 miles across Tennessee. He defeated Blanton, 56%-44%.

After the election, Blanton started issuing many pardons of criminals, who, it turned out, were paying him bribes. The U.S. attorney urged that Alexander be sworn in three days early, and Democratic legislative leaders and the state's chief justice agreed. In a hurried ceremony, Alexander took the oath and announced that he was naming Fred Thompson, famous for his work as Baker's chief counsel in the Senate Watergate hearings, as special prosecutor. In office, Alexander attended a White House meeting where President Jimmy Carter urged governors to get Japanese auto manufacturers to build cars in the United States; he responded by flying to Japan and persuading Nissan to build its first American plant in Rutherford County. He also persuaded General Motors to build its innovative Saturn plant in Williamson County. The plants became the sparkplugs of rapid growth in the counties around Nashville. Alexander was reelected in 1982, 60%-40%. After leaving office he spent six months living in Australia, writing a book appropriately called *Six Months Off*. In 1988, he became president of the University of Tennessee, and in 1991, George H.W. Bush tapped him as Secretary of Education.

In 1996, Alexander sought a bigger prize: the White House. He campaigned as a plaid-shirt-wearing outsider. Of members of Congress, he said, "Cut their pay and bring them home!" He ran on a message of decentralizing government, and he had a superb fundraising organization that made Nashville one of the leading Republican money sources in the nation. He hired top-notch political consultants and organizers in Iowa and New Hampshire. Alexander finished third in the Iowa caucuses, behind Bob Dole and Pat Buchanan and ahead of Steve Forbes. New Hampshire was his best chance for a breakthrough. Five days before the primary, Dole shrewdly ran ads attacking Alexander. Buchanan was likely to do well in New Hampshire, but probably could never be nominated. If Buchanan finished second in New Hampshire, he would likely become Dole's chief rival, smoothing Dole's path to the nomination. It worked: Buchanan won with 27 percent of the vote, edging Dole with 26 percent. Alexander, in third place with 23 percent, dropped by the wayside and Dole cruised to the nomination.

Alexander started to run for president again in 1999, but the shirt grew old and the outsider themes failed to resonate. George W. Bush, with his celebrity and his fundraising, dominated the race, and Forbes' extensive campaigning in Iowa left little room for Alexander. His fundraising faltered, and after his disappointing sixth-place finish in the August 1999 straw poll, he dropped out and endorsed Bush. He was later interviewed by Dick Cheney as a possible vice presidential nominee, but Cheney kept the job for himself. Critical of the front-loaded presidential primary calendar, Alexander in 2007 was a chief co-sponsor of legislation to implement a system of rotating regional primaries.

In March 2002, less than a month before the filing deadline, Thompson, by then a senator, announced that he would not seek reelection. He gave Alexander a heads-up on his decision, allowing Alexander to get his campaign underway shortly after the announcement. Republican Rep. Ed Bryant of suburban Memphis also got into the race, even though some Republicans tried to talk him out of it. On talk radio shows, Alexander ran a series of "plain talk" ads taking conservative stands on taxes, charter schools, and oil drilling in the Arctic National Wildlife Refuge. Bryant's ads urged, "Don't be plaid. Be solid for Bryant." And he emphasized that Alexander increased the sales and gasoline taxes as governor. But Alexander won, 54%-44%.

In the general election, his opponent was Democratic Rep. Bob Clement of Nashville, the state's largest media market. Clement had a relatively moderate voting record, having supported the Bush tax cuts and the 2002 Iraq war resolution. Clement depicted Alexander as a political insider who became wealthy through political connections. Alexander countered that Clement, while public service commissioner in the 1970s, served on the board of one of the banks of Jake Butcher, whose banks imploded in scandal in the 1980s. Clement maintained that it was an advisory board and his work on it occurred a decade before the scandal. Alexander prevailed, 54%-44%, winning 63% in his native (and ancestrally Republican) East Tennessee, which cast nearly 40% of the vote. Clement carried Nashville's Davidson County and rural counties in Middle Tennessee, but Alexander carried the fast-growing ring of suburban counties around Nashville and held Clement to 53% in Middle Tennessee. In West Tennessee, Alexander made some inroads among Memphis blacks and carried the rural counties. On his office wall in the Senate, he mounted not the usual array of framed photographs but a 27-foot authentic barn wall, with 40 antique items (a guitar made of matchsticks, a banjo made from a fruitcake tin) on loan from The Museum of Appalachia in Norris, Tenn. Six years later, his reelection was relatively easy. Prominent Tennessee Democrats passed on the race, and Alexander easily defeated former state Democratic Chairman Robert Tuke, 65%-32%, carrying 94 of 95 counties, including Memphis's black-majority Shelby County. It was the highest percentage ever for a Tennessee Republican senator.

In his early years in the Senate, Alexander sought to become part of his party's leadership. When Senate Republican Leader Frist decided to retire in 2005, GOP Whip Mitch McConnell of Kentucky was poised to replace him as leader. Alexander courted votes to take McConnell's spot as whip. But after the 2006 election, former majority leader Trent Lott of Mississippi got into the contest. Although Alexander claimed he had sufficient votes to win, Lott prevailed, 25-24. When Lott resigned from the Senate in December 2007, GOP Conference Chairman Jon Kyl was elected whip, and Alexander ran for conference chairman. North Carolina's Richard Burr also ran and pulled support from younger conservatives. Alexander won, 31-16, although he showed deference to those on his right by striving to be inclusive; Burr, for example, was assigned to manage promotion of the GOP health care plan.

At times, Alexander has stuck to consensus party positions. He opposed the Democrats' health care overhaul, telling the *Tennessee Tribune* that it was "arrogant in its dumping of 15 million low-income Americans into a medical ghetto called Medicaid that none of us or any of our families would ever want to be a part of for our health care." After the Newtown Connecticut school massacre in 2012 sparked debates over gun control, he told MSNBC: "I think video games are a bigger problem than guns, because video games affect people."

Yet Alexander has also sought out bipartisan alliances, and has often found them. He joined Delaware Democrat Tom Carper's bill to limit emissions of carbon dioxide and other pollutants, and to create a system of emissions trading, both of which the Bush White House opposed. Air pollution had been high in Knoxville and threatening the tourism industry in the Great Smoky Mountains area. To counter the effects of a federal court ruling, he also pushed to restrict emissions from coal-fired power plants. For his ongoing support of the Great Smoky Mountains and its environmental quality, researchers in 2007 named a newly discovered bug in the park after Alexander, calling it the *Cosberalla lamaralexandrei*. (They said that its checkerboard markings reminded them of—yes—Alexander's ubiquitous shirts.) But in 2009, Alexander actively opposed the Democrats' cap-and-trade bill to create a system of emissions trading, even though it was similar to the one he'd supported with Carper.

On immigration reform, Alexander joined another Delaware Democrat, Sen. Chris Coons, to introduce a measure in 2012 to create a new temporary visa for immigrants working in high-tech fields. He was one of 14 Senate Republicans to support the Gang of Eight's comprehensive reform bill that passed the Senate in 2013. Alexander voted for President Barack Obama's Supreme Court nominee, Sonia Sotomayor, in August 2009, although he voted against his other nominee to the high court, Elena Kagan, in August 2010. He cited Kagan's action as Harvard Law School dean barring military recruiters from the school.

In 2011, Alexander helped craft bipartisan legislation to enable states to compel online retailers collect sales taxes from consumers after previous attempts to implement Internet sales taxes failed to get traction. The issue had been especially divisive in Tennessee, where Amazon.com began building distribution centers but dragged its feet on collecting sales taxes until 2014. On the bill, Alexander joined forces with Senate Majority Whip Dick Durbin of Illinois. Alexander also was a co-sponsor of the controversial Stop Online Piracy Act. The bill was opposed by much of Silicon Valley but had the support of Nashville's country music artists and songwriters, who were worried about Internet piracy. When public opposition to the bill grew, with an Internet "black out" day sponsored by Wikipedia and Google, Alexander and Corker conceded that it had little chance of passage.

On the Health, Education, Labor and Pensions committee, Alexander worked on successful bills to help states ensure special education teachers meet federal standards, to give parents more choice in special education services, and to create summer academies for teachers and students to study American history. He also proposed creating $4,000 scholarships for private schools for students in failing public schools. As a former secretary of Education, Alexander opposed greater involvement by the federal government in federal student loans, comparing it to the "European-Soviet higher education model." On a key labor issue for their state, Alexander and fellow Tennessee Republican Bob Corker held up the Federal Aviation Administration authorization in spring 2010 over their opposition to a House provision increasing the power of labor unions to organize Memphis-based FedEx.

In September 2011, Alexander baffled much of Washington by announcing that he was resigning as Republican Conference chairman—a rare move in a town where people seldom relinquish power voluntarily. "Stepping down from the Republican leadership will liberate me to spend more time working for results on issues that I care most about," he said. However, he insisted that he was still a "very Republican Republican."

In 2014, hoping to avoid the fate of Indiana Sen. Richard Lugar, a moderate who had lost a 2012 primary to a tea-party challenger, Alexander kicked off his reelection bid early, announcing a team that included popular Republican Gov. Bill Haslam and the entire GOP Tennessee delegation except for scandal-ridden Rep. Scott DesJarlais. Some worried that a tea party-aligned rival, state Rep. Joe Carr, could catch fire in the increasingly conservative state—commentator Laura Ingraham came to the state to tout Carr's opposition to immigration reform—but Alexander took no chances, spending a combined $8 million in the primary and the general. He won the August primary, 50%-41%, then defeated Knoxville Democratic attorney Gordon Ball by more than 30 points in the fall.

Taking over as HELP chairman in 2015, Alexander planned to push a bill to balance the National Labor Relations Board with an equal number of Democrats and Republicans, and he was expected to play a part in the GOP push to chip away at the Affordable Care Act. But he was especially determined to deal with the No Child Left Behind education law. He had inveighed against the 2001 law's theory that the federal government should hold states accountable for students' progress. In early 2015, Alexander joined with Democratic Sen. Patty Murray of Washington to introduce an overhaul of No Child Left Behind.

In committee, some of the more contentious provisions were stripped out; the panel ended up voting unanimously to send the measure to the floor. In July, the Senate passed the bill, 81-17.

The GOP Senate takeover also elevated Alexander to chairman of the Appropriations Subcommittee on Energy and Water Development, affording him a position to promote nuclear and alternative energy. In 2009, he had called for 100 new nuclear power plants over the next 20 years and conversion of half the country's automobiles to electric power. Alexander bucked his own party on an Environmental Protection Agency smog rule. When the rule, aimed at limiting pollution from power plants, was implemented in 2011, Alexander was one of six Republicans to cross party lines and oppose a move by GOP Sen. Rand Paul of Kentucky to block the regulation from going forward. "There's a lot I admire about our neighbors in Kentucky, including their two distinguished United States senators, but I don't want their dirty air blowing into Tennessee," Alexander said on the Senate floor. In 2015 Alexander also waded into the controversy over Senate filibusters, joining with Utah Sen. Mike Lee on a resolution to abandon the procedure for all nominations, including those to the Supreme Court. But the idea met with fierce resistance from both parties.

Junior Senator

Bob Corker (R)

Elected 2006, term expires Jan., 2019, 2nd term; b. Aug. 24, 1952, Orangeburg, SC; U. of TN, B.S. 1974; Protestant; married (Elizabeth); 2 children.

Elected Office: Chattanooga mayor, 2001-05.

Professional Career: Owner, Bencor Corp., 1978-90; Commissioner, TN Dept. of Fin. & Admin., 1995-96; Owner, Corker Group, 1982-2006.

DC Office: 425 DSOB, 20510, 202-224-3344; Fax: 202-228-0566; Website: corker.senate.gov.

State Offices: Chattanooga, 423-756-2757; Jackson, 731-664-2294; Knoxville, 865-637-4180; Memphis, 901-683-1910; Nashville, 615-279-8125; Tri-Cities, 423-753-2263.

Committees: *Aging (Special). Banking, Housing & Urban Affairs:* Financial Institutions & Consumer Protection; Housing, Transportation & Community Development; Securities, Insurance & Investment. *Foreign Relations* (Chmn, ex officio member of all subcommittees) *Budget.*

Group Ratings

	ADA	ACLU	AFL-CIO	LCV	ITI	COC	HAFA	ACU	CFG	FRC
2014	15%	13%	–	20%	66%	75%	48%	76%	80%	86%
2013	10%	C	33%	15%	C	88%	C	64%	75%	C

National Journal Ratings

	2013 LIB	—	2013 CONS
Economic	33%	—	66%
Social	37%	—	62%
Foreign	34%	—	65%
Composite	35%	—	65%

Key Votes of the 113th Congress

1. Sandy storm spending N	5. Student Loan Rates Y	9. Bipartisan Budget Deal N
2. Chuck Hagel Confirmation N	6. Employee Non-Discrim'n Act N	10. Farm Bill Conference Rept. N
3. Gun Background Checks N	7. Senate Vote on Judgeships Y	11. Unempl. Comp. Extension N
4. Immigration Reform Y	8. Defense Dept. Spending N	12. Keystone Pipeline Y

Election Results

2012 general	Bob Corker (R)	1,506,443	(65%)	$8,472,064	$6,789
	Mark Clayton (D)	705,882	(30%)		
2012 primary	Bob Corker (R)	389,613	(85%)		
	Zach Poskevich (R)	28,311	(6%)		

Prior winning percentage: 2006 (51%)

Republican Bob Corker, elected in 2006, is the junior senator from Tennessee. He has a reputation as a pragmatist, something that in mid-2014 briefly spurred talk of his running for president. He didn't pursue the idea, preferring to use his new status to try to shape his party's often-fractious approach on international affairs. In 2015, he became chairman of the Foreign Relations Committee.

Corker was born in South Carolina, grew up in Chattanooga, and graduated from the University of Tennessee in 1974 with a degree in industrial management. (He roomed with Jimmy Haslam, the older brother of Tennessee Gov. Bill Haslam.) Just a few years out of college, he started a construction company, which he sold before he turned 40 (he was the Senate's fourth-wealthiest member in 2013, with average assets of $54.4 million, according to the Center for Responsive Politics). Before he sold his company, Corker took a church mission trip to Haiti, which inspired him to help create Chattanooga Neighborhood Enterprise, a non-profit organization designed to get low-income families into affordable housing.

In 1994, he ran for the Senate, finishing second in the Republican primary to Bill Frist, who went on to defeat Democratic incumbent Jim Sasser that year and eventually became majority leader. After his defeat, Corker was named state finance commissioner by Republican Gov. Don Sundquist. After 18 months, he returned to private business, purchasing two real estate and development companies in Chattanooga. In 2001, he won election as Chattanooga mayor and got credit for reducing violent crime and revitalizing the city's waterfront.

While still in his first term as mayor, Corker announced in October 2004 that he would run to succeed Frist, who stuck to his initial campaign promise to serve just two terms. By the end of the year, Corker had raised $2 million. Two former Republican congressmen also ran, Ed Bryant, who had lost to Lamar Alexander in the 2002 Senate primary, and Van Hilleary, who had lost to Democrat Phil Bredesen in the 2002 governor's race. Corker drew on his personal wealth, spending $5 million through mid-July to introduce himself to voters and defend against attacks that he was insufficiently conservative. Bryant and Hilleary claimed Corker raised property taxes in Chattanooga and criticized his support for abortion rights during his 1994 Senate campaign. Corker called his opponents "ineffective career politicians" and talked about his background as a successful businessman and mayor. He said he was "wrong" on abortion in 1994 and that he opposed the right to abortion except in cases of rape and incest. Corker ended up winning by a comfortable margin as Bryant and Hilleary split the conservative vote. He carried nearly every county east of Nashville and a half-dozen west of it, winning 48 percent to Bryant's 34 percent; Hilleary finished third with 17 percent.

The Democratic nominee was Rep. Harold Ford, Jr., of Memphis, who, in the absence of serious primary opposition, was able to conserve his resources for the general election. Youthful, ambitious, and telegenic, Ford was an attractive candidate. The son of former Rep. Harold Ford, Sr., he was first elected to the House in 1996, just months after graduating from law school, and his record was sufficiently moderate to make him a competitive statewide candidate. For much of the general election campaign, it appeared Corker might defy Tennessee's recent Republican trend in national elections and lose a seat that was critical to the party's hopes of retaining its Senate majority. Corker struggled to unify the party after the contentious August primary and failed to gain traction in the weeks following the race. Meanwhile, Ford ran a nearly flawless campaign. Corker's efforts to frame Ford as too liberal for Tennessee fell flat in the face of Ford's centrist, even conservative, positions on illegal immigration, the Iraq war, border security, and same-sex marriage. Ford also put Corker on the defensive about his business dealings.

Nevertheless, as the scion of a Memphis political dynasty, Ford had to weather distractions caused by several family members, including his uncle, former state Sen. John Ford, who was indicted on federal corruption charges. Then, John Ford's sister—Harold's aunt—won the special election to replace him, but she was ousted by the state Senate in April amid allegations of voter fraud. Meanwhile, in the racially-charged House race to succeed Harold Ford, his brother, Jake, unexpectedly ran as an independent candidate against white Democratic nominee Steve Cohen. Heading into the final weeks of the campaign, the election appeared to be a dead heat. But Corker gained momentum after Republicans launched a series of attack ads and zeroed in on Ford's personal story, characterizing it as a life of privilege. Corker's ads described his rise from a laborer who poured concrete. In late October, the Republican National Committee weighed in with a controversial ad featuring purported on-the-street interviews with regular people, including an attractive young, blonde, and white woman, claiming that she had "met Harold at the *Playboy* party," a reference to news stories that Ford had attended a Super Bowl party hosted by *Playboy* magazine. The commercial ended with the woman saying, "Harold, call me." Critics called the ad racial politicking, while Republicans insisted it was about values. Corker's campaign asked television stations not to air the spot. Ultimately, Corker won, 51%-48%, with whites voting 59%-40% for Corker, and blacks voting 95%-4% for Ford. Ford took the Memphis area, 61%-38%, while Corker carried the Nashville area, 50%-49%. Corker far outpaced Ford in East Tennessee, winning 58%-40%. Ford carried Middle and West Tennessee 52%-46%.

Corker, who has silver hair straight out of Senate central casting, has amassed a voting record that's conservative, but not overly so. In 2013-14, his legislative score from the conservative group Heritage Action was just 48 percent, well below the average Senate Republican and just two percentage points above his home-state GOP colleague Lamar Alexander. "I can be a conservative Republican, but I can sit down and find common ground with a liberal Democrat on some issues," he told McClatchy newspapers. "For people to look at that as somehow compromising principles is ridiculous."

When he first arrived, Corker tried to further separate himself from the controversial attack ads against Ford. He introduced a bill to allow candidates to approve commercials and direct mail pieces from political parties before they are released to the public. While he was a reliable vote for Republicans on issues such as opposing embryonic stem cell research and troop withdrawal timetables in Iraq, Corker broke with the party on some high-profile issues. He backed an energy bill to raise gas mileage standards for cars and trucks. He joined a bipartisan effort to promote a 2008 energy bill allowing offshore drilling while also emphasizing renewable energy sources. In 2007, he voted for a Democratic bill to expand the State Children's Health Insurance Program and also played a crucial role in negotiations to renew federal funding for the state's TennCare Medicaid program. Such unpredictability has made Corker popular with reporters and a regular guest on Sunday television talk shows.

In 2008, Corker got a seat on the Banking Committee. When committee ranking Republican Richard Shelby of Alabama refused to participate in bipartisan talks about a bailout for the collapsing financial industry, Corker engaged in meetings with Democratic Chairman Christopher Dodd that produced the $700 billion Troubled Asset Relief Program. In late 2008, when the big three domestic automakers sought a multi-billion-dollar bailout, Corker criticized auto executives who appeared before the committee, chiding their plans for securing government loans and waiting for mergers. He told the head of Chrysler: "While this is happening, you're going to be going to spas and getting facials and hopefully finding someone to marry you." In December, Corker offered an alternative proposal that required retiring autoworkers to accept most of their benefits in stock rather than in cash, forced bondholders to accept a steep cut in the value of their bonds, and required wages and benefits comparable to American employees of foreign automakers. Corker's conditions angered big auto's supporters in Detroit, but they were in large part followed by President Barack Obama's task force on the auto companies.

Corker was unusually active for a junior member on financial regulation, the big issue before the Banking Committee, in 2009 and 2010. By then, he had built a good working relationship with Dodd, who encouraged him to engage in informal meetings with Virginia Democrat Mark Warner. "I don't see him as a partisan," Warner later told The Associated Press. "I think he's somebody who's willing to work with anybody who he thinks has a good idea." In early February 2010, when Dodd concluded that negotiations with Shelby on the bill were going nowhere, Corker once again agreed to work with Dodd.

On the sensitive issue of creating a consumer finance protection agency, strongly backed by liberal Democrats, Corker, Dodd, Shelby, and New Hampshire Republican Judd Gregg agreed to put the new agency under the authority of the Federal Reserve. But Corker continued to be troubled by what he regarded as the too-big-to-fail treatment of major banks and other financial institutions. And in March, Dodd announced that he would unveil his own bill without support from Corker or other Republicans. Corker complained that the unilateral action was ordered by the Obama White House, but he was also critical of fellow Republicans, saying they had made a major strategic error in not reaching a compromise and that GOP assertions that the bill would increase the likelihood of bailouts were overstated. In March 2013, when Republican leaders circulated a letter vowing to block any director to lead the consumer agency unless Democrats agreed to restructure it, Corker declined to sign it and expressed hope that a compromise could be reached.

After a report revealed that top executives at mortgage giants Fannie Mae and Freddie Mac were rewarded with some $13 million in bonus pay, Corker introduced a bill in November 2011 to phase out Fannie Mae and Freddie Mac in 10 years and replace them with a private mortgage market. In 2008, the struggling companies were taken over by the federal government in a conservatorship to keep them afloat. In the summer of 2011, Corker joined with Democratic Sen. Jon Tester of Montana in an attempt to delay a rule sponsored by Democratic Sen. Richard Durbin of Illinois that placed limits on bank fees charged to retailers for debit card transactions. Corker argued that the cap on transaction fees would actually hurt small, community banks. The Corker-Tester bill garnered 54 votes, but that was not enough to stop a filibuster. Ultimately, Corker's financial-sector proposals "did not get far," wrote Tennessee journalist Chas Sisk, "but his positions made him a popular guest on the business news channels, where he bantered with the ease of a businessman taking questions from his local Rotary Club."

Corker jumped into the debate over cutting federal spending in 2011, and again, did so in a bipartisan way. He and Missouri Democrat Claire McCaskill sponsored a bill to require reductions of federal spending from 24.7 percent of gross domestic product to the 40-year historic average of 20.6 percent, with the White House budget office charged with making simultaneous cuts in entitlement and discretionary spending if Congress did not meet the targets. When the Republican leadership and Obama brokered a deal to raise the debt ceiling in early August 2011, some hardline conservatives carped that the legislation failed to achieve substantial deficit reduction, but Corker voted for the deal.

His reelection bid in 2012 was far easier than his first. After beating four Republicans in a primary with 85 percent of the vote, he faced Democrat Mark Clayton, a self-described author and anti-gay rights activist. Within days of the primary, the state Democratic Party disavowed Clayton and made it known that it didn't consider him to be a legitimate nominee. Corker won, 65%-30%.

In the 113th Congress, Corker drew attention for a number of iconoclastic moves. He complained in September 2013 that his more junior GOP colleagues Ted Cruz of Texas and Mike Lee of Utah sought a government shutdown for what amounted to publicity purposes. He was the only Senate Republican in April 2013 to vote with Democrats in favor of considering a minimum-wage increase. He and Warner teamed again to tackle housing finance reform, crafting a framework that became incorporated into an April 2014 draft from Banking Chairman Tim Johnson of South Dakota and ranking Republican Mike Crapo of Idaho. He also worked with Connecticut Democrat Chris Murphy on a proposal to boost the federal gasoline tax to save the depleted Highway Trust Fund.

Of special interest at home, Corker worked with fellow Tennessee Republican Lamar Alexander to strip from the 2010 Federal Aviation Administration bill a provision that would facilitate unionization of Memphis-based FedEx. To help Nashville's music industry, he joined Alexander and Utah Republican Orrin Hatch in introducing a bill in May 2014 that would allow songwriters to be paid based on the fair-market value of their songs.

While all of these activities made Corker an unusually busy junior senator, he has made his biggest mark recently as the top Republican on the Senate Foreign Relations Committee. Corker became the ranking Republican after Indiana's Richard Lugar, one of the Senate's most respected voices on foreign policy, lost to tea-party favorite Richard Mourdock in the 2012 GOP primary. Corker has acknowledged that he had initially possessed little practical experience in international relations, but he has made up for lost time: By his count, he had visited 63 countries by January 2015.

At times, Corker has been more tolerant of the Obama administration than others in his party. He was among the Republicans voting to ratify the New START arms-reduction treaty with Russia in 2010 after getting assurances from appropriators of funding for the modernization of nuclear weapons. And in 2013, rather than joining other GOP panel members in pummeling outgoing Secretary of State Hillary Clinton for her handling of the terrorist attacks in Benghazi, Libya, Corker suggested that the incident be used as an opportunity to craft a policy "that reflects the dynamics of the region as they really are today."

As time went on, though, Corker became more critical of the administration's foreign policy. He complained that the Obama administration did not sufficiently consult Congress on military engagement in Libya, and he introduced a resolution with Democratic Sen. Jim Webb of Virginia asking for a detailed justification for the U.S. operation. He was an early backer of arming Syrian rebels opposed to Bashar Assad, and of sending lethal—rather than just non-lethal—aid to Ukraine, in both cases getting out in front of the administration.

By August 2014, Corker's exasperation with Obama reached the point where he wrote a blunt op-ed for *The Washington Post* blasting the president as unreliable on foreign affairs. "Those around the world who are looking to the United States for support against intimidation, oppression or outright massacres have learned a tough lesson in the past few years: This U.S. president, despite his bold pronouncements and moral posturing, cannot be counted on," he wrote. Citing the White House's handling of the situations in Syria, Libya and Eastern Europe, Corker concluded, "More often than not, the president doesn't hit singles and doubles; he just balks. It is hard to watch."

As the panel's newly installed chairman in 2015, Corker faced an immediate dilemma prompted by Obama's nuclear talks with Iran. Just-elected Republican Sen. Tom Cotton of Arkansas circulated a letter written directly to Iran's leaders, warning them that the Senate could undo any deal Obama struck. In all, 47 GOP senators signed on, including key party leaders like Senate Majority Leader Mitch McConnell, but the move, and the letter's seemingly condescending tone, drew fire from many corners, and not just from Democrats. Seven Republicans declined to sign it—including Corker, who had been engaged in less confrontational, bipartisan negotiations to ensure that any final deal be approved by lawmakers first. Corker's ability to craft broadly agreeable terms won over Democrats; his bill ended up passing the Senate 98-1 (with Cotton as the only dissenting vote) and was signed by Obama in May. In an op-ed, Corker wrote that congressional approval was so important because "a nuclear Iran is a threat to every nation and would lead to a less safe and secure world. It also could create a dangerous arms race with the possibility of a nuclear weapon falling into the hands of terrorists." His central role in the Iran bill led *Time* magazine to name Corker one of the 100 most influential people in the world in 2015.

Corker's work on foreign relations has underscored a key duality of his style—a propensity for making impolitic comments on the one hand, and for crafting deals on the other. Corker has called National Security Agency data-mining "malpractice" and "ineptly carried out," and he's been willing to target Republicans for grandstanding (as with Cruz) or for myopia (as when he called Republican strategy on replenishing the highway trust fund "incredibly irresponsible, a total failure, an abdication of leadership"). Corker also blasted Republicans for offering unrealistic solutions to illegal immigration, saying, "I just hope that we don't let demagogues prevail, and that we finally deal with this issue and put it behind us." As it happens, Corker worked closely on that bill with New York Democratic Sen. Charles Schumer to forge a compromise. "Corker understands the value of a glib turn of phrase," wrote Sisk, the Tennessee journalist. "But more often than not, the bluster seems like a bargaining ploy, a way of shaping the negotiations before the real work begins, out of sight and away from the microphones."

FIRST DISTRICT

Phil Roe (R)

Elected 2008, 4th term; b. July 21, 1945, Clarksville; Austin Peay St. U., B.S. 1967, U. of TN, M.D. 1970; Methodist; widower (Pam); 3 children.

Military Career: Army, 1973-74.

Elected Office: Johnson City Commission, 2003-09, vice mayor, 2005-07, mayor, 2007-09.

Professional Career: Obstetrician/gynecologist, 1970-2008.

DC Office: 407 CHOB, 20515, 202-225-6356; Fax: 202-225-5714; Website: roe.house.gov.

State Offices: Kingsport, 423-247-8161; Morristown, 423-254-1400.

Committees: *Education & the Workforce:* Higher Education & Workforce Training; Health, Employment, Labor & Pensions (Chmn). *Veterans' Affairs:* Health; Oversight & Investigations.

Group Ratings

	ADA	ACLU	AFL-CIO	LCV	ITI	COC	HAFA	ACU	CFG	FRC
2014	0%	0%	–	0%	100%	79%	59%	76%	56%	100%
2013	5%	C	10%	0%	C	85%	C	80%	68%	C

National Journal Ratings

	2013 LIB	—	2013 CONS
Economic	31%	—	68%
Social	0%	—	87%
Foreign	5%	—	86%
Composite	16%	—	84%

Key Votes of the 113th Congress

1. Sandy storm spending	N	5. Medical Marijuana	N	9. Syrian Rebels Training	Y
2. Violence Against Women Act	N	6. Farm Bill	Y	10. Keystone pipeline	Y
3. Guantanamo Bay Detainees	N	7. Afghanistan Combat	N	11. Immigration Exec. Action	Y
4. Abortion 20-week ban	Y	8. NSA Phone Data Collection	Y	12. Bipartisan budget deal	Y

Election Results

2014 general	Phil Roe (R)	115,495	(83%)	$426,805	$6,294
	Robert Franklin (I)	9,905	(7%)		
	Robert Smith (Green)	9,869	(7%)		
	Michael Salyer (Lib)	4,145	(3%)		
2014 primary	Phil Roe (R)	72,903	(84%)		
	Daniel Hartley (R)	7,533	(9%)		
	John Rader (R)	6,557	(8%)		

Prior winning percentages: 2012 (76%), 2010 (81%), 2008 (72%)

Population		Race and Ethnicity		Income	
Total:	709,547	White	92.1%	Median income:	$37,176
Urban:	38.4%	Latino	3.2%		(407 of 435)
Suburban:	25.0%	Black	2.3%	Under $50,000	62.4%
Rural:	36.5%	Asian	0.5%	$50,000-$99,999:	26.3%
Land area:	4,100	Two races	1.6%	$100,000-$199,999:	9.8%
Pop/sq. mi.:	173.1	White Ethnic	16.7%	$200,000 or more:	1.4%
Born in state:	62.6%			Poverty Rate	19.5%
		Education			
Age Groups		H.S. grad or less:	55.0%	**Work**	
Under 18:	20.8%	Some college:	26.4%	White collar:	29.2%
18 to 34:	19.6%	College degree, 4 yr.:	11.0%	Blue collar:	44.3%
35 to 64:	41.4%	Post-grad study:	7.5%	Sales and service:	26.5%
Over 64:	18.3%				
		Military		Govt. workers:	15.4%
		Veterans/active duty:	10.9%		

Northeast Tennessee: Kingsport, Bristol, Johnson City

Between the corduroy-like ridges of the Appalachian chains, as they bend west and then south,
the Great Valley of Virginia extends far into northeastern Tennessee. These ridges guide travel today
(even the interstates follow the valleys here) just
as they guided settlement over 200 years ago. The

Voter Turnout	
2013 Total Citizen 18+	550,505
2014 House Turnout	139,470
2014 Turnout as % CVAP	25.3%
2012 Turnout as % CVAP	46.5%

land rush immediately after the Revolutionary War populated the area, mostly with Scots-
Irish immigrants. These settlers and their descendants were often hot-tempered, fierce folk.
In tiny Jonesborough, the early settlers attempted to establish the free state of Franklin
in 1784. The original town had an ordinance requiring settlers "to within three years build
a brick, stone, or well framed house, 20 feet long and 16 feet wide, and at least 10 feet in
the pitche, with a brick or stone chimney"—a sort of early restrictive covenant—and many
pioneer cabins, Federal-style mansions, and Greek Revival churches are lovingly preserved
today. A young Andrew Jackson made his way from North Carolina to the area, set up a legal
practice, and became a (typically irascible) judge before moving westward.

But it was the building of the railroads in the 1850s that determined the winners and losers for the modern era. The small industrial cities that developed—Johnson City, Kingsport,
and Bristol, now collectively known as the Tri-Cities—were on the main lines of national

commerce before the Civil War. The war had a different political effect here than in most of the South: Northeast Tennessee had few slaves and, with its connection to Northern industry, was Union and Republican territory. East Tennesseans twice voted against secession. It remains heavily Republican to this day.

2012 Presidential Vote		
Mitt Romney (R)	186,318	(73%)
Barack Obama (D)	65,782	(26%)
2008 Presidential Vote		
John McCain (R)	188,265	(70%)
Barack Obama (D)	77,100	(29%)
Cook Partisan Voting Index: R+25		

The political continuity may be surprising because the area developed the sort of industrial economy that produced unions and Democrats in the North. Its growth was helped by a skilled labor force, low electric power rates because of the Tennessee Valley Authority, and good transportation routes (rail lines and Interstate 81). Its small cities once boasted major paper and printing plants, although most of them are gone. One of the largest and rapidly expanding employers is Kingsport-based Eastman Chemical Co., which is the world's second largest producer of cigarette filter materials. With companies such as Eastman and Bell Helicopters taking the lead, the area had a 37 percent increase in exports in 2013. In Sevier County near Knoxville, Gatlinburg and Pigeon Forge (home of Dolly Parton's Dollywood theme park) have more than 10,000 hotel rooms at the entry point to the Great Smoky Mountains National Park, the nation's busiest. In 2014, it had 10 million visitors; Grand Canyon was the runner-up with 4.8 million.

The 1st Congressional District takes in the far northeastern end of Tennessee. The district hasn't elected a Democrat to the House in 136 years. It includes Mountain City, where fugitive murderer Tom Dula was captured before being returned to North Carolina for hanging (generations of folk musicians would eventually alter his name to the more familiar "Tom Dooley"). Greeneville was the birthplace of Congressman Davy Crockett and the longtime home of President Andrew Johnson. Over the years, this district's politics haven't budged an inch, and true to its roots, it gave 2012 GOP nominee Mitt Romney 73 per cent of the vote: His highest in Tennessee and in the top three percent of GOP districts nationwide.

Phil Roe (R)

Phil Roe, a conservative Republican elected in 2008, is one of the House's physicians and perhaps the one most closely associated with his former profession. He serves on two committees dealing with health issues, regularly appears on television talk shows to espouse the party's opposition to the Obama administration on health care, and issues his news releases with "M.D." after his name.

Roe grew up in Clarksville and attended a one-room schoolhouse with no running water. He graduated from Austin Peay State University and received a medical degree from the University of Tennessee. He served in the Army Medical Corps and then relocated to Johnson City, setting up practice as an obstetrician/gynecologist for 30 years. In 2003, the political bug bit Roe, and he ran successfully for the Johnson City Commission. Roe was chosen by commission members to be vice mayor in 2005 and mayor 2007. When five-term Rep. Bill Jenkins retired in 2006, Roe competed in a crowded GOP primary but finished fourth with 17% of the vote, behind health care business owner David Davis, who went on to win the general election.

In his first term in the House, Davis quickly gained a reputation as a combative partisan. Roe decided to challenge Davis for reelection in 2008 and embarked on a grass-roots campaign, visiting each county multiple times, talking to voters, stumping in restaurants, and waving signs at busy intersections. In ads featuring an elderly grandmother trying to fill up her car with gas, Roe criticized Davis for accepting money from oil companies, attacks that resonated as gas prices spiked. Davis outspent the challenger 3-to-1. Roe rebounded to narrowly upset Davis, becoming the first challenger in more than 40 years to defeat a sitting House member in Tennessee. His margin of victory was 482 votes. He won the district's two largest counties, Washington and Sullivan, while Davis was strong along the western edge of the district, winning Sevier and Hawkins counties. In November, Roe easily beat Democrat Robert Russell with 72% of the vote. He has been reelected with ease.

Roe's positions mirror the conservative bent of the district. He has an upbeat, folksy demeanor and was among the first House Republicans to join the Tea Party Caucus in 2010.

With the GOP takeover of the House, he became chairman of the Education and Workforce Committee's health panel in 2011 and helped to craft his party's free-market alternatives to the new law. He filed a bill that year seeking to repeal an advisory board that was created to rein in the growth of Medicare spending. The House passed the measure in 2012, but GOP leaders drew criticism from Democrats—including those who supported the bill—for attaching a provision setting caps on medical damage lawsuit awards, and the bill did not move in the Senate. In 2015, he reintroduced that bill with Democrat Linda Sanchez of California. In another bipartisan move, he worked with Democrat Ami Bera of California, another doctor, on a program to limit drug abuse by disposing of prescription drugs that the user no longer needs. Roe also serves on the Health Subcommittee of Veterans' Affairs. After committee hearings revealed problems with the agency's contracting procedures, he won approval in 2012 of a provision barring Veterans' Affairs employees who break the law from receiving bonuses.

With GOP Rep. Austin Scott of Georgia and the backing of the Republican Study Committee, Roe filed in June 2015 a bill that would repeal the health care reform law and replace it with what the authors called patient-centered reforms and free-market solutions. He worked on the bipartisan bill that was enacted in April 2015 to repeal the "doc fix" reducing payments to doctors with Medicare patients and take other steps to strengthen Medicare. He voted in June to give trade promotion authority to President Barack Obama which, Roe said, could help the 800,000 Tennesseans with jobs that benefit from trade. He harshly criticized restrictions on coal-fired utility plants in the Obama administration's "clean power plan" as an attempt to "take one industry and try to put them out of business."

Roe has been reliably conservative on other issues. He supports the fair tax, which would replace the federal income tax with a 23% national retail sales tax, and has a 100% rating from the National Rifle Association. The defense spending bill that was enacted in December 2014 included his provision to authorize a privately funded memorial to members of the military who made sacrifices during the 1991 war to drive Iraqi forces out of Kuwait.

SECOND DISTRICT

John Duncan (R)

Elected Nov. 1988, 14th full term; b. July 21, 1947, Lebanon; U. of TN, B.S. 1969, George Washington U., J.D. 1973; Presbyterian; married (Lynn); 4 children.

Military Career: Army Natl. Guard & Army Reserve, 1970-87.

Professional Career: Practicing atty., 1973-81; Knox Cnty. judge, 1981-88.

DC Office: 2207 RHOB, 20515, 202-225-5435; Fax: 202-225-6440; Website: duncan.house.gov.

State Offices: Knoxville, 865-523-3772; Maryville, 865-984-5464.

Committees: *Oversight & Government Reform:* National Security, Transportation & Public Assets. *Transportation & Infrastructure* (VChmn): Aviation; Highways & Transit; Railroads, Pipelines & Hazardous Materials.

Group Ratings

	ADA	ACLU	AFL-CIO	LCV	ITI	COC	HAFA	ACU	CFG	FRC
2014	20%	27%	–	3%	80%	64%	83%	76%	89%	100%
2013	20%	C	14%	7%	C	69%	C	96%	94%	C

National Journal Ratings

	2013 LIB	—	2013 CONS
Economic	20%	—	79%
Social	34%	—	62%
Foreign	53%	—	47%
Composite	37%	—	64%

Key Votes of the 113th Congress

1. Sandy storm spending	N	5. Medical Marijuana	N
2. Violence Against Women Act	N	6. Farm Bill	N
3. Guantanamo Bay Detainees	Y	7. Afghanistan Combat	Y
4. Abortion 20-week ban	Y	8. NSA Phone Data Collection	Y

9. Syrian Rebels Training	N	
10. Keystone pipeline	Y	
11. Immigration Exec. Action	Y	
12. Bipartisan budget deal	N	

Election Results

2014 general	John J. Duncan, Jr. (R)	120,853	(73%)	$992,997
	Bob Scott (D)	37,599	(23%)	
	Norris Dryer (Green)	4,033	(2%)	
	Casey Gouge (I)	4,222	(3%)	
2014 primary	John Duncan (R)	50,443	(61%)	
	Jason Zachary (R)	32,936	(40%)	

Prior winning percentages: 2012 (74%), 2010 (82%), 2008 (78%), 2006 (78%), 2004 (79%), 2002 (79%), 2000 (89%), 1998 (89%), 1996 (71%), 1994 (90%), 1992 (72%), 1990 (81%), 1988 (57%), 1988 special (56%)

Population		Race and Ethnicity		Income	
Total:	722,761	White	86.8%	Median income:	$46,594
Urban:	54.2%	Black	6.8%		(291 of 435)
Suburban:	33.5%	Latino	3.0%	Under $50,000	53.1%
Rural:	12.4%	Asian	1.7%	$50,000-$99,999:	29.7%
Land area:	2,927	Two races	1.4%	$100,000-$199,999:	13.4%
Pop/sq. mi.:	246.9	White Ethnic	20.2%	$200,000 or more:	3.7%
Born in state:	61.0%			Poverty Rate	16.3%
		Education			
Age Groups		H.S. grad or less:	42.7%	**Work**	
Under 18:	21.3%	Some college:	28.7%	White collar:	35.4%
18 to 34:	23.3%	College degree, 4 yr.:	17.3%	Blue collar:	42.7%
35 to 64:	39.3%	Post-grad study:	11.4%	Sales and service:	21.9%
Over 64:	16.1%			Govt. workers:	13.2%
		Military			
		Veterans/active duty:	9.9%		

East Tennessee: Knoxville

Knoxville, the largest city in East Tennessee, was the state's first capital. It is nestled between mountain ridges where the Holston and French Broad rivers join to form the Tennessee River. It was established not long after the first wave of pioneers came through the gaps and down the mountains of the Appalachian chain. During the Civil War, it was Union territory, and it has remained Republican in allegiance and progressive on civil rights ever since. But its Republican heritage is tempered by another tradition, that of the Tennessee Valley Authority. A venturesome program when created in the 1930s, it is now part of the fabric of life in East Tennessee, sometimes criticized as it has reached capacity to produce hydroelectric power and begun to rely more on expensive and sometimes poorly functioning nuclear power plants. In a competitive electricity market, TVA has labored under billions of dollars in debt mostly incurred in building its nuclear plants. Heavy ozone pollution in Knoxville led the Environmental Protection Agency to impose growth limits, so TVA spent several billion dollars to reduce pollution at its coal-fired power plants. The result has been a marked improvement in recent years in local air quality, and the EPA in 2011 ruled that the Knoxville area had met its ozone standard.

Voter Turnout	
2013 Total Citizen 18+	550,305
2014 House Turnout	166,751
2014 Turnout as % CVAP	30.3%
2012 Turnout as % CVAP	50.6%

Knoxville has overcome other setbacks and grown, at times robustly. *Forbes* magazine ranked it the sixth best city for job growth in 2012. Knoxville's Republican mayor, Bill Haslam, touted his record of promoting economic growth as the centerpiece of his successful 2010 campaign for governor. The University of Tennessee's football complex, Neyland Stadium, on fall Saturdays

2012 Presidential Vote		
Mitt Romney (R)	186,362	(67%)
Barack Obama (D)	85,510	(31%)

2008 Presidential Vote		
John McCain (R)	188,257	(64%)
Barack Obama (D)	101,583	(35%)

Cook Partisan Voting Index: R+20

contains one of the nation's largest crowds, cheering on the Vols. Women's basketball is nearly as popular as football here, and in 2009 Lady Vols' Coach Pat Summitt became the first Division I basketball coach, men's or women's, to win 1,000 career games. She retired in 2012 with a diagnosis of early-onset Alzheimer's disease, after having won 1,098 games and eight national championships. In May 2015, city officials announced plans to build a bridge for walkers and bikers that will cross the Tennessee River from the campus to South Knoxville.

The 2nd Congressional District of Tennessee includes Knoxville and Knox County, plus all or part of six mountainous counties to the north and south. Most of its people live within the Knoxville metro area, where the landmark Sunsphere is still visible from Interstate 40 (the 266-foot tower, topped by a 600-ton ball with facets tinted with 24-karat gold, was erected during the 1982 World's Fair). The heavily Republican district has not elected a Democratic congressman since the early 1850s.

John Duncan (R)

Republican John (Jimmy) Duncan, first elected in 1988, has been a maverick on economic and foreign policy issues, something that has hindered his ascension in the House GOP ranks. He has played a modest legislative role, but he continues to seek opportunities.

His similarly low-profile father, John Duncan, a former mayor of Knoxville who became the senior Republican on the House Ways and Means Committee, had held the seat from 1964 until his death in May 1988. Jimmy Duncan got a bachelor's degree in journalism at the University of Tennessee and a law degree from George Washington University. He practiced law and was a trial judge in the 1980s. When his father died, he won the seat despite a spirited challenge from Democrat Dudley Taylor, a scion of another prominent East Tennessee political family. Taylor attacked Duncan for his ties to scandal-tarred banker and Democratic politician Jake Butcher. Duncan won with 57% of the vote. He has been reelected every two years since with at least 71%.

Duncan is known for his independence, and *Reason* magazine has listed him as one of the consistent libertarians in the House, both at home and abroad. Duncan lacks the appetite for self-promotion but he often speaks his views on the House floor. Duncan has repeatedly called for an end to U.S. involvement in the war in Afghanistan, which he complained in 2011 was "seemingly endless." In October 2002, he was one of six Republicans who voted against the use of force in Iraq. Duncan argued that there was not sufficient proof that Iraqi Leader Saddam Hussein had weapons of mass destruction. In April 2011, he voted against the budget compromise that Republicans struck with President Barack Obama to avert a government shutdown. Duncan has consistently opposed international trade deals, regardless of who controls the White House, on the grounds that they give too much power to the president and they are a boon chiefly to giant multinational companies. He also objects that the trade agreements have led to excessive deficits in the U.S. balance of payments with other large nations.

On domestic issues, he opposed the Bush administration's 2001 No Child Left Behind education law that imposed mandatory testing on schools. The National Taxpayers Union has named him the most fiscally conservative member of the House. He also has been consistently conservative on social issues. Though he voted for the Violence Against Women Act's reauthorization in 2005, he opposed it in 2013 on economic grounds. He raised eyebrows when he told the *Chattanooga Times Free-Press*: "Like most men, I'm more opposed to violence against women than even violence against men. Because most men can handle it a little better than a lot of women can."

In 2011, Duncan became chairman of Transportation and Infrastructure's Subcommittee on Highways and Transit, where he sought to play a major role in getting a multi-year surface transportation bill into law. He slipped a provision into the bill in 2012 barring the use of federal money to buy red-light traffic cameras, though the cameras are funded by violators' fines and safety advocates said it would have little impact. He has disdained "radical environmentalists" whom he accused in June 2010 of being insensitive to rural Americans: "Most of them are city people, anyway. They probably think it would be good if everyone was forced to live in 25 or 30 urban areas, with the country left totally empty."

His contrariness has had its price. Duncan was a candidate for the chairmanship of the Natural Resources Committee in 2003, but Speaker Dennis Hastert skipped over him and five other senior Republicans to give the post to the more loyal Richard Pombo of California. When Republicans recaptured the House in 2010, Speaker John Boehner gave the chairmanship to the more loyal Doc Hastings of Washington. In 2006, Duncan made a big push for the top Republican position on the Transportation and Infrastructure Committee. He lost to John Mica of Florida, who had less seniority but was more of a party regular. In 2013, the less-senior Bill Shuster of Pennsylvania got the gavel. Instead, Duncan became the panel's vice chairman in 2013.

Duncan hasn't been shy about seeking funding for local projects, from resurfacing the Foothills Parkway near the Great Smoky Mountains National Park to a rail and trolley system for downtown Knoxville. Another of his legislative interests has been a bill to require the disclosure of contributions to presidential libraries, which the House passed three times, most recently in 2009 by a 388-31 vote. But the bill died each time in the Senate. He has subsequently reintroduced the measure, though congressional leaders have been reluctant to deny this presidential perk. Duncan also has filed a bill with Democratic Reps. Louise Slaughter of New York and Tim Walz of Minnesota to require disclosure of those who are compensated for providing political intelligence in Washington.

In Knoxville, Duncan's annual barbecue dinner at the downtown coliseum draws as many as 6,000 people and reinforces his local popularity. His father began the event in 1968. Although he shows no signs of retiring, when Duncan decides to leave Congress, his son, John Duncan III, is said to be interested in the seat. The younger Duncan was elected Knox County trustee in 2010. But he left office and pleaded guilty in 2013 to a felony charge of official misconduct for having approved more than $50,000 in official bonuses to himself and several employees. After he completed a year of unsupervised probation, a local judge agreed to dismiss the case.

THIRD DISTRICT

Charles Fleischmann (R)

Elected 2010, 3rd term; b. Oct. 11, 1962, Ooltewah; U. of IL, B.A. 1983, U. of TN, J.D. 1986; Catholic; married (Brenda); 3 children.

Professional Career: Practicing atty., 1987-2010.

DC Office: 230 CHOB, 20515, 202-225-3271; Fax: 202-225-3494; Website: fleischmann.house.gov.

State Offices: Athens, 423-745-4671; Chattanooga, 423-756-2342; Oak Ridge, 865-576-1976.

Committees: *Appropriations:* Energy & Water Development; Homeland Security; Labor, HHS, Education & Related Agencies.

Group Ratings

	ADA	ACLU	AFL-CIO	LCV	ITI	COC	HAFA	ACU	CFG	FRC
2014	5%	0%	–	3%	100%	86%	68%	80%	67%	100%
2013	5%	C	10%	4%	C	85%	C	88%	74%	C

National Journal Ratings

	2013 LIB	—	2013 CONS
Economic	21%	—	77%
Social	0%	—	87%
Foreign	0%	—	95%
Composite	10%	—	90%

Key Votes of the 113th Congress

1. Sandy storm spending	N	5. Medical Marijuana	N	9. Syrian Rebels Training	Y
2. Violence Against Women Act	N	6. Farm Bill	Y	10. Keystone pipeline	Y
3. Guantanamo Bay Detainees	N	7. Afghanistan Combat	N	11. Immigration Exec. Action	Y
4. Abortion 20-week ban	Y	8. NSA Phone Data Collection	Y	12. Bipartisan budget deal	Y

Election Results

2014 general	Charles J. Fleischmann (R)	97,319	(62%)	$1,544,338	$5,496
	Mary Headrick (D)	53,963	(35%)	$177,280	
	Cassandra Mitchell (I)	4,768	(3%)		
2014 primary	Charles Fleischmann (R)	46,556	(51%)		
	Weston Wamp (R)	45,082	(49%)		

Prior winning percentages: 2012 (61%), 2010 (57%)

Population		Race and Ethnicity		Income	
Total:	721,988	White	83.1%	Median income:	$41,906
Urban:	34.8%	Black	10.9%		*(358 of 435)*
Suburban:	41.3%	Latino	3.4%	Under $50,000	57.2%
Rural:	23.9%	Asian	1.1%	$50,000-$99,999:	28.1%
Land area:	4,380	Two races	1.3%	$100,000-$199,999:	12.2%
Pop/sq. mi.;	164.8	White Ethnic	15.3%	$200,000 or more:	2.5%
Born in state:	65.4%			Poverty Rate	18.5%
		Education			
Age Groups		H.S. grad or less:	50.1%	**Work**	
Under 18:	21.4%	Some college:	29.2%	White collar:	32.9%
18 to 34:	20.9%	College degree, 4 yr.:	12.9%	Blue collar:	43.2%
35 to 64:	40.8%	Post-grad study:	7.8%	Sales and service:	23.9%
Over 64:	16.9%			Govt. workers:	15.2%
		Military			
		Veterans/active duty:	9.7%		

East Tennessee: Chattanooga, Oak Ridge

Voter Turnout	
2013 Total Citizen 18+	556,462
2014 House Turnout	156,097
2014 Turnout as % CVAP	28.1%
2012 Turnout as % CVAP	49.9%

Etching its way through the serrated ridges of East Tennessee, with some of the most vivid scenery in the Appalachian Mountain chain, is the river that gave the state its name. From Knoxville, the Tennessee River cuts through a ridge and then plunges down a long valley to the city of Chattanooga at the Georgia line. There it switches course again, winding around the tabletop Lookout Mountain and then moving into northern Alabama before eventually swinging back north to empty into the Ohio River. Chattanooga was just a village when it became a Civil War battlefield. It then grew to be the industrial "Dynamo of Dixie," rising to prominence as a part of the "New South." Four decades ago, it was labeled America's most polluted city. But regional political leaders, prodded by influential and civic-minded scions of its Industrial Age aristocracy, used creative measures, such as locally built electric shuttle buses, to reduce pollution and to spruce up the city's scenic river banks. With big job cuts at the Tennessee Valley Authority, the region has pinned its hopes for economic growth more on the private sector, including tourism and a large food-service industry that includes the MoonPie and Little Debbie confectioners. Downtown Chattanooga features the well-visited Tennessee Aquarium.

Chattanooga is the state's fourth-largest city and in recent years has been challenging Knoxville for third place. After declining in the 1980s and stagnating in the 1990s, the city's population has had a double-digit increase since 2000. As old businesses have shut down, new ones have arrived. In May 2015, Volkswagen announced a $700 million expansion of its plant that was expected to add 2,000 jobs with VW and nearly 8,000 jobs with suppliers. The announcement came a few months after VW workers turned down an organizing campaign by the United Auto Workers at the plant. Amazon.com opened a sprawling distribution center in the area, and said in 2013 that it would expand it from the size of 17 to 28 football fields and eventually employ 5,000 people. The high-tech industry is transforming more than the local economy; the city recently won plaudits for its state-of-the-art, publicly owned, citywide fiber network.

2012 Presidential Vote		
Mitt Romney (R)	172,227	(63%)
Barack Obama (D)	95,014	(35%)

2008 Presidential Vote		
John McCain (R)	175,105	(61%)
Barack Obama (D)	106,491	(37%)

Cook Partisan Voting Index: R+16

Chattanooga is increasingly in the ever-growing orbit of metropolitan Atlanta and has been discussed as a possible site for the latter city's second airport.

The 3rd Congressional District of Tennessee includes Chattanooga, stretches from Georgia to Kentucky, and stops a few miles short of both Alabama and Virginia. The district includes what is now the Oak Ridge National Laboratory, which was secretly constructed during World War II in virgin Appalachian forest to house the facility that made uranium isotopes for the Hiroshima bomb. For years, it did not appear on maps. Today, its location is well-known. In 2012, peace activists broke into the facility, splashed blood on the Enriched Uranium Materials Facility, and hung slogan-filled banners on the walls. The district also contains the Museum of Appalachia in Clinton, which maintains dozens of frontier structures, including a cabin owned by Mark Twain's father. Historically, the area was split politically, with Chattanooga voting Democratic and the mountain counties Republican. Today, it is solidly Republican, although the 63 percent that Mitt Romney won here in 2012 was his smallest vote in the seven Republican-controlled districts in the state.

Charles Fleischmann (R)

Republican Charles (Chuck) Fleischmann was elected in 2010 to succeed GOP Rep. Zach Wamp, who ran unsuccessfully for governor. Fleischmann is more of a team player than the independent-minded Wamp and was rewarded in 2013 with a seat on the Appropriations Committee. But he has contended with two primary challenges from Zach's son Weston, in which Fleischmann narrowly prevailed.

When he was a boy, Fleischmann's father, Max, worked in the food services business. The family moved often, following his father's job opportunities. Fleischmann, an only child, lived in Philadelphia and New Jersey before finishing high school in Chicago. His mother died of cancer when he was 14. He graduated from the University of Illinois in three years with a bachelor's degree in political science. He got his law degree at the University of Tennessee, and started his own firm in Knoxville with his wife, Brenda.

When Zach Wamp opened the seat, Fleischmann decided to run, saying he was "very, very upset with the way things were going in Washington, D.C." In the August primary, his most formidable opponent was health care consultant Robin Smith, a former Republican state party chairwoman. Fleischmann put $544,000 of his own money into the campaign and accused Smith of mismanaging funds when she chaired the GOP.

Smith attacked Fleischmann's record as a personal injury lawyer, saying that he had sued gun clubs, Wal-Mart stores, and churches, all popular institutions in the state. Fleischmann defended himself by saying, "I make a living standing up for the little guy, people who have traditionally not had a voice and who have been dealt injustices and harm." In the end, Fleischmann edged out Smith, 30%-28%. In November, Fleischmann won an easy 57%-28% victory over radio talk show personality John Wolfe, who had twice lost to Wamp.

In the House, Fleischmann has been a reliable GOP vote and a conservative mainstay. He is capable of serving up red-meat rhetoric; asked at a 2012 debate for his views on climate change, he responded: "I think we ought to take Al Gore, put him on an iceberg, and put him way out there." Although he opposed raising the debt ceiling in 2011 and the compromise to avoid the fiscal cliff in 2013, he has been loyal to GOP leaders on other votes. The *Chattanooga Free Press'* editorial page, in endorsing him for reelection, complained that "his unwillingness to vote against his party ... is exasperating."

His position on Appropriations, especially its Energy and Water Development Subcommittee, has given Fleischmann a critical voice on those needs. He joined fellow Tennessee Republican Scott DesJarlais in opposing an Energy Department plan to consolidate management of Oak Ridge's Y-12 weapons plant with the one at Texas' Pantex facility. He has repeatedly stressed the need to replace Chickamauga's deteriorating 75-year-old river lock by overhauling the project's funding mechanism, the Inland Waterway Trust Fund; he has jokingly referred to the prospective $680 million project as the "Chuck" lock. With Democratic Rep. Ben Ray Lujan of New Mexico, he co-chaired the Nuclear Cleanup Caucus.

Fleischmann has survived two grueling primary fights against Weston Wamp. In 2012, he drew spirited challenges from the 25-year-old Wamp and dairy magnate Scottie Mayfield. Neither Wamp nor Mayfield was as polished as Fleischmann, who also raised much more money. He won the primary with 39%, as Mayfield took 31% and Wamp 29%. He narrowly lost Chattanooga-based Hamilton County to Wamp but prevailed in most of the smaller, rural areas. His Democratic general election opponent, acute care physician Mary Headrick, accused him of being in the pocket of special interests and blasted his proposal to cut capital gains tax rates. But she raised just $119,000 to his $1.4 million, and he coasted to a win with 61% of the vote.

Wamp returned for another try in 2014 in what became an even tighter primary. He called himself an "independent-minded conservative," and he courted votes from Democrats, who were eligible to vote in the primary. Fleischmann rebuked him at one debate, saying, "If he wants to run as a Democrat, let him run as a Democrat." Wamp responded that the congressman apparently believed "that Democrats have cooties and you can't talk to them." Fleischmann retorted, "They have got a lot worse than that, Weston." Fleischmann accused Wamp of being a "show horse" and supporting "amnesty" for illegal immigrants. The latter prompted a rebuke from Oklahoma GOP Sen. Tom Coburn, who endorsed the challenger, as did former Pennsylvania Sen. Rick Santorum and the district's two largest newspapers. Fleischmann eked out a win in the August primary, 51%-49%. The outcome in many of the counties was exceedingly close, and neither candidate had an obvious base.

FOURTH DISTRICT

Scott DesJarlais (R)

Elected 2010, 3rd term; b. Feb. 21, 1964, Des Moines, IA; U. of SD, B.S. 1987, M.D. 1991; Episcopalian; married (Amy); 3 children.

Professional Career: Practicing physician, 1993-2010.

DC Office: 413 CHOB, 20515, 202-225-6831; Fax: 202-226-5172; Website: desjarlais.house.gov.

State Offices: Columbia, 931-381-9920; Cleveland, 423-472-7500; Murfreesboro, 615-896-1986; Winchester, 931-962-3180.

Committees: *Agriculture. Oversight & Government Reform:* Health Care, Benefits, & Administrative Rules. Foreign Affairs: Africa, Global Health, Global Human Rights & International Organizations; Asia & the Pacific.

Group Ratings

	ADA	ACLU	AFL-CIO	LCV	ITI	COC	HAFA	ACU	CFG	FRC
2014	5%	0%	–	0%	100%	50%	82%	100%	–	100%
2013	5%	C	14%	4%	C	77%	C	76%	85%	C

National Journal Ratings

	2013 LIB	—	2013 CONS
Economic	8%	—	91%
Social	0%	—	87%
Foreign	0%	—	95%
Composite	6%	—	94%

Key Votes of the 113th Congress

1. Sandy storm spending	N	5. Medical Marijuana	N	9. Syrian Rebels Training	NV
2. Violence Against Women Act	N	6. Farm Bill	Y	10. Keystone pipeline	Y
3. Guantanamo Bay Detainees	N	7. Afghanistan Combat	N	11. Immigration Exec. Action	Y
4. Abortion 20-week ban	Y	8. NSA Phone Data Collection	Y	12. Bipartisan budget deal	N

Election Results

2014 general	Scott DesJarlais (R)	84,781	(58%)	$643,369	$41,481
	Lenda Sherrell (D)	51,338	(35%)	$1,051,312	$77,899
	Robert Doggart (I)	9,238	(6%)		
2014 primary	Scott DesJarlais (R)	34,793	(45%)		
	Jim Tracy (R)	34,755	(45%)		
	John Anderson (R)	4,592	(6%)		

Prior winning percentages: 2012 (56%), 2010 (57%)

Population		Race and Ethnicity		Income	
Total:	726,649	White	82.5%	Median income:	$47,369
Urban:	31.2%	Black	8.2%		*(275 of 435)*
Suburban:	22.8%	Latino	5.4%	Under $50,000	52.5%
Rural:	46.0%	Asian	1.3%	$50,000-$99,999:	33.0%
Land area:	5,685	Two races	2.4%	$100,000-$199,999:	12.7%
Pop/sq. mi.:	127.8	White Ethnic	17.0%	$200,000 or more:	1.8%
Born in state:	60.3%			Poverty Rate	15.5%
		Education			
Age Groups		H.S. grad or less:	49.9%	**Work**	
Under 18:	23.9%	Some college:	28.9%	White collar:	31.6%
18 to 34:	23.4%	College degree, 4 yr.:	14.1%	Blue collar:	40.7%
35 to 64:	39.0%	Post-grad study:	7.0%	Sales and service:	27.7%
Over 64:	13.7%				
		Military		Govt. workers:	13.3%
		Veterans/active duty:	9.0%		

Middle Tennessee: Murfreesboro Area

The invisible line between Republican and Democratic territory during the Civil War in Tennessee ran along Walden Ridge, the westernmost swelling of the Appalachians. This invisible line also separates the Tennessee Valley, which had few slaves and whose economic ties were to the North, from

Voter Turnout	
2013 Total Citizen 18+	533,036
2014 House Turnout	145,418
2014 Turnout as % CVAP	27.3%
2012 Turnout as % CVAP	49.2%

the rolling farmlands of Middle Tennessee, first settled by Andrew Jackson in the 1790s and resolutely Democratic from 1829, when Jackson became the first president to call himself a Democrat. This is an America of small towns, where every hamlet seems to have its own annual festival, like the RC MoonPie Festival in Bell Buckle. Lynchburg is where Jasper Newton Daniel, better known by the nickname "Jack," began brewing his "Old No. 7" whiskey, an operation that continues to this day. Oddly, Moore County, where the distillery is located, is a dry county.

There is an industrial base here as well, particularly in the automobile industry. General Motors launched its Saturn brand in Spring Hill in 1990, igniting growth in the region. When the erstwhile auto giant went bankrupt in 2009, it shut down the factory and furloughed most of its 2,700 employees. Assembly-line production resumed in September 2012 on the Chevrolet Equinox, and the plant produces engines and other components for GM assembly plants elsewhere. Total employment climbed above 2,100 in March 2015. Nissan has a large engine assembly plant in Decherd in Franklin County; the company operates a large vehicle production assembly plant in Smyrna, and opened in 2013 a $1.4 billion facility to manufacture batteries for its Leaf electric cars, which also are assembled in Smyrna. In Murfreesboro, Amazon opened a distribution center in 2012 and has more than 1,000 year-round workers, with many more temporary hires during the holiday season. General Mills announced in April 2015 a $250 million expansion of its local plant, where it already had 900 workers who produced Yoplait yogurt and Toaster Strudel.

The 4th Congressional District of Tennessee takes in all of these places. About 40% of its population is in Rutherford County, which has become part of suburban Nashville. Murfreesboro has more than doubled since 1990, and it is now the sixth-largest city in the state, with a population exceeding 100,000. This is the most blue-collar of Nashville's major suburban counties and the least-heavily Republican. The rest of the district is a scattering of small towns and rural areas. Dayton is where the famous Scopes Monkey Trial was held in 1925; Scopes was convicted of teaching evolution. This was once reliably

2012 Presidential Vote		
Mitt Romney (R)	169,508	(65%)
Barack Obama (D)	86,394	(33%)

2008 Presidential Vote		
John McCain (R)	170,669	(63%)
Barack Obama (D)	97,715	(36%)

Cook Partisan Voting Index: R+18

Democratic territory. But Democrats have become scarce in most of Tennessee outside of Nashville and Memphis. Mitt Romney won the 4th with 65% in 2012.

Scott DesJarlais (R)

Republican Scott DesJarlais was elected in 2010 following one of the year's most negative campaigns. He has overcome explosive accusations about his personal life in subsequent elections, and survived by 38 votes a 2014 primary challenger that he was widely expected to lose.

DesJarlais grew up in Sturgis, South Dakota. His father was a barber, and his mother was a registered nurse at a veterans' hospital. He earned a bachelor's degree in chemistry and psychology from the University of South Dakota in 1987. After receiving his medical degree from the school in 1991, DesJarlais moved to Jasper, where he practiced medicine.

The 2010 House race was DesJarlais' first bid for elected office, and he said it was motivated by his patients' concerns about the foundering economy and their fears about losing their jobs. He challenged Rep. Lincoln Davis, who had been the most conservative Democrat in the Tennessee delegation and had earned the endorsements of the U.S. Chamber of Commerce, the National Rifle Association, and National Right to Life. DesJarlais billed himself as a "doctor, not a politician." Davis made headlines with accusations made by DesJarlais' first wife, Susan, who claimed that he physically intimidated her during their 2000 divorce and threatened to commit suicide.

DesJarlais called the charges "completely false," and the ad exposed Davis to accusations of mudslinging. Davis pointed out his votes against the Democrats' health care overhaul and their cap-and-trade bill to limit greenhouse gas emissions, both unpopular in the district. But even his limited cooperation with President Barack Obama in voting for the $787 billion economic stimulus bill cost him votes. DesJarlais won 57%-39%.

In the House, DesJarlais has been a devout fiscal conservative, and he annually has had a perfect conservative score on social issues, according to *National Journal's* vote ratings. When he suggested cutting the Forest Service's outreach programs for children, environmental groups protested that he was putting Smokey Bear in jeopardy. He joined fellow Tennessee Republican Charles Fleischmann in opposing an Energy Department plan to consolidate management of Oak Ridge's Y-12 weapons plant with the Pantex facility in Texas. He defended as essential outreach his unusually high spending on constituent mailings.

Scandal has so overshadowed DesJarlais' legislative work that survival has seemed his most significant accomplishment. *The Huffington Post* reported in October 2012 that, according to a transcript of a phone recording made prior to his divorce, DesJarlais urged his pregnant mistress—who was one of his medical patients—to get an abortion. He issued a statement accusing opponents of "the same gutter politics" as his earlier race, but he later said in a letter to supporters that he encouraged the abortion because he was trying to get her to admit she wasn't pregnant. Conservatives abandoned him in droves, and national Democrats raced to assist challenger Eric Stewart, who had been seen as a long shot.

The district's conservative voters gave DesJarlais the benefit of the doubt, as he defeated Stewart 56%-44%. He won Rutherford County—the district's largest—by 53%-47%, and he easily won the rest of the district except for three small counties in the Cumberland mountains. After the election, the state Democratic Party released court transcripts showing that DesJarlais and his ex-wife mutually agreed that she would have two abortions, and that he admitted having sex with at least two patients, three coworkers, and a drug company representative. DesJarlais later acknowledged having used "very poor judgment" but dismissed suggestions that he resign or not run again. In 2013, the Tennessee Board of Medical Examiners fined him $500 and reprimanded him for having sex with multiple patients.

In January 2013, state Sen. Jim Tracy announced a primary challenge for 2014 and began to peel off DesJarlais' donors. Tracy told supporters, "I'm a conservative in word and deed. I'm 100 percent pro-life." Tracy outraised DesJarlais and won endorsements from many in the state's GOP establishment; he had run for an open seat in the 6th District in 2010, and finished third in the primary by only 566 votes behind winner Diane Black. He campaigned on bringing "integrity" to the office, but he was slow to attack DesJarlais directly. The incumbent countered that his personal life was old news, noting that he had been married for 12 years to his second wife. "I know God's forgiven me," he told one conservative talk-radio host. "I simply ask my fellow Christians and constituents to [do] the same for me." He ran an active campaign that emphasized his conservative values and efforts in Washington. That message resonated with some voters; Vanderbilt political scientist John Geer told *The Washington Post* that "conservative evangelicals believe in forgiveness."

DesJarlais won the high-turnout primary by 38 votes. Five other GOP candidates split 10 percent of the vote. After 18 days of recounts, Tracy continued to fault the handling of the election but said that further challenges "would not be the right thing for the Republican Party and the conservative cause in Tennessee." In early 2015, he left the door open for another primary challenge in 2016.

In November, DesJarlais faced a competitive challenge from Democrat Lenda Sherrell, an accountant, who spent more than $1 million. But Republicans rallied around DesJarlais and he took every county to win 58%-35%. During the campaign, he underwent treatment for early-stage cancer in his neck.

In January 2015, DesJarlais voted against giving John Boehner another term as speaker, on the basis that "we need a new direction and a fresh approach." Instead, he voted for conservative stalwart Jim Jordan of Ohio, citing Jordan's "steadfast commitment to conservative principles and to holding the White House accountable for their actions." During a February town hall meeting in Columbia, DesJarlais said that Obama should be impeached, though he didn't offer details. According to the *Columbia Daily Herald*, he added, "It's not easy to impeach a president. But if you tell me how to do it, I'll do it."

FIFTH DISTRICT

Jim Cooper (D)

Elected 2002, 13th term; b. June 19, 1954, Nashville; U. of NC, B.A. 1975, Oxford U., B.A./M.A. 1977, Harvard U., J.D. 1980; Episcopalian; married (Martha); 3 children.

Elected Office: U.S. House, 1983-95.

Professional Career: Practicing atty., 1980-82; Investment banker, 1995-99; Founder & partner, investment bank, 1999-2002.

DC Office: 1536 LHOB, 20515, 202-225-4311; Fax: 202-226-1035; Website: cooper.house.gov.

State Offices: Nashville, 615-736-5295.

Committees: *Armed Services:* Oversight & Investigations; Strategic Forces (RMM); Emerging Threats & Capabilities. *Oversight & Government Reform:* Interior; Health Care, Benefits, & Administrative Rules.

Group Ratings

	ADA	ACLU	AFL-CIO	LCV	ITI	COC	HAFA	ACU	CFG	FRC
2014	80%	77%	–	91%	80%	43%	29%	8%	20%	25%
2013	65%	C	75%	89%	C	67%	C	28%	24%	C

National Journal Ratings

	2013 LIB	—	2013 CONS
Economic	60%	—	40%
Social	59%	—	41%
Foreign	61%	—	38%
Composite	60%	—	40%

Key Votes of the 113th Congress

1. Sandy storm spending	N	5. Medical Marijuana	N	9. Syrian Rebels Training	N
2. Violence Against Women Act	Y	6. Farm Bill	N	10. Keystone pipeline	Y
3. Guantanamo Bay Detainees	Y	7. Afghanistan Combat	N	11. Immigration Exec. Action	N
4. Abortion 20-week ban	N	8. NSA Phone Data Collection	N	12. Bipartisan budget deal	Y

Election Results

2014 general	Jim Cooper (D)	95,635	(62%)	$600,091
	Bob Ries (R)	54,939	(36%)	$43,721
	Paul Deakin (I)	3,032	(2%)	
2014 primary	Jim Cooper (D)	unopposed		

Prior winning percentages: 2012 (65%), 2010 (56%), 2008 (66%), 2006 (69%), 2004 (69%), 2002 (64%), 1992 (66%), 1990 (69%), 1988 (100%), 1986 (100%), 1984 (75%), 1982 (66%)

Population		Race and Ethnicity		Income	
Total:	739,937	White	61.0%	Median income:	$47,039
Urban:	59.9%	Black	24.7%		*(280 of 435)*
Suburban:	37.8%	Latino	9.1%	Under $50,000	52.9%
Rural:	2.3%	Asian	2.6%	$50,000-$99,999:	29.7%
Land area:	1,525	Two races	2.1%	$100,000-$199,999:	13.5%
Pop/sq. mi.:	485.3	White Ethnic	16.9%	$200,000 or more:	3.9%
Born in state:	53.8%			Poverty Rate	17.4%
		Education			
Age Groups		H.S. grad or less:	38.8%	**Work**	
Under 18:	22.0%	Some college:	26.1%	White collar:	38.2%
18 to 34:	28.4%	College degree, 4 yr.:	21.9%	Blue collar:	41.8%
35 to 64:	38.5%	Post-grad study:	13.1%	Sales and service:	20.0%
Over 64:	11.1%				
		Military		Govt. workers:	11.6%
		Veterans/active duty:	7.1%		

Nashville Metro

Country music, an art form that emerged from the settlers of the hardscrabble, mountainous counties of East Tennessee, is now a more than $2 billion-a-year business. The heart of country music is located in the city that is increasingly the cultural, political and economic heart of Tennessee: Nashville. Run

Voter Turnout	
2013 Total Citizen 18+	532,860
2014 House Turnout	154,276
2014 Turnout as % CVAP	29%
2012 Turnout as % CVAP	52.4%

out of a series of deceptively modest homes-turned-offices on Music Row, the industry congregated in Nashville because local radio station WSM had a clear channel in the 1920s from which to beam its weekly "barn dances" throughout the South. The broadcasts later became known as the Grand Ole Opry, the nation's longest continuously running radio show.

Music Row has become a corporate juggernaut that views itself as more influential than the entertainment meccas on the East or West Coast. The city has about 200 recording studios, and Nashville music has more than $1 billion in sales each year. The Country Music Hall of Fame and Museum opened as part of a downtown revitalization and completed in April 2014 a $100 million expansion. The city now offers good music of all sorts, sushi bars and a lively cafe scene. The music industry is increasingly intertwined with the television industry here. The Wildhorse Saloon, where a popular CMT show featuring line dancing was taped in the 1990s, is now the venue for the network's popular *Can You Duet?* show. The critically acclaimed ABC musical drama *Nashville* is filmed in the city and features some of the industry's other musical landmarks, such as the Bluebird Cafe, a small venue where many of the industry's biggest stars have been discovered, including Kathy Mattea, Garth Brooks and Taylor Swift.

For years, both the city's elite and its religious leaders resented the growing local influence of country music. But all three made their peace in the 1970s, and since then Nashville has become one of the South's boom cities—one of the fastest-growing metropolitan areas behind the much larger Atlanta and Dallas-Fort Worth Metroplex. In 2014, the Census Bureau listed Nashville as the ninth-fastest growing city in the nation. In 2013, the music industry supported 57,000 jobs here. It is also a center of the for-profit health industry, the area's largest and fastest-growing employer. Goodlettsville-based retail store chain Dollar General is traded on the S&P 500.

An agreeable quality of life, plenty of highly skilled labor, a central location, and absence of urban strife have all enhanced Nashville as the largest metropolitan area in the state, with suburban growth in all directions. In 2011, *Forbes* magazine called it America's No. 3 "boom town," following Austin and Raleigh.

2012 Presidential Vote		
Barack Obama (D)	152,960	(56%)
Mitt Romney (R)	116,289	(43%)

2008 Presidential Vote		
Barack Obama (D)	170,158	(58%)
John McCain (R)	122,210	(41%)

Cook Partisan Voting Index: D+5

The dominant cultural tone in the metropolitan area is conservative—Nashville has more than 700 churches, and is the headquarters for the publishing arms of the Southern Baptist Convention, United Methodist Church, and National Baptist Convention—but Nashville and Davidson County remain Democratic bulwarks. The city's diversity is increasingly reflected in its businesses. Two immigrant sisters from Mexico opened Las Paletas Gourmet Popsicles—it is exactly what it sounds like—while Manuel Cuevas, who designed outfits for acts as diverse as Elvis, Aerosmith and Johnny Cash (including those famous black suits) moved his business, Manuel's Exclusive Clothiers, here from Los Angeles in the late 1980s.

The 5th Congressional District of Tennessee includes all of consolidated Nashville-Davidson County. Neighboring Cheatham and Dickson counties include about 10 percent of the district's population. The 5th is reliably Democratic, one of only two districts in Tennessee where a Democrat has a chance, but it is much more centrist than the Memphis-based 9th District.

Jim Cooper (D)

Jim Cooper, a Democrat elected in 2002 who also served from 1982 to 1994, is a brainy moderate with a tart tongue—especially when it comes to his own party's leadership. Despite the polarized political climate, he persistently seeks bipartisanship on fiscal matters.

His father, Prentice Cooper, was governor for six years. Jim Cooper, educated at the University of North Carolina, Oxford and Harvard Law School, was first elected in 1982 by defeating Republican Cissy Baker, the daughter of then-Senate Majority Leader Howard Baker. During his first stint in Congress, he spoke out against tobacco use and opposed the National Rifle Association in a state where both were popular. He participated actively in the "Group of Nine" Democrats on the Energy and Commerce Committee that produced a compromise between Michigan Democrat John Dingell, an ally of the auto industry, and California's Henry Waxman, who was pro-environmental regulation, on the Clean Air Act of 1990. In 1994, Cooper ran against Republican Fred Thompson for the Senate seat that Democrat Al Gore had vacated when he was elected vice president; Thompson won, 60%-39%.

Cooper then went to work as an investment banker in Nashville and as a teacher at Vanderbilt University's business school. In 2002, when Democratic Rep. Bob Clement jumped into a Senate race, Cooper joined a flurry of Democratic candidates for the seat. His toughest opponent was Davidson County Sheriff Gayle Ray, the first female sheriff in Tennessee, who had support from the Democratic women's fundraising group EMILY's List. Ray attacked Cooper's voting record on abortion. An abortion rights supporter, Cooper said that Ray's charges were inaccurate and ran compelling and positive ads showing his children describing what he does well—banjo playing, helping with homework, getting health care for senior citizens—and what he doesn't do well—cooking, playing basketball.

The AFL-CIO and *The Tennessean* endorsed Ray. Cooper had support from the Sierra Club and several smaller newspapers and raised twice as much money as Ray, including $700,000 of his own money. He won the primary with 47%. Ray got 23% in the seven-candidate field. Cooper won the general election easily and has faced no serious reelection challenges.

Cooper has focused on being a leader of the fiscally conservative Blue Dog Coalition and a consensus-builder within the national Democratic Party. In the dwindling ranks of Blue Dogs, he is co-chair for policy and legislative strategy, and describes himself as "the nerd" of the group. In 2011, he supported fellow Blue Dog Heath Shuler of North Carolina for speaker over California's Nancy Pelosi, whom he disdains for her strong-armed management style. He once said of his fellow Democrats under Pelosi, "We're just told how to vote. We are treated like mushrooms most of the time." Two fellow Blue Dogs, Dan Lipinski of Illinois and Mike McIntyre of North Carolina, voted for him for speaker in 2013; Cooper cast his own vote for former GOP Secretary of State Colin Powell. In the 2015 vote for speaker, freshman Rep. Gwen Graham of Florida voted for him, and Cooper again voted for Powell. "We need a hero now more than ever," he said.

New York Times columnist Joe Nocera, in a 2011 piece titled "The Last Moderate," praised Cooper as "the House's conscience, a lonely voice for civility in this ugly era." He has introduced numerous measures with GOP support. The House-passed bill to temporarily raise the federal debt limit in February 2013 included his provision to withhold lawmakers' pay if a budget isn't passed on time. He said finding Republicans to support him "is really not hard" but gets overlooked. "The press is only focused on the leaders," he said. "They barely know the names of the backbenchers, and those are the people who can make things happen if they choose to." During his second stint in Congress, he joined the Armed Services Committee, where he has been ranking Democrat on the Strategic Forces Subcommittee, which oversees the nation's nuclear arsenal.

One way Cooper builds cooperation is by giving out his cell phone number to everyone. "Phone numbers are kind of a trust issue," he said at a 2013 town hall meeting. "If you trust people, then they will trust you back." It also helps that Cooper eschews name-calling. When others in his party were savaging Republican Paul Ryan of Wisconsin for his budget-cutting proposals in 2011, Cooper said he didn't agree with all of Ryan's proposals but defended him as "genuinely smart and nice and humble and caring." Cooper earlier had joined another conservative Republican, Virginia's Frank Wolf, in calling for a panel to examine entitlement spending—an idea that became reality with President Barack Obama's creation of the Simpson-Bowles commission on the national debt in 2010. Cooper offered an amendment in March 2012 to have a budget resolution based on the commission's recommendations; it drew just 38 votes. During the health care debate in 2009, he worked with Waxman, the Energy and Commerce chairman, to moderate some provisions that conservative Democrats considered government overreach.

Cooper has sought to reform Congress, which he has accused of being "too lazy to prioritize." In 2012, he became the first lawmaker to sign a pledge by the activist group Rootstrikers not to lobby after leaving office. He has sought limits on spending earmarks—before the earmark moratorium, he had refused for years to seek such special-interest funding—and enforcement of pay-as-you-go rules that require tax cuts or spending increases to be offset elsewhere in the budget. Cooper also urged expanded powers for the president to veto specific items in the budget. A longtime proponent of increased government oversight, his bill to strengthen the independence of federal inspectors passed Congress and, despite a veto threat from President George W. Bush, became law in 2008. He has taken the lead in calling for redistricting reform by requiring that each state establish a bipartisan commission to draw House boundaries. In 2015, he added his Redistricting Transparency Act, requiring that such information be made public.

Cooper was mentioned as a candidate to head the White House budget office, but he fell out of favor with the Obama administration early in 2009 during work on the $787 billion economic stimulus bill. Cooper was one of 11 House Democrats to vote against the initial version of the bill and he told a Nashville radio station he had gotten "quiet encouragement" from the White House to oppose it because Obama disagreed with changes in the legislation made by the House Democratic leadership. The White House denied urging Cooper to vote against the leadership-backed bill.

SIXTH DISTRICT

Diane Black (R)

Elected 2010, 3rd term; b. Jan. 16, 1951, Baltimore, MD; Anne Arundel Col., A.S. 1971, Belmont U., B.A. 1992; Lutheran; married (David); 3 children.

Elected Office: TN House, 1998-2004; TN Senate, 2004-10.

Professional Career: Registered nurse, 1969-2010; Dir., Sumner Regional Health Systems, 1993-98; Owner, Ebon-Falcon.

DC Office: 1131 LHOB, 20515, 202-225-4231; Fax: 202-225-6887; Website: black.house.gov.

State Offices: Cookeville, 931-854-0069; Gallatin, 615-206-8204.

Committees: *Budget. Ways & Means:* Health.

Group Ratings

	ADA	ACLU	AFL-CIO	LCV	ITI	COC	HAFA	ACU	CFG	FRC
2014	0%	0%	–	0%	100%	86%	60%	84%	62%	100%
2013	5%	C	10%	0%	C	85%	C	88%	73%	C

National Journal Ratings

	2013 LIB	—	2013 CONS
Economic	18%	—	80%
Social	0%	—	87%
Foreign	0%	—	95%
Composite	9%	—	91%

Key Votes of the 113th Congress

1. Sandy storm spending N	5. Medical Marijuana N	9. Syrian Rebels Training Y
2. Violence Against Women Act N	6. Farm Bill Y	10. Keystone pipeline Y
3. Guantanamo Bay Detainees N	7. Afghanistan Combat N	11. Immigration Exec. Action Y
4. Abortion 20-week ban Y	8. NSA Phone Data Collection Y	12. Bipartisan budget deal Y

Election Results

2014 general	Diane Black (R)	115,190	(71%)	$587,243	$2,906
	Amos Powers (D)	37,215	(23%)		
	Mike Winton (I)	9,630	(6%)		
2014 primary	Diane Black (R)	67,881	(77%)		
	Jerry Lowery (R)	20,660	(23%)		

Prior winning percentages: 2012 (76%), 2010 (67%)

Population		Race and Ethnicity:		Income	
Total:	724,274	White	89.8%	Median income:	$43,709
Urban:	0.0%	Black	4.3%		*(336 of 435)*
Suburban:	45.2%	Latino	3.7%	Under $50,000	55.5%
Rural:	54.8%	Asian	0.8%	$50,000-$99,999:	29.9%
Land area:	6,457	Two races	1.1%	$100,000-$199,999:	12.1%
Pop/sq. mi.:	112.2	White Ethnic	18.4%	$200,000 or more:	2.6%
Born in state:	63.3%			Poverty Rate	16.5%
		Education			
Age Groups		H.S. grad or less:	53.3%	**Work**	
Under 18:	22.9%	Some college:	27.1%	White collar:	30.4%
18 to 34:	20.2%	College degree, 4 yr.:	12.6%	Blue collar:	42.4%
35 to 64:	40.4%	Post-grad study:	6.9%	Sales and service:	27.2%
Over 64:	16.5%				
		Military		Govt. workers:	14.3%
		Veterans/active duty:	9.3%		

Middle Tennessee: Eastern Nashville Suburbs, Cookesville

Middle Tennessee is hilly and fertile, cut by deep, curvy rivers. The terrain was never much suited for plantation crops, and there were few big landholdings. This has long been a land of small farmers and small county-seat towns, nestled amid some of the loveliest scenery in the country. As one of the

Voter Turnout	
2013 Total Citizen 18+	543,438
2014 House Turnout	162,097
2014 Turnout as % CVAP	29.8%
2012 Turnout as % CVAP	51.1%

heartlands of the Democratic Party, it was the political base of President Andrew Jackson and supported him nearly unanimously in his 1832 reelection. For 140 years after Jackson, it voted solidly Democratic and elected as its representatives in Congress some of the luminaries of the national party: Cordell Hull (1907-21, 1923-31), later senator and Secretary of State; Albert Gore Sr. (1939-53), later senator; and Albert Gore Jr. (1977-85), later senator and vice president.

The 6th Congressional District includes 17 Middle Tennessee counties, plus part of Cheatham County and a tip of Van Buren. These counties have a rural heritage. Dan Evans, founder of the Cracker Barrel Old Country Store chain, grew up in Smithville. The populated areas evoke the small-town charm for which those stores are famous. The National Rolley Hole Marble Tournament is held annually at Standing Stone State Park; Jamestown is the headquarters for the World's Longest Yard Sale.

Because this part of Tennessee had few African Americans, the racial politics of the 1960s largely passed the region by, and Democratic loyalties outlasted those in other parts of the South. Bill Clinton swept the area in 1992. But as the Democratic Party

2012 Presidential Vote		
Mitt Romney (R)	192,602	(69%)
Barack Obama (D)	82,276	(30%)

2008 Presidential Vote		
John McCain (R)	188,284	(65%)
Barack Obama (D)	97,110	(34%)

Cook Partisan Voting Index: R+21

became an increasingly urban coalition in the 2000s, the party's fortunes deteriorated. Barack Obama carried only Jackson County in 2008 and lost all of the counties here in 2012.

Just over half of the district's population lives in counties that adjoin Music City, USA. These are generally upscale places with median incomes that are among the highest in the state. The two largest counties have been adding population swiftly: Wilson has grown 37% since 2000, and Sumner by 29%. This is solidly Republican territory, giving Mitt Romney in 2012 and John McCain in 2008 their second-best showings in the state.

Diane Black (R)

Diane Black, a Republican elected in 2010, is an active social conservative and has a background in health care, which has been instrumental in her work on the Ways and Means Committee. She is an avid supporter of tax reform and an outspoken opponent of abortion.

Black was born in Baltimore and lived in the area for most of her early life. She obtained an associate's degree in nursing from a local community college in 1971. In 1985, she and her business executive husband, David Black, moved to Tennessee. Black returned to school to get her bachelor's degree in nursing from Belmont University. She entered politics in 1998, when she was elected to the first of three terms in the Tennessee House. By 2001, she joined an anti-tax protest that foreshadowed her involvement in the tea party eight years later. In 2004, Black moved to the state Senate, where she became the first woman to chair the Senate Republican Caucus. She earned her stripes as a small-government conservative, repeatedly voting against a state income tax and increases to the sales tax. She pushed for a traditional definition of marriage, a zero-tolerance policy for illegal immigrants, and a balanced budget constitutional amendment. Her husband became president of a sports anti-doping laboratory at Vanderbilt University, which the two of them co-founded.

When Democratic Rep. Bart Gordon retired after 13 terms, Black ran for the seat. Her campaign hit a bump when one of her legislative aides sent an email from her government account portraying President Barack Obama as two eyes peering out of a black background in a presidential portrait. The incident received widespread media coverage for its seemingly racist intentions, and Black reprimanded the staffer but did not fire her. Black survived a bruising three-way GOP primary with 31% of the vote, edging out second-place finisher Lou Ann Zelenik by 283 votes. Zelenik, the Rutherford County GOP chair, made her opposition to a local Muslim community center a top issue and accused Black of not taking a strong enough stand against it.

In the general election, Black's conservative views made her a tea party favorite, and she racked up endorsements from Republican luminaries, including former Alaska Gov. Sarah Palin. In calling for repeal of the health care law, Black invoked her experience as a nurse in emergency rooms. She raised $2.4 million, with more than half coming from her own wallet, more than 10 times the amount mustered by her opponent, Iraq war veteran Brett Carter. She won 67%-29%, taking every county in this once-Democratic district.

In the House, Black quickly showed her cachet as a freshman with seats on the Ways and Means and Budget committees and staunchly defended Budget Chairman Paul Ryan's plan to rein in spending. She was named one of four regional directors of the National Republican Congressional Committee in recognition of her fundraising acumen. *Roll Call* has listed her as 20th among the wealthiest members of Congress, with a net worth in 2013 at $21 million. But she cares little for the trappings of wealth; according to Robert Draper's 2012 book *Do Not Ask What Good We Do*, her choice of transportation as a freshman was a well-worn Oldsmobile. She has been among the House's most-conservative members in *National Journal's* rankings.

Her first piece of legislation was a bill to deny federal funding to Planned Parenthood because of the group's involvement with abortion—an issue that eventually became one of the main sticking points in a final budget deal between Obama and House Republicans in 2011. She introduced half a dozen other abortion-related bills. In 2013, she sponsored a measure to give any individual or group that opposes contraception an automatic exemption from the requirement in the health care law that employee health insurance plans provide birth control. In 2015, she filed a bill to block Title X federal funding to organizations that perform abortions, including Planned Parenthood. She was a strong proponent of the House-passed bill barring most abortions after 20 weeks, and she cited growing evidence that such fetuses feel pain. She advocates a flatter, fairer and simpler tax code to help create the conditions for economic growth, and was tapped to chair the Ways and Means Education and Family Benefits Tax Reform Working Group. In July 2015, she voted against the House-passed 21st Century Cures Act because its mandatory spending would add to the federal deficit.

Zelenik returned for another primary challenge in 2012, once again making her opposition to the Islamic Center of Murfreesboro a focal point. She found a wealthy ally in Tennessee multimillionaire Andy Miller, who paid for ads attacking Black for supporting a hike in the federal debt limit. But with Zelenik's base of Rutherford County having been removed from the 6th District by redistricting, Black won a suspense-free 69%-31% primary. Democrats didn't bother to field a general election candidate. In 2014, Democrats ran Amos Powers, who worked for a local radio station and held Black accountable for dysfunction in Washington. It didn't seem to make much difference. Black won, 71%-23%.

SEVENTH DISTRICT

Marsha Blackburn (R)

Elected 2002, 7th term; b. June 6, 1952, Laurel, MS; MS St. U., B.S. 1973; Presbyterian; married (Chuck); 2 children.

Elected Office: TN Senate, 1998-2002.

Professional Career: Retail marketing consultant, 1973-98.

DC Office: 2266 RHOB, 20515, 202-225-2811; Fax: 202-225-3004; Website: blackburn.house.gov.

State Offices: Clarksville, 931-503-0391; Franklin, 615-591-5161.

Committees: *Budget. Energy & Commerce* (VChmn): Commerce, Manufacturing & Trade; Communications & Technology; Health; Oversight & Investigations.

Group Ratings

	ADA	ACLU	AFL-CIO	LCV	ITI	COC	HAFA	ACU	CFG	FRC
2014	5%	0%	–	0%	80%	79%	73%	96%	77%	100%
2013	5%	C	10%	0%	C	83%	C	84%	77%	C

National Journal Ratings

	2013 LIB	—	2013 CONS
Economic	21%	—	77%
Social	13%	—	84%
Foreign	5%	—	86%
Composite	15%	—	85%

Key Votes of the 113th Congress

1. Sandy storm spending	N	5. Medical Marijuana	N	9. Syrian Rebels Training	Y
2. Violence Against Women Act	N	6. Farm Bill	Y	10. Keystone pipeline	Y
3. Guantanamo Bay Detainees	N	7. Afghanistan Combat	N	11. Immigration Exec. Action	Y
4. Abortion 20-week ban	Y	8. NSA Phone Data Collection	Y	12. Bipartisan budget deal	Y

Election Results

2014 general	Marsha Blackburn (R)	110,498	(70%)	$1,444,429 $13,314
	Dan Cramer (D)	42,260	(27%)	
	Lenny Ladner (I)	5,092	(3%)	
2014 primary	Marsha Blackburn (R)	64,969	(84%)	
	Jacob Brimm (R)	12,199	(16%)	

Prior winning percentages: 2012 (71%), 2010 (72%), 2008 (69%), 2006 (66%), 2004 (100%), 2002 (71%)

Population		Race and Ethnicity		Income	
Total:	728,823	White	82.0%	Median income:	$50,273
Urban:	35.6%	Black	9.7%		*(238 of 435)*
Suburban:	16.7%	Latino	4.3%	Under $50,000	49.7%
Rural:	47.7%	Asian	1.3%	$50,000-$99,999:	30.9%
Land area:	8,141	Two races	2.2%	$100,000-$199,999:	14.7%
Pop/sq. mi.:	89.5	White Ethnic	20.7%	$200,000 or more:	4.8%
Born in state:	53.6%			Poverty Rate	14.8%
		Education			
Age Groups		H.S. grad or less:	44.8%	**Work**	
Under 18:	25.3%	Some college:	27.3%	White collar:	37.5%
18 to 34:	21.7%	College degree, 4 yr.:	18.4%	Blue collar:	38.6%
35 to 64:	39.5%	Post-grad study:	9.4%	Sales and service:	23.9%
Over 64:	13.5%				
		Military		Govt. workers:	16.0%
		Veterans/active duty:	13.7%		

Middle Tennessee: Western Nashville Suburbs, Clarksville

Rural Tennessee north of Mississippi is one of the most sparsely settled areas in the state. Along each side of the Tennessee River, as it flows north and widens out into Kentucky Lake, are small rural communities. Many date to pre-Civil War days and have not grown much since. One of these is Waynes-

Voter Turnout	
2013 Total Citizen 18+	533,701
2014 House Turnout	157,907
2014 Turnout as % CVAP	29.6%
2012 Turnout as % CVAP	53.0%

boro, where Davy Crockett delivered campaign speeches from the base of a huge natural stone double bridge overlooking the Buffalo River. Farther west is McNairy County, where Sheriff Buford Pusser of *Walking Tall* fame carried his big stick and fought organized crime until his death in a 1974 car crash. Country music icon Patsy Cline died in a tragic plane crash just outside of Camden. Even some of the roads have changed little; the Natchez Trace Parkway follows the same basic path as the trail carved out by prehistoric bison from Mississippi grazing lands to the salt licks of central Tennessee. Meriwether Lewis met a violent and mysterious death—most likely a suicide—while traveling on the Trace in 1807.

This sparsely populated land is complemented by two urban areas: Greater Nashville to the east and Clarksville to the north. South of Nashville is Williamson County, where the bedroom communities of Franklin and Brentwood are affluent, highly educated, and fast-growing. Nissan North America took advantage of the low cost of doing business in Tennessee by moving its headquarters from California to the Cool Springs area of Franklin. Along the Cumberland River is Clarksville, the fifth-largest city in the state, with many restored 19th-century homes and a large industrial park. Straddling the Kentucky border north of Clarksville is the Army's sprawling Fort Campbell, home of the 101st Airborne Division; it has been termed a military boomtown, though it suffered a setback in 2014 when the 2,400-soldier Combat Aviation Brigade was deactivated. In 2015, the website Credit.com ranked Clarksville as the best place in the nation for first-time home buyers.

The 7th Congressional District of Tennessee covers this territory. Close to 40 percent live in Tennessee's Central Basin, in Williamson County. Another fifth of its population live in Montgomery County, where Clarksville is the county seat. This is the wealthiest county in the state, measured by median income, and is heavily Republican. The remainder live in the lightly populated, rural counties traversing the state from northern border to southern. The area around Clarksville retains some of its historic attachment to the Democratic Party dating to the Civil War; Houston County is

2012 Presidential Vote
Mitt Romney (R).................183,840   (66%)
Barack Obama (D) 91,987   (33%)

2008 Presidential Vote
John McCain (R).................178,275   (62%)
Barack Obama (D) 103,878   (36%)

Cook Partisan Voting Index: R+18

one of six Tennessee counties that Barack Obama carried in 2008. But the district overall is solidly Republican.

Marsha Blackburn (R)

Marsha Blackburn, a Republican elected in 2002, is a conservative firebrand who has become a frequent GOP presence on television. Although her penchant for tossing rhetorical bombs can be divisive, she has been an active lawmaker at the Energy and Commerce Committee, especially on communications issues.

Blackburn grew up in Laurel, Mississippi, where her father sold oil-field production equipment. Her interest in gardening and canning won her a 4-H college scholarship at Mississippi State University, where she majored in merchandising and clothing. She helped pay her way through college by selling books door-to-door. She became a sales manager for Southwestern Co., which sells educational materials, and moved to Williamson County. Her hilltop home is known as "Up Yonder," named by its former owner, Grand Ole Opry star Minnie Pearl. Blackburn became director of retail fashion for a Nashville department store and was appointed by Republican Gov. Don Sundquist as executive director of the Tennessee Film, Entertainment, and Music Commission. In 1992, she was the Republican nominee against Democrat Rep. Bart Gordon and lost 57%-41%. Elected in 1998 to the state Senate, she became an outspoken opponent of Sundquist's proposed income tax. In 2014, Tennessee voters approved a constitutional amendment that expressly prohibited a state income tax.

When the seat opened in 2002, Blackburn was the only well-known candidate from the Nashville area. Of the six other candidates, three were familiar figures in the Memphis area. She benefited from financial support of the national anti-tax Club for Growth and from attacks by the Shelby County candidates on one another. She ran as an anti-abortion rights, pro-gun, and pro-military conservative and won with 40% of the vote. She easily won the general election.

In the House, Blackburn lost in 2006 a bid to chair the Republican Conference. But she has been active on the Republican Study Committee, and in 2012 she co-chaired the GOP convention's Platform Committee. She cosponsored the controversial "birther" bill in 2009 requiring future presidential candidates to prove they were born in the United States, a measure that played off attacks from the right on Obama's legal fitness to hold office, although the measure would not have applied to him. In May 2015, she continued her practice of offering across-the-board cuts to appropriations bills; her proposed 1 percent cut for congressional spending was defeated, 172-250.

A champion of gun owners' rights, Blackburn has boasted about her perfect marksmanship score with her Smith & Wesson .38. After the Newtown Connecticut elementary school massacre, she said the debate should focus on mental health, because disturbed people disposed toward violence could use "a hammer, a hatchet, a car" instead of a gun. Among her admirers is former Vice President Dick Cheney, who told *The Tennessean* of Nashville in 2012 that Blackburn is "relentlessly common-sensible."

When Republicans regained control of the House in 2011, Blackburn assumed a more prominent role on technology policy on Energy and Commerce. A fervent advocate of the Nashville-based music industry and founder of the Congressional Songwriters Caucus, she has fought to protect intellectual property rights of artists against illegal music downloads. In April 2015, she cosponsored the bipartisan Fair Play, Fair Pay bill to assure that musicians are compensated for their work. The recording industry has given her a congressional Grammy.

Blackburn has challenged the Federal Communications Commission. In July 2014, the House passed on a largely party-line vote Blackburn's amendment to prevent the FCC from preempting state laws that block or impede the ability of cities and municipalities to create new local broadband networks; she cited state sovereignty on behalf of her proposal, which was supported by large cable companies. In March 2015, she sought to deny funding for the FCC to implement its net-neutrality rules that were designed to bar tiered pricing for Internet services; she contends that such authority is solely Congress' responsibility. In 2013, she was named the committee's vice chairman, providing reassurance to conservatives who were skeptical about its moderate chairman, Fred Upton of Michigan. She has been active in the failed effort to repeal Obama's health care legislation. Blackburn engaged in some presidential politics with a May 2015 letter to the Internal Revenue Service challenging the tax-exempt status of the Clinton Foundation. She complained when the IRS responded with an unsigned letter that the agency had "an ongoing examination program" of tax-exempt groups.

In 2008, Blackburn faced a primary challenge from Shelby County Register of Deeds Tom Leatherwood, whose campaign gained ammunition when it was revealed Blackburn had misreported more than $440,000 on campaign finance disclosure forms dating to her first House campaign. Blackburn filed amended returns. The underdog Leatherwood charged that Blackburn had used her campaign funds to help her family's businesses and that she hadn't been effective in Washington. She easily won the primary, 62%-38%, carrying every county except Shelby. After redistricting in 2011, her district no longer includes the Shelby area and she has not faced competitive challenges.

In 2009, Blackburn wrote a book, *Life Equity: Realize Your True Value and Pursue Your Passions at Any Stage in Life*. She described it as a "book of encouragement and empowerment for women."

EIGHTH DISTRICT

Stephen Fincher (R)

Elected 2010, 3rd term; b. Feb. 7, 1973, Memphis; Crockett Cnty. H.S. 1990; Methodist; married (Lynn); 3 children.

Professional Career: Partner, Fincher Farms; Singer, Fincher Family.

DC Office: 2452 RHOB, 20515, 202-225-4714; Fax: 202-225-1765; Website: fincher.house.gov.

State Offices: Arlington, 901-581-4718; Dyersburg, 731-285-0910; Jackson, 731-423-4848; Martin, 731-588-5190; Memphis, 901-682-4422.

Committees: *Financial Services:* Capital Markets & Government Sponsored Enterprises; Oversight & Investigations.

Group Ratings

	ADA	ACLU	AFL-CIO	LCV	ITI	COC	HAFA	ACU	CFG	FRC
2014	0%	11%	–	0%	100%	71%	66%	80%	74%	100%
2013	5%	C	10%	4%	C	75%	C	72%	70%	C

National Journal Ratings

	2013 LIB	—	2013 CONS
Economic	21%	—	79%
Social	0%	—	87%
Foreign	14%	—	85%
Composite	14%	—	86%

Key Votes of the 113th Congress

1. Sandy storm spending	N	5. Medical Marijuana	N	9. Syrian Rebels Training	N
2. Violence Against Women Act	N	6. Farm Bill	Y	10. Keystone pipeline	Y
3. Guantanamo Bay Detainees	N	7. Afghanistan Combat	N	11. Immigration Exec. Action	Y
4. Abortion 20-week ban	Y	8. NSA Phone Data Collection	Y	12. Bipartisan budget deal	Y

Election Results

2014 general	Stephen Lee Fincher (R)	122,205	(71%)	$629,223
	Wes Bradley (D)	42,403	(25%)	
	Mark Rawles (CNP)	4,450	(3%)	
	James Hart (I)	3,446	(2%)	
2014 primary	Stephen Fincher (R)	68,465	(79%)	
	Dana Matheny (R)	11,819	(14%)	
	John Mills (R)	6,337	(7%)	

Prior winning percentages: 2012 (68%), 2010 (59%)

Population		Race and Ethnicity		Income	
Total:	710,335	White	74.7%	Median income:	$51,290
Urban:	29.8%	Black	19.3%		*(214 of 435)*
Suburban:	28.1%	Latino	2.6%	Under $50,000	48.6%
Rural:	42.1%	Asian	1.6%	$50,000-$99,999:	28.9%
Land area:	5,372	Two races	1.4%	$100,000-$199,999:	17.2%
Pop/sq. mi.:	132.2	White Ethnic	19.8%	$200,000 or more:	5.3%
Born in state:	65.9%			Poverty Rate	14.4%
		Education			
Age Groups		H.S. grad or less:	44.7%	**Work**	
Under 18:	23.7%	Some college:	26.9%	White collar:	36.5%
18 to 34:	19.6%	College degree, 4 yr.:	17.3%	Blue collar:	40.8%
35 to 64:	41.2%	Post-grad study:	11.1%	Sales and service:	22.7%
Over 64:	15.5%			Govt. workers:	14.3%
		Military			
		Veterans/active duty:	10.1%		

West Tennessee: Memphis Suburbs, Jackson

West of Nashville and north of Memphis, the rivers roll lazily through flat or gently rolling land that has similarities to the northern end of Mississippi. Cotton and soybeans are the main crops—the annual Tennessee Soybean Festival is held in Martin, near the Kentucky border—and they often are

Voter Turnout	
2013 Total Citizen 18+	530,846
2014 House Turnout	172,595
2014 Turnout as % CVAP	32.5%
2012 Turnout as % CVAP	58.5%

abundant. African Americans remain in rural areas here, a reminder of the old plantation economy. Henning is the hometown of Alex Haley, who used to sit on his porch and listen to his aunts tell him stories about slave ships and the Civil War; these became his book *Roots*. The plantation economy also bequeathed a fierce loyalty to the Democratic Party; before 2011, much of this district hadn't been represented by a Republican since Reconstruction. The small towns in this area are sustained by manufacturers such as the NSK automotive plant and light industry such as Dot Foods, the nation's largest food redistributor, both in Dyersburg. Kentucky Lake draws big crowds for its annual BASSfest in Henry County.

Crockett County, with a county seat named Alamo, is named after Davy Crockett, who represented the area for three terms in the House. The area carries the highest earthquake risk in the United States outside of the West Coast. In the early 1800s, four earthquakes rocked the region, permanently altering the topography. Perhaps the most extreme example is Reelfoot Lake, the only large natural lake in Tennessee, which was a dry area before the quakes occurred; the land dropped almost 20 feet in places before the Mississippi River filled in the newly formed depression.

The 8th Congressional District of Tennessee includes much of this West Tennessee farmland. Its largest city is Jackson, founded shortly after the area was opened for white settlement in 1818, and the site of one of Crockett's final speeches before heading west to his doom at the Alamo. Suburban Shelby County east of Memphis includes 40% of the district population. Overall, the population

2012 Presidential Vote		
Mitt Romney (R)................202,041	(66%)
Barack Obama (D)..............99,608	(33%)
2008 Presidential Vote	
John McCain (R)................202,797	(64%)
Barack Obama (D).............109,855	(35%)
Cook Partisan Voting Index: R+19	

is 19% black. Redistricting changes in 2011 dropped President Barack Obama's 2008 vote share by eight percentage points, and this is now a strongly Republican seat, like the six other GOP-held districts in Tennessee. Mitt Romney got 66% of the vote in 2012.

Stephen Fincher (R)

Republican Stephen Fincher, a gospel-singing farmer from Frog Jump, is a rock-solid conservative. He pays attention to agriculture and small business, but also focuses on broader business interests on the Financial Services Committee. He was emblematic of the outsiders who helped to create the GOP's 63-seat House gain in the 2010 election.

Starting at the age of 9, Fincher made the rounds of the gospel-singing circuit as a member of the Fincher Family, performing with his father, a cousin, and an uncle at more than

100 events a year. The group has produced its own music and has made many recordings. (In Washington, he expanded his musical repertoire to play bass guitar in the bipartisan rock band The Second Amendments, led by Democratic Rep. Collin Peterson of Minnesota.) He worked most of his life on the family farm, which produces cotton, corn, soybeans and wheat. Fincher said he had his own crop at age 12 and was developing budgets at 13.

In 2010, he decided to challenge 11-term veteran Democratic Rep. John Tanner. Using the theme "Plow Congress," he raised $300,000 so quickly, and without any staff, that it seemed to prompt Tanner's decision to retire. In the Republican primary, Fincher won with 48% of the vote against Shelby County Commissioner George Flinn and physician Ron Kirkland, each of whom got 24%. The candidates spent $7 million in an area with one of the nation's lowest median incomes.

Democrats nominated state Sen. Roy Herron, who was a farmer, a Methodist preacher, an author, and a lawyer. "No one will out-God me, no one will outgun me," Herron vowed. Democrats criticized Fincher for collecting millions of dollars in federal farm subsidies since 1995. He responded that he needed to participate in the program to earn a living. Still, Fincher was endorsed by several key tea party organizations. Fincher outspent Herron, $2.6 million to $2.1 million. The National Republican Congressional Committee spent more than $850,000 for Fincher, which was part of $3 million spent on his behalf by GOP and other allies; Herron was largely ignored by Democrats and liberal groups. Fincher won a resounding 59%-39% victory.

In the House, Fincher joined the Tea Party Caucus and had a solidly conservative voting record. "We were not sent here to go along and compromise," he said when the Senate balked at a budget deal in 2011. "We were sent to come up here and lead."

Fincher has focused on business-related issues. He enacted his bill that made it easier for small privately held firms to tap public capital markets through initial public offerings. He filed a bill in 2012 to help the manufactured-housing industry—mobile home and house-trailer makers—contend with some requirements of the Dodd-Frank financial regulatory law that the industry complained were overly burdensome. On the Agriculture Committee, he joined conservative complaints about Environmental Protection Agency regulations. "We must cut the EPA's legs off," he said.

When other Republicans on the Financial Services Committee sought to shut down the Export-Import Bank in 2015, Fincher called the agency a "job-creator" and offered amendments to reform the bank, including a proposal that users should first seek private funding. He was unhappy when the leadership of the Republican Study Committee voiced opposition to the agency. Fincher's openness to a middle ground generated complaints by the conservative Club for Growth political action committee, which ran broadcast ads against him in his district in May 2015.

Taking seriously his 2012 reelection bid, Fincher raked in more than $2.2 million. He named his leadership political action committee in honor of his hometown, Funding Republicans Supporting Opportunity and Growth (FROG) Jump PAC. His challenger, Timothy Dixon, raised less than $27,000, and Fincher won 68%-28%. In 2014, his opponent spent even less money and Fincher won with 71% of the vote. He has become entrenched in this former Democratic preserve.

NINTH DISTRICT

Steve Cohen (D)

Elected 2006, 5th term; b. May 24, 1949, Memphis; Vanderbilt U., B.A. 1971, U. of Memphis, J.D. 1973; Jewish; single.

Elected Office: Shelby Cnty. Comm., 1977-78; TN Senate, 1982-2006.

Professional Career: Practicing atty., 1974-2006.

DC Office: 2404 RHOB, 20515, 202-225-3265; Fax: 202-225-5663; Website: cohen.house.gov.

State Offices: Memphis, 901-544-4131.

Committees: *Judiciary:* Constitution & Civil Justice; Courts (RMM), Intellectual Property, & the Internet. *Transportation & Infrastructure:* Aviation; Highways & Transit; Railroads, Pipelines & Hazardous Materials.

Group Ratings

	ADA	ACLU	AFL-CIO	LCV	ITI	COC	HAFA	ACU	CFG	FRC
2014	100%	88%	–	97%	60%	43%	13%	8%	11%	0%
2013	95%	C	95%	96%	C	31%	C	16%	16%	C

National Journal Ratings

	2013 LIB	—	2013 CONS
Economic	91%	—	0%
Social	93%	—	0%
Foreign	90%	—	6%
Composite	95%	—	5%

Key Votes of the 113th Congress

1. Sandy storm spending	Y	5. Medical Marijuana	Y	9. Syrian Rebels Training	Y
2. Violence Against Women Act	Y	6. Farm Bill	N	10. Keystone pipeline	N
3. Guantanamo Bay Detainees	Y	7. Afghanistan Combat	Y	11. Immigration Exec. Action	N
4. Abortion 20-week ban	N	8. NSA Phone Data Collection	Y	12. Bipartisan budget deal	Y

Election Results

2014 general	Steve Cohen (D)	87,308	(75%)	$915,467	$1,906
	Charlotte Bergmann (R)	27,163	(23%)	$53,276	
2014 primary	Steve Cohen (D)	45,366	(66%)		
	Ricky Wilkins (D)	22,311	(33%)		

Prior winning percentages: 2012 (75%), 2010 (74%), 2008 (88%), 2006 (60%)

Population		Race and Ethnicity		Income	
Total:	711,664	Black	63.5%	Median income:	$37,087
Urban:	86.2%	White	25.9%		*(409 of 435)*
Suburban:	13.8%	Latino	7.0%	Under $50,000	62.8%
Rural:	0.0%	Asian	1.9%	$50,000-$99,999:	26.2%
Land area:	605	Two races	1.5%	$100,000-$199,999:	9.2%
Pop/sq. mi.:	1,175.7	White Ethnic	7.5%	$200,000 or more:	1.7%
Born in state:	64.6%			Poverty Rate	27.2%
Age Groups		**Education**			
		H.S. grad or less:	46.4%	**Work**	
Under 18:	25.5%	Some college:	30.6%	White collar:	30.9%
18 to 34:	27.3%	College degree, 4 yr.:	14.8%	Blue collar:	44.0%
35 to 64:	37.0%	Post-grad study:	8.2%	Sales and service:	25.1%
Over 64:	10.3%			Govt. workers:	15.1%
		Military			
		Veterans/active duty:	7.3%		

Memphis Metro

Memphis is the largest city in Tennessee, although its metropolitan area is second to Nashville's. In the state's far southwestern corner, 20 miles from Mississippi's cotton fields and riverboat casinos, metropolitan Memphis has one of the highest per-

Voter Turnout	
2013 Total Citizen 18+	500,428
2014 House Turnout	116,550
2014 Turnout as % CVAP	23.3%
2012 Turnout as % CVAP	50.4%

centages of African Americans in the country, evidence of the city's economic heritage as a capital of the Cotton Kingdom. Big Mississippi planters used to come north to sell their crops in the courtyard of the Peabody Hotel, then make financial arrangements for the next growing season. According to tradition, ducks still famously march daily to the hotel's fountain for a dip.

The city's most celebrated tradition is blues music. Unlike Nashville's country music, which emerged from mountainous East Tennessee, the Memphis sound originated from the self-taught musical stylings of poor, rural blacks in the Mississippi Delta. Throughout the first half of the 20th century, talented black musicians migrated north to Memphis and congregated downtown on Beale Street. The blues sound was later adapted by Elvis Presley, a poor white from rural Mississippi, in pivotal sessions in July 1954 at Sam Phillips' Sun Studio in Memphis—the birth of rock 'n' roll. In the early 1960s, Memphis once again became the crucible of a new sound, soul music, which emerged as a counterpoint to rock, its increasingly white-dominated cousin. Otis Redding, Isaac Hayes, the Staple Singers, and Sam &

Dave made their records at the Stax studio. Competing Hi Records featured Al Green, who changed careers after his girlfriend committed suicide, becoming an ordained minister preaching at the Full Gospel Tabernacle in southern Memphis. For some years, Memphis tried to downplay its musical heritage. Much of Beale Street was razed and set on a misguided path toward urban renewal. But

2012 Presidential Vote
Barack Obama (D) 201,171   (79%)
Mitt Romney (R)...................53,147   (21%)

2008 Presidential Vote
Barack Obama (D) 223,547   (77%)
John McCain (R)...................65,316   (23%)

Cook Partisan Voting Index: D+25

the city came to recognize its history as an asset. Graceland, Presley's garishly decorated mansion, attracts hordes of musical pilgrims from all over the world, and a Museum of American Soul Music opened in 2003 on the site of the Stax studio, demolished in 1989.

Memphis is the home of the first supermarket chain: Piggly Wiggly, founded in 1916 (its symbol, Mr. Pig, has slimmed down since then). It also hosted the first Holiday Inn. The biggest employer by far is FedEx, where 7,000 employees scan, sort, weigh and route 1.5 million packages on 140 aircraft that arrive and depart within a six-hour period almost every night from the world's busiest cargo airport. For some years, racial discord scarred the political life of Memphis. The Rev. Martin Luther King Jr., was assassinated there in 1968, and the site, the Lorraine Motel, has been converted into a civil rights museum. Even today, resurgent Beale Street is one of the few racially integrated spaces in the city, a division that holds equally true in voting. Blacks vote almost unanimously Democratic, and whites vote Republican by margins almost as great. Many African Americans in Memphis have moved into the middle class, although the city continues to be the most impoverished large metropolitan area in the country. The city's recovery from the recession lagged Nashville and Knoxville. In April 2015, the unemployment rate in Memphis was 6.8%, compared with 6 percent statewide.

The black-majority 9th Congressional District of Tennessee remains the strongest Democratic district in the state and is essential to any chance of success for Democrats running statewide. In 2012, Democrat Barack Obama won 79% in the district. African Americans are 65% of the population.

Steve Cohen (D)

Democrat Steve Cohen, elected in 2006, is a rare white member of Congress representing a majority-minority district. He has easily fended off primary challenges from the district's African-American majority by maintaining one of the House's most liberal voting records and concentrating on issues of strong interest to his constituents.

Cohen is a fourth-generation Memphian and the son of a psychiatrist. At age 5, Cohen was diagnosed with polio, an illness that would shift his focus from sports to politics. Cohen studied at Vanderbilt University and went on to law school at the University of Memphis. After graduation, he worked as a legal advisor for the Memphis Police Department and then started a law practice. He was elected to the Shelby County Commission and, in 1982, to the state Senate, where he served for the next 24 years. He became known as the father of the Tennessee State Lottery for his successful efforts in 2002 to pass a referendum repealing a lottery ban and for passing legislation that used the lottery revenue to fund college scholarships.

Cohen wanted to run for Congress in 1996 when 22-year African-American Rep. Harold Ford Sr., announced his retirement, but he found his path blocked by the incumbent's 26-year-old son, who secured the seat. He got a second chance in 2006 when Harold Ford Jr. ran unsuccessfully for the Senate. As the only serious white contender among the 15 candidates who filed to run, Cohen faced criticism from local black leaders, who said that an African American should represent the district. Cohen's supporters charged that another primary foe paid for a push poll that asked, "Are you more likely to vote for a born-again Christian or a Jew?" Cohen quipped that his staunchly liberal record would make people mistake him for a black woman.

The district's black leaders did not sufficiently narrow the field, and the primary results splintered. Cohen won with 31%. Nikki Tinker, the former campaign manager for Ford Jr., finished second with 25%. The incumbent's cousin, Joe Ford Jr., finished third with 12%.

The primary is typically the only election that matters in the solidly Democratic district, but Cohen faced a challenge in November from yet another Ford—Jake Ford, the incumbent's younger brother, who ran as an independent. Jake Ford was a high school drop-out who had had a few scrapes with the law, but he had support from his father and other African-American leaders who opposed Cohen. He argued that he was in better sync with the community, noting that more than two-thirds of the primary vote went against Cohen. Cohen's critics made an issue of the fact that he supported same-sex marriage. He won the general election with 60% of the vote, ending the Ford family's 32-year hold on the district. Cohen wanted to join the Congressional Black Caucus, but he backed off when CBC leaders made it clear he would not be allowed to join.

Cohen worked to quickly secure his hold on the seat, knowing that he faced a near-certain primary challenge in 2008. Among his first moves was a resolution apologizing for slavery. While it seemed like a relatively harmless motion that easily passed the House on a voice vote, Cohen's office was slammed with constituent calls charging the measure was a political ploy. It was approved just days before the August 2008 primary. Cohen also succeeded in naming a Memphis federal building and post offices after prominent African Americans.

Winning a plum seat on the Judiciary Committee, Cohen worked on bills to force radio broadcasters to pay money to performers whose music is played and on studying racial disparities in the criminal justice system. He enacted a measure in 2010 protecting authors and journalists from having foreign libel judgments honored in U.S. courts and another a year later to help members of the National Guard and Reserve obtain bankruptcy relief. He introduced several amendments to reduce spending on the war in Afghanistan; one of them ultimately passed in July 2012. On the Transportation and Infrastructure Committee, Cohen opposed a bill that could have exposed FedEx to worker strikes.

Cohen became the ranking Democrat in 2015 of the Constitution and Civil Justice Sub-committee, whose jurisdiction includes civil rights issues. The chairman of that panel was Trent Franks of Arizona, an arch-conservative who was not likely to find common ground with Cohen on many legislative issues. In March, Cohen filed a bipartisan bill that would make marijuana legal for some medical purposes. Earlier, he urged Attorney General Eric Holder to take executive action to reclassify marijuana as a legal drug. Holder responded that "there is a legitimate debate to be had," but he took no action.

In his 2008 reelection, race was Cohen's biggest obstacle in the primary. African-American leaders in the district coalesced around Tinker, who staged a rematch. "He's not black, and he can't represent me," one minister told the Memphis *Commercial Appeal*. Tinker got financial help from the CBC and EMILY's list, the women's fundraising group. But prominent black leaders from outside the district, including Judiciary Chairman John Conyers of Michigan and Rep. Jesse Jackson Jr. of Illinois, made radio ads for Cohen and donated to his campaign. He outraised Tinker by more than 2-to-1 and crushed her, 79%-19%.

He drew another primary challenge in 2010 from Willie Herenton, Memphis' first elected black mayor. But Cohen once again was ready—he snagged a rare written endorsement from Obama, a hugely popular figure in the district, as well as support from a dozen CBC members. He trounced Herenton, 79%-21%, in the August primary and again sailed to reelection. Two years later, his primary challenger was Memphis School Board member and Memphis Urban League CEO Tomeka Hart. *The Cook Political Report* observed that her campaign "seems to be focusing more on promoting her brand than giving voters a reason to replace Cohen," and the incumbent won 89%-11% before again coasting in the general election. In 2014, against the less well-known Ricky Wilkins, he had his closest primary since he was first elected. Wilkins campaigned publicly on how Cohen's race and ethnicity differed from that of most of his constituents. Cohen won, 66%-33%.

Cohen's personal life became a national story in February 2013 when he sent, and then quickly deleted, seemingly flirtatious tweets to a woman. He initially said the woman was a daughter of a family friend but later told NBC News that she was his daughter, whom he had learned about just three years earlier. "I Googled her mother, found out she had a child, and the math looked pretty accurate," he recalled. "The mom told me we had a lot of catching up to do." A DNA test later showed the woman was not his daughter.

★ TEXAS ★

The Great Recession, a commodity price collapse, illegal immigration, hurricanes, floods: Any two or three of those forces could cripple a state; Texas has faced all five. And yet, the Lone Star State just keeps rising.

At its origin, Texas was an independent republic, freed from Mexico before it agreed to annexation by the United States in 1845. Today it is a nation-state, 26 million strong, larger in area than any of the 28 nations of the European Union and more populous than all but six. In the 13 presidential elections since 1960, Americans have elected Texans four times and Californians four times. The two largest states have put their stamp on national politics in our time, just as New York did from 1900 to 1960, when it produced five of the winners and eight of the losers in 15 presidential elections. Texas has been the second-largest state in area since Alaska was admitted to the Union in 1959, and it became the second largest in population in 1994, when it surpassed New York. A formative strain in the state's history is that it is a society without an aristocratic past, a state not formed by plantation owners or plutocrats, but by dirt farmers and citizen-soldiers like Sam Houston. Texas was founded by Southerners, particularly Tennesseans, who wanted to establish their own enclave within the borders of Mexico, a republic with Anglo-Saxon freedoms and black slavery. They defended their dream to the death at the Alamo and to a bloody victory at San Jacinto. They entered the Union willingly in 1845 and left it enthusiastically in 1861. The Texas that emerged from the Civil War was still young and poor. Not until 1901 was oil discovered at Spindletop, setting Texas wildcatters on the road to riches.

Without the underpinnings and burdens of tradition, 20th century Texas produced fabulous wealth, generously rewarding success while being unforgiving of failure. It has respect for learning and style—think of its great universities and Neiman Marcus—and it revels in rough manners and Western wear. Texans are prone to wild swings in fortune—think of Sam Houston and Lyndon B. Johnson, the Yankee wildcatter George H. W. Bush and his son George W. In the 21st century, Texans, despite their history of slavery and segregation, have proved open to immigrants and friendly to their Mexican neighbors. The North American Free Trade Agreement, the opening up of the border and the coming together of these two countries that are at such different economic levels and have such different cultures, was a project mainly of Texans of both political parties—of Republican President George H. W. Bush and Democratic Treasury Secretary Lloyd Bentsen, of Democratic Gov. Ann Richards and Republican Gov. George W. Bush. At the same time, Texas has become a high-technology powerhouse with some of the nation's most creative businesses. But its success is not just economic. There are elements of heroism—some mythical, some genuine—in the Texas history that every public school student learns. Common Core, the national set of curriculum standards in math and English, is forbidden by Texas law.

Texas started off as a marshland on the border of the Third World, with an economy based on commodities, mainly cotton, when cotton prices were in long-term decline. Its farmers felt as if they were part of a colonial economy controlled by bankers and Wall Street financiers. After Spindletop, Texas became the nation's—and for a time the world's—leading producer of oil. But oil prices, too, fell in free markets and were propped up by politicians. There was the 1935 "hot oil" act that Democrat Sam Rayburn, as chairman of the House Commerce Committee, pushed through. Then came the oil depletion allowance, maintained for years by Rayburn when he was speaker and by Johnson when he was Senate majority leader and later by Bentsen as Senate Finance Committee chairman. These politicians also secured subsidies for cotton growers and contracts for defense plants and space facilities during World War II and through the Cold War years. Most Texas voters stayed Democratic up to 1970 because of Confederate memories, New Deal affections, and the clout and competence of Texas Democratic officeholders.

By the 1970s, Texas was no longer dependent on raw commodities. The "awl bidness" here became less a matter of extracting oil than it was playing host to the greatest concentration of highly skilled specialists in extracting oil and natural gas in any part of the world. Also beginning in the 1960s, Texas became a center for technology with the critical mass of knowledge and finances needed to produce firms like Texas Instruments and Dell Computer and a university infrastructure in the University of Texas and Texas A&M. (A&M educated three of the 2015 Fortune100 CEOs, the only public university to tie the Ivy League

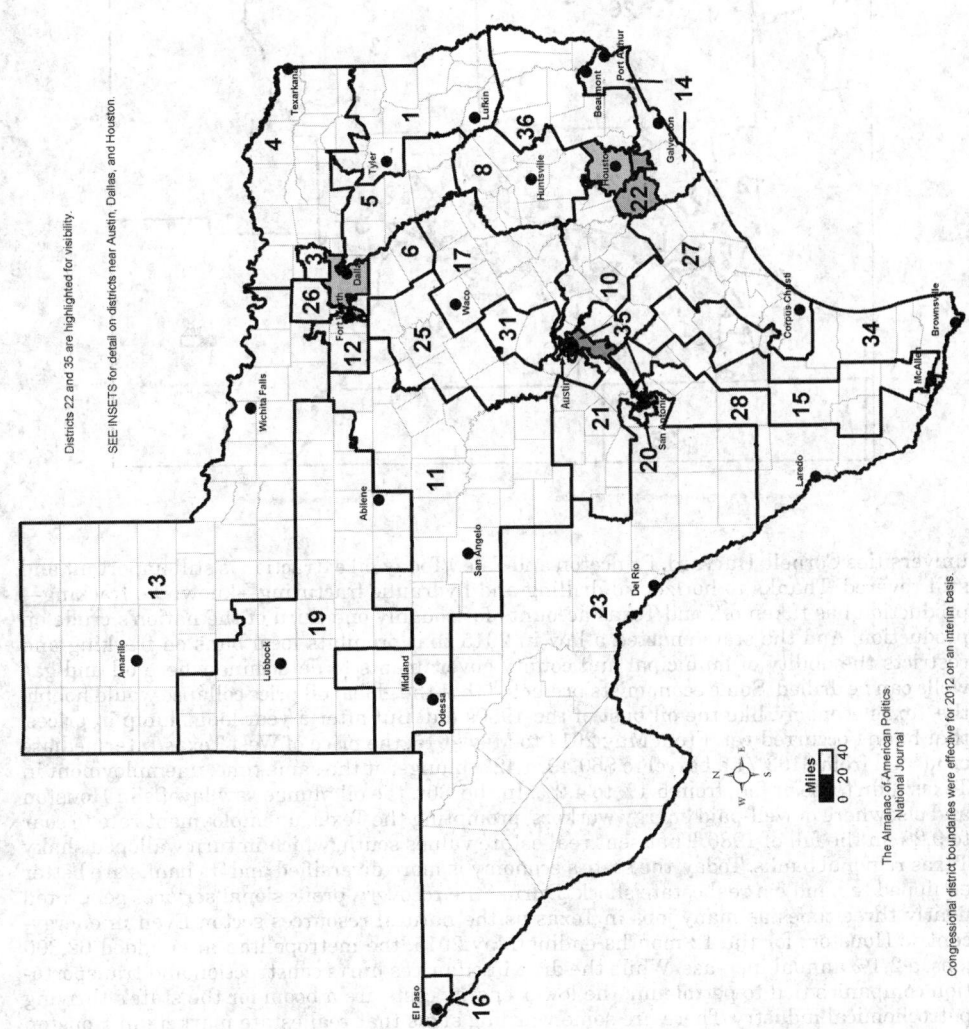

Districts 22 and 35 are highlighted for visibility.

SEE INSETS for detail on districts near Austin, Dallas, and Houston.

Miles
0 20 40

The Almanac of American Politics:
National Journal

Congressional district boundaries were effective for 2012 on an interim basis.

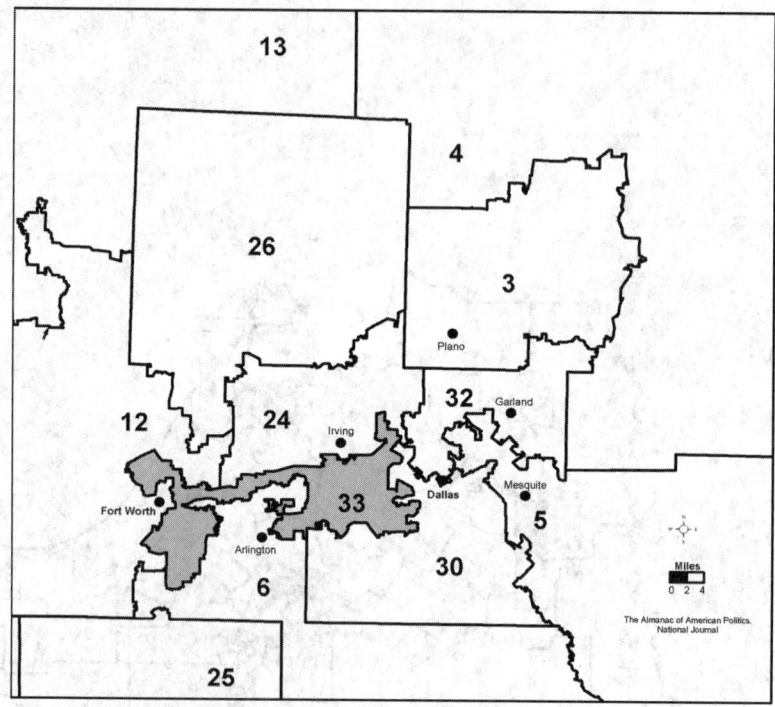

Congressional district boundaries were effective for 2012 on an interim basis.   District 33 is highlighted for visibility.

universities Cornell, Harvard, Princeton and Yale.) Today, oil extraction is still important and still revered. Thanks to horizontal drilling and hydraulic fracturing—known as fracking—production has taken off, and Texas accounts for roughly one third of the nation's crude oil production. And the state enacted a law in 2015 that prohibits local bans on fracking and restricts the ability of municipal and county governments to determine where oil and gas wells can be drilled. Some economists predicted that the global oil price collapse would hobble the Texas economy, like the oil bust of the 1980s did. But after a year-long slump in prices, that hadn't occurred yet. From May 2014 to May 2015, the price of West Texas Intermediate crude fell from $103.71 a barrel to $60.49, a 42% plunge; at the same time, unemployment in Texas didn't rise, it fell, from 5.1% to 4.2%. In the '80s, the oil plunge saw layoffs in Houston and elsewhere of well-paid energy workers, prompting the Texas unemployment rate to soar to 9.2% in the fall of 1986. That sent real estate values south, which in turn walloped shaky Texas regional banks. Today, the state's economy is more diversified and its banks are better equipped to handle a real estate shock. During the recovery, professional services generated nearly three times as many jobs in Texas as the natural resources sector. Even in energy-centric Houston, for the 12 months ending May 2015, the metropolitan area added 62,300 jobs, a 2.1% annual increase. While the drop in oil prices hurts construction and transportation companies tied to petroleum, the lower energy costs are a boom for the state's thriving petrochemical industry. There are some warning signs that real estate markets in Houston and Austin are becoming overvalued, but according to the Federal Reserve Banks of Dallas, less than 1% of state banks had a high amount of nonperforming loans in 2014, compared with 20% in the late 1980s.

The Dallas-Fort Worth Metroplex is rich with defense contractors and with erstwhile small firms that grew large with exports to Mexico. Houston is home to firms like Schlumberger, the global oil services company, to many of the high-tech spinoffs from the space program, and to the enormous Texas Medical Center. (Houston used to be home to oil service giants Halliburton and Weatherford, but those two companies moved their headquarters to Dubai and Ireland, respectively.) San Antonio, with the Air Force's prime hospital, has significant medical technology and biotech industries. As UT doubled its number of engineering

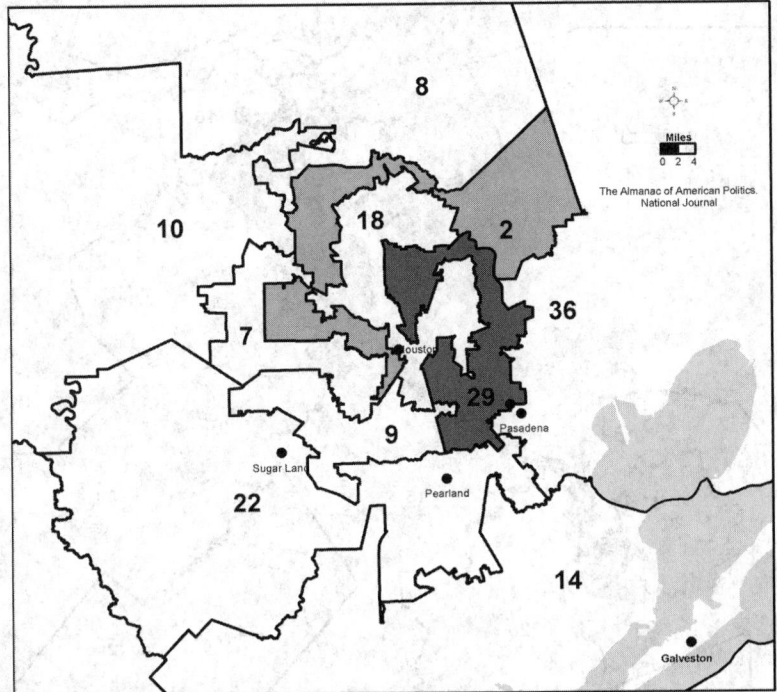

8
18
2
10
36
7
Houston
29
Pasadena
9
Sugar Land
22
Pearland
14
Galveston

The Almanac of American Politics.
National Journal

Miles
0 2 4

Congressional district boundaries were effective for 2012 on an interim basis. Districts 2 and 29 are highlighted for visibility.

professors, Austin became a high-tech center vying for second place after California's Silicon Valley. Texas' low taxes and lack of a state income tax have helped attract corporate headquarters like Exxon Mobil, AT&T, American Airlines, J.C. Penney and the U.S. headquarters of Toyota. Texas ranked second on the 2015 *Fortune* 500 rankings with 54 on that list headquartered there, one ahead of California and one behind New York. Those corporations helped make the Dallas-Fort Worth and Houston metro areas the fourth and fifth largest in the country, ahead of Philadelphia and Washington.

Texas surged ahead despite some formidable obstacles: The crash of oil prices and the savings and loan crisis in the 1980s, the defense cuts of the early 1990s, and the World Trade Organization ruling against cotton subsidies in 2005. It was hit late and only lightly by the 2007-09 recession. Low housing prices, tight lending practices, and tough foreclosure laws meant that Texas did not have much of a housing bubble. Foreclosure rates were well below the national average and far below those in Sunbelt states California, Nevada, Arizona and Florida. The state's unemployment rate remained well under the national average. Texas kept producing an increasing number of jobs during the recession. But by some indicators, the state is underperforming: While its public colleges prosper, the rest of the public school system is cash-starved and Texas still faces a major challenge in health insurance coverage. Although the number of Texans lacking health insurance has fallen from 25% to 17% since the startup of health exchanges established by the Affordable Care Act, Texas remains the state with the highest share of uninsured residents in the nation, according to a 2015 study by the Episcopal Health Foundation and Rice University's Baker Institute for Public Policy. Equally vexing was the less dramatic improvement among the state's poorest population: the uninsured rate for people earning less than $16,000 fell by 20%, while the uninsured rate fell by 45% for those earning more.

Texas has developed a civic culture of adaptability and resilience, as it demonstrated by taking in thousands of Hurricane Katrina evacuees in 2005. Three years later, Houston weathered Hurricane Ike with orderly and timely evacuations. Four weeks of torrential rainstorms in the spring of 2015 required Gov. Greg Abbott to declare 70 counties as disaster areas while flooding claimed the lives of at least 31 people, according to various news reports. The downpours were so great that they brought an end to a four-year water shortage

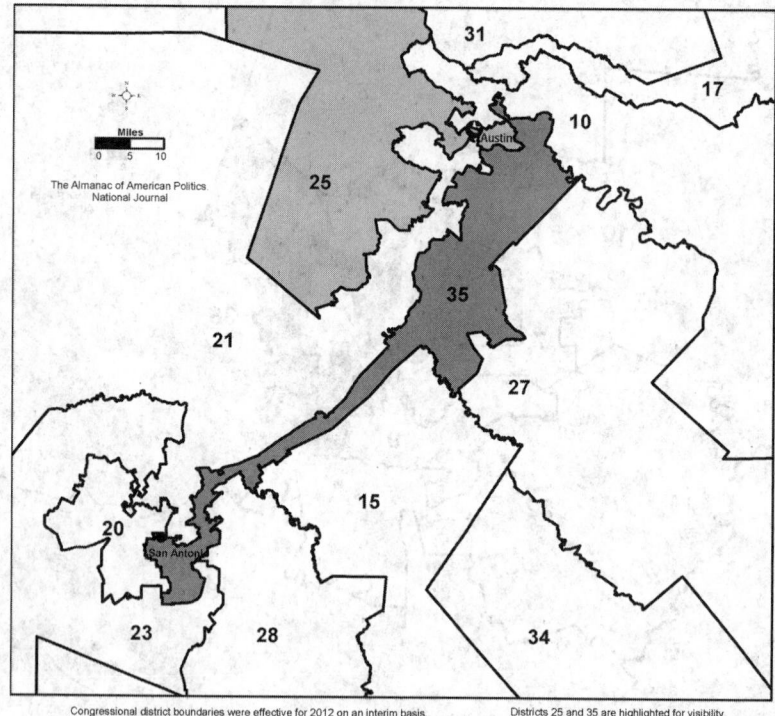

Congressional district boundaries were effective for 2012 on an interim basis.   Districts 25 and 35 are highlighted for visibility.

in the state. Texas has tamed some aspects of nature's force. While other states increasingly look for alternative energy sources, Texas already leads the nation in wind-powered electricity generation, accounting for more than one-fifth of the nation's total, and is the first state to reach 10,000 megawatts of installed wind generation. That's useful because Texas is the largest electricity-consuming state. That's due in part to the size of its population, but also because of high demand for air conditioning during the hot summer months and the widespread use of electricity for home heating in winter. And in typically Texas fashion among the contiguous 48 states, it is the only state that has a stand-alone electric grid entirely within its borders. Texas is largely dependent on its own resources to meet its electricity needs, and that isolation from interstate electrical grids means it is not subject to some federal energy rules.

Newcomers—think of the Bushes—have done much to put the stamp of Texas on the whole of the United States. And people have been voting for Texas with their feet. Its population grew from 21 million in 2000 to 25 million in 2010, a 21% increase. The state accounted for 16% of the population increase of the entire country. Growth came from both immigration and from domestic migration. The U.S. Census Bureau estimates that 933,000 immigrants came to the state between 2000 and 2009 and 849,000 people came from elsewhere in the United States. The reapportionment of House seats among the states reflects relative population growth; after the 2010 census, six states gained one seat, Florida gained two, California for the first time in its history gained none—and Texas gained four. Growth has continued since the 2010 census: The population rose another 1.8 million from 2010 to 2014, 18% of the national population gain. And among cities with a population of at least 50,000, from 2013 to 2014, five of the 10 fastest growing in the country were in Texas: San Marcos (No. 1), south of Austin; Georgetown (No. 2), north of Austin; Frisco (No. 4) and McKinney (No. 7), north of Dallas; and Conroe (No. 6), north of Houston. Those annual growth clips ran from 7.9% in San Marcos to 5.1% in McKinney.

Latino activists note that Hispanics accounted for about half of the state's population increase, and immigration was particularly heavy in Dallas County and Houston's Harris County. Illegal immigration along the state's border with Mexico reached crisis proportions in 2014, when there was a surge of children largely from El Salvador, Guatemala and

Honduras, seeking to escape grinding poverty and gang violence and perhaps to join family members already in the United States. Of the children who were apprehended trying to enter the U.S., more than three quarters were caught crossing along the Rio Grande Valley. The Texas governor at the time, Rick Perry, complained that the federal government had failed to secure the border and dispatched hundreds of Texas National Guard troops and Department of Public Safety officers to provide additional surveillance of the border, deter crossings and interdict the flow of illegal drugs. The effort cost more than $100 million while arrests and citations by Texas Rangers and the Highway Patrol fell. Still, Texas has surged in part because it has nurtured and profited from its relationship with its southern neighbor, Mexico. The border is long, some 1,200 miles, and porous. Southern Texas along the Rio Grande is a transition zone between two very different economies. Nearly half of merchandise exports to Mexico are from Texas. The North American Development Bank is headquartered in San Antonio, the Border Environment Cooperation Commission is in Juarez, across the Rio Grande from El Paso, and the busiest truck crossing between the countries is the new World Trade Bridge near Laredo and Nuevo Laredo.

Politically, Texas is now a predominantly Republican state. Republicans hold both Senate seats, all nine statewide elective offices in the executive branch, all nine elected seats on the state Supreme Court, and all nine statewide elected judges on the Court of Criminal Appeals. Republicans have large margins in both houses of the state legislature. They have carried the state in the last eight presidential elections, starting in 1980, and have won every gubernatorial election since 1990 and every Senate race since 1988. Many commentators have pointed out that demographic factors seem to threaten Republican dominance in the state. Rural, small-town Texas—now the GOP stronghold—is growing less than the rest of the state, and the minority population is increasing, especially Hispanics. But there is still a gap between the make-up of the state's population and the electorate that shows up at the polls. The States of Change study by the Center for American Progress, the American Enterprise Institute and the Brookings Institution, reported that in 2014, 39% of Texas' residents were Hispanic, 11% were black and 6% were Asian or another race. And two-thirds of the state's children were minorities. The white population was 44%, down from 66% in 1980. But among eligible voters, 53% were white and 31% were Hispanic. And in terms of actual voters who cast ballots in the 2012 presidential election, the study found that 59% were white and 22% were Hispanic (15% were black, 4% were Asian or some other race). Right before the 2014 election the Supreme Court allowed Texas to continue requiring voters to show a photo identification such as a Texas driver's or gun license, or a passport, to cast a ballot, but the law remains under court review. Justice Ruth Bader Ginsburg's dissent, joined by Justices Sonia Sotomayor and Elena Kagan, said the court's action "risks denying the right to vote to hundreds of thousands of eligible voters." Still, Texas Republicans would be foolish to ignore the demographics that point to a state whose population is getting younger and less white. In 2020, non-white eligible Texas voters are projected to edge out white eligible voters, 50%-49%. That gap just keeps growing in subsequent elections.

The challenge for Texas Democrats is that they are largely an urban party other than the stretch of rural counties from El Paso to Brownsville in the Rio Grande Valley that have heavy Hispanic populations. They have not figured out a way to break through in the state's

Population		Race and Ethnicity		Income	
Total:	26,448,193	White	44.7%	Median income:	$53,027
Urban:	54.1%	Latino	38.1%		(25 of 50)
Suburban:	31.1%	Black	11.5%	Under $50,000	48.2%
Rural:	14.8%	Asian	3.8%	$50,000-$99,999:	29.2%
Land area:	261,232	Two races	1.4%	$100,000-$199,999:	17.6%
Pop/sq. mi.:	101.2	White Ethnic	14.5%	$200,000 or more:	5.1%
Born in state:	60.2%			Poverty Rate	16.2%
		Education			
Age Groups		H.S. grad or less:	43.3%	**Work**	
Under 18:	26.6%	Some college:	29.1%	White collar:	34.9%
18 to 34:	24.7%	College degree, 4 yr.:	18.3%	Blue collar:	42.2%
35 to 64:	37.4%	Post-grad study:	9.3%	Sales and service:	22.9%
Over 64:	11.2%				
		Military		Govt. workers:	13.5%
		Veterans/active duty:	7.8%		

extensive suburban and exurban turf, let alone vast swaths of West Texas and East Texas. In the 2014 midterm elections, it seemed as though the party had simply given up on many races. Patricia Kilday Hart noted in the *Houston Chronicle* that Democrats didn't field a candidate for any county government office in 86 of the state's 254 coun-

Voter Turnout	
2013 Total Citizen 18+	16,785,829
2014 Highest Statewide Turnout	4,727,208
2014 Turnout as % CVAP	28.2%
2012 Turnout as % CVAP	48.4%
Legislature	
Senate:	20R 11D
House:	98R 52D

ties. In 168 counties, there was no candidate running for the office of county judge. Only 40% of the districts for the 150-seat Texas House of Representatives had a Democratic candidate. The same was true for 15 of the 31 state Senate seats that were up for election in 2014. This is not how you develop a Democratic farm team of office holders that someday might be able to take advantage of favorable demographic trends and win a few statewide offices.

Presidential Politics In presidential general elections, Texas has not voted Democratic since 1976, when Jimmy Carter narrowly won its 26 electoral votes. Since then, the closest a Democratic nominee has come to carrying Texas was in 1996, when Texan Ross Perot split the opposition to Bill Clinton, and Bob Dole carried the state 49%-44%. Not surprisingly, Texas has not been a battleground in this century. George W. Bush carried the state with 59% and 61% of the vote in 2000 and 2004, respectively. In 2008, Barack Obama increased the Democratic percentage, but only to 44%, far behind John McCain's 55%. Obama carried the central city counties including Dallas, Houston, San

2012 Presidential Vote		
Mitt Romney (R)	4,569,843	(57%)
Barack Obama (D)	3,308,124	(41%)
2012 Presidential Primary		
Barack Obama (D)	520,410	(88%)
John Wolfe (D)	29,879	(5%)
2012 Presidential Primary		
Mitt Romney (R)	1,001,387	(69%)
Ron Paul (R)	174,207	(12%)
Rick Santorum (R)	115,584	(8%)
2008 Presidential Vote		
John McCain (R)	4,479,328	(55%)
Barack Obama (D)	3,528,633	(44%)

Antonio, and Austin, something no Democrat had done since Lyndon Johnson swept his home state in 1964. Whites voted 73%-26% for McCain, who also won 83% among white evangelical Protestants and 69% among white voters under 30. African-Americans voted 98%-2% for Obama. Hispanics voted 63%-35% for Obama. Hispanics and upscale white voters were the most likely to have switched from Bush in 2004 to Obama in 2008. In 2012, Mitt Romney carried the state 57%-41%. Romney lost 65%-34% in the Rio Grande Valley and 52%-45% in metro Austin. But he won a solid 56% in the Dallas-Fort Worth Metroplex, 55% in metro Houston, 53% in metro San Antonio, and 72% in rural, small-town Texas.

For the first time in 20 years, Texas was an important state in the presidential nomination process in 2008. Texas voted on March 4, after Obama had won 14 straight Democratic primaries and 11 caucuses in February. So Texas and Ohio, voting on the same day, were must-wins for Hillary Clinton, and Texas got a lot more attention than it would have if the legislature had chosen to set the primary for Super Tuesday, February 5. Obama and Clinton debated and campaigned hard in Texas. Democratic turnout was nearly 2.9 million, more than triple the 839,000 who voted in 2004. The primary was a closer contest than Ohio's. Clinton won by just 51%-47%. She carried women, older voters, downscale and rural whites, and Latinos by wide margins. Obama carried men, younger voters, upscale and urban whites, and blacks by wide margins. Clinton won 61% to 70% of the vote in San Antonio and border state Senate districts. (Texas Democrats elect delegates by state Senate districts.) Obama won 73% in heavily African-American state Senate districts in Houston and Dallas. Rural districts, except for one that includes exurban Austin's Williamson County, voted for Clinton. Obama carried metro Dallas with 56%, metro Houston with 55%, and metro Austin with 60%. Clinton carried 18 Senate districts to Obama's 13, but Obama won more delegates overall because one-third of them were selected in caucuses held on primary night and more Obama voters took the trouble to show up. The caucus counting continued for days after the primary and was never completed, casting doubt on the actual results.

Turnout on the Republican side was much lower, 1.3 million, only slightly above the 1.1 million Republicans who voted in the not seriously contested primary in 2000. McCain beat Mike Huckabee 51%-38%. Huckabee carried only one House district, the 4th, which included Texarkana, right on the border with his native Arkansas. Half the primary voters were white evangelical Protestants, and Huckabee won more than 40% of the vote in the northern, more-Baptist, half of the state, including the Dallas-Fort Worth Metroplex. He won less than 40% in most parts of the southern half of the state. McCain's biggest majorities were in the border areas and in the most upscale districts in Houston and Dallas. The May 29 primary in 2012 was of little consequence, and Romney defeated Ron Paul, 69%-12%.

Congressional Districts Texas redistricting, once the plain prerogative of Anglo Democrats, now involves one of the most complex sets of partisan, racial, and legal considerations in the country. In the 2000 census, Texas gained two seats, and in 2010, another four. The early projection is for another multiple-

114th Congress Lineup	
25 R	11 D
113th Congress Lineup	
24 R	12 D

seat gain in 2020. In 2001, after a split legislature failed to agree on a map, a federal court drew a plan protecting 17 Democratic incumbents and adding two new Republican seats, for a 17-15 breakdown. Since then, as the Republicans' strengthening grip on state politics has coincided with a Hispanic population boom, Texas has endured what seems like a never-ending legislative and legal rollercoaster ride. Between 2000 and 2012, the state held its elections under five separate sets of boundaries, and a sixth is possible by 2016.

Republicans took over the legislature in 2002, and House Majority Leader Tom DeLay (whose 2011 conviction for charges related to his role was overturned by an appeals court) pressured his party to replace the court plan with a design to maximize Republican seats. Famously, 51 Texas House Democrats, who became known as the "Killer D's," fled to Oklahoma to thwart a two-thirds quorum. But Republicans eventually rammed through their map, converting a 15-17 deficit into a 21-11 edge in 2004 by defeating five "WD-40s"—white Democrats over 40—whom DeLay had targeted for extinction. In 2006, the U.S. Supreme Court insisted on minor changes in South Texas to protect Hispanics. But in 2010, Republicans captured 23 of 32 seats, and it was Democrats rather than Republicans who were severely underrepresented.

In early 2011, holding a gluttony of seats, Republicans faced a dilemma. The most rapid growth in the state had taken place in exurban counties, almost all of them Republican. But Hispanics had accounted for 65% of all growth between 2000 and 2010, and the state's plans were subject to review by the Obama administration's Justice Department. The prevailing interpretation of the Voting Rights Act seemed to require maximizing black- and Hispanic-majority seats. So, mindful of federal scrutiny, a group of pragmatic House Republicans led by Rep. Lamar Smith lobbied legislators in Austin to simply shore up incumbents and split the four new seats evenly: two new Democratic-leaning, Hispanic-majority seats, and two new Republican seats in fast-growing exurban areas, for a 25-11 delegation.

Republican legislators, and Perry, were horror-struck by the idea of "giving" Democrats *any* seats. In June, they disregarded their own delegation's advice and passed their own plan to split the Metroplex's Hispanic population six ways, stuff Austin Democrat Lloyd Doggett into a heavily Hispanic seat stretching to San Antonio, and create three new safely Republican enclaves: one in Fort Worth's western suburbs, another in Houston's eastern suburbs, and a third running along the I-35 corridor from the fringes of the Metroplex to the outskirts of Austin. The plan did create one new Democratic seat in the Rio Grande Valley. But it did so by dropping the neighboring 27th District of Republican Blake Farenthold, a surprise 2010 winner, from 73% to 49% Hispanic.

Doggett and Democrats immediately blasted the "Perry-mander" as a gross overreach. Hispanic advocacy groups denounced it as discriminatory and sued in a San Antonio federal court. The groups argued that while Republicans had created a "new" Hispanic majority 35th District stretching from Austin to San Antonio, they had weakened the sprawling 23rd District between El Paso and San Antonio by underhandedly swapping out high-turnout Hispanic precincts for low-turnout precincts to boost freshman Republican Quico Canseco's Anglo share.

The Justice Department declared the map had been drawn with discriminatory intent and assumed the opposition as Attorney General Greg Abbott, in an end-around attempt, sought preclearance from a three-judge panel at the U.S. Court of Appeals in Washington. Back in San Antonio, Republicans weren't faring much better before a separate three-judge panel. The state's own expert witness, Rice University professor John Alford, admitted on the stand the Republican map didn't create an effective new Hispanic seat. The San Antonio panel halted the map's implementation and announced its intent to draw its own interim plan if the state map did not obtain federal preclearance before the December 2011 opening of the candidate filing period.

Sure enough, the D.C. court denied Abbott's request for quick summary judgment, setting up a protracted preclearance trial that couldn't possibly be resolved by a December deadline. So the San Antonio judges delighted Democrats with their own plan: Not only did it preserve Doggett's existing Austin-based 25th District, it essentially drew three of four new seats for Democrats—one minority "coalition" seat in Fort Worth, and one Hispanic majority seat each in the Rio Grande Valley and San Antonio areas. In yet another surprise twist, the high court granted Abbott's request for a stay, in turn forcing Texas to delay its primary until May.

In January 2012, the Supreme Court ruled that the San Antonio court had "exceeded its mission" to fix only the districts that had violated the Voting Rights Act and faulted the court for failing to use an elected legislature's original plan as a baseline for its own. So in February, the San Antonio court issued a second interim map. This time, it resembled Republicans' plan, except it created a new 66% Hispanic seat linking Dallas and Fort Worth and restored Hispanic voting strength in the 23rd District. After nearly a year and millions of dollars in court costs, the end result was nearly identical to what Republican incumbents had lobbied for in the first place: a 2-2 division of new seats. Democrats scored another pickup in November by ousting Canseco in the 23rd, for 12 of 36 seats overall.

In August 2012, the D.C. three-judge panel formally rejected preclearance of the original Republican plan in a 2-1 decision, leaving Texas without a permanent map for 2014. In early 2013, several Republican state legislators, satisfied with a 24-12 breakdown, hinted support for making the 2012 interim map permanent. Democratic plaintiffs, particularly Austinites upset their county had been split five ways, still held out hope for additional winnable seats in Austin and Dallas. That option became less likely when the Supreme Court in 2013, in *Shelby County v. Holder*, struck down the federal preclearance process altogether.

Of note, although the 2012 interim map increased the number of Hispanic majority districts from seven to nine, the number of Hispanics representing them remained at five. Anglo Democrats Doggett and Gene Green won reelection in overwhelmingly Hispanic districts, black Democrat Marc Veasey narrowly captured the new Dallas-area 33rd District, and although Democrat Filemon Vela won the new 34th District in the Rio Grande Valley, Democrat Silvestre Reyes lost a primary challenge to an Anglo, Beto O'Rourke, in the El Paso 16th District. (In a sign of how times have changed, no white Democrat represents an Anglo-majority district in Texas.) In 2014, African-American Republican Will Hurd ousted Hispanic Democrat Pete Gallego in the heavily Hispanic 23rd District. It may take more decades of naturalization, mobilization, and litigation before Texas' share of Hispanic officeholders catches up to the fast-maturing Hispanic share of the state's total residents—38% in 2010.

Governor

Greg Abbott (R)

Elected 2014, term expires Jan. 2019, 1st term; b. Nov. 13, 1957, Wichita Falls; U. of TX, B.B.A. 1981, Vanderbilt U., J.D. 1984; Catholic; married (Cecilia); 1 child.

Elected Office: TX st. trial judge, 129th Dist. Ct., 1992-95; TX Supreme Ct., 1995-2001; TX atty. general, 2002-14.

Professional Career: Practicing atty., Butler & Binion, 1984-1992.

Office: Office of the Governor, PO Box 12428, 78711-2428, 512-463-2000; Fax: 512-463-5571; Website: gov.texas.gov.

Election Results

2014 general	Greg Abbott (R)	2,796,547	(59%)
	Wendy Davis (D)	1,835,596	(39%)
2014 primary	Greg Abbott (R)	1,224,014	(92%)

Republican Greg Abbott once described his job as the state's attorney general this way: "I go into the office in the morning, I sue Barack Obama, and then I go home." It was that reputation that helped Abbott win the governorship in 2014, entrenching Republican domination in a state that has not elected a Democrat to statewide office in two decades.

Abbott was born in Wichita Falls and raised in Duncanville in Dallas County. He earned a bachelor's degree in finance from the University of Texas at Austin and got his law degree from Vanderbilt University in Nashville. The year he finished law school, in 1984, a falling tree injured Abbott while he was out for a run. The incident made him a paraplegic, and he has used a wheelchair ever since.

After a stint in private practice, Abbott became an associate justice on the Texas Supreme Court in 1995, appointed by then-Gov. George W. Bush to fill a vacancy. Abbott won election twice more to the state's highest civil court, and in 2001 he resigned to run for attorney general in 2002. Abbott won reelection twice and became the longest-serving state attorney general in Texas history. As the state's highest law enforcement officer, Abbott was a pure Texas conservative. He sued the federal government more than two dozen times, on issues ranging from the Affordable Care Act to abortion, voter ID, and environmental regulations. In 2005, Abbott appeared before the U.S. Supreme Court to argue in favor of the constitutionality of the Ten Commandments monument on the Texas State Capitol grounds (he won, with the high court ruling 5-4 that the display did not violate the Constitution's Establishment Clause).

Less than a week after Gov. Rick Perry announced he would not seek another term, Abbott declared his candidacy for the job. He faced only token opposition in the GOP primary, which he won with 92% of the vote. His Democratic opponent was state Sen. Wendy Davis, whose supporters hoped would benefit from the national attention she got from her ultimately unsuccessful attempt to filibuster a bill to restrict abortion access. Davis won her primary over nominal opposition with 78% of the vote. Texas, with its growing Hispanic population, is a state that Democrats believe they can carry with the right candidates and that eventually could even become competitive in the presidential election. Davis' running mate was Hispanic state Sen. Leticia Van de Putte. Running with Abbott at the top of the GOP ticket were state Sen. Dan Patrick, the nominee for lieutenant governor, and state Sen. Ken Paxton, the nominee for attorney general, who prevailed in contentious primaries and runoffs over establishment favorites, incumbent Lt. Gov. David Dewhurst and state Rep. Dan Branch, respectively. Tea party activists gave enthusiastic support to both Patrick and Paxton in those contests, but that imprimatur had no apparent drag on Abbott's candidacy.

Davis sought to portray Abbott as an Austin "insider" siding with the interests of his rich and powerful friends at the expense of "hard-working Texans." But Abbott, who significantly outspent Davis, saturated the airwaves with spots that reminded voters how, despite using a wheelchair, he had persevered and succeeded in life. His ads also portrayed Davis as closely aligned with President Barack Obama, who was not popular in the Lone Star State. And he featured his Hispanic mother-in-law in TV ads and on billboards to appeal to Hispanic voters. The flood of children from Central American into the state became a humanitarian crisis in 2014, and made the border and immigration control a top concern of Texans, especially of conservatives. When Obama failed to visit the border during a fundraising swing through Texas in July, he basically punted the issue to Texas Republicans. At the same time, his decision to delay any action on immigration reform that he had said he would deliver in the fall, discouraged many Texas Hispanic activists, whose enthusiasm Davis desperately needed to generate a large turnout of Hispanic voters for her in November.

In October the Davis campaign released the "wheelchair ad." The spot opened with a picture of a wheelchair, noted Abbott's crippling accident and said, "He sued and got millions. Since then he spent his career working against other victims." The ad then cited cases as evidence that Abbott had thwarted or ruled against other victims trying to get compensation. The ad got a lot of attention including criticism that it was in bad taste. But there was probably nothing that was going to save Davis' campaign and Abbott trounced her, 59%-39%. Exit polls showed he won roughly 44% of the Hispanic vote. A group called Battleground Texas, set up by veterans of the 2012 Obama campaign, was supposed to bring its organizational prowess to the governor's race but it ended up severely lacking. Abbott carried 235 of the state's 254 counties, limiting Davis to the Democratic strongholds of Dallas, El Paso and Travis (Austin) counties and 16 others in the heavily Hispanic Rio Grande Valley.

In his first State of the State address, Abbott highlighted five issues that he said were emergency items that warranted expedited action by the legislature: Early education, higher education, transportation, border security and ethics reform. He called for more than doubling state spending on a comprehensive border security initiative that included deploying 500 additional state troopers to the border. In the meantime, Abbott said he would continue the deployment of the Texas National Guard on the border. Hours before his remarks, a federal judge in Brownsville blocked Obama's executive order on immigration, which Abbott, in his waning days as attorney general had fought with his lawsuit. And the newly minted governor could not resist taking a shot at his nemesis. "In Texas, we will not sit idly by while the President ignores the law and fails to secure the border," declared Abbott. On higher education, he called for boosting community colleges and a $500 million effort to raise the status of the state's research universities that includes recruiting Nobel Laureates to Texas campuses. Abbott proposed a $4 billion transportation measure to build and repair roadways without raising taxes or fees. On ethics reform, he called for greater disclosure by lawmakers on their contracts and campaign finances and barring them from voting on legislation that would directly benefit them.

Abbott won early action for a key part of his early education proposals. He signed legislation in May 2015 to provide $130 million in funding to school districts whose pre-kindergarten programs meet standards including having certified teachers and using a state-approved curriculum. The measure won bipartisan approval in the legislature, but it was briefly stalled in the Senate when Lt. Gov. Patrick's "Grassroots Advisory Board," a council of mostly tea party activists, distributed a letter to lawmakers calling the proposal "socialistic" and a "threat to parental rights." Patrick distanced himself from that opposition, and the measure passed the 31-member upper chamber with only six Republican senators who were tea party allies voting no. Even a strong conservative like Abbott, it seems, will have to deal with the GOP's tea party fringe. He certainly played to that crowd earlier in the year, when he asked the State National Guard to monitor a U.S. military summer training exercise in the Southwest named "Jade Helm 15" that Internet conspiracy theorists believed was a pretense for a military takeover.

Senior Senator

John Cornyn (R)

Elected 2002, term expires Jan. 2021, 3rd full term; b. Feb. 2, 1952, Houston; Trinity U., B.A. 1973, St. Mary's Law Schl., J.D. 1977, U. of VA, L.L.M. 1995; non-denominational Christian; married (Sandy); 2 children.

Elected Office: Bexar Cnty. dist. court judge, 1985-91; TX Supreme Court, 1991-97; TX atty. gen., 1999-2002.

Professional Career: Practicing atty., 1977-84.

DC Office: 517 HSOB, 20510, 202-224-2934; Website: cornyn.senate. gov.

State Offices: Austin, 512-469-6034; Dallas, 972-239-1310; Harlingen, 956-423-0162; Houston, 713-572-3337; Lubbock, 806-472-7533; San Antonio, 210-224-7485; Tyler, 903-593-0902.

Committees: Senate Majority Whip. *Finance:* Energy, Natural Resources & Infrastructure; Int'l Trade, Customs & Global Competitiveness (Chmn); Taxation & IRS Oversight. *Judiciary:* Crime & Terrorism; Immigration & the Nat'l Interest; the Constitution (Chmn).

Group Ratings

	ADA	ACLU	AFL-CIO	LCV	ITI	COC	HAFA	ACU	CFG	FRC
2014	5%	0%	–	20%	33%	100%	75%	92%	72%	93%
2013	0%	C	6%	8%	C	75%	C	96%	93%	C

National Journal Ratings

	2013 LIB	—	2013 CONS
Economic	15%	—	80%
Social	10%	—	89%
Foreign	17%	—	82%
Composite	15%	—	85%

Key Votes of the 113th Congress

1. Sandy storm spending	N	5. Student Loan Rates	Y	9. Bipartisan Budget Deal	N
2. Chuck Hagel Confirmation	N	6. Employee Non-Discrim'n Act	N	10. Farm Bill Conference Rept.	N
3. Gun Background Checks	N	7. Senate Vote on Judgeships	Y	11. Unempl. Comp. Extension	N
4. Immigration Reform	N	8. Defense Dept. Spending	NV	12. Keystone Pipeline	Y

Election Results

2014 general	John Cornyn (R)..................... 2,860,678	(62%)	$14,672,004	$635,391	$27,244
	David Alameel (D) 1,597,272	(34%)	$5,715,984		
	Rebecca Paddock (Lib).............. 133,738	(3%)			
2014 primary	John Cornyn (R)......................... 781,259	(59%)			
	Steve Stockman (R) 251,577	(19%)			
	Dwayne Stovall (R)................... 140,794	(11%)			

Prior winning percentages: 2008 (55%), 2002 (55%)

Republican John Cornyn, the senior senator from Texas, was elected to the Senate in 2002. He rose quickly through the party ranks and became minority whip—the second-ranking GOP leadership post—in 2013 after two terms as chairman of the National Republican Senatorial Committee. When his party retook control of the Senate, he retained the whip job behind Majority Leader Mitch McConnell, a similarly savvy inside operator.

Cornyn was born in Houston and spent much of his childhood in San Antonio. His father was an oral pathologist in the Air Force stationed in Japan, where Cornyn went to high school. After his father retired from the service, the family settled in San Antonio. Cornyn graduated from Trinity University and St. Mary's University School of Law, both in San Antonio, in the 1970s. He practiced law for five years with a firm that defended doctors and insurance companies in medical malpractice cases. In 1984, he ran for district court judge on the Republican ticket in Bexar County and, at age 32, upset a strong favorite in the race. In 1990, Cornyn was elected to the state Supreme Court. In 1995, he wrote a 5-4 decision upholding the "Robin Hood" school finance system, in which property-wealthy school districts had to send money to property-poor districts.

In 1997, he resigned from the court to run for attorney general, defeating two better-known opponents in the Republican primary. In the general election, he faced a grizzled veteran of Texas politics, Jim Mattox, a populist Democrat, former House member from Dallas, and the second-place finisher to Ann Richards in the 1990 runoff for Texas governor. Cornyn won 54%-44%, becoming the first Republican attorney general in Texas since Reconstruction. He argued two cases before the U.S. Supreme Court, including the Santa Fe Independent School District's defense of reading the Lord's Prayer at football games. (The high court nixed it.)

When GOP Sen. Phil Gramm announced that he would not seek reelection in 2002, Cornyn got into the contest to succeed him, and had no serious opposition in the Republican primary. Democrats nominated Dallas Mayor Ron Kirk, the son of the first black mailman in Austin, a teacher, and former aide to Sen. Lloyd Bentsen. He had been elected mayor of Dallas in 1995, and reelected in 1999 by a wide margin. In the primary, he overcame challenges from former Rep. Ken Bentsen of Houston, the senator's nephew, and Victor Morales, who had been the Democratic nominee against Gramm in 1996.

In the general election, Cornyn ran as a supporter of President George W. Bush. He called for making Bush's 2001 tax cuts permanent, for extending the research and development tax credit, and for raising Texas' share of gas tax funds from 90.5 cents to 95 cents of each dollar of gas tax revenues. He supported government vouchers for private school tuition, individual investment accounts as part of Social Security, and color-blind standards for college and university admissions. Kirk took opposite stands on most issues, but portrayed himself as a moderate Democrat who would support Bush on many issues.

Republicans ran ads linking Kirk to Hillary Clinton, then a New York senator, and liberal out-of-state contributors. Kirk campaigned with a sense of humor, making fun of his bald pate, but he made some mistakes. He refused to disclose his income tax returns, except for allowing reporters one peek at his 2001 return. Cornyn came out in favor of a bill in the Texas legislature requiring district attorneys to seek the death penalty for killers of law enforcement officials after the Austin-based district attorney had not sought the death penalty for the killer of a Travis County sheriff's deputy. Kirk said Cornyn was acting like he was running for district attorney, and then apologized to a convention of law enforcement officials a few days later. Meanwhile, Cornyn met with the deputy's widow. In the high-spending contest, Kirk spent $8.9 million to Cornyn's $9.5 million.

Democrats operated on the assumption that Kirk had to win 85% of African-Americans, 65% of Hispanics, and 35% of whites to win. He clearly achieved the first and probably achieved the second of those goals, but failed by a solid margin to achieve the third. Cornyn won 55%-43%—almost the same percentages as in his race for attorney general in 1998 and a fair reflection of basic party identification in Texas in recent years. Kirk carried histori-cally Republican Dallas County 50%-49%. But Cornyn carried the entire Dallas-Fort Worth Metroplex, 58%-41%. Cornyn also won metro Houston, 55%-43%, and the combined San Antonio and Austin metro areas, 51%-47%. He became the first Texas senator to come from San Antonio, once the state's largest city and now second behind Houston.

Cornyn often is described as "genial," and generally favors reasoned language over angry rhetoric. "He's quiet by nature and isn't excitable," his friend Jim Lunz, a retired San Antonio businessman, told *The New Republic*. "So when he does speak, you are more inclined to listen to what he has to say." Because of his reputation, South Carolina Repub-lican Sen. Lindsey Graham told NPR in December 2014 that Cornyn was "the best guy in the [GOP] conference to bring us together" as Republicans prepared to assume the majority. "Nobody doubts his conservatism," Graham said. "But he's a very practical, let's-move-the-ball-forward kind of guy."

In a sign of his formidability, Cornyn was named in January 2015 to chair the Finance Committee's panel on international trade, an issue expected to be one of the main areas in which the two parties can find common ground. He promised to focus on patent reform leg-islation, which has stalled despite bipartisan support in recent years.

Cornyn has sought to work with his new GOP colleague Ted Cruz, a tea party favorite who had initially declined to endorse Cornyn's bid for whip. He helped Cruz to land a seat on the Judiciary Committee, and initially signed on to his colleague's effort to shut down the government in an effort to de-fund the Affordable Care Act. Cornyn subsequently withdrew his support and criticized the highly controversial tactic. But *The Dallas Morning News'* edi-torial page said in January 2015 that too often he was guilty of "straying from his signature sound judgment and allowing the party's extremists, including Cruz, to set an agenda that feeds gridlock."

Cornyn had been an early player in working on immigration reform in 2007 before aban-doning the efforts. Arizona Republican John McCain angrily accused him at the time of raising arcane legal issues to scuttle the bill. Cornyn said of the talks, "I didn't so much walk away as got chased away." His amendment to bar illegal immigrants convicted of identity theft from legalization processes was defeated 51-46. From then on, he opposed the larger immigration bill.

As immigration reform heated up in 2013, Cornyn remained a skeptic about a compre-hensive approach, a high priority for the party. He said giving illegal immigrants a path to citizenship remained premature and insisted on focusing on border enforcement. Frank Sharry, founder of the pro-immigration group America's Voice, complained in the *Huffington Post* that Cornyn "is famous for posing as a reformer even as he works to derail reform." Cornyn voted against the bipartisan comprehensive reform bill that passed the Senate in 2013 after the chamber rejected his amendment that would have required 100 percent surveillance of the southern border and 90 percent apprehension of border-crossers before undocumented immigrants could begin a pathway to citizenship.

When a crisis involving Central American refugees along the border became a major controversy in 2014, Cornyn joined with Texas Democratic Rep. Henry Cuellar on a bill expediting the deportation of undocumented children from countries other than Mexico and Canada. Democrats and immigration advocates criticized the bill, saying an easier deporta-tion process would return the children to potentially dangerous situations back home. In January 2015, Cornyn joined Republicans Jeff Flake of Arizona and Ron Johnson of Wiscon-sin on a tough border-security bill similar to one debated in the House.

On a less-contentious issue, Cornyn worked with the Senate Judiciary Committee's top Democrat, Patrick Leahy of Vermont, in 2014 on a measure aimed at strengthening the Freedom of Information Act. The two men agreed to water down the bill in the hope of get-ting it passed in the lame-duck session, but even though it moved through the Senate with-out opposition, House Speaker John Boehner refused to bring it up for a vote.

Cornyn helped strike the compromise to raise the debt ceiling in early 2014, joining McConnell and breaking with most members of the Republican conference to vote for a clean increase after they failed to convince other Republicans to take those votes instead. The vote ended years of repeated brinksmanship over government spending that had often hurt Republicans in the polls.

In 2015, Cornyn took over as chairman of Judiciary's Constitution, Civil Rights and Human Rights Subcommittee, which he had led in his first term. In an early move he changed its name to the Constitution Subcommittee, angering civil rights groups. But as interest mounted in criminal justice reform mounted, Cornyn introduced a bipartisan bill in early 2015 to help prisoners transition back into the community and avoid recidivism in exchange for slightly shortened sentences. And he joined Democrats in backing bills to improve support for mentally ill prisoners and to create a committee to examine the criminal justice system for possible reforms.

But another bipartisan bill Cornyn introduced in 2015 ended up leading to major partisan conflict. His bill targeting sexual abuse and human trafficking passed the Judiciary Committee unanimously before Democrats realized it had language that would limit the ability of victims to receive abortions. An incensed Cornyn pointed out the bill had been public for weeks before Democrats noticed just before it was supposed to be passed by the full Senate. "The idea that there's been some sort of ambush is just preposterous, it's just not credible," he said on the Senate floor. But Democrats refused to accept the language, despite quietly admitting they'd failed to notice it earlier on. Republicans retaliated by holding up the nomination of Loretta Lynch for Attorney General, putting them in the position of blocking the nation's first African-American woman to hold the job over an unrelated issue. Cornyn and Washington Democratic Sen. Patty Murray eventually ironed out compromise language that led to unanimous passage of the bill and paved the way for Lynch's confirmation.

Cornyn emerged as a leading critic of the Obama administration's "Operation Fast and Furious" program, an ill-fated plan that allegedly allowed guns to cross the border into Mexico as a way to track drug cartels, but that were later linked to fatal shootings. In October 2011, Cornyn's bill blocking the Justice Department from undertaking future Fast and Furious-type programs passed the Senate, 99-0. He later called for Attorney General Eric Holder to resign over the matter. Cornyn also exercised his oversight powers in criticizing Ashton Carter, the head of weapons acquisition at the Pentagon. In August 2011, he sent a letter to Carter expressing disappointment for his "lack of commitment to the success" of the F-35 Joint Strike Fighter program, which originated at a Lockheed Martin plant in Fort Worth. After Cornyn said he received assurances from Carter that the "F-35 will form the backbone" of U.S. air combat, he voted to confirm Carter as deputy defense secretary.

Cornyn began his campaign for reelection in 2008 with polls showing he was less popular than his Republican colleague, Kay Bailey Hutchison. But Democratic attempts to attract a well-known challenger failed. Their nominee was Houston state Rep. Rick Noriega, who had served with the Texas Army National Guard in Afghanistan. He set a goal of raising $10 million, but ultimately raised $4 million to Cornyn's $16.5 million. Polls consistently showed Cornyn ahead, and neither national party invested in the contest. Cornyn won 55%-43%, the same margin as in 2002. He won 36% of the Hispanic vote, an improvement over 2002. He carried 223 of the state's 254 counties, running behind only in the Rio Grande Valley and in the counties with the central cities of Houston, Dallas, Austin, and San Antonio.

Cornyn had a major role in the Republican leadership in 2010 as chairman of the National Republican Senatorial Committee, the main political arm of the Senate GOP. Democrats had gained 14 Senate seats in the 2006 and 2008 campaign cycles, when their Senate campaign committee was headed by Chuck Schumer of New York; Cornyn wanted to reverse those results. Cornyn adopted Schumer's strategy of recruiting candidates who could win in states not naturally inclined to his party. He urged Gov. Charlie Crist to run in Florida and Rep. Mike Castle to run in Delaware. He opposed the candidacy of former Rep. Pat Toomey, who announced he was running again in Pennsylvania against Arlen Specter, who had won their 2004 primary by only 51%-49%. But as the tea party movement gained strength and opposition to Obama administration programs grew, conservatives criticized his treatment of Toomey, a staunch conservative. In April 2009, Specter announced he was switching parties, leaving Cornyn in the embarrassing position of having to support Toomey, now the obvious Republican nominee. Toomey went on to win the seat. In Florida, former state House Speaker Marco Rubio gained steam against Crist, eventually forcing him from the party and then crushing his independent bid.

Despite these setbacks, Cornyn succeeded in the chairman's major duty: raising large sums for the candidates. He brought in $115 million for the season and came close to matching the $130 million raised for the 2010 election by the rival Democratic Senatorial Campaign Committee. Cornyn managed to surf the conservative tide when it gained strength. When Joe Miller upset Lisa Murkowski in the August primary in Alaska, the NRSC supported Miller against Murkowski's ultimately successful write-in campaign. (By virtue of party rules, the NRSC had no choice but to support the GOP nominee).When Christine O'Donnell upset Mike Castle in the September primary in Delaware, Cornyn sent in the technical maximum of $42,000 and then left her on her own, correctly calculating that she had no chance of making it a close race. Republicans ended up gaining six seats, many more than seemed likely in January 2009, when insiders were predicting further Democratic gains, but less than seemed possible over the summer and fall. In addition to O'Donnell's defeat in Delaware, where Castle would almost certainly have won, tea party candidates Sharron Angle in Nevada and Ken Buck in Colorado both lost their races.

After the election, Cornyn got another term as NRSC chairman for the 2012 elections without serious opposition. Plainly irritated by South Carolina Republican Jim DeMint's endorsements of candidates whose chances he thought dim in 2010, notably Angle and O'Donnell, he urged colleagues to bring concerns they had about candidates to him. DeMint pledged not to oppose any incumbent Republican senators. Cornyn in turn made it plain that he would be more wary of taking sides in primaries, as he did in the Pennsylvania contest. The result was that a pair of far-right Republicans became nominees: Richard Mourdock in Indiana and Todd Akin in Missouri. Both blew what were seen as nearly sure-thing opportunities for Republicans after they made politically disastrous comments about rape and abortion. Democrats ended up netting two seats in the upper chamber in a year they were expected to lose a handful, winning 22 of the 23 races where they held seats; only Nebraska fell beyond their grasp.

When Republican Whip Jon Kyl of Arizona announced that he would retire at the end of his term in 2012, Cornyn announced that he would run for the position. Lamar Alexander of Tennessee initially said he would run, but later dropped out. Sen. Richard Burr of North Carolina also briefly considered running for whip, but decided against it, leaving Cornyn's claim to the No. 2 post in the minority leadership all but assured.

In 2014, Cornyn's bigger reelection threat appeared to be from the right following Cruz's come-from-behind 2012 primary win over then-Texas Lt. Gov. David Dewhurst, another establishment Republican. But Cornyn assiduously courted conservatives in the state, careful not to split with Cruz's hardline postures on most high-profile votes after the younger senator's election. And he brought in some of the conservative strategists that had helped Cruz win to run his own campaign. His efforts, and huge early fundraising figures, helped scare off any serious challengers.

Even though Cruz declined to endorse him in the primary, Cornyn drew no serious tea-party opposition—just an impulsive last-minute challenge from quirky far-right Rep. Steve Stockman, who made an already uphill task even tougher with accusations of ethics violations against him and a habit of dropping out of sight for days on end. Cornyn cruised with 59% in the primary to Stockman's 19%. In heavily Republican Texas, Cornyn's race against Democratic businessman David Alameel was merely a formality, he cruised to a 62%-34% win.

Cornyn could be in line for the top GOP leadership position should Senate Majority Leader Mitch McConnell decide to retire when his term ends in 2020. He would be 68 then.

Junior Senator

Ted Cruz (R)

Elected 2012, term expires Jan. 2019, 1st term; b. Dec. 22, 1970, Calgary, AB, Canada; Princeton U., B.A. 1992, Harvard U., J.D. 1995; Baptist; married (Heidi); 2 children.

Professional Career: Clerk, U.S. Appeals Court, 1995; Clerk, Supreme Court Justice William Rehnquist, 1996; Atty., Cooper, Carvin & Rosenthal, 1997-99; Domestic policy adviser, Bush-Cheney campaign, 1999-2000; Assoc. deputy U.S. atty. gen., 2001; Policy-planning office dir., Fed. Trade Commission, 2001-02; Texas solicitor gen., 2003-08; Adjunct prof., U. of TX, 2004-09; Atty., Morgan, Lewis & Bockius, 2008-12.

DC Office: 404 RSOB, 20510, 202-224-5922; Website: cruz.senate.gov.

State Offices: Austin, 512-916-5834; Dallas, 214-599-8749; Houston, 713-718-3057; McAllen, 956-686-7339; San Antonio, 210-340-2885; Tyler, 903-593-5130.

Committees: *Armed Services:* Emerging Threats & Capabilities; SeaPower; Strategic Forces. *Commerce, Science & Transportation:* Aviation Operations, Safety & Security; Communications, Technology, Innovation & the Internet; Consumer Protection, Product Safety, Insurance & Data Security; Oceans, Atmosphere, Fisheries & Coast Guard; Space, Science & Competitiveness (Chmn). *Judiciary:* Immigration & the Nat'l Interest; Oversight, Agency Action, Federal Rights & Federal Courts (Chmn); the Constitution. *Rules & Administration. Joint Economic Committee.*

Group Ratings

	ADA	ACLU	AFL-CIO	LCV	ITI	COC	HAFA	ACU	CFG	FRC
2014	10%	20%	–	0%	0%	71%	95%	100%	92%	93%
2013	0%	C	0%	15%	C	63%	C	100%	100%	C

National Journal Ratings

	2013 LIB	—	2013 CONS
Economic	0%	—	95%
Social	11%	—	88%
Foreign	0%	—	98%
Composite	5%	—	95%

Key Votes of the 113th Congress

1. Sandy storm spending	N	5. Student Loan Rates	Y	9. Bipartisan Budget Deal	N
2. Chuck Hagel Confirmation	N	6. Employee Non-Discrim'n Act	N	10. Farm Bill Conference Rept.	N
3. Gun Background Checks	N	7. Senate Vote on Judgeships	Y	11. Unempl. Comp. Extension	N
4. Immigration Reform	N	8. Defense Dept. Spending	NV	12. Keystone Pipeline	Y

Election Results

2012 general	Ted Cruz (R)	4,440,137	(56%)	$14,031,864	$3,160,012	$5,872,431
	Paul Sadler (D)	3,194,927	(41%)	$510,439	$30,867	
	John Jay Myers (Lib)	162,354	(2%)	$15,341		
2012 prim.runoff						
	Ted Cruz (R)	631,812	(57%)			
	David Dewhurst (R)	480,126	(43%)			
2012 primary	David Dewhurst (R)	627,731	(45%)			
	Ted Cruz (R)	480,558	(34%)			
	Tom Leppert (R)	187,900	(13%)			

Cuban-American Ted Cruz is Texas' junior senator and a leading conservative who has been central to some of the Senate's biggest fights since his election. His successful bid in 2012 to replace retiring Sen. Kay Bailey Hutchison—which came after he easily dispatched a wealthy primary opponent who had the strong backing of Texas's Republican establishment—was seen as an affirmation of the tea party movement's power. He became the movement's standard-bearer, dominating national politics soon after his election with a headstrong, take-no-prisoners approach that thrilled tea party activists but infuriated both Democrats and most of his Republican colleagues. Cruz launched his bid for president in March 2015.

Cruz was born in Calgary, Alberta, where his parents worked in the Canadian oil business. His father's life story figures prominently into Cruz's political narrative. Rafael Cruz fought to overthrow the Fulgencio Batista regime in Cuba in the 1950s before fleeing to

Texas at the age of 18, with nothing more than $100 sewn into his underwear. He worked as a dishwasher for 50 cents an hour to put himself through the University of Texas and ultimately started a business in Houston. There, he met Cruz's mother, an Irish-American who studied math at Rice University.

As a high school student, Cruz earned scholarship money by entering speech contests organized by the Free Enterprise Institute, in which participants studied the "Ten Pillars of Economic Wisdom," a libertarian manifesto, and then delivered 20-minute speeches about it. As part of the program, Cruz eventually memorized the Constitution and traveled around Texas discussing conservative ideas. He went on to Princeton, where he was a champion debater. After graduating from Harvard Law School in 1995, he clerked for Supreme Court Chief Justice William Rehnquist.

After a few years spent with the Washington law firm Cooper, Carvin & Rosenthal, Cruz joined George W. Bush's campaign in 2000 as a domestic policy adviser. It was on the campaign trail he met his wife, Heidi Nelson Cruz, another member of the policy team. Both were dispatched to Florida in the chaos of the recount, which then led to jobs in the Bush administration. Cruz admits in his autobiography that he was "far too cocky for my own good" in those years and "burned a fair number of bridges" that hurt his chances at landing a higher-level administration job. Cruz served first as associate deputy attorney general at the Justice Department and then as director of the Office of Policy Planning for the Federal Trade Commission.

He returned to Texas in 2003, when he was appointed state solicitor general, making him the first Hispanic to hold the position. During his five-year tenure, Cruz argued before the U.S. Supreme Court nine times and participated in a number of high-profile cases, including one in which Texas fought to execute a Mexican citizen who raped and murdered two teenage girls and another in which he defended the display of the Ten Commandments on the state Capitol grounds. Cruz in July 2012 told the *Texas Tribune*, "We ended up, year after year, arguing some of the biggest cases in the country. There was a degree of serendipity in that, but there was also a concerted effort to seek out and lead conservative fights." His successor in the job, James Ho, told *The New Yorker:* "He was and is the best appellate litigator in the state of Texas."

Cruz was in private practice when he decided to run for the Senate. He began the race as an underdog against Lt. Gov. David Dewhurst, who not only was much better known and had millions of dollars to throw into the race but also the backing of almost every prominent state Republican, including Texas Gov. Rick Perry. But Cruz attracted the attention of tea party activists and got the backing of such national conservative heavyweights as former Alaska Gov. Sarah Palin, South Carolina Sen. Jim DeMint, former Rep. Ron Paul of Texas and his son, Kentucky Sen. Rand Paul, as well as outside groups such as the Club for Growth and Freedom Works. Cruz sank $1 million of his own money into the contest shortly before the primary to make sure Dewhurst stayed under 50 percent of the vote and thus force a runoff.

Dewhurst sought to cast Cruz as a creature of Washington, given his government experience, and suggested that Cruz did not have the state's best interests in mind. Cruz portrayed Dewhurst as just another moderate Republican. It wasn't so much that Dewhurst was a moderate, but that, as Lieutenant Governor, he served as President of the state Senate, a position that required a lot of deal-cutting and horse trading. Cruz ultimately trounced Dewhurst, 57% to 43%. He took every major Texas county, piling up margins as high as 73%-27% in west Texas' El Paso County. In Houston's Harris County, the state's largest, he won 64%-36%. From there, he had little trouble beating his opponent in the general election, Democrat Paul Sadler, a lawyer from Henderson and a former Texas House member, 56%-41%.

Cruz immediately established himself during his early months in office as a strong intellectual voice for the far right in the Senate, following in the iconoclastic mold of DeMint. Summarizing what he would do to enact a conservative agenda, Cruz told *National Review*, "What it takes is backbone, the willingness to stand and fight for those principles in the face of opposition and derision. Of those who have firm principles, even fewer have the backbones to stand for those principles when the heat is on."

Cruz won ecstatic reviews from conservative activists for his aggressiveness on issues ranging from Obama administration nominees to foreign policy. But his hyper-confident style won him few friends among his new Senate colleagues. When he reviewed the origins of the Bill of Rights to California Democrat Dianne Feinstein at a Judiciary Committee hearing in March, she snapped, "It's fine you want to lecture me on the Constitution. I appreciate it. Just know that I've been here a long time." After he used his initial Senate floor speech to lambast the new health care law, Iowa Democrat Tom Harkin chastised him for continuing the conservative "obsession" with the issue. When Arizona Republican John McCain complained about Cruz lending assistance to Paul during his 13-hour talking filibuster against nominating a new CIA director because of the government's drone policy, he referred to them as "wacko birds."

But Cruz didn't seem to care. At a conservative awards dinner, he joked, "It is wonderful to be among friends or, as some might say, fellow wacko birds." A *Texas Tribune* poll in March showed his favorability rating back home at 39 percent, seven percentage points higher than that of his Texas GOP colleague John Cornyn.

As 2013 progressed, Cruz eclipsed fellow freshman Republican Sen. Marco Rubio, whom *Time* had anointed on its cover as the party's "savior." He opposed Rubio's efforts to enact a comprehensive immigration reform bill while helping to spearhead the fight against expanded background checks on gun sales. But he had an even bigger goal in mind. He sought to block a vote on a continuing resolution to fund the federal government past the Sept. 30 budget deadline unless Congress barred spending any money to implement the Affordable Care Act. "I believe we can win this fight," he told reporters and conservative activists. But other Republicans weren't buying it; North Carolina Sen. Richard Burr called it "the dumbest idea I've ever heard." The resulting government shutdown damaged the GOP brand, and Cruz took a significant share of the blame. In September he staged a 21-hour talking marathon on the Senate floor in which he memorably read portions of Dr. Seuss's "Green Eggs and Ham" as a bedtime story to his two young daughters supposedly watching on C-SPAN.

But the episode thrilled tea party activists who were itching for a confrontation with the president they despised, and caused Cruz's star to shine even brighter in conservative circles—Cruz won a number of straw polls at conservative events during and after the shutdown. He traveled across the country giving speeches, accompanied by his father Rafael, who introduced him with the assertion, "He will not compromise!" His poll numbers as a potential 2016 presidential candidate crept upward, reaching double digits in some mid-2014 surveys. He made what was perceived as one small step toward a race in May 2014, when his Canadian citizenship was officially terminated.

By February 2014, Cruz was emboldened to the point where he objected to a deal crafted by Minority Leader Mitch McConnell of Kentucky that would require 51 votes instead of 60 to raise the debt ceiling. The lower threshold would give senators like McConnell in tough reelection races the political cover to vote against the increase while ensuring the chances that it would pass and government could continue to function. Cruz later said it enraged his colleagues more than any of his actions, but was unrepentant. "It's part of the reason why I've said many times that I think the biggest divide we've got in this country is not between Republicans and Democrats," he told *The New Yorker*. "It's between entrenched politicians in Washington in both parties and the American people."

Cruz again planted himself squarely in the center of a prominent debate in August, when lawmakers were considering legislation to deal with a growing Central American refugee crisis at the borders of Texas and Mexico. Cruz met with a dozen House conservatives urging them to oppose any legislation that continued a program delaying deportation proceedings for certain undocumented immigrants brought to the country illegally as children. House GOP leaders were forced to pull the plan from the floor, delaying the August recess, and eventually passing a bill that was widely seen as too far to the right for the Democratically-controlled Senate to find acceptable. Republican Rep. Peter King of New York, a frequently quoted antagonist of Cruz, told *The Washington Post:* "The Obama White House should put Ted Cruz on the payroll." Cruz helped lead the charge in Republicans' fight to hold up Department of Homeland Security funds unless Obama reversed his executive orders on immigration in early 2015, though he eventually backed down after Senate GOP leaders decided to fold, leading some House conservatives to grumble that he'd abandoned them after pushing them to take up the fight.

Cruz became the first major Republican into the presidential race when he launched his long-expected presidential bid in March 2015 at Liberty University, a hotbed of social conservatism founded by the late Jerry Falwell. But his star had faded somewhat with the base since his first years in office—he began the race in the low single digits in national polling, stuck in the second tier of a crowded GOP field.

Undeterred, Cruz kept up his bomb-throwing rhetorical approach on the campaign trail, seeking to put together a coalition of religious and economic ultra-conservatives. His calls to "abolish the IRS" and Common Core national education standards earned regular cheers on the campaign trail. Cruz leaned hard into religious liberty arguments as well, introducing legislation for a Constitutional amendment that would reinstate states' rights to bar gay marriage just days before the Supreme Court legalized it nationwide. "The way you win [the White House] … is you draw a line in the sand," he declared at the Club for Growth's annual meeting in early 2015.

Cruz's accusation that President Obama had "inflamed racial tensions" with a speech following rioting in Baltimore drew the usual mix of centrist scorn and conservative cheers, and he was one of the few Republicans to defend fellow presidential candidate and media mogul Donald Trump when Trump described most Mexican undocumented immigrants as "rapists" and "criminals."

FIRST DISTRICT

Louie Gohmert (R)

Elected 2004, 6th term; b. Aug. 18, 1953, Pittsburg; TX A&M U., B.A. 1975, Baylor U., J.D. 1977; Baptist; married (Kathy); 3 children.

Military Career: Army, 1978-82.

Elected Office: Smith Cnty. Dist. Court judge, 1993-2002.

Professional Career: Practicing atty., 1982-92; Chief justice, TX 12th Court of Appeals, 2002-03.

DC Office: 2243 RHOB, 20515, 202-225-3035; Fax: 202-226-1230; Website: gohmert.house.gov.

State Offices: Longview, 903-236-8597; Lufkin, 936-632-3180; Marshall, 903-938-8386; Nacogdoches, 936-715-9514; Tyler, 903-561-6349.

Committees: *Judiciary:* Constitution & Civil Justice; Crime, Terrorism, Homeland Security & Investigations (VChmn). *Natural Resources:* Energy & Mineral Resources; Federal Lands; Oversight & Investigations (Chmn).

Group Ratings

	ADA	ACLU	AFL-CIO	LCV	ITI	COC	HAFA	ACU	CFG	FRC
2014	15%	22%	–	3%	60%	50%	91%	96%	97%	100%
2013	10%	C	19%	7%	C	69%	C	96%	94%	C

National Journal Ratings

	2013 LIB	—	2013 CONS
Economic	24%	—	76%
Social	0%	—	87%
Foreign	15%	—	77%
Composite	17%	—	84%

Key Votes of the 113th Congress

1. Sandy storm spending	N	5. Medical Marijuana	N	9. Syrian Rebels Training	N
2. Violence Against Women Act	N	6. Farm Bill	N	10. Keystone pipeline	Y
3. Guantanamo Bay Detainees	N	7. Afghanistan Combat	N	11. Immigration Exec. Action	N
4. Abortion 20-week ban	Y	8. NSA Phone Data Collection	Y	12. Bipartisan budget deal	N

Election Results

2014 general	Louie Gohmert (R)	115,084	(77%)	$690,899	$18,462	$369
	Shirley McKellar (D)	33,476	(23%)	$31,399		
2014 primary	Louie Gohmert (R)	unopposed				

Prior winning percentages: 2012 (71%), 2010 (90%), 2008 (88%), 2006 (68%), 2004 (62%)

Population		Race and Ethnicity		Income	
Total:	712,524	White	63.4%	Median Income:	$43,301
Urban:	35.3%	Black	18.1%		*(340 of 435)*
Suburban:	13.8%	Latino	16.4%	Under $50,000	56.1%
Rural:	50.9%	Asian	1.0%	$50,000-$99,999:	27.9%
Land area:	8,486	Two races	0.8%	$100,000-$199,999:	13.4%
Pop/sq. mi.:	84.0	White Ethnic	17.5%	$200,000 or more:	2.6%
Born in state:	71.0%			Poverty Rate	19.1%
		Education			
Age Groups		H.S. grad or less:	47.2%	**Work**	
Under 18:	25.1%	Some college:	33.0%	White collar:	27.8%
18 to 34:	23.1%	College degree, 4 yr.:	13.6%	Blue collar:	41.5%
35 to 64:	36.7%	Post-grad study:	6.1%	Sales and service:	30.7%
Over 64:	15.1%				
		Military		Govt. workers:	12.1%
		Veterans/active duty:	8.8%		

East Texas: Tyler, Longview

The gently rolling land of East Texas was settled by Tennessee farmers in the years before the Civil War. It sits at the western edge of Scots-Irish America, a swath of territory that starts in the Appalachian ridge and is inhabited by a combative, honor-bound, and highly religious populace. A

Voter Turnout	
2013 Total Citizen 18+	496,754
2014 House Turnout	148,560
2014 Turnout as % CVAP	29.9%
2012 Turnout as % CVAP	51.1%

hundred years ago, this was one of the poorest parts of America, where farmers scratched a living off the land and hoped for good weather and decent prices in the marketplace. When a peach blight in the early 20th century wiped out much of the local fruit industry, many farmers turned to growing roses, which proved ideally suited to the climate and soil of East Texas. By the 1940s, more than half the nation's rose bushes were grown within 10 miles of Tyler, which has become known for its annual Texas Rose Festival. In 2014, the festival drew 120,000 visitors. Today, about 75% of the garden roses in the country find their way through Tyler and are distributed throughout the country.

Longview, which in the 1870s was the western terminus of the Southern Pacific Railroad, became a trading center for wagon trains and local cotton growers and timber cutters. In 1943, the Big Inch pipeline began sending millions of barrels of crude oil from the "Black Giant" oil field near Longview—at the time, the largest ever in the state—to the East for refining. Since then, the Longview area has become an industrial center for earth-moving equipment and chemicals. Eastman Chemical Co., which once produced chemicals for film company Eastman Kodak, has had a booming business because of lower natural gas prices; it recently completed an expansion at its Longview site.

The fields and woodlands around Nacogdoches—the oldest city in Texas—are the site where debris from the Space Shuttle *Columbia* fell in February 2003. An organized search by 25,000 people recovered more than 84,000 pieces—38% of the shuttle. The Keystone XL pipeline runs through the district in eastern Wood and Smith counties and western Nacogdoches County. Unlike the pipeline's northern end, mired in regulatory holdups, oil began flowing through the Gulf Coast portion in January 2014. Supporters claimed that it brought a $3.6 billion boost to the area.

The 1st Congressional District of Texas, covering the heart of East Texas, is made up of 12 counties, the most populous being Tyler's Smith County and Longview's Gregg County. East Texas is ancestrally Democratic, a region that responded to the populist rhetoric of presidential candidate William Jennings Bryan in the 1890s and President Franklin D. Roosevelt in the 1930s and 1940s. But Republicans began making inroads in Tyler and Longview in the 1950s. By the time Republican George W. Bush ran for reelection as Texas governor in 1998, it was solidly Republican. In 2014, singer and conservative activist Ted Nugent was disinvited from

2012 Presidential Vote
Mitt Romney (R)................181,835 (72%)
Barack Obama (D) 69,858 (28%)

2008 Presidential Vote
John McCain (R)................178,520 (69%)
Barack Obama (D) 78,918 (30%)

Cook Partisan Voting Index: R+24

a July Fourth musical festival in Longview after he referred to President Barack Obama as a "subhuman mongrel." The city paid Nugent $16,000 not to attend, which led him to call the mayor a racist.

Democrats held onto the district until the 2003 redistricting, masterminded by former House Majority Leader Tom DeLay of Texas to give the GOP a strong advantage. GOP-friendly Smith and Gregg counties were added to the district, and overall the district today is solidly Republican. In the Cook Political Report's PVI listings, this is the 17th most Republican district in the nation. But it is only the 7th most Republican district in Texas.

Louie Gohmert (R)

Louie Gohmert, a Republican first elected in 2004, is a devout tea party conservative with a knack for provoking Democrats, fellow Republicans, and even the U.S. Park Police. He had his "15 minutes of fame" when he challenged John Boehner for speaker in 2015.

Gohmert grew up in Mount Pleasant and graduated on an Army scholarship at Texas A&M University, where he was class president. He got a law degree from Baylor University, then served as a captain in the Army. He practiced law in Tyler and spent a decade as a district court judge. Republican Gov. Rick Perry named him chief justice of the Texas Appellate Court in 2002. He earned a reputation as a tough law-and-order judge with a knack for attracting attention. In 1996, he ordered an HIV-positive convicted car thief, as a condition of probation, to notify future sexual partners of his HIV status and to obtain written consent from them before engaging in sexual activity.

After the 2003 redistricting in Texas, Gohmert was one of six Republicans to challenge four-term Democratic Rep. Max Sandlin, who had a moderate voting record but was a close ally of Minority Leader Nancy Pelosi. Gohmert led in the primary with 42% of the vote to 30% for lawyer John Graves. In the runoff campaign, few differences separated the two conservatives, and Gohmert prevailed 57%-43%. Graves carried nine of the 13 counties, but Gohmert won 77% of the vote in his home base of Smith County, where half the votes were cast. In the general election, Gohmert linked Sandlin to the national Democratic Party and their 2004 presidential nominee, John Kerry. The result wasn't close. Gohmert beat Sandlin, 61%-38%, with 79% in Smith County.

In the House, Gohmert established a conservative voting record, with occasional dissents from the party line. When the bailout for the financial industry came to the House floor in 2008, he made a motion to adjourn the chamber "so we don't do this terrible thing to our nation." It was defeated 394-8. When the House voted in 2012 to remove the archaic word "lunatic" from laws referring to the mentally ill, there was one dissenting vote—Gohmert's. "Not only should we not eliminate the word 'lunatic' from federal law when the most pressing issue of the day is saving our country from bankruptcy, we should use the word to describe the people who want to continue with business as usual in Washington," he said.

Gohmert has little regard for President Barack Obama. In 2013, he sought to amend a bill to block Obama from using federal funds to play golf until he reinstated White House tours that had fallen victim to budget cuts. In 2012, he drew criticism from Sen. John McCain of Arizona, after Gohmert joined several Republicans in accusing a top State Department official of having ties to the Muslim Brotherhood. He called McCain a "numbnut," and later apologized, but, he said, only for using the word "numb." In March 2013, Gohmert reportedly had a tense encounter with the Park Police—one officer described him as "rude and irate"—after getting ticketed for illegally parking his car at the Lincoln Memorial. He argued that being a House member allowed him to park in an official space.

Gohmert's work on the Judiciary Committee has drawn television talk-show invitations and scorn from liberal blogs for his provocative views. He drew widespread attention for his appearance on CNN in 2010 to discuss "terror babies"—an alleged effort to send pregnant women into the United States to give birth to children eligible for U.S. passports who could be trained to carry out attacks. Anderson Cooper pressed Gohmert to offer proof. "Had somebody done this in your courtroom, you would have asked for evidence, and you have none," Cooper said. An irate Gohmert replied: "This isn't a courtroom. We're trying to protect America." During a September 2013 press conference in Cairo after he and two other House conservatives met with new Egyptian leader Abdel Fatah el-Sissi, the Army general who had ousted the Muslim Brotherhood government in a coup two months earlier, Gohmert compared him to George Washington.

Gohmert, who often speaks to tea party groups, has tangled with House Speaker Boehner. In the usually pro forma election of speaker, Gohmert in 2013 instead voted for Allen West, a Florida Republican and fellow firebrand who had just lost his House seat. Two years later, Gohmert launched his own candidacy as conservative unhappiness with Boehner deepened. He received three votes, including his own, while GOP Rep. Daniel Webster of Florida got 12 votes, though he stepped into the race the morning of the vote. Allies referred to Gohmert as "a stalking horse" who encouraged others to enter the contest. "It was never about me," Gohmert said the next day. His objective, he later said, was to force a second ballot, which might have led Boehner to step aside. To the dismay of some Boehner supporters, Gohmert then became chairman of the Natural Resources Subcommittee on Oversight and Investigations. He said that the Obama administration needed to be "held accountable for their actions that are hindering America's potential of becoming energy independent."

Gohmert has never been reelected with less than 68% of the vote. Former Smith County GOP Chair Marcia Daughtrey told the *Texas Tribune* in 2012 that constituents admire his challenges to political correctness.

SECOND DISTRICT

Ted Poe (R)

Elected 2004, 6th term; b. Sept. 10, 1948, Temple; Abilene Christian U., B.A. 1970, U. of Houston, J.D. 1973; Restorationist; married (Carol); 4 children.

Military Career: U.S. Air Force Reserve, 1970-76.

Elected Office: Harris Cnty. judge, 1981-2003.

Professional Career: Teacher; Practicing atty.; Asst. dist. atty., 1973-81.

DC Office: 2412 RHOB, 20515, 202-225-6565; Fax: 202-225-5547; Website: poe.house.gov.

State Offices: Houston and Kingwood, 281-446-0242.

Committees: *Foreign Affairs:* Europe, Eurasia & Emerging Threats; Terrorism, Nonproliferation & Trade (Chmn). *Judiciary:* Courts, Intellectual Property & the Internet; Crime, Terrorism, Homeland Security & Investigations.

Group Ratings

	ADA	ACLU	AFL-CIO	LCV	ITI	COC	HAFA	ACU	CFG	FRC
2014	5%	5%	–	3%	100%	71%	74%	79%	76%	88%
2013	5%	C	14%	4%	C	69%	C	79%	79%	C

National Journal Ratings

	2013 LIB	—	2013 CONS
Economic	28%	—	72%
Social	41%	—	58%
Foreign	43%	—	56%
Composite	38%	—	62%

Key Votes of the 113th Congress

1. Sandy storm spending	N	5. Medical Marijuana	N	9. Syrian Rebels Training	N
2. Violence Against Women Act	Y	6. Farm Bill	Y	10. Keystone pipeline	Y
3. Guantanamo Bay Detainees	N	7. Afghanistan Combat	N	11. Immigration Exec. Action	Y
4. Abortion 20-week ban	Y	8. NSA Phone Data Collection	Y	12. Bipartisan budget deal	N

Election Results

2014 general	Ted Poe (R)	101,936	(68%)	$507,176 $5,796
	Niko Letsos (D)	44,462	(30%)	
2014 primary	Ted Poe (R)	unopposed		

Prior winning percentages: 2012 (65%), 2010 (89%), 2008 (89%), 2006 (68%), 2004 (56%)

Population		Race and Ethnicity		Income	
Total:	722,575	White	49.5%	Median income:	$69,833
Urban:	59.1%	Latino	29.6%		*(64 of 435)*
Suburban:	40.9%	Black	12.3%	Under $50,000	34.2%
Rural:	0.0%	Asian	6.3%	$50,000-$99,999:	31.9%
Land area:	329	Two races	1.4%	$100,000-$199,999:	24.0%
Pop/sq. mi.:	2,199.1	White Ethnic	20.0%	$200,000 or more:	9.9%
Born in state:	50.2%			Poverty Rate	10.9%
		Education			
Age Groups		H.S. grad or less:	32.3%	**Work**	
Under 18:	24.2%	Some college:	28.2%	White collar:	44.9%
18 to 34:	25.7%	College degree, 4 yr.:	25.2%	Blue collar:	36.3%
35 to 64:	39.8%	Post-grad study:	14.3%	Sales and service:	18.8%
Over 64:	10.3%				
		Military		Govt. workers:	9.1%
		Veterans/active duty:	5.9%		

West Houston and Northern Suburbs

Houston, which remains one of the fastest growing metropolitan areas in the country, has become an internationally renowned energy hub that provides the largest share of the nation's jobs in oil and gas extraction. The city's Energy Corridor, a sprawling 4,000-acre business district on both sides of

Voter Turnout	
2013 Total Citizen 18+	458,439
2014 House Turnout	150,026
2014 Turnout as % CVAP	32.7%
2012 Turnout as % CVAP	53%

the Katy Freeway, is a state-established district whose vision is to become the world's premier location for energy-related businesses. It houses more than 300 companies and 90,000 employees, including U.S. headquarters for BP, ConocoPhillips and Shell. Generation Park, a 4,000-acre master-planned enterprise park for corporate and residential development, is under construction on the Sam Houston Tollway. Phase One began in 2012. Developers have described this area in northeast Houston as a "sleeping giant."

The oil and gas rush in South Texas' Eagle Ford Shale region alone has supported 155,000 jobs in Texas, according to a 2013 University of Texas-San Antonio study. Many of those field operation and management jobs have been centered in Harris County, which grew by 5.5% from 2010 to 2013 to 4.3 million and is the third largest county in the nation. Its rate of growth from 2000 to 2013 was 27%, though many of its most affluent residents are moving to Montgomery County. New office space and condominiums have been concentrated on the west side of Houston, where expanding energy corporate headquarters are found. Ten of the county's top 11 employers are related to the oil-and-gas industry.

The 2nd Congressional District of Texas is a swirl-shaped district located entirely within Harris County. It comes close to the downtown, covering Rice University, the museum district, and Memorial Park, which at 1,466 acres is larger than New York City's Central Park. It also takes in the heavily Democratic neighborhood of Montrose, which is the center of Houston's gay and lesbian community and also claims President Lyndon Baines Johnson (who lived there after he graduated from Southwest Texas State) and Howard Hughes as former residents.

The district includes some of the most Republican precincts in Harris County. It is one of the two—of Houston's seven districts—where whites make up a majority of the population. President Barack Obama

2012 Presidential Vote		
Mitt Romney (R)	157,094	(63%)
Barack Obama (D)	88,751	(36%)
2008 Presidential Vote		
John McCain (R)	150,665	(62%)
Barack Obama (D)	91,087	(37%)
Cook Partisan Voting Index:	R+16	

narrowly carried the county in the 2012 presidential election, but Mitt Romney easily won the 2nd with 63% of the vote.

Ted Poe (R)

Ted Poe, a Republican first elected in 2004, is best known for his loquaciousness on the House floor. He has used his chairmanship of a Foreign Affairs Subcommittee to engage on terrorism issues. As chairman of the all-GOP House Immigration Reform Caucus, he has become an interesting lawmaker to watch as conservatives wrestle with the issue.

A sixth-generation Texan, Poe got a bachelor's degree from Abilene Christian University and enlisted in the Air Force Reserve. He received his law degree from the University of Houston and became a prosecutor in Harris County where, he boasts, he never lost a jury trial. Poe then became a criminal court judge in the county, becoming a judicial celebrity during his 22 years on the bench for meting out humiliating "Poe-tic justice" punishments to criminals. He required murderers to hang pictures of their victims in their prison cells and ordered drunken drivers and shoplifters to stand at the entrances to taverns and stores carrying signs publicizing their offenses. He gained national recognition as a legal commentator on national television.

In 2003, Poe stepped down as a judge to run for Congress. In a six-candidate Republican primary, his high name recognition and bench experience earned him 61% of the vote and the right to challenge Democratic Rep. Nick Lampson. The incumbent was running in largely unfamiliar territory because of the 2003 Republican-engineered redistricting of congressional boundaries. Lampson had a moderate voting record, a low-key style, and was a big booster of NASA. At first, national Republicans fretted about his fundraising and his seemingly complacent campaign. Lampson outspent Poe nearly 2-to-1. On Election Day, the new district's shift of residents and its solid Republican bent were decisive. Lampson led 68%-31% in Jefferson County, the area he had previously represented and where 36% of votes were cast. But Poe won 70%-28% in Harris County, which cast 58% of the votes. Overall, Poe won 56%-43%. He has not been seriously challenged for reelection.

In the House, Poe began with a relatively moderate voting record for a Republican from Texas, but has become a more loyal party vote since President Barack Obama took office. He joined fellow Texas Republicans John Carter and Joe Barton in amending a House-passed spending bill in 2011 to prevent the Environmental Protection Agency from regulating greenhouse gas emissions. Saying that they did not go far enough in reducing spending, he opposed compromises that Republicans struck with Obama on the 2011 budget and the January 2013 tax and spending deal to avert the so-called "fiscal cliff." One of Poe's causes has been the Keystone XL pipeline, designed to bring oil from Canada to Texas refineries; he pushed for legislation to put the decision in the hands of Congress instead of the White House.

In the Immigration Reform Caucus, Poe has sought tighter enforcement at the border with Mexico. He travels regularly to the border to meet directly with local law enforcement officials. In November 2014, he took the lead in advocating legislation to prohibit funding to implement President Barack Obama's executive action on immigration. Federal judges in Texas later delayed its implementation. Poe successfully amended spending bills in both 2011 and 2012 to add $10 million each year for fencing and border infrastructure, but failed to add $100 million for more detention beds for immigrants facing deportation.

In 2013, Poe became chairman of the Foreign Affairs Committee's panel on terrorism, nonproliferation, and trade, giving him a megaphone for his view that Pakistan has done too little to help the U.S. in the war on terror. He has urged Twitter to remove accounts associated with terrorist groups. "Terrorists should not have access to an American-controlled social media platform so they can kill, rape, pillage, and burn," he told the House in February 2015. In April, the panel held hearings on legislation to repeal the ban on exports of crude oil, which he strongly backed. He worked with Democrat Zoe Lofgren of California on early versions of the successful legislation to ban the National Security Agency from searching for data without a search warrant. In May 2015, the House Ethics Committee announced that it was investigating a May 2013 trip to Azerbaijan by a delegation of nine House members, including Poe; he contended that the ethics panel had cleared the trip in advance as part of his work on the Foreign Affairs Committee. In July, the committee dismissed the case.

Poe takes a keen interest in victim's rights causes, something he said stems partly from his maternal grandfather's death at the hands of a drunk driver. In February 2013, he and Blake Farenthold were the only two Texas Republicans to join Democrats in supporting the reauthorization of the Violence Against Women Act. In May 2015, Obama signed the Victims of Human Trafficking Act, which Poe cosponsored with Democratic Rep. Carolyn Maloney of New York. The bill supports victims with a fund collected from trafficking fines.

Poe is perhaps best known to C-SPAN junkies for his loquaciousness. In 2009-10, according to C-SPAN, Poe spoke on 234 of the 317 days that the chamber was in session—far ahead of second-place finisher Democrat Sheila Jackson Lee, who represents an adjacent district in Houston. "The people of Southeast Texas can't come up here and do it, so I speak for them," he told *the Houston Chronicle*. Poe typically ends speeches on the House floor with his trademark, "And that's just the way it is." In 2015, many of his floor speeches focused on the inadequate response to the threat posed by the Islamic State, or ISIS. He said in July, "The President has recently admitted that the United States really doesn't even have a complete strategy against ISIS. Now, isn't that lovely?"

THIRD DISTRICT

Sam Johnson (R)

Elected May 1991, 12th full term; b. Oct. 11, 1930, San Antonio; S. Methodist U., B.B.A. 1951, George Washington U., M.S.I.A. 1974; Methodist; married (Shirley); 3 children (1 deceased).

Military Career: U.S. Air Force, 1950-79 (Korea & Vietnam), Vietnam prisoner of war, 1966-73.

Elected Office: TX House, 1985-91.

Professional Career: Homebuilder.

DC Office: 2304 RHOB, 20515, 202-225-4201; Website: samjohnson. house.gov.

State Offices: Plano, 469-304-0382.

Committees: *Ways & Means:* Health; Social Security (Chmn). *Joint Committee on Taxation*.

Group Ratings

	ADA	ACLU	AFL-CIO	LCV	ITI	COC	HAFA	ACU	CFG	FRC
2014	0%	0%	–	0%	100%	69%	76%	96%	81%	100%
2013	0%	C	15%	4%	C	77%	C	92%	78%	C

National Journal Ratings

	2013 LIB	—	2013 CONS
Economic	12%	—	87%
Social	26%	—	73%
Foreign	24%	—	68%
Composite	22%	—	78%

Key Votes of the 113th Congress

1. Sandy storm spending	N	5. Medical Marijuana	N	9. Syrian Rebels Training	N
2. Violence Against Women Act	NV	6. Farm Bill	Y	10. Keystone pipeline	Y
3. Guantanamo Bay Detainees	N	7. Afghanistan Combat	N	11. Immigration Exec. Action	Y
4. Abortion 20-week ban	Y	8. NSA Phone Data Collection	N	12. Bipartisan budget deal	N

Election Results

2014 general	Sam Johnson (R)	113,404	(82%)	$1,261,812
	Paul Blair (Green)	24,876	(18%)	
2014 primary	Sam Johnson (R)	31,178	(81%)	
	Harry Pierce (R)	3,004	(8%)	
	Cami Dean (R)	2,435	(6%)	
	Josh Loveless (R)	2,086	(5%)	

Prior winning percentages: 2012 (unopposed), 2010 (66%), 2008 (60%), 2006 (63%), 2004 (86%), 2002 (74%), 2000 (72%), 1998 (91%), 1996 (73%), 1994 (91%), 1992 (86%), 1991 special (53%)

Population		Race and Ethnicity		Income	
Total:	765,486	White	61.7%	Median income:	$80,912
Urban:	39.9%	Latino	14.6%		*(29 of 435)*
Suburban:	58.8%	Asian	12.6%	Under $50,000	28.9%
Rural:	1.3%	Black	8.1%	$50,000-$99,999:	31.0%
Land area:	668	Two races	2.4%	$100,000-$199,999:	29.9%
Pop/sq. mi.:	1,145.9	White Ethnic	19.9%	$200,000 or more:	10.2%
Born in state:	45.2%			Poverty Rate	8.0%
		Education			
Age Groups		H.S. grad or less:	20.6%	**Work**	
Under 18:	27.8%	Some college:	27.9%	White collar:	51.6%
18 to 34:	20.8%	College degree, 4 yr.:	33.0%	Blue collar:	38.1%
35 to 64:	42.1%	Post-grad study:	18.4%	Sales and service:	10.3%
Over 64:	9.2%				
		Military		Govt. workers:	9.9%
		Veterans/active duty:	6.1%		

Northern Dallas Suburbs: Plano, McKinney

The Dallas and Fort Worth metropolitan area, once a railroad junction and cotton-shipping center, now has 7 million people, the fourth largest in the nation and more than all of Texas had during World War II. More than two-thirds of them live beyond the city limits of Dallas and Fort Worth.

Voter Turnout	
2013 Total Citizen 18+	485,898
2014 House Turnout	138,280
2014 Turnout as % CVAP	28.5%
2012 Turnout as % CVAP	57.8%

In Dallas, the city's old elite occupies the mansions of Highland Park north of downtown, but its business and professional classes have moved farther up into Collin County's scrub-covered hills. Collin's population exploded from 67,000 in 1970 to 855,000 in 2013, with an 8 percent increase since 2010. It is now the sixth-largest and the second-wealthiest county in Texas. The median income in the county is the highest in the Dallas Metroplex. Its biggest city is Plano, with 274,000 people. The former farming community is the corporate headquarters of Dr. Pepper, J.C. Penney, and HP Enterprise Services. In April 2014, Toyota announced that it was moving its headquarters and 4,000 employees to a state-of-the-art campus in Plano. The relocation will be the largest to Plano since Ross Perot's Electronic Data Systems moved there in the 1980s. Toyota officials reviewed more than 100 other potential sites before they decided to shift from the nation's bluest mega-state to its reddest.

Plano and near-by Richardson have Asian-American populations that are among the highest in the state. Sixty Chinese cultural organizations are based in North Texas, mostly in Collin County, serving more than 30,000 Chinese-American residents. Recruited by then-Gov. Rick Perry, the Chinese telecommunications company Huawei established its North American headquarters in Plano in 2001. More than 20,000 Indian-American residents moved into Collin County from 2000 to 2010, with many working at high-tech firms and medical centers in the region. The state demographer of Texas projected in 2015 that the population will increase to 3.8 million by 2050.

Despite the growing diversity, one traditional Texas pastime continues strong in these parts: high school football. Collin County boasts some of the top high school football programs in the country, and the well-heeled suburb of Allen opened a $60 million high school football stadium in 2012 that seats 18,000 fans, with amenities comparable to many college football facilities. Eagle Stadium reopened in 2015 after more

2012 Presidential Vote		
Mitt Romney (R)	175,383	(64%)
Barack Obama (D)	93,290	(34%)
2008 Presidential Vote		
John McCain (R)	165,158	(62%)
Barack Obama (D)	100,440	(37%)
Cook Partisan Voting Index:	R+17	

than $10 million of concrete and other repairs, which took more than a year.

The 3rd Congressional District of Texas, based entirely within Collin County, includes most of the county and centers on Plano. Collin is heavily Republican, and in 2012, Mitt Romney took 65% of the countywide vote, even as he lost to President Barack Obama in neighboring Dallas County by a 16-point margin.

Sam Johnson (R)

Sam Johnson, a hard-line Republican first elected in 1991, is the only remaining founder of the Republican Study Committee—the influential caucus of House conservatives—still serving in the chamber. As chairman of the Ways and Means Subcommittee on Social Security, he has a prominent perch from which to oversee the program.

Johnson grew up in Dallas and graduated from Southern Methodist University and got a master's degree from George Washington University. He was a director of the Air Force Fighter Weapons (Top Gun) School, and as a fighter pilot, flew 87 combat missions during the wars in Korea and Vietnam. After his F-4 was shot down over North Vietnam during his 25th mission, he was imprisoned from 1966 to 1973 in the "Hanoi Hilton," where he spent 42 months in solitary confinement and was forced into leg stocks for more than two years. He weighed 120 pounds upon his release, having subsisted on river weeds and pig fat, and was left with a slight stoop in his walk and a disfigured hand. "His scars bear witness to his tenacity and toughness," House Speaker John Boehner said in a February 2013 speech honoring the 40th anniversary of his release. In 2009, the Congressional Medal of Honor Society gave Johnson its highest civilian honor, the National Patriots Award.

After his military service, Johnson started a homebuilding company and was elected to the Texas House in 1984. He was elected to Congress in a 1991 special election, after Republican Steve Bartlett resigned to become mayor of Dallas. Johnson ran second in the primary, behind former Peace Corps director Tom Pauken. In the runoff, he emphasized his war record and won 53%-47%. Although his district has shifted substantially from its north Dallas roots, he has not faced a serious challenger since then.

Johnson is among the House's most conservative members. He was a founder of the Conservative Action Team, the precursor to the Republican Study Committee, which has pressed Republican leaders to support goals ranging from a balanced budget amendment to shutting down the National Endowment for the Arts.

Johnson has pushed for lower taxes. Every two years, he offers a constitutional amendment to repeal the 16th Amendment, which authorized the federal income tax. He has supported Boehner on most tax and spending measures, but drew the line at the late 2012 compromise to avert a so-called "fiscal cliff," calling it "a bad bill that raises taxes on families and small businesses." On Ways and Means, where he is the senior Republican behind Chairman Paul Ryan, Johnson has raised the specter of the U.S. "corporate structure" incrementally relocating overseas to avoid high rates if the tax code is not reformed. Earlier, he sponsored the successful repeal in 2000 of the earnings limit for Social Security recipients, and he was a leading proponent of pension reform that was enacted in 2006.

In 2012, he called for Internal Revenue Service Commissioner Douglas Shulman to resign, contending the agency was helping illegal immigrants defraud the government. Johnson cited a report that people sought $4.2 billion in refundable child tax credits using IRS identification numbers, which are issued to non-citizens seeking tax refunds. He spent four years on a bipartisan working group on comprehensive immigration reform legislation. But, with fellow Texas GOP Rep. John Carter, he withdrew in September 2013 with a statement blasting President Barack Obama for his disregard of the Constitution "to advance his political agenda."

Johnson also focuses on military issues. He staunchly opposed setting arbitrary troop withdrawal deadlines in Afghanistan. When Obama announced an economic aid plan for Egypt in 2011, Johnson blasted the idea: "America has no business sending large sums of money to volatile nations in the Middle East that may end up with radical Islamists at the helm." He helped to enact the Military Family Tax Relief Act of 2003, which doubled the death benefit for families of active service members who pass away and also reduced taxes for those families.

Johnson gained national attention in February 2007 when he spoke emotionally on the House floor against a plan by Democratic Speaker Nancy Pelosi to set a timetable to withdraw from Iraq. Invoking his memories of Vietnam, he said, "I know what it's like to be far from home and hear that your country and your Congress don't care about you." In June 2014, he criticized Obama for "ill-advised, inappropriate and immature" actions in the swap for Bowe Bergdahl, a different kind of prisoner of war who had walked away from his base in Afghanistan. Even though he and Sen. John McCain of Arizona, also a well-known Vietnam prisoner of war, shared a cell for 18 months, they have had a chilly political relationship. Johnson strongly backed George W. Bush for the 2000 GOP presidential nomination, stating that McCain "cannot hold a candle to George Bush."

With the reelection defeat in 2014 of Ralph Hall of Texas, Johnson became the oldest Republican in Congress at age 84; three House Democrats are slightly older. He regularly draws GOP primary challengers who seek to get their name in front of the public for the day when he decides to retire.

FOURTH DISTRICT

John Ratcliffe (R)

Elected 2014, 1st term; b. Oct. 20, 1965, Chicago, IL; U. of Notre Dame, B.A. 1987, Southern Methodist U., J.D. 1989; Catholic; married (Michele); 2 children.

Elected Office: Heath City Cncl., 2001-04; Heath mayor, 2004-12.

Professional Career: Practicing atty.; Heath Bd. of Adjustment, 1997-98; Heath Planning & Zoning Comm., 1998-2001; E. TX dist. chief, Anti-Terrorism & Nat'l Security, 2004-07; U.S. atty., TX E. dist., 2007-08.

DC Office: 325 CHOB, 20515, 202-225-6673; Fax: 202-225-3332; Website: ratcliffe.house.gov.

State Offices: Rockwall, 972-771-0100; Sherman, 903-813-5270; Texarkana, 903-823-3173.

Committees: *Homeland Security:* Cybersecurity, Infrastructure Protection & Security Technologies (Chmn); Transportation Security. *Judiciary:* Immigration & Border Security; Regulatory Reform, Commercial & Antitrust Law.

Election Results

2014 general	John Ratcliffe (R)..................unopposed		$1,340,131	$135,673
2014 prim.	John Ratcliffe (R)........................ 22,271	(53%)		
runoff	Ralph Hall (R)............................. 19,899	(47%)		
2014 primary	Ralph Hall (R)............................. 29,848	(45%)		
	John Ratcliffe (R)........................ 18,917	(29%)		
	Lou Gigliotti (R)........................ 10,601	(16%)		

Population		Race and Ethnicity		Income	
Total:	710,641	White	72.6%	Median income:	$45,384
Urban:	22.3%	Latino	12.6%		*(312 of 435)*
Suburban:	32.8%	Black	11.4%	Under $50,000	53.4%
Rural:	44.8%	Asian	0.9%	$50,000-$99,999:	29.0%
Land area:	8,201	Two races	1.6%	$100,000-$199,999:	14.3%
Pop/sq. mi.:	86.7	White Ethnic	19.3%	$200,000 or more:	3.3%
Born in state:	66.8%			Poverty Rate	16.9%
		Education			
Age Groups		H.S. grad or less:	48.6%	**Work**	
Under 18:	24.5%	Some college:	32.2%	White collar:	31.1%
18 to 34:	20.4%	College degree, 4 yr.:	13.0%	Blue collar:	41.3%
35 to 64:	39.2%	Post-grad study:	6.3%	Sales and service:	27.6%
Over 64:	15.9%				
		Military		Govt. workers:	14.4%
		Veterans/active duty:	10.8%		

Northeast Texas: Eastern Dallas Area, Denison

The Red River Valley is hardscrabble farm country along an unnavigable river. First settled in the 1830s, in the days of the Texas Republic, many counties here reached their population peak around 1900, when a large extended farm family worked every 160 acres. It includes towns like Denison, due north of Dallas, best-known as the birthplace of Dwight Eisenhower, and Sherman, which was the site of a major race riot in 1930 when a black farm worker accused of rape was attacked by a white mob. To the east is Texarkana, noteworthy because its neat grid streets cross the Texas-Arkansas state line, which is straddled by the city's downtown post office. The contrast between the laws of the two states has created competition for which side of the border is more attractive. Arkansas accepted the Medicaid expansion of the 2010 health care law, for example, but Texas did not. This small city and its hinterland have produced three recent presidential candidates: Ross Perot grew up in Texarkana, while Bill Clinton and Mike Huckabee hail from Hope, Arkansas, just 30 miles east.

Voter Turnout	
2013 Total Citizen 18+	511,298
2014 House Turnout	115,085
2014 Turnout as % CVAP	22.5%
2012 Turnout as % CVAP	50.8%

Northeast Texas in 1912 sent Democrat Sam Rayburn to Congress, where he became the powerful House speaker from 1940 until his death in 1961 (except for two terms when Republicans had the majority). The region was once a Democratic bastion, with a sentimental regard for Confederate veterans and a seething hatred of Wall Street bankers. That was Rayburn's politics, and he arguably was the most skillful lawmaker of the 20th century. Today, Rayburn's style of politics has almost completely vanished from the area. Rafael de la Garza, a Republican-turned-Democrat who unsuccessfully ran for Collin County district attorney in 2010, told *The Dallas Morning News* he had trouble getting his backers to put up yard signs or publicly endorse him because they feared neighbors would assume they also supported the deeply unpopular President Barack Obama.

The 4th Congressional District of Texas is the lineal descendant of the seat that Rayburn held, and still includes his hometown of Bonham in Fannin County, which houses a Rayburn museum. But it is quite a different district today. In Rayburn's time, it was a farm district, separate and distinct from citified Dallas. Today, it retains its farm counties, but they are only a short hop on the interstate from the Dallas-Fort Worth Metroplex, and about one-third of the district's residents live in the DFW metropolitan area. Rockwall County, at the edge of the Metroplex, is the third-fastest growing county in the nation; its population increased 94% between 2000 and 2013. With one of the highest median

2012 Presidential Vote		
Mitt Romney (R)	189,554	(74%)
Barack Obama (D)	63,559	(25%)

2008 Presidential Vote		
John McCain (R)	180,772	(70%)
Barack Obama (D)	75,910	(29%)

Cook Partisan Voting Index:	R+25

household incomes in the state at just over $86,000, the county is home to upwardly mobile families who lean Republican.

In 1940, the year Rayburn became speaker, his district voted 90% for Franklin D. Roosevelt. In 2012, the 4th District voted 74% for Republican Mitt Romney, which placed it among his top 3% of districts in the nation.

John Ratcliffe (R)

For Republican John Ratcliffe, elected in 2014, the easy part was running unopposed in the general election. But his primary race drew national attention: He ousted 91-year-old incumbent Ralph Hall, the oldest member of Congress, who was seeking his 18th term. With the retirement of Democrat John Dingell, Hall's defeat meant that the 114th Congress became the first since the 1940s without a World War II veteran.

Ratcliffe, the youngest of six children, earned a scholarship to Notre Dame, where he graduated in three years, and got his law degree from Southern Methodist University. He served eight years as mayor in the town of Heath. He took credit for the town being the only municipality in Rockwall County to not have a tax increase during those years.

He was nominated by President George W. Bush as U.S. attorney for northern and eastern Texas, where his caseload included terrorism, illegal immigration, drug trafficking, public corruption and Internet child predators. During that time, he led a national operation, which resulted in the single-day arrest of more than 300 illegal immigrants and the subsequent successful prosecution of hundreds who committed identity theft and Social Security fraud, plus a $4.5 million criminal penalty for the company that hired them. Later, he became a partner in a law firm run by former Attorney General John Ashcroft.

In the primary, Ratcliffe sought to refer to the issue of Hall's age without offending seniors, who make up more than 15 percent of the district's electorate. He told voters he admired Hall as a man and as a politician while portraying the congressman's Washington experience as a liability. After so much time in the nation's capital, "the problems are getting worse, not better," Ratcliffe said in one ad.

In terms of substance, little distinguished the two. Hall, a former Democrat who switched parties following the redistricting in 2003, had one of the most conservative voting records in the House. He won the backing of tea party favorite Rep. Michele Bachmann of Minnesota and former Arkansas Gov. Mike Huckabee. Ratcliffe was endorsed by the Club for Growth and the Senate Conservatives Fund. He opposed raising the debt ceiling. When asked about continuing with John Boehner as House speaker, he said that the House should have "better leadership at the top." A bigger difference was tactical: Ratcliffe pursued a data-driven approach, while Hall favored old-style stumping. He cited his background in law enforcement—particularly, immigration and homeland security—as a chief reason to seek higher office.

In the six-person primary in March, Hall led 45%-29%. That triggered a runoff in May. Turnout was one-third lower this time and committed conservatives flocked to Ratcliffe. He edged out Hall, 52.8%-47.2%, a margin of 2,372 votes.

In the House, Ratcliffe joined the Judiciary Committee plus Homeland Security, where he chaired the Cybersecurity, Infrastructure Protection and Security Technologies Subcommittee, which has a timely portfolio. He worked with Homeland Security Chairman Michael McCaul, a fellow Texan, on bipartisan passage in April of the National Cybersecurity Protection Advancement Act, which Ratcliffe said "will help safeguard personal privacy and prevent cyber intrusions from occurring." He urged the resignation of Katherine Archuleta as director of the Office of Personnel Management before she finally stepped down in July 2015 following revelations of massive data breaches of federal records. Even with her departure, he said, there were "serious vulnerabilities that must be fully addressed."

Contrary to his campaign comments, Ratcliffe voted for Boehner for speaker once he took office. "I certainly don't see myself as an establishment guy or a leadership guy, but I also don't see myself as a bomb-thrower who's anti-establishment or [an] anti-leadership guy," he said in a February 2015 interview with *The Texas Tribune*. "Republicans need a big tent," he added.

FIFTH DISTRICT

Jeb Hensarling (R)

Elected 2002, 7th term; b. May 29, 1957, Stephenville; TX A&M U., B.A. 1979, U. of TX Austin, J.D. 1982; Episcopalian; married (Melissa); 2 children.

Professional Career: Practicing atty., 1982-84; TX dir., U.S. Sen. Phil Gramm, 1985-89; Exec. dir., NRSC, 1991-93; Communications exec., 1993-2002.

DC Office: 2228 RHOB, 20515, 202-225-3484; Fax: 202-226-4888; Website: hensarling.house.gov.

State Offices: Athens, 903-675-8288; Dallas, 214-349-9996.

Committees: *Financial Services* (Chmn: ex officio member of each subcommittee).

Group Ratings

	ADA	ACLU	AFL-CIO	LCV	ITI	COC	HAFA	ACU	CFG	FRC
2014	5%	0%	–	3%	100%	69%	85%	96%	90%	100%
2013	0%	C	10%	7%	C	85%	C	96%	89%	C

National Journal Ratings

	2013 LIB	—	2013 CONS
Economic	5%	—	94%
Social	0%	—	87%
Foreign	5%	—	86%
Composite	7%	—	93%

Key Votes of the 113th Congress

1. Sandy storm spending	N	5. Medical Marijuana	N	9. Syrian Rebels Training	Y
2. Violence Against Women Act	N	6. Farm Bill	N	10. Keystone pipeline	Y
3. Guantanamo Bay Detainees	N	7. Afghanistan Combat	N	11. Immigration Exec. Action	Y
4. Abortion 20-week ban	Y	8. NSA Phone Data Collection	N	12. Bipartisan budget deal	Y

Election Results

2014 general	Jeb Hensarling (R)	88,998	(85%)	$3,408,252	$60
	Ken Ashby (Lib)	15,264	(15%)		
2014 primary	Jeb Hensarling (R)	unopposed			

Prior winning percentages: 2012 (64%), 2010 (71%), 2008 (84%), 2006 (62%), 2004 (65%), 2002 (58%)

Population		Race and Ethnicity		Income	
Total:	726,896	White	56.3%	Median income:	$43,698
Urban:	31.3%	Latino	26.4%		*(337 of 435)*
Suburban:	32.3%	Black	13.6%	Under $50,000	56.0%
Rural:	36.4%	Asian	1.7%	$50,000-$99,999:	26.2%
Land area:	4,053	Two races	1.5%	$100,000-$199,999:	14.8%
Pop/sq. mi.:	179.4	White Ethnic	13.9%	$200,000 or more:	3.0%
Born in state:	64.8%			Poverty Rate	17.3%
		Education			
Age Groups		H.S. grad or less:	50.8%	**Work**	
Under 18:	26.1%	Some college:	29.8%	White collar:	29.3%
18 to 34:	22.8%	College degree, 4 yr.:	12.9%	Blue collar:	44.9%
35 to 64:	38.2%	Post-grad study:	6.5%	Sales and service:	25.8%
Over 64:	12.9%				
		Military		Govt. workers:	14.1%
		Veterans/active duty:	7.4%		

Eastern Dallas Suburbs, Northeast Texas

Not all of Dallas is glitz and postmodern marble. East of downtown is an older Dallas with neighborhoods of old mansions, modest bungalows and shotgun houses. Some of these areas have been renovated and rebuilt, with chic cafes and trendy stores. Other once middle-class neighborhoods are

Voter Turnout	
2013 Total Citizen 18+	467,516
2014 House Turnout	104,262
2014 Turnout as % CVAP	22.3%
2012 Turnout as % CVAP	46.9%

filling up with immigrants from Mexico and are again noisy with children as they were in the 1950s when people moved here not from Mexico or Central America, but from the almost all-Anglo counties of North and Central Texas. In March 2015, the Dallas County Commission voted its approval of President Barack Obama's executive order that halted deportation of illegal immigrants. The measure was approved on a 4-1 party-line vote, with the sole Republican dissenting that the executive action was "an extreme overreach by the president."

The 5th Congressional District includes much of east and southeast Dallas County, including neighborhoods in east Dallas and suburban Mesquite, which has become a destination for immigrants moving up the economic ladder. The population is 28% Hispanic and 14% black. In April 2015, the Breitbart.com website ran a story headlined, "Mesquite Texas—The Gun Show Capital of America," which described its several hundred shows annually as a mix of "trade shows, swap meets and raw capitalism," with crowds that are usually male, white and over 40. The district also covers a more upscale slice of Dallas inside the LBJ freeway, including parts of Lakewood and White Rock Lake.

2012 Presidential Vote		
Mitt Romney (R)	137,239	(65%)
Barack Obama (D)	73,085	(34%)
2008 Presidential Vote		
John McCain (R)	137,698	(62%)
Barack Obama (D)	83,216	(37%)
Cook Partisan Voting Index:	R+17	

About one-third of the district's voters are in Dallas County. The 5th also takes in six other counties in East Texas, the largest of which are Henderson and Kaufman, both high-growth areas. One of the booming small towns is Forney, which has become a destination for young families; it was hit by a powerful cyclone in April 2012. Anderson County was the site in 1910 of the little-noted Slocum Massacre in which a white mob attacked and killed as many as 25 black residents and forced the remainder to flee, according to a January 2015 report on Texas Public Radio. Each of the outlying counties is more heavily Republican than the Dallas portion of the district. As rural areas have swung away from the Democrats, the district switched from being a battleground in the early 1990s to safely Republican. In 2012, Mitt Romney won 65 percent of the presidential vote in the 5th.

Jeb Hensarling (R)

Jeb Hensarling, a Republican first elected in 2002, is a disciplined and politically savvy conservative who is often in the thick of debates on economic policy. He served as Republican Conference chairman before stepping down in 2013 to chair the Financial Services Committee and lead the GOP attacks on the Dodd-Frank financial reform law. His hardline stances occasionally put him at odds with the corporate world, including his initiative to shut down the Export-Import Bank.

Hensarling grew up in Morris County in East Texas. He worked on his father's poultry farm near College Station as a teenager and decided that he did not want to be a farmer. In high school, he started a Republican club and began organizing political events. He graduated from Texas A&M University and got a law degree from the University of Texas. After briefly practicing law, he got a job on the staff of Sen. Phil Gramm. Hensarling rose quickly through the ranks and became Gramm's campaign manager in 1990. When GOP senators chose Gramm to chair the National Republican Senatorial Committee, he named Hensarling as his executive director. Hensarling later returned to Texas to become vice president of communications for Green Mountain Energy, a local utility, and was co-founder of Family Support Assurance, a firm that aided child support collections.

After the redistricting in 2001, Republican Rep. Pete Sessions, who had represented the 5th District, decided to run in the new and more affluent 32nd District on the north side of Dallas. Hensarling became the front-runner for the Republican nomination in the 5th. Like his mentor, Gramm, he listed cutting taxes as his top priority. Against four opponents, he won the nomination with 54% of the vote.

Democrats nominated Ron Chapman, a former Dallas County appellate judge. Hensarling referred to his opponent as "Judge Softie" for his record on capital murder cases. The folksy Chapman tried to paint Hensarling as too extreme for the district, but his message failed to take hold, especially as high-profile Republicans came through the district with endorsements for Hensarling, including President George W. Bush, Vice President Dick Cheney and Gramm. Hensarling won 58%-40% and has been reelected easily since.

In the House, Hensarling was the Texas delegation's most conservative member in 2011-12, according to *National Journal's* annual rankings. But his votes are not always business friendly. He told *Fortune* in 2014: "I do not subscribe to the theory that what is good for GM is necessarily good for America." A *Wall Street Journal* profile in October 2014 wrote that he "may be the most important Republican elected official you've never heard of."

Hensarling frequently pushes Republican leaders to take more conservative positions. He has sometimes differed with John Boehner, most notably in 2006 when he managed Indiana Republican Mike Pence's unsuccessful challenge to Boehner for minority leader. Hensarling was a key ally at the time of another GOP leader, Eric Cantor of Virginia. In 2007, he became chairman of the Republican Study Committee, which typically advocated conservative views. In that role, Hensarling crafted a seven-point strategy for House Republicans that included a constitutional amendment to limit spending and a flat tax on goods and services to replace the federal income tax. The party embraced his platform, except for his call for a moratorium on spending earmarks in appropriations bills. After the 2008 election, Hensarling was named to head fundraising for the National Republican Congressional Committee.

He helped lead the conservative revolt in 2008 against the call by President George W. Bush for the Troubled Asset Relief Program, which Boehner was charged with selling to his caucus. With Cantor's backing, he easily succeeded Pence as conference chairman after the 2010 election. When Hensarling stepped down from that post to become Financial Services chairman, he endorsed Georgia Rep. Tom Price over Washington's Cathy McMorris Rodgers—a Boehner favorite—as his successor. But McMorris Rodgers won.

As Financial Services chairman, Hensarling has been known for firmly standing his ground, whether it's on a cable TV show or at a committee hearing. When he took over in 2013, he clashed on several issues with California's Maxine Waters, the panel's fiery new ranking Democrat who is as liberal as he is conservative. One area of disagreement was the Federal Housing Administration, which Hensarling accused of overextending credit to risky borrowers. He has called for the abolition of the government-sponsored mortgage giants Fannie Mae and Freddie Mac, which he said abused their power. But he predicted that doing so would take several years. "Nobody can wave a magic wand and get this done overnight," he told *The Dallas Morning News* in November 2012.

Hensarling pushed through his committee the Protecting American Taxpayers and Homeowners (PATH) Act in July 2013 on a largely party-line vote. The bill called for winding down Fannie Mae and Freddie Mac and almost completely privatizing the housing finance industry. It drew criticism from the real estate and home-builder lobbies and did not muster enough support to make it to the House floor. His bill to kill the Emergency Homeowners' Relief Program, which was set up to provide loans to recently unemployed homeowners who have missed mortgage payments, prompted a veto threat from Obama. Hensarling ran into another problem in 2013 when he objected to a flood-insurance bill; his erstwhile ally Cantor took it away from him. The bill eventually passed the House, 306-91.

The Wall Street Journal reported in March 2013 that financial industry executives were nervous about Hensarling's plans to push legislation that could require them to hold significantly more capital and set up new barriers between their federally insured deposits and other activities, including trading and investment banking. But Hensarling has been generally supportive of Wall Street. In 2012, he likened the 2010 Dodd-Frank law to "a legislative drive-by shooting," and aggressively criticized the work of the Consumer Financial Protection Bureau created by that law. He later contended that the law's burdensome rules had become a drag on economic growth.

Hensarling has waved off criticism, saying he should be judged by his entire six-year stint as chairman. "I play a long game," he told *National Journal* in September 2014. Oklahoma Republican Frank Lucas, term-limited as chairman of the Agriculture Committee, publicly mulled a challenge that fall to Hensarling for the Financial Services chairmanship, citing frustration among some panel members. Lucas eventually decided against it. Hensarling has remained a prodigious fundraiser, drawing on his financial industry connections to take in more than $4 million during the 2012 election cycle.

Two major tests loomed for Hensarling as 2015 began. One was the Terrorism Risk Insurance Act (TRIA), which backstops financial losses from a terrorist attack. The Senate voted overwhelming in July 2014 to extend the program for seven years, two years longer than Hensarling's committee, and a bipartisan group of TRIA's backers expressed opposition to the changes in the law that he had proposed, such as raising the amount of losses needed to trigger the federal backstop. Several roadblocks, including the view by Hensarling that Senate Democrats had become inflexible, prevented final action in 2014. Congress acted swiftly in early 2015, after the GOP took Senate control, to enact a six-year renewal.

The other challenge for Hensarling was reauthorization of the Export-Import Bank, a government-sponsored agency that helps sell American-made products to businesses and governments with limited or no access to capital. Hensarling and other conservatives disparaged the bank as a shining example of crony capitalism and a precursor to the higher-stakes battle over tax reform. But business interests mounted a sustained lobbying campaign to have its charter extended, and succeeded in getting one until June 2015. At the insistence of Hensarling and other conservatives, Boehner at that point agreed not to bring a renewal to the floor. But with other members remaining supportive of the Ex-Im Bank, including some Republicans on Financial Services, the speaker did not rule out a subsequent House vote.

Hensarling has maintained his focus on fiscal issues. He served on the Simpson-Bowles deficit commission in 2010 and made clear that he preferred that it concentrate on federal spending. He opposed the commission's findings as insufficient in containing health care costs. He disdained the 2011 budget-cutting deal that Obama struck with Republicans, saying it did not cut spending enough and that "we probably all deserve to be tarred and feathered."

After the protracted standoff over raising the federal debt limit in 2011, Boehner selected him to work with Washington Democratic Sen. Patty Murray as co-chairs of the Joint Select Committee on Deficit Reduction, the so-called "super committee," which was given several months to forge a bipartisan deal or face the alternative of more automatic spending "sequesters." The effort proved fruitless, leading to what Hensarling called "a huge blown opportunity." He blamed the Democrats' unwillingness to negotiate and said Republicans were willing to increase taxes if Democrats agreed to pro-growth tax reform. He blamed Obama for trying to fit $450 billion in stimulus spending into the super committee's mandate and vowing to veto any plan that altered Medicare without raising taxes on the highest earners. Having Hensarling as chairman limited Boehner's exposure to conservative second-guessing.

He hasn't hid his continuing ambition for a top leadership post, but he also has failed to step to the plate. In a May 2014 radio interview, he did not rule out a challenge to Boehner for speaker after the November election. "I'm not going to say 'no,' just in case the invitation comes," he told conservative host Hugh Hewitt. When Cantor unexpectedly lost his primary in June 2014, Hensarling declined to run for majority leader despite intensive discussions and encouragement from conservatives who wanted a credible challenger to Majority Whip Kevin McCarthy of California, who did not hesitate in his own bid. "After prayerful reflection, I have come to the conclusion that this is not the right office at the right time for me and my family," Hensarling said. Whether he eventually makes a move that could be a risky career step, or instead remains an influential chairman, likely will come down to whether he can garner the votes.

SIXTH DISTRICT

Joe Barton (R)

Elected 1984, 16th term; b. Sept. 15, 1949, Waco; Texas A&M U., B.A. 1972, Purdue U., M.S. 1973; Methodist; divorced; 6 children.

Professional Career: Asst. to V.P., Ennis Business Forms, 1973-81; White House Fellow, U.S. Dept. of Energy, 1981-82; Consultant, Atlantic Richfield Oil & Gas Co., 1982-84.

DC Office: 2107 RHOB, 20515, 202-225-2002; Fax: 202-225-3052; Website: joebarton.house.gov.

State Offices: Arlington, 817-543-1000; Ennis, 972-875-8488.

Committees: *Energy & Commerce* (Chmn Emeritus): Communications & Technology; Energy & Power; Health; Oversight & Investigations.

Group Ratings

	ADA	ACLU	AFL-CIO	LCV	ITI	COC	HAFA	ACU	CFG	FRC
2014	5%	0%	–	6%	80%	73%	70%	92%	79%	100%
2013	5%	C	20%	0%	C	85%	C	87%	72%	C

National Journal Ratings

	2013 LIB	—	2013 CONS
Economic	16%	—	84%
Social	0%	—	87%
Foreign	15%	—	77%
Composite	14%	—	86%

Key Votes of the 113th Congress

1. Sandy storm spending	N	5. Medical Marijuana	N	9. Syrian Rebels Training	NV
2. Violence Against Women Act	N	6. Farm Bill	Y	10. Keystone pipeline	NV
3. Guantanamo Bay Detainees	N	7. Afghanistan Combat	N	11. Immigration Exec. Action	Y
4. Abortion 20-week ban	Y	8. NSA Phone Data Collection	Y	12. Bipartisan budget deal	N

Election Results

2014 general	Joe Barton (R)	92,334	(61%)	$1,659,549	$1,865
	David Cozad (D)	55,027	(36%)	$12,827	
	Hugh Chauvin (Lib)	3,635	(2%)		
2014 primary	Joe Barton (R)	32,618	(73%)		
	Frank Kuchar (R)	12,272	(27%)		

Prior winning percentages: 2012 (58%), 2010 (66%), 2008 (62%), 2006 (61%), 2004 (66%), 2002 (70%), 2000 (88%), 1998 (73%), 1996 (77%), 1994 (76%), 1992 (72%), 1990 (67%), 1988 (68%), 1986 (56%), 1984 (57%)

Population		Race and Ethnicity		Income	
Total:	730,955	White	51.3%	Median income:	$57,477
Urban:	51.7%	Latino	22.7%		*(146 of 435)*
Suburban:	39.8%	Black	18.9%	Under $50,000	42.6%
Rural:	8.5%	Asian	5.2%	$50,000-$99,999:	31.7%
Land area:	1,607	Two races	1.5%	$100,000-$199,999:	21.8%
Pop/sq. mi.:	454.9	White Ethnic	15.0%	$200,000 or more:	3.9%
Born in state:	59.9%			Poverty Rate	13.6%
		Education			
Age Groups		H.S. grad or less:	37.3%	**Work**	
Under 18:	27.0%	Some college:	33.3%	White collar:	37.2%
18 to 34:	23.2%	College degree, 4 yr.:	21.0%	Blue collar:	40.8%
35 to 64:	39.4%	Post-grad study:	8.4%	Sales and service:	22.1%
Over 64:	10.4%				
		Military		Govt. workers:	13.5%
		Veterans/active duty:	8.7%		

Southwest Metroplex: Arlington, Fort Worth Area

The Dallas-Fort Worth Metroplex—a name even the locals use—has spread outward from its historic nodes in downtown Dallas and downtown Fort Worth. Although Dallas is the larger population center, much of the development has moved west, across the plains and the barely perceptible

Voter Turnout	
2013 Total Citizen 18+	488,111
2014 House Turnout	150,996
2014 Turnout as % CVAP	30.9%
2012 Turnout as % CVAP	53%

Balcones Escarpment, the geologist's boundary between green and grassy East Texas and brown, barren and hilly West Texas. The plains have been filled in with subdivisions and shopping centers under the enormous Texas sky. Among the larger suburbs is Arlington, right between Dallas and Fort Worth and an easy highway commute to both cities. Named in 1877 after Robert E. Lee's hometown in Virginia (another suburb, but not quite so booming as the Texas locale), its location has been ideal as a site for regional attractions like Six Flags over Texas and the Ballpark in Arlington, commissioned by the former part-owner of the Texas Rangers, George W. Bush. In 2009, the Dallas Cowboys opened the $1.1 billion domed AT&T Stadium in Arlington, which hosted the 2011 Super Bowl. (Redistricting in 2011 put both complexes just outside the 6th District.)

The city's population of 380,000 in 2013 was 27% Hispanic, 19% African-American, and 7% Asian. Enrollment at the University of Texas campus in Arlington reached a new high of 36,000 students in 2015, making it the second-largest in the UT system behind Austin. GM's Arlington assembly plant, which produces the company's popular and highly profitable SUVs, employs about 4,200 workers and completed in 2014 a $530 million stamping facility expansion. In April 2015, GM announced plans for a $1.3 billion expansion of the plant. As Arlington has filled up, the big growth now is to the south in Mansfield, where the population more than doubled to 61,000 between 2000 and 2013. Klein Tools, a major tool manufacturer, relocated from the Chicago suburbs in 2013 to set up shop in Mansfield. In 2014, a five-year-old boy found a dinosaur fossil on land behind a shopping center in Mansfield.

The 6th Congressional District of Texas includes most of Arlington and the southern and northeastern fringes of Fort Worth to the west. Nearly three-fourths of the people live in Arlington and Tarrant County, which is the 16th largest in the nation. Much of the rest are in fast-growing Ellis County, directly south of Dallas County. To the southeast, the

2012 Presidential Vote
Mitt Romney (R)................146,985 (58%)
Barack Obama (D) 103,444 (41%)

2008 Presidential Vote
John McCain (R)................148,503 (57%)
Barack Obama (D) 109,854 (42%)

Cook Partisan Voting Index: R+11

district includes small-town Navarro County, home to the Collin Street Bakery, which ships its famed fruitcakes around the world during Christmas season each year. Politically, this territory was ancestrally Democratic for many years, then became solidly Republican, but its growing minority population—non-Hispanic whites are barely a majority—has reduced the GOP margins at the presidential level.

Joe Barton (R)

Republican Joe Barton, first elected in 1984, has been an outspoken champion for the oil industry and a leading global-warming skeptic on Capitol Hill. Barton's influence waned after he was term-limited and lost his bid to remain as chairman of the Energy and Commerce Committee, which followed his unpopular defense of BP during the 2010 oil spill disaster in the Gulf of Mexico.

Barton grew up in Ennis, in then-rural Ellis County. He graduated from Texas A&M and got a master's degree in industrial administration from Purdue, worked as an oil company engineer, and then was a White House fellow at the Energy Department in 1981. When Republican Rep. Phil Gramm ran successfully for the Senate in 1984, Barton ran for his House seat. Barton won the Republican runoff by only 10 votes, and he won the general election with 57% of the vote.

Barton has enjoyed a degree of success on the busy Energy and Commerce Committee. In 1995, he became chairman of the panel's Oversight and Investigations Subcommittee and used the platform to conduct extensive hearings of the nation's food and drug laws. The result was enactment, with bipartisan support, of significant modernization of the Food and Drug Administration, which encouraged the agency to more quickly review innovative drugs and medical devices. In 1999, he became chairman of the Energy and Power Subcommittee with jurisdiction over energy legislation. He managed to reach agreement in 2001 with ranking committee Democrat John Dingell of Michigan on higher fuel economy standards. Barton pressed for action on electricity regulation, but he retreated from requiring utilities to join regional transmission organizations and sought to encourage them to do so. His bill passed the House but died in the Senate.

In 2004, after committee Chairman Billy Tauzin of Louisiana stepped down because of health problems, Barton was his successor. He aroused some partisan ire that September when he blocked committee Democrats' demand for information about Vice President Dick Cheney's 2001 energy task force. But he worked successfully to win Democratic votes on some issues and to defend and expand the committee's jurisdiction. Telecommunications issues are a major responsibility of Energy and Commerce, and in 2006 the House passed Barton's bill to make it easier for telephone companies to enter the broadband market. Influential Democrats opposed the measure, and it died in the Senate. Barton became a leading opponent of a Federal Communications Commission plan to increase regulation of broadband service companies.

Barton fought the Democrats' health care proposals tooth-and-nail in 2009, but was usually outgunned by California's Henry Waxman, who had taken over as chairman of Energy and Commerce. On some issues, Barton sought common ground with Waxman, as he had with Dingell. He worked with committee Democrats on a proposal to approve generic versions of biologic drugs following a 12-year period of exclusivity for the inventor to recoup costs.

Barton's contrariness has sometimes landed him in controversy. Discussing global warming with former Democratic Vice President Al Gore at a hearing in 2007, Barton told Gore, who'd written a book on the topic, "You're not just off a little. You're totally wrong." In a December 2009 C-SPAN interview, Barton said, "There's ample evidence that warming generically, however it is caused, is a net benefit to mankind." He was the party's lead spokesman against the sweeping climate change bill passed by the House in June 2009. He offered his own bill that would have set emission standards for new coal and natural gas plants, but would not have penalized existing plants. Barton's plan failed on a party-line vote. In March 2010, he introduced a bill to prevent the Environmental Protection Agency from regulating greenhouse gases; it passed the House in April 2011 with unanimous GOP support, but did not move in the Democratic-controlled Senate. When some scientists pronounced 2012 the hottest year on record in the continental United States, Barton scoffed to *The Dallas Morning News:* "What are they going to say in the next three or four years when [the temperature] goes down a little bit?"

Barton hoped to retain the committee chairmanship when Republicans regained control in 2010, despite GOP-imposed term limits. He organized an aggressive campaign to boost his chances against Michigan's Fred Upton, the Republican next in line on the panel. A 22-page critique of the moderate Upton's record was circulated that accused him of being a "part-time Republican." Though Barton said he wasn't behind the effort, many Republicans were skeptical. The leadership-controlled GOP Steering Committee picked Upton, and Barton chose not to challenge its decision.

The chairmanship defeat capped what had been a tough year for Barton. News reports surfaced in February that Barton had earned nearly $100,000 from an interest in natural gas wells that he bought from a campaign donor who had given him advice on energy policy. He said his investment was legal and presented no conflict with his legislative responsibilities. Then came the June committee hearing at which BP executives were grilled on the catastrophic spill in the Gulf. Barton apologized to the executives for the Obama administration's decision to force it to establish a $20 billion fund—which he called "a shakedown"—to compensate people who lost their livelihoods in the aftermath. In light of the public's anger over the spill, his remarks sparked a political uproar. GOP leaders threatened to strip him of his ranking spot on the committee, and Barton issued a retraction.

In the past, Barton sometimes strayed to the center on cultural issues. But since Barack Obama became president, he has been a rock-solid conservative. In 2012, most House Republicans sought to end the administration's energy loan guarantee program following the collapse of California solar company Solyndra Corp. Barton, who helped write the 2005 law setting up the program, initially called for reforming it instead. But he ended up voting for the "No More Solyndras" legislation after *The Wall Street Journal's* editorial page and other conservatives ratcheted up pressure on him. The House approved in 2011 his bill to repeal a 2007 law requiring light bulbs to be 25% to 30% more efficient, but the result fell short of the two-thirds support required under House rules. In 2015, he took the lead in seeking to lift the ban on crude-oil exports from the United States, which generated considerable Republican support.

At home, Barton was criticized by Democrats for seeking to keep Ellis County outside the Environmental Protection Agency's Dallas region in applications of the stringent rules of the Clean Air Act. Ellis County is home to three cement producers and other companies whose political action committees and executives were big contributors to Barton's campaigns, and the county produced 40% of the industrial emissions in North Texas. Barton said there was no connection between the contributions and his action and argued that there was no scientific basis for Ellis County's inclusion. In 2004, the EPA decided otherwise and ordered the county to take steps to reduce air pollution.

Barton has had some political disappointments. He ran for the Senate in 1993 after Democrat Lloyd Bentsen resigned to become President Bill Clinton's Treasury secretary. He finished third with 14% of the vote in the all-party primary. In September 2001, when Gramm announced his retirement from the Senate, Barton considered running for his seat. But the Bush White House favored Texas Attorney General John Cornyn and Barton stepped aside. After the 2006 election, he made a bid for minority leader, but discovered that John Boehner of Ohio had wrapped up sufficient votes to win. Barton withdrew after six days.

He has been reelected easily in the 6th District. He suffered a heart attack in December 2005 but made a full recovery. He reportedly got into a spat with fellow Texas Republican Lamar Smith in early 2011 over the state's redistricted congressional boundaries. Smith sought to evenly split four new districts between Republicans and Democrats, giving Texas' booming Hispanic population minority-majority seats in the Dallas and Houston areas. But Barton wanted to keep Republican voters dominant in three of the new districts. His plan passed the state legislature, but ultimately was tossed out in federal court, leading to a court-drawn map that made his 6th District seat more Democratic. He seems secure for now but, with other Republicans, faces demographic challenges in the Metroplex.

SEVENTH DISTRICT

John Culberson (R)

Elected 2000, 8th term; b. Aug. 24, 1956, Houston; Southern Methodist U., B.A. 1981, S. TX Col. of Law, J.D. 1988; Methodist; married (Belinda); 1 child

Elected Office: TX House, 1987-2001, maj. whip, 1999-2001.

Professional Career: Jim Culberson Advertising, 1981-85; Practicing atty., 1988-2000.

DC Office: 2372 RHOB, 20515, 202-225-2571; Fax: 202-225-4381; Website: culberson.house.gov.

State Offices: Houston, 713-682-8828.

Committees: *Appropriations:* Commerce, Justice, Science & Related Agencies (Chmn); Homeland Security; Transportation, HUD & Related Agencies.

Group Ratings

	ADA	ACLU	AFL-CIO	LCV	ITI	COC	HAFA	ACU	CFG	FRC
2014	0%	5%	–	6%	80%	83%	66%	64%	60%	100%
2013	0%	C	20%	11%	C	75%	C	84%	78%	C

National Journal Ratings

	2013 LIB	—	2013 CONS
Economic	31%	—	69%
Social	34%	—	62%
Foreign	5%	—	86%
Composite	26%	—	75%

Key Votes of the 113th Congress

1. Sandy storm spending	Y	5. Medical Marijuana	N	9. Syrian Rebels Training	Y
2. Violence Against Women Act	N	6. Farm Bill	N	10. Keystone pipeline	Y
3. Guantanamo Bay Detainees	N	7. Afghanistan Combat	N	11. Immigration Exec. Action	Y
4. Abortion 20-week ban	Y	8. NSA Phone Data Collection	N	12. Bipartisan budget deal	Y

Election Results

2014 general	John Culberson (R)	90,606	(63%)	$691,304	$20,552
	James Cargas (D)	49,478	(35%)	$74,635	
	Gerald Fowler (Lib)	3,135	(2%)		
2014 primary	John Culberson (R)	unopposed			

Prior winning percentages: 2012 (61%), 2010 (81%), 2008 (56%), 2006 (59%), 2004 (64%), 2002 (89%), 2000 (74%)

Population		Race and Ethnicity		Income	
Total:	741,599	White	44.6%	Median income:	$66,451
Urban:	79.0%	Latino	31.5%		(77 of 435)
Suburban:	21.0%	Black	12.2%	Under $50,000	38.0%
Rural:	0.0%	Asian	9.6%	$50,000-$99,999:	27.2%
Land area:	195	Two races	1.7%	$100,000-$199,999:	21.8%
Pop/sq. mi.:	3,805.1	White Ethnic	15.5%	$200,000 or more:	13.0%
Born in state:	46.2%			Poverty Rate	13.0%
		Education			
Age Groups		H.S. grad or less:	26.5%	**Work**	
Under 18:	26.7%	Some college:	23.6%	White collar:	51.0%
18 to 34:	24.4%	College degree, 4 yr.:	29.5%	Blue collar:	35.8%
35 to 64:	39.4%	Post-grad study:	20.4%	Sales and service:	13.2%
Over 64:	9.4%				
		Military		Govt. workers:	7.9%
		Veterans/active duty:	5.3%		

West Houston and Suburbs

When George H.W. Bush moved from Midland in West Texas to Houston in 1960, he bought a house in Briarwood in what were then the western outskirts of the fast-growing city. He returned to Houston in 1993 after losing his reelection bid for the presidency and built a new house one mile

Voter Turnout	
2013 Total Citizen 18+	433,620
2014 House Turnout	143,219
2014 Turnout as % CVAP	33%
2012 Turnout as % CVAP	57%

from his old one, near lush Memorial Park. The lavish Galleria, one of the largest malls in the United States, draws more than 30 million visitors a year under its impressive glass atriums, and it continues to upgrade. Downtown Houston is sprouting residential apartments. Although the sale of high-priced homes suffered during the recession, the economy of Houston remains relatively strong. Oil company revenues have been up, and many businesses moved here from the New Orleans area following the devastation of Hurricane Katrina in 2005. In 2014, Memorial Park had a double-digit increase in sales of million-dollar homes, many of them bought by energy executives. Record rains in May 2015 caused extensive flooding here, including at the Galleria.

The 7th Congressional District of Texas is the lineal descendant of the district that in 1966 elected Bush as the first Republican to represent Houston in the House. It occupied far more territory then, half of Harris County. It now includes only 17% of Harris County. In successive redistricting rounds, its boundaries have been pared back, as the population of the west side of Houston has

2012 Presidential Vote		
Mitt Romney (R)...............143,631	(60%)
Barack Obama (D) 92,499	(39%)
2008 Presidential Vote		
John McCain (R)................140,692	(59%)
Barack Obama (D) 96,866	(40%)
Cook Partisan Voting Index: R+13		

skyrocketed. Today, more than 1.5 million people live in an area where 350,000 lived when Bush was first elected. The district, based entirely in Harris County, includes most of the territory between the Katy Freeway (Interstate 10) and Westheimer Road from downtown. In Texas fashion, Katy's 26 lanes when it crosses Beltway 8 may be the widest highway in the world. The district takes in the affluent neighborhoods southwest of downtown Houston, Bellaire and a swath of Houston west of the 610 highway loop. Outside the loop is Gulfton, a predominantly Hispanic town that the *Houston Chronicle* called an "ersatz Ellis Island for economic refugees from Mexico and Central America." Continued surges of immigration from Mexico have strained the public schools in Gulfton, whose sprawling apartment complexes have become the most densely populated neighborhood in Houston.

Most of Houston's business and professional elite live within the district's boundaries: the partners of the big law firms, cutting-edge medical researchers, and society mavens. The district is also home to Rev. Joel Osteen's Lakewood evangelical megachurch, which describes itself as the largest congregation in the nation and draws more than 43,000 worshipers a week, with many more viewing the service on an internationally televised Sunday program. The church is housed in the former home of the Houston Rockets basketball team, which underwent a $95 million remodeling.

The 7th District is a solidly Republican district, but its demographics are changing. After redistricting in 2011, this became a majority-minority district: Whites are 45% of the population, Hispanics 32%, blacks 12%, and Asian Americans 10%. Among the voting age population, the growing Hispanic population skews younger and turns out to vote at a lower rate; whites maintain a slim 51% majority. Mitt Romney won 60% here in 2012, down from George W. Bush's 66% in 2004.

John Culberson (R)

John Culberson, a conservative first elected in 2000, calls himself a "Jeffersonian Republican" and is passionate about transferring power to local governments. That causes tension with serving as a senior appropriator who controls funding for several large federal agencies, including NASA, which has a major presence in his district.

Culberson grew up in Houston, the son of the owner of an advertising agency. He graduated from Southern Methodist University, South Texas College of Law, and then worked as a defense lawyer. In 1986, while still in law school at age 29, Culberson won a seat in the Texas House, where he served for 14 years. In 2000, Republican Rep. Bill Archer, who succeeded George H. W. Bush in the House, retired after being term-limited as chairman of the Ways and Means Committee. The front-runners in the GOP primary were Culberson and Peter Wareing, a Houston merchant banker and son-in-law of Texas oilman Jack Blanton. Culberson led Wareing in the first round 38%-27%. Wareing spent nearly $4 million to Culberson's $650,000, but Culberson had an extensive grassroots campaign and won the runoff four weeks later 60%-40%. The general election was no contest in the GOP-dominant district.

Culberson likes to say that his goal is to "let Texans run Texas." He ranks among the House's most conservative members, especially on social issues. When Houston veterans groups in 2011 accused a Veterans Affairs official of banning religious speech—including the words "Jesus" and "God"—during services at the cemetery there, an angry Culberson vowed to zero out the official's salary. VA officials said the claims were inaccurate, but transferred the woman to another job. He cosponsored Florida GOP Rep. Bill Posey's 2009 "birther" bill requiring future presidential candidates to offer proof of citizenship; they were responding to theories, repeatedly proven false, that President Barack Obama was born overseas (the legislation would not have applied to Obama in any case).

Culberson has shown his disdain for how Congress does its work. During the final days of the health care debate in November 2009, he attended a Capitol Hill rally of the bill's opponents and tossed loose pages of the 2,000-page document to the crowd. Like his predecessor, Archer, he dreams of junking the current tax system and replacing it with a national sales tax. Culberson sometimes goes his own way. He ruffled feathers as one of only two Texas Republicans to oppose passage of the $400 billion Medicare expansion and prescription-drug coverage in 2003.

An amateur astronomer and self-proclaimed science buff since he was a kid, Culberson is an enthusiast for NASA and has an interest in nanotechnology research, which is a specialty at Rice University. "I want to get the politicians and knuckleheads out of their way," he told the *Houston Chronicle*. He sponsored a bill in 2012 to give the space agency's administrator a 10-year term similar to that given to the FBI director, which he said would promote better planning and a return to what he believes should be its core mission of scientific research. In 2013, he called for restructuring NASA, saying it lacked vision. He joined several conservatives in getting a provision into a 2011 spending measure that banned NASA from collaborating with China's scientists.

Culberson was once an avid fan of Twitter and in 2009, was the House's top user of the social media service, according to a University of Maryland study. But in recent years he has preferred Facebook, which he said draws fewer deliberately provocative "trolls." He was an early proponent of requiring the House to post all non-emergency legislation online at least 72 hours before debate, a rules change that Republicans approved in 2011.

Culberson has a coveted spot on Appropriations, as chairman of the subcommittee that handles spending for the Commerce and Justice departments and science agencies. He has used his post to secure money for projects in his district, including medical research, flood control projects, and improvements to the Houston Ship Channel. He has fought with Houston officials who wanted money for local light rail projects, filing a formal objection with the Federal Transit Administration in December 2009 to stop a light-rail line because he said the local transit agency was in precarious financial shape—a charge agency officials said was based on outdated information. When he sought in 2012 to block funds from going to an expansion of two rail lines, the *Chronicle's* editorial page rebuked him for "trying to impose his own rules rather than work with local leaders." In May 2015, the *Chronicle* reported that he had called a truce to his war with the Metro agency. Culberson takes some credit for the Katy Freeway expansion, which combined the Interstate highway with several locally owned toll lanes.

In 2008, Culberson faced his first well-financed Democratic challenger. Wind energy executive Michael Skelly spent nearly $3.1 million, including $1 million of his own money. Culberson spent a relatively modest $1.8 million. Skelly criticized Culberson's lack of support for alternative energy and said he was not sufficiently helpful to the space program, citing Culberson's call to reduce the bureaucracy at NASA, which employs about 20,000 people locally. Culberson ran as a strong social and fiscal conservative and won, 56%-42%. Since then, he has had no trouble winning reelection.

EIGHTH DISTRICT

Kevin Brady (R)

Elected 1996, 10th term; b. April 11, 1955, Vermillion, SD; U. of SD, B.A. 1990; Catholic; married (Cathy); 2 children.

Elected Office: TX House, 1991-96.

Professional Career: Exec., The Woodlands Chamber of Commerce, 1978-96.

DC Office: 301 CHOB, 20515, 202-225-4901; Fax: 202-225-5524; Website: kevinbrady.house.gov.

State Offices: Conroe, 936-441-5700; Huntsville, 936-439-9532.

Committees: *Ways & Means:* Health (Chmn); Social Security; Trade. *Joint Committee on Taxation. Joint Economic Committee* (VChmn).

Group Ratings

	ADA	ACLU	AFL-CIO	LCV	ITI	COC	HAFA	ACU	CFG	FRC
2014	0%	0%	–	0%	80%	92%	64%	87%	67%	100%
2013	0%	C	10%	7%	C	85%	C	88%	84%	C

National Journal Ratings

	2013 LIB	—	2013 CONS
Economic	17%	—	83%
Social	16%	—	74%
Foreign	15%	—	77%
Composite	19%	—	81%

Key Votes of the 113th Congress

1. Sandy storm spending	N	5. Medical Marijuana	N	9. Syrian Rebels Training	Y
2. Violence Against Women Act	N	6. Farm Bill	N	10. Keystone pipeline	Y
3. Guantanamo Bay Detainees	NV	7. Afghanistan Combat	N	11. Immigration Exec. Action	Y
4. Abortion 20-week ban	Y	8. NSA Phone Data Collection	N	12. Bipartisan budget deal	Y

Election Results

2014 general	Kevin Brady (R)	125,066	(89%)	$2,184,912	$6,238
	Ken Petty (Lib)	14,947	(11%)		
2014 primary	Kevin Brady (R)	42,368	(68%)		
	Craig McMichael (R)	19,687	(32%)		

Prior winning percentages: 2012 (77%), 2010 (80%), 2008 (73%), 2006 (67%), 2004 (69%), 2002 (93%), 2000 (92%), 1998 (93%), 1996 (59%)

Population		Race and Ethnicity		Income	
Total:	761,764	White	68.0%	Median income:	$61,012
Urban:	15.0%	Latino	20.2%		(116 of 435)
Suburban:	64.7%	Black	7.8%	Under $50,000	41.4%
Rural:	20.3%	Asian	2.0%	$50,000-$99,999:	30.0%
Land area:	5,123	Two races	1.7%	$100,000-$199,999:	20.7%
Pop/sq. mi.:	148.7	White Ethnic	21.5%	$200,000 or more:	7.9%
Born in state:	59.1%			Poverty Rate	14.8%
		Education			
Age Groups		H.S. grad or less:	45.6%	Work	
Under 18:	26.2%	Some college:	27.2%	White collar:	34.5%
18 to 34:	21.9%	College degree, 4 yr.:	18.9%	Blue collar:	43.3%
35 to 64:	39.6%	Post-grad study:	8.2%	Sales and service:	22.2%
Over 64:	12.3%			Govt. workers:	13.5%
		Military			
		Veterans/active duty:	8.7%		

Northern Houston Suburbs: East-Central Texas

Voter Turnout	
2013 Total Citizen 18+	502,915
2014 House Turnout	140,013
2014 Turnout as % CVAP	27.8%
2012 Turnout as % CVAP	51.5%

Montgomery County, to the north of Houston, was once fenceless cattle country, dotted with roadside stands and barbecues. In 1931, wildcatter George Strake struck oil near Conroe. Thousands of other wildcatters and roughnecks quickly joined in the boom, and this became one of the richest oil-producing areas in the nation. Active production continues today. The oil boom centered on Conroe was followed by a population boom. In 1972, construction began on a planned community called The Woodlands, 30 miles north of Houston and 15 miles south of Conroe. Development of this new city has barreled along since then, with corporate parks, glistening condo towers, pristine golf courses, and a man-made waterway. Its real estate, which is the most expensive in the Houston area, is home to 108,000 residents and 1,900 businesses. The Cynthia Woods Mitchell Pavilion in the Woodlands was the second-busiest outdoor concert venue in the world in 2014, selling 488,916 tickets. Exxon Mobil has built a 385-acre campus close to the Woodlands, which is projected to add 10,000 jobs. Parts of the new campus, which plans substantial research of resources, technologies and products, opened in 2014 and it was expected to be completed in 2015. Business leaders view the campus, with about 20 office buildings, as a boon to the Houston economy.

The 8th Congressional District includes all of Montgomery County, which is the sixth fastest-growing county in Texas and contains about two-thirds of the district's people. It includes a small slice of Harris County, not far from George Bush International Airport. The district extends north through parts of the Brazos Valley and covers Sam Houston National Forest and Davy Crockett National Forest.

2012 Presidential Vote		
Mitt Romney (R)	195,742	(77%)
Barack Obama (D)	55,273	(22%)
2008 Presidential Vote		
John McCain (R)	171,408	(73%)
Barack Obama (D)	61,357	(26%)
Cook Partisan Voting Index: R+29		

It spans through all of seven counties and parts of two. The district takes in Huntsville, with one of Texas' oldest prisons and "Big Sam," a 67-foot-tall statue of Sam Houston outside the town along Interstate 45. This is one of the most Republican districts in the country, and it gave Republican Mitt Romney 77 percent of the vote in 2012.

Kevin Brady (R)

Kevin Brady, a Republican first elected in 1996, has leveraged his stature as one of the party's key figures on trade into influence on other economic matters. He chairs the Ways and Means Health Subcommittee, bringing an avidly pro-business focus to the panel. He unsuccessfully vied with the high-profile Paul Ryan of Wisconsin to chair Ways and Means, but he remains well-positioned to eventually take the chairmanship.

Brady grew up and went to college in South Dakota, moved to Montgomery County in 1978, and headed The Woodlands Chamber of Commerce for 18 years. In 1990, he was elected to the Texas House. When Brady ran for the open seat, his main opponent in the decisive Republican primary was Eugene Fontenot, a physician who said he wanted "to restore America to its Christian heritage." Brady was the choice of party regulars; Fontenot was backed by religious conservatives.

Fontenot attacked Brady for being one of two Republicans to vote against the state's concealed weapons law. Brady had opposed most gun control bills but not the concealed weapons bill. When he was 12 years old, his father, an attorney, was shot and killed while trying a case in a South Dakota courtroom. "I couldn't look Mom in the eye and vote for this," he told the *Houston Chronicle* after the vote. (Then, in February 2013, he said he regretted the vote. "I've been remarkably impressed with how well concealed-carry has worked in Texas," he told *National Journal*.) The campaign was grueling. After Fontenot led Brady in the March primary, Brady won the April runoff 53%-47%. After the U.S. Supreme Court in June ordered a redrawing of 13 districts, Brady led Fontenot 41%-39% in an all-party primary in November. Finally, in the December runoff, turnout was sharply down, and Brady won 59%-41%. He has had no problem winning reelection since.

In the House, Brady has compiled a conservative voting record, though he has often been more of a pragmatist than other Texas conservatives. Brady is a deputy whip for the House Republican leadership and in 2011 joined with Oklahoma Republican Tom Cole on a National Republican Congressional Committee effort to raise money from colleagues, which led them to be dubbed "the Dues Brothers." He is known for being easygoing and soft-spoken, but that doesn't mean he never gets mad. His November 2009 showdown with Treasury Secretary Timothy Geithner made national news when Brady savaged Geithner's handling of the Wall Street crisis, saying, "The public has lost all confidence in your ability to do the job." A year earlier, Brady was the only Houston-area member of the House in either party to vote for the financial industry rescue. "As much as I detest this bill, doing nothing is worse," he said.

Brady has focused on economic issues. Taking over the Health Subcommittee in 2013, his agenda included repealing unpopular parts of the 2010 health care law, such as a tax on medical devices and an advisory panel that critics say usurps Congress' responsibilities. He got those bills through the House, but they stalled in the Democratic-controlled Senate. He previously led that panel's trade subcommittee and has persistently fought for more free-trade agreements, which he contends are essential to the U.S. economic recovery. In June 2015, he worked closely with Ways and Means and House GOP leaders to win the House's narrow approval of trade promotion authority for President Barack Obama to submit his Trans-Pacific Partnership.

Brady in May 2014 got a bipartisan bill through the House to make permanent and expand the so-called R&D tax credit. The Obama administration, however, opposed the measure because it would expand the credit without offsetting the cost. Three months later, Brady released the draft text of a bill to find those savings by curtailing Medicare and Medicaid fraud and abuse with bipartisan suggestions that he collected from committee members.

Even before term-limited Ways and Means Chairman Dave Camp of Michigan announced that he wouldn't seek reelection in 2014, Brady publicly made his case for the job in media interviews, saying that he was ready to challenge Ryan, the 2012 vice presidential nominee and a policy maven. "I'm qualified and prepared to lead this committee. At the right time, I'm going to make that case to my colleagues," Brady told Bloomberg TV. "This is all about the ideas and how we can move tax reform, trade, entitlement reform forward, so it's good to have a healthy competition."

Ryan took the gavel after a November 2014 meeting of the House GOP Steering Committee, with less seniority than Brady but support from Speaker John Boehner and at least an implicit disavowal of plans for another national campaign. Brady was the senior committee Republican behind 84-year-old Sam Johnson of Texas, and he retained his Health Subcommittee post and seemed to benefit from running a respectful campaign. Ryan's career options remain abundant, and it is possible that Brady will have another opportunity to take the top committee post before Ryan's six-year term limit expires. Brady has remained active on committee issues. In April 2015, the House passed his bill to repeal the estate tax. In May, he won passage of his measure to make permanent the research and development tax credit and provide more certainty to businesses. White House officials said Obama would veto each bill.

On the Joint Economic Committee, which studies fiscal policy but has no power to pass legislation, Brady as chairman preached the gospel of getting Washington out of the way to let the private sector create jobs. "The 'government spending is the answer' crowd had their chance to jump-start the economy. They failed," he wrote in a *National Review Online* op-ed in February 2013. "It's time for a proven, pro-growth approach." Concerned about the Federal Reserve's repeated lowering of interest rates, he called for reforming the agency and appointing a bipartisan commission to study its operations, though Federal Reserve leaders have taken a dim view of his efforts. The JEC chairmanship rotates every two years between the House and Senate majority parties; in 2015-16, Brady serves as vice-chairman of the panel.

On local matters, Brady was a central figure in the successful effort in 2004 to make state and local sales taxes deductible in the seven states, including Texas, that have no personal income tax. Like Houston-area lawmakers of both parties, Brady jealously guards NASA's Johnson Space Center. When the agency announced in April 2011 that it would not place any of its retired space shuttles at Johnson, he said, "With this White House, I always expect the worst and am rarely disappointed."

NINTH DISTRICT

Al Green (D)

Elected 2004, 6th term; b. Sept. 1, 1947, New Orleans, LA; TX Southern U., J.D. 1973; Baptist; divorced.

Elected Office: Harris Cnty. justice of the peace, 1977-2004.

Professional Career: Practicing atty., 1973-77; Pres., Houston NAACP, 1986-95.

DC Office: 2347 RHOB, 20515, 202-225-7508; Fax: 202-225-2947; Website: algreen.house.gov.

State Offices: Houston, 713-383-9234.

Committees: *Financial Services:* Housing & Insurance; Oversight & Investigations (RMM); Task Force to Investigate Terrorism Financing.

Group Ratings

	ADA	ACLU	AFL-CIO	LCV	ITI	COC	HAFA	ACU	CFG	FRC
2014	85%	72%	–	74%	80%	62%	18%	10%	13%	0%
2013	75%	C	95%	89%	C	54%	C	12%	15%	C

National Journal Ratings

	2013 LIB	—	2013 CONS
Economic	67%	—	32%
Social	84%	—	15%
Foreign	61%	—	39%
Composite	71%	—	29%

Key Votes of the 113th Congress

1. Sandy storm spending	Y	5. Medical Marijuana	NV	9. Syrian Rebels Training Y
2. Violence Against Women Act	Y	6. Farm Bill	N	10. Keystone pipeline Y
3. Guantanamo Bay Detainees	Y	7. Afghanistan Combat	Y	11. Immigration Exec. Action N
4. Abortion 20-week ban	N	8. NSA Phone Data Collection	N	12. Bipartisan budget deal Y

Election Results

2014 general	Al Green (D)	78,109	(91%)	$483,696
	Johnny Johnson (Lib)	7,894	(9%)	
2014 primary	Al Green (D)	unopposed		

Prior winning percentages: 2012 (78%), 2010 (76%), 2008 (94%), 2006 (100%), 2004 (72%)

Population		Race and Ethnicity		Income	
Total:	736,852	Black	38.3%	Median income:	$41,772
Urban:	86.1%	Latino	37.2%		(362 of 435)
Suburban:	13.9%	White	13.6%	Under $50,000	57.8%
Rural:	0.0%	Asian	9.1%	$50,000-$99,999:	26.7%
Land area:	177	Two races	1.4%	$100,000-$199,999:	13.0%
Pop/sq. mi.:	4,160.0	White Ethnic	4.5%	$200,000 or more:	2.6%
Born in state:	50.1%			Poverty Rate	23.3%
		Education			
Age Groups		H.S. grad or less:	47.6%	**Work**	
Under 18:	26.4%	Some college:	25.7%	White collar:	29.4%
18 to 34:	28.0%	College degree, 4 yr.:	18.2%	Blue collar:	46.9%
35 to 64:	37.3%	Post-grad study:	8.6%	Sales and service:	23.7%
Over 64:	8.3%				
		Military		Govt. workers:	11.2%
		Veterans/active duty:	4.7%		

South Houston, Eastern Fort Bend County

A half-century ago, the steaming flatlands south of Houston running down to the Gulf of Mexico did not seem a likely site for one of the world's most advanced civilizations. But spreading out in all directions from its historic center at Allen's Land-ing on Buffalo Bayou, Houston has become one of

Voter Turnout	
2013 Total Citizen 18+	402,499
2014 House Turnout	86,003
2014 Turnout as % CVAP	21.4%
2012 Turnout as % CVAP	47.2%

the great metropolises of North America. Most of the scientific work in NASA's early years was done in Houston, and the first word spoken when man landed on the moon was "Hous-ton." It is the undisputed center of expertise in the oil business and has been at the center of innovations in hydraulic fracking, leading to a resurgence in drilling throughout South Texas. Houston has also become a medical mecca, with the giant Texas Medical Center and its 14 hospitals leaving their mark on the health care statewide. After she was shot in the head by a deranged constituent, former Rep. Gabrielle Giffords spent five months at Memorial Hermann Health System for rehabilitation in 2011; the center, which has 12 hospitals across Houston, announced in 2014 a $650 million expansion. The Reliant Stadium pro football facility in 2014 became NRG Park, sponsored by NRG Energy Inc. The famed Astrodome, which was once the

2012 Presidential Vote		
Barack Obama (D)	145,332	(78%)
Mitt Romney (R)	39,392	(21%)
2008 Presidential Vote		
Barack Obama (D)	144,707	(76%)
John McCain (R)	44,520	(23%)
Cook Partisan Voting Index:	D+25	

"Eighth Wonder of the World" but has been closed since 2009 and had a yard sale in 2013, had an uncertain future after voters in 2013 rejected a referendum to turn it into a giant convention center.

Houston bounced back quickly from the recession, ranking sixth in a 2012 Brookings Institution report assessing the scope of economic recovery in major urban areas. Twenty-six Fortune 500 companies are headquartered in Houston, second only to New York City; all but three of them are chiefly in the energy business. This success is in part a triumph of air conditioning, which made Houston's five-month summer tolerable. Today, it is the fourth-largest city in the nation, with a population that grew 29% from 1990 to 2010. It is also now the most ethnically diverse major metropolitan area, according to a Rice University report, citing its status as an "immigration gateway." Annise Parker, the first openly lesbian mayor of a major American city, was elected to a third term in 2013.

The 9th Congressional District of Texas slices across the southern part of metropolitan Houston in Harris County. It also takes in two wedges of Fort Bend County, which form a crescent around the 22nd District. The 9th includes many African-American neighborhoods, low-income and middle-income, in both counties. Its population is 38% black. Another 14% are Asians, many clustered along Bellaire Boulevard in the Chinese-American community. Entrepreneurial Vietnamese boat people settled in Alief and have created quality schools, an Asian-oriented shopping mall, and businesses that serve one of the largest Vietnamese communities in the nation. Hispanics make up 37% of the district's population, although many are not citizens or do not vote. Several thousand residents arrived after fleeing the devastation of Hurricane Katrina and stayed. Overall, this is a heavily Democratic district, which gave President Barack Obama 78% of the vote in 2012.

Al Green (D)

Democrat Al Green, first elected in 2004, champions the concerns of the homeless and poor. Like his namesake soul-singer-turned-preacher, Green is deeply religious, usually sporting a "God Is Good" lapel pin. His legislative work has focused on the Financial Services Committee, where he represents the interests of low-income groups.

Green grew up in New Orleans. He attended college at Florida A&M University and graduated from Texas Southern University's law school, where he later taught. He was elected justice of the peace for Harris County in 1977 and served 26 years. For a decade, he also was president of the Houston chapter of the NAACP. After the congressional redistricting in 2003 that largely benefited Republicans, Green saw an opening to run for Congress. The representative from the old district that covered much of this area was Chris Bell, a white Democrat elected in 2002, when he ran with liberal support and beat a more conservative black candidate. The primary against Green was a different matter. Green said that he wanted to fight racial profiling and discrimination in law enforcement, and used subtle racial references on the campaign trail, including his promise to bring "a mountain of soul" to the new district. He amassed an impressive roster of endorsements from prominent local and national black leaders.

Bell responded by asking voters "not to focus on the color of my skin, but on the size of my heart." He was endorsed by the AFL-CIO, Texas teachers unions, abortion rights groups, and Democratic Minority Leader Nancy Pelosi. But he struggled as a white candidate running in a heavily minority district. As the primary neared, the racially charged atmosphere intensified. When state Democratic Chairman Charles Soechting endorsed Bell, Green said it reminded him of "the double standards when African Americans had to ride on the back of the bus and drink from colored-only water fountains." Green won the primary in a landslide, 66%-31%, and faced no real opposition in the general election.

In the House, Green began with a relatively moderate voting record, but recently has become a more liberal Democrat. On the Financial Services Committee, where he has become the ranking Democrat on the Oversight and Investigations Subcommittee, he has worked to eliminate housing practices that discriminated against minorities, at times successfully enlisting Republicans in his efforts. In its 2013 oversight plan for the new Congress, the committee approved amendments to cover several of his priorities: Enforcing discrimination violations, ensuring that the Department of Housing and Urban Development pays attention to veterans' housing issues, and maintaining funding of Securities and Exchange Commission enforcement activities. He has regularly introduced his "Homes for Heroes" bill to assist homeless veterans.

Green has focused on a diverse set of social issues. After Democrats were criticized before their 2012 convention for initially leaving the word "God" out of the party platform, Green was added as a speaker to reinforce the party's commitment to religion. "Our faith tells us we have a moral obligation to better our communities, to accept responsibility and care for each other," he said in his remarks. "But these values are not just unique to believers—they are American values, and this is the American way." At a controversial Homeland Security Committee hearing on Muslim extremism in 2011, he passionately told panel members that other groups using religion as the basis for their views, such as the Ku Klux Klan, also should be examined. In October 2013, he was arrested with 200 other activists blocking a street near the Capitol at a rally for immigration legislation.

Like most Texas lawmakers, Green is protective of the oil and gas industry, joining a group of Democrats in 2009 warning that President Barack Obama's proposal to raise taxes and impose new fees on the industry would hamper domestic production. Green broke with most House Democrats by voting in 2012 for a bill to double the number of offshore oil and gas drilling leases, probably the smart vote in a Houston-based district that relies on oil profits. In January 2015, he was one of 28 House Democrats who voted for the Keystone XL oil pipeline.

Green is among the handful of members who stake out an aisle seat in the House chamber hours before the annual State of Union address to ensure getting a few seconds of televised face time with the president. He was reelected in 2014 without Republican opposition in his safe district.

TENTH DISTRICT

Michael McCaul (R)

Elected 2004, 6th term; b. Jan. 14, 1962, Dallas; Trinity U., B.A. 1984, St. Mary's U., J.D. 1987; Catholic; married (Linda); 5 children.

Professional Career: Fed. prosecutor, 1990-99; Deputy atty. gen., 1999-2003; Chief, Western Div. of TX. U.S. Atty's. Office, 2003-04.

DC Office: 131 CHOB, 20515, 202-225-2401; Fax: 202-225-5955; Website: mccaul.house.gov.

State Offices: Austin, 512-473-2357; Brenham, 979-830-8497; Katy, 281-398-1247; Tomball, 281-255-8372.

Committees: *Foreign Affairs:* Western Hemisphere. *Homeland Security* (Chmn: ex officio member of each subcommittee). *Science, Space, & Technology:* Space; Research & Technology.

Group Ratings

	ADA	ACLU	AFL-CIO	LCV	ITI	COC	HAFA	ACU	CFG	FRC
2014	5%	0%	–	6%	100%	93%	64%	76%	70%	100%
2013	0%	C	10%	4%	C	85%	C	84%	74%	C

National Journal Ratings

	2013 LIB	—	2013 CONS
Economic	21%	—	77%
Social	0%	—	87%
Foreign	0%	—	95%
Composite	10%	—	90%

Key Votes of the 113th Congress

1. Sandy storm spending	N	5. Medical Marijuana	N	9. Syrian Rebels Training	Y
2. Violence Against Women Act	N	6. Farm Bill	Y	10. Keystone pipeline	Y
3. Guantanamo Bay Detainees	N	7. Afghanistan Combat	N	11. Immigration Exec. Action	Y
4. Abortion 20-week ban	Y	8. NSA Phone Data Collection	N	12. Bipartisan budget deal	Y

Election Results

2014 general	Michael McCaul (R)..................109,726	(62%)	$1,599,939
	Tawana Walter-Cadien (D)..........60,243	(34%)	$10,501
	Bill Kelsey (Lib)............................6,491	(4%)	
2014 primary	Michael McCaul (R)..............unopposed		

Prior winning percentages: 2012 (61%), 2010 (65%), 2008 (54%), 2006 (55%), 2004 (79%)

Population		Race and Ethnicity		Income	
Total:	758,585	White	57.9%	Median income:	$64,220
Urban:	29.4%	Latino	25.9%		*(84 of 435)*
Suburban:	50.7%	Black	9.6%	Under $50,000	39.5%
Rural:	19.9%	Asian	5.0%	$50,000-$99,999:	31.0%
Land area:	3,495	Two races	1.4%	$100,000-$199,999:	22.3%
Pop/sq. mi.:	217.0	White Ethnic	18.0%	$200,000 or more:	7.2%
Born in state:	58.9%			Poverty Rate	12.6%
		Education			
Age Groups		H.S. grad or less:	35.1%	**Work**	
Under 18:	25.7%	Some college:	28.2%	White collar:	42.3%
18 to 34:	23.9%	College degree, 4 yr.:	24.6%	Blue collar:	38.4%
35 to 64:	39.5%	Post-grad study:	12.1%	Sales and service:	19.3%
Over 64:	11.0%				
		Military		Govt. workers:	13.5%
		Veterans/active duty:	7.2%		

Austin/Houston Corridor

Two of Texas' major cities are named for leaders of the old Texas Republic, Sam Houston and Stephen Austin. They were not entirely attractive characters: Houston had episodes of alcoholic depression, and Austin was a slaveholder who argued that Mexico infringed on Texas' liberty when it freed

Voter Turnout	
2013 Total Citizen 18+	505,213
2014 House Turnout	119,574
2014 Turnout as % CVAP	23.7%
2012 Turnout as % CVAP	46%

its slaves. But they were also men of courage and determination who built a distinctively American culture in what was then the northeast of Mexico. Today, the two metropolises named for them are quite different in character. Houston is about commerce, the capital of the oil business, an entrepreneurial hub spread out over the swampy, humid plains north of the Gulf of Mexico. Austin is the creature of the state government headquartered in the grand Capitol building and of the University of Texas with a huge endowment of land in West Texas that turned out to be full of oil. Former Gov. Rick Perry, who was the state's chief executive for 14 years, told late-night TV host Jimmy Kimmel in March 2014 that Austin was "kind of the blueberry in the tomato soup of the state. It's a little different than the rest of the place."

The historic Austin is a liberal enclave in the heart of a conservative state. But the area around north Austin and its suburbs has taken on some of Houston's character in recent years despite the continuing popularity of "Keep Austin Weird" bumper stickers. North of the Capitol and the university, on land that was vacant when Lyndon Johnson celebrated his 87-vote victory in the 1948 Senate primary in the Driskill Hotel, an entrepreneurial Austin has taken shape, one that embraces technology and the free market, and is a major center for technology start-ups and the manufacturing of computer and electronic products. It is host to the annual South by Southwest music, film and technology conferences, which had 155,000 participants in 2013. Apple is building a new campus in northwest Austin that is expected to double its payroll of 3,600; IBM has a major research lab that employs about 6,000; and not far away, the J.J. Pickle Research Campus of UT-Austin conducts research in areas ranging from archaeology to robots. Curiously, there is no

2012 Presidential Vote		
Mitt Romney (R)	159,714	(59%)
Barack Obama (D)	104,839	(39%)
2008 Presidential Vote		
John McCain (R)	148,867	(56%)
Barack Obama (D)	112,866	(43%)
Cook Partisan Voting Index:	R+11	

superhighway connecting the 160 miles between Austin and Houston, though there has been discussion of a rail line. To get from one to the other, the drive goes through rural counties with monuments and plaques recalling the days of the Texas Republic.

The 10th Congressional District of Texas connects the western suburbs of Houston with the northern precincts of Austin through a corridor of rural counties. It is split into three parts. Approximately 39% of the population lives in Austin and Travis County, where the Democratic arm of the district includes the northern third of Austin, with one tentacle reaching northwest beyond the city limits and another dropping south to Austin State Hospital.

Another 36% lives in the western edge of Houston's Harris County, a fast-growing and overwhelmingly Republican area, with lots of young families, new subdivisions, and mega churches. In between are seven lightly populated GOP-leaning rural counties, including Austin County and its small town of Sealy, where the same-named mattress company was founded. The town of Brenham is home to renowned ice cream manufacturer Blue Bell Creamery, though the company suffered a setback in April 2015 following Listeria contamination that caused several deaths. With its trendy shops, red-brick inns, and fancy restaurants, Brenham is a popular rest stop for travelers between the two cities. Overall, the 10th District is comfortably Republican. With some minority growth on each end, the Hispanic population is 26%.

Michael McCaul (R)

Michael McCaul, a Republican first elected in 2004 as a protégé of Texas GOP Sen. John Cornyn, became chairman of the Homeland Security Committee in 2013. He has pursued an activist agenda of timely issues, usually on a bipartisan basis. He is among the wealthiest members of Congress.

McCaul grew up in Dallas, studied business and history at Trinity University, and got his law degree at St. Mary's University, both in San Antonio. He worked as a federal prosecutor and then moved to Austin in 1999 to be a deputy to state Attorney General Cornyn. In 2002, he joined the U.S. attorney's office and was chief of the Terrorism and National Security Section for West Texas.

McCaul was one of eight candidates in the Republican primary for the newly created congressional district in 2004. The other top Republican contenders were mortgage company owner Ben Streusand, and former Judge John Devine. McCaul focused on his anti-terrorism work, calling himself the only candidate who "won't have a learning curve." Streusand, based in Harris County, called for less government regulation and opposed the Bush administration's immigration proposals. Devine, who had refused to remove a Ten Commandments display from his Harris County courtroom, had the support of Christian conservatives and called for a crackdown on illegal immigration. In the primary, Streusand carried seven of the eight counties to finish with 28% of the vote, to 24% for McCaul, who ran strongly in his Travis County base, and 21% for Devine.

In the runoff campaign, McCaul and Streusand agreed on most issues. McCaul criticized Streusand's past donations to Democratic candidates, while Streusand questioned McCaul's service in the Clinton administration Justice Department. McCaul used his connections—his father-in-law is Clear Channel Communications founder and Chairman Lowry Mays—to collect major Republican endorsements, including from former President George H.W. Bush, Gov. Rick Perry and Sen. Kay Bailey Hutchison. McCaul won 63%-37%, carrying both Travis and Harris counties. He faced no major party opposition in the general election. *Roll Call* lists him as the second wealthiest member of the House with a net worth of at least $118 million.

In the House, McCaul has a conservative voting record. His occasional moderate votes include requiring insurers to treat mental illness the same as other health conditions in 2008, and allowing the Food and Drug Administration to regulate tobacco products in 2009. Since Republicans took control of the House in 2011, his voting record has grown more conservative, particularly on fiscal matters. He has repeatedly introduced legislation banning so-called "monuments to me," landmarks honoring incumbent lawmakers. He worked with Democratic Rep. G.K. Butterfield of North Carolina to enact a bill in 2012 encouraging companies to make drugs for rare childhood cancers and other diseases.

McCaul earned the gratitude of House GOP leaders for leading the protracted 2010 ethics investigation of Democratic Rep. Charles Rangel of New York that culminated in Rangel's censure by the full House. A former chief counsel and staff director on Ethics accused McCaul and then-chairman GOP Rep. Jo Bonner of Alabama of having had secret conversations with two ex-staffers on the committee about the Rangel investigation and a separate probe involving Democratic Rep. Maxine Waters of California. Such interactions are not permitted under Ethics Committee rules in certain circumstances. Both Bonner and McCaul recused themselves in the Waters case.

McCaul chaired Homeland Security's Oversight, Investigations and Management Subcommittee in 2011-12. He filed legislation to have six Mexican drug cartels designated as foreign terrorist organizations, a move that could lead to much stiffer penalties for drug traffickers. Later, he pressed Obama administration officials at a hearing over its failure to define "spill-over violence" from the drug wars in Mexico. McCaul co-sponsored a cyber-security bill with Democratic Rep. Daniel Lipinski of Illinois that would develop standards for dealing with cyberthreats; it passed the House in 2012 but fell victim to partisan squab-bling in the Senate. With Democratic Rep. Jim Langevin of Rhode Island, he founded and co-chairs the Cybersecurity Caucus.

He sought the Homeland Security gavel in 2012 when term limits forced out New York Republican Peter King as chairman. McCaul had less seniority than other contenders, but told the *Houston Chronicle* he put his "prosecutor's hat back on and delivered a closing argument" to colleagues about why he deserved the position. He stressed his desire to avoid incendiary issues such as the high-profile hearings on Islamic extremism that alienated many Democrats and to focus on border security, computer network vulnerabilities, and improving the Homeland Security Department's management. In his narrow victory in the leadership-dominated Republican Steering Committee, it helped that he tapped his wealth to donate more than $60,000 to more than four dozen Republicans in the 2012 election season.

Taking over as chairman, McCaul blasted a Homeland Security Department decision in February 2013 to release hundreds of immigrants from around the country for budgetary reasons as "indicative of the department's weak stance on national security." After former National Security Agency contractor Edward Snowden fled to China and then Russia with a laptop full of secret documents, McCaul speculated that he had been "cultivated by a foreign power" to leak sensitive intelligence information. Following the mysterious disappearance of the Malaysian Airlines flight, he speculated to Fox News in March 2014 that the aircraft could be parked somewhere for use as a huge bomb. "What would be the purpose behind crashing it into the ocean?" he asked rhetorically.

McCaul has been busy moving legislation on several fronts. In December 2014, he worked with a bipartisan group to enact the National Cybersecurity Protection Act, which provided private and government digital networks additional protection against attacks. He worked with the bipartisan coalition that enacted in June 2015 the USA Freedom Act, formerly known as the Patriot Act, to reduce the bulk collection of phone data and other records by the National Security Agency. He helped to preserve and update other key provi-sions, including surveillance of suspected "lone wolf" terrorists who are not affiliated with a government or organized group, plus the "roving wiretap" provision that allowed govern-ment agents to target suspected individuals. In April, he won House passage of the National Cybersecurity Protection Advancement Act that gave the Homeland Security Department authority over cyberthreat data sharing. Early in 2015, he ran into problems in trying to move a border-security bill, the Secure Our Borders First Act. That became part of the sepa-rate debate over the appropriation bill for the Homeland Security Department, where House Republicans ultimately failed to restrict President Barack Obama's executive actions on immigration (which were eventually halted by a federal judge).

McCaul's reelection performances have improved following his first two relatively close campaigns. With his deep pockets and law-enforcement persona, he could be a credible state-wide contender.

ELEVENTH DISTRICT

Mike Conaway (R)

Elected 2004, 6th term; b. June 11, 1948, Borger; TX A&M U., B.B.A. 1970; Baptist; married (Suzanne); 4 children.

Military Career: U.S. Army, 1970-72.

Elected Office: Midland Schl. Bd., 1985-88.

Professional Career: Tax mgr., Price Waterhouse & Co., 1972-80; CFO, Keith G. Graham, 1980-81; CFO, Lantern Petroleum Co., 1981; CFO, Arbusto Energy Inc./Bush Exploration Co., 1982-84; CFO, Spec-trum 7 Energy Corp., 1984-86; CFO, United Bank, 1987-90; Sr. V.P., TX Community Bank, 1990-92; Owner, K. Michael Conaway, CPA, 1993-2004; TX St. Bd. of Public Accountancy, 1995-2002.

DC Office: 2430 RHOB, 20515, 202-225-3605; Fax: 202-225-1783; Website: conaway.house.gov.

State Offices: Brownwood, 325-646-1950; Granbury, 682-936-2577; Llano, 325-247-2826; Midland, 432-687-2390; Odessa, 432-331-9667; San Angelo, 325-659-4010.

Committees: *Agriculture* (Chmn: ex officio member of each subcommittee). *Armed Services:* Oversight & Investigations; Seapower & Projection Forces. *Intelligence (Select).*

Group Ratings

	ADA	ACLU	AFL-CIO	LCV	ITI	COC	HAFA	ACU	CFG	FRC
2014	0%	0%	–	3%	80%	71%	67%	92%	81%	100%
2013	0%	C	14%	0%	C	77%	C	76%	67%	C

National Journal Ratings

	2013 LIB	—	2013 CONS
Economic	13%	—	85%
Social	16%	—	74%
Foreign	24%	—	68%
Composite	21%	—	79%

Key Votes of the 113th Congress

1. Sandy storm spending	N	5. Medical Marijuana	N	9. Syrian Rebels Training	Y
2. Violence Against Women Act	N	6. Farm Bill	Y	10. Keystone pipeline	Y
3. Guantanamo Bay Detainees	N	7. Afghanistan Combat	N	11. Immigration Exec. Action	Y
4. Abortion 20-week ban	Y	8. NSA Phone Data Collection	N	12. Bipartisan budget deal	Y

Election Results

2014 general	Mike Conaway (R)	107,939	(90%)	$1,559,657
	Ryan Lange (Lib)	11,635	(10%)	
2014 primary	Mike Conaway (R)	53,272	(74%)	
	Wade Brown (R)	19,010	(26%)	

Prior winning percentages: 2012 (79%), 2010 (81%), 2008 (88%), 2006 (100%), 2004 (77%)

Population		Race and Ethnicity		Income	
Total:	729,613	White	60.1%	Median income:	$50,412
Urban:	48.8%	Latino	34.0%		*(235 of 435)*
Suburban:	7.0%	Black	3.7%	Under $50,000	49.5%
Rural:	44.2%	Asian	0.6%	$50,000-$99,999:	28.9%
Land area:	25,954	Two races	1.2%	$100,000-$199,999:	16.8%
Pop/sq. mi.:	28.1	White Ethnic	13.8%	$200,000 or more:	4.8%
Born in state:	69.7%			Poverty Rate	14.2%
		Education			
Age Groups		H.S. grad or less:	49.4%	**Work**	
Under 18:	24.9%	Some college:	30.5%	White collar:	28.5%
18 to 34:	24.4%	College degree, 4 yr.:	14.4%	Blue collar:	40.2%
35 to 64:	35.4%	Post-grad study:	5.7%	Sales and service:	31.3%
Over 64:	15.2%			Govt. workers:	13.0%
		Military			
		Veterans/active duty:	9.7%		

West-Central Texas: Midland, Odessa

In the 1540s, the conquistador Francisco Coronado and his men rode their horses over the plains of the land they called the Llano Estacado, or "flat palisades," which is now West Texas. They found a vast emptiness, gradually and imperceptibly rising in elevation to the west, with only scrub vegetation

Voter Turnout	
2013 Total Citizen 18+	495,832
2014 House Turnout	149,049
2014 Turnout as % CVAP	30.1%
2012 Turnout as % CVAP	56.6%

and small bands of Comanche Indians. What they did not see, lying far beneath the surface, was oil, discovered in the 1940s in large amounts in the Permian Basin. When oil was found, two tiny county seats 25 miles apart suddenly became small cities—Odessa, home of the roughneck oil well workers, and Midland, the more upscale town where oil entrepreneurs lived and started their own Petroleum Club. The Permian Basin boomed in the years just after World War II. In 1940, Ector and Midland counties had a population of 26,000. By 1960, they had grown to 159,000. Midland in the 1950s was an affluent town by west Texas standards, but hardly luxurious. Air conditioning had not yet become standard in homes or schools, and there were no mansions at the edge of town, just barren desert and oil derricks. George and Barbara Bush moved to the Permian Basin in 1948 in search of success in the oil industry and room for a growing family. They rented houses in Odessa before upgrading to a series of larger, but by no means grand, ranch houses in Midland. President George W. Bush's wife, Laura, also is from Midland. Odessa is now perhaps best known as the high school football-crazed town depicted in

2012 Presidential Vote		
Mitt Romney (R)................182,438	(79%)
Barack Obama (D) 45,083	(20%)
2008 Presidential Vote		
John McCain (R).................184,238	(76%)
Barack Obama (D) 56,145	(23%)
Cook Partisan Voting Index: R+31		

the 1990 book *Friday Night Lights*, later turned into a movie and hit TV series.

Growth has slowed as new oil discoveries dwindled, but the area still yields much of the state's oil and more than one-quarter of its gas. Midland's unemployment rate in 2008 was among the lowest in the nation following the oil-price boom. Production in the Permian Basin surged in 2012 to its highest level in 14 years, driven by new hydraulic fracturing techniques. As recently as early 2014, 536 of the 1,540 on-shore oil rigs operating in the United States were in the Permian Basin. But the plunge in the price of oil later in 2014 caused at least a short-term drop in shale-oil production and the closing of some small businesses, a boom-and-bust pattern that is common to the area. Midland's population grew at a healthy 18% rate from 2000 to 2010. Optimistic city leaders projected that, if the boom holds, population could double over the next three decades. An impressive 11% growth in the next three years showed that their projections may remain realistic.

The 11th Congressional District of Texas covers much of West Texas. It sweeps through 29 counties and over 300 miles of often barren land from the New Mexico border to the outskirts of both Fort Worth and Austin. Over half the population is in Midland, Ector, and Tom Green (San Angelo) counties. None of the other counties have more than 52,000 people. The district's Hispanic population has steadily increased to 34%, and poverty is a bit above the national average.

West Texas in the 1940s was, like nearly every other part of Texas, almost totally Democratic. That began to change in the 1950s as Midland moved toward Republicans. Newcomers like the Bushes were an important part of this trend. The 11th today is overwhelmingly Republican, giving Mitt Romney 79 percent of the vote in 2012. Slightly behind the adjacent 13th District, it is the second-most Republican district in the nation.

Mike Conaway (R)

Mike Conaway, a Republican first elected in 2004, is a low-profile but well-regarded conservative who has taken on an assortment of chores for his party, including generously fundraising for GOP colleagues and serving as chairman of the House Ethics Committee. He was rewarded in 2015 with the gavel of the Agriculture Committee.

Conaway grew up in Odessa, playing offensive and defensive line on the Odessa Permian High School team that won the 1965 state championship and became the inspiration for the TV show *Friday Night Lights*. He graduated from East Texas State University, before it became known as Texas A&M-Commerce. He worked as a certified public accountant with Price Waterhouse for, among others, George W. Bush, and was chief financial officer in Arbusto/Bush Exploration during the 1980s. After Bush became governor, he named Conaway to the state Board of Public Accountancy, and Conaway later chaired the National Association of State Boards of Accountancy. In May 2003, he finished second in the all-party primary for a special election in the 19th District. In June, he lost by fewer than 600 votes in a hard-fought runoff with Republican Randy Neugebauer of Lubbock, who later won the seat.

After state Republicans pushed through a new redistricting plan in October 2003, Conaway was the obvious front-runner for the seat in the redrawn 11th District, which is immediately south of the 19th. Veteran Democratic Rep. Charles Stenholm, who represented much of the area, decided to run against Neugebauer. Conaway's GOP primary opponent was Bill Lester, a little-known political science professor who campaigned against Bush's proposed guest worker program. Lester called for the militarization of the border with helicopter patrols to stop illegal immigration. Conaway supported increased documentation of people crossing the border. He won 75%- 25%, carrying 33 of the 36 counties. In the general election, he won 77%-22% and has been reelected with ease ever since.

Through 2013, Conaway had a lifetime rating of nearly 93% from the American Conservative Union. He is known for requiring his staff to read and understand the Constitution. "It's only 4,500 words—it's not like reading *War and Peace*," he told the *Houston Chronicle*. He favors state-based regulatory actions over federal ones, arguing that they are far more nimble and responsive. He has been critical of Obama administration efforts to promote renewable energy and sponsored legislation to limit the purchase of biofuels, which compete against his state's oil and natural gas. He voted against the original $700 billion bailout of the financial services industry in 2008, but voted for the final version after his long-time friend President Bush called to urge his support.

As a junior member and accountant, Conaway served on the executive committee of the National Republican Congressional Committee. In 2007, he uncovered an internal fraud scheme by the committee's longtime treasurer, who had embezzled almost $1 million. After the GOP won control of the House in 2010, Conaway was named to a 22-member transition team helping his party adjust to its majority status.

Boehner personally asked Conaway to become chairman in 2013 of the Ethics Committee, an undesirable posting but one that often brings later leadership rewards with other opportunities. Conaway said he sought to enhance Congress' low public standing by conducting investigations thoroughly and fairly. "I have a long history of accepting the responsibilities I have been offered and doing the best I can," he told *The San Angelo Standard-Times* in February 2013. He and California's Linda Sanchez, the panel's top Democrat, declined to act on a recommendation from the Office of Congressional Ethics that the panel set up a special committee to look into allegations that Washington's Cathy McMorris Rodgers, a member of the GOP leadership, improperly used funds in a leadership race and to cover other campaign activities. They also declined to conduct a full-scale investigation into the advocacy of Wisconsin GOP Rep. Tom Petri on behalf of a defense company in which he owned stock.

With Oklahoma's Frank Lucas term-limited as Agriculture's chairman at the end of 2014, speculation mounted about a successor. Tea party favorite Steve King of Iowa was mentioned as one possibility, but Conaway was more reliable and he solidified his hold on the job by raising more than $800,000 for other Republicans during the second quarter of 2014. Already a favorite of Speaker John Boehner, he organized a fundraising event in Texas to benefit Boehner and appeared with the speaker at another farm event.

After easily winning the chairmanship, Conaway noted that there are "fewer and fewer voices" in Congress that represent rural America, and he was honored to be one of those voices. He promised a comprehensive review of the Supplemental Nutrition Assistance Program, also known as food stamps, a target for numerous fiscal conservatives' ire. With immigration on the front burner, he pledged to see how any House legislation would affect farmers, especially their need for workers. Having previously chaired the Agriculture subcommittee on farm commodities and risk management, Conaway has been willing to challenge fellow conservatives who have criticized subsidies for mohair, a fabric yielded from Angora goats. Numerous Angora farmers live in his district. In an ongoing international trade dispute, Conaway has supported repeal of "country of origin labeling" on exports of beef, pork and chicken. In June 2015, the House passed on a 300-131 vote his bill to repeal the labeling requirement.

With Congress having enacted in 2014 a five-year extension of most farm programs, Conaway did not face the pressure of immediate legislative action. He has kept busy on other issues as a member of the Armed Services and Intelligence committees.

TWELFTH DISTRICT

Kay Granger (R)

Elected 1996, 10th term; b. Jan. 18, 1943, Greenville; TX Wesleyan U., B.S. 1965; Methodist; divorced; 3 children.

Elected Office: Ft. Worth City Cncl., 1989-91; Ft. Worth mayor, 1991-96.

Professional Career: Teacher, 1965-78; Life ins. agent, 1978-85; Chmn., Ft. Worth Zoning Comm., 1981-89; Founder & Pres., Kay Granger Ins. Co. Inc.

DC Office: 1026 LHOB, 20515, 202-225-5071; Fax: 202-225-5683; Website: kaygranger.house.gov.

State Offices: Ft. Worth, 817-338-0909.

Committees: *Appropriations:* Defense (VChmn); Energy & Water Development & Related Agencies; State, Foreign Operations & Related Programs (Chmn).

Group Ratings

	ADA	ACLU	AFL-CIO	LCV	ITI	COC	HAFA	ACU	CFG	FRC
2014	0%	0%	–	6%	60%	93%	52%	72%	54%	100%
2013	0%	C	20%	7%	C	75%	C	74%	59%	C

National Journal Ratings

	2013 LIB	—	2013 CONS
Economic	28%	—	71%
Social	29%	—	70%
Foreign	23%	—	76%
Composite	27%	—	73%

Key Votes of the 113th Congress

1. Sandy storm spending	N	5. Medical Marijuana	N	9. Syrian Rebels Training	Y
2. Violence Against Women Act	NV	6. Farm Bill	Y	10. Keystone pipeline	Y
3. Guantanamo Bay Detainees	N	7. Afghanistan Combat	N	11. Immigration Exec. Action	Y
4. Abortion 20-week ban	Y	8. NSA Phone Data Collection	N	12. Bipartisan budget deal	Y

Election Results

2014 general	Kay Granger (R)	113,186	(71%)	$1,317,818
	Mark Greene (D)	41,757	(26%)	$80,204
	Ed Colliver (Lib)	3,787	(2%)	
2014 primary	Kay Granger (R)	unopposed		

Prior winning percentages: 2012 (71%), 2010 (72%), 2008 (68%), 2006 (67%), 2004 (72%), 2002 (92%), 2000 (63%), 1998 (62%), 1996 (58%)

Population		Race and Ethnicity		Income	
Total:	732,246	White	66.2%	Median income:	$58,905
Urban:	62.7%	Latino	20.9%		*(137 of 435)*
Suburban:	32.1%	Black	7.6%	Under $50,000	42.1%
Rural:	5.1%	Asian	2.7%	$50,000-$99,999:	33.3%
Land area:	1,508	Two races	2.1%	$100,000-$199,999:	19.0%
Pop/sq. mi.:	485.7	White Ethnic	19.6%	$200,000 or more:	5.6%
Born in state:	61.4%			Poverty Rate	12.6%
		Education			
Age Groups		H.S. grad or less:	36.5%	**Work**	
Under 18:	24.7%	Some college:	32.3%	White collar:	37.3%
18 to 34:	24.9%	College degree, 4 yr.:	21.0%	Blue collar:	41.0%
35 to 64:	38.5%	Post-grad study:	10.3%	Sales and service:	21.6%
Over 64:	11.8%				
		Military		Govt. workers:	13.9%
		Veterans/active duty:	9.2%		

Fort Worth and Western Suburbs

Fort Worth has a fair claim to being the quintessential mid-American city. It sits halfway across
the continent, just west of the Balcones Escarpment that divides the dry, treeless grazing lands
of West Texas from the humid green croplands of
East Texas, "where the West begins," as its 19th

Voter Turnout	
2013 Total Citizen 18+	504,799
2014 House Turnout	158,730
2014 Turnout as % CVAP	31.4%
2012 Turnout as % CVAP	50.2%

century boosters proclaimed, coining the slogan that's still used by the city. This was the last
stop for cattle drives before they returned to Kansas. It is Southern in heritage and Northern in its advanced post-industrial economy. It has the nation's longest row of Western wear
shops and one of the nation's richest families, the Basses, whose steel skyscrapers dominate
the skyline. The family also developed Sundance Square, a 38-block entertainment, office
and retail district that has helped revive the downtown district. The area was named for the
running mate of famed outlaw Butch Cassidy, who regularly frequented Fort Worth for its
saloons and gambling establishments at the turn of the 20th century.

"Cowtown," as the city is sometimes called, is the 16th most populous city in the nation,
larger than Boston, Memphis and Baltimore. It has a high-tech economy and has been an
aviation center since the 1940s, though one hard hit by defense cuts. The big Lockheed
Martin plant, which employs about 14,000 people, produces numerous bombers and fighter
planes for the armed forces, including the F-35 fighter jet. Next door is the Naval Air Station
Fort Worth Joint Reserve Base, formerly Carswell Air Force Base, the home of B-52 bombers
for years. The city's economy has also benefited recently from the boom in shale gas production. *The New York Times* has called the city "an irresistible combination of cowboys and
culture," in part because it has some of the nation's premier small museums, including the
Amon Carter Museum, the Kimbell Art Museum, the Modern Art Museum of Fort Worth,
and the Sid Richardson Museum. In November 2014, voters approved a referendum for a
$450 million arena in Fort Worth, where the sports events will include rodeos.

The 12th Congressional District includes about half of Fort Worth and western suburban Tarrant County, as well as all of Parker County to the west and part of Wise County
to the northwest. About 80% of the population is in Tarrant, which has grown an impressive 25% since 2000. It has slightly narrowed its long-standing population gap with Dallas County to less than 600,000 residents. The district includes northern and western city
neighborhoods and the affluent southwest quarter beyond Texas Christian University,
downtown and the Stockyards. Parker County was once windswept open land around the
courthouse town of Weatherford, where for-
mer House Speaker Jim Wright, a Democrat,
grew up and was first elected to the House
in 1954. (Facing ethics sanctions, he quit
the House in June 1989 and he returned
to Texas to write and teach; he died in May
2015.) Today, it is sprouting subdivisions and
grew 32% from 2000 to 2010, to a population
of 117,000. Fort Worth and Tarrant County
stayed Democratic in the 1950s when Dallas

2012 Presidential Vote		
Mitt Romney (R)	166,992	(67%)
Barack Obama (D)	79,147	(32%)
2008 Presidential Vote		
John McCain (R)	161,030	(64%)
Barack Obama (D)	89,718	(35%)
Cook Partisan Voting Index:	R+19	

went Republican. With Dallas recently swinging back to Democrats, Fort Worth and Tarrant County have swung Republican. The 12th District, where Wright was elected 18 times
without serious opposition, is now solidly Republican, giving Mitt Romney 67% of the vote in
2012. An important change is that its minority downtown areas have shifted to the heavily
Hispanic 33rd District, which stretches to Dallas. These contrasts highlight the diversity
within the Metroplex.

Kay Granger (R)

Kay Granger, first elected in 1996, is the only Republican woman to represent the Lone Star
State in Congress. Less conservative than her fellow Texans, she has climbed the ladder of
the Appropriations Committee, where she is an expert on defense and chairs the subcommittee that controls spending for the State Department and foreign aid.

Granger grew up in Fort Worth, graduated from Texas Wesleyan College, and worked as a high school journalism and English teacher in North Richland Hills. She raised three children and started her own insurance agency, which she operated for more than 20 years. In 1989, she was elected to the Fort Worth Council, and two years later was elected as the non-partisan mayor. In 1995, when the House seat became open, leaders of both parties tried to recruit Granger. She decided to run in the Republican primary.

In a three-candidate race, she was attacked as a liberal, partly for her support of abortion rights. But she won with 69% of the vote. Her Democratic opponent was Hugh Parmer, a former Fort Worth mayor and the Democratic nominee against Republican Sen. Phil Gramm in 1990. Parmer attacked Republican cuts in Medicare and the stewardship of Republican House Speaker Newt Gingrich. Granger called for a balanced budget and tax cuts for business and ran on her record as mayor. She won 58%-41%, a stunning victory for a Republican in the district held by Speaker Jim Wright seven years earlier.

In the House, Granger's voting record has trended moderate on cultural issues and more conservative on economic issues. She once attended meetings of the centrist Republican Main Street Partnership but never formally joined. In 2007 and 2008, she was vice chair of the Republican Conference, but her leadership ambitions were limited. One of Granger's legislative achievements was enactment of tax-free savings accounts for higher education expenses. She and Democratic Rep. Emanuel Cleaver of Missouri, another former big-city mayor, announced in February 2013 an effort to build bipartisanship in the deeply polarized House. In June 2014, Speaker John Boehner named her to chair a working group on the border crisis, chiefly in the Rio Grande valley. Her proposal a month later was far less costly than the plan submitted by President Barack Obama. She takes her work seriously and she rarely seeks news-media attention. "Kay Granger chooses work over recognition," the *Fort Worth Star-Telegram* headlined a March 2015 news story.

With a seat on Appropriations, including as vice-chair of the Defense Subcommittee, Granger keeps a close eye on local Pentagon spending. She has worked to maintain production of Lockheed Martin planes in her district. In 2012, she successfully opposed a proposal by the Air Force to shift a squadron of C-130 military transport planes from Fort Worth to Montana.

In January 2005, Granger traveled to Iraq, where she and Democratic Rep. Ellen Tauscher of California conducted an election training session for women candidates. In late 2009, she visited U.S. troops in Afghanistan, and was among the Republicans who urged the Obama administration to step up pressure on Afghan President Hamid Karzai to establish a "functional, transparent government that does not condone corruption." She also has served on a private commission that reviewed global health policy.

In 2011, she became chairwoman of the State and Foreign Operations Subcommittee, where her experience with military spending and her interest in human rights are useful to her goals of global security and stability. She warned freshman Republicans against cutting foreign aid too deeply. "I think that there is more pressure [to cut foreign aid] because there's this misunderstanding of how much that part of the budget is," she said on the PBS *NewsHour*. But she has hardly embraced major increases in foreign aid. Despite personal lobbying from U2 singer and human rights activist Bono and former Bush White House Chief of Staff Joshua Bolten, she said that the Agency for International Development's request for a 22 percent increase for fiscal 2012 was "unrealistic in today's budget environment." She backed off slightly to permit Secretary of State John Kerry to announce $250 million in aid to Egypt during his March 2013 trip to Cairo. On her subcommittee, she has formed a close and productive working relationship with Rep. Nita Lowey of New York, the committee's top Democrat.

Granger has been reelected by wide margins. Her moderate tendencies inspired challenges in the 2010 and 2012 Republican primaries by underfunded challengers from her right, whom she dispatched with ease. She wrote a book, *What's Right About America: Celebrating Our Nation's Values*, published in 2006.

THIRTEENTH DISTRICT

Mac Thornberry (R)

Elected 1994, 11th term; b. July 15, 1958, Clarendon; TX Tech. U., B.A. 1980, U. of TX Law Schl., J.D. 1983; Presbyterian; married (Sally); 2 children.

Professional Career: Legis. counsel, Rep. Tom Loeffler, 1983-85; Chief of staff, Rep. Larry Combest, 1985-88; Deputy asst. secy. of st. for legis. affairs, 1988-89; Practicing atty., 1989-94; Rancher, 1989-94.

DC Office: 2208 RHOB, 20515, 202-225-3706; Fax: 202-225-3486; Website: thornberry.house.gov.

State Offices: Amarillo, 806-371-8844; Wichita Falls, 940-692-1700.

Committees: *Armed Services* (Chmn: ex officio member of each subcommittee).

Group Ratings

	ADA	ACLU	AFL-CIO	LCV	ITI	COC	HAFA	ACU	CFG	FRC
2014	0%	0%	–	3%	100%	93%	67%	88%	73%	100%
2013	0%	C	14%	4%	C	77%	C	80%	72%	C

National Journal Ratings

	2013 LIB	—	2013 CONS
Economic	7%	—	92%
Social	27%	—	71%
Foreign	34%	—	60%
Composite	24%	—	76%

Key Votes of the 113th Congress

1. Sandy storm spending	N	5. Medical Marijuana	N	9. Syrian Rebels Training	Y
2. Violence Against Women Act	N	6. Farm Bill	Y	10. Keystone pipeline	Y
3. Guantanamo Bay Detainees	N	7. Afghanistan Combat	N	11. Immigration Exec. Action	Y
4. Abortion 20-week ban	Y	8. NSA Phone Data Collection	N	12. Bipartisan budget deal	Y

Election Results

2014 general	Mac Thornberry (R)	110,842	(84%)	$1,693,677
	Mike Minter (D)	16,822	(13%)	
	Emily Pivoda (Lib)	2,863	(2%)	
2014 primary	Mac Thornberry (R)	45,168	(68%)	
	Elaine Hays (R)	12,330	(19%)	
	Pam Barlow (R)	8,723	(13%)	

Prior winning percentages: 2012 (91%), 2010 (87%), 2008 (78%), 2006 (74%), 2004 (92%), 2002 (79%), 2000 (68%), 1998 (68%), 1996 (67%), 1994 (55%)

Population		Race and Ethnicity		Income	
Total:	700,874	White	65.4%	Median income:	$46,847
Urban:	45.8%	Latino	25.4%		(285 of 435)
Suburban:	5.7%	Black	5.3%	Under $50,000	52.4%
Rural:	48.5%	Asian	1.6%	$50,000-$99,999:	30.3%
Land area:	33,151	Two races	1.8%	$100,000-$199,999:	14.9%
Pop/sq. mi.:	21.1	White Ethnic	14.6%	$200,000 or more:	2.3%
Born in state:	67.3%			Poverty Rate	17.1%
		Education			
Age Groups		H.S. grad or less:	46.6%	**Work**	
Under 18:	25.2%	Some college:	33.4%	White collar:	29.5%
18 to 34:	23.9%	College degree, 4 yr.:	14.1%	Blue collar:	42.8%
35 to 64:	36.7%	Post-grad study:	5.9%	Sales and service:	27.7%
Over 64:	14.3%			Govt. workers:	16.5%
		Military			
		Veterans/active duty:	10.7%		

North Texas/Panhandle: Amarillo, Wichita Falls

The farther west one travels in Texas, the browner the land gets and the smaller the towns get, until you arrive at counties containing only a few hundred people each—plus quite a few more head of cattle. At that point, the land rises nearly 1,000 feet in eleva-tion, up steep hillsides from the gullies along the riv-

Voter Turnout	
2013 Total Citizen 18+	485,436
2014 House Turnout	131,451
2014 Turnout as % CVAP	27.1%
2012 Turnout as % CVAP	47.2%

ers that for most of the year are just trickles, to the tilted tableland that makes up the High Plains of West Texas. The winds here sweep down from the Rockies, the land is barren except where irrigated, often with the now dangerously depleted waters of the Ogallala Aquifer. The land alternates between grazing areas and cotton fields. But here and there in this demanding environment—sticky hot in the summer, swept by north winds from Canada in winter, always threatened by tornadoes—comfortable cities have been built to house the people and businesses that bring forth some of the nation's most abundant oil, natural gas, helium and other elements from the earth. The area produces cotton and milo, a variety of sorghum, and is home to one of the nation's oldest cattle auctions. Severe drought forced Wichita Falls in 2014 to consider dras-tic steps to address water shortages, but floods in the region in May 2015 brought some relief.

Still, the population in the region has been either in decline or stagnant for nearly three decades. Around Wichita Falls is the agricultural land of the Red River Valley. Shep-pard Air Force Base, a medical facility and pilot training center, was hit hard by cutbacks in the 2005 base review. Cadillac Ranch, located just off I-40 west of Amarillo, is a famous roadside sculpture featuring "10 tail-finned, brightly painted Cadillacs planted nose down in a pasture," as *Texas Monthly* describes it. Built in 1974, the attraction inspired the 1980 Bruce Springsteen song "Cadillac Ranch." Archer City, home of novelist Larry McMurtry, was chronicled in *The Last Picture Show* and *Texasville*.

The 13th Congressional District of Texas spans 39 counties and parts of two others, from the New Mexico border to just north of Denton in the Dallas exurbs. That is a Texas-sized drive of more than 450 miles. The area was long dominated by Texas Anglos, but Latinos lately have been moving here in large numbers to work in the fields or in crop processing. Today, the district is 25 percent Hispanic. The largest city here is Amarillo in the heart of cowboy country. It is famously windy—windier than Chicago, in fact. In January 2014, the domestic subsidiary of a French company purchased its fourth wind farm in the Panhandle. Just outside town is the Pantex plant that secretly assem-bled thousands of nuclear warheads and was the epicenter of American defense in the Cold War. Much of the facility has decayed, including leaky roofs, the *Lubbock Avalanche Journal* reported in November 2014. But it has become the site of a renewable energy project that removes carbon dioxide emis-sions from the air. Bell Helicopter, which has built the V-22 Osprey at its plant in Amarillo, announced layoffs in April 2015.

2012 Presidential Vote		
Mitt Romney (R)...............184,104		(80%)
Barack Obama (D) 42,521		(19%)
2008 Presidential Vote		
John McCain (R).................189,600		(77%)
Barack Obama (D) 54,855		(22%)
Cook Partisan Voting Index: R+32		

Settled by Confederate veterans, the valley was heavily Democratic through the 1970s. The High Plains were for years more Republican. Both are now solidly Republican, and so is the 13th District. Mitt Romney got 80 percent of the vote here, which was his strongest performance in the nation.

Mac Thornberry (R)

Mac Thornberry, first elected in 1994, has been one of Congress' brainiest and most thought-ful Republicans on national and domestic security issues. He capped a long tenure with numerous assignments on the House Armed Services Committee when he became chairman in 2015, the first Texan of either party to hold that post.

His great-great-grandfather, Amos Thornberry, a Union Army veteran and staunch Republican, moved to Clay County, just east of Wichita Falls, in the 1880s. A year after Amos died in 1925, his son bought the cattle ranch in Donley County, closer to Amarillo, which Mac Thornberry and his family now run. After college at Texas Tech and law school at the Uni-versity of Texas, Thornberry worked for influential west Texas GOP Reps. Tom Loeffler and

Larry Combest. He returned to practice law in West Texas, and in 1994, challenged Democratic Rep. Bill Sarpalius, whom he attacked for voting for President Bill Clinton's budget and tax legislation. He profited from news stories that Sarpalius failed to pay a company that moved him to Washington, and then accepted a fee for speaking at the company's convention in Las Vegas. Thornberry won 55%-45%, and has rolled up large reelection margins since.

In the House, Thornberry has a solidly conservative voting record, though he is hardly the most ideological Republican in the Texas delegation. In keeping with his scholarly nature, his official website includes a section on "Mac's reading list." He told *National Journal* that he spends an increasing amount of time dispelling inaccurate rumors from constituents that reach his office, such as one in 2012 that the Homeland Security Department was stockpiling ammunition to create a private army. To further discourage such talk, "one thing we can do is not feed the beast," he said. "It's tempting to play to the crowd, and they may whoop and holler and love you for it. But you're doing people a disservice." The *Dallas Morning News*, in a January 2015 profile with a headline saying he brought "expertise, not notoriety" to his work, wrote that his office bookshelves are "filled with tomes on spy craft, military history and strategy."

Thornberry has often been at the forefront of security issues. In 2002, after the Sept. 11 terrorist attacks, he played a key role in the establishment of the new Homeland Security Department. In 2011, he took over as chairman of the Armed Services' terrorism panel and Speaker John Boehner asked him to lead an effort to develop a cybersecurity strategy for the country. The House in 2012 passed a series of bills based on his task force's recommendations that were in keeping with his desire to take up issues in "bite-sized chunks" rather than in a single sweeping measure. But partisan disagreements stalled action in the Senate. Earlier, as a member of the Intelligence Committee, Thornberry criticized delays in integrating computer networks and intelligence analyses at Homeland Security. He also has championed missile defense and called for better coordination of military space programs. In February 2014, he told reporters that the leaks of confidential information by Edward Snowden were acts of espionage that worked to "compromise the military capability and defense of the country" and would cost of billions of dollars to repair.

Thornberry's district includes the aging Pantex Plant, the nation's only nuclear weapons assembly and disassembly facility. He sought in 2013-14 to improve operations at the Energy Department's National Nuclear Security Administration, which has drawn bipartisan criticism for its safety and security policies. He criticized President Barack Obama's arms control deal with Russia in 2010 for precluding the use of nuclear weapons against non-nuclear nations. He also was critical of the limited input that the administration gave Congress about the use of unmanned drone aircraft to attack suspected terrorists and he added language to the defense authorization bill in 2013 to require that lawmakers be promptly notified of sensitive military operations outside of Afghanistan, including drone strikes.

Despite his expertise on security matters, he lost his bid in 2009 to gain the top Republican post on the Armed Services Committee to Buck McKeon of California, who had more seniority. But they developed a good working relationship, and McKeon named Thornberry in October 2013 to lead a long-term effort to reform the Pentagon's acquisition programs. Thornberry told *Federal Computer Week* that he wanted to change the underlying principles of acquisition instead of merely trying to eliminate wasteful programs. "I think the key is looking ... to the incentives that exist in the system, both on the side of government and on the side of industry," he said. "So there's no new oversight office, no new regulation, no elimination of regulation, that's really going to get at the heart of the matter if the incentives for the program manager or for industry are going to stay the way they are."

McKeon made it known that he wanted Thornberry to be his successor, though senior committee Republicans Randy Forbes of Virginia and Mike Turner of Ohio made known their interest. Thornberry elevated his public profile, giving a May 2014 Heritage Foundation speech that amounted to a GOP rebuttal of Obama's address on foreign policy at West Point. He accused the president of believing he could influence security simply by "giving a speech" and that when it came to achieving U.S. objectives in Afghanistan, "his heart just isn't in it." He called for the administration to take a tougher approach against the Islamic State terrorist organization, telling Fox News in August: "The president is going to have to reassure other countries, including the Iraqis, that if we get into this, we're in it to stay; we're not going to cut and run like we have before." His selection as committee chairman after the 2014 election ultimately was widely approved.

In taking over at Armed Services, Thornberry made clear that he would seek to be a firm check on the Obama administration. "Congress is sometimes criticized for exercising its proper role in defense," he said in a forceful January 2015 speech that made clear he would be an activist and cited Capitol Hill's decision to block the Pentagon's decision to shut down the country's lone tank-production line and its insistence on using Predator drones as a weapon against terrorists. At the same time, though, he acknowledged that Congress can be "parochial" and get things wrong. He told *Politico* he was open to "any solution" that would stave off the steep budget cuts under sequestration. He said he wasn't advocating a tax increase, but acknowledged that higher revenues would be part of any conversation with Obama.

Thornberry won House approval in May 2015 of his first authorization bill, which reflected the view of his committee's defense hawks that the Pentagon needed an infusion of funds for new and expanded programs. Many liberals and a few Republican budget hawks complained that he used budget tricks to break spending ceilings. Defense Secretary Ash Carter called the bill "a road to nowhere" that would be vetoed unless Congress revised both domestic and military spending ceilings. An analysis by business consultants that was published by *Defense One* said the bill's overhaul of Pentagon acquisition procedures "makes considerable strides toward disrupting a procurement process that is widely considered broken, but the bill is far from a fix-all." The measure passed on a 269-151 vote.

On domestic issues, Thornberry has pressed for repeal of the estate tax and adoption of a national sales tax. In 2010, he enacted a bill expanding access to state veterans' homes for parents whose children died while serving in the military. He filed a bill in 2011 to help states set up special health care courts staffed by judges with health policy expertise. The judges would serve as an alternative to juries that Republicans say are inclined to award unnecessarily large damage amounts in malpractice cases. He has supported a two-year budget cycle, an idea that reform groups have said would make the budget process run far more smoothly.

FOURTEENTH DISTRICT

Randy Weber (R)

Elected 2012, 2nd term; b. July 2, 1953, Pearland; U. of Houston–Clear Lake, B.S. 1977; Baptist; married (Brenda); 3 children.

Elected Office: Pearland City Cncl., 1990-96; TX House, 2008-2013.

Professional Career: Owner, Weber's Air & Heat, 1981-present.

DC Office: 510 CHOB, 20515, 202-225-2831; Fax: 202-225-0271; Website: weber.house.gov.

State Offices: Beaumont, 409-835-0108; Lake Jackson, 979-285-0231; League City, 281-316-0231.

Committees: *Foreign Affairs:* Europe, Eurasia & Emerging Threats; Middle East & North Africa. *Science, Space, & Technology:* Energy (Chmn); Environment.

Group Ratings

	ADA	ACLU	AFL-CIO	LCV	ITI	COC	HAFA	ACU	CFG	FRC
2014	10%	0%	–	0%	80%	57%	83%	100%	91%	100%
2013	5%	C	10%	4%	C	69%	C	84%	84%	C

National Journal Ratings

	2013 LIB	—	2013 CONS
Economic	3%	—	97%
Social	16%	—	74%
Foreign	5%	—	86%
Composite	11%	—	89%

Key Votes of the 113th Congress

1. Sandy storm spending	N	5. Medical Marijuana	N	9. Syrian Rebels Training	N
2. Violence Against Women Act	N	6. Farm Bill	Y	10. Keystone pipeline	Y
3. Guantanamo Bay Detainees	N	7. Afghanistan Combat	N	11. Immigration Exec. Action	Y
4. Abortion 20-week ban	Y	8. NSA Phone Data Collection	Y	12. Bipartisan budget deal	N

Election Results

2014 general	Randy Weber (R)............................ 90,116	(62%)	$545,588	$8,690
	Donald Brown (D)......................... 52,545	(36%)	$29,083	
	John Wieder (Lib).......................... 3,037	(2%)		
2014 primary	Randy Weber (R).....................unopposed			

Prior winning percentage: 2012 (53%)

Population		Race and Ethnicity		Income	
Total:	716,592	White	52.3%	Median income:	$52,469
Urban:	29.9%	Latino	23.3%		*(196 of 435)*
Suburban:	67.0%	Black	20.4%	Under $50,000	47.7%
Rural:	3.1%	Asian	2.7%	$50,000-$99,999:	29.4%
Land area:	2,146	Two races	0.9%	$100,000-$199,999:	18.4%
Pop/sq. mi.:	333.9	White Ethnic	20.5%	$200,000 or more:	4.5%
Born in state:	66.1%			Poverty Rate	17.5%
		Education			
Age Groups		H.S. grad or less:	44.4%	**Work**	
Under 18:	24.6%	Some college:	33.4%	White collar:	34.7%
18 to 34:	23.0%	College degree, 4 yr.:	15.3%	Blue collar:	41.3%
35 to 64:	40.3%	Post-grad study:	6.8%	Sales and service:	24.0%
Over 64:	12.2%				
		Military		Govt. workers:	15.2%
		Veterans/active duty:	8.7%		

Gulf Coast: Galveston, Beaumont-Port Arthur

The spongy land of the Texas Gulf Coast remained mostly unsettled until well into the 19th century. When oil was found at the Spindletop field near Beaumont in 1901, the area all around it boomed, first with oil exploration, then petroleum refining, and then petrochemical production. The rig work-

Voter Turnout	
2013 Total Citizen 18+	497,215
2014 House Turnout	145,698
2014 Turnout as % CVAP	29.3%
2012 Turnout as % CVAP	50.4%

ers and mechanical engineers they attracted have given a kind of permanent roughneck air to the region, and it's one of the few places in Texas where unions have any strength. The Humble oil field was once the largest in Texas, and the local Humble Oil and Refining Company is now known as Exxon. Galveston, on a barrier island in the Gulf, was an immigrant port until a 1900 hurricane killed thousands and is now guarded by a 17-foot seawall and connected to the mainland by a hurricane-resistant bridge. Its cruise port in 2013 ranked fourth in total passengers and serves several of the largest cruise lines. The nearby refinery town of Texas City was home to one of the state's worst disasters: In April 1947, more than 500 people died after two freighters containing ammonium nitrate fertilizer exploded, demolishing the port. More recently, Hurricanes Gustav and Ike in 2008 shut down oil pipelines for months and toppled some platforms.

The 14th Congressional District of Texas stretches along the southeast Gulf Coast, from Port Arthur and Beaumont to Freeport at its southernmost point. Just over one-third of the district's population lives in and around the highly polluted "Golden Triangle" oil refining area of Beaumont and Port Arthur, both in Jefferson County. Of the two, Port Arthur is smaller and suffered more during the recession, with unemployment rates through 2012 in excess of 16%; by April 2015, the jobless rate was still high at 9.1%. While refineries are Port Arthur's economic lifeline, the city's downtown is virtually abandoned, and over a quarter of residents live below the poverty level. The BP oil spill disaster and subsequent offshore drilling moratorium hurt not only that industry but the local shrimping economy as well. But the economy received a boost from the January 2014 opening of the southern leg of the Keystone XL pipeline from Cushing, Oklahoma, to the Port Arthur refineries. "Beaumont's recent economic growth outpaced every metro area in Texas," the *Beaumont Enterprise* reported in

2012 Presidential Vote		
Mitt Romney (R).................147,213	(59%)
Barack Obama (D) 97,958	(40%)

2008 Presidential Vote		
John McCain (R).................139,304	(57%)
Barack Obama (D) 102,902	(42%)

Cook Partisan Voting Index: R+12

September 2014. Construction of additional terminals and infrastructure ultimately will benefit the area, regardless of the price of oil and its destination. The population in Jefferson County is 34% African American. The remainder of the district's population is south of Houston in the solidly Republican confines of Galveston and inland Brazoria County, home to the first capital of the Republic of Texas.

The 14th is a working-class, ancestrally Democratic district that has become significantly more Republican over the last three decades. Overall, the 23% Latino and 20% black population have not affected the comfortably Republican tilt. After local favorite ex-Rep. Ron Paul lost the nomination, Mitt Romney won 59% of the vote in November 2012.

Randy Weber (R)

Air conditioning contractor Randy Weber in 2012 prevailed in a crowded Republican primary and claimed the seat of retiring libertarian icon Rep. Ron Paul. Although he lacked the fame of his predecessor, he wasn't afraid to speak his mind and soon posed challenges to House GOP leaders.

Before he was elected to Congress, Weber had always resided within a five-mile radius of his hometown of Pearland. (He bought a new home in nearby Alvin in 2012 after his residence just outside the district became a frequent attack issue against him in the campaign.) His father owned a gas station and later ran an RV business. After high school, Weber enrolled in Alvin Junior College, where he says he was a subpar student until he became a born-again Christian. Weber said that his spiritual reawakening happened on his 20th birthday.

Balancing work at his father's RV business with caring for his new family and taking night classes at the University of Houston-Clear Lake, Weber recalls, required that he awake at 4 a.m. to study and take care of the baby on Wednesdays while his wife went to school to earn a teaching degree. After graduating from college, he started Weber's Air and Heat, making all the service calls and putting flyers on every doorstep in town to drum up business. "Did we struggle? Man, did we," Weber said, recalling the number of times the electric company threatened to turn off his power. "Nobody came to bail out Randy Weber. My company, I made it the old fashioned way." The business had 10 employees when he entered Congress.

In the 1980s, President Ronald Reagan's message of limited government inspired Weber to get politically involved. He became an active Republican volunteer, as well as a precinct judge and election official. From 1990 to 1996, he served on the Pearland City Council. Twelve years after that, he was elected to the Texas House, where he worked on issues ranging from veterans affairs to domestic human trafficking—usually with a strongly conservative view.

In the congressional race, Weber emerged from a field of nine GOP contenders. He secured endorsements from Paul and Texas Gov. Rick Perry, both of whom were presidential candidates in 2012. Weber styled himself as a devoted family man and Christian and he ran "to everyone else's right," wrote David Wasserman of the Cook Political Report. He demonstrated his skill as a fundraiser, joining the ranks of "Young Guns" at the National Republican Congressional Committee. After leading the first round of voting with 28% to 19% for Felicia Harris, an attorney and councilwoman from Pearland, he easily won the runoff with 63% of the vote.

In the general election, Weber faced off against former Rep. Nick Lampson, a Democrat who attempted to distance himself from the national party and who retained some of his local popularity from two earlier stints in the House during which he served a total of five terms. The unique makeup of the district—rife with working-class voters—coupled with the political chops of both men, led the *Texas Tribune* to dub it the only "real, true, honest-to-goodness competition" in the deeply red state in 2012. Republicans needed to work harder than expected, especially when Weber ran short of cash in the final weeks of the campaign. Each candidate spent a bit more than a million dollars. Lampson benefited from his name ID and the local Democratic lean to take 58% of the vote in Jefferson, but Weber ran stronger in his base, with 68% in Brazoria. Galveston, which cast 45% of the total vote, became the swing county, and Weber got 57% of its vote. Voters' enmity toward President Barack Obama helped Weber win, 53%-45%. He was reelected in 2014 with 62% of the vote against an opponent whom he outspent nearly 20-to-1.

When he arrived in Washington, he unabashedly said that nobody would "out-conservative" him—unlike Paul, whose libertarian views on some social and foreign policy issues sometimes fit more comfortably with Democrats. In June 2014, Weber filed a resolution condemning Obama for having routinely refused to enforce the law and said that the president was provoking a constitutional crisis. "In my view, the president has not faithfully executed the law," Weber said. He voted for GOP Rep. Louie Gohmert of Texas—and against John Boehner—for House speaker in January 2015, and explained, "I voted according to my constituents' wishes," and that he hoped that his vote sent a signal to GOP leaders that "we need to be more forceful in fighting this president and his liberal agenda." He later told reporters that he paid a price that week when his plan to sponsor a routine bill on Energy Department research was given to another GOP member.

He got an opportunity to deal with important local issues when he became chairman of the Science, Space and Technology Subcommittee on Energy. He listed the removal of the ban on crude-oil exports as an important priority. But it was a good bet that Weber would not be assigned a leadership role on that measure.

FIFTEENTH DISTRICT

Rubén Hinojosa (D)

Elected 1996, 10th term; b. Aug. 20, 1940, Edcouch; U. of TX, B.B.A. 1962, M.B.A. 1980; Catholic; married (Martha); 5 children.

Elected Office: Mercedes Schl. Bd., 1972-74; TX Bd. of Ed., 1974-84.

Professional Career: Pres. & CEO, H&H Foods Inc., 1976-1996; Chmn, Hidalgo & Starr Cnty. Bd. of S. TX Comm. Col., 1993-96; consultant, H&H Foods, 1996-2008.

DC Office: 2262 RHOB, 20515, 202-225-2531; Fax: 202-225-5688; Website: hinojosa.house.gov.

State Offices: Edinburg, 956-682-5545.

Committees: *Education & the Workforce:* Health, Employment, Labor & Pensions; Higher Education & Workforce Training (RMM). *Financial Services:* Capital Markets & Government Sponsored Enterprises; Financial Institutions & Consumer Credit.

Group Ratings

	ADA	ACLU	AFL-CIO	LCV	ITI	COC	HAFA	ACU	CFG	FRC
2014	75%	66%	–	63%	40%	62%	14%	4%	6%	20%
2013	70%	C	100%	82%	C	38%	C	9%	12%	C

National Journal Ratings

	2013 LIB	—	2013 CONS
Economic	65%	—	34%
Social	62%	—	38%
Foreign	69%	—	29%
Composite	66%	—	34%

Key Votes of the 113th Congress

1. Sandy storm spending	Y	5. Medical Marijuana	N	9. Syrian Rebels Training	Y
2. Violence Against Women Act	NV	6. Farm Bill	N	10. Keystone pipeline	Y
3. Guantanamo Bay Detainees	NV	7. Afghanistan Combat	Y	11. Immigration Exec. Action	N
4. Abortion 20-week ban	N	8. NSA Phone Data Collection	N	12. Bipartisan budget deal	Y

Election Results

2014 general	Ruben Hinojosa (D)	48,708	(54%)	$466,828	$2,210
	Eddie Zamora (R)	39,016	(43%)	$129,150	
	Johnny Partain (Lib)	2,460	(3%)		
2014 primary	Ruben Hinojosa (D)	unopposed			

Prior winning percentages: 2012 (61%), 2010 (56%), 2008 (66%), 2006 (62%), 2004 (58%), 2002 (100%), 2000 (88%), 1998 (58%), 1996 (62%)

Population		Race and Ethnicity		Income	
Total:	731,065	Latino	80.2%	Median income:	$40,440
Urban:	54.7%	White	16.4%		*(383 of 435)*
Suburban:	34.0%	Black	1.5%	Under $50,000	59.1%
Rural:	11.4%	Asian	1.3%	$50,000-$99,999:	26.9%
Land area:	6,200	Two races	0.5%	$100,000-$199,999:	12.1%
Pop/sq. mi.:	117.9	White Ethnic	6.2%	$200,000 or more:	1.9%
Born in state:	64.1%			Poverty Rate	29.0%
		Education			
Age Groups		H.S. grad or less:	57.0%	**Work**	
Under 18:	32.1%	Some college:	25.3%	White collar:	27.4%
18 to 34:	24.1%	College degree, 4 yr.:	13.1%	Blue collar:	48.1%
35 to 64:	33.5%	Post-grad study:	4.7%	Sales and service:	24.5%
Over 64:	10.3%				
		Military		Govt. workers:	19.1%
		Veterans/active duty:	6.0%		

McAllen/San Antonio Corridor

A century ago, there was little but desert wilderness in the Lower Rio Grande Valley in South Texas. Only a handful of people lived anywhere near the shallow, sluggish Rio Grande. There was no U.S. Border Patrol because very few people wanted to venture across desert. Then came

Voter Turnout	
2013 Total Citizen 18+	386,355
2014 House Turnout	90,184
2014 Turnout as % CVAP	23.3%
2012 Turnout as % CVAP	40.2%

pioneers like Lloyd Bentsen Sr., father of the former senator and Treasury secretary, who arrived after World War I with $5 in his pocket and became one of the Valley's biggest landowners. Bentsen and others cleared the land and dug canals, hired Mexican and Mexican-American workers, and with irrigated water from the Rio Grande planted citrus groves, cornfields and palm windbreaks, ran cattle and drilled for oil and gas. Along U.S. 83, north of the Rio Grande, these pioneers built a string of towns with Anglo names and storefronts. But most of the people were Latino in culture and language. Wage levels higher than in Mexico, though low by U.S. standards, brought more Mexicans over the border.

The 15th Congressional District of Texas is one of three districts in the Lower Rio Grande Valley that run from the river along the border to just north of San Antonio. The days are past when ranchers and oilmen wielded absolute political power here. There is instead a robust, mostly Hispanic politics. The Hispanic population in the district is 80%, the second-highest in the state. Although the district reaches as far north as the rural area between Corpus Christi and San Antonio, three-quarters of its residents live just north of the river in McAllen-based Hidalgo County. Reasonably priced real estate contributed to fast-paced growth in the region and Hidalgo's population more than doubled from 1990 to 2010, with continuing rapid growth to 816,000 in 2013.

The local infrastructure has barely kept up as subdivisions have replaced citrus groves. In the McAllen area, new suburbanites work just across the border as corporate managers in the low-wage "maquiladoras," or factories. Poverty is pervasive. As of 2012, 34% of residents lived below the poverty line, the second highest rate for a metro area in the nation. The McAllen-Edinburg area also reported the highest obesity rate in the country at 39%, according to a 2012 Gallup survey. The abortion clinic in McAllen has become a flashpoint in the federal litigation

2012 Presidential Vote
Barack Obama (D) 86,941 (57%)
Mitt Romney (R)..................62,885 (42%)

2008 Presidential Vote
Barack Obama (D) 83,924 (57%)
John McCain (R)..................61,282 (42%)

Cook Partisan Voting Index: D+5

over state-imposed restrictions on abortion. The region is struggling to handle crime from the trade in illegal immigration and drugs. Another Gallup survey in April 2014 found that McAllen had the highest rate of fear of walking alone at night.

The district is heavily Democratic in the border areas but more conservative elsewhere. President Barack Obama carried the district with 57% in 2012, a few points less than he got in each of the two adjacent heavily Hispanic districts. The 15th shares Hidalgo with the 28th and 34th Districts, but includes about 70% of the total.

Rubén Hinojosa (D)

Rubén Hinojosa, a Democrat first elected in 1996, has been a staunch advocate for improving education, housing and rural economic development for Hispanics. He served as chairman of the Congressional Hispanic Caucus in 2013-14, hoping for a prominent role on immigration reform, but the House took little action on the issue during that time.

Hinojosa grew up in Mercedes, where his family owned H&H Foods, a company that produced Mexican foods and was one of the largest employers in the Rio Grande Valley. After earning his bachelor's and M.B.A. from the University of Texas, he went into the family business and was active in civic affairs, primarily in education and regional development. He served on the state Board of Education and led an effort to create three regional magnet schools.

When the seat opened in 1996, Hinojosa led initial voting in the Democratic primary against Anglo lawyer Jim Selman 34%-33%. During the runoff campaign, Selman questioned Hinojosa's Democratic credentials and said he profited from government contracts. Hinojosa emphasized his interest in improving educational opportunities and extending highways to the Lower Rio Grande Valley. Hinojosa took some moderate positions, calling for a reduction of the capital gains tax and investment tax credits for those making capital improvements. He won the runoff 52%-48% and easily won the general election.

Hinojosa has had a centrist voting record among House Democrats, especially on economic issues. But he moved more in line with his party to back the Obama administration's major initiatives. He introduced a bill in March 2013 to expand "early college" schools that allow students to earn college credit while getting their high school diplomas. He has sought to protect benefits for legal immigrants, to promote the North American Free Trade Agreement, and to demand that Mexico deliver on its agreement for water to South Texas farmers. He has a proclivity for holding out on votes to make last-minute legislative deals. He supported Republican President George W. Bush's proposal for broader authority to negotiate trade deals after he was promised a job training project for his district.

Hinojosa has struggled to advance in the House at times. Despite support in 2003 from the Texas delegation for a spot on the Ways and Means Committee, Hinojosa was passed over in favor of Texas Rep. Max Sandlin, a Nancy Pelosi ally who lost reelection two years later. In early 2005, Hinojosa made a bid for vice chairman of the Democratic Caucus, but abandoned his candidacy after two weeks because of a lack of support.

After Democrats won control of the House in 2006, Hinojosa chaired the Higher Education, Life Long Learning, and Competitiveness Subcommittee, where he focused on families he said were traditionally left behind in American education. After the GOP regained control in 2010, he became the ranking Democrat on the renamed Higher Education and Workforce Training panel. He joined Democrats in walking out of a March 2013 hearing to consider a Republican worker training bill that he and other committee leaders from his party said "was being advanced for political reasons, not to make the workforce investment system work better." In April 2015, he introduced with Democratic Sen. Mazie Hirono of Hawaii legislative changes to expand the use of Pell grants for university students, including benefits for children brought to the country illegally by their parents.

Taking over as head of the Hispanic Caucus, Hinojosa in 2013 called the bipartisan Senate blueprint on immigration "a good foundation for the legislation that is needed." But a bipartisan House task force was unable to resolve differences, and Republican leaders did not pursue legislative action. He clashed with the conservative Heritage Foundation over its report on the lower intellectual skills of immigrants, which Hinojosa termed "ugly racism and xenophobia dressed up in economic hyperbole." In March 2014, he joined a handful of Hispanic lawmakers who met with President Barack Obama to encourage his plans to suspend deportation of illegal immigrants.

In February 2011, Hinojosa made headlines when, as a member of the Financial Services Committee, he filed for personal bankruptcy. He blamed the problem on a loan that he guaranteed for his family's food products company that led him to owe $2.6 million to Wells Fargo Bank. Republicans discussed making a serious run at Hinojosa in 2012, but their plans fell apart when their preferred candidate, Latina businesswoman Rebecca Cervera, lost in the GOP primary. Hinojosa crushed Republican Dale Brueggemann, 61%-37%, and subsequently emerged from bankruptcy. In 2014, Hinojosa faced a more competitive contest from three-time GOP challenger Eddie Zamora, a local businessman and anti-abortion advocate. Hinojosa outspent him $467,000 to $129,000, and won 54%-43%. Hinojosa took the district overall by about 9,700 votes. He led in Hidalgo by 19,200 votes, which meant that he trailed significantly elsewhere in the district, which cast 40% of the total vote.

In May 2015, Hinojosa was one of nine House members that the House Ethics Committee said it was investigating for accepting extensive gifts during a 2013 visit to Azerbaijan. Hinojosa said the committee had granted prior approval for the trip, but the McAllen *Monitor* newspaper demanded more information. The committee dismissed the case in July 2015.

SIXTEENTH DISTRICT

Beto O'Rourke (D)

Elected 2012, 2nd term; b. Sept. 26, 1972, El Paso; Columbia U., B.A. 1995; Catholic; married (Amy Sanders); 3 children.

Elected Office: El Paso City Cncl., 2005-11.

Professional Career: Owner, Stanton St. Tech. Group, 1999-present

DC Office: 1330 LHOB, 20515, 202-225-4831;Website: orourke.house.gov.

State Offices: El Paso, 915-541-1400.

Committees: *Armed Services:* Military Personnel; Readiness. *Veterans' Affairs:* Health; Oversight & Investigations.

Group Ratings

	ADA	ACLU	AFL-CIO	LCV	ITI	COC	HAFA	ACU	CFG	FRC
2014	85%	94%	–	97%	60%	29%	16%	8%	13%	0%
2013	80%	C	95%	96%	C	46%	C	20%	19%	C

National Journal Ratings

	2013 LIB	—	2013 CONS
Economic	74%	—	25%
Social	93%	—	0%
Foreign	83%	—	15%
Composite	85%	—	15%

Key Votes of the 113th Congress

1. Sandy storm spending	Y	5. Medical Marijuana	Y	9. Syrian Rebels Training N
2. Violence Against Women Act	Y	6. Farm Bill	N	10. Keystone pipeline N
3. Guantanamo Bay Detainees	Y	7. Afghanistan Combat	Y	11. Immigration Exec. Action N
4. Abortion 20-week ban	N	8. NSA Phone Data Collection	Y	12. Bipartisan budget deal Y

Election Results

2014 general	Beto O'Rourke (D)	49,338	(68%)	$409,513
	Corey Roen (R)	21,324	(29%)	
	Jaime Perez (Lib)	2,443	(3%)	
2014 primary	Beto O'Rourke (D)	unopposed		

Prior winning percentage: 2012 (68%)

Population		Race and Ethnicity		Income	
Total:	728,654	Latino	79.3%	Median income:	$41,207
Urban:	97.7%	White	15.3%		*(374 of 435)*
Suburban:	2.3%	Black	3.3%	Under $50,000	59.1%
Rural:	0.0%	Asian	1.2%	$50,000-$99,999:	27.0%
Land area:	688	Two races	0.6%	$100,000-$199,999:	11.7%
Pop/sq. mi.:	1,059.6	White Ethnic	5.5%	$200,000 or more:	2.3%
Born in state:	54.8%			Poverty Rate	21.0%
		Education			
Age Groups		H.S. grad or less:	46.0%	**Work**	
Under 18:	28.5%	Some college:	31.2%	White collar:	32.1%
18 to 34:	26.1%	College degree, 4 yr.:	15.7%	Blue collar:	47.1%
35 to 64:	34.3%	Post-grad study:	7.1%	Sales and service:	20.8%
Over 64:	11.0%				
		Military		Govt. workers:	21.4%
		Veterans/active duty:	12.8%		

El Paso

El Paso, Texas, and Ciudad Juaréz, Mexico, face each other across the narrow Rio Grande, their tree-shaded streets spread out below the rough brown face of Comanche Peak. Downtown El Paso is only a few blocks from the bridge to Ciudad Juaréz. The two border cities are surrounded by

Voter Turnout	
2013 Total Citizen 18+	421,508
2014 House Turnout	73,105
2014 Turnout as % CVAP	17.3%
2012 Turnout as % CVAP	37%

hundreds of miles of some of North America's most rugged and desolate landscape. El Paso is closer to San Diego than to Houston, and it's in a different time zone from the rest of the state. Still, the region has grown significantly. In the 1950s, El Paso and Ciudad Juaréz each had a population around 130,000. In 2014, there were 833,000 people in El Paso County (including 675,000 in the city of El Paso), 81% of them Hispanic, and the Mexican census counted 1.3 million in metro Juaréz. This is a bilingual, bicultural pair of cities, where most people have a Mexican heritage. El Paso is one of the lowest-wage and lowest-education locales in the United States, though statistically it is also one of the safest, with the lowest crime rate of any large U.S. city. Ciudad Juaréz, though struggling with drug cartel violence and crime, is one of the highest-wage cities in Mexico.

In the wake of the North American Free Trade Agreement, *maquiladora* factories created a cross-border economy. Much of the local economy is built on cheap, low-skill labor. South of the border, there is a large General Motors technical center. Many factories on both sides of the border were shuttered during the 2007-09 recession, but trade with Mexico helped shield El Paso from the worst of the economic downturn. The other important factor was Fort Bliss, a big winner in the 2005 base closing review, with a $5 billion expansion and a net gain of nearly 30,000 soldiers. The Milken Institute in January 2012 ranked El Paso's economy as the 18th best-performing among 200 metro areas. But most of its job growth has been in leisure and hospitality, jobs that carry lower wages than new jobs in the rest of the state. Only 72% of El Paso County residents are high school graduates. In September 2012, the Brookings Institution reported that El Paso had the third-largest "workforce education gap" of the 100 biggest metropolitan areas in the country, with demand for jobs outstripping the supply of educated workers. Health care is a growth sector in the district: The Medical Center of Americas, an integrated 440-acre campus of medical facilities in El Paso, in 2014 became fully operational. By April 2015, unemployment in the county had dropped to 4.9%. But there has been deep concern about the potentially devastating impact of an expected nationwide base-

2012 Presidential Vote		
Barack Obama (D) 100,993	(64%)
Mitt Romney (R)...................54,315	(35%)
2008 Presidential Vote		
Barack Obama (D) 109,387	(64%)
John McCain (R)...................58,764	(35%)
Cook Partisan Voting Index: D+12		

closing review in 2017. One in three jobs in El Paso depends directly or indirectly on Fort Bliss. A more immediate fear was reports in April 2015 of an Islamic State terrorist cell operating in Ciudad Juarez, though local authorities have dismissed the concerns.

The 16th Congressional District of Texas is based entirely in El Paso County—the city itself, the suburban fringe, giant Fort Bliss to the north, and rural housing settlements known as *colonias*, most without electricity and running water, spreading out to the east and south. The district is solidly Democratic. The sprawling 23rd District includes the remaining 9% of El Paso voters. In both 2008 and 2012, Barack Obama won the 16th with 64% of the vote.

Beto O'Rourke (D)

Democrat Beto O'Rourke, a sort of preppy Anglo and former El Paso city councilman, won this heavily Latino district in the 2012 season when he defeated eight-term Rep. Silvestre Reyes, who had been chairman of the Intelligence Committee and of the Hispanic Caucus. O'Rourke settled comfortably into an outsider niche.

Born to a family that has lived in El Paso for four generations, O'Rourke's roots in the district run deep. His first name is short for Roberto. His grandmother opened a furniture store there in 1950 that his mother now owns, and his father, also a Democrat, served on the El Paso County Commissioners Court and as a county judge in the 1980s. A self-described "bookish" teenager, O'Rourke spent much of his high school time in the library. "I had a real fascination with books and learning," he said. He attended Woodberry Forest, a preparatory school in Virginia, on a full scholarship and worked in the school library.

At Columbia University, O'Rourke majored in English and worked odd jobs to help pay his way, including delivering newspapers and washing windows. He also played guitar in a rock band called Foss, which did tours and was part of the emerging do-it-yourself punk movement. O'Rourke and his bandmates often were dependent on the goodwill of club owners and nearby residents for meals and places to sleep. He describes it as an "absolutely magical" time in his life. "We met wonderful people involved in that culture of rock 'n' roll and in their community," he said. "It was just awesome."

After college, O'Rourke landed a job in the then-developing Web technology field. He spent three years working in Manhattan, then returned to El Paso to start his own company. Stanton Street Technology Group began in his apartment, with O'Rourke and a couple of his friends mastering HTML and coding work for local websites. Today, the company provides Internet services throughout El Paso and nationally.

O'Rourke became involved in civic work, seeking to reverse a trend of young people leaving El Paso. With an economy dependent on low-wage, low-skill jobs, the city was "not a place you wanted to be," he said. Many jobs had been outsourced to Mexico, and bridges from Ciudad Juárez, Mexico, into El Paso had some of the longest waiting times along the border, threatening tens of thousands of local jobs. O'Rourke served two terms on the City Council. He worked to save Sun Metro, public transportation in El Paso, from a fiscal meltdown. In 2011, *Newsweek* named El Paso the No. 1 "Can-Do City" for its civic progress.

In his June primary challenge, O'Rourke argued that Reyes had accomplished little on the Veterans' Affairs Committee and failed to work on a solution to reduce bridge traffic. Reyes attacked O'Rourke for his support of legalizing marijuana and painted him as unfit for office based on his arrest for drunken driving 16 years earlier. The charge had been dismissed. O'Rourke unexpectedly defeated Reyes 50%-44%, assuring his victory in the heavily Democratic district. He has easily defeated his Republican opponents.

Serving on the Armed Services and Veterans' Affairs committees, O'Rourke was not reluctant to criticize the Obama administration. The more than two months that are required for El Paso veterans to meet with a mental health counselor at the local VA facility, he said, helps to explain the suicides among local veterans.

Eager to move immigration legislation, he told *The Washington Post* in November 2014 that President Barack Obama's proposed executive order was "noble" in its intention, but "terrible" by adding to "the precedent of presidents bypassing Congress to achieve something they think is important to national interest." With Republican Rep. Steve Pearce of New Mexico, he filed a bill that sought to increase transparency and accountability at the Customs and Border Protection agency. He said that he was responding to growing reports of abuses by officers along the border. The Hispanic Caucus determined in 2013 that O'Rourke was not eligible for membership, though his spokeswoman said that he never asked to join.

In a September 2013 interview with the elpasoinc.com web site, he said that the biggest surprise to him about serving in Congress was, "They set your expectations so low when you come in the door." The advice of senior Democrats, he explained, was "You will not pass any legislation or be able to get anything done. You should focus on raising money, winning re-election and returning us to a majority so that you can do those things you ran for in Congress." The most positive surprise, he added, was that he was able to get things done in the Armed Services Committee and on behalf of Fort Bliss. He cited his work with Republican Rep. Joe Wilson of South Carolina to restore tuition assistance that had been eliminated because of tight budgets. In September 2014, O'Rourke was among 22 House Democrats who condemned the Obama administration's handling of the swap of Army deserter Bowe Bergdahl for five Taliban prisoners at Guantanamo.

In another display of independence, O'Rourke joined first-term Republican Rep. Jim Bridenstine of Oklahoma in sponsoring a bill imposing 10-year term limits for members of Congress. "The longer you're there, the more these interests and access agreements you've implicitly developed," he explained. He co-founded with Republican Rep. Rod Blum of Iowa the Congressional Term Limits Caucus, and O'Rourke said that he planned to limit himself to a maximum of eight years.

SEVENTEENTH DISTRICT

Bill Flores (R)

Elected 2010, 3rd term; b. Feb. 25, 1954, Cheyenne, WY; TX A&M U., B.B.A. 1976, Houston Baptist U., M.B.A. 1985; Baptist; married (Gina); 2 children.

Professional Career: Keyes Offshore, 1980-90; Marine Drilling, 1990-97; Western Atlas, 1997-98; Gryphon Exploration, 2001-05; Accountant, financial mgr., Phoenix Exploration, 2006-09.

DC Office: 1030 LHOB, 20515, 202-225-6105; Fax: 202-225-0350; Website: flores.house.gov.

State Offices: Austin, 512-373-3378; Bryan, 979-703-4037; Waco, 254-732-0748.

Committees: *Energy & Commerce:* Energy & Power; Environment & the Economy; Oversight & Investigations.

Group Ratings

	ADA	ACLU	AFL-CIO	LCV	ITI	COC	HAFA	ACU	CFG	FRC
2014	0%	0%	–	0%	80%	71%	71%	92%	76%	100%
2013	0%	C	10%	4%	C	85%	C	88%	83%	C

National Journal Ratings

	2013 LIB — 2013 CONS	
Economic	8% —	91%
Social	16% —	74%
Foreign	0% —	95%
Composite	11% —	89%

Key Votes of the 113th Congress

1. Sandy storm spending	N	5. Medical Marijuana	N	9. Syrian Rebels Training	Y
2. Violence Against Women Act	N	6. Farm Bill	Y	10. Keystone pipeline	Y
3. Guantanamo Bay Detainees	N	7. Afghanistan Combat	N	11. Immigration Exec. Action	Y
4. Abortion 20-week ban	Y	8. NSA Phone Data Collection	N	12. Bipartisan budget deal	Y

Election Results

2014 general	Bill Flores (R)	85,807	(65%)	$809,523	$26,608
	Nick Haynes (D)	43,049	(32%)		
	Shawn Michael Hamilton (Lib)	4,009	(3%)		
2014 primary	Bill Flores (R)	unopposed			

Prior winning percentages: 2012 (80%), 2010 (62%)

Population		Race and Ethnicity		Income	
Total:	726,128	White	58.0%	Median income:	$45,373
Urban:	62.5%	Latino	22.9%		*(313 of 435)*
Suburban:	15.8%	Black	13.2%	Under $50,000	54.0%
Rural:	21.7%	Asian	4.0%	$50,000-$99,999:	29.1%
Land area:	6,702	Two races	1.6%	$100,000-$199,999:	14.1%
Pop/sq. mi.:	108.3	White Ethnic	19.3%	$200,000 or more:	2.9%
Born in state:	66.0%			Poverty Rate	20.7%
		Education			
Age Groups		H.S. grad or less:	41.5%	**Work**	
Under 18:	23.0%	Some college:	30.6%	White collar:	35.9%
18 to 34:	31.4%	College degree, 4 yr.:	17.6%	Blue collar:	43.6%
35 to 64:	34.0%	Post-grad study:	10.3%	Sales and service:	20.5%
Over 64:	11.5%				
		Military		Govt. workers:	19.2%
		Veterans/active duty:	7.7%		

Central Texas: Waco, College Station

Waco, about midway between Dallas and Austin, is deep in the heart of Texas. In the late 19th century, it was one of the largest cotton markets in the world, a rip-roaring town with legalized prostitution. In 1870, Waco opened across the Brazos River what was then the largest single-span suspension bridge in the United States. It became the main depot along the Chisholm Trail, which cattlemen used to drive their longhorns north to Kansas stockyards. In 1885, a Waco pharmacist concocted the first Dr. Pepper. Waco is the home of Baylor University, the oldest

Voter Turnout	
2013 Total Citizen 18+	504,006
2014 House Turnout	132,865
2014 Turnout as % CVAP	26.4%
2012 Turnout as % CVAP	45.3%

college in Texas and the largest Baptist university in the world. The city has embarked on an "Imagine Waco" program to restore a walkable downtown.

Near Waco are the ruins of David Koresh's Branch Davidian compound, the scene of fatal standoff in 1993 between cult extremists and federal agents attempting to execute a search warrant. In Waco's McLennan County is the tiny town of Crawford, where the White House press corps huddled when President George W. Bush stayed at his 1,583-acre Prairie Chapel Ranch.

The 17th Congressional District of Texas includes all of eight counties and parts of four more, but centers on Waco and McLennan County, which has a third of the district's population. The southwestern tip of the district covers a small slice of northern Austin and most of socially diverse suburban Pflugerville, whose population jumped from 4,400 in 1990 to more than 50,000 residents in 2010. The other population center is Brazos County, whose largest city, College Station, is home to Texas A&M University. The school's agricultural and military tradition has given it a much more conservative ambience than the similarly selective University of Texas at Austin. College Station is the site of the George H.W. Bush Presidential Library; former Defense Secretary Robert Gates had been president of A&M until he left for Washington in December 2006. The university is one of three federally funded centers to prepare the country for a biological attack. In May 2015, a bloody war broke out among bikers at a Twin Peaks restaurant, which left nine bikers killed, another 18 injured and resulted in the arrests of 177 motorcyclists from rival gangs.

2012 Presidential Vote		
Mitt Romney (R)................135,309	(60%)
Barack Obama (D) 84,531	(38%)
2008 Presidential Vote		
John McCain (R).................135,738	(58%)
Barack Obama (D) 95,884	(41%)
Cook Partisan Voting Index: R+13		

The political tradition in Central Texas for more than a century after the Civil War was heavily Democratic. This area voted for Hubert Humphrey in 1968, while most of the rural South went for George Wallace and Richard Nixon. As recently as 1990, it voted Democratic for governor, supporting Waco native Ann Richards. Since then, the district has followed most of non-urban Texas to the Republican Party. Mitt Romney won 60 percent of the district-wide vote in 2012.

Bill Flores (R)

Republican Bill Flores, a retired oil and gas executive, won his seat in 2010 by defeating Rep. Chet Edwards, the final remaining "yellow dog" Texas Democrat. In addition to zealously guarding home-state interests with a seat on the Energy and Commerce Committee, Flores was selected after the 2014 election as chairman of the conservative Republican Study Committee. He defeated a more activist contender, which led some to depict Flores as the establishment candidate. He rejected that characterization.

Flores was born at Warren Air Force Base in Cheyenne, Wyoming. After his father's military tour of duty, the family moved back to Stratford, in the northern tip of the Texas Panhandle. From age 9, Flores helped work cattle on the family's ranch. "I was always taught that you don't turn to the government for anything. You create your own opportunities," Flores said in an interview.

Flores helped pay his way through Texas A&M, where he was a member of the Corps of Cadets, the student body government, and the honor guard. He has remained active as an alumnus, donating millions of dollars to his alma mater to fund scholarships. After graduation, he went to work for the KPMG accounting firm and built a career as a financial manager for several large corporations, eventually settling in the oil and gas industry in Houston. He was president and chief executive officer of Phoenix Exploration until late 2009, when he ran for Congress.

He had four opponents in the March 2010 Republican primary. After leading 2008 GOP nominee Rob Curnock in the first round, 33%-29%, Flores won the runoff, 65%-35%. He ran against Edwards, a 20-year incumbent with considerable political skills who had taken care to cast conservative votes on some issues and to tend to the needs of sprawling Fort Hood. But his standing with conservatives was damaged when liberal House Speaker Nancy Pelosi in July 2008 mentioned him as a possible Democratic vice presidential candidate. That year, Republican Curnock held the Democratic incumbent to a 53%-46% victory, even though Edwards outspent him $2 million to $96,000.

In the 2010 general election, Flores targeted Edwards's vote for the 2009 economic stimulus bill. And he emphasized his own business credentials, saying that he would bring to Congress the discipline of a successful accountant. Flores touted his role in the early 1990s helping to turn around a financially struggling oil and gas company called Marine Drilling. However, *The Dallas Morning News* reported that a Marine subsidiary filed for bankruptcy in 1992, leaving the government with $7.5 million in unpaid debt. Edwards assembled a "Vets for Chet" parade with retired generals attesting to his work for Fort Hood and attacked Flores as a Houston interloper.

It was a high-dollar race, with Edwards spending $3.8 million and Flores $3.3 million ($1.5 million of it his own money), with outside groups spending another $720,000 against Edwards and $1 million against Flores. By summer, Edwards was trailing badly in polls, and the Democratic Congressional Campaign Committee mostly pulled out of the race to focus resources on more winnable contests. Flores won by an impressive 62%-37%, carrying all but one small county. He won with just 52% in Waco's McLennan County, but got 64% in College Station's Brazos County and 71% in Johnson County south of Fort Worth.

In the House, Flores' first bills were measures to set more stringent deadlines for government approval of offshore oil and gas drilling and to extend for 12 months all leases in the Gulf of Mexico affected by the Interior Department's drilling moratoriums after the massive BP spill. He later successfully amended several House-passed bills to block a provision in the 2007 energy law promoting the use of alternative fuels in federal vehicles. In one instance involving the Pentagon in June 2011, he said, "The Defense Department should not be wasting its time studying fuel emissions and should not have to be stifled by the arguments over how to interpret a small section of an energy law." He took heat from constituents at home for voting in 2011 to raise the federal debt limit, but opposed the subsequent tax and spending compromise in 2013 to avoid the so-called "fiscal cliff." In 2015, he gained a seat on Energy and Commerce, a valuable niche for a former oil executive from Texas.

Flores became active in the Republican Study Committee, the caucus of the House's most conservative members. He decided to run for chairman after the 2014 election, after years in which the RSC had become increasingly confrontational within the GOP and often spent more time attacking other Republicans than Democrats. He sought a more constructive relationship that would push the party agenda to the right. He also wanted to lower the press profile of the RSC. In the contest for the chairmanship, his chief foe was South Carolina Rep. Mike Mulvaney, who had been a far more outspoken member of the class first elected in 2010. After the easy victory by Flores, which was encouraged by allies of Speaker John Boehner, Mulvaney and other mavericks created the Freedom Caucus to give them a separate forum to challenge Boehner and other GOP leaders.

In an interview with *Roll Call* in July 2015, Flores asserted that the new Freedom Caucus had become "complementary" to the RSC, in part because of their stylistic differences, and that each had been effective in pushing conservative themes. The key for the RSC, according to Flores, was to encourage its members to pursue their personal interests while uniting on issues where they had common ground. He cited their efforts to block the District of Columbia's new Reproductive Health Non-Discrimination Act, which blocked religious employers from refusing to hire workers because of their views on abortions.

At home, he easily deflected a GOP primary challenger in 2012 by getting 83% of the vote. Democrats abandoned what had been a fertile playing ground for them and didn't field a candidate in November. Flores beat Libertarian Ben Easton 80%-20%. In 2014, he had no primary and his reelection was routine.

EIGHTEENTH DISTRICT

Sheila Jackson Lee (D)

Elected 1994, 11th term; b. Jan. 12, 1950, Queens, NY; Yale U., B.A. 1972, U. of VA Law Schl., J.D. 1975; Seventh Day Adventist; married (Elwyn Lee); 2 children.

Elected Office: Houston City Cncl., 1990-94.

Professional Career: Practicing atty., 1975-77, 1978-87; Staff counsel, U.S. House Select Assassinations Cmte., 1977-78; Houston assoc. municipal judge, 1987-90.

DC Office: 2252 RHOB, 20515, 202-225-3816; Fax: 202-225-3317; Website: jacksonlee.house.gov.

State Offices: Acres Home, 713-691-4882; Fifth Ward, 713-227-7740; Heights, 713-861-4070; Houston, 713-655-0050.

Committees: *Homeland Security:* Border & Maritime Security; Cybersecurity, Infrastructure Protection & Security Technologies. *Judiciary:* Crime, Terrorism, Homeland Security & Investigations (RMM); Immigration & Border Security.

Group Ratings

	ADA	ACLU	AFL-CIO	LCV	ITI	COC	HAFA	ACU	CFG	FRC
2014	85%	77%	–	86%	40%	50%	16%	8%	16%	0%
2013	80%	C	100%	82%	C	23%	C	13%	13%	C

National Journal Ratings

	2013 LIB	—	2013 CONS
Economic	72%	—	27%
Social	77%	—	23%
Foreign	65%	—	34%
Composite	72%	—	28%

Key Votes of the 113th Congress

1. Sandy storm spending	NV	5. Medical Marijuana	Y	9. Syrian Rebels Training	Y
2. Violence Against Women Act	Y	6. Farm Bill	N	10. Keystone pipeline	Y
3. Guantanamo Bay Detainees	Y	7. Afghanistan Combat	Y	11. Immigration Exec. Action	N
4. Abortion 20-week ban	N	8. NSA Phone Data Collection	N	12. Bipartisan budget deal	Y

Election Results

2014 general	Sheila Jackson Lee (D)	76,097	(72%)	$384,140
	Sean Seibert (R)	26,249	(25%)	$7,669
	Vince Duncan (I)	2,362	(2%)	
2014 primary	Sheila Jackson Lee (D)	unopposed		

Prior winning percentages: 2012 (75%), 2010 (70%), 2008 (77%), 2006 (77%), 2004 (89%), 2002 (77%), 2000 (76%), 1998 (90%), 1996 (77%), 1994 (73%)

Population		Race and Ethnicity		Income	
Total:	741,385	Latino	41.0%	Median income:	$41,043
Urban:	92.6%	Black	38.2%		(375 of 435)
Suburban:	7.4%	White	15.9%	Under $50,000	58.1%
Rural:	0.0%	Asian	3.9%	$50,000-$99,999:	26.0%
Land area:	228	Two races	0.9%	$100,000-$199,999:	12.5%
Pop/sq. mi.:	3,246.3	White Ethnic	7.3%	$200,000 or more:	3.5%
Born in state:	59.7%			Poverty Rate	24.2%

Age Groups		Education			
Under 18:	26.6%	H.S. grad or less:	52.8%	Work	
18 to 34:	28.5%	Some college:	26.9%	White collar:	27.8%
35 to 64:	36.4%	College degree, 4 yr.:	12.9%	Blue collar:	44.5%
Over 64:	8.5%	Post-grad study:	7.4%	Sales and service:	27.7%

Military			
Veterans/active duty:	4.9%	Govt. workers:	10.6%

Central and Northern Houston

Within its sprawling boundaries, Houston contains income and wealth disparities as striking as any city in America, the product of an expanding city with dynamic economic growth, a high rate of immigration, and the absence of centralized planning. The contrast is most obvious at the edge of

Voter Turnout	
2013 Total Citizen 18+	433,957
2014 House Turnout	106,010
2014 Turnout as % CVAP	24.4%
2012 Turnout as % CVAP	46.9%

Houston's gleaming downtown. Just blocks from the Heritage Plaza, Pennzoil and Bank of America buildings, and the sports complexes for baseball's Astros and basketball's Rockets, are slums where many people live in unpainted frame houses with cracks wide enough to let in Houston's humid, smoggy air.

Half a century ago, Houston had a Third World economy. It was a low-skill producer of basic commodities, where a few got rich and many lived near subsistence level. Since then, Houston has built a high-tech economy offering myriad opportunities and a wider range of economic outcomes. It has also greatly expanded its international trade. Many of Houston's African Americans and Hispanics have moved to comfortable middle-class neighborhoods. In 2007, Hispanics for the first time outnumbered Anglos in Harris County, which grew 20% from 2000 to 2010. The Houston metropolitan area was ranked the most ethnically diverse in the country in a Rice University study in 2012, though many neighborhoods remain largely segregated. While the city has diversified economically, oil is still king. With economic growth getting a lift from the demand for fuel by China and other emerging nations, Houston was largely shielded from the 2007-09 recession. In January 2015, *Forbes* ranked Houston as the fastest-growing city in the nation, though the collapse in the price of oil likely will test how well the city has diversified its economy. The contrasts between rich and poor remain. In a February 2014 report, the Brookings Institution ranked Houston 11th among cities with the highest income inequality. In April 2015, a study by New World Wealth reported that Houston has the fastest growing community of multi-millionaires in the country.

The 18th Congressional District of Texas contains Houston's downtown area and the African-American and Latino neighborhoods immediately south of it. The district has two arms running beyond Loop 610—one is northeast, between the Eastex Freeway and Beaumont Highway, and the larger one is northwest, between the Northwest Freeway and Interstate 45, extending east to take in George Bush Intercontinental Airport. African Americans make up 38% of the district's population and Hispanics 41%. In downtown Houston's St. John's United Methodist Church, the singer Beyoncé sang in the

2012 Presidential Vote
Barack Obama (D) 150,129   (76%)
Mitt Romney (R)...................44,991   (23%)

2008 Presidential Vote
Barack Obama (D) 150,733   (77%)
John McCain (R)...................45,069   (23%)

Cook Partisan Voting Index: D+24

choir as a child; she is still involved in some of the church's charitable outreach. This is the third most Democratic district in Texas. President Barack Obama won 76% of the vote here in 2012.

Sheila Jackson Lee (D)

Sheila Jackson Lee, a Democrat first elected in 1994, is known as one of Congress' most difficult members—she has had more staff turnover than any other lawmaker and fares poorly in *Washingtonian*'s annual survey of Hill aides. But she is hugely popular at home, always winning at least 70% of the vote in elections and rarely facing a primary challenge.

A native of Queens, New York, Jackson Lee graduated from Yale University and the University of Virginia law school. She practiced law in Houston, where she was a local judge and won two terms as an at-large member of the Houston City Council. After a local term-limits law took effect in 1994, she ran against Democratic Rep. Craig Washington, a talented but iconoclastic legislator. He had voted against funding for the space station, a source of many local jobs, and against the 1993 North American Free Trade Agreement, which was a boon to Houston's port traffic. Jackson Lee supported NAFTA and raised a lot of money from business interests that favored it. She won the primary, 63%-37%, and swept the general election.

In the House, Jackson Lee has a liberal voting record, although she has leaned toward the center on economic issues. She is prolific in proposing bills and offering amendments on the floor. Typically, her measures call for studies on one topic or another, add small amounts to spending bills, or are noncontroversial, such as one that called on Afghanistan to prohibit the use of children as soldiers. In the first five months of 2015, she filed 52 bills. Only one made it out of committee: A measure to require the secretary of Homeland Security to prepare a comprehensive assessment of the transportation security card program. Her more substantive proposals—for example, in favor of NASA funding and abortion rights— usually have been defeated. She is known for grabbing a prominent aisle seat for State of the Union addresses, ensuring her a moment of national television time with the president as he enters. In *Washingtonian's* poll, Jackson Lee has won best "Show Horse" regularly since 2000 and has taken top honors in the poll's "Biggest Windbag" and "Meanest" categories. According to C-SPAN records, Jackson Lee in 2014 talked on the House floor for nine hours, which was the most of any Democrat. But she fell far short of Republican Rep. Louie Gohmert of Texas, who clocked in at 29 hours.

Jackson Lee also draws negative reviews for treatment of her staff. She used to have an aide drive her one block to and from her Capitol Hill apartment daily, and she has required aides to drive her to late-night hair styling appointments. A *Washington Times* analysis found that between 2001 and 2011, her annual staff turnover rate was 54 percent. She told the *Houston Chronicle* that while she can ruffle feathers, she is unflagging in her desire to serve constituents. "I just want to be called an Energizer bunny that keeps on working for the people of this great district," she said. She has been active on the Homeland Security Committee, especially the Border and Maritime Security Subcommittee, an assignment that suits a port city.

Jackson Lee gained national prominence as an outspoken defender of President Bill Clinton during his impeachment in 1998. On the Judiciary Committee, she has faced conflicting tensions from Latino constituents, who favor more generous treatment of immigrants, and African-American constituents, who see immigrants as competition for jobs. She frequently takes the pro-immigrant side. She favors an increase in visas and access to permanent resident status. She has vigilantly pursued racial injustices in local courts. In 2015, she became the ranking Democrat on the Subcommittee on Crime, Terrorism, Homeland Security, and Investigations. Among the bills Jackson Lee introduced in January 2015 was the "Build Trust Act," which, she said, was intended to decrease the excessive reliance by some local governments on traffic fines and court costs to generate revenue to fund government operations. She has generated controversy at home with gun-rights groups with her support for universal background checks for firearms purchasers.

Jackson Lee has been mindful to keep her name recognition in the district high, going so far as to call grieving families to ask if she can speak at their funerals. Her most famous eulogy came in July 2009, when Jermaine Jackson asked her to speak at his iconic brother Michael Jackson's memorial service in Los Angeles. She delivered a rambling speech to the crowd of 20,000 who gathered for the pop star's funeral, speaking longer than many of the stars there who knew Jackson personally.

In 2010, Jackson Lee faced a primary challenge from Houston City Councilman Jarvis Johnson, who cited her reputation as difficult to work with, and local lawyer Sean Roberts. Neither, however, came remotely close to her in fundraising, and in February, she unveiled her trump card—an endorsement from President Barack Obama calling her "a tireless champion for Houston's working families." She drew 67% of the vote to Johnson's 28% and Roberts' 5%. She faced no primary challenge in the next two elections. She was diagnosed in 2011 with breast cancer but announced three months before the election that she was cancer-free.

NINETEENTH DISTRICT

Randy Neugebauer (R)

Elected June 2003, 6th full term; b. Dec. 24, 1949, St. Louis, MO; TX Tech. U., B.B.A. 1972; Baptist; married (Dana); 2 children.

Elected Office: Lubbock City Cncl., 1992-98; Mayor pro tem, Lubbock, 1994-96.

Professional Career: Mgr., Sentry Property Mgmt., 1972-75; Instructor, South Plains Col., 1975-78; V.P., First Natl. Bank, 1975-82; Pres., Prestige Homes, 1983-87; Pres., Lubbock Land Co., 1987-2003.

DC Office: 1424 LHOB, 20515, 202-225-4005; Fax: 202-225-9615; Website: randy.house.gov.

State Offices: Abilene, 325-675-9779; Big Spring, 432-264-0722; Lubbock, 806-763-1611.

Committees: *Agriculture* (VChmn); Commodity Exchanges, Energy & Credit; General Farm Commodities & Risk Mgmt.; Nutrition. *Financial Services:* Capital Markets & Government Sponsored Enterprises; Financial Institutions & Consumer Credit (Chmn). *Science, Space, & Technology:* Energy; Environment.

Group Ratings

	ADA	ACLU	AFL-CIO	LCV	ITI	COC	HAFA	ACU	CFG	FRC
2014	0%	0%	–	3%	100%	64%	83%	96%	87%	100%
2013	0%	C	14%	4%	C	77%	C	92%	87%	C

National Journal Ratings

	2013 LIB	—	2013 CONS
Economic	5%	—	94%
Social	13%	—	84%
Foreign	15%	—	77%
Composite	13%	—	87%

Key Votes of the 113th Congress

1. Sandy storm spending	N	5. Medical Marijuana	N	9. Syrian Rebels Training	N
2. Violence Against Women Act	N	6. Farm Bill	Y	10. Keystone pipeline	Y
3. Guantanamo Bay Detainees	N	7. Afghanistan Combat	N	11. Immigration Exec. Action	Y
4. Abortion 20-week ban	Y	8. NSA Phone Data Collection	N	12. Bipartisan budget deal	N

Election Results

2014 general	Randy Neugebauer (R)	89,326	(77%)	$1,883,938
	Neal Marchbanks (D)	21,325	(18%)	$58,682
	Richard Peterson (Lib)	5,120	(4%)	
2014 primary	Randy Neugebauer (R)	39,611	(64%)	
	Donald May (R)	14,498	(24%)	
	Chris Winn (R)	7,429	(12%)	

Prior winning percentages: 2012 (85%), 2010 (78%), 2008 (72%), 2006 (68%), 2004 (58%), 2003 special (51%)

Population		Race and Ethnicity		Income	
Total:	719,455	White	56.2%	Median income:	$46,029
Urban:	57.5%	Latino	34.7%		*(297 of 435)*
Suburban:	1.6%	Black	5.8%	Under $50,000	53.5%
Rural:	40.9%	Asian	1.3%	$50,000-$99,999:	29.7%
Land area:	30,470	Two races	1.5%	$100,000-$199,999:	13.5%
Pop/sq. mi.:	23.6	White Ethnic	12.0%	$200,000 or more:	3.4%
Born in state:	74.7%			Poverty Rate	17.5%
		Education			
Age Groups		H.S. grad or less:	48.8%	**Work**	
Under 18:	24.7%	Some college:	30.0%	White collar:	30.8%
18 to 34:	27.8%	College degree, 4 yr.:	13.9%	Blue collar:	44.0%
35 to 64:	34.5%	Post-grad study:	7.3%	Sales and service:	25.2%
Over 64:	13.0%				
		Military		Govt. workers:	16.6%
		Veterans/active duty:	8.1%		

West Texas: Lubbock, Abilene

Until water was discovered in the giant Ogallala Aquifer that lies under Lubbock and its environs, this was Indian country, a land of Army forts and cattle ranches. When the water was tapped, well into the 20th century, what had been grazing land suddenly became cotton-growing territory, with

Voter Turnout	
2013 Total Citizen 18+	509,752
2014 House Turnout	115,825
2014 Turnout as % CVAP	22.7%
2012 Turnout as % CVAP	43.3%

green crops grown in circles where the sprinklers reached and parched ground beyond. Lubbock became a regional center, the home of Texas Tech University, and grew rapidly at mid-century. Lubbock County's population increased from 101,000 in 1950 to 156,000 in 1960. Since then, the regional economy has grown more slowly, and in 2013, the county's population was 289,000. Cotton growers have struggled with international competitors and adverse trade rulings, as well as pressure to reduce agricultural subsidies. Wind power has become a new industry here, with hundreds of towers between Abilene and Sweetwater. In September 2013, developers promoted a wind farm near Plainview that they described as the largest in the nation, with 340 landowners over 190 square miles. In the first quarter of 2015, economic growth was strong, with a 35 percent increase in home construction. Lubbock and nearby counties have made an outsized contribution to American popular culture with a disproportionate share of renowned musicians: Buddy Holly, Tanya Tucker, Jimmy Dean, Waylon Jennings, Mac Davis, Joe Ely, Roy Orbison, Don Williams and the Dixie Chicks' Natalie Maines.

Nearly 200 miles southeast of Lubbock, over gully-ridden territory, are Abilene and the surrounding Big Country, with ranches specializing in Angora goats and sheep and exotic animals like ostriches, emus and aoudad sheep. Sweetwater, near Abilene, features an annual "rattlesnake roundup," with a noise from thousands of snakes that apparently can be fearsome. There also are cotton fields, pecan trees, mesquite and many oil wells. Some of the nation's B-1 bombers are stationed at Dyess Air Force Base. Like other parts of Texas, Abilene has become a haven for resettlement of refugees. Since 2000, there have been more than 2,000 in Abilene, mostly from the Congo, Bhutan and Burundi.

The 19th Congressional District of Texas takes in the Lubbock and Abilene areas. The two regions combined account for about 59% of the district's population. In 1978, this part of West Texas was Democratic enough that in an open-seat election, voters rejected the candidacy of a young Midland oilman named George W. Bush in favor of Lubbock Democrat Kent Hance. Today, the area is heavily Republican. Bush received 77% of the vote in his 2004 reelection, and Republican candidate Mitt Romney won the district with 74% in 2012—among their highest scores in the nation, but only third-best among districts in west Texas. GOP Gov. Rick Perry's boyhood home is in Haskell

2012 Presidential Vote		
Mitt Romney (R)	160,058	(74%)
Barack Obama (D)	54,448	(25%)
2008 Presidential Vote		
John McCain (R)	168,553	(71%)
Barack Obama (D)	66,122	(28%)
Cook Partisan Voting Index: R+26		

County, and nearby Throckmorton County is the site of his family's hunting camp. It drew controversy during his 2012 presidential campaign after *The Washington Post* reported that a racial epithet was painted on a rock in front of the property.

Randy Neugebauer (R)

Randy Neugebauer, a Republican who won his seat in a June 2003 special election, has been a staunch House conservative. A former developer and banker, he has criticized federal regulations as a senior member of the Financial Services Committee.

Neugebauer graduated from Texas Tech, became a banker, then ran his own land development company, which has made him one of the wealthiest members of Texas' delegation. From 1992 to 1998, he was a Lubbock city councilman. His opportunity for a House seat was prompted by the unexpected resignation of Republican Rep. Larry Combest, who chaired the House Agriculture Committee. In the all-party primary, the four leading contenders to succeed Combest were all Republicans. Neugebauer, the biggest spender, emphasized his positions on national defense and his business connections to oil and farming. He finished first, with 821 more votes than Mike Conaway, a Midland accountant. The runoff featured few differences on the issues, and Neugebauer won 51%-49%. (Following redistricting, Conaway won the neighboring 11th District in 2004.)

He barely had a chance to settle in before the Texas Legislature drew up a new map for congressional districts in October 2003. Those lines placed the home of 13-term Democratic Rep. Charlie Stenholm in the new 13th District, but that district was almost entirely unfamiliar territory for him and heavily Republican to boot, so Stenholm decided to run in the 19th against Neugebauer. Stenholm was the most conservative Democrat from Texas in the House, one of only five Democrats who voted to impeach President Bill Clinton in 1998.

In the 2004 showdown, key factors—the district's partisan tilt, the fact that Neugebauer had represented 58% of its residents and Stenholm only 31%—favored the Republican. Both candidates promised to protect farm subsidies. Stenholm emphasized his social conservatism, his dedication to West Texas constituent services, and his independence as a Democrat. He criticized Neugebauer's ads that suggested he supported abortion rights and he sought to link Neugebauer with then-Majority Leader Tom DeLay of Texas, who was mired in ethics controversies. The Texas Farm Bureau, which earlier honored Stenholm as "one of the giants of Texas agriculture," endorsed Neugebauer. He won 58%-40%, capturing 22 of the 27 counties. In Lubbock, Stenholm trailed 65%-33%. In his base of Abilene, which cast half as many votes as Lubbock, Stenholm led 50%-48%. Neugebauer has been easily reelected since.

In the House, Neugebauer has sought to free the private sector from federal intervention. "A market system that's left alone will reward good behavior and punish bad behavior. When government steps in, we almost try to reverse that," he told *The Texas Tribune* in 2012. But his position is inconsistent on farm subsidies, which are popular in his district and which he has ardently defended as a member of the Agriculture Committee. The Environmental Working Group listed his district as the nation's fourth-highest recipient of crop subsidies, and Neugebauer supports expanded crop insurance coverage for farmers.

Neugebauer has engaged in occasional grandstanding. To show that President Barack Obama shouldn't be immune from cost-cutting, he introduced an amendment to a spending bill in February 2011 to bar any money from being used on White House residence repairs; it was rejected overwhelmingly. He drew substantial attention in March 2010 as the lawmaker who shouted "baby killer" during Michigan Democratic Rep. Bart Stupak's speech on abortion during the final debate before passage of the health care overhaul bill. (Neugebauer apologized for his outburst and said it was not directed at Stupak, who opposes abortion.) A charter member of the Tea Party Caucus, Neugebauer co-sponsored Florida Rep. Bill Posey's "birther" bill in 2009, requiring future presidential candidates to provide a copy of their birth certificate. He unsuccessfully sought to strike everything but tax cuts from the 2009 economic stimulus bill.

On Financial Services, he has sponsored or co-sponsored several measures aimed at reining in government-sponsored mortgage giants Fannie Mae and Freddie Mac. He told an audience of housing experts in 2011 that the federal government should get out of the foreclosure process. Also that year, he chaired Financial Services' oversight and investigations panel and aggressively monitored the new Consumer Financial Protection Bureau (CFPB) established in the Dodd-Frank financial overhaul law. His panel released a report in November 2012 on the collapse of the brokerage firm MF Global and urged lawmakers to consider combining the Securities and Exchange Commission and the Commodity Futures Trading Commission for greater efficiency and investor security.

In January 2015, Neugebauer became chairman of the Financial Institutions and Consumer Credit Subcommittee. He managed the bill to encourage more private sector participation in the terrorism risk insurance market, which became the first law enacted that year. The bill had been largely written in 2014, but ran into stumbling blocks at the close of the previous Congress and the earlier law had expired. In March, he introduced a proposal to reorganize the CFPB to switch from a single director to a bipartisan five-member commission appointed by the president, and he criticized the agency's "regulatory paternalism." He has cosponsored bipartisan legislation to create national standards to protect the security of financial services data. To promote that proposal, he co-founded the Congressional Payments Technology Caucus.

In January 2015, Mike Conaway, former campaign opponent and now colleague from an adjacent district, named Neugebauer vice-chairman of the Agriculture Committee.

TWENTIETH DISTRICT

Joaquin Castro (D)

Elected 2012, 2nd term; b. Sept. 16, 1974, San Antonio; Stanford U., B.A. 1996; Harvard U., J.D. 2000; Catholic; married (Anna Flores); 1 child.

Elected Office: TX House, 2003-13.

Professional Career: Practicing atty., 2000-2013.

DC Office: 212 CHOB, 20515, 202-225-3236; Fax: 202-225-1915; Website: castro.house.gov.

State Offices: San Antonio, 210-348-8216.

Committees: *Armed Services:* Emerging Threats & Capabilities; Readiness. *Foreign Affairs:* Terrorism, Nonproliferation & Trade; Western Hemisphere.

Group Ratings

	ADA	ACLU	AFL-CIO	LCV	ITI	COC	HAFA	ACU	CFG	FRC
2014	80%	83%	–	91%	60%	43%	13%	8%	14%	0%
2013	75%	C	95%	96%	C	42%	C	12%	13%	C

National Journal Ratings

	2013 LIB	—	2013 CONS
Economic	86%	—	13%
Social	69%	—	28%
Foreign	64%	—	36%
Composite	74%	—	26%

Key Votes of the 113th Congress

1. Sandy storm spending	Y	5. Medical Marijuana	Y	9. Syrian Rebels Training	Y
2. Violence Against Women Act	Y	6. Farm Bill	N	10. Keystone pipeline	N
3. Guantanamo Bay Detainees	Y	7. Afghanistan Combat	Y	11. Immigration Exec. Action	N
4. Abortion 20-week ban	N	8. NSA Phone Data Collection	N	12. Bipartisan budget deal	NV

Election Results

2014 general	Joaquin Castro (D)	66,554	(76%)	$1,147,967
	Jeffrey Blunt (Lib)	21,410	(24%)	
2014 primary	Joaquin Castro (D)	unopposed		

Prior winning percentage: 2012 (64%)

Population		Race and Ethnicity		Income	
Total:	752,996	Latino	66.3%	Median income:	$45,222
Urban:	97.9%	White	24.7%		*(317 of 435)*
Suburban:	2.1%	Black	4.4%	Under $50,000	54.6%
Rural:	0.0%	Asian	2.4%	$50,000-$99,999:	29.3%
Land area:	410	Two races	2.0%	$100,000-$199,999:	14.0%
Pop/sq. mi.:	1,838.0	White Ethnic	9.3%	$200,000 or more:	2.1%
Born in state:	65.1%			Poverty Rate	20.2%
		Education			
Age Groups		H.S. grad or less:	46.6%	**Work**	
Under 18:	26.6%	Some college:	29.4%	White collar:	30.8%
18 to 34:	26.9%	College degree, 4 yr.:	15.3%	Blue collar:	50.5%
35 to 64:	36.4%	Post-grad study:	8.7%	Sales and service:	18.7%
Over 64:	10.1%				
		Military		Govt. workers:	13.8%
		Veterans/active duty:	10.9%		

San Antonio

With its antique past and Hispanic heritage, San Antonio is unlike any other city in the United States. It is the home of the Alamo, preserved by the Daughters of the Republic of Texas, where Davy Crockett, Jim Bowie and 184 others were killed in 1836. (Crockett was a Tennessee congressman for three terms; if he had not lost his reelection in 1835, he presumably would not have left Tennessee for Texas.) Its Spanish architecture recalls San Antonio's days as the most important town in Texas, when the state was part of Mexico; it contrasts with the 30-story Tower

Voter Turnout	
2013 Total Citizen 18+	484,260
2014 House Turnout	87,964
2014 Turnout as % CVAP	18.2%
2012 Turnout as % CVAP	39.7%

Life Building and with the armadillo-like Alamodome. Its Paseo del Rio, the Riverwalk along the tiny San Antonio River that was redeveloped in the 1970s, recalls an earlier era.

For most of the 20th century, San Antonio's economy was built on the military. What the locals call "Military City, U.S.A." remains the home of Lackland Air Force Base, Fort Sam Houston and a giant military hospital. San Antonio has many military retirees and is the largest tourist center in Texas. From 2000 to 2013, its population grew 22%, and it has surpassed Dallas as Texas' second-largest city, after Houston. Its metropolitan area population of 2.2 million is only about one-third the size of metro Houston or of the Dallas-Fort Worth Metroplex, but 54% of that total are Hispanic and that share is growing. Its low education and income levels have been partially due to the large numbers of new immigrants in the city. In the metro area, the Anglo growth between 2010 and 2012 was 2.1%; the non-Anglo growth was 5.5%. A January 2015 study by the Migration Policy Institute showed that San Antonio had a disproportionately lower share of foreign-born and undocumented immigrants, compared to other population centers in Texas.

The city's diversifying economy has also attracted good-paying jobs in its booming medical research industry. It is home to the world headquarters of Valero Energy, Clear Channel Communications and USAA. One out of every six San Antonio employees works in the health care and biosciences fields, according to the city's Chamber of Commerce. San Antonio's manufacturing center now contributes over $22 billion to the local economy, more than triple the revenue it generated in 1991. After Washington, D.C., San Antonio has the second-highest concentration of network security professionals in the country.

2012 Presidential Vote		
Barack Obama (D) 110,663		(59%)
Mitt Romney (R)..................74,540		(40%)
2008 Presidential Vote		
Barack Obama (D) 115,579		(58%)
John McCain (R)..................80,667		(41%)
Cook Partisan Voting Index: D+6		

Just under half of San Antonio's population is located in the 20th Congressional District of Texas, which includes its lower-income west side, but not the downtown area where most of the city's attractions are located. The district is wholly contained in Bexar County. With a Hispanic population share of 66%, it is one of the state's nine Hispanic-majority districts. It leans Democratic. President Barack Obama, with strong support among the fast-growing Hispanic population, won 59% of the district vote against Mitt Romney in 2012.

Joaquin Castro (D)

Joaquin Castro is a former Texas legislator who won his San Antonio-based seat in 2012. As a young, telegenic Hispanic, he vaulted into an unusually prominent position along with his twin brother Julián, a former San Antonio mayor who became secretary of Housing and Urban Development in July 2014.

Politics is in Castro's blood. His mother, Rosie Castro, was a noted Latina activist in the 1960s and 1970s, and she instilled a belief in civil rights and equality of opportunity in her sons. "We grew up believing that when government works right, it can help people," Joaquin Castro told *National Journal*.

Both he and his brother went to Stanford University, where they earned degrees in political science. Both continued to Harvard Law School and then returned to San Antonio to work for the politically well-connected Akin, Gump, Strauss, Hauer & Feld law firm and launch their local political careers.

Joaquin Castro challenged a Democratic incumbent for his Texas House seat in 2002, running a successful, change-themed campaign. In the legislature, he focused on education and eventually became the Democratic floor leader. "I've always been in deep minorities" in the legislature, Castro said. "The silver lining is that you learn, almost in a Darwinian way, how to be effective without using sheer force of numbers." That included restoring education funding amid budget-cutting after the 2010 elections.

Castro initially announced he would run in 2012 for Texas' new 35th Congressional District, a thin ribbon of a district from San Antonio's east side to Austin. That pitted Castro against veteran Democratic Rep. Lloyd Doggett and foretold an expensive primary battle dividing the two cities and two ethnic groups of Democrats. But longtime Democratic Rep. Charles Gonzalez later called Castro and said he had decided to retire. "At that point," Castro said, "it became clear I should run for my home district."

No other Democrats filed to run against the popular state legislator and he has faced perfunctory Republican opposition, which has freed Castro to help other Democratic candidates with their campaigns. He delivered more than $100,000 in donations to other 2012 candidates, including 23rd District Democrat Pete Gallego in his primary campaign. National Democrats enlisted Castro to stump for President Barack Obama in battleground states, including Colorado and Florida.

In the House, Castro has been a reliable Democrat, particularly on economic issues. He has focused on education, introducing a bill in June 2014 to expand a pre-kindergarten program that his brother started in San Antonio. It would give cities a direct line to federal funds, bypassing state legislatures. "Local entities must have the ability to step up to the plate and pick up the slack where their state governments are failing," he wrote in a *Dallas Morning News* op-ed column. He pushed on various fronts to urge legislative action on immigration legislation, including a pathway to citizenship for those without legal status. In March 2015, he initiated a letter signed by 72 other House Democrats in which they urged President Barack Obama to take executive action to reduce the backlog of more than 200,000 delayed applications for foreign students and workers seeking visas.

As a member of the Armed Services Committee, Castro voiced disappointment in April 2015 that the panel rejected his efforts to include in the annual spending bill a provision to take military sexual assault prosecutions out of the chain of command to ensure that victims are comfortable in bringing charges. In June 2015, he won voice-vote approval in the House of his amendment that added $10 million to an appropriation bill for police body-worn cameras which, he said, provide "a better indication of the interaction between law enforcement and members of our community."

Castro has drawn more attention for his efforts on behalf of his party. In an essay for *Texas Monthly* about his first year in Congress, he wrote: "The U.S. House of Representatives is designed for fighting." He became an in-demand figure on the political circuit, appearing at such events as the Jefferson-Jackson Dinner in Indiana, the Democratic state convention in New Jersey and South Carolina Rep. James Clyburn's annual fish fry. After the 2014 election, he was widely mentioned as the potential chairman of the Democratic Congressional Campaign Committee. But Minority Leader Nancy Pelosi gave the job to another Latino, Rep. Ben Ray Luján of New Mexico. In March 2015, Minority Whip Steny Hoyer named Castro as a chief deputy whip, which could be his initial step up the Democrats' leadership ladder.

In a 2013 interview with the *Texas Tribune*, Castro said jokingly he was glad to "play the Robert Kennedy" to his brother's John F. Kennedy. But in July 2014, he took the lead role in striking back at Rick Perry when Texas' GOP governor blasted the Obama administration's handling of the thousands of Central American refugees flocking to the U.S. border. When Perry announced he would send National Guard troops to the border, Castro accused him of "militarizing" the region and said he should instead be sending the Red Cross.

Castro leaves no doubt that his political ambition is not confined to the House. A statewide bid remains a daunting challenge for any Texas Democrat, especially after the party's disappointing losses in 2014. But journalists have written about his frequent travels to meet with grass-roots Democrats across the state. Depending on circumstances, he might be well-positioned to challenge Republican Sen. Ted Cruz, who faces reelection in 2018, or to seek what could be an open seat.

TWENTY-FIRST DISTRICT

Lamar Smith (R)

Elected 1986, 15th term; b. Nov. 19, 1947, San Antonio; Yale U., B.A. 1969, S. Methodist U., J.D. 1975; Christian Scientist; married (Beth Schafer); 2 children.

Elected Office: TX House, 1981-82; Bexar Cnty. comm., 1983-85.

Professional Career: U.S. Small Business Admin., 1969-70; Business writer, Christian Science Monitor, 1970-72; Practicing atty., 1975-78.

DC Office: 2409 RHOB, 20515, 202-225-4236; Fax: 202-225-8628; Website: lamarsmith.house.gov.

State Offices: Austin, 512-912-7508; Kerrville, 830-896-0154; San Antonio, 210-821-5024.

Committees: *Homeland Security:* Border & Maritime Security. *Judiciary:* Courts, Intellectual Property & the Internet; Immigration & Border Security. *Science, Space, & Technology* (Chmn: ex officio member of each subcommittee).

Group Ratings

	ADA	ACLU	AFL-CIO	LCV	ITI	COC	HAFA	ACU	CFG	FRC
2014	0%	0%	–	3%	80%	77%	69%	84%	74%	100%
2013	0%	C	14%	7%	C	85%	C	83%	76%	C

National Journal Ratings

	2013 LIB	—	2013 CONS
Economic	13%	—	85%
Social	27%	—	71%
Foreign	15%	—	77%
Composite	20%	—	80%

Key Votes of the 113th Congress

1. Sandy storm spending	N	5. Medical Marijuana	N
2. Violence Against Women Act	N	6. Farm Bill	Y
3. Guantanamo Bay Detainees	N	7. Afghanistan Combat	N
4. Abortion 20-week ban	Y	8. NSA Phone Data Collection	N

9. Syrian Rebels Training	Y
10. Keystone pipeline	Y
11. Immigration Exec. Action	Y
12. Bipartisan budget deal	Y

Election Results

2014 general	Lamar Smith (R)	135,660	(72%)	$1,567,733	$3,500
	Antonio Diaz (G)	27,831	(15%)		
	Ryan Shields (Lib)	25,505	(14%)		
2014 primary	Lamar Smith (R)	40,441	(60%)		
	Matt McCall (R)	22,681	(34%)		
	Michael Smith (R)	3,796	(6%)		

Prior winning percentages: 2012 (61%), 2010 (69%), 2008 (80%), 2006 (60%), 2004 (61%), 2002 (73%), 2000 (76%), 1998 (91%), 1996 (76%), 1994 (90%), 1992 (72%), 1990 (75%), 1988 (93%), 1986 (61%)

Population		Race and Ethnicity		Income	
Total:	743,443	White	64.1%	Median income:	$60,543
Urban:	70.0%	Latino	27.7%		*(121 of 435)*
Suburban:	15.3%	Black	3.2%	Under $50,000	41.5%
Rural:	14.7%	Asian	2.7%	$50,000-$99,999:	30.4%
Land area:	4,666	Two races	1.7%	$100,000-$199,999:	20.8%
Pop/sq. mi.:	159.3	White Ethnic	22.4%	$200,000 or more:	7.4%
Born in state:	57.1%			Poverty Rate	12.4%
		Education			
Age Groups		H.S. grad or less:	26.2%	**Work**	
Under 18:	20.3%	Some college:	29.0%	White collar:	47.0%
18 to 34:	26.6%	College degree, 4 yr.:	28.5%	Blue collar:	40.2%
35 to 64:	38.5%	Post-grad study:	16.3%	Sales and service:	12.8%
Over 64:	14.5%			Govt. workers:	15.2%
		Military			
		Veterans/active duty:	11.6%		

San Antonio/South Austin Corridor

The Balcones Escarpment is a bulwark of cracked and weathered rock that crosses Texas diagonally from the Dallas-Fort Worth Metroplex southwest to Austin and San Antonio and all the way to the Rio Grande. It separates the flatlands of central Texas from the stony hills to the north and west.

Voter Turnout	
2013 Total Citizen 18+	555,358
2014 House Turnout	188,996
2014 Turnout as % CVAP	34%
2012 Turnout as % CVAP	57.3%

It is a boundary between cropland and grazing land, between acres rich with greenery and acres whose rolling brown hills blaze out in color when the wildflowers bloom in early spring. But the Balcones Escarpment is less familiar to Texans today than the highway that runs pretty much along the same line: Interstate 35. This is one of the most heavily traveled and congested interstates in America, thick with truck traffic in the populated stretches between the Metroplex and the Mexican border even as it passes through the lightly populated near-desert between San Antonio and Laredo. I-35 connects Austin and San Antonio, two booming Texan cities with very different beginnings and different characters now.

In the counties between these two cities and in the Hill Country to the west is the Texas German country, originally settled by Germans in the mid-1800s. It consists of economically prosperous communities that were anti-slavery and politically Republican in a state whose enthusiasm for the Democratic Party had roots in Confederate loyalties and populist rebellions. Texas Germans introduced the long-barbecued beef brisket that has become synonymous with Lone Star State cuisine, and an antique German dialect is sometimes heard on the streets of New Braunfels, Boerne and Fredericksburg. These communities, with their neat houses, low cost of living, and Hill Country ambience, are attracting new residents to new subdivisions. More than 3 million tourists visit New Braunfels every year for wine-tasting, tubing, and beer and bratwurst.

The 21st Congressional District of Texas includes much of this territory. One-third of its people are in San Antonio and Bexar County. It includes the northeast corner of the city and county, taking in Fort Sam Houston, and the affluent north-side neighborhoods of Terrell Hills, Olmos Park and Alamo Heights just outside San Antonio. Fort Sam's renowned Brooke Army Medical Center was transformed into a regional military medical center for a net gain of more than 4,000 jobs. Halliburton opened in September 2013 new headquarters in San Antonio with 1,000 workers, many of whom service oil production on the nearby Eagle Ford Shale. In May 2015, 60 of those workers were laid off as the price of oil slid.

In the Hill Country, the district takes in Gillespie County; along the Pedernales River is the LBJ Ranch, where the 36th president was born, vacationed during his presidency, and is buried. He grew up in neighboring Blanco County's Johnson City, where he ran his first race for the House. Another one-fourth of the district is in Travis County, with parts of downtown Austin's central business district that border the University of Texas. Amid the booming corporate development, downtown Austin cherishes its fame of more bars per capita than any other ZIP code in the nation. San Marcos, with an 8 percent increase in the 12 months ending in June 2014, was the fastest-growing city in the nation. The politi-

2012 Presidential Vote		
Mitt Romney (R)	188,241	(60%)
Barack Obama (D)	119,220	(38%)
2008 Presidential Vote		
John McCain (R)	178,531	(56%)
Barack Obama (D)	133,581	(42%)
Cook Partisan Voting Index:	R+12	

cal heritage of the district is mixed. While Travis County was always Democratic and the Texas German country was Republican, San Antonio was mixed. Overall, the district today is solidly Republican.

Lamar Smith (R)

Republican Lamar Smith, first elected in 1986, has long been among his party's most influential conservatives on immigration. He has brought a strong conservative perspective to numerous issues and became chairman of the Science, Space, and Technology Committee in 2013.

Smith is from an old San Antonio and South Texas ranching family. Their Jim Wells County ranch has been in the family for four generations. Smith graduated from Texas Military Institute (now TMI, the Episcopal School of Texas), Yale University, and Southern

Methodist University's law school. He worked as a reporter for the *Christian Science Monitor* and as a lawyer in San Antonio.

He was elected to the Texas House in 1980 and the Bexar County Commissioners Court in 1982. In 1986, Smith ran for the open House seat. He defeated two other San Antonio-based candidates in the primary and won the runoff 54%-46% against a religious conservative. His campaign was run by then little-known Texas political consultant Karl Rove, who became President George W. Bush's top political advisor. Smith has been reelected by wide margins.

In the House, Smith has a conservative voting record and joined the Tea Party Caucus when it was formed in 2010. Like other veteran Republicans, his rhetoric has become noticeably sharper since Barack Obama became president. Smith said on the Family Research Council's radio program in February 2015 that Obama wasn't taking the threat of the Islamic State "seriously" and was doing "nothing" to stop the extremist group because, he contended, the president thinks "America's not exceptional."

Smith was an activist as the top Republican on the Judiciary Committee for six years before he was term-limited in 2012. He pressed for tougher enforcement of immigration laws as an alternative to comprehensive reform, which he and many Republicans insist cannot include provisions giving illegal immigrants a path to citizenship. He is a firm believer in stronger action to stop illegal immigration. Smith irked Democrats in December 2010 when he called the DREAM Act—which would have opened up legal status to some children of illegal immigrants—an "American nightmare." Smith was a leading House Republican voice in support of a controversial Arizona law that allowed police to demand proof of citizenship from people stopped or questioned by police for other reasons. He criticized the Obama administration for suing to stop enforcement of the Arizona law.

In early 2013, Smith blasted a reform initiative offered by a bipartisan group of senators: "By granting amnesty, the Senate proposal actually compounds the problem by encouraging more illegal immigration." As an alternative, he proposed in 2011 a program to bring 500,000 foreign migrant farm workers to the United States each year to placate farmers who complain about shortages of legally authorized labor. At the behest of technology firms, he proposed another bill to provide permanent resident visas for foreigners who graduate from U.S. universities with advanced degrees in science and technology. That measure passed the House in November 2012 on a mostly party-line vote. Democrats opposed the bill because it eliminated a diversity visa lottery, which allocated spots to people from countries with low rates of immigration to the U.S. Smith was sharply critical of Obama's executive order protecting some of the nation's illegal immigrants and joined a group of lawmakers supporting a lawsuit to stop it. "Putting a stop to these overreaching executive actions isn't about Republicans or Democrats; it's about respecting and restoring the rule of law," he said.

Perhaps his most significant achievement in this area was passage of the Illegal Immigration Reform and Immigrant Responsibility Act of 1996. Smith was the chief House architect of several of its provisions, including a dramatic increase in the number of Border Patrol agents, more wiretap authority for law enforcement authorities, and funds for state-of-the-art equipment such as helicopters, four-wheel-drive vehicles and night goggles. The law also greatly increased penalties for illegal entry into the U.S., clamped down on alien smuggling and document fraud, and toughened deportation measures.

Smith found common ground with Democrats at Judiciary on other bills, such as strengthened cybersecurity and intellectual property enforcement. He worked closely with ranking Judiciary Democrat John Conyers of Michigan on patent reform issues, including structural changes at the Patent and Trademark Office aimed at improving review quality, which were enacted in 2011. He joined with then-Senate Judiciary Committee Chairman Patrick Leahy, a Vermont Democrat, to enact a bill that updated patent law by giving priority to the "first inventor to file" for a patent from the previous "first to invent" standard. Smith parted with Conyers and opposed a committee proposal that eliminated mandatory minimum prison sentences for crack cocaine use. A modified version of the bill was eventually signed into law, making crack sentencing closer to the lighter penalties enforced for powder cocaine use.

In taking over as chairman of the Science Committee, his priorities have included cybersecurity and investigating the Obama administration's science-related work. Smith promised an emphasis on the future of NASA, an important agency in Texas that he wants to focus more on space exploration and less on scientific research, where he contends the agency wastes money studying climate change. Smith steered a bipartisan reauthorization bill for the agency through the House in February 2015 that included $540 million more than the Obama administration requested. It required NASA to provide more details on how it envisions sending humans to Mars or one of its moons, perhaps after 2030.

On climate change, Smith is a bit less of a skeptic than other conservatives on the committee, acknowledging that it "has the potential to impact agriculture, ecosystems, sea levels, weather patterns, and human health." But when the Intergovernmental Panel on Climate Change issued a report in November 2014 warning the problem was becoming worse and assigning even more blame to humans, Smith told Bloomberg TV that the report was "clearly biased" and added: "There's still no explanation and no one can tell me yet what percentage of so-called climate change is due to human activity [and] what percentage is due to natural trends, natural cycles."

He introduced a bill with Wyoming GOP Sen. John Barrasso in February 2015 that banned the Environmental Protection Agency from writing any regulations unless they were based on the "best available science" that is made publicly available. The lawmakers said too much of the agency's rulemaking was secret. Smith has publicly rebuked the National Science Foundation for spending money on what he deemed low-priority initiatives, such as China's milk supplies or ancient Icelandic textiles. In 2014, the House passed his bill restricting research by the NSF. In January 2015, he co-authored with Republican Sen. Rand Paul of Kentucky a column for Politico in which they refuted Democratic accusations that Republicans were "at war with science." They demanded that money be spent for "not just any science but the *best* science."

Smith displayed his broad command when he chaired the House Ethics Committee in 1999-2000, an unusual case of a House member chairing three separate House panels.

Smith quarterbacked the 2011 redistricting for Texas Republicans and got into a spat with GOP colleague Joe Barton over the racial makeup of the state's new map. Smith sought to evenly split four new districts between Republicans and Democrats, giving Texas' booming Hispanic population minority-majority seats in the Dallas and south Texas areas. Barton wanted to keep Republican voters dominant in three of the new districts. Barton's plan passed the state legislature, but Smith ultimately prevailed on a court-drawn map that created what appear to be 24 secure Republican seats. Although Smith remains safe at home, he got an unusual warning in 2014, when two third-party candidates held him to 42% of the vote in Democratic-leaning Travis County. Overall, he won the district with 72%.

TWENTY-SECOND DISTRICT

Pete Olson (R)

Elected 2008, 4th term; b. Dec. 9, 1962, Fort Lewis, WA; Rice U., B.A. 1985, U of TX, J.D. 1988; Methodist; married (Nancy); 2 children.

Military Career: Navy 1988-98, Naval Reserves, 1998-Present.

Professional Career: Naval officer, 1995; Staffer, U.S. Sen. Phil Gramm, 1998-2002; Staffer, U.S. Sen. John Cornyn, 2002-07.

DC Office: 2133 RHOB, 20515, 202-225-5951; Fax: 202-225-5241; Website: olson.house.gov.

State Offices: Katy, 281-889-7134; Pearland, 281-485-4855; Sugar Land, 281-494-2690.

Committees: *Energy & Commerce:* Commerce, Manufacturing & Trade; Communications & Technology; Energy & Power (VChmn).

Group Ratings

	ADA	ACLU	AFL-CIO	LCV	ITI	COC	HAFA	ACU	CFG	FRC
2014	0%	5%	–	0%	100%	69%	78%	88%	78%	100%
2013	0%	C	10%	0%	C	85%	C	92%	78%	C

National Journal Ratings

	2013 LIB	—	2013 CONS
Economic	12%	—	88%
Social	0%	—	87%
Foreign	23%	—	77%
Composite	14%	—	86%

Key Votes of the 113th Congress

1. Sandy storm spending	N	5. Medical Marijuana	N	9. Syrian Rebels Training	Y
2. Violence Against Women Act	N	6. Farm Bill	Y	10. Keystone pipeline	Y
3. Guantanamo Bay Detainees	N	7. Afghanistan Combat	N	11. Immigration Exec. Action	Y
4. Abortion 20-week ban	Y	8. NSA Phone Data Collection	N	12. Bipartisan budget deal	N

Election Results

2014 general	Pete Olson (R)............................ 100,861	(67%)	$1,259,370
	Frank Briscoe (D) 47,844	(32%)	
2014 primary	Pete Olson (R) ....unopposed		

Prior winning percentages: 2012 (64%), 2010 (67%), 2008 (52%)

Population		Race and Ethnicity		Income	
Total:	783,172	White	44.4%	Median income:	$86,681
Urban:	33.0%	Latino	25.2%		*(19 of 435)*
Suburban:	64.7%	Asian	17.1%	Under $50,000	29.7%
Rural:	2.3%	Black	11.6%	$50,000-$99,999:	26.8%
Land area:	1,152	Two races	1.4%	$100,000-$199,999:	32.0%
Pop/sq. mi.:	680.0	White Ethnic	15.4%	$200,000 or more:	11.5%
Born in state:	52.2%			Poverty Rate	8.0%
		Education			
Age Groups		H.S. grad or less:	28.4%	**Work**	
Under 18:	28.4%	Some college:	28.2%	White collar:	50.0%
18 to 34:	20.9%	College degree, 4 yr.:	28.0%	Blue collar:	33.4%
35 to 64:	40.8%	Post-grad study:	15.5%	Sales and service:	16.7%
Over 64:	9.9%			Govt. workers:	13.1%
		Military			
		Veterans/active duty:	5.9%		

Southern Houston Area: Sugar Land

The story of the Houston area's booming growth is well captured in a drive out the Southwest Freeway to Sugar Land. Much has changed from the days before the Civil War, when sugar plantations flourished here. Sugar Land is a privately planned city of more than 83,000 people, with privatized water and other services. (In 1990, its population was 45,000.) The surrounding Fort Bend County was fifth in the nation in job growth between 2000 and 2009. In September 2014, *Money* magazine ranked Sugar Land number one in the nation on its list of "Best Places to Find a New Job." The Memorial Hermann hospital in Sugar Land launched a $93 million expansion in 2014. The local baseball team is the Sugar Land Skeeters, a reference to the area's uncomfortable proliferation of the biting insects.

Voter Turnout	
2013 Total Citizen 18+	488,410
2014 House Turnout	151,566
2014 Turnout as % CVAP	31%
2012 Turnout as % CVAP	54.4%

When former House Majority Leader Tom DeLay represented the 22nd Congressional District, whites were a majority. Now suburban Sugar Land and Fort Bend County are among the most-diverse areas in the country. Almost a quarter of the county's population is Hispanic, 21% is African American, and 18% is Asian. Sugar Land has elected a Chinese American to the city council, and a native of India has served on the board of the Chamber of Commerce. The district covers three-quarters of Fort Bend County, including Sugar Land, and half of Brazoria County, centering on fast-growing Pearland, just south of Houston. Although much of Fort Bend's black population resides in the adjacent 9th District, the 22nd is a minority-majority district. Pearland, a sub-

2012 Presidential Vote		
Mitt Romney (R)................158,452	(62%)
Barack Obama (D) 93,582	(37%)

2008 Presidential Vote		
John McCain (R)................142,073	(61%)
Barack Obama (D) 91,137	(39%)

Cook Partisan Voting Index: R+15

urb whose population exploded from 46,000 in 2000 to 100,000 in 2013, is positioning itself as a health care hub for the region. The district also takes in a tiny slice of southwestern Houston. The district remains solidly Republican. Mitt Romney won 62% of the vote in 2012.

Pete Olson (R)

Pete Olson, a Republican elected in 2008, represents the district once overseen by Tom DeLay, the powerful former House majority leader. Olson is every bit as conservative as DeLay and just as vigilant in advocating on behalf of Texas' oil and space interests.

A graduate of Rice University and the University of Texas Law School, Olson entered the Navy on the same day he took the Texas bar exam. He served as a naval aviator and flew anti-submarine missions, including in the Persian Gulf following the war against Iraq in 1991. He finished his military career in Washington, D.C., as a liaison to the Senate (the same job that Arizona Republican Sen. John McCain had before he entered politics). His next job was as a staff member for Republican Sen. Phil Gramm of Texas. After Gramm retired in 2002, Olson was chief of staff for his successor, Republican Sen. John Cornyn.

In 2006, DeLay, at the pinnacle of power as majority leader, resigned his seat after his September 2005 indictment in Texas required him to give up his leadership post. He was convicted in 2011 and sentenced to a three-year prison term for money laundering and conspiracy stemming from his role funneling corporate contributions to Texas state races. The state criminal appeals court in 2014 overturned the conviction on the basis that prosecutors failed to prove that the contributions were illegal. Houston City Council Member Shelley Sekula-Gibbs, a Republican, won a special election for the seat, served for several weeks, then lost in the general election to Democrat Nick Lampson. A legal technicality kept her name off the ballot, and Sekula-Gibbs was forced to run as a write-in candidate.

Two years later, Republicans targeted Lampson for defeat. Olson joined a crowded primary field that included Sekula-Gibbs and Sugar Land Mayor Dean Hrbacek. Sekula-Gibbs finished first in the primary but with only 30% of the vote, far short of the majority needed to avoid a runoff with runner-up Olson. Republicans at the state and national levels regarded Sekula-Gibbs as a weak candidate and coalesced around Olson, who won the runoff with 69% of the vote.

In the general election campaign, Olson touted a conservative message, while Lampson tried to tar Olson with DeLay's image, charging that Olson employed consultants who had previously worked for DeLay. Democratic leaders came to Lampson's aid, saying that if reelected he would chair the House subcommittee with jurisdiction over NASA, an important local employer. But in the end, all of this could not stop the district from returning to its GOP roots on Election Day. Olson won 52%-45%.

In the House, Olson has been a rock-solid conservative. He got a plum seat on the Energy and Commerce Committee in 2011 and joined fellow Texas Republican Joe Barton on the panel as a staunch defender of their state's oil and gas industry. The House passed his bill in August 2012 allowing power companies off the hook if they violate environmental laws while attempting to comply with federal mandates to maintain the reliability of their electricity grids during power emergencies. The Senate did not take it up. Olson was an outspoken advocate of the Keystone XL pipeline, which is designed to carry Canadian oil to Texas refineries. He also sought to permit more oil and gas drilling on public lands. With Democratic Rep. Cedric Richmond of Louisiana, he co-founded the Congressional Refinery Caucus, which was designed to educate lawmakers about the industry's interests.

Olson has pursued various conservative initiatives. In February 2013, he called for the Government Accountability Office to release a study on the use of federal funding by Planned Parenthood and other organizations that perform abortions. In December 2013, he wrote an op-ed for *The Hill* contending that the 2010 health reform law was not intended to expand health care coverage but to "implement government control over our daily lives." In November 2013, he took the lead in filing articles of impeachment against Attorney General Eric Holder for his mismanagement of the "Fast and Furious" gun-running program in Mexico. "The pattern of disregard for the rule of law and refusal to be forthright has only continued," he said in a statement. "The American people deserve answers and accountability."

Olson has been a champion of NASA's Johnson Space Center and has criticized President Barack Obama's budget requests for ignoring Congress' interest in human space flight. He bemoaned what he called Obama's lack of interest in space policy. "Those who argue we do not have the resources or say government should not play a role in space exploration are short-sighted and wrong," he wrote in a 2012 op-ed in which he called for a return to the moon by 2020 to set the stage for an eventual manned mission to Mars.

In March 2009, Olson collapsed while lifting weights in the House gym and underwent emergency surgery to install a pacemaker. He later filed a bill to establish liability protections for businesses that acquire heart defibrillators for emergency use. He fully recovered and had no trouble winning reelection. He twice was opposed by Democrat Kesha Rogers, a Lyndon LaRouche activist. This is another example of Democrats throwing in the towel on an ethnically diverse Republican-leaning seat that they managed to win in the past decade.

TWENTY-THIRD DISTRICT

Will Hurd (R)

Elected 2014, 1st term; b. Aug. 19, 1977, San Antonio; TX A&M U., B.S. 2000; Christian; single.

Elected Office: TX House, 1990-2013.

Professional Career: Operations officer, CIA, 2000-09; Partner, Crumpton Group, 2010-13; Sr. advisor, FusionX, 2010-present.

DC Office: 317 CHOB, 20515, 202-225-4511; Website: hurd.house.gov..

State Offices: Del Rio, 830-422-2040; Eagle Pass, 210-238-4296.

Committees: *Homeland Security:* Border & Maritime Security; Counterterrorism & Intelligence. *Oversight & GovernmentReform:* Information Technology (Chmn); Nat'l Security.

Election Results

2014 general	Will Hurd (R)	57,459	(50%)	$1,437,694	$461,532	$2,373,405
	Pete Gallego (D)	55,037	(48%)	$2,677,653	$260,121	$2,312,203
	Ruben Corvalan (Lib)	2,933	(3%)			
2014 prim. runoff						
	Will Hurd (R)	8,699	(59%)			
	Francisco Canseco (R)	5,930	(41%)			
2014 primary	Will Hurd (R)	10,496	(41%)			
	Francisco Canseco (R)	10,332	(40%)			
	Robert Lowry (R)	4,796	(19%)			

Population		Race and Ethnicity		Income	
Total:	723,867	Latino	70.8%	Median income:	$47,748
Urban:	61.3%	White	24.8%		*(270 of 435)*
Suburban:	7.3%	Black	2.2%	Under $50,000	51.5%
Rural:	31.5%	Asian	1.2%	$50,000-$99,999:	28.9%
Land area:	24,879	Two races	0.5%	$100,000-$199,999:	15.1%
Pop/sq. mi.:	29.1	White Ethnic	8.8%	$200,000 or more:	4.5%
Born in state:	65.4%			Poverty Rate	18.8%
		Education			
Age Groups		H.S. grad or less:	52.6%	**Work**	
Under 18:	28.7%	Some college:	27.5%	White collar:	29.3%
18 to 34:	23.8%	College degree, 4 yr.:	13.0%	Blue collar:	43.1%
35 to 64:	35.3%	Post-grad study:	7.0%	Sales and service:	27.7%
Over 64:	12.2%				
		Military		Govt. workers:	17.3%
		Veterans/active duty:	9.4%		

San Antonio Exurbs, West Texas

Fifty or so miles west of San Antonio, the hills flatten out and become the parched uplands of West Texas. This is a borderland, just north of Mexico, where people are concentrated in tiny hamlets amid the empty ranchlands. Most are Hispanic. Once, Indians were the threat on

Voter Turnout	
2013 Total Citizen 18+	440,336
2014 House Turnout	115,429
2014 Turnout as % CVAP	26.2%
2012 Turnout as % CVAP	44.8%

this frontier. Now the challenge is a lack of water. The aquifers of West Texas are being drained, and state law still permits landowners to pump out as much water as they want. The Rio Grande, dried out by a dam in New Mexico, gets most of its water from the Rio Conchos in the Mexican state of Chihuahua. The mountains of Big Bend National Park rise above the Rio Grande, where in the clean air you can see for 180 miles. Texas' frontier in many ways is thriving; its remote location makes it one of the least-visited national parks. Eccentrics established an art colony in Marfa and stage a chili cook-off in Terlingua. In 2013, the CBS "60 Minutes" program reported on Marfa as "the capital of quirkiness," chiefly because of the gentrification that the new arrivals have brought. Near the Mexican border is Dimmit County, where more than a dozen companies have drilled thousands of wells in an oil and gas field known as the Eagle Ford shale formation. Huge wind farms have flowered along the interstate in Crockett County. Near the New Mexico border is oil-producing Loving County, which is among the least populous counties in the nation. From 2012 to 2013, the population grew from 78 to 95 residents, which made it the fastest-growing county in the nation; Mentone, its only town, remained unincorporated. The increase may have resulted from the local interest in serving as a dump site for radioactive waste.

The 23rd Congressional District of Texas is geographically the largest in the state, stretching from the outskirts of San Antonio to the edge of El Paso, from Eagle Pass and Maverick County to the New Mexico border. It takes in 23% of the state's land area, spanning 800 miles of the Texas-Mexico border and covering 29 counties. About 9% of the district's residents are military veterans, with many working as active duty personnel at Fort Sam Houston, Lackland Air Force Base, and Randolph Air Force Base, all just outside the district in or near San Antonio.

About 48% of the district's population is in Bexar County, chiefly in a C-shaped ring in the county's western suburbs that surround downtown San Antonio and is the more heavily Republican part of the district. The Mexican-American tradition in the part of South Texas radiating from San Antonio is anchored in two culturally conservative institutions: The Catholic Church and the

2012 Presidential Vote		
Mitt Romney (R)	99,666	(51%)
Barack Obama (D)	94,419	(48%)
2008 Presidential Vote		
Barack Obama (D)	96,871	(50%)
John McCain (R)	95,679	(49%)
Cook Partisan Voting Index:	R+3	

U.S. military. San Antonio's Mexican-American community has produced many politicians who are liberal on economic issues and civil rights but also are pro-military and at home with traditional religious and cultural values. Only 6% of the 23rd is in El Paso County, which is disproportionately Democratic, as are most of the rural counties that lie between the urban anchors. The district is 71% Hispanic, but this is still a battleground district. It was one of only nine House seats won by a Democrat in 2012 that Mitt Romney also carried, 51%-48%.

Will Hurd (R)

In a district known for its frequent change of party control, former CIA employee Will Hurd, a Republican, convinced voters in 2014 to toss out the incumbent for the third time in as many elections. The *Houston Chronicle* headlined him as the spy "who came in from the shadows."

Hurd, a native of San Antonio, is the youngest of three children of a mixed-race couple; his father is African American. He graduated from Texas A&M University with a degree in computer science. As student body president, he helped a grieving campus recover from the 1999 collapse of the traditional football bonfire, which killed 12 students and injured 27 others.

He worked as an under-cover CIA officer and was stationed in Afghanistan, Pakistan and India. On the day after the September 11 attacks, he joined a new counter-terrorism unit in Afghanistan. When he left the agency after nine years and returned to Texas, he became a partner in the strategic advisory firm Crumpton Group, founded by former CIA officer and counterterrorism director Henry "Hank" Crumpton. Hurd also was a senior adviser with the cybersecurity firm FusionX.

Hurd ran for the House seat in 2010, and he led the first round of primary voting with 34% of the vote. But he lost the GOP runoff to Francisco "Quico" Canseco, 53%-47%, a margin of 722 votes. Canseco then defeated Democratic Rep. Ciro Rodriguez. In 2012, Pete Gallego, a former prosecutor and former state representative, took the seat back for Democrats,

50%-46%. But the district gave GOP presidential candidate Mitt Romney 51% of the vote and strong support for Sen. Ted Cruz, a tea party Republican.

In 2014, Hurd easily defeated Canseco, 59%-41%, in the runoff after the two ran close to each other in the three-candidate primary. Tea-party supporters backed Hurd's campaign, which emphasized his intelligence service "in this time of heartbreak and troubles throughout the world." Gallego portrayed himself as a moderate Blue Dog Democrat, but Hurd criticized him as too aligned with President Barack Obama and "radical environmentalists." Painting Gallego as a job killer, Hurd attacked his votes against the Keystone XL pipeline and drilling on public lands. In a district that stretches 800 miles along the border with Mexico, Hurd campaigned for stronger border security and said he opposed granting citizenship to undocumented immigrants. He criticized Gallego for supporting Obama's decision not to visit the border in July during a trip to Texas.

The race remained tight to the end. Gallego outspent Hurd, $2.7 million to $1.4 million. Each candidate was helped by more than $2.5 million in spending by national party committees and other outside groups that made huge ad purchases. The *San Antonio Express-News* endorsed Hurd as a young, charismatic conservative "with equal appeal to grizzled West Texas ranchers and upwardly mobile urban twentysomethings." Hurd won by about 2,400 votes, 49.8%-47.7%. In Bexar, which cast nearly half of the votes, Hurd led, 57%-40%. In a district with only a 3% black population, Hurd explained to *The Washington Post* how "the black dude" was successful: "We did it by engaging people on the issues that they care about," notably, a good income, housing and health. "So we have to translate our agenda in a way that hits at those issues."

In the House, Hurd got a plum assignment for a freshman as chairman of the Oversight and Government Reform Subcommittee on Information Technology. In June 2015, he chaired a hearing on the data breach at the Office of Personnel Management that affected millions of federal employees and their family members. "It's no secret that federal agencies need to improve their cybersecurity posture," he said in his opening statement. "Until agency leadership takes control of these basic cybersecurity measures—things like strong authentication, network monitoring, encrypting data, and segmentation—we will always be playing catch-up against our highly sophisticated and well-resourced adversaries." After OPM director Katherine Archuleta resigned a month later, Hurd said that the idea of moving the security clearance database away from OPM was "something to be explored."

Hurd joined Democratic Rep. Ted Lieu of California, another freshman on the Oversight committee with a degree in computer science, in urging caution about new rules that required business to give law-enforcement officials access to their encrypted data. "Any vulnerability to encryption or security technology that can be accessed by law enforcement is one that can be exploited by bad actors such as criminals, spies and those engaged in economic espionage," they wrote to the FBI director. In a February 2015 interview with *Baseline* magazine, Hurd said that the nation needs to do more to prepare against a cyberattack. "We do not have clear rules of engagement for a pure digital-on-digital attack. Knowing the rules of engagement deters some of this undesirable behavior." Hurd, who also joined the Homeland Security Committee, won House passage in May of his bill that clarified that Border Patrol agents would continue to qualify for overtime pay.

Hurd said that he declined an invitation to join the Congressional Black Caucus, which is exclusively Democratic.

Given his tight victory in 2014, it was no surprise that the Democratic Congressional Campaign Committee made him an early target for 2016. In April 2015, Gallego announced that he would seek to reclaim his seat. If he succeeds, it would continue the pattern since 2008 of Democrats winning in presidential-election years and Republicans taking the seat in midterms. As has become the pattern, it might be the only competitive House contest in the state.

TWENTY-FOURTH DISTRICT

Kenny Marchant (R)

Elected 2004, 6th term; b. Feb. 23, 1951, Bonham; South Nazarene U., B.A. 1974; Nazarene; married (Donna); 4 children.

Elected Office: Carrollton City Cncl., 1980-84; Carrolton Mayor, 1984-86; TX House, 1987-2005.

Professional Career: Founder & owner, construction & home building business, 1975-2004.

DC Office: 2313 RHOB, 20515, 202-225-6605; Fax: 202-225-0074; Website: marchant.house.gov.

State Offices: Irving, 972-556-0162.

Committees: *Ethics. Ways & Means:* Health; Trade.

Group Ratings

	ADA	ACLU	AFL-CIO	LCV	ITI	COC	HAFA	ACU	CFG	FRC
2014	0%	5%	–	3%	20%	64%	87%	96%	87%	100%
2013	5%	C	10%	7%	C	69%	C	96%	87%	C

National Journal Ratings

	2013 LIB	—	2013 CONS
Economic	3%	—	97%
Social	0%	—	87%
Foreign	0%	—	95%
Composite	4%	—	96%

Key Votes of the 113th Congress

1. Sandy storm spending	N	5. Medical Marijuana	N	9. Syrian Rebels Training	Y
2. Violence Against Women Act	N	6. Farm Bill	Y	10. Keystone pipeline	Y
3. Guantanamo Bay Detainees	N	7. Afghanistan Combat	N	11. Immigration Exec. Action	Y
4. Abortion 20-week ban	Y	8. NSA Phone Data Collection	Y	12. Bipartisan budget deal	N

Election Results

2014 general	Kenny Marchant (R)	93,712	(65%)	$431,772	$10,291
	Patrick McGehearty (D)	46,548	(32%)	$9,517	
	Mike Kolls (Lib)	3,813	(3%)		
2014 primary	Kenny Marchant (R)	unopposed			

Prior winning percentages: 2012 (61%), 2010 (82%), 2008 (56%), 2006 (60%), 2004 (64%)

Population		Race and Ethnicity		Income	
Total:	741,164	White	52.3%	Median income:	$63,223
Urban:	46.1%	Latino	24.4%		*(91 of 435)*
Suburban:	53.9%	Black	10.5%	Under $50,000	39.7%
Rural:	0.0%	Asian	10.2%	$50,000-$99,999:	31.0%
Land area:	262	Two races	2.1%	$100,000-$199,999:	20.6%
Pop/sq. mi.:	2,831.0	White Ethnic	17.7%	$200,000 or more:	8.7%
Born in state:	45.6%			Poverty Rate	11.1%
		Education			
Age Groups		H.S. grad or less:	26.8%	**Work**	
Under 18:	23.8%	Some college:	30.2%	White collar:	43.4%
18 to 34:	25.7%	College degree, 4 yr.:	28.4%	Blue collar:	40.9%
35 to 64:	40.6%	Post-grad study:	14.5%	Sales and service:	15.7%
Over 64:	9.9%				
		Military		Govt. workers:	7.8%
		Veterans/active duty:	6.9%		

North-Central Metroplex: Fort Worth Suburbs

The gigantic (larger than Manhattan Island) Dallas-Fort Worth International Airport, the third-busiest in the world, bisects the Metroplex and its two adjacent counties with its large terminals and the Texas-sized highway network that feeds them. It has become the largest capacity airport in the world, with seven runways, five terminals and 175 gates. DFW, as the locals call it, has been a focal point for development in both Dallas and Tarrant counties. "DFW is no longer solely an airport. DFW is our home," the *Fort Worth Star-Telegram* wrote. New cities, with as many people as Dallas and Fort Worth had in the 1950s—Grand Prairie and Irving—grew up around the airport during the next two decades in an area that had been an open prairie. Underway is a $2.3 billion upgrade of DFW's terminals, which augurs future growth. The 2012 merger of American Airlines and US Airways was a windfall for the region. The combined company became the largest airline in the country, with its headquarters remaining in Fort Worth; in 2014, it operated more than 80 percent of the flights out of DFW.

Voter Turnout	
2013 Total Citizen 18+	469,817
2014 House Turnout	144,073
2014 Turnout as % CVAP	30.7%
2012 Turnout as % CVAP	54.8%

North of DFW are newer and more upscale suburbs in northeast Tarrant County: Southlake, with huge shopping malls and resort centers, and Grapevine, home to video game retailer GameStop and the largest consumer-judged wine competition in the country. Southlake is home to the headquarters of the online travel agency Travelocity.com. Across the International Parkway in northwest Dallas County are Coppell, Farmers Branch, and Carrollton. To the north are the fast-growing suburbs and exurbs of Denton County. The Dallas-Fort Worth-Arlington Metropolitan Statistical Area has passed Philadelphia as the nation's fourth-largest MSA.

The 24th Congressional District of Texas is based in the suburban territory around DFW Airport, with the most populous sector extending northeast into Dallas County and into Denton County. It includes some of Irving, including ExxonMobil's corporate headquarters, part of Carrolton and all of Farmers Branch and Coppell. To the west, another spoke reaches into Tarrant County

2012 Presidential Vote		
Mitt Romney (R)	150,547	(60%)
Barack Obama (D)	94,634	(38%)
2008 Presidential Vote		
John McCain (R)	152,453	(58%)
Barack Obama (D)	105,822	(41%)
Cook Partisan Voting Index:	R+13	

and includes Grapevine, Bedford, Colleyville and Southlake. The Tarrant County section is a bit more Republican and has a higher voter turnout than the Dallas portion, with about 16 percent in Denton County. This is solidly Republican territory.

Kenny Marchant (R)

Republican Kenny Marchant, elected in 2004, has a prized seat on the Ways and Means Committee, a reward for his loyalty to Speaker John Boehner and the GOP agenda. Mild-mannered and deeply religious, he does not have the sharp rhetorical edge of many Texas conservatives.

Marchant graduated from Southern Nazarene University and became a homebuilder and successful developer. He said that he got involved in politics when the head of the local homebuilders association told him that officials planned to change the construction codes and make it more expensive to build. Marchant served a quarter-century in local elected offices, including stints on the Carrollton City Council, as Carrollton mayor, and then in the state House. (His son, Matthew, became Carrollton's mayor in 2011.) He has been active in humanitarian projects around the world; the Ken Marchant Foundation funds church loans, mission projects and scholarships. He has a ranch about an hour from Dallas, where he maintains 400 cows and likes to fish and hunt. He had a net worth of at least $8.1 million in January 2015, according to *Roll Call*.

In the state House, he enjoyed a reputation on both sides of the aisle as a levelheaded peacemaker. Despite serving in some of the legislature's most partisan leadership posts, Marchant refrained from engaging in the acrimonious battles all around him. Marchant had been chairman of the Banking and Investments Committee, and spent four years as floor leader of the Texas House Republican caucus. He served on the House Redistricting Committee during the bitter 2003 mapping battle.

Unsurprisingly, the redistricting plan couldn't have been more favorable to him. The new 24th District was heavily Republican and inhospitable to Democratic Rep. Martin Frost, an effective partisan who was targeted by then-Majority Leader Tom DeLay of Texas, the mastermind behind the effort. Frost opted to run in the new 32nd District and lost. Meanwhile, Marchant thrived in the newly drawn 24th, which incorporated nearly his entire state legislative district. In the primary, he defeated three other candidates with 73% of the vote, and in the general election he won 64%-34%.

In the House, Marchant has a solidly conservative voting record. He was among the original members of the Tea Party Caucus and a co-sponsor of the so-called "birther" bill in 2009 requiring future presidential candidates to prove U.S. citizenship. "My vision for America is one where government is limited, taxes are low, success is celebrated, and the public sector flourishes," he told the *Fort Worth Star-Telegram* in 2012. He developed a fruitful relationship with Boehner; he joined the Education and the Workforce Committee that Boehner chaired in 2005 and was one of the few Texans to back Boehner when he ran for majority leader in 2006. Marchant serves on the House Ethics Committee.

On Ways and Means in 2013, Marchant chaired the tax reform working group on debt, equity and capital. In response to the recent political targeting controversy at the IRS, which he said jeopardized the security of confidential taxpayer information, he prepared a bill to prohibit IRS employees from using personal email accounts for official business. The House passed the measure on a voice vote in April 2015. He has proposed a phase-out of the $6 billion production tax credit for wind energy. As a member of the Trade Subcommittee, he was an enthusiastic supporter of the prospective Trans-Pacific Partnership agreement.

Marchant in 2011 sponsored a bill to prevent the federal government from subsidizing illegal immigrants' housing purchases by requiring borrowers to submit to the E-Verify background check program. In October 2014, he called on the Centers for Disease Control to set up a quarantine facility at DFW to care for overseas passengers arriving with Ebola.

Marchant drew a spirited GOP primary challenger in 2012 in Grant Stinchfield, a former TV news investigative reporter. He accused Marchant of failing to adequately represent conservatives and chastised him for requesting in an email to a GOP operative that his "grandbabies" schools be included in his district as part of the recent redistricting. Stinchfield won the endorsement of the *Star-Telegram*, which called Marchant "a good argument for term limits" and cited his lack of legislative productivity. Marchant's campaign noted that Stinchfield lived outside the district and that most of his support came from there. Stinchfield spent a relatively modest $239,000. The incumbent won 68%-32%. Marchant has not faced a competitive Democratic challenger.

TWENTY-FIFTH DISTRICT

Roger Williams (R)

Elected 2012, 2nd term; b. Sept. 13, 1949, Evanston, IL; TX Christian U., B.S. 1972; Christian; married (Patty); 2 children.

Professional Career: Owner, Roger Williams Chrysler Dodge Jeep Ram, 1971-present; Atlanta Braves farm team, 1971-74; Baseball coach, TX Christian U., 1974-76; TX secy. of st., 2005-07.

DC Office: 1323 LHOB, 20515, 202-225-9896; Website: williams.house.gov.

State Offices: Austin, 512-473-8910; Cleburne, 817-774-2575.

Committees: *Financial Services:* Financial Institutions & Consumer Credit; Housing & Insurance; Task Force to Investigate Terrorism Financing.

Group Ratings

	ADA	ACLU	AFL-CIO	LCV	ITI	COC	HAFA	ACU	CFG	FRC
2014	5%	0%	–	3%	60%	75%	79%	100%	92%	100%
2013	5%	C	14%	4%	C	77%	C	84%	80%	C

National Journal Ratings

	2013 LIB —	2013 CONS
Economic	10% —	88%
Social	0% —	87%
Foreign	5% —	86%
Composite	9% —	91%

Key Votes of the 113th Congress

1. Sandy storm spending N	5. Medical Marijuana N	9. Syrian Rebels Training N
2. Violence Against Women Act N	6. Farm Bill Y	10. Keystone pipeline Y
3. Guantanamo Bay Detainees N	7. Afghanistan Combat N	11. Immigration Exec. Action Y
4. Abortion 20-week ban Y	8. NSA Phone Data Collection Y	12. Bipartisan budget deal Y

Election Results

2014 general	Roger Williams (R)	107,120	(60%)	$1,234,454
	Marco Montoya (D)	64,463	(36%)	$25,126
	John Betz, Jr. (Lib)	6,300	(4%)	
2014 primary	Roger Williams (R)	unopposed		

Prior winning percentage: 2012 (58%)

Population		Race and Ethnicity		Income	
Total:	731,689	White	70.7%	Median income:	$60,847
Urban:	35.1%	Latino	16.9%		*(117 of 435)*
Suburban:	40.6%	Black	7.4%	Under $50,000	41.4%
Rural:	24.3%	Asian	2.4%	$50,000-$99,999:	29.9%
Land area:	5,209	Two races	1.8%	$100,000-$199,999:	21.2%
Pop/sq. mi.:	140.5	White Ethnic	22.0%	$200,000 or more:	7.6%
Born in state:	58.8%			Poverty Rate	12.1%
		Education			
Age Groups		H.S. grad or less:	33.3%	**Work**	
Under 18:	25.1%	Some college:	31.1%	White collar:	43.7%
18 to 34:	23.3%	College degree, 4 yr.:	22.6%	Blue collar:	37.2%
35 to 64:	38.7%	Post-grad study:	13.0%	Sales and service:	19.1%
Over 64:	13.0%				
		Military		Govt. workers:	17.4%
		Veterans/active duty:	12.3%		

Austin/Fort Worth Suburbs Corridor

Austin, the capital of the second-largest state in the country and the site of the largest capitol building, was laid-back and countrified until fairly recently. Sixty years ago, in Lyndon Johnson's time, Austin had a metropolitan population of just over 130,000. There had never been

Voter Turnout	
2013 Total Citizen 18+	516,540
2014 House Turnout	177,883
2014 Turnout as % CVAP	34.4%
2012 Turnout as % CVAP	53.7%

much commerce and state government provided much of the local employment. Its skies were untainted by industrial smoke. Its biggest industry was the University of Texas, with 50,000 students and an endowment of thousands of West Texas acres that turned out to sit on top of oil. The university has long had a distinguished faculty and some of the world's great scholarly collections, including the LBJ Presidential Library and its 45 million pages of documents. The Austin of old was also the central focus of Texas' hardy but almost always outnumbered liberals, based in the university, state government and *Texas Observer* magazine. They mocked the business lobbyists who called the shots when the "Leg" (pronounced *lej*) was in session.

Today's Austin is quite a different place. The metropolitan area has doubled every 20 years, and today Greater Austin's population stands at 1.9 million, the fourth-largest in the state. In the 12 months ending in June 2014, it was the fastest-growing metro area in the nation with at least 1 million people. In July 2013, *Time* magazine worried about the growing challenge of "keeping Austin weird," which had been a familiar mantra on its T-shirts and bumper stickers. The city core and the university area are still Democratic—President Barack Obama won 60% of the vote in Travis County in 2012. Some businesses cater to the old liberal bastions: The upscale organic-food chain, Whole Foods Market, is based in Austin. But the area overall has become more conservative, especially as its private sector began to make up a larger share of

2012 Presidential Vote		
Mitt Romney (R)	162,279	(60%)
Barack Obama (D)	102,433	(38%)

2008 Presidential Vote		
John McCain (R)	153,998	(56%)
Barack Obama (D)	117,402	(43%)

Cook Partisan Voting Index: R+12

the local economy. The techies who settled in the Silicon Hills extending from Austin's Travis County to once-rural Williamson County have tended to vote Republican. Many of the nation's largest high-tech companies are based there. When Austin's local government in 2014 shifted from at-large to district representation, Republicans picked up seats. Housing prices across the city have grown much higher, though they still seem cheap compared with San Francisco and Boston.

The 25th Congressional District of Texas, which includes the capitol and the UT campus, has about 30 percent of the residents of Travis County. To dilute the liberal votes cast in Austin, they have been split among five districts, of which the 25th has the largest share. That part of the district leans Democratic. To the west of downtown, Mopac Boulevard operates as a dividing line between overwhelmingly Democratic Austin and the more suburban, Republican-leaning areas of Travis County near Lake Travis. The remaining 60% of the district's population resides in a string of Republican-leaning counties that include what was known in LBJ's days as the Hill Country. This stretch, which extends north to Burleson in the Fort Worth suburbs, politically overwhelms the liberal enclaves in Austin. Lampasas, where the first chapter of the Farmers' Alliance, a precursor to the Populists, was founded in 1877; musician and activist Willie Nelson was born in tiny Abbott. The 25th has become a solidly Republican district.

Roger Williams (R)

After dropping a bid for the Senate, Republican Roger Williams, a former Texas secretary of state and prolific fundraiser, easily won a wide-open GOP primary in 2012 to take the district that had become reliably Republican in redistricting. He has quietly gone about his work, which includes a seat on the Financial Services Committee.

Williams grew up in Fort Worth, where his father was a Chevrolet dealer and his mother ran a needlepoint business. He distinctly remembers that, as a 14-year-old, he was the last person to shake President John Kennedy's hand as he left the Texas Hotel in Fort Worth on the morning of Nov. 22, 1963. He attended Texas Christian University on a baseball scholarship. After graduating, he played in the Atlanta Braves minor league system for four years until he injured a shoulder while sliding into first base. He returned home to run the family car dealership and to coach baseball at TCU for three years. "I always thought I'd be a Major League Baseball player," he said. "When you're young, you never think you're going to get hurt or get old." Baseball is still important to Williams; he checks box scores every morning in season and considers pitching legend Nolan Ryan a good friend. He continues to own the dealership.

Their shared love for baseball connected Williams and George W. Bush. A former owner of the Texas Rangers, Bush invited Williams to be a regional finance chairman for his two campaigns for governor, which was Williams' first foray into politics. He made his way to Washington in 2000, when Bush appointed him to the Republican National Committee's Eagles program. He left that position to accept Gov. Rick Perry's appointment as secretary of state. He was also Perry's chief liaison to Mexico.

Williams, who was Sen. John Cornyn's finance chair in 2002, said that political fundraising comes easily to him. Having voiced interest in running for the open Senate seat in 2012, Williams announced in June 2011 that he would instead run for the 25th District seat, which had been altered to become securely Republican. The GOP-engineered changes prompted Democratic Rep. Lloyd Doggett to move to the 35th District. Williams overwhelmingly outspent the GOP primary field and defeated tea party activist Wes Riddle in a runoff, 58%-42%.

Williams ran on what he called a "pretty simple" platform. "It's lower taxes, less government, cut the spending, defend the borders, listen to your generals, and understand the 10th Amendment," he said. He generated controversy when he called President Barack Obama a socialist at a campaign event, but said he saw no reason to apologize. "Here's a man that wants to own the banks, the car manufacturers, the student loan programs," he said. "It's basically socialism versus entrepreneurialism and capitalism. That's what we're fighting." In November, Williams defeated Democrat Elaine Henderson, 58%-37%. He was reelected easily in 2014.

As a new member of the Financial Services Committee in 2015, he joined the terrorism financing task force. He generated some controversy in seeking to give the Medal of Honor to former Navy SEAL Chris Kyle, who inspired the movie "American Sniper" for having killed more than 160 people during combat in Iraq, and then was the victim of a shooting at a Texas rifle range. Critics from some veterans' groups contended that Kyle did not meet the required standard of a single extraordinary act of valor. But Williams disagreed, and filed his bill in February 2015.

Williams became finance chairman of the National Republican Congressional Committee in 2013. From that base, he soon voiced interest in taking over as chairman of the full committee after the 2014 election, regardless of the intentions of then-chairman Greg Walden of Oregon. When House Republicans made a double-digit gain in the 2014 election and Walden made clear that he was not giving up the post, Williams quietly and wisely abandoned his bid. Instead, he was named chairman in 2015 of the House Conservatives Fund, which had been relatively inactive.

TWENTY-SIXTH DISTRICT

Michael Burgess (R)

Elected 2002, 7th term; b. Dec. 23, 1950, Rochester, MN; N. TX St. U., B.S. 1972, M.S. 1976, U. of TX Med. Schl., M.D. 1977, U. of TX Dallas, M.S. 2000; Episcopalian; married (Laura); 3 children.

Professional Career: Practicing obstetrician, 1981-2003.

DC Office: 2336 RHOB, 20515, 202-225-7772; Fax: 202-225-2919; Website: burgess.house.gov.

State Offices: Lake Dallas, 940-497-5031.

Committees: *Energy & Commerce:* Commerce, Manufacturing & Trade (Chmn); Health; Oversight & Investigations. *Rules:* Legislative and Budget Process.

Group Ratings

	ADA	ACLU	AFL-CIO	LCV	ITI	COC	HAFA	ACU	CFG	FRC
2014	15%	0%	–	3%	80%	79%	81%	92%	92%	100%
2013	5%	C	14%	4%	C	85%	C	92%	84%	C

National Journal Ratings

	2013 LIB	—	2013 CONS
Economic	13%	—	85%
Social	0%	—	87%
Foreign	46%	—	54%
Composite	22%	—	78%

Key Votes of the 113th Congress

1. Sandy storm spending	N	5. Medical Marijuana	N	9. Syrian Rebels Training	N
2. Violence Against Women Act	N	6. Farm Bill	Y	10. Keystone pipeline	Y
3. Guantanamo Bay Detainees	N	7. Afghanistan Combat	Y	11. Immigration Exec. Action	Y
4. Abortion 20-week ban	Y	8. NSA Phone Data Collection	Y	12. Bipartisan budget deal	N

Election Results

2014 general	Michael Burgess (R)	116,944	(83%)	$1,068,923
	Mark Boler (Lib)	24,526	(17%)	
2014 primary	Michael Burgess (R)	33,909	(83%)	
	Joel Krause (R)	6,433	(16%)	

Prior winning percentages: 2012 (68%), 2010 (67%), 2008 (60%), 2006 (60%), 2004 (66%), 2002 (75%)

Population		Race and Ethnicity		Income	
Total:	768,246	White	69.6%	Median income:	$80,124
Urban:	7.2%	Latino	16.1%		*(32 of 435)*
Suburban:	90.5%	Black	6.5%	Under $50,000	29.7%
Rural:	2.3%	Asian	4.9%	$50,000-$99,999:	31.6%
Land area:	1,212	Two races	2.3%	$100,000-$199,999:	30.2%
Pop/sq. mi.:	633.8	White Ethnic	24.1%	$200,000 or more:	8.5%
Born in state:	49.9%			Poverty Rate	8.0%
		Education			
Age Groups		H.S. grad or less:	27.3%	**Work**	
Under 18:	28.0%	Some college:	32.2%	White collar:	43.8%
18 to 34:	22.9%	College degree, 4 yr.:	27.7%	Blue collar:	41.1%
35 to 64:	40.9%	Post-grad study:	12.8%	Sales and service:	15.1%
Over 64:	8.2%				
		Military		Govt. workers:	12.6%
		Veterans/active duty:	7.9%		

Northern Metroplex: Denton, Fort Worth Area

Until the Texas Land and Immigration Company settled this portion of northeast Texas with a land grant from the Texas Congress in 1841, settlers were scarce and Indian raids were common. The area now known as Denton County takes its name

Voter Turnout	
2013 Total Citizen 18+	503,248
2014 House Turnout	141,470
2014 Turnout as % CVAP	28.1%
2012 Turnout as % CVAP	53.5%

from John Bunyan Denton, a Methodist pioneer preacher and lawyer killed in a skirmish with Indians. Today, this area on the northern edge of the Dallas-Fort Worth Metroplex is teeming with new arrivals and filling up with young, well-educated, middle-class families. The University of North Texas, with more than 36,000 students, is the fifth-largest in the state, while Texas Woman's University is the largest state-supported university for women in the United States (although it does accept men).

The county's chief cities are Denton, Flower Mound and Lewisville, and there is plenty of room for more growth along Interstates 35E and 35W. In September 2014, GE Transportation hired a second shift for its $200 million facility that is manufacturing rail locomotives in Fort Worth. Truck manufacturer Peterbilt Motors, the largest employer in Denton with 2,100 employees, announced an expansion in February 2015. Near Justin, in the southwest corner of Denton County, a pipeline project was completed in 2010 allowing for the production of up to 1 billion cubic feet of natural gas daily. With sophisticated imaging and drilling technology, other natural gas wells operate within 10 miles of downtown Fort Worth. In 1940, there were 34,000 people in Denton County, and they voted 88% Democratic for president. The county of more than 650,000 people voted 62% for John McCain in 2008 and 65% for Mitt Romney in 2012. The county inflicted an unusual setback on the oil and gas industry, but it didn't last long. Local voters in November 2014 approved a referendum to ban hydraulic fracturing within city limits, but Gov. Greg Abbott in May 2015 signed a law prohibiting such a local ban.

The 26th Congressional District of Texas is at the heart of the northern expansion of the Metroplex. It includes almost all of suburban and exurban Denton County, and a small fragment of urban Tarrant County, including the old railroad town of Keller, now a bustling upscale suburb with a median

2012 Presidential Vote
Mitt Romney (R)................177,941 (68%)
Barack Obama (D) 80,828 (31%)

2008 Presidential Vote
John McCain (R)................166,877 (64%)
Barack Obama (D) 90,791 (35%)

Cook Partisan Voting Index: R+20

family income in excess of $100,000. There are some Democratic areas here, especially around Denton's universities, but overall this is the strongest Republican district in the Metroplex.

Michael Burgess (R)

Michael Burgess, a conservative Republican physician first elected in 2002, is a spokesman for House Republicans on health care issues and has become an active member of the Energy and Commerce Committee.

Burgess grew up in Denton County, the son of a physician, and graduated from the University of North Texas and the University of Texas Medical School in Houston. He trained at Parkland Hospital in Dallas and set up an obstetrics-gynecology practice in Lewisville. After 21 years in practice, Burgess ran for Congress, his first bid for elective office. When Majority Leader Dick Armey announced in 2001 that he would not run again, there was no doubt that a Republican would succeed him. But almost no one expected that the winner would be Burgess. The widespread expectation was that the winner would be the majority leader's son, Scott Armey, a former Denton County judge.

In the primary, Armey outspent Burgess by more than 6-to-1. But turnout was light—only 25,000 people of 456,000 voting-age residents took part. There were no statewide Republican contests, and there didn't seem to be much suspense about the outcome. Armey won 45% of the vote, failing to avoid a runoff. Burgess won 23%. In the four-week runoff campaign, Burgess benefited from a series of hard-hitting articles in the *Dallas Morning News* about Scott Armey's record as a county judge, which suggested he had used his position to steer county jobs and contracts to close friends.

Burgess focused on health care and taxes. He had helped to draft the Texas Patients' Bill of Rights and vowed to do the same on a national level. In another low-turnout affair, Burgess won 55%-45% in the runoff. Armey tellingly lost 60%-40% in Denton County, where he was known best. After the runoff, his powerful father spoke bitterly of the newspaper's "vicious unprofessionalism" and accused the paper of a vendetta against the Armey family. In the general election, Burgess defeated his Democrat opponent, 75%-23%. He has been reelected comfortably since.

In the House, Burgess has a reliably conservative voting record. He joined the Tea Party Caucus when it was formed in 2010. Also that year, he voted "present" on a resolution commemorating the 40th anniversary of the Vietnam-era shootings at Kent State University because he said the measure implied that the National Guard was at fault. He has pushed legislation to implement a flat tax, a popular idea with conservatives that would replace the federal income tax with a 23% sales tax on goods and services. He drew headlines in August 2011 when, while attending a tea party meeting, he responded to a question about whether impeaching President Barack Obama would tie up Obama's agenda by saying there was "no question" that it would. But he said later that he didn't advocate impeachment.

Burgess is best known for his work on health care. On the Energy and Commerce Subcommittee on Health, he has been an effective inquisitor on the 2010 health reform law, and fellow Republicans regularly yielded him their extra time at hearings so he could ask pointed questions of Obama administration officials. He was vocal about seeking to fully defund the law in the fiscal 2011 budget, an idea that House Republican leaders sought to defuse. His nine-part plan for health care includes many ideas that GOP candidates have espoused, including allowing patients to shop for insurance across state lines and limiting damages in malpractice lawsuits. In January 2015, Burgess became chairman of the Subcommittee on Commerce, Manufacturing and Trade, which has jurisdiction over consumer and tourism issues.

Burgess has shown that he is not a reflexive partisan, notably on pharmaceutical issues. In 2009, he joined a bipartisan agreement to permit the Food and Drug Administration to approve generic versions of biologic drugs. He was part of a bipartisan group that filed legislation in 2011 ensuring that seniors who show signs of Alzheimer's receive a formal diagnosis from their doctor. In February 2015, he filed with Democratic Rep. Chris Van Hollen of Maryland the Advancing Research for Neurological Diseases Act of 2015, which would create a national data collection system at the Centers for Disease Control and Prevention for disorders such as Parkinson's disease and multiple sclerosis. He played an active role when Congress finally resolved in April 2015 the "doc fix" issue that limited reimbursements for patients with Medicare coverage. "May we never speak of it again," he concluded. The bipartisan deal, which he called the most significant entitlement reform in years, included other changes in Medicare, such as performance incentives for health care providers.

Burgess has made some inroads into the GOP leadership. He served as vice chairman of the Republican Policy Committee, which hammers out the party's positions on issues. But he has kept his distance from the Texas GOP establishment. He backed Ted Cruz's successful

Senate primary bid against Lt. Gov. David Dewhurst in 2012. While other Lone Star State lawmakers were backing Gov. Rick Perry in that year's presidential race, Burgess came out early for Newt Gingrich. In February 2015, he said that it would be "inappropriate" for vaccination against measles to become an issue in the 2016 presidential campaign.

TWENTY-SEVENTH DISTRICT

Blake Farenthold (R)

Elected 2010, 3rd term; b. Dec. 12, 1961, Corpus Christi; U. of TX, B.S. 1985, St. Mary's U., J.D. 1989; Episcopalian; married (Debbie); 2 children.

Professional Career: Practicing atty., 1989-95; Owner, Farenthold LLC, 1995-2010; Radio host, 1999-2010.

DC Office: 1027 LHOB, 20515, 202-225-7742; Fax: 202-226-1134; Website: farenthold.house.gov.

State Offices: Victoria, 361-894-6446; Corpus Christi, 361-884-2222.

Committees: *Judiciary:* Courts, Intellectual Property & the Internet; Regulatory Reform, Commercial & Antitrust Law (VChmn). *Oversight & Government Reform:* Information Technology; Interior. *Transportation & Infrastructure:* Aviation; Highways & Transit; Railroads, Pipelines & Hazardous Materials.

Group Ratings

	ADA	ACLU	AFL-CIO	LCV	ITI	COC	HAFA	ACU	CFG	FRC
2014	5%	5%	–	0%	100%	79%	64%	80%	72%	88%
2013	5%	C	19%	0%	C	77%	C	76%	66%	C

National Journal Ratings

	2013 LIB	—	2013 CONS
Economic	21%	—	77%
Social	31%	—	67%
Foreign	34%	—	60%
Composite	30%	—	70%

Key Votes of the 113th Congress

1. Sandy storm spending	N	5. Medical Marijuana	N	9. Syrian Rebels Training	Y
2. Violence Against Women Act	Y	6. Farm Bill	Y	10. Keystone pipeline	Y
3. Guantanamo Bay Detainees	N	7. Afghanistan Combat	N	11. Immigration Exec. Action	Y
4. Abortion 20-week ban	Y	8. NSA Phone Data Collection	Y	12. Bipartisan budget deal	Y

Election Results

2014 general	Blake Farenthold (R)................. 83,342	(64%)	$962,434
	Wesley Reed (D).......................... 44,152	(34%)	$315,649
	Roxanne Simonson (Lib) 3,553	(3%)	
2014 primary	Blake Farenthold (R)............unopposed		

Prior winning percentages: 2012 (57%), 2010 (48%)

Population		Race and Ethnicity		Income	
Total:	714,527	Latino	50.8%	Median income:	$49,518
Urban:	54.0%	White	41.4%		*(247 of 435)*
Suburban:	16.4%	Black	4.8%	Under $50,000	50.4%
Rural:	29.6%	Asian	1.4%	$50,000-$99,999:	30.5%
Land area:	8,971	Two races	1.4%	$100,000-$199,999:	16.7%
Pop/sq. mi.:	79.6	White Ethnic	16.8%	$200,000 or more:	2.4%
Born in state:	75.3%			Poverty Rate	17.3%
		Education			
Age Groups		H.S. grad or less:	51.1%	**Work**	
Under 18:	25.4%	Some college:	31.8%	White collar:	25.5%
18 to 34:	22.6%	College degree, 4 yr.:	11.7%	Blue collar:	46.5%
35 to 64:	37.5%	Post-grad study:	5.4%	Sales and service:	27.9%
Over 64:	14.5%				
		Military		Govt. workers:	14.2%
		Veterans/active duty:	10.3%		

Central Gulf Coast: Corpus Christi, Victoria

The Nueces River rises on the Edwards Plateau in Central Texas, almost a half mile above sea level. From there it cascades across the Texas Hill Country and passes through the coastal plain before emptying into the Gulf of Corpus Christi. Early attempts at establishing settlements near the

Voter Turnout	
2013 Total Citizen 18+	500,770
2014 House Turnout	131,047
2014 Turnout as % CVAP	26.2%
2012 Turnout as % CVAP	43.5%

river's terminus were half-hearted and unsuccessful, and the area was uninhabited until Henry Lawrence Kinney and William Aubrey established a trading post on the west shore of the bay in 1839. Growth came slowly here at first; a population of 2,100 in 1870 was barely 11,000 in 1920. Hurricanes, the occasional outbreak of yellow fever and, more importantly, the lack of a deep-water port, frustrated attempts to expand the city.

Then, in 1926, the federal government completed the dredging of a shipping channel and the modern Port of Corpus Christi was born. The city's population almost tripled in the 1920s, then doubled in the 1930s. By 2013, it topped 316,000. The port is the sixth largest in the United States in total tonnage shipped, a center for exporting cotton, sorghum and grains, and importing oil and crude petroleum. Barge traffic of oil has increased greatly along the Gulf Intracoastal Waterway. The Naval Air Station at Corpus Christi is another major contributor to the local economy, while sport fishing is a burgeoning industry. Starting in 2010, the Eagle Ford Shale has yielded more than 1.5 million barrels of daily oil production, though the oil-price slump began to shut down rigs at the end of 2014. The overall economy remained strong, with unemployment at 4% in April 2015. Corpus Christi's population is 60% Hispanic. According to a Pew Research Center report in August 2013, only 8% of them were foreign-born. That is the smallest share for any of the 60 metro areas with sizable Hispanic populations.

The 27th Congressional District of Texas is centered on Corpus Christi, and almost half of its residents live in the city and surrounding Nueces County. The district takes in most of the Gulf Coast north of Corpus Christi, up to Bay City and the outskirts of Houston's suburbs. The only other city of any size in the district is Victoria, an industrial town of 65,000. Formosa Plastics has begun a $1.7 billion expansion of its plastics and petrochemicals site in nearby Point Comfort. An arm of the 27th reaches to Bastrop and Caldwell counties, in the Austin area, and takes in Gonzales, where the first shots of

2012 Presidential Vote		
Mitt Romney (R)	131,803	(61%)
Barack Obama (D)	83,152	(38%)
2008 Presidential Vote		
John McCain (R)	133,839	(59%)
Barack Obama (D)	91,083	(40%)
Cook Partisan Voting Index: R+13		

the Texas Revolution were fired. The redrawn district, unlike its predecessor, is safe Republican territory, even with its 51% Hispanic population.

Blake Farenthold (R)

Republican Blake Farenthold was elected in 2010 with one of the most surprising GOP wins of that cycle, then emerged as a big winner in Texas redistricting with a more solidly Republican district. He has been slow to have much impact in the large Texas delegation.

Farenthold was born and raised in Corpus Christi, where his family has farmed for three generations. His father died when Farenthold was 11 years old, and his mother raised him and his younger sister alone. His family is known for strong women. His grandfather's second wife was Sissy Farenthold, a Democratic state legislator and a pioneer of the women's rights movement who was a serious contender to be George McGovern's presidential running mate in 1972.

Blake Farenthold studied radio, film and television at the University of Texas. After earning his law degree at St. Mary's University, he joined his step-grandfather's law practice, focusing on agricultural law. He became dissatisfied with the legal profession, and launched a computer consulting and website design firm. He also began dabbling in radio, appearing as an occasional guest to talk about computer-related issues. Eventually, he became a sidekick on the morning program of Corpus Christi's news radio station KKTX. Farenthold aired his conservative views and gained name recognition.

Motivated by his opposition to the health care overhaul, he ran in 2010 against 14-term Democratic Rep. Solomon Ortiz. He faced a tough fight for the Republican nomination against Corpus Christi real estate agent James Duerr, who campaigned on a similarly conservative platform, but he prevailed in the April runoff, 51%-49%. Farenthold drew on his personal wealth to outspend Duerr. The Center for Responsive Politics estimated his net worth in 2013 at between $2.3 and $5.6 million.

In the general election against Ortiz, Farenthold was a decided underdog. Ortiz had built a moderate voting record in a Hispanic-majority district, and he was a senior member of the Armed Services Committee who had shepherded money to local projects. The incumbent also had a fundraising advantage. Farenthold raised $616,000, including about $150,000 from his own pocket, compared with Ortiz's $1.2 million.

The Republican's campaign suffered a credibility deficit after images surfaced of Farenthold wearing pajamas featuring yellow ducks while out for a night on the town with a young woman wearing what appeared to be a sheer nightie. (It turned out to be a photo at a costume party, and the woman was a waitress.) Ortiz touted the photograph, which was widely circulated on the Internet, in his campaign ads as evidence that his opponent could not be taken seriously. But Farenthold's campaign picked up steam with the support of local tea party activists in what had become a political swing district. On Election Night, the contest was too close to call. Ortiz conceded on November 22 after the recount showed that the challenger led by 799 votes.

In the House, the first bill filed by Farenthold would require federal agencies to display receipts and expenditures every two weeks on their websites. He pushed for legislative riders on the fiscal 2011 funding bill, including one to ban funding for Planned Parenthood. He became disillusioned with House Republicans' inability to cut spending enough to suit him. "What I'm coming to realize is that all we're really able to do is put the brakes on," he said in Robert Draper's 2012 book *Do Not Ask What Good We Do*. "Imagine going real fast in a *Flintstones* car, and my heel is out there. I went to Washington to change the world, and all I can do is put my heel out." He also lamented what he saw as the party's inability to get its message across: "What the Democrats can say in two emotion-packed sentences take us 10 PowerPoint slides."

He took over in 2013 as chairman of the Oversight and Government Reform Committee's panel on the federal workforce and expressed concerns about agencies' spending on outside conferences. He also sponsored a bill to shield federal workers from furloughs as a result of automatic and steep budget cuts that kicked in that spring after the White House and Congress failed to reach a budget accord. But he lost that post in 2015 when Rep. Jason Chaffetz became chairman of the Oversight committee.

Farenthold initially was a top Democratic target in 2012. But the redistricting changes gave his district—which had been 73% Hispanic—a strong GOP bent by stretching it north along the Gulf Coast. It also did not include precincts in suburban Houston, enabling him to avoid a serious primary challenge from that area. He beat Democrat Rose Meza Harrison 57%-39%. In 2014, he avoided primary opposition and had an easy win in November against former Marine pilot Wesley Reed, 64%-34%.

In December 2014, a 27-year-old former aide on his House staff filed a lawsuit against Farenthold in which she accused him of excessive drinking, flirting and firing her after she complained of a hostile work environment. He told the *Houston Chronicle* that he was shocked by the allegations that were "far out in left field" and that he had "good reason" for the dismissal. His lawyers wrote in a court filing that the aide had failed to report for work. In March 2015, the *Texas Tribune* reported that the Democratic Congressional Campaign Committee saw the lawsuit as an opportunity to seek a credible challenger to Farenthold in 2016. For Democrats, the story asserted, "a competitive race materializing at all in the 27th District would be a moral victory," regardless of the outcome.

TWENTY-EIGHTH DISTRICT

Henry Cuellar (D)

Elected 2004, 6th term; b. Sept. 19, 1955, Laredo; Georgetown U., B.S. 1978, U. of TX Austin, J.D. 1981, Ph.D. 1998, TX A&M U., M.A. 1982; Catholic; married (Imelda); 2 children.

Elected Office: TX House,1987-2001; TX secy. of st., 2001.

Professional Career: Practicing atty., 1981-2004; Adjunct prof., TX A&M U., 1984-86.

DC Office: 2209 RHOB, 20515, 202-225-1640; Fax: 202-225-1641; Website: cuellar.house.gov.

State Offices: Laredo, 956-725-0639; Rio Grande City, 956-487-5603; San Antonio, 210-271-2851; Mission, 956-424-3942.

Committees: *Appropriations:* Homeland Security; Transportation, HUD & Related Agencies.

Group Ratings

	ADA	ACLU	AFL-CIO	LCV	ITI	COC	HAFA	ACU	CFG	FRC
2014	15%	27%	–	31%	80%	100%	22%	36%	18%	75%
2013	35%	C	76%	29%	C	77%	C	20%	17%	C

National Journal Ratings

	2013 LIB	—	2013 CONS
Economic	55%	—	45%
Social	55%	—	45%
Foreign	55%	—	45%
Composite	55%	—	45%

Key Votes of the 113th Congress

1. Sandy storm spending	Y	5. Medical Marijuana	N	9. Syrian Rebels Training	Y
2. Violence Against Women Act	Y	6. Farm Bill	Y	10. Keystone pipeline	Y
3. Guantanamo Bay Detainees	N	7. Afghanistan Combat	N	11. Immigration Exec. Action	N
4. Abortion 20-week ban	Y	8. NSA Phone Data Collection	N	12. Bipartisan budget deal	Y

Election Results

2014 general	Henry Cuellar (D)	62,508	(82%)	$937,078
	Will Aikens (Lib)	10,153	(13%)	
	Michael Cary (G)	3,475	(5%)	
2014 primary	Henry Cuellar (D)	unopposed		

Prior winning percentages: 2012 (68%), 2010 (56%), 2008 (69%), 2006 (68%), 2004 (59%)

Population		Race and Ethnicity		Income	
Total:	724,080	Latino	78.4%	Median income:	$44,275
Urban:	58.8%	White	15.9%		*(331 of 435)*
Suburban:	16.7%	Black	4.0%	Under $50,000	55.8%
Rural:	24.5%	Asian	0.8%	$50,000-$99,999:	28.7%
Land area:	7,721	Two races	0.7%	$100,000-$199,999:	13.8%
Pop/sq. mi.:	93.8	White Ethnic	6.2%	$200,000 or more:	1.8%
Born in state:	63.5%			Poverty Rate	25.9%
		Education			
Age Groups		H.S. grad or less:	57.7%	**Work**	
Under 18:	31.6%	Some college:	25.8%	White collar:	25.0%
18 to 34:	23.0%	College degree, 4 yr.:	11.4%	Blue collar:	48.5%
35 to 64:	34.8%	Post-grad study:	5.1%	Sales and service:	26.5%
Over 64:	10.6%				
		Military		Govt. workers:	17.0%
		Veterans/active duty:	7.9%		

Laredo/San Antonio Corridor

The border country along the Rio Grande is in some ways a region all its own, a mixture of the United States and Mexico. As former Laredo Mayor Betty Flores has said, "The river for us is more like some street that we cross. It's really not a border." This is where, in "Streets of Laredo," singer Johnny Cash

Voter Turnout	
2013 Total Citizen 18+	390,931
2014 House Turnout	76,136
2014 Turnout as % CVAP	19.5%
2012 Turnout as % CVAP	43.3%

(and many others over the years) summoned up images of lonely cowboys on dusty streets outside of saloons in a tiny town. But that is not the Laredo of today. It is the busiest border crossing for U.S.-Mexico trade. Thousands of trucks and railcars cross its four bridges daily; with about $253 billion in two-way trade crossing the Rio Grande in 2013, the Laredo customs district was the third busiest in the nation behind Los Angeles and New York. Laredo grew at a 34% pace in the first decade of the 21st century. Its old downtown streets are filled with Mexicans who cross the border on foot.

Laredo's Webb County had a population of 263,000 in 2013, of which 95% was Hispanic. Local fast-food restaurants feature enchiladas more often than hamburgers. Nearly three-fourths of all businesses are minority owned, which is the largest share in the nation. The region has its problems, including crime from the trade in illegal immigration and drugs; its positioning at the end of Interstate 35 makes it an important point of entry for both. The county retained a 31% poverty rate in 2014, even with the boom in oil drilling at the Eagle Ford Shale. The good news locally is that the shale formation from Laredo to East Texas supported 116,000 jobs in 2012, according to the *Texas Tribune*.

The 28th Congressional District of Texas is centered in Laredo and Webb County, which has the largest population in the district. South along the Rio Grande, it crosses Starr County, one of the poorest counties in Texas and home of many blatant and wealthy drug smugglers. It also takes in Mission in Hidalgo County. These border counties make up about two-thirds of the district. To the north, it extends through thinly settled ranch and oil well country, plus about 160,000 residents on the eastern side of Bexar County, including a small portion of San Antonio. It includes the Joint Base San Antonio, formed from the joining of Randolph and Lackland Air Force bases and Fort Sam Houston in 2010. About

2012 Presidential Vote		
Barack Obama (D)	101,843	(60%)
Mitt Romney (R)	65,372	(39%)
2008 Presidential Vote		
Barack Obama (D)	92,557	(58%)
John McCain (R)	65,066	(41%)
Cook Partisan Voting Index:	D+7	

78% of the residents of the 28th are Hispanic. The district leans Democratic locally, but Republicans sometimes do well. President George W. Bush in 2004 and some state GOP officials have carried the district as currently configured, but Barack Obama won with 58% in 2008 and 60% in 2012.

Henry Cuellar (D)

Henry Cuellar, elected in 2004, is one of the most conservative Hispanic Democrats, with a voting record putting him near the center of the House as a whole. Despite his maverick tendencies, he has shown enough loyalty to his party to earn a coveted seat on the Appropriations Committee. He remains eager for more influence.

Cuellar was the oldest of eight children of migrant workers who had only elementary school educations. He graduated from Georgetown University and the University of Texas law school, and he later got a Ph.D. in government from UT. With his five degrees, he claims to be the "most degreed" member of the House. From his base in Laredo, he served in the Texas House from 1986 to 2000, where he helped to author the Texas Grant college aid program. In 2001, Republican Gov. Rick Perry appointed him secretary of state even though he is a Democrat.

Cuellar resigned in 2002 to run against veteran Republican Rep. Henry Bonilla in the sprawling 23rd District. He got a big boost from a Bonilla gaffe; Bonilla claimed he didn't need Laredo to win, and in response, the Webb County GOP chairman endorsed Cuellar. Cuellar attacked Bonilla for his votes against funding for the State Children's Health Insurance Program, the Family and Medical Leave Act, and Pell grants. Bonilla had the money advantage. Cuellar carried Webb County 84%-15%. When the Bexar County votes were counted a few days later, Bonilla won 52%-47%.

Redistricting in 2003 gave Cuellar an opportunity to run in the 28th against Democratic Rep. Ciro Rodriguez of San Antonio, who had the most liberal voting record of Texas' Hispanic Democrats in Congress and was chairman of the Hispanic Caucus. When Cuellar announced his candidacy, Rodriguez expressed disbelief that a friend and former legislative colleague for whom he had raised money in 2002 would run against him. The ambitious Cuellar explained that primary bids like his were a common political occurrence in South Texas. He sealed the end of the friendship when he told a local reporter, "Nobody died and made him king."

Rodriguez had just five months to get acquainted with and prepare for the primary in the new district. Cuellar criticized Rodriguez for voting against the GOP's 2003 Medicare prescription drug bill, while Rodriguez pointed up Cuellar's collusion with Republicans as secretary of state. A recount put Cuellar ahead by 203 votes. After a lawsuit, a second recount, and a state appellate court ruling in July, Cuellar was declared the Democratic nominee by 58 votes out of 49,000 cast. He went on to win in November 59%-39%. In September 2007, the Federal Election Commission fined Cuellar $28,500 for failing to disclose a $200,000 bank loan in his 2004 campaign.

In the House, Cuellar's voting has placed him among the most conservative Democrats, though he was still more liberal than all House Republicans. Many Democrats were slow to embrace him, given his endorsement of George W. Bush in the 2000 presidential election. He is a member of the shrinking Blue Dog Coalition of his party's fiscal conservatives and was one of just 22 Democrats to support a failed amendment for a fiscal 2013 budget based on the recommendations of the Simpson-Bowles deficit reduction commission. Cuellar was one of 19 Democrats—many of them Blue Dogs—to oppose the Dodd-Frank financial industry overhaul in 2010. He joined Texas delegation members in voting against lifting the financial liability cap on oil spills.

Before joining Appropriations, Cuellar served on the Homeland Security Committee and won the chairmanship of its border security subcommittee in January 2010. He got into a spat with Fox News host Greta Van Susteren in 2011 after two retired generals issued a report characterizing the Texas border as a "war zone." Cuellar aggressively challenged their conclusions, prompting Van Susteren to accuse him of "disgraceful behavior" and being "a phony." His middle ground positions on immigration also have irritated many Democrats, the *Houston Chronicle* reported in September 2014. He was the only House Democrat who voted for a bill that would have made it easier to deport unaccompanied minors from Central America. He hasn't been shy about criticizing President Barack Obama, including for his handling of immigration. On MSNBC, he said that Obama looked "aloof and detached" by not going to the Mexican border when he was in Texas for political fundraisers in 2014. In response to criticism of his independence, Cuellar told a San Antonio audience in September 2014, "I will die as a Democrat."

With his bipartisan approach, Cuellar has had success getting legislation passed. With Republican help, he won passage of a bill to create a national gang intelligence center at the Federal Bureau of Investigation and to toughen penalties for sex offenders who break the terms of their release. He enacted a bill in 2010 requiring federal agencies to establish measurable performance goals and devise systems for tracking them. And in 2012, the House passed his bill requiring the Office of Management and Budget to establish customer service standards for federal agencies. In January 2015, he was one of 28 House Democrats to vote for the Keystone XL pipeline.

In Cuellar's first reelection bid in 2006, Rodriguez was back to challenge him in the primary, but struggled to match him in fundraising. Cuellar won the primary comfortably this time, 53%-40%. He has won reelection easily since. In 2014, he had no major-party opposition. Cuellar told the *Chronicle* that he would like to seek a statewide office, and mentioned the possibility of running for governor or a Senate seat in 2018.

TWENTY-NINTH DISTRICT

Gene Green (D)

Elected 1992, 12th term; b. Oct. 17, 1947, Houston; U. of Houston, B.B.A. 1971; Methodist; married (Helen Albers); 2 children.

Elected Office: TX House, 1973-85; TX Senate, 1985-93.

Professional Career: Practicing atty., 1977-92.

DC Office: 2470 RHOB, 20515, 202-225-1688; Fax: 202-225-9903; Website: green.house.gov.

State Offices: Houston (East), 713-330-0761; Houston (North), 281-999-5879.

Committees: *Energy & Commerce:* Energy & Power; Environment & the Economy; Health (RMM); Oversight & Investigations.

Group Ratings

	ADA	ACLU	AFL-CIO	LCV	ITI	COC	HAFA	ACU	CFG	FRC
2014	80%	55%	–	66%	80%	77%	20%	28%	14%	14%
2013	75%	C	95%	54%	C	50%	C	20%	12%	C

National Journal Ratings

	2013 LIB	—	2013 CONS
Economic	60%	—	39%
Social	58%	—	41%
Foreign	62%	—	37%
Composite	61%	—	40%

Key Votes of the 113th Congress

1. Sandy storm spending	Y	5. Medical Marijuana	Y	9. Syrian Rebels Training	Y
2. Violence Against Women Act	Y	6. Farm Bill	N	10. Keystone pipeline	Y
3. Guantanamo Bay Detainees	NV	7. Afghanistan Combat	N	11. Immigration Exec. Action	N
4. Abortion 20-week ban	N	8. NSA Phone Data Collection	Y	12. Bipartisan budget deal	Y

Election Results

2014 general	Gene Green (D)	41,321	(90%)	$687,926
	James Stanczak (Lib)	4,822	(11%)	
2014 primary	Gene Green (D)	unopposed		

Prior winning percentages: 2012 (90%), 2010 (65%), 2008 (75%), 2006 (74%), 2004 (94%), 2002 (95%), 2000 (73%), 1998 (93%), 1996 (68%), 1994 (73%), 1992 (65%)

Population		Race and Ethnicity		Income	
Total:	729,827	Latino	76.4%	Median income:	$36,628
Urban:	80.9%	White	12.1%		*(412 of 435)*
Suburban:	19.1%	Black	9.3%	Under $50,000	64.2%
Rural:	0.0%	Asian	1.6%	$50,000-$99,999:	26.3%
Land area:	237	Two races	0.3%	$100,000-$199,999:	8.5%
Pop/sq. mi.:	3,082.3	White Ethnic	4.0%	$200,000 or more:	1.0%
Born in state:	57.8%			Poverty Rate	28.3%
Age Groups		**Education**			
Under 18:	32.2%	H.S. grad or less:	70.9%	**Work**	
18 to 34:	27.5%	Some college:	20.1%	White collar:	15.2%
35 to 64:	33.2%	College degree, 4 yr.:	6.7%	Blue collar:	41.7%
Over 64:	7.1%	Post-grad study:	2.3%	Sales and service:	43.2%
		Military		Govt. workers:	8.0%
		Veterans/active duty:	3.2%		

East Houston and Pasadena

Many areas of Texas have large Mexican-American communities that can be traced back to statehood. But not Houston. The swampy area in what was originally called Harrisburg County had few inhabitants of any ethnicity until the 20th century. Houston and its Mexican-American community had to

Voter Turnout	
2013 Total Citizen 18+	329,844
2014 House Turnout	46,143
2014 Turnout as % CVAP	14%
2012 Turnout as % CVAP	35.7%

be built from the ground up. The city's economy was also built from the ground up, based on a combination of cotton, oil and trade via the ship canal. Cotton and oil were gifts of nature, though they required much human effort and ingenuity to produce in commercial quantities. The 52-mile Houston Ship Channel was almost totally man's creation. Along with the unsettled conditions created by the Mexican Revolution of 1910, it provided the impetus for Mexican immigration to the city.

After the sand-spit port of Galveston was destroyed by a hurricane in 1900, Houston's elders decided to dredge out Buffalo Bayou and make their inland city a seaport. When the channel officially opened in November 1914, a sluggish, 6-foot-deep creek had become a 40-foot-deep waterway that would turn Houston into one of the nation's biggest ports. Today, the channel is 45 feet deep and 530 feet wide. To accompany the giant ships that will be arriving through the expanded Panama Canal, which is scheduled to open in 2016, the ports have been increased to 50 feet deep. More than 70 ships come through each day, supporting in 2012 more than 1 million jobs and adding $180 billion to the Texas economy. In 2014, it was the busiest U.S. port in both imports and exports. Exports include rice, wheat, grain sorghum, cotton, caustic soda, cement and petroleum products, while frequent imports include crude oil, iron ore, molasses, coffee, gypsum and automobiles. The port also is the site of the largest petrochemical complex in the nation. On its west side, Houston seems entirely a white-collar, office-bound city. But on the east and north, around the port and through the maze of refinery towers and pipelines, it remains blue-collar and a job magnet for Mexican Americans and workers from the rural South.

The 29th Congressional District of Texas, which is entirely in Harris County, covers much of the ship channel area and working-class Houston. Its unusual shape—some say that it resembles a seated dragon—connects heavily Hispanic sections north of Houston with the Hispanic community around the ship channel and Pasadena. Northside's residents began an effort in 2010 to build more affordable housing, along with parks, hiking and bike trails, and other environmentally sustainable amenities. The district wraps around the Sam Houston Tollway, taking in blue-collar neighborhoods in northeast

2012 Presidential Vote		
Barack Obama (D)	75,720	(66%)
Mitt Romney (R)	37,909	(33%)
2008 Presidential Vote		
Barack Obama (D)	70,286	(62%)
John McCain (R)	41,843	(37%)
Cook Partisan Voting Index:	D+12	

Houston as well. In the southeast, Pasadena, once part of the giant Allen Ranch, is now a working-class city of 153,000 centered on the oil and aerospace industries. The district is 76 percent Hispanic and comfortably Democratic.

Gene Green (D)

Democrat Gene Green, first elected in 1992, is a gregarious centrist with a bipartisan streak. He stays popular in a district that is more than three-fourths Hispanic by paying close attention to constituents: He's known for providing various services to his constituents. But some local activists question how long a Caucasian can continue to be elected in this district.

Green grew up in the largely Hispanic Lindale section of north Houston, the son of a home-improvement business owner who enlisted his sons to provide him with free labor. "The joke in our family was that nobody had enough money to be a Republican," he said. He worked as a printer's apprentice and got business and law degrees from the University of Houston. He was elected to the state House in 1972, at age 25, and to the state Senate in a special election in 1985. He has been a friend to unions and trial lawyers in Austin and Washington, and an opponent of gun control, a politician whose natural political base is Texas' small, unionized blue-collar class.

In the 1992 primary for the House seat, he faced Ben Reyes, a tempestuous Houston councilman who once protested official inaction on crime by demolishing a crack house. Green went door-to-door and carried lawn signs and a hammer in his trunk while appearing as a frequent guest on Spanish-language radio shows. In the primary, Reyes led 34%-28%. But in the runoff, Green came out ahead by 180 votes out of 31,508 cast. Reyes went to court and charged that Republican voters had illegally crossed over to vote in the runoff. That got him a re-runoff, but to no avail. This time, Green won with 52%. He went on to win the general election with 65%.

In the House, Green has a moderate voting record, especially for a member of a heavily minority urban district. He has more often joined Democrats since President Barack Obama took office. He assailed Republican budgets for their impact on senior citizens and low-income residents. But he still goes his own way on occasion. In December 2010, he opposed repealing the military's "don't ask, don't tell" policy barring openly gay service members. He joined most Republicans in defeating a 2012 Democratic amendment to cut $400 million from the missile defense budget and backed a GOP proposal that year to try suspected terrorists at Cuba's Guantanamo Bay rather than in U.S. civilian courts.

Green has a seat on the influential Energy and Commerce Committee, where he naturally has focused on issues important to the oil industry. In 2008, he became chairman of the Environment and Hazardous Materials Subcommittee. But Democrat Henry Waxman of California eliminated the panel—and Green's chairmanship—after taking over as Energy and Commerce chairman in 2009. Green had been an ally of Michigan Democrat John Dingell in the pitched battle for the committee chairmanship in November 2008. He said he patched things up with Waxman after letting him know that he wouldn't stand for being retaliated against for backing Dingell. After the Republican takeover of the House in 2011, Green became ranking Democrat on the newly created Environment and Economy Subcommittee, but only for two years.

In 2009, he got significant concessions from Waxman for oil refineries in the climate change bill the committee produced, which capped emissions and created a system for companies to "trade" emissions limits. Green has had to strike a balance between the industry's desires and quality-of-life issues in the district. For example, he fought Republican proposals to encourage new oil refineries because the environmental exemptions could have jeopardized the clean air program in Houston. But he sided with other Texas delegation members after the 2010 BP oil spill in the Gulf of Mexico and opposed lifting the liability cap on spills. In March 2011, he joined Louisiana GOP Rep. Charles Boustany in sponsoring a resolution to support continued deep-water drilling in the Gulf of Mexico. He has led Democrats who have urged Obama to approve the Keystone XL pipeline, which will bring Canadian oil to Texas refineries.

With Dingell and Waxman both gone in 2015, Green became the ranking Democrat on the Health Subcommittee. More of a liberal Democrat on health care, he backed the government-run "public option" to compete with private insurers that passed the House on the reform bill in 2009 but was stripped from the final version. He voiced willingness to work with members of both parties to find areas to make improvements in the law. With Houston-area Republican Rep. Pete Olson, who also serves on Energy and Commerce, he wrote an op-ed praising the committee's bipartisan 21st Century Cures Act, which encourages more rapid introduction of new pharmaceuticals and other modernizing of health care. They said that the bill will "reverse course on flagging investments and inflexible, sometimes outdated regulation," and bolster medical research, which is vital to Houston.

Despite the fact that the 29th remains an inviting opportunity for an ambitious Hispanic politician, Green has been reelected easily and has had no significant primary challenges. With a population of 2.2 million, of whom 44 percent are Hispanic, Houston is the only city or metro area with a large Hispanic presence that does not have a Hispanic representative in Congress. Green defended his representation and the voters. "We're not South Africa under apartheid. They've had the opportunity, and they made that decision," he told the *Houston Chronicle* in September 2014. "I'm up every two years." But the *Chronicle* wrote that he could be vulnerable in a primary to "the right Hispanic candidate in a presidential election year when minority turnout is generally higher."

THIRTIETH DISTRICT

Eddie Bernice Johnson (D)

Elected 1992, 12th term; b. Dec. 3, 1935, Waco; U. of Notre Dame, B.A. 1955, TX Christian U., B.S. 1967, S. Methodist U., M.P.A. 1976; Baptist; divorced; 1 child.

Elected Office: TX House, 1973-77; TX Senate, 1987-93.

Professional Career: Registered nurse, 1955-72; Regional dir., U.S. Dept. of HEW, 1977-81; Mgmt. consultant, Sammons Corp., 1979-81; Owner, Eddie Bernice Johnson & Assoc.

DC Office: 2468 RHOB, 20515, 202-225-8885; Fax: 202-226-1477; Website: ebjohnson.house.gov.

State Offices: Dallas, 214-922-8885.

Committees: *Science, Space, & Technology* (RMM: ex officio member of each subcommittee). *Transportation & Infrastructure:* Aviation; Highways & Transit; Water Resources & Environment.

Group Ratings

	ADA	ACLU	AFL-CIO	LCV	ITI	COC	HAFA	ACU	CFG	FRC
2014	85%	72%	–	91%	80%	43%	8%	4%	7%	0%
2013	80%	C	100%	93%	C	38%	C	24%	11%	C

National Journal Ratings

	2013 LIB	—	2013 CONS
Economic	88%	—	12%
Social	79%	—	16%
Foreign	69%	—	29%
Composite	80%	—	20%

Key Votes of the 113th Congress

1. Sandy storm spending	Y	5. Medical Marijuana	Y	9. Syrian Rebels Training	N
2. Violence Against Women Act	Y	6. Farm Bill	N	10. Keystone pipeline	N
3. Guantanamo Bay Detainees	Y	7. Afghanistan Combat	N	11. Immigration Exec. Action	NV
4. Abortion 20-week ban	N	8. NSA Phone Data Collection	N	12. Bipartisan budget deal	Y

Election Results

2014 general	Eddie Bernice Johnson (D)	93,041	(88%)	$546,099	$36,142
	Max Koch, II (Lib)	7,153	(7%)		
	Eric LeMonte Williams (I)	5,598	(5%)		
2014 primary	Eddie Bernice Johnson (D)	23,756	(70%)		
	Barbara Mallory Caraway (D)	10,216	(30%)		

Prior winning percentages: 2012 (79%), 2010 (76%), 2008 (82%), 2006 (80%), 2004 (93%), 2002 (74%), 2000 (92%), 1998 (72%), 1996 (55%), 1994 (73%), 1992 (72%)

Population		Race and Ethnicity		Income	
Total:	746,336	Black	44.3%	Median income:	$41,863
Urban:	61.2%	Latino	35.7%		(359 of 435)
Suburban:	38.5%	White	16.9%	Under $50,000	57.8%
Rural:	0.3%	Asian	1.9%	$50,000-$99,999:	28.1%
Land area:	348	Two races	1.0%	$100,000-$199,999:	11.8%
Pop/sq. mi.:	2,144.1	White Ethnic	5.6%	$200,000 or more:	2.3%
Born in state:	64.6%			Poverty Rate	24.8%
		Education			
Age Groups		H.S. grad or less:	50.6%	**Work**	
Under 18:	28.4%	Some college:	29.4%	White collar:	27.8%
18 to 34:	25.3%	College degree, 4 yr.:	13.0%	Blue collar:	45.6%
35 to 64:	37.0%	Post-grad study:	7.1%	Sales and service:	26.6%
Over 64:	9.3%			Govt. workers:	13.7%
		Military			
		Veterans/active duty:	6.0%		

Central and Southern Dallas Metro

In 1923, Texas adopted the "white primary," which barred blacks from participating in statewide Democratic primary elections, although blacks who could pay a poll tax could still vote in general elections, municipal elections, school board elections, special elections and on ballot propositions. In

Voter Turnout	
2013 Total Citizen 18+	446,139
2014 House Turnout	105,793
2014 Turnout as % CVAP	23.7%
2012 Turnout as % CVAP	50.4%

1940, an estimated 40,000 blacks voted in the presidential election, comprising almost 4% of the total electorate, but they represented only about 7% of the potential black electorate at the time; around 33% of eligible whites voted. Texas politicians also overwhelmingly signed on to the "Southern Manifesto," criticizing the Supreme Court's *Brown* decision in 1954 striking down segregation in public schools. But voting participation was accepted enough in Texas that when the Supreme Court struck down the state's white primary law in 1944, polling found public opinion surprisingly closely divided, with 49% of white Texans opposing the decision and 44% favoring it.

By 1947, Dallas County had a majority-black electorate, and yet despite this, there was no congressional district in North Texas that was considered likely to elect a black representative until the creation of the 30th Congressional District of Texas in 1991. Its creation was insisted on by the then-chairman of the Texas Senate's redistricting committee, and the result was a grotesquely shaped district. Its center was south and east Dallas, but it had tentacles as complex as a Portuguese Man O' War. Since then, lawsuits and four more rounds of redistricting have smoothed out the lines and left the 30th as one of two heavily minority Democratic districts in the Dallas-Fort Worth Metroplex.

Today, the 30th District consists of most of the south side of Dallas, with one tentacle running northwest, out Stemmons Freeway to Love Field. In between is the "mixmaster," where three busy highways—Interstates 30, 35E and 45—come together within a square mile, surrounding many of the prominent sites in Dallas. The district, which is entirely in Dallas County, includes The Cedars neighborhood, which is home to Southside on Lamar. A former 10-story Sears, Roebuck building that was transformed into a loft and retail development, it has become one of the foremost centers of Dallas' black community. The century-old Neiman Marcus chain of luxury department stores has its flagship store here, where shoppers can bring their (leashed) dogs along. Further south, it embraces African-American majority towns such as Cedar Hill, Glenn Heights and upscale DeSoto, as well as minority-majority locales like Duncanville and Hutchins.

The court-drawn map in the latest redistricting removed much of the district's previous Hispanic population and placed it in the newly created 33rd District. The 30th District's population is now 44% African American and 36% Hispanic; the latter are mostly young and foreign-born and less likely to vote, and 90% of them are from Mexico. The growing influence of racial minorities in the

2012 Presidential Vote		
Barack Obama (D) 175,637		(80%)
Mitt Romney (R)...................43,333		(20%)
2008 Presidential Vote		
Barack Obama (D) 175,237		(78%)
John McCain (R)...................47,144		(21%)
Cook Partisan Voting Index: D+27		

city has been a major factor in Democrats' gaining control of many Dallas County offices and seats in the Texas Legislature. This district is overwhelmingly Democratic, and the party's strongest in Texas.

Eddie Bernice Johnson (D)

Eddie Bernice Johnson, a Democrat first elected in 1992, is a revered figure in Dallas politics, having spent four decades advocating for the city. Some of her younger rivals and *The Dallas Morning News'* editorial page have suggested it's time for her to step aside, but she remained a potent political force even as she approached age 80.

Johnson grew up in Texas, graduated from Texas Christian University with a nursing degree, and later got a master's degree in public administration at Southern Methodist University. She worked at St. Paul Hospital and was the chief psychiatric nurse at the Veterans Administration Hospital in Dallas. She told *The Morning News* in 1987 that she first got interested in politics in the early 1960s, when she went to buy a new hat and was shocked to learn that blacks in the city weren't allowed to try on such headgear. She organized a boycott of the store. In 1972, she was elected to the Texas House, the first black woman elected to the legislature from Dallas. She became a regional director of the old Health, Education and Welfare Department under Democratic President Jimmy Carter. She was elected to the Texas Senate in 1986. As the Senate's Redistricting Committee chair in 1991, she was instrumental in creating the new 30th District, and she went on to win the Democratic primary with 92% of the vote.

In the House, Johnson—known by her initials "EBJ"—has a mostly liberal voting record. A former chairwoman of the Congressional Black Caucus, she was more supportive of President Barack Obama in 2009 than other caucus members critical of his limited efforts for low-income and unemployed blacks. She has been attentive to business interests in Dallas, though her lifetime voting score from the U.S. Chamber of Commerce is among the Texas House delegation's lowest. Johnson once pledged to labor unions to oppose the North American Free Trade Agreement, but she changed her mind and voted for it in 1993. Dallas probably exports more to Mexico than any other American city, and many jobs depend on those exports. Johnson also sided with business on normalizing trade relations with China, and was one of 28 House Democrats who backed trade promotion authority for Obama in June 2015.

Johnson became ranking Democrat on the Science, Space, and Technology Committee in 2011. What had long been a bipartisan committee has become increasingly polarized, even with fellow Texan Lamar Smith as chairman. At an August 2013 hearing, she accused Smith of representing the interests of "industry hacks." In November 2014, she said that a committee bill to restrict the Environmental Protection Agency would "stifle public health protections." She joined others in her party in lambasting Republican cuts in science funding while seeking to encourage more students to enter science- and technology-related fields. She shared credit for passing the Networking and Information Research and Development Act to double funding for information research. As a health-care professional, she takes an interest in minority health issues. In 2015, she and New York GOP Rep. Peter King reintroduced their bill to have a federal National Nurse for Public Health work alongside the surgeon general.

On the Transportation and Infrastructure Committee, Johnson has worked to secure funds for construction of the Interstate 30 suspension bridge over the Trinity River that opened in 2012, and she continues to support Trinity River projects. The Trinity River Corridor toll-road project, in the works for decades and including three new suspension bridges, remains controversial and unresolved. She also has sought to address the Dallas-Fort Worth area's mass transit needs to alleviate traffic congestion.

Johnson generally has sailed to reelection. But in the months before the 2010 election, the *Morning News* reported that she had awarded college scholarships to four relatives and the two children of a top aide who otherwise would have been ineligible under the Congressional Black Caucus Foundation's guidelines. Johnson said she had not been familiar with the rules and agreed to repay the foundation. But the scandal provided an opening for her Republican challenger, minister Stephen Broden. *The Morning News* endorsed Broden and rebuked Johnson for being among the South Dallas leaders "who treat their districts as if they were their fiefdoms." But whatever chance Broden may have had for an upset vanished a few weeks later when he told a television interviewer that an armed overthrow of the federal government is "on the table." Johnson chalked up another landslide, 76%-22%.

Two years later, Johnson faced two young Democratic challengers in attorney Taj Clayton and state Rep. Barbara Mallory Caraway, who avoided criticizing Johnson directly but made clear their belief that the district needed fresh representation. The *Morning News* endorsed Clayton this time, saying Johnson "once had what it takes, but now it's time for new leadership." The normally even-keeled Johnson ripped into both of her opponents, calling Clayton a stooge for Republicans. She won the primary with ease, reaping 70% to Caraway's 18% and Clayton's 12%, and coasted to another reelection. In a primary rematch in 2014 with just Caraway, whose husband Dwaine Caraway was interim mayor of Dallas in 2011, Johnson again took 70% before winning 88% in November. If nothing else, these futile challenges may be opening the door to Johnson's potential successor.

THIRTY-FIRST DISTRICT

John Carter (R)

Elected 2002, 7th term; b. Nov. 6, 1941, Houston; TX Tech. U., B.A. 1964, U. of TX Austin, J.D. 1969; Lutheran; married (Erika); 4 children.

Elected Office: Williamson Cnty. TX Dist. Court judge, 1981-2001.

Professional Career: Practicing atty., 1969-81.

DC Office: 2110 RHOB, 20515, 202-225-3864; Website: carter.house.gov.

State Offices: Round Rock, 512-246-1600; Temple, 254-933-1392.

Committees: *Appropriations:* Commerce, Justice, Science & Related Agencies; Defense; Homeland Security (Chmn).

Group Ratings

	ADA	ACLU	AFL-CIO	LCV	ITI	COC	HAFA	ACU	CFG	FRC
2014	0%	0%	–	9%	60%	79%	55%	80%	68%	100%
2013	0%	C	9%	7%	C	77%	C	71%	61%	C

National Journal Ratings

	2013 LIB	—	2013 CONS
Economic	36%	—	63%
Social	16%	—	74%
Foreign	24%	—	68%
Composite	29%	—	72%

Key Votes of the 113th Congress

1. Sandy storm spending	N	5. Medical Marijuana	N	9. Syrian Rebels Training	Y
2. Violence Against Women Act	N	6. Farm Bill	Y	10. Keystone pipeline	Y
3. Guantanamo Bay Detainees	N	7. Afghanistan Combat	N	11. Immigration Exec. Action	Y
4. Abortion 20-week ban	Y	8. NSA Phone Data Collection	N	12. Bipartisan budget deal	Y

Election Results

2014 general	John Carter (R)	91,607	(64%)	$862,690	$16,376
	Louie Minor (D)	45,715	(32%)	$65,279	
	Scott Ballard (Lib)	5,706	(4%)		
2014 primary	John Carter (R)	unopposed			

Prior winning percentages: 2012 (61%), 2010 (83%), 2008 (60%), 2006 (58%), 2004 (65%), 2002 (69%)

Population		Race and Ethnicity		Income	
Total:	767,721	White	58.8%	Median income:	$61,693
Urban:	58.3%	Latino	23.1%		*(103 of 435)*
Suburban:	36.5%	Black	10.5%	Under $50,000	39.1%
Rural:	5.2%	Asian	4.2%	$50,000-$99,999:	34.3%
Land area:	2,622	Two races	2.9%	$100,000-$199,999:	21.8%
Pop/sq. mi.:	292.7	White Ethnic	19.0%	$200,000 or more:	4.8%
Born in state:	52.9%			Poverty Rate	10.8%
		Education			
Age Groups		H.S. grad or less:	32.2%	**Work**	
Under 18:	27.3%	Some college:	34.7%	White collar:	40.5%
18 to 34:	25.1%	College degree, 4 yr.:	22.2%	Blue collar:	41.3%
35 to 64:	37.3%	Post-grad study:	10.9%	Sales and service:	18.2%
Over 64:	10.3%			Govt. workers:	18.1%
		Military			
		Veterans/active duty:	15.6%		

Williamson and Bell Counties

In 1932, Williamson County was a rural backwater that cast a little more than 7,000 votes for president; Franklin Roosevelt won all but 431 of them. Today it has become a major population and business center deep in the heart of Texas, casting 163,000 votes in 2012, almost 60 percent of which went for Republican Mitt Romney. Its population has virtually doubled in every recent decade. It had 40,000 people in 1970, 80,000 in 1980, 140,000 in 1990, 250,000 in 2000, and 427,000 in 2010. It grew another 10 percent by 2013, but the increase may be slowing due to local

Voter Turnout	
2013 Total Citizen 18+	520,194
2014 House Turnout	143,028
2014 Turnout as % CVAP	27.5%
2012 Turnout as % CVAP	48.4%

congestion. Williamson County is just north of Austin, and much of this growth has been generated by the area's high-technology boom—Austin's city limits actually now spill over into Williamson. Hugely successful computer producer Dell, with 13,000 local employees, is headquartered in Round Rock (the rock, which served as an important wagon crossing, is in the middle of Brushy Creek, with wheel ruts still visible). Texas 130, a 49-mile, 10-lane toll road with a speed limit of 85 miles per hour in parts, has generated more growth. Rapidly growing Georgetown has become a popular retirement destination and plans to be the first city in Texas to rely entirely on renewable energy, both wind and solar, starting in 2016.

Bell County, just north of Williamson County, is home to part of Fort Hood, the largest U.S. military base in the world in terms of acreage. The base is the only post in the nation capable of supporting two full armored divisions. Its mission—maintaining combat readiness, including training Army reservists in urban combat—explains its size; it covers 218,000 acres, or, 340 square miles, an area larger than New York's five boroughs. Killeen, home of the base, has been growing rapidly and had the most affordable housing of a mid-sized Texas city in 2014. Ford Hood is where Maj. Nidal Malik Hasan in November 2009 killed 13 people and wounded 38 others. That was followed by another bloody rampage in April 2014 when an enlisted man killed three unarmed soldiers and wounded 16 others before he put a bullet in his own head. East of Fort Hood is Temple, a rail center and the birthplace of Miriam "Ma" Ferguson, wife of Gov. James "Pa" Ferguson, who was elected governor in 1925 after her husband was impeached and convicted.

The 31st Congressional District is an unusually compact district by modern Texas standards. It is entirely contained within Bell and Williamson counties, and takes in almost all of each. Williamson has 70 percent of the population. Historically this was solidly Democratic country, devoted to the party of the Confederacy and then the New Deal.

2012 Presidential Vote		
Mitt Romney (R)	144,634	(60%)
Barack Obama (D)	92,842	(38%)
2008 Presidential Vote		
John McCain (R)	135,601	(56%)
Barack Obama (D)	103,359	(43%)
Cook Partisan Voting Index:	R+12	

It was populated by cotton farmers who distrusted Wall Street and railroads and who trusted politicians like Sam Rayburn and Lyndon Johnson and, later, Gov. Ann Richards and Sen. Lloyd Bentsen. But these people took a shine to Ronald Reagan's and George W. Bush's brand of Republicanism, and it is a safely Republican area today. Mitt Romney got 60 percent of the vote in 2012.

John Carter (R)

John Carter, a conservative Republican first elected in 2002, brings an ex-judge's no-nonsense, law-and-order perspective to homeland security and immigration as the chairman of the Appropriations subcommittee with jurisdiction over those issues. He is respected as an informal leader among House Republicans.

Carter grew up in Houston and graduated from Texas Tech University and the University of Texas law school. He practiced law in Williamson County and served as a municipal judge in Round Rock. He was appointed a district judge in 1981 by Republican Gov. Bill Clements and in 1982 stood for election. Judicial elections are partisan in Texas, and Carter was the first GOP judge elected in Williamson County. He became known as the father of the county Republican Party.

In 2001, after a three-judge district court created a new Republican district stretching from Williamson County to Houston, Carter retired from the bench and ran for the seat. The real contest was among the eight candidates for the Republican nomination. Carter's main rivals were Peter Wareing, the son-in-law of Texas oilman Jack Blanton, and Brad Barton, son of Rep. Joe Barton of the 6th District. In the primary, Wareing led with 37% to 26% for Carter and 16% for Barton.

In the runoff campaign, Carter attacked Wareing as a liberal in disguise, pointing to his campaign contributions to Democrats like Rep. Sheila Jackson Lee of Houston. When Wareing proposed that each candidate sign a "clean campaign pledge," Carter offered what he called a "homestead pledge"—a ploy to highlight his charge that Wareing was a Houston carpetbagger who had rented an apartment in the district in order to run for the seat. Rep. Barton endorsed Carter as "the only true conservative in this race." Wareing outspent Carter more than 2-to-1, but Carter won 57%-43%. He got 78% of the vote in Williamson County, which cast 33% of the vote. Carter won the general election easily and has had little trouble winning reelection.

In the House, Carter has been a reliable conservative. With his perspective as an Appropriations Committee member, he opposed some of the more drastic GOP proposals to cut spending in 2012, such as an across-the-board cut in energy and water spending. He fought off a Republican attempt in 2011 to sharply cut spending for military bands, arguing that they "are an integral part to the patriotism that keeps our soldiers' hearts beating fast." He joined the Tea Party Caucus when it formed in 2010 and co-sponsored the "birther" bill in 2009 requiring future presidential candidates to provide proof of U.S. citizenship. Carter accused the Pentagon of watering down a 2010 report on the Fort Hood shootings to avoid discussing Islamic terrorism and has tried since then to award Purple Heart medals to the shooting victims so their families can receive benefits.

Taking over as Homeland Security Subcommittee chairman in 2013, Carter fought for spending more to secure the U.S.-Mexico border, but also acknowledged the need to "show compassion" to immigrants who are already in the United States. In February 2015, he cooperated with Speaker John Boehner on the House GOP leadership strategy to use the Homeland Security spending bill to try to force President Barack Obama to back down on his executive actions to loosen restrictions on immigrants from Mexico. But Senate Democrats held firm against any compromise, and Republicans eventually agreed to approve full-year funding of Carter's bill rather than force a shutdown.

He took part in bipartisan discussions to seek a compromise on a broader immigration measure. With fellow GOP Rep. Sam Johnson of Texas, he quit the group in September 2013 because, they said, President Barack Obama was using the immigration issue to "advance his political agenda." Before he joined Appropriations, Carter served on the Judiciary Committee, where he passed his Terrorist Penalties Enhancement Act and a bill to establish penalties for identity theft. He has served three terms as co-chairman of the bipartisan House Army Caucus. He has been a leader of the Texas Republican delegation and still likes to be called "Judge."

He served three terms in the leadership as House Republican Conference secretary, where he became the chief antagonist on ethics charges against Democratic Rep. Charles Rangel in 2009. He introduced several resolutions seeking to remove the New Yorker as chairman of the Ways and Means Committee during the ethics investigation. Rangel ultimately was removed as head of the committee and censured for transgressions. Carter himself drew Democrats' fire for an alleged ethical lapse after he reportedly failed to disclose nearly $300,000 in profits from sales of oil stocks in 2006 and 2007. Carter responded by taking the offensive, noting that he had paid all taxes on his stock transactions and had admitted his errors, and then challenged Rangel to do the same.

THIRTY-SECOND DISTRICT

Pete Sessions (R)

Elected 1996, 10th term; b. March 22, 1955, Waco; SW U., B.S. 1978; Methodist; married (Karen); 5 children.

Professional Career: Dist. mgr., SW Bell Telephone Co., 1978-93; V.P. public policy, Natl. Ctr. for Policy Analysis, 1994-95.

DC Office: 2233 RHOB, 20515, 202-225-2231; Fax: 202-225-5878; Website: sessions.house.gov.

State Offices: Dallas, 972-392-0505.

Committees: *Rules* (Chmn): Rules and Organization of the House.

Group Ratings

	ADA	ACLU	AFL-CIO	LCV	ITI	COC	HAFA	ACU	CFG	FRC
2014	0%	0%	–	0%	80%	79%	68%	84%	76%	100%
2013	0%	C	15%	4%	C	85%	C	80%	73%	C

National Journal Ratings

	2013 LIB	—	2013 CONS
Economic	27%	—	72%
Social	41%	—	58%
Foreign	5%	—	86%
Composite	26%	—	74%

Key Votes of the 113th Congress

1. Sandy storm spending	N	5. Medical Marijuana		9. Syrian Rebels Training	Y
2. Violence Against Women Act	N	6. Farm Bill	Y	10. Keystone pipeline	Y
3. Guantanamo Bay Detainees	N	7. Afghanistan Combat	N	11. Immigration Exec. Action	Y
4. Abortion 20-week ban	Y	8. NSA Phone Data Collection	N	12. Bipartisan budget deal	Y

Election Results

2014 general	Pete Sessions (R)	96,495	(62%)	$3,015,805	$292,223	$6,527	
	Frank Perez (D)	55,325	(35%)	$8,389			
	Ed Rankin (Lib)	4,276	(3%)				
2014 primary	Pete Sessions (R)	28,981	(64%)				
	Katrina Pierson (R)	16,574	(36%)				

Prior winning percentages: 2012 (58%), 2010 (63%), 2008 (57%), 2006 (56%), 2004 (54%), 2002 (68%), 2000 (54%), 1998 (56%), 1996 (53%)

Population		Race and Ethnicity		Income	
Total:	718,713	White	50.7%	Median income:	$60,247
Urban:	53.0%	Latino	28.3%		*(127 of 435)*
Suburban:	47.0%	Black	10.6%	Under $50,000	42.0%
Rural:	0.0%	Asian	7.0%	$50,000-$99,999:	27.5%
Land area:	204	Two races	2.9%	$100,000-$199,999:	20.3%
Pop/sq. mi.:	3,521.2	White Ethnic	15.4%	$200,000 or more:	10.2%
Born in state:	51.5%			Poverty Rate	14.4%
		Education			
Age Groups		H.S. grad or less:	31.0%	**Work**	
Under 18:	23.8%	Some college:	26.2%	White collar:	43.5%
18 to 34:	25.1%	College degree, 4 yr.:	26.9%	Blue collar:	39.8%
35 to 64:	40.2%	Post-grad study:	15.8%	Sales and service:	16.7%
Over 64:	10.9%				
		Military		Govt. workers:	9.9%
		Veterans/active duty:	6.2%		

Northern Dallas Metro: Dallas, Garland

North Dallas has long been the home of the city's elite and, indeed, a slice of the nation's elite. Early in the 20th century, the richest citizens started moving away from old neighborhoods adjacent to downtown and out past Turtle Creek to the area around the suburbs of Highland Park and Univer-

Voter Turnout	
2013 Total Citizen 18+	465,036
2014 House Turnout	156,096
2014 Turnout as % CVAP	33.6%
2012 Turnout as % CVAP	55.2%

sity Park—the Park Cities. Dallas grew lustily from mid-century. Beyond the Park Cities, miles of affluent neighborhoods were built, especially between the Central Expressway and the Dallas North Tollway. Galleries and office complexes followed. An entertainment and singles apartment corridor runs along Greenville Avenue, plus working-class neighborhoods here and there, and pockets of Latino neighborhoods near the freeways. Overall, the tone has been set by Dallas' upper crust.

Highland Park and University Park are well-heeled and over 90% white. In the 1990s, George W. Bush and Dick Cheney lived in or near the Park Cities. After eight years in the White House, George and Laura Bush returned to their Preston Hollow neighborhood, to an 8,500-square-foot home on an acre of land a few miles from his presidential library at Southern Methodist University, which opened in May 2013.

In 1954, voters here elected strict conservative Rep. Bruce Alger, who was only the third Republican to represent any portion of the state in the 20th century. But North Dallas and the 32nd Congressional District of Texas now reflect the political trends driving 21st century politics: As upper-income suburbanites drifted toward the Democrats and the minority population of north Dallas County increased, the district moved leftward. John McCain won here with only 55% of the vote in 2008, and its Republican congressman was held below 60% in three successive elections.

The latest Republican-engineered redistricting removed many of the heavily minority areas around Irving and Grand Prairie, dropping the Hispanic share of the population from 43% to 28%, and improving Republican performance by a few points. A portion of the district crosses into Collin County to take in some of fast-growing, upscale Wylie, but more than 90% of the 32nd is in Dallas County. The district still has Democratic pockets around racially diverse Richardson and the downtown area, but it is not likely to be a competitive battleground.

Pete Sessions (R)

Pete Sessions, a Republican first elected in 1996, chairs the Rules Committee, a job that allows him to indulge his fondness for ritual sparring with Democrats while upholding the leadership's priorities. He previously chaired the National Republican Congressional Committee, where he guided his party to a 63-seat gain and control of the House in 2010.

Sessions grew up in Waco, graduated from Southwestern University, then worked at Southwestern Bell in Dallas for 16 years. His father is William Sessions, a federal judge who served as director of the Federal Bureau of Investigation from 1987 to 1993. The vagaries of redistricting in Texas have led Sessions to run for Congress in several different House districts. In 1991, he ran and finished sixth in the special election in the 3rd District, which then included much of North Dallas.

In 1993, he resigned from the phone company to run against Democratic Rep. John Bryant in the 5th District, which included much of the east side of Dallas and several rural counties to the south. The district had been drawn to reelect Bryant, a liberal Democrat. Sessions ran a vigorous campaign, making a two-day, 12-city tour of the district's rural portions with a livestock trailer full of horse manure and a sign saying, "The Clinton health care plan stinks worse than this trailer." Although he outspent Sessions 2-to-1 in 1994, Bryant won by just 50%-47%.

Two years later, Bryant ran, unsuccessfully, for the Senate. Sessions ran again for the House seat and won the primary. In the general election, he faced John Pouland, a former regional General Services Administration director. Sessions charged that Pouland was a big-government liberal and would abandon U.S. military bases overseas. Pouland criticized Republican cuts in Medicare. Sessions won 53%-47%.

Sessions' voting record is among the most conservative in the House, though some conservative blogs and websites have questioned whether he is too much a part of the Washington establishment that they loathe. In 1999, he got a seat on Rules and used it to promote the Republican message.

Sessions sponsored the constitutional amendment to require a two-thirds vote to raise taxes, was a leading advocate of the Republican proposal to stop the government from spending Social Security and Medicare surpluses, and called for scrapping the income tax code. He contended in October 2010 that the economic stimulus law actually put Americans out of work. When President Barack Obama laid out a liberal agenda in his 2013 State of the Union address, Sessions told *The New York Times*: "We're now managing America's demise, not America's great future." He is generally tightfisted but is apt to support government spending to help families with disabled children. Sessions has a son with Down syndrome.

Sessions sought to get on the House leadership track by running in 2006 for chairman of the NRCC, which raises money for Republicans and recruits challengers in House races. But he lost to Republican Tom Cole of Oklahoma. After the 2008 election, Sessions won a second try to head the NRCC. He had the strong support of Boehner: Sessions was among the few Texas Republicans who had backed Boehner for party leader against Roy Blunt of Missouri in 2006. Cole wanted a second term as NRCC chairman, but he carried the burden of the party's 21-seat loss in the November 2008 election.

Sessions had a rocky start as chairman. Republicans lost a seat in a special election in upstate New York. He drew criticism for holding fundraisers at risqué venues that were at odds with the party's family-values image. He was lampooned by Democrats for his sometimes odd comments, including his statement that Obama was trying "to inflict damage and hardship on the free enterprise system, if not to kill it." Sessions set a challenging goal of gaining the 40 seats the party needed to recapture the majority in 2010, and reorganized the committee to improve fundraising, communications and candidate recruitment. He was not in complete command of the job, as Boehner reportedly sat in on major strategy meetings. Sessions let other NRCC figures, such as his close friend Greg Walden of Oregon, take on major roles. Sessions was among the first members to join the Tea Party Caucus and, sharing its members' anger at big spending, helped to mesh the GOP message to that theme. The Republicans' huge gain in November was the largest switch since 1948.

Sessions considered using his political capital to run for majority whip in November 2010, but decided against challenging California's politically savvy Kevin McCarthy. Boehner gave Sessions added responsibilities as NRCC chairman to advise new members taking office on how to coordinate their House work schedule with their reelection campaigns.

In the 2012 election season, Sessions predicted that Republicans would pick up as many as seven new seats "because we are playing offense, not trying to protect what we have." Democrats netted eight seats and outgained the GOP in the total popular vote. But the nationwide redistricting gave Republicans the edge, and they retained control—at least until the 2022 redistricting, many House experts believe.

House Speaker John Boehner chose Sessions in November 2012 to succeed retiring Rules Chairman David Dreier of California over Washington's Doc Hastings, another close Boehner ally. Earlier that year, news media accounts said some Republicans privately wondered whether Hastings might be better suited for the job, citing an incident in which Sessions falsely accused Democratic Rep. Jim McGovern of Massachusetts of drinking on the job after McGovern sought to offer an amendment to end U.S. participation in the war in Afghanistan. Minority Whip Steny Hoyer said in a floor speech that the accusation was a cause of "deep disappointment," and Sessions apologized.

Rules Committee meetings can often set off partisan sparks, as was the case in February 2015. Outspoken Democrat Alcee Hastings of Florida declared that Texas is "a crazy state" and that he would never want to live there. Though Sessions wasn't present at the hearing, he took the House floor to defend his state. "Texans are a proud people, and we've been a proud people since the days of the Alamo," Sessions said. "While some people may think that limited government and empowering families is 'crazy,' I disagree."

When Majority Leader Eric Cantor unexpectedly lost his primary in June 2014, Sessions flirted again with seeking a leadership post. He told reporters that he was running and cited the big boost that he expected to receive from the Texas delegation. But less than 48 hours after Cantor's defeat, he changed his mind and decided for a second time not to challenge McCarthy, saying that running a successful campaign "would have created unnecessary and painful division within our party." Other Republicans said that McCarthy already had locked up the needed support. Some conservatives reportedly approached Sessions about running for McCarthy's old whip job, but he declined after brief consideration. A failed leadership bid would have jeopardized his continuation as chairman of Rules, where Sessions remained influential in the business of the House.

Sessions has had his own roller-coaster electoral history. In 2001, he unexpectedly left the safe 5th to run in the newly created and more upscale 32nd, which had no incumbent but included only 16% of his old district. He said he wanted to spend less time traveling around his district—the 32nd was considerably more compact—and he thought it more compatible with his pro-business philosophy. Sessions had only token primary opposition and won the seat, 68%-30%. Ironically, his successor in the 5th was Jeb Hensarling, who has become the influential chairman of the Financial Services Committee and a potential leadership aspirant.

In 2003, Tom DeLay of Texas, the powerful House majority leader, persuaded the Republican-controlled Texas Legislature to draw the lines yet again. Although most GOP members were well-served by the new lines, Sessions wound up in a somewhat less Republican district and with a reelection challenge from 13-term Democratic incumbent Martin Frost, whose 24th District had been shorn of its most Democratic precincts. Frost chose to run in the 32nd because of its Democratic-friendly Jewish population in the Park Cities. Frost also felt that Sessions was too conservative for the new district.

The contest became the most expensive House campaign of 2004. Sessions spent $4.5 million and Frost $4.8 million, and much more was spent by party committees and independent groups. Sessions criticized Frost for scheduling a fundraiser with Peter Yarrow, the Peter, Paul and Mary singer who had been convicted of "taking indecent liberties" with a 14-year-old girl in 1969. Frost cited Sessions' vote against the establishment of new air-passenger security rules after the September 11 attacks and ran an ad with images of the World Trade Center in flames and the message "Protect America. Say No to Pete Sessions." Sessions won 54%-44%, capturing more than 80% of the vote in some Park Cities precincts; Frost failed to get the higher turnout he needed in increasingly Hispanic Oak Cliff.

Sessions has been reelected without difficulty since then. In 2014, he fended off a primary challenge from Katrina Pierson, a tea party activist who was a top volunteer on Republican Ted Cruz's 2012 Senate campaign. But she failed to raise serious money—$144,000 to Sessions' $1.5 million—and Sessions won 64%-36%.

THIRTY-THIRD DISTRICT

Marc Veasey (D)

Elected 2012, 2nd term; b. Jan. 3, 1971, Fort Worth; TX Wesleyan U., B.S. 1995; Baptist; married (Tonya); 1 child.

Elected Office: TX House, 2005-2013.

Professional Career: Staffer, Rep. Martin Frost, 1998-2004; Commercial real-estate broker.

DC Office: 414 CHOB, 20515, 202-225-9897; Website: veasey.house. gov.

State Offices: Dallas, 214-741-1387; Fort Worth, 817-920-9086.

Committees: *Armed Services:* Emerging Threats & Capabilities; Tactical Air & Land Forces. *Science, Space, & Technology:* Energy; Space.

Group Ratings

	ADA	ACLU	AFL-CIO	LCV	ITI	COC	HAFA	ACU	CFG	FRC
2014	85%	77%	–	86%	80%	57%	15%	8%	14%	0%
2013	75%	C	100%	93%	C	46%	C	12%	13%	C

National Journal Ratings

	2013 LIB	—	2013 CONS
Economic	73%	—	27%
Social	63%	—	36%
Foreign	66%	—	32%
Composite	68%	—	32%

Key Votes of the 113th Congress

1. Sandy storm spending	Y	5. Medical Marijuana	Y	9. Syrian Rebels Training	Y
2. Violence Against Women Act	Y	6. Farm Bill	N	10. Keystone pipeline	Y
3. Guantanamo Bay Detainees	Y	7. Afghanistan Combat	Y	11. Immigration Exec. Action	N
4. Abortion 20-week ban	N	8. NSA Phone Data Collection	N	12. Bipartisan budget deal	Y

Election Results

2014 general	Marc Veasey (D)	43,769	(87%)	$1,224,552	$40,930
	Jason Reeves (Lib)	6,823	(14%)		
2014 primary	Marc Veasey (D)	13,292	(74%)		
	Tom Sanchez (D)	4,798	(27%)		

Prior winning percentage: 2012 (73%)

Population		Race and Ethnicity		Income	
Total:	725,761	Latino	65.0%	Median income:	$35,827
Urban:	85.5%	White	16.0%		*(417 of 435)*
Suburban:	14.5%	Black	15.3%	Under $50,000	67.3%
Rural:	0.0%	Asian	2.5%	$50,000-$99,999:	24.7%
Land area:	244	Two races	0.8%	$100,000-$199,999:	7.0%
Pop/sq. mi.:	2,971.0	White Ethnic	4.1%	$200,000 or more:	1.0%
Born in state:	54.7%			Poverty Rate	29.4%
		Education			
Age Groups		H.S. grad or less:	70.6%	**Work**	
Under 18:	32.8%	Some college:	19.9%	White collar:	15.3%
18 to 34:	26.5%	College degree, 4 yr.:	6.5%	Blue collar:	44.5%
35 to 64:	33.2%	Post-grad study:	3.1%	Sales and service:	40.2%
Over 64:	7.6%				
		Military		Govt. workers:	6.4%
		Veterans/active duty:	3.8%		

Central Metroplex: Parts of Fort Worth and Dallas

In the 1950s, the Dallas-Fort Worth Turnpike was built on empty land to link the two cities' downtowns. Over the next three decades, the land filled up, with as many people as the central cities had. Irving, Grand Prairie and Arlington grew up along the highway in the once impoverished area and

Voter Turnout	
2013 Total Citizen 18+	316,653
2014 House Turnout	50,592
2014 Turnout as % CVAP	16%
2012 Turnout as % CVAP	38.5%

became central to one of America's richest and most productive metropolitan areas. Major civic landmarks followed: Rangers Ballpark in Arlington, built by one-time managing partner George W. Bush, and now the domed AT&T Stadium, home of the Dallas Cowboys.

Arlington and Grand Prairie are in their second generation, taking on the patina of age, but above them you still see the big Texas sky and, in the distance, the small bluffs that mark the Balcones Escarpment, the geological divide between flat and lush East Texas and rolling and dry West Texas. The turnover brought newcomers to the area: Arlington is now only 45% non-Hispanic white; Irving is 31%; Grand Prairie 29%.

The 33rd Congressional District of Texas, which covers this suburban zone, is a judicial creation. After the 2010 census, state Republicans in control of redistricting drew a 33rd District that combined Arlington with heavily Republican Parker and Wise counties. The court found that the arrangement violated the Voting Rights Act and created the minority-majority district, which is 65% Hispanic, 15% African American, and 16% Anglo. Its jagged boundaries mesh with those of the African-American-controlled 30th District in Dallas.

It doesn't take in many of the industrial plants in the area, but its blue-collar workforce provides much of the manpower for companies like Northrop Grumman, General Motors, Hughes Training, Bell Textron Helicopter and Lockheed Martin, all of which have facilities in or near the district. It includes a few neighborhoods in western Dallas, including Oak Cliff, a collection of Victorian era mansions near the Trinity River that became heavily African American in the 1970s and 1980s as a result of white flight; it is now heavily Hispanic. Lee Harvey Oswald lived in a rooming house in Oak Cliff. He took a cab the short distance from near Dealey Plaza to his home after killing President John Kennedy in November 1963 and then was arrested in the nearby Texas Theater.

The district also includes much of Grand Prairie and Irving, as well as tiny, almost-entirely Hispanic Cockrell Hill. Across a narrow tentacle of lightly populated precincts, the district has about a third of Fort Worth, including the old stockyards, where cattle drives are still conducted twice a day by real cattle drovers. In June 2014, local media reported that developers had plans to build

2012 Presidential Vote
Barack Obama (D) 86,686 (72%)
Mitt Romney (R)...................32,641 (27%)

2008 Presidential Vote
Barack Obama (D) 90,180 (69%)
John McCain (R)...................40,290 (31%)

Cook Partisan Voting Index: D+18

hotels, restaurants and shops at the stockyards. This Tarrant County section has close to 60 percent of the voters of the 33rd. Overall, the district is strongly Democratic.

Marc Veasey (D)

Democrat Marc Veasey won a hard-fought primary in 2012 to claim the seat in the 33rd District, which was created by the 2011 redistricting. As an African American in this heavily Hispanic district, he has faced challenges. But his deep political background has educated him on those dynamics.

Veasey, a commercial real estate broker, was born and still lives in Fort Worth. He credits his involvement in politics to his uncle, who worked for Fort Worth's Jim Wright, the Democratic speaker of the House from 1987 to 1989. After watching a White House press briefing on television in his mid-teens, Veasey remembers asking his uncle what it would take to get such a job, and his uncle advised he get a college degree.

After graduating from Texas Wesleyan University, Veasey held a string of jobs, including substitute teaching, writing phone-book ads and working for local Democratic Rep. Martin Frost. As a Frost staffer, he worked to attract a grocery store to a poor section of Fort Worth to create jobs and enable residents to buy fresh produce. He also secured transportation funding for the district's roads. Veasey ran for the state House in 2004 out of frustration with an incumbent who refused to join other Texas Democrats in leaving the state to protest GOP-led redistricting. He chaired the Democratic Caucus, served on an environmental regulations committee and dealt with banking and pension issues.

His main competition in the decisive primary for the House seat was Dallas attorney Domingo Garcia. The contest polarized black voters who supported Veasey and Hispanics who largely supported Garcia; it also developed into a regional spat between Veasey from Fort Worth and Garcia from crosstown rival Dallas. In the initial balloting, Veasey bested Garcia, 37%-25%, not enough to avoid a runoff.

In the runoff campaign, Veasey targeted the Democratic base and black voters on his home turf, plus blacks and Hispanics in Dallas County. Garcia accused him of "playing the race card" by spending a lot of time in Fort Worth's black neighborhoods. But it turned out to be a good strategy. Voters in Tarrant County turned out in higher proportions than those in Dallas County. Garcia failed to galvanize Hispanics the way that Veasey excited African Americans as the first black to represent Tarrant County in Congress.

Garcia made costly mistakes in the campaign. He called for scrapping the F-35 plane even though it's responsible for more than 40,000 local jobs. And he labeled Veasey an "errand boy for the establishment"—and then refused to apologize for use of the racially charged term "boy" because, he said, he didn't mean it as a slur.

Veasey won the runoff 53%-47%. He got 68% of the vote in Tarrant County, which cast 59% of the total, and was careful to sound a conciliatory note in his acceptance speech. "Despite what the pundits said, this election was never about Dallas versus Fort Worth. It was never about African Americans versus Hispanics," he said to cheering supporters in Fort Worth, according to *The Dallas Morning News*. "This election was about making sure North Texans were represented fairly and honestly." In November, Veasey had no trouble defeating Republican Chuck Bradley, 73%-26%.

Veasey got a seat on the Armed Services Committee, where he tended to the interests of the many military contractors in or near his district. When the annual defense spending bill passed the House in May 2015, he claimed credit for additional weapons procurement that will benefit his district plus a bipartisan agreement that required the Pentagon to review how illegal immigrants were serving in the military, including their eligibility for service. Veasey supported the merger of Fort Worth-based American Airlines and U.S. Airways as a plus for local jobs, and he broke with the Obama administration in its 2013 objections to the deal on anti-competitive grounds. He was one of five Texas Democrats who split with Obama and their party to support the Keystone XL pipeline.

In a January 2015 interview with the *Texas Tribune*, Veasey conceded that state Democrats were in "a tough place" politically but added that "things are changing." He cited the long-term implications of immigration patterns. In 2014, he faced a well-financed primary challenge from Tom Sanchez, a telecommunications lawyer who self-financed nearly all of his $1.5 million campaign and outspent Veasey. But Veasey won easily, 73%-27%, and showed increased strength in Dallas County where he took 62% of the vote. The turnout in his home base of Tarrant County nearly doubled that in Dallas. Garcia weighed a possible rematch against Veasey in 2016. Local Democrats talked up the possibility that another round of redistricting could create separate minority seats for each of them in the Metroplex, in addition to the long-standing 30th District.

THIRTY-FOURTH DISTRICT

Filemon Vela (D)

Elected 2012, 2nd term; b. Feb. 13, 1963, Harlingen; Georgetown U., B.A. 1985, U. of TX Austin, J.D. 1987; Catholic; married (Rose).

Professional Career: Practicing atty., 1988-2012.

DC Office: 437 CHOB, 20515, 202-225-9901;Website: vela.house.gov.

State Offices: Alice, 361-230-9776; Brownsville, 956-644-8352; San Benito, 956-276-4497; Weslaco, 956-520-8273.

Committees: *Agriculture:* Commodity Exchanges, Energy & Credit; Livestock & Foreign Agriculture. *Homeland Security:* Border & Maritime Security (RMM); Counterterrorism & Intelligence.

Group Ratings

	ADA	ACLU	AFL-CIO	LCV	ITI	COC	HAFA	ACU	CFG	FRC
2014	55%	61%	–	69%	60%	69%	16%	8%	17%	29%
2013	55%	C	81%	46%	C	62%	C	12%	17%	C

National Journal Ratings

	2013 LIB	—	2013 CONS
Economic	56%	—	44%
Social	61%	—	38%
Foreign	56%	—	43%
Composite	58%	—	42%

Key Votes of the 113th Congress

1. Sandy storm spending	Y	5. Medical Marijuana	NV	9. Syrian Rebels Training	Y
2. Violence Against Women Act	Y	6. Farm Bill	Y	10. Keystone pipeline	Y
3. Guantanamo Bay Detainees	N	7. Afghanistan Combat	N	11. Immigration Exec. Action	N
4. Abortion 20-week ban	N	8. NSA Phone Data Collection	Y	12. Bipartisan budget deal	Y

Election Results

2014 general	Filemon Vela (D)	47,503	(60%)	$595,235
	Larry Smith (R)	30,811	(39%)	$120,236
	Ryan Rowley (Lib)	1,563	(2%)	
2014 primary	Filemon Vela (D)	unopposed		

Prior winning percentage: 2012 (62%)

Population		Race and Ethnicity		Income	
Total:	720,005	Latino	82.6%	Median income:	$35,144
Urban:	45.7%	White	15.2%		*(420 of 435)*
Suburban:	33.6%	Black	1.4%	Under $50,000	62.8%
Rural:	20.8%	Asian	0.5%	$50,000-$99,999:	25.0%
Land area:	6,738	Two races	0.2%	$100,000-$199,999:	10.3%
Pop/sq. mi.:	106.9	White Ethnic	4.2%	$200,000 or more:	2.0%
Born in state:	68.5%			Poverty Rate	30.6%
		Education			
Age Groups		H.S. grad or less:	60.6%	**Work**	
Under 18:	30.1%	Some college:	24.9%	White collar:	28.2%
18 to 34:	23.8%	College degree, 4 yr.:	10.1%	Blue collar:	46.4%
35 to 64:	33.5%	Post-grad study:	4.5%	Sales and service:	25.4%
Over 64:	12.7%			Govt. workers:	16.7%
		Military			
		Veterans/active duty:	6.2%		

Southern Gulf Coast: Brownsville, McAllen

At the far southern tip of Texas, just before the waters of the Rio Grande end their 1,900-mile journey from southern Colorado by washing out into the Gulf of Mexico, stands the fast-growing city of Brownsville. Situated across the river from Matamoros Mexico, it is one of the country's major border crossings, and its history has been intertwined with U.S.-Mexican relations for much of its existence. Fort Texas, later renamed Fort Brown, was established in the run-up to the Mexican-American War. After the war ended, land speculators bought up property nearby, and

Voter Turnout	
2013 Total Citizen 18+	406,667
2014 House Turnout	79,877
2014 Turnout as % CVAP	19.6%
2012 Turnout as % CVAP	37%

the town of Brownsville was born. The First and Second Cortina wars took place here, as a private army under Juan Cortina did battle with Texas Rangers over perceived mistreatment of Mexican-American laborers. The last land engagement of the Civil War, the Battle of Palmito Ranch, was fought nearby, more than a month after Robert E. Lee surrendered at Appomattox. Later, Teddy Roosevelt notoriously gave dishonorable discharges to an entire regiment of African-American soldiers stationed in Brownsville for a purported cover-up of a murder. An investigation held more than 60 years later concluded the soldiers were innocent, and President Richard Nixon granted them pardons, all but two of which were issued posthumously.

Fort Brown was decommissioned in 1946, but Brownsville still stands at the crossroads of Mexican-American relations. The 1993 North American Free Trade Agreement has lifted the economy in parts of the area, and there has been a boom in commercial construction. Increased trade is expected to boost the local economy with the completion of parts of Interstate 69 through the redesignation of former state highways; it eventually will link Brownsville with Port Huron, Michigan, and the conclusion of a similar corridor linking Matamoros with Mazatlán on the Pacific Ocean. Despite this development, pockets of poverty remain: Not far from the border is the *colonia* of Cameron Park, where people live in trailers or makeshift structures without water or sewer service. It is rated by the Census Bureau as one of the poorest places in the nation, with an annual per capita income of $7,000. One sign of hope has come from a new niche for Brownsville as the "ship-breaking" capital of the nation. In late 2014, it dismantled a former aircraft carrier, the *Constellation*.

The 34th Congressional District of Texas stretches nearly 300 miles while reaching across 11 counties, with more than half of its population at the far southern end of the district in Brownsville-based Cameron County and another 15 percent in Hidalgo County. The rest of the district is mostly ranching country, with only a handful of small towns that lean heavily Republican. Kleberg County is home to the vast grazing and oil lands of the 825,000-acre—that's 1,289 square miles—King Ranch, which is bigger than Rhode Island. Goliad County, to the north of Corpus Christi, is the site of the infamous Goliad Massacre in the Texas Revolution, when over 300 captured Texan soldiers were executed as bandits by Mexican forces. South Padre Island, a few miles from the border, is a popular spring break beach destination.

2012 Presidential Vote		
Barack Obama (D)	90,885	(61%)
Mitt Romney (R)	57,303	(38%)
2008 Presidential Vote		
Barack Obama (D)	90,178	(60%)
John McCain (R)	58,707	(39%)
Cook Partisan Voting Index: D+8		

In the 2011 redistricting, this new district replaced much of the old Corpus Christi-based 27th District, which has become more Republican. With its 83% Hispanic population and solidly Democratic locales along the border, the 34th is a Democratic district, where President Barack Obama won 61% of the vote in 2012.

Filemon Vela (D)

Democrat Filemon Vela won the 34th District House seat in part on the strength of his illustrious political family. Brownsville's federal courthouse bears the name of his late father, a federal district judge who was nominated by President Jimmy Carter and served more than two decades, and his mother was the city's first elected woman mayor. Their son now holds his first elected position, and the growth of Hispanic political power in Texas could give him opportunities for increased influence.

Vela was born in Harlingen, at the southern tip of Texas, and raised in nearby Brownsville. After receiving a bachelor's degree from Georgetown University and a law degree from the University of Texas, he returned to Brownsville to practice law. As a civil attorney for 25 years, Vela represented school districts seeking restitution for shoddy construction by independent contractors. In one case, he recovered money spent by the district on a poorly built facility; in another, he won recompense for a malfunctioning air-quality control system.

When Vela launched his campaign, some political observers were surprised by the "D" next to his name. His wife was a Republican justice on the Texas Court of Appeals, and Vela acknowledged that he sometimes backed GOP office-seekers. But he aligned himself with the Democratic agenda, calling for "a realistic and fair way" to deal with illegal immigration, protection of Medicare and Social Security benefits, and tax cuts for small businesses as an incentive to hire workers.

His main rival for the Democratic nomination, Cameron County District Attorney Armando Villalobos, led the field in fundraising until he was indicted on federal fraud charges two weeks before the May primary. Vela had a 40%-13% lead in the opening round and got 67% of the vote in the July runoff against Denise Saenz Blanchard, who was a chief of staff to former Democratic Rep. Solomon Ortiz, who had represented the area for 28 years before he was defeated in 2010. Following the runoff, she told the Associated Press, "We now have a Republican who has converted to being a Democrat who I believe is taking a seat from the Democrats."

In the general election, Vela gained the imprimatur of Nancy Pelosi, the House Democratic leader who headlined a fundraiser for Vela in August. His election was never in doubt. He won, 62%-36%.

In the House, he showed a strong interest in immigration issues and in 2015 became the ranking Democrat on the Homeland Security Subcommittee on Border and Maritime Security. He made an unusual decision to resign from the Hispanic Caucus because he felt that the caucus was not objecting strongly enough to a provision in the Senate-passed immigration reform bill in 2013, which he believed was spending too much money on new barriers and border officials. The caucus agreed to his return. In September 2013, he filed with Democratic Rep. Raul Grijalva of Arizona a comprehensive immigration bill in an effort to jump-start the House debate. In May 2015, he filed a bill to require that the secretary of Defense report to Congress on violence and cartel activity in Mexico and its impact on U.S. national security.

In a May 2014 interview with the *Valley Star* newspaper, Vela was asked whether immigration, border security or water was the most important issue for his constituents. "They're all on par in terms of their significance, from an issue standpoint," he responded.

Vela was reelected 59%-39% over Republican Larry Smith, who spent $120,000 and had a small lead among the one-third of district voters who did not reside in Cameron or Hidalgo counties. Vela has become entrenched along the border.

THIRTY-FIFTH DISTRICT

Lloyd Doggett (D)

Elected 1994, 11th term; b. Oct. 6, 1946, Austin; U. of TX Austin, B.A. 1967, J.D. 1970; Methodist; married (Libby Belk); 2 children.

Elected Office: TX Senate, 1973-85; TX Supreme Court justice, 1989-94.

Professional Career: Practicing atty., 1970-89; Adjunct prof., U. of TX Law Schl., 1989-94.

DC Office: 2307 RHOB, 20515, 202-225-4865; Website: doggett.house .gov.

State Offices: Austin, 512-916-5921; San Antonio, 210-704-1080.

Committees: *Ways & Means:* Human Resources (RMM); Oversight; Social Security.

Group Ratings

	ADA	ACLU	AFL-CIO	LCV	ITI	COC	HAFA	ACU	CFG	FRC
2014	95%	83%	–	97%	60%	29%	19%	8%	18%	0%
2013	90%	C	95%	96%	C	46%	C	24%	21%	C

National Journal Ratings

	2013 LIB	—	2013 CONS
Economic	68%	—	32%
Social	79%	—	16%
Foreign	86%	—	13%
Composite	79%	—	21%

Key Votes of the 113th Congress

1. Sandy storm spending	Y	5. Medical Marijuana	Y	9. Syrian Rebels Training	N
2. Violence Against Women Act	Y	6. Farm Bill	N	10. Keystone pipeline	N
3. Guantanamo Bay Detainees	Y	7. Afghanistan Combat	Y	11. Immigration Exec. Action	N
4. Abortion 20-week ban	N	8. NSA Phone Data Collection	Y	12. Bipartisan budget deal	Y

Election Results

2014 general	Lloyd Doggett (D).........................	60,124	(63%)	$630,990	$10
	Susan Narvaiz (R)	32,040	(33%)	$229,450	$42
	Cory Bruner (Lib)	2,767	(3%)		
2014 primary	Lloyd Doggett (D).................unopposed				

Prior winning percentages: 2012 (64%), 2010 (53%), 2008 (66%), 2006 (67%), 2004 (68%), 2002 (84%), 2000 (85%), 1998 (85%), 1996 (56%), 1994 (56%)

Population		Race and Ethnicity		Income	
Total:	752,749	Latino	64.0%	Median income:	$40,714
Urban:	86.6%	White	23.8%		*(381 of 435)*
Suburban:	11.5%	Black	9.3%	Under $50,000	58.6%
Rural:	1.9%	Asian	1.5%	$50,000-$99,999:	30.2%
Land area:	852	Two races	1.0%	$100,000-$199,999:	10.4%
Pop/sq. mi.:	883.7	White Ethnic	9.6%	$200,000 or more:	0.9%
Born in state:	64.9%			Poverty Rate	24.0%
		Education			
Age Groups		H.S. grad or less:	53.0%	**Work**	
Under 18:	26.9%	Some college:	28.4%	White collar:	25.8%
18 to 34:	30.7%	College degree, 4 yr.:	13.6%	Blue collar:	49.6%
35 to 64:	34.3%	Post-grad study:	5.0%	Sales and service:	24.6%
Over 64:	8.2%				
		Military		Govt. workers:	12.6%
		Veterans/active duty:	7.6%		

San Antonio/East Austin Corridor

"There are only four unique cities in America: Boston, New Orleans, San Francisco, and San Antonio." This quote may well be apocryphal—it has been attributed to both Mark Twain and Will Rogers—and today one would have to add a few other cities to the list. But San Antonio still stands as a

Voter Turnout	
2013 Total Citizen 18+	466,693
2014 House Turnout	96,225
2014 Turnout as % CVAP	20.6%
2012 Turnout as % CVAP	36.5%

one-of-a-kind American city. It started out as a collection of five Spanish missions, including the Mission San Antonio de Valero, better known today as the Alamo. From there it grew into a colonial capital, a hub for cattle drives, a railroad base, and eventually the heart of South Texas' increasingly transnational economy. Southerners and Mexicans played a large role in the city's growth, but Germans also settled here in large numbers in the mid-19th century. Frederick Law Olmsted referred to antebellum San Antonio as a "jumble of races, costumes, languages, and buildings," and as late as 1877, German speakers outnumbered Anglos and Mexican Americans.

Even the city's politics ran against the grain. In 1920, a district that included Bexar County elected Republican Harry Wurzbach to Congress, the only member of his party the Lone Star State sent to Congress in the first half of the 20th century. He lost in 1928, but returned to Congress in 1930, even as the country was engaged in a historic shift toward Democrats.

2012 Presidential Vote		
Barack Obama (D)	105,550	(63%)
Mitt Romney (R)..................	58,007	(35%)

2008 Presidential Vote		
Barack Obama (D)	111,790	(63%)
John McCain (R)..................	62,764	(36%)

Cook Partisan Voting Index: D+11

The 35th Congressional District of Texas covers many of the features that helped to make San Antonio unique. After 110 years in which it had been maintained by the private Daughters of the Republic of Texas, state lands commissioner George P. Bush in March 2015 switched management of the Alamo to the state's general land office. The district takes in the 2.5-mile-long River Walk, lined with restaurants, museums, and hotels; the 30-story, octagonal Tower Life Building; and the Alamodome, a 65,000 seat basketball/football stadium and convention center. A little less than half of the district's population lives in Bexar County. Another fifth lives in the strip of precincts running along Interstate 35 through the outskirts of Texas Hill Country, in the German settlement of New Braunfels, the old mill town of San Marcos, and Kyle, a fast-growing suburb of Austin, where most of the housing units have been built since 2000. About 30 percent of the district's population lives in southeastern Travis County, where Austin is located. The Austin airport, once a former military base, had been about even with San Antonio in its passenger load; since 2010, Austin has had a spurt in traffic and has taken a wider lead.

The district owes its unique shape to two goals of Republicans during the 2011 redistricting. They wanted to pack as many Democrats as possible into a single district, and they wanted to make a majority-Hispanic district that would endanger longtime Austin-based Democratic Rep. Lloyd Doggett in a primary. They attained their objective of a district that is 64 percent Hispanic. But Doggett has shown remarkable resilience.

Lloyd Doggett (D)

Lloyd Doggett, first elected in 1994, is a liberal Democrat and a respected voice in his party on tax and poverty issues. His political views and pugnacity have made him a target of Texas' GOP-led redistricting, but he has eluded efforts to draw him out of a seat.

Doggett grew up in Austin, finished first in his class at the University of Texas, and was student body president. At age 26, he was elected to the state Senate. In the 1970s, as part of a large liberal bloc, he pushed for laws against job discrimination plus cop-killer bullets and for generic drugs. He has long been a close ally of trial lawyers, a strong force supporting liberal Democrats in Texas. In the legislature, he was one of the "Killer Bees" who hid out to prevent a quorum on changing the rules in the Democratic primary and filibustered what he called anti-consumer bills.

In 1984, he ran for the Senate, narrowly edging out two House members to win the Democratic nomination. He lost the general election 59%-41% to Rep. Phil Gramm, a former Democrat who had switched parties. Doggett was elected to the Texas Supreme Court in 1988. When Democratic Rep. Jake Pickle retired after 31 years, Doggett ran for his seat. He won the Democratic primary with token opposition and took the general 56%-40%.

In the House, Doggett's voting record has been the most liberal among Texans and near the center of all Democrats. He has been a close ally of Nancy Pelosi of California. In 2002, he was a leader in opposing the resolution authorizing the use of force in Iraq. He is at times highly partisan, and was a frequent critic of Republican Speaker Newt Gingrich and a close ally of Minority Whip David Bonior of Michigan in seeking to diminish Gingrich's power by raising continual questions about his ethics.

When Democrats controlled the House between 2007 and 2010, Doggett was active and often influential on the Ways and Means Committee. His priorities included eliminating tax shelters and loopholes and giving the federal government power to negotiate prescription drug prices for Medicare. He sought tax incentives for purchasers of plug-in hybrid electric cars. In 2009, when President Barack Obama announced his plan to reform international tax policy, he cited Doggett's input on proposals to crack down on overseas tax evasion. Doggett pressed the president's Simpson-Bowles fiscal commission to scrutinize the more than $1 trillion a year that the Internal Revenue Service provides in the form of reduced taxes or refunds to companies and individuals. Doggett refused to back Obama's tax-cut deal with Republicans in the 2010 lame-duck session for its inclusion of tax cuts for high-income taxpayers.

Doggett drew attention in 2010 for a protracted standoff with Texas Republican Gov. Rick Perry over a provision that Doggett added to a House-passed bill giving states aid to hire and retain teachers. The provision, which applied only to Texas, required the governor to maintain the state's current level of education funding over the next three years. Then-Attorney General Greg Abbott filed suit, arguing Texas was unfairly singled out. Doggett was unrepentant: "Instead of running to the courtroom, the governor should focus on our classrooms," he told *The Texas Tribune*. The requirement was eventually removed in the fiscal 2011 budget deal. When Perry decided to run for president later that year, Doggett became a leading Lone Star critic and he pulled no punches in seeking to paint Perry as an extremist. "He's messed with Texas, and we think he shouldn't mess with America," Doggett said in August 2011. When Perry sent National Guard troops to the border in July 2014, Doggett was dismissive. "Our Border Patrol does not need interference from either Gov. Perry or vigilantes."

Despite being in the minority in the House, Doggett has found ways to be effective as the senior Democrat on the Human Resources Subcommittee at Ways and Means. He got a bill into law in January 2013 setting up a national commission to examine ways to reduce the number of children who die from abuse and neglect. Texas has the nation's highest rate of child abuse and neglect fatalities. The tax and spending deal approved that month to avoid a so-called "fiscal cliff" included an extension of a higher-education tax credit he had proposed. He worked with Texas Republican Sam Johnson to get a bill through the House in December 2012 to authorize the phased removal of Social Security numbers from Medicare cards to crack down on identity theft. Although an outspoken foe of Obama's international trade deals, he scored a modest triumph in early 2015 when he convinced White House officials to increase the transparency of the agreements for members of Congress.

Republicans have long been giddy at the prospect that redistricting might end Doggett's congressional career. In 2004, the GOP stretched his district 300 miles south to the Mexican border. But he took up the challenge. As other dislocated Texas Democrats took their fight to the courts, Doggett took his case to the voters of his new district. If he lost, Doggett told voters, "Tom DeLay will have won," a reference to the powerful GOP majority leader from Texas who had orchestrated the remap. Doggett won the primary 64%-36%. He led 88%-12% in Travis County and held Leticia Hinojosa, a former district court judge from McAllen, to a standoff in Hidalgo County. He won handily in November. In 2010, he drew a tough challenge from Republican Donna Campbell, a doctor and hospital emergency department director who raised $765,000. But Doggett spent $1.2 million and won 53%-45%, carrying Travis County by 2-to-1.

In 2011, Texas Republicans again sought to carve up Doggett's stronghold. The eventual map added his liberal Austin base to a predominantly San Antonio district that included some conservative rural counties. Initially, it appeared that state Rep. Joaquin Castro would run here. But when San Antonio Rep. Charlie Gonzalez announced his retirement, Castro decided to move to the 20th District. That enabled Doggett to easily win a three-way Democratic primary with 73% of the vote and then crush Republican San Marcos Mayor Susan Narvaiz in November with 64%. In a 2014 rematch with Narvaiz, Doggett won 62%-33%. He has become more active in the politics of his adopted city, including a September 2013 letter urging the San Antonio City Council to OK a measure barring workplace discrimination against gays; the measure was approved a few days later.

THIRTY-SIXTH DISTRICT

Brian Babin (R)

Elected 2014, 1st term; b. Mar. 23, 1948, Port Arthur; Lamar U., B.S. 1973, U. of TX Houston, D.D.S. 1976; Baptist; married (Roxanne); 5 children.

Military Career: TX Army Nat'l Guard, 1969-71; U.S. Army Reserve, 1971-75; U.S. Air Force, 1976-79.

Elected Office: Woodville City Cncl., 1981-82, 1984-89; Woodville mayor, 1982-84; Woodville Schl. Bd., 1992-95.

Professional Career: Dentist, 1979-2014; TX St. Bd. of Dental Examiners, 1981-87; TX Historical Comm., 1989-95; Lower Neches Valley Authority, 1999-2014.

DC Office: 316 CHOB, 20515, 202-225-1555; Fax: 202-226-0396; Website: babin.house.gov.

State Offices: Deer Park, 832-780-0966; Orange, 409-883-8075; Woodville, 844-303-8934.

Committees: *Science, Space, & Technology:* Environment; Space (Chmn). *Transportation & Infrastructure:* Highways & Transit; Railroads, Pipelines & Hazardous Materials; Water Resources & Environment.

Election Results

2014 general	Brian Babin (R)	101,663	(76%)	$964,205	$131,152
	Michael Cole (D)	29,543	(22%)	$16,651	
2014 prim.	Brian Babin (R)	19,301	(58%)		
runoff	Ben Streusand (R)	14,069	(42%)		
2014 primary	Brian Babin (R)	17,194	(33%)		
	Ben Streusand (R)	12,024	(23%)		
	John Manlove (R)	3,556	(7%)		
	Doug Centilli (R)	3,506	(7%)		
	Phil Fitzgerald (R)	3,388	(7%)		
	Robin Riley (R)	2,648	(5%)		

Population		Race and Ethnicity		Income	
Total:	710,008	White	62.9%	Median income:	$52,708
Urban:	13.6%	Latino	22.9%		*(188 of 435)*
Suburban:	60.4%	Black	9.9%	Under $50,000	46.8%
Rural:	26.1%	Asian	2.3%	$50,000-$99,999:	29.9%
Land area:	5,702	Two races	0.9%	$100,000-$199,999:	19.4%
Pop/sq. mi.:	124.5	White Ethnic	21.5%	$200,000 or more:	3.8%
Born in state:	68.0%			Poverty Rate	14.5%
		Education			
Age Groups		H.S. grad or less:	47.7%	**Work**	
Under 18:	24.7%	Some college:	33.6%	White collar:	31.6%
18 to 34:	22.2%	College degree, 4 yr.:	12.9%	Blue collar:	38.8%
35 to 64:	39.7%	Post-grad study:	5.8%	Sales and service:	29.6%
Over 64:	13.4%			Govt. workers:	14.9%
		Military			
		Veterans/active duty:	8.5%		

Eastern Houston Area, Southeast Texas

East Texas is thick with landmarks of Lone Star history. There's still an Indian reservation in Polk County, and the swampland Big Thicket National Preserve reminds you of what the area looked like before humans first settled the region some 2,500 years ago. (It is called "America's Ark" because of

Voter Turnout	
2013 Total Citizen 18+	492,728
2014 House Turnout	133,842
2014 Turnout as % CVAP	27.2%
2012 Turnout as % CVAP	49.3%

its vast array of animals and plants.) These were some of the first parts of Texas to be settled by Anglos; Anahuac in Chambers County was a port of entry for early colonists, and the Turtle Bayou Resolutions, signed nearby in 1832 and condemning violations of the Mexican Constitution by the government, marked an escalation in tensions between the colonists and Mexico. Later, the area became a destination for colonists during the famed "Runaway Scrape," as they fled eastward, leaving beds unmade and breakfasts sitting on the table, in the face of Santa Anna's approaching army.

Today, much of East Texas looks frozen in time—farm towns that the railroads passed by and the interstates overlooked. One can still get a sense of what the wildcatters saw when they crisscrossed the land buying up mineral rights in Mont Belvieu, hoping to cash in on the oil boom taking place in nearby Spindletop. But of course, some things have changed. Racial segregation has been abolished—this part of the state is home to a large portion of the state's rural black population—and the isolation of the small town has been reduced by television, the regional shopping mall, and the Internet. And urban development, sprinting outward from Houston's loop freeways, is spreading in between

2012 Presidential Vote		
Mitt Romney (R)	175,883	(73%)
Barack Obama (D)	61,786	(26%)

2008 Presidential Vote		
John McCain (R)	165,899	(70%)
Barack Obama (D)	70,543	(30%)

Cook Partisan Voting Index: R+25

the pine forests and reservoirs. The industrial age is prominent in Baytown, where Exxon is building its second refinery; the massive facility, with about 10,000 construction workers, is scheduled to start production in 2017, with the company's promises of a reduction in carbon emissions. Its first refinery, which is the second largest in the nation, has been the target of numerous legal and regulatory challenges.

The 36th Congressional District of Texas is one of four Texas created as a result of population growth revealed in the 2010 Census. It is a compromise: Both suburban Houston Republicans and East Texas Republicans wanted a new congressional district, and the result is one evenly divided between the two groups. About half of the district's population lives in a collection of eight lightly populated counties, where lumbering, farming, ranching, and oil and gas dominate. The district is among the top 5% of the most Republican nationwide. Mitt Romney got 73% in 2012.

Jasper, the "Butterfly Capital of Texas," is on the northern edge of the district; it is also where James Byrd Jr. was fatally dragged behind a truck driven by white supremacists in 1998. The other half of the district's population lives in the suburbs on the eastern edge of Harris County. They include blue-collar Baytown, Deer Park, La Porte and part of Pasadena, near the Houston Ship Channel. Further south are Clear Lake, Taylor Lake Village and part of Webster. They are in the southern end of Harris County, and tend to be more upscale, populated by highly educated employees of the Lyndon B. Johnson Space Center, as well as the space and aeronautics industry that grew up around it. That iconic center, which opened in 1961, has "lost its identity and purpose" with the demise of NASA's manned space flights, the *Houston Press* reported in April 2014. Roughly half of its buildings recently have been torn down or consolidated.

Brian Babin (R)

Brian Babin, a dentist and local Republican leader who made his third run for Congress in 2014, sealed this victory in a primary runoff against tea party favorite Ben Streusand. Babin decisively beat Democrat Michael Cole to succeed retiring GOP conservative firebrand Rep. Steve Stockman, who served two terms separated by 20 years.

Babin grew up in Beaumont, attended Lamar University and got his degree in dentistry at the University of Texas at Houston; friends refer to him as "Doc Babin." After dental school, he served overseas in the Air Force, and later was an airborne artilleryman in the Army Reserve. He settled in Woodville in rural Tyler County, where he has maintained his dental practice. Babin entered local politics by serving as an alderman and mayor of Woodville. He was a regional chairman for Ronald Reagan's 1980 presidential campaign and claims some credit for the shift in local politics to the Republican Party. He has served on various local and state authorities, including a 1999 appointment by Gov. George W. Bush to the Lower Neches Valley Authority.

Not long ago, these parts of east Texas were "yellow dog" conservative Democratic territory and home to the colorful late Democratic Rep. Charlie Wilson, the subject of the book and movie *Charlie Wilson's War*. When Wilson retired in 1996, Babin ran for the seat, only to lose to Democrat Jim Turner 52%-46%. He tried again two years later and lost by a wider margin. With partisan changes, the area covered by the 36th has skewed toward the GOP over the past decade; the outspokenly conservative Stockman was the initial representative of the new district. When Stockman gave up his House seat in a quixotic challenge to Republican Sen. John Cornyn, Babin seized on the chance to convert his decades of local political activism into a viable congressional run. Friends described him as just as conservative as Stockman, but more experienced in the give-and-take of governing.

In a 12-candidate field in the March primary, Babin ran first with 33% of the vote, followed by Streusand at 23%. Failing to secure the required majority, the two competed in the May runoff vote. Their contest proved to be one of the more contentious races of the cycle. Streusand brought up Babin's role in a Texas campaign finance scandal, noting that he received $37,000 in illegal corporate money from his friend, businessman Peter Cloeren, when he made his first House bid in 1996. Cloeren claimed the idea came from GOP Rep. Tom DeLay—the former House majority leader—but DeLay denied any involvement. Cloeren eventually pleaded guilty to campaign violations and paid a fine of $200,000, while the Federal Election Commission dismissed his claim that DeLay was responsible. The FEC gave Babin a relative pass, ordering him to pay $30,000 in civil fines. The official who let him off the hook was Lois Lerner, the embattled former IRS official who recently was accused of giving unfair scrutiny to tea party groups.

By the May runoff election, Babin's years of local political work gave him the edge over Streusand, 58%-42%. Streusand, a Houston banker who lived outside the district, won his base in Harris County with 65% of the vote, but he underperformed on turnout as Harris cast only one-third of the total vote. Babin rolled up huge majorities in the rural areas, including 85% in his native Tyler County. His general election victory was largely a formality.

In the House, Babin won seats on two committees well-suited to his district: Transportation and Infrastructure; and Science, Space and Technology. On his first day in office, Babin voted "present" rather than support John Boehner for House speaker, which he said was a reflection of his constituents' dissatisfaction with the GOP leadership. He was the only member in the chamber not to vote for a candidate. Despite that distancing, Babin was given the chairmanship of the Space Subcommittee when it opened in June 2015, due to a shuffle of other committee assignments. His goal, he said, was to "strengthen NASA's core exploration mission, create an environment for commercial space ventures to thrive, and build a clear vision for America's space program." In an April speech in Pasadena, he said that his goals were to return manned space flight as NASA's top priority, and to end NASA's reliance on other nations to send astronauts to the International Space Station. He also supports expansion of commercial space flight.

With his subcommittee niche, Babin is positioned to bring stability to his House district.

★ UTAH ★

"This is the place," exclaimed Brigham Young, as he stood on the western slope of the Wasatch Range and looked out over the valley of the Great Salt Lake in 1847. Other American states were founded by leaders of religious sects—Massachusetts, Connecticut, Pennsylvania—but only in colonial times and along waters navigable by ocean ships. Utah, a triumph of man over nature, was the creation of a productive and orderly civilization in a remote expanse of desert and mountain, arrayed around a desolate salt sea. It owes its settlement to the Church of Jesus Christ of Latter-day Saints, commonly called "LDS," which was founded in Upstate New York some 185 years ago. There, farmer Joseph Smith said he experienced a vision in which the angel Moroni appeared and told him where to unearth several golden tablets inscribed with hieroglyphic writings. With the aid of special spectacles, Smith translated the tablets and published them as *The Book of Mormon* in 1830; he declared himself to be a prophet. The Mormons he led attracted thousands of converts and created their own communities. Persecuted for their beliefs, they moved west to Ohio, Missouri, and then Nauvoo, Illinois, where some 15,000 members lived under Smith's theocratic rule. It was there that Smith received a revelation sanctioning the practice of polygamy and was murdered by a mob in 1844. The new church president, Brigham Young, decided to move the faithful—"the saints"—farther west into territory that was still part of Mexico and far beyond white settlement. In 1846, Young led a well-organized march across the Great Plains and into the Rocky Mountains and in 1847 stopped in what became Utah.

Utah was transferred from Mexico to the United States by the Treaty of Guadalupe Hidalgo of 1848, but for many years, it lived apart from the rest of the nation. Brigham Young was the first governor of the Utah Territory and most settlers in Utah continued to live by the teachings of the church. The early pioneers laid out towns foursquare to the points of the compass with huge city blocks. They built sturdy houses and planted dozens of trees. Young's home still stands a block away from Temple Square, where the Salt Lake LDS Temple, closed to non-Mormons, stands in gleaming granite, topped by the golden angel Moroni and situated across from the oval Mormon Tabernacle, where its renowned choir sings. For 160 years, this "Zion" has attracted thousands of converts from the Midwest, England, Scandinavia, and all over the world—Utah has the highest percentage of Native Hawaiians and Pacific Islanders outside Hawaii and Alaska. The object of religious fear and prejudice, Utah was not granted statehood until 1896, after the church had renounced polygamy. The state has grown steadily since then and remains heavily Mormon—more than 60%, far ahead of second-place Idaho at 24%. Without the Mormon migration, Utah would probably have remained as unpopulated as Nevada before it legalized gambling; Utah's landscape of sandswept vistas and saline lakes is inhospitable, if also beautiful, playing host to five major national parks (Arches, Bryce Canyon, Capitol Reef, Canyonlands and Zion).

The LDS Church accounts for only about 2 percent of Americans, but it remains distinctive in many ways. It cares deeply about its past. The church preserves America's most complete genealogical records in its Family History Library and has made them available on site and on the Internet. It works hard to spread the faith: The most recent statistics show that a record 85,150 young Mormons did missionary work in the United States and abroad—a number that jumped after the church lowered the minimum age for both men and women. (An ancillary result is that Utah has below-average rates of Army enlistment.) The missionaries' experiences give Utah the broadest inventory of people with knowledge of obscure foreign languages of any state in the union, a nice commercial advantage, and one that played a role in the National Security Agency's decision to build a $2 billion cloud-based facility in Bluffdale, south of Salt Lake City. By law, the state now prioritizes teaching languages in public schools as early as first grade.

Utah, according to Gallup, is the second most religious state in the nation, trailing only Mississippi. The church prohibits the consumption of tobacco, alcohol, coffee, and tea. (A possible side effect: Utahns buy candy at the highest rate in the United States, about 50% higher than the national average.) The church encourages hard work and large families; 31% of Utah residents in 2013 were under 18, compared to the national average of 23%. On average, Mormons are better educated, work longer hours, and earn more money. The LDS Church has no clergy, but members serve in positions for which they are chosen, conducting religious services but also keeping in touch with members and counseling them when they

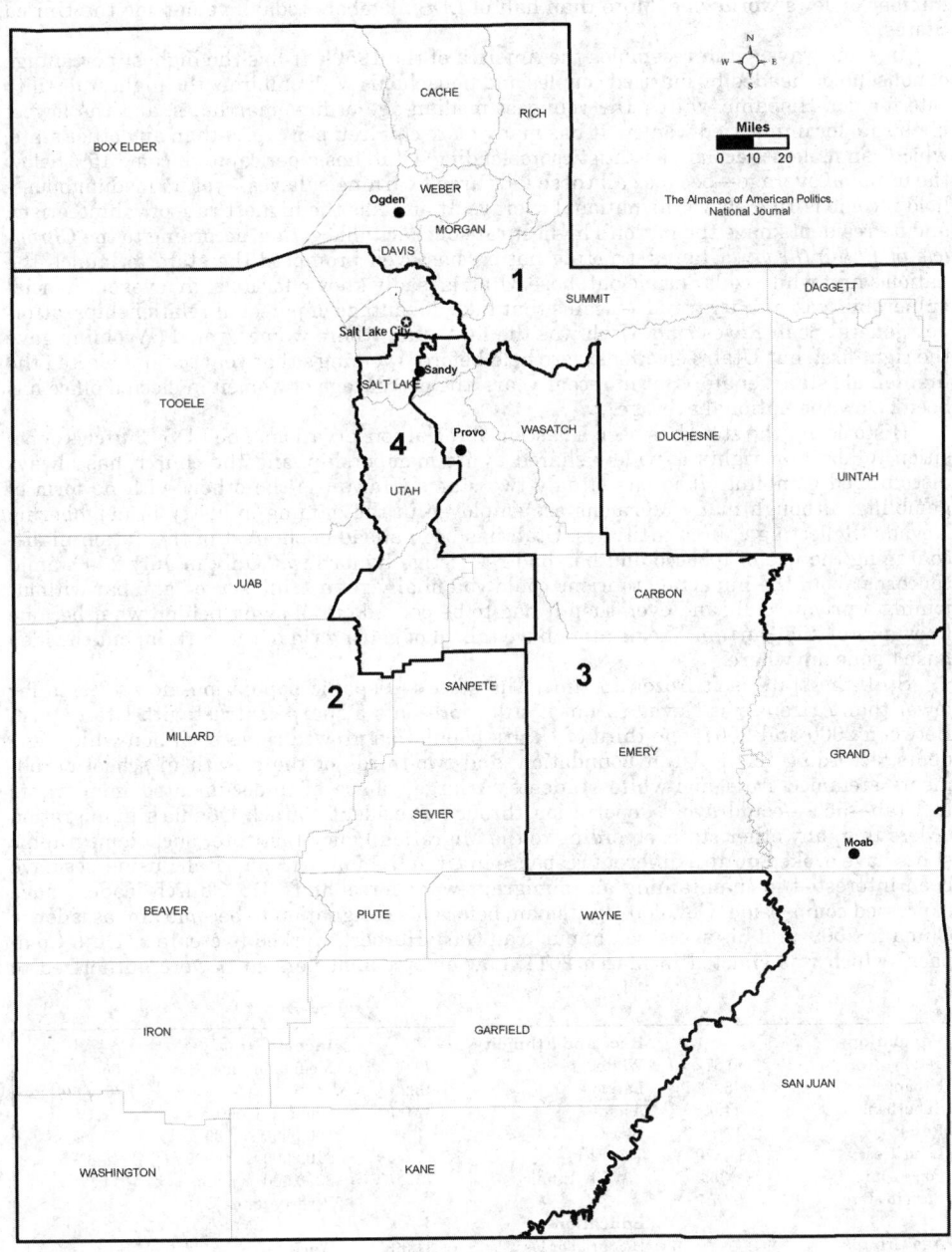

Congressional district boundaries were first effective for 2012.

need help. The church also maintains its own social-service organizations. While American mainline denominations have been losing members, the LDS Church is growing. Starting with just 30 members, the church took a century to reach 1 million. There were 2.9 million Mormons in 1970, 5 million in 1982 and 15 million today—slightly more than the estimated number of Jews worldwide. More than half of LDS members today live outside the United States.

In some ways, Utah resembles the America of the 1950s. It has the highest percentage of households headed by married couples and households with children, the highest fertility rate for non-Hispanic whites, the youngest median age of first marriages, and the lowest birth rate for unmarried women. It has many more children per capita than any other state, which can make its economic statistics misleading: Utah has a per capita income 15% below the national average—because all those kids aren't earning salaries—yet its median household income is 10% above the national average. It also has the highest rate of volunteerism, and its residents have the nation's highest rate of charitable giving, according to the *Chronicle of Philanthropy*. Utahns' trusting nature has even prompted the state to launch the nation's first white-collar-crime database. Utah is "sadly known for its high level of financial vulnerability to affinity fraud"—scams that take advantage of personal relationships, attorney general Sean Reyes said. Utah was the first state where women voted (Wyoming gave the right first, but Utah's elections were held before Wyoming's that year), and it elected the first female state senator. But in recent years, the percentage of women in elected office has been below the national average.

Historically, the state has been a bastion of social conservatism. The LDS Church's opposition to abortion rights is widely shared by its membership, and the church has always discouraged gambling. It is one of only two states (Hawaii is the other) with no form of gambling, although many Mormons are employed in the gaming industry in neighboring Nevada. Reflecting church attitudes, Utah has been ahead of the rest of the nation in discouraging the use of tobacco and has had restrictive liquor laws. Only in July 2009, amid concerns about the impact on tourism, could you finally get a drink served at a bar without joining a private club, and even then it had to be poured out of sight, behind what became known as a "Zion curtain." Legislators have talked of getting rid of the curtain, but the idea hasn't gone anywhere.

Still, the state isn't frozen in time. The state's Hispanic population, now 13%, is far lower than Arizona's or Nevada's, but it still represents a sharp contrast with Utah's past. Between 2000 and 2007, one-third of Utah's population growth came from non-white residents, according to the Utah Foundation, and two-thirds of the growth in school enrollment stemmed from non-white students. A larger share of undocumented immigrants in Utah—55%—could avoid deportation through President Barack Obama's immigration orders than any other state, according to the Migration Policy Institute. Such demographic shifts have evoked quite a different response in Utah than in Arizona. Utah businesses have been interested in maintaining an immigrant work force, and LDS Church leaders have expressed compassion. Gov. Jon Huntsman, before his resignation to become ambassador to China in 2009, and his successor, Republican Gary Herbert, worked to create a "Utah Compact," which was enacted in March 2011. Law-enforcement personnel were authorized to

Population		Race and Ethnicity		Income	
Total:	2,900,872	White	79.9%	Median income:	$62,967
Urban:	45.0%	Latino	13.2%		(6 of 50)
Suburban:	44.0%	Asian	2.0%	Under $50,000	41.1%
Rural:	11.1%	Black	1.0%	$50,000-$99,999:	36.1%
Land area:	82,170	Two races	1.8%	$100,000-$199,999:	18.8%
Pop/sq. mi.:	35.3	White Ethnic	15.2%	$200,000 or more:	4.1%
Born in state:	62.7%			Poverty Rate	9.2%
		Education			
Age Groups		H.S. grad or less:	31.3%	**Work**	
Under 18:	30.9%	Some college:	37.3%	White collar:	37.0%
18 to 34:	26.7%	College degree, 4 yr.:	20.9%	Blue collar:	42.0%
35 to 64:	32.7%	Post-grad study:	10.5%	Sales and service:	21.0%
Over 64:	9.7%			Govt. workers:	15.2%
		Military			
		Veterans/active duty:	6.4%		

check the immigration status only of those arrested for felonies or serious misdemeanors, and illegal immigrants who paid a fine of $2,500 (or $1,000 if they had only overstayed a legal visa) and passed criminal background checks could get work permits. Other provisions allowed Utahns to sponsor an immigrant and established a partnership with the Mexican state of Nuevo León to facilitate visas for workers coming to Utah.

Voter Turnout	
2013 Total Citizen 18+	1,871,465
2014 Highest Statewide Turnout	565,970
2014 Turnout as % CVAP	30.2%
2012 Turnout as % CVAP	55.6%
Legislature	
Senate:	25R 4D
House:	62R 13D

This strain of moderate, tolerant Republicanism has become evident in other areas as well. In 2015, Mormon leaders worked with lawmakers to pass a measure by overwhelming margins that banned employment and housing discrimination against members of the LGBT community while carving out protections for religious institutions that oppose homosexuality—a compromise that satisfied both the church and key gay-rights groups. The law expanded upon earlier nondiscrimination ordinances in Salt Lake City, Ogden, Park City, Moab and more than a dozen other jurisdictions. Meanwhile, the Republican establishment fought tea party influence at the state's longstanding, activist-dominated conventions. Prompted by the 2010 convention in which insurgent tea party-aligned Mike Lee won enough votes to keep incumbent Sen. Robert Bennett off the primary ballot, establishment Republicans pushed successfully to allow candidates alternate paths to the primary, a system that will take effect in 2016.

Overall, Utah has been on a growth spurt. From 2000 to 2010, the state's population rose by 24%, to nearly 2.8 million—the third-highest growth rate in the nation after Nevada and Arizona, and in the succeeding two years, its population increased by 3.3%, more than anywhere else except Washington, D.C., North Dakota, and Texas. Its economy has done well, too: Utah had a much smaller housing bubble than other states, and unemployment peaked at 8.0%, below the national average, and fell to 3.4 by mid-2015, the third-best rate in nation.

Mormons and Utahns are heavily Republican today—Utah is the most Republican state in the nation, according to Gallup, and its legislative chambers are thoroughly dominated by the GOP. But this was not always the case. In the 19th century, Republicans led the fight to keep Utah out of the union, and Democratic President Grover Cleveland signed the statehood act. Before World War II, Utah saw itself as a colonial victim of East Coast bankers and financiers, and Mormons saw themselves as suffering religious discrimination and bigotry—all with some cause. Utah's income levels were well below the national average, and its cost of living was higher. In political terms, this perspective translated into a Democratic allegiance. In 1940, Utah was represented by staunch New Dealers in Congress and voted 62%-38% for Franklin Roosevelt. Since then, Utah has come to see itself as a busy generator of wealth, with a raft of successful businesses, a knack for high-tech innovation, and longer workweeks than the rest of the nation.

In 1960, Utah voted for Richard Nixon by only 55%-45%. It voted 73%-21% for Ronald Reagan in 1980, 67%-26% for George W. Bush in 2000, and 73%-25% for Mitt Romney, America's first Mormon major-party nominee, in 2012. Utah has not voted Democratic for president since 1964, hasn't elected a Democratic governor since Scott Matheson in 1980, and hasn't sent a Democratic senator to Washington since 1970. Utah's last Democratic congressman, Scott Matheson's son Jim, retired in 2014 and was succeeded by Mia Love, a Brooklyn native of Haitian ancestry who had converted to the LDS church. She is the first African-American woman to serve as a Republican in Congress. In 2012, church members were proud that two Mormons, Romney and Huntsman, ran for president. Mormons vote at disproportionately high rates: Though they account for 60% of the population, the 2008 exit poll found that 75% of voters identified as Mormons. (There was no state exit poll four years later.)

Salt Lake City has been the state's primary pocket of liberalism. The neighborhoods close to the church headquarters, with their gracious old houses and a smaller street grid, have attracted academic and professional newcomers and so have become the most heavily "gentile" (the Mormon term for non-Mormons) part of the state. In 2004, the city voted 58% for Democratic presidential nominee John Kerry and in 2008, Salt Lake County went for Obama, albeit by only 296 votes out of 367,000 cast. Democrats that year won control of the county government and elected most of its state legislators. But Democrats won almost no legislative seats in the rest of the state. And Utah County, which takes in Provo and Brigham Young University, voted 78%-19% for John McCain in 2008 and 88%-10% for Romney in 2012. While Salt Lake County grew by 15% from 2000 to 2010, Utah County grew by 40%—and there has been even faster growth in Washington County, in the far southwest corner of the state, just northeast of Las Vegas.

Presidential Politics Utah has been the most Republican state in seven of the last 10 presidential elections. George H.W. Bush won 66% of the vote in 1988, and son George W. Bush got 67% in 2000 and 72% in 2004. In 1992, this was also the least Democratic state: Third-party candidate Ross Perot finished ahead of Bill Clinton, 27% to 25%. But in 2008, the movement toward Democrats in Salt Lake County and widespread enthusi-

2012 Presidential Vote		
Mitt Romney (R)................740,600	(73%)
Barack Obama (D) 251,813	(25%)
2012 Presidential Primary		
Mitt Romney (R)................225,428	(93%)
2008 Presidential Vote		
John McCain (R)................596,030	(63%)
Barack Obama (D) 327,670	(34%)

asm for Barack Obama left John McCain carrying the state by a reduced 63%-34%, behind his showings in Oklahoma and Wyoming. Some 600 Young Democrats campaigned for Obama at Brigham Young University, and during the primary his campaign opened an office in Washington County, a fast-growing area popular among retirees and tourists that has more than 150,000 residents. Obama's showing was the best Democratic performance since Hubert Humphrey won 37% of the vote in Utah in 1968. He carried Salt Lake County, if only by 296 votes. The exit poll showed Mormons voting 78%-19% for McCain. The trend was, unsurprisingly, reversed in 2012, when Republicans nominated Mitt Romney, a Mormon who was widely known for his work in rescuing the 2002 Salt Lake City Winter Olympics. Utah saw the biggest swing toward Romney in the nation, as he carried the state 73%-25% and Salt Lake County 58%-38%.

Utah's attempts to become a force in presidential primaries have not been successful. Republican Gov. Mike Leavitt spent much time and effort promoting a Western regional primary for the Friday following the South-dominated Super Tuesday, March 10, 2000. But only Colorado and Wyoming (with a caucus, not a primary) adopted the date and candidates paid less attention to Western issues than Leavitt had hoped. In 2004, Utah held a Democratic primary on Feb. 24, but the legislature would not pay for it, so the state Democratic Party footed the bill of $50,000. In a state of 2.3 million, 35,000 people voted and John Kerry beat John Edwards 55%-30%. For 2008, the legislature decided to hold state-financed primaries on February 5, which turned out to be Super Tuesday, when many larger states dominated the political stage. Nonetheless, Hillary Clinton and Obama ran television spots, perhaps the first Democratic presidential ads many native Utahns had ever seen. Some 131,000 Utahns voted in the Democratic primary, 57% for Obama and 39% for Clinton.

There was little suspense on the Republican side in either 2008 or 2012. In 2008, Romney won 89% of a robust turnout of 296,000. In 2012, Utah voted on June 26, when the race was long over. Romney won 93% of a turnout of 242,000. His county percentages ranged from 87% to 97%.

Congressional Districts Fast-growing Utah waited longer than expected for a fourth seat in the House. Then, Republicans had to wait another two years. For now, they appear to have a lock on all four seats. Utahns had expected that the 2000 census would boost their delegation from three to four. But under the

114th Congress Lineup	
4 R	0 D
113th Congress Lineup	
3 R	1 D

reapportionment formula, Utah fell 857 residents short of getting a new seat. After growing 24% between 2000 and 2010, Utah was a slam dunk to finally get its fourth seat in 2012. Republicans' safe play would have been to create one solid Democratic district in Salt Lake City—a "doughnut hole"—for Jim Matheson, a savvy centrist Blue Dog, and simply draw a safe new Republican seat somewhere else.

But for decades, many Utah Republicans have argued, in their party's interest, that all the state's districts should contain both urban and rural areas, splitting Salt Lake City like a "pizza pie." The doughnut versus pizza debate raged on in 2011, and at a hearing one rural voter even complained she didn't want a "pie in the face." After lengthy debate and some Republican internal bickering, the state House and Senate passed a map: The new 4th District would be a "doughnut hole," but it would consist of heavily Republican suburbs south of Salt Lake City and the northern reaches of prohibitively Republican northern Utah County.

Matheson's rejiggered 2nd District would continue to stretch to the state's southwestern corner.

Matheson calculated that although he represented only 33% of the new 4th District, it would have given Obama 41% of the vote in 2008. Meanwhile, Republicans had dropped his 2nd District from 40% pro-Obama to 38%. So, he announced he would run in the 4th. In November 2012, Republicans easily picked up the 2nd. But like Houdini, Matheson cheated Republicans' plan, prevailing by 768 votes. The feat was all the more impressive in light of his opponent, Mia Love, a black Mormon small-town mayor who gained a national following. To boot, Mitt Romney atop the ballot won 68% in the 4th. Had Republicans carved just one more Utah County precinct into the 4th, Matheson would have almost certainly lost. Still, Matheson decided that he had struggled enough, including with Democratic leaders in the House. He retired in 2014, and Love prevailed this time—though by an unexpectedly narrow margin.

Governor

Gary Herbert (R)

Assumed office Aug. 2009, term expires Jan. 2017, 1st full term; b. May 7, 1947, American Fork; Brigham Young U., attended 1968-70; Mormon; married (Jeanette); 6 children.

Military Career: UT Natl. Guard, 1970-76.

Elected Office: UT Cnty. commissioner, 1990-2004; UT lt. gov., 2005-09.

Professional Career: Realtor, Herbert & Assocs. Realtors; Co-owner, The Kids Connection, 1985-2008.

Office: 350 N. State St., Suite 200, P.O. Box 142220, Salt Lake City, 84114-2220, 801-538-1000; Fax: 801-538-1528; Website: utah.gov/governor.

Election Results

2012 general	Gary Herbert (R)	688,592	(68%)
	Peter Cooke (D)	277,622	(28%)
	Ken Larsen (Lib)	22,611	(2%)
2012 primary	Gary Herbert (R)	unopposed	

Prior winning percentage: 2010 special (64%)

Republican Gov. Gary Herbert assumed office in August 2009 following the resignation of Republican Gov. Jon Huntsman Jr., who was tapped by President Barack Obama to become U.S. ambassador to China. He was easily elected in 2010 to serve out the remainder of Huntsman's term, then won reelection comfortably on his own in 2012. Herbert has steered a relatively moderate course despite his state's overwhelmingly Republican lean, and his approval ratings have been consistently high.

Herbert was born in American Fork, where his father owned a construction company. He studied engineering and accounting at Brigham Young University but left school before graduating and established Herbert and Associates Realtors. He ran for the Orem City Council in 1989, losing the election by just 32 votes. The next year, he was elected to the Utah County Commission and served as its chairman for 13 years. During his tenure, Utah County had one of the state's lowest tax rates. He entered the 1994 race to unseat Democratic Rep. Bill Orton but dropped out after struggling to raise money. Orton went on to win reelection.

In 2003, Herbert left the Utah County Commission to run for governor. The field for the 2004 Republican primary was crowded with better known politicians, including former Rep. Jim Hansen, former Utah House Speaker Nolan Karras, and Huntsman, the son of industrialist Jon Huntsman Sr., the wealthiest man in Utah, Herbert cast himself as a "David" in a field of "Goliaths" and stressed his rural roots and ties to local government. Unable to generate enough support for his candidacy, Herbert accepted Huntsman's invitation to join his ticket as the nominee for lieutenant governor. At the time, Huntsman was perceived as lacking credibility in state politics and rural issues, two areas where Herbert was strong. The ticket won with 58% of the vote.

Under Utah's Constitution, the lieutenant governor's sole official duty is overseeing the state Elections Office, but Huntsman expanded Herbert's responsibilities to include overseeing the state's public lands policies, transportation plans, and homeland security operations. He pushed for the creation of a Public Lands Policy Coordination Office to help manage the state's role in land-management issues. In 2008, Huntsman won a second term as governor but soon handed the office over to Herbert after accepting the ambassadorship. Herbert is considered unflashy and unpretentious. "He's plainspoken," the *Salt Lake Tribune* said in endorsing him for reelection in 2012. "With Gary, what you see is what you get." Legislatively, Herbert made few changes to Huntsman's cabinet and continued a policy of opposing tax increases. He did, however, agree not to veto a bill that raised the state's cigarette tax by $1 a pack in order to reduce an education budget shortfall from $300 million to around $10 million. He also retained a four-day workweek—since repealed—that his predecessor had initiated as a way to cut costs.

Herbert was strongly favored for election in 2010 and won the GOP nomination at the state party's convention in May with 71% of the vote. He ran on his state's fiscal stability during the 2007-09 recession. His Democratic opponent was Salt Lake County Mayor Peter Corroon, a conservative who tapped Republican state Rep. Sheryl Allen as his running mate and who ran ads vowing to put "ideas ahead of ideology." The state's GOP leanings and the strong election cycle for the party enabled Herbert to easily beat Corroon, 64%-32%, carrying every county except Summit (Park City).

Early in his new term in 2011, Herbert enraged open-government advocates and the news media by signing a bill to restrict disclosure of some state information, such as text messages and instant messages. Three days later, activists filed a petition to start a referendum drive, and newspaper editorials condemned the measure. Herbert agreed to seek repeal, saying the public's response "demands us to push the reset button." The law was overwhelmingly repealed.

On immigration, Herbert signed a package of bills that authorized a guest-worker program that allowed undocumented immigrants to remain in the state if they paid fines. At the same time, it required police to check the legal status of people arrested on felony or serious misdemeanor charges; established a partnership with the Mexican state of Nuevo León to allow workers to come to Utah; and allowed Utah citizens to sponsor immigrants.

Herbert addressed another controversial issue in March 2012, when he vetoed a bill that would have allowed school districts to drop sex education and required abstinence-only instruction in those that kept it. The measure had sparked emotional protests and petition drives, and Herbert argued that it "simply goes too far by constricting parental options." His action displeased conservatives, but they were mollified when he signed another measure asking the federal government to give back more than 20 million acres of land to the state.

In running for a full four-year term of his own in 2012, Herbert drew five Republican challengers but won 58% on the first ballot at the state's GOP convention, then proceeded to trounce runner-up Morgan Philpot, a former state representative, 63%-37%. With Mitt Romney, a Mormon, on the presidential ballot, any Democrat running in 2012 faced overwhelming odds in Utah. Herbert's Democratic opponent, Peter Cooke, was a retired Army Reserve general; Herbert couldn't match Romney's 73% in Utah, but he still won, 68%-28%, carrying every county, including Summit this time by a 50%-47% margin.

After that election, Herbert—and the overwhelmingly Republican Legislature—displayed a moderate streak. He signed a bill urging treatment rather than prison for drug offenders, and he signed another to permit the use of cannabis oil as a medical treatment. He also said he was open to broader medical-marijuana legislation. He created a Clean Air Action Team to craft ideas for improving air quality along the Wasatch Front. He hiked property taxes to benefit education and raised the gasoline tax to boost transportation initiatives. He also worked with the Obama administration to propose a middle ground on the expansion of Medicaid under the Affordable Care Act, something anathema to other Republican governors.

Most strikingly, Herbert worked with leaders of the LDS church and gay-rights groups to enact a measure that simultaneously outlawed discrimination against members of the LGBT community while protecting religious freedoms. The landmark measure was seen as a compromise that might be replicated elsewhere. "I have no doubt the eyes of the nation are upon us," Herbert said at the signing ceremony. "We can do difficult things because we are determined to work together, one with another, as opposed to working against one another."

At the same time, Herbert took some stands that pleased conservatives. He signed a resolution opposing federal protections for two areas, Cedar Mesa and San Rafael Swell, and he enacted a law that allows firing squads for executions if no drugs are available for lethal injections. Herbert can run for another term in 2016, and all indications suggest he will. While he could face a primary challenge from Overstock.com chairman Jonathan Johnson, Herbert looks tough to beat—he received a 74% approval rating in a January 2015 Utah Policy survey, including 89% from Republicans.

Senior Senator

Orrin Hatch (R)

Elected 1976, term expires Jan. 2019, 7th term; b. March 22, 1934, Pittsburgh, PA; Brigham Young U., B.S. 1959, U. of Pittsburgh, J.D. 1962; Mormon; married (Elaine); 6 children.

Professional Career: Practicing atty., 1962-76.

DC Office: 104 HSOB, 20510, 202-224-5251; Fax: 202-224-6331; Website: hatch.senate.gov.

State Offices: Cedar City, 435-586-8435; Ogden, 801-625-5672; Provo, 801-375-7881; Salt Lake City, 801-524-4380; St. George, 435-634-1795.

Committees: *Aging (Special). Finance* (Chmn: ex officio member of each subcommittee). *Health, Education, Labor & Pensions:* Children & Families; Primary Health & Retirement Security. *Judiciary:* Antitrust, Competition Policy & Consumer Rights; Oversight, Federal Rights, & Agency Actions; Privacy, Technology & the Law. *Joint Committee on Taxation.*

Group Ratings

	ADA	ACLU	AFL-CIO	LCV	ITI	COC	HAFA	ACU	CFG	FRC
2014	15%	13%	–	20%	66%	100%	52%	80%	44%	79%
2013	10%	C	29%	8%	C	75%	C	75%	76%	C

National Journal Ratings

	2013 LIB	—	2013 CONS
Economic	26%	—	72%
Social	26%	—	73%
Foreign	36%	—	63%
Composite	30%	—	70%

Key Votes of the 113th Congress

1. Sandy storm spending	N	5. Student Loan Rates	Y	9. Bipartisan Budget Deal	Y
2. Chuck Hagel Confirmation	N	6. Employee Non-Discrim'n Act	Y	10. Farm Bill Conference Rept.	Y
3. Gun Background Checks	N	7. Senate Vote on Judgeships	Y	11. Unempl. Comp. Extension	N
4. Immigration Reform	Y	8. Defense Dept. Spending	N	12. Keystone Pipeline	Y

Election Results

2012 general	Orrin Hatch (R)	657,608	(65%)	$13,140,209	$475,982	$947,793
	Scott Howell (D)	301,873	(30%)	$420,779	$46,209	
	Shaun Lynn McCausland (CNP)	31,905	(3%)			
2012 primary	Orrin Hatch (R)	160,359	(66%)			
	Dan Liljenquist (R)	80,915	(34%)			

Prior winning percentages: 2006 (63%), 2000 (66%), 1994 (69%), 1988 (67%), 1982 (58%), 1976 (54%)

Republican Orrin Hatch, Utah's senior senator, first elected to the Senate in 1976, is president pro tem, his party's longest-serving member in the chamber. Like few others in Congress, he has been consistent in his inconsistency—he veers between collaborating enthusiastically with Democrats and attacking them with vigor. He tacked rightward in the face of a 2012 tea party challenge, but displayed greater bipartisanship after winning a primary to ensure reelection to what he said would be his final term. He took the coveted helm of the Finance Committee in 2015.

Hatch grew up in Pittsburgh, where his father was a metal lather. The family lost their home during the Depression, and lived for a time in a shelter made of salvaged wood and metal and without plumbing. He worked his way through Brigham Young University as a janitor and a metal lather, like his father. He went on to get a law degree from the University of Pittsburgh, and practiced law in the Steel City. He and his wife and their young family later moved to Salt Lake City, and the newly-minted lawyer got interested in politics. In 1976, he ran for the U.S. Senate. An endorsement from Republican presidential candidate Ronald Reagan helped him get attention, and he won the GOP nomination. In the general election, he upset three-term Democrat Frank Moss, defeating him, 54%-45%. His toughest reelection fight came in 1982, when he was opposed by Democratic Salt Lake City Mayor Ted Wilson. Hatch won 58% to 41%.

Hatch is second overall in Senate seniority to Vermont Democrat Patrick Leahy. His ascension to the pro-tem position (technically third in line in presidential succession) earned him a $19,400 raise as well as a security detail. His Senate career has been shaped by two impulses that are sometimes at odds with each other: a strong conservative philosophy and a sense of responsibility to pass meaningful legislation. As the new Finance chairman and a tough critic of the Affordable Care Act, Hatch said one of his top priorities was the repeal of the tax on the sale of medical devices in the law. The courtly senator also took a leadership role on trade, another area in which he has reached across the aisle. He stressed the importance of trade to Utah, which had more than $12 billion in exports in 2014. When the Senate, in 2015, passed legislation to renew Trade Promotion Authority, Hatch called it "perhaps the most important bill we'll pass in the Senate this year."

Another major focus for Hatch is reforming the tax code, which he said in a speech is "essential if we're going to get our economy moving again." He said any reform should promote competitiveness as well as help spur savings and investment but not, of course, raise taxes. In a swipe at President Barack Obama's call to raise taxes on the wealthy, Hatch said that any attempt to use reform as a way to raise taxes on businesses or individuals was "a needless distraction."

When Obama took office in 2009, Hatch expressed a willingness to work with his long-time friend, the seriously-ailing liberal Massachusetts Democrat Edward Kennedy, on comprehensive health care legislation. But even before Kennedy's death in August of that year, Hatch was assailing the measure as big-government overreach. In January 2011, he became the ranking Republican on Finance and took the lead on his party's efforts to repeal the law, sponsoring bills to end both the individual mandate and the employer mandate.

In March, he was one of just nine senators to oppose a fiscal 2011 budget deal that staved off a government shutdown, arguing that it did not cut spending enough. He also called on the Treasury Department to delay implementation of the Dodd-Frank financial services overhaul law. Even though he had voted to confirm Elena Kagan as solicitor general, Hatch opposed her nomination to the Supreme Court in 2010 because, he contended, she "embraces an essentially activist view of judicial power."

Hatch's strong endorsement of conservative positions was an acknowledgment that he had received the message Utah Republicans delivered in 2010, when they dumped three-term Sen. Robert Bennett at the state party nominating convention after he backed the controversial bank bailout legislation as well as the $787 billion stimulus bill favored by Obama. Bennett's perceived apostasy paved the way for conservative Republican Mike Lee to defeat him. With an eye toward the 2012 state party convention, Hatch told a conference of conservatives in Washington in February 2011 that he was so much a deficit hawk that, "I'm prepared to be the most hated man in this Godforsaken city in order to save this country."

Hatch had some vulnerabilities, as the hard-charging conservative activists who dominate the state's nominating convention, knew that he, like Bennett, backed the Wall Street bailout measure and that he has a long history of working across the aisle. So Hatch went into overdrive to emphasize his strong conservative credentials. He may not have been the most hated, but for those two years Hatch was among the most conservative. He cosponsored legislation forcing government-sponsored mortgage giants Fannie Mae and Freddie Mac, both tea party targets, into gradual privatization. At a Finance hearing on oil prices, he made his feelings clear about the event's importance by unveiling a portrait of a dog sitting on a pony.

Hatch scoffed at the idea that he was operating any differently. "The fact of the matter is, I've been a tea party person, I think, since before the tea party came into existence," he told Fox News in August. But given his past work with Democrats, especially Kennedy, that notion was a hard sell. Even his Utah colleague, Lee, declined to endorse him, putting a strain on their relationship. Hatch's shift to the right was reflected in his rating boost from the anti-tax Club for Growth. His rating had been 75 percent during his career through 2010, but it jumped to 99 percent in 2011. In addition, the senator's rhetoric took a noticeably sharper bite. He told Fox News that Obama was a "scaredy cat hiding in some closet in the White House" for not moving faster on the Keystone XL pipeline, designed to bring Canadian oil to U.S. refineries.

Throughout this time, Hatch energetically courted tea party support. But by early 2012, FreedomWorks, one of the largest of the movement's groups and one that has a close relationship with Lee, had raised more than $615,000 to try to oust him. Hatch responded by calling FreedomWorks "the sleaziest bunch I've ever seen in my life." But the group's favored challenger, Rep. Jason Chaffetz, declined to take on Hatch. At the April 2012 convention, Hatch fell just short—with 59.19 percent of the vote during the second round of balloting— to attain the 60 percent threshold to avoid a primary in June. His primary opponent, Dan Liljenquist, a former state senator, accused Hatch of "fiscal child abuse" for repeatedly voting to raise the nation's debt limit. But Liljenquist lacked Chaffetz's star quality with the tea party faithful, and Hatch sailed to a 66% to 34% victory, winning every county and racking up a 2-to-1 margin in populous Salt Lake County. That lopsided win sealed his status in the general election. He beat Democrat Scott Howell, 65% to 30%, with three minor-party candidates splitting the remainder.

After the primary, Hatch showed signs of his former aisle-crossing self. He worked with Finance Committee Chairman Max Baucus of Montana on a bill containing tax breaks for a range of businesses and industries. Five of the committee's 11 Republicans voted against the measure. He was the only member of Utah's delegation to support the tax and spending compromise aimed at avoiding a so-called "fiscal cliff" in early 2013. And he joined a bipartisan group of senators in January 2013 on a bill to nearly double the number of visas available to highly skilled foreign workers. His Club for Growth score for 2013 dipped to 76 percent or roughly the middle of the pack in the Senate.

In October 2013, Hatch was secure enough politically to warn, on MSNBC, that the conservative Heritage Foundation think tank was "in danger of losing its clout and its power" because it had lurched so far rightward. He also had some unsolicited advice for Lee in a radio station interview with KSL in Salt Lake City in 2014, after some Republicans criticized the junior Utah senator, one of the architects of the government shutdown in 2013: "You can't be devoted to just one strain of the Republican Party without making sure you represent everybody, and I think that's where some of this resentment comes." Meanwhile, he declined to endorse Lee's reelection, taking a page from Lee's failure to endorse him as the tea party made him a target in 2012.

In an earlier radio interview with that station in 2014, Hatch also sounded a more pragmatic note than Lee about same sex marriage despite the fact that he, personally, opposed such unions. He predicted that same sex marriages inevitably would become legal, as the Supreme Court would approve it at some point. Lee, by contrast, on the same radio show, did not think such a ruling was inevitable and said that it's wrong for judges to make that call because the decision should rest with the people of the states. When Hatch proved to be prescient and the court, in June 2015, legalized same-sex marriage, Hatch stressed, again, his personal view that marriage should be between a man and a woman. He vowed to "ensure that this decision does not infringe" on "our fundamental right to the free exercise of religion." To that end, Hatch also co-sponsored Lee's bill to prohibit any federal agency from denying a tax exemption or grant a license to an individual or association that believes marriage is a union between a man and a woman.

At the same time, to counter Democrats' criticism that the GOP had no alternative to the Affordable Care Act, Hatch unveiled a proposal in 2014 with Republican Sens. Richard Burr of North Carolina and Tom Coburn of Oklahoma. The bill retained many of the most popular elements of the law but repealed the mandate that Americans obtain insurance or pay a penalty. It also would only guarantee coverage for people with pre-existing medical conditions if they maintained "continuous coverage." The idea drew widespread attention but failed to gain much political traction.

Over many years prior to his primary battle in 2012, Hatch regularly had taken similar surprising and bipartisan positions. In 1997, he joined Kennedy in sponsoring a $24 billion program to get states to provide health insurance for children of low-income working parents who don't qualify for Medicaid. Hatch, however, voted against reauthorizing the State Children's Health Insurance Program in 2009, saying Democrats improperly modified it. In 2004, he gained wide bipartisan support for setting up a trust fund to handle asbestos cases, and two years later, the Senate passed a measure Hatch sponsored with Illinois Democrat Dick Durbin that toughened federal regulation of dietary supplements and over-the-counter drugs. Hatch has expressed doubts about the use of mandatory minimum sentences in some drug cases. And with then-Senator Barack Obama of Illinois, he got a provision in a tax bill to bar bankruptcy courts from preventing the carrying out of charitable and tithing pledges. The title of his 2002 autobiography—*Square Peg*—neatly summed up his idiosyncratic political style.

Yet Hatch also aggressively defends traditional Republican positions, sponsoring bills to restrict class action lawsuits and to set limits on medical malpractice cases. As the ranking minority member of the Judiciary Committee from June 2001 to January 2003, Hatch defended the Bush Justice Department and judicial nominees against Democrats' attacks. He also took them to task for refusing to hold hearings on many nominees. Hatch has opposed federal gun control measures, and in 2003 sponsored a bill to make it easier to carry handguns in the District of Columbia.

Another of Hatch's preoccupations is protecting intellectual property in the face of technological advance. He supported the Digital Millennium Copyright Act of 1998 banning unlawful downloading of copyrighted music and movies, and he backed the record industry against the threat raised by Napster. In 2004, the Senate passed his bill, co-sponsored with Leahy, to authorize the Justice Department to bring civil lawsuits as well as criminal actions for illegal downloading.

Hatch's interest in these issues is not just theoretical. He has long written poetry and hundreds of songs, some of which have been recorded by a Utah firm, including a 13-song album of Christmas music. Some of his songs have been recorded by singer Gladys Knight, a convert to the Mormon Church. His music has earned praise from Bono, the lead singer of the popular and politically-oriented rock band U2. In 2003, the two men met to discuss the AIDS crisis in Africa, and the singer suggested for Hatch the stage name "Johnny Trapdoor." One of his songs, "Souls Along the Way," was written for his friend Kennedy and was used in the movie *Ocean's 12*. In 2009, he even wrote a Jewish holiday tune called "Eight Days of Hanukkah."

On the Judiciary Committee, Hatch has fought abortion rights legislation and a civil rights bill that produced racial quotas and preferences. In earlier major battles over Supreme Court nominees, he staunchly defended conservatives Robert Bork and Clarence Thomas. In 1995, when Hatch became chairman of the committee, he worked on limiting tort liability and regulatory law and managed the balanced budget amendment proposal to one-vote defeats in 1995 and 1997. He also helped draft the 2001 USA Patriot Act, the Bush administration's centerpiece anti-terrorism law, and in 2004 defended it against attempts to eliminate some of its main provisions. During negotiations to reauthorize the Foreign Intelligence Surveillance Act, Hatch supported a provision to grant retroactive immunity to phone companies that had participated in the administration's warrantless wiretapping program. Hatch described the phone companies as "patriotic" in a speech on the Senate floor. The FISA reauthorization passed the Senate in 2008 with retroactive immunity for the companies.

Every senator, it sometimes seems, feels compelled to run for president, and that time came for Hatch with the 2000 election. He argued that he had more experience in federal office than the other candidates and that he was not "beholden to the Republican establishment." In the Iowa caucuses in January 2000, he won only 1 percent of the vote, even fewer than Republican John McCain, who did not campaign in the state. Two days later, he withdrew from the race and endorsed George W. Bush. In the 2008 presidential primaries, Hatch endorsed fellow Mormon Mitt Romney of Massachusetts. But after Romney dropped out, Hatch endorsed his colleague McCain and wrote a patriotic campaign song for him called "Together Forever."

In 2000, Hatch easily defeated former state senator Scott Howell, 66% to 31% (Howell would challenge him again 12 years later), and he became the first Utahn popularly elected five times to the Senate. The only other five-term senator in Utah history, Reed Smoot, who served from 1903 to 1933, was elected to his first term by the legislature. In 2006, Hatch defeated Pete Ashdown, founder of a technology firm, 63% to 31% to become the longest-serving senator in Utah history. He extended that record in 2012.

Junior Senator

Mike Lee (R)

Elected 2010, term expires Jan. 2017, 1st term; b. June 4, 1971, Mesa, AZ; Brigham Young U., B.A. 1994, J.D. 1997; Mormon; married (Sharon); 3 children.

Professional Career: Law clerk, Judge Samuel Alito, U.S. Court of Appeals, 3rd Circuit, 1998-99; Practicing atty., 1999-2002; Asst. U.S. atty., 2002-05; Gen. counsel, Gov. Jon Huntsman, 2005-06; Law clerk, Supreme Court Justice Samuel Alito, 2006-07; Practicing atty., 2007-10.

DC Office: 316A RSOB, 20510, 202-224-5444; Fax: 202-228-1168; Website: lee.senate.gov.

State Offices: Ogden, 801-392-9633; Salt Lake City, 801-524-5933; St. George, 435-628-5514.

Committees: *Armed Services:* Airland; Readiness & Management Support; Strategic Forces. *Energy & Natural Resources:* National Parks; Public Lands, Forests, & Mining; Water & Power (Chmn). *Judiciary:* Antitrust, Competition Policy & Consumer Rights (Chmn); Immigration & the National Interest; Oversight, Agency Action, Federal Rights & Federal Courts; Privacy, Technology & the Law. *Joint Economic Committee.*

Group Ratings

	ADA	ACLU	AFL-CIO	LCV	ITI	COC	HAFA	ACU	CFG	FRC
2014	10%	13%	–	20%	33%	71%	97%	100%	97%	93%
2013	0%	C	0%	0%	C	75%	C	100%	100%	C

National Journal Ratings

	2013 LIB	—	2013 CONS
Economic	0%	—	95%
Social	23%	—	75%
Foreign	0%	—	98%
Composite	9%	—	91%

Key Votes of the 113th Congress

1. Sandy storm spending	N	5. Student Loan Rates	N	9. Bipartisan Budget Deal	N
2. Chuck Hagel Confirmation	N	6. Employee Non-Discrim'n Act	N	10. Farm Bill Conference Rept.	N
3. Gun Background Checks	N	7. Senate Vote on Judgeships	Y	11. Unempl. Comp. Extension	N
4. Immigration Reform	N	8. Defense Dept. Spending	N	12. Keystone Pipeline	Y

Election Results

2010 general	Mike Lee (R)	390,179	(62%)	$1,676,351	$138,218
	Sam Granato (D)	207,685	(33%)	$290,629	$46,822
	Scott Bradley (CNP)	35,937	(6%)		
2010 primary	Mike Lee (R)	98,512	(51%)		
	Tim Bridgewater (R)	93,905	(49%)		

Utah's junior senator is Republican Mike Lee, who toppled 18-year Senate veteran Robert Bennett at the state GOP convention in 2010 and went on to win the seat in the general election. Though low-key and outwardly unassuming, Lee has strong convictions, especially an abiding interest in spreading his tea party-influenced views. He was called "the next Jim DeMint" even before the South Carolina conservative's 2013 departure from the Senate.

Lee grew up in Provo, where his father, Rex Lee, was the founding dean of Brigham Young University law school. He also lived part of the time in McLean Virginia, when Rex Lee was an assistant attorney general from 1975 to 1976 and solicitor general from 1981 to 1985. Senate Democratic Leader Harry Reid of Nevada, then a House member, was his Mormon (Church of Jesus Christ of Latter-day Saints) "home teacher," and he was schoolmates with children of Republican Sen. Strom Thurmond of South Carolina and Democratic Rep. Dick Gephardt of Missouri. As a teenager, Lee remembers watching his father argue cases before the Supreme Court. "It took me a while before I realized it wasn't entirely an ordinary experience to get to do that frequently," he recalled.

Lee returned to Provo at age 14, and later entered Brigham Young University, where he ran for student body president on a platform that the university should end the practice of vetting candidates for student government. "There were a number of people who called me a radical because of that. It's hardly radical to say students ought to be able to conduct their own elections," he said. He graduated from college and law school at Brigham Young, and then served as a law clerk to District Judge Dee Benson in Utah and Third Circuit Court of Appeals Judge Samuel Alito in New Jersey. He went on to practice law in Washington D.C. and Utah. In 2005, he was appointed legal counsel to Republican Gov. Jon Huntsman, and in 2006, after Alito was appointed to the United States Supreme Court, Lee returned to Washington to clerk for him once again.

Lee had joined a Utah law firm by the time the 2010 election rolled around. He said he decided to challenge Bennett after Congress passed the $700 billion bailout of the financial industry and the $787 billion stimulus bill that President Barack Obama sought. "The Republican Party had in so many ways deviated from what it professes," Lee said. Bennett was in his third term and regarded as a solid conservative. But he had voted for the Troubled Asset Relief Program for the financial industry, and he also had been a chief supporter of a bipartisan approach to health care legislation with Oregon Democrat Ron Wyden.

Bennett was endorsed by soon-to-be presidential nominee Mitt Romney and fellow Utah GOP Senator Orrin Hatch. But to get on the primary ballot, he had to finish first or second at the Utah Republican convention in May 2010. In the meantime, Lee had caught the fancy of tea party activists, who were beginning to make inroads with their attacks on government spending and the expanded reach of government into the health care system. He was endorsed by DeMint, who was trying to influence the selection of a more conservative crop of GOP candidates in 2010.

At the convention, involving roughly 3,500 delegates from around the state, Bennett survived a first round of balloting despite being pilloried for backing the TARP, which was decried as a bank bailout, and for working on bipartisan health care legislation. He also was hammered for being a member of the Appropriations Committee at a time when the government debt kept growing. Given those difficult atmospherics, Bennett was swept out in the second round in which business consultant Tim Bridgewater came in first with 37 percent, and Lee was second, with 35 percent of the delegates. Bennett finished third with 27 percent.

The outcome ended Bennett's 18-year Senate career. In a third round of voting, neither Lee nor Bridgewater reached the 60 percent threshold to win outright, and, as a result, the contest went to a primary election. Bennett endorsed Bridgewater in his one-on-one matchup with Lee. But Lee prevailed, 51%-49%. Of the state's two most populous counties, Bridgewater carried Salt Lake County, where relatively less-conservative voters live, but Lee won in Utah County. The general election was anticlimactic in this heavily Republican state. Lee easily defeated Democrat Sam Granato, 62%-33%.

At age 38, Lee was the youngest senator when he took office in January 2011. One of his first moves was to introduce a bill for a balanced budget amendment that would require a two-thirds vote of both houses of Congress to override the limitation on spending. It did not go far in the Democratic-controlled Senate. Lee got some notice when he was one of the few Republicans to vote against extending the USA Patriot Act after expressing concern that it did not sufficiently protect civil liberties and privacy.

In 2011, Lee penned a book titled *The Freedom Agenda: Why a Balanced Budget Amendment is Necessary to Restore Constitutional Government*. During the standoff over raising the debt limit in the summer of 2011, he tried to push the balanced budget amendment as part of any deal. But the Senate eventually approved a plan with more modest deficit reduction. Lee voted against it. In December 2011, he and fellow Utahn Orrin Hatch offered a balanced budget amendment that was rejected, 47-53. In May 2012, Lee offered a proposal to balance the budget in five years, implement a flat tax, and reform health care coverage. The Senate also rejected it, 17-82. After Hurricane Sandy, Lee offered another amendment in January 2013 to cut federal programs across the board by a half of a percentage point through 2021 as a way to prevent disaster aid from raising the debt; it failed 35-62.

Lee also jumped into the fray on judicial nominations. Outraged over President Obama's recess appointments, he voted, from his seat on the Judiciary Committee, against Utah lawyer Robert Shelby for a federal judgeship in April 2012. He made it clear that he supported Shelby, but voted "no" as a protest against the recess appointments.

Lee's effort underscored his willingness to press a fight for a principle, which, in this case, was what he saw as an unconstitutional power grab by the Executive Branch. His persistence was rewarded when the Supreme Court ruled unanimously in 2014 that such recess appointments were unconstitutional if made when the Senate says that it is in session.

Lee's tenacity would also be evident in his battle to dismantle the Affordable Care Act. During the initial legal challenge to the law, Lee was quite visible as the lawsuit wended its way to the Supreme Court. He put out three *YouTube* videos related to the high court and health care, but the Court, in 2012, upheld the law's requirement that individuals must carry health insurance or face a penalty as part of the government's tax authority.

That setback did not stop Lee from continuing his efforts to target the law. He emerged as a leader, along with his friend and ally, Republican Senator Ted Cruz of Texas, in formulating the strategy to defund what came to be derided as Obamacare. That approach eventually led to a government shutdown, much to the consternation of his party's leaders. So when the 16-day shutdown ended without having made a dent in Obamacare, Lee faced a great deal of unhappiness in the Senate from fellow Republicans, as Democrats looked to make political hay from the unpopular maneuver. Lee also suffered back home, where the federal government is the largest employer. Between shutting down national parks and furloughing federal workers, Utah took a hit, and Lee's poll numbers sagged.

But that downturn has proved to be temporary as Lee has rebounded by reaching out to reassure the business community and explain his relentless push for smaller and less meddlesome government. He also has the strong backing of a number of aggressive, well-funded conservative groups that are poised to spend lavishly to help him fend off would-be GOP primary challengers.

Lee also roiled the clubby Senate when he declined to endorse his colleague, Hatch, in 2012 when the long-time incumbent was facing the fight of his political life from tea party-backed challengers. Hatch survived to win a seventh term, but Lee's stance strained the relationship between the two Republican senators.

Lee does not shy from shaking up his party's establishment and has continued to press some controversial stances. With other conservative Republicans, he co-sponsored a bill declaring that the 14th Amendment's birthright citizenship is limited to children of citizens, legal residents, and members of the military, and does not extend to illegal immigrants. But he also pushed for loosening some immigration restrictions. He crossed party lines in an unusual alliance with New York Democratic Senator Charles Schumer to advance a visa reform bill that included helping foreigners who have invested at least $500,000 in a house in the United States. At Schumer's behest, Lee took part in bipartisan talks on a comprehensive immigration reform bill in late 2012 and early 2013, but backed out and refused to sign the group's draft giving immigrants a path to legal citizenship. "Reforms to our complex and dysfunctional immigration system should not in any way favor those who came here illegally over the millions of applicants who seek to come here lawfully," he said.

On foreign policy, Lee has been less hawkish than some other conservatives. In a Senate Foreign Relations Committee vote in June 2011, Lee opposed a congressional resolution authorizing U.S. military involvement in Libya. He was the first GOP senator to join his Kentucky colleague Rand Paul during Paul's 13-hour filibuster in March 2013 that protested the Obama administration's potential use of unmanned drones to attack U.S. citizens.

His ideological kinship with Paul and Cruz, another tea party favorite, also came to the fore when they said they would filibuster any attempt to bring gun-control legislation to the floor. Lee continues to cause some upset with Republican Senate leaders. During the high-stakes fight for trade legislation, the Trans-Pacific Partnership, the junior Utah senator was the subject of a *Politico* story that reported that he had blindsided his party leaders by failing to show up on a critical vote. GOP lawmakers, in an unusual alliance with President Obama, worked assiduously to secure Trade Promotion Authority. Though Lee had stated he backed the effort, he stayed in Utah when the vote was called, because, his office said, he had a family commitment to be with his sons who had just completed their Mormon missions. Though the measure narrowly passed, Lee's absence did not endear him to the GOP Senate leaders, who had counted on his vote.

Like DeMint, Lee has worked hard to elect other tea party-backed candidates. In 2012, he formed a political action committee to support like-minded conservative candidates and also produced a policy blueprint for them to use on the trail. Lee has traveled across the country to campaign with such candidates who are involved in tough party primaries. Whether his independence from the party establishment and his continued alliance with Cruz would draw Republican opposition in Utah or affect his reelection in 2016 remained a mystery during the summer of 2015.

FIRST DISTRICT

Rob Bishop (R)

Elected 2002, 7th term; b. July 13, 1951, Kaysville; U. of UT, B.A. 1974; Mormon; married (Jeralyn Hansen); 5 children.

Elected Office: UT House, 1978-94, speaker 1993-94.

Professional Career: H.S. teacher, 1974-2002; Chair, UT Rep. Party, 1997-2001.

DC Office: 123 CHOB, 20515, 202-225-0453; Fax: 202-225-5857; Website: robbishop.house.gov.

State Offices: Brigham City, 435-734-2270; Ogden, 801-625-0107.

Committees: *Armed Services:* Readiness; Strategic Forces. *Natural Resources* (Chmn: ex officio member of each subcommittee).

Group Ratings

	ADA	ACLU	AFL-CIO	LCV	ITI	COC	HAFA	ACU	CFG	FRC
2014	0%	5%	–	0%	60%	85%	70%	83%	77%	88%
2013	5%	C	24%	4%	C	69%	C	80%	72%	C

National Journal Ratings

	2013 LIB	—	2013 CONS
Economic	26%	—	74%
Social	13%	—	84%
Foreign	0%	—	95%
Composite	14%	—	86%

Key Votes of the 113th Congress

1. Sandy storm spending	N	5. Medical Marijuana		9. Syrian Rebels Training	Y
2. Violence Against Women Act	N	6. Farm Bill	Y	10. Keystone pipeline	Y
3. Guantanamo Bay Detainees	N	7. Afghanistan Combat	N	11. Immigration Exec. Action	NV
4. Abortion 20-week ban	Y	8. NSA Phone Data Collection	Y	12. Bipartisan budget deal	Y

Election Results

2014 general	Rob Bishop (R)	70,240	(64%)	$525,675	$13,600
	Donna McAleer (D)	31,668	(29%)	$268,196	
	Craig Bowden (Lib)	3,941	(4%)	$4,269	
	Dwayne Vance (IAP)	3,538	(3%)		
2014 primary	Rob Bishop (R)	unopposed			

Prior winning percentages: 2012 (71%), 2010 (69%), 2008 (65%), 2006 (63%), 2004 (68%), 2002 (61%)

Population		Race and Ethnicity		Income	
Total:	720,959	White	83.2%	Median income:	$59,760
Urban:	48.4%	Latino	11.5%		(129 of 435)
Suburban:	33.1%	Asian	1.2%	Under $50,000	40.5%
Rural:	18.5%	Black	1.0%	$50,000-$99,999:	37.8%
Land area:	13,361	Two races	2.0%	$100,000-$199,999:	18.3%
Pop/sq. mi.:	54.0	White Ethnic	13.5%	$200,000 or more:	3.4%
Born in state:	65.3%			Poverty Rate	11.2%
		Education			
Age Groups		H.S. grad or less:	33.5%	**Work**	
Under 18:	31.7%	Some college:	37.7%	White collar:	35.7%
18 to 34:	25.8%	College degree, 4 yr.:	20.0%	Blue collar:	39.5%
35 to 64:	33.3%	Post-grad study:	8.8%	Sales and service:	24.8%
Over 64:	9.2%			Govt. workers:	19.1%
		Military			
		Veterans/active duty:	8.8%		

Northern Utah: Ogden, Logan

In May 1869, a motley crowd of Irish and Chinese laborers, teamsters, engineers, train crews, officials, and guests from Salt Lake City gathered at Promontory Summit, Utah, to watch the opening of the transcontinental railroad. Leland Stanford's blow with a silver sledge, intended to drive the ceremonial "Last Spike" into the railroad ties, missed its mark, but in that kinder, gentler media age, telegraphs nevertheless conveyed the word "done" across the nation. It wasn't just the railroad that was complete. As long as America had been America, there had been a

Voter Turnout	
2013 Total Citizen 18+	472,517
2014 House Turnout	130,341
2014 Turnout as % CVAP	27.6%
2012 Turnout as % CVAP	54.5%

frontier, but as the civilized East and the mostly untamed West were finally united, that frontier began to shrink and then vanish.

Ogden, Utah, is in many ways a microcosm of the impact the railway could have. At the time the railroad was completed, it was a small farming community of 1,500 inhabitants. Had it not won the right to become the junction of the Union Pacific and Central Pacific railroads—which meant that all of the passengers and shipping crossing the nation changed trains in Ogden—it might have suffered the same fate as Corinne, the nearby town that lost out to Ogden in the competition for the junction and today has a population of 688. The city adopted the motto, "You

2012 Presidential Vote		
Mitt Romney (R)................193,672	(78%)
Barack Obama (D) 51,098	(20%)
2008 Presidential Vote		
John McCain (R)................160,063	(67%)
Barack Obama (D) 70,257	(30%)
Cook Partisan Voting Index: R+27		

can't get anywhere without coming to Ogden!" Today, with a population approaching 84,000, Ogden has developed as a hub for outdoor sports equipment makers. Amer Sports, founded in Finland and with operations in 34 nations, has consolidated its North American operations in Ogden; it owns Wilson, Atomic and other brands. As a manufacturing center for bicycles, it has become known as "biketown." Like other cities in Utah, Ogden has become a center for high-tech jobs. In May 2015, the Ogden-Clearfield unemployment rate was just 3.6 percent.

The 1st Congressional District of Utah takes in Ogden and areas to the north of Salt Lake City. While its land area sprawls from the Colorado border to Idaho, about two thirds of its residents live in the stretch north of Salt Lake City from Kaysville to Brigham City. Hill Air Force Base, which houses the new F-35 fighter jets, is in the district, as is Utah State University, farther north in Logan. The Great Salt Lake, which is the largest water mass west of the Mississippi River and much of which is in this district, was at record lows in early 2015. Much of the district is farm country and heavily Mormon. An exception is Park City, in the mountains east of Salt Lake City, which is a fashionable ski resort and home of actor Robert Redford's annual Sundance Film Festival, which infuses about $80 million annually to the Utah economy. In January 2015, the event attracted more than 30,000 visitors, including 1,100 journalists. But very few of them vote in this area. Overall, the 1st is among the top 10 most heavily Republican districts in the nation and gave Mitt Romney 78 percent of the vote in 2012.

Rob Bishop (R)

Rob Bishop, a Republican first elected in 2002, is a leading advocate of states' rights and a sharp critic of federal management of public lands, both hot-button issues in the rural West. With Jason Chaffetz, he was one of two Utah Republicans in the House who became "Mr. Chairman" in 2015. An ally of Speaker John Boehner and known for his sarcastic wit, Bishop took over as chairman of the Natural Resources Committee.

Bishop grew up in Davis County and graduated from the University of Utah. He became a high school history and government teacher in Box Elder County. (He remains fond of giving guided historical tours of the Capitol. In one, videotaped for *The Salt Lake Tribune*'s website, he pointed out religious-themed paintings displayed in the Rotunda and quipped, "So much for the separation of church and state.") In 1978, at age 27, he was elected to the state House. In 1993 and 1994, he was House speaker. He continued working as a teacher after leaving the legislature, and also worked as a lobbyist for state Republicans and for the National Rifle Association.

When the House seat became open, both Bishop and former House Majority Leader Kevin Garn ran. As a former state party chair for four years, Bishop won 58% of the vote at the Republican nominating convention. With mostly similar conservative views, their chief difference was a contentious issue in Utah: the ongoing battle between banks and credit unions. The credit union lobby endorsed Bishop who, as a lobbyist in 1999, helped defeat legislation to curtail the credit unions' tax-exempt status. Bishop won the primary 60%-40%.

Democrats believed they had a chance in the general election with nominee Dave Thomas, a wealthy advertising executive and an anti-abortion rights Mormon bishop who presented himself as a fiscal conservative and "a regular guy" not tied to special interests. Bishop won more easily than expected, 61%-37%.

In the House, Bishop has been an active conservative voice. In 2009, he unsuccessfully offered a GOP resolution on the House floor calling for an investigation into Democratic Speaker Nancy Pelosi's claim that the Central Intelligence Agency misled her about the use of enhanced interrogation techniques on suspected terrorists. He started a "10th Amendment Task Force" to advocate for allowing states to assume control of federal programs, and proposed a constitutional amendment to allow any federal law or regulation to be overturned if two-thirds of states opposed it. In the Utah Legislature, "I learned to hate the federal government," he told *The Salt Lake Tribune* in May 2010. "I could point to [highway] overpasses that were made because there was a 10-to-1 [funding] match, or programs we ran simply because the government bribed us with money."

When Obama in 2013 nominated as his new Interior secretary Sally Jewell, CEO of recreational retail chain REI, Bishop contended that REI "has intimately supported several special interest groups and subsequently helped to advance their radical political agendas." Bishop's spokeswoman pointed to the company's support of the Southern Utah Wilderness Alliance and the Outdoor Industry Association. Bishop spoke more positively of Jewell two years later in an interview with *Huffington Post*, saying that she comes from the business world, not politics. "I think she's willing to explore ideas and I think she will just approach them differently than has been done in the past."

But the *Standard-Examiner* of Ogden, in endorsing him for reelection in 2014, said: "Rep. Bishop has matured. He's less of the tea party wannabe and more of a statesman willing to both listen and work hard for his constituents. ... In fact, he expressed concern to us about some of the extreme right-wing conspiracy theories that he sometimes hears at town hall meetings, particularly on immigration."

On Natural Resources, Bishop sometimes has been averse to compromise with Democrats. Soon after taking over as chairman in January 2015, he included in a border-security bill a provision to exempt from some environmental laws immigration enforcement activities within 100 miles of U.S. borders, a move that critics condemned as a ruse to bar any regulation of those lands. He introduced a similar bill that passed the House in 2012 on a nearly party-line vote but died in the Democratic-controlled Senate.

Still, Bishop has demonstrated skill at deal-making during his long legislative career. He accommodated Democrats by agreeing to their request to include climate change on the committee's agenda for 2015-16. He also has signaled that he wants to think broadly and that he sees his chairmanship "as a chance to shake up the way the United States manages federal and Indian lands, from protecting treasured areas to permitting drilling in others," the *Houston Chronicle* reported. As Bishop told the *Chronicle* in March 2015, "We haven't had a change in the way people look at the stewardship of the federal government and land in 50 or 60 years. ... We are timed for a paradigm shift, and I want to be part of that." In April 2015, he and fellow Utah Republican Rep. Chris Stewart created an informal Federal Land Action Group, with a goal of finding ways to transfer federal land to local control.

Bishop has long been highly critical of unilateral presidential attempts to designate new national monuments in the West. He told *The Washington Post* in 2012 that the Park Service, which was struggling to maintain its national parks, should stop acquiring land. "Why don't we prioritize and realize the federal government cannot print money fast enough to do everything that needs to get done?" he asked. In January 2015, after Obama proposed to set aside more than 12 million acres of the Alaska National Wildlife Refuge as wilderness, with tight restrictions on oil and gas leasing, Bishop was livid. "By tightening his grasp on these resources, the president has revealed another lack of leadership on the global stage," he wrote in a *Washington Times* op-ed. "This time, it's America's future leverage in world affairs and our nation's path to energy security that's at stake."

Bishop remains an active member of the Armed Services Committee; the military has numerous facilities in Utah. On the annual defense spending bill the House approved in May 2015, he cited his efforts to "protect the Utah Test and Training Range, Dugway Proving Ground, the Tooele Army Depot, and other lands used for military training, from intrusion by the Obama administration."

Bishop has been comfortably reelected every two years. In 2012, his Democratic rival was Donna McAleer, an Army veteran and technology executive who blamed him for contributing to Congress' gridlock. The *Tribune* called her the best-qualified candidate her party had fielded in years, but it endorsed Bishop, who won 71%-25%. In a 2014 rematch, in which McAleer spent $268,000 to his $526,000, Bishop's victory was a bit tighter at 64%-29%. Short of serious wrongdoing, he seems secure in this district.

SECOND DISTRICT

Chris Stewart (R)

Elected 2012, 2nd term; b. July 15, 1960, Logan; UT St. U., B.S. 1984; Mormon; married (Evie); 6 children.

Military Career: U.S. Air Force, 1984-98.

Professional Career: Owner, Shipley Group, 2000-present.

DC Office: 323 CHOB, 20515, 202-225-9730; Website: stewart.house.gov.

State Offices: Salt Lake City, 801-364-5550; St. George, 435-627-1500.

Committees: *Appropriations:* Homeland Security; Interior, Environment & Related Agencies; State, Foreign Operations & Related Programs. *Intelligence (Select):* Department of Defense Intelligence & Overhead Architecture; Emerging Threats.

Group Ratings

	ADA	ACLU	AFL-CIO	LCV	ITI	COC	HAFA	ACU	CFG	FRC
2014	5%	0%	–	6%	100%	85%	64%	72%	69%	88%
2013	5%	C	14%	4%	C	85%	C	80%	79%	C

National Journal Ratings

	2013 LIB	—	2013 CONS
Economic	24%	—	75%
Social	16%	—	74%
Foreign	15%	—	77%
Composite	22%	—	79%

Key Votes of the 113th Congress

1. Sandy storm spending	N	5. Medical Marijuana	Y	9. Syrian Rebels Training	Y
2. Violence Against Women Act	N	6. Farm Bill	Y	10. Keystone pipeline	Y
3. Guantanamo Bay Detainees	N	7. Afghanistan Combat	N	11. Immigration Exec. Action	Y
4. Abortion 20-week ban	Y	8. NSA Phone Data Collection	Y	12. Bipartisan budget deal	Y

Election Results

2014 general	Chris Stewart (R)	76,966	(60%)	$665,016
	Luz Robles (D)	42,356	(33%)	$147,222
	Shaun McCausland (CNP)	3,821	(3%)	
	Wayne Hill (IAP)	2,913	(2%)	
2014 primary	Chris Stewart (R)	unopposed		

Prior winning percentage: 2012 (62%)

Population		Race and Ethnicity		Income	
Total:	715,552	White	77.5%	Median income:	$55,107
Urban:	49.3%	Latino	14.5%		*(164 of 435)*
Suburban:	35.7%	Asian	2.2%	Under $50,000	45.1%
Rural:	15.0%	Pac. Island	1.4%	$50,000-$99,999:	34.7%
Land area:	13,231	Two races	1.8%	$100,000-$199,999:	16.2%
Pop/sq. mi.:	54.1	White Ethnic	13.8%	$200,000 or more:	4.0%
Born in state:	60.0%			Poverty Rate	14.2%
		Education:			
Age Groups:		H.S. grad or less:	33.2%	**Work:**	
Under 18:	28.5%	Some college:	34.9%	White collar:	36.2%
18 to 34:	26.4%	College degree, 4 yr.:	19.9%	Blue collar:	43.5%
35 to 64:	33.0%	Post-grad study:	12.0%	Sales and service:	20.3%
Over 64:	12.2%			Govt. workers:	16.3%
		Military			
		Veterans/active duty:	7.5%		

Salt Lake City and Western Utah

In Salt Lake City, at the center of the Mormon Church is Temple Square, illuminated by 300,000 lights during Christmas week and nestled beneath the towering mountains that flank Salt Lake City. The Mormon Tabernacle is here, home to the famous choir, as is the Salt Lake LDS Temple itself, crowned with the golden angel Moroni. The area has been the focal point of Utah since Mormon leader Brigham Young, looking down at the valley, said, "This is the place." Ironically, this part of Salt Lake City is the least Mormon and most cosmopolitan part of Utah, with the state university and businesses bringing in outsiders who, flouting Mormon strictures, keep purveyors of alcohol and caffeine in business. The state ended its private club system at bars in 2009, hoping to attract more customers and tourists. Liquor sales went up 6 percent in the year ending June 2014. The state retained prohibitions on bartenders pouring drinks in plain sight.

Voter Turnout	
2013 Total Citizen 18+	472,992
2014 House Turnout	144,695
2014 Turnout as % CVAP	30.6%
2012 Turnout as % CVAP	54.8%

The 2nd Congressional District of Utah consists of most of Salt Lake City, its northern and southwestern suburbs, and the southwestern portion of the state. In Salt Lake, which includes about one-third of the district's population, it takes in the historic downtown, its distinctive Avenues District, and the airport. The county has one Mormon chapel every 1.3 square miles, many of which are relatively small. New suburbs near Interstate 80 have made Tooele, where real estate remains affordable, one of the state's fastest growing counties. The Milken Institute, in its annual report on best-performing cities, ranked Salt Lake City sixth in 2014, with praise as "a financial hub with a highly skilled workforce." Construction began in 2014 on a new $1.8 billion terminal at the airport, which is scheduled to be completed in 2019.

Further west are the desolate Bonneville Salt Flats, where land speed records have been set. This land of stark beauty, much of it federally owned, has been used roughly by man, as a repository for hazardous wastes at civilian and military dumps in Tooele County and as a place for military experimentations at the Dugway Proving Grounds, where scientists test defenses against chemical and biological agents. In February 2015, the facility opened a new center for biological warfare readiness.

The Skull Valley Band of Goshute Indians has pressed for a temporary nuclear waste storage site, near Dugway, but it has remained on hold for years because of Utah's reluctance to take waste from other states. About 15% of the district's residents live in

2012 Presidential Vote		
Mitt Romney (R)	173,513	(68%)
Barack Obama (D)	74,556	(29%)
2008 Presidential Vote		
John McCain (R)	143,656	(59%)
Barack Obama (D)	93,415	(38%)
Cook Partisan Voting Index: R+18		

the stretch of the Wasatch Front, between the mountains and Great Salt Lake, just north of Salt Lake City, in suburban and fairly affluent Davis County. Another one-fourth live in the stretch of lightly populated counties in the southwest corner of the state, chiefly Washington County, which is the home of Zion National Park.

Politically, this is a mostly Republican area, with patches of Democratic strength, chiefly in Salt Lake County. Barack Obama carried the county by 296 votes in 2008. But the rest of the district is heavily Republican. Overall the 2nd voted 59% for Republican John McCain in 2008 and 68% for Mitt Romney, a Mormon, in 2012.

Chris Stewart (R)

Republican Chris Stewart, a former Air Force pilot and author, is a conservative who won election in 2012 in an open seat after Utah gained a House district in the 2010 reapportionment. Following impressive careers in the military and private sector, he moved quickly in the House to establish his credentials as a member of the Appropriations and Intelligence committees.

Stewart and his nine siblings grew up on a dairy farm in southern Idaho. His parents, both Mormon, had moved there from nearby Utah to start a family. Before taking up farming, Stewart's father had served in the Air Force. Stewart enrolled in Utah State University, serving as a Mormon missionary in Texas before completing a degree in economics.

As a teenager, Stewart recalls being skeptical of his father's recommendation that he enlist in the military. But after graduating from college, he entered the service. He was first in his class in both officer training school and undergraduate pilot training. In 14 years in uniform, he attained the rank of major and in 1995 set the world record for the fastest, nonstop flight around the world in a B-1 Lancer. (His crew flew nearly 23,000 miles in just over 36 hours, for an average speed of about 630 mph.) He also flew rescue helicopters. Five of Stewart's six sons have served in the military. Stewart began writing in the military, and after his discharge took it up full time to spend more time with his children. After two years, Stewart says he found himself "bored" and bought the Shipley Group, an energy and environment consulting firm that does government and corporate security work.

While he was running the business, Stewart's writing career flourished. He has written two *New York Times* best sellers, *Seven Miracles That Saved America* in 2009 and *The Miracle of Freedom* in 2011. But he says that he found more meaning in writing a six-part fiction series, *The Great and Terrible*, a religious epic about the struggle between good and evil. In 2012, Stewart, who calls talk show host Glenn Beck a friend, began collaborating with the conservative commentator to adapt *The Great and Terrible* into a 10-volume e-book series aimed at a general audience. In his writing, he favored a balanced-budget amendment, a 25 percent top marginal income-tax rate, and a dramatically reduced federal budget.

Democratic Rep. Jim Matheson's decision to run in 2012 in the newly created 4th District, which was seen as friendlier to Democrats than the redrawn 2nd District, left an open seat in the 2nd. Stewart got into the contest, emerging on top in an acrimonious GOP primary. One of the candidates, Eureka Mayor Milt Hanks, alleged just before delegates began casting ballots at the April party convention that four other contenders tried to pull him into a plan to hit Stewart with negative attacks. The other candidates angrily denied the charges and accused Stewart of starting a rumor of a conspiracy against him to attract voter sympathy. Still, Stewart prevailed with more than 60% of the vote in the only contest that really mattered in the heavily Republican district. A subsequent Utah Republican Party investigation found no evidence of plots among candidates. He had no trouble dispatching Democrat Jay Seegmiller in the general election, 62%-33%.

After the October 2013 government shutdown, which cost local governments and businesses millions of dollars, he filed a bill that would allow states to fund the operations of national parks, monuments and other facilities related to tourism and other commercial activity in the event of a future lapse of federal spending. In November 2014, he brought a bill to the House floor on which he had worked as a subcommittee chairman at the Science, Space and Technology Committee. The bill, which the House passed on a largely party-line vote, revamped the selection of members to the Environmental Protection Agency's scientific advisory board to require more representatives of state and local governments. Following the 2014 election, he wrote in an op-ed that the new Republican-controlled Congress will "move beyond partisan gridlock and reaffirm constitutionally limited government where Congress, not the president, writes law and establishes national spending priorities."

His new assignments in 2015 on the Appropriations Subcommittees on Homeland Security, plus State and Foreign Operations, in addition to the Intelligence Committee, positioned him to use his Air Force experience to oversee national security activities, including the nuclear-arms discussions with Iran. In March, he wrote in *The Wall Street Journal* that, as a B-1 pilot, he was a military representative in arms-reduction talks with the former Soviet Union. Based on that experience, he wrote, negotiating parties must be reliable partners who want an agreement to succeed. On that basis, he contended, "the record is bare" of Iran partnering with the United States or an ally "in a productive way." When the international agreement with Iran was reached in July, he said that President Barack Obama was "naïve." The deal, he added, was "an incredibly dangerous agreement and Congress must do everything in its power to stop it."

Stewart may have lost at least one conservative friend when he voted in January 2015 to give John Boehner another term as House speaker. When Stewart went on Beck's radio show to defend Boehner against attacks that he hasn't been tough enough on Obama, Beck responded, "We think you're losing your soul." But Stewart appeared to have gained a niche in the House.

THIRD DISTRICT

Jason Chaffetz (R)

Elected 2008, 4th term; b. March 26, 1967, Los Gatos, CA; Brigham Young U., B.A. 1989; Mormon; married (Julie); 3 children.

Professional Career: Spokesman & public relations, Nu Skin Intl.; Pres. Maxtera Utah; Chief of staff, Gov. Jon Huntsman, 2005-08.

DC Office: 2236 RHOB, 20515, 202-225-7751; Fax: 202-225-5629; Website: chaffetz.house.gov.

State Offices: Provo, 801-851-2500.

Committees: *Judiciary:* Courts, Intellectual Property & the Internet; Crime, Terrorism, Homeland Security & Investigations. *Oversight & Government Reform* (Chmn: ex officio member of each subcommittee).

Group Ratings

	ADA	ACLU	AFL-CIO	LCV	ITI	COC	HAFA	ACU	CFG	FRC
2014	0%	5%	–	0%	100%	85%	69%	81%	76%	85%
2013	5%	C	15%	4%	C	85%	C	84%	81%	C

National Journal Ratings

	2013 LIB	—	2013 CONS
Economic	8%	—	91%
Social	16%	—	74%
Foreign	41%	—	57%
Composite	24%	—	76%

Key Votes of the 113th Congress

1. Sandy storm spending	N	5. Medical Marijuana	NV
2. Violence Against Women Act	N	6. Farm Bill	Y
3. Guantanamo Bay Detainees	N	7. Afghanistan Combat	N
4. Abortion 20-week ban	Y	8. NSA Phone Data Collection	Y

9. Syrian Rebels Training	Y
10. Keystone pipeline	Y
11. Immigration Exec. Action	Y
12. Bipartisan budget deal	Y

Election Results

2014 general	Jason Chaffetz (R) 94,571	(72%)	$775,881
	Brian Wonnacott (D) 29,575	(23%)	$9,948
	Zack Strong (IAP) 2,930	(2%)	
2014 primary	Jason Chaffetz (R) ....unopposed		

Prior winning percentages: 2012 (77%), 2010 (72%), 2008 (66%)

Population		Race and Ethnicity		Income	
Total:	718,575	White	82.7%	Median income:	$61,875
Urban:	44.1%	Latino	10.6%		(100 of 435)
Suburban:	46.4%	Asian	1.7%	Under $50,000	40.0%
Rural:	9.5%	Amer. Indian	1.6%	$50,000-$99,999:	33.6%
Land area:	10,602	Two races	1.8%	$100,000-$199,999:	20.6%
Pop/sq. mi.:	67.8	White Ethnic	13.4%	$200,000 or more:	5.7%
Born in state:	61.2%			Poverty Rate	13.4%
		Education			
Age Groups		H.S. grad or less:	23.7%	**Work**	
Under 18:	31.5%	Some college:	37.8%	White collar:	40.8%
18 to 34:	28.4%	College degree, 4 yr.:	25.2%	Blue collar:	42.8%
35 to 64:	30.8%	Post-grad study:	13.3%	Sales and service:	16.4%
Over 64:	9.3%				
		Military		Govt. workers:	12.8%
		Veterans/active duty:	5.2%		

Central and East Utah: Provo Area, Salt Lake City Suburbs

Provo is in a geographically isolated valley between 11,000-foot peaks of the Wasatch Range and the shores of Utah Lake. It is the third-largest city in the state and home of Brigham Young University, the heart of Mormonism and an institution long known for old-fashioned moral standards and the

Voter Turnout	
2013 Total Citizen 18+	462,695
2014 House Turnout	142,580
2014 Turnout as % CVAP	30.8%
2012 Turnout as % CVAP	57%

conservative views of its faculty. Its student population in the fall of 2012 was 98.7% Mormon, and 26% were married. Not surprisingly, it is annually ranked as the most sober university in the nation. BYU also is known for its welcoming of technological innovation. The Mormon commonwealth, after all, started off with a huge shortage of both labor and water, and its inhabitants were motivated to use technology to prosper in the fearsome terrain. Provo produced Philo Farnsworth, the inventor of television, and Harvey Fletcher, inventor of the hearing aid. Today, the city is a high-technology center, the home of Novell and hundreds of other computer-related firms. Nearby Lehi is home to a large office site for the software maker Adobe, and to Micron's 735-acre business and residential development, a 25-year project that plans to create thousands of jobs that center around the use of flash memory chips. Provo is also where the vast majority of Mormon missionaries are trained; 36,000 of them annually go through Provo's Missionary Training Center, which has had the effect of producing a disproportionately high number of foreign language speakers in the area. In March 2014, a Gallup poll rated Provo the best city to live in the United States.

The 3rd Congressional District of Utah includes all or part of seven counties in central and eastern Utah. Many of them are remote, and the vast majority of the district's residents live in Utah or Salt Lake counties. The 3rd takes in affluent suburbs southeast of Salt Lake City, including Holladay, Cottonwood Heights and Draper. In Utah County, which grew by 6% from 2010 to 2013, the district takes in Provo and the

2012 Presidential Vote		
Mitt Romney (R)	208,121	(79%)
Barack Obama (D)	51,791	(20%)
2008 Presidential Vote		
John McCain (R)	168,024	(67%)
Barack Obama (D)	73,470	(29%)
Cook Partisan Voting Index: R+28		

string of towns between the mountains and Utah Lake. The area around Moab is a destination for outdoor-loving tourists. The land is mostly owned by one federal agency or another, and there have been bitter fights between locals dependent on mining and environmentalists who want to preserve the scenery, including recently discovered dinosaur tracks. The 3rd, where Mitt Romney got 79% of the vote in 2012, is the most Republican district in Utah and in the top 10 nationwide.

Jason Chaffetz (R)

Republican Jason Chaffetz, a media-savvy conservative, was elected in 2008 and had close kinship with the tea party-backed Republicans who arrived two years later. On the Oversight and Government Reform Committee, where he has been an outspoken critic of the Obama administration, he became chairman in 2015. In a notable change for the panel, Chaffetz pressed for bipartisanship and had some conflicts with conservatives.

Born in Los Gatos, California, Chaffetz grew up in Arizona. His family's politics were Democratic, and they boasted one notable link: His father's first wife, Katharine Dickson, would later enter the national consciousness as "Kitty," whose second husband was Michael Dukakis, the 1988 Democratic presidential nominee. During college, Chaffetz was named an honorary co-chairman of the Dukakis campaign in Utah in 1988.

He won an athletic scholarship to Brigham Young University, where he was the place-kicker for the football team. More significantly, he converted to Mormonism and began what he views in hindsight as a natural movement toward the political right. After college, Chaffetz worked in public relations, first as an executive for Nu Skin Enterprises, a company that sells skin care products, and then at a firm he started with his brother. In 2003, he volunteered for Republican Jon Huntsman Jr.'s gubernatorial campaign. When his campaign manager abruptly resigned, Huntsman asked Chaffetz to replace him. After the election, Chaffetz served a year as the new governor's chief of staff.

Chaffetz sensed an opportunity in early 2007 as perennial discontent with Republican Rep. Chris Cannon simmered among Utah conservatives. Chaffetz entered the race in October, at a steep disadvantage in both cash and name recognition. He criticized Cannon's support of President George W. Bush's proposal for a guest worker program and a path to citizenship for illegal immigrants, both deeply unpopular in the conservative district. He called for immediate deportation of all illegal immigrants and the construction of tent cities, ringed by barbed-wire fences, to detain those who had committed crimes while in the United States. His staunchly conservative platform played well at the state GOP convention in May, where he came 10 votes short of the 60% needed to win the nomination outright.

Bush and most of the state's Republican establishment endorsed Cannon, although Huntsman stayed neutral. Cannon attacked Chaffetz as an opportunist and raised more than $840,000. Chaffetz spent less than $200,000. In the low-turnout June contest, he stacked up big margins in the district's population centers in Salt Lake and Utah counties to win by a whopping 20 percentage points. Although Chaffetz came under fire nationally from some Japanese-American interest groups for his advocacy of tent cities, the outcome of the general election was never in doubt. Chaffetz won with 66%. He has gone unchallenged in his heavily Republican district.

In the House, Chaffetz typically votes the conservative line in accordance with his district's wishes. During the debate over raising the debt limit in the summer of 2011, Chaffetz became a chief sponsor of the "cut, cap, and balance" proposal favored by deficit hawks, which passed the House. The plan, which included a spending cap and a proposed balanced budget amendment to the Constitution, was tabled by the Senate. But he is occasionally unpredictable. He was one of 36 House Republicans who refused to back the December 2010 deal extending the Bush-era tax cuts, contending the move would only contribute to the national debt. An amendment he introduced in 2011 to slash funding for various federal research programs while zeroing out the Food for Peace program proved too much for most Republicans and was resoundingly defeated. And he incensed conservative activists in 2012 with his bill to reduce the royalty rates to musicians for online radio to the same levels paid by satellite and cable companies; they said that the government had no business setting rates for music.

In his early work on Oversight and Government Reform, Chaffetz got a bill through the House in 2009 to bar primary scanning at airports using whole body imaging machines, which he considered unnecessarily intrusive. He had a confrontation at Salt Lake's airport after trying to avoid an image scanner. He also was an outspoken opponent of the District of Columbia's 2009 legalization of same-sex marriage. In 2011, Chaffetz took over the chairmanship of the panel's subcommittee on national security and introduced bills that would allow for the firing of federal workers who are delinquent paying taxes and bar them from receiving government contracts or grants.

Chaffetz, who views accountability as a hallmark of his work, became a leading critic of the administration's response to the deadly September 2012 terrorist attack at the U.S. consulate in Benghazi, Libya. He was among the first congressional investigators to Libya in the weeks following the attack and his concerns became the impetus for a broader investigation and the appointment of a select committee. When his subcommittee publicly released unclassified but sensitive documents a month later that included the names of Libyan human rights activists who had worked with the U.S. government, prompting criticism from the State Department, Chaffetz was unapologetic. "That's right out of the Democrat playbook: Attack the messenger," he told *The Huffington Post.* And when asked on CNN whether he had voted to cut funding for embassy security, he responded, "Absolutely. Look, we have to make priorities and choices in this country."

Chaffetz developed a reputation for his media accessibility and quotability, appearing in a CNN video project highlighting his freshman year and giving numerous interviews to publications, TV stations, and websites. He also regularly posted videos on *YouTube* and collected thousands of followers on Twitter. "He's impossible not to like on a personal level," said South Carolina GOP Rep. Trey Gowdy, another favorite of Hill journalists.

His media savvy was a boost in helping Chaffetz to defeat three more senior members— John Mica of Florida and Jim Jordan and Mike Turner, both of Ohio—who challenged him for the Oversight and Government Reform chairmanship in late 2014. "We as a party often make the mistake of just talking to the same people that agree with us," he said. "We talk a lot about being a big tent, but we tend not to talk to other audiences." Chaffetz brought in dozens of new staffers and reshuffled subcommittees, creating a new panel devoted to information technology. He also gave Jordan, a well-regarded figure among conservatives, an enhanced role in scrutinizing the Obama administration's rules.

The committee's Democrats expressed hope that Chaffetz would take the panel in a new direction after the bruising partisanship of California's Darrell Issa, who was term-limited as committee chairman under House GOP rules. Chaffetz was serious about promoting bipartisanship at the committee. He started by reaching out to ranking Democrat Elijah Cummings of Maryland, and they spent time with each other in visits to each other's district during the summer of 2014. "We're going to disagree on most issues," Chaffetz told *Time*. "I just don't want to be disagreeable." That proved to be no easy matter. At the first committee meeting in January, Chaffetz pushed through a rules package that Cummings complained was "worse than the rules we had under Chairman Issa." Cummings and other Democrats tried and failed to roll back the chairman's ability to subpoena witnesses or documents without obtaining the prior consent of the ranking member, or putting the subpoena request to a vote of the full committee. But Chaffetz also took the symbolic step of removing Issa's portrait from the committee hearing room.

Chaffetz launched an ambitious schedule of investigations and nearly daily committee hearings, much of which he sought to peg to pending controversies. When the Secret Service was plagued by continuing misbehavior within its ranks, including among senior officers, Chaffetz called a hearing to review compliance with the agency's protocols. When Homeland Security Secretary Jeh Johnson objected to open hearings, Chaffetz responded that the objection was "unacceptable." With Cummings, he issued a joint statement in May 2015 that "a major cultural overhaul is essential to restoring the Secret Service to its former stature." Later, Chaffetz held hearings on criminal justice reform at the request of Cummings, who said that he appreciated the cooperation. Following reports of a data breach at the Office of Personnel Management involving the records of millions of federal employees, Chaffetz quickly launched hearings and moved with other committee Republicans to demand the removal of OPM Director Katherine Archuleta from her job. With similar statements from congressional Democrats, she stepped down two weeks later in July 2015. In an unusual move for a Republican, he held hearings in June that were sympathetic with the problems that journalists have faced in gaining compliance with the Freedom of Information Act. He blamed "the yahoos at the White House having to review each and every document."

Probably the most difficult incident for Chaffetz in his initial months at the helm came on his own side of the aisle when he decided in June to remove Rep. Mark Meadows of North Carolina as chairman of the Government Operations Subcommittee for various acts of party disloyalty, including voting against procedural steps on giving trade promotion authority to President Barack Obama. The move, which Speaker John Boehner appeared to have encouraged, sparked a furor by conservatives and lengthy closed-door talks. A few days later, they issued a joint statement restoring Meadows to the post. "I think we both better understand each other" following several discussions, Chaffetz said, "I respect Mark and his approach." Other members said that they had "a family discussion," a sign of how quickly the youthful-looking Chaffetz had moved to become one of the father figures in the House.

Chaffetz has cruised to reelection. An interesting question has been his political future. In early 2011, with strong tea party backing, Chaffetz began testing the waters for a primary challenge to six-term Sen. Orrin Hatch. But in late August, Chaffetz decided against a run, saying that a primary battle with Hatch would be a "multi-million dollar bloodbath." According to Robert Draper's 2012 book *Do Not Ask What Good We Do*, Boehner told him that he would enjoy life more in the House, with its greater turnover and more frequent opportunities to advance. Chaffetz has leadership aspirations and said that they were a factor in his decision to forego a Senate bid. With Hatch expected to retire in 2018 when he will be 84, Chaffetz also might have an opportunity for a smoother ride to the Senate, with additional notches on his belt.

FOURTH DISTRICT

Mia Love (R)

Elected 2014, 1st term; b. Dec. 6, 1975, Brooklyn, NY; U. of Hartford, B.A. 1997; Mormon; married (Jason); 3 children.

Elected Office: Saratoga Springs, UT City Cncl., 2003-09; Saratoga Springs, UT Mayor, 2010-14.

Professional Career: Flight attendant, 1997-98; Call center employee, 1998-2000; Software company marketing director, 2000.

DC Office: 217 CHOB, 20515, 202-225-011; Fax: 202-225-5638; Website: love.house.gov.

State Offices: West Jordan, 801-996-8729.

Committees: *Financial Services:* Financial Institutions & Consumer Credit; Monetary Policy & Trade.

Election Results

2014 general	Mia Love (R)	64,390	(50%)	$5,159,840	$191,113	$41,596
	Doug Owens (D)	60,165	(47%)	$866,595	$95,800	
2014 primary	Mia Love (R)	unopposed				

Population		Race and Ethnicity		Income	
Total:	745,786	White	76.1%	Median income:	$61,788
Urban:	38.4%	Latino	16.3%		*(102 of 435)*
Suburban:	60.0%	Asian	2.7%	Under $50,000	38.3%
Rural:	1.5%	Pac. Island	1.4%	$50,000-$99,999:	38.2%
Land area:	1,574	Two races	1.7%	$100,000-$199,999:	20.2%
Pop/sq. mi.:	473.9	White Ethnic	12.8%	$200,000 or more:	3.3%
Born in state:	64.4%			Poverty Rate	11.9%
		Education			
Age Groups		H.S. grad or less:	34.2%	**Work**	
Under 18:	31.9%	Some college:	38.9%	White collar:	35.7%
18 to 34:	26.0%	College degree, 4 yr.:	18.8%	Blue collar:	42.1%
35 to 64:	33.7%	Post-grad study:	8.1%	Sales and service:	22.2%
Over 64:	8.4%			Govt. workers:	12.9%
		Military			
		Veterans/active duty:	5.5%		

Central Utah: Suburbs of Salt Lake City and Provo

Driving along the Wasatch Front on the 90-mile stretch of Interstate 15 from North Ogden to Provo, one passes within about five miles of two-thirds of the state's population. In Utah, 65% of the people occupy about 2% of the land area. Salt Lake City itself accounts for a

Voter Turnout	
2013 Total Citizen 18+	463,261
2014 House Turnout	147,168
2014 Turnout as % CVAP	31.8%
2012 Turnout as % CVAP	55.1%

surprisingly small portion of this: Its population of 190,000 is only slightly larger than the 180,000 it had in 1950; the population fell to 160,000 in 1990, but then picked up again. Like many Western cities, Salt Lake City mostly grew up with automobiles and suburbs and houses with yards for children in mind, and the settlement patterns reflect that. Suburbs and small cities stretch out to the north, south, and west of the city, and even into the foothills of the Wasatch.

2012 Presidential Vote		
Mitt Romney (R)	165,294	(68%)
Barack Obama (D)	74,368	(30%)
2008 Presidential Vote		
John McCain (R)	124,280	(56%)
Barack Obama (D)	90,486	(41%)
Cook Partisan Voting Index:	R+16	

The 4th Congressional District of Utah, the smallest district in the state, takes in much of the suburban area to the south and southwest of Salt Lake City. Although the city sections of Salt Lake County lean Democratic, about 40% of the district's population is in the county south of the interstate—West Jordan, South Jordan, Sandy and Riverton—all of which are Republican. Sandy was an old mining town and West Jordan was a farming community, but their populations shot up as suburban growth took off in the 1960s. Today, West Jordan has more than 110,000 people. South Jordan and Lehi are the new growth centers. Each was among the five fastest-growing cities in the nation for the year ending in June 2013. Technology-related employment has expanded strongly in this area since 2010. Bluffdale, the site of a new $1.2 billion National Security Agency data center, offered the appeal of low utility rates plus land that belonged to Utah's National Guard. These are all upscale places, with median incomes well above the national average. The district also takes in western Utah County, including Eagle Mountain and Saratoga Springs, which were created in the early 1990s and have grown rapidly.

Overall, this is a solidly Republican district that Mitt Romney won in 2012 with 68 percent of the vote. It is the least Republican district in deep-red Utah, but still very Republican.

Mia Love (R)

The first black Republican woman elected to Congress, Mia Love had been proclaimed a rising star two years ago when she fell 768 votes short of beating Democratic Rep. Jim Matheson. His subsequent decision to retire paved the way for an easier—but hardly automatic—2014 race for Love.

Love was given a prominent speaking slot at the 2012 Republican National Convention to tell her life story. Her parents immigrated to Brooklyn from Haiti with $10 and became legal citizens shortly after she was born. The family then moved to Connecticut, where she stayed until she graduated from the University of Hartford with a degree in fine arts. Love worked as a flight attendant for Continental Airlines. The job allowed her to live almost anywhere, so she decided to move to Utah. She met Jason Love on a Mormon mission, married him and converted to Mormonism. She remembers being upset when hearing news stories about groups trying to remove "under God" from the Pledge of Allegiance and decided to enter politics. In 2003, she won a seat on the Saratoga Springs City Council, where she served for six years before voters elected her mayor.

The first black mayor of a Utah city, Love took a firmly conservative line on limited government, immigration and social issues. When she challenged Matheson, she became a national sensation within the GOP. She won praise for her Republican convention speech in which she said, "Mr. President, I am here to tell you we are not buying what you are selling in 2012." Presidential candidate Mitt Romney picked her to serve on his black leadership council to help foster dialogue between Romney and black community leaders. In the new district lines, Love had been widely expected to win. But Matheson was one of the House's most conservative Democrats, and Republicans found it difficult to tie him closely to President Barack Obama.

Six months after the 2012 election, after appearing at numerous state and local GOP events, Love announced she would run again. Realizing he faced a tougher path to victory in the midterm election with a smaller voter turnout, Matheson decided not to seek an eighth term. Love won the nomination at the state Republican convention in April with 78% of the vote. Democratic nominee Doug Owens campaigned against her in much the way Matheson had, seeking to appeal to moderate Republicans and independents. He blasted Love for statements in 2012 that she would do away with the Department of Education, eliminate federally subsidized student loans and cut other federal programs. Love said those positions weren't etched in stone and accused Owens of resorting to personal attacks. Love spent $5.2 million, compared with only $867,000 for Owens, and she notched a 50%-46% victory. Owens had a 2,100 vote lead in Salt Lake County, which cast more than 80% of the vote. But Love wrapped up her victory with a 3-to-1 lead in Utah County. The day after the election, she told CNN that race and gender had nothing to do with her election. "Principles had everything to do with it," she said.

Upon being sworn into office, Love took part in a ceremonial swearing-in for the Congressional Black Caucus, a Democratic-dominated group, despite having previously accused it of "demagoguery," and told the *Deseret News* in 2012 that she would "take that thing apart from the inside out." She prominently defended Majority Whip Steve Scalise after it was revealed in December 2014 that Scalise had spoken to a white nationalist group while he was serving in the Louisiana Legislature. She told ABC News: "There's one quality that he has that I think is very important in leadership, and that's humility. And he's actually shown that in this case. He's apologized, and I think that we need to move on and get the work of the American people done."

In the House, Love kept a low profile during her opening months. She introduced in May her first bill, "The Student Right to Know Before You Go Act," which was designed to assure that college students and their families understand the consequences of their financial decisions, especially student loans. Florida GOP Sen. Marco Rubio earlier introduced a similar measure in the Senate. Love planned to address other issues related to education and poverty. She gained a seat on the Financial Services Committee.

★ VERMONT ★

Early America and contemporary America come together in Vermont. The state is a mixture of the 19th and 21st centuries—maple syrup and Ben & Jerry's ice cream, tiny clapboard villages and carefully zoned towns with unobtrusively signed outlet malls, covered bridges and same-sex marriages. It was the first state where the legislature passed a full same-sex marriage law rather than its judges decreeing it. Not so long ago, Vermont seemed an antique state, almost as carefully preserved as its Shelburne Museum, with its barn and jail, railroad station and blacksmith shop, and its 37 buildings of folk art; its new Center for Art and Education, by contrast, is sleekly contemporary. In just two decades, Vermont was transformed by newcomers, who were attracted to its throwback look but who have since transformed Vermont's culture in their own image. Now, in-migration is down and the population is aging comfortably—it is the second oldest state, after Maine, and it has the highest percentage of households with cats (almost half).

Vermont was first settled by flinty Yankees from Connecticut, and it showed an independent streak from the beginning. After Ethan Allen's Green Mountain Boys repulsed the British in 1777, Vermont called itself an independent republic for 14 years, claimed, to no avail, by New York and New Hampshire. Allen tried to persuade George Washington to make it a new state, but several histories argue that Vermont never voluntarily joined the United States. In any case, Vermont was admitted as the 14th state in 1791. Its economy then was almost entirely agricultural, as second sons and daughters from small New England farms struggled to scratch out livings from the rocky soil. Eventually many gave up and moved west, while those who remained raised dairy cows, producing milk for the masses in New York City, and harvested maple syrup in the spring.

With their legendary thriftiness, Vermonters accumulated capital that, invested wisely, was used to build the solid stone office buildings and courthouses, the thick-timbered houses, and gold-topped state Capitol in Montpelier that have survived to this day. Vermont also made an economic asset of its maple trees and its quaintness. Beginning in the 1890s, the state government promoted Vermont as a tourist destination and passed a law requiring Vermont maple syrup to be made only from local trees. But the state never developed labor-intensive industry, and so over the years, it exported people and its population aged. From 1850 to the 1960s, as a result of continuous out-migration, Vermont's population hovered between 300,000 and 400,000. Two presidents were born in Vermont, but both made their careers elsewhere—Chester Arthur in New York City and Calvin Coolidge in Massachusetts. Two great foreign writers lived there for years—Rudyard Kipling and Aleksandr Solzhenitsyn—but neither wrote much about Vermont. The 2010 census counted 626,000 Vermonters, 48% of whom were born outside the state. Sheldon has the highest representation of native Vermonters at 83%, and tiny Buels Gore, a sliver of land left out when the first settlers drew town lines, has had a population boom, rising from 12 people in 2000 to 30 in 2010; it exceeded the peak in 1840, when it had 16 people and 3,516 sheep.

Starting in the 1960s—perhaps the key date was 1963, when people first outnumbered cows—Vermont changed rapidly. Its economy boomed, led by leisure-time industries—ski resorts and summer homes—and high-tech companies, starting with IBM in 1957, in and around the Burlington area on the mostly undeveloped shores of glorious Lake Champlain. You can find big-box retailers in Williston, but also ethnic diversity—Vietnamese, Bosnians, and Koreans—in Winooski. Homegrown firms started by baby boom rebels—Ben & Jerry's, founded in 1978, is the archetype—have flourished. There were 45 separate communes in Vermont during the late 1960s and early 1970s, according to the Vermont Historical Society, though they represented just the furthest edge of a much wider movement within the state. Next-door New Hampshire may have trumpeted its low taxes and aversion to government regulation, attracting right-leaning migrants from Massachusetts and elsewhere to settle spanking-new developments, but Vermont, proclaiming its desire to preserve the environment and the past, attracted left-leaning migrants from New York and elsewhere who were willing to pay higher taxes and higher prices and submit to tough environmental restrictions for the privilege of living in a pristine setting. Today, Gallup rates Vermont as the second-most liberal state, slightly behind Massachusetts, as well as the most non-religious state and the state where residents are most likely to eat produce frequently. (Organic, in all likelihood.)

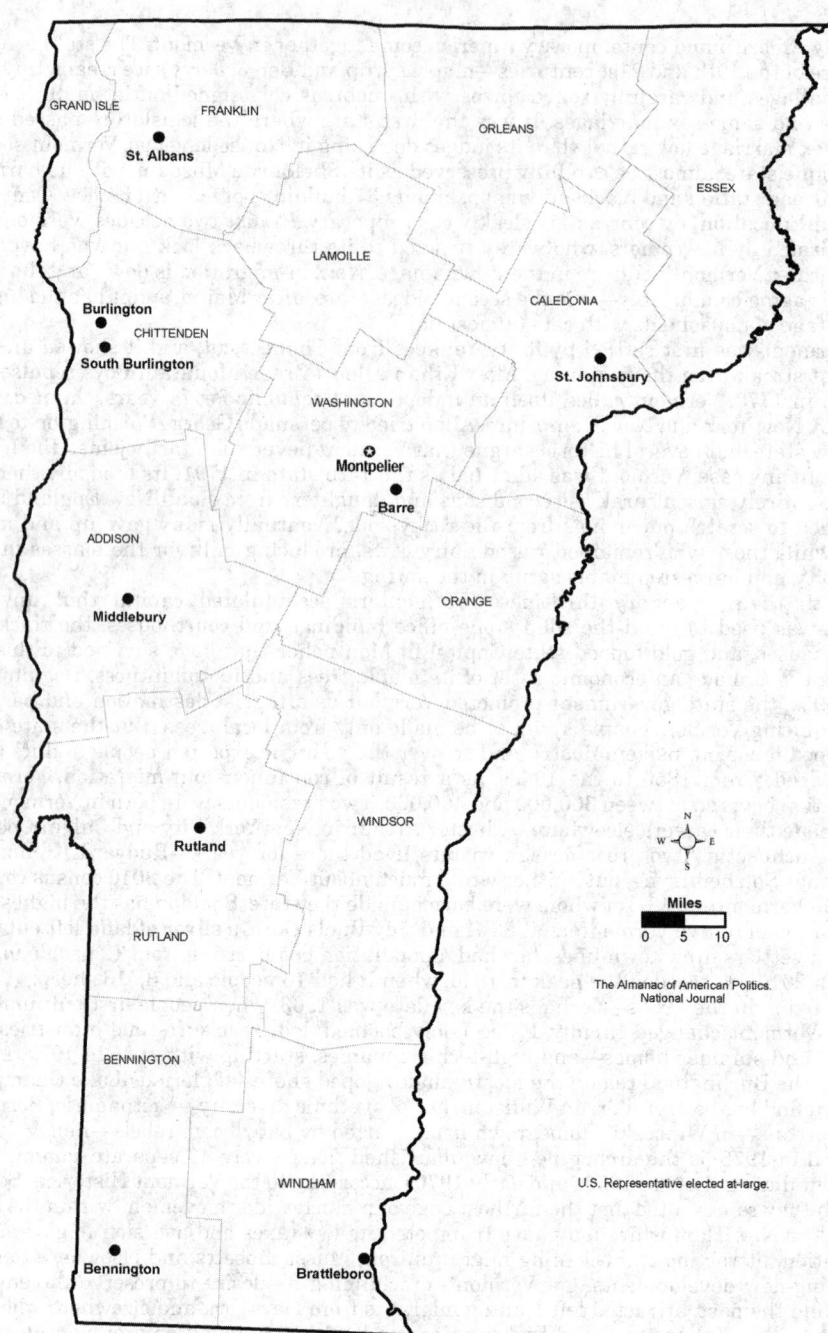

GRAND ISLE   FRANKLIN

St. Albans •

ORLEANS

ESSEX

LAMOILLE

CALEDONIA

Burlington •
CHITTENDEN

South Burlington •

St. Johnsbury •

WASHINGTON

Montpelier ✛

Barre •

ADDISON

ORANGE

Middlebury •

WINDSOR

Rutland •

RUTLAND

Miles
0   5   10

The Almanac of American Politics.
National Journal

BENNINGTON

WINDHAM   U.S. Representative elected at-large.

Bennington •   Brattleboro •

Public policy played a part in the evolution of Vermont. In 1970, Republican Gov. Deane Davis (the last Vermont native to hold the job until Democrat Peter Shumlin was elected in 2010) pushed through Act 250, a sweeping land use law that helped give Vermont its environmental reputation. Housing developments and new ski resorts were required to meet 10 environmental criteria and get the approval of five different commissions, with opponents granted a right to appeal. Later, Vermont passed its own Clean Air Act, levying a tax on new cars that get less than 20 miles to the gallon. It bans billboards and rooftop air conditioning units. Residents also passed Act 60, which attempted to equalize property taxes throughout the state. The state maintains a land trust that buys development rights of farmland to stop the disappearance of family farms. Distressed by the demise of dairy farming—the number of dairy farms declined from 3,300 in 1983 to 992 in 2011—the state government loans money to help farmers buy water buffalo to produce mozzarella cheese. In 2014, two landmark events occurred in the state's energy sector: The Vermont Yankee nuclear power plant on the Connecticut River shut down after more than four decades of operation, and the city of Burlington announced that 100 percent of its electricity came from renewable sources.

The quintessential Vermont commercial strip is the Church Street Marketplace in downtown Burlington, a four-block pedestrian mall known for its tasteful shopping venues and street fairs—the polar opposite of the big-box stores sprouting elsewhere. There were four Walmarts in the state in 2011, but two of them are in pre-existing buildings and the developer trying to expand one in Bennington had to pay $225,000 to refurbish downtown buildings and support watershed development. Dollar General was required to face its Chester store with clapboard wood rather than vinyl siding and keep its shopping carts off the street. Some dairy farmers are processing their animals' solid waste, mixed with bacteria from their digestive systems, into methane fuel. Other farmers are making biodiesel fuel from canola beans, sunflower seeds, and flax. But Vermont does not try to regulate everything. The state has some of the laxest gun-control laws in the country, tolerated even by leading Vermont Democrats, to the consternation of others in their party who represent more urbanized areas.

Vermonters love their natural environment, but nature can sometimes be cruel. In August 2011, Hurricane Irene roared inland and devastated major sections of Vermont. Water crashed down the Green Mountains and the White River crested at 28 feet above normal. Hundreds of miles of roads that followed mountainside streambeds were washed away along with hundreds of dairy cows. Farmers were stranded on hilltops, and 73,000 homes lost electric power. Vermonters responded with Yankee alacrity. Neighbors hiked in with shovels to clear new paths; local fire and rescue squads improvised new roadways; electric power was restored to all but 5,900 homes within three days. State government reopened 500 miles of road, replaced a dozen bridges, and repaired 200 more by December, working with Google to keep maps updated to show passable roads. The new Vermont responded in a way that would make the old Yankee Vermont proud. But the state has also suffered from a scourge that stems from humans rather than nature—drug addiction. In a high-profile speech in 2014, Shumlin said that $2 million worth of heroin enters the state every week, and that heroin addiction had risen a stunning 770 percent since 2000. Heroin is "now easier to find than weed in many parts of Vermont," wrote journalist Gina Tron, a Vermont native,

Population		Race and Ethnicity		Income	
Total:	626,630	White	94.0%	Median income:	$54,842
Urban:	11.6%	Latino	1.5%		(20 of 50)
Suburban:	19.0%	Asian	1.2%	Under $50,000	47.0%
Rural:	69.5%	Black	0.8%	$50,000-$99,999:	32.8%
Land area:	9,217	Two races	2.1%	$100,000-$199,999:	16.4%
Pop/sq. mi.:	68.0	White Ethnic	53.9%	$200,000 or more:	3.8%
Born in state:	50.5%			Poverty Rate	12.3%
		Education			
Age Groups		H.S. grad or less:	39.1%	**Work**	
Under 18:	19.8%	Some college:	25.1%	White collar:	39.5%
18 to 34:	21.8%	College degree, 4 yr.:	21.4%	**Blue collar:**	39.8%
35 to 64:	42.0%	Post-grad study:	14.3%	Sales and service:	20.7%
Over 64:	16.4%			Govt. workers:	14.3%
		Military			
		Veterans/active duty:	7.9%		

in *Politico*. At the same time, Shumlin and
other leading figures in the state are weighing the legalization of marijuana, which is
already consumed widely.

As Vermont has changed culturally, it
has also changed politically. In the 19th century, Yankee Vermont was the most Republican state in the nation, voting Republican
in every presidential election from 1856 to

Voter Turnout	
2013 Total Citizen 18+	492,678
2014 Highest Statewide Turnout	193,087
2014 Turnout as % CVAP	39.2%
2012 Turnout as % CVAP	60.7%

Legislature			
Senate:	20D	9R	1I
House:	85D	53R	12I

1960. In 1936, Vermont and Maine were the only states to resist Franklin D. Roosevelt's
landslide, inspiring Roosevelt's campaign manager, James Farley, to joke, "As Maine goes,
so goes Vermont." For three decades thereafter, Vermont's Yankee Protestant Republicans
outnumbered its French Canadian and Irish Catholic Democrats. As newcomers kept arriving, Vermont was divided politically along different lines: between liberal, highly educated
newcomers and conservative, less educated, old Vermonters. A key figure was Howard Dean,
who grew up on Park Avenue in New York City, was educated at Yale and moved to Vermont,
where he and his wife practiced medicine. He was elected lieutenant governor in 1986 and
became governor when incumbent Republican Richard Snelling died in August 1991, learning of his elevation while treating a patient. He was elected to five terms in his own right
(Vermont and New Hampshire are the last states with two-year gubernatorial terms) and
set out to run for president in January 2003. His campaign took off mainly because of his
full-throated opposition to the Iraq war. This was the point at which Vermont had moved
way to the left on America's political spectrum.

Republicans didn't become extinct in Vermont, but the ones who survived tended to be
much more moderate than their peers within the national GOP, such as Sen. James Jeffords,
whose party switch from Republican to Independent in 2001 enabled the Democrats to take
over the chamber mid-session, and Jim Douglas, who was elected governor in 2002, 2004,
2006 and 2008. But Democrats have done increasingly well in Vermont. Barack Obama
recorded his third-highest margin of victory here in both 2008 and 2012, trailing only the
District of Columbia and Hawaii. Sen. Patrick Leahy—through a combination of the state's
Republican roots, the recent service of two Senate Independents and Leahy's own long tenure in the chamber—oddly remains the only Democratic senator ever elected from Vermont.
He has served seven terms, and in December 2012 became the most senior member of the
Senate. His Senate colleague, Bernie Sanders, a self-styled Socialist and Independent who
caucuses with the Democrats, has managed to hold office almost continuously in Vermont
since 1981, first as Burlington mayor, then as the at-large House member and, since the
2006 election, as a senator. Sanders is an example of the liberal inflow to the state, having graduated from Brooklyn's James Madison High School (the same one as Sen. Charles
Schumer of New York, former Sen. Norm Coleman of Minnesota, and Supreme Court Justice
Ruth Bader Ginsburg). Sanders would later muster an unexpectedly potent presidential bid
in the 2016 Democratic primaries, consolidating a large share of the party's most liberal voters with his anti-Wall Street rhetoric, although back home, Sanders has also garnered surprisingly strong support in the state's rural and conservative Northeast Kingdom, thanks in
part to his anti-establishment persona. In the House, Sanders' Democratic successor, Peter
Welch, has had no trouble winning reelection.

The governor's office has been a somewhat dicier proposition for Democrats. Shumlin
has won three elections, but in two of them—the elections of 2010 and 2014—he failed to
reach 50%. Under Vermont law, his failure to win an absolute majority meant that the legislature had to officially elect the governor. Democrats had huge majorities in both houses, so
Shumlin won both times, but the narrowness of the 2014 victory—46%-45% over Republican
businessman Scott Milne—came as an unpleasant surprise. In office, Shumlin has pursued a
progressive agenda, enacting the highest state minimum wage in the nation ($10.50 an hour
by 2018) and the nation's first labeling law for genetically modified foods. The legislature
also passed a bill shielding doctors and others from liability for helping terminal patients
ingest lethal drugs. But Shumlin also faced the limits of liberalism even in a liberal state:
He pulled back from his proposal for a single-payer health insurance system in 2014, citing
the pitfalls of financing it. "These are simply not tax rates that I can responsibly support or
urge the Legislature to pass," he said. "In my judgment, the potential economic disruption
and risks would be too great to small businesses, working families and the state's economy."
In June 2015, he announced he would not seek reelection.

Presidential Politics Vermont was the most Republican state in the 1936 presidential election, when Franklin Roosevelt's campaign manager had a good laugh updating an old adage to say, "As goes Maine, so goes Vermont." Times have changed. In 2004, Vermont was the fourth-most Democratic state, after the District of Columbia, Massachusetts, and Rhode Island. In 2008 and 2012, it was the third most Democratic, after D.C. and Barack Obama's birthplace of Hawaii. Republican Mitt Romney journeyed to Vermont for debate preparation in 2012, but he

2012 Presidential Vote		
Barack Obama (D) 199,239	(67%)
Mitt Romney (R)...................92,698	(31%)
2012 Presidential Primary		
Mitt Romney (R)...................24,008	(39%)
Ron Paul (R) 15,391	(25%)
Rick Santorum (R) 14,368	(24%)
Newt Gingrich (R) 4,949	(8%)
2008 Presidential Vote		
Barack Obama (D) 219,262	(67%)
John McCain (R)...................98,974	(30%)

carried only two of the state's 251 cities and towns. Vermont has become solidly liberal on cultural and foreign issues and it is not very conservative on economics either.

The Vermont presidential primary, abolished for 1992, reappeared in 1996, but got little notice both that year or in 2000. Turnout in 2000 was light and tilted Republican because the Democratic race was over. Howard Dean's 2004 campaign was headquartered in Burlington, and although Dean was effectively eliminated by the time Vermont voted on March 2, Vermonters still came out in droves to give their former governor his only primary victory. Turnout was 83,000 for the Democrats and 27,000 in the uncontested Republican primary.

In 2008, Vermont voted on March 4, when Obama and Hillary Clinton were locked in a struggle for the nomination. Turnout was 155,000 in the Democratic primary, in which Obama beat Clinton 59%-39%. Each Democrat got more than twice as many votes as John McCain did in winning the light turnout (40,000) Republican primary, 71%-14%. In 2012, Vermont voted on March 6, when the Republican race was still raging, and Republican turnout was 60,000. Romney led with 40% of the votes, to 26% for Ron Paul and 24% for Rick Santorum.

Governor

Peter Shumlin (D)

Elected 2010, term expires Jan. 2017, 3rd term; b. March 24, 1956, Brattleboro; Wesleyan U., B.A. 1979; No religious affiliation; divorced; 2 children.

Elected Office: Putney Select Bd., 1980-90; VT House, 1990-92; VT Senate, 1992-2002, 2006-11.

Professional Career: Co-dir., Putney Student Travel & Nat'l Geographic Student Expeditions, 2003-06; Partner, dairy farm.

Office: 109 State St., Pavilion, Montpelier, 05609, 802-828-3333; Fax: 802-828-3339; Website: governor.vermont.gov.

Election Results

2014 general	Peter Shumlin (D)........................	89,509	(46%)
	Scott Milne (R)............................	87,075	(45%)
	Dan Feliciano (Lib)......................	8,428	(4%)
2014 primary	Peter Shumlin (D)........................	15,260	(77%)
	Brooke Paige (D)...........................	3,199	(16%)

Prior winning percentages: 2012 (58%), 2010 (49%)

Vermont's governor is Peter Shumlin, a Democrat first elected in 2010. A veteran of Vermont state politics, he eked out one of the closest wins of the political season, coasted to reelection in 2012, but sweated through a tough 2014 race in which neither he nor his opponent won a majority of votes cast, forcing the Democratic-dominated legislature to elect him to another two-year term.

Shumlin grew up in Putney, a small town in the state's southeast corner. His parents were educators who started a business matching high school students with academic and community service projects around the world. He suffered from dyslexia as a child, a problem that forced him to work on being articulate—something he said helped him later in politics. "I had to be the guy who was fastest with my tongue," he told the *Burlington Free Press*. After graduating from Wesleyan University, Shumlin and his brother took over their parents' business. In 1980, at age 24, he was elected to the Putney Selectboard.

He was chosen in 1990 to fill an empty seat in the state House of Representatives, and then was elected to the seat the following year. He was elected in 1992 to represent Windham County in the state Senate, becoming the chamber's president pro tempore within five years. He gave up his seat to run in an open-seat lieutenant governor's race, which he lost to Republican Brian Dubie. After four years away from politics, he returned to the Senate, where he was again elected president pro tempore. Around the capital, he was known as a forceful advocate for Democratic causes and for being fast with a sound bite. He was a key sponsor of a comprehensive energy bill for the state in 2007 that sought to cut greenhouse gas emissions blamed for global warming.

Shumlin announced his candidacy for governor in November 2009, stressing his record of running the family business and years as Senate leader. He joined a crowded Democratic field that already included a number of political veterans, including state Senate Appropriations Committee Chairman Susan Bartlett, Secretary of State Deborah Markowitz, and state Sen. Doug Racine, a former lieutenant governor who had lost a gubernatorial bid to Republican Jim Douglas in 2002. The candidates battled to stand out from the pack in the months leading up to the August 2010 primary. The race was so close that a winner couldn't be determined on Election Night, forcing a recount. Shumlin emerged with a 203-vote lead over Racine, who conceded more than two weeks after the polls closed. Shumlin finished with 24.8% to Racine's 24.6%, with Markowitz getting 23.9%. Former state Sen. Matt Dunne won 21% and Bartlett received 5%.

On the Republican side, Brian Dubie, by then the state's lieutenant governor, had raised nearly $1.2 million and had no primary competition. Shumlin had just $61,000 as the general election campaign got underway. Dubie ran on the same small-government, anti-taxation platform as other Republicans around the country, calling for a 2% cap on state spending increases. Shumlin advocated a single-payer health care system as a way of boosting the economy. With help from outside Democratic groups, Shumlin was able to close the financial gap with Dubie, but a Vermont Public Radio survey in October showed the Republican ahead by 1 percentage point. On Election Night, the race was too close to call, but Shumlin pulled out a 49.5%-47.7% victory. Under state law, because neither candidate received 50% plus one vote, the race could have been decided in the legislature. But with Democrats holding solid majorities in the House and Senate, Dubie chose to concede.

Shumlin presented an initial budget intended to reduce general funding more than $80 million, while keeping taxes stable. He named Racine to head the state Agency of Human Services and Bartlett as a special assistant. But he also got off to a rocky start when in March he took a Caribbean vacation as Vermont was hit with two feet of snow. He did not bring along his security detail and did not inform the public of his whereabouts until he returned. He said he had no regrets about not returning sooner, saying his staff kept him abreast of emergency response developments. But Shumlin made sure he took a more hands-on approach to the response to Hurricane Irene in August 2011 by meeting with storm victims in dozens of affected communities; his handling of the crisis won him plaudits.

He also generated good feelings among Republicans by opposing tax increases and by reaching out to Republican Lt. Gov. Phil Scott. A Smith Johnson Research poll in November found that almost 69% of those surveyed either approved or strongly approved of Shumlin's performance. He won a big political victory in April 2012, when he signed into law an overhaul of the state's mental health system. It would replace an existing hospital with a new one, expand psychiatric units in Brattleboro and Rutland, and place the mentally ill in smaller and less-restrictive facilities. Rejecting the path taken by nearby states, Shumlin signed a ban on hydraulic fracturing or "fracking," a method of extracting natural gas that is opposed by many environmentalists. In April 2012, Shumlin unexpectedly made national news when he nearly suffered serious injury after chasing four bears that were raiding birdfeeders at his rented home in Montpelier. Then, in October, his personal finances became an issue when reports surfaced that he had paid $35,000 to buy 27 acres of farmland for a new house in East Montpelier. He insisted there was nothing improper about the deal, but he acknowledged that he'd coordinated with friends who bought the rest of the 180-acre property to help drive down the price.

In Vermont, governors are elected every two years. Republicans were destined to have trouble winning in 2012, a presidential-election year in which Barack Obama was headed toward a rout. The GOP nominee was state Sen. Randy Brock, who criticized Shumlin's pursuit of a single-payer health care system. He also rebuked the administration's energy policy, in particular its support for subsidies for renewable energy. He released a spate of attack ads that drew criticism for making questionable claims. Shumlin got good news in September, when the U.S. Census Bureau's American Community Survey showed Vermont was the only state with an increase in median household income from 2010 to 2011. He won 58%-38%, with three other candidates splitting the rest.

In 2013, Shumlin became chairman of the Democratic Governors Association. In that role, he promoted progressive policies that he said would work well in other states, such as expanding child care programs, issuing driver's licenses to undocumented agricultural workers, decriminalizing marijuana, and legalizing physician-assisted suicide. Shumlin attracted notice by devoting his entire State of the State speech in 2014 to the problem of heroin addiction in the state. He also signed a bill—which would be the first in the nation to take effect—to require labeling of foods with genetically modified ingredients. "Vermonters take our food and how it is produced seriously, and we believe we have a right to know what's in the food we buy," he said. In 2015, a federal district judge rejected an industry request to preliminarily block the law's planned implementation in July 2016. Shumlin also signed an increase in the state's minimum wage to $10.50 an hour—the highest statewide rate in the country.

Shumlin initially seemed to be in good shape for reelection in 2014, when he faced Republican Scott Milne, a travel agent and first-time candidate. Milne argued that property taxes were excessive and that the state needed education reform, though he was criticized for being short on details. Shumlin was attacked for his frequent out-of-state travel as head of the Democratic governors group. Stagnating wages, difficulties implementing the Affordable Care Act in the state, and concerns about wind farms posed problems as well. Six other candidates ended up on the ballot, and on Election Night, Shumlin ended up with 46.5% to Milne's 45.3%. Libertarian Dan Feliciano got 8,000 votes, greater than Shumlin's margin of victory and likely stealing support from Milne. With neither Shumlin nor Milne winning more than 50%, the state's Constitution required the matter to be settled by the legislature, for the 25th time since statehood. Milne did not concede, and for a time, there was talk that the Republican could win, or at least come close, if lawmakers voted as the constituents in their district did, rather than as their own party affiliation dictated. But it didn't affect the final result. In January 2015, Shumlin got 110 votes on green paper ballots while Milne got 69. Shumlin's brush with defeat capped an awful election cycle for the DGA chair, as Democratic candidates lost even in blue states such as Illinois, Maryland and Massachusetts.

Shumlin's near-loss helped close the book on his pursuit of a single-payer health-insurance system. Early in his tenure, Shumlin had succeeded in getting the legislature to pass a bill establishing Green Mountain Care, a single-payer system, with a planned launch in 2017. The proposal was designed to blend universal coverage with cost controls. But despite some seeming advantages—Vermont's small size, its already high coverage rates and its liberal electorate—the complex implementation lagged, and worries grew as it became clear that expanding coverage would require new state payroll and income taxes. In December 2014, Shumlin acknowledged that the revenue increases would be too heavy a lift for the state. Liberals were disappointed, and Shumlin called the scuttling of the plan "the biggest disappointment of my political life."

In May 2015, amid national concern about declining vaccination rates, Shumlin signed a law ending "philosophical" exemptions to vaccination. Vermont had among the highest rates in the country for incomplete childhood immunization regimens. He had supported legislation that included the exemption in 2012, but three years later Shumlin agreed with lawmakers to change course. Also in 2015, Shumlin came out in favor of a proposal to require paid employee sick leave that would be among the nation's strongest. But the National Education Association helped block a Shumlin-backed proposal to ban teacher strikes. In June 2015, with his approval rating under water, Shumlin said he would not seek a fourth term, making him a lame duck for most of his final two years.

Senior Senator

Patrick Leahy (D)

Elected 1974, term expires Jan. 2017, 7th term; b. March 31, 1940, Montpelier; St. Michael's Col., B.A. 1961, Georgetown U., J.D. 1964; Catholic; married (Marcelle); 3 children.

Elected Office: VT st. atty., Chittenden Cnty., 1966-74.

Professional Career: Practicing atty., 1964-74.

DC Office: 437 RSOB, 20510, 202-224-4242; Website: leahy.senate. gov.

State Offices: Burlington, 802-863-2525; Montpelier, 802-229-0569.

Committees: *Agriculture, Nutrition & Forestry:* Conservation, Forestry & Natural Resources; Livestock, Marketing & Ag Security; Nutrition, Specialty Crops & Ag Research. *Appropriations:* Agriculture, Rural Development, FDA & Related Agencies; Commerce, Justice, Science & Related Agencies; Defense; Homeland Security; Interior, Environment & Related Agencies; State, Foreign Operations & Related Programs (RMM). *Judiciary* (RMM): Immigration & the Nat'l Interest. *Rules & Administration. Joint Committee on the Library.*

Group Ratings

	ADA	ACLU	AFL-CIO	LCV	ITI	COC	HAFA	ACU	CFG	FRC
2014	95%	100%	–	80%	100%	25%	3%	0%	2%	0%
2013	100%	C	94%	100%	C	38%	C	4%	0%	C

National Journal Ratings

	2013 LIB	—	2013 CONS
Economic	93%	—	0%
Social	73%	—	0%
Foreign	51%	—	47%
Composite	78%	—	22%

Key Votes of the 113th Congress

1. Sandy storm spending	Y	5. Student Loan Rates	N	9. Bipartisan Budget Deal	Y
2. Chuck Hagel Confirmation	Y	6. Employee Non-Discrim'n Act	Y	10. Farm Bill Conference Rept.	Y
3. Gun Background Checks	Y	7. Senate Vote on Judgeships	N	11. Unempl. Comp. Extension	Y
4. Immigration Reform	Y	8. Defense Dept. Spending	Y	12. Keystone Pipeline	N

Election Results

2010 general	Patrick Leahy (D)	151,281	(64%)	$4,104,770	$4,280
	Len Britton (R)	72,699	(31%)	$231,364	$60,484
2010 primary	Patrick Leahy (D)	64,515	(89%)		
	Daniel Freilich (D)	7,892	(11%)		

Prior winning percentages: 2004 (71%), 1998 (72%), 1992 (54%), 1986 (63%), 1980 (50%), 1974 (50%)

Democrat Patrick Leahy, Vermont's senior senator, was first elected in 1974, and, in late 2012, became the chamber's longest serving current member. For the next two years, while his party held the majority, Leahy was Senate president *pro tempore*—putting him third in the line of succession to the presidency. More significant, however, is the influence he has wielded in his four decades on Capitol Hill over a wide variety of issues—ranging from civil liberties and intellectual property rights to human rights abroad and agriculture policy at home.

Leahy has chaired two Senate committees: the Agriculture Committee, from 1987-1995, and the Judiciary panel, from 2001-2003 and again from 2007-2015. He could have ascended to the chairmanship of a third committee, the influential Appropriations panel, when a vacancy occurred in late 2012. But, as a former prosecuting attorney, Leahy took a pass to stay as Judiciary Committee chairman and continue focusing on a host of legal issues that have been his legislative passion. The Republican takeover of the Senate in the 2014 election cost him the Judiciary Committee gavel, but Leahy has continued to play a key role as the panel's ranking Democrat—notably in the 2015 debate over renewal of the controversial surveillance provisions in the USA Patriot Act, first enacted in the wake of the 9/11 attacks.

As a stalwart progressive, Leahy has been as much of an influential ally of President Barack Obama as he was a stubborn antagonist of President George W. Bush. Bush's vice president, Dick Cheney, infamously told Leahy to "Go f—yourself" following a 2004 picture taking session at the Capitol; Cheney was apparently angered by Leahy's criticism of the activities of Halliburton, a company once headed by Cheney, during the Iraq war. Leahy, too, is known for periodic flashes of temper, but also is credited by Republicans for efforts to reach across the aisle. He has found common ground on civil liberties and criminal justice issues with some of the Senate's most outspoken GOP conservatives, including Kentucky Sen. Rand Paul, and has long enjoyed a good relationship with Iowa Sen. Charles Grassley, who took over the Judiciary chairmanship in 2015. "He's a good listener who will take into account the views of others," Maine Sen. Susan Collins, a GOP moderate, told *The Boston Globe*. The more conservative Mississippi Sen. Thad Cochran, a colleague of Leahy for more than a third of a century, told the *Associated Press*: "I'm fond of him. I shouldn't be, but I am."

Leahy grew up in Vermont at a time when the Green Mountain State—now one of the nation's bluest—was rock-ribbed Republican. He graduated from St. Michael's College in Winooski, just north of where he grew up in Burlington, and earned a law degree at Georgetown University before returning home to practice law. Leahy joined the law firm of Philip Hoff, who, in 1962, had become the first Democrat since before the Civil War to win election as Vermont's governor. In 1966, Hoff appointed Leahy, then just 26, to fill a vacancy as state's attorney for Chittenden County, the jurisdiction that includes Burlington. Leahy was elected to full terms in 1966 and 1970, and still often invokes recollections of his years in that post during congressional hearings and in interviews.

In 1974, after eight years as state's attorney, he ran for the Senate at age 34. The seat was being vacated by George Aiken, a liberal Republican who was first elected to the Senate the year that Leahy was born. Leahy had made a name for himself in the pocket-sized state as a prosecutor who tried all major felony cases personally, and who criticized the big oil companies during the 1970s energy crisis. He had a solid base in predominantly Democratic Burlington, together with the kind of thoughtful temperament Vermonters like in their public officials. In a year when the political fallout from the Watergate scandal benefited Democrats nationwide, Leahy outpolled Republican Rep. Richard Mallary by 50%-46%. Leahy became the first Democrat in history to win a Senate seat from Vermont, and remains the only Democrat ever elected from the state. (His junior home state colleague, Bernie Sanders, caucuses with the Democrats but has been elected twice as a political independent.)

Leahy became the seventh longest-serving senator in history in 2015. A key reason he opted to stay at the helm of the Judiciary Committee—rather than move over to chair the Appropriations panel upon the death of Hawaii Sen. Daniel Inouye in December 2012—was that the Judiciary Committee was confronting two issues that could shape his legacy. One was the first attempt at comprehensive immigration reform in six years, the other the first major gun control legislation in nearly two decades. He was an unlikely figure on the latter issue: An avid gun enthusiast, he was a member of his college shooting team and still enjoys the sport. But he has a mixed legislative record that earned him a "C" rating from the National Rifle Association. In 1993, Leahy voted against passage of the so-called Brady Bill, which requires background checks for individuals purchasing firearms. And, notwithstanding its recent reputation as a bastion of liberalism, Leahy's home state continues to have one of the highest rates of gun ownership in the country, along with some of the least restrictive gun laws of any state.

Nevertheless, with Democrats demanding action in the wake of the December 2012 elementary school shooting in Newtown Connecticut, in which 26 were killed, most of them children, Leahy took up the challenge. He moved a series of bills through his committee to bar the straw purchase and trafficking of guns, and to strengthen other law enforcement tools to assist investigations of those crimes. His legislation also included a ban on assault weapons, which Senate Majority Leader Harry Reid refused to go along with on the grounds that it lacked the votes for passage. Even so, efforts to pass gun control legislation fell apart during floor debate in April 2013: A compromise proposal by West Virginia Democratic Sen. Joe Manchin and Pennsylvania GOP Sen. Pat Toomey to expand the background check process for would-be gun buyers fell five votes short of the 60 votes necessary to end a GOP filibuster.

On immigration, Leahy held a series of hearings to try to build support for reform, while leaving much of the legislative work to a bipartisan group of eight senators. His combative side was on display in April 2013, when he accused Republicans of politicizing the issue by tying their objections to the Boston Marathon bombings—which involved two suspects from Chechnya. No one, Leahy declared at a hearing, should "be so cruel as to try to use the heinous acts of two young men last week to derail the dreams and futures of millions." Leahy guided a major overhaul of the nation's immigration laws, providing a path to citizenship for undocumented residents, through the Judiciary Committee in May 2013—where it garnered the support of all Democrats and three Republicans. The legislation cleared the Senate a month later on a bipartisan 68-32 vote, after provisions were added to beef up security along the U.S.-Mexico border. But the Republican-controlled House never took up the measure, as the immigration issue became increasingly politicized. The combination of a 2014 executive order by Obama that Republicans attacked as an effort to circumvent Congress and the onset of the 2016 presidential election season kept the House from considering the bill.

Leahy's first stint as Judiciary chairman coincided with the Sept. 11, 2001 attacks, as he and his staff worked with the Bush administration to hammer out the USA Patriot Act—the sweeping law that sparked a national debate over whether government investigators should be given broader powers at the expense of individual liberties. It is a debate in which Leahy continued to play a major role nearly a decade and a half later. After onetime National Security Agency contractor Edward Snowden revealed in 2013 that the agency was collecting Americans' phone records, sentiment grew in Congress for restricting such authority, contained in Section 215 of the law. As Section 215 was due to expire at the end of May 2015, Leahy and Utah Republican Sen. Mike Lee, a tea party conservative, introduced legislation to require targeted warrants to obtain phone metadata from telecommunications companies. The legislation attracted 18 co-sponsors, running the gamut from the most liberal to the most conservative members of the Senate, including Texas firebrand Ted Cruz.

As a bill similar to the one proposed by Leahy and Lee moved through the House, Leahy hoped to get Grassley to sign on to the legislation. Grassley ultimately declined, but his failure to move a bill through the Judiciary Committee strengthened the hand of Leahy, as the ranking Democrat on the committee. It left the Leahy-Lee measure and a rival proposal by Senate Majority Leader Mitch McConnell and Senate Intelligence Committee Richard Burr—to continue the law in its current form—as the two major options. A filibuster by McConnell's Kentucky junior colleague, Rand Paul, caused provisions of the USA Patriot Act to lapse for a couple of days. It gave McConnell, who had argued that extending Section 215 was essential to national security, little choice but to concede to the approach passed by the House and contained in the Leahy-Lee bill. "It's historical. It's the first major overhaul of government surveillance in decades," Leahy declared after Congress stripped the NSA of its authority to collect phone records.

Leahy had tried earlier, in November 2014, to pass a similar measure, but it fell a few votes short of the 60-vote supermajority needed to avoid a filibuster. All Democrats had supported it, along with four Republicans—including Lee and Cruz. The original USA Patriot Act, enacted a month after the 9/11 attacks, was essentially the Senate version of the legislation crafted in Leahy's committee, as opposed to the House version of the bill. But Leahy fought the Bush administration when it sought to expand police powers in the wake of the attacks. He opposed a proposal to allow the government to detain and deport immigrants suspected of terrorism without presenting evidence in court. In 2002, he contended the Justice Department should be required to disclose the number of U.S. citizens being spied on, the number of secret foreign intelligence wiretaps that had become part of criminal proceedings, and the total number of persons targeted by foreign intelligence surveillance warrants.

During Bush's second term, Leahy in 2005 objected to the government's surveillance of communications between suspected al-Qaida terrorists abroad and individuals in the United States. Back for a second stint as Judiciary chairman when the Democrats recaptured the Senate majority in 2006, Leahy made life difficult for Attorney General Alberto Gonzales in 2007 by requesting an internal investigation of whether Gonzales had told the truth about the warrantless wiretapping program. Leahy subsequently placed Gonzales's successor, Michael Mukasey, on the spot with demands that he denounce the use of waterboarding, an interrogation tactic that simulates drowning and that has been used on terrorism suspects.

Leahy was an early supporter of Obama in the 2008 presidential primaries, and has largely been in sync with his administration. He helped guide Obama's two Supreme Court nominees, Sonia Sotomayor and Elena Kagan, to swift confirmation, even while working with a new ranking Republican, Alabama's Jeff Sessions, who was considerably more partisan than his predecessor in that role, Pennsylvania's Arlen Specter—who had switched to the Democratic Party in early 2009. Leahy accused Republicans of seeking to play the race card against Sotomayor, the court's first Latina justice, and of gender bias toward Kagan. As Senate Republicans blocked numerous Obama nominees to federal district and appeals courts, Leahy lamented in April 2013, "I have repeatedly asked Senate Republicans to abandon their destructive tactics."

When the Republicans held the congressional majority in the mid-to-late 1990s, Leahy criticized them for stalling President Bill Clinton's judicial appointments, and he stoutly defended Clinton during the impeachment proceedings in 1998 and 1999. But, when Leahy became chairman during the Democrats' year and a half in the majority starting in mid-2001, he, in turn, held up Bush's judicial nominations. Later, as ranking Democrat on the panel from 2003-2007, Leahy led filibusters against 10 appeals court nominees, tactics that the Republicans bitterly attacked. Leahy countered that the committee had approved the vast majority of appellate nominees and almost every trial court nominee, and argued he had been fairer to Bush's appointees than Republicans had been to Clinton's.

In 2005, Leahy led the minority's questioning of Bush's Supreme Court nominees, John Roberts and Samuel Alito, both of whom were confirmed by the Senate. The liberal Leahy surprised many when he voted to approve the conservative Roberts. "I came here to do what I thought was right, and as a Vermonter I can do nothing different," Leahy said. He also asked tough questions of Alito, but voted no in that instance. "This president is in the midst of a radical realignment of the powers of government and its intrusiveness into the private lives of Americans. This nomination is part of that plan," Leahy charged.

Intellectual property rights also have been a major focus for Leahy at the Judiciary Committee, particularly as the dawn of the digital age has posed new challenges in this area. (In 2003, Leahy became the first member of Congress with a blog.) He enacted an overhaul of the nation's patent system in September 2011, ending a seven-year stalemate. But in mid-2014, Leahy was forced to throw in the towel on legislation to rein in so-called patent trolls—firms which accumulate patents not to produce tangible goods, but rather to use the legal system to extract fees and legal judgments from other companies. Leahy reportedly withdrew the measure under pressure from Reid, as the legislation faced opposition from such powerful lobbies as the pharmaceutical industry and the nation's trial lawyers. Leahy also has been frustrated in recent efforts to pass legislation aimed at cracking down on online piracy and counterfeiting.

Leahy is the ranking member of the Appropriations subcommittee with jurisdiction over the State Department and foreign aid programs, and has chaired that subcommittee in the past—giving him a platform to advance several foreign policy-related causes. He has been a major force behind the Trafficking Victims Protection Act, first passed in 2000 and reauthorized several times since; the law is designed to pressure foreign countries engaged in human trafficking, while providing legal recourse to victims of the practice in the United States. Another Leahy cause is the elimination of land mines. Since 1989, he has been crusading against the export and use of such devices, which are easy and cheap to implant yet difficult and expensive to remove. In 1994, he persuaded the United Nations to unanimously call for the eventual elimination of land mines. He pushed Obama in 2010 to join an international treaty banning the mines, and in 2011 and 2013 introduced bills to restrict the use of cluster bombs.

As an opponent of the U.S. embargo against Cuba, Leahy was actively involved in the successful effort to free government contractor Alan Gross from a Cuban prison at the end of 2014—a move that paved the way for Obama's decision to restore diplomatic relations. Leahy was among several lawmakers who flew to Cuba to bring Gross home, and later for the opening of the U.S. Embassy. He took aim at critics of Obama's initiative to normalize relations, accusing them of applying a "flagrant double standard." In an op-ed in his hometown newspaper, the *Burlington Free Press*, Leahy noted the critics had not raised objections to U.S. engagement with allies, such as Egypt and Saudi Arabia, despite their poor human rights records. "The critics apparently believe that engagement through diplomatic relations and trade everywhere except Cuba is in our national interest, despite the repressive and corrupt policies of other governments." Leahy gibed.

Earlier in his career, Leahy became one of the few senators to chair the Agriculture Committee who did not represent a state with crops such as wheat, corn or cotton. Later, as the panel's ranking Democrat, he worked with Indiana Republican Richard Lugar in the 1990s to phase out the subsidy system. But after their success in passing the Freedom to Farm Act of 1996, crop prices fell, and lawmakers' resolve dissipated. Congress took to supporting large annual subsidies in the form of emergency relief to farmers, and in 2002, largely rolled back the 1996 act. Closer to home, Leahy has used his perch on the Agriculture panel to deliver for the roughly 1,000 dairy farms in Vermont. He got an extension of a safety net program for dairy farmers into the January 2013 tax and spending bill that averted the so-called "fiscal cliff." His Appropriations Committee membership also has yielded some parochial benefits. In 2010, he secured more than $57 million in earmarks for his state—the 10th highest total among senators, according to Taxpayers for Common Sense. There has been an informal ban on earmarks since, due to opposition from the White House and House Republicans.

Around the Capitol, Leahy is known for his hobbies. He is a gadgeteer and an accomplished amateur photographer, despite being legally blind in his left eye since birth; his work has been published in *The New York Times, USAToday* and several news magazines. He is also an avid student of popular culture, and a huge fan of the *Batman* movies. (He appeared briefly in three of the films, with a speaking part in 2008's *The Dark Knight*. Leahy tells the Joker, "We're not intimidated by thugs.") He has been a high-profile fan of the Grateful Dead, and can recite lyrics from their songs—along with verses from Shakespeare.

Leahy had a close call in his first reelection bid, surviving a 1980 challenge from Republican Stewart Ledbetter, then the state's banking and insurance commissioner, by 50%-49% amid a national Republican landslide. Six years later, in a year more favorable for Democrats, he had little trouble defeating popular Gov. Richard Snelling, 63%-35%. In 1992, Leahy was held to 54 percent by Jim Douglas, who was later elected governor—and among the few Republicans to achieve electoral success in Vermont in recent years. That was the last time Leahy faced a competitive race, as he easily won reelection in 1998, 2004, and 2010, garnering more than 70 percent of the vote on a couple of occasions.

Leahy, who turned 75 in 2015, put out the word early in the year that he planned to seek an eighth term, and is not likely to be seriously challenged in 2016, either. But speculation persisted he may yet opt to retire, following the pattern of several other senior senators in recent years who initially announced plans to run—only later to change their minds. If Leahy decides to leave, Democratic Rep. Peter Welch, who has held the state's at-large House seat since 2006, would top the list of possible successors. In June 2015, Welch passed on an opportunity to run to succeed retiring Gov. Peter Shumlin, making him available if a Senate seat comes open.

Junior Senator

Bernie Sanders (I)

Elected 2006, term expires Jan. 2019, 2nd term; b. Sept. 8, 1941, Brooklyn, NY; U. of Chicago, B.S. 1964; Jewish; married (Jane O'Meara); 4 children.

Elected Office: Elected Office: Burlington mayor, 1981-89; U.S. House, 1991-2007.

Professional Career: Writer; Dir., American People's Historical Soc., 1977-81; Lecturer, Harvard U., 1989; Lecturer, Hamilton Col., 1990.

DC Office: 332 DSOB, 20510, 202-224-5141; Fax: 202-228-0776; Website: sanders.senate.gov.

State Offices: Burlington, 802-862-0697 or 800-339-9834; St. Johnsbury, 802-748-0191 or 802-748-9269.

Committees: *Budget* (RMM). *Energy & Natural Resources:* Energy; Nat'l Parks; Water & Power. *Environment & Public Works:* Clean Air & Nuclear Safety; Fisheries, Water & Wildlife; Transportation & Infrastructure. *Health, Education, Labor & Pensions:* Children & Families; Primary Health & Retirement Security (RMM). *Veterans' Affairs*.

Group Ratings

	ADA	ACLU	AFL-CIO	LCV	ITI	COC	HAFA	ACU	CFG	FRC
2014	95%	100%	–	80%	100%	14%	7%	4%	7%	0%
2013	100%	C	100%	100%	C	38%	C	0%	0%	C

National Journal Ratings

	2013 LIB	—	2013 CONS
Economic	82%	—	8%
Social	66%	—	32%
Foreign	51%	—	47%
Composite	69%	—	31%

Key Votes of the 113th Congress

1. Sandy storm spending	Y	5. Student Loan Rates	N	9. Bipartisan Budget Deal	Y
2. Chuck Hagel Confirmation	Y	6. Employee Non-Discrim'n Act	Y	10. Farm Bill Conference Rept.	Y
3. Gun Background Checks	Y	7. Senate Vote on Judgeships	N	11. Unempl. Comp. Extension	Y
4. Immigration Reform	Y	8. Defense Dept. Spending	Y	12. Keystone Pipeline	N

Election Results

2012 general	Bernie Sanders (I)..................... 207,848	(71%)	$3,247,555
	John MacGovern (R)................... 72,898	(25%)	$131,927
	Cris Ericson (UMJ)........................ 5,924	(2%)	
2012 primary	Bernie Sanders (D) ....unopposed		

Prior winning percentages: 2006 (65%); House: 2004 (67%), 2002 (64%), 2000 (69%), 1998 (63%), 1996 (55%), 1994 (50%), 1992 (58%), 1990 (56%)

A couple of months after announcing his candidacy for the 2016 Democratic presidential nomination, Bernie Sanders—a self-styled socialist who since 2006 has been Vermont's junior senator—made an appearance on CBS' "Face The Nation", during which he criticized President Barack Obama's efforts to compromise early in his White House tenure. Sanders made clear he felt Obama had wasted time trying to engage Republican congressional leaders, asserting: "The truth is Republicans never wanted to negotiate. All they wanted to do was obstruct."

Such comments—while hardly in keeping with the more compromising tones usually adopted by presidential contenders—are nonetheless consistent with Sanders' long-time public persona. The latter was elevated nationally in December 2010, when he delivered an eight-hour, often apoplectic Senate floor speech against extending tax cuts for the wealthy enacted early in the administration of President George W. Bush. Sanders' unapologetic stance was also reflective of his fiery rhetoric since hitting the presidential campaign trail, where he early on drew large crowds—and pulled even with frontrunner Hillary Clinton in one poll of New Hampshire primary voters—by railing against the "billionaire class" and urging a "political revolution."

But the reality of Sanders' long tenure on Capitol Hill, which began with his election to the House in 1990, is more complex. He has won praise from Senate colleagues for his willingness to—yes, compromise, and forge legislative deals. Taking over the chairmanship of the Senate Veterans' Affairs Committee in 2013, he steered an overhaul of the VA into law a year later, making it one of the few major bipartisan accomplishments of a politically gridlocked Congress. Shortly after closing that legislative deal in 2014—and a year before his comments on "Face The Nation"—Sanders adopted a more conciliatory tone as he harkened back to his days as the first socialist mayor of Burlington, in the 1980s. "When I took office, [in terms of] people who supported me on the city council, we had two out of 13, and I had to make things happen while being in the minority," Sanders told *Roll Call*. "So I do know how to negotiate fairly. Negotiation is part of the political process. I certainly have been prepared to do that since day one."

As his still-thick Brooklyn accent indicates, Sanders grew up in the Flatbush section of New York City's largest borough, the son of a paint salesman who had emigrated from Poland; his mother died when he was a teenager. He attended Brooklyn College before graduating from the University of Chicago, where he became involved in radical leftist politics. Sanders then moved to Vermont as part of the hippie migration of 1968—part of the influx of urbanites in the 1960s and 1970s that transformed the once solidly Republican state into the deep blue bastion it is today. Sanders worked as a carpenter after arriving in Vermont. In 1971, he ran in a special election for the Senate to replace Republican Winston Prouty, who died in office in 1971. Sanders won just 2 percent of the vote as the candidate of the Liberty Union Party. He went on to lose four more statewide races (including a 1974 Senate bid when, running against Democrat Patrick Leahy, now his senior colleague from the Green Mountain State, Sanders raised his share of the vote on the Liberty Union line to 4 percent.)

Sanders' rumpled, tieless, earnest persona finally won over the people of Burlington, who elected him mayor in 1981 by just 10 votes. "There was anger in the air, plenty of it," the *Burlington Free Press* recalled more than three decades later. "Bernie Sanders, a self-proclaimed socialist of all people, had somehow stolen City Hall from [the Democrats]." He served as mayor until 1989, winning reelection three times. "I am a socialist, of course I am a socialist," Sanders declared during a 1983 mayoral debate, according to an *Associated Press* account at the time. He added, "To hold a vision that society can be fundamentally different, to believe that all people can be equal, that is not a new idea." He called a change he had made to give city employees input into policies such as sick leave and grievance procedures "a socialist idea."

In 1988, when Republican Rep. James Jeffords ran for the Senate, Sanders made a bid for the House as an independent, but lost to Republican Peter Smith in a close, three-way race: 41 percent for Smith to 38 percent for Sanders, a margin of about 9,000 votes. Two years later, Sanders ran again, and this time defeated Smith, 56%-40%, becoming only the third socialist ever elected to the House, after Victor Berger of Milwaukee (1911-13, 1923-29) and Meyer London of Manhattan's Lower East Side (1915-23).

Sanders benefited politically in 1990 from his opposition to gun control: Smith had voted to ban semi-automatic weapons, and the National Rifle Association came out against him. Three years later, in 1993, Sanders voted against the so-called Brady Bill requiring background checks for individuals purchasing firearms. It is a vote that has haunted him politically; in 2015, a political action committee backing one of his presidential rivals, former Maryland Gov. Martin O'Malley, ran ads attacking Sanders' gun control stance. In recent years, Sanders has shifted his position, voting in 2013 in favor of legislation to expand background checks in the wake of the Newtown Connecticut school shootings. But he represents a state where gun ownership is widespread, and Sanders appeared to be playing the role of pragmatic politician during his successful 1990 campaign. "Bernie's response is that he doesn't just represent liberals and progressives. He was sent to Washington to represent all of Vermont," Sanders' chief of staff was quoted as saying shortly after he won. "It's not inappropriate for a congressman to support a majority position, particularly on something Vermonters have been very clear about."

During his 16 years in the House, Sanders was Vermont's single, at-large member. Democrats initially balked at accepting a socialist in their caucus, but they granted him seniority as a Democrat after he arrived on Capitol Hill in early 1991. He amassed a heavily liberal voting record and formed a Progressive Caucus with a quixotic agenda: progressive tax reform, a Canada-style single-payer health care system, a 50-percent cut in military spending, a national energy policy, and—a Vermont touch—support for family farms. A number of these ideas formed the heart of his presidential bid. After announcing, Sanders called for significantly raising tax rates on the highest earners and instituting a government-run single-payer system for health care; a similar public option was considered as part of the debate over the Affordable Care Act in 2009-2010, but dropped for lack of support.

However, Sanders exhibited his more practical side as a legislator at times during his House tenure. He gained Republican allies in targeting so-called corporate welfare—government benefits to well-heeled companies. With Republican Chris Smith of New Jersey, he won passage of an amendment barring spending for defense contractor mergers. In 2001, he proposed a $300-per-person income tax rebate. It quickly became Democratic Party policy, and Republicans, in assembling majorities for the Bush tax cuts, included it in diluted form—a $300 rebate for income-tax-paying adults. Sanders and the Democrats noted ruefully that Bush took credit for a tax-cutting proposal that was initially theirs. As much as any member of Congress, Sanders made the cost of prescription drugs a national issue. Since the 1980s, he had called for government programs to pay for prescription drugs, and he was the first member of Congress to lead bus trips to Canada to buy lower cost pharmaceuticals there.

All of this played well with Vermont voters, and by the late 1990s, Sanders was winning reelection by large margins, regularly garnering more than 60 percent of the vote. In May 2001, Jeffords left the Republican Party, an event that gave Democrats a majority in the Senate for 19 months. Like Sanders in the House, Jeffords called himself an independent, but caucused with the Democrats. In April 2005, Jeffords announced he would not run for another term in 2006. Sanders became the early frontrunner and quickly amassed endorsements from top Vermont Democrats, including Burlington Mayor Peter Clavelle and state Senate President Pro Tempore Peter Welch (who succeeded Sanders in the state's at-large House seat). With Sanders' consent, Democrats ran his name on their primary ballot, and he won 94 percent of the vote, although he formally declined the nomination and petitioned the state to list him on the general election ballot as an independent.

On the GOP side, Gov. Jim Douglas was considered the one Republican with a real shot at defeating Sanders, but Douglas declined to run. Richard Tarrant, a multi-millionaire businessman and former high school basketball star, became the nominee. His ads sought to portray Sanders as an ineffective radical who was soft on sexual predators and drug dealers. The strategy might have worked elsewhere, but not in Vermont, where voters were well-acquainted with Sanders and his iconoclastic ways. Despite the harsh attacks—or perhaps because of them—Tarrant was never able to close the gap in the polls. He outspent Sanders, but Sanders raised and spent over $6 million, many times more than ever before and enough to make it the costliest race in state history. Sanders won handily, 65%-32%. Sanders had even less trouble winning election to a second term in 2012, easily dispatching underfunded Republican John MacGovern, 71%-25%.

After crossing over to the other side of the Capitol, Sanders settled with surprising ease into the Senate's more structured ways, and grew more sensitive to his reputation as a troublemaker. Leahy told a Vermont reporter that other senators—presumably expecting a political bomb-thrower in their midst—had confided to him "what a pleasant surprise [Sanders] has turned out to be" with his willingness to craft legislative deals. With seats on committees that deal with energy and environmental issues, Sanders worked for deep cuts in industrial pollution in the global warming bill. He sought to promote new technology to reduce emissions in the automobile and energy industries. In 2007, the Senate passed his amendment to the energy bill to encourage universities to support energy-efficient projects.

But the feisty liberal side of Sanders that would later be on prominent display in the presidential contest remained very much in evidence—as he at one point likened skeptics of human-caused global warming to non-Germans who had denied the spread of Nazism before World War II. When Obama nominated Ben Bernanke in 2009 as chairman of the Federal Reserve, Sanders bristled, "When the people voted for change in 2008, they did not vote to have one of the key architects of the Bush economy be reappointed." In June 2012, Sanders released the names of 18 Federal Reserve regional bank directors (current and former) whose businesses had received close to zero interest loans from the Federal Reserve. A couple of years earlier, as Congress debated the so-called Dodd-Frank bill overhauling regulation of the financial industry, Sanders got a provision into the Senate version ordering an audit of the Fed.

When in 2011 the "Occupy Wall Street" protest movement energized the American left, Sanders endorsed the goals of the upstart movement. "I am very supportive of the protests because they are focusing attention on an issue that needs a lot of discussion: not only the greed of Wall Street and the reckless behavior that has caused this recession, but also the growing inequality in the United States," Sanders told the *Burlington Free Press*. None of his efforts, however, drew as much attention as the marathon floor speech at the end of 2010 when he excoriated the extension of the Bush tax cuts for the wealthy as "Robin Hood in reverse." At one point, Sanders sarcastically asked: "How can I get by on one house? I need five houses, 10 houses! I need three jet planes to take me all over the world! Sorry, American people. We've got the money, we've got the power, we've got the lobbyists here and on Wall Street. Tough luck."

The speech proved so popular that it temporarily shut down the Senate video server and put his name atop Twitter's list of trending topics. In early 2011, it was sold as a book, *The Speech: A Historic Filibuster on Corporate Greed and the Decline of Our Middle Class*, with the proceeds going to Vermont charities. In the months following the speech, Sanders made the rounds of television shows ranging from MSNBC to *The Daily Show with Jon Stewart*. He was picked as the keynote speaker at California's Democratic Party convention, as he released a list of 10 large corporations that he said had paid disproportionately low taxes, including GE, Exxon Mobil, and Bank of America.

Sanders drew attention in fall 2013 when he toured several Southern states and declared he would consider running for president in 2016. "Anyone who really, really wants to be president is slightly crazy because this is an unbelievably difficult job given the crises that this country faces today," he said during one appearance. Nevertheless, he said that if no one else with his views ended up in the race, he would contemplate it to ensure someone raised the issues important to him—reining in Wall Street, addressing the "collapse" of the middle class and fighting the spread of poverty. He took the plunge after the first choice of the party's left wing, Massachusetts Sen. Elizabeth Warren, spent a year insisting she had no plans to mount a White House bid. But his prospective entry into the race prompted a rebuke of sorts from a former left-wing third party presidential candidate, consumer activist Ralph Nader. "You are a Lone Ranger, unable even to form a core progressive force within the Senate," Nader declared in an April 2014 letter chastising Sanders for his work on Capitol Hill.

Back in Washington, Sanders found himself in a somewhat unexpected position of influence as Veterans' Affairs chairman in 2014. Revelations about the poor treatment that veterans faced forced out Secretary Eric Shinseki and led to considerable pressure to pass a reform bill. Over several months, Sanders engaged in a regular and bitter war of words with his conservative House counterpart, Jeff Miller of Florida, but the two men struck a compromise at the conclusion of what Sanders called "a very, very difficult process." The $17 billion package sailed through the House unanimously and drew just three dissenting votes in the Senate. It represented one of the largest expansions of the federal government since the Republicans had taken over the House majority at the beginning of 2011.

Despite statements by Sanders that he's in it to win, virtually no one else saw a prospect of Sanders capturing the Democratic presidential nomination in 2016, albeit the early enthusiasm for his candidacy was credited with pulling Clinton to the left. Meanwhile, at the beginning of 2015, Sanders became ranking Democrat on the Budget Committee. If the Democrats regain majority control of the Senate in the 2016 election, Sanders could hold the influential post of Budget Committee chairman. It may not be the Oval Office, but it nevertheless would make for a high profile consolation prize.

In a June 2015 interview with *The Washington Post*, Sanders sought to define himself as a liberal version of a "deficit hawk," declaring, "Very often at budget hearings you will hear me say 'as the major deficit hawk in the committee'...I refer to myself as that because I voted against the war in Iraq, I voted against tax breaks for millionaires, I voted against the Medicare prescription drug program [adopted by the Republican-controlled Congress in 2003], I voted against the deregulation of Wall Street, which has caused so many problems." He continued: "The question is how do you do deficit reduction in a way that is fair? I'm a deficit hawk when I say we have to ask the wealthiest people and the largest corporations to pay their fair share. That's a deficit hawk."

Sanders has been a steadfast opponent of proposals to privatize Social Security. Throughout his career, retiree groups have been his leading campaign contributor, according to the Center for Responsive Politics. In March 2011, Sanders introduced a bill that would make it out of order in the Senate or House to consider any legislation that would increase the retirement age for Social Security eligibility. In August 2011, he made a public plea to lift the cap on payroll taxes that underwrite Social Security. Such a move would provide additional revenue that could be used to increase benefits, a move Sanders has included in his presidential campaign platform. Such a proposal comes at a time when the focus of discussion in recent years has been on ways to restrain the growth of entitlements. However, when Obama expressed a willingness to discuss entitlement reform as part of deficit talks, Sanders quickly pointed out that the president had vowed not to cut Social Security during the 2008 campaign.

On another fiscal front, after Hurricane Irene hit his state hard in the summer of 2011, Sanders led the way in attacking then-House Majority Leader Eric Cantor of Virginia for suggesting that offsetting cuts should be made in conjunction with the release of federal disaster relief funds. In a *USA Today* op-ed, an outraged Sanders declared, "This absurd logic means that whether it is Hurricane Irene today or any future disaster, we might have to cut nutrition programs, Medicare, Medicaid or education before we can rebuild a devastated community."

REPRESENTATIVE-AT-LARGE

Peter Welch (D)

Elected 2006, 5th term; b. May 2, 1947, Springfield, MA; Col. of the Holy Cross, B.A. 1969, U. of CA Berkeley, J.D. 1973; Catholic; married (Margaret Cheney); 8 children.

Elected Office: Elected Office: VT Senate, 1981-89, 2002-07, min. ldr., 1983-85, pres. pro tem, 1985-89, 2003-07.

Professional Career: Robert F. Kennedy fellow, 1969-70; Practicing atty., 1974-2006.

DC Office: 2303 RHOB, 20515, 202-225-4115; Website: welch.house. gov.

State Offices: Burlington, 802-652-2450 or 888-605-7270.

Committees: Energy & Commerce: *Energy & Commerce:* Commerce, Manufacturing & Trade; Communications & Technology; Energy & Power; Oversight & Investigations. *Oversight & Government Reform.*

Group Ratings

	ADA	ACLU	AFL-CIO	LCV	ITI	COC	HAFA	ACU	CFG	FRC
2014	85%	88%	–	91%	60%	29%	10%	4%	10%	0%
2013	95%	C	90%	93%	C	31%	C	12%	10%	C

National Journal Ratings

	2013 LIB	—	2013 CONS
Economic	90%	—	9%
Social	93%	—	0%
Foreign	94%	—	0%
Composite	95%	—	5%

Key Votes of the 113th Congress

1. Sandy storm spending	Y	5. Medical Marijuana	Y	9. Syrian Rebels Training	N
2. Violence Against Women Act	Y	6. Farm Bill	N	10. Keystone pipeline	N
3. Guantanamo Bay Detainees	Y	7. Afghanistan Combat	Y	11. Immigration Exec. Action	N
4. Abortion 20-week ban	N	8. NSA Phone Data Collection	Y	12. Bipartisan budget deal	Y

Election Results

2014 general	Peter Welch (D) 123,349	(64%)	$700,783	$7,696
	Mark Donka (R) 59,432	(31%)	$4,558	
2014 primary	Peter Welch (D) .... unopposed			

Prior winning percentages: 2012 (72%), 2010 (65%), 2008 (83%), 2006 (53%)

Population		Race and Ethnicity		Income	
Total:	626,630	White	94.0%	Median income:	$54,842
Urban:	11.6%	Latino	1.5%		*(190 of 435)*
Suburban:	19.0%	Asian	1.2%	Under $50,000	47.0%
Rural:	69.5%	Black	0.8%	$50,000-$99,999:	32.8%
Land area:	9,217	Two races	2.1%	$100,000-$199,999:	16.4%
Pop/sq. mi.:	68.0	White Ethnic	53.9%	$200,000 or more:	3.8%
Born in state:	50.5%			Poverty Rate	12.3%
		Education			
Age Groups		H.S. grad or less:	39.1%	**Work**	
Under 18:	19.8%	Some college:	25.1%	White collar:	39.5%
18 to 34:	21.8%	College degree, 4 yr.:	21.4%	Blue collar:	39.8%
35 to 64:	42.0%	Post-grad study:	14.3%	Sales and service:	20.7%
Over 64:	16.4%				
		Military		Govt. workers:	14.3%
		Veterans/active duty:	8.2%		

Peter Welch (D)

Vermont's only House member is Peter Welch, a Democrat first elected in 2006. He is highly regarded within his party as a strategist and spokesman. He serves as a chief deputy whip and has been active on energy and health care issues.

Welch grew up in Springfield Massachusetts, the son of a dentist, and graduated from the College of the Holy Cross. The summer before his junior year, he worked for a Jesuit group that did community outreach in poor black neighborhoods in Chicago, where he was inspired by a speech by the

Voter Turnout	
2013 Total Citizen 18+	492,678
2014 House Turnout	191,504
2014 Turnout as % CVAP	38.9%
2012 Turnout as % CVAP	60.7%

Rev. Martin Luther King Jr. After graduating from law school at the University of California, Berkeley, Welch backpacked down the Pan-American Highway to Santiago, Chile, went overland to Brazil, then worked on a freighter that sailed to Portugal. After that, he was ready to practice law, and chose White River Junction, Vermont, as his home. He worked as a public defender before founding his small firm.

In 1980, Welch became the first Democrat to represent Windsor County in the state Senate since the Civil War. Two years later, he was made Senate minority leader. In 1984, after Democrats won a majority in the Senate for the first time ever, he was elected Senate president pro tem. He focused on environment, education, and tax issues and helped establish the Housing and Land Conservation Trust, which worked to create affordable housing and to conserve farmland and forests. In 1988, when Republican Rep. James Jeffords ran for the Senate, Welch aimed for the House but lost the Democratic primary by 266 votes. In 1990, he ran for governor, but lost 52%-46% to Republican Richard Snelling. For some years after that, Welch was out of political life. His wife, Joan, who had been his closest adviser and campaign manager, fought cancer for nine years, and Welch at times was her full-time caregiver. She died in 2004.

In 2001, Democratic Gov. Howard Dean appointed Welch to the state Senate to fill a vacancy in Windsor County. In 2003, he became president pro tem once again and focused on health care issues. He helped negotiate a deal for the storage of spent nuclear fuel on the site of the Vermont Yankee nuclear power plant. In the spring of 2005, Jeffords announced that he would not seek reelection in 2006. Socialist Rep. Bernie Sanders, after 15 years in the House, ran for the Senate and attracted little opposition. Welch decided to run again for the House.

Other potential Democratic candidates canvassed for support, but no one else ran and Welch won the primary unopposed. Martha Rainville, commander of the Vermont National Guard, won the Republican primary 71%-28%. In the general election, Welch ran as an opponent—from the start—of military action in Iraq, and he condemned the "corrupt" Republicans in Washington. He supported a universal health care program. Rainville said she would have voted for military action in Iraq in 2002 given what was known then, but she also criticized some of the Bush administration's decisions since. Both candidates favored access to abortion.

Following an agreement by the candidates, this was probably the only seriously contested House race in 2006 without a single negative ad. But there was some dispute. Welch called Rainville the "hand-picked" candidate of the unpopular national Republicans. Rainville countered that Vermont Republicans are "something very different," and insisted that "the party has a lot of room for diversity." Welch spent $1.7 million to Rainville's $1.1 million. But the House Republican campaign committee outspent its Democratic counterpart, $750,000 to $300,000. This was one of the few Democratic seats that Republicans thought they had a good chance to pick up. The contest was close in the polls throughout the summer, but by late September, Welch opened up a lead. Rainville was embarrassed when she was forced to fire a speechwriter in early October for plagiarizing from Democratic Sen. Hillary Clinton of New York. Welch won, 53%-45%.

In the House, Welch has become known for legislative skill, which features an understated and collegial style. He joined the Energy and Commerce Committee in 2009, just in time to help shape energy and climate-change legislation. He got a provision in the House-passed bill to invest billions of dollars in energy-efficiency efforts. A year later, he won committee approval of a measure to provide tax rebates to consumers for installing upgraded insulation, storm windows and other energy-efficiency aids. Practicing what he preached, he made his office the first in the House to install new lights and water fixtures to reduce energy use.

After the GOP takeover of the House, he became a chief deputy for Minority Whip Steny Hoyer. He helped liberals articulate their opposition to both the tax cut extension deal between President Barack Obama and House Republicans in December 2010 as well as the GOP's vote to repeal health care reform the following month. The Democrats' move to the minority forced him to give up his Energy and Commerce seat for two years until there was a slot for Welch to return.

Welch is not a strict partisan. He worked with Republicans on a measure in early 2013 to allow states to ensure online merchants collect sales taxes in return for simplified tax procedures. In 2011, his bill to prevent the Afghan government from taxing American companies delivering U.S. aid to that country drew support from several conservatives. Retaining his interest in energy efficiency, he joined Republican Rep. David McKinley of West Virginia on a broad package that includes efficiency standards for utility companies and a requirement that federally backed home mortgages must include efficiency ratings for the property. The House passed the bill in April 2015. Welch has been a member of the bipartisan citizen activist effort No Labels.

Overseas, he broke with Obama in September 2014 on the call to train and equip rebels opposing the Islamic State and the regime in Syria. "I do not believe that that plan has any reasonable prospect of success," Welch said. Two months later, he said that it was "an abdication of congressional responsibility" for lawmakers to take no action on Obama's request for authorization of force against ISIS.

At home, Welch has faced no serious reelection threats. In 2009, he married state Rep. Margaret Cheney, who later became a member of the Vermont Public Service Board. After Gov. Peter Shumlin announced that he would not seek reelection in 2016, Welch said that he would not seek to replace him in Montpelier. But he is considered a distinct possibility to run for the Senate if an opening occurs.

★ VIRGINIA ★

What we now know as the United States originated in Virginia—in 1607, with the first permanent English settlement in North America at Jamestown. The colony had its struggles—with food, weather and Indians—but ultimately persevered, producing twin, contradictory legacies that shaped the nation: representative democracy and slavery. Virginia's capital moved to Williamsburg in 1699, becoming the locus of commercial, cultural and intellectual life of the colonial era, all the way through the American Revolution. In the early Republic, Virginia was the leading state, with the largest population, the greatest wealth, and the most illustrious political figures—a state that seemed destined to lead and shape a nation. From this tobacco-growing region emerged a group of leaders—George Washington, George Mason, Patrick Henry, Thomas Jefferson, Richard Henry Lee, and James Madison—that in learning, wisdom, and strength of character equaled any group from any polity since Periclean Athens or Republican Rome. The Virginia they led into the American Revolution was the indispensable creator of the republic and the Constitution that has held together the world's greatest democracy. But these men embodied ideals that were profoundly dichotomous. They were slaveholders who insisted on liberty, armed men who insisted on the rule of law, and believers in racial inequality who set forth principles of equality that would in time form the basis of a society that rejected racism.

After the Revolutionary War, seven of the first dozen presidents hailed from Virginia. But in the first half of the 19th century, the state was eclipsed in population and wealth by Pennsylvania and New York. During the Civil War, Virginia had two great heroes, Robert E. Lee and Stonewall Jackson, but they fought for their state rather than the larger nation. Much of that fighting took place in Virginia, as Union forces tried to storm Richmond—by then the Confederate capital—and Lee's forces started to break through to the North. In the process, many of Virginia's mountain counties broke off and joined the Union as the separate state of West Virginia. After the war, Virginia's leadership class was impoverished and embittered. Industrialization was haphazard. Railroads were constructed to ship cotton up from the South and coal east to the seaports. Textile mills were built in Southside towns and tobacco factories in Richmond. Railroad magnate Collis Huntington built the giant Newport News Shipbuilding & Drydock Co. Politically, Virginia was ruled by local gentry who worshipped their revolutionary past and mourned the "Lost Cause" of the Confederacy. They were pessimists, looking not for economic growth but for stability, bent on maintaining Virginia's segregation and content with its second-class economy. County courthouse organizations were united in a political machine by Harry Byrd Sr., who ran Virginia politics from 1925, when he was elected governor, to 1965, when he retired from the U.S. Senate. In national politics, this machine lost battles more often than Lee lost on the battlefield, and less gallantly. For years, the Byrd machine succeeded in keeping most vestiges of racial equality out of Virginia, to the point of closing public schools in Prince Edward County in the 1950s rather than obeying a federal court desegregation order.

This "massive resistance" collapsed in the late 1950s. The many federal employees in the bedroom communities of Northern Virginia, combined with workers in the industrial Hampton Roads region around Norfolk and Newport News and the enfranchisement of African-Americans, provided a new political base for Democrats, though suburban growth also kept the Republicans strong; the state would vote Republican for president from 1968 to 2004. In 1970, Virginia was roughly split between its major metropolitan areas—Northern Virginia, Hampton Roads and Richmond—and the rest of Virginia, consisting of rural areas, small towns, and small industrial and textile-mill cities. The latter were solidly conservative. Most African-Americans didn't vote, and the poll tax held down voting among poor whites until it was found unconstitutional. With less than half of Virginia's population, but hardly any African-Americans, West Virginia cast more votes than Virginia did in 1960.

A half-century later, Northern Virginia had spread inexorably into once-rural counties, some of which became the nation's fastest-growing exurbs in the 1990s and 2000s, and which accounted for 33% of the state's population. Hampton Roads, growing out into swampy lands on either side of the James River and swelled because of a large military presence, accounted for another 21%. Metropolitan Richmond, undeterred by the increasing marginalization of tobacco, expanded outward in every direction and accounted for 16% of the state's population. The traditional Virginia had shrunk geographically, limited to the Northern Neck, the

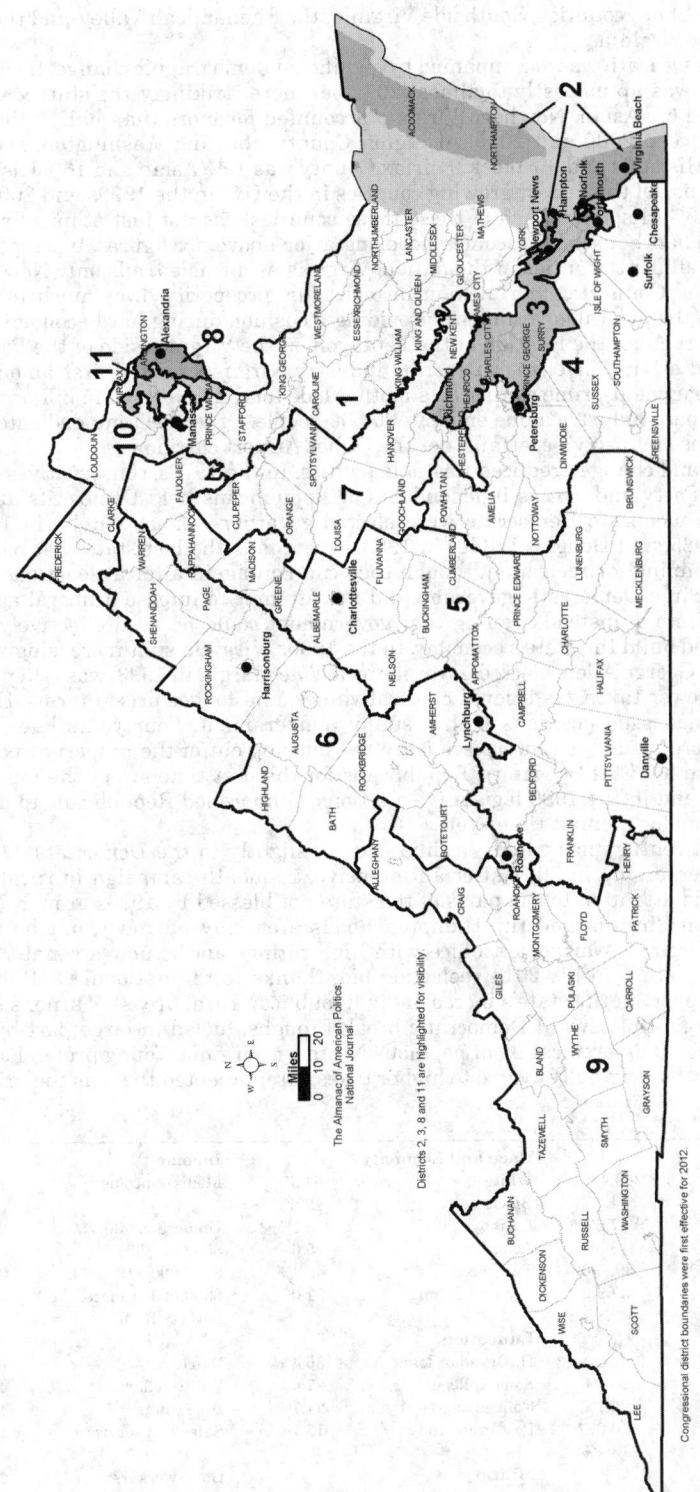

The Almanac of American Politics.
National Journal.

Miles
0 10 20

Districts 2, 3, 8 and 11 are highlighted for visibility.

Congressional district boundaries were first effective for 2012.

two Eastern Shore counties, Southside Virginia, the Shenandoah Valley, and the mountains of Southwest Virginia.

Virginia's growth was accompanied by significant demographic change. Its black population in 2014 was up modestly to almost 20%, but more strikingly, the state was almost 9% Hispanic and 6% Asian. Northern Virginia accounted for more than half of the population increase between 2000 and 2010. Arlington County, abutting Washington, D.C., was 10% Asian, 16% Hispanic and 9% black. Fairfax County was 19% Asian and 16% Hispanic. Loudoun County, one of the fastest growing counties in the U.S. in the 1990s and 2000s, was 17% Asian and 13% Hispanic. Each of these three counties was not just ethnically diverse but also had median household incomes hovering at or above six figures, placing them in the top 10 most affluent counties in the nation. Virginia as a whole trails only New Hampshire, Maryland and Connecticut in median income. This prosperity owes much to the region's proximity to the federal government, providing a cushion during hard economic times elsewhere. In particular, the location of the Pentagon on the Virginia side of the Potomac River has spawned a large defense-contracting industry. Virginia ranked first among states for Defense Department prime contracts, a mother lode totaling almost $45 billion in 2013. The state's aerospace industry alone employs 30,500 people. Other tech-minded enterprises, riding the defense industry's coattails, dot the Dulles Airport corridor.

Growth and change produced unstable politics. In the 1970s, conservatives who left the Democratic Party and ran as independents or Republicans held Democrats at bay. In the 1980s, three moderate Democrats were elected governor—Charles Robb in 1981, Gerald Baliles in 1985, and Douglas Wilder in 1989. (Virginia is the last state that bars its governors from running for reelection, though they can run again after at least one term out of office.) The three Democratic governors did not attempt to impose a liberal agenda on an unwilling Virginia, instead arguing that government could be used effectively to improve education and build the state's economy. In the 1990s, Virginia split increasingly along ideological lines. George Allen, elected governor by a wide margin in 1993, was a Republican who believed in lower taxes, traditional cultural values, and longer prison terms. He combined confrontational issue positions with a sunny temperament. Four years later, Republican James Gilmore made his centerpiece issue the phasing-out of the property tax on automobiles and won a 56%-43% victory. Republicans for the first time swept the top three statewide offices, and in the 1999 legislative elections, Gilmore led Republicans to majorities in both chambers for the first time ever.

The 21st century has tilted Virginia ever so slightly to the Democrats. Mark Warner won the governorship in 2001 after an intensive, 18-month campaign in rural Virginia in which he paid attention to the parts of the state not blessed by 1990s growth. Warner carried Northern Virginia and the Hampton Roads area only narrowly, but he also carried non-urban Virginia. Warner left office with high ratings and is now a senator (though he experienced a scare in his 2014 reelection bid, thanks to the national GOP wave and an erosion of support in the state's increasingly Republican rural areas). Warner's success represented the first of several Democratic breakthroughs, fueled in large part by the ethnic and generational diversification of populous Northern Virginia. Young professionals moving into the suburbs, originally averse to higher taxes, later accepted them as the price of easing

Population		Race and Ethnicity		Income	
Total:	8,260,405	White	64.3%	Median income:	$67,620
Urban:	34.2%	Black	19.2%		(3 of 50)
Suburban:	47.5%	Latino	8.0%	Under $50,000	39.9%
Rural:	18.3%	Asian	5.6%	$50,000-$99,999:	30.2%
Land area:	39,490	Two races	2.4%	$100,000-$199,999:	22.1%
Pop/sq. mi.:	209.2	White Ethnic	21.0%	$200,000 or more:	7.8%
Born in state:	49.8%			Poverty Rate	9.2%
		Education			
Age Groups		H.S. grad or less:	36.4%	**Work**	
Under 18:	22.6%	Some college:	27.4%	White collar:	42.2%
18 to 34:	24.1%	College degree, 4 yr.:	21.1%	Blue collar:	40.1%
35 to 64:	40.0%	Post-grad study:	15.1%	Sales and service:	17.7%
Over 64:	13.4%				
		Military		Govt. workers:	20.0%
		Veterans/active duty:	12.0%		

their rigorous commuting. Many suburban voters were also repelled by the Republicans' social conservatism, which was punctuated by a turn to the right within the party apparatus, which turned toward nominating conventions dominated by hard-core activists.

While George W. Bush carried Northern Virginia in 2000, he lost it four years later, 51%-48%. The trend accelerated as Democrat

Voter Turnout		
2013 Total Citizen 18+	5,966,761	
2014 Highest Statewide Turnout	2,184,473	
2014 Turnout as % CVAP	36.6%	
2012 Turnout as % CVAP	65.5%	
Legislature		
Senate:	21R	19D
House:	67R	32D	1V

Tim Kaine was elected governor in 2005 over Republican Jerry Kilgore, whose conservative stands were a tough sell in Northern Virginia as well as suburban Richmond and Hampton Roads. Three years later, Barack Obama became the first Democratic presidential candidate to carry Virginia since 1964, and he did so by his national average of 53%-46%. To do it, his campaign masterfully registered African-American voters all over the state, as well as new, young voters in Northern Virginia and in college towns. "Old Virginny is dead. We are a new and dynamic and exciting commonwealth," Kaine, an early Obama backer, proclaimed on Election Night. Obama installed Kaine as Democratic National Committee chairman.

Virginia politics zig-zagged back, at least temporarily, in 2009, amid dissatisfaction with Obama's agenda. Attorney General Bob McDonnell, elected in 2005 by just 323 votes over state Sen. Creigh Deeds, was the Republican nominee. McDonnell deemphasized the cultural issues he had focused on for years, running instead as a job-creating candidate ready to tackle the recession. His low-key demeanor and steady concentration on economic issues won him a smashing 59%-41% victory, the biggest margin for any Virginia governor since the last big victory of the Byrd machine in 1961. He carried through on his pragmatic approach, irking some Republicans by pushing through a transportation-funding bill for the congestion-plagued state in 2013; he also benefited from the economy, which remained relatively healthy during the recession, thanks in part to federal spending. Unemployment in the state hit 7.4% during the Great Recession, but that was still well below the national peak; by mid-2015, it had fallen below 5%, also lower than the national average. Virginia's relative prosperity—plus a never-ending organization, with 60 offices, 20,000 volunteers, and 580,000 door knocks—enabled Obama to carry the commonwealth again in 2012, though by the reduced margin of 51%-47%. The following year, amid a metastasizing money-and-influence scandal surrounding McDonnell and his wife, voters returned the governor's mansion to the Democrats, as national party fixer Terry McAuliffe defeated socially conservative attorney general Ken Cuccinelli. But wary about trusting one party with all levers of power, voters continued to give Republicans a large margin in the state House and a narrow one in the state Senate.

Presidential Politics Long ignored in presidential politics, Virginia suddenly became a national bellwether in 2008 and 2012, when its 53%-46% and 51%-47% margins for Barack Obama were the same as those in the nation as a whole. In the first half of the 20th century, it was part of the solid Democratic South. From 1952 to 1960, it obeyed the "golden silence" of Democratic Sen. Harry Byrd Sr. and voted Republican. It voted for Democrat Lyndon Johnson

2012 Presidential Vote		
Barack Obama (D) 1,971,820	(51%)
Mitt Romney (R).............1,822,522	(47%)
2012 Presidential Primary		
Mitt Romney (R).................158,119	(60%)
Ron Paul (R) 107,451	(40%)
2008 Presidential Vote		
Barack Obama (D) 1,959,532	(53%)
John McCain (R).............1,725,005	(46%)

for president in 1964 and then voted Republican in the next 10 elections. But over time, the margins narrowed. Democrat Bill Clinton lost here by only 47%-45% in 1996. In 2000, George W. Bush won 53%-44%. In 2004, Democrats, heartened by Mark Warner's election as governor in 2001, targeted the state early. John Kerry spent $1 million in advertising in the spring and early summer. But August polls showed Bush well ahead, and Virginia dropped out of the Democrat's focus. Even so, Bush lost the increasingly Democratic close-in D.C. suburbs in Northern Virginia 57%-42%, and his statewide margin was reduced to 54%-46%.

In 2008, Barack Obama targeted Virginia from start to finish, with satisfying results. His organizing efforts for the February 12 primary gave him a head start. He won the primary 64%-35% over Hillary Clinton. Republicans had difficulty believing polls showing Obama leading throughout most of the summer and fall, but the polls proved accurate. Obama ran seven percentage points ahead of Kerry's showing in 2004. Another way to look at it: John McCain got 8,000 more votes than Bush did in 2004; Obama got 505,000 more votes than Kerry.

In Northern Virginia, the Obama campaign registered immigrants and young singles and carried not only the close-in D.C. suburbs by a whopping 63%-36% spread, he also captured the Northern Virginia exurbs that stretch all the way to Frederick County on the border with West Virginia and south to Spotsylvania County, 51%-48%. In the Tidewater region (Hampton Roads) and metro Richmond, there was more emphasis on registering African-Americans, and turnout rose 19% and 20%, way ahead of population growth. Obama ran 10 points ahead of Kerry in the Tidewater, winning 57%-43%, and 10 points ahead of Kerry in metro Richmond, winning an area once staunchly Republican, 53%-46%. In the rest of the state, Obama ran five points ahead of Kerry. The county returns show sharp improvement in areas with many African-Americans. The Obama campaign opened offices and canvassed in counties where no one had ever seen a Democratic operation before. But that was not effective everywhere. In the Shenandoah Valley, where there are few blacks, he ran only slightly ahead of Kerry. In Southwest Virginia, where there are almost none, turnout was down, and Obama's percentages were lower than Kerry's, as was the case in adjacent Appalachian areas of West Virginia, Kentucky and Tennessee. The impact of Obama's organization was apparent from the exit poll showing that 50% of voters were contacted by his campaign, compared to 38% contacted by McCain's.

In 2012, intensive campaigning—national candidates made some 90 appearances in Virginia—didn't change the result appreciably. Obama's margin over Republican Mitt Romney was reduced to 51%-47%; he won 12,000 more votes than four years before, while Romney won 98,000 more votes than McCain. The patterns of support were similar. Close-in Northern Virginia D.C. suburbs voted 62%-36% for Obama, and he narrowly carried the Northern Virginia exurbs, 50%-49%. The vote was almost identical to 2008 in the Tidewater and metro Richmond, while Romney increased the Republican margin in the rest of the state to 57%-41%. Even without Northern Virginia, Obama would have barely won the state in 2008, by 50%-49%, and barely lost it in 2012, by 50%-48%.

Virginia has not had much of a tradition of presidential primaries, but that changed in 2008 as well. It did hold primaries on the original Super Tuesday in March 1988, when it voted for George H.W. Bush and Jesse Jackson, but it then switched back to choosing delegates at state conventions. Republicans held a primary in 2000 in which George W. Bush beat McCain 53%-44%. In 2004, Virginia held its presidential primary in February in order to gain the attention of presidential candidates and the national media, but Wesley Clark and John Edwards largely ceded Virginia to Kerry. Kerry carried every part of the state and won 52% of the vote to 27% for Edwards and 9% for Clark.

For 2008, Virginia scheduled primaries for Feb. 12, one week after Super Tuesday. Many people had expected both nominations to be settled by then, but the Democratic nomination was still very much in play, and the Republican nomination, though obviously headed to McCain, was still being contested by Mike Huckabee. Obama showed his mettle in this contest, out-organizing the Clinton campaign and, with his big victories the same day in Maryland and the District of Columbia, generating an enthusiasm that proved to be contagious for the rest of the month, as he won 11 straight February contests. Turnout was 986,000, more than double the 396,000 in 2004. Obama won 64%-35%, his biggest percentage in any primary except for those in the District of Columbia (75%), Georgia (66%), and Illinois (65%). He carried Northern Virginia 61%-39%, running well in upscale areas. But he also won over 70% of the vote in the Tidewater and metro Richmond, reflecting a major effort at turning out black voters. He even prevailed 54%-45% in the rest of the state. Clinton carried only one of the 11 congressional districts, the "Fighting 9th" in southwest Virginia.

The Republican contest attracted less attention and, significantly in a state with no party registration, only 489,000 votes. McCain beat Huckabee 50%-41%. Most of McCain's margin came from Northern Virginia, where he won 65% in the close-in D.C. suburbs and 53% in the exurbs. He got 49% in the Tidewater, 52% in metro Richmond, and only 41% in the rest of the state, while Huckabee carried almost everything west of the big metro areas. McCain's high mark was in Alexandria, just outside Washington, where he got 70% of the vote. Huckabee's was in Campbell County, just outside of Lynchburg and near the late Rev. Jerry Falwell's Liberty University, where he got 71% of the vote.

In 2012, the Republican primary was held on March 6. But only two candidates amassed the number of signatures required to get on the ballot; Rick Santorum, who lives in the state and whose campaign was headquartered there, failed to do so. Romney beat Ron Paul 60%-40%. This was Paul's highest percentage in any primary, but he won only three delegates.

Congressional Districts Despite above national average population growth, Virginia failed to gain a seat in the reapportionment following the 2010 census. In early 2011, Republicans controlled the governorship and the House of Delegates 59-39, but Democrats held a 22-18 majority in the Senate. By March,

114th Congress Lineup	
8 R	3 D
113th Congress Lineup	
8 R	3 D

Virginia's House incumbents had agreed on a mutual protection plan for both parties: Fairfax County Democrat Gerry Connolly, who had won reelection in the 11th by just 981 votes in 2010, would shed his toughest precincts to Republican Frank Wolf, whose exurban 10th District Republicans wanted to shore up in anticipation of Wolf's looming retirement. In the 9th District, freshman Morgan Griffith would pick up his hometown of Salem from the 6th. And Republican Randy Forbes would shed the 78% black city of Petersburg to the black-majority 3rd District. In April, Republicans in the House of Delegates dutifully passed the plan.

But in June, Senate Democrats, grimacing at the prospect of a solid 8-3 Republican delegation, passed a competing plan converting Forbes' 4th District into a second minority-majority seat. Rather than negotiate, Republicans stonewalled, shrewdly waiting to see whether they could take back the Senate in November 2011 (Virginia holds odd-year elections). Sure enough, Republicans picked up two seats—allowing Republican Lt. Gov. Bill Bolling to break a tie—and passed their map in January. In November, Republicans easily kept their 8-3 edge.

The Senate Democrats' plan took on new life in October 2014, when a three-judge federal court panel ruled that the state's map was an unconstitutional violation of the 14th Amendment's civil rights protections. The court ordered the Republican-controlled legislature to draw a new map by September 2015. Additional litigation remained a strong possibility.

Governor

Terry McAuliffe (D)

Elected 2013, term expires Jan. 2018, 1st term; b. Feb. 9, 1957, Syracuse, NY; Catholic U., B.A. 1979, Georgetown U., J.D. 1984; Catholic; married (Dorothy); 5 children.

Professional Career: Founder, McAuliffe Driveway Maintenance, 1971; Bd. member & chmn, Federal City Nat'l Bank, 1987-91; Campaign finance dir., U.S. Rep. Richard Gephardt, 1988; Co-founder & partner, McAuliffe, Kelly, Raffaelli, 1990-94; Co-dir., Pres. Bill Clinton re-election campaign, 1996; Chmn, Democratic Natl. Committee, 2001-05; Dir., Hilary Clinton presidential campaign, 2008; Chmn, GreenTech Automotive, 2009.

Office: State Capitol, 3rd floor, Richmond, 23219, 804-786-2211; Fax: 804-371-6351; Website: governor.virginia.gov.

Election Results

2013 general	Terry McAuliffe (D)	1,069,789	(48%)
	Ken Cuccinelli (R)	1,013,354	(45%)
	Robert Sarvis (Lib)	146,084	(7%)
2013 primary	Terry McAuliffe (D)	unopposed	

Democrat Terry McAuliffe was elected Virginia governor in 2013. A longtime fundraiser and all-around Democratic impresario known for his aggressive, wheeler-dealer style, McAuliffe finally became a candidate himself in 2009, losing Virginia's Democratic gubernatorial primary. Four years later, he won in an epic contest against Ken Cuccinelli, a state attorney general known for his fiery conservatism. It was widely believed during the campaign that, because of their polarizing natures, each man may have been the only one the other could have defeated.

McAuliffe was born in Syracuse New York, son of the treasurer of the Onondaga County Democratic Committee, whom he began helping collect money at the age of 8. At 14, McAuliffe built a driveway-tarring company—the first of many businesses he's been involved with during his career, from banking to real estate to investing to manufacturing. Whatever the business, McAuliffe has always kept a foot—or more—in politics. He gravitated to Washington early on, attending Catholic University as an undergraduate and then Georgetown for law school. He served as finance director of the Jimmy Carter-Walter Mondale reelection committee, as national finance chairman of Rep. Richard Gephardt's presidential committee, as national co-chairman of the Bill Clinton-Al Gore reelection committee and as chairman of Hillary Clinton's 2008 presidential campaign. McAuliffe has chaired party conventions and inaugurations, and between 2001 and 2005 he chaired the Democratic National Committee.

But such resume entries don't fully capture what sets McAuliffe apart—his eccentrically effective skills at separating political donors from their money. By the time he was elected governor, McAuliffe's aggressive salesmanship had been the stuff of legend for more than a quarter-century. In 1984, a Seattle newspaper said McAuliffe "could sell an icebox to an Eskimo or soda water to W. C. Fields." In 1987, the *New York Times'* Maureen Dowd noted that McAuliffe alternately cajoled and sweet-talked donors and their gatekeepers using the peppy language of a 1930s screwball-comedy character. He was known, she wrote, to lurk "in the dim light of dawn in driveways and on airport taxiways, interrupting dinners and vacations" just to bag an elusive donation, once even wrestling an alligator in Florida to secure a $15,000 check. His infectious enthusiasm and optimism got people to open their checkbooks; in his autobiography, he dubbed himself a "huckster." McAuliffe grew particularly close to Bill and Hillary Clinton; in addition to golfing and vacationing with them, he put up $1.35 million in cash to backstop the couple's mortgage when they purchased their post-presidential home in Chappaqua New York.

In 2009, McAuliffe moved beyond being a surrogate and a strategist by seeking the Democratic nomination for governor. McAuliffe's connections were golden, and he was extraordinarily well prepared for the nitty-gritty of running for office. But his stature within the national party wasn't enough to scare off challengers in Virginia, where he was seen as something of a carpetbagger. In the primary, he faced former state Del. Brian Moran from northern Virginia—the brother of Rep. James Moran—and state Sen. Creigh Deeds from the Shenandoah Valley, who four years earlier had lost an excruciatingly close race for attorney general to Republican Bob McDonnell. With the campaign under way during the Great Recession, McAuliffe touted his business background, but this proved to be a double-edged sword. To some, McAuliffe's wheeler-dealer style was off-putting, and his opponents reinforced this part of his background.

It became clear during the campaign that with McAuliffe, the lines between politicians, political donors and business partners had often become blurred. The *Washington Post* in 2013 detailed a "pattern of investments in which McAuliffe has used government programs, political connections and access to wealthy investors of both parties in pursuit of big profits for himself. ... A review of McAuliffe's business history shows him often coming out ahead personally, even if some investments fail or become embroiled in controversy." One such deal was a $100,000 investment in Global Crossing Holdings that earned him a reported $8 million, even though the company eventually flamed out. His opponents questioned whether the deals he put together actually created significant numbers of new jobs, as opposed to helping his own bottom line. Ultimately, primary voters gave the low-key, little-known Deeds the nod with a surprisingly large 50% of the vote. McAuliffe drew 26% and Moran took 24%. In the general election, Deeds faced McDonnell. The Republican came into the race known for his strong socially conservative views, but he ran a campaign that downplayed social issues in favor of economic ones, and that proved attractive to swing voters. Just as he did against Deeds four years earlier, McDonnell prevailed in the gubernatorial race, but this time his margin was much larger—59%-41%. The Republican won such northern Virginia swing counties as Loudoun and Prince William, both easily, and Fairfax, more narrowly.

With Deeds' second consecutive statewide loss, McAuliffe became the presumed front-runner for the Democratic gubernatorial nomination in 2013, and he devoted significant effort to retail politicking over the next four years, aiming to build up his credibility with Virginia voters. It eventually became clear that his general-election opponent would be Cuccinelli, producing a clash of titans, each with strikingly high negatives. Virginia gubernatorial elections usually attract special attention nationally because they occur in off-years, with only New Jersey voting on the same schedule. But this national focus was heightened in 2013 because of the ideological gap between McAuliffe and Cuccinelli, the pivotal role Virginia had come to play in presidential elections, and the intense competitiveness displayed by both men.

As attorney general, Cuccinelli had taken an aggressively conservative approach, often in tune with the tea party. He focused on such social issues as abortion and gay rights, and he hammered away at President Barack Obama's health care law and sought to probe a University of Virginia climate-change scientist. Cuccinelli won the nomination at a convention—one that he himself had pushed the state party to hold, rather than holding a nominating primary. The convention was dominated by conservative activists to a greater degree than a primary would have been, giving Cuccinelli such an edge over his leading rival, the more moderate Lt. Gov. Bill Bolling, that Bolling exited the race before it was even held. The convention also nominated other statewide Republicans who tilted heavily to the right. McAuliffe, for his part, ran further to the left on social issues than previous statewide Democratic nominees had—openly backing gun control, same-sex marriage and abortion rights—while taking a more moderate approach to economic issues. He promoted investments in such areas as alternative energy, cybersecurity and biotechnology. He also backed a roads bill popular in suburban areas that McDonnell had pushed and that Cuccinelli had opposed.

McAuliffe took some hits, several self-inflicted. Critics noted that in his 2007 memoir, he had bragged about leaving his wife Dorothy in the middle of childbirth in order to attend a party for a *Washington Post* reporter, and he added that he'd stopped on the way home from the hospital with another newborn in order to attend a fundraiser. ("I felt bad for Dorothy," McAuliffe wrote, "but it was a million bucks for the Democratic Party and by the time we got home and the kids had their new little brother in their arms, Dorothy was all smiles and we were one big happy family again.") He also attracted negative attention over GreenTech, an electric car company he had founded. McAuliffe took heat for planning to build a facility in Mississippi instead of Virginia. The company also caused problems for McAuliffe after news reports of federal investigations into possible irregularities in special visas the firm had sought for some of its foreign investors. In April 2013, McAuliffe stepped away from the company. As in the past, McAuliffe was never charged with any wrongdoing.

Despite such challenges for McAuliffe, Cuccinelli was unable to take full advantage because he had his own problem—a metastasizing scandal surrounding McDonnell, the outgoing governor. McDonnell and his wife, Maureen, had been wooed by Jonnie R. Williams Sr., the CEO of a dietary supplement company who hoped that McDonnell could provide credibility for his business. Williams gave the first family $177,000 in loans and gifts, ranging from catering to fancy vacations to a Rolex watch. Ten days after the election, McDonnell and his wife were indicted; eventually, they were both convicted of public corruption, and the former governor was sentenced to two years in prison, a conviction upheld on appeal in July 2015. Cuccinelli was never charged with anything related to the case, but he had to disclose during the campaign that he'd received more than $18,000 from Williams. The spiraling allegations about McDonnell also became a more generalized problem for the Republican slate.

In surveys, McAuliffe led Cuccinelli modestly going into the homestretch. Not surprisingly given his background, McAuliffe amassed a fundraising advantage—$34.4 million to $19.7 million. He successfully drew a contrast with Cuccinelli's tea party views, which worried elements of the business establishment and which were punctuated when Cuccinelli appeared with Republican Sen. Ted Cruz of Texas just as a government shutdown led by Cruz was under way; the shutdown was hurting federal workers in northern Virginia, and Cruz' appearance only rubbed salt in the wound. Even so, Cuccinelli appeared to gain ground in the final week or two, perhaps because of rising discontent with Obama's health care law. The law had just become fully implemented, and operational problems with the healthcare. gov website were emerging. The fact that the election was not held any later was fortuitous for McAuliffe; in the end, he won, 48%-45%, with Libertarian Robert Sarvis taking 7%. The most striking finding by political analysts was that McAuliffe had managed to draw an off-year electorate that looked more like a presidential-year electorate—one much more favorable to Democrats. Exit polls found that voters were less white and less Republican than when McDonnell won in 2009; African-Americans accounted for about 20% of voters, and about one in five voters cited abortion as their top concern, of which McAuliffe won a big majority. It was the first time in three and a half decades that Virginia voters chose a governor from the same party as the one controlling the White House.

After being sworn in, McAuliffe quickly signed executive orders establishing a gift ban and protecting state employees from discrimination based on sexual orientation or gender identity. He proposed bringing back a one-gun-per-month purchase limit and an end to the "gun show" loophole, and he added abortion-rights supporters to a state health board in a bid to undo anti-abortion policies instituted under Cuccinelli. He also sought to allow same-sex marriage in the state. But with Republicans holding key levers of power in the legislature, McAuliffe's most liberal efforts were largely stymied. This was seen most clearly in his bid to expand Medicaid under Obama's health care law. Despite an aggressive effort to sell the policy, McAuliffe drew fierce opposition in the GOP-held House of Delegates. He then faced an endgame when Democratic state Sen. Phillip Puckett resigned amid controversy surrounding a job offer and a judgeship for his daughter; Puckett's departure tipped the chamber to the GOP, putting the kibosh on any hopes for Medicaid expansion. McAuliffe did what he could on health care by using executive orders to enact a "Healthy Virginia" agenda, but in 2015, the Medicaid expansion was once again blocked by the GOP in both chambers.

Senior Senator

Mark Warner (D)

Elected 2008, term expires Jan. 2021, 2nd term; b. Dec. 15, 1954, Indianapolis, IN; George Washington U., B.A. 1977, Harvard U., J.D. 1980; Presbyterian; married (Lisa Collis); 3 children.

Elected Office: VA gov., 2002-06.

Professional Career: Fundraiser, Democratic Natl. Committee, 1980-82; Venture capitalist, 1982-89; Mng. dir., Columbia Capital Corp., 1989-2001; Commonwealth Transportation Bd., 1990-94; Chmn., VA Democratic Party, 1993-95; Chmn, Nat'l Governors Assoc., 2004-05.

DC Office: 475 RSOB, 20510, 202-224-2023; Website: warner.senate.gov.

State Offices: State Offices: Abingdon, 276-628-8158; Norfolk, 757-441-3079; Richmond, 804-775-2314; Roanoke, 540-857-2676; Vienna, 703-442-0670.

Committees: *Banking, Housing & Urban Affairs:* Financial Institutions & Consumer Protection; Nat'l Security & Int'l Trade & Finance; Securities, Insurance & Investment (RMM). *Budget. Finance:* Fiscal Responsibility and Economic Growth (RMM); Health Care; Taxation and IRS Oversight. *Intelligence (Select). Rules & Administration.*

Group Ratings

	ADA	ACLU	AFL-CIO	LCV	ITI	COC	HAFA	ACU	CFG	FRC
2014	85%	93%	–	60%	100%	50%	3%	8%	16%	0%
2013	65%	C	89%	85%	C	63%	C	4%	11%	C

National Journal Ratings

	2013 LIB	—	2013 CONS
Economic	58%	—	41%
Social	55%	—	44%
Foreign	54%	—	44%
Composite	56%	—	44%

Key Votes of the 113th Congress

1. Sandy storm spending	Y	5. Student Loan Rates	Y	9. Bipartisan Budget Deal	Y
2. Chuck Hagel Confirmation	Y	6. Employee Non-Discrim'n Act	Y	10. Farm Bill Conference Rept.	Y
3. Gun Background Checks	Y	7. Senate Vote on Judgeships	N	11. Unempl. Comp. Extension	Y
4. Immigration Reform	Y	8. Defense Dept. Spending	NV	12. Keystone Pipeline	Y

Election Results

2014 general	Mark Warner (D)	1,073,667	(49%)	$18,114,108	$345,891	$321,800
	Ed Gillespie (R)	1,055,940	(48%)	$7,875,545	$486,890	$1,827,242
	Robert Sarvis (Lib)	53,102	(2%)	$84,949		
2014 primary	Mark Warner (D)	unopposed				

Prior winning percentages: 2008 (65%); Governor: 2001 (52%)

Democrat Mark Warner, Virginia's senior senator, is a former governor whose tenure in Richmond was widely seen as a template for fellow Democrats seeking ways to win and effectively govern in the states of the Old Confederacy. Warner's success in his 2001-2005 gubernatorial tenure was such that many viewed him as a leading presidential contender in 2008, an option he seriously considered. Warner instead ran for an open Senate set that year, and won by a 2-1 margin, carrying all but a handful of counties in the state. But Warner's political career was almost cut short in 2014, when he sought a second term and sweated out a close win in what was originally thought to be an easy reelection bid.

Warner was born in Indianapolis, where his father was a safety evaluator for Aetna Life & Casualty Inc. The family moved to Vernon Connecticut, when Warner was in the eighth grade. He graduated from George Washington University, the first college graduate in his family, and from Harvard Law School. Although he has emphasized his business experience in his campaigns, his first love appears to have been politics: Soon after graduating from law school in 1980, he took a job fundraising for the Democratic National Committee. And in 1989, he managed Democrat Douglas Wilder's successful campaign to become not only Virginia's first African-American governor, but the first African-American elected governor anywhere in the nation since Reconstruction.

Warner spent most of the 1980s and 1990s as a highly successful venture capitalist, with the origins of that success the result of his political contacts. While working for the DNC, Warner met Rep. Tom McMillen, a Maryland Democrat, who told him about the potential of cell phone markets just as the Reagan administration was about to award 1,500 free licenses for metropolitan markets. Warner cobbled together investor groups and packaged their applications in exchange for a fee and a 5-percent ownership stake if they received the licenses. The best known of these ventures was Nextel, and Warner soon became a wealthy man. His average net worth in 2013 was estimated at $254 million, making him the second wealthiest member of Congress, according to an analysis of financial disclosure reports by the nonpartisan Center for Responsive Politics.

But a political career remained very much on Warner's mind. From 1993-1995, he was Virginia Democratic chairman. In 1996, he ran against Republican Sen. John Warner in what seemed a quixotic race: The senior Warner, elected narrowly in 1978, had won reelection in a landslide in 1984 and had no Democratic opponent in 1990. Mark Warner pitched his campaign not to his home turf in northern Virginia, but to the Shenandoah Valley and southwest Virginia. He carried southwest Virginia, and lost the part of the state outside the three big metropolitan areas by only 51%-49%, a considerable achievement for a Democrat. But John Warner's strength among moderates enabled him to carry northern Virginia 55%-45% and to win the Tidewater region and metropolitan Richmond with smaller majorities. The result was a 52%-47% statewide win for John Warner, but certainly not an end to upstart Mark Warner's electoral ambitions.

In the late 1990s, Mark Warner put millions of dollars into philanthropic efforts and set up four regional business investment funds in Tidewater, Richmond, and Southside—the area south of Richmond—as well as southwest Virginia. By 1999, he had an eye on running for governor in 2001 as an entrepreneur who could bring savvy business methods to government. He picked a good year. Republican Gov. Jim Gilmore had helped to elect Republican majorities in both houses of the legislature, but then battled with them over the budget. Republicans had an intraparty fight over the gubernatorial nomination in 2001 between Lt. Gov. John Hager and Attorney General Mark Earley. Earley resigned as attorney general immediately after winning the nomination to focus on the campaign, but had little money and no clear strategy. Warner poured $5 million of his own money into his candidacy.

Warner lived in a mansion in Old Town Alexandria but avoided being typecast as an urban liberal. He characterized himself as a fiscal conservative and pledged not to raise income or sales taxes. Responding to complaints from traffic-choked northern Virginia and Tidewater, he called for regional referenda on local sales tax increases for transportation. He opposed any new gun control laws and wooed the National Rifle Association, which remained neutral in the contest. Warner ran ads featuring old pickup trucks and bluegrass music, and he sponsored a NASCAR race truck. He traveled to all parts of rural Virginia, much as Wilder had in 1989, to show he was in touch with everyday folks and to remind them of his investment funds and philanthropic initiatives.

Warner won, but not resoundingly, by 52%-47%, a reversal of the numbers in the 1996 Senate race. He carried all major regions of the state, albeit by narrow margins. And he attracted notice from national Democrats for winning a Southern state through business-friendly, fiscally responsible policies combined with cultural conservatism—a combination Warner dubbed "radical centrism."

Once in office, Warner convinced the legislature to approve transportation tax referenda in northern Virginia and Tidewater, but the House of Delegates rejected his education initiative in 2002. As a budget shortfall grew, Warner cut more than $850 million in spending and laid off 1,800 state employees. In November 2003, after the legislative elections and when Virginia seemed to be in danger of losing its AAA bond rating, Warner presented his new fiscal plan: a $1 billion tax increase, with increases in the income, sales, and cigarette taxes, and tax reductions for those with low incomes and in car and food taxes. In early 2004, his plan was rejected by the heavily Republican House of Delegates, which increased taxes by just $520 million and provided few spending increases. But House Speaker William Howell was unable to hold his Republicans in line, and 17 of them abandoned their anti-tax positions. The Senate agreed to a $1.3 billion tax increase, more than Warner had requested, and the House went along, a major victory for the governor.

By December 2004, the fiscal picture had changed: State government was facing a $1.2 billion surplus, and Warner called for more spending. Barred from seeking a second consecutive term, he sought a larger national profile before his term came to a close at the end of 2005. He became chairman of the National Governors Association, urged 2004 Democratic presidential candidate John Kerry to target Virginia (which Kerry did, until August), and advised other Democrats around the country about how to win support in rural areas and woo conservative voters on social issues. While speculation increased about Warner seeking the presidency in 2008 as a Democrat, he announced in October 2006 that he would not run—citing the impact a national campaign would have on his family.

When John Warner in August 2007 announced his retirement from the Senate after five terms, Mark Warner's next career move seemed obvious. He had no serious opposition for the Democratic nomination. On the Republican side, Gilmore, Warner's predecessor as governor, decided to run. At the 2008 state GOP nominating convention, he barely prevailed after being challenged from the right because of his support for abortion rights in some cases. It turned out not to be a seriously contested campaign. Warner argued Gilmore had left the state in poor fiscal shape, and that he had been able to turn things around as Gilmore's successor. Warner won 65%-34%, losing only two counties in the Shenandoah Valley, two exurban Richmond counties, and two small independent cities. He ran far ahead of Democratic presidential nominee Barack Obama, even as Obama was carrying the state by 6 points. For the first time since 1970, when Harry Byrd, Jr. declared himself an independent, Virginia had two Democratic senators.

In the Senate, Warner lamented the adjustment ex-governors face in becoming one of 100 legislators. (In 2013, he toyed with running again for governor, which he called "the best job I ever had," but ultimately opted against it.) His driven and frenetic personality became a source of humor among his colleagues. In a "Secret Santa" gift exchange in 2011, Nebraska Republican Mike Johanns presented him with a large Energizer bunny. "Mark never stops," Johanns said. In recounting his close working relationship with the laid-back Republican Saxby Chambliss of Georgia, Warner told reporters in January 2013, "The way he starts each day is, 'Well, Mark, did you take your Ritalin today?'"

Warner's voting habits have put him in the political center. He was the 44th most liberal senator in 2012 and the 46th most liberal in 2013, placing him to the right of all but a handful of his Democratic colleagues. He has supported President Barack Obama on some major legislation, notably the health care overhaul in 2009; during that debate, he led 11 freshman Democrats in proposing a series of amendments intended to control costs and boost accountability of the new program. He also backed the Budget Control Act of 2011 and other Obama administration efforts to raise the federal debt ceiling, but has joined Republicans in backing caps on discretionary spending. On the environmental front, Warner parted ways with the White House in June 2012 when he was one of just five Senate Democrats to vote in favor of taking up a failed GOP resolution to overturn a regulation cutting mercury and other toxic emissions from coal-fired power plants. A year earlier, he called for Virginia to become the first East Coast state to allow offshore drilling, which he saw as a way to bring in jobs and new revenue.

Despite his "A" rating from the NRA, Warner declared after the December 2012 Newtown Connecticut school shooting in which 26 were killed that "the status quo isn't acceptable" on guns. "There needs to be appropriate restrictions on these tools of mass-killing," he said. In April 2013, Warner joined most Democrats in backing a compromise measure—opposed by the NRA—to expand background checks on gun buyers. But he was among 15 Democrats to vote against an assault weapons ban, and one of 10 Democrats to oppose a ban on high-capacity magazines. Warner took blowback from the party's liberal wing, as the president of MoveOn.org called Warner's votes on the latter issues "shameful," and told *U.S. News & World Report*, "He better hope he has another opportunity to weigh in on those measures to rectify his vote if he wants to be a presidential candidate."

As he frequently reached across the political aisle, Warner became best known for joining forces with Chambliss—Warner's closest Republican friend until retiring at the end of 2014—in leading the "Gang of Six." The group, consisting of three Republicans and three Democrats, came together in 2011 in the hope of putting the recommendations of the bipartisan Simpson-Bowles deficit reduction commission into legislation. To keep the group's closed-door meetings from becoming too partisan, Warner reportedly would occasionally push a comic buzzer that sounded the message: "Bull—detected. Take precautions."

By July 2011, as the House and Senate faced a controversial increase in the federal debt limit, the Warner-Chambliss group had developed a $3.7 trillion deficit-reduction plan. Of that total, $2.7 trillion in cuts came from adjustments to Medicaid and Social Security. Meanwhile, federal revenues would be increased $1.1 trillion over 10 years through changes to tax deductions for home mortgage interest, charitable giving, and health care insurance. But Republicans remained resolutely opposed to any revenue increases, and the deficit-reduction "supercommittee"—formed by the Budget Control Act that provided for a 2011 increase in the federal debt ceiling—failed to make headway in addressing the partisan deadlock. The Gang of Six proposal never became formal legislation, and the leadership of both parties paid the group scant attention.

Warner repeatedly expressed frustration over his inability to get a deal. "In Washington there is no support group, or institutional structure, to support people doing the right thing," he complained at a June 2012 gathering in Richmond. When lack of an agreement triggered steep automatic budget cuts in March 2013, he acknowledged at a meeting of defense and technology executives that Congress had "muffed this thing." But he also pinned blame on the executives. "Every time there's been efforts to try to build a broader coalition … most of y'all have said, 'Well, I don't want to piss off this guy or that guy or this chairman or that chairman,'" he told them.

Tennessee Republican Bob Corker also has been a frequent Warner collaborator. As fellow members of the Banking Committee, they worked together on ways to prevent financial institutions from becoming "too big to fail" as part of the crafting of the 2010 Dodd-Frank bill overhauling the federal financial regulatory structure. Later, Warner and Corker coauthored legislation to wind down mortgage giants Fannie Mae and Freddie Mac and make changes to the mortgage finance system. A similar measure cleared the Banking Committee in May 2014, but stalled due to the opposition of liberal Democrats including Charles Schumer of New York and Elizabeth Warren of Massachusetts, amid concerns it might limit access to mortgages by middle-income Americans. Meanwhile, Warner won a seat on the Finance Committee in 2014, a plum assignment he had pursued for years. It provided him with an influential platform to pursue long-time interests in reforming the tax code and curbing entitlement spending.

After the 2010 election, Warner had a chance to become part of the Senate leadership when he was offered the chairmanship of the Democratic Senatorial Campaign Committee. His business connections made him a highly desirable candidate. but he turned down the post—which would have required him to become much more of a partisan. In late 2014, Warner was given a place at the leadership table as a "policy development advisor" to the Democratic Policy and Communications Center. The appointment came despite the fact Warner was one of a handful of moderate Democrats to vote against the re-election of Senate Democratic Leader Harry Reid, with whom Warner has had a bumpy relationship.

The vote against Reid occurred shortly after Warner came within a percentage point of losing his seat in the 2014 election. He started the campaign as a prohibitive favorite, and polls as late as September showed him up by 20 points over his challenger, former Republican National Committee Chairman Ed Gillespie. By the end of the campaign, Warner had outspent Gillespie by almost 2-1, $15.7 million to $7.9 million. Warner's money underwrote an effective ad campaign in which he attacked Gillespie, founder of a major Washington lobbying firm, for lobbying on behalf of Enron—the Texas-based energy firm that collapsed amid scandal in 2001. Gillespie, meanwhile, in 2010 had helped to found American Crossroads, an outside group that pumped millions into Republican campaigns around the country. But he was unable to attract the group's interest to his seemingly long-shot bid, and his own campaign couldn't afford to go on the air until October.

But two major factors conspired almost to do in Warner. One was turnout. Democratic turnout was off in 2014 around the country—but especially so in Virginia, and particularly in Democratic leaning areas such as the northern Virginia suburbs. Warner was later criticized in Democratic circles for not doing more to turn out the vote in such areas. And Gillespie relentlessly tied Warner to Obama, pointing to a *CQ/Roll Call* analysis that found Warner had voted with Obama 97 percent of the time. *PolitiFact* noted the 97 percent figure was based on just 419 of the 1,473 votes Warner had cast in the Senate, and that more than half of the 419 votes came on presidential nominations. But this line of attack proved potent in Virginia—where Obama's approval ratings had sunk to 40 percent after he carried the state in 2008 and 2012. University of Virginia political scientist Larry Sabato told *Politico* that Gillespie's focus on the 97 percent figure "nearly killed" Warner. Warner eked out a win, 49%-48%, a statewide margin of less than 17,000 votes.

Warner, who focused heavily during the campaign on the centrist, fiscally responsible persona he had developed during his time as governor, afterward brushed aside suggestions that the election results were an indication his moderate stance no longer plays well in an increasingly polarized state. "I'm going to continue to be bipartisan," he said. But he also vowed to be more of a "disrupter" in his second term. In comments to *The Washington Post*, Warner noted his personal approval ratings remained high, but attributed his close call to voters "grumpy" over congressional inaction and saying that "they want results." The voters, he added, were telling him: "'Warner, show us some more of being that change agent.' I'm taking that message to heart."

Junior Senator

Tim Kaine (D)

Elected 2012, term expires Jan. 2019, 1st term; b. Feb. 26, 1958, St. Paul, MN; U. of MO, B.A. 1979, Harvard U., J.D. 1983; Catholic; married (Anne Holton); 3 children.

Elected Office: Richmond City Cncl., 1994-98; Richmond mayor, 1998-2001; VA lt.gov., 2002-06; VA gov., 2006-10.

Professional Career: Practicing atty., 1983-2000; Lecturer, U. of Richmond, 1987-93, 2010-12; Chmn., Democratic Natl. Committee, 2009-11.

DC Office: 231 RSOB, 20510, 202-224-4024; Fax: 202-228-6363; Website: kaine.senate.gov.

State Offices: Abingdon, 276-525-4790; Manassas, 703-361-3192; Richmond, 804-771-2221; Roanoke, 540-682-5693; Virginia Beach, 757-518-1674.

Committees: *Aging (Special). Armed Services:* Emerging Threats & Capabilities; Readiness & Mgmt. Support (RMM); SeaPower. *Budget. Foreign Relations:* Europe & Regional Security Cooperation; Near East, South Asia, Central Asia, & Counterterrorism; State Department and USAID Management, International Operations, and Bilateral International Development; Western Hemisphere, Transnational Crime, Civilian Security, Democracy, Human Rights & Global Women's Issues.

Group Ratings

	ADA	ACLU	AFL-CIO	LCV	ITI	COC	HAFA	ACU	CFG	FRC
2014	90%	93%	–	80%	100%	50%	3%	0%	0%	0%
2013	85%	C	94%	100%	C	50%	C	0%	6%	C

National Journal Ratings

	2013 LIB	—	2013 CONS
Economic	53%	—	46%
Social	68%	—	29%
Foreign	71%	—	0%
Composite	70%	—	31%

Key Votes of the 113th Congress

1. Sandy storm spending	Y	5. Student Loan Rates	Y	9. Bipartisan Budget Deal	Y
2. Chuck Hagel Confirmation	Y	6. Employee Non-Discrim'n Act	Y	10. Farm Bill Conference Rept.	Y
3. Gun Background Checks	Y	7. Senate Vote on Judgeships	N	11. Unempl. Comp. Extension	Y
4. Immigration Reform	Y	8. Defense Dept. Spending	Y	12. Keystone Pipeline	N

Election Results

2012 general	Tim Kaine (D)	2,010,067	(53%)	$17,918,247	$3,220,901	$28,008,366
	George Allen (R)	1,785,542	(47%)	$14,392,354	$2,782,563	$18,399,356
2012 primary	Tim Kaine (D)	unopposed				

Prior winning percentage: Governor: 2005 (52%)

Democrat Tim Kaine, a former Virginia governor, became the state's junior senator after defeating another former Virginia governor, Republican George Allen, in a high-priced campaign in 2012. Also a former mayor of Richmond, Virginia's capital city, Kaine says he numbers among just 20 individuals in U.S. history to have served as mayor, governor and senator. Kaine has been close to President Barack Obama, a fellow Harvard Law School graduate.

He was on the short list of possible vice presidential running mates in 2008, and was later Obama's choice to chair the Democratic National Committee. While his decision to run for the Senate was at Obama's urging, a high-profile difference of opinion between the two emerged early in Kaine's Senate term, as Kaine questioned the White House's authority to conduct military operations in the Middle East without authorization from Congress.

Born in St. Paul Minnesota, Kaine grew up in Overland Park Kansas, a suburb of Kansas City. His father ran his own ironworking and welding shop, with Kaine and his younger brothers frequently helping out. Kaine attended the University of Missouri, where he graduated in three years, before going on to Harvard Law School. Midway through law school, Kaine left to spend nine months teaching at a Jesuit mission in Honduras. In a *Washington Post* interview three decades later, Kaine said of his time in Honduras: "It made a public servant out of me...And the Jesuits themselves kind of became my heroes." It also gave him fluency in Spanish. As the Senate debated a major immigration overhaul bill in 2013, Kaine became the first senator ever to deliver a floor speech entirely in Spanish. "I think people were probably surprised," Kaine told *The New York Times* afterward. "One of my people got a call by a Latino staffer in the House [who] said, 'I have waited 20 years to see this happen.'"

Kaine returned to Harvard from Honduras to complete his law degree in 1983. It was there that he met his wife, Anne Holton, a daughter of A. Linwood Holton, Virginia's first Republican governor since Reconstruction. Anne Holton made national headlines as a child when her father, as governor from 1969-1973, declared an end to the state's policy of resistance to desegregation—and enrolled his children in Richmond's public schools, whose student population was largely African-American. For a time, Kaine worked for a federal judge in Macon Georgia, while Holton was working for a federal judge in Richmond. They decided to get married and settle in Richmond. Kaine subsequently worked as a civil rights lawyer, specializing in representing those who had been denied housing due to race or disability. In 1994, he won a seat on the Richmond City Council and four years later was elected mayor. In 2001, he was elected lieutenant governor. (Holton worked as a legal aid attorney before serving as a juvenile court judge; she is currently Virginia's secretary of education.)

Kaine ran for governor in 2005 against former state Attorney General Jerry Kilgore. Kaine, a former big city mayor who held positions well to the left of Kilgore, pitched a quality-of-life agenda designed to appeal to urban and suburban voters. He emphasized tax relief for homeowners, a statewide pre-kindergarten initiative, a balanced approach to growth, and new transportation solutions. Kilgore relied on hot-button issues such as the death penalty and illegal immigration, while dismissing Kaine as "too liberal for Virginia." In one Kilgore ad, a man whose son and daughter-in-law were murdered criticized Kaine for opposing the death penalty for "the worst mass murderer in modern times." Kaine said his opposition to capital punishment was based on religious convictions, and the issue gave him an opportunity to talk about his Catholic faith. However, Kaine also emphasized that, despite his personal beliefs, he would allow executions as governor.

Kaine won 52%-46%, a victory powered by large margins in suburban northern Virginia. Kaine's focus on managing growth enabled him to carry six of the state's 10 fastest-growing counties, including two in the Washington D.C. suburbs, Loudoun and Prince William, that were among the fastest-growing in the nation. In his first year, Kaine had some successes dealing with the Republican-controlled legislature, including passage of a bill requiring rigorous teacher evaluations. But he was unable to deliver on his primary objective of finding a reliable source of transportation financing to relieve traffic congestion. Kaine did not stand in the way of four executions of death row inmates, although he delayed the execution of a fifth after questions were raised about the inmate's mental capacity. He symbolically refused to sign a proposed constitutional amendment banning same-sex marriage that was approved by the General Assembly for placement on the November 2006 ballot.

A year later, he made progress on the transportation front, reaching agreement with the Republican-controlled House and Senate in 2007 on a $1 billion compromise bill, representing the state's biggest transportation funding increase in two decades. Since Republicans would not agree to a significant statewide tax increase, the scheme called for borrowing up to $3 billion over 10 years and giving taxing powers to regional authorities in the two traffic-choked big metro areas, northern Virginia and Tidewater. But the plan was frustrated when the state Supreme Court ruled that the regional authorities couldn't raise taxes. As part of his $78 billion, two-year budget in 2008, Kaine proposed $1.1 billion for transportation, with a penny sales tax increase in northern Virginia and Tidewater. But House Republicans steadfastly resisted it.

Much of Kaine's second year as governor was dominated by the mass shootings at Virginia Tech in April 2007. He was in Japan on an overseas trade mission at the time a deranged Virginia Tech student opened fire on fellow students during classes, killing 32 before taking his own life. He immediately flew back home and won praise for his handling of the tragedy. Unable to succeed himself under Virginia law barring a governor from serving two consecutive terms, Kaine in his last year in office reached agreement with House Speaker William Howell, a Republican, on a ban on smoking in bars and restaurants—which passed in February 2009. But Kaine failed to get the legislature to agree to proposals for background checks on sales at gun shows and universal pre-kindergarten.

In February 2007, Kaine endorsed Obama for the Democratic presidential nomination, the first governor to do so outside of Obama's home state. He campaigned heavily for Obama in Virginia and helped him win one of his biggest primary victories there. He was regarded as a possibility for the vice presidential nomination. Named chairman of the Democratic National Committee in 2009, Kaine held the post until 2011—juggling his responsibilities as governor with his party post during the first year of his tenure at the DNC.

When Democratic Sen. Jim Webb decided not to seek reelection in 2012 after serving just one term, Kaine got into the Senate race at the urging of Obama and other leading Democrats eager to find a high-profile challenger to George Allen. The son and namesake of a legendary football coach, Allen was first elected to the Senate in 2000, and his name was frequently mentioned as a potential presidential candidate in 2008. But he narrowly lost reelection in 2006 to Webb in a major upset, after Allen sparked widespread controversy when he referred to an Indian-American aide to Webb—who had been assigned to tape Allen's public campaign appearances—with the racially derogatory term "macaca."

Kaine and Allen flooded the airwaves with ads. By the end of the campaign, Kaine had raised and spent nearly $18 million, as compared to about $14.4 million for Allen. But Allen also benefited from the outside group Crossroads GPS, organized by Republican strategist Karl Rove, which spent millions attacking Kaine. Allen ridiculed Kaine for accepting a position to head the DNC while still governor; Kaine criticized Allen for increased spending while in the statehouse. Kaine also hit Allen for past support of partial privatization of Social Security. Allen said he did not support changes for current retirees, but was open to a voluntary retirement investment plan as a supplement. During one debate, the normally disciplined Kaine made a rare gaffe. After Republican presidential candidate Mitt Romney was caught on tape complaining about 47 percent of Americans not paying taxes, Kaine said he was "open to a proposal that would have some minimum tax level for everyone." Republicans jumped on the comment, and Allen ran ads highlighting it. But Kaine started to pull ahead in the polls in the fall and scored a big victory for Democrats when he won, 53%-47%.

Once sworn in, Kaine was assigned to seats on the Foreign Relations and Armed Services committees. The latter panel is of key importance to his home state, given the large Navy presence in the Tidewater area. While preoccupied with issues related to transportation and budgets while governor, he shifted his focus to national security—and, specifically, the process for authorizing the United States to engage in military action. Kaine and Arizona Republican John McCain, now the chairman of the Armed Services Committee and Obama's 2008 opponent, in January 2014 introduced legislation to clarify the 40-year old War Powers Act—and the underlying question of the degree to which the president and Congress possess, or share, the power to initiate military action abroad.

In addition, Kaine has pushed repeatedly for congressional debate and a vote on a new authorization for U.S. military action against the Islamic State, or ISIS. This stance has put him at odds with Obama, who has asserted that an Authorization for Use of Military Force (AUMF) passed in 2001, a week after the 9/11 attacks, is sufficient for current U.S. military activities in and around Syria and Iraq. But Kaine has contended that current military action against ISIS "goes well beyond the intent" of the 2001 AUMF. In June 2014, after writing an op-ed piece arguing for constraints on the president's unilateral power to conduct war, Kaine engaged Obama at the White House in what the senator later referred to as a "spirited discussion." Kaine is reported to have firmly told Obama that, if he intended to go to war, he would need Congress' permission, while the president—politely, but just as firmly—disagreed.

Kaine, in an interview with the *New York Times* in late 2014, said that his adamant position on this issue grew not only out of the large military presence in his home state, but also Virginia's unique place in the nation's founding. "They know I feel strongly about this because I'm a Virginian," Kaine said of the White House. "Until we have a vote, and we live by that vote, I am going to keep pushing them hard." Kaine has been consulting regularly on the matter with former Virginia Sen. John Warner, a Republican who is also a former Navy secretary. "Kaine was very close to the president, but he courageously went out, and I think properly so, demanded that Congress participate," Warner told the *Times*.

Virginia has become a purple state, and it seems a fair bet Kaine will face a competitive reelection race in 2018, particularly in light of his senior colleague, Democrat Mark Warner, barely eking out a win in the 2014 election. One possibility is former Republican National Chairman Ed Gillespie, a lobbyist and former congressional aide who came close to ousting Warner. Gillespie is also mentioned as a prospect for the gubernatorial seat that will open up in 2017. In the wake of the Democrats' loss of the Senate majority in the 2014 election, Kaine and his colleague, Mark Warner, were among a half-dozen Democrats to vote against the election of Sen. Harry Reid of Nevada as minority leader. An aide said Kaine had "voted no because he believes the caucus should have had a more thorough discussion on strategy before taking a leadership vote."

"...The way I look at it is, in politics you've got to have a fallback in our line of work because your career can be over in an instant—not that I would make much money playing a harmonica," Kaine chuckled when asked by the *Washington Post* in 2015 about one of his hobbies—playing the harmonica in bluegrass bands. Does anyone tell a senator to stop playing his harmonica, he was asked. "I've had people comment less than favorably on my quality," Kaine replied. "My wife is the most honest. She says, 'Hey, you ought to play anytime they ask you because as soon as you're not in elected office, they're not going to ask you anymore'."

FIRST DISTRICT

Rob Wittman (R)

Elected Dec. 2007, 4th full term; b. Feb. 3, 1959, Washington, D.C.; VA Polytech Inst., B.S. 1981, U. of NC Chapel Hill, M.P.H. 1990, VA Commonwealth U., Ph.D. 2002; Episcopalian; married (Kathyrn); 2 children.

Elected Office: Montross Town Cncl., 1986-96; Montross mayor, 1992-96; Westmoreland Cnty. Bd. of Supervisors, 1996-2005, chmn, 2004-05; VA House, 2006-07.

Professional Career: Environmental health specialist, VA health dept.; Field dir., VA Health Dept. Div. of Shellfish Sanitation.

DC Office: 2454 RHOB, 20515, 202-225-4261; Fax: 202-225-4382; Website: wittman.house.gov.

State Offices: Stafford, 540-659-2734; Tappahannock, 804-443-0668; Yorktown, 757-874-6687.

Committees: *Armed Services:* Readiness (Chmn); Seapower & Projection Forces. *Natural Resources:* Energy & Mineral Resources; Water, Power & Oceans.

Group Ratings

	ADA	ACLU	AFL-CIO	LCV	ITI	COC	HAFA	ACU	CFG	FRC
2014	0%	0%	–	3%	100%	71%	62%	72%	71%	100%
2013	0%	C	24%	4%	C	92%	C	76%	63%	C

National Journal Ratings

	2013 LIB	—	2013 CONS
Economic	38%	—	61%
Social	16%	—	74%
Foreign	40%	—	59%
Composite	33%	—	67%

Key Votes of the 113th Congress

1. Sandy storm spending	N	5. Medical Marijuana	N	9. Syrian Rebels Training	Y
2. Violence Against Women Act	N	6. Farm Bill	Y	10. Keystone pipeline	Y
3. Guantanamo Bay Detainees	N	7. Afghanistan Combat	N	11. Immigration Exec. Action	Y
4. Abortion 20-week ban	Y	8. NSA Phone Data Collection	N	12. Bipartisan budget deal	Y

Election Results

2014 general	Robert J. Wittman (R)................ 131,861	(63%)	$866,738	$5,255
	Norm Mosher (D)......................... 72,059	(34%)	$108,214	
	Gail Parker (I).............................. 5,097	(2%)		
2014 primary	Rob Wittman (R)......................... 13,414	(76%)		
	Anthony Riedel (R) 4,128	(24%)		

Prior winning percentages: 2012 (56%), 2010 (64%), 2008 (57%), 2007 special (61%)

Population		Race and Ethnicity		Income	
Total:	763,763	White	67.1%	Median income:	$75,485
Urban:	4.1%	Black	17.2%		(42 of 435)
Suburban:	78.9%	Latino	9.5%	Under $50,000	31.2%
Rural:	16.9%	Asian	3.3%	$50,000-$99,999:	32.5%
Land area:	2,802	Two races	2.4%	$100,000-$199,999:	28.1%
Pop/sq. mi.:	272.5	White Ethnic	24.1%	$200,000 or more:	8.2%
Born in state:	45.5%			Poverty Rate	8.9%
		Education			
Age Groups		H.S. grad or less:	34.0%	**Work**	
Under 18:	24.2%	Some college:	30.2%	White collar:	42.0%
18 to 34:	21.4%	College degree, 4 yr.:	22.0%	Blue collar:	40.5%
35 to 64:	40.8%	Post-grad study:	13.8%	Sales and service:	17.4%
Over 64:	13.5%				
		Military		Govt. workers:	24.2%
		Veterans/active duty:	17.0%		

Eastern Virginia: DC Exurbs, Hampton Roads Area

When the English first sailed up the estuaries that flow into the Chesapeake Bay, they were searching for gold. But they couldn't help noticing that the spot where the James River fed into the bay, now Hampton Roads, was a fine natural harbor with calm, deep water and good anchorages. So some of

Voter Turnout	
2013 Total Citizen 18+	548,578
2014 House Turnout	209,621
2014 Turnout as % CVAP	38.2%
2012 Turnout as % CVAP	67.8%

them stayed and established communities farther up the river that achieved not only the high craftsmanship of Williamsburg, but endured the pitiless hardship of Jamestown and other early settlements. Tidewater Virginia brought slavery to America and tobacco to the world, and slave-raised tobacco was the center of its economy in the colonial era and in the years afterward. Today, more than 1.7 million people live in the area. Because of the heavy military presence, it's a population collected from all over the country. So, like most of Northern Virginia, it has less of a Southern atmosphere than other regions of the Old Dominion.

About half of the population of the 1st Congressional District of Virginia lives south and east of Fredericksburg, the unofficial southern terminus of Northern Virginia. The residents here are scattered across Virginia's three necks (peninsulas to outsiders). Most of the major Hampton Roads military installations are in surrounding congressional districts, but the 1st remains steeped in military culture, and the Department of Defense and NASA are significant employers. Historic Yorktown, the site of the decisive battle of the Revolutionary War in 1781, is adjacent to a naval weapons station on the banks of the York River. To the north, in Caroline County, Fort A.P. Hill serves as a training site for active and reserve-component units. Not far from there is the Naval Surface Warfare Center in Dahlgren, located on the Potomac River, originally established as the Navy's main proving ground for large-caliber guns. Major parts of Williamsburg have been restored to look as they did in colonial times, with actors playing the roles of colonists, which is a major tourist draw. Also in Williamsburg is the College of William & Mary. America's second-oldest college claims as alumni presidents Thomas Jefferson, James Monroe and John Tyler, as well as Chief Justice John Marshall.

The other half of the district's population lives in the southern reaches of exurban Washington D.C., effectively making its representative the fourth member of Congress from Northern Virginia. Unlike other parts of the region, this part leans Republican with Fredericksburg, Stafford County and portions of Prince William and Fauquier counties. Prince William and Stafford are the two largest counties in the district, and they comprise nearly

40 percent of the population. The district has a large military presence here as well, including the Quantico Marine Corps base. Drivers in this area have some of the worst commutes in the nation, which prompts continued discussion of high-speed rail between Richmond and Washington. With its military population and growing retirement communities, the 1st is reliably Republican in most

2012 Presidential Vote		
Mitt Romney (R)................193,647	(53%)
Barack Obama (D) 166,510	(46%)
2008 Presidential Vote		
John McCain (R)................180,029	(52%)
Barack Obama (D) 161,417	(47%)
Cook Partisan Voting Index: R+6		

elections; statewide Republicans won the district with about 57% of the vote on average from 2000 through 2009.

Rob Wittman (R)

Republican Rob Wittman, who won the seat in a 2007 special election, has engaged on national security, with a focus that goes beyond the parochial concerns of his district. He combines military expertise with a professional interest in environmental protection, a pairing not often found among either conservative Republicans like Wittman or liberal Democrats.

Wittman was born in Washington D.C., and became a marine scientist. He has a Ph.D. in public policy and administration from Virginia Commonwealth University. Wittman served for many years as an environmental health specialist in the Northern Neck and Peninsula regions, including as field director for the state's shellfish sanitation division. His first public office was a seat on the Montross Town Council, where he served for 10 years, including four as mayor. In 1995, he began a decade on the Westmoreland County Board of Supervisors. In 2005, he was elected to the Virginia House of Delegates.

In 2007, five weeks after GOP Rep. Jo Ann Davis died of breast cancer, Republicans held a convention to choose their nominee. Wittman's chief opponent was Paul Jost, a businessman and anti-tax activist who lost the 2000 primary to Davis 35%-30%. Wittman cited his experience in public office and "the basics of good government." With help from several busloads of supporters, Jost led in early balloting, which began with 11 candidates. The key moment came after five ballots, when Davis' widower, Chuck Davis, threw his support to Wittman.

Democrats nominated Philip Forgit, a school teacher and Navy reservist who won a Bronze Star in Iraq. He described himself as a centrist and called for improved training to bring strategic change in Iraq. Wittman emphasized his conservative credentials, including his support for gun rights and his opposition to abortion. He touted the fact that House Minority Leader John Boehner had pledged to give him a seat on the Armed Services Committee. The Democratic Congressional Campaign Committee paid little attention to the heavily Republican district, and Wittman won the low-turnout contest 61%-37%, carrying all 18 counties.

In the House, Wittman got a seat on Armed Services as promised, and also a seat on the Natural Resources Committee, another good fit for his district. He usually sticks with Republicans on major issues but is not an automatic vote. He bucked his party as one of 33 House Republicans to support the creation of an Office of Congressional Ethics, which for the first time would give an outside panel the power to investigate the alleged misdeeds of lawmakers. Coming from a district with a large government presence, he is less enamored of eliminating federal programs and dramatically reducing spending than other conservatives. The House in 2009 passed his bill to improve management of efforts to clean up Chesapeake Bay, but it died in the Senate. He won Natural Resources approval in 2011 of his bill to streamline the process to develop offshore wind energy.

Wittman took over the chairmanship of Armed Services' Oversight and Investigations Subcommittee in 2011 and delved into the management scandal at Arlington National Cemetery, where an Army report found mismarked graves and numerous other problems. In 2013, when more senior fellow Virginia Rep. Randy Forbes claimed the Seapower Subcommittee, Wittman took over as chairman of the Readiness Subcommittee. Like others from his state and the committee, he aggressively advocates expanding the Navy's fleet and co-chairs the Congressional Shipbuilding Caucus. He maintains that it is more critical than ever for the military to project power around the world. During a November 2014 visit by a delegation of House members with King Abdullah of Jordan, Wittman said the United States can assist in the fight against the Islamic State but added, "this effort needs an Arab face."

Wittman has not been seriously threatened for reelection even as his district has moved north. In 2012, he lost Prince William County to Democrat Adam Cook, along with the cities of Fredericksburg, Newport News and Williamsburg, but he won reelection with 56% of the vote. He is young enough and respected enough that he eventually could be positioned to chair one of his two committees.

SECOND DISTRICT

Scott Rigell (R)

Elected 2010, 3rd term; b. May 28, 1960, Titusville, FL; Mercer U., B.B.A. 1983, Regent U., M.B.A. 1990; Christian; married (Teri); 4 children.

Military Career: U.S. Marine Corps Reserves, 1978-84.

Professional Career: Salesman Ford dealership, 1983-86; Pres., Freedom Automotive, 1991-2010; VA Motor Vehicle Dealer Bd., 1995-99.

DC Office: 418 CHOB, 20515, 202-225-4215; Fax: 202-225-4218; Website: rigell.house.gov.

State Offices: Belle Haven, 757-442-4790; Hampton, 757-687-8290; Virginia Beach, 757-687-8290.

Committees: *Appropriations:* Financial Services & General Gov't; Labor, HHS, Education & Related Agencies; Legislative Branch.

Group Ratings

	ADA	ACLU	AFL-CIO	LCV	ITI	COC	HAFA	ACU	CFG	FRC
2014	5%	5%	–	3%	80%	86%	63%	72%	61%	50%
2013	0%	C	19%	7%	C	85%	C	84%	68%	C

National Journal Ratings

	2013 LIB	—	2013 CONS
Economic	36%	—	64%
Social	34%	—	62%
Foreign	24%	—	68%
Composite	33%	—	67%

Key Votes of the 113th Congress

1. Sandy storm spending	N	5. Medical Marijuana	Y	9. Syrian Rebels Training	Y
2. Violence Against Women Act	Y	6. Farm Bill	N	10. Keystone pipeline	Y
3. Guantanamo Bay Detainees	N	7. Afghanistan Combat	Y	11. Immigration Exec. Action	Y
4. Abortion 20-week ban	Y	8. NSA Phone Data Collection	N	12. Bipartisan budget deal	Y

Election Results

2014 general	Scott Rigell (R)	101,558	(59%)	$1,405,821	$211,724	$6,118
	Suzanne Patrick (D)	71,178	(41%)	$859,160		
2014 primary	Scott Rigell (R)	unopposed				

Prior winning percentages: 2012 (54%), 2010 (53%)

Population		Race and Ethnicity		Income	
Total:	738,759	White	63.2%	Median income:	$59,435
Urban:	87.3%	Black	21.3%		*(130 of 435)*
Suburban:	8.2%	Latino	7.3%	Under $50,000	40.6%
Rural:	4.5%	Asian	4.9%	$50,000-$99,999:	35.7%
Land area:	756	Two races	2.9%	$100,000-$199,999:	19.3%
Pop/sq. mi.:	977.2	White Ethnic	23.2%	$200,000 or more:	4.3%
Born in state:	42.3%			Poverty Rate	10.8%
		Education			
Age Groups		H.S. grad or less:	31.7%	**Work**	
Under 18:	21.8%	Some college:	35.9%	White collar:	37.8%
18 to 34:	28.2%	College degree, 4 yr.:	20.5%	Blue collar:	42.7%
35 to 64:	37.3%	Post-grad study:	11.9%	Sales and service:	19.5%
Over 64:	12.7%			Govt. workers:	21.6%
		Military			
		Veterans/active duty:	24.3%		

Hampton Roads: Virginia Beach, Parts of Newport News and Norfolk

The U.S. Navy Atlantic fleet berthed in its home port of Norfolk is one of the most awe-inspiring sights in America, or anywhere. Norfolk has been a Navy port since 1801 and has long been recognized as having one of the best natural harbors on the East Coast, one that never freezes, has a channel

Voter Turnout	
2013 Total Citizen 18+	554,925
2014 House Turnout	173,060
2014 Turnout as % CVAP	31.2%
2012 Turnout as % CVAP	59.5%

50 feet deep, and is within 750 miles of three-quarters of U.S. manufacturing capacity. The Norfolk Naval Station is the world's largest naval base, situated on 4,300 acres on Sewell's Point. Almost a quarter of the nation's uniformed military personnel are stationed in the Hampton Roads area, and the aggregation of destructive power in the line of towering gray ships is probably greater than in any other single port. Once a small city, Norfolk is now part of a metropolitan area of 1.7 million people, anchored by Virginia Beach. The local Navy community—active duty and civilian personnel, dependents, retirees, and workers at the Newport News Shipyard—is estimated at more than 300,000, and military spending pours some $11 billion annually into the local economy.

Virginia Beach, once a sleepy beach resort, is now the state's largest city, with 448,000 people. It began attracting tourists when rail service to Norfolk began in 1883. It is home to the headquarters of the Christian Broadcasting Network, which produces "The 700 Club" and features evangelist Pat Robertson, the son of former Democratic Sen. A. Willis Robertson of Virginia. In 1974, the city converted a local landfill into a grass-covered park, and Mount Trashmore Park was born, with its basketball courts, walking trails and fishing in the adjoining Lake Trashmore. The city has a growing industrial base, including a large power tool plant of the German-based Stihl company. Like Norfolk, Virginia Beach is infused with military culture. The city is the base of East Coast Navy SEAL teams; these elite commandos endure punishing training, and they took on some of the military's most secretive and daring missions in Iraq and Afghanistan, including participating in the Pakistan compound raid that killed Osama bin Laden in May 2011.

The 2nd Congressional District of Virginia includes all of Virginia Beach, plus a wedge of Norfolk, including the navy base. On the peninsula, it takes in parts of the city of Hampton, including Langley Air Force Base and, on a spit of land in the bay, Fort Monroe, where Jefferson Davis was confined after the Civil War. It crosses over into Newport News, where it includes the middle third of the city, where most of the Republican voters reside. Newport News and Norfolk each include a bit more than 10 percent of the district. Across the Chesapeake Bay Bridge-Tunnel, the district transforms into a more placid area, including the two Virginia counties of the Delmarva Peninsula, the site of the annual roundup of wild Chincoteague ponies in the national wildlife refuge. In February 2015, Accomack County approved what was promoted as the largest solar power facility on the East Coast. More than 60 percent of the district's population is in Virginia Beach, and it leans Republican.

2012 Presidential Vote		
Barack Obama (D) 159,695	(50%)
Mitt Romney (R).................154,935	(49%)

2008 Presidential Vote		
Barack Obama (D) 163,767	(50%)
John McCain (R).................158,259	(49%)

Cook Partisan Voting Index: R+2

George W. Bush carried it handily twice, but Democrat Barack Obama also carried the district twice, each time by a few thousand votes.

Scott Rigell (R)

Republican Scott Rigell is a car dealer who won the seat in 2010 over Democratic freshman Glenn Nye. He has shown a repeated willingness to take centrist stands that inflame conservatives in his party. But he moved to the right in January 2015 to vote against another term for John Boehner as House speaker, a signal that he was worried about internal Republican politics.

Rigell hails from Titusville Florida, near the Kennedy Space Center, where his father was an engineer and director of NASA's launch-vehicle operations. Rigell got his bachelor's degree from Mercer University and soon returned to Titusville to work at a Ford dealership run by his father-in-law. He later enrolled in business school at Regent University, a private Christian college founded by televangelist Pat Robertson. After getting a master's degree in business administration, Rigell purchased Freedom Automotive in 1991 and became rich;

Roll Call estimated his net worth in 2013 at $11.3 million. Soon afterward, he met Bob McDonnell, later the Republican governor of Virginia and then convicted for corruption, on the showroom floor of his auto dealership, and the two became friends. Over the years, Rigell helped McDonnell in his campaigns and contributed to other Republican candidates. He also gave $1,000 to Democrat Barack Obama's presidential campaign in 2008, which conservatives cited as proof that he is too moderate for the district.

When he challenged Nye, Rigell competed first against five other candidates in the GOP primary. He ran as the establishment candidate, with the most cash in the field. Though McDonnell remained neutral, his politically active daughter, Jeanine, ran an ad for Rigell calling him a "longtime friend" of the family. Rigell won with 40% of the vote to 27% for Ben Loyola, the tea party favorite.

In the general election, Rigell pledged to adhere to a 12-year term limit and to extend the Bush-era tax cuts for all income levels. Nye said he, too, favored extending the tax cuts for everyone, and he won the endorsement of the U.S. Chamber of Commerce, which called him a "pro-business" Democrat. Rigell spent $4.4 million, nearly twice as much as the incumbent, and rode the 2010 Republican wave to a 53%-42% victory. During his House career, he has spent $3.3 million of his own money, according to the Center for Responsive Politics.

In Washington, Rigell has taken a centrist approach, particularly on economic issues. He is a co-founder of the Fix Congress Now Caucus, and his first official act was to unveil a 10-point proposal for scaling back congressional perks that he said have fostered "a culture of privilege." His plan included cutting lawmakers' budgets to 2008 levels, replacing their pensions with 401(k) plans, limiting congressionally funded franked mail to two pieces a year, banning travel paid by lobbyists, and prohibiting lawmakers and their staffs from working as lobbyists for five years after leaving government employment. In the highly likely event that Congress declined to adopt his ideas, Rigell said he would abide by them voluntarily. He was one of two House Republicans in 2012 to vote against a criminal contempt citation against Attorney General Eric Holder in connection with the "Operation Fast and Furious" gun-tracing operation. He enacted a bill in January 2013 setting chemical standards for domestic and imported drywall.

On the Budget Committee, Rigell became an outspoken critic of conservative lobbyist Grover Norquist's no-new-taxes pledge during the 2012 tax and spending negotiations aimed at avoiding a so-called "fiscal cliff." In 2013, Norquist criticized him as a "cheap date" when Rigell joined Obama on Air Force One on a visit to the area shipyard.

Rigell won additional attention on gun control. A National Rifle Association member, he nonetheless joined with Democrats in early 2013 to sponsor a bill creating a federal gun-trafficking law imposing a prison sentence of up to 20 years for straw purchases of guns. He said it was a "common ground" issue on which both parties should agree. But Karen Miner Hurd, chairman emeritus of the Virginia Tea Party Alliance PAC, accused him in *The Washington Post* of "caving to the politically correct left." The National Association for Gun Rights aired radio ads and sent direct-mail fliers accusing Rigell of backing a federal registry system and working with Obama to seize guns, both of which Rigell denied. He asked Kentucky GOP Sen. Rand Paul, a supporter of the group, to denounce its attacks, but Paul declined.

In November 2014, with the support of the Virginia delegation, Rigell filled a vacancy on the Appropriations Committee that resulted from the retirement of veteran Virginia Rep. Frank Wolf. That made it all the more surprising that Rigell voted a few weeks later against giving John Boehner another term as House speaker. In explaining his decision, Rigell said that "Boehner has served the House well and will continue to do so with great integrity," but he said that he voted for Rep. Daniel Webster of Florida because of "his dedication to reforming the institutional dysfunction in Congress." During debate in June 2015 on the defense appropriations bill, Rigell sided with the leaders on that committee and was the only member from Virginia to oppose an amendment from Virginia GOP Rep. Randy Forbes to secure permanent funding for a new class of submarines, which likely would bring major financial benefits to the Tidewater area.

Democrats initially hoped to reclaim Rigell's seat in 2012. Democrat Paul Hirschbiel, a venture capitalist, spent more than $400,000 on his campaign. But he couldn't make a dent in Rigell's poll numbers, and by October the Democratic Congressional Campaign Committee canceled its air time in the Hampton Roads market. Rigell won, 54%-46%. In 2014, he had an easier time, with 59% of the vote against retired Navy commander Suzanne Patrick, who spent $859,000. "Voters in Virginia Beach don't seem to be yearning to replace Rigell, who strikes a conciliatory tone," wrote David Wasserman of the Cook Political Report.

Like others in the Virginia delegation, Rigell faced uncertainty in the 2016 campaign after a federal court in June 2015 maintained that the 3rd District was an unconstitutional racial gerrymander and ordered the state to redraw the map by Sept. 1. That placed Rigell and Forbes of the 4th District at the greatest risk that the redrawn map would force one of them to run in a more Democratic-leaning district, or they might run against each other. Additional legal and political maneuvering were expected to play out. But the uncertainty might help to explain Rigell's shifting House votes in early 2015.

THIRD DISTRICT

Bobby Scott (D)

Elected 1992, 12th term; b. April 30, 1947, Washington, D.C.; Harvard U., B.A. 1969, Boston Col., J.D. 1973; Episcopalian; divorced.

Military Career: U.S. Army Reserve, 1970-74; MA Army Nat'l Guard, 1974-76.

Elected Office: VA House, 1978-83; VA Senate, 1983-93.

Professional Career: Practicing atty., 1973-91.

DC Office: 1201 LHOB, 20515, 202-225-8351; Fax: 202-225-8354; Website: bobbyscott.house.gov.

State Offices: Newport News, 757-380-1000; Richmond, 804-644-4845.

Committees: *Education & the Workforce* (RMM): Health, Employment, Labor & Pensions.

Group Ratings

	ADA	ACLU	AFL-CIO	LCV	ITI	COC	HAFA	ACU	CFG	FRC
2014	80%	94%	–	94%	40%	43%	12%	4%	4%	0%
2013	85%	C	90%	96%	C	31%	C	8%	14%	C

National Journal Ratings

	2013 LIB	—	2013 CONS
Economic	83%	—	16%
Social	93%	—	0%
Foreign	66%	—	32%
Composite	82%	—	18%

Key Votes of the 113th Congress

1. Sandy storm spending	Y	5. Medical Marijuana	Y	9. Syrian Rebels Training	Y
2. Violence Against Women Act	Y	6. Farm Bill	N	10. Keystone pipeline	N
3. Guantanamo Bay Detainees	Y	7. Afghanistan Combat	Y	11. Immigration Exec. Action	N
4. Abortion 20-week ban	N	8. NSA Phone Data Collection	Y	12. Bipartisan budget deal	Y

Election Results

2014 general	Bobby Scott (D)	139,197	(94%)	$473,415
2014 primary	Bobby Scott (D)	unopposed	

Prior winning percentages: 2012 (81%), 2010 (70%), 2008 (97%), 2006 (96%), 2004 (69%), 2002 (96%), 2000 (100%), 1998 (76%), 1996 (82%), 1994 (79%), 1992 (79%)

Population		Race and Ethnicity		Income	
Total:	742,782	Black	56.3%	Median income:	$38,885
Urban:	54.6%	White	33.1%		(399 of 435)
Suburban:	42.8%	Latino	5.2%	Under $50,000	60.7%
Rural:	2.5%	Asian	2.0%	$50,000-$99,999:	27.4%
Land area:	1,062	Two races	2.7%	$100,000-$199,999:	10.3%
Pop/sq. mi.:	699.5	White Ethnic	10.3%	$200,000 or more:	1.6%
Born in state:	62.1%			Poverty Rate	23.8%
		Education			
Age Groups		H.S. grad or less:	46.1%	**Work**	
Under 18:	21.9%	Some college:	31.8%	White collar:	30.6%
18 to 34:	31.0%	College degree, 4 yr.:	14.4%	Blue collar:	48.1%
35 to 64:	35.7%	Post-grad study:	7.6%	Sales and service:	21.4%
Over 64:	11.4%			Govt. workers:	20.5%
		Military			
		Veterans/active duty:	14.0%		

Richmond/Norfolk Corridor

The history of American slavery literally began
along the tidal expanse of the James River. Only
a dozen years after the founding of Jamestown
in 1607, the first slave ship sailed up the James
and offloaded its human cargo, giving birth to the
slave-based economy of the American South. In the

Voter Turnout	
2013 Total Citizen 18+	559,381
2014 House Turnout	147,402
2014 Turnout as % CVAP	26.4%
2012 Turnout as % CVAP	59%

21st century, some of the big plantation houses of the Tidewater still dot the banks of the
James. Charles City County—the site of William Byrd II's Westover, Benjamin Harrison III's
Berkeley, and John Carter's Shirley—also was the birthplace of two successive presidents,
William Henry Harrison and John Tyler. Virginia famously produced a total of eight U.S.
presidents—almost 20% of the individuals to serve—but none for almost a century.

The 3rd Congressional District of Virginia includes all of the majority-black city of
Portsmouth, a Navy port and industrial town with a charming old section. It travels back
and forth across the James River to string together black precincts and communities in
Norfolk, Hampton and Newport News. The economy here depends heavily on the Newport
News Shipyard. Upriver on the south bank of the James, it takes in 79% African-American
Petersburg, where much of the movie *Lincoln* was filmed, as well as eastern Henrico County.
Most of Richmond is in the district, including the state's 224-year-old Capitol, designed by
Thomas Jefferson; the historic Jefferson Hotel; and the African-American neighborhoods
around Church Hill, where Patrick Henry gave his famous speech. Monument Avenue has
statues of Confederate luminaries and tennis player Arthur Ashe. Old tobacco warehouses
on the banks of the James have been converted into loft apartments. Hollywood Cemetery
is where Presidents James Monroe and John Tyler share a final resting place with 25 Confederate generals, Jefferson Davis, and Davis' son, Joseph, who died at age 5 in 1864 after
falling from the Confederate White House balcony.

The district also takes in areas with high
concentrations of white liberals, such as the
Fan in Richmond and Ghent in Norfolk, placing the greatest possible number of Democrats in a single district. In 2012, President
Barack Obama carried the 3rd District, 79%-
20%, one of his best showings in the South.
As a three-judge federal court affirmed in its
June 2015, the district is an unconstitutional
racial gerrymander and must be redrawn so

2012 Presidential Vote		
Barack Obama (D) 262,265		(79%)
Mitt Romney (R)...................66,391		(20%)
2008 Presidential Vote		
Barack Obama (D) 258,668		(78%)
John McCain (R)...................68,806		(21%)
Cook Partisan Voting Index: D+27		

that the 2016 election will be held with new boundaries. That likely will make the 3rd District less overwhelmingly Democratic, but it has plenty of votes for Democrats to share with
adjacent districts.

Bobby Scott (D)

Bobby Scott, a Democrat first elected in 1992, is an influential civil libertarian, an intellectual force in the Congressional Black Caucus, and an important figure in Virginia politics.
He became the Education and Workforce Committee's top Democrat in January 2015.

Scott grew up in Newport News, the son of a doctor. His maternal grandfather is Fili-
pino, which led him to join the Congressional Asian Pacific American Caucus upon coming to
Capitol Hill. He went to Harvard University, where he was a classmate of future Democratic
Vice President Al Gore, and then on to Boston College law school. He served in the National
Guard and Army Reserves and returned home to practice law. In 1977, he was elected to the
Virginia House of Delegates, and in 1983 to the state Senate, representing a multi-racial dis-
trict in a community where, because of the military tradition of integration, biracial politics
came more naturally than in other places.

In 1986, he ran a credible race for Congress and lost to Republican Herb Bateman, 56%-
44%. In 1992, with his base on the Peninsula in a district that had been redrawn to become
African-American majority, Scott won the Democratic primary with 67% of the vote against
two Richmond-based candidates. He won the general election easily to become the first African-
American elected from Virginia since 1891. He has been reelected by overwhelming margins.

Scott has a solidly liberal voting record, with occasional exceptions on economic and defense issues, and he is one of the House's most outspoken civil libertarians. He joined like-minded Reps. Jerrold Nadler of New York and John Conyers of Michigan in 2012 in calling for greater scrutiny of the Obama administration's use of unmanned drones to kill suspected terrorists. When bipartisan coalitions passed legislation to permit states to display the Ten Commandments in schools or government buildings, he raised First Amendment objections. After the September 11 attacks, he opposed the USA Patriot Act, the nation's tough new anti-terrorism law, arguing that it might promote racial profiling. Scott was one of three lawmakers to oppose condemnation of a federal court decision declaring unconstitutional the words "one nation under God" in the Pledge of Allegiance. "We ought to be standing up for unpopular decisions" and not voting for a resolution that "everyone knows is stupid, but it sounds popular," he said.

After the Newtown Connecticut, elementary school massacre, Minority Leader Nancy Pelosi named Scott vice chair of the Democrats' gun-violence prevention task force. One of Scott's legislative successes was the bipartisan Death in Custody Reporting Act, which requires states to report deaths of arrestees and prisoners. He also enacted in 2010 the Fair Sentencing Act to narrow the discrepancies between sentences for powder and crack cocaine, an issue he had long contended led to blacks receiving disproportionately longer sentences. In May 2009, the CBC urged President Barack Obama to select Scott to replace retiring Supreme Court Justice David Souter, although Obama ultimately settled on federal appellate Judge Sonia Sotomayor.

Scott took over as Education and the Workforce's ranking member following the retirement of California's George Miller. Scott has had a longtime interest in K-12 education, with a special focus on equity. He introduced a bill in 2014 to authorize the Obama administration's "Promise Neighborhood" program, augmenting K-12 classes with health and arts programs. As Republicans sought to rewrite the No Child Left Behind education law in 2015, Scott took a dim view of panel Chairman John Kline's ideas. "There is broad agreement that No Child Left Behind is outdated," Scott said. "But rather than building upon the advancements we've made since the last rewrite, the Republican [bill] would turn back the clock on our public education system."

Scott has joined others in the Black Caucus in opposing the administration's gainful-employment regulation, which many other Democrats back. The rule aims to force colleges to overhaul or shut down career-training programs that leave low-salaried students with large amounts of debt. He and other caucus members fear any tightening could unfairly limit minority students who attend career-training colleges.

Scott is a fervent advocate of boosting funding in an effort to reduce juvenile crime. "We have to end the cradle-to-prison pipeline," he told *The Daily Press* of Newport News in 2012. With Idaho GOP Rep. Raul Labrador in February 2015, he introduced a measure to reduce certain mandatory drug sentences, restore judicial discretion in sentencing for some offenses, and promote alternatives to incarceration. He worked with members of both parties in the Judiciary Committee to reduce national security collection of telephone metadata records, as part of a revision of the Patriot Act that was enacted in June 2015.

In 2007, Scott joined with then-Sens. Obama of Illinois and Joe Biden of Delaware in pushing legislation to compensate black farmers who had been victims of government discrimination; the bill was enacted in 2010. Scott opposed the so-called fiscal cliff budget deal in 2012 that extended most of the Bush-era tax cuts, and he has been the prime sponsor of the CBC's alternative budget plan that would phase out those tax cuts for upper-income taxpayers to finance more spending on domestic programs. The House has routinely defeated his annual proposal.

Scott hosts an annual Labor Day picnic that has become a required stop for Democratic candidates for state and federal office. He used the 2011 picnic to announce that he wouldn't run for retiring Democrat Jim Webb's Senate seat, clearing the way for former Gov. Tim Kaine to get the nomination. Earlier that year, he said he was considering a Senate bid because he had become disenchanted with the "fiscal insanity" in the House and the scant opportunity for debate and compromise.

He and his district became the focal point of redistricting litigation that threw out the congressional map that Republicans approved in 2011. Even though a second district in the Tidewater area with a substantial minority presence would likely remove from his district African-American locales, perhaps including Portsmouth and Petersburg, Scott has consistently encouraged that step. He has not personally been part of the litigation.

FOURTH DISTRICT

Randy Forbes (R)

Elected June 2001, 7th full term; b. Feb. 17, 1952, Chesapeake; Randolph-Macon Col., B.A. 1974, U. of VA, J.D. 1977; Baptist; married (Shirley); 4 children.

Elected Office: VA House, 1990-97; VA Senate, 1997-2001.

Professional Career: Practicing atty., 1977-2001; Chmn, VA Republican Party, 1996-2000.

DC Office: 2135 RHOB, 20515, 202-225-6365; Fax: 202-226-1170; Website: forbes.house.gov.

State Offices: Chesapeake, 757-382-0080; Chesterfield, 804-318-1363.

Committees: *Armed Services:* Seapower & Projection Forces (Chmn); Strategic Forces. *Judiciary:* Courts, Intellectual Property & the Internet; Crime, Terrorism, Homeland Security & Investigations.

Group Ratings

	ADA	ACLU	AFL-CIO	LCV	ITI	COC	HAFA	ACU	CFG	FRC
2014	0%	0%	–	3%	80%	86%	52%	60%	54%	100%
2013	0%	C	29%	4%	C	77%	C	68%	62%	C

National Journal Ratings

	2013 LIB	—	2013 CONS
Economic	40%	—	59%
Social	16%	—	74%
Foreign	34%	—	60%
Composite	33%	—	67%

Key Votes of the 113th Congress

1. Sandy storm spending		N	5. Medical Marijuana	N	9. Syrian Rebels Training	Y
2. Violence Against Women Act	N	6. Farm Bill	Y	10. Keystone pipeline	Y
3. Guantanamo Bay Detainees	N	7. Afghanistan Combat	N	11. Immigration Exec. Action	Y
4. Abortion 20-week ban	Y	8. NSA Phone Data Collection	N	12. Bipartisan budget deal	Y

Election Results

2014 general	Randy Forbes (R)	120,684	(60%)	$1,082,780
	Elliott Fausz (D)	75,270	(38%)	$30,934
	Bo Brown (Lib)	4,427	(2%)	
2014 primary	Randy Forbes (R)	unopposed		

Prior winning percentages: 2012 (57%), 2010 (62%), 2008 (60%), 2006 (76%), 2004 (64%), 2002 (98%), 2001 special (52%)

Population		Race and Ethnicity		Income	
Total:	739,602	White	59.2%	Median income:	$60,216
Urban:	7.6%	Black	31.1%		(128 of 435)
Suburban:	77.6%	Latino	4.7%	Under $50,000	41.3%
Rural:	14.9%	Asian	2.0%	$50,000-$99,999:	33.1%
Land area:	3,888	Two races	2.4%	$100,000-$199,999:	21.6%
Pop/sq. mi.:	190.2	White Ethnic	17.0%	$200,000 or more:	3.9%
Born in state:	59.8%			Poverty Rate	12.5%
Age Groups		**Education**			
Under 18:	23.8%	H.S. grad or less:	42.5%	**Work**	
18 to 34:	21.6%	Some college:	32.7%	White collar:	36.6%
35 to 64:	41.4%	College degree, 4 yr.:	15.2%	Blue collar:	41.4%
Over 64:	13.2%	Post-grad study:	9.5%	Sales and service:	22.0%
		Military		Govt. workers:	21.3%
		Veterans/active duty:	14.5%		

Southeast Virginia: Richmond Suburbs, Chesapeake

The clash of arms resounds through much of the history of Tidewater and Southside Virginia. During the Revolutionary War, the Battle of Great Bridge, near Chesapeake, forced British forces to evacuate Norfolk. During the Civil War, the Blackwater River was a prominent dividing line between

Voter Turnout	
2013 Total Citizen 18+	549,952
2014 House Turnout	200,638
2014 Turnout as % CVAP	36.5%
2012 Turnout as % CVAP	65.9%

Union and Confederate troops. Numerous engagements from that conflict raged south of the James River: Drewry's Bluff, Hill's Point, the Siege of Suffolk, White Oak Road, Dinwiddie Court House, to name a few. The region hasn't seen much fighting since then, but the Tidewater still boasts one of the densest concentrations of military power in the world. Fort Lee, the big Army base near Petersburg, met its goal of doubling in size by 2011 and contributes $2.4 billion annually to the area's economy.

The 4th Congressional District of Virginia includes much of the Tidewater south of the James River. About half of its people are in the Hampton Roads area, mostly in the fast-growing suburbs of Chesapeake and Suffolk. *Money* magazine in 2010 named Chesapeake one of the best places to live in the country, with its quality schools, open local government, and ample green space; it has come close to passing Norfolk as the state's second largest city, though its population growth slowed to 12 percent from 2000 to 2010. The city has pioneered the use of police body cameras, which have generated more interest since 2014 following a wave of controversial police practices in minority communities. Suffolk is the original home of the Planters Nut and Chocolate Co. on the eastern edge of Virginia's Peanut Belt. Growth in Suffolk has centered on high-tech defense contracting firms, which were threatened by automatic budget cuts in 2013 after the two parties failed to reach an agreement on deficit reduction but then were deferred for two years.

The district also takes in the flat lands of Southside Virginia. These were tobacco lands after the English first settled them in the 17th century. Today, they also produce Smithfield hams in an area that calls itself the "Ham Capital of the World." The tiny town of Wakefield is home to the Shad Planking, the fishing event where Virginia politicians still make pilgrimages every spring to meet and greet each other and voters. The remainder of the district is in suburban and exurban Richmond, including fast-growing Chesterfield County, where the population increased by 26% from 2000 to 2013 and surpassed neighboring Henrico County. The district includes all of the city of Hopewell, with its Honeywell plant and 18th century plantations. But there are signs of the new economy in this part of the district as well: Amazon opened two distribution centers in the district, each measuring over 1 million square feet, and Northrop Grumman has a huge data center in Chesterfield. The district is 31% African American, but that minority population has been reduced by the removal of majority-black Portsmouth and Petersburg to the 3rd District during the

2012 Presidential Vote		
Mitt Romney (R)	181,265	(50%)
Barack Obama (D)	176,311	(49%)
2008 Presidential Vote		
John McCain (R)	175,685	(50%)
Barack Obama (D)	170,315	(49%)
Cook Partisan Voting Index:	R+4	

past two redistricting cycles, which has become a focus during discussions to comply with court-ordered redistricting for the 2016 election. Democrat Barack Obama twice lost the district 50%-49%.

Randy Forbes (R)

Republican Randy Forbes, who came to office in a June 2001 special election, is a defense hawk and advocate of a stronger Navy who in 2013 became chairman of the Armed Services Subcommittee on Seapower and Projection Forces. He is at risk that redistricting will jeopardize his district or force him to run against another House Republican.

Forbes grew up in Chesapeake, majored in government at Randolph-Macon College, and got his law degree from the University of Virginia. He started a law firm in Chesapeake that later merged with a larger one in Norfolk. His first job in politics was as an aide to a Democratic from Chesapeake in the House of Delegates. When his boss retired in 1989, Forbes won the seat as a Republican. Four years later, when Republicans were still in the minority, he became the party's floor leader. In 1997, he was elected to the state Senate. A law school classmate and friend of Govs. George Allen and Jim Gilmore, Allen made him state Republican chairman in 1996. In that job, he helped to engineer the historic Republican 1997 sweep of all three statewide offices.

When 10-term Democratic Rep. Norman Sisisky died after cancer surgery in 2001, national and state Republican leaders asked Forbes to run for the competitive seat. He was nominated at a GOP convention and then caught a break when the strongest Democrat, Sisisky's son, Mark, declined to run. Democrats chose state Sen. Louise Lucas of Portsmouth, an African American who held a majority-black seat. Both national parties and their interest-group allies spent heavily on the race. Republicans attacked Lucas for opposing repeal of the sales tax on non-prescription drugs and for supporting a gasoline tax increase. Democrats criticized Forbes for his position in support of President George W. Bush's plan to create individual investment accounts in Social Security. Lucas carried Portsmouth 63%-37%. But Forbes won in more populous Chesapeake, 61%-39%, and in rural counties for an overall victory of 52%-48%.

In the House, the conservative Forbes sometimes goes his own way on domestic spending when he deems it too costly. On the Judiciary Committee, he has led an effort to halt the removal of references to God in public dialogue. Emphasizing the importance of "In God We Trust" as the national motto, he noted that President Barack Obama, during a 2010 Indonesia trip, said that the national motto is "E Pluribus Unum." After the House passed his resolution in November 2011 on a 396-9 vote, Obama retorted that lawmakers had more important things to do.

His chief work has been on Armed Services, where he deftly combines his personal interests with those of the many military service members and contractors in his Tidewater district. As Seapower Subcommittee chairman, he sharply rebuked the Pentagon in February 2013 for what he said was its unwillingness to disclose the impact of steep automatic budget cuts that kicked in after Congress and the president were unable to reach a long-term spending deal. He earlier fought the Obama administration over its plans to close the Joint Forces Command in Norfolk, attaching a provision to a House-passed spending bill in February 2011 that delayed the move. He was part of the Virginia delegation's efforts to try to stop the Navy's plans to shift an aircraft carrier from Norfolk to Jacksonville, Florida. He has cited China's growing economic and military strength as a reason for a U.S. military buildup. "If they (the Chinese) perceive a power vacuum, they get more bold," he told a Hampton Roads audience.

Forbes made known his interest in the opening for Armed Services Committee chairman after the 2014 election. But he ultimately deferred to the more senior Mac Thornberry of Texas, and the two have had a good relationship in which the committee head defers to Forbes on some naval issues. Their teamwork has been evident in an attempt by Armed Services to lock in spending for a new *Ohio*-class nuclear submarine, with an estimated cost exceeding $80 billion, including $10 billion in the program's first five years. Under Forbes' leadership, the 2014 defense spending bill created a National Sea-Based Deterrent Fund to fund the submarines outside of the usual appropriation process. "This is a national project and requires a national effort to implement," Forbes said. Noting that the overall fleet has dropped from nearly 600 ships in the late 1980s to 275, he told the *New York Times* that it is urgent to stop "the precipitous decline of our Navy."

In the House-passed defense bill for fiscal 2016, Forbes and his allies began to put money into the fund. In June 2015, House appropriators challenged what they viewed as a budget gimmick and sought to defend their control of spending. But in a striking setback for the appropriators, the House on a 321-111 vote passed a Forbes amendment to remove a prohibition on the transfer of funds to the Deterrent Fund. All House members from Virginia voted with Forbes except for Scott Rigell, who serves on Appropriations. His proposal has gained bipartisan support from other members who represent areas with shipyards and submarine facilities.

Forbes is also interested in energy issues. He has introduced a bill calling for a new Manhattan Project of scientists to make the United States free of dependence on foreign oil within two decades.

In 2008, Forbes was held to a 60%-40% reelection victory against poorly funded Democrat Andrea Miller, a former regional director for MoveOn.org who benefited from the local strength of Obama and Senate candidate Mark Warner. He had an easier time in 2010, winning 62%-37% over retired physician Wynne LeGrow. Republican redistricters in 2011 gave him a boost with tweaks that reduced the African-American population in his district. But he has not exceeded 60% in his wins since then.

Forbes faced the political challenge that a new redistricting map for Virginia—to address what a federal court has ruled is a racial gerrymander in the adjacent 3rd District—likely will increase the number of black voters in his district. That could play out in various ways, with the possibility that Forbes will be at odds with Rigell, whose 2nd district also borders the 3rd, or perhaps with first-term GOP Rep. Dave Brat of the 7th District.

FIFTH DISTRICT

Robert Hurt (R)

Elected 2010, 3rd term; b. June 16, 1969, New York, NY; Hampden-Sydney Col., B.A. 1991, MS Col., J.D. 1995; Presbyterian; married (Kathy); 3 children.

Elected Office: Chatham Town Cncl., 2000-01; VA House, 2002-07; VA Senate, 2008-11.

Professional Career: Chief asst., Pittsylvania Cnty. Commonwealth's atty., 1996-99; Practicing atty., 1999-2010

DC Office: 125 CHOB, 20515, 202-225-4711; Fax: 202-225-5681; Website: hurt.house.gov.

State Offices: Charlottesville, 434-973-9631; Danville, 434-791-2596; Farmville, 434-395-0120.

Committees: *Financial Services:* Capital Markets & Gov't Sponsored Enterprises (VChmn); Housing & Insurance; Oversight & Investigations.

Group Ratings

	ADA	ACLU	AFL-CIO	LCV	ITI	COC	HAFA	ACU	CFG	FRC
2014	0%	0%	–	3%	80%	64%	68%	83%	81%	100%
2013	0%	C	10%	7%	C	85%	C	88%	83%	C

National Journal Ratings

	2013 LIB	—	2013 CONS
Economic	17%	—	83%
Social	16%	—	74%
Foreign	5%	—	86%
Composite	16%	—	84%

Key Votes of the 113th Congress

1. Sandy storm spending	N	5. Medical Marijuana	N	9. Syrian Rebels Training	N
2. Violence Against Women Act	N	6. Farm Bill	N	10. Keystone pipeline	Y
3. Guantanamo Bay Detainees	N	7. Afghanistan Combat	N	11. Immigration Exec. Action	Y
4. Abortion 20-week ban	Y	8. NSA Phone Data Collection	N	12. Bipartisan budget deal	Y

Election Results

2014 general	Robert Hurt (R)	124,735	(61%)	$1,227,681
	Lawrence Gaughan (D)	73,482	(36%)	$86,054
	Paul Jones (Lib)	4,298	(2%)	$2,837
2014 primary	Robert Hurt (R)	unopposed		

Prior winning percentages: 2012 (55%), 2010 (51%)

Population		Race and Ethnicity		Income	
Total:	735,799	White	72.9%	Median income:	$47,972
Urban:	18.9%	Black	20.8%		*(268 of 435)*
Suburban:	24.7%	Latino	2.9%	Under $50,000	51.7%
Rural:	56.4%	Asian	1.4%	$50,000-$99,999:	29.6%
Land area:	9,089	Two races	1.6%	$100,000-$199,999:	15.2%
Pop/sq. mi.:	81.0	White Ethnic	18.9%	$200,000 or more:	3.6%
Born in state:	65.5%			Poverty Rate	15.1%
		Education			
Age Groups		H.S. grad or less:	46.3%	**Work**	
Under 18:	21.1%	Some college:	26.8%	White collar:	37.4%
18 to 34:	21.3%	College degree, 4 yr.:	15.5%	Blue collar:	39.5%
35 to 64:	39.9%	Post-grad study:	11.4%	Sales and service:	23.0%
Over 64:	17.7%			Govt. workers:	19.1%
		Military			
		Veterans/active duty:	9.6%		

Southside: Charlottesville, Lynchburg, Danville

Southside Virginia is technically defined as the parts of the commonwealth east of the Blue Ridge, west of the Fall Line, and south of the James River. But it really is a cultural designation: an outcropping of Deep South culture in the Old Dominion. The eastern counties are flat and humid—frontier

Voter Turnout	
2013 Total Citizen 18+	567,072
2014 House Turnout	204,945
2014 Turnout as % CVAP	36.1%
2012 Turnout as % CVAP	64.5%

in the late-colonial period, plantation country by 1800, and now peanut fields and pine forests. Along U.S. 58, which snakes across southern Virginia from Virginia Beach almost to the Cumberland Gap, are the vestiges of the state's Tobacco Road, including the Tobacco Farm Life Museum of Virginia in South Hill. Further west, into the Piedmont, the land gradually gets hillier. The largest metropolitan area here is Danville, where the tobacco auction originated in 1858. Tobacco magnates later built "Millionaire's Row," one of the finest extant collections of Edwardian and Victorian architecture. Two of the most important battles for African-American equality were won northeast of Danville. The first was at Appomattox Court House, the serene little hamlet where Robert E. Lee surrendered to his onetime subordinate Ulysses S. Grant. The second was in Prince Edward County, where one of the five cases consolidated into the landmark *Brown v. Board of Education* case arose. There is a D-Day memorial in Bedford, which lost more men per capita (23 of its 35 soldiers) in the Normandy invasion than any other town in the country.

Today, the local economies are in transition. Danville was jolted when Dan River Mills was purchased by an Indian chemical firm that moved its remaining jobs overseas in 2006. But Ikea opened a furniture factory in 2008. The unemployment rate, which reached 13% in 2010, remained at 8.3% in April 2015. In Pittsylvania County, which is home to a large undeveloped uranium deposit, Virginia Uranium Inc. said in December 2013 that it was abandoning its mining plans because of the opposition of newly elected Gov. Terry McAuliffe. Since 2010, Microsoft has opened three data centers in Mecklenburg County for a total cost of $1 billion. In April 2015, Duke Energy agreed to pay $2.5 million for a coal ash spill that coated 70 miles of the Dan River with a gray sludge. The Dan River Business Development Center has 2,300 jobs in Danville, many of them in high tech and biomedicine.

The 5th District of Virginia covers most of Southside Virginia west of metro Richmond, spreading out to the Blue Ridge Mountains. This is still the heart of the district; about two-thirds of its population lives south of the James River. The district also includes overwhelmingly liberal Charlottesville and Thomas Jefferson's University of Virginia, and surrounding Albemarle County, but their 20 percent of the vote has little impact in this district. An arm extends north to the western part of Fauquier County in the Washington D.C., exurbs. Southside Virginia was long conservative and Democratic; it was the last part of Virginia to elect a Republican to Congress. In recent decades, the district has mostly voted Republican. Virginia's recent Democratic governors, Mark Warner and Tim Kaine, energized Charlottesville and Albemarle County liberals, and Democrat

2012 Presidential Vote		
Mitt Romney (R)	188,485	(53%)
Barack Obama (D)	164,555	(46%)

2008 Presidential Vote		
John McCain (R)	178,887	(51%)
Barack Obama (D)	167,861	(48%)

Cook Partisan Voting Index: R+5

Barack Obama's presidential campaign in 2008 registered thousands of Southside blacks. Still, Republican John McCain won the district, 51%-48%. Mitt Romney raised the GOP vote to 53% four years later.

Robert Hurt (R)

Republican Robert Hurt, who reclaimed the 5th District for the GOP in 2010, shares with his Class of 2010 colleagues a strong conservative bent. With his mild manner, he has shunned declamatory rhetoric and intra-party conflicts.

Hurt was born in New York City, the son of Henry Hurt, a journalist, nonfiction author, and editor for *Reader's Digest*. While Henry Hurt was writing in rural Chatham Virginia, his son went to a local boarding school and then on to Episcopal High School in Alexandria. He got his bachelor's at Hampden-Sydney College and then a law degree at Mississippi College before returning to Chatham to practice law. Hurt was the chief assistant attorney for Pittsylvania County and, in 2001, began his political career with his election to the Chatham

Town Council. Later that year, he was elected to the Virginia House of Delegates. In 2007, he ran successfully for the state Senate. His brother, Charlie Hurt, has been a conservative political columnist and a writer for the Drudge Report.

In 2010, Rep. Tom Perriello was among the most vulnerable freshman lawmakers. In 2008, he had snatched the Republican-leaning district away by only 727 votes from Rep. Virgil Goode, a six-term conservative Republican who left the Democratic Party in 2000. Hurt won the primary with 48% of the vote, nearly double the runner-up.

In the general election, Hurt slammed Perriello for his support of President Barack Obama's $787 billion economic stimulus bill, the Democrats' health care overhaul, and their legislation to cap carbon emissions. He said he would try to reduce the size of the federal budget with free-market solutions rather than stimulus spending. Perriello attacked Hurt for supporting then-Democratic Gov. Mark Warner's 2004 budget, which increased state taxes by $1.4 billion. Hurt responded that as a state legislator he had voted against more than two dozen tax increases. Perriello outspent Hurt $3.8 million to $2.5 million and also had the edge in spending by national party and ideological groups. Hurt lost out on the endorsement of the National Rifle Association, which backed Perriello in accordance with its policy of supporting gun rights-friendly incumbents. But Hurt benefited from the wave of opposition to Democrats, especially in rural areas, and he prevailed 51%-47%.

In Washington, Hurt got a seat on the Financial Services Committee and won early House passage in 2011 of his amendment that mandated that any savings from a bill to terminate an Obama-backed mortgage aid program go to deficit reduction. He introduced a bill to require Fannie Mae and Freddie Mac to develop a plan to sell non-critical assets, such as patents and historical mortgage data, in a move to shrink the two government-sponsored mortgage giants. With Democratic Rep. Kyrsten Sinema of Arizona, he introduced in May 2015 a bill to require the Securities and Exchange Commission to conduct a broad review of its regulations to encourage streamlining and a removal of outdated rules.

In 2012, Democrats persuaded John Douglass, a retired Air Force brigadier general, to take on Hurt. Douglass spent $1.1 million. He focused on his opposition to uranium mining and blasted Hurt for his father's investment in a company hoping to mine and mill a uranium ore deposit in the district. Hurt, with $2 million, ran a series of ads accusing Douglass of being a "D.C. insider," citing his tenure as the head of the Aerospace Industries Association, a Washington trade group. Douglass got 73% of the vote in liberal Charlottesville, but it wasn't nearly enough to stop Hurt, who won 55%-43%. In 2014, Hurt had an easier campaign and got 61% of the vote. Pending the potential ripple effect of expected redistricting changes in the nearby Tidewater area, he appears to have locked down this district.

SIXTH DISTRICT

Bob Goodlatte (R)

Elected 1992, 12th term; b. Sept. 22, 1952, Holyoke, MA; Bates Col., B.A. 1974, Washington & Lee U., J.D. 1977; Christian Scientist; married (Maryellen); 2 children.

Professional Career: Dist. dir., U.S. Rep. Caldwell Butler, 1977-79; Practicing atty., 1979-92; Partner, Bird, Kinder & Huffman, 1981-92.

DC Office: 2309 RHOB, 20515, 202-225-5431; Fax: 202-225-9681; Website: goodlatte.house.gov.

State Offices: Harrisonburg, 540-432-2391; Lynchburg, 434-845-8306; Roanoke, 540-857-2672; Staunton, 540-885-3861.

Committees: *Agriculture:* Commodity Exchanges, Energy & Credit; Livestock & Foreign Agriculture. *Judiciary* (Chmn).

Group Ratings

	ADA	ACLU	AFL-CIO	LCV	ITI	COC	HAFA	ACU	CFG	FRC
2014	0%	0%	–	3%	100%	85%	70%	84%	73%	100%
2013	0%	C	14%	7%	C	85%	C	84%	81%	C

National Journal Ratings

	2013 LIB	—	2013 CONS
Economic	26%	—	74%
Social	13%	—	84%
Foreign	5%	—	86%
Composite	17%	—	83%

Key Votes of the 113th Congress

1. Sandy storm spending	N	5. Medical Marijuana	N	9. Syrian Rebels Training	Y
2. Violence Against Women Act	N	6. Farm Bill	N	10. Keystone pipeline	Y
3. Guantanamo Bay Detainees	N	7. Afghanistan Combat	N	11. Immigration Exec. Action	Y
4. Abortion 20-week ban	Y	8. NSA Phone Data Collection	N	12. Bipartisan budget deal	Y

Election Results

2014 general	Bob Goodlatte (R)......................	133,898	(75%)	$1,554,911
	Will Hammer (Lib).....................	22,161	(12%)	
	Elaine Hildebrandt (G)...............	21,447	(12%)	
2014 primary	Bob Goodlatte (R).................unopposed			

Prior winning percentages: 2012 (65%), 2010 (76%), 2008 (62%), 2006 (75%), 2004 (97%), 2002 (97%), 2000 (100%), 1998 (69%), 1996 (67%), 1994 (100%), 1992 (60%)

Population		Race and Ethnicity		Income	
Total:	735,143	White	81.1%	Median income:	$46,862
Urban:	48.6%	Black	11.1%		(284 of 435)
Suburban:	22.6%	Latino	3.9%	**Under $50,000**	52.9%
Rural:	28.8%	Asian	1.7%	$50,000-$99,999:	30.5%
Land area:	6,004	Two races	2.0%	$100,000-$199,999:	13.9%
Pop/sq. mi.:	122.4	White Ethnic	18.4%	$200,000 or more:	2.7%
Born in state:	65.0%			Poverty Rate	15.2%
		Education			
Age Groups		H.S. grad or less:	47.9%	**Work**	
Under 18:	20.4%	Some college:	26.7%	**White collar:**	34.1%
18 to 34:	24.2%	College degree, 4 yr.:	16.2%	Blue collar:	43.7%
35 to 64:	38.6%	Post-grad study:	9.1%	Sales and service:	22.2%
Over 64:	16.8%				
		Military		Govt. workers:	15.7%
		Veterans/active duty:	9.4%		

Shenandoah Valley: Roanoke, Harrisonburg

The sturdy men and women who settled the Shenandoah Valley of Virginia west of the Blue Ridge were quite different from the "second sons" of the European aristocracy who cleared the marshy forests of the Tidewater and built grand planta-tions. Even before the Revolutionary War, Scots and

Voter Turnout	
2013 Total Citizen 18+	564,273
2014 House Turnout	179,708
2014 Turnout as % CVAP	31.8%
2012 Turnout as % CVAP	59.5%

Scots-Irish, German Protestants, and Mennonites and Moravians—members of religious communities and fiercely independent farmers—poured down the Great Wagon Road from Pennsylvania to the valley, planting farms and founding towns with names like Strasburg, Edinburg, Mount Jackson, and Glasgow. They were looking not for the flat, mahogany col-ored land that Eastern tobacco growers sought, but for land that could support wheat, corn and hay—crops that could be rotated and that an individual farmer and his family could handle. A young George Washington surveyed portions of the land; what are believed to be his carved initials are still visible on Natural Bridge, in Rockbridge County.

The same independent spirit nurtured the growth of higher education here. In Lexing-ton alone are Washington and Lee University, which Robert E. Lee headed, and the Vir-ginia Military Institute, where Stonewall Jackson taught philosophy and artillery tactics and which did not admit women until required by the U.S. Supreme Court in 1996. A trio of distinguished women's colleges is nearby: Mary Baldwin College in Staunton, Hollins University in Roanoke and Sweet Briar College in Sweet Briar, which came close to shutting down in June 2015 because of financial woes. President Woodrow Wilson's birthplace is in Staunton.

Industry flourished here more than in most of Virginia east of the Blue Ridge. In the 19th century, the Norfolk and Western Railway established its chief junction at Roanoke, and as the years passed, the city became the headquarters of the railroad, now Norfolk Southern, and many other companies. But the city's population has remained flat since the 1970s.

2012 Presidential Vote		
Mitt Romney (R)..................197,045	(59%)
Barack Obama (D) 132,153	(39%)
2008 Presidential Vote		
John McCain (R).................186,868	(57%)
Barack Obama (D) 137,684	(42%)
Cook Partisan Voting Index: R+12		

The 6th Congressional District of Virginia covers the heart of the Valley of Virginia, from Strasburg to Roanoke. It crosses over the Blue Ridge to take in Lynchburg, the home of Liberty University, a fundamentalist Baptist college where Sen. Ted Cruz launched his presidential campaign in March 2015. In recent decades, the ancestral conservatism of the region and the feisty politics of the mountain rebels have melded into a single conservative Republicanism, more populist than elitist in tone, as concerned with moral values as with economic freedom, and prickly about interference from Washington and Richmond. Those roots here go deep: Many of these counties have shown Republican tendencies dating back over 100 years, and in 1952, the district's voters did something extremely rare at the time: They voted out an incumbent Southern Democrat in favor of a Republican. The GOP has held the seat ever since, save for an interlude in the 1980s.

Bob Goodlatte (R)

Bob Goodlatte, a Republican first elected in 1992, took over in 2013 as chairman of the Judiciary Committee. He has found common ground with Democrats on technology and patent matters, plus national security, but not on gun control, immigration and other hot-button social issues. Earlier, he chaired the Agriculture Committee.

Goodlatte grew up in Holyoke Massachusetts, the son of a Friendly's ice cream store manager and a part-time retail clerk. He attended Bates College in Maine, where he was president of the College Republicans, then went to law school at Washington and Lee University. After college, he became an aide to Republican Rep. Caldwell Butler of Roanoke. Goodlatte practiced law in Roanoke and stayed active in politics. In 1992, when Democrat Jim Olin retired, Goodlatte was nominated by the Republican convention; he won in November 60%-40%.

Goodlatte has been conservative on most fiscal and social issues. He jumped into the "birther" controversy in 2009 by co-sponsoring a bill to require presidential candidates to make their birth certificates public—a reaction to a discredited theory that President Barack Obama is foreign-born. In 2011 and 2013, Goodlatte introduced bills to abolish the tax code. He has sponsored measures to implement a constitutional balanced-budget amendment, which fell short of the two-thirds majority required for passage in 2011, and to stop the Environmental Protection Agency from implementing steps aimed at cleaning up Chesapeake Bay by regulating stormwater runoff. In recent years, Goodlatte's zeal for deficit reduction has made him more willing to break with his party on foreign policy. He joined a majority of Democrats in supporting an unsuccessful 2012 amendment to reduce defense spending by $7.6 billion.

Goodlatte got the Judiciary gavel after Texas Republican Rep. Lamar Smith was term-limited. As comprehensive immigration reform heated up in the Senate in early 2013, Goodlatte threw cold water on a central sticking point, whether to grant illegal immigrants a potential path to citizenship. "I don't think [it's] going to happen," he told National Public Radio in February. Seven months later, he said that so-called "dreamers" who were brought in illegally by their parents should get an "earned pathway to citizenship." When waves of migrants from Central America sparked a crisis at the U.S.-Mexico border in mid-2014, Goodlatte blasted Obama's request for $3.7 billion as a "slap in the face" and a "blank check" without any limits. And he was incensed when Obama issued an executive order protecting some categories of illegal immigrants, saying that overturning it would be his top priority. "We cannot allow one man to nullify the law of the land with either a stroke of his pen or a phone call," he said after a federal judge prevented the order from taking effect in February 2015.

He has been outspoken on other issues at Judiciary. On gun control, Goodlatte said in 2013 that a Democratic push for universal background checks is "not a very practical thing to do." In 2015, he circulated a draft bill allowing states to collect sales taxes on out-of-state Internet purchases—though he stirred controversy among retailers and their allies by basing the taxes on the seller's location instead of the buyer's. In 2003, he sponsored the House-passed bill to limit class action lawsuits against tobacco companies, gun makers and other companies.

Goodlatte has a less partisan side. The usually low-key lawmaker co-chairs the bipartisan Congressional Internet Caucus and often has worked with its Democratic members. He also chairs the House Republican Technology Working Group. He was a vocal proponent of the bipartisan Stop Online Piracy Act (SOPA) aimed at cracking down on foreign-based websites offering pirated movies, music and other content. The bill received strong backing from movie studios and unions, both traditional Democratic allies, but ran into fierce opposition in 2012 from Internet giants such as Google and did not advance. He joined Democrats in expressing skepticism about the proposed merger of phone giants AT&T and T-Mobile, which AT&T abandoned in 2011. He and California Democrat Anna Eshoo pushed for a permanent ban on Internet taxes. When he failed to achieve that goal, he helped to broker in 2007 an agreement for a four-year prohibition. "I don't think there is a single issue related to tech that isn't bipartisan," Goodlatte has said.

The House in December 2013 approved on a 325-91 vote his Innovation Act to fight abusive patent litigation. To combat so-called "patent trolls" seeking to hide behind shell companies, the bill required plaintiffs to disclose who is the owner of a patent before filing litigation. Goodlatte's Democratic counterpart in the Senate, Vermont's Patrick Leahy, refused to move it. Goodlatte reintroduced his proposal in 2015, with hopes for a more sympathetic reaction from the Senate's new GOP majority.

In early 2015, Goodlatte was part of a wide-ranging bipartisan group that worked to revise and extend the Patriot Act, but with limits on the government's collection of phone metadata from telecommunications companies. He worked closely with Republican Jim Sensenbrenner of Wisconsin and Democrat John Conyers of Michigan, both former chairmen of the committee who had earlier helped to enact the measure, and with former Senate Judiciary Chairman Leahy. Their new USA Freedom Act, enacted in June 2015, contained the most sweeping reforms of government surveillance practices since the 1970s.

"The ceaseless effort to restrain the reach of government is in our DNA as Americans. And for 225 years, we have refused to accept the idea that in order to have national security, we must sacrifice our personal freedoms," Goodlatte and Sensenbrenner wrote in an op-ed for *The Hill* newspaper in May 2015. "The USA Freedom Act lives up to these ideals, proving once again that we can protect both Americans' civil liberties and our national security without compromising either one." The libertarian approach by these two GOP old bulls was well-received by House Republicans, including party leaders, who had voiced growing concerns about Big Government. Their effort played well with the *Lynchburg News & Advance*, Goodlatte's local newspaper, which editorialized that he "knows America has mortal enemies abroad who must be dealt with," but has also been "a staunch defender of the individual when confronted by the power of the central government."

In May 2015, Goodlatte won House passage of a bill that would ban most abortions after 20 weeks. The bill, which passed on a nearly party-line 242-184 vote, had been slightly modified to respond to the concerns of some women in the Republican Conference who objected that the bill was too far-reaching. The Pain-Capable Unborn Child Protection Act faced an uncertain future in the Senate and a guaranteed veto from Obama. But Goodlatte viewed his position as a persistent measure of his beliefs and in line with a growing consensus in public opinion, as well as a political talking point for conservatives. "Current medical research tells us that late-term abortions are cruel to unborn children and do not exist in the gray areas of morality," he said.

On the Agriculture Committee, which he chaired from 2003 to 2007, Goodlatte worked closely with Democratic Chairman Collin Peterson of Minnesota to enact the 2008 farm bill, serving as the committee's informal liaison with the Bush White House. He helped to broker a compromise on country-of-origin labeling of meat in the bill. In 2008, he joined 50 other House Republicans in urging the Environmental Protection Agency to reduce ethanol production requirements. Colleagues praise him for being fair-minded. "When you're around Bob, you just get the sense that he's listening, he's genuinely interested in your point of view, and that his objective is to come to an outcome that is going to move things forward," Democratic Rep. Peter Welch of Vermont told *The Hill* newspaper in 2013.

Goodlatte has been consistently reelected without difficulty. He encountered no problem in 2002 when he abandoned his pledge to serve no more than 12 years. His support of SOPA prompted a primary challenge in 2012 from libertarian Karen Kwiatkowski, who lost 65%-35%. He was reelected without major party opposition in 2014.

SEVENTH DISTRICT

Dave Brat (R)

Elected Nov. 2014, 1st term; b. July 27, 1964, Detroit, MI; Hope Col, B.A. 1986, Princeton Theological Seminary, M. Div. 1990, American U., Ph.D. 1995; Presbyterian; married (Laura); 2 children.

Professional Career: Consultant, Arthur Anderson, 1986-88; Economic consultant, World Bank, 1993-95; Faculty, Randolph-Macon Col., 1996-present; VA Governor Bd. of Economic Advisors, 2006-13.

DC Office: 330 CHOB, 20515, 202-225-2815; Fax: 202-225-0011; Website: brat.house.gov.

State Offices: Glen Allen, 804-747-4073; Spotsylvania, 540-507-7216.

Committees: *Budget. Education & the Workforce:* Early Childhood, Elementary & Secondary Education; Workforce Protections. *Small Business:* Agriculture, Energy & Trade; Economic Growth, Tax & Capital Access.

Election Results

2014 general	David Brat (R)	148,026	(61%)	$1,408,693	$76,894
	Jack Trammell (D)	89,914	(37%)	$534,106	$10,233
	James Carr (Lib)	5,086	(2%)	$7,024	
2014 primary	David Brat (R)	36,110	(56%)		
	Eric Cantor (R)	28,898	(44%)		

Prior winning percentage: 2014 special (62%)

Population		Race and Ethnicity		Income	
Total:	760,928	White	74.2%	Median income:	$68,761
Urban:	18.3%	Black	14.3%		*(66 of 435)*
Suburban:	66.5%	Latino	5.0%	Under $50,000	34.4%
Rural:	15.2%	Asian	4.0%	$50,000-$99,999:	33.8%
Land area:	2,771	Two races	2.0%	$100,000-$199,999:	24.5%
Pop/sq. mi.:	274.6	White Ethnic	22.4%	$200,000 or more:	7.3%
Born in state:	55.8%			Poverty Rate	7.4%
		Education			
Age Groups		H.S. grad or less:	33.7%	**Work**	
Under 18:	23.4%	Some college:	27.9%	White collar:	44.0%
18 to 34:	20.7%	College degree, 4 yr.:	24.0%	Blue collar:	40.7%
35 to 64:	41.7%	Post-grad study:	14.4%	Sales and service:	15.3%
Over 64:	14.1%			Govt. workers:	16.6%
		Military			
		Veterans/active duty:	10.0%		

Central Virginia: Richmond Suburbs

Richmond, the centrally located capital of Virginia, still sets the tone for the Commonwealth. It is home to many of the state's great institutions—Dominion Resources, Main Street banks, big law firms, and the *Richmond Times-Dispatch*. Its metro area, now the third-largest in the commonwealth, has grown far past its city borders, covering almost all of suburban Henrico and Chesterfield counties and spreading into what was, until recently, countryside in Hanover and New Kent counties.

The 7th Congressional District of Virginia sprawls over 100 miles from the Tidewater to the outer reaches of the Washington, D.C. exurbs.

Voter Turnout	
2013 Total Citizen 18+	557,548
2014 House Turnout	243,351
2014 Turnout as % CVAP	43.6%
2012 Turnout as % CVAP	73.7%

Almost 70% of its population lives in the Richmond area. In the West End section of the city, the district takes in the University of Richmond and the terminus of historic Monument Avenue. This is an area of upscale young professionals, tending to spacious older homes, mostly located on quiet, tree-lined side streets. The large houses west of Interstate 195, mostly built in the inter-war period, lack the architectural grandeur of the Victorian- and Edwardian-era mansions of eastern Monument Avenue but are built on more spacious lots set back from the street.

Henrico County was once a linchpin of the state Republican coalition—it gave GOP nominee Barry Goldwater 70% of the vote in 1964—but demographic change, especially in the eastern portion of the county, and the movement of suburbanites toward the Democrats in the past two decades have changed its makeup. In 2008, Barack Obama became the first Democrat to carry Henrico since Franklin Roosevelt, a feat he repeated in 2012, though he suffered double-digit losses in the district. The 7th District takes in Henrico's Republican-leaning areas—the upscale Tuckahoe and Glen Allen and the fast-growing Short Pump area—and also Hanover, New Kent and Chesterfield counties, which are exurban and largely Republican. A smaller share of Henrico and all of Richmond are part of the black-majority 3rd District, which a federal court has ruled must be redrawn for the 2016 election because it is a racial gerrymander. For now, the 7th is a safe Republican district. But its boundaries may shift before the 2016 election.

2012 Presidential Vote		
Mitt Romney (R)...............222,915	(57%)
Barack Obama (D) 163,331	(42%)

2008 Presidential Vote		
John McCain (R)................207,023	(56%)
Barack Obama (D) 162,704	(44%)

Cook Partisan Voting Index: R+10

Dave Brat (R)

Republican Dave Brat pulled off the greatest political shock in the 2014 congressional election cycle—and arguably in years—with his June primary upset of House Majority Leader Eric Cantor. It was a shock not least to Cantor, who spent the morning of the primary at routine meetings in Washington. An obscure college professor, Brat tapped into voters' anti-Washington mood to topple the House's No. 2 Republican before coasting to victory over Democrat Jack Trammell in the general election. Because Cantor resigned his seat in August, Brat also won a special election to fill the remainder of Cantor's term and took office on Nov. 12, 2014.

Brat was an unlikely tea party hero. Born and raised in Dearborn Michigan, he studied business and religion before completing a Ph.D. in economics at American University. He taught economics at Randolph-Macon College, focusing on the ethics of capitalism. Apart from a failed run in 2011 for the state House of Delegates, he stayed out of politics and led the quiet life of an academic.

But Brat's political timing was impeccable. After redistricting, the 7th became more conservative and rural, dropping parts of Richmond and taking in more of New Kent County. Cantor had thought that would shore up his reelection, but in fact it brought in more blue-collar voters amenable to the tea party message rather than white-collar professionals who had made up his base. Many felt that Cantor's leadership duties and fundraising increasingly kept him away from the retail politics that his constituents expected.

The race ultimately turned on the issue of immigration. Although the House GOP refused to take up a bipartisan bill that the Senate passed in 2013, Cantor staked out a position to the left of many in his party when he proposed limited legal immigration status for children of undocumented workers who were brought into the United States as minors. Conservatives saw that as a bridge too far, and Brat picked up on their anger.

As the primary campaign progressed, Cantor committed several unforced errors. He used much of his huge cash advantage to launch a negative ad campaign that increased Brat's name recognition rather than hurting him. Cantor also took comfort from the only two polls issued, both of which happened to be favorable, while ignoring the outsized attention that Brat was getting from conservative media stars such as Laura Ingraham. Although Brat got little formal support from the tea party movement, which largely saw his campaign as hopeless, he benefited from a powerful local grass-roots conservative movement, abetted by a rallying cry from conservative media personalities such as Ingraham and Mark Levin, another national radio host. Cantor spent $6 million through the primary, some of which went for leadership activities not related to his district; Brat spent $392,000 on the primary.

In June, Brat defeated Cantor by a stunning 11 percentage points. The first House party leader to lose a primary, Cantor soon resigned his seat to take a job with an investment bank, while Brat settled into the role of a front-runner. Cantor's resignation meant that the November election also became a special election, allowing Brat to be sworn in right away and acquire several weeks' seniority over other freshmen. As expected, Brat handily beat Trammell—he took 62% in the special election and 61% in the general election—to become the only House member with a Ph.D. in economics.

Former Rep. Tom Davis, a Republican from Virginia, wrote a perceptive analysis of Cantor's defeat in a book, *The Partisan Divide*, that he co-authored. With his role as a national party leader, Davis wrote, it became hard to argue that he was using his clout to help his local district. "Cantor was defeated because he was viewed as too soft on Obama, too willing to compromise, and too eager to abandon conservative principles by a constituency (particularly the primary voting universe) that wanted the opposite."

In the January 2015 vote for speaker, Brat was the only member who voted for Republican Rep. Jeff Duncan of South Carolina. Given that he had taken out the No. 2 GOP leader, it was no surprise that he voted against another term for John Boehner. He was assigned to the Budget Committee, where he praised chairman Tom Price of Georgia for "demonstrating that House Republicans are here to govern," plus the Education and the Workforce and Small Business panels.

Brat pledged to serve no more than 12 years in Congress. Before being sworn in, he said: "I will focus on keeping the promises I made during the campaign, including sponsoring or co-sponsoring bills to repeal or defund Obamacare in the House, to pass a flat or fair tax, and to secure the southern border. Later, I will also work to pass constitutional amendments to balance the budget and to term-limit members of Congress." Brat is hardly the first House member to introduce such proposals. And once he took office, he rarely sought or received news-media attention. But his route to Congress surely was unique.

EIGHTH DISTRICT

Don Beyer (D)

Elected 2014, 1st term; b. June 20, 1950, Trieste, Italy; Williams Col., B.A. 1972; Episcopalian; married (Megan Carroll); 4 children.

Elected Office: VA lt. gov., 1990-98.

Professional Career: Automobile dealer; Chmn, Jobs for VA Graduates, 1999-2013; U.S. Ambassador to Switzerland and Liechtenstein, 2009-13.

DC Office: 431 CHOB, 20515, 202-225-4376; Fax: 202-225-0017; Website: beyer.house.gov.

State Offices: Alexandria, 703-658-5403.

Committees: *Natural Resources:* Energy & Mineral Resources; Federal Lands. *Science, Space & Technology:* Environment; Oversight (RMM); Space.

Election Results

2014 general	Don Beyer (D) 128,102	(63%)	$2,688,020	$43,455	
	Micah Edmond (R)....................... 63,810	(31%)	$115,578	$4,952	
	Gwendolyn Beck (I) 5,420	(3%)	$28,572		
	Jeffrey Carson (Lib)....................... 4,409	(2%)	$23,937		
2014 primary	Don Beyer (D) 17,780	(46%)			
	Patrick Hope (D) 7,092	(18%)			
	Adam Ebbin (D) 5,272	(14%)			
	William Euille (D) 3,251	(8%)			
	Mark Levine (D) 2,613	(7%)			
	Lavern Chatman (D) 2,116	(5%)			

Population		Race and Ethnicity		Income	
Total:	774,396	White	53.9%	Median income:	$97,323
Urban:	85.1%	Latino	18.0%		(8 of 435)
Suburban:	14.9%	Black	14.1%	Under $50,000	23.0%
Rural:	0.0%	Asian	10.9%	$50,000-$99,999:	28.3%
Land area:	173	Two races	2.3%	$100,000-$199,999:	32.3%
Pop/sq. mi.:	4,475.2	White Ethnic	24.4%	$200,000 or more:	16.4%
Born in state:	23.4%			Poverty Rate	7.7%
		Education			
Age Groups		H.S. grad or less:	21.5%	**Work**	
Under 18:	21.0%	Some college:	17.1%	White collar:	56.7%
18 to 34:	28.0%	College degree, 4 yr.:	30.3%	Blue collar:	33.3%
35 to 64:	40.9%	Post-grad study:	31.1%	Sales and service:	10.0%
Over 64:	10.1%				
		Military		Govt. workers:	23.6%
		Veterans/active duty:	10.2%		

Northern Virginia: Fairfax, Arlington, Alexandria

When George Washington strolled the brick side-walks of Alexandria on his way to market or church or Gadsby's Tavern (where he celebrated his final two birthdays), it was the largest city in Northern Virginia, and larger than Georgetown just up the Potomac River. The areas that are now Capitol Hill

Voter Turnout	
2013 Total Citizen 18+	505,032
2014 House Turnout	203,076
2014 Turnout as % CVAP	40.2%
2012 Turnout as % CVAP	72.4%

and downtown Washington D.C., were hills above the river's mud flats. But Washington became the national capital, and as it grew, Northern Virginia seemed left behind. In 1846, the District of Columbia retroceded its land south of the Potomac—now Alexandria and Arlington—to Virginia because it seemed then that the federal government would never need it. It would be another 97 years before the first federal building was constructed on the Virginia side—the Pentagon. When that occurred, Alexandria and the rural countryside of Northern Virginia were represented in Congress by Judge Howard W. Smith, for many years the influential chairman of the House Rules Committee, a Democrat who saw as his mission the maintenance of the standards of George Washington, Thomas Jefferson and Robert E. Lee. Yet by the 1940s, the area was changing around him.

New subdivision dwellers with white-collar jobs wanted schools with good academic programs, not the segregated schoolhouses Judge Smith's friends were willing to finance. The new generation wanted freeways, parks and recreation facilities. Today, the onetime suburbs of Arlington and Alexandria are "edge cities." Arlington County has the third highest median household income, $103,208, of any county in the nation and has a greater share of people with college degrees, 72%, than any other county. Cranes dot its cityscape, as giant office and housing developments have sprung up from rail yards in Crystal City and from used car lots upriver in Rosslyn. Commuters find roads jammed: Washington has the worst traffic congestion in the country, although Virginia officials hope that new transportation spending by Richmond will alleviate some of it. The nearby federal government insulated the region from the worst of the economic downturn, and Arlington's unemployment rate sat at 2.9% in April 2014, the lowest in the state.

The 8th Congressional District of Virginia consists of Arlington County and the cities of Alexandria and Falls Church, where slightly more than half of its population resides. The district covers all of Virginia that is inside the Capital Beltway except for small pockets in Annandale and McLean. The balance lives in Fairfax County, either in precincts near the perimeter of Arlington/Falls Church/Alexandria or in areas south of the Beltway. The district also takes in George Washington's Mount Vernon estate and the more rural areas around Fort Belvoir. The district is solidly Democratic. Barack Obama twice won 68 percent of the local vote.

2012 Presidential Vote		
Barack Obama (D) 243,746	(68%)
Mitt Romney (R)................111,518	(31%)
2008 Presidential Vote		
Barack Obama (D) 236,148	(68%)
John McCain (R)................105,507	(31%)
Cook Partisan Voting Index: D+16		

Don Beyer (D)

Democrat Don Beyer easily won the primary and general elections to take his district, which covers the wealthy and heavily Democratic Northern Virginia suburbs, giving him the shortest commute to his district and home of any member—around "18 minutes," he says. Although he has a long record as a successful businessman and public official, this was his first election to an office in Northern Virginia

Beyer was born in Trieste, Italy, where his father was serving as an Army officer, grew up in Washington, went to Gonzaga High School in the shadow of the Capitol, and got his bachelor's degree from Williams College. American politics is rich in examples of second and third chances, and Beyer is no exception. He built a reputation as an affable deal-maker who could work with both sides of the aisle when he served two terms as Virginia's lieutenant governor, starting in 1990. But in 1997, when he sought the prize of the governorship, he floundered in his campaign against Republican James Gilmore III, stumbling in particular over the issue of the state's contested car tax. When he lost by 10 percentage points, many Virginians thought it would mark the end of Beyer's political career.

Beyer turned toward building his family's car-dealership business, which features Volvos, but he found he couldn't stay away from politics for good. In 2004, he served as campaign treasurer for Howard Dean's presidential campaign, and in 2008, he helped raise substantial sums for the Obama campaign. He led the new administration's transition planning at the Commerce Department. He was rewarded with a plum ambassadorship to Switzerland and Liechtenstein, where he represented the United States for four years.

Beyer's next big chance came when 12-term Democratic Rep. Jim Moran announced his retirement. Beyer promptly launched his bid and tapped his extensive network of high-level Democratic contacts. His name recognition—due in part to the car dealerships that bear the family name—and his connections proved to be an advantage in a crowded primary race that drew six other Democrats. Of the $2.7 million that he spent, $415,000 was self-financed.

Although all the primary candidates endorsed staunchly progressive ideals and the Obama administration, Beyer stood out in candidate forums by demonstrating a strong grasp of both foreign and domestic policy. In the June primary, he topped the field with 46% of the vote, followed by state Del. Patrick Hope at 18%.

In the House, he got seats on the Natural Resources Committee, and on Science, Space and Technology, where he became the ranking Democrat on the Oversight Subcommittee. In May, the House passed his Science Prize Competition Act, which encourages federal agencies to use prize competitions as incentives for innovative scientific research and development. He said that he identified with the more than 70,000 federal employees in his district: Three of his four grandparents were federal employees. To the dismay of labor unions that had supported him, he was an enthusiastic backer of Obama's request for trade promotion authority and the prospective trans-Pacific trade deal. Beyer praised the July nuclear-arms agreement with Iran, and took a bit of credit. As Ambassador to Switzerland, he recounted, he hosted the initial discussions with Iran that launched the broader negotiations.

Beyer is a close fit for his deep-blue district, but many in Virginia have asked how the state will fare with their loss of seniority in the House. The retirements of Moran and

Republican Frank Wolf from the neighboring 10th District left the area without two veteran appropriators. Beyer has responded that his deep ties to the Obama administration will benefit his district—for two years, anyway.

NINTH DISTRICT

Morgan Griffith (R)

Elected 2010, 3rd term; b. March 15, 1958, Philadelphia, PA; Emory & Henry Col., B.A. 1980, Washington and Lee U., J.D. 1983; Episcopalian; married (Hilary); 3 children..

Elected Office: VA House, 1994-2010, maj.ldr., 2000-10.

Professional Career: Practicing atty., 2008-10.

DC Office: 1108 LHOB, 20515, 202-225-3861; Fax: 202-225-0076; Website: morgangriffith.house.gov.

State Offices: Abingdon, 276-525-1405; Christiansburg, 540-381-5671; Big Stone Gap, 275-525-14051.

Committees: *Energy & Commerce:* Energy & Power; Health; Oversight & Investigations.

Group Ratings

	ADA	ACLU	AFL-CIO	LCV	ITI	COC	HAFA	ACU	CFG	FRC
2014	5%	16%	–	3%	100%	79%	54%	63%	57%	100%
2013	20%	C	14%	4%	C	69%	C	72%	66%	C

National Journal Ratings

	2013 LIB	—	2013 CONS
Economic	38%	—	61%
Social	42%	—	57%
Foreign	53%	—	46%
Composite	45%	—	55%

Key Votes of the 113th Congress

1. Sandy storm spending	N	5. Medical Marijuana	N	9. Syrian Rebels Training	Y
2. Violence Against Women Act	N	6. Farm Bill	Y	10. Keystone pipeline	Y
3. Guantanamo Bay Detainees	N	7. Afghanistan Combat	N	11. Immigration Exec. Action	Y
4. Abortion 20-week ban	Y	8. NSA Phone Data Collection	Y	12. Bipartisan budget deal	Y

Election Results

2014 general	Morgan Griffith (R)	117,465	(72%)	$889,987
	William Carr (I)	39,412	(24%)	
2014 primary	Morgan Griffith (R)	unopposed		

Prior winning percentages: 2012 (61%), 2010 (51%)

Population		Race and Ethnicity		Income	
Total:	721,531	White	90.0%	Median income:	$39,427
Urban:	25.3%	Black	5.8%		(395 of 435)
Suburban:	10.1%	Latino	1.7%	Under $50,000	60.9%
Rural:	64.7%	Asian	1.2%	$50,000-$99,999:	27.5%
Land area:	9,634	Two races	1.0%	$100,000-$199,999:	9.6%
Pop/sq. mi.:	74.9	White Ethnic	16.2%	$200,000 or more:	2.0%
Born in state:	66.6%			Poverty Rate	18.1%
		Education			
Age Groups		H.S. grad or less:	52.5%	**Work**	
Under 18:	18.8%	Some college:	28.6%	White collar:	30.2%
18 to 34:	23.3%	College degree, 4 yr.:	10.9%	Blue collar:	42.5%
35 to 64:	39.7%	Post-grad study:	8.1%	Sales and service:	27.3%
Over 64:	18.1%				
		Military		Govt. workers:	19.3%
		Veterans/active duty:	8.0%		

Southwest Virginia: Blacksburg, Bristol

As early as 1765, settlements were carved out of the great Valley of Virginia, bending westward and south toward Tennessee and the Cumberland Gap. Most of these founders were of Scots-Irish lineage, and they moved to a mountainous area that devel-

Voter Turnout	
2013 Total Citizen 18+	575,703
2014 House Turnout	162,815
2014 Turnout as % CVAP	28.3%
2012 Turnout as % CVAP	54.5%

oped almost apart from the rest of Virginia. The fiercely independent settlers eventually spilled over the ridges that bound the valley to the west and into the heart of the Appalachian Mountains. Here, they followed the same political and economic development patterns as those in West Virginia, which wasn't a separate state until 1863. They were first farmers and later coal miners. Politically, this virtually all-white area opposed slavery and was skeptical, if not hostile, to the Confederacy. It is a long way from here to plantation country—the state's extreme southwest corner is closer to nine other state capitals than to Richmond. Out of the crucible of struggle between secessionists and unionists, Southwest Virginia developed a robust two-party politics after the Civil War, sooner than in the rest of the state.

The 9th Congressional District covers all of Southwest Virginia west of Roanoke; the city and most of Roanoke County are in the 6th District. Over the years, it became known as the "Fighting Ninth" because of its taste for raucous politics, which by and large were culturally conservative and economically populist. This is also NASCAR country; Martinsville's speedway is here, and Bristol's is just across the Tennessee line. Blacksburg, with a population of 44,000 plus the 31,000 students at Virginia Tech University, is the largest city in the area. *Big Stone Gap*, a movie that was shot in the coal-mining town with the same name in the southwest corner of the state and stars Ashley Judd seeking love and herself, was scheduled for release in October 2015.

In recent decades, as development has moved down Interstate 81, the region has become more like the rest of Virginia. With encouragement from state officials, businesses have created jobs at high-tech companies and telephone call centers. Agriculture has been thriving, especially produce and dairy, while the role of coal mining has diminished. Buchanan County, in the far western part of the district, shows how the political winds have shifted here. It gave Bill Clinton 63% of the vote in both 1992 and 1996, but the Democrats' vote share dropped about five percentage points in each succeeding election

2012 Presidential Vote		
Mitt Romney (R)	196,354	(63%)
Barack Obama (D)	108,641	(35%)
2008 Presidential Vote		
John McCain (R)	178,998	(58%)
Barack Obama (D)	123,420	(40%)
Cook Partisan Voting Index:	R+15	

through 2008. As Democratic support collapsed, this has become easily the most Republican district in the state. Mitt Romney won 63%-35% in 2012.

Morgan Griffith (R)

Republican Morgan Griffith, a former Virginia House majority leader, uses his Energy and Commerce Committee seat to protect his region's coal industry and inveigh against the Environmental Protection Agency. Following his election in 2010, he has quickly become entrenched in a district that Democrat Rick Boucher had held for 28 years.

Griffith was born in Philadelphia and moved to Salem as a child. He was president of his high school student body and an avid swimmer. He attended Emory & Henry College, in part because it had just completed a new pool. He graduated in 1980 and received a law degree three years later from Washington and Lee University. Griffith opened a private practice in Salem and joined a statewide firm in 2008. After winning a seat in the state House of Delegates in 1994, Griffith pursued conservative efforts to repeal restrictions on gun ownership, limit abortion rights, and block a $1.4 billion tax increase. In 2000, he became the first Republican in Virginia to serve as the House majority leader and earned a reputation as a skilled parliamentarian. Occasionally, Griffith bucked his party, as when he helped draft a bill in 2010 to legalize marijuana for medicinal use.

In the House race, Griffith easily won the Republican nomination on the first ballot at a party convention in May. He was at a significant financial disadvantage in the general election, outspent by Boucher 3-to-1. But Boucher, though he sought a middle ground, had been a leader at the Energy and Commerce Committee on the party's cap-and-trade bill aimed at limiting greenhouse gas emissions, which passed the House in 2009. The bill was unpopular in Appalachia's coal country, and Griffith made Boucher's work on the bill a centerpiece of his campaign. He argued that the measure would have killed jobs and raised electricity costs. Boucher framed his support for the bill as a way to ensure that Congress—and not conservatives' nemesis, the Environmental Protection Agency—had regulatory power over carbon emissions. But this bill was crafted and embraced mostly by coastal Democrats.

Griffith ran an ad in 2010 with a video clip of President Barack Obama saying, "I love Rick Boucher." Boucher attacked Griffith as a carpetbagger who lived outside the district, running a television ad that said, "Morgan Griffith: He's not from here ... and it shows." Boucher outspent the challenger $3.3 million to $1 million, though Griffith was bolstered by nearly $2 million in spending by national party and conservative groups. As Republicans swept across the country, especially in rural areas, Griffith won 51%-46%.

In the House, Griffith has mostly been a loyal Republican, though less of an ideologue than many of his GOP classmates. He joined most Democrats in voting against a House-passed 2012 amendment requiring trials for terrorism detainees to be held at Cuba's Guantanamo Bay instead of in civilian courts. Though he expressed interest in filing a medical-marijuana bill similar to the one he crafted in Virginia, he told *The Hill* newspaper in 2012 that he was hesitant. "Here's the problem: Everybody hears medical marijuana and they think California—'Hey, if it makes you feel good, do it,'" he said.

He followed Boucher with a plum seat on Energy and Commerce, rare for a freshman, and steered a bill through the House in 2011 that sought to limit EPA's power to regulate boilers. He and West Virginia Republican David McKinley complained in a January 2013 op-ed about "the destructive consequences of this administration's regulatory assault" on the coal industry. He also contended in 2011 that EPA regulations treated dairy milk spills the same as oil spills, an assertion that the fact-checking site *PolitiFact* labeled false. When Appalachian Power in June 2015 shut down two coal-fired power plants in Virginia and three in West Virginia in response to an EPA mandate of stricter emissions standards, Griffith said that the EPA was threatening the stability of the electrical grid. "It puts people at risk during peak periods," he said, while voicing hope that Congress and the courts, especially with a Republican president, could limit the damage to coal country. He added that Virginia Gov. Terry McAuliffe had joined the "war on coal," which was jeopardizing the economy of Southwest Virginia.

With Boucher uninterested in a 2012 rematch, Democrats had no one of his stature to face Griffith, and he steamrolled political novice Anthony Flaccavento, 61%-39%. In 2014, Democrats had no challenger and Griffith won with 72% against William Carr, a retired insurance agent with no political experience.

In supporting the reelection of Speaker John Boehner in January 2015, Griffith issued a lengthy statement that no viable candidate had circulated plans or sought his support in the days prior to the vote and that he would have given serious consideration to such a contender "due to my frustrations with the leadership style of John Boehner." A legislative leader must have a plan for leadership, Griffith added. "While I do not completely agree with John Boehner's leadership style or plan, at least he has one."

TENTH DISTRICT

Barbara Comstock (R)

Elected 2014, 1st term; b. June 30, 1959, Springfield, MA; Middlebury Col., B.A. 1981, Georgetown U., J.D. 1986; Catholic; married (Chip); 3 children.

Elected Office: VA House, 2010-15.

Professional Career: Practicing atty.; Staffer, U.S. Rep. Frank Wolf, 1991-95; Staff, U.S. House Oversight & Gov't Reform Committee, 1995-99; Dir., U.S. Dept. of Justice Office of Public Affairs, 2002-03; Sr. partner & principal, Blank Rome LLP & Blank Rome Gov't Relations LLC, 2003-06; Founding partner, Corallo Comstock; Founding partner, Comstock Strategies, present.

DC Office: 226 CHOB, 20515, 202-225-5136; Fax: 202-225-0437; Website: comstock.house.gov.

State Offices: Sterling, 703-404-6903; Winchester, 540-773-3600.

Committees: *House Administration. Science, Space & Technology:* Energy; Research & Technology (RMM). *Transportation & Infrastructure:* Aviation; Economic Development, Public Buildings & Emergency Mgmt.; Highways & Transit.

Election Results

2014 general	Barbara Comstock (R)	125,914	(57%)	$3,403,550	$1,588,914	$1,692,713
	John Foust (D)	89,957	(40%)	$3,022,597	$134,761	$2,374,958
2014 primary	Barbara Comstock (R)	7,337	(54%)			
	Bob Marshall (R)	3,829	(28%)			
	Howie Lind (R)	1,108	(8%)			
	Stephen Hollingshead (R)	816	(6%)			

Population		Race and Ethnicity		Income	
Total:	781,947	White	65.1%	Median income:	$110,444
Urban:	15.3%	Latino	12.2%		(1 of 435)
Suburban:	83.2%	Asian	11.8%	Under $50,000	19.9%
Rural:	1.4%	Black	7.4%	$50,000-$99,999:	24.3%
Land area:	1,056	Two races	3.1%	$100,000-$199,999:	35.0%
Pop/sq. mi.:	740.4	White Ethnic	27.4%	$200,000 or more:	20.7%
Born in state:	37.2%			Poverty Rate	4.6%
		Education			
Age Groups		H.S. grad or less:	23.7%	**Work**	
Under 18:	27.6%	Some college:	22.6%	White collar:	53.1%
18 to 34:	19.6%	College degree, 4 yr.:	31.6%	Blue collar:	34.7%
35 to 64:	42.9%	Post-grad study:	22.2%	Sales and service:	12.2%
Over 64:	9.9%				
		Military		Govt. workers:	16.8%
		Veterans/active duty:	9.8%		

Northern Virginia: Loudoun and Fairfax Counties

What we think of today as the outer suburbs and exurbs of Washington D.C., was still open country as late as World War II. Gen. George Marshall, driving from his office in the Pentagon to the old house he bought in Leesburg 40 miles away, would pass a few gas stations, crossroads villages and countless

Voter Turnout	
2013 Total Citizen 18+	506,342
2014 House Turnout	222,910
2014 Turnout as % CVAP	44.0%
2012 Turnout as % CVAP	76.9%

acres of farm fields. If Marshall made the trip today, his drive would take much more time and he would see something very different. As the federal government grew, Fairfax County population doubled in the 1940s and very nearly tripled in the 1950s. It has continued to grow, though at a much slower rate, passing 1 million in 2002 and 1.1 million in 2011. Loudoun County, just past Dulles International Airport, lately has experienced that type of explosive growth. Its population fell just short of doubling in the 1990s and grew from 174,000 people in 2000 to 350,000 in 2013. This has become one of the richest areas of the country: Loudoun and Fairfax counties ranked first and second, respectively, in the nation in median household income in 2011. Growth continues apace, and the Washington metro area now extends past those two counties and over the Blue Ridge into the Shenandoah Valley.

No longer simply a collection of bedroom communities, Northern Virginia has become a booming employment center and focus of innovation in its own right. The Dulles Access Road is lined with high-tech firms and entrepreneurial startups, defense contractors and "Beltway bandit" lobbying firms. There have been growing pains: Traffic is mightily congested and Loudoun has taken steps to curb sprawl. This is family country: 46% of households have children under 18, in contrast to 15% in gentrified Arlington County.

The 10th Congressional District covers much of Northern Virginia's western suburbs. It includes most of well-heeled McLean, home of many of Washington's political and lawyer-lobbyist elites, but it skirts the booming and increasingly liberal residential enclaves in the Tysons commercial area. It includes the conservative Clifton area of southwest Fairfax, northern Prince William County, and the cities of Manassas and Manassas Park, which were both hard-hit by the housing collapse. Beyond the Beltway, it takes in woodsy Great Falls and the Dulles Airport corridor. It includes all of Loudoun County, which is heavily built-up in the east with some still-rural areas west of Leesburg. Middleburg, with both old and new money, is horse country with many gated mansions. Beyond the Blue Ridge, it takes in the fast-growing, Republican Winchester area. About 40% of the population is in Loudoun, and 30% in Fairfax.

The district was once reliably Republican; it gave George W. Bush 56% of the vote in 2000 and 55% in 2004. With an influx of immigrants and federal workers, Northern Virginia is becoming friendlier to Democrats.

2012 Presidential Vote		
Mitt Romney (R)..............186,650	(50%)
Barack Obama (D) 182,432	(49%)
2008 Presidential Vote		
Barack Obama (D) 172,622	(51%)
John McCain (R)................163,148	(48%)
Cook Partisan Voting Index: R+2		

But redistricting in 2011 shed some Democratic parts of Fairfax County, increasing John McCain's vote in 2008 by two percentage points. Barack Obama narrowly lost the district in 2012, while the three statewide Republican candidates in 2009 all won it by double-digits.

Barbara Comstock (R)

Virginia's 10th District in 2014 replaced a longtime Republican lawmaker with another political veteran, Barbara Comstock, a state delegate and former congressional staffer and lobbyist. Comstock had an easier time than expected in a contest that both parties from the outset had viewed as a toss-up in this wealthy Northern Virginia district.

Comstock was born in Springfield Massachusetts, and was once an intern for the late Democratic Sen. Edward Kennedy. After getting her bachelor's from Middlebury College and her law degree from Georgetown, Comstock went into private practice as an attorney. She worked for four years for GOP Rep. Frank Wolf, whom she would later succeed, and then spent another four years as chief investigative counsel and senior counsel for the House Oversight and Government Reform Committee.

Comstock became a valuable strategic and legal operative for Republicans, including opposition research on Vice President Al Gore for George W. Bush's 2000 presidential campaign. She was director of public affairs at the Justice Department from 2002 to 2003, and returned to the private sector to help the legal defense of former House Majority Leader Tom DeLay and Scooter Libby, the former aide to Vice President Dick Cheney. Comstock worked as a lobbyist for the Motion Picture Association of America, was a consultant for the Mitt Romney campaign in 2012 and for the Workplace Fairness Institute, which opposes the Democratic-supported, pro-union Employee Free Choice Act.

Comstock was elected to Virginia's House of Delegates in 2009, ousting a Democratic incumbent. When Wolf announced he would retire after 34 years, Comstock ran, as many had long expected. In a January "firehouse primary"—one that allows the nominee to be chosen earlier and get a head start on general-election campaigning—Comstock won in a crowded field with 54 percent of the vote.

With Northern Virginia trending more Democratic, that party eyed the seat as a possible pickup and joined Republicans in dumping early money into the race. Democrats believed that they could use Comstock's votes in Richmond against transportation funding and for anti-abortion legislation against her. Democrat John Foust attacked Comstock as a creature of Washington, and cited her for failing to disclose the Workplace Fairness Institute as a client even as she was sponsoring bills the group supported. The Comstock campaign called it an oversight, which it corrected. Foust made a critical mistake when he put down his opponent to a campaign audience, "I don't think that she has even had a real job." The comment was obviously inaccurate. Comstock called it, "offensive and demeaning." It seemed to take the wind out of Foust's campaign and the Democrats' "war on women" rhetoric. Later, Foust told an interviewer that he had misspoke, and that he had intended to say that the jobs were hyper-partisan. In October, the Democratic Congressional Campaign Committee pulled its ads from the contest. Comstock outspent Foust, $3.4 million to $3 million, and had another $4 million spent on her behalf. She won with a surprisingly easy 57%-40%, and she took all five counties by comfortable margins.

In the House, she got seats on Transportation and Infrastructure, House Administration, and Science, Space and Technology, where she became chairwoman of the Research and Technology Subcommittee. With the many technology firms and entrepreneurs in her district, she described the latter assignment as an opportunity to address "innovation issues that can revolutionize our education, economy, health care, and national security." She calibrated some of her House votes to appeal to moderates and government workers, much as her predecessor Wolf had done. She voted against the House Republican budget, for example, because she said that its employee benefit changes were unfair to federal employees. She criticized GOP appropriators for their $75 million cut in transit funds for Metro.

Comstock likely will face a competitive challenger in 2016. But her opposition may not clarify until after state and local elections in November 2015 and resolution of the federal court's requirement for a new redistricting map, which could affect Northern Virginia.

ELEVENTH DISTRICT

Gerald Connolly (D)

Elected 2008, 4th term; b. March 30, 1950, Boston, MA; Maryknoll Col., B.A. 1971, Harvard U., M.P.A. 1979; Catholic; married (Cathy); 1 child.

Elected Office: Fairfax Cnty. Bd. of Supervisors, 1995-2009, chmn., 2004-09.

Professional Career: Non-profit exec.; U.S. Senate aide; Defense contractor.

DC Office: 2238 RHOB, 20515, 202-225-1492; Website: connolly. house.gov.

State Offices: Annandale, 703-256-3071; Woodbridge, 571-408-4407.

Committees: *Foreign Affairs:* Asia & the Pacific; Middle East & North Africa. *Oversight & Gov't Reform:* Government Operations (RMM); Information Technology.

Group Ratings

	ADA	ACLU	AFL-CIO	LCV	ITI	COC	HAFA	ACU	CFG	FRC
2014	85%	72%	–	94%	100%	57%	14%	4%	7%	0%
2013	70%	C	86%	96%	C	62%	C	24%	13%	C

National Journal Ratings

	2013 LIB	—	2013 CONS
Economic	64%	—	35%
Social	66%	—	32%
Foreign	75%	—	23%
Composite	69%	—	31%

Key Votes of the 113th Congress

1. Sandy storm spending	Y	5. Medical Marijuana	Y	9. Syrian Rebels Training	Y
2. Violence Against Women Act	Y	6. Farm Bill	N	10. Keystone pipeline	N
3. Guantanamo Bay Detainees	Y	7. Afghanistan Combat	N	11. Immigration Exec. Action	N
4. Abortion 20-week ban	N	8. NSA Phone Data Collection	Y	12. Bipartisan budget deal	Y

Election Results

2014 general	Gerald Connolly (D).................	106,780	(57%)	$1,455,123	
	Suzanne Scholte (R)....................	75,796	(40%)	$269,142	$9,927
2014 primary	Gerald Connolly (D)..............unopposed				

Prior winning percentages: 2012 (61%), 2010 (49%), 2008 (55%)

Population		Race and Ethnicity		Income	
Total:	765,755	White	49.1%	Median income:	$101,226
Urban:	11.1%	Asian	17.6%		*(4 of 435)*
Suburban:	88.9%	Latino	17.3%	Under $50,000	19.6%
Rural:	0.0%	Black	11.6%	$50,000-$99,999:	29.6%
Land area:	296	Two races	4.0%	$100,000-$199,999:	34.9%
Pop/sq. mi.:	2,587.8	White Ethnic	22.3%	$200,000 or more:	15.9%
Born in state:	28.4%			Poverty Rate	6.5%
		Education			
Age Groups		H.S. grad or less:	23.7%	**Work**	
Under 18:	23.8%	Some college:	22.8%	White collar:	51.1%
18 to 34:	25.4%	College degree, 4 yr.:	29.4%	Blue collar:	37.6%
35 to 64:	40.7%	Post-grad study:	24.1%	Sales and service:	11.3%
Over 64:	10.2%				
		Military		Govt. workers:	20.7%
		Veterans/active duty:	11.0%		

Northern Virginia: Fairfax and Prince William Counties

Rising on a hill west of Washington D.C., Tysons Corner was a back-country intersection 50 years ago. By the late 1980s, it was an edge city, with the largest concentration of office space to be found anywhere between Washington and Atlanta, and with a modern skyline and busy multi-lane ave-

Voter Turnout	
2013 Total Citizen 18+	477,955
2014 House Turnout	187,805
2014 Turnout as % CVAP	39.3%
2012 Turnout as % CVAP	70.3%

nues that served as arteries to the Capital Beltway. Fairfax County, which includes Tysons Corner, had been a typical postwar suburb. It had only 99,000 people in 1950, far fewer than Washington's 802,000. But in the years that followed, the trickle moving into Fairfax became a gusher. In 2012, it had 1.1 million people, nearly twice as many as Washington. Today, it is packed with mostly affluent communities, with dazzlingly high percentages of residents with college degrees and two or more cars.

In the last decade, Fairfax County has once again changed. Just as Tysons Corner (now referred to as simply Tysons) made it a major corporate and shopping center, plans are underway to transform that complex to approximate a walkable, downtown urban area. By 2050, planners envision 100,000 residents and 200,000 jobs in Tysons, which will become a 24-hour urban center. Population growth has slowed since the 1980s; the 12% growth rate of the 2000s was the slowest since the 1910s. Meanwhile, Prince William County has been growing at a fast clip, 54% between 2000 and 2013, attracting the young families that Fairfax once did. Immigrants—Koreans and Vietnamese, Ethiopians and Afghans, Salvadorans and Mexicans—have put their stamp in Fairfax on what once were mostly white, heavily Protestant neighborhoods. George Mason University economist Tyler Cowen runs a popular website that reviews the area's best ethnic dining spots, including Burmese, Tunisian and Palestinian restaurants.

The federal government still provides a solid base for the local economy, and the 2007-09 recession hit Fairfax with less force than most other locales; its jobless rate was 3.6% in April 2015. The Federal Transit Administration in August 2008 approved the nearly $5.2 billion Silver Line extension of the Washington-area Metrorail system from Tysons to Dulles Airport; the initial 11.7 mile segment, with four stations in Tysons, opened to Reston in July 2014. Unlike nearby Loudoun and Prince William counties, Fairfax has declined to pass ordinances denying services to illegal immigrants, although local law enforcement annually have turned over hundreds of suspected illegal residents to federal immigration officials.

The 11th Congressional District of Virginia consists of much of Fairfax County and southeastern Prince William County. Republicans in control of redistricting packed as many Democratic voters into the district as possible in order to shore up neighboring Republican districts. The 11th takes in sprawling Tysons, parts of Annandale that are the only part of the district inside the

2012 Presidential Vote		
Barack Obama (D) 212,181	(62%)
Mitt Romney (R).................123,317	(36%)
2008 Presidential Vote		
Barack Obama (D) 205,422	(62%)
John McCain (R).................122,085	(37%)
Cook Partisan Voting Index:　D+10		

Capital Beltway, and also Oakton, Vienna, Fairfax City, Lorton, Burke and part of Centreville. An arm extends west to the heavily Democratic planned community of Reston and neighboring Herndon. In Prince William County, it includes Woodbridge and Dale City, areas with large Latino immigrant populations. The district is 18% Asian, 17% Hispanic, and 12% African American; in Virginia, only the 3rd District has a smaller non-Hispanic white population. It is solidly Democratic, as intended.

Gerald Connolly (D)

Democrat Gerald (Gerry) Connolly, elected in 2008, is a former Capitol Hill staffer who remains an ardent champion of the federal workers and government contractors who populate his Northern Virginia district, which is almost entirely outside the Capital Beltway.

Connolly grew up in the Boston area and graduated from Maryknoll College. He considered joining the priesthood and studied for six years at a Catholic seminary. But his interest in public policy led him to Washington D.C., where in the 1970s he managed the American Freedom from Hunger Foundation and the U.S. Committee for Refugees. He got a master's degree from Harvard and worked for a decade on the staff of the Senate Foreign Relations Committee, where he specialized in Middle Eastern affairs and foreign aid. He left Capitol Hill to run the Washington office of Stanford Research Institute International and then became vice president of the San Diego-based defense contractor SAIC. In 1995, Connolly won a seat on the Fairfax County Board of Supervisors, and in 2003, he was elected board chairman, putting him in charge of a large local government at a time of rapid growth. Transportation was a major preoccupation, and his biggest project was the Metrorail extension to Tysons Corner and Dulles.

In these battles, Connolly worked with then-Republican Rep. Tom Davis, who continued to pay close attention to local issues as well as playing a major national role as chairman of the National Republican Congressional Committee in the 2000 and 2002 election seasons. Davis, an expert on political demographics, could see that Northern Virginia was moving away from the GOP; he also was term-limited as the top Republican on the Oversight and Government Reform Committee. In 2008, he decided not to seek reelection.

In the primary, Connolly faced former Rep. Leslie Byrne, whom Davis defeated in 1994. She had the backing of the national women's fundraising group EMILY's List, but Connolly outpaced her finances, in part because of his support from defense contractors. In a low-turnout June primary, Connolly won by a solid 58%-33%. The Republican nominee was Keith Fimian, a businessman and newcomer to Northern Virginia politics who self-financed much of his campaign. Democrats attacked Fimian as a conservative on cultural issues, in contrast to Davis' moderate record, and Fimian got little help from national Republicans. Connolly won 55%-43%.

In the House, Connolly has been a leader of the dwindling centrist New Democrat Coalition and established a moderate voting record. He was among the Democrats who joined a majority of Republicans in backing free-trade deals with Colombia, Panama and South Korea in 2011. In June 2015, he was an enthusiastic supporter among an even smaller number of House Democrats who supported trade promotion authority for President Barack Obama and his prospective trans-Pacific partnership deal. In turn, he was strongly criticized by labor and liberal groups that opposed the measure.

Connolly generally works well with Republicans, though he clashed occasionally with Oversight and Government Reform Committee Chairman Darrell Issa of California. When the Republican criticized the heavy-handed approach of Nuclear Regulatory Commission Chairman Gregory Jaczko in 2011, Connolly said on Twitter it was "ironic" that Issa accused someone else of a "bullying management style." The two of them set aside their differences in

2014 to enact the landmark Federal Information Technology Acquisition Reform Act, which was the first major overhaul of federal IT management since 1996.

In 2013, Connolly became ranking Democrat on the Oversight Subcommittee on Government Operations. He has blasted Republican budget-cutting efforts that he said unfairly target government workers. "Federal employees are now fair game, because [Republicans] see some short-term political advantage in making them a scapegoat," he said in 2012. He enacted a bill in 2010 to encourage teleworking, one method to reduce traffic congestion in his district, as well as another measure in 2011 to help agencies identify qualified interns who can become full-time workers

He has taken an interest in other issues. With Virginia Democratic Sen. Mark Warner, he introduced bills in 2012 calling for an initiative on election reform modeled after the "Race to the Top" competition for education funds, with federal grants going to states that devise innovative efforts to improve the voting process. Following up on his work as a Senate staffer, he is an active member of the House Foreign Affairs Committee, where he tends to voice an internationalist view.

At home, Fimian returned for a rematch in 2010, which had become perilous for Democrats. This time, Fimian did not have to rely on self-financing and spent $2.8 million to Connolly's $2.4 million. Fimian stuck to the national Republican message of "outrageous spending" and rising deficits and attacked Connolly as a "career politician." The Democrat's lead shrunk to single digits by the closing weeks of the race. Five days after the election, Fimian conceded, having won 48.8% to his opponent's 49.2%—a margin of 981 votes out of 227,000 cast.

Connolly has had it easier since then, with assistance from new district lines and Obama's political domination of Northern Virginia. In 2014, he had a 57%-40% win over Republican Suzanne Scholte, a human-rights activist who has worked with political refugees.

★ WASHINGTON ★

Off in the far northwest corner of the continental United States, Washington likes to think of itself as a national trendsetter and model for the rest of the nation. As the headquarters of Microsoft, Starbucks, and Amazon, Washington has been on the cutting edge of innovation for the past two decades. An unusual environment and human creativity combined to produce these achievements. Seattle's cold, misty air and 225 overcast days a year stimulate the appetite for strong, aromatic coffee, and the torn blue jeans and flannel shirts worn year-round in this moist climate by professionals and teenagers alike created the trend made famous in the 1990s by Seattle-based grunge musicians. Boeing's airframe business took off during World War II because the Pacific Northwest's abundant hydroelectric power made cheap aluminum possible, and the boom in air travel in the 1980s and 1990s kept Boeing's huge assembly lines humming. Microsoft, founded by the usually tie-less and tousle-haired Bill Gates and based in Redmond, across Lake Washington from Seattle, became one of America's great success stories as its software became embedded in the vast majority of the world's computers. Washington set a tone for the late 1990s, an ordinariness so hip it is no longer ordinary. Grunge rock is no longer in the vanguard, but it's had a lasting influence on rock music; similarly, Washington's innovators have survived government lawsuits and rollicking, turbulent cycles.

In the two decades after it became a state in 1889, it built a new civilization as transcontinental railroads reached the great ports of Puget Sound, the wheat-processing city of Spokane, and the region's orchard towns, fishing ports, and lumber settlements. Shielded from the storms of the Pacific Ocean by the Olympic Mountains and the sound, Seattle quickly became a serious American city, a lusty town full of lumbermen and railroad workers. When gold was struck in the Klondike and in Alaska, Seattle became a metropolis of miners, prospectors, and get-rich-quick operators, the site of the original "Skid Road," where logs were rolled downhill to the port. (Today it's in gentrified Pioneer Square.) In the years before World War I, thriving young Seattle's politics were turbulent, as class warfare pitted the Industrial Workers of the World (the IWW, or Wobblies) against city business and civic leaders. The businessmen, after some violence, prevailed. Adding to the area's distinctiveness was its large number of Scandinavian immigrants, with their favorable views of cooperative enterprises and government ownership.

Over time, Washington was transformed by a series of national decisions that set its course. One was government development of hydroelectric power. The Columbia River and its tributary, the Snake River, falling thousands of feet in a relatively short distance, had far greater hydroelectric potential than any other American river system, and Franklin Roosevelt, who grew up in another scenic river valley, was interested in these aqueous projects. In 1937, Bonneville Dam was completed on the lower Columbia, followed three years later by Grand Coulee Dam, the largest man-made structure in the world at the time and still the nation's single greatest producer of electricity; its old generators are being replaced on an ongoing, multi-year basis. When war came, Washington's hydroelectric power—the cheapest electricity in the country—made it the natural site for huge aluminum plants, which required vast amounts of electricity. The Seattle area became the home not only of shipbuilders, but also of the biggest aircraft manufacturer in the country, Boeing. William Boeing founded the company in 1916 in a converted shipyard on the Duwamish River. The Navy had a large presence as well, with depots in Seattle, Bremerton and other locations. Further inland, the Hanford plant on the Columbia was secretly one of the government's main nuclear weapons manufacturing sites; it is currently undergoing a multi-decade, multi-billion-dollar cleanup. Cheap power, aluminum, aircraft, nuclear weapons, and high unionized wages—these became the starting point for the state's post-World War II economy.

Today, Washington lives less off the brawn of hydroelectric power and rail and ship tonnage, and more off the brains that made Boeing the world leader in aircraft and Microsoft the world leader in software. Yet it ran into trouble at the turn of the 21st century. Violent demonstrators trashed the streets of Seattle during the World Trade Organization meeting in December 1999, keeping Bill Clinton and other world leaders indoors, while the city's police chief and mayor, showing an abundance of tolerance, did little to stop the violence. In March 2000, the high-tech bubble, inflated as businesses retooled to avoid Y2K problems, suddenly burst. Microsoft was fending off an antitrust suit initiated in 1998 by the Clinton

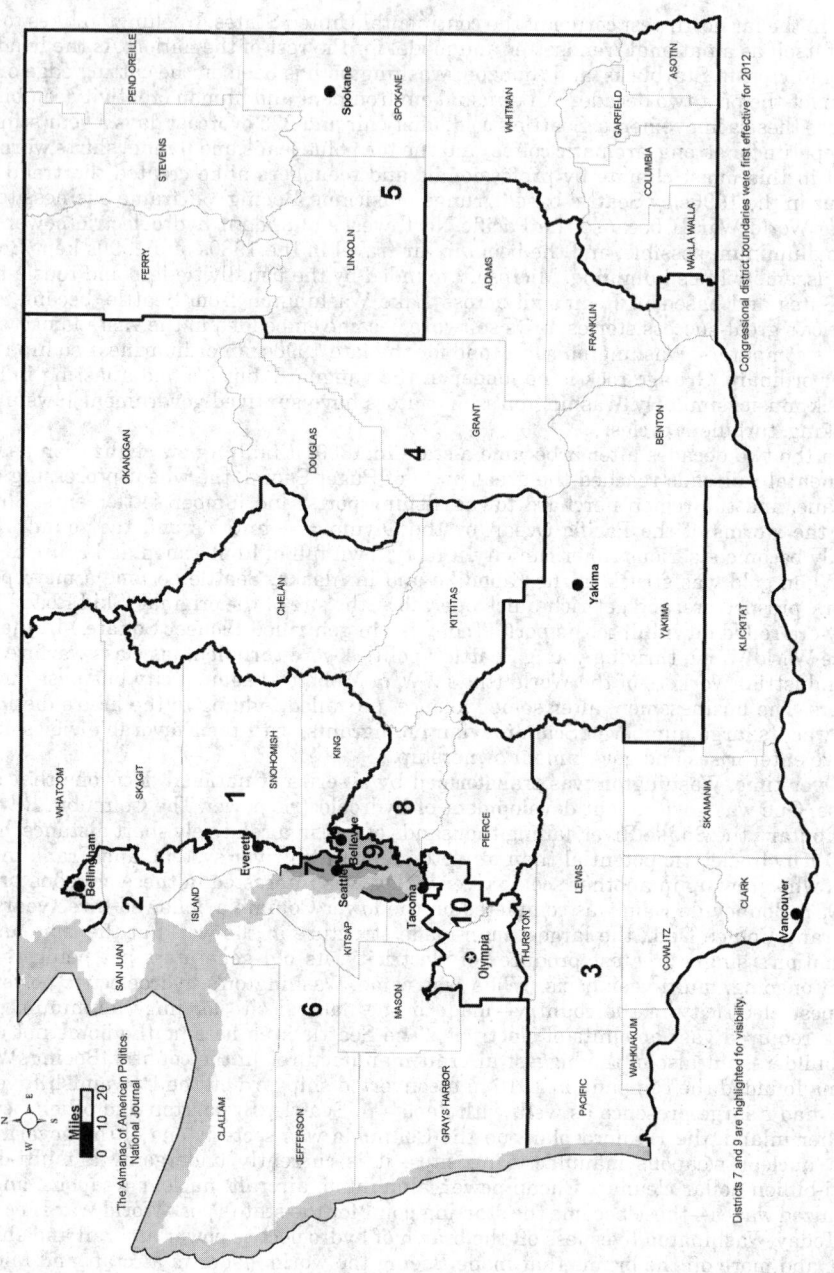

Congressional district boundaries were first effective for 2012

Districts 7 and 9 are highlighted for visibility.

The Almanac of American Politics,
National Journal

Miles
0 10 20

administration, and over the next decade, the company failed to achieve the dominance in computer games and search engines that it has enjoyed in PC software. In March 2001, Boeing announced it was moving its headquarters (though not its factories) to Chicago; then it saw its order book go blank after the September 11 attacks. In the recession of the early 2000s Washington's unemployment was the second highest in the nation, after Oregon's.

Washington has bounced back pretty well. Its population increased 14% between 2000 and 2010, more than Oregon's or California's, and its numbers of Hispanics and Asians shot up, so that the state's population was a bit under 4% black, 12% Hispanic, 8% Asian, and 2% American Indian. Unemployment during the recession peaked at 10.4% and fell back to 5.4% in May 2015, tracking the nationwide pattern pretty closely. Boeing's 787 Dreamliner was introduced, although the plane was grounded temporarily in 2013 while a problem with recurring battery fires was remedied. And the company finally got the controversial contract for the Air Force's KC-46 refueling tanker. Microsoft survived the federal antitrust case, a huge fine from European Union antitrust authorities, Gates' retirement, and vigorous competition from California-based Apple and Google. By 2014, after acquiring Nokia's handset and services business, Microsoft had 125,000 full-time employees, though 18,000 jobs made redundant by the merger were scheduled to be eliminated; in metro Seattle, the company employs roughly 40,000 people. Starbucks cut back during the recession but started expanding again, abroad and at home, in 2012. Amazon was transformed from an Internet bookseller that wreaked havoc on the big bookstores to an all-purpose retailer threatening almost every big-box outfit; it expanded into streaming video and even toyed with the idea of delivery by drones. Washington's exports to China tripled in a decade, and it is estimated that exports drive 40% of its economy.

Politically, Washington, with its Scandinavian and labor union heritage, was one of the most Democratic northern states in the 1930s. Roosevelt's campaign manager, James Farley, used to refer to "the 47 states and the Soviet of Washington." Its mainstream Democrats—notably Warren Magnuson and Henry "Scoop" Jackson, who represented the state in Congress for a cumulative 87 years—believed in an active and compassionate federal government that built dams, bought military aircraft, and pursued an internationalist, anti-Communist foreign policy abroad. Their political strength came out of a blue-collar base, augmented by the respect big business had for their political clout. Today, the state remains one of the most unionized in the nation, but the fulcrum of the electorate has moved from blue collar to white collar, and from economic class warfare to culture wars, with the Democrats benefiting, on balance; according to Gallup, Washington ranks fifth nationally in the percentage of nonreligious residents. In presidential races, Washington has voted exclusively Democratic since 1988 and has elected only Democratic governors since 1984. For eight years from 2004 to 2012, Washington's governor and both of its senators were Democratic women.

Still, there has been some strenuous competition for other offices, with Democrats sometimes coming out ahead only narrowly. The 2004 gubernatorial race was especially close, and the official count, after many shenanigans and legal challenges, declared Democrat Christine Gregoire the winner over Republican Dino Rossi by just 129 votes. Here as elsewhere, 2006 was a banner Democratic year, with Sen. Maria Cantwell reelected by a solid 57%-40% and the party substantially increasing its majorities in the legislature. In 2008, Gregoire was reelected in a rematch 53%-47%, while Republican Attorney General Rob McKenna was reelected 59%-41%. In 2010, Rossi ran against Sen. Patty Murray and, despite her work steering federal money to Washington, she won by only 52%-48%, while Republicans made significant gains in the legislature. One ballot issue may have helped Republicans: the initiative advanced by William Gates Sr. to impose a 5% tax on income over $200,000 and a 9% tax on income over $500,000. It was supported by his son, Bill Gates, but encountered plenty of other opposition among Washington's business elite. They argued that once the state had an income tax, the legislature would not be able to resist extending it to households with lower incomes. The anti-tax campaign prevailed by a crushing 64%-36%, passing only in the central city of Seattle and in San Juan County. A measure to make it more difficult for the legislature to raise taxes passed by an identical margin. Gregoire was compelled to make tough spending cuts, which led her to say, "I hate my budget."

In 2012, Barack Obama carried the state 56%-41%, a two-point decline from his 2008 share, and Cantwell was reelected 60%-40%. The governor's race was closer: Democratic Rep. Jay Inslee defeated McKenna 52%-48%. But Democrats lost ground in the state Senate, and in December, two Democratic senators joined forces with Senate Republicans to take control by a 26-23 margin. Also in 2012, Washington joined Maine and Maryland in endorsing same-sex marriage, 54%-46%; it passed with 67% in King County but was rejected by 60% in eastern Washington. A second ballot question proposed legalizing possession of up to one ounce of marijuana, along with a prohibition on drugged driving; it was endorsed by the King County

Voter Turnout		
2013 Total Citizen 18+		4,915,887
2014 Highest Statewide Turnout		2,029,189
2014 Turnout as % CVAP		41.3%
2012 Turnout as % CVAP		64.1%
Legislature		
Senate:	25R	24D
House:	51D	47R

sheriff and the Bush-appointed U.S. attorney in Seattle, and it passed, 56%-44%. In November 2014, voters passed Initiative 594 with 59% of the vote; it mandated background checks on all gun sales and transfers, joining California, Colorado, Connecticut, Delaware, New York, Rhode Island, and Washington, D.C.

Politically, Washington is divided. The immediate Seattle area casts about 30% of the state's votes. Growth in King County, which includes metro Seattle, has been consistently high; it had the fourth-biggest population gains of any large county in the nation in 2013. In the 1980s, King County was closely divided, with higher-income suburbs voting Republican and working-class neighborhoods in Seattle voting Democratic. But Seattle has become a relatively childless city with a small black population. Hispanics have been moving to southern King County suburbs, and a rising number of Asians have been relocating to suburbs like Bellevue and Redmond east of Lake Washington. All these groups tend to vote heavily Democratic. Obama won King County in 2012 by a 69%-28% margin. In recent years, Seattle has pursued a particularly liberal course, raising its minimum wage to $15 and even electing Kshama Sawant, an Indian-born Trotskyist socialist, to the city council.

By contrast, the area east of the Cascade Range, which casts 20% of the state's votes, voted 56%-41% for Republican Mitt Romney, who fared a bit better there than John McCain four years earlier. There are large numbers of Hispanics in apple-growing Yakima County and the Tri-Cities area in eastern Washington, but relatively few are eligible to vote. The remaining half of the state's votes are cast west of the Cascades but outside King County. Historically, the blue-collar and flannel-shirt country west of Seattle was Democratic, as were working-class Tacoma's Pierce County and, to a lesser extent, Everett's Snohomish County north of Seattle. In recent years, however, the area west of Seattle and Pierce County has trended toward Republicans. The movement has been greater in Clark County, just north of Portland, which has been rapidly gaining population. (Washington has no income tax and Oregon no sales tax, so you can avoid lots of taxes by living in Clark County and shopping across the line in Oregon.) Snohomish County, with high-tech overflow from King County, has trended Democratic. In 2012, Obama carried western Washington outside of King County by a 54%-43% margin. In the closer 2012 gubernatorial and 2010 Senate races, the area split 50%-50%.

A worry only just now starting to register is the region's potential for a colossal natural disaster—either a major volcanic event at Mount Rainier, just 60 miles away from Seattle and Tacoma, or an earthquake and tsunami stemming from the little known Cascadia subduction zone. A regional director of the Federal Emergency Management Agency told the

Population		Race and Ethnicity		Income	
Total:	6,971,406	White	71.9%	Median income:	$60,106
Urban:	45.1%	Latino	11.6%		*(12 of 50)*
Suburban:	39.7%	Asian	7.3%	Under $50,000	42.7%
Rural:	15.2%	Black	3.4%	$50,000-$99,999:	31.6%
Land area:	66,456	Two races	3.9%	$100,000-$199,999:	20.5%
Pop/sq. mi.:	104.9	White Ethnic	23.9%	$200,000 or more:	5.2%
Born in state:	47.4%			Poverty Rate	10.2%
Age Groups		**Education**			
Under 18:	22.9%	H.S. grad or less:	33.1%	**Work**	
18 to 34:	23.8%	Some college:	34.1%	White collar:	38.5%
35 to 64:	39.6%	College degree, 4 yr.:	20.9%	Blue collar:	40.5%
Over 64:	13.6%	Post-grad study:	11.8%	Sales and service:	21.0%
		Military		Govt. workers:	15.9%
		Veterans/active duty:	10.6%		

New Yorker in 2015 that, in the worst-case scenario, "our operating assumption is that everything west of Interstate 5 will be toast," meaning 140,000 square miles and 7 million people living in and around Seattle, Tacoma and Olympia in Washington and Portland, Eugene and Salem in Oregon.

Presidential Politics For three decades, Washington was one of the most contrarian states in presidential politics, voting for Republican losers Richard Nixon in 1960 and Gerald Ford in 1976 and Democratic losers Hubert Humphrey in 1968 and Michael Dukakis in 1988. In the 1990s, it was more in sync with the nation, voting for Bill Clinton twice. Since then, it has moved significantly toward the Democrats, voting 50%-45% for Al Gore in 2000, 53%-46% for John Kerry in 2004, and 58%-40% and 56%-41% for Barack

2012 Presidential Vote		
Barack Obama (D) 1,755,396		(56%)
Mitt Romney (R).............1,290,670		(41%)

2012 Presidential Caucus		
Mitt Romney (R)...................19,111		(38%)
Ron Paul (R) 12,594		(25%)
Rick Santorum (R) 12,089		(24%)
Newt Gingrich (R)..................5,221		(10%)

2008 Presidential Vote		
Barack Obama (D) 1,750,848		(58%)
John McCain (R).............1,229,216		(40%)

Obama in 2008 and 2012, respectively. These results are more similar than may appear. In 2000, 4% voted for third-party candidate Ralph Nader; if you add those votes to Gore's, both parties' percentages in the four contests fall within a 4% range. Voting behavior seems to be a function more of cultural values than of economic status. In 2012, college graduates gave Obama an 18% margin, non-graduates just a 10% margin. Among those with a post-graduate degree, he won by 24%. Unmarried voters went 72%-26% for Obama; married voters went 53%-46% for Mitt Romney. The 29% who never attend religious services voted 77%-19% for Obama, the 33% who attend weekly voted 65%-33% for Romney.

Washington adopted a presidential primary in 1992, after conservative evangelical candidate Pat Robertson won among Republicans and civil rights leader Jesse Jackson finished a solid second among Democrats in the 1988 party caucuses. But Democrats have never chosen to allocate delegates according to the results, preferring to use the results of the caucuses. In 2000, Democrat Bill Bradley, having lost in Iowa and New Hampshire and having no other states to contest for five weeks, came to Washington for the February 29 contest, to no avail; Gore won the caucus by about 2-to-1. On the Republican side, George W. Bush beat John McCain by a razor-thin margin in a primary that counted a little toward delegate selection. In 2004, Washington Democrats held caucuses on February 7, and Kerry defeated Howard Dean.

In 2008, Republicans decided to allocate about half their delegates based on primary results; Democrats decided to use only the caucus results to allocate delegates. When Democrats caucused on the Saturday after Super Tuesday, Obama beat Hillary Clinton 68%-31%, carrying every county. In the non-binding primary 10 days later, Obama prevailed by a much narrower 51%-46%, illustrating the huge advantage he and his organization had in caucus states. Turnout was 691,000; Obama got 56% of the vote in King County and barely won the rest of the state, running behind in less upscale areas like Pierce County (Tacoma) and Clark County (Vancouver).

The Republican contests produced murkier results. In the February 9 caucus, McCain got 26% of the vote, Mike Huckabee 24%, and Ron Paul 22%. All three, unlike the Democrats, campaigned in the 10 days before the primary. In that contest, McCain won 50% of the vote, Huckabee 24%, Romney 16%, and Paul 8%. McCain carried every county. Turnout was 530,000; McCain did better in King County and the rest of western Washington than in the eastern part of the state. In 2012, Republicans ran a caucus on March 3 and held a state convention. Romney prevailed in all the big counties and won with 38% of the vote; Paul had 25% and Rick Santorum 24%.

Congressional Districts Washington gained a House seat in the reapportionment following the 2010 census. In 1983, voters approved a constitutional amendment that created a bipartisan redistricting commission, made up of two Democrats and two Republicans appointed by legislative leaders. If the com-

114th Congress Lineup	
4 R	6 D
113th Congress Lineup	
4 R	6 D

mission deadlocks, the issue goes to the Supreme Court; lines can also be changed by a two-thirds vote in both houses of the legislature. The Washington plan is often lauded for encouraging cooperation and creating more districts that both parties can win. But unlike

Iowa or California, where commissions are not supposed to take political considerations into account, the result in Washington is often incumbent protection.

Democrats are increasingly dominant in statewide elections, but in 2011, Democrats held just a 5-4 lead in House seats, and 56% of the state's growth between 2000 and 2010 had taken place in the four Republican-held districts. In September 2011, the two Republican commissioners, including former three-term U.S. Sen. Slade Gorton, proposed placing a new "fair fight" 10th District in the state's highly competitive northwest and North Puget Sound. The two Democrats countered with proposals putting the new 10th District in the more reliably Democratic South Puget Sound area around Olympia.

Three days before their New Year's Eve deadline, the commissioners forged a compromise in a display of bipartisanship rare for the 2012 cycle. The new 10th District went to the South Sound and was a perfect fit for Democrat Denny Heck, who had lost to Republican Rep. Jaime Herrera Beutler in 2010. In exchange, Democrats strengthened two incumbent Republicans, and stretched the suburban Seattle 1st District of Democrat Jay Inslee, who was leaving to run for governor, all the way north to the Canadian border to make it marginally more competitive. In November 2012, Heck won the 10th, Democrat Suzan DelBene comfortably won the 1st, and every other incumbent won reelection, for a 6-4 Democratic lead. This self-styled good-government state, with its bipartisan commission, reduced the prospect of competitive elections for the next decade.

Governor

Jay Inslee (D)

Elected 2012, term expires Jan. 2017, 1st term; b. Feb. 9, 1951, Seattle; Stanford U., 1969-70, U. of WA, B.A. 1973, Willamette U., J.D. 1976; Protestant; married (Trudi); 3 children.

Elected Office: WA House, 1988-92; U.S. House, 1993-95, 1999-2012.

Professional Career: City prosecutor, Selah, WA, 196-84; Practicing atty., 1976-92, 1995-96; Regional dir., U.S. Dept. of H.H.S., 1997-98.

Office: Office of the Governor, P.O. Box 40002, Olympia, 98504, 360-902-4111; Fax: 360-753-4110; Website: governor.wa.gov.

Election Results

2012 general	Jay Inslee (D)	1,582,802	(52%)
	Rob McKenna (R)	1,488,245	(48%)
2012 primary	Jay Inslee (D)	664,534	(47%)
	Rob McKenna (R)	604,872	(43%)

Prior winning percentages: House: 2010 (58%), 2008 (68%), 2006 (68%), 2004 (62%), 2002 (56%), 2000 (55%), 1998 (50%), 1992 (51%)

Democrat Jay Inslee was narrowly elected Washington's governor in 2012 after serving 15 years in the House.

Inslee grew up in north Seattle, the son of a high school biology teacher and football coach. He graduated from the University of Washington and Willamette University College of Law. He moved to Selah, in Yakima County east of the Cascades, to practice law and served on the State Trial Lawyers Association board of directors. In 1988, at age 37, he was elected to the state House over a former Yakima mayor.

In 1992, when 4th District Rep. Sid Morrison ran for governor, Inslee won the general election to succeed him, 51%-49%, over Doc Hastings, a conservative supported by the Christian Coalition. In the House, Inslee voted for the Clinton budget and tax increase and for a crime bill with a ban on assault weapons. In 1994, Hastings challenged Inslee and beat him, 53%-47%. After his defeat, Inslee moved to Bainbridge Island and practiced law in Seattle. In 1996, he ran for governor and finished fifth, with 10% of the total vote, in the all-party primary. He briefly served as regional director of the U.S. Health and Human Services Department.

In 1998, Inslee decided to run for Congress again, this time in the 1st District against Republican incumbent Rick White, an economic conservative with liberal votes on some cultural issues. Inslee attacked White for voting to reduce spending on education and the environment and for supporting electricity deregulation, claiming that White was "willing to sell our reasonably priced electricity to California." White painted Inslee as a carpetbagger. In the September all-party primary, White led 50%-44%. But by November, with the two pitted head to head exclusively, two issues changed the balance. One stemmed from White's divorce. Inslee ran ads claiming that White intended to spend 10 years in the House and then become a lobbyist, a charge his ex-wife had made in divorce papers. He also ran ads highlighting White's vote to impeach President Bill Clinton. In the acrimony, the primary numbers were reversed in November, and Inslee won 50%-44%. A conservative Christian candidate, Bruce Craswell, was on the ballot in both the primary and the general on the American Heritage Party line, receiving over 6 percent of the vote both times and aiding Inslee's election.

In Congress, Inslee was a moderate-to-liberal Democrat. He joined in protecting the privacy of consumer financial records—an issue important to Microsoft, his largest single source of campaign funds as a congressman. He and Democratic Sen. Maria Cantwell of Washington pressed the Federal Communications Commission in December 2010 for stricter rules on the FCC's proposed net-neutrality order that some Republicans said was already too unfriendly to business. When security experts reported in 2011 that Apple's iPhone could secretly track its users' movements, Inslee called for greater government oversight of data collection. In February 2011, Inslee seconded the GOP's alarm about growing budget deficits and called for closing tax loopholes. On the Energy and Commerce Committee, Inslee focused on conservation and increasing renewable energy sources. As early as 2005, he introduced bills to address global warming and reduce U.S. dependence on foreign oil (a topic he explored in a 2007 book). When Republicans skeptical of climate change took control of the House, Inslee criticized what he called the GOP's "allergy to science," and toted a stack of more than 20 books to a March 2011 hearing, saying they contained irrefutable evidence of the problem.

When two-term Democratic Gov. Christine Gregoire decided to retire in 2012, Inslee already had laid the groundwork for a bid, alerting his campaign donors of the possibility. Nine months after launching his candidacy, he decided in March 2012 to resign his House seat to campaign full-time, saying, "I am not one for half measures or half-hearted efforts." The situation created a dilemma for state officials, who had not budgeted the $1 million needed to hold a special election. They decided to leave the seat vacant until November, with the winner serving the remaining two months of his unexpired term.

Inslee's stature cleared the field of any other top-tier contenders, and he won the state's top-two primary in August with 47% of the vote. That set up a general-election matchup against Republican Rob McKenna, the state's attorney general, who took 43% in the all-party primary. Republicans accused Inslee of notching no significant legislative accomplishments or attaining a leadership position. But with the state tilting Democratic, especially in presidential politics, Inslee was regarded as having a slight edge. He focused on four main themes: Streamlining state government to support job creation in targeted industries, especially in alternative energy; lowering high school dropout rates; protecting Washington's quality of life, especially its cherished natural environment; and eliminating government waste and improving the quality of services. He unveiled a detailed plan to create a cabinet-level Office of Economic Competitiveness and Development that would focus on aerospace, agriculture, information technology, life sciences, defense, and small businesses.

Even though a Republican hadn't won a gubernatorial race in the state since 1980, the GOP liked McKenna's chances. As attorney general, he focused on consumer protection issues and, as president of the National Association of Attorneys General, played a key role in a $25-billion, multi-state settlement with banks over their mortgage practices. Democrats sought to tie him to the tea party movement, citing his decision to join other states in challenging the federal health care law. But McKenna campaigned as a business-friendly moderate who promised to reprioritize government spending and devote more money to education without raising taxes. He played up his pro-environment beliefs and said that, in contrast to several GOP governors elected in 2010, he did not oppose collective bargaining and would work with unions if elected. He said he personally opposed abortion, but that ultimately it was up to the woman to decide. He got help from state Republicans who played up the failure of some of the clean-energy companies that Inslee had highlighted in his book.

Polls showed the race to be close. But Barack Obama's strong reelection showing in the state—he won with 56% of the vote—helped put Inslee over the top with a 52%-48% victory. McKenna eked out a 52%-48% win in Tacoma's Pierce County and dominated the rural eastern half of the state. But Inslee decisively won Seattle's King County, 62%-38%, and took Everett's Snohomish County 51%-49%. He also joined Obama in winning the Asian and Hispanic vote by large margins.

As governor in 2013, Inslee floated extending tax breaks for Boeing past 2024 to 2040, as long as the company agreed to build its next-generation plane, the 777X, in Washington rather than elsewhere, such as South Carolina, where the company had recently been expanding. In February 2014, Inslee established a moratorium on the death penalty, covering the nine men on death row in the state. "There have been too many doubts raised about capital punishment," he said. "There are too many flaws in the system. And when the ultimate decision is death, there is too much at stake to accept an imperfect system." In 2015, Senate Republicans blocked his bid for a $12 statewide minimum wage; Inslee floated the idea of sending the proposal to the voters as a ballot measure instead. Meanwhile, on taxes, Inslee in December 2014 proposed a roughly $1.5 billion package that would include a capital gains tax, a carbon tax, a hike in the cigarette tax and a tax on e-cigarettes, along with several narrower provisions. None were voted on in the Democratic-controlled state House, and six months later, following an unexpectedly strong revenue forecast, he said a tax package that extensive was no longer necessary, though individual elements might remain on the table. The final budget was closer to the one passed in April by the Republican majority in the state Senate.

For much of his term, Inslee grappled with the issue of carbon emission cuts—a signature accomplishment if he could achieve it. In April 2014, Inslee proposed a cap-and-trade program aimed at reducing greenhouse gases in 2020, 2035 and 2050 in order to reach target levels that had been enacted in 2008. He also urged phasing out coal-derived electricity, reducing vehicular emissions, increasing investment in clean energy and curbing emissions by state government. But the centerpiece of his agenda—the cap-and-trade plan—faced resistance, not only from Republicans but also from some Democrats in the legislature. By June 2015, even modified versions of the cap-and-trade proposal appeared to be dead for the year. On a different environmental front, Inslee in May 2015 signed a statewide emergency declaration in the wake of a historically low snowpack. This freed up aid for fighting wildfires and helping the agricultural and fishery sectors. As the 2016 election cycle approached, Inslee seemed to be in reasonably good shape, particularly given the prospect of running for a second term during a presidential cycle, when the Democratic nominee should give him a boost. While a May 2015 Public Policy Polling survey found Inslee's job approval and disapproval statistically tied, two potential Republican challengers tested in the poll—Seattle Port Commissioner Bill Bryant and state Sen. Andy Hill—both trailed Inslee by double digits.

Senior Senator

Patty Murray (D)

Elected 1992, term expires Jan. 2017, 4th term; b. Oct. 11, 1950, Bothell; WA St. U., B.A. 1972; Catholic; married (Rob); 2 children.

Elected Office: Shoreline Schl. Bd., 1985-89, pres., 1985-86; WA Senate, 1988-92.

DC Office: 154 RSOB, 20510, 202-224-2621; Fax: 202-224-0238; Website: murray.senate.gov.

State Offices: Everett, 425-259-6515; Seattle, 206-553-5545; Spokane, 509-624-9515; Tacoma, 253-572-3636; Vancouver, 360-696-7797; Yakima, 509-453-7462.

Committees: *Appropriations:* Defense; Energy & Water Development; Homeland Security; Labor, Health & Human Services, Education & Related Agencies (RMM); Military Construction, Veterans Affairs & Related Agencies; Transportation, HUD & Related Agencies. *Budget. Health, Education, Labor & Pensions* (RMM: ex officio member of each subcommittee). *Veterans' Affairs.*

Group Ratings

	ADA	ACLU	AFL-CIO	LCV	ITI	COC	HAFA	ACU	CFG	FRC
2014	90%	100%	–	80%	100%	50%	0%	0%	0%	0%
2013	95%	C	100%	85%	C	43%	C	5%	0%	C

National Journal Ratings

	2013 LIB — 2013 CONS	
Economic	71%	28%
Social	73%	0%
Foreign	71%	0%
Composite	81%	19%

Key Votes of the 113th Congress

1. Sandy storm spending	NV	5. Student Loan Rates	Y	9. Bipartisan Budget Deal	Y
2. Chuck Hagel Confirmation	Y	6. Employee Non-Discrim'n Act	Y	10. Farm Bill Conference Rept.	Y
3. Gun Background Checks	Y	7. Senate Vote on Judgeships	N	11. Unempl. Comp. Extension	Y
4. Immigration Reform	Y	8. Defense Dept. Spending	Y	12. Keystone Pipeline	N

Election Results

2010 general	Patty Murray (D)	1,314,930	(52%)	$17,279,813	$1,929,582	$8,716,706
	Dino Rossi (R)	1,196,164	(48%)	$9,571,313	$2,331,450	$7,164,909
2010 primary	Patty Murray (D)	670,284	(46%)			
	Dino Rossi (R)	483,305	(33%)			
	Clint Didier (R)	185,304	(13%)			

Prior winning percentages: 2004 (55%), 1998 (58%), 1992 (54%)

Patty Murray is the senior senator from Washington, first elected in 1992. She has come a long way from her entry into politics as a parent-activist. Even as Murray maintains a low-key, plainspoken style, she has become a powerful backroom player, with a seat at her party's leadership table. She plays a key role in advancing the Democrats' positions—a lofty status she ascribes partly to her training as an educator of young children. "You don't walk into a class with 4-year-olds without a direction of where you're going to go," she told *The Huffington Post* in 2013.

Murray grew up in the Seattle suburb of Bothell, one of seven children of a disabled World War II veteran. She graduated from Washington State University in 1972, married, and stayed home to raise her children. In 1980, she was in Olympia trying to save a parent education class she was teaching at Shoreline Community College, which was the target of budget cuts. A state legislator told her gruffly, "You're just a mom in tennis shoes. You can't make a difference." As she said later, "Almost every woman I've ever met in politics got into it because she was mad about something." She won her fight over the parents' class and then ran for the Shoreline School District board. She eventually was chosen board president. In 1988, she challenged a Republican state senator, knocked on 17,000 doors and won the seat. While there, she worked on a raft of issues that resonated with voters, from school bus safety to extending a family leave bill to include leave for a parent whose child is ill or dying. Then, in late 1991, Murray decided to run against Sen. Brock Adams, a Democrat who was under a cloud following charges of sexual molestation. He ultimately decided not to seek reelection.

Amid a crowd of better-known, conventional male politicians, Murray, with her flat, Midwestern-style accent and "mom in tennis shoes" line, attracted most of the attention. In the 1992 all-party primary, her main Democratic opponent was former Rep. Don Bonker, who had narrowly lost a Senate nomination in 1988. But Murray won 28 percent of the vote to Bonker's 19 percent. She then sprinted to a big lead in polls against Republican Rep. Rod Chandler, who had served his district for a decade. She went on to win, 54% to 46% in November in what came to be called "the year of the woman."

In the Senate, Murray has had a largely liberal voting record. But she is known for being attuned to the needs of more conservative members, for being adept at ingratiating herself with her more senior colleagues, and for recognizing and exploiting the possibility of a deal for legislation even in a very partisan environment. "She's a pretty good arbiter and proxy for the caucus as a whole," Rich Tarplin, a lobbyist close to Senate Democrats, told *National Journal*. Murray generally leaves the spotlight to others, but does not shy from taking on administration officials. In what she calls her "angry mom" voice, she has rebuked Republican and Democratic secretaries of the Department of Veterans Affairs for proposals that would make veterans pay more for health care. "Ask my kids about it," she said of such confrontations to *The Olympian* newspaper in October 2010. "There is a line they knew they shouldn't cross."

Murray assumed the chairmanship of the Budget Committee in January 2013, replacing Democrat Kent Conrad of North Dakota, who had retired in 2012. To counter the controversial budget proposal offered by her House counterpart, Wisconsin Republican Paul Ryan, she unveiled a proposed fiscal 2014 budget that was the first from her party since 2009. It included about $1 trillion in new revenues while advocating the closing of tax loopholes and incentives to match about $1 trillion in spending cuts. Unlike Ryan's budget, which some House GOP moderates found draconian, her plan was geared toward getting broad Democratic support. It included $100 billion for a new "economic recovery protection plan" that would fund infrastructure projects and education programs. But in something of a surprise, it contained more than double the cuts to the biggest health entitlement, Medicare, than Ryan's. Though Republicans vilified her proposal as unworkable, they said Murray was easy to work with. "You've allowed us to have free ability to speak out; you've been respectful," Budget ranking Republican Jeff Sessions of Alabama told her at a hearing.

Murray also was able to forge a working relationship with Ryan through a combination of affability and a can-do, pragmatic style that she has used to good effect with other Republicans as well. Her development of a partnership with Ryan enabled them in December 2013 to strike a two-year budget deal that called for raising new revenue through fee increases without tax increases or controversial reforms to Social Security or Medicare. It also replaced steep budget cuts under the looming "sequester" in January with targeted spending cuts. Democrats groused about the deal, which didn't add much money for party priorities such as infrastructure spending, and it failed to close any of the tax loopholes they sought to close. But it easily passed both chambers and was signed into law.

The Budget chairmanship represented Murray's second turn as a leader on the issue. After the protracted standoff over raising the federal debt limit in 2011, she and Texas Republican Rep. Jeb Hensarling were named as co-chairs of the Joint Select Committee on Deficit Reduction, the "super committee" charged with finding a bipartisan consensus on future spending in just a few months. To almost no one's surprise, the effort was fruitless, but, in this case, she had less maneuverability. It was important for her to stick to her guns. "The one thing the Republicans wouldn't put on the table was revenue," Murray told *The Seattle Times* about her experience. "I knew what a bad deal would mean for the middle class in this country. Many of us are where we are in our lives because we had a country that was there for us."

On the Appropriations Committee, Murray also is influential and makes a point of getting along with more senior senators. After Alaska's Ted Stevens, the former GOP chairman, lost his bid for reelection in 2008, he gave Murray the desk that once belonged to legendary Washington Democrat Warren Magnuson (1944-81). And when West Virginia Democrat Robert Byrd was too ill in 2007 and 2008 to manage spending bills on the floor as chairman, he gave Murray the task ahead of more senior members. Murray chaired the Appropriations subcommittee on transportation, housing and urban development. She has delivered for her state and then some: $219 million in home-state projects in 2010, which was the ninth highest amount among senators that year. The Washington watchdog group Taxpayers for Common Sense dubbed her the "Queen of Pork." Despite a subsequent ban on earmarking, Murray still worked to include funding for a variety of Washington projects in the fiscal 2013 bill, including money for a Seattle light-rail system and a bridge over the Columbia River.

Murray moved over to take the top Democratic seat in 2015 on the panel dealing with the departments of Labor, Health and Human Services and Education. With the retirement of Iowa Sen. Tom Harkin, she also claimed the ranking-member post on the Health, Education, Labor and Pensions Committee.

From that perch, she worked closely with Tennessee Republican Sen. Lamar Alexander, the chairman of the committee, on a measure to overhaul No Child Left Behind. She dissuaded him from writing his own bill and then seeking some moderate Democrats' support and, instead, he agreed to develop a bipartisan proposal from the start. No Child Left Behind had become very unpopular because of its heavy reliance on standardized testing. "I've heard from parent after parent and teacher after teacher in Washington state who has told me that not only are students taking too many tests, oftentimes the tests are of low quality or redundant," Murray said.

Though previous efforts to reform the law in earlier Congresses repeatedly failed, Alexander and Murray led the way to craft a proposal to cut back on the heavy reliance on testing and to give states and local school districts more say-so over academic standards and teacher and school performance. Their measure would shift responsibility out of Washington and back to the states for determinations of how to use the basic federally-required tests to ensure accountability of teachers and schools. Remarkably, the HELP Committee, whose members' views span the ideological spectrum, voted unanimously for the bill in April. When the Senate passed the measure overwhelmingly—81-17—in July, Murray made clear that any final measure must also address inequality, "where some schools are unable to offer the same opportunities as other schools do."

A few months earlier, Murray also worked with Senate Republican Whip John Cornyn of Texas to end a stalemate over a noncontroversial measure to combat human trafficking that became ensnared in the always-combustible abortion debate. Democrats objected to what they saw as an anti-abortion provision in the legislation that would prevent money from the victims' fund from being used for abortions in keeping with the Hyde Amendment's prevention of taxpayer funds from being used for abortion services. Murray and Cornyn led the way to clarifying that money from the fines would go to non-health care concerns, which would not be subject to the Hyde prohibition, and federal funds, which are subject to the prohibition, would cover heath care. The measure then passed 99-0—a move that then paved the way for a vote on the nomination of Loretta Lynch to be attorney general which had been held up until the dispute over the trafficking bill was resolved.

Murray was praised by her colleagues for helping to pull off the education bill as well as her role in ending the impasse over the human trafficking measure. She already had earned chits with them when she agreed, in the 2012 election cycle, to head the Democratic Senatorial Campaign Committee, the party's campaign recruiting and fundraising arm. She took the post only after several of her colleagues had reportedly turned it down. Majority Leader Harry Reid and others leaned on Murray and made the case that she could succeed. The assignment was daunting: Twenty-three Democratic senators faced reelection in 2012. But even her political opponents predicted that she would not be outworked. "She's a mechanic, not a visionary. But she's really good at it," said Chris Vance, a former chairman of Washington's Republican Party. Not only were Murray and fellow Democrats able to hold the Senate, they picked up two seats. They got some fortunate breaks, most notably the disastrous comments on rape and abortion by Republicans Todd Akin in Missouri and Richard Mourdock in Indiana that spelled their political doom in those races. But Murray also recruited a number of successful female candidates, such as Massachusetts' Elizabeth Warren, Wisconsin's Tammy Baldwin, and North Dakota's Heidi Heitkamp. "Oftentimes, when you're looking at people to run, they rule the women out, saying they can't win," Murray told *The Oregonian* of Portland. "I ruled them in."

It was Murray's second stint in the role. She led the DSCC in the 2002 election cycle and had less good fortune then. She nearly doubled the committee's fundraising, bringing in $158 million during the cycle, and her recruiting efforts were mostly successful. But the results were disappointing. Democrats lost more seats than they won, and they lost their Senate majority. Still, Murray's efforts got high marks. In 2004, Reid appointed Murray assistant floor leader, and after Democrats won back the majority in 2006, her colleagues elected her Democratic Conference Secretary, the fourth-ranking position in the leadership.

To take the Budget chairmanship, Murray gave up the helm of the Veterans' Affairs Committee. She has long been one of the most persistent advocates for veterans' funding, and during the 2011 debt-limit negotiations she aggressively rejected a Republican proposal to expose veterans' benefits to steep domestic and military spending cuts. Murray has sponsored bills for more benefits for National Guard and Reserve troops called up to active duty, and she successfully fought for more health care funding for veterans of the Iraq and Afghanistan conflicts. Republicans initially rejected her attempt to add $2 billion for veterans' health care, but relented and added $1.5 billion after it was revealed that the VA was using dated cost estimates and expected a shortfall.

In her first years on Capitol Hill, Murray was criticized as too staff reliant, but she grew into the role of senator. She immersed herself in Washington state issues, becoming one of the Senate's staunchest proponents of normal trade relations with China, a position strongly backed by Boeing, a major Washington-based company. Murray also has worked to remove restrictions on abortion rights and has prevailed in the Senate on legislation allowing abortions in military hospitals. With then-Democratic Sen. Hillary Clinton of New York, she waged a fight with the Bush administration regarding the approval of over-the-counter sales of the Plan B contraceptive.

Murray has won reelection three times by steadily diminishing margins. In 1998, she was challenged by Rep. Linda Smith, a Republican and a strong opponent of abortion and free trade deals. Murray raised far more money than Smith and won 58% to 42%. In 2004, she faced Republican George Nethercutt, another House member, who in 1994 earned a reputation as a giant killer by defeating Democratic House Speaker Tom Foley. But the former mom in tennis shoes had become a hardball fundraiser: An aide put out the word to lobbyists that the senator would regard contributions to Nethercutt as hostile, even if contributors gave to her too. Murray raised $11.5 million, much more than Nethercutt's $7.7 million. He campaigned vigorously, and big-name Republicans came in for him. On Election Day, Murray won 55% to 43%. It was almost as if the election had been held in two states: Nethercutt carried every county east of the Cascades, and Murray carried all but two counties to the west.

Republicans initially considered Murray vulnerable in 2010. They landed a top-tier recruit in former state Sen. Dino Rossi, a fiscal conservative who had twice run impressive but losing campaigns against Democratic Gov. Christine Gregoire. He criticized her involvement in shaping the Democratic agenda. But Murray did not back down from her record and said Rossi would bankrupt the nation by giving tax breaks to the wealthy. She got a substantial boost from Boeing, whose machinists' union called her reelection its top priority, and from campaign stops by Vice President Joe Biden and first lady Michelle Obama. She won 52% to 48%. Exit polls showed Murray beating Rossi among women, 56% to 44%. And even though national Republicans won the senior citizens' vote by 19 percentage points, Murray carried it by 10 points.

Murray announced in February 2014 that she would seek a fifth term, and she is a clear favorite for reelection absent a top-tier competitor and a GOP wave in 2016.

When Reid announced in March that he would not seek reelection, Murray saw an opening and did not rule out a move to climb up the Democratic leadership ladder. Though she endorsed New York Sen. Chuck Schumer to succeed Reid in the top post in 2017, the senior Washington senator declined to back Sen. Dick Durbin of Illinois to retain his position as Democratic whip. When pressed by reporters about whether she planned to seek the whip post, Murray sidestepped the question, saying that her first priority and focus was her own reelection. Still, having served as Budget Committee chairman, ranking member on HELP and twice as chair of the campaign committee, Murray has a strong following among her colleagues and would be a formidable candidate if she decides to pursue the Number Two Democratic post in the Senate.

Junior Senator

Maria Cantwell (D)

Elected 2000, term expires Jan. 2019, 3rd term; b. Oct. 13, 1958, Indianapolis, IN; Miami U. (OH), B.A. 1980; Catholic; single.

Elected Office: WA House, 1987-93; U.S. House, 1993-95.

Professional Career: Owner, Cantwell & Assoc. PR firm, 1985-91; RealNetworks, 1995-2000.

DC Office: 511 HSOB, 20510, 202-224-3441; Fax: 202-228-0514; Website: cantwell.senate.gov.

State Offices: Everett, 425-303-0114; Richland, 509-946-8106; Seattle, 206-220-6400; Spokane, 509-353-2507; Tacoma, 253-572-2281; Vancouver, 360-696-7838.

Committees: *Commerce, Science & Transportation:* Aviation Operations, Safety & Security (RMM); Communications, Technology & the Internet; Oceans, Atmosphere, Fisheries & Coast Guard; Surface Transportation & Merchant Marine Infrastructure, Safety & Security. *Energy & Natural Resources* (RMM: ex officio member of each subcommittee). *Finance:* Energy, Natural Resources & Infrastructure; Health Care; International Trade, Customs & Global Competitiveness. *Indian Affairs. Small Business & Entrepreneurship.*

Group Ratings

	ADA	ACLU	AFL-CIO	LCV	ITI	COC	HAFA	ACU	CFG	FRC
2014	90%	100%	–	80%	100%	38%	0%	4%	7%	0%
2013	100%	C	100%	100%	C	38%	C	4%	0%	C

National Journal Ratings

	2013 LIB	—	2013 CONS
Economic	82%	—	8%
Social	73%	—	0%
Foreign	71%	—	0%
Composite	86%	—	14%

Key Votes of the 113th Congress

1. Sandy storm spending	Y	5. Student Loan Rates	Y	9. Bipartisan Budget Deal	Y
2. Chuck Hagel Confirmation	Y	6. Employee Non-Discrim'n Act	Y	10. Farm Bill Conference Rept.	Y
3. Gun Background Checks	Y	7. Senate Vote on Judgeships	N	11. Unempl. Comp. Extension	Y
4. Immigration Reform	Y	8. Defense Dept. Spending	Y	12. Keystone Pipeline	N

Election Results

2012 general	Maria Cantwell (D)	1,855,493	(60%)	$11,198,862	$183,709
	Michael Baumgartner (R)	1,213,924	(40%)	$998,360	
2012 primary	Maria Cantwell (D)	772,058	(56%)		
	Michael Baumgartner (R)	417,141	(30%)		
	Art Coday (R)	79,727	(6%)		

Prior winning percentages: 2006 (57%), 2000 (49%); House: 1992 (55%)

Democrat Maria Cantwell, Washington's junior senator, was elected in 2000. She is active on energy, technology, and tax matters, often working with Republicans, and is known for her tough tenacity. She assumed the ranking-member slot on the Energy and Natural Resources Committee in 2015, having previously chaired the Indian Affairs and Small Business and Entrepreneurship committees.

Cantwell grew up in Indianapolis, where her father, Paul Cantwell, a construction worker, served as county commissioner, a city councilman, and a state legislator. As a child, Cantwell observed politics firsthand as her father dispensed advice to the union members, laborers, and politicians who stopped by to talk politics. During her father's stint as an aide to Democratic Rep. Andy Jacobs of Indiana, she awoke one morning to the distinctive Boston accent of Sen. Edward Kennedy of Massachusetts downstairs.

Cantwell graduated from Miami University of Ohio in 1980, the first in her family to graduate from college. She worked in Ohio for television personality Jerry Springer's 1982 campaign for governor. (In 2003, when Springer was considering running for senator in Ohio, she said, "I think people will be surprised by his intellect. There's much more to him than his TV show.") Then she worked for California Democratic Sen. Alan Cranston's presidential campaign in 1984, going to Seattle to set up a regional campaign office. The Cranston campaign went nowhere, but Cantwell loved the Pacific Northwest and decided to stay. She moved to Mountlake Terrace, a suburb in Snohomish County just north of Seattle, where she organized a coalition to build a new library. In 1986, at age 28, she was elected to the Washington state House.

In 1992, Cantwell ran for an open House seat and won a solid 55% to 42% victory—the first Democrat to prevail in the district in 40 years. In the House, she showed her independence by not supporting President Bill Clinton's health care plan, but she did back the family and medical leave bill, the Clinton economic plan and NAFTA. Cantwell was a strong supporter of abortion rights and an unwavering champion of stands backed by environmental advocacy groups. She also sounded early alarms about encroachments on privacy, and persuaded the Clinton administration to drop its support for the "clipper chip," which would have enabled the government to monitor personal electronic communications. Still, she lost her 1994 bid for reelection to Republican Rick White, 52% to 48%, in a huge wave year for the GOP. It was an acrimonious campaign in which White contrasted his attractive family—he and his wife and four children—with Cantwell, who was single with no family in the district.

Back in the Seattle area, Cantwell joined a start-up firm called Progressive Networks in 1995. Five years later, it had become RealNetworks, a leader in Internet-based audio and visual software. In late 1999, her stock was worth about $40 million, and Cantwell was ready to resume her political career. She decided to run against Republican Sen. Slade Gorton. Microsoft's leading advocate on Capitol Hill, Gorton had an increasingly conservative record on environmental and economic issues. Insurance Commissioner Deborah Senn, who also was running, was widely considered too liberal to win. Cantwell called herself a New

Democrat in the Clinton mode and backed permanent normal trade relations with China—a move that Senn opposed. But the real difference was money. Cantwell, who liquidated more than $5 million in stock, spent freely, while Senn was on television only during the last two weeks before the September all-party primary. In the first round of balloting, Gorton got the most votes, 44 percent of the total, but fell short of a majority. Cantwell got 37 percent, and Senn received only 13 percent. Gorton, a brainy and hard-working veteran of Washington state and Capitol Hill politics, who was close to GOP Senate leader Trent Lott of Mississippi, faced off against Cantwell in the general election.

Cantwell said she would spend "whatever it takes" to win. At the same time, she made her support of McCain-Feingold-type campaign finance regulation a major issue and refused to take contributions from political action committees or large donations known as "soft money" from the Democratic Party (though it put $640,000 into the state before Cantwell won the primary). She charged that Gorton was beholden to special interest contributors, singling out his late-night amendment that paved the way for a cyanide-leach gold mine in rural Okanogan County, which environmentalists were fighting. She also spoke of her work in high-tech and contrasted her experience with his, saying: "I've just spent the last five years in the private sector learning how to do things on the outside. Senator Gorton's been in office for 41 years. He seems to like government a lot." Gorton countered by describing Cantwell as an old-style liberal Democrat who would have government meddling in health care, education, and local environmental issues. Overall, she spent $11.5 million, $10.3 million of it her own money, to Gorton's $6.4 million. Gorton also was hurt when Indian tribes, some flush with casino cash, weighed in against him as they felt that he did not respect their sovereignty when he sought to have them bound by the same laws that bind other people.

Gorton led on Election Night, but not by much. That year, 54 percent of the votes were cast absentee, and it took three weeks to count them. The last two days' worth of absentee ballots from heavily Democratic King County put Cantwell over the top by 1,953 votes. A mandated recount left the margin at 2,229 for Cantwell, out of 2.4 million cast, the closest Senate contest of 2000. Cantwell carried only five counties: King, Snohomish, Thurston, which includes the state capital of Olympia, and two small counties in the west. Gorton carried eastern Washington with 61 percent, not quite enough to win. Cantwell's victory created a tie in the Senate, until Vermont's James Jeffords became an independent in May 2001 and gave Democrats a razor-thin majority.

Cantwell is known for being intense, though some aides say she is as demanding of herself as she is of them. Her voting record is consistently liberal on social issues, but more moderate on economic and foreign policy matters. Through 2012, her lifetime score from the anti-tax group Club for Growth was 14 percent, seventh highest among active Democratic senators. She was one of just nine Senate Democrats to oppose the 2008 law creating the Troubled Asset Relief Fund for ailing financial institutions, saying the government had no business getting so deeply involved with the private sector. Three years later, she was one of six Democrats to support a failed GOP amendment to halt tax breaks and incentives for corn-based ethanol products popular with farm-state lawmakers.

During the 2010 debate on overhauling the banking and financial services regulatory system, Cantwell pushed for more radical reforms. She co-sponsored a bill with GOP Sen. John McCain of Arizona that would have reinstated the Glass-Steagall Banking Act of 1933, which created a wall between commercial and investment banking. She also wanted to close loopholes on unregulated derivatives trading. Cantwell was one of only two Democrats to vote against the White House-backed banking reform bill in May 2010. However, she joined her party in July in voting for the final conference report version of the bill, reasoning that the updated bill offered at least tougher regulation and greater transparency of the derivatives market.

Cantwell took over in 2013 as chair of Indian Affairs, becoming the first woman to lead the panel. When Oklahoma GOP Sen. Tom Coburn sought in February 2013 to amend the Violence Against Women Act to eliminate a section that covered Indian tribes, Cantwell spoke out forcefully against the idea, saying that it would treat Indians "like second-class citizens." The measure was defeated. Later, she drew attention for circulating a letter imploring NFL Commissioner Roger Goodell to formally call on the Washington Redskins to change the team's name, which the letter called "a racial slur."

When Montana Sen. Max Baucus' decision to leave the Senate in early 2014 led Oregon's Ron Wyden to take over the Finance Committee and Louisiana's Mary Landrieu to move into Wyden's chair on Energy and Natural Resources, Cantwell assumed the gavel at the Small Business Committee. She worked with Jim Risch of Idaho, the panel's ranking Republican, on a measure to renew the State Trade and Export Promotion program, which awards grants to states to help small businesses begin or expand exports of their products. She also held separate hearings on helping veteran as well as women entrepreneurs.

To help her state's hydropower industry, which produces almost three-fourths of Washington's electricity, Cantwell has been active in efforts to remove barriers to licensing new facilities. She also called in 2012 for a Federal Trade Commission investigation into her state's high gasoline prices. When the Obama administration and Democrats in Congress pushed for ultimately unsuccessful legislation aimed at curbing greenhouse gases, Cantwell jumped into the debate. The Obama White House bill, which allowed energy efficient companies to trade credits to larger greenhouse gas emitters as a way to reduce overall levels of carbon dioxide emissions, proved a hard sell. By mid-2010, Cantwell and GOP Sen. Susan Collins of Maine stepped up efforts to push their "cap-and-dividend" bill that skirted the idea of a carbon trading market. Instead, their bill would cap emissions from sources such as coal mines and oil refineries, and those emitters would be required to purchase carbon permits. The Senate failed to take action on the bill. There was more political momentum for curbing offshore drilling in the aftermath of the BP oil rig explosion in the Gulf of Mexico. Cantwell offered a bill in 2010 and again in 2012 requiring the oil drilling industry to continually integrate the latest technology into efforts at spill prevention.

An energy bill passed by Congress in December 2008 contained Cantwell's provision to give the Federal Trade Commission authority to fine companies or individuals that manipulate petroleum markets. She has backed extending tax credits for wind, solar, and other sources of renewable energy and told the *Tri-City Herald* in November 2010 that green energy could be a $6 trillion sector of the economy that is "bigger than the Internet." A few years earlier, in 2005, Cantwell waged a series of floor fights with then-Senate Commerce Chairman Ted Stevens over drilling in the Arctic National Wildlife Refuge that antagonized the powerful Alaska senator, who was of the take-no-prisoners school.

Cantwell, in 2006, was given a coveted seat on the Finance Committee—a perch from which she secured passage of a 2008 measure to temporarily extend the deductibility of state sales taxes, a popular tax break in Washington as it doesn't have a personal income tax. Her other committee assignment is Commerce, where she chairs the aviation panel and keeps a close eye out for Boeing Co. and the rest of her state's aerospace businesses. In 2012, Cantwell was the point person on the ambitious NextGen air traffic control modernization effort, which was part of the Federal Aviation Administration reauthorization bill that became law. "She's brilliant on technology and all those things, and she's very organized," then-Commerce Committee Chairman Jay Rockefeller of West Virginia, said at a hearing in praise of her efforts.

Although a strong supporter of campaign finance regulation, Cantwell has had campaign finance problems of her own. To fund her 2000 campaign, she had sold $5.6 million of her RealNetworks stock and had borrowed $3.8 million from a bank using the company's stock as collateral. That enabled her to run the last-minute ads that surely were essential to her victory. The Federal Election Commission ruled in January 2004 that she had violated the law by failing to disclose the terms of the loans, but it took no punitive action. Paying off the loans should have been easy; Cantwell's net worth at one point was around $40 million. But RealNetworks, like other high-tech firms, saw its stock price plummet, from $80 per share in spring 2000 to $6 in spring 2001. Suddenly Cantwell owed far more than the collateral was worth. She negotiated another loan that would come due December 2001, guaranteed by the DSCC. Over the course of the next several years, she paid off the debt. Cantwell's top campaign contributor has been Microsoft.

Cantwell's narrow victory in 2000 placed her high on the Republicans target list for 2006. National Republicans recruited Mike McGavick, chairman and chief executive officer at Safeco insurance. McGavick, a successful businessman, with moderate positions and political smarts developed while he managed Gorton's 1988 campaign and served as his chief of staff, appeared formidable. But McGavick also acknowledged that he had been charged with drunken driving in 1993. Cantwell faced lingering discontent from liberals in the party for her 2002 vote in favor of the Iraq war resolution. But her earlier, well-publicized dustup with Stevens helped boost the reserved and cautious senator, allowing her to show she could stand up to the pugnacious Stevens and the oil lobby in defense of

Washington's environment. McGavick poured $2.5 million of his own money into the race, but in the end Cantwell outspent him $14 million to $10.8 million. In a Democratic year in a Democratic-leaning state, she won 57 percent to 40 percent.

In 2012, another good year for Democrats, Cantwell had an easy race against Republican state Sen. Michael Baumgartner. Not only was Baumgartner from eastern Washington, which hadn't produced a senator since 1934, he was unable to raise the kind of money necessary to compete with Cantwell. It hardly helped him that Washington Republicans were more focused on the concurrent governor's race. She won 60 percent to 40 percent.

Cantwell wasted no time after her return for a third term, scolding the Obama Administration in January for not moving fast enough on oil train safety rules. Noting that "rail cars are going through every major population center in our state," Cantwell said at a Commerce Committee hearing that the Transportation Department should issue its safety rules for tanker cars pronto and enforce them. "We should go faster," she said.

Cantwell opposed legislation to authorize the Keystone XL pipeline, and worked with Democratic Sen. Ron Wyden of Oregon to close a loophole in the measure that would free the TransCanada Pipeline Co. from having to pay into the federal Oil Spill Liability Trust Fund. "I hope we can get our colleagues around the fact that the number of crude oil spills has been growing since 2009," she said. Their bill failed.

Cantwell fought in 2015 to extend the life of the U.S. Export-Import Bank, which expired as Congress went on its July 4 recess. The bank, which finances U.S. exports abroad, became the center of a fierce political debate pitting tea-party conservatives who argue that it is a prime example of corporate cronyism and welfare to companies that don't need it against its defenders, like Cantwell, who see it as a critical element to U.S. competitiveness. About 85 other countries have similar agencies to boost their export sales, and Cantwell plus her Washington colleague Patty Murray led the charge for its renewal as a way for the U.S. to remain competitive and to promote U.S. jobs, including at small businesses. Cantwell and Murray played tough with GOP Senate leader Mitch McConnell, according to the *Seattle Post-Intelligencer*, and won a promise for a floor vote on renewal of the bank in return for which they supported legislation to give President Obama fast-track authority to negotiate new trade deals. "What is frustrating in America's trade debate is that the far-right conservatives are trying to get rid of trade tools that allow American companies to compete," Cantwell said. The bank has provided millions of dollars in assistance to Washington-based Boeing's jet sales, and, in 2014, it supported 3,340 small-business transactions, $27 billion in total U.S. export sales and 164,000 jobs, according to Cantwell's website.

FIRST DISTRICT

Suzan DelBene (D)

Elected Nov. 2012, 2nd full term; b. Feb. 17, 1962, Selma, AL; Reed Col., B.A. 1983, U. of WA, M.B.A. 1990; Episcopalian; married (Kurt); 2 children.

Professional Career: Director of Marketing, Microsoft, 1989-98; V.P., Drugstore.com, 1998-2000; Pres., CEO, Nimble Tech., 2000-03; V.P., Microsoft, 2004-07; Consultant, Global Partnerships, 2008-09; Dir., WA Dept. of Revenue, 2010-12.

DC Office: 318 CHOB, 20515, 202-225-6311; Fax: 202-226-1606; Website: delbene.house.gov.

State Offices: Bothell, 425-485-0085; Mount Vernon, 360-416-7879.

Committees: *Agriculture:* Biotechnology, Horticulture & Research (RMM); Conservation & Forestry; Nutrition. *Judiciary:* Courts, Intellectual Property & the Internet; Regulatory Reform, Commercial & Antitrust Law.

Group Ratings

	ADA	ACLU	AFL-CIO	LCV	ITI	COC	HAFA	ACU	CFG	FRC
2014	75%	83%	–	89%	80%	50%	10%	4%	6%	0%
2013	65%	C	95%	96%	C	46%	C	12%	12%	C

National Journal Ratings

	2013 LIB	—	2013 CONS
Economic	64%	—	36%
Social	69%	—	28%
Foreign	81%	—	18%
Composite	72%	—	28%

Key Votes of the 113th Congress

1. Sandy storm spending	Y 5. Medical Marijuana	Y 9. Syrian Rebels Training Y
2. Violence Against Women Act	Y 6. Farm Bill	N 10. Keystone pipeline N
3. Guantanamo Bay Detainees	Y 7. Afghanistan Combat	Y 11. Immigration Exec. Action N
4. Abortion 20-week ban	N 8. NSA Phone Data Collection	Y 12. Bipartisan budget deal Y

Election Results

2014 general	Suzan DelBene (D)	124,151	(55%)	$2,289,913	$5,858
	Pedro Celis (R)	101,428	(45%)	$701,553	
2014 primary	Suzan DelBene (D)	59,798	(51%)		
	Pedro Celis (R)	19,407	(16%)		
	Robert Sutherland (R)	18,424	(16%)		
	John Orlinski (R)	11,891	(10%)		
	Edwin Moats (R)	5,225	(4%)		

Prior winning percentages: 2012 (54%), 2012 special (60%)

Population		Race and Ethnicity		Income	
Total:	709,693	White	77.0%	Median income:	$79,145
Urban:	22.7%	Asian	8.9%		*(34 of 435)*
Suburban:	71.1%	Latino	8.1%	Under $50,000	30.7%
Rural:	6.3%	Black	1.0%	$50,000-$99,999:	30.2%
Land area:	4,315	Two races	3.5%	$100,000-$199,999:	29.8%
Pop/sq. mi.:	164.5	White Ethnic	24.8%	$200,000 or more:	9.3%
Born in state:	48.5%			Poverty Rate	9.2%
		Education			
Age Groups		H.S. grad or less:	26.7%	**Work**	
Under 18:	24.1%	Some college:	32.9%	White collar:	46.1%
18 to 34:	21.1%	College degree, 4 yr.:	26.2%	Blue collar:	35.9%
35 to 64:	42.7%	Post-grad study:	14.1%	Sales and service:	17.9%
Over 64:	12.1%				
		Military		Govt. workers:	12.1%
		Veterans/active duty:	8.1%		

Interior Northwest Washington: Seattle and Everett Suburbs

In the past 30 years, metropolitan Seattle grew to the north and to the east, as a wave of newcomers arrived seeking the area's distinctive blend of natural beauty, robust and creative economic expansion, and freewheeling culture. The heart of the new Seattle is east of Lake Washington, in the edge city

Voter Turnout	
2013 Total Citizen 18+	485,099
2014 House Turnout	225,579
2014 Turnout as % CVAP	46.5%
2012 Turnout as % CVAP	72%

of Redmond. That is where you find the turquoise, pine-shaded, low-rise buildings of the Microsoft campus—a tranquil environment for a booming and boisterously aggressive company. With 41,700 employees in the Puget Sound area in June 2015, which was down 1,300 in the previous year chiefly from the consolidation of staff with the former Nokia phone company, the company has expanded its campus in Redmond and leased major chunks of office space in Seattle and Bellevue. Microsoft has fueled Redmond's transformation from a sleepy hamlet of 1,426 people in 1960 to a hip center of commerce with a population of more than 57,000. Not far away, on the eastern shore of Lake Washington, are the homes and estates of the "Microsoft millionaires," many of whom exercised company stock options before the economic bust.

The 1st Congressional District of Washington includes most of Redmond and many of the other King County suburbs east of Seattle. Technology is a huge factor in the local economy: Redmond is also home of Nintendo of North America, while neighboring Kirkland is where Google's research and development center came up with Google Maps. The district includes affluent suburbs on Lake Washington—Medina, Clyde Hill, Yarrow Point and Hunts Point—as well as Bill Gates' $60 million, 66,000-square-foot home.

2012 Presidential Vote
Barack Obama (D) 183,802   (54%)
Mitt Romney (R).................147,074   (43%)

2008 Presidential Vote
Barack Obama (D) 183,396   (56%)
John McCain (R).................136,881   (42%)

Cook Partisan Voting Index: D+4

The 1st goes through the Cascades to take in the eastern extremities of King County. It also takes in the interior portions away from coastline of Snohomish, Skagit and Whatcom counties, all the way to the Canadian border. Along the way, the economy gradually shifts from software code to raspberries and dairy farming. At the far north end of the district is the fishing and lumber town of Blaine, with America's most attractively landscaped border crossing and the International Peace Arch, just south of British Columbia. About 40 percent of the population is in King, and 35 percent in Snohomish. The overall economy remained strong, with unemployment in April 2015 at 3.3 percent in King and 3.6 percent in Snohomish.

The King County areas of the district are strongly Democratic, while the inland portions are swing territory. The resulting district leans Democratic, but can be competitive. Barack Obama won here in 2012 with 54 percent of the vote, which was his smallest win in the state's six Democratic-held districts. Democrat Jay Inslee, who represented the former metro-based 1st in Congress, lost the expanded district by 4 points in his successful run for governor.

Suzan DelBene (D)

Former Microsoft executive Suzan DelBene, a Democrat, touted her business experience to win Washington's open 1st District in 2012. It was her second try for a seat in Congress. She settled in with the dwindling ranks of business-oriented Democrats in the House, and backed President Barack Obama's international trade agenda.

DelBene was born in Selma, Alabama. When she was a toddler, her parents divorced and DelBene lived with her mother, who married an airline pilot. The family moved often. When she was in high school, DelBene's stepfather got a job with Iran Air and her parents relocated overseas. She majored in biology at Reed College, originally hoping to become a veterinarian. Undergraduate research changed her career interests and her first job after college was with a biotechnology firm in Seattle. She went back to school to get her master's degree in business administration and interned at Microsoft. She landed a full-time job there and met and married her husband, Kurt, president of Microsoft's Office division. She spent 12 years at Microsoft, rising to the position of corporate vice president of the company's mobile communications business. DelBene left Microsoft in 1998 and was involved with two high-tech startups. She later worked on microfinance with an international nonprofit, a job that she said taught her the ways in which policy could create opportunities for families. DelBene is a marathon runner.

Inspired to run for Congress, she spent more than $2 million of her own money in 2010, but lost a challenge to Republican Rep. Dave Reichert in the east Seattle suburbs. Her narrow 52%-48% loss in the GOP-leaning district was impressive in what was a disastrous election for Democrats. Shortly after that setback, Democratic Gov. Christine Gregoire appointed DelBene director of the state Department of Revenue, where she helped to enact a tax amnesty program that generated $345 million to help close the state's budget gap. But that job didn't last long. In 2012, DelBene was one of five Democrats running in a crowded primary for the newly drawn 1st District. With a reported net worth of more than $50 million, her personal wealth was a prime topic in the race. Her Democratic opponents cast her as just another millionaire running for Congress. Her background was appealing to the Democratic establishment for her ability to self-fund, and she was endorsed by Gregoire and Rep. Rick Larsen. DelBene's campaign aired a series of biographical ads that focused on the financial struggles of her youth. Her platform spotlighted support for added economic stimulus spending and for Obama's plan to allow the Bush-era tax cuts for the highest earners to expire.

DelBene's chief Democratic opponent was liberal Darcy Burner, also a Microsoft executive. The only Republican in the all-party primary was state legislator John Koster, who had lost two earlier contests a decade apart in the adjacent 2nd District. Koster finished first with 45% of vote. DelBene won the battle to enter the runoff with 22% to 14% for Burner. In the general election, Koster was endorsed by notable conservatives such as former Arkansas Gov. Mike Huckabee. DelBene consolidated support among Democrats and won, 54%-46%. She got 60% in King County, and 52% in Snohomish; Koster took 55% in Whatcom, which cast 15% of the vote.

On the same day, DelBene won a special election to fill the remainder of the term of Democratic Rep. Jay Inslee, who had resigned to run for governor. In that contest, she defeated Koster by the wider margin of 60%-40%. The chief explanation for the unusual difference is that the special election was waged in the more Democratic boundaries prior to redistricting and consequently had a different electorate.

DelBene got seats on the Agriculture and Judiciary committees, though she didn't follow the conventional routes to those panels of being a farmer or a lawyer. On Judiciary, she spoke out on technology and privacy and she advocated greater transparency and oversight of the National Security Agency. In June 2015, she voted to give trade promotion authority to Obama, noting that "Washington is the most trade-dependent state in the nation and 40 percent of our jobs depend on trade." She filed a bill with California Democratic Rep. Ted Lieu to create a federal ban on conversion therapy for gays and lesbians. DelBene spent much of her time during her first year tending to two unexpected local disasters and their follow-up: the collapse of a bridge on Interstate 5 in Skagit Valley and a destructive mudslide in rural Oso.

She had a relatively easy reelection campaign against Latino businessman Pedro Celis, who was a political neophyte. He spent $702,000 but got off to a bad start when he barely was the Republican front-runner in the primary against a largely unknown contender. DelBene spent $2.3 million, though did not self-finance as in her earlier campaigns. Following the initial computer snafus, DelBene's husband Kurt took on the challenging job as an executive with the government website for citizen enrollment in the Affordable Care Act.

SECOND DISTRICT

Rick Larsen (D)

Elected 2000, 8th term; b. June 15, 1965, Arlington; Pacific Lutheran U., B.A. 1987, U. of MN, M.P.A. 1990; Methodist; married (Tiia); 2 children.

Elected Office: Snohomish City Cncl., 1998-2000, pres., 1999-2000.

Professional Career: Econ. dev. official, Port of Everett, 1990-91; Dir. pub. affairs, WA St. Dental Assn., 1991-98.

DC Office: 2113 RHOB, 20515, 202-225-2605; Fax: 202-225-4420; Website: larsen.house.gov.

State Offices: Bellingham, 360-733-4500; Everett, 425-252-3188.

Committees: *Armed Services:* Seapower & Projection Forces; Strategic Forces. *Transportation & Infrastructure:* Aviation (RMM); Railroads, Pipelines & Hazardous Materials.

Group Ratings

	ADA	ACLU	AFL-CIO	LCV	ITI	COC	HAFA	ACU	CFG	FRC
2014	70%	72%	–	91%	80%	50%	11%	4%	12%	25%
2013	55%	C	90%	89%	C	50%	C	5%	6%	C

National Journal Ratings

	2013 LIB	—	2013 CONS
Economic	65%	—	35%
Social	77%	—	23%
Foreign	75%	—	25%
Composite	72%	—	28%

Key Votes of the 113th Congress

1. Sandy storm spending	Y	5. Medical Marijuana	Y	9. Syrian Rebels Training	Y
2. Violence Against Women Act	Y	6. Farm Bill	NV	10. Keystone pipeline	N
3. Guantanamo Bay Detainees	Y	7. Afghanistan Combat	Y	11. Immigration Exec. Action	N
4. Abortion 20-week ban	NV	8. NSA Phone Data Collection	N	12. Bipartisan budget deal	Y

Election Results

2014 general	Rick Larsen (D)	122,173	(61%)	$1,112,278
	B.J. Guillot (R)	79,518	(39%)	$9,985
2014 primary	Rick Larsen (D)	44,718	(57%)	
	B.J. Guillot (R)	25,449	(32%)	
	Mike Lapointe (I)	8,946	(11%)	

Prior winning percentages: 2012 (61%), 2010 (51%), 2008 (62%), 2006 (64%), 2004 (64%), 2002 (50%), 2000 (50%)

Population		Race and Ethnicity		Income	
Total:	692,085	White	74.2%	Median income:	$56,236
Urban:	29.5%	Latino	10.3%		(157 of 435)
Suburban:	54.8%	Asian	7.7%	Under $50,000	44.1%
Rural:	15.6%	Black	2.1%	$50,000-$99,999:	33.6%
Land area:	1,390	Two races	3.7%	$100,000-$199,999:	19.2%
Pop/sq. mi.:	498.0	White Ethnic	25.7%	$200,000 or more:	3.1%
Born in state:	48.2%			Poverty Rate	14.4%
Age Groups		**Education**			
		H.S. grad or less;	31.0%	**Work**	
Under 18:	21.4%	Some college:	39.2%	White collar:	34.5%
18 to 34:	25.3%	College degree, 4 yr.:	20.5%	Blue collar:	42.7%
35 to 64:	39.1%	Post-grad study:	9.3%	Sales and service:	22.8%
Over 64:	14.1%				
		Military		Govt. workers:	14.9%
		Veterans/active duty:	11.7%		

Upper Puget Sound: Everett Metro

The Seattle metropolitan area has marched north along the shore of Puget Sound, beyond the old lumber port and railroad terminus of Everett, where the huge Boeing plant produces 747s, 767s, 777s, and the new long-range 787s. Sales of the 787 Dreamliner, which made its maiden flight in

Voter Turnout	
2013 Total Citizen 18+	507,344
2014 House Turnout	201,691
2014 Turnout as % CVAP	39.8%
2012 Turnout as % CVAP	63%

2009, have been especially strong, although the Federal Aviation Administration grounded the Dreamliner in early 2013 after two incidents involving battery failures. In a May 2015 interview with the *Seattle Times*, a Boeing executive said that the company will be hiring as many as 30,000 workers in the next few years because of expected retirements. Further north is Bellingham, which grew up as a supply station for gold miners in the 1850s and was the source of much of the lumber used to rebuild San Francisco after the 1906 earthquake. It still plays an important role in the local fishing industry. Officials at the region's deepwater ports, two days closer to Asia than Southern California's ports, are nervous about the widening of the competing Panama Canal.

In the waters of Puget Sound are the 176 San Juan Islands, which were the last part of the continental United States to be turned over to this country. The waters were great whaling grounds, and not until 1860 did the British relinquish them. Today, ferryboats ply the waters of the sound, connecting the islands to mainland Washington and to British Columbia, directly to the west. The publicly operated Washington State Ferries system in 2014 had more than 23 million passengers to 20 ports, the largest ferry operator in the United States. Whale-watching is popular not only with tourists but among scientists on both sides of the border. This is some of the most beautiful coastline in North America: the steely blue sound with forested hills rising behind it, shielded from the full force of Pacific rains by the Olympic Mountains,

2012 Presidential Vote		
Barack Obama (D)	185,771	(59%)
Mitt Romney (R)	119,266	(38%)

2008 Presidential Vote		
Barack Obama (D)	187,392	(61%)
John McCain (R)	116,288	(38%)

Cook Partisan Voting Index: D+8

though still seldom dry. The little towns, on bits of level land between the water and the mountains, have the look of pristine New England villages, and the stores are stocked with fresh produce and local seafood.

The 2nd Congressional District of Washington encompasses the San Juan Islands, including 45-mile-long Whidbey Island, and most of the mainland along the sound. The district has several military installations, including a Navy base at Everett and a naval air station on Whidbey. The political tradition in most of the lumbering and fishing areas here is Democratic, as is the political culture in Everett. In addition to Everett, the district takes in most of the major ports on Puget Sound. The 2nd leans strongly Democratic.

Rick Larsen (D)

Rick Larsen, a moderate Democrat first elected in 2000, takes an avid interest in issues related to China, a country that does substantial business with his state. He is well-positioned in the House on aviation matters to assist Boeing Co., the largest employer in his district.

Larsen grew up in Arlington, in Snohomish County, graduated from Pacific Lutheran University, and got a master's degree at the University of Minnesota. He spent a year doing research on economic development for the Port of Everett. For six years, he was director of public affairs for the Washington State Dental Association. In 1998, he won a seat on the Snohomish County Council and later became its president.

In 2000, Republican Jack Metcalf kept his promise to retire after three terms in Congress. The Democratic field was cleared for Larsen when a state legislator unpopular with labor leaders withdrew. Republicans nominated state Rep. John Koster. The general election became a battleground for political action committees and one of the premier contests in the nation. Anti-abortion rights groups and the National Rifle Association backed Koster, and unions and abortion rights groups fought for Larsen. Larsen said that the contest offered "a clear choice" on abortion, and he criticized Koster for referring to "our American holocaust," a fairly common term among anti-abortion activists. Larsen won 50%-46%.

In the House, Larsen joined the New Democrat Coalition and leans toward the center in his voting record, although he has been more reliably Democratic since President Barack Obama took office. He backed the president's 2009 economic stimulus and 2010 health care legislation. Earlier, he voted for the Bush-era tax cuts in 2001, but later opposed extending the cuts for upper-income taxpayers. Though he opposed the 2005 Central America Free Trade Agreement, he joined with most Republicans six years later to back free-trade pacts with Korea, Panama and Colombia. In June 2015, he was one of 28 House Democrats who voted to give trade promotion authority to Obama, especially for the prospective trans-Pacific partnership. He was one of 22 Democrats in 2012 to support a failed plan for a budget along the lines of the Simpson-Bowles deficit reduction commission.

Larsen co-chairs the U.S.-China Working Group, a bipartisan group of House members that seeks to build lasting diplomatic ties with China. Washington state exports to China nearly quadrupled from 2000 to 2009. The group met with Chinese military officials in May 2011 and was permitted to tour a Chinese navy attack submarine. The same year, Larsen got a bill into law creating a new type of business card aimed at expediting travel in the Asia-Pacific region for qualified American travelers. In 2013, he joined Republican Rep. Charles Boustany of Louisiana, the group's other co-chair, in calling for greater U.S. engagement with China on military issues, despite reports of widespread computer-security breaches that were blamed on that nation's army.

As the "Congressman from Boeing," Larsen won a plum assignment in 2013 as the top Democrat on the Transportation and Infrastructure Committee's aviation panel. Boeing and its employees are among his major campaign contributors. He supported the Federal Aviation Administration's decision in January 2013 to ground the company's new 787 Dreamliner fleet over concerns about the plane's fire-plagued batteries, saying that safety should be paramount. When the review was completed, he said that Congress must assure that the FAA is "positioned to understand and challenge assumptions put forward by manufacturers regarding new technologies."

On other issues, Larsen has pushed to secure funds for upgraded border security at Bellingham and helped get a pipeline safety bill into law in 2002 after a lethal explosion in his district. He co-founded the Congressional Arctic Working Group, with the chief focus of protecting U.S. environmental, economic and strategic interests in the region.

Larsen won reelection easily until 2010, when he was challenged by Koster, his opponent of a decade earlier. Koster won endorsements from leading national conservatives, which inspired tea party activists to pump hundreds of thousands of dollars into the Republican's campaign. Larsen outspent the challenger $2.1 million to $1.1. million. Their second battle was a microcosm of the two major parties' talking points that year: Koster blasted the Democrats' "socialist" health care bill and the rising federal debt, while Larsen stressed job creation and expanding credit for small business. On Election Night, Larsen trailed by about 1,200 votes, but gained ground as more ballots were counted. He declared victory a week later with a 51%-49% edge, a margin of 6,500 votes.

After the 2011 redistricting boosted the Democratic base in the district by five percentage points, Larsen returned to form by gaining more than 60% of the vote in each of the next two elections.

THIRD DISTRICT

Jaime Herrera Beutler (R)

Elected 2010, 3rd term; b. Nov. 3, 1978, Glendale, CA; Bellevue Comm. Col., A.A. 2003, U. of WA, B.A. 2004; Protestant; married (Daniel Beutler); 1 child.

Elected Office: WA House, 2007-11.

Professional Career: Legis. aide, Rep. Cathy McMorris Rodgers, 2005-07.

DC Office: 1130 LHOB, 20515, 202-225-3536; Fax: 202-225-3478; Website: herrerabeutler.house.gov.

State Offices: Vancouver, 360-695-6292.

Committees: *Appropriations:* Commerce, Justice, Science & Related Agencies; Energy & Water Development & Related Agencies; Financial Services & General Government (VChmn).

Group Ratings

	ADA	ACLU	AFL-CIO	LCV	ITI	COC	HAFA	ACU	CFG	FRC
2014	5%	5%	–	11%	40%	93%	42%	60%	52%	88%
2013	0%	C	25%	4%	C	60%	C	59%	44%	C

National Journal Ratings

	2013 LIB	—	2013 CONS
Economic	52%	—	48%
Social	30%	—	69%
Foreign	48%	—	52%
Composite	44%	—	57%

Key Votes of the 113th Congress

1. Sandy storm spending	Y	5. Medical Marijuana	N	9. Syrian Rebels Training	Y
2. Violence Against Women Act	Y	6. Farm Bill	Y	10. Keystone pipeline	Y
3. Guantanamo Bay Detainees	N	7. Afghanistan Combat	N	11. Immigration Exec. Action	Y
4. Abortion 20-week ban	Y	8. NSA Phone Data Collection	NV	12. Bipartisan budget deal	Y

Election Results

2014 general	Jaime Herrera Beutler (R)	124,796	(62%)	$944,901
	Bob Dingethal (D)	78,018	(39%)	$202,059
2014 primary	Jaime Herrera Beutler (R)	45,065	(48%)	
	Bob Dingethal (D)	36,115	(39%)	
	Michael Delavar (R)	12,000	(13%)	

Prior winning percentages: 2012 (60%), 2010 (53%)

Population		Race and Ethnicity		Income	
Total:	691,968	White	82.7%	Median income:	$52,172
Urban:	54.7%	Latino	8.0%		*(205 of 435)*
Suburban:	25.6%	Asian	3.0%	Under $50,000	47.5%
Rural:	19.7%	Black	1.2%	$50,000-$99,999:	32.3%
Land area:	9,061	Two races	3.8%	$100,000-$199,999:	17.2%
Pop/sq. mi.:	76.4	White Ethnic	25.5%	$200,000 or more:	3.1%
Born in state:	40.9%			Poverty Rate	13.9%
		Education			
Age Groups		H.S. grad or less:	38.2%	**Work**	
Under 18:	24.3%	Some college:	39.3%	White collar:	32.5%
18 to 34:	20.2%	College degree, 4 yr.:	14.7%	Blue collar:	42.2%
35 to 64:	40.1%	Post-grad study:	7.8%	Sales and service:	25.3%
Over 64:	15.4%				
		Military		Govt. workers:	14.6%
		Veterans/active duty:	11.3%		

Southwest Washington: Vancouver

From the Pacific Ocean to the majestic row of active and inactive volcanoes of the Cascades, southwest Washington was long one of America's most productive lumber areas. The moist air and almost constant rain blown in from the Pacific have kept the trees on the coast growing rapidly. Precipitation is

Voter Turnout	
2013 Total Citizen 18+	497,930
2014 House Turnout	202,814
2014 Turnout as % CVAP	40.7%
2012 Turnout as % CVAP	61.7%

heavy in the valleys just past the Coast Range, and the forests there are also fast growing. Then come the high mountains. The Cascades are a genuine divide, wringing almost all of the moisture out of the atmosphere and making an arid climate eastward for a thousand miles. Americans had long been taught that the lower 48 states had no active volcanoes, but Mount St. Helens proved that wrong in 1980 when it erupted after laying dormant for 123 years, killing 57 people, destroying its own peak, and paving the land around it with lava. Plants, animals and fish have been slowly coming back.

For many years, this part of Washington was sparsely settled, with lumber-mill and fishing-boat towns scattered between mountains and water. It was flannel shirt country, Democratic since New Deal days. In the early 1990s, its resource-based economy was threatened by the environmental movement, which restricted fishing practices and produced a court decision shutting down logging in old-growth forests to save spotted owl habitat. This roiled local politics and gave Republicans an opening. The GOP's efforts in the region have been assisted by the growth of Clark County, across the Columbia River from Portland, Oregon, which has filled with new residents eager to avoid Oregon's income tax but who want to make big purchases in Oregon free of sales tax. Clark County, where one-third of the residents commute to work in Portland, grew by 28% from 2000 to 2013.

The 3rd Congressional District of Washington covers the southwestern corner of the state, between the ocean and the Cascades. Economic growth and diversification and the arrival of many new residents with no roots in the old industries have made the area

2012 Presidential Vote		
Mitt Romney (R)................150,409	(50%)
Barack Obama (D) 145,442	(48%)
2008 Presidential Vote		
Barack Obama (D) 151,269	(51%)
John McCain (R)................139,866	(47%)
Cook Partisan Voting Index: R+2		

politically marginal. About 60% of the district's residents live in Clark County. The district now leans Republican by a few percentage points; Mitt Romney won here 50%-48% in 2012, while GOP gubernatorial nominee Rob McKenna carried the area by almost 9 points.

Jaime Herrera Beutler (R)

Republican Jaime Herrera Beutler, elected in 2010, is a young Latina—exactly the kind of politician that her party wants in its ranks. She assists the GOP in its outreach while compiling a business-friendly centrist voting record. She has reaped the benefit of a seat on the Appropriations Committee.

Herrera Beutler grew up in the region. Her father was a printer, her parents raised six children, and finances were tight. It was a blended family: Her parents took in an uncle's children to shelter them from gangs and violence in Southern California. She took a job as a nanny to help pay her way through college. She started with nursing classes, but suspended her studies after concluding that nursing wasn't the right field for her. Herrera Beutler eventually got a degree in communications from the University of Washington. She got involved in politics as a teenager, knocking on doors for Republican candidates in 1994. While in college, she scored a prestigious White House internship.

After graduating, she worked as a legislative aide to Rep. Cathy McMorris Rodgers of Washington, who became her mentor. When a seat unexpectedly opened up in the state legislature in 2007, she was appointed, and she won election in her own right the next year with 60% of the vote. She served on the health, transportation, and human services committees and became the assistant floor leader, the only woman and minority on the Republican leadership team.

When six-term Democratic Rep. Brian Baird announced that he would retire in 2010, Herrera Beutler, then 31 and a newlywed, discussed getting into the race with her husband, Daniel Beutler, who was about to start law school. They decided to delay his plans so she could run. "We didn't want to look back in 10 or 20 years and say to our children we were too comfortable to do what was right," she said. In the all-party primary, Herrera Beutler led a crowded Republican field that included two tea party-backed candidates, with 28% of the vote; runner-up David Hendrick got 14%. She got help in the primary from the National Republican Congressional Committee, which put her on its "Young Guns" list of candidates worthy of funding and advertising.

In the general, Herrera Beutler was outspent. Media and technology entrepreneur Denny Heck spent $2 million, including $350,000 of his own money, to her $1.5 million. But national party and interest-group money helped to close the gap. Heck ran as a moderate Democrat and emphasized his experience creating jobs. Still, she remained competitive. She criticized Heck for his support of the health care overhaul championed by Democrats in Congress and of President Barack Obama's $787 billion economic stimulus bill. Her television ads concluded, "For fiscal sanity, Jaime Herrera for Congress." Riding that year's GOP tidal wave, she won 53%-47%.

Herrera Beutler has been among the moderate members of the Class of 2010. She has been loyal to the GOP leadership on most major votes, partly with a boost from McMorris Rodgers. In her first year, she opposed conservative attempts to eliminate or drastically reduce funding for agencies such as the Legal Services Corporation and Foreign Agricultural Service. She joined most Democrats in protecting funding for the Endangered Species Act. Oregon GOP Rep. Greg Walden, taking over in 2013 as chairman of the National Republican Congressional Committee, appointed her vice chair of his minority outreach effort. "I think we can do a better job of tone," she told *The Columbian* of Vancouver about her party's relationship with Hispanics. She expressed reservations about legislative proposals to restrict gun rights, citing her own experience in her early 20s when a man repeatedly tried to break into her house. She said owning a gun gave her peace of mind. On immigration, she favors comprehensive reform, but has opposed Obama's unilateral efforts to impose changes.

On the Transportation and Infrastructure Committee she joined Oregon Democrat Kurt Schrader in leading objections to a federal court's 2011 decision that water runoff from forest roads must be regulated the same as runoff from factories and sewage treatment plants. The Supreme Court in 2013 reversed the decision. She switched in 2013 to her plum seat on Appropriations.

Herrera Beutler has coasted to reelection with 60% and 61% of the vote, and has entrenched herself in the previously Democratic district. In January 2015, some conservative Republicans unhappy with her House votes for additional spending and regulations discussed calls for a censure by the Clark County GOP. Instead, they reconsidered and agreed to a mechanism to monitor the votes of all elected officials. For now, her political future remains bright.

In 2013, her daughter Abigail was born premature and without kidneys. Herrera Beutler took six months away from the Capitol to be with her daughter, who unexpectedly has survived, though with the need for a kidney transplant. As a result of that experience, she has pushed for a bill to help create a nationwide network of providers to assist medically complex children.

FOURTH DISTRICT

Dan Newhouse (R)

Elected 2014, 1st term; b. July 10, 1955, Sunnyside; WA St. U., B.S. 1977; Presbyterian; married (Carol); 2 children.

Elected Office: WA House, 2003-09.

Professional Career: Farmer; WA Director of Agriculture, 2009-13.

DC Office: 1641 LHOB, 20515, 202-225-5816; Fax: 202-225-3251; Website: newhouse.house.gov.

State Offices: Richland, 509-713-7374; Yakima, 509-452-3243.

Committees: *Agriculture:* Biotechnology, Horticulture & Research; Livestock & Foreign Agriculture. *Natural Resources:* Federal Lands; Water, Power & Oceans. *Rules:* Legislative and Budget Process; Rules of the House. *Science, Space & Technology:* Energy (VChmn); Environment.

Election Results

2014 general	Dan Newhouse (R)	77,772	(51%)	$981,595	$44,040
	Clint Didier (R)	75,307	(49%)	$578,734	$114,492	$117,411
2014 primary	Clint Didier (R)	22,304	(30%)		
	Dan Newhouse (R)	19,517	(27%)		
	Estakio Beltran (D)	8,298	(11%)		
	Janea Holmquist (R)	7,720	(11%)		
	Tony Sandoval (D)	5,076	(7%)		
	George Cicotte (R)	4,733	(7%)		

Population		Race and Ethnicity		Income	
Total:	698,426	White	56.3%	Median income:	$48,691
Urban:	41.1%	Latino	36.8%		*(262 of 435)*
Suburban:	19.4%	Amer. Indian	2.0%	Under $50,000	51.2%
Rural:	39.5%	Asian	1.9%	$50,000-$99,999:	32.7%
Land area:	20,060	Two races	1.9%	$100,000-$199,999:	13.5%
Pop/sq. mi.:	34.8	White Ethnic	16.0%	$200,000 or more:	2.5%
Born in state:	55.9%			Poverty Rate	17.9%
		Education			
Age Groups		H.S. grad or less:	49.5%	**Work**	
Under 18:	29.5%	Some college:	31.5%	White collar:	27.4%
18 to 34:	22.6%	College degree, 4 yr.:	12.4%	Blue collar:	38.9%
35 to 64:	35.5%	Post-grad study:	6.7%	Sales and service:	33.7%
Over 64:	12.5%				
		Military		Govt. workers:	15.3%
		Veterans/active duty:	8.5%		

Central Washington: Richland, Yakima

The rugged peaks of the Cascade Mountains divide the State of Washington into two starkly different climate zones and two almost as starkly different political cultures. West of the Cascades, Washington is moist, green and crammed with watery inlets. To the east, it is barren and brown, except

Voter Turnout	
2013 Total Citizen 18+	411,716
2014 House Turnout	153,079
2014 Turnout as % CVAP	37.2%
2012 Turnout as % CVAP	56.9%

where irrigation ditches channel the water of the Columbia River into thirsty valleys and where the mountaintop waters fall east, as they do above the apple orchards in the Yakima Valley. As Washington has become mostly Democratic west of the Cascades, it has become mostly Republican on the eastern side.

This shift in political inclinations has followed the development of national politics and the local economy. The federal government has been a presence east of the Cascades since the 1930s, when it began to build dams to provide cheap power and boost economic development in this forbidding landscape. A giant bust of Franklin D. Roosevelt gazes out from a bluff on the Columbia over 550-foot-high Grand Coulee Dam, one of Roosevelt's favorite projects.

Other dams are strung along the Columbia to Bonneville Dam near Portland, where the river breaks through the Cascades. This was Democratic territory then; Grant County gave Franklin Roosevelt 86% of the vote in 1936, his best showing in the state. But as the region became wealthier—in part because of the federal projects—and as the nation's politics took on a cultural cast in the 1960s, the area shifted toward the Republicans. The environmentalism of the Democratic Party shaped political views here. Farmers in the Yakima Valley, which produces most of the nation's apples and many other crops, were enraged when environmentalists proposed breaching the Snake River dams upriver to save salmon. Lumber towns in the Cascades responded angrily when the logging business was harmed by efforts to preserve the spotted owl.

The 4th Congressional District of Washington covers much of the center of the state east of the Cascades, running from the vast wilderness of Okanogan County, which has long been gold country, past the Grand Coulee and the Columbia River. The biggest population center here is the Tri-Cities of Richland, Kennewick and Pasco in Benton County. Like Benton, Yakima County includes about one-third of the district. The region suffered economically in the recession, with the unemployment rate in both counties above 10% in 2012. Since then, the rate has dropped below 7% in each county.

The district's population is 38% Hispanic; many are farm workers or the children of farm workers who have picked fruit for generations. The area was narrowly split

2012 Presidential Vote		
Mitt Romney (R)................142,741		(60%)
Barack Obama (D) 90,612		(38%)
2008 Presidential Vote		
John McCain (R)................135,149		(59%)
Barack Obama (D) 89,870		(39%)
Cook Partisan Voting Index: R+13		

between the parties as recently as the 1990s, but the 4th now is the most Republican district in the state, and the cultural liberalism of Seattle seems very far away from here.

Dan Newhouse (R)

Dan Newhouse prevailed in 2014 over fellow Republican Clint Didier in the top-two general election campaign in the 4th District with a promise of greater bipartisanship. Newhouse described himself as "someone that's not afraid to work with anybody, if there's a good idea on the table."

Newhouse grew up in a Yakima Valley family that was active in local politics. His father, Irv, was a state legislator for 34 years. The younger Newhouse and his wife operate a 600-acre farm where they grow hops, grapes and alfalfa. He got his bachelor's degree in agricultural economics from Washington State University and is a former president of the Hop Growers of America. Newhouse won election to the state House in 2002. Democratic Gov. Christine Gregoire named him state agriculture director, calling him "the best person for the job." He served four years in the position. When Gregoire's successor, Democrat Jay Inslee, declined to keep Newhouse in the position, he became a frequent television spokesman for opponents of a failed 2013 state ballot initiative that would have required labeling of genetically modified food products.

When Republican Rep. Doc Hastings, a close confidant of House Speaker John Boehner and chairman of the Natural Resources Committee, announced his retirement after 20 years, Republicans were confident they would keep the seat. In the all-party primary, Didier and Newhouse led the field with 31% and 26%, respectively. It marked the first time in state history that two Republicans faced off in the general election. That left voters a choice between two starkly different Republicans. Didier, a former tight end in the National Football League who ran for the Senate in 2010 and finished third in the all-party primary with 13% of the vote, was a significant figure in the state's tea party movement. He drew endorsements from former Alaska Gov. Sarah Palin and former Rep. Ron Paul of Texas, and emphasized the importance of gun rights, patriotism and religion.

Newhouse won endorsements from Hastings as well as the National Rifle Association. His campaign criticized Didier for reporting $291,000 in federal farm subsidies between 1995 and 2010, alleging the payments were at odds with his limited-government message. In its endorsement of Newhouse, the *Yakima Herald-Republic* noted the importance of the federal government in the district, which includes multiple federal dams. "Newhouse by far shows a better grasp of the federal government's influence and the need to work with others for the interests of Central Washington, all while representing the region's conservative slant," the newspaper said.

Newhouse outspent Didier, $982,000 to $579,000, and won 51%-49%, a margin of 2,465 votes. Didier led in six of the eight counties. But Newhouse led in Benton and Yakima counties, which cast 64% of the total votes. He won 60% in his Yakima base, which was the deciding factor.

In the House, Newhouse did well in his committee assignments, with the district-connected Agriculture and Natural Resources panels. When an opening occurred after the start of the new Congress, he was named by Boehner as the only freshman on the Rules Committee, which operates as an arm of the leadership. He supported the renewal of the Export-Import Bank, a split with many junior Republicans but a popular move in his home state, where Boeing-manufactured aircraft are major beneficiaries of the loans, as are many farmers. "It's something I've seen as a very effective tool to help increase the exports coming out of the state of Washington," Newhouse said.

FIFTH DISTRICT

Cathy McMorris Rodgers (R)

Elected 2004, 6th term; b. May 22, 1969, Salem, OR; Pensacola Christian Col., B.A. 1990, U. of WA, M.B.A. 2002; Christian; married (Brian Rodgers); 3 children.

Elected Office: WA House, 1994-2004, min. ldr., 2002-04.

Professional Career: Owner-operator, Peachcrest Fruit Basket orchard, 1984-98; St. legis. aide, 1990-94.

DC Office: 203 CHOB, 20515, 202-225-2006; Fax: 202-225-3392; Website: mcmorris.house.gov.

State Offices: Colville, 509-684-3481; Spokane, 509-353-2374; Walla Walla, 509-529-9358.

Committees: *Energy & Commerce:* Health.

Group Ratings

	ADA	ACLU	AFL-CIO	LCV	ITI	COC	HAFA	ACU	CFG	FRC
2014	0%	0%	–	6%	80%	93%	49%	72%	62%	88%
2013	5%	C	14%	4%	C	83%	C	72%	59%	C

National Journal Ratings

	2013 LIB	—	2013 CONS
Economic	37%	—	63%
Social	16%	—	74%
Foreign	33%	—	67%
Composite	30%	—	70%

Key Votes of the 113th Congress

1. Sandy storm spending	N	5. Medical Marijuana	N	9. Syrian Rebels Training	Y
2. Violence Against Women Act	Y	6. Farm Bill	Y	10. Keystone pipeline	Y
3. Guantanamo Bay Detainees	N	7. Afghanistan Combat	N	11. Immigration Exec. Action	Y
4. Abortion 20-week ban	Y	8. NSA Phone Data Collection	Y	12. Bipartisan budget deal	Y

Election Results

2014 general	Cathy McMorris Rodgers (R)	135,470	(61%)	$2,910,112	$9,961
	Joseph Pakootas (D)	87,772	(39%)	$188,062	
2014 primary	Cathy McMorris Rodgers (R)	59,173	(52%)		
	Joseph Pakootas (D)	33,302	(29%)		
	Dave Wilson (I)	12,984	(11%)		
	Tom Horne (R)	9,328	(8%)		

Prior winning percentages: 2012 (62%), 2010 (68%), 2008 (65%), 2006 (56%), 2004 (60%)

Population		Race and Ethnicity		Income	
Total:	681,812	White	85.2%	Median income:	$46,009
Urban:	59.3%	Latino	5.8%		*(298 of 435)*
Suburban:	15.7%	Asian	2.1%	Under $50,000	53.7%
Rural:	24.9%	Black	1.6%	$50,000-$99,999:	30.5%
Land area:	18,428	Two races	3.1%	$100,000-$199,999:	13.7%
Pop/sq. mi.:	37.0	White Ethnic	27.0%	$200,000 or more:	2.1%
Born in state:	53.8%			Poverty Rate	17.8%
		Education			
Age Groups		H.S. grad or less:	35.6%	**Work**	
Under 18:	21.9%	Some college:	37.5%	White collar:	35.2%
18 to 34:	25.3%	College degree, 4 yr.:	17.1%	Blue collar:	44.6%
35 to 64:	37.7%	Post-grad study:	9.8%	Sales and service:	20.2%
Over 64:	15.1%				
		Military		Govt. workers:	18.6%
		Veterans/active duty:	11.8%		

Eastern Washington: Spokane

Eastern Washington is a land of great rivers and bare parched land, where the Columbia, Spokane and Snake rivers wind among vast plateaus, bringing water from the Rockies to the desert. Spokane grew up at the falls of the Spokane River when the railroads first came through. It was initially a gold

Voter Turnout	
2013 Total Citizen 18+	510,941
2014 House Turnout	223,242
2014 Turnout as % CVAP	43.7%
2012 Turnout as % CVAP	61.9%

rush town, and later became a major wheat, mining and railroad center. Nearby are some of the most fascinating landscapes in the United States: undulating yellow wheat fields on the rolling ridges of the Palouse, where the wheat-growing topsoil is 200 feet deep; acres of protected forestland in Colville National Forest, home to the last surviving herd of caribou in the lower 48 states; and bare-rock coulees rising above dammed-up lakes and barren desert. Much of this area is remote and inhospitable. The summers can be blazingly hot and the winters bitterly cold. But the water from the Grand Coulee and other dams irrigates some of the richest farmland in the country.

The 5th Congressional District of Washington covers the easternmost part of the state. About two-thirds of the people live in Spokane County, where the voting habits have grown apart from the Washington west of the Cascades, especially on natural resource issues. Several Spokane-area politicians have called for creating a 51st state of Eastern Washington, which would cover 60 percent of the state. The upcoming round of base closures has residents concerned about the fate of Fairchild Air Force Base, the area's largest employer. But there are some positive signs: Caterpillar recently opened a $37 million distribution center. In December 2014, JP Morgan Chase & Co. took majority control of the Palouse wind farm that has powered 30,000 homes. Near the Oregon border is Walla Walla, long dependent on wheat and sweet onions but now attracting tourists with its budding wine industry; *USA Today* rated Walla Walla the friendliest small town in America in 2011.

The district's political inclinations lean Republican. Spokane County voted for Democrat Bill Clinton in 1992 and 1996, but Republicans have won it since then. When

2012 Presidential Vote		
Mitt Romney (R).................168,671	(54%)
Barack Obama (D) 137,771	(44%)
2008 Presidential Vote		
John McCain (R).................159,523	(51%)
Barack Obama (D) 144,118	(46%)
Cook Partisan Voting Index: R+7		

30-year Democratic Rep. Tom Foley was defeated for reelection in 1994, some of the local voters reportedly were surprised that his Republican successor did not automatically replace him as House Speaker.

Cathy McMorris Rodgers (R)

Cathy McMorris Rodgers, elected in 2004, took over in 2013 as head of the House Republican Conference, the fourth-ranking post in the GOP leadership. She is the top woman among House Republican leaders and a trusted on-message lieutenant of House Speaker John Boehner.

McMorris Rodgers spent much of her childhood in northern British Columbia but moved with her family to Kettle Falls, where her parents bought a fruit orchard and operated a stand selling apples, peaches, cherries and strawberries. Her father was a county Republican chairman. She graduated from Pensacola Christian College in Florida and got an M.B.A. from the University of Washington. After college, she became a legislative assistant to Bob Morton, a state House member. "Bob Morton was always encouraging me: 'Go represent me at this meeting,' 'Go give this speech.' You know, I was, like, 'Huh?' And I look back on it now and I think he saw something in me that I didn't see in myself, really," she recalled. McMorris Rodgers was appointed to her state House seat at age 24, and later, was elected in her own right. She served for 10 years and chaired the Commerce and Labor Committee. She eventually rose to minority leader, the first woman to hold such a post in state history.

In 2004, George Nethercutt, who defeated Democratic House Speaker Tom Foley in 1994, ran for the Senate. He encouraged her to run for his House seat: "Without being rancorous, it's hard to run against a woman. It's different, I'll say. I thought that might give her a little bit of edge," he said. McMorris Rodgers and two other Republicans competed in the primary. They agreed on most major issues, including opposing abortion and favoring a constitutional amendment banning same-sex marriage. McMorris Rodgers won 50% of the vote in the primary to 27% for state Sen. Larry Sheahan.

The Democratic nominee, Don Barbieri, a wealthy businessman, had a geographical edge over McMorris Rodgers. He was from Spokane, while she was from rural northeastern Washington. Barbieri also had a heavy financial advantage and no primary opposition. The National Republican Congressional Committee spent heavily for McMorris Rodgers, including an ad charging that Barbieri had put "profits before jobs" when his hotel development company laid off workers following a merger. McMorris Rodgers highlighted her pro-business credentials and agricultural background. That was enough to give her a comfortable victory, 60%-40%, a sign of the change in Foley's old district.

In the House, she initially leaned toward the center on some issues. In 2007, she voted to expand the State Children's Health Insurance Plan, a move favored by Democrats but opposed by President George W. Bush. (She opposed the final version that became law in 2009.) She backed Bush's Iraq war policies, but also criticized the administration on veterans' health care and on a delay in rules for country-of-origin meat labeling. She has a seat on the Energy and Commerce Committee and has worked across the aisle on several issues. With Democratic Rep. Diana DeGette, she enacted in 2013 the Hydropower Regulatory Efficiency Act, which streamlined the permitting process for small hydropower projects as a tool to expand clean energy.

McMorris Rodgers became an acolyte of Boehner, with whom she served on the Education and the Workforce Committee. She was chosen the conference vice chair with his backing and took on several tasks. He selected her in 2009 to head a GOP task force that sought to develop a policy on earmarks. She has helped to recruit women to run and has served as a liaison to newly elected Republican women, including with fund-raising. McMorris Rodgers also has broadened her party's use of social media tools. During the 2012 presidential campaign, Mitt Romney tapped McMorris Rodgers to serve as his House liaison, partly as a reward for her early endorsement.

She pitched to move up to Republican Conference chair after the 2012 election, stressing her communications skills and her recruiting of successful candidates. She touted raising more than $1 million for the National Republican Congressional Committee and contributing more than $300,000 to candidates. She defeated Tom Price of Georgia, a favorite of the tea party who had the backing of Paul Ryan of Wisconsin.

The Office of Congressional Ethics recommended that the Ethics Committee investigate whether McMorris Rodgers improperly used official funds in that leadership contest as well as to cover campaign-related activities. The allegations came from a former aide, who told OCE investigators that he wrote campaign speeches and did other political work on official time. Her attorney denied the allegations, and in March 2014 the committee said it would not appoint a special investigative panel on the matter.

Along with senior GOP leaders, she considered the party's perceived weaknesses to be less about its policies than about how it conveys its message. "I don't think it's about the Republican Party needing to become more moderate," she told CNN. "I really believe it's the Republican Party becoming more modern." She hired a Hispanic staffer to provide the party's message to Spanish-language television networks and set up a Twitter feed in Spanish. Eventually she brought in four full-time staffers dedicated to creating video products for other members to use on social media and in their districts.

She hosted meetings between groups of young Republican voters and younger members of Congress. Much of her work remained behind the scenes. "I'm trying to promote a Republican cause," she said. "And part of that is [about] message as well as messengers. It's not about me, it's not about my profile, it is about doing that which I think is going to help our overall effort to advance the conservative cause." In May 2015, McMorris Rodgers was instrumental in crafting a compromise between GOP women and pro-life conservatives on a House-passed abortion bill that stopped most abortions after 20 weeks.

Her voting record has become more conservative. Though *The Spokesman-Review* of Spokane endorsed her in 2012, it added, "Too often she appears the ideologue in her solidarity with House leadership." She was chosen to give the GOP response to Obama's 2014 State of the Union address and played up her party's attempt to "trust people" to make their own economic decisions. "The president talks a lot about income inequality," she said. "But the real gap we face today is one of opportunity inequality … and with this administration's policies, that gap has become far too wide. We see this gap growing every single day."

Republican colleagues praised McMorris Rodgers for her hard work. But when Majority Leader Eric Cantor's unexpected primary defeat in June 2014 opened two GOP leadership seats, she quickly said she would not run for either of them. Her staffers said that the timing wasn't right and that she remained open to pursuing a higher post.

In April 2007, McMorris Rodgers and her husband had their first child, a boy, Cole McMorris Rodgers, who was born four weeks premature and was diagnosed with Down syndrome. She subsequently gave birth to two daughters, making her the first member of Congress to deliver multiple babies while in office. She formed the Congressional Down Syndrome Caucus in 2008 to raise awareness about institutional barriers that face individuals with Down syndrome, and she became a leader in the disabilities community. In 2013, she enacted her National Pediatric Research Network Act.

SIXTH DISTRICT

Derek Kilmer (D)

Elected 2012, 2nd term; b. Jan. 1, 1974, Port Angeles; Princeton U., B.A. 1996, Oxford U., Ph.D. 2003; Methodist; married (Jennifer); 2 children.

Elected Office: WA House, 2005-07; WA Senate, 2007-13.

Professional Career: Mgmt. consultant, McKinsey & Co., 1999-2002; V.P., Economic Development Bd., Tacoma-Pierce Cnty., 2002-12.

DC Office: 1520 LHOB, 20515, 202-225-5916; Website: kilmer.house. gov.

State Offices: Bremerton, 360-373-9725; Port Angeles, 360-797-3623; Tacoma, 253-272-3515.

Committees: *Armed Services:* Intelligence, Emerging Threats & Capabilities; Seapower & Projection Forces. *Science, Space, & Technology:* Space; Technology.

Group Ratings

	ADA	ACLU	AFL-CIO	LCV	ITI	COC	HAFA	ACU	CFG	FRC
2014	75%	77%	–	83%	100%	50%	13%	4%	6%	13%
2013	60%	C	90%	93%	C	69%	C	20%	16%	C

National Journal Ratings

	2013 LIB	—	2013 CONS
Economic	66%	—	34%
Social	59%	—	40%
Foreign	65%	—	35%
Composite	64%	—	37%

Key Votes of the 113th Congress

1. Sandy storm spending	Y	5. Medical Marijuana	Y	9. Syrian Rebels Training	Y
2. Violence Against Women Act	Y	6. Farm Bill	N	10. Keystone pipeline	N
3. Guantanamo Bay Detainees	Y	7. Afghanistan Combat	Y	11. Immigration Exec. Action	N
4. Abortion 20-week ban	N	8. NSA Phone Data Collection	N	12. Bipartisan budget deal	Y

Election Results

2014 general	Derek Kilmer (D) 141,265	(63%)	$1,239,106	$3,676
	Marty McClendon (R) 83,025	(37%)	$23,310	
2014 primary	Derek Kilmer (D) 66,932	(59%)		
	Marty McClendon (R) 38,720	(34%)		
	W. McPherson (I) 3,978	(4%)		
	Douglas Milholland (G) 3,845	(3%)		

Prior winning percentage: 2012 (59%)

Population		Race and Ethnicity		Income	
Total:	682,280	White	77.6%	Median income:	$54,049
Urban:	39.3%	Latino	6.7%		*(177 of 435)*
Suburban:	32.9%	Asian	4.4%	Under $50,000	45.6%
Rural:	27.8%	Black	3.6%	$50,000-$99,999:	32.7%
Land area:	5,367	Two races	5.0%	$100,000-$199,999:	17.9%
Pop/sq. mi.:	127.1	White Ethnic	26.4%	$200,000 or more:	3.7%
Born in state:	48.5%			Poverty Rate	14.7%
		Education			
Age Groups		H.S. grad or less:	32.9%	**Work**	
Under 18:	20.0%	Some college:	38.7%	White collar:	35.6%
18 to 34:	22.1%	College degree, 4 yr.:	18.1%	Blue collar:	43.4%
35 to 64:	40.3%	Post-grad study:	10.3%	Sales and service:	21.0%
Over 64:	17.6%				
		Military		Govt. workers:	22.2%
		Veterans/active duty:	17.5%		

Central Tacoma, Olympic Peninsula

The rainiest part of the continental United States is its far northwest corner, where the Olympic Mountains of Washington jut into the Pacific Ocean. The waters of the Pacific evaporate, condense, and then mist or rain on the hills and mountains along Puget Sound. The mountains here are always green, the

Voter Turnout	
2013 Total Citizen 18+	528,738
2014 House Turnout	224,290
2014 Turnout as % CVAP	42.4%
2012 Turnout as % CVAP	62.3%

trees that line the inlets towering, and during heavy rain falls, the rivers can rise six feet in a day. (The winter of 2015 was unusually dry and raised local concerns of water shortages.) This has long been lumbering and fishing country, where people start work at 6 a.m. and where the vagaries of nature and environmental laws—like the ban on old-growth logging to protect the habitat of the spotted owl—have strengthened a traditional surly independence and suspicion of authority. Still, respect for the beauty of nature endures, including at the 3,310-square-mile Olympic Coast National Marine Sanctuary, a vast underwater reserve. There are some local fears that too much land has been bought to build subdivisions and second homes. The small city of Forks is where the "Twilight" teen vampire novels were set, and some of the locals complain about the influx of outsiders who visit the scenery firsthand. But the local Chamber of Commerce operates a welcoming station for the tourism boomlet to give out maps of the can't-miss locales in the novels.

The many inlets of Puget Sound, winding sinuously through mountains, are among America's most picturesque waterways and strategically among its most important. During World War II, shipyards were built to shelter much of the Navy's Pacific fleet. During the Cold War, some of the nuclear submarine fleet was anchored at the giant Kitsap Navy base. The shipyard employed 12,800 in May 2015, with plans to add a few hundred more workers. The Tacoma Narrows Bridge replaced the original bridge which, in a scene preserved on newsreel and still viewed by civil engineering students, started vibrating

2012 Presidential Vote

Barack Obama (D) 184,820	(56%)
Mitt Romney (R) 135,573	(41%)

2008 Presidential Vote

Barack Obama (D) 186,366	(57%)
John McCain (R) 133,682	(41%)

Cook Partisan Voting Index: D+5

on the wrong harmonic in high winds and collapsed in 1940. On the other side is Tacoma, long the second city on Puget Sound, with its massive docks, former pulp mills, pleasant hilly residential neighborhoods, and recently revived waterfront. On the northern coast, across from British Columbia, Port Angeles has had an economic revival and is ranked among the nation's best small towns.

The 6th Congressional District of Washington includes the Olympic Peninsula, Bremerton, and about 30 percent of Tacoma. Kitsap is the largest population center, including Bainbridge Island, where residents commute by ferry to downtown Seattle. About two-thirds of the 6th's residents live in Kitsap or in Tacoma's Pierce County. Politically, the Olympic Peninsula and Tacoma are working-class Democrat, as is the district overall, though not overwhelmingly so.

Derek Kilmer (D)

Democrat Derek Kilmer succeeded his political mentor, Rep. Norm Dicks, who retired in 2012 from the 6th District seat after serving 36 years. After two years, Kilmer took another step in his predecessor's path with a seat on the Appropriations Committee, where Dicks had been the senior Democrat.

Kilmer grew up as the son of two public school teachers in Port Angeles, where he first met Dicks at age 18. "He's been a really great mentor for me over the years," Kilmer said. Watching the town's economic struggles in the wake of the timber industry's decline led Kilmer to pursue a career linking public policy and economic development. He got a bachelor's degree in public policy from Princeton University and a doctorate in social policy from the University of Oxford in England, with a focus on economic development.

After working as a business consultant for McKinsey and Co., he went to work for the nonprofit Economic Development Board for Tacoma-Pierce County. As a vice president, he talked with 200 businesses a year in an effort to broaden the economies of communities like Port Angeles, long dependent on timber. "How do you put more legs on the stool so it's more stable," he said. "How do you diversify a local economy to help it prosper?"

Kilmer was elected to the state House in 2004 and two years later moved to the state Senate. He rose to chair the chamber's Capital Budget Committee, where he was the chief author of the state's capital budget and promoted legislation to create jobs by borrowing money for public construction. In addition to economic development and education, Kilmer focused on veterans' affairs. With Naval Base Kitsap in the 6th District, veterans make up more than 15 percent of the population.

Dicks gave his protégé early word in March 2012 that he would not seek a 19th term. "He told me, 'In about an hour I'm going to announce my retirement, and you should figure out what you're going to do,'" Kilmer recalled. He moved quickly and was the only Democratic contender. In the all-party primary, Kilmer got 53% of the total vote and Republican businessman Bill Driscoll led the six Republican candidates with 18%. Driscoll had served with the Marines in Iraq and Afghanistan and also worked in the timber and real estate industries. He called the federal deficit the biggest threat to national security and departed from Republican orthodoxy in calling for tax increases tied to specific spending cuts. Driscoll also supported abortion rights and same-sex marriage.

Kilmer made sure to let voters know that he was running with Dicks' backing. *The Seattle Times* endorsed him as "a problem solver who can be bipartisan," and *The News Tribune* of Tacoma praised him for having "an uncommon understanding of trade, business taxation, smart regulation, job creation, and other fundamentals of economic growth." Each candidate spent close to $2 million. Kilmer won 59%-41%, including 58% in Kitsap and 64% in Pierce.

In the House, Kilmer made an early effort at consensus-building with the Bipartisan Working Group and the Problem Solvers Caucus, which have tried to forge greater consensus on a variety of issues. He helped to organize the Puget Sound Recovery Caucus to bring increased focus and attention to cleanup work that needs to be done. He enacted a bill in September 2014 that renamed a memorial on Bainbridge Island in honor of Japanese Americans who were forced from their local homes during World War II. In May 2015, he called for a "neutral" review of military jet noise over Olympic National Park. In June, he filed legislation to reorganize the selection of members to the Federal Election Commission in a bid to break its typically deadlocked status. He also sought to limit contributions and increase transparency in federal campaigns.

With his new seat on Appropriations in 2015, he moved quickly to add provisions to subcommittee bills and to issue public statements about those details. He seemed ready to follow in Dicks' footsteps with a long run on the committee, much as Dicks earlier was mentored as an aide to Sen. Warren Magnuson of Washington, who chaired the Senate Appropriations Committee.

At home, Kilmer outspent by more than 50-to-1 his Republican opponent, Marty McClendon, a real estate agent and church pastor, and was reelected with 63% of the vote.

SEVENTH DISTRICT

Jim McDermott (D)

Elected 1988, 14th term; b. Dec. 28, 1936, Chicago, IL; Wheaton Col., B.S. 1958, U. of IL, M.D. 1963; Episcopalian; divorced; 2 children.

Military Career: U.S. Navy Med. Corps, 1968-70.

Elected Office: WA House, 1970-72; WA Senate, 1975-87.

Professional Career: Asst. prof., U. of WA; Practicing psychiatrist, 1970-83; Med. officer, U.S. Foreign Svc., Zaire, 1987-88.

DC Office: 1035 LHOB, 20515, 202-225-3106; Fax: 202-225-6197; Website: mcdermott.house.gov.

State Offices: Seattle, 206-553-7170.

Committees: *Budget. Ways & Means:* Health (RMM).

Group Ratings

	ADA	ACLU	AFL-CIO	LCV	ITI	COC	HAFA	ACU	CFG	FRC
2014	95%	77%	–	97%	40%	29%	15%	8%	15%	0%
2013	100%	C	100%	96%	C	23%	C	8%	10%	C

National Journal Ratings

	2013 LIB	—	2013 CONS
Economic	91%	—	0%
Social	85%	—	13%
Foreign	94%	—	0%
Composite	93%	—	7%

Key Votes of the 113th Congress

1. Sandy storm spending	Y	5. Medical Marijuana	Y	9. Syrian Rebels Training	N
2. Violence Against Women Act	Y	6. Farm Bill	N	10. Keystone pipeline	N
3. Guantanamo Bay Detainees	Y	7. Afghanistan Combat	Y	11. Immigration Exec. Action	N
4. Abortion 20-week ban	N	8. NSA Phone Data Collection	Y	12. Bipartisan budget deal	Y

Election Results

2014 general	Jim McDermott (D)	203,954	(81%)	$581,723
	Craig Keller (R)	47,921	(19%)	$6,229
2014 primary	Jim McDermott (D)	95,708	(77%)	
	Craig Keller (R)	11,687	(9%)	
	Scott Sutherland (R)	8,443	(7%)	
	Doug McQuaid (I)	7,973	(6%)	

Prior winning percentages: 2012 (80%), 2010 (83%), 2008 (84%), 2006 (79%), 2004 (81%), 2002 (74%), 2000 (73%), 1998 (88%), 1996 (81%), 1994 (75%), 1992 (78%), 1990 (72%), 1988 (76%)

Population		Race and Ethnicity		Income	
Total:	706,603	White	71.6%	Median income:	$70,596
Urban:	91.6%	Asian	10.4%		*(61 of 435)*
Suburban:	8.3%	Latino	7.3%	Under $50,000	35.7%
Rural:	0.0%	Black	5.2%	$50,000-$99,999:	29.8%
Land area:	151	Two races	4.1%	$100,000-$199,999:	25.0%
Pop/sq. mi.:	4,683.9	White Ethnic	28.5%	$200,000 or more:	9.4%
Born in state:	41.0%			Poverty Rate	12.2%
		Education			
Age Groups		H.S. grad or less:	17.1%	**Work**	
Under 18:	16.0%	Some college:	25.4%	White collar:	54.9%
18 to 34:	30.8%	College degree, 4 yr.:	34.5%	Blue collar:	35.0%
35 to 64:	40.9%	Post-grad study:	23.0%	Sales and service:	10.2%
Over 64:	12.4%				
		Military		Govt. workers:	14.1%
		Veterans/active duty:	6.5%		

Seattle

Seattle rises from the Puget Sound harbor of Elliott Bay on steep hills once covered with 300-foot-high Douglas firs. Behind the hills and buildings, on a clear day you can see the nimbus of Mount Rainier. On the picturesque waterfront, below gleaming high-rises, is Pike Place Market, where you can get

Voter Turnout	
2013 Total Citizen 18+	541,902
2014 House Turnout	251,875
2014 Turnout as % CVAP	46.5%
2012 Turnout as % CVAP	72.8%

fresh salmon and Dungeness crabs. Nearby, where the ferries from Bainbridge and Vashon Islands and Bremerton Dock in the nation's busiest ferry system, is Pioneer Square, where stores and warehouses from the turn of the 20th century have been restored. Yesler Way was America's original Skid Road—literally a path for skidding newly cut logs to transportation terminals. It remains a haven for the homeless and a frequent locale for open-air drug dealing.

Seattle has some old ethnic neighborhoods, like the once heavily Scandinavian Ballard, which now features boutiques and nightspots, and the countercultural Capitol Hill, where shoppers jam busy stores, galleries, and clubs. Highly educated, affluent single professionals have made the Victorian houses overlooking the harbor and the 1940s houses in Capitol Hill among the nation's highest-priced residential real estate. But the city also has a new ethnic mix, with thousands of Asian immigrants. Boeing has remained a major presence in the Seattle area since moving its headquarters to Chicago in 2001 and is a prime exporter. Seattle is the headquarters, in an old industrial district, of Starbucks coffee. In 2014, Starbucks had 7,300 company-owned stores, about the same as in 2008; the number of licensed stores had increased 7 percent to more than 4,600. The company announced plans in March 2015 to add 3,500 stores in the "Americas region," with a new emphasis on smaller express locations.

Seattle ranks as one of the nation's most desirable cities, but it has its flaws. The Justice Department investigated the city's police after several episodes in which officers were accused of using unnecessary force and discriminating against minorities, and concluded that the department had engaged in a pattern of excessive force that violated the Constitution and federal law. The city's professional basketball team, the SuperSonics, moved to Oklahoma City after Starbucks owner Howard Schultz sold the team to a group of Oklahoma businessmen who broke a promise to keep the team in the Northwest. In 2009, the *Seattle Post-Intelligencer* stopped its printing presses and began publishing exclusively online, leaving *The Seattle Times* as the city's only daily newspaper.

Still, the city's economic foundation is sound, and parts are bustling. Rejecting Microsoft's local model of a suburban campus, the robust Amazon has expanded into a huge new campus with three new office towers in the South Lake Union area. Amazon founder and CEO Jeff Bezos checks in occasionally with the other Washington on his part-time investment property, *The Washington Post*. Microsoft founder Bill Gates' decision to turn his attention to global health philanthropy has made Seattle the Davos of health care, drawing experts in malaria, tuberculosis, AIDS and other global scourges. The city is a growing haven for young singles, as married couples with children make up only 13 percent of Seattle households. In June 2014, the city council spurred a nation-wide movement when it increased Seattle's minimum wage to $15 per hour, on a phased timetable from 2017 to 2021, depending on the size of a business. In June 2015, Seattle was the best city in the nation to find a new job, according to WalletHub.com.

The 7th Congressional District of Washington includes nearly all of the city of Seattle, some industrial suburban fringe to the

2012 Presidential Vote		
Barack Obama (D) 310,828		(79%)
Mitt Romney (R)..................70,973		(18%)
2008 Presidential Vote		
Barack Obama (D) 302,549		(80%)
John McCain (R)..................67,882		(18%)
Cook Partisan Voting Index: D+29		

south, a white-collar suburban fringe to the north, and artsy, bucolic Vashon Island in Puget Sound. It is a Democratic enclave, where President Barack Obama got 79 percent of the vote in 2012.

Jim McDermott (D)

Democrat Jim McDermott, first elected in 1988, has been one of Congress' most liberal members and a persistent attack dog against Republican policies that he complains, often caustically, are unfair to the middle class. Serving on the Ways and Means Committee, he has had an impact in debates on topics such as inequality and taxes.

McDermott grew up in the Chicago suburb of Downers Grove and was the first in his family to attend college. His father, a fundamentalist Christian, ministered in a church run out of the garage. McDermott graduated from conservative Christian Wheaton College, the alma mater of the Rev. Billy Graham. He got a medical degree from the University of Illinois and completed his psychiatric residency at the University of Washington. He fell in love with the area and made it his home. With the Vietnam War under way, he volunteered for a stint in the Navy as a psychiatrist, where he served at the Long Beach Naval Station and treated servicemen returning from the war. The experience left him adamantly opposed to the war.

When he returned to Seattle, he got involved in politics. In 1970, while he was operating his medical practice, he was elected to the state House, and four years later to the Senate. He ran for governor three times and lost each time. In 1987, he retired from the legislature and went to Zaire (now the Democratic Republic of the Congo) as a medical officer in the Foreign Service providing psychiatric services. When the House seat opened in 1988, he returned to Seattle and defeated Norm Rice 38%-29% in the primary and took 76% in the general; Rice later served eight years as Seattle mayor. Among the 17 physicians in Congress, McDermott is the only psychiatrist.

In his early years in the House, McDermott rose quickly in influence. House Speaker Tom Foley of Washington tapped him for influential assignments. McDermott is upfront that his legislative interests tend not to include the parochial matters that consume some of his congressional colleagues. He has promoted health issues overseas; he founded and chaired the Congressional Task Force on International HIV/AIDS. He also sponsored a measure that at first seemed quixotic but was enacted in 2000: The African Growth and Opportunity Act, which reduced import quotas and tariffs on African goods and included investment funds. More recently, he has introduced bills requiring the Internal Revenue Service to provide to taxpayers a detailed breakdown of how their money is spent.

A longtime ally of Nancy Pelosi, he was an activist during her four years as House Speaker. In 2007, he helped shape the House-passed bill to rescind some tax breaks for oil companies. Between 2008 and 2010, he was the lead sponsor of bills that extended unemployment benefits. He shepherded to enactment legislation aimed at improving foster care programs.

McDermott's great cause has been health care, but he has shared the frustration many have felt in dealing with the issue. He has long backed a single-payer, Canadian-style national health insurance program. During the health care debate in 2009 and 2010, he pushed for a government-run "public option" to compete with private insurers. He became ranking Democrat in 2013 on the Ways and Means health panel, an added platform for his rejoinders to GOP criticisms of the health care law. In June 2015, he opposed the request from President Barack Obama for trade promotion authority to expedite the Trans-Pacific trade agreement. Despite the expected benefits for Seattle and its port, he said that he worried about Americans who would suffer when jobs went overseas.

McDermott also is upfront in voicing his displeasure with the GOP. During debate over the fiscal 2014 budget, he mocked the Republicans' oft-stated talking point that no family would run its household finances like the federal government. "I don't know any family in America that would use their children's lunch money to pay down their credit cards," he said on the House floor. In April 2011, he said on the floor, "The difference between a Boy Scout troop and this House of Representatives is that the Boy Scout troop has adult leadership." He issued a video calling the tea party "the most nonsensical display of people not thinking" that he had seen in decades.

McDermott was harshly critical of the Bush administration on a number of fronts, especially the war in Iraq. In September 2002, with a congressional delegation in Baghdad, McDermott said in a statement broadcast on ABC's *This Week* that Bush was willing to "mislead the American people," and that he found Iraqi Leader Saddam Hussein to be more credible than Bush. He took some heat when he returned home. But his antiwar sentiments have been bipartisan: He has castigated the Obama administration for its Middle East policies, though not nearly as crudely.

He has had more than his share of conflicts within the House. In 2004, McDermott stirred controversy in 2004 when he omitted the words "under God" as he led the House in its daily Pledge of Allegiance to the flag. After leaders of both parties criticized him, he replied that his omission had not been deliberate. In 2007, he was attacked by conservatives for voting against a House resolution recognizing the importance of Christmas.

He was bogged down in an unusual years-long battle with House Republicans stemming from an incident when he was ranking minority member on the Ethics Committee in 1997 as it was reviewing charges against Republican Speaker Newt Gingrich. Two Democratic activists in Florida taped from a police scanner a cell phone conversation between Ohio Republican John Boehner and other GOP leaders. They gave the tape to McDermott. A few days later, excerpts from it appeared in newspapers. Boehner sued McDermott in federal court for invasion of privacy, and the case lingered in the courts for years.

McDermott approached Boehner in 2002—they had not spoken in the 12 years they served together—and sought to settle the case. He agreed to one of Boehner's demands, that he apologize to the House. But he would not agree to the other two: admit that he was wrong and make a contribution to charity. In 2004, the judge found McDermott guilty of violating the federal wiretapping law and ordered him to pay $60,000 in damages and $500,000 in attorneys' fees. McDermott appealed the ruling. But the case took yet another turn against him in 2007, when the divided D.C. Circuit Court concluded that House rules on confidentiality barred him from disclosing the contents of the tape. The judges ordered payment of the damages to Boehner. McDermott claimed the ruling infringed on his free speech rights and took his case to the Supreme Court, which refused to hear it. In April 2008, a federal judge ordered McDermott to pay Boehner more than $1.2 million in legal fees.

His outspokenness has not hurt McDermott in Seattle, where he has never been reelected with less than 72% of the vote. He considered running against Republican Sen. Slade Gorton in 2000, but backed away soon after he underwent open heart surgery, saying he didn't want to raise the $8 million that would be required. During his 2012 race, he had to deal with headlines about a messy divorce from his second wife. He won that November with 81%.

EIGHTH DISTRICT

Dave Reichert (R)

Elected 2004, 6th term; b. Aug. 29, 1950, Detroit Lakes, MN; Concordia Lutheran Col., A.A. 1970; Lutheran; married (Julie); 3 children. .

Military Career: Air Force Reserve, 1971-76.

Elected Office: King Cnty. sheriff, 1997-2004.

Professional Career: King Cnty. police officer, 1972-97.

DC Office: 1127 LHOB, 20515, 202-225-7761; Fax: 202-225-4282; Website: reichert.house.gov.

State Offices: Issaquah, 425-677-7414; Wenatchee, 509-885-6615.

Committees: *Ways & Means:* Select Revenue Measures (Chmn); Trade.

Group Ratings

	ADA	ACLU	AFL-CIO	LCV	ITI	COC	HAFA	ACU	CFG	FRC
2014	10%	5%	–	14%	100%	100%	38%	56%	29%	88%
2013	5%	C	43%	21%	C	100%	C	48%	52%	C

National Journal Ratings

	2013 LIB	—	2013 CONS
Economic	52%	—	48%
Social	46%	—	53%
Foreign	34%	—	60%
Composite	45%	—	55%

Key Votes of the 113th Congress

1. Sandy storm spending	Y	5. Medical Marijuana	N	9. Syrian Rebels Training	Y
2. Violence Against Women Act	Y	6. Farm Bill	Y	10. Keystone pipeline	Y
3. Guantanamo Bay Detainees	N	7. Afghanistan Combat	N	11. Immigration Exec. Action	Y
4. Abortion 20-week ban	Y	8. NSA Phone Data Collection	N	12. Bipartisan budget deal	Y

Election Results

2014 general	Dave Reichert (R)	125,741	(63%)	$991,617	$2,825	$6,118
	Jason Ritchie (D)	73,003	(37%)	$235,196		
2014 primary	Dave Reichert (R)	53,907	(63%)			
	Jason Ritchie (D)	24,368	(28%)			
	Keith Arnold (D)	7,540	(9%)			

Prior winning percentages: 2012 (60%), 2010 (52%), 2008 (53%), 2006 (51%), 2004 (52%)

Population		Race and Ethnicity		Income	
Total:	701,614	White	76.4%	Median income:	$71,033
Urban:	12.3%	Latino	9.2%		*(60 of 435)*
Suburban:	72.3%	Asian	6.7%	Under $50,000	34.0%
Rural:	15.4%	Black	2.3%	$50,000-$99,999:	32.4%
Land area:	5,335	Two races	3.9%	$100,000-$199,999:	26.2%
Pop/sq. mi.:	131.5	White Ethnic	23.8%	$200,000 or more:	7.3%
Born in state:	52.1%			Poverty Rate	11.4%
		Education			
Age Groups		H.S. grad or less:	35.5%	**Work**	
Under 18:	25.3%	Some college:	32.5%	White collar:	37.4%
18 to 34:	20.1%	College degree, 4 yr.:	21.1%	Blue collar:	39.5%
35 to 64:	42.7%	Post-grad study:	10.9%	Sales and service:	23.1%
Over 64:	11.9%			Govt. workers:	14.6%
		Military			
		Veterans/active duty:	10.1%		

Outer Seattle-Tacoma Suburbs

In the shadow of the majestic 14,410-foot Mount Rainier, Seattle in the last 50 years has spread out to all four points of the compass. In 1960, surrounding King County had 935,000 residents, 557,000 of whom lived in Seattle. Since then, the city has added about 95,000 people, but the county has more

Voter Turnout	
2013 Total Citizen 18+	484,602
2014 House Turnout	198,744
2014 Turnout as % CVAP	41%
2012 Turnout as % CVAP	66.3%

than doubled to 2 million. At first these newcomers moved into places like Bellevue, Redmond and Renton, on the flat lands to the north and west of Cougar Mountain. But as those places have filled in, the metropolitan area expanded out past Lake Sammamish and into the foothills of the Cascades, the valleys between the peaks of the Issaquah Alps, and the southern flatlands of the Puget Trough. Auburn, an old center for hop farming that became a factory town for Boeing in the 1960s, increased its population by one-third since 2000 as a new super mall attracted businesses, jobs, and new residents. Upscale Sammamish, a town of 50,000 that was incorporated just in 1999, was rated "the friendliest town in the United States" by *Forbes* magazine in 2012.

The 8th Congressional District of Washington takes in much of this new frontier in greater Seattle's development, as well as some of its last remaining areas of undeveloped land. It encompasses all of Mount Rainier, as well as one of the nation's last inland old-growth rain forests. Other areas include the southern edge of King County, including Auburn and smaller towns like Algona, Milton and Lakeland North. The district extends into Pierce County, where it includes some of the suburbs around Tacoma, including parts of fast-growing South Hill. And it takes in three agricultural counties that extend east of the Cascades. Kittitas County is a major producer of hay, most of which is shipped overseas, to Japan, South Korea, China and the United Arab Emirates. In Chelan County, growers in May 2015 replaced a camp area with a state-required $6 million facility to

2012 Presidential Vote		
Barack Obama (D)	155,982	(50%)
Mitt Romney (R)	151,069	(48%)
2008 Presidential Vote		
Barack Obama (D)	154,604	(51%)
John McCain (R)	140,634	(47%)
Cook Partisan Voting Index: R+1		

house seasonal workers who pick cherries, apples and pears. About 55% of the district is in King, 20% in Pierce, and the remainder is in or beyond the Cascades.

The 8th had become increasingly Democratic during the 2000s—President Barack Obama won it by 15% in 2008 under the old lines. But that margin reduced to 4% under the newly drawn lines, and the district is now marginal. Obama carried it by 2% in 2012.

Dave Reichert (R)

Dave Reichert, a Republican elected in 2004, is a party loyalist on economic matters but regularly joins Democrats on environmental issues. That approach, along with a seat on the powerful Ways and Means Committee that opened fundraising doors, enabled him to thwart Democratic attempts to unseat him in close contests.

Reichert was born in Detroit Lakes, Minnesota, and his family moved to the Seattle area when he was an infant. He graduated from Concordia Lutheran College in Portland and then joined the Air Force Reserve. He worked for 32 years in the King County sheriff's office and was elected sheriff in 1997. He became a national leader on firearms reduction and methamphetamine prevention. During the riots that hampered the 1999 international trade meeting in Seattle, he criticized city leaders and the police force for inadequate preparation. He gained national attention for capturing Gary Ridgway, the "Green River Killer" who had terrorized the Seattle area with a two-decade murder spree that left 48 women dead. After Ridgway's capture in 2001, Reichert was featured on television shows and in documentaries. He published a book about the experience, *Chasing the Devil: My Twenty-Year Quest to Capture the Green River Killer*.

When the long-time GOP seat opened, Republicans recruited Reichert. He defeated three opponents in the September primary, with 43% of the vote. The Democratic nominee was Dave Ross, a veteran Seattle radio talk show host. In the general election, the national parties spent well over $5 million and organized visits by party leaders. Each candidate tried to portray the other as lacking policy experience and holding views too extreme for the district. Both Seattle newspapers, with strong liberal traditions, endorsed Ross for his greater familiarity with issues and suggested that Reichert was too conservative for the district. Still, Reichert won 52%-47%.

Reichert has been one of the House's most environmentally friendly Republicans, according to the League of Conservation Voters' scorecard. He was among eight Republicans who voted for the 2009 House-passed bill to cap carbon dioxide emissions blamed for global warming. In April 2011, he was the lone Republican to support a Democratic amendment putting the House on record as accepting the scientific view that human beings are a major cause of global warming. He co-sponsored a 2005 bill to designate wilderness in Washington state as off-limits to development, and he opposed oil drilling in Alaska's Arctic National Wildlife Refuge. He later voted with his party to block enforcement by the Environmental Protection Agency of air pollution requirements for many older coal-fired power plants, and to block the Obama administration's oceans management policy. In a February 2015 interview with the *Seattle Times*, Reichert said that Republicans need to "fill the room" with more conservationists in their ranks.

When Reichert arrived in the House, he was rewarded with the chairmanship of the Homeland Security Subcommittee on Emergency Preparedness, making him the only freshman in his class to chair a subcommittee. He won enactment of a bill that established standards for interoperable communications. He later sponsored a successful bill to fund programs that foster intelligence-sharing with state and local governments. In May 2015, following a series of controversial police incidents in cities run by Democrats, he urged Republicans to conduct more oversight of local police departments.

Reichert has opposed President Barack Obama's major economic initiatives, and in 2009 gained a prized seat on Ways and Means. He served as chairman of its Human Resources Subcommittee, which deals with job creation, and took over in 2015 as head of the Select Revenue Measures Subcommittee, which handles tax legislation. In 2012, he advocated an extension of the wind-energy tax credit, which became part of the budget deal to avoid the "fiscal cliff" of automatic spending cuts and tax hikes. In 2011, he joined several Republicans in releasing a committee report critical of AARP's venture into the for-profit insurance business, which was an argument for potential revocation of the giant senior organization's tax-exempt status. His district depends heavily on trade, and he has led Ways and Means Republicans in prodding Obama to move on free-trade agreements.

National Democrats consistently targeted Reichert for reelection, but he has defeated well-financed challengers who had been top managers at Microsoft. In 2006, former Microsoft executive Darcy Burner, the Democratic nominee, dubbed him "Rubber Stamp Reichert" for his support of President George W. Bush. The candidates each spent $3 million, and together, the national parties poured in more than $4 million. In a tough year for Republicans, Reichert won 51%-49%. Two years later, he was the 53%-47% winner of a rematch in which Burner outspent him by more than $1 million. In 2010, his Democratic opponent was Suzan DelBene, who had been a Microsoft executive. She ran a strong campaign in which she outspent him and got substantial national party help, but Reichert again won, 52%-48%. (DelBene won election in 2012 in the open 1st District.) Since then, he has benefited from redistricting that moved his district to conservative areas across the Cascades, and has won with at least 60% of the vote against weaker challengers.

Reichert has fanned local speculation by saying that he was "keeping my option open" to run statewide in 2016. That would require him to relinquish his seniority at Ways and Means in exchange for what likely would be an uphill challenge against either Sen. Patty Murray or Gov. Jay Inslee.

NINTH DISTRICT

Adam Smith (D)

Elected 1996, 10th term; b. June 15, 1965, Washington, D.C.; Fordham U., B.A. 1987, U. of WA, J.D. 1990; Episcopalian; married (Sara); 2 children.

Elected Office: WA Senate, 1990-96.

Professional Career: Practicing atty., 1991-92; City prosecutor, 1993-95.

DC Office: 2264 RHOB, 20515, 202-225-8901; Fax: 202-225-5893; Website: adamsmith.house.gov.

State Offices: Renton, 425-793-5180.

Committees: *Armed Services* (RMM). *Select Benghazi Committee.*

Group Ratings

	ADA	ACLU	AFL-CIO	LCV	ITI	COC	HAFA	ACU	CFG	FRC
2014	80%	83%	–	80%	60%	55%	11%	4%	9%	0%
2013	85%	C	89%	89%	C	46%	C	12%	16%	C

National Journal Ratings

	2013 LIB	—	2013 CONS
Economic	76%	—	24%
Social	87%	—	7%
Foreign	68%	—	32%
Composite	78%	—	22%

Key Votes of the 113th Congress

1. Sandy storm spending	Y	5. Medical Marijuana	Y
2. Violence Against Women Act	Y	6. Farm Bill	N
3. Guantanamo Bay Detainees	Y	7. Afghanistan Combat	N
4. Abortion 20-week ban	N	8. NSA Phone Data Collection	N

9. Syrian Rebels Training	Y
10. Keystone pipeline	NV
11. Immigration Exec. Action	N
12. Bipartisan budget deal	Y

Election Results

2014 general	Adam Smith (D)	118,132	(71%)	$795,120
	Doug Basler (R)	48,662	(29%)	$11,665
2014 primary	Adam Smith (D)	46,251	(63%)	
	Doug Basler (R)	20,674	(28%)	
	Don Rivers (D)	4,190	(6%)	

Prior winning percentages: 2012 (72%), 2010 (55%), 2008 (65%), 2006 (66%), 2004 (63%), 2002 (59%), 2000 (62%), 1998 (65%), 1996 (50%)

Population		Race and Ethnicity		Income	
Total:	705,731	White	49.4%	Median income:	$61,060
Urban:	50.8%	Asian	21.1%		(113 of 435)
Suburban:	49.2%	Latino	12.4%	Under $50,000	41.7%
Rural:	0.0%	Black	10.5%	$50,000-$99,999:	28.3%
Land area:	248	Two races	4.5%	$100,000-$199,999:	22.5%
Pop/sq. mi.:	2,845.2	White Ethnic	17.5%	$200,000 or more:	7.5%
Born in state:	39.0%			Poverty Rate	15.4%
		Education			
Age Groups		H.S. grad or less:	32.5%	**Work**	
Under 18:	22.1%	Some college:	27.6%	White collar:	40.2%
18 to 34:	25.5%	College degree, 4 yr.:	25.0%	Blue collar:	41.6%
35 to 64:	39.5%	Post-grad study:	14.9%	Sales and service:	18.2%
Over 64:	12.9%				
		Military		Govt. workers:	10.3%
		Veterans/active duty:	6.9%		

Southern and Eastern Seattle Metro

The misty shores of Puget Sound have seen some of America's most vibrant economic growth over the past two decades. It has spread south and west from Seattle, over suburban territory to the outskirts of the once-industrial city of Tacoma. The subdivisions along the sound, which have some

Voter Turnout	
2013 Total Citizen 18+	451,201
2014 House Turnout	166,794
2014 Turnout as % CVAP	37%
2012 Turnout as % CVAP	63.5%

of the loveliest views in the U.S., tend to be high-income. But much of greater Seattle's prime industrial territory lies between the ridges that run north and south inland. Weyerhaeuser, the world's largest private owner of softwood timber, is headquartered in Federal Way. Boeing is a major presence in Renton, on the south end of Lake Washington. Boeing's aircraft and electronic components plants have made it the nation's No. 1 exporter for many years. Renton, which gained renown as the home of 1960s guitarist Jimi Hendrix, manufactures 737s, the best-selling commercial jet in history. It has a backlog of 2,700 orders and is increasing production to 52 monthly, the *Seattle Times* reported in April 2015. A host of smaller factories cluster near the rail lines that are the terminus from Minneapolis-St. Paul across the Great Plains to Puget Sound.

The 9th Congressional District of Washington covers much of this area. It includes Sea-Tac Airport and Renton, just south of Seattle, as well as Des Moines, and most of Kent and Federal Way. It includes the container port of Tacoma, though most of the rest of that city is in the 6th District. The district extends northward from the south Seattle suburbs, where it takes in the southeastern neighborhoods of Seattle proper. It also pushes into the eastern suburbs. As the city grew over the years, newcomers crossed the pontoon bridge across Mercer Island to Bellevue and made that area one of the most vibrant parts of metropolitan Seattle; Bellevue's population almost quintupled in the 1960s and then doubled again over the next 40 years, but recently has flattened. It now has a vibrant downtown of its own. Online auction house eBay has its operations there. Plans were underway in 2014 for new office towers and residential high-rises in what today is an "edge city." In October 2014, the long-time rival Seattle and Tacoma ports announced an alliance to compete more effectively, including against nearby British Columbia. Their container cargo made the combined ports the third-largest in the United States, with 48,000 jobs.

2012 Presidential Vote		
Barack Obama (D)	195,863	(68%)
Mitt Romney (R)	84,828	(30%)
2008 Presidential Vote		
Barack Obama (D)	187,672	(68%)
John McCain (R)	81,964	(30%)
Cook Partisan Voting Index:	D+17	

Following redistricting changes that removed most of Pierce County, the 9th takes in much of Seattle's minority population, and is the city's first majority-minority district. It is 22% Asian, 12% Hispanic, 11% African American, and just under 50% non-Hispanic white. The district is no longer competitive. President Barack Obama won each of his elections here by the same 68%-30%.

Adam Smith (D)

Adam Smith, a Democrat first elected in 1996, has been a thoughtful, pro-business moderate who isn't shy about expressing his irritations with both political parties. He is the Armed Services Committee's ranking Democrat, giving his state added clout on defense matters. He was floated as a prospect for secretary of Defense in late 2014.

Smith grew up in the Sea-Tac area. His father, a baggage handler for United Airlines who was active in the Machinists Union, died when Smith was 17. The family went on welfare. Smith worked his way through Fordham University driving trucks for UPS, and got his law degree at the University of Washington. He worked as a Seattle prosecutor, handling drunk-driving and domestic-abuse cases. In 1990, at age 25, he was elected to the state Senate, beating an incumbent Republican by canvassing the district door-to-door.

In 1996, he ran against first-term Republican Rep. Randy Tate. The two had similar backgrounds. They had been born in the same year to families of modest means, were elected to office at a young age, and were firm believers in grassroots campaigning. Tate was a religious conservative and a strong supporter of House Speaker Newt Gingrich, while Smith campaigned as a moderate Democrat, supporting the death penalty and tougher penalties for criminals. He attacked Tate for his support of Gingrich and for backing cuts in Medicare. Tate attacked Smith for his opposition to assigning youthful offenders to adult courts and prisons and for voting for a tax increase in 1993. This was one of the closest races in the country. In the September all-party primary, Smith led 49%-48%. In November, he won 50%-47%.

In the House, Smith joined the New Democrat Coalition, established a moderate voting record, and showed a willingness to take on established interests in his party. He voted to authorize military action in Iraq and sought to improve compensation and other quality-of-life benefits for military personnel. In 2004, he was one of four Democrats who opposed a provision in the USA Patriot Act to bar law enforcement access to library and bookstore records. He joined Republicans in 2011 in voting to extend several key expiring provisions of the anti-terrorism law. He supported the House-passed health care overhaul in 2009, but remained neutral on the final version until the very end in March 2010, finally agreeing to back it after pleas from President Barack Obama and others. In 2012, he lamented "the hyper-partisanship that is making Congress so dysfunctional." In opposing the New Year's Day 2013 tax and spending deal to avoid the so-called fiscal cliff, he accused Obama of "bad math" and of being unrealistic. "His insistence that we only tax the rich has put us in a box," he told *The Seattle Times.* In June 2015, Smith cited problems for workers and the environment when he voted against giving trade promotion authority to Obama, a switch in his customary free-trade view.

On the Armed Services Committee, Smith rose quickly and earned praise for his work as chairman of two of its subcommittees. He served on the Intelligence Committee, further bolstering his credentials on military and foreign affairs issues. When Armed Services Chairman Ike Skelton lost his reelection bid in 2010, Smith jumped into the race to succeed the Missourian as the senior Democrat on the panel. Intelligence Committee Chairman Silvestre Reyes of Texas was the early favorite for the job, and California Rep. Loretta Sanchez also got into the race. When the House Democratic Caucus voted, Sanchez and Smith tied at 64 votes apiece, while Reyes got 53. In the two-person runoff, Smith won by 11 votes.

He joined efforts to help the military adapt to automatic spending cuts that took effect in 2013 after Obama and Congress failed to reach a budget accord. He introduced a bill calling for spending reductions to be split about evenly between defense and domestic spending programs. Republican Rep. Mac Thornberry of Texas, who took over in 2015 as Armed Services' chairman, said that Smith has helped make the committee less partisan. Ironically, Smith for the first time voted in May 2015 against passage of the defense spending bill, and called it "extremely damaging" to national security because it did not remove the budgetary spending caps and shifted some funding off-budget.

Smith has generally supported the Obama administration's defense and foreign policies, telling *The New York Times* in May 2012 that they were "pragmatic and practical." He occasionally appears on Fox News to try to refute its conservative hosts, and in 2014 was appointed to the select committee investigating the terrorist attacks at U.S. facilities in Benghazi, Libya. "This is a committee that should not have been formed," he said when it was unveiled. "But since the Republicans chose to form it, I think we have to participate to do our best to bring out the correct arguments." Earlier, he said Obama "could have done a better job" in working with Congress before taking military action against Libya in March 2011 as part of a NATO coalition, but he backed the president's strategy. When Chuck Hagel stepped down as Defense secretary in November 2014, Smith was mentioned as a possible successor. "I'm open to it, but I don't anticipate being asked," he told a broadcast interviewer in Seattle. "It would be a difficult decision." Evidently, he was not forced to choose.

As concerns rose over the influence of the Islamic State, he dismissed conservative hawks' calls for swift military action against the terrorist group, saying that the administration needed time to build coalitions. "We need reliable partners to work with in the region," Smith told CBS News. "We can't simply bomb first and ask questions later." But he joined Republicans in urging the administration to better outline its approach. "I think too often the president does sound like he's in the ... camp that 'we don't want to do this because we know it's hard and we know you [the public] don't like it,'" he said. He subsequently said that a formal request to involve the military—known as an Authorization for Use of Military Force (AUMF)—should be sharply limited in how much power it gave to the president. "I would support a more limited version and if in a few years from now, new situations emerge Congress can pass it again," he said. "I don't think we should give the executive a blank check."

Smith's independence has worked well for him at home, and he has won reelection easily. In 2008, he chaired Obama's presidential campaign in Washington state. His closest contest was a 55%-45% win over Pierce County Council member Dick Muri during the Republican wave in 2010. Redistricting changes then removed much of what had been his base in Pierce County and gave him a King County-based district that was ethnically diverse and almost three-fifths new to him, but more safely Democratic.

TENTH DISTRICT

Denny Heck (D)

Elected 2012, 2nd term; b. July 29, 1952, Vancouver; Evergreen St. Col., B.A. 1973; Lutheran; married (Paula); 2 children. .

Elected Office: WA House, 1976-86.

Professional Career: Chief of staff, Gov. Booth Gardner, 1989-93; Co-founder & CEO, TVW, 1993-2003; Co-founder, bd. member, Intrepid Learning Solutions, 1999-2012.

DC Office: 425 CHOB, 20515, 202-225-9740; Fax: 202-225-0129; Website: dennyheck.house.gov.

State Offices: Lacey, 360-459-8514; Tacoma, 253-722-5860.

Committees: *Financial Services:* Financial Institutions & Consumer Credit; Monetary Policy & Trade; Oversight & Investigations.

Group Ratings

	ADA	ACLU	AFL-CIO	LCV	ITI	COC	HAFA	ACU	CFG	FRC
2014	80%	77%	–	94%	100%	38%	15%	4%	6%	0%
2013	60%	C	90%	96%	C	62%	C	12%	16%	C

National Journal Ratings

	2013 LIB	—	2013 CONS
Economic	68%	—	32%
Social	61%	—	38%
Foreign	81%	—	18%
Composite	70%	—	30%

Key Votes of the 113th Congress

1. Sandy storm spending	Y	5. Medical Marijuana	Y	9. Syrian Rebels Training	Y
2. Violence Against Women Act	Y	6. Farm Bill	Y	10. Keystone pipeline	N
3. Guantanamo Bay Detainees	Y	7. Afghanistan Combat	Y	11. Immigration Exec. Action	N
4. Abortion 20-week ban	N	8. NSA Phone Data Collection	N	12. Bipartisan budget deal	Y

Election Results

2014 general	Denny Heck (D)	99,279	(55%)	$1,705,018	$6,426
	Joyce McDonald (R)	82,213	(45%)	$87,818	$5,298
2014 primary	Denny Heck (D)	39,866	(51%)		
	Joyce McDonald (R)	32,119	(41%)		
	Jennifer Ferguson (I)	3,730	(5%)		

Population		Race and Ethnicity		Income	
Total:	701,194	White	69.8%	Median income:	$54,735
Urban:	50.0%	Latino	10.5%		(169 of 435)
Suburban:	46.0%	Asian	6.3%	Under $50,000	44.5%
Rural:	4.0%	Black	5.2%	$50,000-$99,999:	34.4%
Land area:	1,258	Two races	5.5%	$100,000-$199,999:	18.2%
Pop/sq. mi.:	557.5	White Ethnic	23.6%	$200,000 or more:	3.0%
Born in state:	46.4%			Poverty Rate	14.8%
		Education			
Age Groups		H.S. grad or less:	35.8%	**Work**	
Under 18:	24.4%	Some college:	38.0%	White collar:	33.4%
18 to 34:	25.3%	College degree, 4 yr.:	16.8%	Blue collar:	44.3%
35 to 64:	37.7%	Post-grad study:	9.4%	Sales and service:	22.2%
Over 64:	12.7%				
		Military		Govt. workers:	25.2%
		Veterans/active duty:	18.6%		

Southwest Washington: Tacoma Metro, Olympia

Beginning at Deception Pass, near present-day Mount Vernon and Anacortes, Puget Sound winds its way southward from the Strait of Juan de Fuca for over 100 miles, through an intricate latticework of bays, straits and islands. At the far southern end of the sound, off of Budd Inlet, is Olympia, the capital of Washington. In 1846, two New England natives, Lathrop Smith and Edmund Sylvester, hoping to take advantage of the location near the end of the Cowlitz Trail, platted a town in the New England style: a town square, carefully planned streets, and land reserved for schools. They initially opted to name the town Smithster—a portmanteau of their surnames—but eventually opted for Olympia, after the mountains that are visible to the north on a clear day. It soon thereafter became the capital of Washington territory. As late as 1880, Olympia's population rivaled that of other major Washington cities. But the railroads passed it by, and other ports were developed in more advantageous positions closer to the mouth of Puget Sound. Olympia grew at a relatively slow but steady pace, sustained mostly by the lumber industry and state government.

Voter Turnout	
2013 Total Citizen 18+	496,414
2014 House Turnout	181,492
2014 Turnout as % CVAP	36.6%
2012 Turnout as % CVAP	59.2%

Today, the lumber industry is in decline in Olympia; the Simpson, Georgia Pacific, and St. Regis mills are all long closed. Olympia is a relatively small city, with an economy that revolves mostly around government. This recently proved to be a boon; compared to other Washington cities, it was less affected by the recession and its unemployment rate stayed relatively low. The city is trying to diversify into tourism and as a potential hub for hydraulic fracturing, known as "fracking," a technique for extracting oil and natural gas. In 2014, environmentalists protested shipments through the Olympia port of materials for fracking. Under renovation is the waterfront park of Percival Landing, which features a mile-long boardwalk, restaurants, and piers for boats. Since 2000, Thurston County has grown by 26%, twice the rate of Olympia; nearby Lacey has been fast-growing and is almost as large as Olympia.

2012 Presidential Vote		
Barack Obama (D)	164,505	(56%)
Mitt Romney (R)	120,066	(41%)
2008 Presidential Vote		
Barack Obama (D)	163,612	(57%)
John McCain (R)	117,348	(41%)
Cook Partisan Voting Index:	D+5	

The 10th Congressional District centers around Olympia-based Thurston County and Tacoma-based Pierce County. A small fraction lives in Mason County, to the northwest. That county takes in the town of Shelton, where a local lumber mill with 270 employees announced in April 2015 that it was shutting down. Sierra Pacific also planned to shut down two other nearby mills and build a state-of-the-art facility along the waterfront in Shelton. A bit more than half of the population is in Pierce and 40% in Thurston. Politically, the district leans comfortably toward Democrats. President Barack Obama won with 56% in 2012.

Denny Heck (D)

Democrat Denny Heck's path to Congress was much easier in 2012 than in 2010, when he lost a tough race in a nearby marginal district to Jaime Herrera Beutler, a rising star in the Republican Party. The second time around, Heck ran in the new, more Democratic-friendly and Olympia-based 10th District. He has had a long and diverse career in politics and business.

Heck had a working-class upbringing in Vancouver. His father was a truck driver, and Heck began working at a nearby strawberry farm at age 9. After graduating from Evergreen State College, he applied for a position as an assistant to a school district superintendent. At the school board meeting where Heck was officially hired, he met his wife, Paula, who was monitoring the meeting as a local union representative. In 1976, he was elected to the state House, where he became an author of the state's Basic Education Act and its funding formula. He became House majority leader before retiring in 1986 at age 34. Two years later, he became chief of staff to Democratic Gov. Booth Gardner.

In the 1990s, Heck cofounded TVW, a statewide public affairs network modeled after C-SPAN. He hosted a public-affairs program and won an Emmy for a documentary that he produced. Soon afterward, one of TVW's board members, Rob Glaser, created RealNetworks, an early audio and video Internet service. Glaser convinced Heck to invest in RealNetworks, which pioneered streaming video. "He said, 'Do you want to get in on this idea I've got for a software that pushes audio and video over the Internet?' And my question was, 'What's the Internet?' I mean, this was really early," Heck recalled. Later, Heck cofounded an education and worker training company called Intrepid Learning Solutions.

By 2010, Heck hadn't worked in politics in years. He entered the race for the open 3rd District, which had been Democratic-held. Heck had a cash advantage over Herrera Beutler, raising almost $2 million to her $1.5 million. She criticized Heck for his support of President Barack Obama's health care overhaul and $787 billion economic stimulus bill. Heck ran as a moderate Democrat and emphasized his experience in business creating jobs. Herrera Beutler ran on a campaign of "fiscal sanity," a message that resonated that year, and won, 53%-47%.

Not discouraged, Heck had another opportunity when Washington in 2012 gained a new district in more favorable territory. In the all-party primary with six candidates, he led Republican Dick Muri 40%-28%. As a veteran of the 1991 Gulf War and a retired Air Force lieutenant colonel, Muri's military experience was a strong selling point in a district that includes Joint Base Lewis-McChord. Muri called for a constitutional amendment to balance the budget and signed anti-tax activist Grover Norquist's pledge never to raise taxes. Heck called for phasing out tax breaks for households earning more than $250,000 a year, but he also pushed for a lower estate-tax rate. He outspent Muri nearly 8-to-1 in the campaign, and national funding groups showed little interest. Heck met expectations for the new district and won, 59%-41%. He ran more strongly in Thurston with 63% than in Pierce, where he got 55%.

In the House, he gained a seat on the Financial Services Committee and found some areas of bipartisan cooperation. With Republican Rep. Robert Pittenger of North Carolina, Heck moved legislation that gave small businesses a formal advisory role at the Consumer Financial Protection Bureau. Heck opposed other changes to the 2010 Dodd-Frank law that he contended were designed to undermine its banking regulatory reforms. He was an outspoken advocate for extending the authority of the Export-Import Bank of the United States. He worked with Republican Rep. Bradley Byrne of Alabama to re-launch the Congressional Singapore Caucus to encourage bilateral relations. But Heck opposed legislation to provide trade promotion authority to Obama because, he said, prospective trade deals would not do enough to protect workers or the environment.

At home, he under-performed in the 2014 election against Joyce McDonald, a former member of the Pierce County Council. The two candidates agreed on limiting cuts at Joint Base Lewis-McChord, whose future was a major local concern. McDonald, a native of Scotland who became a naturalized citizens and served in the state House, called for tighter limits on federal spending. She spent only $88,000, while Heck spent $1.7 million. But McDonald held him to a 55%-45% win. The two candidates were less than 400 votes apart in Pierce, but Heck took 60% of the vote in his base of Thurston.

★ WEST VIRGINIA ★

"**A**lmost heaven"—that's what the song says about West Virginia. And there's something to it, at least in the minds of West Virginians who have never lost their affection for the hills and mountains that make this the most unhorizontal state in the nation. The late Sen. Robert Byrd, working in a shipyard in Baltimore in 1944, once painted a landscape of the mountains. (Lithographs of it sometimes appear on eBay.) But West Virginia has had more than its share of tragedy and heartbreak. It was first settled by Scots-Irish immigrants, fresh from internecine fighting in the British Isles and determined to stake out comfortable homesteads. The state slogan is *Montani semper liberi:* Mountaineers are always free. West Virginia was created as a separate state during the Civil War, when a Republican Congress recognized that 55 mountain counties with few slaves had seceded from Virginia and admitted them to the Union in 1863. It has made a living most of the years since from that cruelest of minerals, coal. The state flag features a farmer and a coal miner, and the state's hills and mountains are laced with coal. There are coal seams in 53 of its 55 counties, and today, even after many mines have closed, production continues in 28 counties. Coal kept the sons of large mountaineer families here for much of the 20th century, men who would otherwise have left for big cities. Coal brought immigrants from odd corners of Europe. But more people came from adjacent areas of the South, where the local farming economies were stagnant as West Virginia's coal economy was booming. In the mid-20th century, the availability of coal and local rock salt and brines led to the building of chemical plants in the Kanawha Valley around Charleston. Steel mills and glass factories were established in the Panhandle and in the Monongahela River valley south of Pittsburgh. An ugly reminder of these industrial operations came in 2014, when 10,000 gallons of a toxic chemical smelling like licorice spilled into the Elk River, leaving 300,000 people temporarily without water.

But resource extraction has not produced a steady or reliable economy. Demand for coal skyrocketed during World War II, and just after the war, West Virginia coal production peaked at 179 million tons a year, coal mine jobs peaked at 125,000, and the state's population peaked at 2 million in the 1950 census. But demand for coal plunged as houses switched to oil heat. Mechanization, especially in strip mines, reduced the demand for labor. West Virginia had about 50,000 coal mining jobs in the 1960s and early 1970s, and just 22,000 in 2012. The United Mine Workers' membership has declined even more: Its rolls included 90% of the state's miners when it staged a black lung strike in 1969 but only 32% in 2012. West Virginia University's Bureau of Business and Economic Research projects that coal production will drop by 29% by 2035. Still, coal remains a major industry and it's still big for generating electricity. Coal also provides solid wages, with the average West Virginia coal miner making $68,000 a year. And while the coal industry is threatened by competition from cheap natural gas, West Virginia has some of that, too, in the Marcellus Shale Formation under some of the state's northern counties.

The decline of coal mining jobs has meant that West Virginia has a stagnating population, wobbling up and down beneath the 1950 peak, with an estimated 1.85 million in 2014. Of the state's 55 counties, 38 had fewer people in 2010 than they did in 1950, and West Virginia was one of just six states to lose population between 2013 and 2014. There have been population increases recently in the Eastern Panhandle, now a long-distance suburb of Washington, D.C.; in Morgantown, home of WVU; and in several Ohio River counties below Charleston and around Parkersburg. Out-migration is much lower than it was in the 1960s or 1980s, but it nonetheless has left West Virginia with an elderly population—it has the second-highest percentage of residents 65 and older of any state. It ranks near the bottom of states in household income, while ranking high in diabetes and disability payments. West Virginia ranks dead last in the percentage of residents with a bachelor's degree. It has attracted few immigrants since the 1920s, and its population is only 3% African-American and 1% Hispanic. West Virginians who remained have a strong attachment to this unique state, where the accent sounds Southern and the early 20th century factories and houses look Northern, where the landscape is rural and the economy is industrial.

Mining for natural gas through hydraulic fracturing and horizontal drilling in the Marcellus Shale that underlies most of West Virginia could create 20,000 jobs in the state by 2015. Forest products are replacing coal in rural counties, while the health care and telemarketing industries are growing. In 2010, Macy's announced it would build a new distribution

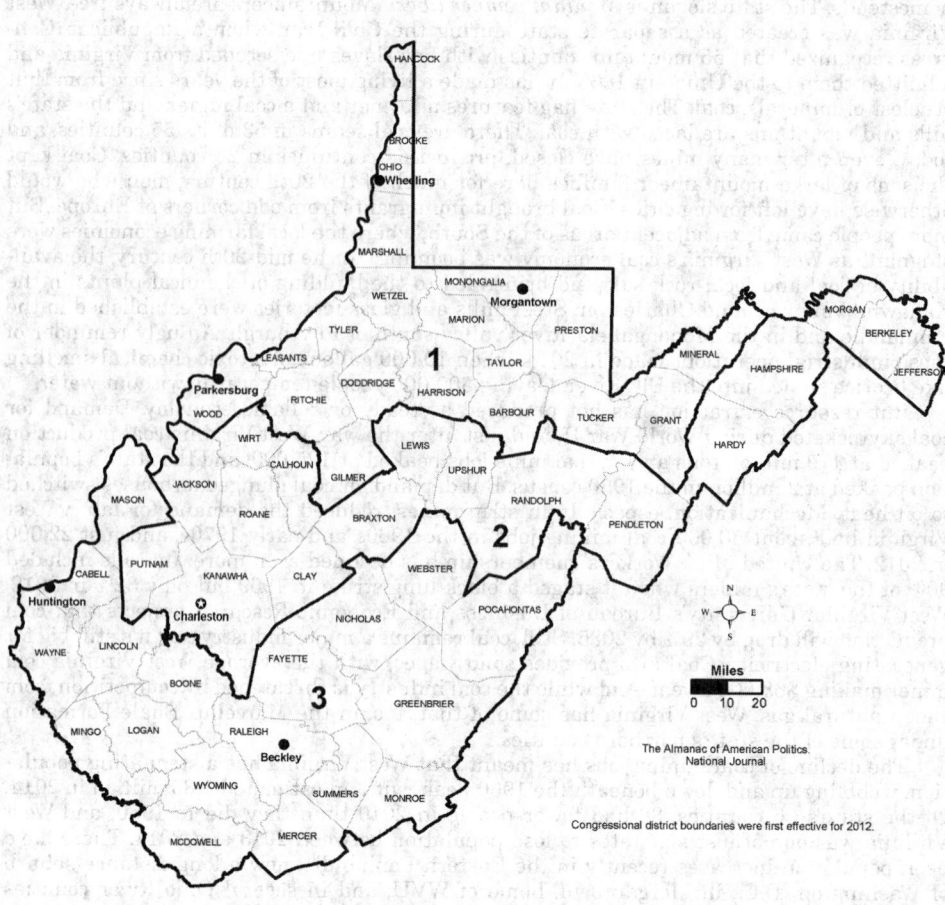

The Almanac of American Politics.
National Journal

Congressional district boundaries were first effective for 2012.

center for online sales in Martinsburg in the Eastern Panhandle, while Walmart, the state's largest private employer, broke ground on its 38th store in the state. The Boy Scouts of America chose a site in the Glen Jean-Mount Hope area of Fayette County to hold their Boy Scouts Jamboree every four years. And between 2000 and 2012, exports rose from 5.4% of the state's GDP to 16.3%. Still, government has inevitably played a role. During his 50 years on the Senate Appropriations Committee, Byrd exceeded his goal of steering $1 billion of federal projects into the state, such as the FBI's biggest division, with 2,600 workers plus contractors, in Clarksburg, W.Va.

Between 2013 and 2014, West Virginia's GDP grew 5.1%, but if you subtract mining, GDP actually shrank. During the recession, West Virginia's unemployment peaked at 8.8%, which was below the national average—but by mid-2015, it had fallen only to 7.2%, a point and a half above the national average. That was a far cry from the state's pre-recession low of 4.1%. Meanwhile, incomes ranked in the bottom five states from 2011 to 2013, and more than a quarter of personal income in the state comes from government transfer payments, according to the U.S. Agriculture Department's Economic Research Service. Almost one of every five residents receives food stamps.

West Virginia's political heritage from the Civil War days was Republican, though some counties tilted toward the Confederacy and the Democrats. The United Mine Workers organized most of the West Virginia mines by 1902, and there were bloody strikes in 1912-13 and 1920-21. Under the UMW's John L. Lewis, the coal country shifted toward the New Deal Democrats, and West Virginia for more than half a century was one of the most Democratic states, deserting the national ticket only in Republican landslide years (1956, 1972, 1984). But in the 21st century, it has swung to the Republicans. One reason has been the national party leaders' attitudes toward coal. In the 2000 presidential race, George W. Bush's strategist Karl Rove ignored precedent and targeted West Virginia, smartly calculating that Bush's support for mountaintop mining and his opposition to gun control could make the state winnable for a Republican. In office, Bush continued to push Congress to spend billions of dollars on clean coal technology and backed import quotas to help the steel industry, still a major coal user. That helped Bush and John McCain carry the state by almost identical margins in 2004 and 2008.

After Barack Obama took office, the Environmental Protection Agency revoked a 2007 permit issued to Arch Coal for mountaintop mining in Logan County—the first time such a permit had been denied under clean water rules. Democratic Gov. Joe Manchin sued to overturn federal rules on mountaintop mining in October 2010, when he was running in the special election to fill Byrd's Senate seat. An ad that helped him clinch the election showed Manchin taking aim with a rifle and shooting a hole in a copy of the cap-and-trade energy bill that Democrats passed in the House in June 2009. Manchin won 53%-43% over self-financing Republican John Raese. In 2012, West Virginians' anger at Obama administration policies was apparent in the May presidential primary, in which 41% of registered Democrats voted for a convict instead of the president, and in the general election, in which Mitt Romney won the state 62%-36% and carried all 55 counties. For many years, West Virginians stuck with the political party representing local Civil War loyalties; it was considered remarkable when Byrd became the first statewide candidate to carry every county. But culture and coal have evidently trumped the Civil War if a candidate as little attuned to

Population		Race and Ethnicity		Income	
Total:	1,854,304	White	93.1%	Median income:	$40,241
Urban:	29.9%	Black	3.0%		(48 of 50)
Suburban:	22.6%	Latino	1.1%	Under $50,000	58.3%
Rural:	47.4%	Asian	0.6%	$50,000-$99,999:	28.0%
Land area:	24,038	Two races	2.0%	$100,000-$199,999:	11.6%
Pop/sq. mi.:	77.1	White Ethnic	25.2%	$200,000 or more:	2.1%
Born in state:	70.0%			Poverty Rate	15.4%
		Education			
Age Groups		H.S. grad or less:	55.6%	**Work**	
Under 18:	20.6%	Some college:	25.4%	White collar:	30.9%
18 to 34:	21.1%	College degree, 4 yr.:	11.3%	Blue collar:	43.3%
35 to 64:	41.0%	Post-grad study:	7.6%	Sales and service:	25.8%
Over 64:	17.3%				
		Military		Govt. workers:	19.0%
		Veterans/active duty:	10.0%		

West Virginia culture as Romney can sweep the Mountain State.

The 2014 election was a watershed. The legislature had been Democratic since the 1930s, but in 2014, the GOP won control of the state House, and ultimately the state Senate, after a post-election party switch. Also in 2014, Republicans won all of the state's House seats for the first time

Voter Turnout	
2013 Total Citizen 18+	1,461,521
2014 Highest Statewide Turnout	451,498
2014 Turnout as % CVAP	30.9%
2012 Turnout as % CVAP	45.9%

Legislature		
Senate:	18R	16D
House:	64R	36D

since 1921, and they flipped the seat held by five-term Democratic Sen. John (Jay) Rockefeller. Despite the state's longstanding reliance on the federal government, West Virginia "has become an extreme example of the hostility that shows up in every national poll when people are asked how they feel about the federal government," Karen Tumulty wrote in the *Washington Post*. "Many here now speak of Washington as an enemy that threatens their economy and their way of life, that traps them into dependency."

Presidential Politics West Virginia has voted Republican in the last four presidential elections. This can be explained by two factors: culture and coal. West Virginians tend to be more religious and tradition-minded than Americans generally, more supportive of gun ownership, and more skeptical of environmental regulation that affects the economy. At a time when national Democrats are bent on reducing carbon emissions to address climate change, West Virginia has an economy that is growing enough to sustain an aging population and that depends heavily on coal. Political reporters were puzzled when Republican candidate George W. Bush targeted West Virginia in his 2000 campaign.

2012 Presidential Vote		
Mitt Romney (R)	417,655	(62%)
Barack Obama (D)	238,269	(36%)

2012 Presidential Primary		
Barack Obama (D)	106,770	(59%)
Keith Judd (D)	73,138	(41%)

2012 Presidential Primary		
Mitt Romney (R)	78,197	(70%)
Rick Santorum (R)	13,590	(12%)
Ron Paul (R)	12,412	(11%)
Newt Gingrich (R)	7,076	(6%)

2008 Presidential Vote		
John McCain (R)	397,466	(56%)
Barack Obama (D)	303,857	(43%)

Between 1928 and 2000, the only Republican nominees it voted for were incumbents headed for landslide victories—Dwight Eisenhower in 1956, Richard Nixon in 1972, and Ronald Reagan in 1984. But Bush's support of mountaintop mining and his promotion of clean coal technology enabled him to beat Al Gore 52%-46% in 2000 and John Kerry 56%-43% in 2004. It also helped that about half of West Virginia voters were white evangelical Protestants and about 70% were gun owners. Its five electoral votes were crucial for Bush in 2000: Without them, it would not have mattered who won Florida.

In 2008, the result in West Virginia was not in doubt once Barack Obama clinched the Democratic nomination. Obama visited the state only twice during the primary season and not at all after his nomination. General election turnout in West Virginia was 715,000, down 6% from 2004. John McCain beat Obama 56%-43%, carrying 48 of 55 counties. McCain ran well ahead of Bush four years earlier in the southern coal counties and behind in the fast-growing Eastern Panhandle, part of which is now officially part of the Washington, D.C., metro area. McCain carried both the young and the elderly and ran best among voters 30 to 44 years old. Obama carried union members by only 54%-43% and lost white evangelical Protestants 66%-32%. Among those who voted for Hillary Clinton in the primary, 32% voted for McCain, one of the largest defection rates in the country. In 2012, the coal country swung even more heavily Republican. Mitt Romney carried the state 62%-36%, winning all 55 counties—the first nominee of either party to do so since the Civil War.

West Virginia's presidential primary, held in May, has not attracted much attention since 1960, when John Kennedy took on Hubert Humphrey and beat him with 61% of the vote, proving that a Catholic could carry a virtually all-Protestant state. For 2008, West Virginia Republicans chose delegates in a party convention on February 5, Super Tuesday. Thanks to some last-minute switches by McCain supporters, Mike Huckabee won 52%-47% over Romney. Republicans also voted in the May 13 primary, two months after Huckabee's withdrawal. McCain got 76% of the vote. In 2012, the Republican race was over by the time West Virginia voted. Mitt Romney won 70%, Rick Santorum captured 12% and Ron Paul took 11%.

The 2008 Democratic contest was not an epic battle as in 1960, but it was hard fought nonetheless by Hillary Clinton, with Bill Clinton campaigning extensively in the state and hoping for a win that would provide her with a significant delegate edge. Turnout was a robust 356,000, well above the levels in the three previous primaries. Clinton won 67%-26%, her biggest victory except for Arkansas, carrying every county. The results were close only in Jefferson County, in the far end of the Eastern Panhandle. In 2012, Obama won the West Virginia primary, but Keith Judd, a serial presidential candidate who at the time of the primary was incarcerated at the Federal Correctional Institution in Texarkana, Texas, serving a 210-month sentence for extortion, received 41% of the vote and carried 10 counties.

Congressional Districts West Virginia elected six members of the House in 1960 but only three in 1992, and may be on the cusp of losing another district in the 2020 reapportionment. As recently as 1998, the state elected three Democrats. With increasing voter hostility to the national party, Republicans

114th Congress Lineup	
3 R	0 D
113th Congress Lineup	
2 R	1 D

took two of those seats by 2010. That year, Democrat Nick Rahall, who had held the southern 3rd District since 1976, won with just 56%. Still, Democrats held onto the governorship and both houses of the legislature, and with them, control over redistricting.

Beltway Democratic strategists pressured West Virginia's legislators to be aggressive. In early August 2011, Democratic state Sen. John Unger unveiled a proposal to keep Rahall's district untouched but run the 1st and 2nd districts north-south rather than east-west, in effect pairing Shelley Moore Capito and David McKinley and creating an open Eastern Panhandle seat. Furious Republicans pointed out that moving Mason County, population 27,324, from the 2nd District to the 3rd District was all that was needed to equalize seats. And the Unger plan earned tepid reception from Democrats, too: Some were fearful that rocking the boat would prompt Capito to run for governor or Senate; others didn't see the need to satisfy their party's Washington, D.C., leaders.

So a few days later, the legislature passed and Democratic Gov. Earl Ray Tomblin signed the "Mason County flip" into law. In November, commissioners in the Eastern Panhandle's Jefferson County voted to challenge it in federal court, arguing the elongated 2nd District violated compactness standards, diluted the Panhandle's influence, and resulted in the largest population deviation between districts in the country—4,871 people. In September 2012, the Supreme Court ruled the deviation was permissible to attain the goal of keeping counties whole. Redistricting notwithstanding, Rahall lost reelection in 2014. Nothing could save him from the unpopularity of the Democratic brand.

Governor

Earl Ray Tomblin (D)

Assumed office Nov. 2010, term expires Jan. 2017, 1st full term; b. March 15, 1952, Chapmanville; WV U., B.S. 1974, Marshall U., M.B.A. 1975; Presbyterian; married (Joanne); 1 child.

Elected Office: WV House, 1974-80; WV Senate, 1980-2011, pres., 1995-2011.

Professional Career: Restaurant owner; Farmer.

Office: State Capitol, 1900 Kanawha Blvd. East, Charleston, 25305, 304-558-2000; Website: governor.wv.gov.

Election Results

2012 general	Earl Ray Tomblin (D)	335,468	(50%)
	Bill Maloney (R)	303,291	(46%)
	Jesse Johnson (G)	16,791	(3%)
2012 primary	Earl Ray Tomblin (D)	170,481	(84%)
	Arne Moltis (D)	31,587	(16%)

Prior winning percentage: 2011 special (50%)

West Virginia's governor is Earl Ray Tomblin, a culturally conservative Democrat who assumed office on Nov. 15, 2010. The former president of the state Senate, Tomblin succeeded Democrat Joe Manchin, who stepped down as governor to run successfully for the late Sen. Robert Byrd's seat in the U.S. Senate. Tomblin won an October 2011 special election to serve the remaining year of Manchin's unexpired term and 13 months later won a four-year term of his own. Like many other West Virginia Democrats, he opposes abortion rights and disdains many of the national Democratic Party's other priorities.

Tomblin was born in Logan County, in southwestern West Virginia's coal country. His parents ran a restaurant in Chapmanville, and he bussed tables there in addition to selling eggs and rabbits and mowing lawns for income. He attended West Virginia University and ran for the state House of Delegates as a college senior, winning election in 1974 at age 22. He served until 1980, when he was elected to the state Senate. He became the Senate's president in January 1995 after chairing its Finance Committee.

When Byrd died in June 2010 after a 51-year career, Manchin, who had easily been reelected to a second term as governor in 2008, declined to appoint himself as Byrd's successor. Instead, the governor named his legal adviser, Carte Goodwin, to the job in a caretaker capacity, and then announced his candidacy four days later. Manchin beat Republican John Raese in the general election that November, and under state law, Tomblin was next in line of succession. But Manchin's vacancy as the state's chief executive immediately raised a series of legal questions. He ruled out the possibility of calling a special legislative session to resolve the issue of succession because he said there was no consensus among state officials about whether one was needed. Tomblin contended that he could serve in the job until the next general election in 2012. The matter went to the state Supreme Court, which issued a unanimous opinion in January 2011 that said the state constitution never intended for an acting governor to serve more than one year without an election.

A primary election was scheduled for May 2011. Tomblin campaigned on his experience as a lawmaker and stressed his ability to work with members of both parties. He promised to promote the state to attract large corporations while keeping taxes low and improving the state's schools. Tomblin took 40% of the vote against five Democratic opponents, including Secretary of State Natalie Tennant, State Treasurer John Perdue, and state House Speaker Rick Thompson. Tomblin's victory set up a general election matchup with Morgantown GOP businessman Bill Maloney. Maloney sought to nationalize the race, tying Tomblin to President Barack Obama, who is deeply unpopular in most of the state. The strategy appeared to work, as Maloney climbed in the polls. Outside Republican groups poured millions into the race. The Republican Governors Association ran an ad in late September attacking Tomblin for implementing the Obama administration's 2010 health care reform law and not challenging it in court. Tomblin did keep his distance from Obama, and would not even commit to voting for him in the 2012 presidential race. Endorsements from the National Rifle Association and the West Virginia Coal Association made it difficult to characterize him as an Obama-style Democrat, and in the end he narrowly defeated Maloney, 50%-47%.

In contrast to the Republican-led states that targeted public employees, such as Wisconsin, Michigan, and Ohio, Tomblin during the 2011 legislative session agreed to a $67 million pay raise—about a 2% increase—for teachers, judicial officers, and other state employees. Initially left unresolved was whether to increase regulation of drilling in the Marcellus Shale gas wells in the state. A special legislative session was called in November 2011, and Tomblin eventually signed a regulatory bill that included higher permitting fees, buffer zones around wells, and advance notice to property owners near drilling sites. Although the governor called the measure "a milestone piece of legislation," environmentalists and property owners' groups complained that it watered down regulations that had been developed by a House-Senate select committee.

Maloney returned for another challenge in 2012. As he did in the special election, Tomblin touted the progress the state had made in improving its finances by balancing the budget, adding to the rainy day fund, and seeing improvement in the state's credit rating. He also noted that he had made good on his promise to eliminate the sales tax on food, which was cut in half in 2012 and would be eliminated entirely in 2013. Maloney again tried to link Tomblin to Obama, running ads that constantly mentioned the president. The governor maintained a steady lead in fundraising and picked up most of the state's newspaper endorsements, though the *Charleston Gazette* damned with faint praise, saying Maloney "is so unpalatable that we have no choice but to back Tomblin." The governor won a close race again, 50%-46%.

In February 2013, after months of remaining mum on the subject, Tomblin agreed to establish a federal-state partnership as part of the insurance exchanges created under Obama's health care law. Then, in May, he approved an expansion of Medicaid under the health care law. In the first year under the law, enrollment outpaced the state's initial projections—130,000 new signups, well beyond the expected 63,000. The state also took part in a voluntary federal program to automatically sign up food stamp recipients for the Medicaid expansion if they responded to a letter.

In January 2014, the state faced a major disaster—10,000 gallons of a toxic chemical used for coal washing that smelled like licorice spilled from a ruptured storage tank into the Elk River, only a mile and a half from a water treatment plant. The spill left 300,000 people in and around the capital of Charleston without water for drinking, brushing teeth and even showering. Several executives of the company, Freedom Industries, eventually faced criminal charges, and the company, which had allegedly ignored advance warnings about the risk of an accident, filed for bankruptcy. Tomblin signed legislation that placed tighter regulations on the chemical industry and raised safety standards for water utilities. On the personal front, Tomblin's brother Carl pleaded guilty to selling prescription painkillers to support his own addiction; he was sentenced to eight months of home confinement and three years of probation.

In 2015, Tomblin vetoed two conservative bills from the newly Republican legislature that he said went too far. Two years earlier, Tomblin had cheered the NRA by signing a pair of pro-gun laws, but in 2015 he vetoed a measure that would have allowed concealed carry without a permit or safety training. "Throughout my career, I have strongly supported the Second Amendment, as demonstrated by my repeated endorsements and high grades from the National Rifle Association," Tomblin said in a statement. "However, I must also be responsive to the apprehension of law enforcement officers from across the state, who have concerns about the bill as it relates to the safety of their fellow officers." Meanwhile, the legislature overrode Tomblin's veto of a measure to ban abortions after 20 weeks, even in cases of rape and incest.

Tomblin faces a gubernatorial term limit in 2016, and some have speculated that he might run for the House against first-year GOP Rep. Evan Jenkins. But the district, like the state, increasingly leans Republican, so neither a bid nor a victory would be assured.

Senior Senator

Joe Manchin (D)

Elected Nov. 2010, term expires Jan. 2019, 1st full term; b. Aug. 24, 1947, Farmington; WV U., B.A. 1970; Catholic; married (Gayle); 3 children.

Elected Office: WV House, 1982-86; WV Senate, 1986-96; WV secy. of st., 2000-04; WV gov., 2004-10.

Professional Career: Co-owner, Manchin's Carpet & Tile, 1968-82; Owner, Enersystems, 1989-2000.

DC Office: 306 HSOB, 20510, 202-224-3954; Fax: 202-228-0002; Website: manchin.senate.gov.

State Offices: Charleston, 304-342-5855; Martinsburg, 304-264-4626; Morgantown, 304-284-8663.

Committees: *Armed Services:* Airland (RMM); Emerging Threats & Capabilities; Strategic Forces. *Commerce, Science & Transportation.* Aviation Operations, Safety & Security; Communications, Technology, Innovation & the Internet. *Energy & Natural Resources:* Energy (RMM); Public Lands, Forests & Mining; Water & Power. *Veterans' Affairs.*

Group Ratings

	ADA	ACLU	AFL-CIO	LCV	ITI	COC	HAFA	ACU	CFG	FRC
2014	80%	73%	–	20%	100%	13%	14%	32%	20%	40%
2013	50%	C	89%	38%	C	50%	C	28%	20%	C

National Journal Ratings

	2013 LIB	—	2013 CONS
Economic	45%	—	54%
Social	43%	—	56%
Foreign	47%	—	52%
Composite	46%	—	55%

Key Votes of the 113th Congress

1. Sandy storm spending	Y	5. Student Loan Rates	Y	9. Bipartisan Budget Deal	Y
2. Chuck Hagel Confirmation	Y	6. Employee Non-Discrim'n Act	Y	10. Farm Bill Conference Rept.	Y
3. Gun Background Checks	Y	7. Senate Vote on Judgeships	Y	11. Unempl. Comp. Extension	Y
4. Immigration Reform	Y	8. Defense Dept. Spending	Y	12. Keystone Pipeline	Y

Election Results

2012 general	Joe Manchin (D).........................399,908	(61%)	$7,678,708	$204,219	$97,225
	John Raese (R)..........................240,787	(36%)	$1,610,493	$40,392	$89,252
	Bob Henry Baber (G)...................19,517	(3%)			
2012 primary	Joe Manchin (D).........................163,891	(80%)			
	Sheirl Fletcher (D)......................41,118	(20%)			

Prior winning percentages: 2010 special (53%); Governor: 2008 (70%), 2004 (64%)

Democrat Joe Manchin, elected in a special election in 2010 to succeed the late, legendary Robert Byrd, is West Virginia's senior senator. A popular former governor, he has used his political capital to try to break through the Senate's gridlock, most notably on gun control and student loan rates.

Manchin hails from a prominent political family. He grew up in Farmington, a few miles up Buffalo Creek from the industrial city of Fairmont on the Monongahela River. Manchin took a semester off from college to help his father rebuild his carpet and furniture store after a fire. His grandfather and father both served as mayor of Farmington. His uncle, A. James Manchin, was elected to the West Virginia House of Delegates and was also secretary of state and state treasurer.

After graduating from West Virginia University, Joe Manchin went to work in the carpet and furniture business, helping to send his four siblings to college. Then he started a coal brokerage company and eventually moved to Fairmont. Manchin was elected to the House of Delegates in 1982 and the state Senate in 1986. He then ran for governor, only to lose in the Democratic primary to legislator Charlotte Pritt. When Secretary of State Ken Hechler ran for the House in 2000, Manchin ran to succeed him, as did Pritt. This time, Manchin beat her in the primary, 51% to 29%. He went on to win the general election.

In May 2003, Manchin announced that he would challenge Democratic Gov. Bob Wise in the 2004 primary. Later that month, Wise admitted that he'd had an extramarital affair and would not seek reelection. Manchin worked successfully to get support from both unions and business. His stands on cultural issues were impeccably conservative and in line with state preferences: He was opposed to abortion rights, gun control, and same sex marriage. Manchin won the Democratic primary with 53 percent, and he went on to defeat Republican Monty Warner in the general election, 64% to 34%, carrying 52 of 55 counties.

Manchin had been in office for just one year when he gained renown as the public face of desperate attempts to rescue 13 trapped coal miners after the January 2006 explosion at the Sago Mine in central West Virginia. Manchin, whose uncle was killed in a 1968 mine accident that claimed 78 lives, gave numerous televised interviews from the mine site. But he also mistakenly announced "the miracle of all miracles"—that 12 of the miners had survived—when in fact they had died. The blunder could have been career-ending. But Manchin's standing skyrocketed in the polls, partly because West Virginia Republicans decided that invoking the accident politically was a line that they would not cross. After two other deadly mining accidents, Manchin ordered safety inspections at all mines in the state. In 2007, he signed new safety laws mandating certain ventilation practices and giving the state authority to temporarily shut down mines with violations.

Manchin had success on other issues. In 2006, he signed into law eight bills designed to improve health care in the state, including giving low-income families basic care at clinics and creating a catastrophic health care insurance program and a new mental health commission. But his tenure was also marred by a controversy involving his daughter and politically potent institutions in the state. The *Pittsburgh Post-Gazette* reported that the governor's daughter, Heather Bresch, falsely claimed to have earned a master's degree in business in 1998 at West Virginia University. The school then awarded her the degree in 2007 even though she had completed only about half the required 48 credit hours. Under pressure, several top university officials, including the school's president, resigned. Bresch—a high-level executive at Mylan, a large generic drug maker that had donated heavily to the university and, through its top executives, to Manchin's campaigns—never admitted wrongdoing. Manchin expressed support for Bresch, and although the scandal was making headlines in 2008, he did not have serious competition for reelection that year. He won, 70% to 26%.

His popularity prompted speculation about his political future. When Byrd died in June 2010—after 51 years in the Senate and six more in the House—Manchin was seen as the Democrats' best hope for keeping the seat. Although he would have been able to appoint himself to the Senate pending a special election, Manchin declined to do so. Instead, he appointed his former chief counsel, Carte Goodwin, as a placeholder pending a 2010 special election. Republicans initially hadn't planned to invest in the race. In September, a Rasmussen survey showed Manchin with a soaring job approval rating of 69 percent. His GOP opponent was John Raese, a wealthy businessman whom Byrd had defeated four years earlier by a nearly 2-to-1 margin. But Raese, who poured his own money into the contest, had the wind at his back in a strong election cycle for the GOP. He ran ads seeking to tie Manchin to President Barack Obama, and the National Republican Senatorial Committee launched its own ads portraying Manchin as a rubber stamp for Obama's agenda. Before long, the race was a toss-up.

Manchin distanced himself from the president, even to the extent of flip-flopping. After saying early in 2010 that he supported Obama's health care overhaul, by October, Manchin was saying he would have voted against it had he been serving as a senator at the time. The Democrats' cap-and-trade bill to curb carbon emissions was also highly unpopular in West Virginia coal country. Manchin famously ran an ad in which he shot a mock copy of the carbon emissions bill with a rifle. Manchin raised questions about Raese's commitment to the state, pointing out repeatedly on the stump and in television ads that the steel and limestone magnate owned a home in Palm Beach, Florida (complete with a pink marble driveway) and that his wife was registered to vote there. Manchin also hammered Raese for his support for eliminating the minimum wage and abolishing the Education Department. Although he was outspent $6.3 million to $4.4 million, Manchin won, 53% to 43%.

Manchin went to Washington immediately after the election to begin serving the final two years of Byrd's term. He voted on a proposal to extend the Bush-era tax cuts except for taxpayers earning over $1 million, although he had said during his campaign he favored the Republican position of extending them for all taxpayers. But he was the only Democrat to vote "no" on a proposal to repeal the ban on openly gay members in the military. Still, Manchin was roundly criticized back home for missing a final vote on repeal of "don't ask, don't tell," and also for missing a major vote on a bill to give legal status to the children of some illegal immigrants. *The Charleston Gazette* called him "absolutely gutless." Manchin apologized publicly, saying he missed the December votes to be with his grandchildren over the holidays. He further angered the newspaper in 2012 when he declined to say whether he would vote for Obama's reelection. It refused to endorse him in that April's Democratic primary, questioning whether he was "on course to follow Connecticut's Joe Lieberman and register as independent." It hardly mattered; Manchin beat former Monongalia County legislator Sheirl Fletcher with 80 percent of the vote. His win set up a general-election rematch with Raese for a full six-year term. Raese resurrected his main campaign theme that Manchin was an Obama rubber stamp, but the senator now had a voting record that demonstrated otherwise. Manchin easily improved upon his earlier victory, winning 61%-36% in a state in which GOP presidential nominee Mitt Romney took 62 percent of the vote.

Even before his reelection, Manchin showed signs of wanting to change the Senate's stalemated course. In September, he blasted the chamber for adjourning six weeks before the election. He then teamed up with former Utah Gov. Jon Huntsman to form a "Problem Solvers" initiative enlisting lawmakers from both parties through the group NoLabels.org. "We will either work across the aisle to fix problems or we will achieve nothing," Manchin and Huntsman wrote in a January 2013 op-ed column.

In April 2013, after several months of taking colleagues out on his boat *Black Tie* for evenings of beer and pizza, Manchin announced a compromise on gun control with Republicans Mark Kirk of Illinois—his best friend in the chamber—and Pat Toomey of Pennsylvania. Its most significant feature was a proposal to expand background checks for gun buyers to cover transactions at gun shows and Internet sales. It did not go as far as Obama wanted—it exempted sales between private citizens in some instances—but was seen as the best chance to advance gun control legislation in years. "This is common sense," said Manchin, who previously had boasted of his "A" rating from the National Rifle Association. "This is gun sense." But the measure couldn't attract enough votes to overcome a GOP filibuster, and some gun control proponents said Manchin didn't handle the issue with enough finesse. They noted that his spokesman had said the NRA was "neutral" on the measure when it was unveiled; the powerful group denied that was the case. The NRA ended up taking its attacks on the proposal to Manchin's home state, spending six figures on ads.

Manchin had more success attacking political gridlock during the student loan debate in the summer of 2013. The two parties had spent months bickering about how to prevent an automatic doubling of student-loan rates from 3.4% to 6.8% by a statutory deadline of July 1. Manchin was a key negotiator in a deal that brought the rates back down and tied them to the market. He said he got involved after Senate Democratic leaders presented a doomed plan to temporarily extend lower rates. "You want me to vote for the extension. You know it's going to fail, but you just want to make a political point with the extension like we're trying to keep the rates down. And I said ... I know that we can do so much better, we can reduce everybody's rates," Manchin told *National Journal*. The deal that passed, and was ultimately signed into law, brought rates down for undergraduates to 3.9 percent. It was crafted by a bipartisan group of senators, including Manchin, and the Obama White House.

In the Senate, Manchin serves on the Energy and Natural Resources Committee, where he's the ranking member on the energy subcommittee. In line with the economy of his state, he backed the Keystone XL pipeline and became the only Democrat to co-sponsor the Affordable Reliable Energy Now Act of 2015, a bill shepherded by his fellow West Virginia senator, Republican Shelley Moore Capito. The law—which Obama would almost certainly veto—pushes back against efforts by the administration's Environmental Protection Agency to curb carbon emissions. Manchin also co-sponsored a measure to lift the ban on exporting domestic crude oil, joining several Republicans and one other Democratic senator, Heidi Heitkamp, who represents oil and gas behemoth North Dakota. Manchin also serves on the Armed Services Committee, where he has expressed concern about the effectiveness of U.S. efforts in the Middle East. "Past results have not been very good," Manchin said on MSNBC's *Morning Joe*. "I would think that basically, insanity is doing the same thing over and over and thinking you're going to change and have a different result." Manchin, a member of the Commerce, Science and Transportation Committee, formed an unlikely partnership with Senate liberal icon Elizabeth Warren to offer legislation that would publicize the details of trade deals before lawmakers were asked to approve presidential fast-track trade authority.

After the Democrats lost the Senate in the 2014 election—a development Manchin called "a real ass-whuppin'"—he expressed deep frustration to the *Washington Post* about Obama and Senate Democratic Leader Harry Reid of Nevada, and said he might not back Reid for party leader. But he did recommit to remaining with his party rather than switching to the GOP. "I'm a moderate Democrat, proud West Virginian. If you don't have moderates on both sides, you don't get anything done," he said. As for Obama, Manchin told *Time* magazine that "people just don't believe he cares." Expressing continued frustration with the way the Senate operated, Manchin toyed with leaving the chamber two years early in 2016 to run instead for governor, a job that would provide him with executive powers he had enjoyed before. But in the spring of 2015, Manchin announced that he would remain in the Senate— a big boost for Democrats, who had few other options for winning his seat in increasingly Republican West Virginia. "The 2018 Senate landscape is absolutely terrible for Democrats, and they need every break they can possibly manage," wrote the *Washington Post*'s Chris Cillizza in explaining the importance of Manchin's decision. Meanwhile, isolated chatter about a 2016 presidential bid also came to naught.

Junior Senator

Shelley Moore Capito (R)

Elected 2014, 1st term; b. Nov. 26, 1953, Glen Dale; Duke U., B.S. 1975, U. of VA, M.Ed. 1976; Presbyterian; married (Charles); 3 children.

Elected Office: WV House, 1997-2001; US House, 2001-2015.

Professional Career: Career counselor, WV St. Col., 1976-78; Dir., Ed. Info. Ctr., WV Bd. of Regents, 1978-81.

DC Office: 172 RSOB, 20515, 202-224-6472; Website: capito.senate.gov.

State Offices: Charleston, 304-347-5372; Martinsburg, 304-262-9285.

Committees: *Appropriations:* Commerce, Justice, Science & Related Agencies; Labor, Health & Human Services, Education & Related Agencies; Legislative Branch (Chmn); Military Construction, Veteran Affairs & Related Agencies; Transportation, Housing & Urban Development & Related Agencies. *Energy & Natural Resources:* Energy; National Parks; Public Lands, Forests & Mining. *Environment & Public Works:* Clean Air & Nuclear Safety (Chmn); Fisheries, Water & Wildlife; Transportation & Infrastructure. *Rules & Administration.*

Group Ratings (House)

	ADA	ACLU	AFL-CIO	LCV	ITI	COC	HAFA	ACU	CFG	FRC
2014	0%	5%	–	6%	100%	86%	47%	48%	42%	75%
2013	5%	C	38%	4%	C	92%	C	56%	49%	C

National Journal Ratings (House)

	2013 LIB	—	2013 CONS
Economic	47%	—	53%
Social	43%	—	54%
Foreign	15%	—	77%
Composite	37%	—	63%

Key Votes of the 113th Congress (House)

1. Sandy storm spending	Y	5. Medical Marijuana	NV	9. Syrian Rebels Training	Y
2. Violence Against Women Act	Y	6. Farm Bill	Y	10. Keystone pipeline	Y
3. Guantanamo Bay Detainees	N	7. Afghanistan Combat	N	11. Immigration Exec. Action	Y
4. Abortion 20-week ban	Y	8. NSA Phone Data Collection	N	12. Bipartisan budget deal	Y

Election Results

2014 general	Shelley Moore Capito (R)	 280,400	(62%)	$8,779,918	$640,871	$227,388
	Natalie Tennant (D)	 155,730	(35%)	$3,499,419	$34,000	$290,776
2014 primary	Shelley Moore Capito (R)	 74,655	(88%)			
	Matthew Dodrill (R)	 7,072	(8%)			

Prior winning percentages: 2012 (70%), 2010 (68%), 2008 (57%), 2006 (57%), 2004 (57%), 2002 (60%), 2000 (48%)

Republican Shelley Moore Capito was elected West Virginia's junior senator in 2014 after serving seven terms in the House. She became the state's first female senator and its first Republican in the Senate since the 1950s. She is a well-liked moderate who is unwavering in her advocacy of West Virginia's coal industry.

Capito grew up in northern West Virginia and in the Washington, D.C. area, where her father, Arch Moore, served in the House from 1957 to 1969. He was elected governor of West Virginia in 1968 and 1972, and then again in 1984. Capito graduated from Duke University and received a master's degree in education from the University of Virginia, and she was the first Cherry Blossom Princess elected to Congress. She worked for two years as a career counselor at West Virginia State University and then as director of the state's Educational Information Center from 1978 to 1981. She served two terms in the West Virginia House of Delegates.

Capito's opportunity to follow in her father's footsteps came when Democratic Rep. Bob Wise ran for governor in 2000. She benefited from a divisive Democratic primary won by Jim Humphreys, a former state senator and a lawyer. Capito, who supported abortion rights, started off as the underdog, but Humphreys proved to be a poor candidate despite spending $6 million of his own money in the general election. Capito won, 48% to 46%.

In the House, Capito had a more moderate voting record than many in her caucus; she was a member of the centrist Republican Main Street Caucus. She broke from conservatives to support programs important to her state, such as continued funding of rural air service and opposing drastic cutbacks in food stamps. In a rare encounter with controversy in 2006, Capito had to deal with the fallout from revelations of inappropriate sexual advances by GOP Rep. Mark Foley of Florida, which included contact with House pages. Capito, a member of the three-lawmaker board that oversaw the teenage page program, said she was not informed of the allegations until after the scandal became public.

Capito became more inclined to side with her party after the election of President Barack Obama, who was highly unpopular in West Virginia. Meanwhile, in 2011, she took over as chairwoman of the Financial Services Subcommittee on Financial Institutions and Consumer Credit. She focused on the regulatory burdens facing community banks and credit unions. Her husband, Charles, is a longtime banking executive, which has raised eyebrows among watchdog groups. Capito has said she makes her own decisions, telling *Esquire* magazine in 2010 that "no matter what your decisions are, no matter what your votes are, if you're not playing by the rules you're taking a big risk."

After winning a seventh term in November 2012, Capito announced she would challenge Democratic Sen. Jay Rockefeller for his seat when it came up in 2014. Conservative groups grumbled about her moderate record, but Rockefeller, in his mid-70s, clearly wanted no part of a tough race against Capito and announced his retirement after a poll showed her with a slight lead in a head-to-head matchup. Capito caught a break when Pat McGeehan, a former state House member to her ideological right, exited the race early on.

In the general, Capito's opponent was Natalie Tennant, West Virginia's secretary of state and a former television reporter. (Tennant's husband, Erik Wells, had failed to oust Capito from her House seat in a 2004 challenge.) Tennant sought to make an issue of Capito and her spouse's close ties to banking interests, saying her own "West Virginia first" approach contrasted with Capito's record "working for Wall Street banks where her husband works." But Capito ran a quietly effective campaign, largely overshadowed nationally by more intensely watched races elsewhere, and was aided by Obama's deep unpopularity among West Virginians. Indeed, her ascension from the House to the Senate was seen as such a certainty that by July, friends and colleagues reportedly began addressing her as "Senator." In November, she defeated Tennant by an even larger margin than expected, 62%-35%.

In the Senate, Capito secured a seat on the influential Appropriations Committee, becoming the only new senator tapped as a "cardinal," or subcommittee chair; she took charge of the panel that funds congressional operations. She was also assigned to join two panels of great importance to coal-producing West Virginia—the Energy and Natural Resources Committee and the Environment and Public Works Committee. In that capacity, she became lead sponsor of the Affordable Reliable Energy Now Act. The measure seeks to preempt the Obama administration's proposed program for tackling climate change, which could pose additional costs on the coal industry. "We're asking for a common-sense agreement that assures reliable and affordable energy, protects our economy and jobs and allows states to make their own decisions," she told reporters. The measure won co-sponsorship of almost three dozen senators, including one Democrat, Joe Manchin, Capito's West Virginia colleague.

FIRST DISTRICT

David McKinley (R)

Elected 2010, 3rd term; b. March 28, 1947, Wheeling; Purdue U., B.S. 1969; Episcopalian; married (Mary); 4 children.

Elected Office: WV House, 1980-94.

Professional Career: Principal, McKinley & Assoc., 1981-2010; Chair, WV GOP, 1990-94.

DC Office: 412 CHOB, 20515, 202-225-4172; Fax: 202-225-7564; Website: mckinley.house.gov.

State Offices: Morgantown, 304-284-8506; Parkersburg, 304-422-5972; Wheeling, 304-232-3801.

Committees: *Energy & Commerce:* Energy & Power; Environment & the Economy; Oversight & Investigations (VChmn).

Group Ratings

	ADA	ACLU	AFL-CIO	LCV	ITI	COC	HAFA	ACU	CFG	FRC
2014	5%	5%	–	9%	100%	79%	52%	52%	54%	88%
2013	0%	C	48%	7%	C	85%	C	64%	60%	C

National Journal Ratings

	2013 LIB	—	2013 CONS
Economic	45%	—	54%
Social	48%	—	50%
Foreign	15%	—	77%
Composite	38%	—	62%

Key Votes of the 113th Congress

1. Sandy storm spending	Y	5. Medical Marijuana	N	9. Syrian Rebels Training	Y
2. Violence Against Women Act	Y	6. Farm Bill	Y	10. Keystone pipeline	Y
3. Guantanamo Bay Detainees	N	7. Afghanistan Combat	N	11. Immigration Exec. Action	Y
4. Abortion 20-week ban	Y	8. NSA Phone Data Collection	N	12. Bipartisan budget deal	N

Election Results

2014 general	David McKinley (R)	91,843	(64%)	$2,021,174	$8,217
	Glen Gainer (D)	51,842	(36%)	$447,557	
2014 primary	David McKinley (R)	unopposed			

Prior winning percentages: 2012 (62%), 2010 (50%)

Population		Race and Ethnicity		Income	
Total:	617,842	White	94.3%	Median income:	$41,436
Urban:	36.4%	Black	2.3%		(369 of 435)
Suburban:	15.6%	Latino	1.0%	Under $50,000	57.8%
Rural:	48.0%	Asian	0.8%	$50,000-$99,999:	27.7%
Land area:	6,974	Two races	1.4%	$100,000-$199,999:	12.3%
Pop/sq. mi.:	88.6	White Ethnic	33.3%	$200,000 or more:	2.2%
Born in state:	68.2%			Poverty Rate	17.1%
		Education			
Age Groups		H.S. grad or less:	53.3%	**Work**	
Under 18:	19.7%	Some college:	25.6%	White collar:	31.6%
18 to 34:	23.3%	College degree, 4 yr.:	12.2%	Blue collar:	42.1%
35 to 64:	39.9%	Post-grad study:	8.9%	Sales and service:	26.3%
Over 64:	17.1%			Govt. workers:	17.2%
		Military			
		Veterans/active duty:	9.9%		

Northern West Virginia: Morgantown, Parkersburg

The northern part of West Virginia is in many ways an extension of the Pittsburgh metropolitan area. People here are Steelers and Pirates fans, they drink Iron City and Rolling Rock beer, they watch Pittsburgh television, and they live in the crevasses

Voter Turnout	
2013 Total Citizen 18+	491,997
2014 House Turnout	143,685
2014 Turnout as % CVAP	29.2%
2012 Turnout as % CVAP	46.7%

between hills cut by the Monongahela and Ohio rivers. The terrain here would seem to forbid manufacturing and urban development, yet this has been one of America's prime industrial areas. Northern West Virginia is part of the same coal-and-steel economy that made Pittsburgh one of the nation's largest cities and filled the narrow bottomlands along the rivers with steel and glass factories, foundries and coal yards. As in Pennsylvania, these industries have been declining and they have become far less labor-intensive. Since 1980, the 12,000 mining jobs in this part of West Virginia have dropped by more than two-thirds, with comparable fall-offs in manufacturing. The Weirton tin and steel mill (now called Arcelor Mittal and owned by an integrated steel and mining company headquartered in Luxembourg) employed 14,000 workers in the mid-1970s and was down to fewer than 1,000 in 2013. Service jobs have replaced some of these losses. Walmart has been West Virginia's largest employer since 1998, and the government has brought in thousands more jobs, compliments of the late Sen. Robert Byrd, the West Virginia Democrat and powerful Senate appropriator. One of the largest employers in Harrison

County has been the U.S. Department of Justice. The county has become the state's leader in Marcellus Shale natural gas boom, with an influx of jobs and money.

The 1st Congressional District of West Virginia includes 20 counties in the northern third of the state. On the Panhandle along the Ohio River is Victorian Wheeling, once one of the richest cities in the country with its steel and glass companies. There is Weirton, named for Ernest T. Weir, the anti-union Pittsburgh industrialist who transformed it from a farming community to a steel town in the early 1900s. South of Pittsburgh on the Monongahela River is Morgantown, with human capital from West Virginia University and a popular white-water rafting destination; in 2014, the Milken Institute ranked the city seventh best-performing among 179 small metro areas. On the Ohio River is the former oil-refining and shipping center of Parkersburg, which has become a plastics and manufacturing hub. Parts of the district are stagnant while others are on a growth path. Morgantown's population grew nearly 14% from 2000 to 2013, while Wheeling's fell by 10%—part of a consistent decline since the 1930s—and Parkersburg's decreased by 6%.

2012 Presidential Vote		
Mitt Romney (R)..................141,736	(62%)
Barack Obama (D) 81,017	(36%)
2008 Presidential Vote		
John McCain (R)..................140,421	(57%)
Barack Obama (D) 102,826	(42%)
Cook Partisan Voting Index: R+14		

To the west, the district includes three lonely mountain counties—Doddridge, Ritchie and Tyler—that were never heavily industrialized and have remained firmly Republican since the Civil War. Doddridge was the only one of West Virginia's 55 counties to vote against Byrd in 2006. For most of the 20th century, much of the territory in the 1st District was solidly Democratic. But dissatisfaction with the Clinton-Gore policies on coal mining and the environment helped Republican George W. Bush carry the district twice, and the local hostility accelerated with Obama policies. Mitt Romney took at least 60 percent of the vote in each of West Virginia's three districts, with 62% in the 1st.

David McKinley (R)

Republican David McKinley captured his seat for the GOP in 2010 after it had been in Democratic hands for 40 years. McKinley is a coal-championing centrist along the lines of home-state GOP Sen. Shelley Moore Capito, but he shows more independence from the party on big issues.

McKinley is a seventh-generation native of Wheeling. McKinley's great-grandfather ran for West Virginia governor as a Democrat in 1908. His father was a civil engineer who taught him to read blueprints when he was in third grade. He majored in civil engineering at Purdue University. After college, McKinley worked for several engineering and construction companies until he founded his own firm, McKinley & Associates, which restores historic properties and does other construction work. McKinley has suffered from hearing loss since his 20s; today he is deaf in one ear and has partial hearing in the other.

After he won a seat in West Virginia's House of Delegates in 1981, McKinley pushed for a bill to allow school and prison cafeterias to donate unused food to homeless shelters, and authored a law that prohibits insurance companies from canceling policies of people diagnosed with HIV. He ran for governor in 1996 but lost the primary to Cecil Underwood, who went on to win the general election.

In his House bid, McKinley had the backing of national Republicans in the primary and won with 35% of the vote. In the general election, he faced state Sen. Mike Oliverio, who had toppled 14-term Democratic Rep. Alan Mollohan in the primary after several newspaper accounts raised questions about whether Mollohan profited personally from business deals with people and nonprofit groups that got federal funds that he earmarked in appropriations bills.

McKinley's ads labeled Oliverio as a "career politician" who supported "job-killing liberal Nancy Pelosi," a reference to the then House speaker. McKinley emphasized his opposition to the Democrats' energy bill that would limit carbon emissions, arguing that it would hurt West Virginia's coal industry. But Oliverio also opposed the bill. Oliverio charged that McKinley got rich from government contracts even as he criticized government spending, citing federal economic stimulus money that McKinley's architectural and engineering firm received to design a Marshall County school. Despite his call for repeal of President Barack Obama's health care overhaul, he supported the provision that prohibits insurance companies from denying coverage to people with preexisting conditions. McKinley eked out a victory of 1,440 votes out of 179,880 cast, a split of 50.4%-49.6%.

In Washington, McKinley was one of a handful of Republicans in 2011 and 2012 to vote against Budget Committee Chairman Paul Ryan's controversial budget blueprint, complaining that it did not adequately protect Medicare. Among Class of 2010 GOP members, only Illinois' Robert Dold scored lower than McKinley on the anti-tax Club for Growth's legislative scorecard in those two years. He got a plum seat on the Energy and Commerce Committee and co-founded a Marcellus Shale Caucus to oppose regulation of drilling in the oil-rich area stretching along the East Coast.

McKinley's chief cause has been fighting so-called coal ash rules that affect such industries as concrete production and manufacturing of wallboard. He introduced a bill in 2011 to create an enforceable minimum standard for the regulation of coal ash by the states, allowing its use in a manner that he said would protect jobs. It passed the House but stalled in the Senate. When House Republicans sought in 2012 to add the measure to the surface transportation bill, West Virginia Democratic Sen. Jay Rockefeller—who earlier co-sponsored similar legislation—blocked the move, saying it would jeopardize the bill's passage. McKinley told *The Charleston Gazette* he was "frankly shocked" at Rockefeller's decision, but Rockefeller prevailed. McKinley won Energy and Commerce approval of a similar measure in 2015.

Serving on Energy and Commerce has enabled McKinley to stockpile large contributions from coal interests. In 2012, Democrat Susan Thorn spent just $166,000 to his $1.3 million, and he overpowered her, 62%-38%. In 2014, Democratic nominee Glen Gainer, who had been state auditor since 1992, styled himself as the candidate of change. McKinley outspent him $2 million to $448,000 and won, 64%-36%. In June 2015, after extensive review, he ruled out a run in 2016 for the open seat for governor. After the layoffs of more than 1,400 mine workers in the state, McKinley said he decided, "I can do much more for West Virginia right here in Congress."

SECOND DISTRICT

Alex Mooney (R)

Elected 2014, 1st term; b. June 5, 1971, Washington D.C.; Dartmouth Col., B.A. 1993; Catholic; married (Grace Gonzalez); 3 children.

Elected Office: MD Senate, 1999-2010.

Professional Career: Aide, Rep. Roscoe Bartlett, 1993-95; Exec., Council for National Policy Action, Inc, 1995-98; Dir., The National Journalism Center, 2005-12; Chair, MD GOP, 2010-13; Owner, consulting firm, 2011-14.

DC Office: 1232 LHOB, 20515, 202-225-2711; Fax: 202-225-7856; Website: mooney.house.gov.

State Offices: Charleston, 304-925-5964; Martinsburg, 304-264-8810.

Committees: *Budget. Natural Resources:* Energy & Mineral Resources; Oversight & Investigations.

Election Results

2014 general	Alex Mooney (R)	72,042	(47%)	$2,008,181	$540,886	$792,431
	Nick Casey (D)	67,210	(44%)	$1,993,276	$91,931	$1,006,931
	Davy Jones (Lib)	7,614	(5%)			
	Ed Rabel (I)	6,226	(4%)	$19,027		
2014 primary	Alex Mooney (R)	12,678	(36%)			
	Ken Reed (R)	7,848	(22%)			
	Charlotte Lane (R)	6,358	(18%)			
	Steve Harrison (R)	3,885	(11%)			
	Ron Walters Jr. (R)	2,125	(6%)			
	Jim Moss (R)	1,684	(5%)			

Population		Race and Ethnicity		Income	
Total:	626,979	White	91.2%	Median income:	$45,474
Urban:	30.0%	Black	3.1%		*(310 of 435)*
Suburban:	33.8%	Latino	1.7%	Under $50,000	54.5%
Rural:	36.2%	Asian	0.6%	$50,000-$99,999:	30.1%
Land area:	9,164	Two races	3.1%	$100,000-$199,999:	12.8%
Pop/sq. mi.:	68.4	White Ethnic	19.4%	$200,000 or more:	2.6%
Born in state:	65.1%			Poverty Rate	15.2%
		Education			
Age Groups		H.S. grad or less:	53.7%	**Work**	
Under 18:	21.6%	Some college:	25.7%	White collar:	32.1%
18 to 34:	19.9%	College degree, 4 yr.:	12.5%	Blue collar:	42.6%
35 to 64:	41.7%	Post-grad study:	8.0%	Sales and service:	25.3%
Over 64:	16.8%				
		Military		Govt. workers:	21.0%
		Veterans/active duty:	11.1%		

Central West Virginia: Charleston, Martinsburg

Not all of West Virginia has been coal country, and not all of its hills have been scarred by strip mining. Large parts of this naturally beautiful state look as verdant and unchanged as they must have when George Washington was speculating in land here. For miles, there are gentle hills and rugged moun-

Voter Turnout	
2013 Total Citizen 18+	487,935
2014 House Turnout	153,092
2014 Turnout as % CVAP	31.4%
2012 Turnout as % CVAP	48.1%

tains. Yet over another hill you may find, amid scenery primeval and rural, sudden evidence of industrialization: a pulp mill or charcoal factory in a clearing scraped out of the forest; a small factory town, built close to a river in a cleft bordered with hills; the entrance to an underground coal mine or a mountaintop blasted open to allow surface mining.

The 2nd Congressional District of West Virginia is a central slice of the state, from Berkeley Springs and Harpers Ferry in the Washington D.C. exurbs, more than 300 miles to beyond Charleston and the Ohio River town of Ravenswood. The district includes fast-growing parts of the state: the Eastern Panhandle counties, which are part of the Washington metropolitan area, and chemical-producing Putnam County, which is increasingly home to suburbanites commuting to Charleston. The local Toyota engine plant employs more than 1,200 people. In Charleston, the major urban center in the district, the state Capitol sits on the banks of the Kanawha River, designed by Cass Gilbert with a dome higher than that of the U.S. Capitol. With no advance notice in July 2015, the owners of the city's two quality newspapers—*The Charleston Gazette*, which leans Democratic, and the Republican-tilting *Charleston Daily Mail*—combined them into the *Charleston Gazette-Mail*, with one news staff but two separate editorial pages.

In the 1940s, the area produced all of the nation's Lucite, polyethylenes and nylon, as well as much of its artificial rubber and antifreeze. Today, the state boasts that it is home to more polymer producers than any other place on the planet; the chemical industry makes products used in the manufacturing of cosmetics, detergents, shampoo and other products. Those chemical plants can be hazardous. In January 2014, a spill from a chemi-cal tank farm on the Elk River just north of Charleston caused more than 300,000 people in the metropolitan area to lose fresh drink-ing water for days or weeks in some cases. Charleston is West Virginia's professional center, with a few downtown office towers and some affluent residential districts. Politi-cally, this ancestrally Democratic district is now trending Republican. Berkeley County, which has commuter rail to Washington and

2012 Presidential Vote		
Mitt Romney (R)................140,783	(60%)
Barack Obama (D) 89,079	(38%)

2008 Presidential Vote		
John McCain (R)................136,259	(55%)
Barack Obama (D) 109,369	(44%)

Cook Partisan Voting Index: R+11

a 25% African-American population, has grown 42% since 2000 to become the second-largest county in the state. Mitt Romney in 2012 won here with 60% of the vote, his weakest per-formance in the state.

Alex Mooney (R)

Republican Alex Mooney, a onetime Marylander, found a receptive home in West Virginia in 2014 when he won an open seat after GOP Rep. Shelley Moore Capito ran successfully for the Senate. Mooney, who has run for office in three states, beat Democrat Nick Casey in a costly and contentious contest in the sprawling 2nd District.

Mooney was born in Washington D.C., to a Cuban refugee mother and a father from an Irish immigrant family who served in Vietnam. He graduated from Dartmouth College; during his time there, he ran for the New Hampshire House of Representatives but got just 8 percent of the vote and finished last of the seven candidates in the general election. After college, he was an aide to GOP Rep. Roscoe Bartlett of Maryland. Mooney won a Maryland Senate seat in 1998 at age 27, and became Maryland GOP chairman after he lost reelection to the Senate in 2010. (His official bio says that he served in the state Senate, but it doesn't identify the state.) He set his sights on Bartlett's House seat and started raising money for a potential run in 2012. But he abandoned the effort after Bartlett announced he would run in what turned out to be a losing effort. Mooney kept the campaign cash, saying he would run in 2014, and went back to work for Bartlett part-time in 2012. But he had a change of plan and moved to West Virginia, where he entered a seven-way GOP primary. He won with 36% of the vote to 22% for Ken Reed, a pharmacist.

In the general election, Mooney campaigned on an anti-Obama platform, vowing to repeal the health reform law and pledging to fight any government overreach. Casey said that he wanted to scrap some parts of the health care law, such as the mandate for employers to provide coverage, and argued that Washington needed more moderate voices. Both candidates pledged strong support for coal, a key litmus test in West Virginia. The central fight was over whether geography or ideology mattered more. Casey, a former Democratic state chairman calling himself a "true West Virginian," branded Mooney a carpetbagger and opportunist. Mooney countered that he was a "West Virginian by choice," and therefore more committed to his adopted district's conservative values. He also said that his Maryland state Senate seat bordered West Virginia and that the two areas are similar. He presumably did not tout the virtues of working in Annapolis, compared to Charleston.

The district agreed with Mooney, though some voters undoubtedly were turned off by his river-crossing. Neil Berch, a West Virginia University political science professor told *The New York Times* before the election that a segment of voters would believe that "the best preacher's a convert" who "wrapped himself in West Virginia values." Each candidate spent about $2 million. Mooney benefited from more than $2.3 million in additional spending from Republican and conservative groups, compared with less than $900,000 that national Democrats delivered to Casey. Mooney won, 47%-44%.

In the House, Mooney joined the Budget Committee, where he supported the Republicans' budget plan and took credit for provisions that opposed funding of ozone standards by the Environmental Protection Agency and blocked regulations that would prohibit surface mining in West Virginia. On the Natural Resources Committee, he maintained attacks against Obama administration initiatives that were designed to limit the mining and use of coal. "West Virginia is blessed to be abundant in natural resources," Mooney said in April 2015. "Unfortunately, the president is intent on destroying coal as a domestic energy source."

Casey left the door open to a rematch in 2016.

THIRD DISTRICT

Evan Jenkins (R)

Elected 2014, 1st term; b. Sept. 12, 1960, Huntington; U. of FL., B.S. 1983, Cumberland Schl. of Law, Samford U., J.D. 1987; Presbyterian; married (Elizabeth Weiler); 3 children.

Elected Office: WV House 1994-2000; WV Senate 2002-14.

Professional Career: Practicing atty., Business law instructor, Marshall U., Exec. dir., West Virginia State Medical Association.

DC Office: 502 CHOB, 20515, 202-225-3452; Fax: 202-225-9061; Website: evanjenkins.house.gov.

State Offices: Beckley, 304-250-6177; Bluefield, 304-325-6800; Huntington, 304-522-2201.

Committees: *Appropriations:* Interior, Environment & Related Agencies; Legislative Branch; Transportation, Housing & Urban Development & Related Agencies.

Election Results

2014 general	Evan Jenkins (R)	77,713	(55%)	$1,645,575	$453,003	$4,500,753
	Nick Rahall (D)	62,688	(45%)	$2,645,214	$643,623	$4,711,585
2014 primary	Evan Jenkins (R)	unopposed				

Population		Race and Ethnicity		Income	
Total:	609,483	White	93.8%	Median income:	$36,473
Urban:	23.3%	Black	3.5%		*(413 of 435)*
Suburban:	18.3%	Latino	0.7%	Under $50,000	62.7%
Rural:	58.5%	Asian	0.4%	$50,000-$99,999:	26.1%
Land area:	12,923	Two races	1.4%	$100,000-$199,999:	9.6%
Pop/sq. mi.:	47.2	White Ethnic	21.1%	$200,000 or more:	1.6%
Born in state:	76.8%			Poverty Rate	23.2%
		Education			
Age Groups		H.S. grad or less:	59.9%	**Work**	
Under 18:	20.6%	Some college:	25.0%	White collar:	28.5%
18 to 34:	20.1%	College degree, 4 yr.:	9.3%	Blue collar:	45.7%
35 to 64:	41.4%	Post-grad study:	5.9%	Sales and service:	25.8%
Over 64:	17.9%				
		Military		Govt. workers:	18.8%
		Veterans/active duty:	9.9%		

Southern West Virginia: Huntington, Beckley

Early in the 20th century, the coal fields of southern West Virginia were one of America's boom areas. Into rural farmland and hollows, inhabited by the same families that settled the mountains 100 years before, came coal company lawyers with mineral rights' leases to sign, coal company engineers to

Voter Turnout	
2013 Total Citizen 18+	481,589
2014 House Turnout	139,681
2014 Turnout as % CVAP	29%
2012 Turnout as % CVAP	43%

design and sink mineshafts, and men from other mountain counties to work the mines. Company houses were built, company stores were stocked with goods as the company dictated, and company paymasters kept close tabs on the finances of every employee. These conditions bred discontent, which ignited into the fire of industrial unionism. The Battle of Blair Mountain in Logan County, where 10,000 armed unionists faced off against 3,000 law enforcement officers and strikebreakers, presaged later efforts at organization by John L. Lewis, president of the United Mine Workers. Lewis was not only a militant unionist, but also an isolationist. During and after World War II, he called out his coal miners on strikes, to the fury of Democratic Presidents Franklin Roosevelt and Harry Truman. The national war effort and postwar economic recovery were threatened by these labor stoppages involving some 300,000 workers, centered in back corners of the country like southern West Virginia.

Coal is still the dominant U.S. source of electricity and is likely to remain that way for a while, even as other sources become more popular. The share of electricity that comes from coal is expected to fall to 38% by 2035, a 4 percentage point decline from 2011. Most of the coal mining in this region is done in Boone, Logan, Raleigh and Mingo counties, each of which produced more than 10 million tons of coal in 2009. Raleigh County is the site of Massey Energy's Upper Big Branch Mine, where an April 2010 disaster killed 29 miners in the worst industry accident in four decades. A tragedy of a different kind was the loss of 6,700 jobs in the West Virginia mines from late 2011 until early 2015, with a 15% drop in coal that was mined during that timeframe. In 2012, Boone had been overtaken by Marshall County in the northern part of the state as the county that produced the most coal. Production in the southern part of the state dropped from 116 million tons in 2008 to 79 million tons in 2012, while the northern counties had a slight increase.

2012 Presidential Vote		
Mitt Romney (R)	135,136	(65%)
Barack Obama (D)	68,173	(33%)
2008 Presidential Vote		
John McCain (R)	120,786	(56%)
Barack Obama (D)	91,662	(42%)
Cook Partisan Voting Index:	R+14	

The 3rd Congressional District of West Virginia includes most of the mountainous coal country in the southern part of the state, which for years was heavily Democratic. But the coal mining counties make up less than half of the district. About a quarter of the population is in and around the industrial city of Huntington on the Ohio River, which includes Marshall University. Another quarter is to the east, in Beckley and the farming uplands. (Also located there is the Greenbrier Resort, where the government built a massive secret fallout shelter, code-named "Project Greek Island," to house the entire Congress in the event of nuclear war.) The district has shifted to Republicans in the past decade. In 2012, Republican Mitt Romney won here by over 30 percentage points, a remarkable historical turnaround that resulted largely from discontent with the energy and environmental policies of national Democrats.

Evan Jenkins (R)

Republican Evan Jenkins comfortably defeated 19-term Democratic Rep. Nick Rahall in one of the marquee House contests of 2014 by convincing voters that he would be a better protector of the 3rd District's most precious and defining resource: coal.

Jenkins, born in Huntington, earned his bachelor's degree from the University of Florida and a law degree from the Cumberland School of Law at Samford University. He was the CEO of the West Virginia Medical Foundation and taught business law at Marshall University.

He was first elected to office as a Democrat in 1994, serving three terms in the state House of Delegates. In 2002, he won a state Senate seat after defeating the Democratic incumbent in the primary. Jenkins went on to win two more terms in the Senate. Jenkins told *The Register-Herald* of Beckley that he was most proud of his work to create the Hatfield-McCoy Trail System, 700-plus miles of off-road trails designed to bring an economic boost to nine counties. He also cited his actions on newborn-infant hearing tests, drug-abuse prevention, and a sex-offender registry database. In 2013, he announced that he was changing his party registration to Republican so he could challenge Rahall, one of the most senior members of the House. He was nominated without opposition.

Jenkins and Rahall had similar views on issues such as gun control and gay marriage (both of which each opposed). But it was Jenkins's repeated mentions of two highly charged issues in West Virginia—President Barack Obama and coal—that drove this contest and gave the GOP a pickup of the final House Democratic seat in a state delegation that had been solidly Democratic in 2000 but had become increasingly conservative. Jenkins pledged to lead the effort to repeal the Affordable Care Act, a law Rahall supported. When Rahall emphasized the value his seniority brought to the state, Jenkins dismissed the longtime incumbent as just another vote for a president who did not win a single county in West Virginia in 2012 (and who lost 41 percent of the Democratic primary vote to a prisoner). "West Virginia," Jenkins said as he announced his candidacy, "is under attack from President Obama and a Democratic Party that our parents and grandparents would not recognize." Rahall shot back that Jenkins was "spineless" and "two-faced."

Both candidates and their parties devoted lavish funds to this low-cost media market. Rahall outspent Jenkins $2.6 million to $1.6 million, while each national party and its allies spent a bit more than $5 million for their candidate. The fight came down to which man voters believed was more committed to reversing the decline of the state's coal industry. Jenkins accused Rahall of backing a carbon tax (which Rahall denied), while the incumbent retorted that Jenkins would vote to cut black-lung benefits (which Jenkins denied). Obama's unpopularity put the Republican on top 55%-45%.

House Republicans rewarded Jenkins with a seat on the Appropriations Committee, including its Interior Subcommittee, which oversees the active federal regulations that many West Virginians view as burdensome. As one of two freshmen to get a seat on that panel, he said he planned "to use the power of the purse in fighting the anti-coal agenda of Barack Obama through the EPA's budget." Jenkins also set a priority of financing new highway projects in southern West Virginia. That objective seemed ironic given that Rahall had served as the senior Democrat on the House Transportation and Infrastructure Committee.

In June 2015, Jenkins took credit for the $1.2 billion that the committee cut from EPA. He also cited legislative restrictions that the Interior Subcommittee wrote into its bill, including prohibitions on the implementation of new greenhouse gas regulations and on expanded regulatory authority under the Clean Water Act.

★ WISCONSIN ★

Wisconsin has long been one of America's premier "laboratories of reform," in Justice Louis Brandeis' phrase, a state developing new public policies, debating them vigorously, and even tumultuously, observing whether they worked, and serving as an example for other states. North of the dominant westward paths of migration, the state was sparsely settled first by New England Yankees and then by waves of immigrants from Germany and Scandinavia. The German language is seldom heard now, but German place names and surnames are common and, like the once plainly German beer and brat brands, now seem quintessentially American. But from the 1840s into the 20th century, Germans were the most distinctive immigrants. On the rolling dairy land of Wisconsin and the orderly streets of Milwaukee, they built their own churches, kept their own language, and maintained old customs, from country weddings to Christmas trees to beer gardens—a source of friction in temperance-minded America. Wisconsin still has an orderliness and steadiness that owes something to its Germanic heritage, evident in its excellence in precision manufacturing, low crime rates, respect for higher learning, and its hold on its people—the state ranks No. 5 in the percentage of people born there who are still living there. About half of Wisconsin residents, more than in any other state, reported in the 2010 census that they are of German descent.

Wisconsin's reputation for innovative public policy was established during the Progressive Era that began around 1900 and owes its development to an extraordinary governor, Robert La Follette Sr., and the state's German heritage. This is one of the two states that gave birth to the Republican Party in 1854 (the other is Michigan), and Germans, then arriving in America in vast numbers, heavily favored the GOP. They opposed slavery and welcomed the free lands Republicans delivered in the Homestead Act, the free education provided by land grant colleges, and the transportation routes constructed by subsidized railroad builders. This was the seedbed from which sprouted the Progressive movement founded and symbolized by La Follette. At a time when Germany was the world's leader in graduate education and the application of science to government, La Follette had professors at the University of Wisconsin help develop the state workmen's compensation system and income tax. The Progressive movement favored rational use of government to improve the lot of ordinary citizens, an idea borrowed partly from German liberals and adopted by the New Dealers a generation later.

La Follette became a national figure. He tried to run for president in 1912 as a Progressive, but was shoved aside by Theodore Roosevelt. He did run in 1924 on his Progressive ticket and won 17% of the popular vote, the best third-candidate showing between 1912 and 1992. He ran strongest in the northern tier of states from Wisconsin west, the part of the U.S. with the strongest German and Scandinavian heritage, and along the West Coast, the same area of strength of later liberal Democrats like George McGovern, Walter Mondale, Michael Dukakis, and John Kerry. After La Follette died in 1925, his sons carried on his tradition, progressive at home and isolationist abroad. Robert La Follette Jr. served 22 years in the Senate; Philip La Follette was elected governor in 1930, 1934, and 1936. Robert Jr. ran for reelection in 1946 as a Republican but lost in the primary to Joseph McCarthy, the Wisconsin senator famous for fanning the flames of the Red Scare. McCarthy's national prominence made Wisconsin seem like a Republican state. But he won only two elections in heavily Republican years by narrow margins, and the La Follette progressive tradition was taken up by liberal Democrats such as Sens. William Proxmire and Gaylord Nelson and Gov. Patrick Lucey. Like most liberals of their era, these progressives saw Washington rather than Madison as the main site of their laboratory of reform. Mostly a GOP state in the mostly Democratic presidential years from 1944 to 1964, Wisconsin became a mostly Democratic state in the mostly Republican years from 1968 to 1988.

Wisconsin also has a long history of labor activism. Before the violence of the 1892 Homestead steel strike in Pittsburgh, and Colorado's Ludlow Massacre in 1914, Milwaukee saw bloodshed on May 5, 1886, when 1,500 tradesmen and Polish immigrants demanding an eight-hour work day marched on the Rolling Mills iron plant in the city's Bay View neighborhood. Gov. Jeremiah Rusk, who had served as a U.S. Army general in the Civil War, was in Milwaukee commanding 700 Wisconsin National Guard troops and gave the order to fire upon the workers if they approached the iron works. Seven people, including a young boy,

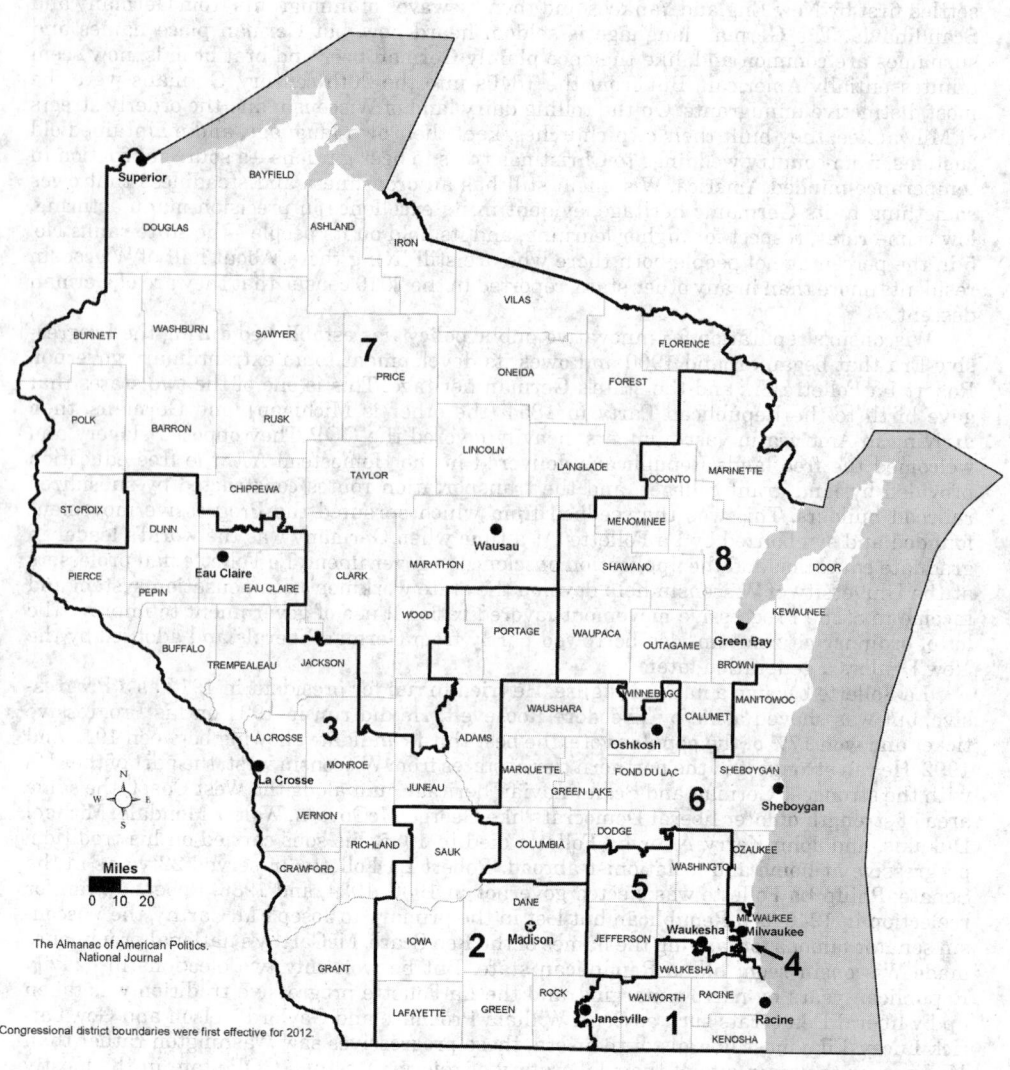

The Almanac of American Politics.
National Journal

Congressional district boundaries were first effective for 2012.

were killed. After the incident, Rusk famously said, "I seen my duty, and I done it." South of downtown Milwaukee, a memorial stands in the Bay View area not far from where the blood was spilled. Local union activists and others gather at the memorial every year to commemorate the anniversary of the tragedy. Wisconsin was the first state in the nation to grant collective-bargaining rights to public employees, in 1959.

Wisconsin's economy has been an outgrowth of its immigrant and manufacturing heritage. Its high-skill, precision instrument production at companies like Johnson Controls and Rockwell Automation jumped into gear in the late 1980s, and helped lead the nation's export boom of the 1990s. Wisconsin ranks No. 2 in milk and butter production and No. 1 in cheese production. But, as a consequence of improved productivity and competition from foreign countries and California's giant agribusiness enterprises, the number of dairy farms has declined from 105,000 in 1960 to 12,700 in 2010. Wisconsin feeds the country in other ways as well. It's No. 1 in the production of cranberries, carrots and snap beans; it's a major harvester of oats, peas, and sweet corn and a leader in food processing—not to mention a prime source of beer and sausage. Pabst, which began in Milwaukee in 1844, but closed its operations there in 1996, plans to return in 2016, opening a craft brewery. Over time, Wisconsin's economy has trailed the nation in some ways, but not dramatically. In 2014, Wisconsin's per capita personal income was $44,585, 97% of the national average, and ranked 26th among all states. In 2004, the per capita personal income of Wisconsin was $33,393 and ranked 23rd among the states. From 2004 to 2014, the compound annual growth rate of Wisconsin's per-capita personal income was 2.9%, while the compound annual growth rate for the nation was 3.0%. At the same time, Wisconsin's unemployment rate has been lower than the national average, but its pace of job creation has lagged during the economic recovery. The state dropped to 50th from 45th last year in the 2015 Ewing Marion Kaufman Foundation ranking for start-up activity in the states.

In the 1990s, Wisconsin was a laboratory for reforms of a different nature. The motivating force was another Republican governor, Tommy Thompson, who beat a liberal Democrat in 1986 and was reelected three times. He cut taxes, sponsored a school choice program, and passed a series of welfare programs—the nation's most sweeping—that dramatically cut caseloads by equipping recipients to work. Across the nation, other governors and Republicans in Congress watched Wisconsin's experiment with interest. It's a fair question whether the 1996 overhaul of federal welfare policy would have passed without Wisconsin's example to give its backers confidence. When Thompson left to become George W. Bush's Health and Human Services secretary in 2001, Wisconsin moved back toward Democrats. It was a battleground state in the 2000 and 2004 presidential races, and in both instances the Democrats won. And in 2008, it gave a resounding majority to Barack Obama. From 1992 to 2006, it elected only Democratic senators, although sometimes by narrow margins, and Democrat Jim Doyle was elected governor in 2002 and 2006. The 2010 election produced another experiment in the laboratory of reform. The winner was Republican Scott Walker, a former Milwaukee County executive who called for curbing the powers of public employee unions. Shortly after taking office, Walker set off a firestorm in the state with a proposal to limit collective bargaining with public employee unions to the issue of wages and to end the practice of sending dues payments directly to the unions. The effort ultimately resulted in a recall election in June 2012 that he won by a wider margin than his 2010 victory. Once known for liberal leaders like the La Follettes and Democratic Sens. Nelson and Proxmire, Wisconsin has turned out a trio of impressive 40-something, Generation X GOP politicians who are hardly slackers: Gov. Walker, a leading 2016 Republican presidential contender; Rep. Paul Ryan, a sharp policy wonk who was the party's 2012 vice presidential nominee and currently chairs the House Ways and Means Committee; and Reince Priebus, the former Wisconsin GOP state chair, who is now the longest-serving chairman of the Republican National Committee in modern times, having rebuilt the party apparatus after the desultory chairmanship of Michael Steele.

Wisconsin's political pattern is unlike most other Great Lakes states, where the major metropolitan areas are comfortably Democratic and the countryside is traditionally Republican. The three large suburban counties around Milwaukee—Ozaukee, Washington and Waukesha—are so heavily Republican that although Milwaukee County voted almost 2-to-1 for John Kerry in 2004, George W. Bush carried the overall Milwaukee metro area. In 2010 a similar pattern held for Walker and the GOP Senate candidate, businessman Ron Johnson, who won his election. Eastern Wisconsin—the counties along Lake Michigan and two or three counties inland, with small industrial cities in the Fox River Valley like Kenosha, Sheboygan, Appleton, and Green Bay—is Republican turf that voted solidly for Walker and Johnson. Western and northern Wisconsin—areas along the Mississippi River, the small inland cities such as Wausau and Eau Claire and the counties along Lake Superior—are more

Voter Turnout	
2013 Total Citizen 18+	4,298,617
2014 Highest Statewide Turnout	2,410,314
2014 Turnout as % CVAP	56.1%
2012 Turnout as % CVAP	71.9%
Legislature	
Senate:	19R 14D
House:	63R 36D

Democratic, voting for now Sen. Tammy Baldwin in 2012 and Doyle for governor in 2006. The *Milwaukee Journal Sentinel's* Craig Gilbert, in his fine-grained analysis of Wisconsin election results, has suggested that this represents ethnic differences: Eastern Wisconsin is more German, and western and northern Wisconsin more Scandinavian. The most Democratic region by far is around Madison (Dane County), the state capital and home of the huge University of Wisconsin, whose college-town atmosphere and unionized state employees have spread to rural counties to the south and northeast. La Crosse and Eau Claire host University of Wisconsin system campuses, as does Rock County (Janesville) that also contains the liberal arts school, Beloit College. The band from Janesville northeast to Eau Claire creates a university belt that also helps this territory lean Democratic.

With statewide races in Wisconsin frequently won by 10 percent of the vote or less, there's a significant number of Wisconsinites who can cross over the ideological and partisan divides, providing the margin of victory in elections. In April 2015, the state held judicial elections that featured two important statewide contests: an officially non-partisan election for the state Supreme Court that pitted sitting Justice Ann Walsh Bradley, a member of the court's liberal bloc, against James Daley, a local judge backed by conservatives; and an amendment to the state constitution that would allow the seven jurists on the state's high court to select their chief justice, rather than let that post be determined by seniority. The effect of voting for the amendment meant that the four conservative judges on the state Supreme Court would be able to replace 81-year-old liberal Wisconsin Chief Justice Shirley Abrahamson with a conservative from their own ranks. Just over 800,000 ballots were cast in both contests and Wisconsin voters delivered a split decision: they reelected Bradley, who made her opposition to the constitutional amendment well known, with 58% of the vote, and then they backed the constitutional amendment with 53% of the vote. Nine counties around Milwaukee and in the lower Fox River Valley voted against Bradley and for the constitutional amendment, and 14 counties including Milwaukee and those in the eastern university belt voted for Bradley and against the amendment. But the 49 other counties in the state were ideologically inconsistent, voting to keep Bradley on the bench but also supporting the amendment that would displace the state Supreme Court's liberal chief. This is not unusual for Wisconsin: In 2010, voters there elected to the Senate GOP entrepreneur Johnson, who turned out to be the most conservative member in that chamber in 2011, according to *National Journal's* annual rankings. In 2012, Wisconsin voters promoted liberal Democratic Rep. Baldwin to be the first openly gay person to serve in the Senate.

Population		Race and Ethnicity		Income	
Total:	5,742,713	White	83.0%	Median income:	$55,258
Urban:	39.3%	Black	6.1%		*(18 of 50)*
Suburban:	26.8%	Latino	6.0%	Under $50,000	48.4%
Rural:	33.9%	Asian	2.3%	$50,000-$99,999:	32.6%
Land area:	54,158	Two races	1.7%	$100,000-$199,999:	16.0%
Pop/sq. mi.:	106.0	White Ethnic	31.0%	$200,000 or more:	3.0%
Born in state:	71.8%			Poverty Rate	10.2%
		Education			
Age Groups		H.S. grad or less:	41.1%	**Work**	
Under 18:	22.7%	Some college:	31.2%	White collar:	33.9%
18 to 34:	22.5%	College degree, 4 yr.:	18.4%	Blue collar:	40.7%
35 to 64:	40.0%	Post-grad study:	9.4%	Sales and service:	25.5%
Over 64:	14.8%				
		Military		Govt. workers:	12.2%
		Veterans/active duty:	8.1%		

Presidential Politics Wisconsin has voted Democratic in the last seven presidential elections, starting in 1988. But sometimes the margin has been quite narrow. Al Gore carried Wisconsin 47.8%-47.6%, a margin of only 5,708 votes in 2000, and John Kerry won it 49.7%-49.3%, a margin of only 11,384 votes in 2004. In both races, some historic patterns were reversed. George W. Bush carried eastern Wisconsin and metro Milwaukee both times, while Gore and Kerry carried western and northern Wisconsin. From 1992 to 2006, it elected only Democratic senators, although sometimes by narrow margins.

2012 Presidential Vote		
Barack Obama (D) 1,620,985	(53%)
Mitt Romney (R)..............1,407,966	(46%)

2012 Presidential Primary		
Mitt Romney (R).................346,876	(44%)
Rick Santorum (R) 290,139	(37%)
Ron Paul (R) 87,858	(11%)
Newt Gingrich (R)...............45,978	(6%)

2008 Presidential Vote		
Barack Obama (D) 1,677,211	(56%)
John McCain (R)..............1,262,393	(42%)

In 2008, Wisconsin was not a presidential battleground, and Obama ended up winning a solid 56%-42% over John McCain, carrying 59 of 72 counties—the largest number of counties in any state switching from one party to the other between 2004 and 2008. Obama made especially large gains over previous Democrats in the Fox River Valley. His victory would seem to have put the state out of Republicans' reach in 2012. But GOP Gov. Scott Walker's victory in the recall election in June and Mitt Romney's selection of Wisconsin Rep. Paul Ryan as the Republican vice presidential nominee put it in play. Wisconsin that year was also the scene of a spirited Senate race between liberal 2nd District Rep. Tammy Baldwin and former Gov. Tommy Thompson.

Romney improved on McCain's performance in Wisconsin, but still fell well short as Obama won 53%-46%, while Baldwin won 51%-46%. Obama increased his lead in Milwaukee County but lost ground in the Fox River Valley and the north-central region. Exit polls tell some of the story. The June recall election exit poll showed Obama with a 51%-44% job approval rating. The November exit poll showed Walker with a 52%-46% job approval rating. While the ardent partisans dominated the political dialogue, a decisive number of Wisconsin voters apparently approved of both their president and their governor.

Wisconsin once had one of the nation's most influential presidential primaries. It knocked Wendell Willkie out of the race in 1944, helped John Kennedy establish his lead over Hubert Humphrey in 1960, prompted Lyndon Johnson to withdraw as Eugene McCarthy was about to beat him here in 1968, gave George McGovern his first victory in 1972, gave Jimmy Carter a key victory in 1976—after ABC and NBC mistakenly called the primary for Mo Udall—and chose "New Democrat" Gary Hart over Minnesota neighbor Walter Mondale in 1984. Later, Wisconsin's primary, even after it was moved from April to March, tended to be ignored. So for the 2004 election, the legislature moved the date up another month, to February 17, the only primary held that day. Wisconsin saw heavier campaigning than it had in years, at least for a few days, and it may have proved crucial. In the Democratic primary, Kerry led John Edwards 40%-34%, with Howard Dean in third place with 18%. Dean ended his campaign, while Edwards failed to get the momentum a victory here might have given him. Wisconsin does not have party registration, and few people bothered to vote in the uncontested Republican primary that year.

Wisconsin scheduled its 2008 primary on February 19. A week earlier, Obama had swept the primaries in Maryland, Virginia, and the District of Columbia. Gov. Jim Doyle campaigned for Obama, who was also backed by longtime Rep. David Obey, the dean of the Wisconsin congressional delegation. Obama outspent Hillary Clinton on television ads 5-to-1 and won a smashing 58%-41% victory, demonstrating, as he did in the Iowa caucuses, that he could prevail among a mostly white electorate. He lost only 10 counties, mostly at the edge of the state and presumably out of range of most Wisconsin television stations. Clinton got the votes of 50% of women, but Obama got the votes of 67% of men. He won 68% of the vote in Dane County, home to Madison and the University of Wisconsin, and 64% in Milwaukee County, with its large African-American population. Turnout topped 1 million, far above that in recent years, though just slightly below the turnout in 1972, when McGovern was in the race.

There was less action on the Republican side. McCain had serious opposition only from Mike Huckabee, who was far behind in delegates. Turnout was 410,000, below that of the previous contested primaries and less than half the turnout in 1980. McCain beat Huckabee

55%-37%. Huckabee did well in the central and western parts of the state, and McCain ran best in the Milwaukee suburbs.

In 2012, Wisconsin voted on April 3 and delivered the final blow to Rick Santorum's chances for the GOP nomination. With March victories in southern primaries and rural caucus states, Santorum established himself as the only viable option to Romney, who had narrow primary wins in Ohio and Michigan and a larger win in Illinois under his belt. Walker, facing the recall election, remained neutral, but Ryan endorsed Romney and stumped for him around the state. Santorum was able to carry most rural counties, but Romney won big margins in Milwaukee and affluent suburbs and won the state, 44%-37%. Santorum insisted he would remain in the race through the primary in his native Pennsylvania, but he ran poorly in polls there and suspended his campaign before the voting.

Congressional Districts Wisconsin lost a congressional district in the 2000 census. After Democratic Rep. Tom Barrett retired to run for governor, his north Milwaukee district was easy to eliminate. The resulting consensus plan enabled all four Democrats and four Republicans running for reelection

114th Congress Lineup	
5 R	3 D
113th Congress Lineup	
5 R	3 D

to win in 2002. The balance tipped in 2006, when Democrat Steve Kagen captured the Green Bay 8th District, but tipped the other way in 2010, when Republican Reid Ribble defeated Kagen and Scott Duffy picked up retiring Democrat David Obey's northwestern 7th District.

In 2011, Republicans had total control over redistricting. Democrats, enraged by the Republicans' bill to curtail collective bargaining rights in Wisconsin, had petitioned to oust six state senators in recall elections on August 9. With the Senate under siege, Gov. Scott Walker quietly signed a pro-Republican map into law the same day. The map shored up Duffy, giving him friendly St. Croix County in the Twin Cities exurbs and trading the liberal cities of Stevens Point and Wisconsin Rapids to 3rd District Democrat Ron Kind. It also boosted Republicans Paul Ryan in the 1st District and Tom Petri in the 6th District with an eye toward possible future open seats. In November 2012, Republicans won 49% of all votes cast for the House but kept their 5-3 edge. Following his retirement in 2014, Petri was replaced by the more conservative Glenn Grothman.

Governor

Scott Walker (R)

Elected 2010, term expires Jan. 2019, 2nd term; b. Nov. 2, 1967, Colorado Springs, CO; Marquette U., attended 1986-90; Christian; married (Tonette); 2 children.

Elected Office: WI Assembly, 1993-2002; Milwaukee Cnty. Exec., 2002-10.

Professional Career: Salesman, IBM Corp., 1988-90; Financial developer, American Red Cross, 1990-94.

Office: 115 E. Capitol, Madison, 53702, 608-266-1212; Website: wisgov. state.wi.us.

Election Results

2014 general	Scott Walker (R)	1,259,706	(52%)
	Mary Burke (D)	1,122,913	(47%)

Prior winning percentages: 2012 (54%), 2010 (52%)

An adroit politician and campaigner, Republican Scott Walker won three elections for Wisconsin's governorship in the space of four years. And his victory in the 2012 recall contest stemming from his success in taming union power in Wisconsin vaulted him to the top ranks of the 2016 GOP White House hopefuls.

Walker was born in Colorado Springs, Colo., and moved with his family at age 10 to Delavan, a small town 60 miles southeast of Madison. His mother kept the books for a local department store and his father was a Baptist preacher who Walker stood next to on Sundays to help greet worshippers. Walker was an Eagle Scout and represented Wisconsin at the Boys Nation student government program in Washington D.C. in 1985, an achievement that he says spurred his interest in politics. Republican Ronald Reagan was president at the time and served as an inspiration to him. He attended Marquette University and left before graduating to take a job in his senior year with the American Red Cross in marketing and development.

Walker ran for the state Assembly in 1990 but lost to Democratic incumbent Gwen Moore, who went on to serve in the U.S. House. Three years later, he tried again and won. He reportedly considered running for governor, but a pension scandal that led to Tom Ament's resignation as Milwaukee County executive changed Walker's plans. Promising to run a clean government, Walker was elected to that job in 2002. Liberal Democrats had previously held the nonpartisan county executive's post and Walker put a fiscally conservative stamp on the job. He cut the workforce by 20% and used his veto more than 100 times to force $44 million in spending cuts. Each of his budgets held property taxes in check, and he returned a portion of his salary to the county's coffers. Some Democrats accused him of being overly stingy in financing basic services. But others hailed his low-key personality and political skills. Walker "has that ability to disagree without being disagreeable, which is important," University of Wisconsin-Milwaukee political scientist Mordecai Lee told the *Wisconsin State Journal* in 2010. "He is probably the best politician I have seen in a generation."

Walker entered the race for governor in 2006, but backed out after 14 months, saying that he had trouble raising enough money to compete. In hindsight, that was a wise call as 2006 turned out to be a banner year for Democrats. In April 2009, he announced his second bid, criticizing Democratic Gov. Jim Doyle for increased spending and taxes. He emphasized what he called a common-sense, "brown bag" approach to making cutbacks; a philosophy he said was reflected in his frequent routine of packing his own lunch. Four months after Walker entered the race, Doyle, who trailed Walker in some polls, announced he would not seek a third term. Walker faced a GOP primary challenger in Mark Neumann, a homebuilder and developer who served two terms in the U.S. House in the 1990s. Despite Neumann's reputation as a budget hawk, Walker accused his opponent of having voted for a transportation bill that included $9 billion in pork-barrel spending—an attack that Neumann said he initially thought was a joke. Neumann remained ahead in fundraising throughout the race, drawing from his personal wealth. But Walker continued to blast Neumann as a "career politician," a charge that resonated in an anti-incumbent political year. He handily beat Neumann in the September 2010 primary, 59%-39%.

Walker's Democratic opponent was another former House member—Tom Barrett, a representative from 1993 to 2003 before winning election as Milwaukee's mayor. He lost the 2002 Democratic primary for governor to Doyle. Barrett touted his economic program, which included targeted tax credits for companies hiring more workers and a proposal to commit $100 million in state funds to private venture capital firms over five years, a move he said would raise at least $500 million. Walker scoffed at the idea, saying it would expand government and hike spending. Barrett began the race with a considerable fundraising edge, but Walker raised $2.8 million from September to mid-October. Wisconsin Republicans were clearly more energized than Democrats in the election, charged up by their efforts to oust veteran Democratic Sen. Russ Feingold, who was up for reelection. They propelled Walker to a 52%-47% victory on his 43rd birthday. Though Barrett carried Milwaukee County 62%-38%, Dane County (Madison) 68%-31%, as well as Eau Clair, La Crosse and Rock Counties, Walker won the Milwaukee suburbs, the Fox River Valley and most of the rest of the state.

On his first official day in office, Walker called the legislature into session to address the state's economy and swiftly won two victories. Republicans passed bills to tighten personal injury laws and to provide tax breaks for people with health savings accounts. He also shuttered the state's Department of Commerce and replaced it with a public-private agency, the Wisconsin Economic Development Corporation. And in a state with same-day voter registration and a large transitory college student population, Walker and the GOP legislature tightened state voter ID laws to require a current or recently expired Wisconsin driver's license, another form of government identification, like a passport, or certain Wisconsin student IDs, to cast a ballot.

But the attention those measures received paled in comparison to the uproar over his attempts to close a $137 million gap in the budget. He called for curtailing collective bargaining rights for many of the state's public employees, describing those rights as an obstacle to reducing state and local budget deficits. Outraged by the assault on unions, 14 Senate Democrats traveled to Illinois to stall a vote. Union workers showed up at the Capitol by the tens of thousands, carrying angry signs and inspiring similar protests against GOP governors' tactics in other states. Activists gathered petitions to recall eight GOP Wisconsin state senators. Walker became an instant political celebrity. Prospective Republican presidential candidates stampeded to support him, he appeared on national television shows, and he even was mentioned as a possible vice presidential candidate for 2012.

In the face of the noisy protests, Walker refused to back down, saying repeatedly that the state was "broke"—an assertion that the politics watchdog *PolitiFact* declared false, noting that the state still had money to pay its bills and enjoyed a high credit rating. State Senate Republicans in March passed a bill with the collective bargaining provisions without Democratic senators present. A *Milwaukee Journal Sentinel* poll that month showed just how polarizing the governor had become: 90% of Republicans approved of his job performance, while 91% of Democrats disapproved. In April, an election for state Supreme Court judges turned into a proxy for the battling sides. Justice David Prosser, a self-described judicial conservative, defeated challenger JoAnne Kloppenburg after a concerted effort by liberal interest groups to topple Prosser in retaliation for Walker's crackdown on unions. Republicans maintained their 4-3 majority on the court.

Walker's collective bargaining changes survived a court challenge and became law in June 2011. But the anger that flared up over the changes did not subside. In July, a report prepared by the state National Guard and Wisconsin Emergency Management criticized the state's handling of the union protests and concluded that no chain of command existed between the governor's office and law enforcement. With the help of labor groups, Democrats tried to gain control of the state Senate by attempting to recall six Republican incumbents, all Walker allies, in August 2011. But four of the six Republicans survived, and the GOP maintained a thin 17-16 majority. Also percolating was an investigation into whether Milwaukee County staffers in Walker's former office did political work with taxpayer money. In early 2012, two of Walker's appointees were charged with embezzling money and spending the money on trips and personal items after one of his staffers noticed missing funds; eventually, they and four other aides and associates of the governor were convicted as part of the state probe. Walker supporters said the outcome showed that the governor was never a target of the investigation, while critics said it demonstrated he was at least guilty of bad judgment.

An official movement to recall Walker over the collective bargaining controversy began in late 2011. United Wisconsin, the group managing the recall and working with the state Democratic Party, announced in January 2012 that it had collected 1 million signatures to put the issue on the ballot, far above the 540,208 required. Subsequent polls showed that the public narrowly opposed the recall, with even some of Walker's opponents saying they preferred to settle differences through the regular election process. But the effort forged ahead and the June recall became the most expensive election in Wisconsin history. Candidates and outside groups poured in more than $63 million, according to the Center for Public Integrity, compared to the $37.4 million spent in the 2010 race. Barrett won a five-way primary to take on Walker again, but suffered a substantial fundraising disadvantage. Walker notched a 53%-46% triumph, improving on his 2010 showing by 1 percentage point and becoming the first governor in history to avoid a recall. "Tonight we tell Wisconsin, we tell our country, and we tell people all across the globe that voters really do want leaders that stand up and make the tough decisions," crowed Walker in his victory speech. The vast campaign spending on Walker's behalf by conservative groups, including the Wisconsin Club for Growth and Wisconsin Manufacturers & Commerce, prompted the state's Government Accountability Board to authorize a so-called "John Doe" investigation—which requires strict secrecy and can prohibit targets of the probe from discussing it—to see if campaign contribution limits or laws barring coordination between candidates and independent groups had been breached. John Chisholm, the Democratic Milwaukee County district attorney who had investigated Walker county executive staffers earlier, was given the initial responsibility for the new probe.

Walker, for his part, kept a lower public profile nationally, though he did reveal in March 2013 that he was writing a book called *Unintimidated: A Governor's Story and a Nation's Challenge*. The book renewed speculation about his presidential ambitions, though he would first have to win reelection in 2014: His approval rating in a Marquette University's survey that month was 50%. His political success over the unions and in the recall earned him a spot on *Time* magazine's list of the 100 most influential people of 2014 and he began that year signing a $541 million tax cut for families and businesses while state officials forecast a $1 billion surplus for the coming year. Unable to entice a marquee candidate to take on Walker against that backdrop, Democrats nominated Mary Burke, a former state Commerce secretary and a millionaire former executive at her family's business, Trek Bicycle Co. She easily beat out state Rep. Brett Hulsey in the primary and then waged a fiercely competitive race against Walker that drew national attention. President Barack Obama, former President Bill Clinton, and First Lady Michelle Obama, twice, campaigned in Wisconsin for Burke, who promised to bring to the state problem-solving skills and moderate views.

Burke didn't dwell on the 2012 recall campaign and the issues that led to it, and instead charged Walker with making deep education cuts and blamed him for the decline in workers' incomes. Outside groups and unions joined the fray on Burke's behalf, helping to highlight Walker's failure to meet his 2010 pledge to create 250,000 new jobs in Wisconsin, and pushing other attacks. Democrats also painted Walker as a social extremist. The groups, led by Emily's List, an organization that backs pro-choice female Democratic candidates, attacked the governor for signing into law a bill requiring women to get an ultrasound before having an abortion, cutting funding for Planned Parenthood and making it harder to advance pay-equity lawsuits. Walker responded by portraying Burke as a liberal, and his campaign ran negative ads mocking Burke's wealth while her family business outsourced jobs by building bikes overseas. Under fire on abortion, Walker appeared in a sober campaign ad that he reportedly crafted himself, defending his proposals as only intended to promote safety and more information that "leaves the final decision to a woman and her doctor." He defeated Burke 52%-47%, carrying almost the exact same counties he did in 2010. While narrow, his victory was comprehensive as exit poll readings showed that he carried college and non-college voters, every age group except for those between 25 and 39, and swept independents. He only narrowly lost self-described moderates to Burke, 52%-46%, an uncommonly good showing for a Republican and three percentage points better than in his 2010 race. During the campaign, Walker had refused to say he would serve a full four-year term if reelected, and the exit poll found that voters weren't eager for a potential White House run by Walker: 55% said they did not think he would make a good president, compared to 42% who said he would.

Walker got plenty of good news in 2015 in that regard: Polls showed him an early favorite in Iowa, whose caucuses kick off the presidential nominating contest. Perhaps just as important, in July the Wisconsin Supreme Court brought a halt to the "John Doe" investigation that had been pursuing Walker and his allies since the 2012 recall. It was a 4-2 ruling by the conservative bloc of the polarized court (one justice recused herself), but it was unambiguous and it rebuked investigators for their overzealous tactics and flimsy legal reasoning. Not long after the verdict, Walker declared he wanted to shut down the Government Accountability Board that had authorized the probe and replace it with an entity "truly accountable" to the state's citizenry. Liberals alleged that idea was motivated by a sense of spite. On fiscal matters, Walker was less fortunate. The $1 billion projected surplus from the previous year never materialized and he was forced to cope with a shortfall of about $280 billion. His proposals to slash funding for the University of Wisconsin system and state aid to education were met with resistance from the GOP-controlled legislature. Republican lawmakers pruned his cuts to the university system, which still took a $250 million hit, and they blocked his proposed reduction in K-12 education funding. But Walker was able to sign a new budget without raising taxes and used his line-item veto pen on more than 100 items in the measure. The two-year, $73-billion budget removed tenure protections for state university professors from state law and repealed the state's prevailing wage law, making Wisconsin a right-to-work state, a proposal Walker hadn't campaigned on but was quick to embrace once it gained momentum among the GOP legislators.

Walker also signed a bill that banned abortion after the 20th week of pregnancy with no exceptions for rape or incest, permitting it only in case of a medical emergency. Notwithstanding his defensiveness on the issue during his reelection campaign, Republican lawmakers said Walker invited them to send such a proposal. One potential blemish on his presidential candidacy, which had garnered generally favorable early reviews, was an ongoing series of audits of the Wisconsin Economic Development Corporation, which Walker established in his first year in office. Reports described a sloppily run agency that handed out grants and loans to unqualified businesses, some with ties to the governor's financial supporters. Walker cannily called on the legislature to reform the beleaguered agency and remove all elected officials from its board, which he chaired. The state lawmakers revised Walker's proposal so that it removed only the governor from the board. His resignation took effect on July 12, when he signed the state budget filled with other measures he can tout on the 2016 campaign trail.

Senior Senator

Ron Johnson (R)

Elected 2010, term expires Jan., 2017, 1st term; b. April 8, 1955, Mankato, MN; U. of MN, B.S. 1977; Lutheran; married (Jane); 3 children.

Professional Career: Owner, PACUR; Accountant, Josten's.

DC Office: 328 HSOB, 20510, 202-224-5323; Fax: 202-228-6965; Website: ronjohnson.senate.gov.

State Offices: Milwaukee, 414-276-7282; Oshkosh, 920-230-7250.

Committees: *Budget. Commerce, Science & Transportation:* Aviation Operations, Safety & Security; Communications, Technology & the Internet; Surface Transportation & Merchant Marine Infrastructure, Safety & Security; Oceans, Atmosphere, Fisheries, & Coast Guard. *Foreign Relations:* European & Regional Security Cooperation (Chmn); Near East, South Asia, Central Asia, & Counterterrorism; East Asian, the Pacific, & International Cybersecurity Policy; State Department & USAID Management, International Operations, & Bilateral International Development. *Homeland Security & Governmental Affairs* (Chmn): Federal Spending Oversight & Emergency Management; Regulatory Affairs & Federal Management; Investigations (Permanent).

Group Ratings

	ADA	ACLU	AFL-CIO	LCV	ITI	COC	HAFA	ACU	CFG	FRC
2014	0%	0%	–	20%	33%	88%	81%	96%	95%	93%
2013	0%	C	0%	8%	C	75%	C	96%	87%	C

National Journal Ratings

	2013 LIB	—	2013 CONS
Economic	8%	—	91%
Social	8%	—	91%
Foreign	14%	—	85%
Composite	11%	—	90%

Key Votes of the 113th Congress

1. Sandy storm spending	N	5. Student Loan Rates	Y	9. Bipartisan Budget Deal	Y
2. Chuck Hagel Confirmation	N	6. Employee Non-Discrim'n Act	N	10. Farm Bill Conference Rept.	N
3. Gun Background Checks	N	7. Senate Vote on Judgeships	Y	11. Unempl. Comp. Extension	N
4. Immigration Reform	N	8. Defense Dept. Spending	N	12. Keystone Pipeline	Y

Election Results

2010 general	Ron Johnson (R)	1,125,999 (52%)	$15,043,252	$1,774,332	$286,373
	Russ Feingold (D)	1,020,958 (47%)	$20,342,208	$1,003,697	$776,209
2010 primary	Ron Johnson (R)	504,644 (85%)			
	Dave Westlake (R)	61,633 (10%)			

Republican Ron Johnson, Wisconsin's senior senator, won his seat in one of 2010's biggest upsets, dispatching 18-year Democratic Sen. Russ Feingold. Johnson has made waves in the Senate, unsuccessfully seeking a GOP leadership post within a year of being elected, taking a hard-line stance on curtailing federal spending and filing a lawsuit over the Affordable Care Act. He became chairman of the Homeland Security and Governmental Affairs Committee in 2015 but faced a tough reelection against the man he ousted.

Johnson grew up in Mankato, Minn. He says he developed a strong work ethic at an early age, delivering newspapers, caddying at a golf course, and baling hay on his uncle's dairy farm. He was a restaurant dishwasher at 15 and within a year won a promotion to night manager. Although Johnson didn't finish high school, he attended college, working full-time and graduating with $7,000 in the bank. While working as an accountant, Johnson went to night school to earn an MBA. Just short of a degree in 1979, he decided to move to Oshkosh to start a plastics company, PACUR, with his brother-in-law. Their first customer was a company co-founded by his father-in-law. Since then, the business has become a major producer of specialty packaging for medical devices, employing about 120 workers.

Johnson has said his political views have been influenced by Ayn Rand's 1957 novel *Atlas Shrugged*, which argues that civilization cannot exist where men are slaves to society and government. Johnson said that his motivation to run against Feingold was the senator's support of the Democrats' 2010 health care overhaul, which he called "the single greatest assault to our freedom in my lifetime."

He entered the race in May, just days before the state Republican nominating convention. Three GOP candidates were already competing, including beer mogul and former state Commerce Secretary Dick Leinenkugel and Madison developer Terrence Wall. But Johnson's ability to self-finance made an immediate impact. At the convention, Leinenkugel surprised everyone, including Johnson, by taking his turn at the lectern to drop out and endorse Johnson, saying, "It's not my time ... it's Ron Johnson's time." Wall then reluctantly followed suit. Spending more than $4 million of his own money, Johnson went on to crush Watertown businessman Dave Westlake in the September primary with 85 percent of the vote.

In the general election, Johnson began with backing from tea party activists. "America needs to be pulled back from the brink of socialism and state control," Johnson told a tea party gathering in May 2010. But some conservative groups developed second thoughts about his readiness for the Senate. Early in the campaign, he acknowledged that he was still developing his views on issues. One state group, the Rock River Patriots, declined to endorse him, saying they were unimpressed with his knowledge of the Constitution. But the National Republican Senatorial Committee, sensing an opportunity, jumped in to help, as did conservative kingmaker Jim DeMint, a Republican senator from South Carolina.

The campaign between Johnson and Feingold—a liberal with a quirky, maverick streak—was nasty, especially by Wisconsin's normally civil standards. Without a legislative record of his opponent to mine, Feingold sought to concentrate on Johnson's record in business, attempting to depict him as someone more concerned about profits than people—someone "with a country club view of reality." Feingold also called Johnson a hypocrite for opposing federal economic stimulus funds and then allegedly seeking those funds for renovation of an opera house.

Johnson fought back, noting in an ad that the Senate had 57 lawyers, including Feingold, but just one accountant and no manufacturers like himself. His GOP allies also did a textbook job of depicting the incumbent—who had contemplated running for president in 2008—as an entrenched Washington insider supportive of deficit spending. Johnson called for a "hard spending cap" in the federal budget, while Feingold said he would support giving the president line-item veto power over appropriations bills. Feingold had $21 million to Johnson's $15 million, but it was not enough in a Republican wave year. Johnson won, 52% to 47%.

Johnson initially got seats on the Appropriations and Budget committees, but he left Appropriations for Foreign Relations in 2013 after saying he was tired of being the only committee member opposed to more spending. In May 2011, he notably did not support fellow Wisconsin Republican Paul Ryan's controversial budget plan to dramatically reduce the deficit and transform Medicare, arguing that Ryan's proposal did not cut spending enough. In late June 2011, Johnson blocked a resolution to support military action in Libya as a way of calling attention to debt reduction, saying on the floor that the debt is "the single most important issue facing this nation." Hoping for more radical spending cuts, he joined 18 other Senate Republicans in opposing the August 2011 deal that raised the debt limit.

In December 2011, Johnson launched a bid for a Senate Republican leadership post as conference vice chairman. The race was a classic outsider-vs.-insider battle, with Johnson the maverick running against the establishment candidate, Roy Blunt of Missouri. The conference ended up electing Blunt over Johnson, 25-22. When *Roll Call* reported that Johnson had alienated some Senate Republicans, he blasted the article, telling the *Milwaukee Journal Sentinel* that "it's pretty clear there is some discomfort with an independent voice pushing for solutions."

In Washington, Johnson has been blunt; a former strategist of his, Brad Todd, has described him as "straight as a shot of uncut whiskey." He's showed little interest in the chamber's usual courtesies, drawing particular attention for grilling outgoing Secretary of State Hillary Clinton at a Foreign Relations Committee hearing in January 2013 on the deadly terrorist attack at the U.S. consulate in Benghazi, Libya. Johnson complained that lawmakers had been "misled" about the incident, and when Clinton said it would have been inappropriate to contact diplomatic staff for details immediately afterward because of an FBI investigation, he replied, "I realize that's a good excuse." An exasperated Clinton retorted: "No, it's a fact ... What difference, at this point, does it make?" After *The Washington Post* awarded Johnson its "Worst Week in Washington" accolade for his aggressiveness, the senator said, "In Washington, demanding the truth is apparently a sin." In the long run, however, Johnson may have fought to at least a draw: The footage of Clinton's incensed answer has been unspooled repeatedly by conservatives to remind voters of the likely Democratic nominee's biggest foreign policy blemish.

Johnson also tangled publicly with another high-profile Democrat. At a hearing in May 2014, Sen. John D. Rockefeller IV of West Virginia, said Republican opposition to the health-care law stemmed from the fact that Obama was "the wrong color." That led an angry Johnson to respond to Rockefeller: "It was regrettable and I would say it was offensive ... that you would play the race card." Johnson's enmity toward the Affordable Care Act led him to file a lawsuit challenging the provision that lawmakers and some of their employees obtain insurance through the state exchanges that the law created. A federal judge in July 2014 dismissed the suit, saying Johnson could not prove that the policy legally impaired him; the ruling was upheld on appeal in April 2015.

As a senator, Johnson has compiled a conservative voting record. His lifetime score from the anti-tax group Club for Growth is 95 percent, one of the chamber's highest. In *Politico* reporter Kenneth P. Vogel's 2014 book *Big Money*, he said he heard a person who attended a seminar organized by influential billionaires Charles and David Koch describe Johnson as the Kochs' "model legislator." But when tea party-backed candidates failed to topple incumbent GOP senators in several primary elections in 2014, Johnson drew attention for emphasizing pragmatism over political purity. "I think the conservative movement may just be maturing a little bit," he said at the Republican Leadership Conference in New Orleans. "You can be very doctrinaire, you can demand purity, but in the end if you want to advance policy that you want enacted, you have to win elections."

And in advance of his difficult reelection campaign, Johnson has softened his approach. He said that he no longer believes that the Affordable Care Act can be "repealed and replaced," a stance that put him at odds with the rhetoric of many in his party, and he was one of the leading voices within the GOP calling for a backup plan if the Supreme Court had overturned extensive portions of the health care law in the case *King v. Burwell*. (The court instead upheld the law as written.) At the Homeland Security panel, Johnson has pointed admiringly to the bipartisan teamwork at the committee's helm by moderates Republican Sen. Susan Collins of Maine and then-Sen. Joe Lieberman of Connecticut. Following their example, Johnson won Senate passage of the Integrated Public Alert and Warning System Modernization Act of 2015 by unanimous consent. And rhetorically, he put some distance between himself and the tea party. "I sprang out of the tea-party movement, no question," he told *National Journal*, but he emphasized that "I've never joined any kind of tea-party caucus or tea-party group."

The rematch with Feingold was poised to become one of the marquee Senate races of 2016, pitting the senator who may be the Republicans' most vulnerable incumbent against his strongest possible Democratic contender, during a presidential election year that should offer Feingold a more favorable turnout pattern than he had in 2010. A challenge for Feingold is that he has largely been out of the state since his loss, teaching at Stanford University and serving as a special State Department envoy in Africa.

Republican leaders were concerned that Johnson did not spend the first four years of his term laying the groundwork for what was destined to be a tough re-election contest. At the same time, Feingold has some history working against him. According to political analyst Nathan Gonzales, it is rare for a fallen incumbent to avenge his loss against the candidate who defeated him. The last time it happened was in 1934. In 1928, two-term Sen. Peter Gerry, a Democrat from Rhode Island, lost re-election to Republican Felix Hebert. Six years later, Gerry came back to handily defeat Heber.

Junior Senator

Tammy Baldwin (D)

Elected 2012, term expires Jan., 2019, 1st term; b. Feb. 11, 1962, Madison; Smith Col., B.A. 1984, U. of WI, J.D. 1989; No religious affiliation; single.

Elected Office: Dane Cnty. Bd. of Supervisors, 1986-94; WI Assembly, 1992-98; U.S. House, 1998-2012.

Professional Career: Practicing atty., 1989-92.

DC Office: 717 HSOB, 20510, 202-224-5653; Website: baldwin.senate. gov.

State Offices: Eau Claire, 715-832-8424; La Crosse, 608-796-0045; Madison, 608-264-5338; Milwaukee, 414-297-4451; Wausau, 715-261-2611.

Committees: *Appropriations*: Agriculture, Rural Development, FDA & Related Agencies; Commerce, Justice, Science & Related Agencies; Homeland Security; Labor, Health & Human Services, Education & Related Agencies; Military Construction, Veterans' Affairs & Related Agencies. *Budget. Health, Education, Labor & Pensions:* Employment & Workplace Safety; Primary Health & Retirement Security. *Homeland Security & Governmental Affairs:* Federal Spending Oversight & Emergency Management (RMM); Investigations (Permanent).

Group Ratings

	ADA	ACLU	AFL-CIO	LCV	ITI	COC	HAFA	ACU	CFG	FRC
2014	85%	100%	–	80%	100%	38%	3%	0%	6%	0%
2013	90%	C	100%	100%	C	50%	C	4%	2%	C

National Journal Ratings

	2013 LIB	—	2013 CONS
Economic	82%	—	8%
Social	73%	—	0%
Foreign	71%	—	0%
Composite	86%	—	14%

Key Votes of the 113th Congress

1. Sandy storm spending	Y	5. Student Loan Rates	N	9. Bipartisan Budget Deal	Y
2. Chuck Hagel Confirmation	Y	6. Employee Non-Discrim'n Act	Y	10. Farm Bill Conference Rept.	Y
3. Gun Background Checks	Y	7. Senate Vote on Judgeships	N	11. Unempl. Comp. Extension	Y
4. Immigration Reform	Y	8. Defense Dept. Spending	Y	12. Keystone Pipeline	N

Election Results

2012 general	Tammy Baldwin (D) 1,547,104	(51%)	$15,204,940	$3,269,678	$15,461,680
	Tommy Thompson (R)............. 1,380,126	(46%)	$9,582,888	$4,030,898	$19,024,651
	Joseph Kexel (I) 62,240	(2%)			
2012 primary	Tammy Baldwin (D) ....unopposed				

Prior winning percentages: House: 2010 (62%), 2008 (69%), 2006 (63%), 2004 (63%), 2002 (66%), 2000 (51%), 1998 (53%)

Democrat Tammy Baldwin, Wisconsin's junior senator, is the first openly gay person to serve in the Senate, and she is the first woman elected to the chamber from Wisconsin. In 2012, the former House member defeated former Gov. Tommy Thompson for the open seat of retiring Democratic Sen. Herb Kohl.

Baldwin grew up in Madison, where she was raised mostly by her maternal grandparents, a University of Wisconsin biochemist and the theater department's head costume designer. Her mother, who was 19 and a UW student when she was born, was "in the middle of a divorce and overwhelmed," Baldwin told the *New York Times*, adding that her mother had long battles with pain and addiction. "My grandparents were there, and I'm very, very grateful." Baldwin graduated first in her class at Madison West High School and went on to Smith College and UW law school. It was in college that it became "very clear" that she was gay. Her grandfather was deceased by the time she came out, but her grandmother was supportive.

In 1986, at age 24 and still in law school, Baldwin was elected to the Board of Supervisors of Dane County (Madison). In 1992, she was elected to the Wisconsin Assembly. Six years later, when moderate Republican Scott Klug honored his promise to serve only four terms in the U.S. House, Baldwin got into the race, along with three other Democrats and six Republicans.

As a woman who favored abortion rights, she was supported by EMILY's List, which helped her raise about one-quarter of her $1.5 million campaign chest. Baldwin won with 37 percent of the vote; then, in the general election, she beat former state Insurance Commissioner Jo Musser. This made her the first openly gay non-incumbent to win a seat in the House.

Baldwin's voting record was consistently one of the most liberal in the House. She secured a coveted seat on the Energy and Commerce Committee, but with the chamber in Republican hands for most of her House years, her ability to accomplish many of her progressive goals was limited. She was sharply critical of many GOP proposals, including the controversial budget proposal of fellow Wisconsin Rep. Paul Ryan and of Republican Gov. Scott Walker's equally controversial but successful effort to limit collective bargaining rights for state workers, the issue that touched off a recall campaign against Walker. (Baldwin told the *Times* that Walker had been "a nice guy" when they served together in the Assembly and that she felt "deceived" by his agenda as governor.)

Baldwin's driving issue has been guaranteed health care for all Americans. The issue was personal: A serious illness as a child kept her in the hospital for three months, making her a patient with a pre-existing condition. Baldwin supported the Democrats' 2010 overhaul of the health insurance system even though it did not include a government-run "public option" to compete with private insurers, a provision she had favored. She was also a leading advocate for the right to same-sex marriage. In 2008, she and Massachusetts Democrat Barney Frank, another gay lawmaker, established the House Lesbian, Gay, Bisexual, and Transgender Equality Caucus. An outspoken opponent of the Iraq war, Baldwin signed on as a cosponsor of Democrat Dennis Kucinich's 2007 resolution to impeach Vice President Dick Cheney for "deceptive actions leading up to the Iraq war" and other suspected crimes.

After Baldwin decided to run for Kohl's seat, she was unchallenged in the Democratic primary, giving her ample time to organize her campaign and raise money. Tommy Thompson, meanwhile, had to first get past three more conservative candidates in the Republican primary. Nevertheless, Thompson—a popular former governor known as a pragmatic conservative—started with a lead over Baldwin in the general election campaign. But she and her allies outspent Thompson and his backers by 3-to-1 in the weeks after the primary. It turned into an unrelentingly negative race.

Baldwin ran a disciplined campaign, seeking to convince voters that she would be more attuned to the needs of Wisconsin than the 70-year-old Thompson, a former Health and Human Services secretary under George W. Bush who hadn't been a candidate for office in 14 years. Realizing it made little sense to attack Thompson's gubernatorial record, which many Wisconsinites of both parties still remembered fondly, Baldwin instead blasted Thompson with negative television ads about his post-gubernatorial career, highlighting his work for a Washington D.C. lobbying firm. Her attacks caused Thompson's negatives to skyrocket. Meanwhile, Baldwin downplayed her liberal views and highlighted her populist stands against China's trade policies and her efforts at bipartisanship.

Thompson and Republicans accused Baldwin of being a radical, with his campaign releasing an ad citing her 2006 vote against a resolution honoring victims of the 9/11 attacks. Baldwin countered that Republicans had added provisions to the resolution commending other policies that she opposed, such as the USA PATRIOT Act. Her campaign fired back with an ad of its own, accusing Thompson of profiting off the victims. One outside analysis of both campaigns' ads found that over a 30-day period, 99 percent were negative. As the race neared its conclusion, Thompson turned to the right—he told a tea party group that he wanted to "do away with the Medicare and Medicaid," a stark departure from his previous positions—but the maneuver rang hollow with voters. The former governor failed to attract a significant number of Democratic crossover voters, and Baldwin won, 51% to 46%.

In the Senate, Baldwin secured seats on Appropriations; Budget; Health, Education, Labor, and Pensions; and Homeland Security and Governmental Affairs committees. She has voted a consistently liberal line, almost always taking the opposite stance from the state's senior senator, conservative Republican Ron Johnson. As Craig Gilbert noted in the Milwaukee *Journal Sentinel*, the two Wisconsin senators have split over the Affordable Care Act, fast-track trade authority, the Keystone XL pipeline, gun control, immigration, the minimum wage and a host of other issues. In fact, Baldwin and Johnson only voted together on six of *National Journal*'s 117 key votes in 2013, Gilbert noted. "Most of these disagreements reflect the huge abyss between the two parties," Gilbert wrote. A rare point of unison, Gilbert found, was a shared vote in favor of ensuring that same-sex spouses have access to Social Security and veterans' benefits.

FIRST DISTRICT

Paul Ryan (R)

Elected 1998, 9th term; b. Jan. 29, 1970, Janesville; Miami U. OH, B.A. 1992; Catholic; married (Janna); 3 children.

Professional Career: Aide, U.S. Sen. Bob Kasten, 1992; Advisor & speechwriter, Empower America, 1993-95; Legis. dir., U.S. Sen. Sam Brownback, 1995-97; Mktg. consultant, Ryan Inc. Central, 1997-98.

DC Office: 1233 LHOB, 20515, 202-225-3031; Fax: 202-225-3393; Website: paulryan.house.gov.

State Offices: Janesville, 608-752-4050; Kenosha, 262-654-1901; Racine, 262-637-0510.

Committees: *Ways & Means* (Chmn).

Group Ratings

	ADA	ACLU	AFL-CIO	LCV	ITI	COC	HAFA	ACU	CFG	FRC
2014	0%	0%	–	3%	80%	79%	58%	80%	69%	88%
2013	0%	C	14%	4%	C	85%	C	84%	79%	C

National Journal Ratings

	2013 LIB	—	2013 CONS
Economic	7%	—	92%
Social	38%	—	59%
Foreign	5%	—	86%
Composite	19%	—	81%

Key Votes of the 113th Congress

1. Sandy storm spending	N	5. Medical Marijuana	N	9. Syrian Rebels Training	Y
2. Violence Against Women Act	Y	6. Farm Bill	N	10. Keystone pipeline	Y
3. Guantanamo Bay Detainees	N	7. Afghanistan Combat	N	11. Immigration Exec. Action	Y
4. Abortion 20-week ban	Y	8. NSA Phone Data Collection	N	12. Bipartisan budget deal	Y

Election Results

2014 general	Paul Ryan (R)	182,316	(63%)	$8,041,590
	Rob Zerban (D)	105,552	(37%)	$704,510
2014 primary	Paul Ryan (R)	40,813	(94%)	
	Jeremy Ryan (R)	2,450	(6%)	

Prior winning percentages: 2012 (55%), 2010 (68%), 2008 (64%), 2006 (63%), 2004 (65%), 2002 (67%), 2000 (67%), 1998 (57%)

Population		Race and Ethnicity		Income	
Total:	709,472	White	81.7%	Median income:	$57,471
Urban:	35.0%	Latino	9.0%		(147 of 435)
Suburban:	50.2%	Black	5.4%	Under $50,000	43.6%
Rural:	14.8%	Asian	1.8%	$50,000-$99,999:	32.3%
Land area:	1,604	Two races	1.5%	$100,000-$199,999:	20.4%
Pop/sq. mi.:	442.4	White Ethnic	36.3%	$200,000 or more:	3.6%
Born in state:	66.9%			Poverty Rate	11.8%
		Education			
		H.S. grad or less:	41.3%	**Work**	
Age Groups		Some college:	32.5%	White collar:	34.4%
Under 18:	23.7%	College degree, 4 yr.:	17.1%	Blue collar:	40.0%
18 to 34:	20.0%	Post-grad study:	9.0%	Sales and service:	25.6%
35 to 64:	42.3%				
Over 64:	14.0%			Govt. workers:	10.9%
		Military			
		Veterans/active duty:	8.4%		

Southeast Wisconsin: Janesville, Kenosha, Kenosha

The southern tier of Wisconsin, from Lake Michigan to the Rock River Valley, is some of America's prime industrial country. Settled by Yankee and German farmers 170 years ago, it was once primarily dairy land. By the early 20th century, the steady habits and high skills of the local dairy farmers had made them a good labor pool for factories. There are still major plants here, including the headquarters of S. C. Johnson in Racine, with its Frank Lloyd Wright–designed tower. But the collapse of the domestic auto industry had a powerful impact on the local economy. In

Voter Turnout	
2013 Total Citizen 18+	521,810
2014 House Turnout	288,170
2014 Turnout as % CVAP	55.2%
2012 Turnout as % CVAP	72.7%

December 2008, General Motors closed its Janesville plant, laying off more than 5,000 workers, and in 2010, Chrysler shuttered its Kenosha plant, which once employed 14,000. (The GM layoffs became a line of attack for 2012 GOP vice presidential nominee Paul Ryan, of Janesville, who slammed President Barack Obama for saying in 2008 that the plant would "be here for another hundred years.") But local innovation was not dead. From a high of over 15% in 2009, the local unemployment rate fell to 4.9% in April 2015, a notable improvement though still a bit above the Wisconsin rate of 4.4%.

Kenosha, once primarily a factory town, has undergone a transformation, with some of the old smokestacks and shipyards along its lakefront replaced with museums, a marina, restaurants and boutiques that attract Chicagoans on weekends. Kenosha is competing with other towns in the region in trying to lure Chicago businesses north with lower tax rates. Most of the region is becoming metropolitan, part of the almost continuously suburban zone where metro Milwaukee melds into metro Chicago. But there are still some thriving old lake resorts, most notably Lake

2012 Presidential Vote		
Mitt Romney (R)	195,835	(52%)
Barack Obama (D)	179,872	(47%)
2008 Presidential Vote		
Barack Obama (D)	185,855	(51%)
John McCain (R)	176,152	(48%)
Cook Partisan Voting Index:	R+3	

Geneva, long a favorite weekend getaway for Chicagoans. In nearby Williams Bay is the University of Chicago's historic Yerkes Observatory, one of the nation's largest astronomy research centers.

The 1st Congressional District of Wisconsin runs from Lake Michigan west to Janesville in Rock County and encompasses all of Racine and Kenosha counties on Lake Michigan as well as parts of Walworth County, including Lake Geneva. It also takes in the southern Milwaukee County suburbs of Oak Creek and Greenfield and the southern tier of townships in suburban Waukesha County, including New Berlin.

The district tilts Republican. Waukesha County is heavily Republican, but Kenosha and Racine counties backed Obama in 2012. Rock County, where Janesville is located, gave Obama 61% of the vote. Boosted a bit by Ryan's presence on the ticket, the 1st District gave Mitt Romney 52% of the vote in 2012. In 2008, Obama won the district with 51%.

Paul Ryan (R)

Paul Ryan, a Republican elected in 1998, became chairman in 2015 of the powerful Ways and Means Committee, at age 44. He already had served four years as chairman of the Budget Committee where he was regarded as an intellectual leader in the GOP with unrivaled influence on fiscal matters, demonstrated the requisite political skills in his quick run as the GOP's vice presidential nominee, and provided much of his party's fresh thinking on domestic issues. In January 2015, he took himself out of the running for president in 2016. "Our party has a responsibility to offer a real alternative," he said. "So I'm going to do what I can to lay out conservative solutions and to help our nominee lead us to victory." Meanwhile, he remained well-positioned to secure added authority in either Congress or the executive branch during the coming years. Or, as he has said, he could move to the private sector.

Ryan grew up in Janesville, where in 1884 his great-grandfather started a family construction firm, now run by his cousins. His father, a Republican lawyer, and former Democratic Sen. Russ Feingold's father had law offices in the same building, and the two sons were friends in Congress before Feingold's 2010 defeat. Ryan got started in politics early, as a staffer for Republican Sen. Bob Kasten while attending college at Miami University in Ohio. During summers, he was a salesman for Oscar Mayer and can boast that he once drove the company's incomparable Wienermobile. He planned to apply to the University of Chicago and eventually become an economist, but says he "just kept getting really interesting jobs" in politics.

Ryan was hired as a speechwriter for Republican Rep. Jack Kemp of New York and then worked for the think tank Empower America founded by Kemp and conservative pundit

William Bennett. He later was legislative director for GOP Sen. Sam Brownback of Kansas. In his days as a poorly paid congressional staffer, Ryan moonlighted as a waiter and fitness trainer. His father and grandfather both died of heart attacks in their 50s, making Ryan, the father of three young children, particularly mindful of a healthy diet and an exercise regimen. *Washingtonian* magazine's survey of anonymous congressional staffers in 2010 named him the House's biggest "gym rat." In 2012 and 2014, he won the "workhorse" category.

In 1998, Ryan returned to the 1st District to run for the House when GOP Rep. Mark Neumann ran for the Senate (Neumann lost to Feingold). Ryan won the Republican primary with 81% of the vote. Democrats nominated Kenosha County official Lydia Spottswood, who had lost to Neumann in 1996. Ryan campaigned against tax increases and in favor of gun ownership rights. In a district that liberal Democrat Les Aspin held for a quarter-century before he became Bill Clinton's first Defense secretary, this was a strenuously contested election, one of the Democrats' top 10 priorities in the nation that year. Spottswood spent $1.33 million, and Ryan spent $1.24 million. But the outcome was not close. Ryan won 57%-43%.

In the House, Ryan has been a loyal conservative, especially since Barack Obama became president. Previously he had a reputation as someone who occasionally bucked his party and took centrist positions on foreign policy and some social issues. In 2007, he voted for a bill to prohibit employment discrimination on the basis of sexual orientation and later said he supported the bill because he had friends "who didn't choose to be gay ... they were just created that way." He said he "took a lot of crap" for the vote from social conservatives. He also voted for the 2008 government bailout of the domestic auto industry, citing mounting hardships in his district because of factory layoffs.

Ryan has been the top Republican on Budget since 2007, when he vaulted over 12 more senior Republicans on the committee. Like his political mentor, the late supply-sider Kemp, Ryan advocated tax cuts to spur economic growth but said his views have evolved to put equal weight on keeping deficits low and government growth in check. His beliefs drew widespread attention in 2009, when he began warning of future fiscal problems in dire terms. The debt, he told *The Washington Post*, was "completely unsustainable" and would "crash our economy." Democrats said such rhetoric came to typify Ryan's approach. Though they praised his affability, they accused him of overstating budgetary hazards and then refusing to accept any solutions other than his own. "It's very important not to mistake congeniality with compromise," Rep. Chris Van Hollen of Maryland, the ranking Democrat on Budget, told the *Los Angeles Times* in 2012.

In 2009, Ryan helped write the Republicans' alternative to Obama's first budget, along with Republican Conference Chairman Mike Pence of Indiana and Minority Whip Eric Cantor of Virginia, a close ally of Ryan. They pushed House Minority Leader John Boehner to include details about how the party would control spending and trim the deficit, but Boehner steered them away from specifics that could be picked apart by Democratic critics. The plan ultimately was panned in the press for lacking detail, and the effort was scrapped.

Undeterred, Ryan in 2010 produced a detailed "roadmap" to economic recovery as an alternative to the majority Democrats' budget, which he said was chock full of "reckless borrowing." His document called for a dramatically simpler tax code of two rates, 10% on annual income up to $100,000 for joint filers and 25% on income above that. Ryan's plan also called for breaking the link between employment and health insurance by switching from tax incentives for employer-provided insurance plans to tax credits for individual purchases of insurance. It would transform Medicare for Americans younger than 55 into a voucher system providing an average $11,000 for the purchase of government-approved policies. Most of the Republicans who won House seats in 2010, when the GOP scored a historic 63-seat gain, campaigned on Ryan's message of immediate and bold action on the deficit.

In 2011, Ryan pronounced himself highly disappointed with Obama's fiscal 2012 budget proposal, contending it did little to rein in spending over 10 years. Answering Democratic taunts that Republicans had no detailed response of their own, Ryan rolled out an alternative to much conservative fanfare. Titled "The Path to Prosperity," it called for freezing most domestic spending for five years and repealing the economic stimulus law in the course of cutting spending more than $6 trillion over 10 years, shrinking federal spending as a percentage of the economy to its lowest level since 1949.

The most immediately controversial feature of Ryan's budget was its plan for Medicare. As with his earlier "roadmap," individuals who turned 65 before 2022 would continue under the current program, while new seniors would get a government subsidy to buy private insurance. Many Democrats and some economic commentators sharply questioned the impact its cuts would have on the poor and middle class. In an April speech, Obama said Ryan's approach would lead to a country that is "fundamentally different than what we've known throughout our history." The House passed the budget in April, with 235 of the chamber's 239 Republicans backing it and every single Democrat opposing it.

Polls showed strong majorities of Americans opposed to the Medicare aspects of his budget. Democrats quickly began incorporating such sentiments into their effort to retake control of the House in 2012. Even some Republicans grew uneasy. Former Speaker Newt Gingrich, fresh from announcing his intention to run for president, called the budget "radical" in May and added, "I don't think right-wing social engineering is any more desirable than left-wing social engineering." Ryan responded to a conservative talk-radio host, "Hardly is that social engineering and radical. What's radical is kicking the can down the road."

In March 2012, Ryan offered another budget plan that cut discretionary spending below the levels agreed upon by Congress in 2011. It would have overhauled Medicare and Medicaid and repealed the 2010 health care law signed by Obama. His budget squeaked out of committee and passed the full House, 228-191; it later failed in the Democratic-controlled Senate, 41-58, with five Republicans opposing the measure.

Despite the recent history of his district as a swing seat, Ryan has remained secure at home, where he cruised to reelection in 2010 with 68% of the vote. As his political stock rose, he was mentioned as a possible 2012 presidential candidate, but Ryan told numerous interviewers in 2010, including *The New York Times* and a Milwaukee television station, that he wasn't interested: "My head's not that big, and my kids are too small."

Still, Ryan emerged as a potential vice presidential pick during the summer of 2012. Likely nominee Mitt Romney reportedly was also considering Ohio Sen. Rob Portman and Minnesota Gov. Tim Pawlenty. He eventually selected Ryan, viewed by some political observers as a dark horse and a riskier choice given Ryan's controversial views on the budget and his willingness to enact sweeping entitlement reforms. But Ryan and Romney had a strong working rapport. Aides to Ryan said later that before he accepted the offer, he received assurances that he would play a central role on economic matters, as Vice President Dick Cheney did on national security during George W. Bush's presidency.

The selection of Ryan kicked off a debate about Medicare that hindered Republicans' desire to make the election a referendum on Obama's handling of the economy. The Romney-Ryan plan called for a new premium support plan beginning with new Medicare beneficiaries in 2023. Seniors would pick from private plans or could choose traditional Medicare, all of which would be offered on a new Medicare exchange. Democrats portrayed those efforts as intended to dismantle the social safety net, leading Ryan to respond that Obama "robbed Medicare" to pay for his health care law. Fact-checking sites such as *PolitFact.com* noted that, although Obama's health care law was slated to reduce the amount of future spending growth in Medicare, it did not actually cut Medicare. The Obama campaign pointed out that Ryan's own past budget plan had relied on the same $700 billion savings in Medicare.

Democrats portrayed Ryan as someone who couldn't be trusted to tell the truth. His address to the Republican National Convention fed that narrative. Ryan mentioned the shuttered General Motors auto plant in his hometown that he said Obama had promised to keep open; the plant had closed in December 2008, a month after the president was elected.

Despite the carping from Democrats, Ryan drew mostly positive marks for his spirited performance on the stump. But his presence on the ticket didn't enable Romney to win Wisconsin. Obama prevailed there by 7 percentage points, which was half of his 56%-42% win there in 2008. Because he was already on the ballot for reelection to his House seat when Romney chose him, he stayed in that race and defeated Democrat Rob Zerban, 55%-43%, which was his closest victory margin in eight House races.

Back in Washington in 2013, Ryan asked for and received a waiver from GOP term limits to continue as Budget chairman—a request that Boehner had denied to less prominent Republicans, though the speaker has more authority to select the Budget chairman. In response to criticism that his earlier budgets took too long to get into balance, his fiscal 2014 proposal called for reaching that level within a decade, again through steep spending cuts. It passed the House on a 221-207 vote with no Democratic support.

But Ryan offered powerful evidence later that year that he was willing and able to work with Democrats. He and Senate Democratic Budget Committee Chairman Patty Murray of Washington struck a two-year budget deal that called for raising new revenue through fee hikes, without tax increases or controversial reforms to Social Security or Medicare. It also deferred for two years steep budget cuts under the looming "sequester" and replaced them with targeted spending cuts. Despite criticism from conservative groups such as the Club For Growth and Heritage Action, Ryan's clout helped it pass the House on a 332-94 vote, with 169 Republicans voting in favor.

Ryan's work on the budget deal, and his informal discussions in search of a deal to get an immigration overhaul through the chamber, sparked speculation that he might one day seek to become speaker of the House. But Ryan told a San Antonio luncheon audience that he wasn't interested. "I could've decided to go on the elected leadership route years ago," he said. "I'm more of a policy person." He already had made clear his goal to take over Ways and Means after term limits forced Chairman Dave Camp of Michigan to step down in 2015.

In 2014, Ryan's visits to the crucial presidential states of Iowa and New Hampshire spurred renewed talk about his future. He said he hadn't made any decisions about 2016, but reportedly told a group of donors at a private meeting in New York to "keep their powder dry" as he considered his options. But he decided that it wasn't worth entering a crowded GOP field. In any case, he would have other opportunities. And he kept the door open to seeking to influence the selection of the nominee, and perhaps working with another prospective Republican president.

Ryan affirmed his considerable fundraising prowess by taking in $9.4 million during the 2013-14 cycle. But he touched off renewed partisan criticism when he said he was looking at overhauling poverty programs to address the "real culture problem ... of men not working." He also said safety-net programs such as unemployment insurance were a "hammock that ends up lulling people in their lives into dependency and complacency."

He subsequently released his anti-poverty plan, which called for giving states more autonomy to administer their own programs. "We don't want to have a poverty management system that simply perpetuates poverty," he said on NBC's *Meet the Press*. "We want to get at the root causes of poverty." To receive so-called "opportunity grants" offering federal assistance, poor families would be required to work with government agencies, nonprofit or for-profit groups to develop "life plans" that would include time limits for receiving money and sanctions for not meeting goals. Democratic critics said while the plan offered some positive ideas, such as reforming mandatory sentences to reduce prison overcrowding and expanding the Earned Income Tax Credit, it amounted to a fresh repackaging of old conservative ideas.

As he took over Ways and Means, Ryan signaled his strong desire to find agreement with Obama on a few potential areas, including tax reform, trade and infrastructure. He provoked Democrats when the committee approved routine extensions of tax breaks despite the minority's objections. "I think it goes counter to tax reform," Michigan's Sander Levin, Ways and Means' top Democrat, told *The Hill*. "Because you're sending the wrong signal, that somehow you're going to do this piecemeal instead of sending the signal that, let's do something comprehensively." The few Democratic proponents of tax reform, for their part, had been advocating a tax overhaul that would raise taxes on the highest earners.

But it was Ryan, not Levin, with whom Obama worked on his administration's top legislative priority in 2015: Congressional approval in June of trade promotion authority, which was expected to open the door for "fast-track" congressional consideration of international trade deals that Obama and most Republicans saw as a spur to economic growth. Ryan worked for months, with little public attention, to craft the details of the trade legislation that would satisfy Obama and his aides, plus Republican leaders, and the rank-and-file Republicans and Democrats whose support was needed to reach the crucial 218 votes. "Probably being part of the national conversation has made him battle-tested" to handle these complex issues, Republican Sen. Tim Scott of South Carolina told The Associated Press.

With action expected later in the year by Congress and Obama on a new budget framework, possibly including tax changes and a sweeping highway bill, Ryan found himself unexpectedly positioned as the "gate-keeper" for Obama's agenda, potentially "to burnish the president's legacy," as *The New York Times* described in February 2015. Ryan seemed comfortable with the potential irony as he and other Republicans made plans for what they hoped would be a GOP takeover of the White House in the following year.

SECOND DISTRICT

Mark Pocan (D)

Elected 2012, 2nd term; b. Aug. 14, 1964, Kenosha; U. of WI, B.A. 1986; No religious affiliation; married (Philip Frank).

Elected Office: Dane Cnty. Bd. of Supervisors, 1991-96; WI Assembly, 1998-2012.

Professional Career: Owner, Budget Signs & Specialties, 1988-present; Public-relations specialist, WI Realtors Assoc., 1986-88.

DC Office: 313 CHOB, 20515, 202-225-2906; Fax: 202-225-6942; Website: pocan.house.gov.

State Offices: Beloit, 608-395-8001; Madison, 608-258-9800.

Committees: *Budget. Education & the Workforce:* Workforce Protections; Health, Employment, Labor & Pensions.

Group Ratings

	ADA	ACLU	AFL-CIO	LCV	ITI	COC	HAFA	ACU	CFG	FRC
2014	100%	94%	–	97%	40%	29%	16%	8%	13%	0%
2013	100%	C	100%	96%	C	23%	C	12%	16%	C

National Journal Ratings

	2013 LIB	—	2013 CONS
Economic	91%	—	0%
Social	93%	—	0%
Foreign	90%	—	6%
Composite	95%	—	5%

Key Votes of the 113th Congress

1. Sandy storm spending	Y	5. Medical Marijuana	Y	9. Syrian Rebels Training	N
2. Violence Against Women Act	Y	6. Farm Bill	N	10. Keystone pipeline	N
3. Guantanamo Bay Detainees	Y	7. Afghanistan Combat	Y	11. Immigration Exec. Action	N
4. Abortion 20-week ban	N	8. NSA Phone Data Collection	Y	12. Bipartisan budget deal	N

Election Results

2014 general	Mark Pocan (D)	224,920	(68%)	$896,400
	Peter Theron (R)	103,619	(32%)	$25,733
2014 primary	Mark Pocan (D)	unopposed		

Prior winning percentage: 2012 (68%)

Population		Race and Ethnicity		Income	
Total:	733,541	White	83.9%	Median income:	$56,861
Urban:	47.0%	Latino	5.9%		*(152 of 435)*
Suburban:	29.4%	Black	4.2%	Under $50,000	44.6%
Rural:	23.6%	Asian	3.5%	$50,000-$99,999:	32.0%
Land area:	5,024	Two races	2.2%	$100,000-$199,999:	19.3%
Pop/sq. mi.:	146.0	White Ethnic	28.7%	$200,000 or more:	4.2%
Born in state:	65.4%			Poverty Rate	14.1%
		Education			
Age Groups		H.S. grad or less:	31.6%	**Work**	
Under 18:	22.0%	Some college:	29.2%	White collar:	43.0%
18 to 34:	26.2%	College degree, 4 yr.:	23.6%	Blue collar:	38.2%
35 to 64:	39.1%	Post-grad study:	15.6%	Sales and service:	18.8%
Over 64:	12.7%			Govt. workers:	18.7%
		Military			
		Veterans/active duty:	6.8%		

South-Central Wisconsin: Madison

On a narrow isthmus between Lakes Mendota and Monona is the center of Madison, and in many ways, the center of Wisconsin. The state Capitol rises at one end of State Street, and at the other end is the main campus of the University of Wisconsin, in a beautiful, park-like setting above Lake Mendota. For most of the 20th century, Wisconsin politics was dominated by the Madison-based La Follettes and their liberal Democratic successors. University faculty were devoted to Robert LaFollette's "Wisconsin idea" of a supposedly apolitical bureaucracy and to his Wisconsin Tax Commission and workmen's compensation law—both firsts in the nation and conceived of by the former governor and senator. Madison spawned an activist and sometimes

Voter Turnout	
2013 Total Citizen 18+	541,859
2014 House Turnout	328,847
2014 Turnout as % CVAP	60.7%
2012 Turnout as % CVAP	76.5%

violent student movement during the Vietnam War. A graduate student was killed in a laboratory by a bomb set off by a protester. In recent years, the liberal campus opposed the welfare reform and school choice laws enacted while Republican Tommy Thompson was governor, and was the center of vocal opposition to Gov. Scott Walker's plan to end collective bargaining for most state workers and the unsuccessful recall effort to replace him in June 2012. The labor and student protests continued, with a renewed focus in early 2015 on GOP right-to-work legislation. Walker took revenge of sorts with the July 2015 enactment of a plan for the state to wield more control over the university, including faculty hiring, through its Board of Regents.

Madison is the center of Wisconsin's 2nd Congressional District, which is roughly equal parts urban, suburban, and rural. It includes surrounding Dane County and dairy and alfalfa country to the north and south, as well as several rural dairy counties that have traditionally been Republican. It takes in the birthplace of the Ringling Brothers Circus in Baraboo, and the Swiss-settled town of New Glarus, known for the brewing company that makes Fat Squirrel and Spotted Cow beers. Prairie du Sac, to the north of Madison, is home to the corporate headquarters of the rapidly expanding Culver's fast-food chain, famous for its quintessentially Wisconsin butter burgers, with an optional side of fried cheese curds. Dodgeville, in Iowa County (not on the Iowa border), is the headquarters of Lands' End, the catalog retailer.

Madison remains economically vibrant. Its unemployment rate in April 2015 was an impressively low 2.9%. Jobs at the university and in state government have been recession-resistant. The Madison metropolitan area boasts one of the best-educated workforces in the country—51% of residents hold a college degree and 17% have a graduate degree. The growth industries include health care (Madison is home to American Family Insurance) and biotechnology start-ups tied to the university.

In the early 1990s, rural Dane County

2012 Presidential Vote		
Barack Obama (D)	284,084	(68%)
Mitt Romney (R)	126,688	(30%)
2008 Presidential Vote		
Barack Obama (D)	274,372	(70%)
John McCain (R)	111,956	(29%)
Cook Partisan Voting Index: D+17		

was open to Republicans like Thompson. But the rural areas have become bluer as Madison-area liberals move to the countryside, even as other parts of the state have become more crimson. The 2nd is a heavily Democratic district. In 2012, President Barack Obama won 68%-30%. People take voting seriously here: Two-thirds of voting-age adults in Dane County voted in the recall (and 70% of them voted to recall Walker).

Mark Pocan (D)

Democrat Mark Pocan is cut from the same political cloth as his predecessor, Democrat Tammy Baldwin, whom he also succeeded in the Wisconsin State Assembly. Like Baldwin, who ran successfully for the Senate, Pocan is openly gay and progressive. After winning a nasty primary campaign in August, Pocan had an easy path to Congress.

Pocan was born and raised in Kenosha, the child of two small-business owners. His father ran a specialty print shop, and his mother owned a beauty-supply store. Pocan's father served on the Kenosha City Council, and as a kid, Pocan campaigned with him and attended council meetings. At the University of Wisconsin, Pocan said, "I started out as a poli-sci major until I took my first poli-sci class that talked about the Ottoman Empire and not political campaigns. So I decided to switch" to journalism. He helped pay for college by working as a magician and tending bar.

After graduating, Pocan worked in public relations. Then, he followed in his father's footsteps and opened his own Madison-based print shop. Around that time, Pocan dealt with personal trauma. After leaving a gay bar one night, he was physically assaulted by two men and needed stitches. "I was not out to everyone, to friends, mostly. ... But that was kind of a turning point because after that happened, that's when I got very active with a number of LGBT nonprofits," he said. Since gay marriage was not legal in Wisconsin in 2006, Pocan married in Canada. He still dabbles as a magician for a hobby.

In 1991, Pocan won a seat on the Dane County Board of Supervisors, where he got to know Baldwin. He later spent 14 years in the state Assembly. He landed a seat on the influential Joint Finance Committee and co-chaired the panel for two years. Among his legislative activities, Pocan helped expand health care coverage for children and extend domestic-partner benefits for gay couples. He coauthored the Compassionate Care for Rape Victims Act, signed into law in 2008, to ensure that hospitals provide information on emergency contraception to victims of sexual assault. *Milwaukee Magazine* named him "best legislator" in 2009.

In the contest for Baldwin's House seat, the four-way primary quickly turned acrimonious. Pocan's chief rival was Kelda Helen Roys, a fellow Madison-area state representative. Pocan had support from unions and much of the party establishment, plus a roughly 2-to-1 fundraising advantage. Roys attacked him for compromising with Republicans and for taking money from political action committees. She also criticized his votes for two business tax credit bills, describing them as Republican Gov. Scott Walker's "corporate tax giveaways."

Pocan did not back away from his image as a strong progressive willing to work across the aisle. "There are those who scream and holler and put out a press release," he told the *Wisconsin State Journal*. "I decided I wanted to be the kind that gets things done." He tried to stay above the fray and emphasized his roots as a small businessman. Pocan won with 72% of the vote to Roys' 22%. In the general election, he got 68% against Chad Lee, a 29-year-old businessman who had lost to Baldwin in 2010.

In the House, Pocan has emphasized the need for bipartisanship, which is the only way that he can get much done in a Republican-controlled House. He serves on the Budget Committee, which rarely works across the aisle. But he has gained more opportunity on the Education and the Workforce Committee. With Republican Rep. Luke Messer of Indiana, he introduced in June 2015 a resolution to support continuation of the Perkins student loan program. He and conservative Republican Rep. Glenn Grothman of Wisconsin have discussed their mutual interest in reducing student loan debt; Pocan says loan-holders should be permitted to refinance. With Rep. Reid Ribble, another Wisconsin Republican, he filed a bill to change the congressional budget cycle from annual to biennial, as is the case in many state legislatures, including Wisconsin.

Pocan sought opportunities to pursue his liberal agenda as the first vice chair of the Progressive Caucus. In May 2015, he joined New York City Mayor Bill de Blasio and others to launch The Progressive Agenda to Combat Income Inequality, which Pocan said would "put meat on the bone of our progressive values." As a chair of the LGBT Equality Caucus, he drew attention to the problem of LGBT youth homelessness.

Pocan was reelected uneventfully with 68 percent of the vote in 2014. He had no primary opposition.

THIRD DISTRICT

Ron Kind (D)

Elected 1996, 10th term; b. March 16, 1963, La Crosse; Harvard U., B.A. 1985, London Schl. of Econ. 1986, U. of MN, J.D. 1990; Lutheran; married (Tawni); 2 children.

Professional Career: Practicing atty., 1990-92; Asst. st. prosecutor, La Crosse Cnty., 1992-96.

DC Office: 1502 LHOB, 20515, 202-225-5506; Fax: 202-225-5739; Website: kind.house.gov.

State Offices: Eau Claire, 715-831-9214; La Crosse, 608-782-2558.

Committees: *Ways & Means:* Health; Trade.

Group Ratings

	ADA	ACLU	AFL-CIO	LCV	ITI	COC	HAFA	ACU	CFG	FRC
2014	75%	77%	–	89%	40%	57%	10%	8%	9%	0%
2013	60%	C	86%	89%	C	62%	C	20%	17%	C

National Journal Ratings

	2013 LIB	—	2013 CONS
Economic	59%	—	41%
Social	61%	—	38%
Foreign	83%	—	15%
Composite	68%	—	32%

Key Votes of the 113th Congress

1. Sandy storm spending	5. Medical Marijuana Y	9. Syrian Rebels Training Y
2. Violence Against Women Act Y	6. Farm Bill Y	10. Keystone pipeline N
3. Guantanamo Bay Detainees Y	7. Afghanistan Combat N	11. Immigration Exec. Action N
4. Abortion 20-week ban N	8. NSA Phone Data Collection N	12. Bipartisan budget deal Y

Election Results

2014 general	Ron Kind (D)	155,368	(57%)	$1,162,176
	Tony Kurtz (R)	119,540	(43%)	$304,791
2014 primary	Ron Kind (D)	unopposed		

Prior winning percentages: 2012 (64%), 2010 (50%), 2008 (63%), 2006 (65%), 2004 (56%), 2002 (63%), 2000 (64%), 1998 (71%), 1996 (52%)

Population		Race and Ethnicity		Income	
Total:	711,620	White	92.9%	Median income:	$49,461
Urban:	24.9%	Asian	2.0%		*(250 of 435)*
Suburban:	9.7%	Latino	2.0%	Under $50,000	50.5%
Rural:	65.4%	Black	0.9%	$50,000-$99,999:	34.6%
Land area:	12,595	Two races	1.4%	$100,000-$199,999:	13.0%
Pop/sq. mi.:	56.5	White Ethnic	29.2%	$200,000 or more:	2.0%
Born in state:	72.3%			Poverty Rate	13.9%
		Education			
Age Groups		H.S. grad or less:	43.0%	**Work**	
Under 18:	21.4%	Some college:	33.6%	White collar:	31.0%
18 to 34:	24.9%	College degree, 4 yr.:	15.8%	Blue collar:	41.6%
35 to 64:	38.0%	Post-grad study:	7.7%	Sales and service:	27.5%
Over 64:	15.7%				
		Military		Govt. workers:	13.6%
		Veterans/active duty:	9.4%		

West-Central Wisconsin: Eau Claire, La Crosse

On the rolling land of western Wisconsin, in the knobby hills just east of the Mississippi River, is some of the most beautiful river landscape in the country. This is where author Laura Ingalls Wilder's family built their little house in the big woods in the 1870s, before the first railroad came steaming up the narrow floodplain alongside the Mississippi River. Today, it is hard to imagine the big woods. The trees have long since been cut down, and the hillsides are covered with grass grazed by placid dairy cattle. Where the pioneers tried to scratch out diversified crops, later generations of farmers created America's premier dairy region, producing milk, butter and cheese. Some Amish communities from Pennsylvania have relocated here in recent years because land is cheaper than in the East. But since 1980, the dairy economy here has been in flux. Numerous dairy farmers have gone out of business. Cows have become more productive, and demand for milk has decreased. Wisconsin also has had trouble competing against the European Union's subsidized cheese and butter, and more recently, with products from California's large-scale agribusiness. In the 1980s, many communities here lost population, but there has been some growth since then. Eau Claire County's population hit 100,000 for the first time in 2012.

Voter Turnout	
2013 Total Citizen 18+	554,064
2014 House Turnout	275,161
2014 Turnout as % CVAP	49.7%
2012 Turnout as % CVAP	66%

2012 Presidential Vote		
Barack Obama (D)	199,188	(55%)
Mitt Romney (R)	159,205	(44%)

2008 Presidential Vote		
Barack Obama (D)	215,429	(59%)
John McCain (R)	141,922	(39%)

Cook Partisan Voting Index: D+5

The 3rd Congressional District of Wisconsin follows the Mississippi from the border with Illinois north to Dunn County, covering the western edge of the state. The district's two largest cities are La Crosse and Eau Claire, home to home-improvement giant Menards. Both cities have won recognition for their livability. The district now stretches east to Democratic-leaning Portage County and Stevens Point, whose lakes, streams and trails make the area a recreational hotspot.

Settled largely by German and Scandinavian immigrants, the region once consistently voted for Wisconsin's La Follette Progressives and its voters cannot be taken for granted. Recently, the district has leaned Democratic at the presidential level. Western Wisconsin was one of the few segments of rural America where President Barack Obama in 2012 ran even with historic Democratic percentages, which was vital to his statewide victory. Still, Obama carried the district with only 55 percent of the vote, a four-point drop from his 2008 performance. This area was a bulwark for Republican Gov. Scott Walker in his 2010 election and his June 2012 recall, when he won every county in the district except La Crosse. One reason for the surge in rural support for Walker was that, in the run-up to the recall election, the National Rifle Association targeted the La Crosse-Eau Claire media market with ads attacking the Democratic nominee, Milwaukee mayor Tom Barrett, over his liberal record on guns.

Ron Kind (D)

Ron Kind, a Democrat elected in 1996, is a moderate who focuses on health and agriculture issues on the Ways and Means Committee. He is chairman of the New Democrat Coalition, a business-oriented group that attempts to break through partisan gridlock. In June 2015, he was the leading Democratic proponent in the bitter intra-party battle to give trade promotion authority to President Barack Obama.

Kind grew up in a large family in La Crosse, the son of a telephone repairman and a secretary in the local schools. He went to Harvard University on a scholarship and played quarterback. He was a summer intern for Democratic Sen. William Proxmire, doing research for Proxmire's Golden Fleece awards pointing out wasteful government spending. Kind attended the London School of Economics and the University of Minnesota's law school, practiced law in a large firm in Milwaukee, then returned home to La Crosse to work as an assistant prosecutor on rape and sexual abuse cases.

Kind ran for Congress after moderate Republican Steve Gunderson announced that he would not seek reelection. Former state Sen. Jim Harsdorf won the Republican primary and made a case for a balanced budget and for Republican Gov. Tommy Thompson's "Wisconsin Works" welfare reform program. Kind presented his own balanced budget proposal and urged reform of campaign finances. Kind won, 52%-48%.

Kind got an early start on the health care overhaul debate in 2009, co-sponsoring a bill to put greater emphasis on quality and coordination of care in reimbursing health care providers. He was dissatisfied with the version that Ways and Means approved the next month and was one of three Democrats who joined committee Republicans in opposing it. After lengthy meetings that he and others held with Pelosi on containing the spiraling costs of Medicare, he pronounced himself satisfied with the legislation. He succeeded in getting $800 million in immediate payments for doctors and hospitals as well as a commitment for a value-based system for paying providers, and he backed the version that became law.

Early in his House career, Kind took an interest in improving the health of the upper Mississippi River, which is vital to the well-being of his district. He has worked to restore the river, combat invasive species, and ensure that it remains a resource for recreation and transportation.

With dairy farming prominent in his district, Kind is vitally interested in issues affecting farmers. In 2007, he joined with conservative deficit hawks and suburban and urban Democrats in an attempt to add provisions to the farm bill that would have changed federal policy for agricultural subsidies and provided more funds for land conservation and school nutrition. "For too long, we've had large taxpayer subsidies going to a few very large farming entities to the disadvantage of family farmers," Kind said. Kind won 200 votes for similar provisions in the 2002 farm bill, but this time around, the Democratic leadership was worried about angering farmers' groups in rural swing districts and refused to allow a vote by the full House. The plan died in committee. Kind voted against the final version of the farm bill, calling it a "nightmare." In July 2012, he complained in a letter to colleagues that the GOP-written farm bill that passed the House Agriculture Committee "takes us backward in terms of budget-busting crop subsidies, unlimited insurance subsidies, and trade-distorting programs."

Despite the farm subsidies that flow to the district, he said that the vast majority of producers he represents don't get huge agriculture subsidies because they're not large agri-businesses. When Obama unveiled a plan in April 2009 to save nearly $10 billion by putting strict limits on subsidies, Kind worked with the White House to revamp the measure. On Ways and Means, he also has championed tax credits aimed at encouraging farmers to control animal waste while producing renewable biogas energy. He told *The Stevens Point Journal* in 2012 that Wisconsin could see "a manufacturing renaissance" with more public-private sector partnerships.

In 2013, Kind took over as head of the New Democrat Coalition. "We want to work hard to find that sensible center on policy and move the ball," he told *The Hill* newspaper. He formerly co-chaired the Congressional Sportsmen's Caucus of pro-conservation hunters and received the National Rifle Association's endorsement in 2010. Following the Democrats' disastrous 2010 election performance, he refused to support liberal Nancy Pelosi in her bid for minority leader in January 2011, casting his vote for Tennessee Democrat Jim Cooper, another moderate. He subsequently has backed Pelosi. But he irked his party after becoming one of the 17 House Democrats to vote in favor of criminal contempt charges in 2012 against Attorney General Eric Holder in connection with the "Fast and Furious" gun-tracing operation.

Kind was instrumental in quietly and methodically assembling Democratic support for trade promotion authority in 2015. He faced fierce opposition from labor unions and many of his Democratic colleagues in his advocacy of Obama's top legislative priority of the year. Working closely with home-state Ways and Means Chairman Paul Ryan and other GOP leaders, he preserved cohesion among the depleted but still vital Democratic supporters of international trade engagement. In a retrospective on the complex handling of the trade bill, *Roll Call* described Kind's role as "integral"—starting with guest speakers to discuss the framework months in advance at lunch meetings of the New Democrat Coalition and continuing with his whip check and one-on-one discussions with dozens of Democratic members who were potential supporters. He compared notes daily with White House officials. "Sometimes the phone rang and it was Obama himself," *Roll Call* reported.

At home, Kind in 2004 had his first credible challenger, Republican state Sen. Dale Schultz, a moderate in the Wisconsin legislature. Schultz ran with an unlikely Republican theme, criticizing Kind as a free trader who had sent jobs overseas. Kind affirmed his support for trade agreements, but he criticized the Bush administration for failing to enforce their labor and environmental protection terms. Kind won, 56%-43%. In 2010, another serious challenger emerged, Dan Kapanke, a Republican state senator who lambasted Kind for his support of the health care bill and Obama's economic agenda. Less than a week before the election, Wisconsin Republicans alleged that a Kind staffer asked for campaign contributions in 2007 to arrange a meeting between the congressman and a group of doctors. Kind called the charge "blatant lies" and questioned the timing of the complaint. He survived with a 50%-46% win. He has won comfortably since 2012 with the district's redrawn lines.

Kind has considered runs for statewide office, and could be a strong contender. But he likely would face problems in a primary with a liberal from Milwaukee or Madison.

FOURTH DISTRICT

Gwen Moore (D)

Elected 2004, 6th term; b. April 18, 1951, Racine; Marquette U., B.A. 1978; Baptist; single; 3 children.

Elected Office: WI Assembly, 1989-92; WI Senate, 1992-2004, pres. pro tem, 1997-98.

Professional Career: Housing & urban dev. specialist, 1985-89.

DC Office: 2245 RHOB, 20515, 202-225-4572; Fax: 202-225-8135; Website: gwenmoore.house.gov.

State Offices: Milwaukee, 414-297-1140.

Committees: *Budget. Financial Services:* Monetary Policy & Trade (RMM); Housing & Insurance.

Group Ratings

	ADA	ACLU	AFL-CIO	LCV	ITI	COC	HAFA	ACU	CFG	FRC
2014	95%	83%	–	94%	20%	43%	12%	8%	13%	0%
2013	85%	C	90%	93%	C	38%	C	8%	14%	C

National Journal Ratings

	2013 LIB	—	2013 CONS
Economic	69%	—	31%
Social	85%	—	13%
Foreign	86%	—	13%
Composite	81%	—	20%

Key Votes of the 113th Congress

1. Sandy storm spending	Y	5. Medical Marijuana	Y	9. Syrian Rebels Training	N
2. Violence Against Women Act	Y	6. Farm Bill	N	10. Keystone pipeline	N
3. Guantanamo Bay Detainees	Y	7. Afghanistan Combat	Y	11. Immigration Exec. Action	N
4. Abortion 20-week ban	N	8. NSA Phone Data Collection	Y	12. Bipartisan budget deal	Y

Election Results

2014 general	Gwen Moore (D)	179,045	(70%)	$1,045,919
	Dan Sebring (R)	68,490	(27%)	$21,964
	Robert Raymond (I)	7,002	(3%)	
2014 primary	Gwen Moore (D)	52,408	(71%)	
	Gary George (D)	21,242	(29%)	

Prior winning percentages: 2012 (72%), 2010 (69%), 2008 (88%), 2006 (71%), 2004 (70%)

Population		Race and Ethnicity		Income	
Total:	715,840	White	43.9%	Median income:	$38,242
Urban:	87.9%	Black	33.3%		(403 of 435)
Suburban:	12.1%	Latino	16.3%	Under $50,000	61.1%
Rural:	0.0%	Asian	3.1%	$50,000-$99,999:	26.6%
Land area:	178	Two races	2.8%	$100,000-$199,999:	10.3%
Pop/sq. mi.:	4,025.9	White Ethnic	24.4%	$200,000 or more:	1.9%
Born in state:	66.7%			Poverty Rate	26.1%
		Education			
Age Groups		H.S. grad or less:	44.6%	**Work**	
Under 18:	25.4%	Some college:	28.7%	White collar:	31.6%
18 to 34:	28.1%	College degree, 4 yr.:	17.2%	Blue collar:	46.0%
35 to 64:	35.7%	Post-grad study:	9.6%	Sales and service:	22.4%
Over 64:	10.8%				
		Military		Govt. workers:	12.2%
		Veterans/active duty:	6.1%		

Milwaukee Metro

Milwaukee is America's most German city, with an ethnic heritage noticeable not just in the names of its beers and its old German restaurants, but in the sturdiness of its houses and the orderliness of its streets. Until World War I inflamed sensitivities to all things German, the language was spoken on the

Voter Turnout	
2013 Total Citizen 18+	498,095
2014 House Turnout	254,892
2014 Turnout as % CVAP	51.2%
2012 Turnout as % CVAP	73.5%

streets and read in city newspapers; German beer was produced in dozens of breweries. A huge four-sided clock, nearly twice the size of London's Big Ben, rises above the Allen-Bradley factory, looking out over the industrial city. It is an apt symbol, a piece of precision engineering in this high-skill manufacturing town, with its skyline of smokestacks and church steeples—the closest thing in America to the German factory cities that inspired Milwaukee's early citizens. The city has led the nation in beer brewing, industrial control equipment, mining gear, cranes and independent foundries. Master Lock, headquartered in Milwaukee since 1921, was operating its plant at capacity in 2012 for the first time in 15 years. In February 2012, President Barack Obama visited its headquarters to argue that manufacturing was on the rebound, praising it for bringing jobs back from overseas.

But like other Rust Belt cities, many of the plants in Milwaukee have shut down over the past three decades. It hemorrhaged population in the 1990s, though it has stopped shrinking, thanks in part to a rapidly expanding Hispanic population. For the most part, the city has embraced Latinos. A chorizo sausage now competes against the bratwurst, Polish sausage, and Italian sausage mascots during the famous Sausage Race at Milwaukee Brewers baseball games. Many Hispanics have settled in the old immigrant neighborhoods of the city's South Side. The West Side and North Side are home to many of the city's African-American neighborhoods, such as Sherman Park and Bronzeville. Some of those areas struggled against a record-low employment rate that for black men dropped to 45% in Milwaukee in 2010—a level better than only Detroit and Buffalo, according to a 2012 University of Wisconsin-Milwaukee study. Unemployment, which remained in double digits in mid-2013, fell to 6.3% in April 2015. The city is focusing on becoming a global hub for water technology and research, with the University of Wisconsin-Milwaukee opening the first graduate school in the nation dedicated solely to the study of freshwater.

2012 Presidential Vote		
Barack Obama (D)	268,440	(75%)
Mitt Romney (R)	84,751	(24%)
2008 Presidential Vote		
Barack Obama (D)	254,712	(74%)
John McCain (R)	84,390	(25%)
Cook Partisan Voting Index:	D+23	

The 4th District of Wisconsin covers the entire city of Milwaukee and a few of its working-class suburbs—St. Francis, Cudahy and South Milwaukee on Lake Michigan, and West Milwaukee and part of West Allis. It includes to the north tonier suburbs along the lake, many with sizable Jewish populations—Shorewood, Whitefish Bay and Fox Point. These communities are politically competitive and closely attuned to state politics. In Whitefish Bay, 84% of registered voters cast ballots during the 2012 recall of Republican Gov. Scott Walker—unheard of turnout for a special election—and favored keeping Walker in office by a narrow margin. About 30% of Milwaukee County voters reside in parts of three other districts in Wisconsin. In the 4th, blacks make up 34% of the population, while Hispanics comprise another 16%. It is easily Wisconsin's most Democratic district, with President Barack Obama getting 75% of the vote here in 2012.

Gwen Moore (D)

Gwen Moore, a Democrat elected in 2004, is Wisconsin's first African-American member of Congress. A former welfare recipient, she often recounts her struggles in spirited and candid detail of standing up for the poor, homeless and victims of domestic violence.

Moore was born in Racine, the eighth of nine children, and raised on the North Side of Milwaukee. As an 18-year-old college freshman, she became a single mother who relied on welfare to help support her daughter. She graduated from Marquette University and worked as a housing and urban development specialist. Moore said she got active in politics when a rent-to-own center repossessed her washer and dryer even though she had paid three times their value in interest rates. She led an effort to establish a community credit union. Elected to the state Assembly in 1989 and the Senate in 1992, she was the state's first black woman senator. In 1990, she defeated Republican Scott Walker, the only election defeat for the future governor of Wisconsin.

In 2003, when Democratic Rep. Gerald Kleczka announced that he was retiring after 20 years, Moore was the front-runner. She had serious competition in the Democratic primary from two political veterans, state Sen. Tim Carpenter and former state party Chairman Matt Flynn, both white. The candidates agreed on most issues: All three supported abortion rights, focused on jobs and economic concerns, and called for eliminating the Bush administration's tax cuts for people with incomes exceeding $200,000 a year. Absent significant ideological clashes, the fallout from Milwaukee's mayoral primary earlier that year played a role. The nonpartisan election had pitted former Rep. Tom Barrett, who is white, against acting Mayor Marvin Pratt, vying to become the city's first black elected mayor. Barrett won, but the vote was split along racial lines and caused hard feelings in the African-American community.

Moore took advantage of the energized black voter base, and she leveraged financial support from national women's organizations, teachers' unions, and other liberal groups. Flynn was endorsed by Kleczka and boasted that he had backed Pratt for mayor. But he was damaged politically by his work as general counsel for the local Roman Catholic archdiocese in a priest sex abuse scandal. Carpenter was the only openly gay member of the Senate and had the support of national gay rights groups. Moore won 64% of the vote to 25% for Flynn and 10% for Carpenter. In the general election, Republican Gerald Boyle tried to win over Democrats disaffected with Moore. But he got no support from the national party and Moore won easily, 70%-28%.

Moore has a staunchly liberal voting record and often is passionate in her criticism of Republican policies. She said in 2012 that a Wisconsin voter ID law "does nothing but attempt to return us to an era of Jim Crow politics." When House Republicans sought to defund Planned Parenthood during the 2011 budget debate, Moore drew on her own unwelcome experience of an unplanned pregnancy at age 18. "I just want to tell you a little bit about what it's like to not have Planned Parenthood," she said on the House floor. "You have to add water to the formula to make it stretch. You have to give your kids Ramen noodles at the end of the month to fill up their little bellies so they won't cry. You have to give them mayonnaise sandwiches." When she joined the commemoration in Selma, Alabama, of the 50th anniversary of the civil rights protest, she wrote in an op-ed for the *Milwaukee Journal Sentinel* that Wisconsin has been "the Selma of the North" because of alleged voting rights abuses.

She has introduced legislation to help the poor through school lunch funding, crackdown on foreclosure fraud, and grants to crime-ravaged communities. In 2005, the House incorporated provisions of her Shield Act into the reauthorization of the Violence Against Women Act, to protect the identity of domestic-violence victims who receive homeless assistance. When the domestic violence law came up for another reauthorization in 2012, Moore stunned House colleagues by taking to the floor to graphically recount how a group of young men once discussed having sex with her. "The appointed boy, when he saw that I wasn't going to be so willing, completed a date rape and then took my underwear to display it to the rest of the boys. I mean, this is what American women are facing," she said. On the Financial Services Committee, she moved up in 2015 to ranking member of the Monetary Policy and Trade Subcommittee, where she took an interest in the World Bank and International Monetary Fund.

Since Walker's emergence as one of the nation's most polarizing governors, Moore has been among his most vocal critics. When he reportedly considered turning down federal education funding in 2011, Moore accused him of "channeling Sarah Palin." She took to Twitter to accuse Walker in 2012 of eliminating a women's cancer screening program "for political gain," an assertion that the website *PolitiFact* called "false and ridiculous." On the *Colbert Report* in 2013, she criticized Walker for having thrown many groups "under the bus." But at a 2011 Oversight and Government Reform hearing at which he appeared, Moore said that she considers Walker a friend. "I'm crazy about his kids and his wife," she said. "But I'm not going to spend my five minutes pretending we agree on anything."

Moore remains well-established in her district and was reelected with 70% of the vote in 2014.

FIFTH DISTRICT

Jim Sensenbrenner (R)

Elected 1978, 19th term; b. June 14, 1943, Chicago, IL; Stanford U., A.B. 1965, U. of WI, J.D. 1968; Episcopalian; married (Cheryl); 2 children.

Elected Office: WI Assembly, 1968-74; WI Senate, 1974-78.

Professional Career: Staff asst., U.S. Rep. Arthur Younger, 1965; Practicing atty., 1968-69.

DC Office: 2449 RHOB, 20515, 202-225-5101; Fax: 202-225-3190; Website: sensenbrenner.house.gov.

State Offices: Brookfield, 262-784-1111.

Committees: *Judiciary:* Courts, Intellectual Property & the Internet; Crime, Terrorism, Homeland Security & Investigations (Chmn). *Science, Space & Technology:* Environment; Oversight.

Group Ratings

	ADA	ACLU	AFL-CIO	LCV	ITI	COC	HAFA	ACU	CFG	FRC
2014	15%	11%	–	6%	80%	64%	78%	100%	93%	100%
2013	5%	C	0%	11%	C	62%	C	96%	88%	C

National Journal Ratings

	2013 LIB	—	2013 CONS
Economic	4%	—	96%
Social	31%	—	67%
Foreign	47%	—	52%
Composite	28%	—	72%

Key Votes of the 113th Congress

1. Sandy storm spending	N	5. Medical Marijuana	N	9. Syrian Rebels Training	N
2. Violence Against Women Act	N	6. Farm Bill	N	10. Keystone pipeline	Y
3. Guantanamo Bay Detainees	N	7. Afghanistan Combat	Y	11. Immigration Exec. Action	Y
4. Abortion 20-week ban	Y	8. NSA Phone Data Collection	Y	12. Bipartisan budget deal	Y

Election Results

2014 general	Jim Sensenbrenner (R)	231,160	(70%)	$326,996
	Chris Rockwood (D)	101,190	(30%)	$13,917
2014 primary	Jim Sensenbrenner (R)	unopposed		

Prior winning percentages: 2012 (68%), 2010 (69%), 2008 (80%), 2006 (62%), 2004 (67%), 2002 (87%), 2000 (74%), 1998 (91%), 1996 (74%), 1994 (100%), 1992 (70%), 1990 (100%), 1988 (75%), 1986 (78%), 1984 (73%), 1982 (100%), 1980 (78%), 1978 (61%)

Population		Race and Ethnicity		Income	
Total:	723,153	White	89.8%	Median income:	$62,665
Urban:	32.6%	Latino	4.8%		(95 of 435)
Suburban:	48.0%	Asian	2.2%	Under $50,000	39.9%
Rural:	19.4%	Black	1.8%	$50,000-$99,999:	33.6%
Land area:	1,955	Two races	1.3%	$100,000-$199,999:	22.0%
Pop/sq. mi.:	369.8	White Ethnic	37.0%	$200,000 or more:	4.5%
Born in state:	76.2%			Poverty Rate	8.7%
		Education			
Age Groups		H.S. grad or less:	34.6%	**Work**	
Under 18:	22.2%	Some college:	30.3%	White collar:	38.6%
18 to 34:	20.8%	College degree, 4 yr.:	23.9%	Blue collar:	40.0%
35 to 64:	41.3%	Post-grad study:	11.3%	Sales and service:	21.3%
Over 64:	15.7%			Govt. workers:	9.2%
		Military			
		Veterans/active duty:	7.9%		

Western Milwaukee Suburbs, Waukesha

For decades, the orderly, heavily German-American factory city of Milwaukee has been spreading slowly, mostly west and north, into Wisconsin dairy country. There are high-income enclaves here, such as close-in Elm Grove and exurban Oconomowoc, halfway to Madison and tucked in around numerous lakes. There is office development in Brookfield, and subdivisions have spread to Menomonee Falls and farther, reaching small towns with roots in the 19th century. This is comfortable but not fancy territory, and the economy is still based heavily on skilled manufacturing. It felt the effects of the recession, but less than other areas. Not far from Milwaukee are West Bend, with West Bend kitchen appliances; and Pewaukee, with Harken sailboat hardware. Closer to the city in Wauwatosa, Harley-Davidson began manufacturing on the city's West Side a century ago.

Voter Turnout

2013 Total Citizen 18+	547,004
2014 House Turnout	332,826
2014 Turnout as % CVAP	60.8%
2012 Turnout as % CVAP	77.6%

2012 Presidential Vote

Mitt Romney (R)	257,017	(61%)
Barack Obama (D)	158,226	(38%)

2008 Presidential Vote

John McCain (R)	230,500	(57%)
Barack Obama (D)	168,328	(42%)

Cook Partisan Voting Index: R+13

The 5th Congressional District of Wisconsin includes most of the western and northwestern suburbs of Milwaukee, spanning the Milwaukee County suburbs of Wauwatosa, Greenfield and West Allis; the northern half of Waukesha County, including New Berlin; and Jefferson County farther west. To the north, it includes all of Washington County and part of Dodge County. Nearly half the population is in Waukesha. This is by far the most Republican district in the state, and voters here tend to be better-off than Republicans elsewhere in Wisconsin. The median household income is over $61,000, the highest of any district in the state, even the well-educated, Madison-based 2nd District.

Waukesha County is the conservative core of the state, providing the grassroots energy that fueled Gov. Scott Walker's victory during the June 2012 recall campaign. Waukesha, which gave Walker 72% of the vote in the recall, reported the second highest countywide turnout in the state. Overall, the district voted 61% for Mitt Romney in the 2012 presidential race, and these conservative suburbs were a stronghold for him in the April 2012 primary against Rick Santorum. People here habitually turn out in large numbers for elections, and the district cast the second-most Republican votes of any district in the country—more than 257,000, trailing only Montana's at-large district, which has a larger population.

Jim Sensenbrenner (R)

Republican Jim Sensenbrenner, first elected in 1978, is a forceful conservative whose prickly personality can rankle liberals, but he has racked up a number of impressive legislative accomplishments. He is the second most-senior Republican, and one of only four House members who served before the election of Ronald Reagan.

Sensenbrenner was born in Chicago and grew up in the Milwaukee area, with strong Wisconsin roots. His great-grandfather was a founder of Kimberly-Clark, which invented the sanitary napkin, and Sensenbrenner is an heir to the paper and cellulose fortune. He graduated from Stanford University and the University of Wisconsin Law School, and has spent most of his adult life in politics. He served briefly as a staffer in the House, then was elected to the Wisconsin Assembly in 1968 and to the Senate in 1974. (His son, Bob, is general counsel of the House Administration Committee.) When Republican Rep. Bob Kasten ran for governor, Sensenbrenner ran to succeed him and won the Republican primary by 589 votes. He was elected in November with 61 percent of the vote, which was the lowest vote of his career. His net worth exceeds $19 million, according to the Center for Responsive Politics. As an example of how the rich get richer, he won $250,000 in the District of Columbia lottery after buying two tickets while picking up some beer for an office party at a Capitol Hill liquor store.

Sensenbrenner's pugnaciousness has endeared him to conservatives. *Human Events* named him as its man of the year in 2006. And his legislative skills have earned him respect on Capitol Hill. He was one of the first to urge that Congress apply to itself the same laws it imposes on the rest of the country. Despite his conservatism, he occasionally opposes his party on principle. In 2003, he said he saw no need to amend the Constitution to ban same-sex marriages. He was one of 17 House Republicans to vote against a 2012 amendment to bar the Obama administration from using taxpayer funds to defend its health care law in court.

He chaired the Judiciary Committee for six years starting in 2001. Sensenbrenner is best known for his work after the September 11 attacks. He pressed for a thorough congressional review of Attorney General John Ashcroft's proposal for beefed-up investigative powers for law enforcement. Concerned about possible violations of civil liberties, he insisted on a sunset provision for the USA Patriot Act, the anti-terrorism law passed just after the attacks on New York and Washington, ensuring it would expire in four years and giving Congress a chance to study its impact.

By 2005, he decided that his concerns about civil liberties had been addressed and he pushed to make most of the law permanent. After a difficult conference committee with the Senate, he won an extension of the law for the Bush administration. But Sensenbrenner had differences with Attorney General Alberto Gonzales over the scope of the domestic surveillance program and demanded steps to protect "the freedoms we cherish." Sensenbrenner pushed for a permanent extension of the law's so-called "lone wolf" provision allowing the government to monitor terrorists even if they are not suspected of ties to a specific group.

In 2015, he was instrumental in reducing the sweep of the Patriot Act, which had become unpopular with both tea party conservatives suspicious of government and civil libertarians. Following revelations of the National Security Agency's bulk collection of data, Sensenbrenner authored what became known as the USA Freedom Act, a bipartisan, bicameral and comprehensive measure that put an end to collection of meta-data, increased the transparency of the Foreign Intelligence Surveillance Court and found a new balance between national security and privacy. "Sensenbrenner could savor the kind of victory that doesn't come along too often in a polarized, party-line political world," the *Milwaukee Journal Sentinel* wrote after the bill was enacted in June. "[President Obama and I] both realized there was a problem that had to be fixed. And we worked together to fix it," he said.

Sensenbrenner worked steadily for years on some bills. One of them was bankruptcy reform, which was enacted in 2005 after being held up for years by a Democratic provision preventing abortion protesters from filing for bankruptcy to avoid fines and damages in attacks on abortion clinics. He has backed limitations in tort law on class action, medical malpractice and asbestos liability, and has sought to increase penalties for frivolous lawsuits. He was instrumental in passing the first congressional authorization of the Department of Justice in many years, citing the vital role that it gave the Judiciary Committee in improving oversight of the department. He was instrumental in enacting in 2003 the Child Abduction Prevention Act, which enhanced the AMBER Alert system. One of his final actions as chairman was the bipartisan extension of the Voting Rights Act.

Another of Sensenbrenner's focused efforts has been on immigration. In 2004, he successfully added to the intelligence reorganization bill provisions setting national standards for driver's licenses that denied licenses to illegal immigrants, prohibited the use of Mexican *matricula consular* cards for identification, tightened standards for asylum, and overrode state laws and regulations blocking border barriers. He took a skeptical view in January 2013 of bipartisan efforts to pass a comprehensive immigration reform bill, saying, "extending amnesty to those who came here illegally or overstayed their visas is dangerous waters."

The House Republicans' six-year term limit for senior committee members forced Sensenbrenner to give up the top Republican spot on Judiciary in January 2007. In March, Minority Leader John Boehner named Sensenbrenner the ranking Republican on the Select Committee on Energy Independence and Global Warming, which Speaker Nancy Pelosi had created to accommodate environmentalists. A global warming skeptic, Sensenbrenner had voted against the creation of the panel, saying it was nothing more than a publicity stunt, but he promised to participate in the debate. He protested in late 2010 when the new Republican majority abolished the committee—which he would have chaired—saying the panel was still needed as a check on the Obama administration.

As chairman of the Science, Space, and Technology Committee in the late 1990s, he attacked climate science. He sought to regain that chairmanship in 2013, but lost out to Lamar Smith of Texas. He now chairs the Judiciary Subcommittee on Crime, Terrorism, Homeland Security and Investigations.

Sensenbrenner occasionally displays a rough and often partisan edge, which grates on colleagues and others. He apologized in 2011 for remarks he made about first lady Michelle Obama, who has made fighting the nation's high obesity rate one of her priorities. Attempting to make a point about hypocrisy while speaking at a church bazaar, Sensenbrenner said that she had a "big butt." Fellow Republican Dan Lungren of California told *The New York Times* in 2006 that Sensenbrenner "treats us all like dogs." The watchdog group Citizens for Responsibility and Ethics in Washington in 2010 criticized his role after the BP oil spill in the Gulf of Mexico. Sensenbrenner owned more than 3,600 shares of the company's stock, which he disclosed, but did not recuse himself from an investigation of the incident or from votes relating to it. He was not required to do so under House rules, but CREW said his activity created an appearance of impropriety.

Sensenbrenner has been reelected easily every two years. In 2009, he announced his plans for reelection at the same time he made it known that he had prostate cancer. He prided himself on not missing votes, scheduling his cancer treatments around the House schedule and holding his customary schedule of town meetings in his district.

SIXTH DISTRICT

Glenn Grothman (R)

Elected 2014; 1st term; b. July 3, 1955, Milwaukee; U., of WI—Madison, B.A. 1978, J.D. 1983; Lutheran; single.

Elected Office: WI Assembly, 1994-2004; Asst. Minority Leader, WI State Senate, 2012-13; Asst. Majority Leader, WI State Senate 2013; Member WI State Senate (District 20), 2004-14.

Professional Career: Atty.

DC Office: 501 CHOB, 20515; 202-225-2476; Fax: 202-225-2356; Website: grothman.house.gov.

State Offices: Fond du Lac, 920-907-0624.

Committees: *Budget. Education & the Workforce:* Early Childhood, Elementary, & Secondary Education; Health, Employment, Labor & Pensions. *Oversight & Government Reform:* Government Operations; Transportation & Public Assets.

Election Results

2014 general	Glenn Grothman (R)	169,767	(57%)	$1,162,106	$51,202
	Mark Harris (D)	122,212	(41%)	$272,123	
	Gus Fahrendorf (Lib)	6,865	(2%)		
2014 primary	Glenn Grothman (R)	23,247	(36%)		
	Joe Leibham (R)	23,028	(36%)		
	Duey Stroebel (R)	15,873	(25%)		

Population		Race and Ethnicity		Income	
Total:	713,224	White	91.0%	Median income:	$51,404
Urban:	36.6%	Latino	4.0%		*(212 of 435)*
Suburban:	24.9%	Asian	2.0%	Under $50,000	48.3%
Rural:	38.5%	Black	1.5%	$50,000-$99,999:	34.0%
Land area:	4,914	Two races	1.1%	$100,000-$199,999:	15.0%
Pop/sq. mi.:	145.2	White Ethnic	28.6%	$200,000 or more:	2.7%
Born in state:	79.9%			Poverty Rate	10.2%
		Education			
Age Groups		H.S. grad or less:	45.0%	**Work**	
Under 18:	21.7%	Some college:	30.6%	White collar:	29.4%
18 to 34:	20.6%	College degree, 4 yr.:	16.9%	Blue collar:	39.4%
35 to 64:	41.2%	Post-grad study:	7.5%	Sales and service:	31.2%
Over 64:	16.5%				
		Military		Govt. workers:	9.9%
		Veterans/active duty:	9.2%		

East-Central Wisconsin: Oshkosh, Sheboygan

Central Wisconsin is a producer of basic commodities—milk, butter, cheese, Kleenex, Mercury Marine outboard motors and military trucks. This is where the rolling hills and prairies of southern Wisconsin begin to give way to the pine and hardwood forests and glacial lakes of the Northwoods. First settled

Voter Turnout	
2013 Total Citizen 18+	547,737
2014 House Turnout	299,033
2014 Turnout as % CVAP	54.6%
2012 Turnout as % CVAP	70.6%

by Yankee Protestants, the 1850s brought the first large surge of German migration into the United States, and central Wisconsin was a favorite destination. They built the dairy farms and factory towns that seemed steadfastly prosperous, and they developed a manufacturing economy. The German influence is still felt. Sheboygan is the Bratwurst Capital of the World, though the city and surrounding county in 2014 were home to more than 5,300 Asians, mostly Hmong, and 6,300 Hispanics. Johnsonville Foods, which began as a small family-owned company in 1945, now employs over 1,500 workers and sells more sausage than any of its national competitors. Oshkosh is no longer the place where children's clothing maker Oshkosh B'Gosh manufactures its products. But it is home to the Oshkosh Corp., which produces everything from dump trucks to military vehicles.

Central Wisconsin was also one of the birthplaces of the Republican Party, when a group of Whigs, Free Soilers and anti-slavery Democrats met in February 1854 in a small white schoolhouse in Ripon and proclaimed themselves Republicans. (A similar gathering took place in Jackson, Michigan, which also claims to be the birthplace of the party.) The party grew rapidly, winning a near majority in the House in that year's elections.

2012 Presidential Vote		
Mitt Romney (R)..............202,979	(53%)
Barack Obama (D) 174,988	(46%)
2008 Presidential Vote		
Barack Obama (D) 184,881	(49%)
John McCain (R)................184,230	(49%)
Cook Partisan Voting Index: R+5		

The 6th Congressional District is a slice of central Wisconsin from Lake Michigan to the Wisconsin River. It takes in the conservative, northern Milwaukee suburbs in Ozaukee County, including Port Washington. It includes Oshkosh, the largest city in the district, on the west shore of Lake Winnebago; Sheboygan and Manitowoc on Lake Michigan; and Fond du Lac on the south shore of Lake Winnebago. The district also includes four rural counties plus the Wisconsin Dells and its giant water park, a longtime family vacation destination for city dwellers in Milwaukee and Chicago.

Oshkosh, a working-class city, used to be solidly Republican but now favors Democrats. Even Oshkosh resident Sen. Ron Johnson won his hometown by only 305 votes in 2010. Overall, the district has been Republican territory since that first meeting in Ripon. In 2012, it was Mitt Romney's second-best performing district in Wisconsin. He won 53% of the vote after President Barack Obama barely won it four years earlier.

Glenn Grothman (R)

Republican Glenn Grothman was elected in 2014 to succeed Republican Rep. Tom Petri, who retired after 35 years in office. Though the two men share a party, the moderate low-profile Petri had little in common with his successor. Grothman is a staunch conservative with a lengthy record of provocative comments that raised national GOP concerns.

Born in Milwaukee, Grothman earned his bachelor's and law degrees from the University of Wisconsin. He won a special election to the Wisconsin Assembly in 1993, then easily took the GOP nomination for a Senate seat in 2004, arguing that the incumbent was insufficiently conservative. He became assistant Republican leader in 2009, and was a vocal supporter of GOP Gov. Scott Walker's budget and policy changes.

In April 2014, Grothman said that he would challenge Petri, who decided to retire. In the closest congressional race in Wisconsin since 1970, Grothman won the primary over state Sen. Joe Leibham by 219 votes, with 36% each. State Rep. Duey Stroebel finished third with 25%. Leibham declined to ask for a recount. The primary results showed unusual disparities in voting. Grothman led Liebham nearly 4-to-1 in Ozaukee County and 3-to-2 in Fond du Lac. Liebham led 2-to-1 in Sheboygan and 5-to-1 in Manitowoc. Strobel won two small counties in the western part of the district.

Grothman was a dream candidate for opposition researchers. In the legislature, he supported Walker's decision to repeal the state's Equal Pay Enforcement Act, saying that "you could argue that money is more important for men." He introduced a bill that would have required a state board to list single parenthood as a contributor to child abuse. He opposed increasing funding for antismoking programs because, he said, "everyone knows you're not supposed to smoke." Grothman also proposed an unsuccessful amendment to delete language prohibiting sex-education teachers from displaying "bias" against gay and lesbian students. He told *The Capital Times* that when he was in high school, "Homosexuality was not on anybody's radar. And that's a good thing." He coauthored a law to legalize concealed carry of firearms.

On national issues, Grothman takes strongly conservative views on spending, tax reform, education and abortion. He has opposed Martin Luther King Day as a public holiday and called the promotion of Kwanzaa "deplorable," urging people to "treat Kwanzaa with the contempt it deserves before it becomes a permanent part of our culture." He described welfare programs as "a bribe not to work that hard or a bribe not to marry someone with a full-time job."

Both Grothman and Winnebago County Executive Mark Harris, the Democratic nominee, argued that the other was too extreme for the district. Harris said Grothman was weak on women's issues, while Grothman in a fundraising email labeled Harris a "far-left politician." Harris cast himself as being more like Petri—a "thoughtful, quiet moderate." But Grothman had demographics and money on his side. Newly drawn boundaries made the 6th District the second-most Republican of the state's eight congressional districts. Grothman spent $1.2 million, more than four times as much as Harris. Neither national party showed much interest in this contest. Grothman won 57%-41%—four percentage points better than Romney in 2012. He took 9 of the 11 counties; Harris narrowly won Columbia and Winnebago.

During his early months in the House, Grothman attracted relatively little attention and kept busy with work on his committees: Budget, Education and the Workforce, and Oversight and Government Reform. Like the other four Republicans from Wisconsin, he voted for John Boehner for speaker, despite a campaign pledge that he "would have no problem looking for an alternative." After two months, the *Milwaukee Journal Sentinel* reported, "we've hardly heard a word from him."

SEVENTH DISTRICT

Sean Duffy (R)

Elected 2010, 3rd term; b. Oct. 3, 1971, Hayward; St. Mary's Col. MN, B.A. 1994, William Mitchell Col. of Law, J.D. 1999; Catholic; married (Rachel Campos-Duffy); 6 children.

Elected Office: Dist. atty., Ashland Cnty., 2002-10.

Professional Career: Practicing atty., 1999-2000; Special prosecutor, Ashland Cnty., 2000-02.

DC Office: 1208 LHOB, 20515, 202-225-3365; Fax: 202-225-3240; Website: duffy.house.gov.

State Offices: Wausau, 715-298-9344; Superior, 715-392-3984; Hudson, 715-808-8160.

Committees: *Financial Services:* Oversight & Investigations (Chmn); Capital Markets & Government Sponsored Enterprises.

Group Ratings

	ADA	ACLU	AFL-CIO	LCV	ITI	COC	HAFA	ACU	CFG	FRC
2014	5%	0%	–	0%	80%	77%	57%	73%	70%	88%
2013	5%	C	15%	4%	C	77%	C	72%	67%	C

National Journal Ratings

	2013 LIB	—	2013 CONS
Economic	18%	—	82%
Social	43%	—	54%
Foreign	24%	—	68%
Composite	30%	—	70%

Key Votes of the 113th Congress

1. Sandy storm spending N	5. Medical Marijuana N	9. Syrian Rebels Training N
2. Violence Against Women Act Y	6. Farm Bill Y	10. Keystone pipeline Y
3. Guantanamo Bay Detainees N	7. Afghanistan Combat N	11. Immigration Exec. Action Y
4. Abortion 20-week ban Y	8. NSA Phone Data Collection Y	12. Bipartisan budget deal Y

Election Results

2014 general	Sean Duffy (R)............................ 169,891	(59%)	$1,970,453	$4,933	$30,376
	Kelly Westlund (D) 112,949	(39%)	$526,935		
2014 primary	Sean Duffy (R)............................. 25,707	(88%)			
	Don Raihala (R) 3,607	(12%)			

Prior winning percentages: 2012 (56%), 2010 (52%)

Population		Race and Ethnicity		Income	
Total:	715,263	White	92.6%	Median income:	$47,849
Urban:	7.7%	Amer. Indian	2.0%		*(269 of 435)*
Suburban:	18.9%	Latino	1.8%	Under $50,000	51.6%
Rural:	73.4%	Asian	1.4%	$50,000-$99,999:	32.8%
Land area:	21,506	Two races	1.6%	$100,000-$199,999:	13.2%
Pop/sq. mi.:	33.3	White Ethnic	31.2%	$200,000 or more:	2.3%
Born in state:	67.7%			Poverty Rate	12.3%
		Education			
		H.S. grad or less:	46.1%	**Work**	
Age Groups		Some college:	32.8%	White collar:	30.0%
Under 18:	22.3%	College degree, 4 yr.:	14.1%	Blue collar:	40.8%
18 to 34:	18.3%	Post-grad study:	7.1%	Sales and service:	29.2%
35 to 64:	41.4%				
Over 64:	18.0%			Govt. workers:	11.9%
		Military			
		Veterans/active duty:	10.1%		

North-Central Wisconsin

In the late 19th century, thousands of migrants traveled the rail lines radiating northwest from Chicago and Milwaukee to settle the northern reaches of Wisconsin, the most thickly settled land this far north in the United States and east of the

Voter Turnout	
2013 Total Citizen 18+	549,787
2014 House Turnout	286,603
2014 Turnout as % CVAP	52.1%
2012 Turnout as % CVAP	68.9%

Mississippi. What attracted them was not cropland—there are no large wheat farms as in the Red River Valley of North Dakota—but trees, iron and cows. This was one of America's largest virgin timberlands, and the river towns are still dotted with paper mills. Farther north, iron brought Finns and Italians to the port of Superior, across the St. Louis Bay from Duluth, Minnesota, and to smaller towns on the chilly lake. Nearby Apostle Islands National Lakeshore has eight lighthouses and breeding grounds for 240 species of birds that migrate through the archipelago. The cleared forest lands became dairy farms. Dairy cattle, properly cared for, thrived in these northern uplands, and the sons of Wisconsin dairymen, many of them immigrants from Germany and Norway, moved their dairy herds even farther north toward Canada. Small cities grew, and some became home to big enterprises.

Wausau has paper mills, but the city's eponymous paper industry has shrunk, as has household income in surrounding Marathon County. In 2011, Wausau Paper Corp. closed its mill in Brokaw, shedding 450 jobs. The number of dairy farmers in the region is in sharp decline, as the economics of their business became less attractive; some farmers have turned to potatoes, vegetables, cranberries, and even ginseng. Wausau, which the 1980 census found to be the most ethnically homogeneous city in the nation, now has a sizeable immigrant community. Many Hmong refugees moved there in the 1980s; as of 2010, 11% of the city's population was Asian.

2012 Presidential Vote		
Mitt Romney (R)..................190,364	(51%)
Barack Obama (D) 178,841	(48%)

2008 Presidential Vote		
Barack Obama (D) 198,323	(53%)
John McCain (R)..................169,076	(45%)

Cook Partisan Voting Index: R+2

This region makes up Wisconsin's 7th Congressional District, which stretches more than 200 miles from Lake Superior in the north to Monroe County, next to La Crosse. Commuter-oriented St. Croix County, part of the Minneapolis-St. Paul metro area, was the fastest-growing county in Wisconsin from 2000 to 2010, with the population approaching 86,000. In rural Iron and Ashland counties, developers have been eager to mine a 22-mile long strip of land rich with iron ore, arguing it would create at least 700 jobs in the region. Democratic state legislators have blocked the project, fearing negative environmental impact, which led the company to propose in September 2014 a scaled-down proposal for an open-pit mine solely in Iron County.

The politics of the 7th District have a rough-hewn quality, a lumberjack-populist flavor. Ancestrally Republican, the area favored the progressivism of Wisconsin's LaFollettes. Today, Superior-based Douglas County is the chief Democratic outpost, while Marathon, St. Croix and many of the smaller counties have leaned Republican. Barack Obama carried it with 53% of the vote in 2008, and did three percentage points better with the old boundaries. Four years later, Mitt Romney won it with 51% of the vote.

Sean Duffy (R)

Republican Sean Duffy succeeded retiring Democratic stalwart David Obey, the House Appropriations Committee chairman, in a stunning turnaround in 2010. The telegenic Duffy, a former prosecutor, has largely avoided the intra-party conflicts that have consumed many of his classmates and he has tended to his work on the Financial Services Committee.

Duffy hails from the sparsely populated, thickly forested northern end of the state, the 10th of 11 children. He became adept at the local craft of lumberjacking, eventually earning multiple world-champion titles in the 60-foot and 90-foot pole speed climb. At St. Mary's College in Minnesota, he got his degree in business marketing. On a lark after graduation, Duffy joined the cast of MTV's *The Real World: Boston*, one of the earliest reality-TV series. The program brought young people with diverse backgrounds together to live as roommates, with the aim of spurring lively confrontations. Duffy was cast as the conservative in the show, and he frequently sparred with a liberal roommate. Around that time, he met his future wife, Rachel Campos-Duffy, a Latina who had been cast as the conservative foil in the *Real World* season taped in San Francisco.

Duffy got a law degree from William Mitchell College of Law in St. Paul. He returned to Wisconsin to work briefly for his family's law firm before becoming a prosecutor. In 2002, Republican Gov. Scott McCallum appointed Duffy as Ashland County district attorney. In that role, he boasted a 90% success rate in jury trials and prosecuting child sex offenders. He was serving his fourth term when he resigned to challenge Obey in the 2010 election. Then, Obey unexpectedly announced that he would not seek reelection, removing himself as a target for Duffy and his conservative, anti-government message in the increasingly anti-incumbent climate. Instead of facing an old-time appropriator who had been in Washington for four decades, Duffy drew as an opponent a young Washington outsider like himself, Democratic state Sen. Julie Lassa.

In his campaign, Duffy made an issue of big-spending government and, specifically, the $787 billion economic stimulus bill that Obey had initially crafted and pushed to passage. Duffy was adept at raising money, and he ran as an unabashedly family-values and small-government conservative. Campos-Duffy, a conservative activist who made many appearances on "The View," the Barbara Walters syndicated talk show, wrote a book in 2009, *Stay Home, Stay Happy: 10 Secrets to Loving At-Home Motherhood*, which she calls "a love letter to at-home moms." The couple has seven young children.

Lassa accused Duffy of supporting deep cuts in entitlement spending after he embraced Wisconsin Rep. Paul Ryan's budget plan. She campaigned as a champion of the middle class, calling for a first-time home buyers' tax credit, a payroll tax holiday for businesses that hire new workers, and a 10% pay cut for members of Congress until the unemployment rate dropped. But Lassa had difficulty connecting with voters, giving stump speeches that were heavily reliant on notes. By contrast, Duffy was at ease and even charming in a crowd. On Election Day, he won, 52%-44%.

In the House, Duffy has backed his party on big votes, especially on fiscal issues, but has shown greater independence on matters that touch on his district. He refused to join most other tea party-backed freshmen in voting to end subsidies to rural airports and to defund National Public Radio, which maintains a strong audience in some non-urban regions. He formed a close friendship with South Carolina's Trey Gowdy, a fellow freshman and ex-prosecutor, and the two cosponsored each other's legislation aimed at reining in spending.

Duffy became active as a member of the Financial Services Committee. In 2015, he took over as chairman of the Oversight and Investigations Subcommittee. In March, he won bipartisan committee approval of his bill to require transparency at meetings of the advisory board of the Consumer Financial Protection Bureau. With committee Chairman Jeb Hensarling of Texas, he announced in May an investigation of a leak of market-sensitive information from the Federal Open Market Committee of the Federal Reserve. In June, he continued a series of hearings exploring allegations of discrimination and retaliation by CFPB managers against the agency's employees.

Duffy made occasional statements that Democrats eagerly turned against him. Nothing brought Duffy more attention than his attempt to show empathy with an economically struggling constituent at a 2011 town hall meeting. When the man pointed out that Duffy's salary was "three times what I make," Duffy responded, "If you think I'm living high off the hog, I've got one paycheck. ... I struggle to meet my bills right now." Democrats pounced on the comment, contending that it illustrated how out of touch Duffy was, and launched an aggressive attempt to unseat him.

Pat Kreitlow, a former Democratic state senator, spent a respectable $1.3 million in his 2012 challenge. But Duffy drew on the financial industry's largesse and spent twice that amount. Each national party spent more than $2 million for its candidate. With an additional boost from redistricting, Duffy won, 56%-44%. In 2014, Duffy faced Kelly Westlund, a 30-year-old liberal activist who served on the city council in Ashland and spent $527,000. Duffy increased his win to 59%-39%, winning every county except for Douglas in the northwest corner. He seems to have secured his district, and opened the door to additional political options.

EIGHTH DISTRICT

Reid Ribble (R)

Elected 2010, 3rd term; b. April 5, 1956, Neenah; H.S. diploma 1974, Grand Rapids Bible and Music Schl., attended; Baptist; married (DeaNa); 2 children.

Professional Career: Pres., The Ribble Group, 1981-2009.

DC Office: 1513 LHOB, 20515, 202-225-5665; Fax: 202-225-5729; Website: ribble.house.gov.

State Offices: Appleton, 920-380-0061; Green Bay, 920-471-1950.

Committees: *Transportation & Infrastructure:* Aviation; Highways & Transit; Water Resources & Environment; *Foreign Affairs:* Europe, Eurasia & Emerging Threats; Terrorism, Nonproliferation & Trade.

Group Ratings

	ADA	ACLU	AFL-CIO	LCV	ITI	COC	HAFA	ACU	CFG	FRC
2014	0%	11%	–	3%	100%	64%	68%	88%	84%	75%
2013	10%	C	14%	4%	C	92%	C	80%	72%	C

National Journal Ratings

	2013 LIB	—	2013 CONS
Economic	12%	—	88%
Social	16%	—	74%
Foreign	48%	—	51%
Composite	27%	—	73%

Key Votes of the 113th Congress

1. Sandy storm spending	N	5. Medical Marijuana	Y	9. Syrian Rebels Training	N
2. Violence Against Women Act	N	6. Farm Bill	Y	10. Keystone pipeline	Y
3. Guantanamo Bay Detainees	N	7. Afghanistan Combat	N	11. Immigration Exec. Action	Y
4. Abortion 20-week ban	Y	8. NSA Phone Data Collection	Y	12. Bipartisan budget deal	Y

Election Results

2014 general	Reid Ribble (R)	188,553	(65%)	$1,066,298	$8,572	$11,676
	Ron Gruett (D)	101,345	(35%)	$22,206		
2014 primary	Reid Ribble (R)	unopposed				

Prior winning percentages: 2012 (56%), 2010 (55%)

Population		Race and Ethnicity		Income	
Total:	720,600	White	88.5%	Median income:	$52,169
Urban:	42.1%	Latino	4.4%		*(206 of 435)*
Suburban:	21.3%	Asian	2.2%	Under $50,000	47.6%
Rural:	36.7%	Amer. Indian	2.1%	$50,000-$99,999:	34.4%
Land area:	6,644	Two races	1.5%	$100,000-$199,999:	15.1%
Pop/sq. mi.:	108.5	White Ethnic	30.2%	$200,000 or more:	2.9%
Born in state:	79.3%			Poverty Rate	11.1%
		Education			
Age Groups		H.S. grad or less:	43.3%	**Work**	
Under 18:	23.3%	Some college:	31.5%	White collar:	31.4%
18 to 34:	20.6%	College degree, 4 yr.:	18.1%	Blue collar:	40.3%
35 to 64:	41.1%	Post-grad study:	7.2%	Sales and service:	28.3%
Over 64:	15.0%				
		Military		Govt. workers:	10.8%
		Veterans/active duty:	9.0%		

Northeast Wisconsin: Green Bay, Appleton

In 1673, the French Catholic missionary and explorer Jacques Marquette sailed from the open waters of Lake Michigan into what is now the expansive Green Bay. He had hoped to find the Northwest Passage to the Pacific. Instead, he found the Fox River, which leads to Lake Winnebago and,

Voter Turnout	
2013 Total Citizen 18+	538,261
2014 House Turnout	290,048
2014 Turnout as % CVAP	53.9%
2012 Turnout as % CVAP	69.6%

after a not-too-difficult portage, the Wisconsin River, which flows into the Mississippi. Green Bay and the Fox River Valley remained mostly wilderness and Indian country for more than 150 years. But once settled by Europeans, they became, as Father Marquette would have liked, one of the most heavily Catholic parts of the United States. The area thrived economically, with paper mills, a busy port, and high-skill manufacturing in Green Bay and Appleton. The 2007-09 recession caused a slowdown in Port of Green Bay shipping, as did lowered demand for the region's timber. The port economy has rebounded since 2010 with double-digit annual percentage increases in domestic cargo, mostly imports. In Marinette County, located on the bay, the Marinette Marine shipyard is spurring an economic boomlet with a multibillion dollar Navy contract to build 10 new littoral combat ships by 2030, with a workforce of more than 2,000.

No reference to Green Bay is complete without a mention of professional football's Packers, the locally beloved franchise owned by 110,000 shareholding Wisconsinites and unlikely ever to move. Under the team's charter, if the Packers are sold, the proceeds would go to the local Sullivan-Wallen American Legion Post 11 "for the purposes of erecting a proper soldier's memorial." The city, by far the smallest with an NFL franchise, has earned the nickname "Titletown" for the Packers' numerous championships, including the 2011 Super Bowl. Thirty miles south is Appleton, which has produced famous, and infamous, Americans: novelist Edna Ferber, escape artist

2012 Presidential Vote		
Mitt Romney (R)...............191,127		(51%)
Barack Obama (D) 177,346		(48%)
2008 Presidential Vote		
Barack Obama (D) 195,295		(54%)
John McCain (R)................164,160		(45%)
Cook Partisan Voting Index: R+2		

Harry Houdini, and demagogue Sen. Joseph McCarthy, the central figure in the "red scare" of the 1950s. Both Green Bay and Appleton are growing, thanks in part to surging Hispanic populations. Green Bay's Latino community has increased from approximately 1,000 people in 1990 to nearly 14,000; the city is now more than 13% Hispanic.

The 8th Congressional District of Wisconsin includes Green Bay and the Fox River Valley south to Appleton. It also includes the inland dairy counties and the Northwoods, which has hundreds of pine-ringed lakes where city dwellers keep summer homes. The Door County peninsula, which extends from Green Bay into Lake Michigan, is a more upscale summer destination, with art galleries, boutiques and restaurants.

Politically, this has often been malleable territory and is one of the must-win regions in this traditional swing state. Green Bay was one of the most-heavily advertised media markets in the country during the 2012 presidential race, and both President Barack Obama and GOP vice-presidential nominee Paul Ryan campaigned in the city. Obama carried the district with 54% of the vote in 2008, but Romney won it with 51% in 2012—not enough to swing the state to Republicans.

Reid Ribble (R)

Republican Reid Ribble defeated two-term Democratic Rep. Steve Kagen in 2010 in his first bid for political office. Ribble has become known for his straight-talking manner, particularly when it comes to decrying partisan gridlock. He has taken control of the 8th District, which had experienced frequent shifts in partisan control.

Ribble was raised in Appleton as the youngest of eight children. He says that he often got beaten up as a youth, a consequence of his tendency to say exactly what was on his mind. His father was a World War II-era Marine who started a roofing business that still bears the family name. After high school, Ribble enrolled in Grand Rapids Bible and Music School, planning to join the Baptist ministry. When he was age 20, his father asked him to take over the business. Ribble left school and spent five years learning the ropes from his father. Then he became president of the company. He ran the firm for almost 30 years, until he sold it to his nephew in 2009.

Ribble lodged his challenge to Kagen as "just an American who is frustrated with the overall condition of the economy and state of the union." He campaigned as a conservative and an outsider. His campaign website included detailed position papers, which he said his professional consultants advised against posting. "I decided to go out on a limb and be a different type of candidate, and trust people to make the decision," Ribble said. GOP recruiters viewed him as an attractive prospect because he lacked a voting record and had the ability to self-fund his campaign. In the Republican primary, Ribble dispatched two more-seasoned candidates who served in the Wisconsin House, with a hefty 48 percent of the vote.

In the general election, Ribble criticized Kagen for his support of President Barack Obama's health care overhaul and the Democratic energy bill that would put limits on carbon emissions. Kagen outspent Ribble, $2.1 million to $1.3 million. The Democratic Congressional Campaign Committee stepped in with an ad asserting that Ribble's construction firm had gotten $300,000 in federal stimulus money to replace a school roof. While some endangered Democrats that year ran away from the party's agenda, Kagen defended his vote for the health care bill, and he reminded voters that Republican President George W. Bush was in charge when the economy went south in 2007. Ribble won 55%-45%.

In the House, Ribble generally has been a loyal Republican soldier, especially on fiscal issues. He has shown an independent streak on other matters. In 2012, he was one of 11 Republicans to join most Democrats in opposing an amendment to try suspected terrorists at Cuba's Guantanamo Bay instead of in U.S. civilian courts. He also accepted an offer from liberal Wisconsin Rep. Tammy Baldwin that year to work on a successful effort to restore trade sanctions against several made-in-China paper products. "I knew she was going to run for the U.S. Senate," he later told the *Milwaukee Journal Sentinel*. "But I cared more about solving a problem than the politics."

Ribble joined the bipartisan Problem Solvers group spearheaded by former Utah GOP Gov. Jon Huntsman and West Virginia Democratic Sen. Joe Manchin. In a December 2012 op-ed column, Ribble pointed the finger at those in his party whom he deemed inflexible on striking a budget deal. "Republicans must confront their own conventional wisdom that says, 'The only way to shrink government is to starve it of resources,'" he wrote. In February 2015, as a member of the Transportation and Infrastructure Committee, he spearheaded a bipartisan group that urged quick action to approve a long-term extension of the highway trust fund with "a long-term sustainable revenue source," and end the cycle of brief extensions that kick the can down the road. In May 2015, Ribble launched a "Save the Bay" initiative to focus on environmental issues jeopardizing the waters of Green Bay.

His goal, Ribble said, is "to get our fiscal house back in order with responsible spending priorities and long-term budgeting that will give families and businesses the certainty they need." In 2013, he warned that partisanship and institutional incompetence were setting the stage for a third and possibly a fourth major political party to emerge. "I think we're at the precipice of a breakdown of the two-party system," he said.

Ribble's 2012 opponent was Jamie Wall, a business consultant who accused him of failing to fight the planned closure of the Kewaunee Power Station while accepting contributions from the plant's owner, Dominion Resources Inc. Ribble brushed off the allegation and charged that Wall's campaign was "stalking" him after the Democrat's supporters posted an online video of Ribble's house. Wall spent $1 million, half of Ribble's total. National Democrats turned their attention to other races, and Ribble won a comfortable 56%-44% reelection. In 2014, he sailed to reelection with 65% of the vote against a challenger with scant funding.

★ WYOMING ★

America's frontier disappeared in 1890, according to the Census Bureau and historian Frederick Jackson Turner, but some people still believe they are living on the frontier in Wyoming. This is "the land of the cowboy," as the *WPA Guide* said more than 70 years ago. "Its mountains, plains, and valleys are essentially livestock country. A cowboy astride a bucking bronco greets the visitor from enameled license plates, from newspapers, magazines, and painted signs." The cowboy is still on the license plates, and Wyoming remains the most western of states in spirit—largely unsettled, with a thin veneer of civilization stretched over a forbidding and beautiful land. After the open range era, cattle ranches were made possible by the barbed wire that could fence in roaming herds and the steam locomotives that could carry cattle to markets in the East.

Wyoming is still stretched thinly in some places: The Census Bureau missed three of the four people in Lost Springs in 2000 but got them all in 2010, and the one-person town of Buford was sold in 2012 to a Vietnamese investor. Though Wyoming is still the least populous state—Washington D.C. is 7% bigger in population despite being 1,400 times smaller in area—its population grew by 14% to 564,000 in the decade ending in 2010, and then an additional 3% through 2013. Historically, Wyoming was one of the few states with more men than women, which was one reason that Wyoming, when it was still a territory in 1869, was the first to give women the vote. (The exception: New Jersey allowed women with property to vote between 1776 and 1807, but there weren't many women with property.)

Wyoming is more than the land of the cowboy now—it is the land of the oil and gas worker, of the coal mine operator, and of the tourism executive. Its dependence on mining and minerals is not exactly new; the first oil well here was drilled in 1884, six years before statehood, and the Teapot Dome scandal in the 1920s involved Wyoming oil fields. The state boomed with oil prospectors during the energy price surge of the 1970s, but was hit hard by steep drops in oil prices in the early 1980s and again in the late 1990s. As oil exploration slumped, the production of other minerals surged. The 1970 Clean Air Act put a premium on Wyoming's low-sulfur coal, and it is now the No. 1 coal state, producing more than 40% of the nation's output. In the Powder River Basin, 30-story-high machines blast away the topsoil and scoop out coal. It is then hauled away by 60-some Burlington Northern Santa Fe and Union Pacific trains every day, each carrying 15,000 to 20,000 tons of coal. Two surface mines in Campbell County—Peabody's North Antelope Rochelle mine and Arch Coal's Black Thunder mine—produce more than 20% of America's coal.

The state is also eighth in crude oil production and fifth in natural gas. Much of the natural gas is coal-bed methane, mixed with water next to coal seams. Only in 1989 did engineers figure out how to separate the natural gas from the water, and now 200-foot drilling rigs are sinking wells as deep as 25,000 feet. Wyoming has 70% of the world supply of bentonite, which can swell to 16 times its weight or grow 10 times its size in water; it is used in oil drilling, cosmetics, and cat litter. It has the nation's largest uranium reserves, and its Shute Creek natural gas plant produces 20% of the nation's helium. The state is also hedging its bets with renewable energy, particularly wind farms; some are already operating, while another, an $8 billion project that would include a cavern-based energy-storage site and a 525-mile transmission line, has been proposed. (One downside: The renewable-energy division of Duke Energy pleaded guilty to killing eagles and other birds at two wind farms in the state between 2009 and 2013, agreeing to pay $1 million in damages.)

The mineral industry has made Wyoming an unusually prosperous state, but it is not the only source of income. Unemployment peaked at only 7.2% during the recession, and by mid-2015, it had fallen to 4.1%, well below the national average. With fiber optic linkages, some of the nation's lowest electricity rates, and a cool climate, Wyoming has proved a good site for giant data centers—Microsoft is expanding its already significant data-center presence around Cheyenne, and the National Center for Atmospheric Research has a $30 million supercomputer in the state.

Wyoming's other big industry is tourism. Its amazing landscape has long elicited national notice. Yellowstone, established in 1872, was the nation's first national park; it draws more than 3 million visitors a year, and Grand Teton National Park draws nearly that many. Jackson Hole, just south of the parks, has become one of America's elite year-round resort areas, with the state's busiest airport. There has been growth as well in the scenic

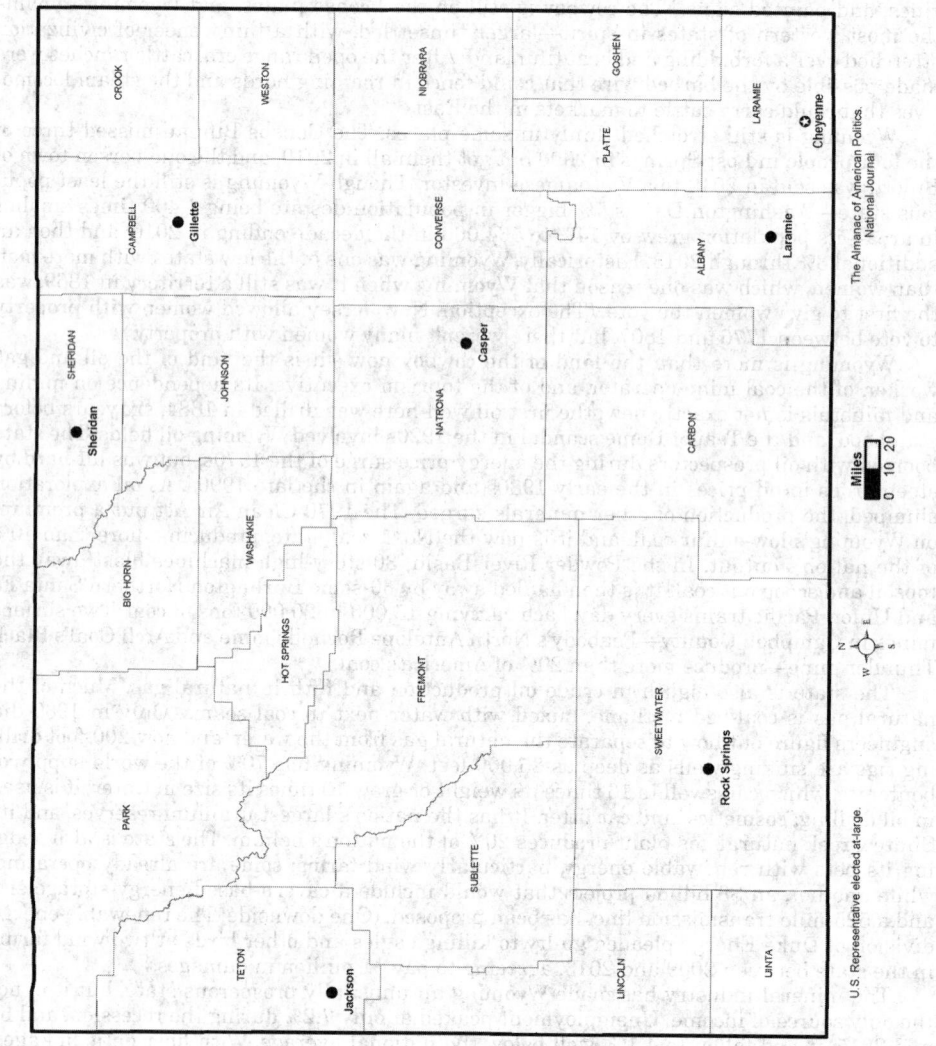

The Almanac of American Politics,
National Journal

CROOK

WESTON

NIOBRARA

GOSHEN

LARAMIE

✪ Cheyenne

PLATTE

CAMPBELL

● Gillette

CONVERSE

ALBANY

● Laramie

SHERIDAN

JOHNSON

NATRONA

● Casper

CARBON

● Sheridan

BIG HORN

WASHAKIE

HOT SPRINGS

FREMONT

SWEETWATER

Rock Springs ●

PARK

SUBLETTE

TETON

LINCOLN

UINTA

● Jackson

Miles

0 10 20

N
W—E
S

U.S. Representative elected at-large

and pastoral country on the eastern slope of the Big Horn Mountains around Buffalo and Sheridan. And agriculture remains significant. Wyoming ranks high in wool production and sheep inventory. It also produces hay, sugar beets, barley, pinto beans, and beef cattle.

The juxtaposition of civilization and wilderness has created some thorny policy issues. For years, the state has run feeding grounds for elk near Jackson Hole, and the herd has grown to tens of thousands. Environmental groups, worried about the spread of chronic wasting disease, want the feeding stopped, though thousands of elk induced over generations to depend on the feeding grounds likely will die. Local ranchers want it continued, to keep the elk away from their cattle, especially in winter. Grizzly bears, once endangered and protected in Yellowstone, have now increased in number and have been removed from the endangered list. The Interior Department agreed that the wolves previously reintroduced into the state and protected could be shot on sight, as long as the state committed to preserve 10 breeding pairs and 100 wolves outside Yellowstone. After protests from locals, the National Park Service agreed to allow 480 snowmobiles and 60 snow coaches into Yellowstone, and the National Forest Service permitted ice climbs on the Shoshone River to the east. On petition from the Northern Arapaho, the Fish and Wildlife Service granted the tribe permits to kill bald eagles. Meanwhile, nine Wyoming landowners agreed to take steps to preserve the endangered sage grouse, in exchange for flexibility in the face of regulations if the bird is placed on the endangered species list. Wyoming has 37 percent of the world's sage grouse habitat, accounting for about a quarter of the state's land area.

The state takes a hard line on resource extraction. The state sued the federal Bureau of Land Management over new rules governing the gas drilling method known as "fracking," arguing that the state, not the federal government, should take regulatory precedence. And Wyoming has gone to court to take issue with the Environmental Protection Agency over air quality, emissions and water quality. "Shouldn't we say that coal is a valuable resource that we want to use today and for the next 300 or 400 years or whatever it may be?" said Gov. Matt Mead. "So let's find solutions. You are not going to find solutions by putting unreasonable rules or regulations that prevent new coal-fired power plants from being produced."

The settled part of Wyoming consists of medium-sized towns, which are the state's largest cities. It is a small state, a single community really, where people remember who played what position, when and how well, and for what high school football team. The locals set the tone of life in Wyoming. There was once a sharp economic and regional split reflected in its partisan politics. The big economic interests—cattle ranchers, organized in the Wyoming Stock Growers Association, and the Union Pacific Railroad management—favored the Republicans, as did the wildcatters, independent producers, and oil company geologists. The main Democratic constituency was the Union Pacific Railroad workers who built the first transcontinental line across southern Wyoming in the 1860s. (Cheyenne was established because it was the midpoint between the UP's operations in Omaha and Ogden, Utah.) The southern tier of counties, from Cheyenne through Laramie to Evanston, once voted Democratic. But now the Democrats are strongest in Teton County, the home of Jackson Hole, the state's only county to vote for Barack Obama in both 2008 and 2012, and in Albany County, home of Laramie and the University of Wyoming, which Obama carried in 2008. Every other county voted between 59% and 85% for John McCain in 2008 and Mitt Romney in 2012.

Population		Race and Ethnicity		Income	
Total:	582,658	White	85.6%	Median income:	$55,700
Urban:	15.8%	Latino	9.1%		(17 of 50)
Suburban:	0.0%	Amer. Indian	1.8%	Under $50,000	43.1%
Rural:	84.2%	Black	0.9%	$50,000-$99,999:	33.6%
Land area:	97,093	Two races	1.8%	$100,000-$199,999:	19.8%
Pop/sq. mi.:	6.0	White Ethnic	23.1%	$200,000 or more:	3.5%
Born in state:	41.9%			Poverty Rate	10.9%
		Education			
Age Groups		H.S. grad or less:	34.9%	**Work**	
Under 18:	24.0%	Some college:	38.5%	White collar:	34.1%
18 to 34:	24.1%	College degree, 4 yr.:	17.8%	Blue collar:	39.1%
35 to 64:	38.6%	Post-grad study:	8.8%	Sales and service:	26.8%
Over 64:	13.3%			Govt. workers:	23.5%
		Military			
		Veterans/active duty:	11.2%		

Wyoming hasn't elected a Democrat to the Senate since 1970, or to the House since 1976, though it has had Democratic governors over that time, thanks to the importance of personal campaigning in such a tight-knit state. Democrats Ed Herschler, Mike Sullivan, and Dave Freudenthal have occupied the governor's chair for 28 of the past 40 years. But it may be a while before the Democrats win the governorship—or any state-wide office—again. In 2014, the Democrats couldn't even field a candidate for secretary of state, state treasurer and state auditor, and their candidate for education secretary, a credible business executive, won less than 40 percent of the vote. Both chambers of the legislature have Democratic caucuses numbering in the single digits. In 2008, Wyoming cast the lowest percentage for Obama—33%—of any state, and in two Senate races, it voted 76% and 73% for Republicans Mike Enzi and John Barrasso, respectively.

Voter Turnout	
2013 Total Citizen 18+	425,511
Highest Statewide Turnout	168,390
2014 Turnout as % CVAP	38.9%
2012 Turnout as % CVAP	58.1%

Legislature		
Senate:	26R	4D
House:	51R	9D

Still, compared to other solidly Republican states where religious conservatives are dominant, Wyoming has a libertarian, live-and-let-live ethos. In 1994, on the same Election Day when the GOP was winning a competitive gubernatorial race by a 3- 2 margin (and rolling to big gains nationally), Wyoming voters rejected a tough anti-abortion ballot measure by an equivalent 3- 2 margin. Wyoming attracted negative attention with the gruesome 1998 murder of Matthew Shepard, a gay college student, in Laramie. But more recently, Laramie, home of the University of Wyoming, approved an ordinance that banned discrimination on the basis of sexual orientation or gender identity, the first such ban in the state.

Presidential Politics Wyoming is one of the least likely states in the nation to be seriously contested in presidential general elections. It is too Republican, too remote, and has only three electoral votes. Candidates have seldom visited, except when Vice President Dick Cheney was at his home in Jackson. This was George W. Bush's best state in 2000, when he carried it 68%-28%, and it was his second best state in 2004, when he carried it 69%-29%. It was Mitt Romney's No. 2 state in 2012, when he carried it 69%-28%.

2012 Presidential Vote		
Mitt Romney (R)	170,962	(69%)
Barack Obama (D)	69,286	(28%)
Gary Johnson (Lib)	5,326	(2%)

2012 Presidential Caucus		
Mitt Romney (R)	822	(39%)
Rick Santorum (R)	673	(32%)
Ron Paul (R)	439	(21%)
Newt Gingrich (R)	165	(8%)

2008 Presidential Vote		
John McCain (R)	164,958	(65%)
Barack Obama (D)	82,868	(33%)

Wyoming has typically held presidential caucuses in early March, with no significant impact on the presidential nominating process. In early 2007, Wyoming Republicans pledged to caucus on the same date as the New Hampshire Republican primary. They settled on Jan. 5, which turned out to be two days after the Iowa caucuses and three days before the New Hampshire primary. The date was against party rules and cost the state half of its 28 delegates, but state party leaders evidently decided it was a minimal price to pay. In initial results, Romney won eight delegates, to three for Fred Thompson, and one for Duncan Hunter. In retrospect, it was a high watermark for the Thompson and Hunter campaigns.

Wyoming Democrats held their caucuses on March 8, a date on which most observers thought the nomination would be determined. Not so. Barack Obama's brilliant February, with 11 straight primary and caucus wins, was followed by Hillary Clinton's victories in Ohio and Texas on March 4. Anticipating a prolonged campaign, Obama opened a Cheyenne office in mid-February and ran television ads. The Clinton campaign, caught short-funded, sent in Bill Clinton and daughter Chelsea and ran radio spots. The Wyoming media wrote stories about state Democrats being energized, and Obama half-filled the University of Wyoming's auditorium in Laramie. Obama won 68%-31%, thanks in large part to big percentages in affluent Jackson Hole's Teton County (80%) and in the University of Wyoming's Albany County (74%). Clinton carried the Democrats' historical base, the Union Pacific Railroad worker counties of Carbon and Sweetwater that cover most of the southern half of the state.

In the February 29, 2012, GOP caucuses, Romney led with 39% of the vote, to 32% for Rick Santorum and 21% for Ron Paul. In the county conventions, Romney beat Santorum by a wider margin, 50%-32%, with only 10% for Paul.

Governor

Matt Mead (R)

Elected 2010, term expires Jan. 2019, 2nd term; b. March 11, 1962, Jackson; Trinity U. TX, B.A. 1984, U. of WY, J.D. 1987; Episcopalian; married (Carol); 2 children.

Professional Career: Campbell Cnty. prosecutor, 1987-90; Fed. prosecutor, U.S. atty., Cheyenne, 1991-94; Special asst. U.S. atty., 1994-95; Special asst. atty. gen., WY, 1998-2001; Practicing atty., 1995-2001; U.S. atty., WY, 2001-07; Farm/ranch operator, 2007-present.

Office: State Capitol, 200 W. 24th St., Cheyenne, 82002-0010, 307-777-7434; Fax: 307-632-3909; Website: governor.wy.gov.

Election Results

2014 general	Matt Mead (R)	99,700	(59%)
	Pete Gosar (D)	45,752	(27%)
	Don Wills (I)	9,895	(6%)
	Dee Cozzens (Lib)	4,040	(2%)
2014 primary	Matt Mead (R)	53,673	(55%)
	Taylor Haynes (R)	31,532	(32%)
	Cindy Hill (R)	12,464	(13%)

Prior winning percentage: 2010 (66%)

Wyoming's governor is Matt Mead, a Republican elected in 2010 to succeed two-term Democrat Dave Freudenthal. Mead drew positive reviews and easily won a second term in 2014.

Mead was born in Jackson and raised on his family's Teton County ranch. He is the grandson of Clifford Hansen, a former Republican governor of Wyoming (1963-67) and a senator (1967-78). Mead's mother, Mary, ran unsuccessfully for governor in 1990, six years before her death in a horseback riding accident. After receiving a bachelor's degree from Trinity University in San Antonio, Mead returned home to attend the University of Wyoming's law school. He worked as a prosecutor in Campbell County and in the U.S. Attorney's office in Cheyenne, and he practiced law for six years at a Cheyenne firm. He was chosen to serve as U.S. attorney for Wyoming in 2001 and spent nearly six years in the job. When Republican Sen. Craig Thomas died in 2007, Mead resigned his position to run for the Senate. But the Republican State Central Committee instead picked three other candidates, including state Sen. John Barrasso, whom Freudenthal subsequently appointed. Barrasso won a 2008 special election to serve the remaining four years of Thomas' term.

After the Senate setback, Mead returned to working in his family's ranching business. Meanwhile, Freudenthal—who had won reelection in 2006 with an impressive 70% of the vote—weighed a possible third term, which may or may not have been allowed under the constitution. That became moot when he decided against running again. Mead got into a crowded Republican field for governor, emphasizing his family's record of service. His opponents included state Auditor Rita Meyer, who served as GOP Gov. Jim Geringer's chief of staff; former state Rep. Ron Micheli; and state House Speaker Colin Simpson, son of former Sen. Alan Simpson. The candidates shared similar conservative views. Meyer got the endorsement of former Alaska Gov. Sarah Palin, while Simpson used his family connections to win the backing of former President George H.W. Bush. But Mead put nearly $900,000 of his own money into the contest to give him a 2-1 cash advantage, and that helped him build name recognition against his better-known competitors. He won 29% of the vote in the September primary, to Meyer's 28%. Micheli took 26%, and Simpson won 16%. In the general election, Mead benefited from running as a Republican at a time when Wyoming was increasingly negative about the Democratic Party. Mead easily defeated Leslie Petersen, Wyoming's former state Democratic Party chairman, by a 66%-23% margin, carrying every county.

Taking office, Mead noted that Wyoming's relatively sound fiscal health made it the envy of other states coping with severe budget shortfalls. He displayed his fiscal conservatism by trimming the payroll in the governor's office by about $100,000 a year. And he signed into law $15 million in incentives to entice large computer data centers to the state. He also proposed investing more state money in highways by taking a portion of the proceeds from Wyoming's statutory severance tax on minerals. The state legislature rejected the idea but committed to an interim study to look at new non-tax and non-toll-based revenue sources to fund roads.

On other issues, Mead signed into law a bill that would eliminate the right of suspected drunk drivers to refuse testing, and a measure that enabled Wyoming to join Alaska, Arizona, and Vermont in allowing residents to carry concealed guns without a permit. He called this "an appropriate law for Wyoming." He won praise for his dealings with the federal government, particularly on the U.S. Fish and Wildlife Service's agreement to remove some wolves from the endangered species list. By January 2012, his approval rating in a Colorado College poll stood at an astronomical 77%, the highest of any Rocky Mountain governor.

In 2012, Mead urged lawmakers to adopt a budget plan that financed one-time expenses in construction projects, highway maintenance, and aid to local governments for infrastructure needs. He later called on agency heads to cut 8% of their budget for fiscal year 2014, as a hedge against fluctuating coal and natural gas prices, and froze $4.4 million planned for a new state office building. At year's end, he proposed raising the state fuels tax by 10 cents, quickly expanding its rainy-day fund, and slightly shrinking the size of its operating budget. Lawmakers gave him most of what he wanted. In 2013, a Wyoming House-passed bill that drew national publicity sought to exempt the state from new federal laws. But after Mead raised concerns about potentially pitting police against federal agents charged with enforcing those laws, the measure died in the state Senate.

Mead feuded with Cindy Hill, the state superintendent of schools whose stormy tenure included accusations that she had exercised poor management skills; Hill was ousted following passage of a bill signed by Mead, then reinstated after the courts deemed it unconstitutional. Hill sought revenge against Mead by running in the 2014 gubernatorial primary. She had a base in the tea party, and in the state GOP convention, her supporters nearly succeeded in tagging Mead with a censure resolution. But Mead consolidated establishment support and won the primary. In the general, Mead was the overwhelming favorite over Democrat Pete Gosar, Libertarian Dee Cozzens, and independents Don Wills and Taylor Haynes, ultimately winning with nearly 60% of the vote.

Mead's view on the Affordable Care Act has evolved somewhat. He had said in November 2012 that Wyoming would decline to set up a state insurance exchange under the federal health care law, defaulting to a federally operated exchange. He also recommended that the state not participate in an expansion of Medicaid. But in his State of the State Address in 2015, Mead made the case for negotiations to expand Medicaid that were already under way with the federal government. "The fact is many of us don't like the ACA, including me," Mead said. "But here's another fact: Our federal tax dollars help pay for the ACA, and Wyoming tax dollars pay for the ACA. Do we choose to have that Wyoming money be returned to Colorado, California or Wyoming? I say Wyoming." However, the legislature put the kibosh on the idea, at least for 2015. Mead also warned of "turmoil" if the Supreme Court decided the case *King v. Burwell* by ending subsidies for people buying insurance on the federal exchanges. (The court's June 2015 ruling supported the subsidies.)

On other issues, Mead has also taken a more pragmatic approach than some fellow Republican governors, particularly those seeking a national profile with presidential bids. On climate change, Mead has leavened his defense of fossil fuels by urging practical solutions for the next generation of energy. He also signed a repeal of a ban on adopting science-education standards that say global warming is caused by humans. And Mead worked with the legislature and Hill's successor as schools superintendent to navigate the controversies over Common Core; the state, with support from local school-district leaders, is poised to implement the standards within a strengthened oversight regime. In Wyoming, Mead told the *Casper Star-Tribune*, voters "stay away from fringes on either side, and they want to see somebody who gets stuff done and doesn't approach everything through a completely partisan lens."

Senior Senator

Michael Enzi (R)

Elected 1996, term expires Jan., 2021, 4th term; b. Feb. 1, 1944, Bremerton, WA; George Washington U., B.S. 1966, Denver U., M.B.A. 1968; Presbyterian; married (Diana); 3 children.

Military Career: WY Natl. Guard, 1967-73.

Elected Office: Gillette mayor, 1975-82; WY House, 1986-90; WY Senate, 1990-96.

Professional Career: Owner, NZ Shoes, 1969-95; Dir. & chmn., First WY Bank of Gillette, 1978-88; Accounting mgr. & computer programmer, Dunbar Well Service, 1985-97; Ed. Comm. of States, 1989-93; Dir., Black Hills Corp., 1992-96; Western Interstate Comm. for Higher Ed., 1995-96.

DC Office: 379-A RSOB, 20510, 202-224-3424; Fax: 202-228-0359; Website: enzi.senate.gov.

State Offices: Casper, 307-261-6572; Cheyenne, 307-772-2477; Cody, 307-527-9444; Gillette, 307-682-6268; Jackson, 307-739-9507.

Committees: *Budget.* (Chmn) *Finance:* Energy, Natural Resources & Infrastructure; Health Care; Taxation & IRS Oversight. *Health, Education, Labor & Pensions:* Primary Health & Retirement (Chmn). *Homeland Security & Governmental Affairs:* Federal Spending Oversight & Emergency Management; Regulatory Affairs & Federal Management. *Small Business & Entrepreneurship.*

Group Ratings

	ADA	ACLU	AFL-CIO	LCV	ITI	COC	HAFA	ACU	CFG	FRC
2014	15%	6%	–	20%	33%	88%	70%	80%	68%	93%
2013	5%	C	17%	0%	C	63%	C	88%	94%	C

National Journal Ratings

	2013 LIB	—	2013 CONS
Economic	0%	—	95%
Social	0%	—	92%
Foreign	5%	—	93%
Composite	4%	—	96%

Key Votes of the 113th Congress

1. Sandy storm spending	N	5. Student Loan Rates	Y	9. Bipartisan Budget Deal	N
2. Chuck Hagel Confirmation	N	6. Employee Non-Discrim'n Act	N	10. Farm Bill Conference Rept.	Y
3. Gun Background Checks	N	7. Senate Vote on Judgeships	Y	11. Unempl. Comp. Extension	N
4. Immigration Reform	N	8. Defense Dept. Spending	N	12. Keystone Pipeline	Y

Election Results

2014 general	Mike Enzi (R)	121,554	(72%)	$3,486,953
	Charlie Hardy (D)	29,377	(17%)	$88,284
	Curt Gottshall (I)	13,311	(8%)	$76,431
	Joe Porambo (Lib)	3,677	(2%)	
2014 primary	Mike Enzi (R)	77,965	(82%)	
	Bryan Miller (R)	9,330	(10%)	

Prior winning percentages: 2008 (76%), 2002 (73%), 1996 (54%)

Michael Enzi, the senior senator from Wyoming, was elected in 1996. He is a mild-mannered conservative who's skillful at both working with Democrats and winning back-room battles. His widespread support among Republicans thwarted a potential 2014 primary challenge from ex-Vice President Dick Cheney's daughter Liz, and in 2015 he took over as chairman of the Budget Committee after asserting his seniority over the higher-profile Sen. Jeff Sessions of Alabama.

Enzi grew up in Thermopolis and Sheridan, the son of a shoe salesman. He earned degrees in accounting and retail marketing, moved to Gillette, and became an accountant for an oil well servicing company. He and his wife, Diana, started a small business, NZ Shoes. In the 1970s, at a meeting of his local Jaycee business group, Enzi met Republican Sen. Alan Simpson, who was impressed by his volunteerism and suggested he run for public office. In 1975, Enzi was elected mayor of Gillette, the center of Wyoming's coal belt and its fastest-growing town. He was mayor for eight years. In 1986, he was elected to the Wyoming state House and in 1990 to the state Senate.

After Simpson announced his retirement in December 1995, Enzi was one of nine Republicans and two Democrats who ran for the seat. With support from a grassroots network of conservatives, Enzi finished first in a straw poll at the May 1996 Republican state convention. His key contrast with second-place finisher John Barrasso was on abortion rights—Enzi opposed abortion rights, and Barrasso did not. Barrasso had more money, but Enzi won 32%-30%. (Barrasso later became a friendly colleague with Enzi in the Senate.) In the general, the Democratic nominee, former Secretary of State Kathy Karpan, opposed gun control and abortion rights, but it was her support for President Bill Clinton and his Interior Secretary, former Arizona Gov. Bruce Babbitt, that doomed her candidacy in solidly Republican Wyoming. Enzi led from the outset and won, 54%-42%.

In the Senate, Enzi was named "nicest senator" in *Washingtonian's* annual anonymous survey of congressional staffers. He has been a conservative stalwart—his lifetime rating from the anti-tax Club for Growth through 2013 was 94 percent, one of the highest among senators. Enzi and GOP Rep. Rob Bishop of Utah pleased tea party activists in May 2011 when they introduced the "Repeal Amendment," a measure enabling states to repeal any federal law.

Despite this, Enzi has regularly sought common ground. As the only accountant in the Senate at the time, Enzi played a key role on a major corporate accountability bill in 2002. He opposed a move by the Securities and Exchange Commission to bar accounting firms from doing auditing and consulting work for the same corporation. Enzi and Banking, Housing, and Urban Affairs Committee Chairman Paul Sarbanes of Maryland worked out a compromise establishing an accounting board independent of the SEC with power to oversee accounting firms. The Senate later passed the bill that became known as the Sarbanes-Oxley corporate accounting law.

With California Democrat Dianne Feinstein, Enzi worked in 2010 to limit the use of the controversial chemical bisphenol A as part of food safety legislation, though the chemical industry successfully blocked the move. He also joined North Dakota Democrat Byron Dorgan that year in pushing a bill to lift the U.S. travel ban on Cuba. He would later join a similar bipartisan effort in 2015. Enzi and Democratic Sen. Bob Casey of Pennsylvania co-sponsored a bill that aimed to help small businesses pool together as regional associations to secure federal government contracts. He also offered a bill with Democratic Sen. Herb Kohl of Wisconsin in May 2011 that would allow more time for displaced workers to repay loans to their 401(k) accounts.

However, it was on the Health, Education, Labor, and Pensions Committee where Enzi left his biggest mark. Despite his ideological differences with the late Sen. Edward M. Kennedy of Massachusetts, Enzi forged a productive relationship with the liberal lion. They operated on the "80-20 principle"—reach broad agreement on 80 percent of an issue and leave out the 20 percent where no agreement can be found. The two successfully pushed through the committee a bill requiring insurance companies to treat mental illness the same as other ailments in coverage decisions. They also agreed on reauthorization of Head Start early education programs and on renewal of college programs.

Enzi chaired the HELP panel in 2005; he did not always follow the Bush administration's lead. He sided with ranking minority member Kennedy in opposing a White House proposal to encourage more use of government vouchers for private school tuition in Gulf states recovering from Hurricane Katrina. He put together the reauthorization of the Carl D. Perkins Vocational and Technical Education Act, which passed the Senate 99-0 and was enacted that August. Enzi also won passage of renewed versions of a major jobs training bill and the higher education law. On an issue of special interest back home, Enzi helped to enact a bill to expedite the cleanup of abandoned coal mines. In the closing days of the Republican majority, he was instrumental in resolving conflicts over the funding formula to renew domestic AIDS programs.

In 2011, HELP Chairman Tom Harkin of Iowa worked with Enzi to try to rewrite the No Child Left Behind federal education law. But other Republicans on the committee derailed a scheduled bill-drafting session in October, complaining that they were left out of the process. Despite the objections, the bill passed the committee 15-7, with Enzi and two other Republicans joining all committee Democrats in supporting it. The bill never came to a vote on the Senate floor. On other education issues, Enzi disagreed sharply with Harkin. When Harkin planned a hearing examining controversial for-profit colleges, Enzi sent two letters to Harkin urging him to broaden the hearing to include all higher education institutions. When Harkin went ahead with the hearing, Enzi led other Republicans in a boycott of the meeting in June 2011.

When Obama's health care proposal was being crafted in the Senate in 2009, Enzi was a key negotiator. His own health care proposal called for tax credits for buying health care, assistance to help small businesses provide coverage for their employees, and requirements for the states to reduce the cost of medical malpractice insurance. He was one of the "Gang of Six" senators that met during the summer of 2009 in an unsuccessful effort to hammer out a solution acceptable to both parties. Since then, Enzi has been a critic of the Obama administration's efforts on health care.

Enzi briefly considered retirement after being passed over twice for appointment to the Finance Committee. In 2007, GOP Senate leaders gave a committee vacancy to the less-senior John Ensign of Nevada as a reward for Ensign's work leading the National Republican Senatorial Committee. Enzi tried again when another seat opened in late 2007, but the spot instead went to New Hampshire Sen. John Sununu, who also had less seniority but was facing a difficult reelection in 2008. Sununu lost in 2008, and Enzi finally got a seat on the powerful Finance panel.

He has not had serious opposition in his reelection races, though in 2013 it appeared that Liz Cheney might be his first real challenger. Cheney, the daughter of the onetime vice president and a former State Department official and prominent conservative activist in her own right, declared that "the Washington establishment is the problem." But Cheney was tagged as a carpetbagger, having lived extensively in the Washington area, and her candidacy led to a damaging intra-family split over same-sex marriage with her sister Mary, who is a lesbian. Enzi won the immediate and unwavering public backing of colleagues of all stripes. Republican Sen. Orrin Hatch of Utah told *Politico* that Enzi is "honest and decent, hard-working; he's got very important positions in the Senate. He's highly respected. And these are all things that would cause anybody to say: 'Why would anybody run against him?'" A poll in November of 2013 showed Enzi ahead by more than 50 percentage points. Liz Cheney ended her bid in January 2014, citing "serious health issues" in her family. Enzi subsequently won the primary and clobbered Democrat Charlie Hardy by 55 percentage points in November.

After Enzi's 2014 win—and the GOP's seizure of the majority—an unexpected battle broke out over the chairmanship of the Budget Committee. Sessions, a staunch conservative and outspoken partisan, had been the top Republican on the panel and was widely expected to take over as chairman. But the lower-key Enzi startled fellow senators when he decided to use his edge in seniority over Sessions to claim the slot. (His seniority edge had been determined by a coin flip, since the two men entered the Senate at the same time.) Ultimately, Sessions deferred to Enzi, avoiding what could have been a nasty battle. In taking over as Budget chairman, Enzi told reporters that he would seek to offer a blueprint bringing the budget into balance within 10 years "without gimmicks and bad accounting."

Junior Senator

John Barrasso (R)

Appointed June 2007, term expires Jan., 2019, 2nd term; b. July 21, 1952, Reading, PA; Georgetown U., B.A. 1974, M.D. 1978; Presbyterian; married (Bobbi); 3 children.

Elected Office: WY Senate, 2002-07.

Professional Career: Orthopedic surgeon, 1983-2007; RNC Committeeman, 1992-96; Chief of staff, WY Med. Ctr., 2003-05.

DC Office: 307 DSOB, 20510, 202-224-6441; Fax: 202-224-1724; Website: barrasso.senate.gov.

State Offices: Casper, 307-261-6413; Cheyenne, 307-772-2451; Riverton, 307-856-6642; Rock Springs, 307-362-5012; Sheridan, 307-672-6456.

Committees: *Energy & Natural Resources:* National Parks; Public Lands, Forests, & Mining (Chmn); Water & Power. *Environment & Public Works:* Clean Air & Nuclear Safety; Transportation & Infrastructure; Fisheries, Water & Wildlife. *Foreign Relations:* African & Global Health Policy; Europe & Regional

Security Cooperation; Multilateral International Development, Multilateral Institutions & International Economic, Energy & Environmental Policy (Chmn.). *Indian Affairs* (Chmn).

Group Ratings

	ADA	ACLU	AFL-CIO	LCV	ITI	COC	HAFA	ACU	CFG	FRC
2014	15%	0%	–	20%	33%	86%	68%	84%	71%	93%
2013	0%	C	18%	0%	C	75%	C	88%	85%	C

National Journal Ratings

	2013 LIB	—	2013 CONS
Economic	10%	—	87%
Social	0%	—	92%
Foreign	5%	—	93%
Composite	7%	—	93%

Key Votes of the 113th Congress

1. Sandy storm spending	N	5. Student Loan Rates	Y	9. Bipartisan Budget Deal	N
2. Chuck Hagel Confirmation	N	6. Employee Non-Discrim'n Act	NV	10. Farm Bill Conference Rept.	N
3. Gun Background Checks	N	7. Senate Vote on Judgeships	Y	11. Unempl. Comp. Extension	N
4. Immigration Reform	N	8. Defense Dept. Spending	N	12. Keystone Pipeline	Y

Election Results

2012 general	John Barrasso (R)	185,250	(76%)	$4,511,679	$14,534
	Tim Chesnut (D)	53,019	(22%)		
	Joel Otto (Country)	6,176	(3%)		
2012 primary	John Barrasso (R)	73,516	(90%)		
	Thomas Bleming (R)	5,080	(6%)		

Prior winning percentage: 2008 special (73%)

Republican John Barrasso, Wyoming's junior senator, was appointed in June 2007 after Republican Sen. Craig Thomas died in office of leukemia. Barrasso was then elected in November 2008 to fill the remaining four years of Craig's unexpired term. He won a full six-year term in 2012. Barrasso's intellect and unwavering conservatism have helped him quickly climb the GOP leadership ladder; he is chairman of the Senate Republican Policy Committee and in 2015 took the helm of the Indian Affairs Committee.

Barrasso grew up in Reading Pennsylvania, the son of a World War II veteran who made a living as a cement finisher and who took his family to Washington every four years for the president's inauguration. John Barrasso got his undergraduate and medical degrees from Georgetown University, moved to Wyoming in the 1980s, and set up practice as an orthopedic surgeon in Casper. Barrasso quickly made his name in local Republican politics, serving as a Republican national committeeman and as state party treasurer. He also was a local radio and television personality, dispensing practical medical advice on news programs and in public service announcements. He hosted the annual Jerry Lewis telethon for muscular dystrophy.

In 1996, Barrasso ran for the Senate when Republican Alan Simpson retired. He faced then-state Sen. Michael Enzi in a crowded GOP primary where abortion played a key role. Running as a moderate, Barrasso favored abortion rights and had opposed a 1994 constitutional amendment to ban most abortions. Enzi, who had support from social conservatives, opposed abortion rights and narrowly edged out Barrasso 32% to 30%. The two then joined forces for the general election, with Barrasso serving as Enzi's finance chairman in the fall.

In 2002, Barrasso won election to the state Senate, where he worked on health care issues and chaired the Transportation, Highways, and Military Affairs Committee. He sponsored a bill to increase the criminal penalty for killing a pregnant woman, but then-Democratic Gov. Dave Freudenthal vetoed it. He occasionally crossed the political aisle to join with Democrats, backing a bill to exempt food from the state sales tax and supporting a ban on smoking in public buildings. He also sponsored a law enabling physicians to talk freely with patients about medical complications, without the risk that the conversations could be used against them in a lawsuit.

After Thomas died on June 4, 2007, Wyoming's Republican State Central Committee had 15 days to select three candidates to fill the vacancy, from which the governor was required to pick the successor. That triggered a scramble by 31 candidates who applied for consideration. They conducted a week-long beauty pageant among the 71 members of the party committee. The roster of applicants included state Rep. Colin Simpson, the son of former Sen.

Simpson, and numerous state legislators, lawyers, ranchers, and other professionals. Unlike in his Senate bid 11 years earlier, Barrasso emphasized his conservative credentials, saying in a statement to the committee, "I believe in limited government, lower taxes, less spending, traditional family values, local control, and a strong national defense." He noted that he had an "A" rating from the National Rifle Association, voted for prayer in public schools, sponsored legislation "to protect the sanctity of life," and opposed gay marriage.

The Republican committee named three finalists: Barrasso; Cynthia Lummis, who had served 14 years in the legislature and two terms as state treasurer; and Tom Sansonetti, who had been Thomas' chief of staff and an assistant attorney general in the Bush administration. But Lummis was not on good terms with the governor, and Sansonetti had been a lobbyist for mining and ranching interests at a time influence-peddling in Congress was not a plus. Barrasso, by contrast, had worked with Freudenthal on health care issues, and on June 22, the governor tapped him for the seat. He needed to quickly run for the seat in 2008 to fill out Thomas' term. Barrasso was unopposed in the Republican primary; in the general he defeated Democratic lawyer Nick Carter, an underfunded political newcomer, 73%-27%.

While Barrasso opposed the Democratic proposal to extend the State Children's Health Insurance Program in 2009, he successfully included a provision in the bill to benefit rural doctors and hospitals. He broke with many conservatives in calling for lifting the U.S. ban on travel to Cuba, saying U.S. citizens should be free to visit relatives in the communist country. Continuing work on an issue that was dear to Thomas' heart, he pushed for greater protection of Wyoming wilderness and wildlife. He proposed legislation to protect undeveloped areas of the Wyoming range from oil and gas development and to preserve 387 miles around the Snake River. It became law as part of a larger land management bill in March 2009. Barrasso introduced a bipartisan bill in April 2011 that became law a year later, paving the way for Indian tribes to pursue homeownership and other economic development opportunities on tribal lands. As Indian Affairs chairman, he and Montana Democrat Jon Tester, the committee's vice chairman, reintroduced a bill they had sponsored to streamline federal reviews of Indian energy projects. Meanwhile, he worked on a bipartisan compromise aimed at tamping down Republicans' widespread use of filibusters, telling the *New York Times*: "I hope we're more functional. I want (the Senate) to function."

Other stances had a distinct conservative lean. Among his first bills was a proposal to withhold 10 percent of highway funds from states that issue driver's licenses to illegal immigrants. In 2013, he angered Indian tribes when he opposed a reauthorization of the Violence Against Women Act that would have allowed tribal courts to have jurisdiction over non-Indians who commit crimes against Indians on reservations. As a member of the Energy and Natural Resources Committee and the Environment and Public Works Committee, Barrasso has reflected the views of constituents and industries back home by expressing skepticism about federal regulation, and in this area, he's found some success legislatively. Barrasso supported removing gray wolves from the Endangered Species List, telling the Associated Press, "This is a Wyoming concern that requires a Wyoming solution. It does not require interference from Washington." The U.S. Fish and Wildlife Service eventually removed gray wolves from the list. Barrasso also objected loudly to a CIA center on climate change, an area that experts increasingly regard as a national security challenge. The agency closed the center in 2012.

Barrasso said the cap-and-trade bill regulating carbon emissions that failed to get through the Senate in 2009 would have unfairly punished his state's farmers and ranchers. In opposing similar legislation in 2008, he said the bill would harm Wyoming's coal industry. He also lashed out at Obama's nominee to head the Environmental Protection Agency, Gina McCarthy, at an April 2013 confirmation hearing, asserting that the EPA was "making it impossible for our coal miners to feed their families." Barrasso also introduced a bill in February 2011 to bar the EPA from regulating greenhouse gases blamed for global warming. "This is not your parents' EPA," he said in a May 2011 speech. "Your parents' EPA focused on rebuilding the environment. This EPA is focused on remaking society."

Washingtonian magazine's anonymous survey of Capitol Hill staffers named him "brainiest senator" in 2010, along with Rhode Island Democrat Sheldon Whitehouse. Barrasso climbed the leadership ranks, becoming a firm ally of Republican Leader Mitch McConnell of Kentucky. He became Republican Conference vice chairman in September 2010, and then, just over a year later, he took control of the Republican Policy Committee, making him the fourth-ranking leader among Senate Republicans.

As he's risen within the Senate GOP, Barrasso has become one of the most frequent—and outspoken—lawmakers opposing President Barack Obama and his policies, particularly on health care. When Barrasso attacked the Democrats' health care law in a closed-door meeting that Obama held with Republicans, the president became so irked that he reportedly reminded him there were no TV cameras in the room, prompting the senator to answer, "I'm saying this out of my most firm beliefs." In 2013, he attacked Obama for saying people could keep their insurance plans if they liked them, and he knocked then-Health and Human Services Secretary Kathleen Sebelius—who was under fire for the problematic launch of the federal health care exchange—as the "laughingstock of America." A few months later, he accused the Obama administration of "cooking the books" on Affordable Care Act enrollment statistics.

Barrasso attacked Obama on other issues as well. On CNBC, he said of Obama's executive actions on undocumented immigrants, "Once again we have a situation where the president is intentionally misleading the people, misdirecting, saying one thing and doing another, (and) setting himself up as some kind of judge and jury and executioner, which is not what you would expect in a democracy. It's what you would see in a dictatorship." He also accused Obama of "bullying the Supreme Court" and he told high-school students in Kemmerer that "we are at war with the president. He has gone beyond the law to enforce his own agenda, and it affects Wyoming." A member of the Foreign Relations Committee, Barrasso also took an early and high-profile rhetorical stance against a nuclear deal with Iran, saying, "The White House seemed fixated on getting a deal, even a bad deal."

REPRESENTATIVE-AT-LARGE

Cynthia Lummis (R)

Elected 2008, 4th term; b. Sept. 10, 1954, Cheyenne; U. of WY, B.S. 1976, B.S. 1978, J.D. 1985; Lutheran; widow (Alvin Wiederspahn); 1 child.

Elected Office: WY House, 1979-83, 1985-93; WY Senate, 1994-95; WY treas., 1998-2006.

Professional Career: WY Supreme Court law clerk, 1985-86; Wiederspahn Lummis & Liepas P.C., 1986-96; Lummis Livestock Co. LLC, 1976-present.

DC Office: 2433 RHOB, 20515, 202-225-2311; Fax: 202-225-3057; Website: lummis.house.gov.

State Offices: Casper, 307-261-6595; Cheyenne, 307-772-2595; Sheridan, 307-673-4608.

Committees: *Natural Resources* (VChmn): Energy & Mineral Resources; Water, Power & Oceans; Federal Lands. *Oversight & Government Reform:* Health Care, Benefits, & Administrative Rules; Interior (Chmn.).

Group Ratings

	ADA	ACLU	AFL-CIO	LCV	ITI	COC	HAFA	ACU	CFG	FRC
2014	5%	5%	–	3%	80%	64%	72%	92%	84%	88%
2013	5%	C	5%	0%	C	69%	C	88%	73%	C

National Journal Ratings

	2013 LIB	—	2013 CONS
Economic	16%	—	84%
Social	47%	—	53%
Foreign	32%	—	67%
Composite	32%	—	68%

Key Votes of the 113th Congress

1. Sandy storm spending	N	5. Medical Marijuana	Y	9. Syrian Rebels Training	N
2. Violence Against Women Act	N	6. Farm Bill	Y	10. Keystone pipeline	Y
3. Guantanamo Bay Detainees	N	7. Afghanistan Combat	N	11. Immigration Exec. Action	Y
4. Abortion 20-week ban	Y	8. NSA Phone Data Collection	Y	12. Bipartisan budget deal	N

Election Results

2014 general	Cynthia Lummis (R)	113,038	(69%)	$300,949
	Richard Grayson (D)	37,803	(23%)	
	Richard Brubaker (Lib)	7,112	(4%)	
	Daniel Clyde Cummings (CNP)	6,749	(4%)	
2014 primary	Cynthia Lummis (R)	70,918	(76%)	
	Jason Senteney (R)	22,251	(24%)	

Prior winning percentages: 2012 (69%), 2010 (70%), 2008 (53%)

Population		Race and Ethnicity		Income	
Total:	582,658	White	85.6%	Median income:	$55,700
Urban:	15.8%	Latino	9.1%		*(138 of 435)*
Suburban:	0.0%	Amer. Indian	1.8%	Under $50,000	43.1%
Rural:	84.2%	Black	0.9%	$50,000-$99,999:	33.6%
Land area:	97,093	Two races	1.8%	$100,000-$199,999:	19.8%
Pop/sq. mi.:	6.0	White Ethnic	23.1%	$200,000 or more:	3.5%
Born in state:	41.9%			Poverty Rate	10.9%
		Education			
Age Groups		H.S. grad or less:	34.9%	**Work**	
Under 18:	24.0%	Some college:	38.5%	White collar:	34.1%
18 to 34:	24.1%	College degree, 4 yr.:	17.8%	Blue collar:	39.1%
35 to 64:	38.6%	Post-grad study:	8.8%	Sales and service:	26.8%
Over 64:	13.3%			Govt. workers:	23.5%
		Military			
		Veterans/active duty:	11.7%		

Cynthia Lummis, a Republican elected in 2008, is a rancher and former state treasurer whose background reflects Wyoming's rural and fiscal conservative underpinnings. She is vice chair of the House Natural Resources Committee, which she terms "Wyoming's committee" because the state has so much public land. She has shown her independence among House Republicans.

Voter Turnout	
2013 Total Citizen 18+	432,511
2014 House Turnout	165,100
2014 Turnout as % CVAP	38.2%
2012 Turnout as % CVAP	58.1%

Lummis grew up on her family's ranch in Cheyenne. She earned two bachelor's degrees and a law degree at the University of Wyoming. When she won a seat in the state House at age 24, Lummis was the youngest woman ever elected to the Wyoming Legislature. She chaired the Revenue Committee and helped revise state taxation of the mining industry, which is the state's chief source of revenue. She served in the state Senate briefly and went on to become state treasurer in 1998. In that office, she diversified the state's investment portfolio, which at the time was heavily invested in mortgage giants Fannie Mae and Freddie Mac. Lummis said that the move helped Wyoming weather the 2007-09 economic downturn spurred by the credit crisis in the home mortgage market.

In 2007, the Wyoming Republican Party placed Lummis on a list of three potential candidates to succeed Sen. Craig Thomas, a Republican who died of leukemia that year. Under state law, if a senator leaves office prematurely, his political party must nominate three possible replacements. The governor then chooses a successor from among the candidates. Lummis' poor relationship with then-Gov. Dave Freudenthal made her an underdog candidate. Freudenthal selected state Sen. John Barrasso for the Senate seat, but Lummis says the experience encouraged her to seek federal office. She ran for the state's House seat, which came open in 2008 when Republican Barbara Cubin retired.

In the Republican primary, Lummis faced rancher Mark Gordon, who outspent Lummis by 4-to-1, including $1 million of his own money. Gordon ran as a political outsider, but Lummis criticized him for supporting Democratic presidential nominee John Kerry in 2004 and Democrat Gary Trauner in his 2006 race against Cubin. Lummis won with 46% of the vote to Gordon's 37%.

In the general election, Lummis faced Trauner, a businessman who had used a well-financed grassroots campaign to nearly unseat Cubin. The Democratic Congressional Campaign Committee put Trauner on their top-priority "Red to Blue" list, but his chances of winning in a heavily Republican state diminished with the prospect of having to face a candidate other than Cubin, whose poor attendance record and penchant for outlandish comments had weakened her. Lummis ran as a staunch conservative, pledging to oppose new taxes and calling for making the Bush-era tax cuts permanent. Trauner claimed that Lummis would threaten the stability of the country's Social Security system by investing money from the program in unstable capital markets, which she denied. Lummis won 53%-43%.

In the House, Lummis showed enough party loyalty to land a spot on the Appropriations Committee after the House GOP takeover in 2010. But she took the unusual step of leaving the panel two years later to rejoin the Natural Resources Committee, explaining that it was a better fit for her state. As Western Caucus co-chair with New Mexico Republican Rep. Steve Pearce, she leads the 40-member group in assailing administration policies. When President Barack Obama released his fiscal 2014 budget proposal, she blasted what she called its excessive taxes and fees. "It's as if they sit around and try to out-do each other on how badly they can hurt Western economies and communities," she said. In January 2015, she became chairman of the newly created Interior Subcommittee on Oversight and Government Reform, where she planned to work on issues such the Endangered Species Act and regulation of coal-fired power plants. With her expanded role on Natural Resources, she saw herself as both writing and enforcing laws that affect the West, including Wyoming. Her goal, she said, was to "improve the stewardship of natural resources and at the same time alleviate the overreach of federal agencies," including the Environmental Protection Agency.

Lummis has been a proponent of firearms. She has filed multiple measures to prevent the State Department from interfering with imports of U.S.-made collectable firearms from overseas. Earlier, she co-sponsored a successful proposal to allow gun owners to carry concealed weapons in national parks. It was signed into law by Obama as part of a credit cardholders' consumer protection bill. But showing that she is not always predictable, she joined with liberal Democratic Rep. Carolyn Maloney of New York in a new push for an Equal Rights Amendment to the Constitution. Recalling that after she graduated from college she was denied a job as a bank teller because of her gender, Lummis said, "When you face those kinds of realities in life, they stay with you."

Lummis ran into trouble with Republican leaders in June 2015 after she split with most Republicans and opposed giving trade promotion authority to President Barack Obama, including on procedural votes. She was one of three members removed from the GOP Whip team by Majority Whip Steve Scalise. Publicly at least, she voiced no hard feelings and a spokesman said that Lummis understood that leadership members were expected to be team players. But more rebellious conservatives were angered by the crackdown.

In 2010, Lummis faced competition in her first reelection bid from Democrat David Wendt, president of the Jackson Hole Center for Global Affairs. The *Wyoming Tribune-Eagle* of Cheyenne endorsed Lummis but also scolded what it called her "partisan stridency" and tea party affiliation. "We suggest Ms. Lummis find her way back to the Wyoming mainstream," the newspaper wrote. She soundly defeated Wendt, 70%-24%, and has had comparable victory margins since.

THE INSULAR
★ TERRITORIES ★

AMERICAN SAMOA

American Samoa, the only American territory south of the Equator, remains almost as Polynesian today as it was when the United States took possession of it in 1900 at the request of tribal chiefs. These seven hot, rainy islands are 2,500 miles southwest of Hawaii, 1,700 miles northeast of New Zealand, and have a land area slightly larger than the District of Columbia.

American Samoa has 56,000 people, 98% of them on the island of Tutuila. The islands' population doubled in the last quarter century, and fear that outsiders will change the culture has prompted demands for stricter immigration standards. An estimated 50,000 Samoans live on the U.S. mainland and 20,000 in Hawaii, including former Honolulu Mayor Mufi Hannemann. A federal law from 1940 classifies American Samoans as U.S. nationals but not as U.S. citizens; they can serve in the military, but not as officers. In 2012, a group of American Samoans, including several veterans, challenged the law by arguing that it violated the 14th Amendment. The territorial government, however, refused to back them over fears that automatic citizenship could dilute what Samoans call *fa'asamoa*, or the "Samoan way of life." An appellate court in June 2015 rejected the plaintiffs' interpretation of the 14th Amendment and voiced its reluctance to "impose citizenship over the objections of the American Samoan people themselves, as expressed through their democratically elected representatives."

The Interior Department has overseen the administration of American Samoa since 1956, and it authorized the territory to adopt its own constitution in 1967. The territory elects a governor and a two-house legislature known as the Fono. The secretary of the Interior appoints the chief justice and associate justice of the High Court. American Samoa is a largely Christian and bilingual society and government. Government is mostly conducted in English, Fono proceedings are in Samoan, and court sessions are conducted in English but translated into Samoan. The territory sent its first non-voting delegate to Congress in 1981. Within this governmental framework, older Samoan traditions and politics continue to exist. Local chiefs, or *matai*, still oversee communal lands and kinship systems called *aigas*.

Pago Pago, the largest town in American Samoa, has one of the finest natural harbors in the Pacific. But the market economy has not made much progress here. American Samoa lives primarily off the federal government, which contributes more than half of its total government revenues. The territorial government employs almost 30 percent of the workforce. Local agriculture is minimal. For years, the private sector economy consisted of two big StarKist and Chicken of the Sea tuna canneries, which provided one-third of all U.S. canned tuna and employed over 5,000 workers. But demand for tuna has been stagnant in recent years, while tuna workers' wages have gone up. In 2007, Congress passed a law raising the minimum wage in American Samoa to $7.25 an hour by 2014, though federally mandated delays temporarily froze wages for cannery workers at $4.76 an hour between 2009 and 2015. Chicken of the Sea in 2009 announced the closing of its Samoa packing plant, with 2,100 jobs lost. StarKist, owned by the Korean firm Dongwon, reduced its workforce of 3,000 to 1,200 by late 2010. But some new enterprises have moved into the islands recently. Tri Marine International, a tuna company that opened in January, announced its intentions to employ 1,500 workers upon becoming fully operational, and a Filipino company has planned a $106 million food-processing plant that government officials hope will create 1,000 jobs. Wages, however, are still a concern. In May, Tri Marine International said it could not afford a wage increase scheduled for September.

Health is a major issue in American Samoa. The territory has one of the highest obesity rates in the world, and along with obesity have come diabetes and heart disease. One in five babies born in American Samoa is overweight, and usually within a year most infants are obese, according to a Brown University study. Despite this, American Samoans have developed a reputation for athleticism, most notably in regards to their success in American football. In 1960, Washington Redskins player Al Lolotai brought the game to the island, and since then, American Samoa has sent 30 players to the NFL. Top coaches make the long flight to Pago Pago to scout high school players.

American Samoa does not cast electoral votes for president, but it does send delegates to the major parties' national conventions. In 2008, Hillary Clinton edged out Barack Obama, receiving two convention votes split among four delegates, while Obama got one vote and two delegates. John McCain swept the Republican caucus, receiving all nine delegates. Mitt Romney's campaign sent his son, Matt, to campaign in the March 2012 contests in American Samoa, Guam, and the Northern Marianas, and Romney won all nine delegates in each territory.

Governor   Independent Lolo Letalu Matalasi Moliga was elected governor of American Samoa in 2012 to succeed Togiola Tulafono, who was term-limited. He was a High Talking Chief (Lolo) in the village of Sili in the Manu'a islands and High Chief (Letalu) from Ta'u, the largest island in the Manu'a group. He received an education degree from Chadron State College in Nebraska and an M.P.A. in 2012 from San Diego State University. He worked as a teacher and then as assistant principal and principal at Manu'a High School. He later became a school administrator, head of the American Samoa budget office, and chief procurement officer for the territory. He was elected to four terms in the territorial House of Representatives and to the Senate. In the November 2012 election for governor, he led Democrat Faoa Aitofele T. F. Sunia by 34%-33%, and in the runoff, he won 53%-47%.

As governor, Moliga has sought increased autonomy for the territorial government in American Samoan affairs. In February 2014, he wrote in *The Hill*, "We are tethered to Mainland-based federal policies that work well in the lower forty-eight. After they travel the more than 7,000 miles to get to our shores, these policies become attenuated, dissipated and oftentimes inflict more harm than good." He supported a federal court's decision in 2015 not to grant automatic citizenship rights to American Samoans. He has also been critical of federal aviation laws and minimum wage hikes, which he once called "well intentioned" but "inappropriate for our small economy." In June 2015, he requested that the U.S. government subsidize a wage increase scheduled for September 2015. His administration has been active on immigration issues and sees reform as a way to bolster the territory's stagnant population growth. Under Moliga, American Samoa has granted amnesty to more than 4,000 foreigners living illegally on the islands.

DELEGATE

Aumua Amata Coleman Radewagen (R)

Elected 2014, 1st term; b. Dec. 29, 1947, Washington, D.C.; U. of Guam, B.A. 1975; Catholic; married (Fred); 3 children.

Professional Career: Journalist; Trainer; Staff, U.S. Rep. Philip Crane (IL), 1997-99; Staff, U.S. Rep. J.C. Watts Jr. (OK), 1999-2003; White House Commissioner for Asian Americans & Pacific Islanders, 2001.

DC Office: 1339 LHOB, 20515, 202-225-8577, Fax: 202-225-8757; Website: radewagen.house.gov.

State Offices: Pago Pago 684-633-3601.

Committees: *Natural Resources:* Indian, Insular & Alaska Native Affairs (VChmn); Oversight & Investigations. *Small Business:* Economic Growth, Tax & Capital Access; Health & Technology (Chmn). *Veterans' Affairs:* Economic Opportunity.

Aumua Amata Coleman Radewagen, a Republican, became the first woman to represent American Samoa in Congress after defeating 13-term Democrat Eni F. H. Faleomavaega. She comes from a family with deep roots in Samoan politics and is the longest serving member of the Republican National Committee. Her father, Peter Tali Coleman, was the first Samoan appointed to serve as governor of the territory and its first popularly elected governor. Collectively, his tenure spanned five decades, from 1956 to 1993, and he founded the territory's Republican Party. Radewagen, a cancer survivor, grew up with 12 siblings and earned a degree from the University of Guam. From 1997 to 2003, she served on the staffs of Reps. Philip Crane of Illinois and J.C. Watts of Oklahoma. In 2001, President George W. Bush appointed her to serve as a White House Commissioner for Asian Americans and Pacific Islanders. At the RNC, she has served on the Executive Council and the Standing Committee on Rules, and in 2013 she received the organization's Trailblazer Award.

Radewagen challenged Faleomavaega on eight different occasions, beginning in 1994. In her 2008, 2010, and 2012 attempts, she came up short by 16 points or more in each contest. But in 2013, Faleomavaega began experiencing complications from exposure to Agent Orange in the Vietnam War and his health became a major issue. In 2014, he faced a field of eight challengers, and Radewagen was able to pull in 42% of the vote to Faleomavaega's 30%.

In the House, Radewagen is vice-chair of the Natural Resources subcommittee responsible for insular affairs. She has pushed for postponing minimum wage increases in American Samoa and for giving the territory more control over future increases. In April 2015, the House passed her bill reducing the holding periods that territorial banks are required to place on off-island checks. She supported a U.S. appellate court's decision in June 2015 not to grant birthright citizenship status to American Samoans, saying in a press release that the decision reaffirmed "the bedrock principle that the American Samoan people, and not outside interest groups or federal courts, should have the final say in matters concerning their political status."

GUAM

Some 6,300 miles west of Los Angeles and 3,800 miles west of Hawaii, 17 hours of flying time from Washington, D.C., is Guam, an American possession since 1898. Geographically, this island is in the center of the Marianas Islands, though Guam is legally separate. It was acquired from Spain after the Spanish-American War, while the U.S. was happy to let Germany acquire the rest of the Mariana chain. It was ruled by Navy captains from 1898 to 1949, except for 31 months of Japanese occupation during World War II. In 1950, the Guam Organic Act made Guamanians U.S. citizens. Carlton Skinner, who as a captain integrated the crew of his Navy ship in 1943, became the first civilian governor in 1949 and helped write the constitution. The local government is known as GovGuam, but Congress retains final power over the territory. It gave Guam a non-voting delegate to the House in 1972.

Guam, as *The Washington Post's* Blaine Harden put it, "marries the beauty of Bali with the banality of Kmart." It is 36 miles long by four to nine miles wide, with about 165,000 people. Some 37% are Chamorro (descendants of the original islanders) or from elsewhere in Micronesia; 26% are Filipino; 12% other Pacific Islander; 6% other Asian; and 7% white. The population is politically mixed and overwhelmingly Catholic, yet in 2015 Guam became the first U.S. territory to recognize same-sex marriage. The island's tropical environment can be dangerous. In August 1993, it lived through an earthquake rated at 8.2 on the Richter scale, comparable to San Francisco's in 1906. In 2002, a typhoon with winds up to 184 miles per hour caused hundreds of millions of dollars in damage. And Guam suffers from an invasive species, the semi-poisonous brown tree snake, which has killed off nearly all of the island's bird population and severely disrupted the ecosystem. The latest attempt to eradicate the 10-foot long snakes consisted of dropping dead mice packed with acetaminophen from helicopters.

Guam depends heavily on tourism—especially from Japan—and service businesses, but most of all on the U.S. military. It is America's forward position in Asia; in March 2013, North Korean dictator Kim Jong Un threatened to rain nuclear weapons on Guam's Andersen Air Force Base. Bases occupy one-third of the land, and 60% of the island's income derives from the federal government. In 2013, the Pentagon announced plans to relocate some 5,000 marines and 1,300 dependents from Okinawa to Guam, a move that defense officials predict could add upwards of $37 million per year to Guam's economy. After several years of deficits and borrowing, the island's finances have stabilized. A $336 million deficit at the start of 2011 became a $30 million surplus by the end of 2012, and the government began issuing tax refunds for the first time in more than two decades. Meanwhile, unemployment fell from 14.6% in June 2013 to 7.4% less than a year later, and Guam's first new luxury resort in 15 years opened in 2015.

Guam does not cast any electoral votes for president, but elects delegates to national party conventions. In the 2008 primary, Barack Obama stressed his Hawaiian roots and ties to the Pacific islands and won 2,264 votes to Hillary Clinton's 2,257. Under Democrats' proportional representation delegate allocation rules, they evenly split Guam's four delegate votes. Guam Republicans held a convention that year after John McCain clinched the Republican nomination. All nine delegates supported him. In 2012, Mitt Romney sent his son, Matt, to campaign in Guam, the Northern Marianas, and American Samoa. Romney won all nine delegates. In lieu of a general election, Guam began holding non-binding straw polls every four years in 1984; and every four years since then it has accurately predicted the next president.

Governor Eddie Calvo, a Republican, was elected governor of Guam in 2010 and won a second term in 2014. Calvo grew up in Guam and south of San Francisco, where he graduated from a Catholic high school in Mountain View and Notre Dame de Namur University in Belmont. His father, Paul Calvo, was elected governor in 1978. After school, Eddie Calvo returned to Guam and worked for the Pacific Construction Co. and as general manager of the Pepsi Bottling Co. of Guam. In 1998, he was elected senator in the Guam legislature. In 2002, he ran for lieutenant governor as the running mate of Tony Unpingco, who lost to Felix Camacho, also a Republican. In April 2010, with Camacho term-limited, Calvo announced he was running for governor and chose Sen. Ray Tenorio as his running mate. In the Republican primary, he was opposed by Lt. Gov. Mike Cruz. The Calvo-Tenorio ticket won 59%-41% out of 15,679 votes cast. The results of the general election were exceedingly close; Calvo won by just 487 votes, 20,066 to 19,579 for former Gov. Carl Gutierrez, an independent. Calvo faced Gutierrez again in 2014. This time, he won 63%-35%.

Calvo faced major fiscal problems, but has managed to turn the territory's finances around. The 2012 general fund saw a $30 million surplus and the budget has remained in the black since he took office. Calvo suspended employee pay increases, appointed new management at Guam Memorial Hospital, and proposed to sell $343 million of bonds to pay overdue tax refunds. The legislature pushed back, but enough bonds were sold to satisfy a court requirement that refunds be paid within a year of when they were owed. Since then, issuing tax refunds on time has become a focal point of his administration, once saying in an official statement, "Last year, this year, and for every year that Eddie Calvo is governor, tax refunds will be paid on time." In 2015, Calvo tussled with Guam Attorney General Elizabeth Barrett-Anderson when she refused to defend the territory against a lawsuit brought by a gay couple to whom Calvo's administration had refused to issue a marriage license. A U.S. district judge ruled in favor of the couple in June, prompting Calvo to claim that the territory's laws were "being challenged by federal judges that were nominated by a U.S. president and confirmed by a U.S Senate, none of whom were elected through a process that included the people of Guam."

DELEGATE

Madeleine Bordallo (D)

Elected 2002, 7th term; b. May 31, 1933, Graceville, MN; St. Mary's Col., attended, St. Katherine's Col., attended; Catholic; widowed; 1 child.

Elected Office: GU Senate, 1981-82, 1987-94; GU lt. gov., 1995-2002.

Professional Career: Radio & TV broadcaster KUAM, 1954.

DC Office: 2441 RHOB, 20515, 202-225-1188; Fax: 202-226-0341; Website: bordallo.house.gov.

State Offices: Hagåtña, 671-477-4272.

Committees: *Armed Services:* Readiness (RMM); Seapower & Projection Forces. *Natural Resources:* Indian, Insular & Alaskan Native Affairs; Water, Power & Oceans.

Madeleine Bordallo, a Democrat, was first elected as the delegate from Guam in 2002. She grew up in Minnesota and, after age 14, in Guam. She studied vocal music at St. Catherine's College in St. Paul and worked for Guam radio stations. She was elected to the Guam legislature in 1980. Her husband, Ricardo Bordallo, was elected governor in 1974, was defeated for reelection in 1978 by Paul Calvo, the father of current Gov. Eddie Calvo, and was elected governor again in 1982. Then, in a tragic turn of events, Ricardo Bordallo, facing a prison term for bribery in 1990, chained himself to the statue of Chief Quipuha and shot himself in the head, dying later that day. Madeleine Bordallo was a candidate for governor that year, and lost 57%-43% to incumbent Republican Joseph Ada. In 1994, she was elected lieutenant governor and was reelected in 1998.

In 2002, when Del. Robert Underwood decided to run for governor, Bordallo ran for delegate. In the primary, she faced Judith Won Pat, daughter of Guam's first delegate, Antonio

Borja Won Pat, after whom Guam's international airport is named. In this contest between longtime friends, Bordallo won 59%-41%. In the general election, she once again faced Ada. This time, Bordallo won 65%-35%.

Bordallo is the ranking Democrat on the Readiness Subcommittee of the House Armed Services Committee. She has strongly supported the military buildup on Guam and has sought aid for infrastructure. In 2014, she angered both environmentalists and land-rights advocates by proposing a wildlife refuge and Chamorro archaeological site in Guam as a potential site for a Marines' live-fire training range. The year before, she sparred with Republican Sen. John McCain of Arizona, accusing him of lacking a "sense of history" when he opposed $120 million for Guam wastewater treatment, water infrastructure and a public health laboratory. She has resisted base closings and supports more Aegis ground interceptors for Guam. Bordallo has sought reparations for human rights abuses suffered during Japan's occupation during World War II, even though the 1951 treaty between the United States and Japan absolved Japan of any claims. The House approved her bill for reparations in 2009, but the Senate limited it to living survivors and relatives of those killed—terms that Bordallo rejected. She has reintroduced the bill.

Bordallo did not face major party opposition from 2004 to 2010. In 2012, she was opposed for the Democratic nomination by Karlo Dizon, a Philippine-born Guamanian and graduate of Yale and the London School of Economics. She won 73%-26%. In the general election, she easily defeated Republican Frank Blas Jr., 58%-38%. In 2014, she won by a similar margin against Republican Margaret Metcalfe.

NORTHERN MARIANA ISLANDS

The Commonwealth of the Northern Mariana Islands (CNMI), in American hands since 1944, gained representation in Congress for the first time in January 2009. This is a chain of 14 islands, only three permanently inhabited, running north from Guam in the Western Pacific. The northern islands are volcanic and the southern islands are limestone and fringed with coral reefs. They are much closer to mainland Asia than to the mainland U.S. and sit some 7,800 miles southwest of Los Angeles.

The Northern Marianas have a storied history. They were first peopled by Micronesians three millennia ago and were visited by Magellan in 1521. Spanish Jesuits arrived in 1668, and the islands were a possession of Spain until the Spanish-American War in 1898. Over the centuries, they became depopulated, and then in the middle 19th century, began to be settled by Chamorros from Guam. In 1898, the United States acquired Guam as a coaling station but was content to see the Northern Marianas sold to Germany in 1899. They were seized by Japan in 1914 soon after it entered World War I, and the League of Nations gave Japan legal claim to them in 1920.They were occupied by U.S. forces in 1944, in the midst of World War II. In August 1945, the *Enola Gay* took off from Tinian on its mission to drop the atomic bomb on Hiroshima. That same year, the Northern Marianas were put in the custody of the new United Nations Security Council, and in 1947 they were declared part of the U.S. Trust Territory of the Pacific Islands. While the other islands in time opted for independence, the Northern Marianas voted in 1975 to approve a covenant with the United States creating the Commonwealth of the Northern Mariana Islands (CNMI), which went into effect in March 1976. Under its terms, the CNMI was not subject to federal immigration or labor laws and not obliged to pay U.S. taxes, but it deferred entirely to the United States in foreign and military affairs. Foreign investors were limited to a 49% share of businesses or property, and land could be owned only by "persons of Northern Marianas descent." The CNMI government started operating after the 1977 elections.

In the early 1970s, the Northern Marianas had only 12,000 people. There were no modern runways and only one rickety flight a day from Guam. Then, in the mid-1980s, the CNMI government opened up the economy to foreign investment and wrote its immigration laws to permit an influx of guest workers. This resulted in heavy investment in garment factories that imported guest workers, mostly female, from low-wage countries such as the Philippines, China and Vietnam. Products made here could be labeled "Made in U.S.A." and imported into the United States without being subject to textile import quotas. By the mid-1990s, there were some 34 garment factories, employing 17,000 guest workers. Japanese investors also began building tourist destinations, with many low-wage jobs for guest workers.

The result was a population boom. The 2000 census counted 69,000 people in the Northern Marianas, with more than 90% on Saipan. Only 44% were U.S. citizens. Conservatives hailed the booming garment industry and tourism business as a triumph of free enterprise. House Majority Leader Tom DeLay was a strong booster of the CNMI's exemption from federal immigration laws and minimum wage. Other members of Congress objected to what they termed the exploitation of the mostly female Chinese and Filipina guest workers, who were often required to work long hours in difficult conditions to pay off recruiting fees needed to get such jobs. The Senate voted unanimously in 1995 and 2000 to deny the "Made in U.S.A." label to clothing manufactured in the CNMI. But DeLay kept the measure from coming to a vote in the House.

Two outside developments transformed the situation. In January 2005, a treaty that had set quotas on textile imports into the United States expired. Suddenly the CNMI's exemption from those quotas became irrelevant, and Saipan was subject to lower-wage competition from Vietnam, Cambodia and China. Then in October 2005, Japan Airlines canceled its daily flights to Saipan after nearly 30 years of direct service. Japanese investors sold three hotels, a golf course and a shopping center. Tourism, which had employed half the workforce, nosedived.

The increase in the federal minimum wage that passed in 2007 included a gradual increase of $.50 per hour for the CNMI until its minimum wage reached $7.25. A law from 2013, however, temporarily delayed scheduled increases, and the wage has held steady at $5.55 since 2012. Regardless, by January 2009, all of the islands' garment factories were shuttered. Congress in 2008 brought the CNMI under federal immigration law, at the same time phasing out the current guest worker program by 2017 and providing worker protections. Most CNMI politicians opposed the bill but had little power to stop it. It also gave the CNMI its first-ever delegate in Congress.

The U.S. military presence in the Northern Marianas has been more limited than in nearby Guam since the CIA closed its covert training base on Saipan in 1962. But the Obama administration's efforts to realign U.S. military operations in the Pacific could change that. The Marine Corps recently announced its intention to use the island of Pagan for live-fire amphibious training. Locals have hotly protested the plan, citing historical and environmental concerns.

The Northern Marianas' economy began to decline in 2002, with gross domestic product dropping about 20% in 2009, and its population decreased from a high of 74,000 in 2002 to less than 54,000 a decade later. The CNMI hit a low in 2012, when its pension fund became the first public pension fund in the U.S. to file for bankruptcy. But signs of a recovery have been appearing. Tourism, building activity and automobile purchases have noticeably increased. A Hong Kong-based company announced plans in 2014 to build a multi-billion dollar casino resort on Saipan, the first-of-its-kind on the island, with more than 4,000 hotel rooms. In 2013 the GDP reversed course and grew 4.4%, and the CNMI has been inching toward finding a solution to its pension crisis.

The CNMI does not vote for president and plays less of a role in presidential politics than the other territories represented in Congress. In 2008, all nine of its delegates to the Republican National Convention decided to vote as a team for John McCain. In 2012, Mitt Romney won all nine delegates after his son, Matt, campaigned in the Islands. The national Democratic Party did not officially recognize the CNMI Democratic Party until 2012.

Governor   After serving four years as lieutenant governor, Eloy Inos became governor of the CNMI in February 2013, following the resignation of Republican Beningo Fitial, who left office that same month amid impeachment proceedings and multiple allegations of corruption and misconduct. Inos, a Republican and former Covenant Party member, has been involved in government and public affairs since before the establishment of the CNMI. He held positions in the government of the Pacific Trust Territories and the CNMI from 1971 to 1983 and was CNMI finance director from 1983 to 1994. In 2006 Fitial appointed him CNMI secretary of finance, and in 2009 he tapped him to serve as lieutenant governor. Inos won election to a full term in 2014, defeating former CNMI House Speaker Heinz Sablan Hofschneider 57%-43%.

As governor, Inos has sought to distance himself from his predecessor's administration by removing many of Fitial's appointees and requiring his cabinet to undergo ethics training. He has focused heavily on the economy and reviving the Northern Marianas' tourism industry. Inos has championed the development of a controversial resort casino on the island of Saipan, arguing that it will be a critical source of revenue and will help the CNMI pay off its pension obligations. In 2013, he expressed concerns over the potential impact of U.S. military operations on tourism, wildlife, and the islands' archaeological sites.

DELEGATE

Gregorio Kilili Camacho Sablan (D)

Elected 2008, 4th term; b. Jan. 19, 1955, Saipan; U. of Guam, attended 1972; Armstrong U., attended 1973-74; U. of HI Manoa, attended 1989-90; Catholic; married (Andrea); 6 children.

Military Career: U.S. Army Reserve, 1982-86.

Elected Office: N. Marianas Islands Legislature, 1982-86.

Professional Career: Gov.'s deputy chief admin. officer, CNMI govt., 1980-81; Special asst. for mgmt. & budget, CNMI govt., 1994-95; Exec. dir., Commonwealth Election Commission, 1999-2008.

DC Office: 423 CHOB, 20515, 202-225-2646; Fax: 202-226-4249; Website: sablan.house.gov.

State Offices: Rota, 670-532-2647; Saipan, 670-323-2647/8; Tinian, 670-433-2647.

Committees: *Education & the Workforce:* Early Childhood, Elementary & Secondary Education; Health, Employment, Labor & Pensions. *Natural Resources:* Indian, Insular & Alaska Native Affairs; Water, Power & Oceans.

The first delegate to the House from the Commonwealth of the Northern Mariana Islands was Gregorio Kilili Camacho Sablan, elected in November 2008.

He grew up in Saipan in an extended family much involved in politics. His grandfather was the first elected mayor of Saipan, and his uncle was the city's longest-serving mayor. At age 11, Sablan moved to the Federated States of Micronesia and attended boarding school, the only ethnic Chamorro there. He attended the University of Guam and the University of California, Berkeley, but did not get a degree.

He worked for Democratic Gov. Carlos Camacho, the CNMI's first elected governor, then served in the legislature from 1982 to 1986. Sablan also worked for 18 months on the Washington staff of former Hawaii Democratic Sen. Daniel Inouye, who long had an interest in the Pacific territories. When he returned to Saipan, Sablan worked as special assistant for management and budget for Democratic Gov. Froilan Tenorio. Later, he was appointed executive director of the Commonwealth Election Commission and won praise for his conduct of CNMI's closely contested election in 2006.

After Congress voted in April 2008 to give the CNMI a non-voting delegate in Congress, Sablan joined a field of nine candidates seeking the seat. Two of them spent large sums—large for the CNMI, at least—on their campaigns. Retired Judge Juan Tudela Lizama spent $52,000, and seven-year CNMI Washington representative Pete A. Tenorio, a Republican, spent $37,000. Sablan ran as an independent rather than as a Democrat because, he said, the local Democratic Party was "not organized," and spent $15,000. Of 10,161 votes cast, Sablan received 2,474, edging his nearest competition, Tenorio, by 357 votes. Sablan has been reelected by increasingly wide margins.

Sablan has had some legislative successes, including enactment of a measure in 2013 giving the CNMI ownership of submerged lands three miles out to sea and a December 2012 amendment to the defense authorization bill requiring that the flags of the CNMI and other territories be displayed whenever military units display all of the states' flags. In 2014, he secured an exemption for the CNMI from caps on the admittance of foreign workers and he helped prolong a visa program that allows long-term foreign investors to reside on the islands. Sablan came one step closer to his goal of creating a national park on the island of Rota in December 2014 when he added an amendment to the final version of the defense authorization bill instructing the Department of the Interior to conduct a feasibility study. The House had previously passed his bill on this issue three times, most recently in June 2013, though the Senate never took it up. Sablan has called for extending U.S. voting rights protections to the territories and has urged the Census Bureau to include the territories in its Census of Governments, which it hasn't done since 1982. He has been an opponent of militarizing the island of Pagan, saying in April 2015 that "I have made my personal position on Pagan clear for over two years: I oppose the bombing of Pagan."

PUERTO RICO

Puerto Rico has a unique history. From Columbus' landing in 1493 until the Spanish-American War of 1898, it was a Spanish colony—and an important one in the three centuries when the port of San Juan was the gathering place for its annual convoy of gold and silver from the Americas to Spain. From the time it became an American territory in 1898 to the 1950s, it was considered "the poorhouse of the Caribbean," a sugar-producing island with a tiny elite. In the second half of the 20th century, it developed a recognizably First World economy and a solidly democratic—though sometimes turbulent—political system.

In the 21st century, however, Puerto Rico's forward momentum came to a halt. Its economy shrank by more than 16% between 2004 and 2013, and unemployment soared to double digits. Meanwhile, the government borrowed. By May 2015, its debt had reached $72 billion, four times the amount that brought Detroit to its knees in 2013, prompting some to refer to Puerto Rico as the "Greece of the Caribbean." Prohibited by U.S. law from declaring Chapter 9 bankruptcy, the governor and legislator in San Juan have looked to spending cuts and tax hikes to slow the bleeding, causing anti-austerity protests to erupt in the capital, as worried residents have left in droves. 110,000 people left the commonwealth between 2010 and 2013, with many of them relocating to the mainland. The island's future became even more uncertain in June 2015, when Gov. Alejandro García Padilla concluded that Puerto Rico could not pay off its debts, an outcome that many fear could send shockwaves through the municipal bond market and raise borrowing costs for state and local governments. The financial crisis has given new life to the fundamental question of status—whether Puerto Rico should seek statehood, continue its current commonwealth status, or, in what is very much a minority view, declare independence. Its resident commissioner, Pedro Pierluisi, who views statehood as key to pulling the island out of debt, introduced a bill in Congress in 2015 calling for a formal vote on the issue by the end of the decade.

Puerto Rico has elected a resident commissioner to Congress since 1900, the only member of Congress with a four-year term, and residents of Puerto Rico have been American citizens since 1917. But it didn't elect its own governor until 1948. From the 1940s until the early 1960s, Puerto Rico was transformed by Gov. Luis Muñoz Marín and his Popular Democratic Party. Muñoz initiated "Operation Bootstrap" to lure businesses to Puerto Rico with promises of low-wage labor, government-built factories and tax exemptions. Muñoz also developed Puerto Rico's commonwealth form of government—in Spanish, Estado Libre Asociado, or, ELA, meaning Free Associated State—that was approved by referendum in 1952. Puerto Rico is part of the United States for purposes of international trade, foreign policy and war, but it has its own laws, taxes and representative government. It is not subject to federal income taxes and is not eligible for all federal benefits, though some have been approved by Congress. In 2014, the Obama administration ruled that U.S. territories were not required to follow the 2010 health care overhaul. The legislature adopted most of the law anyway, with the exception of the individual mandate. But because Puerto Ricans are ineligible to receive the federal subsidies to help pay for coverage, few have bothered to sign up and some have begun to call for the law's repeal. The island has also developed its own political parties: Muñoz's Popular Democrats (the Spanish acronym is PPD), the New Progressives (PNP) who favor statehood, and two small pro-independence parties.

For many years, as Puerto Rico's economy grew, there seemed to be gradual movement toward statehood. In a 1967 referendum, Puerto Ricans voted to continue commonwealth status over statehood 60%-39%. In a 1993 referendum, the vote was 48% for continuing the commonwealth and 46% for statehood. In a 1998 referendum, the vote was 47% for statehood and 50% for "none of the above," the option favored by the PPD. Independence has low levels of support (4% in 2008). PPD politicians have long been affiliated with the mainland Democratic Party, while PNP politicians have been split, with some favoring mainland Democrats and some favoring mainland Republicans. As a result, Republican presidential hopefuls often pledge support for statehood, while Democrats take more ambiguous positions. A task force appointed by the George W. Bush administration recommended a two-step referendum, with Puerto Ricans both on the island and on the mainland first voting on whether to consider a change in the current ELA (commonwealth) status, and then choosing between statehood and independence. In April 2010, the House passed a bill providing for a two-step referendum, but the Senate declined to act.

In the absence of action from Washington, the PNP government took action. Gov. Luis Fortuño signed a measure for a two-step referendum in the November 2012 election. The first question was whether to continue the present status. The second was a choice between statehood, independence, or a "sovereign commonwealth." On the first question, 52% of those who turned out voted against the current status and 44% voted for it; 4% presented blank ballots and 1% of ballots were void. On the second question, statehood won a plurality. But, taking into account all those who turned out, it got only 44% of the vote—roughly comparable to statehood's showing in past referenda. One percent of the ballots were void; 4% voted for independence, 24% voted for "sovereign commonwealth," and 27% left their ballots blank. Statehood advocates such as Commissioner Pedro Pierluisi, argued that a majority of those voting were for statehood. Statehood opponents such as Gov. Alejandro García Padilla, argued that a clear majority had not endorsed statehood.

When President Barack Obama visited Puerto Rico in June 2011, the first president to do so since Gerald Ford in 1976, he said, "When the people of Puerto Rico make a clear decision, I will stand by you." In 2014, his administration allocated $2.5 million to help the island hold a vote on its status. In the 2012 presidential contest, Republicans Mitt Romney and Rick Santorum, seeking delegates in Puerto Rico, pledged to support statehood. In 2015, former Florida governor Jeb Bush voiced his support in Spanish. But House Republicans seem unlikely to raise the issue for fear that Puerto Rico as a state would elect five Democratic House members and cast seven Democratic electoral votes. And members of both parties may be wary of statehood for a territory in which there is no overwhelming consensus for that status, as there was in Alaska and Hawaii in the 1950s.

Puerto Rico does not vote for president, but it elects delegations to the Democratic and Republican National Conventions. In 2008, Hillary Clinton, who as a senator from New York had many constituents with roots in Puerto Rico, campaigned heavily and won a solid 68%-32% victory, winning 38 delegates to Obama's 17.

In 2012, Republicans switched from a caucus to a primary. Romney was supported by Fortuño and campaigned around the island, as did Rick Santorum. Both supported statehood, but Santorum raised hackles when he said that as a state, Puerto Rico would have to use English as its primary language. Romney got 85% of the vote and Santorum 8%, and Romney picked up 20 delegates.

Governor Alejandro García Padilla, a member of the Popular Democratic Party (PPD), was elected Puerto Rico's 11th governor in 2012. He grew up in a political family in the interior town of Coamo, the youngest of six brothers, one of whom is now the city's mayor. He attended college and graduate school on the island, at the University of Puerto Rico and Interamerican University Law School. He served from 2005 to 2007 as Gov. Aníbal Acevedo's secretary of consumer affairs. In 2012, he defeated PNP Gov. Luis Fortuño, who was elected in 2008, but only narrowly, 48%-47%.

Financial crisis has dominated Padilla's tenure. To address the territory's $72 billion debt, his administration has looked to tax hikes and spending cuts, including an increase in the sales tax from 7% to 11.5% in 2015, and a proposed $166 million reduction in state higher-education spending. Padilla has also pushed for a debt-exchange program with the island's creditors and has been a vocal advocate for bankruptcy legislation in Congress that would allow Puerto Rican corporations and municipalities to restructure their debts. In June 2015 he stated that "the debt is not payable. There is no other option. I would love to have an easier option. This is not politics, this is math." He is an ardent opponent of statehood, once saying that annexation would turn Puerto Rico into a "Latin American ghetto," though in 2014 he pledged there would be a plebiscite, with multiple options, on the issue by 2016.

RESIDENT COMMISSIONER

Pedro Pierluisi (D)

Elected 2008, term expires Jan. 2016, 2nd term; b. April 26, 1959, San Juan; Tulane U., B.A. 1981, George Washington U., J.D. 1984; Catholic; married (Maria Elena Carrión); 4 children.

Elected Office: PR secy. of justice, 1993-96.

Professional Career: Practicing atty., 1997-2007.

DC Office: 2410 RHOB, 20515, 202-225-2615; Fax: 202-225-2154; Website: pierluisi.house.gov.

State Offices: San Juan, 787-723-6333.

Committees: *Judiciary:* Crime, Terrorism, Homeland Security & Investigations; Immigration & Border Security. *Natural Resources:* Federal Lands; Indian, Insular & Alaskan Native Affairs.

Pedro Pierluisi, a member of Puerto Rico's New Progressive Party (PNP) which aligns with mainland Democrats, was elected resident commissioner in November 2008 and reelected in 2012. He is a strong supporter of Puerto Rican statehood and holds seats on the Judiciary and Natural Resources committees.

Pierluisi grew up in San Juan, the son of former Puerto Rico Housing Secretary Jorge Pierluisi. He graduated from Tulane University and George Washington University Law School in the early 1980s and served as an aide to Resident Commissioner Baltasar Corrada del Río of the PNP. He then practiced law for six years in Washington. In 1993, Gov. Pedro Rosselló of the PNP appointed him attorney general of Puerto Rico. He argued two constitutional cases before the Puerto Rico Supreme Court. He left Rosselló's scandal-plagued administration in 1996 and practiced law in Puerto Rico.

After the PNP's Luis Fortuño gave up the resident commissioner post to run for governor, Pierluisi ran for the vacancy. Although the two had different mainland party affiliations (Fortuño is a Republican), both were strong backers of statehood for Puerto Rico and ran on a united ticket. Pierluisi spent $1.5 million, while his PPD opponent, Alfredo Salazar, spent $530,000. Pierluisi won 53%-42%, an almost identical result as Fortuño's victory, and carried 71 of Puerto Rico's 78 municipalities. It was the biggest win for either party in Puerto Rico since 1964. Four years later, however, he was narrowly reelected, defeating PPD candidate Rafael Cox Alomar 48-47%.

In the House, Pierluisi has been active on Puerto Rico statehood issues. In 2009, he introduced a bill for a two-stage referendum on Puerto Rico's status. The measure passed the House 223-169 in April 2010, but the Senate declined to take it up. In 2015, Pierluisi called the "root cause" of Puerto Rico's financial crisis "our political status" and authored a bill aimed at transitioning the Commonwealth to statehood by 2020. Within four months, it had attracted 108 co-sponsors. (The 2009 bill had 123 when it passed the House). Pierlusi also drafted legislation in 2014 and 2015 to allow government-owned utilities and municipalities in Puerto Rico to restructure their debt under Chapter 9 of the U.S. Bankruptcy Code.

On other issues, Pierluisi responded furiously in 2011 when Rep. Luis Gutierrez, who is of Puerto Rican descent and represents a Chicago district, criticized Puerto Rican police for misconduct. He has called for a study of the Jones Act, backed by maritime unions, that raises the price of consumer goods on the island. He criticized the 2012 House Republican budget for cuts in Medicaid for Puerto Rico and supported a surge of Department of Homeland Security personnel to the island in February 2013 to combat drug-related violence.

VIRGIN ISLANDS

The U.S. Virgin Islands, acquired from Denmark in 1917, are near the northern end of the Antilles chain between the Caribbean Sea and the Atlantic Ocean. They were settled by the Dutch and Danish and had a polyglot colonial society, with one of the oldest Jewish communities in the Western Hemisphere. Their most famous son is Alexander Hamilton, who grew up on St. Croix but moved to New York and never came back. Almost all of the islands' 106,000 people live on the three main islands of St. Thomas, St. John and St. Croix.

The Virgin Islands have lived primarily off tourism and, until 2013, an oil refinery. St. Thomas has long been one of the top cruise ship destinations in the world, with more than

2 million visitors a year, and tourism, together with shopping, accounts for 80 percent of the islands' economy. Tourism numbers fluctuated throughout the recession, but 2013 saw a return to healthy revenues from hotel occupancy taxes and tourist spending. Advocates for tourism in the area scored a legislative victory in 2014 when Congress amended a 1993 law that prohibited charter yachts operating in the islands from carrying more than six passengers without inspection. Opponents of the law argued that it had the effect of redirecting tourists to the British Virgin Islands. It was amended to allow for 12 passengers.

The refinery was built on St. Croix by Hess Oil in 1966 and was expanded to handle 650,000 barrels a day in 1974, making it the largest refinery in the world. It handled heavy Venezuelan crude and, in 1998, joined with the Venezuelan state firm PDVSA to form Hovensa. But as fuel costs increased and Venezuelan production declined under the regime of Hugo Chavez, Hovensa cut capacity to 350,000 barrels a day and in early 2012 announced plans to close the refinery, with the loss of 2,200 jobs and $100 million revenue to the territorial government. "Even after the terrible economic realities of the last few years, it's hard to imagine any single piece of economic news worse for this territory," Gov. John de Jongh said. Another firm, Atlantic Basic Refining Inc., negotiated with Hess to reopen the refinery in 2015, but the islands' legislature voted against the deal, effectively killing it.

Unemployment in the Virgin Islands has remained above 10 percent since 2012. One-third of workers on the islands are employed by government, and the territorial government has been running structural deficits of about one-eighth of spending. That's on top of the crushing burden of $2.4 billion in bond debt, which requires millions of dollars in debt service. The financial troubles of nearby Puerto Rico have only increased anxieties over the territory's future.

Rum sales in the Virgin Islands have spurred some renewed economic activity. Rum-producing territories have been receiving $13.25 of the $13.50 per-gallon federal tax on rum since 1999. In 2008, the Virgin Islands government made a deal with the British-based liquor company Diageo to move its Captain Morgan rum operations from Puerto Rico to a new $165 million distillery in the Virgin Islands. The islands' government estimated it would get $119 million in annual revenue, of which $36 million would go to Diageo as an incentive to move. (The Virgin Islands has a similar arrangement with its other major rum company, Cruzan). Not surprisingly, Puerto Rican politicians were unhappy with the plan and argued that it was illegitimate to use rum tax funds to lure a distillery operation from one territory to another. In 2009, Puerto Rico Resident Commissioner Pedro Pierluisi sponsored a bill to limit payment to liquor companies to 10 percent of rum tax funds. It won bipartisan support, but Virgin Island Del. Donna Christensen rounded up support from the Congressional Black Caucus and the bill failed. The rum tax rebate has been renewed every two years, though criticism of the practice from fiscal hawks in Congress have been growing louder.

The Virgin Islands play a small role in the presidential selection process. The territory held a Democratic presidential primary in 2008 in which Barack Obama beat Hillary Clinton 90%-8% and got all three pledged delegates. Republicans held a tiny caucus in a local restaurant after John McCain had already locked up the nomination. In March 2012, Republicans voted again, and Mitt Romney won all the delegates.

Governor Kenneth Mapp, an independent, was elected to replace term-limited Democrat John de Jongh in 2014, in an upset over Donna Christensen, the territory's long-time delegate to Congress. Christensen entered the race as the favorite, but trailed Mapp by almost nine points in the first round of voting and suffered a crushing defeat in the runoff. Mapp, running on an economic platform that included a plan to create 1,000 jobs during his first year in office, won 62%-37%. He is the Virgin Islands' first non-Democratic governor since 1999.

A former police officer in New York City, Mapp served three terms as a Republican in the Virgin Islands Legislature and one term as lieutenant governor from 1995 to 1999 under Roy Lester Schneider. He ran as an independent for governor in 2006 and 2010, losing both times to de Jongh. Mapp earned a masters in public administration from Harvard University and worked in the administration of Gov. Charles Turnbull as director of finance and administration for the Virgin Islands Public Finance Authority from 2002 to 2006.

In office, Mapp has tangled with Hovensa over the fate of its shuttered oil refinery on St. Croix. He has pushed to remove the company from the property, and in March he proposed repurposing the refinery as a military installation, similar to—or as a potential replacement for—Guantanamo Bay. He has also sought increased funding from Washington for highways and infrastructure projects in the Virgin Islands. In May, Mapp was criticized for the $12,500 per month price tag of his government-provided rental property on St. Thomas. He vacated the property at the end of the month, saying, "I suspect that I may be the only governor that does not have a home in the capital in the jurisdiction in which he presides."

DELEGATE

Stacey Plaskett (D)

Elected 2014, 1st term; b. May 13, 1966, Brooklyn, NY; Georgetown U., B.S.F.S. 1988, American U., J.D. 1994; Lutheran; married (Jonathan Buckney-Small); 5 children.

Professional Career: Asst. dist. atty., Bronx; Consultant & legal counsel, Mitchel Madison Group; Practicing atty.; Staff, U.S. Dept. of Justice, 2002-04; General counsel, Virgin Isl. econ. dev't. auth. 2007-14.

DC Office: 509 CHOB, 20515, 202-225-1790; Fax: 202-225-5517; Website: plaskett.house.gov.

State Offices: St. Croix, 340-778-5900; St. Thomas, 340-774-4408.

Committees: *Agriculture:* Livestock & Foreign Agriculture; Nutrition. *Oversight & Gov't Reform:* Gov't Operations; Interior.

Stacey Plaskett, a Democrat, was elected delegate from the Virgin Islands in 2014. Plaskett grew up in Brooklyn, raised by parents who migrated to New York from the Virgin Islands in the 1950s. She attended Choate Rosemary Hall, where a young John F. Kennedy was voted "most likely to succeed" by his graduating class in 1935 (the school became co-educational in the 1970s). She earned a degree in history and diplomacy from Georgetown University and a law degree from American University. Afterwards, she worked as an assistant district attorney in the Bronx and later as counsel to the House Ethics Committee. Before relocating to the Virgin Islands, Plaskett was a political appointee in the Department of Justice from 2002 to 2004 and served on the staff of Deputy Attorney General Larry Thompson.

Plaskett first ran for the delegate seat in 2012 when she lost to incumbent Donna Christensen in the primary 57%-42%. In 2014, Christensen vacated the seat to run for governor. Plaskett ran again and defeated Virgin Islands State Senate President Shawn-Michael Malone in the Democratic primary 50%-41%. She won the general election with more than 90% of the vote.

In the House, Plaskett serves on the Oversight and Government Reform Committee and is the first delegate from the Virgin Islands to hold a seat on the Agriculture Committee. She has been active on territorial issues. In May, she introduced a bill to raise the rebate that the Virgin Islands receives from federal taxes on rum sales from $13.25 per gallon to $13.50. The increase, it has been argued, would generate an additional $5 million in rum tax revenues for the territory per year. Plaskett has also sponsored legislation calling attention to the centennial anniversary of the U.S. acquisition of the Virgin Islands in 1917, and on the House floor she has advocated increased voting rights for the insular territories.

LEADERSHIP

The 114th Congress
2015-2016

U.S. Senate

54 R, 44 D, 2 I

Republicans

Majority Leader	Mitch McConnell (KY)
President Pro Tempore	Orrin Hatch (UT)
Majority Whip & Assistant Majority Leader	John Cornyn (TX)
Republican Conference Chairman	John Thune (SD)
Republican Policy Committee Chairman	John Barrasso (WY)
Republican Conference Vice Chairman	Roy Blunt (MO)
National Republican Senatorial Committee Chairman	Roger Wicker (MS)

Democrats

Minority Leader	Harry Reid (NV)
Minority Whip	Dick Durbin (IL)
Democratic Conference Vice Chairman, Policy and Communications Center Chairman	Charles Schumer (NY)
Democratic Conference Secretary	Patty Murray (WA)
Democratic Senatorial Campaign Committee Chairman	Jon Tester (MT)
Democratic Steering and Outreach Committee Chairman	Amy Klobuchar (MN)
Democratic Policy and Communications Center Vice Chairman	Deborah Stabenow (MI)

U.S. House of Representatives

246 R, 188 D, 1 V

Republicans

Speaker of the House	John Boehner (OH-8)
Majority Leader	Kevin McCarthy (CA-23)
Majority Whip	Steve Scalise (LA-1)
Chief Deputy Whip	Patrick McHenry (NC-10)
Republican Conference Chairman	Cathy McMorris Rodgers (WA-5)
National Republican Congressional Committee Chairman	Greg Walden (OR-2)
Republican Conference Vice Chairman	Lynn Jenkins (KS-2)
Republican Conference Secretary	Virginia Foxx (NC-5)

Democrats

Minority Leader	Nancy Pelosi (CA-12)
Minority Whip	Steny Hoyer (MD-5)
Democratic Caucus Chairman	Xavier Becerra (CA-34)
Democratic Congressional Campaign Committee Chairman	Ben Ray Luján (NM-3)
Assistant Democratic Leader	James Clyburn (SC-6)
Democratic Caucus Vice Chairman	Joseph Crowley (NY-14)
Democratic Steering & Policy Committee Co-Chairman	Rosa DeLauro (CT-3)
Democratic Steering & Policy Committee Co-Chairman	Donna Edwards (MD-4)
Senior Chief Deputy Whip	John Lewis (GA-5)

Chief Deputy Whips:
> Jan Schakowsky (IL-9), Diana DeGette (CO-1), G.K. Butterfield (NC-1), Debbie Wasserman Schultz (FL-23), Peter Welch (VT-AL), Keith Ellison (MN-5), Terri Sewell (AL-7), Kyrsten Sinema (AZ-9), Joaquin Castro (TX-20)

SENATE SENIORITY

Senators are ranked by length of consecutive service in the Senate. If necessary, ties are broken based on previous public service and state population. The Senate seniority list was provided by the Senate Press Gallery and was compiled from Senate Historical Office records. It is current as of August 6, 2015.

Senator (Party and State)	Start of Service	Senator (Party and State)	Start of Service
Patrick Leahy (D-VT)	Jan. 3, 1975	Jeff Merkley (D-OR)	Jan. 6, 2009
Orrin Hatch (R-UT)	Jan. 3, 1977	Michael Bennet (D-CO)	Jan. 22, 2009
Thad Cochran (R-MS)	Dec. 27, 1978	Kirsten Gillibrand (D-NY)	Jan. 27, 2009
Charles Grassley (R-IA)	Jan. 3, 1981	Al Franken (D-MN)	Jul. 7, 2009
Mitch McConnell (R-KY)	Jan. 3, 1985	Joe Manchin (D-WV)	Nov. 15, 2010
Barbara Mikulski (D-MD)	Jan. 3, 1987	Christopher Coons (D-DE)	Nov. 15, 2010
Richard Shelby (R-AL)	Jan. 3, 1987	Mark Kirk (R-IL)	Nov. 29, 2010
John McCain (R-AZ)	Jan. 3, 1987	Dan Coats (R-IN)[1]	Jan. 3, 2011
Harry Reid (D-NV)	Jan. 3, 1987	Roy Blunt (R-MO)	Jan. 3, 2011
Dianne Feinstein (D-CA)	Nov. 4, 1992	Jerry Moran (R-KS)	Jan. 3, 2011
Barbara Boxer (D-CA)	Jan. 3, 1993	Rob Portman (R-OH)	Jan. 3, 2011
Patty Murray (D-WA)	Jan. 3, 1993	John Boozman (R-AR)	Jan. 3, 2011
James Inhofe (R-OK)	Nov. 16, 1994	Pat Toomey (R-PA)	Jan. 3, 2011
Ron Wyden (D-OR)	Feb. 6, 1996	John Hoeven (R-ND)	Jan. 3, 2011
Pat Roberts (R-KS)	Jan. 3, 1997	Marco Rubio (R-FL)	Jan. 3, 2011
Richard Durbin (D-IL)	Jan. 3, 1997	Ron Johnson (R-WI)	Jan. 3, 2011
Jack Reed (D-RI)	Jan. 3, 1997	Rand Paul (R-KY)	Jan. 3, 2011
Jeff Sessions (R-AL)	Jan. 3, 1997	Richard Blumenthal (D-CT)	Jan. 3, 2011
Susan Collins (R-ME)	Jan. 3, 1997	Mike Lee (R-UT)	Jan. 3, 2011
Michael Enzi (R-WY)	Jan. 3, 1997	Kelly Ayotte (R-NH)	Jan. 3, 2011
Charles Schumer (D-NY)	Jan. 3, 1999	Dean Heller (R-NV)	May 9, 2011
Michael Crapo (R-ID)	Jan. 3, 1999	Brian Schatz (D-HI)	Dec. 27, 2012
Bill Nelson (D-FL)	Jan. 3, 2001	Tim Scott (R-SC)	Jan. 3, 2013
Thomas Carper (D-DE)	Jan. 3, 2001	Tammy Baldwin (D-WI)	Jan. 3, 2013
Debbie Stabenow (D-MI)	Jan. 3, 2001	Jeff Flake (R-AZ)	Jan. 3, 2013
Maria Cantwell (D-WA)	Jan. 3, 2001	Joe Donnelly (D-IN)	Jan. 3, 2013
Lisa Murkowski (R-AK)	Dec. 20, 2002	Chris Murphy (D-CT)	Jan. 3, 2013
Lindsey Graham (R-SC)	Jan. 3, 2003	Mazie Hirono (D-HI)	Jan. 3, 2013
Lamar Alexander (R-TN)	Jan. 3, 2003	Martin Heinrich (D-NM)	Jan. 3, 2013
John Cornyn (R-TX)	Dec. 2, 2002	Angus King (I-ME)	Jan. 3, 2013
Richard Burr (R-NC)	Jan. 3, 2005	Tim Kaine (D-VA)	Jan. 3, 2013
John Thune (R-SD)	Jan. 3, 2005	Ted Cruz (R-TX)	Jan. 3, 2013
John Isakson (R-GA)	Jan. 3, 2005	Elizabeth Warren (D-MA)	Jan. 3, 2013
David Vitter (R-LA)	Jan. 3, 2005	Deb Fischer (R-NE)	Jan. 3, 2013
Robert Menendez (D-NJ)	Jan. 18, 2006	Heidi Heitkamp (D-ND)	Jan. 3, 2013
Ben Cardin (D-MD)	Jan. 3, 2007	Edward Markey (D-MA)	Jul. 16, 2013
Bernie Sanders (I-VT)	Jan. 3, 2007	Cory Booker (D-NJ)	Oct. 31, 2013
Sherrod Brown (D-OH)	Jan. 3, 2007	Shelley Moore Capito (R-WV)	Jan. 3, 2015
Robert Casey (D-PA)	Jan. 3, 2007	Gary Peters (D-MI)	Jan. 3, 2015
Bob Corker (R-TN)	Jan. 3, 2007	Bill Cassidy (R-LA)	Jan. 3, 2015
Claire McCaskill (D-MO)	Jan. 3, 2007	Cory Gardner (R-CO)	Jan. 3, 2015
Amy Klobuchar (D-MN)	Jan. 3, 2007	James Lankford (R-OK)	Jan. 3, 2015
Sheldon Whitehouse (D-RI)	Jan. 3, 2007	Tom Cotton (R-AR)	Jan. 3, 2015
Jon Tester (D-MT)	Jan. 3, 2007	Steve Daines (R-MT)	Jan. 3, 2015
John Barrasso (R-WY)	June 22, 2007	Mike Rounds (R-SD)	Jan. 6, 2015
Roger Wicker (R-MS)	Dec. 31, 2007	David Perdue (R-GA)	Jan. 3, 2015
Tom Udall (D-NM)	Jan. 6, 2009	Thom Tillis (R-NC)	Jan. 3, 2015
Jeanne Shaheen (D-NH)	Jan. 6, 2009	Joni Ernst (R-IA)	Jan. 3, 2015
Mark Warner (D-VA)	Jan. 6, 2009	Ben Sasse (R-NE)	Jan. 3, 2015
James Risch (R-ID)	Jan. 6, 2009	Dan Sullivan (R-AK)	Jan. 3, 2015

[1] Also served 1989-1999.

HOUSE SENIORITY

Representatives are ranked by the total length of time served in the House. Members are given credit for prior service, and ties are broken alphabetically. The House seniority list was provided by the House Press Gallery and was compiled from information provided by the office of the Clerk of the House. It is current as of August 6, 2015.

Member (Party and State)	Start of Service	Member (Party and State)	Start of Service
John Conyers Jr. (D-MI)	Jan. 3, 1965	Ed Royce (R-CA)	Jan. 3, 1993
Charles Rangel (D-NY)	Jan. 3, 1971	Bobby Rush (D-IL)	Jan. 3, 1993
Don Young (R-AK)	March 6, 1973	Bobby Scott (D-VA)	Jan. 3, 1993
Jim Sensenbrenner Jr. (R-WI)	Jan. 3, 1979	Nydia Velázquez (D-NY)	Jan. 3, 1993
Harold Rogers (R-KY)	Jan. 3, 1981	Bennie Thompson (D-MS)	April 13, 1993
Chris Smith (R-NJ)	Jan. 3, 1981	Sam Farr (D-CA)	June 8, 1993
Steny Hoyer (D-MD)	May 19, 1981	Frank Lucas (R-OK)	May 10, 1994
Marcy Kaptur (D-OH)	Jan. 3, 1983	Lloyd Doggett (D-TX)	Jan. 3, 1995
Sander Levin (D-MI)	Jan. 3, 1983	Mike Doyle (D-PA)	Jan. 3, 1995
Joe Barton (R-TX)	Jan. 3, 1985	Chaka Fattah (D-PA)	Jan. 3, 1995
Peter Visclosky (D-IN)	Jan. 3, 1985	Rodney Frelinghuysen (R-NJ)	Jan. 3, 1995
Peter DeFazio (D-OR)	Jan. 3, 1987	Sheila Jackson Lee (D-TX)	Jan. 3, 1995
John Lewis (D-GA)	Jan. 3, 1987	Walter Jones (R-NC)	Jan. 3, 1995
Louise Slaughter (D-NY)	Jan. 3, 1987	Frank LoBiondo (R-NJ)	Jan. 3, 1995
Lamar Smith (R-TX)	Jan. 3, 1987	Zoe Lofgren (D-CA)	Jan. 3, 1995
Fred Upton (R-MI)	Jan. 3, 1987	Mac Thornberry (R-TX)	Jan. 3, 1995
Nancy Pelosi (D-CA)	Jun. 2, 1987	Ed Whitfield (R-KY)	Jan. 3, 1995
Frank Pallone (D-NJ)	Nov. 8, 1988	Elijah Cummings (D-MD)	April 16, 1996
John Duncan (R-TN)	Nov. 8, 1988	Earl Blumenauer (D-OR)	May 21, 1996
Eliot Engel (D-NY)	Jan. 3, 1989	Robert Aderholt (R-AL)	Jan. 3, 1997
Nita Lowey (D-NY)	Jan. 3, 1989	Kevin Brady (R-TX)	Jan. 3, 1997
Jim McDermott (D-WA)	Jan. 3, 1989	Danny Davis (D-IL)	Jan. 3, 1997
Richard Neal (D-MA)	Jan. 3, 1989	Diana DeGette (D-CO)	Jan. 3, 1997
Dana Rohrabacher (R-CA)	Jan. 3, 1989	Kay Granger (R-TX)	Jan. 3, 1997
Ileana Ros-Lehtinen (R-FL)	Aug. 29, 1989	Rubén Hinojosa (D-TX)	Jan. 3, 1997
Jose Serrano (D-NY)	March 20, 1990	Ron Kind (D-WI)	Jan. 3, 1997
David Price (D-NC)[1]	Jan. 3, 1997	Jim McGovern (D-MA)	Jan. 3, 1997
John Boehner (R-OH)	Jan. 3, 1991	Bill Pascrell (D-NJ)	Jan. 3, 1997
Rosa DeLauro (D-CT)	Jan. 3, 1991	Joe Pitts (R-PA)	Jan. 3, 1997
Collin Peterson (D-MN)	Jan. 3, 1991	Loretta Sanchez (D-CA)	Jan. 3, 1997
Maxine Waters (D-CA)	Jan. 3, 1991	Pete Sessions (R-TX)	Jan. 3, 1997
Sam Johnson (R-TX)	May 18, 1991	Brad Sherman (D-CA)	Jan. 3, 1997
Jerrold Nadler (D-NY)	Nov. 4, 1992	John Shimkus (R-IL)	Jan. 3, 1997
Jim Cooper (D-TN)[2]	Jan. 3, 2003	Adam Smith (D-WA)	Jan. 3, 1997
Xavier Becerra (D-CA)	Jan. 3, 1993	Gregory Meeks (D-NY)	Feb. 3, 1998
Sanford Bishop (D-GA)	Jan. 3, 1993	Lois Capps (D-CA)	March 10, 1998
Corrine Brown (D-FL)	Jan. 3, 1993	Barbara Lee (D-CA)	April 7, 1998
Ken Calvert (R-CA)	Jan. 3, 1993	Robert Brady (D-PA)	May 19, 1998
James Clyburn (D-SC)	Jan. 3, 1993	Steve Chabot (R-OH)[3]	Jan. 5, 2011
Anna Eshoo (D-CA)	Jan. 3, 1993	Michael Capuano (D-MA)	Jan. 3, 1999
Bob Goodlatte (R-VA)	Jan. 3, 1993	Joseph Crowley (D-NY)	Jan. 3, 1999
Gene Green (D-TX)	Jan. 3, 1993	John Larson (D-CT)	Jan. 3, 1999
Luis Gutierrez (D-IL)	Jan. 3, 1993	Grace Napolitano (D-CA)	Jan. 3, 1999
Alcee Hastings (D-FL)	Jan. 3, 1993	Paul Ryan (R-WI)	Jan. 3, 1999
Eddie Bernice Johnson (D-TX)	Jan. 3, 1993	Jan Schakowsky (D-IL)	Jan. 3, 1999
Peter King (R-NY)	Jan. 3, 1993	Mike Simpson (R-ID)	Jan. 3, 1999
Carolyn Maloney (D-NY)	Jan. 3, 1993	Mike Thompson (D-CA)	Jan. 3, 1999
John Mica (R-FL)	Jan. 3, 1993	Greg Walden (R-OR)	Jan. 3, 1999
Lucille Roybal-Allard (D-CA)	Jan. 3, 1993	William Lacy Clay Jr. (D-MO)	Jan. 3, 2001

[1]Also served 1987-1995.
[2]Also served 1983-1995.
[3]Also served 1995-2009.

Member (Party and State)	Start of Service	Member (Party and State)	Start of Service
Ander Crenshaw (R-FL)	Jan. 3, 2001	Cathy McMorris Rodgers (R-WA)	Jan. 3, 2005
John Culberson (R-TX)	Jan. 3, 2001	Gwen Moore (D-WI)	Jan. 3, 2005
Susan Davis (D-CA)	Jan. 3, 2001	Ted Poe (R-TX)	Jan. 3, 2005
Sam Graves Jr. (R-MO)	Jan. 3, 2001	Tom Price (R-GA)	Jan. 3, 2005
Mike Honda (D-CA)	Jan. 3, 2001	Dave Reichert (R-WA)	Jan. 3, 2005
Steve Israel (D-NY)	Jan. 3, 2001	Debbie Wasserman Schultz (D-FL)	Jan. 3, 2005
Darrell Issa (R-CA)	Jan. 3, 2001	Lynn Westmoreland (R-GA)	Jan. 3, 2005
Jim Langevin (D-RI)	Jan. 3, 2001	Doris Matsui (D-CA)	March 8, 2005
Rick Larsen (D-WA)	Jan. 3, 2001	Albio Sires (D-NJ)	Nov. 13, 2006
Betty McCollum (D-MN)	Jan. 3, 2001	Steve Pearce (R-NM)[4]	Jan. 5, 2011
Adam Schiff (D-CA)	Jan. 3, 2001	Gus Bilirakis (R-FL)	Jan. 4, 2007
Pat Tiberi (R-OH)	Jan. 3, 2001	Vern Buchanan (R-FL)	Jan. 4, 2007
Bill Shuster (R-PA)	May 15, 2001	Kathy Castor (D-FL)	Jan. 4, 2007
Randy Forbes (R-VA)	June 19, 2001	Yvette Clarke (D-NY)	Jan. 4, 2007
Stephen Lynch (D-MA)	Oct. 16, 2001	Steve Cohen (D-TN)	Jan. 4, 2007
Jeff Miller (R-FL)	Oct. 16, 2001	Joe Courtney (D-CT)	Jan. 4, 2007
Joe Wilson (R-SC)	Dec. 18, 2001	Keith Ellison (D-MN)	Jan. 4, 2007
Rob Bishop (R-UT)	Jan. 3, 2003	Hank Johnson (D-GA)	Jan. 4, 2007
Marsha Blackburn (R-TN)	Jan. 3, 2003	Jim Jordan (R-OH)	Jan. 4, 2007
Michael Burgess (R-TX)	Jan. 3, 2003	Doug Lamborn (R-CO)	Jan. 4, 2007
John Carter (R-TX)	Jan. 3, 2003	Dave Loebsack (D-IA)	Jan. 4, 2007
Tom Cole (R-OK)	Jan. 3, 2003	Kevin McCarthy (R-CA)	Jan. 4, 2007
Mario Diaz-Balart (R-FL)	Jan. 3, 2003	Jerry McNerney (D-CA)	Jan. 4, 2007
Trent Franks (R-AZ)	Jan. 3, 2003	Ed Perlmutter (D-CO)	Jan. 4, 2007
Scott Garrett (R-NJ)	Jan. 3, 2003	Peter Roskam (R-IL)	Jan. 4, 2007
Raúl Grijalva (D-AZ)	Jan. 3, 2003	John Sarbanes (D-MD)	Jan. 4, 2007
Jeb Hensarling (R-TX)	Jan. 3, 2003	Adrian Smith (R-NE)	Jan. 4, 2007
Steve King (R-IA)	Jan. 3, 2003	Tim Walz (D-MN)	Jan. 4, 2007
John Kline (R-MN)	Jan. 3, 2003	Peter Welch (D-VT)	Jan. 4, 2007
Candice Miller (R-MI)	Jan. 3, 2003	John Yarmuth (D-KY)	Jan. 4, 2007
Tim Murphy (R-PA)	Jan. 3, 2003	Niki Tsongas (D-MA)	Oct. 18, 2007
Devin Nunes (R-CA)	Jan. 3, 2003	Bob Latta (R-OH)	Dec. 13, 2007
Mike Rogers (R-AL)	Jan. 3, 2003	Rob Wittman (R-VA)	Dec. 13, 2007
Dutch Ruppersberger (D-MD)	Jan. 3, 2003	André D. Carson (D-IN)	March 13, 2008
Tim Ryan (D-OH)	Jan. 3, 2003	Jackie Speier (D-CA)	April 10, 2008
Linda Sánchez (D-CA)	Jan. 3, 2003	Steve Scalise (R-LA)	May 7, 2008
David Scott (D-GA)	Jan. 3, 2003	Donna Edwards (D-MD)	June 19, 2008
Mike Turner (R-OH)	Jan. 3, 2003	Marcia Fudge (D-OH)	Nov. 19, 2008
Chris Van Hollen (D-MD)	Jan. 3, 2003	Rick Nolan (D-MN) [5]	Jan. 3, 2013
Randy Neugebauer (R-TX)	June 3, 2003	Matt Salmon (R-AZ) [6]	Jan. 3, 2013
G.K. Butterfield (D-NC)	July 20, 2004	Mark Sanford (R-SC)[7]	May 15, 2013
Charles Boustany (R-LA)	Jan. 3, 2005	Jason Chaffetz (R-UT)	Jan. 6, 2009
Emanuel Cleaver (D-MO)	Jan. 3, 2005	Mike Coffman (R-CO)	Jan. 6, 2009
Mike Conaway (R-TX)	Jan. 3, 2005	Gerald Connolly (D-VA)	Jan. 6, 2009
Jim Costa (D-CA)	Jan. 3, 2005	John Fleming (R-LA)	Jan. 6, 2009
Henry Cuellar (D-TX)	Jan. 3, 2005	Brett Guthrie (R-KY)	Jan. 6, 2009
Charie Dent (R-PA)	Jan. 3, 2005	Gregg Harper (R-MS)	Jan. 6, 2009
Jeff Fortenberry (R-NE)	Jan. 3, 2005	Jim Himes (D-CT)	Jan. 6, 2009
Virginia Foxx (R-NC)	Jan. 3, 2005	Duncan D. Hunter (R-CA)	Jan. 6, 2009
Louie Gohmert (R-TX)	Jan. 3, 2005	Lynn Jenkins (R-KS)	Jan. 6, 2009
Al Green (D-TX)	Jan. 3, 2005	Leonard Lance (R-NJ)	Jan. 6, 2009
Brian Higgins (D-NY)	Jan. 3, 2005	Blaine Luetkemeyer (R-MO)	Jan. 6, 2009
Dan Lipinski (D-IL)	Jan. 3, 2005	Ben Ray Luján (D-NM)	Jan. 6, 2009
Kenny Marchant (R-TX)	Jan. 3, 2005	Cynthia Lummis (R-WY)	Jan. 6, 2009
Michael McCaul (R-TX)	Jan. 3, 2005	Tom McClintock (R-CA)	Jan. 6, 2009
Patrick McHenry (R-NC)	Jan. 3, 2005	Pete Olson (R-TX)	Jan. 6, 2009

[4] Also served 2003-2009.
[5] Also served 1975-1981.
[6] Also served 1995-2001.
[7] Also served 1995-2001.

Member (Party and State)	Start of Service	Member (Party and State)	Start of Service
Erik Paulsen (R-MN)	Jan. 6, 2009	Raúl Labrador (R-ID)	Jan. 5, 2011
Chellie Pingree (D-ME)	Jan. 6, 2009	Billy Long (R-MO)	Jan. 5, 2011
Jared Polis (D-CO)	Jan. 6, 2009	Tom Marino (R-PA)	Jan. 5, 2011
Bill Posey (R-FL)	Jan. 6, 2009	David McKinley (R-WV)	Jan. 5, 2011
Phil Roe (R-TN)	Jan. 6, 2009	Pat Meehan (R-PA)	Jan. 5, 2011
Tom Rooney (R-FL)	Jan. 6, 2009	Mick Mulvaney (R-SC)	Jan. 5, 2011
Kurt Schrader (D-OR)	Jan. 6, 2009	Kristi Noem (R-SD)	Jan. 5, 2011
Glenn Thompson (R-PA)	Jan. 6, 2009	Richard Nugent (R-FL)	Jan. 5, 2011
Paul Tonko (D-NY)	Jan. 6, 2009	Steven Palazzo (R-MS)	Jan. 5, 2011
Mike Quigley (D-IL)	April 21, 2009	Mike Pompeo (R-KS)	Jan. 5, 2011
Judy Chu (D-CA)	July 16, 2009	Jim Renacci (R-OH)	Jan. 5, 2011
John Garamendi (D-CA)	Nov. 5, 2009	Reid Ribble (R-WI)	Jan. 5, 2011
Ted Deutch (D-FL)	April 15, 2010	Cedric Richmond (D-LA)	Jan. 5, 2011
Tom Graves (R-GA)	June 14, 2010	Scott Rigell (R-VA)	Jan. 5, 2011
Tom Reed (R-NY)	Nov. 2, 2010	Martha Roby (R-AL)	Jan. 5, 2011
Marlin Stutzman (R-IN)	Nov. 2, 2010	Todd Rokita (R-IN)	Jan. 5, 2011
Mike Fitzpatrick (R-PA)[8]	Jan. 5, 2011	Dennis Ross (R-FL)	Jan. 5, 2011
Tim Walberg (R-MI)[9]	Jan. 5, 2011	David Schweikert (R-AZ)	Jan. 5, 2011
Bill Foster (D-IL)	Jan. 3, 2013	Austin Scott (R-GA)	Jan. 5, 2011
Justin Amash (R-MI)	Jan. 5, 2011	Terri Sewell (D-AL)	Jan. 5, 2011
Lou Barletta (R-PA)	Jan. 5, 2011	Steve Stivers (R-OH)	Jan. 5, 2011
Karen Bass (D-CA)	Jan. 5, 2011	Scott Tipton (R-CO)	Jan. 5, 2011
Dan Benishek (R-MI)	Jan. 5, 2011	Daniel Webster (R-FL)	Jan. 5, 2011
Diane Black (R-TN)	Jan. 5, 2011	Frederica Wilson (D-FL)	Jan. 5, 2011
Mo Brooks Jr. (R-AL)	Jan. 5, 2011	Steve Womack (R-AR)	Jan. 5, 2011
Larry Bucshon (R-IN)	Jan. 5, 2011	Rob Woodall (R-GA)	Jan. 5, 2011
John Carney (D-DE)	Jan. 5, 2011	Kevin Yoder (R-KS)	Jan. 5, 2011
David Cicilline (D-RI)	Jan. 5, 2011	Todd Young (R-IN)	Jan. 5, 2011
Rick Crawford (R-AR)	Jan. 5, 2011	Janice Hahn (D-CA)	July 19, 2011
Jeff Denham (R-CA)	Jan. 5, 2011	Mark Amodei (R-NV)	Sept. 15, 2011
Scott DesJarlais (R-TN)	Jan. 5, 2011	Suzanne Bonamici (D-OR)	Feb. 7, 2012
Sean Duffy (R-WI)	Jan. 5, 2011	Suzan DelBene (D-WA)	Nov. 13, 2012
Jeff Duncan (R-SC)	Jan. 5, 2011	Thomas Massie (R-KY)	Nov. 13, 2012
Renee Ellmers (R-NC)	Jan. 5, 2011	Donald Payne Jr. (D-NJ)	Nov. 15, 2012
Blake Farenthold (R-TX)	Jan. 5, 2011	Alan Grayson (D-FL)[10]	Jan. 3, 2013
Stephen Fincher (R-TN)	Jan. 5, 2011	Ann Kirkpatrick (D-AZ)[11]	Jan. 3, 2013
Chuck Fleischmann (R-TN)	Jan. 5, 2011	Dina Titus (D-NV)[12]	Jan. 3, 2013
Bill Flores (R-TX)	Jan. 5, 2011	Andy Barr (R-KY)	Jan. 3, 2013
Bob Gibbs (R-OH)	Jan. 5, 2011	Joyce Beatty (D-OH)	Jan. 3, 2013
Chris Gibson (R-NY)	Jan. 5, 2011	Ami Bera (D-CA)	Jan. 3, 2013
Paul Gosar (R-AZ)	Jan. 5, 2011	Jim Bridenstine (R-OK)	Jan. 3, 2013
Trey Gowdy (R-SC)	Jan. 5, 2011	Susan Brooks (R-IN)	Jan. 3, 2013
Morgan Griffith (R-VA)	Jan. 5, 2011	Julia Brownley (D-CA)	Jan. 3, 2013
Richard Hanna (R-NY)	Jan. 5, 2011	Cheri Bustos (D-IL)	Jan. 3, 2013
Andy Harris (R-MD)	Jan. 5, 2011	Tony Cárdenas (D-CA)	Jan. 3, 2013
Vicky Hartzler (R-MO)	Jan. 5, 2011	Matt Cartwright (D-PA)	Jan. 3, 2013
Joe Heck (R-NV)	Jan. 5, 2011	Joaquin Castro (D-TX)	Jan. 3, 2013
Jaime Herrera Beutler (R-WA)	Jan. 5, 2011	Chris Collins (R-NY)	Jan. 3, 2013
Tim Huelskamp (R-KS)	Jan. 5, 2011	Doug Collins (R-GA)	Jan. 3, 2013
Bill Huizenga (R-MI)	Jan. 5, 2011	Paul Cook (R-CA)	Jan. 3, 2013
Randy Hultgren (R-IL)	Jan. 5, 2011	Kevin Cramer (R-ND)	Jan. 3, 2013
Robert Hurt (R-VA)	Jan. 5, 2011	Rodney Davis (R-IL)	Jan. 3, 2013
Bill Johnson (R-OH)	Jan. 5, 2011	John Delaney (D-MD)	Jan. 3, 2013
William Keating (D-MA)	Jan. 5, 2011	Ron DeSantis (R-FL)	Jan. 3, 2013
Mike Kelly (R-PA)	Jan. 5, 2011	Tammy Duckworth (D-IL)	Jan. 3, 2013
Adam Kinzinger (R-IL)	Jan. 5, 2011	Elizabeth Esty (D-CT)	Jan. 3, 2013

[8] Also served 2005-2007.
[9] Also served 2007-2009.
[10] Also served 2009-2011.
[11] Also served 2009-2011.
[12] Also served 2009-2011.

Member (Party and State)	Start of Service	Member (Party and State)	Start of Service
Lois Frankel (D-FL)	Jan. 3, 2013	Rick Allen (R-GA)	Jan. 6, 2015
Tulsi Gabbard (D-HI)	Jan. 3, 2013	Brad Ashford (D-NE)	Jan. 6, 2015
Denny Heck (D-WA)	Jan. 3, 2013	Brian Babin (R-TX)	Jan. 6, 2015
George Holding (R-NC)	Jan. 3, 2013	Don Beyer (D-VA)	Jan. 6, 2015
Richard Hudson (R-NC)	Jan. 3, 2013	Mike Bishop (R-MI)	Jan. 6, 2015
Jared Huffman (D-CA)	Jan. 3, 2013	Rod Blum (R-IA)	Jan. 6, 2015
Hakeem Jeffries (D-NY)	Jan. 3, 2013	Michael Bost (R-IL)	Jan. 6, 2015
David Joyce (R-OH)	Jan. 3, 2013	Brendan Boyle (D-PA)	Jan. 6, 2015
Joe Kennedy (D-MA)	Jan. 3, 2013	Ken Buck (R-CO)	Jan. 6, 2015
Dan Kildee (D-MI)	Jan. 3, 2013	Buddy Carter (R-GA)	Jan. 6, 2015
Derek Kilmer (D-WA)	Jan. 3, 2013	Barbara Comstock (R-VA)	Jan. 6, 2015
Ann McLane Kuster (D-NH)	Jan. 3, 2013	Ryan Costello (R-PA)	Jan. 6, 2015
Doug LaMalfa (R-CA)	Jan. 3, 2013	Carlos Curbelo (R-FL)	Jan. 6, 2015
Alan Lowenthal (D-CA)	Jan. 3, 2013	Mark DeSaulnier (D-CA)	Jan. 6, 2015
Michelle Lujan Grisham (D-NM)	Jan. 3, 2013	Debbie Dingell (D-MI)	Jan. 6, 2015
Sean Patrick Maloney (D-NY)	Jan. 3, 2013	Tom Emmer (R-MN)	Jan. 6, 2015
Mark Meadows (R-NC)	Jan. 3, 2013	Ruben Gallego (D-AZ)	Jan. 6, 2015
Grace Meng (D-NY)	Jan. 3, 2013	Gwen Graham (D-FL)	Jan. 6, 2015
Luke Messer (R-IN)	Jan. 3, 2013	Garret Graves (R-LA)	Jan. 6, 2015
Markwayne Mullin (R-OK)	Jan. 3, 2013	Glenn Grothman (R-WI)	Jan. 6, 2015
Patrick Murphy (D-FL)	Jan. 3, 2013	Cresent Hardy (R-NV)	Jan. 6, 2015
Beto O'Rourke (D-TX)	Jan. 3, 2013	Jody Hice (R-GA)	Jan. 6, 2015
Scott Perry (R-PA)	Jan. 3, 2013	French Hill (R-AR)	Jan. 6, 2015
Scott Peters (D-CA)	Jan. 3, 2013	Will Hurd (R-TX)	Jan. 6, 2015
Robert Pittenger (R-NC)	Jan. 3, 2013	Evan Jenkins (R-WV)	Jan. 6, 2015
Mark Pocan (D-WI)	Jan. 3, 2013	John Katko (R-NY)	Jan. 6, 2015
Tom Rice (R-SC)	Jan. 3, 2013	Steve Knight (R-CA)	Jan. 6, 2015
Keith Rothfus (R-PA)	Jan. 3, 2013	Brenda Lawrence (D-MI)	Jan. 6, 2015
Raul Ruiz (D-CA)	Jan. 3, 2013	Ted Lieu (D-CA)	Jan. 6, 2015
Kyrsten Sinema (D-AZ)	Jan. 3, 2013	Barry Loudermilk (R-GA)	Jan. 6, 2015
Chris Stewart (R-UT)	Jan. 3, 2013	Mia Love (R-UT)	Jan. 6, 2015
Eric Swalwell (D-CA)	Jan. 3, 2013	Tom MacArthur (R-NJ)	Jan. 6, 2015
Mark Takano (D-CA)	Jan. 3, 2013	Martha McSally (R-AZ)	Jan. 6, 2015
David Valadao (R-CA)	Jan. 3, 2013	John Moolenaar (R-MI)	Jan. 6, 2015
Juan Vargas (D-CA)	Jan. 3, 2013	Alex Mooney (R-WV)	Jan. 6, 2015
Marc Veasey (D-TX)	Jan. 3, 2013	Seth Moulton (D-MA)	Jan. 6, 2015
Filemon Vela (D-TX)	Jan. 3, 2013	Dan Newhouse (R-WA)	Jan. 6, 2015
Ann Wagner (R-MO)	Jan. 3, 2013	Gary Palmer (R-AL)	Jan. 6, 2015
Jackie Walorski (R-IN)	Jan. 3, 2013	Bruce Poliquin (R-ME)	Jan. 6, 2015
Randy Weber (R-TX)	Jan. 3, 2013	John Ratcliffe (R-TX)	Jan. 6, 2015
Brad Wenstrup (R-OH)	Jan. 3, 2013	Kathleen Rice (D-NY)	Jan. 6, 2015
Roger Williams (R-TX)	Jan. 3, 2013	David Rouzer (R-NC)	Jan. 6, 2015
Ted Yoho (R-FL)	Jan. 3, 2013	Steve Russell (R-OK)	Jan. 6, 2015
Robin Kelly (D-IL)	April 11, 2013	Elise Stefanik (R-NY)	Jan. 6, 2015
Jason Smith (R-MO)	June 5, 2013	Mark Takai (D-HI)	Jan. 6, 2015
Katherine Clark (D-MA)	Dec. 12, 2013	Norma Torres (D-CA)	Jan. 6, 2015
Bradley Byrne (R-AL)	Jan. 8, 2014	Dave Trott (R-MI)	Jan. 6, 2015
David Jolly (R-FL)	March 13, 2014	Mark Walker (R-NC)	Jan. 6, 2015
Curt Clawson (R-FL)	June 25, 2014	Mimi Walters (R-CA)	Jan. 6, 2015
Alma Adams (D-NC)	Nov. 12, 2014	Bonnie Watson Coleman (D-NJ)	Jan. 6, 2015
Dave Brat (R-VA)	Nov. 12, 2014	Bruce Westerman (R-AR)	Jan. 6, 2015
Donald Norcross (D-NJ)	Nov. 12, 2014	David Young (R-IA)	Jan. 6, 2015
Bob Dold (R-IL)	Jan. 6, 2015	Lee Zeldin (R-NY)	Jan. 6, 2015
Frank Guinta (R-NH)	Jan. 6, 2015	Ryan Zinke (R-MT)	Jan. 6, 2015
Ralph Abraham (R-LA)	Jan. 6, 2015	Dan Donovan (R-NY)	May 12, 2015
Pete Aguilar (D-CA)	Jan. 6, 2015	Trent Kelly (R-MS)	June 9, 2015

SENATE COMMITTEES

Agriculture, Nutrition & Forestry
ag.senate.gov

328A Russell
202-224-2035

Majority (R 11): Roberts (KS), Chmn; Cochran (MS), McConnell (KY), Boozman (AR), Hoeven (ND), Perdue (GA), Ernst (IA), Tillis (NC), Sasse (NE), Grassley (IA), Thune (SD)
Minority (D 9): Stabenow (MI), RMM; Leahy (VT), Brown (OH), Klobuchar (MN), Bennet (CO), Gillibrand (NY), Donnelly (IN), Heitkamp (ND), Casey (PA)

SUBCOMMITTEES

Commodities, Risk Management & Trade
Majority (R 7): Boozman, Chmn; Cochran, Hoeven, Perdue, Grassley, Thune, Roberts
Minority (D 6): Donnelly, RMM; Heitkamp, Brown, Gillibrand, Bennet, Stabenow

Conservation, Forestry & Natural Resources
Majority (R 7): Perdue, Chmn; Cochran, McConnell, Boozman, Sasse, Grassley, Roberts
Minority (D 6): Bennet, RMM; Klobuchar, Leahy, Heitkamp, Casey, Stabenow

Livestock, Marketing & Agriculture Security
Majority (R 7): Sasse, Chmn; McConnell, Ernst, Tillis, Thune, Grassley, Roberts
Minority (D 6): Gillibrand, RMM; Leahy, Klobuchar, Donnelly, Casey, Stabenow

Nutrition, Specialty Crops & Agricultural Research
Majority (R 7): Hoeven, Chmn; McConnell, Boozman, Ernst, Tillis, Sasse, Roberts
Minority (D 6): Casey, RMM; Leahy, Brown, Gillibrand, Bennet, Stabenow

Rural Development & Energy
Majority (R 7): Ernst, Chmn; Cochran, Hoeven, Perdue, Tillis, Thune, Roberts
Minority (D 6): Heitkamp, RMM; Brown, Klobuchar, Bennet, Donnelly, Stabenow

Appropriations
appropriations.senate.gov

S-128 The Capitol
202-224-7257

Majority (R 16): Cochran (MS), Chmn; McConnell (KY), Shelby (AL), Alexander (TN), Collins (ME), Murkowski (AK), Graham (SC), Kirk (IL), Blunt (MO), Moran (KS), Hoeven (ND), Boozman (AR), Capito (WV), Cassidy (LA), Lankford (OK), Daines (MT)
Minority (D 14): Mikulski (MD), RMM; Leahy (VT), Murray (WA), Feinstein (CA), Durbin (IL), Reed (RI), Tester (MT), Udall (NM), Shaheen (NH), Merkley (OR), Coons (DE), Schatz (HI), Baldwin (WI), Murphy (CT)

SUBCOMMITTEES

Agriculture, Rural Development, FDA & Related Agencies
Majority (R 7): Moran, Chmn; Blunt, Cochran, McConnell, Collins, Hoeven, Daines
Minority (D 7): Merkley, RMM; Feinstein, Tester, Udall, Leahy, Baldwin, Mikulski

Commerce, Justice, Science & Related Agencies
Majority (R 10): Shelby, Chmn; Alexander, Murkowski, Collins, Graham, Kirk, Boozman, Capito, Lankford, Cochran
Minority (D 8): Mikulski, RMM; Leahy, Feinstein, Reed, Shaheen, Coons, Baldwin, Murphy

Defense
Majority (R 10): Cochran, Chmn; McConnell, Shelby, Alexander, Collins, Murkowski, Graham, Blunt, Daines, Moran
Minority (D 9): Durbin, RMM; Leahy, Feinstein, Mikulski, Murray, Reed, Tester, Udall, Schatz

Energy & Water Development
Majority (R 9): Alexander, Chmn; Cochran, McConnell, Shelby, Collins, Murkowski, Graham, Hoeven, Lankford
Minority (D 9): Feinstein, RMM; Murray, Tester, Durbin, Udall, Shaheen, Merkley, Coons, Mikulski

Financial Services & General Government
Majority (R 4): Boozman, Chmn; Moran, Lankford, Cochran
Minority (D 3): Coons, RMM; Durbin, Mikulski

Homeland Security
Majority (R 6): Hoeven, Chmn; Cochran, Shelby, Murkowski, Graham, Cassidy
Minority (D 6): Shaheen, RMM; Leahy, Murray, Tester, Baldwin, Mikulski

Interior, Environment & Related Agencies
Majority (R 8): Murkowski, Chmn; Alexander, Cochran, Blunt, Hoeven, McConnell, Daines, Cassidy
Minority (D 7): Udall, RMM; Feinstein, Leahy, Reed, Tester, Merkley, Mikulski

Labor, HHS & Education & Related Agencies
Majority (R 10): Blunt, Chmn; Moran, Shelby, Cochran, Alexander, Graham, Kirk, Cassidy, Capito, Lankford
Minority (D 8): Murray, RMM; Durbin, Reed, Mikulski, Shaheen, Merkley, Schatz, Baldwin

Legislative Branch
Majority (R 4): Capito, Chmn; Kirk, Moran, Cochran
Minority (D 3): Schatz, RMM; Murphy, Mikulski

Military Construction & Veteran Affairs & Related Agencies
Majority (R 9): Kirk, Chmn; McConnell, Murkowski, Hoeven, Collins, Boozman, Capito, Cassidy, Cochran
Minority (D 8): Tester, RMM; Murray, Reed, Udall, Schatz, Baldwin, Murphy, Mikulski

State, Foreign Operations & Related Programs
Majority (R 9): Graham, Chmn; McConnell, Kirk, Blunt, Boozman, Moran, Lankford, Daines, Cochran
Minority (D 7): Leahy, RMM; Mikulski, Durbin, Shaheen, Coons, Merkley, Murphy

Transportation, HUD & Related Agencies
Majority (R 10): Collins, Chmn; Shelby, Alexander, Kirk, Blunt, Boozman, Capito, Cassidy, Daines, Cochran
Minority (D 8): Reed, RMM; Mikulski, Murray, Durbin, Feinstein, Coons, Schatz, Murphy

Armed Services
armed-services.senate.gov

228 Russell
202-224-3871

Majority (R 14): McCain (AZ), Chmn; Inhofe (OK), Sessions (AL), Wicker (MS), Ayotte (NH), Fischer (NE), Cotton (AR), Rounds (SD), Ernst (IA), Tillis (NC), Sullivan (AK), Lee (UT), Graham (SC), Cruz (TX)
Minority (D 12): Reed (RI), RMM; Nelson (FL), McCaskill (MO), Manchin (WV), Shaheen (NH), Gillibrand (NY), Blumenthal (CT), Donnelly (IN), Hirono (HI), Kaine (VA), King (ME), Heinrich (NM)

SUBCOMMITTEES

Airland
Majority (R 9): Cotton, Chmn; Inhofe, Sessions, Wicker, Rounds, Ernst, Sullivan, Lee, McCain
Minority (D 8): Manchin, RMM; McCaskill, Gillibrand, Blumenthal, Donnelly, Hirono, Heinrich, Reed

Emerging Threats & Capabilities
Majority (R 8): Fischer, Chmn; Ayotte, Cotton, Ernst, Tillis, Graham, Cruz, McCain
Minority (D 7): Nelson, RMM; Manchin, Shaheen, Gillibrand, Donnelly, Kaine, Reed

Personnel
Majority (R 6): Graham, Chmn; Wicker, Cotton, Tillis, Sullivan, McCain
Minority (D 5): Gillibrand, RMM; McCaskill, Blumenthal, King, Reed

Readiness & Management Support
Majority (R 7): Ayotte, Chmn; Inhofe, Fischer, Rounds, Ernst, Lee, McCain
Minority (D 6): Kaine, RMM; McCaskill, Shaheen, Hirono, Heinrich, Reed,

Seapower
Majority (R 8): Wicker, Chmn; Sessions, Ayotte, Rounds, Tillis, Sullivan, Cruz, McCain,
Minority (D 7): Hirono, RMM; Nelson, Shaheen, Blumenthal, Kaine, King, Reed,

Strategic Forces
Majority (R 7): Sessions, Chmn; Inhofe, Fischer, Lee, Graham, Cruz, McCain,
Minority (D 6): Donnelly, RMM; Nelson, Manchin, King, Heinrich, Reed

Banking, Housing & Urban Affairs
banking.senate.gov

534 Dirksen
202-224-7391

Majority (R 12): Shelby (AL), Chmn; Crapo (ID), Corker (TN), Vitter (LA), Toomey (PA), Kirk (IL), Heller (NV), Scott (SC), Sasse (NE), Cotton (AR), Rounds (SD), Moran (KS)

Minority (D 10): Brown (OH), RMM; Reed (RI), Schumer (NY), Menendez (NJ), Tester (MT), Warner (VA), Merkley (OR), Warren (MA), Heitkamp (ND), Donnelly (IN)

SUBCOMMITTEES

Economic Policy
Majority (R 7): Heller, Chmn; Toomey, Cotton, Rounds, Sasse, Moran, Shelby
Minority (D 5): Warren, RMM; Tester, Merkley, Heitkamp, Brown

Financial Institutions & Consumer Protection
Majority (R 9): Toomey, Chmn; Crapo, Heller, Rounds, Scott, Corker, Vitter, Kirk, Shelby
Minority (D 8): Merkley, RMM; Reed, Schumer, Menendez, Warner, Warren, Donnelly, Brown

Housing, Transportation & Community Development
Majority (R 9): Scott, Chmn; Crapo, Heller, Moran, Corker, Cotton, Rounds, Vitter, Shelby
Minority (D 8): Menendez, RMM; Reed, Schumer, Tester, Merkley, Heitkamp, Donnelly, Brown

National Security & International Trade & Finance
Majority (R 4): Kirk, Chmn; Cotton, Sasse, Shelby
Minority (D 3): Heitkamp, RMM; Warner, Brown

Securities, Insurance & Investment
Majority (R 9): Crapo, Chmn; Corker, Vitter, Toomey, Kirk, Scott, Sasse, Moran, Shelby
Minority (D 8): Warner, RMM; Reed, Schumer, Menendez, Tester, Warren, Donnelly, Brown

Budget
budget.senate.gov

624 Dirksen
202-224-0642

Majority (R 12): Enzi (WY), Chmn; Grassley (IA), Sessions (AL), Crapo (ID), Graham (SC), Portman (OH), Toomey (PA), Johnson (WI), Ayotte (NH), Wicker (MS), Corker (TN), Perdue (GA),
Minority (D 10): Sanders (VT), RMM; Murray (WA), Wyden (OR), Stabenow (MI), Whitehouse (RI), Warner (VA), Merkley (OR), Baldwin (WI), Kaine (VA), King (ME)

Commerce, Science & Transportation
commerce.senate.gov

512 Dirksen
202-224-1251

Majority (R 13): Thune (SD), Chmn; Wicker (MS), Blunt (MO), Rubio (FL), Ayotte (NH), Heller (NV), Cruz (TX), Fischer (NE), Sullivan (AK), Moran (KS), Johnson (WI), Gardner (CO), Daines (MT)
Minority (D 11): Nelson (FL), RMM; Cantwell (WA), McCaskill (MO), Klobuchar (MN), Blumenthal (CT), Schatz (HI), Markey (MA), Booker (NJ), Udall (NM), Manchin (WV), Peters (MI)

Aviation Operations, Safety & Security
Majority (R 12): Ayotte, Chmn; Wicker, Blunt, Rubio, Cruz, Fischer, Moran, Sullivan, Johnson, Heller, Gardner, Thune
Minority (D 10): Cantwell, RMM; Klobuchar, Blumenthal, Schatz, Markey, Booker, Udall, Manchin, Peters, Nelson

Communications, Technology, Innovation & the Internet
Majority (R 13): Wicker, Chmn; Blunt, Rubio, Ayotte, Cruz, Fischer, Moran, Sullivan, Johnson, Heller, Gardner, Daines, Thune
Minority (D 11): Schatz, RMM; Cantwell, McCaskill, Klobuchar, Blumenthal, Markey, Booker, Udall, Manchin, Peters, Nelson

Consumer Protection, Product Safety, Ins & Data Security
Majority (R 8): Moran, Chmn; Blunt, Cruz, Fischer, Heller, Gardner, Daines, Thune
Minority (D 7): Blumenthal, RMM; McCaskill, Klobuchar, Markey, Booker, Udall, Nelson

Oceans, Atmosphere, Fisheries & Coast Guard
Majority (R 7): Rubio, Chmn; Wicker, Ayotte, Cruz, Sullivan, Johnson, Thune
Minority (D 7): Booker, RMM; Cantwell, Blumenthal, Markey, Schatz, Peters, Nelson

Space, Science & Competitiveness
Majority (R 7): Cruz, Chmn; Rubio, Moran, Sullivan, Gardner, Daines, Thune
Minority (D 6): Peters, RMM; Markey, Booker, Udall, Schatz, Nelson

Surface Transportation & Merchant Marine Infrastructure, Safety & Security

Majority (R 10): Fischer, Chmn; Wicker, Blunt, Ayotte, Moran, Sullivan, Johnson, Heller, Daines, Thune
Minority (D 9): Booker, RMM; Cantwell, McCaskill, Klobuchar, Blumenthal, Schatz, Markey, Udall, Nelson

Energy & Natural Resources
energy.senate.gov

304 Dirksen
202-224-4971

Majority (R 12): Murkowski (AK), Chmn; Barrasso (WY), Risch (ID), Lee (UT), Flake (AZ), Cassidy (LA), Gardner (CO), Daines (MT), Portman (OH), Hoeven (ND), Alexander (TN), Capito (WV)
Minority (D 10): Cantwell (WA), RMM; Wyden (OR), Sanders (VT), Stabenow (MI), Franken (MN), Manchin (WV), Heinrich (NM), Hirono (HI), King (ME), Warren (MA)

SUBCOMMITTEES

Energy

Majority (R 10): Risch, Chmn; Flake, Daines, Cassidy, Gardner, Hoeven, Alexander, Portman, Capito, Murkowski
Minority (D 9): Manchin, RMM; Sanders, Stabenow, Franken, Heinrich, Hirono, King, Warren, Cantwell

National Parks

Majority (R 8): Cassidy, Chmn; Portman, Barrasso, Alexander, Lee, Hoeven, Capito, Murkowski
Minority (D 7): Heinrich, RMM; Wyden, Sanders, Stabenow, King, Warren, Cantwell

Public Lands, Forests & Mining

Majority (R 11): Barrasso, Chmn; Capito, Risch, Lee, Daines, Cassidy, Gardner, Hoeven, Flake, Alexander, Murkowski
Minority (D 8): Wyden, RMM; Stabenow, Franken, Manchin, Heinrich, Hirono, Warren, Cantwell

Water & Power

Majority (R 8): Lee, Chmn; Flake, Barrasso, Risch, Daines, Gardner, Portman, Murkowski
Minority (D 7): Hirono, RMM; Wyden, Sanders, Franken, Manchin, King, Cantwell

Environment & Public Works
epw.senate.gov

410 Dirksen
202-224-6176

Majority (R 11): Inhofe (OK), Chmn; Vitter (LA), Barrasso (WY), Capito (WV), Crapo (ID), Boozman (AR), Sessions (AL), Wicker (MS), Fischer (NE), Rounds (SD), Sullivan (AK)
Minority (D 9): Boxer (CA), RMM; Carper (DE), Cardin (MD), Sanders (VT), Whitehouse (RI), Merkley (OR), Gillibrand (NY), Booker (NJ), Markey (MA)

SUBCOMMITTEES

Clean Air & Nuclear Safety

Majority (R 8): Capito, Chmn; Vitter, Barrasso, Crapo, Sessions, Wicker, Fischer, Inhofe
Minority (D 7): Carper, RMM; Cardin, Sanders, Whitehouse, Merkley, Markey, Boxer

Fisheries, Water, and Wildlife

Majority (R 9): Sullivan, Chmn; Barrasso, Capito, Boozman, Sessions, Wicker, Fischer, Rounds, Inhofe
Minority (D 8): Whitehouse, RMM; Carper, Cardin, Sanders, Gillibrand, Booker, Markey, Boxer

Superfund, Waste Management, & Regulatory Oversight

Majority (R 6): Rounds, Chmn; Vitter, Crapo, Boozman, Sullivan, Inhofe
Minority (D 5): Markey, RMM; Carper, Merkley, Booker, Boxer

Transportation & Infrastructure

Majority (R 9): Vitter, Chmn; Barrasso, Capito, Crapo, Boozman, Sessions, Wicker, Fischer, Inhofe
Minority (D 7): Boxer, RMM; Carper, Cardin, Sanders, Whitehouse, Merkley, Gillibrand

Finance
finance.senate.gov

219 Dirksen
202-224-4515

Majority (R 14): Hatch (UT), Chmn; Grassley (IA), Crapo (ID), Roberts (KS), Enzi (WY), Cornyn (TX), Thune (SD), Burr (NC), Isakson (GA), Portman (OH), Toomey (PA), Coats (IN), Heller (NV), Scott (SC)
Minority (D 12): Wyden (OR), RMM; Schumer (NY), Stabenow (MI), Cantwell (WA), Nelson (FL), Menendez (NJ), Carper (DE), Cardin (MD), Brown (OH), Bennet (CO), Casey (PA), Warner (VA)

SUBCOMMITTEES

Energy, Natural Resources & Infrastructure
Majority (R 8): Coats, Chmn; Grassley, Crapo, Enzi, Cornyn, Thune, Burr, Hatch
Minority (D 6): Bennet, RMM; Cantwell, Nelson, Carper, Casey, Wyden

Fiscal Responsibility & Economic Growth
Majority (R 4): Portman, Chmn; Crapo, Burr, Hatch
Minority (D 2): Warner, RMM; Wyden

Health Care
Majority (R 9): Toomey, Chmn; Grassley, Roberts, Enzi, Burr, Coats, Heller, Scott, Hatch
Minority (D 7): Stabenow, RMM; Cantwell, Menendez, Cardin, Brown, Warner, Wyden

International Trade, Customs & Global Competitiveness
Majority (R 7): Cornyn, Chmn; Grassley, Roberts, Thune, Isakson, Portman, Hatch
Minority (D 4): Wyden, RMM; Schumer, Stabenow, Nelson

Social Security, Pensions & Family Policy
Majority (R 5): Heller, Chmn; Isakson, Toomey, Scott, Hatch
Minority (D 3): Brown, RMM; Schumer, Wyden

Taxation & IRS Oversight
Majority (R 12): Crapo, Chmn; Roberts, Enzi, Cornyn, Thune, Isakson, Portman, Toomey, Coats, Heller, Scott, Hatch
Minority (D 9): Casey, RMM; Schumer, Nelson, Menendez, Carper, Cardin, Bennet, Warner, Wyden

Foreign Relations
foreign.senate.gov

423 Dirksen
202-224-4651

Majority (R 10): Corker (TN), Chmn; Risch (ID), Rubio (FL), Johnson (WI), Flake (AZ), Gardner (CO), Perdue (GA),
   Isakson (GA), Paul (KY), Barrasso (WY)
Minority (D 9): Cardin (MD), RMM; Boxer (CA), Menendez (NJ), Shaheen (NH), Coons (DE), Udall (NM),
   Murphy (CT), Kaine (VA), Markey (MA)

SUBCOMMITTEES

Africa & Global Health Policy
Majority (R 6): Flake, Chmn; Isakson, Paul, Barrasso, Rubio, Corker
Minority (D 5): Markey, RMM; Coons, Udall, Cardin, Menendez

East Asia, the Pacific & International Cybersecurity Policy
Majority (R 6): Gardner, Chmn; Rubio, Johnson, Isakson, Flake, Corker
Minority (D 5): Cardin, RMM; Boxer, Coons, Udall, Menendez

Europe & Regional Security Cooperation
Majority (R 6): Johnson, Chmn; Paul, Risch, Gardner, Barrasso, Corker
Minority (D 5): Shaheen, RMM; Murphy, Kaine, Markey, Menendez

Multilateral International Development, Multilateral Institutions, & International Economic, Energy, & Environmental Policy
Majority (R 6): Barrasso, Chmn; Perdue, Risch, Flake, Gardner, Corker
Minority (D 5): Udall, RMM; Boxer, Shaheen, Markey, Menendez

Near East, South Asia, Central Asia & Counterterrorism
Majority (R 6): Risch, Chmn; Perdue, Paul, Rubio, Johnson, Corker
Minority (D 5): Murphy, RMM; Cardin, Shaheen, Kaine, Menendez

State Dept & USAID Management, International Operations, & Bilateral International Development
Majority (R 6): Perdue, Chmn; Risch, Isakson, Johnson, Paul, Corker
Minority (D 5): Kaine, RMM; Boxer, Coons, Murphy, Menendez

Western Hemisphere, Transational Crime, Civilian Security, Democracy, Human Rights, & Global Women's Issues
Majority (R 6): Rubio, Chmn; Flake, Gardner, Perdue, Isakson, Corker
Minority (D 5): Boxer, RMM; Udall, Kaine, Markey, Menendez

Health, Education, Labor & Pensions
help.senate.gov

835 Hart
202-224-5375

Majority (R 12): Alexander (TN), Chmn; Enzi (WY), Burr (NC), Isakson (GA), Paul (KY), Collins (ME), Murkowski (AK), Kirk (IL), Scott (SC), Hatch (UT), Roberts (KS), Cassidy (LA)
Minority (D 10): Murray (WA), RMM; Mikulski (MD), Sanders (VT), Casey (PA), Franken (MN), Bennet (CO), Whitehouse (RI), Baldwin (WI), Murphy (CT), Warren (MA)

SUBCOMMITTEES

Children & Families
Majority (R 8): Paul, Chmn; Murkowski, Burr, Kirk, Hatch, Roberts, Cassidy, Alexander
Minority (D 6): Casey, RMM; Mikulski, Sanders, Franken, Bennet, Murray

Employment & Workplace Safety
Majority (R 7): Isakson, Chmn; Paul, Scott, Kirk, Roberts, Cassidy, Alexander
Minority (D 5): Franken, RMM; Casey, Whitehouse, Baldwin, Murray

Primary Health & Retirement Security
Majority (R 10): Enzi, Chmn; Burr, Collins, Kirk, Scott, Hatch, Roberts, Cassidy, Murkowski, Alexander
Minority (D 8): Sanders, RMM; Mikulski, Bennet, Whitehouse, Baldwin, Murphy, Warren, Murray

Homeland Security & Government Affairs
hsgac.senate.gov

340 Dirksen
202-224-4751

Majority (R 9): Johnson (WI), Chmn; McCain (AZ), Portman (OH), Paul (KY), Lankford (OK), Enzi (WY), Ayotte (NH), Ernst (IA), Sasse (NE)
Minority (D 7): Carper (DE), RMM; McCaskill (MO), Tester (MT), Baldwin (WI), Heitkamp (ND), Booker (NJ), Peters (MI)

SUBCOMMITTEES

Federal Spending Oversight & Emergency Management
Majority (R 7): Paul, Chmn; Lankford, Enzi, Ayotte, Ernst, Sasse, Johnson
Minority (D 5): Baldwin, RMM; McCaskill, Booker, Peters, Carper

Investigations
Majority (R 7): Portman, Chmn; McCain, Paul, Lankford, Ayotte, Sasse, Johnson
Minority (D 5): McCaskill, RMM; Tester, Baldwin, Heitkamp, Carper

Regulatory Affairs & Federal Management
Majority (R 7): Lankford, Chmn; McCain, Portman, Enzi, Ernst, Sasse, Johnson
Minority (D 5): Heitkamp, RMM; Tester, Booker, Peters, Carper

Judiciary
judiciary.senate.gov

224 Dirksen
202-224-5225

Majority (R 11): Grassley (IA), Chmn; Hatch (UT), Sessions (AL), Graham (SC), Cornyn (TX), Lee (UT), Cruz (TX), Flake (AZ), Vitter (LA), Perdue (GA), Tillis (NC)
Minority (D 9): Leahy (VT), RMM; Feinstein (CA), Schumer (NY), Durbin (IL), Whitehouse (RI), Klobuchar (MN), Franken (MN), Coons (DE), Blumenthal (CT)

SUBCOMMITTEES

Antitrust, Competition Policy & Consumer Rights
Majority (R 5): Lee, Chmn; Perdue, Tillis, Grassley, Hatch
Minority (D 4): Klobuchar, RMM; Coons, Franken, Blumenthal

Constitution
Majority (R 5): Cornyn, Chmn; Tillis, Graham, Cruz, Vitter
Minority (D 4): Durbin, RMM; Whitehouse, Coons, Franken

Crime & Terrorism
Majority (R 5): Graham, Chmn; Vitter, Sessions, Cornyn, Flake
Minority (D 4): Whitehouse, RMM; Schumer, Klobuchar, Franken

Immigration & the National Interest
Majority (R 8): Sessions, Chmn; Vitter, Perdue, Grassley, Cornyn, Lee, Cruz, Tillis
Minority (D 7): Schumer, RMM; Leahy, Feinstein, Durbin, Klobuchar, Franken, Blumenthal

Oversight, Agency Action, Federal Rights & Federal Courts
Majority (R 8): Cruz, Chmn; Grassley, Hatch, Sessions, Flake, Graham, Lee, Vitter
Minority (D 7): Coons, RMM; Feinstein, Durbin, Schumer, Whitehouse, Klobuchar, Blumenthal

Privacy, Technology & the Law
Majority (R 6): Flake, Chmn; Hatch, Perdue, Lee, Tillis, Graham
Minority (D 5): Franken, RMM; Feinstein, Schumer, Whitehouse, Coons

Rules & Administration
rules.senate.gov

305 Russell
202-224-6352

Majority (R 10): Blunt (MO), Chmn; Alexander (TN), McConnell (KY), Cochran (MS), Roberts (KS), Shelby (AL), Cruz (TX), Capito (WV), Boozman (AR), Wicker (MS)
Minority (D 8): Schumer (NY), RMM; Feinstein (CA), Durbin (IL), Udall (NM), Warner (VA), Leahy (VT), Klobuchar (MN), King (ME)

Small Business & Entrepreneurship
sbc.senate.gov

428A Russell
202-224-5175

Majority (R 10): Vitter (LA), Chmn; Risch (ID), Rubio (FL), Paul (KY), Scott (SC), Fischer (NE), Gardner (CO), Ernst (IA), Ayotte (NH), Enzi (WY)
Minority (D 9): Shaheen (NH), RMM; Cantwell (WA), Cardin (MD), Heitkamp (ND), Markey (MA), Booker (NJ), Coons (DE), Hirono (HI), Peters (MI)

Veterans' Affairs
veterans.senate.gov

412 Russell
202-224-9126

Majority (R 8): Isakson (GA), Chmn; Moran (KS), Boozman (AR), Heller (NV), Cassidy (LA), Rounds (SD), Tillis (NC), Sullivan (AK)
Minority (D 7): Blumenthal (CT), RMM; Murray (WA), Sanders (VT), Brown (OH), Tester (MT), Hirono (HI), Manchin (WV)

SPECIAL AND SELECT

Aging (Special)
aging.senate.gov

G31 Dirksen
202-224-5364

Majority (R 11): Collins (ME), Chmn; Hatch (UT), Kirk (IL), Flake (AZ), Corner (TN), Heller (NV), Scott (SC), Cotton (AR), Perdue (GA), Tillis (NC), Sasse (NE)
Minority (D 9): McCaskill (MO), RMM; Nelson (FL), Casey (PA), Whitehouse (RI), Gillibrand (NY), Blumenthal (CT), Donnelly (IN), Warren (MA), Kaine (VA)

Ethics (Select)
ethics.senate.gov

220 Hart
202-224-2981

Majority (R 3): Isakson (GA), Chmn; Roberts (KS), Risch (ID)
Minority (D 3): Boxer (CA), RMM; Coons (DE), Schatz (HI)

Indian Affairs (Special)
indian.senate.gov

838 Hart
202-224-2251

Majority (R 8): Barrasso (WY), Chmn; McCain (AZ), Murkowski (AK), Hoeven (ND), Lankford (OK), Daines (MT), Crapo (ID), Moran (KS)
Minority (D 6): Tester (MT), RMM ; Cantwell (WA), Udall (NM), Franken (MN), Schatz (HI), Heitkamp (ND)

Intelligence (Select)
intelligence.senate.gov

211 Hart
202-224-1700

Majority (R 8): Burr (NC), Chmn; Risch (ID), Coats (IN), Rubio (FL), Collins (ME), Blunt (MO), Lankford (OK), Cotton (AR)
Minority (D 7): Feinstein (CA), RMM; Wyden (OR), Mikulski (MD), Warner (VA), Heinrich (NM), King (ME), Hirono (HI)

HOUSE COMMITTEES

Agriculture
agriculture.house.gov

1301 LHOB
202-225-2171

Majority (R 25): Conaway (TX), Chmn; Neugebauer (TX), Goodlatte (VA), Lucas (OK), King (IA), Rogers (AL), Thompson (PA), Gibbs (OH), Scott (GA), Crawford (AR), DesJarlais (TN), Gibson (NY), Hartzler (MO), Benishek (MI), Denham (CA), LaMalfa (CA), Davis (IL), Yoho (FL), Walorski (IN), Allen (GA), Bost (IL), Rouzer (NC), Abraham (LA), Moolenaar (MI), Newhouse (WA)

Minority (D 19): Peterson (MN), RMM; Scott (GA), Costa (CA), Walz (MN), Fudge (OH), McGovern (MA), DelBene (WA), Vela (TX), Lujan Grisham (NM), Kuster (NH), Nolan (MN), Bustos (IL), Maloney (NY), Kirkpatick (AZ), Aguilar (CA), Plaskett (VI), Adams (NC), Graham (FL), Ashford (NE)

SUBCOMMITTEES

Biotechnology, Horticulture & Research
Majority (R 8): Davis (IL), Chmn; Thompson (PA), Scott (GA), Gibson (NY), Denham (CA), Yoho (FL), Moolenaar (MI), Newhouse (WA)
Minority (D 5): DelBene (WA), RMM; Fudge (OH), McGovern (MA), Kuster (NH), Graham (FL)

Commodity Exchanges, Energy & Credit
Majority (R 7): Scott, Austin (GA), Chmn; Goodlatte (VA), Lucas (OK), Neugebauer (TX), Rogers (AL), LaMalfa (CA), Davis (IL)
Minority (D 5): Scott, David (GA), RMM; Vela (TX), Maloney (NY), Kirkpatick (AZ), Aguilar (CA)

Conservation & Forestry
Majority (R 8): Thompson (PA), Chmn; Lucas (OK), King (IA), DesJarlais (TN), Gibson (NY), Benishek (MI), Allen (GA), Bost (IL)
Minority (D 5): Lujan Grisham (NM), RMM; Kuster (NH), Nolan (MN), DelBene (WA), Kirkpatick (AZ)

General Farm Commodities & Risk Management
Majority (R 12): Crawford (AR), Chmn; Lucas (OK), Neugebauer (TX), Rogers (AL), Gibbs (OH), Scott (GA), Denham (CA), LaMalfa (CA), Walorski (IN), Allen (GA), Bost (IL), Abraham (LA)
Minority (D 8): Walz (MN), RMM; Bustos (IL), Graham (FL), Ashford (NE), Scott (GA), Costa (CA), Maloney (NY), Kirkpatick (AZ)

Livestock & Foreign Agriculture
Majority (R 7): Rouzer (NC), Chmn; Goodlatte (VA), King (IA), DesJarlais (TN), Hartzler (MO), Yoho (FL), Newhouse (WA)
Minority (D 5): Costa (CA), RMM; Plaskett (VI), Vela (TX), Nolan (MN), Bustos (IL)

Nutrition
Majority (R 12): Walorski (IN), Chmn; Neugebauer (TX), Thompson (PA), Gibbs (OH), Crawford (AR), Hartzler (MO), Benishek (MI), Davis (IL), Yoho (FL), Rouzer (NC), Abraham (LA), Moolenaar (MI)
Minority (D 8): McGovern (MA), RMM; Fudge (OH), Adams (NC), Lujan Grisham (NM), Aguilar (CA), Plaskett (VI), Ashford (NE), DelBene (WA)

Appropriations
appropriations.house.gov

H-305 The Capitol
202-225-2771

Majority (R 30): Rogers (KY), Chmn; Frelinghuysen (NJ), Aderholt (AL), Granger (TX), Simpson (ID), Culberson (TX), Crenshaw (FL), Carter (TX), Calvert (CA), Cole (OK), Diaz-Balart (FL), Dent (PA), Graves (GA), Yoder (KS), Womack (AR), Fortenberry (NE), Rooney (FL), Fleischmann (TN), Herrera Beutler (WA), Joyce (OH), Valadao (CA), Harris (MD), Roby (AL), Amodei (NV), Stewart (UT), Rigell (VA), Jolly (FL), Young (IA), Jenkins (WV), Palazzo (MS)

Minority (D 21): Lowey (NY), RMM; Kaptur (OH), Visclosky (IN), Serrano (NY), DeLauro (CT), Price (NC), Roybal-Allard (CA), Farr (CA), Fattah (PA), Bishop (GA), Lee (CA), Honda (CA), McCollum (MN), Israel (NY), Ryan (OH), Ruppersberger (MD), Wasserman Schultz (FL), Cuellar (TX), Pingree (ME), Quigley (IL), Kilmer (WA)

SUBCOMMITTEES

Agriculture, Rural Development, FDA & Related Agencies
Majority (R 8): Aderholt (AL), Chmn; Valadao (CA), Yoder (KS), Rooney (FL), Harris (MD), Young (IA), Palazzo (MS), Rogers (KY)
Minority (D 5): Farr (CA), RMM; DeLauro (CT), Bishop (GA), Pingree (ME), Lowey (NY)

Commerce, Justice, Science & Related Agencies
Majority (R 8): Culberson (TX), Chmn; Aderholt (AL), Carter (TX), Herrera Beutler (WA), Roby (AL), Jolly (FL), Palazzo (MS), Rogers (KY)
Minority (D 5): Honda (CA), RMM; Fattah (PA), Serrano (NY), Kilmer (WA), Lowey (NY)

Defense
Majority (R 11): Frelinghuysen (NJ), Chmn; Granger (TX), Crenshaw (FL), Calvert (CA), Cole (OK), Womack (AR), Aderholt (AL), Carter (TX), Diaz-Balart (FL), Graves (GA), Rogers (KY)
Minority (D 7): Visclosky (IN), RMM; McCollum (MN), Israel (NY), Ryan (OH), Ruppersberger (MD), Kaptur (OH), Lowey (NY)

Energy & Water Development & Related Agencies
Majority (R 9): Simpson (ID), Chmn; Fleischmann (TN), Frelinghuysen (NJ), Calvert (CA), Fortenberry (NE), Granger (TX), Herrera Beutler (WA), Valadao (CA), Rogers (KY)
Minority (D 5): Kaptur (OH), RMM; Visclosky (IN), Honda (CA), Roybal-Allard (CA), Lowey (NY)

Financial Services & General Government
Majority (R 8): Crenshaw (FL), Chmn; Herrera Beutler (WA), Graves (GA), Yoder (KS), Womack (AR), Amodei (NV), Rigell (VA), Rogers (KY)
Minority (D 5): Serrano (NY), RMM; Quigley (IL), Fattah (PA), Bishop (GA), Lowey (NY)

Homeland Security
Majority (R 26): Carter (TX), Chmn; Frelinghuysen (NJ), Culberson (TX), Fleischmann (TN), Harris (MD), Stewart (UT), Young (IA), Rogers (KY)
Minority (D 17): Roybal-Allard (CA), RMM; Price (NC), Cuellar (TX), Kaptur (OH), Lowey (NY)

Interior, Environment & Related Agencies
Majority (R 8): Calvert (CA), Chmn; Simpson (ID), Cole (OK), Joyce (OH), Stewart (UT), Amodei (NV), Jenkins (WV), Rogers (KY)
Minority (D 5): McCollum (MN), RMM; Pingree (ME), Kilmer (WA), Israel (NY), Lowey (NY)

Labor, Health & Human Services, Education & Related Agencies
Majority (R 9): Cole (OK), Chmn; Womack (AR), Simpson (ID), Fleischmann (TN), Harris (MD), Roby (AL), Dent (PA), Rigell (VA), Rogers (KY)
Minority (D 5): DeLauro (CT), RMM; Roybal-Allard (CA), Lee (CA), Fattah (PA), Lowey (NY)

Legislative Branch
Majority (R 6): Graves (GA), Chmn; Amodei (NV), Rigell (VA), Jenkins (WV), Palazzo (MS), Rogers (KY)
Minority (D 4): Wasserman Schultz (FL), RMM; Farr (CA), McCollum (MN), Lowey (NY)

Military Construction, Veterans Affairs & Related Agencies
Majority (R 8): Dent (PA), Chmn; Fortenberry (NE), Rooney (FL), Roby (AL), Valadao (CA), Joyce (OH), Jolly (FL), Rogers (KY)
Minority (D 5): Bishop (GA), RMM; Farr (CA), Price (NC), Lee (CA), Lowey (NY)

State, Foreign Operations & Related Programs
Majority (R 8): Granger (TX), Chmn; Dent (PA), Diaz-Balart (FL), Crenshaw (FL), Rooney (FL), Fortenberry (NE), Stewart (UT), Rogers (KY)
Minority (D 5): Lowey (NY), RMM; Lee (CA), Ruppersberger (MD), Wasserman Schultz (FL), Serrano (NY)

Transportation, HUD & Related Agencies
Majority (R 8): Diaz-Balart (FL), Chmn; Yoder (KS), Joyce (OH), Culberson (TX), Jolly (FL), Young (IA), Jenkins (WV), Rogers (KY)
Minority (D 5): Price (NC), RMM; Quigley (IL), Ryan (OH), Cuellar (TX), Lowey (NY)

Armed Services
armedservices.house.gov

2216 RHOB
202-225-4151

Majority (R 36): Thornberry (TX), Chmn; Jones (NC), Forbes (VA), Miller (FL), Wilson (SC), LoBiondo (NJ), Bishop (UT), Turner (OH), Kline (MN), Rogers (AL), Franks (AZ), Shuster (PA), Conaway (TX), Lamborn (CO), Wittman (VA), Hunter (CA), Fleming (LA), Coffman (CO), Gibson (NY), Hartzler (MO), Heck (NV), Scott (GA), Brooks (AL), Nugent (FL), Cook (CA), Bridenstine (OK), Wenstrup (OH), Walorski (IN), Byrne (AL), Graves (MO), Zinke (MT), Stefanik (NY), McSally (AZ), Knight (CA), MacArthur (NJ), Russell (OK)

Minority (D 27): Smith (WA), RMM; Sanchez, Loretta (CA), Brady (PA), Davis (CA), Langevin (RI), Larsen (WA), Cooper (TN), Bordallo (GU), Courtney (CT), Tsongas (MA), Garamendi (CA), Johnson (GA), Speier (CA), Castro (TX), Duckworth (IL), Peters (CA), Veasey (TX), Gabbard (HI), Walz (MN), O'Rourke (TX), Norcross (NJ), Gallego (AZ), Takai (HI), Graham (FL), Ashford (NE), Moulton (MA), Aguilar (CA)

SUBCOMMITTEES

Emerging Threats & Capabilities
Majority (R 11): Wilson (SC), Chmn; Franks (AZ), Kline (MN), Shuster (PA), Hunter (CA), Nugent (FL), Zinke (MT), Lamborn (CO), Brooks (AL), Byrne (AL), Stefanik (NY)

Minority (D 8): Langevin (RI), RMM; Cooper (TN), Garamendi (CA), Castro (TX), Veasey (TX), Norcross (NJ), Ashford (NE), Aguilar (CA)

Military Personnel
Majority (R 8): Heck (NV), Chmn; MacArthur (NJ), Jones (NC), Kline (MN), Coffman (CO), Stefanik (NY), Cook (CA), Knight (CA)

Minority (D 6): Davis (CA), RMM; Brady (PA), Tsongas (MA), Speier (CA), Walz (MN), O'Rourke (TX)

Oversight & Investigations
Majority (R 6): Hartzler (MO), Chmn; Miller (FL), Conaway (TX), Heck (NV), Scott (GA), McSally (AZ)

Minority (D 4): Speier (CA), RMM; Cooper (TN), Johnson (GA), Graham (FL)

Readiness
Majority (R 12): Wittman (VA), Chmn; Stefanik (NY), Bishop (UT), Hartzler (MO), Scott (GA), LoBiondo (NJ), Rogers (AL), Gibson (NY), Nugent (FL), Wenstrup (OH), Graves (MO), Russell (OK)

Minority (D 9): Bordallo (GU), RMM; Davis (CA), Courtney (CT), Castro (TX), Duckworth (IL), Peters (CA), Gabbard (HI), O'Rourke (TX), Gallego (AZ)

Seapower & Projection Forces
Majority (R 12): Forbes (VA), Chmn; Hunter (CA), Conaway (TX), Byrne (AL), Wittman (VA), Hartzler (MO), Cook (CA), Bridenstine (OK), Walorski (IN), Zinke (MT), Knight (CA), Russell (OK)

Minority (D 9): Courtney (CT), RMM; Langevin (RI), Larsen (WA), Bordallo (GU), Johnson (GA), Peters (CA), Gabbard (HI), Graham (FL), Moulton (MA)

Strategic Forces
Majority (R 10): Rogers (AL), Chmn; Lamborn (CO), Franks (AZ), Coffman (CO), Brooks (AL), Bridenstine (OK), Forbes (VA), Bishop (UT), Turner (OH), Fleming (LA)

Minority (D 7): Cooper (TN), RMM; Sanchez, Loretta (CA), Larsen (WA), Garamendi (CA), Takai (HI), Ashford (NE), Aguilar (CA)

Tactical Air & Land Forces
Majority (R 13): Turner (OH), Chmn; Cook (CA), LoBiondo (NJ), Fleming (LA), Gibson (NY), Wenstrup (OH), Walorski (IN), Graves (MO), McSally (AZ), Knight (CA), MacArthur (NJ), Jones (NC), Wilson (SC)

Minority (D 11): Sanchez, Loretta (CA), RMM; Tsongas (MA), Johnson (GA), Duckworth (IL), Veasey (TX), Walz (MN), Norcross (NJ), Gallego (AZ), Takai (HI), Graham (FL), Moulton (MA)

Budget
budget.house.gov

207 CHOB
202-226-7270

Majority (R 22): Price (GA), Chmn; Rokita (IN), Garrett (NJ), Diaz-Balart (FL), Cole (OK), McClintock (CA), Black (TN), Woodall (GA), Blackburn (TN), Hartzler (MO), Rice (SC), Stutzman (IN), Sanford (SC), Womack (AR), Brat (VA), Blum (IA), Mooney (WV), Grothman (WI), Palmer (AL), Moolenaar (MI), Westerman (AR), Buchanan (FL)

Minority (D 14): Van Hollen (MD), RMM; Yarmuth (KY), Pascrell (NJ), Ryan (OH), Moore (WI), Castor (FL), McDermott (WA), Lee (CA), Pocan (WI), Lujan Grisham (NM), Dingell (MI), Lieu (CA), Norcross (NJ), Moulton (MA)

Education & the Workforce
edworkforce.house.gov

2181 RHOB
202-225-4527

Majority (R 22): Kline (MN), Chmn; Wilson (SC), Foxx (NC), Hunter (CA), Roe (TN), Thompson (PA), Walberg
(MI), Salmon (AZ), Guthrie (KY), Rokita (IN), Barletta (PA), Heck (NV), Messer (IN), Byrne (AL), Brat (VA),
Carter (GA), Bishop (MI), Grothman (WI), Russell (OK), Curbelo (FL), Stefanik (NY), Allen (GA)
Minority (D 16): Scott (VA), RMM; Hinojosa (TX), Davis (CA), Grijalva (AZ), Courtney (CT), Fudge (OH), Polis
(CO), Sablan (MP), Wilson (FL), Bonamici (OR), Pocan (WI), Takano (CA), Jeffries (NY), Clark (MA), Adams
(NC), DeSaulnier (CA)

SUBCOMMITTEES

Early Childhood, Elementary & Secondary Education
Majority (R 9): Rokita (IN), Chmn; Hunter (CA), Thompson (PA), Brat (VA), Carter (GA), Bishop (MI),
Grothman (WI), Russell (OK), Curbelo (FL)
Minority (D 7): Fudge (OH), RMM; Davis (CA), Grijalva (AZ), Sablan (MP), Bonamici (OR), Takano (CA), Clark (MA)

Health, Employment, Labor & Pensions
Majority (R 13): Roe (TN), Chmn; Wilson (SC), Foxx (NC), Walberg (MI), Salmon (AZ), Guthrie (KY), Barletta
(PA), Heck (NV), Messer (IN), Byrne (AL), Carter (GA), Grothman (WI), Allen (GA)
Minority (D 10): Polis (CO), RMM; Courtney (CT), Pocan (WI), Hinojosa (TX), Sablan (MP), Wilson (FL),
Bonamici (OR), Takano (CA), Jeffries (NY), Scott (VA)

Higher Education & Workforce Training
Majority (R 11): Foxx (NC), Chmn; Roe (TN), Salmon (AZ), Guthrie (KY), Barletta (PA), Heck (NV), Messer
(IN), Byrne (AL), Curbelo (FL), Stefanik (NY), Allen (GA)
Minority (D 8): Hinojosa (TX), RMM; Jeffries (NY), Adams (NC), DeSaulnier (CA), Davis (CA), Grijalva (AZ),
Courtney (CT), Polis (CO)

Workforce Protections
Majority (R 8): Walberg (MI), Chmn; Hunter (CA), Thompson (PA), Rokita (IN), Brat (VA), Bishop (MI), Russell
(OK), Stefanik (NY)
Minority (D 6): Wilson (FL), RMM; Pocan (WI), Clark (MA), Adams (NC), DeSaulnier (CA), Fudge (OH)

Energy & Commerce
energycommerce.house.gov

2125 RHOB
202-225-2927

Majority (R 31): Upton (MI), Chmn; Blackburn (TN), Barton (TX), Whitfield (KY), Shimkus (IL), Pitts (PA),
Walden (OR), Murphy (PA), Burgess (TX), Scalise (LA), Latta (OH), McMorris Rodgers (WA), Harper (MS),
Lance (NJ), Guthrie (KY), Olson (TX), McKinley (WV), Pompeo (KS), Kinzinger (IL), Griffith (VA), Bilirakis
(FL), Johnson (OH), Long (MO), Ellmers (NC), Bucshon (IN), Flores (TX), Brooks (IN), Mullin (OK), Hudson
(NC), Collins (NY), Cramer (ND)
Minority (D 23): Pallone (NJ), RMM; Rush (IL), Eshoo (CA), Engel (NY), Green (TX), DeGette (CO), Capps
(CA), Doyle (PA), Schakowsky (IL), Butterfield (NC), Matsui (CA), Castor (FL), Sarbanes (MD), McNerney
(CA), Welch (VT), Lujan (NM), Tonko (NY), Yarmuth (KY), Clarke (NY), Loebsack (IA), Schrader (OR),
Kennedy (MA), Cardenas (CA)

SUBCOMMITTEES

Commerce, Manufacturing & Trade
Majority (R 12): Burgess (TX), Chmn; Lance (NJ), Blackburn (TN), Harper (MS), Guthrie (KY), Olson (TX),
Pompeo (KS), Kinzinger (IL), Bilirakis (FL), Brooks (IN), Mullin (OK), Upton (MI)
Minority (D 8): Schakowsky (IL), RMM; Clarke (NY), Kennedy (MA), Cardenas (CA), Rush (IL), Butterfield
(NC), Welch (VT), Pallone (NJ)

Communications & Technology
Majority (R 18): Walden (OR), Chmn; Latta (OH), Shimkus (IL), Blackburn (TN), Scalise (LA), Lance (NJ),
Guthrie (KY), Olson (TX), Pompeo (KS), Kinzinger (IL), Bilirakis (FL), Johnson (OH), Long (MO), Ellmers
(NC), Collins (NY), Cramer (ND), Barton (TX), Upton (MI)
Minority (D 13): Eshoo (CA), RMM; Doyle (PA), Welch (VT), Yarmuth (KY), Clarke (NY), Loebsack (IA), Rush
(IL), DeGette (CO), Butterfield (NC), Matsui (CA), McNerney (CA), Lujan (NM), Pallone (NJ)

Energy & Power
Majority (R 18): Whitfield (KY), Chmn; Olson (TX), Shimkus (IL), Pitts (PA), Latta (OH), Harper (MS),
McKinley (WV), Pompeo (KS), Kinzinger (IL), Griffith (VA), Johnson (OH), Long (MO), Ellmers (NC), Flores
(TX), Mullin (OK), Hudson (NC), Barton (TX), Upton (MI)

Minority (D 13): Rush (IL), RMM; McNerney (CA), Tonko (NY), Engel (NY), Green (TX), Capps (CA), Doyle (PA), Castor (FL), Sarbanes (MD), Welch (VT), Yarmuth (KY), Loebsack (IA), Pallone (NJ)

Environment & Economy
Majority (R 13): Shimkus (IL), Chmn; Harper (MS), Whitfield (KY), Pitts (PA), Murphy (PA), Latta (OH), McKinley (WV), Johnson (OH), Bucshon (IN), Flores (TX), Hudson (NC), Cramer (ND), Upton (MI)
Minority (D 9): Tonko (NY), RMM; Schrader (OR), Green (TX), DeGette (CO), Capps (CA), Doyle (PA), McNerney (CA), Cardenas (CA), Pallone (NJ)

Health
Majority (R 18): Pitts (PA), Chmn; Guthrie (KY), Whitfield (KY), Shimkus (IL), Murphy (PA), Burgess (TX), Blackburn (TN), McMorris Rodgers (WA), Lance (NJ), Griffith (VA), Bilirakis (FL), Long (MO), Ellmers (NC), Bucshon (IN), Brooks (IN), Collins (NY), Barton (TX), Upton (MI)
Minority (D 13): Green (TX), RMM; Engel (NY), Capps (CA), Schakowsky (IL), Butterfield (NC), Castor (FL), Sarbanes (MD), Matsui (CA), Lujan (NM), Schrader (OR), Kennedy (MA), Cardenas (CA), Pallone (NJ)

Ethics
ethics.house.gov

1015 LHOB
202-225-7103

Majority (R 5): Dent (PA), Chmn; Meehan (PA), Gowdy (SC), Brooks (IN), Marchant (TX)
Minority (D 5): Sanchez, Linda (CA), RMM; Capuano (MA), Clarke (NY), Deutch (FL), Larson (CT)

Financial Services
financialservices.house.gov

2129 RHOB
202-225-7502

Majority (R 34): Hensarling (TX), Chmn; McHenry (NC), King (NY), Royce (CA), Lucas (OK), Garrett (NJ), Neugebauer (TX), Pearce (NM), Posey (FL), Fitzpatrick (PA), Westmoreland (GA), Luetkemeyer (MO), Huizenga (MI), Duffy (WI), Hurt (VA), Stivers (OH), Fincher (TN), Stutzman (IN), Mulvaney (SC), Hultgren (IL), Ross (FL), Pittenger (NC), Wagner (MO), Barr (KY), Rothfus (PA), Messer (IN), Schweikert (AZ), Guinta (NH), Tipton (CO), Williams (TX), Poliquin (ME), Love (UT), Hill (AR), Emmer (MN)
Minority (D 26): Waters (CA), RMM; Maloney (NY), Velazquez (NY), Sherman (CA), Meeks (NY), Capuano (MA), Hinojosa (TX), Clay (MO), Lynch (MA), Scott (GA), Green (TX), Cleaver (MO), Moore (WI), Ellison (MN), Perlmutter (CO), Himes (CT), Carney (DE), Sewell (AL), Foster (IL), Kildee (MI), Murphy (FL), Delaney (MD), Sinema (AZ), Beatty (OH), Heck (WA), Vargas (CA)

SUBCOMMITTEES

Capital Markets & Government Sponsored Enterprises
Majority (R 18): Garrett (NJ), Chmn; Hurt (VA), King (NY), Royce (CA), Neugebauer (TX), McHenry (NC), Huizenga (MI), Duffy (WI), Stivers (OH), Fincher (TN), Hultgren (IL), Ross (FL), Wagner (MO), Messer (IN), Schweikert (AZ), Poliquin (ME), Hill (AR), Hensarling (TX)
Minority (D 14): Maloney (NY), RMM; Sherman (CA), Hinojosa (TX), Lynch (MA), Perlmutter (CO), Scott (GA), Himes (CT), Ellison (MN), Foster (IL), Meeks (NY), Carney (DE), Sewell (AL), Murphy (FL), Waters (CA)

Financial Institutions & Consumer Credit
Majority (R 18): Neugebauer (TX), Chmn; Pearce (NM), Lucas (OK), Posey (FL), Fitzpatrick (PA), Westmoreland (GA), Luetkemeyer (MO), Stutzman (IN), Mulvaney (SC), Pittenger (NC), Barr (KY), Rothfus (PA), Guinta (NH), Tipton (CO), Williams (TX), Love (UT), Emmer (MN), Hensarling (TX)
Minority (D 14): Clay (MO), RMM; Meeks (NY), Hinojosa (TX), Scott (GA), Maloney (NY), Velazquez (NY), Sherman (CA), Lynch (MA), Capuano (MA), Delaney (MD), Heck (WA), Sinema (AZ), Vargas (CA), Waters (CA)

Housing & Insurance
Majority (R 13): Luetkemeyer (MO), Chmn; Westmoreland (GA), Royce (CA), Garrett (NJ), Pearce (NM), Posey (FL), Hurt (VA), Stivers (OH), Ross (FL), Barr (KY), Rothfus (PA), Williams (TX), Hensarling (TX)
Minority (D 10): Cleaver (MO), RMM; Velazquez (NY), Capuano (MA), Clay (MO), Green (TX), Moore (WI), Ellison (MN), Beatty (OH), Kildee (MI), Waters (CA)

Monetary Policy & Trade
Majority (R 13): Huizenga (MI), Chmn; Mulvaney (SC), Lucas (OK), Pearce (NM), Westmoreland (GA), Stutzman (IN), Pittenger (NC), Messer (IN), Schweikert (AZ), Guinta (NH), Love (UT), Emmer (MN), Hensarling (TX)
Minority (D 10): Moore (WI), RMM; Foster (IL), Perlmutter (CO), Himes (CT), Carney (DE), Sewell (AL), Murphy (FL), Kildee (MI), Heck (WA), Waters (CA)

Foreign Affairs
foreignaffairs.house.gov

2170 RHOB
202-225-5021

Majority (R 25): Royce (CA), Chmn; Smith (NJ), Ros-Lehtinen (FL), Rohrabacher (CA), Chabot (OH), Wilson (SC), McCaul (TX), Poe (TX), Salmon (AZ), Issa (CA), Marino (PA), Duncan (SC), Brooks (AL), Cook (CA), Weber (TX), Perry (PA), DeSantis (FL), Meadows (NC), Yoho (FL), Clawson (FL), DesJarlais (TN), Ribble (WI), Trott (MI), Zeldin (NY), Donovan (NY)

Minority (D 19): Engel (NY), RMM; Sherman (CA), Meeks (NY), Sires (NJ), Connolly (VA), Deutch (FL), Higgins (NY), Bass (CA), Keating (MA), Cicilline (RI), Grayson (FL), Bera (CA), Lowenthal (CA), Meng (NY), Frankel (FL), Gabbard (HI), Castro (TX), Kelly (IL), Boyle (PA)

SUBCOMMITTEES

Africa, Global Health, Global Human Rights & Internat'l Orgs
Majority (R 5): Smith (NJ), Chmn; Meadows (NC), Clawson (FL), DesJarlais (TN), Royce (CA)
Minority (D 4): Bass (CA), RMM; Cicilline (RI), Bera (CA), Engel (NY)

Asia & the Pacific
Majority (R 9): Salmon (AZ), Chmn; Rohrabacher (CA), Chabot (OH), Marino (PA), Duncan (SC), Brooks (AL), Perry (PA), DesJarlais (TN), Royce (CA)
Minority (D 7): Sherman (CA), RMM; Bera (CA), Gabbard (HI), Lowenthal (CA), Connolly (VA), Meng (NY), Engel (NY)

Europe, Eurasia & Emerging Threats
Majority (R 9): Rohrabacher (CA), Chmn; Poe (TX), Marino (PA), Brooks (AL), Cook (CA), Weber (TX), Ribble (WI), Trott (MI), Royce (CA)
Minority (D 7): Meeks (NY), RMM; Sires (NJ), Deutch (FL), Keating (MA), Frankel (FL), Gabbard (HI), Engel (NY)

Middle East & North Africa
Majority (R 12): Ros-Lehtinen (FL), Chmn; Chabot (OH), Wilson (SC), Issa (CA), Weber (TX), DeSantis (FL), Meadows (NC), Yoho (FL), Clawson (FL), Trott (MI), Zeldin (NY), Royce (CA)
Minority (D 9): Deutch (FL), RMM; Connolly (VA), Higgins (NY), Cicilline (RI), Grayson (FL), Meng (NY), Frankel (FL), Boyle (PA), Engel (NY)

Terrorism, Nonproliferation & Trade
Majority (R 8): Poe (TX), Chmn; Wilson (SC), Issa (CA), Cook (CA), Perry (PA), Ribble (WI), Zeldin (NY), Royce (CA)
Minority (D 6): Keating (MA), RMM; Sherman (CA), Higgins (NY), Castro (TX), Kelly (IL), Engel (NY)

Western Hemisphere
Majority (R 8): Duncan (SC), Chmn; Smith (NJ), Ros-Lehtinen (FL), McCaul (TX), Salmon (AZ), DeSantis (FL), Yoho (FL), Royce (CA)
Minority (D 7): Sires (NJ), RMM; Castro (TX), Kelly (IL), Meeks (NY), Grayson (FL), Lowenthal (CA), Engel (NY)

Homeland Security
homeland.house.gov

H2-176 FHOB
202-226-8417

Majority (R 26): McCaul (TX), Chmn; Miller (MI), Smith (TX), King (NY), Rogers (AL), Duncan (SC), Marino (PA), Barletta (PA), Perry (PA), Clawson (FL), Katko (NY), Hurd (TX), Carter (GA), Walker (NC), Loudermilk (GA), McSally (AZ), Ratcliffe (TX), Donovan (NY)

Minority (D 17): Thompson (MS), RMM; Sanchez (CA), Jackson Lee (TX), Langevin (RI), Higgins (NY), Richmond (LA), Keating (MA), Payne (NJ), Vela (TX), Watson Coleman (NJ), Rice (NY), Torres (CA)

SUBCOMMITTEES

Border & Maritime Security
Majority (R 8): Miller (MI), Chmn; Smith (TX), Rogers (AL), Duncan (SC), Barletta (PA), Hurd (TX), McSally (AZ), McCaul (TX)
Minority (D 6): Vela (TX), RMM; Sanchez (CA), Jackson Lee (TX), Higgins (NY), Torres (CA), Thompson (MS)

Counterterrorism & Intelligence
Majority (R 6): King (NY), Chmn; Miller (MI), Barletta (PA), Katko (NY), Hurd (TX), McCaul (TX)
Minority (D 4): Higgins (NY), RMM; Keating (MA), Vela (TX), Thompson (MS)

Cybersecurity, Infrastructure Protection & Security Technologies
Majority (R 7): Ratcliffe (TX), Chmn; King (NY), Marino (PA), Perry (PA), Clawson (FL), Donovan (NY), McCaul (TX)
Minority (D 5): Richmond (LA), RMM; Sanchez (CA), Jackson Lee (TX), Langevin (RI), Thompson (MS)

Emergency Preparedness, Response & Communications
Majority (R 6): McSally (AZ), Chmn; Marino (PA), Walker (NC), Loudermilk (GA), Donovan (NY), McCaul (TX)
Minority (D 4): Payne (NJ), RMM; Watson Coleman (NJ), Rice (NY), Thompson (MS)

Oversight & Management Efficiency
Majority (R 6): Perry (PA), Chmn; Duncan (SC), Clawson (FL), Carter (GA), Loudermilk (GA), McCaul (TX)
Minority (D 4): Watson Coleman (NJ), RMM; Richmond (LA), Torres (CA), Thompson (MS)

Transportation Security
Majority (R 6): Katko (NY), Chmn; Rogers (AL), Carter (GA), Walker (NC), Ratcliffe (TX), McCaul (TX)
Minority (D 4): Rice (NY), RMM; Keating (MA), Payne (NJ), Thompson (MS)

House Administration
cha.house.gov

1309 LHOB
202-225-8281

Majority (R 6): Miller (MI), Chmn; Harper (MS), Nugent (FL), Davis (IL), Comstock (VA), Walker (NC)

Minority (D 3): Brady (PA), RMM; Lofgren (CA), Vargas (CA)

Judiciary
judiciary.house.gov

2138 RHOB
202-225-3951

Majority (R 23): Goodlatte (VA), Chmn; Sensenbrenner (WI), Smith (TX), Chabot (OH), Issa (CA), Forbes (VA), King (IA), Franks (AZ), Gohmert (TX), Jordan (OH), Poe (TX), Chaffetz (UT), Marino (PA), Gowdy (SC), Labrador (ID), Farenthold (TX), Collins (GA), DeSantis (FL), Walters (CA), Buck (CO), Ratcliffe (TX), Trott (MI), Bishop (MI)
Minority (D 16): Conyers (MI), RMM; Nadler (NY), Lofgren (CA), Jackson Lee (TX), Cohen (TN), Johnson (GA), Pierluisi (PR), Chu (CA), Deutch (FL), Gutierrez (IL), Bass (CA), Richmond (LA), DelBene (WA), Jeffries (NY), Cicilline (RI), Peters (CA)

SUBCOMMITTEES

Constitution & Civil Justice
Majority (R 6): Franks (AZ), Chmn; DeSantis (FL), King (IA), Gohmert (TX), Jordan (OH), Goodlatte (VA)
Minority (D 4): Cohen (TN), RMM; Nadler (NY), Deutch (FL), Conyers (MI)

Courts, Intellectual Property & Internet
Majority (R 15): Issa (CA), Chmn; Collins (GA), Sensenbrenner (WI), Smith (TX), Chabot (OH), Forbes (VA), Franks (AZ), Jordan (OH), Poe (TX), Chaffetz (UT), Marino (PA), Farenthold (TX), DeSantis (FL), Walters (CA), Goodlatte (VA)
Minority (D 13): Nadler (NY), RMM; Chu (CA), Deutch (FL), Bass (CA), Richmond (LA), DelBene (WA), Jeffries (NY), Cicilline (RI), Peters (CA), Lofgren (CA), Cohen (TN), Johnson (GA), Conyers (MI)

Crime, Terrorism, Homeland Security & Investigations
Majority (R 11): Sensenbrenner (WI), Chmn; Gohmert (TX), Chabot (OH), Forbes (VA), Poe (TX), Chaffetz (UT), Gowdy (SC), Labrador (ID), Buck (CO), Bishop (MI), Goodlatte (VA)
Minority (D 7): Jackson Lee (TX), RMM; Pierluisi (PR), Chu (CA), Gutierrez (IL), Bass (CA), Richmond (LA), Conyers (MI)

Immigration & Border Security
Majority (R 8): Gowdy (SC), Chmn; Labrador (ID), Smith (TX), King (IA), Buck (CO), Ratcliffe (TX), Trott (MI), Goodlatte (VA)
Minority (D 5): Lofgren (CA), RMM; Gutierrez (IL), Jackson Lee (TX), Pierluisi (PR), Conyers (MI)

Regulatory Reform, Commercial & Antitrust Law
Majority (R 9): Marino (PA), Chmn; Farenthold (TX), Issa (CA), Collins (GA), Walters (CA), Ratcliffe (TX), Trott (MI), Bishop (MI), Goodlatte (VA)
Minority (D 6): Johnson (GA), RMM; DelBene (WA), Jeffries (NY), Cicilline (RI), Peters (CA), Conyers (MI)

Natural Resources
naturalresources.house.gov

1324 LHOB
202-225-2761

Majority (R 25): Bishop (UT), Chmn; Lummis (WY), Young (AK), Gohmert (TX), Lamborn (CO), Wittman (VA), Fleming (LA), McClintock (CA), Thompson (PA), Benishek (MI), Duncan (SC), Gosar (AZ), Labrador (ID), LaMalfa (CA), Denham (CA), Cook (CA), Westerman (AR), Graves (LA), Newhouse (WA), Zinke (MT), Hice (GA), Radewagen (AS), MacArthur (NJ), Mooney (WV), Hardy (NV)

Minority (D 17): Grijalva (AZ), RMM; Napolitano (CA), Bordallo (GU), Costa (CA), Sablan (MP), Tsongas (MA), Pierluisi (PR), Huffman (CA), Ruiz (CA), Lowenthal (CA), Cartwright (PA), Beyer (VA), Gallego (AZ), Torres (CA), Dingell (MI), Capps (CA), Polis (CO)

SUBCOMMITTEES

Energy & Mineral Resources
Majority (R 17): Lamborn (CO), Chmn; Duncan (SC), Gohmert (TX), Wittman (VA), Fleming (LA), Thompson (PA), Lummis (WY), Benishek (MI), Gosar (AZ), Labrador (ID), Cook (CA), Graves (LA), Zinke (MT), Hice (GA), Mooney (WV), Hardy (NV), Bishop (UT)

Minority (D 9): Lowenthal (CA), RMM; Costa (CA), Tsongas (MA), Cartwright (PA), Beyer (VA), Gallego (AZ), Capps (CA), Polis (CO), Grijalva (AZ)

Federal Lands
Majority (R 14): McClintock (CA), Chmn; LaMalfa (CA), Young (AK), Gohmert (TX), Thompson (PA), Lummis (WY), Labrador (ID), Westerman (AR), Newhouse (WA), Zinke (MT), Hice (GA), MacArthur (NJ), Hardy (NV), Bishop (UT)

Minority (D 10): Tsongas (MA), RMM; Cartwright (PA), Beyer (VA), Pierluisi (PR), Huffman (CA), Lowenthal (CA), Dingell (MI), Capps (CA), Polis (CO), Grijalva (AZ)

Indian, Insular & Alaska Native Affairs
Majority (R 8): Young (AK), Chmn; Radewagen (AS), Benishek (MI), Gosar (AZ), LaMalfa (CA), Denham (CA), Cook (CA), Bishop (UT)

Minority (D 6): Ruiz (CA), RMM; Bordallo (GU), Sablan (MP), Pierluisi (PR), Torres (CA), Grijalva (AZ)

Water, Power & Oceans
Majority (R 13): Fleming (LA), Chmn; Gosar (AZ), Young (AK), Wittman (VA), McClintock (CA), Lummis (WY), Duncan (SC), LaMalfa (CA), Denham (CA), Graves (LA), Newhouse (WA), MacArthur (NJ), Bishop (UT)

Minority (D 11): Huffman (CA), RMM; Napolitano (CA), Costa (CA), Gallego (AZ), Bordallo (GU), Sablan (MP), Ruiz (CA), Lowenthal (CA), Torres (CA), Dingell (MI), Grijalva (AZ)

Oversight & Government Reform
oversight.house.gov

2157 RHOB
202-225-5074

Majority (R 25): Chaffetz (UT), Chmn; Mica (FL), Turner (OH), Duncan (TN), Jordan (OH), Walberg (MI), Amash (MI), Gosar (AZ), DesJarlais (TN), Gowdy (SC), Farenthold (TX), Lummis (WY), Massie (KY), Meadows (NC), DeSantis (FL), Mulvaney (SC), Buck (CO), Walker (NC), Blum (IA), Hice (GA), Russell (OK), Carter (GA), Grothman (WI), Hurd (TX), Palmer (AL)

Minority (D 18): Cummings (MD), RMM; Maloney (NY), Norton (DC), Clay (MO), Lynch (MA), Cooper (TN), Connolly (VA), Cartwright (PA), Duckworth (IL), Kelly (IL), Lawrence (MI), Lieu (CA), Watson Coleman (NJ), Plaskett (VI), DeSaulnier (CA), Boyle (PA), Welch (VT), Lujan Grisham (NM)

SUBCOMMITTEES

Government Operations
Majority (R 10): Meadows (NC), Chmn; Walberg (MI), Carter (GA), Grothman (WI), Jordan (OH), Buck (CO), Mulvaney (SC), Massie (KY), Gowdy (SC), Chaffetz (UT)

Minority (D 7): Connolly (VA), RMM; Maloney (NY), Norton (DC), Plaskett (VI), Lynch (MA), Clay (MO), Cummings (MD)

Health Care, Benefits & Administrative Rules
Majority (R 12): Jordan (OH), Chmn; Mulvaney (SC), Carter (GA), Lummis (WY), Hice (GA), Meadows (NC), Walker (NC), DeSantis (FL), DesJarlais (TN), Walberg (MI), Gowdy (SC), Chaffetz (UT)

Minority (D 8): Cartwright (PA), RMM; Watson Coleman (NJ), Boyle (PA), Norton (DC), Cooper (TN), DeSaulnier (CA), Lujan Grisham (NM), Cummings (MD)

Information Technology
Majority (R 6): Hurd (TX), Chmn; Farenthold (TX), Walker (NC), Gosar (AZ), Blum (IA), Chaffetz (UT)
Minority (D 5): Kelly (IL), RMM; Connolly (VA), Duckworth (IL), Lieu (CA), Cummings (MD)

Interior
Majority (R 7): Lummis (WY), Chmn; Buck (CO), Farenthold (TX), Palmer (AL), Gosar (AZ), Russell (OK), Chaffetz (UT)
Minority (D 5): Lawrence (MI), RMM; Cooper (TN), Cartwright (PA), Plaskett (VI), Cummings (MD)

National Security
Majority (R 7): DeSantis (FL), Chmn; Russell (OK), Hice (GA), Duncan (TN), Mica (FL), Hurd (TX), Chaffetz (UT)
Minority (D 5): Lynch (MA), RMM; Lawrence (MI), Kelly (IL), Lieu (CA), Cummings (MD)

Transportation & Public Assets
Majority (R 7): Mica (FL), Chmn; Grothman (WI), Duncan (TN), Amash (MI), Turner (OH), Massie (KY), Chaffetz (UT)
Minority (D 5): Duckworth (IL), RMM; Watson Coleman (NJ), Boyle (PA), DeSaulnier (CA), Cummings (MD)

Rules
rules.house.gov

H-312, The Capitol
202-225-9191

Majority (R 9): Sessions (TX), Chmn; Foxx (NC), Cole (OK), Woodall (GA), Burgess (TX), Stivers (OH), Collins (GA), Byrne (AL), Newhouse (WA)
Minority (D 4): Slaughter (NY), RMM; McGovern (MA), Hastings (FL), Polis (CO)

SUBCOMMITTEES

Legislative and Budget Process
Majority (R 5): Woodall (GA), Chmn; Foxx (NC), Burgess (TX), Byrne (AL), Newhouse (WA),
Minority (D 2): Hastings (FL), RMM; Polis (CO)

Rules and Organization of the House
Majority (R 5): Stivers (OH), Chmn; Collins (GA), Byrne (AL), Newhouse (WA), Sessions (TX)
Minority (D 2): Slaughter (NY), RMM; McGovern (MA)

Science, Space & Technology
science.house.gov

2321 RHOB
202-225-6371

Majority (R 22): Smith (TX), Chmn; Lucas (OK), Sensenbrenner (WI), Rohrabacher (CA), Neugebauer (TX), McCaul (TX), Brooks (AL), Hultgren (IL), Posey (FL), Massie (KY), Bridenstine (OK), Weber (TX), Johnson (OH), Moolenaar (MI), Knight (CA), Babin (TX), Westerman (AR), Comstock (VA), Newhouse (WA), Palmer (AL), Loudermilk (GA), Abraham (LA)
Minority (D 16): Johnson (TX), RMM; Lofgren (CA), Lipinski (IL), Edwards (MD), Bonamici (OR), Swalwell (CA), Grayson (FL), Bera (CA), Esty (CT), Veasey (TX), Clark (MA), Beyer (VA), Perlmutter (CO), Tonko (NY), Takano (CA), Foster (IL)

SUBCOMMITTEES

Energy
Majority (R 10): Weber (TX), Chmn; Newhouse (WA), Rohrabacher (CA), Neugebauer (TX), Brooks (AL), Hultgren (IL), Massie (KY), Comstock (VA), Loudermilk (GA), Smith (TX)
Minority (D 7): Grayson (FL), RMM; Swalwell (CA), Veasey (TX), Lipinski (IL), Clark (MA), Perlmutter (CO), Johnson (TX)

Environment
Majority (R 10): Bridenstine (OK), Chmn; Westerman (AR), Sensenbrenner (WI), Neugebauer (TX), Weber (TX), Moolenaar (MI), Babin (TX), Newhouse (WA), Palmer (AL), Smith (TX)
Minority (D 7): Bonamici (OR), RMM; Edwards (MD), Grayson (FL), Bera (CA), Takano (CA), Foster (IL), Johnson (TX)

Oversight
Majority (R 15): Loudermilk (GA), Chmn; Johnson (OH), Sensenbrenner (WI), Posey (FL), Massie (KY), Bridenstine (OK), Smith (TX)
Minority (D 9): Beyer (VA), RMM; Grayson (FL), Lofgren (CA), Johnson (TX)

Research & Technology

Majority (R 10): Comstock (VA), Chmn; Moolenaar (MI), Lucas (OK), McCaul (TX), Palazzo (MS), Hultgren (IL), Knight (CA), Westerman (AR), Palmer (AL), Smith (TX)

Minority (D 7): Lipinski (IL), RMM; Esty (CT), Clark (MA), Tonko (NY), Bonamici (OR), Swalwell (CA), Johnson (TX)

Space

Majority (R 10): Babin (TX), Chmn; Brooks (AL), Rohrabacher (CA), Lucas (OK), McCaul (TX), Posey (FL), Bridenstine (OK), Johnson (OH), Knight (CA), Smith (TX)

Minority (D 7): Edwards (MD), RMM; Bera (CA), Lofgren (CA), Perlmutter (CO), Veasey (TX), Beyer (VA), Johnson (TX)

Small Business
smallbusiness.house.gov

2361 RHOB
202-225-5821

Majority (R 13): Chabot (OH), Chmn; Luetkemeyer (MO), King (IA), Hanna (NY), Huelskamp (KS), Rice (SC), Gibson (NY), Brat (VA), Radewagen (AS), Knight (CA), Curbelo (FL), Bost (IL), Hardy (NV)

Minority (D 10): Velazquez (NY), RMM; Chu (CA), Hahn (CA), Payne (NJ), Meng (NY), Lawrence (MI), Takai (HI), Clarke (NY), Adams (NC), Moulton (MA)

SUBCOMMITTEES

Agriculture, Energy & Trade

Majority (R 5): Curbelo (FL), Chmn; King (IA), Luetkemeyer (MO), Huelskamp (KS), Brat (VA)

Minority (D 2): Meng (NY), RMM; Takai (HI)

Contracting & Workforce

Majority (R 5): Hanna (NY), Chmn; King (IA), Gibson (NY), Knight (CA), Hardy (NV)

Minority (D 1): Takai (HI), RMM

Economic Growth, Tax & Capital Access

Majority (R 5): Rice (SC), Chmn; Hanna (NY), Huelskamp (KS), Brat (VA), Radewagen (AS)

Minority (D 1): Chu (CA), RMM

Health & Technology

Majority (R 5): Radewagen (AS), Chmn; Luetkemeyer (MO), Rice (SC), Curbelo (FL), Bost (IL)

Minority (D 1): Moulton (MA), RMM

Investigations, Oversight & Regulations

Majority (R 5): Hardy (NV), Chmn; Rice (SC), Gibson (NY), Knight (CA), Bost (IL)

Minority (D 1): Adams (NC), RMM

Transportation & Infrastructure
transportation.house.gov

2251 RHOB
202-225-9446

Majority (R 34): Shuster (PA), Chmn; Duncan (TN), Young (AK), Mica (FL), LoBiondo (NJ), Graves (MO), Miller (MI), Hunter (CA), Crawford (AR), Barletta (PA), Farenthold (TX), Gibbs (OH), Hanna (NY), Webster (FL), Denham (CA), Ribble (WI), Massie (KY), Rice (SC), Meadows (NC), Perry (PA), Davis (IL), Sanford (SC), Woodall (GA), Rokita (IN), Katko (NY), Babin (TX), Hardy (NV), Costello (PA), Graves (LA), Walters (CA), Comstock (VA), Curbelo (FL), Rouzer (NC), Zeldin (NY)

Minority (D 25): DeFazio (OR), RMM; Norton (DC), Nadler (NY), Brown (FL), Johnson (TX), Cummings (MD), Larsen (WA), Capuano (MA), Napolitano (CA), Lipinski (IL), Cohen (TN), Sires (NJ), Edwards (MD), Garamendi (CA), Carson (IN), Hahn (CA), Nolan (MN), Kirkpatrick (AZ), Titus (NV), Maloney (NY), Esty (CT), Frankel (FL), Bustos (IL), Huffman (CA), Brownley (CA)

SUBCOMMITTEES

Aviation

Majority (R 20): LoBiondo (NJ), Chmn; Young (AK), Duncan (TN), Mica (FL), Graves (MO), Miller (MI), Farenthold (TX), Hanna (NY), Ribble (WI), Meadows (NC), Davis (IL), Sanford (SC), Woodall (GA), Rokita (IN), Costello (PA), Walters (CA), Comstock (VA), Curbelo (FL), Zeldin (NY), Shuster (PA)

Minority (D 15): Larsen (WA), RMM; Norton (DC), Johnson (TX), Lipinski (IL), Carson (IN), Kirkpatrick (AZ), Titus (NV), Maloney (NY), Bustos (IL), Brownley (CA), Capuano (MA), Cohen (TN), Nolan (MN), Garamendi (CA), DeFazio (OR)

Coast Guard & Maritime Transportation
Majority (R 10): Hunter (CA), Chmn; Young (AK), LoBiondo (NJ), Gibbs (OH), Sanford (SC), Graves (LA), Curbelo (FL), Rouzer (NC), Zeldin (NY), Shuster (PA)
Minority (D 7): Garamendi (CA), RMM; Cummings (MD), Brown (FL), Hahn (CA), Frankel (FL), Brownley (CA), DeFazio (OR)

Economic Development, Public Buildings & Emergency Management
Majority (R 10): Barletta (PA), Chmn; Crawford (AR), Massie (KY), Meadows (NC), Perry (PA), Costello (PA), Comstock (VA), Curbelo (FL), Rouzer (NC), Shuster (PA)
Minority (D 6): Carson (IN), RMM; Norton (DC), Sires (NJ), Edwards (MD), Titus (NV), DeFazio (OR)

Highways & Transit
Majority (R 28): Graves (MO), Chmn; Young (AK), Duncan (TN), Mica (FL), LoBiondo (NJ), Hunter (CA), Crawford (AR), Barletta (PA), Farenthold (TX), Gibbs (OH), Hanna (NY), Webster (FL), Denham (CA), Ribble (WI), Massie (KY), Rice (SC), Meadows (NC), Perry (PA), Davis (IL), Woodall (GA), Katko (NY), Babin (TX), Hardy (NV), Costello (PA), Graves (LA), Walters (CA), Comstock (VA), Shuster (PA)
Minority (D 21): Norton (DC), RMM; Nadler (NY), Johnson (TX), Cohen (TN), Sires (NJ), Edwards (MD), Hahn (CA), Nolan (MN), Kirkpatrick (AZ), Titus (NV), Maloney (NY), Esty (CT), Frankel (FL), Bustos (IL), Huffman (CA), Brownley (CA), Capuano (MA), Napolitano (CA), Brown (FL), Lipinski (IL), DeFazio (OR)

Railroads, Pipelines & Hazardous Materials
Majority (R 18): Denham (CA), Chmn; Duncan (TN), Mica (FL), Graves (MO), Miller (MI), Barletta (PA), Farenthold (TX), Hanna (NY), Webster (FL), Rice (SC), Perry (PA), Rokita (IN), Katko (NY), Babin (TX), Hardy (NV), Walters (CA), Zeldin (NY), Shuster (PA)
Minority (D 13): Capuano (MA), RMM; Brown (FL), Lipinski (IL), Nadler (NY), Cummings (MD), Larsen (WA), Cohen (TN), Sires (NJ), Nolan (MN), Esty (CT), Napolitano (CA), Hahn (CA), DeFazio (OR)

Water Resources & Environment
Majority (R 18): Gibbs (OH), Chmn; Miller (MI), Hunter (CA), Crawford (AR), Webster (FL), Denham (CA), Ribble (WI), Massie (KY), Rice (SC), Davis (IL), Sanford (SC), Rokita (IN), Katko (NY), Babin (TX), Hardy (NV), Graves (LA), Rouzer (NC), Shuster (PA)
Minority (D 13): Napolitano (CA), RMM; Edwards (MD), Garamendi (CA), Frankel (FL), Huffman (CA), Johnson (TX), Kirkpatrick (AZ), Titus (NV), Maloney (NY), Esty (CT), Norton (DC), Nolan (MN), DeFazio (OR)

Veterans' Affairs
veterans.house.gov

335 CHOB
202-225-3527

Majority (R 14): Miller (FL), Chmn; Lamborn (CO), Bilirakis (FL), Roe (TN), Benishek (MI), Huelskamp (KS), Coffman (CO), Wenstrup (OH), Walorski (IN), Abraham (LA), Zeldin (NY), Costello (PA), Radewagen (AS), Bost (IL)
Minority (D 10): Brown (FL), RMM; Takano (CA), Brownley (CA), Titus (NV), Ruiz (CA), Kuster (NH), O'Rourke (TX), Rice (NY), Walz (MN), McNerney (CA)

SUBCOMMITTEES

Disability Assistance & Memorial Affairs
Majority (R 5): Abraham (LA), Chmn; Lamborn (CO), Zeldin (NY), Costello (PA), Bost (IL)
Minority (D 3): Titus (NV), RMM; Brownley (CA), Ruiz (CA)

Economic Opportunity
Majority (R 5): Wenstrup (OH), Chmn; Zeldin (NY), Radewagen (AS), Costello (PA), Bost (IL)
Minority (D 4): Takano (CA), RMM; Titus (NV), Rice (NY), McNerney (CA)

Health
Majority (R 7): Benishek (MI), Chmn; Bilirakis (FL), Roe (TN), Huelskamp (KS), Coffman (CO), Wenstrup (OH), Abraham (LA)
Minority (D 5): Brownley (CA), RMM; Takano (CA), Ruiz (CA), Kuster (NH), O'Rourke (TX)

Oversight & Investigations
Majority (R 6): Coffman (CO), Chmn; Lamborn (CO), Roe (TN), Benishek (MI), Huelskamp (KS), Walorski (IN)
Minority (D 4): Kuster (NH), RMM; O'Rourke (TX), Rice (NY), Walz (MN)

Ways & Means
waysandmeans.house.gov

1102 LHOB
202-225-3625

Majority (R 24): Ryan (WI), Chmn; Johnson (TX), Brady (TX), Nunes (CA), Tiberi (OH), Reichert (WA), Boustany (LA), Roskam (IL), Price (GA), Buchanan (FL), Smith (NE), Jenkins (KS), Paulsen (MN), Marchant (TX), Black (TN), Reed (NY), Young (IN), Kelly (PA), Renacci (OH), Meehan (PA), Noem (SD), Holding (NC), Smith (MO), Dold (IL)
Minority (D 15): Levin (MI), RMM; Rangel (NY), McDermott (WA), Lewis (GA), Neal (MA), Becerra (CA), Doggett (TX), Thompson (CA), Larson (CT), Blumenauer (OR), Kind (WI), Pascrell (NJ), Crowley (NY), Davis (IL), Sanchez, Linda (CA)

SUBCOMMITTEES

Health
Majority (R 10): Brady (TX), Chmn; Johnson (TX), Nunes (CA), Roskam (IL), Price (GA), Buchanan (FL), Smith (NE), Jenkins (KS), Marchant (TX), Black (TN)
Minority (D 6): McDermott (WA), RMM; Thompson (CA), Kind (WI), Blumenauer (OR), Pascrell (NJ), Davis (IL)

Human Resources
Majority (R 8): Boustany (LA), Chmn; Young (IN), Noem (SD), Meehan (PA), Holding (NC), Smith (MO), Dold (IL), Ryan (WI)
Minority (D 5): Doggett (TX), RMM; Lewis (GA), Crowley (NY), Davis (IL), Levin (MI)

Oversight
Majority (R 7): Roskam (IL), Chmn; Kelly (PA), Meehan (PA), Holding (NC), Smith (MO), Noem (SD), Renacci (OH)
Minority (D 4): Lewis (GA), RMM; Crowley (NY), Rangel (NY), Doggett (TX)

Select Revenue Measures
Majority (R 8): Reichert (WA), Chmn; Tiberi (OH), Paulsen (MN), Reed (NY), Young (IN), Kelly (PA), Renacci (OH), Ryan (WI)
Minority (D 5): Neal (MA), RMM; Larson (CT), Sanchez, Linda (CA), Thompson (CA), Levin (MI)

Social Security
Majority (R 8): Johnson (TX), Chmn; Reed (NY), Dold (IL), Young (IN), Kelly (PA), Renacci (OH), Brady (TX), Ryan (WI)
Minority (D 5): Becerra (CA), RMM; Doggett (TX), Larson (CT), Blumenauer (OR), Levin (MI)

Trade
Majority (R 11): Tiberi (OH), Chmn; Nunes (CA), Brady (TX), Reichert (WA), Buchanan (FL), Smith (NE), Jenkins (KS), Boustany (LA), Paulsen (MN), Marchant (TX), Ryan (WI)
Minority (D 7): Rangel (NY), RMM; Neal (MA), Blumenauer (OR), Kind (WI), Becerra (CA), Pascrell (NJ), Levin (MI)

SELECT COMMITTEES

Benghazi (Select)
benghazi.house.gov

202-226-710

Majority (R 7): Gowdy (SC), Chmn; Brooks (IN), Jordan (OH), Pompeo (KS), Roby (AL), Roskam (IL), Westmoreland (GA)
Minority (D 5): Cummings (MD), RMM; Smith (WA), Schiff (CA), Sanchez, Linda (CA), Duckworth (IL)

Intelligence (Permanent Select)
intelligence.house.gov

202-225-4121
HVC-304 The Capitol

Majority (R 13): Nunes (CA), Chmn; Miller (FL), Conaway (TX), King (NY), LoBiondo (NJ), Westmoreland (GA), Rooney (FL), Heck (NV), Pompeo (KS), Ros-Lehtinen (FL), Turner (OH), Wenstrup (OH), Stewart (UT)
Minority (D 9): Schiff (CA), RMM; Gutierrez (IL), Himes (CT), Sewell (AL), Carson (IN), Speier (CA), Quigley (IL), Swalwell (CA), Murphy (FL)

JOINT COMMITTEES

Economic (Joint)
jec.senate.gov

G-01 Dirksen
202-224-5171

House (10): Brady (TX), VChmn; Amash (MI), Paulsen (MN), Hanna (NY), Schweikert (AZ), Grothman (WI), Maloney (NY) RM; Delaney (MD), Adams (NC), Beyer (VA)
Senate (10): Coats (IN), Chmn; Lee (UT), Cotton (AR), Sasse (NE), Cruz (TX), Cassidy (LA), Klobuchar (MN), Casey (PA), Heinrich (NM), Peters (MI)

Library (Joint)
cha.house.gov

1309 Longworth
202-225-8281

House (5): Harper (MS), VChmn; Miller (MI), Graves (GA), Brady (PA), Lofgren (CA)
Senate (5): Blunt (MO), Chmn; Roberts (KS), Capito (WV), Schumer (NY), Leahy (VT)

Printing (Joint)
cha.house.gov

1309 Longworth
202-225-8281

House (5): Harper (MS), Chmn; Miller (MI), Davis (IL), Brady (PA), Vargas (CA)
Senate (5): Blunt (MO), VChmn; Roberts (KS); Boozman (AR); Schumer (NY), Udall (NM)

Taxation (Joint)
jct.gov

H2-502 Ford
202-225-3621

House (5): Ryan (WI), Chmn; Johnson (TX), Brady (TX), Levin (MI), Rangel (NY)
Senate (5): Hatch (UT), VChmn; Grassley (IA), Crapo (ID), Wyden (OR), Stabenow (MI)

PROFILE LIST

A

Abbott, Greg, 1710–1712
Abraham, Ralph, 808–810
Adams, Alma, 1378–1380
Aderholt, Robert, 48–51
Aguilar, Pete, 256–258
Alexander, Lamar, 1667–1671
Allen, Rick, 543–545
Amash, Justin, 936–939
Amodei, Mark, 1124–1127
Ashford, Brad, 1102–1104
Ayotte, Kelly, 1146–1149

B

Babin, Brian, 1824–1827
Baker, Charlie, 881–883
Baldwin, Tammy, 1997–1998
Barletta, Lou, 1565–1567
Barr, Andy, 777–779
Barrasso, John, 2033–2036
Barton, Joe, 1735–1738
Bass, Karen, 272–275
Beatty, Joyce, 1420–1423
Becerra, Xavier, 264–267
Benishek, Dan, 930–933
Bennet, Michael, 330–333
Bentley, Robert, 30–32
Bera, Ami, 179–181
Beshear, Steve, 749–752
Beyer, Don, 1909–1912
Bilirakis, Gus, 455–457
Bishop, Mike, 951–953
Bishop, Rob, 1842–1845
Bishop, Sanford, 517–520
Black, Diane, 1690–1693
Blackburn, Marsha,
    1693–1696
Blum, Rod, 708–710
Blumenauer, Earl, 1511–1514
Blumenthal, Richard,
    364–366
Blunt, Roy, 1048–1052
Boehner, John, 1435–1441
Bonamici, Suzanne,
    1505–1508
Booker, Cory, 1170–1173
Boozman, John, 126–128
Bordallo, Madeleine,
    2042–2043
Bost, Mike, 635–637
Boustany, Charles, 802–805
Boxer, Barbara, 158–162
Boyle, Brendan, 1570–1572
Brady, Kevin, 1741–1744
Brady, Robert, 1536–1539
Branstad, Terry, 699–701
Brat, Dave, 1907–1909
Bridenstine, Jim, 1476–1479
Brooks, Mo, 51–54
Brooks, Susan, 679–681

Brown, Corrine, 433–436
Brown, Jerry, 151–154
Brown, Kate, 1496–1498
Brown, Sherrod, 1406–1410
Brownback, Sam, 724–726
Brownley, Julia, 241–243
Bryant, Phil, 1016–1017
Buchanan, Vern, 466–469
Buck, Ken, 345–347
Bucshon, Larry, 687–689
Bullock, Steve, 1080–1081
Burgess, Michael, 1795–1798
Burr, Richard, 1340–1344
Bustos, Cheri, 649–651
Butterfield, G.K., 1346–1348
Byrne, Bradley, 39–41

C

Calvert, Ken, 286–289
Cantwell, Maria, 1932–1936
Capito, Shelley Moore,
    1975–1976
Capps, Lois, 236–239
Capuano, Michael, 906–909
Cárdenas, Tony, 250–253
Cardin, Ben, 844–847
Carney, John, 397–398
Carper, Thomas, 391–394
Carson, André, 684–686
Carter, Buddy, 515–517
Carter, John, 1810–1812
Cartwright, Matt, 1580–1583
Casey Jr., Robert, 1528–1532
Cassidy, Bill, 792–794
Castor, Kathy, 460–463
Castro, Joaquin, 1778–1780
Chabot, Steve, 1414–1417
Chaffetz, Jason, 1848–1851
Christie, Chris, 1162–1165
Chu, Judy, 244–246
Cicilline, David, 1599–1601
Clark, Katherine, 902–904
Clarke, Yvette, 1273–1276
Clawson, Curt, 474–477
Clay, William Lacy,
    1052–1055
Cleaver, Emanuel, 1064–1067
Clyburn, James, 1636–1640
Coats, Dan, 662–664
Cochran, Thad, 1018–1021
Coffman, Mike, 350–353
Cohen, Steve, 1698–1701
Cole, Tom, 1485–1488
Collins, Chris, 1329–1331
Collins, Doug, 536–539
Collins, Susan, 819–823
Comstock, Barbara,
    1915–1917
Conaway, Mike, 1750–1753
Connolly, Gerald, 1917–1920

Conyers, John, 964–968
Cook, Paul, 182–184
Coons, Christopher, 394–397
Cooper, Jim, 1687–1690
Corker, Bob, 1671–1675
Cornyn, John, 1712–1716
Costa, Jim, 211–213
Costello, Ryan, 1551–1553
Cotton, Tom, 129–131
Courtney, Joe, 372–375
Cramer, Kevin, 1395–1397
Crapo, Mike, 575–577
Crawford, Rick, 131–134
Crenshaw, Ander, 430–433
Crowley, Joseph, 1291–1295
Cruz, Ted, 1717–1720
Cuellar, Henry, 1801–1803
Culberson, John, 1738–1741
Cummings, Elijah, 867–871
Cuomo, Andrew, 1236–1240
Curbelo, Carlos, 496–498

D

Daines, Steve, 1085–1086
Dalrymple, Jack, 1387–1389
Daugaard, Dennis, 1648–1649
Davis, Danny, 621–624
Davis, Rodney, 637–640
Davis, Susan, 319–322
Dayton, Mark, 977–979
Deal, Nathan, 508–510
DeFazio, Peter, 1514–1517
DeGette, Diana, 335–338
Delaney, John, 864–867
DeLauro, Rosa, 375–378
DelBene, Suzan, 1936–1939
Denham, Jeff, 187–190
Dent, Charlie, 1575–1577
DeSantis, Ron, 437–439
DeSaulnier, Mark, 191–193
DesJarlais, Scott, 1684–1687
Deutch, Ted, 480–483
Diaz-Balart, Mario, 493–496
Dingell, Debbie, 962–964
Doggett, Lloyd, 1821–1824
Dold, Bob, 630–632
Donnelly, Joe, 665–667
Donovan, Daniel, 1280–1283
Doyle, Mike, 1572–1574
Ducey, Doug, 83–85
Duckworth, Tammy, 624–627
Duffy, Sean, 2018–2021
Duncan, Jeff, 1627–1629
Duncan, John, 1678–1681
Durbin, Richard, 595–599

E

Edwards, Donna, 856–860
Ellison, Keith, 999–1002
Ellmers, Renee, 1349–1352

Emmer, Tom, 1002–1004
Engel, Eliot, 1298–1301
Enzi, Michael, 2031–2033
Ernst, Joni, 706–707
Eshoo, Anna, 217–220
Esty, Elizabeth, 381–384

F

Fallin, Mary, 1469–1471
Farenthold, Blake, 1798–1800
Farr, Sam, 223–225
Fattah, Chaka, 1539–1542
Feinstein, Dianne, 154–158
Fincher, Stephen, 1696–1698
Fischer, Deb, 1094–1097
Fitzpatrick, Mike, 1556–1558
Flake, Jeff, 92–94
Fleischmann, Charles,
  1681–1684
Fleming, John, 805–808
Flores, Bill, 1769–1771
Forbes, Randy, 1898–1901
Fortenberry, Jeff, 1099–1102
Foster, Bill, 632–635
Foxx, Virginia, 1358–1361
Frankel, Lois, 483–486
Franken, Al, 983–986
Franks, Trent, 115–118
Frelinghuysen, Rodney,
  1202–1205
Fudge, Marcia, 1447–1450

G

Gabbard, Tulsi, 565–568
Gallego, Ruben, 112–115
Garamendi, John, 168–170
Gardner, Cory, 333–335
Garrett, Scott, 1185–1187
Gibbs, Bob, 1432–1435
Gibson, Chris, 1307–1310
Gillibrand, Kirsten,
  1246–1250
Gohmert, Louie, 1720–1723
Goodlatte, Bob, 1903–1907
Gosar, Paul, 103–106
Gowdy, Trey, 1629–1633
Graham, Gwen, 425–428
Graham, Lindsey, 1613–1617
Granger, Kay, 1754–1756
Grassley, Charles, 701–705
Graves, Garret, 810–812
Graves, Sam, 1067–1070
Graves, Tom, 548–551
Grayson, Alan, 446–448
Green, Al, 1744–1747
Green, Gene, 1804–1806
Griffith, Morgan, 1912–1914
Grijalva, Raúl, 100–103
Grothman, Glenn, 2016–2018
Guinta, Frank, 1149–1152
Guthrie, Brett, 764–767
Gutierrez, Luis, 612–615

H

Hahn, Janice, 293–296
Haley, Nikki, 1610–1613
Hanna, Richard, 1315–1318
Hardy, Cresent, 1130–1133
Harper, Gregg, 1031–1033
Harris, Andy, 847–850
Hartzler, Vicky, 1061–1064
Haslam, Bill, 1664–1667
Hassan, Maggie, 1140–1141
Hastings, Alcee, 477–480
Hatch, Orrin, 1835–1838
Heck, Denny, 1962–1964
Heck, Joe, 1127–1130
Heinrich, Martin, 1217–1219
Heitkamp, Heidi, 1392–1395
Heller, Dean, 1119–1121
Hensarling, Jeb, 1731–1735
Herbert, Gary, 1833–1835
Herrera Beutler, Jaime,
  1942–1944
Hice, Jody, 539–541
Hickenlooper, John, 327–330
Higgins, Brian, 1326–1329
Hill, French, 134–136
Himes, Jim, 378–381
Hinojosa, Rubén, 1763–1766
Hirono, Mazie, 561–563
Hoeven, John, 1389–1392
Hogan, Larry, 837–840
Holding, George, 1380–1382
Honda, Mike, 214–216
Hoyer, Steny, 860–864
Hudson, Richard, 1366–1368
Huelskamp, Tim, 733–736
Huffman, Jared, 165–167
Huizenga, Bill, 933–936
Hultgren, Randy, 640–643
Hunter, Duncan D., 311–313
Hurd, Will, 1787–1789
Hurt, Robert, 1901–1903
Hutchinson, Asa, 125–126

I

Ige, David, 557–559
Inhofe, James, 1471–1474
Inslee, Jay, 1926–1928
Isakson, Johnny, 510–513
Israel, Steve, 1256–1259
Issa, Darrell, 307–310

J

Jackson Lee, Sheila,
  1772–1774
Jeffries, Hakeem, 1271–1273
Jenkins, Evan, 1982–1984
Jenkins, Lynn, 736–738
Jindal, Bobby, 785–788
Johnson, Bill, 1429–1432
Johnson, Eddie Bernice,
  1807–1809
Johnson, Hank, 522–525

Johnson, Ron, 1994–1996
Johnson, Sam, 1726–1729
Jolly, David, 458–460
Jones, Walter, 1352–1355
Jordan, Jim, 1423–1426
Joyce, David, 1456–1459

K

Kaine, Tim, 1886–1889
Kaptur, Marcy, 1441–1444
Kasich, John, 1404–1406
Katko, John, 1321–1323
Keating, William, 913–915
Kelly, Mike, 1542–1544
Kelly, Robin, 606–608
Kelly, Trent, 1025–1027
Kennedy, Joe, 899–901
Kildee, Dan, 941–944
Kilmer, Derek, 1950–1953
Kind, Ron, 2006–2009
King, Angus, 823–825
King, Peter, 1253–1256
King, Steve, 716–719
Kinzinger, Adam, 646–649
Kirk, Mark, 599–602
Kirkpatrick, Ann, 94–97
Kline, John, 990–993
Klobuchar, Amy, 980–983
Knight, Steve, 239–241
Kuster, Ann McLane,
  1152–1155

L

Labrador, Raúl, 580–583
LaMalfa, Doug, 162–165
Lamborn, Doug, 347–350
Lance, Leonard, 1191–1193
Langevin, Jim, 1602–1604
Lankford, James, 1474–1476
Larsen, Rick, 1939–1942
Larson, John, 369–372
Latta, Bob, 1426–1429
Lawrence, Brenda, 968–971
Leahy, Patrick, 1862–1866
Lee, Barbara, 201–204
Lee, Mike, 1839–1841
LePage, Paul, 817–819
Levin, Sander, 953–956
Lewis, John, 525–528
Lieu, Ted, 261–263
Lipinski, Daniel, 609–612
LoBiondo, Frank, 1176–1179
Loebsack, Dave, 710–713
Lofgren, Zoe, 220–222
Long, Billy, 1070–1073
Loudermilk, Barry, 541–543
Love, Mia, 1852–1854
Lowenthal, Alan, 301–304
Lowey, Nita, 1301–1304
Lucas, Frank, 1482–1485
Luetkemeyer, Blaine,
  1058–1061

Lujan Grisham, Michelle, 1219–1222
Luján, Ben Ray, 1225–1227
Lummis, Cynthia, 2036–2038
Lynch, Stephen, 910–912

M

MacArthur, Tom, 1179–1181
Malloy, Dannel, 361–364
Maloney, Carolyn, 1283–1286
Maloney, Sean Patrick, 1304–1307
Manchin, Joe, 1971–1974
Marchant, Kenny, 1790–1792
Marino, Tom, 1562–1564
Markell, Jack, 389–391
Markey, Edward, 887–890
Martinez, Susana, 1212–1214
Massie, Thomas, 770–772
Matsui, Doris, 176–178
McAuliffe, Terry, 1879–1882
McCain, John, 85–91
McCarthy, Kevin, 232–236
McCaskill, Claire, 1044–1048
McCaul, Michael, 1747–1750
McClintock, Tom, 170–173
McCollum, Betty, 996–999
McConnell, Mitch, 752–757
McCrory, Pat, 1337–1339
McDermott, Jim, 1953–1956
McGovern, James, 893–896
McHenry, Patrick, 1371–1374
McKinley, David, 1976–1979
McMorris Rodgers, Cathy, 1947–1950
McNerney, Jerry, 184–187
McSally, Martha, 97–100
Mead, Matt, 2029–2030
Meadows, Mark, 1375–1377
Meehan, Pat, 1553–1556
Meeks, Gregory, 1262–1265
Menendez, Robert, 1165–1169
Meng, Grace, 1265–1267
Merkley, Jeff, 1502–1505
Messer, Luke, 681–684
Mica, John, 439–442
Mikulski, Barbara, 840–844
Miller, Candice, 956–959
Miller, Jeff, 422–425
Moolenaar, John, 939–941
Mooney, Alex, 1979–1981
Moore, Gwen, 2009–2012
Moran, Jerry, 730–733
Moulton, Seth, 904–906
Mullin, Markwayne, 1479–1481
Mulvaney, Mick, 1633–1636
Murkowski, Lisa, 68–71
Murphy, Chris, 366–369
Murphy, Patrick, 472–474
Murphy, Tim, 1583–1585
Murray, Patty, 1928–1932

N

Nadler, Jerrold, 1277–1280
Napolitano, Grace, 259–261
Neal, Richard, 890–893
Nelson, Bill, 415–418
Neugebauer, Randy, 1775–1777
Newhouse, Dan, 1945–1947
Nixon, Jay, 1041–1044
Noem, Kristi, 1656–1658
Nolan, Rick, 1008–1011
Norcross, Donald, 1173–1176
Norton, Eleanor Holmes, 401–403
Nugent, Richard, 452–455
Nunes, Devin, 229–232

O

O'Rourke, Beto, 1766–1768
Olson, Pete, 1784–1787
Otter, Butch, 573–575

P

Palazzo, Steven, 1033–1036
Pallone, Frank, 1188–1191
Palmer, Gary, 54–57
Pascrell, Bill, 1197–1199
Paul, Rand, 758–761
Paulsen, Erik, 993–995
Payne Jr., Donald, 1200–1202
Pearce, Steve, 1222–1224
Pelosi, Nancy, 193–201
Pence, Mike, 660–662
Perdue, David, 513–515
Perlmutter, Ed, 353–356
Perry, Scott, 1545–1547
Peters, Gary, 928–930
Peters, Scott, 316–319
Peterson, Collin, 1004–1008
Pierluisi, Pedro, 2048
Pingree, Chellie, 826–828
Pittenger, Robert, 1368–1371
Pitts, Joe, 1578–1580
Plaskett, Stacey, 2050
Pocan, Mark, 2004–2006
Poe, Ted, 1723–1726
Poliquin, Bruce, 829–831
Polis, Jared, 338–341
Pompeo, Mike, 741–744
Portman, Rob, 1410–1414
Posey, Bill, 443–445
Price, David, 1355–1358
Price, Tom, 528–531

Q

Quigley, Mike, 615–618

R

Radewagen, Aumua Amata Coleman, 2040–2041
Raimondo, Gina, 1590–1592
Rangel, Charles, 1287–1291
Ratcliffe, John, 1729–1731
Rauner, Bruce, 593–595
Reed, Jack, 1592–1595
Reed, Tom, 1318–1321
Reichert, Dave, 1956–1959
Reid, Harry, 1115–1118
Renacci, Jim, 1461–1464
Ribble, Reid, 2021–2024
Rice, Kathleen, 1259–1262
Rice, Tom, 1640–1642
Richmond, Cedric, 799–802
Ricketts, Pete, 1092–1094
Rigell, Scott, 1892–1895
Risch, James, 578–580
Roberts, Pat, 726–730
Roby, Martha, 42–44
Roe, Phil, 1675–1678
Rogers, Harold, 773–776
Rogers, Mike, 44–47
Rohrabacher, Dana, 304–307
Rokita, Todd, 676–678
Rooney, Tom, 469–472
Roskam, Peter, 618–621
Ros-Lehtinen, Ileana, 499–502
Ross, Dennis, 463–465
Rothfus, Keith, 1567–1570
Rounds, Mike, 1654–1656
Rouzer, David, 1363–1365
Roybal-Allard, Lucille, 281–283
Royce, Ed, 278–281
Rubio, Marco, 418–422
Ruiz, Raul, 270–272
Ruppersberger, Dutch, 850–853
Rush, Bobby, 602–605
Russell, Steve, 1489–1491
Ryan, Paul, 1999–2003
Ryan, Tim, 1453–1456

S

Sablan, Gregorio Kilili Camacho, 2045–2046
Salmon, Matt, 106–109
Sánchez, Linda, 275–278
Sanchez, Loretta, 298–301
Sanders, Bernie, 1866–1870
Sandoval, Brian, 1113–1114
Sanford, Mark, 1620–1623
Sarbanes, John, 853–856
Sasse, Ben, 1097–1099
Scalise, Steve, 794–798
Schakowsky, Jan, 627–630
Schatz, Brian, 559–561
Schiff, Adam, 247–250
Schrader, Kurt, 1517–1520
Schumer, Charles, 1240–1246
Schweikert, David, 109–112
Scott, Austin, 534–536
Scott, Bobby, 1895–1897
Scott, David, 545–548

Scott, Rick, 411–415
Scott, Tim, 1617–1620
Sensenbrenner, Jim, 2012–2015
Serrano, José, 1295–1298
Sessions, Jeff, 36–39
Sessions, Pete, 1812–1816
Sewell, Terri, 57–60
Shaheen, Jeanne, 1142–1145
Shelby, Richard, 32–36
Sherman, Brad, 253–256
Shimkus, John, 643–646
Shumlin, Peter, 1859–1861
Shuster, Bill, 1559–1562
Simpson, Mike, 583–586
Sinema, Kyrsten, 118–120
Sires, Albio, 1194–1196
Slaughter, Louise, 1323–1326
Smith, Adam, 1959–1962
Smith, Adrian, 1105–1107
Smith, Chris, 1181–1184
Smith, Jason, 1073–1075
Smith, Lamar, 1781–1784
Snyder, Rick, 922–924
Speier, Jackie, 205–208
Stabenow, Debbie, 924–927
Stefanik, Elise, 1313–1315
Stewart, Chris, 1845–1847
Stivers, Steve, 1459–1461
Stutzman, Marlin, 673–676
Sullivan, Dan, 72–73
Swalwell, Eric, 208–210

T
Takai, Mark, 563–565
Takano, Mark, 284–286
Tester, Jon, 1081–1084
Thompson, Bennie, 1027–1030

Thompson, Glenn, 1548–1550
Thompson, Mike, 173–176
Thornberry, Mac, 1757–1760
Thune, John, 1650–1654
Tiberi, Pat, 1450–1453
Tillis, Thom, 1344–1345
Tipton, Scott, 341–344
Titus, Dina, 1121–1124
Tomblin, Earl Ray, 1969–1971
Tonko, Paul, 1310–1313
Toomey, Pat, 1532–1536
Torres, Norma, 267–269
Trott, Dave, 960–962
Tsongas, Niki, 896–899
Turner, Mike, 1444–1447

U
Udall, Tom, 1214–1217
Upton, Fred, 944–947

V
Valadao, David, 226–228
Van Hollen, Chris, 871–875
Vargas, Juan, 314–316
Veasey, Marc, 1816–1818
Vela, Filemon, 1819–1821
Velázquez, Nydia, 1268–1270
Visclosky, Peter, 667–670
Vitter, David, 788–791

W
Wagner, Ann, 1056–1058
Walberg, Tim, 948–950
Walden, Greg, 1508–1511
Walker, Bill, 66–67
Walker, Mark, 1361–1363
Walker, Scott, 1990–1993
Walorski, Jackie, 670–673
Walters, Mimi, 296–298

Walz, Tim, 986–989
Warner, Mark, 1882–1886
Warren, Elizabeth, 883–886
Wasserman Schultz, Debbie, 486–490
Waters, Maxine, 289–293
Watson Coleman, Bonnie, 1206–1207
Weber, Randy, 1760–1763
Webster, Daniel, 449–452
Welch, Peter, 1871–1873
Wenstrup, Brad, 1417–1420
Westerman, Bruce, 139–141
Westmoreland, Lynn, 520–522
Whitehouse, Sheldon, 1595–1598
Whitfield, Ed, 761–764
Wicker, Roger, 1021–1024
Williams, Roger, 1792–1795
Wilson, Frederica, 490–493
Wilson, Joe, 1624–1626
Wittman, Rob, 1889–1892
Wolf, Tom, 1527–1528
Womack, Steve, 136–139
Woodall, Rob, 531–534
Wyden, Ron, 1498–1502

Y
Yarmuth, John, 767–770
Yoder, Kevin, 739–741
Yoho, Ted, 428–430
Young, David, 713–715
Young, Don, 74–77
Young, Todd, 690–692

Z
Zeldin, Lee, 1250–1252
Zinke, Ryan, 1086–1087